BARRON'S
PROFILES OF AMERICAN COLLEGES

2007 27TH EDITION

Compiled and Edited by the College Division of
Barron's Educational Series

BARRON'S

All inquiries should be addressed to:
Barron's Educational Series, Inc.
250 Wireless Boulevard
Hauppauge, New York 11788
www.barronseduc.com

ISBN-13: 978-0-7641-7903-7
ISBN-10: 0-7641-7903-9

International Standard Serial No. 1065-5026

PRINTED IN THE UNITED STATES OF AMERICA
9 8 7 6 5 4 3 2 1

CONTENTS

PREFACE

Barron's *Profiles of American Colleges* is the most all-encompassing, easy-to-use guide available. All four-year institutions that offer bachelor's degrees are described if they are fully accredited or are recognized candidates for accreditation. The comprehensive, concise capsule and detailed essay on each school give an easy-to-absorb, complete picture of the colleges that interest the reader. And the attractive graphic design provides added readability.

The capsule of each profile lists important information for quick reference: address and phone and fax numbers; enrollment; calendar; fall application deadline; size and salary level of the faculty; percentage of faculty members who hold doctorates; student/faculty ratio; tuition and fees; room-and-board costs; the number of students who applied to the freshman class, were accepted, and enrolled; the median SAT* and/or ACT scores; and finally, the College Admissions Selector Rating for the school. The information in the essay portion of each profile ranges from available housing and the financial aid climate to admissions requirements and the success of graduates. There are twenty-one categories of information under eight main headings: Student Life, Programs of Study, Admissions, Financial Aid, International Students, Computers, Graduates, and Admissions Contact. The Admissions Contact section also gives Internet addresses and video availability.

We are confident that the features we have added in recent years, along with those that have appeared in previous editions of Barron's *Profiles*, will make this twenty-seventh edition the most thorough guide available to the college-bound student.

A Word of Thanks

To all the college admissions officers, to participating high school advisers, to the students, parents, and other supporters of Barron's *Profiles of American Colleges*, we offer our sincere thanks.

Grateful acknowledgment is made to the late Gloria M. Barron, who inspired the editors and production personnel to create a book that would offer every possible assistance in selecting the best college.

We acknowledge with thanks the demanding editing tasks performed by Editor Darrell Buono, College Division Coordinator Kathy Ammirati, and Editorial Assistants Erin Glynn and Lena Perfetto, along with the database designers and our hardworking editing and keyboarding staff.

CONTRIBUTORS

Steven R. Antonoff, Ph.D.
Educational Consultant
Antonoff Associates, Inc.
Denver, Colorado

Barbara J. Aronson
Career Center Coordinator
Miramonte High School
Orinda, California

Anthony F. Capraro, III, Ph.D.
President, Teach Inc.
College Counseling
Larchmont, New York

Marguerite J. Dennis
Vice President for
Development and
Enrollment
Suffolk University
Boston, Massachusetts

Benjamin W. Griffith
Former Dean of the
Graduate School
West Georgia College
Carrolton, Georgia

Sheldon Halpern
Former Dean
Enrollment Management
Caldwell College
Caldwell, New Jersey

Ira Wolf, Ph.D.
President
PowerPrep, Inc.
Roslyn Heights, New York

---

*SAT is a registered trademark owned by the College Entrance Examination Board. No endorsement of this product is implied or given.

AN EXPLANATION OF THE BOOK

You have been thinking about going to college within the next couple of years, and now you're convinced that it's time to get somewhat serious about your plans, and take some steps that will lead to your ultimate college decisions, right?

But how do you go about taking these steps? How much does college cost? How can you and your parents afford it? What about entrance exams? How can you possibly know where you want to go and even if you decide *that,* how do you apply with any degree of assurance that you will be accepted? What if you decide, apply, and then get turned down? How can you ensure that *that* doesn't happen? And if you do get past all those hurdles, how can you determine your college major, when you don't have a clue as to what you want to do *after* college?

But right now—where do you begin? In addition to hundreds of two-year schools, there are more than 1600 accredited four-year colleges in the United States, and your options are almost unlimited. But Barron's *Profiles of American Colleges* can point you in the right direction, and help you through the coming months of decision making.

You will find articles that will guide you in evaluating your own needs and interests, selecting the college, filling out the application, writing the essay, having the interview, finding the money, and surviving the freshman year.

There is advice on selecting a major and a career, and the Index of College Majors—a helpful aid for students who want to know which colleges offer the major they have selected. More than 600 majors are listed, along with the in-state costs and the Admissions Selector Rating in easy-to-read columns.

There is advice for international students, as well as a list of schools' in-state costs from least to most expensive. There is also a geographic chart that gives students quick information about schools on a state-by-state basis.

The College Admissions Selector Ratings give applicants an idea of the competition they will encounter when applying to a particular school. And you will find a key to abbreviations and an explanation of the actual college entries.

The heart of the book, of course, is the detailed descriptions of the colleges, including a special section of religious schools that prepare students for careers in the clergy and related fields. The college Profiles are presented alphabetically by state, and the states are also arranged in alphabetical order. Maps of the states begin each chapter. Actually, Barron's *Profiles of American Colleges* covers more than the fifty states; it also describes colleges in the District of Columbia, Puerto Rico, and selected universities in Canada and abroad (along with advice for international students) as well as state and private systems of higher education, for a total of approximately 1700 Profile entries.

This expanded and updated edition of *Profiles of American Colleges* will answer all of your questions as you embark on this most significant experience—college application, acceptance, and enrollment.

KEY TO ABBREVIATIONS

DEGREES

A.A.—Associate of Arts
A.A.S.—Associate of Applied Science
A.B. or B.A.—Bachelor of Arts
A.B.J.—Bachelor of Arts in Journalism
A.S.—Associate of Science

B.A.—Bachelor of Arts
B.A.A.—Bachelor of Applied Arts
B.A.A.S. or B.Applied A.S.—Bachelor of Applied Arts and Sciences
B.Ac. or B.Acc.—Bachelor of Accountancy
B.A.C.—Bachelor of Science in Air Commerce
B.A.C.V.I.—Bachelor of Arts in Computer and Video Imaging
B.A.E. or B.A.Ed.—Bachelor of Arts in Education
B.A.G.E.—Bachelor of Arts in General Education
B.Agri.—Bachelor of Agriculture
B.A.G.S.—Bachelor of Arts in General Studies
B.A.J.S.—Bachelor of Arts in Judaic Studies
B.A.M.—Bachelor of Arts in Music
B.Applied Sc.—Bachelor of Applied Science
B.A.R.—Bachelor of Religion
B.Arch.—Bachelor of Architecture
B.Arch.Hist.—Bachelor of Architectural History
B.Arch.Tech.—Bachelor of Architectural Technology
B.Ar.Sc.—Baccalaurium Artium et Scientiae (honors college degree) (Bachelor of Arts & Sciences)
B.Art.Ed.—Bachelor of Art Education
B.A.S.—Bachelor of Applied Science
B.A.S.—Bachelor of Arts and Sciences
B.A.Sec.Ed.—Bachelor of Arts in Secondary Ed.
B.A.S.W.—B.A. in Social Work
B.A.T.—Bachelor of Arts in Teaching
B.B. or B.Bus.—Bachelor of Business
B.B.A.—Bachelor of Business Administration
B.B.E.—Bachelor of Business Education
B.C. or B.Com. or B.Comm.—Bachelor of Commerce
B.C.A.—Bachelor of Creative Arts
B.C.E.—Bachelor of Civil Engineering
B.C.E.—Bachelor of Computer Engineering
B.Ch. or B.Chem.—Bachelor of Chemistry
B.Ch.E.—Bachelor of Chemical Engineering
B.C.J.—Bachelor of Criminal Justice
B.C.M.—Bachelor of Christian Ministries
B.Church Mus.—Bachelor of Church Music
B.C.S.—Bachelor of College Studies
B.E.—Bachelor of English
B.E. or B.Ed.—Bachelor of Education
B.E.—Bachelor of Engineering
B.E.D.—Bachelor of Environmental Design
B.E.E.—Bachelor of Electrical Engineering
B.En. or B.Eng.—Bachelor of Engineering
B.E.S. or B.Eng.Sc.—Bachelor of Engineering Science
B.E.T.—Bachelor of Engineering Technology
B.F.A.—Bachelor of Fine Arts
B.G.S.—Bachelor of General Studies
B.G.S.—Bachelor of Geological Sciences
B.H.E.—Bachelor of Health Education
B.H.P.E.—Bachelor of Health and Physical Education
B.H.S.—Bachelor of Health Science
B.I.D.—Bachelor of Industrial Design
B.I.M.—Bachelor of Industrial Management
B.Ind.Tech.—Bachelor of Industrial Technology
B.Int.Arch.—Bachelor of Interior Architecture
B.Int.Design—Bachelor of Interior Design
B.I.S.—Bachelor of Industrial Safety
B.I.S.—Bachelor of Interdisciplinary Studies
B.J.—Bachelor of Journalism
B.J.S.—Bachelor of Judaic Studies
B.L.A. or B.Lib.Arts—Bachelor of Liberal Arts
B.L.A. or B.Land.Arch.—Bachelor in Landscape Architecture
B.L.I.—Bachelor of Literary Interpretation
B.L.S.—Bachelor of Liberal Studies
B.M. or B.Mus. or Mus.Bac.—Bachelor of Music
B.M.E.—Bachelor of Mechanical Engineering

B.M.E. or B.M.Ed. or B.Mus.Ed.—Bachelor of Music Education
B.Med.Lab.Sc.—Bachelor of Medical Laboratory Science
B.Min—Bachelor of Ministry
B.M.P. or B.Mu.—Bachelor of Music in Performance
B.Mus.A.—Bachelor of Applied Music
B.M.T.—Bachelor of Music Therapy
B.O.T.—Bachelor of Occupational Therapy
B.P.A.—Bachelor of Public Administration
B.P.E.—Bachelor of Physical Education
B.Perf.Arts—Bachelor of Performing Arts
B.Ph.—Bachelor of Philosophy
B.Pharm.—Bachelor of Pharmacy
B.Phys.Hlth.Ed.—Bachelor of Physical Health Education
B.P.S.—Bachelor of Professional Studies
B.P.T.—Bachelor of Physical Therapy
B.R.E.—Bachelor of Religious Education
B.R.T.—Bachelor of Respiratory Therapy
B.S. or B.Sc. or S.B.—Bachelor of Science
B.S.A. or B.S.Ag. or B.S.Agr.—Bachelor of Science in Agriculture
B.Sacred Mus.—Bachelor of Sacred Music
B.Sacred Theol.—Bachelor of Sacred Theology
B.S.A.E.—Bachelor of Science in Agricultural Engineering
B.S.A.E. or B.S.Art Ed.—Bachelor of Science in Art Education
B.S.Ag.E.—Bachelor of Science in Agricultural Engineering
B.S.A.S.—Bachelor of Science in Administrative Sciences
B.S.A.T.—Bachelor of Science in Athletic Training
B.S.B.—Bachelor of Science (business)
B.S.B.A. or B.S.Bus. Adm.—Bachelor of Science in Business Administration
B.S.Bus.—Bachelor of Science in Business
B.S.Bus.Ed.—Bachelor of Science in Business Education
B.S.C.—Bachelor of Science in Commerce
B.S.C.E. or B.S.C.I.E.—Bachelor of Science in Civil Engineering
B.S.C.E.T—B.S. in Computer Engineering Technology
B.S.Ch. or B.S.Chem. or B.S. in Ch.—Bachelor of Science in Chemistry
B.S.C.H.—Bachelor of Science in Community Health
B.S.Ch.E.—Bachelor of Science in Chemical Engineering
B.S.C.I.S.—Bachelor of Science in Computer Information Sciences
B.S.C.J.—Bachelor of Science in Criminal Justice
B.S.C.L.S.—Bachelor of Science in Clinical Laboratory Science
B.S.Comp.Eng.—Bachelor of Science in Computer Engineering
B.S.Comp.Sci. or B.S.C.S.—Bachelor of Science in Computer Science
B.S.Comp.Soft—Bachelor of Science in Computer Software
B.S.Comp.Tech.—Bachelor of Science in Computer Technology
B.Sc.(P.T.)—Bachelor of Science in Physical Therapy
B.S.C.S.T.—Bachelor of Science in Computer Science Technology
B.S.D.H.—Bachelor of Science in Dental Hygiene
B.S.Die—Bachelor of Science in Dietetics
B.S.E. or B.S.Ed. or B.S.Educ.—Bachelor of Science in Education
B.S.E. or B.S in E. or B.S. in Eng.—Bachelor of Science in Engineering
B.S.E.E.—Bachelor of Science in Electrical Engineering
B.S.E.E.T.—Bachelor of Science in Electrical Engineering Technology
B.S.E.H.—Bachelor of Science in Environmental Health
B.S.Elect.T.—Bachelor of Science in Electronics Technology
B.S.El.Ed. or B.S. in Elem. Ed.—Bachelor of Science in Elementary Education
B.S.E.P.H.—Bachelor of Science in Environmental and Public Health
B.S.E.S.—Bachelor of Science in Engineering Science
B.S.E.S.—Bachelor of Science in Environmental Studies
B.S.E.T.—Bachelor of Science in Engineering Technology
B.S.F.—Bachelor of Science in Forestry
B.S.F.R.—Bachelor of Science in Forestry Resources
B.S.F.W.—Bachelor of Science in Fisheries and Wildlife
B.S.G.—Bachelor of Science in Geology

B.S.G.—Bachelor of Science in Gerontology
B.S.G.E.—Bachelor of Science in Geological Engineering
B.S.G.S.—Bachelor of Science in General Studies
B.S.H.C.A.—Bachelor of Science in Health Care Administration
B.S.H.E.—Bachelor of Science in Home Economics
B.S.H.F.—Bachelor of Science in Health Fitness
B.S.H.M.S.—Bachelor of Science in Health Management Systems
B.S.H.S.—Bachelor of Science in Health Sciences
B.S.H.S.—Bachelor of Science in Human Services
B.S.I.A.—Bachelor of Science in Industrial Arts
B.S.I.E.—Bachelor of Science in Industrial Engineering
B.S.I.M.—Bachelor of Science in Industrial Management
B.S. in Biomed.Eng.—Bachelor of Science in Biomedical Engineering
B.S. in C.D.—Bachelor of Science in Communication Disorders
B.S.Ind.Ed.—Bachelor of Science in Industrial Education
B.S.Ind.Tech.—Bachelor of Science in Industrial Technology
B.S. in Sec.Ed.—Bachelor of Science in Secondary Education
B.S.I.S.—Bachelor of Science in Interdisciplinary Studies
B.S.I.T.—Bachelor of Science in Industrial Technology
B.S.J.—Bachelor of Science in Journalism
B.S.L.E.—Bachelor of Science in Law Enforcement
B.S.M.—Bachelor of Science in Management
B.S.M.—Bachelor of Science in Music
B.S.M.E.—Bachelor of Science in Mechanical Engineering
B.S.Med.Tech. or B.S.M.T.—Bachelor of Science in Medical Technology
B.S.Met.E.—Bachelor of Science in Metallurgical Engineering
B.S.M.R.A.—Bachelor of Science in Medical Records Administration
B.S.M.T.—Bachelor of Science in Medical Technology
B.S.M.T.—Bachelor of Science in Music Therapy
B.S.Mt.E.—Bachelor of Science in Materials Engineering
B.S.Mus.Ed.—Bachelor of Science in Music Education
B.S.N.—Bachelor of Science in Nursing
B.S.Nuc.T.—Bachelor of Science in Nuclear Technology
B.S.O.A.—Bachelor of Science in Office Administration
B.S.O.E.—Bachelor of Science in Occupational Education
B.S.O.T.—Bachelor of Science in Occupational Therapy
B.S.P. or B.S.Pharm—Bachelor of Science in Pharmacy
B.S.P.A.—Bachelor of Science in Public Administration
B.S.Pcs.—Bachelor of Science in Physics
B.S.P.E.—Bachelor of Science in Physical Education
B.S.P.T.—Bachelor of Science in Physical Therapy
B.S.Rad.Tech.—Bachelor of Science in Radiation Technology
B.S.R.C.—Bachelor of Science in Respiratory Care
B.S.R.S.—Bachelor of Science in Radiological Science
B.S.R.T.T.—Bachelor of Science in Radiation Therapy Technology
B.S.S.—Bachelor of Science in Surveying
B.S.S.—Bachelor of Special Studies
B.S.S.A.—Bachelor of Science in Systems Analysis
B.S.Soc. Work or B.S.S.W.—Bachelor of Science in Social Work
B.S.Sp.—Bachelor of Science in Speech
B.S.S.T.—Bachelor of Science in Surveying and Topography
B.S.T. or B.S.Tech.—Bachelor of Science in Technology
B.S.S.W.E.—Bachelor of Science in Software Engineering
B.S.V.T.E.—Bachelor of Science in Vocational Technical Education
B.S.W.—Bachelor of Social Work
B.T. or B.Tech.—Bachelor of Technology
B.Th.—Bachelor of Theology
B.T.S.—Bachelor of Technical Studies
B.U.S.—Bachelor of Urban Studies
B.V.M.—Bachelor of Veterinarian Medicine
B.Voc.Arts or B.V.A.—Bachelor of Vocational Arts
B.V.E.D. or B.Voc.Ed.—Bachelor of Vocational Education

D.D.S.—Doctor of Dental Surgery

Ed.S.—Education Specialist

J.D.—Doctor of Jurisprudence

LL.B.—Bachelor of Laws

M.A.—Master of Arts
  M.A.Ed.—Master of Arts in Education
M.A.T.—Master of Arts in Teaching
M.B.A.—Master of Business Administration
M.D.—Doctor of Medicine
M.F.A.—Master of Fine Arts
M.P.A.—Master of Public Administration
M.S.—Master of Science
Mus.B. or Mus.Bac.—Bachelor of Music

Ph.D.—Doctor of Philosophy

R.N.—Registered Nurse

S.B. or B.S. or B.Sc.—Bachelor of Science

OTHER ABBREVIATIONS

AABC—Accrediting Association of Bible Colleges
AACN—American Association of Colleges of Nursing
AACSB—American Assembly of Collegiate Schools of Business
AAFCS—American Association of Family and Consumer Sciences
AALE—American Academy for Liberal Education
AALS—Association of American Law Schools
AAMFT—American Association for Marriage and Family Therapy
ABA—American Bar Association
ABET—Accreditation Board for Engineering and Technology
ABFSE—American Board of Funeral Service Education
ABHES—Accrediting Bureau of Health Education Schools
ACBSP—Association of Collegiate Business Schools and Programs
ACCE—American Council for Construction Education
ACE HSA—Accrediting Commission on Education for Health Services Administration
ACE JMC—American Council on Education in Journalism and Mass Communication
ACOTE—American Council for Occupational Therapy Education
ACPE—Association for Clinical Pastoral Education, Inc.
ACPE—American Council on Pharmaceutical Education
ACS—American Chemical Society
ACT—American College Testing Program
ADA—American Dietetic Association
ADA—American Dental Association
ADDA—American Design Drafting Association
AFSA—Application for Federal Student Aid
AHEA—American Home Economics Association
AHIMA—American Health Information Management Association
ALA—American Library Association
ALIGU—American Language Institute of Georgetown University
AMAC AHEA—American Medical Association Committee on Allied Health Education and Accreditation
AOA—American Osteopathic Association
AOA—American Optometric Association
AOTA—American Occupational Therapy Association
AP—Advanced Placement
APA—American Podiatry Association
APA—American Psychological Association
APET—Asset Placement Evaluation Test
APIEL—Advance Placement International English Language Exam
APTA—American Physical Therapy Association
ASHA—American School Health Association

ASLA—American Society of Landscape Architects
ASLHA—American Speech-Language-Hearing Association
ATSUSC—Association of Theological Schools in the United States and Canada
AUCC—Association of Universities and Colleges of Canada
AVMA—American Veterinary Medical Association

BEOG—Basic Educational Opportunity Grant (now Pell Grant)

CAA—Council on Aviation Accreditation
CAADE—California Association for Alcohol/Drug Educators
CAAHEP—Commission on Accreditation of Allied Health Education Programs
CAAP—College Achievement Admission Program
CACREP—Council for Accreditation of Counseling and Related Educational Programs
CADE—Commission on Accreditation for Dietetics Education
CAPTE—Commission on Accreditation in Physical Therapy Education
CAS—Certificate of Advanced Study
CCE—Council on Chiropractic Education
CCNE—Commission on Collegiate Nursing Education
CCTE—California Commission on Teacher Credentialing
CDN—Canadian
CED—Council for Education of the Deaf
CEEB—College Entrance Examination Board
CELT—Comprehensive English Language Test
CEPH—Council on Education for Public Health
CLAST—College Level Academic Skills Test
CLEP—College-Level Examination Program
COE—Council on Occupational Education
CRDA—Candidates Reply Date Agreement
CRE—Council on Rehabilitation Education
CSAB—Computing Science Accreditation Board
CSS—College Scholarship Service
CSS/Profile—College Scholarship Service Financial Aid Profile
CSWE—Council on Social Work Education
CWS—College Work-Study

EESL—Examination of English as a Second Language
ELPT—English Language Proficiency Test (SAT II)
ELS/ALA—English Language Services/American Language Academy
EMH—Educable Mentally Handicapped
EOP—Equal Opportunity Program
ESL—English as a Second Language
ETS—Educational Testing Service

FAFSA—Free Application for Federal Student Aid
FET—Full-time equivalent
FFS—Family Financial Statement
FIDER—Foundation for Interior Design Education Research
FISL—Federally Insured Student Loan
FTE—Full-Time Equivalent

GED—General Educational Development (high school equivalency examination)
GPA—Grade Point Average
GRE—Graduate Record Examination
GSLP—Guaranteed Student Loan Program
G-STEP—Georgia State Test for English Proficiency

HEOP—Higher Equal Opportunity Program
HPER—Health, Physical Education, and Recreation

IACBE—International Assembly for Collegiate Business Education
IAME—International Association for Management Education
IB—International Baccalaureate
IELTS—International English Language Testing System

JRCERT—Joint Review Committee on Education in Radiologic Technology
JRCNMT—Joint Review Committee on Educational Programs in Nuclear Medicine Technology

LCME—Liaison Committee on Medical Education

MAPS—Multiple Assessment Program/Services
MELAB—Michigan English Language Assessment Battery
MUSIC—Multi User System for Interactive Computing

NAAB—National Architectural Accrediting Board
NAACLS—National Accrediting Agency for Clinical Laboratory Educators
NAIT—National Association of Industrial Technology
NAPNES—National Association for Practical Nurse Education and Service
NASAD—National Association of Schools of Art and Design
NASD—National Association of Schools of Dance
NASDTEC—National Association of State Development Teacher Education
NASM—National Association of Schools of Music
NASPAA—National Association of Schools of Public Affairs and Administration
NASPE—National Association of Sport and Physical Education
NAST—National Association of Schools of Theatre
NCATE—National Council for Accreditation of Teacher Education
NCCAA—National Christian College Athletic Association
NCOPE—National Commission on Orthotic and Prosthetic Education
NDEA—National Defense Education Act
NLN—National League for Nursing
NRPA—National Recreation and Park Association

PCS—Parents' Confidential Statement
PAIR—PHEAA Aid Information Request
PEP—Proficiency Examination Program
PHEAA—Pennsylvania Higher Education Assistance Agency
PSAT/NMSQT—Preliminary Scholastic Aptitude Test/National Merit Scholarship Qualifying Test

ROTC—Reserve Officers Training Corps
RSE—Regents Scholarship Examination (New York State)

SAAC—Student Aid Application for California
SACU—Service for Admission to College and University (Canada)
SAF—Society of American Foresters
SAM—Single Application Method
SAR—Student Aid Report
SAT—Scholastic Assessment Testing (formerly ATP–Admissions Testing Program)
SCAT—Scholastic College Aptitude Test
SCS—Students' Confidential Statement
SEOG—Supplementary Educational Opportunity Grant
SOA—Society of Actuaries

TAP—Tuition Assistance Program (New York State)
TDD—Telecommunication Device for the Deaf
TEAC—Teacher Education Accreditation Council
TOEFL—Test of English as a Foreign Language
TTY—Talking Typewriter

UAP—Undergraduate Assessment Program
UP—Undergraduate Program (area tests)

VFAF—Virginia Financial Assistance Form

WPCT—Washington Pre-College Test

PART I

AN INTRODUCTION

TO COLLEGE

You'll soon be on your way to college—but how much thought have you given it so far? Have you started thinking about the career that's in your future?

- Which college will help you make the most of your natural abilities and interests, and get you ready for life?
- Which courses should you take?

This section will help you find answers to these questions. It will also give you advice on:

- how to apply to schools
- how to increase your chances of acceptance
- how to finance your education

And just as important, this introductory section will give you valuable tips on how to get through that critical freshman year.

You have in your hands a book that will give you answers to your questions about the qualities and features of more than 1650 colleges. But before you start reading the descriptions and getting the answers, you need to know what questions to ask about finding the college that is right for you. Although you need to ask questions about "getting in" i.e., exploring colleges in terms of ease of admission for you, most of your questions should focus on the more significant issue of "fitting in." Fitting in means finding a college where you will be comfortable; where you are compatible with your peers, and where the overall atmosphere encourages your growth as a student and as a person.

This article is designed to help you assess some values and attitudes that will help you determine where you will fit in. It will enable you to ask the right questions. Not all colleges are for everyone; careful thinking about your interests, ideals, and values will lead you to find the college that is right *for you*. Colleges are not "good" or "bad" in a generic sense; they are either good or bad matches for you.

The two assessments that follow will be helpful in thinking about yourself as a future college student; they should help you make the right college choice.

THE COLLEGE PLANNING VALUES ASSESSMENT

Students have different reasons for going to college. Eleven reasons or values are found to be most important to students as they think about college. Knowing about your values is the important first step in identifying the colleges where you will fit in and be happy.

To complete the assessment, read through the list of ten values—A through K. Think about the outcomes you hope college will produce for you. Each student will rank them differently; hence, there are no "right" answers. Whereas several, or even most, of these values may be significant for you in one way or another, the goal is to decide which three are the most important. After you read each of the values, go back and circle the THREE most important ones on the basis of the following question:

What do you want college to do for you?

—— A. To provide me with a place to learn and study.
—— B. To provide me with opportunities to interact with teachers inside and outside the classroom.
—— C. To provide me with lots of fun experiences.
—— D. To prepare me to make a lot of money.
—— E. To provide me with recognition for accomplishments.
—— F. To get politically involved and/or to use much of my college years to help those who are disadvantaged.
—— G. To help me prepare for a career.
—— H. To enable me to be more independent.
—— I. To provide opportunities for me to grow religiously or spiritually.
—— J. To provide me with a variety of new experiences.
—— K. To enable me to receive a degree from a prestigious school.

What do your college planning values say about you?

If **A** was among the top three priorities on your list, you will want to explore the academic character of the colleges you are considering. Although all colleges are, by definition, intellectual centers, some put more priority on challenging students and pushing them to their limits. Reading about the academic features of the colleges you are considering will be important. (In the college Profiles, pay attention to the *special* section to learn about these features.) Your high ranking of this value says that you will be able to take advantage of intellectual opportunities at college. You may want to select a college where your SAT scores are similar to or slightly above the ranges of other admitted students—at those colleges you will be able to shine academically. You may desire to take an active part in classroom discussions and will want a college where the student faculty ratio is low.

If **B** was among your top three priorities, you feel challenged and stimulated by academics and classroom learning. You will want to find a college where your mind will be stretched. You will want to choose a college where you can explore a range of new academic subjects. A liberal arts and sciences college may give you an enriching breadth of academic offerings. You will want to look for a college where academic clubs are popular and where you have a good chance of knowing professors and sharing ideas with them. Access to faculty is important to you and you will want to look at the student faculty ratio in colleges you consider. Also note the ratio of undergraduate students to graduate students. Primarily undergraduate institutions will be the colleges that may best be able to meet your needs, because you will be the focus of teachers' attention. Teachers at such colleges place their priority on teaching and are not distracted by the needs of graduate students or by pressure to balance teaching and student time with research and writing.

If **C** was circled, you derive satisfaction from social opportunities. You will want a college where the academic demands will not diminish your ability to socialize. You likely will want a good balance between the social and academic sides of campus life. You will want to explore the percentage of students who get involved in intramural sports, clubs, or fraternities and sororities. (This information is listed in each college profile.) Look at your college choices on the basis of school spirit and sporting events offered. The profiles list popular campus events—see if they sound exciting to you. Also look at the percentage of students who stay on campus over the weekend. You will also want a college where it is easy to make friends. Both small and larger colleges would be appropriate for you. Although a larger college would expose you to more students and a larger quantity of potential friends, studies show that students at smaller colleges become more involved in activities and build deep friendships more quickly. Look for supportiveness and camaraderie in the student body.

If **D** is circled, you will want to consider earning potential, advancement opportunities, and the future market for the careers you consider. You will want to consider this value in your career planning. Remember, however, that there is no sure road to riches! You not only must pick a career direction carefully, but must choose a college where the potential for academic success—good grades—is high. The name of a particular college is less important than good grades or contributions to campus life when securing a good job or being admitted to graduate school. Even if you find that a particular career has tremendous earning potential, those earnings may come to only those who are most successful in the profession. Look at average salaries, but also consider your interests, values, and personality before making your final career choice. Be sure to take advantage of hands-on learning opportunities. Perhaps, for example, there are internships that meet your needs. Also, finding good, career-focused summer jobs can be helpful.

If **E** is high on your list, you take pleasure in being known for your success in an area of interest. For instance, you might feel good about being recognized or known in school as a good student, a top athlete, or a leader in a club. No doubt this type of recognition contributes to your confidence. You might look for colleges where you will be able to acquire or continue to receive this recognition. Often, recognition is easier to achieve at smaller colleges where you would not be competing against large numbers of students hoping to achieve the same recognition. You will also want to choose colleges where it is easy to get involved and where the activities offered are appealing to you. You may want to consider the benefits of being a "big fish in a small pond."

If **F** is important, that value will no doubt guide your vocational or avocational pursuits. You may find yourself choosing a career in which this value can be fulfilled, or you may seek opportunities on a college campus where you can be of service to others. You will want to choose a college where community service is valued. Look at the *activities* section and note whether community service-related involvements are available. Colleges vary a great deal in terms of political awareness. At some colleges, students are attuned to national and international events, often express feelings about current issues and policies, and in general, show interest in political affairs. Students at other colleges show little or no interest in these matters and find other ways to interact with peers.

If **G** was circled, you may know what career you want to pursue or you may be concerned but uncertain about your career decision. If you have tentatively selected a career, you will want to choose a college where you can take courses leading to the attainment of a degree in your chosen field. Explore the *programs of study* section in the profiles to determine whether a college you are considering offers the course work you desire. You will want to make a note of the most popular majors and the strongest majors as they are listed. If you don't yet know what career would suit you, remember, that for most careers, a broad, solid liberal arts foundation is considered good preparation. You will want to look at opportunities for internships and take advantage of the career planning and placement office at your chosen college. Finding a career that will be fulfilling is one of the most important choices you will make in your life. Your selection of a college will be your first step toward achieving your career goal.

If **H** is circled, it suggests that personal autonomy is important to you. College is, in general, a time for independence, and students are often anxious to make their own decisions without parental involvement. If you feel you can handle lots of independence, you will want to look for colleges where there is some freedom in choosing courses and where students are given responsibility for their own lives. Colleges vary in terms of these factors. Note particularly the *required* section under *programs of study*, which tells you the courses that must be fulfilled by all students. Be certain that you will not be stifled by too many rules and regulations. You may also want to look for colleges where the personal development of students receives high priority. A priority on independence also suggests that you will be comfortable being away from home and on your own.

If **I** is one of your top three choices, you will want to look first at the religious affiliation of each of your college options. There are two ways to consider religious life on college campuses. First is the question of how religion affects the day-to-day life of the college. For example, are biblical references made in class? Are religious convocations mandatory? Second is the question of whether there is a religious heritage at the college. Many hundreds of colleges have historical relationships with a religious denomination, but this tie does not affect the rules or the general life of the students. (For example, the college may have a certain number of religion classes required to graduate, but these classes are typically broad-based and not doctrinal.) You may want a college that has a relationship with your particular religious group. Or you may desire a large number of students who belong to the same denomination as you do. The profiles will also give you the percentage of students who are members of the major religious denominations. As you explore colleges, you will also want to see if the college has a commitment to the values and ideals held by you or your family.

If **J** is appealing, you like newness and will likely be stimulated by new experiences and new activities. You are in for a treat at most colleges. New experiences are the "stuff" of which college life is made. You may see college-going as an adventure and will want to pick colleges where you can meet your need for stimulation and excitement. Because you value newness, you should not hesitate to attend college in a different part of the country or to experience an environment or a climate that is quite different from your high school. You will also want to look for evidence of diversity in the student body. As you read the descriptions, look for colleges with lots of new opportunities for growth and for personal expansion.

If **K** is appealing, be cautious. Students who are overly concerned about this value might find college planning traumatic, and even painful, because of the admission

selectivity of "name brand" colleges. Even though it is perfectly acceptable for students to be attuned to the overall excellence of a college, academic quality and prestige are not the same thing. Some colleges are well-known because of, say, a fine football team or because of academic excellence in a subject like psychology or physics. Although it is appropriate to look for a strong faculty and a highly regarded college, you want a college that will give you the greatest chance of academic success. It is success in college, not just academic reputation or prestige, that will lead to admission into graduate school or a broad selection of jobs.

Now that you've read about your top three values, answer the following question on a separate sheet of paper: In your own words, what do your top three values say about what you are looking for in a college? Then, share that information with your college adviser as he or she assists you in finding colleges that are right for you.

SELF-KNOWLEDGE QUESTIONNAIRE

The following seven items—A–G—will help you in thinking about yourself as a college student and the ease with which you will likely proceed through the college selection process. Read each statement and determine whether it is true or not true of you. After each question, you will see numbers ranging from 1 to 5. Circle 1 if the statement is very true of you. Circle 5 if the statement is not true of you. Use 2, 3, or 4 to reflect varying levels of preference. Be realistic and honest.

A. My academic abilities for college (such as reading, writing, and note taking) are good.

Very true of me   1   2   3   4   5   Not true of me

Academic abilities such as reading speed and comprehension, writing, note taking, calculating, speaking, and listening are important for college students. You will be called upon to use such skills in your college classes. If you are confident about your academic skills, you can approach picking a college with the ease of knowing that you will be able to master the academic rigors of college life. If you circled 3, 4, or 5 you will want to work on these skills in your remaining days in high school. You will want to choose colleges where you can work to strengthen these skills. Some colleges provide a learning skills center in which you are able to get help if you are having difficulty writing a paper or understanding the content of a class. If you are less than confident, you might look to colleges where you will not be intimidated by the skills of the other students.

B. My study skills and time management are good.

Very true of me   1   2   3   4   5   Not true of me

Study skills and time management are two of the most important qualities for an efficient and productive college student. Successful college students are average or above in organizing themselves for studying, scheduling, and using study time productively, and differentiating important content of a lecture or a book from supplementary information. In addition, they complete assignments on time and don't get flustered if they have several papers or a couple of tests due on the same day. If you circled 3, 4, or 5, it is important to work on improving these skills during your remaining high school days. You might consider the following:

- Seek help from your parents, a teacher, a counselor, or a learning specialist in becoming more organized.
- Try keeping a calendar. Anticipate each step necessary in preparing for every test and every paper.
- Be responsible for your own appointments.
- Check to see if a study skills course is offered at a local community college or university. Or consider reading a book on study skills.

C. I am motivated to succeed in college.

Very true of me   1   2   3   4   5   Not true of me

Motivation is definitely the most important skill you bring to college. Those students who want to succeed do succeed! Studies show that it is motivation, not your SAT scores, that determines academic success in college. And motivation means knowing not only that you want to go to college, but that you also want to be a student. Some students want to go to college for the fun aspects, but forget that college is primarily an academic experience. So if you circled 1 or 2, great, you're off to a good start. If you circled 3, 4, or 5, it may be an appropriate time to consider your wants and needs in a college. What sort of college would help motivate you? Would a college with a balance between academics and social life be appealing? Would you be more motivated if you were near a large and interesting city? Would nice weather be a distraction rather than an energizer? Is a trade or technical school best for you? Have you considered taking some time off between high school and college? Considering such questions is important, and the time to do that exploration is now.

D. I am a good decision maker.

Very true of me   1   2   3   4   5   Not true of me

Decisions, decisions, decisions. The college selection process is full of decisions! What colleges will I initially consider? To which colleges will I apply for admission? What college will I eventually attend? You will be facing these decisions in the upcoming months. If you circled 1 or 2, you are on your way. If you circled 3, 4, or 5, think about an important decision you made recently. Why didn't it go well? If you can analyze your decision-making weakness in that situation, it may help to avoid any potential pitfalls in your college decision-making. The following suggestions will help you improve your ability to make the right college choice:

- Clearly articulate what you're looking for in a college. Write down those features that will make a college right for you.
- Involve lots of people and resources in your search for a college. Your parents, counselors, and friends can help you.
- List and compare pros and cons of alternative colleges. Every college has both.
- Evaluate each college on the basis of the criteria you set for yourself.

Remember, you're looking for a college where you will get in *and* fit in.

E. I'm a good information gatherer; for example, I am usually able to find books, articles, and so on to help me do a research paper for, say, a history class.

Very true of me   1   2   3   4   5   Not true of me

Finding a college requires you to be a good researcher. There is so much information about colleges to sort through and analyze. If you feel you can do good research, fine, you're on your way. If you circled 3, 4, or 5, the following ideas may be helpful:

- Start with this book and look for colleges that are consistent with what you want. Remember that your primary concern is where you will fit in. Use your college-going values and your responses in this questionnaire to guide your thinking about colleges that will match you.
- Work closely with your college counselor, and seek impressions from students and others with reliable and up-to-date information about colleges of interest. You will make a better decision with credible and extensive input.
- Look for differences in features that are important to you. Is ease of making friends important to you? What about balance between academics and social life? Do you want teachers to know you?

F. I feel I adapt to new situations easily.

Very true of me   1   2   3   4   5   Not true of me

Everyone goes through changes in life. Some move through transition periods with great ease, others find them more difficult. You may have experienced the changes that come after a change of schools (even from middle school to high school), the illness or death of a relative, or the divorce of your parents. If you circled 1 or 2, you are not likely to be intimidated by a college in another part of the country or a college very different from your high school. If you circled 3, 4, or 5, you may want to carefully look at colleges that are a bit closer to home or colleges where the same values, perceptions, and attitudes exist as were true in your high school. Almost everyone has fear and apprehension about leaving for college. But if that fear is significant, you will want to choose a college where you will feel comfortable. Visits to college campuses may be particularly significant in feeling good about potential choices.

G. It is easy for me to meet people and establish friendships.

Very true of me   1   2   3   4   5   Not true of me

Identifying and nurturing friendships is an important skill for college adjustment. If you circled 3, 4, or 5, you will want to look carefully at colleges where there are few cliques, where there is an atmosphere of sharing, and where students report that it is relatively easy to integrate into the campus environment. Your choice of a college is a quest for a good social fit. Your thorough review of the profiles and even visits to college campuses will be helpful in assuring your ability to fit in and be comfortable.

FINAL THOUGHTS

If you took time to carefully consider the issues raised in both the Values Assessment and the Self-Knowledge Questionnaire, you should have gained new insights and perspectives about yourself. You will want to share these results with your parents and with your guidance counselor. Elicit their help in getting more insight as to how they see you as a prospective college student. Finally, two suggestions:

- As you research colleges, consider what you have learned about yourself. You want a college that is a good match with your values and interests.
- Spend time on your college search. It will take many hours of organized planning and investigation. But the time spent will result in a better choice and a greater likelihood that you will spend four productive and exciting years in college.

Good luck. There are lots of colleges out there that want you. Let your knowledge of yourself and your objective analysis of potential college options guide you to college environments where you will be able to shine. Success in college is in your hands. Make the most of the opportunity.

Steven R. Antonoff, Ph.D., Certified Educational Planner
Educational Consultant
Antonoff Associates, Inc.
Denver, Colorado

Start your college search positively. Start with the knowledge that there are many schools out there that want you. Start with the idea that there are many good college choices for every student. Too often these days, articles on college admission make students and their parents apprehensive. You can have choices. You can get financial aid. You can have a happy, successful college career.

When you begin to think about college, you are embarking on a major research project. You have many choices available to you in order to get the best possible education for which you are qualified. This article is intended to help you think of some of the important variables in your college search.

Let us help make the book work for you!

THE CURRENT ADMISSION SCENE

Today there are approximately 1,650 four-year colleges and universities accredited. Most existing institutions have grown larger, and many have expanded their programs, offering master's and doctoral degrees as well as bachelor's.

Total graduate and undergraduate students has also grown, from under 4 million in 1960 to more than 16 million today. In fact, between 2000 and 2013 total enrollment at U.S. colleges and universities is expected to rise 19 percent, to 18.2 million students. Almost 40 percent are part-time students, including many working adults. Part-time enrollments are mostly concentrated in the two-year colleges, which enroll about a third of all students.

What does this all mean to you? There is good news and bad news. The good news is that most of the colleges you will read about in this book are colleges you can get into! In other words, the vast majority of colleges in the U.S. admit more than 70 percent of those who apply. Many hundreds admit all of those who apply. So, on one level, you shouldn't worry that you won't be able to get a college education. The bad news is for the student with extremely high grades who seeks admission to the 50 or so most competitive colleges in the country. These "brand name" colleges have many times more candidates than they admit. Even incredibly qualified students are sometimes denied admission.

The key to good college planning is, as mentioned above, research. Find out about what makes one college different from another. Find out what students say about their experiences. Rely on many sources of information—many people, many books, many web sites, and so on. There are lots of people and materials available to help you. This book is one of them. Let the information be your guide. But also let your instincts and your sense of what's best for you play a part. The higher education opportunities in the U.S. are unlimited. The opportunity to let education help pave the way to achieving your dreams is a worthy goal of your college search.

MAKING A SHORT LIST

You have probably already started a list of colleges you know about from friends or relatives who have attended them, from recommendations by counselors or teachers, or by their academic or social reputations. This list will grow as you read the Profiles, receive college mailings, and attend college fairs. If you are interested in preparing for a very specific career, such as engineering, agriculture, nursing, or architecture, you should add only institutions that offer that program. If you want to study business, teacher education, or the arts and sciences, almost every college can provide a suitable major. Either way, your list will soon include dozens of institutions. Most students apply to between four and seven colleges. To narrow your list, you should keep the following process in mind:

- As you explore, be attuned to the admission requirements. You will want to have colleges on your list that span the admission selectivity continuum—from "reach" colleges (those where your grades, test scores, etc., suggest less chance of admission) to "safety" schools (those where your credentials are a bit better than the average student admitted), eliminating colleges at which you clearly would not qualify for admission.
- You also will want to keep an eye on cost. You want to consider colleges that are generally in line with your family's ability to finance your education. Be very cautious as you do this. Literally millions of dollars are available each year for students. There is both "need-based" aid (aid based on your family's ability to pay) and "merit-based" aid (aid based on such things as grades, test scores, and leadership ability).
- Screen the list according to your preferences, such as size, academic competitiveness, religious focus, and location.
- Make quality judgments, using published information and campus visits, to decide which colleges can give you the best quality and value.

The following sections are organized around the factors most important in researching a college. Discussion of admission competitiveness and cost comes first. After that, a wide range of factors important to consider as you evaluate colleges is examined. These include size, housing, the faculty, academic programs, internships, accreditation, libraries and computer technology, and religious/racial considerations. The final two sections are a discussion of campus visits and, finally, a checklist of 25 important questions to ask about each of the colleges you are exploring.

In the end, you must allow yourself to be a good decision maker. You will have to make some quality judgments. It is not as difficult as you may think. You have to be willing to read the information in this book and the literature that the schools make available, to visit a few campuses, and to ask plenty of questions. Usually you can ask questions of the admissions office by regular mail, e-mail, or in person during a campus visit. Because colleges sincerely are interested in helping you make the right choice, they generally will welcome your questions and answer them politely and honestly. In addition, your high school counselor is a key person who can offer advice and guidance. Finally, there are many resources available, in printed form and on the web, to help you.

SELECTION FACTORS

Admissions Competitiveness

The first question most students ask about a college is, "How hard is it to get in?" It should certainly not be the last question. Admissions competitiveness is not the only, or even the most important, measurement of institutional quality. It makes sense to avoid wasting time, money, and useless disappointment applying to institutions for which you clearly are not qualified. Nevertheless, there are many colleges for which you are qualified, and you can make a good choice from among them. The most prestigious institutions are rarely affected by market conditions. Most of the better known private and public colleges and universities have raised their admission standards in recent years. But there remain hundreds of fine public and private colleges, with good local reputations, that will welcome your application.

Use the College Admissions Selector to compare your qualifications to the admissions competitiveness of the institutions of your list. Make sure you read the descriptions of standards very carefully. Even if you meet the stated qualifications for *Most Competitive* or *Highly Competitive* institutions, you cannot assume that you will be offered admission. These colleges receive applications from many more students than they can enroll and reject far more than they accept. When considering colleges rated *Very Competitive* or *Competitive*, remember that the median test scores identify the middle of the most recent freshman class; half of the admitted students had scores lower than the median, and half were above. Students of average ability are admissible to most of the colleges and universities rated as *Competitive* and to virtually all of those rated as *Less Competitive*.

Cost

The basic cost of the most expensive colleges and universities can exceed $40,000 a year. This is widely publicized and very frightening, especially to your parents. But you don't have to spend that much for a good education. Private colleges charge an average of nearly $30,000 a year for tuition and room and board. Public institutions generally cost an average of $14,000 a year for in-state residents. Because many states have been cutting budgets in recent years, tuition at public institutions is now rising faster than at private ones. If you can commute to school from home, you can save about $6000 to $7000 in room and board, but should add the cost of transportation. The least expensive option is to attend a local community college for two years, at about $1500 a year, and then transfer to a four-year institution to complete your bachelor's degree. Depending on what you may qualify for in financial aid, and what your family is willing to sacrifice, you may have more choices than you think.

Size

Only one-fifth of American colleges and universities have enrollments of 5000 or more, but they account for more than half the ten million plus students who are pursuing bachelor's degrees. The rest are spread out among more than 1000 smaller schools. There are advantages and disadvantages that go with size.

At a college of 5000 or fewer students, you will get to know the campus quickly. You will not have to compete with many other students when registering for courses or for use of the library or other facilities. You can get to know your professors personally and become familiar with most of your fellow students. On the other hand, the school may not have as many majors and it may have less emphasis on spectator sports. Students at small schools are not able to be as "anonymous" as those at larger schools.

As colleges and universities enroll more students, they offer more courses and activities. Within a large campus community, you can probably find others who share your special interests and form a circle of good friends. But you may also find the facilities more crowded, classes closed out, and competition very stiff for athletic teams or musical groups.

Many of the largest institutions are universities offering medical, law, or other doctoral programs as well as bachelor's and master's degrees. Many colleges that do not offer these programs call themselves universities; and a few universities, Dartmouth among them, continue to call themselves colleges. Don't go by the name, but by the academic program. Universities emphasize research. University faculty need specialized laboratory equipment, computers, library material, and technical assistance for their research. Colleges tend to emphasize teaching.

Because research is very expensive, universities usually charge higher tuition than colleges, even to their undergraduate students. In effect, undergraduates at universities subsidize the high cost of graduate programs. Freshmen and sophomores usually receive some instruction from graduate student assistants and fellows, who are paid to be apprentice faculty members.

Of course, many larger private universities, and many public ones, have fine reputations. They have larger and more up-to-date libraries, laboratories, computers, and other special resources than colleges. They attract students from many states and countries and provide a rich social and cultural environment.

Housing

Deciding whether you will stay in a residence hall or at home is more than a matter of finances or how close to the college you live. You should be aware that students who live on campus, especially during the freshman year, are more likely to pass their courses and graduate than students who commute from home. Campus residents spend more time with faculty members, have more opportunity to use the library and laboratories, and are linked to other students who help one another with their studies. Residence hall life usually helps students mature faster as they participate in social and organizational activities.

If you commute to school, you can get maximum benefits from your college experience by spending time on campus between and after classes. If you need a part-time job, get employment in the college library, offices, or dining halls. Use the library to do homework in an environment that may be less distracting than home. If possible, have some dinners on campus, to make friends with other students and participate in evening social and cultural events. Get involved in campus activities, participating in athletics, working on the newspaper, attending a meeting, or rehearsing a play.

You will have a choice of food plans. Most meal plans include a certain number of meals per week. Other plans allow you to prepay a fixed dollar amount and purchase food by the item rather than by the meal. Choose a meal plan that fits your own eating habits. Most colleges today offer a tremendous variety of food and are accommodating to most diets and preferences.

Many students live off campus after their freshman or sophomore year, either by choice or because the school does not have room for them on campus. Schools try to provide listings of available off-campus rooms and apartments that meet good standards for safety and cleanliness. Many colleges also offer health care and food services to students who live off campus.

It is usually more expensive to live in an apartment than in a residence hall, especially if you plan to prepare your own meals. But that option is appealing to some students, particularly those in their junior or senior years.

The Faculty

The most important resources of any college or university are its professors. Admissions brochures usually point out the strengths of the faculty, but provide little detail. You should direct your questions about the faculty and other academic matters to the specific department or to the office that coordinates academic advising. Recruiting brochures also emphasize faculty research, because the prestige of professors depends largely on the books and articles they have published. Good researchers may or may not make good teachers. Ask how often the best researchers teach undergraduate courses, and whether they instruct small as well as large classes. For example, a Nobel prize chemist may lecture to 500 students at a time but never show up in the laboratories where graduate assistants actually teach individual students.

Also ask about class size, because this determines the amount of individual attention students get from professors. Student/faculty ratios, which usually range from 10 to 20 students per professor, don't really tell you much. Every school offers a mixture of large and small classes. Ask admission officers for the average size of a freshman class. You will want to look for such factors as those that follow:

- Science and technology courses should enroll only 25 to 30 students in each laboratory session, but may combine a number of laboratory classes for large weekly lectures.
- Skill development courses such as speech, foreign language, English composition, and fine and performing arts should have classes of 25 or fewer. Mathematics and computer science require considerable graded homework, and classes should be no larger than 35.
- Most other courses in humanities, social sciences, and professional areas are taught by classroom lectures and discussion. Classes should average 35 to 45 in introductory courses such as general psychology or American government. They should be smaller in advanced or specialized courses, such as Shakespeare or tax accounting.
- Many introductory courses, especially at universities, are taught in lecture classes of 100 or more. This is acceptable, if those courses also include small weekly discussion groups for individual instruction. Sometimes these discussion groups are taught by graduate student assistants rather than regular professors. Although graduate assistants lack teaching experience, they are very often highly

capable. You should ask whether the teaching done by graduate assistants is closely supervised by regular faculty members.

Academic Programs

Even colleges and universities that boast fine and well qualified faculties can be short of professors in certain programs. Some schools depend on instruction by part-time faculty members or fill in with available teachers from other specializations. Many international students are enrolled in technical doctoral programs, so you may find yourself being taught mathematics or engineering by a teaching assistant who is not a native English speaker. If you are interested in these subjects, check to see whether full-time faculty members teach the majority of the courses.

Other programs may have sufficient faculty but too few student majors. Majors such as physics and philosophy, for example, often have many students in required introductory courses, but few taking the major. Because of small enrollments, these departments may not be able to offer their advanced and specialized courses on a regular basis.

Academic departments give strength to the program by bringing together faculty members who share a common area of study and make sure their students get the classes they need. Some programs, usually called interdisciplinary, are taught by groups of faculty members from several departments. These programs generally have the word *studies* in their titles; for example, Middle-Eastern Studies, Communication Studies, Women's Studies, or Ethnic Studies. If you are enrolled in one of these programs, be sure to ask about the student advising. (Sometimes, advising suffers if faculty members are primarily loyal to their own department.)

Internships

Internships are available at many colleges. They provide an opportunity to experience work in your major and learn from experienced people in your field. Many students have received job offers after participating in an internship program during the school year or during summer vacation. These internships can make a big difference as you enter the job market.

Accreditation

General standards of academic quality are established by associations of colleges and universities through a process called voluntary accreditation. The criteria include: standards for admission of students; faculty qualifications; content of courses; grading standards; professional success of alumni; adequacy of libraries, laboratories, computers, and other support facilities; administrative systems and policy decision making; and financial support.

Six regional associations (New England, Middle States, Southern, North Central, Northwest, and Western) evaluate and accredit colleges as total institutions. Bible colleges have their own accrediting association. Other organizations evaluate and accredit specific programs, primarily in technical fields, like engineering and architecture; or those that require licensing, such as teaching and health care.

Libraries and Computer Technology

Most people judge libraries by the size of the collection, the bigger the better. Collection size is important, but only in relation to the variety and level of programs offered. A small liberal arts college can support its baccalaureate programs with a collection of 200,000 to 400,000 volumes. A university with many professional schools and doctoral programs may require over 2 million. Many books and journals are available through various methods of information technology, computer storage, and the Internet.

The main stacks should be open to students, with the possible exception of rare books, bound journals, and other special items. Open stacks encourage browsing and save students from waiting on line while a library assistant fetches a few books at a time. Instead, assistants constantly should be picking up unused materials from reading desks or carts and putting them back on the shelves.

Good circulation policies encourage students to check materials out for short periods and to return them promptly. One week or less loans are appropriate for books regularly used in courses, and four week loans should be the maximum for other materials. A recall system should be available to get back borrowed material when it is needed. Journals, reference material, or books placed on reserve for assigned reading should be used within the library while it is open, and circulated overnight only at closing time.

Using a computer is integral to university study. Some institutions require students to have personal computers. Colleges often offer the best price for new computers. You may want to check out the options on campus before you purchase a computer elsewhere. Many residence hall rooms are wired for computers and direct connections are linked to the main campus system. More and more campuses have wireless capability.

Religious/Ethnic Considerations

For some students, the religious life of the campus is important as college choices are reviewed. Religious life can vary from being pervasive to being absent. Most colleges are independent of religious influence. Some are historically affiliated with a religious group, yet religious matters are not part of student life. Other schools exist, in part, to educate students in the doctrine and the practices of their own religious perspective. Information you find on these pages will give you answers to some of your initial questions about religious life at particular schools.

If connecting with and learning from members of your racial/ethnic heritage is important, you will find many colleges and universities from which to choose. Again, this guide provides information about the diversity of the campus and the composition of students who are white, African-American, Hispanic, Asian-American, Latino, and so forth.

GETTING THE MOST FROM YOUR CAMPUS VISIT

It is best not to eliminate any options without at least visiting a few campuses of different types to judge their feeling and style first hand.

To learn everything important about a college, you need more than the standard presentation and tour given to visiting students and parents. Plan your visit for a weekday during the school term. This will let you see how classes are taught and how students live. It also is the best time to meet faculty and staff members. If the college does not schedule group presentations or tours at the time you want, call the office of admissions to arrange for an individual tour and interview. (This is more likely at a small college.) At the same time, ask the admissions office to make appointments with people you want to meet.

To find out about a specific academic program, ask to meet the department chairperson or a professor. If you are interested in athletics, religion, or music, arrange to meet with the coach, the chaplain, or the conductor of the orchestra. Your parents will also want to talk to a financial aid counselor about scholarships, grants, and loans. The office of academic affairs can help with your questions about courses or the faculty. The office of student affairs is in charge of residence halls, health services, and extracurricular activities. Each of these areas has a dean or vice president and a number of assistants, so you should be able to get your questions answered even if you go in without an appointment.

Take advantage of a group presentation and tour if one is scheduled on the day of your visit. Much of what you learn may be familiar, but other students and parents will ask about some of the same things you want to know. Student tour guides are also good sources of information. They love to talk about their own courses, professors, and campus experiences.

Finally, explore the campus on your own. Check the condition of the buildings and the grounds. If they appear well maintained, the college probably has good overall management. If they look run down, the college may have financial problems that also make it scrimp on the book budget or laboratory supplies. Visit a service office, such as the registrar, career planning, or academic advising. Observe whether they treat students courteously and seem genuinely interested in helping them. Look at bulletin boards for signs of campus activities.

And, perhaps most importantly, talk to some of the students who are already enrolled at the college. They will usually speak frankly about weekend activities, whether they find it easy to talk to professors out of class, and how much drinking or drug abuse there is on campus. Most importantly, meeting other students will help you discover how friendly the campus is and whether the college will suit you socially and intellectually.

More than buildings and courses of study, a college is a community of people. Only during a campus visit can you experience the human environment in which you will live and work during four critical years.

25 CRITICAL QUESTIONS

The following questions form a checklist to evaluate each college or university you are considering. Use the profiles, material from the colleges, and your own inquiries and observations to get the answers.

1. Do I have a reasonable chance of being admitted?
2. Can my family manage the costs?
3. Is the overall size of the school right for my personality?
4. Is the location right? (Consider such specifics as region, distance from a major city, distance from home, and weather.)
5. Are class sizes right for my learning style and my need for involvement in class?
6. Will I be comfortable with the setting of the campus?
7. Are the housing and food services suitable?
8. Does the college offer the program I want to study? (Or, often more importantly, does the college offer people and classes that will help me decide what I want to study?)
9. Will the college push me academically, but not shove me?
10. Do the best professors teach undergraduate courses?
11. Can I change majors easily, if I need to?
12. Do students say the majority of classes are taught by fun, stimulating, interesting professors?
13. Is the library collection adequate and accessible?
14. Are computer facilities readily available and are campus networking opportunities up-to-date?
15. Is the connection to the Internet adequate?
16. Are there resources for career development?
17. Do the people in the financial aid, housing, and other service offices seem attentive and genuinely interested in helping students?
18. Will I find activities that meet my interests?
19. Does the campus seem well maintained and managed?
20. Will the college meet my religious and/or ethnic needs?

And, finally, the five most critical questions:
21. Is there a good chance I will be academically successful there?
22. Will I be happy as a student there?
23. Do I seem compatible with the student population? Do they seem to enjoy what I enjoy?
24. Does the student life seem in sync with my personality and my goals? Is the student life what I'm looking for in a college?
25. Does the college "feel" right for me?

Steven R. Antonoff
Sheldon Halpern
Barbara Aronson

COLLEGE ENTRANCE EXAMINATIONS

By providing you with exactly the same information about each of the colleges in which you are interested, the book you are now reading, *Profiles of American Colleges*, will help you narrow down the list of colleges to which you will apply. Of course, your final decision will be influenced by many other factors, many of which are far more important: actual visits to the colleges; virtual visits on the Internet; viewings of videotapes; advice from guidance counselors, parents, teachers, and friends.

In much the same way, by providing college admissions officers with the same information about thousands of applicants, the results of college entrance exams can help them narrow down the list of students they are considering accepting. The results of these exams help admissions officers compare students with widely differing backgrounds. Students from different high schools in different states who earn the same grade in their biology classes, B+ say, have used different textbooks, have performed different labs, have taken different tests, and in general often exhibit great disparity in their level of mastery of the subject; indeed, even within the same school, a grade of B+ from one teacher might not represent the same level of accomplishment as a B+ from another teacher. However, a grade of 650 on the Biology SAT Subject Test, or a 4 on the Biology AP test means the same thing whether it was earned by a student from a rural community in Idaho, an inner-city school in New York, or a private prep school in Massachusetts. Because students all across the country take the same standardized test on the same day, colleges can give greater credence to the results, than they can to the results of final exams from different schools.

KINDS OF COLLEGE ENTRANCE EXAMINATIONS

Although some students who go from high school to two-year community colleges do not take any college entrance tests, most do, and virtually all students who are applying to four-year colleges will take some of the following exams:

- PSAT/NMSQT or the Preliminary SAT/National Merit Scholarship Qualifying Test.
- SAT Reasoning Test.
- SAT Subject Tests.
- Advanced Placement (AP) Examinations.
- The ACT Assessment.

The PSAT/NMSQT

The PSAT/NMSQT measures verbal and mathematical reasoning necessary for success in college. It is a standardized test taken by students in high schools throughout the country, in October of their junior year. The test consists of five sections: two 25-minute critical reading sections, two 25-minute math sections, and one 30-minute writing section.

This Preliminary SAT is also the qualifying test for the scholarship competition conducted by the National Merit Scholarship Corporation, an independent, nonprofit organization supported by grants from over 600 corporations, private foundations, colleges, and universities. All students whose scores are in the top 5% of students taking the exam that year receive National Merit Letters of Commendation. In addition, students whose scores are in the top 1% of those taking the exam that year become National Merit Semifinalists. Those who advance to finalist standing by meeting additional requirements compete for one-time National Merit $2000 Scholarships and renewable four-year Merit Scholarships, which may be worth as much as $2000 a year or more for four years.

In addition, this test is used by the National Achievement Scholarship Program for outstanding African American students. Top-scoring black students in each of the regional selection units established for the competition continue in the competition for nonrenewable National Achievement $2000 Scholarships and for four-year Achievement Scholarships sponsored by more than 175 organizations.

Test-Taking Strategies for the PSAT/NMSQT

1. Know what to expect. Each critical reading section has sentence completion questions and reading comprehension questions. A few of the reading questions are based on short passages (often a single paragraph), whereas most are based on longer passages (typically four to seven paragraphs). The first math section has 20 multiple-choice questions; the second math section has 8 quantitative comparison questions and 10 questions for which no choices are provided and whose answers must be entered in a special grid. Calculators may be used on any question in the math sections. The writing skills section, which does *not* have an essay, has three types of multiple-choice questions that test your knowledge of standard written English (grammar and usage).

2. On average, wild guessing has no effect on your score. Educated guessing, on the other hand, can improve your score dramatically. On all multiple-choice questions, try to eliminate as many obviously incorrect answer choices as possible, and then guess from among the choices still remaining.

3. Expect easy questions at the beginning of each set of the same question type. Within each set (except for the reading comprehension questions), the questions progress from easy to difficult. In other words, the first sentence completion questions in a set will be easier than the last sentence completion questions in that set; the first grid-in questions will be easier than the last ones.

4. Take advantage of the easy questions to boost your score. Remember: each question is worth the same number of points. Whether it is easy or difficult, whether it takes you ten seconds or two minutes to answer, you get the same number of points for each question you answer correctly. Your job is to answer as many questions as you can without rushing so fast that you make careless errors. Take enough time to get those easy questions right!

The SAT

The SAT is a reasoning test consisting of three parts—critical reading, mathematical reasoning, and writing. It is designed to measure your ability to do college work. Part of the test deals with verbal skills with an emphasis on critical reading including a double passage with different points of view. The critical reading sections measure the extent of your vocabulary, your ability to interpret and create ideas, and your ability to reason logically and draw conclusions correctly. The mathematics part measures your ability to reason with numbers and mathematical concepts. It tests your ability to handle general number concepts rather than specific achievement in mathematics. Calculators are permitted on each math section.

The writing part consists of a short essay and multiple-choice questions that test your knowledge of standard written English (grammar and usage).

The SAT is given on seven Saturdays during the year—once each in January, March, May, June, October, November, and December. Applicants may request, for religious reasons, to take the test on the Sunday following the regularly scheduled date.

You can register online at *www.collegeboard.org* or by mail by using the registration form available at your school.

On each part of the SAT—critical reading, math, and writing—you will receive a scaled score between 200 and 800. On each part the national mean is approximately 500.

Test-Taking Strategies for the SAT

1. Pace yourself properly. It is much better to slow down and avoid careless errors than it is to speed up in an effort to answer all the questions. You can earn an above-average score (over 1000) by correctly answering fewer than half of the questions on the test and omitting the rest. Even scores of 1300 can be achieved by omitting more than 20% of the questions.

2. Read carefully. Make sure you are answering the question asked, not a similar one you once encountered. Underline key words (e.g., NOT and EXCEPT) to make sure you do not answer the opposite of the question asked.

3. Learn the directions for each type of question before taking the test. During the test, do not waste even one second reading the directions or looking at the sample questions.

4. Always answer the easy questions first (the ones at the beginning of each section). Do not panic if you can't answer a question. Do not spend too much time on any one question. If you are truly stuck, make an educated guess if possible (see below), and move on. Remember that each question is worth the same one point, and the next few questions may be much easier for you.

5. On average, wild guessing does not affect your score—it is unlikely to help, but it is equally unlikely to hurt you. The choice is yours. However, educated guessing—when you can eliminate one or more of the answer choices—can significantly increase your score! In particular, don't omit critical reading questions if you have read the passage; you can always eliminate some of the choices. Most math questions contain at least one or two choices that are absurd (for example, negative choices when you know that the answer must be positive); eliminate them and guess.

SAT Subject Tests

These tests are one-hour, multiple-choice question tests. You may take one, two, or three tests on any one test date. Some colleges do not require SAT Subject Tests. Of those that do, some colleges require specific subject tests, whereas others allow applicants to choose the ones they wish to present with the admission application. Those colleges that do require these tests may use them to determine acceptance or placement in college courses. The tests in foreign language not only are used for placement, but also for possible exemption from a foreign language requirement. If the college of your choice does not require these tests, but you would like to demonstrate proficiency in a particular field, take the test anyway and have your scores sent. Tests are given in literature, history, mathematics, sciences, and several foreign languages.

Advanced Placement (AP) Examinations

The College Board also conducts Advanced Placement tests, given to high school students who have completed advanced or honors courses and wish to get college credit. Many secondary schools offer college-level courses in calculus, statistics, art, psychology, European history, American history, Latin, Spanish, French, German, biology, chemistry, and physics. As a result of scores obtained on these tests, colleges grant credit or use the results for placement in advanced college courses.

The ACT Assessment

The registration form for the ACT includes a detailed questionnaire that takes about one hour to complete. As a result of the answers to those questions about your high school courses, personal interests, and career plans, plus the scores on your ACT, an ACT Assessment Student Report is produced. This is made available to you, your high school, and to any college or scholarship source that you request. Decisions regarding college acceptance and award of scholarships are the result. This information is kept confidential and is released only according to your written instructions. To obtain an ACT application form, write or call ACT Registration, P.O. Box 414, Iowa City, Iowa 52243, telephone (319) 337-1270.

The ACT measures knowledge, understanding, and skills acquired in the educational process. The test is made up of four distinct sections: English, mathematics, reading, and science reasoning.

In addition, you may register to take an optional fifth section: a 30-minute writing test. Some colleges require their applicants to take the writing test, but most do not. Check with the colleges to which you will be applying to know whether you need to take the writing part of the ACT.

On the ACT, you should answer all questions, because your score is based on the number of questions you answer correctly. There is no penalty for wrong answers. For each of the four tests the total number of correct responses yields a raw score. A table is used to convert the raw scores to *scaled scores*. The highest possible scaled score for each test is 36. The average of the four scaled scores yields the *composite score*.

The ACT English Test is a 75-question, 45-minute test that measures punctuation, grammar, usage, and sentence structure. The test consists of five passages, each accompanied by multiple-choice test items.

Test-Taking Strategies for the ACT English Test

1. Pace yourself. You have 45 minutes to complete 75 questions.
2. Read the sentences immediately before and after the one containing an underlined portion.

The ACT Mathematics Test has 60 questions to answer in 60 minutes. The test emphasizes quantitative reasoning rather than memorized formulas. Five content areas are included in the mathematics test. About 14 questions deal with pre-algebra topics, such as operations with whole numbers, decimals, fractions, and integers and about 10 questions deal with elementary algebra. Usually 18 questions are based on intermediate algebra and coordinate geometry. About 14 questions are based on plane geometry and usually four items are based on right triangle trigonometry and basic trigonometric identities.

Test-Taking Strategies for the ACT Mathematics Test

1. Spend an average of one minute on each question, less on the easy questions, more on the difficult ones.
2. Be sure to answer each question even if you have to guess.
3. Make sure your answers are reasonable.

The ACT Reading Test is a 40-question, 35-minute test that measures reading comprehension. Three scores are reported for this test: a total score, a subscore based on the 20 items in the social studies and natural sciences sections, and a subscore on the 20 items in the prose fiction and humanities sections.

Test-Taking Strategies for the ACT Reading Test

1. Read each passage carefully. Underline important ideas in the passage.
2. Pace yourself. You have 40 questions to answer in 35 minutes.

3. Refer to the passage and in particular to your underlined sections when answering the questions.

The ACT Science Reasoning Test presents seven sets of scientific information in three different formats: data representations (graphs, tables, and other schematic forms); research summaries (description of experiments); and conflicting viewpoints. The 40 questions are to be answered in 35 minutes. The content of the test is drawn from biology, chemistry, physics, geology, astronomy, and meteorology. Background knowledge at the level of a high school general science course is all that is needed to answer these questions. The test emphasizes scientific reasoning skills rather than recall of scientific content, skill in mathematics, or reading ability.

Test-Taking Strategies for the ACT Science Reasoning Test

1. Read the scientific material before you begin answering a question. Read tables and text carefully, underlining important ideas.
2. Look for flaws in the experiments and devise ways of improving the experiments.
3. When you are asked to compare viewpoints, make notes in the margin of the printed material summarizing each viewpoint.

A FINAL WORD

Don't take any examination without preparation, even though you will find descriptions of these tests that say they test skills developed over years of study both in and out of school. Don't walk in cold, even though you believe that you meet all the qualities colleges are looking for.

Although the College Board suggests no special preparation, it does distribute to applicants the booklet, "Taking the SAT Reasoning Test." It also makes available other publications containing former test questions along with advice on how to cope with the questions. Evidently, all candidates need some form of preparation.

The American College Testing Program furnishes the booklet, "Preparing for the ACT Assessment." This gives specific information about the test, test questions, and strategies for taking each of the four parts. It also describes what to expect on the test day and gives practice with typical questions.

Barron's Educational Series publishes books to help you prepare for these tests. They are available at all bookstores and in many libraries. You should be sure to use them before taking any of these tests.

Although no high school student takes all of the college-entrance exams described above, virtually all students planning to attend a four-year college take at least one of them—the SAT or ACT. Prepare conscientiously for each exam that you take and you will provide the colleges to which you are applying with valuable information about your abilities. Good luck!

Ira K. Wolf
President
PowerPrep, Inc.

The college admission process—getting in—begins the minute you start making your first choices in course selection and in cocurricular activities in junior high school, middle school, and high school. These initial and ongoing decisions are crucial to your future well-being. They lay the groundwork for the curriculum you will follow throughout your high school career: they are not easily reversed. These are the decisions that will allow you to market yourself to the colleges of your choice.

STUDENTS TAKE NOTE!

There is a myth prevalent among college-bound students throughout the country that the best way to gain entrance to the selective colleges is to be well rounded. This term usually refers to students who have earned good grades in high school (B+ or better) and participated in a wide range of cocurricular activities.

However, most admission officers at the selective colleges prefer applications from candidates they term angular—students who have demonstrated solid academic achievement in and out of school *and* who have developed one or two particularly strong cocurricular skills, interests, and activities. These angular students are very different in character from the well-rounded students who are very good at everything, yet excel at little, if anything.

William Fitzsimmons, Dean of Admission at Harvard, says that Harvard is looking for a well-rounded class, which means Harvard is most interested in admitting angular students—students who have excelled at something. He cautions, though, that "...It is a mistake to denigrate or underestimate that persuasive power of high grades, rank, triple 800s on the SAT, 36 on the ACT, and equally impressive SAT Subject Test scores. The selective colleges take many of these academically high profile applicants. But the numbers game alone often won't get you in! It would be fairly simple for Harvard to enroll an entire freshman class with a superior academic profile and little depth of quality in areas that make up the personality of the class. We just would not do that!"

Dean Fitzsimmons is saying that the majority of the successful applicants to selective colleges must have some major commitment(s) combined with excellent academic qualities. A strong impact results from quality involvements rather than a proliferation of joinings and transient interests. Essentially, the angular applicant is a committed individual, while the well-rounded candidate is merely involved.

STUDENTS AND PARENTS TAKE AN EARLY, ACTIVE ROLE

Students and parents must make time to ensure an early, active role in the college admissions process. Each year, starting in the seventh grade, students and parents should take the time to sit down with the student's guidance counselor and talk meaningfully about the following:

- selection and level of courses, projecting through the senior year of high school;
- cocurricular activities available, such as drama, music, athletics, academic clubs, community activities, student government, and other special interest groups; and
- summer study, work, or recreation.

Why is this important to getting in? As sure as taxes and death, there is going to come a time in your senior year when you, the college-bound student, will be asked to choose colleges, complete the college application, write your college essay(s), and have an interview—either on the college campus, or in your hometown.

You must create the personal marketing, which will take place during the application process in your senior year, long before your senior year starts. By the time you reach that long-awaited dream of being a senior, you and you alone have created the person you must market to the colleges of your choice. You must understand that the person you have created is the only person you have to market. There is no Madison Avenue glitz involved in this marketing process! You don't create a pseudo marketing campaign that shows you jumping off a bridge with a bungee cord tied to your sneakers. Admission counselors can tell the difference between a real marketing effort and a pseudo marketing campaign.

THE APPLICATION FORM

Today colleges are offering their application on hard copy, computer disk, E-mail, or through on-line services of the Internet. Each application form differs from college to college, with the exception of those colleges that use the common application. When you start to work, be sure to note all deadlines, follow all directions, be complete, be neat, fill out the geographical data with accurate facts, and type it all (unless you print exceptionally well). Always review the entire application before you start to fill it out, and complete the entire application before you start the next one. Remember the application is *you* to the admissions committee member reading it. Even though "a book should not be judged by its cover," appearances do influence opinions.

It is best to work through a rough draft of the application before you actually work on the application copy to be submitted. Remember to make a copy of all parts of the finished application in the event that yours gets lost and a replacement must be sent.

You are responsible for giving the Secondary School Report, found in each application, directly to your high school guidance counselor. Your counselor is responsible for sending official copies of grades, rank in class (if any), the school's profile, and a written recommendation regarding you. It also is your responsibility to call or fill out the appropriate forms for either the SAT and/or SAT Subject Tests or the ACT, to send the appropriate test information directly to each college to which you have applied, even if your scores are on your high school transcript. Your college file will not be considered complete, and will not be sent to the admission committee for a decision, without these official scores. Additionally, many colleges want recommendations from one or two teachers. Choose wisely and allow each teacher plenty of time. Request letters from teachers who know you best. If English is your interest, be sure to choose an English teacher. If you are fluent in Spanish and have future interest in Spanish at college, ask the Spanish teacher. Remember, though you have many interests and have participated in many activities—you are developing an admissions package as part of your marketing of yourself. Emphasize your strengths and show how they are integrated into your activities and achievements.

Cocurricular activities usually are athletic or nonathletic. If you have won athletic awards, note them. If you have had the starring role in the spring musical for the last two years, say so. If you are an editor on the school newspaper, specify this. Admissions people view your activities with special interest. They realize how very time consuming these activities can be and how they sometimes bring very few accolades. List these activities in the order of importance to you. If you do not believe that the application allows you the opportunity to show your depth of commitment to one or two cocurricular areas, you may add an addendum. Use the KISS (Keep It Short and Simple) method. This is an addendum, not an essay, letter, or dissertation. Be honest!

Some applications have mini essays. When space is provided, be sure you are concise, clear, and grammatically correct. Here, less is more. Your ability to organize your thoughts and present them concisely is being tested. You will receive your chance to impress each college with your prose in the long essay segment of the application. Some colleges have as many as four long essays, whereas some require none. In addition to the short and long essay questions, some colleges ask the student for a graded paper signed by the teacher.

Some colleges encourage you to support your application with additional materials. If you are given this option, consider what will strengthen your application: musical tapes, art and/or photography portfolios, published writings, an exceptional graded term paper, all the additional opportunities for the college to get to know you better and for you to increase your image as an angular candidate. Such additions help the admissions committee to get a better handle on who you are in relation to other applicants. Be sure your presentation is clear and as professional as possible. These additions are not going to be evaluated by the admissions committee. Your material will be directed to the appropriate department for evaluation and an evaluative note will be sent back to the admissions committee. It is this note that will become part of your admissions package, the same way an athletic coach evaluates potential student/athletes.

Proofread all parts of the application. Be sure you, the student, place your signature where it is required. If you are not sending your application on-line, then place everything, including the registration fee check, in a large manila envelope and give it to your college guidance counselor. After adding the completed Secondary School Report to the application, your guidance counselor will mail it. Your job is now finished and the waiting begins!

E-Mail, On-line Services through the College or the Internet

We have joined the 21st century with E-mail and on-line services of the Internet offering college applications. This movement promises to be the wave of the future. Certainly ecologically correct, by producing as close to a paperless process as possible, this method is still in cyberspace. Be sure you know what you are doing when you use any of these methods. It is seriously suggested that you take the time to call the college shortly after sending this type of application, to ensure that your application is on file. If you have an addendum or two, you may want to speak to an admission clerk to make sure each addendum has reached the office of admission in the format you desired. If it were my application and I chose any of these methods, I'd still send my musical tape, the slides for my art portfolio, and such, by certified or registered mail. Clarity is so important to the professionals who will be evaluating these addenda for your college admission process!

PC- and Mac-Based Computer Disk Applications

Since the emergence of on-line applications, fewer colleges have a computer disk application. If you wish to apply this way, make sure that your target college has authorized the disk: there are a number of organizations selling computer disk applications without the consent of the college. Make sure the service to which you have subscribed allows you to print a hard copy of the application, even if they want you to send the disk back to the service or to the college. Do yourself a favor and print an extra copy of the application for your personal college file—it is very easy for the post office or college to lose your information. It is also wise, if you have to send the disk with the application, to write, "DO NOT SCAN" on the envelope. It is highly probable that the information on the disk will be lost if it is passed through a scanning machine.

The Common Application

About 200 colleges in the United States have agreed that students may apply to their colleges by completing one common application. Some of the colleges using the common application also have their own application. Students applying to a college that allows an applicant a choice of using either the college's own application or the common application, obviously face a choice. The use of the common application substantially reduces the time spent composing different essay answers and neatly typing separate application forms. If you are one of those who must make a choice between the common application and the application of the college, you should understand that each college using the common application (either as its only application or as an alternative application) has the right to ask for a supplement. If you choose the common application, be very sure to read the pages surrounding the common application carefully.

Each college has a paragraph in which they discuss their deadlines, requirements for admission, and specify if they require supplemental information. The supplemental information can range from an additional essay or two, to additional information about your cocurricular activities.

All the colleges participating in the common application have each member of their admission staff sign a statement that they will NOT discriminate in the admissions process among students who submit the common application versus students who submit the college's application. However, there are counselors who believe that when there is a choice, the applicant has a better chance of conveying information by using the college's application; there is a vast difference in format between the two applications, even if the college requires a supplement. Check with your guidance counselor if you are unsure regarding your choice of format. To access the common application online, go to:
www.commonapp.org

College Web Sites

Most colleges today have their own web site. Here you will find a wealth of information. Some colleges have even put their viewbook, course curriculum guide, a campus tour, as well as their application, on their site. Visit each college's web page—the addresses are in the Admissions Contact section of the college Profiles in this book. You'll be a much better informed consumer.

THE INTERVIEW

The interview is a contrived situation that few people enjoy, of which many people misunderstand the value, and about which everyone is apprehensive. However, no information from a college catalog, no friend's friend, no high school guidance counselor's comments, and no parental remembrances from bygone days can surpass the value of your college campus visit and interview. This first hand opportunity to assess your future alma mater will confirm or contradict other impressions and help you make a sound college acceptance.

Many colleges will recommend or request a personal interview. It is best to travel to the campus to meet with a member of the admissions staff if you can; however, if you can't, many colleges will arrange to have one of their representatives, usually an alumnus, interview you in your hometown.

Even though the thought of an interview might give you enough butterflies to lift you to the top of your high school's flagpole, here are some tips that might make it a little easier.

1. **Go prepared.** Read the college's catalog and this book's Profile ahead of time so you won't ask "How many books are in your library?" or "How many students do you have?" Ask intelligent questions that introduce a topic of conversation that you want the interviewer to know about you. The key is to distinguish yourself in a positive way from thousands of other applicants. Forge the final steps in the marketing process you have been building since your first choices in the college admission process back in junior high school. The interview is your chance to enhance those decisions.

2. **Nervousness** is absolutely and entirely normal. The best way to handle it is to admit it, out loud, to the interviewer. Richard Shaw, Dean of Admission at Yale University, sometimes relates this true story to his apprehensive applicants. One extremely agitated young applicant sat opposite him for her interview with her legs crossed, wearing loafers on her feet. She swung her top leg back and forth to some inaudible rhythm. The loafer on her top foot flew off her foot, hit him in the head, ricocheted to the desk lamp and broke it. She looked at him in terror, but when their glances met, they both dissolved in

laughter. The moral of the story—the person on the other side of the desk is also a human being and wants to put you at ease. So admit to your anxiety, and don't swing your foot if you're wearing loafers! (And by the way, she was admitted.)

3. **Be yourself.** Nobody's perfect, and everyone knows nobody's perfect, so admit to a flaw or two before the interviewer goes hunting for them. The truly impressive candidate will convey a thorough knowledge of self.

4. **Interview the interviewer.** Don't passively sit there and allow the interviewer to ask all the questions and direct the conversation. Participate in this responsibility by assuming an active role. A thoughtful questioner will accomplish three important tasks in a successful interview:

   demonstrate interest, initiative, and maturity for taking partial responsibility for the content of the conversation; **guide the conversation** to areas where he/she feels most secure and accomplished; and **obtain answers.** Use your genuine feelings to react to the answers you hear. If you are delighted to learn of a certain program or activity, show it. If you are curious, ask more questions. If you are disappointed by something you learn, try to find a path to a positive answer. Then consider yourself lucky that you discovered this particular inadequacy in time.

5. **Parents** do belong in your college decision process as your advisers! Often it is they who spend the megabucks for your next four years. They can provide psychological support and a stabilizing influence for sensible, rational decisions. However, they do NOT belong in your interview session. In essence, the sage senior will find constructive ways to include parents in the decision-making process as catalysts, without letting them take over (as many are apt to do) the interview process. You may want your parents to meet and speak briefly to your interviewer prior to your interview and that is fine, but parents may not accompany you into the interview session! Arrange with your parents to meet somewhere out of the interview building after your interview is over. You do not want the interviewer inviting your parents back to the interview room. As intelligent as parents may be, they do not perceive the answers to questions the same way you do. The worst scenario I can imagine is the interviewer asking your parents some of the same questions that were asked you, and that is highly likely. Parents just answer questions differently than teenagers. At best, the scenario creates a long, long ride home, and when you get home you can't punish your parents by taking the car keys away from them, or grounding them for a week. At worst, the scenario has caused a blight in your admissions file. This is your time! Keep it that way!

6. **Practice makes perfect.** Begin your interviews at colleges that are low on your list of preferred choices, and leave your first-choice colleges until last. If you are shy, you will have a chance to practice vocalizing what your usually silent inner voice tells you. Others will have the opportunity to commit their inevitable first blunders where they won't count as much.

7. **Departing impressions.** There is a remarkable tendency for the student to base final college preferences on the quality of the interview only, or on the personal reaction to the interviewer as the personification of the entire institution. Do not do yourself the disservice of letting it influence an otherwise rational selection, one based on institutional programs, students, services, and environment. After the last good-bye and thank you has been smiled, and you exhale deeply on your way out the door, go ahead and congratulate yourself. If you used the interview properly, you will know whether or not you wish to attend that college and why.

8. **Send a thank-you note** to your interviewer. A short and simple handwritten or typed note will do—and if you forgot to mention something important about yourself at the interview, here's your chance.

WRITING THE COLLEGE ESSAY

Do the colleges read the essays you write on their applications? You bet your diploma they do. Here is your chance to strut your stuff, stand up, be counted, and stylize your way into the hearts of the decision makers.

Write it, edit it, review it. Rewrite it. Try to show why you are unique and how the college will benefit having you in its student body. This is not a routine homework assignment, but a college level essay that will be carefully examined for spelling, grammar, content, and style of a high school senior. As strenuous an effort as it may be, completing the essay gives the admissions committee a chance to know the real you, a three-dimensional human being with passions, preferences, strengths, weaknesses, imagination, energy, and ambition. Your ability to market yourself will help the deans and directors of admission remember your application from among the sea of thousands that flood their offices each year.

First, maximize your strengths—use your essays to say what you want to say. The answer to a specific question on the college's part still provides an opening for you to furnish background information about yourself, your interests, ambitions, and insights. For example, the essay that asks you to name your favorite book and the reason for your selection could be answered with the title of a Dr. Seuss book because you are considering a career as an elementary school teacher. If you are interested in business, read about a famous businessman you admire and then discuss your interest in business.

Whatever the essay questions are, autobiographical or otherwise, select the person or issue that puts you in the position to discuss the subject in which you are the most well versed. In essence, all of your essay responses are autobiographical in the sense that they will illustrate something important about yourself, your values, and the kind of person you are (or hope to become). If personal values are important to you, and they should be, then here is your opportunity to stress their importance.

Because many colleges will ask for more than one essay, make sure that the *sum* of the essays in any one college application covers your best points. Do not repeat your answers, even if the questions sound alike. Cover the most important academic and cocurricular activities (most important meaning the one in which you excelled and/or in which you spent the most quality time).

If you are fortunate to have a cooperative English teacher, you might request a critique of your first draft, but be sure to allow enough time for a careful evaluation and your revision.

Write the essays yourself—no substitutes or stand-ins. College admission professionals can discern mature adult prose from student prose.

PARTING WORDS

You may wish to ask yourself the following questions to help you decide which is your Paradise College. Most of this information is in the individual college Profiles in this book.

1. **Caliber of School Programs** Is the college known for its English department or chemistry department? What are its strengths?

2. **Selectivity of Admissions** Is the college Most Competitive, Highly Competitive, Very Competitive, Competitive, Less Competitive or Noncompetitive? Check the Selector Ratings.

3. **Chances of Admission** Be realistic. What are your chances of getting in? How far can you reach? Listen when you are given advice!

4. **Location of the School**   Is the school near home, one hour away, 300 miles away, or across the United States?

5. **Rural, Suburban, Urban Campus**   Is the school in the city or in a rural area?

6. **Size of the School**   Can you spend four years at a small liberal arts college of 800 undergraduates? Do you need the larger atmosphere of a university? Do not equate size with social life!

7. **State College vs. Private College**   Is the college a large state university with most of the student population from the state where it's located? Is it one of the public "Ivies"? Will you be a minority in the state school?

8. **Geographical Diversity**   Is the college a regional one attracting students from the same state or region? Or is it a college, regardless of its size, which attracts students from all over the United States, or the world at large?.

9. **Cost of College**   What is the tuition? What are the living costs? What travel costs are there from home to campus? Are there hidden costs?

10. **Financial Aid**   With a great percentage of undergraduates at many private colleges on financial aid of some type, where do you fit? What monies are available for the students at the schools of your choice? Is the college need blind in its admission program?

11. **Living Conditions**   Is housing on campus guaranteed for all four years? Are the dorms coed? Are there single-sex dorms? Are alternatives in housing available?

12. **Socialization**   Is it a grind school—all work, work, work? Is it fraternity- and sorority-oriented? What are the on-campus facilities for socialization?

13. **Safety on Campus**   Are the dorms secure and locked? What's the safety system on the campus?

14. **Core Curriculum—Distribution Credits**   Does the college require (for graduation) a specific number of credits in different academic disciplines? For example, does the student have to take six credits in philosophy before graduating? Is a self-designed curriculum possible?

15. **Sophomore Standing**   Does the college accept AP credits? Does it offer advanced standing for an AP course, or just a credit toward graduation?

16. **Junior Year Abroad**   Are there opportunities to study in Italy, Japan, or Australia, for example, while you are an undergraduate?

17. **Internships**   Are there opportunities for hands-on experience while in college? Which departments have formal internship opportunities?

18. **Graduate School After College**   What percentage of its graduates go on to graduate school immediately upon graduation, or within five years? What is the record of those who successfully get into the law, medical, or business school of their choice?

19. **Placement After Graduation**   Is there an office for job placement after college? Is there an alumni network that helps in job placement?

20. **Weekend College**   Do the students remain on campus on weekends, or is it a suitcase college?

21. **Minorities**   What percentage of the students are minorities? Reflect on the racial, ethnic, and religious minority roles in the college you are considering. How would you feel being Jewish at a Roman Catholic college for example—or Catholic at a Jewish college?

22. **Sports Facilities**   Is there a swimming pool? Are there horse stables? Is there an ice hockey rink on campus?

23. **Library Facilities**   How many books are in the library? Is it computerized? Is the campus library tied into a larger network?

24. **Athletic Programs**   Is the ice hockey team a varsity sport? Does the lacrosse team play Division I or III? Is basketball strong? Do they have a women's squash team?

25. **Honors Programs**   Are honors programs available? What are they? Who is eligible?

26. **Student Body**   Are the students politically active? Are they professional in orientation?

27. **Faculty**   Are all classes taught by full professors? Or are TAs (teaching assistants) the norm?

28. **Computer Labs**   Are computers required of incoming freshmen? What are the facilities on campus? Can you have your own PC in your room?

29. **Campus Visits**   If possible, make a visit to the campus. Spend some time talking to students for a feel of the campus.

30. **Special Talents**   Recognize your special talents and discover where they fit best. Often, a special talent becomes a scale-tipper in the admissions process.

31. **Special Family Circumstances**   Talk with your parents about their expectations. Discuss your needs as well as their thoughts.

32. **Legacy**   Does your family have a history at a specific school? Are you interested in continuing the tradition?

33. **Note Well—Final List**   Be sure the final list is a realistic one. It should include "reaches," "targets," and "safeties." No matter which one admits you—it must fit!

Finding and applying to the best colleges for you is not supposed to be easy, but it can be fun. Parents, guidance counselors, and teachers are there to help you, so don't struggle alone. Keep your sense of humor and a smile on your face as you go about researching, exploring, and discovering your ideal college.

Last but not least is The Parent Credo: The right college is the one where your child will fit in scholastically and socially. Be realistic in your aspirations and support the child's choice!

Anthony F. Capraro, III, Ph.D.
President, Teach Inc.
College Counseling
Purchase, New York

Postsecondary education is a major American industry. A greater proportion of students pursue postsecondary education in the United States than in any other industrialized country. Annually, more than 13 million students study at over 8000 institutions of higher learning. The diversity of our system of higher education is admired by educators and students throughout the world. There is no reason to believe that this system will change in the future. However, college costs and the resources available to parents and students to meet those costs have changed.

Unfortunately, many high school students and their parents believe either that there is no financial aid available or that they will not qualify for any type of financial assistance from any source. Neither assumption is correct. College costs have increased and will continue to increase. Federal allocations, for some financial aid programs, have decreased. But this decline has been met with generous increases in financial aid from state and school sources.

American students and their parents should realize that they must assume the primary role in planning to meet their future college costs and that the family financial planning process must begin much earlier than has been the case.

COLLEGE COSTS

- Nearly all parents believe college costs are too expensive.
- Currently, the average cost of education, including tuition, fees, and room and board for one year at a public college would have been about $10,000 and for a private college and university, the total cost could have exceeded $20,000.
- While college costs will increase each year, it is important to remember that currently nearly 3/4 of all college students attend schools with tuition costs below $10,000.

STUDENT FINANCIAL AID

- In 2006, the total amount of financial aid available from federal, state, and institutional sources to postsecondary students is over $100 billion.
- A majority of all students enrolled in higher education receive some type of financial assistance.
- Federal student aid remains the largest source of funding.
- Not long ago the majority of federal financial assistance was grants. Today, a greater amount of financial aid is from loan money.

TIMETABLE FOR APPLYING FOR FINANCIAL AID

Sophomore Year of High School

Most families wait until a child has been accepted into a college or university to begin planning on how the family will meet those college costs. However, a family's college financial planning should begin much earlier.

Students, as early as the sophomore year of high school, should begin a systematic search for colleges that offer courses of study that are of interest. There are many computer programs that can be helpful in this process. These programs can match a student's interest with colleges fitting the profile. Considering that half of all students who enter college either drop out or transfer to another school, this type of early selection analysis can be invaluable.

After selecting certain schools for further consideration, you should write to the school and request a viewbook, catalog, and financial aid brochure. After receiving this information, you and your family should compare the schools. Your comparison should include academic considerations as well as financial. Don't rule out a school because you think you can't afford it. Remember the financial aid programs at that school may be more generous than at a lower-priced school. If possible, visit the college and speak with both an admission and financial aid counselor. If it is not possible to visit all the schools, call the schools and obtain answers to your questions about admission, financial aid, and placement after graduation.

Junior Year of High School

The comparative analysis of colleges and universities that you began in your sophomore year should continue in your junior year. By the completion of your junior year, you and your parents should have some idea of what it will cost to attend and the financial aid policies of each of the schools you are considering.

Some colleges and universities offer prospective applicants an early estimate of their financial aid award. This estimate is based upon information supplied by the family and can provide assistance in planning a family's budget. Remember that for most families, financial aid from federal, state, and school sources will probably not meet the total cost of attendance.

Families should remember that college costs can be met over the course of the academic year. It is not necessary to have all of the money needed to attend school available at the beginning of the academic year. Student and family savings, as well as student employment throughout the year, can be used to meet college costs.

Senior Year of High School

January

By January of your senior year of high school you should know which colleges and universities you want to receive your financial aid application forms. Be certain that you have completed not only the federal financial aid application form, but also any necessary state or school forms. Read carefully all of the instructions. Application methods and deadline dates may differ from one college to another. Submit an application clean of erasures or notations in the margins, and sign all of the application forms.

February

Approximately six weeks after you submit your application for financial aid, you will receive a report from the service agency you selected containing information on your family's expected contribution and your eligibility for financial aid. You and your parents should discuss the results of the financial aid application with regard to family contribution, educational costs, and how those costs can be met.

March

Beginning in March, most colleges begin to make financial aid decisions. If your application is complete, your chances of receiving an award letter early are greater than if additional information is required.

The financial aid award letter you receive from your school serves as your official document indicating the amount of financial aid you will receive for the year. You must sign and return a copy of the award letter to your school if you agree to accept their offer of financial aid.

If your family's financial circumstances change and you need additional funding, you should make an appointment to speak with your school's financial aid director or counselor. College financial aid personnel are permitted to exercise professional judgment and make adjustments to a student's financial need. Your letter of appeal should state explicitly how much money you need and why you need it.

TIPS ON APPLYING FOR FINANCIAL AID

1. Families can no longer wait until a child is accepted into college before deciding how they will finance that education. Earlier college financial planning is necessary.

2. Families should assume a much more active role in locating the resources necessary to fund future college costs.

3. Families should assume that college costs will continue to increase.

4. Families should assume that in the future the federal government will not substantially increase financial aid allocations.

5. Families should obtain information on a wide range of colleges including the many excellent low-cost schools.

6. Families should seek information about all of the funding sources available at each school they are considering.

7. Families should seek the advice and expertise of financial experts for college financing strategies. College financial planning should specify the amount of money a family should invest or save each month in order to meet future college bills.

8. Families should investigate all of the legitimate ways of reducing their income and assets before filing for financial aid.

9. Families should know how financial aid is awarded and the financial aid policies and programs of each school they are considering.

10. Families should realize that although the job of financing a college education rests primarily with them, they probably will not be able to save the entire cost of their child's college education. They probably will be eligible to receive some type of financial aid from some source and they will have to borrow a portion of their child's college education costs.

11. Families should be advised that the federal government frequently changes the rules and regulations governing financial aid eligibility. Check with your high school guidance counselor or college financial aid administrator for the latest program qualifications.

Marguerite J. Dennis
Vice President for Development
and Enrollment
Suffolk University
Boston, Massachusetts

COLLEGE: IT'S DIFFERENT

In college you are likely to hear fellow students say, "I don't know what that prof *wants*, and she won't *tell* me." "I wrote about three papers in high school, and now they want one every week." Though these students may be exaggerating a bit, college *is* different, both in the quality and the amount of work expected. Sometimes in high school the basic concepts of a course are reduced to a set of facts on a study sheet, handed to students to be reviewed and learned for a test.

In college, it is the concepts and ideas that are most important. These can only be grasped through a real understanding of the facts as they interrelate and form larger patterns. Writing papers and answering essay questions on tests can demonstrate a genuine understanding of the concepts, and this is why they are so important to college instructors. Learning to deal with ideas in this way can be a long-term asset, developing your independence, intellectual interests, and self-awareness.

Don't be discouraged; you are not alone. Most of your fellow students are having equally difficult times adjusting to a new learning method. Persist, and you will improve, leading to a lifetime habit of critical thinking and problem solving that can benefit you in many important ways.

College is also different outside of classes. Now that you have the freedom to choose how to spend time and what types of relationships to make, you have a bewildering number of possibilities.

MAKING A GOOD IMPRESSION

Here you are, plopped down in a strange place, feeling a bit like Dorothy transported to Oz. Your first goal is to make a good impression, showing your best self to those who will be important in your life for the next four years and even longer.

Impressing Faculty Members Favorably

Faculty members come in all ranks, from the graduate assistant, who teaches part-time while pursuing a degree, to a lofty full professor, who teaches primarily graduate students. Though different in rank and seniority, they respond to their students in roughly the same ways. They are, after all, people, with families and relationships much like your own. To have a good working relationship with them, try the following suggestions:

- **Make up your own mind about your instructors.** Listening to other students talk about teachers can be confusing. If you listen long enough, you will hear arguments for and against each of them. Don't allow hearsay to affect your own personal opinion.
- **Get to know your instructors firsthand.** Set up a meeting, during regular office hours. Don't try to settle important issues in the few moments before and after class.
- **Approach a discussion of grades carefully.** If you honestly believe that you have been graded too low, schedule a conference. Do not attack your instructor's integrity or judgment. Instead, say that you had expected your work to result in a better grade and would like to know ways to improve. Be serious about overcoming faults.
- **Don't make excuses.** Instructors have heard them all and can rarely be fooled. Accept responsibility for your mistakes, and learn from them.
- **Pay attention in class.** Conversing and daydreaming can insult your instructor and inhibit the learning process.
- **Arrive ahead of time for class.** You will be more relaxed, and you can use these moments to review notes or talk with classmates. You also demonstrate to your instructor a commitment to the class.

- **Participate in class discussions.** Ask questions and give answers to the instructor's questions. Nothing pleases an instructor more than an intelligent question that proves you are interested and prepared.
- **Learn from criticism.** It is an instructor's job to correct your errors in thinking. Don't take in-class criticism personally.

Impressing Fellow Students Favorably

Relationships with other students can be complex, but there are some basic suggestions that may make life easier in the residence halls and classrooms:

- **Don't get into the habit of bragging.** Frequent references to your wealth, your outstanding friends, your social status, or your family's successes are offensive to others.
- **Don't pry.** When your fellow students share their feelings and problems, listen carefully and avoid any tendency to intrude or ask embarrassing questions.
- **Don't borrow.** Borrowing a book, a basketball, or a few bucks may seem like a small thing to you, but some people who have trouble saying no may resent your request.
- **Divide chores.** Do your part; agree on a fair division of work in a lab project or a household task.
- **Support others.** Respect your friends' study time and the "Do not disturb" signs on their doors. Helping them to reach their goals will help you as well.
- **Allow others to be upset.** Sometimes, turning someone's anger into a joke, minimizing their difficulties, or belittling their frustration is your worst response. Support them by letting them release their emotions.
- **Don't preach.** Share your opinions when asked for, but don't try to reform the world around you.
- **Tell the truth.** Your reputation is your most important asset. When you make an agreement, keep it.

MANAGING YOUR TIME

Everyone, no matter how prominent or how insignificant, has 168 hours a week to spend. In this one asset we are all equal. There are students on every college campus, however, who seem to accomplish all their goals and still find time for play and socializing. There are others who seem to be alternating between frantic dashes and dull idleness, accomplishing very little. To the first group, college is a happy, fulfilling experience; to the latter, it is maddeningly frustrating. The first group has gained control of time, the second is controlled by that elusive and precious commodity.

- **Know where your time goes.** Unfortunately, we cannot store up time as we do money, to be used when the need is greatest. We use it as it comes, and it is amazing how it sometimes comes slowly (as in the last five minutes of a Friday afternoon class) or quickly (as in the last hour before a final exam). The first step in controlling time is to determine exactly how you use it. For a while, at least, you should carefully record how much time you spend in class, going to and from class, studying, sleeping, eating, listening to music, watching television, and running errands. You need to know what happens to your 168 hours. Only then can you make sensible decisions about managing them.
- **Make a weekly schedule.** You can schedule your routine for the week, using the time plan forms available at most college bookstores or by making your own forms.
- **First schedule the inflexible blocks of time.** Your class periods, transportation time, sleeping, and eating will form relatively routine patterns throughout the week. Trying to shave minutes off these important activities is often a mistake.

- **Plan your study time.** It is preferable, though not always possible, to set your study hours at the same time every weekday. Try to make your study time *prime time*, when your body and mind are ready for a peak performance.

- **Plan time for fun.** No one should plan to spend four years of college as a working robot. Fun and recreation are important, but they can be enjoyed in short periods just as well as long. For example, jogging with friends for 30 minutes can clear the mind, tone up the muscles, and give you those all-important social contacts. Parties and group activities can be scheduled for weekends.

- **Be reasonable in your time allotments.** As you progress through your freshman year, you will learn more precisely how much time is required to write a paper or complete a book report. Until then, schedule some extra minutes for these tasks. You are being unfair to yourself by planning one hour for a job that requires two.

- **Allow flexibility.** The unexpected is to be expected. There will be interruptions to your routine and errands that must be run at certain times. Allow for these unforeseen circumstances.

STUDYING EFFECTIVELY

Your most important activity in college is studying. Efficient study skills separate the inept student (who may spend just as many hours studying as an "A" student) from the excellent student, who thinks while studying and who uses common sense strategies to discover the important core of courses. The following suggested game plan for good study has worked in the past; it can work for you.

- **Make a commitment.** It is universally recommended that you spend two hours studying for every hour in class. At the beginning of your college career, be determined to do just that. It doesn't get easy until you make up your mind to do it.

- **Do the tough jobs first.** If certain courses are boring or particularly difficult, study them first. Don't read the interesting, enjoyable materials first, saving the toughies for the last sleepy twinges of your weary brain.

- **Study in short sessions.** Three two-hour sessions, separated from each other by a different activity, are much better than a long six-hour session.

- **Use your bits of time.** Use those minutes when you're waiting for a bus, a return call, laundry to wash, or a friend to arrive. Some of the best students I know carry 3 × 5 cards filled with definitions, formulas, or equations and learn during brief waiting periods. Most chief executives form the habit early of using bits of time wisely.

Digesting a Textbook

1. **Preview chapters.** Before you read a chapter in your textbook, preview it. Quickly examine the introductory paragraphs, headings, tables, illustrations, and other features of the chapter. The purpose is to discover the major topics. Then you can read with increased comprehension because you know where the author is leading.

2. **Underline the important points as you read.** Underlining should never be overdone; it can leave your textbook almost completely marked and less legible to read. Only the major ideas and concepts should be highlighted.

3. **Seven categories of information are commonly found in textbooks.** Be particularly alert when you see the following; get your marking pen ready.
   Definitions of terms.
   Types or *categories* of items.
   Methods of accomplishing certain tasks.
   Sequences of events or stages in a process.
   Reasons or *causes*.
   Results or *effects*.
   Contrasts or *comparisons* between items.

4. **Repeat information you need to learn.** When the object is to learn information, nothing is so effective as reciting the material, either silently or aloud.

5. **Don't read all material the same way.** Decide what you need to learn from the material and read accordingly. You read a work of fiction to learn the characters and the narrative; a poem, to learn an idea, an emotion, or a theme; a work of history, to learn the interrelationships of events. Do not read every sentence with the same speed and concentration; learn when to skim rapidly along. Remember, your study time is limited and the trick is to discriminate between the most important and the least important. No one can learn *everything* equally well.

6. **The five-minute golden secret.** As soon as possible after class is over—preferably at your desk in the classroom—skim through the chapter that has just been covered, marking the points primarily discussed. Copy what was written on the board. Now you know what the professor thinks is important!

TAKING TESTS SKILLFULLY

Try to predict the test questions. At some college libraries, copies of old examinations are made available to students. If you can legally find out your professor's previous test methods do so.

Ask your professor to describe the format of the upcoming test: multiple-choice? true-false? essay questions? problems? Adjust your study to the format described.

Listen for clues in the professor's lecture. Sometimes the questions posed in class have a way of reappearing on tests. If a statement is repeated several times or recurs in a subsequent lecture, note it as important.

As you review for the test, devise questions based on the material, and answer them. If you are part of a study group, have members ask questions of the others.

Common Sense Tactics

Arrive on the scene early; relax by breathing deeply. If the instructor gives instructions while distributing the test, listen very carefully.

- **Scan the whole test first.** Notice the point value for each section and budget your time accordingly.

- **Read the directions carefully** and then reread them. Don't lose points because you misread the directions.

- **Answer the short, easy questions first.** A bit of early success stimulates the mind and builds your confidence.

- **Leave space between answers.** You may think of a brilliant comment to add later.

- **Your first instinct is often the best** in answering true-false and multiple-choice questions. Look for qualifiers such as *never, all, often,* or *seldom* in true-false statements. Usually a qualifier that is absolute (*never, all,* or *none*) will indicate a false statement. Work fast on short-answer questions: they seldom count many points.

- **Open-book tests are no picnic.** Don't think that less study is required for an open-book test. They are often the most difficult of all examinations. If the material is unfamiliar, you won't have time to locate it and learn it during the test period.

Important Essay Strategies

- **Read the question carefully** and find out exactly what is asked for. If you are asked to contrast the French Revolution with the American Revolution and you spend your time describing each, without any contrasting references, your grade will be lowered.

- **Know the definitions of key words** used in essay questions:
   analyze: discuss the component parts.
   compare: examine for similarities.
   criticize: give a judgment or evaluation.
   define: state precise meaning of terms.

describe: give a detailed picture of qualities and characteristics.

discuss: give the pros and cons: debate them, and come to a conclusion.

enumerate: briefly mention a number of ideas, things, or events.

evaluate: give an opinion, with supporting evidence.

illustrate: give examples (illustrations) relating to a general statement.

interpret: usually means to state in other words, to explain, make clear.

outline: another way of asking for brief listings of principal ideas or characteristics. Normally the sentence or topic outline format is not required.

prove: give evidence and facts to support the premise stated in the test.

summarize: give an abbreviated account, with your conclusions.

- **Write a short outline** before you begin your essay. This organizes your thinking, making you less likely to leave out major topics.
- **Get to the point immediately.** Don't get bogged down in a lengthy introduction.
- **Read your essay over** before you hand it in. Words can be left out or misspelled. Remember that essay answers are graded somewhat subjectively, and papers that are correctly and neatly written make a better impression.
- **Learn from your test paper** when it is returned. Students who look at a test grade and discard the paper are throwing away a valuable tool. Analyze your mistakes honestly; look for clues for improvement in the professor's comments.

WRITING A TERM PAPER

Doing convincing library research and writing a term paper with correct footnotes and bibliography is a complicated procedure. Most first-year English composition courses include this process. Good students will work hard to master this skill because they know that research papers are integral parts of undergraduate and graduate courses.

Many students make the mistake of waiting until near the deadline to begin a term paper. At the busy end of the term, with final exams approaching, they embark on the uncertain time span of research and writing. Begin your term paper early, when the library staff is unhurried and ready to help and when you are under less pressure. It will pay dividends.

REGULATING YOUR RELATIONSHIPS

Find your special friends who believe in your definition of success. In a fast-paced environment like college, it is important to spend most of your time with people who share your ideas toward learning, where you can be yourself, without defensiveness. To find your kind of friends, first ask yourself: What is success? Is it a secure position and a comfortable home? A life of serving others? A position of power with a commodious executive suite? A challenging job that allows you to be creative? When you have answered honestly, you will have a set of long-range personal goals, and you can begin looking for kindred souls to walk with you on the road to success.

There will be, of course, some persons around you who are determined not to succeed, who for some reason program their lives for failure. Many college freshmen never receive a college degree; some may start college with no intention of passing courses. Their goal is to spend one hectic term as a party animal. If you intend to succeed at college, spending time among this type will be a considerable handicap. Consider making friends who will be around longer than the first year.

If possible, steer clear of highly emotional relationships during your first year of college. You don't have time for a broken heart, and relationships that begin with a rush often end that way.

MAINTAINING YOUR HEALTH

Poor health can threaten your success in the first year of college as nothing else can. No matter how busy you are, you must not forget your body and its needs: proper food, sufficient sleep, and healthy exercise. Many students, faced with the stress of college life, find themselves overmunching junk foods and gaining weight. Guard against this. Drugs and alcohol threaten the health and the success of many college students.

A FINAL WORD

So there it is. If you have read this far, you probably have a serious interest in succeeding in your first year of college. You probably have also realized that these suggestions, even if they sound a bit preachy, are practical and workable. They are based on many years of observing college students.

Benjamin W. Griffith
Former Dean, Graduate School
West Georgia College
Carrollton, Georgia

PART II

COLLEGE FACTS

AND FINANCES

Now that you've read through Part I, you'll need specific information on the colleges that best match your needs and aptitudes. Here's where you'll find essential information in a nutshell.

Facts and figures on all schools are listed in chart form to help you make quick and easy comparisons. Thumbnail data include:

- campus environment
- degrees offered
- composition of the student body
- enrollment figures
- test scores of entering freshmen
- fall application deadlines

You'll also see at a glance how much it's going to cost you for tuition, room-and-board, and related expenses. In-state costs are broken down on a state-by-state basis, each range starting with colleges that don't charge tuition and going up the scale to the most expensive schools.

COLLEGES AT A GLANCE

The charts on these pages present some of the basic data that initially concerns many students. All of the four-year accredited schools in the United States are listed here alphabetically by state. The type of college environment (from urban to rural) is given, followed by degrees offered and whether the institution is public or private. Information about whether the student body is coed or primarily men or women, and whether fraternities or sororities are on campus follows. The undergraduate enrollment for the fall of 2005 is given as well as the median test scores for freshmen who took the ACT or the SAT. Finally, the fall admissions deadline is shown. "Open" usually indicates that admission applications will be accepted until a few weeks before classes begin.

Column key: ENVIRONMENT (U-Urban, R-Rural, SU-Suburban, SM-Small Town); DEGREES AWARDED (A-Associate, B-Bachelor, M-Master, D-Doctorate); CONTROL (Pri-Private, Pub-Public); FRATERNITIES AND SORORITIES (F-Fraternities, S-Sororities, No-Neither); STUDENTS (C-Coed, M-Men, W-Women).

Name of School	Town	Env	Degrees	Control	Frat/Sor	Students	Enroll Fall 2005	ACT Median	ACT Below 21	ACT 21-23	ACT 24-26	ACT 27-28	ACT Above 28	SATV Median	SATV Below 500	SATV 500-599	SATV 600-700	SATV Above 700	SATM Median	SATM Below 500	SATM 500-599	SATM 600-700	SATM Above 700	Deadline
Alabama																								
Alabama Agricultural and Mechanical University	Normal	SU	A,M,D	Pub	F,S	C	4,375																	7/15
Alabama State University	Montgomery	U	B,M,D	Pub	F,S	C	4,485																	7/30
Auburn University	Auburn	SM	B,M,D	Pub	F,S	C	19,254	24	17	31	26	12	14	550	22	51	24	3	560	13	49	33	5	8/1
Auburn University Montgomery	Montgomery	U	B,M,D	Pub	F,S	C	4,300		65	19	10	2	2											Open
Birmingham-Southern College	Birmingham	U	B,M	Pri	F,S	C	1,324	26	8	22	26	15	28	600	15	35	40	10	580	13	40	38	10	1/15
Concordia College	Selma	SM	A,B	Pri	No	C	875																	Open
Faulkner University	Montgomery	U	A,B,M,D		F,S	C	2,225	22	36	32	16	8	8	527	37	44	12	7	525	32	46	21	1	Open
Huntingdon College	Montgomery	SU	A		F,S	C	835																	Open
Jacksonville State University	Jacksonville	SM	B,M	Pub	F,S	C	7,285	17	63	18	13	4	2	480	62	29	8	1	460	64	30	6		Open
Judson College	Marion	SM	B	Pri	No	W	331	22	40	27	17	7	9			29	43	14		14	43	29	29	Open
Miles College	Birmingham	U	B	Pri	F,S	C	1,716														43	29	29	Open
Oakwood College	Huntsville	SU	A,B		No	C	1,775																	Open
Samford University	Birmingham	SU	A,B,M,D	Pri	F,S	C	2,856	25	9	31	23	16	21	570	17	44	34	5	570	14	51	31	4	8/1
Southern Christian University	Montgomery	U	B,M,D	Pri	No	C	342																	Open
Spring Hill College	Mobile	SU	A,B,M	Pri	F,S	C	1,299	23	24	32	23	15	6	540	30	41	25	4	540	39	30	28	3	7/1
Stillman College	Tuscaloosa	SM	B		F,S	C	1,480																	
Talladega College	Talladega	SM	B		F,S	C	680																	Open
Troy University	Troy	R	A,B,M	Pub	F,S	C	13,868																	Open
Troy University Dothan Campus	Dothan	U	A,B,M	Pub	No	C	1,469	21	45	27	25	2												Open
Troy University Montgomery Campus	Montgomery	U	A,B,M	Pub	No	C	3,661																	Open
Tuskegee University	Tuskegee	R	B,M,D	Pri	F,S	C	2,400																	Open
University of Alabama	Tuscaloosa	SU	B,M,D	Pub	F,S	C	17,553	23	26	30	20	11	13	550	24	39	28	8	550	23	42	26	9	4/1
University of Alabama at Birmingham	Birmingham	U	B,M,D	Pub	F,S	C	11,470	22	30	28	21	10	11											3/1
University of Alabama in Huntsville	Huntsville	SU	B,M,D	Pub	F,S	C	5,475																	7/1
University of Mobile	Mobile	SU	A,B,M	Pri	No	C	1,549	22	49	21	15	7	8											9/10
University of Montevallo	Montevallo	SM	B,M	Pub	F,S	C	2,571																	8/1
University of North Alabama	Florence	U	B,M	Pub	F,S	C	5,417	21	49	22	19	6	4											7/1
University of South Alabama	Mobile	SU	B,M,D	Pub	F,S	C	10,144	22																8/10
University of West Alabama	Livingston	SM	A,B,M	Pub	F,S	C	1,625																	Open
Alaska																								
Alaska Pacific University	Anchorage	SU	A,B,M	Pri	No	C	580	21	39	22	28	6	6	520	40	48	12		490	52	32	12	4	2/1
Sheldon Jackson College	Sitka	SM	A,B		No	C	250																	Open
University of Alaska Anchorage	Anchorage	U	A,B,M	Pub	No	C	9,861																	
University of Alaska Fairbanks	Fairbanks	SM	A,B,M,D	Pub	F,S	C	7,136	20	53	19	18	4	4	530	38	35	21	6	510	41	40	17	2	8/1
University of Alaska Southeast	Juneau	SU	A,B,M	Pub	No	C	2,010																	Open
Arizona																								
American Indian College of the Assemblies of God	Phoenix	U	A,B		No	C	80																	Open
Arizona State University-Tempe	Tempe	SU	B,M,D	Pub	F,S	C	41,256	23	27	27	24	11	11	549	28	43	23	6	559	23	42	28	7	Open
DeVry University/Phoenix	Phoenix	SU	A,B,M		No	C	2,000																	Open
Embry-Riddle Aeronautical University	Prescott	R	B,M	Pri	F,S	C	1,653	24	18	26	21	18	17	560	23	40	31	6	590	15	37	39	9	Open
Grand Canyon University	Phoenix	SU	B,M		No	C	1,615																	Open
Northern Arizona University	Flagstaff	R	B,M,D	Pub	F,S	C	13,252	22	39	29	20	8	4	524	34	45	20	2	520	34	44	20	2	3/1
Prescott College	Prescott	SM	B,M,D	Pri	No	C	752																	8/15
University of Arizona	Tucson	U	B,M,D		F,S	C	27,800																	4/1
Arkansas																								
Arkansas Baptist College	Little Rock	U	A,B		F,S	C	360																	
Arkansas State University	State University	SM	A,B,M,D	Pub	F,S	C	9,138	21	44	25	19	9	4											
Arkansas Tech University	Russellville	SM	A,B,M	Pub	F,S	C	6,328	22																Open
Harding University	Searcy	SM	B,M		F,S	C	4,092	23	26	25	24	10	14	560	24	39	25	12	550	28	35	27	10	6/1
Henderson State University	Arkadelphia	SM	A,B,M		F,S	C	3,025																	Open
Hendrix College	Conway	SU	B,M	Pri	No	C	1,022	28	2	10	28	17	43	636	7	20	48	25	611	8	33	45	14	Open
John Brown University	Siloam Springs	SM	A,B,M	Pri	No	C	1,659	25	14	26	28	13	19	590	14	40	37	9	580	20	40	34	6	
Lyon College	Batesville	SM	B	Pri	F,S	C	488	25	5	23	34	17	22	590	25	25	20	30	585	15	40	45		8
Ouachita Baptist University	Arkadelphia	SM	A,B	Pri	F,S	C	1,520																	Open
Philander Smith College	Little Rock	U	B		F,S	C	785																	7/15
Southern Arkansas University	Magnolia	SM	A,B,M	Pub	F,S	C	2,876		54	21	15	7	3											Open
University of Arkansas	Fayetteville	U	B,M,D		F,S	C	14,281	24	15	28	27	11	19	570	20	39	32	9	570	18	40	33	9	8/15
University of Arkansas at Little Rock	Little Rock	U	A,B,M,D	Pub	F,S	C	9,200																	Open
University of Arkansas at Monticello	Monticello	SM	A,B,M	Pub	F,S	C	2,911																	Open
University of Arkansas at Pine Bluff	Pine Bluff	SM	A,B,M	Pub	F,S	C	3,075																	
University of Central Arkansas	Conway	SM	A,B,M,D	Pub	F,S	C	9,969	23	32	20	20	15	13	490	57	33	10		515	38	38	24		8/1

TEST SCORES

Name of School	Town	Environment	Degrees Awarded	Control	Fraternities and Sororities	Students	Undergrad. Enrollment Fall 2005	ACT Median	ACT Below 21	ACT 21-23	ACT 24-26	ACT 27-28	ACT Above 28	SAT I Verbal Median	Verbal Below 500	Verbal 500-599	Verbal 600-700	Verbal Above 700	SAT I Math Median	Math Below 500	Math 500-599	Math 600-700	Math Above 700	Application Deadline Month/Day
University of the Ozarks	Clarksville	SM	B	Pri	No	C	628																	4/1
Williams Baptist College	Walnut Ridge	R	A,B		No	C	610	21																Open

California

Name of School	Town	Environment	Degrees Awarded	Control	Fraternities and Sororities	Students	Undergrad. Enrollment Fall 2005	ACT Median	ACT Below 21	ACT 21-23	ACT 24-26	ACT 27-28	ACT Above 28	SAT I Verbal Median	Verbal Below 500	Verbal 500-599	Verbal 600-700	Verbal Above 700	SAT I Math Median	Math Below 500	Math 500-599	Math 600-700	Math Above 700	Application Deadline Month/Day
Art Center College of Design	Pasadena	SU	B,M	Pri	No	C	1,512																	Open
Azusa Pacific University	Azusa	U	B,M,D	Pri	No	C	4,602																	2/15
Biola University	La Mirada	SU	B,M,D	Pri	No	C	3,663	24						563					555					12/1
California Baptist University	Riverside	SU	B,M	Pri	No	C	2,415	21						500					500					Open
California College of the Arts	San Francisco	U	B,M	Pri	No	C	1,312	22						547					507					2/1
California Institute of Technology	Pasadena	SU	B,M,D	Pri	No	C	896																	1/1
California Institute of the Arts	Valencia	SU	B,M	Pri	No	C	821																	1/5
California Lutheran University	Thousand Oaks	SU	B,M,D	Pri	No	C	1,920																	
California Maritime Academy	Vallejo	SU	B	Pub	No	C	739																	
California Polytechnic State University	San Luis Obispo	SU	B,M	Pub	F,S	C	17,385	25	7	20	33	21	19	575	9	47	37	7	590	4	31	49	15	11/30
California State Polytechnic University, Pomona	Pomona	SU	B,M	Pub	F,S	C	17,974	20	51	25	14	6	4	480	50	37	12	1	520	32	39	25	4	11/1
California State University, Bakersfield	Bakersfield	U	B,M	Pub	F,S	C	5,240																	Open
California State University, Chico	Chico	SM	B,M	Pub	F,S	C	14,526	22	35	36	21	6	2	520	35	49	15	1	550	29	48	21	2	11/30
California State University, Dominguez Hills	Carson	U	B,M	Pub	F,S	C	7,700																	4/1
California State University East Bay	Hayward	SU	B,M	Pub	F,S	C	9,425																	8/31
California State University, Fresno	Fresno	SU	B,M,D	Pub	F,S	C	15,575																	
California State University, Fullerton	Fullerton	SU	B,M	Pub	F,S	C	29,462	20	60	23	12	4	1	480	56	35	9		500	46	39	15	1	11/30
California State University, Long Beach	Long Beach	SU	B,M	Pub	F,S	C	28,514								48	39	12	1		38	43	17	2	11/30
California State University, Los Angeles	Los Angeles	U	B,M,D	Pub	F,S	C	14,400																	6/15
California State University, Monterey Bay	Seaside	SU	B,M	Pub	F,S	C	3,407	20	54	22	20	2	2	490	51	37	11	1	490	51	38	11	1	3/15
California State University, Northridge	Northridge	SU	B,M	Pub	F,S	C	25,475																	
California State University, Sacramento	Sacramento	SU	B,M,D	Pub	F,S	C	23,028	19	63	25	10	3		480	58	33	9		500	50	37	13	1	11/30
California State University, San Bernardino	San Bernardino	SU	B,M	Pub	F,S	C	12,464	19	71	17	8	2	1	455	70	24	6		468	65	28	7		Open
California State University, San Marcos	San Marcos	SU	B,M	Pub	F,S	C	5,757																	7/1
California State University, Stanislaus	Turlock	SU	B,M	Pub	F,S	C	6,483	19	61	24	11	4	1	469	45	47	8	1	479	42	49	8	1	1/31
Chapman University	Orange	SU	B,M,D	Pri		C	3,450																	1/1
Claremont McKenna College	Claremont	SM	B	Pri	No	C	1,140	31		2	10	19	69	700			12	38	700			7	40	1/1
Cogswell Polytechnical College	Sunnyvale	SU	B		No	C	500																	Open
Concordia University	Irvine	SU	A,B,M	Pri	No	C	1,357	22	31	33	25	7	5	520	36	49	13	2	530	35	46	18	1	5/1
DeVry University/Fremont	Fremont	SU	A,B,M		No	C	1,655																	Open
DeVry University/Long Beach	Long Beach	U	A,B,M		No	C	1,930																	Open
DeVry University/Pomona	Pomona	U	A,B,M		No	C	2,400																	Open
DeVry University/West Hills	West Hills	SU	A,B,M		No	C	1,170																	Open
Dominican University of California	San Rafael	SU	B,M	Pri	No	C	1,391	21	40	35	14	9	5	500	45	36	17	2	500	46	41	11	2	3/2
Fresno Pacific University	Fresno	SU	A,B,M	Pri	No	C	1,453	21	51	26	13	6	4	500	50	36	12	2	510	46	38	15	1	7/31
Golden Gate University	San Francisco	U	B,M,D		No	C	567																	
Harvey Mudd College	Claremont	SU	B		No	C	751							720					760					1/15
Holy Names College	Oakland	U	B,M	Pri	No	C	593																	8/1
Hope International University	Fullerton	U	A,B,M		No	C	840																	
Humboldt State University	Arcata	SM	B,M	Pub	F,S	C	6,395	22	41	24	22	8	5	530	37	39	21	3	510	41	43	15	1	6/1
Humphreys College	Stockton	SU	A,B,D		No	C	760																	Open
La Sierra University	Riverside	SU	A,B,M,D		No	C	1,638	19	67	16	7	7	3	480	58	32	9	1	490	53	34	11	2	8/15
Laguna College of Art and Design	Laguna Beach	SM	B		No	C	210																	2/2
Loyola Marymount University	Los Angeles	SU	B,M	Pri	F,S	C	5,490																	1/15
Master's College and Seminary, The	Santa Clarita	R	B,M		No	C	1,160	24	31	16	27	8	19	576	19	47	25	9	556	26	38	32	5	3/2
Menlo College	Atherton	SU	A,B	Pri	No	C	769	21	59	31	6		4	520	61	35	4		530	62	32	4	2	Open
Mills College	Oakland	U	B,M,D		No	W	881	23						529	19	35	29	17	555	27	46	24	3	2/1
Mount Saint Mary's College	Los Angeles	U	A,B,M		S	PW	952																	2/15
National University	La Jolla	U	A,B,M	Pri	No	C	5,820																	Open
New College of California	San Francisco	U	B,M		No	C	649																	8
Notre Dame de Namur University	Belmont	SU	A,B,M		No	C	890	19	63	10	17	10		480	58	29	12	1	490	51	37	11	1	
Occidental College	Los Angeles	U	B,M	Pri	F,S	C	1,819	29						640	3	20	55	22	650	2	18	56	24	1/10
Otis College of Art and Design	Los Angeles	U	B,M		No	C	1,035																	Open
Pacific Union College	Angwin	R	A,B,M	Pri	No	C	1,422	23	42	23	23	6	5	585	42	36	19	3	525	42	36	19	3	1/15
Pepperdine University	Malibu	SU	B,M,D		F,S	C	3,201							625	11	37	42	10	610	6	36	45	13	1/15
Pitzer College	Claremont	SU	B		No	C	963								5	27	50	18		5	35	49	11	1/1
Point Loma Nazarene University	San Diego	SU	B,M		F,S	C	2,360	25						570	16	43	34	7	580	15	43	34	8	3/1
Pomona College	Claremont	SU	B		F	C	1,565																	1/2
Saint Mary's College of California	Moraga	SU	B,M,D	Pri	No	C	3,291	23	29	28	19	11	13	540	26	46	25	3	540	26	45	26	3	1/15
San Diego Christian College	El Cajon	SU	A,B	Pri	No	C	600																	Open
San Diego State University	San Diego	U	B,M,D	Pub	F,S	C	26,690	22	31	32	27	7	4	530	33	49	18	1	550	24	48	27	1	11/30
San Francisco Art Institute	San Francisco	U	B,M		No	C	505																	2/15
San Francisco Conservatory of Music	San Francisco	U	B,M		No	C	145																	1/15
San Francisco State University	San Francisco	U	A,B,M,D	Pub	F,S	C	21,000																	Open
San Jose State University	San Jose	U	B,M	Pub	F,S	C	21,450																	
Santa Clara University	Santa Clara	SU	B,M,D	Pri	No	C	4,638	25						619	7	38	41	14	598	4	33	47	16	1/15
Scripps College	Claremont	SU	B	Pri	No	W	878	30		4	17	30	49	690	1	5	51	43	670	1	11	59	29	1/1
Simpson University	Redding	SU	A,B,M	Pri	No	C	924	21	47	22	13	13	5	520	43	45	11	1	500	49	43	7	1	Open
Sonoma State University	Rohnert Park	SU	B,M	Pub	F,S	C	7,000																	11
Stanford University	Stanford	SU	B,M,D		F,S	C	6,576							680		5	27	67	700		3	23	74	12/15
Thomas Aquinas College	Santa Paula	R	B	Pri	No	C	359	26	13		38	13	38	680		11	48	40	610	3	42	44	11	Open
University of California at Davis	Davis	SU	B,M,D	Pub	F,S	C																		
University of California at Berkeley	Berkeley	U	B,M,D	Pub	F,S	C	22,880							653	8	21	41	30	691	4	15	35	46	11/30
University of California at Irvine	Irvine	SU	B,M,D	Pub	F,S	C	19,200																	11/30

Column key — ENVIRONMENT: U-Urban, R-Rural, SU-Suburban, SM-Small Town · DEGREES AWARDED: A-Associate, B-Bachelor, M-Master, D-Doctorate · CONTROL: Pri-Private, Pub-Public · FRATERNITIES AND SORORITIES: F-Fraternities, S-Sororities, F,S-Both, No-Neither · STUDENTS: C-Coed, M-Men, W-Women, PM-Primarily Men, PW-Primarily Women

NAME OF SCHOOL	TOWN	ENVIR.	DEGREES	CONTROL	FRAT/SOR	STUDENTS	UNDERGRAD ENROLL FALL 2005	ACT Med	ACT Below 21	ACT 21-23	ACT 24-26	ACT 27-28	ACT Above 28	SAT V Med	V Below 500	V 500-599	V 600-700	V Above 700	SAT M Med	M Below 500	M 500-599	M 600-700	M Above 700	APPL. DEADLINE
University of California at Los Angeles	Los Angeles	U	B,M,D	Pub	F,S	C	24,811	27						630	8	30	44	18	670	5	20	40	34	11/30
University of California at Riverside	Riverside	SU	B,M,D	Pub	F,S	C	14,571	21	46	30	15	5	4	517	42	39	16	3	557	26	38	29	7	11/30
University of California at San Diego	La Jolla	SU	B,M,D	Pub	F,S	C	20,339	26	3	25	20	33	19	598	12	37	39	10	644	1	23	47	25	11/30
University of California at Santa Barbara	Santa Barbara	SU	B,M,D	Pub	F,S	C	17,730																	11/30
University of California at Santa Cruz	Santa Cruz	SM	B,M,D	Pub	F,S	C	13,625	23						572	18	38	35	9	577	14	40	38	8	11/30
University of Judaism College of Arts and Sciences	Bel Air	SU	B,M		No	C	108																	1/31
University of La Verne	La Verne	SU	A,B,M,D	Pri	F,S	C	1,685	21	45	31	21	3		510	45	42	13	1	510	39	46	15		2/1
University of Redlands	Redlands	SU	B,M	Pri	F,S	C	2,362	24	18	29	29	13	11	579	9	51	34	6	581	8	49	38	5	2/1
University of San Diego	San Diego	U	B,M,D	Pri	F,S	C	4,970																	1/5
University of San Francisco	San Francisco	U	B,M,D	Pri	F,S	C	4,967																	
University of Southern California	Los Angeles	U	B,M,D	Pri	F,S	C	16,897	30		3	12	18	67	668	1	13	51	35	690		7	43	50	1/10
University of the Pacific	Stockton	SU	B,M,D	Pri	F,S	C	3,457	25	9	25	28	20	19	580	14	41	40	5	610	9	35	43	14	1/15
Vanguard University of Southern California	Costa Mesa	SU	B,M	Pri	No	C	1,814	21						509	36	42	19	3	502	41	41	16	2	12/1
Westmont College	Santa Barbara	SU	B	Pri	No	C	1,354	26	4	14	34	25	23	620	6	34	43	17	610	7	37	40	16	2/15
Whittier College	Whittier	SU	B,M,D		F,S	C	1,270																	2/1
Woodbury University	Burbank	SU	B,M	Pri	F,S	C	1,268	19						464	68	24	7	1	465	57	30	12	1	Open

Colorado

NAME OF SCHOOL	TOWN	ENVIR.	DEGREES	CONTROL	FRAT/SOR	STUDENTS	UNDERGRAD ENROLL FALL 2005	ACT Med	ACT Below 21	ACT 21-23	ACT 24-26	ACT 27-28	ACT Above 28	SAT V Med	V Below 500	V 500-599	V 600-700	V Above 700	SAT M Med	M Below 500	M 500-599	M 600-700	M Above 700	APPL. DEADLINE
Adams State College	Alamosa	SM	A,B,M	Pub	No	C	2,338	19	67	18	11	2	2	490	57	31	9	3	510	47	43	10		8/1
Colorado Christian University	Lakewood	SU	A,B,M	Pri	No	C	1,462	24	24	25	28	15	8	550	18	47	25	10	550	31	40	25	4	8/1
Colorado College	Colorado Springs	SU	B,M	Pri	F,S	C	1,928																	12/20
Colorado School of Mines	Golden	SM	B,M,D	Pub	F,S	C	3,098	27	1	11	27	22	39	595	10	38	41	11	660	2	17	56	25	6/1
Colorado State University-Fort Collins	Fort Collins	SU	B,M,D	Pub	F,S	C	20,720	24	16	32	29	12	11	550	24	45	27	4	560	20	45	32	3	7/1
Colorado State University-Pueblo	Pueblo	U	B,M	Pub	F,S	C	5,324																	7/28
Colorado Technical University	Colorado Springs	SU	A,B,M,D	Pri	No	C	1,206																	Open
DeVry University/Colorado Springs	Colorado Springs		A,B,M		No	C	320																	Open
DeVry University/Westminster	Westminster		A,B		No	C	680																	Open
Fort Lewis College	Durango	SM	A,B	Pub	No	C	3,946	21	51	30	14	4	3	510	42	45	11	2	503	47	39	12	2	8/1
Johnson and Wales University/ Denver Campus	Denver	SU	A,B	Pri	F,S	C	1,544							500	49	38	13	1	500	47	39	14	1	
Mesa State College	Grand Junction	SM	A,B,M	Pub	No	C	5,297																	7/31
Metropolitan State College of Denver	Denver	U	B	Pub	No	C	18,445																	8/12
Naropa University	Boulder	U	B,M	Pri	No	C	451	24	14	43	14	14	14	582	10	60	15	15	547	10	75	15		1/15
Regis University	Denver	SU	B,M		No	C	1,550	23	24	29	26	7	14	530	37	37	21	5	530	36	43	18	3	Open
United States Air Force Academy	USAFA	SU	B	Pub	No	C	4,157							630	2	32	51	15	663	1	20	54	25	1/31
University of Colorado at Boulder	Boulder	SU	B,M,D	Pub	F,S	C	25,205	25	9	24	33	17	17	570	14	46	35	5	600	10	39	44	7	1/15
University of Colorado at Colorado Springs	Colorado Springs	U	B,M,D	Pub	F,S	C	6,119	23	24	21	38	9	8	531	29	47	19	5	540	28	41	29	2	7/1
University of Colorado at Denver and Health Sciences Center	Denver	U	B,M,D	Pub	No	C	9,921	22						539	34	42	20	4	540	37	42	16	5	7/22
University of Denver	Denver	U	B,M,D	Pri	F,S	C	4,611	26						580					585					1/15
University of Northern Colorado	Greeley	SU	B,M,D	Pub	F,S	C	10,811	22	33	34	22	7	4	530	33	47	18	2	520	35	46	16	1	8/1
Western State College of Colorado	Gunnison	R	B	Pub	F,S	C	2,000	21	49	27	15	7	2	520	41	41	17	1	505	43	45	12		

Connecticut

NAME OF SCHOOL	TOWN	ENVIR.	DEGREES	CONTROL	FRAT/SOR	STUDENTS	UNDERGRAD ENROLL FALL 2005	ACT Med	ACT Below 21	ACT 21-23	ACT 24-26	ACT 27-28	ACT Above 28	SAT V Med	V Below 500	V 500-599	V 600-700	V Above 700	SAT M Med	M Below 500	M 500-599	M 600-700	M Above 700	APPL. DEADLINE
Albertus Magnus College	New Haven	SU	A,B,M		No	C	1,892							460	62	30	7	1	496	70	21	8	1	Open
Central Connecticut State University	New Britain	SU	B,M,D	Pub	F,S	C	9,678							516	39	49	12	1	516	38	47	13	1	5/1
Charter Oak State College	New Britain	SU	A,B	Pub	No	C	1,902																	Open
Connecticut College	New London	SM	B,M	Pri	No	C	1,887	27						670	2	10	58	30	660		13	62	25	1/1
Eastern Connecticut State University	Willimantic	SU	A,B,M	Pub	No	C	4,745							514					507					5/1
Fairfield University	Fairfield	SU	A,B,M	Pri	No	C	4,073	26						587	6	49	36	5	601	4	41	44	7	1/15
Mitchell College	New London	SU	A,B	Pri	No	C	745																	8/30
Post University	Waterbury	U	A,B		No	C	1,101																	
Quinnipiac University	Hamden	SU	B,M,D	Pri	F,S	C	5,706	25	6	29	34	25	6	547	19	58	21	2	564	14	55	29	2	2/1
Sacred Heart University	Fairfield	SU	A,B,M,D	Pri	F,S	C	4,104							530	30	54	15	1	540	21	59	19	1	
Saint Joseph College	West Hartford	SU	B,M	Pri	No	PW	1,159							500	48	39	12	1	490	54	38	7	1	
Southern Connecticut State University	New Haven	U	A,B,M	Pub	F,S	C	8,316																	Open
Trinity College	Hartford	U	B,M		F	C	2,188	27	5	12	23	25	35	650	3	26	54	15	660	4	22	55	20	1/15
United States Coast Guard Academy	New London	SU	B	Pub	No	C	1,052	27		14	63	23		630	1	29	53	17	650		10	70	20	3/1
University of Bridgeport	Bridgeport	U	A,B,M,D	Pri	F,S	C	1,676	18						430	78	19	3		440	77	17	5	1	4/1
University of Connecticut	Storrs	R	B,M,D	Pub	F,S	C	16,112							585	10	45	38	7	604	7	38	44	11	2/1
University of Hartford	West Hartford	SU	A,B,M,D		F,S	C	5,592	23						530	30	49	19	2	540	25	48	24	3	Open
University of New Haven	West Haven	SU	A,B,M		F,S	C	2,625																	Open
Wesleyan University	Middletown	SU	B,M,D	Pri	F,S	C	2,751	31	1	2	11	11	70	700	2	10	33	55	700		8	38	54	1/1
Western Connecticut State University	Danbury	SU	A,B,M,D	Pub	F,S	C	5,195							504	50	37	12	1	494	53	38	8	1	Open
Yale University	New Haven	U	B,M,D	Pri	F,S	C	5,268	32						750			2	24	750		2	26	72	12/31

Delaware

NAME OF SCHOOL	TOWN	ENVIR.	DEGREES	CONTROL	FRAT/SOR	STUDENTS	UNDERGRAD ENROLL FALL 2005	ACT Med	ACT Below 21	ACT 21-23	ACT 24-26	ACT 27-28	ACT Above 28	SAT V Med	V Below 500	V 500-599	V 600-700	V Above 700	SAT M Med	M Below 500	M 500-599	M 600-700	M Above 700	APPL. DEADLINE
Delaware State University	Dover	SU	B,M	Pub	F,S	C	2,280																	6/1
Goldey-Beacom College	Wilmington	SU	A,B,M		F,S		1,290																	Open
University of Delaware	Newark	SM	A,B,M,D	Pub	F,S	C	16,939	27	5	14	33	27	21	590	13	45	35	7	610	10	35	44	11	1/15
Wesley College	Dover	SM	A,B,M		F,S	C	1,591																	Open
Wilmington College	New Castle	U	A,B,M,D		No		3,977																	Open

District of Columbia

NAME OF SCHOOL	TOWN	ENVIR.	DEGREES	CONTROL	FRAT/SOR	STUDENTS	UNDERGRAD ENROLL FALL 2005	ACT Med	ACT Below 21	ACT 21-23	ACT 24-26	ACT 27-28	ACT Above 28	SAT V Med	V Below 500	V 500-599	V 600-700	V Above 700	SAT M Med	M Below 500	M 500-599	M 600-700	M Above 700	APPL. DEADLINE
American University	Washington	U	A,B,M,D	Pri	F,S	C	5,921	28		7	28	26	39	640	1	20	58	21	630	1	29	59	11	1/15

Legend — ENVIRONMENT: U-Urban, R-Rural, SU-Suburban, SM-Small Town. DEGREES AWARDED: A-Associate, B-Bachelor, M-Master, D-Doctorate. CONTROL: Pri-Private, Pub-Public. FRATERNITIES AND SORORITIES: F-Fraternities, S-Sororities, F,S-Both, No-Neither. STUDENTS: C-Coed, M-Men, W-Women, PM-Primarily Men, PW-Primarily Women. UNDERGRADUATE ENROLLMENT FALL 2005. TEST SCORES. APPLICATION DEADLINE Month/Day.

NAME OF SCHOOL	TOWN	ENV	DEGREES	CONTROL	FRAT/SOR	STUDENTS	UNDERGRAD ENROLL	ACT Median	ACT Below 21	ACT 21-23	ACT 24-26	ACT 27-28	ACT Above 28	SAT V Median	SAT V Below 500	SAT V 500-599	SAT V 600-700	SAT V Above 700	SAT M Median	SAT M Below 500	SAT M 500-599	SAT M 600-700	SAT M Above 700	APP DEADLINE
Catholic University of America	Washington	U	B,M,D	Pri	F,S	C	3,053	24	20	22	27	18	13	580	14	43	35	8	570	18	46	31	5	2/15
Corcoran School of Art and Design	Washington	U	A,B,M	Pri	No	C	393																	Open
Gallaudet University	Washington	U	A,B,M,D		F,S	C	1,250																	Open
George Washington University	Washington	U	A,B,M,D		F,S	C	10,761	28						650	3	20	51	25	650	1	19	56	23	1/15
Georgetown University	Washington	U	B,M,D	Pri	No	C	6,719	29										51					51	1/10
Howard University	Washington	U	B,M,D	Pri	F,S	C	7,164	22	35	32	21	8	4	544	26	47	23	4	537	32	44	20	4	2/2
Southeastern University	Washington	U	A,B,M		F,S	C	513																	Open
Strayer University	Washington	U	A,B,M		No	C	11,785																	Open
Trinity College	Washington	U	B,M	Pri	No	W	1,011																	Open
University of the District of Columbia	Washington	SU	A,B,M	Pub	F,S	C	5,006																	Open

Florida

NAME OF SCHOOL	TOWN	ENV	DEGREES	CONTROL	FRAT/SOR	STUDENTS	UNDERGRAD ENROLL	ACT Median	ACT Below 21	ACT 21-23	ACT 24-26	ACT 27-28	ACT Above 28	SAT V Median	SAT V Below 500	SAT V 500-599	SAT V 600-700	SAT V Above 700	SAT M Median	SAT M Below 500	SAT M 500-599	SAT M 600-700	SAT M Above 700	APP DEADLINE
Barry University	Miami Shores	SU	B,M,D		F,S	C	6,006																	Open
Beacon College	Leesburg	SM	A,B		S	C	101																	Open
Bethune-Cookman College	Daytona Beach	U	B	Pri	F,S	C	3,090		96	4				410	87	11	1		410	89	9	1		7/30
Carlos Albizu University	Miami	U	B,M,D		No	C	453																	Open
Clearwater Christian College	Clearwater	SM	A,B		No	C	640																	
DeVry University/Orlando	Orlando		A,B,M		No	C	1,395																	4/1
Eckerd College	St. Petersburg	SU	B		No	C	1,778	24	14	25	32	17	14	560	16	47	28	9	570	20	46	29	5	4/1
Edward Waters College	Jacksonville	U	B	Pri	F,S	C	1,300																	7/1
Embry-Riddle Aeronautical University	Daytona Beach	U	A,B,M		F,S	C	4,382	23	24	27	24	14	11	540	31	44	22	4	570	18	41	34	7	3/1
Flagler College	St. Augustine	SM	B		No	C	2,157	24	8	39	35	13	5	570	6	58	31	5	560	13	61	22	4	3/1
Florida Agricultural and Mechanical University	Tallahassee	U	A,B,M,D	Pub	F,S	C	10,806																	5/15
Florida Atlantic University	Boca Raton	SU	A,B,M,D	Pub	F,S	C	21,505	22	40	35	16	6	3	528	36	48	14	2	530	34	49	16	3	6/1
Florida Gulf Coast University	Fort Myers	R	A,B,M	Pub	F,S	C	6,118	21	44	34	16	4	2	510	40	48	11	1	520	36	49	14	1	6/1
Florida Hospital College of Health Sciences	Orlando	U	A,B	Pri	No	C	1,021																	7/18
Florida Institute of Technology	Melbourne	SM	B,M,D		F,S	C	2,358	25	12	23	26	12	27	570	18	42	32	8	610	8	36	43	13	Open
Florida International University	Miami	U	A,B,M,D	Pub	F,S	C	30,684	23	1	24	50	14	11	560	17	55	25	3	557	16	56	25	3	Open
Florida Memorial College	Miami	U	B		No	C																		Open
Florida Southern College	Lakeland	SU	B,M	Pri	F,S	C	1,816	23	29	28	22	11	10	528	37	43	17	3	539	33	43	20	4	8/1
Florida State University	Tallahassee	SU	A,B,M,D	Pub	F,S	C	29,630																	3/1
International College	Naples	SU	A,B,M		No	C	1,477																	Open
Jacksonville University	Jacksonville	SU	B,M	Pri	F,S	C	2,214																	Open
Johnson and Wales University/ North Miami Campus	North Miami	U	A,B	Pri	F,S	C	2,452							450	70	26	3		440	70	26	5		Open
Lynn University	Boca Raton	SU	A,B,M,D	Pri	F,S	C	1,903																	Open
New College of Florida	Sarasota	SU	B	Pub	No	C	692	28		8	26	27	39	680	1	5	57	37	630	1	28	53	18	5/1
Northwood University	West Palm Beach	SU	A,B	Pri	No	C	685																	
Nova Southeastern University	Fort Lauderdale	SU	A,B,M,D	Pri	F,S	C	5,325	21						510	42	47	9	1	520	41	40	17	2	Open
Palm Beach Atlantic University	West Palm Beach	U	A,B,M,D	Pri	No	C	2,486	23	26	35	24	10	5	580	29	46	22	3	575	29	47	22	2	Open
Ringling School of Art and Design	Sarasota	U	B	Pri	F,S	C	1,088	23						540	32	38	26	4	510	44	35	20	1	2/1
Rollins College	Winter Park	SU	B,M	Pri	F,S	C	1,719	25	12	30	27	15	16	590	7	48	38	7	590	9	42	41	8	2/15
Saint Leo University	Saint Leo	R	A,B,M	Pri	F,S	C	1,384	21	47	26	18	8	1	510	43	47	10		500	45	46	9		Open
Saint Thomas University	Miami	SU	B,M	Pri	No	C	1,169	17						440					450					Open
Southeastern University	Lakeland	SM	B		No	C	2,297																	
Stetson University	Deland	SM	B,M	Pri	F,S	C	2,234	24	17	27	30	17	9	573	14	49	33	4	572	13	52	31	5	3/1
University of Central Florida	Orlando	U	A,B,M,D	Pub	F,S	C	37,796	24	9	23	39	18	11	582	15	53	28	4	595	10	50	35	5	5/1
University of Florida	Gainesville	SU	B,M,D	Pub	F,S	C	49,693	27	1	10	24	27	38	625	4	30	52	14	642	2	23	56	19	1/13
University of Miami	Coral Gables	SU	B,M,D	Pri	F,S	C	10,537	27																2/1
University of North Florida	Jacksonville	U	A,B,M,D	Pub	F,S	C	13,735	22	28	50	16	4	2	583	7	52	38	3	577	7	54	37	2	7/2
University of South Florida	Tampa	U	A,B,M,D	Pub	F,S	C	33,702	24		52	42		5	560	17	55	25	3	570	13	55	29	4	5/1
University of Tampa	Tampa	U	A,B,M	Pri	F,S	C	4,636	23	26	35	26	8	5	539	26	54	18	2	542	23	57	19	1	Open
University of West Florida	Pensacola	SU	A,B,M,D	Pub	F,S	C	7,781	23	20	30	30	15		550	23	48	25	4	545	28	45	23	4	6/30
Warner Southern College	Lake Wales	R	A,B,M	Pri	No	C	1,090																	Open
Webber International University	Babson Park	SM	A,B,M	Pri	No	C	557																	8/1

Georgia

NAME OF SCHOOL	TOWN	ENV	DEGREES	CONTROL	FRAT/SOR	STUDENTS	UNDERGRAD ENROLL	ACT Median	ACT Below 21	ACT 21-23	ACT 24-26	ACT 27-28	ACT Above 28	SAT V Median	SAT V Below 500	SAT V 500-599	SAT V 600-700	SAT V Above 700	SAT M Median	SAT M Below 500	SAT M 500-599	SAT M 600-700	SAT M Above 700	APP DEADLINE
Agnes Scott College	Decatur	U	B,M		No	W	1,003	26	7	16	32	19	26	630	4	30	43	22	600	7	44	43	7	3/1
Albany State University	Albany	U	A,B,M	Pub	F,S	C	3,025																	
American InterContinental University	Atlanta	U	A,B		No	C	1,000																	Open
Armstrong Atlantic State University	Savannah	U	A,B,M	Pub	F,S	C	5,915	19	64	23	10	2	1	500	47	41	11	1	490	54	38	8	1	7/1
Art Institute of Atlanta	Atlanta	SU	A,B	Pri	No	C	2,540																	Open
Atlanta College of Art	Atlanta	U	B		No	C	445																	Open
Augusta State University	Augusta	U	A,B,M	Pub	F,S	C	5,482		74	18	6	1	1	492	56	32	11	1	487	55	34	10	1	7/21
Berry College	Mount Berry	SU	B,M	Pri	No	C	1,864																	2/1
Brenau University Women's College	Gainesville	SU	B,M	Pri	S	W	711																	Open
Brewton-Parker College	Mt. Vernon	R	A,B	Pri	F,S	C	1,080																	Open
Clark Atlanta University	Atlanta	U	B,M,D		F,S	C	3,671																	6/1
Clayton College and State University	Morrow	SU	A,B	Pub	No	C	5,220																	
Columbus State University	Columbus	SU	A,B,M	Pub	F,S	C	6,624	20						503	46	41	11	2	493	52	36	10	2	5/1
Covenant College	Lookout Mountain	SU	A,B,M		No	C	902	26	18	17	22	21	25	610	14	28	42	16	590	19	32	39	10	5/1
DeVry University/Alpharetta	Alpharetta	SU	A,B,M		No	C	1,290																	Open
DeVry University/Decatur	Decatur	SU	A,B,M		No	C	2,570																	Open
Emory University	Atlanta	SU	A,B,M,D		F,S	C	5,665	29		4	15	20	61	670		10	55	35	690		8	47	45	1/15
Fort Valley State University	Fort Valley	R	A,B,M		F,S	C	2,305																	
Georgia College and State University	Milledgeville	SM	B,M	Pub	F,S	C	4,801	22	26	39	26	6	4	550	12	60	25	3	550	14	60	24	2	4/1
Georgia Institute of Technology	Atlanta	U	B,M,D	Pub	F,S	C	11,841	28	1	6	29	23	41	641	2	22	59	17	687	1	6	56	37	1/15
Georgia Southern University	Statesboro	SM	B,M,D	Pub	F,S	C	14,650	22	30	42	18	4	3	546	19	60	19	2	552	17	58	23	2	7/1
Georgia Southwestern State University	Americus	SM	A,B,M	Pub	F,S	C	1,955																	

Column key:
ENVIRONMENT: U-Urban, R-Rural, SU-Suburban, SM-Small Town — DEGREES AWARDED: A-Associate, B-Bachelor, M-Master, D-Doctorate — CONTROL: Pri-Private, Pub-Public — FRATERNITIES AND SORORITIES: F-Fraternities, S-Sororities, F,S-Both, No-Neither — STUDENTS: C-Coed, M-Men, W-Women, PM-Primarily Men, PW-Primarily Women — UNDERGRADUATE ENROLLMENT FALL 2005 — APPLICATION DEADLINE: Month/Day

NAME OF SCHOOL	TOWN	ENV	DEGREES	CTRL	FRAT	STU	ENROLL	ACT Median	ACT Below 21	ACT 21-23	ACT 24-26	ACT 27-28	ACT Above 28	SAT V Median	SAT V Below 500	SAT V 500-599	SAT V 600-700	SAT V Above 700	SAT M Median	SAT M Below 500	SAT M 500-599	SAT M 600-700	SAT M Above 700	APP DEADLINE
Georgia State University	Atlanta	U	B,M,D	Pub	F,S	C	18,960																	3/1
Kennesaw State University	Kennesaw	SU	B,M	Pub	F,S	C	16,739							535	27	57	15	1	532	28	58	13	1	1
LaGrange College	LaGrange	SM	A,B,M	Pri	F,S	C	986	21	50	20	20	11		515	44	42	14	1	500	44	43	11	2	Open
Mercer University	Macon	SU	B,M,D		F,S	C	4,595																	2/15
Morehouse College	Atlanta	U	B		F	M	3,028	21	41	28	19	9	3	565	38	40	21	1	523	36	41	22	1	2/15
North Georgia College and State University	Dahlonega	SM	A,B,M	Pub	No	C	3,965																	
Oglethorpe University	Atlanta	SU	B,M	Pri	F,S	C	945	25	17	28	22	18	15	560	23	41	26	10	540	30	40	27	3	
Paine College	Augusta	U	B	Pri	F,S	C	828	16	94	4		1		410	87	9	3	1	400	85	13	2		8/1
Piedmont College	Demorest	SM	B,M		No	C	939																	Open
Reinhardt College	Waleska	SM	A,B		No	C	1,090																	Open
Savannah College of Art and Design	Savannah	U	B,M	Pri	No	C	6,136	24	24	26	24	9	18	550	28	42	24	6	536	32	43	21	3	Open
Savannah State University	Savannah	SU	B,M	Pub	F,S	C	2,975	17						440	82	16	2		430	82	16	2		7/1
Shorter College	Rome	SM	B	Pri	F,S	C	967	21	46	28	19	7		515	43	39	16	2	510	43	41	15	1	Open
South University	Savannah	U	A,B,M,D	Pri	No	C																		Open
Southern Polytechnic State University	Marietta	SU	A,B,M	Pub	F,S	C	3,299	21	35	38	22	3	2	540	22	51	25	2	570	8	55	34	3	8/1
Spelman College	Atlanta	U	B		S	W	2,318	23						1101	23	57	17	3		28	55	16	1	2/1
Thomas University	Thomasville	R	A,B,M		No	C	690																	Open
Toccoa Falls College	Toccoa Falls	SM	A,B	Pri	No	C	870	22	43	18	18	11	10	524	42	33	21	4	499	47	35	17	1	8/1
University of Georgia	Athens	SM	A,B,M,D		F,S	C	25,204	27	4	11	33	23	30	620	5	33	47	16	620	4	31	50	15	1/15
University of West Georgia	Carrollton	SU	B,M,D	Pub	F,S	C	8,346	20	59	26	11	3	1	520	44	41	14	1	511	47	41	10	2	7/1
Valdosta State University	Valdosta	SU	A,B,M,D	Pub	F,S	C	9,093	21		11	78	12		511	43	45	10	1	504	45	43	11		7/1
Wesleyan College	Macon	SU	B,M	Pri	No	W	551	22	36	27	25	7	5	540	24	44	26	6	500	48	38	12	2	2/1

Hawaii

NAME OF SCHOOL	TOWN	ENV	DEGREES	CTRL	FRAT	STU	ENROLL	ACT Median	ACT Below 21	ACT 21-23	ACT 24-26	ACT 27-28	ACT Above 28	SAT V Median	SAT V Below 500	SAT V 500-599	SAT V 600-700	SAT V Above 700	SAT M Median	SAT M Below 500	SAT M 500-599	SAT M 600-700	SAT M Above 700	APP DEADLINE
Brigham Young University/Hawaii	Laie	SM	A,B		No	C	2,492	23	32	19	27	9	13	585	21	29	43	7	595	7	43	43	7	2/15
Chaminade University of Honolulu	Honolulu	U	A,B,M		No	C	1,106	22						480	58	3	9	1	470	58	32	9	1	Open
Hawaii Pacific University	Honolulu	U	A,B,M		No	C	5,111	22	34	24	31	5	6	508	46	39	13	2	510	45	37	17	1	Open
University of Hawaii at Hilo	Hilo	SM	B,M	Pub	No	C	2,840																	
University of Hawaii at Manoa	Honolulu	U	B,M,D	Pub	F,S	C	14,351	23	19	36	31	8	7	530	31	49	18	2	570	14	51	31	4	5/1

Idaho

NAME OF SCHOOL	TOWN	ENV	DEGREES	CTRL	FRAT	STU	ENROLL	ACT Median	ACT Below 21	ACT 21-23	ACT 24-26	ACT 27-28	ACT Above 28	SAT V Median	SAT V Below 500	SAT V 500-599	SAT V 600-700	SAT V Above 700	SAT M Median	SAT M Below 500	SAT M 500-599	SAT M 600-700	SAT M Above 700	APP DEADLINE
Albertson College of Idaho	Caldwell	SM	B		F,S	C	788	25	8	21	32	15	24	590	16	36	35	14	580	16	40	33	11	6/1
Boise State University	Boise	U	A,B,M,D	Pub	F,S	C	16,925	22	51	22	12	8	7	520	38	45	16	1	525	36	43	19	2	7/12
Idaho State University	Pocatello	SM	A,B,M,D	Pub	F,S	C	11,899	21	50	24	16	5	4	510	45	37	14	4	540	30	44	22	4	8/1
Lewis-Clark State College	Lewiston	U	A,B	Pub	No	C	3,485																	Open
Northwest Nazarene University	Nampa	SM	A,B,M	Pri	No	C	1,167	23	35	30	18	10	8											8/8
University of Idaho	Moscow	SM	B,M,D	Pub	F,S	C	9,550	23	32	26	23	9	11	550	26	42	26	6	550	25	43	26	6	8/1

Illinois

NAME OF SCHOOL	TOWN	ENV	DEGREES	CTRL	FRAT	STU	ENROLL	ACT Median	ACT Below 21	ACT 21-23	ACT 24-26	ACT 27-28	ACT Above 28	SAT V Median	SAT V Below 500	SAT V 500-599	SAT V 600-700	SAT V Above 700	SAT M Median	SAT M Below 500	SAT M 500-599	SAT M 600-700	SAT M Above 700	APP DEADLINE
Augustana College	Rock Island	SU	B		F,S	C	2,386	26	4	11	30	22	33											Open
Aurora University	Aurora	SU	B,M,D		F,S	C	1,670																	Open
Benedictine University	Lisle	SU	A,B,M,D	Pri	No	C	2,320	23	37	24	23	6	10											Open
Blackburn College	Carlinville	R	B		No	C	575																	Open
Bradley University	Peoria	U	B,M		F,S	C	5,369	25	10	23	33	16	17	560	25	41	30	4	570	13	43	38	6	Open
Chicago State University	Chicago	U	B,M	Pub	F,S	C	4,920																	Open
Columbia College Chicago	Chicago	U	B,M		No	C	9,280																	Open
Concordia University, River Forest	River Forest	SU	B,M,D	Pri	No	C	1,032		36	23	20	9	12											Open
DePaul University	Chicago	U	B,M,D	Pri	F,S	C	14,740	24	25	22	28	14	11	570	17	48	30	5	560	23	47	26	4	2/1
DeVry University/Addison (DuPage County)	Addison	SU	A,B		No	C	4,835																	Open
DeVry University/Chicago	Chicago	U	A,B		No	C	2,905																	Open
DeVry University/Tinley Park	Tinley Park		A,B,M		No	C	1,445																	Open
Dominican University	River Forest	SU	B,M	Pri	No	C	1,287	23	34	29	23	8	5											Open
Eastern Illinois University	Charleston	SM	B,M	Pub	F,S	C	10,375	22	39	33	19	8	4											Open
East-West University	Chicago	U	A,B		No	C	1,020																	Open
Elmhurst College	Elmhurst	SU	B,M	Pri	F,S	C	2,405																	Open
Eureka College	Eureka	SM	B	Pri	F,S	C	550	23																8/1
Greenville College	Greenville	SM	B,M		No	C	1,215	22	35	21	27	9	8	518	54	26	18	2	496	54	38	3	5	8/1
Illinois College	Jacksonville	SM	B	Pri	No	C	1,030	24	22	23	27	16	11	550	12	47	35	6	580	6	41	47	6	Open
Illinois Institute of Technology	Chicago	U	B,M,D		F,S	C	1,985																	Open
Illinois State University	Normal	U	B,M,D	Pub	F,S	C	17,858	24	13	35	35	11	6											3/1
Illinois Wesleyan University	Bloomington	SU	B	Pri	F,S	C	246	29		6	20	24	50	630	1	23	53	23	645	2	25	49	24	3/1
Judson College	Elgin	SU	B,M	Pri	No	C	1,195	23																Open
Kendall College	Chicago	U	A,B	Pri	No	C	780	22	37	35	22	4	1	515					520					Open
Knox College	Galesburg	SM	B	Pri	F,S	C	1,205	28	3	14	18	21	44	640	7	22	42	29	600	7	39	39	15	2/1
Lake Forest College	Lake Forest	SU	B,M	Pri	F,S	C	1,418	25	12	21	32	14	21	590	10	42	36	12	590	10	42	35	13	2/15
Lewis University	Romeoville	SU	A,B,M	Pri	F,S	C	3,230																	Open
Loyola University Chicago	Chicago	U	B,M,D		F,S	C	9,240	25	12	25	29	17	18	590	11	41	40	8	585	14	42	36	8	4/1
MacMurray College	Jacksonville	SM	A,B		F,S	C	701	21	50	28	15	4	3	470	17	75	8		600	17	75	8		Open
McKendree College	Lebanon	SU	B,M	Pri	F,S	C	2,257	25	21	27	27	13	10											Open
Millikin University	Decatur	SU	B,M		F,S	C	2,610																	Open
Monmouth College	Monmouth	SM	B	Pri	F,S	C	1,167																	Open
NAES College of Eastern Illinios University	Chicago	U	B		No	C	90																	Open
National-Louis University	Chicago	SU	B,M,D	Pri	No	PW	2,084																	Open
North Central College	Naperville	SU	B,M	Pri	No	C	2,133	24	15	29	25	13	17	570	16	44	35	5	590	13	42	36	9	Open
North Park University	Chicago	U	B,M	Pri	No	C	1,590																	Open
Northeastern Illinois University	Chicago	U	B,M	Pub	S	C	9,418	21	40	49	9	9	1											7/1
Northern Illinois University	DeKalb	SM	B,M,D	Pub	F,S	C	18,467	22	35	32	23	7	4											8/1

NAME OF SCHOOL	TOWN	ENVIRONMENT	DEGREES AWARDED	CONTROL	FRATERNITIES AND SORORITIES	STUDENTS	UNDERGRADUATE ENROLLMENT FALL 2005	ACT Median	Below 21	21-23	24-26	27-28	Above 28	SAT I VERBAL Median	Below 500	500-599	600-700	Above 700	SAT I MATH Median	Below 500	500-599	600-700	Above 700	APPLICATION DEADLINE Month/Date
Northwestern University	Evanston	SU	B,M,D	Pri	F,S	C	8,010																	5/15
Olivet Nazarene University	Bourbonnais	SU	A,B,M	Pri	No	C	2,402	23	29	25	26	10	10	550	29	39	29	3	540	30	45	19	6	3/1
Principia College	Elsah	R	B	Pri	No	C	536																	Open
Quincy University	Quincy	SM	A,B,M		F,S	C	1,075	23	36	35	20	6	3											Open
Rockford College	Rockford	SU	B,M		No	C	910																	Open
Roosevelt University	Chicago	U	B,M,D		F,S	C	4,300																	Open
Saint Xavier University	Chicago	U	B,M		No	C	3,070																	
School of the Art Institute of Chicago	Chicago	U	B,M		No	C	2,008																	9/1
Shimer College	Waukegan	U	B	Pri	No	C	107																	7/31
Southern Illinois University Carbondale	Carbondale	R	A,B,M,D	Pub	F,S	C	16,697	23	21	38	25	9	7											Open
Southern Illinois University Edwardsville	Edwardsville	SU	B,M	Pub	F,S	C	10,945		29	34	23	7	6											5/1
Trinity Christian College	Palos Heights	SU	B	Pri	No	C	1,280	22	34	29	20	7	10											8/15
Trinity College of Nursing and Health Sciences	Rock Island	U	A,B	Pri	No	C	190																	Open
Trinity International University	Deerfield	SU	B,M,D	Pri	No	C	1,254	23	26	34	20	7	13	519	44	38	13	5	545	23	56	15	6	Open
University of Chicago	Chicago	U	B,M,D		F,S	C	4,638	30		4	9	13	74	720		4	28	68	708		5	31	64	1/1
University of Illinois at Chicago	Chicago	U	B,M,D	Pub	F,S	C	15,150	23	27	27	26	10	10											1/15
University of Illinois at Urbana-Champaign	Urbana	SM	B,M,D		F,S	C	30,453	28	5	11	27	23	33	620	11	33	42	14	680	3	17	41	39	1/2
University of Saint Francis	Joliet	SU	B,M	Pri	No	C	1,276	22	39	31	19	9	2											8/1
VanderCook College of Music	Chicago	U	B,M		F,S	C	89																	
Western Illinois University	Macomb	R	B,M	Pub	F,S	C	11,284	22	46	32	16	4	2											5/15
Wheaton College	Wheaton	SU	B,M,D	Pri	No	C	2,392																	1/15

Indiana

NAME OF SCHOOL	TOWN	ENVIRONMENT	DEGREES AWARDED	CONTROL	FRATERNITIES AND SORORITIES	STUDENTS	UNDERGRADUATE ENROLLMENT FALL 2005	ACT Median	Below 21	21-23	24-26	27-28	Above 28	SAT I VERBAL Median	Below 500	500-599	600-700	Above 700	SAT I MATH Median	Below 500	500-599	600-700	Above 700	APPLICATION DEADLINE Month/Date
Anderson University	Anderson	SU	A,B,M,D	Pri	No	C	2,337							525					526					Open
Ball State University	Muncie	SU	A,B,M,D	Pub	F,S	C	15,903	22						525					526					3/1
Bethel College	Mishawaka	SU	A,B,M	Pri	No	C	1,745																	Open
Butler University	Indianapolis	SU	B,M,D	Pri	F,S	C	3,879	27	3	14	29	22	32	592	7	48	37	8	599	9	37	44	10	Open
Calumet College of St. Joseph	Whiting	U	A,B,M		No	C	1,170																	Open
DePauw University	Greencastle	SM	B		F,S	C	2,375																	
Earlham College	Richmond	SM	B,M	Pri	No	C	1,185	26						640	9	24	40	27	600	17	31	43	9	2/15
Franklin College	Franklin	SM	B	Pri	F,S	C	1,003	21	35	30	19	11	5	510	43	42	13	2	520	37	45	17	1	Open
Goshen College	Goshen	SM	B		No	C	930																	
Grace College	Winona Lake	SM	A,B,M	Pri	No	C	868	23	25	29	28	8	10	532	32	44	19	5	579	36	40	21	3	8/1
Hanover College	Hanover	R	B		Pri	C	1,008	26	2	25	25	14	34	590	9	42	34	15	600	7	42	43	8	3/1
Huntington University	Huntington	SM	A,B,M	Pri	S	C	949		31	29	18	11	11		33	42	18	7		33	41	19	7	8/15
Indiana Institute of Technology	Fort Wayne	U	A,B,M		F,S	C	2,828	18	65	21	3	8		460	63	30	6	1	500	47	34	18	1	Open
Indiana State University	Terre Haute	U	A,B,M,D	Pub	F,S	C	8,670	20	61	16	17	4	2	477	60	32	7	1	473	62	30	7	1	8/1
Indiana University Bloomington	Bloomington	SM	A,B,M,D	Pub	F,S	C	29,562	24	18	24	29	14	15	550	27	44	25	4	560	23	43	29	5	2/1
Indiana University East	Richmond	SM	A,B	Pub	F,S	C	2,392	19	78	13	4	4		470	67	26	7		450	68	26	5	1	Open
Indiana University Kokomo	Kokomo	SM	A,B,M	Pub	No	C	2,737	19	69	19	10	2		490	56	34	9	1	490	52	40	7		8/3
Indiana University Northwest	Gary	U	A,B,M	Pub	F,S	C	4,387	18	65	23	8	4		450	70	25	5		450	68	26	6		8/1
Indiana University South Bend	South Bend	SU	A,B,M	Pub	S	C	6,324	20	60	20	17	3		480	57	34	8	1	480	57	34	8		Open
Indiana University Southeast	New Albany	SU	A,B,M	Pub	F,S	C	3,500	20	58	28	10	4		480	59	31	10		470	60	34	6		7/15
Indiana University-Purdue University Fort Wayne	Fort Wayne	SU	A,B,M	Pub	F	C	11,028	21	48	26	18	5	3	485	58	31	9	2	497	51	36	11	2	8/1
Indiana University-Purdue University Indianapolis	Indianapolis	U	A,B,M,D	Pub	F,S	C	21,438	20	54	25	12	7	2	490	52	36	11	1	500	49	38	12	1	Open
Indiana Wesleyan University	Marion	U	A,B,M,D		No	C	2,830	24	12	26	28	23	11	544	30	42	24	4	541	28	45	24	3	8/1
Manchester College	North Manchester	SM	A,B,M		No	C	1,120																	Open
Marian College	Indianapolis	SU	A,B,M	Pri	No	C	1,666	21	48	26	20	3	3	520	39	47	13	1	520	33	48	17	2	8/1
Martin University	Indianapolis	U	B,M	Pri	No	C	590																	Open
Oakland City University	Oakland City	SM	A,B,M	Pri	No	C	1,900																	Open
Purdue University/Calumet	Hammond	U	A,B,M	Pub	F,S	C	8,359																	
Purdue University/West Lafayette	West Lafayette	SU	A,B,M,D	Pub	F,S	C	30,875	25	12	22	29	17	20	557	27	47	22	4	593	17	40	33	10	Open
Rose-Hulman Institute of Technology	Terre Haute	SU	B,M		F,S	C	1,768	29	1	5	18	20	56	630	2	33	52	13	680		10	55	35	3/1
Saint Joseph's College	Rensselaer	SM	A,B,M		No	C	1,003	22	35	36	13	14	2	499	49	37	13	1	498	48	43	9		Open
Saint Mary-of-the-Woods College	St. Mary-of-the-Woods	R	A,B,M	Pri	No	W	1,626	21						516					499					7/15
Saint Mary's College	Notre Dame	SU	B	Pri	No	W	1,397	25	7	28	34	19	12	570	15	47	32	6	570	15	52	32	2	3/1
Taylor University	Upland	R	A,B,M	Pri	No	C	1,853	26	9	16	26	23	25	590	10	41	35	14	610	11	34	39	16	1/15
Tri-State University-Main Campus	Angola	SM	A,B,M		F,S	C	1,168																	6/1
University of Evansville	Evansville	U	A,B,M		F,S	C	2,552	25	14	24	25	14	23	580	17	40	34	8	570	20	38	35	7	2/1
University of Indianapolis	Indianapolis	SU	A,B,M,D	Pri	No	C	3,361	22	42	26	15	14	3	510	40	39	15	2	510	40	43	16	1	Open
University of Notre Dame	Notre Dame	SU	B,M,D		No	C	8,275	31						667		12	41	47	693		6	37	57	12/31
University of Saint Francis	Fort Wayne	U	A,B,M	Pri	No	C	1,615																	Open
University of Southern Indiana	Evansville	SU	A,B,M	Pub	F,S	C	9,252	20	55	25	14	3	3	476	61	31	7	1	483	56	34	9	1	
Valparaiso University	Valparaiso	SM	A,B,M,D		F,S	C	2,966																	8/15
Wabash College	Crawfordsville	SM	B		F	M	877	26						592	11	40	41	8	604	10	33	45	12	2/1

Iowa

NAME OF SCHOOL	TOWN	ENVIRONMENT	DEGREES AWARDED	CONTROL	FRATERNITIES AND SORORITIES	STUDENTS	UNDERGRADUATE ENROLLMENT FALL 2005	ACT Median	Below 21	21-23	24-26	27-28	Above 28	SAT I VERBAL Median	Below 500	500-599	600-700	Above 700	SAT I MATH Median	Below 500	500-599	600-700	Above 700	APPLICATION DEADLINE Month/Date
Allen College	Waterloo	SU	A,B,M	Pri	No	PW	374	22	44	44	6	6												3/1
Ashford University	Clinton	SM	A,B,M	Pri	No	C	376																	8/15
Briar Cliff University	Sioux City	SU	A,B,M	Pri	No	C	1,096	22	45	27	16	8	5	498	57	29	14		435	63	38			Open
Buena Vista University	Storm Lake	SM	B,M	Pri	No	C	1,214	22	35	29	23	5	8											3/1
Central College	Pella	SU	B	Pri	F,S	C	1,635																	3/1
Clarke College	Dubuque	U	A,B,M,D		No	C	1,021	23						559	40	30	10	20	548	50	10	20	20	Open
Coe College	Cedar Rapids	U	B,M	Pri		C	1,295																	
Cornell College	Mount Vernon	SM	B		F,S	C	1,179	26	2	23	28	17	30	630	5	29	49	17	620	6	34	45	15	2/1
Dordt College	Sioux Center	R	A,B,M		No	C	1,300																	3/1
Drake University	Des Moines	SU	B,M,D		F,S	C	3,141	26	4	18	21	31	25	600	14	34	43	10	590	9	32	37	14	3/1

TEST SCORES

Legend — ENVIRONMENT: U-Urban, R-Rural, SU-Suburban, SM-Small Town · DEGREES AWARDED: A-Associate, B-Bachelor, M-Master, D-Doctorate · CONTROL: Pri-Private, Pub-Public · FRATERNITIES AND SORORITIES: F-Fraternities, S-Sororities, PM-Primarily Men, PW-Primarily Women, B-Both, No-Neither · STUDENTS: C-Coed, M-Men, W-Women

Name of School	Town	Env.	Degrees Awarded	Control	Frat./Sor.	Students	Undergrad Enroll. Fall 2005	ACT Median	ACT Below 21	ACT 21-23	ACT 24-26	ACT 27-28	ACT Above 28	SAT V Median	SAT V Below 500	SAT V 500-599	SAT V 600-700	SAT V Above 700	SAT M Median	SAT M Below 500	SAT M 500-599	SAT M 600-700	SAT M Above 700	App Deadline
Graceland University	Lamoni	SM	B,M	Pri	No	C	2,045																	
Grand View College	Des Moines	U	A,B	Pri	No	C	1,761	20	60	25	11	3	1											Open
Grinnell College	Grinnell	SM	B	Pri	No	C	1,577	31			7	28	66	695	3	13	32	53	685	3	11	41	44	1/20
Iowa State University	Ames	U	B,M,D	Pub	F,S	C	21,354	24	15	25	26	16	17		19	35	33	13		12	28	40	21	8/1
Iowa Wesleyan College	Mount Pleasant	SM	B		F,S	C	849	19	80	11	9													Open
Loras College	Dubuque	SM	A,B,M		S	C	1,594	22	34	34	19	9	6	517	39	44	17		556	22	39	39		Open
Luther College	Decorah	SM	B	Pri	No	C	2,545	26	11	21	25	18	24	610	12	26	45	17	630	7	30	47	16	Open
Maharishi University of Management	Fairfield	SM	B,M,D	Pri	No	C	260																	Open
Mercy College of Health Sciences	Des Moines	U	A,B		No	C	656																	
Morningside College	Sioux City	SU	B,M		F,S	C	1,149	22	38	28	21	7	6		47	26	26			42	26	26	5	Open
Mount Mercy College	Cedar Rapids	U	B		No	C	1,490	22	41	33	20	4	2											8/15
Northwestern College of Iowa	Orange City	SM	B		No	C	1,273	24	18	25	27	13	17											Open
Saint Ambrose University	Davenport	U	B,M,D	Pri	No	C	2,699	22	41	25	18	7	9											Open
Simpson College	Indianola	SU	B		F,S	C	2,035	24	12	28	33	13	14											Open
University of Dubuque	Dubuque	SU	A,B,M,D	Pri	F,S	C	1,179	23						500	26	64	9	1	500	17	68	15		5/1
University of Iowa	Iowa City	SM	B,M,D	Pub	F,S	C	20,300	25	11	25	33	16	13	590	16	36	36	12	600	12	34	39	15	4/1
University of Northern Iowa	Cedar Falls	SM	B,M,D	Pub	F,S	C	10,952	23	28	31	26	9	6	549	35	40	17	8	568	12	29	37	26	8/15
Upper Iowa University	Fayette	R	A,B,M		F,S	C	700																	Open
Wartburg College	Waverly	SM	B	Pri	No	C	1,811	23	23	28	24	13	12	560	20	44	24	12	600	20	28	36	16	9/1
William Penn University	Oskaloosa	R	A,B		F,S	C	1,555																	Open
Kansas																								
Baker University	Baldwin City	R	B,M	Pri	F,S	C	916	23	25	28	28	8	11		44	35	18	3		53	24	21	3	Open
Benedictine College	Atchison	SM	A,B,M		No	C	1,393																	Open
Bethany College	Lindsborg	SM	B	Pri	F,S	C	588																	5/1
Bethel College	North Newton	SU	B	Pri	No	C	514																	Open
Emporia State University	Emporia	SM	B,M,D	Pub	F,S	C	4,351	22	38	28	21	9	4											Open
Fort Hays State University	Hays	SM	A,B,M	Pub	F,S	C	7,755	22	47	24	18	6	5											Open
Friends University	Wichita	U	A,B,M	Pri	F,S	C	1,025																	Open
Kansas State University	Manhattan	SU	A,B,M,D	Pub	F,S	C	18,838		23	26	26	11	13											Open
Kansas Wesleyan University	Salina	U	A,B,M	Pri	F,S	C	791	22																Open
McPherson College	McPherson	SM	B		No	C	466	21	37	31	20	6	8	485	58	25	17		495	63	21	12	4	Open
MidAmerica Nazarene University	Olathe	SU	A,B,M		No	C	1,390																	8/1
Newman University	Wichita	U	A,B,M	Pri	No	C	1,732	23	26	33	25	7	9	600	45	31	17	7	500	45	41	7	7	Open
Ottawa University	Ottawa	SM	B		No	C	475																	Open
Pittsburg State University	Pittsburg	SM	A,B,M	Pub	F,S	C	5,543	22	40	29	20	6	5											Open
Southwestern College	Winfield	SM	B,M	Pri	F,S	C	1,263	22	37	20	26	10	5	480	58	37		5	490	58	26	11	5	8/1
Sterling College	Sterling	R	B		No	C	516	21	40	28	18	6	8						470	67	29	5		Open
Tabor College	Hillsboro	R	A,B	Pri	No	C	596							470	62	69	10							Open
University of Kansas	Lawrence	SU	B,M,D	Pub	F,S	C	21,343	24	15	27	28	13	17											4/1
University of Saint Mary	Leavenworth	SM	A,B,M		No	C	590																	Open
Washburn University	Topeka	U	A,B,M,D	Pub	F,S	C	6,424																	8/1
Wichita State University	Wichita	U	A,B,M,D	Pub	F,S	C	11,710																	Open
Kentucky																								
Alice Lloyd College	Pippa Passes	R	B	Pri	No	C	612	20	48	35	13	3	1											Open
Asbury College	Wilmore	SM	B,M	Pri	No	C	1,229	24	21	27	19	13	19	593	17	32	35	16	560	22	37	33	8	Open
Bellarmine University	Louisville	SU	B,M	Pri	F,S	C	2,004	24	20	32	28	12	10	551	26	49	19	6	552	20	48	27	5	2/1
Berea College	Berea	SM	B		No	C	1,595	23	22	35	29	9	5	565	18	40	33	9	550	20	48	27	6	Open
Brescia University	Owensboro	U	A,B,M		No	C	710																	Open
Campbellsville University	Campbellsville	SM	A,B,M		No	C	1,831	21	47	30	17	3	3											
Centre College	Danville	SM	B	Pri	F,S	C	1,065																	2/1
Eastern Kentucky University	Richmond	SM	A,B,M	Pub	F,S	C	13,380																	
Georgetown College	Georgetown	SU	B,M	Pri	F,S	C	1,332	25	22	31	26	11	10											
Kentucky Christian College	Grayson	SM	A,B,M		No	C	585																	Open
Kentucky State University	Frankfort	SM	A,B,M			C	2,251	17						418					426					Open
Kentucky Wesleyan College	Owensboro	U	B		F,S	C	755	21	44	26	18	7	5	490	50	36	14		520	36	39	22	3	Open
Lindsey Wilson College	Columbia	SM	A,B,M		No	C	1,390																	Open
Midway College	Midway	R	A,B		No	PW	1,279	20	62	21	10	3	4	576	31	31	13	25	529	49	13	25	13	Open
Morehead State University	Morehead	SM	A,B,M	Pub	F,S	C	7,550	20	55	26	13	4	2											8/1
Murray State University	Murray	SM	A,B,M	Pub	F,S	C	8,467	23	20	30	30	12	8											
Northern Kentucky University	Highland Heights	SU	A,B,M	Pub	F,S	C	10,840																	
Pikeville College	Pikeville	SM	A,B	Pri	No	C	844	19	62	23	10	3	2											8/16
Spalding University	Louisville	U	A,B,M,D	Pri	No	C	903																	Open
Thomas More College	Crestview Hills	SU	A,B,M		No	C	1,342	22	37	34	16	6	7	537	34	36	25	5	538	36	39	22	3	8/15
Transylvania University	Lexington	U	B		F,S	C	1,151	26	6	15	27	23	29	599	15	35	35	15	589	17	33	39	11	2/1
Union College	Barbourville	SM	A,B,M		No	C	611																	Open
University of Kentucky	Lexington	SU	B,M,D	Pub	F,S	C	16,865																	
University of Louisville	Louisville	U	A,B,M,D	Pub	F,S	C	13,893	23	25	30	23	11	11											8/21
University of the Cumberlands	Williamsburg	SM	B,M	Pri	No	C	1,630	22	43	29	16	8	4	510	47	40	13	1	520	44	39	16	1	Open
Western Kentucky University	Bowling Green	SU	A,B,M	Pub	F,S	C	15,978	20	52	24	14	6	4	500	48	35	17		500	45	41	11	3	8/1
Louisiana																								
Centenary College of Louisiana	Shreveport	U	B,M		F,S	C	904	25	13	23	31	14	1	580	22	30	37	11	570	22	39	37	2	8/1
Dillard University	New Orleans	U	B		F,S	C	2,315																	
Grambling State University	Grambling	SM	A,B,M,D	Pub	F,S	C	4,700																	Open
Louisiana College	Pineville	SM	B	Pri	F,S	C	1,055																	Open
Louisiana State University and Agricultural and Mechanical College	Baton Rouge	U	B,M,D	Pub	F,S	C	25,705	25	5	28	34	17	16	589	11	42	40	7	608	6	36	49	9	4/15
Louisiana State University in Shreveport	Shreveport	U	B,M	Pub	F,S	C	3,675																	

TEST SCORES

Column legend (from rotated header labels):
- ENVIRONMENT: U-Urban, R-Rural, SU-Suburban, SM-Small Town
- DEGREES AWARDED: A-Associate, B-Bachelor, M-Master, D-Doctorate
- CONTROL: Pri-Private, Pub-Public
- FRATERNITIES AND SORORITIES: F-Fraternities, S-Sororities, No-Neither
- STUDENTS: C-Coed, M-Men, W-Women, PM-Primarily Men, PW-Primarily Women
- UNDERGRADUATE ENROLLMENT FALL 2005
- APPLICATION DEADLINE Month/Day

NAME OF SCHOOL	TOWN	ENV	DEGREES	CTRL	FRAT	STUD	ENROLL 2005	ACT Med	ACT <21	ACT 21-23	ACT 24-26	ACT 27-28	ACT >28	SATV Med	SATV <500	SATV 500-599	SATV 600-700	SATV >700	SATM Med	SATM <500	SATM 500-599	SATM 600-700	SATM >700	DEADLINE
Louisiana Tech University	Ruston	SM	A,B,M,D	Pub	F,S	C	9,750																	
Loyola University New Orleans	New Orleans	U	B,M	Pri	F,S	C	3,660																	
McNeese State University	Lake Charles	SU	A,B,M	Pub	F,S	C	6,855																	Open
Nicholls State University	Thibodaux	SM	A,B,M	Pub	F,S	C	6,535																	Open
Northwestern State University of Louisiana	Natchitoches	SM	A,B,M	Pub	F,S	C	8,788	20	58	24	12	3	2	500	45	36	17	1	500	44	43	11	2	7/6
Our Lady of Holy Cross College	New Orleans	U	A,B,M	Pri	No	C	1,312																	7/20
Southeastern Louisiana University	Hammond	SM	A,B,M	Pub	F,S	C	14,363	21	49	32	14	3	2											7/15
Southern University and A&M College	Baton Rouge	U	A,B,M,D	Pub	F,S	C	8,576	18	85	11	3	1	1	433	80	15	2		427	80	15	2		7/1
Southern University at New Orleans	New Orleans	SU	B	Pub	No	C	450																	
Tulane University	New Orleans	U	A,B,M,D	Pri	F,S	C	7,978								4	8	52	36		2	18	47	33	1/15
University of Louisiana at Lafayette	Lafayette	U	B,M,D	Pub	F,S	C	14,590																	Open
University of Louisiana at Monroe	Monroe	U	A,B,M,D	Pub	F,S	C	8,376		56	26	12	4	3		61	32	6	1		63	24	11	2	Open
University of New Orleans	New Orleans	U	B,M,D	Pub	F,S	C	13,350																	
Xavier University of Louisiana	New Orleans	U	B,M,D	Pri	F,S	C	3,160																	

Maine

NAME OF SCHOOL	TOWN	ENV	DEGREES	CTRL	FRAT	STUD	ENROLL 2005	ACT Med	ACT <21	ACT 21-23	ACT 24-26	ACT 27-28	ACT >28	SATV Med	SATV <500	SATV 500-599	SATV 600-700	SATV >700	SATM Med	SATM <500	SATM 500-599	SATM 600-700	SATM >700	DEADLINE
Bates College	Lewiston	SM	B		No	C	1,684							675		7	55	37	680		6	65	29	1/1
Bowdoin College	Brunswick	SM	B	Pri	No	C	1,666							700	1	5	52	42	700		9	44	47	1/1
Colby College	Waterville	SM	B	Pri	No	C	1,871	29		3	17	23	57	680	1	9	48	42	680	1	8	55	36	1/1
College of the Atlantic	Bar Harbor	SM	B	Pri	No	C	305	26	9	18	32	23	18	627	4	27	54	15	579	10	50	27	12	2/15
Husson College	Bangor	U	A,B,M,D	Pri	F,S	C	1,877	20	88	8	4			459	74	23	3		469	66	29	5		Open
Maine College of Art	Portland	U	B,M	Pri	No	C	400							520					540					7/1
Maine Maritime Academy	Castine	SM	A,B,M	Pub	F	C	805	21						518	50	38	12		521	53	36	11		Open
Saint Joseph's College of Maine	Standish	R	A,B		No	C	955	21						464	67	27	5	1	468	64	28	7	1	Open
Thomas College	Waterville	R	A,B,M	Pri	F,S	C	732		100					510	48	32	17	1	500	50	43	7		Open
Unity College	Unity	R	A,B	Pri	No	C	527																	Open
University of Maine	Orono	SM	B,M,D	Pub	F,S	C	9,179	23	30	28	25	11	6	540	28	48	21	3	540	27	46	22	5	Open
University of Maine at Augusta	Augusta	SM	A,B	Pub	No	C	5,494							460					440					6/15
University of Maine at Farmington	Farmington	SM	B	Pub	No	C	2,452							528	42	37	18	2	511	47	37	13	1	Open
University of Maine at Fort Kent	Fort Kent	SM	A,B	Pub	F,S	C	1,193	20	100					444	70	24	6		445	71	21	6		Open
University of Maine at Machias	Machias	R	B	Pub	F,S	C	1,149	22	43	14	29	7	7	500	49	36	13	2	480	59	30	9	1	Open
University of Maine at Presque Isle	Presque Isle	R	A,B	Pub	F,S	C	1,548							461	65	27	8		453	69	29	1	1	Open
University of New England	Biddeford	R	A,B,M,D	Pri	No	C	1,736							520	36	50	13	2	520	35	45	19	1	Open
University of Southern Maine	Gorham	U	A,B,M,D	Pub	F,S	C	8,622	20	54	25	15	5		510	46	38	14	1	501	48	40	12	1	2/15

Maryland

NAME OF SCHOOL	TOWN	ENV	DEGREES	CTRL	FRAT	STUD	ENROLL 2005	ACT Med	ACT <21	ACT 21-23	ACT 24-26	ACT 27-28	ACT >28	SATV Med	SATV <500	SATV 500-599	SATV 600-700	SATV >700	SATM Med	SATM <500	SATM 500-599	SATM 600-700	SATM >700	DEADLINE
Baltimore Hebrew University	Baltimore	U	B,M,D	Pri	No	C	90																	
Bowie State University	Bowie	SU	B,M,D	Pub	F,S	C	4,000																	
Capitol College	Laurel	R	A,B,M		No	C	310																	Open
College of Notre Dame of Maryland	Baltimore	SU	B,M		No	PW	1,601																	Open
Columbia Union College	Takoma Park	SU	A,B		No	C	318	19																8/1
Coppin State College	Baltimore	U	B,M	Pub	F,S	C	3,285																	
Frostburg State University	Frostburg	SM	B,M	Pub	F,S	C	4,321		64	16	13	5	2		52	37	10	1		46	42	11	1	Open
Goucher College	Baltimore	SU	B,M		No	C	1,346		14	22	31	15	18	616	6	34	41	19	592	9	45	36	10	2/1
Hood College	Frederick	SU	B,M	Pri	No	C	1,183	22	33	33	20	9	5	559	19	51	27	3	553	21	50	26	3	2/15
Johns Hopkins University	Baltimore	SU	B,M,D		F,S	C	4,417	30	1	3	13	14	69	685	2	10	48	40	710	1	5	40	54	1/1
Loyola College in Maryland	Baltimore	U	B,M,D	Pri	F,S	C	3,533	25	5	19	42	19	16	600	6	38	48	9	590	6	31	53	10	1/15
Maryland Institute College of Art	Baltimore	U	B,M	Pri	No	C	1,497							590	10	43	33	14	570	19	45	29	7	2/15
McDaniel College	Westminster	SU	B,M	Pri	F,S	C	1,695							550	26	46	23	5	560	21	45	27	6	2/1
Morgan State University	Baltimore	SU	B,M,D	Pub	F,S	C	5,820																	
Mount Saint Mary's University	Emmitsburg	R	B,M		No	C	1,656							540	24	49	25	2	540	25	47	25	3	3/1
Saint John's College	Annapolis	SM	B,M	Pri	No	C	479																	Open
Saint Mary's College of Maryland	St. Marys City	R	B	Pub	No	C	1,964							630	7	27	48	18	610	7	36	51	6	1/15
Salisbury University	Salisbury	SM	B,M		F,S	C	6,437	24	30	18	33	14	5	560	13	59	26	2	570	9	55	34	2	1/15
Sojourner-Douglass College	Baltimore	U	B		No	C	250																	
Towson University	Towson	SU	B,M,D	Pub	F,S	C	14,495							540	27	53	18	2	550	21	53	25	2	5/2
United States Naval Academy	Annapolis	SM	B		No	C	4,200	29						650	2	25	45	28	670			53	34	Open
University of Maryland/Baltimore County	Baltimore	SU	B,M,D	Pub	F,S	C	9,670																	
University of Maryland/College Park	College Park	SU	B,M,D	Pub	F,S	C	25,442								7	22	51	17		5	17	49	29	1/20
University of Maryland/Eastern Shore	Princess Anne	R	B,M,D	Pub	F,S	C	3,335																	
University of Maryland/University College	Adelphi	U	A,B,M,D	Pub	No	C	19,000																	Open
Villa Julie College	Stevenson	SU	B,M	Pri	S	C	2,807							500	45	42	12	1	500	44	41	14	1	Open
Washington College	Chestertown	SM	B,M	Pri	No	C	1,341	23						578	12	48	29	11	567	12	54	30	4	3/1

Massachusetts

NAME OF SCHOOL	TOWN	ENV	DEGREES	CTRL	FRAT	STUD	ENROLL 2005	ACT Med	ACT <21	ACT 21-23	ACT 24-26	ACT 27-28	ACT >28	SATV Med	SATV <500	SATV 500-599	SATV 600-700	SATV >700	SATM Med	SATM <500	SATM 500-599	SATM 600-700	SATM >700	DEADLINE
American International College	Springfield	U	A,B,M,D	Pri	No	C	1,398	20	15	80	5			475	50	40	10	1	505	50	45	5		Open
Amherst College	Amherst	SM	B	Pri	No	C	1,623				4	13	83			4	29	67			6	26	68	1/1
Anna Maria College	Paxton	R	A,B,M	Pri	No	C	637	19	84	8				470	71	25	3		460	64	32	3	1	Open
Art Institute of Boston at Lesley University	Boston	U	B,M	Pri	No	C	531																	
Assumption College	Worcester	SU	B,M	Pri	No	C	2,105	21	40	38	16	5	1	540	27	52	19	2	540	27	50	22	1	2/15
Atlantic Union College	South Lancaster	SM	A,B,M	Pri	No	C	431	17	64	24	6	3	3	430	60	32	6		400	72	21	4		8/1
Babson College	Babson Park	SU	B,M	Pri	F,S	C	1,725																	
Bay Path College	Longmeadow	SU	A,B,M		No	W	1,343							515	39	47	14		495	56	38	6		Open
Becker College	Worcester	U	A,B		No	C	1,480																	Open
Benjamin Franklin Institute of Technology	Boston	U	A,B	Pri	No	C	388																	8/15
Bentley College	Waltham	SU	A,B,M	Pri	F,S	C	4,294							590	7	48	42	3	630	1	21	63	15	2/1
Berklee College of Music	Boston	U	B,M	Pri	No	C	4,037																	2/1

TEST SCORES

Column key:
- ENVIRONMENT: U-Urban, R-Rural, SU-Suburban, SM-Small Town
- DEGREES AWARDED: A-Associate, B-Bachelor, M-Master, D-Doctorate
- CONTROL: Pri-Private, Pub-Public
- FRATERNITIES AND SORORITIES: F-Fraternities, S-Sororities, F,S-Both, No-Neither
- STUDENTS: C-Coed, M-Men, W-Women, PM-Primarily Men, PW-Primarily Women
- UNDERGRADUATE ENROLLMENT FALL 2005
- APPLICATION DEADLINE: Month/Day

Name of School	Town	Env	Degrees	Ctrl	Frat	Stu	Enroll	ACT Med	ACT <21	ACT 21-23	ACT 24-26	ACT 27-28	ACT >28	SATV Med	V<500	V500-599	V600-700	V>700	SATM Med	M<500	M500-599	M600-700	M>700	Deadline
Boston Architectural Center	Boston	U	B,M		No	C	495																	Open
Boston College	Chestnut Hill	SU	B,M,D	Pri	No	C	9,019																	1/2
Boston Conservatory	Boston	U	B		F,S	C	365																	Open
Boston University	Boston	U	B,M,D	Pri	F,S	C	18,694	28	1	9	27	22	41	630	4	27	54	15	650		21	60	19	1/1
Brandeis University	Waltham	SU	B,M,D	Pri	No	C	3,267							680	2	11	50	37	690	3	10	46	41	1/15
Bridgewater State College	Bridgewater	SU	B,M	Pub	F,S	C	7,851	21	53	23	23			510	43	45	11	1	509	42	45	12	1	2/15
Cambridge College	Cambridge	U	B,M	Pri	No	C	1,423																	Open
Clark University	Worcester	U	B,M,D	Pri	No	C	2,255	26	9	15	35	21	20	610	10	36	44	10	590	12	39	40	9	1/15
College of Our Lady of the Elms	Chicopee	SU	A,B,M		No	C	640																	Open
College of the Holy Cross	Worcester	SU	B	Pri	No	C	2,816							632	4	23	54	19	634	3	20	57	20	1/15
Curry College	Milton	SU	B,M		No	C	2,315																	
Eastern Nazarene College	Quincy	SU	A,B,M		No	C	640																	
Emerson College	Boston	U	B,M,D		F,S	C	3,373	27	3	12	40	27	18	630	1	26	56	17	605	4	43	45	8	1/5
Emmanuel College	Boston	U	B,M	Pri	No	C	2,096	22	30	28	26	12	4	531	26	46	23	5	510	35	43	20	2	3/1
Endicott College	Beverly	SU	A,B,M		No	C	1,897							535	27	57	15	1	537	25	57	17	1	2/15
Fitchburg State College	Fitchburg	SU	B,M	Pub	F,S	C	3,660	20	55	25	14	3	3	510	44	42	13	1	500	43	44	12	1	4/1
Framingham State College	Framingham	SU	B,M	Pub	No	C	3,772							532	27	57	15	1	530	29	55	15	1	2/15
Gordon College	Wenham	SM	B,M	Pri	No	C	1,617	25						607	8	33	48	11	593	10	34	49	7	3/1
Hampshire College	Amherst	R	B		No	C	1,335																	
Harvard University/Harvard College	Cambridge	U	B,M,D		No	C	6,660																	
Hellenic College/Holy Cross Greek Orthodox School of Theology	Brookline	U	B,M	Pri	No	C	84								30	50	20			40	30	30		5/1
Lasell College	Newton	SU	B,M	Pri	No	C	1,095																	Open
Lesley University	Cambridge	U	A,B,M,D	Pri	No	PW	1,265							538	30	43	26	1	510	42	43	15		3/1
Massachusetts College of Art	Boston	U	B,M	Pub	No	C	1,549	23	9	45	36	10		570	17	50	29	4	540	32	49	18	1	2/15
Massachusetts College of Liberal Arts	North Adams	R	B,M	Pub	F,S	C	1,400																	
Massachusetts College of Pharmacy and Health Sciences	Boston	U	A,B,M,D	Pri	F,S	C	1,886	22	34	38	19	7	2	532	32	51	16	1	575	13	50	32	5	2/1
Massachusetts Institute of Technology	Cambridge	U	B,M,D	Pri	F,S	C	4,066	33		1	1	4	94	730	1	4	27	68	780			7	92	1/1
Massachusetts Maritime Academy	Buzzards Bay	SM	B,M	Pub	No	C	969	21						520	48	42	9	1	540	36	47	16	1	Open
Merrimack College	North Andover	SU	A,B,M	Pri	F,S	C	2,154	21	38	34	22	4	2	540	18	67	12	3	540	14	65	15	6	2/1
Montserrat College of Art	Beverly	SU	B	Pri	No	C	299																	Open
Mount Holyoke College	South Hadley	SM	B,M		No	W	2,125	29		5	14	20	60	667	1	10	56	33	650	2	15	59	24	1/15
Mount Ida College	Newton	SU	A,B	Pri	No	C	1,130																	Open
New England Conservatory of Music	Boston	U	B,M,D		No	C	383																	12/1
Newbury College	Brookline	SU	A,B		No	C	1,340	20																3/1
Nichols College	Dudley	R	A,B,M		No	C	1,400																	Open
Northeastern University	Boston	U	A,B,M,D	Pri	F,S	C	14,730							603	8	34	48	10	623	5	26	55	14	1/15
Pine Manor College	Chestnut Hill	SU	A,B	Pri	No	W	455																	Open
Regis College	Weston	SU	A,B,M	Pri	No	W	843							480	55	40	4	1	460	62	32	6		Open
Salem State College	Salem	U	B,M	Pub	No	C	7,296							490	52	38	9	1	480	56	36	7	1	Open
Simmons College	Boston	U	B,M,D	Pri	No	PW	1,965	23						561	18	49	29	4	545	23	55	21	1	4/1
Simon's Rock College of Bard	Great Barrington	SM	A,B	Pri	No	C	389	23		53	13	13	20	645	1	31	44	24	605	22	26	31	21	
Smith College	Northampton	SM	B,M,D	Pri	No	W	2,665	28	10	12	12	13	53	660	2	23	45	30	640	5	34	44	17	1/16
Springfield College	Springfield	SU	B,M,D		No	C	2,200																	
Stonehill College	Easton	SU	B,M	Pri	No	C	2,431	25	8	18	46	19	9	590	5	46	45	4	600	5	40	50	5	1/15
Suffolk University	Boston	U	A,B,M,D	Pri	F,S	C	4,340	21	38	36	18	7	1	520	39	44	15	2	510	42	45	13		3/1
Tufts University	Medford	SU	B,M,D	Pri	F,S	C	5,078	30																1/1
University of Massachusetts Amherst	Amherst	SM	A,B,M,D	Pub	F,S	C	18,812							560					580					
University of Massachusetts Boston	Boston	U	B,M,D	Pub	No	C	8,958							510	42	41	13	4	510	39	46	13	2	1/1
University of Massachusetts Dartmouth	North Dartmouth	SU	B,M,D	Pub	F,S	C	7,519	21	34	40	20	2	4	530	34	49	16	1	540	27	50	22	1	Open
University of Massachusetts Lowell	Lowell	U	A,B,M,D	Pub	No	C	8,301																	Open
Wellesley College	Wellesley	SU	B		No	W	2,300	30					69	700		7	55	38	685		6	45	49	1/15
Wentworth Institute of Technology	Boston	U	A,B	Pri	No	C	3,636	23						517					556					Open
Western New England College	Springfield	SU	A,B,M	Pri	No	C	2,855							520	33	51	15	1	540	29	43	26	2	Open
Westfield State College	Westfield	R	B,M	Pub	No	C	4,305																	Open
Wheaton College	Norton	SU	B	Pri	No	C	1,568	28			35	28	37	640	4	21	55	20	620	1	33	52	14	1/15
Wheelock College	Boston	U	A,B,M	Pri	No	C	675							509	44	43	12	1	485	54	38	8	1	3/1
Williams College	Williamstown	SM	B,M	Pri	No	C	2,154	31	1	1	13	13	72	710		11	35	54	710		9	36	56	1/1
Worcester Polytechnic Institute	Worcester	SU	B,M,D	Pri	F,S	C	2,806	27	5	11	31	24	28	620	6	34	44	16	670		13	53	34	2/1
Worcester State College	Worcester	U	B,M	Pub	No	C	4,598	20	60	30	4	6	2	504	47	41	12		510	42	50	8		Open

Michigan

Name of School	Town	Env	Degrees	Ctrl	Frat	Stu	Enroll	ACT Med	ACT <21	ACT 21-23	ACT 24-26	ACT 27-28	ACT >28	SATV Med	V<500	V500-599	V600-700	V>700	SATM Med	M<500	M500-599	M600-700	M>700	Deadline
Adrian College	Adrian	SU	A,B		F,S	C	950																	
Albion College	Albion	SM	B		F,S	C	1,610																	
Alma College	Alma	SM	B	Pri	F,S	C	1,284	25	19	25	28	14	14	586	17	35	26	22	574	22	22	39	15	Open
Andrews University	Berrien Springs	R	A,B,M,D	Pri	F,S	C	1,726	23	28	31	21	7	13	540	37	42	23	4	520	41	35	20	4	Open
Aquinas College	Grand Rapids	SU	A,B,M		No	C	1,782	22	35	25	24	9	7											Open
Baker College of Flint	Flint	U	A,B		No	C	4,400																	Open
Calvin College	Grand Rapids	SU	B,M	Pri	No	C	4,125	26	9	20	26	21	24	610	12	34	38	16	610	9	33	41	17	8/15
Central Michigan University	Mount Pleasant	SM	B,M,D	Pub	F,S	C	18,100	22	39	30	21	7	3	510	45	34	18	4	520	37	42	14	8	Open
Cleary College	Ann Arbor	SU	A,B		No	C	700																	Open
College for Creative Studies	Detroit	U	B		No	C	1,200																	
Concordia University, Ann Arbor	Ann Arbor	SU	A,B,M	Pri	No	C	559	22	37	24	20	9	10	570	38	25	33	4	575	21	38	33	8	Open
Cornerstone University and Grand Rapids Theological Seminary	Grand Rapids	SU	A,B,M	Pri	No	C	2,177	23																Open
Davenport University	Grand Rapids	U	A,B,M	Pri	No	C	12,062																	9
Eastern Michigan University	Ypsilanti	SU	B,M,D	Pub	F,S	C	18,578	21	49	24	17	5	4	520	39		16	2	510	41	41	15	3	7/31
Ferris State University	Big Rapids	SM	A,B,M	Pub	F,S	C	11,051	21	50	25	16	5	3											8/4
Grace Bible College	Grand Rapids	SU	A,B	Pri	No	C	161	20	63	21	8	8		584		57	43		534	29	43	28		
Grand Valley State University	Allendale	SM	B,M	Pub	F,S	C	17,400	23																Open

TEST SCORES

Legend — ENVIRONMENT: U-Urban, R-Rural, SU-Suburban, SM-Small Town · DEGREES AWARDED: A-Associate, B-Bachelor, M-Master, D-Doctorate · CONTROL: Pri-Private, Pub-Public · FRATERNITIES AND SORORITIES: F-Fraternities, S-Sororities, F,S-Both, N-Neither · STUDENTS: C-Coed, M-Men, W-Women, PM-Primarily Men, PW-Primarily Women · APPLICATION DEADLINE: Month/Day

NAME OF SCHOOL	TOWN	ENV	DEG	CTRL	FRAT	STU	ENROLL FALL 2005	ACT Median	ACT Below 21	ACT 21-23	ACT 24-26	ACT 27-28	ACT Above 28	SAT V Median	SAT V Below 500	SAT V 500-599	SAT V 600-700	SAT V Above 700	SAT M Median	SAT M Below 500	SAT M 500-599	SAT M 600-700	SAT M Above 700	APP DEADLINE
Hillsdale College	Hillsdale	SM	B		F,S	C	1,304	27	4	15	28	20	32	660					620					2/15
Hope College	Holland	SU	B	Pri	F,S	C	3,141	26	7	19	28	28	18	614	8	36	37	20	618	6	34	40	20	2/15
Kalamazoo College	Kalamazoo	SU	B		No	C	1,263	28			10	60	30	631	1	13	60	26	630	1	22	51	26	2/15
Kendall College of Art and Design of Ferris State University	Grand Rapids	U	B,M	Pub	No	C	1,036																	Open
Kettering University	Flint	SU	B,M	Pri	F,S	C	2,376	26	5	20	29	24	23	580	10	46	34	10	650	1	20	56	23	Open
Lake Superior State University	Sault Sainte Marie	SM	A,B,M	Pub	F,S	C	2,888																	Open
Lawrence Technological University	Southfield	SU	A,B,M,D		F,S	C	2,906	22	35	25	20	10	10	530	38	28	30	4	560	26	28	40	6	Open
Madonna University	Livonia	U	A,B,M		No	C	3,376	23	22	35	24	8	11	533					518					Open
Marygrove College	Detroit	U	A,B,M	Pri	No	C	732	18	86	9	1	4												8/15
Michigan State University	East Lansing	SU	B,M,D		F,S	C	35,678	24	14	26	32	14	14	560	26	39	26	9	590	16	36	35	13	7/25
Michigan Technological University	Houghton	SM	A,B,M,D	Pub	F,S	C	5,614	25	12	22	29	17	20	587	15	36	40	9	630	6	26	49	19	Open
Northern Michigan University	Marquette	U	A,B,M	Pub	F,S	C	8,714																	
Northwood University	Midland	SU	A,B,M	Pri	F,S	C	1,750																	
Oakland University	Rochester	SU	B,M,D	Pub	F,S	C	13,448	22	40	30	20	6	4											
Olivet College	Olivet	SM	B,M	Pri	F,S	C	1,042	19	25	40	15	15	5											Open
Rochester College	Rochester Hills	SU	A,B,M	Pri	F,S	C	1,051	21	45	25	17	6	7	620	21	21	43	15	570	29	43	21	7	8/30
Saginaw Valley State University	University Center	SU	B,M	Pub	F,S	C	7,929	21	48	25	17	5	5											Open
Siena Heights University	Adrian	SM	A,B,M		F,S	C	1,100																	Open
Spring Arbor University	Spring Arbor	SM	A,B,M	Pri	No	C	1,588																	Open
University of Detroit Mercy	Detroit	U	A,B,M,D	Pri	F,S	C	3,400																	
University of Michigan/Ann Arbor	Ann Arbor	SU	B,M,D	Pub	F,S	C	25,467	28	3					640	3	24	47	26	690	2	12	42	44	2/1
University of Michigan/Dearborn	Dearborn	SU	B,M	Pub	F,S	C	6,400																	
University of Michigan/Flint	Flint	U	B,M	Pub	F,S	C	5,671	21	43	26	21	5	5	495	58	21	16	5	475	58	32	10		9/15
Wayne State University	Detroit	U	B,M,D	Pub	F,S	C	20,155																	
Western Michigan University	Kalamazoo	U	B,M,D	Pub	F,S	C	21,434	22	37	30	21	7	5											Open
William Tyndale College	Farmington Hills	SU	A,B		No	C	290	23																Open

Minnesota

NAME OF SCHOOL	TOWN	ENV	DEG	CTRL	FRAT	STU	ENROLL FALL 2005	ACT Median	ACT Below 21	ACT 21-23	ACT 24-26	ACT 27-28	ACT Above 28	SAT V Median	SAT V Below 500	SAT V 500-599	SAT V 600-700	SAT V Above 700	SAT M Median	SAT M Below 500	SAT M 500-599	SAT M 600-700	SAT M Above 700	APP DEADLINE
Augsburg College	Minneapolis	U	B,M	Pri	No	C	2,808	23	26	25	28	11	9	541	18	42	35	5	542	15	55	25	5	5/1
Bemidji State University	Bemidji	SM	A,B,M	Pub	F,S	C	4,522																	2/1
Bethel University	St. Paul	SU	A,B,M	Pri	No	C	3,284	25	14	26	24	18	18	580	15	36	33	16	580	15	35	35	10	12/1
Carleton College	Northfield	SM	B	Pri	No	C	1,959																	1/15
College of Saint Benedict	St. Joseph	SM	B	Pri	No	W	2,045	25	8	25	36	14	17	580	18	39	39	4	570	15	44	35	6	Open
College of Saint Catherine	St. Paul	U	A,B,M	Pri	S	W	3,511	23	23	30	26	13	8	605	13	28	50	9	590	25	28	25	22	Open
College of Saint Scholastica	Duluth	SU	B,M,D	Pri	No	C	2,613	23	22	30	28	13	7	560	25	47	12	16	570	12	47	28	13	Open
College of Visual Arts	St. Paul	U	B	Pri	No	C	194	21	55	24	12	9												3/1
Concordia College: Moorhead	Moorhead	U	B,M	Pri	No	C	1,796	24	19	28	29	13	11	570	21	39	28	11	545	23	43	19	15	Open
Concordia University St.Paul	St. Paul	U	A,B,M	Pri	No	C	1,736	22	43	24	17	10	6	490	50	16	17	17	550	42	16	42		8/1
Gustavus Adolphus College	St. Peter	SM	B	Pri	F,S	C	2,571	26	8	22	28	18	24	625	6	29	47	18	615	7	33	46	14	4/1
Hamline University	St. Paul	U	B,M,D	Pri	S	C	1,944	24						598					589					Open
Macalester College	St. Paul	U	B	Pri	No	C	1,869	30		3		41	56	700	3	12	35	50	670		12	51	37	1/15
Metropolitan State University	St. Paul	U	B,M	Pub	No	C	5,959	21																6/15
Minneapolis College of Art and Design	Minneapolis	U	B,M	Pri	No	C	656	23	10	40	40	7	3	550	20	40	30	10	525	30	35	25	10	2/15
Minnesota State University, Mankato	Mankato	R	A,B,M	Pub	F,S	C	12,684	21	40	36	18	5	2											Open
Minnesota State University, Moorhead	Moorhead	SU	A,B,M	Pub	F,S	C	5,920																	
North Central University	Minneapolis	U	A,B		No	C	1,225	21	25	50	10	10	5	555	25	50	25		370	25	50	25		6/1
Northwestern College	St. Paul	SU	A,B		No	C	1,767	23	35	23	23	12	7											8/1
Saint Cloud State University	St. Cloud	SU	A,B,M,D	Pub	F,S	C	14,486	22																Open
Saint John's University	Collegeville	R	B,M	Pri	No	M	1,875	25	7	25	31	18	19	590	12	39	36	13	610	14	26	51	9	Open
Saint Mary's University of Minnesota	Winona	SM	B,M,D	Pri	F,S	C	1,251	22	34	27	21	10	8	570	11	63	16	11	580	16	37	42	5	5/1
Saint Olaf College	Northfield	SM	B	Pri	No	C	3,058	27						644	4	24	42	30	635	5	27	44	24	2/1
Southwest Minnesota State University	Marshall	R	A,B,M	Pub	No	C	2,692	22	49	28	15	4	4											8/15
University of Minnesota/Crookston	Crookston	SM	A,B	Pub	No	C	2,134	21	46	29	17	4	4	475	50	10	40		460	56	33	11		Open
University of Minnesota/Duluth	Duluth	SU	B,M	Pub	F,S	C	9,538	23	12	48	24	13	3											8/1
University of Minnesota/Morris	Morris	SM	B	Pub	No	C	1,843	24	10	25	36	15	14	600	15	35	35	15	600	12	35	40	13	2/1
University of Minnesota/Twin Cities	Minneapolis	U	B,M,D	Pub	F,S	C	28,958	25	13	20	29	17	21	600	12	34	41	13	600	8	28	47	17	Open
University of Saint Thomas	St. Paul	U	B,M,D		No	C	5,200																	Open
Winona State University	Winona	SM	A,B,M		F,S	C	7,447	23	27	41	22	6	3	524	27	18	18	4	540	27	40	20	7	1/30

Mississippi

NAME OF SCHOOL	TOWN	ENV	DEG	CTRL	FRAT	STU	ENROLL FALL 2005	ACT Median	ACT Below 21	ACT 21-23	ACT 24-26	ACT 27-28	ACT Above 28	SAT V Median	SAT V Below 500	SAT V 500-599	SAT V 600-700	SAT V Above 700	SAT M Median	SAT M Below 500	SAT M 500-599	SAT M 600-700	SAT M Above 700	APP DEADLINE
Alcorn State University	Alcorn State	R	A,B,M	Pub	F,S	C	2,962																	Open
Belhaven College	Jackson	U	A,B,M		No	C	1,714	23	9	29	27	10	25	560	10	32	32	26	560	8	45	39	8	2/1
Blue Mountain College	Blue Mountain	R	B		No	PW	365																	Open
Delta State University	Cleveland	SM	B,M,D	Pub	F,S	C	3,257	20	62	22	9	5	2											8/1
Jackson State University	Jackson	U	B,M,D	Pub	F,S	C	6,310																	Open
Millsaps College	Jackson	U	B,M	Pri	F,S	C	1,085	27	9	19	18	19	33	610	11	33	42	14	585	15	41	35	9	2/1
Mississippi College	Clinton	SU	B,M		No	C	2,553	23	31	26	25	7	11	571	17	49	30	7	563	23	40	28	9	Open
Mississippi State University	Mississippi State	SM	B,M,D	Pub	F,S	C	12,555	23	33	21	20	10	16											8/1
Mississippi University for Women	Columbus	SM	A,B,M	Pub	F,S	C	3,200																	Open
Mississippi Valley State University	Itta Bena	SM	B,M	Pub	F,S	C	2,748	17	91	6	3													8/10
Rust College	Holly Springs	SM	A,B		F,S	C	1,001		47	22		3												7/15
Tougaloo College	Tougaloo	SU	A,B	Pri	F,S	C	940																	Open
University of Mississippi	University	SM	B,M,D	Pub	F,S	C	9,800																	
University of Southern Mississippi	Hattiesburg	SU	B,M,D	Pub	F,S	C	12,468	21	47	26	14	6	7	520	40	41	15	4	520	34	48	14	4	
William Carey College	Hattiesburg	SM	B,M		F,S	C	1,850																	

TEST SCORES

Column key:
- **ENVIRONMENT:** U-Urban R-Rural SU-Suburban SM-Small Town
- **DEGREES AWARDED:** A-Associate B-Bachelor M-Master D-Doctorate
- **CONTROL:** Pri-Private Pub-Public
- **FRATERNITIES AND SORORITIES:** F-Fraternities S-Sororities F,S-Both No-Neither
- **STUDENTS:** C-Coed M-Men W-Women PM-Primarily Men PW-Primarily Women

Name of School	Town	Env.	Degrees	Control	Frat/Sor.	Students	Undergrad Enroll. Fall 2005	ACT Median	ACT Below 21	ACT 21-23	ACT 24-26	ACT 27-28	ACT Above 28	SAT V Median	SAT V Below 500	SAT V 500-599	SAT V 600-700	SAT V Above 700	SAT M Median	SAT M Below 500	SAT M 500-599	SAT M 600-700	SAT M Above 700	Appl. Deadline Month/Day
Missouri																								
Avila University	Kansas City	SU	B,M		No	C	1,214	21	53	25	16	3	4	490	55	18	27		490	55	18	18	9	
Central Methodist University	Fayette	SM	A,B		F,S	C	850																	Open
Central Missouri State University	Warrensburg	SM	A,B,M	Pub		C	8,700																	Open
College of the Ozarks	Point Lookout	SM	B	Pri	No	C	1,348	22	40	33	18	5	4											2/1
Columbia College	Columbia	U	A,B,M	Pri	No	C	1,009	22	41	22	20	10	7	530	20	50	30		520	20	60	20		Open
Culver-Stockton College	Canton	R	B	Pri	F,S	C	840	22	45	27	16	9	3						520	20	60	20		Open
Deaconess College of Nursing	St. Louis	U	A,B		No	C	400																	Open
DeVry University/Kansas City	Kansas City	U	A,B		No	C	1,927																	Open
Drury University	Springfield	U	B,M	Pri	F,S	C	1,580	25	11	24	29	13	23	580	19	38	36	7	590	13	44	33	10	8/1
Evangel University	Springfield	U	A,B,M		No	C	1,735	21	37	29	18	9	7											8/1
Fontbonne University	St. Louis	SU	B,M	Pri	F	C	2,078	21	42	31	18	7	2											8/1
Hannibal-LaGrange College	Hannibal	SM	A,B	Pri	No	C	1,056		20	43	27	4	6											8/29
Harris-Stowe State College	St. Louis	U	B	Pub	F,S	C	1,255																	Open
Jewish Hospital College of Nursing and Allied Health	St. Louis	U	A,B,M		No	C	670																	Open
Kansas City Art Institute	Kansas City	U	B	Pri	No	C	601	22	24	39	24	8	5	559	27	41	27	6	523	35	43	19	3	
Lester L. Cox College of Nursing and Health Sciences	Springfield	U	A,B		No	C	592																	2/1
Lincoln University	Jefferson City	SM	A,B,M		F,S	C	3,125																	Open
Lindenwood University	St. Charles	SU	B,M	Pri	F,S	C	5,728	23	21	47	16	10	6											Open
Maryville University of Saint Louis	St. Louis	SU	B,M		No	C	2,700																	
Missouri Baptist University	St. Louis	SU	A,B,M		No	C	3,484	20	55	20	15	4	6											Open
Missouri Southern State University	Joplin	SM	A,B,M	Pub	F,S	C	5,473	22	37	30	22	6	5											8/21
Missouri State University	Springfield	SU	B,M,D	Pub	F,S	C	14,463	24	19	32	25	12	11											7/20
Missouri Valley College	Marshall	SM	A,B		F,S	C	1,565																	Open
Missouri Western State University	St. Joseph	SU	A,B	Pub	F,S	C	5,248	19	63	20	11	4	2											5/1
Northwest Missouri State University	Maryville	R	B,M	Pub	F,S	C	5,650																	Open
Park University	Parkville	SU	A,B,M		No	C	12,688	20	52	24	13	6	4											8/15
Research College of Nursing	Kansas City	U	B	Pri	No	C	246	23	25	25	38	5	7											6/30
Rockhurst University	Kansas City	U	B,M,D		F,S	C	2,091	25	14	25	26	15	20	570	14	41	43	1	570	12	43	41	4	6/30
Saint Louis University	St. Louis	U	B,M,D	Pri	F,S	C	7,421	26	7	18	29	18	29		8	39	44	9		9	34	43	14	8/1
Southeast Missouri State University	Cape Girardeau	SM	A,B,M	Pub	F,S	C	3,041	22	40	26	20	7	7											8/1
Southwest Baptist University	Bolivar	SM	A,B,M,D	Pri	No	C	2,449	23	32	26	22	9	11	536	38	34	26	2	533	32	43	21	4	Open
Stephens College	Columbia	U	A,B,M	Pri	S	W	754																	Open
Truman State University	Kirksville	SM	B,M	Pub	F,S	C	5,567	27	1	12	27	22	38	630	5	29	50	16	610	7	33	48	12	3/1
University of Missouri/Columbia	Columbia	SU	B,M,D	Pub	F,S	C	21,375	25	6	24	30	18	22											5/1
University of Missouri/Kansas City	Kansas City	U	B,M,D	Pub	F,S	C	5,141																	Open
University of Missouri/Rolla	Rolla	SM	B,M,D	Pub	F,S	C	4,100																	7/1
University of Missouri/St. Louis	St. Louis	U	B,M,D	Pub	F,S	C	12,619	24	22	31	27	10	10	550	36	32	26	6	540	32	38	28	2	7/1
Washington University in Saint Louis	St. Louis	SU	B,M,D	Pri	F,S	C	7,466				3	9	88			3	38	59			1	26	73	1/15
Webster University	St. Louis	SU	B,M,D		No	C	4,899	24	18	30	27	12	13	610	10	38	45	7	540	22	44	28	6	3/1
Westminster College	Fulton	SM	B		F,S	C	891	24	13	27	37	10	13	530	37	38	21	4	560	28	32	35	5	8/15
William Jewell College	Liberty	SU	B	Pri	F,S	C	1,331																	
William Woods University	Fulton	SM	A,B,M	Pri	F,S	C	1,151	22	39	26	21	7	7	529	36	41	14	9	501	48	38	14		Open
Montana																								
Carroll College	Helena	SM	A,B		No	C	1,499	24	23	25	35	9	7	534	30	45	22	3	540	28	44	27	1	6/1
Montana State University-Billings	Billings	U	A,B,M	Pub	No	C	4,407	21	57	20	15	5	3	500	44	46	9	1	513	43	41	16		Open
Montana State University-Bozeman	Bozeman	SM	B,M,D	Pub	F,S	C	10,842	23	27	28	22	12	11	550	27	42	26	5	570	22	39	32	7	Open
Montana State University-Northern	Havre	SM	A,B,M	Pub	No	C	1,400																	Open
Montana Tech of The University of Montana	Butte	SM	A,B	Pub	No	C	2,094	22	25	37	12	25		530	34	40	23	2	549					Open
Rocky Mountain College	Billings	SM	A,B,M	Pri	No	C	964	22	34	29	27		2	525	37	41	15	7	527	32	47	19	2	8/1
University of Great Falls	Great Falls	U	A,B,M		No	C	800																	8/1
University of Montana	Missoula	U	A,B,M,D	Pub	F,S	C	11,504	23															4	3/1
University of Montana—Western	Dillon	SM	A,B	Pub	No	C	1,159																	7/1
Nebraska																								
Bellevue University	Bellevue	SU	B,M		No	C	3,666																	Open
Chadron State College	Chadron	SM	B,M	Pub	No	C	2,305																	Open
Clarkson College	Omaha	U	B,M		No	PW	330																	Open
College of Saint Mary	Omaha	SU	A,B,M		No	W	939	20	54	34	8	3	1											Open
Concordia University Nebraska	Seward	SM	B,M		No	C	1,180																	Open
Creighton University	Omaha	U	A,B,M,D	Pri	F,S	C	3,988	26	7	19	29	19	25	600	12	37	44	8	610	9	33	47	11	8/1
Dana College	Blair	SM	B		No	C	676	22	51	25	21	3	2	480	61	22	11	6	475	58	28	8	6	8/1
Doane College	Crete	SM	B,M	Pri	F,S	C	973	23	30	25	19	13	13											8/15
Hastings College	Hastings	R	B,M	Pri	F,S	C	1,144	23	11	27	28	19	15											8/1
Midland Lutheran College	Fremont	SM	A,B		F,S	C	950								13	43	28	16		19	36	26	19	8/1
Nebraska Methodist College of Nursing and Allied Health	Omaha	U	A,B,M	Pri	S		500	20	55	25	20													3/1
Nebraska Wesleyan University	Lincoln	SU	B,M		F,S	C	1,842	24	19	30	28	12	12											5/1
Peru State College	Peru	R	B,M	Pub	No	C	1,455																	Open
Union College	Lincoln	SU	A,B		No	C	885	22	40	30	17	8	5											Open
University of Nebraska at Kearney	Kearney	SM	B,M	Pub	F,S	C	6,100																	Open
University of Nebraska at Lincoln	Lincoln	U	A,B,M,D	Pub	F,S	C	17,037	25	14	18	26	25	17	590	16	35	36	13	610	13	30	39	17	6/30
University of Nebraska at Omaha	Omaha	SU	B,M,D	Pub	F,S	C	11,329	23	34	27	21	7	10	552	30	33	31	6	548	27	46	20	7	8/1
Wayne State College	Wayne	R	B,M	Pub	F,S	C	2,706	21	45	23	20	7	5											Open
York College	York	SM	A,B		F,S	C	452	21	45	24	20	7	4	520	41	42	17		490	59	25	8	8	Open

TEST SCORES

Name of School	Town	Environment	Degrees Awarded	Fraternities/Sororities	Control	Students	Undergrad Enrollment Fall 2005	ACT Median	ACT Below 21	ACT 21-23	ACT 24-26	ACT 27-28	ACT Above 28	SAT I Verbal Median	SAT I Verbal Below 500	SAT I Verbal 500-599	SAT I Verbal 600-700	SAT I Verbal Above 700	SAT I Math Median	SAT I Math Below 500	SAT I Math 500-599	SAT I Math 600-700	SAT I Math Above 700	Application Deadline Month/Day
Nevada																								
Sierra Nevada College	Incline Village	R	B	No		C	320							500					490					2/15
University of Nevada/Las Vegas	Las Vegas	U	B,M,D	F,S	Pub	C	20,680																	4/2
University of Nevada/Reno	Reno	U	B,M,D	F,S	Pub	C	12,404	22	31	32	27	8	2	526	36	44	18	2	533	32	44	22	2	2/1
New Hampshire																								
Colby-Sawyer College	New London	SM	A,B	No		C	901																	Open
Daniel Webster College	Nashua	SU	A,B	No		C	578																	Open
Dartmouth College	Hanover	R	B,M,D	No		C	4,079							713		7	27	65	719	1	5	25	70	1/1
Franklin Pierce College	Rindge	R	B,M	No	Pri	C	1,635																	Open
Granite State College	Concord	SM	A,B	No	Pub	C	1,364																	Open
Hesser College	Manchester		A,B	No		C	770																	
Keene State College	Keene	SU	A,B,M	F,S	Pub	C	4,370	20	100					500	46	42	11	1	500	48	40	11	1	4/1
New England College	Henniker	SM	A,B,M	F,S	Pri	C	1,020							450	72	24	3	1	440	77	18	5		Open
Plymouth State University	Plymouth	SM	B,M	F,S	Pub	C	3,980																	
Rivier College	Nashua	SU	A,B,M	No		C	1,600																	Open
Saint Anselm College	Manchester	SU	B	No	Pri	C	1,987							560	18	54	26	2	560	17	57	24	2	3/1
Southern New Hampshire University	Manchester	SU	A,B,M,D	F,S	Pri	C	1,706		63	14	14	4	4	495	52	39	8	1	498	50	40	11		
Thomas More College of Liberal Arts	Merrimack	SU	B	No		C	70																	Open
University of New Hampshire	Durham	R	A,B,M,D	F,S		C	11,083							560	21	51	25	3	570	18	49	29	4	2/1
New Jersey																								
Bloomfield College	Bloomfield	SU	B	F,S		C	2,212																	3/14
Caldwell College	Caldwell	SU	B,M	No		C	1,684							460	65	27	8	1	450	67	23	9	1	Open
Centenary College	Hackettstown	SU	A,B,M	F,S	Pri	C	1,887	19	10					460	68	28	3	1	460	86	13	1		Open
College of New Jersey, The	Ewing	SU	B,M	F,S	Pub	C	5,895							630	8	25	53	14	650	5	18	54	23	2/15
College of Saint Elizabeth	Morristown	SU	B,M	No		PW	1,205							480	59	30	8	3	460	61	32	6	1	8/15
DeVry College of Technology/North Brunswick	North Brunswick	SM	A,B	No		C	2,500																	Open
Drew University/College of Liberal Arts	Madison	SM	B,M,D	No	Pri	C	1,613	25	14	21	27	17	22	608	8	35	42	15	596	8	44	38	10	2/15
Fairleigh Dickinson University/College at Florham	Madison	SU	A,B,M	F,S	Pri	C	2,660							517	40	44	14	1	515	41	43	15	1	3/1
Fairleigh Dickinson University/Metropolitan Campus	Teaneck	SU	A,B,M,D	F,S	Pri	C	5,744							498	51	39	9	1	507	46	41	12	1	3/15
Felician College	Lodi	SU	A,B,M	No		C	1,416							440	75	21	4		440	71	24	5		Open
Georgian Court College	Lakewood	SU	B,M	No		PW	1,550																	
Kean University	Union	SU	B,M	F,S	Pub	C	10,035							490	57	37	6		500	45	46	9		5/31
Monmouth University	West Long Branch	SU	A,B,M	F,S	Pri	C	4,555	23	33	25	25	13	4	528	30	56	13	1	548	21	56	22	1	3/1
Montclair State University	Upper Montclair	SU	B,M	F,S	Pub	C	12,174							537	25	58	14	3	548	18	60	21	2	3/1
New Jersey City University	Jersey City	U	B,M	F,S	Pub	C	5,969							440	79	16	4		440	74	23	3		4/1
New Jersey Institute of Technology	Newark	U	B,M,D	No	Pub	C	5,800																	
Princeton University	Princeton	SM	B,M,D	No	Pri	C	4,710										4	23	73			2	24	74	1/2
Ramapo College of New Jersey	Mahwah	SU	B,M	F,S	Pub	C	5,233																	3/1
Richard Stockton College of New Jersey	Pomona	SU	B,M	F,S	Pub	C	6,550																	
Rider University	Lawrenceville	SU	A,B,M	F,S	Pri	C	4,049	22	50	50				530	28	53	17	3	540	22	53	23	2	Open
Rowan University	Glassboro	SU	B,M,D	F,S	Pub	C	8,000																	
Rutgers, The State University of New Jersey/Camden Campus	Camden	U	B,M	No		C	3,774							560	18	51	28	3	560	17	49	28	6	Open
Rutgers, The State University of New Jersey/New Brunswick/Piscataway Campus	Piscataway	SM	B,M,D	F,S		C	26,172							590	9	44	37	9	620	5	32	43	19	Open
Rutgers, The State University of New Jersey/Newark Campus	Newark	U	B,M,D	No		C	5,963							540	22	54	21	4	570	15	47	31	7	Open
Saint Peter's College	Jersey City	U	A,B,M	No		C	2,800																	Open
Seton Hall University	South Orange	SU	B,M,D	F,S	Pri	C	5,335							550	21	48	26	5	560	16	50	31	3	3/1
Stevens Institute of Technology	Hoboken	U	B,M,D	F,S	Pri	C	1,789																	2/15
Thomas Edison State College	Trenton	U	A,B,M	No	Pub	C	10,904																	Open
Westminster Choir College	Princeton	SU	B,M	No	Pri	C	334							550	25	39	26	10	540	26	43	29	2	
William Paterson University of New Jersey	Wayne	SU	B,M	F,S	Pub	C	9,110								36	51	12	1		30	55	14	1	5/1
New Mexico																								
College of Santa Fe	Santa Fe	SU	A,B,M	No	Pri	C	1,342	23	36	22	24	9	9	580	16	46	31	7	520	33	51	15	1	
College of the Southwest	Hobbs	SM	B,M	No	Pri	C	528	19	76	20	2		2	431	77	23			456	61	35	3		Open
Eastern New Mexico University	Portales	SM	A,B,M	No	Pub	C	3,303	19	68	20	10	2	1	475	62	23	13	2	479	56	33	9	2	Open
New Mexico Highlands University	Las Vegas	SM	A,B,M	No	Pub	C	1,992	18	82	10	5			447	76	24			442	76	12	12		Open
New Mexico Institute of Mining and Technology	Socorro	SM	A,B,M,D	No	Pub	C	1,386	26		1	30	52	17	620	10	25	48	17	630	6	31	44	20	8/1
New Mexico State University	Las Cruces	U	A,B,M,D	F,S		C	12,656	21	50	26	16	5	3											Open
Saint John's College	Santa Fe	SU	B,M	No		C	442																	
University of New Mexico	Albuquerque	U	A,B,M,D	F,S	Pub	C	20,358	21	40	28	19	8	2	550	31	40	24	4	540	33	40	24	3	6/15
Western New Mexico University	Silver City	SM	A,B,M	F,S	Pub	C	620																	7/21
New York																								
Adelphi University	Garden City	SU	A,B,M,D	F,S	Pri	C	4,130																	Open
Albany College of Pharmacy	Albany	U	B,M,D	F,S	Pri	C	872	26						560	11	57	28	4	600	5	44	44	7	2/1
Albert A. List College of Jewish Studies	New York	U	B	No		C	180																	
Alfred University	Alfred	R	B,M,D	No	Pri	C	1,961		18	30	24	16	12	562	20	47	27	6	570	15	48	32	5	2/1

Legend: ENVIRONMENT — U-Urban, R-Rural, SU-Suburban, SM-Small Town. DEGREES AWARDED — A-Associate, B-Bachelor, M-Master, D-Doctorate. FRATERNITIES AND SORORITIES — F-Fraternities, S-Sororities. CONTROL — Pri-Private, Pub-Public. STUDENTS — C-Coed, M-Men, W-Women, PM-Primarily Men, PW-Primarily Women.

NAME OF SCHOOL	TOWN	ENV	DEGREES	CONTROL	FRAT/SOR	STUDENTS	ENROLL 2005	ACT Median	ACT <21	ACT 21-23	ACT 24-26	ACT 27-28	ACT >29	SAT V Median	SAT V <500	SAT V 500-599	SAT V 600-700	SAT V >700	SAT M Median	SAT M <500	SAT M 500-599	SAT M 600-700	SAT M >700	DEADLINE
Bard College	Annandale-on-Hudson	R	A,B,M,D	Pri	No	C	1,585							680		9	44	47	650		23	50	27	1/15
Berkeley Colleg/Westchester Campus	White Plains	SU	A,B		No	C	610																	Open
Berkeley College/New York City	New York	U	A,B		No	C	2,321																	Open
Boricua College	New York	U	B		No	C	1,150																	Open
Canisius College	Buffalo	U	B,M	Pri	F,S	C	3,591	24	19	33	25	11	11	550	23	50	23	3	561	19	50	27	4	5/1
Cazenovia College	Cazenovia	SM	B	Pri	No	C	989																	Open
City University of New York/Baruch College	New York	U	B,M,D	Pub	F,S	C	12,844							520	44	40	14	2	580	15	46	32	7	2/1
City University of New York/Brooklyn College	Brooklyn	U	B,M	Pub	F,S	C	11,364																	Open
City University of New York/City College	New York	U	B,M	Pub	No	C	9,494							471	63	22	11	4	514	45	31	20	4	12/1
City University of New York/College of Staten Island	Staten Island	U	A,B,M,D	Pub	No	C	10,920							516	36	50	14	1	532	29	52	16	2	Open
City University of New York/Herbert H. Lehman College	Bronx	U	B,M	Pub	S	C	7,200																	
City University of New York/Hunter College	New York	U	B,M	Pub	F,S	C	15,900																	Open
City University of New York/John Jay College of Criminal Justice	New York	U	A,B,M	Pub	No	C	11,449																	Open
City University of New York/Medgar Evers College	Brooklyn	U	A,B	Pub	F,S	C	5,212							340	96	3	1		430	92	7	1		Open
City University of New York/New York City College of Technology	Brooklyn	U	A,B	Pub	No	C	12,443																	Open
City University of New York/Queens College	Flushing	U	B,M	Pub	F,S	C	13,018							509	50	37	11	3	545	33	45	18	3	
City University of New York/York College	Jamaica	U	B	Pub	No	C	5,900																	Open
Clarkson University	Potsdam	R	B,M,D	Pri	F,S	C	2,648							570	15	47	32	6	620	4	32	49	15	3/1
Colgate University	Hamilton	R	B,M		F,S	C	2,749	31		3	4	10	83	666	2	12	49	37	681		10	46	44	1/15
College of Mount Saint Vincent	Riverdale	U	A,B,M	Pri	No	C	1,325																	3/1
College of New Rochelle	New Rochelle	SU	B,M	Pri	No	PW	1,106	18						500	37	51	9	3	480	43	46	10	1	8/15
College of New Rochelle - School of New Resources	New Rochelle	U	B	Pri	No	C	4,344																	8/15
College of Saint Rose	Albany	SU	B,M		No	C	3,004																	2/1
Columbia University/Barnard College	New York	U	B		No	W	2,350																	
Columbia University/Columbia College	New York	U	B	Pri	F,S	C	4,225	30	1	5	14	17	64	720	1	7	26	67	710		5	35	60	1/2
Columbia University/Fu Foundation School of Engineering and Applied Science	New York	U	B,M,D	Pri	F,S	C	1,436	34			6	11	83	700	1	6	35	58	760		1	8	91	1/2
Columbia University/School of General Studies	New York	U	B,M,D	Pri	F,S	C	1,146																	6/1
Concordia College-New York	Bronxville	SU	A,B	Pri	F,S	C	713	18	90	10				480	57	36	7		470	65	27	8		3/15
Cooper Union for the Advancement of Science and Art	New York	U	B,M	Pri	F,S	C	924							670	4	16	50	30	700	5	12	25	58	1/1
Cornell University	Ithaca	R	B,M,D	Pri	F,S	C	13,684	30		4	14	14	68	680	1	13	50	34	710	1	6	41	53	1/1
Daemen College	Amherst	SU	B,M,D	Pri	F,S	C	1,603	22	35	32	22	7	4	520	36	53	11		520	27	57	15	1	Open
DeVry Institute of Technology/New York	Long Island City	U	A,B,M		No	C	1,840																	Open
Dominican College	Orangeburg	SU	A,B,M	Pri	No	C	1,383							440	75	22	3		450	75	21	4		Open
Dowling College	Oakdale	SU	B,M,D	Pri	No	C	3,627							460	63	28	8	1	470	57	31	9	1	Open
D'Youville College	Buffalo	U	B,M,D	Pri	No	C	1,478	21	35	35	26	1	3	490	52	38	9	1	500	49	40	10	1	Open
Eastman School of Music	Rochester	U	B,M,D	Pri	F,S	C	505																	
Elmira College	Elmira	SU	A,B,M	Pri	No	C	1,497	25	2	29	42	20	7	580	23	51	22	4	560	25	51	20	4	
Eugene Lang College New School for Liberal Arts	New York	U	B	Pri	No	C	985	25						617					570					2/1
Excelsior College	Albany	SU	A,B,M	Pri	No	C	26,311																	Open
Farmingdale State University of New York	Farmingdale	SU	A,B	Pub	No	C	6,461							478	62	33	4	1	494	49	42	8	1	Open
Fashion Institute of Technology/State University of New York	New York	U	A,B,M	Pub	No	C	10,700																	
Five Towns College	Dix Hills	SU	A,B,M,D		No	C	1,088	21	99	1				484	74	24	2		470	73	25	2		3
Fordham University	Bronx	U	B,M,D	Pri	No	C	7,750																	
Hamilton College	Clinton	R	B		F,S	C	1,814							690	2	14	49	35	680	1	9	59	31	1/1
Hartwick College	Oneonta	SM	B	Pri	F,S	C	1,463	24						570	13	53	30	4	565	17	47	30	5	2/15
Hilbert College	Hamburg	U	A,B	Pri	No	C	1,105																	Open
Hobart and William Smith Colleges	Geneva	SM	B,M		F	C	1,868							585	10	49	35	6	590	8	47	42	4	2/1
Hofstra University	Hempstead	SU	B,M,D	Pri	F,S	C	8,884	23	22	29	28	11	11	570	11	54	34	2	580	8	52	38	3	
Houghton College	Houghton	R	A,B,M		No	C	1,401	26	9	23	29	17	22	593	13	39	33	14	574	19	38	36	7	Open
Iona College	New Rochelle	SU	B,M	Pri	F,S	C	3,365	21	10	36	33	21		550	26	45	28	1	540	25	47	27	1	2/15
Ithaca College	Ithaca	SM	B,M	Pri	F,S	C	6,098							590	9	45	39	7	590	7	46	41	6	2/1
Juilliard School	New York	U	B,M,D	Pri	No	C	478																	12/1
Keuka College	Keuka Park	R	B		No	C	1,267	20	31	29	23	16	1	483	56	35	8	1	487	56	38	6	1	
Laboratory Institute of Merchandising	New York	U	A,B		No	C	493																	Open
Le Moyne College	Syracuse	SU	B,M	Pri	No	C	2,789	23	17	34	31	10	8	550	23	50	25	2	570	16	51	31	2	2/1
Long Island University/Brooklyn Campus	Brooklyn	U	A,B,M,D	Pri	F,S	C	5,350																	Open
Long Island University/C.W. Post Campus	Brookville	SU	A,B,M,D		F,S	C	6,600																	Open
Manhattan College	Riverdale	U	B,M		F,S	C	2,900																	3/1
Manhattan School of Music	New York	U	B,M,D		F,S	C	400																	
Manhattanville College	Purchase	SU	B,M	Pri	No	C	1,685																	Open
Mannes College of Music	New York	U	B,M	Pri	No	C	130																	
Marist College	Poughkeepsie	SU	B,M	Pri	F,S	C	4,896	25	7	16	44	17	16	580	10	50	36	4	590	5	45	43	7	2/15
Marymount Manhattan College	New York	U	A,B	Pri	S	C	2,007	24	25	18	50	7		550	26	47	23	4	510	40	44	16		

TEST SCORES

Column key:
- ENVIRONMENT: U-Urban R-Rural SU-Suburban SM-Small Town
- DEGREES AWARDED: A-Associate B-Bachelor M-Master D-Doctorate
- CONTROL: Pri-Private, Pub-Public
- FRATERNITIES AND SORORITIES: F-Fraternities S-Sororities F,S-Both No-Neither
- STUDENTS: C-Coed M-Men W-Women PM-Primarily Men PW-Primarily Women

NAME OF SCHOOL	TOWN	ENV	DEGREES	CONTROL	FRAT/SOR	STUD	UNDERGRAD ENROLL FALL 2005	ACT Median	ACT Below 21	ACT 21-23	ACT 24-26	ACT 27-28	ACT Above 28	SAT V Median	SAT V Below 500	SAT V 500-599	SAT V 600-700	SAT V Above 700	SAT M Median	SAT M Below 500	SAT M 500-599	SAT M 600-700	SAT M Above 700	APPLICATION DEADLINE
Medaille College	Buffalo	U	A,B,M	Pri	No	C	1,640																	
Mercy College	Dobbs Ferry	SU	A,B,M	Pri	No	C	6,500																	Open
Metropolitan College of New York	New York	U	A,B,M	Pri	No	C	1,300																	
Molloy College	Rockville Centre	SU	A,B,M		No	C	2,589							505	38	47	14	1	518	37	46	15	2	Open
Monroe College	Bronx		A,B,M	Pri	No	C	5,450																	8/15
Mount Saint Mary College	Newburgh	SU	B,M	Pri	No	C	2,039																	Open
Nazareth College of Rochester	Rochester	SU	A,B,M,D	Pri	No	C	2,057	25	12	26	39	13	9	576	12	48	34	5	576	13	45	38	3	2/15
New York Institute of Technology	Old Westbury	SU	A,B,M,D	Pri	F,S	C	6,486	22						530	34	42	21	3	580	20	33	31	16	2/1
New York University	New York	U	A,B,M,D	Pri	F,S	C	20,566	30			16	21	63	680	1	13	53	33	690	1	13	51	35	1/15
Niagara University	Niagara University	SU	A,B,M	Pri	F	C	2,942	23	34	30	21	5		523	36	49	14	1	528	33	49	16	2	
Nyack College	Nyack	SU	A,B,M		No	C	1,897																	Open
Pace University	New York	U	A,B,M,D	Pri	F,S	C	8,900																	Open
Parsons School of Design	New York	U	A,B,M		No	C	2,311																	Open
Polytechnic University/Brooklyn	Brooklyn	U	B,M,D	Pri	F,S	C	1,519							540	20	52	26	2	640	5	31	48	16	Open
Pratt Institute	Brooklyn	U	A,B,M	Pri	F,S	C	3,052	25	2	46	39	13		573	16	46	32	6	561	19	45	31	5	2/1
Rensselaer Polytechnic Institute	Troy	SU	B,M,D	Pri	F,S	C	4,951	26	2	19	35	27	16	630	3	26	49	22	690		8	46	46	2/1
Roberts Wesleyan College	Rochester	SU	A,B,M		No	C	1,408								29	42	27	2		26	47	25	2	1/1
Rochester Institute of Technology	Rochester	SU	A,B,M,D		F,S	C	12,933	26	10	18	28	20	24	590	10	44	37	9	620	4	32	49	15	Open
Russell Sage College	Troy	U	B,M		No	W	850																	
Saint Bonaventure University	St. Bonaventure	SM	B,M	Pri	No	C	2,141	21	49	26	13	6	7	520	36	48	15	2	520	36	47	16	1	4/1
Saint Francis College	Brooklyn	U	A,B,M	Pri	No	C	2,209							480	60	31	9		490	54	37	9		4/1
Saint John Fisher College	Rochester	SU	B,M	Pri	No	C	2,696	23	27	31	30	9		530	28	52	19	1	540	21	53	25	1	Open
Saint John's University	Queens	SU	A,B,M,D	Pri	F,S	C	15,092							520	38	42	17	3	500	34	39	21	6	Open
Saint Joseph's College, New York, Brooklyn Campus	Brooklyn	U	B,M		F,S	C	1,122							491	56	38	6		502	51	40	4		8/1
Saint Joseph's College, New York, Suffolk Campus	Patchogue	SU	B,M	Pri	F,S	C	2,810																	
Saint Lawrence University	Canton	R	B,M		F,S	C	2,131							570	15	47	33	5	580	11	46	37	6	2/15
Saint Thomas Aquinas College	Sparkill	SU	A,B,M		No	C	2,010																	
Sarah Lawrence College	Bronxville	SU	B,M	Pri	No	C	1,270																	
School of Visual Arts	New York	U	B,M		No	C	3,003	22	32	23	10	33	1	530	35	40	20	5	520	40	36	21	3	3/15
Siena College	Loudonville	SU	B		No	C	3,336	26						554	18	55	25	1	570	11	54	32	3	3/1
Skidmore College	Saratoga Springs	SM	B,M	Pri	No	C	2,773	27	2	11	31	34	23	630	5	27	51	17	630	3	29	57	12	1/15
State University of New York at Oswego	Oswego	SM	B,M	Pub	F,S	C	7,134	21	14	50	17	17	2	540	24	57	18	1	550	21	58	20	1	1/15
State University of New York at Potsdam	Potsdam	R	B,M	Pub	F,S	C	3,619	22	48	11	20	11	10	530	39	39	19	3	530	39	42	16	3	Open
State University of New York/College at Brockport	Brockport	SM	B,M	Pub	F,S	C	6,965	23	18	36	32	12	2	560	13	58	28	2	540	23	60	16	1	Open
State University of New York/College at Buffalo	Buffalo	U	B,M	Pub	F,S	C	9,010							500	52	39	8	1	500	46	46	7	1	
State University of New York/College at Cortland	Cortland	SM	B,M	Pub	F,S	C	5,787																	
State University of New York/College at Fredonia	Fredonia	SM	B,M	Pub	F,S	C	5,043	24	8	38	32	13	9	560	21	55	21	2	560	16	58	24	1	
State University of New York/College at Geneseo	Geneseo	SM	B,M	Pub	F,S	C	5,307	28	3	2	25	47	23	634	1	20	65	14	647		13	71	16	1/15
State University of New York/College at Old Westbury	Old Westbury	SU	B,M	Pub	F,S	C	3,373	19	74	16	5	5		480	62	34	3	1	490	58	36	5	1	Open
State University of New York/College at Oneonta	Oneonta	R	B,M	Pub	F,S	C	5,649	23	8	20	39	23	10	552	16	62	20	2	563	10	62	27	1	5/1
State University of New York/College at Plattsburgh	Plattsburgh	SU	B,M	Pub	F,S	C	5,394	22	36	35	21	7	1	510	41	47	11	1	510	39	48	12	1	8/1
State University of New York/College at Purchase	Purchase	SU	B,M	Pub	No	C	3,688							570					540	28	44	25	3	8/15
State University of New York/College of Agriculture and Technology at Cobleskill	Cobleskill	R	A,B	Pub	No	C	2,482																	Open
State University of New York/College of Environmental Science and Forestry	Syracuse	U	A,B,M,D	Pub	F,S	C	1,510																	
State University of New York/College of Technology at Alfred	Alfred	R	A,B	Pub	F,S	C	3,500																	Open
State University of New York/Empire State College	Saratoga Springs		A,B,M	Pub	No	C	9,522																	
State University of New York/Institute of Technology	Utica	SU	B,M	Pub	No	C	2,019	23	21	60	40			535	24	53	23	1	590	5	49	42	4	
State University of New York/Maritime College	Throggs Neck	SU	A,B,M	Pub	No	C	1,150	21	46	40	11	3		520	30	56	13	1	560	13	56	27	3	Open
State University of New York/University at Albany	Albany	SU	B,M,D	Pub	F,S	C	12,013							560	12	61	24	3	570	4	58	35	3	3/1
State University of New York/University at Binghamton	Binghamton	SU	B,M,D	Pub	F,S	C	11,174	27	3	12	26	29	30	620	5	34	49	12	650	1	19	56	24	1/15
State University of New York/University at Buffalo	Buffalo	SU	B,M,D	Pub	F,S	C	18,165	26		16	38	17	29	570	9	53	34	4	610	2	41	50	7	
State University of New York/University at New Paltz	New Paltz	SM	B,M	Pub	F,S	C	6,421							545	17	53	26	4	550	16	53	29	2	4/1
State University of New York/University at Stony Brook	Stony Brook	SU	B,M,D	Pub	F,S	C	14,287							580	7	51	34	8	620	1	34	48	17	3/1
Syracuse University	Syracuse	U	B,M,D	Pri	F,S	C	11,441								4	42	45	9		5	32	49	14	1/1
Touro College	New York	U	A,B,M,D	Pri	No	C	9,700																	Open
Union College	Schenectady	U	B	Pri	F,S	C	2,252	27	1	9	29	29	31	620	2	30	55	26	640	1	20	55	26	1/15
United States Merchant Marine Academy	Kings Point	SU	B	Pub	No	C	1,021	28			37	47	16	620	3	46	37	14	608					3/1
United States Military Academy	West Point	SM	B	Pub	No	C	4,165																	

NAME OF SCHOOL	TOWN	ENVIRONMENT	DEGREES AWARDED	CONTROL	FRATERNITIES AND SORORITIES	STUDENTS	UNDERGRADUATE ENROLLMENT FALL 2005	ACT						SAT I VERBAL REASONING					SAT I MATHEMATICAL REASONING					APPLICATION DEADLINE Month/Day
								Median	Below 21	21-23	24-26	27-28	Above 29	Median	Below 500	500-599	600-700	Above 700	Median	Below 500	500-599	600-700	Above 700	
University of Rochester	Rochester	SU	B,M,D	Pri	F,S	C	4,696							637	5	23	48	24	667	2	16	51	31	1/15
Utica College	Utica	SU	B,M,D	Pri	F,S	C	2,413	21						480	58	35	7		500	50	42	8	1	Open
Vassar College	Poughkeepsie	SU	B,M	Pri	No	C	2,378	30						700		3	43	55	686		5	53	42	1/1
Vaughn College of Aeronautics and Technology	Flushing	U	A,B	Pri	No	C	1,126							470					560					Open
Wagner College	Staten Island	SU	B,M	Pri	F,S	C	1,962	24	9	29	42	17	3	560	19	50	29	2	560	19	55	24	2	2/15
Webb Institute	Glen Cove	SU	B	Pri	No	C	75							680		5	60	35	740			30	70	2/15
Wells College	Aurora	SM	B	Pri	No	W	417	23	28	26	29	11	6	580	18	41	36	5	540	34	45	19	2	3/1
Yeshiva University	New York	U	A,B		No	C	2,360																	

North Carolina

NAME OF SCHOOL	TOWN	ENVIRONMENT	DEGREES AWARDED	CONTROL	FRATERNITIES AND SORORITIES	STUDENTS	UNDERGRADUATE ENROLLMENT FALL 2005	ACT Median	Below 21	21-23	24-26	27-28	Above 29	SATV Median	Below 500	500-599	600-700	Above 700	SATM Median	Below 500	500-599	600-700	Above 700	APPLICATION DEADLINE
Appalachian State University	Boone	R	B,M,D	Pub	F,S	C	13,001																	Open
Barber-Scotia College	Concord	SU	B		F,S	C	710																	
Barton College	Wilson	SU	B	Pri	F,S	C	1,189							470	63	28	7	2	480	57	30	11	2	Open
Belmont Abbey College	Belmont	SU	B		F,S	C	887	21	55	23	14	6	2	510	47	39	12	2	510	48	39	12	1	
Bennett College	Greensboro	U	A,B		S	W	510																	Open
Cabarrus College of Health Sciences	Concord	SU	A,B	Pri	No	C	255																	
Campbell University	Buies Creek	R	A,B,M,D	Pri	No	C	2,678							539	29	46	21	4	564	23	45	29	3	Open
Catawba College	Salisbury	SM	B,M		No	C	1,256	22	35	26	30	3	6	510	42	43	12	3	520	33	51	15	1	3/15
Davidson College	Davidson	SM	B		F	C	1,683	30	1	3	10	22	64	680	1	10	52	37	680	1	6	59	34	1/2
Duke University	Durham	SU	B,M,D	Pri	F,S	C	6,259	31		2		40	58	720	1	5	31	63	740	1	4	23	72	1/2
East Carolina University	Greenville	U	B,M,D	Pub	F,S	C	16,800																	
Elizabeth City State University	Elizabeth City	SM	B	Pub	F,S	C	1,975																	Open
Elon University	Elon	SU	B,M,D	Pri	F,S	C	4,702							600	6	42	46	6	610	5	35	54	7	1/10
Fayetteville State University	Fayetteville	U	B,M	Pub	F,S	C	3,800																	
Gardner-Webb University	Boiling Springs	SM	A,B,M,D	Pri	No	C	2,626	21						510	46	35	16	3	510	43	41	15	1	Open
Greensboro College	Greensboro	U	B,M	Pri	F,S	C	1,150																	
Guilford College	Greensboro	SU	B	Pri	No	C	2,101	24	21	22	33	9	15	580	19	37	32	13	560	21	44	30	5	2/15
High Point University	High Point	SU	B,M	Pri	F,S	C	2,524	21	42	30	16	10	2	510	43	41	14	2	500	47	39	12	2	8/15
Johnson and Wales University/ Charlotte Campus	Charlotte	U	A,B	Pri	No	C	2,156							480	54	39	6		470	59	32	9	1	Open
Johnson C. Smith University	Charlotte	U	B	Pri	F,S	C	1,480																	Open
Lees-McRae College	Banner Elk	R	B		No	C	874	23	20	57	13	8	2	540	25	55	19	1	530	26	56	17	1	Open
Lenoir-Rhyne College	Hickory	SU	B,M		F,S	C	1,426	21	43	26	20	10	1	522	41	40	17	2	543	31	44	22	3	Open
Livingstone College	Salisbury	SM	B		F,S	C	895	15						370					375					6
Mars Hill College	Mars Hill	R	B		F,S	C	1,240																	Open
Meredith College	Raleigh	U	B,M	Pri	No	W	2,015	20	54	27	10	3	6	530	37	47	15	1	510	39	46	14	1	2/15
Methodist College	Fayetteville	SU	A,B,M		F,S	C	1,900																	Open
Montreat College	Montreat	R	A,B,M		No	C	950																	Open
Mount Olive College	Mount Olive	SM	A,B		No	C	1,800																	Open
North Carolina Agricultural and Technical State University	Greensboro	U	B,M,D	Pub	F,S	C	6,610																	
North Carolina Central University	Durham	U	B,M	Pub	F,S	C	5,300																	
North Carolina School of the Arts	Winston-Salem	U	B,M	Pub	No	C	779																	3/1
North Carolina State University	Raleigh	U	A,B,M,D		F,S	C	22,767	25	2	37	47	14		580	12	50	33	5	615	5	35	48	12	2/1
North Carolina Wesleyan College	Rocky Mount	SU	B	Pri	F,S	C	1,752																	
Pfeiffer University	Misenheimer	R	B,M	Pri	No	C	1,196	21	72	14	9	5		490	54	37	8		510	42	45	12	1	8/25
Queens University of Charlotte	Charlotte	SU	A,B,M	Pri	F,S	C	1,623		25	39	28	7	1		39	43	15	3		36	49	14	1	Open
Saint Andrews Presbyterian College	Laurinburg	SM	B	Pri	No	C	781	20	51	31	3	11	4	500	47	27	23	3	500	42	45	13		Open
Saint Augustine's College	Raleigh	U	B		F,S	C	1,350																	
Salem College	Winston-Salem	U	B,M	Pri	No	PW	868	28						570	18	41	32	9	550	25	37	35	3	Open
Shaw University	Raleigh	U	A,B,M	Pri	F,S	C	2,565	14																7/30
University of North Carolina at Asheville	Asheville	SU	B,M	Pub	F,S	C	3,476	24	15	26	32	11	16	600	13	35	39	13	590	10	46	38	6	3/1
University of North Carolina at Chapel Hill	Chapel Hill	SU	B,M,D	Pub	F,S	C	16,764	28	4	10	24	20	41	643	3	22	55	20	656	2	16	58	24	1/15
University of North Carolina at Charlotte	Charlotte	SU	B,M,D	Pub	F,S	C	16,555	21	42	32	19	5	2	520	34	50	14	2	550	21	53	24	2	7/1
University of North Carolina at Greensboro	Greensboro	U	B,M,D	Pub	F,S	C	12,291							530	38	41	16	5	530	34	46	16	4	8/1
University of North Carolina at Pembroke	Pembroke	SM	B,M	Pub	F,S	C	4,963	18	80	14	3	3		462	75	23	2		476	69	27	4		7/15
University of North Carolina at Wilmington	Wilmington	SU	B,M	Pub	F,S	C	1,949	23	20	40	27	9	4	560	19	57	22	2	574	11	59	28	2	2/1
Wake Forest University	Winston-Salem	SU	B,M,D	Pri	F,S	C	4,263								2	13	57	29		2	11	50	38	1/15
Warren Wilson College	Asheville	SM	B,M	Pri	No	C	832	24						616	5	36	39	20	567	18	41	37	4	3/15
Western Carolina University	Cullowhee	R	B,M,D	Pub	F,S	C	6,200																	
Wingate University	Wingate	SM	B,M	Pri	F,S	C	1,341	20	38	23	23	10	7	510	50	37	13	1	520	38	42	19	1	Open
Winston-Salem State University	Winston-Salem	SU	B,M	Pub	F,S	C	3,932																	Open

North Dakota

NAME OF SCHOOL	TOWN	ENVIRONMENT	DEGREES AWARDED	CONTROL	FRATERNITIES AND SORORITIES	STUDENTS	UNDERGRADUATE ENROLLMENT FALL 2005	ACT Median	Below 21	21-23	24-26	27-28	Above 29	SATV Median	Below 500	500-599	600-700	Above 700	SATM Median	Below 500	500-599	600-700	Above 700	APPLICATION DEADLINE
Dickinson State University	Dickinson	R	A,B	Pub	No	C	2,516	22	51	25	15	3	3	460	48	45	6		490	51	39	9		8/15
Jamestown College	Jamestown	SM	B	Pri	No	C	1,026	22	35	29	20	8	8											Open
Mayville State University	Mayville	R	A,B	Pub	No	C	912	19	71	17	6	7												Open
Minot State University	Minot	SM	A,B,M	Pub	No	C	3,600																	Open
North Dakota State University	Fargo	U	B,M,D	Pub	F,S	C	10,160																	
University of Mary	Bismarck	SU	B,M		No	C	2,197		45	20	23	8	4											8/15
University of North Dakota	Grand Forks	U	B,M,D	Pub	F,S	C	10,498	23	22	34	25	10	9											7/1
Valley City State University	Valley City	SM	A,B	Pub	F,S	C	413	20	54	24	14	5	2	515	45	40	15		505	45	40	15		Open

		ENVIRONMENT U-Urban R-Rural SU-Suburban SM-Small Town	DEGREES AWARDED A-Associate B-Bachelor M-Master D-Doctorate	CONTROL Pri-Private Pub-Public	FRATERNITIES AND SORORITIES F-Fraternities S-Sororities	STUDENTS: C-Coed M-Men W-Women PM-Primarily Men PW-Primarily Women	UNDERGRADUATE ENROLLMENT FALL 2005	TEST SCORES ACT						SAT I VERBAL REASONING					SAT I MATHEMATICAL REASONING					APPLICATION DEADLINE Month/Day
NAME OF SCHOOL	TOWN							Median	Below 21	21-23	24-26	27-28	Above 28	Median	Below 500	500-599	600-700	Above 700	Median	Below 500	500-599	600-700	Above 700	

Ohio

NAME OF SCHOOL	TOWN	Env	Deg	Ctrl	Frat	Stu	Enroll	ACT Med	<21	21-23	24-26	27-28	>28	SATV Med	<500	500-599	600-700	>700	SATM Med	<500	500-599	600-700	>700	Deadline
Antioch College	Yellow Springs	SM	B	Pri	No	C	379																	2/1
Art Academy of Cincinnati	Cincinnati	U	A,B,M	Pri	No	C	163	21	57	19	19	5		514	25	25	44	1	500	44	37	19		6/30
Ashland University	Ashland	SM	A,B,M,D		F,S	C	2,785	22																Open
Baldwin-Wallace College	Berea	SU	B,M		F,S	C	3,675	23	23	27	29	14	7	547	25	45	26	4	557	25	43	28	4	5/1
Bluffton College	Bluffton	SM	B,M	Pri	No	C	1,079	23	24	30	33	10	3	536	37	46	14	3	529	41	32	24	3	5/31
Bowling Green State University	Bowling Green	SM	B,M,D	Pub	F,S	C	16,079	22	40	31	16	6	7	516	44	38	14	4	516	43	37	17	3	7/15
Capital University	Columbus	SU	B,M	Pri	F,S	C	2,862	23	26	31	24	10	9	541	30	42	24	4	526	28	45	22	5	4/15
Case Western Reserve University	Cleveland	U	B,M,D	Pri	F,S	C	3,949	29	2	6	15	17	60	660	3	18	48	31	690	1	11	42	46	1/15
Cedarville University	Cedarville	SM	A,B,M		No	C	3,090	25	8	27	30	17	18	600	9	39	41	11	580	15	41	37	7	Open
Central State University	Wilberforce	R	B,M	Pub	F,S	C	1,335																	
Cincinnati College of Mortuary Science	Cincinnati	U	A,B		No	C	137																	
Cleveland Institute of Art	Cleveland	U	B,M	Pri	No	C	540	21	37	28	21	9	5	580	23	41	27	9	494	55	27	18		7/1
Cleveland Institute of Music	Cleveland	U	B,M,D		No	C	225																	
Cleveland State University	Cleveland	U	B,M,D	Pub	F,S	C	9,155	19	65	19	10	4	2	490	53	35	12	1	480	54	30	14	2	8
College of Mount St. Joseph	Cincinnati	SU	A,B,M		No	C	1,901	21	43	32	17	5	2	500	50	37	13		490	55	34	9	2	8/15
College of Wooster	Wooster	SU	B	Pri	F,S	C	1,810	26	7	22	31	16	24	620	7	31	44	18	610	5	38	45	12	2/15
Columbus College of Art and Design	Columbus	U	B	Pri	No	C	1,750																	Open
David N. Myers College	Cleveland	U	A,B,M		No	C	1,096																	Open
Defiance College	Defiance	SM	A,B,M	Pri	F,S	C	828	21	47	25	17	10		484	51	45	4		480	55	33	12		Open
Denison University	Granville	SU	B	Pri	F,S	C	2,329	27	6	13	25	25	31	615	5	36	51	8	620	6	29	57	8	2/15
DeVry University/Columbus	Columbus	U	A,B,M		No	C	3,155																	Open
Franciscan University of Steubenville	Steubenville	SM	A,B,M	Pri	No	C	1,844	24						580	12	41	37	10	560	18	47	31	4	6/30
Franklin University	Columbus	U	A,B,M		No	C	5,318																	Open
Heidelberg College	Tiffin	SM	B,M	Pri	F,S	C	1,121	22	51	23	16	5	5	510	50	36	14		520	50	34	16		5/1
Hiram College	Hiram	R	B		No	C	1,120																	
John Carroll University	University Heights	SU	B,M		F,S	C	3,449	24	22	25	34	11	8	570	14	51	26	6	580	16	43	34	7	2/1
Kent State University	Kent	SU	A,B,M,D	Pub	F,S	C	18,745	22	42	30	17	6	5	517	39	43	16	1	517	43	39	16	2	5/1
Kenyon College	Gambier	R	B	Pri	F,S	C	1,661	29		4	9	23	64	670	1	8	50	41	660	1	14	60	25	2/2
Lake Erie College	Painesville	SM	A,B,M	Pri	S	C																		Open
Lourdes College	Sylvania	SU	A,B,M		No	C	1,210																	Open
Malone College	Canton	SU	B,M	Pri	No	C	1,920	23	27	30	25	11	7	530	28	49	23		520	38	40	21	1	7/1
Marietta College	Marietta	SM	A,B,M	Pri	F,S	C	1,421	23	30	27	22	15	6	534	31	44	21	5	530	33	41	22	4	4/15
Miami University	Oxford	SM	B,M,D	Pub	F,S	C	14,643	27	2	14	38	23	23	590	5	41	45	9	610	3	27	56	14	1/31
Mount Union College	Alliance	SU	B	Pri	F,S	C	2,205	22	34	31	22	8	5	500	47	38	14	2	520	41	41	17	1	5/1
Mount Vernon Nazarene University	Mt. Vernon	SM	A,B,M	Pri	No	C	2,212	22	34	28	23	8	7	537	31	50	16	3	517	40	40	18	1	5/1
Muskingum College	New Concord	SM	B,M	Pri	F,S	C	1,684	22	40	32	18	5	5	529	36	39	22	3	522	37	41	18	4	8/15
Notre Dame College	South Euclid	SU	A,B,M		No	C	800																	Open
Oberlin College	Oberlin	SM	B,M		No	C	2,845	30						698	1	8	42	49	663	2	13	54	31	1/15
Ohio Dominican University	Columbus	U	A,B,M		No	C	2,559		49	35	11	4	1											Open
Ohio Northern University	Ada	SM	B,D		F,S	C	2,296																	8/1
Ohio State University	Columbus	U	B,M,D	Pub	F,S	C	37,411	26	5	19	35	18	23	590	11	43	39	8	610	7	35	46	12	2/1
Ohio State University at Lima	Lima	SU	A,B,M	Pub	No	C	2,339																	7/1
Ohio State University at Mansfield	Mansfield	SU	A,B	Pub	No	C	1,230																	Open
Ohio State University at Marion	Marion	R	A,B,M	Pub	No	C	1,365																	Open
Ohio State University at Newark	Newark	SU	A,B	Pub	No	C	2,088	20	54	29	13	3	1	490	54	35	11		500	46	41	12		7/1
Ohio University	Athens	SM	A,B,M,D	Pub	F,S	C	17,191	23	23	36	25	9	8	540	28	46	22	4	540	26	45	25	4	2/1
Ohio Wesleyan University	Delaware	SM	B	Pri	F,S	C	1,976	26		21	32	21	26	605	8	35	41	16	610	7	34	44	16	3/1
Otterbein College	Westerville	SU	B,M	Pri	F,S	C	2,724																	3/1
Shawnee State University	Portsmouth	SM	A,B	Pub	F,S	C	3,820	19	68	21	7	3	1											Open
Tiffin University	Tiffin	SM	A,B,M	Pri	F,S	C	1,030																	Open
Union Institute & University	Cincinnati	U	B,M,D	Pri	No	C	1,122																	10/1
University of Akron	Akron	U	A,B,M,D	Pub	F,S	C	18,723	21	54	23	14	6	4	505	46	37	15	2	515	42	36	20	2	Open
University of Cincinnati	Cincinnati	U	A,B,M,D	Pub	F,S	C	19,512	22	36		20	11	10	540	32	39	25	4	550	30	36	28	6	7/31
University of Dayton	Dayton	SU	B,M,D	Pri	F,S	C	7,426	25	8	24	30	16	22	560	16	47	33	4	580	10	40	40	10	Open
University of Findlay	Findlay	SM	A,B,M		F,S	C	4,600	22	41	26	18	10	5	520	38	43	16	3	530	34	46	19	1	6/1
University of Rio Grande	Rio Grande	R	A,B,M		F,S	C	1,855																	Open
University of Toledo	Toledo	SU	A,B,M,D	Pub	F,S	C	16,058	22	38	27	21	7	7	510	42	39	17	1	530	34	39	24	2	Open
Urbana University	Urbana	SM	A,B,M	Pri	No	C	1,447																	Open
Ursuline College	Pepper Pike	SU	B,M	Pri	No	PW	1,152	21	51	28	15	5	1	480	62	33	5		480	59	34	7		Open
Walsh University	North Canton	SM	A,B,M		No	C	1,869	22	42	31	18	6	3		49	31	18	2		46	35	17	2	Open
Wilberforce University	Wilberforce	R	B		F,S	C	800																	Open
Wilmington College	Wilmington	SM	B,M	Pri	F,S	C	1,723																	Open
Wittenberg University	Springfield	SU	B,M	Pri	F,S	C	2,115	24	19	29	23	14	15	571	20	41	32	7	564	22	41	31	6	3/15
Wright State University	Dayton	SU	B,M,D	Pub	F,S	C	12,268	21	50	25	15	6	4	500	50	33	15	2	500	49	34	15	2	Open
Xavier University	Cincinnati	SU	A,B,M,D	Pri	No	C	3,879	26	9	21	25	21	24	593	10	43	38	9	591	11	42	37	11	2/1
Youngstown State University	Youngstown	U	A,B,M,D	Pub	F,S	C	11,702	20	59	19	12	5	5	490	55	29	14	2	490	52	31	14	3	8/15

Oklahoma

NAME OF SCHOOL	TOWN	Env	Deg	Ctrl	Frat	Stu	Enroll	ACT Med	<21	21-23	24-26	27-28	>28	SATV Med	<500	500-599	600-700	>700	SATM Med	<500	500-599	600-700	>700	Deadline
Cameron University	Lawton	SU	A,B,M	Pub	F,S	C	5,403	19	64	19	11	4	4											Open
East Central University	Ada	SM	A,B,M	Pub	F,S	C	3,803	20	52	26	16	4	2											Open
Langston University	Langston	R	A,B,M	Pub	F,S	C	4,020																	Open
Northeastern State University	Tahlequah	SM	B,M,D	Pub	F,S	C	8,625	24																Open
Northwestern Oklahoma State University	Alva	SM	A,B,M	Pub	F,S	C	1,861	20	59	26	9	5	2											Open
Oklahoma Baptist University	Shawnee	SM	A,B,M		F,S	C	1,649	24	10	30	25	16	19	590	16	36	36	12	560	19	43	29	9	8/1
Oklahoma Christian University	Oklahoma City	SU	B,M		F,S	C	1,835	23	27	26	19	13	15	551	27	35	27	10	618	27	33	29	10	Open
Oklahoma City University	Oklahoma City	U	B,M	Pri	F,S	C	1,911	24	17	24	26	15	18	580	16	42	35	7	555	22	45	29	4	8/20
Oklahoma Panhandle State University	Goodwell	R	A,B	Pub	No	C	1,144	21	72	18	8	1	1											Open
Oklahoma State University	Stillwater	SM	B,M,D		F,S	C	18,909	24	14	29	29	11	17	550	22	48	25	5	570	19	44	30	7	Open
Oklahoma Wesleyan University	Bartlesville	SU	A,B,M		No	C	816																	Open

NAME OF SCHOOL	TOWN	ENVIRONMENT	DEGREES AWARDED	CONTROL	FRATERNITIES AND SORORITIES	STUDENTS	UNDERGRAD ENROLLMENT FALL 2005	ACT Median	ACT Below 21	ACT 21-23	ACT 24-26	ACT 27-28	ACT Above 28	SAT I VERBAL Median	Below 500	500-599	600-700	Above 700	SAT I MATH Median	Below 500	500-599	600-700	Above 700	APPLICATION DEADLINE
Oral Roberts University	Tulsa	U	B,M,D	Pri	No	C	3,265	21	30	24	27	8	11	520	35	39	19	7	510	33	41	23	3	Open
Saint Gregory's University	Shawnee	SU	A,B,M		F,S	C	757																	Open
Southeastern Oklahoma State University	Durant	R	B,M	Pub	F,S	C	3,738	20	60	23	12	4	1											Open
Southern Nazarene University	Bethany	SU	A,B,M		No	C	1,705																	
Southwestern Oklahoma State University	Weatherford	SM	A,B,M,D	Pub	F,S	C	3,858																	8/5
University of Central Oklahoma	Edmond	SU	B,M	Pub	F,S	C	14,628																	8/15
University of Oklahoma	Norman	SU	B,M,D	Pub	F,S	C	20,424	26	9	16	34	17	24	591					600					4/1
University of Science and Arts of Oklahoma	Chickasha	SM	B	Pub	F,S	C	1,430	21	48	21	18	7	6											9/8
University of Tulsa	Tulsa	U	B,M,D	Pri	F,S	C	2,796	26	6	20	24	14	36	620	12	30	32	28	620	10	30	34	26	Open

Oregon

NAME OF SCHOOL	TOWN	ENVIRONMENT	DEGREES AWARDED	CONTROL	FRATERNITIES AND SORORITIES	STUDENTS	UNDERGRAD ENROLLMENT FALL 2005	ACT Median	ACT Below 21	ACT 21-23	ACT 24-26	ACT 27-28	ACT Above 28	SAT I VERBAL Median	Below 500	500-599	600-700	Above 700	SAT I MATH Median	Below 500	500-599	600-700	Above 700	APPLICATION DEADLINE
Art Institute of Portland	Portland	U	A,B		No	C	1,327																	Open
Cascade College	Portland	SU	B	Pri	No	C	286	20	49	22	22	6	1	490	47	42	11		500	45	41	14		Open
Concordia University	Portland	U	A,B,M	Pri	No	C	1,006	21	40	35	16	9	2	500	50	34	15	1	520	44	39	17		
Eastern Oregon University	La Grande	R	B,M	Pub	No	C	3,050																	Open
George Fox University	Newberg	SM	B,M,D	Pri	No	C	1,860	23	29	23	33	9	6	560	27	40	29	4	560	24	43	30	3	2/1
Lewis and Clark College	Portland	SU	B,M	Pri	No	C	1,909	26	3	12	18	23	44	600	1	21	48	30	570	1	31	51	17	2/1
Linfield College	McMinnville	SM	B	Pri	F,S	C	1,750	24	11	38	23	13	15	560	19	46	31	5	580	17	40	37	7	2/15
Marylhurst University	Marylhurst	SU	B,M		No	C	817																	Open
Northwest Christian College	Eugene	U	A,B,M	Pri	No	C	402	20	57	21	7	14		500	50	27	23		460	61	30	9		
Oregon Institute of Technology	Klamath Falls	SM	A,B,M	Pub	F,S	C	3,086																	6/1
Oregon State University	Corvallis	SM	B,M,D	Pub	F,S	C	15,599		31	28	22	9	10		35	42	21	2		29	42	26	3	
Pacific Northwest College of Art	Portland	U	B	Pri	No	C	291		25	25	50				37	25	38			50	25	25		8/15
Pacific University	Forest Grove	SM	B,M,D	Pri	F,S	C	1,075																	2/15
Portland State University	Portland	U	B,M,D	Pub	No	C	15,917																	Open
Reed College	Portland	U	B,M	Pri	No	C	1,309	30	1	2	6	14	77	710		6	37	57	670	1	13	53	33	1/15
Southern Oregon University	Ashland	SM	B,M	Pub	No	C	4,438	21	24	34	32	5	5	520	32	45	19	4	510	39	45	15	1	Open
University of Oregon	Eugene	SU	B,M,D	Pub	F,S	C	16,473							560	24	43	27	6	580	22	44	28	5	1/15
University of Portland	Portland	U	B,M	Pri	No	C	2,860							591	10	44	36	10	591	8	43	41	8	2/1
Warner Pacific College	Portland	U	A,B,M	Pri	No	C	645																	Open
Western Baptist College	Salem	SU	A,B	Pri	No	C	737	21	7	60	6	7	20	550	24	45	28	3	540	31	44	22	3	8/1
Western Oregon University	Monmouth	R	A,B,M	Pub	No	C	4,480	21	23	50	23	2	2	495	52	37	11		485	55	35	9	1	Open
Willamette University	Salem	U	B,M,D	Pri	F,S	C	1,954	27	5	11	28	27	29	620	7	30	46	17	620	6	33	48	13	2/1

Pennsylvania

NAME OF SCHOOL	TOWN	ENVIRONMENT	DEGREES AWARDED	CONTROL	FRATERNITIES AND SORORITIES	STUDENTS	UNDERGRAD ENROLLMENT FALL 2005	ACT Median	ACT Below 21	ACT 21-23	ACT 24-26	ACT 27-28	ACT Above 28	SAT I VERBAL Median	Below 500	500-599	600-700	Above 700	SAT I MATH Median	Below 500	500-599	600-700	Above 700	APPLICATION DEADLINE
Albright College	Reading	SU	B,M	Pri	F,S	C	2,165							520	41	42	16	1	510	38	44	17	1	Open
Allegheny College	Meadville	SM	B	Pri	F,S	C	2,053	25	9	21	30	21	19	610	6	31	49	14	610	4	36	51	9	2/15
Alvernia College	Reading	SU	A,B,M	Pri	No	C	1,996								58	31	11			61	33	6		Open
Arcadia University	Glenside	SU	B,M,D	Pri	No	C	1,955	25						569	18	47	30	5	553	22	47	28	3	Open
Bloomsburg University of Pennsylvania	Bloomsburg	SM	A,B,M,D	Pub	F,S	C	7,783							500	48	43	9		510	41	47	12		Open
Bryn Athyn College of the New Church	Bryn Athyn	SU	A,B,M	Pri	S	C	142						50	550	35	20	33	5	530	35	31		4	2/1
Bryn Mawr College	Bryn Mawr	SU	B,M,D	Pri	No	W	1,334							670	2	16	44	38	630	1	31	53	15	1/15
Bucknell University	Lewisburg	SM	B,M	Pri	F,S	C	3,505	29	1	5	15	21	59	640	2	22	56	20	670	1	11	55	34	1/1
Cabrini College	Radnor	SU	B,M	Pri	No	C	1,739							490	52	38	10	1	480	58	34	9	1	Open
California University of Pennsylvania	California	SM	A,B,M	Pub	F,S	C	5,943	20	68	21	7	3	1	493	57	36	6	1	493	55	36	8	1	Open
Carlow University	Pittsburgh	U	B,M	Pri	No	PW	1,623	21	45	23	18	9	5	520	37	49	12	2	500	44	42	13	1	7/1
Carnegie Mellon University	Pittsburgh	SU	B,M,D	Pri	F,S	C	5,155																	Open
Cedar Crest College	Allentown	SU	A,B	Pri	No	W	1,821	23	15	35	25	15	10	480	35	39	24	2	460	40	40	18	2	Open
Chatham College	Pittsburgh	U	B,M,D	Pri	No	W	675																	Open
Chestnut Hill College	Philadelphia	SU	A,B,M,D	Pri	No	C	915								1	4								Open
Cheyney University of Pennsylvania	Cheyney	SU	A,B,M	Pub	F,S	C	1,401																	5/30
Clarion University of Pennsylvania	Clarion	SM	A,B,M	Pub	F,S	C	5,744							505	56	35	8	1	502	57	35	7	1	Open
College Misericordia	Dallas	SU	B,M,D	Pri	No	C	2,072	20	60	30		10		500	48	43	8	1	510	44	44	12		Open
Curtis Institute of Music	Philadelphia	U	B		No	C	130																	Open
De Sales University	Center Valley	SU	B,M	Pri	S	C	2,284	22						548	26	52	19	3	541	30	48	21	1	Open
Delaware Valley College	Doylestown	SU	A,B,M	Pri	F,S	C	2,000	22	38	25	25	13		510	43	43	13	1	510	41	46	12	1	Open
DeVry University/Fort Washington	Fort Washington		A,B,M		No	C	675																	Open
Dickinson College	Carlisle	SU	B	Pri	No	C	2,352	28	1	4	23	29	43	640	2	21	52	25	650	1	21	59	19	2/1
Drexel University	Philadelphia	U	B,M,D	Pri	F,S	C	11,030																	3/1
Duquesne University	Pittsburgh	U	B,M,D	Pri	F,S	C	5,650																	7/1
East Stroudsburg University of Pennsylvania	East Stroudsburg	SM	B,M	Pub	F,S	C	5,135							490	57	36	6	1	490	53	38	8	1	3/1
Eastern University	St. Davids	SM	A,B,M		No	C	1,920																	Open
Edinboro University of Pennsylvania	Edinboro	SM	A,B,M	Pub	F,S	C	6,450																	Open
Elizabethtown College	Elizabethtown	SM	A,B,M		No	C	2,206							560	25	46	26	3	550	21	46	27	6	Open
Franklin and Marshall College	Lancaster	SU	B	Pri	F,S	C	2,025							630	3	26	50	20	640	3	20	59	18	2/1
Gannon University	Erie	U	A,B,M,D	Pri	F,S	C	2,574	21	41	30	18	7	4	520	38	49	12	2	530	34	45	19	2	Open
Geneva College	Beaver Falls	SM	A,B,M	Pri	No	C	1,385									45	4							Open
Gettysburg College	Gettysburg	SU	B	Pri	F,S	C	2,616							640		22	63	15	640		19	70	11	2/15
Grove City College	Grove City	SM	B	Pri	F,S	C	2,310	28	2	7	29	20	42	640	5	25	47	23	640	3	24	50	23	2/1
Gwynedd-Mercy College	Gwynedd Valley	SU	A,B,M	Pri	No	C	2,180							490	51	38	10	1	490	51	41	8		8/1
Haverford College	Haverford	SU	B	Pri	No	C	1,168							690		8	44	48	690		10	43	47	1/15
Holy Family University	Philadelphia	SU	A,B,M	Pri	No	C	2,065							505					495					Open
Immaculata University	Immaculata	SU	A,B,M,D	Pri	No	W	390																	
Indiana University of Pennsylvania	Indiana	SM	A,B,M,D	Pub	F,S	C	12,047							536	35	48	15	2	532	38	48	13	1	Open
Juniata College	Huntingdon	SM	B	Pri	No	C	1,449							570	9	51	31	8	600	7	40	46	7	3/15
Keystone College	La Plume	R	A,B	Pri	No	C	1,718	17	75	17	8			450	74	23	3		440	74	23	3		Open
King's College	Wilkes Barre	U	B,M	Pri	No	C	2,105							520	38	46	14	2	530	35	46	17	2	Open
Kutztown University of Pennsylvania	Kutztown	SM	B,M	Pub	F,S	C	8,065																	Open
La Roche College	Pittsburgh	SU	A,B,M	Pri	No	C	1,500	20	52	24	12	12		490	53	40	6	1	480	57	36	6	1	Open

TEST SCORES

NAME OF SCHOOL	TOWN	ENV	DEGREES	CONTROL	FRAT/SOR	STUDENTS	ENROLL FALL 2005	ACT Median	ACT Below 21	ACT 21-23	ACT 24-26	ACT 27-28	ACT Above 28	SAT V Median	SAT V Below 500	SAT V 500-599	SAT V 600-700	SAT V Above 700	SAT M Median	SAT M Below 500	SAT M 500-599	SAT M 600-700	SAT M Above 700	APPL DEADLINE
La Salle University	Philadelphia	U	A,B,M,D	Pri	F,S	C	4,339							550	25	45	29	2	550	23	50	24	3	4/1
Lafayette College	Easton	SU	B		F,S	C	2,346																	1/1
Lebanon Valley College	Annville	SM	A,B,M,D	Pri	F,S	C	1,774							554	22	50	26	2	569	18	44	34	4	Open
Lehigh University	Bethlehem	SU	B,M,D		F,S	C	4,679							625	1	23	57	18	670		9	51	40	1/1
Lincoln University	Lincoln University	R	B,M	Pub	F,S	C	1,714							410	84	14	2		400	86	12	2		Open
Lock Haven University of Pennsylvania	Lock Haven	R	A,B,M	Pub	F,S	C	4,977																	Open
Lycoming College	Williamsport	SM	B		F,S	C	1,485	24	14	29	43	14		530	30	49	19	2	530	28	53	18	1	4/1
Mansfield University	Mansfield	R	A,B,M	Pub	F,S	C	2,886		50	30	14	3	3	500	38	48	13	1	490	39	46	13	2	Open
Marywood University	Scranton	SU	A,B,M,D	Pri	S	C	1,867	22	59	18	14		9	527	37	46	14	3	521	41	42	15	2	Open
Mercyhurst College	Erie	SU	A,B,M		No	C	3,840		21	46	33				31	46	20	3		29	47	22	2	Open
Messiah College	Grantham	SM	B	Pri	No	C	2,916	26	11	17	28	20	24	600	8	39	40	12	590	12	41	39	9	Open
Millersville University of Pennsylvania	Millersville	SM	A,B,M	Pub	F,S	C	6,935							520	33	50	16	1	540	28	52	19	1	Open
Moore College of Art and Design	Philadelphia	U	B	Pri	No	W	630																	Open
Moravian College	Bethlehem	SU	B,M	Pri	F,S	C	1,850																	
Mount Aloysius College	Cresson	SM	A,B,M	Pri	No	C	1,482	18	84	15	1			460	67	30	3		460	67	28	5		Open
Muhlenberg College	Allentown	SU	B		F,S	C	2,457	28		7	30	26	37	610	3	40	45	12	620	4	28	58	10	2/15
Neumann College	Aston	SU	A,B,M	Pri	No	C	2,313							450	81	16	2	1	430	81	17	2		Open
Peirce College	Philadelphia	U	A,B	Pri	No	C	1,962																	
Penn State Erie/The Behrend College	Erie	SU	A,B,M	Pub	F,S	C	3,440								38	47	14	1		27	48	22	3	Open
Penn State University/Altoona	Altoona	SU	A,B		F,S	C	3,825																	Open
Penn State University/University Park Campus	University Park	SU	A,B,M,D	Pub	F,S	C	34,637							580	12	44	36	8	620	6	32	47	15	Open
Pennsylvania College of Technology	Williamsport	U	A,B,M	Pub	No	C	6,537							460					460					7/1
Philadelphia Biblical University	Langhorne	SU	B,M	Pri	No	C	1,063	23	25	29	17	21	8	540	29	50	19	2	520	42	41	15	2	Open
Philadelphia University	Philadelphia	SU	B,M,D	Pri	F,S	C	2,703							535	27	56	16	1	542	26	51	20	3	Open
Point Park University	Pittsburgh	U	A,B,M	Pri	No	C	2,962	22	32	37	21	7	3	524	37	44	17	2	501	46	41	12	1	Open
Robert Morris University	Moon Township	SU	B,M,D		F,S	C	3,971	21						500	48	42	10		520	38	46	14	2	7/1
Rosemont College	Rosemont	SU	B,M	Pri	No	PW	644	21		100				509	24	44	25	4	493	38	42	15	3	Open
Saint Francis University	Loretto	R	B,M	Pri	F,S	C	1,340																	
Saint Joseph's University	Philadelphia	SU	A,B,M,D	Pri	F,S	C	5,143	25						570					570					2/1
Saint Vincent College	Latrobe	SU	B,M	Pri	No	C	1,445	22	32	20	30	9	9	540	27	50	19	4	540	31	44	22	3	Open
Seton Hill University	Greensburg	SM	B,M	Pri	No	C	1,526																	Open
Shippensburg University of Pennsylvania	Shippensburg	R	B,M	Pub	F,S	C	6,459							520	38	47	14	1	520	34	50	16	1	Open
Slippery Rock University of Pennsylvania	Slippery Rock	SM	B,M,D	Pub	F,S	C	7,065																	3/1
Susquehanna University	Selinsgrove	SM	A,B		F,S	C	1,989																	3/1
Swarthmore College	Swarthmore	SU	B	Pri	F	C	1,479							730	1	4	26	69	710		5	33	62	1/1
Temple University	Philadelphia	U	A,B,M,D	Pub	F,S	C	24,194		32	37	19	8	4	540	24	51	23	2	540	21	52	24	3	4/1
Thiel College	Greenville	R	A,B	Pri	F,S	C	1,320	19	66	21	9	2	2	480	58	34	7	1	480	56	35	8	1	
University of Pennsylvania	Philadelphia	U	A,B,M,D	Pri	F,S	C	9,841	31		3	8	13	76	700		6	46	48	720		3	34	63	1/1
University of Pittsburgh at Bradford	Bradford	SM	A,B	Pub	F,S	C	1,301	21	41	45	7	7	2	510	47	42	11	1	520	43	49	7		Open
University of Pittsburgh at Greensburg	Greensburg	SU	B	Pub	No	C	1,795							519	34	52	13	1	520	26	58	15	1	Open
University of Pittsburgh at Johnstown	Johnstown	SU	A,B	Pub	F,S	C	3,146	21	52	36	10	1	1	506	42	47	10	1	517	36	47	16	1	Open
University of Pittsburgh at Pittsburgh	Pittsburgh	U	B,M,D	Pub	F,S	C	17,024							610	5	39	42	14	620	4	32	49	15	Open
University of Scranton	Scranton	U	A,B,M,D	Pri	No	C	4,090																	
University of the Arts	Philadelphia	U	B,M	Pri	No	C	2,079	22	48	11	27	7	7	550	31	42	24	3	520	44	40	15	1	Open
University of the Sciences in Philadelphia	Philadelphia	U	B,M,D	Pri	F,S	C	2,468	25	14	24	30	26	6	560	10	58	30	2	600	5	42	48	5	Open
Ursinus College	Collegeville	SU	B	Pri	F,S	C	1,571	23						596	9	40	38	13	600	12	29	47	12	2/15
Villanova University	Villanova	SU	A,B,M,D	Pri	F,S	C	7,087	28		4	14	41	41	620	5	29	54	13	650	3	18	58	22	1/7
Washington and Jefferson College	Washington	SM	A,B	Pri	F,S	C	1,418	25	8	25	41	14	11	560	12	57	26	5	570	11	51	32	6	3/1
Waynesburg College	Waynesburg	SM	A,B,M		No	C	1,614																	Open
West Chester University of Pennsylvania	West Chester	SU	A,B,M	Pub	F,S	C	10,838							530	28	56	16	1	530	26	57	16	1	Open
Westminster College	New Wilmington	R	B,M		F,S	C	1,464	24	73	13	8	2	3	544	32	44	21	3	543	31	44	23	2	Open
Widener University	Chester	SU	A,B,M,D		F,S	C	2,340							505	51	37	11	1	510	43	39	16	2	2/15
Wilkes University	Wilkes Barre	U	B,M		F,S	C	320							520	33	47	19	1	540	30	42	26	2	Open
Wilson College	Chambersburg	SM	A,B	Pri	No	W	732	22	50	10	30		10	530	36	42	15	7	500	45	40	15		Open
York College of Pennsylvania	York	SU	A,B,M		F,S	C	5,405	23						544	17	55	24	4	551	17	60	21	2	Open

Puerto Rico

NAME OF SCHOOL	TOWN	ENV	DEGREES	CONTROL	FRAT/SOR	STUDENTS	ENROLL FALL 2005	ACT Median	ACT Below 21	ACT 21-23	ACT 24-26	ACT 27-28	ACT Above 28	SAT V Median	SAT V Below 500	SAT V 500-599	SAT V 600-700	SAT V Above 700	SAT M Median	SAT M Below 500	SAT M 500-599	SAT M 600-700	SAT M Above 700	APPL DEADLINE
American University of Puerto Rico	Bayamon	U	A,B	Pri	No	C	3,050																	Open
Caribbean University	Bayamon	U	B		No		3,100																	Open
Central University of Bayamon	Bayamon	U	A,B,M		No	C	2,885																	
Conservatory of Music of Puerto Rico	San Juan	U	B	Pub	No	C	255																	
Escuela de Artes Plasticas de Puerto Rico	San Juan	U	B	Pub	No	C	471																	5/16
Inter American University of Puerto Rico/Aguadilla Campus	Aguadilla	SU	A,B,M	Pri	No	C	4,086																	5/1
Inter American University of Puerto Rico/Arecibo Campus	Arecibo	SU	A,B,M		F,S	C	3,935																	
Inter American University of Puerto Rico/Barranquitas Regional College	Barranquitas	SM	A,B		No	C	1,720																	
Inter American University of Puerto Rico/Bayamon University College	Bayamon	U	A,B		No	C	5,090																	5/1
Inter American University of Puerto Rico/Fajardo Campus	Fajardo	U	A,B,M,D	Pri	No	C	2,240																	8/15
Inter American University of Puerto Rico/Metropolitan Campus	San Juan	U	A,B,M,D	Pri	No	C	7,100																	
Inter American University of Puerto Rico/Ponce Regional College	Ponce	U	B		No	C																		

TEST SCORES

NAME OF SCHOOL	TOWN	ENVIRONMENT U-Urban R-Rural SU-Suburban SM-Small Town	DEGREES AWARDED A-Associate B-Bachelor M-Master D-Doctorate	CONTROL Pri-Private, Pub-Public	FRATERNITIES AND SORORITIES F-Fraternities S-Sororities F,S-Both No-Neither	STUDENTS: C-Coed M-Men W-Women PM-Primarily Men PW-Primarily Women	UNDERGRADUATE ENROLLMENT FALL 2005	ACT Median	ACT Below 21	ACT 21-23	ACT 24-26	ACT 27-28	ACT Above 28	SAT I VERBAL REASONING Median	Below 500	500-599	600-700	Above 700	SAT I MATHEMATICAL REASONING Median	Below 500	500-599	600-700	Above 700	APPLICATION DEADLINE Month / Day
Inter American University of Puerto Rico/San German	San Germ·n	R	A,B,M,D		No	C	5,090																	
Pontifical Catholic University of Puerto Rico/Ponce	Ponce	U	A,B,M,D	Pri	F,S	C	8,020																	
Turabo University	Gurabo	SU	A,B,M		No																			
Universidad Adventista de las Antillas	Mayaguez	SM	A,B,M	Pri	F,S	C	760																	Open
Universidad Metropolitana	Rio Piedras	U	A,B,M		No	C																		Open
Universidad Politecnica de Puerto Rico	Hato Rey	U	B,M	Pri	No	C	5,180																	
University of Puerto Rico at Humacao	Humacao	SU	A,B	Pub	S	C	4,282							525	39	46	14	1	539	34	43	21	2	11/14
University of Puerto Rico/Arecibo	Arecibo	U	A,B	Pub	No	C	4,146																	11/30
University of Puerto Rico/ Bayamon University College Campus	Bayamon	SU	A,B	Pub	No	C	5,324																	
University of Puerto Rico/ Cayey University College	Cayey	U	A,B	Pub	F	C	3,995																	
University of Puerto Rico/Mayaguez	Mayaguez	U	A,B,M,D	Pub	F,S	C	11,095							550					550					
University of Puerto Rico/Rio Piedras	San Juan	U	B,M,D	Pub	F,S	C	17,860																	
University of the Sacred Heart	Santurce	U	A,B,M		No	C	4,565																	

Rhode Island

NAME OF SCHOOL	TOWN																							
Brown University	Providence	U	B,M,D	Pri	F,S	C	6,176	30		7	16	15	62	720		8	28	64	720		5	29	66	1/1
Bryant College	Smithfield	SU	B,M	Pri	F,S	C	3,203	23	15	37	33	4	11	540	21	60	18	1	570	9	53	35	3	2/15
Johnson and Wales University/ Providence Campus	Providence	U	A,B,M,D	Pri	F,S	C	9,337							470	65	28	7		470	61	33	6	1	Open
Providence College	Providence	SU	A,B,M	Pri	No	C	4,587	25	9	22	32	23	14	597	7	42	43	8	606	7	35	48	10	1/15
Rhode Island College	Providence	SU	B,M,D	Pub	No	C	7,320																	
Rhode Island School of Design	Providence	U	B,M	Pri	No	C	2,258							600	12	35	37	15	620	10	35	43	12	2/15
Roger Williams University	Bristol	SM	B,M	Pri	No	C	3,440																	
Salve Regina University	Newport	SU	A,B,M,D	Pri	No	C	2,091	23	24	37	27	11		544	23	56	20	2	540	22	59	18	1	3/1
University of Rhode Island	Kingston	SM	B,M,D	Pub	F,S	C	11,546							540	21	54	22	3	560	16	52	28	4	2/1

South Carolina

NAME OF SCHOOL	TOWN																							
Allen University	Columbia	SM	A,B	Pri	F,S	C	350																	Open
Benedict College	Columbia	U	B	Pri	F,S	C	2,552																	Open
Charleston Southern University	Charleston	SU	A,B,M		No	C	2,480																	Open
Citadel, The	Charleston	SU	B,M	Pub	No	C	2,176								33	41	22	4		21	54	23	3	Open
Claflin University	Orangeburg	SU	B,M	Pri	F,S	C	1,678	18						463	51	41	7	1	460	69	22	8	1	Open
Clemson University	Clemson	SM	B,M,D	Pub	F,S	C	13,936	26	8	15	31	15	31	600	8	45	40	7	625	5	32	50	13	5/1
Coastal Carolina University	Conway	SU	B,M	Pub	F,S	C	6,397	22	42	33	17	5	3	510	41	49	9	1	520	31	53	15	1	8/15
Coker College	Hartsville	SM	B	Pri	No	C	489																	Open
College of Charleston	Charleston	U	B,M	Pub	F,S	C	9,878	24	7	43	41	7	2	609	1	41	50	8	604	2	40	52	6	4/1
Columbia College	Columbia	U	B,M	Pri	No	PW	1,108																	2/15
Converse College	Spartanburg	U	B,M	Pri	No	W	720																	
Erskine College	Due West	R	B,M,D	Pri	No	C	594	24	26	22	26	13	13	550	28	35	29	8	570	19	48	29	3	Open
Francis Marion University	Florence	R	B,M	Pub	F,S	C	3,500	20	73	13	10	3	1	491	57	32	10	1	490	53	38	8	1	Open
Furman University	Greenville	SU	B,M	Pri	F,S	C	2,803	28	4	10	23	22	41	650	2	20	56	22	650	2	19	61	18	1/15
Lander University	Greenwood	SM	B,M	Pub	F,S	C	2,650																	Open
Limestone College	Gaffney	SU	A,B	Pri	S	C	677	19	71	21	6	2		480	63	32	5		490	53	34	13		Open
Morris College	Sumter	U	B		F,S	C	863																	4/30
Newberry College	Newberry	SM	B	Pri	F,S	C	785																	Open
Presbyterian College	Clinton	SM	B		F,S		1,196	23	20	31	31	8	10	567	22	43	30	5	570	17	44	35	3	Open
South Carolina State University	Orangeburg	SM	B,M,D		F,S	C	4,020																	7/31
Southern Wesleyan University	Central	SM	A,B,M	Pri	No	C	1,995	21	29	47	24			520	37	47	15	2	510	38	45	15	1	
University of South Carolina at Aiken	Aiken	SU	B,M	Pub	F,S	C	3,151	20	63	25	11	1		490	57	35	7	1	505	47	43	10		Open
University of South Carolina at Columbia	Columbia	U	A,B,M,D	Pub	F,S	C	18,362	25	12	26	30	15	17	570	14	47	31	9	590	10	44	37	9	12/1
University of South Carolina Upstate	Spartanburg	U	A,B,M	Pub	F,S	C	4,332	19	66	23	7	2	2	490	55	35	9	1	500	50	38	12		Open
Voorhees College	Denmark	R	B		F,S	C	890																	
Winthrop University	Rock Hill	SM	B,M	Pub	F,S	C	5,200	21	41	28	21	6	4	530	33	45	19	3	520	33	48	17	2	
Wofford College	Spartanburg	U	B	Pri	F,S		1,174	25	15	23	33	12	17	616	5	43	43	9	628	5	35	49	11	2/1

South Dakota

NAME OF SCHOOL	TOWN																							
Augustana College	Sioux Falls	SU	B,M	Pri	No	C	1,714	24	15	28	29	16	12	595	12	38	38	12	595	25	25	38	12	Open
Black Hills State University	Spearfish	SM	A,B,M	Pub	F,S	C	3,720																	Open
Dakota State University	Madison	SM	A,B,M	Pub	No	C	2,110																	Open
Dakota Wesleyan University	Mitchell	SM	A,B,M		No	C	760																	8/25
Huron University	Huron	SM	A,B,M		No	C	555																	
Mount Marty College	Yankton	SM	A,B,M		No	C	1,089		10	50	30	5	5											Open
National American University	Rapid City	SM	A,B,M	Pri	No	C	463																	Open
Northern State University	Aberdeen	U	A,B,M	Pub	No	C	2,425	21						550					525					8/15
Oglala Lakota College	Kyle	R	B		No	C																		Open
Presentation College	Aberdeen	SM	A,B		No	C	630	21																
Sinte Gleska University	Rosebud	R	A,B,M		No	C	341																	Open
South Dakota School of Mines and Technology	Rapid City	SU	A,B,M,D	Pub	F,S	C	2,057	25	20	29	26	13	11	555					555					8/15
South Dakota State University	Brookings	SM	A,B,M,D		F,S	C	9,594	23	33	23	28	10	6											Open
University of Sioux Falls	Sioux Falls	SU	A,B,M		No	C	1,262																	Open
University of South Dakota	Vermillion	R	A,B,M,D	Pub	F,S	C	6,408	22	33	28	26	6	6	535	42	25	28	3	535	33	38	18	8	Open

Tennessee

NAME OF SCHOOL	TOWN																							
Aquinas College	Nashville	U	A,B		No	C	520																	Open

NAME OF SCHOOL	TOWN	ENVIRONMENT	DEGREES AWARDED	CONTROL	FRAT./SOR.	STUDENTS	UNDERGRAD ENROLLMENT FALL 2005	ACT Median	ACT Below 21	ACT 21-23	ACT 24-26	ACT 27-28	ACT Above 28	SAT V Median	SAT V Below 500	SAT V 500-599	SAT V 600-700	SAT V Above 700	SAT M Median	SAT M Below 500	SAT M 500-599	SAT M 600-700	SAT M Above 700	APPLICATION DEADLINE
Austin Peay State University	Clarksville	U	A,B,M	Pub	F,S	C	8,216	21	29	46	16	5	4	500	42	34	21	3	485	53	29	15	2	7/29
Belmont University	Nashville	U	B,M	Pri	F,S	M	3,645	25	7	26	32	16	19	580	9	47	36	8	580	11	47	32	9	8/1
Bethel College	McKenzie	SM	B,M	Pri	F,S	C	1,226																	8/30
Bryan College	Dayton	SM	A,B	Pri	No	C	775																	Open
Carson-Newman College	Jefferson City	SM	A,B,M	Pri	F,S	C	1,960																	Open
Christian Brothers University	Memphis	U	B,M	Pri	F,S	C	1,493	24	17	32	21	16	14	539	30	46	20	4	544	29	41	30		8/1
Crichton College	Memphis	U	B	Pri	No	C	885																	Open
Cumberland University	Lebanon	SM	A,B,M	Pri	F,S	C	1,083	21	62	22	12	3	1	490	60	30	10		485	65	25	10		Open
East Tennessee State University	Johnson City	SM	A,B,M,D	Pub	F,S	C	9,576	22	40	24	20	9	7	520	41	39	18	2	520	43	39	16	2	Open
Fisk University	Nashville	U	B,M		F,S	C	866	20	60	21	14	3	1	480	53	33	13	1	470	57	33	10	1	Open
Freed-Hardeman University	Henderson	SM	B,M		No	C	1,455																	Open
King College	Bristol	SM	B,M	Pub	No	C	867	22	28	39	20	7	6	515	40	43	16	1	524	26	63	11		Open
Knoxville College	Knoxville	U	A,B		No	C																		Open
Lambuth University	Jackson	U	B	Pri	F,S	C	805	24	19	32	27	12	10	548	31	43	24	2	551	24	52	21	3	Open
Lane College	Jackson	SM	B	Pri	F,S	C	965	16																Open
Lee University	Cleveland	SU	B,M	Pri	No	C	3,348	23	35	21	20	16	8	538	32	39	24	5	524	40	33	21	6	9/1
LeMoyne-Owen College	Memphis	U	B	Pri	F,S	C	785																	Open
Lincoln Memorial University	Harrogate	R	A,B,M	Pri	F,S	C	1,316																	Open
Lipscomb University	Nashville	SU	B,M		No	C	2,297	24	22	27	25	10	15	570	23	36	34	7	550	27	37	30	6	Open
Maryville College	Maryville	SU	B	Pri	No	C	1,146	24	20	28	18	17	17	560	28	37	27	8	530	38	35	24	3	3/1
Memphis College of Art	Memphis	U	B,M	Pri	No	C	314	21	46	26	24	2	2											Open
Middle Tennessee State University	Murfreesboro	U	B,M,D	Pub	F,S	C	20,279	22	31	36	21	7	5	540	30	46	21	3	530	36	47	17		7/1
Milligan College	Milligan College	SU	B,M		No	C	753	24	12	37	27	14	10	560	20	51	23	6	550	27	49	22	2	8/15
Rhodes College	Memphis	U	B,M	Pri	F,S	C	1,709	27		9	31	23	37	630	3	28	50	19	630	4	27	49	19	2/1
Southern Adventist University	Collegedale	SM	A,B,M	Pri	No	C		21	43	26	19	7	5											Open
Tennessee State University	Nashville	U	A,B,M,D	Pub	F,S	C	7,118	18	77	17	5	1	1	441	76	21	4		440	74	23	3		8/1
Tennessee Technological University	Cookeville	SM	B,M,D	Pub	F,S	C	7,205	23	30	25	23	12	10		26	46	23	5		23	40	29	8	8/1
Tennessee Wesleyan College	Athens	SM	B	Pri	S	C	865	21	49	28	13	9	2											Open
Trevecca Nazarene University	Nashville	U	A,B,M,D	Pri	No	C	1,245	22	36	29	15	11	8	510					510					Open
Tusculum College	Greeneville	SM	B,M	Pri	No	C	2,289	20	56	26	12	4	2	470					470	60	30	9		Open
Union University	Jackson	SU	A,B,M,D	Pri	F,S	C	2,086	24	20	25	26	12	17	560	15	41	32	11	550	22	41	30	7	Open
University of Memphis	Memphis	U	B,M,D	Pub	F,S	C	15,765	21	44	28	16	7	5	525	37	36	23	3	530	34	41	22	3	7/1
University of Tennessee at Chattanooga	Chattanooga	U	B,M,D	Pub	F,S	C	7,125																	
University of Tennessee at Knoxville	Knoxville	U	B,M,D	Pub	F,S	C	20,052																	2/1
University of Tennessee at Martin	Martin	R	B,M	Pub	F,S	C	5,942	21	37	32	20	7	5											Open
University of the South	Sewanee	SM	B,M,D	Pri	F,S	C	1,405		1	22	20	43	14		4	31	52	13		3	37	50	10	2/1
Vanderbilt University	Nashville	U	B,M,D	Pri	F,S	C	6,286																	1/3

Texas

NAME OF SCHOOL	TOWN	ENVIRONMENT	DEGREES AWARDED	CONTROL	FRAT./SOR.	STUDENTS	UNDERGRAD ENROLLMENT FALL 2005	ACT Median	ACT Below 21	ACT 21-23	ACT 24-26	ACT 27-28	ACT Above 28	SAT V Median	SAT V Below 500	SAT V 500-599	SAT V 600-700	SAT V Above 700	SAT M Median	SAT M Below 500	SAT M 500-599	SAT M 600-700	SAT M Above 700	APPLICATION DEADLINE
Abilene Christian University	Abilene	U	A,B,M,D		F,S	C	4,120	23	30	27	25	8	11	559	27	40	26	7	560	26	38	31	5	Open
Angelo State University	San Angelo	U	A,B,M	Pub	F,S	C	5,709	20	53	27	13	4	3	480	56	32	11	1	490	51	35	13	1	8/9
Austin College	Sherman	SU	B,M	Pri	F,S	C	1,298	26	6	21	33	17	22	628	3	30	47	19	623	3	31	50	16	3/1
Baylor University	Waco	U	A,B,M,D		F,S	C	11,825	25	1	30	32	20	17	600	7	43	39	11	610	4	37	49	10	Open
Concordia University at Austin	Austin	U	A,B,M	Pri	No	C	1,021																	8/15
Dallas Baptist University	Dallas	SU	A,B,M,D	Pri	No	C	3,567	23	27	37	25	6	7	550	19	55	21	5	540	20	51	22	7	Open
DeVry University/Dallas	Irving	SU	A,B,M		No	C	2,510																	Open
East Texas Baptist University	Marshall	SM	A,B	Pri	F,S	C	1,326	21	48	25	17	4	6	480	61	30	7	2	490	55	31	14		Open
Hardin-Simmons University	Abilene	U	A,B,M,D		F,S	C	1,991	22	40	28	18	8	6	517	41	42	17		520	38	45	14	3	Open
Houston Baptist University	Houston	U	A,B,M		F,S	C	1,934	22	39	24	23	8	6	540	24	47	23	6	560	23	42	30	5	Open
Howard Payne University	Brownwood	SM	A,B		F,S	C	1,364	21	47	29	14	7	3	495	52	32	11	5	500	56	29	13	2	8/1
Huston-Tillotson University	Austin	U	B	Pri	F,S	C	674	14	92	4	4			406	83	16	1		403	85	12	3		3/1
Jarvis Christian College	Hawkins	R	B		F,S	C	572	15	98	2				360	99	1			350	99	2			8/1
Lamar University	Beaumont	U	A,B,M,D	Pub	F,S	C	8,430																	
LeTourneau University	Longview	U	A,B,M	Pri	No	C	3,190																	
Lubbock Christian University	Lubbock	SU	A,B,M	Pri	F,S	C	1,835	20	52	18	19	7	4	490	52	31	14	3	490	50	34	15	1	Open
McMurry University	Abilene	U	B	Pri	F,S	C	1,420																	
Midwestern State University	Wichita Falls	U	A,B,M	Pub	F,S	C	5,537	19	60	26	10	3	2	480	57	35	7	1	480	56	35	9		8/7
Northwood University	Cedar Hill	SU	A,B	Pri	No	C	661																1	
Our Lady of the Lake University of San Antonio	San Antonio	U	B,M,D		No	C	1,792	19	68	23	6	2		460	66	29	5		450	67	29	4		Open
Paul Quinn College	Dallas	U	B		F,S	C	790																	
Prairie View A&M University	Prairie View	SM	B,M,D		F,S	C	5,702																	7/1
Rice University	Houston	U	B,M,D	Pri	No	C	2,966																	
Saint Edward's University	Austin	U	B,M	Pri	No	C	3,964	23	24	32	23	17	4	560	17	48	30	5	545	21	55	22	2	5/1
Saint Mary's University of San Antonio	San Antonio	SU	B,M,D		F,S	C	2,600																	Open
Sam Houston State University	Huntsville	SM	B,M,D	Pub	F,S	C	13,193	20	53	28	13	4	2	500	54	37	8	1	510	44	43	12	1	Open
Schreiner University	Kerrville	SM	A,B,M		F,S	C	760																	
Southern Methodist University	Dallas	SU	B,M,D	Pri	F,S	C	6,494	26	1	23	61	15		610	7	39	43	11	620	5	32	47	16	1/15
Southwestern Adventist University	Keene	R	A,B,M	Pri	No	C	880																	9/5
Southwestern University	Georgetown	SU	B		F,S	C	1,309	26	3	21	28	22	26	620	7	31	47	16	610	6	29	51	14	2/15
Stephen F. Austin State University	Nacogdoches	SM	B,M,D	Pub	F,S	C	9,806	21	52	27	15	5	2	502	48	39	13	1	503	47	42	11		Open
Sul Ross State University	Alpine	R	A,B,M	Pub	No	C	1,510																	Open
Tarleton State University	Stephenville	SM	B,M	Pub	F,S	C	7,614	20	55	25	14	4	2	484	58	33	8	1	465	55	35	9	1	8/1
Texas A&M University	College Station	U	B,M,D	Pub	F,S	C	36,368	26	10	20	30	15	25	587	15	40	37	8	616	9	31	45	15	2/15
Texas A&M University at Commerce	Commerce	SM	B,M,D	Pub	F,S	C	6,314	20																8/6
Texas A&M University at Galveston	Galveston	SU	B,M	Pub	No	C	1,385																	
Texas A&M University at Kingsville	Kingsville	SU	B,M,D	Pub	F,S	C	5,580																	Open
Texas Christian University	Fort Worth	SU	B,M,D	Pri	F,S	C	7,171	26						570					590					2/15
Texas Lutheran University	Seguin	SU	B	Pri	F,S	C	1,430	22						528					528					6/1
Texas Southern University	Houston	U	B,M,D	Pub	F,S	C	9,760																	8/13
Texas State University - San Marcos	San Marcos	SU	B,M,D	Pub	F,S	C	23,022	23	29	37	26	6	3	530	32	50	18	1	540	25	54	21	1	6/1
Texas Tech University	Lubbock	U	B,M,D	Pub	F,S	C	23,002	24	15	32	29	12	12	556	20	52	25	3	576	11	51	34	4	5/1

TEST SCORES

Legend:
- **Environment:** U-Urban R-Rural SU-Suburban SM-Small Town
- **Degrees Awarded:** A-Associate B-Bachelor M-Master D-Doctorate
- **Control:** Pri-Private, Pub-Public
- **Fraternities and Sororities:** F-Fraternities S-Sororities F,S-Both No-Neither
- **Students:** C-Coed M-Men W-Women PM-Primarily Men PW-Primarily Women

Name of School	Town	Environment	Degrees Awarded	Control	Fraternities & Sororities	Students	Undergraduate Enrollment Fall 2005	ACT Median	ACT Below 21	ACT 21-23	ACT 24-26	ACT 27-28	ACT Above 28	SAT I Verbal Median	SAT V Below 500	SAT V 500-599	SAT V 600-700	SAT V Above 700	SAT I Math Median	SAT M Below 500	SAT M 500-599	SAT M 600-700	SAT M Above 700	Application Deadline Month/Day
Texas Wesleyan University	Fort Worth	U	B,M		F,S	C	1,348																	Open
Texas Woman's University	Denton	U	B,M,D	Pub	S	PW	5,345	19	64	15	10	2	1	460	64	29	7		450	71	24	5		7/15
Trinity University	San Antonio	SU	B,M	Pri	F,S	C	2,453	29	1	3	19	26	51	649	1	21	53	25	648		20	60	20	2/1
University of Dallas	Irving	U	B,M,D	Pri	No	C	1,166	26	9	17	24	17	33	650	5	24	44	27	600	9	37	44	10	8/1
University of Houston	Houston	U	B,M,D	Pub	F,S	C	27,000																	4/1
University of Houston-Downtown	Houston	U	B,M	Pub		C	11,359																	7/1
University of Mary Hardin-Baylor	Belton	SM	B,M	Pri	No	C	2,588	22	29	30	28	8	5	530	28	57	14	1	530	26	57	16	1	Open
University of North Texas	Denton	U	B,M,D	Pub	F,S	C	21,750																	Open
University of Saint Thomas	Houston	U	B,M,D	Pri	No	C	1,884	24	16	28	26	12	19	580	14	44	35	8	570	16	42	37	6	Open
University of Texas at Arlington	Arlington	U	B,M,D	Pub	F,S	C	16,450	21	44	30	19	5	3	520	39	45	16	1	530	34	45	20	1	6/1
University of Texas at Austin	Austin	U	B,M,D	Pub	F,S	C	36,878	26	10	16	26	18	30	608	12	31	40	18	634	7	25	43	26	2/1
University of Texas at Dallas	Richardson	SU	B,M,D	Pub	F,S	C	9,343	26	8	16	30	16	30	610	10	34	42	14	640	4	26	49	21	8/1
University of Texas at El Paso	El Paso	U	B,M,D	Pub	F,S	C	15,806																	7/31
University of Texas at San Antonio	San Antonio	SU	B,M,D	Pub	F,S	C	23,684	20	53	27	14	4	2	500	46	40	13	1	520	39	43	17	1	7/1
University of Texas-Pan American	Edinburg	SM	B,M,D	Pub	F,S	C	14,942	20	57	28	11	3	1	480	59	33	7	1	490	51	37	11	1	7
University of the Incarnate Word	San Antonio	U	B,M,D	Pri	No	C	4,370	20	60	24	11	3	2	480	58	32	9	1	470	58	34	8		Open
Wayland Baptist University	Plainview	SM	A,B,M		F,S	C	1,004																	Open
West Texas A&M University	Canyon	SM	B,M,D	Pub	F,S	C	5,588	21	49	28	15	5	2	500	50	35	14	2	510	44	42	14		Open
Wiley College	Marshall	SM	B		No																			Open

Utah

Name of School	Town	Environment	Degrees Awarded	Control	Fraternities & Sororities	Students	Undergraduate Enrollment Fall 2005	ACT Median	ACT Below 21	ACT 21-23	ACT 24-26	ACT 27-28	ACT Above 28	SAT I Verbal Median	SAT V Below 500	SAT V 500-599	SAT V 600-700	SAT V Above 700	SAT I Math Median	SAT M Below 500	SAT M 500-599	SAT M 600-700	SAT M Above 700	Application Deadline Month/Day
Brigham Young University	Provo	SU	B,M,D	Pri	No	C	30,798			1	16	61	23		9	35	41	15		6	32	4	18	2/15
Southern Utah University	Cedar City	SM	A,B,M	Pub	F,S	C	4,988	22						512					510					8/1
University of Utah	Salt Lake City	U	B,M,D	Pub	F,S	C	22,661	24	21	28	24	12	15											4/1
Utah State University	Logan	SM	A,B,M,D	Pub	F,S	C	12,737	24	24	25	25	14	12	540	33	36	25	6	570	21	43	32	4	7/1
Weber State University	Ogden	U	A,B,M	Pub	F,S	C	17,628	22	38	24	27	7	4	506	45	39	13	3	497	48	34	16	2	7/1
Westminster College	Salt Lake City	SU	B,M	Pri	No	C	1,842	23	22	28	28	11	11	550	25	34	32	9	540	34	36	22	8	4/15

Vermont

Name of School	Town	Environment	Degrees Awarded	Control	Fraternities & Sororities	Students	Undergraduate Enrollment Fall 2005	ACT Median	ACT Below 21	ACT 21-23	ACT 24-26	ACT 27-28	ACT Above 28	SAT I Verbal Median	SAT V Below 500	SAT V 500-599	SAT V 600-700	SAT V Above 700	SAT I Math Median	SAT M Below 500	SAT M 500-599	SAT M 600-700	SAT M Above 700	Application Deadline Month/Day
Bennington College	Bennington	SM	B,M		No	C	571	27	4	12	24	36	24	660		15	61	24	590	11	44	40	5	1/1
Burlington College	Burlington	U	A,B	Pri	No	C	184																	8
Castleton State College	Castleton	R	A,B,M	Pub	No	C	1,891																	Open
Champlain College	Burlington	SU	A,B,M	Pri	No	C	2,296	20	59	26	11	4		510	30	58	11	1	520	30	48	22		Open
College of Saint Joseph	Rutland	R	A,B,M		No	C	271				100				25	75				25	75			Open
Goddard College	Plainfield	R	B,M		No	C	320																	Open
Green Mountain College	Poultney	SM	B	Pri	No	C	684	20	41	39	11	8	1	520	36	39	23	1	490	51	38	10	1	Open
Johnson State College	Johnson	SM	A,B,M	Pub	No	C	1,540																	Open
Lyndon State College	Lyndonville	SM	A,B,M	Pub	No	C	1,430																	Open
Marlboro College	Marlboro	R	B,M		No	C	336	25		35	29	29	7	660	4	10	57	29	580	9	51	35	5	2/15
Middlebury College	Middlebury	SM	B,M,D	Pri	No	C	2,455	32	2	4	11	20	63	740	1	4	22	73	730	1	3	32	64	12/15
Norwich University	Northfield	R	A,B	Pri	No	C	1,903	22	40	28	20	7	5	532	36	40	22	3	540	31	42	24	3	Open
Saint Michael's College	Colchester	SU	B,M	Pri	No	C	2,006							570	15	50	30	5	568	14	50	32	4	2/1
Southern Vermont College	Bennington	SM	A,B	Pri	No	C	475																	Open
Sterling College	Craftsbury Common	R	A,B		No	C	98																	Open
University of Vermont	Burlington	SU	A,B,M,D	Pub	F,S	C	9,859	25	11	26	32	19	12	580	11	37	37	7	580	11	45	38	6	1/15
Vermont Technical College	Randolph Center	R	A,B	Pub	No	C	1,356							480	56	30	13	1	500	45	42	12	1	Open
Woodbury College	Montpelier	SM	A,B		No	C	131																	Open

Virginia

Name of School	Town	Environment	Degrees Awarded	Control	Fraternities & Sororities	Students	Undergraduate Enrollment Fall 2005	ACT Median	ACT Below 21	ACT 21-23	ACT 24-26	ACT 27-28	ACT Above 28	SAT I Verbal Median	SAT V Below 500	SAT V 500-599	SAT V 600-700	SAT V Above 700	SAT I Math Median	SAT M Below 500	SAT M 500-599	SAT M 600-700	SAT M Above 700	Application Deadline Month/Day
Averett University	Danville	SM	A,B,M	Pri	F,S	C	1,788	19	71	13	15	2		480	56	35	9	1	500	47	45	7		7/15
Bluefield College	Bluefield	SM	B	Pri	F,S	C	776	21	57	20	13	3	7	487	65	22	12	1	475	67	26	7		Open
Bridgewater College	Bridgewater	SM	B	Pri	No	C	1,506	22	37	36	11	8	8	520	35	46	17	2	530	31	49	17	3	Open
Christendom College	Front Royal	R	A,B,M		No	C	379	25	16	16	23	16	29	659	2	19	47	32	581	13	48	33	6	3/1
Christopher Newport University	Newport News	SU	B,M	Pub	F,S	C	5,210																	3/1
College of William and Mary	Williamsburg	SM	B,M,D	Pub	F,S	C	5,790																	1/5
DeVry University/Crystal City	Arlington		A,B,M		No	C	625																	Open
Eastern Mennonite University	Harrisonburg	SM	A,B,M	Pri	No	C	897	25	17	21	30	9	23	545	32	34	24	10	550	31	35	31	3	Open
Emory & Henry College	Emory	R	B,M	Pri	F,S	C	1,027	23							33	44	19	4		36	43	19	2	4/15
Ferrum College	Ferrum	R	B	Pri	No	C	991																	Open
George Mason University	Fairfax	SU	B,M,D	Pub	F,S	C	18,090							547	26	48	22	4	560	21	51	25	3	2/1
Hampden-Sydney College	Hampden-Sydney	R	B		F	M	1,050																	3/1
Hampton University	Hampton	U	B,M,D		F,S	C	4,956																	4/15
Hollins University	Roanoke	SU	B,M		No	PW	848																	2/15
James Madison University	Harrisonburg	SM	B,M,D	Pub	F,S	C	15,618							570	15	53	29	3	580	13	50	34	3	1/15
Liberty University	Lynchburg	SU	A,B,M,D		No	C	6,330																	Open
Longwood University	Farmville	SM	B,M	Pub	F,S	C	3,751							543	33	51	14	2	535	37	50	13	1	3/1
Lynchburg College	Lynchburg	SU	B,M	Pri	F,S	C	2,049	20	53	33	8	2	4	515	44	43	11	2	510	43	43	11	1	
Mary Baldwin College	Staunton	SM	B,M	Pri	No	PW	1,535	23	46	11	23	17	3	550	33	32	26	9	510	43	41	13	3	4/15
Marymount University	Arlington	SU	A,B,M,D	Pri	No	C	2,327	20	54	32	11	1	1	510	46	36	17	1	490	51	38	11		Open
Norfolk State University	Norfolk	U	A,B,M,D	Pub	F,S	C	5,337	18	81	13	6			450	79	18	2	1	440	81	17	2		5/31
Old Dominion University	Norfolk	U	B,M,D	Pub	F,S	C	14,605	21	47	32	14	3	2	530	32	50	17	1	530	33	48	17	1	3/15
Radford University	Radford	SM	B,M	Pub	F,S	C	8,482		57	28	11	4		500	47	41	11	1	500	47	42	10	1	
Randolph-Macon College	Ashland	SU	B	Pri	F,S	C	1,125							560	20	54	23	3	550	21	59	18	2	3/1
Randolph-Macon Woman's College	Lynchburg	SU	B		No	W	735																	3/1
Roanoke College	Salem	SU	B		F,S	C	1,936							560	15	54	27	4	550	20	51	27	2	3/15
Saint Paul's College	Lawrenceville	SM	B		No	C	690																	Open
Shenandoah University	Winchester	SM	A,B,M,D	Pri	F,S	C	1,606	20	56	17	20	6	2	515	46	35	19	1	513	45	35	19	1	
Sweet Briar College	Sweet Briar	R	B,M	Pri	No	W	739	24	14	29	32	16	9	570	15	45	33	7	550	23	53	22	2	2/1
University of Mary Washington	Fredericksburg	SM	B,M	Pub	No	C	3,882	27						617	3	28	52	17	606	5	41	47	7	2/1
University of Richmond	University of Richmond	SU	A,B,M		F,S	C	2,920		6	8	13	25	48		4	19	56	21		3	14	57	26	1/15

TEST SCORES

Legend:
- ENVIRONMENT: U-Urban R-Rural SU-Suburban SM-Small Town
- DEGREES AWARDED: A-Associate B-Bachelor M-Master D-Doctorate
- CONTROL: Pri-Private, Pub-Public
- FRATERNITIES AND SORORITIES: F-Fraternities S-Sororities F,S-Both No-Neither
- STUDENTS: C-Coed M-Men W-Women, PM-Primarily Men PW-Primarily Women
- UNDERGRADUATE ENROLLMENT FALL 2005
- APPLICATION DEADLINE: Month/Day

Name of School	Town	Environment	Degrees Awarded	Control	Frats/Sors	Students	Undergrad Enroll Fall 2005	ACT Median	ACT Below 21	ACT 21-23	ACT 24-26	ACT 27-28	ACT Above 28	SAT Verbal Median	SATV Below 500	SATV 500-599	SATV 600-700	SATV Above 700	SAT Math Median	SATM Below 500	SATM 500-599	SATM 600-700	SATM Above 700	App Deadline
University of Virginia	Charlottesville	SU	B,M,D	Pub	F,S	C	14,213	28	7	8	20	21	43	660	4	18	45	32	670	3	14	44	39	1/2
University of Virginia's College at Wise	Wise	SM	B	Pub	F,S	C	1,892	20	58	24	11	4	3	496	52	38	9	2	485	57	37	6	2	8/1
Virginia Commonwealth University	Richmond	U	B,M,D	Pub	F,S	C	20,508	21	49	27	16	4	4	540	30	44	23	3	530	32	46	20	2	2/1
Virginia Intermont College	Bristol	U	A,B	Pri	No	C	1,138	20	60	21	16	2	1	490	63	24	12	1	480	69	23	6	2	Open
Virginia Military Institute	Lexington	SM	B	Pub	No	C	1,369								17	43	36	5		12	50	35	4	4/1
Virginia Polytechnic Institute and State University	Blacksburg	R	B,M,D	Pub	F,S	C	21,625	24	9	28	33	16	14	590	8	46	41	5	620	3	36	50	11	1/15
Virginia State University	Petersburg	SU	B,M		F,S	C	3,550																	
Virginia Union University	Richmond	U	B,M,D		F,S	C	1,380																	
Virginia Wesleyan College	Norfolk	SU	B	Pri	F,S	C	1,392	20	55	23	19	2	2	522	42	40	16	2	520	38	43	17	2	Open
Washington and Lee University	Lexington	SM	B,D	Pri	F,S	C	1,770	29		2		12	85	690		4	55	40	690		3	58	39	1/15

Washington

Name of School	Town	Environment	Degrees Awarded	Control	Frats/Sors	Students	Undergrad Enroll Fall 2005	ACT Median	ACT Below 21	ACT 21-23	ACT 24-26	ACT 27-28	ACT Above 28	SAT Verbal Median	SATV Below 500	SATV 500-599	SATV 600-700	SATV Above 700	SAT Math Median	SATM Below 500	SATM 500-599	SATM 600-700	SATM Above 700	App Deadline
Central Washington University	Ellensburg	R	B,M	Pub	No	C	9,617	20	51	23	12	12	2	490	44	40	15	2	490	44	40	15	1	4/1
City University	Renton	SU	A,B,M		No	C	3,005																	Open
Cornish College of the Arts	Seattle	U	B	Pri	No	C	710																	8/15
DeVry University/Seattle	Federal Way		A,B,M		No	C	1,080																	Open
Eastern Washington University	Cheney	SM	B,M	Pub	F,S	C	9,090																	
Evergreen State College	Olympia	SM	B,M	Pub	No	C	4,171	24	22	24	27	14	14	600	15	32	42	11	530	32	42	24	2	3/1
Gonzaga University	Spokane	U	B,M,D		No	C	4,171	26	4	18	30	19	29	593	9	45	36	10	598	8	40	43	10	2/1
Henry Cogswell College	Everett	SU	B	Pri	No	C	100	20			100			540		100			580			60	40	Open
Heritage University	Toppenish	R	A,B,M	Pri	No	C	750																	Open
Northwest University	Kirkland	SU	A,B,M	Pri	No	C	1,057								33	45	19	3		40	42	15	3	8/1
Pacific Lutheran University	Tacoma	SU	B,M		No	C	3,270																	Open
Saint Martin's University	Lacey	SU	B,M	Pri	No	C	1,178	20	63	17	12	2	6	497	46	39	13	2	489	51	30	17	2	3/1
Seattle Pacific University	Seattle	U	B,M,D	Pri	No	C	2,978																	3/1
Seattle University	Seattle	U	B,M,D		No	C	4,110																	3/1
University of Puget Sound	Tacoma	SU	B,M		F,S	C	2,589	27	3	14	31	20	32	635	4	27	50	19	615	6	35	48	11	2/1
University of Washington	Seattle	U	B,M,D	Pub	F,S	C	25,660																	
Walla Walla College	College Place	SM	A,B,M	Pri	No	C	1,670	22	40	21	24	8	7	490	31	38	29	2	490	36	36	24	4	Open
Washington State University	Pullman	SM	B,M,D	Pub	F,S	C	19,585																3	
Western Washington University	Bellingham	SM	B,M	Pub	No	C	13,002	24						569	20	43	30	7	567	16	48	32	4	3/1
Whitman College	Walla Walla	SM	B	Pri	F,S	C	1,512	29	1	8	11	20	60	670	2	15	46	37	660	1	12	56	31	1/15
Whitworth College	Spokane	SU	B,M		No	C	2,226	26						595	9	46	38	7	610	10	48	37	6	3/1

West Virginia

Name of School	Town	Environment	Degrees Awarded	Control	Frats/Sors	Students	Undergrad Enroll Fall 2005	ACT Median	ACT Below 21	ACT 21-23	ACT 24-26	ACT 27-28	ACT Above 28	SAT Verbal Median	SATV Below 500	SATV 500-599	SATV 600-700	SATV Above 700	SAT Math Median	SATM Below 500	SATM 500-599	SATM 600-700	SATM Above 700	App Deadline
Alderson-Broaddus College	Philippi	SM	A,B,M		F,S	C	745																	8/1
Bethany College	Bethany	SM	B	Pri	F,S	C	902	22	30	41	21	6	3	510	48	37	11	4	500	43	42	10	4	Open
Bluefield State College	Bluefield	SM	A,B	Pub	F,S	C	1,708	18	73	17	8	1	1											Open
Concord College	Athens	SM	A,B	Pub	F,S	C	3,100																	Open
Davis and Elkins College	Elkins	SM	A,B		F,S	C	660																	Open
Fairmont State	Fairmont	SM	A,B,M	Pub	F,S	C	7,450																	Open
Glenville State College	Glenville	R	A,B	Pub	F,S	C	1,392	19	68	19	11	2		452	72	23	5		461	78	22			Open
Marshall University	Huntington	U	A,B,M,D	Pub	F,S	C	10,030																	
Mountain State University	Beckley	SM	A,B,M	Pri	No	C	3,268	19	70	20	6	3		475	70	30			495	50	30	10	10	Open
Ohio Valley University	Vienna	SU	A,B	Pri	No	C	542	23	75	25	9	3	2	510	75	25	10	3	460	75	25	7		Open
Salem International University	Salem	R	A,B,M	Pri	No	C	340																	Open
Shepherd University	Shepherdstown	SM	B,M		F,S	C	3,809	22	37	33	21	6	3	516	41	47	10	2	506	44	48	8		Open
University of Charleston	Charleston	U	A,B,M		F,S	C	987	22	42	23	20	9	6	478	67	25	8		488	56	33	10	1	Open
West Liberty State College	West Liberty	R	A,B	Pub	F,S	C	2,374																	
West Virginia State University	Institute	SU	A,B	Pub	F,S	C	3,455	19																
West Virginia University	Morgantown	SM	B,M,D	Pub	F,S	C	19,510	23	26	30	25	10	9	510	41	45	12	2	520	33	46	18	3	8/1
West Virginia University Institute of Technology	Montgomery	SM	A,B,M	Pub	F,S	C	2,400																	
West Virginia Wesleyan College	Buckhannon	SM	B,M	Pri	F,S	C	1,324	23	18	19	16	6	4	512	26	26	10		510	25	25	11		8/1
Wheeling Jesuit University	Wheeling	SU	B,M		No	C	1,218	21	41	27	22	5	5	520	41	41	14	4	500	46	34	19	1	Open

Wisconsin

Name of School	Town	Environment	Degrees Awarded	Control	Frats/Sors	Students	Undergrad Enroll Fall 2005	ACT Median	ACT Below 21	ACT 21-23	ACT 24-26	ACT 27-28	ACT Above 28	SAT Verbal Median	SATV Below 500	SATV 500-599	SATV 600-700	SATV Above 700	SAT Math Median	SATM Below 500	SATM 500-599	SATM 600-700	SATM Above 700	App Deadline
Alverno College	Milwaukee	U	A,B,M	Pri	S	W	2,176																	Open
Beloit College	Beloit	SM	B	Pri	F,S	C	1,385	27	3	11	24	23	39	640	6	23	43	28	620	7	32	51	10	1/15
Cardinal Stritch University	Milwaukee	SU	A,B,M,D		No	C	3,130																	
Carroll College	Waukesha	SU	B,M	Pri	F,S	C	2,861	23	31	34	22	9	4											Open
Carthage College	Kenosha	SU	B,M	Pri	F,S	C	2,265																	Open
Concordia University Wisconsin	Mequon	SU	A,B,M		No	C	3,982	22																8/1
Edgewood College	Madison	SU	A,B,M		No	C	2,023	22	38	31	22	7	3											8/25
Lakeland College	Sheboygan	R	B,M		F,S	C	840																	
Lawrence University	Appleton	U	B		F,S	C	1,405	28	4	10	22	21	43	650	5	25	46	24	640	2	27	50	21	1/15
Marian College of Fond du Lac	Fond du Lac	SM	B,M,D	Pri	F,S	C	2,077	20	56	26	13	5	1											Open
Marquette University	Milwaukee	U	A,B,M,D		F,S	C	8,010	27	8	12	29	23	28	600	9	40	40	11	600	8	39	38	15	12/1
Milwaukee Institute of Art and Design	Milwaukee	U	B		No	C	670																	Open
Milwaukee School of Engineering	Milwaukee	U	B,M	Pri	No	C	2,092	26	1	21	29	33	16	580	17	43	34	6	610	6	30	60	4	Open
Mount Mary College	Milwaukee	U	B,M	Pri	No	PW	1,452		61	23	10	3	3											8
Northland College	Ashland	SM	B		F,S	C	739	23	27	20	28	10	15	576	20	55	20	5	561	22	58	15	5	
Ripon College	Ripon	SM	B	Pri	F,S	C	979	24	21	23	26	13	1	579	27	18	41	14	570	20	36	36	8	8/1
Saint Norbert College	De Pere	SU	B,M	Pri	F,S	C	1,987	24	19	30	29	10	12											Open
Silver Lake College of the Holy Family	Manitowoc	R	A,B,M	Pri	No	C	790																	Open
University of Wisconsin/Eau Claire	Eau Claire	U	A,B,M	Pub	F,S	C	10,063	24	6	36	36	13	9	560	16	44	30	10	570	12	47	32	9	Open
University of Wisconsin/Green Bay	Green Bay	SU	A,B,M	Pub	F,S	C	5,622	23	24	40	22	8	6	520	23	71	6		560	18	53	29		2/1
University of Wisconsin/La Crosse	La Crosse	SM	A,B,M	Pub	F,S	C	7,908	25	5	28	41	17	9	570	23	32	45		590	21	30	40	9	Open
University of Wisconsin/Madison	Madison	U	B,M,D	Pub	F,S	C	30,106	28						610	10	30	44	16	650	2	19	50	29	2/1

Legend:
- **ENVIRONMENT:** U-Urban R-Rural SU-Suburban SM-Small Town
- **DEGREES AWARDED:** A-Associate B-Bachelor M-Master D-Doctorate
- **CONTROL:** Pri-Private, Pub-Public
- **FRATERNITIES AND SORORITIES:** F-Fraternities S-Sororities F,S-Both No-Neither
- **STUDENTS:** C-Coed M-Men W-Women PM-Primary Men PW-Primary Women
- **APPLICATION DEADLINE:** Month / Day

NAME OF SCHOOL	TOWN	ENVIRONMENT	DEGREES AWARDED	CONTROL	FRATERNITIES AND SORORITIES	STUDENTS	UNDERGRADUATE ENROLLMENT FALL 2005	ACT						SAT I VERBAL REASONING					SAT I MATHEMATICAL REASONING					APPLICATION DEADLINE
								Median	Below 21	21-23	24-26	27-28	Above 28	Median	Below 500	500-599	600-700	Above 700	Median	Below 500	500-599	600-700	Above 700	Month / Day
University of Wisconsin/Milwaukee	Milwaukee	U	B,M,D	Pub	F,S	C	19,900																	
University of Wisconsin/Oshkosh	Oshkosh	U	A,B,M	Pub	F,S	C	9,290																	
University of Wisconsin/Parkside	Kenosha	SU	B,M	Pub	No	C	4,370																	8/1
University of Wisconsin/Platteville	Platteville	SM	A,B,M	Pub	F,S	C	5,775	22	29	33	26	8	4											Open
University of Wisconsin/River Falls	River Falls	SU	B,M	Pub	F,S	C	5,490																	Open
University of Wisconsin/Stevens Point	Stevens Point	SM	A,B,M	Pub	F,S	C	8,353	22	26	36	25	8	5	505	50	32	18		520	32	46	5	18	Open
University of Wisconsin/Stout	Menomonie	R	B,M	Pub	F,S	C	7,248	21	42	35	17	5	2											Open
University of Wisconsin/Superior	Superior	U	A,B,M	Pub	No	C	2,450																	4/1
University of Wisconsin/Whitewater	Whitewater	SM	A,B,M	Pub	F,S	C	9,350																	Open
Viterbo University	LaCrosse	SU	B,M	Pri	No	C	1,850																	Open
Wisconsin Lutheran College	Milwaukee	SU	B	Pri	No	C	710																	

Wyoming

NAME OF SCHOOL	TOWN	ENVIRONMENT	DEGREES AWARDED	CONTROL	FRATERNITIES AND SORORITIES	STUDENTS	UNDERGRADUATE ENROLLMENT FALL 2005	ACT Median	Below 21	21-23	24-26	27-28	Above 28	SAT V Median	Below 500	500-599	600-700	Above 700	SAT M Median	Below 500	500-599	600-700	Above 700	Month / Day
University of Wyoming	Laramie	SM	B,M,D	Pub	F,S	C	9,583	23	29	27	23	10	10	530	32	43	23	3	540	29	42	26	3	8/10

IN-STATE COST RANGES DIRECTORY

The breakdown of in-state tuition, room, and board costs for the 2005-2006 academic year is arranged from least expensive to most expensive. Within each range are lists of schools that don't charge for tuition or room and board, and those that do.

Less Than $2000

Colleges without Tuition, Room, and Board

California State University, San Marcos, CA (no R & B)
Charter Oak State College, CT (no R & B)
University of Puerto Rico/Bayamon University College Campus, PR (no R & B)

Colleges with Tuition, Room, and Board

Conservatory of Music of Puerto Rico, PR (no R & B)
Curtis Institute of Music, PA
Excelsior College, NY (no R & B)
Montana State University-Bozeman, MT
Oglala Lakota College, SD (no R & B)
Southern University at New Orleans, LA (no R & B)
United States Air Force Academy, CO (no R & B)
United States Coast Guard Academy, CT (no R & B)
United States Military Academy, NY (no R & B)
United States Naval Academy, MD (no R & B)
University of Puerto Rico at Humacao, PR (no R & B)
University of Puerto Rico/Cayey University College, PR (no R & B)
University of Puerto Rico/Mayaguez, PR (no R & B)
Webb Institute, NY

$2000-$3999

Colleges without Tuition, Room, and Board

Augusta State University, GA (no R & B)
Bluefield State College, WV (no R & B)
Caribbean University, PR (no R & B)
Central University of Bayamon, PR (no R & B)
Clayton College and State University, GA (no R & B)
Escuela de Artes Plasticas de Puerto Rico, PR (no R & B)
Harris-Stowe State College, MO (no R & B)
Inter American University of Puerto Rico/Aguadilla Campus, PR (no R & B)
Inter American University of Puerto Rico/Arecibo Campus, PR (no R & B)
Inter American University of Puerto Rico/Barranquitas Regional College, PR (no R & B)
Langston University, OK (no R & B)
Louisiana State University in Shreveport, LA (no R & B)
Metropolitan State College of Denver, CO (no R & B)
Ohio State University at Mansfield, OH (no R & B)
Sinte Gleska University, SD (no R & B)
University of Houston-Downtown, TX (no R & B)
University of the District of Columbia, DC (no R & B)

Colleges with Tuition, Room, and Board

Inter American University of Puerto Rico/Bayamon University College, PR (no R & B)
Inter American University of Puerto Rico/Ponce Regional College, PR (no R & B)
Northeastern Illinois University, IL (no R & B)
Thomas Edison State College, NJ (no R & B)
Universidad Metropolitana, PR (no R & B)
Wilmington College, OH

$4000-$5999

Colleges without Tuition, Room, and Board

Bellevue University, NE (no R & B)
City University of New York/Brooklyn College, NY (no R & B)
City University of New York/City College, NY (no R & B)
City University of New York/Herbert H. Lehman College, NY (no R & B)
City University of New York/John Jay College of Criminal Justice, NY (no R & B)
City University of New York/Queens College, NY (no R & B)
City University of New York/York College, NY (no R & B)
Granite State College, NH (no R & B)
Inter American University of Puerto Rico/Fajardo Campus, PR (no R & B)
Metropolitan State University, MN (no R & B)
NAES College of Eastern Illinios University, IL (no R & B)
Ohio State University at Lima, OH (no R & B)
Ohio State University at Marion, OH (no R & B)
Sojourner-Douglass College, MD (no R & B)
Troy University Montgomery Campus, AL (no R & B)
Universidad Politecnica de Puerto Rico, PR (no R & B)
University of Colorado at Denver and Health Sciences Center, CO (no R & B)
University of Maine at Augusta, ME (no R & B)
University of Maryland/University College, MD (no R & B)
Wilmington College, DE (no R & B)

Colleges with Tuition, Room, and Board

Albany State University, GA
Alice Lloyd College, KY
American University of Puerto Rico, PR (no R & B)
Arkansas Baptist College, AR
Berea College, KY
California State University, Los Angeles, CA
City University of New York/Baruch College, NY (no R & B)
City University of New York/College of Staten Island, NY (no R & B)
City University of New York/Medgar Evers College, NY (no R & B)
City University of New York/New York City College of Technology, NY (no R & B)
College of the Ozarks, MO
Elizabeth City State University, NC
Indiana University East, IN (no R & B)
Indiana University Kokomo, IN (no R & B)
Indiana University Northwest, IN (no R & B)
Indiana University South Bend, IN (no R & B)
Indiana University Southeast, IN (no R & B)
Indiana University-Purdue University Fort Wayne, IN (no R & B)
Inter American University of Puerto Rico/Metropolitan Campus, PR (no R & B)
McNeese State University, LA
Northeastern State University, OK
Southwestern Oklahoma State University, OK
State University of New York/Empire State College, NY (no R & B)
Trinity College of Nursing and Health Sciences, IL (no R & B)
Troy University Dothan Campus, AL (no R & B)
Turabo University, PR (no R & B)
University of Louisiana at Lafayette, LA
University of Puerto Rico/Rio Piedras, PR
University of the Sacred Heart, PR

$6000-$7999

Colleges without Tuition, Room, and Board

Boston Architectural Center, MA (no R & B)
City University, WA (no R & B)
College of New Rochelle - School of New Resources, NY (no R & B)
Franklin University, OH (no R & B)
Heritage University, WA (no R & B)
Humphreys College, CA (no R & B)
University of Michigan/Flint, MI (no R & B)

Colleges with Tuition, Room, and Board

Alabama State University, AL
Armstrong Atlantic State University, GA
Austin Peay State University, TN
Baker College of Flint, MI
Black Hills State University, SD
Brigham Young University/Hawaii, HI
California State University, Bakersfield, CA
Cameron University, OK
Chadron State College, NE
Colorado State University-Pueblo, CO
Dakota State University, SD
Delta State University, MS
Dickinson State University, ND
East Central University, OK
Eastern Kentucky University, KY
Eastern New Mexico University, NM
Fayetteville State University, NC
Florida Memorial College, FL (no R & B)
Fort Hays State University, KS
Fort Valley State University, GA
Georgia Southwestern State University, GA
Grambling State University, LA
Henderson State University, AR
Inter American University of Puerto Rico/San Germ·n, PR
Jacksonville State University, AL
Knoxville College, TN (no R & B)
Lamar University, TX
Lewis-Clark State College, ID
Louisiana Tech University, LA
Minnesota State University, Moorhead, MN
Minot State University, ND
Mississippi University for Women, MS
Mississippi Valley State University, MS
New Mexico Highlands University, NM
Nicholls State University, LA
North Carolina School of the Arts, NC

North Georgia College and State University, GA
Northern Kentucky University, KY
Northwestern Oklahoma State University, OK
Northwestern State University of Louisiana, LA
Oklahoma Panhandle State University, OK
Peru State College, NE
Pontifical Catholic University of Puerto Rico/Ponce, PR
Savannah State University, GA
South Carolina State University, SC
South Dakota School of Mines and Technology, SD
Southeastern Oklahoma State University, OK
Southern Arkansas University, AR
Southern Polytechnic State University, GA
Stephen F. Austin State University, TX
Sul Ross State University, TX
Texas A&M University at Kingsville, TX
Texas Woman's University, TX
United States Merchant Marine Academy, NY (no R & B)
Universidad Adventista de las Antillas, PR
University of Arkansas at Little Rock, AR
University of Arkansas at Monticello, AR
University of Hawaii at Hilo, HI
University of Houston, TX
University of Kentucky, KY
University of Louisiana at Monroe, LA
University of Michigan/Dearborn, MI (no R & B)
University of New Orleans, LA
University of North Carolina at Pembroke, NC
University of North Texas, TX
University of Science and Arts of Oklahoma, OK
University of Tennessee at Chattanooga, TN
University of Texas at Arlington, TX
University of Texas-Pan American, TX
University of West Alabama, AL
Western Carolina University, NC
Western New Mexico University, NM

$8000-$9999

Colleges without Tuition, Room, and Board

Baltimore Hebrew University, MD (no R & B)
Boricua College, NY (no R & B)
Calumet College of St. Joseph, IN (no R & B)
Colorado Technical University, CO
National University, CA (no R & B)
Southeastern University, DC (no R & B)
Strayer University, DC (no R & B)
Union Institute & University, OH (no R & B)
University of Massachusetts Boston, MA (no R & B)

Colleges with Tuition, Room, and Board

Adams State College, CO
Alabama Agricultural and Mechanical University, AL
Alcorn State University, MS
American Indian College of the Assemblies of God, AZ
Angelo State University, TX
Appalachian State University, NC
Arkansas State University, AR
Arkansas Tech University, AR
Auburn University Montgomery, AL
Boise State University, ID
Brigham Young University, UT

Cabarrus College of Health Sciences, NC (no R & B)
California State University, Long Beach, CA
California State University, Northridge, CA
Central State University, OH
City University of New York/Hunter College, NY
Columbus State University, GA
Concord College, WV
David N. Myers College, OH (no R & B)
Delaware State University, DE
East Tennessee State University, TN
Emporia State University, KS
Fairmont State, WV
Florida Agricultural and Mechanical University, FL
Florida International University, FL
Florida State University, FL
Georgia Southern University, GA
Glenville State College, WV
Idaho State University, ID
International College, FL (no R & B)
Jackson State University, MS
Lincoln University, MO
Marshall University, WV
Massachusetts College of Liberal Arts, MA
Mayville State University, ND
Mesa State College, CO
Middle Tennessee State University, TN
Midwestern State University, TX
Miles College, AL
Mississippi State University, MS
Missouri Southern State University, MO
Missouri Western State University, MO
Montana State University-Billings, MT
Morehead State University, KY
Murray State University, KY
New Mexico Institute of Mining and Technology, NM
New Mexico State University, NM
North Carolina Agricultural and Technical State University, NC
North Carolina Central University, NC
North Dakota State University, ND
Northern State University, SD
Oregon Institute of Technology, OR
Our Lady of Holy Cross College, LA (no R & B)
Paul Quinn College, TX
Pittsburg State University, KS
Rust College, MS
Sam Houston State University, TX
South Dakota State University, SD
Southeastern Louisiana University, LA
Southern Christian University, AL (no R & B)
Southern University and A&M College, LA
Tarleton State University, TX
Tennessee State University, TN
Texas A&M University at Commerce, TX
Texas Southern University, TX
Troy University, AL
University of Alabama, AL
University of Alabama in Huntsville, AL
University of Alaska Southeast, AK
University of Arkansas at Pine Bluff, AR
University of Central Arkansas, AR
University of Central Oklahoma, OK
University of Florida, FL
University of Idaho, ID
University of Mississippi, MS
University of Montana—Western, MT
University of Montevallo, AL
University of Nebraska at Kearney, NE
University of North Alabama, AL
University of North Carolina at Asheville, NC
University of North Carolina at Charlotte, NC
University of North Carolina at Greensboro, NC
University of North Florida, FL
University of Puerto Rico/Arecibo, PR
University of Rio Grande, OH
University of South Alabama, AL
University of South Dakota, SD
University of Tennessee at Martin, TN
University of Texas at El Paso, TX
University of West Florida, FL
University of West Georgia, GA
University of Wisconsin/Eau Claire, WI
University of Wisconsin/Green Bay, WI
University of Wisconsin/Milwaukee, WI

University of Wisconsin/Platteville, WI
University of Wisconsin/River Falls, WI
University of Wisconsin/Stevens Point, WI
University of Wisconsin/Superior, WI
University of Wisconsin/Whitewater, WI
University of Wyoming, WY
Utah State University, UT
Valdosta State University, GA
Valley City State University, ND
Washburn University, KS
Wayne State College, NE
Weber State University, UT
West Liberty State College, WV
West Texas A&M University, TX
West Virginia State University, WV
West Virginia University Institute of Technology, WV
Western State College of Colorado, CO
Wichita State University, KS
Wiley College, TX (no R & B)
Winston-Salem State University, NC

$10,000-$11,999

Colleges without Tuition, Room, and Board

Cleary College, MI (no R & B)
DeVry College of Technology/North Brunswick, NJ (no R & B)
DeVry University/Chicago, IL (no R & B)
DeVry University/Columbus, OH (no R & B)
DeVry University/Dallas, TX (no R & B)
DeVry University/Decatur, GA (no R & B)
DeVry University/Phoenix, AZ (no R & B)
East-West University, IL (no R & B)
Kendall College of Art and Design of Ferris State University, MI (no R & B)
Martin University, IN (no R & B)
Mercy College of Health Sciences, IA (no R & B)

Colleges with Tuition, Room, and Board

Allen University, SC
Aquinas College, TN (no R & B)
Arizona State University-Tempe, AZ
Bemidji State University, MN
Bennett College, NC
Bloomsburg University of Pennsylvania, PA
Blue Mountain College, MS
Bowie State University, MD
California State University, Chico, CA
California State University, Dominguez Hills, CA
California State University, East Bay, CA
California State University, Fresno, CA
California State University, Fullerton, CA
California State University, Monterey Bay, CA
California State University, Sacramento, CA
California State University, Stanislaus, CA
Cambridge College, MA (no R & B)
Carlos Albizu University, FL (no R & B)
Central Missouri State University, MO
Central Washington University, WA
Cheyney University of Pennsylvania, PA
Chicago State University, IL
Clarion University of Pennsylvania, PA
Cleveland State University, OH
Colorado State University-Fort Collins, CO
Concordia College, AL
Coppin State College, MD
DeVry University/Addison (DuPage County), IL (no R & B)
DeVry University/Alpharetta, GA (no R & B)
DeVry University/Kansas City, MO (no R & B)
East Carolina University, NC

East Stroudsburg University of Pennsylvania, PA
Eastern Oregon University, OR
Eastern Washington University, WA
Edinboro University of Pennsylvania, PA
Evergreen State College, WA
Fashion Institute of Technology/State University of New York, NY
Fitchburg State College, MA
Florida Atlantic University, FL
Florida Gulf Coast University, FL
Florida Hospital College of Health Sciences, FL
Fort Lewis College, CO
Framingham State College, MA
Francis Marion University, SC
George Mason University, VA
Georgia College and State University, GA
Georgia Institute of Technology, GA
Georgia State University, GA
Goldey-Beacom College, DE
Humboldt State University, CA
Huron University, SD
Indiana State University, IN
Indiana University of Pennsylvania, PA
Indiana University-Purdue University Indianapolis, IN
Iowa State University, IA
Jarvis Christian College, TX
Johnson State College, VT
Kansas State University, KS
Kentucky State University, KY
Kutztown University of Pennsylvania, PA
Lander University, SC
Lane College, TN
Louisiana State University and Agricultural and Mechanical College, LA
Mansfield University, PA
Massachusetts Maritime Academy, MA
Minnesota State University, Mankato, MN
Missouri State University, MO
Montana State University-Northern, MT
Montana Tech of The University of Montana, MT
Morris College, SC
Mountain State University, WV
New College of Florida, FL
Norfolk State University, VA
North Carolina State University, NC
Northern Arizona University, AZ
Northwest Missouri State University, MO
Oakland University, MI
Ohio State University at Newark, OH
Oklahoma State University, OK
Old Dominion University, VA
Oregon State University, OR
Park University, MO
Prairie View A&M University, TX
Purdue University/Calumet, IN
Rhode Island College, RI
Saginaw Valley State University, MI
Saint Cloud State University, MN
San Jose State University, CA
Shepherd University, WV
Shippensburg University of Pennsylvania, PA
Slippery Rock University of Pennsylvania, PA
Southeast Missouri State University, MO
Southern Connecticut State University, CT
Southern Illinois University Edwardsville, IL
Southwest Minnesota State University, MN
State University of New York/College at Buffalo, NY
State University of New York/College at Purchase, NY
Stillman College, AL
Talladega College, AL
Tennessee Technological University, TN
Texas A&M University at Corpus Christi, TX
Texas A&M University at Galveston, TX
Texas State University - San Marcos, TX
Thomas University, GA
Truman State University, MO

University of Alaska Anchorage, AK
University of Alaska Fairbanks, AK
University of Arizona, AZ
University of Arkansas, AR
University of California at Santa Barbara, CA
University of Central Florida, FL
University of Colorado at Colorado Springs, CO
University of Georgia, GA
University of Hawaii at Manoa, HI
University of Kansas, KS
University of Louisville, KY
University of Maine at Farmington, ME
University of Maine at Fort Kent, ME
University of Maine at Machias, ME
University of Maine at Presque Isle, ME
University of Mary Washington, VA
University of Maryland/Eastern Shore, MD
University of Memphis, TN
University of Montana, MT
University of Nebraska at Lincoln, NE
University of Nebraska at Omaha, NE
University of Nevada/Las Vegas, NV
University of New Mexico, NM
University of North Carolina at Chapel Hill, NC
University of North Carolina at Wilmington, NC
University of North Dakota, ND
University of Northern Colorado, CO
University of Northern Iowa, IA
University of Oklahoma, OK
University of South Carolina at Aiken, SC
University of South Carolina Upstate, SC
University of South Florida, FL
University of Southern Mississippi, MS
University of Tennessee at Knoxville, TN
University of Texas at San Antonio, TX
University of Utah, UT
University of Virginia's College at Wise, VA
University of Washington, WA
University of Wisconsin/La Crosse, WI
University of Wisconsin/Oshkosh, WI
University of Wisconsin/Parkside, WI
University of Wisconsin/Stout, WI
Virginia Polytechnic Institute and State University, VA
Virginia State University, VA
Voorhees College, SC
Wayne State University, MI
West Virginia University, WV
Western Kentucky University, KY
Western Oregon University, OR
Western Washington University, WA
Westfield State College, MA
William Carey College, MS
Winona State University, MN
Winthrop University, SC

$12,000-$13,999

Colleges without Tuition, Room, and Board

American InterContinental University, GA (no R & B)
Cogswell Polytechnical College, CA (no R & B)
DeVry University/Fremont, CA (no R & B)
DeVry University/Long Beach, CA (no R & B)
DeVry University/Pomona, CA (no R & B)
New College of California, CA (no R & B)
Peirce College, PA (no R & B)
Prescott College, AZ (no R & B)
Saint Joseph's College, New York, Brooklyn Campus, NY (no R & B)

Colleges with Tuition, Room, and Board

Auburn University, AL
Ball State University, IN
Blackburn College, IL
Bridgewater State College, MA
California Maritime Academy, CA
California Polytechnic State University, CA

California State University, San Bernardino, CA
Castleton State College, VT
Central Connecticut State University, CT
Central Michigan University, MI
Christopher Newport University, VA
Cincinnati College of Mortuary Science, OH (no R & B)
Clarkson College, NE
Clearwater Christian College, FL
Clemson University, SC
Coastal Carolina University, SC
College of Charleston, SC
College of the Southwest, NM
Cooper Union for the Advancement of Science and Art, NY
DeVry Institute of Technology/New York, NY (no R & B)
DeVry University/Colorado Springs, CO (no R & B)
DeVry University/Crystal City, VA (no R & B)
DeVry University/Fort Washington, PA (no R & B)
DeVry University/Miramar, FL (no R & B)
DeVry University/Orlando, FL (no R & B)
DeVry University/Seattle, WA (no R & B)
DeVry University/Tinley Park, IL (no R & B)
DeVry University/West Hills, CA (no R & B)
DeVry University/Westminster, CO (no R & B)
Eastern Connecticut State University, CT
Eastern Illinois University, IL
Eastern Michigan University, MI
Farmingdale State University of New York, NY
Ferris State University, MI
Flagler College, FL
Frostburg State University, MD
Golden Gate University, CA (no R & B)
Grand Valley State University, MI
Illinois State University, IL
Indiana University Bloomington, IN
James Madison University, VA
Jewish Hospital College of Nursing and Allied Health, MO
Keene State College, NH
Kennesaw State University, GA
Kentucky Christian College, KY
Lake Superior State University, MI
LeMoyne-Owen College, TN
Lester L. Cox College of Nursing and Health Sciences, MO
Lincoln University, PA
Lock Haven University of Pennsylvania, PA
Longwood University, VA
Louisiana College, LA
Michigan State University, MI
Millersville University of Pennsylvania, PA
Morgan State University, MD
Nebraska Methodist College of Nursing and Allied Health, NE
New Jersey City University, NJ
Northern Illinois University, IL
Northern Michigan University, MI
Ottawa University, KS (no R & B)
Penn State University/Altoona, PA
Philander Smith College, AR
Plymouth State University, NH
Portland State University, OR
Purdue University/West Lafayette, IN
Radford University, VA
Saint Joseph's College, New York, Suffolk Campus, NY (no R & B)
Salem State College, MA
Salisbury University, MD
San Diego State University, CA
San Francisco State University, CA
Shawnee State University, OH
Southern Illinois University Carbondale, IL
Southern Oregon University, OR
State University of New York at Oswego, NY
State University of New York at Potsdam, NY
State University of New York/College at Brockport, NY

State University of New York/College at Cortland, NY
State University of New York/College at Fredonia, NY
State University of New York/College at Geneseo, NY
State University of New York/College at Old Westbury, NY
State University of New York/College at Oneonta, NY
State University of New York/College at Plattsburgh, NY
State University of New York/College of Agriculture and Technology at Cobleskill, NY
State University of New York/Institute of Technology, NY
State University of New York/Maritime College, NY
State University of New York/University at Albany, NY
State University of New York/University at Binghamton, NY
State University of New York/University at Buffalo, NY
State University of New York/University at New Paltz, NY
State University of New York/University at Stony Brook, NY
Texas A&M University, TX
Texas Tech University, TX
Towson University, MD
University of Alabama at Birmingham, AL
University of Colorado at Boulder, CO
University of Iowa, IA
University of Maine, ME
University of Minnesota/Crookston, MN
University of Minnesota/Duluth, MN
University of Minnesota/Twin Cities, MN
University of Missouri/Columbia, MO
University of Missouri/Rolla, MO
University of Nevada/Reno, NV
University of Oregon, OR
University of South Carolina at Columbia, SC
University of Southern Indiana, IN
University of Southern Maine, ME
University of Texas at Dallas, TX
University of Virginia, VA
University of Wisconsin/Madison, WI
Vaughn College of Aeronautics and Technology, NY (no R & B)
Virginia Commonwealth University, VA
Virginia Military Institute, VA
Washington State University, WA
Wayland Baptist University, TX
West Chester University of Pennsylvania, PA
Western Connecticut State University, CT
Western Illinois University, IL
Western Michigan University, MI
William Tyndale College, MI
Williams Baptist College, AR
Worcester State College, MA
Wright State University, OH
Youngstown State University, OH

$14,000-$15,999

Colleges without Tuition, Room, and Board
Burlington College, VT (no R & B)
Lourdes College, OH (no R & B)

Colleges with Tuition, Room, and Board
Barber-Scotia College, NC
Bowling Green State University, OH
Brescia University, KY
Brewton-Parker College, GA
Bryn Athyn College of the New Church, PA
California University of Pennsylvania, PA
College of William and Mary, VA
Colorado School of Mines, CO
Crichton College, TN
Davenport University, MI
Deaconess College of Nursing, MO
Edward Waters College, FL
Faulkner University, AL
Grove City College, PA

Huston-Tillotson University, TX
Jamestown College, ND
Kean University, NJ
Kent State University, OH
Lee University, TN
Lyndon State College, VT
Maine Maritime Academy, ME
Marylhurst University, OR (no R & B)
Michigan Technological University, MI
Mississippi College, MS
Monroe College, NY
National American University, SD
Oakwood College, AL
Ohio State University, OH
Ohio University, OH
Paine College, GA
Presentation College, SD
Richard Stockton College of New Jersey, NJ
Rochester College, MI
Rutgers, The State University of New Jersey/Camden Campus, NJ
Rutgers, The State University of New Jersey/New Brunswick/Piscataway Campus, NJ
Rutgers, The State University of New Jersey/Newark Campus, NJ
Saint Augustine's College, NC
Shaw University, NC
Sonoma State University, CA
Southern Nazarene University, OK
State University of New York/College of Environmental Science and Forestry, NY
State University of New York/College of Technology at Alfred, NY
Tougaloo College, MS
University of Akron, OH
University of at California Davis, CA
University of Delaware, DE
University of Illinois at Urbana-Champaign, IL
University of Mary, ND
University of Massachusetts Amherst, MA
University of Massachusetts Dartmouth, MA
University of Massachusetts Lowell, MA
University of Minnesota/Morris, MN
University of Missouri/Kansas City, MO
University of Missouri/St. Louis, MO
University of Rhode Island, RI
University of Texas at Austin, TX
University of Toledo, OH
Vermont Technical College, VT
Wilberforce University, OH
Woodbury College, VT (no R & B)

$16,000-$17,999

Colleges without Tuition, Room, and Board
Metropolitan College of New York, NY (no R & B)
Molloy College, NY (no R & B)

Colleges with Tuition, Room, and Board
Atlantic Union College, MA
Berkeley College/New York City, NY (no R & B)
Bethel College, TN
Bethune-Cookman College, FL
Bluefield College, VA
Carson-Newman College, TN
Cascade College, OR
Charleston Southern University, SC
Claflin University, SC
Columbia College, MO
Dakota Wesleyan University, SD
Dallas Baptist University, TX
Dillard University, LA
East Texas Baptist University, TX
Evangel University, MO
Freed-Hardeman University, TN
Friends University, KS
Gallaudet University, DC
Hannibal-LaGrange College, MO
Harding University, AR
Henry Cogswell College, WA (no R & B)
Hesser College, NH
Howard Payne University, TX
Husson College, ME
Judson College, AL

Laguna College of Art and Design, CA (no R & B)
Lindsey Wilson College, KY
Livingstone College, NC
Lubbock Christian University, TX
Madonna University, MI
Massachusetts College of Art, MA
Montclair State University, NJ
Mount Olive College, NC
National-Louis University, IL (no R & B)
New Jersey Institute of Technology, NJ
North Central University, MN
Ohio Valley University, WV
Oklahoma Baptist University, OK
Pacific Northwest College of Art, OR (no R & B)
Penn State Erie/The Behrend College, PA
Pennsylvania College of Technology, PA
Pikeville College, KY
Ramapo College of New Jersey, NJ
Rowan University, NJ
Saint Gregory's University, OK
Saint Paul's College, VA
Sheldon Jackson College, AK
Siena Heights University, MI
Southeastern University, FL
Temple University, PA
Thomas More College of Liberal Arts, NH
Toccoa Falls College, GA
Touro College, NY
University of California at Irvine, CA
University of California at Los Angeles, CA
University of California at Riverside, CA
University of California at San Diego, CA
University of Cincinnati, OH
University of Connecticut, CT
University of Great Falls, MT
University of Illinois at Chicago, IL
University of Maryland/Baltimore County, MD
University of Maryland/College Park, MD
University of Michigan/Ann Arbor, MI
University of Mobile, AL
University of New Hampshire, NH
University of Pittsburgh at Bradford, PA
University of Pittsburgh at Greensburg, PA
University of Pittsburgh at Johnstown, PA
Webber International University, FL
William Paterson University of New Jersey, NJ
William Penn University, IA
Xavier University of Louisiana, LA
York College, NE
York College of Pennsylvania, PA

$18,000-$19,999

Colleges with Tuition, Room, and Board
Allen College, IA
Art Academy of Cincinnati, OH (no R & B)
Atlanta College of Art, GA
Belhaven College, MS
Benedict College, SC
Bethel College, IN
Bryan College, TN
Central Methodist University, MO
College of New Jersey, The, NJ
College of Visual Arts, MN (no R & B)
Cumberland University, TN
Eastern Nazarene College, MA
Eureka College, IL
Fisk University, TN
Grace Bible College, MI
Graceland University, IA
Hampton University, VA
Hardin-Simmons University, TX
Houston Baptist University, TX
Howard University, DC
Kentucky Wesleyan College, KY
Liberty University, VA
Limestone College, SC
Lincoln Memorial University, TN
Lindenwood University, MO
Lyon College, AR

Mars Hill College, NC
Marygrove College, MI
McMurry University, TX
Midland Lutheran College, NE
Missouri Baptist University, MO
Missouri Valley College, MO
Northwest University, WA
Nyack College, NY
Oakland City University, IN
Oklahoma Christian University, OK
Oklahoma Wesleyan University, OK
Olivet College, MI
Penn State University/University Park
    Campus, PA
Saint Francis College, NY
Saint Mary's College of Maryland, MD
Salem International University, WV
Shorter College, GA
Silver Lake College of the Holy Family,
    WI
Southern Adventist University, TN
Southwest Baptist University, MO
Southwestern Adventist University, TX
Spalding University, KY
Sterling College, KS
Tennessee Wesleyan College, TN
Texas Wesleyan University, TX
Tiffin University, OH
Trevecca Nazarene University, TN
Tuskegee University, AL
Union College, KY
Union College, NE
University of California at Berkeley, CA
University of California at Santa Cruz,
    CA
University of Mary Hardin-Baylor, TX
University of Pittsburgh at Pittsburgh,
    PA
University of Saint Mary, KS
University of the Cumberlands, KY
University of the Ozarks, AR
University of Vermont, VT
VanderCook College of Music, IL
Virginia Union University, VA
Warner Southern College, FL
Wesley College, DE
Wesleyan College, GA
Westminster College, MO

$20,000-$21,999

Colleges with Tuition, Room, and Board

Abilene Christian University, TX
Albert A. List College of Jewish
    Studies, NY
Albertson College of Idaho, ID
Alverno College, WI
Andrews University, MI
Ashford University, IA
Aurora University, IL
Benedictine College, KS
Bethany College, KS
Bethany College, WV
Bethel College, KS
Campbell University, NC
Campbellsville University, KY
Capitol College, MD
Cardinal Stritch University, WI
Cedarville University, OH
Christendom College, VA
Clark Atlanta University, GA
Coker College, SC
College of Our Lady of the Elms, MA
College of Saint Joseph, VT
Colorado Christian University, CO
Concordia University Nebraska, NE
Cornerstone University and Grand
    Rapids Theological Seminary, MI
Cornish College of the Arts, WA
    (no R & B)
Culver-Stockton College, MO
Dordt College, IA
Drury University, MO
Franciscan University of Steubenville,
    OH
Gardner-Webb University, NC
Geneva College, PA
Georgian Court College, NJ
Goddard College, VT
Grand View College, IA
Hawaii Pacific University, HI
Hilbert College, NY
Illinois College, IL
John Brown University, AR
Johnson C. Smith University, NC
Kansas Wesleyan University, KS

Lambuth University, TN
LeTourneau University, TX
Lipscomb University, TN
MacMurray College, IL
Marian College of Fond du Lac, WI
McPherson College, KS
Medaille College, NY
Mercy College, NY
Methodist College, NC
MidAmerica Nazarene University, KS
Midway College, KY
Milligan College, TN
Montreat College, NC
Mount Aloysius College, PA
Mount Marty College, SD
Mount Vernon Nazarene University,
    OH
Newman University, KS
Northwood University, FL
Northwood University, MI
Northwood University, TX
Notre Dame College, OH
Ouachita Baptist University, AR
Pfeiffer University, NC
Piedmont College, GA
Reinhardt College, GA
Rocky Mountain College, MT
Samford University, AL
Schreiner University, TX
Southern Vermont College, VT
Southern Wesleyan University, SC
Southwestern College, KS
Tabor College, KS
Tusculum College, TN
Union University, TN
University of Saint Francis, IN
University of Sioux Falls, SD
Upper Iowa University, IA
Urbana University, OH
Viterbo University, WI
Warner Pacific College, OR
Waynesburg College, PA
Western Baptist College, OR
William Woods University, MO

$22,000-$23,999

Colleges with Tuition, Room, and Board

Adrian College, MI
Aquinas College, MI
Art Institute of Atlanta, GA
Art Institute of Portland, OR
Asbury College, KY
Avila University, MO
Baker University, KS
Barton College, NC
Benjamin Franklin Institute of
    Technology, MA
Bloomfield College, NJ
Brenau University Women's College,
    GA
Briar Cliff University, IA
California Baptist University, CA
Carroll College, MT
Chaminade University of Honolulu, HI
College of Saint Mary, NE
Columbia Union College, MD
Concordia College: Moorhead, MN
Concordia University at Austin, TX
Concordia University Wisconsin, WI
Dana College, NE
Davis and Elkins College, WV
Doane College, NE
Dowling College, NY
D'Youville College, NY
Edgewood College, WI
Fontbonne University, MO
Goshen College, IN
Grace College, IN
Greensboro College, NC
Greenville College, IL
Hastings College, NE
Heidelberg College, OH
Hope International University, CA
Huntingdon College, AL
Indiana Institute of Technology, IN
Indiana Wesleyan University, IN
Iowa Wesleyan College, IA
Keystone College, PA
King College, TN
LaGrange College, GA
Lakeland College, WI
Lees-McRae College, NC
Lewis University, IL
Malone College, OH
Manchester College, IN

Maryville University of Saint Louis, MO
Monmouth College, IL
Morningside College, IA
Mount Mary College, WI
Mount Mercy College, IA
Muskingum College, OH
Nebraska Wesleyan University, NE
Newberry College, SC
North Carolina Wesleyan College, NC
Northwest Nazarene University, ID
Northwestern College of Iowa, IA
Oklahoma City University, OK
Olivet Nazarene University, IL
Oral Roberts University, OK
Our Lady of the Lake University of
    San Antonio, TX
Palm Beach Atlantic University, FL
Philadelphia Biblical University, PA
Robert Morris University, PA
Roosevelt University, IL
Saint Andrews Presbyterian College,
    NC
Saint Edward's University, TX
Saint Leo University, FL
Saint Mary's University of Minnesota,
    MN
Saint Mary's University of San Antonio,
    TX
Saint Thomas Aquinas College, NY
Saint Thomas University, FL
Saint Xavier University, IL
Simpson University, CA
Spring Arbor University, MI
Sterling College, VT
Texas Christian University, TX
Texas Lutheran University, TX
Thomas College, ME
Trinity Christian College, IL
University of Dubuque, IA
University of Saint Thomas, TX
University of the Incarnate Word, TX
Virginia Intermont College, VA
Walsh University, OH
Wells College, NY
Wingate University, NC
Wisconsin Lutheran College, WI
Yeshiva University, NY

$24,000-$25,999

Colleges without Tuition, Room, and Board

San Francisco Art Institute, CA
    (no R & B)

Colleges with Tuition, Room, and Board

Alaska Pacific University, AK
Albany College of Pharmacy, NY
Albertus Magnus College, CT
Alderson-Broaddus College, WV
Anderson University, IN
Ashland University, OH
Augustana College, SD
Averett University, VA
Barry University, FL
Becker College, MA
Belmont Abbey College, NC
Belmont University, TN
Benedictine University, IL
Berry College, GA
Bradley University, IL
Calvin College, MI
Carlow University, PA
Carroll College, WI
Catawba College, NC
Centenary College of Louisiana, LA
Champlain College, VT
Christian Brothers University, TN
Clarke College, IA
Cleveland Institute of Music, OH
College for Creative Studies, MI
College of Mount St. Joseph, OH
College of Saint Rose, NY
Columbia College, SC
Columbia College Chicago, IL
Columbus College of Art and Design,
    OH
Concordia University, OR
Concordia University, Ann Arbor, MI
Converse College, SC
Daemen College, NY
Daniel Webster College, NH
Defiance College, OH
Eastern Mennonite University, VA
Eastern University, PA

Elmhurst College, IL
Elon University, NC
Erskine College, SC
Felician College, NJ
Ferrum College, VA
Five Towns College, NY
Florida Southern College, FL
Fresno Pacific University, CA
Georgetown College, KY
Hellenic College/Holy Cross Greek
    Orthodox School of Theology, MA
High Point University, NC
Hillsdale College, MI
Holy Family University, PA
Houghton College, NY
Huntington University, IN
Immaculata University, PA
Jacksonville University, FL
Judson College, IL
La Roche College, PA
La Sierra University, CA
Laboratory Institute of Merchandising,
    NY
Lawrence Technological University, MI
Lenoir-Rhyne College, NC
Long Island University/Brooklyn
    Campus, NY
Marymount University, VA
Master's College and Seminary, The,
    CA
McKendree College, IL
Memphis College of Art, TN
Meredith College, NC
Millikin University, IL
Montserrat College of Art, MA
Morehouse College, GA
Mount Saint Mary College, NY
Mount Union College, OH
Neumann College, PA
Newbury College, MA
North Park University, IL
Northwest Christian College, OR
Northwestern College, MN
Nova Southeastern University, FL
Ohio Dominican University, OH
Pacific Union College, CA
Pacific University, OR
Pine Manor College, MA
Point Park University, PA
Post University, CT
Queens University of Charlotte, NC
Quincy University, IL
Research College of Nursing, MO
Rockhurst University, MO
Saint Ambrose University, IA
Saint Francis University, PA
Saint Mary-of-the-Woods College, IN
San Diego Christian College, CA
Spelman College, GA
Springfield College, MA
Thiel College, PA
Thomas Aquinas College, CA
Thomas More College, KY
Trinity College, DC
Trinity International University, IL
Unity College, ME
University of Indianapolis, IN
University of Saint Francis, IL
University of Tampa, FL
University of Tulsa, OK
Ursuline College, OH
Villa Julie College, MD
Walla Walla College, WA
Warren Wilson College, NC
Webster University, MO
Westminster College, UT
William Jewell College, MO

$26,000-$29,999

Colleges without Tuition, Room, and Board

Art Center College of Design, CA
    (no R & B)
Otis College of Art and Design, CA
    (no R & B)

Colleges with Tuition, Room, and Board

Adelphi University, NY
Albion College, MI
Alma College, MI
Alvernia College, PA
American International College, MA
Anna Maria College, MA

Art Institute of Boston at Lesley
University, MA
Augsburg College, MN
Augustana College, IL
Austin College, TX
Azusa Pacific University, CA
Baldwin-Wallace College, OH
Bay Path College, MA
Baylor University, TX
Beacon College, FL
Bellarmine University, KY
Berkeley Colleg/Westchester Campus,
NY
Bethel University, MN
Biola University, CA
Birmingham-Southern College, AL
Bluffton College, OH
Boston Conservatory, MA
Bridgewater College, VA
Buena Vista University, IA
Caldwell College, NJ
California Lutheran University, CA
Carthage College, WI
Cazenovia College, NY
Centenary College, NJ
Central College, IA
Chatham College, PA
Chestnut Hill College, PA
Coe College, IA
Colby-Sawyer College, NH
College Misericordia, PA
College of Mount Saint Vincent, NY
College of New Rochelle, NY
College of Notre Dame of Maryland,
MD
College of Saint Catherine, MN
College of Saint Elizabeth, NJ
College of Saint Scholastica, MN
College of Santa Fe, NM
Concordia College-New York, NY
Concordia University, CA
Concordia University St.Paul, MN
Concordia University, River Forest, IL
Covenant College, GA
Creighton University, NE
Curry College, MA
De Sales University, PA
Delaware Valley College, PA
DePaul University, IL
Dominican College, NY
Dominican University, IL
Drake University, IA
Drexel University, PA
Duquesne University, PA
Emory & Henry College, VA
Fairleigh Dickinson
University/Metropolitan Campus, NJ
Florida Institute of Technology, FL
Gannon University, PA
George Fox University, OR
Gordon College, MA
Guilford College, NC
Gwynedd-Mercy College, PA
Hamline University, MN
Hanover College, IN
Hendrix College, AR
Hiram College, OH
Holy Names College, CA
Hope College, MI
Illinois Institute of Technology, IL
John Carroll University, OH
Johnson and Wales
University/Charlotte Campus, NC
Johnson and Wales University/Denver
Campus, CO
Johnson and Wales
University/Providence Campus, RI
Kansas City Art Institute, MO
Kendall College, IL
Kettering University, MI
Keuka College, NY
King's College, PA
Lake Erie College, OH
Lasell College, MA
Le Moyne College, NY
Linfield College, OR
Long Island University/C.W. Post
Campus, NY
Loras College, IA
Luther College, IA
Maharishi University of Management,
IA
Maine College of Art, ME
Manhattan College, NY
Marian College, IN
Marietta College, OH
Mary Baldwin College, VA
Maryville College, TN
Mercer University, GA

Mercyhurst College, PA
Messiah College, PA
Miami University, OH
Millsaps College, MS
Milwaukee Institute of Art and Design,
WI
Milwaukee School of Engineering, WI
Mitchell College, CT
Monmouth University, NJ
Moore College of Art and Design, PA
Moravian College, PA
Mount Ida College, MA
Naropa University, CO
Nazareth College of Rochester, NY
New York Institute of Technology, NY
Niagara University, NY
Nichols College, MA
North Central College, IL
Northland College, WI
Norwich University, VT
Ohio Northern University, OH
Otterbein College, OH
Pacific Lutheran University, WA
Point Loma Nazarene University, CA
Principia College, IL
Ripon College, WI
Rivier College, NH
Roberts Wesleyan College, NY
Rockford College, IL
Rosemont College, PA
Russell Sage College, NY
Saint Bonaventure University, NY
Saint John Fisher College, NY
Saint John's University, MN
Saint Joseph's College, IN
Saint Joseph's College of Maine, ME
Saint Martin's University, WA
Saint Norbert College, WI
Saint Vincent College, PA
Salem College, NC
San Francisco Conservatory of Music,
CA (no R & B)
Seattle Pacific University, WA
Seton Hill University, PA
Shenandoah University, VA
Shimer College, IL
Siena College, NY
Simpson College, IA
Southern New Hampshire University,
NH
Southwestern University, TX
Spring Hill College, AL
Stephens College, MO
Taylor University, IN
Transylvania University, KY
Tri-State University-Main Campus, IN
University of Bridgeport, CT
University of Charleston, WV
University of Dallas, TX
University of Dayton, OH
University of Detroit Mercy, MI
University of Evansville, IN
University of Findlay, OH
University of Saint Thomas, MN
Valparaiso University, IN
Vanguard University of Southern
California, CA
Virginia Wesleyan College, VA
Wartburg College, IA
Wentworth Institute of Technology, MA
West Virginia Wesleyan College, WV
Wheaton College, IL
Wheeling Jesuit University, WV
Whittier College, CA
Whitworth College, WA
Widener University, PA
Wilson College, PA

$30,000 and over

**Colleges without Tuition, Room, and
Board**

Middlebury College, VT (no R & B)

**Colleges with Tuition, Room, and
Board**

Agnes Scott College, GA
Albright College, PA
Alfred University, NY
Allegheny College, PA
American University, DC
Amherst College, MA
Antioch College, OH
Arcadia University, PA
Assumption College, MA
Babson College, MA

Bard College, NY
Bates College, ME
Beloit College, WI
Bennington College, VT
Bentley College, MA
Berklee College of Music, MA
Boston College, MA
Boston University, MA
Bowdoin College, ME
Brandeis University, MA
Brown University, RI
Bryant College, RI
Bryn Mawr College, PA
Bucknell University, PA
Butler University, IN
Cabrini College, PA
California College of the Arts, CA
California Institute of Technology, CA
California Institute of the Arts, CA
California State Polytechnic University,
Pomona, CA
Canisius College, NY
Capital University, OH
Carleton College, MN
Carnegie Mellon University, PA
Case Western Reserve University, OH
Catholic University of America, DC
Cedar Crest College, PA
Centre College, KY
Chapman University, CA
Claremont McKenna College, CA
Clark University, MA
Clarkson University, NY
Cleveland Institute of Art, OH
Colby College, ME
Colgate University, NY
College of Saint Benedict, MN
College of the Atlantic, ME
College of the Holy Cross, MA
College of Wooster, OH
Colorado College, CO
Columbia University/Barnard College,
NY
Columbia University/Columbia
College, NY
Columbia University/Fu Foundation
School of Engineering and Applied
Science, NY
Columbia University/School of General
Studies, NY
Connecticut College, CT
Corcoran School of Art and Design,
DC
Cornell College, IA
Cornell University, NY
Dartmouth College, NH
Davidson College, NC
Denison University, OH
DePauw University, IN
Dickinson College, PA
Dominican University of California, CA
Drew University/College of Liberal
Arts, NJ
Duke University, NC
Earlham College, IN
Eastman School of Music, NY
Eckerd College, FL
Elizabethtown College, PA
Elmira College, NY
Embry-Riddle Aeronautical University,
AZ
Embry-Riddle Aeronautical University,
FL
Emerson College, MA
Emmanuel College, MA
Emory University, GA
Endicott College, MA
Eugene Lang College New School for
Liberal Arts, NY
Fairfield University, CT
Fairleigh Dickinson University/College
at Florham, NJ
Fordham University, NY
Franklin and Marshall College, PA
Franklin Pierce College, NH
Furman University, SC
George Washington University, DC
Georgetown University, DC
Gettysburg College, PA
Gonzaga University, WA
Goucher College, MD
Grand Canyon University, AZ
Green Mountain College, VT
Grinnell College, IA
Gustavus Adolphus College, MN
Hamilton College, NY
Hampden-Sydney College, VA
Hampshire College, MA
Hartwick College, NY

Harvard University/Harvard College,
MA
Harvey Mudd College, CA
Haverford College, PA
Hobart and William Smith Colleges,
NY
Hofstra University, NY
Hollins University, VA
Hood College, MD
Illinois Wesleyan University, IL
Iona College, NY
Ithaca College, NY
Johns Hopkins University, MD
Johnson and Wales University/North
Miami Campus, FL
Juilliard School, NY
Juniata College, PA
Kalamazoo College, MI
Kenyon College, OH
Knox College, IL
La Salle University, PA
Lafayette College, PA
Lake Forest College, IL
Lawrence University, WI
Lebanon Valley College, PA
Lehigh University, PA
Lesley University, MA
Lewis and Clark College, OR
Loyola College in Maryland, MD
Loyola Marymount University, CA
Loyola University Chicago, IL
Loyola University New Orleans, LA
Lycoming College, PA
Lynchburg College, VA
Lynn University, FL
Macalester College, MN
Manhattan School of Music, NY
Manhattanville College, NY
Mannes College of Music, NY
Marist College, NY
Marlboro College, VT
Marquette University, WI
Maryland Institute College of Art, MD
Marymount Manhattan College, NY
Marywood University, PA
Massachusetts College of Pharmacy
and Health Sciences, MA
Massachusetts Institute of Technology,
MA
McDaniel College, MD
Menlo College, CA
Merrimack College, MA
Mills College, CA
Minneapolis College of Art and Design,
MN
Mount Holyoke College, MA
Mount Saint Mary's College, CA
Mount Saint Mary's University, MD
Muhlenberg College, PA
New England College, NH
New England Conservatory of Music,
MA
New York University, NY
Northeastern University, MA
Northwestern University, IL
Notre Dame de Namur University, CA
Oberlin College, OH
Occidental College, CA
Oglethorpe University, GA
Ohio Wesleyan University, OH
Pace University, NY
Parsons School of Design, NY
Pepperdine University, CA
Philadelphia University, PA
Pitzer College, CA
Polytechnic University/Brooklyn, NY
Pomona College, CA
Pratt Institute, NY
Presbyterian College, SC
Princeton University, NJ
Providence College, RI
Quinnipiac University, CT
Randolph-Macon College, VA
Randolph-Macon Woman's College,
VA
Reed College, OR
Regis College, MA
Regis University, CO
Rensselaer Polytechnic Institute, NY
Rhode Island School of Design, RI
Rhodes College, TN
Rice University, TX
Rider University, NJ
Ringling School of Art and Design, FL
Roanoke College, VA
Rochester Institute of Technology, NY
Roger Williams University, RI
Rollins College, FL

Rose-Hulman Institute of Technology, IN
Sacred Heart University, CT
Saint Anselm College, NH
Saint John's College, MD
Saint John's College, NM
Saint John's University, NY
Saint Joseph College, CT
Saint Joseph's University, PA
Saint Lawrence University, NY
Saint Louis University, MO
Saint Mary's College, IN
Saint Mary's College of California, CA
Saint Michael's College, VT
Saint Olaf College, MN
Saint Peter's College, NJ
Salve Regina University, RI
Santa Clara University, CA
Sarah Lawrence College, NY
Savannah College of Art and Design, GA
School of the Art Institute of Chicago, IL
School of Visual Arts, NY
Scripps College, CA
Seattle University, WA

Seton Hall University, NJ
Sierra Nevada College, NV
Simmons College, MA
Simon's Rock College of Bard, MA
Skidmore College, NY
Smith College, MA
Southern Methodist University, TX
Stanford University, CA
Stetson University, FL
Stevens Institute of Technology, NJ
Stonehill College, MA
Suffolk University, MA
Susquehanna University, PA
Swarthmore College, PA
Sweet Briar College, VA
Syracuse University, NY
Trinity College, CT
Trinity University, TX
Tufts University, MA
Tulane University, LA
Union College, NY
University of Chicago, IL
University of Denver, CO
University of Hartford, CT
University of Judaism College of Arts and Sciences, CA

University of La Verne, CA
University of Miami, FL
University of New England, ME
University of New Haven, CT
University of Notre Dame, IN
University of Pennsylvania, PA
University of Portland, OR
University of Puget Sound, WA
University of Redlands, CA
University of Richmond, VA
University of Rochester, NY
University of San Diego, CA
University of San Francisco, CA
University of Scranton, PA
University of Southern California, CA
University of the Arts, PA
University of the Pacific, CA
University of the Sciences in Philadelphia, PA
University of the South, TN
Ursinus College, PA
Utica College, NY
Vanderbilt University, TN
Vassar College, NY
Villanova University, PA
Wabash College, IN

Wagner College, NY
Wake Forest University, NC
Washington and Jefferson College, PA
Washington and Lee University, VA
Washington College, MD
Washington University in Saint Louis, MO
Wellesley College, MA
Wesleyan University, CT
Western New England College, MA
Westminster Choir College, NJ
Westminster College, PA
Westmont College, CA
Wheaton College, MA
Wheelock College, MA
Whitman College, WA
Wilkes University, PA
Willamette University, OR
Williams College, MA
Wittenberg University, OH
Wofford College, SC
Woodbury University, CA
Worcester Polytechnic Institute, MA
Xavier University, OH
Yale University, CT

PART III

INDEX OF

COLLEGE MAJORS

By now, you either have a clear idea about what your college major will be, or you are worrying about it. This section presents an overview of academic majors as well as information about some of the careers for which each major prepares you.

Majors are listed alphabetically in chart form. This lets you compare the various schools that offer the majors that interest you. You'll also be able to compare each school's Selector Rating and in-state costs.

After you've found a representative sampling of the schools that offer majors in the fields you may want to pursue, go on to the college Profiles that make up this book's main section.

DECIDING ON A COLLEGE MAJOR AND CAREER

What Is a College Major? A major is a field of study in which a student chooses an academic specialty to receive a college degree. A major consists of a concentration of specialized subject matter in a field of study. Most majors occupy about one-quarter to two-thirds of courses in that subject. Most college and university students must complete a required number of courses in their major to earn a Bachelor of Arts (B.A.) or a Bachelor of Science (B.S.) degree. The other twenty-five to fifty percent of courses are occupied by "general education" requirements for graduation, or electives that enhance and broaden a student's academic knowledge. Students' choice of major should be made carefully considering their interests and special talents.

What Is a College Minor? A minor in a field of study usually consists of a number of courses in a field of study other than the major. However, the required units of study are fewer than those required of the major. Many colleges today do not require a formal minor for graduation. The practical reason for a minor is to supplement and strengthen a major. For example, a computer science major may require specified courses in mathematics that, when totaled up, meet the definition of a minor, or perhaps a dual major.

Majors and Careers. Choosing a field of study is one of the most important decisions a student will make in the process of choosing a college major leading to an associate or bachelor's degree. A major with a structured course of study not only provides for intellectual growth, self-improvement, general knowledge, and a search for truth and understanding, but often provides the required technical training to enter and become successful in the world of work. Personal enlightenment is a noble goal, but most students no longer can afford the monetary expenses and the time to pursue courses that do not lead to a major that ties into career goals. Information on majors and careers is presented here to help students to make wise educational and career decisions. Informed educational and career decisions should include interests, academic abilities, and work values.

WHAT ARE SOME DIFFERENT APPROACHES TO CHOOSING A COLLEGE MAJOR?

JOB TRAINING: A student may want to go to college for one main reason: to acquire specific job skills to qualify for direct job entry. Job training course work is usually work-related and technical and it is evident that the skills learned in class can be directly applied to an occupation. For example, students who want to work as engineers in one of the many engineering specialties should pursue a two-year program course work as engineering technicians, or a four- to five-year engineering curriculum to become professional engineers.

Technical preparation: Technical preparation students generally enroll in associate degree programs that provide them with advanced skills through studies and experiences in applied academics, skills, and advanced technology. These students join the workforce after grade 14 or continue their formal preparation by working toward a baccalaureate degree in applied technology. Technical majors can be planned in agriculture, arts and communications, business, engineering and mechanics, health, human service, and natural science.

A general approach: Students may want to pursue a more general major that may not directly tie in to job entry, but will improve their general knowledge and prepare them as generalists with intellectual and problem-solving skills rather than technical training. This kind of major is often referred to as liberal arts, humanities, or general studies. Liberal arts majors can be planned in Social and Behavioral Sciences, The Arts, Communications, Humanities, and Ethnic Studies. A liberal arts major, leading to a baccalaureate degree, may not guarantee direct entry into an occupation associated with the major.

Special talent approach: Students may want to select a major because of a special talent and a strong interest in a certain field of study. Students with a strong interest in writing, drama, music, art, or an academic subject should select a major that helps to further the talent. College life will be more enjoyable if students select majors that will provide personal satisfaction. Designing a career plan that will allow a lifestyle compatible with the special talent will also provide personal satisfaction.

Double major approach: Students often decide to choose two majors in preparation for a career. A double major may be necessary in preparing for occupations in the science field where it is essential to be well-grounded in both the physical and biological sciences.

Independent approach: Students may have highly divergent interests that cut across two or more fields of study. Many colleges allow students to design a major to satisfy their goals. For example, students may have artistic talents and scientific interests. They might combine the two interests and design a scientific illustration major that meets faculty approval.

CONNECTING COLLEGE MAJOR PLANNING AND CAREER PLANNING

All students from the ninth grade through postsecondary school should be following a program of study that will prepare them for specific careers—studies that blend appropriate academics with appropriate skills and knowledge in a particular career area. All students in postsecondary studies should be preparing for life and work after completing their studies. This assertion eliminates a justification for a "general plan" of studies that in theory "leads anywhere," but in fact "leads nowhere." Students should either be in a postsecondary associate, technical, or baccalaureate educational plan that leads to a satisfying career.

The next section presents relevant educational and career information on 14 fields of study from which students may choose a major based on career plans. Each of the 14 fields of study has specific information on majors and careers that students should consider carefully when choosing a college major. Information about employment, growth, and earnings is taken from the Department of Labor figures for 2002, with growth projected to 2012.

1. AGRICULTURAL SCIENCES

Agriculture is a broad and diverse field of study that trains scientists for many rewarding and satisfying careers. These play an important part in maintaining the nation's food supply through ensuring agricultural productivity and the safety of the food supply. Agricultural scientists engage in research, development, and production of farm crops and animals, food sciences, plant sciences, and soil sciences. Others manage marketing or production operations in companies that produce food products or agricultural chemicals, supplies, and machinery. Other agricultural scientists are consultants to business firms, private clients, or governmental agencies.

Interests: Agricultural research, development, and production of farm crops and animals, and development of ways to improve their quantity and quality

Popular majors in this field of study: Agribusiness, Agricultural Education, Agronomy, Animal Science, Entomology, Farm and Ranch Management, Fisheries and Wildlife, Food Sciences, Forestry, Horticultural Science, and Soil Sciences

Employment information/outlook: More than 335,000 people worked in related occupations in this field of study in 2002. The 2002–2012 employment growth is expected to be 12.6%. Median annual earnings are $48,717.

Agribusiness

Agribusiness majors will learn the business aspect of farms, firms, and industries that supply and service the farmer and other farm-related businesses. They will study merchandising, advertising, finance, marketing, and international trade.

Interests: Taking initiative, leadership, decision making, problem solving, analyzing data, global interdependence, working with people

Skills and abilities: Planning, organizing, making business decisions, leadership, teamwork, creative and critical thinking, working with people, written and verbal skills, adapting to change

Occupations related to this major: Agricultural Crop Farm Managers, Farm Products Purchasing Agents and Buyers, Farm and Ranch Managers, Fish Hatchery Managers, Farmers and Ranchers, Agricultural Statisticians, and Farm and Home Management advisers

Agricultural Education

Agricultural Education majors will study those basic courses in agriculture that will prepare them to teach agricultural science in high schools, community colleges, or universities. They will also complete general preparation for a service-type career in agriculture, such as extension services. They will learn to supervise youth and adult groups and to direct programs in both agricultural and human resources.

Interests: Working with people, working with plants, working with animals

Skills and abilities: Communication, science (especially natural sciences and chemistry)

Occupations related to this major: Farm and Home Management Advisers, Park Naturalists, Farmers and Ranchers, Agricultural Science Teachers, and 4-H and Agricultural Extension Agents

Agronomy

Agronomy majors will learn about three basic natural elements—crops, soils, and climates—and their interdependence in producing food, feed, fiber, and fuel. Agronomists study theory and practices for improving crop production while conserving natural resources and maintaining environmental quality.

Interests: Nature and the outdoors, environmental quality (soil, water, and air), conservation of natural resources, biological and physical sciences, problem solving, plant growth and experimentation, weather, climate, geologic formations

Skills and qualities: Oral and written communication skills, group dynamics, leadership, organizational (interpersonal) skills, analytic reasoning, creative thinking

Occupations related to this major: Agricultural Climatologists, Agrochemical Technologists, Environmental Technicians, Food and Drug Inspectors, Farm or Ranch Managers, Plant Breeders, Agricultural Technicians, Soil and Water Conservationists, and Greenhouse Managers

Animal Science

Animal Science majors will learn how to manage livestock and poultry. They will study the role of animals in the economy, how animal products influence eating habits and are part of the global food supply, and how animals help serve people's recreation needs. They will carry out investigations and experiments in the areas of breeding, feeding, management, and disease control in farm and domestic animals.

Interests: Working with plants, working with animals, working with people

Skills and abilities: Speaking and writing effectively

Occupations related to this major: Animal Scientists, Soil and Plant Scientists, Park Naturalists, Biologists, Farm and Ranch Managers, and Soil Conservationists

Entomology

Entomology majors will study the biology, ecology, classification, distribution, physiology, economic importance, and management of insects and their relation to plant and animal life. They will learn to identify species of insects and allied forms, such as mites and spiders. They will study methods of controlling and eliminating agricultural, structural, and forest pests by developing new and improved pesticides and cultural and biological methods, including using natural enemies of pests. They will also study insect distribution and habitat, and methods to prevent importation and spread of injurious species.

Interests: Science, techniques of scientific research, the environment, the health and well-being of people

Skills and abilities: Curiosity, rational thinking, objective thinking, performing laboratory tasks carefully

Occupations related to this major: Entomologists, Environmental Scientists, Soil and Plant Scientists, Biologists, Clinical Laboratory Technologists, and Pest Control Workers

Farm and Ranch Management

Farm and Ranch Management majors will learn to guide and assist farmers and ranchers in maximizing the financial returns to their land by managing the day-to-day activities. Duties and responsibilities may vary widely. For example, the owner of a very large livestock farm may employ a farm manager to oversee a single activity, such as feeding livestock. When managing a small crop farm, on the other hand, a farm manager may assume responsibility for all functions, from selecting the crop to participating in planting and harvesting.

Interests: Directing and coordinating worker activities, decision making, problem solving, nature and the outdoors, conservation of natural resources, biological and physical science

Skills and abilities: Speaking, motivating people, creative and critical thinking, oral and written expression and comprehension, organizational skills, leadership

Occupations related to this major: Agricultural Crop Farm Managers, Farm and Ranch Managers, Foresters, Dairy Farm Managers, Poultry Farm Managers, and Farm and Home Management Advisers

Fisheries and Wildlife

Fisheries and Wildlife majors will learn about fish eggs, larvae, fish parasites, and diseases. They will learn to operate fish culture facilities, tag and mark fish, detect problems of water pollution, analyze, identify, collect, control, and preserve populations of fur and game animals.

Interests: Nature and the outdoors, science, research

Skills and abilities: Solving problems, communicating effectively, working with others

Occupations related to this major: Fish Culturists, Fish Hatchery Managers, Environmental Scientists, Zoo Workers, Fisheries and Wildlife Biologists, and Park Naturalists

Food Sciences

Food Science majors will learn to use biological, physical, and social sciences to transform raw materials into safe, nutritious, and economical foods. They will learn to apply scientific and engineering principles in research, development, and food production technology. They will also work to improve methods of processing, preserving, packaging, distributing, and preparing food.

Interests: Biological and physical science, public well-being, teamwork, observing details, solving complex problems

Skills and abilities: Good laboratory technique, oral and written expression and comprehension, mathematical reasoning

Occupations related to this major: Food Scientists, Food Science Technicians, Food Chemists, Food Plant Managers, Food Microbiologists, and Biological and Agricultural Technologists

Forestry

Forestry majors will learn to manage, protect, and develop forest lands and other resources for economic and recreational purposes; plan and supervise the cutting and harvesting of timber; carry out forestation and reforestation activities and manage parks and camps.

Interests: Nature and the outdoors, working with people, planning activities, investigative research, solving problems

Skills and abilities: Communicating effectively, working with quantitative and qualitative problems, presenting ideas to others

Occupations related to this major: Foresters, Soil Conservationists, Environmental Scientists, Biologists, Range Managers, Nursery and Greenhouse Managers, Agricultural Engineers, and Forest and Conservation Technicians

Horticultural Science

Horticultural Science majors will study problems of plant production, processing, and disease resistance. They will also study soil and climate to learn the conditions in which different types of plants thrive. They will be concerned with orchards, garden plants, flowers, ornamental plants, and nursery stock.

Interests: Science, working with plants, business, working with people, solving problems, improving the environment

Skills and abilities: Biological and physical sciences, written and oral communication, organization, creativity, quantitative thinking, computer competency, working with people

Occupations related to this major: Horticulturists, Foresters, Conservation Scientists, Landscape Architects, Plant Scientists, Farmers, and Farm Managers

Soil Sciences

Soil Science majors will study the physical, chemical, and geological characteristics and behaviors of soils. They will learn how to investigate soil both in the field and in the lab, and to classify soils in terms of their capability in producing crops, grasses, and trees. They also will learn how to make land appraisals.

Interests: Nature and the outdoors, conservation of natural resources, the environment, science

Skills and abilities: Quantitative reasoning, keen observation of natural phenomena, oral and written communication, applying scientific knowledge to complex systems

Occupations related to this major: Plant Scientists, Conservation Scientists, Botanists, Biochemists, Park Naturalists, and Farm and Range Managers

2. ARCHITECTURE AND DESIGN

Architects learn to plan, design, and supervise the construction of buildings, houses, factories, skyscrapers, schools, and other structures. They learn to make them attractive, usable, energy efficient, and economical. Architects must qualify for a state license after graduation. Most architects work for architectural firms. Others work directly for builders, real estate developers, or large construction projects, as well as governmental agencies responsible for housing and community planning, such as the Department of Defense, Interior, and Housing and Urban Development. Students interested in the field of architecture will do well in such courses as architectural theory design, computer graphics, computer science, general engineering urban planning, mathematics, physics, and economics.

Interests: Architects have an interest in planning, designing, and supervising the construction of buildings, houses, factories, skyscrapers, schools, and other structures.

Popular majors in this field of study: Architectural Engineering, Architecture, City and Regional Planning, Construction Science, Interior Design, Landscape Architecture, Marine Architecture, and Surveying

Employment information/outlook: More than 255,000 people worked in related occupations in this field of study in 2002. The 2002–2012 employment growth is expected to be 15.3%. Median annual earnings are $45,256.

Architectural Engineering

Architectural Engineering majors will learn how different materials interact. They also will learn to calculate loads and stress and study the strength, durability, and safety-factor of materials. They will use artistic, applied physics, and material science skills in the design of buildings.

Interests: Mathematics, physical science, building things, applying mathematics and science to practical use, design, computers

Skills and abilities: Oral and written expression and comprehension, speech clarity, logical thinking, interpersonal skills, teamwork

Occupations related to this major: Architects, Civil Engineers, Marine Architects, Materials Engineers, and Architectural Drafters

Architecture

Architecture majors learn to plan, design, and supervise the construction of buildings, houses, factories, skyscrapers, schools, and other structures. They learn to make them attractive, usable, energy efficient, and economical. They must qualify for a license after graduation. They work in design studios that develop skills and foster creative expression. Architecture students also study the history of the building environment (rooms, buildings, landscapes, cities), the technology required to create it, and related graphic communication.

Interests: The formation of the physical environment; the history of buildings, cities, and landscapes; applied creative expression

Skills and abilities: Communicating by sketching and drafting; solving spatial problems; sensitivity to visual forms, proportions, and colors

Occupations related to this major: Architects, Naval Architects, Landscape Architects, Civil Engineers, Industrial Designers, Interior Designers, and Drafters

City and Regional Planning

City and Regional Planning majors learn to deal with land use and environmental issues created by population movements. They learn how to draw plans for new city environments including streets, sewers, water, and electricity. They also learn to zone areas for residential, commercial, or industrial use. Students commit themselves, through planning, to the future, and to social and environmental improvement.

Interests: Solving problems, working with people, helping groups, communities, and organizations improve people's lives

Skills and abilities: Working with numbers, listening, interpreting and communicating what was observed or heard

Occupations related to this major: Urban and Regional Planners, Architects, Landscape Architects, City Managers, Civil Engineers, and Environmental Engineers

Construction Science

Construction Science majors learn about all areas of construction technology. These areas include contracting, remodeling, cabinet making, building inspection, carpentry, and estimating the costs of building projects.

Interests: Starting and completing projects; leading people and making decisions; risk taking; activities that include practical, hands-on problems and solutions

Skills and abilities: Listening to and understanding information; reading and understanding information; managing one's own time and the time of others; communicating information and ideas in writing

Occupations related to this major: Architects, Property and Real Estate Managers, Real Estate Appraisers, Construction and Building Inspectors, and Industrial Engineers

Interior Design

Interior Design majors learn to arrange the interiors of buildings to fit the functional and aesthetic needs of their owners. They will design everything from lighting and furniture to home decorating accessories. Interior design majors study all aspects of the building environment: scale, proportion, arrangement, light, acoustics, temperature, textures, colors, and materials. They learn how to develop surroundings that are satisfying, creative, and appropriate to human needs.

Interests: Architecture, design (interior, industrial, graphic), building construction, interaction of colors, nature of materials, and textures

Skills and abilities: Design, organization, working with people, drawing, communicating ideas

Occupations related to this major: Interior Designers, Fashion, Furniture, Textile, and Floral Designers, Exhibition Designers, Architects, and Landscape Architects

Landscape Architecture

Landscape Architecture majors learn skills and techniques for planning, designing, and managing the land. They learn about weather, drainage, botany, and construction. They are frequently involved in mapping and consultation. They creatively apply information and principles drawn from both the arts and the sciences to reshape and conserve landscapes.

Interests: Visual arts, ecology, nature, environmental issues

Skills and abilities: Drawing and graphic expression, problem solving, written communication

Occupations related to this major: Landscape Architects, Architects, Surveyors, Civil Engineers, Urban and Regional Planners, Botanists, and Park Naturalists

Marine Architecture

Marine Architecture majors learn to design and oversee construction and repair of marine craft and floating structures, such as ships, barges, tugs, dredges, submarines, torpedoes, floats, and buoys. May confer with marine engineers.

Interests: Design techniques, engineering science and technology, building materials, construction and repair of structures

Skills and abilities: Problem solving, listening and understanding information and ideas, creativity, communicating information and ideas in writing, fluency of ideas

Occupations related to this major: Marine Architects, Aerospace Engineers, Civil Engineers, Materials Engineers, Engineering Technicians, and Drafters

Surveying

Surveying majors learn to make exact measurements and determine property boundaries. They learn to provide data relevant to the shape, contour, gravitation, location, elevation, or dimension of land, or land features on or near the earth's surface, for engineering, mapping, mining, land evaluation, construction, and other purposes.

Interests: Shapes and elevations of geomorphic and topographic features, geography, and methods for describing the features of land, sea, and air masses

Skills and abilities: Communicating effectively in writing; using mathematics to solve problems; understanding written information; using scientific methods to solve problems; motivating, developing, and directing people as they work

Occupations related to this major: Surveyors, Cartographers, Urban Planners, Civil Drafters, Agricultural Engineers, and Landscape Architects

3. THE ARTS

The Arts is a field of study that includes a wider range of subjects than found in other areas of concentration. If students major in one of the arts, they will learn to design products, articles, and materials; they will develop talents as actors; they will study the theory and practice of film production; they will develop talents to draw, paint, or design interpretations of objects, people, and nature, or they will develop talents dealing with the art of sound that express ideas and emotions either by song, dance, or by instrumental musical instruments. This field, in contrast to a liberal arts education, is often thought of as professional training. A major in this field gives information, methods, procedures, and techniques needed in a career. A professional program in this field will offer students good training to make a contribution in the world of art.

Interests: Developing talents to draw, paint, or design interpretations of objects, people, and nature; or developing the art of sound that expresses ideas and emotions either by speech, song, dance, or musical instruments.

Popular majors in this field of study: Art Education, Art History, Arts Management, Dance, Dramatic Arts, Film Arts, Fine Arts, Graphic Design, Music Business Management, Music Education, Music Performance, Music Therapy, Photography, Religious Music, and Studio Art

Employment information/outlook: More than 733,000 people worked in related occupations in this field of study in 2002. The 2002–2012 employment growth is expected to be 17.4%. Median annual earnings are $42,972.

Art Education

Art Education majors learn to develop their artistic talents and gain the knowledge and skills needed to teach art at various education levels. They will explore the value of art both to the individual and to various cultures throughout history.

Interests: Visual arts, creating art, teaching

Skills and abilities: Working with others, solving problems creatively, manipulating materials creatively, responding to other people's art with sensitivity

Occupations related to this major: Art Teachers, Curriculum Specialists, Art Administrators, Manual Arts Therapists, Craft Demonstrators, Curators, Archivists, and Museum Research Workers

Art History

Art History majors study works of art—how they came about and what they mean. They will examine works of art as they appear now and also consider appearance and function in their original contexts. Through their visual analysis and extensive reading and writing, students explore the traditions of appearance and technique that guided the creation of art in different cultures.

Interests: Visual arts, past civilizations, the connections between different aspects of a civilization, artists, art technique

Skills and abilities: Observing carefully, information gathering, reading critically, written expression and comprehension

Occupations related to this major: High School Teachers, College Teachers, Curators, Archivists, Conservators, Museum Directors, and Museum Technicians

Arts Management

Arts Management majors learn to organize and manage art organizations and facilities. They receive instruction in business and financial management and labor relations, event promotion and management, public relations and arts advocacy, and arts law. They will learn to analyze and address the issues concerning the health of theaters, dance companies, museums, and other arts organizations.

Interests: Visual and performance arts, leadership, working with people

Skills and abilities: Oral and written communication, organizational ability, creative thinking, critical thinking

Occupations related to this major: Theater Managers, Symphony Orchestra Managers, Dance Company Managers, Curators, and Museum Technicians and Conservators

Dance

Dance majors learn to interpret an idea or a story through physical expression or rhythm and/or sound. Dance forms vary from ballet and modern interpretative dance to tap and chorus lines. Dance is a demanding discipline. Students learn to develop their bodies as articulate instruments for dance expression: to understand contributions that dance has made to the arts, and to create their own dances.

Interests: Dance, other arts, the physicality of movement

Skills and abilities: Sense of rhythm and musicality, physical stamina, dynamic strength, speed of limb movement, gross body coordination

Occupations related to this major: Dance Teachers, Actors and Performers, Choreographers, Dance Researchers, and Dance Therapists

Dramatic Arts

Dramatic Arts majors learn how to play a part to entertain, inform, or instruct an audience. They learn to be involved in interpreting plays or scripts, selecting plays or scripts, or planning and supervising performances. They gain breadth of knowledge about past and present culture, art, literature, politics, psychology, and philosophy.

Interests: Self-expression, communication of ideas and feelings, literature and language, art and music, human personality and motivation

Skills and abilities: Speech clarity, memorization, originality, oral and written expression and comprehension, emotional openness

Occupations related to this major: Actors, Directors, Designers, Playwrights, Stage Managers, Talent Directors, and Teachers

Film Arts

Film Arts majors study the theory and practice of film production and the techniques used in this medium of communication. They learn to do creative work, as well as learn the rapidly changing technology. They study cinema history, screenwriting, and the aesthetic and technical aspects of cinema production, including directing, cinematography, and editing. They also examine the economic, technical, social, cultural, and ideological aspects of film as a medium for communication and personal expression.

Interests: Film literature, psychology, theater, music, art history, biography, current events

Skills and abilities: Creativity, ability to express oneself verbally and visually, self-discipline, understanding of human psychology, organization, attention to detail, flexibility, working with people

Occupations related to this major: Directors—Stage, Motion Pictures, Television and Radio, Cinematographers, Technical Directors, Programming and Script Editors, Production Assistants

Fine Arts

Fine Arts majors learn to draw or design their interpretations of objects, people, and nature, using a wide variety of materials from watercolors and oils to stone and metal. They learn to create art to satisfy their own need for self-expression. They learn about the creation of art historically, in contemporary society, and through their own efforts in studio classes. They may display their work in museums, art galleries, corporate collections, and private homes.

Interests: Making things with the hands, other cultures, history, paintings, sculpture, film, self-expression

Skills and abilities: Oral and written expression and comprehension, fluency of ideas, originality, visual color discrimination, manual and finger dexterity

Occupations related to this major: Fine Artists, Graphic Artists, Sculptors, Painters, Illustrators, and Cartoonists and Animators

Graphic Design

Graphic Design majors study the principles of design to learn how to create attractive and effective advertisements, flyers, brochures, logos, magazines, or books. They learn how to create images through the use of silkscreen, computers, and printing presses. Students learn to communicate information visually using words and images. They also study how people perceive and interpret information.

Interests: Visual arts, creativity, critical thinking, working with people

Skills and abilities: Drawing, photography, originality, fluency of ideas, oral expression, visual color discrimination

Occupations related to this major: Graphic Designers, Painters, Illustrators, Cartoonists, Animators, Fashion Designers, and Interior Designers

Music Business Management

Music Business Management majors learn to organize and manage music operations, facilities, and personnel. They receive instruction in business and financial management, personnel management and labor relations, event promotion, and music products merchandising. They study the functional area of business as well as music performance, history, and theory.

Interests: Music, leadership, organizing people, business, solving problems, negotiating

Skills and abilities: Oral expression and comprehension, written expression and comprehension, leadership, organization, creative thinking

Occupations related to this major: Music Facilities Managers, Recording Studio Managers, Artists' Representatives, Orchestra Managers, Music Directors, and Concert Booking Agents

Music Education

Music Education majors learn to become music teachers in public and private schools. They learn the basics of music and the fundamentals of teaching to share music with people of all ages and abilities.

Interests: Listening to music, performing, working with young people, leadership

Skills and abilities: Musical ability, a sense of rhythm and pitch, oral and written expression and comprehension, speech clarity, discriminating listening

Occupations related to this major: Music Teachers, Music Therapists, Choir Directors, Conductors, Composers, Arrangers, and Music Librarians

Music Performance

Music Performance majors learn to develop a high level of performance skill and musical understanding. They reach a high level of technical proficiency and musical sensitivity as music performance majors. They become well-rounded musicians through the study of core music theory and history courses.

Interests: Communicating through music performance, the theoretical and historical aspects of musical structure and style, the relation of music to society

Skills and abilities: Natural aptitude for music, technical skill, strong background in piano

Occupations related to this major: Musicians, Singers, Music Directors, Music Composers, Music Teachers, and Positions with Orchestras and Ensembles

Music Therapy

Music Therapy majors learn to design music experiences and activities to the treatment of individuals and groups in all age categories who have psychological, emotional, physical, social, intellectual, or medical disorders.

Interests: Music, the arts, behavioral and life sciences, helping others

Skills and abilities: Competency in music performance and theory, oral and written expression and comprehension, working with people

Occupations related to this major: Music Therapists, Occupational Therapists, Physical Therapists, Musicians, Singers, and Music Directors

Photography

Photography majors learn the use of camera and film to portray people, places, and events. They become involved in everything from creating motion pictures and video/television to still, portrait, aerial, and commercial photography. They learn both the artistic and technical aspects of photography and a broad understanding of the social, political, and interpersonal aspects of society.

Interests: Expressing oneself in a visual medium, creating images from ideas, helping people see and understand subjects to which they might not otherwise have access

Skills and abilities: Visualization, far vision, fluency of ideas, arm-hand steadiness, control precision, color discrimination

Occupations related to this major: Commercial Photographers, Portrait Photographers, Graphic Designers, Photojournalists, Photo Editors, and Technical and Science Photographers

Religious Music

Religious Music majors develop their skills and interests as musicians and learn to use music in religious celebrations while focusing on the role and history of music in worship. They study the history, theory, composition, and performance of music for religious or sacred purposes.

Interests: Music, music history, the fine arts, the place of music in religious celebrations, matters of faith, working with people

Skills and abilities: Ability to listen carefully, hearing sensitivity, auditory attention, oral expression and comprehension, working with people

Occupations related to this major: Music Directors, Music Teachers, Music Conductors, Organists, Cantors, Musicians, and Singers

Studio Art

Studio Art majors learn to create works of art by exploring a variety of techniques and materials. They learn to focus on learning to master new media, discovering unique solutions to visual problems, exploring fresh ways to create satisfying images, and evaluating what is worth doing.

Interests: Visual arts, manipulating materials, observing visual phenomena in nature and works of art, communicating and experimenting with forms, colors, images, and symbols

Skills and abilities: Working independently, creativity, problem solving, oral and written expression and comprehension

Occupations related to this major: Fine Artists, Commercial Artists, Graphic Designers, Art Teachers, Exhibit Designers, and Set Designers

4. BIOLOGICAL AND LIFE SCIENCES

Biological and Life Sciences majors are concerned with the world of living things—people and microbes, wild and domestic animals, plants and insects, birds and fish. Some biological scientists conduct research. Still others apply biological knowledge to the solution of practical problems, such as the development of new drugs and vaccines or new strains of plants. Biological scientists, who may also be called life scientists, study the structure of living organisms, their life processes, and evolutionary development. They may be classified into groups characterized by the type of organism with which they work or the specific activity they perform. Examples of these groups are botanists who study plants, microbiologists who work with microorganisms, and zoologists who work with animals.

Interests: The world of living things—people and microbes, wild and domestic animals, plants and insects, birds and fish—or the evolutionary development of living organisms.

Popular majors in this field of study: Biochemistry, Biology, Biophysics, Biotechnology, Botany, Marine/Aquatic Biology, Microbiology, Molecular and Cell Biology, Science Education, Wildlife Management, and Zoology

Employment information/outlook: More than 94,000 people worked in related occupations in this field of study in 2002. The 2002–2012 employment growth is expected to be 21.9%. Median annual earnings are $54,252.

Biochemistry

Biochemistry majors learn how chemical substances enter into or are created in living things; how drugs, foods, hormones, serums, and other substances can influence organisms. They perform tests to identify, classify, and analyze various chemical reactions. They learn to use the physical and biological sciences to explore the nature of living organisms. They study the structure and behavior of complex molecules and how they interact to form cells, tissues, and entire organisms. They also gain a fundamental grasp of metabolism, energy flow, and the regulation of various life processes.

Interests: Nature, problem solving, investigative research

Skills and abilities: Using information from many areas of science, inductive and deductive reasoning, handling and interpreting data, written expression and comprehension

Occupations related to this major: Microbiologists, Biologists, Toxicologists, Plant Pathologists, Physiologists, Cytologists, and Food Scientists

Biology

Biology majors learn about the structure of living organisms, their life processes and evolutionary development, and the relation between these organisms and their environment. They may specialize in research centering on plants, animals, or human organisms. They study animals, plants, and microorganisms that constitute the living world at the levels of molecule, cell, organism, and population.

Interests: Quality of life, investigative laboratory work, fieldwork

Skills and abilities: Problem solving, deductive and inductive reasoning, information gathering, written expression and comprehension

Occupations related to this major: Biologists, Biochemists, Botanists, Microbiologists, Geneticists, and Zoologists

Biophysics

Biophysics majors learn to apply the laws of physics to biological systems. They study vision, hearing, nerve action, blood flow, and even the behavior of DNA. They also study the effects of radiation and radioactivity on biological systems, and the use of ultrasound scanners to construct images of body interiors. They use biology, physics, chemistry, and mathematics to explore the properties of biological molecules and groups of molecules. They study the inner workings of biological systems with precision to learn how proteins fold, how genes are switched on and off, how organisms respond to light, how cells move, and how the nervous system works.

Interests: Natural history, investigative problem solving

Skills and abilities: Curiosity, deductive and inductive reasoning, written expression and comprehension, information ordering, manual dexterity

Occupations related to this major: Biophysicists, Biologists, Botanists, Geneticists, Microbiologists, and Soil Scientists

Biotechnology

Biotechnology is an interdisciplinary field of study involving the molecular life sciences and engineering fields of study. Students learn techniques for using living matter to develop new products and services in agriculture (plant growth hormones, food additives), health care (vaccines, improved drugs and vitamins), the environment (detoxification of chemicals), and other areas.

Interests: Science, treating and preventing disease, investigative research, and problem solving

Skills and abilities: Creative thinking, oral and written expression and comprehension, deductive and inductive reasoning, problem sensitivity

Occupations related to this major: Biological Technologists, Agricultural Technologists, Environmental Scientists, Food Scientists, Animal Scientists, Botanists, and Microbiologists

Botany

Botany majors focus on all aspects of plant life including taxonomy, genetics, physiology, and plant anatomy. They learn about the economic value of plants in their application to agronomy, forestry, horticulture, and pharmacology. Students study all aspects of plant biology to become familiar with the cellular and molecular functioning of life.

Interests: Nature, investigative problem solving, analytic reasoning

Skills and abilities: Deductive and inductive reasoning, information ordering, written expression and comprehension

Occupations related to this major: Botanists, Agricultural Scientists, Soil Scientists, Ecologists, Microbiologists, Physiologists

Marine/Aquatic Biology

Marine/Aquatic Biology majors learn to research and study marine organisms and their environments. They receive instruction in freshwater and saltwater organisms, physiological and anatomical marine adaptations, ocean and freshwater ecologies, marine microbiology, marine mammalogy, ichthyology, marine botany, and biochemical products of marine life used by humans. They learn about the diversity of life in the ocean, how ocean species relate to each other as food and prey, and how different species depend on and use the physical and chemical structures of the ocean.

Interests: Life in the ocean, how organisms use the sea as a habitat

Skills and abilities: Quantitative thinking, deductive and inductive reasoning, information ordering, written expression and comprehension

Occupations related to this major: Marine Biologists, Aquatic Biologists, Biochemists, Botanists, Agricultural Scientists, and Zoologists

Microbiology

Microbiology majors concentrate on microorganisms, bacteria, yeasts, fungi, protozoa, and one-celled algae. They learn about the application of these organisms in the production of food products, antibiotics, and industrial chemicals. They learn to use the basic knowledge acquired from other biological sciences, chemistry/biochemistry, and physics to study microscopic organisms such as bacteria, yeasts, molds, viruses, rickettsia, and protozoa.

Interests: Biological sciences, health and medicine, ecology, food production, investigative research

Skills and abilities: Working with detail, analytic thinking, deductive and inductive reasoning, information ordering

Occupations related to this major: Microbiologists, Botanists, Medical Scientists, Zoologists, Physiologists, and Geneticists

Molecular and Cell Biology

Molecular and Cell Biology majors study the nature of biological phenomena at the molecular level through the study of DNA proteins and other macromolecules relating to genetic information and cell function. They study what cells are, how they are put together, what makes them work, what makes them differ from each other, how they associate and interact, what goes wrong in disease states, and how they can intervene beneficially in these processes. They study how molecular biology underlies many aspects of genetic engineering, protein engineering, and other new approaches to improving upon nature.

Interests: Organisms and their development, how things work, the molecular basis of plant, animal, and human disease, disease prevention

Skills and abilities: Investigative research, laboratory skills, information gathering, deductive and inductive reasoning, oral and written expression and comprehension

Occupations related to this major: Molecular Biologists, Medical Doctors, Toxicologists, Botanists, Plant Pathologists, and Biologists

Science Education

Science Education majors prepare to teach science in grades 7 through 12. Students typically major in one science and take additional course work in two other sciences. They learn techniques for teaching science.

Interests: Working with young people, helping others, the learning process, solving practical problems, understanding complex processes, learning how things work

Skills and abilities: Oral and written expression and comprehension, speech clarity, fluency of ideas, deductive reasoning, working with numbers

Occupations related to this major: Biological Technicians, Health Specialties Teachers, Elementary School Teachers, Dietitians, Nutritionists, Pharmacists, Psychiatrists, Veterinarians, and Medical and Clinical Laboratory Technologists

Wildlife Management

Wildlife Management majors receive a solid background in basic biology. They study natural resources and wildlife management. They study conservation of animal populations and their habitats, paying special attention to species that are hunted regularly and species that are threatened or endangered. They learn to analyze characteristics of animals to identify and classify them; to conduct experimental studies with live animals in controlled or natural surroundings; to study animals in their natural habitats; and to study characteristics of animals such as origin, interrelationships, classification, life histories and diseases, development, genetics, and distribution.

Interests: Nature, conservation of natural resources, hunting, bird-watching

Skills and abilities: Using scientific rules and methods to solve problems, mathematics, deductive and inductive reasoning, problem sensitivity

Occupations related to this major: Wildlife Biologists, Environmental Scientists, Park Naturalists, and Research Wildlife Biologists

Zoology

Zoology majors study the identification, description, and classification of animals. They study life histories, habits, diseases, life processes, and distribution of animal species within the environment. They study living organisms in the animal kingdom, exploring their form and function, chemistry and structure, growth, reproduction, maintenance, and interactions with each other and their world. They study the transmission of characteristics from one generation to the next (genetics and evolution).

Interests: Natural history, wildlife, the outdoors, bird-watching, how things work, living things, fossils, working with animals

Skills and abilities: Deductive and inductive reasoning, synthesizing information, gathering and analyzing information, working with numbers

Occupations related to this major: Zoologists, Ecologists, Agricultural Scientists, Physiologists, Cytologists, Microbiologists, and Botanists

5. BUSINESS AND MANAGEMENT

Business and Management majors are found in every industry. Business executives, administrators, managers, and support staff are found in every organization. They direct and coordinate operations and activities of an organization. Business majors must be comfortable with numbers and the manipulation of data, enjoy working with a computer, and have good communication skills, both written and oral. Business majors deal with large amounts of information to make production, personnel, financial, and marketing decisions.

Interests: Business managers and support workers have an interest in directing and coordinating operations and activities of a business or organization; an interest in making production, personnel, financial, and market decisions of a business.

Popular majors in this field of study: Accounting, Business Administration, Business Education, Finance, Human Resource Management, Insurance and Risk Management, International Business Management, Labor Relations Management, Management, Management Information Systems, Management Science, Marketing, and Real Estate

Employment information/outlook: More than 10,332,000 people worked in related occupations in this field of study in 2002. The 2002–2012 employment growth is expected to be 18.8%. Median annual earnings are $57,196.

Accounting

Accounting majors learn to keep track of expenditures, income, profit and loss, prepare financial reports, and calculate taxes. They may specialize in auditing, taxes, or consulting. Many accountants seek Certified Public Accountant (CPA) certification after graduation. Students will learn to apply this knowledge in all areas of business, government, and nonprofit enterprises.

Interests: Working with numbers, competition, economics, computers, mathematics, entrepreneurship, social and political activism, moral and ethical responsibility

Skills and abilities: Mathematical reasoning, written and oral expression and comprehension, working with people, leadership

Occupations related to this major: Accountants, Auditors, Loan Officers, Loan Counselors, Credit Analysts, Tax Preparers, Budget Analysts, and Marketing Managers

Business Administration

Business Administration majors learn about a variety of managerial opportunities in finance, accounting, marketing, information management, operations and production, general management, retailing, and consulting. They learn the fundamental principles, concepts, and applications of accounting, finance, and management.

Interests: Leadership, organizing people, taking initiative, starting and running a business, working with numbers, solving problems, competing, taking risks, working with people

Skills and abilities: Oral and written expression and comprehension, speech clarity, inductive reasoning, creative and critical thinking

Occupations related to this major: Private Sector Executives, Administrative Services Managers, Human Resources Specialists, Production Managers, Labor Relations Specialists, and Financial Analysts

Business Education

Business Education majors learn to teach vocational business programs at various education levels. They develop instructional methods and training techniques including curriculum design principles, learning theory, group and individual teaching techniques, design of individual development plans, and test design principles.

Interests: Teaching young people, helping people develop their academic interests in business, and helping people develop career plans

Skills and abilities: Working with young people, speech clarity, oral and written expression and comprehension, teaching, learning, understanding human behavior

Occupations related to this major: Business Education Teacher, Education Administrators, Training and Development Managers, and Educational Program Directors

Finance

Finance majors study financial and accounting information, economic models, and analytic techniques that can be applied to financing problems. They learn to determine prices of assets such as stocks, bonds, and businesses, and to manage assets to maximize their economic value.

Interests: Business, the stock market, the economy, budgets

Skills and abilities: Logical thinking, organizational skills, oral and written expression and comprehension, problem sensitivity, mathematical reasoning, working with people, solving problems with computers

Occupations related to this major: Financial Managers, Financial Planners, Treasurers, Controllers, Chief Financial Officers, and Loan Officers and Counselors

Human Resource Management

Human Resource Management majors learn to deal with many personnel activities, including hiring competent workers and dismissing workers when necessary, keeping records, classifying jobs, evaluating and properly placing workers, analyzing and assisting in morale and discipline problems, and promoting and rewarding employees. They learn to deal with issues that affect men and women at work.

Interests: Solving problems, working with numbers, working with people of different ages and backgrounds, leadership

Skills and abilities: Logical and critical thinking, speech clarity, oral and written expression and comprehension, analyzing numerical data, teamwork

Occupations related to this major: Human Resource Specialists, Training and Development Managers, Labor Relations Managers, Employee Assistance Specialists, Employee Benefits Managers, and Career Planning and Placement Counselors

Insurance and Risk Management

Insurance and Risk Management majors learn to analyze and solve problems involving loss of personal and corporate assets. They study programs, integrate knowledge from finance, quantitative analysis, and management, and include study of the legal, social, and institutional environment in which losses may occur.

Interests: Working with numbers, solving problems, competing, leadership, taking initiative

Skills and abilities: Oral and written expression and comprehension, fluency of ideas, problem sensitivity, deductive and inductive reasoning, creative and critical thinking

Occupations related to this major: Insurance Adjusters, Insurance Appraisers, Risk Managers, Insurance Brokers, Insurance Sales Representatives, and Insurance Underwriters

International Business Management

International Business Management majors learn to determine and formulate policies, and provide the overall direction of international companies or private and public sector organizations with international business activities. They learn to conduct management guidelines set up by a board of directors or similar governing body. They learn basic business management techniques and practices and how business is conducted in other countries and between different countries.

Interests: Business operations, other cultures, different people and environments

Skills and abilities: Learning languages, organizing and managing people, oral and written expression and comprehension, deductive and inductive reasoning, fluency of ideas

Occupations related to this major: International Business Managers, International Purchasing Agents and Buyers, International Marketing Managers, International Advertising and Promotions Managers, Compliance Officers and Inspectors, and Investment Bankers

Labor Relations Management

Labor Relations Management majors learn to deal with various aspects of employer-employee relations. They learn to deal with wage and salary negotiations, benefits and welfare, affirmative action, grievances, abuses and demands, labor laws, union organization, and collective bargaining. Particular attention is given to government policies, labor unions, and human resources management.

Interests: The employment relationship, human behavior, problem solving

Skills and abilities: Working with people, oral and written expression and comprehension, problem sensitivity, inductive reasoning

Occupations related to this major: Labor Relations Managers, Human Resource Managers, Training and Development Managers, Employee Assistance Specialists, Employee Benefits Managers, and Union Organizers

Management

Management majors study courses designed for the generalist who wants a broad business background. They take courses in business areas, such as accounting, marketing, finance, and business law, and courses that prepare them to function as managers in any organization.

Interests: Working with people, listening, persuading, leading, starting new systems

Skills and abilities: Thinking analytically, problem sensitivity, oral and written expression and comprehension, speech clarity

Occupations related to this major: General and Operations Managers, Marketing Managers, Public Relations Managers, Corporate Communications Specialists, Human Resource Specialists, and Human Resources Recruiters

Management Information Systems

Management Information Systems majors unite studies in computer science and business knowledge. They learn to act as intermediaries between persons with information needs and the computer programmers who provide the solutions to the problems.

Interests: Computer languages, computer programming, problem solving, logic, taking initiative, organizing groups

Skills and abilities: Oral and written expression and comprehension, deductive and inductive reasoning, information ordering, fluency of ideas, creativity

Occupations related to this major: Management Information Systems Managers, Systems Analysts, Computer Support Specialists, Database Administrators, and Computer Programmers

Management Science

Management Science majors learn to plan, organize, direct, and control the functions and processes of a business firm or organization. They learn about management theory, human resources, management and behavior, accounting and other quantitative methods, purchasing and logistics organization and production, marketing and business decision making. They learn to use mathematics, computers, and statistical and economic analysis to solve managerial and business problems.

Interests: Mathematics, solving business and management problems, computer languages, computer programming

Skills and abilities: Quantitative thinking, computer programming, creativity, oral and written expression and comprehension, speech clarity

Occupations related to this major: Employee Training Specialists, Administrative Service Managers, Purchasing Managers, Association Managers, and Property Managers

Marketing

Marketing majors learn to increase sales of products or services by analyzing and compiling data, and researching and influencing the purchasing power of the public through inventory procedures. They study trend forecasting, product development, management, wholesale selling, and operations. They learn how to display and to buy and sell items through showrooms, department stores, and specialty shops. They learn to make decisions about product design and quality, pricing, advertising, selling, and distribution.

Interests: Running a business, economic issues, social issues, working on new products, problem solving, analyzing data, understanding how people buy, use, and sell products and services

Skills and abilities: Oral and written expression and comprehension, speech clarity, originality, fluency of ideas, mathematical reasoning, persuasion

Occupations related to this major: Marketing Managers, Sales Managers, Public Relations Representatives, Advertising and Promotions Managers, Market Research Analysts, and Advertising Account Executives

Real Estate

Real Estate majors learn to show real estate properties to clients, evaluate and list properties for sale, and advise and arrange financing. They study property management and insurance. They act as independent agents, brokers, or appraisers. They gain an understanding of and proficiency in the business and social principles that affect how real property—buildings and land—is developed, operated, and traded.

Interests: Business, people and social conditions, the economy, public affairs

Skills and abilities: Oral and written expression and comprehension, mathematical reasoning, working independently, critical and analytic thinking

Occupations related to this major: Property Managers, Real Estate Sales Agents, Real Estate Financial Analysts, Real Estate Brokers, Loan Processors, and Real Estate Appraisers

6. COMMUNICATIONS

Communications is the giving or exchanging of information. It is a way to share facts, experiences, or emotions with others. A message can be conveyed through a wide variety of means. These can include writing, speaking, drawing, or using face, hand, and body movements. People receive messages through each of the five senses: taste, touch, sight, smell, and hearing. Communications studies involve the understanding of the role of mass communication in society; broadcast satellites, cable television transmitters, computer networks, and other mass media technology provide a global communication system. The field of communications includes training for those occupations necessary for the system to work efficiently.

Interests: The ways and means of exchanging information; an interest in broadcast satellites, television transmitters, computer networks, and other mass media technology.

Popular majors in this field of study: Advertising, Communications, Creative Writing, Journalism, Public Relations, Radio/Television Broadcasting, and Speech

Employment information/outlook: More than 562,000 people worked in related occupations in this field of study in 2002. The 2002–2012 employment growth is expected to be 18.1%. Median annual earnings are $43,364.

Advertising

Advertising majors learn to plan and prepare advertisements for newspapers, magazines, radio, television, billboards, and brochures. They may specialize in writing copy, layout, or research. They use creative talents to market a product to prospective clients. They learn how advertising campaigns are produced, how advertising is coordinated with marketing, and how advertising strategies develop from research. They learn to write advertising copy for broadcasting and print, and to select media for advertising campaigns.

Interests: Writing, art and design, analysis, knowing something about lots of things, investigative research

Skills and abilities: Oral and written expression and comprehension, originality, fluency of ideas, analytic reasoning, public speaking, art and design

Occupations related to this major: Advertising and Promotions Managers, Advertising Agency Account Executives, Marketing Managers, Sales Managers, Fund-raising Directors, and Advertising Research Specialists

Communications

Communications majors study the role of mass communication in society. They study the nature, function, content, values, and effects of communication on public policy and opinion. They study the nature of language and how it is communicated. They study the history of political and religious oratory; explore the sociology of interpersonal relations, group dynamics, and messages; examine ways of thinking about human symbol systems (semiotics); and examine the ethics of communication.

Interests: Politics, presentations, advertising, television, film, analyzing oral and electronic messages

Skills and abilities: Oral and written expression and comprehension, critical listening, logical analysis, leadership

Occupations related to this major: Communications Managers, Public Relations Specialists, Television Producers and Directors, Press Secretaries, Reporters, and Speech Writers

Creative Writing

Creative Writing majors study the processes and techniques of original composition in various literary forms, such as short stories, novels, biographies, articles, plays, and scripts. They receive instruction in technical and editorial skills, criticism, and the marketing of finished manuscripts.

Interests: Reading, fiction and nonfiction prose, writing, factual information, English language, critical thinking, computers

Skills and abilities: Written and oral expression and comprehension, information ordering, deductive and inductive reasoning, fluency of ideas

Occupations related to this major: Radio and Television Announcers, Broadcast News Analysts, Reporters and Correspondents, Editors, Technical Writers, and Poets and Lyricists

Journalism

Journalism majors learn to write, edit, manage, and produce newspapers and magazines. They learn to interview people, review records, observe events, and conduct journalistic research. They study the liberal arts and sciences to acquire the depth and breadth of knowledge they need to understand the world better and communicate information about it to others. They learn special skills needed by reporters, editors, broadcasters, and photojournalists.

Interests: Human psychology and behavior, reading widely, photography, world events

Skills and abilities: Writing, oral and written expression and comprehension, speech clarity, learning quickly about a wide range of topics

Occupations related to this major: Reporters and Correspondents, Magazine Writers and Editors, Columnists, Critics, Commentators, Creative Writers, Radio and Television Reporters, and Photojournalists

Public Relations

Public Relations majors learn how to manage an organization's or an individual's communication and relationship with others. They develop skills to build trust between an organization and the public. They learn how to write news articles and press releases, give speeches, and create audiovisual presentations designed to build trust. They learn technical and managerial skills, such as writing and producing printed and visual materials, and study strategic planning and problem solving.

Interests: Solving problems, mediating between opposing groups, writing, public speaking, giving advice

Skills and abilities: Communicating clearly, oral and written expression and comprehension, speech clarity, fluency of ideas, creative and critical thinking

Occupations related to this major: Public Relations Specialists, Publicity Writers, Advertising and Promotions Managers, Corporate Video Producers, Staff Writers and Editors, Special Events Planners, and Reporters and Correspondents

Radio/Television Broadcasting

Radio/Television Broadcasting majors learn about the planning,

preparation, and production of radio and television programs. They may specialize in announcing, programming, engineering, or sales. They study the relationship between the mass media and society and develop skills in such specialties as reporting, performance, production, sales, and management

Interests: Writing, speaking, editing words, pictures, or sound; operating a camera; sound recording

Skills and abilities: Interviewing people, oral and written expression and comprehension, speech clarity, persuasion, operating technical equipment

Occupations related to this major: Broadcast News Analysts, Reporters and Correspondents, Radio/Television Announcers, Radio/Television Producers, Station Managers, Radio/Television Writers

Speech

Speech majors learn about the human communication process. They learn the principles and practical application of speech communication, and the skills and techniques essential for effective interpersonal communication. They learn to develop listening skills.

Interests: Public speaking, human behavior

Skills and abilities: Working with people, oral and written expression and comprehension, speech clarity

Occupations related to this major: Speech Teachers, Speech Writers, Public Relations Specialists, Journalists, Writers, Editors, and Radio and Television Reporters

7. COMPUTER AND INFORMATION SCIENCES

Computer and Information Sciences field of study prepares students for a wide variety of occupations in most sectors of the economy. This field of study prepares a wide range of professionals who design computers and the software that runs them. Information technology occupations are comprised of computer-related occupations engaged in either managing, storing, transmitting, or generating the information organizations use to make decisions, as well as installing and repairing computer hardware and software used to perform such tasks. Computer science is distinguished by a high level of theoretical expertise and innovation applied to complex problems, as well as the creation or application of new technology. Computer scientists and technicians can be theorists, researchers, or inventors. They may work at an academic institution on theory, hardware, or language design. Others work in industry to apply theory, develop specialized languages, or design programming tools and knowledge-based systems.

Interests: Designing computers and the software that runs them; managing, storing, transmitting, or generating and repairing computer hardware and software used to perform such tasks

Popular majors in this field of study: Computer Software Engineering, Computer Science, Information Sciences and Systems, Computer Programming, Mathematics, Mathematics Education, and Statistics

Employment information/outlook: More than 2,026,000 people worked in related occupations in this field of study in 2002. The 2002–2012 employment growth is expected to be 21.1%. Median annual earnings are $65,988.

Computer Software Engineering

Computer Software Engineering majors study applied mathematical and scientific principles to the design, development, and operational evaluation of computer hardware and software systems and related equipment and facilities. They learn to develop, create, and test applications software and/or operating systems level software. They learn to analyze specific problems in computer applications.

Interests: Computers and electronics, computer programming, problem solving, engineering technology, design

Skills and abilities: Using mathematics to solve problems, computer programming, critical thinking, oral and written expression and comprehension, speech clarity, problem sensitivity

Occupations related to this major: Computer Support Specialists, Mathematical Technicians, Computer Science Teachers, and Numerical Tool and Process Control Programmers

Computer Science

Computer Science majors learn to design new computers, computer languages, and related devices, and research new ways to use computers effectively. They become involved in aspects of artificial intelligence, from pattern recognition to problem solving. They learn how computers work and how to program computers to perform tasks and provide services. They study the physical hardware components of computer systems and software procedures for making computers work.

Interests: Mathematics, electronics, investigative research

Skills and abilities: Oral and written expression and comprehension, mathematical reasoning, problem solving, abstract reasoning, working with people

Occupations related to this major: Computer Scientists, Computer Engineers, Computer Science Teachers, Computer Programmers, Software and Hardware Developers

Information Sciences and Systems

Information Sciences and Systems majors receive broad exposure to computer and programming concepts. They learn to bring people and computers together to solve problems in businesses and other organizations. They learn to plan, direct, and coordinate activities in such fields as electronic data processing, information systems, systems analysis, and computer programming.

Interests: Solving problems, working with details, taking initiative, working with numbers, organizing information, working with people

Skills and abilities: Oral and written expression and comprehension, mathematical reasoning, deductive reasoning, critical and logical thinking, working with changing technology

Occupations related to this major: Computer Programmers, Information Systems Designers, Information Systems Analysts, Computer Security Specialists, Database Administrators

Computer Programming

Computer Programming majors learn to write step-by-step instructions in several computer languages and create video games and software packages. They learn how to write software to handle specific jobs. They learn to convert project specifications and statements of problems and procedures to detailed logical flowcharts for coding into computer language. They learn to develop and write computer programs to store, locate, and retrieve specific documents, data, and information. They learn how to maintain software that controls the operations of entire computer systems.

Interests: Mathematics, electronics, using computers, investigative research, problem solving

Skills and abilities: Programming, critical thinking, active listening, oral and written expression and comprehension, mathematical reasoning, fluency of ideas, problem sensitivity

Occupations related to this major: Computer Programmers, Computer and Information Systems Managers, Computer Support Specialists, Computer Systems Analysts, Numerical Tool and Process Control Programmers, and Computer Science Teachers

Mathematics

Mathematics majors learn to solve both theoretical and practical problems that can be explained in mathematical terms. They study all aspects of algebra, geometry, advanced mathematics, and computer languages. They develop the abilities to explore, conjecture, and reason logically as well as the ability to use various mathematical methods effectively to solve problems.

Interests: Problem solving, working with numbers, games requiring analytic reasoning, investigative research

Skills and abilities: Oral and written comprehension, number facility, mathematical reasoning, deductive reasoning, analytic skills

Occupations related to this major: Mathematicians, Statisticians, Mathematics Teachers, and Financial Analysts

Mathematics Education

Mathematics Education majors learn to teach mathematics at the high school or middle school level. They learn techniques to help students develop skills and knowledge in the field of mathematics; they also take professional education courses.

Interests: Problem solving, analytic reasoning, working with young students, working with computers, leadership, organizing people

Skills and abilities: Oral and written expression and comprehension, speech clarity, organizational skills, creativity, using computers

Occupations related to this major: Middle School Teachers, High School Teachers, Insurance Underwriters, Business Training Specialists, and Education Administrators

Statistics

Statistics majors learn the science of dealing with data. They learn to design efficient data collection systems and to analyze and interpret information derived from the data. They learn to use mathematical theory or apply statistical theory and methods to collect, organize, interpret, and summarize numerical data to provide usable information. They may specialize in fields such as biostatistics, agricultural statistics, business statistics, economic statistics, or other fields.

Interests: Mathematics, working with numbers, problem solving, quantitative problems

Skills and abilities: Mathematical reasoning, computer operations, critical thinking, deductive and inductive reasoning, written expression

Occupations related to this major: Statisticians, Actuaries, Mathematicians, Operations Research Analysts, and Cost Estimators

8. EDUCATION

Education is a people-oriented field of study providing teachers, librarians, and school counselors involved in helping others to learn, acquire information, or gain insight into it. There are many levels on which one can teach. These include preschool and day care facilities, elementary schools, secondary schools, colleges and universities, as well as public and private vocational education institutions, dance, music, and art studios, and many other places. Librarianship and counseling are smaller fields than teaching. Archivists and curators are more involved with things than people. They may also help people learn and gain information, but they do not usually work as closely with people as do teachers, librarians, and counselors. All of these professions usually require a bachelor's degree, although some require a master's or doctoral degree.

Interest: Helping others learn, acquire information; teaching, counseling, or librarianship

Popular majors in this field of study: Early Childhood Education, Elementary School Education, Library Science, Middle School Education, Parks and Recreation Management, Physical Education, Secondary School Education, Special Education, Technology Education, and Vocational and Educational Counseling

Employment information/outlook: More than 7,550,000 people worked in related occupations in this field of study in 2002. The 2002–2012 employment growth is expected to be 21.1%. Median annual earnings are $43,612.

Early Childhood Education

Early Childhood Education majors learn to teach preschool students through art, music, play, poetry, and stories to prepare for learning language, science, numbers, and social studies. They learn to design programs to develop students' mental capacities, learning abilities, and emotional health. They learn a variety of appropriate teaching methods and strategies.

Interests: Childhood development, working with children, communicating with children and their parents

Skills and abilities: Oral expression and comprehension, speech clarity, problem sensitivity, time sharing, creativity, music or artistic ability

Occupations related to this major: Preschool Teachers, Kindergarten Teachers, Elementary School Teachers, Early Childhood Education Program Directors, Child Care Administrators, and Family Service Coordinators

Elementary School Education

Elementary School Education majors learn to teach young students (kindergarten through grade 6) basic academic, social, and manipulative skills. They learn to instill good study and work habits and an appreciation for learning. They learn to prepare lesson plans, tests, records, and reports, and to conduct conferences with parents. They learn a variety of methods for understanding how and why children develop socially and intellectually, and get professional experience that includes research in teaching and learning.

Interests: Communication, creativity, problem solving, flexibility, ability to organize, energy, enthusiasm

Skills and abilities: Oral and written expression and comprehension, speech clarity, problem sensitivity

Occupations related to this major: Elementary School Teachers, Kindergarten Teachers, Middle School Teachers, Secondary School Teachers, Special Education Teachers, and School Counselors

Library Science

Library Science majors learn the science of acquiring and organizing collections of books, pamphlets, manuscripts, clippings, and reports, and assisting readers in their use. They learn how to analyze reader needs, prepare bibliographies, and organize films, tapes, and maps.

Interests: Reading, multimedia communication, working with people, computers

Skills and abilities: Reading comprehension, active listening, oral and written expression and comprehension, speech clarity, fluency of ideas, information ordering

Occupations related to this major: Librarians, Computer and Information Systems Managers, Elementary School Teachers, Secondary School Teachers, and School Administrators

Middle School Education

Middle School Education majors learn to develop a wide array of instructional skills, which include multimedia approaches, classroom management, advisory ability, effective communication, and alternatives to teacher-centered instruction. They learn to build on and extend basic academic skills developed in elementary school students, and introduce them to the world of more abstract thinking and knowledge that they will encounter in high school.

Interests: Helping or providing service to others, communicating with young people, teaching young people, working with ideas

Skills and abilities: Instructing others, active listening, social perceptiveness, oral and written expression and comprehension, speech clarity, problem sensitivity

Occupations related to this major: Middle School Teachers, High School Teachers, Vocational Education Teachers, School Counselors, and Librarians

Parks and Recreation Management

Parks and Recreation Management majors study how individuals and communities pursue leisure and recreation. They explore what recreation is, investigate what motivates people's recreational choices, and develop skills to manage a variety of leisure and recreation enterprises and organizations.

Interests: Working with people; scientific, historic, and natural features of parks, forests, and other attractions

Skills and abilities: Helping others, leadership, solving problems, oral and written expression, speech clarity, problem sensitivity

Occupations related to this major: Community Recreation Planners/Directors, Social Directors, Park Naturalists, Forest Rangers, Amusement and Recreation Establishment Managers, and Camp Directors

Physical Education

Physical Education majors learn to teach and supervise individual and team sports. They learn to demonstrate sports techniques, analyze physical capabilities and needs of students, and administer corrective exercises and physical conditioning. They learn to provide students with activities to maximize physical fitness.

Interests: Physical activity, sports, working with people, health-related issues, biological science

Skills and abilities: Physical stamina, leadership, oral expression, speech clarity, multilimb coordination

Occupations related to this major: Physical Education Teachers, Sports Coaches, Physical Training Instructors, Aerobic Dance Instructors, Athletic Trainers, Fitness Directors, and Athletic Administrators

Secondary School Education

Secondary School Education majors learn to teach one or more high school subjects using various teaching methods. They learn to develop and plan teaching materials and assignments. They learn to construct tests to evaluate learning. They gain depth of knowledge in the subject they intend to teach and develop teaching skills in subject matters such as science, mathematics, social studies, English, music, art, business, physical education, or other subjects.

Interests: Serving others, teaching young people and helping them develop their academic interests and career choices

Skills and abilities: Working with people, teaching, learning, understanding human behavior, oral and written expression and comprehension, speech clarity

Occupations related to this major: Secondary School Teachers, Middle School Teachers, Special Education Teachers, Vocational Education Teachers, and Vocational and Educational School Counselors

Special Education

Special Education majors prepare for a career working with disabled children and adults in a variety of settings. They learn to coordinate the services available to people with disabilities, and provide appropriate educational experiences for people with varying disabilities, including deafness, blindness, aphasia, and mobility impairments.

Interests: Helping others, working with people

Skills and abilities: Accepting differences in people, communicating effectively, teaching, oral and written expression and comprehension, speech clarity, problem sensitivity

Occupations related to this major: Special Education Teachers; Teachers of the Emotionally and Mentally Impaired; Teachers of the Physically, Visually, and Hearing Impaired; Rehabilitation Counselors

Technology Education

Technology Education majors are trained to teach the design, operation, and impact of technological systems to students. They learn technical skills to be used in advanced communication, applied higher mathematics, and science. This major prepares students to teach technical pathway programs found in middle schools, high schools, and colleges. Technical majors can be planned in agriculture, arts, communication, business, engineering, information science, mechanics, and other fields.

Interests: Helping people, design, technological systems, network technology, graphics and multimedia, system designs, programming, teaching

Skills and abilities: Working with people, oral and written expression and comprehension, analyzing and describing technological systems

Occupations related to this major: Agriculture Teachers, Art Teachers, Computer Science Teachers, Business Teachers, Engineering Technology Teachers, and Science Teachers

Vocational and Educational Counseling

Vocational and Educational Counseling majors learn to counsel individuals and provide group educational and vocational guidance services. They learn to promote and enhance student learning through three broad and interrelated areas of student development: academic development, career development, and personal/social development.

Interests: Working with, communicating with, and teaching people; providing service to others

Skills and abilities: Speaking, active listening, oral and written expression and comprehension, problem sensitivity, speech clarity, fluency of ideas

Occupations related to this major: Educational and Vocational School Counselors, Child, Family, and School Social Workers, Health Educators, and Probation Officers

9. ENGINEERING

Engineering field of study involves planning and designing various things. Engineers design machines, processes, systems, and structures. They apply physical laws and mathematical theories and principles to solve practical technical problems. Engineers work in research, development, design, manufacturing and construction, operations, management, technical sales, teaching, and consulting services.

Interests: Designing machines, processes, systems and structures; research, development, design, manufacturing and construction, operations, management, and technical consulting services

Popular majors in this field of study: Aerospace/Aeronautical Engineering, Agricultural Engineering, Chemical Engineering, Civil Engineering, Computer Engineering, Electrical Engineering, Industrial Engineering, Materials Engineering, Mechanical Engineering, and Petroleum Engineering

Employment information/outlook: More than 1,663,000 people worked in related occupations in this field of study in 2002. The 2001–2012 employment growth is expected to be 5.9%. Median annual earnings are $71,437.

Aerospace/Aeronautical Engineering

Aerospace/Aeronautical Engineering majors learn to perform a variety of engineering work in designing, constructing, and testing aircraft, missiles, and spacecraft. They learn to conduct basic and applied research to evaluate adaptability of materials and equipment to aircraft design and manufacture. They learn to make improvements in testing equipment and techniques.

Interests: Model aircraft and rocketry, astronomy, piloting, space exploration, computers, problem solving, working with people

Skills and abilities: Leadership, computer technology, physical science, oral and written expression and comprehension, mathematical reasoning, deductive and inductive reasoning

Occupations related to this major: Aerospace/Aeronautical Engineers, Electronics Engineers, Nuclear Engineers, Ceramic Engineers, Chemical Engineers, and Civil Engineers

Agricultural Engineering

Agricultural Engineering majors learn to apply knowledge of engineering technology and biological science to agricultural problems concerned with power and machinery, electrification, structures, soil and water conservation, and processing of agricultural products.

Interests: Solving problems, improving the quality of life, computers, leadership

Skills and abilities: Problem solving, oral and written expression and comprehension, computer operation, deductive and inductive reasoning, number facility

Occupations related to this major: Soil Conservationists, Landscape Architects, Geoscientists, Foresters, Chemical Engineers, Industrial Engineers, and Mechanical Engineers

Chemical Engineering

Chemical Engineering majors learn to turn chemicals into products through research and development. They learn to devise economical and efficient production processes. They learn to work in a number of fields, such as cosmetics, fertilizers, paints, dyes, pesticides, oil refining, and pollution prevention.

Interests: Science, chemistry, mathematics

Skills and abilities: Applying knowledge of science and mathematics to real-world problems, written expression and comprehension, mathematical reasoning, originality, deductive reasoning

Occupations related to this major: Chemical Engineers, Nuclear Engineers, Civil Engineers, Petroleum Engineers, Agricultural Engineers, and Electrical Engineers

Civil Engineering

Civil Engineering majors learn to solve technical problems involved in providing buildings, bridges, airports, transportation systems, foundations, coastal facilities, environmental control systems, and water supply and purification systems. They become involved in the conception, planning, design, construction, operation, and maintenance of these important public facilities. Studies will include soil mechanics, hydraulics, and structural engineering.

Interests: Mathematics, physical sciences, computers, building things, public service, applying mathematics and science to practical uses

Skills and abilities: Mathematics, physical sciences, logical thinking, interpersonal skills, oral and written expression and comprehension, inductive and deductive reasoning

Occupations related to this major: Civil Engineers, Civil Engineering Technicians, Architectural Engineers, Nuclear Engineers, Electrical Engineers, and Industrial Engineers

Computer Engineering

Computer Engineering majors learn to design and develop computer and computer-related systems. These systems include software systems, hardware systems, and combined hardware/software systems. Students take courses in basic sciences, mathematics, and engineering science and design.

Interests: Mathematics, science, computing, investigative research

Skills and abilities: Mathematics, computer operations, oral and written expression and comprehension, inductive and deductive reasoning

Occupations related to this major: Computer Hardware Engineers, Computer Software Engineers, Electronics Engineers, and Computer Service Technicians

Electrical Engineering

Electrical Engineering majors learn to design, develop, test, or supervise the manufacturing and installation of electrical equipment components or systems for commercial, industrial, military, or scientific use. They learn to design and manufacture a broad array of electrical and electronic devices and systems to meet society's needs.

Interests: Computer languages, computer programming, electronic equipment

Skills and abilities: Mathematics, physical science, oral and written expression and comprehension, deductive reasoning

Occupations related to this major: Electrical Engineers, Electronics Engineers, Mechanical Engineers, Electricians, Nuclear Engineers, and Production Engineers

Industrial Engineering

Industrial Engineering majors learn to plan, design, and implement complex systems for industry that take into account the availability, capabilities, and needs of people, machines, and materials. They learn to plan the layout of factories for efficiency, and engage in time, motion, and incentive studies. They learn about safety studies, cost, and quality control measures, and long-range planning goals.

Interests: Problem solving, leadership

Skills and abilities: Working with people, critical thinking, written and oral expression and comprehension, fluency of ideas, mathematical reasoning

Occupations related to this major: Aerospace Engineers, Materials Engineers, Petroleum Engineers, Industrial Engineers, Mechanical Engineers, and Engineering Technicians

Materials Engineering

Materials Engineering majors learn to evaluate properties of materials used to manufacture products that must meet specialized design and performance criteria. They learn to develop machinery and processes to manufacture materials, such as polymers, plastics, and alloys.

Interests: Nature and the physical sciences, problem solving, computer operations, working with ideas

Skills and abilities: Creative and critical thinking, problem sensitivity, oral and written expression and comprehension, deductive and inductive reasoning

Occupations related to this major: Materials Engineers, Marine Architects, Mechanical Engineers, Electrical Drafters, and Electrical Engineering Technicians

Mechanical Engineering

Mechanical Engineering majors learn to plan and design tools, engines, machines, and other mechanically functioning equipment. They learn to oversee installation, operation, maintenance, and repair of such equipment as centralized heat, gas, water, and steam systems. They learn to create and build machines, devices, and systems that perform useful services.

Interests: Mechanical devices, computers, cars, solving problems, mathematics, physical science

Skills and abilities: Mathematics, critical thinking, complex problem solving, mathematical reasoning, deductive and inductive reasoning, oral and written comprehension

Occupations related to this major: Mechanical Engineers, Marine Architects, Materials Engineers, Petroleum Engineers, Engineering Technicians, and Mechanical Drafters

Petroleum Engineering

Petroleum Engineering majors learn about exploring and drilling for fossil fuel, both on land and under the sea, and how to maximize the recovery of oil and gas through engineering processes. They learn methods of searching for new sources of energy, for example, geothermal energy. They learn to devise methods to improve oil and gas well production and determine the need for new or modified tool designs.

Interests: Solving problems, working with others, using computers, outdoor activities

Skills and abilities: Mathematics, physics, oral and written expression and comprehension, inductive and deductive reasoning, problem sensitivity, fluency of ideas

Occupations related to this major: Petroleum Engineers, Aerospace Engineers, Marine Engineers, Materials Engineers, Mining and Geological Engineers, and Geologists

10. FAMILY AND CONSUMER SCIENCES

Family and Consumer Sciences majors concentrate on issues concerning feeding, clothing, and caring for children, managing resources, and providing housing for individuals and families. Family and Consumer Science majors provide information, gained through research, about families and individuals as consumers and decision makers. These majors provide information about child care, elder care, food, clothing, housing, finance, and other issues of resource management.

Interests: Issues concerning feeding, clothing, and caring for children, managing resources, and providing housing for individuals and families; an interest in families as consumers and decision makers.

Popular majors in this field of study: Day Care Administration, Family and Consumer Education, Fashion Merchandising, Food Science and Nutrition, Hotel and Motel Management, Housing and Human Development, Individual and Family Development, Leisure Studies, Textile Sciences, and Tourism

Employment information/outlook: More than 1,571,000 people worked in related occupations in this field of study in 2002. The 2001–2012 employment growth is expected to be 19.9%. Median annual earnings are $44,137.

Day Care Administration

Day Care Administration majors learn to manage programs that provide education or social services to young children and their families. They gain knowledge of child development and develop skills in teaching young children, in supervising staff, and in business management.

Interests: Leadership, management, supervising people, administering programs, working with children

Skills and abilities: Organizational and managerial skills, program development, oral and written expression and comprehension, speech clarity

Occupations related to this major: Day Care Director, Preschool Director, Head Start Directors, Early Childhood Education Program Directors, and Child Care Workers

Family and Consumer Education

Family and Consumer Education majors learn to use community resources to meet the needs of the individual and the family in the management of time, energy, and money. They learn about parenting skills, communication skills, relationship skills, wellness, foods and nutrition, consumerism, clothing selection, and job skills. They prepare to become family and consumer teachers for preschool through adult education in subjects related to the family. They study various aspects of family life including human development, nutrition, and decision making, in addition to teaching strategies.

Interests: Family life, using current technology, working with people

Skills and abilities: Critical and analytical thinking, oral and written expression and comprehension, speech clarity

Occupations related to this major: Family and Consumer Science Teachers, Consumer Advocates, Education Consultants, Extension Agents, Financial Planners, Housing Administrators

Fashion Merchandising

Fashion Merchandising majors study how to manufacture fashions for consumers and effectively sell those fashions.

Interests: Current trends in apparel, arts, furnishings, travel and leisure, food business trends, fabrics, fashion and fashion designers

Skills and abilities: Motivating people, leadership, organizational ability, originality, fluency of ideas, color discrimination, oral comprehension

Occupations related to this major: Retail Buyers, Manufacturers' Representatives, Product Designer-Pattern Makers, and Fashion Designers

Food Science and Nutrition

Food Science and Nutrition majors study the nature of foods, the causes of their deterioration, and the principles of food processing. They will learn about the selection, preservation, processing, packaging, distribution, and use of safe, nutritious, and wholesome food.

Interests: Social, health, economic, and political issues involved in food production and availability; chemical reactions and what happens to food when it enters the human body; solving problems

Skills and abilities: Organizational abilities, critical thinking, oral and written expression and comprehension, speech clarity, mathematical reasoning

Occupations related to this major: Dietitians, Nutritionists, Nutrition Educators, and Food Scientists and Technicians

Hotel and Motel Management

Hotel Management majors learn the operation of a hotel. They learn the principles of managing lodging facilities efficiently and profitably. They learn about personnel management, services, supplies, business aspects, decision making, accounting, and public relations. They are introduced to the principles of managing these key components of the hospitality industry.

Interests: Working with people, problem solving, attention to detail, leadership

Skills and abilities: Organization ability, creativity, oral and written expression and comprehension, speech clarity, speech recognition

Occupations related to this major: Lodging Managers, Food Service Managers, Retail Store Managers, and Office Managers

Housing and Human Development

Housing and Human Development majors learn to analyze the use of investment in housing and its impact on families, the community, and the larger economy and society.

Interests: Working with people, serving others, real estate, home automation, the family, marketing, management, interior design, environmental design, finance

Skills and abilities: Computer skills, analytical skills, oral and written expression and comprehension, problem sensitivity

Occupations related to this major: Real Estate Managers, Property Managers, Consumer Affairs Specialists, Extension Agents, and Financial/Mortgage Specialists

Individual and Family Development

Individual and Family Development majors study interpersonal relationships and human development from infancy to old age. They study theories of development with an emphasis on techniques to improve quality of life for individuals and families.

Interests: Helping others, family and individual well-being, prevention and elimination of problems facing people in their daily lives

Skills and abilities: Working with people, critical thinking, oral and written expression and comprehension, curiosity about interpersonal and family dynamics, speech clarity

Occupations related to this major: Child Life Specialists, Day Care Teachers, Recreation Activities Directors, Drug and Alcohol Rehabilitation Counselors, and Crisis Center Directors

Leisure Studies

Leisure Studies majors learn to design, manage, and deliver leisure services to a variety of people in diverse settings. They learn about the impact of leisure services upon individual satisfaction and the quality of life.

Interests: Helping people, leadership, organizing individual and group activities

Skills and abilities: Working with people, oral and written expression and comprehension, speech clarity, problem sensitivity, fluency of ideas, memorization

Occupations related to this major: Amusement and Recreation Establishment Managers, Recreation Workers, Tour Guides and Escorts, Social and Community Service Managers, and Meeting and Convention Planners

Textile Sciences

Textile Sciences majors learn how to design fabrics for garments, upholstery, rugs, and other products. They study print, woven, and embroidery styles, and learn how to buy and sell certain fabrics and trims. They learn how to analyze fabric performance in the marketplace.

Interests: Fashion design, garment fashion, art, history of textiles, textile technology, design principles

Skills and abilities: Originality, visualization, visual color discrimination, fluency of ideas, oral expression and comprehension

Occupations related to this major: Textile Designers, Fashion Designers, Quality Control Analysts, Sales Representatives, and Wardrobe Planners

Tourism

Tourism majors study how to manage travel-related enterprises and conventions and tour services. They learn about travel agency management, travel industry operations and procedures, tourism marketing and promotion strategies, and travel industry law.

Interests: Travel, tourism planning, human resource management, travel industry operations, marketing

Skills and abilities: Oral and written expression and comprehension, mathematical reasoning, speech clarity, fluency of ideas

Occupations related to this major: Travel Agents, Travel Guides, Tour Guides and Escorts, Reservation and Transportation Ticket Agents, and Amusement and Recreation Establishment Managers

11. HEALTH SCIENCE

The **Health Science** field of study trains workers in a vast array of occupations. Occupational titles vary, and the training necessary to fill these occupations requires lengthy postgraduate education. Health practitioners diagnose, treat, and prevent illness and disease. While all health practitioners practice the art of healing, they differ in methods of treatment and areas of specialization. Training for this profession is more rigorous than training for most other professional occupations, but practice also offers unusual rewards. Incomes of health practitioners generally are higher than those of other professional workers with similar years of education. Furthermore, most health practitioners derive considerable satisfaction from knowing that their work contributes directly to the well-being of others. Workers in the industry must have the ability and perseverance to complete the years of study required. They should be emotionally stable, able to make decisions in emergencies, and have a strong desire to help the sick and injured. Sincerity and an ability to gain the confidence of patients are important qualities.

Interests: Diagnosing, treating, and preventing illness and disease; an interest in the well-being of others and a desire to help the sick and injured

Popular majors in this field of study: Athletic Training, Clinical Laboratory Science, Dental Hygiene, Health Services Management, Medical Record Administration, Nuclear Medical Technology, Nursing, Occupational Therapy, Pharmacy, and Physical Therapy

Employment information/outlook: More than 2,367,000 people worked in related occupations in this field of study in 2002. The 2002–2012 employment growth is expected to be 25.4%. Median annual earnings are $65,823.

Athletic Training

Athletic Training majors learn to prevent, recognize, refer, and treat injuries and illnesses sustained by athletes. They learn about the administration of athletic training programs in public and private schools, colleges, universities, and with professional teams. They study exercise sciences and the medical aspects of sport. Together with clinical experience, this prepares students for national certification in the field.

Interests: Sports, helping others, health and medicine, physical fitness and exercise, anatomy, nutrition, first aid

Skills and abilities: Manual skills, science, problem solving, interpersonal communication, integrity, oral expression, speech clarity, physical strength

Occupations related to this major: Athletic Trainers, Sports Medicine Clinic Administrators, Exercise Physiologists, Physical and Corrective Therapists, and Occupational Therapists

Clinical Laboratory Science

Clinical Laboratory Science majors learn to perform medical tests to determine the presence and cause of disease. They study sophisticated instrumentation used to perform a variety of laboratory procedures. They study blood and other body fluids that aid in the diagnosis of disease and the maintenance of health.

Interests: Solving problems, working with complex machinery, computer science, laboratory work, helping others, medicine, biological science

Skills and abilities: Computer skills, analytic skills, oral and written expression and comprehension, arm-hand steadiness, visual color discrimination

Occupations related to this major: Laboratory Technologists and Technicians, Research Analysts, Coroners, Clinical Scientists, Environmental Health Officers, and Toxicologists

Dental Hygiene

Dental Hygiene majors learn to work under the supervision of a dentist to clean and polish teeth, massage gums, apply fluoride to prevent decay, and provide dental health education. They obtain the knowledge and clinical skills needed to provide preventive oral health care. They learn skills as an assistant to a dentist performing a number of duties.

Interests: Working with people, helping individuals maintain their health, science

Skills and abilities: Critical thinking, oral expression, arm-hand steadiness, manual dexterity, near vision

Occupations related to this major: Dental Hygienists, Dental Assistants, Dentists, and Medical Assistants

Health Services Management

Health Services Management majors prepare for entry-level positions managing a wide variety of health care organizations such as hospitals, nursing homes, insurance companies, and public agencies. They learn to direct the many activities of health care organizations and coordinate administrative duties with medical services. They learn about space needs, staffing, and supplies. They learn to supervise personnel, prepare budgets, and direct the policies of the organization.

Interests: Working with people, taking initiative, solving problems, working with data

Skills and abilities: Oral and written expression and comprehension, speech clarity, organizational skills, interpersonal skills, critical thinking

Occupations related to this major: Medical and Health Services Managers, Public Health Directors, Educational Program Directors, Nursing Directors, Social Welfare Administrators, and Health Insurance Underwriters

Medical Record Administration

Medical Record Administration majors learn to supervise and manage the preparation, storage, and use of medical records and related information systems. They study the legal and technical aspects of medical records, and the design and management of secure data systems. They learn to merge the study of business and medicine. Students prepare to direct medical record departments in varied health care settings by exploring the health care environment, health care organizations, clinical information systems, medical record department operations, and health care reimbursement systems.

Interests: Leadership, working with people, designing and implementing systems, problem solving, working with detail

Skills and abilities: Writing and speaking effectively, working in a changing environment, oral and written expression and comprehension, near vision, mathematical reasoning

Occupations related to this major: Medical Records Administrators and Directors, Quality Assurance Coordinators, Health Care Administrators, Medical Records Educators, and Research Coordinators

Nuclear Medicine Technology

Nuclear Medicine Technology majors learn how to administer radionuclides to patients and to monitor the characteristics and functions of tissues or organs in which they localize. They learn to operate the cameras that detect the radionuclides and maintain patient records. They learn to prepare and administer radioactive drugs to patients, operate radiation detection equipment, and perform the calculations or computer analysis needed to complete the patient's examination.

Interests: Biological sciences, new technologies, helping others, working in a medical setting, working with people

Skills and abilities: Biological and physical science, working with others, oral and written expression and comprehension, problem sensitivity

Occupations related to this major: Nuclear Medicine Technologists, Radiation Therapists, Radiologic Technologists, Electroneurodiagnostic Technologists, and Medical and Clinical Laboratory Technologists

Nursing

Nursing majors learn to administer nursing care to ill or injured persons. They learn to administer medication and treatments prescribed by medical doctors, observe and record symptoms and behaviors of patients, and promote good health. They learn how to rehabilitate, counsel, and educate patients, and how to work as part of a health care team in many settings. They study humanities, natural sciences, and nursing theory to serve individuals, families, groups, and communities.

Interests: Provide intimate helping services to people, ethical care, chemistry, physics, anatomy, biology

Skills and abilities: Clear thinking, oral and written expression and comprehension, problem sensitivity, speech clarity

Occupations related to this major: Registered Nurses, Doctors of Medicine, Nursing Instructors, Physical Therapists, Medical Assistants, Chiropractors, and Podiatrists

Occupational Therapy

Occupational Therapy majors learn to determine the educational, recreational, and vocational activities needed to hasten a patient's recovery from physical, psychological, social, or developmental problems. They learn to instruct patients in the use of artificial limbs or to regain the use of muscles. They learn to help patients function independently so that they may work, play, take care of themselves, and relate to others in a productive and satisfying manner.

Interests: Solving problems, anatomy, working with people, medicine, health, rehabilitation

Skills and abilities: Logical thinking, working with others, oral and written expression and comprehension, deductive reasoning

Occupations related to this major: Occupational Therapists, Respiratory Therapists, Physical Therapists, Speech-Language Pathologists and Audiologists, Recreational Therapists, and Exercise Physiologists

Pharmacy

Pharmacy majors study the science of drugs, including their chemical and physical properties and composition. They learn to understand the effects of drugs, to test those drugs for purity and strength. They learn to provide drug products and drug information in all areas of patient care. They learn to monitor drug therapy to ensure that the treatment is appropriate, safe, therapeutically effective, and cost-effective.

Interests: Chemistry, biology, mathematics, solving problems, helping others

Skills and abilities: Patience, tact, adapting to change, working carefully, oral and written expression and comprehension, information ordering, mathematical reasoning

Occupations related to this major: Pharmacists, Pharmacy Technicians, Physician Assistants, Opticians, Licensed Practical Nurses, and Dietitians and Nutritionists

Physical Therapy

Physical Therapy majors learn to assist and help persons with injuries, muscle, nerve, and joint problems, burns, and bone diseases. They learn to use exercise, massage, and heat and light to assist in healing. They prepare to take state licensure examinations in this field and qualify for service in the prevention of disabilities and the rehabilitation of the disabled. They learn to test, evaluate, and plan a treatment program for patients who are physically incapacitated as the result of accidents or disease, and for healthy individuals who wish to prevent injuries in work or recreational settings.

Interests: Biological and physical sciences, exercise and fitness, people, analytic reasoning

Skills and abilities: Interpersonal communication, problem solving, visual spatial perception, emotional sensitivity, oral and written expression, speech clarity, problem sensitivity, manual dexterity

Occupations related to this major: Physical Therapists, Occupational Therapists, Respiratory Therapists, Manual Arts Therapists, Corrective Therapists, and Speech-Language Pathologists and Audiologists

Speech Pathology/Audiology

Speech Pathology majors learn to treat people with speech, language, voice, hearing, and communication disorders. These disorders may be the result of hearing loss, brain injury or deterioration, cerebral palsy, stroke, cleft palate, mental retardation, or emotional problems. They receive training in the identification and treatment of human communication disorders. They learn about the normal processes of speech and language development, why problems may occur, and what can be done to minimize their impact.

Interests: Working with children, working with adults, identifying and solving behavioral problems, applying technology to human needs

Skills and abilities: Oral and written expression and comprehension, speech clarity, creativity, working cooperatively in groups

Occupations related to this major: Speech-Language Pathologists and Audiologists, Recreation Therapists, Corrective Therapists, Exercise Physiologists, Occupational Therapists, and Respiratory Therapists

12. HUMANITIES

Humanities students explore thought and expression through aesthetic, historical, philosophical, social, political, psychological, and symbolic contexts. Humanities studies serve as a liberal and broad training for professional careers. Students will enjoy courses in English, literature, history, classics, culture studies, history of art and music, philosophy, foreign language, social and natural sciences. Graduates with a bachelor's degree may qualify for management trainee positions in corporations, banks, and federal and state governmental agencies. Many students use humanities as an undergraduate degree for the teaching or law professions. Other students may become writers or communications specialists in humanistic endeavors.

Interests: Exploring thoughts and expressions through aesthetic, historical, philosophical, social, political, psychological and symbolic contests; literature, history, foreign language, social and natural sciences

Popular majors in this field of study: American Literature, Anthropology, Classics, Comparative Literature, English, English Education, Foreign Language, History, Linguistics, Philosophy, Religion, and Sociology

Employment information/outlook: More than 1,162,000 people worked in related occupations in this field of study in 2002. The 2002–2012 employment growth is expected to be 14.8%. Median annual earnings are $42,552.

American Literature

American Literature majors study the historical development of the culture in which they live. They study the literature and literary development of the United States from the Colonial Era to the present. They learn about the forces—intellectual, economic, geographic, and social—that have shaped their own character. They study periods and genres, authors, literary criticism, and regional and oral traditions.

Interests: Sensitivity to language, the power of ideas, exploring the development of different regional and ethnic traditions that make up American culture

Skills and abilities: Assessing conflicting points of view, oral and written expression and comprehension, speech clarity

Occupations related to this major: English Teachers, Creative Writers, Art, Drama, and Music Teachers, Reporters and Correspondents, and Publicity Writers

Anthropology

Anthropology majors learn to make comparative studies of the distribution, origin, and evolution of man, cultures that man has created, and their social and physical characteristics. Studies include ancient as well as modern man.

Interests: Writing, archeology, sociology, social sciences, investigative research

Skills and abilities: Writing, science, critical thinking, oral and written expression and comprehension, inductive reasoning, fluency of ideas

Occupations related to this major: Anthropologists, Archeologists, Historians, Sociologists, Linguistic Scientists, and Genealogists

Classics

Classics majors immerse themselves in two cultures fundamental to the West—the cultures of ancient Greece and ancient Rome. Students explore the literature, history, art, philosophy, and architecture of those civilizations. Connecting with the past creates a sense of belonging to humanity and participating in human achievement and evokes reflections on the present. Students will explore their poetry, prose, and drama, and consider the relation of literature to other arts and to other fields of study.

Interests: Language, literature, exploring the past, acquiring a broad liberal education

Skills and abilities: Oral and written expression and comprehension, information ordering, skills of analysis and criticism

Occupations related to this major: Classicists, Anthropologists, Art History Teachers, English Teachers, Foreign Language Teachers, and Literature Teachers

Comparative Literature

Comparative Literature majors study the literature of different countries, cultures, and languages. They explore their poetry, prose, and drama, and consider the relation of literature to other arts and to other fields of study.

Interests: Literature, foreign languages, differences between cultures as expressed in their languages and works of art

Skills and abilities: Reading critically, speaking, active listening, oral and written expression and comprehension, speech recognition, information ordering

Occupations related to this major: English Teachers, Foreign Language Teachers, Postsecondary Teachers, Journalists, Lawyers, Reporters and Correspondents, and Writers

English

English majors study the linguistic and literary richness of the English language as well as some of the cultural history of the English-speaking world. They concentrate on specific areas such as creative writing, comparative or American literature, or semantics. They study important works of literature—drama, prose, and poetry—focusing on the point of view, organization, and language of the works. They develop critical and analytical reading skills, and practice language use and composition.

Interests: Reading, talking, writing about literature; music, theater, and film

Skills and abilities: Speaking, writing, oral and written expression and comprehension, speech clarity

Occupations related to this major: English Teachers, Teachers, Journalists, Publishers, Radio and Television Broadcasters, and Social Workers

English Education

English Education majors learn to teach students about English grammar and linguistics. They learn to instruct students in different types of literature such as poetry, short stories, plays, and novels. They learn how to teach students to research and prepare research papers. They learn how to teach public speaking, drama, and English as a second language

Interests: Nature and history of languages, reading, literature, journalism, creative writing, linguistic development of children and teenagers

Skills and abilities: Speaking, working with students, art, guiding discussions

Occupations related to this major: Elementary School Teachers, Secondary School Teachers, Postsecondary School Teachers, Linguistic Scientists, and Speech-Language Pathologists and Audiologists

Foreign Language

Foreign Language majors study foreign languages (French, German, Italian, Japanese, Russian, Spanish, etc.). They study the language, literature, and culture of the country where the language is spoken.

Interests: Literature, history, culture of a language

Skills and abilities: Fluency in speaking and writing, learning languages, oral and written expression and comprehension, speech clarity

Occupations related to this major: Foreign Language Teachers, Translators, Journalists, Foreign Travel Consultants, Diplomats, and Linguists

History

History majors study the social, economic, and political developments of societies. They learn to analyze historical happenings and, as reporters, writers, or teachers, report on their significance. Students expand their knowledge and understanding of the past. Working with written, oral, visual, and art factual evidence they examine the causes, contexts, and chronologies of historical events, thus cultivating a sense of continuity and change in human experiences.

Interests: Curiosity about when, where, and why historical happenings occurred; what it was like to have lived in different times and places

Skills and abilities: Reading carefully, writing clearly, speaking articulately, thinking analytically, oral and written expression and comprehension, expressing ideas with clarity and precision

Occupations related to this major: Historians, Archeologists, Anthropologists, Genealogists, Curators, Archivists, and Teachers

Linguistics

Linguistics majors study the common properties of the world's languages. They study the structure and development of a specific language or language group. They trace the origin and evolution of words through comparative analysis of ancient parent languages and modern language groups. They study word and structural characteristics, such as phonetics and phonology, morphology, syntax, and semantics.

Interests: Language, foreign languages, how people talk and express themselves

Skills and abilities: Learning foreign languages, problem solving, oral and written expression and comprehension, speech recognition

Occupations related to this major: Linguistic Scientists, English as a Second Language Teachers, English Teachers, Foreign Language Teachers, Interpreters, Translators, Public Relations Specialists, and Speech Pathologists

Philosophy

Philosophy majors learn the process of developing a philosophy. They gain insight into how the great minds of the past and present have attempted to answer the most serious questions of the universe. They participate in a tradition of thought as old as civilized life and as new as artificial intelligence and medical ethics. They examine issues of morality, reality, and knowledge. Philosophy is a foundation for teaching, religion, wisdom, and logical thinking.

Interests: Solitary meditation, argument with family and friends, reading, asking the "why" question, seeing the connections between different things

Skills and abilities: Writing, debating, thinking logically, mathematics, oral and written expression and comprehension, speech recognition, information ordering

Occupations related to this major: Philologists, Political Scientists, Anthropologists, Psychologists, Sociologists, and Historians

Religion

Religion majors study and compare the major world religions, as well as many of the lesser-known religions. They study the various branches, sects, and denominations of particular religions. They learn how religion plays an integral part in all societies. They learn to use a range of approaches when examining religion—historical, textual, psychological, philosophical, sociological, and anthropological.

Interests: Different cultures and societies, world religions, human problems and mysteries, such as birth, growth, love, death, grief

Skills and abilities: Reading carefully and critically, foreign languages, oral and written expression and comprehension, problem sensitivity, speech clarity

Occupations related to this major: Clergy, Directors of Religious Activities and Education, Therapists and Counselors, Psychologists, Social Workers, and Teachers

Sociology

Sociology majors study the origin, development, organization, and functions of human society. They trace the origin and growth of human organizations and the behavior and interaction within social groups. They analyze the influence of group activities on individual and group behavior.

Interests: Anthropology, geography, criminology, psychology, investigative research, politics

Skills and abilities: Reading critically, critical thinking, solving problems, oral and written expression and comprehension, deductive reasoning

Occupations related to this major: Sociologists, Anthropologists, Political Scientists, Counseling Psychologists, Historians, and Linguistic Scientists

13. PHYSICAL SCIENCES

Physical Sciences majors in this field of study investigate the structure and composition of the Earth and the universe. Everything in our physical environment, whether naturally occurring or of human design, is composed of chemicals. Chemists search for, and put to practical use, new knowledge about chemicals. Geological scientists play an important role in preserving and cleaning up the environment. Meteorologists forecast the weather. Physicists design and perform experiments with lasers, cyclotrons, telescopes, mass spectrometers, and other equipment. Physical science technicians use the principles and theories of science and mathematics to solve problems in research and development and to help invent and improve products and processes.

Interests: The structure and composition of the Earth and the universe; an interest in our physical environment, whether naturally occurring or of human design

Popular majors in this field of study: Astronomy, Atmospheric Sciences, Chemistry, Environmental Sciences, Geology, Geophysics, and Physics

Employment information/outlook: More than 310,000 people worked in related occupations in this field of study in 2002. The 2002–2012 employment growth is expected to be 8.2%. Median earnings are $68,427.

Astronomy

Astronomy majors study the sizes, shapes, motions, and all other physical properties of the sun, moon, stars, and planets. They may use knowledge of astronomy in space exploration and the development of space technology. Students seek to understand the entire universe—its constituent parts, such as the stars and planets, and the physical and mathematical laws that govern them.

Interests: Nature, the night sky, the expanding universe, physical science, astronomical science

Skills and abilities: Mathematics, science, computers, inductive and deductive reasoning, written comprehension

Occupations related to this major: Astronomers, Geophysicists, Physicists, Geologists, Chemists, and Atmospheric and Space Scientists

Atmospheric Sciences

Atmospheric Sciences majors learn to investigate atmospheric phenomena and interpret meteorological data gathered by surface and air stations, satellites, and radar to prepare reports and weather forecasts for public and other uses. They study the basic principles of atmospheric physics and dynamics and are concerned with understanding and forecasting weather.

Interests: Weather, environment, climate, science, mathematics, computer science, geography, serving the public

Skills and abilities: Analytic reasoning, mechanical reasoning, problem solving, oral and written expression and comprehension, speech clarity, inductive reasoning

Occupations related to this major: Atmospheric Scientists, Space Scientists, Climatologists, Geophysicists, Astronomers, and Meteorologists

Chemistry

Chemistry majors study the sciences of physical substances, atoms, molecules, elements, and compounds. They learn to perform chemical tests, develop new chemical products, and monitor the purity of air, food, and drugs. Because it is an experimental science, students learn to design and perform the experiments that allow a better understanding of the physical world.

Interests: Investigative research, problem solving, curiosity about how things work

Skills and abilities: Analytic and mathematical skills, oral and written expression and comprehension, deductive reasoning, mathematical reasoning

Occupations related to this major: Chemists, Chemical Engineers, Chemical Engineering Technicians, Agricultural Scientists, Biological Scientists, and Physicists

Environmental Sciences

Environmental Sciences majors study the biological and physical aspects of the environment. They learn about the conservation and/or improvement of natural resources, such as air, soil, water, land, fish, and wildlife, as well as methods of controlling environmental pollution. They conduct research or perform investigation for the purpose of identifying, abating, or eliminating sources of pollutants or hazards that affect either the environment or the health of the population.

Interests: Investigative research, solving problems, working with ideas

Skills and abilities: Working with others, oral and written expression and comprehension, problem sensitivity, mathematical reasoning, inductive reasoning

Occupations related to this major: Environmental Scientists, Materials Scientists, Geographers, Geologists, Atmospheric Scientists, and Space Scientists

Geology

Geology majors study the Earth's structure, composition, and history. They examine rocks, minerals, and fossils. They record data, prepare maps, conduct surveys, and advise suitability of sites. They develop skills that are useful for basic research and applied problem solving.

Interests: The outdoors, remote places, problem solving, collecting minerals or fossils

Skills and abilities: Reasoning ability, critical thinking, mathematics, oral and written expression and comprehension, number facility, inductive reasoning

Occupations related to this major: Geologists, Physicists, Geophysicists, Materials Scientists, Geological Data Technicians, and Geographers

Geophysics

Geophysics majors study aspects of the earth, including the atmosphere and hydrosphere. They investigate and measure seismic, gravitational, electrical, thermal, and magnetic forces affecting the Earth, and utilize principles of physics, mathematics, and chemistry. They study the Earth and its atmosphere by physical measurements. Students learn to use mathematics and physics, along with electrical engineering, computer science, geology, and other earth sciences to analyze measurements taken at the surface to infer properties and processes deep within the Earth's complex interior.

Interests: The outdoors, travel, taking measurements, computer languages, graphics, computer programming

Skills and abilities: Natural curiosity, mathematics, physical science, computers, oral and written comprehension, mathematical reasoning, deductive reasoning

Occupations related to this major: Geophysicists, Geologists, Astronomers, Physicists, Atmospheric Scientists, Space Scientists, and Chemists

Physics

Physics majors learn to explore and identify the basic principles of the structure and behavior of matter, the generation and transfer of energy, and the interaction of matter and energy. They learn to use these principles in theoretical areas such as the origin of the universe, or in practical areas to develop advanced materials, electronic devices, or medical equipment.

Interests: Investigative research, mathematics, problem solving, improving the quality of life

Skills and abilities: Computational skills, reasoning logically, solving problems, oral and written expression and comprehension, mathematical reasoning

Occupations related to this major: Physicists, Astronomers, Geologists, Atmospheric Scientists, Space Scientists, Geophysicists, and Environmental Scientists

14. SOCIAL AND BEHAVIORAL SCIENCES

Social and Behavioral Sciences majors learn about the social needs of people. Clinical psychologists help the mentally or emotionally disturbed adjust to life through behavior modification programs and other techniques. Social workers address the needs of individuals, families, groups, and communities. Their work may involve everything from helping an elderly person adjust to life in a nursing home, to organizing fund-raising for community social welfare activities. Other social scientists conduct basic and applied research in the social sciences. They use established methods to assemble a body of fact and theory that contributes to human knowledge. Social scientists investigate all aspects of human society—from anthropologists studying the origins of the human race, or historians studying an ancient civilization—to political scientists analyzing the results of presidential elections.

Interests: Social and emotional needs of people; an interest in all aspects of society—from the origins of the human race, or an ancient civilization, to political results of presidential elections

Popular majors in this field of study: Criminal Justice Studies, Economics, Geography, Gerontology, Political Sciences, Psychology, Public Administration, Social Studies Education, and Social Work

Employment information/outlook: More than 1,731,000 people worked in related occupations in this field of study in 2002. The 2002–2012 employment growth is expected to be 16.1%. Median annual earnings are $49,417.

Criminal Justice Studies

Criminal Justice Studies majors learn about the dimensions and causes of crime and delinquency; the structure of the American criminal justice system; the operation of criminal courts; and the techniques and theories of law enforcement.

Interests: Serving others, court procedures, criminal law, private security, criminal justice

Skills and abilities: Working with others, making decisions, oral and written expression and comprehension, inductive reasoning, speech clarity, problem sensitivity

Occupations related to this major: Criminal Investigators, United States Marshals, Police Detectives, Sheriffs and Deputy Sheriffs, Correction Officers and Jailers, and Child Support and Missing Persons Investigators

Economics

Economics majors learn to plan, design, and conduct research into activities devoted to satisfying human wants. They learn to analyze the relationship between supply and demand. They study the problems of inflation, unemployment, tariffs, taxation, and foreign trade. They learn to analyze such issues as inflation, unemployment, monopoly, and economic growth. They study theory, policy, and trends and explore ways to deal with the economic problems of society and the individual.

Interests: Current issues such as taxes, poverty, health, inflation, the environment, human behavior

Skills and abilities: Solving problems, oral and written expression and comprehension, mathematical reasoning, logical reasoning

Occupations related to this major: Economists, Market Research Analysts, Urban and Regional Planners, Financial Managers, Financial Analysts, and Underwriters

Geography

Geography majors study the activities of people. Students study where people live, why they are located there, and how they earn a living. Students study the physical characteristics of the Earth, such as landforms, vegetation, climate, locale, and mineral and water resources. They study how people relate to and are shaped by their environment. They gain a broad perspective on the world's environments and its peoples while gaining a strong background in the physical and social sciences.

Interests: Analyzing and solving social and environmental problems, doing social and physical scientific research, the relationship between people and their environment

Skills and abilities: Oral and written expression and comprehension, spatial orientation, working individually and in groups, information gathering, working with computers

Occupations related to this major: Geographers, Geophysicists, Geologists, Atmospheric and Space Scientists, Environmental Scientists, and Materials Scientists

Gerontology

Gerontology majors learn about aging and older persons. They study physical, emotional, and intellectual changes in the elderly,

cultural aspects of aging, and governmental policies and programs for the aging.

Interests: Helping people, human development, older people, family relations, improving the quality of life

Skills and abilities: Oral and written expression and comprehension, listening, objectivity, deductive reasoning, determining needs and interests, organizing and managing projects

Occupations related to this major: Gerontologists, Geriatric Nurses, Nursing Home Administrators, Social Welfare Administrators, and Occupational and Physical Therapists

Political Sciences

Political Sciences majors study government and the nature of politics. They analyze the operations of different forms of government, and attempt to find theoretical and practical solutions to political problems. Students learn about the origins, historical development, and social functions of government. They study how electoral, legislative, judicial, and administrative structures and processes vary from one country and one age to another; how and why governments change, fall, and engage in wars. They study the behavior of public officials and other citizens involved in politics.

Interests: Public policy issues such as health care and environmental protection; politicians and public figures, justice, good and bad government, law, criminal justice, the legal system

Skills and abilities: Reading critically, thinking analytically, oral and written expression and comprehension, understanding graphic material

Occupations related to this major: Political Scientists, Legislators, Sociologists, Historians, Anthropologists, and Political Science Teachers

Psychology

Psychology majors learn to collect and interpret scientific data relating to human behavior to understand people and explain their actions. They learn to interview patients, give diagnostic tests, and offer therapy to help people make behavioral adjustments. Students study human and animal behavior and explore the processes involved in normal and abnormal thoughts, feelings, and actions. They increase their understanding of behavior while learning psychological facts, methods, principles, and generalizations about individuals and groups.

Interests: Working with people, scientific method, human and animal behavior

Skills and abilities: Critical thinking, oral and written expression and comprehension, inductive reasoning

Occupations related to this major: Developmental Psychologists, Experimental Psychologists, Educational Psychologists, Social Psychologists, Clinical Psychologists, and Counseling Psychologists

Public Administration

Public Administration majors may study in five areas of specialization: personnel, management, public relations, finance, and planning. They learn to establish government policy, and develop laws, rules and regulations. These studies will prepare students to find positions managing public agencies. Students deal with the operations of all forms and levels of government. Students learn about the many skills and challenges associated with implementing public policy in government and in nonprofit organizations.

Interests: Public and community service, organizing people, leadership, working with people from different backgrounds

Skills and abilities: Leadership, organizational ability, problem solving, oral and written expression and comprehension, inductive reasoning

Occupations related to this major: Government Service Executives, City Managers, Management Analysts, Government Affairs Specialists, and Legislators

Social Studies Education

Social Studies Education majors learn to teach courses pertaining to human society and its characteristic elements. They learn to teach subjects such as psychology, economics, history, political science, and sociology. They learn to teach students in middle school and high school courses in history, citizenship, and other social sciences.

Interests: Serving people, working with people, history, social sciences

Skills and abilities: Speaking, organizing working with people, oral and written expression and comprehension, speech clarity

Occupations related to this major: Middle School Teachers, High School Teachers, Postsecondary School Teachers, Historians, Sociologists, and Psychologists

Social Work

Social Work majors study many types of social issues and needs. They learn to aid families with physical, mental, or social problems, such as poverty, unemployment, illness, broken homes, various disabilities, antisocial behavior, and inadequate housing. Students acquire the knowledge and skills to assist individuals, families, groups, and communities in preventing and alleviating the problems of a modern, rapidly changing society. They learn to help others and to modify harmful social conditions, promote social and economic well being, and increase opportunities for all people to live with dignity and freedom.

Interests: Helping those in need, particularly children, the poor, minorities, the aged, the disabled, and women, enabling others to develop unique, positive responses and solutions to their problems

Skills and abilities: Objectivity, ability to listen, analytic ability, oral and written expression and comprehension, problem sensitivity

Occupations related to this major: Social Workers, Medical and Psychiatric Social Workers, Community Organization Social Workers, Residential Counselors, Probation and Correctional Treatment Specialists, and Human Services Workers

LOCATING OCCUPATIONAL INFORMATION RELATED TO YOUR MAJOR

Students may find occupations in a Field of Study in which they have a work interest. They may wish to conduct research to find specific information about an occupation. Good sources for occupational information are public libraries, high school and college career resource centers, One-Stop Career Centers, America's InfoNet (*www.acinet.org*) and O*Net (*www.online.onetcenter.org*), the occupational information Network.

Recommended books for occupations and college entry research:

Occupational Outlook Handbook, 2004–2005 Edition, U.S. Bureau of Labor Statistics, 2 Massachussetts Avenue, NE, Ste. 2135, Washington, DC 20212 *www.bls.gov*

A Guide to the College Admission Process, National Association for College Admissions Counseling, 1631 Prince Street, Alexandria, VA 22314–2818

College Major Handbook, 3rd Edition, CFKR Career Materials, 11860 Kemper Road, Unit 7, Auburn, CA 95603 *www.cfkr.com*

Federal Student Financial Aid, The Student Guide, Federal Student Aid Information Center, P.O. Box 84, Washington, DC 20044 *www.fafsa.ed.gov*

CHOOSING A COLLEGE

A student's choice of institution may depend on individual needs and talents. A person's career goals, career plans, and choice of college major are very important criteria in choosing a college. A student's choice may be limited by financial or other considerations. However, if at all possible, students should give high priority to their career plans and choice of a college major when choosing a college that best matches their career plans. Students' choice of their college major may influence their final college choice.

Some majors are rare and specialized. Special attention must be given to those majors that are fairly rare and specialized. Students will be limited in the number of colleges from which to choose. There are more than 1800 four-year colleges in the United States; only 78 offer aerospace engineering; 42 offer landscape architecture; 81 offer astronomy; 24 offer petroleum engineering; 8 offer statistics; 8 offer business statistics; 26 offer oceanography; 59 offer pharmacy; and 115 offer occupational therapy majors. This is a partial listing. A student who chooses a specialized major may find it necessary to travel a distance to find a college offering that major. School career centers and public libraries may carry listings of colleges that offer the major of the student's choice.

The most widely offered baccalaureate-level majors are found in four-year colleges. No college, not even the largest university, offers every major; some offer relatively few. Students will want to attend a college that offers several of the majors they are considering. Students can keep their choice of major open by selecting a university or college that offers a wide range of majors. The most common majors are found in the Art, Business, Computer and Information Science, Education, Engineering, Health, Humanities, and the Social and Behavioral Science fields of study.

MAKING THE FINAL DECISION

Making important decisions and setting long-range goals is never an easy task. Making a decision on what to study in college for four or more years, and how this will fit into students' lifestyles and career goals is very important and very personal. With the soaring costs of education and the increasing complexity of the job market, students cannot afford the luxury of trial and error in preparing for a career that requires college training; entering college without a career or major in mind can add time and expense to the entire journey. Good decision-making calls for awareness of one's needs and the matching of those needs with a wide variety of alternate choices. It is to this end that sufficient information has been explored for making a final decision.

In making a final decision, students must take a broad view of the fourteen Fields of Study. They should look carefully at all career and major options within the fourteen fields. Students should not limit themselves to a career or major that has been recommended to them by family or friends. The final decision should be the student's, along with the responsibility to reach their goals. In the final analysis, students will have to look at themselves. As Plato once said, "Know thyself, and to thine own self be true."

- **Assess work interests.** Identify work-related interests. Discover the type of work activities and occupations that match work interests. Identify and learn about the most relevant broad interest areas. Use interest results to explore the world of work.
- **Assess work values.** Pinpoint what is important in a job. Identify occupations that provide satisfaction based on the similarity among work values, conditions of work, and the characteristics of an occupation.
- **Assess work abilities.** Identify user ability strength, parts of work that the user likes to do, parts of work that the user finds important, and training needs of the user.

The more students know about their interests, work values, abilities, and career goals, the better their decisions will be. In the final analysis, good decision-making by students is based on knowing oneself and being flexible enough to sense whether they are on the right track, and to alter decisions when they are not in their best interest. No matter what major is chosen, students must keep in ming that intellectual flexibility is the skill that enables them to work productively when the knowledge they have mastered is challenged or replaced by new ideas.

We wish all students well in their college studies and in the career path that they have chosen.

Robert Kauk and Francis Ferry

Occupational information was gathered from O*Net, U.S. Department of Labor.

INDEX OF COLLEGE MAJORS

This section of *Profiles of American Colleges* will help you quickly determine which schools offer the major in which you are interested, the in-state tuition, room and board costs, and the Selector Rating. The colleges are listed alphabetically and the first column indicates the state where each is located. These data reflect the 2005-2006 academic year.

You will be able to compare schools offering those majors that interest you the most and see what their in-state costs and Selector Ratings are, before reading the Profiles in the main section of the book (see page 239 for Selector Rating details). You may also discover some new schools or majors that interest you.

ACCOUNTING

School	ST	$IS	SR
Abilene Christian Univ	TX	20,830	C
Adams State College	CO	8,613	C
Adelphi Univ	NY	27,000	VC
Adrian College	MI	23,000	C
Alabama A&M Univ	AL	8,890	LC
Alabama State Univ	AL	7,658	C
Albany State Univ	GA	5,770	C+
Albertus Magnus College	CT	25,336	C
Albright College	PA	33,920	C
Alcorn State Univ	MS	8,190	LC
Alderson-Broaddus College	WV	24,006	C
Alfred Univ	NY		VC
Alvernia College	PA	26,388	C
American International College	MA	28,710	C
Anderson Univ	IN	25,050	LC
Andrews Univ	MI	21,786	C
Angelo State Univ	TX	8,340	NC
Appalachian State Univ	NC	8,000	VC
Aquinas College	MI	23,750	C
Arcadia Univ	PA	33,570	VC
Arizona State Univ-Tempe	AZ	11,174	C
Arkansas Baptist College	AR	5,600	NC
Arkansas State Univ	AR	9,630	C
Arkansas Tech Univ	AR	8,108	VC
Asbury College	KY	23,762	VC
Ashford Univ	IA	20,370	C
Ashland Univ	OH	25,000	C
Assumption College	MA	32,875	C
Atlantic Union College	MA	17,600	LC
Auburn Univ	AL	12,230	VC
Auburn Univ Montgomery	AL	9,530	NC
Augsburg College	MN	28,300	C
Augusta State Univ	GA	2,920	C
Augustana College	IL	29,862	VC+
Augustana College	SD	24,380	VC
Aurora Univ	IL	20,645	C
Austin Peay State Univ	TN	7,535	C
Averett Univ	VA	24,920	C
Avila Univ	MO	22,100	C
Azusa Pacific Univ	CA	28,546	VC
Baker College of Flint	MI	7,800	NC
Baker Univ	KS	22,190	C
Baldwin-Wallace College	OH	27,256	VC
Ball State Univ	IN	13,138	C
Barry Univ	FL	24,100	LC
Barton College	NC	22,316	C
Baylor Univ	TX	27,555	HC
Becker College	MA	24,300	LC
Belhaven College	MS	19,530	NC
Bellarmine Univ	KY	27,650	C+
Bellevue Univ	NE	4,440	NC
Belmont Abbey College	NC	25,314	C
Belmont Univ	TN	24,110	VC
Bemidji State Univ	MN	11,180	LC
Benedict College	SC	19,114	LC
Benedictine College	KS	21,968	C
Benedictine Univ	IL	25,710	C
Bennett College	NC	11,500	C
Bentley College	MA	38,784	HC
Berkeley Coleg/ Westchester Campus	NY	26,700	LC
Berkeley College/New York City	NY	16,950	LC
Berry College	GA	24,342	VC
Bethany College	WV	21,395	C
Bethel College	IN	19,680	C
Bethel Univ	MN	29,840	VC
Bethune-Cookman College	FL	17,922	LC
Biola Univ	CA	29,372	VC
Birmingham-Southern College	AL	28,494	VC+
Black Hills State Univ	SD	7,800	LC
Blackburn College	IL	13,690	C
Bloomfield College	NJ	22,500	LC
Bloomsburg Univ of Pennsylvania	PA	11,602	C
Bluefield State College	WV	3,140	LC
Bluffton College	OH	26,110	C
Boise State Univ	ID	9,438	LC
Boston College	MA	41,608	MC
Boston Univ	MA	42,046	HC+
Bowling Green State Univ	OH	14,994	C
Bradley Univ	IL	25,280	VC
Brenau Univ Women's College	GA	23,950	VC
Brescia Univ	KY	14,240	C
Brewton-Parker College	GA	14,220	LC
Briar Cliff Univ	IA	23,550	LC
Bridgewater State College	MA	12,120	C

School	ST	$IS	SR
Brigham Young Univ	UT	9,200	VC
Brigham Young Univ/Hawaii	HI	7,740	HC+
Bucknell Univ	PA	39,660	MC
Buena Vista Univ	IA	27,742	C
Butler Univ	IN	31,944	VC+
Cabrini College	PA	33,340	C
Caldwell College	NJ	26,450	LC
Calif Lutheran Univ	CA	27,800	LC
Calif State Polytechnic Univ, Pomona	CA	18,053	C+
Cal State East Bay	CA	10,856	LC
Cal State, Fullerton	CA	10,990	C
Cal State, Long Beach	CA	9,512	C
Cal State, Northridge	CA	9,036	LC
Cal State, Sacramento	CA	11,122	C
Cal State, San Bernardino	CA	12,563	LC
Calif Univ of Pennsylvania	PA	14,217	C
Calumet College of St. Joseph	IN	9,500	LC
Calvin College	MI	25,735	VC
Cameron Univ	OK	6,314	NC
Campbell Univ	NC	21,137	VC
Campbellsville Univ	KY	21,328	C
Canisius College	NY	32,257	VC
Capital Univ	OH	30,444	C
Cardinal Stritch Univ	WI	21,910	C
Caribbean Univ	PR	3,000	
Carlow Univ	PA	24,313	C
Carroll College	MT	23,324	C+
Carroll College	WI	24,860	C
Carson-Newman College	TN	16,800	C
Carthage College	WI	26,000	C
Case Western Reserve Univ	OH	37,314	MC
Catawba College	NC	25,000	C
Catholic Univ of America	DC	35,838	VC
Cedar Crest College	PA	30,615	C
Cedarville Univ	OH	21,904	VC
Centenary College	NJ	28,870	LC
Centenary College of Louisiana	LA	24,760	VC
Central College	IA	26,774	VC
Central Conn State Univ	CT	13,620	C
Central Methodist Univ	MO	18,000	C
Central Mich Univ	MI	12,244	C
Central Missouri State Univ	MO	10,000	C
Central State Univ	OH	9,010	C+
Central Univ of Bayamon	PR	3,335	
Central Washington Univ	WA	11,730	C
Chaminade Univ of Honolulu	HI	23,320	LC
Champlain College	VT	24,605	C
Chapman Univ	CA	37,550	VC
Chatham College	PA	27,290	C
Chestnut Hill College	PA	26,600	LC
Chicago State Univ	IL	10,915	C+
Christopher Newport Univ	VA	13,326	VC
City Univ	WA	7,425	NC
CUNY/Baruch College	NY	4,320	VC+
CUNY/Brooklyn College	NY	4,377	C+
CUNY/College of Staten Island	NY	4,328	NC
CUNY/Herbert H. Lehman College	NY	4,000	LC
CUNY/Hunter College	NY	8,000	C+
CUNY/Medgar Evers College	NY	4,250	NC
CUNY/Queens College	NY	4,356	C
CUNY/York College	NY	4,242	NC
Clarion Univ of Pennsylvania	PA	11,844	C
Clark Atlanta Univ	GA	20,960	LC
Clarke College	IA	25,390	C
Clarkson Univ	NY	34,930	VC
Clayton College and State Univ	GA	2,445	LC
Clearwater Christian College	FL	13,160	LC
Cleary College	MI	11,000	LC
Clemson Univ	SC	13,366	HC
Cleveland State Univ	OH	10,798	NC
Coastal Carolina Univ	SC	13,140	C
Coe College	IA	27,440	VC
College Misericordia	PA	27,950	C
College of Charleston	SC	13,616	VC
College of Mount St. Joseph	OH	24,860	C
College of New Jersey	NJ	18,315	MC
College of Notre Dame of Maryland	MD	27,700	C
College of Our Lady of the Elms	MA	21,000	C
College of St. Benedict	MN	30,091	VC

School	ST	$IS	SR
College of St. Catherine	MN	27,505	VC
College of St. Joseph	VT	20,900	NC
College of St. Rose	NY	25,684	C
College of St. Scholastica	MN	28,456	C+
College of Santa Fe	NM	28,978	C
College of the Ozarks	MO	4,130	VC+
College of the Southwest	NM	12,420	C+
Colo Christian Univ	CO	21,182	VC
Colo State Univ-Fort Collins	CO	10,878	C+
Colo State Univ-Pueblo	CO	7,821	LC
Columbia College	MO	16,900	C
Columbia College	SC	24,982	VC
Columbia Union College	MD	23,536	LC
Columbus State Univ	GA	8,664	C
Concord College	WV	9,708	C
Concordia College: Moorhead	MN	22,475	VC
Concordia Univ at Austin	TX	23,640	LC
Concordia Univ Nebr	NE	20,500	C+
Concordia Univ St.Paul	MN	27,776	C
Concordia Univ Wisc	WI	22,660	VC
Concordia Univ, River Forest	IL	26,300	C
Converse College	SC	24,800	VC
Cornerstone Univ and Grand Rapids Theological Seminary	MI	21,350	NC
Creighton Univ	NE	29,918	VC+
Culver-Stockton College	MO	20,625	C
Cumberland Univ	TN	18,894	C
Daemen College	NY	24,580	C
Dakota Wesleyan Univ	SD	17,832	C
Dallas Baptist Univ	TX	17,040	NC
Dana College	NE	22,390	C
Davenport Univ	MI	15,205	NC
David N. Myers College	OH	9,475	C
Davis and Elkins College	WV	22,416	C
De Sales Univ	PA	28,580	VC
Defiance College	OH	24,790	C
Delaware State Univ	DE	8,130	LC
Delaware Valley College	PA	29,944	C
Delta State Univ	MS	7,709	C
DePaul Univ	IL	29,835	VC
Dickinson State Univ	ND	7,847	NC
Dillard Univ	LA	17,500	VC
Doane College	NE	22,458	C
Dominican College	NY	26,630	LC
Dominican Univ	IL	26,370	C
Dordt College	IA	20,325	VC
Dowling College	NY	22,110	LC
Drake Univ	IA	27,632	VC+
Drury Univ	MO	20,117	VC
Duquesne Univ	PA	29,534	VC
D'Youville College	NY	23,660	C
East Carolina Univ	NC	10,000	C
East Central Univ	OK	6,207	C
East Tenn State Univ	TN	8,497	C
East Texas Baptist Univ	TX	16,713	C
Eastern Conn State Univ	CT	13,554	C
Eastern Illinois Univ	IL	12,569	C
Eastern Kentucky Univ	KY	7,725	C
Eastern Mennonite Univ	VA	25,450	VC
Eastern Mich Univ	MI	12,897	C
Eastern Nazarene College	MA	19,500	LC
Eastern New Mexico Univ	NM	7,264	C
Eastern Oregon Univ	OR	10,400	NC
Eastern Univ	PA	24,075	C
Eastern Washington Univ	WA	10,608	C
Edgewood College	WI	22,862	C
Edinboro Univ of Pennsylvania	PA	11,809	LC
Edward Waters College	FL	14,374	LC
Elizabeth City State Univ	NC	5,700	LC
Elizabethtown College	PA	32,100	VC
Elmhurst College	IL	24,685	C
Elmira College	NY	37,200	VC
Elon Univ	NC	25,371	HC
Emory Univ	GA	40,546	MC
Emporia State Univ	KS	8,093	C
Eureka College	IL	19,280	C
Evangel Univ	MO	17,380	C
Excelsior College	NY	995	SP
Fairfield Univ	CT	39,835	HC
Fairleigh Dickinson Univ/ College at Florham	NJ	30,130	C
Fairleigh Dickinson Univ/ Metropolitan Campus	NJ	28,590	C
Fairmont State	WV	8,400	LC
Fayetteville State Univ	NC	6,000	LC
Ferris State Univ	MI	13,698	C
Ferrum College	VA	24,290	LC
Flagler College	FL	13,790	VC+
Florida A&M Univ	FL	8,344	C

School	ST	$IS	SR
Florida Atlantic Univ	FL	11,221	C
Florida Gulf Coast Univ	FL	10,833	C
Florida Inst of Technology	FL	29,720	VC
Florida International Univ	FL	9,245	VC
Florida Memorial College	FL	6,000	LC
Florida Southern College	FL	25,965	C
Florida State Univ	FL	9,028	HC
Fordham Univ	NY	36,000	HC
Fort Hays State Univ	KS	7,638	C
Fort Lewis College	CO	11,852	C
Fort Valley State Univ	GA	6,975	C
Francis Marion Univ	SC	11,114	C
Franciscan Univ of Steubenville	OH	20,300	VC
Franklin College	IN		C
Franklin Pierce College	NH	31,700	C
Franklin Univ	OH	6,720	SP
Freed-Hardeman Univ	TN	16,370	NC
Fresno Pacific Univ	CA	25,454	C
Friends Univ	KS	16,250	LC
Frostburg State Univ	MD	12,672	C
Furman Univ	SC	33,264	HC+
Gallaudet Univ	DC	16,554	
Gannon Univ	PA	26,100	C
Gardner-Webb Univ	NC	21,500	C
Geneva College	PA	21,850	C
George Mason Univ	VA	10,850	VC
George Washington Univ	DC	48,820	MC
Georgetown College	KY	24,950	C+
Georgetown Univ	DC	43,183	MC
Georgia College and State Univ	GA	11,020	C
Georgia Southern Univ	GA	9,762	C
Georgia Southwestern State Univ	GA	6,035	C
Georgia State Univ	GA	11,444	VC
Georgian Court College	NJ	20,000	LC
Glenville State College	WV	8,778	NC
Golden Gate Univ	CA	12,150	LC
Goldey-Beacom College	DE	11,440	C
Gonzaga Univ	WA	30,218	HC
Gordon College	MA	29,194	C+
Goshen College	IN	22,850	VC
Grace College	IN	22,170	C
Graceland Univ	IA	19,700	C
Grambling State Univ	LA	6,538	NC
Grand Canyon Univ	AZ	32,000	LC
Grand Valley State Univ	MI	12,000	VC
Grand View College	IA	21,482	C
Greensboro College	NC	23,000	C
Greenville College	IL	23,146	C
Grove City College	PA	15,784	HC+
Guilford College	NC	28,160	C+
Gustavus Adolphus College	MN	30,920	HC
Gwynedd-Mercy College	PA	26,080	C
Hampton Univ	VA	19,868	C+
Hannibal-LaGrange College	MO	16,390	C
Harding Univ	AR	16,512	VC
Hardin-Simmons Univ	TX	18,641	C
Hartwick College	NY	36,065	C+
Hastings College	NE	22,218	VC
Hawaii Pacific Univ	HI	21,080	C
Heidelberg College	OH	23,242	C
Henderson State Univ	AR	7,600	C
Hendrix College	AR	27,646	HC+
Hesser College	NH	17,700	LC
High Point Univ	NC	25,720	C
Hilbert College	NY	20,480	LC
Hillsdale College	MI	24,160	HC
Hofstra Univ	NY	32,630	VC
Holy Family Univ	PA	25,740	C
Hope College	MI	28,208	VC+
Houghton College	NY	25,980	VC+
Houston Baptist Univ	TX	18,660	C
Howard Payne Univ	TX	17,115	C
Howard Univ	DC	18,481	C+
Humphreys College	CA	7,000	NC
Huntingdon College	AL	23,090	VC
Husson College	ME	17,410	LC
Idaho State Univ	ID	9,030	C
Illinois College	IL	21,900	C+
Illinois State Univ	IL	12,839	C+
Illinois Wesleyan Univ	IL	34,050	HC+
Immaculata Univ	PA	25,350	C
Indiana Inst of Technology	IN	23,430	C
Indiana State Univ	IN	11,604	C
Indiana Univ Bloomington	IN	13,356	VC
Indiana Univ Kokomo	IN	4,835	LC
Indiana Univ Northwest	IN	4,902	LC
Indiana Univ of Pennsylvania	PA	11,209	C
Indiana Univ South Bend	IN	4,989	LC
Indiana Univ Southeast	IN	4,880	LC

ST = STATE   **$IS** = IN-STATE COSTS   **SR** = SELECTOR RATING

INDEX OF COLLEGE MAJORS

School	ST	$IS	SR
Indiana Univ-Purdue Univ Fort Wayne	IN	5,067	LC
Indiana Univ-Purdue Univ Indianapolis	IN	10,959	C
Indiana Wesleyan Univ	IN	22,074	C+
Inter American Univ of PR/ Aguadilla Campus	PR	3,784	
Inter American Univ of PR/ Arecibo Campus	PR	3,350	
Inter American Univ of PR/ Barranquitas Regional College	PR	3,350	
Inter American Univ of PR/ Bayamon Univ College	PR	3,522	
Inter American Univ of PR/ Fajardo Campus	PR	4,000	
Inter American Univ of PR/ Metropolitan Campus	PR	4,320	
Inter American Univ of PR/ Ponce Regional College	PR	3,700	
Inter American Univ of PR/ San German	PR	6,720	
International College	FL	9,500	NC
Iona College	NY	30,878	VC
Iowa State Univ	IA	11,831	VC
Iowa Wesleyan College	IA	22,140	C
Ithaca College	NY	35,144	VC
Jackson State Univ	MS	8,500	C
Jacksonville State Univ	AL	7,618	LC
Jacksonville Univ	FL	24,040	C
James Madison Univ	VA	12,010	VC
Jamestown College	ND	14,130	NC
John Brown Univ	AR	20,910	VC
John Carroll Univ	OH	27,658	C+
Johnson and Wales Univ/ Charlotte Campus	NC	29,121	LC
Johnson and Wales Univ/ North Miami Campus	FL	30,126	LC
Johnson and Wales Univ/ Providence Campus	RI	28,126	LC
Johnson State College	VT	11,830	LC
Judson College	IL	25,130	C
Juniata College	PA	33,130	VC
Kansas State Univ	KS	10,516	C
Kansas Wesleyan Univ	KS	21,400	VC
Kean Univ	NJ	15,880	C
Kennesaw State Univ	GA	12,152	C
Kent State Univ	OH	14,594	C
Kentucky Wesleyan College	KY	18,590	C
Keuka College	NY	26,050	C
Keystone College	PA	22,810	LC
King's College	PA	29,810	C
Knoxville College	TN	6,200	LC
Kutztown Univ of Pennsylvania	PA	10,820	C
La Roche College	PA	24,724	LC
La Salle Univ	PA	34,950	C
La Sierra Univ	CA	24,327	C+
LaGrange College	GA	22,874	C+
Lake Erie College	OH	27,725	C
Lake Superior State Univ	MI	12,842	LC
Lakeland College	WI	22,990	C
Lamar Univ	TX	6,820	LC
Langston Univ	OK	2,308	LC
Lasell College	MA	26,250	C
Le Moyne College	NY	29,570	VC
Lebanon Valley College	PA	31,700	VC
Lee Univ	TN	14,780	NC
Lehigh Univ	PA	42,690	HC+
LeMoyne-Owen College	TN	13,150	LC
Lenoir-Rhyne College	NC	25,580	C
LeTourneau Univ	TX	21,200	C
Lewis Univ	IL	23,050	C
Liberty Univ	VA	19,101	C
Limestone College	SC	19,840	C
Lincoln Memorial Univ	TN	18,144	C
Lincoln Univ	MO	8,000	NC
Lincoln Univ	PA	13,658	C
Lindenwood Univ	MO	18,600	VC
Lindsey Wilson College	KY	16,425	LC
Linfield College	OR	29,632	VC
Lipscomb Univ	TN	20,967	VC
Livingstone College	NC	17,815	LC
LIU/Brooklyn Campus	NY	25,000	C
LIU/C.W. Post Campus	NY	28,282	C
Loras College	IA	27,193	C
Louisiana State Univ and A&M College	LA	10,749	VC
Louisiana State Univ in Shreveport	LA	2,900	NC
Louisiana Tech Univ	LA	7,370	C
Lourdes College	OH	15,300	LC
Loyola College in Maryland	MD	38,898	HC
Loyola Marymount Univ	CA	36,321	VC
Loyola Univ Chicago	IL	32,896	VC
Loyola Univ New Orleans	LA	31,050	VC+
Lubbock Christian Univ	TX	16,960	C
Luther College	IA	28,800	VC+
Lycoming College	PA	30,797	C
Lynchburg College	VA	30,645	C
Lyndon State College	VT	14,233	LC
Lynn Univ	FL	30,750	C
Lyon College	AR	19,990	VC
MacMurray College	IL	20,755	C
Madonna Univ	MI	16,068	VC
Malone College	OH	23,040	C
Manchester College	IN	23,470	C
Manhattan College	NY	29,000	VC
Mansfield Univ	PA	11,300	C
Marian College	IN	26,160	C
Marian College of Fond du Lac	WI	21,775	LC
Marietta College	OH	29,327	C
Marist College	NY	30,566	VC
Marquette Univ	WI	31,066	HC
Mars Hill College	NC	19,000	LC
Marshall Univ	WV	9,116	C
Martin Univ	IN	10,300	SP
Marymount Manhattan College	NY	30,049	VC
Marymount Univ	VA	25,934	C
Maryville Univ of St. Louis	MO	23,000	VC
Marywood Univ	PA	30,680	C
McKendree College	IL	24,800	VC
McMurry Univ	TX	18,100	LC
McNeese State Univ	LA	5,270	LC
McPherson College	KS	21,010	C
Mercer Univ	GA	27,525	VC+
Mercy College	NY	20,000	NC
Mercyhurst College	PA	28,633	VC
Meredith College	NC	25,600	C
Merrimack College	MA	34,380	C
Mesa State College	CO	8,051	C
Messiah College	PA	28,910	VC+
Methodist College	NC	21,000	C
Metropolitan State College of Denver	CO	2,338	VC
Metropolitan State Univ	MN	4,682	SP
Miami Univ	OH	29,097	HC
Mich State Univ	MI	13,689	VC
MidAmerica Nazarene Univ	KS	20,584	LC
Middle Tenn State Univ	TN	8,540	C
Midland Lutheran College	NE	18,600	C
Midwestern State Univ	TX	9,381	LC
Miles College	AL	9,922	NC
Milligan College	TN	21,990	VC
Millikin Univ	IL	25,590	C
Millsaps College	MS	28,256	VC+
Minn State Univ, Mankato	MN	10,276	LC
Minn State Univ, Moorhead	MN	7,000	LC
Minot State Univ	ND	6,700	LC
Miss College	MS	14,574	VC
Miss State Univ	MS	9,577	C
Miss Univ for Women	MS	6,000	LC
Miss Valley State Univ	MS	7,970	C
Missouri Baptist Univ	MO	19,640	C
Missouri Southern State Univ	MO	8,396	NC
Missouri State Univ	MO	10,748	C+
Missouri Valley College	MO	18,500	C
Missouri Western State Univ	MO	9,534	NC
Molloy College	NY	16,510	C
Monmouth College	IL	23,700	C
Monmouth Univ	NJ	28,956	C
Monroe College	NY	15,960	LC
Montclair State Univ	NJ	16,327	C
Moravian College	PA	28,950	VC
Morehead State Univ	KY	9,150	C
Morehouse College	GA	25,082	C
Morgan State Univ	MD	12,080	C
Morningside College	IA	23,704	C
Mount Aloysius College	PA	20,900	LC
Mount Marty College	SD	20,590	C
Mount Mary College	WI	22,895	C
Mount Mercy College	IA	23,670	C
Mount Olive College	NC	16,000	LC
Mount St. Mary College	NY	25,250	C
Mount St. Mary's Univ	MD	30,930	C
Mount Union College	OH	25,840	C
Mount Vernon Nazarene Univ	OH	20,810	C
Mountain State Univ	WV	11,406	NC
Muhlenberg College	PA	36,030	HC+
Murray State Univ	KY	8,900	NC
Muskingum College	OH	22,970	C
National American Univ	SD	14,820	NC
National Univ	CA	8,412	SP
Nazareth College of Rochester	NY	28,175	VC
Nebr Wesleyan Univ	NE	23,415	C+
Neumann College	PA	25,996	LC
New Mexico Highlands Univ	NM	6,272	NC
New Mexico State Univ	NM	9,250	C
New York Inst of Technology	NY	28,126	VC
New York Univ	NY	43,170	MC
Newbury College	MA	25,600	C
Newman Univ	KS	21,106	C
Niagara Univ	NY	28,250	C
Nicholls State Univ	LA	6,560	NC
Nichols College	MA	28,000	LC
Norfolk State Univ	VA	10,531	LC
N Car Agricultural and Technical State Univ	NC	8,000	LC
N Car Central Univ	NC	9,000	LC
N Car State Univ	NC	11,824	HC
N Car Wesleyan College	NC	22,670	C
North Central College	IL	28,926	VC
N Dak State Univ	ND	8,500	C
North Georgia College and State Univ	GA	7,000	C
North Park Univ	IL	24,050	C
Northeastern Illinois Univ	IL	3,000	NC
Northeastern State Univ	OK	5,896	LC
Northeastern Univ	MA	35,742	HC
Northern Arizona Univ	AZ	10,353	C
Northern Illinois Univ	IL	13,178	C
Northern Kentucky Univ	KY	6,670	NC
Northern Mich Univ	MI	12,340	LC
Northern State Univ	SD	8,257	C
Northwest Christian College	OR	24,298	C
Northwest Missouri State Univ	MO	10,000	C
Northwest Nazarene Univ	ID	22,590	NC
Northwestern College	MN	25,220	NC
Northwestern College of Iowa	IA	22,174	C+
Northwestern Okla State Univ	OK	6,250	NC
Northwestern State Univ of Louisiana	LA	7,144	C
Northwood Univ	FL	21,040	C
Northwood Univ	MI	21,000	LC
Northwood Univ	TX	20,135	LC
Norwich Univ	VT	28,212	C
Notre Dame College	OH	20,425	C
Notre Dame de Namur Univ	CA	32,790	LC
Nova Southeastern Univ	FL	24,320	C
Nyack College	NY	18,540	C
Oakland City Univ	IN	19,620	NC
Oakland Univ	MI	11,936	C
Oakwood College	AL	14,904	C
Oglethorpe Univ	GA	30,300	VC
Ohio Dominican Univ	OH	25,954	C
Ohio Northern Univ	OH	27,765	VC
Ohio State Univ	OH	15,357	HC
Ohio State Univ at Marion	OH	4,801	NC
Ohio Univ	OH	15,921	C
Ohio Valley Univ	WV	17,752	C
Ohio Wesleyan Univ	OH	35,830	VC+
Okla Baptist Univ	OK	17,986	VC
Okla Christian Univ	OK	18,992	NC
Okla City Univ	OK	23,965	VC
Okla Panhandle State Univ	OK	7,635	NC
Okla State Univ	OK	10,213	VC
Okla Wesleyan Univ	OK	18,950	NC
Old Dominion Univ	VA	11,907	C
Olivet College	MI	19,984	C+
Olivet Nazarene Univ	IL	22,590	C
Oral Roberts Univ	OK	22,650	C
Oregon State Univ	OR	11,055	C
Ottawa Univ	KS	12,000	LC
Otterbein College	OH	28,986	C
Ouachita Baptist Univ	AR	21,900	VC
Our Lady of Holy Cross College	LA	8,090	LC
Our Lady of the Lake Univ of San Antonio	TX	22,430	LC
Pace Univ	NY	30,000	VC
Park Univ	MO	11,592	C
Paul Quinn College	TX	8,300	LC
Peirce College	PA	12,760	NC
Penn State Erie/The Behrend College	PA	16,256	C
Penn State Univ/Univ Park Campus	PA	18,038	HC
Pennsylvania College of Technology	PA	16,980	LC
Pepperdine Univ	CA	39,960	HC
Peru State College	NE	6,350	NC
Pfeiffer Univ	NC	21,900	C
Philadelphia Univ	PA	30,006	C
Pittsburg State Univ	KS	8,112	C
Plymouth State Univ	NH	12,298	LC
Point Loma Nazarene Univ	CA	27,610	VC
Point Park Univ	PA	24,160	C
Pontifical Catholic Univ of PR/Ponce	PR	7,310	
Portland State Univ	OR	12,453	C
Post Univ	CT	24,875	C
Prairie View A&M Univ	TX	11,110	LC
Presbyterian College	SC	30,044	VC
Providence College	RI	34,580	HC
Purdue Univ/Calumet	IN	10,891	C
Purdue Univ/West Lafayette	IN	13,458	VC
Queens Univ of Charlotte	NC	24,528	C
Quincy Univ	IL	24,920	C
Quinnipiac Univ	CT	34,640	VC
Radford Univ	VA	13,145	C
Ramapo College of New Jersey	NJ	16,630	VC
Randolph-Macon College	VA	31,250	C
Regis Univ	CO	31,890	C
Rhode Island College	RI	11,570	C
Richard Stockton College of New Jersey	NJ	14,000	VC
Rider Univ	NJ	32,560	C
Robert Morris Univ	PA	22,822	C
Roberts Wesleyan College	NY	26,378	C
Rochester College	MI	15,636	C+
Rochester Inst of Technology	NY	32,070	VC+
Rockford College	IL	28,330	VC
Rocky Mountain College	MT	20,805	C
Roger Williams Univ	RI	30,500	C
Roosevelt Univ	IL	22,605	VC
Rosemont College	PA	29,350	C
Rowan Univ	NJ	16,000	VC
Rutgers, The State Univ of New Jersey/Camden Campus	NJ	15,000	VC
Rutgers, The State Univ of New Jersey/New Brunswick/Piscataway Campus	NJ	15,810	HC
Rutgers, The State Univ of New Jersey/Newark Campus	NJ	15,640	VC
Sacred Heart Univ	CT	33,404	C
Saginaw Valley State Univ	MI	11,432	C
St. Ambrose Univ	IA	25,495	C
St. Anselm College	NH	33,810	C
St. Augustine's College	NC	14,000	LC
St. Bonaventure Univ	NY	28,785	LC
St. Cloud State Univ	MN	10,010	C
St. Edward's Univ	TX	23,560	C
St. Francis College	NY	19,974	LC
St. Francis Univ	PA	25,880	LC
St. John Fisher College	NY	27,860	C
St. John's Univ	MN	29,749	VC
St. John's Univ	NY	34,370	C
St. Joseph's College	IN	26,600	C
St. Joseph's College, New York, Brooklyn Campus	NY	12,206	C
St. Joseph's College, New York, Suffolk Campus	NY	12,000	C
St. Joseph's Univ	PA	37,428	VC
St. Leo Univ	FL	22,140	C+
St. Martin's Univ	WA	27,555	C
St. Mary-of-the-Woods College	IN	25,480	C
St. Mary's College	MD	32,538	VC
St. Mary's College of Calif	CA	37,290	C
St. Mary's Univ of Minn	MN	23,857	VC
St. Mary's Univ of San Antonio	TX	22,444	C
St. Michael's College	VT	33,330	VC
St. Norbert College	WI	28,577	C+
St. Peter's College	NJ	30,160	LC
St. Thomas Aquinas College	NY	22,000	LC
St. Thomas Univ	FL	23,490	C
St. Vincent College	PA	26,160	VC
St. Xavier Univ	IL	23,160	C
Salem College	NC	26,226	VC+
Salem State College	MA	13,161	LC
Salisbury Univ	MD	13,128	VC
Salve Regina Univ	RI	33,450	C
Sam Houston State Univ	TX	8,000	C
Samford Univ	AL	20,258	VC
San Diego State Univ	CA	12,971	C
San Francisco State Univ	CA	13,000	C
San Jose State Univ	CA	11,707	C
Santa Clara Univ	CA	38,931	VC
Savannah State Univ	GA	7,772	LC
Schreiner Univ	TX	20,600	C
Seattle Pacific Univ	WA	29,355	C
Seattle Univ	WA	30,063	VC
Seton Hall Univ	NJ	33,622	VC
Seton Hill Univ	PA	28,810	C
Shaw Univ	NC	15,488	LC
Shepherd Univ	WV	10,066	C
Shippensburg Univ of Pennsylvania	PA	11,621	C
Shorter College	GA	19,700	C
Siena College	NY	28,260	VC+
Siena Heights Univ	MI	17,000	LC
Silver Lake College of the Holy Family	WI	18,500	LC
Simpson College	IA	26,833	VC
Simpson Univ	CA	22,900	C
Slippery Rock Univ of Pennsylvania	PA	10,360	LC
S Car State Univ	SC	6,700	LC
Southeast Missouri State Univ	MO	10,596	C
Southeastern Louisiana Univ	LA	8,521	LC
Southeastern Okla State Univ	OK	6,147	C
Southeastern Univ	DC	9,000	NC
Southeastern Univ	FL	17,180	LC
Southern Adventist Univ	TN	18,500	C
Southern Arkansas Univ	AR	6,956	C
Southern Conn State Univ	CT	10,310	C
Southern Illinois Univ Carbondale	IL	12,391	C
Southern Illinois Univ Edwardsville	IL	11,022	C
Southern Methodist Univ	TX	36,088	VC+
Southern Nazarene Univ	OK	14,634	NC
Southern New Hampshire Univ	NH	28,764	C
Southern Oregon Univ	OR	12,186	C
Southern Univ and A&M College	LA	8,238	LC
Southern Univ at New Orleans	LA	1,000	NC
Southern Utah Univ	UT		C
Southern Wesleyan Univ	SC	21,675	C
Southwest Baptist Univ	MO	18,300	C
Southwest Minn State Univ	MN	10,975	C
Southwestern College	KS	21,476	C

ST = STATE   **$IS** = IN-STATE COSTS   **SR** = SELECTOR RATING

School	ST	$IS	SR
Southwestern Okla State Univ	OK	4,801	C
Southwestern Univ	TX	26,767	HC
Spalding Univ	KY	18,882	C
Spring Arbor Univ	MI	22,476	C
Spring Hill College	AL	28,678	C
SUNY at Oswego	NY	13,662	VC
SUNY/College at Brockport	NY	12,747	VC
SUNY/College at Fredonia	NY	12,771	VC
SUNY/College at Geneseo	NY	12,910	HC+
SUNY/College at Old Westbury	NY	13,154	C
SUNY/College at Oneonta	NY	12,905	VC
SUNY/College at Plattsburgh	NY	12,362	C
SUNY/Inst of Technology	NY	12,575	VC
SUNY/Univ at Albany	NY	13,860	VC
SUNY/Univ at Binghamton	NY	13,988	HC
SUNY/Univ at New Paltz	NY	12,480	VC
Stephen F. Austin State Univ	TX	7,930	C
Stephens College	MO	26,930	VC
Stetson Univ	FL	32,725	VC
Stonehill College	MA	36,104	HC
Strayer Univ	DC	8,789	SP
Suffolk Univ	MA	33,160	C
Sul Ross State Univ	TX	6,600	LC
Susquehanna Univ	PA	33,465	VC
Syracuse Univ	NY	38,655	HC
Tabor College	KS	21,614	NC
Talladega College	AL	11,240	LC
Tarleton State Univ	TX	8,952	C
Taylor Univ	IN	26,376	VC+
Temple Univ	PA	17,438	C
Tenn State Univ	TN	9,048	LC
Tenn Tech Univ	TN	10,044	C
Tenn Wesleyan College	TN	18,650	C
Texas A&M Univ	TX	13,351	HC
Texas A&M Univ at Commerce	TX	9,020	C
Texas A&M Univ at Corpus Christi	TX	10,280	LC
Texas A&M Univ at Kingsville	TX	6,800	LC
Texas Christian Univ	TX	23,410	VC+
Texas Lutheran Univ	TX	23,530	C
Texas Southern Univ	TX	9,828	C
Texas State Univ - San Marcos	TX	10,862	C
Texas Tech Univ	TX	13,026	VC
Texas Wesleyan Univ	TX	18,700	C
Texas Woman's Univ	TX	7,804	LC
Thiel College	PA	24,580	C
Thomas College	ME	23,770	LC
Thomas Edison State College	NJ	3,780	SP
Thomas More College	KY	24,470	C
Tiffin Univ	OH	19,490	LC
Touro College	NY	17,000	VC
Towson Univ	MD	13,924	VC
Transylvania Univ	KY	26,240	VC+
Trevecca Nazarene Univ	TN	19,594	C
Trinity Christian College	IL	23,645	C
Trinity International Univ	IL	25,686	C
Tri-State Univ-Main Campus	IN	26,200	C
Troy Univ	AL	8,916	C
Troy Univ Dothan Campus	AL	4,678	C
Troy Univ Montgomery Campus	AL	4,104	NC
Truman State Univ	MO	11,242	HC
Tulane Univ	LA	41,098	MC
Turabo Univ	PR	4,110	
Tuskegee Univ	AL	18,860	LC
Union College	KY	18,920	C
Union College	NE	18,710	C
Union Univ	TN	20,750	VC
Universidad Metropolitana	PR	3,330	
Univ of Akron	OH	15,166	NC
Univ of Alabama	AL	9,888	C
Univ of Alabama at Birmingham	AL	13,716	C
Univ of Alabama in Huntsville	AL	9,516	VC
Univ of Alaska Anchorage	AK	11,275	NC
Univ of Alaska Fairbanks	AK	10,101	C
Univ of Alaska Southeast	AK	8,050	LC
Univ of Arizona	AZ	11,958	VC
Univ of Arkansas	AR	11,859	VC
Univ of Arkansas at Little Rock	AR	7,230	NC
Univ of Arkansas at Monticello	AR	7,325	NC
Univ of Arkansas at Pine Bluff	AR	8,300	C
Univ of Bridgeport	CT	29,595	LC
Univ of Central Arkansas	AR	9,984	C
Univ of Central Florida	FL	10,739	VC
Univ of Central Okla	OK	8,094	C
Univ of Charleston	WV	27,600	C
Univ of Cincinnati	OH	17,682	C
Univ of Colo at Boulder	CO	13,352	C+
Univ of Conn	CT	16,628	HC
Univ of Dayton	OH	28,826	VC
Univ of Delaware	DE	14,142	HC
Univ of Denver	CO	36,376	VC+

School	ST	$IS	SR
Univ of Detroit Mercy	MI	27,000	C
Univ of Dubuque	IA	23,390	C
Univ of Evansville	IN	28,320	VC
Univ of Findlay	OH	29,238	C
Univ of Florida	FL	9,354	HC
Univ of Georgia	GA	11,004	HC
Univ of Great Falls	MT	17,000	C
Univ of Hartford	CT	34,044	C
Univ of Hawaii at Manoa	HI	10,413	VC
Univ of Houston	TX	7,000	C
Univ of Houston-Downtown	TX	3,326	NC
Univ of Idaho	ID	9,310	NC
Univ of Illinois at Chicago	IL	16,256	VC
Univ of Illinois at Urbana-Champaign	IL	15,800	HC+
Univ of Indianapolis	IN	25,090	C
Univ of Iowa	IA	12,172	VC
Univ of Kansas	KS	10,915	VC
Univ of Kentucky	KY	7,800	C
Univ of La Verne	CA	33,470	C
Univ of Louisiana at Lafayette	LA	5,830	C
Univ of Louisiana at Monroe	LA	7,103	C
Univ of Louisville	KY	10,400	VC
Univ of Maine at Augusta	ME	5,025	NC
Univ of Maine at Machias	ME	10,523	C
Univ of Maine at Presque Isle	ME	10,066	LC
Univ of Mary	ND	15,374	C
Univ of Mary Hardin-Baylor	TX	19,428	C
Univ of Maryland/College Park	MD	16,036	HC
Univ of Maryland/Eastern Shore	MD	11,210	C
Univ of Maryland/Univ College	MD	5,640	SP
Univ of Mass Amherst	MA	15,973	C+
Univ of Mass Dartmouth	MA	15,985	C
Univ of Memphis	TN	11,153	C
Univ of Miami	FL	38,397	MC
Univ of Mich/Flint	MI	6,398	C
Univ of Minn/Crookston	MN	13,157	LC
Univ of Minn/Twin Cities	MN	13,165	HC
Univ of Miss	MS	9,000	C
Univ of Missouri/Columbia	MO	13,500	VC
Univ of Missouri/Kansas City	MO	15,000	VC
Univ of Missouri/St. Louis	MO	14,046	VC
Univ of Mobile	AL	16,880	C
Univ of Montana	MT	10,602	C
Univ of Montevallo	AL	9,630	C
Univ of Nebr at Kearney	NE	9,000	NC
Univ of Nebr at Lincoln	NE	11,401	VC
Univ of Nebr at Omaha	NE	11,235	C
Univ of Nevada/Las Vegas	NV	11,566	C
Univ of Nevada/Reno	NV	12,155	NC
Univ of New Haven	CT	31,794	C
Univ of New Mexico	NM	11,253	C
Univ of New Orleans	LA	7,370	C
Univ of North Alabama	AL	8,992	C
Univ of N Car at Asheville	NC	9,237	VC
Univ of N Car at Chapel Hill	NC	11,129	MC
Univ of N Car at Charlotte	NC	9,101	C
Univ of N Car at Greensboro	NC	8,993	C
Univ of N Car at Pembroke	NC	7,940	LC
Univ of N Car at Wilmington	NC	10,107	VC
Univ of N Dak	ND	10,114	VC
Univ of North Florida	FL	9,908	VC
Univ of North Texas	TX	7,800	C
Univ of Northern Colo	CO	10,249	C
Univ of Northern Iowa	IA	11,133	C
Univ of Notre Dame	IN	39,552	MC
Univ of Okla	OK	10,769	VC+
Univ of Oregon	OR	13,108	VC
Univ of Pennsylvania	PA	41,766	MC
Univ of Pittsburgh at Greensburg	PA	17,640	C
Univ of Pittsburgh at Johnstown	PA	16,740	LC
Univ of Pittsburgh at Pittsburgh	PA	18,866	HC
Univ of Portland	OR	32,300	VC
Univ of PR at Humacao	PR	1,707	
Univ of PR/Arecibo	PR	8,327	
Univ of PR/Bayamon Univ College Campus	PR	1,600	
Univ of PR/Cayey Univ College	PR	1,250	
Univ of PR/Mayaguez	PR	1,250	
Univ of PR/Rio Piedras	PR	5,750	
Univ of Redlands	CA	36,160	VC
Univ of Rhode Island	RI	15,398	C
Univ of Richmond	VA	40,510	MC
Univ of Rio Grande	OH	8,728	NC
Univ of St. Francis	IL	25,430	C
Univ of St. Francis	IN	20,970	C
Univ of St. Mary	KS	18,900	C
Univ of St. Thomas	MN	28,000	VC
Univ of St. Thomas	TX	23,810	VC
Univ of San Diego	CA	40,620	HC
Univ of San Francisco	CA	37,560	VC
Univ of Scranton	PA	31,100	VC
Univ of Sioux Falls	SD	20,800	C
Univ of South Alabama	AL	8,930	LC
Univ of S Car at Columbia	SC	13,397	VC

School	ST	$IS	SR
Univ of S Car Upstate	SC	11,957	C
Univ of S Dak	SD	9,068	C
Univ of South Florida	FL	10,284	VC
Univ of Southern Calif	CA	41,618	MC
Univ of Southern Indiana	IN	12,590	LC
Univ of Southern Maine	ME	12,614	C
Univ of Southern Miss	MS	10,112	C
Univ of Tampa	FL	25,784	C
Univ of Tenn at Knoxville	TN	11,720	C
Univ of Tenn at Martin	TN	8,693	C
Univ of Texas at Arlington	TX	7,195	LC
Univ of Texas at Austin	TX	14,610	HC
Univ of Texas at Dallas	TX	13,244	HC
Univ of Texas at El Paso	TX	8,764	NC
Univ of Texas at San Antonio	TX	11,325	LC
Univ of Texas-Pan American	TX	7,290	C+
Univ of the Cumberlands	KY	18,184	C
Univ of the District of Columbia	DC	2,070	LC
Univ of the Ozarks	AR	19,250	C
Univ of the Sacred Heart	PR	5,590	
Univ of Toledo	OH	15,806	NC
Univ of Tulsa	OK	25,348	HC
Univ of Utah	UT	10,162	C
Univ of Virginia's College at Wise	VA	11,076	C
Univ of Washington	WA	10,400	VC
Univ of West Alabama	AL	7,611	C
Univ of West Florida	FL	8,559	C
Univ of West Georgia	GA	8,838	C
Univ of Wisc/Eau Claire	WI	9,915	VC
Univ of Wisc/Green Bay	WI	9,415	VC
Univ of Wisc/La Crosse	WI	10,045	VC
Univ of Wisc/Madison	WI	13,117	HC
Univ of Wisc/Milwaukee	WI	9,427	LC
Univ of Wisc/Oshkosh	WI	10,426	LC
Univ of Wisc/Platteville	WI	9,779	NC
Univ of Wisc/River Falls	WI	9,722	LC
Univ of Wisc/Stevens Point	WI	9,384	C
Univ of Wisc/Superior	WI	9,610	C+
Univ of Wisc/Whitewater	WI	9,274	C
Univ of Wyoming	WY	9,666	C
Upper Iowa Univ	IA	20,130	C
Ursuline College	OH	25,456	C
Utah State Univ	UT	8,002	VC
Utica College	NY	31,396	C
Valdosta State Univ	GA	8,802	C
Valparaiso Univ	IN	28,970	VC+
Vanguard Univ of Southern Calif	CA	27,071	C
Villanova Univ	PA	38,672	HC+
Virginia Commonwealth Univ	VA	12,987	C
Virginia Polytechnic Inst and State Univ	VA	10,834	VC
Virginia State Univ	VA	11,318	C
Virginia Union Univ	VA	18,432	LC
Viterbo Univ	WI	21,670	C
Voorhees College	SC	11,800	LC
Wagner College	NY	33,300	VC
Wake Forest Univ	NC	38,290	MC
Walsh Univ	OH	23,440	C
Warner Southern College	FL	18,000	LC
Wartburg College	IA	27,315	NC
Washburn Univ	KS	9,734	NC
Washington and Jefferson College	PA	33,490	VC
Washington and Lee Univ	VA	35,880	MC
Washington State Univ	WA	12,260	C
Washington Univ in St. Louis	MO	42,106	MC
Wayne State Univ	MI	11,905	C
Waynesburg College	PA	21,230	C
Webber International Univ	FL	17,580	LC
Weber State Univ	UT	9,635	NC
Webster Univ	MO	24,280	VC
Wesley College	DE	19,905	C
West Chester Univ of Pennsylvania	PA	12,355	C+
West Liberty State College	WV	9,142	LC
West Texas A&M Univ	TX	8,452	C
West Virginia State Univ	WV	8,378	NC
West Virginia Univ	WV	10,506	C
West Virginia Univ Inst of Technology	WV	8,788	NC
West Virginia Wesleyan College	WV	26,880	C
Western Baptist College	OR	21,808	C
Western Carolina Univ	NC	7,000	C
Western Conn State Univ	CT	12,993	C
Western Illinois Univ	IL	13,042	C
Western Kentucky Univ	KY	10,192	C
Western Mich Univ	MI	13,299	C
Western New England College	MA	32,054	C
Western New Mexico Univ	NM	7,233	LC
Western State College of Colo	CO	9,942	C
Western Washington Univ	WA	11,262	VC
Westminster College	MO	19,060	VC
Westminster College	PA	31,290	C+
Westminster College	UT	25,656	C
Wheeling Jesuit Univ	WV	26,910	C
Whitworth College	WA	29,428	VC+

School	ST	$IS	SR
Wichita State Univ	KS	8,500	C
Widener Univ	PA	27,275	C
Wilberforce Univ	OH	14,937	LC
Wilkes Univ	PA	30,886	C
William Jewell College	MO	24,340	C
William Paterson Univ of New Jersey	NJ	17,810	C+
William Penn Univ	IA	17,685	C
William Woods Univ	MO	21,020	C
Wilmington College	DE	5,594	NC
Wilmington College	OH	2,806	NC
Wilson College	PA	27,660	C
Wingate Univ	NC	23,300	C
Winona State Univ	MN	11,333	C
Winston-Salem State Univ	NC	8,960	LC
Wofford College	SC	30,935	HC
Woodbury Univ	CA	30,176	LC
Wright State Univ	OH	13,616	C
Xavier Univ	OH	30,490	HC
Xavier Univ of Louisiana	LA	17,600	C
Yeshiva Univ	NY	22,000	C
York College	NE	16,330	NC
York College of Pennsylvania	PA	16,550	VC
Youngstown State Univ	OH	12,613	NC

ACTUARIAL SCIENCE

School	ST	$IS	SR
Ball State Univ	IN	13,138	C
Bellarmine Univ	KY	27,650	C+
Bradley Univ	IL	25,280	VC
Brigham Young Univ	UT	9,200	VC
Butler Univ	IN	31,944	VC+
Carroll College	WI	24,860	C
Central Mich Univ	MI	12,244	C
Central Missouri State Univ	MO	10,000	C
Central Washington Univ	WA	11,730	C
CUNY/Baruch College	NY	4,320	VC+
CUNY/Queens College	NY	4,356	C
Drake Univ	IA	27,632	VC+
Eastern Mich Univ	MI	12,897	C
Elizabethtown College	PA	32,100	VC
Florida A&M Univ	FL	8,344	C
Florida State Univ	FL	9,028	HC
Georgia State Univ	GA	11,444	VC
Indiana Univ Northwest	IN	4,902	LC
Indiana Univ South Bend	IN	4,989	LC
Kent State Univ	OH	14,594	C
Lebanon Valley College	PA	31,700	VC
Lincoln Univ	PA	13,658	C+
Maryville Univ of St. Louis	MO	23,000	VC
Missouri Valley College	MO	18,500	C
New York Univ	NY	43,170	MC
North Central College	IL	28,926	VC
N Dak State Univ	ND	8,500	C
Northwestern College of Iowa	IA	22,174	C+
Ohio State Univ	OH	15,357	HC
Ohio Univ	OH	15,921	C
Penn State Univ/Univ Park Campus	PA	18,038	HC
Purdue Univ/West Lafayette	IN	13,458	VC
Rider Univ	NJ	32,560	C
Robert Morris Univ	PA	22,822	C
Roosevelt Univ	IL	22,605	VC
St. John's Univ	NY	34,370	C
St. Joseph's Univ	PA	37,428	VC
Seton Hill Univ	PA	28,810	C
Southern Adventist Univ	TN	18,500	C
SUNY/Univ at Albany	NY	13,860	VC
SUNY/Univ at Binghamton	NY	13,988	HC
Temple Univ	PA	17,438	C
Thiel College	PA	24,580	C
Univ of Central Okla	OK	8,094	C
Univ of Illinois at Urbana-Champaign	IL	15,800	HC+
Univ of Iowa	IA	12,172	VC
Univ of Minn/Twin Cities	MN	13,165	HC
Univ of Nebr at Lincoln	NE	11,401	VC
Univ of Pennsylvania	PA	41,766	MC
Univ of St. Thomas	MN	28,000	VC
Univ of Texas at San Antonio	TX	11,325	LC
Univ of Wisc/Madison	WI	13,117	HC
Valparaiso Univ	IN	28,970	VC+
Worcester Polytechnic Inst	MA	40,450	VC+

ADDICTION STUDIES

School	ST	$IS	SR
Alvernia College	PA	26,388	C
Graceland Univ	IA	19,700	C
Indiana Wesleyan Univ	IN	22,074	C+
Kansas Wesleyan Univ	KS	21,400	VC
Kent State Univ	OH	14,594	C
Metropolitan State Univ	MN	4,682	SP
Minot State Univ	ND	6,700	LC
Missouri Valley College	MO	18,500	C
Northwestern State Univ of Louisiana	LA	7,144	C
Southern Univ at New Orleans	LA	1,000	NC
Univ of Central Okla	OK	8,094	C
Univ of Detroit Mercy	MI	27,000	C
Univ of Mary	ND	15,374	C
Univ of S Dak	SD	9,068	C

ST = STATE   **$IS** = IN-STATE COSTS   **SR** = SELECTOR RATING

School	ST	$IS	SR
Univ of Memphis	TN	11,153	C
Univ of Miami	FL	38,397	MC
Univ of Mich/Ann Arbor	MI	16,587	HC+
Univ of Minn/Twin Cities	MN	13,165	HC
Univ of Nebr at Omaha	NE	11,235	C
Univ of New Mexico	NM	11,253	C
Univ of N Car at Chapel Hill	NC	11,129	MC
Univ of N Car at Charlotte	NC	9,101	C
Univ of N Car at Greensboro	NC	8,993	C
Univ of Northern Colo	CO	10,249	C
Univ of Okla	OK	10,769	VC+
Univ of Pennsylvania	PA	41,766	MC
Univ of Pittsburgh at Pittsburgh	PA	18,866	HC
Univ of S Car at Columbia	SC	13,397	VC
Univ of South Florida	FL	10,284	VC
Univ of Southern Calif	CA	41,618	MC
Univ of Tenn at Knoxville	TN	11,720	C
Univ of Virginia	VA	13,759	MC
Univ of Washington	WA	10,400	VC
Univ of Wisc/Madison	WI	13,117	HC
Univ of Wisc/Milwaukee	WI	9,427	LC
Vanderbilt Univ	TN	41,986	MC
Virginia Commonwealth Univ	VA	12,987	C
Washington Univ in St. Louis	MO	42,106	MC
Wellesley College	MA	41,030	MC
Wesleyan Univ	CT	42,122	MC
William Paterson Univ of New Jersey	NJ	17,810	C+
Yale Univ	CT	41,000	MC

AFRICAN LANGUAGES

School	ST	$IS	SR
Duke Univ	NC	41,239	MC
Univ of Calif at Los Angeles	CA	17,681	VC
Univ of Wisc/Madison	WI	13,117	HC

AFRICAN STUDIES

School	ST	$IS	SR
Bard College	NY	41,800	HC+
Bowdoin College	ME	41,660	MC
Bowling Green State Univ	OH	14,994	C
Brandeis Univ	MA	41,551	MC
Brown Univ	RI	42,015	MC
Cal State, Dominguez Hills	CA	10,220	LC
Carleton College	MN	40,467	MC
CUNY/Brooklyn College	NY	4,377	C+
CUNY/Queens College	NY	4,356	C
Colgate Univ	NY	41,170	MC
Conn College	CT	41,975	MC
Cornell Univ	NY	41,717	MC
Creighton Univ	NE	29,918	VC+
Dartmouth College	NH	39,465	MC
Dillard Univ	LA	17,500	VC
Drew Univ/College of Liberal Arts	NJ	39,698	VC
Duke Univ	NC	41,239	MC
Emory Univ	GA	40,546	MC
Fordham Univ	NY	36,000	MC
Franklin and Marshall College	PA	40,590	HC
Hamilton College	NY	41,660	MC
Hampshire College	MA	37,120	HC
Hobart and William Smith Colleges	NY	41,123	VC
Hofstra Univ	NY	32,630	VC
Howard Univ	DC	18,481	C+
Johns Hopkins Univ	MD	42,044	MC
Lafayette College	PA	39,267	MC
Lehigh Univ	PA	42,690	HC+
New York Univ	NY	43,170	MC
Ohio Univ	OH	15,921	C
St. Lawrence Univ	NY	40,545	VC
San Diego State Univ	CA	12,971	C
Shaw Univ	NC	15,488	LC
SUNY/College at Brockport	NY	12,747	VC
SUNY/College at Oneonta	NY	12,905	VC
SUNY/Univ at Stony Brook	NY	13,625	HC
Tenn State Univ	TN	9,048	LC
Tulane Univ	LA	41,098	MC
Univ of at Calif Davis	CA	15,010	VC
Univ of Kansas	KS	10,915	VC
Univ of Louisville	KY	10,400	VC
Univ of Mich/Ann Arbor	MI	16,587	HC+
Univ of Minn/Twin Cities	MN	13,165	HC
Univ of N Car at Chapel Hill	NC	11,129	MC
Univ of Pennsylvania	PA	41,766	MC
Univ of Pittsburgh at Pittsburgh	PA	18,866	HC
Vassar College	NY	41,700	MC
Washington Univ in St. Louis	MO	42,106	MC
Wayne State Univ	MI	11,805	C
Western Mich Univ	MI	13,299	C
Youngstown State Univ	OH	12,613	NC

AGRICULTURAL BUSINESS MANAGEMENT

School	ST	$IS	SR
Alabama A&M Univ	AL	8,890	LC
Angelo State Univ	TX	8,340	NC
Arkansas State Univ	AR	9,630	C
Arkansas Tech Univ	AR	8,108	VC
Auburn Univ	AL	12,230	VC
Brigham Young Univ	UT	9,200	VC
Calif Polytechnic State Univ	CA	12,390	VC
Calif State Polytechnic Univ, Pomona	CA	18,053	C+
Cal State, Chico	CA	11,395	C
Cal State, Fresno	CA	10,037	LC
Central Missouri State Univ	MO	10,000	C
College of the Ozarks	MO	4,130	VC+
Colo State Univ-Fort Collins	CO	10,878	C+
Cornell Univ	NY	41,717	MC
Delaware State Univ	DE	8,130	C
Dickinson State Univ	ND	7,847	NC
Eastern New Mexico Univ	NM	7,264	C
Eastern Oregon Univ	OR	10,400	NC
Fort Hays State Univ	KS	7,638	C
Freed-Hardeman Univ	TN	16,370	NC
Hardin-Simmons Univ	TX	18,641	C
Iowa State Univ	IA	11,831	VC
Kansas State Univ	KS	10,516	VC
Lindenwood Univ	MO	18,600	VC
Louisiana State Univ and A&M College	LA	10,749	VC
Louisiana Tech Univ	LA	7,370	C
Lubbock Christian Univ	TX	16,960	C
McNeese State Univ	LA	5,270	C
Middle Tenn State Univ	TN	8,540	C
Miss State Univ	MS	9,577	C
Missouri Valley College	MO	18,500	C
Montana State Univ-Bozeman	MT	1,137	C
New Mexico State Univ	NM	9,250	C
Nicholls State Univ	LA	6,500	NC
N Car Agricultural and Technical State Univ	NC	8,000	LC
N Car State Univ	NC	11,824	HC
N Dak State Univ	ND	8,500	C
Northwest Missouri State Univ	MO	10,000	C
Northwestern College of Iowa	IA	22,174	C+
Northwestern Okla State Univ	OK	6,250	NC
Okla Panhandle State Univ	OK	7,635	NC
Okla State Univ	OK	10,213	VC
Oregon State Univ	OR	11,055	C
Penn State Univ/Univ Park Campus	PA	18,038	HC
Prairie View A&M Univ	TX	11,110	LC
Purdue Univ/West Lafayette	IN	13,458	VC
S Car State Univ	SC	6,700	LC
S Dak State Univ	SD	9,815	C
Southeast Missouri State Univ	MO	10,596	C
Southern Arkansas Univ	AR	6,956	C
Southwest Minn State Univ	MN	10,975	C
SUNY/College of Agriculture and Technology at Cobleskill	NY	12,915	C
Stephen F. Austin State Univ	TX	7,930	C
Sul Ross State Univ	TX	6,600	LC
Tarleton State Univ	TX	8,952	C
Texas A&M Univ	TX	13,351	HC
Texas A&M Univ at Kingsville	TX	6,800	LC
Texas State Univ - San Marcos	TX	10,862	C
Texas Tech Univ	TX	13,026	VC
Univ of Arkansas	AR	11,859	VC
Univ of at Calif Davis	CA	15,010	VC
Univ of Delaware	DE	14,142	HC
Univ of Florida	FL	9,354	HC
Univ of Georgia	GA	11,004	HC
Univ of Idaho	ID	9,310	NC
Univ of Illinois at Urbana-Champaign	IL	15,800	HC+
Univ of Louisiana at Monroe	LA	7,103	C
Univ of Maryland/College Park	MD	16,036	HC
Univ of Minn/Crookston	MN	13,157	LC
Univ of Minn/Twin Cities	MN	13,165	HC
Univ of Missouri/Columbia	MO	13,500	VC
Univ of Nebr at Lincoln	NE	11,401	VC
Univ of Tenn at Martin	TN	8,693	C
Univ of Wisc/Madison	WI	13,117	HC
Univ of Wisc/Platteville	WI	9,779	NC
Univ of Wisc/River Falls	WI	9,722	LC
Univ of Wyoming	WY	9,666	C
Utah State Univ	UT	8,002	VC
Washington State Univ	WA	12,260	C
West Texas A&M Univ	TX	8,452	C
West Virginia Univ	WV	10,506	C

AGRICULTURAL COMMUNICATIONS

School	ST	$IS	SR
Texas Tech Univ	TX	13,026	VC
Univ of Georgia	GA	11,004	HC
Univ of Illinois at Urbana-Champaign	IL	15,800	HC+
Univ of Nebr at Lincoln	NE	11,401	VC
Univ of Wyoming	WY	9,666	C

AGRICULTURAL ECONOMICS

School	ST	$IS	SR
Alabama A&M Univ	AL	8,890	LC
Alcorn State Univ	MS	8,190	LC
Central Missouri State Univ	MO	10,000	C
Colo State Univ-Fort Collins	CO	10,878	C+
Cornell Univ	NY	41,717	MC
Eastern Oregon Univ	OR	10,400	NC
Fort Valley State Univ	GA	6,975	C
Kansas State Univ	KS	10,516	VC
Langston Univ	OK	2,308	LC
McPherson College	KS	21,010	C
Miss State Univ	MS	9,577	C
New Mexico State Univ	NM	9,250	C
N Car Agricultural and Technical State Univ	NC	8,000	LC
N Car State Univ	NC	11,824	HC
N Dak State Univ	ND	8,500	C
Ohio State Univ	OH	15,357	HC
Okla State Univ	OK	10,213	VC
Oregon State Univ	OR	11,055	C
Prairie View A&M Univ	TX	11,110	LC
Purdue Univ/West Lafayette	IN	13,458	VC
S Dak State Univ	SD	9,815	C
Southern Illinois Univ Carbondale	IL	12,391	C
Southern Univ and A&M College	LA	8,238	LC
Tarleton State Univ	TX	8,952	C
Tenn Tech Univ	TN	10,044	C
Texas A&M Univ	TX	13,351	HC
Texas A&M Univ at Commerce	TX	9,020	C
Texas Tech Univ	TX	13,026	VC
Truman State Univ	MO	11,242	HC
Univ of Arizona	AZ	11,958	VC
Univ of Arkansas	AR	11,859	VC
Univ of at Calif Davis	CA	15,010	VC
Univ of Conn	CT	16,628	HC
Univ of Delaware	DE	14,142	HC
Univ of Georgia	GA	11,004	HC
Univ of Idaho	ID	9,310	NC
Univ of Illinois at Urbana-Champaign	IL	15,800	HC+
Univ of Kentucky	KY	7,800	C
Univ of Maryland/College Park	MD	16,036	HC
Univ of Minn/Twin Cities	MN	13,165	HC
Univ of Missouri/Columbia	MO	13,500	VC
Univ of Nebr at Lincoln	NE	11,401	VC
Univ of Nevada/Reno	NV	12,155	NC
Univ of Tenn at Knoxville	TN	11,720	C
Univ of Wisc/Madison	WI	13,117	HC
Utah State Univ	UT	8,002	VC
Virginia Polytechnic Inst and State Univ	VA	10,834	VC
Washington State Univ	WA	12,260	C
West Texas A&M Univ	TX	8,452	C

AGRICULTURAL EDUCATION

School	ST	$IS	SR
Alabama A&M Univ	AL	8,890	LC
Arkansas State Univ	AR	9,630	C
Cal State, Fresno	CA	10,037	LC
Central Missouri State Univ	MO	10,000	C
Clemson Univ	SC	13,366	HC
College of the Ozarks	MO	4,130	VC+
Colo State Univ-Fort Collins	CO	10,878	C+
Delaware State Univ	DE	8,130	C
Eastern New Mexico Univ	NM	7,264	C
Fort Valley State Univ	GA	6,975	C
Iowa State Univ	IA	11,831	VC
Kansas State Univ	KS	10,516	VC
Kent State Univ	OH	14,594	C
Mich State Univ	MI	13,689	VC
Miss State Univ	MS	9,577	C
Missouri State Univ	MO	10,748	C+
Montana State Univ-Bozeman	MT	1,137	C
Morehead State Univ	KY	9,150	C
Murray State Univ	KY	8,900	VC
New Mexico State Univ	NM	9,250	C
N Car Agricultural and Technical State Univ	NC	8,000	LC
N Car State Univ	NC	11,824	HC
N Dak State Univ	ND	8,500	C
Northwest Missouri State Univ	MO	10,000	C
Ohio State Univ	OH	15,357	HC
Okla Panhandle State Univ	OK	7,635	NC
Okla State Univ	OK	10,213	VC
Penn State Univ/Univ Park Campus	PA	18,038	HC
Purdue Univ/West Lafayette	IN	13,458	VC
S Dak State Univ	SD	9,815	C
Southern Arkansas Univ	AR	6,956	C
SUNY at Oswego	NY	13,662	VC
Stephen F. Austin State Univ	TX	7,930	C
Tarleton State Univ	TX	8,952	C
Tenn Tech Univ	TN	10,044	C
Texas A&M Univ at Commerce	TX	9,020	C
Texas A&M Univ at Kingsville	TX	6,800	LC
Univ of Arizona	AZ	11,958	VC
Univ of Arkansas	AR	11,859	VC
Univ of Arkansas at Pine Bluff	AR	8,300	C
Univ of Conn	CT	16,628	HC
Univ of Delaware	DE	14,142	HC
Univ of Florida	FL	9,354	HC
Univ of Georgia	GA	11,004	HC
Univ of Idaho	ID	9,310	NC
Univ of Illinois at Urbana-Champaign	IL	15,800	HC+
Univ of Kentucky	KY	7,800	C
Univ of Louisiana at Lafayette	LA	5,830	C
Univ of Maryland/Eastern Shore	MD	11,210	C
Univ of Minn/Crookston	MN	13,157	LC
Univ of Minn/Twin Cities	MN	13,165	HC
Univ of Nebr at Lincoln	NE	11,401	VC
Univ of Tenn at Knoxville	TN	11,720	C
Univ of Wisc/Madison	WI	13,117	HC
Univ of Wisc/Platteville	WI	9,779	NC
Univ of Wisc/River Falls	WI	9,722	LC
Univ of Wyoming	WY	9,666	C
Utah State Univ	UT	8,002	VC
Virginia Polytechnic Inst and State Univ	VA	10,834	VC
Washington State Univ	WA	12,260	C
West Virginia Univ	WV	10,506	C

AGRICULTURAL ENGINEERING

School	ST	$IS	SR
Auburn Univ	AL	12,230	VC
Calif Polytechnic State Univ	CA	12,390	VC
Clemson Univ	SC	13,366	HC
Colo State Univ-Fort Collins	CO	10,878	C+
Cornell Univ	NY	41,717	MC
Iowa State Univ	IA	11,831	VC
Kansas State Univ	KS	10,516	VC
N Car State Univ	NC	11,824	HC
N Dak State Univ	ND	8,500	C
Penn State Univ/Univ Park Campus	PA	18,038	HC
S Dak State Univ	SD	9,815	C
Texas A&M Univ	TX	13,351	HC
Univ of Arkansas	AR	11,859	VC
Univ of at Calif Davis	CA	15,010	VC
Univ of Florida	FL	9,354	HC
Univ of Georgia	GA	11,004	HC
Univ of Idaho	ID	9,310	NC
Univ of Illinois at Urbana-Champaign	IL	15,800	HC+
Univ of Minn/Twin Cities	MN	13,165	HC
Univ of Nebr at Lincoln	NE	11,401	VC
Univ of Tenn at Knoxville	TN	11,720	C
Univ of Wisc/River Falls	WI	9,722	LC
Utah State Univ	UT	8,002	VC
Virginia Polytechnic Inst and State Univ	VA	10,834	VC
Washington State Univ	WA	12,260	C

AGRICULTURAL ENGINEERING TECHNOLOGY

School	ST	$IS	SR
Central Missouri State Univ	MO	10,000	C
Fort Valley State Univ	GA	6,975	C
Kansas State Univ	KS	10,516	VC
Miss State Univ	MS	9,577	C
Montana State Univ-Bozeman	MT	1,137	C
S Dak State Univ	SD	9,815	C
Univ of Arizona	AZ	11,958	VC

AGRICULTURAL MECHANICS

School	ST	$IS	SR
Montana State Univ-Northern	MT	10,000	NC
Murray State Univ	KY	8,900	VC
N Dak State Univ	ND	8,500	C
Northwest Missouri State Univ	MO	10,000	C
Purdue Univ/West Lafayette	IN	13,458	VC
SUNY/College of Agriculture and Technology at Cobleskill	NY	12,915	C
Stephen F. Austin State Univ	TX	7,930	C
Tarleton State Univ	TX	8,952	C
Univ of Idaho	ID	9,310	NC
Univ of Illinois at Urbana-Champaign	IL	15,800	HC+
Univ of Nebr at Lincoln	NE	11,401	VC
Washington State Univ	WA	12,260	C

AGRICULTURE

School	ST	$IS	SR
Alcorn State Univ	MS	8,190	LC
Andrews Univ	MI	21,786	C
Arkansas State Univ	AR	9,630	C
Auburn Univ	AL	12,230	VC
Austin Peay State Univ	TN	7,535	C
Berea College	KY	5,496	VC+

School	ST	$IS	SR
Calif Polytechnic State Univ	CA	12,390	VC
Calif State Polytechnic Univ, Pomona	CA	18,053	C+
Cal State, Chico	CA	11,395	C
Cal State, Stanislaus	CA	11,283	C
Cameron Univ	OK	6,314	NC
Clemson Univ	SC	13,366	HC
College of the Ozarks	MO	4,130	VC+
Cornell Univ	NY	41,717	MC
Eastern Kentucky Univ	KY	7,725	C
Eastern New Mexico Univ	NM	7,264	C
Ferrum College	VA	24,290	LC
Fort Hays State Univ	KS	7,638	C
Hampshire College	MA	37,120	HC
Hardin-Simmons Univ	TX	18,641	C
Illinois State Univ	IL	12,839	C+
Iowa State Univ	IA	11,831	C
Lincoln Univ	MO	8,000	NC
McNeese State Univ	LA	5,270	C
Mich State Univ	MI	13,689	VC
Miss State Univ	MS	9,577	C
Missouri State Univ	MO	10,748	C
Morehead State Univ	KY	9,150	C
Murray State Univ	KY	8,900	VC
New Mexico State Univ	NM	9,250	C
N Car State Univ	NC	11,824	HC
N Dak State Univ	ND	8,500	C
Northwest Missouri State Univ	MO	10,000	C
Northwestern Okla State Univ	OK	6,250	NC
Oregon State Univ	OR	11,055	C
Penn State Univ/Univ Park Campus	PA	18,038	HC
Purdue Univ/West Lafayette	IN	13,458	VC
Rutgers, The State Univ of New Jersey/New Brunswick/Piscataway Campus	NJ	15,810	HC
Sam Houston State Univ	TX	8,000	C
S Dak State Univ	SD	9,815	C
Southeast Missouri State Univ	MO	10,596	C
Southern Arkansas Univ	AR	6,956	C
Southern Illinois Univ Carbondale	IL	12,391	C
Southern Nazarene Univ	OK	14,634	NC
Southern Univ and A&M College	LA	8,238	LC
Southern Utah Univ	UT		C
Stephen F. Austin State Univ	TX	7,930	C
Tarleton State Univ	TX	8,952	C
Tenn State Univ	TN	9,048	LC
Tenn Tech Univ	TN	10,044	C
Texas A&M Univ at Commerce	TX	9,020	C
Texas State Univ - San Marcos	TX	10,862	C
Truman State Univ	MO	11,242	HC
Univ of Arkansas at Monticello	AR	7,325	NC
Univ of Arkansas at Pine Bluff	AR	8,300	C
Univ of Conn	CT	16,628	HC
Univ of Delaware	DE	14,142	HC
Univ of Hawaii at Hilo	HI	6,500	C
Univ of Idaho	ID	9,310	NC
Univ of Kentucky	KY	7,800	C
Univ of Maine	ME	13,642	C
Univ of Maryland/College Park	MD	16,036	HC
Univ of Maryland/Eastern Shore	MD	11,210	C
Univ of Missouri/Columbia	MO	13,500	VC
Univ of Nebr at Lincoln	NE	11,401	VC
Univ of Tenn at Knoxville	TN	11,720	C
Univ of Tenn at Martin	TN	8,693	C
Univ of Vermont	VT	18,080	VC
Univ of Wyoming	WY	9,666	C
Virginia State Univ	VA	11,318	C
Washington State Univ	WA	12,260	C
West Texas A&M Univ	TX	8,452	C
West Virginia Univ	WV	10,506	C
Western Illinois Univ	IL	13,042	C
Western Kentucky Univ	KY	10,192	C
Wilmington College	OH	2,806	NC

AGRONOMY

School	ST	$IS	SR
Alabama A&M Univ	AL	8,890	LC
Calif State Polytechnic Univ, Pomona	CA	18,053	C+
College of the Ozarks	MO	4,130	VC+
Colo State Univ-Fort Collins	CO	10,878	C+
Cornell Univ	NY	41,717	MC
Delaware Valley College	PA	29,944	C
Iowa State Univ	IA	11,831	VC
Kansas State Univ	KS	10,516	VC
McPherson College	KS	21,010	C
Miss State Univ	MS	9,577	C
Missouri State Univ	MO	10,748	C+
New Mexico State Univ	NM	9,250	C
N Car State Univ	NC	11,824	HC
Northwest Missouri State Univ	MO	10,000	C
Okla Panhandle State Univ	OK	7,635	NC
Penn State Univ/Univ Park Campus	PA	18,038	HC
Prairie View A&M Univ	TX	11,110	LC
Purdue Univ/West Lafayette	IN	13,458	VC
S Dak State Univ	SD	9,815	C
Southeast Missouri State Univ	MO	10,596	C
Stephen F. Austin State Univ	TX	7,930	C
Tarleton State Univ	TX	8,952	C
Texas Tech Univ	TX	13,026	VC
Truman State Univ	MO	11,242	HC
Univ of Conn	CT	16,628	HC
Univ of Florida	FL	9,354	HC
Univ of Illinois at Urbana-Champaign	IL	15,800	HC+
Univ of Nebr at Lincoln	NE	11,401	VC
Univ of Wisc/River Falls	WI	9,722	LC
Univ of Wyoming	WY	9,666	C
Washington State Univ	WA	12,260	C
West Virginia Univ	WV	10,506	C

AIR TRAFFIC CONTROL

School	ST	$IS	SR
Daniel Webster College	NH	24,870	C
Embry-Riddle Aeronautical Univ	FL	30,280	C
Florida Memorial College	FL	6,000	LC
Thomas Edison State College	NJ	3,780	SP
Univ of N Dak	ND	10,114	VC

AIRCRAFT MECHANICS

School	ST	$IS	SR
Andrews Univ	MI	21,786	C
Averett Univ	VA	24,920	C
Kent State Univ	OH	14,594	C
Lewis Univ	IL	23,050	C+
Pennsylvania College of Technology	PA	16,980	LC
St. Louis Univ	MO	33,158	VC+
Vaughn College of Aeronautics and Technology	NY	13,680	SP
Western Mich Univ	MI	13,299	C

AIRLINE PILOTING AND NAVIGATION

School	ST	$IS	SR
Averett Univ	VA	24,920	C
Baylor Univ	TX	27,555	HC
Daniel Webster College	NH	24,870	C
Eastern Kentucky Univ	KY	7,725	C
Indiana State Univ	IN	11,604	C
Kansas State Univ	KS	10,516	VC
Lewis Univ	IL	23,050	C+
Louisiana Tech Univ	LA	7,370	C
Metropolitan State College of Denver	CO	2,338	LC
Ohio Univ	OH	15,921	C
Pacific Union College	CA	24,555	VC+
Univ of Illinois at Urbana-Champaign	IL	15,800	HC+
Univ of N Dak	ND	10,114	VC
Univ of Texas at Dallas	TX	13,244	HC
Vaughn College of Aeronautics and Technology	NY	13,680	SP
Western Mich Univ	MI	13,299	C

ALLIED HEALTH

School	ST	$IS	SR
Adams State College	CO	8,613	C
Albany State Univ	GA	5,770	C+
Andrews Univ	MI	21,786	C
Bloomfield College	NJ	22,500	LC
Bridgewater College	VA	27,790	C
Clark Atlanta Univ	GA	20,960	LC
Clayton College and State Univ	GA	2,445	LC
College of Mount St. Vincent	NY	28,000	C
East Stroudsburg Univ of Pennsylvania	PA	10,336	C
East Tenn State Univ	TN	8,497	C
Eastern Mich Univ	MI	12,897	C
Elizabethtown College	PA	32,100	VC
Fairleigh Dickinson Univ/College at Florham	NJ	30,130	C
Fairleigh Dickinson Univ/Metropolitan Campus	NJ	28,590	C
Hofstra Univ	NY	32,630	VC
Indiana Univ South Bend	IN	4,989	LC
Ithaca College	NY	35,144	VC
Johnson State College	VT	11,830	LC
Kent State Univ	OH	14,594	C
Madonna Univ	MI	16,068	VC
Mars Hill College	NC	19,000	LC
Merrimack College	MA	34,380	C
Montclair State Univ	NJ	16,327	C
National American Univ	SD	14,820	NC
National Univ	CA	8,412	SP
Ramapo College of New Jersey	NJ	16,630	VC
Rochester Inst of Technology	NY	32,070	VC+
Roosevelt Univ	IL	22,605	VC
Rutgers, The State Univ of New Jersey/Newark Campus	NJ	15,640	VC
Saginaw Valley State Univ	MI	11,432	C
San Francisco State Univ	CA	13,000	C
Univ of Florida	FL	9,354	HC
Univ of Northern Colo	CO	10,249	C
Univ of St. Francis	IL	25,430	C
Univ of Texas at El Paso	TX	8,764	NC
Ursuline College	OH	25,456	C
West Texas A&M Univ	TX	8,452	C
Youngstown State Univ	OH	12,613	NC

AMERICAN INDIAN STUDIES

School	ST	$IS	SR
Arizona State Univ-Tempe	AZ	11,174	C
Black Hills State Univ	SD	7,800	LC
Sonoma State Univ	CA	14,732	C
Univ of Calif at Los Angeles	CA	17,681	MC
Univ of Minn/Twin Cities	MN	13,165	HC
Univ of N Car at Pembroke	NC	7,940	LC
Univ of N Dak	ND	10,114	VC
Univ of Science and Arts of Okla	OK	7,650	C
Univ of S Dak	SD	9,068	C
Univ of Wisc/Eau Claire	WI	9,915	VC

AMERICAN LITERATURE

School	ST	$IS	SR
Bard College	NY	41,800	HC+
Bennington College	VT	41,890	HC
Blackburn College	IL	13,690	C
Brandeis Univ	MA	41,551	MC
Brown Univ	RI	42,015	MC
Eastern Mich Univ	MI	12,897	C
Florida State Univ	FL	9,028	HC
Hofstra Univ	NY	32,630	VC
Middlebury College	VT	42,120	MC
New York Univ	NY	43,170	MC
Univ of Calif at Los Angeles	CA	17,681	MC
Univ of Southern Calif	CA	41,618	MC
Washington Univ in St. Louis	MO	42,106	MC

AMERICAN SIGN LANGUAGE

School	ST	$IS	SR
College of St. Catherine	MN	27,505	VC
Gardner-Webb Univ	NC	21,500	C
Goshen College	IN	22,850	VC
Indiana Univ-Purdue Univ Indianapolis	IN	10,959	C
Keuka College	NY	26,050	C
Maryville College	TN	29,224	VC
Univ of New Mexico	NM	11,253	C
Univ of Rochester	NY	41,135	MC
Valdosta State Univ	GA	8,802	C
Western Oregon Univ	OR	10,295	C

AMERICAN STUDIES

School	ST	$IS	SR
Albion College	MI	26,000	VC
Albright College	PA	33,920	C
American Univ	DC	38,719	HC+
Amherst College	MA	41,590	MC
Ashland Univ	OH	25,000	C
Austin College	TX	27,871	HC
Bard College	NY	41,800	HC+
Bates College	ME	42,100	MC
Baylor Univ	TX	27,555	HC
Boston Univ	MA	42,046	HC+
Bowling Green State Univ	OH	14,994	C
Brandeis Univ	MA	41,551	MC
Brigham Young Univ	UT	9,200	VC
Brown Univ	RI	42,015	MC
Cabrini College	PA	33,340	C
Cal State, Chico	CA	11,395	C
Cal State, Fullerton	CA	10,990	C
Cal State, San Bernardino	CA	12,563	C
Carleton College	MN	40,467	MC
Case Western Reserve Univ	OH	37,314	MC
Cedarville Univ	OH	21,904	VC
CUNY/Brooklyn College	NY	4,377	C+
CUNY/City College	NY		C
CUNY/College of Staten Island	NY	4,328	NC
CUNY/Herbert H. Lehman College	NY	4,000	LC
CUNY/Queens College	NY	4,356	C
Claflin Univ	SC	16,798	C+
Claremont McKenna College	CA	42,920	MC
Coe College	IA	27,440	VC
Colby College	ME	41,770	MC
College of Our Lady of the Elms	MA	21,000	C
College of St. Elizabeth	NJ	28,495	C
College of St. Rose	NY	25,684	C
College of William and Mary	VA	14,147	MC
Columbia Univ/Barnard College	NY	38,000	MC
Columbia Univ/Columbia College	NY	42,584	MC
Conn College	CT	41,975	MC
Cornell Univ	NY	41,717	MC
Creighton Univ	NE	29,918	VC+
Cumberland Univ	TN	18,894	C
DePaul Univ	IL	29,835	VC
Dickinson College	PA	40,170	HC+
Dominican Univ	IL	26,370	C
Eastern Conn State Univ	CT	13,554	C
Eckerd College	FL	35,492	VC
Elmhurst College	IL	24,685	C
Elmira College	NY	37,200	VC
Emmanuel College	MA	32,000	C+
Emory Univ	GA	40,546	MC
Erskine College	SC	25,468	VC
Fairfield Univ	CT	39,835	HC
Florida State Univ	FL	9,028	HC
Fordham Univ	NY	36,000	HC
Franklin and Marshall College	PA	40,590	HC
Franklin College	IN		C
Franklin Pierce College	NH	31,700	C
George Washington Univ	DC	48,820	MC
Georgetown College	KY	24,950	C+
Georgetown Univ	DC	43,183	MC
Goucher College	MD	36,225	VC
Hamilton College	NY	41,660	MC
Hampshire College	MA	37,120	HC
Harding Univ	AR	16,512	VC
Harvard Univ/Harvard College	MA	45,860	MC
Hendrix College	AR	27,646	HC+
High Point Univ	NC	25,720	C
Hillsdale College	MI	24,160	HC
Hobart and William Smith Colleges	NY	41,123	VC
Hofstra Univ	NY	32,630	VC
Huntingdon College	AL	23,090	VC
Idaho State Univ	ID	9,030	C
Illinois Wesleyan Univ	IL	34,050	HC+
Keene State College	NH	13,836	C
Kent State Univ	OH	14,594	C
King College	TN	23,400	C
Knox College	IL	32,385	C+
Lafayette College	PA	39,267	MC
Lake Forest College	IL	33,860	VC
Lebanon Valley College	PA	31,700	VC
Lehigh Univ	PA	42,690	HC+
Lenoir-Rhyne College	NC	25,580	C
Lindsey Wilson College	KY	16,425	LC
Lipscomb Univ	TN	20,967	VC
Macalester College	MN	36,500	MC
Manhattanville College	NY	32,500	C+
Marist College	NY	30,566	VC
Meredith College	NC	25,600	C
Miami Univ	OH	29,097	HC
Mich State Univ	MI	13,689	VC
Middlebury College	VT	42,120	MC
Millikin Univ	IL	25,590	C
Mills College	CA	39,870	C
Minn State Univ, Moorhead	MN	7,000	LC
Miss College	MS	14,574	VC
Montreat College	NC	21,440	C
Mount Holyoke College	MA	42,148	HC+
Mount St. Mary's College	CA	32,086	VC
Mount Union College	OH	25,840	C
Muhlenberg College	PA	36,030	HC+
Muskingum College	OH	22,970	C
Nazareth College of Rochester	NY	28,175	VC
Northwestern Univ	IL	37,595	MC
Oberlin College	OH	40,904	MC
Occidental College	CA	40,185	MC
Oglethorpe Univ	GA	30,300	VC
Okla State Univ	OK	10,213	VC
Oregon State Univ	OR	11,055	C
Penn State Univ/Univ Park Campus	PA	18,038	HC
Pfeiffer Univ	NC	21,900	C
Pitzer College	CA	41,644	HC
Pomona College	CA	40,774	MC
Providence College	RI	34,580	HC
Purdue Univ/West Lafayette	IN	13,458	VC
Queens Univ of Charlotte	NC	24,528	C
Ramapo College of New Jersey	NJ	16,630	VC
Randolph-Macon Woman's College	VA	31,160	VC+
Rider Univ	NJ	32,560	C
Roger Williams Univ	RI	30,500	C
Roosevelt Univ	IL	22,605	VC
Rutgers, The State Univ of New Jersey/New Brunswick/Piscataway Campus	NJ	15,810	HC
Rutgers, The State Univ of New Jersey/Newark Campus	NJ	15,640	C
St. John Fisher College	NY	27,860	C
St. Joseph College	CT	32,050	C
St. Louis Univ	MO	33,158	VC+
St. Michael's College	VT	33,330	VC
St. Olaf College	MN	32,800	HC
St. Peter's College	NJ	30,160	LC
Salem College	NC	26,226	VC+

School	ST	$IS	SR
Salve Regina Univ	RI	33,450	C
San Diego State Univ	CA	12,971	C
San Francisco State Univ	CA	13,000	C
Scripps College	CA	41,000	MC
Siena College	NY	28,260	VC+
Siena Heights Univ	MI	17,000	LC
Simon's Rock College of Bard	MA	41,988	VC+
Skidmore College	NY	41,779	HC
Smith College	MA	41,474	MC
Southwestern Univ	TX	26,767	HC
Stanford Univ	CA	41,557	MC
SUNY at Oswego	NY	13,662	VC
SUNY/College at Geneseo	NY	12,910	HC+
SUNY/College at Old Westbury	NY	13,154	C
SUNY/Univ at Buffalo	NY	13,694	VC
SUNY/Univ at Stony Brook	NY	13,625	HC
Stetson Univ	FL	32,725	VC
Stonehill College	MA	36,104	HC
Suffolk Univ	MA	33,160	C
Syracuse Univ	NY	38,655	HC
Temple Univ	PA	17,438	C
Texas State Univ - San Marcos	TX	10,862	C
Trinity College	CT	38,040	HC+
Tufts Univ	MA	42,018	MC
Tulane Univ	LA	41,098	MC
Union College	NY	41,595	HC
Univ of Alabama	AL	9,888	C
Univ of Arkansas	AR	11,859	VC
Univ of at Calif Davis	CA	15,010	VC
Univ of Calif at Berkeley	CA	18,141	HC+
Univ of Calif at Los Angeles	CA	17,681	MC
Univ of Calif at Santa Cruz	CA	19,174	VC
Univ of Dayton	OH	28,826	VC
Univ of Florida	FL	9,354	MC
Univ of Hawaii at Manoa	HI	10,413	VC
Univ of Idaho	ID	9,310	NC
Univ of Iowa	IA	12,172	VC
Univ of Kansas	KS	10,915	VC
Univ of Mary Washington	VA	11,636	HC
Univ of Maryland/Baltimore County	MD	16,642	VC+
Univ of Maryland/College Park	MD	16,036	HC
Univ of Mass Boston	MA	8,024	C
Univ of Mass Lowell	MA	14,327	VC
Univ of Miami	FL	38,397	MC
Univ of Mich/Ann Arbor	MI	16,587	HC+
Univ of Mich/Dearborn	MI	7,000	C
Univ of Minn/Twin Cities	MN	13,165	HC
Univ of Missouri/Kansas City	MO	15,000	VC
Univ of New England	ME	31,005	C
Univ of New Mexico	NM	11,253	C
Univ of N Car at Chapel Hill	NC	11,129	MC
Univ of Northern Iowa	IA	11,133	C
Univ of Notre Dame	IN	39,552	MC
Univ of Pittsburgh at Greensburg	PA	17,640	C
Univ of Pittsburgh at Johnstown	PA	16,740	LC
Univ of Richmond	VA	40,510	MC
Univ of Rio Grande	OH	8,728	NC
Univ of South Florida	FL	10,284	VC
Univ of Southern Calif	CA	41,618	MC
Univ of Texas at Austin	TX	14,610	HC
Univ of Texas at Dallas	TX	13,244	HC
Univ of Texas at San Antonio	TX	11,325	LC
Univ of the South	TN	34,645	HC
Univ of Wyoming	WY	9,666	C
Upper Iowa Univ	IA	20,130	C
Ursinus College	PA	38,950	VC
Ursuline College	OH	25,456	C
Utah State Univ	UT	8,002	VC
Valparaiso Univ	IN	28,970	VC+
Vanderbilt Univ	TN	41,986	MC
Vassar College	NY	41,700	MC
Virginia Wesleyan College	VA	28,433	C
Warner Pacific College	OR	21,900	C
Washington College	MD	34,990	VC
Washington State Univ	WA	12,260	MC
Washington Univ in St. Louis	MO	42,106	MC
Wayne State Univ	MI	11,805	C
Wellesley College	MA	41,030	MC
Wells College	NY	23,070	VC
Wesley College	DE	19,905	C
Wesleyan College	GA	19,560	C
Wesleyan Univ	CT	42,122	MC
West Chester Univ of Pennsylvania	PA	12,355	C+
Western Conn State Univ	CT	12,993	C
Western Mich Univ	MI	13,299	C
Wheaton College	MA	40,180	HC+
Whitworth College	WA	29,428	VC+
Willamette Univ	OR	35,416	VC+
Williams College	MA	40,310	MC
Wingate Univ	NC	23,300	C
Wittenberg Univ	OH	34,596	VC
Yale Univ	CT	41,000	MC
Youngstown State Univ	OH	12,613	NC

ANATOMY

School	ST	$IS	SR
Andrews Univ	MI	21,786	C
Duke Univ	NC	41,239	MC
Kent State Univ	OH	14,594	C

ANIMAL SCIENCE

School	ST	$IS	SR
Abilene Christian Univ	TX	20,830	C
Alabama A&M Univ	AL	8,890	LC
Alcorn State Univ	MS	8,190	LC
Andrews Univ	MI	21,786	C
Angelo State Univ	TX	8,340	NC
Arkansas State Univ	AR	9,630	C
Auburn Univ	AL	12,230	VC
Berry College	GA	24,342	VC
Calif State Polytechnic Univ, Pomona	CA	18,053	C+
Cal State, Fresno	CA	10,037	LC
Clemson Univ	SC	13,366	HC
College of the Ozarks	MO	4,130	VC+
Colo State Univ-Fort Collins	CO	10,878	C+
Cornell Univ	NY	41,717	MC
Delaware Valley College	PA	29,944	C
Florida A&M Univ	FL	8,344	C
Fort Valley State Univ	GA	6,975	C
Hampshire College	MA	37,120	HC
Hardin-Simmons Univ	TX	18,641	C
Iowa State Univ	IA	11,831	VC
Kansas State Univ	KS	10,516	VC
Kent State Univ	OH	14,594	C
Langston Univ	OK	2,308	LC
Louisiana State Univ and A&M College	LA	10,749	VC
Louisiana Tech Univ	LA	7,370	C
Lubbock Christian Univ	TX	16,960	C
McNeese State Univ	LA	5,270	LC
McPherson College	KS	21,010	C
Mich State Univ	MI	13,689	VC
Middle Tenn State Univ	TN	8,540	C
Miss State Univ	MS	9,577	C
Missouri State Univ	MO	10,748	C+
Montana State Univ-Bozeman	MT	1,137	C
Murray State Univ	KY	8,900	VC
New Mexico State Univ	NM	9,250	C
N Car Agricultural and Technical State Univ	NC	8,000	LC
N Car State Univ	NC	11,824	HC
N Dak State Univ	ND	8,500	C
Northwest Missouri State Univ	MO	10,000	C
Ohio State Univ	OH	15,357	HC
Okla Panhandle State Univ	OK	7,635	NC
Okla State Univ	OK	10,213	VC
Oregon State Univ	OR	11,055	C
Penn State Univ/Univ Park Campus	PA	18,038	HC
Prairie View A&M Univ	TX	11,110	LC
Purdue Univ/West Lafayette	IN	13,458	VC
Rutgers, The State Univ of New Jersey/New Brunswick/Piscataway Campus	NJ	15,810	HC
Sam Houston State Univ	TX	8,000	C
S Dak State Univ	SD	9,815	C
Southeast Missouri State Univ	MO	10,596	C
Southern Illinois Univ Carbondale	IL	12,391	C
Southwestern Univ	TX	26,767	HC
SUNY/College of Agriculture and Technology at Cobleskill	NY	12,915	C
SUNY/College of Environmental Science and Forestry	NY	15,000	VC
Stephen F. Austin State Univ	TX	7,930	C
Sul Ross State Univ	TX	6,600	LC
Tarleton State Univ	TX	8,952	C
Tenn Tech Univ	TN	10,044	C
Texas A&M Univ	TX	13,351	HC
Texas A&M Univ at Commerce	TX	9,020	C
Texas A&M Univ at Kingsville	TX	6,800	LC
Texas State Univ - San Marcos	TX	10,862	C
Texas Tech Univ	TX	13,026	VC
Thomas Edison State College	NJ	3,780	SP
Truman State Univ	MO	11,242	HC
Tuskegee Univ	AL	18,860	LC
Univ of Arizona	AZ	11,958	VC
Univ of Arkansas	AR	11,859	VC
Univ of Calif at Davis	CA	15,010	VC
Univ of Conn	CT	16,628	HC
Univ of Delaware	DE	14,142	HC
Univ of Florida	FL	9,354	MC
Univ of Georgia	GA	11,004	HC
Univ of Hawaii at Manoa	HI	10,413	VC
Univ of Idaho	ID	9,310	NC
Univ of Illinois at Urbana-Champaign	IL	15,800	HC+
Univ of Kentucky	KY	7,800	C
Univ of Maine	ME	13,642	C
Univ of Maryland/College Park	MD	16,036	HC
Univ of Mass Amherst	MA	15,973	C+
Univ of Minn/Crookston	MN	13,157	LC
Univ of Missouri/Columbia	MO	13,500	C
Univ of Nebr at Lincoln	NE	11,401	VC
Univ of Nevada/Reno	NV	12,155	NC
Univ of New Hampshire	NH	16,810	VC
Univ of PR/Mayaguez	PR	1,250	
Univ of Rhode Island	RI	15,398	C
Univ of Tenn at Knoxville	TN	11,720	C
Univ of Tenn at Martin	TN	8,693	C
Univ of Vermont	VT	18,080	VC
Univ of Wisc/Madison	WI	13,117	HC
Univ of Wisc/Platteville	WI	9,779	NC
Univ of Wisc/River Falls	WI	9,722	LC
Univ of Wyoming	WY	9,666	C
Utah State Univ	UT	8,002	VC
Virginia Polytechnic Inst and State Univ	VA	10,834	VC
Washington State Univ	WA	12,260	MC
West Texas A&M Univ	TX	8,452	C
West Virginia Univ	WV	10,506	C

ANIMATION

School	ST	$IS	SR
Art Inst of Atlanta	GA	23,220	SP
Art Inst of Portland	OR	23,040	SP
Brigham Young Univ	UT	9,200	VC
Cal State, Fullerton	CA	10,990	C
Cogswell Polytechnical College	CA	13,760	LC
College for Creative Studies	MI	24,000	SP
Kansas City Art Inst	MO	29,542	SP
Laguna College of Art and Design	CA	17,600	SP
Maryland Inst College of Art	MD	34,450	SP
Mass College of Art	MA	16,650	SP
Minneapolis College of Art and Design	MN	31,110	SP
Rochester Inst of Technology	NY	32,070	VC+
Savannah College of Art and Design	GA	30,800	SP
School of Visual Arts	NY	32,580	SP
Southern Adventist Univ	TN	18,500	C
Woodbury Univ	CA	30,176	LC

ANTHROPOLOGY

School	ST	$IS	SR
Adelphi Univ	NY	27,000	VC
Agnes Scott College	GA	32,070	HC
Albertson College of Idaho	ID	21,095	VC
Albion College	MI	26,000	VC
Alma College	MI	28,544	VC
American Univ	DC	38,719	HC+
Amherst College	MA	41,590	MC
Andrews Univ	MI	21,786	C
Appalachian State Univ	NC	8,000	VC
Arizona State Univ-Tempe	AZ	11,174	C
Auburn Univ	AL	12,230	VC
Ball State Univ	IN	13,138	C
Bard College	NY	41,800	HC+
Bates College	ME	42,100	MC
Baylor Univ	TX	27,555	HC
Beloit College	WI	32,808	HC
Bennington College	VT	41,890	HC
Biola Univ	CA	29,372	VC
Bloomsburg Univ of Pennsylvania	PA	11,602	C
Boise State Univ	ID	9,438	LC
Boston Univ	MA	42,046	HC+
Bowdoin College	ME	41,660	MC
Brandeis Univ	MA	41,551	MC
Bridgewater State College	MA	12,120	C
Brigham Young Univ	UT	9,200	VC
Brown Univ	RI	42,015	MC
Bryn Mawr College	PA	42,780	HC+
Bucknell Univ	PA	39,660	MC
Butler Univ	IN	31,944	VC+
Calif State Polytechnic Univ, Pomona	CA	18,053	C+
Cal State East Bay	CA	10,856	LC
Cal State, Bakersfield	CA	6,125	LC
Cal State, Chico	CA	11,395	C
Cal State, Dominguez Hills	CA	10,220	LC
Cal State, Fresno	CA	10,037	LC
Cal State, Fullerton	CA	10,990	C
Cal State, Long Beach	CA	9,512	C
Cal State, Los Angeles	CA	5,900	C
Cal State, Northridge	CA	9,036	LC
Cal State, Sacramento	CA	11,122	C+
Cal State, San Bernardino	CA	12,563	LC
Cal State, Stanislaus	CA	11,283	C
Canisius College	NY	32,257	VC
Carleton College	MN	40,467	MC
Case Western Reserve Univ	OH	37,314	MC
Catholic Univ of America	DC	35,838	VC
Central College	IA	26,774	VC
Central Conn State Univ	CT	13,620	C
Central Mich Univ	MI	12,244	C
Central Washington Univ	WA	11,730	C
Centre College	KY	30,810	VC
CUNY/Brooklyn College	NY	4,377	C+
CUNY/City College	NY		C
CUNY/Herbert H. Lehman College	NY	4,000	LC
CUNY/Hunter College	NY	8,000	C+
CUNY/Queens College	NY	4,356	C
CUNY/York College	NY	4,242	NC
Clarion Univ of Pennsylvania	PA	11,844	C
Cleveland State Univ	OH	10,798	NC
Colby College	ME	41,770	MC
College of Charleston	SC	13,616	VC
College of the Holy Cross	MA	40,664	MC
College of William and Mary	VA	14,147	MC
College of Wooster	OH	31,310	VC+
Colo College	CO	37,668	HC
Colo State Univ-Fort Collins	CO	10,878	C+
Columbia Univ/Barnard College	NY	38,000	MC
Columbia Univ/Columbia College	NY	42,584	MC
Columbia Univ/School of General Studies	NY	41,516	C
Conn College	CT	41,975	MC
Cornell College	IA	30,110	VC+
Cornell Univ	NY	41,717	MC
Creighton Univ	NE	29,918	VC+
Dartmouth College	NH	39,465	MC
Davidson College	NC	36,825	MC
Denison Univ	OH	37,040	MC
DePauw Univ	IN	32,100	HC
Dickinson College	PA	40,170	HC+
Drew Univ/College of Liberal Arts	NJ	39,698	VC
Duke Univ	NC	41,239	MC
Earlham College	IN	33,604	HC
East Carolina Univ	NC	10,000	C
Eastern Kentucky Univ	KY	7,725	C
Eastern Mich Univ	MI	12,897	C
Eastern New Mexico Univ	NM	7,264	C
Eastern Oregon Univ	OR	10,400	NC
Eastern Washington Univ	WA	10,608	C
Eckerd College	FL	35,492	VC
Edinboro Univ of Pennsylvania	PA	11,809	LC
Elmira College	NY	37,200	VC
Emory Univ	GA	40,546	MC
Florida Atlantic Univ	FL	11,221	C
Florida Gulf Coast Univ	FL	10,833	C
Florida State Univ	FL	9,028	HC
Fordham Univ	NY	36,000	HC
Fort Lewis College	CO	11,852	C
Franciscan Univ of Steubenville	OH	20,300	VC
Franklin and Marshall College	PA	40,590	HC
Franklin Pierce College	NH	31,700	C
George Mason Univ	VA	10,850	VC
George Washington Univ	DC	48,820	MC
Georgetown Univ	DC	43,183	MC
Georgia Southern Univ	GA	9,762	C
Georgia State Univ	GA	11,444	VC
Gettysburg College	PA	39,864	HC
Goucher College	MD	36,225	VC
Grand Valley State Univ	MI	12,000	VC
Grinnell College	IA	34,814	HC+
Guilford College	NC	28,160	C+
Gustavus Adolphus College	MN	30,920	HC
Hamilton College	NY	41,660	MC
Hamline Univ	MN	27,070	VC
Hampshire College	MA	37,120	HC
Hanover College	IN	28,150	HC
Hartwick College	NY	36,065	C+
Harvard Univ/Harvard College	MA	45,860	MC
Haverford College	PA	41,600	MC
Hawaii Pacific Univ	HI	21,080	C
Heidelberg College	OH	23,242	C
Hobart and William Smith Colleges	NY	41,123	VC
Hofstra Univ	NY	32,630	VC
Howard Univ	DC	18,481	C+
Humboldt State Univ	CA	11,176	C
Idaho State Univ	ID	9,030	C
Illinois State Univ	IL	12,839	C+
Illinois Wesleyan Univ	IL	34,050	HC+
Indiana State Univ	IN	11,604	C
Indiana Univ Bloomington	IN	13,356	VC
Indiana Univ of Pennsylvania	PA	11,209	C
Indiana Univ-Purdue Univ Fort Wayne	IN	5,067	LC
Indiana Univ-Purdue Univ Indianapolis	IN	10,959	C
Iowa State Univ	IA	11,831	VC
Ithaca College	NY	35,144	VC
James Madison Univ	VA	12,010	VC
Johns Hopkins Univ	MD	42,044	MC
Johnson State College	VT	11,830	LC
Judson College	IL	25,130	C
Juniata College	PA	33,130	VC
Kalamazoo College	MI	32,442	VC+
Kansas State Univ	KS	10,516	VC
Kent State Univ	OH	14,594	C

INDEX OF COLLEGE MAJORS

School	ST	$IS	SR
Kenyon College	OH	39,500	MC
Knox College	IL	32,385	VC+
Kutztown Univ of Pennsylvania	PA	10,820	C
Lafayette College	PA	39,267	MC
Lake Forest College	IL	33,860	VC
Lawrence Univ	WI	33,958	HC+
Lehigh Univ	PA	42,690	HC+
Lewis and Clark College	OR	35,358	VC+
Lincoln Univ	PA	13,658	C+
Linfield College	OR	29,632	VC
LIU/Brooklyn Campus	NY	25,000	C
Longwood Univ	VA	12,426	C
Louisiana State Univ and A&M College	LA	10,749	VC
Loyola Univ Chicago	IL	32,896	VC
Loyola Univ New Orleans	LA	31,050	VC+
Luther College	IA	28,800	VC+
Lycoming College	PA	30,797	C+
Macalester College	MN	36,500	MC
Mansfield Univ	PA	11,300	C
Marlboro College	VT	35,980	VC+
Marquette Univ	WI	31,066	HC
Marylhurst Univ	OR	14,220	NC
Mass Inst of Technology	MA	41,800	MC
Mercyhurst College	PA	28,633	VC
Metropolitan State College of Denver	CO	2,338	LC
Miami Univ	OH	29,097	HC
Mich State Univ	MI	13,689	VC
Middle Tenn State Univ	TN	8,540	C
Middlebury College	VT	42,120	MC
Millersville Univ of Pennsylvania	PA	12,113	C
Mills College	CA	39,870	C
Millsaps College	MS	28,256	VC+
Minn State Univ, Mankato	MN	10,276	LC
Minn State Univ, Moorhead	MN	7,000	LC
Miss State Univ	MS	9,577	C
Missouri State Univ	MO	10,748	C+
Monmouth College	IL	23,700	C
Monmouth Univ	NJ	28,956	C
Montana State Univ-Bozeman	MT	1,137	HC
Montclair State Univ	NJ	16,327	C
Mount Holyoke College	MA	42,148	HC+
Muhlenberg College	PA	36,030	HC+
National-Louis Univ	IL	16,915	LC
Nazareth College of Rochester	NY	28,175	VC
New College of Calif	CA	12,842	NC
New College of Florida	FL	10,009	HC
New Mexico Highlands Univ	NM	6,272	NC
New Mexico State Univ	NM	9,250	C
New York Univ	NY	43,170	MC
North Central College	IL	28,926	VC
N Dak State Univ	ND	8,500	C
North Park Univ	IL	24,050	C
Northeastern Illinois Univ	IL	3,000	NC
Northeastern Univ	MA	35,742	HC
Northern Arizona Univ	AZ	10,353	C
Northern Illinois Univ	IL	13,178	C
Northern Kentucky Univ	KY	6,670	NC
Northwestern Univ	IL	37,595	MC
Oakland Univ	MI	11,936	C
Oberlin College	OH	40,904	MC
Occidental College	CA	40,185	MC
Ohio State Univ	OH	15,357	HC
Ohio Univ	OH	15,921	C
Ohio Wesleyan Univ	OH	35,830	VC+
Old Dominion Univ	VA	11,907	C
Olivet College	MI	19,984	C+
Oregon State Univ	OR	11,055	C
Pacific Lutheran Univ	WA	28,805	VC
Penn State Univ/Univ Park Campus	PA	18,038	HC
Pitzer College	CA	41,644	HC
Plymouth State Univ	NH	12,298	LC
Pomona College	CA	40,774	MC
Portland State Univ	OR	12,453	C
Prescott College	AZ	13,445	LC
Princeton Univ	NJ	40,213	MC
Purdue Univ/West Lafayette	IN	13,458	VC
Radford Univ	VA	13,145	C
Reed College	OR	41,106	MC
Rhode Island College	RI	11,570	C
Rhodes College	TN	32,860	HC
Rice Univ	TX	32,290	MC
Richard Stockton College of New Jersey	NJ	14,000	VC
Ripon College	WI	27,160	C+
Rockford College	IL	28,330	VC
Rocky Mountain College	MT	20,805	C
Rollins College	FL	38,366	VC
Rutgers, The State Univ of New Jersey/New Brunswick/Piscataway Campus	NJ	15,810	HC
Rutgers, The State Univ of New Jersey/Newark Campus	NJ	15,640	VC
St. Cloud State Univ	MN	10,010	C
St. John Fisher College	NY	27,860	C
St. John's Univ	NY	34,370	C
St. Lawrence Univ	NY	40,545	VC
St. Mary's College of Calif	CA	37,290	C
St. Mary's College of Maryland	MD	18,876	VC+
St. Michael's College	VT	33,330	VC
St. Vincent College	PA	26,160	VC
San Diego State Univ	CA	12,971	C
San Francisco State Univ	CA	13,000	C
San Jose State Univ	CA	11,707	C
Santa Clara Univ	CA	38,931	VC
Sarah Lawrence College	NY	42,000	HC
Scripps College	CA	41,000	MC
Seton Hall Univ	NJ	33,622	VC
Skidmore College	NY	41,779	HC
Slippery Rock Univ of Pennsylvania	PA	10,360	LC
Smith College	MA	41,474	MC
Sonoma State Univ	CA	14,732	C
Southeast Missouri State Univ	MO	10,596	C
Southern Illinois Univ Carbondale	IL	12,391	C
Southern Illinois Univ Edwardsville	IL	11,022	C
Southern Methodist Univ	TX	36,088	VC+
Southern Oregon Univ	OR	12,186	C
Spelman College	GA	24,650	VC
Stanford Univ	CA	41,557	MC
SUNY at Oswego	NY	13,662	VC
SUNY at Potsdam	NY	12,959	C
SUNY/College at Brockport	NY	12,747	VC
SUNY/College at Buffalo	NY	11,903	C+
SUNY/College at Cortland	NY	12,095	C
SUNY/College at Geneseo	NY	12,910	HC+
SUNY/College at Oneonta	NY	12,905	VC
SUNY/College at Plattsburgh	NY	12,362	C
SUNY/College at Purchase	NY	11,989	VC+
SUNY/Univ at Albany	NY	13,860	VC
SUNY/Univ at Binghamton	NY	13,988	HC
SUNY/Univ at Buffalo	NY	13,694	VC
SUNY/Univ at New Paltz	NY	12,480	VC
SUNY/Univ at Stony Brook	NY	13,625	HC
Swarthmore College	PA	41,280	MC
Sweet Briar College	VA	31,460	VC
Syracuse Univ	NY	38,655	HC
Temple Univ	PA	17,438	C
Texas A&M Univ	TX	13,351	HC
Texas A&M Univ at Commerce	TX	9,020	C
Texas A&M Univ at Kingsville	TX	6,800	LC
Texas Christian Univ	TX	23,410	VC+
Texas State Univ - San Marcos	TX	10,862	C
Texas Tech Univ	TX	13,026	VC
Thomas Edison State College	NJ	3,780	SP
Towson Univ	MD	13,924	VC
Transylvania Univ	KY	26,240	VC+
Trinity College	CT	38,040	HC+
Trinity Univ	TX	30,157	HC+
Truman State Univ	MO	11,242	HC
Tufts Univ	MA	42,018	MC
Tulane Univ	LA	41,098	MC
Union College	NY	41,595	HC
Univ of Akron	OH	15,166	NC
Univ of Alabama	AL	9,888	C
Univ of Alabama at Birmingham	AL	13,716	C
Univ of Alaska Anchorage	AK	11,275	NC
Univ of Alaska Fairbanks	AK	10,101	C
Univ of Arizona	AZ	11,958	VC
Univ of Arkansas	AR	11,859	VC
Univ of at Calif Davis	CA	15,010	VC
Univ of Calif at Berkeley	CA	18,141	HC+
Univ of Calif at Irvine	CA	16,475	HC
Univ of Calif at Los Angeles	CA	17,681	MC
Univ of Calif at Riverside	CA	16,625	C
Univ of Calif at San Diego	CA	16,102	HC
Univ of Calif at Santa Barbara	CA	11,800	VC
Univ of Calif at Santa Cruz	CA	19,174	VC
Univ of Central Florida	FL	10,739	VC
Univ of Chicago	IL	42,369	MC
Univ of Cincinnati	OH	17,682	C
Univ of Colo at Boulder	CO	13,352	C+
Univ of Colo at Colo Springs	CO	11,517	VC
Univ of Colo at Denver and Health Sciences Center	CO	5,021	C
Univ of Conn	CT	16,628	HC
Univ of Delaware	DE	14,142	HC
Univ of Denver	CO	36,376	VC+
Univ of Florida	FL	9,354	HC
Univ of Georgia	GA	11,004	HC
Univ of Hawaii at Hilo	HI	6,500	C
Univ of Hawaii at Manoa	HI	10,413	VC
Univ of Houston	TX	7,000	C
Univ of Idaho	ID	9,310	NC
Univ of Illinois at Chicago	IL	16,256	VC
Univ of Illinois at Urbana-Champaign	IL	15,800	HC+
Univ of Indianapolis	IN	25,090	C
Univ of Iowa	IA	12,172	VC
Univ of Kansas	KS	10,915	VC
Univ of Kentucky	KY	7,800	VC
Univ of La Verne	CA	33,470	C
Univ of Louisiana at Lafayette	LA	5,830	C
Univ of Louisville	KY	10,400	VC
Univ of Maine	ME	13,642	C
Univ of Mary Washington	VA	11,636	HC
Univ of Maryland/Baltimore County	MD	16,642	VC+
Univ of Maryland/College Park	MD	16,036	HC
Univ of Mass Amherst	MA	15,973	C+
Univ of Mass Boston	MA	8,024	C
Univ of Mass Dartmouth	MA	15,985	C
Univ of Memphis	TN	11,153	C
Univ of Miami	FL	38,397	MC
Univ of Mich/Ann Arbor	MI	16,587	HC+
Univ of Mich/Dearborn	MI	7,000	VC
Univ of Mich/Flint	MI	6,398	C
Univ of Minn/Duluth	MN	13,974	C
Univ of Minn/Morris	MN	15,472	VC
Univ of Minn/Twin Cities	MN	13,165	HC
Univ of Miss	MS	9,000	C
Univ of Missouri/Columbia	MO	13,500	VC
Univ of Missouri/St. Louis	MO	14,046	VC
Univ of Montana	MT	10,602	C
Univ of Nebr at Lincoln	NE	11,401	VC
Univ of Nevada/Las Vegas	NV	11,566	C
Univ of Nevada/Reno	NV	12,155	NC
Univ of New Hampshire	NH	16,810	VC
Univ of New Mexico	NM	11,253	C
Univ of New Orleans	LA	7,370	C
Univ of N Car at Chapel Hill	NC	11,129	MC
Univ of N Car at Charlotte	NC	9,101	C
Univ of N Car at Greensboro	NC	8,993	C
Univ of N Car at Wilmington	NC	10,107	VC
Univ of N Dak	ND	10,114	VC
Univ of North Florida	FL	9,908	VC
Univ of North Texas	TX	7,800	C
Univ of Northern Iowa	IA	11,133	C
Univ of Notre Dame	IN	39,552	MC
Univ of Okla	OK	10,769	VC+
Univ of Oregon	OR	13,108	VC
Univ of Pennsylvania	PA	41,766	MC
Univ of Pittsburgh at Greensburg	PA	17,640	C
Univ of Pittsburgh at Pittsburgh	PA	18,866	HC
Univ of PR/Rio Piedras	PR	5,750	
Univ of Redlands	CA	36,160	VC
Univ of Rhode Island	RI	15,398	C
Univ of Rochester	NY	41,135	MC
Univ of San Diego	CA	40,620	HC
Univ of South Alabama	AL	8,930	LC
Univ of S Car at Columbia	SC	13,397	VC
Univ of S Dak	SD	9,068	C
Univ of South Florida	FL	10,284	VC
Univ of Southern Calif	CA	41,618	MC
Univ of Southern Maine	ME	12,614	C
Univ of Southern Miss	MS	10,112	C
Univ of Tenn at Knoxville	TN	11,720	C
Univ of Texas at Arlington	TX	7,195	LC
Univ of Texas at Austin	TX	14,610	HC
Univ of Texas at El Paso	TX	8,764	NC
Univ of Texas at San Antonio	TX	11,325	LC
Univ of Texas-Pan American	TX	7,290	C+
Univ of the South	TN	34,645	HC
Univ of Toledo	OH	15,806	NC
Univ of Tulsa	OK	25,348	HC
Univ of Utah	UT	10,162	VC
Univ of Vermont	VT	18,080	VC
Univ of Virginia	VA	13,759	MC
Univ of Washington	WA	10,400	VC
Univ of West Georgia	GA	8,838	C
Univ of Wisc/Madison	WI	13,117	HC
Univ of Wisc/Milwaukee	WI	9,427	LC
Univ of Wisc/Oshkosh	WI	10,426	LC
Univ of Wyoming	WY	9,666	C
Ursinus College	PA	38,950	VC
Valdosta State Univ	GA	8,802	C
Vanderbilt Univ	TN	41,986	MC
Vanguard Univ of Southern Calif	CA	27,071	C
Vassar College	NY	41,700	MC
Virginia Commonwealth Univ	VA	12,987	C
Wagner College	NY	33,300	VC
Wake Forest Univ	NC	38,290	MC
Warren Wilson College	NC	24,382	VC
Washburn Univ	KS	9,734	NC
Washington and Lee Univ	VA	35,880	MC
Washington College	MD	34,990	VC
Washington State Univ	WA	12,260	C
Washington Univ in St. Louis	MO	42,106	MC
Wayne State Univ	MI	11,805	C
Webster Univ	MO	24,280	VC
Wellesley College	MA	41,030	MC
Wells College	NY	23,070	VC
Wesleyan Univ	CT	42,122	MC
West Chester Univ of Pennsylvania	PA	12,355	C+
West Virginia Univ	WV	10,506	C
Western Carolina Univ	NC	7,000	C
Western Conn State Univ	CT	12,993	C
Western Kentucky Univ	KY	10,192	C
Western Mich Univ	MI	13,299	C
Western Oregon Univ	OR	10,295	C
Western State College of Colo	CO	9,942	C
Western Washington Univ	WA	11,262	VC
Westminster College	MO	19,060	VC
Wheaton College	IL	27,760	HC
Wheaton College	MA	40,180	HC+
Whitman College	WA	36,110	HC+
Wichita State Univ	KS	8,500	C
Widener Univ	PA	27,275	C
Willamette Univ	OR	35,416	VC+
William Paterson Univ of New Jersey	NJ	17,810	C+
Williams College	MA	40,310	MC
Wright State Univ	OH	13,616	LC
Yale Univ	CT	41,000	MC
Youngstown State Univ	OH	12,613	NC

APPAREL AND ACCESSORIES MARKETING

School	ST	$IS	SR
Bluffton College	OH	26,110	C
Bowling Green State Univ	OH	14,994	C
Calif State Polytechnic Univ, Pomona	CA	18,053	C+
Colo State Univ-Fort Collins	CO	10,878	C+
Fashion Inst of Technology/SUNY	NY	11,600	C+
Indiana Univ Bloomington	IN	13,356	VC
Kansas State Univ	KS	10,516	VC
Kentucky State Univ	KY	10,089	LC
Northwood Univ	TX	20,135	LC
S Dak State Univ	SD	9,815	C
Univ of Arkansas	AR	11,859	VC
Virginia Polytechnic Inst and State Univ	VA	10,834	VC
Youngstown State Univ	OH	12,613	NC

APPAREL DESIGN

School	ST	$IS	SR
Art Inst of Portland	OR	23,040	SP
Boston Univ	MA	42,046	HC+
Central Mich Univ	MI	12,244	C
Concordia College: Moorhead	MN	22,475	VC
Florida State Univ	FL	9,028	HC
Gallaudet Univ	DC	16,554	
Kansas State Univ	KS	10,516	VC
Oregon State Univ	OR	11,055	C
Purdue Univ/West Lafayette	IN	13,458	VC
Rhode Island School of Design	RI	38,130	SP
Texas Tech Univ	TX	13,026	VC
Univ of Hawaii at Manoa	HI	10,413	VC
Univ of Wisc/Stout	WI	11,164	C

APPLIED ART

School	ST	$IS	SR
Centenary College	NJ	28,870	LC
Cleveland Inst of Art	OH	34,109	SP
Daemen College	NY	24,580	C
Edinboro Univ of Pennsylvania	PA	11,809	LC
Minn State Univ, Mankato	MN	10,276	LC
Oral Roberts Univ	OK	22,650	C
Point Park Univ	PA	24,160	C
Rochester Inst of Technology	NY	32,070	VC+
Shenandoah Univ	VA	27,600	C
Tabor College	KS	21,614	VC
Texas State Univ - San Marcos	TX	10,862	C
Univ of North Texas	TX	7,800	C
West Texas A&M Univ	TX	8,452	C

APPLIED AVIATION

School	ST	$IS	SR
Univ of Minn/Crookston	MN	13,157	LC

APPLIED MATHEMATICS

School	ST	$IS	SR
American Univ	DC	38,719	HC+
Andrews Univ	MI	21,786	C
Asbury College	KY	23,762	VC
Auburn Univ	AL	12,230	VC
Baylor Univ	TX	27,555	HC
Biola Univ	CA	29,372	VC
Bloomfield College	NJ	22,500	LC
Brown Univ	RI	42,015	MC
Cal State, Long Beach	CA	9,512	C
Case Western Reserve Univ	OH	37,314	MC
CUNY/New York City College of Technology	NY	4,269	NC
Clarkson Univ	NY	34,930	VC
Colby College	ME	41,770	MC
Columbia Univ/Fu Foundation School of Engineering and Applied Science	NY	42,584	MC
Columbia Univ/School of General Studies	NY	41,516	C
Dowling College	NY	22,110	LC

ST = STATE   **$IS** = IN-STATE COSTS   **SR** = SELECTOR RATING

School	ST	$IS	SR
East Central Univ	OK	6,207	C
Eastern Mich Univ	MI	12,897	C
Ferris State Univ	MI	13,698	C
Florida Inst of Technology	FL	29,720	VC
Florida International Univ	FL	9,215	VC
Florida State Univ	FL	9,028	HC
Geneva College	PA	21,850	C
George Washington Univ	DC	48,820	MC
Georgia Inst of Technology	GA	11,450	HC+
Grand View College	IA	21,482	C
Hampden-Sydney College	VA	31,148	VC
Harvard Univ/Harvard College	MA	45,860	MC
Hawaii Pacific Univ	HI	21,080	C
Hofstra Univ	NY	32,630	VC
Illinois Inst of Technology	IL	26,465	HC+
Indiana Univ of Pennsylvania	PA	11,209	C
Indiana Univ South Bend	IN	4,989	LC
Johns Hopkins Univ	MD	42,044	MC
Johnson C. Smith Univ	NC	20,000	C
Kent State Univ	OH	14,594	C
Kentucky State Univ	KY	10,089	LC
Kettering Univ	MI	29,338	HC
King College	TN	23,400	C
Le Moyne College	NY	29,570	VC
Mary Baldwin College	VA	26,465	C
Metropolitan State Univ	MN	4,682	SP
Montclair State Univ	NJ	16,327	C
New Jersey Inst of Technology	NJ	16,396	VC
North Central College	IL	28,926	VC
Northwestern Univ	IL	37,595	MC
Ohio Univ	OH	15,921	C
Pacific Union College	CA	24,555	VC+
Purdue Univ/West Lafayette	IN	13,458	VC
Rice Univ	TX	32,290	MC
Rochester Inst of Technology	NY	32,070	VC+
Rutgers, The State Univ of New Jersey/Newark Campus	NJ	15,640	VC
Saginaw Valley State Univ	MI	11,432	C
St. Augustine's College	NC	14,000	LC
St. Louis Univ	MO	33,158	VC+
San Francisco State Univ	CA	13,000	C
Simon's Rock College of Bard	MA	41,988	VC+
SUNY at Oswego	NY	13,662	VC
SUNY/Inst of Technology	NY	12,575	VC
SUNY/Univ at Albany	NY	13,860	VC
SUNY/Univ at Stony Brook	NY	13,625	HC
Univ of Arkansas at Pine Bluff	AR	8,300	C
Univ of Calif at Berkeley	CA	18,141	HC+
Univ of Calif at Los Angeles	CA	17,681	MC
Univ of Calif at San Diego	CA	16,102	HC
Univ of Chicago	IL	42,369	MC
Univ of Colo at Boulder	CO	13,352	C+
Univ of Evansville	IN	28,320	VC
Univ of Houston-Downtown	TX	3,326	NC
Univ of Idaho	ID	9,310	NC
Univ of Mass Lowell	MA	14,327	VC
Univ of Miami	FL	38,397	MC
Univ of Missouri/Rolla	MO	13,332	HC
Univ of New Haven	CT	31,794	C
Univ of Pittsburgh at Greensburg	PA	17,640	C
Univ of Pittsburgh at Pittsburgh	PA	18,866	HC
Univ of PR/Rio Piedras	PR	5,750	
Univ of Rochester	NY	41,135	MC
Univ of S Car at Aiken	SC	11,718	LC
Univ of Tenn at Chattanooga	TN	7,790	C
Univ of Texas at Dallas	TX	13,244	NC
Univ of Texas at El Paso	TX	8,764	NC
Univ of the Pacific	CA	34,380	VC
Univ of Wisc/Madison	WI	13,117	HC
Univ of Wisc/Milwaukee	WI	9,427	C
Univ of Wisc/Stout	WI	11,164	C
Valdosta State Univ	GA	8,802	C
Villa Julie College	MD	25,222	C
Washington Univ in St. Louis	MO	42,106	MC
West Virginia State Univ	WV	8,378	NC
Wingate Univ	NC	23,000	C
Yale Univ	CT	41,000	MC

APPLIED MUSIC

School	ST	$IS	SR
Baylor Univ	TX	27,555	HC
Concordia College-New York	NY	27,740	C
Covenant College	GA	26,460	VC+
Dallas Baptist Univ	TX	17,040	VC
DePaul Univ	IL	29,835	VC
Eastern Mich Univ	MI	12,897	C
Geneva College	PA	21,850	C
Grand Canyon Univ	AZ	32,000	LC
Inter American Univ of PR/ Fajardo Campus	PR	4,000	
Inter American Univ of PR/ Ponce Regional College	PR	3,700	
Judson College	AL	16,522	C
Kansas State Univ	KS	10,516	VC

School	ST	$IS	SR
Lenoir-Rhyne College	NC	25,580	C
Meredith College	NC	25,600	C
Miss College	MS	14,574	VC
Nebr Wesleyan Univ	NE	23,415	C+
New England Conservatory of Music	MA	38,750	SP
Newberry College	SC	23,000	LC
Sul Ross State Univ	TX	6,600	LC
Trinity Christian College	IL	23,645	C
Univ of Houston	TX	7,000	C
Univ of Idaho	ID	9,310	NC
Univ of Memphis	TN	11,153	C
Univ of Mich/Ann Arbor	MI	16,587	HC+
Univ of Nevada/Reno	NV	12,155	NC
Univ of Texas at Austin	TX	14,610	HC
Viterbo Univ	WI	21,670	C
Wartburg College	IA	27,315	NC

APPLIED PHYSICS

School	ST	$IS	SR
Angelo State Univ	TX	8,340	NC
Armstrong Atlantic State Univ	GA	7,394	C
Beloit College	WI	32,808	HC
Bethel College	IN	19,680	C
Bridgewater College	VA	27,790	C
Cal State, San Bernardino	CA	12,563	LC
Cal State, Stanislaus	CA	11,283	C
Columbia Univ/Fu Foundation School of Engineering and Applied Science	NY	42,584	MC
East Carolina Univ	NC	10,000	C
Georgia Inst of Technology	GA	11,450	HC+
Hiram College	OH	28,700	VC
Hofstra Univ	NY	32,630	VC
Indiana Univ of Pennsylvania	PA	11,209	C
Kettering Univ	MI	29,338	HC
Linfield College	OR	29,632	VC
Marietta College	OH	29,327	C
Mich Tech Univ	MI	14,569	VC
New Jersey Inst of Technology	NJ	16,396	VC
Northeastern Univ	MA	35,742	HC
Ohio Univ	OH	15,921	C
Pacific Lutheran Univ	WA	28,805	VC
Providence College	RI	34,580	HC
Purdue Univ/West Lafayette	IN	13,458	VC
Rensselaer Polytechnic Inst	NY	41,288	HC+
Rutgers, The State Univ of New Jersey/Newark Campus	NJ	15,640	VC
Saginaw Valley State Univ	MI	11,432	C
Shippensburg Univ of Pennsylvania	PA	11,621	C
SUNY/College at Geneseo	NY	12,910	HC+
Tufts Univ	MA	42,018	MC
Univ of Alaska Fairbanks	AK	10,101	C
Univ of Calif at San Diego	CA	16,102	HC
Univ of Nevada/Las Vegas	NV	11,566	C
Univ of Notre Dame	IN	39,552	MC
Whitworth College	WA	29,428	VC+
Xavier Univ	OH	30,490	HC

APPLIED PSYCHOLOGY

School	ST	$IS	SR
Bryant College	RI	34,330	VC
Champlain College	VT	24,605	C
Christian Brothers Univ	TN	24,650	VC
College of Santa Fe	NM	28,978	C
Georgia Inst of Technology	GA	11,450	HC+
Indiana Univ South Bend	IN	4,989	LC
Loyola Univ Chicago	IL	32,896	VC
New York Univ	NY	43,170	MC
Robert Morris Univ	PA	22,822	C
Russell Sage College	NY	27,000	C
Univ of St. Mary	KS	18,900	C

APPLIED SCIENCE

School	ST	$IS	SR
Aquinas College	MI	23,750	C
Lehigh Univ	PA	42,690	HC+
Madonna Univ	MI	16,068	VC
Southwest Minn State Univ	MN	10,975	C
Univ of Arizona	AZ	11,958	VC
Univ of Maine at Augusta	ME	5,025	NC
Univ of Mich/Flint	MI	6,398	C
Univ of N Car at Chapel Hill	NC	11,129	MC
Univ of Wisc/Stout	WI	11,164	C

ARABIC

School	ST	$IS	SR
Dartmouth College	NH	39,465	MC
Georgetown Univ	DC	43,183	MC
Ohio State Univ	OH	15,357	HC
SUNY/Univ at Binghamton	NY	13,988	HC
Univ of Calif at Los Angeles	CA	17,681	MC
Univ of Texas at Austin	TX	14,610	HC
Washington Univ in St. Louis	MO	42,106	MC
Wayne State Univ	MI	11,805	C

ARCHEOLOGY

School	ST	$IS	SR
Bard College	NY	41,800	HC+
Baylor Univ	TX	27,555	HC
Boston Univ	MA	42,046	HC+
Bowdoin College	ME	41,660	MC
Brandeis Univ	MA	41,551	MC
Brigham Young Univ	UT	9,200	VC
Brown Univ	RI	42,015	MC
Bryn Mawr College	PA	42,780	HC+
CUNY/Brooklyn College	NY	4,377	C+
CUNY/Hunter College	NY	8,000	C
College of Wooster	OH	31,310	VC+
Columbia Univ/Columbia College	NY	42,584	MC
Columbia Univ/School of General Studies	NY	41,516	C
Cornell Univ	NY	41,717	MC
Dickinson College	PA	40,170	HC+
George Washington Univ	DC	48,820	MC
Hamilton College	NY	41,660	MC
Haverford College	PA	41,600	MC
Hood College	MD	30,085	VC
Mass Inst of Technology	MA	41,800	MC
Mercyhurst College	PA	28,633	VC
Oberlin College	OH	40,904	MC
Princeton Univ	NJ	40,213	MC
Stanford Univ	CA	41,557	MC
SUNY at Potsdam	NY	12,959	C
Texas A&M Univ at Galveston	TX	10,000	C+
Tufts Univ	MA	42,018	MC
Univ of Evansville	IN	28,320	VC
Univ of Indianapolis	IN	25,090	C
Univ of Kansas	KS	10,915	VC
Univ of Mich/Ann Arbor	MI	16,587	HC+
Univ of Missouri/Columbia	MO	13,500	VC
Univ of Texas at Austin	TX	14,610	HC
Univ of Wisc/La Crosse	WI	10,045	VC
Washington and Lee Univ	VA	35,880	MC
Washington Univ in St. Louis	MO	42,106	MC
Wellesley College	MA	41,030	MC
Wesleyan Univ	CT	42,122	MC
Wheaton College	IL	27,760	HC
Yale Univ	CT	41,000	MC

ARCHITECTURAL ENGINEERING

School	ST	$IS	SR
Calif Polytechnic State Univ	CA	12,390	VC
Drexel Univ	PA	27,700	VC
Illinois Inst of Technology	IL	26,465	HC+
Kansas State Univ	KS	10,516	VC
Milwaukee School of Engineering	WI	29,847	VC+
N Car Agricultural and Technical State Univ	NC	8,000	LC
Okla State Univ	OK	10,213	VC
Parsons School of Design	NY	32,242	SP
Penn State Univ/Univ Park Campus	PA	18,038	HC
Princeton Univ	NJ	40,213	MC
Purdue Univ/West Lafayette	IN	13,458	VC
Rice Univ	TX	32,290	MC
Tenn State Univ	TN	9,048	LC
Univ of Cincinnati	OH	17,682	C
Univ of Colo at Boulder	CO	13,352	C+
Univ of Hartford	CT	34,044	C
Univ of Houston	TX	7,000	C
Univ of Idaho	ID	9,310	NC
Univ of Illinois at Urbana-Champaign	IL	15,800	HC+
Univ of Kansas	KS	10,915	VC
Univ of Miami	FL	38,397	MC
Univ of Missouri/Rolla	MO	13,332	HC
Univ of Nebr at Lincoln	NE	11,401	VC
Univ of Nevada/Las Vegas	NV	11,566	C
Univ of Okla	OK	10,769	VC+
Univ of Texas at Austin	TX	14,610	HC
Univ of Wyoming	WY	9,666	C
Vermont Technical College	VT	15,751	C

ARCHITECTURAL HISTORY

School	ST	$IS	SR
Cornell Univ	NY	41,717	MC
Lehigh Univ	PA	42,690	HC+
Middlebury College	VT	42,120	C
Savannah College of Art and Design	GA	30,800	SP

ARCHITECTURAL TECHNOLOGY

School	ST	$IS	SR
Brown Univ	RI	42,015	MC
CUNY/New York City College of Technology	NY	4,269	NC
Fairmont State	WV	8,400	LC
Florida International Univ	FL	9,215	VC
Keene State College	NH	13,836	C
SUNY/College of Technology at Alfred	NY	14,000	C
SUNY/Univ at Buffalo	NY	13,694	VC
Univ of Cincinnati	OH	17,682	C
Univ of Memphis	TN	11,153	C

School	ST	$IS	SR
Univ of Southern Miss	MS	10,112	C
Washington Univ in St. Louis	MO	42,106	MC
Wentworth Inst of Technology	MA	27,500	C

ARCHITECTURE

School	ST	$IS	SR
Andrews Univ	MI	21,786	C
Arizona State Univ-Tempe	AZ	11,174	C
Auburn Univ	AL	12,230	VC
Ball State Univ	IN	13,138	C
Baylor Univ	TX	27,555	HC
Bennington College	VT	41,890	VC
Boston Architectural Center	MA	6,500	SP
Brown Univ	RI	42,015	MC
Calif College of the Arts	CA	34,325	SP
Calif Polytechnic State Univ	CA	12,390	VC
Calif State Polytechnic Univ, Pomona	CA	18,053	C+
Case Western Reserve Univ	OH	37,314	MC
Catholic Univ of America	DC	35,838	VC
CUNY/City College	NY		C
Columbia Univ/Barnard College	NY	38,000	MC
Columbia Univ/Columbia College	NY	42,584	MC
Columbia Univ/School of General Studies	NY	41,516	C
Conn College	CT	41,975	MC
Cooper Union for the Advancement of Science and Art	NY	12,450	MC
Cornell Univ	NY	41,717	MC
Drexel Univ	PA	27,700	VC
Drury Univ	MO	20,117	VC
Florida Atlantic Univ	FL	11,221	C
Georgia Inst of Technology	GA	11,450	HC+
Hampshire College	MA	37,120	HC
Hampton Univ	VA	19,468	C+
Hobart and William Smith Colleges	NY	41,123	VC
Howard Univ	DC	18,481	C+
Illinois Inst of Technology	IL	26,465	HC+
Iowa State Univ	IA	11,831	VC
Kansas State Univ	KS	10,516	VC
Kent State Univ	OH	14,594	C
Lawrence Tech Univ	MI	25,475	VC
Lehigh Univ	PA	42,690	HC+
Louisiana State Univ and A&M College	LA	10,749	VC
Louisiana Tech Univ	LA	7,370	C
Mass College of Art	MA	16,650	SP
Mass Inst of Technology	MA	41,800	MC
Miami Univ	OH	29,097	HC
Miss State Univ	MS	9,577	C
Mount Holyoke College	MA	42,148	HC+
New Jersey Inst of Technology	NJ	16,396	VC
New York Inst of Technology	NY	28,126	VC
N Car State Univ	NC	11,824	HC
N Dak State Univ	ND	8,500	C
Northeastern Univ	MA	35,742	HC
Norwich Univ	VT	28,212	C
Ohio State Univ	OH	15,357	HC
Okla State Univ	OK	10,213	VC
Penn State Univ/Univ Park Campus	PA	18,038	HC
Philadelphia Univ	PA	30,006	C
Portland State Univ	OR	12,453	C
Prairie View A&M Univ	TX	11,110	LC
Pratt Inst	NY	36,156	SP
Princeton Univ	NJ	40,213	MC
Rensselaer Polytechnic Inst	NY	41,288	HC+
Rhode Island School of Design	RI	38,130	SP
Rice Univ	TX	32,290	MC
Roger Williams Univ	RI	30,500	C
Savannah College of Art and Design	GA	30,800	SP
Smith College	MA	41,474	MC
Southern Illinois Univ Carbondale	IL	12,391	C
Southern Polytechnic State Univ	GA	7,640	VC
Southern Univ and A&M College	LA	8,238	LC
SUNY/Univ at Buffalo	NY	13,694	VC
Syracuse Univ	NY	38,655	HC
Temple Univ	PA	17,438	C
Texas Tech Univ	TX	13,026	VC
Thomas Edison State College	NJ	3,780	SP
Tufts Univ	MA	42,018	MC
Tulane Univ	LA	41,098	MC
Univ of Arizona	AZ	11,958	VC
Univ of Arkansas	AR	11,859	VC
Univ of Calif at Berkeley	CA	18,141	HC+
Univ of Detroit Mercy	MI	27,000	C
Univ of Florida	FL	9,354	HC
Univ of Houston	TX	7,000	C
Univ of Illinois at Chicago	IL	16,256	VC
Univ of Illinois at Urbana-Champaign	IL	15,800	HC+

School	ST	$IS	SR
Univ of Kansas	KS	10,915	VC
Univ of Maine at Augusta	ME	5,025	NC
Univ of Maryland/College Park	MD	16,036	HC
Univ of Memphis	TN	11,153	C
Univ of Miami	FL	38,397	MC
Univ of Mich/Ann Arbor	MI	16,587	HC+
Univ of Minn/Twin Cities	MN	13,165	HC
Univ of Nebr at Lincoln	NE	11,401	VC
Univ of New Mexico	NM	11,253	C
Univ of N Car at Charlotte	NC	9,101	C
Univ of N Car at Greensboro	NC	8,993	C
Univ of Notre Dame	IN	39,552	MC
Univ of Okla	OK	10,769	VC+
Univ of Oregon	OR	13,108	VC
Univ of Pennsylvania	PA	41,766	MC
Univ of Pittsburgh at Pittsburgh	PA	18,866	HC
Univ of San Francisco	CA	37,560	VC
Univ of Southern Calif	CA	41,618	MC
Univ of Tenn at Knoxville	TN	11,720	C
Univ of Texas at Arlington	TX	7,195	LC
Univ of Texas at Austin	TX	14,610	HC
Univ of Texas at San Antonio	TX	11,325	LC
Univ of the District of Columbia	DC	2,070	LC
Univ of Utah	UT	10,162	VC
Univ of Virginia	VA	13,759	MC
Univ of Wisc/Milwaukee	WI	9,427	LC
Virginia Polytechnic Inst and State Univ	VA	10,834	VC
Washington State Univ	WA	12,260	C
Washington Univ in St. Louis	MO	42,106	MC
Wellesley College	MA	41,030	MC
Wentworth Inst of Technology	MA	27,500	C
Woodbury Univ	CA	30,176	LC
Yale Univ	CT	41,000	MC

AREA STUDIES

School	ST	$IS	SR
American Univ	DC	38,719	HC+
Bard College	NY	41,800	HC+
Calvin College	MI	25,735	NC
CUNY/City College	NY		C
College of Wooster	OH	31,310	VC+
Columbia Univ/Columbia College	NY	42,584	MC
Duke Univ	NC	41,239	MC
Eastern Mich Univ	MI	12,897	C
Lake Forest College	IL	33,860	VC
New York Univ	NY	43,170	MC
Sterling College	VT	23,286	VC
Univ of Alaska Fairbanks	AK	10,101	C
Univ of Miss	MS	9,000	C
Univ of Nebr at Lincoln	NE	11,401	VC
Univ of Okla	OK	10,769	VC+
Univ of Virginia	VA	13,759	MC
Washington State Univ	WA	12,260	C
Washington Univ in St. Louis	MO	42,106	MC

ART

School	ST	$IS	SR
Abilene Christian Univ	TX	20,830	C
Adams State College	CO	8,613	C
Adrian College	MI	23,000	C
Alabama A&M Univ	AL	8,890	LC
Alabama State Univ	AL	7,658	C
Albany State Univ	GA	5,770	C+
Albertson College of Idaho	ID	21,095	VC
Albion College	MI	26,000	VC
Albright College	PA	33,920	C
Allegheny College	PA	33,500	HC
Alma College	MI	28,544	VC
Alverno College	WI	21,088	C
Andrews Univ	MI	21,786	C
Angelo State Univ	TX	8,340	NC
Anna Maria College	MA	29,815	LC
Appalachian State Univ	NC	8,000	VC
Aquinas College	MI	23,750	C
Arizona State Univ-Tempe	AZ	11,174	C
Arkansas State Univ	AR	9,630	C
Arkansas Tech Univ	AR	8,108	VC
Armstrong Atlantic State Univ	GA	7,394	C
Asbury College	KY	23,762	VC
Ashland Univ	OH	25,000	C
Atlantic Union College	MA	17,600	LC
Augusta State Univ	GA	2,920	C
Augustana College	IL	29,862	VC+
Augustana College	SD	24,380	VC
Austin College	TX	27,871	VC
Austin Peay State Univ	TN	7,535	C
Averett Univ	VA	24,920	C
Avila Univ	MO	22,100	C
Ball State Univ	IN	13,138	C
Barry Univ	FL	24,100	LC
Bates College	ME	42,100	MC
Baylor Univ	TX	27,555	HC
Belhaven College	MS	19,530	NC
Bellarmine Univ	KY	27,650	C+
Benedictine College	KS	21,968	C

School	ST	$IS	SR
Bennington College	VT	41,890	HC
Berea College	KY	5,496	VC+
Berry College	GA	24,342	VC
Bethany College	KS	20,660	LC
Bethel College	IN	19,680	C
Bethel College	KS	21,650	C
Biola Univ	CA	29,372	VC
Black Hills State Univ	SD	7,800	LC
Blackburn College	IL	13,690	C
Bluffton College	OH	26,110	C
Boise State Univ	ID	9,438	LC
Bowling Green State Univ	OH	14,994	C
Brescia Univ	KY	14,240	C
Briar Cliff Univ	IA	23,550	LC
Bridgewater College	VA	27,790	C
Bridgewater State College	MA	12,120	C
Brigham Young Univ	UT	9,200	VC
Brigham Young Univ/Hawaii	HI	7,740	HC+
Brown Univ	RI	42,015	MC
Bucknell Univ	PA	39,660	MC
Buena Vista Univ	IA	27,742	C
Caldwell College	NJ	26,450	LC
Calif College of the Arts	CA	34,325	SP
Calif Lutheran Univ	CA	27,800	LC
Calif State Polytechnic Univ, Pomona	CA	18,053	C+
Cal State East Bay	CA	10,856	LC
Cal State, Bakersfield	CA	6,125	LC
Cal State, Chico	CA	11,395	C
Cal State, Dominguez Hills	CA	10,220	LC
Cal State, Fresno	CA	10,037	LC
Cal State, Long Beach	CA	9,512	C
Cal State, Northridge	CA	9,036	LC
Cal State, San Bernardino	CA	12,563	LC
Cal State, Stanislaus	CA	11,283	C
Calif Univ of Pennsylvania	PA	14,217	C
Calvin College	MI	25,735	NC
Cameron Univ	OK	6,314	NC
Campbell Univ	NC	21,137	VC
Campbellsville Univ	KY	21,328	C
Cardinal Stritch Univ	WI	21,910	C
Carlow Univ	PA	24,313	C
Carroll College	WI	24,860	C
Carthage College	WI	26,000	C
Castleton State College	VT	13,158	C
Catholic Univ of America	DC	35,838	VC
Cedar Crest College	PA	30,615	C
Centenary College of Louisiana	LA	24,760	VC
Central Conn State Univ	CT	13,620	C
Central Mich Univ	MI	12,244	C
Central Washington Univ	WA	11,730	C
Chadron State College	NE	6,360	NC
Chapman Univ	CA	37,550	VC
Chicago State Univ	IL	10,915	C+
CUNY/Brooklyn College	NY	4,377	C+
CUNY/City College	NY		C
CUNY/College of Staten Island	NY	4,328	NC
CUNY/Queens College	NY	4,356	C
Claflin Univ	SC	16,798	C+
Clarion Univ of Pennsylvania	PA	11,844	C
Clark Atlanta Univ	GA	20,960	LC
Clarke College	IA	25,390	C
Cleveland State Univ	OH	10,798	NC
Coe College	IA	27,440	C
Coker College	SC	21,600	C
Colby College	ME	41,770	MC
Colby-Sawyer College	NH	27,850	C
College of Mount St. Joseph	OH	24,860	C
College of New Jersey	NJ	18,315	MC
College of St. Benedict	MN	30,091	VC
College of St. Catherine	MN	27,505	VC
College of St. Elizabeth	NJ	28,495	C
College of St. Mary	NE	23,938	C
College of the Ozarks	MO	4,130	VC+
Colo Christian Univ	CO	21,182	VC
Colo State Univ-Fort Collins	CO	10,878	C+
Colo State Univ-Pueblo	CO	7,821	LC
Columbia College	MO	16,900	C
Columbia College Chicago	IL	25,125	LC
Columbus State Univ	GA	8,664	C
Concordia Univ	CA	26,780	C
Concordia Univ St.Paul	MN	27,776	C
Concordia Univ Wisc	WI	22,640	VC
Concordia Univ, Ann Arbor	MI	25,153	C
Concordia Univ, River Forest	IL	26,300	C
Conn College	CT	41,975	MC
Covenant College	GA	26,460	VC+
Creighton Univ	NE	29,918	VC+
Culver-Stockton College	MO	20,625	C
Daemen College	NY	24,580	C
Dakota Wesleyan Univ	SD	17,832	C
Dana College	NE	22,390	C
Davidson College	NC	36,825	MC
Davis and Elkins College	WV	22,416	C
Defiance College	OH	24,790	C
Delta State Univ	MS	7,709	C
DePaul Univ	IL	29,835	VC
Dillard Univ	LA	17,500	VC
Doane College	NE	22,458	C
Dominican Univ	IL	26,370	C
Dominican Univ of Calif	CA	36,836	C

School	ST	$IS	SR
Drew Univ/College of Liberal Arts	NJ	39,698	VC
Earlham College	IN	33,604	HC
East Carolina Univ	NC	10,000	C
East Central Univ	OK	6,207	C
East Stroudsburg Univ of Pennsylvania	PA	10,336	C
East Tenn State Univ	TN	8,497	C
Eastern Illinois Univ	IL	12,569	C
Eastern Kentucky Univ	KY	7,725	C
Eastern Mennonite Univ	VA	25,450	VC
Eastern Mich Univ	MI	12,897	C
Eastern New Mexico Univ	NM	7,264	C
Eastern Oregon Univ	OR	10,400	NC
Eastern Washington Univ	WA	10,608	C
Edgewood College	WI	22,862	C
Edinboro Univ of Pennsylvania	PA	11,809	LC
Elizabeth City State Univ	NC	5,700	LC
Elizabethtown College	PA	32,100	VC
Elmhurst College	IL	24,685	C
Elmira College	NY	37,200	VC
Elon Univ	NC	25,371	HC
Emory & Henry College	VA	26,570	C
Emory Univ	GA	40,546	MC
Emporia State Univ	KS	8,093	C
Erskine College	SC	25,468	VC
Evangel Univ	MO	17,380	C
Felician College	NJ	24,300	C
Ferrum College	VA	24,290	LC
Florida Atlantic Univ	FL	11,221	C
Florida International Univ	FL	9,215	VC
Fontbonne Univ	MO	23,308	C
Fort Hays State Univ	KS	7,638	C
Fort Lewis College	CO	11,852	C
Freed-Hardeman Univ	TN	16,370	NC
Friends Univ	KS	16,250	LC
Furman Univ	SC	33,264	HC+
Gardner-Webb Univ	NC	21,500	C
George Fox Univ	OR	28,490	C
Georgetown College	KY	24,950	C+
Georgia College and State Univ	GA	11,020	C
Georgia Southern Univ	GA	9,762	C
Georgia State Univ	GA	11,444	VC
Georgian Court College	NJ	20,000	LC
Gonzaga Univ	WA	30,218	HC
Gordon College	MA	29,194	C+
Goucher College	MD	36,225	VC
Grace College	IN	22,170	C
Grambling State Univ	LA	6,538	NC
Green Mountain College	VT	32,164	C
Greensboro College	NC	23,000	C
Greenville College	IL	23,146	C
Grinnell College	IA	34,814	HC+
Guilford College	NC	28,160	C+
Hamilton College	NY	41,660	MC
Hamline Univ	MN	27,070	VC
Hampton Univ	VA	19,468	C+
Hannibal-LaGrange College	MO	16,390	C
Hanover College	IN	28,150	HC
Harding Univ	AR	16,512	VC
Hardin-Simmons Univ	TX	18,641	C
Hartwick College	NY	36,065	C+
Hendrix College	AR	27,646	HC+
High Point Univ	NC	25,720	C
Hiram College	OH	28,700	VC
Holy Family Univ	PA	25,740	C
Hood College	MD	30,085	VC
Houghton College	NY	25,980	VC+
Houston Baptist Univ	TX	18,660	C
Howard Payne Univ	TX	17,115	C
Humboldt State Univ	CA	11,176	C
Huntingdon College	AL	23,090	VC
Huntington Univ	IN	24,830	C
Idaho State Univ	ID	9,030	C
Illinois State Univ	IL	12,839	C+
Indiana Univ of Pennsylvania	PA	11,209	C
Indiana Wesleyan Univ	IN	22,074	C+
Ithaca College	NY	35,144	VC
Jackson State Univ	MS	8,506	C
James Madison Univ	VA	12,010	VC
Johnson State College	VT	11,830	LC
Judson College	AL	16,522	C
Kalamazoo College	MI	32,442	VC+
Kansas State Univ	KS	10,516	VC
Keene State College	NH	13,836	C
Kennesaw State Univ	GA	12,152	C
Kentucky State Univ	KY	10,089	LC
Kentucky Wesleyan College	KY	18,590	C
La Sierra Univ	CA	24,327	C+
Lafayette College	PA	39,267	MC
LaGrange College	GA	22,874	C+
Lake Forest College	IL	33,860	VC
Lakeland College	WI	22,990	C
Lebanon Valley College	PA	31,700	VC
LeMoyne-Owen College	TN	13,150	LC
Lincoln Univ	MO	8,000	NC
Lindsey Wilson College	KY	16,425	LC
Linfield College	OR	29,632	VC
Lipscomb Univ	TN	20,967	VC
Longwood Univ	VA	12,426	C
Lourdes College	OH	15,300	LC
Luther College	IA	28,800	VC+

School	ST	$IS	SR
Lynchburg College	VA	30,645	C
Lyon College	AR	19,990	VC
Macalester College	MN	36,500	MC
MacMurray College	IL	20,755	C
Madonna Univ	MI	16,068	VC
Malone College	OH	23,040	C
Manchester College	IN	23,470	C
Manhattanville College	NY	32,500	C+
Marian College of Fond du Lac	WI	21,775	LC
Mary Baldwin College	VA	26,465	C
Marygrove College	MI	19,310	C+
Marylhurst Univ	OR	14,220	NC
Marymount Univ	VA	25,934	C
Maryville College	TN	29,224	VC
McKendree College	IL	24,800	VC
McMurry Univ	TX	18,100	LC
McPherson College	KS	21,010	C
Meredith College	NC	25,600	C
Methodist College	NC	21,000	C
Metropolitan State College of Denver	CO	2,338	LC
Miami Univ	OH	29,097	HC
Millersville Univ of Pennsylvania	PA	12,113	C
Millikin Univ	IL	25,590	C
Millsaps College	MS	28,256	VC+
Minn State Univ, Mankato	MN	10,276	LC
Minot State Univ	ND	6,700	LC
Miss College	MS	14,574	VC
Miss State Univ	MS	9,577	C
Miss Valley State Univ	MS	7,970	C
Missouri Southern State Univ	MO	8,396	NC
Missouri State Univ	MO	10,748	C+
Missouri Valley College	MO	18,500	C
Molloy College	NY	16,510	C
Monmouth College	IL	23,700	C
Monmouth Univ	NJ	28,956	C
Montana State Univ-Billings	MT	8,906	C
Montana State Univ-Bozeman	MT	1,137	C
Montclair State Univ	NJ	16,327	C
Morehouse College	GA	25,082	C
Morningside College	IA	23,704	C
Mount Mercy College	IA	23,670	C
Mount Olive College	NC	16,000	LC
Mount St. Mary's College	CA	32,086	VC
Mount Union College	OH	25,840	C
Mount Vernon Nazarene Univ	OH	20,810	C
Muhlenberg College	PA	36,030	HC+
Muskingum College	OH	22,970	C
Nazareth College of Rochester	NY	28,175	VC
Nebr Wesleyan Univ	NE	23,415	C+
New Mexico Highlands Univ	NM	6,272	NC
New Mexico State Univ	NM	9,250	C
Newberry College	SC	23,000	LC
Newman Univ	KS	21,106	C
Nicholls State Univ	LA	6,500	NC
N Car Central Univ	NC	9,000	LC
N Dak State Univ	ND	8,500	C
North Georgia College and State Univ	GA	7,000	C
Northeastern Univ	MA	35,742	HC
Northern Illinois Univ	IL	13,178	C
Northern Kentucky Univ	KY	6,670	NC
Northwest Missouri State Univ	MO	10,000	C
Northwest Nazarene Univ	ID	22,590	VC
Northwestern Univ	IL	37,595	MC
Notre Dame College	OH	20,425	C
Notre Dame de Namur Univ	CA	32,790	LC
Oberlin College	OH	40,904	MC
Oglethorpe Univ	GA	30,300	VC
Ohio Dominican Univ	OH	25,954	C
Ohio State Univ	OH	15,357	HC
Ohio Univ	OH	15,921	C
Okla Christian Univ	OK	18,992	NC
Okla City Univ	OK	23,965	VC
Okla State Univ	OK	10,213	VC
Olivet Nazarene Univ	IL	22,590	C
Oregon State Univ	OR	11,055	C
Ottawa Univ	KS	12,000	LC
Otterbein College	OH	28,986	C
Our Lady of the Lake Univ of San Antonio	TX	22,430	LC
Pacific Lutheran Univ	WA	28,805	VC
Palm Beach Atlantic Univ	FL	23,597	VC
Penn State Univ/Univ Park Campus	PA	18,038	HC
Pepperdine Univ	CA	39,960	HC
Piedmont College	GA	20,500	C
Pikeville College	KY	16,500	NC
Pine Manor College	MA	25,038	LC
Pittsburg State Univ	KS	8,112	C
Pitzer College	CA	41,644	HC
Plymouth State Univ	NH	12,298	LC
Point Loma Nazarene Univ	CA	27,610	VC
Prairie View A&M Univ	TX	11,110	LC
Presbyterian College	SC	30,044	VC
Quincy Univ	IL	24,920	C
Radford Univ	VA	13,145	C
Ramapo College of New Jersey	NJ	16,630	VC

School	ST	$IS	SR
Randolph-Macon Woman's College	VA	31,160	VC+
Reed College	OR	41,106	MC
Rhodes College	TN	32,860	HC
Rider Univ	NJ	32,560	C
Ripon College	WI	27,160	C+
Roanoke College	VA	30,748	VC
Rockford College	IL	28,330	VC
Rocky Mountain College	MT	20,805	C
Rowan Univ	NJ	16,000	VC
Rutgers, The State Univ of New Jersey/Camden Campus	NJ	15,000	VC
Rutgers, The State Univ of New Jersey/New Brunswick/Piscataway Campus	NJ	15,810	HC
Rutgers, The State Univ of New Jersey/Newark Campus	NJ	15,640	VC
Sacred Heart Univ	CT	33,404	C
Saginaw Valley State Univ	MI	11,432	C
St. Edward's Univ	TX	23,560	C
St. John's Univ	MN	29,749	VC
St. Joseph's College	IN	26,600	C
St. Lawrence Univ	NY	40,545	VC
St. Mary's College	IN	32,538	VC
St. Mary's College of Calif	CA	37,290	C
St. Mary's College of Maryland	MD	18,876	VC+
St. Mary's Univ of Minn	MN	23,857	VC
St. Norbert College	WI	28,577	C+
St. Olaf College	MN	32,800	HC
St. Vincent College	PA	26,160	VC
Salisbury Univ	MD	13,128	VC
Sam Houston State Univ	TX	8,000	C
Samford Univ	AL	20,258	VC
Savannah College of Art and Design	GA	30,800	SP
Schreiner Univ	TX	20,600	C
Seattle Pacific Univ	WA	29,355	C
Seton Hall Univ	NJ	33,622	VC
Shepherd Univ	WV	10,066	C
Shippensburg Univ of Pennsylvania	PA	11,621	C
Shorter College	GA	19,700	C
Simmons College	MA	35,640	VC
Simon's Rock College of Bard	MA	41,988	VC+
Simpson College	IA	26,833	VC
Sinte Gleska Univ	SD	2,300	NC
Skidmore College	NY	41,779	HC
Sonoma State Univ	CA	14,732	C
S Dak State Univ	SD	9,815	C
Southeast Missouri State Univ	MO	10,596	C
Southeastern Louisiana Univ	LA	8,521	LC
Southeastern Okla State Univ	OK	6,147	C
Southern Adventist Univ	TN	18,500	C
Southern Arkansas Univ	AR	6,956	C
Southern Illinois Univ Carbondale	IL	12,391	C
Southern Illinois Univ Edwardsville	IL	11,022	C
Southern Oregon Univ	OR	12,186	C
Southern Utah Univ	UT		C
Southwest Baptist Univ	MO	18,300	C
Southwest Minn State Univ	MN	10,975	C
Southwestern Univ	TX	26,767	HC
Spelman College	GA	24,650	VC
Spring Arbor Univ	MI	22,476	C
Stanford Univ	CA	41,557	MC
SUNY at Oswego	NY	13,662	VC
SUNY/College at Buffalo	NY	11,903	C+
SUNY/College at Cortland	NY	12,095	C
SUNY/College at Oneonta	NY	12,905	VC
SUNY/Univ at Binghamton	NY	13,988	HC
Stephen F. Austin State Univ	TX	7,930	C
Sterling College	KS	19,992	C
Stetson Univ	FL	32,725	VC
Stillman College	AL	11,475	LC
Susquehanna Univ	PA	33,465	VC
Swarthmore College	PA	41,280	MC
Syracuse Univ	NY	38,655	HC
Tarleton State Univ	TX	8,952	C
Taylor Univ	IN	26,376	VC+
Temple Univ	PA	17,438	C
Tenn State Univ	TN	9,048	LC
Texas A&M Univ at Corpus Christi	TX	10,280	C
Texas Lutheran Univ	TX	23,530	C
Texas Southern Univ	TX	9,828	C
Texas State Univ - San Marcos	TX	10,862	C
Texas Wesleyan Univ	TX	18,700	C
Texas Woman's Univ	TX	7,804	LC
Thiel College	PA	24,580	C
Thomas Edison State College	NJ	3,780	SP
Thomas More College	KY	24,470	C
Tougaloo College	MS	15,975	NC
Towson Univ	MD	13,924	VC
Trinity Christian College	IL	23,645	C

School	ST	$IS	SR
Troy Univ	AL	8,916	C
Truman State Univ	MO	11,242	HC
Union Univ	TN	20,750	C
Univ of Akron	OH	15,166	NC
Univ of Alabama at Birmingham	AL	13,716	C
Univ of Alaska Anchorage	AK	11,275	NC
Univ of Alaska Fairbanks	AK	10,101	C
Univ of Alaska Southeast	AK	8,050	LC
Univ of Arkansas	AR	11,859	VC
Univ of Arkansas at Little Rock	AR	7,230	NC
Univ of Arkansas at Monticello	AR	7,325	NC
Univ of Arkansas at Pine Bluff	AR	8,300	C
Univ of Calif at Berkeley	CA	18,141	HC+
Univ of Calif at Los Angeles	CA	17,681	MC
Univ of Calif at Riverside	CA	16,625	C
Univ of Calif at Santa Barbara	CA	11,800	VC
Univ of Calif at Santa Cruz	CA	19,174	VC
Univ of Central Florida	FL	10,739	VC
Univ of Charleston	WV	27,600	C
Univ of Conn	CT	16,628	HC
Univ of Delaware	DE	14,142	HC
Univ of Denver	CO	36,376	VC+
Univ of Evansville	IN	28,320	VC
Univ of Florida	FL	9,354	HC
Univ of Georgia	GA	11,004	HC
Univ of Great Falls	MT	17,000	C
Univ of Hawaii at Hilo	HI	6,500	C
Univ of Hawaii at Manoa	HI	10,413	VC
Univ of Houston	TX	7,000	C
Univ of Idaho	ID	9,310	NC
Univ of Indianapolis	IN	25,090	C
Univ of Iowa	IA	12,172	VC
Univ of Kansas	KS	10,915	VC
Univ of La Verne	CA	33,470	C
Univ of Louisiana at Monroe	LA	7,103	C
Univ of Louisville	KY	10,400	VC
Univ of Maine	ME	13,642	C
Univ of Maine at Augusta	ME	5,025	NC
Univ of Maine at Farmington	ME	11,515	C
Univ of Maine at Presque Isle	ME	10,066	LC
Univ of Mary Hardin-Baylor	TX	19,428	C
Univ of Mass Boston	MA	8,024	C
Univ of Memphis	TN	11,153	C
Univ of Miami	FL	38,397	MC
Univ of Mich/Flint	MI	6,398	C
Univ of Minn/Duluth	MN	13,974	C
Univ of Miss	MS	9,000	C
Univ of Missouri/Kansas City	MO	15,000	VC
Univ of Montana--Western	MT	8,406	NC
Univ of Montevallo	AL	9,630	C
Univ of Nebr at Lincoln	NE	11,401	VC
Univ of Nebr at Omaha	NE	11,235	C
Univ of Nevada/Reno	NV	12,155	NC
Univ of New Haven	CT	31,794	C
Univ of New Mexico	NM	11,253	C
Univ of New Orleans	LA	7,370	C
Univ of North Alabama	AL	8,992	C
Univ of N Car at Asheville	NC	9,237	VC
Univ of N Car at Charlotte	NC	9,101	C
Univ of N Car at Greensboro	NC	8,993	C
Univ of N Car at Pembroke	NC	7,940	LC
Univ of North Florida	FL	9,908	VC
Univ of North Texas	TX	7,800	C
Univ of Northern Colo	CO	10,249	C
Univ of Okla	OK	10,769	VC+
Univ of Pittsburgh at Pittsburgh	PA	18,866	HC
Univ of Puget Sound	WA	35,600	HC
Univ of Redlands	CA	36,160	VC
Univ of Rhode Island	RI	15,398	C
Univ of Rio Grande	OH	8,728	NC
Univ of St. Mary	KS	18,900	C
Univ of Science and Arts of Okla	OK	7,650	C
Univ of S Dak	SD	9,068	C
Univ of Tampa	FL	25,784	C
Univ of Texas at El Paso	TX	8,764	NC
Univ of Texas at San Antonio	TX	11,325	LC
Univ of Texas-Pan American	TX	7,290	C+
Univ of the Cumberlands	KY	18,184	C
Univ of the Incarnate Word	TX	23,306	C
Univ of the Ozarks	AR	19,250	C
Univ of the Pacific	CA	34,380	VC
Univ of the South	TN	34,645	HC
Univ of Tulsa	OK	25,348	HC
Univ of Utah	UT	10,162	VC
Univ of Vermont	VT	18,080	VC
Univ of Virginia	VA	13,759	MC
Univ of Virginia's College at Wise	VA	11,076	C
Univ of West Georgia	GA	8,838	C
Univ of Wisc/Eau Claire	WI	9,915	VC
Univ of Wisc/La Crosse	WI	10,045	VC
Univ of Wisc/Madison	WI	13,117	HC
Univ of Wisc/Oshkosh	WI	10,426	LC

School	ST	$IS	SR
Univ of Wisc/River Falls	WI	9,722	LC
Univ of Wisc/Stout	WI	11,164	C
Univ of Wyoming	WY	9,666	C
Upper Iowa Univ	IA	20,130	C
Ursinus College	PA	38,950	VC
Ursuline College	OH	25,456	C
Valdosta State Univ	GA	8,802	C
Valley City State Univ	ND	9,854	LC
Valparaiso Univ	IN	28,970	VC+
Vassar College	NY	41,700	MC
Virginia Intermont College	VA	22,200	C
Virginia Polytechnic Inst and State Univ	VA	10,834	VC
Virginia Wesleyan College	VA	28,433	C
Wabash College	IN	30,116	HC
Wake Forest Univ	NC	38,290	MC
Walla Walla College	WA	24,489	NC
Warren Wilson College	NC	24,382	VC
Wartburg College	IA	27,315	NC
Washburn Univ	KS	9,734	NC
Washington and Jefferson College	PA	33,490	VC
Washington College	MD	34,990	VC
Wayland Baptist Univ	TX	13,484	C
Wayne State College	NE	8,033	NC
Wayne State Univ	MI	11,805	C
Waynesburg College	PA	21,230	C
Webster Univ	MO	24,280	VC
West Chester Univ of Pennsylvania	PA	12,355	C+
West Texas A&M Univ	TX	8,452	C
West Virginia Univ	WV	10,506	C
Western Carolina Univ	NC	7,000	C
Western Conn State Univ	CT	12,993	C
Western Illinois Univ	IL	13,042	C
Western Mich Univ	MI	13,299	C
Western Oregon Univ	OR	10,295	C
Western State College of Colo	CO	9,942	C
Western Washington Univ	WA	11,262	VC
Westminster College	PA	31,290	C+
Westmont College	CA	36,672	HC
Wheaton College	IL	27,760	HC
Whittier College	CA	29,108	C
Whitworth College	WA	29,428	VC+
Wichita State Univ	KS	8,500	C
William Carey College	MS	11,000	LC
William Jewell College	MO	24,340	C
William Woods Univ	MO	21,020	C
Williams Baptist College	AR	13,450	C
Williams College	MA	40,310	MC
Wilmington College	OH	2,806	NC
Wingate Univ	NC	23,300	C
Winston-Salem State Univ	NC	8,960	LC
Winthrop Univ	SC	11,302	C
Wisc Lutheran College	WI	23,510	VC
Xavier Univ	OH	30,490	HC
Yale Univ	CT	41,000	MC
Youngstown State Univ	OH	12,613	NC

ART EDUCATION

School	ST	$IS	SR
Abilene Christian Univ	TX	20,830	C
Adams State College	CO	8,613	C
Adelphi Univ	NY	27,000	VC
Alabama A&M Univ	AL	8,890	C
Alabama State Univ	AL	7,658	C
Alfred Univ	NY		VC
Alverno College	WI	21,088	C
Anderson Univ	IN	25,050	LC
Andrews Univ	MI	21,786	C
Anna Maria College	MA	29,815	LC
Appalachian State Univ	NC	8,000	VC
Arcadia Univ	PA	33,570	VC
Arkansas State Univ	AR	9,630	C
Arkansas Tech Univ	AR	8,108	VC
Armstrong Atlantic State Univ	GA	7,394	C
Asbury College	KY	23,762	VC
Ashland Univ	OH	25,000	C
Augustana College	IL	29,862	VC+
Averett Univ	VA	24,920	C
Azusa Pacific Univ	CA	28,546	VC
Baker Univ	KS	22,190	C
Baldwin-Wallace College	OH	27,256	VC
Ball State Univ	IN	13,138	C
Barton College	NC	22,316	C
Baylor Univ	TX	27,555	HC
Beloit College	WI	32,808	HC
Bemidji State Univ	MN	11,180	LC
Berea College	KY	5,496	VC+
Berry College	GA	24,342	VC
Bethany College	KS	20,660	LC
Bethel Univ	MN	29,840	VC
Birmingham-Southern College	AL	28,494	VC+
Black Hills State Univ	SD	7,800	LC
Blackburn College	IL	13,690	C
Boise State Univ	ID	9,438	LC
Boston Univ	MA	42,046	HC+
Bowling Green State Univ	OH	14,994	C
Bradley Univ	IL	25,280	VC
Brenau Univ Women's College	GA	23,950	VC
Brescia Univ	KY	14,240	C
Brigham Young Univ	UT	9,200	VC

School	ST	$IS	SR
Brigham Young Univ/Hawaii	HI	7,740	HC+
Buena Vista Univ	IA	27,742	C
Cal State, Fullerton	CA	10,990	C
Calvin College	MI	25,735	NC
Carlow Univ	PA	24,313	C
Carroll College	WI	24,860	C
Carson-Newman College	TN	16,800	C
Case Western Reserve Univ	OH	37,314	MC
Catholic Univ of America	DC	35,838	VC
Central Conn State Univ	CT	13,620	C
Central Mich Univ	MI	12,244	C
Central Missouri State Univ	MO	10,000	C
Central State Univ	OH	9,010	C+
Central Washington Univ	WA	11,730	C
Chicago State Univ	IL	10,915	C+
CUNY/Brooklyn College	NY	4,377	C+
CUNY/City College	NY		C
CUNY/Herbert H. Lehman College	NY	4,000	LC
CUNY/Hunter College	NY	8,000	C+
CUNY/Queens College	NY	4,356	C
Claflin College	SC	16,798	C+
Clarke College	IA	25,390	C
Coker College	SC	21,600	C
Colby-Sawyer College	NH	27,850	LC
College for Creative Studies	MI	24,000	SP
College of Mount St. Joseph	OH	24,860	C
College of New Jersey	NJ	18,315	MC
College of New Rochelle	NY	28,396	C+
College of Notre Dame of Maryland	MD	27,700	C
College of St. Catherine	MN	27,505	VC
College of St. Rose	NY	25,684	C
College of the Ozarks	MO	4,130	VC+
Columbus State Univ	GA	8,664	C
Concord College	WV	9,708	C
Concordia College: Moorhead	MN	22,475	VC
Converse College	SC	24,800	VC
Corcoran School of Art and Design	DC	32,850	SP
Cornell College	IA	30,110	VC+
Culver-Stockton College	MO	20,625	C
Daemen College	NY	24,580	C
Dakota State Univ	SD	7,466	C
Dana College	NE	22,390	C
Defiance College	OH	24,790	C
Delaware State Univ	DE	8,130	LC
Dickinson State Univ	ND	7,847	NC
Dordt College	IA	20,325	VC
Dowling College	NY	22,110	LC
East Carolina Univ	NC	10,000	C
East Central Univ	OK	6,207	C
Eastern Kentucky Univ	KY	7,725	C
Eastern Mich Univ	MI	12,897	C
Eastern Washington Univ	WA	10,608	C
Edinboro Univ of Pennsylvania	PA	11,809	LC
Elmhurst College	IL	24,685	C
Elmira College	NY	37,200	VC
Emporia State Univ	KS	8,093	C
Escuela de Artes Plasticas de PR	PR	2,372	
Fairmont State	WV	8,400	LC
Fisk Univ	TN	19,830	C
Flagler College	FL	13,790	VC+
Florida A&M Univ	FL	8,344	C
Florida International Univ	FL	9,215	VC
Florida Southern College	FL	25,965	C
Florida State Univ	FL	9,028	HC
Fontbonne Univ	MO	23,308	C
Fort Hays State Univ	KS	7,638	C
Francis Marion Univ	SC	11,114	C
Freed-Hardeman Univ	TN	16,370	NC
Friends Univ	KS	16,250	LC
Gallaudet Univ	DC	16,554	
Georgia Southern Univ	GA	9,762	C
Georgia Southwestern State Univ	GA	6,035	C
Georgia State Univ	GA	11,444	VC
Goshen College	IN	22,850	VC
Grace College	IN	22,170	C
Grambling State Univ	LA	6,538	NC
Grand Canyon Univ	AZ	32,000	LC
Grand Valley State Univ	MI	12,000	VC
Grand View College	IA	21,482	C
Green Mountain College	VT	32,164	C
Greensboro College	NC	23,000	C
Gustavus Adolphus College	MN	30,920	HC
Hardin-Simmons Univ	TX	18,641	C
Hastings College	NE	22,218	VC
High Point Univ	NC	25,720	C
Hillsdale College	MI	24,160	HC
Hofstra Univ	NY	32,630	VC
Hope College	MI	28,208	VC+
Houston Baptist Univ	TX	18,660	C
Howard Univ	DC	18,481	C+
Huntingdon College	AL	23,090	VC
Huntington Univ	IN	24,830	C
Indiana State Univ	IN	11,604	C
Indiana Univ of Pennsylvania	PA	11,209	C
Indiana Univ-Purdue Univ Fort Wayne	IN	5,067	LC

INDEX OF COLLEGE MAJORS

School	ST	$IS	SR
Indiana Univ-Purdue Univ Indianapolis	IN	10,959	C
Indiana Wesleyan Univ	IN	22,074	C+
Inter American Univ of PR/ San German	PR	6,720	
Iowa Wesleyan College	IA	22,140	C
Ithaca College	NY	35,144	VC
Jacksonville Univ	FL	24,040	C
Johnson State College	VT	11,830	LC
Kansas State Univ	KS	10,516	VC
Kansas Wesleyan Univ	KS	21,400	VC
Kendall College of Art and Design of Ferris State Univ	MI	11,870	SP
Kennesaw State Univ	GA	12,152	C
Kent State Univ	OH	14,594	C
Kentucky State Univ	KY	10,089	LC
Kentucky Wesleyan College	KY	18,590	C
Keystone College	PA	22,810	C
Kutztown Univ of Pennsylvania	PA	10,820	C
Lamar Univ	TX	6,820	C
Lawrence Univ	WI	33,958	HC+
Lenoir-Rhyne College	NC	25,580	C
Limestone College	SC	19,840	C
Lincoln Univ	MO	8,000	NC
Lindenwood Univ	MO	18,600	VC
Lipscomb Univ	TN	20,967	VC
LIU/Brooklyn Campus	NY	25,000	C
LIU/C.W. Post Campus	NY	28,282	C
Longwood Univ	VA	12,426	C
Loras College	IA	27,193	C
Louisiana College	LA	13,450	C
Louisiana State Univ in Shreveport	LA	2,900	NC
Louisiana Tech Univ	LA	7,370	C
Lubbock Christian Univ	TX	16,960	C
Madonna Univ	MI	16,068	VC
Malone College	OH	23,040	C
Manchester College	IN	23,470	C
Mansfield Univ	PA	11,300	C
Marian College of Fond du Lac	WI	21,775	C
Mars Hill College	NC	19,000	LC
Marymount Univ	VA	25,934	C
Maryville Univ of St. Louis	MO	23,000	VC
Marywood Univ	PA	30,680	C
Mass College of Art	MA	16,650	SP
McKendree College	IL	24,800	VC
McMurry Univ	TX	18,100	LC
Mercyhurst College	PA	28,633	VC
Messiah College	PA	28,910	VC+
Methodist College	NC	21,000	C
Miami Univ	OH	29,097	HC
Mich State Univ	MI	13,689	VC
Middle Tenn State Univ	TN	8,540	C
Midland Lutheran College	NE	18,600	C
Millersville Univ of Pennsylvania	PA	12,113	C
Millikin Univ	IL	25,590	C
Minn State Univ, Mankato	MN	10,276	LC
Minn State Univ, Moorhead	MN	7,000	LC
Miss College	MS	14,574	VC
Miss Univ for Women	MS	6,000	LC
Missouri Southern State Univ	MO	8,396	NC
Missouri State Univ	MO	10,748	C+
Missouri Western State Univ	MO	9,534	NC
Monmouth Univ	NJ	28,956	C
Montana State Univ-Billings	MT	8,906	C
Montclair State Univ	NJ	16,327	C
Montserrat College of Art	MA	25,929	SP
Moore College of Art and Design	PA	27,200	SP
Moravian College	PA	28,950	VC
Morningside College	IA	23,704	C
Mount Mary College	WI	22,895	C
Mount Vernon Nazarene Univ	OH	20,810	C
Murray State Univ	KY	8,900	VC
Nazareth College of Rochester	NY	28,175	VC
New Jersey City Univ	NJ	13,695	LC
New York Inst of Technology	NY	28,126	VC
New York Univ	NY	43,170	MC
N Car Agricultural and Technical State Univ	NC	8,000	LC
North Georgia College and State Univ	GA	7,000	C
Northeastern State Univ	OK	5,896	LC
Northern Arizona Univ	AZ	10,353	C
Northern Illinois Univ	IL	13,178	C
Northern Kentucky Univ	KY	6,670	NC
Northern Mich Univ	MI	12,340	LC
Northern State Univ	SD	8,257	C
Northwest Missouri State Univ	MO	10,000	C
Northwest Nazarene Univ	ID	22,590	VC
Northwestern College	MN	25,220	NC
Northwestern College of Iowa	IA	22,174	C+
Oakland City Univ	IN	19,620	NC
Ohio State Univ	OH	15,357	HC
Ohio Univ	OH	15,921	C
Ohio Wesleyan Univ	OH	35,830	VC+
Okla Baptist Univ	OK	17,986	VC
Okla Christian Univ	OK	18,992	NC
Old Dominion Univ	VA	11,907	C
Oral Roberts Univ	OK	22,650	C
Ouachita Baptist Univ	AR	21,900	VC
Our Lady of the Lake Univ of San Antonio	TX	22,430	LC
Palm Beach Atlantic Univ	FL	23,597	VC
Penn State Univ/Univ Park Campus	PA	18,038	HC
Peru State College	NE	6,350	NC
Pittsburg State Univ	KS	8,112	C
Plymouth State Univ	NH	12,298	LC
Pontifical Catholic Univ of PR/Ponce	PR	7,310	
Pratt Inst	NY	36,156	SP
Prescott College	AZ	13,445	LC
Purdue Univ/West Lafayette	IN	13,458	VC
Radford Univ	VA	13,145	C
Rhode Island College	RI	11,570	C
Rivier College	NH	26,600	C
Roberts Wesleyan College	NY	26,378	C
Rocky Mountain College	MT	20,805	C
Rosemont College	PA	29,350	C
Saginaw Valley State Univ	MI	11,432	C
St. Ambrose Univ	IA	25,495	C
St. Cloud State Univ	MN	10,010	C
St. Edward's Univ	TX	23,560	C
St. Joseph's College	IN	26,600	C
St. Mary-of-the-Woods College	IN	25,480	C
St. Michael's College	VT	33,330	VC
St. Thomas Aquinas College	NY	22,000	LC
St. Vincent College	PA	26,160	VC
St. Xavier Univ	IL	23,160	C
Salem State College	MA	13,161	LC
School of the Art Inst of Chicago	IL	37,800	SP
Schreiner Univ	TX	20,600	C
Seattle Pacific Univ	WA	29,355	C
Seton Hill Univ	PA	28,810	C
Shepherd Univ	WV	10,066	C
Shippensburg Univ of Pennsylvania	PA	11,621	C
Silver Lake College of the Holy Family	WI	18,500	LC
S Car State Univ	SC	6,700	LC
S Dak State Univ	SD	9,815	C
Southeast Missouri State Univ	MO	10,596	C
Southeastern Louisiana Univ	LA	8,521	LC
Southeastern Okla State Univ	OK	6,147	C
Southern Arkansas Univ	AR	6,956	C
Southern Conn State Univ	CT	10,310	C
Southern Methodist Univ	TX	36,088	VC+
Southern Univ at New Orleans	LA	1,000	NC
Southern Utah Univ	UT		C
Southwest Baptist Univ	MO	18,300	C
Southwest Minn State Univ	MN	10,975	C
Southwestern Okla State Univ	OK	4,801	C
Spelman College	GA	24,650	VC
SUNY/College at Buffalo	NY	11,903	C+
SUNY/Univ at New Paltz	NY	12,480	VC
Sul Ross State Univ	TX	6,600	LC
Syracuse Univ	NY	38,655	HC
Tarleton State Univ	TX	8,952	C
Taylor Univ	IN	26,376	VC+
Temple Univ	PA	17,438	C
Tenn Tech Univ	TN	10,044	C
Texas Christian Univ	TX	23,410	VC+
Towson Univ	MD	13,924	VC
Trinity Christian College	IL	23,645	C
Trinity Univ	TX	30,157	HC+
Troy Univ	AL	8,916	C
Union College	NE	18,710	C
Univ of Akron	OH	15,166	NC
Univ of Arizona	AZ	11,958	VC
Univ of Arkansas at Pine Bluff	AR	8,300	C
Univ of Central Arkansas	AR	9,984	C
Univ of Central Florida	FL	10,739	VC
Univ of Central Okla	OK	8,094	C
Univ of Cincinnati	OH	17,682	C
Univ of Dallas	TX	27,432	VC+
Univ of Dayton	OH	28,826	VC
Univ of Evansville	IN	28,320	VC
Univ of Findlay	OH	29,238	C
Univ of Florida	FL	9,354	HC
Univ of Georgia	GA	11,004	HC
Univ of Idaho	ID	9,310	NC
Univ of Illinois at Chicago	IL	16,256	VC
Univ of Illinois at Urbana-Champaign	IL	15,800	HC+
Univ of Indianapolis	IN	25,090	C
Univ of Iowa	IA	12,172	VC
Univ of Kansas	KS	10,915	VC
Univ of Kentucky	KY	7,800	VC
Univ of Louisiana at Lafayette	LA	5,830	C
Univ of Louisiana at Monroe	LA	7,103	C
Univ of Louisville	KY	10,400	VC
Univ of Maine	ME	13,642	C
Univ of Mary Hardin-Baylor	TX	19,428	C
Univ of Maryland/College Park	MD	16,036	HC
Univ of Maryland/Eastern Shore	MD	11,210	C
Univ of Mass Dartmouth	MA	15,985	C
Univ of Mich/Ann Arbor	MI	16,587	HC+
Univ of Minn/Duluth	MN	13,974	C
Univ of Minn/Twin Cities	MN	13,165	HC
Univ of Missouri/Columbia	MO	13,500	VC
Univ of Montana--Western	MT	8,406	NC
Univ of Montevallo	AL	9,630	C
Univ of Nebr at Kearney	NE	9,000	NC
Univ of Nebr at Lincoln	NE	11,401	VC
Univ of New England	ME	31,005	C
Univ of New Mexico	NM	11,253	C
Univ of North Alabama	AL	8,992	C
Univ of N Car at Charlotte	NC	9,101	C
Univ of N Car at Pembroke	NC	7,940	LC
Univ of North Florida	FL	9,908	VC
Univ of Northern Iowa	IA	11,133	C
Univ of Rio Grande	OH	8,728	NC
Univ of St. Francis	IN	20,970	C
Univ of Sioux Falls	SD	20,800	C
Univ of S Car at Columbia	SC	13,397	VC
Univ of S Dak	SD	9,068	C
Univ of South Florida	FL	10,284	VC
Univ of Southern Indiana	IN	12,590	LC
Univ of Southern Miss	MS	10,112	C
Univ of Tenn at Chattanooga	TN	7,790	C
Univ of Tenn at Knoxville	TN	11,720	C
Univ of the Cumberlands	KY	18,184	C
Univ of the Incarnate Word	TX	23,306	C
Univ of Toledo	OH	15,806	NC
Univ of Vermont	VT	18,080	VC
Univ of West Florida	FL	8,559	C
Univ of West Georgia	GA	8,838	C
Univ of Wisc/Eau Claire	WI	9,915	VC
Univ of Wisc/Madison	WI	13,117	HC
Univ of Wisc/Milwaukee	WI	9,427	C
Univ of Wisc/Oshkosh	WI	10,426	LC
Univ of Wisc/Platteville	WI	9,779	NC
Univ of Wisc/River Falls	WI	9,722	C
Univ of Wisc/Stout	WI	11,164	C
Univ of Wisc/Superior	WI	9,610	C+
Univ of Wisc/Whitewater	WI	9,274	C
Utah State Univ	UT	8,002	VC
Valdosta State Univ	GA	8,802	C
Virginia Commonwealth Univ	VA	12,987	C
Virginia Union Univ	VA	18,432	LC
Virginia Wesleyan College	VA	28,433	C
Viterbo Univ	WI	21,670	C
Wartburg College	IA	27,315	NC
Washburn Univ	KS	9,734	NC
Washington and Jefferson College	PA	33,490	VC
Washington Univ in St. Louis	MO	42,106	MC
Wayne State Univ	MI	11,805	C
Weber State Univ	UT	9,635	NC
West Liberty State College	WV	9,142	LC
West Texas A&M Univ	TX	8,452	C
West Virginia State Univ	WV	8,378	NC
West Virginia Wesleyan College	WV	26,880	C
Western Carolina Univ	NC	7,000	C
Western Kentucky Univ	KY	10,192	C
Western Mich Univ	MI	13,299	C
Western New Mexico Univ	NM	7,233	C
Western State College of Colo	CO	9,942	C
Western Washington Univ	WA	11,262	VC
Westfield State College	MA	10,200	C
Westmont College	CA	36,672	HC
Wichita State Univ	KS	8,500	C
Wingate Univ	NC	23,300	C
Winona State Univ	MN	11,333	C
Wright State Univ	OH	13,616	LC
Xavier Univ of Louisiana	LA	17,600	C
Youngstown State Univ	OH	12,613	NC

ART HISTORY AND APPRECIATION

School	ST	$IS	SR
Adelphi Univ	NY	27,000	VC
Albion College	MI	26,000	VC
Allegheny College	PA	33,500	HC
American Univ	DC	38,719	HC+
Aquinas College	MI	23,750	C
Arcadia Univ	PA	33,570	VC
Art Academy of Cincinnati	OH	18,100	SP
Augsburg College	MN	28,300	C
Augustana College	IL	29,862	VC+
Baker Univ	KS	22,190	C
Baldwin-Wallace College	OH	27,256	VC
Bard College	NY	41,800	HC+
Baylor Univ	TX	27,555	VC
Beloit College	WI	32,808	HC
Birmingham-Southern College	AL	28,494	VC+
Bloomsburg Univ of Pennsylvania	PA	11,602	C
Boston College	MA	41,608	MC
Bowdoin College	ME	41,660	MC
Bowling Green State Univ	OH	14,994	C
Bradley Univ	IL	25,280	VC
Brandeis Univ	MA	41,551	MC
Brigham Young Univ	UT	9,200	VC
Brown Univ	RI	42,015	MC
Bryn Mawr College	PA	42,780	HC+
Bucknell Univ	PA	39,660	MC
Cal State, Fullerton	CA	10,990	C
Cal State, San Bernardino	CA	12,563	LC
Cal State, Stanislaus	CA	11,283	C
Calvin College	MI	25,735	NC
Canisius College	NY	32,257	VC
Carleton College	MN	40,467	MC
Carlow Univ	PA	24,313	C
Case Western Reserve Univ	OH	37,314	MC
Catholic Univ of America	DC	35,838	VC
Chapman Univ	CA	37,550	VC
Chatham Univ	PA	27,290	C+
Chestnut Hill College	PA	26,600	LC
CUNY/Brooklyn College	NY	4,377	C+
CUNY/Queens College	NY	4,356	C
CUNY/York College	NY	4,242	NC
Clark Univ	MA	35,165	VC+
Clarke College	IA	25,390	C
Colgate Univ	NY	41,170	MC
College of Charleston	SC	13,616	VC
College of New Rochelle	NY	28,396	C+
College of Notre Dame of Maryland	MD	27,700	C
College of Santa Fe	NM	28,978	C
College of the Holy Cross	MA	40,664	MC
Colo College	CO	37,668	HC
Columbia Univ/Barnard College	NY	38,000	MC
Columbia Univ/Columbia College	NY	42,584	MC
Columbia Univ/School of General Studies	NY	41,516	C
Concordia College: Moorhead	MN	22,475	VC
Conn College	CT	41,975	MC
Cornell Univ	NY	41,717	MC
Dartmouth College	NH	39,465	MC
Denison Univ	OH	37,040	HC
DePauw Univ	IN	32,100	HC
Dominican Univ of Calif	CA	36,836	C
Drake Univ	IA	27,632	VC+
Drew Univ/College of Liberal Arts	NJ	39,698	VC
Drury Univ	MO	20,117	VC
Duke Univ	NC	41,239	MC
Duquesne Univ	PA	29,534	VC
East Carolina Univ	NC	10,000	C
Eastern Univ	PA	24,075	C
Eastern Washington Univ	WA	10,608	C
Edinboro Univ of Pennsylvania	PA	11,809	LC
Emory Univ	GA	40,546	MC
Florida International Univ	FL	9,215	VC
Florida State Univ	FL	9,028	HC
Fordham Univ	NY	36,000	HC
Framingham State College	MA	11,156	C
Franklin and Marshall College	PA	40,590	HC
Gallaudet Univ	DC	16,554	
George Mason Univ	VA	10,850	VC
George Washington Univ	DC	48,820	MC
Georgia State Univ	GA	11,444	VC
Georgian Court College	NJ	20,000	LC
Gettysburg College	PA	39,864	HC
Hamilton College	NY	41,660	MC
Hamline Univ	MN	27,070	VC
Hampshire College	MA	37,120	HC
Hanover College	IN	28,150	HC
Hartwick College	NY	36,065	C+
Harvard Univ/Harvard College	MA	45,860	MC
Haverford College	PA	41,600	MC
Hiram College	OH	28,700	VC
Hobart and William Smith Colleges	NY	41,123	VC
Hofstra Univ	NY	32,630	VC
Hollins Univ	VA	31,105	C
Howard Univ	DC	18,481	C+
Indiana State Univ	IN	11,604	C
Indiana Univ Bloomington	IN	13,356	VC
Indiana Univ-Purdue Univ Indianapolis	IN	10,959	C
Ithaca College	NY	35,144	VC
Jacksonville Univ	FL	24,040	C
James Madison Univ	VA	12,010	VC
John Carroll Univ	OH	27,658	C+
Johns Hopkins Univ	MD	42,044	MC
Juniata College	PA	33,130	VC
Kalamazoo College	MI	32,442	VC+
Kansas City Art Inst	MO	29,542	SP
Kean Univ	NJ	15,880	C
Kendall College of Art and Design of Ferris State Univ	MI	11,870	SP
Kent State Univ	OH	14,594	C
Kenyon College	OH	39,500	MC
Knox College	IL	32,385	VC+

ST = STATE   **$IS** = IN-STATE COSTS   **SR** = SELECTOR RATING

School	ST	$IS	SR
Lawrence Univ	WI	33,958	HC+
Lehigh Univ	PA	42,690	HC+
Lewis and Clark College	OR	35,358	VC+
Lindenwood Univ	MO	18,600	VC
Lourdes College	OH	15,300	LC
Loyola Marymount Univ	CA	36,321	VC
Lycoming College	PA	30,797	C+
Manhattanville College	NY	32,500	C+
Mansfield Univ	PA	11,300	C
Marian College	IN	26,160	C
Mars Hill College	NC	19,000	LC
Mary Baldwin College	VA	26,465	C
Maryville College	TN	29,224	VC
Mass College of Art	MA	16,650	SP
McDaniel College	MD	31,610	VC
Messiah College	PA	28,910	VC+
Miami Univ	OH	29,097	HC
Mich State Univ	MI	13,689	VC
Mills College	CA	39,870	C
Monmouth Univ	NJ	28,956	C
Montclair State Univ	NJ	16,327	C
Moravian College	PA	28,950	VC
Mount Holyoke College	MA	42,148	HC+
Nazareth College of Rochester	NY	28,175	VC
New College of Florida	FL	10,009	HC+
New England College	NH	31,466	C
New York Univ	NY	43,170	MC
Northern Arizona Univ	AZ	10,353	C
Northern Illinois Univ	IL	13,178	C
Northwestern Univ	IL	37,595	MC
Oakland Univ	MI	11,936	C
Occidental College	CA	40,185	MC
Oglethorpe Univ	GA	30,300	VC
Ohio Univ	OH	15,921	C
Old Dominion Univ	VA	11,907	C
Penn State Univ/Univ Park Campus	PA	18,038	HC
Pomona College	CA	40,774	MC
Portland State Univ	OR	12,453	C
Pratt Inst	NY	36,156	SP
Providence College	RI	34,580	HC
Purdue Univ/West Lafayette	IN	13,458	VC
Randolph-Macon College	VA	31,250	C
Rice Univ	TX	32,290	MC
Ripon College	WI	27,160	C+
Rockford College	IL	28,330	VC
Roger Williams Univ	RI	30,500	C
Rollins College	FL	38,366	VC
Roosevelt Univ	IL	22,605	VC
Rutgers, The State Univ of New Jersey/Camden Campus	NJ	15,000	VC
Rutgers, The State Univ of New Jersey/New Brunswick/Piscataway Campus	NJ	15,810	HC
St. Joseph College	CT	32,050	C
St. Lawrence Univ	NY	40,545	VC
St. Louis Univ	MO	33,158	VC+
St. Mary's College of Maryland	MD	18,876	VC+
St. Olaf College	MN	32,800	HC
St. Peter's College	NJ	30,160	LC
St. Vincent College	PA	26,160	VC
Salem College	NC	26,226	VC+
Salve Regina Univ	RI	33,450	C
Santa Clara Univ	CA	38,931	VC
Sarah Lawrence College	NY	42,000	HC
Savannah College of Art and Design	GA	30,800	SP
School of the Art Inst of Chicago	IL	37,800	SP
Scripps College	CA	41,000	MC
Seton Hill Univ	PA	28,810	C
Siena Heights Univ	MI	17,000	LC
Simon's Rock College of Bard	MA	41,988	VC+
Skidmore College	NY	41,779	HC
Smith College	MA	41,474	MC
Southern Conn State Univ	CT	10,310	C
Southern Methodist Univ	TX	36,088	VC+
SUNY/College at Buffalo	NY	11,903	C
SUNY/College at Geneseo	NY	12,910	HC+
SUNY/College at Purchase	NY	11,989	VC+
SUNY/Univ at Albany	NY	13,860	VC
SUNY/Univ at Binghamton	NY	13,988	HC
SUNY/Univ at Buffalo	NY	13,694	VC
SUNY/Univ at New Paltz	NY	12,480	VC
SUNY/Univ at Stony Brook	NY	13,625	HC
Suffolk Univ	MA	33,160	C
Susquehanna Univ	PA	33,465	VC
Swarthmore College	PA	41,280	MC
Sweet Briar College	VA	31,460	VC
Syracuse Univ	NY	38,655	HC
Temple Univ	PA	17,438	C
Texas Christian Univ	TX	23,410	VC+
Texas Tech Univ	TX	13,026	VC
Trinity College	CT	38,040	HC+
Troy Univ	AL	8,916	C
Truman State Univ	MO	11,242	HC
Tufts Univ	MA	42,018	MC
Tulane Univ	LA	41,098	MC
Univ of Alabama	AL	9,888	C
Univ of Arizona	AZ	11,958	VC
Univ of Arkansas at Little Rock	AR	7,230	NC
Univ of at Calif Davis	CA	15,010	VC
Univ of Calif at Berkeley	CA	18,141	HC+
Univ of Calif at Irvine	CA	16,475	HC
Univ of Calif at Los Angeles	CA	17,681	MC
Univ of Calif at Riverside	CA	16,625	C
Univ of Calif at San Diego	CA	16,102	HC
Univ of Calif at Santa Barbara	CA	11,800	VC
Univ of Calif at Santa Cruz	CA	19,174	VC
Univ of Chicago	IL	42,369	MC
Univ of Colo at Boulder	CO	13,352	C+
Univ of Conn	CT	16,628	HC
Univ of Dallas	TX	27,432	VC+
Univ of Dayton	OH	28,826	VC
Univ of Delaware	DE	14,142	HC
Univ of Denver	CO	36,376	VC+
Univ of Evansville	IN	28,320	VC
Univ of Florida	FL	9,354	HC
Univ of Georgia	GA	11,004	HC
Univ of Hartford	CT	34,044	C
Univ of Houston	TX	7,000	C
Univ of Illinois at Chicago	IL	16,256	VC
Univ of Illinois at Urbana-Champaign	IL	15,800	HC+
Univ of Iowa	IA	12,172	VC
Univ of Kansas	KS	10,915	VC
Univ of Kentucky	KY	7,800	C
Univ of La Verne	CA	33,470	C
Univ of Louisville	KY	10,400	VC
Univ of Mary Washington	VA	11,636	HC
Univ of Maryland/College Park	MD	16,036	HC
Univ of Mass Amherst	MA	15,973	C+
Univ of Mass Dartmouth	MA	15,985	C
Univ of Memphis	TN	11,153	C
Univ of Miami	FL	38,397	MC
Univ of Mich/Ann Arbor	MI	16,587	HC+
Univ of Mich/Dearborn	MI	7,000	VC
Univ of Minn/Morris	MN	15,472	VC
Univ of Minn/Twin Cities	MN	13,165	HC
Univ of Miss	MS	9,000	C
Univ of Missouri/Columbia	MO	13,500	C
Univ of Missouri/Kansas City	MO	15,000	VC
Univ of Missouri/St. Louis	MO	14,046	VC
Univ of Nebr at Lincoln	NE	11,401	VC
Univ of Nebr at Omaha	NE	11,235	C
Univ of Nevada/Las Vegas	NV	11,566	C
Univ of New Hampshire	NH	16,810	VC
Univ of New Mexico	NM	11,253	C
Univ of N Car at Chapel Hill	NC	11,129	MC
Univ of N Car at Wilmington	NC	10,107	VC
Univ of North Texas	TX	7,800	C
Univ of Northern Iowa	IA	11,133	C
Univ of Notre Dame	IN	39,552	MC
Univ of Okla	OK	10,769	VC+
Univ of Oregon	OR	13,108	VC
Univ of Pennsylvania	PA	41,766	MC
Univ of Richmond	VA	40,510	MC
Univ of Rochester	NY	41,135	MC
Univ of St. Thomas	MN	28,000	VC
Univ of San Francisco	CA	37,560	VC
Univ of S Car at Columbia	SC	13,397	VC
Univ of Southern Calif	CA	41,618	MC
Univ of Tenn at Knoxville	TN	11,720	C
Univ of Texas at Arlington	TX	7,195	LC
Univ of Texas at Austin	TX	14,610	HC
Univ of the South	TN	34,645	HC
Univ of Toledo	OH	15,806	NC
Univ of Utah	UT	10,162	VC
Univ of Vermont	VT	18,080	VC
Univ of Washington	WA	10,400	VC
Univ of Wisc/Madison	WI	13,117	HC
Univ of Wisc/Milwaukee	WI	9,427	LC
Univ of Wisc/Superior	WI	9,610	C+
Univ of Wisc/Whitewater	WI	9,274	C
Villanova Univ	PA	38,672	HC+
Virginia Commonwealth Univ	VA	12,987	C
Washburn Univ	KS	9,734	NC
Washington and Lee Univ	VA	35,880	MC
Washington Univ in St. Louis	MO	42,106	MC
Wayne State Univ	MI	11,805	C
Wellesley College	MA	41,030	MC
Wesleyan College	GA	19,560	C
Wesleyan Univ	CT	42,122	MC
Western Mich Univ	MI	13,299	C
Wheaton College	MA	40,180	HC+
Whitman College	WA	36,110	HC+
Wichita State Univ	KS	8,500	C
Willamette Univ	OR	35,416	VC+
William Paterson Univ of New Jersey	NJ	17,810	C+
Williams College	MA	40,310	MC
Winthrop Univ	SC	11,302	C
Wofford College	SC	30,935	HC
Wright State Univ	OH	13,616	LC
Yale Univ	CT	41,000	MC
Youngstown State Univ	OH	12,613	NC

ART THERAPY

School	ST	$IS	SR
Albertus Magnus College	CT	25,336	C
Alverno College	WI	21,088	C
Andrews Univ	MI	21,786	C
Anna Maria College	MA	29,815	LC
Arcadia Univ	PA	33,570	VC
Brescia Univ	KY	14,240	C
Capital Univ	OH	30,444	C
College of New Rochelle	NY	28,396	C+
Converse College	SC	24,800	VC
Edgewood College	WI	22,862	C
Emmanuel College	MA	32,000	C+
LIU/C.W. Post Campus	NY	28,282	C
Marian College of Fond du Lac	WI	21,775	LC
Marygrove College	MI	19,310	C+
Marylhurst Univ	OR	14,220	NC
Marywood Univ	PA	30,680	C
Mercyhurst College	PA	28,633	VC
Millikin Univ	IL	25,590	C
Mount Mary College	WI	22,895	C
Russell Sage College	NY	27,000	C
Seton Hill Univ	PA	28,810	C
Spring Hill College	AL	28,678	C
Springfield College	MA	25,000	C
Univ of Indianapolis	IN	25,090	C
Univ of Wisc/Superior	WI	9,610	C+

ARTS ADMINISTRATION/MANAGEMENT

School	ST	$IS	SR
Adrian College	MI	23,000	C
Appalachian State Univ	NC	8,000	VC
Bellarmine Univ	KY	27,650	C+
Benedictine Univ	IL	25,710	C
Bennett College	NC	11,500	C
Brenau Univ Women's College	GA	23,950	VC
Buena Vista Univ	IA	27,742	C
Butler Univ	IN	31,944	VC+
Cal State East Bay	CA	10,856	LC
Chatham College	PA	27,290	C+
College of Charleston	SC	13,616	VC
College of Santa Fe	NM	28,978	C
Concordia College-New York	NY	27,740	C
Culver-Stockton College	MO	20,625	C
Drury Univ	MO	20,117	VC
Eastern Mich Univ	MI	12,897	VC
Franklin Pierce College	NH	31,700	C
Green Mountain College	VT	32,164	C
Huntingdon College	AL	23,090	VC
Lake Erie College	OH	27,725	C
Lees-McRae College	NC	23,000	C
LIU/C.W. Post Campus	NY	28,282	C
Mary Baldwin College	VA	26,465	C
Marywood Univ	PA	30,680	C
Millikin Univ	IL	25,590	C
North Georgia College and State Univ	GA	7,000	C
Northern Arizona Univ	AZ	10,353	C
Pfeiffer Univ	NC	21,900	C
Point Park Univ	PA	24,160	C
Randolph-Macon College	VA	31,250	C
Salem College	NC	26,226	VC+
Seton Hill Univ	PA	28,810	C
Shenandoah Univ	VA	27,600	C
Simmons College	MA	35,640	VC
Southeastern Louisiana Univ	LA	8,521	LC
Spring Hill College	AL	28,678	C
Univ of Findlay	OH	29,238	C
Univ of Kentucky	KY	7,800	C
Univ of Mich/Dearborn	MI	7,000	VC
Univ of San Francisco	CA	37,560	VC
Univ of Tulsa	OK	25,348	HC
Univ of Wisc/Stevens Point	WI	9,384	VC
Upper Iowa Univ	IA	20,130	C
Viterbo Univ	WI	21,670	C
Wagner College	NY	33,300	VC
Wartburg College	IA	27,315	NC
Waynesburg College	PA	21,230	C
Wright State Univ	OH	13,616	LC

ASIAN/AMERICAN STUDIES

School	ST	$IS	SR
Brigham Young Univ	UT	9,200	VC
Cal State, Fullerton	CA	10,990	C
Cal State, Northridge	CA	9,036	LC
Columbia Univ/Columbia College	NY	42,584	MC
Emory Univ	GA	40,546	MC
Pitzer College	CA	41,644	HC
Purdue Univ/West Lafayette	IN	13,458	VC
St. Olaf College	MN	32,800	HC
Scripps College	CA	41,000	MC
SUNY/Univ at Binghamton	NY	13,988	HC
Univ of Calif at Berkeley	CA	18,141	HC+
Univ of Calif at Los Angeles	CA	17,681	MC
Univ of Calif at Riverside	CA	16,625	C
Univ of Calif at Santa Barbara	CA	11,800	VC
Univ of Southern Calif	CA	41,618	MC
Univ of Washington	WA	10,400	VC

ASIAN/ORIENTAL STUDIES

School	ST	$IS	SR
Amherst College	MA	41,590	MC
Augustana College	IL	29,862	VC+
Bard College	NY	41,800	HC+
Baylor Univ	TX	27,555	HC
Birmingham-Southern College	AL	28,494	VC+
Boston Univ	MA	42,046	HC+
Bowdoin College	ME	41,660	MC
Bowling Green State Univ	OH	14,994	C
Brigham Young Univ	UT	9,200	VC
Cal State, Chico	CA	11,395	C
Cal State, Long Beach	CA	9,512	C
Calvin College	MI	25,735	NC
Carleton College	MN	40,467	MC
Case Western Reserve Univ	OH	37,314	MC
Central Washington Univ	WA	11,730	C
CUNY/City College	NY		C
Claremont McKenna College	CA	42,920	MC
Coe College	IA	27,440	VC
Colgate Univ	NY	41,170	MC
College of the Holy Cross	MA	40,664	MC
Colo College	CO	37,668	HC
Columbia Univ/Columbia College	NY	42,584	MC
Cornell Univ	NY	41,717	MC
Dartmouth College	NH	39,465	MC
Duke Univ	NC	41,239	MC
Emory Univ	GA	40,546	MC
Florida International Univ	FL	9,215	VC
Florida State Univ	FL	9,028	NC
Furman Univ	SC	33,264	HC+
Hamilton College	NY	41,660	MC
Hampshire College	MA	37,120	HC
Harvard Univ/Harvard College	MA	45,860	MC
Hobart and William Smith Colleges	NY	41,123	VC
Hofstra Univ	NY	32,630	VC
Lake Forest College	IL	33,860	VC
Lehigh Univ	PA	42,690	HC+
Loyola Marymount Univ	CA	36,321	VC
Macalester College	MN	36,500	MC
Manhattanville College	NY	32,500	C+
Mary Baldwin College	VA	26,465	C
Mount Holyoke College	MA	42,148	HC+
Oakland Univ	MI	11,936	C
Occidental College	CA	40,185	MC
Old Dominion Univ	VA	11,907	C
Pacific Lutheran Univ	WA	28,805	VC
Pitzer College	CA	41,644	HC
Pomona College	CA	40,774	MC
Rice Univ	TX	32,290	MC
Rutgers, The State Univ of New Jersey/New Brunswick/Piscataway Campus	NJ	15,810	HC
St. Andrews Presbyterian College	NC	23,530	C
St. John's Univ	NY	34,370	C
St. Lawrence Univ	NY	40,545	VC
Samford Univ	AL	20,258	VC
San Diego State Univ	CA	12,971	C
Sarah Lawrence College	NY	42,000	HC
Scripps College	CA	41,000	MC
Seton Hall Univ	NJ	33,622	VC
Simon's Rock College of Bard	MA	41,988	VC+
Skidmore College	NY	41,779	HC
SUNY/Univ at Albany	NY	13,860	VC
SUNY/Univ at Buffalo	NY	13,694	VC
SUNY/Univ at New Paltz	NY	12,480	VC
Swarthmore College	PA	41,280	MC
Temple Univ	PA	17,438	C
Texas State Univ - San Marcos	TX	10,862	C
Tufts Univ	MA	42,018	MC
Tulane Univ	LA	41,098	MC
Univ of Calif at Berkeley	CA	18,141	HC+
Univ of Calif at Riverside	CA	16,625	C
Univ of Calif at Santa Barbara	CA	11,800	VC
Univ of Chicago	IL	42,369	MC
Univ of Cincinnati	OH	17,682	C
Univ of Colo at Boulder	CO	13,352	C+
Univ of Denver	CO	36,376	VC+
Univ of Florida	FL	9,354	HC
Univ of Hawaii at Manoa	HI	10,413	VC
Univ of Iowa	IA	12,172	VC
Univ of New Mexico	NM	11,253	C
Univ of N Car at Chapel Hill	NC	11,129	MC
Univ of Northern Iowa	IA	11,133	C
Univ of Okla	OK	10,769	VC+
Univ of Oregon	OR	13,108	VC
Univ of Pennsylvania	PA	41,766	MC
Univ of Redlands	CA	36,160	VC
Univ of Tenn at Knoxville	TN	11,720	C
Univ of Texas at Austin	TX	14,610	HC
Univ of the South	TN	34,645	HC
Univ of Utah	UT	10,162	VC
Univ of Vermont	VT	18,080	VC
Univ of Washington	WA	10,400	VC

ST = STATE **$IS** = IN-STATE COSTS **SR** = SELECTOR RATING

School	ST	$IS	SR
Univ of Wisc/Madison	WI	13,117	HC
Valparaiso Univ	IN	28,970	VC+
Vassar College	NY	41,700	MC
Washington State Univ	WA	12,260	C
Washington Univ in St. Louis	MO	42,106	MC
Wellesley College	MA	41,030	MC
Wesleyan Univ	CT	42,122	MC
Wheaton College	MA	40,180	MC
Whitman College	WA	36,110	HC+
Willamette Univ	OR	35,416	VC+
Williams College	MA	40,310	MC

ASTRONOMY

School	ST	$IS	SR
Amherst College	MA	41,590	MC
Benedictine College	KS	21,968	C
Bennington College	VT	41,890	MC
Boston Univ	MA	42,046	HC+
Brigham Young Univ	UT	9,200	VC
Bryn Mawr College	PA	42,780	HC+
Calif Inst of Technology	CA	36,123	MC
Case Western Reserve Univ	OH	37,314	MC
Central Mich Univ	MI	12,244	C
Colgate Univ	NY	41,170	MC
Columbia Univ/Barnard College	NY	38,000	MC
Columbia Univ/Columbia College	NY	42,584	MC
Columbia Univ/School of General Studies	NY	41,516	C
Cornell Univ	NY	41,717	MC
Earlham College	IN	33,604	HC
Eastern Mich Univ	MI	12,897	C
Eastern Univ	PA	24,075	C
Franklin and Marshall College	PA	40,590	MC
George Mason Univ	VA	10,850	VC
Harvard Univ/Harvard College	MA	45,860	MC
Haverford College	PA	41,600	MC
Indiana Univ Bloomington	IN	13,356	VC
Lehigh Univ	PA	42,690	HC+
Lycoming College	PA	30,797	C+
Minn State Univ, Mankato	MN	10,276	LC
Montclair State Univ	NJ	16,327	C
Mount Holyoke College	MA	42,148	HC+
Mount Union College	OH	25,840	C
Northwestern Univ	IL	37,595	MC
Oberlin College	OH	40,904	MC
Ohio State Univ	OH	15,357	HC
Penn State Univ/Univ Park Campus	PA	18,038	HC
San Diego State Univ	CA	12,971	C
Smith College	MA	41,474	MC
SUNY/Univ at Stony Brook	NY	13,625	HC
Swarthmore College	PA	41,280	MC
Union College	NY	41,595	HC
Univ of Arizona	AZ	11,958	VC
Univ of Chicago	IL	42,369	MC
Univ of Colo at Boulder	CO	13,352	C+
Univ of Delaware	DE	14,142	HC
Univ of Denver	CO	36,376	VC+
Univ of Florida	FL	9,354	HC
Univ of Georgia	GA	11,004	HC
Univ of Hawaii at Hilo	HI	6,500	C
Univ of Illinois at Urbana-Champaign	IL	15,800	HC+
Univ of Iowa	IA	12,172	VC
Univ of Kansas	KS	10,915	VC
Univ of Maryland/College Park	MD	16,036	HC
Univ of Mass Amherst	MA	15,973	C+
Univ of Mich/Ann Arbor	MI	16,587	HC+
Univ of Minn/Twin Cities	MN	13,165	VC
Univ of Okla	OK	10,769	VC+
Univ of Pittsburgh at Pittsburgh	PA	18,866	HC
Univ of Southern Calif	CA	41,618	MC
Univ of Texas at Austin	TX	14,610	VC
Univ of Virginia	VA	13,759	MC
Univ of Washington	WA	10,400	VC
Univ of Wisc/Madison	WI	13,117	HC
Univ of Wyoming	WY	9,666	C
Valdosta State Univ	GA	8,802	C
Vassar College	NY	41,700	MC
Villanova Univ	PA	38,672	HC+
Wellesley College	MA	41,030	MC
Wesleyan Univ	CT	42,122	MC
Wheaton College	MA	40,180	HC+
Williams College	MA	40,310	MC
Yale Univ	CT	41,000	MC
Youngstown State Univ	OH	12,613	NC

ASTROPHYSICS

School	ST	$IS	SR
Agnes Scott College	GA	32,070	HC
Boston Univ	MA	42,046	HC+
Cal State, Northridge	CA	9,036	LC
Colgate Univ	NY	41,170	MC
Columbia Univ/Columbia College	NY	42,584	MC
Conn College	CT	41,975	MC
Florida Inst of Technology	FL	29,720	VC

School	ST	$IS	SR
Franklin and Marshall College	PA	40,590	HC
Indiana Univ Bloomington	IN	13,356	VC
Lehigh Univ	PA	42,690	HC+
Mich State Univ	MI	13,689	VC
Ohio Univ	OH	15,921	C
Princeton Univ	NJ	40,213	MC
Rutgers, The State Univ of New Jersey/New Brunswick/Piscataway Campus	NJ	15,810	HC
Swarthmore College	PA	41,280	MC
Texas Christian Univ	TX	23,410	VC+
Tufts Univ	MA	42,018	MC
Univ of Calif at Berkeley	CA	18,141	HC+
Univ of Calif at Los Angeles	CA	17,681	MC
Univ of Chicago	IL	42,369	MC
Univ of Mich/Ann Arbor	MI	16,587	HC+
Univ of Minn/Twin Cities	MN	13,165	VC
Univ of New Mexico	NM	11,253	C
Univ of Okla	OK	10,769	VC+
Villanova Univ	PA	38,672	HC+
Wellesley College	MA	41,030	MC
Williams College	MA	40,310	MC

ATHLETIC TRAINING

School	ST	$IS	SR
Adams State College	CO	8,613	C
Alderson-Broaddus College	WV	24,006	C
Alfred Univ	NY		VC
Alvernia College	PA	26,388	C
Angelo State Univ	TX	8,340	NC
Arkansas State Univ	AR	9,630	C
Ashland Univ	OH	25,000	C
Augustana College	SD	24,380	VC
Averett Univ	VA	24,920	C
Baldwin-Wallace College	OH	27,256	VC
Barton College	NC	22,316	C
Baylor Univ	TX	27,555	HC
Belhaven College	MS	19,530	NC
Benedictine College	KS	21,968	C
Bethany College	KS	20,660	LC
Bethel College	KS	21,650	C
Bethel Univ	MN	29,840	VC
Boston Univ	MA	42,046	HC+
Bridgewater College	VA	27,790	C
Bryan College	TN	19,270	C
Calif Univ of Pennsylvania	PA	14,217	C
Campbell Univ	NC	21,137	VC
Campbellsville Univ	KY	21,328	C
Canisius College	NY	32,257	VC
Carroll College	WI	24,860	C
Castleton State College	VT	13,158	C
Catawba College	NC	25,000	C
Cedarville Univ	OH	21,904	VC
Central Conn State Univ	CT	13,620	C
Central Methodist Univ	MO	18,000	C
Central Mich Univ	MI	12,244	C
Chapman Univ	CA	37,550	VC
Clarion Univ of Pennsylvania	PA	11,844	C
Coe College	IA	27,440	VC
Colby-Sawyer College	NH	27,850	LC
College of Charleston	SC	13,616	VC
College of Mount St. Joseph	OH	24,860	C
Concordia Univ Wisc	WI	22,660	VC
Creighton Univ	NE	29,918	VC+
Culver-Stockton College	MO	20,625	C
Dakota Wesleyan Univ	SD	17,832	C
Defiance College	OH	24,790	C
Delta State Univ	MS	7,709	C
Dominican College	NY	26,630	LC
Duquesne Univ	PA	29,534	VC
East Carolina Univ	NC	10,000	C
East Central Univ	OK	6,207	C
East Texas Baptist Univ	TX	16,713	C
Eastern Nazarene College	MA	19,500	LC
Elmhurst College	IL	24,685	C
Emporia State Univ	KS	8,093	C
Endicott College	MA	30,156	C+
Erskine College	SC	25,468	VC
Eureka College	IL	19,280	C
Florida Gulf Coast Univ	FL	10,833	C
Florida Southern College	FL	25,965	C
Florida State Univ	FL	9,028	HC
Gardner-Webb Univ	NC	21,500	C
George Mason Univ	VA	10,850	VC
Georgetown College	KY	24,950	C+
Graceland Univ	IA	19,700	C
Greensboro College	NC	23,000	C
Guilford College	NC	28,160	C+
Hamline Univ	MN	27,070	VC
Harding Univ	AR	16,512	VC
Hardin-Simmons Univ	TX	18,641	C
Heidelberg College	OH	23,242	C
Henderson State Univ	AR	7,600	C
High Point Univ	NC	25,720	C
Hofstra Univ	NY	32,630	VC
Howard Payne Univ	TX	17,115	C
Huntingdon College	AL	23,090	VC
Illinois State Univ	IL	12,839	C+
Indiana Univ Bloomington	IN	13,356	VC
Indiana Wesleyan Univ	IN	22,074	C+
Ithaca College	NY	35,144	VC
James Madison Univ	VA	12,010	VC

School	ST	$IS	SR
Johnson State College	VT	11,830	LC
Kansas State Univ	KS	10,516	VC
Kent State Univ	OH	14,594	C
Lake Superior State Univ	MI	12,842	LC
Lasell College	MA	26,250	C
Lewis Univ	IL	23,050	C+
Liberty Univ	VA	19,101	C
Limestone College	SC	19,840	C
Lincoln Memorial Univ	TN	18,144	C
Lindenwood Univ	MO	18,600	VC
Linfield College	OR	29,632	VC
Lipscomb Univ	TN	20,967	VC
Longwood Univ	VA	12,426	C
Loras College	IA	27,193	C
Louisiana College	LA	13,450	C
Luther College	IA	28,800	VC+
Lynchburg College	VA	30,645	C
Marietta College	OH	29,327	C
Marist College	NY	30,566	VC
Mars Hill College	NC	19,000	LC
Marywood Univ	PA	30,680	C
McKendree College	IL	24,800	VC
McMurry Univ	TX	18,100	LC
Mercyhurst College	PA	28,633	VC
Messiah College	PA	28,910	VC+
Methodist College	NC	21,000	C
Miami Univ	OH	29,097	HC
MidAmerica Nazarene Univ	KS	20,584	LC
Middle Tenn State Univ	TN	8,540	C
Minn State Univ, Mankato	MN	10,276	LC
Missouri Baptist Univ	MO	19,640	C
Missouri State Univ	MO	10,748	C+
Montclair State Univ	NJ	16,327	C
Mount Marty College	SD	20,590	C
Mount Union College	OH	25,840	C
National American Univ	SD	14,820	NC
Nebr Wesleyan Univ	NE	23,415	C+
Neumann College	PA	25,996	LC
New Mexico State Univ	NM	9,250	C
N Dak State Univ	ND	8,500	C
Northeastern Univ	MA	35,742	HC
Northwestern College of Iowa	IA	22,174	C+
Nova Southeastern Univ	FL	24,320	C
Ohio Northern Univ	OH	27,765	VC
Ohio Univ	OH	15,921	C
Olivet College	MI	19,984	C+
Otterbein College	OH	28,986	C
Palm Beach Atlantic Univ	FL	23,597	VC
Park Univ	MO	11,592	C
Pfeiffer Univ	NC	21,900	C
Plymouth State Univ	NH	12,298	LC
Purdue Univ/West Lafayette	IN	13,458	VC
Roanoke College	VA	30,748	VC
Rockford College	IL	28,330	VC
Russell Sage College	NY	27,000	C
Saginaw Valley State Univ	MI	11,432	C
Salem International Univ	WV	18,020	C
Salisbury Univ	MD	13,128	VC
Samford Univ	AL	20,258	VC
Shaw Univ	NC	15,488	LC
Simpson College	IA	26,833	VC
S Dak State Univ	SD	9,815	C
Southeast Missouri State Univ	MO	10,596	C
Southeastern Louisiana Univ	LA	8,521	LC
Southern Nazarene Univ	OK	14,634	NC
Southern Utah Univ	UT		C
Southwest Baptist Univ	MO	18,300	C
Southwestern College	KS	21,476	C
Southwestern Okla State Univ	OK	4,801	C
SUNY/College at Cortland	NY	12,095	C
SUNY/Univ at Stony Brook	NY	13,625	VC
Sterling College	KS	19,992	C
Tabor College	KS	21,614	NC
Texas Christian Univ	TX	23,410	VC+
Texas Lutheran Univ	TX	23,530	C
Texas State Univ - San Marcos	TX	10,862	C
Towson Univ	MD	13,924	VC
Trinity International Univ	IL	25,686	C
Troy Univ	AL	8,916	C
Univ of Akron	OH	15,166	NC
Univ of Alabama	AL	9,888	C
Univ of Central Arkansas	AR	9,984	C
Univ of Conn	CT	16,628	HC
Univ of Delaware	DE	14,142	HC
Univ of Evansville	IN	28,320	VC
Univ of Findlay	OH	29,238	C
Univ of Illinois at Urbana-Champaign	IL	15,800	HC+
Univ of Indianapolis	IN	25,090	C
Univ of Kansas	KS	10,915	VC
Univ of La Verne	CA	33,470	C
Univ of Mary	ND	15,374	C
Univ of Mary Hardin-Baylor	TX	19,428	C
Univ of Miami	FL	38,397	MC
Univ of Minn/Duluth	MN	13,974	C
Univ of Nebr at Lincoln	NE	11,401	VC
Univ of New England	ME	31,005	C
Univ of New Hampshire	NH	16,810	VC
Univ of New Mexico	NM	11,253	C
Univ of N Car at Charlotte	NC	9,101	C
Univ of N Car at Pembroke	NC	7,940	LC

School	ST	$IS	SR
Univ of N Car at Wilmington	NC	10,107	VC
Univ of N Dak	ND	10,114	VC
Univ of North Florida	FL	9,908	VC
Univ of Northern Iowa	IA	11,133	C
Univ of Pittsburgh at Bradford	PA	17,008	C
Univ of San Francisco	CA	37,560	VC
Univ of the Incarnate Word	TX	23,306	C
Univ of Tulsa	OK	25,348	HC
Univ of Vermont	VT	18,080	VC
Univ of West Alabama	AL	7,611	C
Univ of Wisc/Eau Claire	WI	9,915	VC
Univ of Wisc/La Crosse	WI	10,045	VC
Univ of Wisc/Stevens Point	WI	9,384	VC
Upper Iowa Univ	IA	20,130	C
Virginia State Univ	VA	11,318	C
Washington State Univ	WA	12,260	C
Waynesburg College	PA	21,230	C
Weber State Univ	UT	9,635	NC
West Chester Univ of Pennsylvania	PA	12,355	C+
West Texas A&M Univ	TX	8,452	C
West Virginia Univ	WV	10,506	C
Western Mich Univ	MI	13,299	C
Whitworth College	WA	29,428	VC+
William Woods Univ	MO	21,020	C
Wilmington College	OH	2,806	NC
Wingate Univ	NC	23,300	C
Xavier Univ	OH	30,490	HC

ATMOSPHERIC SCIENCES AND METEOROLOGY

School	ST	$IS	SR
CUNY/City College	NY		C
Cornell Univ	NY	41,717	VC
Creighton Univ	NE	29,918	VC+
Embry-Riddle Aeronautical Univ	AZ	30,280	C+
Embry-Riddle Aeronautical Univ	FL	30,280	C
Florida Inst of Technology	FL	29,720	VC
Florida State Univ	FL	9,028	HC
Indiana Univ Bloomington	IN	13,356	VC
Iowa State Univ	IA	11,831	VC
Jackson State Univ	MS	8,500	C
Lewis Univ	IL	23,050	C+
Lyndon State College	VT	14,233	LC
Metropolitan State College of Denver	CO	2,338	LC
Millersville Univ of Pennsylvania	PA	12,113	C
N Car State Univ	NC	11,824	HC
Northern Illinois Univ	IL	13,178	C
Northland College	WI	26,680	VC
Ohio Univ	OH	15,921	C
Penn State Univ/Univ Park Campus	PA	18,038	HC
Plymouth State Univ	NH	12,298	LC
Purdue Univ/West Lafayette	IN	13,458	VC
St. Cloud State Univ	MN	10,010	C
St. Louis Univ	MO	33,158	VC+
SUNY at Oswego	NY	13,662	VC
SUNY/College at Brockport	NY	12,747	VC
SUNY/College at Oneonta	NY	12,905	VC
SUNY/Maritime College	NY	12,475	C
SUNY/Univ at Albany	NY	13,860	VC
SUNY/Univ at Stony Brook	NY	13,625	HC
Texas A&M Univ	TX	13,351	HC
United States Air Force Academy	CO		HC+
Univ of Arizona	AZ	11,958	VC
Univ of at Calif Davis	CA	15,010	VC
Univ of Calif at Los Angeles	CA	17,681	MC
Univ of Hawaii at Manoa	HI	10,413	VC
Univ of Kansas	KS	10,915	VC
Univ of Louisiana at Monroe	LA	7,103	C
Univ of Mich/Ann Arbor	MI	16,587	HC+
Univ of Missouri/Columbia	MO	13,500	VC
Univ of Nebr at Lincoln	NE	11,401	VC
Univ of N Car at Asheville	NC	9,237	VC
Univ of N Car at Charlotte	NC	9,101	C
Univ of N Dak	ND	10,114	VC
Univ of Northern Colo	CO	10,249	C
Univ of Okla	OK	10,769	VC+
Univ of South Alabama	AL	8,930	LC
Univ of Utah	UT	10,162	VC
Univ of Washington	WA	10,400	VC
Univ of Wisc/Madison	WI	13,117	HC
Valparaiso Univ	IN	28,970	VC+
Western Conn State Univ	CT	12,993	C

AUDIO TECHNOLOGY

School	ST	$IS	SR
American Univ	DC	38,719	HC+
Berklee College of Music	MA	37,779	SP
Brigham Young Univ	UT	9,200	VC
Cogswell Polytechnical College	CA	13,760	LC
Columbia College Chicago	IL	25,125	LC
Five Towns College	NY	24,600	SP
Hofstra Univ	NY	32,630	VC
Indiana Univ Bloomington	IN	13,356	VC
Ithaca College	NY	35,144	VC
Kent State Univ	OH	14,594	C
Lebanon Valley College	PA	31,700	VC

School	ST	$IS	SR
Mich Tech Univ	MI	14,569	VC
Savannah College of Art and Design	GA	30,800	SP
School of the Art Inst of Chicago	IL	37,800	SP
SUNY/College at Fredonia	NY	12,771	VC
Texas State Univ - San Marcos	TX	10,862	C
Univ of Hartford	CT	34,044	C
Univ of Miami	FL	38,397	MC
Univ of New Haven	CT	31,794	VC
Webster Univ	MO	24,280	VC

AUTOMOTIVE TECHNOLOGY

School	ST	$IS	SR
Benjamin Franklin Inst of Technology	MA	23,039	SP
Central Missouri State Univ	MO	10,000	C
Colo State Univ-Pueblo	CO	7,821	LC
Farmingdale SUNY	NY	13,521	C
Minn State Univ, Mankato	MN	10,276	LC
Montana State Univ-Northern	MT	10,000	NC
Pennsylvania College of Technology	PA	16,980	LC
Pittsburg State Univ	KS	8,112	C
Southern Illinois Univ Carbondale	IL	12,391	C
Walla Walla College	WA	24,489	NC
Weber State Univ	UT	9,635	NC

AVIAN SCIENCES

School	ST	$IS	SR
Minn State Univ, Mankato	MN	10,276	LC
Southern Illinois Univ Carbondale	IL	12,391	C
Univ of at Calif Davis	CA	15,010	VC
Univ of Georgia	GA	11,004	HC

AVIATION ADMINISTRATION/ MANAGEMENT

School	ST	$IS	SR
Andrews Univ	MI	21,786	C
Auburn Univ	AL	12,230	VC
Averett Univ	VA	24,920	C
Baker College of Flint	MI	7,800	NC
Bridgewater State College	MA	12,120	C
Central Washington Univ	WA	11,730	C
Daniel Webster College	NH	24,870	C
Delta State Univ	MS	7,709	C
Dowling College	NY	22,110	LC
Eastern Mich Univ	MI	12,897	C
Embry-Riddle Aeronautical Univ	AZ	30,280	C+
Farmingdale SUNY	NY	13,521	C
Florida Inst of Technology	FL	29,720	VC
Florida Memorial College	FL	6,000	LC
Geneva College	PA	21,850	C
Henderson State Univ	AR	7,600	C
Inter American Univ of PR/ Bayamon Univ College	PR	3,522	
Jacksonville Univ	FL	24,040	C
Lewis Univ	IL	23,050	C+
Louisiana Tech Univ	LA	7,370	C
Lynn Univ	FL	30,750	C
Marywood Univ	PA	30,680	C
Metropolitan State College of Denver	CO	2,338	LC
Minn State Univ, Mankato	MN	10,276	LC
Mountain State Univ	WV	11,406	NC
Ohio Univ	OH	15,921	C
Park Univ	MO	11,592	C
Purdue Univ/West Lafayette	IN	13,458	VC
Quincy Univ	IL	24,920	C
Robert Morris Univ	PA	22,822	C
Rocky Mountain College	MT	20,805	C
St. Cloud State Univ	MN	10,010	C
St. Louis Univ	MO	33,158	VC+
Salem International Univ	WV	18,020	C
San Diego Christian College	CA	24,172	C
Southeastern Okla State Univ	OK	6,147	C
Southern Illinois Univ Carbondale	IL	12,391	C
Southern Nazarene Univ	OK	14,634	NC
Texas Southern Univ	TX	9,828	C
Univ of Dubuque	IA	23,390	C
Univ of Illinois at Urbana-Champaign	IL	15,800	HC+
Univ of Louisiana at Monroe	LA	7,103	C
Univ of Nebr at Omaha	NE	11,235	C
Univ of New Haven	CT	31,794	C
Univ of N Dak	ND	10,114	VC
Univ of Okla	OK	10,769	VC+
Univ of the District of Columbia	DC	2,070	LC
Vaughn College of Aeronautics and Technology	NY	13,680	SP
Western Mich Univ	MI	13,299	C
Westminster College	UT	25,656	C
Wilmington College	DE	5,594	NC

AVIATION COMPUTER TECHNOLOGY

School	ST	$IS	SR
Andrews Univ	MI	21,786	C
Central Missouri State Univ	MO	10,000	C
Florida Inst of Technology	FL	29,720	VC
Florida Memorial College	FL	6,000	LC
Inter American Univ of PR/ Bayamon Univ College	PR	3,522	
Metropolitan State College of Denver	CO	2,338	LC
Okla State Univ	OK	10,213	VC
Purdue Univ/West Lafayette	IN	13,458	VC
Southern Illinois Univ Carbondale	IL	12,391	C
Thomas Edison State College	NJ	3,780	SP
Walla Walla College	WA	24,489	NC

AVIATION MAINTENANCE MANAGEMENT

School	ST	$IS	SR
Averett Univ	VA	24,920	C
Central Washington Univ	WA	11,730	C
Embry-Riddle Aeronautical Univ	AZ	30,280	C+
Embry-Riddle Aeronautical Univ	FL	30,280	C
Thomas Edison State College	NJ	3,780	SP
Univ of N Dak	ND	10,114	VC
Univ of Texas at Dallas	TX	13,244	HC

BACTERIOLOGY

School	ST	$IS	SR
Univ of at Calif Davis	CA	15,010	VC
Univ of Wisc/Madison	WI	13,117	HC

BALLET

School	ST	$IS	SR
Belhaven College	MS	19,530	NC
Friends Univ	KS	16,250	LC
Indiana Univ Bloomington	IN	13,356	VC
N Car School of the Arts	NC	7,401	SP
Texas Christian Univ	TX	23,410	VC+
Univ of Utah	UT	10,162	VC

BANKING AND FINANCE

School	ST	$IS	SR
Abilene Christian Univ	TX	20,830	C
Adams State College	CO	8,613	C
Adelphi Univ	NY	27,000	VC
Alabama A&M Univ	AL	8,890	LC
Alabama State Univ	AL	7,658	C
Alfred Univ	NY		VC
Anderson Univ	IN	25,050	LC
Andrews Univ	MI	21,786	C
Angelo State Univ	TX	8,340	NC
Appalachian State Univ	NC	8,000	VC
Arcadia Univ	PA	33,570	VC
Arizona State Univ-Tempe	AZ	11,174	C
Arkansas State Univ	AR	9,630	C
Ashland Univ	OH	25,000	C
Auburn Univ	AL	12,230	VC
Auburn Univ Montgomery	AL	9,530	NC
Augusta State Univ	GA	2,920	C
Austin Peay State Univ	TN	7,535	C
Avila Univ	MO	22,100	C
Baldwin-Wallace College	OH	27,256	VC
Ball State Univ	IN	13,138	C
Baylor Univ	TX	27,555	HC
Becker College	MA	24,300	LC
Benedictine Univ	IL	25,710	C
Bentley College	MA	38,784	HC
Berry College	GA	24,342	VC
Bethel Univ	MN	29,840	VC
Boise State Univ	ID	9,438	LC
Boston College	MA	41,608	MC
Boston Univ	MA	42,046	HC+
Bowling Green State Univ	OH	14,994	C
Bradley Univ	IL	25,280	VC
Brescia Univ	KY	14,240	C
Buena Vista Univ	IA	27,742	C
Butler Univ	IN	31,944	VC+
Cabrini College	PA	33,340	C
Calif State Polytechnic Univ, Pomona	CA	18,053	C+
Cal State, Fullerton	CA	10,990	C
Cal State, Long Beach	CA	9,512	C
Cal State, Northridge	CA	9,036	LC
Cal State, Sacramento	CA	11,122	C+
Cal State, San Bernardino	CA	12,563	LC
Canisius College	NY	32,257	VC
Caribbean Univ	PR	3,000	
Catholic Univ of America	DC	35,838	VC
Cedarville Univ	OH	21,904	VC
Centenary College of Louisiana	LA	24,760	VC
Central Conn State Univ	CT	13,620	C
Central Mich Univ	MI	12,244	C
Central Missouri State Univ	MO	10,000	C
Central State Univ	OH	9,010	C+
Central Washington Univ	WA	11,730	C
Chestnut Hill College	PA	26,600	LC
Chicago State Univ	IL	10,915	C+
Christopher Newport Univ	VA	13,326	VC
CUNY/Brooklyn College	NY	4,377	C+
Clarion Univ of Pennsylvania	PA	11,844	C
Cleary College	MI	11,000	LC
Clemson Univ	SC	13,366	HC
Cleveland State Univ	OH	10,798	NC
Coastal Carolina Univ	SC	13,140	C
College of New Jersey	NJ	18,315	MC
College of Notre Dame of Maryland	MD	27,700	C
Colo State Univ-Fort Collins	CO	10,878	C+
Columbia College	MO	16,900	C
Columbus State Univ	GA	8,664	C
Concord College	WV	9,708	C
Concordia Univ St.Paul	MN	27,776	C
Concordia Univ Wisc	WI	22,660	VC
Creighton Univ	NE	29,918	VC+
Culver-Stockton College	MO	20,625	C
Dallas Baptist Univ	TX	17,040	VC
Davenport Univ	MI	15,205	NC
De Sales Univ	PA	28,580	VC
Defiance College	OH	24,790	C
DePaul Univ	IL	29,835	VC
Dominican College	NY	26,630	LC
Dowling College	NY	22,110	LC
Drake Univ	IA	27,632	VC+
Duquesne Univ	PA	29,534	VC
East Carolina Univ	NC	10,000	C
East Central Univ	OK	6,207	C
East Texas Baptist Univ	TX	16,713	C
Eastern Illinois Univ	IL	12,569	C
Eastern Kentucky Univ	KY	7,725	C
Eastern Mich Univ	MI	12,897	C
Eastern New Mexico Univ	NM	7,264	C
Eastern Washington Univ	WA	10,608	C
Edinboro Univ of Pennsylvania	PA	11,809	LC
Elmhurst College	IL	24,685	C
Emory Univ	GA	40,546	MC
Excelsior College	NY	995	SP
Fairfield Univ	CT	39,835	HC
Fairmont State	WV	8,400	LC
Fayetteville State Univ	NC	6,000	LC
Ferris State Univ	MI	13,698	C
Florida A&M Univ	FL	8,344	C
Florida Atlantic Univ	FL	11,221	C
Florida Gulf Coast Univ	FL	10,833	C
Florida International Univ	FL	9,215	VC
Florida Southern College	FL	25,965	C
Florida State Univ	FL	9,028	HC
Fort Hays State Univ	KS	7,638	C
Francis Marion Univ	SC	11,114	C
Franklin Pierce College	NH	31,700	C
Franklin Univ	OH	6,720	SP
Freed-Hardeman Univ	TN	16,370	NC
Gannon Univ	PA	26,100	C
George Mason Univ	VA	10,850	VC
George Washington Univ	DC	48,820	MC
Georgetown College	KY	24,950	C+
Georgetown Univ	DC	43,183	MC
Georgia Southern Univ	GA	9,762	C
Georgia State Univ	GA	11,444	VC
Glenville State College	WV	8,778	NC
Golden Gate Univ	CA	12,150	LC
Goldey-Beacom College	DE	11,440	C
Gordon College	MA	29,194	C+
Grand Canyon Univ	AZ	32,000	LC
Grand Valley State Univ	MI	12,000	VC
Grove City College	PA	15,784	VC+
Gwynedd-Mercy College	PA	26,080	C
Hampton Univ	VA	19,468	C+
Hardin-Simmons Univ	TX	18,641	C
Hawaii Pacific Univ	HI	21,080	C
Hillsdale College	MI	24,160	HC
Hofstra Univ	NY	32,630	VC
Houston Baptist Univ	TX	18,660	C
Howard Univ	DC	18,481	C+
Huron Univ	SD	10,700	C
Husson College	ME	17,410	LC
Idaho State Univ	ID	9,030	C
Illinois State Univ	IL	12,839	C+
Immaculata Univ	PA	25,350	C
Indiana State Univ	IN	11,604	C
Indiana Univ Bloomington	IN	13,356	VC
Indiana Univ of Pennsylvania	PA	11,209	C
Indiana Univ South Bend	IN	4,989	LC
Indiana Univ Southeast	IN	4,880	LC
Indiana Univ-Purdue Univ Fort Wayne	IN	5,067	LC
Indiana Univ-Purdue Univ Indianapolis	IN	10,959	C
Indiana Wesleyan Univ	IN	22,074	C+
Inter American Univ of PR/ Bayamon Univ College	PR	3,522	
Inter American Univ of PR/ Fajardo Campus	PR	4,000	
Inter American Univ of PR/ Metropolitan Campus	PR	4,320	
Inter American Univ of PR/ Ponce Regional College	PR	3,700	
Inter American Univ of PR/ San German	PR	6,720	
Iona College	NY	30,878	VC
Iowa State Univ	IA	11,831	VC
Ithaca College	NY	35,144	VC
Jackson State Univ	MS	8,500	C
Jacksonville State Univ	AL	7,618	LC
Jacksonville Univ	FL	24,040	C
James Madison Univ	VA	12,010	VC
John Carroll Univ	OH	27,658	C+
Juniata College	PA	33,130	VC
Kansas State Univ	KS	10,516	VC
Kean Univ	NJ	15,880	C
Kennesaw State Univ	GA	12,152	C
King's College	PA	29,810	C
Kutztown Univ of Pennsylvania	PA	10,820	C
La Roche College	PA	24,724	LC
La Salle Univ	PA	34,950	C
La Sierra Univ	CA	24,327	C+
Lasell College	MA	26,250	C
Lehigh Univ	PA	42,690	HC+
Lewis Univ	IL	23,050	C+
Lincoln Univ	PA	13,658	C+
Lindenwood Univ	MO	18,600	VC
Linfield College	OR	29,632	VC
Lipscomb Univ	TN	20,967	VC
LIU/Brooklyn Campus	NY	25,000	C
LIU/C.W. Post Campus	NY	28,282	C
Loras College	IA	27,193	C
Louisiana State Univ and A&M College	LA	10,749	VC
Louisiana State Univ in Shreveport	LA	2,900	NC
Louisiana Tech Univ	LA	7,370	C
Loyola Univ Chicago	IL	32,896	VC
Loyola Univ New Orleans	LA	31,050	VC+
Lubbock Christian Univ	TX	16,960	C
Manchester College	IN	23,470	C
Manhattan College	NY	29,000	VC
Manhattanville College	NY	32,500	C+
Marian College	IN	26,160	C
Marietta College	OH	29,327	C
Marquette Univ	WI	31,066	HC
Marshall Univ	WV	9,116	C
Marymount Univ	VA	25,934	C
Marywood Univ	PA	30,680	C
McKendree College	IL	24,800	VC
McMurry Univ	TX	18,100	C
McNeese State Univ	LA	5,270	C
Medaille College	NY	21,000	C
Mercer Univ	GA	27,525	VC+
Mercyhurst College	PA	28,633	VC
Metropolitan State College of Denver	CO	2,338	LC
Metropolitan State Univ	MN	4,682	SP
Miami Univ	OH	29,097	HC
Mich State Univ	MI	13,689	VC
Middle Tenn State Univ	TN	8,540	C
Midwestern State Univ	TX	9,381	LC
Millikin Univ	IL	25,590	C
Minn State Univ, Mankato	MN	10,276	C
Minn State Univ, Moorhead	MN	7,000	LC
Minot State Univ	ND	6,700	LC
Miss State Univ	MS	9,577	C
Missouri Southern State Univ	MO	8,396	NC
Missouri State Univ	MO	10,748	C+
Monmouth Univ	NJ	28,956	C
Montclair State Univ	NJ	16,327	C
Morehead State Univ	KY	9,150	C
Morehouse College	GA	25,082	C
Mountain State Univ	WV	11,406	NC
Murray State Univ	KY	8,900	VC
National Univ	CA	8,412	SP
New Mexico Highlands Univ	NM	6,272	NC
New Mexico State Univ	NM	9,250	C
New York Inst of Technology	NY	28,126	VC
New York Univ	NY	43,170	MC
Newman Univ	KS	21,106	C
Nicholls State Univ	LA	6,500	NC
Nichols College	MA	28,000	LC
Norfolk State Univ	VA	10,531	LC
North Central College	IL	28,926	VC
North Georgia College and State Univ	GA	7,000	C
North Park Univ	IL	24,050	C
Northeastern State Univ	OK	5,896	LC
Northern Arizona Univ	AZ	10,353	C
Northern Illinois Univ	IL	13,178	C
Northern Mich Univ	MI	12,340	LC
Northern State Univ	SD	8,257	C
Northwest Missouri State Univ	MO	10,000	C
Northwestern College	MN	25,220	NC
Northwood Univ	FL	21,040	C
Northwood Univ	MI	21,000	LC
Northwood Univ	TX	20,135	LC
Notre Dame de Namur Univ	CA	32,790	LC
Nova Southeastern Univ	FL	24,320	C
Oakland Univ	MI	11,936	C
Ohio Dominican Univ	OH	25,954	C
Ohio State Univ	OH	15,357	HC
Ohio Univ	OH	15,921	C
Okla Baptist Univ	OK	17,986	VC
Okla City Univ	OK	23,965	VC
Okla State Univ	OK	10,213	VC
Old Dominion Univ	VA	11,907	C

BEHAVIORAL SCIENCE (continued)

School	ST	$IS	SR
Oral Roberts Univ	OK	22,650	C
Pace Univ	NY	30,000	VC
Palm Beach Atlantic Univ	FL	23,597	VC
Penn State Erie/The Behrend College	PA	16,256	C
Penn State Univ/Univ Park Campus	PA	18,038	HC
Pennsylvania College of Technology	PA	16,980	LC
Philadelphia Univ	PA	30,006	C
Pittsburg State Univ	KS	8,112	C
Pontifical Catholic Univ of PR/Ponce	PR	7,310	
Post Univ	CT	24,875	C
Prairie View A&M Univ	TX	11,110	LC
Providence College	RI	34,580	HC
Purdue Univ/Calumet	IN	10,891	LC
Quincy Univ	IL	24,920	C
Quinnipiac Univ	CT	34,640	VC
Radford Univ	VA	13,145	C
Richard Stockton College of New Jersey	NJ	14,000	VC
Rider Univ	NJ	32,560	C
Robert Morris Univ	PA	22,822	C
Rochester Inst of Technology	NY	32,070	VC+
Roger Williams Univ	RI	30,500	C
Roosevelt Univ	IL	22,605	VC
Rutgers, The State Univ of New Jersey/Camden Campus	NJ	15,000	VC
Rutgers, The State Univ of New Jersey/New Brunswick/Piscataway Campus	NJ	15,810	HC
Rutgers, The State Univ of New Jersey/Newark Campus	NJ	15,640	VC
Sacred Heart Univ	CT	33,404	C
Saginaw Valley State Univ	MI	11,432	C
St. Anselm College	NH	33,810	C
St. Bonaventure Univ	NY	28,785	LC
St. Cloud State Univ	MN	10,010	C
St. Edward's Univ	TX	23,560	C
St. John's Univ	NY	34,370	C
St. Joseph's Univ	PA	37,428	VC
St. Martin's Univ	WA	27,555	C
St. Mary's Univ of San Antonio	TX	22,444	C
St. Thomas Aquinas College	NY	22,000	C
St. Thomas Univ	FL	23,490	C
St. Vincent College	PA	26,160	VC
St. Xavier Univ	IL	23,160	C
Salem State College	MA	13,161	LC
Salisbury Univ	MD	13,128	VC
Sam Houston State Univ	TX	8,000	C
San Diego State Univ	CA	12,917	C
San Francisco State Univ	CA	13,000	C
San Jose State Univ	CA	11,707	C
Santa Clara Univ	CA	38,931	VC
Seattle Univ	WA	30,063	VC
Seton Hall Univ	NJ	33,622	VC
Shippensburg Univ of Pennsylvania	PA	11,621	C
Siena College	NY	28,260	VC+
Simmons College	MA	35,640	VC
Southeast Missouri State Univ	MO	10,596	C
Southeastern Louisiana Univ	LA	8,521	LC
Southeastern Univ	DC	9,000	NC
Southeastern Univ	FL	17,180	LC
Southern Adventist Univ	TN	18,500	C
Southern Conn State Univ	CT	10,310	C
Southern Illinois Univ Carbondale	IL	12,391	C
Southern Methodist Univ	TX	36,088	VC+
Southern Nazarene Univ	OK	14,634	NC
Southern Univ and A&M College	LA	8,238	LC
Southern Utah Univ	UT		C
Southwestern Okla State Univ	OK	4,801	C
Spring Hill College	AL	28,678	C
SUNY at Oswego	NY	13,662	VC
SUNY/College at Old Westbury	NY	13,154	C
SUNY/Inst of Technology	NY	12,575	VC
SUNY/Univ at New Paltz	NY	12,480	VC
Stephen F. Austin State Univ	TX	7,930	C
Stetson Univ	FL	32,725	VC
Stonehill College	MA	36,104	HC
Suffolk Univ	MA	33,160	C
Syracuse Univ	NY	38,655	HC
Talladega College	AL	11,240	LC
Tarleton State Univ	TX	8,952	C
Taylor Univ	IN	26,376	VC+
Temple Univ	PA	17,438	C
Tenn Tech Univ	TN	10,044	C
Texas A&M Univ	TX	13,351	HC
Texas A&M Univ at Commerce	TX	9,020	C
Texas A&M Univ at Corpus Christi	TX	10,280	LC
Texas A&M Univ at Kingsville	TX	6,800	LC
Texas Christian Univ	TX	23,410	VC+
Texas Southern Univ	TX	9,828	C
Texas State Univ - San Marcos	TX	10,862	C
Texas Tech Univ	TX	13,026	VC
Thomas Edison State College	NJ	3,780	SP
Tiffin Univ	OH	19,490	LC
Touro College	NY	17,000	VC
Tri-State Univ-Main Campus	IN	26,200	C
Troy Univ	AL	8,916	C
Troy Univ Dothan Campus	AL	4,678	C
Troy Univ Montgomery Campus	AL	4,104	NC
Tuskegee Univ	AL	18,860	LC
Union College	NE	18,710	C
Union Univ	TN	20,750	VC
Univ of Akron	OH	15,166	NC
Univ of Alabama at Birmingham	AL	13,716	C
Univ of Alabama in Huntsville	AL	9,516	VC
Univ of Alaska Anchorage	AK	11,275	NC
Univ of Arizona	AZ	11,958	VC
Univ of Arkansas	AR	11,859	VC
Univ of Arkansas at Little Rock	AR	7,230	NC
Univ of Bridgeport	CT	29,595	LC
Univ of Central Arkansas	AR	9,984	C
Univ of Central Florida	FL	10,739	VC
Univ of Central Okla	OK	8,094	C
Univ of Charleston	WV	27,600	C
Univ of Cincinnati	OH	17,682	C
Univ of Colo at Boulder	CO	13,352	C+
Univ of Conn	CT	16,628	HC
Univ of Dayton	OH	28,826	VC
Univ of Delaware	DE	14,142	HC
Univ of Denver	CO	36,376	VC+
Univ of Evansville	IN	28,320	VC
Univ of Findlay	OH	29,238	C
Univ of Florida	FL	9,354	HC
Univ of Georgia	GA	11,004	HC
Univ of Hartford	CT	34,044	C
Univ of Hawaii at Manoa	HI	10,413	VC
Univ of Houston	TX	7,000	C
Univ of Houston-Downtown	TX	3,326	NC
Univ of Idaho	ID	9,310	NC
Univ of Illinois at Chicago	IL	16,256	VC
Univ of Illinois at Urbana-Champaign	IL	15,800	HC+
Univ of Indianapolis	IN	25,090	C
Univ of Iowa	IA	12,172	VC
Univ of Kansas	KS	10,915	VC
Univ of Kentucky	KY	7,800	C
Univ of Louisiana at Lafayette	LA	5,830	C
Univ of Louisiana at Monroe	LA	7,103	C
Univ of Louisville	KY	10,400	VC
Univ of Mary Hardin-Baylor	TX	19,428	C
Univ of Maryland/College Park	MD	16,036	HC
Univ of Mass Amherst	MA	15,973	C+
Univ of Mass Dartmouth	MA	15,985	C
Univ of Memphis	TN	11,153	C
Univ of Miami	FL	38,397	MC
Univ of Mich/Flint	MI	6,398	C
Univ of Miss	MS	9,000	C
Univ of Missouri/Columbia	MO	13,500	VC
Univ of Montana	MT	10,602	C
Univ of Montevallo	AL	9,630	C
Univ of Nebr at Kearney	NE	9,000	NC
Univ of Nebr at Lincoln	NE	11,401	VC
Univ of Nebr at Omaha	NE	11,235	C
Univ of Nevada/Las Vegas	NV	11,566	C
Univ of Nevada/Reno	NV	12,155	NC
Univ of New Haven	CT	31,794	C
Univ of New Mexico	NM	11,253	C
Univ of New Orleans	LA	7,370	C
Univ of North Alabama	AL	8,992	C
Univ of N Car at Charlotte	NC	9,101	C
Univ of N Car at Greensboro	NC	8,993	C
Univ of N Car at Wilmington	NC	10,107	VC
Univ of N Dak	ND	10,114	VC
Univ of North Florida	FL	9,908	VC
Univ of North Texas	TX	7,800	VC
Univ of Northern Iowa	IA	11,133	C
Univ of Notre Dame	IN	39,552	MC
Univ of Okla	OK	10,769	VC+
Univ of Pennsylvania	PA	41,766	MC
Univ of Pittsburgh at Johnstown	PA	16,740	C
Univ of Pittsburgh at Pittsburgh	PA	18,866	HC
Univ of Portland	OR	32,300	VC
Univ of PR/Arecibo	PR	8,327	
Univ of PR/Bayamon Univ College Campus	PR	1,600	
Univ of PR/Mayaguez	PR	1,250	
Univ of PR/Rio Piedras	PR	5,750	
Univ of Rhode Island	RI	15,398	C
Univ of St. Francis	IL	25,430	C
Univ of St. Thomas	MN	28,000	VC
Univ of St. Thomas	TX	23,810	VC
Univ of San Francisco	CA	37,560	VC
Univ of Scranton	PA	31,100	VC
Univ of South Alabama	AL	8,930	VC
Univ of S Car at Columbia	SC	13,397	VC
Univ of South Florida	FL	10,284	VC
Univ of Southern Indiana	IN	12,590	LC
Univ of Southern Miss	MS	10,112	C
Univ of Tampa	FL	25,784	C
Univ of Tenn at Knoxville	TN	11,720	C
Univ of Texas at Arlington	TX	7,195	LC
Univ of Texas at Austin	TX	14,610	NC
Univ of Texas at El Paso	TX	8,764	NC
Univ of Texas at San Antonio	TX	11,325	LC
Univ of Texas-Pan American	TX	7,290	C+
Univ of the District of Columbia	DC	2,070	LC
Univ of Toledo	OH	15,806	NC
Univ of Tulsa	OK	25,348	HC
Univ of Utah	UT	10,162	VC
Univ of Washington	WA	10,400	VC
Univ of West Florida	FL	8,559	C
Univ of West Georgia	GA	8,838	C
Univ of Wisc/Eau Claire	WI	9,915	VC
Univ of Wisc/La Crosse	WI	10,045	VC
Univ of Wisc/Madison	WI	13,117	HC
Univ of Wisc/Milwaukee	WI	9,427	C
Univ of Wisc/Oshkosh	WI	10,426	LC
Univ of Wisc/Whitewater	WI	9,274	C
Univ of Wyoming	WY	9,666	VC
Upper Iowa Univ	IA	20,130	C
Utah State Univ	UT	8,002	VC
Valdosta State Univ	GA	8,802	C
Valparaiso Univ	IN	28,970	VC+
Villanova Univ	PA	38,672	HC+
Virginia Polytechnic Inst and State Univ	VA	10,834	VC
Virginia Union Univ	VA	18,432	LC
Wake Forest Univ	NC	38,290	MC
Walsh Univ	OH	23,440	C
Warner Southern College	FL	18,000	LC
Wartburg College	IA	27,315	NC
Washburn Univ	KS	9,734	NC
Washington State Univ	WA	12,260	C
Washington Univ in St. Louis	MO	42,106	MC
Wayne State Univ	MI	11,805	C
Waynesburg College	PA	21,230	C
Webber International Univ	FL	17,580	LC
Weber State Univ	UT	9,635	NC
West Liberty State College	WV	9,142	LC
West Texas A&M Univ	TX	8,452	C
West Virginia State Univ	WV	8,378	NC
West Virginia Univ	WV	10,506	C
Western Carolina Univ	NC	7,000	C
Western Conn State Univ	CT	12,993	C
Western Illinois Univ	IL	13,042	C
Western Kentucky Univ	KY	10,192	C
Western Mich Univ	MI	13,299	C
Western New England College	MA	32,054	C
Westminster College	PA	31,290	C+
Wichita State Univ	KS	8,500	C
Wilberforce Univ	OH	14,937	LC
William Paterson Univ of New Jersey	NJ	17,810	C+
Wilmington College	DE	5,594	NC
Wingate Univ	NC	23,300	C
Winona State Univ	MN	11,333	C
Wofford College	SC	30,935	HC
Wright State Univ	OH	13,616	LC
Xavier Univ	OH	30,490	NC
Xavier Univ of Louisiana	LA	17,600	C
York College of Pennsylvania	PA	16,550	VC
Youngstown State Univ	OH	12,613	NC

BEHAVIORAL SCIENCE

School	ST	$IS	SR
Andrews Univ	MI	21,786	C
Calif Baptist Univ	CA	23,780	C
Calif State Polytechnic Univ, Pomona	CA	18,053	C+
Cal State, Dominguez Hills	CA	10,220	LC
Cal State, Monterey Bay	CA	10,099	C
Capital Univ	OH	30,444	C
Chaminade Univ of Honolulu	HI	23,320	LC
College of St. Scholastica	MN	28,456	C+
Concordia College-New York	NY	27,740	C
Concordia Univ	CA	26,780	C
Concordia Univ at Austin	TX	23,640	LC
Concordia Univ Nebr	NE	20,500	C+
Dakota Wesleyan Univ	SD	17,832	C
Drew Univ/College of Liberal Arts	NJ	39,698	VC
East-West Univ	IL	10,375	LC
Erskine College	SC	25,468	VC
Glenville State College	WV	8,778	NC
Granite State College	NH	4,800	SP
Green Mountain College	VT	32,164	C
Indiana Univ East	IN	4,806	LC
Indiana Univ Kokomo	IN	4,835	LC
Iona College	NY	30,878	VC
Johnson State College	VT	11,830	LC
King College	TN	23,400	C
Lakeland College	WI	22,990	C
Lehigh Univ	PA	42,690	HC+
Mercy College	NY	20,000	NC
Metropolitan State College of Denver	CO	2,338	LC
Missouri Baptist Univ	MO	19,640	C
Mount Marty College	SD	20,590	C
Mount Mary College	WI	22,895	C
National Univ	CA	8,412	SP
New York Inst of Technology	NY	28,126	VC
North Central Univ	MN	16,646	LC
Northwest Univ	WA	18,854	C
Oglethorpe Univ	GA	30,300	VC
Okla Wesleyan Univ	OK	18,950	NC
Our Lady of Holy Cross College	LA	8,090	LC
Our Lady of the Lake Univ of San Antonio	TX	22,430	LC
Point Park Univ	PA	24,160	C
Rochester College	MI	15,636	C+
Southern Adventist Univ	TN	18,500	C
Spring Arbor Univ	MI	22,476	C
Sterling College	KS	19,992	C
Tenn Wesleyan College	TN	18,650	C
Trevecca Nazarene Univ	TN	19,594	C
United States Air Force Academy	CO		HC+
United States Military Academy	NY		MC
Univ of at Calif Davis	CA	15,010	VC
Univ of Kansas	KS	10,915	VC
Univ of La Verne	CA	33,470	C
Univ of Maine at Fort Kent	ME	10,832	LC
Univ of Maine at Machias	ME	10,523	C
Univ of Maine at Presque Isle	ME	10,066	LC
Univ of Mary	ND	15,374	C
Univ of Mich/Dearborn	MI	7,000	VC
Univ of Rio Grande	OH	8,728	NC
Univ of Utah	UT	10,162	VC
Warren Wilson College	NC	24,382	VC
Widener Univ	PA	27,275	C
Wilmington College	DE	5,594	NC
York College of Pennsylvania	PA	16,550	VC

BIBLICAL LANGUAGES

School	ST	$IS	SR
Abilene Christian Univ	TX	20,830	C
Asbury College	KY	23,762	VC
Baylor Univ	TX	27,555	HC
Concordia Univ Wisc	WI	22,660	VC
Concordia Univ, Ann Arbor	MI	25,153	C+
Cornerstone Univ and Grand Rapids Theological Seminary	MI	21,350	NC
Houston Baptist Univ	TX	18,660	C
Luther College	IA	28,800	VC+
North Central Univ	MN	16,646	LC
Southern Nazarene Univ	OK	14,634	NC
Union Univ	TN	20,750	VC
Walla Walla College	WA	24,489	NC

BIBLICAL STUDIES

School	ST	$IS	SR
Abilene Christian Univ	TX	20,830	C
Albert A. List College of Jewish Studies	NY	20,000	HC+
Asbury College	KY	23,762	VC
Azusa Pacific Univ	CA	28,546	VC
Belhaven College	MS	19,530	NC
Bethel College	IN	19,680	C
Biola Univ	CA	29,372	VC
Blue Mountain College	MS	11,086	C
Cascade College	OR	17,980	NC
Cedarville Univ	OH	21,904	VC
Clearwater Christian College	FL	13,160	LC
Colo Christian Univ	CO	21,182	VC
Cornerstone Univ and Grand Rapids Theological Seminary	MI	21,350	NC
Covenant College	GA	26,460	VC+
Crichton College	TN	15,300	C
Dallas Baptist Univ	TX	17,040	VC
Eastern Mennonite Univ	VA	25,450	VC
Eastern Univ	PA	24,075	C
Evangel Univ	MO	17,380	C
Faulkner Univ	AL	15,600	C
Freed-Hardeman Univ	TN	16,370	NC
Geneva College	PA	21,850	C
George Fox Univ	OR	28,490	C
Gordon College	MA	29,194	C+
Goshen College	IN	22,850	VC
Grace College	IN	22,170	C
Hannibal-LaGrange College	MO	16,390	C
Hardin-Simmons Univ	TX	18,641	C
Hope International Univ	CA	23,760	NC
Houghton College	NY	25,980	VC+
Huntington Univ	IN	24,830	C
Indiana Wesleyan Univ	IN	22,074	C+
John Brown Univ	AR	20,910	VC

School	ST	$IS	SR
Kentucky Christian College	KY	12,680	C
King College	TN	23,400	C
LeTourneau Univ	TX	21,200	C
Lipscomb Univ	TN	20,967	VC
Lubbock Christian Univ	TX	16,960	C
Malone College	OH	23,040	C
Master's College and Seminary	CA	25,850	VC
Messiah College	PA	28,910	VC+
Milligan College	TN	21,990	C
Montreat College	NC	21,440	C
Northwest Univ	WA	18,854	C
Northwestern College	MN	25,220	NC
Nyack College	NY	18,540	C
Ohio Valley Univ	WV	17,752	C
Okla Christian Univ	OK	18,992	NC
Oral Roberts Univ	OK	22,650	C
Ouachita Baptist Univ	AR	21,900	VC
Palm Beach Atlantic Univ	FL	23,597	VC
Philadelphia Biblical Univ	PA	22,425	C
Rochester College	MI	15,636	C+
San Diego Christian College	CA	24,172	C
Simpson Univ	CA	22,900	C
Southeastern Univ	FL	17,180	LC
Southern Christian Univ	AL	9,440	LC
Southwest Baptist Univ	MO	18,300	C
Tabor College	KS	21,614	NC
Taylor Univ	IN	26,376	VC+
Toccoa Falls College	GA	17,125	C
Trinity Bible College	ND		
Trinity Christian College	IL	23,645	C
Trinity International Univ	IL	25,686	C
Union Univ	TN	20,750	VC
Univ of Evansville	IN	28,320	VC
Univ of Mary Hardin-Baylor	TX	19,428	C
Univ of Mich/Ann Arbor	MI	16,587	HC+
Vanguard Univ of Southern Calif	CA	27,071	C
Warner Southern College	FL	18,000	LC
Western Baptist College	OR	21,808	C
Wheaton College	IL	27,760	HC
William Tyndale College	MI	13,000	NC
York College	NE	16,330	NC

BILINGUAL/BICULTURAL EDUCATION

School	ST	$IS	SR
Boston Univ	MA	42,046	HC+
Cal State, San Bernardino	CA	12,563	LC
Chicago State Univ	IL	10,915	C+
CUNY/Brooklyn College	NY	4,377	C+
CUNY/City College	NY		C
College of Our Lady of the Elms	MA	21,000	C
Eastern Mich Univ	MI	12,897	C
Kent State Univ	OH	14,594	C
Loyola Univ Chicago	IL	32,896	VC
McMurry Univ	TX	18,100	LC
Mount Mary College	WI	22,895	C
Northeastern Illinois Univ	IL	3,000	NC
St. John's Univ	NY	34,370	C
St. Thomas Aquinas College	NY	22,000	LC
SUNY/College at Old Westbury	NY	13,154	C
Texas Christian Univ	TX	23,410	VC+
Texas Southern Univ	TX	9,828	C
Univ of Findlay	OH	29,238	C
Univ of Houston-Downtown	TX	3,326	NC
Univ of Minn/Twin Cities	MN	13,165	HC
Univ of New Mexico	NM	11,253	C
Washington State Univ	WA	12,260	C
Western Illinois Univ	IL	13,042	C

BIOCHEMISTRY

School	ST	$IS	SR
Abilene Christian Univ	TX	20,830	C
Adelphi Univ	NY	27,000	VC
Agnes Scott College	GA	32,070	HC
Albright College	PA	33,920	C
Allegheny College	PA	33,500	HC
Alma College	MI	28,544	VC
Alvernia College	PA	26,388	C
American International College	MA	28,710	LC
American Univ	DC	38,719	HC+
Andrews Univ	MI	21,786	C
Angelo State Univ	TX	8,340	NC
Arizona State Univ-Tempe	AZ	11,174	C
Asbury College	KY	23,762	VC
Auburn Univ	AL	12,230	VC
Austin College	TX	27,871	HC
Averett Univ	VA	24,920	C
Azusa Pacific Univ	CA	28,546	VC
Bard College	NY	41,800	HC+
Bates College	ME	42,100	MC
Baylor Univ	TX	27,555	HC
Beloit College	WI	32,808	HC
Benedictine College	KS	21,968	C
Benedictine Univ	IL	25,710	C
Bethany College	WV	21,395	C
Bethel Univ	MN	29,840	VC
Biola Univ	CA	29,372	VC
Boston College	MA	41,608	MC
Boston Univ	MA	42,046	HC+
Bowdoin College	ME	41,660	MC
Bradley Univ	IL	25,280	VC
Brandeis Univ	MA	41,551	MC
Brigham Young Univ	UT	9,200	VC
Brown Univ	RI	42,015	MC
Bucknell Univ	PA	39,660	MC
Calif Lutheran Univ	CA	27,800	LC
Calif Polytechnic State Univ	CA	12,390	VC
Cal State East Bay	CA	10,856	LC
Cal State, Fullerton	CA	10,990	C
Cal State, Long Beach	CA	9,512	C
Cal State, Los Angeles	CA	5,900	C
Cal State, Northridge	CA	9,036	LC
Cal State, San Bernardino	CA	12,563	LC
Calvin College	MI	25,735	NC
Campbell Univ	NC	21,137	VC
Canisius College	NY	32,257	VC
Capital Univ	OH	30,444	C
Carroll College	WI	24,860	C
Case Western Reserve Univ	OH	37,314	MC
Catholic Univ of America	DC	35,838	VC
Cedar Crest College	PA	30,615	C
Centenary College of Louisiana	LA	24,760	VC
Centre College	KY	30,810	VC
Charleston Southern Univ	SC	17,800	C
Chatham College	PA	27,290	C+
Chestnut Hill College	PA	26,600	LC
Chicago State Univ	IL	10,915	C+
CUNY/College of Staten Island	NY	4,328	NC
CUNY/Queens College	NY	4,356	C
Claflin Univ	SC	16,798	C+
Claremont McKenna College	CA	42,920	MC
Clark Univ	MA	35,165	VC+
Clarke College	IA	25,390	C
Clemson Univ	SC	13,366	HC
Coe College	IA	27,440	VC
Colgate Univ	NY	41,170	MC
College Misericordia	PA	27,950	C
College of Charleston	SC	13,616	VC
College of Mount St. Vincent	NY	28,000	C
College of Mount St. Joseph	OH	24,860	C
College of St. Benedict	MN	30,091	VC
College of St. Catherine	MN	27,505	VC
College of St. Elizabeth	NJ	28,495	C
College of St. Rose	NY	25,684	C
College of St. Scholastica	MN	28,456	C+
College of Wooster	OH	31,310	VC+
Colo College	CO	37,668	HC
Colo State Univ-Fort Collins	CO	10,878	C+
Colo State Univ-Pueblo	CO	7,821	LC
Columbia Union College	MD	23,536	LC
Columbia Univ/Barnard College	NY	38,000	MC
Columbia Univ/Columbia College	NY	42,584	MC
Conn College	CT	41,975	MC
Cornell Univ	NY	41,717	MC
Daemen College	NY	24,580	C
Dartmouth College	NH	39,465	MC
Denison Univ	OH	37,040	HC
DePauw Univ	IN	32,100	HC
Dickinson College	PA	40,170	HC+
Dominican Univ	IL	26,370	C
Drew Univ/College of Liberal Arts	NJ	39,698	VC
Duquesne Univ	PA	29,534	VC
Earlham College	IN	33,604	HC
East Carolina Univ	NC	10,000	C
East Stroudsburg Univ of Pennsylvania	PA	10,336	C
Eastern Conn State Univ	CT	13,554	C
Eastern Mennonite Univ	VA	25,450	VC
Eastern Mich Univ	MI	12,897	C
Eastern Univ	PA	24,075	C
Eastern Washington Univ	WA	10,608	C
Edinboro Univ of Pennsylvania	PA	11,809	LC
Elizabethtown College	PA	32,100	VC
Elmira College	NY	37,200	VC
Emmanuel College	MA	32,000	C+
Fairleigh Dickinson Univ/Metropolitan Campus	NJ	28,590	C
Florida Inst of Technology	FL	29,720	VC
Florida State Univ	FL	9,028	HC
Franklin and Marshall College	PA	40,590	HC
Georgetown Univ	DC	43,183	MC
Georgian Court College	NJ	20,000	LC
Gettysburg College	PA	39,864	HC
Gonzaga Univ	WA	30,218	HC
Grinnell College	IA	34,814	HC+
Grove City College	PA	15,784	HC+
Gustavus Adolphus College	MN	30,920	HC
Hamilton College	NY	41,660	MC
Harding Univ	AR	16,512	VC
Hardin-Simmons Univ	TX	18,641	C
Hartwick College	NY	36,065	C+
Harvard Univ/Harvard College	MA	45,860	MC
Hofstra Univ	NY	32,630	VC
Holy Family Univ	PA	25,740	C
Hood College	MD	30,085	VC
Hope College	MI	28,208	VC+
Idaho State Univ	ID	9,030	C
Illinois Inst of Technology	IL	26,465	HC+
Illinois State Univ	IL	12,839	C+
Immaculata Univ	PA	25,350	C
Indiana Univ Bloomington	IN	13,356	VC
Indiana Univ of Pennsylvania	PA	11,209	C
Iona College	NY	30,878	VC
Iowa State Univ	IA	11,831	VC
Ithaca College	NY	35,144	VC
Jamestown College	ND	14,130	NC
John Brown Univ	AR	20,910	VC
Juniata College	PA	33,130	VC
Kansas State Univ	KS	10,516	VC
Kennesaw State Univ	GA	12,152	C
Kenyon College	OH	39,500	MC
Keuka College	NY	26,050	C
King College	TN	23,400	C
Knox College	IL	32,385	VC+
La Salle Univ	PA	34,950	C
La Sierra Univ	CA	24,327	C+
Lafayette College	PA	39,267	MC
LaGrange College	GA	22,874	C
Lawrence Tech Univ	MI	25,475	VC
Le Moyne College	NY	29,570	VC
Lebanon Valley College	PA	31,700	VC
Lehigh Univ	PA	42,690	HC+
Lewis and Clark College	OR	35,358	VC+
Lewis Univ	IL	23,050	C+
Lipscomb Univ	TN	20,967	VC
Loras College	IA	27,193	C
Louisiana State Univ and A&M College	LA	10,749	VC
Louisiana State Univ in Shreveport	LA	2,900	VC
Loyola Marymount Univ	CA	36,321	VC
Madonna Univ	MI	16,068	VC
Manchester College	IN	23,470	C
Manhattan College	NY	29,000	VC
Manhattanville College	NY	32,500	C+
Mansfield Univ	PA	11,300	C
Marietta College	OH	29,327	C
Marlboro College	VT	35,980	VC+
Marquette Univ	WI	31,066	HC
Mary Baldwin College	VA	26,465	C
Maryville College	TN	29,224	VC
McMurry Univ	TX	18,100	LC
Mercyhurst College	PA	28,633	VC
Merrimack College	MA	34,380	C
Messiah College	PA	28,910	VC+
Miami Univ	OH	29,097	NC
Mich State Univ	MI	13,689	VC
Middlebury College	VT	42,120	MC
Mills College	CA	39,870	C
Minn State Univ, Mankato	MN	10,276	LC
Miss College	MS	14,574	VC
Miss State Univ	MS	9,577	C
Monmouth College	IL	23,700	C
Montclair State Univ	NJ	16,327	C
Mount Holyoke College	MA	42,148	HC+
Mount St. Mary's College	CA	32,086	VC
Mount St. Mary's Univ	MD	30,930	C
Mount Union College	OH	25,840	C
Muhlenberg College	PA	36,030	HC+
Murray State Univ	KY	8,900	VC
Nazareth College of Rochester	NY	28,175	VC
Nebr Wesleyan Univ	NE	23,415	C+
New Mexico State Univ	NM	9,250	C
New York Univ	NY	43,170	MC
Newman Univ	KS	21,106	C
Niagara Univ	NY	28,250	C
N Car State Univ	NC	11,824	HC
North Central College	IL	28,926	VC
Northeastern Univ	MA	35,742	HC
Northern Mich Univ	MI	12,340	LC
Northwest Nazarene Univ	ID	22,590	VC
Norwich Univ	VT	28,212	C
Notre Dame de Namur Univ	CA	32,790	LC
Oakland Univ	MI	11,936	C
Oakwood College	AL	14,904	C
Oberlin College	OH	40,904	MC
Occidental College	CA	40,185	MC
Ohio Northern Univ	OH	27,765	VC
Ohio State Univ	OH	15,357	HC
Ohio Univ	OH	15,921	C
Ohio Wesleyan Univ	OH	35,830	VC+
Okla Christian Univ	OK	18,992	NC
Okla City Univ	OK	23,965	VC
Okla State Univ	OK	10,213	VC
Old Dominion Univ	VA	11,907	C
Olivet College	MI	19,984	C+
Oregon State Univ	OR	11,055	C
Otterbein College	OH	28,986	C
Penn State Univ/Univ Park Campus	PA	18,038	HC
Philadelphia Univ	PA	30,006	C
Pitzer College	CA	41,644	HC
Portland State Univ	OR	12,453	C
Providence College	RI	34,580	HC
Purdue Univ/West Lafayette	IN	13,458	VC
Queens Univ of Charlotte	NC	24,528	C
Quinnipiac Univ	CT	34,640	VC
Ramapo College of New Jersey	NJ	16,630	VC
Regis College	MA	31,350	LC
Regis Univ	CO	31,890	C
Rensselaer Polytechnic Inst	NY	41,288	HC+
Richard Stockton College of New Jersey	NJ	14,000	VC
Rider Univ	NJ	32,560	C
Ripon College	WI	27,160	C+
Roanoke College	VA	30,748	VC
Roberts Wesleyan College	NY	26,378	C
Rochester Inst of Technology	NY	32,070	VC+
Rockhurst Univ	MO	25,440	VC
Rocky Mountain College	MT	20,805	C
Rollins College	FL	38,366	VC
Rosemont College	PA	29,350	C
Russell Sage College	NY	27,000	C
Rutgers, The State Univ of New Jersey/Camden Campus	NJ	15,000	VC
Rutgers, The State Univ of New Jersey/New Brunswick/Piscataway Campus	NJ	15,810	HC
Saginaw Valley State Univ	MI	11,432	C
St. Anselm College	NH	33,810	C
St. Bonaventure Univ	NY	28,785	LC
St. Edward's Univ	TX	23,560	C
St. John's Univ	MN	29,749	VC
St. Lawrence Univ	NY	40,545	VC
St. Louis Univ	MO	33,158	VC+
St. Mary's College of Maryland	MD	18,876	VC+
St. Mary's Univ of Minn	MN	23,857	VC
St. Mary's Univ of San Antonio	TX	22,444	C
St. Michael's College	VT	33,330	VC
St. Peter's College	NJ	30,160	LC
St. Vincent College	PA	26,160	VC
Samford Univ	AL	20,258	VC
San Francisco State Univ	CA	13,000	C
San Jose State Univ	CA	11,707	C
Schreiner Univ	TX	20,600	C
Seattle Pacific Univ	WA	29,355	C
Seattle Univ	WA	30,063	VC
Seton Hall Univ	NJ	33,622	VC
Seton Hill Univ	PA	28,810	C
Siena College	NY	28,260	VC+
Simmons College	MA	35,640	VC
Simpson College	IA	26,833	VC
Skidmore College	NY	41,779	HC
Smith College	MA	41,474	MC
S Dak State Univ	SD	9,815	C
Southern Conn State Univ	CT	10,310	C
Southern Methodist Univ	TX	36,088	VC+
Southwestern College	KS	21,476	C
Spelman College	GA	24,650	VC
Spring Arbor Univ	MI	22,476	C
Spring Hill College	AL	28,678	C
Springfield College	MA	25,000	C
SUNY at Oswego	NY	13,662	VC
SUNY at Potsdam	NY	12,959	C
SUNY/College at Fredonia	NY	12,771	VC
SUNY/College at Geneseo	NY	12,910	HC+
SUNY/College at Old Westbury	NY	13,154	C
SUNY/College at Plattsburgh	NY	12,362	C
SUNY/Univ at Albany	NY	13,860	VC
SUNY/Univ at Binghamton	NY	13,988	VC
SUNY/Univ at Buffalo	NY	13,694	VC
SUNY/Univ at Stony Brook	NY	13,625	HC
Stetson Univ	FL	32,725	VC
Stevens Inst of Technology	NJ	40,935	HC
Stonehill College	MA	36,104	HC
Suffolk Univ	MA	33,160	C
Susquehanna Univ	PA	33,465	VC
Swarthmore College	PA	41,280	MC
Sweet Briar College	VA	31,460	VC
Temple Univ	PA	17,438	C
Tenn Tech Univ	TN	10,044	C
Texas A&M Univ	TX	13,351	HC
Texas Christian Univ	TX	23,410	VC+
Texas State Univ - San Marcos	TX	10,862	C
Texas Tech Univ	TX	13,026	VC
Texas Wesleyan Univ	TX	18,700	C
Trinity College	CT	38,040	HC+
Trinity College	DC	24,150	LC
Trinity Univ	TX	30,157	HC+
Tufts Univ	MA	42,018	MC
Tulane Univ	LA	41,098	MC
Union College	NY	41,595	VC
Univ of Arizona	AZ	11,958	VC
Univ of Calif at Davis	CA	15,010	VC
Univ of Calif at Los Angeles	CA	17,681	HC
Univ of Calif at Riverside	CA	16,625	C
Univ of Calif at San Diego	CA	16,102	HC
Univ of Calif at Santa Barbara	CA	11,800	VC
Univ of Calif at Santa Cruz	CA	19,174	VC
Univ of Chicago	IL	42,369	MC
Univ of Cincinnati	OH	17,682	C
Univ of Colo at Boulder	CO	13,352	C+

ST = STATE   **$IS** = IN-STATE COSTS   **SR** = SELECTOR RATING

School	ST	$IS	SR
Univ of Dallas	TX	27,432	VC+
Univ of Dayton	OH	28,826	VC
Univ of Delaware	DE	14,142	VC
Univ of Denver	CO	36,376	VC+
Univ of Detroit Mercy	MI	27,000	C
Univ of Evansville	IN	28,320	VC
Univ of Georgia	GA	11,004	HC
Univ of Houston	TX	7,000	C
Univ of Illinois at Chicago	IL	16,256	VC
Univ of Iowa	IA	12,172	VC
Univ of Kansas	KS	10,915	VC
Univ of Maine	ME	13,642	C
Univ of Maryland/Baltimore County	MD	16,642	VC+
Univ of Maryland/College Park	MD	16,036	HC
Univ of Mass Amherst	MA	15,973	C+
Univ of Mass Boston	MA	8,024	C
Univ of Mass Dartmouth	MA	15,985	C
Univ of Miami	FL	38,397	MC
Univ of Mich/Ann Arbor	MI	16,587	HC+
Univ of Mich/Dearborn	MI	7,000	VC
Univ of Minn/Twin Cities	MN	13,165	VC
Univ of Missouri/Columbia	MO	13,500	VC
Univ of Nebr at Lincoln	NE	11,401	VC
Univ of Nevada/Reno	NV	12,155	NC
Univ of New England	ME	31,005	C
Univ of New Hampshire	NH	16,810	VC
Univ of New Mexico	NM	11,253	C
Univ of N Car at Greensboro	NC	8,993	C
Univ of North Texas	TX	7,800	C
Univ of Northern Colo	CO	10,249	C
Univ of Notre Dame	IN	39,552	MC
Univ of Okla	OK	10,769	VC+
Univ of Oregon	OR	13,108	VC
Univ of Pennsylvania	PA	41,766	MC
Univ of PR/Mayaguez	PR	1,250	
Univ of Redlands	CA	36,160	VC
Univ of Richmond	VA	40,510	MC
Univ of Rochester	NY	41,135	MC
Univ of St. Thomas	MN	28,000	VC
Univ of Scranton	PA	31,100	VC
Univ of Tampa	FL	25,784	C
Univ of Tenn at Knoxville	TN	11,720	C
Univ of Texas at Arlington	TX	7,195	LC
Univ of Texas at Austin	TX	14,610	HC
Univ of Texas at Dallas	TX	13,244	VC
Univ of the Pacific	CA	34,380	VC
Univ of the Sciences in Philadelphia	PA	33,380	VC
Univ of Tulsa	OK	25,348	HC
Univ of Vermont	VT	18,080	VC
Univ of Washington	WA	10,400	VC
Univ of Wisc/Eau Claire	WI	9,915	VC
Univ of Wisc/Madison	WI	13,117	HC
Univ of Wisc/Milwaukee	WI	9,427	LC
Ursinus College	PA	38,950	VC
Utah State Univ	UT	8,002	VC
Valparaiso Univ	IN	28,970	VC+
Vassar College	NY	41,700	VC
Virginia Polytechnic Inst and State Univ	VA	10,834	VC
Walla Walla College	WA	24,489	NC
Wartburg College	IA	27,315	NC
Washington and Jefferson College	PA	33,490	VC
Washington and Lee Univ	VA	35,880	MC
Washington State Univ	WA	12,260	C
Washington Univ in St. Louis	MO	42,106	MC
Wellesley College	MA	41,030	VC
Wells College	NY	23,070	VC
Wesleyan Univ	CT	42,122	MC
West Chester Univ of Pennsylvania	PA	12,355	C+
Western Kentucky Univ	KY	10,192	C
Western Mich Univ	MI	13,299	C
Western Washington Univ	WA	11,262	VC
Wheaton College	MA	40,180	HC+
Whittier College	CA	29,108	C
Widener Univ	PA	27,275	C
Wilkes Univ	PA	30,886	C
William Jewell College	MO	24,340	C
Worcester Polytechnic Inst	MA	40,450	VC+
Xavier Univ of Louisiana	LA	17,600	C
Yale Univ	CT	41,000	MC

BIOENGINEERING

School	ST	$IS	SR
Arizona State Univ-Tempe	AZ	11,174	C
Cornell Univ	NY	41,717	MC
Florida State Univ	FL	9,028	HC
Lehigh Univ	PA	42,690	HC+
Louisiana State Univ and A&M College	LA	10,749	VC
Miss State Univ	MS	9,577	C
Okla State Univ	OK	10,213	VC
Oral Roberts Univ	OK	22,650	C
Rice Univ	TX	32,290	MC
SUNY/Univ at Binghamton	NY	13,988	HC
Syracuse Univ	NY	38,655	HC
Texas A&M Univ	TX	13,351	HC
Univ of Arizona	AZ	11,958	VC
Univ of Arkansas	AR	11,859	VC
Univ of at Calif Davis	CA	15,010	VC
Univ of Calif at Berkeley	CA	18,141	HC+
Univ of Calif at Los Angeles	CA	17,681	MC
Univ of Calif at Riverside	CA	16,625	C
Univ of Calif at San Diego	CA	16,102	HC
Univ of Delaware	DE	14,142	VC
Univ of Georgia	GA	11,004	HC
Univ of Hawaii at Manoa	HI	10,413	VC
Univ of Idaho	ID	9,310	NC
Univ of Illinois at Chicago	IL	16,256	VC
Univ of Illinois at Urbana-Champaign	IL	15,800	HC+
Univ of Maine	ME	13,642	C
Univ of Nebr at Lincoln	NE	11,401	VC
Univ of Pennsylvania	PA	41,766	MC
Univ of Pittsburgh at Pittsburgh	PA	18,866	HC
Univ of Toledo	OH	15,806	NC
Univ of Utah	UT	10,162	VC
Univ of Wisc/Madison	WI	13,117	HC
Vanderbilt Univ	TN	41,986	MC
Walla Walla College	WA	24,489	NC
Washington Univ in St. Louis	MO	42,106	MC
Western New England College	MA	32,054	C

BIOINFORMATICS

School	ST	$IS	SR
Baylor Univ	TX	27,555	HC
Brigham Young Univ	UT	9,200	VC
Canisius College	NY	32,257	VC
Chatham College	PA	27,290	C+
Claflin Univ	SC	16,798	C+
Clarke College	IA	25,390	C
DeVry Univ/Alpharetta	GA	10,675	LC
DeVry Univ/Dallas	TX	10,700	LC
DeVry Univ/Decatur	GA	10,680	LC
DeVry Univ/Fremont	CA	13,060	LC
DeVry Univ/Kansas City	MO	10,670	LC
DeVry Univ/Long Beach	CA	12,450	LC
DeVry Univ/Phoenix	AZ	11,790	LC
DeVry Univ/Westminster	CO	10,200	LC
Gannon Univ	PA	26,100	C
Inter American Univ of PR/Bayamon Univ College	PR	3,522	
Loyola Univ Chicago	IL	32,896	VC
Mich State Univ	MI	13,689	VC
Mich Tech Univ	MI	14,569	VC
Rochester Inst of Technology	NY	32,070	VC+
Rockhurst Univ	MO	25,440	VC
St. Edward's Univ	TX	23,560	C
Stevens Inst of Technology	NJ	40,935	HC
Univ of Calif at San Diego	CA	16,102	HC
Univ of Calif at Santa Cruz	CA	19,174	VC
Univ of Nebr at Omaha	NE	11,235	C
Univ of Northern Iowa	IA	11,133	C
Univ of the Sciences in Philadelphia	PA	33,380	VC

BIOLOGY/BIOLOGICAL SCIENCE

School	ST	$IS	SR
Abilene Christian Univ	TX	20,830	C
Adams State College	CO	8,613	C
Adelphi Univ	NY	27,000	VC
Adrian College	MI	23,000	C
Agnes Scott College	GA	32,070	HC
Alabama A&M Univ	AL	8,890	LC
Alabama State Univ	AL	7,658	C
Albany State Univ	GA	5,770	C+
Albertson College of Idaho	ID	21,095	VC
Albertus Magnus College	CT	25,336	C
Albion College	MI	26,000	VC
Albright College	PA	33,920	C
Alcorn State Univ	MS	8,190	LC
Alderson-Broaddus College	WV	24,006	C
Alfred Univ	NY		VC
Alice Lloyd College	KY	4,900	C
Allegheny College	PA	33,500	HC
Allen Univ	SC	10,500	NC
Alma College	MI	28,544	VC
Alvernia College	PA	26,388	C
Alverno College	WI	21,088	C
American International College	MA	28,710	LC
American Univ	DC	38,719	HC+
Amherst College	MA	41,590	MC
Anderson Univ	IN	25,050	LC
Andrews Univ	MI	21,786	C
Angelo State Univ	TX	8,340	NC
Anna Maria College	MA	29,815	LC
Appalachian State Univ	NC	8,000	VC
Aquinas College	MI	23,750	C
Arcadia Univ	PA	33,570	VC
Arizona State Univ-Tempe	AZ	11,174	C
Arkansas State Univ	AR	9,630	C
Arkansas Tech Univ	AR	8,108	VC
Armstrong Atlantic State Univ	GA	7,394	C
Asbury College	KY	23,762	VC
Ashford Univ	IA	20,370	C
Ashland Univ	OH	25,000	C
Assumption College	MA	32,875	C
Atlantic Union College	MA	17,600	LC
Auburn Univ	AL	12,230	VC
Auburn Univ Montgomery	AL	9,530	NC
Augsburg College	MN	28,300	C
Augusta State Univ	GA	2,920	C
Augustana College	IL	29,862	VC+
Augustana College	SD	24,380	VC
Aurora Univ	IL	20,645	C
Austin College	TX	27,871	HC
Austin Peay State Univ	TN	7,535	C
Averett Univ	VA	24,920	C
Avila Univ	MO	22,100	C
Azusa Pacific Univ	CA	28,546	VC
Baker Univ	KS	22,190	C
Baldwin-Wallace College	OH	27,256	VC
Ball State Univ	IN	13,138	C
Barber-Scotia College	NC	15,000	LC
Bard College	NY	41,800	HC+
Barry Univ	FL	24,100	LC
Barton College	NC	22,316	C
Bates College	ME	42,100	MC
Bay Path College	MA	29,362	C
Baylor Univ	TX	27,555	HC
Belhaven College	MS	19,530	NC
Bellarmine Univ	KY	27,650	VC
Belmont Abbey College	NC	25,314	C
Belmont Univ	TN	24,110	VC
Beloit College	WI	32,808	HC
Bemidji State Univ	MN	11,180	LC
Benedict College	SC	19,114	LC
Benedictine College	KS	21,968	C
Benedictine Univ	IL	25,710	C
Bennett College	NC	11,500	C
Bennington College	VT	41,890	HC
Berea College	KY	5,496	VC+
Berry College	GA	24,342	VC
Bethany College	KS	20,660	LC
Bethany College	WV	21,395	C
Bethel College	IN	19,680	C
Bethel College	KS	21,500	C
Bethel College	TN	16,066	NC
Bethel Univ	MN	29,840	VC
Bethune-Cookman College	FL	17,922	LC
Biola Univ	CA	29,372	VC
Birmingham-Southern College	AL	28,494	VC+
Black Hills State Univ	SD	7,800	LC
Blackburn College	IL	13,690	C
Bloomfield College	NJ	22,500	LC
Bloomsburg Univ of Pennsylvania	PA	11,602	C
Blue Mountain College	MS	11,086	C
Bluefield College	VA	17,230	C+
Bluefield State College	WV	3,140	NC
Bluffton College	OH	26,110	C
Boise State Univ	ID	9,438	LC
Boston College	MA	41,608	MC
Boston Univ	MA	42,046	HC+
Bowdoin College	ME	41,660	MC
Bowie State Univ	MD	10,880	C+
Bowling Green State Univ	OH	14,994	C
Bradley Univ	IL	25,280	VC
Brandeis Univ	MA	41,551	MC
Brenau Univ Women's College	GA	23,950	VC
Brescia Univ	KY	14,240	C
Brewton-Parker College	GA	14,220	LC
Briar Cliff Univ	IA	23,550	LC
Bridgewater College	VA	27,790	C
Bridgewater State College	MA	12,120	C
Brigham Young Univ	UT	9,200	VC
Brigham Young Univ/Hawaii	HI	7,740	HC+
Brown Univ	RI	42,015	MC
Bryan College	TN	19,270	C
Bryn Athyn College of the New Church	PA	14,999	NC
Bryn Mawr College	PA	42,780	HC+
Bucknell Univ	PA	39,660	MC
Buena Vista Univ	IA	27,742	C
Butler Univ	IN	31,944	VC+
Cabrini College	PA	33,340	C
Caldwell College	NJ	26,450	LC
Calif Baptist Univ	CA	23,780	C
Calif Inst of Technology	CA	36,123	MC
Calif Lutheran Univ	CA	27,800	LC
Calif Polytechnic State Univ	CA	12,390	VC
Calif State Polytechnic Univ, Pomona	CA	18,053	C+
Cal State East Bay	CA	10,856	LC
Cal State, Bakersfield	CA	6,125	LC
Cal State, Chico	CA	11,395	C
Cal State, Dominguez Hills	CA	10,220	LC
Cal State, Fresno	CA	10,037	LC
Cal State, Fullerton	CA	10,990	C
Cal State, Long Beach	CA	9,512	C
Cal State, Los Angeles	CA	5,900	C
Cal State, Northridge	CA	9,036	LC
Cal State, Sacramento	CA	11,122	C+
Cal State, San Bernardino	CA	12,563	LC
Cal State, San Marcos	CA	11,283	C
Cal State, Stanislaus	CA	11,283	C
Calif Univ of Pennsylvania	PA	14,217	C
Calvin College	MI	25,735	NC
Cameron Univ	OK	6,314	NC
Campbell Univ	NC	21,137	VC
Campbellsville Univ	KY	21,328	C
Canisius College	NY	32,257	VC
Capital Univ	OH	30,444	C
Cardinal Stritch Univ	WI	21,910	C
Caribbean Univ	PR	3,000	
Carleton College	MN	40,467	MC
Carlow Univ	PA	24,313	C
Carnegie Mellon Univ	PA	32,700	MC
Carroll College	MT	23,324	C+
Carroll College	WI	24,860	C
Carson-Newman College	TN	16,800	C
Carthage College	WI	26,000	C
Case Western Reserve Univ	OH	37,314	MC
Castleton State College	VT	13,158	C
Catawba College	NC	25,000	C
Catholic Univ of America	DC	35,838	VC
Cedar Crest College	PA	30,615	C
Cedarville Univ	OH	21,904	VC
Centenary College	NJ	28,870	LC
Centenary College of Louisiana	LA	24,760	VC
Central College	IA	26,774	VC
Central Conn State Univ	CT	13,620	C
Central Methodist Univ	MO	18,000	C
Central Mich Univ	MI	12,244	VC
Central Missouri State Univ	MO	10,000	C
Central State Univ	OH	9,010	C+
Central Univ of Bayamon	PR	3,335	
Central Washington Univ	WA	11,730	C
Centre College	KY	30,810	VC
Chadron State College	NE	6,350	NC
Chaminade Univ of Honolulu	HI	23,320	LC
Chapman Univ	CA	37,550	VC
Charleston Southern Univ	SC	17,800	C
Chatham College	PA	27,290	C+
Chestnut Hill College	PA	26,600	C
Cheyney Univ of Pennsylvania	PA	11,497	LC
Chicago State Univ	IL	10,915	C+
Christian Brothers Univ	TN	24,650	VC
Christopher Newport Univ	VA	13,326	VC
Citadel, The	SC		C
CUNY/Brooklyn College	NY	4,377	C+
CUNY/City College	NY		C
CUNY/College of Staten Island	NY	4,328	NC
CUNY/Herbert H. Lehman College	NY	4,000	LC
CUNY/Hunter College	NY	8,000	C+
CUNY/Medgar Evers College	NY	4,250	NC
CUNY/Queens College	NY	4,356	C
CUNY/York College	NY	4,242	NC
Claflin Univ	SC	16,798	C+
Claremont McKenna College	CA	42,920	MC
Clarion Univ of Pennsylvania	PA	11,844	C
Clark Atlanta Univ	GA	20,960	LC
Clark Univ	MA	35,165	VC+
Clarke College	IA	25,390	C
Clarkson Univ	NY	34,930	VC
Clearwater Christian College	FL	13,160	LC
Clemson Univ	SC	13,366	HC
Cleveland State Univ	OH	10,798	NC
Coastal Carolina Univ	SC	13,140	C
Coe College	IA	27,440	VC
Coker College	SC	21,600	C
Colby College	ME	41,770	MC
Colby-Sawyer College	NH	27,850	LC
Colgate Univ	NY	41,170	MC
College Misericordia	PA	27,950	C
College of Charleston	SC	13,616	C
College of Mount St. Vincent	NY	28,000	C
College of Mount St. Joseph	OH	24,860	C
College of New Jersey	NJ	18,315	MC
College of New Rochelle	NY	28,396	C+
College of Notre Dame of Maryland	MD	27,700	C
College of Our Lady of the Elms	MA	21,000	C
College of St. Benedict	MN	30,091	VC
College of St. Catherine	MN	27,505	VC
College of St. Elizabeth	NJ	28,495	C
College of St. Mary	NE	23,938	C
College of St. Rose	NY	25,684	C
College of St. Scholastica	MN	28,456	C+
College of the Holy Cross	MA	40,664	MC
College of the Ozarks	MO	4,130	VC+
College of the Southwest	NM	12,420	LC
College of William and Mary	VA	14,147	NC
Colo Christian Univ	CO	21,182	VC
Colo College	CO	37,668	HC
Colo State Univ-Fort Collins	CO	10,878	C+
Colo State Univ-Pueblo	CO	7,821	C
Columbia College	MO	16,900	C
Columbia College	SC	24,982	C
Columbia Univ/Barnard College	NY	38,000	MC
Columbia Univ/Columbia College	NY	42,584	MC

School	ST	$IS	SR
Columbia Univ/School of General Studies	NY	41,516	C
Columbus State Univ	GA	8,664	C
Concord College	WV	9,708	C
Concordia College: Moorhead	MN	22,475	VC
Concordia College-New York	NY	27,740	C
Concordia Univ	CA	26,780	C
Concordia Univ	OR	24,400	C
Concordia Univ Nebr	NE	20,500	C+
Concordia Univ St.Paul	MN	27,776	C
Concordia Univ Wisc	WI	22,660	VC
Concordia Univ, Ann Arbor	MI	25,153	C+
Concordia Univ, River Forest	IL	26,300	C
Conn College	CT	41,975	MC
Converse College	SC	24,800	VC
Coppin State College	MD	10,200	LC
Cornell College	IA	30,110	VC+
Cornell Univ	NY	41,717	MC
Cornerstone Univ and Grand Rapids Theological Seminary	MI	21,350	NC
Covenant College	GA	26,460	VC+
Creighton Univ	NE	29,918	VC+
Crichton College	TN	15,300	C
Culver-Stockton College	MO	20,625	C
Cumberland Univ	TN	18,894	C
Curry College	MA	26,100	LC
Daemen College	NY	24,580	C
Dakota State Univ	SD	7,466	C
Dakota Wesleyan Univ	SD	17,832	C
Dallas Baptist Univ	TX	17,040	VC
Dana College	NE	22,390	C
Dartmouth College	NH	39,465	MC
Davidson College	NC	36,825	MC
Davis and Elkins College	WV	22,416	C
De Sales Univ	PA	28,580	VC
Defiance College	OH	24,790	C
Delaware State Univ	DE	8,130	LC
Delaware Valley College	PA	29,944	C
Delta State Univ	MS	7,709	C
Denison Univ	OH	37,040	HC
DePaul Univ	IL	29,835	VC
DePauw Univ	IN	32,100	HC
Dickinson College	PA	40,170	HC+
Dickinson State Univ	ND	7,847	NC
Dillard Univ	LA	17,500	VC
Doane College	NE	22,458	C
Dominican College	NY	26,630	C
Dominican Univ	IL	26,370	C
Dominican Univ of Calif	CA	36,836	C
Dordt College	IA	20,325	VC
Dowling College	NY	22,110	LC
Drake Univ	IA	27,632	VC+
Drew Univ/College of Liberal Arts	NJ	39,698	VC
Drexel Univ	PA	27,700	VC
Drury Univ	MO	20,117	VC
Duke Univ	NC	41,239	MC
Duquesne Univ	PA	29,534	VC
D'Youville College	NY	23,660	C
Earlham College	IN	33,604	HC
East Carolina Univ	NC	10,000	VC
East Central Univ	OK	6,207	C
East Stroudsburg Univ of Pennsylvania	PA	10,336	C
East Tenn State Univ	TN	8,497	C
East Texas Baptist Univ	TX	16,713	C
Eastern Conn State Univ	CT	13,554	C
Eastern Illinois Univ	IL	12,569	C
Eastern Kentucky Univ	KY	7,725	C
Eastern Mennonite Univ	VA	25,450	VC
Eastern Mich Univ	MI	12,897	C
Eastern Nazarene College	MA	19,500	LC
Eastern New Mexico Univ	NM	7,264	C
Eastern Oregon Univ	OR	10,400	NC
Eastern Univ	PA	24,075	C
Eastern Washington Univ	WA	10,608	C
Eckerd College	FL	35,492	VC
Edgewood College	WI	22,862	C
Edinboro Univ of Pennsylvania	PA	11,809	LC
Edward Waters College	FL	14,374	LC
Elizabeth City State Univ	NC	5,700	LC
Elizabethtown College	PA	32,100	VC
Elmhurst College	IL	24,685	VC
Elmira College	NY	37,200	VC
Elon Univ	NC	25,371	HC
Emmanuel College	MA	32,000	C+
Emory & Henry College	VA	26,570	C
Emory Univ	GA	40,546	MC
Emporia State Univ	KS	8,093	C
Erskine College	SC	25,468	VC
Eureka College	IL	19,280	C
Evangel Univ	MO	17,380	C
Excelsior College	NY	995	SP
Fairfield Univ	CT	39,835	HC
Fairleigh Dickinson Univ/ College at Florham	NJ	30,130	C
Fairleigh Dickinson Univ/ Metropolitan Campus	NJ	28,590	C
Fairmont State	WV	8,400	LC
Farmingdale SUNY	NY	13,521	C
Faulkner Univ	AL	15,600	C
Fayetteville State Univ	NC	6,000	LC
Felician College	NJ	24,300	C
Ferris State Univ	MI	13,698	C
Ferrum College	VA	24,290	LC
Fisk Univ	TN	19,830	C
Fitchburg State College	MA	11,276	C
Florida A&M Univ	FL	8,344	C
Florida Atlantic Univ	FL	11,221	C
Florida Inst of Technology	FL	29,720	VC
Florida International Univ	FL	9,215	VC
Florida Memorial Univ	FL	6,000	LC
Florida Southern College	FL	25,965	C
Florida State Univ	FL	9,028	HC
Fontbonne Univ	MO	23,308	C
Fordham Univ	NY	36,000	HC
Fort Hays State Univ	KS	7,638	C
Fort Lewis College	CO	11,852	C
Fort Valley State Univ	GA	6,975	C
Framingham State College	MA	11,156	C
Francis Marion Univ	SC	11,114	C
Franciscan Univ of Steubenville	OH	20,300	VC
Franklin and Marshall College	PA	40,590	HC
Franklin College	IN		C
Franklin Pierce Univ	NH	31,700	C
Freed-Hardeman Univ	TN	16,370	NC
Fresno Pacific Univ	CA	25,454	C
Friends Univ	KS	16,250	LC
Frostburg State Univ	MD	12,672	C
Furman Univ	SC	33,264	HC+
Gallaudet Univ	DC	16,554	
Gannon Univ	PA	26,100	C
Gardner-Webb Univ	NC	21,500	C
Geneva College	PA	21,850	C
George Fox Univ	OR	28,490	C
George Mason Univ	VA	10,850	VC
George Washington Univ	DC	48,820	MC
Georgetown College	KY	24,950	C+
Georgetown Univ	DC	43,183	MC
Georgia College and State Univ	GA	11,020	C
Georgia Inst of Technology	GA	11,450	HC+
Georgia Southern Univ	GA	9,762	C
Georgia Southwestern State Univ	GA	6,035	C
Georgia State Univ	GA	11,444	VC
Georgian Court College	NJ	20,000	LC
Gettysburg College	PA	39,864	HC
Glenville State College	WV	8,778	NC
Gonzaga Univ	WA	30,218	HC
Gordon College	MA	29,194	C+
Goshen College	IN	22,850	VC
Goucher College	MD	36,225	VC
Grace College	IN	22,170	C
Graceland Univ	IA	19,700	C
Grambling State Univ	LA	6,538	NC
Grand Canyon Univ	AZ	32,000	LC
Grand Valley State Univ	MI	12,000	VC
Grand View College	IA	21,482	C
Green Mountain College	VT	32,164	C
Greensboro College	NC	23,000	C
Greenville College	IL	23,146	C
Grinnell College	IA	34,814	HC+
Grove City College	PA	15,784	HC+
Guilford College	NC	28,160	C+
Gustavus Adolphus College	MN	30,920	HC
Gwynedd-Mercy College	PA	26,080	C
Hamilton College	NY	41,660	MC
Hamline Univ	MN	27,070	VC
Hampden-Sydney College	VA	31,148	VC
Hampshire College	MA	37,120	HC
Hampton Univ	VA	19,468	C+
Hannibal-LaGrange College	MO	16,390	C
Hanover College	IN	28,150	HC
Harding Univ	AR	16,512	VC
Hardin-Simmons Univ	TX	18,641	C
Hartwick College	NY	36,065	C+
Harvard Univ/Harvard College	MA	45,860	MC
Harvey Mudd College	CA	42,352	MC
Hastings College	NE	22,218	VC
Haverford College	PA	41,600	MC
Hawaii Pacific Univ	HI	21,080	VC
Heidelberg College	OH	23,242	C
Henderson State Univ	AR	7,600	C
Hendrix College	AR	27,646	HC+
High Point Univ	NC	25,720	C
Hillsdale College	MI	24,160	HC
Hiram College	OH	28,700	VC
Hobart and William Smith Colleges	NY	41,123	VC
Hofstra Univ	NY	32,630	VC
Hollins Univ	VA	31,105	C
Holy Family Univ	PA	25,740	C
Holy Names College	CA	27,980	NC
Hood College	MD	30,085	VC
Hope College	MI	28,208	VC+
Houghton College	NY	25,980	VC+
Houston Baptist Univ	TX	18,660	C
Howard Payne Univ	TX	17,115	C
Howard Univ	DC	18,481	C+
Humboldt State Univ	CA	11,176	C
Huntingdon College	AL	23,090	VC
Huntington Univ	IN	24,830	C
Husson College	ME	17,410	LC
Huston-Tillotson Univ	TX	14,232	LC
Idaho State Univ	ID	9,030	C
Illinois College	IL	21,900	C+
Illinois Inst of Technology	IL	26,465	HC+
Illinois State Univ	IL	12,839	C+
Illinois Wesleyan Univ	IL	34,050	HC+
Immaculata Univ	PA	25,350	C
Indiana State Univ	IN	11,604	C
Indiana Univ Bloomington	IN	13,356	VC
Indiana Univ East	IN	4,806	LC
Indiana Univ Kokomo	IN	4,835	LC
Indiana Univ Northwest	IN	4,902	LC
Indiana Univ of Pennsylvania	PA	11,209	C
Indiana Univ South Bend	IN	4,989	LC
Indiana Univ Southeast	IN	4,880	LC
Indiana Univ-Purdue Univ Fort Wayne	IN	5,067	LC
Indiana Univ-Purdue Univ Indianapolis	IN	10,959	C
Indiana Wesleyan Univ	IN	22,074	C+
Inter American Univ of PR/ Aguadilla Campus	PR	3,784	
Inter American Univ of PR/ Arecibo Campus	PR	3,350	
Inter American Univ of PR/ Bayamon Univ College	PR	3,522	
Inter American Univ of PR/ Fajardo Campus	PR	4,000	
Inter American Univ of PR/ Metropolitan Campus	PR	4,320	
Inter American Univ of PR/ Ponce Regional College	PR	3,700	
Inter American Univ of PR/ San German	PR	6,720	
Iona College	NY	30,878	VC
Iowa State Univ	IA	11,831	VC
Iowa Wesleyan College	IA	22,140	C
Ithaca College	NY	35,144	VC
Jackson State Univ	MS	8,500	C
Jacksonville State Univ	AL	7,618	LC
Jacksonville Univ	FL	24,040	C
James Madison Univ	VA	12,010	VC
Jamestown College	ND	14,130	NC
Jarvis Christian College	TX	11,136	NC
John Brown Univ	AR	20,910	VC
John Carroll Univ	OH	27,658	C+
Johns Hopkins Univ	MD	42,044	MC
Johnson C. Smith Univ	NC	20,000	C
Johnson State College	VT	11,830	LC
Judson College	AL	16,522	C
Judson College	IL	25,130	C
Juniata College	PA	33,130	VC
Kalamazoo College	MI	32,442	VC+
Kansas State Univ	KS	10,516	VC
Kansas Wesleyan Univ	KS	21,400	VC
Kean Univ	NJ	15,880	C
Keene State College	NH	13,836	C
Kennesaw State Univ	GA	12,152	C
Kent State Univ	OH	14,594	C
Kentucky State Univ	KY	10,089	LC
Kentucky Wesleyan College	KY	18,590	C
Kenyon College	OH	39,500	MC
Keuka College	NY	26,050	C
King College	TN	23,400	C
King's College	PA	29,810	C
Knox College	IL	32,385	VC+
Knoxville College	TN	6,200	LC
Kutztown Univ of Pennsylvania	PA	10,820	C
La Roche College	PA	24,724	LC
La Salle Univ	PA	34,950	C
La Sierra Univ	CA	24,327	C+
Lafayette College	PA	39,267	MC
LaGrange College	GA	22,874	C+
Lake Erie College	OH	27,725	C
Lake Forest College	IL	33,860	VC
Lake Superior State Univ	MI	12,842	LC
Lakeland College	WI	22,990	C
Lamar Univ	TX	6,820	LC
Lambuth Univ	TN	21,700	C+
Lander Univ	SC	10,600	C
Lane College	TN	11,220	C+
Langston Univ	OK	2,308	LC
Lawrence Univ	WI	33,958	HC
Le Moyne College	NY	29,570	VC
Lebanon Valley College	PA	31,700	VC
Lee Univ	TN	14,780	NC
Lees-McRae College	NC	23,000	C
Lehigh Univ	PA	42,690	HC+
LeMoyne-Owen College	TN	13,150	LC
LeTourneau Univ	TX	21,200	C
Lewis and Clark College	OR	35,358	VC+
Lewis Univ	IL	23,550	C+
Lewis-Clark State College	ID	6,990	C
Liberty Univ	VA	19,101	C
Limestone College	SC	19,840	C
Lincoln Memorial Univ	TN	18,144	C
Lincoln Univ	MO	8,000	NC
Lincoln Univ	PA	13,658	C+
Lindenwood Univ	MO	18,600	VC
Lindsey Wilson College	KY	16,425	LC
Linfield College	OR	29,632	VC
Lipscomb Univ	TN	20,967	VC
Livingstone College	NC	17,815	LC
Lock Haven Univ of Pennsylvania	PA	12,098	LC
LIU/Brooklyn Campus	NY	25,000	C
LIU/C.W. Post Campus	NY	28,282	C
Longwood Univ	VA	12,426	C
Loras College	IA	27,193	C
Louisiana College	LA	13,450	C
Louisiana State Univ and A&M College	LA	10,749	VC
Louisiana State Univ in Shreveport	LA	2,900	NC
Louisiana Tech Univ	LA	7,370	C
Lourdes College	OH	15,300	LC
Loyola College in Maryland	MD	38,898	HC
Loyola Marymount Univ	CA	36,321	VC
Loyola Univ Chicago	IL	32,896	VC
Loyola Univ New Orleans	LA	31,050	VC+
Lubbock Christian Univ	TX	16,960	C
Luther College	IA	28,800	VC+
Lycoming College	PA	30,797	C+
Lynchburg College	VA	30,645	C
Lyon College	AR	19,990	VC
Macalester College	MN	36,500	MC
MacMurray College	IL	20,755	C
Madonna Univ	MI	16,068	VC
Malone College	OH	23,040	C
Manchester College	IN	23,470	C
Manhattan College	NY	29,000	C
Manhattanville College	NY	32,500	C+
Mansfield Univ	PA	11,300	C
Marian College	IN	26,160	C
Marian College of Fond du Lac	WI	21,775	LC
Marietta College	OH	29,327	C
Marist College	NY	30,566	VC
Marlboro College	VT	35,980	VC+
Marquette Univ	WI	31,066	HC
Mars Hill College	NC	19,000	LC
Marshall Univ	WV	9,116	C
Martin Univ	IN	10,300	SP
Mary Baldwin College	VA	26,465	C
Marygrove College	MI	19,310	C+
Marymount Manhattan College	NY	30,049	VC
Marymount Univ	VA	25,934	C
Maryville College	TN	29,224	VC
Maryville Univ of St. Louis	MO	23,000	VC
Marywood Univ	PA	30,680	C
Mass College of Liberal Arts	MA	8,725	LC
Mass Inst of Technology	MA	41,800	MC
Master's College and Seminary	CA	25,850	VC
Mayville State Univ	ND	8,667	NC
McDaniel College	MD	31,610	VC
McKendree College	IL	24,800	VC
McMurry Univ	TX	18,100	LC
McNeese State Univ	LA	5,270	LC
McPherson College	KS	21,010	C
Medaille College	NY	21,000	C
Mercer Univ	GA	27,525	VC+
Mercy College	NY	20,000	NC
Mercyhurst College	PA	28,633	VC
Meredith College	NC	25,600	C
Merrimack College	MA	34,380	C
Mesa State College	CO	8,051	C
Messiah College	PA	28,910	VC+
Methodist College	NC	21,000	C
Metropolitan State College of Denver	CO	2,338	LC
Metropolitan State Univ	MN	4,682	SP
Miami Univ	OH	29,970	HC
Mich State Univ	MI	13,689	VC
Mich Tech Univ	MI	14,569	VC
MidAmerica Nazarene Univ	KS	20,584	LC
Middle Tenn State Univ	TN	8,540	C
Middlebury College	VT	42,120	MC
Midland Lutheran College	NE	18,600	C
Midway College	KY	20,150	C
Midwestern State Univ	TX	9,381	LC
Miles College	AL	9,922	NC
Millersville Univ of Pennsylvania	PA	12,113	C
Milligan College	TN	21,990	VC
Millikin Univ	IL	25,590	C
Mills College	CA	39,870	C
Millsaps College	MS	28,256	VC+
Minn State Univ, Mankato	MN	10,276	LC
Minn State Univ, Moorhead	MN	7,000	LC
Minot State Univ	ND	6,700	LC
Miss College	MS	14,574	VC
Miss State Univ	MS	9,577	C
Miss Univ for Women	MS	6,000	LC
Miss Valley State Univ	MS	7,970	C
Missouri Baptist Univ	MO	19,640	C
Missouri Southern State Univ	MO	8,396	NC
Missouri State Univ	MO	10,748	C+
Missouri Valley College	MO	18,500	C
Missouri Western State Univ	MO	9,534	NC
Molloy College	NY	16,510	C
Monmouth College	IL	23,700	C
Monmouth Univ	NJ	28,956	C
Montana State Univ-Billings	MT	8,906	C

ST = STATE   **$IS** = IN-STATE COSTS   **SR** = SELECTOR RATING

ST = STATE **$IS** = IN-STATE COSTS **SR** = SELECTOR RATING

School	ST	$IS	SR
Univ of Alaska Fairbanks	AK	10,101	C
Univ of Alaska Southeast	AK	8,050	LC
Univ of Arizona	AZ	11,958	VC
Univ of Arkansas	AR	11,859	VC
Univ of Arkansas at Little Rock	AR	7,230	NC
Univ of Arkansas at Monticello	AR	7,325	NC
Univ of Arkansas at Pine Bluff	AR	8,300	C
Univ of at Calif Davis	CA	15,010	C
Univ of Bridgeport	CT	29,595	LC
Univ of Calif at Berkeley	CA	18,141	HC+
Univ of Calif at Irvine	CA	16,475	HC
Univ of Calif at Los Angeles	CA	17,681	VC
Univ of Calif at Riverside	CA	16,625	C
Univ of Calif at San Diego	CA	16,102	HC
Univ of Calif at Santa Barbara	CA	11,800	VC
Univ of Calif at Santa Cruz	CA	19,174	VC
Univ of Central Arkansas	AR	9,984	C
Univ of Central Florida	FL	10,739	VC
Univ of Central Okla	OK	8,094	C
Univ of Charleston	WV	27,600	C
Univ of Chicago	IL	42,369	MC
Univ of Cincinnati	OH	17,682	C
Univ of Colo at Colo Springs	CO	11,517	VC
Univ of Colo at Denver and Health Sciences Center	CO	5,021	C
Univ of Conn	CT	16,628	HC
Univ of Dallas	TX	27,432	VC+
Univ of Dayton	OH	28,826	VC
Univ of Delaware	DE	14,142	HC
Univ of Denver	CO	36,376	VC+
Univ of Detroit Mercy	MI	27,000	C
Univ of Dubuque	IA	23,390	C
Univ of Evansville	IN	28,320	VC
Univ of Findlay	OH	29,238	C
Univ of Georgia	GA	11,004	VC
Univ of Great Falls	MT	17,000	C
Univ of Hartford	CT	34,044	C
Univ of Hawaii at Hilo	HI	6,500	C
Univ of Hawaii at Manoa	HI	10,413	VC
Univ of Houston	TX	7,000	C
Univ of Idaho	ID	9,310	NC
Univ of Illinois at Chicago	IL	16,256	VC
Univ of Illinois at Urbana-Champaign	IL	15,800	HC+
Univ of Indianapolis	IN	25,090	C
Univ of Iowa	IA	12,172	VC
Univ of Kansas	KS	10,915	VC
Univ of Kentucky	KY	7,800	C
Univ of La Verne	CA	33,470	C
Univ of Louisiana at Monroe	LA	7,103	C
Univ of Louisville	KY	10,400	VC
Univ of Maine	ME	13,642	C
Univ of Maine at Augusta	ME	5,025	NC
Univ of Maine at Farmington	ME	11,515	C
Univ of Maine at Fort Kent	ME	10,832	LC
Univ of Maine at Machias	ME	10,523	C
Univ of Maine at Presque Isle	ME	10,066	LC
Univ of Mary	ND	15,374	C
Univ of Mary Hardin-Baylor	TX	19,428	C
Univ of Mary Washington	VA	11,636	HC
Univ of Maryland/Baltimore County	MD	16,642	VC+
Univ of Maryland/College Park	MD	16,036	HC
Univ of Maryland/Eastern Shore	MD	11,210	C
Univ of Mass Amherst	MA	15,973	C+
Univ of Mass Boston	MA	8,024	C
Univ of Mass Dartmouth	MA	15,985	C
Univ of Mass Lowell	MA	14,327	VC
Univ of Memphis	TN	11,153	C
Univ of Miami	FL	38,397	MC
Univ of Mich/Ann Arbor	MI	16,587	HC+
Univ of Mich/Dearborn	MI	7,000	VC
Univ of Mich/Flint	MI	6,398	C
Univ of Minn/Duluth	MN	13,974	C
Univ of Minn/Morris	MN	15,472	VC
Univ of Minn/Twin Cities	MN	13,165	VC
Univ of Miss	MS	9,000	C
Univ of Missouri/Columbia	MO	13,500	VC
Univ of Missouri/Kansas City	MO	15,000	VC
Univ of Missouri/Rolla	MO	13,332	HC
Univ of Missouri/St. Louis	MO	14,046	VC
Univ of Mobile	AL	16,880	C
Univ of Montana	MT	10,602	C
Univ of Montevallo	AL	9,630	C
Univ of Nebr at Kearney	NE	9,000	NC
Univ of Nebr at Lincoln	NE	11,401	VC
Univ of Nebr at Omaha	NE	11,235	C
Univ of Nevada/Las Vegas	NV	11,566	C
Univ of Nevada/Reno	NV	12,155	NC
Univ of New England	ME	31,005	C
Univ of New Hampshire	NH	16,810	VC
Univ of New Haven	CT	31,794	C
Univ of New Mexico	NM	11,253	C
Univ of New Orleans	LA	7,370	C
Univ of North Alabama	AL	8,992	C
Univ of N Car at Asheville	NC	9,237	LC
Univ of N Car at Chapel Hill	NC	11,129	MC
Univ of N Car at Charlotte	NC	9,101	C
Univ of N Car at Greensboro	NC	8,993	C
Univ of N Car at Pembroke	NC	7,940	LC
Univ of N Car at Wilmington	NC	10,107	VC
Univ of N Dak	ND	10,114	VC
Univ of North Florida	FL	9,908	VC
Univ of North Texas	TX	7,800	C
Univ of Northern Colo	CO	10,249	C
Univ of Northern Iowa	IA	11,133	C
Univ of Notre Dame	IN	39,552	MC
Univ of Oregon	OR	13,108	VC
Univ of Pennsylvania	PA	41,766	MC
Univ of Pittsburgh at Bradford	PA	17,008	C
Univ of Pittsburgh at Greensburg	PA	17,640	C
Univ of Pittsburgh at Johnstown	PA	16,740	LC
Univ of Pittsburgh at Pittsburgh	PA	18,866	HC
Univ of Portland	OR	32,300	VC
Univ of PR at Humacao	PR	1,707	
Univ of PR/Cayey Univ College	PR	1,250	
Univ of PR/Mayaguez	PR	1,250	
Univ of PR/Rio Piedras	PR	5,750	
Univ of Puget Sound	WA	35,600	HC
Univ of Redlands	CA	36,160	VC
Univ of Rhode Island	RI	15,398	C
Univ of Richmond	VA	40,510	MC
Univ of Rio Grande	OH	8,728	NC
Univ of Rochester	NY	41,135	MC
Univ of St. Francis	IL	25,430	C
Univ of St. Francis	IN	20,970	C
Univ of St. Mary	KS	18,900	C
Univ of St. Thomas	MN	28,000	VC
Univ of St. Thomas	TX	23,810	VC
Univ of San Diego	CA	40,620	HC
Univ of San Francisco	CA	37,560	VC
Univ of Science and Arts of Okla	OK	7,650	C
Univ of Scranton	PA	31,100	VC
Univ of Sioux Falls	SD	20,800	C
Univ of South Alabama	AL	8,930	LC
Univ of S Car at Aiken	SC	11,718	LC
Univ of S Car at Columbia	SC	13,397	VC
Univ of S Car Upstate	SC	11,957	C
Univ of S Dak	SD	9,068	C
Univ of South Florida	FL	10,284	VC
Univ of Southern Calif	CA	41,618	MC
Univ of Southern Indiana	IN	12,590	LC
Univ of Southern Maine	ME	12,614	C
Univ of Southern Miss	MS	10,112	C
Univ of Tampa	FL	25,784	C
Univ of Tenn at Chattanooga	TN	7,790	C
Univ of Tenn at Knoxville	TN	11,720	C
Univ of Tenn at Martin	TN	8,693	C
Univ of Texas at Arlington	TX	7,195	LC
Univ of Texas at Austin	TX	14,610	HC
Univ of Texas at Dallas	TX	13,244	HC
Univ of Texas at El Paso	TX	8,764	NC
Univ of Texas at San Antonio	TX	11,325	LC
Univ of Texas-Pan American	TX	7,290	C+
Univ of the Cumberlands	KY	18,184	C
Univ of the District of Columbia	DC	2,070	LC
Univ of the Incarnate Word	TX	23,306	C
Univ of the Ozarks	AR	19,250	C
Univ of the Pacific	CA	34,380	VC
Univ of the Sacred Heart	PR	5,590	
Univ of the Sciences in Philadelphia	PA	33,380	VC
Univ of the South	TN	34,645	HC
Univ of Toledo	OH	15,806	NC
Univ of Tulsa	OK	25,348	HC
Univ of Utah	UT	10,162	VC
Univ of Vermont	VT	18,080	VC
Univ of Virginia	VA	13,759	MC
Univ of Virginia's College at Wise	VA	11,076	C
Univ of Washington	WA	10,400	VC
Univ of West Alabama	AL	7,611	C
Univ of West Florida	FL	8,559	C
Univ of West Georgia	GA	8,838	C
Univ of Wisc/Eau Claire	WI	9,915	VC
Univ of Wisc/Green Bay	WI	9,415	VC
Univ of Wisc/La Crosse	WI	10,045	VC
Univ of Wisc/Madison	WI	13,117	HC
Univ of Wisc/Milwaukee	WI	9,427	LC
Univ of Wisc/Oshkosh	WI	10,426	LC
Univ of Wisc/Parkside	WI	10,181	LC
Univ of Wisc/Platteville	WI	9,779	NC
Univ of Wisc/River Falls	WI	9,722	LC
Univ of Wisc/Stevens Point	WI	9,384	VC
Univ of Wisc/Superior	WI	9,610	C+
Univ of Wisc/Whitewater	WI	9,274	C
Univ of Wyoming	WY	9,666	C
Upper Iowa Univ	IA	20,130	C
Ursinus College	PA	38,950	VC
Ursuline College	OH	25,456	C
Utah State Univ	UT	8,002	VC
Utica College	NY	31,396	C
Valdosta State Univ	GA	8,802	C
Valley City State Univ	ND	9,854	LC
Valparaiso Univ	IN	28,970	VC+
Vanderbilt Univ	TN	41,986	MC
Vanguard Univ of Southern Calif	CA	27,071	C
Vassar College	NY	41,700	MC
Villa Julie College	MD	25,222	C
Villanova Univ	PA	38,672	HC+
Virginia Commonwealth Univ	VA	12,987	C
Virginia Intermont College	VA	22,200	LC
Virginia Military Inst	VA	12,654	C
Virginia Polytechnic Inst and State Univ	VA	10,834	VC
Virginia State Univ	VA	11,318	C
Virginia Union Univ	VA	18,432	LC
Virginia Wesleyan College	VA	28,433	C
Viterbo Univ	WI	21,670	C
Voorhees College	SC	11,800	LC
Wabash College	IN	30,116	HC
Wagner College	NY	33,300	VC
Wake Forest Univ	NC	38,290	MC
Walla Walla College	WA	24,489	NC
Walsh Univ	OH	23,440	C
Warner Pacific College	OR	21,900	C
Warner Southern College	FL	18,000	LC
Warren Wilson College	NC	24,382	VC
Wartburg College	IA	27,315	NC
Washburn Univ	KS	9,734	NC
Washington and Jefferson College	PA	33,490	VC
Washington and Lee Univ	VA	35,880	MC
Washington College	MD	34,990	VC
Washington State Univ	WA	12,260	C
Washington Univ in St. Louis	MO	42,106	MC
Wayland Baptist Univ	TX	13,484	C
Wayne State College	NE	8,033	NC
Wayne State Univ	MI	11,805	C
Waynesburg College	PA	21,230	C
Weber State Univ	UT	9,635	NC
Webster Univ	MO	24,280	VC
Wellesley College	MA	41,030	MC
Wells College	NY	23,070	VC
Wesley College	DE	19,905	C
Wesleyan College	GA	19,560	C
Wesleyan Univ	CT	42,122	MC
West Chester Univ of Pennsylvania	PA	12,355	C+
West Liberty State College	WV	9,142	LC
West Texas A&M Univ	TX	8,452	C
West Virginia State Univ	WV	8,378	NC
West Virginia Univ	WV	10,506	C
West Virginia Univ Inst of Technology	WV	8,788	NC
West Virginia Wesleyan College	WV	26,880	C
Western Carolina Univ	NC	7,000	C
Western Conn State Univ	CT	12,993	C
Western Illinois Univ	IL	13,042	C
Western Kentucky Univ	KY	10,192	C
Western Mich Univ	MI	13,299	C
Western New England College	MA	32,054	C
Western New Mexico Univ	NM	7,233	LC
Western Oregon Univ	OR	10,295	C
Western State College of Colo	CO	9,942	C
Western Washington Univ	WA	11,262	VC
Westfield State College	MA	10,200	C
Westminster College	MO	19,060	VC
Westminster College	PA	31,290	C+
Westminster College	UT	25,656	C
Westmont College	CA	36,672	HC
Wheaton College	IL	27,760	HC
Wheaton College	MA	40,180	HC+
Wheeling Jesuit Univ	WV	26,910	C
Whitman College	WA	36,110	HC+
Whittier College	CA	29,108	C
Whitworth College	WA	29,428	VC+
Wichita State Univ	KS	8,500	C
Widener Univ	PA	27,275	C
Wilberforce Univ	OH	14,937	LC
Wiley College	TX	8,100	LC
Wilkes Univ	PA	30,886	C
Willamette Univ	OR	35,416	VC+
William Carey College	MS	11,000	LC
William Jewell College	MO	24,340	C
William Paterson Univ of New Jersey	NJ	17,810	C+
William Penn Univ	IA	17,685	LC
William Woods Univ	MO	21,020	C
Williams Baptist College	AR	13,450	C
Williams College	MA	40,310	MC
Wilmington College	OH	2,806	NC
Wilson College	PA	27,660	C
Wingate Univ	NC	23,300	C
Winona State Univ	MN	11,333	C
Winston-Salem State Univ	NC	8,960	LC
Winthrop Univ	SC	11,302	C
Wisc Lutheran College	WI	23,510	VC
Wittenberg Univ	OH	34,596	VC
Wofford College	SC	30,935	HC
Worcester State College	MA	12,499	C
Wright State Univ	OH	13,616	LC
Xavier Univ	OH	30,490	MC
Xavier Univ of Louisiana	LA	17,600	C
Yale Univ	CT	41,000	MC
Yeshiva Univ	NY	22,000	C
York College	NE	16,330	NC
York College of Pennsylvania	PA	16,550	VC
Youngstown State Univ	OH	12,613	NC

BIOMATHEMATICS

School	ST	$IS	SR
Rutgers, The State Univ of New Jersey/New Brunswick/Piscataway Campus	NJ	15,810	HC

BIOMEDICAL ENGINEERING

School	ST	$IS	SR
Boston Univ	MA	42,046	HC+
Bucknell Univ	PA	39,660	MC
Case Western Reserve Univ	OH	37,314	MC
Catholic Univ of America	DC	35,838	VC
CUNY/City College	NY		C
College of New Jersey	NJ	18,315	MC
Columbia Univ/Fu Foundation School of Engineering and Applied Science	NY	42,584	MC
DeVry Univ/Dallas	TX	10,700	LC
DeVry Univ/Decatur	GA	10,680	LC
DeVry Univ/Fremont	CA	13,060	LC
DeVry Univ/Kansas City	MO	10,670	LC
DeVry Univ/Phoenix	AZ	11,790	LC
DeVry Univ/Pomona	CA	12,450	LC
DeVry Univ/West Hills	CA	12,450	LC
DeVry Univ/Westminster	CO	12,000	LC
Drexel Univ	PA	27,700	VC
Duke Univ	NC	41,239	MC
Florida International Univ	FL	9,215	VC
Florida State Univ	FL	9,028	HC
Georgia Inst of Technology	GA	11,450	HC+
Hofstra Univ	NY	32,630	VC
Indiana Inst of Technology	IN	23,430	C
Indiana Univ-Purdue Univ Indianapolis	IN	10,959	C
Johns Hopkins Univ	MD	42,044	MC
Lawrence Tech Univ	MI	25,475	VC
Louisiana Tech Univ	LA	7,370	C
Marquette Univ	WI	31,066	HC
Mercer Univ	GA	27,525	VC+
Mich Tech Univ	MI	14,569	VC
Milwaukee School of Engineering	WI	29,847	VC+
New Jersey Inst of Technology	NJ	16,396	VC
New York Inst of Technology	NY	28,126	VC
Northwestern Univ	IL	37,595	MC
Purdue Univ/West Lafayette	IN	13,458	VC
Rensselaer Polytechnic Inst	NY	41,288	HC+
Rochester Inst of Technology	NY	32,070	VC+
Rose-Hulman Inst of Technology	IN	34,557	HC+
St. Louis Univ	MO	33,158	VC+
SUNY/Univ at Stony Brook	NY	13,625	HC
Stevens Inst of Technology	NJ	40,935	HC
Tufts Univ	MA	42,018	MC
Tulane Univ	LA	41,098	MC
Univ of Akron	OH	15,166	NC
Univ of Alabama at Birmingham	AL	13,716	C
Univ of Conn	CT	16,628	HC
Univ of Hartford	CT	34,044	C
Univ of Iowa	IA	12,172	VC
Univ of Memphis	TN	11,153	C
Univ of Miami	FL	38,397	VC
Univ of Missouri/Columbia	MO	13,500	VC
Univ of Rhode Island	RI	15,398	C
Univ of Rochester	NY	41,135	VC
Univ of Southern Calif	CA	41,618	MC
Univ of Texas at Austin	TX	14,610	VC
Univ of Utah	UT	10,162	VC
Univ of Virginia	VA	13,759	MC
Univ of Wisc/Madison	WI	13,117	HC
Virginia Commonwealth Univ	VA	12,987	C
Washington Univ in St. Louis	MO	42,106	MC
Western New England College	MA	32,054	C
Worcester Polytechnic Inst	MA	40,450	VC+
Wright State Univ	OH	13,616	LC
Yale Univ	CT	41,000	MC

BIOMEDICAL EQUIPMENT TECHNOLOGY

School	ST	$IS	SR
Andrews Univ	MI	21,786	C
Thomas Edison State College	NJ	3,780	SP
Univ of Houston	TX	7,000	C

ST = STATE $IS = IN-STATE COSTS   SR = SELECTOR RATING

School	ST	$IS	SR

BIOMEDICAL SCIENCE

School	ST	$IS	SR
Albany College of Pharmacy	NY	25,090	SP
Andrews Univ	MI	21,786	C
Averett Univ	VA	24,920	C
Brown Univ	RI	42,015	MC
Cal State, Northridge	CA	9,036	LC
Central Mich Univ	MI	12,244	C
CUNY/City College	NY		
Kent State Univ	OH	14,594	C
LIU/C.W. Post Campus	NY	28,282	C
Lynchburg College	VA	30,645	C
Marquette Univ	WI	31,066	MC
Mountain State Univ	WV	11,406	NC
Okla State Univ	OK	10,213	VC
Oral Roberts Univ	OK	22,650	C
Rutgers, The State Univ of New Jersey/New Brunswick/Piscataway Campus	NJ	15,810	HC
St. Peter's College	NJ	30,160	LC
Texas A&M Univ	TX	13,351	HC
Univ of Illinois at Urbana-Champaign	IL	15,800	HC+
Univ of Mich/Ann Arbor	MI	16,587	HC+
Univ of Miss	MS	9,000	C
Univ of New England	ME	31,005	C
Univ of Pennsylvania	PA	41,766	MC
Univ of South Alabama	AL	8,930	LC
Univ of Vermont	VT	18,080	VC
Western Mich Univ	MI	13,299	C

BIOMETRICS AND BIOSTATISTICS

School	ST	$IS	SR
Cornell Univ	NY	41,717	MC
La Sierra Univ	CA	24,327	C+
Univ of N Car at Chapel Hill	NC	11,129	MC
Univ of Pennsylvania	PA	41,766	MC

BIOPHYSICS

School	ST	$IS	SR
Andrews Univ	MI	21,786	C
Brandeis Univ	MA	41,551	MC
Brigham Young Univ	UT	9,200	VC
Brown Univ	RI	42,015	MC
Centenary College of Louisiana	LA	24,760	VC
Columbia Univ/Columbia College	NY	42,584	MC
Harvard Univ/Harvard College	MA	45,860	MC
Illinois Inst of Technology	IL	26,465	HC+
Iowa State Univ	IA	11,831	VC
Johns Hopkins Univ	MD	42,044	MC
La Sierra Univ	CA	24,327	C+
Okla City Univ	OK	23,965	VC
Oregon State Univ	OR	11,055	C
Pacific Union College	CA	24,555	VC+
Rensselaer Polytechnic Inst	NY	41,288	HC+
St. Bonaventure Univ	NY	28,516	C
St. Mary's Univ of Minn	MN	23,857	VC
Southwestern Okla State Univ	OK	4,801	C
SUNY/College at Geneseo	NY	12,910	HC+
SUNY/Univ at Buffalo	NY	13,694	VC
Temple Univ	PA	17,438	C
Univ of Calif at Los Angeles	CA	17,681	MC
Univ of Calif at San Diego	CA	16,102	HC
Univ of Conn	CT	16,628	HC
Univ of Houston	TX	7,000	C
Univ of Illinois at Urbana-Champaign	IL	15,800	HC+
Univ of Mich/Ann Arbor	MI	16,587	HC+
Univ of Pennsylvania	PA	41,766	MC
Univ of Scranton	PA	31,100	VC
Univ of Southern Calif	CA	41,618	MC
Univ of Southern Indiana	IN	12,590	LC
Walla Walla College	WA	24,489	NC
Washington and Jefferson College	PA	33,490	VC
Washington Univ in St. Louis	MO	42,106	MC
Yale Univ	CT	41,000	MC

BIOPSYCHOLOGY

School	ST	$IS	SR
Averett Univ	VA	24,920	C
Columbia Univ/Barnard College	NY	38,000	MC
Messiah College	PA	28,910	VC+
Mills College	CA	39,870	C
Monmouth College	IL	23,700	C
Nebr Wesleyan Univ	NE	23,415	VC
Oglethorpe Univ	GA	30,300	VC
Philadelphia Univ	PA	30,006	C
Rider Univ	NJ	32,560	C
Russell Sage College	NY	27,000	C
Tufts Univ	MA	42,018	MC
Univ of Calif at Santa Barbara	CA	11,800	VC
Univ of Mich/Ann Arbor	MI	16,587	HC+
Univ of Texas at Dallas	TX	13,244	HC
Vassar College	NY	41,700	MC

School	ST	$IS	SR
Washington Univ in St. Louis	MO	42,106	MC
York College	NE	16,330	NC

BIORESOURCE ENGINEERING

School	ST	$IS	SR
Rutgers, The State Univ of New Jersey/New Brunswick/Piscataway Campus	NJ	15,810	HC
Univ of Maryland/College Park	MD	16,036	HC

BIOTECHNOLOGY

School	ST	$IS	SR
Brigham Young Univ	UT	9,200	VC
Cabrini College	PA	33,340	C
Calif State Polytechnic Univ, Pomona	CA	18,053	C+
Calvin College	MI	25,735	NC
CUNY/York College	NY	4,242	NC
Claflin Univ	SC	16,798	C+
Colo State Univ-Pueblo	CO	7,821	LC
Cornell Univ	NY	41,717	MC
Elizabethtown College	PA	32,100	VC
Florida Gulf Coast Univ	FL	10,833	C
Fontbonne Univ	MO	23,308	C
Gannon Univ	PA	26,100	C
Inter American Univ of PR/Bayamon Univ College	PR	3,522	C
James Madison Univ	VA	12,010	VC
Kennesaw State Univ	GA	12,152	C
Kent State Univ	OH	14,594	C
Marywood Univ	PA	30,680	C
Mich State Univ	MI	13,689	VC
Minn State Univ, Mankato	MN	10,276	LC
Missouri Southern State Univ	MO	8,396	NC
Montana State Univ-Bozeman	MT	1,137	C
N Dak State Univ	ND	8,500	C
Plymouth State Univ	NH	12,298	LC
Point Park Univ	PA	24,160	C
Purdue Univ/Calumet	IN	10,891	LC
Quinnipiac Univ	CT	34,640	VC
Rochester Inst of Technology	NY	32,070	VC+
Rutgers, The State Univ of New Jersey/New Brunswick/Piscataway Campus	NJ	15,810	HC
Southeastern Okla State Univ	OK	6,147	C
Springfield College	MA	25,000	C
SUNY/Univ at Buffalo	NY	13,694	VC
Suffolk Univ	MA	33,160	C
Tufts Univ	MA	42,018	MC
Univ of Calif at San Diego	CA	16,102	HC
Univ of Delaware	DE	14,142	HC
Univ of Georgia	GA	11,004	HC
Univ of Illinois at Urbana-Champaign	IL	15,800	HC+
Univ of Maine	ME	13,642	C
Univ of Nebr at Omaha	NE	11,235	C
Univ of New Haven	CT	31,794	C
Univ of N Car at Pembroke	NC	7,940	LC
Univ of Northern Iowa	IA	11,133	C
Univ of PR/Mayaguez	PR	1,250	
Univ of Wisc/River Falls	WI	9,722	LC
Ursuline College	OH	25,456	C
Villa Julie College	MD	25,222	C
West Texas A&M Univ	TX	8,452	C
William Paterson Univ of New Jersey	NJ	17,810	C+
William Penn Univ	IA	17,685	LC
Worcester Polytechnic Inst	MA	40,450	VC+
Worcester State College	MA	12,499	C

BOTANY

School	ST	$IS	SR
Andrews Univ	MI	21,786	C
Auburn Univ	AL	12,230	VC
Ball State Univ	IN	13,138	C
Brigham Young Univ	UT	9,200	VC
Calif State Polytechnic Univ, Pomona	CA	18,053	C+
Cal State, Long Beach	CA	9,512	C
Colo State Univ-Fort Collins	CO	10,878	C+
Conn College	CT	41,975	MC
Cornell Univ	NY	41,717	MC
Delaware State Univ	DE	8,130	LC
Eastern Mich Univ	MI	12,897	C
Eastern Washington Univ	WA	10,608	C
Hampshire College	MA	37,120	HC
Humboldt State Univ	CA	11,176	VC
Idaho State Univ	ID	9,030	C
Juniata College	PA	33,130	VC
Kent State Univ	OH	14,594	C
Marlboro College	VT	35,980	VC+
Mars Hill College	NC	19,000	LC
Miami Univ	OH	29,097	HC
Mich State Univ	MI	13,689	VC
N Car State Univ	NC	11,824	HC
N Dak State Univ	ND	8,500	C
Northern Arizona Univ	AZ	10,353	C
Northern Mich Univ	MI	12,340	LC
Northwest Missouri State Univ	MO	10,000	C
Ohio Wesleyan Univ	OH	35,830	VC+
Okla State Univ	OK	10,213	VC
Oregon State Univ	OR	11,055	C
Rutgers, The State Univ of New Jersey/New Brunswick/Piscataway Campus	NJ	15,810	HC
Rutgers, The State Univ of New Jersey/Newark Campus	NJ	15,640	VC
San Francisco State Univ	CA	13,000	C
San Jose State Univ	CA	11,707	C
Southern Illinois Univ Carbondale	IL	12,391	C
SUNY/College of Environmental Science and Forestry	NY	15,000	VC
Texas A&M Univ	TX	13,351	HC
Texas A&M Univ at Commerce	TX	9,020	C
Texas State Univ - San Marcos	TX	10,862	C
Univ of Akron	OH	15,166	NC
Univ of at Calif Davis	CA	15,010	VC
Univ of Calif at Riverside	CA	16,625	C
Univ of Florida	FL	9,354	HC
Univ of Great Falls	MT	17,000	C
Univ of Hawaii at Manoa	HI	10,413	VC
Univ of Idaho	ID	9,310	NC
Univ of Illinois at Urbana-Champaign	IL	15,800	HC+
Univ of Kentucky	KY	7,800	C
Univ of Maine	ME	13,642	C
Univ of Mich/Ann Arbor	MI	16,587	HC+
Univ of Minn/Twin Cities	MN	13,165	HC
Univ of Montana	MT	10,602	C
Univ of Okla	OK	10,769	VC+
Univ of Tenn at Knoxville	TN	11,720	C
Univ of Vermont	VT	18,080	VC
Univ of Washington	WA	10,400	VC
Univ of Wisc/Madison	WI	13,117	HC
Univ of Wisc/Milwaukee	WI	9,427	LC
Univ of Wyoming	WY	9,666	C
Weber State Univ	UT	9,635	NC
Western New Mexico Univ	NM	7,233	LC

BRITISH STUDIES

School	ST	$IS	SR
Bard College	NY	41,800	HC+

BROADCASTING

School	ST	$IS	SR
Abilene Christian Univ	TX	20,830	C
Alabama State Univ	AL	7,658	C
Asbury College	KY	23,762	VC
Ashland Univ	OH	25,000	C
Baldwin-Wallace College	OH	27,256	VC
Ball State Univ	IN	13,138	C
Barry Univ	FL	24,100	LC
Baylor Univ	TX	27,555	HC
Bemidji State Univ	MN	11,180	LC
Biola Univ	CA	29,372	VC
Black Hills State Univ	SD	7,800	LC
Bowie State Univ	MD	10,880	C+
Bowling Green State Univ	OH	14,994	C
Cal State East Bay	CA	10,856	LC
Cal State, Fullerton	CA	10,990	C
Campbell Univ	NC	21,137	VC
Central Methodist Univ	MO	18,000	C
Central Mich Univ	MI	12,244	C
Central Missouri State Univ	MO	10,000	C
Central State Univ	OH	9,010	C+
Central Washington Univ	WA	11,730	C
Champlain College	VT	24,605	C
Chicago State Univ	IL	10,915	C+
CUNY/Brooklyn College	NY	4,377	C+
College of the Ozarks	MO	4,130	VC+
Colo State Univ-Pueblo	CO	7,821	LC
Concord College	WV	9,708	C
Dordt College	IA	20,325	VC
Drake Univ	IA	27,632	VC+
Drury Univ	MO	20,117	VC
Eastern Kentucky Univ	KY	7,725	C
Eastern Nazarene Univ	MA	19,560	LC
Eastern Washington Univ	WA	10,608	C
Edinboro Univ of Pennsylvania	PA	11,809	LC
Elon Univ	NC	25,371	HC
Emerson College	MA	35,076	HC
Evangel Univ	MO	17,380	C
Florida State Univ	FL	9,028	HC
Fontbonne Univ	MO	23,308	C
Fordham Univ	NY	36,000	HC
Freed-Hardeman Univ	TN	16,370	NC
Geneva College	PA	21,850	C
George Washington Univ	DC	48,820	MC
Georgia Southern Univ	GA	9,762	C
Gonzaga Univ	WA	30,218	HC
Grand Valley State Univ	MI	12,000	VC
Grand View College	IA	21,482	C
Harding Univ	AR	16,512	VC
Hardin-Simmons Univ	TX	18,641	C
Hastings College	NE	22,218	VC
Indiana State Univ	IN	11,604	C
Indiana Univ-Purdue Univ Fort Wayne	IN	5,067	LC
Ithaca College	NY	35,144	VC
John Brown Univ	AR	20,910	VC
Lewis Univ	IL	23,050	C+
Lincoln Memorial Univ	TN	18,144	C
LIU/Brooklyn Campus	NY	25,000	C
LIU/C.W. Post Campus	NY	28,282	C
Loras College	IA	27,193	C
Mansfield Univ	PA	11,300	C
Marietta College	OH	29,327	C
Marquette Univ	WI	31,066	MC
McNeese State Univ	LA	5,270	LC
Mercyhurst College	PA	28,633	VC
Messiah College	PA	28,910	VC+
Miami Univ	OH	29,097	HC
Minn State Univ, Moorhead	MN	7,000	LC
Minot State Univ	ND	6,700	LC
Missouri State Univ	MO	10,748	C+
Montclair State Univ	NJ	16,327	C
Morris College	SC	11,999	LC
Murray State Univ	KY	8,900	VC
North Central College	IL	28,926	VC
Northern Arizona Univ	AZ	10,353	C
Northern Mich Univ	MI	12,340	LC
Northwest Missouri State Univ	MO	10,000	C
Northwestern College	MN	25,220	NC
Northwestern Okla State Univ	OK	6,250	NC
Ohio Northern Univ	OH	27,765	VC
Ohio Univ	OH	15,921	C
Okla Baptist Univ	OK	17,986	VC
Okla Christian Univ	OK	18,992	NC
Okla City Univ	OK	23,965	VC
Oral Roberts Univ	OK	22,650	C
Otterbein College	OH	28,986	C
Palm Beach Atlantic Univ	FL	23,597	VC
Penn State Univ/Univ Park Campus	PA	18,038	HC
Point Park Univ	PA	24,160	C
Prairie View A&M Univ	TX	11,110	LC
Purdue Univ/Calumet	IN	10,891	LC
Radford Univ	VA	13,145	C
Rider Univ	NJ	32,560	C
Roosevelt Univ	IL	22,605	VC
Rowan Univ	NJ	16,000	VC
St. Cloud State Univ	MN	10,010	C
San Diego State Univ	CA	12,971	C
San Francisco State Univ	CA	13,000	C
San Jose State Univ	CA	11,707	C
Savannah College of Art and Design	GA	30,800	SP
Savannah State Univ	GA	7,772	LC
Seton Hall Univ	NJ	33,622	VC
Shaw Univ	NC	15,488	LC
Sojourner-Douglass College	MD	4,200	LC
Southeastern Univ	FL	17,180	LC
Southern Adventist Univ	TN	18,500	C
Southern Arkansas Univ	AR	6,956	C
Southern Illinois Univ Carbondale	IL	12,391	C
Southern Methodist Univ	TX	36,088	VC+
Southwestern Adventist Univ	TX	18,290	LC
SUNY at Oswego	NY	13,662	VC
SUNY/College at Buffalo	NY	11,903	C+
SUNY/Univ at New Paltz	NY	12,480	VC
Stephen F. Austin State Univ	TX	7,930	C
Suffolk Univ	MA	33,160	C
Syracuse Univ	NY	38,655	HC
Temple Univ	PA	17,438	C
Texas A&M Univ at Commerce	TX	9,020	C
Texas Christian Univ	TX	23,410	VC+
Texas State Univ - San Marcos	TX	10,862	C
Texas Tech Univ	TX	13,026	VC
Trevecca Nazarene Univ	TN	19,594	C
Troy Univ	AL	8,916	C
Union Univ	TN	20,750	VC
Univ of Akron	OH	15,166	NC
Univ of Central Florida	FL	10,739	VC
Univ of Central Okla	OK	8,094	C
Univ of Cincinnati	OH	17,682	C
Univ of Colo at Boulder	CO	13,352	C+
Univ of Dayton	OH	28,826	VC
Univ of Findlay	OH	29,238	C
Univ of Georgia	GA	11,004	HC
Univ of Illinois at Urbana-Champaign	IL	15,800	HC+
Univ of Indianapolis	IN	25,090	C
Univ of Iowa	IA	12,172	VC
Univ of La Verne	CA	33,470	C
Univ of Louisiana at Lafayette	LA	5,830	C
Univ of Miami	FL	38,397	MC
Univ of Miss	MS	9,000	C
Univ of Missouri/Columbia	MO	13,500	VC
Univ of Nebr at Kearney	NE	9,000	C
Univ of Nebr at Lincoln	NE	11,401	VC
Univ of Nebr at Omaha	NE	11,235	C
Univ of Northern Iowa	IA	11,133	C
Univ of Okla	OK	10,769	VC+

School	ST	$IS	SR
Univ of S Car at Columbia	SC	13,397	VC
Univ of Southern Calif	CA	41,618	MC
Univ of Southern Indiana	IN	12,590	LC
Univ of Tenn at Knoxville	TN	11,720	C
Univ of Texas at Arlington	TX	7,195	LC
Univ of Wisc/Eau Claire	WI	9,915	VC
Wartburg College	IA	27,315	NC
Washington State Univ	WA	12,260	C
Wayne State Univ	MI	11,805	C
Waynesburg College	PA	21,230	C
Webster Univ	MO	24,280	VC
West Texas A&M Univ	TX	8,452	C
West Virginia Univ	WV	10,506	C
Western Kentucky Univ	KY	10,192	C
Western Mich Univ	MI	13,299	C
Westminster College	PA	31,290	C+
Winona State Univ	MN	11,333	C
York College of Pennsylvania	PA	16,550	VC
Youngstown State Univ	OH	12,613	NC

BUSINESS ADMINISTRATION AND MANAGEMENT

School	ST	$IS	SR
Adams State College	CO	8,613	C
Adelphi Univ	NY	27,000	VC
Adrian College	MI	23,000	C
Alabama A&M Univ	AL	8,890	LC
Alabama State Univ	AL	7,658	C
Alaska Pacific Univ	AK	25,142	C
Albertson College of Idaho	ID	21,095	VC
Albertus Magnus College	CT	25,336	C
Albright College	PA	33,920	C
Alcorn State Univ	MS	8,190	LC
Alderson-Broaddus College	WV	24,006	C
Alfred Univ	NY		VC
Alice Lloyd College	KY	4,900	C
Allen Univ	SC	10,500	NC
Alma College	MI	28,544	VC
Alvernia College	PA	26,388	C
Alverno College	WI	21,088	C
American InterContinental Univ	GA	12,100	NC
American International College	MA	28,710	LC
American Univ	DC	38,719	HC+
Anderson Univ	IN	25,050	LC
Andrews Univ	MI	21,786	C
Angelo State Univ	TX	8,340	NC
Anna Maria College	MA	29,815	C
Aquinas College	MI	23,750	C
Aquinas College	TN	10,660	LC
Arcadia Univ	PA	33,570	VC
Arkansas Baptist College	AR	5,600	NC
Arkansas State Univ	AR	9,630	C
Asbury College	KY	23,762	VC
Ashford Univ	IA	20,370	C
Ashland Univ	OH	25,000	C
Assumption College	MA	32,875	C
Atlantic Union College	MA	17,600	LC
Auburn Univ	AL	12,230	VC
Auburn Univ Montgomery	AL	9,530	NC
Augsburg College	MN	28,300	C
Augusta State Univ	GA	2,920	C
Augustana College	IL	29,862	VC+
Augustana College	SD	24,380	VC
Aurora Univ	IL	20,645	C
Austin College	TX	27,871	HC
Austin Peay State Univ	TN	7,535	C
Averett Univ	VA	24,920	C
Avila Univ	MO	22,100	C
Azusa Pacific Univ	CA	28,546	VC
Babson College	MA	41,288	HC
Baker College of Flint	MI	7,800	NC
Baker Univ	KS	22,190	C
Baldwin-Wallace College	OH	27,256	VC
Ball State Univ	IN	13,138	C
Barber-Scotia College	NC	15,000	LC
Barton College	NC	22,316	C
Bay Path College	MA	29,362	C
Baylor Univ	TX	27,555	HC
Becker College	MA	24,300	LC
Belhaven College	MS	19,530	NC
Bellarmine Univ	KY	27,650	C+
Bellevue Univ	NE	4,440	NC
Belmont Abbey College	NC	25,314	C
Belmont Univ	TN	24,110	VC
Beloit College	WI	32,808	HC
Bemidji State Univ	MN	11,180	LC
Benedict College	SC	19,114	LC
Benedictine College	KS	21,968	C
Benedictine Univ	IL	25,710	C
Bennett College	NC	11,500	C
Bentley College	MA	38,784	HC
Berea College	KY	5,496	VC+
Berkeley College/ Westchester Campus	NY	26,700	LC
Berkeley College/New York City	NY	16,950	LC
Berry College	GA	24,342	VC
Bethany College	KS	20,660	LC
Bethel College	IN	19,680	C
Bethel College	KS	21,650	C
Bethel College	TN	16,066	NC
Bethel Univ	MN	29,840	VC
Bethune-Cookman College	FL	17,922	LC
Biola Univ	CA	29,372	VC
Birmingham-Southern College	AL	28,494	VC+
Black Hills State Univ	SD	7,800	LC
Blackburn College	IL	13,690	C
Bloomfield College	NJ	22,500	LC
Bloomsburg Univ of Pennsylvania	PA	11,602	C
Blue Mountain College	MS	11,086	C
Bluefield College	VA	17,230	C
Bluefield State College	WV	3,140	LC
Bluffton College	OH	26,110	C
Boise State Univ	ID	9,438	LC
Boricua College	NY	8,000	C
Boston College	MA	41,608	MC
Boston Univ	MA	42,046	HC+
Bowie State Univ	MD	10,880	C
Bowling Green State Univ	OH	14,994	C
Bradley Univ	IL	25,280	VC
Brenau Univ Women's College	GA	23,950	VC
Brescia Univ	KY	14,240	C
Brewton-Parker College	GA	14,220	LC
Briar Cliff Univ	IA	23,550	C
Bridgewater College	VA	27,790	C
Brigham Young Univ	UT	9,200	VC
Bryan College	TN	19,270	C
Bryant College	RI	34,330	VC
Bucknell Univ	PA	39,660	MC
Buena Vista Univ	IA	27,742	C
Cabrini College	PA	33,340	C
Caldwell College	NJ	26,450	LC
Calif Baptist Univ	CA	23,780	C
Calif Lutheran Univ	CA	27,800	LC
Calif Maritime Academy	CA	13,490	C
Calif Polytechnic State Univ	CA	12,390	VC
Calif State Polytechnic Univ, Pomona	CA	18,053	C+
Cal State East Bay	CA	10,856	LC
Cal State, Bakersfield	CA	6,125	LC
Cal State, Chico	CA	11,395	C
Cal State, Dominguez Hills	CA	10,220	LC
Cal State, Fresno	CA	10,037	LC
Cal State, Fullerton	CA	10,990	C
Cal State, Long Beach	CA	9,512	C
Cal State, Los Angeles	CA	5,900	C
Cal State, Monterey Bay	CA	10,099	C
Cal State, Northridge	CA	9,036	LC
Cal State, Sacramento	CA	11,122	C+
Cal State, San Bernardino	CA	12,563	LC
Cal State, San Marcos	CA	1,800	C
Cal State, Stanislaus	CA	11,283	C
Calif Univ of Pennsylvania	PA	14,217	C
Calumet College of St. Joseph	IN	9,500	LC
Calvin College	MI	25,735	NC
Cameron Univ	OK	6,314	NC
Campbell Univ	NC	21,137	VC
Campbellsville Univ	KY	21,328	C
Canisius College	NY	32,257	VC
Capital Univ	OH	30,444	C
Cardinal Stritch Univ	WI	21,910	C
Caribbean Univ	PR	3,000	
Carlos Albizu Univ	FL	11,109	C
Carlow Univ	PA	24,313	C
Carnegie Mellon Univ	PA	32,700	MC
Carroll College	MT	23,324	C+
Carroll College	WI	24,860	C
Carson-Newman College	TN	16,800	C
Carthage College	WI	26,000	C
Cascade College	OR	17,980	NC
Case Western Reserve Univ	OH	37,314	MC
Castleton State College	VT	13,158	C
Catawba College	NC	25,000	C
Catholic Univ of America	DC	35,838	VC
Cazenovia College	NY	26,900	C
Cedar Crest College	PA	30,615	C
Cedarville Univ	OH	21,904	VC
Centenary College	NJ	28,870	LC
Centenary College of Louisiana	LA	24,760	VC
Central College	IA	26,774	VC
Central Conn State Univ	CT	13,620	C
Central Methodist Univ	MO	18,000	C
Central Mich Univ	MI	12,244	C
Central Missouri State Univ	MO	10,000	C
Central State Univ	OH	9,010	C+
Central Univ of Bayamon	PR	3,335	
Central Washington Univ	WA	11,730	C
Chadron State College	NE	6,350	NC
Champlain College	VT	24,605	C
Chapman Univ	CA	37,550	VC
Charleston Southern Univ	SC	17,800	C
Chatham College	PA	27,290	C+
Chestnut Hill College	PA	26,600	LC
Cheyney Univ of Pennsylvania	PA	11,497	LC
Chicago State Univ	IL	10,915	C+
Christian Brothers Univ	TN	24,650	VC
Christopher Newport Univ	VA	13,326	VC
Citadel, The	SC		C+
City Univ	WA	7,425	NC
CUNY/Brooklyn College	NY	4,377	C
CUNY/City College	NY		C
CUNY/College of Staten Island	NY	4,328	NC
CUNY/Herbert H. Lehman College	NY	4,000	NC
CUNY/Medgar Evers College	NY	4,250	NC
CUNY/Queens College	NY	4,356	C
CUNY/York College	NY	4,242	NC
Claflin Univ	SC	16,798	C+
Clarion Univ of Pennsylvania	PA	11,844	C
Clark Atlanta Univ	GA	20,960	LC
Clark Univ	MA	35,165	VC+
Clarke College	IA	25,390	C
Clarkson College	NE	13,000	C
Clarkson Univ	NY	34,930	VC
Clayton College and State Univ	GA	2,445	LC
Clearwater Christian College	FL	13,160	LC
Cleary College	MI	11,000	LC
Clemson Univ	SC	13,366	HC
Coastal Carolina Univ	SC	13,140	C
Coe College	IA	27,440	VC
Coker College	SC	21,600	C
Colby-Sawyer College	NH	27,850	LC
College Misericordia	PA	27,950	C
College of Charleston	SC	13,616	VC
College of Mount St. Vincent	NY	28,000	C
College of Mount St. Joseph	OH	24,860	C
College of New Jersey	NJ	18,315	MC
College of New Rochelle	NY	28,396	C+
College of Notre Dame of Maryland	MD	27,700	C
College of Our Lady of the Elms	MA	21,000	C
College of St. Catherine	MN	27,505	VC
College of St. Elizabeth	NJ	28,495	C
College of St. Joseph	VT	20,900	NC
College of St. Mary	NE	23,938	C
College of St. Rose	NY	25,684	C
College of St. Scholastica	MN	28,456	C+
College of Santa Fe	NM	28,978	C
College of the Ozarks	MO	4,130	VC+
College of the Southwest	NM	12,420	C+
College of William and Mary	VA	14,147	MC
Colo Christian Univ	CO	21,182	VC
Colo State Univ-Fort Collins	CO	10,878	C+
Colo State Univ-Pueblo	CO	7,821	C
Colo Technical Univ	CO	9,500	LC
Columbia College	MO	16,900	C
Columbia College	SC	24,982	LC
Columbia Union College	MD	23,536	LC
Columbus State Univ	GA	8,664	C
Concord College	WV	9,708	C
Concordia College	AL	10,500	NC
Concordia College: Moorhead	MN	22,475	VC
Concordia College-New York	NY	27,740	C
Concordia Univ	CA	26,780	C
Concordia Univ	OR	24,400	C
Concordia Univ at Austin	TX	23,640	LC
Concordia Univ Nebr	NE	20,500	C+
Concordia Univ St.Paul	MN	27,776	C
Concordia Univ Wisc	WI	22,660	VC
Concordia Univ, Ann Arbor	MI	25,153	C+
Concordia Univ, River Forest	IL	26,300	C
Converse College	SC	24,800	VC
Coppin State College	MD	10,200	LC
Cornerstone Univ and Grand Rapids Theological Seminary	MI	21,350	NC
Covenant College	GA	26,460	VC+
Creighton Univ	NE	29,918	VC+
Crichton College	TN	15,300	C
Culver-Stockton College	MO	20,625	C
Cumberland Univ	TN	18,894	C
Curry College	MA	26,100	C
Daemen College	NY	24,580	C
Dakota State Univ	SD	7,466	C
Dakota Wesleyan Univ	SD	17,832	C
Dallas Baptist Univ	TX	17,040	VC
Dana College	NE	22,390	C
Daniel Webster College	NH	24,870	C
David N. Myers College	OH	9,475	C
Davis and Elkins College	WV	22,416	C
De Sales Univ	PA	28,580	VC
Defiance College	OH	24,790	C
Delaware State Univ	DE	8,130	LC
Delaware Valley College	PA	29,944	C
Delta State Univ	MS	7,709	C
DePaul Univ	IL	29,835	VC
DeVry/New York	NY	12,000	LC
DeVry Univ/Addison (DuPage County)	IL	10,800	LC
DeVry Univ/Alpharetta	GA	10,675	LC
DeVry Univ/Chicago	IL	10,800	LC
DeVry Univ/Colo Springs	CO	12,000	LC
DeVry Univ/Columbus	OH	11,000	C
DeVry Univ/Crystal City	VA	12,000	LC
DeVry Univ/Dallas	TX	10,700	LC
DeVry Univ/Decatur	GA	10,680	LC
DeVry Univ/Fort Washington	PA	12,000	LC
DeVry Univ/Fremont	CA	13,060	LC
DeVry Univ/Kansas City	MO	10,670	LC
DeVry Univ/Long Beach	CA	12,450	LC
DeVry Univ/Miramar	FL	12,000	LC
DeVry Univ/Orlando	FL	12,000	LC
DeVry Univ/Phoenix	AZ	11,790	LC
DeVry Univ/Pomona	CA	12,450	LC
DeVry Univ/Seattle	WA	12,000	LC
DeVry Univ/Tinley Park	IL	12,000	LC
DeVry Univ/West Hills	CA	12,450	LC
DeVry Univ/Westminster	CO	12,000	LC
Dickinson State Univ	ND	7,847	NC
Dillard Univ	LA	17,500	VC
Doane College	NE	22,458	C
Dominican College	NY	26,630	LC
Dominican Univ	IL	26,370	C
Dominican Univ of Calif	CA	36,836	C
Dordt College	IA	20,325	VC
Dowling College	NY	22,110	LC
Drake Univ	IA	27,632	VC+
Drexel Univ	PA	27,700	VC
Drury Univ	MO	20,117	VC
Duquesne Univ	PA	29,534	VC
D'Youville College	NY	23,660	C
Earlham College	IN	33,604	HC
East Carolina Univ	NC	10,000	C
East Central Univ	OK	6,207	C
East Stroudsburg Univ of Pennsylvania	PA	10,336	C
East Texas Baptist Univ	TX	16,713	C
Eastern Conn State Univ	CT	13,554	C
Eastern Illinois Univ	IL	12,569	C
Eastern Kentucky Univ	KY	7,725	C
Eastern Mennonite Univ	VA	25,450	VC
Eastern Mich Univ	MI	12,897	C
Eastern Nazarene College	MA	19,500	LC
Eastern New Mexico Univ	NM	7,264	C
Eastern Oregon Univ	OR	10,400	NC
Eastern Univ	PA	24,075	C
Eastern Washington Univ	WA	10,608	C
East-West Univ	IL	10,375	C
Eckerd College	FL	35,492	VC
Edgewood College	WI	22,862	C
Edinboro Univ of Pennsylvania	PA	11,809	LC
Edward Waters College	FL	14,374	LC
Elizabeth City State Univ	NC	5,700	LC
Elizabethtown College	PA	32,100	VC
Elmhurst College	IL	24,685	C
Elmira College	NY	37,200	VC
Elon Univ	NC	25,371	HC
Embry-Riddle Aeronautical Univ	FL	30,280	C
Emmanuel College	MA	32,000	C+
Emory & Henry College	VA	26,570	C
Emory Univ	GA	40,546	MC
Emporia State Univ	KS	8,093	C
Endicott College	MA	30,156	C+
Erskine College	SC	25,468	VC
Eureka College	IL	19,280	C
Excelsior College	NY	995	SP
Fairfield Univ	CT	39,835	HC
Fairleigh Dickinson Univ/ College at Florham	NJ	30,130	C
Fairleigh Dickinson Univ/ Metropolitan Campus	NJ	28,590	C
Fairmont State	WV	8,400	LC
Faulkner Univ	AL	15,600	C
Fayetteville State Univ	NC	6,000	LC
Felician College	NJ	24,300	C
Ferris State Univ	MI	13,698	C
Ferrum College	VA	24,290	LC
Fisk Univ	TN	19,830	C
Fitchburg State College	MA	11,276	C
Flagler College	FL	13,790	VC+
Florida A&M Univ	FL	8,344	C
Florida Atlantic Univ	FL	11,221	C
Florida Gulf Coast Univ	FL	10,833	C
Florida Inst of Technology	FL	29,720	VC
Florida International Univ	FL	9,215	VC
Florida Memorial College	FL	6,000	LC
Florida Southern College	FL	25,965	C
Florida State Univ	FL	9,028	HC
Fontbonne Univ	MO	23,308	C
Fordham Univ	NY	36,000	HC
Fort Hays State Univ	KS	7,638	C
Fort Lewis College	CO	11,852	C
Fort Valley State Univ	GA	6,975	C
Framingham State College	MA	11,156	C
Francis Marion Univ	SC	11,114	C
Franciscan Univ of Steubenville	OH	20,300	VC
Franklin and Marshall College	PA	40,590	HC
Franklin College	IN		C
Franklin Pierce College	NH	31,700	C
Franklin Univ	OH	6,720	SP
Freed-Hardeman Univ	TN	16,370	NC
Fresno Pacific Univ	CA	25,454	C
Friends Univ	KS	16,250	LC
Frostburg State Univ	MD	12,672	C
Furman Univ	SC	33,264	HC+
Gallaudet Univ	DC	16,554	
Gannon Univ	PA	26,100	C

ST = STATE   **$IS** = IN-STATE COSTS   **SR** = SELECTOR RATING

School	ST	$IS	SR
Gardner-Webb Univ	NC	21,500	C
Geneva College	PA	21,850	C
George Mason Univ	VA	10,850	VC
George Washington Univ	DC	48,820	MC
Georgetown Univ	DC	43,183	MC
Georgia College and State Univ	GA	11,020	C
Georgia Inst of Technology	GA	11,450	HC+
Georgia Southwestern State Univ	GA	6,035	C
Georgia State Univ	GA	11,444	VC
Georgian Court College	NJ	20,000	LC
Gettysburg College	PA	39,864	HC
Glenville State College	WV	8,778	NC
Gonzaga Univ	WA	30,218	HC
Gordon College	MA	29,194	C+
Goshen College	IN	22,850	VC
Grace Bible College	MI	18,810	C
Grace College	IN	22,170	C
Graceland Univ	IA	19,700	C
Grambling State Univ	LA	6,538	NC
Grand Canyon Univ	AZ	32,000	LC
Grand Valley State Univ	MI	12,000	VC
Grand View College	IA	21,482	C
Green Mountain College	VT	32,164	C
Greensboro College	NC	23,000	C
Greenville College	IL	23,146	C
Grove City College	PA	15,784	HC+
Guilford College	NC	28,160	C+
Gustavus Adolphus College	MN	30,920	HC
Gwynedd-Mercy College	PA	26,080	C
Hamline Univ	MN	27,070	VC
Hampton Univ	VA	19,468	C+
Hannibal-LaGrange College	MO	16,390	C
Hanover College	IN	28,150	HC
Harding Univ	AR	16,512	VC
Hardin-Simmons Univ	TX	18,641	C
Harris-Stowe State College	MO	3,200	SP
Hartwick College	NY	36,065	C+
Hastings College	NE	22,218	VC
Hawaii Pacific Univ	HI	21,080	C
Heidelberg College	OH	23,242	C
Hellenic College/Holy Cross Greek Orthodox School of Theology	MA	24,975	C
Henderson State Univ	AR	7,600	C
Henry Cogswell College	WA	16,680	SP
Heritage Univ	WA	6,800	NC
Hesser College	NH	17,700	LC
High Point Univ	NC	25,720	C
Hilbert College	NY	20,480	LC
Hillsdale College	MI	24,160	HC
Hofstra Univ	NY	32,630	VC
Hollins Univ	VA	31,105	C
Holy Family Univ	PA	25,740	C
Holy Names College	CA	27,980	NC
Hood College	MD	30,085	VC
Hope College	MI	28,208	VC+
Hope International Univ	CA	23,700	NC
Houghton College	NY	25,980	VC+
Houston Baptist Univ	TX	18,660	C
Howard Payne Univ	TX	17,115	C
Howard Univ	DC	18,481	C+
Humboldt State Univ	CA	11,176	C
Humphreys College	CA	7,000	NC
Huntingdon College	AL	23,090	VC
Huntington Univ	IN	24,830	C
Huron Univ	SD	10,700	C
Husson College	ME	17,410	LC
Huston-Tillotson Univ	TX	14,232	LC
Idaho State Univ	ID	9,030	C
Illinois College	IL	21,900	C+
Illinois State Univ	IL	12,839	C+
Illinois Wesleyan Univ	IL	34,050	HC+
Immaculata Univ	PA	25,350	C
Indiana Inst of Technology	IN	23,430	C
Indiana State Univ	IN	11,604	C
Indiana Univ Bloomington	IN	13,356	VC
Indiana Univ East	IN	4,806	LC
Indiana Univ Kokomo	IN	4,835	LC
Indiana Univ Northwest	IN	4,902	LC
Indiana Univ of Pennsylvania	PA	11,209	C
Indiana Univ South Bend	IN	4,989	LC
Indiana Univ Southeast	IN	4,880	LC
Indiana Univ-Purdue Univ Indianapolis	IN	10,959	C
Indiana Wesleyan Univ	IN	22,074	C+
Inter American Univ of PR/ Aguadilla Campus	PR	3,784	
Inter American Univ of PR/ Arecibo Campus	PR	3,350	
Inter American Univ of PR/ Barranquitas Regional College	PR	3,350	
Inter American Univ of PR/ Bayamon Univ College	PR	3,522	
Inter American Univ of PR/ Fajardo Campus	PR	4,000	
Inter American Univ of PR/ Metropolitan Campus	PR	4,320	
Inter American Univ of PR/ Ponce Regional College	PR	3,700	
Inter American Univ of PR/ San German	PR	6,720	
International College	FL	9,500	NC
Iona College	NY	30,878	VC
Iowa State Univ	IA	11,831	VC
Iowa Wesleyan College	IA	22,140	C
Ithaca College	NY	35,144	VC
Jackson State Univ	MS	8,500	C
Jacksonville Univ	FL	24,040	C
James Madison Univ	VA	12,010	VC
Jamestown College	ND	14,130	NC
John Brown Univ	AR	20,910	VC
John Carroll Univ	OH	27,658	C+
Johnson and Wales Univ/ Charlotte Campus	NC	29,121	LC
Johnson and Wales Univ/ North Miami Campus	FL	30,126	LC
Johnson and Wales Univ/ Providence Campus	RI	28,126	LC
Johnson C. Smith Univ	NC	20,000	C
Johnson State College	VT	11,830	VC
Judson College	AL	16,522	C
Judson College	IL	25,130	C
Juniata College	PA	33,130	VC
Kansas State Univ	KS	10,516	VC
Kean Univ	NJ	15,880	C
Kendall College	IL	28,800	NC
Kent State Univ	OH	14,594	C
Kentucky Christian College	KY	12,680	C
Kentucky State Univ	KY	10,089	LC
Kentucky Wesleyan College	KY	18,590	C
Kettering Univ	MI	29,338	HC
Keuka College	NY	26,050	C
Keystone College	PA	22,810	LC
King College	TN	23,400	C
King's College	PA	29,810	C
Knoxville College	TN	6,200	LC
Kutztown Univ of Pennsylvania	PA	10,820	C
La Roche College	PA	24,724	LC
La Salle Univ	PA	34,950	C
La Sierra Univ	CA	24,327	C+
LaGrange College	GA	22,874	C+
Lake Erie College	OH	27,725	C
Lake Superior State Univ	MI	12,842	LC
Lakeland College	WI	22,990	C
Lamar Univ	TX	6,820	LC
Lambuth Univ	TN	21,700	C+
Lander Univ	SC	10,600	C
Lane College	TN	11,220	C+
Langston Univ	OK	2,308	LC
Lasell College	MA	26,250	C
Lawrence Tech Univ	MI	25,475	VC
Le Moyne College	NY	29,570	VC
Lebanon Valley College	PA	31,700	VC
Lee Univ	TN	14,780	NC
Lees-McRae College	NC	23,000	C
Lehigh Univ	PA	42,690	HC+
LeMoyne-Owen College	TN	13,150	LC
Lenoir-Rhyne College	NC	25,580	C
LeTourneau Univ	TX	21,200	C
Lewis Univ	IL	23,050	C+
Lewis-Clark State College	ID	6,990	C
Liberty Univ	VA	19,101	C
Limestone College	SC	19,840	C
Lincoln Memorial Univ	TN	18,144	C
Lincoln Univ	MO	8,000	NC
Lincoln Univ	PA	13,658	C+
Lindenwood Univ	MO	18,600	VC
Lindsey Wilson College	KY	16,425	LC
Linfield College	OR	29,632	VC
Lipscomb Univ	TN	20,967	VC
Livingstone College	NC	17,815	LC
Lock Haven Univ of Pennsylvania	PA	12,098	LC
LIU/Brooklyn Campus	NY	25,000	C
LIU/C.W. Post Campus	NY	28,282	C
Longwood Univ	VA	12,426	C
Loras College	IA	27,193	C
Louisiana College	LA	13,450	C
Louisiana State Univ and A&M College	LA	10,749	VC
Louisiana State Univ in Shreveport	LA	2,900	NC
Louisiana Tech Univ	LA	7,370	C
Lourdes College	OH	15,300	LC
Loyola College in Maryland	MD	38,898	HC
Loyola Marymount Univ	CA	36,321	VC
Loyola Univ Chicago	IL	32,896	VC
Loyola Univ New Orleans	LA	31,050	VC+
Lubbock Christian Univ	TX	16,960	C
Lycoming College	PA	30,797	C+
Lynchburg College	VA	30,645	C
Lyndon State College	VT	14,233	LC
Lynn Univ	FL	30,750	C
Lyon College	AR	19,990	VC
MacMurray College	IL	20,755	C
Madonna Univ	MI	16,068	VC
Malone College	OH	23,040	C
Manchester College	IN	23,470	C
Mansfield Univ	PA	11,300	C
Marian College	IN	26,160	C
Marian College of Fond du Lac	WI	21,775	LC
Marietta College	OH	29,237	C
Marist College	NY	30,566	VC
Marquette Univ	WI	31,066	HC
Mars Hill College	NC	19,500	LC
Martin Univ	IN	10,300	SP
Mary Baldwin College	VA	26,465	C
Marygrove College	MI	19,310	C+
Marylhurst Univ	OR	14,220	NC
Marymount Manhattan College	NY	30,049	VC
Marymount Univ	VA	25,934	C
Maryville College	TN	29,224	VC
Maryville Univ of St. Louis	MO	23,000	C
Marywood Univ	PA	30,680	C
Mass College of Liberal Arts	MA	8,725	LC
Master's College and Seminary	CA	25,850	VC
Mayville State Univ	ND	8,667	NC
McDaniel College	MD	31,610	VC
McKendree College	IL	24,800	VC
McMurry Univ	TX	18,100	LC
McNeese State Univ	LA	5,270	LC
McPherson College	KS	21,010	C
Medaille College	NY	21,000	C
Menlo College	CA	33,600	C
Mercer Univ	GA	27,525	VC+
Mercy College	NY	20,000	NC
Mercyhurst College	PA	28,633	VC
Meredith College	NC	25,600	C
Merrimack College	MA	34,380	C
Mesa State College	CO	8,051	C
Messiah College	PA	28,910	VC+
Methodist College	NC	21,000	C
Metropolitan College of New York	NY	16,000	C
Metropolitan State Univ	MN	4,682	SP
Miami Univ	OH	29,097	HC
Mich State Univ	MI	13,689	VC
Mich Tech Univ	MI	14,569	VC
MidAmerica Nazarene Univ	KS	20,584	LC
Middle Tenn State Univ	TN	8,540	C
Midland Lutheran College	NE	18,600	C
Midway College	KY	20,150	C
Midwestern State Univ	TX	9,381	LC
Miles College	AL	9,922	NC
Millersville Univ of Pennsylvania	PA	12,113	C
Milligan College	TN	21,990	VC
Millikin Univ	IL	25,590	C
Millsaps College	MS	28,256	VC+
Milwaukee School of Engineering	WI	29,847	VC+
Minn State Univ, Mankato	MN	10,276	LC
Minn State Univ, Moorhead	MN	7,000	LC
Miss College	MS	14,574	VC
Miss State Univ	MS	9,577	C
Miss Univ for Women	MS	6,000	LC
Miss Valley State Univ	MS	7,970	C
Missouri Baptist Univ	MO	19,640	C
Missouri Southern State Univ	MO	8,396	NC
Missouri State Univ	MO	10,748	C+
Missouri Valley College	MO	18,500	C
Missouri Western State Univ	MO	9,534	NC
Mitchell College	CT	26,396	C
Molloy College	NY	16,510	C
Monmouth College	IL	23,700	C
Monmouth Univ	NJ	28,956	C
Monroe College	NY	15,960	LC
Montana State Univ-Billings	MT	8,906	C
Montana State Univ-Bozeman	MT	1,137	C
Montclair State Univ	NJ	16,327	C
Montreat College	NC	21,440	C
Moravian College	PA	28,950	VC
Morehouse College	GA	25,082	C
Morgan State Univ	MD	12,080	C
Morningside College	IA	23,704	C
Morris College	SC	11,999	LC
Mount Aloysius College	PA	20,900	C
Mount Ida College	MA	26,000	C
Mount Marty College	SD	20,590	C
Mount Mary College	WI	22,895	C
Mount Mercy College	IA	23,670	C
Mount Olive College	NC	16,000	LC
Mount St. Mary College	NY	25,250	C
Mount St. Mary's College	CA	32,086	VC
Mount St. Mary's Univ	MD	30,930	C
Mount Union College	OH	25,840	C
Mount Vernon Nazarene Univ	OH	20,810	C
Mountain State Univ	WV	11,406	NC
Muhlenberg College	PA	36,030	HC+
Murray State Univ	KY	8,900	VC
Muskingum College	OH	22,970	C
National American Univ	SD	14,820	NC
National-Louis Univ	IL	16,915	LC
Nazareth College of Rochester	NY	28,175	VC
Nebr Wesleyan Univ	NE	23,415	C+
Neumann College	PA	25,996	LC
New England College	NH	31,466	C
New Jersey City Univ	NJ	13,695	LC
New Mexico Highlands Univ	NM	6,272	NC
New Mexico Inst of Mining and Technology	NM	8,510	VC+
New Mexico State Univ	NM	9,250	C
New York Inst of Technology	NY	28,126	VC
New York Univ	NY	43,170	MC
Newberry College	SC	23,000	LC
Newbury College	MA	25,600	C
Newman Univ	KS	21,106	C
Niagara Univ	NY	28,250	C
Nicholls State Univ	LA	6,500	NC
Nichols College	MA	28,000	LC
N Car Agricultural and Technical State Univ	NC	8,000	LC
N Car Central Univ	NC	9,000	LC
N Car State Univ	NC	11,824	HC
N Car Wesleyan College	NC	22,670	C
North Central College	IL	28,926	VC
N Dak State Univ	ND	8,500	C
North Georgia College and State Univ	GA	7,000	C
North Park Univ	IL	24,050	C
Northeastern Illinois Univ	IL	3,000	NC
Northeastern State Univ	OK	5,896	LC
Northeastern Univ	MA	35,742	HC
Northern Arizona Univ	AZ	10,353	C
Northern Illinois Univ	IL	13,178	C
Northern Mich Univ	MI	12,340	LC
Northern State Univ	SD	8,257	C
Northland College	WI	26,680	C+
Northwest Christian College	OR	24,298	C
Northwest Missouri State Univ	MO	10,000	C
Northwest Nazarene Univ	ID	22,590	VC
Northwest Univ	WA	18,854	C
Northwestern College	MN	25,220	NC
Northwestern College of Iowa	IA	22,174	C+
Northwestern Okla State Univ	OK	6,250	NC
Northwestern State Univ of Louisiana	LA	7,144	C
Northwood Univ	FL	21,040	C
Northwood Univ	MI	21,000	LC
Northwood Univ	TX	20,135	LC
Norwich Univ	VT	28,212	C
Notre Dame de Namur Univ	CA	32,790	LC
Nova Southeastern Univ	FL	24,320	C
Nyack College	NY	18,540	C
Oakland City Univ	IN	19,620	NC
Oakland Univ	MI	11,936	C
Oakwood College	AL	14,904	C
Oglala Lakota College	SD	1,950	NC
Oglethorpe Univ	GA	30,300	VC
Ohio Dominican Univ	OH	25,954	C
Ohio Northern Univ	OH	27,765	VC
Ohio State Univ at Lima	OH	4,416	NC
Ohio State Univ at Newark	OH	11,347	NC
Ohio Valley Univ	WV	17,752	C
Okla Baptist Univ	OK	17,986	VC
Okla Christian Univ	OK	18,992	NC
Okla City Univ	OK	23,965	VC
Okla Panhandle State Univ	OK	7,635	NC
Okla State Univ	OK	10,213	VC
Okla Wesleyan Univ	OK	18,950	NC
Old Dominion Univ	VA	11,907	C
Olivet College	MI	19,984	C+
Olivet Nazarene Univ	IL	22,590	C
Oral Roberts Univ	OK	22,650	C
Oregon State Univ	OR	11,055	C
Ottawa Univ	KS	12,000	LC
Otterbein College	OH	28,986	C
Ouachita Baptist Univ	AR	21,900	VC
Our Lady of Holy Cross College	LA	8,090	LC
Our Lady of the Lake Univ of San Antonio	TX	22,430	C
Pacific Lutheran Univ	WA	28,805	VC
Pacific Union College	CA	24,555	VC+
Pacific Univ	OR	24,250	C
Paine College	GA	14,418	LC
Palm Beach Atlantic Univ	FL	23,597	VC
Park Univ	MO	11,592	C
Paul Quinn College	TX	8,300	LC
Peirce College	PA	12,760	NC
Penn State Erie/The Behrend College	PA	16,256	C
Penn State Univ/Altoona	PA	12,635	C
Penn State Univ/Univ Park Campus	PA	18,038	HC
Pennsylvania College of Technology	PA	16,980	LC
Pepperdine Univ	CA	39,960	HC
Peru State College	NE	6,350	NC
Pfeiffer Univ	NC	21,900	C
Philadelphia Biblical Univ	PA	22,425	C
Philander Smith College	AR	13,230	LC
Piedmont College	GA	20,500	C
Pikeville College	KY	16,500	NC
Pine Manor College	MA	25,038	LC
Pittsburg State Univ	KS	8,112	C
Plymouth State Univ	NH	12,298	LC
Point Loma Nazarene Univ	CA	27,610	VC
Point Park Univ	PA	24,160	C
Pontifical Catholic Univ of PR/Ponce	PR	7,310	
Portland State Univ	OR	12,453	C
Post Univ	CT	24,875	C
Prairie View A&M Univ	TX	11,110	C
Presbyterian College	SC	30,044	VC
Presentation College	SD	14,800	LC

ST = STATE   **$IS** = IN-STATE COSTS   **SR** = SELECTOR RATING

School	ST $IS	SR
Principia College	IL 27,765	VC+
Providence College	RI 34,580	HC
Queens Univ of Charlotte	NC 24,528	C
Quincy Univ	IL 24,920	C
Quinnipiac Univ	CT 34,640	VC
Radford Univ	VA 13,145	C
Ramapo College of New Jersey	NJ 16,630	VC
Regis Univ	CO 31,890	C
Reinhardt College	GA 20,870	C
Rhode Island College	RI 11,570	C
Rhodes College	TN 32,860	HC
Richard Stockton College of New Jersey	NJ 14,000	VC
Rider Univ	NJ 32,560	C
Ripon College	WI 27,160	C+
Rivier College	NH 26,600	C
Roanoke College	VA 30,748	VC
Robert Morris Univ	PA 22,822	C
Roberts Wesleyan College	NY 26,378	C
Rochester Inst of Technology	NY 32,070	VC+
Rockford College	IL 28,330	VC
Rockhurst Univ	MO 25,440	VC
Rocky Mountain College	MT 20,805	C
Roger Williams Univ	RI 30,500	C
Roosevelt Univ	IL 22,605	VC
Rosemont College	PA 29,350	C
Rowan Univ	NJ 16,000	VC
Russell Sage College	NY 27,000	C
Rust College	MS	C+
Rutgers, The State Univ of New Jersey/New Brunswick/Piscataway Campus	NJ 15,810	HC
Rutgers, The State Univ of New Jersey/Newark Campus	NJ 15,640	VC
Sacred Heart Univ	CT 33,404	C
Saginaw Valley State Univ	MI 11,432	C
St. Ambrose Univ	IA 25,495	C
St. Andrews Presbyterian College	NC 23,530	C
St. Anselm College	NH 33,810	C
St. Augustine's College	NC 14,000	LC
St. Cloud State Univ	MN 10,010	C
St. Edward's Univ	TX 23,560	C
St. John's Univ	NY 34,370	C
St. Joseph's College	IN 26,600	C
St. Joseph's College of Maine	ME 29,185	C
St. Joseph's College, New York, Brooklyn Campus	NY 12,206	C
St. Joseph's College, New York, Suffolk Campus	NY 12,000	C
St. Joseph's Univ	PA 37,428	VC
St. Leo Univ	FL 22,140	C+
St. Louis Univ	MO 33,158	VC+
St. Mary-of-the-Woods College	IN 25,480	C
St. Mary's College	IN 32,538	C
St. Mary's College of Calif	CA 37,290	C
St. Mary's Univ of San Antonio	TX 22,444	C
St. Michael's College	VT 33,330	VC
St. Norbert College	WI 28,577	C+
St. Paul's College	VA 16,030	NC
St. Peter's College	NJ 30,160	LC
St. Thomas Aquinas College	NY 22,000	LC
St. Thomas Univ	FL 23,490	C
St. Vincent College	PA 26,160	VC
St. Xavier Univ	IL 23,160	C
Salem College	NC 26,226	VC+
Salem International Univ	WV 18,020	LC
Salem State College	MA 13,161	LC
Salisbury Univ	MD 13,128	VC
Salve Regina Univ	RI 33,450	C
Sam Houston State Univ	TX 8,000	C
San Diego Christian College	CA 24,172	C
San Diego State Univ	CA 12,971	C
San Francisco State Univ	CA 13,000	C
San Jose State Univ	CA 11,707	C
Santa Clara Univ	CA 38,931	VC
Schreiner Univ	TX 20,600	C
Seattle Pacific Univ	WA 29,355	C
Seattle Univ	WA 30,063	VC
Seton Hall Univ	NJ 33,622	VC
Seton Hill Univ	PA 28,810	C
Shaw Univ	NC 15,488	LC
Shawnee State Univ	OH 12,237	NC
Shenandoah Univ	VA 27,600	C
Shepherd Univ	WV 10,066	
Shippensburg Univ of Pennsylvania	PA 11,621	C
Shorter College	GA 19,700	C
Siena Heights Univ	MI 17,000	LC
Sierra Nevada College	NV 30,235	C
Silver Lake College of the Holy Family	WI 18,500	LC
Simpson Univ	CA 22,900	C
Skidmore College	NY 41,779	HC
Slippery Rock Univ of Pennsylvania	PA 10,360	LC
Sojourner-Douglass College	MD 4,200	LC

School	ST $IS	SR
Sonoma State Univ	CA 14,732	C
S Car State Univ	SC 6,700	LC
South Univ	GA	LC
Southeastern Louisiana Univ	LA 8,521	LC
Southeastern Okla State Univ	OK 6,147	C
Southeastern Univ	DC 9,000	NC
Southeastern Univ	FL 17,180	LC
Southern Adventist Univ	TN 18,500	C
Southern Arkansas Univ	AR 6,956	C
Southern Conn State Univ	CT 10,310	C
Southern Illinois Univ Carbondale	IL 12,391	C
Southern Illinois Univ Edwardsville	IL 11,022	C
Southern Methodist Univ	TX 36,088	VC+
Southern Nazarene Univ	OK 14,634	NC
Southern New Hampshire Univ	NH 28,764	C
Southern Oregon Univ	OR 12,186	C
Southern Polytechnic State Univ	GA 7,640	VC
Southern Univ and A&M College	LA 8,238	LC
Southern Univ at New Orleans	LA 1,000	NC
Southern Utah Univ	UT	C
Southern Vermont College	VT 21,322	C
Southern Wesleyan Univ	SC 21,675	C
Southwest Baptist Univ	MO 18,300	C
Southwest Minn State Univ	MN 10,975	C
Southwestern Adventist Univ	TX 18,290	LC
Southwestern College	KS 21,476	C
Southwestern Okla State Univ	OK 4,801	C
Southwestern Univ	TX 26,767	HC
Spalding Univ	KY 18,882	C
Spring Arbor Univ	MI 22,476	C
Spring Hill College	AL 28,678	C
Springfield College	MA 25,000	C
SUNY at Oswego	NY 13,662	VC
SUNY at Potsdam	NY 12,959	C
SUNY/College at Brockport	NY 12,747	VC
SUNY/College at Buffalo	NY 11,903	C+
SUNY/College at Fredonia	NY 12,771	VC
SUNY/College at Geneseo	NY 12,910	HC+
SUNY/College at Old Westbury	NY 13,154	C
SUNY/College at Plattsburgh	NY 12,362	C
SUNY/Empire State College	NY 4,575	SP
SUNY/Inst of Technology	NY 12,575	VC
SUNY/Maritime College	NY 12,475	C
SUNY/Univ at Albany	NY 13,860	VC
SUNY/Univ at Binghamton	NY 13,988	HC
SUNY/Univ at Buffalo	NY 13,694	VC
SUNY/Univ at New Paltz	NY 12,480	VC
SUNY/Univ at Stony Brook	NY 13,625	HC
Stephen F. Austin State Univ	TX 7,930	C
Stephens College	MO 26,930	VC
Sterling College	KS 19,992	C
Stetson Univ	FL 32,725	VC
Stevens Inst of Technology	NJ 40,935	HC
Stillman College	AL 11,475	LC
Stonehill College	MA 36,104	HC
Strayer Univ	DC 8,789	SP
Sul Ross State Univ	TX 6,600	LC
Susquehanna Univ	PA 34,395	VC
Sweet Briar College	VA 31,460	VC
Syracuse Univ	NY 38,655	HC
Tabor College	KS 21,614	NC
Talladega College	AL 11,240	LC
Tarleton State Univ	TX 8,952	C
Temple Univ	PA 17,438	C
Tenn State Univ	TN 9,048	LC
Tenn Tech Univ	TN 10,044	C
Tenn Wesleyan College	TN 18,650	C
Texas A&M Univ at Commerce	TX 9,020	C
Texas A&M Univ at Corpus Christi	TX 10,280	LC
Texas A&M Univ at Kingsville	TX 6,800	LC
Texas Christian Univ	TX 23,410	VC+
Texas Lutheran Univ	TX 23,530	C
Texas Southern Univ	TX 9,828	C
Texas State Univ - San Marcos	TX 10,862	C
Texas Tech Univ	TX 13,026	VC
Texas Wesleyan Univ	TX 18,700	C
Texas Woman's Univ	TX 7,804	C
Thiel College	PA 24,580	C
Thomas College	ME 23,770	LC
Thomas More College	KY 24,470	C
Thomas Univ	GA 11,520	NC
Tiffin Univ	OH 19,490	LC
Toccoa Falls College	GA 17,125	C
Touro College	NY 17,000	VC
Towson Univ	MD 13,924	VC
Transylvania Univ	KY 26,240	VC+
Trevecca Nazarene Univ	TN 19,594	C
Trinity Christian College	IL 23,645	C
Trinity College	DC 24,150	LC

School	ST $IS	SR
Trinity International Univ	IL 25,686	C
Trinity Univ	TX 30,157	HC+
Tri-State Univ-Main Campus	IN 26,200	C
Troy Univ	AL 8,916	C
Troy Univ Dothan Campus	AL 4,678	C
Troy Univ Montgomery Campus	AL 4,104	NC
Truman State Univ	MO 11,242	HC
Tulane Univ	LA 41,098	MC
Turabo Univ	PR 4,110	
Tuskegee Univ	AL 18,860	LC
Union College	KY 18,920	C
Union College	NE 18,710	C
Union Inst & Univ	OH 8,912	SP
Union Univ	TN 20,750	C
Universidad Adventista de las Antillas	PR 7,360	
Universidad Metropolitana	PR 3,330	
Universidad Politecnica de PR	PR 5,400	
Univ of Akron	OH 15,166	NC
Univ of Alabama at Birmingham	AL 13,716	C
Univ of Alabama in Huntsville	AL 9,516	VC
Univ of Alaska Anchorage	AK 11,275	NC
Univ of Alaska Fairbanks	AK 10,101	C
Univ of Alaska Southeast	AK 8,050	LC
Univ of Arizona	AZ 11,958	VC
Univ of Arkansas	AR 11,859	VC
Univ of Arkansas at Little Rock	AR 7,230	NC
Univ of Arkansas at Monticello	AR 7,325	NC
Univ of Arkansas at Pine Bluff	AR 8,300	C
Univ of Bridgeport	CT 29,595	LC
Univ of Calif at Berkeley	CA 18,141	HC+
Univ of Calif at Riverside	CA 16,625	C
Univ of Central Arkansas	AR 9,984	C
Univ of Central Florida	FL 10,739	VC
Univ of Central Okla	OK 8,094	C
Univ of Charleston	WV 27,600	C
Univ of Cincinnati	OH 17,682	C
Univ of Colo at Boulder	CO 13,352	C+
Univ of Colo at Colo Springs	CO 11,517	VC
Univ of Colo at Denver and Health Sciences Center	CO 5,021	C
Univ of Conn	CT 16,628	HC
Univ of Dallas	TX 27,432	VC+
Univ of Delaware	DE 14,142	HC
Univ of Denver	CO 36,376	VC+
Univ of Detroit Mercy	MI 27,000	C
Univ of Dubuque	IA 23,390	C
Univ of Evansville	IN 28,320	VC
Univ of Findlay	OH 29,238	C
Univ of Florida	FL 9,354	HC
Univ of Georgia	GA 11,004	HC
Univ of Great Falls	MT 17,000	C
Univ of Hartford	CT 34,044	C
Univ of Hawaii at Hilo	HI 6,500	C
Univ of Hawaii at Manoa	HI 10,413	VC
Univ of Houston	TX 7,000	C
Univ of Houston-Downtown	TX 3,326	NC
Univ of Indianapolis	IN 25,090	C
Univ of Iowa	IA 12,172	VC
Univ of Judaism College of A&S	CA 30,010	C
Univ of Kansas	KS 10,915	VC
Univ of La Verne	CA 33,470	C
Univ of Louisiana at Lafayette	LA 5,830	C
Univ of Louisiana at Monroe	LA 7,103	C
Univ of Louisville	KY 10,400	VC
Univ of Maine	ME 13,642	VC
Univ of Maine at Augusta	ME 5,025	NC
Univ of Maine at Fort Kent	ME 10,832	LC
Univ of Maine at Machias	ME 10,523	C
Univ of Maine at Presque Isle	ME 10,066	LC
Univ of Mary	ND 15,374	C
Univ of Mary Hardin-Baylor	TX 19,428	C
Univ of Mary Washington	VA 11,636	HC
Univ of Maryland/College Park	MD 16,036	HC
Univ of Maryland/Eastern Shore	MD 11,210	C
Univ of Maryland/Univ College	MD 5,640	SP
Univ of Mass Amherst	MA 15,973	C+
Univ of Mass Dartmouth	MA 15,985	C
Univ of Mass Lowell	MA 14,327	VC
Univ of Memphis	TN 11,153	C
Univ of Miami	FL 38,397	MC
Univ of Mich/Ann Arbor	MI 16,587	HC+
Univ of Mich/Dearborn	MI 7,000	VC
Univ of Mich/Flint	MI 6,398	C
Univ of Minn/Crookston	MN 13,157	LC
Univ of Minn/Duluth	MN 13,974	C
Univ of Minn/Twin Cities	MN 13,165	HC
Univ of Miss	MS 9,000	C
Univ of Missouri/Columbia	MO 13,500	VC
Univ of Missouri/Kansas City	MO 15,000	VC

School	ST $IS	SR
Univ of Missouri/Rolla	MO 13,332	HC
Univ of Missouri/St. Louis	MO 14,046	VC
Univ of Mobile	AL 16,880	C
Univ of Montana	MT 10,602	C
Univ of Montevallo	AL 9,630	C
Univ of Nebr at Kearney	NE 9,000	NC
Univ of Nebr at Lincoln	NE 11,401	VC
Univ of New England	ME 31,005	C
Univ of New Hampshire	NH 16,810	VC
Univ of New Haven	CT 31,794	C
Univ of New Mexico	NM 11,253	C
Univ of New Orleans	LA 7,370	C
Univ of N Car at Asheville	NC 9,237	VC
Univ of N Car at Chapel Hill	NC 11,129	MC
Univ of N Car at Charlotte	NC 9,101	C
Univ of N Car at Greensboro	NC 8,993	C
Univ of N Car at Pembroke	NC 7,940	LC
Univ of N Car at Wilmington	NC 10,107	VC
Univ of North Florida	FL 9,908	VC
Univ of North Texas	TX 7,800	C
Univ of Northern Colo	CO 10,249	C
Univ of Okla	OK 10,769	VC+
Univ of Oregon	OR 13,108	VC
Univ of Pennsylvania	PA 41,766	MC
Univ of Pittsburgh at Bradford	PA 17,008	C
Univ of Pittsburgh at Johnstown	PA 16,740	LC
Univ of Pittsburgh at Pittsburgh	PA 18,866	HC
Univ of PR at Humacao	PR 1,707	
Univ of PR/Arecibo	PR 8,327	
Univ of PR/Bayamon Univ College Campus	PR 1,600	
Univ of PR/Cayey Univ College	PR 1,250	
Univ of PR/Mayaguez	PR 1,250	
Univ of PR/Rio Piedras	PR 5,750	
Univ of Puget Sound	WA 35,600	HC
Univ of Redlands	CA 36,160	VC
Univ of Rhode Island	RI 15,398	C
Univ of Richmond	VA 40,510	MC
Univ of Rio Grande	OH 8,728	NC
Univ of St. Francis	IL 25,430	C
Univ of St. Francis	IN 20,970	C
Univ of St. Mary	KS 18,900	C
Univ of St. Thomas	MN 28,000	VC
Univ of St. Thomas	TX 23,810	VC
Univ of San Diego	CA 40,620	HC
Univ of San Francisco	CA 37,560	VC
Univ of Science and Arts of Okla	OK 7,650	C
Univ of Scranton	PA 31,100	C
Univ of Sioux Falls	SD 20,800	C
Univ of South Alabama	AL 8,930	LC
Univ of S Car at Aiken	SC 11,718	LC
Univ of S Car at Columbia	SC 13,397	VC
Univ of S Car Upstate	SC 11,957	C
Univ of South Florida	FL 10,284	VC
Univ of Southern Calif	CA 41,618	MC
Univ of Southern Indiana	IN 12,590	LC
Univ of Southern Maine	ME 12,614	C
Univ of Southern Miss	MS 10,112	C
Univ of Tampa	FL 25,784	C
Univ of Tenn at Chattanooga	TN 7,790	C
Univ of Tenn at Knoxville	TN 11,720	C
Univ of Tenn at Martin	TN 8,693	C
Univ of Texas at Arlington	TX 7,195	LC
Univ of Texas at Austin	TX 14,610	HC
Univ of Texas at Dallas	TX 13,244	HC
Univ of Texas at San Antonio	TX 11,325	C
Univ of the Cumberlands	KY 18,184	C
Univ of the District of Columbia	DC 2,070	LC
Univ of the Incarnate Word	TX 23,306	C
Univ of the Ozarks	AR 19,250	C
Univ of the Pacific	CA 34,380	VC
Univ of the Sacred Heart	PR 5,590	
Univ of Toledo	OH 15,806	NC
Univ of Utah	UT 10,162	VC
Univ of Vermont	VT 18,080	VC
Univ of Virginia	VA 13,759	MC
Univ of Virginia's College at Wise	VA 11,076	C
Univ of Washington	WA 10,400	VC
Univ of West Alabama	AL 7,611	C
Univ of West Florida	FL 8,559	C
Univ of Wisc/Eau Claire	WI 9,915	VC
Univ of Wisc/Green Bay	WI 9,415	VC
Univ of Wisc/La Crosse	WI 10,045	VC
Univ of Wisc/Milwaukee	WI 9,427	LC
Univ of Wisc/Oshkosh	WI 10,426	LC
Univ of Wisc/Parkside	WI 10,181	C
Univ of Wisc/Platteville	WI 9,779	NC
Univ of Wisc/River Falls	WI 9,722	LC
Univ of Wisc/Stevens Point	WI 9,384	C
Univ of Wisc/Stout	WI 11,164	C
Univ of Wisc/Superior	WI 9,610	C+
Univ of Wisc/Whitewater	WI 9,274	C
Univ of Wyoming	WY 9,666	C
Upper Iowa Univ	IA 20,130	C
Urbana Univ	OH 21,190	C
Ursuline College	OH 25,456	C

ST = STATE $IS = IN-STATE COSTS   SR = SELECTOR RATING

Business communications (continued)

School	ST	$IS	SR
Utah State Univ	UT	8,002	VC
Utica College	NY	31,396	C
Valdosta State Univ	GA	8,802	C
Valley City State Univ	ND	9,854	LC
Valparaiso Univ	IN	28,970	VC+
Vanguard Univ of Southern Calif	CA	27,071	C
Villa Julie College	MD	25,222	C
Villanova Univ	PA	38,672	HC+
Virginia Commonwealth Univ	VA	12,987	C
Virginia Intermont College	VA	22,200	LC
Virginia State Univ	VA	11,318	C
Virginia Union Univ	VA	18,432	LC
Virginia Wesleyan College	VA	28,433	C
Viterbo Univ	WI	21,670	C
Voorhees College	SC	11,800	LC
Wagner College	NY	33,300	VC
Wake Forest Univ	NC	38,290	MC
Walla Walla College	WA	24,489	NC
Walsh Univ	OH	23,440	C
Warner Pacific College	OR	21,900	C
Warner Southern College	FL	18,000	LC
Wartburg College	IA	27,315	NC
Washburn Univ	KS	9,734	NC
Washington and Jefferson College	PA	33,490	VC
Washington and Lee Univ	VA	35,880	MC
Washington College	MD	34,990	VC
Washington State Univ	WA	12,260	C
Washington Univ in St. Louis	MO	42,106	MC
Wayland Baptist Univ	TX	13,484	C
Wayne State College	NE	8,033	NC
Webber International Univ	FL	17,580	LC
Weber State Univ	UT	9,635	NC
Webster Univ	MO	24,280	VC
Wells College	NY	23,070	VC
Wesley College	DE	19,905	C
Wesleyan College	GA	19,560	C
West Chester Univ of Pennsylvania	PA	12,355	C
West Liberty State College	WV	9,142	LC
West Texas A&M Univ	TX	8,452	C
West Virginia State Univ	WV	8,378	NC
West Virginia Univ	WV	10,506	C
West Virginia Univ Inst of Technology	WV	8,788	NC
West Virginia Wesleyan College	WV	26,880	C
Western Baptist College	OR	21,808	C
Western Conn State Univ	CT	12,993	C
Western Illinois Univ	IL	13,042	C
Western Mich Univ	MI	13,299	C
Western New England College	MA	32,054	C
Western New Mexico Univ	NM	7,233	LC
Western Oregon Univ	OR	10,295	C
Western State College of Colo	CO	9,942	C
Western Washington Univ	WA	11,262	VC
Westfield State College	MA	10,200	C
Westminster College	MO	19,060	VC
Westminster College	PA	31,290	C+
Westminster College	UT	25,656	C
Whittier College	CA	29,108	C
Whitworth College	WA	29,428	VC+
Wichita State Univ	KS	8,500	C
Widener Univ	PA	27,275	C
Wilberforce Univ	OH	14,937	LC
Wiley College	TX	8,100	LC
Wilkes Univ	PA	30,886	C
William Carey College	MS	11,000	LC
William Jewell College	MO	24,340	C
William Paterson Univ of New Jersey	NJ	17,810	C+
William Penn Univ	IA	17,685	LC
William Tyndale College	MI	13,000	NC
William Woods Univ	MO	21,020	C
Williams Baptist College	AR	13,450	C
Wilmington College	DE	5,594	NC
Wilmington College	OH	2,806	NC
Wingate Univ	NC	23,300	C
Winona State Univ	MN	11,333	C
Winston-Salem State Univ	NC	8,960	LC
Winthrop Univ	SC	11,302	C
Wittenberg Univ	OH	34,596	VC
Woodbury Univ	CA	30,176	LC
Worcester Polytechnic Inst	MA	40,450	VC+
Worcester State College	MA	12,499	C
Xavier Univ	OH	30,490	HC
Xavier Univ of Louisiana	LA	17,600	C
Yeshiva Univ	NY	22,000	C
York College	NE	16,330	NC
York College of Pennsylvania	PA	16,550	VC
Youngstown State Univ	OH	12,613	NC
Southwestern College	KS	21,476	C
Univ of Indianapolis	IN	25,090	C
Univ of Mary	ND	15,374	C
Univ of Nebr at Omaha	NE	11,235	C
Western Mich Univ	MI	13,299	C

BUSINESS COMMUNICATIONS

School	ST	$IS	SR
Bentley College	MA	38,784	HC
Calvin College	MI	25,735	NC
Chestnut Hill College	PA	26,600	LC
Mount Vernon Nazarene Univ	OH	20,810	C
Rockhurst Univ	MO	25,440	VC

BUSINESS DATA PROCESSING

School	ST	$IS	SR
Eastern Mich Univ	MI	12,897	C
Faulkner Univ	AL	15,600	C

BUSINESS ECONOMICS

School	ST	$IS	SR
Adams State College	CO	8,613	C
Alabama State Univ	AL	7,658	C
American International College	MA	28,710	LC
Andrews Univ	MI	21,786	C
Aquinas College	MI	23,750	C
Arkansas State Univ	AR	9,630	C
Ashland Univ	OH	25,000	C
Auburn Univ	AL	12,230	VC
Auburn Univ Montgomery	AL	9,530	NC
Aurora Univ	IL	20,645	C
Baker Univ	KS	22,190	C
Ball State Univ	IN	13,138	C
Baylor Univ	TX	27,555	HC
Benedictine Univ	IL	25,710	C
Bentley College	MA	38,784	HC
Bethany College	KS	20,660	LC
Bethany College	WV	21,395	C
Bloomsburg Univ of Pennsylvania	PA	11,602	C
Boston College	MA	41,608	MC
Bowling Green State Univ	OH	14,994	C
Brescia Univ	KY	14,240	C
Buena Vista Univ	IA	27,742	C
Cal State, Fullerton	CA	10,990	C
Cal State, San Bernardino	CA	12,563	LC
Canisius College	NY	32,257	VC
Carnegie Mellon Univ	PA	32,700	MC
Carson-Newman College	TN	16,800	C
Centenary College of Louisiana	LA	24,760	VC
Central Mich Univ	MI	12,244	C
Central Washington Univ	WA	11,730	C
Christopher Newport Univ	VA	13,326	VC
Clarion Univ of Pennsylvania	PA	11,844	C
Cleveland State Univ	OH	10,798	NC
College of the Ozarks	MO	4,130	VC
College of Wooster	OH	31,310	VC+
DePaul Univ	IL	29,835	VC
Dominican College	NY	26,630	LC
Eastern Mich Univ	MI	12,897	C
Eastern New Mexico Univ	NM	7,264	C
Elmira College	NY	37,200	VC
Emory Univ	GA	40,546	MC
Eureka College	IL	19,280	C
Fairmont State	WV	8,400	LC
Fayetteville State Univ	NC	6,000	LC
Florida A&M Univ	FL	8,344	C
Florida Southern College	FL	25,965	C
Fordham Univ	NY	36,000	HC
Francis Marion Univ	SC	11,114	C
Franklin Pierce College	NH	31,700	C
George Fox Univ	OR	28,490	C
George Washington Univ	DC	48,820	MC
Georgetown College	KY	24,950	C+
Georgia State Univ	GA	11,444	VC
Gonzaga Univ	WA	30,218	HC
Grambling State Univ	LA	6,538	NC
Grand Valley State Univ	MI	12,000	VC
Gustavus Adolphus College	MN	30,920	HC
Hampden-Sydney College	VA	31,148	VC
Harding Univ	AR	16,512	VC
Hawaii Pacific Univ	HI	21,080	C
Heidelberg College	OH	23,242	C
Hendrix College	AR	27,646	HC+
Humboldt State Univ	CA	11,176	C
Indiana Univ Bloomington	IN	13,356	VC
Indiana Univ Kokomo	IN	4,835	LC
Indiana Univ Southeast	IN	4,880	LC
Indiana Univ-Purdue Univ Fort Wayne	IN	5,067	LC
Indiana Univ-Purdue Univ Indianapolis	IN	10,959	C
Inter American Univ of PR/ Bayamon Univ College	PR	3,522	
Ithaca College	NY	35,144	VC
James Madison Univ	VA	12,010	VC
Johnson C. Smith Univ	NC	20,000	C
Kalamazoo College	MI	32,442	VC+
Kansas Wesleyan Univ	KS	21,400	C
Kennesaw State Univ	GA	12,152	C
Kent State Univ	OH	14,594	C
Kentucky Wesleyan College	KY	18,590	C
King College	TN	23,400	C
Kutztown Univ of Pennsylvania	PA	10,820	C
Lafayette College	PA	39,267	MC
Lake Forest College	IL	33,860	VC
Lakeland College	WI	22,990	C
Lamar Univ	TX	6,820	LC
Lehigh Univ	PA	42,690	HC+
Limestone College	SC	19,840	C
Louisiana State Univ and A&M College	LA	10,749	VC
Louisiana State Univ in Shreveport	LA	2,900	NC
Louisiana Tech Univ	LA	7,370	C
Loyola Univ Chicago	IL	32,896	VC
Manhattan College	NY	29,000	VC
Mansfield Univ	PA	11,300	C
Marquette Univ	WI	31,066	HC
Marshall Univ	WV	9,116	C
Marymount Univ	VA	25,934	C
McMurry Univ	TX	18,100	LC
Merrimack College	MA	34,380	C
Messiah College	PA	28,910	VC+
Miami Univ	OH	29,097	HC
Midland Lutheran College	NE	18,600	C
Midwestern State Univ	TX	9,381	C
Mills College	CA	39,870	C
Missouri Southern State Univ	MO	8,396	NC
Monmouth College	IL	23,700	C
Monmouth Univ	NJ	28,956	C
Montclair State Univ	NJ	16,327	C
Moravian College	PA	28,950	VC
Morehead State Univ	KY	9,150	C
Mount Vernon Nazarene Univ	OH	20,810	C
Murray State Univ	KY	8,900	VC
New Mexico State Univ	NM	9,250	C
New York Univ	NY	43,170	MC
Niagara Univ	NY	28,250	C
N Car State Univ	NC	11,824	HC
North Georgia College and State Univ	GA	7,000	C
Northern Arizona Univ	AZ	10,353	C
Northern State Univ	SD	8,257	C
Northland College	WI	26,680	C+
Northwest Missouri State Univ	MO	10,000	C
Northwestern College of Iowa	IA	22,174	C+
Northwood Univ	MI	21,000	LC
Norwich Univ	VT	28,212	C
Notre Dame College	OH	20,425	C
Notre Dame de Namur Univ	CA	32,790	LC
Ohio Northern Univ	OH	27,765	VC
Ohio State Univ	OH	15,357	HC
Ohio Univ	OH	15,921	C
Ohio Wesleyan Univ	OH	35,830	VC+
Okla State Univ	OK	10,213	VC
Old Dominion Univ	VA	11,907	C
Ouachita Baptist Univ	AR	21,900	VC
Pace Univ	NY	30,000	VC
Park Univ	MO	11,592	C
Penn State Erie/The Behrend College	PA	16,256	C
Pontifical Catholic Univ of PR/Ponce	PR	7,310	
Purdue Univ/Calumet	IN	10,891	LC
Quinnipiac Univ	CT	34,640	VC
Randolph-Macon College	VA	31,250	C
Regis Univ	CO	31,890	C
Rhode Island College	RI	11,570	C
Rider Univ	NJ	32,560	C
Rockhurst Univ	MO	25,440	VC
Rocky Mountain College	MT	20,805	C
Sacred Heart Univ	CT	33,404	C
Saginaw Valley State Univ	MI	11,432	C
St. Ambrose Univ	IA	25,495	C
St. Cloud State Univ	MN	10,010	C
St. John's Univ	NY	34,370	C
Santa Clara Univ	CA	38,931	VC
Seattle Univ	WA	30,063	VC
Seton Hall Univ	NJ	33,622	VC
Seton Hill Univ	PA	28,810	C
Siena College	NY	28,260	VC+
Skidmore College	NY	41,779	HC
S Car State Univ	SC	6,700	LC
Southeast Missouri State Univ	MO	10,596	C
Southern Conn State Univ	CT	10,310	C
Southern Illinois Univ Carbondale	IL	12,391	C
Southern Illinois Univ Edwardsville	IL	11,022	C
Southern Nazarene Univ	OK	14,634	NC
Southern Univ and A&M College	LA	8,238	LC
SUNY at Potsdam	NY	12,959	C
SUNY/College at Fredonia	NY	12,771	VC
SUNY/College at Oneonta	NY	12,905	VC
SUNY/College at Plattsburgh	NY	12,362	C
Stetson Univ	FL	32,725	VC
Temple Univ	PA	17,438	VC
Tenn State Univ	TN	9,048	LC
Texas A&M Univ at Kingsville	TX	6,800	C
Texas State Univ - San Marcos	TX	10,862	C
Texas Tech Univ	TX	13,026	VC
Texas Wesleyan Univ	TX	18,700	C
Thomas College	ME	23,770	LC
Trinity College	DC	24,150	LC
Troy Univ Dothan Campus	AL	4,678	C
Tuskegee Univ	AL	18,860	LC
Union College	NY	41,595	HC
Univ of Akron	OH	15,166	NC
Univ of Alaska Fairbanks	AK	10,101	C
Univ of Arizona	AZ	11,958	VC
Univ of Arkansas	AR	11,859	VC
Univ of Calif at Los Angeles	CA	17,681	MC
Univ of Calif at Riverside	CA	16,625	C
Univ of Calif at Santa Barbara	CA	11,800	VC
Univ of Calif at Santa Cruz	CA	19,174	VC
Univ of Central Arkansas	AR	9,984	C
Univ of Central Okla	OK	8,094	C
Univ of Dayton	OH	28,826	VC
Univ of Denver	CO	36,376	VC+
Univ of Findlay	OH	29,238	C
Univ of Indianapolis	IN	25,090	C
Univ of Iowa	IA	12,172	VC
Univ of Kentucky	KY	7,800	C
Univ of La Verne	CA	33,470	C
Univ of Louisville	KY	10,400	C
Univ of Maine	ME	13,642	C
Univ of Maine at Farmington	ME	11,515	C
Univ of Memphis	TN	11,153	C
Univ of Miss	MS	9,000	C
Univ of Missouri/Columbia	MO	13,500	C
Univ of Nebr at Kearney	NE	9,000	NC
Univ of Nebr at Lincoln	NE	11,401	VC
Univ of Nevada/Reno	NV	12,155	NC
Univ of New Haven	CT	31,794	C
Univ of New Orleans	LA	7,370	C
Univ of North Alabama	AL	8,992	C
Univ of N Car at Charlotte	NC	9,101	C
Univ of N Car at Wilmington	NC	10,107	VC
Univ of N Dak	ND	10,114	VC
Univ of North Florida	FL	9,908	VC
Univ of North Texas	TX	7,800	C
Univ of Okla	OK	10,769	VC+
Univ of Pittsburgh at Johnstown	PA	16,740	LC
Univ of PR/Mayaguez	PR	1,250	
Univ of PR/Rio Piedras	PR	5,750	
Univ of Richmond	VA	40,510	MC
Univ of Rio Grande	OH	8,728	NC
Univ of San Diego	CA	40,620	HC
Univ of Scranton	PA	31,100	VC
Univ of Sioux Falls	SD	20,800	C
Univ of South Alabama	AL	8,930	C
Univ of S Car at Columbia	SC	13,397	VC
Univ of South Florida	FL	10,284	VC
Univ of Southern Indiana	IN	12,590	C
Univ of Southern Miss	MS	10,112	C
Univ of Tampa	FL	25,784	C
Univ of Tenn at Knoxville	TN	11,720	C
Univ of Tenn at Martin	TN	8,693	C
Univ of Texas at Arlington	TX	7,195	LC
Univ of Texas at El Paso	TX	8,764	NC
Univ of Texas at San Antonio	TX	11,325	LC
Univ of Utah	UT	10,162	VC
Univ of Washington	WA	10,400	VC
Univ of West Florida	FL	8,559	C
Univ of Wisc/Eau Claire	WI	9,915	VC
Univ of Wisc/Platteville	WI	9,779	NC
Univ of Wisc/Whitewater	WI	9,274	C
Univ of Wyoming	WY	9,666	C
Ursinus College	PA	38,950	VC
Utah State Univ	UT	8,002	VC
Utica College	NY	31,396	C
Valdosta State Univ	GA	8,802	C
Villanova Univ	PA	38,672	HC+
Virginia Military Inst	VA	12,654	VC
Virginia Polytechnic Inst and State Univ	VA	10,834	VC
Warren Wilson College	NC	24,382	VC
Washburn Univ	KS	9,734	NC
Washington State Univ	WA	12,260	C
Washington Univ in St. Louis	MO	42,106	MC
Wayne State Univ	MI	11,805	C
Weber State Univ	UT	9,635	NC
West Chester Univ of Pennsylvania	PA	12,355	C+
West Liberty State College	WV	9,142	LC
West Texas A&M Univ	TX	8,452	C
Western Kentucky Univ	KY	10,192	VC
Western Mich Univ	MI	13,299	C
Westmont College	CA	36,672	HC
Wheaton College	IL	27,760	HC
Widener Univ	PA	27,275	C
Wilberforce Univ	OH	14,937	LC
William Jewell College	MO	24,340	C
Wilson College	PA	27,660	C
Wingate Univ	NC	23,300	C
Winona State Univ	MN	11,333	C
Wisc Lutheran College	WI	23,510	VC
Wofford College	SC	30,935	HC
Wright State Univ	OH	13,616	LC
Xavier Univ	OH	30,490	HC
Xavier Univ of Louisiana	LA	17,600	C
Youngstown State Univ	OH	12,613	NC

ST = STATE   **$IS** = IN-STATE COSTS   **SR** = SELECTOR RATING

BUSINESS EDUCATION

School	ST	$IS	SR
Abilene Christian Univ	TX	20,830	C
Adams State College	CO	8,613	C
Alabama State Univ	AL	7,658	C
Alfred Univ	NY		VC
Appalachian State Univ	NC	8,000	C
Arkansas State Univ	AR	9,630	C
Arkansas Tech Univ	AR	8,108	VC
Armstrong Atlantic State Univ	GA	7,394	C
Ashford Univ	IA	20,370	C
Auburn Univ	AL	12,230	VC
Avila Univ	MO	22,100	C
Baker Univ	KS	22,190	C
Ball State Univ	IN	13,138	C
Baylor Univ	TX	27,555	HC
Bethany College	KS	20,660	LC
Bethel College	IN	19,680	C
Bethel Univ	MN	29,840	VC
Bethune-Cookman College	FL	17,922	LC
Black Hills State Univ	SD	7,800	LC
Bloomsburg Univ of Pennsylvania	PA	11,602	C
Blue Mountain College	MS	11,086	C
Bowling Green State Univ	OH	14,994	C
Brigham Young Univ/Hawaii	HI	7,740	HC+
Buena Vista Univ	IA	27,742	C
Cal State, Northridge	CA	9,036	LC
Cal State, Sacramento	CA	11,122	C+
Caribbean Univ	PR	3,000	
Central Mich Univ	MI	12,244	C
Central Missouri State Univ	MO	10,000	C
Central Washington Univ	WA	11,730	C
Chicago State Univ	IL	10,915	C+
CUNY/Herbert H. Lehman College	NY	4,000	LC
Clark Atlanta Univ	GA	20,960	LC
College of the Ozarks	MO	4,130	VC+
Concord Univ	WV	9,708	C
Concordia College: Moorhead	MN	22,475	VC
Concordia Univ Nebr	NE	20,500	C+
Dakota State Univ	SD	7,466	C
Dana College	NE	22,390	C
Delaware State Univ	DE	8,130	LC
Delta State Univ	MS	7,709	C
Dickinson State Univ	ND	7,847	NC
Dordt College	IA	20,325	VC
D'Youville College	NY	23,660	C
East Carolina Univ	NC	10,000	C
East Central Univ	OK	6,207	C
Eastern Kentucky Univ	KY	7,725	C
Eastern Mich Univ	MI	12,897	C
Eastern New Mexico Univ	NM	7,264	C
Elizabeth City State Univ	NC	5,700	LC
Emporia State Univ	KS	8,093	C
Evangel Univ	MO	17,380	C
Fairmont State	WV	8,400	LC
Fayetteville State Univ	NC	6,000	LC
Ferris State Univ	MI	13,698	C
Florida A&M Univ	FL	8,344	C
Framingham State College	MA	11,156	C
Friends Univ	KS	16,250	LC
Georgia Southern Univ	GA	9,762	C
Georgia Southwestern State Univ	GA	6,035	C
Glenville State College	WV	8,778	NC
Goshen College	IN	22,850	VC
Grace College	IN	22,170	C
Grambling State Univ	LA	6,538	NC
Grand Canyon Univ	AZ	32,000	LC
Gustavus Adolphus College	MN	30,920	HC
Gwynedd-Mercy College	PA	26,080	C
Hardin-Simmons Univ	TX	18,641	C
Hastings College	NE	22,218	VC
Henderson State Univ	AR	7,600	C
Hofstra Univ	NY	32,630	VC
Humboldt State Univ	CA	11,176	C
Illinois State Univ	IL	12,839	C+
Indiana State Univ	IN	11,604	C
Indiana Univ of Pennsylvania	PA	11,209	C
Jackson State Univ	MS	8,500	C
James Madison Univ	VA	12,010	VC
Kent State Univ	OH	14,594	C
Knoxville College	TN	6,200	LC
Lakeland College	WI	22,990	C
Langston Univ	OK	2,308	LC
Lenoir-Rhyne College	NC	25,580	C
LeTourneau Univ	TX	21,200	C
Lincoln Memorial Univ	TN	18,144	C
Lincoln Univ	MO	8,000	NC
Lindenwood Univ	MO	18,600	VC
LIU/Brooklyn Campus	NY	25,000	C
Louisiana College	LA	13,450	C
Lubbock Christian Univ	TX	16,960	C
Mayville State Univ	ND	8,667	NC
McKendree College	IL	24,800	VC
McNeese State Univ	LA	5,270	LC
Mercyhurst College	PA	28,633	VC
MidAmerica Nazarene Univ	KS	20,584	LC
Middle Tenn State Univ	TN	8,540	C
Midland Lutheran College	NE	18,600	C
Minot State Univ	ND	6,700	LC
Miss College	MS	14,574	VC
Miss State Univ	MS	9,577	C
Missouri Southern State Univ	MO	8,396	NC
Missouri State Univ	MO	10,748	C+
Montana State Univ-Northern	MT	10,000	NC
Montclair State Univ	NJ	16,327	LC
Morehead State Univ	KY	9,150	C
Morningside College	IA	23,704	C
Mount Mary College	WI	22,895	C
Mount Vernon Nazarene Univ	OH	20,810	C
Murray State Univ	KY	8,900	VC
Nazareth College of Rochester	NY	28,175	VC
New York Inst of Technology	NY	28,126	VC
Niagara Univ	NY	28,250	C
Nicholls State Univ	LA	6,500	NC
Norfolk State Univ	VA	10,531	LC
N Car Agricultural and Technical State Univ	NC	8,000	LC
Northern Kentucky Univ	KY	6,670	NC
Northern Mich Univ	MI	12,340	LC
Northern State Univ	SD	8,257	C
Northwest Missouri State Univ	MO	10,000	C
Northwestern College of Iowa	IA	22,174	C+
Northwestern Okla State Univ	OK	6,250	NC
Oakland City Univ	IN	19,620	NC
Oakwood College	AL	14,904	C
Oglala Lakota College	SD	1,950	NC
Ohio Univ	OH	15,921	C
Okla Panhandle State Univ	OK	7,635	NC
Okla Wesleyan Univ	OK	18,950	NC
Oral Roberts Univ	OK	22,650	C
Ouachita Baptist Univ	AR	21,900	VC
Pace Univ	NY	30,000	VC
Philander Smith College	AR	13,230	LC
Pontifical Catholic Univ of PR/Ponce	PR	7,310	
Rider Univ	NJ	32,560	C
Robert Morris Univ	PA	22,822	C
Rust College	MS		C+
St. Augustine's College	NC	14,000	LC
St. Mary's Univ of San Antonio	TX	22,444	C
St. Paul's College	VA	16,030	NC
St. Vincent College	PA	26,160	VC
Salem State College	MA	13,161	LC
Shippensburg Univ of Pennsylvania	PA	11,621	C
Siena Heights Univ	MI	17,000	LC
Simpson College	IA	26,833	VC
S Car State Univ	SC	6,700	LC
Southeast Missouri State Univ	MO	10,596	C
Southeastern Okla State Univ	OK	6,147	C
Southern Arkansas Univ	AR	6,956	C
Southern Illinois Univ Carbondale	IL	12,391	C
Southern Nazarene Univ	OK	14,634	NC
Southern New Hampshire Univ	NH	28,764	C
Southern Univ at New Orleans	LA	1,000	NC
Southern Utah Univ	UT		C
Southwestern Adventist Univ	TX	18,290	LC
Southwestern College	KS	21,476	C
SUNY at Oswego	NY	13,662	VC
SUNY/College at Buffalo	NY	11,903	C+
SUNY/College at Oneonta	NY	12,905	VC
Suffolk Univ	MA	33,160	C
Tabor College	KS	21,614	NC
Tarleton State Univ	TX	8,952	C
Temple Univ	PA	17,438	C
Texas A&M Univ at Commerce	TX	9,020	C
Texas Wesleyan Univ	TX	18,700	C
Thomas College	ME	23,770	LC
Union College	NE	18,710	C
Univ of Akron	OH	15,166	NC
Univ of Arkansas at Pine Bluff	AR	8,300	C
Univ of Central Florida	FL	10,739	VC
Univ of Central Okla	OK	8,094	C
Univ of Cincinnati	OH	17,682	C
Univ of Findlay	OH	29,238	C
Univ of Georgia	GA	11,004	HC
Univ of Idaho	ID	9,310	C
Univ of Indianapolis	IN	25,090	C
Univ of Kentucky	KY	7,800	C
Univ of Louisville	KY	10,400	C
Univ of Maine at Machias	ME	10,523	C
Univ of Mary Hardin-Baylor	TX	19,428	C
Univ of Maryland/Eastern Shore	MD	11,210	C
Univ of Minn/Twin Cities	MN	13,165	HC
Univ of Montana--Western	MT	8,406	NC
Univ of Nebr at Kearney	NE	9,306	NC
Univ of Nebr at Lincoln	NE	11,401	VC
Univ of New Orleans	LA	7,370	C
Univ of North Alabama	AL	8,992	C
Univ of N Dak	ND	10,114	VC
Univ of North Texas	TX	7,800	C
Univ of Northern Iowa	IA	11,133	C
Univ of Rio Grande	OH	8,728	NC
Univ of St. Francis	IN	20,970	C
Univ of South Florida	FL	10,284	VC
Univ of Southern Indiana	IN	12,590	LC
Univ of Southern Miss	MS	10,112	C
Univ of the Cumberlands	KY	18,184	C
Univ of the Ozarks	AR	19,250	C
Univ of Toledo	OH	15,806	NC
Univ of West Georgia	GA	8,838	C
Univ of Wisc/Whitewater	WI	9,274	C
Utah State Univ	UT	8,002	VC
Valdosta State Univ	GA	8,802	C
Valley City State Univ	ND	9,854	LC
Vermont Technical College	VT	15,751	C
Virginia Polytechnic Inst and State Univ	VA	10,834	VC
Virginia State Univ	VA	11,318	C
Virginia Union Univ	VA	18,432	LC
Viterbo Univ	WI	21,670	C
Walla Walla College	WA	24,489	NC
Warner Southern College	FL	18,000	C
Washburn Univ	KS	9,734	NC
Wayne State Univ	MI	11,805	C
Weber State Univ	UT	9,635	NC
West Texas A&M Univ	TX	8,452	C
Western Kentucky Univ	KY	10,192	C
Western Mich Univ	MI	13,299	C
Western New Mexico Univ	NM	7,233	LC
Westfield State College	MA	10,200	C
Wiley College	TX	8,100	LC
Winona State Univ	MN	11,333	C
Wright State Univ	OH	13,616	LC
York College of Pennsylvania	PA	16,550	LC
Youngstown State Univ	OH	12,613	NC

BUSINESS LAW

School	ST	$IS	SR
Bowling Green State Univ	OH	14,994	C
Hofstra Univ	NY	32,630	VC
Lamar Univ	TX	6,820	LC
Marymount Univ	VA	25,934	C
Mountain State Univ	WV	11,406	NC
Ohio Univ	OH	15,921	C
Peirce College	PA	12,760	NC
Saginaw Valley State Univ	MI	11,432	C
Temple Univ	PA	17,438	C
Univ of Pennsylvania	PA	41,766	MC
Warner Southern College	FL	18,000	LC
Washington State Univ	WA	12,260	C
Western Carolina Univ	NC	7,000	C

BUSINESS STATISTICS

School	ST	$IS	SR
Baylor Univ	TX	27,555	HC
Univ of PR/Rio Piedras	PR	5,750	
Univ of Texas at San Antonio	TX	11,325	LC
Washington State Univ	WA	12,260	C

BUSINESS SYSTEMS ANALYSIS

School	ST	$IS	SR
Arkansas State Univ	AR	9,630	C
Baylor Univ	TX	27,555	HC
Canisius College	NY	32,257	VC
Clarkson Univ	NY	34,930	VC
Eastern Mich Univ	MI	12,897	C
Husson College	ME	17,410	LC
Idaho State Univ	ID	9,030	C
Johnson State College	VT	11,830	C
Kent State Univ	OH	14,594	C
Lehigh Univ	PA	42,690	HC+
Louisiana Tech Univ	LA	7,370	C
Messiah College	PA	28,910	VC+
Montana Tech of The Univ of Montana	MT	10,434	C
Rochester Inst of Technology	NY	32,070	VC+
Shippensburg Univ of Pennsylvania	PA	11,621	C
Southern Illinois Univ Carbondale	IL	12,391	C
Texas A&M Univ	TX	13,351	HC
Univ of Findlay	OH	29,238	C
Univ of N Car at Wilmington	NC	10,107	VC
Univ of St. Mary	KS	18,900	C
Villa Julie College	MD	25,222	C

CANADIAN STUDIES

School	ST	$IS	SR
Duke Univ	NC	41,239	MC
Franklin College	IN		C
St. Lawrence Univ	NY	40,545	VC
SUNY/College at Plattsburgh	NY	12,362	C
Univ of Vermont	VT	18,080	VC
Univ of Washington	WA	10,400	VC
Western Washington Univ	WA	11,262	VC

CARIBBEAN STUDIES

School	ST	$IS	SR
CUNY/Brooklyn College	NY	4,377	C+
Emory Univ	GA	40,546	MC
Florida State Univ	FL	9,028	HC
Hofstra Univ	NY	32,630	VC
Pitzer College	CA	41,644	HC
SUNY/Univ at Albany	NY	13,860	VC
SUNY/Univ at Binghamton	NY	13,988	HC

CARTOGRAPHY

School	ST	$IS	SR
East Central Univ	OK	6,207	C
Missouri State Univ	MO	10,748	C+
Ohio Univ	OH	15,921	C
Salem State College	MA	13,161	LC
Texas State Univ - San Marcos	TX	10,862	C
Univ of Idaho	ID	9,310	NC
Univ of Wisc/Madison	WI	13,117	HC

CELL BIOLOGY

School	ST	$IS	SR
Ball State Univ	IN	13,138	C
Bard College	NY	41,800	HC+
Beloit College	WI	32,808	HC
Bucknell Univ	PA	39,660	MC
Cal State, Long Beach	CA	9,512	C
Florida State Univ	FL	9,028	HC
Johns Hopkins Univ	MD	42,044	MC
Johnson State College	VT	11,830	LC
Kent State Univ	OH	14,594	C
Mansfield Univ	PA	11,300	C
Missouri State Univ	MO	10,748	C+
Montana State Univ-Bozeman	MT	1,137	C
Ohio Univ	OH	15,921	C
Okla State Univ	OK	10,213	VC
Purdue Univ/West Lafayette	IN	13,458	VC
Rutgers, The State Univ of New Jersey/New Brunswick/Piscataway Campus	NJ	15,810	HC
San Francisco State Univ	CA	13,000	C
SUNY/College at Plattsburgh	NY	12,362	C
Texas Tech Univ	TX	13,026	VC
Tulane Univ	LA	41,098	MC
Univ of Calif at Riverside	CA	16,625	C
Univ of Calif at Santa Barbara	CA	11,800	VC
Univ of Colo at Boulder	CO	13,352	C+
Univ of Georgia	GA	11,004	HC
Univ of Illinois at Urbana-Champaign	IL	15,800	HC+
Univ of Maine	ME	13,642	C
Univ of Mich/Ann Arbor	MI	16,587	HC+
Univ of Minn/Twin Cities	MN	13,165	HC
Univ of Rochester	NY	41,135	MC
Washington State Univ	WA	12,260	C

CELTIC STUDIES

School	ST	$IS	SR
Bard College	NY	41,800	HC+
Univ of Calif at Berkeley	CA	18,141	HC+

CERAMIC ART AND DESIGN

School	ST	$IS	SR
Alfred Univ	NY		VC
Andrews Univ	MI	21,786	C
Aquinas College	MI	23,750	C
Bennington College	VT	41,890	HC
Calif College of the Arts	CA	34,325	SP
Cal State, Fullerton	CA	10,990	C
Cal State, San Bernardino	CA	12,563	LC
College for Creative Studies	MI	24,000	SP
Edinboro Univ of Pennsylvania	PA	11,809	LC
Hofstra Univ	NY	32,630	VC
Indiana Univ Bloomington	IN	13,356	VC
Indiana Univ-Purdue Univ Indianapolis	IN	10,959	C
Indiana Wesleyan Univ	IN	22,074	C+
Kansas City Art Inst	MO	29,542	SP
Maryland Inst College of Art	MD	34,450	SP
Mass College of Art	MA	16,650	SP
McMurry Univ	TX	18,100	LC
Northwest Nazarene Univ	ID	22,590	VC
Ohio Northern Univ	OH	27,765	VC
Ohio Univ	OH	15,921	C
Rhode Island School of Design	RI	38,130	SP
Rochester Inst of Technology	NY	32,070	VC+
School of the Art Inst of Chicago	IL	37,800	SP
Syracuse Univ	NY	38,655	HC
Univ of Dallas	TX	27,432	VC+
Univ of Georgia	GA	11,004	HC
Univ of Hartford	CT	34,044	C
Univ of Kansas	KS	10,915	VC
Univ of Mass Dartmouth	MA	15,985	C
Univ of Miami	FL	38,397	MC
Univ of Mich/Ann Arbor	MI	16,587	HC+

School	ST	$IS	SR
Univ of North Texas	TX	7,800	C
Univ of Oregon	OR	13,108	VC
Washington Univ in St. Louis	MO	42,106	MC

CERAMIC ENGINEERING

School	ST	$IS	SR
Alfred Univ	NY		VC
Clemson Univ	SC	13,366	HC
Ohio State Univ	OH	15,357	HC
Rutgers, The State Univ of New Jersey/New Brunswick/Piscataway Campus	NJ	15,810	HC
Univ of Illinois at Urbana-Champaign	IL	15,800	HC+
Univ of Missouri/Rolla	MO	13,332	HC
Univ of Washington	WA	10,400	VC

CERAMIC SCIENCE

School	ST	$IS	SR
Maine College of Art	ME	28,820	SP

CHEMICAL ENGINEERING

School	ST	$IS	SR
Arizona State Univ-Tempe	AZ	11,174	C
Auburn Univ	AL	12,230	VC
Bethel College	IN	19,680	C
Brigham Young Univ	UT	9,200	VC
Bucknell Univ	PA	39,660	MC
Calif Inst of Technology	CA	36,123	MC
Calif State Polytechnic Univ, Pomona	CA	18,053	C+
Cal State, Long Beach	CA	9,512	C
Calvin College	MI	25,735	NC
Carnegie Mellon Univ	PA	32,700	MC
Case Western Reserve Univ	OH	37,314	MC
Christian Brothers Univ	TN	24,650	VC
CUNY/City College	NY		C
Clarkson Univ	NY	34,930	VC
Clemson Univ	SC	13,366	HC
Cleveland State Univ	OH	10,798	NC
Colo School of Mines	CO	14,893	HC
Colo State Univ-Fort Collins	CO	10,878	C+
Columbia Univ/Fu Foundation School of Engineering and Applied Science	NY	42,584	MC
Cooper Union for the Advancement of Science and Art	NY	12,450	MC
Cornell Univ	NY	41,717	MC
Delaware State Univ	DE	8,130	LC
Dordt College	IA	20,325	VC
Drexel Univ	PA	27,700	VC
Florida A&M Univ	FL	8,344	C
Florida Inst of Technology	FL	29,720	VC
Florida International Univ	FL	9,215	VC
Florida State Univ	FL	9,028	NC
Geneva College	PA	21,850	C
Georgia Inst of Technology	GA	11,450	HC+
Hampton Univ	VA	19,468	C+
Howard Univ	DC	18,481	C+
Illinois Inst of Technology	IL	26,465	HC+
Iowa State Univ	IA	11,831	VC
Johns Hopkins Univ	MD	42,044	MC
Kansas State Univ	KS	10,516	VC
Lafayette College	PA	39,267	MC
Lamar Univ	TX	6,820	LC
Lehigh Univ	PA	42,690	HC+
Louisiana State Univ and A&M College	LA	10,749	VC
Louisiana Tech Univ	LA	7,370	C
Manhattan College	NY	29,000	VC
Mass Inst of Technology	MA	41,800	MC
McNeese State Univ	LA	5,270	LC
Mich State Univ	MI	13,689	VC
Mich Tech Univ	MI	14,569	VC
Miss State Univ	MS	9,577	C
Montana State Univ-Bozeman	MT	1,137	C
New Jersey Inst of Technology	NJ	16,396	VC
New Mexico Inst of Mining and Technology	NM	8,510	VC+
New Mexico State Univ	NM	9,250	C
N Car Agricultural and Technical State Univ	NC	8,000	LC
N Car State Univ	NC	11,824	HC
Northeastern Univ	MA	35,742	HC
Northwestern Univ	IL	37,595	MC
Oakland Univ	MI	11,936	VC
Ohio State Univ	OH	15,357	HC
Ohio Univ	OH	15,921	C
Okla State Univ	OK	10,213	VC
Oregon State Univ	OR	11,055	C
Penn State Univ/Univ Park Campus	PA	18,038	HC
Polytechnic Univ/Brooklyn	NY	37,150	VC
Prairie View A&M Univ	TX	11,110	LC
Princeton Univ	NJ	40,213	MC
Purdue Univ/West Lafayette	IN	13,458	VC
Rensselaer Polytechnic Inst	NY	41,288	HC+
Rice Univ	TX	32,290	MC
Rose-Hulman Inst of Technology	IN	34,557	HC+
Rutgers, The State Univ of New Jersey/New Brunswick/Piscataway Campus	NJ	15,810	HC
San Jose State Univ	CA	11,707	C
Savannah State Univ	GA	7,772	LC
S Dak School of Mines and Technology	SD	7,624	C+
Stanford Univ	CA	41,557	MC
SUNY/College of Environmental Science and Forestry	NY	15,000	VC
SUNY/Univ at Buffalo	NY	13,694	VC
SUNY/Univ at Stony Brook	NY	13,625	HC
Stevens Inst of Technology	NJ	40,935	HC
Syracuse Univ	NY	38,655	HC
Tenn Tech Univ	TN	10,044	C
Texas A&M Univ	TX	13,351	HC
Texas A&M Univ at Kingsville	TX	6,800	LC
Texas Tech Univ	TX	13,026	VC
Tri-State Univ-Main Campus	IN	26,200	C
Tufts Univ	MA	42,018	MC
Tulane Univ	LA	41,098	MC
Tuskegee Univ	AL	18,860	LC
Universidad Politecnica de PR	PR	5,400	
Univ of Akron	OH	15,166	NC
Univ of Alabama	AL	9,888	C
Univ of Alabama in Huntsville	AL	9,516	VC
Univ of Arizona	AZ	11,958	VC
Univ of Arkansas	AR	11,859	VC
Univ of at Calif Davis	CA	15,010	VC
Univ of Calif at Berkeley	CA	18,141	HC+
Univ of Calif at Irvine	CA	16,475	HC
Univ of Calif at Los Angeles	CA	17,681	MC
Univ of Calif at Riverside	CA	16,625	C
Univ of Calif at San Diego	CA	16,102	HC
Univ of Calif at Santa Barbara	CA	11,800	VC
Univ of Cincinnati	OH	17,682	C
Univ of Colo at Boulder	CO	13,352	C+
Univ of Conn	CT	16,628	HC
Univ of Dayton	OH	28,826	VC
Univ of Delaware	DE	14,142	HC
Univ of Florida	FL	9,354	HC
Univ of Houston	TX	7,000	C
Univ of Idaho	ID	9,310	NC
Univ of Illinois at Chicago	IL	16,256	VC
Univ of Illinois at Urbana-Champaign	IL	15,800	HC+
Univ of Iowa	IA	12,172	VC
Univ of Kansas	KS	10,915	VC
Univ of Kentucky	KY	7,800	C
Univ of Louisiana at Lafayette	LA	5,830	C
Univ of Louisville	KY	10,400	VC
Univ of Maine	ME	13,642	C
Univ of Maryland/Baltimore County	MD	16,642	VC+
Univ of Maryland/College Park	MD	16,036	HC
Univ of Mass Amherst	MA	15,973	C+
Univ of Mass Lowell	MA	14,327	VC
Univ of Mich/Ann Arbor	MI	16,587	HC+
Univ of Minn/Duluth	MN	13,974	C
Univ of Minn/Twin Cities	MN	13,165	HC
Univ of Miss	MS	9,000	C
Univ of Missouri/Columbia	MO	13,500	VC
Univ of Missouri/Rolla	MO	13,332	HC
Univ of Nebr at Lincoln	NE	11,401	VC
Univ of Nevada/Reno	NV	12,155	NC
Univ of New Hampshire	NH	16,810	VC
Univ of New Haven	CT	31,794	C
Univ of New Mexico	NM	11,253	C
Univ of N Dak	ND	10,114	VC
Univ of Notre Dame	IN	39,552	MC
Univ of Okla	OK	10,769	VC+
Univ of Pennsylvania	PA	41,766	MC
Univ of Pittsburgh at Pittsburgh	PA	18,866	HC
Univ of PR/Mayaguez	PR	1,250	
Univ of Rhode Island	RI	15,398	C
Univ of Rochester	NY	41,135	MC
Univ of South Alabama	AL	8,930	LC
Univ of S Car at Columbia	SC	13,397	VC
Univ of South Florida	FL	10,284	VC
Univ of Southern Calif	CA	41,618	VC
Univ of Tenn at Knoxville	TN	11,720	C
Univ of Texas at Austin	TX	14,610	HC
Univ of Toledo	OH	15,806	NC
Univ of Tulsa	OK	25,348	HC
Univ of Utah	UT	10,162	VC
Univ of Virginia	VA	13,759	MC
Univ of Washington	WA	10,400	VC
Univ of Wisc/Madison	WI	13,117	HC
Univ of Wyoming	WY	9,666	C
Vanderbilt Univ	TN	41,986	MC
Villanova Univ	PA	38,672	HC+
Virginia Commonwealth Univ	VA	12,987	C
Virginia Polytechnic Inst and State Univ	VA	10,834	VC
Washington and Lee Univ	VA	35,880	MC
Washington State Univ	WA	12,260	C
Washington Univ in St. Louis	MO	42,106	MC
Wayne State Univ	MI	11,805	C
West Virginia Univ	WV	10,506	C
West Virginia Univ Inst of Technology	WV	8,788	NC
Western Mich Univ	MI	13,299	C
Widener Univ	PA	27,275	C
Worcester Polytechnic Inst	MA	40,450	VC+
Xavier Univ	OH	30,490	HC
Yale Univ	CT	41,000	MC
Youngstown State Univ	OH	12,613	NC

CHEMICAL ENGINEERING TECHNOLOGY

School	ST	$IS	SR
Univ of Hartford	CT	34,044	C
Univ of PR/Arecibo	PR	8,327	

CHEMICAL PHYSICS

School	ST	$IS	SR
Bowdoin College	ME	41,660	MC
Brown Univ	RI	42,015	MC
Maryville College	TN	29,224	VC
Mich State Univ	MI	13,689	VC
Saginaw Valley State Univ	MI	11,432	C

CHEMICAL TECHNOLOGY

School	ST	$IS	SR
Florida State Univ	FL	9,028	NC
Gallaudet Univ	DC	16,554	
Inter American Univ of PR/Arecibo Campus	PR	3,350	
Inter American Univ of PR/Bayamon Univ College	PR	3,522	
Inter American Univ of PR/Fajardo Campus	PR	4,000	
Inter American Univ of PR/Ponce Regional College	PR	3,700	
Midwestern State Univ	TX	9,381	LC
Univ of Cincinnati	OH	17,682	C

CHEMISTRY

School	ST	$IS	SR
Abilene Christian Univ	TX	20,830	C
Adams State College	CO	8,613	C
Adelphi Univ	NY	27,000	VC
Adrian College	MI	23,000	C
Agnes Scott College	GA	32,070	HC
Alabama A&M Univ	AL	8,890	LC
Alabama State Univ	AL	7,658	C
Albany State Univ	GA	5,770	C+
Albertson College of Idaho	ID	21,095	VC
Albion College	MI	26,000	VC
Albright College	PA	33,920	C
Alcorn State Univ	MS	8,190	LC
Alderson-Broaddus College	WV	24,006	C
Alfred Univ	NY		VC
Allegheny College	PA	33,500	HC
Alma College	MI	28,544	VC
Alvernia College	PA	26,388	C
Alverno College	WI	21,088	C
American International College	MA	28,710	LC
American Univ	DC	38,719	HC+
Amherst College	MA	41,590	MC
Anderson Univ	IN	25,050	LC
Andrews Univ	MI	21,786	C
Angelo State Univ	TX	8,340	NC
Appalachian State Univ	NC	8,000	VC
Aquinas College	MI	23,750	C
Arcadia Univ	PA	33,570	VC
Arizona State Univ-Tempe	AZ	11,174	C
Arkansas State Univ	AR	9,630	C
Arkansas Tech Univ	AR	8,108	VC
Armstrong Atlantic State Univ	GA	7,394	C
Asbury College	KY	23,762	VC
Ashland Univ	OH	25,000	C
Assumption College	MA	32,875	C
Auburn Univ	AL	12,230	VC
Augsburg College	MN	28,300	C
Augusta State Univ	GA	2,920	C
Augustana College	IL	29,862	VC+
Augustana College	SD	24,380	VC
Austin College	TX	27,871	HC
Austin Peay State Univ	TN	7,565	C
Averett Univ	VA	24,920	C
Avila Univ	MO	22,100	C
Azusa Pacific Univ	CA	28,546	VC
Baker Univ	KS	22,190	C
Baldwin-Wallace College	OH	27,256	VC
Ball State Univ	IN	13,138	C
Bard College	NY	41,800	HC+
Barry Univ	FL	24,100	LC
Barton College	NC	22,316	C
Bates College	ME	42,100	MC
Baylor Univ	TX	27,555	HC
Belhaven College	MS	19,530	NC
Bellarmine Univ	KY	27,613	C+
Belmont Univ	TN	24,110	VC
Beloit College	WI	32,808	HC
Bemidji State Univ	MN	11,180	LC
Benedict College	SC	19,114	LC
Benedictine College	KS	21,968	C
Benedictine Univ	IL	25,710	C
Bennett College	NC	11,500	C
Bennington College	VT	41,890	HC
Berea College	KY	5,496	VC+
Berry College	GA	24,342	VC
Bethany College	KS	20,660	LC
Bethany College	WV	21,395	C
Bethel College	IN	19,680	C
Bethel College	KS	21,650	C
Bethel College	TN	16,066	NC
Bethel Univ	MN	29,840	VC
Bethune-Cookman College	FL	17,922	LC
Birmingham-Southern College	AL	28,494	VC+
Black Hills State Univ	SD	7,800	LC
Blackburn College	IL	13,690	C
Bloomfield College	NJ	22,500	LC
Bloomsburg Univ of Pennsylvania	PA	11,602	C
Blue Mountain College	MS	11,086	C
Bluefield College	VA	17,230	C+
Bluffton Univ	OH	26,110	C
Boise State Univ	ID	9,438	LC
Boston College	MA	41,608	MC
Boston Univ	MA	42,046	HC+
Bowdoin College	ME	41,660	MC
Bowling Green State Univ	OH	14,994	C
Bradley Univ	IL	25,280	VC
Brandeis Univ	MA	41,551	MC
Brescia Univ	KY	14,240	C
Briar Cliff Univ	IA	23,550	LC
Bridgewater College	VA	27,790	C
Bridgewater State College	MA	12,120	C
Brigham Young Univ	UT	9,200	VC
Brown Univ	RI	42,015	MC
Bryn Mawr College	PA	42,780	HC+
Bucknell Univ	PA	39,660	MC
Buena Vista Univ	IA	27,742	C
Butler Univ	IN	31,944	VC+
Cabrini College	PA	33,340	C
Caldwell College	NJ	26,450	LC
Calif Inst of Technology	CA	36,123	MC
Calif Lutheran Univ	CA	27,800	LC
Calif Polytechnic State Univ	CA	12,390	VC
Calif State Polytechnic Univ, Pomona	CA	18,053	C+
Cal State East Bay	CA	10,856	LC
Cal State, Bakersfield	CA	6,125	LC
Cal State, Chico	CA	11,395	C
Cal State, Dominguez Hills	CA	10,220	LC
Cal State, Fresno	CA	10,037	LC
Cal State, Fullerton	CA	10,990	C
Cal State, Long Beach	CA	9,512	C
Cal State, Los Angeles	CA	5,900	C
Cal State, Northridge	CA	9,036	LC
Cal State, Sacramento	CA	11,122	C+
Cal State, San Bernardino	CA	12,563	LC
Cal State, San Marcos	CA	1,800	LC
Cal State, Stanislaus	CA	11,283	C
Calif Univ of Pennsylvania	PA	14,217	C
Calvin College	MI	25,735	NC
Cameron Univ	OK	6,314	NC
Campbell Univ	NC	21,137	VC
Campbellsville Univ	KY	21,328	C
Canisius College	NY	32,257	VC
Capital Univ	OH	30,444	C
Cardinal Stritch Univ	WI	21,910	C
Carleton College	MN	40,467	MC
Carlow Univ	PA	24,313	C
Carnegie Mellon Univ	PA	32,700	MC
Carroll College	MT	23,324	C+
Carroll College	WI	24,860	C
Carthage College	WI	26,000	C
Case Western Reserve Univ	OH	37,314	MC
Catawba College	NC	25,000	C
Catholic Univ of America	DC	35,838	VC
Cedar Crest College	PA	30,615	C
Cedarville Univ	OH	21,904	VC
Centenary College of Louisiana	LA	24,760	VC
Central College	IA	26,774	VC
Central Conn State Univ	CT	13,620	C
Central Methodist Univ	MO	18,000	C
Central Mich Univ	MI	12,244	C
Central Missouri State Univ	MO	10,000	C
Central State Univ	OH	9,010	C+
Central Univ of Bayamon	PR	3,335	
Central Washington Univ	WA	11,730	C
Centre College	KY	30,810	VC
Chadron State College	NE	6,350	NC
Chapman Univ	CA	37,550	VC
Charleston Southern Univ	SC	17,800	C
Chatham College	PA	27,290	C+
Chestnut Hill College	PA	26,600	LC
Cheyney Univ of Pennsylvania	PA	11,497	LC
Chicago State Univ	IL	10,915	C+
Christian Brothers Univ	TN	24,650	VC
Citadel, The	SC		C+
CUNY/Brooklyn College	NY	4,377	C+
CUNY/City College	NY		C

ST = STATE $IS = IN-STATE COSTS   SR = SELECTOR RATING

School	ST	$IS	SR
CUNY/College of Staten Island	NY	4,328	NC
CUNY/Herbert H. Lehman College	NY	4,000	LC
CUNY/Hunter College	NY	8,000	C+
CUNY/Queens College	NY	4,356	C
CUNY/York College	NY	4,242	NC
Claflin Univ	SC	16,798	C+
Claremont McKenna College	CA	42,920	MC
Clarion Univ of Pennsylvania	PA	11,844	C
Clark Atlanta Univ	GA	20,960	LC
Clark Univ	MA	35,165	VC+
Clarke College	IA	25,390	C
Clarkson Univ	NY	34,930	VC
Clemson Univ	SC	13,366	HC
Cleveland State Univ	OH	10,798	NC
Coastal Carolina Univ	SC	13,140	C
Coe College	IA	27,440	VC
Coker College	SC	21,600	C
Colby College	ME	41,770	MC
Colgate Univ	NY	41,170	MC
College Misericordia	PA	27,950	C
College of Charleston	SC	13,616	VC
College of Mount St. Vincent	NY	28,000	C
College of Mount St. Joseph	OH	24,860	C
College of New Jersey	NJ	18,315	MC
College of New Rochelle	NY	28,396	C+
College of Notre Dame of Maryland	MD	27,700	C
College of Our Lady of the Elms	MA	21,000	C
College of St. Benedict	MN	30,091	VC
College of St. Catherine	MN	27,505	VC
College of St. Elizabeth	NJ	28,495	C
College of St. Mary	NE	23,938	C
College of St. Rose	NY	25,684	C
College of St. Scholastica	MN	28,546	C+
College of the Holy Cross	MA	40,664	MC
College of the Ozarks	MO	4,130	VC+
College of William and Mary	VA	14,147	MC
College of Wooster	OH	31,310	VC
Colo School of Mines	CO	14,893	HC
Colo State Univ-Fort Collins	CO	10,878	C+
Colo State Univ-Pueblo	CO	7,821	LC
Columbia College	MO	16,900	C
Columbia College	SC	24,982	LC
Columbia Union College	MD	23,536	C
Columbia Univ/Barnard College	NY	38,000	MC
Columbia Univ/Columbia College	NY	42,584	MC
Columbia Univ/School of General Studies	NY	41,516	C
Columbus State Univ	GA	8,664	C
Concord College	WV	9,708	C
Concordia College: Moorhead	MN	22,475	VC
Concordia Univ	CA	26,780	C
Concordia Univ	OR	24,400	C
Concordia Univ Nebr	NE	20,500	C+
Concordia Univ, River Forest	IL	26,300	C
Conn College	CT	41,975	MC
Converse College	SC	24,800	VC
Coppin State College	MD	10,200	LC
Cornell College	IA	30,110	VC+
Cornell Univ	NY	41,717	MC
Covenant College	GA	26,460	VC+
Creighton Univ	NE	29,918	VC+
Crichton College	TN	15,300	C
Curry College	MA	26,100	C
Dakota State Univ	SD	7,466	C
Dana College	NE	22,390	C
Dartmouth College	NH	39,465	MC
Davidson College	NC	36,825	MC
Davis and Elkins College	WV	22,416	C
De Sales Univ	PA	28,580	VC
Delaware State Univ	DE	8,130	LC
Delaware Valley College	PA	29,944	C
Delta State Univ	MS	7,709	C
Denison Univ	OH	37,040	HC
DePaul Univ	IL	29,835	VC
DePauw Univ	IN	32,100	HC
Dickinson College	PA	40,170	HC+
Dickinson State Univ	ND	7,847	NC
Dillard Univ	LA	17,500	VC
Doane College	NE	22,458	C
Dominican Univ	IL	26,370	C
Dordt College	IA	20,325	VC
Drake Univ	IA	27,632	VC+
Drew Univ/College of Liberal Arts	NJ	39,698	VC
Drexel Univ	PA	27,700	VC
Drury Univ	MO	20,117	VC
Duke Univ	NC	41,239	MC
Duquesne Univ	PA	29,534	VC
Earlham College	IN	33,604	HC
East Carolina Univ	NC	10,000	C
East Central Univ	OK	6,207	C
East Stroudsburg Univ of Pennsylvania	PA	10,336	C
East Tenn State Univ	TN	8,497	C
East Texas Baptist Univ	TX	16,713	C
Eastern Illinois Univ	IL	12,569	C
Eastern Kentucky Univ	KY	7,725	C
Eastern Mennonite Univ	VA	25,450	VC
Eastern Mich Univ	MI	12,897	C
Eastern Nazarene College	MA	19,500	LC
Eastern New Mexico Univ	NM	7,264	C
Eastern Oregon Univ	OR	10,400	NC
Eastern Univ	PA	24,075	C
Eastern Washington Univ	WA	10,608	C
Eckerd College	FL	35,492	VC
Edgewood College	WI	22,862	C
Edinboro Univ of Pennsylvania	PA	11,809	LC
Elizabeth City State Univ	NC	5,700	LC
Elizabethtown College	PA	32,100	VC
Elmhurst College	IL	24,685	C
Elmira College	NY	37,200	VC
Elon Univ	NC	25,371	HC
Emmanuel College	MA	32,000	C+
Emory & Henry College	VA	26,570	C
Emory Univ	GA	40,546	MC
Emporia State Univ	KS	8,093	C
Erskine College	SC	25,468	VC
Eureka College	IL	19,280	C
Evangel Univ	MO	17,380	C
Excelsior College	NY	995	SP
Fairfield Univ	CT	39,835	HC
Fairleigh Dickinson Univ/College at Florham	NJ	30,130	C
Fairleigh Dickinson Univ/Metropolitan Campus	NJ	28,590	C
Fairmont State	WV	8,400	LC
Fayetteville State Univ	NC	6,000	LC
Ferrum College	VA	24,290	LC
Fisk Univ	TN	19,830	C
Florida A&M Univ	FL	8,344	C
Florida Atlantic Univ	FL	11,221	C
Florida Inst of Technology	FL	29,720	VC
Florida International Univ	FL	9,215	VC
Florida Memorial College	FL	6,000	LC
Florida Southern College	FL	25,965	C
Florida State Univ	FL	9,028	NC
Fordham Univ	NY	36,000	HC
Fort Hays State Univ	KS	7,638	C
Fort Lewis College	CO	11,852	C
Fort Valley State Univ	GA	6,975	C
Framingham State College	MA	11,156	C
Francis Marion Univ	SC	11,114	C
Franciscan Univ of Steubenville	OH	20,300	VC
Franklin and Marshall College	PA	40,590	HC
Franklin College	IN		C
Freed-Hardeman Univ	TN	16,370	NC
Fresno Pacific Univ	CA	25,454	C
Friends Univ	KS	16,250	LC
Frostburg State Univ	MD	12,672	C
Furman Univ	SC	33,264	HC+
Gallaudet Univ	DC	16,554	
Gannon Univ	PA	26,100	C
Gardner-Webb Univ	NC	21,500	C
Geneva College	PA	21,850	C
George Fox Univ	OR	28,490	C
George Mason Univ	VA	10,850	VC
George Washington Univ	DC	48,820	MC
Georgetown College	KY	24,950	C+
Georgetown Univ	DC	43,183	MC
Georgia College and State Univ	GA	11,020	C
Georgia Inst of Technology	GA	11,450	HC+
Georgia Southern Univ	GA	9,762	C
Georgia Southwestern State Univ	GA	6,035	C
Georgia State Univ	GA	11,444	VC
Georgian Court College	NJ	20,000	LC
Gettysburg College	PA	39,864	HC
Glenville State College	WV	8,778	NC
Gonzaga Univ	WA	30,218	HC
Gordon College	MA	29,194	C+
Goshen College	IN	22,850	VC
Goucher College	MD	36,225	VC
Graceland Univ	IA	19,700	C
Grambling State Univ	LA	6,538	NC
Grand Canyon Univ	AZ	32,000	LC
Grand Valley State Univ	MI	12,000	VC
Greensboro College	NC	23,000	C
Greenville College	IL	23,146	C
Grinnell College	IA	34,814	HC+
Grove City College	PA	15,784	HC+
Guilford College	NC	28,160	C
Gustavus Adolphus College	MN	30,920	HC
Hamilton College	NY	41,660	MC
Hamline Univ	MN	27,070	VC
Hampden-Sydney College	VA	31,148	VC
Hampshire College	MA	37,120	HC
Hampton Univ	VA	19,468	C+
Hanover College	IN	28,150	HC
Harding Univ	AR	16,512	VC
Hardin-Simmons Univ	TX	18,641	C
Hartwick College	NY	36,065	C
Harvard Univ/Harvard College	MA	45,860	MC
Harvey Mudd College	CA	42,352	MC
Hastings College	NE	22,218	VC
Haverford College	PA	41,600	MC
Heidelberg College	OH	23,242	C
Henderson State Univ	AR	7,600	C
Hendrix College	AR	27,646	HC+
High Point Univ	NC	25,720	C
Hillsdale College	MI	24,160	HC
Hiram College	OH	28,700	VC
Hobart and William Smith Colleges	NY	41,123	VC
Hofstra Univ	NY	32,630	VC
Hollins Univ	VA	31,105	C
Holy Family Univ	PA	25,740	C
Hood College	MD	30,085	VC
Hope College	MI	28,208	VC+
Houghton College	NY	25,980	VC+
Houston Baptist Univ	TX	18,660	C
Howard Payne Univ	TX	17,115	C
Howard Univ	DC	18,481	C+
Humboldt State Univ	CA	11,176	C
Huntingdon College	AL	23,090	VC
Huntington Univ	IN	24,830	C
Huston-Tillotson Univ	TX	14,232	LC
Idaho State Univ	ID	9,030	C
Illinois College	IL	21,900	C+
Illinois Inst of Technology	IL	26,465	HC+
Illinois State Univ	IL	12,839	C+
Illinois Wesleyan Univ	IL	34,050	HC+
Indiana State Univ	IN	11,604	C
Indiana Univ Bloomington	IN	13,356	VC
Indiana Univ Kokomo	IN	4,835	LC
Indiana Univ Northwest	IN	4,902	LC
Indiana Univ of Pennsylvania	PA	11,209	C
Indiana Univ South Bend	IN	4,989	LC
Indiana Univ Southeast	IN	4,880	LC
Indiana Univ-Purdue Univ Fort Wayne	IN	5,067	LC
Indiana Univ-Purdue Univ Indianapolis	IN	10,959	C
Indiana Wesleyan Univ	IN	22,074	C+
Inter American Univ of PR/Arecibo Campus	PR	3,350	
Inter American Univ of PR/Bayamon Univ College	PR	3,522	
Inter American Univ of PR/Fajardo Campus	PR	4,000	
Inter American Univ of PR/Metropolitan Campus	PR	4,320	
Inter American Univ of PR/Ponce Regional College	PR	3,700	
Inter American Univ of PR/San German	PR	6,720	
Iona College	NY	30,878	VC
Iowa State Univ	IA	11,831	VC
Iowa Wesleyan College	IA	22,140	C
Ithaca College	NY	35,144	VC
Jackson State Univ	MS	8,500	C
Jacksonville State Univ	AL	7,618	LC
Jacksonville Univ	FL	24,040	C
James Madison Univ	VA	12,010	VC
Jamestown College	ND	14,130	NC
Jarvis Christian College	TX	11,136	NC
John Brown Univ	AR	20,910	VC
John Carroll Univ	OH	27,658	C+
Johns Hopkins Univ	MD	42,044	MC
Johnson C. Smith Univ	NC	20,000	C
Judson College	AL	16,522	C
Judson College	IL	25,130	C
Juniata College	PA	33,130	C
Kalamazoo College	MI	32,442	VC+
Kansas State Univ	KS	10,516	VC
Kansas Wesleyan Univ	KS	21,400	VC
Kean Univ	NJ	15,880	C
Keene State College	NH	13,836	C
Kennesaw State Univ	GA	12,152	C
Kent State Univ	OH	14,594	C
Kentucky State Univ	KY	10,089	LC
Kentucky Wesleyan College	KY	18,590	C
Kenyon College	OH	39,500	MC
Kettering Univ	MI	29,338	HC
King College	TN	23,400	C
King's College	PA	29,810	C
Knox College	IL	32,385	VC+
Knoxville College	TN	6,200	LC
Kutztown Univ of Pennsylvania	PA	10,820	C
La Roche College	PA	24,724	LC
La Salle Univ	PA	34,950	C
La Sierra Univ	CA	24,327	C+
Lafayette College	PA	39,267	MC
LaGrange College	GA	22,874	C+
Lake Erie College	OH	27,725	C
Lake Forest College	IL	33,860	VC
Lakeland College	WI	22,990	C
Lamar Univ	TX	6,820	C
Lambuth University	TN	21,700	C+
Lander Univ	SC	10,600	C
Lane College	TN	11,220	C+
Langston Univ	OK	2,308	LC
Lawrence Tech Univ	MI	25,475	VC
Lawrence Univ	WI	33,958	HC+
Lebanon Valley College	PA	31,700	VC
Lee Univ	TN	14,780	NC
Lehigh Univ	PA	42,690	HC+
LeMoyne-Owen College	TN	13,150	LC
Lenoir-Rhyne College	NC	25,580	C
LeTourneau Univ	TX	21,200	C
Lewis and Clark College	OR	35,358	VC+
Lewis Univ	IL	23,050	C+
Lewis-Clark State College	ID	6,990	C
Limestone College	SC	19,840	C
Lincoln Memorial Univ	TN	18,144	C
Lincoln Univ	MO	8,000	NC
Lincoln Univ	PA	13,658	C+
Lindenwood Univ	MO	18,600	VC
Linfield College	OR	29,632	VC
Lipscomb Univ	TN	20,967	VC
Livingstone College	NC	17,815	LC
Lock Haven Univ of Pennsylvania	PA	12,098	LC
LIU/Brooklyn Campus	NY	25,000	C
LIU/C.W. Post Campus	NY	28,282	C
Longwood Univ	VA	12,426	C
Loras College	IA	27,193	C
Louisiana College	LA	13,450	C
Louisiana State Univ and A&M College	LA	10,749	VC
Louisiana State Univ in Shreveport	LA	2,900	NC
Louisiana Tech Univ	LA	7,370	C
Loyola College in Maryland	MD	38,898	HC
Loyola Marymount Univ	CA	36,321	VC
Loyola Univ Chicago	IL	32,896	VC
Loyola Univ New Orleans	LA	31,050	VC+
Lubbock Christian Univ	TX	16,960	C
Luther College	IA	28,800	VC+
Lycoming College	PA	30,797	C+
Lynchburg College	VA	30,645	C
Lyon College	AR	19,990	VC
Macalester College	MN	36,500	MC
MacMurray College	IL	20,755	C
Madonna Univ	MI	16,068	VC
Malone College	OH	23,040	C
Manchester College	IN	23,470	C
Manhattan College	NY	29,000	VC
Manhattanville College	NY	32,500	C+
Mansfield Univ	PA	11,300	C
Marian College	IN	26,160	C
Marian College of Fond du Lac	WI	21,775	LC
Marietta College	OH	29,327	C
Marist College	NY	30,566	VC
Marlboro College	VT	35,980	VC+
Marquette Univ	WI	31,066	HC
Mars Hill College	NC	19,000	LC
Marshall Univ	WV	9,116	C
Martin Univ	IN	10,300	SP
Mary Baldwin College	VA	26,465	C
Marygrove College	MI	19,310	C+
Maryville College	TN	29,224	VC
Maryville Univ of St. Louis	MO	23,000	VC
Mass College of Pharmacy and Health Sciences	MA	32,020	SP
Mass Inst of Technology	MA	41,800	MC
Mayville State Univ	ND	8,667	NC
McDaniel College	MD	31,610	VC
McKendree College	IL	24,800	VC
McMurry Univ	TX	18,100	LC
McNeese State Univ	LA	5,270	LC
McPherson College	KS	21,010	C
Mercer Univ	GA	27,525	VC+
Mercyhurst College	PA	28,633	VC
Meredith College	NC	25,600	C
Merrimack College	MA	34,380	C
Messiah College	PA	28,910	VC+
Methodist College	NC	21,000	C
Metropolitan State College of Denver	CO	2,338	LC
Miami Univ	OH	29,097	HC
Mich State Univ	MI	13,689	VC
Mich Tech Univ	MI	14,569	VC
MidAmerica Nazarene Univ	KS	20,584	C
Middle Tenn State Univ	TN	8,540	C
Middlebury College	VT	42,120	MC
Midland Lutheran College	NE	18,600	C
Midway College	KY	20,150	C
Midwestern State Univ	TX	9,381	LC
Miles College	AL	9,922	NC
Millersville Univ of Pennsylvania	PA	12,113	C
Milligan College	TN	21,990	VC
Millikin Univ	IL	25,590	C
Mills College	CA	39,870	C
Millsaps College	MS	28,256	VC+
Minn State Univ, Mankato	MN	10,276	LC
Minn State Univ, Moorhead	MN	7,000	LC
Minot State Univ	ND	6,700	LC
Miss College	MS	14,574	VC
Miss State Univ	MS	9,577	C
Miss Univ for Women	MS	6,000	LC
Miss Valley State Univ	MS	7,970	C
Missouri Baptist Univ	MO	19,640	C
Missouri Southern State Univ	MO	8,396	NC
Missouri State Univ	MO	10,748	C+
Missouri Western State Univ	MO	9,534	NC
Monmouth College	IL	23,700	C
Monmouth Univ	NJ	28,956	C
Montana State Univ-Billings	MT	8,906	C

School	ST	$IS	SR
Montana State Univ-Bozeman	MT	1,137	C
Montana State Univ-Northern	MT	10,000	NC
Montana Tech of The Univ of Montana	MT	10,434	C
Montclair State Univ	NJ	16,327	C
Moravian College	PA	28,950	VC
Morehead State Univ	KY	9,150	C
Morehouse College	GA	25,082	C
Morgan State Univ	MD	12,080	C
Morningside College	IA	23,704	C
Mount Holyoke College	MA	42,148	HC+
Mount Marty College	SD	20,590	C
Mount Mary College	WI	22,895	C
Mount St. Mary College	NY	25,250	C
Mount St. Mary's College	CA	32,086	VC
Mount St. Mary's Univ	MD	30,930	C
Mount Union College	OH	25,840	C
Mount Vernon Nazarene Univ	OH	20,810	C
Muhlenberg College	PA	36,030	HC+
Murray State Univ	KY	8,900	C
Muskingum College	OH	22,970	C
Nazareth College of Rochester	NY	28,175	VC
Nebr Wesleyan Univ	NE	23,415	C+
New College of Florida	FL	10,009	HC+
New Jersey City Univ	NJ	13,695	LC
New Jersey Inst of Technology	NJ	16,396	VC
New Mexico Highlands Univ	NM	6,272	NC
New Mexico Inst of Mining and Technology	NM	8,510	VC+
New Mexico State Univ	NM	9,250	C
New York Inst of Technology	NY	28,126	VC
New York Univ	NY	43,170	MC
Newberry College	SC	23,000	LC
Newman Univ	KS	21,106	C
Niagara Univ	NY	28,250	C
Nicholls State Univ	LA	6,500	NC
Norfolk State Univ	VA	10,531	LC
N Car Agricultural and Technical State Univ	NC	8,000	LC
N Car Central Univ	NC	9,000	LC
N Car State Univ	NC	11,824	NC
N Car Wesleyan College	NC	22,670	C
North Central College	IL	28,926	VC
N Dak State Univ	ND	8,500	C
North Georgia College and State Univ	GA	7,000	C
North Park Univ	IL	24,050	C
Northeastern Illinois Univ	IL	3,000	NC
Northeastern State Univ	OK	5,896	LC
Northeastern Univ	MA	35,742	HC
Northern Arizona Univ	AZ	10,353	C
Northern Illinois Univ	IL	13,178	C
Northern Kentucky Univ	KY	6,670	NC
Northern Mich Univ	MI	12,340	LC
Northern State Univ	SD	8,257	C
Northland College	WI	26,680	C+
Northwest Missouri State Univ	MO	10,000	C
Northwest Nazarene Univ	ID	22,590	VC
Northwestern College of Iowa	IA	22,174	C+
Northwestern Okla State Univ	OK	6,250	NC
Northwestern State Univ of Louisiana	LA	7,144	C
Northwestern Univ	IL	37,595	MC
Norwich Univ	VT	28,212	C
Notre Dame College	OH	20,425	C
Oakland Univ	MI	11,936	C
Oakwood Univ	AL	14,904	C
Oberlin College	OH	40,904	MC
Occidental College	CA	40,185	MC
Oglethorpe Univ	GA	30,300	VC
Ohio Dominican Univ	OH	25,954	C
Ohio Northern Univ	OH	27,765	VC
Ohio State Univ	OH	15,357	HC
Ohio Univ	OH	15,921	C
Ohio Wesleyan Univ	OH	35,830	VC+
Okla Baptist Univ	OK	17,986	VC
Okla Christian Univ	OK	18,992	NC
Okla City Univ	OK	23,965	VC
Okla Panhandle State Univ	OK	7,635	NC
Okla State Univ	OK	10,213	VC
Okla Wesleyan Univ	OK	18,950	NC
Old Dominion Univ	VA	11,907	C
Olivet College	MI	19,984	C+
Olivet Nazarene Univ	IL	22,590	C
Oral Roberts Univ	OK	22,650	C
Oregon State Univ	OR	11,055	C
Ottawa Univ	KS	12,000	LC
Otterbein College	OH	28,986	C
Ouachita Baptist Univ	AR	21,900	VC
Our Lady of the Lake Univ of San Antonio	TX	22,430	LC
Pace Univ	NY	30,000	VC
Pacific Lutheran Univ	WA	28,805	VC
Pacific Union College	CA	24,555	VC+
Pacific Univ	OR	24,250	C
Paine College	GA	14,418	LC
Park Univ	MO	11,592	C

School	ST	$IS	SR
Penn State Erie/The Behrend College	PA	16,256	C
Penn State Univ/Univ Park Campus	PA	18,038	HC
Pepperdine Univ	CA	39,960	HC
Pfeiffer Univ	NC	21,900	C
Philadelphia Univ	PA	30,006	C
Philander Smith College	AR	13,230	LC
Piedmont College	GA	20,500	C
Pikeville College	KY	16,500	NC
Pittsburg State Univ	KS	8,112	C
Pitzer College	CA	41,644	HC
Plymouth State Univ	NH	12,298	LC
Point Loma Nazarene Univ	CA	27,610	VC
Polytechnic Univ/Brooklyn	NY	37,150	VC
Pomona College	CA	40,774	MC
Pontifical Catholic Univ of PR/Ponce	PR	7,310	
Portland State Univ	OR	12,453	C
Prairie View A&M Univ	TX	11,110	LC
Presbyterian College	SC	30,044	VC
Princeton Univ	NJ	40,213	MC
Principia College	IL	27,765	VC+
Providence College	RI	34,580	HC
Purdue Univ/Calumet	IN	10,891	LC
Purdue Univ/West Lafayette	IN	13,458	VC
Quincy Univ	IL	24,920	C
Quinnipiac Univ	CT	34,640	VC
Radford Univ	VA	13,145	C
Ramapo College of New Jersey	NJ	16,630	VC
Randolph-Macon College	VA	31,250	C
Randolph-Macon Woman's College	VA	31,160	VC+
Reed College	OR	41,106	MC
Regis Univ	CO	31,890	C
Rensselaer Polytechnic Inst	NY	41,288	HC+
Rhode Island College	RI	11,570	C
Rhodes College	TN	32,860	HC
Rice Univ	TX	32,290	MC
Richard Stockton College of New Jersey	NJ	14,000	VC
Rider Univ	NJ	32,560	C
Ripon College	WI	27,160	C+
Roanoke College	VA	30,748	VC
Roberts Wesleyan College	NY	26,378	C
Rochester Inst of Technology	NY	32,070	VC+
Rockford College	IL	28,330	VC
Rockhurst Univ	MO	25,440	VC
Rocky Mountain College	MT	20,805	C
Roger Williams Univ	RI	30,500	C
Rollins College	FL	38,366	VC
Roosevelt Univ	IL	22,605	VC
Rose-Hulman Inst of Technology	IN	34,557	HC+
Rosemont College	PA	29,350	C
Rowan Univ	NJ	16,000	VC
Russell Sage College	NY	27,000	C
Rust College	MS		C+
Rutgers, The State Univ of New Jersey/Camden Campus	NJ	15,000	C
Rutgers, The State Univ of New Jersey/New Brunswick/Piscataway Campus	NJ	15,810	HC
Rutgers, The State Univ of New Jersey/Newark Campus	NJ	15,640	VC
Sacred Heart Univ	CT	33,404	C
Saginaw Valley State Univ	MI	11,432	C
St. Ambrose Univ	IA	25,495	C
St. Andrews Presbyterian College	NC	23,530	C
St. Anselm College	NH	33,810	C
St. Augustine's College	NC	14,000	VC
St. Bonaventure Univ	NY	28,785	LC
St. Cloud State Univ	MN	10,010	C
St. Edward's Univ	TX	23,560	C
St. Francis Univ	PA	25,880	LC
St. John Fisher College	NY	27,860	C
St. John's Univ	MN	29,749	VC
St. John's Univ	NY	34,370	C
St. Joseph College	CT	32,050	C
St. Joseph's College	IN	26,600	C
St. Joseph's College of Maine	ME	29,185	C
St. Joseph's College, New York, Brooklyn Campus	NY	12,206	C
St. Joseph's Univ	PA	37,428	VC
St. Lawrence Univ	NY	40,545	VC
St. Louis Univ	MO	33,158	VC+
St. Martin's Univ	WA	27,555	C
St. Mary's College	IN	32,538	VC
St. Mary's College of Calif	CA	37,290	C
St. Mary's College of Maryland	MD	18,876	VC+
St. Mary's Univ of Minn	MN	23,857	VC
St. Mary's Univ of San Antonio	TX	22,444	C
St. Michael's College	VT	33,330	VC
St. Norbert College	WI	28,577	C+
St. Olaf College	MN	32,800	HC
St. Peter's College	NJ	30,160	LC
St. Vincent College	PA	26,160	VC

School	ST	$IS	SR
St. Xavier Univ	IL	23,160	C
Salem College	NC	26,226	VC+
Salem State College	MA	13,161	LC
Salisbury Univ	MD	13,128	VC
Salve Regina Univ	RI	33,450	C
Sam Houston State Univ	TX	8,000	C
Samford Univ	AL	20,258	VC
San Diego State Univ	CA	12,971	C
San Francisco State Univ	CA	13,000	C
San Jose State Univ	CA	11,707	C
Santa Clara Univ	CA	38,931	VC
Sarah Lawrence College	NY	42,000	HC
Savannah State Univ	GA	7,772	LC
Schreiner Univ	TX	20,600	C
Scripps College	CA	41,000	MC
Seattle Pacific Univ	WA	29,355	C
Seattle Univ	WA	30,063	VC
Seton Hall Univ	NJ	33,622	VC
Seton Hill Univ	PA	28,810	C
Shaw Univ	NC	15,488	LC
Shawnee State Univ	OH	12,237	NC
Shenandoah Univ	VA	27,600	C
Shepherd Univ	WV	10,066	C
Shippensburg Univ of Pennsylvania	PA	11,621	C
Shorter College	GA	19,700	C
Siena College	NY	28,260	VC+
Siena Heights Univ	MI	17,000	LC
Simmons College	MA	35,640	VC
Simon's Rock College of Bard	MA	41,988	VC+
Simpson College	IA	26,833	VC
Skidmore College	NY	41,779	HC
Slippery Rock Univ of Pennsylvania	PA	10,360	LC
Smith College	MA	41,474	MC
Sonoma State Univ	CA	14,732	C
S Car State Univ	SC	6,700	LC
S Dak School of Mines and Technology	SD	7,624	C+
S Dak State Univ	SD	9,815	C
Southeast Missouri State Univ	MO	10,596	C
Southeastern Louisiana Univ	LA	8,521	LC
Southeastern Okla State Univ	OK	6,147	C
Southern Adventist Univ	TN	18,500	C
Southern Arkansas Univ	AR	6,956	C
Southern Conn State Univ	CT	10,310	C
Southern Illinois Univ Carbondale	IL	12,391	C
Southern Illinois Univ Edwardsville	IL	11,022	C
Southern Methodist Univ	TX	36,088	VC+
Southern Nazarene Univ	OK	14,634	NC
Southern Oregon Univ	OR	12,186	C
Southern Univ and A&M College	LA	8,238	LC
Southern Univ at New Orleans	LA	1,000	NC
Southern Utah Univ	UT		C
Southern Wesleyan Univ	SC	21,675	C
Southwest Baptist Univ	MO	18,300	C
Southwest Minn State Univ	MN	10,975	C
Southwestern Adventist Univ	TX	18,290	LC
Southwestern College	KS	21,476	C
Southwestern Okla State Univ	OK	4,801	C
Southwestern Univ	TX	26,767	HC
Spelman College	GA	24,650	VC
Spring Arbor Univ	MI	22,476	C
Spring Hill College	AL	28,678	C
Springfield College	MA	25,000	C
Stanford Univ	CA	41,557	MC
SUNY at Oswego	NY	13,662	VC
SUNY at Potsdam	NY	12,959	C
SUNY/College at Brockport	NY	12,747	VC
SUNY/College at Buffalo	NY	11,903	C+
SUNY/College at Cortland	NY	12,095	C
SUNY/College at Fredonia	NY	12,771	VC
SUNY/College at Geneseo	NY	12,910	HC+
SUNY/College at Old Westbury	NY	13,154	C
SUNY/College at Oneonta	NY	12,905	VC
SUNY/College at Plattsburgh	NY	12,362	C
SUNY/College at Purchase	NY	11,989	VC+
SUNY/College of Environmental Science and Forestry	NY	15,000	VC
SUNY/Univ at Albany	NY	13,860	VC
SUNY/Univ at Binghamton	NY	13,988	HC
SUNY/Univ at Buffalo	NY	13,694	VC
SUNY/Univ at New Paltz	NY	12,480	VC
SUNY/Univ at Stony Brook	NY	13,625	HC
Stephen F. Austin State Univ	TX	7,930	C
Sterling College	KS	19,992	C
Stetson Univ	FL	32,725	VC
Stevens Inst of Technology	NJ	40,935	HC
Stonehill College	MA	36,104	HC
Suffolk Univ	MA	33,160	C
Sul Ross State Univ	TX	6,600	LC
Susquehanna Univ	PA	33,465	VC

School	ST	$IS	SR
Swarthmore College	PA	41,280	MC
Sweet Briar College	VA	31,460	VC
Syracuse Univ	NY	38,655	HC
Tabor College	KS	21,614	NC
Talladega College	AL	11,240	LC
Tarleton State Univ	TX	8,952	C
Taylor Univ	IN	26,376	VC+
Temple Univ	PA	17,438	C
Tenn State Univ	TN	9,048	LC
Tenn Tech Univ	TN	10,044	C
Tenn Wesleyan College	TN	18,650	C
Texas A&M Univ	TX	13,351	HC
Texas A&M Univ at Commerce	TX	9,020	C
Texas A&M Univ at Corpus Christi	TX	10,280	LC
Texas A&M Univ at Kingsville	TX	6,800	LC
Texas Christian Univ	TX	23,410	VC+
Texas Lutheran Univ	TX	23,530	C
Texas Southern Univ	TX	9,828	C
Texas State Univ - San Marcos	TX	10,862	C
Texas Tech Univ	TX	13,026	VC
Texas Wesleyan Univ	TX	18,700	C
Texas Woman's Univ	TX	7,804	LC
Thiel College	PA	24,580	C
Thomas More College	KY	24,470	C
Tougaloo College	MS	15,975	NC
Touro College	NY	17,000	C
Towson Univ	MD	13,924	VC
Transylvania Univ	KY	26,240	VC+
Trevecca Nazarene Univ	TN	19,594	C
Trinity Christian College	IL	23,645	C
Trinity College	CT	38,040	HC+
Trinity College	DC	24,150	LC
Trinity International Univ	IL	25,686	C
Trinity Univ	TX	30,157	HC+
Tri-State Univ-Main Campus	IN	26,200	C
Troy Univ	AL	8,916	C
Troy Univ Dothan Campus	AL	4,678	C
Truman State Univ	MO	11,242	HC
Tufts Univ	MA	42,018	MC
Tulane Univ	LA	41,098	HC
Turabo Univ	PR	4,110	
Tuskegee Univ	AL	18,860	LC
Union College	KY	18,920	C
Union College	NE	18,710	C
Union College	NY	41,595	HC
Union Univ	TN	20,750	VC
United States Air Force Academy	CO		HC+
United States Military Academy	NY		MC
United States Naval Academy	MD		MC
Univ of Akron	OH	15,166	NC
Univ of Alabama	AL	9,888	C
Univ of Alabama at Birmingham	AL	13,716	C
Univ of Alabama in Huntsville	AL	9,516	VC
Univ of Alaska Anchorage	AK	11,275	NC
Univ of Alaska Fairbanks	AK	10,101	C
Univ of Arizona	AZ	11,958	VC
Univ of Arkansas	AR	11,859	VC
Univ of Arkansas at Little Rock	AR	7,230	NC
Univ of Arkansas at Monticello	AR	7,325	NC
Univ of Arkansas at Pine Bluff	AR	8,300	C
Univ of at Calif Davis	CA	15,010	VC
Univ of Calif at Berkeley	CA	18,141	HC+
Univ of Calif at Irvine	CA	16,475	HC
Univ of Calif at Los Angeles	CA	17,681	MC
Univ of Calif at Riverside	CA	16,625	C
Univ of Calif at San Diego	CA	16,102	HC
Univ of Calif at Santa Barbara	CA	11,800	VC
Univ of Calif at Santa Cruz	CA	19,174	VC
Univ of Central Arkansas	AR	9,984	C
Univ of Central Florida	FL	10,739	VC
Univ of Central Okla	OK	8,094	C
Univ of Charleston	WV	27,600	C
Univ of Chicago	IL	42,369	MC
Univ of Cincinnati	OH	17,682	C
Univ of Colo at Boulder	CO	13,352	C+
Univ of Colo at Colo Springs	CO	11,517	VC
Univ of Colo at Denver and Health Sciences Center	CO	5,021	C
Univ of Conn	CT	16,628	HC
Univ of Dallas	TX	27,432	VC+
Univ of Dayton	OH	28,826	VC
Univ of Delaware	DE	14,142	HC
Univ of Denver	CO	36,376	VC+
Univ of Detroit Mercy	MI	27,000	C
Univ of Evansville	IN	28,320	VC
Univ of Findlay	OH	29,238	C
Univ of Florida	FL	9,354	HC
Univ of Georgia	GA	11,004	HC
Univ of Hartford	CT	34,044	C
Univ of Hawaii at Hilo	HI	6,500	C
Univ of Hawaii at Manoa	HI	10,413	VC

ST = STATE   **$IS** = IN-STATE COSTS   **SR** = SELECTOR RATING

School	ST	$IS	SR
Univ of Houston	TX	7,000	C
Univ of Idaho	ID	9,310	NC
Univ of Illinois at Chicago	IL	16,256	VC
Univ of Illinois at Urbana-Champaign	IL	15,800	HC+
Univ of Indianapolis	IN	25,090	C
Univ of Iowa	IA	12,172	VC
Univ of Kansas	KS	10,915	VC
Univ of Kentucky	KY	7,800	C
Univ of La Verne	CA	33,470	C
Univ of Louisiana at Lafayette	LA	5,830	C
Univ of Louisiana at Monroe	LA	7,103	C
Univ of Louisville	KY	10,400	VC
Univ of Maine	ME	13,642	C
Univ of Mary Hardin-Baylor	TX	19,428	C
Univ of Mary Washington	VA	11,636	HC
Univ of Maryland/Baltimore County	MD	16,642	VC+
Univ of Maryland/College Park	MD	16,036	HC
Univ of Maryland/Eastern Shore	MD	11,210	C
Univ of Mass Amherst	MA	15,973	C+
Univ of Mass Boston	MA	8,024	C
Univ of Mass Dartmouth	MA	15,985	C
Univ of Mass Lowell	MA	14,327	VC
Univ of Memphis	TN	11,153	C
Univ of Miami	FL	38,397	MC
Univ of Mich/Ann Arbor	MI	16,587	HC+
Univ of Mich/Dearborn	MI	7,000	VC
Univ of Mich/Flint	MI	6,398	C
Univ of Minn/Duluth	MN	13,974	C
Univ of Minn/Morris	MN	15,472	VC
Univ of Minn/Twin Cities	MN	13,165	HC
Univ of Miss	MS	9,000	C
Univ of Missouri/Columbia	MO	13,500	VC
Univ of Missouri/Kansas City	MO	15,000	VC
Univ of Missouri/Rolla	MO	13,332	HC
Univ of Missouri/St. Louis	MO	14,046	VC
Univ of Montana	MT	10,602	C
Univ of Montevallo	AL	9,630	C
Univ of Nebr at Kearney	NE	9,000	NC
Univ of Nebr at Lincoln	NE	11,401	VC
Univ of Nebr at Omaha	NE	11,235	C
Univ of Nevada/Las Vegas	NV	11,566	C
Univ of Nevada/Reno	NV	12,155	VC
Univ of New England	ME	31,005	C
Univ of New Hampshire	NH	16,810	VC
Univ of New Haven	CT	31,794	C
Univ of New Mexico	NM	11,253	C
Univ of New Orleans	LA	7,370	C
Univ of North Alabama	AL	8,992	C
Univ of N Car at Asheville	NC	9,237	VC
Univ of N Car at Chapel Hill	NC	11,129	MC
Univ of N Car at Charlotte	NC	9,101	C
Univ of N Car at Greensboro	NC	8,993	C
Univ of N Car at Pembroke	NC	7,940	LC
Univ of N Car at Wilmington	NC	10,107	VC
Univ of N Dak	ND	10,114	VC
Univ of North Florida	FL	9,908	VC
Univ of North Texas	TX	7,800	C
Univ of Northern Colo	CO	10,249	C
Univ of Northern Iowa	IA	11,133	C
Univ of Notre Dame	IN	39,552	MC
Univ of Okla	OK	10,769	VC+
Univ of Oregon	OR	13,108	VC
Univ of Pennsylvania	PA	41,766	MC
Univ of Pittsburgh at Bradford	PA	17,008	C
Univ of Pittsburgh at Johnstown	PA	16,740	C
Univ of Pittsburgh at Pittsburgh	PA	18,866	HC
Univ of Portland	OR	32,300	C
Univ of PR at Humacao	PR	1,707	
Univ of PR/Cayey Univ College	PR	1,250	
Univ of PR/Mayaguez	PR	1,250	
Univ of PR/Rio Piedras	PR	5,750	
Univ of Puget Sound	WA	35,600	HC
Univ of Redlands	CA	36,160	VC
Univ of Rhode Island	RI	15,398	C
Univ of Richmond	VA	40,510	MC
Univ of Rio Grande	OH	8,728	NC
Univ of Rochester	NY	41,135	MC
Univ of St. Francis	IN	20,970	C
Univ of St. Mary	KS	18,900	C
Univ of St. Thomas	MN	28,000	VC
Univ of St. Thomas	TX	23,810	VC
Univ of San Diego	CA	40,620	HC
Univ of San Francisco	CA	37,560	VC
Univ of Science and Arts of Okla	OK	7,650	C
Univ of Scranton	PA	31,100	C
Univ of Sioux Falls	SD	20,800	C
Univ of South Alabama	AL	8,930	LC
Univ of S Car at Aiken	SC	11,718	LC
Univ of S Car at Columbia	SC	13,397	VC
Univ of S Car Upstate	SC	11,957	C
Univ of S Dak	SD	9,068	C
Univ of South Florida	FL	10,284	VC
Univ of Southern Calif	CA	41,618	MC
Univ of Southern Indiana	IN	12,590	LC

School	ST	$IS	SR
Univ of Southern Maine	ME	12,614	C
Univ of Southern Miss	MS	10,112	C
Univ of Tampa	FL	25,784	C
Univ of Tenn at Chattanooga	TN	7,790	C
Univ of Tenn at Knoxville	TN	11,720	C
Univ of Tenn at Martin	TN	8,693	C
Univ of Texas at Arlington	TX	7,195	LC
Univ of Texas at Austin	TX	14,610	HC
Univ of Texas at Dallas	TX	13,244	HC
Univ of Texas at El Paso	TX	8,764	NC
Univ of Texas at San Antonio	TX	11,325	LC
Univ of Texas-Pan American	TX	7,290	C+
Univ of the Cumberlands	KY	18,184	C
Univ of the District of Columbia	DC	2,070	LC
Univ of the Incarnate Word	TX	23,306	C
Univ of the Ozarks	AR	19,250	C
Univ of the Pacific	CA	34,380	VC
Univ of the Sacred Heart	PR	5,590	
Univ of the Sciences in Philadelphia	PA	33,380	VC
Univ of the South	TN	34,645	HC
Univ of Toledo	OH	15,806	NC
Univ of Tulsa	OK	25,348	HC
Univ of Utah	UT	10,162	VC
Univ of Vermont	VT	18,080	VC
Univ of Virginia	VA	13,759	MC
Univ of Virginia's College at Wise	VA	11,076	C
Univ of West Alabama	AL	7,611	C
Univ of West Florida	FL	8,559	C
Univ of West Georgia	GA	8,838	C
Univ of Wisc/Eau Claire	WI	9,915	VC
Univ of Wisc/Green Bay	WI	9,415	VC
Univ of Wisc/La Crosse	WI	10,045	VC
Univ of Wisc/Madison	WI	13,117	HC
Univ of Wisc/Milwaukee	WI	9,427	LC
Univ of Wisc/Oshkosh	WI	10,426	LC
Univ of Wisc/Parkside	WI	10,181	LC
Univ of Wisc/Platteville	WI	9,779	NC
Univ of Wisc/River Falls	WI	9,722	LC
Univ of Wisc/Stevens Point	WI	9,384	VC
Univ of Wisc/Superior	WI	9,610	C+
Univ of Wisc/Whitewater	WI	9,274	C
Univ of Wyoming	WY	9,666	C
Upper Iowa Univ	IA	20,130	C
Ursinus College	PA	38,950	VC
Utah State Univ	UT	8,002	VC
Utica College	NY	31,396	C
Valdosta State Univ	GA	8,802	C
Valley City State Univ	ND	9,854	LC
Valparaiso Univ	IN	28,970	VC+
Vanderbilt Univ	TN	41,986	MC
Vanguard Univ of Southern Calif	CA	27,071	C
Vassar College	NY	41,700	MC
Villa Julie College	MD	25,222	C
Villanova Univ	PA	38,672	HC+
Virginia Commonwealth Univ	VA	12,987	C
Virginia Military Inst	VA	12,654	VC
Virginia Polytechnic Inst and State Univ	VA	10,834	VC
Virginia State Univ	VA	11,318	C
Virginia Union Univ	VA	18,432	LC
Virginia Wesleyan College	VA	28,433	C
Viterbo Univ	WI	21,670	C
Wabash College	IN	30,116	HC
Wagner College	NY	33,300	VC
Wake Forest Univ	NC	38,290	MC
Walla Walla College	WA	24,489	NC
Walsh Univ	OH	23,440	C
Warren Wilson College	NC	24,382	VC
Wartburg College	IA	27,315	NC
Washburn Univ	KS	9,734	NC
Washington and Jefferson College	PA	33,490	VC
Washington and Lee Univ	VA	35,880	MC
Washington College	MD	34,990	VC
Washington State Univ	WA	12,260	C
Washington Univ in St. Louis	MO	42,106	MC
Wayland Baptist Univ	TX	13,484	C
Wayne State College	NE	8,033	NC
Wayne State Univ	MI	11,805	C
Waynesburg College	PA	21,230	C
Weber State Univ	UT	9,635	NC
Wellesley College	MA	41,030	MC
Wells College	NY	23,070	VC
Wesleyan College	GA	19,560	C
Wesleyan Univ	CT	42,122	MC
West Chester Univ of Pennsylvania	PA	12,355	C+
West Liberty State College	WV	9,142	LC
West Texas A&M Univ	TX	8,452	C
West Virginia State Univ	WV	8,378	NC
West Virginia Univ	WV	10,506	C
West Virginia Univ Inst of Technology	WV	8,788	NC
West Virginia Wesleyan College	WV	26,880	C
Western Carolina Univ	NC	7,000	C
Western Conn State Univ	CT	12,993	C

School	ST	$IS	SR
Western Illinois Univ	IL	13,042	C
Western Kentucky Univ	KY	10,192	C
Western Mich Univ	MI	13,299	C
Western New England College	MA	32,054	C
Western New Mexico Univ	NM	7,233	LC
Western Oregon Univ	OR	10,295	C
Western State College of Colo	CO	9,942	C
Western Washington Univ	WA	11,262	VC
Westminster College	MO	19,060	VC
Westminster College	PA	31,290	C+
Westminster College	UT	25,656	C
Westmont College	CA	36,672	HC
Wheaton College	IL	27,760	HC
Wheaton College	MA	40,180	HC+
Wheeling Jesuit Univ	WV	26,910	C
Whitman College	WA	36,110	HC+
Whittier College	CA	29,108	C
Whitworth College	WA	29,428	VC+
Wichita State Univ	KS	8,500	C
Widener Univ	PA	27,275	C
Wilberforce Univ	OH	14,937	LC
Wiley College	TX	8,100	LC
Wilkes Univ	PA	30,886	C
Willamette Univ	OR	35,416	VC+
William Carey College	MS	11,000	C
William Jewell College	MO	24,340	C
William Paterson Univ of New Jersey	NJ	17,810	C+
Williams College	MA	40,310	MC
Wilmington College	OH	2,806	NC
Wilson College	PA	27,660	C
Wingate Univ	NC	23,300	C
Winona State Univ	MN	11,333	C
Winston-Salem State Univ	NC	8,960	LC
Winthrop Univ	SC	11,302	C
Wisc Lutheran College	WI	23,510	VC
Wittenberg Univ	OH	34,596	VC
Wofford College	SC	30,935	HC
Worcester Polytechnic Inst	MA	40,450	VC+
Worcester State College	MA	12,499	C
Wright State Univ	OH	13,616	C
Xavier Univ	OH	30,490	HC
Xavier Univ of Louisiana	LA	17,600	C
Yale Univ	CT	41,000	MC
Yeshiva Univ	NY	22,000	C
York College of Pennsylvania	PA	16,550	VC
Youngstown State Univ	OH	12,613	NC

CHILD CARE/CHILD AND FAMILY STUDIES

School	ST	$IS	SR
Albright College	PA	33,920	C
Alcorn State Univ	MS	8,190	LC
Ashland Univ	OH	25,000	C
Baylor Univ	TX	27,555	HC
Berea College	KY	5,496	VC+
Bowling Green State Univ	OH	14,994	C
Central Missouri State Univ	MO	10,000	C
Chestnut Hill College	PA	26,600	LC
Concordia Univ St.Paul	MN	27,776	C
East Carolina Univ	NC	10,000	C
Eastern Kentucky Univ	KY	7,725	C
Edgewood College	WI	22,862	C
Eureka College	IL	19,280	C
Florida State Univ	FL	9,028	HC
Freed-Hardeman Univ	TN	16,370	NC
Gallaudet Univ	DC	16,554	
Georgia Southern Univ	GA	9,762	C
Harding Univ	AR	16,512	VC
Indiana State Univ	IN	11,604	C
Indiana Univ of Pennsylvania	PA	11,209	C
Iowa State Univ	IA	11,831	VC
Jackson State Univ	MS	8,500	C
Kent State Univ	OH	14,594	C
Lasell College	MA	26,250	C
Medaille College	NY	21,000	C
Metropolitan College of New York	NY	16,000	C
Missouri State Univ	MO	10,748	C+
Mount Vernon Nazarene Univ	OH	20,810	C
N Car Central Univ	NC	9,000	LC
N Dak State Univ	ND	8,500	C
Northern Illinois Univ	IL	13,178	C
Northwest Missouri State Univ	MO	10,000	C
Okla Christian Univ	OK	18,992	NC
Okla State Univ	OK	10,213	VC
Park Univ	MO	11,592	C
Plymouth State Univ	NH	12,298	LC
Portland State Univ	OR	12,453	C
Purdue Univ/West Lafayette	IN	13,458	VC
St. Joseph's College, New York, Suffolk Campus	NY	12,000	C
Seton Hill Univ	PA	28,810	C
Southeast Missouri State Univ	MO	10,596	C
SUNY/College at Oneonta	NY	12,905	VC
SUNY/College at Plattsburgh	NY	12,362	C

School	ST	$IS	SR
SUNY/College of Agriculture and Technology at Cobleskill	NY	12,915	C
Syracuse Univ	NY	38,655	HC
Tenn Tech Univ	TN	10,044	C
Texas A&M Univ at Kingsville	TX	6,800	LC
Texas State Univ - San Marcos	TX	10,862	C
Univ of Arizona	AZ	11,958	VC
Univ of Georgia	GA	11,004	HC
Univ of Louisiana at Monroe	LA	7,103	C
Univ of Maine	ME	13,642	C
Univ of Nevada/Reno	NV	12,155	NC
Univ of New Mexico	NM	11,253	C
Univ of N Car at Chapel Hill	NC	11,129	MC
Univ of N Car at Charlotte	NC	9,101	C
Univ of Tenn at Knoxville	TN	11,720	C
Univ of Tenn at Martin	TN	8,693	C
Univ of Texas at Austin	TX	14,610	HC
Univ of the Incarnate Word	TX	23,306	C
Univ of Wisc/Madison	WI	13,117	HC
Univ of Wisc/Stout	WI	11,164	C
Ursuline College	OH	25,456	C
Utah State Univ	UT	8,002	VC
West Virginia Univ	WV	10,506	C
Wheelock College	MA	33,075	C
Youngstown State Univ	OH	12,613	NC

CHILD PSYCHOLOGY/ DEVELOPMENT

School	ST	$IS	SR
Alverno College	WI	21,088	C
Angelo State Univ	TX	8,340	NC
Appalachian State Univ	NC	8,000	VC
Bay Path College	MA	29,362	C
Bethel College	TN	16,066	NC
Bluffton College	OH	26,110	C
Cal State, Bakersfield	CA	6,125	LC
Cal State, Chico	CA	11,395	C
Cal State, Fresno	CA	10,037	LC
Cal State, Fullerton	CA	10,990	C
Cal State, Los Angeles	CA	5,900	C
Cal State, Northridge	CA	9,036	LC
Cal State, San Bernardino	CA	12,563	LC
Cal State, Stanislaus	CA	11,283	C
Central Mich Univ	MI	12,244	C
Colby-Sawyer College	NH	27,850	LC
College of the Ozarks	MO	4,130	VC+
East Tenn State Univ	TN	8,497	C
Eastern Nazarene College	MA	19,500	LC
Fort Valley State Univ	GA	6,975	C
Hope International Univ	CA	23,700	NC
Humboldt State Univ	CA	11,176	C
Iowa State Univ	IA	11,831	VC
Kansas State Univ	KS	10,516	VC
Madonna Univ	MI	16,068	VC
Marygrove College	MI	19,310	C+
Meredith College	NC	25,600	C
Metropolitan State Univ	MN	4,682	SP
Mich State Univ	MI	13,689	VC
Mills College	CA	39,870	C
Missouri Baptist Univ	MO	19,640	C
Mount Ida College	MA	26,000	LC
Mount St. Mary's College	CA	32,086	VC
New Mexico State Univ	NM	9,250	C
N Car Agricultural and Technical State Univ	NC	8,000	LC
N Car Central Univ	NC	9,000	LC
Point Loma Nazarene Univ	CA	27,610	VC
St. Joseph College	CT	32,050	C
San Diego State Univ	CA	12,971	C
Siena Heights Univ	MI	17,000	LC
Southeast Missouri State Univ	MO	10,596	C
Southern New Hampshire Univ	NH	28,764	C
Spelman College	GA	24,650	VC
Stephen F. Austin State Univ	TX	7,930	C
Texas Woman's Univ	TX	7,804	LC
Thomas Edison State College	NJ	3,780	SP
Tougaloo College	MS	15,975	NC
Tufts Univ	MA	42,018	MC
Univ of Illinois at Urbana-Champaign	IL	15,800	HC+
Univ of La Verne	CA	33,470	C
Univ of Minn/Twin Cities	MN	13,165	HC
Univ of North Texas	TX	7,800	C
Univ of St. Mary	KS	18,900	C
Utica College	NY	31,396	C
Vanderbilt Univ	TN	41,986	MC
Whittier College	CA	29,108	C

CHINESE

School	ST	$IS	SR
Arizona State Univ-Tempe	AZ	11,174	C
Bard College	NY	41,800	HC+
Bates College	ME	42,100	MC
Bennington College	VT	41,890	NC
Brigham Young Univ	UT	9,200	VC
Central Washington Univ	WA	11,730	C
CUNY/Hunter College	NY	8,000	C+
Colgate Univ	NY	41,170	MC

Chiropractic (continued)

School	ST	$IS	SR
Conn College	CT	41,975	MC
Dartmouth College	NH	39,465	MC
Drew Univ/College of Liberal Arts	NJ	39,698	VC
Emory Univ	GA	40,546	MC
George Washington Univ	DC	48,820	MC
Georgetown Univ	DC	43,183	MC
Grinnell College	IA	34,814	HC+
Harvard Univ/Harvard College	MA	45,860	MC
Middlebury College	VT	42,120	MC
Oakland Univ	MI	11,936	C
Ohio State Univ	OH	15,357	MC
Pomona College	CA	40,774	MC
Portland State Univ	OR	12,453	C
Reed College	OR	41,106	MC
Rutgers, The State Univ of New Jersey/New Brunswick/Piscataway Campus	NJ	15,810	HC
San Francisco State Univ	CA	13,000	C
Stanford Univ	CA	41,557	MC
SUNY/Univ at Albany	NY	13,860	VC
Swarthmore College	PA	41,280	MC
Tufts Univ	MA	42,018	MC
Univ of Calif Davis	CA	15,010	VC
Univ of Calif at Berkeley	CA	18,141	HC+
Univ of Calif at Irvine	CA	16,475	HC
Univ of Calif at Los Angeles	CA	17,681	MC
Univ of Calif at San Diego	CA	16,102	HC
Univ of Calif at Santa Barbara	CA	11,800	VC
Univ of Colo at Boulder	CO	13,352	C+
Univ of Hawaii at Manoa	HI	10,413	VC
Univ of Maryland/College Park	MD	16,036	HC
Univ of Mass Amherst	MA	15,973	C+
Univ of Mich/Ann Arbor	MI	16,587	HC+
Univ of Minn/Twin Cities	MN	13,165	HC
Univ of Notre Dame	IN	39,552	MC
Univ of Oregon	OR	13,108	VC
Univ of Pittsburgh at Pittsburgh	PA	18,866	HC
Univ of Utah	UT	10,162	VC
Univ of Wisc/Madison	WI	13,117	HC
Vassar College	NY	41,700	MC
Washington Univ in St. Louis	MO	42,106	MC
Wellesley College	MA	41,030	MC
Yale Univ	CT	41,000	MC

CHIROPRACTIC

School	ST	$IS	SR
Colo State Univ-Pueblo	CO	7,821	LC
Juniata College	PA	33,130	VC

CHORAL MUSIC

School	ST	$IS	SR
Baylor Univ	TX	27,555	HC

CHRISTIAN EDUCATION

School	ST	$IS	SR
Anderson Univ	IN	25,050	LC
Bethany College	KS	20,660	LC
Biola Univ	CA	29,372	VC
Catawba College	NC	25,000	C
Cedarville Univ	OH	21,904	VC
Columbia College	SC	24,982	LC
Concordia Univ	CA	26,780	C
Concordia Univ Nebr	NE	20,500	C+
Defiance College	OH	24,790	C
Erskine College	SC	25,468	VC
Hannibal-LaGrange College	MO	16,390	C
Malone College	OH	23,040	C
MidAmerica Nazarene Univ	KS	20,584	LC
Mount Vernon Nazarene Univ	OH	20,810	C
Muskingum College	OH	22,970	C
Northwestern College	MN	25,220	NC
Northwestern College of Iowa	IA	22,174	C+
Olivet Nazarene Univ	IL	22,590	C
Pfeiffer Univ	NC	21,900	C
Philander Smith College	AR	13,230	LC
Seattle Pacific Univ	WA	29,355	C
Spring Arbor Univ	MI	22,476	C
Taylor Univ	IN	26,376	VC+
Toccoa Falls College	GA	17,125	C
Westminster College	PA	31,290	C+

CHRISTIAN STUDIES

School	ST	$IS	SR
Alderson-Broaddus College	WV	24,006	C
Bluefield College	VA	17,230	C+
Brewton-Parker College	GA	14,220	LC
Bryan College	TN	19,270	C
Calif Baptist Univ	CA	23,780	C
Campbellsville Univ	KY	21,328	C
Eastern Nazarene College	MA	19,500	LC
Grand Canyon Univ	AZ	32,000	LC
Hillsdale College	MI	24,160	HC
Houston Baptist Univ	TX	18,660	C
Howard Payne Univ	TX	17,115	C
Lewis Univ	IL	23,050	C+
Miss College	MS	14,574	VC
Palm Beach Atlantic Univ	FL	23,597	VC
Seton Hall Univ	NJ	33,622	VC
Shorter College	GA	19,700	C
Texas Wesleyan Univ	TX	18,700	C
Trinity International Univ	IL	25,686	C
Union Univ	TN	20,750	VC
Univ of Chicago	IL	42,369	MC
Univ of Mary Hardin-Baylor	TX	19,428	C
Univ of St. Thomas	MN	28,000	VC
William Tyndale College	MI	13,000	NC

CITY/COMMUNITY/REGIONAL PLANNING

School	ST	$IS	SR
Alabama A&M Univ	AL	8,890	LC
Brigham Young Univ	UT	9,300	VC
Calif Polytechnic State Univ	CA	12,390	VC
Cornell Univ	NY	41,717	MC
East Carolina Univ	NC	10,000	C
Eastern Mich Univ	MI	12,897	C
Eastern Univ	PA	24,075	C
Indiana Univ of Pennsylvania	PA	11,209	C
Iowa State Univ	IA	11,831	VC
Kent State Univ	OH	14,594	C
Mansfield Univ	PA	11,300	C
Mich State Univ	MI	13,689	VC
New Mexico State Univ	NM	9,250	C
Plymouth State Univ	NH	12,298	LC
Texas State Univ - San Marcos	TX	10,862	C
Univ of Arizona	AZ	11,958	VC
Univ of Cincinnati	OH	17,682	C
Univ of Illinois at Urbana-Champaign	IL	15,800	HC+
Univ of New Hampshire	NH	16,810	VC
Univ of Virginia	VA	13,759	MC

CIVIL ENGINEERING

School	ST	$IS	SR
Alabama A&M Univ	AL	8,890	LC
Arizona State Univ-Tempe	AZ	11,174	C
Auburn Univ	AL	12,230	VC
Bethel College	IN	19,680	C
Bradley Univ	IL	25,280	VC
Brigham Young Univ	UT	9,200	VC
Bucknell Univ	PA	39,660	MC
Calif Inst of Technology	CA	36,123	MC
Calif Polytechnic State Univ	CA	12,390	VC
Calif State Polytechnic Univ, Pomona	CA	18,053	C+
Cal State, Chico	CA	11,395	C
Cal State, Fresno	CA	10,037	LC
Cal State, Fullerton	CA	10,990	C
Cal State, Long Beach	CA	9,512	C
Cal State, Los Angeles	CA	5,900	C
Cal State, Sacramento	CA	11,122	C+
Calvin College	MI	25,735	NC
Caribbean Univ	PR	3,000	C
Carnegie Mellon Univ	PA	32,700	MC
Carroll College	MT	23,324	C+
Case Western Reserve Univ	OH	37,314	MC
Catholic Univ of America	DC	35,838	VC
Christian Brothers Univ	TN	24,650	VC
Citadel, The	SC		C+
CUNY/City College	NY		C
Clarkson Univ	NY	34,930	VC
Clemson Univ	SC	13,366	HC
Cleveland State Univ	OH	10,798	NC
College of New Jersey	NJ	18,315	MC
Colo State Univ-Fort Collins	CO	10,878	C+
Columbia Univ/Fu Foundation School of Engineering and Applied Science	NY	42,584	MC
Cooper Union for the Advancement of Science and Art	NY	12,450	MC
Cornell Univ	NY	41,717	MC
Delaware State Univ	DE	8,130	LC
Drexel Univ	PA	27,700	VC
Duke Univ	NC	41,239	MC
Embry-Riddle Aeronautical Univ	FL	30,280	C
Florida A&M Univ	FL	8,344	C
Florida Atlantic Univ	FL	11,221	C
Florida Inst of Technology	FL	29,720	VC
Florida International Univ	FL	9,215	VC
Florida State Univ	FL	9,028	HC
George Mason Univ	VA	10,850	VC
George Washington Univ	DC	48,820	MC
Georgia Inst of Technology	GA	11,450	HC+
Gonzaga Univ	WA	30,218	VC
Hofstra Univ	NY	32,630	VC
Howard Univ	DC	18,481	C+
Idaho State Univ	ID	9,030	C
Illinois Inst of Technology	IL	26,465	HC+
Iowa State Univ	IA	11,831	VC
Johns Hopkins Univ	MD	42,044	MC
Kansas State Univ	KS	10,516	VC
Lafayette College	PA	39,267	MC
Lamar Univ	TX	6,820	LC
Lawrence Tech Univ	MI	25,475	VC
Lehigh Univ	PA	42,690	HC+
Louisiana State Univ and A&M College	LA	10,749	VC
Louisiana Tech Univ	LA	7,370	C
Loyola Marymount Univ	CA	36,321	VC
Manhattan College	NY	29,000	VC
Marquette Univ	WI	31,066	HC
Mass Inst of Technology	MA	41,800	MC
McNeese State Univ	LA	5,270	LC
Merrimack College	MA	34,380	C
Mich State Univ	MI	13,689	VC
Mich Tech Univ	MI	14,569	VC
Minn State Univ, Mankato	MN	10,276	LC
Miss State Univ	MS	9,557	C
Montana State Univ-Bozeman	MT	1,137	C
Morgan State Univ	MD	12,080	C
New Jersey Inst of Technology	NJ	16,396	VC
New Mexico Inst of Mining and Technology	NM	8,510	VC+
New Mexico State Univ	NM	9,250	C
N Car Agricultural and Technical State Univ	NC	8,000	LC
N Car State Univ	NC	11,824	HC
N Dak State Univ	ND	8,500	C
Northeastern Univ	MA	35,742	HC
Northern Arizona Univ	AZ	10,353	C
Northwestern Univ	IL	37,595	MC
Norwich Univ	VT	28,212	C
Ohio Northern Univ	OH	27,765	VC
Ohio State Univ	OH	15,357	HC
Ohio Univ	OH	15,921	C
Okla State Univ	OK	10,213	VC
Old Dominion Univ	VA	11,907	C
Oregon Inst of Technology	OR	8,718	C
Oregon State Univ	OR	11,055	C
Penn State Univ/Univ Park Campus	PA	18,038	HC
Pennsylvania College of Technology	PA	16,980	LC
Polytechnic Univ/Brooklyn	NY	37,150	VC
Portland State Univ	OR	12,453	C
Prairie View A&M Univ	TX	11,110	LC
Princeton Univ	NJ	40,213	MC
Purdue Univ/West Lafayette	IN	13,458	VC
Rensselaer Polytechnic Inst	NY	41,288	HC+
Rice Univ	TX	32,290	MC
Rose-Hulman Inst of Technology	IN	34,557	HC+
Rowan Univ	NJ	16,000	VC
Rutgers, The State Univ of New Jersey/New Brunswick/Piscataway Campus	NJ	15,810	HC
St. Martin's Univ	WA	27,555	C
San Diego State Univ	CA	12,971	C
San Francisco State Univ	CA	13,000	C
San Jose State Univ	CA	11,707	C
Santa Clara Univ	CA	38,931	VC
Savannah State Univ	GA	7,772	LC
Seattle Univ	WA	30,063	VC
S Dak School of Mines and Technology	SD	7,624	C+
S Dak State Univ	SD	9,815	C
Southern Illinois Univ Carbondale	IL	12,391	C
Southern Illinois Univ Edwardsville	IL	11,022	C
Southern Methodist Univ	TX	36,088	VC+
Southern Univ and A&M College	LA	8,238	LC
Stanford Univ	CA	41,557	MC
SUNY/Univ at Buffalo	NY	13,694	VC
Stevens Inst of Technology	NJ	40,935	HC
Syracuse Univ	NY	38,655	HC
Temple Univ	PA	17,438	C
Tenn State Univ	TN	9,048	LC
Tenn Tech Univ	TN	10,044	C
Texas A&M Univ	TX	13,351	HC
Texas A&M Univ at Galveston	TX	10,000	C
Texas A&M Univ at Kingsville	TX	6,800	LC
Texas Tech Univ	TX	13,026	VC
Tri-State Univ-Main Campus	IN	26,200	C
Tufts Univ	MA	42,018	MC
Tulane Univ	LA	41,098	MC
United States Air Force Academy	CO		HC+
United States Coast Guard Academy	CT		HC
United States Military Academy	NY		MC
Universidad Politecnica de PR	PR	5,400	C
Univ of Akron	OH	15,166	NC
Univ of Alabama	AL	9,888	C
Univ of Alabama at Birmingham	AL	13,716	C
Univ of Alabama in Huntsville	AL	9,516	VC
Univ of Alaska Anchorage	AK	11,275	NC
Univ of Alaska Fairbanks	AK	10,101	C
Univ of Arizona	AZ	11,958	VC
Univ of Arkansas	AR	11,859	VC
Univ of at Calif Davis	CA	15,010	VC
Univ of Calif at Berkeley	CA	18,141	HC+
Univ of Calif at Irvine	CA	16,475	HC
Univ of Calif at Los Angeles	CA	17,681	MC
Univ of Central Florida	FL	10,739	VC
Univ of Cincinnati	OH	17,682	C
Univ of Colo at Boulder	CO	13,352	C+
Univ of Colo at Denver and Health Sciences Center	CO	5,021	C
Univ of Conn	CT	16,628	HC
Univ of Dayton	OH	28,826	VC
Univ of Delaware	DE	14,142	HC
Univ of Detroit Mercy	MI	27,000	C
Univ of Evansville	IN	28,320	VC
Univ of Florida	FL	9,354	HC
Univ of Hartford	CT	34,044	C
Univ of Hawaii at Manoa	HI	10,413	VC
Univ of Houston	TX	7,000	C
Univ of Idaho	ID	9,310	NC
Univ of Illinois at Chicago	IL	16,256	VC
Univ of Illinois at Urbana-Champaign	IL	15,800	HC+
Univ of Iowa	IA	12,172	VC
Univ of Kansas	KS	10,915	VC
Univ of Kentucky	KY	7,800	C
Univ of Louisiana at Lafayette	LA	5,830	C
Univ of Louisville	KY	10,400	VC
Univ of Maine	ME	13,642	C
Univ of Maryland/College Park	MD	16,036	HC
Univ of Mass Amherst	MA	15,973	C+
Univ of Mass Dartmouth	MA	15,985	C
Univ of Mass Lowell	MA	14,327	VC
Univ of Memphis	TN	11,153	C
Univ of Miami	FL	38,397	MC
Univ of Mich/Ann Arbor	MI	16,587	HC+
Univ of Minn/Twin Cities	MN	13,165	HC
Univ of Miss	MS	9,000	C
Univ of Missouri/Columbia	MO	13,500	VC
Univ of Missouri/Kansas City	MO	15,000	VC
Univ of Missouri/Rolla	MO	13,332	HC
Univ of Missouri/St. Louis	MO	14,046	VC
Univ of Nebr at Lincoln	NE	11,401	VC
Univ of Nevada/Las Vegas	NV	11,566	C
Univ of Nevada/Reno	NV	12,155	NC
Univ of New Hampshire	NH	16,810	VC
Univ of New Haven	CT	31,794	C
Univ of New Mexico	NM	11,253	C
Univ of New Orleans	LA	7,370	C
Univ of N Car at Charlotte	NC	9,101	C
Univ of N Dak	ND	10,114	VC
Univ of North Florida	FL	9,908	VC
Univ of Notre Dame	IN	39,552	MC
Univ of Okla	OK	10,769	VC+
Univ of Pennsylvania	PA	41,766	MC
Univ of Pittsburgh at Pittsburgh	PA	18,866	HC
Univ of Portland	OR	32,300	VC
Univ of PR/Mayaguez	PR	1,250	
Univ of Rhode Island	RI	15,398	C
Univ of South Alabama	AL	8,930	LC
Univ of S Car at Columbia	SC	13,397	VC
Univ of South Florida	FL	10,284	VC
Univ of Southern Calif	CA	41,618	MC
Univ of Tenn at Knoxville	TN	11,720	C
Univ of Texas at Arlington	TX	7,195	LC
Univ of Texas at Austin	TX	14,610	HC
Univ of Texas at El Paso	TX	8,764	NC
Univ of Texas at San Antonio	TX	11,325	LC
Univ of the District of Columbia	DC	2,070	LC
Univ of the Pacific	CA	34,380	VC
Univ of Toledo	OH	15,806	NC
Univ of Utah	UT	10,162	VC
Univ of Vermont	VT	18,080	VC
Univ of Virginia	VA	13,759	MC
Univ of Washington	WA	10,400	VC
Univ of Wisc/Madison	WI	13,117	HC
Univ of Wisc/Milwaukee	WI	9,427	C
Univ of Wisc/Platteville	WI	9,779	NC
Univ of Wyoming	WY	9,666	C
Utah State Univ	UT	8,002	VC
Valparaiso Univ	IN	28,970	VC+
Vanderbilt Univ	TN	41,986	MC
Villanova Univ	PA	38,672	HC+
Virginia Military Inst	VA	12,654	VC
Virginia Polytechnic Inst and State Univ	VA	10,834	VC
Washington State Univ	WA	12,260	C
Washington Univ in St. Louis	MO	42,106	MC
Wayne State Univ	MI	11,805	C
West Virginia Univ	WV	10,506	C
West Virginia Univ Inst of Technology	WV	8,788	NC
Western Kentucky Univ	KY	10,192	C
Western Mich Univ	MI	13,299	C
Widener Univ	PA	27,275	C
Worcester Polytechnic Inst	MA	40,450	VC+
Youngstown State Univ	OH	12,613	NC

ST = STATE $IS = IN-STATE COSTS   SR = SELECTOR RATING

School	ST	$IS	SR

CIVIL ENGINEERING TECHNOLOGY

School	ST	$IS	SR
Alabama A&M Univ	AL	8,890	LC
Central Conn State Univ	CT	13,620	C
Colo State Univ-Pueblo	CO	7,821	LC
Fairleigh Dickinson Univ/ Metropolitan Campus	NJ	28,590	C
Fairmont State	WV	8,400	LC
Georgia Southern Univ	GA	9,762	C
Lincoln Univ	MO	8,000	NC
Metropolitan State College of Denver	CO	2,338	LC
Montana State Univ-Northern	MT	10,000	NC
Murray State Univ	KY	8,900	NC
Old Dominion Univ	VA	11,907	C
Pennsylvania College of Technology	PA	16,980	C
Point Park Univ	PA	24,160	C
Rochester Inst of Technology	NY	32,070	VC+
S Car State Univ	SC	6,700	LC
Southern Polytechnic State Univ	GA	7,640	VC
SUNY/Inst of Technology	NY	12,575	NC
Texas Southern Univ	TX	9,828	C
Thomas Edison State College	NJ	3,780	SP
Univ of Houston	TX	7,000	C
Univ of N Car at Charlotte	NC	9,101	C
Univ of Pittsburgh at Johnstown	PA	16,740	LC
Wentworth Inst of Technology	MA	27,500	C
Youngstown State Univ	OH	12,613	NC

CLASSICAL LANGUAGES

School	ST	$IS	SR
Agnes Scott College	GA	32,070	HC
Asbury College	KY	23,762	VC
Ball State Univ	IN	13,138	C
Bard College	NY	41,800	HC+
Beloit College	WI	32,808	HC
Berea College	KY	5,496	VC+
Brigham Young Univ	UT	9,200	VC
Bryn Mawr College	PA	42,780	HC+
Calvin College	MI	25,735	NC
Carroll College	MT	23,324	C+
Concordia College: Moorhead	MN	22,475	VC
DePauw Univ	IN	32,100	HC
Dickinson College	PA	40,170	HC+
Duke Univ	NC	41,239	MC
Duquesne Univ	PA	29,534	VC
Eastern Mich Univ	MI	12,897	C
Fordham Univ	NY	36,000	HC
La Salle Univ	PA	34,950	C
Luther College	IA	28,800	VC+
Marquette Univ	WI	31,066	HC
Ohio Univ	OH	15,921	C
Rockford College	IL	28,330	VC
St. Bonaventure Univ	NY	28,785	LC
St. Louis Univ	MO	33,158	VC+
St. Mary's College of Calif	CA	37,290	C
St. Peter's College	NJ	30,160	LC
Santa Clara Univ	CA	38,931	VC
Scripps College	CA	41,000	MC
Siena College	NY	28,260	VC+
Univ of Calif at Berkeley	CA	18,141	HC+
Univ of Calif at Santa Cruz	CA	19,174	VC
Univ of Houston	TX	7,000	C
Univ of Kansas	KS	10,915	VC
Univ of Mass Boston	MA	8,024	C
Univ of Mich/Ann Arbor	MI	16,587	HC+
Univ of Minn/Twin Cities	MN	13,165	VC
Univ of St. Thomas	MN	28,000	VC
Vanderbilt Univ	TN	41,986	MC
Washington Univ in St. Louis	MO	42,106	MC
Wright State Univ	OH	13,616	LC
Yeshiva Univ	NY	22,000	C

CLASSICAL/ANCIENT CIVILIZATION

School	ST	$IS	SR
Agnes Scott College	GA	32,070	HC
Bates College	ME	42,100	MC
Beloit College	WI	32,808	HC
Boston College	MA	41,608	MC
Boston Univ	MA	42,046	HC+
Bowdoin College	ME	41,660	MC
Bowling Green State Univ	OH	14,994	C
Brigham Young Univ	UT	9,200	VC
Brown Univ	RI	42,015	MC
Carleton College	MN	40,467	MC
Centre College	KY	30,810	VC
Christendom College	VA	21,594	VC+
CUNY/Queens College	NY	4,356	C
Clark Univ	MA	35,165	VC+
Cleveland State Univ	OH	10,798	NC
Coe College	IA	27,440	VC
Colby College	ME	41,770	MC
Columbia Univ/Barnard College	NY	38,000	MC

School	ST	$IS	SR
Columbia Univ/Columbia College	NY	42,584	MC
Columbia Univ/School of General Studies	NY	41,516	C
Cornell College	IA	30,110	VC+
Cornell Univ	NY	41,717	MC
Creighton Univ	NE	29,918	VC+
Dartmouth College	NH	39,465	MC
Denison Univ	OH	37,040	HC
DePauw Univ	IN	32,100	HC
Dickinson College	PA	40,170	HC+
Duke Univ	NC	41,239	MC
Duquesne Univ	PA	29,534	VC
Earlham College	IN	33,604	HC
Emory Univ	GA	40,546	MC
Florida State Univ	FL	9,028	HC
Fordham Univ	NY	36,000	HC
Gonzaga Univ	WA	30,218	HC
Hamilton College	NY	41,660	MC
Hawaii Pacific Univ	HI	21,080	C
Hollins Univ	VA	31,105	C
Indiana Univ Bloomington	IN	13,356	VC
Kalamazoo College	MI	32,442	VC+
Lehigh Univ	PA	42,690	HC+
Loras College	IA	27,193	C
Loyola College in Maryland	MD	38,898	HC
Loyola Marymount Univ	CA	36,321	VC
Loyola Univ Chicago	IL	32,896	VC
Loyola Univ New Orleans	LA	31,050	VC+
Miami Univ	OH	29,097	HC
Mich State Univ	MI	13,689	VC
Mount Holyoke College	MA	42,148	HC+
New York Univ	NY	43,170	MC
North Central College	IL	28,926	VC
Ohio Univ	OH	15,921	C
Rhodes College	TN	32,860	HC
Rice Univ	TX	32,290	MC
Rollins College	FL	38,366	VC
St. Louis Univ	MO	33,158	VC+
St. Olaf College	MN	32,800	HC
St. Peter's College	NJ	30,160	LC
Santa Clara Univ	CA	38,931	VC
Scripps College	CA	41,000	MC
Seton Hall Univ	NJ	33,622	VC
Smith College	MA	41,474	MC
SUNY/Univ at Albany	NY	13,860	VC
SUNY/Univ at Binghamton	NY	13,988	VC
Swarthmore College	PA	41,280	MC
Sweet Briar College	VA	31,460	VC
Syracuse Univ	NY	38,655	HC
Trinity College	CT	38,040	HC+
Univ of at Calif Davis	CA	15,010	VC
Univ of Calif at Berkeley	CA	18,141	HC+
Univ of Calif at Irvine	CA	16,475	HC
Univ of Calif at Los Angeles	CA	17,681	MC
Univ of Calif at Riverside	CA	16,625	C
Univ of Chicago	IL	42,369	MC
Univ of Cincinnati	OH	17,682	C
Univ of Evansville	IN	28,320	VC
Univ of Florida	FL	9,354	VC
Univ of Georgia	GA	11,004	HC
Univ of Idaho	ID	9,310	NC
Univ of Illinois at Chicago	IL	16,256	VC
Univ of Iowa	IA	12,172	VC
Univ of Maryland/Baltimore County	MD	16,642	VC+
Univ of Mich/Ann Arbor	MI	16,587	HC+
Univ of Miss	MS	9,000	C
Univ of N Dak	ND	10,114	VC
Univ of Notre Dame	IN	39,552	MC
Univ of Oregon	OR	13,108	VC
Univ of Richmond	VA	40,510	MC
Univ of St. Thomas	MN	28,000	VC
Univ of Tenn at Knoxville	TN	11,720	C
Univ of Texas at Arlington	TX	7,195	LC
Univ of Texas at Austin	TX	14,610	HC
Vassar College	NY	41,700	MU
Wellesley College	MA	41,030	MC
Wesleyan Univ	CT	42,122	MC
Wheaton College	MA	40,180	HC
Willamette Univ	OR	35,416	VC+
Yale Univ	CT	41,000	MC

CLASSICS

School	ST	$IS	SR
Agnes Scott College	GA	32,070	HC
Amherst College	MA	41,590	MC
Assumption College	MA	32,875	C
Augustana College	IL	29,862	VC+
Austin College	TX	27,871	HC
Ball State Univ	IN	13,138	C
Bard College	NY	41,800	HC+
Baylor Univ	TX	27,555	HC
Boston College	MA	41,608	MC
Boston Univ	MA	42,046	HC+
Bowdoin College	ME	41,660	MC
Brandeis Univ	MA	41,551	MC
Brigham Young Univ	UT	9,200	VC
Brown Univ	RI	42,015	MC
Bryn Mawr College	PA	42,780	HC+
Bucknell Univ	PA	39,660	HC
Calvin College	MI	25,735	NC
Carleton College	MN	40,467	MC
Case Western Reserve Univ	OH	37,314	MC
Catholic Univ of America	DC	35,838	VC

School	ST	$IS	SR
CUNY/Brooklyn College	NY	4,377	C+
CUNY/Hunter College	NY	8,000	C+
Colby College	ME	41,770	MC
Colgate Univ	NY	41,170	MC
College of Charleston	SC	13,616	VC
College of New Rochelle	NY	28,396	C+
College of Notre Dame of Maryland	MD	27,700	C
College of St. Benedict	MN	30,091	VC
College of the Holy Cross	MA	40,664	MC
College of William and Mary	VA	14,147	MC
Colo College	CO	37,668	HC
Columbia Univ/Barnard College	NY	38,000	MC
Columbia Univ/Columbia College	NY	42,584	MC
Columbia Univ/School of General Studies	NY	41,516	C
Conn College	CT	41,975	MC
Cornell Univ	NY	41,717	MC
Dartmouth College	NH	39,465	MC
Davidson College	NC	36,825	MC
Drew Univ/College of Liberal Arts	NJ	39,698	VC
Duquesne Univ	PA	29,534	VC
Elmira College	NY	37,200	VC
Emory Univ	GA	40,546	MC
Florida State Univ	FL	9,028	HC
Franciscan Univ of Steubenville	OH	20,300	VC
Franklin and Marshall College	PA	40,590	HC
George Washington Univ	DC	48,820	MC
Georgetown Univ	DC	43,183	MC
Georgia State Univ	GA	11,444	VC
Gettysburg College	PA	39,864	HC
Grinnell College	IA	34,814	HC+
Gustavus Adolphus College	MN	30,920	HC
Hamilton College	NY	41,660	MC
Hampden-Sydney College	VA	31,148	VC
Hanover College	IN	28,150	HC
Harvard Univ/Harvard College	MA	45,860	MC
Haverford College	PA	41,600	MC
Hellenic College/Holy Cross Greek Orthodox School of Theology	MA	24,975	C
Hillsdale College	MI	24,160	HC
Hiram College	OH	28,700	VC
Hobart and William Smith Colleges	NY	41,123	VC
Hofstra Univ	NY	32,630	VC
Howard Univ	DC	18,481	C+
Indiana Univ Bloomington	IN	13,356	VC
Johns Hopkins Univ	MD	42,044	MC
Kenyon College	OH	39,500	MC
Knox College	IL	32,385	VC+
Lawrence Univ	WI	33,958	HC+
Lehigh Univ	PA	42,690	HC+
Lenoir-Rhyne College	NC	25,580	C
Loyola Marymount Univ	CA	36,321	VC
Macalester College	MN	36,500	MC
Manhattanville College	NY	32,500	C
Marquette Univ	WI	31,066	HC
Middlebury College	VT	42,120	MC
Millsaps College	MS	28,256	VC+
Monmouth College	IL	23,700	C
Montclair State Univ	NJ	16,327	C
Moravian College	PA	28,950	VC
Mount Holyoke College	MA	42,148	HC+
New College of Florida	FL	10,009	HC
New York Univ	NY	43,170	MC
Northwestern Univ	IL	37,595	MC
Oberlin College	OH	40,904	MC
Ohio State Univ	OH	15,357	HC
Pacific Lutheran Univ	WA	28,805	VC
Penn State Univ/Univ Park Campus	PA	18,038	HC
Pitzer College	CA	41,644	HC
Pomona College	CA	40,774	MC
Princeton Univ	NJ	40,213	MC
Purdue Univ/West Lafayette	IN	13,458	VC
Randolph-Macon College	VA	31,250	C
Randolph-Macon Woman's College	VA	31,160	VC+
Reed College	OR	41,106	MC
Rice Univ	TX	32,290	MC
Rutgers, The State Univ of New Jersey/New Brunswick/Piscataway Campus	NJ	15,810	HC
St. Anselm College	NH	33,810	C
St. John's Univ	MN	29,749	VC
St. Olaf College	MN	32,800	HC
Samford Univ	AL	20,258	VC
San Diego State Univ	CA	12,971	C
San Francisco State Univ	CA	13,000	C
Santa Clara Univ	CA	38,931	VC
Sarah Lawrence College	NY	42,000	HC
Seattle Pacific Univ	WA	29,355	C
Skidmore College	NY	41,779	HC
Smith College	MA	41,474	MC
Southern Illinois Univ Carbondale	IL	12,391	C
Southwestern Univ	TX	26,767	HC
Stanford Univ	CA	41,557	MC

School	ST	$IS	SR
SUNY/Univ at Binghamton	NY	13,988	VC
SUNY/Univ at Buffalo	NY	13,694	VC
Swarthmore College	PA	41,280	MC
Syracuse Univ	NY	38,655	HC
Temple Univ	PA	17,438	C
Texas Tech Univ	TX	13,026	VC
Trinity College	CT	38,040	HC+
Truman State Univ	MO	11,242	HC
Tufts Univ	MA	42,018	MC
Tulane Univ	LA	41,098	MC
Union College	NY	41,595	HC
Univ of Akron	OH	15,166	NC
Univ of Alabama	AL	9,888	C
Univ of Arizona	AZ	11,958	VC
Univ of Arkansas	AR	11,859	VC
Univ of Calif at Irvine	CA	16,475	HC
Univ of Calif at Riverside	CA	16,625	C
Univ of Calif at San Diego	CA	16,102	HC
Univ of Calif at Santa Barbara	CA	11,800	VC
Univ of Chicago	IL	42,369	MC
Univ of Colo at Boulder	CO	13,352	C+
Univ of Conn	CT	16,628	HC
Univ of Dallas	TX	27,432	VC+
Univ of Hawaii at Manoa	HI	10,413	VC
Univ of Houston	TX	7,000	C
Univ of Illinois at Chicago	IL	16,256	VC
Univ of Illinois at Urbana-Champaign	IL	15,800	HC+
Univ of Iowa	IA	12,172	VC
Univ of Mary Washington	VA	11,636	HC
Univ of Maryland/College Park	MD	16,036	HC
Univ of Mass Amherst	MA	15,973	C+
Univ of Mass Boston	MA	8,024	C
Univ of Missouri/Columbia	MO	13,500	VC
Univ of Montana	MT	10,602	C
Univ of Nebr at Lincoln	NE	11,401	VC
Univ of New Hampshire	NH	16,810	VC
Univ of New Mexico	NM	11,253	C
Univ of N Car at Asheville	NC	9,237	VC
Univ of N Car at Chapel Hill	NC	11,129	MC
Univ of N Car at Greensboro	NC	8,993	C
Univ of Okla	OK	10,769	VC+
Univ of Oregon	OR	13,108	VC
Univ of Pennsylvania	PA	41,766	MC
Univ of Pittsburgh at Pittsburgh	PA	18,866	HC
Univ of Puget Sound	WA	35,600	HC
Univ of Rhode Island	RI	15,398	C
Univ of Rochester	NY	41,135	MC
Univ of S Car at Columbia	SC	13,397	VC
Univ of South Florida	FL	10,284	VC
Univ of Southern Calif	CA	41,618	MC
Univ of Tenn at Knoxville	TN	11,720	C
Univ of Texas at Austin	TX	14,610	HC
Univ of Texas at San Antonio	TX	11,325	LC
Univ of Utah	UT	10,162	VC
Univ of Vermont	VT	18,080	VC
Univ of Virginia	VA	13,759	MC
Univ of Washington	WA	10,400	VC
Univ of Wisc/Madison	WI	13,174	HC
Univ of Wisc/Milwaukee	WI	9,427	LC
Ursinus College	PA	38,950	VC
Valparaiso Univ	IN	28,970	VC+
Vanderbilt Univ	TN	41,986	MC
Villanova Univ	PA	38,672	HC+
Virginia Wesleyan College	VA	28,433	C
Wabash College	IN	30,116	VC
Wake Forest Univ	NC	38,290	MC
Washington and Lee Univ	VA	35,880	MC
Washington State Univ	WA	12,260	C
Washington Univ in St. Louis	MO	42,106	MC
Wayne State Univ	MI	11,805	C
Wesleyan Univ	CT	42,122	MC
Wheaton College	MA	40,180	HC+
Whitman College	WA	36,110	HC+
Williams College	MA	40,310	MC
Xavier Univ	OH	30,490	HC
Yale Univ	CT	41,000	MC

CLINICAL PSYCHOLOGY

School	ST	$IS	SR
Averett Univ	VA	24,920	C
Bard College	NY	41,800	HC+
Crichton College	TN	15,300	C
Eastern Nazarene College	MA	19,500	LC
Kent State Univ	OH	14,594	C
Marywood Univ	PA	30,680	C
Tufts Univ	MA	42,018	MC
Univ of New Haven	CT	31,794	C

CLINICAL SCIENCE

School	ST	$IS	SR
Appalachian State Univ	NC	8,000	VC
Arizona State Univ-Tempe	AZ	11,174	C
Arkansas State Univ	AR	9,630	C
Ashford Univ	IA	20,370	C
Benedictine Univ	IL	25,710	C
Bethune-Cookman Univ	FL	17,922	LC
Bloomfield College	NJ	22,500	LC
Brigham Young Univ	UT	9,200	VC
Cal State, Bakersfield	CA	6,125	LC

School	ST	$IS	SR
Cal State, Dominguez Hills	CA	10,220	LC
Campbell Univ	NC	21,137	VC
Canisius College	NY	32,257	VC
Carroll College	MT	23,324	C+
Carroll College	WI	24,860	C
Elizabethtown College	PA	32,100	VC
Fairleigh Dickinson Univ/ College at Florham	NJ	30,130	C
Fairleigh Dickinson Univ/ Metropolitan Campus	NJ	28,590	C
Felician College	NJ	24,300	C
George Washington Univ	DC	48,820	MC
Gwynedd-Mercy College	PA	26,080	C
Indiana Univ Southeast	IN	4,880	LC
Indiana Univ-Purdue Univ Indianapolis	IN	10,959	C
Ithaca College	NY	35,144	VC
Jamestown College	ND	14,130	NC
Jewish Hospital College of Nursing and Allied Health	MO	12,000	SP
Kent State Univ	OH	14,594	C
Maryville Univ of St. Louis	MO	23,000	VC
Mich State Univ	MI	13,689	VC
Mich Tech Univ	MI	14,569	VC
Minn State Univ, Mankato	MN	10,276	LC
Monmouth Univ	NJ	28,956	C
New York Inst of Technology	NY	28,126	VC
N Dak State Univ	ND	8,500	C
Northern Illinois Univ	IL	13,178	C
Northern Mich Univ	MI	12,340	LC
Olivet Nazarene Univ	IL	22,590	C
Ramapo College of New Jersey	NJ	16,630	VC
Rockhurst Univ	MO	25,440	VC
Rutgers, The State Univ of New Jersey/Newark Campus	NJ	15,640	VC
St. Louis Univ	MO	33,158	VC+
San Francisco State Univ	CA	13,000	C
S Dak State Univ	SD	9,815	C
SUNY/Univ at Stony Brook	NY	13,625	VC
Texas A&M Univ at Corpus Christi	TX	10,280	LC
Texas State Univ - San Marcos	TX	10,862	C
Thomas Edison State College	NJ	3,780	SP
Univ of Kansas	KS	10,915	VC
Univ of Louisiana at Monroe	LA	7,103	C
Univ of Maine	ME	13,642	C
Univ of Mass Lowell	MA	14,327	VC
Univ of Nevada/Las Vegas	NV	11,566	C
Univ of N Car at Chapel Hill	NC	11,129	MC
Univ of N Car at Wilmington	NC	10,107	VC
Univ of N Dak	ND	10,114	VC
Univ of Pittsburgh at Pittsburgh	PA	18,866	HC
Univ of Rhode Island	RI	15,398	C
Univ of South Alabama	AL	8,930	LC
Univ of Texas at El Paso	TX	8,764	NC
Univ of Texas at San Antonio	TX	11,325	LC
Univ of Wisc/Milwaukee	WI	9,427	LC
Univ of Wisc/Stevens Point	WI	9,384	VC
Walsh Univ	OH	23,440	C
Weber State Univ	UT	9,635	NC
West Liberty State College	WV	9,142	LC
Western Carolina Univ	NC	7,000	C
Youngstown State Univ	OH	12,613	NC

CLOTHING AND TEXTILES MANAGEMENT/ PRODUCTION/SERVICES

School	ST	$IS	SR
Appalachian State Univ	NC	8,000	VC
Cheyney Univ of Pennsylvania	PA	11,497	LC
College of the Ozarks	MO	4,130	VC+
East Carolina Univ	NC	10,000	VC
Eastern Mich Univ	MI	12,897	C
Florida State Univ	FL	9,028	HC
Johnson and Wales Univ/ Charlotte Campus	NC	29,121	LC
Johnson and Wales Univ/ North Miami Campus	FL	30,126	LC
Johnson and Wales Univ/ Providence Campus	RI	28,126	LC
Louisiana State Univ and A&M College	LA	10,749	VC
Miss Univ for Women	MS	6,000	LC
Missouri State Univ	MO	10,748	C+
N Car Agricultural and Technical State Univ	NC	8,000	LC
N Car State Univ	NC	11,824	HC
Northwest Missouri State Univ	MO	10,000	C
Ohio State Univ	OH	15,357	HC
San Francisco State Univ	CA	13,000	C
Seattle Pacific Univ	WA	29,355	C
Southern Illinois Univ Carbondale	IL	12,391	C
Texas Tech Univ	TX	13,026	VC
Univ of Alabama	AL	9,888	C
Univ of North Texas	TX	7,800	C
Univ of Northern Iowa	IA	11,133	C
Washington State Univ	WA	12,260	C

COGNITIVE SCIENCE

School	ST	$IS	SR
Averett Univ	VA	24,920	C
Brown Univ	RI	42,015	MC
Cal State, Stanislaus	CA	11,283	C
Case Western Reserve Univ	OH	37,314	MC
Central Mich Univ	MI	12,244	C
Dartmouth College	NH	39,465	MC
George Fox Univ	OR	28,490	C
Hampshire College	MA	37,120	HC
Indiana Univ Bloomington	IN	13,356	VC
Johns Hopkins Univ	MD	42,044	MC
Lehigh Univ	PA	42,690	HC+
Mass Inst of Technology	MA	41,800	MC
Mount Union College	OH	25,840	C
Northwestern Univ	IL	37,595	MC
Occidental College	CA	40,185	MC
Rice Univ	TX	32,290	MC
SUNY at Oswego	NY	13,662	VC
Tulane Univ	LA	41,098	MC
Univ of Calif at Berkeley	CA	18,141	HC+
Univ of Calif at Los Angeles	CA	17,681	MC
Univ of Calif at San Diego	CA	16,102	HC
Univ of Denver	CO	36,376	VC+
Univ of Evansville	IN	28,320	VC
Univ of Georgia	GA	11,004	HC
Univ of Pennsylvania	PA	41,766	MC
Univ of Rochester	NY	41,135	MC
Univ of Texas at Dallas	TX	13,244	HC
Vanderbilt Univ	TN	41,986	MC
Vassar College	NY	41,700	MC
Wellesley College	MA	41,030	MC

COLLABORATIVE EDUCATION

School	ST	$IS	SR
Birmingham-Southern College	AL	28,494	VC+
Troy Univ	AL	8,916	C

COMMERCIAL ART

School	ST	$IS	SR
American InterContinental Univ	GA	12,100	NC
Ashland Univ	OH	25,000	C
Brenau Univ Women's College	GA	23,950	VC
Calif Univ of Pennsylvania	PA	14,217	C
Cazenovia College	NY	26,900	C
Central Missouri State Univ	MO	10,000	C
Fort Valley State Univ	GA	6,975	C
Graceland Univ	IA	19,700	C
Kent State Univ	OH	14,594	C
Madonna Univ	MI	16,068	VC
Millikin Univ	IL	25,590	C
Oral Roberts Univ	OK	22,650	C
Pittsburg State Univ	KS	8,112	C
St. Norbert College	WI	28,577	C+
St. Thomas Aquinas College	NY	22,000	LC
Southwest Baptist Univ	MO	18,300	C
Univ of Indianapolis	IN	25,090	C
Univ of North Texas	TX	7,800	C
Univ of S Car Upstate	SC	11,957	C
Washington Univ in St. Louis	MO	42,106	MC

COMMUNICATIONS

School	ST	$IS	SR
Abilene Christian Univ	TX	20,830	C
Adelphi Univ	NY	27,000	VC
Adrian College	MI	23,000	C
Alabama State Univ	AL	7,658	C
Albertus Magnus College	CT	25,336	C
Albright College	PA	33,920	C
Alcorn State Univ	MS	8,190	LC
Alderson-Broaddus College	WV	24,006	C
Alfred Univ	NY		C
Allegheny College	PA	33,500	HC
Alma College	MI	28,544	VC
Alvernia College	PA	26,388	C
Alverno College	WI	21,088	C
American International College	MA	28,710	LC
American Univ	DC	38,719	HC+
Anderson Univ	IN	25,050	LC
Andrews Univ	MI	21,786	C
Angelo State Univ	TX	8,340	NC
Antioch College	OH	33,700	C
Appalachian State Univ	NC	8,000	VC
Aquinas College	MI	23,750	C
Arcadia Univ	PA	33,570	VC
Arizona State Univ-Tempe	AZ	11,174	C
Asbury College	KY	23,762	VC
Ashland Univ	OH	25,000	C
Auburn Univ	AL	12,230	VC
Auburn Univ Montgomery	AL	9,530	NC
Augsburg College	MN	28,300	C
Augusta State Univ	GA	2,920	C
Augustana College	SD	24,380	VC
Aurora Univ	IL	20,645	C
Austin College	TX	28,871	HC
Austin Peay State Univ	TN	7,535	C
Avila Univ	MO	22,100	C
Azusa Pacific Univ	CA	28,546	VC
Baker Univ	KS	22,190	C
Baldwin-Wallace College	OH	27,256	VC
Ball State Univ	IN	13,138	C
Barber-Scotia College	NC	15,000	LC
Barry Univ	FL	24,100	LC
Barton College	NC	22,316	C
Bay Path College	MA	29,362	C
Baylor Univ	TX	27,555	HC
Becker College	MA	24,300	C
Belhaven College	MS	19,530	NC
Bellarmine Univ	KY	27,650	C+
Bellevue Univ	NE	4,440	NC
Belmont Univ	TN	24,110	VC
Bemidji State Univ	MN	11,180	LC
Benedictine Univ	IL	25,710	C
Bennett College	NC	11,500	C
Bentley College	MA	38,784	HC
Berry College	GA	24,342	VC
Bethany College	KS	20,660	LC
Bethany College	WV	21,395	C
Bethel College	IN	19,680	C
Bethel College	KS	21,650	C
Bethel College	MN	29,840	VC
Bethune-Cookman College	FL	17,922	VC
Biola Univ	CA	29,372	VC
Black Hills State Univ	SD	7,800	LC
Bloomsburg Univ of Pennsylvania	PA	11,602	C
Bluefield College	VA	17,230	C+
Bluffton College	OH	26,110	C
Boise State Univ	ID	9,438	LC
Boston College	MA	41,608	MC
Boston Univ	MA	42,046	HC+
Bowling Green State Univ	OH	14,994	C
Bradley Univ	IL	25,280	VC
Brenau Univ Women's College	GA	23,950	VC
Briar Cliff Univ	IA	23,550	LC
Bridgewater College	VA	27,790	C
Bridgewater State College	MA	12,120	C
Brigham Young Univ	UT	9,200	VC
Bryan College	TN	19,270	C
Bryant College	RI	34,330	VC
Buena Vista Univ	IA	27,742	C
Butler Univ	IN	31,944	VC+
Cabrini College	PA	33,340	C
Caldwell College	NJ	26,450	LC
Calif Lutheran Univ	CA	27,800	C
Calif State Polytechnic Univ, Pomona	CA	18,053	C+
Cal State East Bay	CA	10,856	LC
Cal State, Bakersfield	CA	6,125	LC
Cal State, Chico	CA	11,395	C
Cal State, Dominguez Hills	CA	10,220	LC
Cal State, Fresno	CA	10,037	LC
Cal State, Fullerton	CA	10,990	C
Cal State, Long Beach	CA	9,512	C
Cal State, Sacramento	CA	11,122	C+
Cal State, San Bernardino	CA	12,563	LC
Cal State, San Marcos	CA	1,800	LC
Cal State, Stanislaus	CA	11,283	C
Calvin College	MI	25,735	NC
Cameron Univ	OK	6,314	NC
Campbell Univ	NC	21,137	VC
Campbellsville Univ	KY	21,328	C
Canisius College	NY	32,257	VC
Capital Univ	OH	30,444	C
Cardinal Stritch Univ	WI	21,910	C
Carlow Univ	PA	24,313	C
Carnegie Mellon Univ	PA	32,700	MC
Carroll College	MT	23,324	C+
Carroll College	WI	24,860	C
Carson-Newman College	TN	16,800	C
Cascade College	OR	17,980	NC
Castleton State College	VT	13,158	C
Catawba College	NC	25,000	C
Catholic Univ of America	DC	35,838	VC
Cazenovia College	NY	26,900	C
Cedar Crest College	PA	30,615	C
Cedarville Univ	OH	21,904	VC
Centenary College	NJ	28,870	C
Centenary College of Louisiana	LA	24,760	VC
Central College	IA	26,974	VC
Central Conn State Univ	CT	13,620	C
Central Methodist Univ	MO	18,000	C
Central Mich Univ	MI	12,244	C
Central Missouri State Univ	MO	10,000	C
Central Washington Univ	WA	11,730	C
Chaminade Univ of Honolulu	HI	23,320	LC
Chapman Univ	CA	37,550	VC
Chatham College	PA	27,290	C+
Cheyney Univ of Pennsylvania	PA	11,497	LC
Christopher Newport Univ	VA	13,326	NC
CUNY/Baruch College	NY	4,320	VC+
CUNY/City College	NY		C
CUNY/College of Staten Island	NY	4,328	NC
CUNY/Herbert H. Lehman College	NY	4,000	LC
CUNY/New York City College of Technology	NY	4,269	NC
CUNY/Queens College	NY	4,356	C
Clarion Univ of Pennsylvania	PA	11,844	C
Clark Atlanta Univ	GA	20,960	LC
Clark Univ	MA	35,165	VC+
Clarke College	IA	25,390	C
Clearwater Christian College	FL	13,160	LC
Clemson Univ	SC	13,366	HC
Cleveland State Univ	OH	10,798	LC
Coastal Carolina Univ	SC	13,140	C
Coker College	SC	21,600	C
Colby-Sawyer College	NH	27,850	LC
College Misericordia	PA	27,950	C
College of Charleston	SC	13,616	VC
College of Mount St. Vincent	NY	28,000	C
College of Mount St. Joseph	OH	24,860	C
College of New Jersey	NJ	18,315	MC
College of New Rochelle	NY	28,396	C+
College of Notre Dame of Maryland	MD	27,700	C
College of St. Benedict	MN	30,091	VC
College of St. Catherine	MN	27,505	VC
College of St. Elizabeth	NJ	28,495	C
College of St. Joseph	VT	20,900	NC
College of St. Rose	NY	25,684	C
College of St. Scholastica	MN	28,456	C+
College of Santa Fe	NM	28,978	C
College of the Ozarks	MO	4,130	VC+
College of Wooster	OH	31,310	VC+
Colo Christian Univ	CO	21,182	VC
Colo State Univ-Pueblo	CO	7,821	C
Columbia College	SC	24,982	LC
Columbia Union College	MD	23,536	LC
Columbus State Univ	GA	8,664	C
Concord College	WV	9,708	C
Concordia College: Moorhead	MN	22,475	VC
Concordia Univ	CA	26,780	C
Concordia Univ at Austin	TX	23,640	LC
Concordia Univ Nebr	NE	20,500	C+
Concordia Univ St.Paul	MN	27,776	C
Concordia Univ Wisc	WI	22,660	VC
Concordia Univ, Ann Arbor	MI	25,153	C+
Concordia Univ, River Forest	IL	26,300	C
Cornell Univ	NY	41,717	MC
Cornerstone Univ and Grand Rapids Theological Seminary	MI	21,350	NC
Creighton Univ	NE	29,918	VC+
Culver-Stockton College	MO	20,625	C
Curry College	MA	26,100	LC
Dakota Wesleyan Univ	SD	17,832	C
Dallas Baptist Univ	TX	17,040	VC
Dana College	NE	22,390	C
Davis and Elkins College	WV	22,416	C
De Sales Univ	PA	28,580	VC
Defiance College	OH	24,790	C
Denison Univ	OH	37,040	HC
DePaul Univ	IL	29,835	VC
DePauw Univ	IN	32,100	HC
Dickinson State Univ	ND	7,847	NC
Dillard Univ	LA	17,500	VC
Doane College	NE	22,458	C
Dominican Univ	IL	26,370	C
Dominican Univ of Calif	CA	36,836	C
Dordt College	IA	20,325	VC
Dowling College	NY	22,110	LC
Drake Univ	IA	27,632	VC+
Drexel Univ	PA	27,700	VC
Drury Univ	MO	20,117	VC
Duquesne Univ	PA	29,534	VC
East Carolina Univ	NC	10,000	C
East Central Univ	OK	6,207	C
East Stroudsburg Univ of Pennsylvania	PA	10,336	C
East Tenn State Univ	TN	8,497	C
Eastern Conn State Univ	CT	13,554	C
Eastern Illinois Univ	IL	12,569	C
Eastern Mennonite Univ	VA	25,450	VC
Eastern Mich Univ	MI	12,897	C
Eastern Nazarene College	MA	19,500	LC
Eastern New Mexico Univ	NM	7,264	C
Eastern Univ	PA	24,075	C
Eastern Washington Univ	WA	10,608	C
East-West Univ	IL	10,375	LC
Eckerd College	FL	35,492	VC
Edward Waters College	FL	14,374	LC
Elizabethtown College	PA	32,100	VC
Elmhurst College	IL	24,685	C
Elon Univ	NC	25,371	HC
Embry-Riddle Aeronautical Univ	AZ	30,280	C+
Embry-Riddle Aeronautical Univ	FL	30,280	C
Emerson College	MA	35,076	HC
Emmanuel College	MA	32,000	C
Emory & Henry College	VA	26,570	C
Emporia State Univ	KS	8,093	C
Endicott College	MA	30,156	C+
Eureka College	IL	19,280	C
Evangel Univ	MO	17,380	C
Excelsior College	NY	995	SP

School	ST	$IS	SR
Fairfield Univ	CT	39,835	HC
Fairleigh Dickinson Univ/ College at Florham	NJ	30,130	C
Fairleigh Dickinson Univ/ Metropolitan Campus	NJ	28,590	C
Fairmont State	WV	8,400	LC
Fitchburg State College	MA	11,276	C
Five Towns College	NY	24,600	SP
Flagler College	FL	13,790	VC+
Florida Atlantic Univ	FL	11,221	C
Florida Inst of Technology	FL	29,720	VC
Florida International Univ	FL	9,215	VC
Florida Southern College	FL	25,965	C
Florida State Univ	FL	9,028	HC
Fontbonne Univ	MO	23,308	C
Fordham Univ	NY	36,000	HC
Fort Hays State Univ	KS	7,638	C
Fort Valley State Univ	GA	6,975	C
Framingham State College	MA	11,156	C
Francis Marion Univ	SC	11,114	C
Franciscan Univ of Steubenville	OH	20,300	VC
Franklin Pierce College	NH	31,700	C
Freed-Hardeman Univ	TN	16,370	NC
Frostburg State Univ	MD	12,672	C
Furman Univ	SC	33,264	HC+
Gallaudet Univ	DC	16,554	
Gannon Univ	PA	26,100	C
Gardner-Webb Univ	NC	21,500	C
Geneva College	PA	21,850	C
George Fox Univ	OR	28,490	C
George Mason Univ	VA	10,850	VC
George Washington Univ	DC	48,820	MC
Georgetown College	KY	24,950	C+
Georgia College and State Univ	GA	11,020	C
Georgia Southern Univ	GA	9,762	C
Gonzaga Univ	WA	30,218	HC
Gordon College	MA	29,194	C+
Goshen College	IN	22,850	VC
Goucher College	MD	36,225	VC
Grace College	IN	22,170	C
Graceland Univ	IA	19,700	C
Grambling State Univ	LA	6,538	NC
Grand Canyon Univ	AZ	32,000	LC
Grand Valley State Univ	MI	12,000	VC
Grand View College	IA	21,482	C
Green Mountain College	VT	32,164	C
Greenville College	IL	23,146	C
Grove City College	PA	15,784	HC+
Gustavus Adolphus College	MN	30,920	HC
Gwynedd-Mercy College	PA	26,080	C
Hamilton College	NY	41,660	MC
Hamline Univ	MN	27,070	VC
Hampshire College	MA	37,120	HC
Hampton Univ	VA	19,468	C+
Hannibal-LaGrange College	MO	16,390	C
Hanover College	IN	28,150	HC
Harding Univ	AR	16,512	VC
Hardin-Simmons Univ	TX	18,641	C
Hastings College	NE	22,218	VC
Hawaii Pacific Univ	HI	21,080	C
Heidelberg College	OH	23,242	C
Henderson State Univ	AR	7,600	C
Hiram College	OH	28,700	VC
Hollins Univ	VA	31,105	C
Holy Names College	CA	27,980	NC
Hood College	MD	30,085	VC
Hope College	MI	28,208	VC+
Houghton College	NY	25,980	VC+
Houston Baptist Univ	TX	18,660	C
Howard Payne Univ	TX	17,115	C
Howard Univ	DC	18,481	C+
Humboldt State Univ	CA	11,176	C
Huntingdon College	AL	23,090	VC
Huntington Univ	IN	24,830	C
Huston-Tillotson Univ	TX	14,232	LC
Idaho State Univ	ID	9,030	C
Illinois College	IL	21,900	C+
Illinois State Univ	IL	12,839	C+
Indiana Inst of Technology	IN	23,430	C
Indiana State Univ	IN	11,604	C
Indiana Univ Bloomington	IN	13,356	VC
Indiana Univ East	IN	4,806	LC
Indiana Univ Kokomo	IN	4,835	LC
Indiana Univ Northwest	IN	4,902	LC
Indiana Univ of Pennsylvania	PA	11,209	C
Indiana Univ South Bend	IN	4,989	LC
Indiana Univ Southeast	IN	4,880	LC
Indiana Univ-Purdue Univ Fort Wayne	IN	5,067	LC
Indiana Univ-Purdue Univ Indianapolis	IN	10,959	C
Indiana Wesleyan Univ	IN	22,074	C+
Iona College	NY	30,878	VC
Iowa State Univ	IA	11,831	VC
Iowa Wesleyan College	IA	22,140	C
Ithaca College	NY	35,144	VC
Jackson State Univ	MS	8,500	C
Jacksonville State Univ	AL	7,618	LC
Jacksonville Univ	FL	24,040	C
James Madison Univ	VA	12,010	VC
Jamestown College	ND	14,130	NC
John Carroll Univ	OH	27,658	C+
Johnson C. Smith Univ	NC	20,000	C
Judson College	IL	25,130	C
Juniata College	PA	33,130	VC
Kansas State Univ	KS	10,516	VC
Kansas Wesleyan Univ	KS	21,400	VC
Kean Univ	NJ	15,880	C
Keene State College	NH	13,836	C
Kennesaw State Univ	GA	12,152	C
Kent State Univ	OH	14,594	C
Kentucky Wesleyan College	KY	18,590	C
Keuka College	NY	26,050	C
Keystone College	PA	22,810	LC
King's College	PA	29,810	C
La Roche College	PA	24,724	LC
La Salle Univ	PA	34,950	C
La Sierra Univ	CA	24,327	C+
Lake Erie College	OH	27,725	C
Lake Forest College	IL	33,860	VC
Lamar Univ	TX	6,820	LC
Lambuth Univ	TN	21,700	C+
Lander Univ	SC	10,600	C
Lane College	TN	11,220	C+
Le Moyne College	NY	29,570	VC
Lee Univ	TN	14,780	NC
Lees-McRae College	NC	23,000	C
Lenoir-Rhyne Univ	NC	25,580	C
Lewis and Clark College	OR	35,358	VC+
Lewis Univ	IL	23,050	C+
Lewis-Clark State College	ID	6,990	C
Liberty Univ	VA	19,101	C
Lincoln Memorial Univ	TN	18,144	C
Lincoln Univ	PA	13,658	C+
Lindenwood Univ	MO	18,600	VC
Lindsey Wilson College	KY	16,425	LC
Linfield College	OR	29,632	VC
Lipscomb Univ	TN	20,967	VC
Lock Haven Univ of Pennsylvania	PA	12,098	LC
LIU/Brooklyn Campus	NY	25,000	C
LIU/C.W. Post Campus	NY	28,282	C
Longwood Univ	VA	12,426	C
Louisiana College	LA	13,450	C
Louisiana State Univ and A&M College	LA	10,749	VC
Louisiana State Univ in Shreveport	LA	2,900	NC
Loyola College in Maryland	MD	38,898	VC
Loyola Marymount Univ	CA	36,321	VC
Loyola Univ Chicago	IL	32,896	VC
Loyola Univ New Orleans	LA	31,050	VC+
Lubbock Christian Univ	TX	16,960	C
Luther College	IA	28,800	VC+
Lycoming College	PA	30,797	C+
Lynchburg College	VA	30,645	C
Lyndon State College	VT	14,233	LC
Lynn Univ	FL	30,750	C
Madonna Univ	MI	16,068	VC
Malone College	OH	23,040	C
Manchester College	IN	23,470	C
Manhattan College	NY	29,000	VC
Marian College	IN	26,160	C
Marian College of Fond du Lac	WI	21,775	LC
Marietta College	OH	29,327	C
Marist College	NY	30,566	VC
Marquette Univ	WI	31,066	HC
Mars Hill College	NC	19,000	LC
Marshall Univ	WV	9,116	C
Martin Univ	IN	10,300	SP
Mary Baldwin College	VA	26,465	C
Marylhurst Univ	OR	14,220	NC
Marymount Manhattan College	NY	30,049	VC
Marymount Univ	VA	25,934	C
Maryville Univ of St. Louis	MO	23,000	VC
Marywood Univ	PA	30,680	C
Master's College and Seminary	CA	25,850	VC
McDaniel College	MD	31,610	VC
McMurry Univ	TX	18,100	C
McNeese State Univ	LA	5,270	LC
Medaille College	NY	21,000	C
Menlo College	CA	33,600	C
Mercyhurst College	PA	28,633	VC
Meredith College	NC	25,600	C
Merrimack College	MA	34,380	C
Mesa State College	CO	8,051	C
Messiah College	PA	28,910	VC+
Methodist College	NC	21,000	C
Metropolitan State College of Denver	CO	2,338	LC
Metropolitan State Univ	MN	4,682	SP
Miami Univ	OH	29,097	HC
Mich State Univ	MI	13,689	VC
Mich Tech Univ	MI	14,569	VC
MidAmerica Nazarene Univ	KS	20,584	LC
Middle Tenn State Univ	TN	8,340	C
Midland Lutheran College	NE	18,600	C
Midwestern State Univ	TX	9,381	LC
Miles College	AL	9,922	NC
Millersville Univ of Pennsylvania	PA	12,113	C
Milligan College	TN	21,990	C
Millikin Univ	IL	25,590	C
Minn State Univ, Mankato	MN	10,276	LC
Minn State Univ, Moorhead	MN	7,000	LC
Minot State Univ	ND	6,700	LC
Miss College	MS	14,574	VC
Miss State Univ	MS	9,577	C
Miss Univ for Women	MS	6,000	LC
Miss Valley State Univ	MS	7,970	C
Missouri Baptist Univ	MO	19,640	C
Missouri Southern State Univ	MO	8,396	NC
Missouri State Univ	MO	10,748	C+
Missouri Valley College	MO	18,500	C
Missouri Western State Univ	MO	9,534	NC
Molloy College	NY	16,510	C
Monmouth College	IL	23,700	C
Monmouth Univ	NJ	28,956	C
Montana State Univ-Billings	MT	8,906	C
Montana State Univ-Northern	MT	10,000	NC
Montana Tech of The Univ of Montana	MT	10,434	C
Montclair State Univ	NJ	16,327	C
Morehead State Univ	KY	9,150	C
Morningside College	IA	23,704	C
Mount Ida College	MA	26,000	LC
Mount Mary College	WI	22,895	C
Mount Mercy College	IA	23,670	C
Mount Olive College	NC	16,000	C
Mount St. Mary College	NY	25,250	C
Mount St. Mary's Univ	MD	30,930	C
Mount Union College	OH	25,840	C
Mount Vernon Nazarene Univ	OH	20,810	C
Mountain State Univ	WV	11,406	NC
Muhlenberg College	PA	36,030	HC+
Murray State Univ	KY	8,900	C
Muskingum College	OH	22,970	C
Nebr Wesleyan Univ	NE	23,415	C+
Neumann College	PA	25,996	LC
New England College	NH	31,466	C
New Jersey Inst of Technology	NJ	16,396	VC
New Mexico Highlands Univ	NM	6,272	NC
New Mexico State Univ	NM	9,250	C
New York Inst of Technology	NY	28,126	VC
New York Univ	NY	43,170	MC
Newberry College	SC	23,000	LC
Newbury College	MA	25,600	C
Newman Univ	KS	21,106	C
Niagara Univ	NY	28,250	C
Nicholls State Univ	LA	6,500	NC
Norfolk State Univ	VA	10,531	LC
N Car Agricultural and Technical State Univ	NC	8,000	LC
N Car State Univ	NC	11,824	HC
North Central College	IL	28,926	VC
North Central Univ	MN	16,646	LC
N Dak State Univ	ND	8,500	C
North Park Univ	IL	24,050	C
Northeastern State Univ	OK	5,896	LC
Northeastern Univ	MA	35,742	HC
Northern Arizona Univ	AZ	10,353	C
Northern Illinois Univ	IL	13,178	C
Northern Mich Univ	MI	12,340	LC
Northwest Christian College	OR	24,298	C
Northwest Missouri State Univ	MO	10,000	C
Northwest Nazarene Univ	ID	22,590	VC
Northwest Univ	WA	18,854	C
Northwestern College	MN	25,220	NC
Northwestern College of Iowa	IA	22,174	C+
Northwestern Okla State Univ	OK	6,250	NC
Northwestern Univ	IL	37,595	MC
Norwich Univ	VT	28,212	C
Notre Dame College	OH	20,425	C
Notre Dame de Namur Univ	CA	32,790	LC
Nyack College	NY	18,540	C
Oakland Univ	MI	11,936	C
Oakwood College	AL	14,904	C
Oglethorpe Univ	GA	30,300	VC
Ohio Dominican Univ	OH	25,954	C
Ohio Northern Univ	OH	27,765	VC
Ohio State Univ	OH	15,357	HC
Ohio Univ	OH	15,921	C
Okla Baptist Univ	OK	17,986	VC
Okla Christian Univ	OK	18,992	NC
Okla City Univ	OK	23,965	VC
Okla State Univ	OK	10,213	VC
Okla Wesleyan Univ	OK	18,950	NC
Old Dominion Univ	VA	11,907	C
Olivet College	MI	19,984	C+
Oral Roberts Univ	OK	22,650	C
Ottawa Univ	KS	12,000	LC
Otterbein College	OH	28,986	C
Ouachita Baptist Univ	AR	21,900	VC
Our Lady of the Lake Univ of San Antonio	TX	22,430	LC
Pace Univ	NY	30,000	VC
Pacific Lutheran Univ	WA	28,805	VC
Pacific Union College	CA	24,555	VC+
Paine College	GA	14,418	LC
Palm Beach Atlantic Univ	FL	23,597	VC
Park Univ	MO	11,592	C
Penn State Erie/The Behrend College	PA	16,256	C
Penn State Univ/Univ Park Campus	PA	18,038	HC
Pepperdine Univ	CA	39,960	HC
Pfeiffer Univ	NC	21,900	C
Piedmont College	GA	20,500	C
Pikeville College	KY	16,500	NC
Pine Manor College	MA	25,038	LC
Pittsburg State Univ	KS	8,112	C
Plymouth State Univ	NH	12,298	LC
Point Loma Nazarene Univ	CA	27,610	VC
Point Park Univ	PA	24,160	C
Pontifical Catholic Univ of PR/Ponce	PR	7,310	
Prairie View A&M Univ	TX	11,110	LC
Pratt Inst	NY	36,156	SP
Prescott College	AZ	13,445	LC
Presentation College	SD	14,800	LC
Principia College	IL	27,765	VC+
Purdue Univ/Calumet	IN	10,891	LC
Purdue Univ/West Lafayette	IN	13,458	VC
Queens Univ of Charlotte	NC	24,528	C
Quincy Univ	IL	24,920	C
Quinnipiac Univ	CT	34,640	VC
Radford Univ	VA	13,145	C
Ramapo College of New Jersey	NJ	16,630	VC
Randolph-Macon Woman's College	VA	31,160	VC+
Regis College	MA	31,350	LC
Regis Univ	CO	31,890	C
Reinhardt College	GA	20,870	C
Rensselaer Polytechnic Inst	NY	41,288	HC+
Rhode Island College	RI	11,570	C
Rider Univ	NJ	32,560	C
Ripon College	WI	27,160	C+
Rivier College	NH	26,600	C
Robert Morris Univ	PA	22,822	C
Roberts Wesleyan College	NY	26,378	C
Rochester College	MI	15,636	C+
Rochester Inst of Technology	NY	32,070	VC+
Rockhurst Univ	MO	25,440	VC
Rocky Mountain College	MT	20,805	C
Roger Williams Univ	RI	30,500	C
Roosevelt Univ	IL	22,605	VC
Rosemont College	PA	29,350	C
Rowan Univ	NJ	16,000	VC
Russell Sage College	NY	27,000	C
Rust College	MS		C+
Rutgers, The State Univ of New Jersey/New Brunswick/Piscataway Campus	NJ	15,810	HC
Saginaw Valley State Univ	MI	11,432	C
St. Ambrose Univ	IA	25,495	C
St. Andrews Presbyterian College	NC	23,530	C
St. Augustine's College	NC	14,000	LC
St. Cloud State Univ	MN	10,010	C
St. Edward's Univ	TX	23,560	C
St. Francis College	NY	19,974	LC
St. Francis Univ	PA	25,880	LC
St. John Fisher College	NY	27,860	C
St. John's Univ	MN	29,749	VC
St. John's Univ	NY	34,370	C
St. Joseph's College of Maine	ME	29,185	C
St. Joseph's Univ	PA	37,428	VC
St. Lawrence Univ	NY	40,545	VC
St. Leo Univ	FL	22,140	C+
St. Louis Univ	MO	33,158	VC+
St. Mary's College	IN	32,538	VC
St. Mary's College of Calif	CA	37,290	C
St. Mary's Univ of San Antonio	TX	22,444	C
St. Norbert College	WI	28,577	C+
St. Peter's College	NJ	30,160	LC
St. Thomas Aquinas College	NY	22,000	LC
St. Thomas Univ	FL	23,490	C
St. Vincent College	PA	26,160	VC
St. Xavier Univ	IL	23,160	C
Salem College	NC	26,226	VC+
Salem International Univ	WV	18,020	C
Salem State College	MA	13,161	LC
Salisbury Univ	MD	13,128	VC
Salve Regina Univ	RI	33,450	C
Samford Univ	AL	20,258	VC
San Diego Christian College	CA	24,172	C
San Diego State Univ	CA	12,971	C
Santa Clara Univ	CA	38,931	VC
Savannah State Univ	GA	7,772	LC
Seattle Pacific Univ	WA	29,355	C
Seattle Univ	WA	30,063	VC
Seton Hall Univ	NJ	33,622	VC
Seton Hill Univ	PA	28,810	C
Shenandoah Univ	VA	27,600	C
Shepherd Univ	WV	10,066	C
Shippensburg Univ of Pennsylvania	PA	11,621	C
Shorter College	GA	19,700	C
Siena Heights Univ	MI	17,000	LC
Simmons College	MA	35,640	VC
Simpson College	IA	26,833	VC
Simpson Univ	CA	22,900	C

ST = STATE   **$IS** = IN-STATE COSTS   **SR** = SELECTOR RATING

School	ST	$IS	SR
Slippery Rock Univ of Pennsylvania	PA	10,360	LC
Sonoma State Univ	CA	14,732	C
S Dak State Univ	SD	9,815	C
Southeast Missouri State Univ	MO	10,596	C
Southeastern Louisiana Univ	LA	8,521	LC
Southeastern Okla State Univ	OK	6,147	C
Southeastern Univ	FL	17,180	LC
Southern Adventist Univ	TN	18,500	C
Southern Arkansas Univ	AR	6,956	C
Southern Conn State Univ	CT	10,310	C
Southern Illinois Univ Edwardsville	IL	11,022	C
Southern Methodist Univ	TX	36,088	VC+
Southern Nazarene Univ	OK	14,634	NC
Southern New Hampshire Univ	NH	28,764	C
Southern Oregon Univ	OR	12,186	C
Southern Univ and A&M College	LA	8,238	LC
Southern Utah Univ	UT		C
Southern Vermont College	VT	21,322	LC
Southwest Baptist Univ	MO	18,300	C
Southwest Minn State Univ	MN	10,975	C
Southwestern Adventist Univ	TX	18,290	LC
Southwestern College	KS	21,476	C
Southwestern Okla State Univ	OK	4,801	C
Southwestern Univ	TX	26,767	HC
Spalding Univ	KY	18,882	C
Spring Arbor Univ	MI	22,476	C
Spring Hill College	AL	28,678	C
Stanford Univ	CA	41,557	MC
SUNY at Oswego	NY	13,662	VC
SUNY/College at Brockport	NY	12,747	VC
SUNY/College at Buffalo	NY	11,903	C+
SUNY/College at Cortland	NY	12,095	C
SUNY/College at Fredonia	NY	12,771	VC
SUNY/College at Geneseo	NY	12,910	HC+
SUNY/College at Old Westbury	NY	13,154	C
SUNY/College at Oneonta	NY	12,905	VC
SUNY/College at Plattsburgh	NY	12,362	C
SUNY/Univ at Albany	NY	13,860	VC
SUNY/Univ at Buffalo	NY	13,694	VC
SUNY/Univ at New Paltz	NY	12,480	VC
Stephen F. Austin State Univ	TX	7,930	C
Sterling College	KS	19,992	C
Stetson Univ	FL	32,725	VC
Stonehill College	MA	36,104	HC
Suffolk Univ	MA	33,160	C
Sul Ross State Univ	TX	6,600	LC
Susquehanna Univ	PA	33,465	VC
Syracuse Univ	NY	38,655	HC
Tabor College	KS	21,614	NC
Taylor Univ	IN	26,376	VC+
Temple Univ	PA	17,438	C
Texas A&M Univ at Corpus Christi	TX	10,280	LC
Texas A&M Univ at Kingsville	TX	6,800	C
Texas Christian Univ	TX	23,410	VC+
Texas Lutheran Univ	TX	23,530	C
Texas Southern Univ	TX	9,828	C
Texas State Univ - San Marcos	TX	10,862	C
Texas Tech Univ	TX	13,026	VC
Texas Wesleyan Univ	TX	18,700	C
Texas Woman's Univ	TX	7,804	LC
Thiel College	PA	24,580	C
Thomas College	ME	23,770	LC
Thomas Edison State College	NJ	3,780	SP
Thomas More College	KY	24,470	C
Toccoa Falls College	GA	17,125	C
Tougaloo College	MS	15,975	NC
Towson Univ	MD	13,924	VC
Trevecca Nazarene Univ	TN	19,594	C
Trinity Christian College	IL	23,645	C
Trinity College	DC	24,150	LC
Trinity International Univ	IL	25,686	C
Trinity Univ	TX	30,157	HC+
Tri-State Univ-Main Campus	IN	26,200	C
Troy Univ	AL	8,916	C
Truman State Univ	MO	11,242	HC
Tulane Univ	LA	41,098	MC
Union College	NE	18,710	C
Union Inst & Univ	OH	8,912	SP
Union Univ	TN	20,750	VC
Univ of Akron	OH	15,166	NC
Univ of Alabama	AL	9,888	C
Univ of Alabama at Birmingham	AL	13,716	C
Univ of Alabama in Huntsville	AL	9,516	VC
Univ of Alaska Anchorage	AK	11,275	NC
Univ of Alaska Fairbanks	AK	10,101	C
Univ of Alaska Southeast	AK	8,050	LC
Univ of Arizona	AZ	11,958	VC

School	ST	$IS	SR
Univ of Arkansas	AR	11,859	VC
Univ of at Calif Davis	CA	15,010	VC
Univ of Bridgeport	CT	29,595	LC
Univ of Calif at Berkeley	CA	18,141	HC+
Univ of Calif at Los Angeles	CA	17,681	MC
Univ of Calif at San Diego	CA	16,102	HC
Univ of Calif at Santa Barbara	CA	11,800	VC
Univ of Central Arkansas	AR	9,984	C
Univ of Central Florida	FL	10,739	VC
Univ of Central Okla	OK	8,094	C
Univ of Charleston	WV	27,600	C
Univ of Cincinnati	OH	17,682	C
Univ of Colo at Boulder	CO	13,352	C+
Univ of Colo at Colo Springs	CO	11,517	VC
Univ of Colo at Denver and Health Sciences Center	CO	5,021	C
Univ of Conn	CT	16,628	HC
Univ of Dayton	OH	28,826	VC
Univ of Delaware	DE	14,142	HC
Univ of Denver	CO	36,376	VC+
Univ of Detroit Mercy	MI	27,000	C
Univ of Evansville	IN	28,320	VC
Univ of Findlay	OH	29,238	C
Univ of Hartford	CT	34,044	C
Univ of Hawaii at Hilo	HI	6,500	C
Univ of Hawaii at Manoa	HI	10,413	VC
Univ of Houston	TX	7,000	C
Univ of Idaho	ID	9,310	NC
Univ of Illinois at Urbana-Champaign	IL	15,800	HC+
Univ of Indianapolis	IN	25,090	C
Univ of Iowa	IA	12,172	VC
Univ of Kentucky	KY	7,800	C
Univ of La Verne	CA	33,470	C
Univ of Louisiana at Lafayette	LA	5,830	C
Univ of Louisiana at Monroe	LA	7,103	C
Univ of Louisville	KY	10,400	VC
Univ of Maine	ME	13,642	C
Univ of Mary	ND	15,374	C
Univ of Mary Hardin-Baylor	TX	19,428	C
Univ of Maryland/College Park	MD	16,036	HC
Univ of Maryland/Univ College	MD	5,640	SP
Univ of Mass Amherst	MA	15,973	C+
Univ of Memphis	TN	11,153	C
Univ of Miami	FL	38,397	MC
Univ of Mich/Ann Arbor	MI	16,587	HC+
Univ of Mich/Flint	MI	6,398	C
Univ of Minn/Crookston	MN	13,157	LC
Univ of Minn/Duluth	MN	13,974	C
Univ of Missouri/Columbia	MO	13,500	VC
Univ of Missouri/Kansas City	MO	15,000	VC
Univ of Missouri/St. Louis	MO	14,046	VC
Univ of Mobile	AL	16,880	C
Univ of Montana	MT	10,602	C
Univ of Montana--Western	MT	8,406	NC
Univ of Montevallo	AL	9,630	C
Univ of Nebr at Kearney	NE	9,000	NC
Univ of Nebr at Lincoln	NE	11,401	VC
Univ of Nebr at Omaha	NE	11,235	C
Univ of Nevada/Las Vegas	NV	11,566	C
Univ of New England	ME	31,005	C
Univ of New Hampshire	NH	16,810	VC
Univ of New Haven	CT	31,794	C
Univ of New Mexico	NM	11,253	C
Univ of New Orleans	LA	7,370	C
Univ of North Alabama	AL	8,992	C
Univ of N Car at Asheville	NC	9,237	VC
Univ of N Car at Chapel Hill	NC	11,129	MC
Univ of N Car at Charlotte	NC	9,101	C
Univ of N Car at Greensboro	NC	8,993	C
Univ of N Car at Pembroke	NC	7,940	LC
Univ of N Dak	ND	10,114	VC
Univ of North Florida	FL	9,908	C
Univ of North Texas	TX	7,800	C
Univ of Northern Colo	CO	10,249	C
Univ of Northern Iowa	IA	11,133	C
Univ of Okla	OK	10,769	VC+
Univ of Pennsylvania	PA	41,766	MC
Univ of Pittsburgh at Bradford	PA	17,008	C
Univ of Pittsburgh at Greensburg	PA	17,640	C
Univ of Pittsburgh at Johnstown	PA	16,740	LC
Univ of Pittsburgh at Pittsburgh	PA	18,866	HC
Univ of Portland	OR	32,300	VC
Univ of Puget Sound	WA	35,600	HC
Univ of Rhode Island	RI	15,398	C
Univ of Rio Grande	OH	8,728	NC
Univ of St. Francis	IL	25,430	C
Univ of St. Francis	IN	20,970	C
Univ of St. Thomas	MN	28,000	VC
Univ of St. Thomas	TX	23,810	VC
Univ of San Diego	CA	42,620	HC
Univ of San Francisco	CA	37,560	VC
Univ of Science and Arts of Okla	OK	7,650	C
Univ of Scranton	PA	31,100	VC

School	ST	$IS	SR
Univ of Sioux Falls	SD	20,800	C
Univ of South Alabama	AL	8,930	LC
Univ of S Car at Aiken	SC	11,718	LC
Univ of S Car at Columbia	SC	13,397	VC
Univ of S Car Upstate	SC	11,957	C
Univ of South Florida	FL	10,284	VC
Univ of Southern Calif	CA	41,618	MC
Univ of Southern Indiana	IN	12,590	LC
Univ of Southern Maine	ME	12,614	C
Univ of Southern Miss	MS	10,112	C
Univ of Tampa	FL	25,784	C
Univ of Tenn at Chattanooga	TN	7,790	C
Univ of Tenn at Martin	TN	8,693	C
Univ of Texas at Arlington	TX	7,195	LC
Univ of Texas at El Paso	TX	8,764	NC
Univ of Texas at San Antonio	TX	11,325	LC
Univ of Texas-Pan American	TX	7,290	C+
Univ of the Arts	PA	32,330	SP
Univ of the Cumberlands	KY	18,184	C
Univ of the Incarnate Word	TX	23,306	C
Univ of the Ozarks	AR	19,250	C
Univ of the Pacific	CA	34,380	VC
Univ of the Sacred Heart	PR	5,590	
Univ of Toledo	OH	15,806	NC
Univ of Tulsa	OK	25,348	NC
Univ of Utah	UT	10,162	VC
Univ of Virginia's College at Wise	VA	11,076	C
Univ of Washington	WA	10,400	VC
Univ of West Florida	FL	8,559	C
Univ of West Georgia	GA	8,838	C
Univ of Wisc/Eau Claire	WI	9,915	VC
Univ of Wisc/Green Bay	WI	9,415	VC
Univ of Wisc/La Crosse	WI	10,045	VC
Univ of Wisc/Madison	WI	13,117	HC
Univ of Wisc/Milwaukee	WI	9,427	LC
Univ of Wisc/Parkside	WI	10,181	LC
Univ of Wisc/Platteville	WI	9,779	NC
Univ of Wisc/River Falls	WI	9,722	LC
Univ of Wisc/Stevens Point	WI	9,384	VC
Univ of Wisc/Stout	WI	11,164	C
Univ of Wisc/Superior	WI	9,610	C
Univ of Wisc/Whitewater	WI	9,274	C
Univ of Wyoming	WY	9,666	C
Upper Iowa Univ	IA	20,130	C
Urbana Univ	OH	21,190	C
Ursinus College	PA	38,950	VC
Utica College	NY	31,396	C
Valparaiso Univ	IN	28,970	VC+
Vanderbilt Univ	TN	41,986	MC
Vanguard Univ of Southern Calif	CA	27,071	C
Villanova Univ	PA	38,672	HC+
Virginia Commonwealth Univ	VA	12,987	C
Virginia Polytechnic Inst and State Univ	VA	10,834	VC
Virginia Wesleyan College	VA	28,433	C
Wake Forest Univ	NC	38,290	MC
Walla Walla College	WA	24,489	NC
Walsh Univ	OH	23,440	C
Warner Southern College	FL	18,000	LC
Wartburg College	IA	27,315	NC
Washburn Univ	KS	9,734	NC
Washington State Univ	WA	12,260	C
Washington Univ in St. Louis	MO	42,106	MC
Wayland Baptist Univ	TX	13,484	C
Wayne State College	NE	8,033	NC
Wayne State Univ	MI	11,805	C
Waynesburg College	PA	21,230	C
Weber State Univ	UT	9,635	NC
Webster Univ	MO	24,280	VC
Wesley College	DE	19,905	C
Wesleyan College	GA	19,560	C
West Chester Univ of Pennsylvania	PA	12,355	C+
West Liberty State College	WV	9,142	LC
West Virginia State Univ	WV	8,378	NC
West Virginia Univ	WV	10,506	C
Western Baptist College	OR	21,808	C
Western Carolina Univ	NC	7,000	C
Western Conn State Univ	CT	12,993	C
Western Illinois Univ	IL	13,042	C
Western Kentucky Univ	KY	10,192	C
Western Mich Univ	MI	13,299	C
Western New England College	MA	32,054	C
Western State College of Colo	CO	9,942	C
Western Washington Univ	WA	11,262	VC
Westfield State College	MA	10,200	C
Westminster College	PA	31,290	C+
Westminster College	UT	25,656	C
Westmont College	CA	36,672	HC
Wheaton College	IL	27,760	HC
Whitworth College	WA	29,428	VC+
Wichita State Univ	KS	8,500	C
Widener Univ	PA	27,275	C
Wilberforce Univ	OH	14,937	LC
Wiley College	TX	8,100	LC
William Carey College	MS	11,000	LC

School	ST	$IS	SR
William Jewell College	MO	24,340	C
William Paterson Univ of New Jersey	NJ	17,810	C+
William Penn Univ	IA	17,685	LC
William Tyndale College	MI	13,000	NC
William Woods Univ	MO	21,020	C
Wilmington College	OH	2,806	NC
Wilson College	PA	27,660	C
Wingate Univ	NC	23,300	C
Winona State Univ	MN	11,333	C
Winston-Salem State Univ	NC	8,960	LC
Winthrop Univ	SC	11,302	C
Wisc Lutheran College	WI	23,510	VC
Wittenberg Univ	OH	34,596	VC
Woodbury Univ	CA	30,176	LC
Worcester State College	MA	12,499	C
Wright State Univ	OH	13,616	LC
Xavier Univ	OH	30,490	HC
Xavier Univ of Louisiana	LA	17,600	C
Yeshiva Univ	NY	22,000	C
York College	NE	16,330	NC
York College of Pennsylvania	PA	16,550	VC
Youngstown State Univ	OH	12,613	NC

COMMUNICATIONS TECHNOLOGY

School	ST	$IS	SR
Alverno College	WI	21,088	C
Cal State, Monterey Bay	CA	10,099	C
Champlain College	VT	24,605	C
Chestnut Hill College	PA	26,600	C
Eastern Mich Univ	MI	12,897	C
Inter American Univ of PR/ Bayamon Univ College	PR	3,522	
James Madison Univ	VA	12,010	VC
Lebanon Valley College	PA	31,700	VC
Lewis Univ	IL	23,050	C+
Loyola Univ New Orleans	LA	31,050	VC+
Montana Tech of The Univ of Montana	MT	10,434	C
Montclair State Univ	NJ	16,327	C
New York Univ	NY	43,170	MC
Northwestern Univ	IL	37,595	MC
Rochester Inst of Technology	NY	32,070	VC+
Sacred Heart Univ	CT	33,404	C
Salve Regina Univ	RI	33,450	C
Southern Methodist Univ	TX	36,088	VC+
SUNY/Inst of Technology	NY	12,575	VC
Trevecca Nazarene Univ	TN	19,594	C
Univ of S Dak	SD	9,068	C
Wilmington College	DE	5,594	NC

COMMUNITY HEALTH WORK

School	ST	$IS	SR
Baylor Univ	TX	27,555	HC
Brown Univ	RI	42,015	MC
Central Washington Univ	WA	11,730	C
CUNY/York College	NY	4,242	NC
Delaware State Univ	DE	8,130	LC
Florida Gulf Coast Univ	FL	10,833	C
Florida State Univ	FL	9,028	HC
Georgia Southern Univ	GA	9,762	C
Hofstra Univ	NY	32,630	VC
Ithaca College	NY	35,144	VC
John Brown Univ	AR	20,910	VC
Lewis Univ	IL	23,050	C+
Liberty Univ	VA	19,101	C
Longwood Univ	VA	12,426	C
Malone College	OH	23,040	C
Montclair State Univ	NJ	16,327	C
Morris College	SC	11,999	C
New Mexico State Univ	NM	9,250	C
Northern Illinois Univ	IL	13,178	C
Ohio Univ	OH	15,921	C
Purdue Univ/West Lafayette	IN	13,458	VC
St. Joseph's College, New York, Brooklyn Campus	NY	12,206	C
Slippery Rock Univ of Pennsylvania	PA	10,360	LC
SUNY at Potsdam	NY	12,959	C
SUNY/College at Old Westbury	NY	13,154	C
Texas State Univ - San Marcos	TX	10,862	C
Univ of at Calif Davis	CA	15,010	VC
Univ of Central Okla	OK	8,094	C
Univ of Illinois at Urbana-Champaign	IL	15,800	HC+
Univ of Kansas	KS	10,915	VC
Univ of Maine at Farmington	ME	11,515	C
Univ of Maryland/College Park	MD	16,036	HC
Univ of Mass Lowell	MA	14,327	VC
Univ of Nebr at Lincoln	NE	11,401	VC
Univ of Nebr at Omaha	NE	11,235	C
Univ of N Car at Pembroke	NC	7,940	VC
Univ of N Dak	ND	10,114	VC
Univ of Northern Colo	CO	10,249	C
Univ of St. Thomas	MN	28,000	VC
Univ of Tenn at Knoxville	TN	11,720	C
Univ of Wisc/La Crosse	WI	10,045	VC
Univ of Wisc/Superior	WI	9,610	C+

ST = STATE   **$IS** = IN-STATE COSTS   **SR** = SELECTOR RATING

School	ST	$IS	SR
Western Conn State Univ	CT	12,993	C
Western Mich Univ	MI	13,299	C
William Paterson Univ of New Jersey	NJ	17,810	C+
Youngstown State Univ	OH	12,613	NC

COMMUNITY PSYCHOLOGY

School	ST	$IS	SR
East Texas Baptist Univ	TX	16,713	C
Kent State Univ	OH	14,594	C
Southwestern Okla State Univ	OK	4,801	C
Univ of Mich/Flint	MI	6,398	C
Univ of New Haven	CT	31,794	C

COMMUNITY SERVICES

School	ST	$IS	SR
Alverno College	WI	21,088	C
Aquinas College	MI	23,750	C
Bemidji State Univ	MN	11,180	LC
Central Mich Univ	MI	12,244	C
Emory & Henry College	VA	26,570	C
Guilford College	NC	28,160	C+
Humphreys College	CA	7,000	NC
Martin Univ	IN	10,300	SP
Metropolitan College of New York	NY	16,000	C
Midland Lutheran College	NE	18,600	C
NAES College of Eastern Illinois Univ	IL	5,150	SP
Northern State Univ	SD	8,257	C
Ohio Univ	OH	15,921	C
Portland State Univ	OR	12,453	C
Prescott College	AZ	13,445	LC
Providence College	RI	34,580	HC
St. Martin's Univ	WA	27,555	C
Samford Univ	AL	20,258	VC
Southern Arkansas Univ	AR	6,956	C
SUNY/College at Plattsburgh	NY	12,362	C
SUNY/Empire State College	NY	4,575	SP
Thomas Edison State College	NJ	3,780	SP
Univ of Calif at Santa Cruz	CA	19,174	VC
Univ of Delaware	DE	14,142	HC
Univ of Mass Boston	MA	8,024	C
Univ of Toledo	OH	15,806	NC
Winona State Univ	MN	11,333	C
Woodbury College	VT	15,150	LC

COMPARATIVE LITERATURE

School	ST	$IS	SR
Beloit College	WI	32,808	HC
Bennington College	VT	41,890	HC
Brandeis Univ	MA	41,551	MC
Brigham Young Univ	UT	9,200	VC
Brown Univ	RI	42,015	MC
Bryn Mawr College	PA	42,780	HC+
Cal State, Fullerton	CA	10,990	C
Cal State, Long Beach	CA	9,512	C
Case Western Reserve Univ	OH	37,314	MC
Cedar Crest College	PA	30,615	C
CUNY/Brooklyn College	NY	4,377	C+
CUNY/City College	NY		C
CUNY/Herbert H. Lehman College	NY	4,000	LC
CUNY/Hunter College	NY	8,000	C+
CUNY/Queens College	NY	4,356	C
Clark Univ	MA	35,165	VC+
College of Wooster	OH	31,310	VC+
Colo College	CO	37,668	HC
Columbia Univ/Barnard College	NY	38,000	MC
Columbia Univ/Columbia College	NY	42,584	MC
Columbia Univ/School of General Studies	NY	41,516	C
Conn College	CT	41,975	MC
Cornell Univ	NY	41,717	MC
Dartmouth College	NH	39,465	MC
DePaul Univ	IL	29,835	VC
Eckerd College	FL	35,492	VC
Emory Univ	GA	40,546	MC
Fordham Univ	NY	36,000	HC
Georgetown Univ	DC	43,183	MC
Hamilton College	NY	41,660	MC
Hampshire College	MA	37,120	HC
Haverford College	PA	41,600	MC
Hillsdale College	MI	24,160	HC
Hobart and William Smith Colleges	NY	41,123	VC
Hofstra Univ	NY	32,630	VC
Indiana Univ Bloomington	IN	13,356	VC
Mills College	CA	39,870	C
New England College	NH	31,466	C
New York Univ	NY	43,170	MC
Northwestern Univ	IL	37,595	MC
Oberlin College	OH	40,904	MC
Occidental College	CA	40,185	MC
Penn State Univ/Univ Park Campus	PA	18,038	HC
Princeton Univ	NJ	40,213	MC
Purdue Univ/West Lafayette	IN	13,458	VC

School	ST	$IS	SR
Rutgers, The State Univ of New Jersey/New Brunswick/Piscataway Campus	NJ	15,810	HC
San Diego State Univ	CA	12,971	C
San Francisco State Univ	CA	13,000	C
Smith College	MA	41,474	MC
Stanford Univ	CA	41,557	MC
SUNY/College at Geneseo	NY	12,910	HC+
SUNY/Univ at Binghamton	NY	13,988	HC
SUNY/Univ at Stony Brook	NY	13,625	HC
Swarthmore College	PA	41,280	MC
Syracuse Univ	NY	38,655	HC
Trinity College	CT	38,040	HC+
Univ of at Calif Davis	CA	15,010	VC
Univ of Calif at Berkeley	CA	18,141	HC+
Univ of Calif at Irvine	CA	16,475	HC
Univ of Calif at Los Angeles	CA	17,681	MC
Univ of Calif at Riverside	CA	16,625	C
Univ of Calif at Santa Barbara	CA	11,800	VC
Univ of Chicago	IL	42,369	MC
Univ of Cincinnati	OH	17,682	C
Univ of Delaware	DE	14,142	HC
Univ of Georgia	GA	11,004	HC
Univ of Illinois at Urbana-Champaign	IL	15,800	HC+
Univ of Iowa	IA	12,172	VC
Univ of La Verne	CA	33,470	C
Univ of Mass Amherst	MA	15,973	C+
Univ of Mich/Ann Arbor	MI	16,587	HC+
Univ of New Mexico	NM	11,253	C
Univ of N Car at Chapel Hill	NC	11,129	NC
Univ of Oregon	OR	13,108	VC
Univ of Pennsylvania	PA	41,766	MC
Univ of PR/Rio Piedras	PR	5,750	
Univ of Rhode Island	RI	15,398	C
Univ of Rochester	NY	41,135	MC
Univ of S Car at Columbia	SC	13,397	VC
Univ of Southern Calif	CA	41,618	MC
Univ of Tenn at Knoxville	TN	11,720	C
Univ of Virginia	VA	13,759	MC
Univ of Washington	WA	10,400	VC
Univ of Wisc/Madison	WI	13,117	HC
Univ of Wisc/Milwaukee	WI	9,427	LC
Washington Univ in St. Louis	MO	42,106	MC
Wellesley College	MA	41,030	MC
West Chester Univ of Pennsylvania	PA	12,355	C+
Willamette Univ	OR	35,416	VC+

COMPUTATIONAL SCIENCES

School	ST	$IS	SR
Brown Univ	RI	42,015	MC
Mich State Univ	MI	13,689	VC
Park Univ	MO	11,592	C
SUNY/College at Brockport	NY	12,747	VC
Stevens Inst of Technology	NJ	40,935	HC
Univ of Illinois at Urbana-Champaign	IL	15,800	HC+

COMPUTER EDUCATION

School	ST	$IS	SR
Averett Univ	VA	24,920	C
Baylor Univ	TX	27,555	HC
College of St. Joseph	VT	20,900	NC
Concordia Univ, River Forest	IL	26,300	C
Eastern Mich Univ	MI	12,897	C
Eastern Washington Univ	WA	10,608	C
Florida Inst of Technology	FL	29,720	VC
Hardin-Simmons Univ	TX	18,641	C
Marymount Univ	VA	25,934	C
Northern Mich Univ	MI	12,340	LC
St. Martin's Univ	WA	27,555	C
Union College	NE	18,710	C
Univ of Illinois at Urbana-Champaign	IL	15,800	HC+
Viterbo Univ	WI	21,670	C
Youngstown State Univ	OH	12,613	NC

COMPUTER ENGINEERING

School	ST	$IS	SR
Arizona State Univ-Tempe	AZ	11,174	C
Auburn Univ	AL	12,230	VC
Baylor Univ	TX	27,555	HC
Bellarmine Univ	KY	27,650	C+
Benedict College	SC	19,114	LC
Bethune-Cookman College	FL	17,922	LC
Boston Univ	MA	42,046	HC+
Brigham Young Univ	UT	9,200	VC
Bucknell Univ	PA	39,660	MC
Calif Polytechnic State Univ	CA	12,390	VC
Cal State, Chico	CA	11,395	C
Cal State, Fresno	CA	10,037	LC
Cal State, Long Beach	CA	9,512	C
Cal State, Sacramento	CA	11,122	C
Capitol College	MD	21,250	C
Carnegie Mellon Univ	PA	32,700	MC
Case Western Reserve Univ	OH	37,314	MC
Cedarville Univ	OH	21,904	VC
Christopher Newport Univ	VA	13,326	VC
CUNY/City College	NY		C

School	ST	$IS	SR
CUNY/New York City College of Technology	NY	4,269	NC
Claflin Univ	SC	16,798	C+
Clarkson Univ	NY	34,930	VC
Clemson Univ	SC	13,366	HC
Cogswell Polytechnical College	CA	13,760	LC
College of New Jersey	NJ	18,315	MC
Colo Technical Univ	CO	9,500	LC
Columbia Univ/Fu Foundation School of Engineering and Applied Science	NY	42,584	MC
Cornell Univ	NY	41,717	MC
DeVry Univ/Addison (DuPage County)	IL	10,800	LC
DeVry Univ/Alpharetta	GA	10,675	LC
DeVry Univ/Chicago	IL	10,800	LC
DeVry Univ/Columbus	OH	11,000	LC
DeVry Univ/Crystal City	VA	12,000	C
DeVry Univ/Dallas	TX	10,700	LC
DeVry Univ/Decatur	GA	10,680	LC
DeVry Univ/Fort Washington	PA	12,000	LC
DeVry Univ/Fremont	CA	13,060	LC
DeVry Univ/Kansas City	MO	10,670	LC
DeVry Univ/Long Beach	CA	12,450	LC
DeVry Univ/Miramar	FL	12,000	C
DeVry Univ/Orlando	FL	12,000	LC
DeVry Univ/Phoenix	AZ	11,790	LC
DeVry Univ/Pomona	CA	12,450	LC
DeVry Univ/Seattle	WA	12,000	LC
DeVry Univ/Tinley Park	IL	12,000	LC
DeVry Univ/West Hills	CA	12,450	LC
DeVry Univ/Westminster	CO	12,000	LC
Drexel Univ	PA	27,700	VC
Eastern Nazarene College	MA	19,500	LC
Elizabethtown College	PA	32,100	C
Embry-Riddle Aeronautical Univ	AZ	30,280	C+
Embry-Riddle Aeronautical Univ	FL	30,280	C
Fairfield Univ	CT	39,835	HC
Florida Atlantic Univ	FL	11,221	C
Florida Inst of Technology	FL	29,720	VC
Florida International Univ	FL	9,215	VC
Florida State Univ	FL	9,028	HC
George Mason Univ	VA	10,850	VC
George Washington Univ	DC	48,820	MC
Georgia Inst of Technology	GA	11,450	HC+
Gonzaga Univ	WA	30,218	HC
Harding Univ	AR	16,512	VC
Hofstra Univ	NY	32,630	VC
Illinois Inst of Technology	IL	26,465	HC+
Indiana Inst of Technology	IN	23,430	C
Indiana Univ-Purdue Univ Fort Wayne	IN	5,067	LC
Indiana Univ-Purdue Univ Indianapolis	IN	10,959	C
Iowa State Univ	IA	11,831	VC
Johns Hopkins Univ	MD	42,044	MC
Johnson C. Smith Univ	NC	20,000	C
Kansas State Univ	KS	10,516	VC
Kettering Univ	MI	29,338	HC
Lawrence Tech Univ	MI	25,475	VC
Lehigh Univ	PA	42,690	HC+
LeTourneau Univ	TX	21,200	C
Lipscomb Univ	TN	20,967	VC
Louisiana State Univ and A&M College	LA	10,749	VC
Marquette Univ	WI	31,066	HC
Mich State Univ	MI	13,689	VC
Mich Tech Univ	MI	14,569	VC
Milwaukee School of Engineering	WI	29,847	VC+
Minn State Univ, Mankato	MN	10,276	LC
Miss State Univ	MS	9,577	C
Montana State Univ-Bozeman	MT	1,137	C
Montana Tech of The Univ of Montana	MT	10,434	C
New Jersey Inst of Technology	NJ	16,396	VC
New York Inst of Technology	NY	28,126	VC
New York Univ	NY	43,170	MC
N Car State Univ	NC	11,824	HC
N Dak State Univ	ND	8,500	C
Northeastern Univ	MA	35,742	HC
Northern Arizona Univ	AZ	10,353	C
Northwestern Univ	IL	37,595	MC
Norwich Univ	VT	28,212	C
Oakland Univ	MI	11,936	C
Ohio Northern Univ	OH	27,765	VC
Ohio State Univ	OH	15,357	HC
Ohio Univ	OH	15,921	C
Okla Christian Univ	OK	18,992	NC
Oregon State Univ	OR	11,055	C
Pacific Lutheran Univ	WA	28,805	VC
Penn State Erie/The Behrend College	PA	16,256	C
Penn State Univ/Univ Park Campus	PA	18,038	HC

School	ST	$IS	SR
Pennsylvania College of Technology	PA	16,980	LC
Polytechnic Univ/Brooklyn	NY	37,150	VC
Portland State Univ	OR	12,453	C
Prairie View A&M Univ	TX	11,110	LC
Purdue Univ/Calumet	IN	10,891	LC
Purdue Univ/West Lafayette	IN	13,458	VC
Rensselaer Polytechnic Inst	NY	41,288	HC+
Rochester Inst of Technology	NY	32,070	VC+
Roger Williams Univ	RI	30,500	C
Rose-Hulman Inst of Technology	IN	34,557	HC+
St. Mary's Univ of Minn	MN	23,857	VC
St. Mary's Univ of San Antonio	TX	22,444	C
San Diego State Univ	CA	12,971	C
San Jose State Univ	CA	11,707	C
Santa Clara Univ	CA	38,931	VC
S Dak School of Mines and Technology	SD	7,624	C+
Southern Illinois Univ Carbondale	IL	12,391	C
Southern Illinois Univ Edwardsville	IL	11,022	C
Southern Methodist Univ	TX	36,088	VC+
Southern Polytechnic State Univ	GA	7,640	VC
Southwestern Okla State Univ	OK	4,801	C
SUNY/Univ at Binghamton	NY	13,988	HC
SUNY/Univ at Buffalo	NY	13,694	VC
SUNY/Univ at New Paltz	NY	12,480	VC
SUNY/Univ at Stony Brook	NY	13,625	VC
Stevens Inst of Technology	NJ	40,935	HC
Stonehill College	MA	36,104	HC
Suffolk Univ	MA	33,160	C
Syracuse Univ	NY	38,655	HC
Taylor Univ	IN	26,376	VC+
Texas A&M Univ	TX	13,351	HC
Tri-State Univ-Main Campus	IN	26,200	C
Tufts Univ	MA	42,018	MC
Tulane Univ	LA	41,098	MC
Union College	NY	41,595	HC
United States Air Force Academy	CO		HC+
Univ of Akron	OH	15,166	NC
Univ of Alabama in Huntsville	AL	9,516	VC
Univ of Arizona	AZ	11,958	VC
Univ of Arkansas	AR	11,859	VC
Univ of at Calif Davis	CA	15,010	VC
Univ of Bridgeport	CT	29,555	LC
Univ of Calif at Berkeley	CA	18,141	HC+
Univ of Calif at Irvine	CA	16,475	HC
Univ of Calif at Los Angeles	CA	17,681	MC
Univ of Calif at Riverside	CA	16,625	C
Univ of Calif at San Diego	CA	16,102	HC
Univ of Calif at Santa Cruz	CA	19,174	VC
Univ of Central Florida	FL	10,739	VC
Univ of Cincinnati	OH	17,682	C
Univ of Colo at Boulder	CO	13,352	C+
Univ of Conn	CT	16,628	HC
Univ of Dayton	OH	28,826	VC
Univ of Delaware	DE	14,142	HC
Univ of Denver	CO	36,376	VC+
Univ of Evansville	IN	28,320	VC
Univ of Florida	FL	9,354	HC
Univ of Hartford	CT	34,044	C
Univ of Houston	TX	7,000	C
Univ of Idaho	ID	9,310	NC
Univ of Illinois at Chicago	IL	16,256	VC
Univ of Illinois at Urbana-Champaign	IL	15,800	HC+
Univ of Iowa	IA	12,172	VC
Univ of Kansas	KS	10,915	VC
Univ of La Verne	CA	33,470	C
Univ of Louisiana at Lafayette	LA	5,830	C
Univ of Louisville	KY	10,400	VC
Univ of Maine	ME	13,642	C
Univ of Maryland/Baltimore County	MD	16,642	VC+
Univ of Maryland/College Park	MD	16,036	HC
Univ of Mass Amherst	MA	15,973	C+
Univ of Mass Dartmouth	MA	15,985	C
Univ of Memphis	TN	11,153	C
Univ of Miami	FL	38,397	MC
Univ of Mich/Ann Arbor	MI	16,587	HC+
Univ of Mich/Dearborn	MI	7,000	VC
Univ of Minn/Duluth	MN	13,974	C
Univ of Missouri/Columbia	MO	13,500	VC
Univ of Missouri/Rolla	MO	13,332	HC
Univ of Nebr at Lincoln	NE	11,401	VC
Univ of Nevada/Las Vegas	NV	11,566	C
Univ of New Hampshire	NH	16,810	VC
Univ of New Haven	CT	31,794	C
Univ of New Mexico	NM	11,253	C
Univ of N Car at Charlotte	NC	9,101	C
Univ of Notre Dame	IN	39,552	MC
Univ of Okla	OK	10,769	VC+
Univ of Pennsylvania	PA	41,766	MC
Univ of Pittsburgh at Pittsburgh	PA	18,866	HC

School	ST	$IS	SR
Univ of PR/Mayaguez	PR	1,250	
Univ of Rhode Island	RI	15,398	C
Univ of South Alabama	AL	8,930	LC
Univ of S Car at Columbia	SC	13,397	VC
Univ of South Florida	FL	10,284	VC
Univ of Southern Calif	CA	41,618	MC
Univ of Texas at Arlington	TX	7,195	VC
Univ of the Pacific	CA	34,380	VC
Univ of Toledo	OH	15,806	NC
Univ of Utah	UT	10,162	VC
Univ of Washington	WA	10,400	VC
Univ of West Florida	FL	8,559	C
Univ of Wisc/Madison	WI	13,117	HC
Univ of Wyoming	WY	9,666	C
Valparaiso Univ	IN	28,970	VC+
Vanderbilt Univ	TN	41,986	MC
Vermont Technical College	VT	15,751	C
Villanova Univ	PA	38,672	HC+
Virginia Commonwealth Univ	VA	12,987	C
Virginia Polytechnic Inst and State Univ	VA	10,834	VC
Washington State Univ	WA	12,260	C
Washington Univ in St. Louis	MO	42,106	MC
West Virginia Univ	WV	10,506	C
Western Mich Univ	MI	13,299	C
Western New England College	MA	32,054	C
Wichita State Univ	KS	8,500	C
Wright State Univ	OH	13,616	LC

COMPUTER GRAPHICS

School	ST	$IS	SR
Andrews Univ	MI	21,786	C
Art Inst of Atlanta	GA	23,220	SP
Ashford Univ	IA	20,370	C
Atlanta College of Art	GA	18,630	SP
Carlow Univ	PA	24,313	C
Cogswell Polytechnical College	CA	13,760	LC
Columbia College Chicago	IL	25,125	LC
Dakota State Univ	SD	7,466	C
Eastern Mich Univ	MI	12,897	C
Embry-Riddle Aeronautical Univ	FL	30,280	C
Escuela de Artes Plasticas de PR	PR	2,372	
Fashion Inst of Technology/ SUNY	NY	11,600	C+
Huntingdon College	AL	23,090	VC
Indiana Univ-Purdue Univ Indianapolis	IN	10,959	C
Indiana Wesleyan Univ	IN	22,074	C+
Jacksonville Univ	FL	24,040	C
La Salle Univ	PA	34,950	C
Lewis Univ	IL	23,050	C+
Loyola Marymount Univ	CA	36,321	VC
Monmouth Univ	NJ	28,956	C
New York Inst of Technology	NY	28,126	VC
Pennsylvania College of Technology	PA	16,980	LC
Pratt Inst	NY	36,156	SP
Purdue Univ/Calumet	IN	10,891	LC
Purdue Univ/West Lafayette	IN	13,458	VC
Ringling School of Art and Design	FL	31,013	SP
Rochester Inst of Technology	NY	32,070	VC+
Savannah College of Art and Design	GA	30,800	SP
School of Visual Arts	NY	32,580	SP
Springfield College	MA	25,000	C
Syracuse Univ	NY	38,655	HC
Taylor Univ	IN	26,376	VC+
Univ of Dubuque	IA	23,390	C
Univ of Great Falls	MT	17,000	C
Univ of Mary Hardin-Baylor	TX	19,428	C
Univ of Tampa	FL	25,784	C

COMPUTER MANAGEMENT

School	ST	$IS	SR
Caldwell College	NJ	26,450	LC
College of St. Mary	NE	23,938	C
Colo Christian Univ	CO	21,182	VC
Eastern Mennonite Univ	VA	25,450	VC
Emory & Henry College	VA	26,570	C
Johnson and Wales Univ/ Providence Campus	RI	28,126	LC
Johnson State College	VT	11,830	LC
Metropolitan State College of Denver	CO	2,338	LC
Mount Olive College	NC	16,000	LC
New Jersey Inst of Technology	NJ	16,396	VC
Northwest Missouri State Univ	MO	10,000	C
Northwest Univ	WA	18,854	C
Northwood Univ	MI	21,000	C
Northwood Univ	TX	20,135	LC
Okla City Univ	OK	23,965	VC
Peirce College	PA	12,760	NC
Peru State College	NE	6,350	NC
Rochester College	MI	15,636	C+
Southern Adventist Univ	TN	18,500	C

School	ST	$IS	SR
Univ of Great Falls	MT	17,000	C
Univ of Illinois at Urbana-Champaign	IL	15,800	HC+
Univ of New Haven	CT	31,794	C
Univ of Northern Iowa	IA	11,133	C
Univ of Scranton	PA	31,100	VC

COMPUTER MATHEMATICS

School	ST	$IS	SR
Ashford Univ	IA	20,370	C
Colo College	CO	37,668	HC
Hollins Univ	VA	31,105	C
Ithaca College	NY	35,144	VC
Keene State College	NH	13,836	C
LeTourneau Univ	TX	21,200	C
Loyola Univ Chicago	IL	32,896	VC
Marist College	NY	30,566	VC
Mary Baldwin College	VA	26,465	C
Missouri Southern State Univ	MO	8,396	NC
New York Univ	NY	43,170	MC
Oakwood College	AL	14,904	C
Piedmont College	GA	20,500	C
Rochester Inst of Technology	NY	32,070	VC+
Saginaw Valley State Univ	MI	11,432	C
Salem International Univ	WV	18,020	C
Univ of Illinois at Urbana-Champaign	IL	15,800	HC+
Univ of S Car at Aiken	SC	11,728	LC
Western Conn State Univ	CT	12,993	C
Wheaton College	MA	40,180	HC+
Wingate Univ	NC	23,300	C

COMPUTER PROGRAMMING

School	ST	$IS	SR
Baker College of Flint	MI	7,800	NC
Caribbean Univ	PR	3,000	
Carnegie Mellon Univ	PA	32,700	MC
Central Washington Univ	WA	11,730	C
City Univ	WA	7,425	NC
Cogswell Polytechnical College	CA	13,760	LC
Concord College	WV	9,708	C
Concordia Univ, River Forest	IL	26,300	C
Dakota State Univ	SD	7,466	C
DeVry Univ/Pomona	CA	12,450	LC
Dickinson State Univ	ND	7,847	NC
Dordt College	IA	20,325	VC
Eastern Kentucky Univ	KY	7,725	C
Eastern Mich Univ	MI	12,897	C
Ferris State Univ	MI	13,698	C
Freed-Hardeman Univ	TN	16,370	NC
Georgia Southwestern State Univ	GA	6,035	C
Goldey-Beacom College	DE	11,440	C
Goshen College	IN	22,850	VC
Hannibal-LaGrange College	MO	16,390	C
Hawaii Pacific Univ	HI	21,080	C
Husson College	ME	17,410	C
Indiana Univ-Purdue Univ Fort Wayne	IN	5,067	LC
Kent State Univ	OH	14,594	C
Lamar Univ	TX	6,820	LC
Lee Univ	TN	14,780	NC
Limestone College	SC	19,840	C
Mayville State Univ	ND	8,667	NC
Midland Lutheran College	NE	18,600	C
Missouri Western State Univ	MO	9,534	NC
Monmouth College	IL	23,700	C
Montana Tech of The Univ of Montana	MT	10,434	C
Murray State Univ	KY	8,900	VC
Nebr Wesleyan Univ	NE	23,415	C+
Northeastern Univ	MA	35,742	HC
Northern Mich Univ	MI	12,340	LC
Pacific Lutheran Univ	WA	28,805	VC
Peirce College	PA	12,760	NC
Pennsylvania College of Technology	PA	16,980	LC
Peru State College	NE	6,350	NC
Pontifical Catholic Univ of PR/Ponce	PR	7,310	
Purdue Univ/Calumet	IN	10,891	LC
Rhode Island College	RI	11,570	C
St. Louis Univ	MO	33,158	VC+
St. Thomas Univ	FL	23,490	C
Salem State College	MA	13,161	NC
Southwestern College	KS	21,476	C
Southwestern Okla State Univ	OK	4,801	C
Stephen F. Austin State Univ	TX	7,930	C
Suffolk Univ	MA	33,160	C
Tarleton State Univ	TX	8,952	C
Turabo Univ	PR	4,110	
Univ of Great Falls	MT	17,000	C
Univ of Illinois at Urbana-Champaign	IL	15,800	HC+
Univ of Nebr at Kearney	NE	10,900	C
Univ of St. Francis	IL	25,430	C
Univ of Wisc/Eau Claire	WI	9,915	VC
Univ of Wisc/River Falls	WI	9,722	LC
Univ of Wisc/Whitewater	WI	9,274	C

School	ST	$IS	SR
Washburn Univ	KS	9,734	NC
Washington Univ in St. Louis	MO	42,106	MC
Weber State Univ	UT	9,635	NC
West Virginia Univ Inst of Technology	WV	8,788	NC
York College of Pennsylvania	PA	16,550	VC
Youngstown State Univ	OH	12,613	NC

COMPUTER SCIENCE

School	ST	$IS	SR
Abilene Christian Univ	TX	20,830	C
Adams State College	CO	8,613	C
Adelphi Univ	NY	27,000	VC
Alabama A&M Univ	AL	8,890	C
Albany State Univ	GA	5,770	C
Albion College	MI	26,000	VC
Albright College	PA	33,920	C
Alcorn State Univ	MS	8,190	LC
Alderson-Broaddus College	WV	24,006	C
Allegheny College	PA	33,500	HC
Alma College	MI	28,544	VC
Alverno College	WI	21,088	C
American Univ	DC	38,719	HC+
Amherst College	MA	41,590	MC
Anderson Univ	IN	25,050	LC
Andrews Univ	MI	21,786	C
Angelo State Univ	TX	8,340	NC
Appalachian State Univ	NC	8,000	VC
Arcadia Univ	PA	33,570	VC
Arizona State Univ-Tempe	AZ	11,174	C
Arkansas Baptist College	AR	5,600	NC
Arkansas State Univ	AR	9,630	C
Arkansas Tech Univ	AR	8,108	VC
Armstrong Atlantic State Univ	GA	7,394	C
Ashford Univ	IA	20,370	C
Ashland Univ	OH	25,000	C
Assumption College	MA	32,875	C
Atlantic Union College	MA	17,600	LC
Auburn Univ	AL	12,230	VC
Augsburg College	MN	28,300	C
Augusta State Univ	GA	2,920	C
Augustana College	IL	29,862	VC+
Augustana College	SD	24,380	VC
Aurora Univ	IL	20,645	C
Austin College	TX	27,871	HC
Austin Peay State Univ	TN	7,535	C
Averett Univ	VA	24,920	C
Avila Univ	MO	22,100	C
Azusa Pacific Univ	CA	28,546	VC
Baker Univ	KS	22,190	C
Baldwin-Wallace College	OH	27,256	VC
Ball State Univ	IN	13,138	C
Barry Univ	FL	24,100	LC
Baylor Univ	TX	27,555	HC
Belhaven College	MS	19,530	NC
Bellarmine Univ	KY	27,650	C+
Belmont Univ	TN	24,110	VC
Beloit College	WI	32,808	HC
Bemidji State Univ	MN	11,180	LC
Benedict College	SC	19,114	LC
Benedictine College	KS	21,968	C
Benedictine Univ	IL	25,710	C
Bennett College	NC	11,500	C
Bennington College	VT	41,890	HC
Berry College	GA	24,342	VC
Bethany College	WV	21,395	C
Bethel College	IN	19,680	C
Bethel College	KS	21,650	C
Bethel Univ	MN	29,840	VC
Bethune-Cookman Univ	FL	17,922	LC
Biola Univ	CA	29,372	VC
Birmingham-Southern College	AL	28,494	VC+
Blackburn College	IL	13,690	C
Bloomsburg Univ of Pennsylvania	PA	11,602	C
Bluefield State College	WV	3,140	LC
Bluffton College	OH	26,110	C
Boston College	MA	41,608	MC
Boston Univ	MA	42,046	HC+
Bowdoin College	ME	41,660	MC
Bowie State Univ	MD	10,880	C+
Bowling Green State Univ	OH	14,994	C
Bradley Univ	IL	25,280	VC
Brandeis Univ	MA	41,551	MC
Brescia Univ	KY	14,240	C
Briar Cliff Univ	IA	23,550	C
Bridgewater College	VA	27,790	C
Bridgewater State College	MA	12,120	C
Brigham Young Univ	UT	9,200	VC
Brigham Young Univ/Hawaii	HI	7,740	HC+
Brown Univ	RI	42,015	MC
Bryan College	TN	19,270	C
Bucknell Univ	PA	39,660	MC
Buena Vista Univ	IA	27,742	C
Butler Univ	IN	31,944	VC+
Caldwell College	NJ	26,450	LC
Calif Lutheran Univ	CA	27,800	VC
Calif Polytechnic State Univ	CA	12,390	VC
Calif State Polytechnic Univ, Pomona	CA	18,053	C+
Cal State East Bay	CA	10,856	VC
Cal State, Bakersfield	CA	6,125	LC

School	ST	$IS	SR
Cal State, Chico	CA	11,395	C
Cal State, Dominguez Hills	CA	10,220	LC
Cal State, Fresno	CA	10,037	C
Cal State, Fullerton	CA	10,990	C
Cal State, Long Beach	CA	9,512	C
Cal State, Los Angeles	CA	5,900	C
Cal State, Monterey Bay	CA	10,099	C
Cal State, Northridge	CA	9,036	LC
Cal State, Sacramento	CA	11,122	C+
Cal State, San Bernardino	CA	12,563	LC
Cal State, San Marcos	CA	1,800	LC
Cal State, Stanislaus	CA	11,283	C
Calvin College	MI	25,735	NC
Cameron Univ	OK	6,314	NC
Campbell Univ	NC	21,137	VC
Canisius College	NY	32,257	VC
Capital Univ	OH	30,444	C
Cardinal Stritch Univ	WI	21,910	C
Caribbean Univ	PR	3,000	
Carleton College	MN	40,467	MC
Carlow Univ	PA	24,313	C
Carnegie Mellon Univ	PA	32,700	MC
Carroll College	MT	23,324	C+
Carroll College	WI	24,860	C
Case Western Reserve Univ	OH	37,314	MC
Castleton State College	VT	13,158	C
Catholic Univ of America	DC	35,838	VC
Cedar Crest College	PA	30,615	C
Cedarville Univ	OH	21,904	VC
Central College	IA	26,774	VC
Central Conn State Univ	CT	13,620	C
Central Methodist Univ	MO	18,000	C
Central Mich Univ	MI	12,244	C
Central Missouri State Univ	MO	10,000	C
Central State Univ	OH	9,010	C+
Central Univ of Bayamon	PR	3,335	
Central Washington Univ	WA	11,730	C
Centre College	KY	30,810	VC
Chaminade Univ of Honolulu	HI	23,320	LC
Chapman Univ	CA	37,550	VC
Charleston Southern Univ	SC	17,800	C
Chatham College	PA	27,290	C+
Chestnut Hill College	PA	26,600	C
Cheyney Univ of Pennsylvania	PA	11,497	LC
Chicago State Univ	IL	10,915	C+
Christian Brothers Univ	TN	24,650	VC
Christopher Newport Univ	VA	13,326	VC
Citadel, The	SC		C+
CUNY/Brooklyn College	NY	4,377	C+
CUNY/City College	NY		C
CUNY/College of Staten Island	NY	4,328	NC
CUNY/Herbert H. Lehman College	NY	4,000	LC
CUNY/Hunter College	NY	8,000	C+
CUNY/Medgar Evers College	NY	4,250	NC
CUNY/Queens College	NY	4,356	C+
Claflin Univ	SC	16,798	C+
Clarion Univ of Pennsylvania	PA	11,844	C
Clark Atlanta Univ	GA	20,960	LC
Clark Univ	MA	35,165	VC+
Clarke College	IA	25,390	C
Clarkson Univ	NY	34,930	VC
Clemson Univ	SC	13,366	HC
Cleveland State Univ	OH	10,798	NC
Coastal Carolina Univ	SC	13,140	C
Coe College	IA	27,440	VC
Coker College	SC	21,600	C
Colby College	ME	41,770	MC
Colgate Univ	NY	41,170	MC
College Misericordia	PA	27,950	C
College of Charleston	SC	13,616	VC
College of Mount St. Vincent	NY	28,000	C
College of New Jersey	NJ	18,315	MC
College of Notre Dame of Maryland	MD	27,700	C
College of Our Lady of the Elms	MA	21,000	C
College of St. Benedict	MN	30,091	VC
College of St. Elizabeth	NJ	28,495	C
College of St. Joseph	VT	20,900	NC
College of St. Scholastica	MN	28,456	C+
College of Santa Fe	NM	28,978	C
College of the Holy Cross	MA	40,664	MC
College of the Ozarks	MO	4,130	VC+
College of William and Mary	VA	14,147	MC
College of Wooster	OH	31,310	VC+
Colo State Univ-Fort Collins	CO	10,878	C+
Colo Technical Univ	CO	9,500	LC
Columbia College	MO	16,900	C
Columbia Union College	MD	23,536	LC
Columbia Univ/Barnard College	NY	38,000	MC
Columbia Univ/Columbia College	NY	42,584	MC
Columbia Univ/Fu Foundation School of Engineering and Applied Science	NY	42,584	MC

ST = STATE   **$IS** = IN-STATE COSTS   **SR** = SELECTOR RATING

ST = STATE **$IS** = IN-STATE COSTS **SR** = SELECTOR RATING

School	ST	$IS	SR
Oakwood College	AL	14,904	C
Oberlin College	OH	40,904	MC
Ohio Dominican Univ	OH	25,954	C
Ohio Northern Univ	OH	27,765	VC
Ohio State Univ	OH	15,357	HC
Ohio Univ	OH	15,921	C
Ohio Wesleyan Univ	OH	35,830	VC+
Okla Baptist Univ	OK	17,986	VC
Okla Christian Univ	OK	18,992	NC
Okla City Univ	OK	23,965	VC
Okla State Univ	OK	10,213	VC
Old Dominion Univ	VA	11,907	C
Olivet College	MI	19,984	C+
Olivet Nazarene Univ	IL	22,590	C
Oral Roberts Univ	OK	22,650	C
Oregon State Univ	OR	11,055	C
Otterbein College	OH	28,986	C
Ouachita Baptist Univ	AR	21,900	VC
Pace Univ	NY	30,000	VC
Pacific Lutheran Univ	WA	28,805	VC
Pacific Union College	CA	24,555	VC+
Pacific Univ	OR	24,250	C
Palm Beach Atlantic Univ	FL	23,597	VC
Park Univ	MO	11,592	C
Paul Quinn College	TX	8,300	LC
Penn State Erie/The Behrend College	PA	16,256	C
Penn State Univ/Univ Park Campus	PA	18,038	HC
Pepperdine Univ	CA	39,960	HC
Peru State College	NE	6,350	NC
Philander Smith College	AR	13,230	LC
Pikeville College	KY	16,500	NC
Pittsburg State Univ	KS	8,112	C
Plymouth State Univ	NH	12,298	C
Point Loma Nazarene Univ	CA	27,610	VC
Point Park Univ	PA	24,160	C
Polytechnic Univ/Brooklyn	NY	37,150	VC
Pomona College	CA	40,774	MC
Portland State Univ	OR	12,453	C
Prairie View A&M Univ	TX	11,110	LC
Presbyterian College	SC	30,044	VC
Princeton Univ	NJ	40,213	MC
Principia College	IL	27,765	VC+
Providence College	RI	34,580	HC
Purdue Univ/Calumet	IN	10,891	LC
Purdue Univ/West Lafayette	IN	13,458	VC
Quincy Univ	IL	24,920	C
Quinnipiac Univ	CT	34,640	VC
Radford Univ	VA	13,145	C
Ramapo College of New Jersey	NJ	16,630	VC
Randolph-Macon College	VA	31,250	C
Regis College	MA	31,350	C
Regis Univ	CO	31,890	C
Rensselaer Polytechnic Inst	NY	41,288	HC+
Rhode Island College	RI	11,570	C
Rhodes College	TN	32,860	HC
Rice Univ	TX	32,290	MC
Richard Stockton College of New Jersey	NJ	14,000	VC
Ripon College	WI	27,160	C+
Rivier College	NH	26,600	C
Roanoke College	VA	30,748	VC
Roberts Wesleyan College	NY	26,378	C
Rochester Inst of Technology	NY	32,070	VC+
Rockford College	IL	28,330	VC
Rockhurst Univ	MO	25,440	VC
Rocky Mountain College	MT	20,805	C
Roger Williams Univ	RI	30,500	C
Rollins College	FL	38,366	VC
Roosevelt Univ	IL	22,605	VC
Rose-Hulman Inst of Technology	IN	34,557	HC+
Rowan Univ	NJ	16,000	VC
Russell Sage College	NY	27,000	C
Rust College	MS		C+
Rutgers, The State Univ of New Jersey/Camden Campus	NJ	15,000	VC
Rutgers, The State Univ of New Jersey/New Brunswick/Piscataway Campus	NJ	15,810	HC
Rutgers, The State Univ of New Jersey/Newark Campus	NJ	15,640	VC
Sacred Heart Univ	CT	33,404	C
Saginaw Valley State Univ	MI	11,432	C
St. Ambrose Univ	IA	25,495	C
St. Anselm College	NH	33,810	C
St. Augustine's College	NC	14,600	LC
St. Bonaventure Univ	NY	28,785	C
St. Cloud State Univ	MN	10,010	C
St. Edward's Univ	TX	23,560	C
St. Francis Univ	PA	25,880	LC
St. John Fisher College	NY	27,860	C
St. John's Univ	MN	29,749	VC
St. John's Univ	NY	34,370	C
St. Joseph's College	IN	26,600	C
St. Joseph's Univ	PA	37,428	VC
St. Lawrence Univ	NY	40,545	VC
St. Louis Univ	MO	33,158	VC+
St. Martin's Univ	WA	27,555	C
St. Mary-of-the-Woods College	IN	25,480	C
St. Mary's College of Maryland	MD	18,876	VC+
St. Mary's Univ of Minn	MN	23,857	VC
St. Mary's Univ of San Antonio	TX	22,444	VC
St. Michael's College	VT	33,330	VC
St. Norbert College	WI	28,577	C+
St. Olaf College	MN	32,800	HC
St. Peter's College	NJ	30,160	LC
St. Thomas Univ	FL	23,490	C
St. Vincent College	PA	26,160	VC
St. Xavier Univ	IL	23,160	C
Salisbury Univ	MD	13,128	VC
Sam Houston State Univ	TX	8,000	C
Samford Univ	AL	20,258	VC
San Diego State Univ	CA	12,971	C
San Francisco State Univ	CA	13,000	C
San Jose State Univ	CA	11,707	C
Santa Clara Univ	CA	38,931	VC
Savannah State Univ	GA	7,772	LC
Scripps College	CA	41,000	MC
Seattle Pacific Univ	WA	29,355	C
Seattle Univ	WA	30,063	VC
Seton Hall Univ	NJ	33,622	VC
Seton Hill Univ	PA	28,810	C
Shaw Univ	NC	15,488	LC
Shepherd Univ	WV	10,066	C
Shippensburg Univ of Pennsylvania	PA	11,621	C
Siena College	NY	28,260	VC+
Silver Lake College of the Holy Family	WI	18,500	LC
Simmons College	MA	35,640	VC
Simpson College	IA	26,833	VC
Skidmore College	NY	41,779	HC
Slippery Rock Univ of Pennsylvania	PA	10,360	LC
Smith College	MA	41,474	MC
Sonoma State Univ	CA	14,732	C
S Car State Univ	SC	6,700	LC
S Dak School of Mines and Technology	SD	7,624	C+
S Dak State Univ	SD	9,815	C
Southeast Missouri State Univ	MO	10,596	C
Southeastern Louisiana Univ	LA	8,521	LC
Southeastern Okla State Univ	OK	6,147	C
Southern Adventist Univ	TN	18,500	C
Southern Arkansas Univ	AR	6,956	C
Southern Conn State Univ	CT	10,310	C
Southern Illinois Univ Carbondale	IL	12,391	C
Southern Illinois Univ Edwardsville	IL	11,022	C
Southern Methodist Univ	TX	36,088	VC+
Southern Nazarene Univ	OK	14,634	NC
Southern New Hampshire Univ	NH	28,764	C
Southern Oregon Univ	OR	12,186	C
Southern Polytechnic State Univ	GA	7,640	VC
Southern Univ and A&M College	LA	8,238	LC
Southern Univ at New Orleans	LA	1,000	NC
Southern Utah Univ	UT		C
Southwest Baptist Univ	MO	18,300	C
Southwest Minn State Univ	MN	10,975	C
Southwestern Adventist Univ	TX	18,290	LC
Southwestern College	KS	21,476	C
Southwestern Okla State Univ	OK	4,801	C
Southwestern Univ	TX	26,767	NC
Spelman College	GA	24,650	VC
Spring Arbor Univ	MI	22,476	C
Spring Hill College	AL	28,678	C
Stanford Univ	CA	41,557	MC
SUNY at Oswego	NY	13,662	VC
SUNY at Potsdam	NY	12,959	C
SUNY/College at Brockport	NY	12,747	VC
SUNY/College at Fredonia	NY	12,771	VC
SUNY/College at Geneseo	NY	12,910	HC+
SUNY/College at Old Westbury	NY	13,154	C
SUNY/College at Oneonta	NY	12,905	VC
SUNY/College at Plattsburgh	NY	12,362	C
SUNY/Inst of Technology	NY	12,575	VC
SUNY/Univ at Albany	NY	13,860	VC
SUNY/Univ at Binghamton	NY	13,988	HC
SUNY/Univ at Buffalo	NY	13,694	VC
SUNY/Univ at New Paltz	NY	12,480	VC
SUNY/Univ at Stony Brook	NY	13,625	HC
Stephen F. Austin State Univ	TX	7,930	C
Sterling College	KS	19,992	C
Stetson Univ	FL	32,725	VC
Stevens Inst of Technology	NJ	40,935	HC
Stillman College	AL	11,475	LC
Stonehill College	MA	36,104	HC
Suffolk Univ	MA	33,160	C
Sul Ross State Univ	TX	6,600	LC
Susquehanna Univ	PA	33,465	VC
Swarthmore College	PA	41,280	MC
Sweet Briar College	VA	31,460	VC
Syracuse Univ	NY	38,655	HC
Tabor College	KS	21,614	NC
Talladega College	AL	11,240	LC
Tarleton State Univ	TX	8,952	C
Taylor Univ	IN	26,376	VC+
Temple Univ	PA	17,438	C
Tenn State Univ	TN	9,048	LC
Tenn Tech Univ	TN	10,044	C
Texas A&M Univ	TX	13,351	HC
Texas A&M Univ at Commerce	TX	9,020	C
Texas A&M Univ at Corpus Christi	TX	10,280	LC
Texas A&M Univ at Kingsville	TX	6,800	LC
Texas Christian Univ	TX	23,410	VC+
Texas Lutheran Univ	TX	23,530	C
Texas Southern Univ	TX	9,828	C
Texas State Univ - San Marcos	TX	10,862	C
Texas Tech Univ	TX	13,026	VC
Texas Wesleyan Univ	TX	18,700	C
Texas Woman's Univ	TX	7,804	LC
Thiel College	PA	24,580	C
Thomas Edison State College	NJ	3,780	SP
Thomas More College	KY	24,470	C
Tougaloo College	MS	15,975	NC
Touro College	NY	17,000	VC
Towson Univ	MD	13,924	VC
Transylvania Univ	KY	26,240	VC+
Trinity Christian College	IL	23,645	C
Trinity College	CT	38,040	HC+
Trinity College	DC	24,150	LC
Trinity Univ	TX	30,157	HC+
Tri-State Univ-Main Campus	IN	26,200	C
Troy Univ	AL	8,916	C
Troy Univ Dothan Campus	AL	4,678	C
Troy Univ Montgomery Campus	AL	4,104	NC
Truman State Univ	MO	11,242	HC
Tufts Univ	MA	42,018	MC
Tulane Univ	LA	41,098	MC
Tusculum College	TN	21,340	LC
Tuskegee Univ	AL	18,860	LC
Union College	NE	18,710	C
Union College	NY	41,595	HC
Union Inst & Univ	OH	8,912	SP
Union Univ	TN	20,750	VC
United States Air Force Academy	CO		HC+
United States Military Academy	NY		MC
United States Naval Academy	MD		MC
Universidad Adventista de las Antillas	PR	7,360	
Univ of Akron	OH	15,166	NC
Univ of Alabama	AL	9,888	C
Univ of Alabama at Birmingham	AL	13,716	C
Univ of Alabama in Huntsville	AL	9,516	VC
Univ of Alaska Anchorage	AK	11,275	NC
Univ of Alaska Fairbanks	AK	10,101	C
Univ of Arizona	AZ	11,958	VC
Univ of Arkansas	AR	11,859	VC
Univ of Arkansas at Little Rock	AR	7,230	NC
Univ of Arkansas at Pine Bluff	AR	8,300	C
Univ of at Calif Davis	CA	15,010	VC
Univ of Bridgeport	CT	29,595	LC
Univ of Calif at Berkeley	CA	18,141	HC+
Univ of Calif at Los Angeles	CA	17,681	MC
Univ of Calif at Riverside	CA	16,625	C
Univ of Calif at San Diego	CA	16,102	HC
Univ of Calif at Santa Barbara	CA	11,800	VC
Univ of Calif at Santa Cruz	CA	19,174	VC
Univ of Central Arkansas	AR	9,984	C
Univ of Central Florida	FL	10,739	VC
Univ of Central Okla	OK	8,094	C
Univ of Chicago	IL	42,369	MC
Univ of Cincinnati	OH	17,682	C
Univ of Colo at Boulder	CO	13,352	C+
Univ of Colo at Colo Springs	CO	11,517	VC
Univ of Colo at Denver and Health Sciences Center	CO	5,021	C
Univ of Conn	CT	16,628	HC
Univ of Dayton	OH	28,826	VC
Univ of Delaware	DE	14,142	HC
Univ of Denver	CO	36,976	VC+
Univ of Detroit Mercy	MI	27,000	C
Univ of Dubuque	IA	23,390	C
Univ of Evansville	IN	28,320	VC
Univ of Findlay	OH	29,238	C
Univ of Florida	FL	9,354	HC
Univ of Georgia	GA	11,004	HC
Univ of Great Falls	MT	17,000	C
Univ of Hartford	CT	34,044	C
Univ of Hawaii at Hilo	HI	6,500	C
Univ of Hawaii at Manoa	HI	10,413	VC
Univ of Houston	TX	7,000	C
Univ of Houston-Downtown	TX	3,326	NC
Univ of Idaho	ID	9,310	NC
Univ of Illinois at Chicago	IL	16,256	VC
Univ of Indianapolis	IN	25,090	C
Univ of Iowa	IA	12,172	VC
Univ of Kansas	KS	10,915	VC
Univ of Kentucky	KY	7,800	C
Univ of La Verne	CA	33,470	C
Univ of Louisiana at Lafayette	LA	5,830	C
Univ of Louisiana at Monroe	LA	7,103	C
Univ of Louisville	KY	10,400	VC
Univ of Maine	ME	13,642	C
Univ of Maine at Farmington	ME	11,515	C
Univ of Maine at Fort Kent	ME	10,832	LC
Univ of Mary Hardin-Baylor	TX	19,428	C
Univ of Mary Washington	VA	11,636	HC
Univ of Maryland/Baltimore County	MD	16,642	VC+
Univ of Maryland/College Park	MD	16,036	HC
Univ of Maryland/Eastern Shore	MD	11,210	C
Univ of Maryland/Univ College	MD	5,640	SP
Univ of Mass Amherst	MA	15,973	C+
Univ of Mass Boston	MA	8,024	C
Univ of Mass Dartmouth	MA	15,985	C
Univ of Mass Lowell	MA	14,327	VC
Univ of Memphis	TN	11,153	C
Univ of Miami	FL	38,397	MC
Univ of Mich/Ann Arbor	MI	16,587	HC+
Univ of Mich/Dearborn	MI	7,000	VC
Univ of Mich/Flint	MI	6,398	C
Univ of Minn/Duluth	MN	13,974	C
Univ of Minn/Morris	MN	15,472	VC
Univ of Minn/Twin Cities	MN	13,165	HC
Univ of Miss	MS	9,000	C
Univ of Missouri/Columbia	MO	13,500	C
Univ of Missouri/Kansas City	MO	15,000	VC
Univ of Missouri/Rolla	MO	13,332	HC
Univ of Missouri/St. Louis	MO	14,046	VC
Univ of Mobile	AL	16,880	C
Univ of Montana	MT	10,602	C
Univ of Nebr at Kearney	NE	9,000	NC
Univ of Nebr at Lincoln	NE	11,401	VC
Univ of Nebr at Omaha	NE	11,235	C
Univ of Nevada/Las Vegas	NV	11,566	C
Univ of Nevada/Reno	NV	12,155	NC
Univ of New Hampshire	NH	16,810	VC
Univ of New Haven	CT	31,794	C
Univ of New Mexico	NM	11,253	C
Univ of New Orleans	LA	7,370	C
Univ of North Alabama	AL	8,992	C
Univ of N Car at Asheville	NC	9,237	VC
Univ of N Car at Chapel Hill	NC	11,129	MC
Univ of N Car at Charlotte	NC	9,101	C
Univ of N Car at Greensboro	NC	8,993	C
Univ of N Car at Pembroke	NC	7,940	LC
Univ of N Car at Wilmington	NC	10,107	VC
Univ of N Dak	ND	10,114	VC
Univ of North Florida	FL	9,908	VC
Univ of North Texas	TX	7,800	C
Univ of Northern Colo	CO	10,249	C
Univ of Northern Iowa	IA	11,133	C
Univ of Notre Dame	IN	39,552	MC
Univ of Okla	OK	10,769	VC+
Univ of Oregon	OR	13,108	VC
Univ of Pennsylvania	PA	41,766	MC
Univ of Pittsburgh at Bradford	PA	17,008	C
Univ of Pittsburgh at Johnstown	PA	16,740	LC
Univ of Pittsburgh at Pittsburgh	PA	18,866	HC
Univ of Portland	OR	32,300	VC
Univ of PR/Arecibo	PR	8,327	
Univ of PR/Bayamon Univ College Campus	PR	1,600	
Univ of PR/Mayaguez	PR	1,250	
Univ of PR/Rio Piedras	PR	5,750	
Univ of Puget Sound	WA	35,600	VC
Univ of Redlands	CA	36,160	VC
Univ of Rhode Island	RI	15,398	C
Univ of Richmond	VA	40,510	MC
Univ of Rio Grande	OH	8,728	NC
Univ of Rochester	NY	41,135	MC
Univ of St. Francis	IL	25,430	C
Univ of St. Thomas	MN	28,000	VC
Univ of San Diego	CA	40,620	HC
Univ of San Francisco	CA	37,560	VC
Univ of Science and Arts of Okla	OK	7,650	C
Univ of Scranton	PA	31,100	VC
Univ of Sioux Falls	SD	20,800	C
Univ of South Alabama	AL	8,930	LC
Univ of S Car at Columbia	SC	13,397	VC
Univ of S Car Upstate	SC	11,957	C
Univ of S Dak	SD	9,068	C

School	ST	$IS	SR
Univ of Southern Calif	CA	41,618	MC
Univ of Southern Maine	ME	12,614	C
Univ of Southern Miss	MS	10,112	C
Univ of Tenn at Chattanooga	TN	7,790	C
Univ of Tenn at Knoxville	TN	11,720	C
Univ of Tenn at Martin	TN	8,693	C
Univ of Texas at Arlington	TX	7,195	LC
Univ of Texas at Austin	TX	14,610	HC
Univ of Texas at Dallas	TX	13,244	HC
Univ of Texas at El Paso	TX	8,764	NC
Univ of Texas at San Antonio	TX	11,325	LC
Univ of Texas-Pan American	TX	7,290	C+
Univ of the District of Columbia	DC	2,070	LC
Univ of the Pacific	CA	34,380	C
Univ of the Sacred Heart	PR	5,590	
Univ of the Sciences in Philadelphia	PA	33,380	VC
Univ of the South	TN	34,645	HC
Univ of Toledo	OH	15,806	NC
Univ of Tulsa	OK	25,348	HC
Univ of Utah	UT	10,162	VC
Univ of Vermont	VT	18,080	VC
Univ of Virginia	VA	13,759	MC
Univ of Washington	WA	10,400	VC
Univ of West Alabama	AL	7,611	C
Univ of West Florida	FL	8,559	C
Univ of West Georgia	GA	8,838	C
Univ of Wisc/Eau Claire	WI	9,915	VC
Univ of Wisc/Green Bay	WI	9,415	VC
Univ of Wisc/La Crosse	WI	10,045	VC
Univ of Wisc/Madison	WI	13,117	HC
Univ of Wisc/Milwaukee	WI	9,427	LC
Univ of Wisc/Oshkosh	WI	10,426	LC
Univ of Wisc/Parkside	WI	10,181	LC
Univ of Wisc/Platteville	WI	9,779	NC
Univ of Wisc/Superior	WI	9,610	C+
Univ of Wyoming	WY	9,666	C
Ursinus College	PA	38,950	VC
Utah State Univ	UT	8,002	VC
Utica College	NY	31,396	C
Valdosta State Univ	GA	8,802	C
Valparaiso Univ	IN	28,970	VC+
Vassar College	NY	41,700	MC
Villanova Univ	PA	38,672	HC+
Virginia Commonwealth Univ	VA	12,987	C
Virginia Military Inst	VA	12,654	VC
Virginia Polytechnic Inst and State Univ	VA	10,834	VC
Virginia Wesleyan College	VA	28,433	C
Voorhees College	SC	11,800	C
Wagner College	NY	33,300	VC
Wake Forest Univ	NC	38,290	MC
Walla Walla College	WA	24,489	VC
Walsh Univ	OH	23,440	C
Wartburg College	IA	27,315	VC
Washburn Univ	KS	9,734	NC
Washington and Lee Univ	VA	35,880	MC
Washington College	MD	34,990	VC
Washington State Univ	WA	12,260	C
Washington Univ in St. Louis	MO	42,106	MC
Wayne State College	NE	8,033	NC
Wayne State Univ	MI	11,805	C
Waynesburg College	PA	21,230	C
Weber State Univ	UT	9,635	NC
Webster Univ	MO	24,280	VC
Wellesley College	MA	41,030	MC
Wells College	NY	23,070	VC
Wentworth Inst of Technology	MA	27,500	C
Wesleyan Univ	CT	42,122	HC
West Chester Univ of Pennsylvania	PA	12,355	C+
West Texas A&M Univ	TX	8,452	C
West Virginia Univ	WV	10,506	C
West Virginia Univ Inst of Technology	WV	8,788	NC
West Virginia Wesleyan College	WV	26,880	C
Western Baptist College	OR	21,808	C
Western Carolina Univ	NC	7,000	C
Western Conn State Univ	CT	12,993	C
Western Illinois Univ	IL	13,042	C
Western Kentucky Univ	KY	10,192	C
Western Mich Univ	MI	13,299	C
Western New England College	MA	32,054	C
Western New Mexico Univ	NM	7,233	LC
Western Oregon Univ	OR	10,295	C
Western State College of Colo	CO	9,942	C
Western Washington Univ	WA	11,262	VC
Westfield State College	MA	10,200	C
Westminster College	MO	19,060	VC
Westminster College	PA	31,290	C+
Westminster College	UT	25,656	C
Westmont College	CA	36,672	HC
Wheaton College	IL	27,760	HC
Wheaton College	MA	40,180	HC+
Wheeling Jesuit Univ	WV	26,910	C
Whitworth College	WA	29,428	VC+

School	ST	$IS	SR
Wichita State Univ	KS	8,500	C
Widener Univ	PA	27,275	C
Wilberforce Univ	OH	14,937	LC
Wiley College	TX	8,100	LC
Wilkes Univ	PA	30,886	C
Willamette Univ	OR	35,416	VC+
William Jewell College	MO	24,340	C
William Paterson Univ of New Jersey	NJ	17,810	C+
William Penn Univ	IA	17,685	LC
William Woods Univ	MO	21,020	C
Williams Baptist College	AR	13,450	C
Williams College	MA	40,310	MC
Wilmington College	OH	2,806	NC
Wingate Univ	NC	23,300	C
Winona State Univ	MN	11,333	C
Winston-Salem State Univ	NC	8,960	LC
Winthrop Univ	SC	11,302	C
Wittenberg Univ	OH	34,596	VC
Wofford College	SC	30,935	HC
Worcester Polytechnic Inst	MA	40,450	VC+
Worcester State College	MA	12,499	C
Wright State Univ	OH	13,616	LC
Xavier Univ	OH	30,490	HC
Xavier Univ of Louisiana	LA	17,600	C
Yale Univ	CT	41,000	MC
Yeshiva Univ	NY	22,000	C
Youngstown State Univ	OH	12,613	NC

COMPUTER SECURITY AND INFORMATION ASSURANCE

School	ST	$IS	SR
Champlain College	VT	24,605	C
Loyola Univ Chicago	IL	32,896	VC
Metropolitan State Univ	MN	4,682	SP
Minn State Univ, Mankato	MN	10,276	LC
Norwich Univ	VT	28,212	C
SUNY/Inst of Technology	NY	12,575	VC
Stevens Inst of Technology	NJ	40,935	HC

COMPUTER TECHNOLOGY

School	ST	$IS	SR
Andrews Univ	MI	21,786	C
Averett Univ	VA	24,920	C
Bentley College	MA	38,784	HC
Bowie State Univ	MD	10,880	C+
Calif State Polytechnic Univ, Pomona	CA	18,053	C+
Calif Univ of Pennsylvania	PA	14,217	C
Central Mich Univ	MI	12,244	C
Daniel Webster College	NH	24,870	C
DeVry/New York	NY	12,000	LC
Eastern Mich Univ	MI	12,897	C
Eastern Washington Univ	WA	10,608	C
Excelsior College	NY	995	SP
Farmingdale SUNY	NY	13,521	C
Georgia Southwestern State Univ	GA	6,035	C
Guilford College	NC	28,160	C+
Indiana State Univ	IN	11,604	C
Indiana Univ-Purdue Univ Indianapolis	IN	10,959	C
Inter American Univ of PR/ Bayamon Univ College	PR	3,522	
International College	FL	9,500	NC
Kent State Univ	OH	14,594	C
LeTourneau Univ	TX	21,200	C
Martin Univ	IN	10,300	SP
Methodist College	NC	21,000	C
Minn State Univ, Mankato	MN	10,276	LC
Missouri Southern State Univ	MO	8,396	NC
Mountain State Univ	WV	11,406	NC
Murray State Univ	KY	8,900	VC
New Jersey Inst of Technology	NJ	16,396	VC
Norfolk State Univ	VA	10,531	LC
Northeastern Univ	MA	35,742	HC
Oregon Inst of Technology	OR	8,718	C
Peirce College	PA	12,760	NC
Pennsylvania College of Technology	PA	16,980	LC
Purdue Univ/Calumet	IN	10,891	LC
Purdue Univ/West Lafayette	IN	13,458	VC
Rochester Inst of Technology	NY	32,070	VC+
Rockhurst Univ	MO	25,440	VC
St. Louis Univ	MO	33,158	VC+
Shawnee State Univ	OH	12,237	NC
Southwestern College	KS	21,476	C
SUNY/College of Technology at Alfred	NY	14,000	C
SUNY/Inst of Technology	NY	12,575	VC
Texas Christian Univ	TX	23,410	VC+
Thomas Edison State College	NJ	3,780	SP
Union College	KY	18,920	C
Univ of Arkansas at Little Rock	AR	7,230	NC
Univ of Dayton	OH	28,826	VC
Univ of Houston	TX	7,000	C
Univ of Illinois at Urbana-Champaign	IL	15,800	HC+
Univ of Maryland/Univ College	MD	5,640	SP

School	ST	$IS	SR
Univ of Memphis	TN	11,153	C
Univ of Northern Iowa	IA	11,133	C
Univ of Rio Grande	OH	8,728	NC
Univ of St. Francis	IL	25,430	C
Univ of Southern Miss	MS	10,112	C
Univ of Texas at Dallas	TX	13,244	HC
Wayne State Univ	MI	11,805	C
Wentworth Inst of Technology	MA	27,500	C
Youngstown State Univ	OH	12,613	NC

CONSERVATION AND REGULATION

School	ST	$IS	SR
Austin Peay State Univ	TN	7,535	C
Central Missouri State Univ	MO	10,000	C
College of the Ozarks	MO	4,130	VC+
Kent State Univ	OH	14,594	C
LIU/C.W. Post Campus	NY	28,282	C
Missouri State Univ	MO	10,748	C+
Muskingum College	OH	22,970	C
N Car State Univ	NC	11,824	HC
Northwest Missouri State Univ	MO	10,000	C
Northwestern Okla State Univ	OK	6,250	NC
Purdue Univ/West Lafayette	IN	13,458	VC
Southeastern Okla State Univ	OK	6,147	C
Sterling College	VT	23,286	VC
Texas Tech Univ	TX	13,026	VC
Unity College	ME	24,320	C
Univ of Arkansas at Pine Bluff	AR	8,300	C
Univ of Calif at Berkeley	CA	18,141	HC+
Univ of Wisc/Madison	WI	13,117	HC
Univ of Wisc/Milwaukee	WI	9,427	LC
Univ of Wisc/River Falls	WI	9,722	LC
Upper Iowa Univ	IA	20,130	C

CONSTRUCTION ENGINEERING

School	ST	$IS	SR
Arizona State Univ-Tempe	AZ	11,174	C
Bradley Univ	IL	25,280	VC
Fairleigh Dickinson Univ/ Metropolitan Campus	NJ	28,590	C
Iowa State Univ	IA	11,831	VC
Lehigh Univ	PA	42,690	HC+
Louisiana Tech Univ	LA	7,370	C
Minn State Univ, Moorhead	MN	7,000	LC
Montana State Univ-Bozeman	MT	1,137	C
National Univ	CA	8,412	SP
N Dak State Univ	ND	8,500	C
Purdue Univ/West Lafayette	IN	13,458	VC
Rensselaer Polytechnic Inst	NY	41,288	HC+
Southern Illinois Univ Edwardsville	IL	11,022	C
Southern Polytechnic State Univ	GA	7,640	VC
Texas A&M Univ	TX	13,351	HC
Thomas Edison State College	NJ	3,780	SP
Univ of Florida	FL	9,354	HC
Univ of New Mexico	NM	11,253	C
Univ of the District of Columbia	DC	2,070	LC
Univ of Washington	WA	10,400	VC
Virginia Polytechnic Inst and State Univ	VA	10,834	VC
Western Mich Univ	MI	13,299	C

CONSTRUCTION MANAGEMENT

School	ST	$IS	SR
Auburn Univ	AL	12,230	VC
Boise State Univ	ID	9,438	LC
Brigham Young Univ	UT	9,200	VC
Calif Polytechnic State Univ	CA	12,390	VC
Cal State, Chico	CA	11,395	C
Cal State, Fresno	CA	10,037	LC
Central Missouri State Univ	MO	10,000	C
Central Washington Univ	WA	11,730	C
Clemson Univ	SC	13,366	NC
Colo State Univ-Fort Collins	CO	10,878	C+
Drexel Univ	PA	27,700	VC
East Carolina Univ	NC	10,000	C
Eastern Mich Univ	MI	12,897	C
Farmingdale SUNY	NY	13,521	C
Ferris State Univ	MI	13,698	C
Florida International Univ	FL	9,215	VC
Georgia Inst of Technology	GA	11,450	HC+
Georgia Southern Univ	GA	9,762	C
John Brown Univ	AR	20,910	VC
Kansas State Univ	KS	10,516	VC
Lawrence Tech Univ	MI	25,475	VC
Louisiana State Univ and A&M College	LA	10,749	VC
Mich State Univ	MI	13,689	VC
Mich Tech Univ	MI	14,569	VC
Milwaukee School of Engineering	WI	29,847	VC+
Minn State Univ, Mankato	MN	10,276	LC
Missouri State Univ	MO	10,748	C+

School	ST	$IS	SR
National Univ	CA	8,412	SP
N Car State Univ	NC	11,824	HC
N Dak State Univ	ND	8,500	C
Northern Mich Univ	MI	12,340	LC
Okla State Univ	OK	10,213	VC
Oregon State Univ	OR	11,055	C
Pennsylvania College of Technology	PA	16,980	LC
Pittsburg State Univ	KS	8,112	C
Pratt Inst	NY	36,156	SP
Roger Williams Univ	RI	30,500	C
S Dak State Univ	SD	9,815	C
Southern Utah Univ	UT		C
SUNY/College of Environmental Science and Forestry	NY	15,000	VC
SUNY/College of Technology at Alfred	NY	14,000	C
Tuskegee Univ	AL	18,860	LC
Univ of Cincinnati	OH	17,682	C
Univ of Denver	CO	36,376	VC+
Univ of Houston	TX	7,000	C
Univ of Nebr at Lincoln	NE	11,401	VC
Univ of Nevada/Las Vegas	NV	11,566	C
Univ of New Mexico	NM	11,253	C
Univ of North Florida	FL	9,908	VC
Univ of Northern Iowa	IA	11,133	C
Univ of Okla	OK	10,769	VC+
Univ of Texas at San Antonio	TX	11,325	LC
Virginia Polytechnic Inst and State Univ	VA	10,834	VC
Washington State Univ	WA	12,260	C
Weber State Univ	UT	9,635	NC
Wentworth Inst of Technology	MA	27,500	C
Western Carolina Univ	NC	7,000	C
Western Kentucky Univ	KY	10,192	C

CONSTRUCTION TECHNOLOGY

School	ST	$IS	SR
Appalachian State Univ	NC	8,000	VC
Calif State Polytechnic Univ, Pomona	CA	18,053	C+
Central Conn State Univ	CT	13,620	C
Eastern Kentucky Univ	KY	7,725	C
Indiana State Univ	IN	11,604	C
Indiana Univ-Purdue Univ Indianapolis	IN	10,959	C
Montana State Univ-Northern	MT	10,000	NC
Murray State Univ	KY	8,900	VC
Norfolk State Univ	VA	10,531	LC
Northern Kentucky Univ	KY	6,670	NC
Pennsylvania College of Technology	PA	16,980	LC
Purdue Univ/Calumet	IN	10,891	LC
Purdue Univ/West Lafayette	IN	13,458	VC
Texas State Univ - San Marcos	TX	10,862	C
Texas Tech Univ	TX	13,026	VC
Univ of Akron	OH	15,166	NC
Univ of Arkansas at Little Rock	AR	7,230	NC
Univ of Houston	TX	7,000	C
Univ of Maine	ME	13,642	C
Univ of Maryland/Eastern Shore	MD	11,210	C
Univ of Mass Amherst	MA	15,973	C+
Univ of Nebr at Lincoln	NE	11,401	VC
Univ of Southern Miss	MS	10,112	C
Univ of Wisc/Stout	WI	11,164	C
Wentworth Inst of Technology	MA	27,500	C

CONSUMER SERVICES

School	ST	$IS	SR
Cornell Univ	NY	41,717	MC
Indiana Univ of Pennsylvania	PA	11,209	C
Purdue Univ/West Lafayette	IN	13,458	VC
S Dak State Univ	SD	9,815	C
Syracuse Univ	NY	38,655	HC
Texas Woman's Univ	TX	7,804	LC
Univ of Delaware	DE	14,142	HC
Univ of Georgia	GA	11,004	HC
Univ of Memphis	TN	11,153	C
Univ of Wisc/Madison	WI	13,117	HC

CONTEMPORARY CHRISTIAN MUSIC

School	ST	$IS	SR
Greenville College	IL	23,146	C
Spring Arbor Univ	MI	22,476	C

CORRECTIONS

School	ST	$IS	SR
CUNY/John Jay College of Criminal Justice	NY	5,000	C
College of the Ozarks	MO	4,130	VC+
Eastern Kentucky Univ	KY	7,725	C
Hardin-Simmons Univ	TX	18,641	C
Jackson State Univ	MS	8,500	C
Limestone College	SC	19,840	C

ST = STATE   **$IS** = IN-STATE COSTS   **SR** = SELECTOR RATING

INDEX OF COLLEGE MAJORS

School	ST	$IS	SR
Minn State Univ, Mankato	MN	10,276	LC
Southeast Missouri State Univ	MO	10,596	C
Stephen F. Austin State Univ	TX	7,930	C
Texas State Univ - San Marcos	TX	10,862	C
Tiffin Univ	OH	19,490	LC
Univ of Indianapolis	IN	25,090	C
Univ of New Haven	CT	31,794	C
Univ of Texas-Pan American	TX	7,290	C+
Washburn Univ	KS	9,734	NC
Western Oregon Univ	OR	10,295	C
Youngstown State Univ	OH	12,613	NC

COUNSELING/PSYCHOLOGY

School	ST	$IS	SR
Averett Univ	VA	24,920	C
College of Santa Fe	NM	28,978	C
Crichton College	TN	15,300	C
Dallas Baptist Univ	TX	17,040	C
Eastern Mich Univ	MI	12,897	C
Emmanuel College	MA	32,000	C+
Geneva College	PA	21,850	C
Goddard College	VT	21,100	C
Grace College	IN	22,170	C
Indiana Univ South Bend	IN	4,989	LC
Kent State Univ	OH	14,594	C
Kentucky Christian College	KY	12,680	C
Limestone College	SC	19,840	C
Martin Univ	IN	10,300	SP
Moravian College	PA	28,950	VC
Newman Univ	KS	21,106	C
Northwest Univ	WA	18,854	C
Rochester College	MI	15,636	C+
Samford Univ	AL	20,258	VC
Toccoa Falls College	GA	17,125	C
Univ of Great Falls	MT	17,000	C
Univ of North Texas	TX	7,800	C
Wayne State College	NE	8,033	NC
Williams Baptist College	AR	13,450	C

COURT REPORTING

School	ST	$IS	SR
Humphreys College	CA	7,000	NC
Northwood Univ	TX	20,135	LC
Univ of Miss	MS	9,000	C

CRAFTS

School	ST	$IS	SR
Cal State, Fullerton	CA	10,990	C
Kent State Univ	OH	14,594	C
Kutztown Univ of Pennsylvania	PA	10,820	C
Purdue Univ/West Lafayette	IN	13,458	VC
Rochester Inst of Technology	NY	32,070	VC+
Univ of Illinois at Urbana-Champaign	IL	15,800	HC+

CREATIVE WRITING

School	ST	$IS	SR
Agnes Scott College	GA	32,070	HC
Albertson College of Idaho	ID	21,095	VC
Alderson-Broaddus College	WV	24,006	C
Andrews Univ	MI	21,786	C
Arkansas Tech Univ	AR	8,108	VC
Ashland Univ	OH	25,000	C
Bard College	NY	41,800	HC+
Baylor Univ	TX	27,555	VC
Belhaven College	MS	19,530	NC
Beloit College	WI	32,808	HC
Bennington College	VT	41,890	HC
Bluffton College	OH	26,110	C
Bowling Green State Univ	OH	14,994	C
Burlington College	VT	14,670	SP
Calif College of the Arts	CA	34,325	SP
Cal State, San Marcos	CA	1,800	C
Cardinal Stritch Univ	WI	21,910	C
Carlow Univ	PA	24,313	C
Carroll College	MT	23,324	C+
Central Mich Univ	MI	12,244	C
Chapman Univ	CA	37,550	VC
Christopher Newport Univ	VA	13,326	VC
CUNY/Brooklyn College	NY	4,377	C+
CUNY/Hunter College	NY	8,000	C+
Colby College	ME	41,770	MC
College of Santa Fe	NM	28,978	C
Colo College	CO	37,668	HC
Columbia College Chicago	IL	25,125	LC
Concordia College: Moorhead	MN	22,475	VC
Dartmouth College	NH	39,465	MC
Dominican Univ of Calif	CA	36,836	C
Drexel Univ	PA	27,700	VC
Eastern Washington Univ	WA	10,608	C
Eckerd College	FL	35,492	VC
Edinboro Univ of Pennsylvania	PA	11,809	LC
Emerson College	MA	35,076	HC
Emory & Henry College	VA	26,570	C
Emory Univ	GA	40,546	MC
Eugene Lang College New School for Liberal Arts	NY	38,800	C+

School	ST	$IS	SR
Fairleigh Dickinson Univ/ College at Florham	NJ	30,130	C
Florida State Univ	FL	9,028	HC
Geneva College	PA	21,850	C
Goddard College	VT	21,100	C
Green Mountain College	VT	32,164	C
Hamilton College	NY	41,660	MC
Hampshire College	MA	37,120	HC
Harvard Univ/Harvard College	MA	45,860	MC
Hofstra Univ	NY	32,630	VC
Hollins Univ	VA	31,105	C
Indiana Univ Bloomington	IN	13,356	VC
Indiana Wesleyan Univ	IN	22,074	C+
Ithaca College	NY	35,144	VC
Johns Hopkins Univ	MD	42,044	MC
Johnson State College	VT	11,830	C
Kansas City Art Inst	MO	29,542	SP
Kent State Univ	OH	14,594	C
Knox College	IL	32,385	VC+
La Roche College	PA	24,724	LC
Lakeland College	WI	22,990	C
Le Moyne College	NY	29,570	VC
Lindenwood Univ	MO	18,600	VC
Linfield College	OR	29,632	VC
Loras College	IA	27,193	C
Loyola College in Maryland	MD	38,898	HC
Loyola Univ New Orleans	LA	31,050	VC+
Marlboro College	VT	35,980	VC+
Maryville College	TN	29,224	VC
Mass Inst of Technology	MA	41,800	MC
Methodist College	NC	21,000	C
Millikin Univ	IL	25,590	C
Mills College	CA	39,870	C
Montclair State Univ	NJ	16,327	C
Mount Union College	OH	25,840	C
New England College	NH	31,466	C
New York Univ	NY	43,170	MC
Northland College	WI	26,680	C+
Oberlin College	OH	40,904	MC
Ohio Northern Univ	OH	27,765	VC
Ohio Univ	OH	15,921	C
Okla Christian Univ	OK	18,992	NC
Old Dominion Univ	VA	11,907	C
Pacific Univ	OR	24,250	C
Pratt Inst	NY	36,156	SP
Purdue Univ/West Lafayette	IN	13,458	VC
Roger Williams Univ	RI	30,500	C
St. Andrews Presbyterian College	NC	23,530	C
St. Edward's Univ	TX	23,560	C
St. Joseph's College	IN	26,600	C
St. Lawrence Univ	NY	40,545	VC
Sarah Lawrence College	NY	42,000	HC
School of the Art Inst of Chicago	IL	37,800	SP
Seattle Univ	WA	30,063	VC
Seton Hill Univ	PA	28,810	C
Simon's Rock College of Bard	MA	41,988	VC+
Southern Methodist Univ	TX	36,088	VC+
Southern Nazarene Univ	OK	14,634	NC
Southern New Hampshire Univ	NH	28,764	C
Southern Vermont College	VT	21,322	LC
Southwest Minn State Univ	MN	10,975	C
Spring Hill College	AL	28,678	C
SUNY/College at Purchase	NY	11,989	VC+
Stephens College	MO	26,930	VC
Suffolk Univ	MA	33,160	C
Susquehanna Univ	PA	33,465	VC
Sweet Briar College	VA	31,460	VC
Univ of Arizona	AZ	11,958	VC
Univ of Calif at Riverside	CA	16,625	C
Univ of Central Okla	OK	8,094	C
Univ of Colo at Denver and Health Sciences Center	CO	5,021	C
Univ of Evansville	IN	28,320	VC
Univ of Houston	TX	7,000	C
Univ of Maine at Farmington	ME	11,515	C
Univ of Miami	FL	38,397	MC
Univ of Mich/Ann Arbor	MI	16,587	HC+
Univ of Montana--Western	MT	8,406	NC
Univ of Nebr at Omaha	NE	11,235	C
Univ of New Haven	CT	31,794	C
Univ of N Car at Wilmington	NC	10,107	VC
Univ of Pittsburgh at Bradford	PA	17,008	C
Univ of Pittsburgh at Greensburg	PA	17,640	C
Univ of Pittsburgh at Johnstown	PA	16,740	LC
Univ of Redlands	CA	36,160	VC
Univ of Southern Calif	CA	41,618	MC
Univ of Tampa	FL	25,784	C
Valparaiso Univ	IN	28,970	VC+
Warren Wilson College	NC	24,382	VC
Wartburg College	IA	27,315	NC
Washington Univ in St. Louis	MO	42,106	MC
Waynesburg College	PA	21,230	C
Wheaton College	MA	40,180	HC+

CRIMINAL JUSTICE

School	ST	$IS	SR
Abilene Christian Univ	TX	20,830	C
Adrian College	MI	23,000	C
Alabama State Univ	AL	7,658	C
Albany State Univ	GA	5,770	C+
Albright College	PA	33,920	C
Alcorn State Univ	MS	8,190	LC
Alfred Univ	NY		VC
Alvernia College	PA	26,388	C
American International College	MA	28,710	LC
American Univ	DC	38,719	HC+
Anderson Univ	IN	25,050	LC
Angelo State Univ	TX	8,340	NC
Anna Maria College	MA	29,815	LC
Appalachian State Univ	NC	8,000	VC
Arcadia Univ	PA	33,570	VC
Arizona State Univ-Tempe	AZ	11,174	C
Armstrong Atlantic State Univ	GA	7,394	C
Ashford Univ	IA	20,370	C
Ashland Univ	OH	25,000	C
Auburn Univ Montgomery	AL	9,530	NC
Augusta State Univ	GA	2,920	C
Aurora Univ	IL	20,645	C
Averett Univ	VA	24,920	C
Baldwin-Wallace College	OH	27,256	VC
Ball State Univ	IN	13,138	C
Barton College	NC	22,316	C
Bay Path College	MA	29,362	C
Becker College	MA	24,300	LC
Bellarmine Univ	KY	27,650	C+
Bellevue Univ	NE	4,440	NC
Bemidji State Univ	MN	11,180	LC
Benedict College	SC	19,114	LC
Bethany College	KS	20,660	LC
Bethel College	IN	19,680	C
Bethune-Cookman College	FL	17,922	LC
Bloomsburg Univ of Pennsylvania	PA	11,602	C
Bluefield College	VA	17,230	C+
Bluefield State College	WV	3,140	LC
Bluffton College	OH	26,110	C
Boise State Univ	ID	9,438	LC
Bowie State Univ	MD	10,880	C+
Bowling Green State Univ	OH	14,994	C
Bradley Univ	IL	25,280	VC
Briar Cliff Univ	IA	23,550	LC
Bridgewater State College	MA	12,120	C
Buena Vista Univ	IA	27,742	C
Butler Univ	IN	31,944	VC+
Cabrini College	PA	33,340	C
Caldwell College	NJ	26,450	LC
Calif Baptist Univ	CA	23,780	C
Calif Lutheran Univ	CA	27,800	LC
Cal State East Bay	CA	10,856	LC
Cal State, Bakersfield	CA	6,125	LC
Cal State, Fullerton	CA	10,990	C
Cal State, Los Angeles	CA	5,900	C
Cal State, Sacramento	CA	11,122	C+
Cal State, San Bernardino	CA	12,563	LC
Cal State, Stanislaus	CA	11,283	C
Calif Univ of Pennsylvania	PA	14,217	C
Calumet College of St. Joseph	IN	9,500	LC
Cameron Univ	OK	6,314	NC
Campbell Univ	NC	21,137	VC
Canisius College	NY	32,257	VC
Capital Univ	OH	30,444	C
Caribbean Univ	PR	3,000	
Carlow Univ	PA	24,313	C
Carroll College	WI	24,860	C
Carthage College	WI	26,000	C
Castleton State College	VT	13,158	C
Cedarville Univ	OH	21,904	VC
Centenary College	NJ	28,870	LC
Central Methodist Univ	MO	18,000	C
Central Mich Univ	MI	12,244	C
Central Missouri State Univ	MO	11,730	C
Central Washington Univ	WA	11,730	C
Chadron State College	NE	6,350	NC
Chaminade Univ of Honolulu	HI	23,320	LC
Champlain College	VT	24,605	C
Charleston Southern Univ	SC	17,800	C
Chestnut Hill College	PA	26,600	LC
Chicago State Univ	IL	10,915	C+
Christopher Newport Univ	VA	13,326	VC
Citadel, The	SC		C+
CUNY/John Jay College of Criminal Justice	NY	5,000	C
Claflin Univ	SC	16,798	C+
College of New Jersey	NJ	18,315	MC
College of St. Rose	NY	25,684	C
College of Santa Fe	NM	28,978	C
College of the Ozarks	MO	4,130	VC+
College of the Southwest	NM	12,420	C
Colo Technical Univ	CO	9,500	LC
Columbia College	MO	16,900	C
Columbus State Univ	GA	8,664	C
Concordia Univ St.Paul	MN	27,776	C
Concordia Univ Wisc	WI	22,660	VC
Concordia Univ, Ann Arbor	MI	25,153	C+
Coppin State College	MD	10,200	LC

School	ST	$IS	SR
Culver-Stockton College	MO	20,625	C
Cumberland Univ	TN	18,894	C
Curry College	MA	26,100	LC
Dakota Wesleyan Univ	SD	17,832	C
Dallas Baptist Univ	TX	17,040	C
Dana College	NE	22,390	C
De Sales Univ	PA	28,580	VC
Defiance College	OH	24,790	C
Delaware Valley College	PA	29,944	C
Delta State Univ	MS	7,709	C
Dordt College	IA	20,325	C
East Carolina Univ	NC	10,000	C
East Central Univ	OK	6,207	C
East Tenn State Univ	TN	8,497	C
Eastern Mich Univ	MI	12,897	C
Eastern New Mexico Univ	NM	7,264	C
Eastern Washington Univ	WA	10,608	C
Edgewood College	WI	22,862	C
Edinboro Univ of Pennsylvania	PA	11,809	LC
Edward Waters College	FL	14,374	LC
Elizabeth City State Univ	NC	5,700	LC
Elizabethtown College	PA	32,100	VC
Elmira College	NY	37,200	VC
Endicott College	MA	30,156	C+
Evangel Univ	MO	17,380	C
Excelsior College	NY	995	SP
Fairleigh Dickinson Univ/ Metropolitan Campus	NJ	28,590	C
Fairmont State	WV	8,400	LC
Fayetteville State Univ	NC	6,000	LC
Ferris State Univ	MI	13,698	C
Ferrum College	VA	24,290	LC
Fitchburg State College	MA	11,276	C
Florida A&M Univ	FL	8,344	C
Florida Atlantic Univ	FL	11,221	C
Florida Gulf Coast Univ	FL	10,833	C
Florida International Univ	FL	9,215	VC
Florida Memorial College	FL	6,000	LC
Florida Southern College	FL	25,965	C
Fort Hays State Univ	KS	7,638	C
Fort Valley State Univ	GA	6,975	C
Franklin Pierce College	NH	31,700	C
Frostburg State Univ	MD	12,672	C
Gannon Univ	PA	26,100	C
George Mason Univ	VA	10,850	VC
George Washington Univ	DC	48,820	MC
Georgia College and State Univ	GA	11,020	C
Georgia Southern Univ	GA	9,762	C
Georgia State Univ	GA	11,444	VC
Gonzaga Univ	WA	30,218	VC
Grace College	IN	22,170	C
Graceland Univ	IA	19,700	C
Grambling State Univ	LA	6,538	NC
Grand Canyon Univ	AZ	32,000	LC
Grand Valley State Univ	MI	12,000	VC
Grand View College	IA	21,482	C
Granite State College	NH	4,800	SP
Greenville College	IL	23,146	C
Guilford College	NC	28,160	C+
Gustavus Adolphus College	MN	30,920	HC
Gwynedd-Mercy College	PA	26,080	C
Hamline Univ	MN	27,070	VC
Hannibal-LaGrange College	MO	16,390	C
Harding Univ	AR	16,512	VC
Hardin-Simmons Univ	TX	18,641	C
Hawaii Pacific Univ	HI	21,080	C
Hesser College	NH	17,700	LC
High Point Univ	NC	25,720	C
Hilbert College	NY	20,480	LC
Holy Family Univ	PA	25,740	C
Howard Univ	DC	18,481	C+
Huron Univ	SD	10,700	C
Husson College	ME	17,410	LC
Illinois State Univ	IL	12,839	C+
Indiana Inst of Technology	IN	23,430	C
Indiana Univ Bloomington	IN	13,356	VC
Indiana Univ East	IN	4,806	LC
Indiana Univ Kokomo	IN	4,835	LC
Indiana Univ Northwest	IN	4,902	LC
Indiana Univ South Bend	IN	4,989	LC
Indiana Univ Southeast	IN	4,880	LC
Indiana Univ-Purdue Univ Fort Wayne	IN	5,067	LC
Indiana Univ-Purdue Univ Indianapolis	IN	10,959	C
Indiana Wesleyan Univ	IN	22,074	C+
Inter American Univ of PR/ Aguadilla Campus	PR	3,784	
Inter American Univ of PR/ Arecibo Campus	PR	3,350	
Inter American Univ of PR/ Barranquitas Regional College	PR	3,350	
Inter American Univ of PR/ Fajardo Campus	PR	4,000	
Inter American Univ of PR/ Metropolitan Campus	PR	4,320	
Inter American Univ of PR/ Ponce Regional College	PR	3,700	
International College	FL	9,500	NC
Iona College	NY	30,878	VC
Iowa Wesleyan College	IA	22,140	C
Jackson State Univ	MS	8,500	C
Jacksonville State Univ	AL	7,618	LC

ST = STATE   **$IS** = IN-STATE COSTS   **SR** = SELECTOR RATING

ST = STATE   **$IS** = IN-STATE COSTS   **SR** = SELECTOR RATING

School	ST	$IS	SR
Cal State, Fresno	CA	10,037	LC
Cal State, Northridge	CA	9,036	LC
Cazenovia College	NY	26,900	C
Central Conn State Univ	CT	13,620	C
Christopher Newport Univ	VA	13,326	VC
CUNY/John Jay College of Criminal Justice	NY	5,000	C
Coker College	SC	21,600	C
College of Mount St. Joseph	OH	24,860	C
College of the Ozarks	MO	4,130	VC+
Colo State Univ-Pueblo	CO	7,821	LC
Dominican Univ	IL	26,370	C
Drury Univ	MO	20,117	VC
Florida Gulf Coast Univ	FL	10,833	C
Florida State Univ	FL	9,028	HC
Hilbert College	NY	20,480	LC
Indiana State Univ	IN	11,604	C
Indiana Univ of Pennsylvania	PA	11,209	C
Le Moyne College	NY	29,570	VC
Limestone College	SC	19,840	C
Longwood Univ	VA	12,426	C
Marquette Univ	WI	31,066	HC
Maryville Univ of St. Louis	MO	23,000	VC
Mount Aloysius College	PA	20,900	LC
Ohio State Univ	OH	15,357	HC
Ohio Univ	OH	15,921	C
Pontifical Catholic Univ of PR/Ponce	PR	7,310	
St. Ambrose Univ	IA	25,495	C
St. Edward's Univ	TX	23,560	C
Southeast Missouri State Univ	MO	10,596	C
Southern Oregon Univ	OR	12,186	C
SUNY/College at Old Westbury	NY	13,154	C
Stonehill College	MA	36,104	HC
Tiffin Univ	OH	19,490	LC
Turabo Univ	PR	4,110	
Univ of Calif at Irvine	CA	16,475	HC
Univ of Florida	FL	9,354	HC
Univ of La Verne	CA	33,470	C
Univ of Maryland/College Park	MD	16,036	HC
Univ of Memphis	TN	11,153	C
Univ of Miami	FL	38,397	MC
Univ of Minn/Duluth	MN	13,974	C
Univ of Northern Iowa	IA	11,133	C
Univ of South Florida	FL	10,284	VC
Univ of Tampa	FL	25,784	C
Univ of Texas at Dallas	TX	13,244	VC
Univ of West Georgia	GA	8,838	C
Upper Iowa Univ	IA	20,130	C
Valparaiso Univ	IN	28,970	VC+
Virginia Union Univ	VA	18,432	LC
Wilkes Univ	PA	30,886	C
William Penn Univ	IA	17,685	LC

CROSSCULTURAL STUDIES

School	ST	$IS	SR
Alfred Univ	NY		VC
Andrews Univ	MI	21,786	C
Antioch College	OH	33,700	C
Biola Univ	CA	29,372	VC
Chatham College	PA	27,290	C+
Columbia College Chicago	IL	25,125	LC
Eugene Lang College New School for Liberal Arts	NY	38,800	C+
Goddard College	VT	21,100	C
Hampshire College	MA	37,120	HC
Hope International Univ	CA	23,700	NC
Houghton College	NY	25,980	VC+
John Brown Univ	AR	20,910	VC
Lee Univ	TN	14,780	NC
Murray State Univ	KY	8,900	VC
National-Louis Univ	IL	16,915	LC
Northwestern College	MN	25,220	NC
Nyack College	NY	18,540	C
Palm Beach Atlantic Univ	FL	23,597	VC
Simon's Rock College of Bard	MA	41,988	VC+
Stanford Univ	CA	41,557	MC
Toccoa Falls College	GA	17,125	C
Towson Univ	MD	13,924	VC
Univ of Calif at Irvine	CA	16,475	HC
Washington State Univ	WA	12,260	C
Waynesburg College	PA	21,230	C
Western Baptist College	OR	21,808	C
Whitworth College	WA	29,428	VC+
Wofford College	SC	30,935	HC

CULINARY ARTS

School	ST	$IS	SR
Art Inst of Atlanta	GA	23,220	SP
Atlantic Union College	MA	17,600	LC
Kendall College	IL	28,800	NC
Mountain State Univ	WV	11,406	NC
Pennsylvania College of Technology	PA	16,980	LC
Southern New Hampshire Univ	NH	28,764	C
Virginia Intermont College	VA	22,200	LC

CYBERNETICS

School	ST	$IS	SR
Univ of Calif at Los Angeles	CA	17,681	MC

CYTOTECHNOLOGY

School	ST	$IS	SR
Alderson-Broaddus College	WV	24,006	C
Ashford Univ	IA	20,370	C
Barry Univ	FL	24,100	LC
Bellarmine Univ	KY	27,650	C+
College of St. Rose	NY	25,684	C
Edgewood College	WI	22,862	C
Indiana Univ Kokomo	IN	4,835	LC
Indiana Univ-Purdue Univ Indianapolis	IN	10,959	C
Jewish Hospital College of Nursing and Allied Health	MO	12,000	SP
Marian College of Fond du Lac	WI	21,775	LC
Marshall Univ	WV	9,116	C
Northern Mich Univ	MI	12,340	LC
Old Dominion Univ	VA	11,907	C
St. Mary's Univ of Minn	MN	23,857	VC
Salve Regina Univ	RI	33,450	C
SUNY/Univ at Stony Brook	NY	13,625	HC
Thiel College	PA	24,580	C
Thomas Edison State College	NJ	3,780	SP
Univ of Alabama at Birmingham	AL	13,716	C
Univ of Conn	CT	16,628	HC
Univ of Kansas	KS	10,915	VC
Univ of N Dak	ND	10,114	VC
Univ of North Texas	TX	7,800	C
Winona State Univ	MN	11,333	C

DAIRY SCIENCE

School	ST	$IS	SR
Calif Polytechnic State Univ	CA	12,390	VC
Delaware Valley College	PA	29,944	C
Iowa State Univ	IA	11,831	VC
Louisiana State Univ and A&M Univ	LA	10,749	VC
Penn State Univ/Univ Park Campus	PA	18,038	HC
S Dak State Univ	SD	9,815	C
Texas A&M Univ	TX	13,351	HC
Univ of Florida	FL	9,354	HC
Univ of Georgia	GA	11,004	HC
Univ of New Hampshire	NH	16,810	VC
Univ of Wisc/Madison	WI	13,117	HC
Utah State Univ	UT	8,002	VC
Virginia Polytechnic Inst and State Univ	VA	10,834	VC

DANCE

School	ST	$IS	SR
Adelphi Univ	NY	27,000	VC
Amherst College	MA	41,590	MC
Arizona State Univ-Tempe	AZ	11,174	C
Ball State Univ	IN	13,138	C
Bard College	NY	41,800	HC+
Belhaven College	MS	19,530	NC
Bennington College	VT	41,890	HC
Birmingham-Southern College	AL	28,494	VC+
Boston Conservatory	MA	27,500	SP
Bowling Green State Univ	OH	14,994	C
Brenau Univ Women's College	GA	23,950	VC
Brigham Young Univ	UT	9,200	VC
Butler Univ	IN	31,944	VC+
Calif Inst of the Arts	CA	35,725	SP
Cal State, Fullerton	CA	10,990	C
Cal State, Long Beach	CA	9,512	C
Cal State, Northridge	CA	9,036	LC
Cal State, San Bernardino	CA	12,563	LC
Cedar Crest College	PA	30,615	C
Centenary College of Louisiana	LA	24,760	VC
Chapman Univ	CA	37,550	VC
CUNY/Herbert H. Lehman College	NY	4,000	LC
CUNY/Hunter College	NY	8,000	C+
CUNY/Queens College	NY	4,356	C
Coker College	SC	21,600	C
Colo College	CO	37,668	HC
Columbia College	SC	24,982	LC
Columbia College Chicago	IL	25,125	LC
Columbia Univ/Barnard College	NY	38,000	MC
Columbia Univ/Columbia College	NY	42,584	MC
Columbia Univ/School of General Studies	NY	41,516	C
Conn College	CT	41,975	MC
Cornell Univ	NY	41,717	MC
Cornish College of the Arts	WA	21,200	SP
Creighton Univ	NE	29,918	VC+
De Sales Univ	PA	28,580	VC
Denison Univ	OH	37,040	HC
Dickinson College	PA	40,170	HC+
East Carolina Univ	NC	10,000	C
Eastern Mich Univ	MI	12,897	C
Eastern Univ	PA	24,075	C

School	ST	$IS	SR
Eastern Washington Univ	WA	10,608	C
Elon Univ	NC	25,371	HC
Emory Univ	GA	40,546	MC
Florida International Univ	FL	9,215	VC
Florida State Univ	FL	9,028	HC
Fordham Univ	NY	36,000	HC
George Mason Univ	VA	10,850	VC
George Washington Univ	DC	48,820	MC
Goucher College	MD	36,225	VC
Gustavus Adolphus College	MN	30,920	HC
Hamilton College	NY	41,660	MC
Hampshire College	MA	37,120	HC
Hobart and William Smith Colleges	NY	41,123	VC
Hofstra Univ	NY	32,630	VC
Hollins Univ	VA	31,105	C
Hope College	MI	28,208	VC+
Howard Univ	DC	18,481	C+
Huntingdon College	AL	23,090	VC
Jacksonville Univ	FL	24,040	C
James Madison Univ	VA	12,010	VC
Juilliard School	NY	37,620	SP
Keene State College	NH	13,836	C
Kent State Univ	OH	14,594	C
Kenyon College	OH	39,500	MC
La Roche College	PA	24,724	LC
Lindenwood Univ	MO	18,600	VC
LIU/C.W. Post Campus	NY	28,282	C
Loyola Marymount Univ	CA	36,321	VC
Luther College	IA	28,800	VC+
Manhattanville College	NY	32,500	C+
Marlboro College	VT	35,980	VC+
Marygrove College	MI	19,310	C+
Marymount Manhattan College	NY	30,049	VC
Mercyhurst College	PA	28,633	VC
Meredith College	NC	25,600	C
Middlebury College	VT	42,120	MC
Mills College	CA	39,870	C
Minn State Univ, Mankato	MN	10,276	LC
Missouri State Univ	MO	10,748	C+
Montclair State Univ	NJ	16,327	C
Mount Holyoke College	MA	42,148	HC+
Muhlenberg College	PA	36,030	HC+
New Mexico State Univ	NM	9,250	C
New York Univ	NY	43,170	MC
N Car School of the Arts	NC	7,401	SP
Northwestern Univ	IL	37,595	MC
Oberlin College	OH	40,904	MC
Ohio State Univ	OH	15,357	HC
Ohio Univ	OH	15,921	C
Okla City Univ	OK	23,965	VC
Old Dominion Univ	VA	11,907	C
Palm Beach Atlantic Univ	FL	23,597	VC
Pitzer College	CA	41,644	HC
Point Park Univ	PA	24,160	C
Radford Univ	VA	13,145	C
Randolph-Macon Woman's College	VA	31,160	VC+
Richard Stockton College of New Jersey	NJ	14,000	VC
Rider Univ	NJ	32,560	C
Roger Williams Univ	RI	30,500	C
Rutgers, The State Univ of New Jersey/New Brunswick/Piscataway Campus	NJ	15,810	HC
St. Olaf College	MN	32,800	HC
Sam Houston State Univ	TX	8,000	C
San Diego State Univ	CA	12,971	C
San Francisco State Univ	CA	13,000	C
San Jose State Univ	CA	11,707	C
Sarah Lawrence College	NY	42,000	HC
Scripps College	CA	41,000	MC
Shenandoah Univ	VA	27,600	C
Simon's Rock College of Bard	MA	41,988	VC+
Skidmore College	NY	41,779	HC
Slippery Rock Univ of Pennsylvania	PA	10,360	LC
Smith College	MA	41,474	MC
Southern Illinois Univ Edwardsville	IL	11,022	C
Southern Methodist Univ	TX	36,088	VC+
Southern Utah Univ	UT		C
SUNY at Potsdam	NY	12,959	C
SUNY/College at Brockport	NY	12,747	VC
SUNY/College at Purchase	NY	11,989	VC+
SUNY/Univ at Buffalo	NY	13,694	VC
Stephen F. Austin State Univ	TX	7,930	C
Stephens College	MO	26,930	VC
Swarthmore College	PA	41,280	MC
Sweet Briar College	VA	31,460	VC
Temple Univ	PA	17,438	C
Texas Christian Univ	TX	23,410	VC+
Texas State Univ - San Marcos	TX	10,862	C
Texas Tech Univ	TX	13,026	VC
Texas Woman's Univ	TX	7,804	LC
Towson Univ	MD	13,924	VC
Trinity Univ	CT	38,040	HC
Tulane Univ	LA	41,098	MC
Univ of Akron	OH	15,166	NC
Univ of Alabama	AL	9,888	C
Univ of Arizona	AZ	11,958	VC

School	ST	$IS	SR
Univ of Calif at Berkeley	CA	18,141	HC+
Univ of Calif at Irvine	CA	16,475	HC
Univ of Calif at Riverside	CA	16,625	C
Univ of Calif at San Diego	CA	16,102	HC
Univ of Calif at Santa Barbara	CA	11,800	VC
Univ of Cincinnati	OH	17,682	C
Univ of Colo at Boulder	CO	13,352	C+
Univ of Florida	FL	9,354	HC
Univ of Georgia	GA	11,004	HC
Univ of Hartford	CT	34,044	C
Univ of Hawaii at Manoa	HI	10,413	VC
Univ of Idaho	ID	9,310	VC
Univ of Illinois at Urbana-Champaign	IL	15,800	HC+
Univ of Iowa	IA	12,172	VC
Univ of Kansas	KS	10,915	VC
Univ of Louisiana at Lafayette	LA	5,830	C
Univ of Maryland/Baltimore County	MD	16,642	VC+
Univ of Maryland/College Park	MD	16,036	HC
Univ of Mass Amherst	MA	15,973	C+
Univ of Mich/Ann Arbor	MI	16,587	HC+
Univ of Minn/Twin Cities	MN	13,165	VC
Univ of Missouri/Kansas City	MO	15,000	VC
Univ of Missouri/St. Louis	MO	14,046	VC
Univ of Nebr at Lincoln	NE	11,401	VC
Univ of Nevada/Las Vegas	NV	11,566	C
Univ of New Mexico	NM	11,253	C
Univ of N Car at Charlotte	NC	9,101	C
Univ of N Car at Greensboro	NC	8,993	C
Univ of North Texas	TX	7,800	C
Univ of Northern Colo	CO	10,249	C
Univ of Okla	OK	10,769	VC+
Univ of Oregon	OR	13,108	VC
Univ of S Car at Columbia	SC	13,597	VC
Univ of South Florida	FL	10,284	VC
Univ of Southern Miss	MS	10,112	C
Univ of Texas at Austin	TX	14,610	HC
Univ of the Arts	PA	32,330	SP
Univ of Utah	UT	10,162	VC
Univ of Washington	WA	10,400	VC
Univ of Wisc/Madison	WI	13,117	HC
Univ of Wisc/Milwaukee	WI	9,427	C
Univ of Wisc/Stevens Point	WI	9,384	VC
Univ of Wyoming	WY	9,666	C
Ursinus College	PA	38,950	VC
Utah State Univ	UT	8,002	VC
Virginia Commonwealth Univ	VA	12,987	C
Virginia Intermont College	VA	22,200	LC
Washington Univ in St. Louis	MO	42,106	MC
Wayne State Univ	MI	11,805	C
Weber State Univ	UT	9,635	NC
Webster Univ	MO	24,280	VC
Wells College	NY	23,070	VC
Wesleyan Univ	CT	42,122	MC
West Texas A&M Univ	TX	8,452	C
Western Mich Univ	MI	13,299	C
Western Oregon Univ	OR	10,295	VC
Winthrop Univ	SC	11,302	C
Wright State Univ	OH	13,616	LC

DANCE EDUCATION

School	ST	$IS	SR
Birmingham-Southern College	AL	28,494	VC+
Brenau Univ Women's College	GA	23,950	VC
Brigham Young Univ	UT	9,200	VC
Columbia College	SC	24,982	LC
East Carolina Univ	NC	10,000	C
Huntingdon College	AL	23,090	VC
Jacksonville Univ	FL	24,040	C
Ohio State Univ	OH	15,357	HC
Old Dominion Univ	VA	11,907	C
Point Park Univ	PA	24,160	C
Shenandoah Univ	VA	27,600	C
Southern Methodist Univ	TX	36,088	VC+
Southern Utah Univ	UT		C
Towson Univ	MD	13,924	VC
Univ of Central Okla	OK	8,094	C
Univ of N Car at Charlotte	NC	9,101	C
Univ of N Car at Greensboro	NC	8,993	C
Univ of the Arts	PA	32,330	SP

DENTAL HYGIENE

School	ST	$IS	SR
Armstrong Atlantic State Univ	GA	7,394	C
Clayton College and State Univ	GA	2,445	LC
East Tenn State Univ	TN	8,497	C
Eastern Washington Univ	WA	10,608	C
Idaho State Univ	ID	9,030	C
Indiana Univ-Purdue Univ Indianapolis	IN	10,959	C
Mass College of Pharmacy and Health Sciences	MA	32,020	SP
Midwestern State Univ	TX	9,381	LC

ST = STATE   **$IS** = IN-STATE COSTS   **SR** = SELECTOR RATING

School	ST	$IS	SR
Minn State Univ, Mankato	MN	10,276	LC
New York Univ	NY	43,170	MC
Ohio State Univ	OH	15,357	HC
Old Dominion Univ	VA	11,907	C
Oregon Inst of Technology	OR	8,718	C
Pennsylvania College of Technology	PA	16,980	LC
Southern Illinois Univ Carbondale	IL	12,391	C
Tenn State Univ	TN	9,048	LC
Texas Woman's Univ	TX	7,804	LC
Thomas Edison State College	NJ	3,780	SP
Univ of Bridgeport	CT	29,595	LC
Univ of Detroit Mercy	MI	27,000	C
Univ of Hawaii at Manoa	HI	10,413	VC
Univ of Louisiana at Monroe	LA	7,103	C
Univ of Maine at Augusta	ME	5,025	NC
Univ of Mich/Ann Arbor	MI	16,587	HC+
Univ of Minn/Twin Cities	MN	13,165	HC
Univ of Missouri/Kansas City	MO	15,000	VC
Univ of New England	ME	31,005	C
Univ of New Haven	CT	31,794	C
Univ of New Mexico	NM	11,253	C
Univ of N Car at Chapel Hill	NC	11,129	MC
Univ of Pittsburgh at Pittsburgh	PA	18,866	NC
Univ of Rhode Island	RI	15,398	C
Univ of S Dak	SD	9,068	C
Univ of Southern Calif	CA	41,618	MC
Univ of Washington	WA	10,400	VC
Univ of Wyoming	WY	9,666	C
Virginia Commonwealth Univ	VA	12,987	C
Weber State Univ	UT	9,635	NC
West Liberty State College	WV	9,142	LC
West Virginia Univ	WV	10,506	C
Western Kentucky Univ	KY	10,192	C

DENTAL LABORATORY TECHNOLOGY

School	ST	$IS	SR
Minot State Univ	ND	6,700	LC
Southern Illinois Univ Carbondale	IL	12,391	C
Southwest Minn State Univ	MN	10,975	C

DESIGN

School	ST	$IS	SR
Abilene Christian Univ	TX	20,830	C
Adelphi Univ	NY	27,000	VC
Alma College	MI	28,544	VC
Andrews Univ	MI	21,786	C
Art Center College of Design	CA	26,370	SP
Art Inst of Boston at Lesley Univ	MA	28,200	SP
Atlanta College of Art	GA	18,630	SP
Auburn Univ	AL	12,230	VC
Becker College	MA	24,300	LC
Bentley College	MA	38,784	VC
Bowling Green State Univ	OH	14,994	C
Cal State, Long Beach	CA	9,512	C
Carnegie Mellon Univ	PA	32,700	MC
Clemson Univ	SC	13,366	NC
Cleveland Inst of Art	OH	34,109	SP
Colby-Sawyer College	NH	27,850	LC
Cornell Univ	NY	41,717	MC
Cornish College of the Arts	WA	21,200	SP
Drexel Univ	PA	27,700	VC
East Carolina Univ	NC	10,000	C
Eastern Mich Univ	MI	12,897	C
Evangel Univ	MO	17,380	C
Fashion Inst of Technology/SUNY	NY	11,600	C+
Frostburg State Univ	MD	12,672	C
Grand Valley State Univ	MI	12,000	VC
Harding Univ	AR	16,512	VC
Hofstra Univ	NY	32,630	VC
Howard Univ	DC	18,481	C+
Iowa State Univ	IA	11,831	VC
John Brown Univ	AR	20,910	VC
Kansas City Art Inst	MO	29,542	SP
Lamar Univ	TX	6,820	LC
Lehigh Univ	PA	42,690	HC+
Lynn Univ	FL	30,750	C
Marywood Univ	PA	30,680	C
Memphis College of Art	TN	24,960	SP
Minneapolis College of Art and Design	MN	31,110	SP
Missouri State Univ	MO	10,748	C+
National Univ	CA	8,412	SP
New Jersey City Univ	NJ	13,695	LC
New York Univ	NY	43,170	MC
N Car State Univ	NC	11,824	HC
Northern Arizona Univ	AZ	10,353	C
Northern Mich Univ	MI	12,340	LC
Okla Christian Univ	OK	18,992	NC
Okla State Univ	OK	10,213	VC
Olivet College	MI	19,984	C+
Otis College of Art and Design	CA	27,546	SP
Parsons School of Design	NY	32,242	SP
Purdue Univ/West Lafayette	IN	13,458	VC
Radford Univ	VA	13,145	C
Rochester Inst of Technology	NY	32,070	VC+
Saginaw Valley State Univ	MI	11,432	C
Salem State College	MA	13,161	LC
San Jose State Univ	CA	11,707	C
Savannah College of Art and Design	GA	30,800	SP
School of the Art Inst of Chicago	IL	37,800	SP
Shenandoah Univ	VA	27,600	C
Southern Illinois Univ Carbondale	IL	12,391	C
Southern Illinois Univ Edwardsville	IL	11,022	C
SUNY/College at Buffalo	NY	11,903	C+
SUNY/Univ at New Paltz	NY	12,480	VC
Syracuse Univ	NY	38,655	VC
Texas Tech Univ	TX	13,026	VC
Troy Univ	AL	8,916	C
Univ of Akron	OH	15,166	NC
Univ of at Calif Davis	CA	15,010	VC
Univ of Calif at Los Angeles	CA	17,681	VC
Univ of Cincinnati	OH	17,682	C
Univ of Dayton	OH	28,826	VC
Univ of Georgia	GA	11,004	HC
Univ of Hartford	CT	34,044	C
Univ of Idaho	ID	9,310	NC
Univ of Illinois at Chicago	IL	16,256	VC
Univ of Kansas	KS	10,915	VC
Univ of Mass Amherst	MA	15,973	C+
Univ of Mass Dartmouth	MA	15,985	C
Univ of Mich/Ann Arbor	MI	16,587	HC+
Univ of Miss	MS	9,000	C
Univ of Missouri/Columbia	MO	13,500	VC
Univ of Nebr at Lincoln	NE	11,401	VC
Univ of Oregon	OR	13,108	VC
Univ of Southern Miss	MS	10,112	C
Univ of Texas at Austin	TX	14,610	HC
Villa Julie College	MD	25,222	C
Virginia Commonwealth Univ	VA	12,987	C
Washington Univ in St. Louis	MO	42,106	MC
Wayne State Univ	MI	11,805	C
Western Kentucky Univ	KY	10,192	C

DEVELOPMENT ECONOMICS

School	ST	$IS	SR
Eastern Mennonite Univ	VA	25,450	VC

DEVELOPMENTAL PSYCHOLOGY

School	ST	$IS	SR
Bard College	NY	41,800	HC+
Cal State, Stanislaus	CA	11,283	C
Emmanuel College	MA	32,000	C+
Metropolitan State Univ	MN	4,682	SP
Moravian College	PA	28,950	VC

DIETETICS

School	ST	$IS	SR
Andrews Univ	MI	21,786	C
Ball State Univ	IN	13,138	C
Baylor Univ	TX	27,555	HC
Bennett College	NC	11,500	C
Berea College	KY	5,496	VC+
Bradley Univ	IL	25,280	VC
Brigham Young Univ	UT	9,200	VC
Cal State, Los Angeles	CA	5,900	C
Central Mich Univ	MI	12,244	C
Central Missouri State Univ	MO	10,000	C
CUNY/Herbert H. Lehman College	NY	4,000	LC
College of St. Benedict	MN	30,091	VC
College of St. Catherine	MN	27,505	VC
College of the Ozarks	MO	4,130	C+
Concordia College: Moorhead	MN	22,475	VC
Dominican Univ	IL	26,370	C
D'Youville College	NY	23,660	C
East Carolina Univ	NC	10,000	C
Eastern Kentucky Univ	KY	7,725	C
Eastern Mich Univ	MI	12,897	C
Florida International Univ	FL	9,215	VC
Florida State Univ	FL	9,028	HC
Fontbonne Univ	MO	23,308	C
Gannon Univ	PA	26,100	C
Harding Univ	AR	16,512	VC
Howard Univ	DC	18,481	C+
Idaho State Univ	ID	9,030	C
Immaculata Univ	PA	25,350	C
Indiana State Univ	IN	11,604	C
Indiana Univ Bloomington	IN	13,356	VC
Indiana Univ of Pennsylvania	PA	11,209	C
Iowa State Univ	IA	11,831	VC
James Madison Univ	VA	12,010	VC
Kansas State Univ	KS	10,516	VC
Keene State College	NH	13,836	C
Lipscomb Univ	TN	20,967	VC
Louisiana Tech Univ	LA	7,370	C
Loyola Univ Chicago	IL	32,896	VC
Madonna Univ	MI	16,068	VC
Mansfield Univ	PA	11,300	C
Marshall Univ	WV	9,116	C
Marywood Univ	PA	30,680	C
Mercyhurst College	PA	28,633	VC
Messiah College	PA	28,910	VC+
Miami Univ	OH	29,097	HC
Mich State Univ	MI	13,689	VC
Minn State Univ, Mankato	MN	10,276	C+
Missouri State Univ	MO	10,748	C+
Mount Mary College	WI	22,895	C
Murray State Univ	KY	8,900	VC
Nicholls State Univ	LA	6,500	NC
Northern Illinois Univ	IL	13,178	C
Oakwood College	AL	14,904	C
Ohio Univ	OH	15,921	C
Olivet Nazarene Univ	IL	22,590	C
Ouachita Baptist Univ	AR	21,900	VC
Point Loma Nazarene Univ	CA	27,610	VC
Prairie View A&M Univ	TX	11,110	C
Purdue Univ/West Lafayette	IN	13,458	VC
Rochester Inst of Technology	NY	32,070	VC+
St. John's Univ	MN	29,749	VC
St. Joseph College	CT	32,050	C
San Francisco State Univ	CA	13,000	C
Seton Hill Univ	PA	28,810	C
Simmons College	MA	35,640	VC
Southern Illinois Univ Carbondale	IL	12,391	C
SUNY/College at Buffalo	NY	11,903	C+
SUNY/College at Oneonta	NY	12,905	VC
SUNY/College at Plattsburgh	NY	12,362	C
Stephen F. Austin State Univ	TX	7,930	C
Syracuse Univ	NY	38,655	HC
Tarleton State Univ	TX	8,952	C
Texas Christian Univ	TX	23,410	VC+
Texas Southern Univ	TX	9,828	C
Texas Tech Univ	TX	13,026	VC
Texas Woman's Univ	TX	7,804	LC
Tuskegee Univ	AL	18,860	LC
Univ of Akron	OH	15,166	NC
Univ of at Calif Davis	CA	15,010	VC
Univ of Central Arkansas	AR	9,984	C
Univ of Conn	CT	16,628	HC
Univ of Dayton	OH	28,826	VC
Univ of Delaware	DE	14,142	HC
Univ of Georgia	GA	11,004	HC
Univ of Idaho	ID	9,310	NC
Univ of Illinois at Urbana-Champaign	IL	15,800	HC+
Univ of Louisiana at Lafayette	LA	5,830	C
Univ of Maryland/College Park	MD	16,036	HC
Univ of Nebr at Lincoln	NE	11,401	VC
Univ of New Haven	CT	31,794	C
Univ of N Dak	ND	10,114	VC
Univ of Northern Colo	CO	10,249	C
Univ of Northern Iowa	IA	11,133	C
Univ of Rhode Island	RI	15,398	C
Univ of Texas at Austin	TX	14,610	HC
Univ of Texas-Pan American	TX	7,290	C+
Univ of Vermont	VT	18,080	VC
Univ of Wisc/Stevens Point	WI	9,384	VC
Univ of Wisc/Stout	WI	11,164	C
Virginia Polytechnic Inst and State Univ	VA	10,834	VC
Viterbo Univ	WI	21,670	C
Wayne State Univ	MI	11,805	C
Western Carolina Univ	NC	7,000	C
Western Mich Univ	MI	13,299	C
Youngstown State Univ	OH	12,613	NC

DIGITAL ARTS/TECHNOLOGY

School	ST	$IS	SR
Arkansas State Univ	AR	9,630	C
Bennington College	VT	41,890	HC
Bethel College	IN	19,680	C
Cal State, Dominguez Hills	CA	10,220	LC
Calvin College	MI	25,735	NC
Canisius College	NY	32,257	VC
Clarkson Univ	NY	34,930	VC
Cogswell Polytechnical College	CA	13,760	LC
College for Creative Studies	MI	24,000	SP
College of New Jersey	NJ	18,315	MC
Dominican Univ of Calif	CA	36,836	C
Drexel Univ	PA	27,700	VC
Grace Bible College	MI	18,810	C
Greenville College	IL	23,146	C
Henry Cogswell College	WA	16,680	SP
Huntingdon College	AL	23,090	VC
Illinois State Univ	IL	12,839	C+
Indiana Univ Bloomington	IN	13,356	VC
Indiana Univ South Bend	IN	4,989	LC
John Brown Univ	AR	20,910	VC
Kendall College of Art and Design of Ferris State Univ	MI	11,870	SP
Marist College	NY	30,566	VC
Minneapolis College of Art and Design	MN	31,110	SP
New York Univ	NY	43,170	MC
Northwestern College	MN	25,220	NC
Otis College of Art and Design	CA	27,546	SP
Philadelphia Univ	PA	30,006	C
Point Park Univ	PA	24,160	C
Quinnipiac Univ	CT	34,640	VC
School of the Art Inst of Chicago	IL	37,800	SP
Southern New Hampshire Univ	NH	28,764	C
Southwestern College	KS	21,476	C
Stetson Univ	FL	32,725	VC
Stevens Inst of Technology	NJ	40,935	HC
Texas State Univ - San Marcos	TX	10,862	C
Univ of Central Florida	FL	10,739	VC
Univ of Denver	CO	36,376	VC+
Univ of Oregon	OR	13,108	VC
Univ of Pennsylvania	PA	41,766	MC
Viterbo Univ	WI	21,670	C
Walla Walla College	WA	24,489	NC
Western Mich Univ	MI	13,299	C

DIGITAL COMMUNICATIONS

School	ST	$IS	SR
Albright College	PA	33,920	C
Marywood Univ	PA	30,680	C
Univ of Georgia	GA	11,004	HC
Washington State Univ	WA	12,260	C

DRAFTING AND DESIGN

School	ST	$IS	SR
Appalachian State Univ	NC	8,000	VC
Missouri State Univ	MO	10,748	C+
Pennsylvania College of Technology	PA	16,980	LC
Thomas Edison State College	NJ	3,780	SP

DRAFTING AND DESIGN TECHNOLOGY

School	ST	$IS	SR
Alabama A&M Univ	AL	8,890	LC
Baker College of Flint	MI	7,800	NC
Central Missouri State Univ	MO	10,000	C
Montana State Univ-Northern	MT	10,000	NC
Norfolk State Univ	VA	10,531	LC
School of the Art Inst of Chicago	IL	37,800	SP
Texas Southern Univ	TX	9,828	C
Tri-State Univ-Main Campus	IN	26,200	C
Univ of Houston	TX	7,000	C
Univ of Rio Grande	OH	8,728	NC
Western Mich Univ	MI	13,299	C

DRAMA EDUCATION

School	ST	$IS	SR
Appalachian State Univ	NC	8,000	VC
Augustana College	SD	24,380	VC
Averett Univ	VA	24,920	C
Baylor Univ	TX	27,555	HC
Bennington College	VT	41,890	HC
Boston Univ	MA	42,046	HC+
Bradley Univ	IL	25,280	VC
Brigham Young Univ	UT	9,200	VC
Catholic Univ of America	DC	35,838	VC
Columbus State Univ	GA	8,664	C
Culver-Stockton College	MO	20,625	C
Dana College	NE	22,390	C
East Carolina Univ	NC	10,000	C
East Central Univ	OK	6,207	C
East Texas Baptist Univ	TX	16,713	C
Eastern Mich Univ	MI	12,897	C
Elmhurst College	IL	24,685	C
Grambling State Univ	LA	6,538	NC
Greensboro College	NC	23,000	C
Hardin-Simmons Univ	TX	18,641	C
Indiana Univ-Purdue Univ Indianapolis	IN	10,959	C
Kean Univ	NJ	15,880	C
Mars Hill College	NC	19,000	LC
Minot State Univ	ND	6,700	LC
Missouri Southern State Univ	MO	8,396	NC
Old Dominion Univ	VA	11,907	C
Oral Roberts Univ	OK	22,650	C
Palm Beach Atlantic Univ	FL	23,597	VC
Point Park Univ	PA	24,160	C
St. Edward's Univ	TX	23,560	C
Simpson College	IA	26,833	VC
Southern Utah Univ	UT		C
Southwestern College	KS	21,476	C
Univ of Arizona	AZ	11,958	VC
Univ of Evansville	IN	28,320	VC
Univ of Indianapolis	IN	25,090	C
Univ of Mary Hardin-Baylor	TX	19,428	C
Univ of Maryland/College Park	MD	16,036	HC
Univ of N Car at Charlotte	NC	9,101	C
Univ of N Car at Greensboro	NC	8,993	C
Viterbo Univ	WI	21,670	C
West Texas A&M Univ	TX	8,452	C
York College	NE	16,330	NC

School	ST	$IS	SR
Youngstown State Univ	OH	12,613	NC

DRAMATIC ARTS

School	ST	$IS	SR
Abilene Christian Univ	TX	20,830	C
Adams State College	CO	8,613	C
Adelphi Univ	NY	27,000	VC
Adrian College	MI	23,000	C
Agnes Scott College	GA	32,070	HC
Alabama A&M Univ	AL	8,890	LC
Alabama State Univ	AL	7,658	C
Albany State Univ	GA	5,770	C+
Albertson College of Idaho	ID	21,095	VC
Albertus Magnus College	CT	25,336	C
Albright College	PA	33,920	C
Alfred Univ	NY		VC
Allegheny College	PA	33,500	HC
Alma College	MI	28,544	VC
American Univ	DC	38,719	HC+
Amherst College	MA	41,590	MC
Anderson Univ	IN	25,050	LC
Angelo State Univ	TX	8,340	NC
Appalachian State Univ	NC	8,000	VC
Arcadia Univ	PA	33,570	C
Arizona State Univ-Tempe	AZ	11,174	C
Armstrong Atlantic State Univ	GA	7,394	C
Ashland Univ	OH	25,000	C
Auburn Univ	AL	12,230	VC
Augsburg College	MN	28,300	C
Augustana College	IL	29,862	VC+
Augustana College	SD	24,380	VC
Averett Univ	VA	24,920	C
Avila Univ	MO	22,100	C
Baker Univ	KS	22,190	C
Ball State Univ	IN	13,138	C
Bard College	NY	41,800	HC+
Barry Univ	FL	24,100	LC
Barton College	NC	22,316	C
Bates College	ME	42,100	MC
Baylor Univ	TX	27,555	HC
Belhaven College	MS	19,530	NC
Beloit College	WI	32,808	HC
Benedictine College	KS	21,968	C
Bennington College	VT	41,890	HC
Berea College	KY	5,496	VC+
Berry College	GA	24,342	VC
Bethel College	IN	19,680	C
Bethel Univ	MN	29,840	VC
Bethune-Cookman College	FL	17,922	LC
Birmingham-Southern College	AL	28,494	VC+
Bloomsburg Univ of Pennsylvania	PA	11,602	C
Blue Mountain College	MS	11,086	C
Boise State Univ	ID	9,438	LC
Boston College	MA	41,608	MC
Boston Univ	MA	42,046	HC+
Bowdoin College	ME	41,660	MC
Bowling Green State Univ	OH	14,994	C
Bradley Univ	IL	25,280	VC
Brandeis Univ	MA	41,551	MC
Brenau Univ Women's College	GA	23,950	VC
Briar Cliff Univ	IA	23,550	LC
Brigham Young Univ	UT	9,200	VC
Bucknell Univ	PA	39,660	MC
Butler Univ	IN	31,944	VC+
Calif Inst of the Arts	CA	35,725	SP
Calif Lutheran Univ	CA	27,800	LC
Calif State Polytechnic Univ, Pomona	CA	18,053	C+
Cal State East Bay	CA	10,856	LC
Cal State, Bakersfield	CA	6,125	LC
Cal State, Chico	CA	11,395	C
Cal State, Dominguez Hills	CA	10,220	LC
Cal State, Fresno	CA	10,037	LC
Cal State, Fullerton	CA	10,990	C
Cal State, Long Beach	CA	9,512	C
Cal State, Los Angeles	CA	5,900	C
Cal State, Northridge	CA	9,036	LC
Cal State, Sacramento	CA	11,122	C+
Cal State, San Bernardino	CA	12,563	LC
Cal State, Stanislaus	CA	11,283	C
Calif Univ of Pennsylvania	PA	14,217	C
Calvin College	MI	25,735	NC
Campbell Univ	NC	21,137	VC
Capital Univ	OH	30,444	C
Cardinal Stritch Univ	WI	21,910	C
Carnegie Mellon Univ	PA	32,700	MC
Carroll College	MT	23,324	C+
Carroll College	WI	24,860	C
Case Western Reserve Univ	OH	37,314	MC
Castleton State College	VT	13,158	C
Catawba College	NC	25,000	C
Catholic Univ of America	DC	35,838	VC
Cedar Crest College	PA	30,615	C
Cedarville Univ	OH	21,904	VC
Centenary College	NJ	28,870	LC
Centenary College of Louisiana	LA	24,760	VC
Central College	IA	26,774	VC
Central Conn State Univ	CT	13,620	C
Central Methodist Univ	MO	18,000	C
Central Mich Univ	MI	12,244	NC
Central Washington Univ	WA	11,730	C
Centre College	KY	30,810	VC
Chadron State College	NE	6,350	NC
Chapman Univ	CA	37,550	VC
Charleston Southern Univ	SC	17,800	C
Chatham College	PA	27,290	C+
Cheyney Univ of Pennsylvania	PA	11,497	LC
Christopher Newport Univ	VA	13,326	VC
CUNY/City College	NY		C
CUNY/College of Staten Island	NY	4,328	NC
CUNY/Hunter College	NY	8,000	C+
CUNY/Queens College	NY	4,356	C
CUNY/York College	NY	4,242	C
Clarion Univ of Pennsylvania	PA	11,844	C
Clark Univ	MA	35,165	VC+
Clarke College	IA	25,390	C
Cleveland State Univ	OH	10,798	NC
Coastal Carolina Univ	SC	13,140	C
Coe College	IA	27,440	VC
Coker College	SC	21,600	C
Colgate Univ	NY	41,170	MC
College of Charleston	SC	13,616	VC
College of St. Benedict	MN	30,091	VC
College of St. Catherine	MN	27,505	VC
College of Santa Fe	NM	28,978	C
College of the Holy Cross	MA	40,664	MC
College of the Ozarks	MO	4,130	VC+
College of Wooster	OH	31,310	VC+
Colo College	CO	37,668	HC
Columbia College Chicago	IL	25,125	LC
Columbia Univ/Barnard College	NY	38,000	MC
Columbia Univ/Columbia College	NY	42,584	MC
Columbia Univ/School of General Studies	NY	41,516	C
Columbus State Univ	GA	8,664	C
Concordia College: Moorhead	MN	22,475	VC
Concordia Univ	CA	26,780	C
Concordia Univ Nebr	NE	20,500	C+
Concordia Univ St.Paul	MN	27,776	C
Concordia Univ, Ann Arbor	MI	25,153	C+
Conn College	CT	41,975	MC
Cornell College	IA	30,110	VC
Cornell Univ	NY	41,717	MC
Cornish College of the Arts	WA	21,200	SP
Creighton Univ	NE	29,918	VC+
Culver-Stockton College	MO	20,625	C
Dakota Wesleyan Univ	SD	17,832	C
Dartmouth College	NH	39,465	MC
Davidson College	NC	36,825	MC
Davis and Elkins College	WV	22,416	C
De Sales Univ	PA	28,580	VC
Denison Univ	OH	37,040	HC
DePaul Univ	IL	29,835	VC
Dickinson College	PA	40,170	HC+
Doane College	NE	22,458	C
Dominican Univ	IL	26,370	C
Dordt College	IA	20,325	VC
Drake Univ	IA	27,632	VC+
Drew Univ/College of Liberal Arts	NJ	39,698	VC
Drury Univ	MO	20,117	VC
Duke Univ	NC	41,239	MC
Duquesne Univ	PA	29,534	VC
Earlham College	IN	33,604	HC
East Carolina Univ	NC	10,000	C
East Central Univ	OK	6,207	C
East Stroudsburg Univ of Pennsylvania	PA	10,336	C
East Texas Baptist Univ	TX	16,713	C
Eastern Illinois Univ	IL	12,569	C
Eastern Kentucky Univ	KY	7,725	C
Eastern Mennonite Univ	VA	25,450	VC
Eastern Mich Univ	MI	12,897	C
Eastern Nazarene College	MA	19,500	LC
Eastern New Mexico Univ	NM	7,264	C
Eastern Oregon Univ	OR	10,400	NC
Eastern Washington Univ	WA	10,608	C
Eckerd College	FL	35,492	VC
Edinboro Univ of Pennsylvania	PA	11,809	LC
Elizabethtown College	PA	32,100	VC
Elmhurst College	IL	24,685	C
Elmira College	NY	37,200	VC
Elon Univ	NC	25,371	HC
Emerson College	MA	35,076	HC
Emory & Henry College	VA	26,570	C
Emory Univ	GA	40,546	MC
Emporia State Univ	KS	8,093	C
Eugene Lang College New School for Liberal Arts	NY	38,800	C+
Eureka College	IL	19,280	C
Evangel Univ	MO	17,380	C
Fairleigh Dickinson Univ/College at Florham	NJ	30,130	C
Fairleigh Dickinson Univ/Metropolitan Campus	NJ	28,590	C
Fayetteville State Univ	NC	6,000	LC
Ferrum College	VA	24,290	LC
Fisk Univ	TN	19,830	C
Five Towns College	NY	24,600	SP
Flagler College	FL	13,790	VC+
Florida A&M Univ	FL	8,344	C
Florida Atlantic Univ	FL	11,221	C
Florida International Univ	FL	9,215	VC
Florida Southern College	FL	25,965	C
Florida State Univ	FL	9,028	NC
Fordham Univ	NY	36,000	MC
Fort Lewis College	CO	11,852	C
Francis Marion Univ	SC	11,114	C
Franklin and Marshall College	PA	40,590	HC
Franklin College	IN		C
Franklin Pierce College	NH	31,700	C
Freed-Hardeman Univ	TN	16,370	NC
Frostburg State Univ	MD	12,672	C
Furman Univ	SC	33,264	HC+
Gallaudet Univ	DC	16,554	
Gannon Univ	PA	26,100	C
George Mason Univ	VA	10,850	VC
George Washington Univ	DC	48,820	MC
Georgetown College	KY	24,950	C+
Georgia College and State Univ	GA	11,020	C
Georgia Southern Univ	GA	9,762	C
Gettysburg College	PA	39,864	HC
Gonzaga Univ	WA	30,218	HC
Gordon College	MA	29,194	C+
Goshen College	IN	22,850	VC
Goucher College	MD	36,225	VC
Graceland Univ	IA	19,700	C
Grambling State Univ	LA	6,538	NC
Grand Canyon Univ	AZ	32,000	LC
Grand Valley State Univ	MI	12,000	VC
Greensboro College	NC	23,000	C
Greenville College	IL	23,146	C
Grinnell College	IA	34,814	HC+
Guilford College	NC	28,160	C+
Gustavus Adolphus College	MN	30,920	HC
Hamilton College	NY	41,660	MC
Hamline Univ	MN	27,070	VC
Hampshire College	MA	37,120	HC
Hampton Univ	VA	19,468	C
Hannibal-LaGrange College	MO	16,390	C
Hanover College	IN	28,150	HC
Harding Univ	AR	16,512	NC
Hardin-Simmons Univ	TX	18,641	C
Hartwick College	NY	36,065	C+
Hastings College	NE	22,218	VC
Heidelberg College	OH	23,242	C
Henderson State Univ	AR	7,600	C
Hendrix College	AR	27,646	HC+
High Point Univ	NC	25,722	C
Hillsdale College	MI	24,160	HC
Hiram College	OH	28,700	VC
Hofstra Univ	NY	32,630	VC
Hollins Univ	VA	31,105	C
Hope College	MI	28,208	VC+
Howard Payne Univ	TX	17,115	C
Howard Univ	DC	18,481	C+
Humboldt State Univ	CA	11,176	C
Huntingdon College	AL	23,090	VC
Huntington Univ	IN	24,830	C
Idaho State Univ	ID	9,030	C
Illinois College	IL	21,900	C+
Illinois State Univ	IL	12,839	C+
Illinois Wesleyan Univ	IL	34,050	HC+
Indiana State Univ	IN	11,604	C
Indiana Univ Bloomington	IN	13,356	VC
Indiana Univ Northwest	IN	4,902	LC
Indiana Univ of Pennsylvania	PA	11,209	C
Indiana Univ South Bend	IN	4,989	LC
Indiana Univ-Purdue Univ Fort Wayne	IN	5,067	LC
Iona College	NY	30,878	VC
Ithaca College	NY	35,144	VC
Jacksonville State Univ	AL	7,618	LC
Jacksonville Univ	FL	24,040	C
James Madison Univ	VA	12,010	VC
Judson College	IL	25,130	C
Juilliard School	NY	37,620	SP
Kalamazoo College	MI	32,442	VC+
Kansas State Univ	KS	10,516	VC
Kansas Wesleyan Univ	KS	21,400	VC
Kean Univ	NJ	15,880	C
Kennesaw State Univ	GA	12,512	C
Kent State Univ	OH	14,594	C
Kentucky Wesleyan College	KY	18,590	C
Kenyon College	OH	39,500	MC
King's College	PA	29,810	C
Knox College	IL	32,385	VC+
Kutztown Univ of Pennsylvania	PA	10,820	C
LaGrange College	GA	22,874	C+
Lakeland College	WI	22,990	C
Lamar Univ	TX	6,820	LC
Lambuth Univ	TN	21,700	C
Lander Univ	SC	10,600	C
Langston Univ	OK	2,308	LC
Lawrence Univ	WI	33,958	HC+
Le Moyne College	NY	29,570	VC
Lees-McRae College	NC	23,000	C
Lehigh Univ	PA	42,690	HC+
Lenoir-Rhyne College	NC	25,580	C
Lewis and Clark College	OR	35,358	VC+
Lewis Univ	IL	23,050	C+
Limestone College	SC	19,840	C
Lindenwood Univ	MO	18,600	VC
Linfield College	OR	29,632	VC
Livingstone College	NC	17,815	LC
LIU/C.W. Post Campus	NY	28,282	C
Louisiana College	LA	13,450	C
Louisiana State Univ and A&M College	LA	10,749	VC
Loyola Marymount Univ	CA	36,321	VC
Loyola Univ Chicago	IL	32,896	VC
Loyola Univ New Orleans	LA	31,050	VC+
Luther College	IA	28,800	VC+
Lycoming College	PA	30,797	C+
Lynchburg College	VA	30,645	C
Lyon College	AR	19,990	VC
Macalester College	MN	36,500	MC
MacMurray College	IL	20,755	C
Maharishi Univ of Management	IA	29,450	VC
Mansfield Univ	PA	11,300	C
Marietta College	OH	29,327	C
Marlboro College	VT	35,980	VC+
Marquette Univ	WI	31,066	HC
Mars Hill College	NC	19,000	LC
Mary Baldwin College	VA	26,465	C
Marymount Manhattan College	NY	30,049	VC
Maryville College	TN	29,224	VC
Marywood Univ	PA	30,680	C
McDaniel College	MD	31,610	VC
McMurry Univ	TX	18,100	LC
McNeese State Univ	LA	5,270	LC
Meredith College	NC	25,600	C
Messiah College	PA	28,910	VC+
Methodist College	NC	21,000	C
Metropolitan State Univ	MN	4,682	SP
Miami Univ	OH	29,097	HC
Mich State Univ	MI	13,689	VC
MidAmerica Nazarene Univ	KS	20,584	LC
Middlebury College	VT	42,120	MC
Midwestern State Univ	TX	9,381	LC
Millikin Univ	IL	25,590	C
Millsaps College	MS	28,256	VC+
Minn State Univ, Mankato	MN	10,276	LC
Minn State Univ, Moorhead	MN	7,000	LC
Missouri Southern State Univ	MO	8,396	NC
Missouri State Univ	MO	10,748	C+
Missouri Valley College	MO	18,500	C
Monmouth College	IL	23,700	C
Montana State Univ-Billings	MT	8,906	C
Montana State Univ-Northern	MT	10,000	NC
Montclair State Univ	NJ	16,327	C
Moravian College	PA	28,950	VC
Morehead State Univ	KY	9,150	C
Morgan State Univ	MD	12,080	C
Morningside College	IA	23,704	C
Mount Holyoke College	MA	42,148	HC+
Mount Mercy College	IA	23,670	C
Mount Union College	OH	25,840	C
Murray State Univ	KY	8,900	C
Muskingum College	OH	22,970	C
Nazareth College of Rochester	NY	28,175	VC
Nebr Wesleyan Univ	NE	23,415	C+
New College of Calif	CA	12,842	NC
New College of Florida	FL	10,009	HC+
New England College	NH	31,466	C
New Mexico State Univ	NM	9,250	C
New York Univ	NY	43,170	MC
Newberry College	SC	23,000	LC
Niagara Univ	NY	28,250	C
N Car Agricultural and Technical State Univ	NC	8,000	LC
N Car Central Univ	NC	9,000	LC
N Car School of the Arts	NC	7,401	SP
N Car Wesleyan College	NC	22,670	C
N Dak State Univ	ND	8,500	C
Northeastern Univ	MA	35,742	HC
Northern Arizona Univ	AZ	10,353	C
Northern Illinois Univ	IL	13,178	C
Northern Kentucky Univ	KY	6,670	NC
Northern Mich Univ	MI	12,340	LC
Northwest Missouri State Univ	MO	10,000	C
Northwestern College of Iowa	IA	22,174	C+
Northwestern Okla State Univ	OK	6,250	NC
Northwestern State Univ of Louisiana	LA	7,144	C
Northwestern Univ	IL	37,595	MC
Notre Dame de Namur Univ	CA	32,790	LC
Nova Southeastern Univ	FL	24,320	C
Oberlin College	OH	40,904	MC
Occidental College	CA	40,185	MC
Ohio Northern Univ	OH	27,765	VC
Ohio Univ	OH	15,921	C
Ohio Wesleyan Univ	OH	35,830	VC+
Okla Baptist Univ	OK	17,986	VC
Okla City Univ	OK	23,965	VC
Okla State Univ	OK	10,213	C
Old Dominion Univ	VA	11,907	C
Oral Roberts Univ	OK	22,650	C
Oregon State Univ	OR	11,055	C

ST = STATE   **$IS** = IN-STATE COSTS   **SR** = SELECTOR RATING

ST = STATE $IS = IN-STATE COSTS SR = SELECTOR RATING

School	ST	$IS	SR
Alfred Univ	NY		VC
American International College	MA	28,710	LC
Anna Maria College	MA	29,815	LC
Appalachian State Univ	NC	8,000	VC
Arcadia Univ	PA	33,570	VC
Arizona State Univ-Tempe	AZ	11,174	C
Arkansas State Univ	AR	9,630	C
Ashland Univ	OH	25,000	C
Atlantic Union College	MA	17,600	LC
Auburn Univ	AL	12,230	VC
Augusta State Univ	GA	2,920	C
Baldwin-Wallace College	OH	27,256	VC
Ball State Univ	IN	13,138	C
Barber-Scotia College	NC	15,000	LC
Barry Univ	FL	24,100	LC
Bay Path College	MA	29,362	C
Becker College	MA	24,300	LC
Bemidji State Univ	MN	11,180	LC
Benedict College	SC	19,114	LC
Bennett College	NC	11,500	C
Bennington College	VT	41,890	HC
Berea College	KY	5,496	VC+
Berry College	GA	24,342	VC
Bethany College	WV	21,395	C
Bethel College	TN	16,066	NC
Bethel Univ	MN	29,840	VC
Bloomsburg Univ of Pennsylvania	PA	11,602	C
Bluffton College	OH	26,110	C
Boston College	MA	41,608	MC
Boston Univ	MA	42,046	HC+
Bowie State Univ	MD	10,880	C+
Bowling Green State Univ	OH	14,994	C
Bradley Univ	IL	25,280	VC
Brenau Univ Women's College	GA	23,950	VC
Brewton-Parker College	GA	14,220	LC
Bridgewater State College	MA	12,120	C
Brigham Young Univ	UT	9,200	VC
Bucknell Univ	PA	39,660	MC
Cabrini College	PA	33,340	C
Cal State, Sacramento	CA	11,122	C+
Calif Univ of Pennsylvania	PA	14,217	C
Canisius College	NY	32,257	VC
Cardinal Stritch Univ	WI	21,910	C
Carlow Univ	PA	24,313	C
Carroll College	WI	24,860	C
Carson-Newman College	TN	16,800	C
Catholic Univ of America	DC	35,838	VC
Cazenovia College	NY	26,900	C
Cedarville Univ	OH	21,904	VC
Central Methodist Univ	MO	18,000	C
Central Missouri State Univ	MO	10,000	C
Central Washington Univ	WA	11,730	C
Chadron State College	NE	6,350	NC
Chaminade Univ of Honolulu	HI	23,320	LC
Champlain College	VT	24,605	C
Charleston Southern Univ	SC	17,800	C
Chestnut Hill College	PA	26,600	LC
Cheyney Univ of Pennsylvania	PA	11,497	LC
Chicago State Univ	IL	10,915	C+
Christopher Newport Univ	VA	13,326	VC
CUNY/Brooklyn College	NY	4,377	C+
CUNY/City College	NY		C
CUNY/Herbert H. Lehman College	NY	4,000	LC
CUNY/Hunter College	NY	8,000	C+
CUNY/Queens College	NY	4,356	C
Claflin Univ	SC	16,798	C+
Clarion Univ of Pennsylvania	PA	11,844	C
Clark Atlanta Univ	GA	20,960	LC
Clemson Univ	SC	13,366	NC
Cleveland State Univ	OH	10,798	NC
Coastal Carolina Univ	SC	13,140	C
Coker College	SC	21,600	C
Colby-Sawyer College	NH	27,850	C
College Misericordia	PA	27,950	C
College of Charleston	SC	13,616	VC
College of Mount St. Joseph	OH	24,860	C
College of New Jersey	NJ	18,315	MC
College of Notre Dame of Maryland	MD	27,700	C
College of Our Lady of the Elms	MA	21,000	C
College of St. Catherine	MN	27,505	VC
College of St. Elizabeth	NJ	28,495	C
College of St. Joseph	VT	20,900	NC
College of St. Mary	NE	23,938	C
College of St. Rose	NY	25,684	C
College of the Ozarks	MO	4,130	VC+
Columbia College	SC	24,982	LC
Columbia College Chicago	IL	25,125	LC
Columbus State Univ	GA	8,664	C
Concord College	WV	9,708	C
Concordia College	AL	10,500	NC
Concordia College-New York	NY	27,740	C
Concordia Univ	CA	26,780	C
Concordia Univ	OR	24,400	C
Concordia Univ Nebr	NE	20,500	C+
Concordia Univ St.Paul	MN	27,776	C
Concordia Univ Wisc	WI	22,660	VC
Concordia Univ, River Forest	IL	26,300	C
Converse College	SC	24,800	VC
Curry College	MA	26,100	LC
Daemen College	NY	24,580	C
Defiance College	OH	24,790	C
Delaware State Univ	DE	8,130	LC
DePaul Univ	IL	29,835	VC
Dickinson State Univ	ND	7,847	NC
Duquesne Univ	PA	29,534	VC
East Carolina Univ	NC	10,000	C
East Central Univ	OK	6,207	C
East Stroudsburg Univ of Pennsylvania	PA	10,336	C
Eastern Conn State Univ	CT	13,554	C
Eastern Illinois Univ	IL	12,569	C
Eastern Mennonite Univ	VA	25,450	VC
Eastern Mich Univ	MI	12,897	C
Edgewood College	WI	22,862	C
Edinboro Univ of Pennsylvania	PA	11,809	LC
Edward Waters College	FL	14,374	LC
Elizabethtown College	PA	32,100	VC
Elmhurst College	IL	24,685	C
Erskine College	SC	25,468	VC
Evangel Univ	MO	17,380	C
Fairmont State	WV	8,400	LC
Fayetteville State Univ	NC	6,000	LC
Fitchburg State College	MA	11,276	C
Florida A&M Univ	FL	8,344	C
Florida Gulf Coast Univ	FL	10,833	C
Florida Southern College	FL	25,965	C
Florida State Univ	FL	9,028	HC
Fontbonne Univ	MO	23,308	C
Fort Valley State Univ	GA	6,975	C
Framingham State College	MA	11,156	C
Francis Marion Univ	SC	11,114	C
Freed-Hardeman Univ	TN	16,370	NC
Frostburg State Univ	MD	12,672	C
Gallaudet Univ	DC	16,554	
Gannon Univ	PA	26,100	C
Georgia College and State Univ	GA	11,020	C
Georgia Southern Univ	GA	9,762	C
Georgia Southwestern State Univ	GA	6,035	C
Georgia State Univ	GA	11,444	VC
Glenville State College	WV	8,778	NC
Gordon College	MA	29,194	C+
Grambling State Univ	LA	6,538	NC
Greensboro College	NC	23,000	C
Greenville College	IL	23,146	C
Hannibal-LaGrange College	MO	16,390	C
Harding Univ	AR	16,512	VC
Hardin-Simmons Univ	TX	18,641	C
Harris-Stowe State College	MO	3,200	SP
Hillsdale College	MI	24,160	HC
Hofstra Univ	NY	32,630	VC
Holy Family Univ	PA	25,740	C
Hood College	MD	30,085	VC
Houston Baptist Univ	TX	18,660	C
Howard Univ	DC	18,481	C+
Humphreys College	CA	7,000	NC
Idaho State Univ	ID	9,030	C
Illinois State Univ	IL	12,839	C+
Immaculata Univ	PA	25,350	C
Indiana State Univ	IN	11,604	C
Indiana Univ Bloomington	IN	13,356	VC
Indiana Univ of Pennsylvania	PA	11,209	C
Indiana Univ South Bend	IN	4,989	LC
Indiana Univ-Purdue Univ Fort Wayne	IN	5,067	LC
Inter American Univ of PR/Aguadilla Campus	PR	3,784	
Inter American Univ of PR/Barranquitas Regional College	PR	3,350	
Inter American Univ of PR/Fajardo Campus	PR	4,000	
Inter American Univ of PR/Metropolitan Campus	PR	4,320	
Inter American Univ of PR/Ponce Regional College	PR	3,700	
Inter American Univ of PR/San German	PR	6,720	
Iona College	NY	30,878	VC
Iowa State Univ	IA	11,831	VC
Iowa Wesleyan College	IA	22,140	C
Jacksonville State Univ	AL	7,618	LC
John Brown Univ	AR	20,910	VC
John Carroll Univ	OH	27,658	C+
Judson College	IL	25,130	C
Juniata College	PA	33,130	VC
Kean Univ	NJ	15,880	C
Keene State College	NH	13,836	C
Kendall College	IL	28,800	NC
Kennesaw State Univ	GA	12,152	C
Kent State Univ	OH	14,594	C
Kentucky State Univ	KY	10,089	LC
Keystone College	PA	22,810	LC
King's College	PA	29,810	C
Knoxville College	TN	6,200	LC
Kutztown Univ of Pennsylvania	PA	10,820	C
LaGrange College	GA	22,874	C+
Lake Erie College	OH	27,725	C
Lake Superior State Univ	MI	12,842	LC
Lakeland College	WI	22,990	C
Lamar Univ	TX	6,820	LC
Lander Univ	SC	10,600	C
Lasell College	MA	26,250	C
LeMoyne-Owen College	TN	13,150	LC
Lenoir-Rhyne College	NC	25,580	C
Lesley Univ	MA	34,950	C
Lincoln Memorial Univ	TN	18,144	C
Lincoln Univ	PA	13,658	C+
Lindenwood Univ	MO	18,600	VC
Livingstone College	NC	17,815	LC
Lock Haven Univ of Pennsylvania	PA	12,098	LC
LIU/Brooklyn Campus	NY	25,000	C
LIU/C.W. Post Campus	NY	28,282	C
Loras College	IA	27,193	C
Louisiana Tech Univ	LA	7,370	C
Lubbock Christian Univ	TX	16,960	C
Lyndon State College	VT	14,233	LC
Lynn Univ	FL	30,750	C
Malone College	OH	23,040	C
Manhattan College	NY	29,000	VC
Mansfield Univ	PA	11,300	C
Marian College of Fond du Lac	WI	21,775	LC
Marietta College	OH	29,327	C
Martin Univ	IN	10,300	SP
Marygrove College	MI	19,310	C+
Maryville Univ of St. Louis	MO	23,000	VC
Marywood Univ	PA	30,680	C
Mayville State Univ	ND	8,667	NC
McNeese State Univ	LA	5,270	C
Mercer Univ	GA	27,525	VC+
Mercyhurst College	PA	28,633	VC
Messiah College	PA	28,910	VC+
Metropolitan College of New York	NY	16,000	C
Metropolitan State Univ	MN	4,682	SP
Miami Univ	OH	29,097	HC
Middle Tenn State Univ	TN	8,540	C
Midland Lutheran College	NE	18,600	C
Miles College	AL	9,922	NC
Milligan College	TN	21,990	VC
Minn State Univ, Mankato	MN	10,276	LC
Minn State Univ, Moorhead	MN	7,000	LC
Miss Valley State Univ	MS	7,970	C
Missouri Baptist Univ	MO	19,640	C
Missouri Southern State Univ	MO	8,396	NC
Missouri State Univ	MO	10,748	C+
Missouri Western State Univ	MO	9,534	NC
Mitchell College	CT	26,396	C
Montana State Univ-Billings	MT	8,906	C
Montclair State Univ	NJ	16,327	C
Morris College	SC	11,999	LC
Mount Ida College	MA	26,000	LC
Mount Mary College	WI	22,895	C
Mount Union College	OH	25,840	C
Mount Vernon Nazarene Univ	OH	20,810	C
Murray State Univ	KY	8,900	VC
Muskingum College	OH	22,970	C
Naropa Univ	CO	26,302	SP
National-Louis Univ	IL	16,915	LC
Neumann College	PA	25,996	LC
New Jersey City Univ	NJ	13,695	LC
New Mexico Highlands Univ	NM	4,222	NC
New Mexico State Univ	NM	9,250	C
New York Univ	NY	43,170	MC
Newberry College	SC	23,000	LC
Niagara Univ	NY	28,250	C
Norfolk State Univ	VA	10,531	LC
N Car Agricultural and Technical State Univ	NC	8,000	LC
North Georgia College and State Univ	GA	7,000	LC
North Park Univ	IL	24,050	C
Northeastern Illinois Univ	IL	3,000	NC
Northeastern State Univ	OK	5,896	LC
Northeastern Univ	MA	35,742	HC
Northern Arizona Univ	AZ	10,353	C
Northern Illinois Univ	IL	13,178	C
Northern State Univ	SD	8,257	C
Northwest Missouri State Univ	MO	10,000	C
Northwestern College	MN	25,220	NC
Northwestern College of Iowa	IA	22,174	C+
Northwestern Okla State Univ	OK	6,250	NC
Northwestern State Univ of Louisiana	LA	7,144	C
Notre Dame College	OH	20,425	C
Nova Southeastern Univ	FL	24,320	C
Ohio Dominican Univ	OH	25,954	C
Ohio Northern Univ	OH	27,765	VC
Ohio Univ	OH	15,921	C
Ohio Wesleyan Univ	OH	35,830	VC+
Okla Baptist Univ	OK	17,986	VC
Okla Christian Univ	OK	18,992	NC
Okla City Univ	OK	23,965	VC
Old Dominion Univ	VA	11,907	C
Olivet Nazarene Univ	IL	22,590	C
Oral Roberts Univ	OK	22,650	C
Ouachita Baptist Univ	AR	21,900	VC
Our Lady of the Lake Univ of San Antonio	TX	22,430	LC
Pace Univ	NY	30,000	VC
Pacific Union College	CA	24,555	VC+
Paine College	GA	14,418	LC
Park Univ	MO	11,592	C
Philander Smith College	AR	13,230	LC
Piedmont College	GA	20,500	C
Point Park Univ	PA	24,160	C
Presbyterian College	SC	30,044	VC
Prescott College	AZ	13,445	LC
Purdue Univ/Calumet	IN	10,891	LC
Purdue Univ/West Lafayette	IN	13,458	VC
Rhode Island College	RI	11,570	C
Rider Univ	NJ	32,560	C
Ripon College	WI	27,160	C+
Rivier College	NH	26,600	C
Rockford College	IL	28,330	VC
Roosevelt Univ	IL	22,605	VC
Rowan Univ	NJ	16,000	VC
St. Ambrose Univ	IA	25,495	C
St. Cloud State Univ	MN	10,010	C
St. John Fisher College	NY	27,860	C
St. John's Univ	NY	34,370	C
St. Joseph's College, New York, Brooklyn Campus	NY	12,206	C
St. Mary-of-the-Woods College	IN	25,480	C
St. Xavier Univ	IL	23,160	C
Salve Regina Univ	RI	33,450	C
Samford Univ	AL	20,258	VC
San Francisco State Univ	CA	13,000	C
San Jose State Univ	CA	11,707	C
Schreiner Univ	TX	20,600	C
Seton Hill Univ	PA	28,810	C
Shawnee State Univ	OH	12,237	NC
Shorter College	GA	19,700	C
Silver Lake College of the Holy Family	WI	18,500	LC
Simmons College	MA	35,640	VC
Sinte Gleska Univ	SD	2,300	NC
Slippery Rock Univ of Pennsylvania	PA	10,360	LC
Smith College	MA	41,474	MC
Sojourner-Douglass College	MD	4,200	LC
S Car State Univ	SC	6,700	LC
S Dak State Univ	SD	9,815	C
Southeast Missouri State Univ	MO	10,596	C
Southeastern Louisiana Univ	LA	8,521	LC
Southeastern Okla State Univ	OK	6,147	C
Southern Conn State Univ	CT	10,310	C
Southern Illinois Univ Carbondale	IL	12,391	C
Southern Illinois Univ Edwardsville	IL	11,022	C
Southern Nazarene Univ	OK	14,634	NC
Southern New Hampshire Univ	NH	28,764	C
Southern Univ and A&M College	LA	8,238	LC
Southwest Baptist Univ	MO	18,300	C
Southwest Minn State Univ	MN	10,975	C
Southwestern College	KS	21,476	C
Spring Hill College	AL	28,678	C
Springfield College	MA	25,000	C
SUNY at Potsdam	NY	12,959	C
SUNY/College at Fredonia	NY	12,771	VC
SUNY/College at Geneseo	NY	12,910	HC+
SUNY/College at Old Westbury	NY	13,154	C
SUNY/Univ at New Paltz	NY	12,480	VC
Stephens College	MO	26,930	VC
Susquehanna Univ	PA	33,465	VC
Syracuse Univ	NY	38,655	HC
Taylor Univ	IN	26,376	VC+
Temple Univ	PA	17,438	C
Tenn State Univ	TN	9,048	LC
Texas A&M Univ at Commerce	TX	9,020	C
Texas Christian Univ	TX	23,410	VC+
Texas Southern Univ	TX	9,828	C
Texas State Univ - San Marcos	TX	10,862	C
Texas Tech Univ	TX	13,026	VC
Texas Wesleyan Univ	TX	18,700	C
Thomas Univ	GA	11,520	NC
Toccoa Falls College	GA	17,125	C
Towson Univ	MD	13,924	VC
Trevecca Nazarene Univ	TN	19,594	C
Troy Univ	AL	8,916	C
Troy Univ Dothan Campus	AL	4,678	C
Tufts Univ	MA	42,018	MC
Tusculum College	TN	21,340	LC
Tuskegee Univ	AL	18,860	LC
Univ of Akron	OH	15,166	NC
Univ of Alabama	AL	9,888	C
Univ of Alabama at Birmingham	AL	13,716	C
Univ of Arizona	AZ	11,958	VC
Univ of Arkansas	AR	11,859	VC

ST = STATE   **$IS** = IN-STATE COSTS   **SR** = SELECTOR RATING

School	ST	$IS	SR
Univ of Arkansas at Little Rock	AR	7,230	NC
Univ of Arkansas at Monticello	AR	7,325	NC
Univ of Arkansas at Pine Bluff	AR	8,300	C
Univ of Central Arkansas	AR	9,984	C
Univ of Central Florida	FL	10,739	VC
Univ of Central Okla	OK	8,094	C
Univ of Cincinnati	OH	17,682	C
Univ of Dayton	OH	28,826	VC
Univ of Delaware	DE	14,142	HC
Univ of Detroit Mercy	MI	27,000	C
Univ of Georgia	GA	11,044	HC
Univ of Hartford	CT	34,044	C
Univ of Idaho	ID	9,310	NC
Univ of Illinois at Urbana-Champaign	IL	15,800	HC+
Univ of Kentucky	KY	7,800	C
Univ of Louisiana at Monroe	LA	7,103	C
Univ of Louisville	KY	10,400	VC
Univ of Maine at Farmington	ME	11,515	C
Univ of Mary	ND	15,374	C
Univ of Mary Hardin-Baylor	TX	19,428	C
Univ of Maryland/College Park	MD	16,036	HC
Univ of Mass Amherst	MA	15,973	C+
Univ of Mich/Dearborn	MI	7,000	VC
Univ of Mich/Flint	MI	6,398	C
Univ of Minn/Crookston	MN	13,157	C
Univ of Minn/Twin Cities	MN	13,165	HC
Univ of Missouri/Columbia	MO	13,500	VC
Univ of Missouri/St. Louis	MO	14,046	VC
Univ of Mobile	AL	16,880	C
Univ of Montevallo	AL	9,630	C
Univ of Nebr at Kearney	NE	9,000	NC
Univ of Nebr at Lincoln	NE	11,401	VC
Univ of New Mexico	NM	11,253	C
Univ of North Alabama	AL	8,992	C
Univ of N Car at Pembroke	NC	7,940	LC
Univ of N Car at Wilmington	NC	10,107	VC
Univ of N Dak	ND	10,114	VC
Univ of North Texas	TX	7,800	C
Univ of Northern Iowa	IA	11,133	C
Univ of Okla	OK	10,769	VC+
Univ of PR/Bayamon Univ College Campus	PR	1,600	
Univ of Rio Grande	OH	8,728	NC
Univ of Science and Arts of Okla	OK	7,650	C
Univ of Scranton	PA	31,100	VC
Univ of Sioux Falls	SD	20,800	C
Univ of South Alabama	AL	8,930	LC
Univ of S Car at Aiken	SC	11,718	LC
Univ of S Car at Columbia	SC	13,397	VC
Univ of S Car Upstate	SC	11,957	C
Univ of Southern Miss	MS	10,112	C
Univ of Tenn at Martin	TN	8,693	C
Univ of the District of Columbia	DC	2,070	LC
Univ of the Ozarks	AR	19,250	C
Univ of Toledo	OH	15,806	NC
Univ of Vermont	VT	18,080	VC
Univ of West Alabama	AL	7,611	C
Univ of West Florida	FL	8,559	C
Univ of West Georgia	GA	8,838	C
Univ of Wisc/Stevens Point	WI	9,384	C
Univ of Wisc/Stout	WI	11,164	C
Univ of Wisc/Whitewater	WI	9,274	C
Ursuline College	OH	25,456	C
Utah State Univ	UT	8,002	VC
Valdosta State Univ	GA	8,802	C
Vanderbilt Univ	TN	41,986	VC
Virginia Union Univ	VA	18,432	LC
Walsh Univ	OH	23,440	C
Washburn Univ	KS	9,734	NC
Washington State Univ	WA	12,260	C
Weber State Univ	UT	9,635	NC
Wesleyan College	GA	19,560	C
West Chester Univ of Pennsylvania	PA	12,355	C+
West Liberty State College	WV	9,142	LC
West Virginia State Univ	WV	8,378	NC
Western Carolina Univ	NC	7,000	C
Western Kentucky Univ	KY	10,192	C
Western Washington Univ	WA	11,262	VC
Westfield State College	MA	10,200	C
Westminster College	UT	25,656	C
Wheelock College	MA	33,075	C
Widener Univ	PA	27,275	C
William Woods Univ	MO	21,020	C
Wilmington College	DE	5,594	NC
Wilmington College	OH	2,806	NC
Winona State Univ	MN	11,333	C
Winthrop Univ	SC	11,302	C
Worcester State College	MA	12,499	C
Xavier Univ	OH	30,490	NC
Xavier Univ of Louisiana	LA	17,600	C
Youngstown State Univ	OH	12,613	NC

EARLY CHILDHOOD STUDIES

School	ST	$IS	SR
Alfred Univ	NY		VC
Bowling Green State Univ	OH	14,994	C
Central Mich Univ	MI	12,244	C

School	ST	$IS	SR
Grace Bible College	MI	18,810	C
Kentucky Wesleyan College	KY	18,590	C
Langston Univ	OK	2,308	LC
Louisiana State Univ and A&M College	LA	10,749	VC
Metropolitan State Univ	MN	4,682	SP
National Univ	CA	8,412	SP
Northern Illinois Univ	IL	13,178	C
Plymouth State Univ	NH	12,298	LC
Rochester College	MI	15,636	C+
St. Mary's Univ of Minn	MN	23,857	VC
Southwestern Univ	TX	26,767	HC
Univ of Minn/Duluth	MN	13,974	C
Wayne State College	NE	8,033	NC
Weber State Univ	UT	9,635	NC
Youngstown State Univ	OH	12,613	NC

EARTH SCIENCE

School	ST	$IS	SR
Adams State College	CO	8,613	C
Adelphi Univ	NY	27,000	VC
Adrian College	MI	23,000	C
Albion College	MI	26,000	VC
Augustana College	IL	29,862	VC+
Baylor Univ	TX	27,555	HC
Bemidji State Univ	MN	11,180	LC
Bloomsburg Univ of Pennsylvania	PA	11,602	C
Boston Univ	MA	42,046	HC+
Bridgewater State College	MA	12,120	C
Cal State, Long Beach	CA	9,512	C
Cal State, Monterey Bay	CA	10,099	C
Cal State, Northridge	CA	9,036	LC
Central Conn State Univ	CT	13,620	C
Central Mich Univ	MI	12,244	C
Central Missouri State Univ	MO	10,000	C
Central Washington Univ	WA	11,730	C
CUNY/City College	NY		C
Clarion Univ of Pennsylvania	PA	11,844	C
Columbia Univ/Columbia College	NY	42,584	MC
Cornell Univ	NY	41,717	MC
Dartmouth College	NH	39,465	MC
DePauw Univ	IN	32,100	HC
Dickinson State Univ	ND	7,847	NC
East Stroudsburg Univ of Pennsylvania	PA	10,336	C
Eastern Mich Univ	MI	12,897	C
Edinboro Univ of Pennsylvania	PA	11,809	LC
Emporia State Univ	KS	8,093	C
Fitchburg State College	MA	11,276	C
George Mason Univ	VA	10,850	VC
Georgia Inst of Technology	GA	11,450	HC+
Guilford College	NC	28,160	C+
Indiana Univ-Purdue Univ Fort Wayne	IN	5,067	LC
Iowa State Univ	IA	11,831	VC
Johns Hopkins Univ	MD	42,044	MC
Juniata College	PA	33,130	VC
Kean Univ	NJ	15,880	C
Lock Haven Univ of Pennsylvania	PA	12,098	LC
Mass Inst of Technology	MA	41,800	MC
Mercyhurst College	PA	28,633	VC
Mich State Univ	MI	13,689	VC
Millersville Univ of Pennsylvania	PA	12,113	C
Minn State Univ, Mankato	MN	10,276	LC
Minot State Univ	ND	6,700	LC
Missouri State Univ	MO	10,748	C+
Montana State Univ-Bozeman	MT	1,137	C
Morehead State Univ	KY	9,150	C
Murray State Univ	KY	8,900	VC
Muskingum College	OH	22,970	C
National Univ	CA	8,412	SP
New Mexico Inst of Mining and Technology	NM	8,510	VC+
New York Univ	NY	43,170	MC
N Car State Univ	NC	11,824	HC
N Dak State Univ	ND	8,500	C
Northeastern Illinois Univ	IL	3,000	NC
Northern Mich Univ	MI	12,340	LC
Northland College	WI	26,680	C+
Northwest Missouri State Univ	MO	10,000	C
Ohio Univ	OH	15,921	C
Ohio Wesleyan Univ	OH	35,830	VC+
Old Dominion Univ	VA	11,907	C
Penn State Univ/Univ Park Campus	PA	18,038	HC
Prescott College	AZ	13,445	LC
Purdue Univ/West Lafayette	IN	13,458	VC
Rice Univ	TX	32,290	MC
St. Cloud State Univ	MN	10,010	C
St. Louis Univ	MO	33,158	VC+
St. Mary's Univ of San Antonio	TX	22,444	C
Salem State College	MA	13,161	LC
Shippensburg Univ of Pennsylvania	PA	11,621	C
Slippery Rock Univ of Pennsylvania	PA	10,360	LC

School	ST	$IS	SR
Southeast Missouri State Univ	MO	10,596	C
Southern Conn State Univ	CT	10,310	C
Stanford Univ	CA	41,557	MC
SUNY/College at Brockport	NY	12,747	VC
SUNY/College at Buffalo	NY	11,903	C+
SUNY/College at Fredonia	NY	12,771	VC
SUNY/College at Oneonta	NY	12,905	VC
SUNY/Univ at Albany	NY	13,860	VC
SUNY/Univ at Stony Brook	NY	13,625	HC
Susquehanna Univ	PA	33,465	VC
Tarleton State Univ	TX	8,952	C
Temple Univ	PA	17,438	C
Texas A&M Univ at Commerce	TX	9,020	C
Texas A&M Univ at Galveston	TX	10,000	C+
Texas Wesleyan Univ	TX	18,700	C
Towson Univ	MD	13,924	VC
Tulane Univ	LA	41,098	MC
Univ of Akron	OH	15,166	NC
Univ of Alaska Fairbanks	AK	10,101	C
Univ of Arizona	AZ	11,958	VC
Univ of Arkansas	AR	11,859	VC
Univ of Calif at Berkeley	CA	18,141	HC+
Univ of Calif at Los Angeles	CA	17,681	MC
Univ of Calif at San Diego	CA	16,102	HC
Univ of Calif at Santa Cruz	CA	19,174	VC
Univ of Florida	FL	9,354	HC
Univ of Houston	TX	7,000	C
Univ of Indianapolis	IN	25,090	C
Univ of Maine	ME	13,642	C
Univ of Mass Amherst	MA	15,973	C+
Univ of Mass Boston	MA	8,024	C
Univ of Minn/Duluth	MN	13,974	C
Univ of Nebr at Lincoln	NE	11,401	VC
Univ of Nevada/Las Vegas	NV	11,566	C
Univ of New Hampshire	NH	16,810	VC
Univ of New Mexico	NM	11,253	C
Univ of N Car at Charlotte	NC	9,101	C
Univ of Northern Colo	CO	10,249	C
Univ of Northern Iowa	IA	11,133	C
Univ of S Dak	SD	9,068	C
Univ of Texas at El Paso	TX	8,764	NC
Univ of West Georgia	GA	8,838	C
Univ of Wisc/Green Bay	WI	9,415	VC
Univ of Wyoming	WY	9,666	C
Utah State Univ	UT	8,002	VC
Virginia Wesleyan College	VA	28,433	C
Washington Univ in St. Louis	MO	42,106	MC
Weber State Univ	UT	9,635	NC
Wesleyan Univ	CT	42,122	MC
West Chester Univ of Pennsylvania	PA	12,355	C+
Western Conn State Univ	CT	12,993	C
Western Mich Univ	MI	13,299	C
Western Oregon Univ	OR	10,295	C
Whittier College	CA	29,108	C
Wilkes Univ	PA	30,886	C
Winona State Univ	MN	11,333	C
Youngstown State Univ	OH	12,613	NC

EAST ASIAN LANGUAGES AND LITERATURE

School	ST	$IS	SR
Beloit College	WI	32,808	HC
Boston Univ	MA	42,046	HC+
Indiana Univ Bloomington	IN	13,356	VC
Mich State Univ	MI	13,689	VC
Rutgers, The State Univ of New Jersey/New Brunswick/Piscataway Campus	NJ	15,810	VC
Smith College	MA	41,474	MC
Univ of Chicago	IL	42,369	MC
Univ of Florida	FL	9,354	HC
Univ of Illinois at Urbana-Champaign	IL	15,800	HC+
Univ of Kansas	KS	10,915	VC
Univ of Pennsylvania	PA	41,766	MC
Univ of Southern Calif	CA	41,618	MC
Washington Univ in St. Louis	MO	42,106	MC

EAST ASIAN STUDIES

School	ST	$IS	SR
Augsburg College	MN	28,300	C
Bates College	ME	42,100	MC
Boston Univ	MA	42,046	HC+
Brown Univ	RI	42,015	MC
Bryn Mawr College	PA	42,780	HC+
Bucknell Univ	PA	39,660	MC
CUNY/Queens College	NY	4,356	C
Colby College	ME	41,770	MC
Columbia Univ/Barnard College	NY	38,000	MC
Columbia Univ/Columbia College	NY	42,584	MC
Columbia Univ/School of General Studies	NY	41,516	C
Conn College	CT	41,975	MC
Denison Univ	OH	37,040	HC
DePauw Univ	IN	32,100	HC
Dickinson College	PA	40,170	HC+

School	ST	$IS	SR
Emory & Henry College	VA	26,570	C
George Washington Univ	DC	48,820	MC
Hamline Univ	MN	27,070	VC
Haverford College	PA	41,600	MC
Indiana Univ Bloomington	IN	13,356	VC
Johns Hopkins Univ	MD	42,044	MC
Lawrence Univ	WI	33,958	HC+
Lewis and Clark College	OR	35,358	VC+
Middlebury College	VT	42,120	MC
Naropa Univ	CO	26,302	SP
New York Univ	NY	43,170	MC
Oakland Univ	MI	11,936	C
Oberlin College	OH	40,904	MC
Penn State Univ/Univ Park Campus	PA	18,038	HC
Princeton Univ	NJ	40,213	MC
Simmons College	MA	35,640	VC
Simon's Rock College of Bard	MA	41,988	VC+
Stanford Univ	CA	41,557	MC
Univ of Arizona	AZ	11,958	VC
Univ of at Calif Davis	CA	15,010	VC
Univ of Calif at Irvine	CA	16,475	HC
Univ of Calif at Los Angeles	CA	17,681	MC
Univ of Illinois at Urbana-Champaign	IL	15,800	HC+
Univ of Minn/Twin Cities	MN	13,165	HC
Univ of Pennsylvania	PA	41,766	MC
Univ of St. Thomas	MN	28,000	VC
Univ of Southern Calif	CA	41,618	MC
Ursinus College	PA	38,950	VC
Vanderbilt Univ	TN	41,986	VC
Washington and Lee Univ	VA	35,880	MC
Washington Univ in St. Louis	MO	42,106	MC
Western Washington Univ	WA	11,262	VC
Wittenberg Univ	OH	34,596	VC
Yale Univ	CT	41,000	MC

EASTERN EUROPEAN STUDIES

School	ST	$IS	SR
Bard College	NY	41,800	HC+
Boston Univ	MA	42,046	HC+
Florida State Univ	FL	9,028	HC
Rutgers, The State Univ of New Jersey/Newark Campus	NJ	15,640	VC
Simon's Rock College of Bard	MA	41,988	VC+
SUNY/Univ at Albany	NY	13,860	VC
Univ of Okla	OK	10,769	VC+
Univ of Texas at Austin	TX	14,610	VC
Washington Univ in St. Louis	MO	42,106	MC
Yale Univ	CT	41,000	MC

ECOLOGY

School	ST	$IS	SR
Adams State College	CO	8,613	C
Appalachian State Univ	NC	8,000	VC
Bard College	NY	41,800	HC+
Beloit College	WI	32,808	HC
Bennington College	VT	41,890	HC
Boston Univ	MA	42,046	HC+
Calif Polytechnic State Univ	CA	12,390	VC
Cal State, Long Beach	CA	9,512	C
Claremont McKenna College	CA	42,920	MC
Cornell Univ	NY	41,717	MC
Defiance College	OH	24,790	C
Florida Inst of Technology	FL	29,720	VC
Florida State Univ	FL	9,028	HC
Hampshire College	MA	37,120	HC
Idaho State Univ	ID	9,030	C
Indiana Univ Bloomington	IN	13,356	VC
Iona College	NY	30,878	VC
Juniata College	PA	33,130	VC
Kent State Univ	OH	14,594	C
Lehigh Univ	PA	42,690	HC+
Mich Tech Univ	MI	14,569	VC
Missouri Southern State Univ	MO	8,396	NC
Montana State Univ-Northern	MT	10,000	NC
Morehead State Univ	KY	9,150	C
Mountain State Univ	WV	11,406	VC
New Mexico State Univ	NM	9,250	C
Northern Mich Univ	MI	12,340	LC
Northwestern Univ	IL	37,595	MC
Penn State Univ/Univ Park Campus	PA	18,038	HC
Princeton Univ	NJ	40,213	MC
Purdue Univ/West Lafayette	IN	13,458	VC
Rutgers, The State Univ of New Jersey/New Brunswick/Piscataway Campus	NJ	15,810	HC
St. John's Univ	NY	34,370	C
San Francisco State Univ	CA	13,000	C
Seattle Univ	WA	30,063	VC
Simon's Rock College of Bard	MA	41,988	VC+

INDEX OF COLLEGE MAJORS

School	ST	$IS	SR
SUNY/College of Environmental Science and Forestry	NY	15,000	VC
Susquehanna Univ	PA	33,465	VC
Tulane Univ	LA	41,098	MC
Unity College	ME	24,320	C
Univ of Arizona	AZ	11,958	VC
Univ of at Calif Davis	CA	15,010	VC
Univ of Calif at Irvine	CA	14,675	HC
Univ of Calif at Los Angeles	CA	17,681	HC
Univ of Calif at San Diego	CA	16,102	HC
Univ of Georgia	GA	11,004	HC
Univ of Mich/Flint	MI	6,398	C
Univ of Minn/Twin Cities	MN	13,165	HC
Univ of Pittsburgh at Pittsburgh	PA	18,866	VC
Univ of Rochester	NY	41,135	MC

ECONOMICS

School	ST	$IS	SR
Adelphi Univ	NY	27,000	VC
Adrian College	MI	23,000	C
Agnes Scott College	GA	32,070	HC
Alabama A&M Univ	AL	8,890	VC
Albertson College of Idaho	ID	21,095	VC
Albion College	MI	26,000	VC
Albright College	PA	33,920	C
Alcorn State Univ	MS	8,190	LC
Alfred Univ	NY		VC
Allegheny College	PA	33,500	HC
Alma College	MI	28,544	VC
American International College	MA	28,710	LC
American Univ	DC	38,719	HC+
Amherst College	MA	41,590	MC
Anderson Univ	IN	25,050	LC
Andrews Univ	MI	21,786	C
Appalachian State Univ	NC	8,000	VC
Aquinas College	MI	23,750	C
Arizona State Univ-Tempe	AZ	11,174	C
Arkansas State Univ	AR	9,630	C
Arkansas Tech Univ	AR	8,108	VC
Armstrong Atlantic State Univ	GA	7,394	C
Ashland Univ	OH	25,000	C
Assumption College	MA	32,875	C
Auburn Univ	AL	12,230	VC
Augsburg College	MN	28,300	C
Augustana College	IL	29,862	VC+
Augustana College	SD	24,380	VC
Austin College	TX	27,871	HC
Austin Peay State Univ	TN	7,535	C
Baker Univ	KS	22,190	C
Baldwin-Wallace College	OH	27,256	VC
Ball State Univ	IN	13,138	C
Bard College	NY	41,800	HC+
Barry Univ	FL	24,100	LC
Barton College	NC	22,316	C
Bates College	ME	42,100	MC
Baylor Univ	TX	27,555	HC
Bellarmine Univ	KY	27,650	C+
Belmont Abbey College	NC	25,314	C
Belmont Univ	TN	24,110	VC
Beloit College	WI	32,808	VC
Bemidji State Univ	MN	11,180	LC
Benedict College	SC	19,114	LC
Benedictine College	KS	21,968	C
Benedictine Univ	IL	25,710	C
Berea College	KY	5,496	VC+
Berry College	GA	24,342	VC
Bethany College	KS	20,660	LC
Bethany College	WV	21,395	C
Bethel Univ	MN	29,840	VC
Birmingham-Southern College	AL	28,494	VC+
Bloomsburg Univ of Pennsylvania	PA	11,602	C
Bluffton College	OH	26,110	C
Boise State Univ	ID	9,438	LC
Boston College	MA	41,608	MC
Boston Univ	MA	42,046	HC+
Bowdoin College	ME	41,660	MC
Bowling Green State Univ	OH	14,994	C
Bradley Univ	IL	25,280	VC
Brandeis Univ	MA	41,551	MC
Bridgewater Univ	VA	27,790	C
Bridgewater State College	MA	12,120	C
Brigham Young Univ	UT	9,200	VC
Brown Univ	RI	42,015	MC
Bryn Mawr College	PA	42,780	VC+
Bucknell Univ	PA	39,660	MC
Buena Vista Univ	IA	27,742	C
Butler Univ	IN	31,944	VC+
Calif Inst of Technology	CA	36,123	MC
Calif Lutheran Univ	CA	27,800	C
Calif Polytechnic State Univ	CA	12,390	VC
Calif State Polytechnic Univ, Pomona	CA	18,053	C
Cal State East Bay	CA	10,856	LC
Cal State, Bakersfield	CA	6,125	LC
Cal State, Chico	CA	11,395	C
Cal State, Dominguez Hills	CA	10,220	LC
Cal State, Fresno	CA	10,037	LC
Cal State, Fullerton	CA	10,990	C
Cal State, Long Beach	CA	9,512	C
Cal State, Los Angeles	CA	5,900	C
Cal State, Northridge	CA	9,036	LC
Cal State, Sacramento	CA	11,122	C+
Cal State, San Bernardino	CA	12,563	LC
Cal State, San Marcos	CA	1,800	LC
Cal State, Stanislaus	CA	11,283	C
Calvin College	MI	25,735	NC
Campbell Univ	NC	21,137	VC
Campbellsville Univ	KY	21,328	C
Canisius College	NY	32,257	VC
Capital Univ	OH	30,444	C
Carleton College	MN	40,467	MC
Carnegie Mellon Univ	PA	32,700	MC
Carson-Newman College	TN	16,800	C
Carthage College	WI	26,000	C
Case Western Reserve Univ	OH	37,314	MC
Catholic Univ of America	DC	35,838	VC
Centenary College of Louisiana	LA	24,760	VC
Central College	IA	26,774	VC
Central Conn State Univ	CT	13,620	C
Central Methodist Univ	MO	18,000	C
Central Mich Univ	MI	12,244	VC
Central Missouri State Univ	MO	10,000	C
Central State Univ	OH	9,010	C+
Central Washington Univ	WA	11,730	C
Centre College	KY	30,810	VC
Chapman Univ	CA	37,550	VC
Charleston Southern Univ	SC	17,800	C
Chatham College	PA	27,290	C+
Cheyney Univ of Pennsylvania	PA	11,497	LC
Chicago State Univ	IL	10,915	C+
Christopher Newport Univ	VA	13,326	VC
CUNY/Baruch College	NY	4,320	VC+
CUNY/Brooklyn College	NY	4,377	C+
CUNY/City College	NY		C
CUNY/College of Staten Island	NY	4,328	NC
CUNY/Herbert H. Lehman College	NY	4,000	LC
CUNY/Hunter College	NY	8,000	C+
CUNY/Queens College	NY	4,356	C
CUNY/York College	NY	4,242	NC
Claremont McKenna College	CA	42,920	MC
Clarion Univ of Pennsylvania	PA	11,844	C
Clark Atlanta Univ	GA	20,960	LC
Clark Univ	MA	35,165	VC+
Clemson Univ	SC	13,366	HC
Cleveland State Univ	OH	10,798	NC
Coastal Carolina Univ	SC	13,140	C
Coe College	IA	27,440	VC
Colby College	ME	41,770	MC
Colgate Univ	NY	41,170	MC
College of Charleston	SC	13,616	VC
College of Mount St. Vincent	NY	28,000	C
College of New Jersey	NJ	18,315	MC
College of New Rochelle	NY	28,396	C+
College of Notre Dame of Maryland	MD	27,700	C
College of St. Benedict	MN	30,091	VC
College of St. Catherine	MN	27,505	VC
College of St. Elizabeth	NJ	28,495	C
College of St. Scholastica	MN	28,456	C+
College of the Holy Cross	MA	40,664	MC
College of William and Mary	VA	14,147	MC
College of Wooster	OH	31,310	VC+
Colo College	CO	37,668	HC
Colo School of Mines	CO	14,893	HC
Colo State Univ-Fort Collins	CO	10,878	C+
Colo State Univ-Pueblo	CO	7,821	LC
Columbia Univ/Barnard College	NY	38,000	MC
Columbia Univ/Columbia College	NY	42,584	MC
Columbia Univ/School of General Studies	NY	41,516	C
Concordia College: Moorhead	MN	22,475	VC
Conn College	CT	41,975	MC
Converse College	SC	24,800	VC
Cornell College	IA	30,110	VC+
Cornell Univ	NY	41,717	MC
Creighton Univ	NE	29,918	VC+
Dartmouth College	NH	39,465	MC
David N. Myers College	OH	9,475	C
Davidson College	NC	36,825	MC
Davis and Elkins College	WV	22,416	C
Delaware State Univ	DE	8,130	LC
Denison Univ	OH	37,040	HC
DePaul Univ	IL	28,935	VC
DePauw Univ	IN	32,100	VC
Dickinson College	PA	40,170	HC+
Dillard Univ	LA	17,500	VC
Doane College	NE	22,458	C
Dowling College	NY	22,110	LC
Drake Univ	IA	27,632	VC+
Drew Univ/College of Liberal Arts	NJ	39,698	VC
Drury Univ	MO	20,117	VC
Duke Univ	NC	41,239	MC
Duquesne Univ	PA	29,534	VC
Earlham College	IN	33,604	HC
East Carolina Univ	NC	10,000	C
East Stroudsburg Univ of Pennsylvania	PA	10,336	C
East Tenn State Univ	TN	8,497	C
Eastern Conn State Univ	CT	13,554	C
Eastern Illinois Univ	IL	12,569	C
Eastern Kentucky Univ	KY	7,725	C
Eastern Mennonite Univ	VA	25,450	VC
Eastern Mich Univ	MI	12,897	C
Eastern New Mexico Univ	NM	7,264	C
Eastern Washington Univ	WA	10,608	C
Eckerd College	FL	35,492	VC
Edgewood College	WI	22,862	C
Edinboro Univ of Pennsylvania	PA	11,809	LC
Elizabethtown College	PA	32,100	VC
Elmhurst College	IL	24,685	C
Elon Univ	NC	25,371	HC
Emory & Henry College	VA	26,570	C
Emory Univ	GA	40,546	MC
Emporia State Univ	KS	8,093	C
Eugene Lang College New School for Liberal Arts	NY	38,800	C+
Excelsior College	NY	995	SP
Fairfield Univ	CT	39,835	HC
Fairleigh Dickinson Univ/ College at Florham	NJ	30,130	C
Fairleigh Dickinson Univ/ Metropolitan Campus	NJ	28,590	C
Fayetteville State Univ	NC	6,000	LC
Fisk Univ	TN	19,830	C
Fitchburg State College	MA	11,276	C
Florida A&M Univ	FL	8,344	C
Florida Atlantic Univ	FL	11,221	C
Florida International Univ	FL	9,215	VC
Florida Southern College	FL	25,965	C
Florida State Univ	FL	9,028	HC
Fordham Univ	NY	36,000	HC
Fort Hays State Univ	KS	7,638	C
Fort Lewis College	CO	11,852	C
Fort Valley State Univ	GA	6,975	C
Framingham State College	MA	11,156	C
Francis Marion Univ	SC	11,114	C
Franciscan Univ of Steubenville	OH	20,300	VC
Franklin and Marshall College	PA	40,590	HC
Franklin College	IN		C
Frostburg State Univ	MD	12,672	C
Furman Univ	SC	33,264	HC+
Gallaudet Univ	DC	16,554	
George Fox Univ	OR	28,490	C
George Mason Univ	VA	10,850	VC
George Washington Univ	DC	48,820	MC
Georgetown Univ	DC	43,183	MC
Georgia College and State Univ	GA	11,020	C
Georgia Inst of Technology	GA	11,450	HC+
Georgia Southern Univ	GA	9,762	C
Georgia State Univ	GA	11,444	VC
Gettysburg College	PA	39,864	HC
Gonzaga Univ	WA	30,218	HC
Gordon College	MA	29,194	C+
Goucher College	MD	36,225	VC
Graceland Univ	IA	19,700	C
Grand Canyon Univ	AZ	32,000	VC
Grand Valley State Univ	MI	12,000	VC
Grinnell College	IA	34,814	HC+
Grove City College	PA	15,784	HC+
Guilford College	NC	28,160	C+
Gustavus Adolphus College	MN	30,920	HC
Hamilton College	NY	41,660	MC
Hamline Univ	MN	27,070	VC
Hampden-Sydney College	VA	31,148	VC
Hampshire College	MA	37,120	HC
Hampton Univ	VA	19,468	C+
Hanover College	IN	28,150	HC
Harding Univ	AR	16,512	VC
Hardin-Simmons Univ	TX	18,641	C
Hartwick College	NY	36,065	C+
Harvard Univ/Harvard College	MA	45,860	MC
Hastings College	NE	22,218	VC
Haverford College	PA	41,600	MC
Hawaii Pacific Univ	HI	21,080	C
Heidelberg College	OH	23,242	C
Hendrix College	AR	27,646	HC+
Hillsdale College	MI	24,160	VC
Hiram College	OH	28,700	VC
Hobart and William Smith Colleges	NY	41,123	VC
Hofstra Univ	NY	32,630	VC
Hollins Univ	VA	31,105	C
Holy Family Univ	PA	25,740	C
Hood College	MD	30,085	VC
Hope College	MI	28,208	VC+
Houston Baptist Univ	TX	18,660	C
Howard Univ	DC	18,481	C+
Idaho State Univ	ID	9,030	C
Illinois College	IL	21,900	C+
Illinois State Univ	IL	12,839	C+
Illinois Wesleyan Univ	IL	34,050	HC+
Immaculata Univ	PA	25,350	C
Indiana State Univ	IN	11,604	C
Indiana Univ Bloomington	IN	13,356	VC
Indiana Univ Northwest	IN	4,902	LC
Indiana Univ of Pennsylvania	PA	11,209	C
Indiana Univ South Bend	IN	4,989	LC
Indiana Univ Southeast	IN	4,880	LC
Indiana Univ-Purdue Univ Fort Wayne	IN	5,067	LC
Indiana Univ-Purdue Univ Indianapolis	IN	10,959	C
Indiana Wesleyan Univ	IN	22,074	C+
Inter American Univ of PR/ San German	PR	6,720	
Iona College	NY	30,878	VC
Iowa State Univ	IA	11,831	VC
Ithaca College	NY	35,144	VC
Jackson State Univ	MS	8,500	C
Jacksonville State Univ	AL	7,618	LC
Jacksonville Univ	FL	24,040	C
James Madison Univ	VA	12,010	VC
Jamestown College	ND	14,130	NC
John Carroll Univ	OH	27,658	C+
Johns Hopkins Univ	MD	42,044	MC
Johnson C. Smith Univ	NC	20,000	C
Juniata College	PA	33,130	VC
Kansas State Univ	KS	10,516	VC
Kean Univ	NJ	15,880	C
Keene State College	NH	13,836	C
Kent State Univ	OH	14,594	C
Kenyon College	OH	39,500	MC
King's College	PA	29,810	C
Knox College	IL	32,385	VC+
La Salle Univ	PA	34,950	C
Lafayette College	PA	39,267	MC
Lake Forest College	IL	33,860	HC
Lake Superior State Univ	MI	12,842	LC
Lakeland College	WI	22,990	C
Lamar Univ	TX	6,820	LC
Langston Univ	OK	2,308	LC
Lawrence Univ	WI	33,958	HC+
Le Moyne College	NY	29,570	VC
Lebanon Valley College	PA	31,700	VC
Lehigh Univ	PA	42,690	HC+
Lenoir-Rhyne College	NC	25,580	C
Lewis and Clark College	OR	35,358	VC+
Lewis Univ	IL	23,050	C+
Lincoln Univ	MO	8,000	NC
Lincoln Univ	PA	13,658	C+
Linfield College	OR	29,632	VC
Lipscomb Univ	TN	20,967	VC
Lock Haven Univ of Pennsylvania	PA	12,098	LC
LIU/Brooklyn Campus	NY	25,000	C
LIU/C.W. Post Campus	NY	28,282	C
Longwood Univ	VA	12,426	C
Loras College	IA	27,193	C
Louisiana College	LA	13,450	C
Louisiana State Univ and A&M College	LA	10,749	VC
Louisiana State Univ in Shreveport	LA	2,900	NC
Loyola College in Maryland	MD	38,898	HC
Loyola Marymount Univ	CA	36,321	VC
Loyola Univ Chicago	IL	32,896	VC
Loyola Univ New Orleans	LA	31,050	VC+
Luther College	IA	28,800	VC+
Lycoming College	PA	30,797	C+
Lynchburg College	VA	30,645	C
Lyon College	AR	19,990	VC
Macalester College	MN	36,500	MC
Manchester College	IN	23,470	C
Manhattan College	NY	29,000	VC
Manhattanville College	NY	32,500	C+
Mansfield Univ	PA	11,300	C
Marian College	IN	26,160	C
Marian College of Fond du Lac	WI	21,775	C
Marietta College	OH	29,327	C
Marist College	NY	30,566	VC
Marlboro College	VT	35,980	VC+
Marquette Univ	WI	31,066	HC
Marshall Univ	WV	9,116	C
Mary Baldwin College	VA	26,465	C
Marymount Univ	VA	25,934	C
Maryville College	TN	29,224	VC
Mass Inst of Technology	MA	41,800	MC
McDaniel College	MD	31,610	VC
McKendree College	IL	24,800	VC
McMurry Univ	TX	18,100	LC
McNeese State Univ	LA	5,270	LC
Mercer Univ	GA	27,525	VC+
Meredith College	NC	25,600	C
Merrimack College	MA	34,380	C
Messiah College	PA	28,910	VC+
Methodist College	NC	21,000	C
Metropolitan State College of Denver	CO	2,338	LC
Metropolitan State Univ	MN	4,682	SP
Miami Univ	OH	29,097	HC
Mich State Univ	MI	13,689	VC
Mich Tech Univ	MI	14,569	VC
Middle Tenn State Univ	TN	8,540	C
Middlebury College	VT	42,120	MC
Midland Lutheran College	NE	18,600	C
Midwestern State Univ	TX	9,381	LC
Millersville Univ of Pennsylvania	PA	12,113	C
Millikin Univ	IL	25,590	C

ST = STATE $IS = IN-STATE COSTS   SR = SELECTOR RATING

School	ST	$IS	SR
Mills College	CA	39,870	C
Millsaps College	MS	28,256	VC+
Minn State Univ, Mankato	MN	10,276	LC
Minn State Univ, Moorhead	MN	7,000	LC
Minot State Univ	ND	6,700	LC
Miss State Univ	MS	9,577	C
Missouri Southern State Univ	MO	8,396	NC
Missouri State Univ	MO	10,748	C+
Missouri Valley College	MO	18,500	C
Missouri Western State Univ	MO	9,534	NC
Montana State Univ-Bozeman	MT	1,137	C
Montclair State Univ	NJ	16,327	C
Moravian College	PA	28,950	VC
Morehouse College	GA	25,082	C
Morgan State Univ	MD	12,080	C
Mount Holyoke College	MA	42,148	HC+
Mount St. Mary's Univ	MD	30,930	C
Mount Union College	OH	25,840	C
Muhlenberg College	PA	36,030	HC+
Murray State Univ	KY	8,900	VC
Muskingum College	OH	22,970	C
Nazareth College of Rochester	NY	28,175	VC
Nebr Wesleyan Univ	NE	23,415	C+
New College of Florida	FL	10,009	HC+
New Jersey City Univ	NJ	13,695	LC
New Mexico State Univ	NM	9,250	C
New York Univ	NY	43,170	MC
Nichols College	MA	28,000	C
N Car Agricultural and Technical State Univ	NC	8,000	LC
N Car State Univ	NC	11,824	HC
North Central College	IL	28,926	VC
N Dak State Univ	ND	8,500	C
North Park Univ	IL	24,050	C
Northeastern Illinois Univ	IL	3,000	NC
Northeastern Univ	MA	35,742	HC
Northern Arizona Univ	AZ	10,353	C
Northern Illinois Univ	IL	13,178	C
Northern Kentucky Univ	KY	6,670	VC
Northern Mich Univ	MI	12,340	LC
Northern State Univ	SD	8,257	C
Northwest Missouri State Univ	MO	10,000	C
Northwest Nazarene Univ	ID	22,590	VC
Northwestern College of Iowa	IA	22,174	C+
Northwestern Okla State Univ	OK	6,250	NC
Northwestern Univ	IL	37,595	MC
Notre Dame College	OH	20,425	C
Oakland Univ	MI	11,936	C
Oberlin College	OH	40,904	MC
Occidental College	CA	40,185	MC
Oglethorpe Univ	GA	30,300	VC
Ohio Dominican Univ	OH	25,954	C
Ohio State Univ	OH	15,357	HC
Ohio Univ	OH	15,921	C
Ohio Wesleyan Univ	OH	35,830	VC+
Okla City Univ	OK	23,965	VC
Okla State Univ	OK	10,213	VC
Old Dominion Univ	VA	11,907	C
Olivet College	MI	19,984	C+
Olivet Nazarene Univ	IL	22,590	C
Oregon State Univ	OR	11,055	C
Otterbein College	OH	28,986	C
Ouachita Baptist Univ	AR	21,900	VC
Pace Univ	NY	30,000	VC
Pacific Lutheran Univ	WA	28,805	VC
Pacific Univ	OR	24,250	C
Park Univ	MO	11,592	C
Penn State Erie/The Behrend College	PA	16,256	C
Penn State Univ/Univ Park Campus	PA	18,038	HC
Pepperdine Univ	CA	39,960	HC
Pfeiffer Univ	NC	21,900	C
Pittsburg State Univ	KS	8,112	C
Pitzer College	CA	41,644	HC
Plymouth State Univ	NH	12,298	LC
Point Loma Nazarene Univ	CA	27,610	VC
Pomona College	CA	40,774	MC
Portland State Univ	OR	12,453	C
Presbyterian College	SC	30,044	VC
Prescott College	AZ	13,445	LC
Princeton Univ	NJ	40,213	MC
Principia College	IL	27,765	VC+
Providence College	RI	34,580	LC
Purdue Univ/West Lafayette	IN	13,458	VC
Quinnipiac Univ	CT	34,640	VC
Radford Univ	VA	13,145	C
Ramapo College of New Jersey	NJ	16,630	VC
Randolph-Macon College	VA	31,250	C
Randolph-Macon Woman's College	VA	31,160	VC+
Reed College	OR	41,106	MC
Regis Univ	CO	31,890	C
Rensselaer Polytechnic Inst	NY	41,288	VC+
Rhode Island College	RI	11,570	C
Rhodes College	TN	32,860	HC
Rice Univ	TX	32,290	MC
Richard Stockton College of New Jersey	NJ	14,000	VC
Rider Univ	NJ	32,560	C
Ripon College	WI	27,160	C+
Roanoke College	VA	30,748	VC
Robert Morris Univ	PA	22,822	C
Rochester Inst of Technology	NY	32,070	VC+
Rockford College	IL	28,330	VC
Rockhurst Univ	MO	25,440	VC
Rollins College	FL	38,366	VC
Roosevelt Univ	IL	22,605	VC
Rose-Hulman Inst of Technology	IN	34,557	HC+
Rosemont College	PA	29,350	C
Rowan Univ	NJ	16,000	VC
Rutgers, The State Univ of New Jersey/Camden Campus	NJ	15,000	VC
Rutgers, The State Univ of New Jersey/New Brunswick/Piscataway Campus	NJ	15,810	HC
Rutgers, The State Univ of New Jersey/Newark Campus	NJ	15,640	VC
Saginaw Valley State Univ	MI	11,432	C
St. Ambrose Univ	IA	25,495	C
St. Anselm College	NH	33,810	C
St. Cloud State Univ	MN	10,010	C
St. Edward's Univ	TX	23,560	C
St. Francis College	NY	19,974	C
St. Francis Univ	PA	25,880	LC
St. John Fisher College	NY	27,860	C
St. John's Univ	MN	29,749	VC
St. John's Univ	NY	34,370	C
St. Joseph College	CT	32,050	C
St. Joseph's College	IN	26,600	C
St. Joseph's Univ	PA	37,428	VC
St. Lawrence Univ	NY	40,545	VC
St. Louis Univ	MO	33,158	VC+
St. Martin's Univ	WA	27,555	C
St. Mary's College	IN	32,538	VC
St. Mary's College of Calif	CA	37,290	C
St. Mary's College of Maryland	MD	18,876	VC+
St. Mary's Univ of San Antonio	TX	22,444	C
St. Michael's College	VT	33,330	VC
St. Norbert College	WI	28,577	C+
St. Olaf College	MN	32,800	HC
St. Peter's College	NJ	30,160	LC
St. Vincent College	PA	26,160	VC
Salem College	NC	26,226	VC+
Salem State College	MA	13,161	LC
Salisbury Univ	MD	13,128	VC
Salve Regina Univ	RI	33,450	C
Sam Houston State Univ	TX	8,000	C
San Diego State Univ	CA	12,971	C
San Francisco State Univ	CA	13,000	C
San Jose State Univ	CA	11,707	C
Santa Clara Univ	CA	38,931	VC
Sarah Lawrence College	NY	42,000	HC
Scripps College	CA	41,000	MC
Seattle Pacific Univ	WA	29,355	C
Seattle Univ	WA	30,063	VC
Seton Hall Univ	NJ	33,622	VC
Seton Hill Univ	PA	28,810	C
Shepherd Univ	WV	10,066	C
Shippensburg Univ of Pennsylvania	PA	11,621	C
Shorter College	GA	19,700	C
Siena College	NY	28,260	VC+
Simmons College	MA	35,640	VC
Simpson College	IA	26,833	VC
Skidmore College	NY	41,779	HC
Slippery Rock Univ of Pennsylvania	PA	10,360	LC
Smith College	MA	41,474	MC
Sonoma State Univ	CA	14,732	C
S Dak State Univ	SD	9,815	C
Southeast Missouri State Univ	MO	10,596	C
Southeastern Okla State Univ	OK	6,147	C
Southern Conn State Univ	CT	10,310	C
Southern Illinois Univ Carbondale	IL	12,391	C
Southern Illinois Univ Edwardsville	IL	11,022	C
Southern Methodist Univ	TX	36,088	VC+
Southern Oregon Univ	OR	12,186	C
Southern Univ at New Orleans	LA	1,000	NC
Southern Utah Univ	UT		
Southwestern Univ	TX	26,767	HC
Spelman College	GA	24,650	VC
Spring Hill College	AL	28,678	C
Stanford Univ	CA	41,557	MC
SUNY at Oswego	NY	13,662	VC
SUNY at Potsdam	NY	12,959	C
SUNY/College at Buffalo	NY	11,903	C+
SUNY/College at Cortland	NY	12,095	C
SUNY/College at Geneseo	NY	12,910	HC+
SUNY/College at Old Westbury	NY	13,154	C
SUNY/College at Oneonta	NY	12,905	VC
SUNY/College at Plattsburgh	NY	12,362	C
SUNY/College at Purchase	NY	11,989	VC+
SUNY/Empire State College	NY	4,575	SP
SUNY/Univ at Albany	NY	13,860	VC
SUNY/Univ at Binghamton	NY	13,988	HC
SUNY/Univ at Buffalo	NY	13,694	VC
SUNY/Univ at New Paltz	NY	12,480	VC
SUNY/Univ at Stony Brook	NY	13,625	HC
Stephen F. Austin State Univ	TX	7,930	C
Stetson Univ	FL	32,725	VC
Stonehill College	MA	36,104	HC
Strayer Univ	DC	8,789	SP
Suffolk Univ	MA	33,160	C
Susquehanna Univ	PA	33,465	VC
Swarthmore College	PA	41,280	MC
Sweet Briar College	VA	31,460	VC
Syracuse Univ	NY	38,655	HC
Talladega College	AL	11,240	LC
Tarleton State Univ	TX	8,952	C
Taylor Univ	IN	26,376	VC+
Temple Univ	PA	17,438	C
Tenn Tech Univ	TN	10,044	C
Texas A&M Univ	TX	13,351	HC
Texas A&M Univ at Commerce	TX	9,020	C
Texas Christian Univ	TX	23,410	VC+
Texas Lutheran Univ	TX	23,530	C
Texas Southern Univ	TX	9,828	C
Texas State Univ - San Marcos	TX	10,862	C
Texas Tech Univ	TX	13,026	VC
Texas Wesleyan Univ	TX	18,700	C
Thomas Edison State College	NJ	3,780	SP
Thomas More College	KY	24,470	C
Tougaloo College	MS	15,975	NC
Touro College	NY	17,000	VC
Towson Univ	MD	13,924	VC
Transylvania Univ	KY	26,240	VC+
Trinity College	CT	38,040	HC+
Trinity College	DC	24,150	LC
Trinity Univ	TX	30,157	HC+
Truman State Univ	MO	11,242	HC
Tufts Univ	MA	42,018	MC
Tulane Univ	LA	41,098	MC
Turabo Univ	PR	4,110	
Union College	NY	41,595	HC
Union Univ	TN	20,750	C
United States Air Force Academy	CO		HC+
United States Military Academy	NY		MC
United States Naval Academy	MD		MC
Univ of Akron	OH	15,166	NC
Univ of Alabama	AL	9,888	C
Univ of Alabama at Birmingham	AL	13,716	C
Univ of Alaska Anchorage	AK	11,275	NC
Univ of Arizona	AZ	11,596	VC
Univ of Arkansas	AR	11,859	VC
Univ of Arkansas at Little Rock	AR	7,230	NC
Univ of at Calif Davis	CA	15,010	VC
Univ of Calif at Berkeley	CA	18,141	HC+
Univ of Calif at Irvine	CA	16,475	HC
Univ of Calif at Los Angeles	CA	17,681	MC
Univ of Calif at Riverside	CA	16,625	C
Univ of Calif at San Diego	CA	16,102	HC
Univ of Calif at Santa Barbara	CA	11,800	VC
Univ of Calif at Santa Cruz	CA	19,174	VC
Univ of Central Arkansas	AR	9,984	C
Univ of Central Florida	FL	10,739	VC
Univ of Central Okla	OK	8,094	C
Univ of Chicago	IL	42,369	MC
Univ of Cincinnati	OH	17,682	C
Univ of Colo at Boulder	CO	13,352	C+
Univ of Colo at Colo Springs	CO	11,517	VC
Univ of Colo at Denver and Health Sciences Center	CO	5,021	C
Univ of Conn	CT	16,628	HC
Univ of Dallas	TX	27,432	VC+
Univ of Dayton	OH	28,826	VC
Univ of Delaware	DE	14,142	HC
Univ of Denver	CO	36,376	VC+
Univ of Detroit Mercy	MI	27,000	C
Univ of Evansville	IN	28,320	VC
Univ of Findlay	OH	29,238	C
Univ of Florida	FL	9,354	HC
Univ of Georgia	GA	11,004	HC
Univ of Hartford	CT	34,044	C
Univ of Hawaii at Hilo	HI	6,500	C
Univ of Hawaii at Manoa	HI	10,413	VC
Univ of Houston	TX	7,000	VC
Univ of Idaho	ID	9,310	NC
Univ of Illinois at Chicago	IL	16,256	VC
Univ of Illinois at Urbana-Champaign	IL	15,800	HC+
Univ of Indianapolis	IN	25,090	C
Univ of Iowa	IA	12,172	VC
Univ of Kansas	KS	10,915	VC
Univ of Kentucky	KY	7,800	C
Univ of Louisiana at Lafayette	LA	5,830	C
Univ of Louisiana at Monroe	LA	7,103	C
Univ of Maine	ME	13,642	C
Univ of Mary Hardin-Baylor	TX	19,428	C
Univ of Mary Washington	VA	11,636	HC
Univ of Maryland/Baltimore County	MD	16,642	VC+
Univ of Maryland/College Park	MD	16,036	HC
Univ of Mass Amherst	MA	15,973	C+
Univ of Mass Boston	MA	8,024	C
Univ of Mass Dartmouth	MA	15,985	C
Univ of Mass Lowell	MA	14,327	VC
Univ of Memphis	TN	11,153	C
Univ of Miami	FL	38,397	MC
Univ of Mich/Ann Arbor	MI	16,587	HC+
Univ of Mich/Dearborn	MI	7,000	VC
Univ of Mich/Flint	MI	6,398	C
Univ of Minn/Duluth	MN	13,974	C
Univ of Minn/Morris	MN	15,472	VC
Univ of Minn/Twin Cities	MN	13,165	HC
Univ of Miss	MS	9,000	C
Univ of Missouri/Columbia	MO	13,500	C
Univ of Missouri/Kansas City	MO	15,000	VC
Univ of Missouri/Rolla	MO	13,332	HC
Univ of Missouri/St. Louis	MO	14,046	VC
Univ of Mobile	AL	16,880	C
Univ of Montana	MT	10,602	C
Univ of Nebr at Kearney	NE	9,000	NC
Univ of Nebr at Lincoln	NE	11,401	VC
Univ of Nebr at Omaha	NE	11,235	C
Univ of Nevada/Las Vegas	NV	11,566	C
Univ of New Hampshire	NH	16,810	VC
Univ of New Mexico	NM	11,253	C
Univ of New Orleans	LA	7,370	C
Univ of N Car at Asheville	NC	9,237	VC
Univ of N Car at Chapel Hill	NC	11,129	MC
Univ of N Car at Charlotte	NC	9,101	C
Univ of N Car at Greensboro	NC	8,993	C
Univ of N Car at Wilmington	NC	10,107	VC
Univ of N Dak	ND	10,114	VC
Univ of North Florida	FL	9,908	VC
Univ of North Texas	TX	7,800	C
Univ of Northern Colo	CO	10,249	C
Univ of Northern Iowa	IA	11,133	C
Univ of Notre Dame	IN	39,552	MC
Univ of Okla	OK	10,769	VC+
Univ of Oregon	OR	13,108	VC
Univ of Pennsylvania	PA	41,766	MC
Univ of Pittsburgh at Bradford	PA	17,008	C
Univ of Pittsburgh at Johnstown	PA	16,740	LC
Univ of Pittsburgh at Pittsburgh	PA	18,866	HC
Univ of PR/Cayey Univ College	PR	1,250	
Univ of PR/Mayaguez	PR	1,250	
Univ of PR/Rio Piedras	PR	5,750	
Univ of Puget Sound	WA	35,600	HC
Univ of Redlands	CA	36,160	VC
Univ of Rhode Island	RI	15,398	C
Univ of Richmond	VA	40,510	MC
Univ of Rio Grande	OH	8,728	NC
Univ of Rochester	NY	41,135	MC
Univ of St. Thomas	MN	28,000	VC
Univ of St. Thomas	TX	23,810	VC
Univ of San Diego	CA	40,620	HC
Univ of San Francisco	CA	37,560	VC
Univ of Science and Arts of Okla	OK	7,650	C
Univ of Scranton	PA	31,100	VC
Univ of S Car at Columbia	SC	13,397	VC
Univ of S Car Upstate	SC	11,957	C
Univ of S Dak	SD	9,068	C
Univ of South Florida	FL	10,284	VC
Univ of Southern Calif	CA	41,618	MC
Univ of Southern Indiana	IN	12,590	LC
Univ of Southern Maine	ME	12,614	C
Univ of Southern Miss	MS	10,112	C
Univ of Tampa	FL	25,784	C
Univ of Tenn at Chattanooga	TN	7,790	C
Univ of Tenn at Knoxville	TN	11,720	C
Univ of Tenn at Martin	TN	8,693	C
Univ of Texas at Arlington	TX	7,195	C
Univ of Texas at Austin	TX	14,610	C
Univ of Texas at Dallas	TX	13,244	C
Univ of Texas at El Paso	TX	8,764	NC
Univ of Texas at San Antonio	TX	11,325	LC
Univ of Texas-Pan American	TX	7,290	C+
Univ of the District of Columbia	DC	2,070	LC
Univ of the Ozarks	AR	19,250	C
Univ of the Pacific	CA	34,380	VC
Univ of the South	TN	34,645	VC
Univ of Toledo	OH	15,806	NC
Univ of Tulsa	OK	25,348	HC
Univ of Utah	UT	10,162	VC
Univ of Vermont	VT	18,080	VC

ST = STATE $IS = IN-STATE COSTS   SR = SELECTOR RATING

School	ST	$IS	SR
Univ of Virginia	VA	13,759	MC
Univ of Virginia's College at Wise	VA	11,076	C
Univ of Washington	WA	10,400	VC
Univ of West Georgia	GA	8,838	C
Univ of Wisc/Eau Claire	WI	9,915	VC
Univ of Wisc/Green Bay	WI	9,415	VC
Univ of Wisc/La Crosse	WI	10,045	VC
Univ of Wisc/Madison	WI	13,117	HC
Univ of Wisc/Milwaukee	WI	9,427	LC
Univ of Wisc/Oshkosh	WI	10,426	LC
Univ of Wisc/Parkside	WI	10,181	LC
Univ of Wisc/Platteville	WI	9,779	NC
Univ of Wisc/River Falls	WI	9,722	LC
Univ of Wisc/Stevens Point	WI	9,384	VC
Univ of Wisc/Whitewater	WI	9,274	C
Univ of Wyoming	WY	9,666	C
Utah State Univ	UT	8,002	VC
Utica College	NY	31,396	C
Valparaiso Univ	IN	28,970	VC+
Vanderbilt Univ	TN	41,986	MC
Vassar College	NY	41,700	MC
Villanova Univ	PA	38,672	HC+
Virginia Commonwealth Univ	VA	12,987	C
Virginia Polytechnic Inst and State Univ	VA	10,834	VC
Virginia State Univ	VA	11,318	C
Wabash College	IN	30,116	HC
Wake Forest Univ	NC	38,290	MC
Wartburg College	IA	27,315	NC
Washburn Univ	KS	9,734	NC
Washington and Jefferson College	PA	33,490	VC
Washington and Lee Univ	VA	35,880	MC
Washington College	MD	34,990	VC
Washington State Univ	WA	12,260	C
Washington Univ in St. Louis	MO	42,106	MC
Wayne State Univ	MI	11,805	C
Weber State Univ	UT	9,635	NC
Webster Univ	MO	24,280	VC
Wellesley College	MA	41,030	MC
Wells College	NY	23,070	VC
Wesleyan College	GA	19,560	C
Wesleyan Univ	CT	42,122	MC
West Chester Univ of Pennsylvania	PA	12,355	C+
West Liberty State College	WV	9,142	LC
West Texas A&M Univ	TX	8,452	C
West Virginia State Univ	WV	8,378	NC
West Virginia Univ	WV	10,506	C
West Virginia Wesleyan College	WV	26,880	C
Western Conn State Univ	CT	12,993	C
Western Illinois Univ	IL	13,042	C
Western Kentucky Univ	KY	10,192	C
Western Mich Univ	MI	13,299	C
Western New England College	MA	32,054	C
Western Oregon Univ	OR	10,295	C
Western State College of Colo	CO	9,942	C
Western Washington Univ	WA	11,262	VC
Westfield State College	MA	10,200	C
Westminster College	MO	19,060	VC
Westminster College	PA	31,290	C
Westminster College	UT	25,656	C
Wheaton College	IL	27,760	HC
Wheaton College	MA	40,180	HC+
Whitman College	WA	36,110	HC+
Whittier College	CA	29,108	C
Whitworth College	WA	29,428	VC+
Wichita State Univ	KS	8,500	C
Widener Univ	PA	27,275	C
Wilberforce Univ	OH	14,937	LC
Willamette Univ	OR	35,416	VC+
William Paterson Univ of New Jersey	NJ	17,810	C+
Williams College	MA	40,310	MC
Winona State Univ	MN	11,333	C
Winston-Salem State Univ	NC	8,960	LC
Wittenberg Univ	OH	34,596	VC
Wofford College	SC	30,935	HC
Worcester Polytechnic Inst	MA	40,450	VC+
Worcester State College	MA	12,499	C
Wright State Univ	OH	13,616	LC
Xavier Univ	OH	30,490	HC
Yale Univ	CT	41,000	MC
Yeshiva Univ	NY	22,000	C
York College of Pennsylvania	PA	16,550	VC
Youngstown State Univ	OH	12,613	NC

EDUCATION

School	ST	$IS	SR
Albertus Magnus College	CT	25,336	C
Aquinas College	MI	23,750	C
Averett Univ	VA	24,920	C
Belmont Abbey College	NC	25,314	C
Beloit College	WI	32,808	HC
Bennington College	VT	41,890	HC
Bethune-Cookman College	FL	17,922	LC
Bloomfield College	NJ	22,500	LC
Boise State Univ	ID	9,438	LC
Boston Univ	MA	42,046	HC+
Brewton-Parker College	GA	14,220	LC
Brown Univ	RI	42,015	MC
Bryn Athyn College of the New Church	PA	14,999	NC
Bucknell Univ	PA	39,660	MC
Cabrini College	PA	33,340	C
Calif Lutheran Univ	CA	27,800	LC
Cal State, Monterey Bay	CA	10,099	C
Calif Univ of Pennsylvania	PA	14,217	C
Case Western Reserve Univ	OH	37,314	MC
Catawba College	NC	25,000	C
Catholic Univ of America	DC	35,838	VC
Central Mich Univ	MI	12,244	C
Chatham Univ	PA	27,290	C+
CUNY/College of Staten Island	NY	4,328	NC
Coker College	SC	21,600	C
Colgate Univ	NY	41,170	MC
College of St. Mary	NE	23,938	C
College of St. Scholastica	MN	28,456	C+
Columbia Univ/Columbia College	NY	42,584	MC
Concordia College-New York	NY	27,740	C
Cornell Univ	NY	41,717	MC
Denison Univ	OH	37,040	HC
Drexel Univ	PA	27,700	VC
Duquesne Univ	PA	29,534	VC
East Texas Baptist Univ	TX	16,713	C
Eastern Mich Univ	MI	12,897	C
Eastern Nazarene College	MA	19,500	LC
Eastern Oregon Univ	OR	10,400	NC
Endicott College	MA	30,156	C+
Eugene Lang College New School for Liberal Arts	NY	38,800	C+
Eureka College	IL	19,280	C
Franklin Pierce College	NH	31,700	C
Furman Univ	SC	33,264	HC+
Goddard College	VT	21,100	C
Guilford College	NC	28,160	C+
Hampshire College	MA	37,120	HC
Hardin-Simmons Univ	TX	18,641	C
Harris-Stowe State College	MO	3,200	SP
Hope International Univ	CA	23,700	NC
Huntington Univ	IN	24,830	C
Huston-Tillotson Univ	TX	14,232	LC
Ithaca College	NY	35,144	VC
Johnson State College	VT	11,830	LC
Keene State College	NH	13,836	C
Kent State Univ	OH	14,594	C
Lake Forest College	IL	33,860	VC
Lipscomb Univ	TN	20,967	C
Lourdes College	OH	15,300	LC
Lynchburg College	VA	30,645	C
Lynn Univ	FL	30,750	C
Maharishi Univ of Management	IA	29,450	VC
Manhattanville College	NY	32,500	C+
Martin Univ	IN	10,300	SP
Mary Baldwin College	VA	26,465	C
Mass College of Liberal Arts	MA	8,725	LC
Mich State Univ	MI	13,689	VC
Midway College	KY	20,150	C
Miss State Univ	MS	9,577	C
Montana State Univ-Billings	MT	8,906	C
Mount Holyoke College	MA	42,148	HC+
New York Inst of Technology	NY	28,126	VC
N Car State Univ	NC	11,824	HC
Northwest Christian College	OR	24,298	C
Northwest Univ	WA	18,854	C
Northwestern Univ	IL	37,595	MC
Ohio State Univ at Lima	OH	4,416	NC
Pacific Lutheran Univ	WA	28,805	VC
Philadelphia Biblical Univ	PA	22,425	C
Prescott College	AZ	13,445	LC
Rocky Mountain College	MT	20,805	C
St. John Fisher College	NY	27,860	C
St. Louis Univ	MO	33,158	VC+
St. Mary's College of Maryland	MD	18,876	VC+
Salem State College	MA	13,161	LC
San Diego Christian College	CA	24,172	C
Schreiner Univ	TX	20,600	C
Shawnee State Univ	OH	12,237	NC
Smith College	MA	41,474	MC
Southern New Hampshire Univ	NH	28,764	C
Spalding Univ	KY	18,882	C
SUNY/Empire State College	NY	4,575	SP
Stonehill College	MA	36,104	HC
Susquehanna Univ	PA	33,615	VC
Swarthmore College	PA	41,280	MC
Temple Univ	PA	17,438	C
Texas A&M Univ at Corpus Christi	TX	10,280	LC
Texas Lutheran Univ	TX	23,530	C
Towson Univ	MD	13,924	VC
Trevecca Nazarene Univ	TN	19,594	C
Trinity Christian College	IL	23,645	C
Trinity College	CT	38,040	HC+
Tusculum College	TN	21,340	LC
Union College	KY	18,920	C
Union Inst & Univ	OH	8,912	SP
Union Univ	TN	20,750	VC
Univ of Alabama in Huntsville	AL	9,516	VC
Univ of Conn	CT	16,628	HC
Univ of Delaware	DE	14,142	HC
Univ of Dubuque	IA	23,390	C
Univ of Illinois at Chicago	IL	16,256	VC
Univ of Illinois at Urbana-Champaign	IL	15,800	HC+
Univ of La Verne	CA	33,470	C
Univ of Maryland/College Park	MD	16,036	HC
Univ of Memphis	TN	11,153	C
Univ of Mich/Flint	MI	6,398	C
Univ of Missouri/Columbia	MO	13,500	VC
Univ of Missouri/St. Louis	MO	14,046	VC
Univ of Nebr at Lincoln	NE	11,401	VC
Univ of New England	ME	31,005	C
Univ of N Car at Chapel Hill	NC	11,129	MC
Univ of Oregon	OR	13,108	VC
Univ of Pennsylvania	PA	41,766	MC
Univ of Pittsburgh at Pittsburgh	PA	18,866	HC
Univ of PR/Rio Piedras	PR	5,750	
Univ of St. Thomas	TX	23,810	VC
Univ of South Alabama	AL	8,930	LC
Univ of South Florida	FL	10,284	VC
Univ of Tenn at Chattanooga	TN	7,790	C
Univ of Texas at Dallas	TX	13,244	HC
Univ of the Pacific	CA	34,380	VC
Univ of Tulsa	OK	25,348	HC
Univ of Vermont	VT	18,080	VC
Univ of Wisc/Green Bay	WI	9,415	VC
Univ of Wisc/Milwaukee	WI	9,427	LC
Univ of Wisc/Parkside	WI	10,181	LC
Vanderbilt Univ	TN	41,986	MC
Virginia Intermont College	VA	22,200	LC
Wake Forest Univ	NC	38,290	MC
Washburn Univ	KS	9,734	NC
Washington State Univ	WA	12,260	C
Washington Univ in St. Louis	MO	42,106	MC
Webster Univ	MO	24,280	VC
Western Baptist College	OR	21,808	C
Western Oregon Univ	OR	10,295	C
Xavier Univ	OH	30,490	HC
York College	NE	16,330	NC
York College of Pennsylvania	PA	16,550	VC
Youngstown State Univ	OH	12,613	NC

EDUCATION ADMINISTRATION

School	ST	$IS	SR
Ashland Univ	OH	25,000	C
Le Moyne College	NY	29,570	VC
Philander Smith College	AR	13,230	LC
Southwestern Okla State Univ	OK	4,801	C
Univ of Tenn at Martin	TN	8,693	C

EDUCATION OF THE DEAF AND HEARING IMPAIRED

School	ST	$IS	SR
Adelphi Univ	NY	27,000	VC
Augustana College	SD	24,380	VC
Ball State Univ	IN	13,138	C
Barton College	NC	22,316	C
Boston Univ	MA	42,046	HC+
Cal State, Northridge	CA	9,036	LC
CUNY/Brooklyn College	NY	4,377	C+
College of New Jersey	NJ	18,315	MC
Eastern Kentucky Univ	KY	7,725	C
Eastern Mich Univ	MI	12,897	C
Flagler College	FL	13,790	VC+
Fontbonne Univ	MO	23,308	C
Indiana Univ of Pennsylvania	PA	11,209	C
Ithaca College	NY	35,144	VC
Kent State Univ	OH	14,594	C
Lenoir-Rhyne College	NC	25,580	C
MacMurray College	IL	20,755	C
Mercy College	NY	20,000	NC
Minot State Univ	ND	6,700	LC
Rochester Inst of Technology	NY	32,070	VC+
St. John's Univ	NY	34,370	C
Southern Univ at New Orleans	LA	1,000	NC
SUNY/College at Plattsburgh	NY	12,362	C
Texas Christian Univ	TX	23,410	VC+
Towson Univ	MD	13,924	VC
Univ of Arkansas at Little Rock	AR	7,230	NC
Univ of Montevallo	AL	9,630	C
Univ of Nebr at Lincoln	NE	11,401	VC
Univ of N Car at Greensboro	NC	8,993	C
Univ of Science and Arts of Okla	OK	7,650	C
Univ of Tulsa	OK	25,348	HC

EDUCATION OF THE EMOTIONALLY HANDICAPPED

School	ST	$IS	SR
Central Mich Univ	MI	12,244	C
CUNY/City College	NY		C
East Carolina Univ	NC	10,000	C
Eastern Mich Univ	MI	12,897	C
Florida International Univ	FL	9,215	VC
Florida State Univ	FL	9,028	HC
Univ of South Florida	FL	10,284	VC
Youngstown State Univ	OH	12,613	C

EDUCATION OF THE EXCEPTIONAL CHILD

School	ST	$IS	SR
Ashland Univ	OH	25,000	C
Bethel College	TN	16,066	NC
Bethune-Cookman College	FL	17,922	LC
Edgewood College	WI	22,862	C
Flagler College	FL	13,790	VC+
Jacksonville Univ	FL	24,040	C
Mansfield Univ	PA	11,300	C
Minot State Univ	ND	6,700	LC
Nova Southeastern Univ	FL	24,320	C
St. Augustine's College	NC	14,000	LC
Southeast Missouri State Univ	MO	10,596	C
Southeastern Univ	FL	17,180	LC
Texas Christian Univ	TX	23,410	VC+
Univ of Central Arkansas	AR	9,984	C
Univ of Central Florida	FL	10,739	VC
Univ of Great Falls	MT	17,000	C
Univ of Wisc/Stevens Point	WI	9,384	VC
Warner Southern College	FL	18,000	LC
Western Kentucky Univ	KY	10,192	C

EDUCATION OF THE MENTALLY HANDICAPPED

School	ST	$IS	SR
Augusta State Univ	GA	2,920	C
Central Mich Univ	MI	12,244	C
CUNY/City College	NY		C
East Carolina Univ	NC	10,000	C
Eastern Mich Univ	MI	12,897	C
Florida International Univ	FL	9,215	VC
Florida State Univ	FL	9,028	HC
Indiana Univ of Pennsylvania	PA	11,209	C
Minot State Univ	ND	6,700	LC
Northern Mich Univ	MI	12,340	C
Northwest Missouri State Univ	MO	10,000	C
Southeastern Okla State Univ	OK	6,147	C
Univ of N Car at Charlotte	NC	9,101	C
Univ of Rio Grande	OH	8,728	NC
Univ of South Florida	FL	10,284	VC
Youngstown State Univ	OH	12,613	NC

EDUCATION OF THE MULTIPLY HANDICAPPED

School	ST	$IS	SR
Eastern Mich Univ	MI	12,897	C
Ohio Univ	OH	15,921	C
Univ of Illinois at Urbana-Champaign	IL	15,800	HC+
Youngstown State Univ	OH	12,613	NC

EDUCATION OF THE PHYSICALLY HANDICAPPED

School	ST	$IS	SR
Aquinas College	MI	23,750	C
Eastern Mich Univ	MI	12,897	C
Indiana Univ of Pennsylvania	PA	11,209	C
Ohio Univ	OH	15,921	C

EDUCATION OF THE VISUALLY HANDICAPPED

School	ST	$IS	SR
Eastern Mich Univ	MI	12,897	C
Florida State Univ	FL	9,028	HC

EDUCATION SERVICES

School	ST	$IS	SR
Birmingham-Southern College	AL	28,494	VC+

EDUCATIONAL MEDIA

School	ST	$IS	SR
Ball State Univ	IN	13,138	C
College of St. Scholastica	MN	28,456	C+
Duquesne Univ	PA	29,534	VC
Eastern Mich Univ	MI	12,897	C
Indiana State Univ	IN	11,604	C
Indiana Univ Bloomington	IN	13,356	VC
Ithaca College	NY	35,144	VC
Purdue Univ/West Lafayette	IN	13,458	VC
Weber State Univ	UT	9,635	NC

School	ST	$IS	SR

EDUCATIONAL STATISTICS AND RESEARCH

School	ST	$IS	SR
Bucknell Univ	PA	39,660	MC
Emory Univ	GA	40,546	MC

ELECTRICAL/ELECTRONICS ENGINEERING

School	ST	$IS	SR
Alabama A&M Univ	AL	8,890	LC
Alfred Univ	NY		VC
Andrews Univ	MI	21,786	C
Arizona State Univ-Tempe	AZ	11,174	C
Auburn Univ	AL	12,230	VC
Baylor Univ	TX	27,555	HC
Benedict College	SC	19,114	LC
Bethel College	IN	19,680	C
Bloomsburg Univ of Pennsylvania	PA	11,602	C
Boston Univ	MA	42,046	HC+
Bradley Univ	IL	25,280	VC
Brigham Young Univ	UT	9,200	VC
Bucknell Univ	PA	39,660	MC
Calif Inst of Technology	CA	36,123	MC
Calif Polytechnic State Univ	CA	12,390	VC
Calif State Polytechnic Univ, Pomona	CA	18,053	C+
Cal State, Chico	CA	11,395	C
Cal State, Fresno	CA	10,037	LC
Cal State, Fullerton	CA	10,990	C
Cal State, Long Beach	CA	9,512	C
Cal State, Los Angeles	CA	5,900	C
Cal State, Sacramento	CA	11,122	C
Calvin College	MI	25,735	NC
Capitol College	MD	21,250	C
Carnegie Mellon Univ	PA	32,700	MC
Case Western Reserve Univ	OH	37,314	MC
Catholic Univ of America	DC	35,838	VC
Cedarville Univ	OH	21,904	VC
Central Mich Univ	MI	12,244	C
Central Missouri State Univ	MO	10,000	C
Central Washington Univ	WA	11,730	VC
Christian Brothers Univ	TN	24,650	VC
Citadel, The	SC		C+
CUNY/City College	NY		C
Clarkson Univ	NY	34,930	VC
Clemson Univ	SC	13,366	HC
Cleveland State Univ	OH	10,798	NC
Cogswell Polytechnical College	CA	13,760	LC
College of New Jersey	NJ	18,315	MC
Colo State Univ-Fort Collins	CO	10,878	C+
Colo Technical Univ	CO	9,500	LC
Columbia Univ/Fu Foundation School of Engineering and Applied Science	NY	42,584	MC
Cooper Union for the Advancement of Science and Art	NY	12,450	MC
Cornell Univ	NY	41,717	MC
Delaware State Univ	DE	8,130	LC
Dordt College	IA	20,325	VC
Drexel Univ	PA	27,700	VC
Duke Univ	NC	41,239	MC
Embry-Riddle Aeronautical Univ	AZ	30,280	C+
Embry-Riddle Aeronautical Univ	FL	30,280	C
Fairfield Univ	CT	39,835	HC
Fairleigh Dickinson Univ/Metropolitan Campus	NJ	28,590	C
Florida A&M Univ	FL	8,344	C
Florida Atlantic Univ	FL	11,221	C
Florida Inst of Technology	FL	29,720	VC
Florida International Univ	FL	9,215	VC
Florida State Univ	FL	9,028	HC
Gannon Univ	PA	26,100	C
George Mason Univ	VA	10,850	VC
George Washington Univ	DC	48,820	MC
Georgia Inst of Technology	GA	11,450	HC+
Gonzaga Univ	WA	30,218	HC
Grove City College	PA	15,784	HC+
Hampton Univ	VA	19,468	C+
Harding Univ	AR	16,512	VC
Henry Cogswell College	WA	16,680	SP
Hofstra Univ	NY	32,630	VC
Howard Univ	DC	18,481	C+
Idaho State Univ	ID	9,030	C
Illinois Inst of Technology	IL	26,465	HC+
Indiana Inst of Technology	IN	23,430	C
Indiana Univ-Purdue Univ Fort Wayne	IN	5,067	LC
Indiana Univ-Purdue Univ Indianapolis	IN	10,959	C
Inter American Univ of PR/Bayamon Univ College	PR	3,522	
Iowa State Univ	IA	11,831	VC
Jacksonville Univ	FL	24,040	C
John Brown Univ	AR	20,910	VC
Johns Hopkins Univ	MD	42,044	MC
Johnson and Wales Univ/North Miami Campus	FL	30,126	LC
Johnson and Wales Univ/Providence Campus	RI	28,126	LC
Kansas State Univ	KS	10,516	VC
Kettering Univ	MI	29,338	VC
Lafayette College	PA	39,267	MC
Lake Superior State Univ	MI	12,842	LC
Lamar Univ	TX	6,820	LC
Lawrence Tech Univ	MI	25,475	VC
Lehigh Univ	PA	42,690	HC+
LeTourneau Univ	TX	21,200	C
Loras College	IA	27,193	C
Louisiana State Univ and A&M College	LA	10,749	VC
Loyola College in Maryland	MD	38,898	HC
Loyola Marymount Univ	CA	36,321	VC
Manhattan College	NY	29,000	VC
Marquette Univ	WI	31,066	HC
Mass Inst of Technology	MA	41,800	MC
McNeese State Univ	LA	5,270	VC
Mercer Univ	GA	22,525	VC+
Merrimack College	MA	34,380	C
Miami Univ	OH	29,097	HC
Mich State Univ	MI	13,689	VC
Mich Tech Univ	MI	14,569	VC
Milwaukee School of Engineering	WI	29,847	VC+
Minn State Univ, Mankato	MN	10,276	LC
Miss State Univ	MS	9,577	C
Montana State Univ-Bozeman	MT	1,137	C
Morgan State Univ	MD	12,080	C
New Jersey Inst of Technology	NJ	16,396	VC
New Mexico Inst of Mining and Technology	NM	8,510	VC+
New Mexico State Univ	NM	9,250	C
New York Inst of Technology	NY	28,126	VC
N Car Agricultural and Technical State Univ	NC	8,000	LC
N Car State Univ	NC	11,824	HC
N Dak State Univ	ND	8,500	C
Northeastern Univ	MA	35,742	HC
Northern Arizona Univ	AZ	10,353	C
Northern Illinois Univ	IL	13,178	C
Northwestern Univ	IL	37,595	MC
Norwich Univ	VT	28,212	C
Oakland Univ	MI	11,936	C
Ohio Northern Univ	OH	27,765	VC
Ohio State Univ	OH	15,357	HC
Ohio Univ	OH	15,921	C
Okla Christian Univ	OK	18,992	NC
Okla State Univ	OK	10,213	VC
Old Dominion Univ	VA	11,907	C
Oral Roberts Univ	OK	22,650	C
Penn State Univ/Univ Park Campus	PA	18,038	HC
Polytechnic Univ/Brooklyn	NY	37,150	VC
Portland State Univ	OR	12,453	C
Prairie View A&M Univ	TX	11,110	LC
Princeton Univ	NJ	40,213	MC
Purdue Univ/Calumet	IN	10,891	LC
Purdue Univ/West Lafayette	IN	13,458	VC
Rensselaer Polytechnic Inst	NY	41,288	HC+
Rice Univ	TX	32,290	MC
Rochester Inst of Technology	NY	32,070	VC+
Rose-Hulman Inst of Technology	IN	34,557	HC+
Rutgers, The State Univ of New Jersey/New Brunswick/Piscataway Campus	NJ	15,810	HC
Saginaw Valley State Univ	MI	11,432	C
St. Cloud State Univ	MN	10,010	C
St. Louis Univ	MO	33,158	VC+
St. Mary's Univ of San Antonio	TX	22,444	C
San Diego State Univ	CA	12,971	C
San Francisco State Univ	CA	13,000	C
San Jose State Univ	CA	11,707	C
Santa Clara Univ	CA	38,931	VC
Seattle Pacific Univ	WA	29,355	C
Seattle Univ	WA	30,063	VC
S Dak School of Mines and Technology	SD	7,624	C+
S Dak State Univ	SD	9,815	C
Southern Illinois Univ Carbondale	IL	12,391	C
Southern Illinois Univ Edwardsville	IL	11,022	C
Southern Methodist Univ	TX	36,088	VC+
Southern Univ and A&M College	LA	8,238	LC
Stanford Univ	CA	41,557	MC
SUNY/Inst of Technology	NY	12,575	VC
SUNY/Maritime College	NY	12,425	C
SUNY/Univ at Binghamton	NY	13,988	HC
SUNY/Univ at Buffalo	NY	13,694	VC
SUNY/Univ at New Paltz	NY	12,480	VC
SUNY/Univ at Stony Brook	NY	13,625	VC
Stevens Inst of Technology	NJ	40,935	HC
Suffolk Univ	MA	33,160	C
Syracuse Univ	NY	38,655	VC
Temple Univ	PA	17,438	C
Tenn State Univ	TN	9,048	LC
Tenn Tech Univ	TN	10,044	C
Texas A&M Univ	TX	13,351	HC
Texas A&M Univ at Kingsville	TX	6,800	LC
Texas Tech Univ	TX	13,026	VC
Tri-State Univ-Main Campus	IN	26,200	C
Tufts Univ	MA	42,018	MC
Tulane Univ	LA	41,098	MC
Tuskegee Univ	AL	18,860	LC
Union College	NY	41,595	HC
United States Air Force Academy	CO		HC+
United States Coast Guard Academy	CT		HC
United States Military Academy	NY		MC
United States Naval Academy	MD		MC
Universidad Politecnica de PR	PR	5,400	
Univ of Akron	OH	15,166	NC
Univ of Alabama	AL	9,888	C
Univ of Alabama at Birmingham	AL	13,716	C
Univ of Alabama in Huntsville	AL	9,516	VC
Univ of Alaska Fairbanks	AK	10,101	C
Univ of Arizona	AZ	11,958	VC
Univ of Arkansas	AR	11,859	VC
Univ of at Calif Davis	CA	15,010	VC
Univ of Calif at Berkeley	CA	18,141	HC+
Univ of Calif at Irvine	CA	16,475	HC
Univ of Calif at Los Angeles	CA	17,681	MC
Univ of Calif at Riverside	CA	16,625	C
Univ of Calif at San Diego	CA	16,102	HC
Univ of Calif at Santa Barbara	CA	11,800	VC
Univ of Central Florida	FL	10,739	VC
Univ of Cincinnati	OH	17,682	C
Univ of Colo at Boulder	CO	13,352	C+
Univ of Colo at Colo Springs	CO	11,517	VC
Univ of Colo at Denver and Health Sciences Center	CO	5,021	C
Univ of Conn	CT	16,628	HC
Univ of Dayton	OH	28,826	VC
Univ of Delaware	DE	14,142	HC
Univ of Denver	CO	36,376	VC+
Univ of Detroit Mercy	MI	27,000	C
Univ of Evansville	IN	28,320	VC
Univ of Florida	FL	9,354	HC
Univ of Hartford	CT	34,044	C
Univ of Hawaii at Manoa	HI	10,413	VC
Univ of Houston	TX	7,000	C
Univ of Idaho	ID	9,310	NC
Univ of Illinois at Chicago	IL	16,256	VC
Univ of Illinois at Urbana-Champaign	IL	15,800	HC+
Univ of Indianapolis	IN	25,090	C
Univ of Iowa	IA	12,172	VC
Univ of Kansas	KS	10,915	VC
Univ of Kentucky	KY	7,800	C
Univ of Louisiana at Lafayette	LA	5,830	C
Univ of Louisville	KY	10,400	VC
Univ of Maine	ME	13,642	C
Univ of Maryland/College Park	MD	16,036	HC
Univ of Mass Amherst	MA	15,973	C+
Univ of Mass Dartmouth	MA	15,985	C
Univ of Mass Lowell	MA	14,327	VC
Univ of Memphis	TN	11,153	C
Univ of Miami	FL	38,397	MC
Univ of Mich/Ann Arbor	MI	16,587	HC+
Univ of Mich/Dearborn	MI	7,000	VC
Univ of Minn/Duluth	MN	13,974	C
Univ of Minn/Twin Cities	MN	13,165	HC
Univ of Miss	MS	9,000	C
Univ of Missouri/Columbia	MO	13,500	VC
Univ of Missouri/Kansas City	MO	15,000	VC
Univ of Missouri/Rolla	MO	13,332	HC
Univ of Missouri/St. Louis	MO	14,046	VC
Univ of Nebr at Lincoln	NE	11,401	VC
Univ of Nevada/Las Vegas	NV	11,566	C
Univ of Nevada/Reno	NV	12,155	NC
Univ of New Hampshire	NH	16,810	VC
Univ of New Haven	CT	31,794	C
Univ of New Mexico	NM	11,253	C
Univ of New Orleans	LA	7,370	C
Univ of N Car at Charlotte	NC	9,101	C
Univ of N Dak	ND	10,114	VC
Univ of North Florida	FL	9,908	VC
Univ of Notre Dame	IN	39,552	MC
Univ of Okla	OK	10,769	VC+
Univ of Pennsylvania	PA	41,766	MC
Univ of Pittsburgh at Pittsburgh	PA	18,866	HC
Univ of Portland	OR	32,300	VC
Univ of PR/Mayaguez	PR	1,250	
Univ of Rhode Island	RI	15,398	C
Univ of Rochester	NY	41,135	HC
Univ of St. Thomas	MN	28,000	VC
Univ of San Diego	CA	40,620	HC
Univ of Scranton	PA	31,100	VC
Univ of South Alabama	AL	8,930	LC
Univ of S Car at Columbia	SC	13,397	VC
Univ of South Florida	FL	10,284	VC
Univ of Southern Calif	CA	41,618	MC
Univ of Southern Maine	ME	12,614	C
Univ of Tenn at Knoxville	TN	11,720	C
Univ of Texas at Arlington	TX	7,195	LC
Univ of Texas at Austin	TX	14,610	HC
Univ of Texas at Dallas	TX	13,244	HC
Univ of Texas at El Paso	TX	8,764	NC
Univ of Texas at San Antonio	TX	11,325	LC
Univ of Texas-Pan American	TX	7,290	C+
Univ of the District of Columbia	DC	2,070	LC
Univ of the Pacific	CA	34,380	VC
Univ of Toledo	OH	15,806	NC
Univ of Tulsa	OK	25,348	VC
Univ of Utah	UT	10,162	VC
Univ of Vermont	VT	18,080	VC
Univ of Virginia	VA	13,759	MC
Univ of Washington	WA	10,400	VC
Univ of West Florida	FL	8,559	C
Univ of Wisc/Madison	WI	13,117	HC
Univ of Wisc/Milwaukee	WI	9,427	LC
Univ of Wisc/Platteville	WI	9,779	LC
Univ of Wyoming	WY	9,666	C
Utah State Univ	UT	8,002	VC
Valparaiso Univ	IN	28,970	VC+
Vanderbilt Univ	TN	41,986	MC
Villanova Univ	PA	38,672	HC+
Virginia Commonwealth Univ	VA	12,987	C
Virginia Military Inst	VA	12,654	VC
Virginia Polytechnic Inst and State Univ	VA	10,834	VC
Washington State Univ	WA	12,260	C
Washington Univ in St. Louis	MO	42,106	MC
Wayne State Univ	MI	11,805	C
West Virginia Univ	WV	10,506	C
West Virginia Univ Inst of Technology	WV	8,788	NC
Western Kentucky Univ	KY	10,192	C
Western Mich Univ	MI	13,299	C
Western New England College	MA	32,054	C
Wichita State Univ	KS	8,500	C
Widener Univ	PA	27,275	C
Wilkes Univ	PA	30,886	C
Worcester Polytechnic Inst	MA	40,450	VC+
Wright State Univ	OH	13,616	LC
Yale Univ	CT	41,000	MC
Youngstown State Univ	OH	12,613	NC

ELECTRICAL/ELECTRONICS ENGINEERING TECHNOLOGY

School	ST	$IS	SR
Alabama A&M Univ	AL	8,890	LC
Appalachian State Univ	NC	8,000	VC
Baker College of Flint	MI	7,800	VC
Brigham Young Univ	UT	9,200	VC
Calif Univ of Pennsylvania	PA	14,217	C
Central Conn State Univ	CT	13,620	C
Central Missouri State Univ	MO	10,000	C
Colo State Univ-Pueblo	CO	7,821	LC
Colo Technical Univ	CO	9,500	LC
DeVry College of Technology/North Brunswick	NJ	10,500	LC
DeVry/New York	NY	12,000	LC
DeVry Univ/Addison (DuPage County)	IL	10,800	LC
DeVry Univ/Alpharetta	GA	10,675	LC
DeVry Univ/Chicago	IL	10,800	LC
DeVry Univ/Columbus	OH	11,000	LC
DeVry Univ/Crystal City	VA	12,000	C
DeVry Univ/Dallas	TX	10,700	LC
DeVry Univ/Decatur	GA	10,680	LC
DeVry Univ/Fort Washington	PA	12,000	LC
DeVry Univ/Fremont	CA	13,060	LC
DeVry Univ/Kansas City	MO	10,670	LC
DeVry Univ/Long Beach	CA	12,450	LC
DeVry Univ/Miramar	FL	12,000	LC
DeVry Univ/Orlando	FL	12,000	LC
DeVry Univ/Phoenix	AZ	11,790	LC
DeVry Univ/Pomona	CA	12,450	LC
DeVry Univ/Seattle	WA	12,000	LC
DeVry Univ/Tinley Park	IL	12,000	LC
DeVry Univ/West Hills	CA	12,450	LC
DeVry Univ/Westminster	CO	12,000	LC
East Carolina Univ	NC	10,000	C
Eastern New Mexico Univ	NM	7,264	C
East-West Univ	IL	10,375	LC
Excelsior College	NY	995	SP
Fairleigh Dickinson Univ/Metropolitan Campus	NJ	28,590	C
Fairmont State Univ	WV	8,400	LC
Farmingdale SUNY	NY	13,521	C
Fort Valley State Univ	GA	6,975	C
Georgia Southern Univ	GA	9,762	C
Indiana State Univ	IN	11,604	C

Electromechanical (continued)

School	ST	$IS	SR
Indiana Univ-Purdue Univ Indianapolis	IN	10,959	C
Inter American Univ of PR/ Aguadilla Campus	PR	3,784	
Inter American Univ of PR/ Bayamon Univ College	PR	3,522	
Inter American Univ of PR/ Fajardo Campus	PR	4,000	
Inter American Univ of PR/ Ponce Regional College	PR	3,700	
Kansas State Univ	KS	10,516	C
Kent State Univ	OH	14,594	C
Louisiana Tech Univ	LA	7,370	C
Metropolitan State College of Denver	CO	2,338	LC
Mich Tech Univ	MI	14,569	VC
Minn State Univ, Mankato	MN	10,276	LC
Missouri State Univ	MO	10,748	C+
Montana State Univ- Northern	MT	10,000	NC
Murray State Univ	KY	8,900	VC
New York Inst of Technology	NY	28,126	VC
Norfolk State Univ	VA	10,531	LC
Northeastern Univ	MA	35,742	HC
Northern Mich Univ	MI	12,340	VC
Northwestern State Univ of Louisiana	LA	7,144	C
Okla State Univ	OK	10,213	VC
Old Dominion Univ	VA	11,907	C
Oregon Inst of Technology	OR	8,718	C
Pacific Union College	CA	24,555	VC+
Pennsylvania College of Technology	PA	16,980	LC
Pittsburg State Univ	KS	8,112	C
Point Park Univ	PA	24,160	C
Purdue Univ/Calumet	IN	10,891	LC
Purdue Univ/West Lafayette	IN	13,458	VC
Rochester Inst of Technology	NY	32,070	VC+
Roosevelt Univ	IL	22,605	VC
Savannah State Univ	GA	7,772	LC
S Car State Univ	SC	6,700	LC
S Dak State Univ	SD	9,815	C
Southern Illinois Univ Carbondale	IL	12,391	C
Southern Polytechnic State Univ	GA	7,640	VC
Southwestern Okla State Univ	OK	4,801	C
SUNY/College at Buffalo	NY	11,903	C+
SUNY/College of Technology at Alfred	NY	14,000	C
SUNY/Inst of Technology	NY	12,575	VC
Temple Univ	PA	17,438	C
Texas A&M Univ at Galveston	TX	10,000	C+
Texas Southern Univ	TX	9,828	C
Texas Tech Univ	TX	13,026	VC
Thomas Edison State College	NJ	3,780	SP
Univ of Arkansas at Little Rock	AR	7,230	NC
Univ of Central Florida	FL	10,739	VC
Univ of Cincinnati	OH	17,682	C
Univ of Dayton	OH	28,826	VC
Univ of Hartford	CT	34,044	C
Univ of Houston	TX	7,000	C
Univ of Maine	ME	13,642	VC
Univ of Memphis	TN	11,153	C
Univ of Nebr at Lincoln	NE	11,401	VC
Univ of N Car at Charlotte	NC	9,101	C
Univ of Pittsburgh at Johnstown	PA	16,740	LC
Univ of PR/Bayamon Univ College Campus	PR	1,600	
Univ of Rio Grande	OH	8,728	NC
Univ of Southern Miss	MS	10,112	C
Weber State Univ	UT	9,635	NC
Wentworth Inst of Technology	MA	27,500	C
West Virginia Univ Inst of Technology	WV	8,788	NC
Western Carolina Univ	NC	7,000	C
Western Washington Univ	WA	11,262	NC
Youngstown State Univ	OH	12,613	NC
Western Kentucky Univ	KY	10,192	C

ELECTROMECHANICAL TECHNOLOGY

School	ST	$IS	SR
CUNY/New York City College of Technology	NY	4,269	NC
Cleveland State Univ	OH	10,798	NC
Penn State Univ/Altoona	PA	12,635	C
SUNY/College of Technology at Alfred	NY	14,000	C
Texas A&M Univ at Galveston	TX	10,000	C+
Univ of Houston	TX	7,000	C+
Univ of Northern Iowa	IA	11,133	C
Univ of the District of Columbia	DC	2,070	LC
Univ of Toledo	OH	15,806	NC
Vermont Technical College	VT	15,751	C
Wentworth Inst of Technology	MA	27,500	C

ELECTRONIC BUSINESS

School	ST	$IS	SR
Champlain College	VT	24,605	C
Clarkson Univ	NY	34,930	VC
Dakota State Univ	SD	7,466	C
Davenport Univ	MI	15,205	NC
De Sales Univ	PA	28,580	VC
Dominican Univ of Calif	CA	36,836	C
Indiana Univ Kokomo	IN	4,835	LC
Ithaca College	NY	35,144	VC
King College	TN	23,400	C
La Sierra Univ	CA	24,327	C+
Maryville Univ of St. Louis	MO	23,000	VC
Messiah College	PA	28,910	VC+
Mountain State Univ	WV	11,406	NC
Old Dominion Univ	VA	11,907	C
St. Mary-of-the-Woods College	IN	25,480	C
St. Mary's Univ of Minn	MN	23,857	VC
Southern Univ and A&M College	LA	8,238	LC
Stetson Univ	FL	32,725	VC
Temple Univ	PA	17,438	C
Texas Christian Univ	TX	23,410	VC+
Thiel College	PA	24,580	C
Univ of La Verne	CA	33,470	C
Univ of Missouri/Rolla	MO	13,332	HC
Univ of Pennsylvania	PA	41,766	MC
Univ of Scranton	PA	31,100	VC
Univ of South Alabama	AL	8,930	LC
Univ of Southern Indiana	IN	12,590	LC

ELEMENTARY EDUCATION

School	ST	$IS	SR
Abilene Christian Univ	TX	20,830	C
Adams State College	CO	8,613	C
Adelphi Univ	NY	27,000	VC
Adrian College	MI	23,000	C
Alabama A&M Univ	AL	8,890	LC
Alabama State Univ	AL	7,658	C
Alaska Pacific Univ	AK	25,142	C
Albright College	PA	33,920	C
Alcorn State Univ	MS	8,190	LC
Alderson-Broaddus College	WV	24,006	C
Alice Lloyd College	KY	4,900	C
Alma College	MI	28,544	VC
Alvernia College	PA	26,388	C
Alverno College	WI	21,088	C
American Indian College of the Assemblies of God	AZ	9,405	LC
American International College	MA	28,710	LC
American Univ	DC	38,719	HC+
Anderson Univ	IN	25,050	LC
Andrews Univ	MI	21,786	C
Anna Maria College	MA	29,815	LC
Appalachian State Univ	NC	8,000	LC
Aquinas College	TN	10,660	LC
Arcadia Univ	PA	33,570	VC
Arizona State Univ-Tempe	AZ	11,174	C
Arkansas Baptist College	AR	5,600	NC
Armstrong Atlantic State Univ	GA	7,394	C
Asbury College	KY	23,762	VC
Ashford Univ	IA	20,370	C
Ashland Univ	OH	25,000	C
Atlantic Union College	MA	17,600	LC
Auburn Univ	AL	12,230	VC
Auburn Univ Montgomery	AL	9,530	NC
Augsburg College	MN	28,300	C
Augusta State Univ	GA	2,920	C
Augustana College	IL	29,862	VC+
Augustana College	SD	24,380	VC
Aurora Univ	IL	20,645	C
Austin Peay State Univ	TN	7,535	C
Averett Univ	VA	24,920	C
Avila Univ	MO	22,100	C
Baker Univ	KS	22,190	C
Ball State Univ	IN	13,138	C
Barton College	NC	22,316	C
Bay Path College	MA	29,362	C
Baylor Univ	TX	27,555	HC
Becker College	MA	24,300	LC
Belhaven College	MS	19,530	NC
Bellarmine Univ	KY	27,650	C+
Belmont Abbey College	NC	25,314	C
Belmont Univ	TN	24,110	VC
Bemidji State Univ	MN	11,180	LC
Benedict College	SC	19,114	LC
Benedictine College	KS	21,968	C
Benedictine Univ	IL	25,710	C
Bennett College	NC	11,500	C
Berea College	KY	5,496	VC+
Bethany College	KS	20,660	LC
Bethany College	WV	21,395	C
Bethel College	IN	19,680	C
Bethel College	KS	21,650	C
Bethel Univ	MN	29,840	VC
Bethune-Cookman College	FL	17,922	LC
Black Hills State Univ	SD	7,800	LC
Blackburn College	IL	13,690	C
Bloomsburg Univ of Pennsylvania	PA	11,602	C
Blue Mountain College	MS	11,086	C
Bluefield State College	WV	3,140	LC
Boise State Univ	ID	9,438	LC
Boricua College	NY	8,000	C
Boston College	MA	41,608	MC
Boston Univ	MA	42,046	HC+
Bowie State Univ	MD	10,880	C+
Bradley Univ	IL	25,280	VC
Brescia Univ	KY	14,240	C
Briar Cliff Univ	IA	23,550	LC
Bridgewater State College	MA	12,120	C
Brigham Young Univ	UT	9,200	VC
Brigham Young Univ/Hawaii	HI	7,740	HC+
Bryan College	TN	19,270	C
Bucknell Univ	PA	39,660	MC
Buena Vista Univ	IA	27,742	C
Butler Univ	IN	31,944	VC+
Cabrini College	PA	33,340	C
Caldwell College	NJ	26,450	LC
Cal State, Long Beach	CA	9,512	C
Calif Univ of Pennsylvania	PA	14,217	C
Calumet College of St. Joseph	IN	9,500	LC
Calvin College	MI	25,735	NC
Cameron Univ	OK	6,314	NC
Campbell Univ	NC	21,137	VC
Campbellsville Univ	KY	21,328	C
Capital Univ	OH	30,444	C
Cardinal Stritch Univ	WI	21,910	C
Caribbean Univ	PR	3,000	
Carlos Albizu Univ	FL	11,109	C
Carlow Univ	PA	24,313	C
Carroll College	MT	23,324	C+
Carroll College	WI	24,860	C
Carson-Newman College	TN	16,800	C
Carthage College	WI	26,000	C
Catawba College	NC	25,000	C
Catholic Univ of America	DC	35,838	VC
Cazenovia College	NY	26,900	C
Cedar Crest College	PA	30,615	C
Centenary College	NJ	28,870	LC
Centenary College of Louisiana	LA	24,760	VC
Central College	IA	26,774	VC
Central Conn State Univ	CT	13,620	C
Central Methodist Univ	MO	18,900	C
Central Mich Univ	MI	12,244	C
Central Missouri State Univ	MO	10,000	C
Central State Univ	OH	9,010	C+
Central Univ of Bayamon	PR	3,335	
Central Washington Univ	WA	11,730	C
Centre College	KY	30,810	VC
Chadron State College	NE	6,350	NC
Chaminade Univ of Honolulu	HI	23,320	LC
Champlain College	VT	24,605	C
Charleston Southern Univ	SC	17,800	C
Chestnut Hill College	PA	26,600	LC
Cheyney Univ of Pennsylvania	PA	11,497	LC
Chicago State Univ	IL	10,915	C+
City Univ	WA	7,425	NC
CUNY/Brooklyn College	NY	4,377	C+
CUNY/City College	NY		C
CUNY/Herbert H. Lehman College	NY	4,000	LC
CUNY/Hunter College	NY	8,000	C+
CUNY/Medgar Evers College	NY	4,250	NC
CUNY/Queens College	NY	4,356	C
Claflin Univ	SC	16,798	C+
Clarion Univ of Pennsylvania	PA	11,844	C
Clarke College	IA	25,390	C
Clearwater Christian College	FL	13,160	LC
Clemson Univ	SC	13,366	NC
Cleveland State Univ	OH	10,798	NC
Coastal Carolina Univ	SC	13,140	C
Coe College	IA	27,440	VC
Coker College	SC	21,600	C
College Misericordia	PA	27,950	C
College of Charleston	SC	13,616	VC
College of Mount St. Joseph	OH	24,860	C
College of New Jersey	NJ	18,315	MC
College of Notre Dame of Maryland	MD	27,700	C
College of Our Lady of the Elms	MA	21,000	C
College of St. Benedict	MN	30,091	VC
College of St. Catherine	MN	27,505	VC
College of St. Elizabeth	NJ	28,495	C
College of St. Joseph	VT	20,900	NC
College of St. Mary	NE	23,938	C
College of St. Rose	NY	25,684	C
College of Santa Fe	NM	28,978	C
College of the Ozarks	MO	4,130	VC+
College of the Southwest	NM	12,420	NC
Colo Christian Univ	CO	21,182	VC
Columbia College	MO	16,900	C
Columbia College	SC	24,982	LC
Columbia Union College	MD	23,536	LC
Concord College	WV	9,708	C
Concordia College	AL	10,500	NC
Concordia College: Moorhead	MN	22,475	VC
Concordia College-New York	NY	27,740	C
Concordia Univ	OR	24,400	C
Concordia Univ at Austin	TX	23,640	VC
Concordia Univ Nebr	NE	20,500	C+
Concordia Univ St.Paul	MN	27,776	C
Concordia Univ Wisc	WI	22,660	VC
Concordia Univ, Ann Arbor	MI	25,153	C+
Concordia Univ, River Forest	IL	26,300	C
Converse College	SC	24,800	VC
Coppin State College	MD	10,200	LC
Cornell Univ	IA	30,110	VC+
Cornerstone Univ and Grand Rapids Theological Seminary	MI	21,350	NC
Covenant College	GA	26,460	VC+
Creighton Univ	NE	29,918	VC+
Crichton College	TN	15,300	C
Culver-Stockton College	MO	20,625	C
Cumberland Univ	TN	18,894	C
Curry College	MA	26,100	LC
Daemen College	NY	24,580	C
Dakota State Univ	SD	7,466	C
Dakota Wesleyan Univ	SD	17,832	C
Dallas Baptist Univ	TX	17,040	VC
Dana College	NE	22,390	C
Davis and Elkins College	WV	22,416	C
De Sales Univ	PA	28,580	VC
Defiance College	OH	24,790	C
Delaware State Univ	DE	8,130	LC
Delta State Univ	MS	7,709	C
DePaul Univ	IL	29,835	VC
DePauw Univ	IN	32,100	HC
Dickinson State Univ	ND	7,847	NC
Dillard Univ	LA	17,500	C
Doane College	NE	22,458	C
Dominican College	NY	26,630	LC
Dordt College	IA	20,325	VC
Dowling College	NY	22,110	LC
Drake Univ	IA	27,632	VC+
Drury Univ	MO	20,117	VC
Duquesne Univ	PA	29,534	VC
D'Youville College	NY	23,660	C
East Carolina Univ	NC	10,000	C
East Central Univ	OK	6,207	C
East Stroudsburg Univ of Pennsylvania	PA	10,336	C
East Texas Baptist Univ	TX	16,713	C
Eastern Conn State Univ	CT	13,554	C
Eastern Illinois Univ	IL	12,569	C
Eastern Kentucky Univ	KY	7,725	C
Eastern Mennonite Univ	VA	25,450	VC
Eastern Mich Univ	MI	12,897	C
Eastern Nazarene College	MA	19,500	LC
Eastern New Mexico Univ	NM	7,264	C
Eastern Univ	PA	24,075	C
Eastern Washington Univ	WA	10,608	C
Edgewood College	WI	22,862	C
Edinboro Univ of Pennsylvania	PA	11,809	LC
Edward Waters College	FL	14,374	LC
Elizabeth City State Univ	NC	5,700	LC
Elizabethtown College	PA	32,100	VC
Elmhurst College	IL	24,685	C
Elmira College	NY	37,200	VC
Elon Univ	NC	25,371	HC
Emmanuel College	MA	32,000	C+
Emporia State Univ	KS	8,093	C
Erskine College	SC	25,468	VC
Eureka College	IL	19,280	C
Evangel Univ	MO	17,380	C
Fairmont State	WV	8,400	LC
Faulkner Univ	AL	15,600	C
Fayetteville State Univ	NC	6,000	LC
Felician College	NJ	24,300	C
Fitchburg State College	MA	11,276	C
Five Towns College	NY	24,600	SP
Flagler College	FL	13,790	VC+
Florida A&M Univ	FL	8,344	C
Florida Atlantic Univ	FL	11,221	C
Florida Gulf Coast Univ	FL	10,833	C
Florida International Univ	FL	9,215	VC
Florida Memorial College	FL	6,000	LC
Florida Southern College	FL	25,965	C
Florida State Univ	FL	9,028	HC
Fontbonne Univ	MO	23,308	C
Fort Hays State Univ	KS	7,638	C
Framingham State College	MA	11,156	C
Francis Marion Univ	SC	11,114	C
Franciscan Univ of Steubenville	OH	20,300	VC
Franklin College	IN		C
Franklin Pierce College	NH	31,700	C
Freed-Hardeman Univ	TN	16,370	NC
Friends Univ	KS	16,250	LC
Frostburg State Univ	MD	12,672	C
Furman Univ	SC	33,264	HC+
Gallaudet Univ	DC	16,554	
Gannon Univ	PA	26,100	C
Gardner-Webb Univ	NC	21,500	C
Geneva College	PA	21,853	C
George Fox Univ	OR	28,490	C
Georgetown College	KY	24,950	C+
Georgia Southwestern State Univ	GA	6,035	C

School	ST	$IS	SR
Georgian Court College	NJ	20,000	LC
Gettysburg College	PA	39,864	HC
Glenville State College	WV	8,778	NC
Gordon College	MA	29,194	C+
Goshen College	IN	22,850	VC
Goucher College	MD	36,225	VC
Grace Bible College	MI	18,810	C
Grace College	IN	22,170	C
Graceland Univ	IA	19,700	C
Grambling State Univ	LA	6,538	NC
Grand Canyon Univ	AZ	32,000	LC
Grand Valley State Univ	MI	10,000	VC
Grand View College	IA	21,482	C
Green Mountain College	VT	32,164	C
Greensboro College	NC	23,000	C
Greenville College	IL	23,146	C
Grove City College	PA	15,784	HC+
Gustavus Adolphus College	MN	30,920	HC
Gwynedd-Mercy College	PA	26,080	C
Hamline Univ	MN	27,070	VC
Hannibal-LaGrange College	MO	16,390	C
Harding Univ	AR	16,512	LC
Hardin-Simmons Univ	TX	18,641	C
Harris-Stowe State College	MO	3,200	SP
Hastings College	NE	22,218	VC
Heidelberg College	OH	23,242	C
Hellenic College/Holy Cross Greek Orthodox School of Theology	MA	24,975	C
Henderson State Univ	AR	7,600	C
Hendrix College	AR	27,646	HC+
Heritage Univ	WA	6,800	NC
High Point Univ	NC	25,720	C
Hillsdale College	MI	24,160	HC
Hiram College	OH	28,700	VC
Hofstra Univ	NY	32,630	VC
Holy Family Univ	PA	25,740	C
Hood College	MD	30,085	HC
Hope College	MI	28,208	VC+
Houghton College	NY	25,980	VC+
Houston Baptist Univ	TX	18,660	C
Howard Payne Univ	TX	17,115	C
Howard Univ	DC	18,481	C+
Humboldt State Univ	CA	11,176	C
Huntington Univ	IN	24,830	C
Huron Univ	SD	10,700	C
Huston-Tillotson Univ	TX	14,232	LC
Idaho State Univ	ID	9,030	C
Illinois College	IL	21,900	C+
Illinois State Univ	IL	12,839	C+
Immaculata Univ	PA	25,350	C
Indiana State Univ	IN	11,604	C
Indiana Univ Bloomington	IN	13,356	VC
Indiana Univ East	IN	4,806	LC
Indiana Univ Kokomo	IN	4,835	LC
Indiana Univ Northwest	IN	4,902	LC
Indiana Univ of Pennsylvania	PA	11,209	C
Indiana Univ South Bend	IN	4,989	LC
Indiana Univ Southeast	IN	4,880	LC
Indiana Univ-Purdue Univ Fort Wayne	IN	5,067	LC
Indiana Univ-Purdue Univ Indianapolis	IN	10,959	C
Indiana Wesleyan Univ	IN	22,074	C+
Inter American Univ of PR/ Aguadilla Campus	PR	3,784	
Inter American Univ of PR/ Arecibo Campus	PR	3,350	
Inter American Univ of PR/ Barranquitas Regional College	PR	3,350	
Inter American Univ of PR/ Fajardo Campus	PR	4,000	
Inter American Univ of PR/ Metropolitan Campus	PR	4,320	
Inter American Univ of PR/ Ponce Regional College	PR	3,700	
Inter American Univ of PR/ San German	PR	6,720	
Iona College	NY	30,878	VC
Iowa State Univ	IA	11,831	VC
Iowa Wesleyan College	IA	22,140	C
Jackson State Univ	MS	8,500	C
Jacksonville State Univ	AL	7,618	LC
Jacksonville Univ	FL	24,040	C
Jamestown College	ND	14,130	NC
Jarvis Christian College	TX	11,136	NC
John Brown Univ	AR	20,910	VC
John Carroll Univ	OH	27,658	C+
Johnson C. Smith Univ	NC	20,000	C
Johnson State College	VT	11,830	VC
Judson College	AL	16,522	C
Judson College	IL	25,130	C
Juniata College	PA	33,130	LC
Kansas State Univ	KS	10,516	VC
Kean Univ	NJ	15,880	C
Keene State College	NH	13,836	C
Kennesaw State Univ	GA	12,152	C
Kent State Univ	OH	14,594	C
Kentucky Christian College	KY	12,680	C
Kentucky State Univ	KY	10,089	LC
Kentucky Wesleyan College	KY	18,590	C
Keuka College	NY	26,050	C
Keystone College	PA	22,810	LC
King College	TN	23,400	C
King's College	PA	29,810	C
Knox College	IL	32,385	VC+
Knoxville College	TN	6,200	LC
Kutztown Univ of Pennsylvania	PA	10,820	C
La Roche College	PA	24,724	LC
La Salle Univ	PA	34,950	C
La Sierra Univ	CA	24,327	C+
Lake Superior State Univ	MI	12,842	LC
Lakeland College	WI	22,990	C
Lamar Univ	TX	6,820	LC
Lambuth Univ	TN	21,700	C+
Lander Univ	SC	10,600	C
Langston Univ	OK	2,308	LC
Lasell College	MA	26,250	C
Le Moyne College	NY	29,570	VC
Lebanon Valley College	PA	31,700	VC
Lee Univ	TN	14,780	NC
Lees-McRae College	NC	23,000	C
Lenoir-Rhyne College	NC	25,580	C
Lesley Univ	MA	34,950	C
LeTourneau Univ	TX	21,200	C
Lewis Univ	IL	23,050	C+
Lewis-Clark State College	ID	6,990	C
Liberty Univ	VA	19,101	C
Limestone College	SC	19,840	C
Lincoln Memorial Univ	TN	18,144	C
Lincoln Univ	MO	8,000	NC
Lincoln Univ	PA	13,658	C+
Lindenwood Univ	MO	18,600	VC
Lindsey Wilson College	KY	16,425	LC
Linfield College	OR	29,632	VC
Lipscomb Univ	TN	20,967	VC
Livingstone College	NC	17,815	LC
Lock Haven Univ of Pennsylvania	PA	12,098	LC
LIU/Brooklyn Campus	NY	25,000	C
LIU/C.W. Post Campus	NY	28,282	C
Longwood Univ	VA	12,426	C
Loras College	IA	27,193	C
Louisiana College	LA	13,450	C
Louisiana State Univ and A&M College	LA	10,749	VC
Louisiana State Univ in Shreveport	LA	2,900	NC
Louisiana Tech Univ	LA	7,370	C
Loyola College in Maryland	MD	38,898	HC
Loyola Univ Chicago	IL	32,896	VC
Loyola Univ New Orleans	LA	31,050	VC+
Lubbock Christian Univ	TX	16,960	C
Luther College	IA	28,800	VC+
Lyndon State College	VT	14,233	LC
Lynn Univ	FL	30,750	C
MacMurray College	IL	20,755	C
Manchester College	IN	23,470	C
Manhattan College	NY	29,000	VC
Mansfield Univ	PA	11,300	C
Marian College	IN	26,160	C
Marian College of Fond du Lac	WI	21,775	LC
Mars Hill College	NC	19,000	LC
Marshall Univ	WV	9,116	C
Marymount Manhattan College	NY	30,049	VC
Maryville College	TN	29,224	VC
Maryville Univ of St. Louis	MO	23,000	C
Marywood Univ	PA	30,680	C
Master's College and Seminary	CA	25,850	VC
Mayville State Univ	ND	8,667	NC
McKendree College	IL	24,800	VC
McMurry Univ	TX	18,100	LC
McNeese State Univ	LA	5,270	LC
McPherson College	KS	21,010	C
Medaille College	NY	21,000	C
Mercer Univ	GA	27,525	VC+
Mercy College	NY	20,000	NC
Mercyhurst College	PA	28,633	VC
Merrimack College	MA	34,380	C
Messiah College	PA	28,910	VC+
Methodist College	NC	21,000	C
Miami Univ	OH	29,097	HC
MidAmerica Nazarene Univ	KS	20,584	LC
Midland Lutheran College	NE	18,600	C
Miles College	AL	9,922	NC
Millersville Univ of Pennsylvania	PA	12,113	C
Millikin Univ	IL	25,590	C
Millsaps College	MS	28,256	VC+
Minn State Univ, Mankato	MN	10,276	LC
Minn State Univ, Moorhead	MN	7,000	LC
Minot State Univ	ND	6,700	LC
Miss College	MS	14,574	VC
Miss State Univ	MS	9,577	C
Miss Univ for Women	MS	6,000	LC
Miss Valley State Univ	MS	7,970	C
Missouri Baptist Univ	MO	19,640	C
Missouri Southern State Univ	MO	8,396	NC
Missouri State Univ	MO	10,748	C+
Missouri Valley College	MO	18,500	C
Missouri Western State Univ	MO	9,534	NC
Molloy College	NY	16,510	C
Monmouth College	IL	23,700	C
Montana State Univ-Billings	MT	8,906	C
Montana State Univ-Bozeman	MT	1,137	C
Montana State Univ-Northern	MT	10,000	NC
Montreat College	NC	21,440	C
Moravian College	PA	28,950	VC
Morehead State Univ	KY	9,150	C
Morgan State Univ	MD	12,080	C
Morningside College	IA	23,704	C
Morris College	SC	11,999	C
Mount Aloysius College	PA	20,900	LC
Mount Marty College	SD	20,590	C
Mount Mary College	WI	22,895	C
Mount Mercy College	IA	23,670	C
Mount St. Mary College	NY	25,250	C
Mount St. Mary's College	CA	32,086	VC
Mount St. Mary's Univ	MD	30,930	C
Mount Union College	OH	25,840	C
Mount Vernon Nazarene Univ	OH	20,810	C
Murray State Univ	KY	8,900	NC
Muskingum College	OH	22,970	C
National-Louis Univ	IL	16,915	LC
Nazareth College of Rochester	NY	28,175	VC
Nebr Wesleyan Univ	NE	23,415	C+
Neumann College	PA	25,996	LC
New England College	NH	31,466	C
New Jersey City Univ	NJ	13,695	LC
New Mexico Highlands Univ	NM	6,272	NC
New Mexico State Univ	NM	9,250	C
New York Inst of Technology	NY	28,126	VC
New York Univ	NY	43,170	MC
Newberry College	SC	23,000	C
Newman Univ	KS	21,106	C
Niagara Univ	NY	28,250	C
Nicholls State Univ	LA	6,500	NC
N Car Central Univ	NC	9,000	LC
N Car Wesleyan College	NC	22,670	C
North Central College	IL	28,926	VC
North Central Univ	MN	16,646	LC
N Dak State Univ	ND	8,500	C
North Georgia College and State Univ	GA	7,000	C
North Park Univ	IL	24,050	C
Northeastern Illinois Univ	IL	3,000	NC
Northeastern State Univ	OK	5,896	LC
Northeastern Univ	MA	35,742	NC
Northern Arizona Univ	AZ	10,353	C
Northern Illinois Univ	IL	13,178	C
Northern Kentucky Univ	KY	6,670	NC
Northern Mich Univ	MI	12,340	LC
Northern State Univ	SD	8,257	C
Northland College	WI	26,680	C+
Northwest Christian College	OR	24,298	C
Northwest Missouri State Univ	MO	10,000	C
Northwest Nazarene Univ	ID	22,590	VC
Northwest Univ	WA	18,854	C
Northwestern College	MN	25,220	NC
Northwestern College of Iowa	IA	22,174	C+
Northwestern Okla State Univ	OK	6,250	NC
Northwestern State Univ of Louisiana	LA	7,144	C
Notre Dame College	OH	20,425	C
Nova Southeastern Univ	FL	24,320	C
Nyack College	NY	18,540	C
Oakland City Univ	IN	19,620	NC
Oakland Univ	MI	11,936	C
Oakwood College	AL	14,904	C
Oglala Lakota College	SD	1,950	NC
Ohio State Univ at Mansfield	OH	3,606	NC
Ohio State Univ at Marion	OH	4,801	NC
Ohio State Univ at Newark	OH	11,347	NC
Ohio Univ	OH	15,921	C
Ohio Valley Univ	WV	17,752	C
Ohio Wesleyan Univ	OH	35,830	VC+
Okla Baptist Univ	OK	17,986	VC
Okla Christian Univ	OK	18,992	NC
Okla City Univ	OK	23,965	VC
Okla Panhandle State Univ	OK	7,635	NC
Okla State Univ	OK	10,213	VC
Okla Wesleyan Univ	OK	18,950	NC
Old Dominion Univ	VA	11,907	C
Olivet College	MI	19,984	C+
Olivet Nazarene Univ	IL	22,590	C
Oral Roberts Univ	OK	22,650	C
Ottawa Univ	KS	12,000	LC
Otterbein College	OH	28,986	C
Ouachita Baptist Univ	AR	21,900	C
Our Lady of Holy Cross College	LA	8,090	LC
Pace Univ	NY	30,000	VC
Palm Beach Atlantic Univ	FL	23,597	VC
Park Univ	MO	11,592	C
Penn State Univ/Univ Park Campus	PA	18,038	HC
Pepperdine Univ	CA	39,960	HC
Peru State College	NE	6,350	NC
Pfeiffer Univ	NC	21,900	C
Pikeville College	KY	16,500	NC
Pittsburg State Univ	KS	8,112	C
Point Park Univ	PA	24,160	C
Pontifical Catholic Univ of PR/Ponce	PR	7,310	
Presbyterian College	SC	30,044	VC
Prescott College	AZ	13,445	LC
Principia College	IL	27,765	VC+
Providence College	RI	34,580	HC
Purdue Univ/Calumet	IN	10,891	LC
Purdue Univ/West Lafayette	IN	13,458	VC
Queens Univ of Charlotte	NC	24,528	C
Quincy Univ	IL	24,920	C
Rhode Island College	RI	11,570	C
Rider Univ	NJ	32,560	C
Ripon College	WI	27,160	C+
Rivier College	NH	26,600	C
Robert Morris Univ	PA	22,822	C
Roberts Wesleyan College	NY	26,378	C
Rockford College	IL	28,330	VC
Rockhurst Univ	MO	25,440	VC
Rocky Mountain College	MT	20,805	C
Roger Williams Univ	RI	30,500	C
Rollins College	FL	38,366	VC
Roosevelt Univ	IL	22,605	VC
Rowan Univ	NJ	16,000	VC
Russell Sage College	NY	27,000	C
Rust College	MS		C+
Saginaw Valley State Univ	MI	11,432	C
St. Ambrose Univ	IA	25,495	C
St. Andrews Presbyterian College	NC	23,530	C
St. Augustine's College	NC	14,100	LC
St. Bonaventure Univ	NY	28,785	C
St. Cloud State Univ	MN	10,010	C
St. Francis College	NY	19,974	LC
St. Francis Univ	PA	25,880	LC
St. John's Univ	MN	29,749	VC
St. John's Univ	NY	34,370	C
St. Joseph's College	IN	26,600	C
St. Joseph's College of Maine	ME	29,185	C
St. Joseph's College, New York, Brooklyn Campus	NY	12,206	C
St. Joseph's Univ	PA	37,428	VC
St. Leo Univ	FL	22,140	C+
St. Martin's Univ	WA	27,555	C
St. Mary-of-the-Woods College	IN	25,480	C
St. Mary's College	IN	32,538	VC
St. Mary's Univ of San Antonio	TX	22,444	C
St. Michael's College	VT	33,330	VC
St. Norbert College	WI	28,577	C+
St. Paul's College	VA	16,030	NC
St. Peter's College	NJ	30,160	LC
St. Thomas Aquinas College	NY	22,000	LC
St. Thomas Univ	FL	23,490	C
St. Xavier Univ	IL	23,160	C
Salem International Univ	WV	18,020	C
Salisbury Univ	MD	13,128	NC
Salve Regina Univ	RI	33,450	C
Samford Univ	AL	20,258	VC
San Francisco State Univ	CA	13,000	C
Schreiner Univ	TX	20,600	C
Seton Hall Univ	NJ	33,622	VC
Seton Hill Univ	PA	28,810	C
Shaw Univ	NC	15,488	LC
Shawnee State Univ	OH	12,237	NC
Sheldon Jackson College	AK	17,900	LC
Shepherd Univ	WV	10,066	C
Shippensburg Univ of Pennsylvania	PA	11,621	C
Siena Heights Univ	MI	17,000	C
Silver Lake College of the Holy Family	WI	18,500	LC
Simmons College	MA	35,640	VC
Simpson College	IA	26,833	VC
Simpson Univ	CA	22,900	C
Sinte Gleska Univ	SD	2,300	NC
Skidmore College	NY	41,779	HC
Slippery Rock Univ of Pennsylvania	PA	10,360	LC
Smith College	MA	41,474	MC
S Car State Univ	SC	6,700	LC
Southeast Missouri State Univ	MO	10,596	C
Southeastern Louisiana Univ	LA	8,521	LC
Southeastern Okla State Univ	OK	6,147	C
Southeastern Univ	FL	17,180	LC
Southern Adventist Univ	TN	18,500	C
Southern Arkansas Univ	AR	6,956	C
Southern Conn State Univ	CT	10,310	C
Southern Illinois Univ Carbondale	IL	12,391	C
Southern Illinois Univ Edwardsville	IL	11,022	C
Southern Methodist Univ	TX	36,088	VC+
Southern Nazarene Univ	OK	14,634	NC
Southern New Hampshire Univ	NH	28,764	C
Southern Univ and A&M College	LA	8,238	LC
Southern Univ at New Orleans	LA	1,000	NC

ST = STATE $IS = IN-STATE COSTS   SR = SELECTOR RATING

School	ST	$IS	SR
Southern Utah Univ	UT		C
Southern Wesleyan Univ	SC	21,675	C
Southwest Baptist Univ	MO	18,300	C
Southwest Minn State Univ	MN	10,975	C
Southwestern Adventist Univ	TX	18,290	LC
Southwestern College	KS	21,476	C
Southwestern Okla State Univ	OK	4,801	C
Spalding Univ	KY	18,882	C
Spring Hill College	AL	28,678	C
Springfield College	MA	25,000	C
SUNY at Oswego	NY	13,662	VC
SUNY at Potsdam	NY	12,959	C
SUNY/College at Buffalo	NY	11,903	C+
SUNY/College at Fredonia	NY	12,771	VC
SUNY/College at Geneseo	NY	12,910	HC+
SUNY/College at Old Westbury	NY	13,154	C
SUNY/College at Oneonta	NY	12,905	VC
SUNY/College at Plattsburgh	NY	12,362	C
SUNY/Univ at New Paltz	NY	12,480	VC
Stephens College	MO	26,930	VC
Sterling College	KS	19,992	C
Stetson Univ	FL	32,725	VC
Stillman College	AL	11,475	LC
Suffolk Univ	MA	33,160	C
Sul Ross State Univ	TX	6,600	LC
Susquehanna Univ	PA	33,465	VC
Syracuse Univ	NY	38,655	HC
Tabor College	KS	21,614	NC
Taylor Univ	IN	26,376	VC+
Temple Univ	PA	17,438	C
Texas A&M Univ	TX	13,351	HC
Texas A&M Univ at Commerce	TX	9,020	C
Texas A&M Univ at Kingsville	TX	6,800	LC
Texas Christian Univ	TX	23,410	VC+
Texas State Univ - San Marcos	TX	10,862	C
Texas Wesleyan Univ	TX	18,700	C
Thiel College	PA	24,580	C
Thomas College	ME	23,770	LC
Thomas More College	KY	24,470	C
Tougaloo College	MS	15,975	NC
Touro College	NY	17,000	VC
Towson Univ	MD	13,924	VC
Transylvania Univ	KY	26,240	VC+
Trinity Bible College	ND		
Trinity Christian College	IL	23,645	C
Trinity College	DC	24,150	LC
Trinity International Univ	IL	25,686	C
Tri-State Univ-Main Campus	IN	26,200	C
Troy Univ	AL	8,916	C
Troy Univ Dothan Campus	AL	4,678	C
Turabo Univ	PR	4,110	C
Tusculum College	TN	21,340	LC
Tuskegee Univ	AL	18,860	LC
Union College	KY	18,920	C
Union College	NE	18,710	C
Union Univ	TN	20,750	VC
Universidad Adventista de las Antillas	PR	7,360	
Universidad Metropolitana	PR	3,330	
Univ of Akron	OH	15,166	NC
Univ of Alabama	AL	9,888	C
Univ of Alabama at Birmingham	AL	13,716	C
Univ of Alaska Anchorage	AK	11,275	NC
Univ of Alaska Fairbanks	AK	10,101	C
Univ of Alaska Southeast	AK	8,050	LC
Univ of Arizona	AZ	11,958	VC
Univ of Arkansas	AR	11,859	VC
Univ of Arkansas at Little Rock	AR	7,230	NC
Univ of Central Arkansas	AR	9,984	C
Univ of Central Florida	FL	10,739	VC
Univ of Central Okla	OK	8,094	C
Univ of Cincinnati	OH	17,682	C
Univ of Conn	CT	16,628	HC
Univ of Dallas	TX	27,432	VC+
Univ of Dayton	OH	28,826	VC
Univ of Delaware	DE	14,142	HC
Univ of Detroit Mercy	MI	27,000	C
Univ of Evansville	IN	28,320	VC
Univ of Findlay	OH	29,238	C
Univ of Florida	FL	9,354	HC
Univ of Great Falls	MT	17,000	C
Univ of Hartford	CT	34,044	C
Univ of Hawaii at Manoa	HI	10,413	VC
Univ of Houston-Downtown	TX	3,326	NC
Univ of Idaho	ID	9,310	NC
Univ of Illinois at Chicago	IL	16,256	VC
Univ of Illinois at Urbana-Champaign	IL	15,800	HC+
Univ of Indianapolis	IN	25,090	C
Univ of Iowa	IA	12,172	VC
Univ of Kansas	KS	10,915	VC
Univ of Kentucky	KY	7,800	VC
Univ of Louisiana at Lafayette	LA	5,830	C
Univ of Louisiana at Monroe	LA	7,103	C
Univ of Louisville	KY	10,400	VC

School	ST	$IS	SR
Univ of Maine	ME	13,642	C
Univ of Maine at Farmington	ME	11,515	C
Univ of Maine at Fort Kent	ME	10,832	LC
Univ of Maine at Machias	ME	10,523	C
Univ of Maine at Presque Isle	ME	10,066	LC
Univ of Mary	ND	15,374	C
Univ of Mary Hardin-Baylor	TX	19,428	C
Univ of Maryland/College Park	MD	16,036	HC
Univ of Maryland/Eastern Shore	MD	11,210	C
Univ of Mass Amherst	MA	15,973	C+
Univ of Memphis	TN	11,153	C
Univ of Miami	FL	38,397	MC
Univ of Mich/Ann Arbor	MI	16,587	HC+
Univ of Mich/Dearborn	MI	7,000	VC
Univ of Mich/Flint	MI	6,398	C
Univ of Minn/Duluth	MN	13,974	C
Univ of Minn/Morris	MN	15,472	VC
Univ of Minn/Twin Cities	MN	13,165	HC
Univ of Miss	MS	9,000	C
Univ of Missouri/Columbia	MO	13,500	VC
Univ of Missouri/Kansas City	MO	15,000	VC
Univ of Missouri/St. Louis	MO	14,046	VC
Univ of Mobile	AL	16,880	C
Univ of Montana	MT	10,602	C
Univ of Montana--Western	MT	8,406	NC
Univ of Montevallo	AL	9,630	C
Univ of Nebr at Kearney	NE	9,000	VC
Univ of Nebr at Lincoln	NE	11,401	VC
Univ of Nebr at Omaha	NE	11,235	C
Univ of Nevada/Las Vegas	NV	11,566	C
Univ of Nevada/Reno	NV	12,155	NC
Univ of New England	ME	31,005	C
Univ of New Mexico	NM	11,253	C
Univ of New Orleans	LA	7,370	C
Univ of North Alabama	AL	8,992	C
Univ of N Car at Chapel Hill	NC	11,129	MC
Univ of N Car at Charlotte	NC	9,101	C
Univ of N Car at Greensboro	NC	8,993	C
Univ of N Car at Pembroke	NC	7,940	LC
Univ of N Car at Wilmington	NC	10,107	VC
Univ of N Dak	ND	10,114	VC
Univ of North Florida	FL	9,908	VC
Univ of North Texas	TX	7,800	C
Univ of Northern Iowa	IA	11,133	C
Univ of Okla	OK	10,769	VC+
Univ of Pennsylvania	PA	41,766	MC
Univ of Pittsburgh at Bradford	PA	17,008	C
Univ of Pittsburgh at Johnstown	PA	16,740	LC
Univ of Portland	OR	32,300	VC
Univ of PR at Humacao	PR	1,707	C
Univ of PR/Arecibo	PR	8,327	
Univ of PR/Bayamon Univ College Campus	PR	1,600	
Univ of PR/Cayey Univ College	PR	1,250	
Univ of PR/Rio Piedras	PR	5,750	
Univ of Rhode Island	RI	15,398	C
Univ of Rio Grande	OH	8,728	NC
Univ of St. Francis	IL	25,430	C
Univ of St. Francis	IN	20,970	C
Univ of St. Mary	KS	18,900	C
Univ of St. Thomas	MN	28,000	VC
Univ of San Diego	CA	40,620	HC
Univ of San Francisco	CA	37,560	VC
Univ of Science and Arts of Okla	OK	7,650	C
Univ of Scranton	PA	31,100	VC
Univ of Sioux Falls	SD	20,800	C
Univ of South Alabama	AL	8,930	C
Univ of S Car at Aiken	SC	11,718	LC
Univ of S Car at Columbia	SC	13,397	VC
Univ of S Car Upstate	SC	11,957	C
Univ of S Dak	SD	9,068	C
Univ of South Florida	FL	10,284	VC
Univ of Southern Indiana	IN	12,590	LC
Univ of Southern Miss	MS	10,112	C
Univ of Tampa	FL	25,784	C
Univ of Tenn at Knoxville	TN	11,720	C
Univ of Tenn at Martin	TN	8,693	C
Univ of the Cumberlands	KY	18,184	C
Univ of the District of Columbia	DC	2,070	LC
Univ of the Incarnate Word	TX	23,306	C
Univ of the Sacred Heart	PR	5,590	
Univ of Toledo	OH	15,806	NC
Univ of Tulsa	OK	25,348	NC
Univ of Utah	UT	10,162	VC
Univ of Vermont	VT	18,080	VC
Univ of West Alabama	AL	7,611	C
Univ of West Florida	FL	8,559	C
Univ of Wisc/Eau Claire	WI	9,915	VC
Univ of Wisc/La Crosse	WI	10,045	VC
Univ of Wisc/Madison	WI	13,117	HC
Univ of Wisc/Oshkosh	WI	10,426	LC
Univ of Wisc/Platteville	WI	9,779	NC
Univ of Wisc/River Falls	WI	9,722	LC
Univ of Wisc/Stevens Point	WI	9,384	VC
Univ of Wisc/Superior	WI	9,610	C

School	ST	$IS	SR
Univ of Wisc/Whitewater	WI	9,274	C
Univ of Wyoming	WY	9,666	C
Upper Iowa Univ	IA	20,130	C
Urbana Univ	OH	21,190	C
Ursuline College	OH	25,456	C
Utah State Univ	UT	8,002	VC
Valley City State Univ	ND	9,854	LC
Valparaiso Univ	IN	28,970	VC+
Vanderbilt Univ	TN	41,986	MC
Vanguard Univ of Southern Calif	CA	27,071	C
Villa Julie College	MD	25,222	C
Villanova Univ	PA	38,672	HC+
Virginia Union Univ	VA	18,432	LC
Virginia Wesleyan College	VA	28,433	C
Viterbo Univ	WI	21,670	C
Wagner College	NY	33,300	VC
Walla Walla College	WA	24,489	NC
Walsh Univ	OH	23,440	VC
Warner Southern College	FL	18,000	LC
Warren Wilson College	NC	24,382	VC
Wartburg College	IA	27,315	NC
Washburn Univ	KS	9,734	VC
Washington Univ in St. Louis	MO	42,106	MC
Wayne State College	NE	8,033	NC
Wayne State Univ	MI	11,805	C
Waynesburg College	PA	21,230	C
Weber State Univ	UT	9,635	NC
Wells College	NY	23,070	VC
Wesley College	DE	19,905	C
West Chester Univ of Pennsylvania	PA	12,355	C+
West Liberty State College	WV	9,142	LC
West Virginia State Univ	WV	8,378	NC
West Virginia Wesleyan College	WV	26,880	C
Western Carolina Univ	NC	7,000	C
Western Conn State Univ	CT	12,993	C
Western Illinois Univ	IL	13,042	C
Western Kentucky Univ	KY	10,192	C
Western Mich Univ	MI	13,299	C
Western New England College	MA	32,054	C
Western New Mexico Univ	NM	7,233	LC
Western State College of Colo	CO	9,942	C
Western Washington Univ	WA	11,262	VC
Westfield State College	MA	10,200	C
Westminster College	MO	19,060	VC
Westminster College	PA	31,290	C+
Westminster College	UT	25,656	C
Wheaton College	IL	27,760	HC
Wheelock College	MA	33,075	C
Whitworth College	WA	29,428	VC+
Wichita State Univ	KS	8,500	C
Widener Univ	PA	27,275	C
Wiley College	TX	8,100	LC
Wilkes Univ	PA	30,886	C
William Carey College	MS	11,000	LC
William Jewell College	MO	24,340	C
William Penn Univ	IA	17,685	LC
William Woods Univ	MO	21,020	C
Williams Baptist College	AR	13,450	C
Wilmington College	DE	5,594	NC
Wilmington College	OH	2,806	NC
Wilson College	PA	27,660	C
Wingate Univ	NC	23,300	C
Winona State Univ	MN	11,333	C
Winston-Salem State Univ	NC	8,960	LC
Winthrop Univ	SC	11,302	C
Wisc Lutheran College	WI	23,510	VC
Wittenberg Univ	OH	34,596	VC
Worcester State College	MA	12,499	C
Wright State Univ	OH	13,616	LC
Xavier Univ of Louisiana	LA	17,600	C
York College	NE	16,330	NC
York College of Pennsylvania	PA	16,550	VC
Youngstown State Univ	OH	12,613	NC

ELEMENTARY PARTICLE PHYSICS

School	ST	$IS	SR
Catholic Univ of America	DC	35,838	VC

EMERGENCY MEDICAL TECHNOLOGIES

School	ST	$IS	SR
Central Washington Univ	WA	11,730	C
Creighton Univ	NE	29,918	VC+
George Washington Univ	DC	48,820	MC
Kent State Univ	OH	14,594	C
Mountain State Univ	WV	11,406	NC
Springfield College	MA	25,000	C
Univ of Akron	OH	15,166	NC
Univ of Maryland/Baltimore County	MD	16,642	VC+
Univ of New Mexico	NM	11,253	C
Univ of Pittsburgh at Pittsburgh	PA	18,866	HC
Western Carolina Univ	NC	7,000	C

EMERGENCY/DISASTER SCIENCE

School	ST	$IS	SR
Arkansas Tech Univ	AR	8,108	VC
Thomas Edison State College	NJ	3,780	SP
Univ of Akron	OH	15,166	NC
Univ of Florida	FL	9,354	HC
Univ of North Texas	TX	7,800	C
West Texas A&M Univ	TX	8,452	C
Western Carolina Univ	NC	7,000	C

ENERGY MANAGEMENT TECHNOLOGY

School	ST	$IS	SR
CUNY/Hunter College	NY	8,000	C+
Penn State Univ/Univ Park Campus	PA	18,038	HC
Univ of Northern Iowa	IA	11,133	C

ENGINEERING

School	ST	$IS	SR
Alabama State Univ	AL	7,658	C
Andrews Univ	MI	21,786	C
Arcadia Univ	PA	33,570	VC
Arizona State Univ-Tempe	AZ	11,174	C
Arkansas State Univ	AR	9,630	C
Bates College	ME	42,100	MC
Baylor Univ	TX	27,555	HC
Boston Univ	MA	42,046	HC+
Brown Univ	RI	42,015	MC
Bucknell Univ	PA	39,660	MC
Calif Inst of Technology	CA	36,123	MC
Calif Polytechnic State Univ	CA	12,390	VC
Cal State East Bay	CA	10,856	LC
Cal State, Los Angeles	CA	5,900	C
Cal State, Northridge	CA	9,036	LC
Calvin College	MI	25,735	NC
Carnegie Mellon Univ	PA	32,700	MC
Case Western Reserve Univ	OH	37,314	MC
Catholic Univ of America	DC	35,838	VC
Central Missouri State Univ	MO	10,000	C
Clark Atlanta Univ	GA	20,960	C
Colo School of Mines	CO	14,893	HC
Cooper Union for the Advancement of Science and Art	NY	12,450	MC
Dominican Univ	IL	26,370	C
Dordt College	IA	20,325	VC
Elizabethtown College	PA	32,100	VC
Elon Univ	NC	25,371	HC
Florida Gulf Coast Univ	FL	10,833	C
Geneva College	PA	21,850	C
George Fox Univ	OR	28,490	C
George Washington Univ	DC	48,820	MC
Grand Valley State Univ	MI	12,000	VC
Harvard Univ/Harvard College	MA	45,860	MC
Harvey Mudd College	CA	42,352	MC
Hope College	MI	28,208	VC+
Idaho State Univ	ID	9,030	C
Indiana Univ-Purdue Univ Fort Wayne	IN	5,067	LC
Indiana Univ-Purdue Univ Indianapolis	IN	10,959	C
Iowa State Univ	IA	11,831	VC
John Brown Univ	AR	20,910	VC
Johns Hopkins Univ	MD	42,044	MC
Johnson C. Smith Univ	NC	20,000	C
Kent State Univ	OH	14,594	C
Lafayette College	PA	39,267	MC
Lake Superior State Univ	MI	12,842	LC
Lehigh Univ	PA	42,690	HC+
LeTourneau Univ	TX	21,200	C
Lincoln Univ	MO	8,000	NC
Lindenwood Univ	MO	18,600	VC
Lipscomb Univ	TN	20,967	VC
Loyola College in Maryland	MD	38,898	HC
Lubbock Christian Univ	TX	16,960	C
Lynchburg College	VA	30,645	C
Maine Maritime Academy	ME	14,340	C
Manchester College	IN	23,470	C
Marquette Univ	WI	31,066	HC
Maryville Univ	TN	29,224	VC
Messiah College	PA	28,910	VC+
Miami Univ	OH	29,097	HC
Mich State Univ	MI	13,689	VC
Mich Tech Univ	MI	14,569	VC
Montana Tech of The Univ of Montana	MT	10,434	C
Mount Holyoke College	MA	42,148	HC+
Mountain State Univ	WV	11,406	NC
New Mexico Highlands Univ	NM	6,272	VC
N Car State Univ	NC	11,824	HC
Northeastern Univ	MA	35,742	HC
Northern Arizona Univ	AZ	10,353	C
Northwestern Univ	IL	37,595	MC
Okla State Univ	OK	10,213	VC
Olivet Nazarene Univ	IL	22,590	C
Oral Roberts Univ	OK	22,650	C
Penn State Erie/The Behrend College	PA	16,256	C
Penn State Univ/Univ Park Campus	PA	18,038	HC

School	ST	$IS	SR
Pennsylvania College of Technology	PA	16,980	LC
Pepperdine Univ	CA	39,960	HC
Philadelphia Univ	PA	30,006	C
Purdue Univ/Calumet	IN	10,891	LC
Purdue Univ/West Lafayette	IN	13,458	VC
Regis Univ	CO	31,890	C
Rensselaer Polytechnic Inst	NY	41,288	HC+
Robert Morris Univ	PA	22,822	C
Rochester Inst of Technology	NY	32,070	VC+
Roger Williams Univ	RI	30,500	C
Rowan Univ	NJ	16,000	HC
St. Anselm College	NH	33,810	C
St. Mary's Univ of San Antonio	TX	22,444	C
San Francisco State Univ	CA	13,000	C
San Jose State Univ	CA	11,707	C
Santa Clara Univ	CA	38,931	VC
Scripps College	CA	41,000	MC
Seton Hill Univ	PA	28,810	C
Smith College	MA	41,474	MC
Spelman College	GA	24,650	VC
Spring Hill College	AL	28,678	C
Stanford Univ	CA	41,557	MC
SUNY/Maritime College	NY	12,475	C
Swarthmore College	PA	41,280	MC
Temple Univ	PA	17,438	C
Tenn Tech Univ	TN	10,044	C
Texas Christian Univ	TX	23,410	VC+
Texas Tech Univ	TX	13,026	VC
Trinity College	CT	38,040	HC+
Trinity College	DC	24,150	LC
Tufts Univ	MA	42,018	MC
Tulane Univ	LA	41,098	MC
United States Air Force Academy	CO		HC+
United States Merchant Marine Academy	NY	6,516	HC+
United States Naval Academy	MD		MC
Univ of Arizona	AZ	11,958	VC
Univ of Calif at Irvine	CA	16,475	HC
Univ of Calif at San Diego	CA	16,102	HC
Univ of Cincinnati	OH	17,682	C
Univ of Colo at Boulder	CO	13,352	C+
Univ of Detroit Mercy	MI	27,000	C
Univ of Hartford	CT	34,044	C
Univ of Illinois at Urbana-Champaign	IL	15,800	HC+
Univ of Iowa	IA	12,172	VC
Univ of Louisville	KY	10,400	VC
Univ of Maryland/College Park	MD	16,036	HC
Univ of Mass Boston	MA	8,024	C
Univ of Miami	FL	38,397	MC
Univ of Mich/Ann Arbor	MI	16,587	HC+
Univ of Mich/Flint	MI	6,398	C
Univ of Miss	MS	9,000	C
Univ of Missouri/Rolla	MO	13,332	HC
Univ of New Haven	CT	31,794	C
Univ of N Car at Greensboro	NC	8,993	C
Univ of Okla	OK	10,769	VC+
Univ of Pennsylvania	PA	41,766	MC
Univ of Pittsburgh at Bradford	PA	17,008	C
Univ of Portland	OR	32,300	VC
Univ of PR/Mayaguez	PR	1,250	
Univ of South Florida	FL	10,284	VC
Univ of Southern Indiana	IN	12,590	LC
Univ of Tenn at Chattanooga	TN	7,790	C
Univ of Tenn at Knoxville	TN	11,720	C
Univ of Tenn at Martin	TN	8,693	C
Univ of Toledo	OH	15,806	NC
Univ of Utah	UT	10,162	VC
Univ of Washington	WA	10,400	VC
Univ of Wisc/Milwaukee	WI	9,427	LC
Univ of Wisc/Platteville	WI	9,779	NC
Utah State Univ	UT	8,002	VC
Walla Walla College	WA	24,489	NC
Washington Univ in St. Louis	MO	42,106	MC
Waynesburg College	PA	21,230	C
West Virginia Univ	WV	10,506	C
Yale Univ	CT	41,000	MC
York College of Pennsylvania	PA	16,550	VC
Youngstown State Univ	OH	12,613	NC

ENGINEERING AND APPLIED SCIENCE

School	ST	$IS	SR
Abilene Christian Univ	TX	20,830	C
Benedictine Univ	IL	25,710	C
Bethel Univ	MN	29,840	VC
Calif Inst of Technology	CA	36,123	MC
Cal State, Fullerton	CA	10,990	C
CUNY/College of Staten Island	NY	4,328	NC
College of New Jersey	NJ	18,315	MC
Colo State Univ-Fort Collins	CO	10,878	C
Dartmouth College	NH	39,465	MC
Franciscan Univ of Steubenville	OH	20,300	VC

School	ST	$IS	SR
New Jersey Inst of Technology	NJ	16,396	VC
Pacific Lutheran Univ	WA	28,805	VC
Rutgers, The State Univ of New Jersey/New Brunswick/Piscataway Campus	NJ	15,810	HC
Seattle Pacific Univ	WA	29,355	C
Southern Polytechnic State Univ	GA	7,640	VC
SUNY/Univ at Stony Brook	NY	13,625	HC
Sweet Briar College	VA	31,460	VC
Trinity Univ	TX	30,157	HC+
Tufts Univ	MA	42,018	MC
United States Air Force Academy	CO		HC+
Univ of Calif at Berkeley	CA	18,141	HC+
Univ of Florida	FL	9,354	HC
Univ of Mary	ND	15,374	C
Univ of Mich/Ann Arbor	MI	16,587	HC+
Univ of Rochester	NY	41,135	MC
Univ of Tenn at Knoxville	TN	11,720	C
Univ of Virginia	VA	13,759	MC
Vanderbilt Univ	TN	41,986	MC
Wartburg College	IA	27,315	NC
Wilkes Univ	PA	30,886	C
Yale Univ	CT	41,000	MC

ENGINEERING CHEMISTRY

School	ST	$IS	SR
Cleveland Inst of Art	OH	34,109	SP
Oakland Univ	MI	11,936	C
SUNY/Univ at Stony Brook	NY	13,625	HC

ENGINEERING MANAGEMENT

School	ST	$IS	SR
Clarkson Univ	NY	34,930	VC
Columbia Univ/Fu Foundation School of Engineering and Applied Science	NY	42,584	MC
Idaho State Univ	ID	9,030	C
Kansas State Univ	KS	10,516	VC
Lake Superior State Univ	MI	12,842	LC
Miami Univ	OH	29,097	HC
N Dak State Univ	ND	8,500	C
Oral Roberts Univ	OK	22,650	C
Park Univ	MO	11,592	C
Point Park Univ	PA	24,160	C
Southern Illinois Univ Carbondale	IL	12,391	C
Southern Methodist Univ	TX	36,088	VC+
Stevens Inst of Technology	NJ	40,935	HC
Sweet Briar College	VA	31,460	VC
Texas A&M Univ at Kingsville	TX	6,800	LC
Tri-State Univ-Main Campus	IN	26,200	C
United States Military Academy	NY		MC
Univ of Evansville	IN	28,320	VC
Univ of Illinois at Chicago	IL	16,256	VC
Univ of Louisville	KY	10,400	VC
Univ of Missouri/Rolla	MO	13,332	HC
Univ of Portland	OR	32,300	VC
Univ of Tenn at Chattanooga	TN	7,790	C
Univ of the Incarnate Word	TX	23,306	C
Univ of the Pacific	CA	34,380	VC
Univ of Vermont	VT	18,080	VC
Western Mich Univ	MI	13,299	C
Wilkes Univ	PA	30,886	C
York College of Pennsylvania	PA	16,550	VC

ENGINEERING MECHANICS

School	ST	$IS	SR
Columbia Univ/Fu Foundation School of Engineering and Applied Science	NY	42,584	MC
Johns Hopkins Univ	MD	42,044	MC
Lehigh Univ	PA	42,690	HC+
Lipscomb Univ	TN	20,967	VC
Mich State Univ	MI	13,689	VC
New Mexico Inst of Mining and Technology	NM	8,510	VC+
United States Air Force Academy	CO		HC+
Univ of Cincinnati	OH	17,682	C
Univ of Illinois at Urbana-Champaign	IL	15,800	HC+
Univ of Missouri/Rolla	MO	13,332	HC
Univ of Wisc/Madison	WI	13,117	HC
Virginia Polytechnic Inst and State Univ	VA	10,834	VC
Washington Univ in St. Louis	MO	42,106	MC

ENGINEERING PHYSICS

School	ST	$IS	SR
Abilene Christian Univ	TX	20,830	C
Augustana College	IL	29,862	VC+
Augustana College	SD	24,380	VC
Bradley Univ	IL	25,280	VC

School	ST	$IS	SR
Case Western Reserve Univ	OH	37,314	MC
Christian Brothers Univ	TN	24,650	VC
Conn College	CT	41,975	MC
Cornell Univ	NY	41,717	MC
Dartmouth College	NH	39,465	MC
Eastern Nazarene College	MA	19,500	LC
Edinboro Univ of Pennsylvania	PA	11,809	LC
Elizabethtown College	PA	32,100	C
Embry-Riddle Aeronautical Univ	AZ	30,280	C+
Embry-Riddle Aeronautical Univ	FL	30,280	C
Jacksonville Univ	FL	24,040	C
John Carroll Univ	OH	27,658	C+
Juniata College	PA	33,130	VC
Lehigh Univ	PA	42,690	HC+
Loyola Marymount Univ	CA	36,321	VC
Miami Univ	OH	29,097	HC
Miss College	MS	14,574	VC
Missouri State Univ	MO	10,748	C+
Morgan State Univ	MD	12,080	C
New Mexico State Univ	NM	9,250	C
N Car Agricultural and Technical State Univ	NC	8,000	LC
Northwest Nazarene Univ	ID	22,590	VC
Oakland Univ	MI	11,936	C
Ohio State Univ	OH	15,357	HC
Okla Christian Univ	OK	18,992	NC
Point Loma Nazarene Univ	CA	27,610	VC
Rensselaer Polytechnic Inst	NY	41,288	HC+
Rose-Hulman Inst of Technology	IN	34,557	HC+
St. Ambrose Univ	IA	25,495	C
St. Bonaventure Univ	NY	28,785	LC
St. Mary's Univ of Minn	MN	23,857	VC
Samford Univ	AL	20,258	VC
Santa Clara Univ	CA	38,931	VC
S Dak State Univ	SD	9,815	C
Southeast Missouri State Univ	MO	10,596	C
Southwestern Okla State Univ	OK	4,801	C
SUNY/Univ at Buffalo	NY	13,694	VC
Stevens Inst of Technology	NJ	40,935	HC
Syracuse Univ	NY	38,655	HC
Taylor Univ	IN	26,376	VC+
Texas Tech Univ	TX	13,026	VC
Tufts Univ	MA	42,018	MC
United States Military Academy	NY		MC
Univ of Arizona	AZ	11,958	VC
Univ of Calif at Berkeley	CA	18,141	HC+
Univ of Calif at San Diego	CA	16,102	HC
Univ of Central Okla	OK	8,094	C
Univ of Colo at Boulder	CO	13,352	C+
Univ of Illinois at Chicago	IL	16,256	VC
Univ of Illinois at Urbana-Champaign	IL	15,800	HC+
Univ of Kansas	KS	10,915	VC
Univ of Maine	ME	13,642	C
Univ of Mass Boston	MA	8,024	C
Univ of Mich/Ann Arbor	MI	16,587	HC+
Univ of Nebr at Omaha	NE	11,235	C
Univ of Nevada/Reno	NV	12,155	NC
Univ of Okla	OK	10,769	VC+
Univ of Pittsburgh at Pittsburgh	PA	18,866	HC
Univ of Tenn at Knoxville	TN	11,720	C
Univ of the Pacific	CA	34,380	VC
Univ of Tulsa	OK	25,348	HC
Univ of Wisc/Madison	WI	13,117	HC
Washington and Lee Univ	VA	35,880	MC
Washington Univ in St. Louis	MO	42,106	MC
West Virginia Wesleyan College	WV	26,880	C
Westmont College	CA	36,672	HC
Worcester Polytechnic Inst	MA	40,450	HC+
Wright State Univ	OH	13,616	LC

ENGINEERING TECHNOLOGY

School	ST	$IS	SR
Austin Peay State Univ	TN	7,535	C
Bluefield State College	WV	3,140	LC
Calif Maritime Academy	CA	13,490	C
Calif State Polytechnic Univ, Pomona	CA	18,053	C+
Cal State, Long Beach	CA	9,512	C
Cal State, Sacramento	CA	11,122	C+
Calif Univ of Pennsylvania	PA	14,217	C
Capitol College	MD	21,250	C
Central Mich Univ	MI	12,244	C
Central Missouri State Univ	MO	10,000	C
Central Washington Univ	WA	11,730	C
East Tenn State Univ	TN	8,497	C
Embry-Riddle Aeronautical Univ	FL	30,280	C
Fairmont State	WV	8,400	C
Ferris State Univ	MI	13,698	C
Florida A&M Univ	FL	8,344	C
Gallaudet Univ	DC	16,554	
Georgia Southern Univ	GA	9,762	C
Grambling State Univ	LA	6,538	NC
Indiana Univ Northwest	IN	4,902	LC

School	ST	$IS	SR
Indiana Univ-Purdue Univ Fort Wayne	IN	5,067	LC
Iowa State Univ	IA	11,831	VC
Kansas State Univ	KS	10,516	VC
Kent State Univ	OH	14,594	C
Lake Superior State Univ	MI	12,842	LC
Lawrence Tech Univ	MI	25,475	VC
LeTourneau Univ	TX	21,200	C
Maine Maritime Academy	ME	14,340	C
Miami Univ	OH	29,097	HC
Middle Tenn State Univ	TN	8,540	C
Midwestern State Univ	TX	9,381	LC
Milwaukee School of Engineering	WI	29,847	VC+
Minn State Univ, Mankato	MN	10,276	LC
Missouri Western State Univ	MO	9,534	NC
Montana State Univ-Northern	MT	10,000	NC
Murray State Univ	KY	8,900	VC
New Jersey Inst of Technology	NJ	16,396	VC
New Mexico State Univ	NM	9,250	C
New York Inst of Technology	NY	28,126	VC
Northeastern Univ	MA	35,742	HC
Old Dominion Univ	VA	11,907	C
Oregon Inst of Technology	OR	8,718	C
Penn State Erie/The Behrend College	PA	16,256	C
Pittsburg State Univ	KS	8,112	C
Prairie View A&M Univ	TX	11,110	LC
Purdue Univ/Calumet	IN	10,891	LC
Rochester Inst of Technology	NY	32,070	VC+
Saginaw Valley State Univ	MI	11,432	C
St. Cloud State Univ	MN	10,010	C
Savannah State Univ	GA	7,772	LC
Shawnee State Univ	OH	12,237	NC
S Car State Univ	SC	6,700	LC
S Dak State Univ	SD	9,815	C
Southern Illinois Univ Carbondale	IL	12,391	C
Southern Univ and A&M College	LA	8,238	LC
Southern Utah Univ	UT		C
Southwestern Okla State Univ	OK	4,801	C
Temple Univ	PA	17,438	C
Texas A&M Univ	TX	13,351	HC
Texas A&M Univ at Commerce	TX	9,020	C
Texas A&M Univ at Corpus Christi	TX	10,280	LC
Texas Southern Univ	TX	9,828	C
Texas State Univ - San Marcos	TX	10,862	C
Texas Tech Univ	TX	13,026	VC
Univ of Central Florida	FL	10,739	VC
Univ of Cincinnati	OH	17,682	C
Univ of Dayton	OH	28,826	VC
Univ of Delaware	DE	14,142	HC
Univ of Hartford	CT	34,044	C
Univ of Houston-Downtown	TX	3,326	NC
Univ of Maryland/Eastern Shore	MD	11,210	C
Univ of Mass Lowell	MA	14,327	VC
Univ of North Texas	TX	7,800	C
Univ of Southern Miss	MS	10,112	C
Univ of Toledo	OH	15,806	NC
Univ of Wisc/Stout	WI	11,164	C
Virginia State Univ	VA	11,318	C
West Texas A&M Univ	TX	8,452	C
West Virginia Univ Inst of Technology	WV	8,788	NC
Western Carolina Univ	NC	7,000	C
Western Washington Univ	WA	11,262	VC
Youngstown State Univ	OH	12,613	NC

ENGLISH

School	ST	$IS	SR
Abilene Christian Univ	TX	20,830	C
Adams State College	CO	8,613	C
Adelphi Univ	NY	27,000	VC
Adrian College	MI	23,000	C
Agnes Scott College	GA	32,070	VC
Alabama A&M Univ	AL	8,890	LC
Alabama State Univ	AL	7,658	C
Albany State Univ	GA	5,770	C
Albertson College of Idaho	ID	21,095	VC
Albertus Magnus College	CT	25,336	C
Albion College	MI	26,000	VC
Albright College	PA	33,920	C
Alcorn State Univ	MS	8,190	LC
Alfred Univ	NY		VC
Alice Lloyd College	KY	4,900	C
Allegheny College	PA	33,500	VC
Allen Univ	SC	10,500	NC
Alma College	MI	28,544	VC
Alvernia College	PA	26,388	C
Alverno College	WI	21,088	C
American International College	MA	28,710	LC
Amherst College	MA	41,590	MC
Anderson Univ	IN	25,050	LC
Andrews Univ	MI	21,786	C

School	ST	$IS	SR
Idaho State Univ	ID	9,030	C
Illinois College	IL	21,900	C+
Illinois State Univ	IL	12,839	C+
Illinois Wesleyan Univ	IL	34,050	HC+
Immaculata Univ	PA	25,350	C
Indiana State Univ	IN	11,604	C
Indiana Univ Bloomington	IN	13,356	VC
Indiana Univ East	IN	4,806	LC
Indiana Univ Kokomo	IN	4,835	LC
Indiana Univ Northwest	IN	4,902	LC
Indiana Univ of Pennsylvania	PA	11,209	C
Indiana Univ South Bend	IN	4,989	LC
Indiana Univ Southeast	IN	4,880	LC
Indiana Univ-Purdue Univ Fort Wayne	IN	5,067	LC
Indiana Univ-Purdue Univ Indianapolis	IN	10,959	C
Indiana Wesleyan Univ	IN	22,074	C+
Inter American Univ of PR/ San German	PR	6,720	
Iona College	NY	30,878	VC
Iowa State Univ	IA	11,831	VC
Iowa Wesleyan College	IA	22,140	C
Ithaca College	NY	35,144	VC
Jackson State Univ	MS	8,500	C
Jacksonville State Univ	AL	7,618	LC
Jacksonville Univ	FL	24,040	C
James Madison Univ	VA	12,010	VC
Jamestown College	ND	14,130	NC
Jarvis Christian College	TX	11,136	NC
John Brown Univ	AR	20,910	VC
John Carroll Univ	OH	27,658	C+
Johns Hopkins Univ	MD	42,044	MC
Johnson C. Smith Univ	NC	20,000	C
Johnson State College	VT	11,830	LC
Judson College	AL	16,522	C
Judson College	IL	25,130	C
Juniata College	PA	33,130	VC
Kalamazoo College	MI	32,442	VC+
Kansas State Univ	KS	10,516	VC
Kansas Wesleyan Univ	KS	21,400	VC
Kean Univ	NJ	15,880	C
Keene State College	NH	13,836	VC
Kennesaw State Univ	GA	12,152	C
Kent State Univ	OH	14,594	C
Kentucky State Univ	KY	10,089	LC
Kentucky Wesleyan College	KY	18,590	C
Kenyon College	OH	39,500	MC
Keuka College	NY	26,050	C
King College	TN	23,400	C
King's College	PA	29,810	C
Knoxville College	TN	6,200	LC
Kutztown Univ of Pennsylvania	PA	10,820	C
La Roche College	PA	24,724	LC
La Salle Univ	PA	34,950	C
La Sierra Univ	CA	24,327	C+
Lafayette College	PA	39,267	MC
LaGrange College	GA	22,874	C+
Lake Erie College	OH	27,725	C
Lake Forest College	IL	33,860	VC
Lake Superior State Univ	MI	12,842	LC
Lakeland College	WI	22,990	C
Lamar Univ	TX	6,820	LC
Lambuth Univ	TN	21,700	C+
Lander Univ	SC	10,600	C
Lane College	TN	11,220	C+
Langston Univ	OK	2,308	LC
Lawrence Univ	WI	33,958	HC+
Le Moyne College	NY	29,570	VC
Lebanon Valley College	PA	31,700	VC
Lee Univ	TN	14,780	NC
Lees-McRae College	NC	23,000	C
Lehigh Univ	PA	42,690	HC+
LeMoyne-Owen College	TN	13,150	LC
Lenoir-Rhyne College	NC	25,580	C
LeTourneau Univ	TX	21,200	C
Lewis and Clark College	OR	35,358	VC+
Lewis Univ	IL	23,050	C
Lewis-Clark State College	ID	6,990	C
Liberty Univ	VA	19,101	C
Limestone College	SC	19,840	C
Lincoln Memorial Univ	TN	18,144	C
Lincoln Univ	MO	8,000	NC
Lincoln Univ	PA	13,658	C+
Lindenwood Univ	MO	18,600	VC
Lindsey Wilson College	KY	16,425	LC
Linfield College	OR	29,632	VC
Lipscomb Univ	TN	20,967	VC
Livingstone College	NC	17,815	LC
Lock Haven Univ of Pennsylvania	PA	12,098	LC
LIU/Brooklyn Campus	NY	25,000	C
LIU/C.W. Post Campus	NY	28,282	C
Longwood Univ	VA	12,426	C
Louisiana College	LA	13,450	C
Louisiana State Univ and A&M College	LA	10,749	VC
Louisiana State Univ in Shreveport	LA	2,900	NC
Louisiana Tech Univ	LA	7,370	C
Lourdes College	OH	15,300	LC
Loyola College in Maryland	MD	38,898	HC
Loyola Marymount Univ	CA	36,321	VC
Loyola Univ Chicago	IL	32,896	VC
Loyola Univ New Orleans	LA	31,050	VC+
Luther College	IA	28,800	VC+
Lycoming College	PA	30,797	C+
Lynchburg College	VA	30,645	C
Lyndon State College	VT	14,233	LC
Lyon College	AR	19,990	VC
Macalester College	MN	36,500	MC
MacMurray College	IL	20,755	C
Madonna Univ	MI	16,068	VC
Malone College	OH	23,040	C
Manchester College	IN	23,470	C
Manhattan College	NY	29,000	VC
Manhattanville College	NY	32,500	C+
Mansfield Univ	PA	11,300	C
Marian College	IN	26,160	C
Marian College of Fond du Lac	WI	21,775	LC
Marietta College	OH	29,327	C
Marist College	NY	30,566	VC
Marlboro College	VT	35,980	VC+
Marquette Univ	WI	31,066	HC
Mars Hill College	NC	19,000	LC
Marshall Univ	WV	9,116	C
Mary Baldwin College	VA	26,465	C
Marygrove College	MI	19,310	C+
Marymount Manhattan College	NY	30,049	VC
Marymount Univ	VA	25,934	C
Maryville College	TN	29,224	VC
Maryville Univ of St. Louis	MO	23,000	VC
Marywood Univ	PA	30,680	C
Mass College of Liberal Arts	MA	8,725	LC
Master's College and Seminary	CA	25,850	VC
Mayville State Univ	ND	8,667	NC
McDaniel College	MD	31,610	VC
McKendree College	IL	24,800	VC
McMurry Univ	TX	18,100	LC
McNeese State Univ	LA	5,270	LC
McPherson College	KS	21,010	C
Mercer Univ	GA	27,525	VC+
Mercy College	NY	20,000	NC
Mercyhurst College	PA	28,633	VC
Meredith College	NC	25,600	C
Merrimack College	MA	34,380	C
Mesa State College	CO	8,051	C
Messiah College	PA	28,910	VC+
Methodist College	NC	21,000	C
Metropolitan State College of Denver	CO	2,338	LC
Metropolitan State Univ	MN	4,682	SP
Miami Univ	OH	29,097	HC
Mich State Univ	MI	13,689	VC
MidAmerica Nazarene Univ	KS	20,584	LC
Middle Tenn State Univ	TN	8,540	C
Middlebury College	VT	42,120	MC
Midland Lutheran College	NE	18,600	C
Midway College	KY	20,150	C
Midwestern State Univ	TX	9,381	LC
Miles College	AL	9,922	NC
Millersville Univ of Pennsylvania	PA	12,113	C
Milligan College	TN	21,990	VC
Millikin Univ	IL	25,590	C
Mills College	CA	39,870	C
Millsaps College	MS	28,256	VC+
Minn State Univ, Mankato	MN	10,276	LC
Minn State Univ, Moorhead	MN	7,000	LC
Minot State Univ	ND	6,700	LC
Miss College	MS	14,574	VC
Miss State Univ	MS	9,577	C
Miss Univ for Women	MS	6,000	LC
Miss Valley State Univ	MS	7,970	C
Missouri Baptist Univ	MO	19,640	C
Missouri Southern State Univ	MO	8,396	NC
Missouri State Univ	MO	10,748	C+
Missouri Valley College	MO	18,500	C
Missouri Western State Univ	MO	9,534	NC
Molloy College	NY	16,510	C
Monmouth College	IL	23,700	C
Monmouth Univ	NJ	28,956	C
Montana State Univ-Billings	MT	8,906	C
Montana State Univ-Bozeman	MT	1,137	C
Montana State Univ-Northern	MT	10,000	NC
Montclair State Univ	NJ	16,327	C
Montreat College	NC	21,440	C
Moravian College	PA	28,950	VC
Morehead State Univ	KY	9,150	C
Morehouse College	GA	25,082	C
Morgan State Univ	MD	12,080	C
Morningside College	IA	23,704	C
Morris College	SC	11,999	LC
Mount Aloysius College	PA	20,900	LC
Mount Holyoke College	MA	42,148	HC+
Mount Marty College	SD	20,590	C
Mount Mary College	WI	22,895	C
Mount Mercy College	IA	23,672	C
Mount Olive College	NC	16,000	LC
Mount St. Mary College	NY	25,250	C
Mount St. Mary's College	CA	32,086	VC
Mount St. Mary's Univ	MD	30,930	C
Mount Union College	OH	25,840	C
Mount Vernon Nazarene Univ	OH	20,810	C
Muhlenberg College	PA	36,030	HC+
Murray State Univ	KY	8,900	VC
Muskingum College	OH	22,970	C
National Univ	CA	8,412	SP
National-Louis Univ	IL	16,915	LC
Nazareth College of Rochester	NY	28,175	VC
Nebr Wesleyan Univ	NE	23,415	C+
Neumann College	PA	25,996	LC
New College of Calif	CA	12,842	NC
New College of Florida	FL	10,009	HC+
New Jersey City Univ	NJ	13,695	LC
New Mexico Highlands Univ	NM	6,272	NC
New Mexico State Univ	NM	9,250	C
New York Inst of Technology	NY	28,126	VC
New York Univ	NY	43,170	MC
Newberry College	SC	23,000	LC
Newman Univ	KS	21,106	C
Niagara Univ	NY	28,250	C
Nicholls State Univ	LA	6,500	NC
Nichols College	MA	28,000	LC
Norfolk State Univ	VA	10,531	C
N Car Agricultural and Technical State Univ	NC	8,000	LC
N Car Central Univ	NC	9,000	LC
N Car State Univ	NC	11,824	HC
N Car Wesleyan College	NC	22,670	C
North Central College	IL	28,926	VC
N Dak State Univ	ND	8,500	C
North Georgia College and State Univ	GA	7,000	C
North Park Univ	IL	24,050	C
Northeastern Illinois Univ	IL	3,000	NC
Northeastern State Univ	OK	5,896	LC
Northeastern Univ	MA	35,742	HC
Northern Arizona Univ	AZ	10,353	C
Northern Illinois Univ	IL	13,178	C
Northern Kentucky Univ	KY	6,670	NC
Northern Mich Univ	MI	12,340	LC
Northern State Univ	SD	8,257	C
Northland College	WI	26,680	C+
Northwest Missouri State Univ	MO	10,000	C
Northwest Nazarene Univ	ID	22,590	NC
Northwest Univ	WA	18,854	C
Northwestern College	MN	25,220	NC
Northwestern Okla State Univ	OK	6,250	NC
Northwestern State Univ of Louisiana	LA	7,144	C
Northwestern Univ	IL	37,595	MC
Norwich Univ	VT	28,212	C
Notre Dame College	OH	20,425	C
Notre Dame de Namur Univ	CA	32,790	LC
Nova Southeastern Univ	FL	24,320	C
Nyack College	NY	18,540	C
Oakland City Univ	IN	19,620	NC
Oakland Univ	MI	11,936	C
Oakwood College	AL	14,904	C
Oberlin College	OH	40,904	MC
Oglethorpe Univ	GA	30,300	VC
Ohio Dominican Univ	OH	25,954	C
Ohio Northern Univ	OH	27,765	VC
Ohio State Univ	OH	15,357	HC
Ohio State Univ at Lima	OH	4,416	NC
Ohio State Univ at Marion	OH	4,801	NC
Ohio State Univ at Newark	OH	11,347	NC
Ohio Univ	OH	15,921	C
Ohio Wesleyan Univ	OH	35,830	VC+
Okla Baptist Univ	OK	17,986	VC
Okla Christian Univ	OK	18,992	NC
Okla City Univ	OK	23,965	VC
Okla Panhandle State Univ	OK	7,635	NC
Okla State Univ	OK	10,213	VC
Okla Wesleyan Univ	OK	18,950	NC
Old Dominion Univ	VA	11,907	C
Olivet College	MI	19,984	C+
Olivet Nazarene Univ	IL	22,590	C
Oral Roberts Univ	OK	22,650	C
Oregon State Univ	OR	11,055	C
Ottawa Univ	KS	12,000	LC
Otterbein College	OH	28,986	C
Ouachita Baptist Univ	AR	21,900	VC
Our Lady of Holy Cross College	LA	8,090	LC
Our Lady of the Lake Univ of San Antonio	TX	22,430	LC
Pace Univ	NY	30,000	VC
Pacific Lutheran Univ	WA	28,805	VC
Pacific Union College	CA	24,555	VC+
Paine College	GA	14,418	LC
Palm Beach Atlantic Univ	FL	23,597	VC
Park Univ	MO	11,592	C
Paul Quinn College	TX	8,300	LC
Penn State Erie/The Behrend College	PA	16,256	C
Penn State Univ/Altoona	PA	12,635	C
Penn State Univ/Univ Park Campus	PA	18,038	HC
Pepperdine Univ	CA	39,960	HC
Peru State College	NE	6,350	NC
Piedmont College	GA	20,500	C
Pikeville College	KY	16,500	NC
Pine Manor College	MA	25,038	LC
Pittsburg State Univ	KS	8,112	C
Pitzer College	CA	41,644	HC
Plymouth State Univ	NH	12,298	LC
Point Park Univ	PA	24,160	C
Pomona College	CA	40,774	MC
Pontifical Catholic Univ of PR/Ponce	PR	7,310	
Portland State Univ	OR	12,453	C
Post Univ	CT	24,875	C
Prairie View A&M Univ	TX	11,110	LC
Presbyterian College	SC	30,044	VC
Prescott College	AZ	13,445	LC
Princeton Univ	NJ	40,213	MC
Principia College	IL	27,765	VC+
Providence College	RI	34,580	HC
Purdue Univ/Calumet	IN	10,891	LC
Purdue Univ/West Lafayette	IN	13,458	VC
Queens Univ of Charlotte	NC	24,528	C
Quincy Univ	IL	24,920	C
Quinnipiac Univ	CT	34,640	VC
Radford Univ	VA	13,145	C
Randolph-Macon College	VA	31,250	C
Randolph-Macon Woman's College	VA	31,160	VC+
Regis College	MA	31,350	LC
Regis Univ	CO	31,890	C
Rhode Island College	RI	11,570	C
Rhodes College	TN	32,860	HC
Rice Univ	TX	32,290	MC
Rider Univ	NJ	32,560	C
Ripon College	WI	27,160	C+
Rivier College	NH	26,600	C
Roanoke College	VA	30,748	VC
Robert Morris Univ	PA	22,822	C
Roberts Wesleyan College	NY	26,378	C
Rochester College	MI	15,636	C+
Rockford College	IL	28,330	VC
Rockhurst Univ	MO	25,440	VC
Roger Williams Univ	RI	30,500	C
Rollins College	FL	38,366	VC
Roosevelt Univ	IL	22,605	VC
Rosemont College	PA	29,350	C
Rowan Univ	NJ	16,000	VC
Russell Sage College	NY	27,000	C
Rust College	MS		C+
Rutgers, The State Univ of New Jersey/Camden Campus	NJ	15,000	VC
Rutgers, The State Univ of New Jersey/New Brunswick/Piscataway Campus	NJ	15,810	HC
Rutgers, The State Univ of New Jersey/Newark Campus	NJ	15,640	VC
Sacred Heart Univ	CT	33,404	C
Saginaw Valley State Univ	MI	11,432	C
St. Ambrose Univ	IA	25,495	C
St. Andrews Presbyterian College	NC	23,530	C
St. Anselm College	NH	33,810	C
St. Augustine's College	NC	14,000	LC
St. Bonaventure Univ	NY	28,785	LC
St. Cloud State Univ	MN	10,010	C
St. Francis College	NY	19,974	LC
St. Francis Univ	PA	25,880	C
St. John Fisher College	NY	27,860	C
St. John's Univ	MN	29,749	VC
St. John's Univ	NY	34,370	C
St. Joseph College	CT	32,050	C
St. Joseph's College	IN	26,600	C
St. Joseph's College of Maine	ME	29,185	C
St. Joseph's College, New York, Brooklyn Campus	NY	12,206	C
St. Joseph's College, New York, Suffolk Campus	NY	12,000	C
St. Joseph's Univ	PA	37,428	VC
St. Lawrence Univ	NY	40,545	VC
St. Leo Univ	FL	22,140	C+
St. Louis Univ	MO	33,158	VC+
St. Martin's Univ	WA	27,555	C
St. Mary-of-the-Woods College	IN	25,480	C
St. Mary's College	IN	32,538	VC
St. Mary's College of Calif	CA	37,290	C
St. Mary's College of Maryland	MD	18,876	VC+
St. Mary's Univ of San Antonio	TX	22,444	C
St. Michael's College	VT	33,330	VC
St. Norbert College	WI	28,577	C+
St. Olaf College	MN	32,800	HC
St. Paul's College	VA	16,030	NC
St. Peter's College	NJ	30,160	LC
St. Thomas Aquinas College	NY	22,000	LC
St. Thomas Univ	FL	23,490	C
St. Vincent College	PA	26,160	VC
St. Xavier Univ	IL	23,160	C
Salem College	NC	26,226	VC+
Salem State College	MA	13,161	LC
Salisbury Univ	MD	13,128	VC
Salve Regina Univ	RI	33,450	C

ST = STATE　　**$IS** = IN-STATE COSTS　　**SR** = SELECTOR RATING

School	ST	$IS	SR
Sam Houston State Univ	TX	8,000	C
Samford Univ	AL	20,258	VC
San Diego Christian College	CA	24,172	C
San Diego State Univ	CA	12,971	C
San Francisco State Univ	CA	13,000	C
San Jose State Univ	CA	11,707	C
Santa Clara Univ	CA	38,931	VC
Sarah Lawrence College	NY	42,000	HC
Savannah State Univ	GA	7,772	LC
Schreiner Univ	TX	20,600	C
Scripps College	CA	41,000	MC
Seattle Pacific Univ	WA	29,355	C
Seattle Univ	WA	30,063	VC
Seton Hall Univ	NJ	33,622	VC
Seton Hill Univ	PA	28,810	C
Shaw Univ	NC	15,488	LC
Shawnee State Univ	OH	12,237	NC
Shenandoah Univ	VA	27,600	C
Shepherd Univ	WV	10,066	C
Shippensburg Univ of Pennsylvania	PA	11,621	C
Shorter College	GA	19,700	C
Siena College	NY	28,260	VC+
Siena Heights Univ	MI	17,000	C
Silver Lake College of the Holy Family	WI	18,500	C
Simmons College	MA	35,640	VC
Simpson College	IA	26,833	VC
Simpson Univ	CA	22,900	C
Skidmore College	NY	41,779	HC
Slippery Rock Univ of Pennsylvania	PA	10,360	LC
Smith College	MA	41,474	MC
Sonoma State Univ	CA	14,732	C
S Car State Univ	SC	6,700	LC
S Dak State Univ	SD	9,815	C
Southeast Missouri State Univ	MO	10,596	C
Southeastern Louisiana Univ	LA	8,521	LC
Southeastern Okla State Univ	OK	6,147	C
Southeastern Univ	FL	17,180	LC
Southern Adventist Univ	TN	18,500	C
Southern Arkansas Univ	AR	6,956	C
Southern Conn State Univ	CT	10,310	C
Southern Illinois Univ Carbondale	IL	12,391	C
Southern Illinois Univ Edwardsville	IL	11,022	C
Southern Methodist Univ	TX	36,088	VC+
Southern Nazarene Univ	OK	14,634	NC
Southern New Hampshire Univ	NH	28,764	C
Southern Oregon Univ	OR	12,186	C
Southern Univ and A&M College	LA	8,238	LC
Southern Univ at New Orleans	LA	1,000	NC
Southern Utah Univ	UT		C
Southern Vermont College	VT	21,322	LC
Southern Wesleyan Univ	SC	21,675	C
Southwest Baptist Univ	MO	18,300	C
Southwestern Adventist Univ	TX	18,290	LC
Southwestern College	KS	21,476	~C
Southwestern Okla State Univ	OK	4,801	C
Southwestern Univ	TX	26,767	HC
Spelman College	GA	24,650	VC
Spring Arbor Univ	MI	22,476	C
Spring Hill College	AL	28,678	C
Springfield College	MA	25,000	C
Stanford Univ	CA	41,557	MC
SUNY at Oswego	NY	13,562	VC
SUNY at Potsdam	NY	12,959	C
SUNY/College at Brockport	NY	12,747	VC
SUNY/College at Buffalo	NY	11,903	C+
SUNY/College at Cortland	NY	12,095	C
SUNY/College at Fredonia	NY	12,771	VC
SUNY/College at Geneseo	NY	12,910	HC+
SUNY/College at Oneonta	NY	12,905	VC
SUNY/College at Plattsburgh	NY	12,362	C
SUNY/Univ at Albany	NY	13,860	VC
SUNY/Univ at Binghamton	NY	13,988	VC
SUNY/Univ at Buffalo	NY	13,694	VC
SUNY/Univ at New Paltz	NY	12,480	VC
SUNY/Univ at Stony Brook	NY	13,625	HC
Stephen F. Austin State Univ	TX	7,930	C
Stephens College	MO	26,930	VC
Sterling College	KS	19,992	C
Stetson Univ	FL	32,725	VC
Stillman College	AL	11,475	LC
Stonehill College	MA	36,164	HC
Suffolk Univ	MA	33,160	C
Sul Ross State Univ	TX	6,600	LC
Susquehanna Univ	PA	33,645	VC
Sweet Briar College	VA	31,460	VC
Syracuse Univ	NY	38,655	VC
Tabor College	KS	21,614	NC
Talladega College	AL	11,240	LC
Tarleton State Univ	TX	8,952	C
Taylor Univ	IN	26,376	VC+
Temple Univ	PA	17,438	C
Tenn State Univ	TN	9,048	LC
Tenn Tech Univ	TN	10,044	C
Tenn Wesleyan College	TN	18,650	C
Texas A&M Univ	TX	13,351	HC
Texas A&M Univ at Commerce	TX	9,020	C
Texas A&M Univ at Corpus Christi	TX	10,280	LC
Texas A&M Univ at Kingsville	TX	6,800	LC
Texas Christian Univ	TX	23,410	VC+
Texas Lutheran Univ	TX	23,530	C
Texas Southern Univ	TX	9,828	C
Texas State Univ - San Marcos	TX	10,862	C
Texas Tech Univ	TX	13,026	VC
Texas Wesleyan Univ	TX	18,700	C
Texas Woman's Univ	TX	7,804	LC
Thiel College	PA	24,580	C
Thomas Edison State College	NJ	3,780	SP
Thomas More College	KY	24,470	C
Thomas Univ	GA	11,520	NC
Toccoa Falls College	GA	17,125	C
Tougaloo College	MS	15,975	NC
Touro College	NY	17,000	C
Towson Univ	MD	13,924	VC
Transylvania Univ	KY	26,240	VC+
Trevecca Nazarene Univ	TN	19,594	C
Trinity Christian College	IL	23,645	C
Trinity College	CT	38,040	HC+
Trinity College	DC	24,150	LC
Trinity International Univ	IL	25,686	C
Trinity Univ	TX	30,157	HC+
Troy Univ	AL	8,916	C
Troy Univ Dothan Campus	AL	4,678	C
Troy Univ Montgomery Campus	AL	4,104	NC
Truman State Univ	MO	11,242	HC
Tufts Univ	MA	42,018	MC
Tulane Univ	LA	41,098	MC
Turabo Univ	PR	4,110	
Tusculum College	TN	21,340	LC
Tuskegee Univ	AL	18,860	LC
Union College	KY	18,920	C
Union College	NE	18,710	C
Union College	NY	41,595	HC
Union Univ	TN	20,750	VC
United States Air Force Academy	CO		HC+
United States Naval Academy	MD		MC
Univ of Akron	OH	15,166	NC
Univ of Alabama	AL	9,888	C
Univ of Alabama at Birmingham	AL	13,716	C
Univ of Alabama in Huntsville	AL	9,516	VC
Univ of Alaska Anchorage	AK	11,275	NC
Univ of Alaska Fairbanks	AK	10,101	C
Univ of Arizona	AZ	11,958	VC
Univ of Arkansas	AR	11,859	VC
Univ of Arkansas at Little Rock	AR	7,230	NC
Univ of Arkansas at Monticello	AR	7,325	NC
Univ of Arkansas at Pine Bluff	AR	8,300	C
Univ of at Calif Davis	CA	15,010	VC
Univ of Bridgeport	CT	29,595	LC
Univ of Calif at Berkeley	CA	18,141	HC+
Univ of Calif at Irvine	CA	16,475	HC
Univ of Calif at Los Angeles	CA	17,681	MC
Univ of Calif at Riverside	CA	16,625	C
Univ of Calif at Santa Barbara	CA	11,800	VC
Univ of Central Arkansas	AR	9,984	C
Univ of Central Florida	FL	10,739	VC
Univ of Central Okla	OK	8,094	C
Univ of Chicago	IL	42,369	MC
Univ of Cincinnati	OH	17,682	C
Univ of Colo at Boulder	CO	13,352	C+
Univ of Colo at Colo Springs	CO	11,517	VC
Univ of Colo at Denver and Health Sciences Center	CO	5,021	C
Univ of Conn	CT	16,628	HC
Univ of Dallas	TX	27,432	VC+
Univ of Dayton	OH	28,826	VC
Univ of Delaware	DE	14,142	HC
Univ of Denver	CO	36,376	VC+
Univ of Detroit Mercy	MI	27,000	C
Univ of Dubuque	IA	23,390	C
Univ of Findlay	OH	29,238	C
Univ of Florida	FL	9,354	HC
Univ of Georgia	GA	11,004	HC
Univ of Great Falls	MT	17,000	C
Univ of Hartford	CT	34,044	C
Univ of Hawaii at Hilo	HI	6,500	C
Univ of Hawaii at Manoa	HI	10,413	VC
Univ of Houston	TX	7,000	C
Univ of Houston-Downtown	TX	3,326	NC
Univ of Idaho	ID	9,310	NC
Univ of Illinois at Urbana-Champaign	IL	15,800	HC+
Univ of Indianapolis	IN	25,090	C
Univ of Iowa	IA	12,172	VC
Univ of Kansas	KS	10,915	VC
Univ of Kentucky	KY	7,800	C
Univ of La Verne	CA	33,470	C
Univ of Louisiana at Lafayette	LA	5,830	C
Univ of Louisiana at Monroe	LA	7,103	C
Univ of Louisville	KY	10,400	VC
Univ of Maine	ME	13,642	C
Univ of Maine at Augusta	ME	5,025	NC
Univ of Maine at Farmington	ME	11,515	C
Univ of Maine at Fort Kent	ME	10,832	LC
Univ of Maine at Machias	ME	10,523	C
Univ of Maine at Presque Isle	ME	10,066	LC
Univ of Mary	ND	15,374	C
Univ of Mary Hardin-Baylor	TX	19,428	C
Univ of Mary Washington	VA	11,636	HC
Univ of Maryland/Baltimore County	MD	16,642	VC+
Univ of Maryland/College Park	MD	16,036	HC
Univ of Maryland/Eastern Shore	MD	11,210	C
Univ of Maryland/Univ College	MD	5,640	SP
Univ of Mass Amherst	MA	15,973	C+
Univ of Mass Boston	MA	8,024	C
Univ of Mass Dartmouth	MA	15,985	C
Univ of Mass Lowell	MA	14,327	VC
Univ of Memphis	TN	11,153	C
Univ of Miami	FL	38,397	MC
Univ of Mich/Ann Arbor	MI	16,587	HC+
Univ of Mich/Dearborn	MI	7,000	VC
Univ of Mich/Flint	MI	6,398	C
Univ of Minn/Duluth	MN	13,974	C
Univ of Minn/Morris	MN	15,472	VC
Univ of Minn/Twin Cities	MN	13,165	HC
Univ of Miss	MS	9,000	C
Univ of Missouri/Columbia	MO	13,500	VC
Univ of Missouri/Kansas City	MO	15,000	VC
Univ of Missouri/Rolla	MO	13,332	HC
Univ of Missouri/St. Louis	MO	14,046	VC
Univ of Mobile	AL	16,880	C
Univ of Montana	MT	10,602	C
Univ of Montevallo	AL	9,630	C
Univ of Nebr at Kearney	NE	9,000	NC
Univ of Nebr at Lincoln	NE	11,401	VC
Univ of Nebr at Omaha	NE	11,235	C
Univ of Nevada/Las Vegas	NV	11,566	C
Univ of Nevada/Reno	NV	12,155	NC
Univ of New England	ME	31,005	C
Univ of New Hampshire	NH	16,810	VC
Univ of New Haven	CT	31,794	C
Univ of New Mexico	NM	11,253	C
Univ of New Orleans	LA	7,370	C
Univ of North Alabama	AL	8,992	C
Univ of N Car at Chapel Hill	NC	11,129	MC
Univ of N Car at Charlotte	NC	9,101	C
Univ of N Car at Greensboro	NC	8,993	C
Univ of N Car at Pembroke	NC	7,940	LC
Univ of N Car at Wilmington	NC	10,107	VC
Univ of N Dak	ND	10,114	VC
Univ of North Florida	FL	9,908	VC
Univ of North Texas	TX	7,800	VC
Univ of Northern Colo	CO	10,249	C
Univ of Northern Iowa	IA	11,133	C
Univ of Notre Dame	IN	39,552	MC
Univ of Okla	OK	10,769	VC+
Univ of Oregon	OR	13,108	VC
Univ of Pennsylvania	PA	41,766	MC
Univ of Pittsburgh at Bradford	PA	17,008	C
Univ of Pittsburgh at Johnstown	PA	16,740	LC
Univ of Portland	OR	32,300	VC
Univ of PR at Humacao	PR	1,707	
Univ of PR/Cayey Univ College	PR	1,250	
Univ of PR/Mayaguez	PR	1,250	
Univ of PR/Rio Piedras	PR	5,750	
Univ of Puget Sound	WA	35,600	HC
Univ of Redlands	CA	36,160	VC
Univ of Rhode Island	RI	15,398	C
Univ of Richmond	VA	40,510	MC
Univ of Rio Grande	OH	8,728	NC
Univ of Rochester	NY	41,135	MC
Univ of St. Francis	IL	25,430	C
Univ of St. Francis	IN	20,970	C
Univ of St. Mary	KS	18,900	C
Univ of St. Thomas	MN	28,000	VC
Univ of St. Thomas	TX	23,810	VC
Univ of San Diego	CA	40,620	HC
Univ of San Francisco	CA	37,560	VC
Univ of Science and Arts of Okla	OK	7,650	C
Univ of Scranton	PA	31,100	VC
Univ of Sioux Falls	SD	20,800	C
Univ of South Alabama	AL	8,930	C
Univ of S Car at Aiken	SC	11,718	LC
Univ of S Car at Columbia	SC	13,397	VC
Univ of S Car Upstate	SC	11,957	C
Univ of S Dak	SD	9,068	C
Univ of Southern Calif	CA	41,618	MC
Univ of Southern Indiana	IN	12,590	LC
Univ of Southern Maine	ME	12,614	C
Univ of Southern Miss	MS	10,112	C
Univ of Tampa	FL	25,784	C
Univ of Tenn at Chattanooga	TN	7,790	C
Univ of Tenn at Knoxville	TN	11,720	C
Univ of Tenn at Martin	TN	8,693	C
Univ of Texas at Arlington	TX	7,195	LC
Univ of Texas at Austin	TX	14,610	HC
Univ of Texas at El Paso	TX	8,764	C
Univ of Texas at San Antonio	TX	11,325	LC
Univ of Texas-Pan American	TX	7,290	C+
Univ of the Cumberlands	KY	18,184	C
Univ of the District of Columbia	DC	2,070	LC
Univ of the Incarnate Word	TX	23,306	C
Univ of the Ozarks	AR	19,250	C
Univ of the Pacific	CA	34,380	VC
Univ of the South	TN	34,645	HC
Univ of Toledo	OH	15,806	NC
Univ of Tulsa	OK	25,348	HC
Univ of Utah	UT	10,162	VC
Univ of Vermont	VT	18,080	VC
Univ of Virginia	VA	13,759	VC
Univ of Virginia's College at Wise	VA	11,076	C
Univ of Washington	WA	10,400	VC
Univ of West Alabama	AL	7,611	C
Univ of West Florida	FL	8,559	C
Univ of West Georgia	GA	8,838	C
Univ of Wisc/Eau Claire	WI	9,915	VC
Univ of Wisc/Green Bay	WI	9,415	VC
Univ of Wisc/La Crosse	WI	10,045	VC
Univ of Wisc/Madison	WI	13,117	HC
Univ of Wisc/Milwaukee	WI	9,427	C
Univ of Wisc/Oshkosh	WI	10,426	LC
Univ of Wisc/Parkside	WI	10,181	LC
Univ of Wisc/Platteville	WI	9,779	NC
Univ of Wisc/River Falls	WI	9,722	C
Univ of Wisc/Stevens Point	WI	9,384	VC
Univ of Wisc/Superior	WI	9,610	C+
Univ of Wisc/Whitewater	WI	9,274	C
Univ of Wyoming	WY	9,666	C
Upper Iowa Univ	IA	20,130	C
Urbana Univ	OH	21,190	C
Ursinus College	PA	38,950	VC
Ursuline College	OH	25,456	C
Utah State Univ	UT	8,002	VC
Utica College	NY	31,396	C
Valdosta State Univ	GA	8,802	C
Valley City State Univ	ND	9,854	LC
Valparaiso Univ	IN	28,970	VC+
Vanderbilt Univ	TN	41,986	MC
Vanguard Univ of Southern Calif	CA	27,071	C
Vassar College	NY	41,700	MC
Villa Julie College	MD	25,222	C
Villanova Univ	PA	38,672	HC+
Virginia Commonwealth Univ	VA	12,987	C
Virginia Intermont College	VA	22,200	LC
Virginia Military Inst	VA	12,654	VC
Virginia Polytechnic Inst and State Univ	VA	10,834	VC
Virginia Union Univ	VA	18,432	VC
Virginia Wesleyan College	VA	28,433	C
Viterbo Univ	WI	21,670	C
Voorhees College	SC	11,800	LC
Wabash College	IN	30,116	HC
Wagner College	NY	33,300	VC
Wake Forest Univ	NC	38,290	MC
Walla Walla College	WA	24,489	NC
Walsh Univ	OH	23,440	C
Warner Pacific College	OR	21,900	C
Warner Southern College	FL	18,000	C
Warren Wilson College	NC	24,382	VC
Wartburg College	IA	27,315	NC
Washburn Univ	KS	9,734	NC
Washington and Jefferson College	PA	33,490	VC
Washington and Lee Univ	VA	35,880	MC
Washington College	MD	34,990	VC
Washington State Univ	WA	12,260	C
Washington Univ in St. Louis	MO	42,106	MC
Wayland Baptist Univ	TX	13,484	C
Wayne State College	NE	8,033	NC
Wayne State Univ	MI	11,805	C
Waynesburg College	PA	21,230	C
Weber State Univ	UT	9,635	NC
Webster Univ	MO	24,280	VC
Wellesley College	MA	41,030	MC
Wells College	NY	23,070	VC
Wesley College	DE	19,905	C
Wesleyan College	GA	19,560	C
Wesleyan Univ	CT	42,122	MC
West Chester Univ of Pennsylvania	PA	12,355	C+
West Liberty State College	WV	9,142	LC
West Texas A&M Univ	TX	8,452	C
West Virginia State Univ	WV	8,378	NC

ST = STATE $IS = IN-STATE COSTS   SR = SELECTOR RATING

School	ST	$IS	SR
West Virginia Univ	WV	10,506	C
West Virginia Wesleyan College	WV	26,880	C
Western Baptist College	OR	21,808	C
Western Carolina Univ	NC	7,000	C
Western Conn State Univ	CT	12,993	C
Western Illinois Univ	IL	13,042	C
Western Kentucky Univ	KY	10,192	C
Western Mich Univ	MI	13,299	C
Western New England College	MA	32,054	C
Western New Mexico Univ	NM	7,233	LC
Western Oregon Univ	OR	10,295	C
Western State College of Colo	CO	9,942	C
Western Washington Univ	WA	11,262	VC
Westfield State College	MA	10,200	C
Westminster College	MO	19,060	VC
Westminster College	PA	31,290	C+
Westminster College	UT	25,656	C
Westmont College	CA	36,672	HC
Wheaton College	IL	27,760	HC
Wheaton College	MA	40,180	HC+
Wheeling Jesuit Univ	WV	26,910	C
Whitman College	WA	36,110	HC+
Whittier College	CA	29,108	C
Whitworth College	WA	29,428	VC+
Wichita State Univ	KS	8,500	C
Widener Univ	PA	27,275	C
Wiley College	TX	8,100	LC
Wilkes Univ	PA	30,886	C
Willamette Univ	OR	35,416	VC+
William Carey College	MS	11,000	LC
William Jewell College	MO	24,340	C
William Paterson Univ of New Jersey	NJ	17,810	C+
William Penn Univ	IA	17,685	LC
William Tyndale College	MI	13,000	NC
William Woods Univ	MO	21,020	C
Williams Baptist College	AR	13,450	C
Williams College	MA	40,310	MC
Wilmington College	OH	2,806	NC
Wilson College	PA	27,660	C
Wingate Univ	NC	23,300	C
Winona State Univ	MN	11,333	C
Winston-Salem State Univ	NC	8,960	LC
Winthrop Univ	SC	11,302	C
Wisc Lutheran College	WI	23,510	VC
Wittenberg Univ	OH	34,596	VC
Wofford College	SC	30,935	HC
Worcester State College	MA	12,499	C
Wright State Univ	OH	13,616	C
Xavier Univ	OH	30,490	HC
Xavier Univ of Louisiana	LA	17,600	C
Yale Univ	CT	41,000	MC
Yeshiva Univ	NY	22,000	C
York College	NE	16,330	NC
York College of Pennsylvania	PA	16,550	VC
Youngstown State Univ	OH	12,613	NC

ENGLISH AS A SECOND/FOREIGN LANGUAGE

School	ST	$IS	SR
Doane College	NE	22,458	C
Eastern Mich Univ	MI	12,897	C
Holy Names College	CA	27,980	NC
La Sierra Univ	CA	24,327	C+
Liberty Univ	VA	19,101	C
Marylhurst Univ	OR	14,220	NC
Maryville College	TN	29,224	VC
Northwestern College	MN	25,220	NC
Salem International Univ	WV	18,020	C
Simmons College	MA	35,640	VC
Union Univ	TN	20,750	VC
Univ of Findlay	OH	29,238	C
Univ of Hawaii at Manoa	HI	10,413	VC
Univ of Nebr at Lincoln	NE	11,401	VC

ENGLISH EDUCATION

School	ST	$IS	SR
Adams State College	CO	8,613	C
Adelphi Univ	NY	27,000	VC
Alabama State Univ	AL	7,658	C
Andrews Univ	MI	21,786	C
Arkansas State Univ	AR	9,630	C
Asbury College	KY	23,762	VC
Ashland Univ	OH	25,000	C
Auburn Univ	AL	12,230	C
Averett Univ	VA	24,920	C
Baylor Univ	TX	27,555	HC
Bennett College	NC	11,500	C
Bethany College	KS	20,660	LC
Bethany College	WV	21,395	C
Bethel College	IN	19,680	C
Bethune-Cookman College	FL	17,922	LC
Blackburn College	IL	13,690	C
Blue Mountain College	MS	11,086	C
Boise State Univ	ID	9,438	LC
Boston Univ	MA	42,046	HC+
Bowie State Univ	MD	10,880	C+
Brigham Young Univ	UT	9,200	VC
Brigham Young Univ/Hawaii	HI	7,740	HC+
Carthage College	WI	26,000	C
Catholic Univ of America	DC	35,838	VC

School	ST	$IS	SR
Cedarville Univ	OH	21,904	VC
Central Mich Univ	MI	12,244	C
Central Missouri State Univ	MO	10,000	C
Central Univ of Bayamon	PR	3,335	
Central Washington Univ	WA	11,730	C
CUNY/Brooklyn College	NY	4,377	C+
CUNY/City College	NY		C
Claflin Univ	SC	16,798	C+
Coker College	SC	21,600	C
Colby-Sawyer College	NH	27,850	LC
College of New Jersey	NJ	18,315	MC
College of St. Rose	NY	25,684	C
College of the Ozarks	MO	4,130	VC+
Columbia Union College	MD	23,536	LC
Concordia Univ St.Paul	MN	27,776	C
Daemen College	NY	24,580	C
Dakota State Univ	SD	7,466	C
Dana College	NE	22,390	C
Delta State Univ	MS	7,709	C
Duquesne Univ	PA	29,534	VC
East Carolina Univ	NC	10,000	C
East Central Univ	OK	6,207	C
East Texas Baptist Univ	TX	16,713	C
Eastern Mich Univ	MI	12,897	C
Eastern Univ	PA	24,075	C
Edinboro Univ of Pennsylvania	PA	11,809	LC
Emory & Henry College	VA	26,570	C
Florida Atlantic Univ	FL	11,221	C
Florida International Univ	FL	9,215	VC
Florida State Univ	FL	9,028	HC
Franklin College	IN		C
Fresno Pacific Univ	CA	25,454	C
Friends Univ	KS	16,250	LC
Georgia Southern Univ	GA	9,762	C
Georgia Southwestern State Univ	GA	6,035	C
Grace College	IN	22,170	C
Grambling State Univ	LA	6,538	NC
Green Mountain College	VT	32,164	C
Greensboro College	NC	23,000	C
Greenville College	IL	23,146	C
Hardin-Simmons Univ	TX	18,641	C
Hofstra Univ	NY	32,630	VC
Hood College	MD	30,085	VC
Humboldt State Univ	CA	11,176	C
Huntington Univ	IN	24,830	C
Indiana Univ of Pennsylvania	PA	11,209	C
Indiana Univ South Bend	IN	4,989	LC
Indiana Univ Southeast	IN	4,880	LC
Indiana Univ-Purdue Univ Indianapolis	IN	10,959	C
Indiana Wesleyan Univ	IN	22,074	C+
Ithaca College	NY	35,144	VC
Johnson C. Smith Univ	NC	20,000	C
Johnson State College	VT	11,830	LC
Judson College	AL	16,522	C
Judson College	IL	25,130	C
Juniata College	PA	33,130	VC
Kennesaw State Univ	GA	12,152	C
La Roche College	PA	24,724	LC
Le Moyne College	NY	29,570	VC
Limestone College	SC	19,840	C
Lincoln Univ	PA	13,658	C+
Lipscomb Univ	TN	10,967	VC
LIU/C.W. Post Campus	NY	28,282	C
Louisiana College	LA	13,450	C
Lyndon State College	VT	14,233	LC
Mansfield Univ	PA	11,300	C
Marian College of Fond du Lac	WI	21,775	C
Marymount Univ	VA	25,934	C
Messiah College	PA	28,910	VC+
MidAmerica Nazarene Univ	KS	20,584	LC
Minot State Univ	ND	6,700	LC
Miss Valley State Univ	MS	7,970	C
Missouri Southern State Univ	MO	8,396	NC
Monmouth Univ	NJ	28,956	C
Morningside College	IA	23,704	C
Morris College	SC	11,999	LC
Mount Mary College	WI	22,895	C
Mount Vernon Nazarene Univ	OH	20,810	C
Nazareth College of Rochester	NY	28,175	VC
Nebr Wesleyan Univ	NE	23,415	C+
New York Univ	NY	43,170	MC
Niagara Univ	NY	28,250	C
N Car Agricultural and Technical State Univ	NC	8,000	LC
Northwest Nazarene Univ	ID	22,590	VC
Northwestern College	MN	25,220	NC
Northwestern Okla State Univ	OK	6,250	NC
Oakwood College	AL	14,904	C
Okla Christian Univ	OK	18,992	NC
Okla Panhandle State Univ	OK	7,635	NC
Okla Wesleyan Univ	OK	18,950	NC
Old Dominion Univ	VA	11,907	C
Oral Roberts Univ	OK	22,650	C
Palm Beach Atlantic Univ	FL	23,597	VC
Pittsburgh State Univ	KS	8,112	C
Providence College	RI	34,580	HC
Purdue Univ/West Lafayette	IN	13,458	VC

School	ST	$IS	SR
Rider Univ	NJ	32,560	C
Rivier College	NH	26,600	C
Rocky Mountain College	MT	20,805	C
Rust College	MS		C+
Saginaw Valley State Univ	MI	11,432	C
St. Augustine's College	NC	14,000	LC
St. Edward's Univ	TX	23,560	C
St. John Fisher College	NY	27,860	C
St. John's Univ	NY	34,370	C
St. Mary's Univ of Minn	MN	23,857	VC
Schreiner Univ	TX	20,600	C
Seattle Pacific Univ	WA	29,355	C
Seton Hill Univ	PA	28,810	C
Shaw Univ	NC	15,488	LC
Shepherd Univ	WV	10,066	C
Shippensburg Univ of Pennsylvania	PA	11,621	C
Southeast Missouri State Univ	MO	10,596	C
Southeastern Louisiana Univ	LA	8,521	LC
Southern New Hampshire Univ	NH	28,764	C
Southern Univ at New Orleans	LA	1,000	NC
Southern Utah Univ	UT		C
Southwestern College	KS	21,476	C
Southwestern Okla State Univ	OK	4,801	C
SUNY at Potsdam	NY	12,959	C
SUNY/College at Oneonta	NY	12,905	VC
SUNY/College at Plattsburgh	NY	12,362	C
SUNY/Univ at Albany	NY	13,860	VC
Suffolk Univ	MA	33,160	C
Syracuse Univ	NY	38,655	HC
Taylor Univ	IN	26,376	VC+
Temple Univ	PA	17,438	C
Texas Christian Univ	TX	23,410	VC+
Texas Southern Univ	TX	9,828	C
Tougaloo College	MS	15,975	NC
Trevecca Nazarene Univ	TN	19,594	C
Tri-State Univ-Main Campus	IN	26,200	C
Troy Univ	AL	8,916	C
Troy Univ Dothan Campus	AL	4,678	C
Turabo Univ	PR	4,110	
Union College	NE	18,710	C
Univ of Arkansas at Pine Bluff	AR	8,300	C
Univ of Central Florida	FL	10,739	VC
Univ of Central Okla	OK	8,094	C
Univ of Conn	CT	16,628	HC
Univ of Delaware	DE	14,142	HC
Univ of Evansville	IN	28,320	VC
Univ of Georgia	GA	11,004	HC
Univ of Illinois at Chicago	IL	16,256	VC
Univ of Illinois at Urbana-Champaign	IL	15,800	HC+
Univ of Indianapolis	IN	25,090	C
Univ of Louisiana at Lafayette	LA	5,830	C
Univ of Louisiana at Monroe	LA	7,103	C
Univ of Mary	ND	15,374	C
Univ of Mary Hardin-Baylor	TX	19,428	C
Univ of Maryland/College Park	MD	16,036	HC
Univ of Minn/Duluth	MN	13,974	C
Univ of Minn/Twin Cities	MN	13,165	HC
Univ of Miss	MS	9,000	C
Univ of New Hampshire	NH	16,810	VC
Univ of New Orleans	LA	7,370	C
Univ of N Car at Chapel Hill	NC	11,129	MC
Univ of N Car at Charlotte	NC	9,101	C
Univ of N Car at Pembroke	NC	7,940	LC
Univ of Pittsburgh at Johnstown	PA	16,740	LC
Univ of Rio Grande	OH	8,728	NC
Univ of St. Francis	IN	20,970	C
Univ of S Car Upstate	SC	11,957	C
Univ of South Florida	FL	10,284	VC
Univ of the Cumberlands	KY	18,184	C
Univ of Vermont	VT	18,080	VC
Warner Southern College	FL	18,000	LC
Warren Wilson College	NC	24,382	VC
Wartburg College	IA	27,315	NC
Washington State Univ	WA	12,260	VC
Wesley College	DE	19,905	C
West Texas A&M Univ	TX	8,452	C
West Virginia Univ	WV	10,506	C
Western Carolina Univ	NC	7,000	C
Westmont College	CA	36,672	HC
Whitworth College	WA	29,428	VC+
Wiley College	TX	8,100	LC
Wingate Univ	NC	23,300	C
Xavier Univ of Louisiana	LA	17,600	C
York College	NE	16,330	NC
Youngstown State Univ	OH	12,613	NC

ENGLISH LITERATURE

School	ST	$IS	SR
Bard College	NY	41,800	HC+
Blackburn College	IL	13,690	C
Brandeis Univ	MA	41,551	MC
Central Mich Univ	MI	12,244	C
Chatham College	PA	27,290	C+

School	ST	$IS	SR
Christopher Newport Univ	VA	13,326	VC
CUNY/Hunter College	NY	8,000	C+
Claremont McKenna College	CA	42,920	MC
Columbia Univ/School of General Studies	NY	41,516	C
Dartmouth College	NH	39,465	MC
DePauw Univ	IN	32,100	HC
Dominican Univ of Calif	CA	36,836	C
Eastern Mich Univ	MI	12,897	C
Eastern Univ	PA	24,075	C
Edinboro Univ of Pennsylvania	PA	11,809	LC
Elmira College	NY	37,200	VC
Emmanuel College	MA	32,000	C+
Emory & Henry College	VA	26,570	C
Excelsior College	NY	995	SP
Fairleigh Dickinson Univ/Metropolitan Campus	NJ	28,590	C
Hofstra Univ	NY	32,630	VC
Kent State Univ	OH	14,594	C
Knox College	IL	32,385	VC+
Loras College	IA	27,193	C
Mountain State Univ	WV	11,406	NC
New England College	NH	31,466	C
New York Univ	NY	43,170	MC
Oral Roberts Univ	OK	22,650	C
Pfeiffer Univ	NC	21,900	C
Purdue Univ/Calumet	IN	10,891	C
Reed College	OR	41,106	MC
Rider Univ	NJ	32,560	C
St. Edward's Univ	TX	23,560	C
Samford Univ	AL	20,258	VC
Simon's Rock College of Bard	MA	41,988	VC+
Southern Illinois Univ Carbondale	IL	12,391	C
Southern New Hampshire Univ	NH	28,764	C
Swarthmore College	PA	41,280	MC
Syracuse Univ	NY	38,655	HC
Union Univ	TN	20,750	VC
Univ of Calif at San Diego	CA	16,102	HC
Univ of Illinois at Urbana-Champaign	IL	15,800	HC+
Univ of Maryland/College Park	MD	16,036	HC
Univ of Montana--Western	MT	8,406	NC
Univ of New Hampshire	NH	16,810	VC
Univ of Pittsburgh at Greensburg	PA	17,640	C
Univ of Pittsburgh at Pittsburgh	PA	18,866	HC
Univ of Redlands	CA	36,160	VC
Univ of South Florida	FL	10,284	VC
Univ of Southern Calif	CA	41,618	MC
Virginia State Univ	VA	11,318	C
Washington Univ in St. Louis	MO	42,106	MC

ENTOMOLOGY

School	ST	$IS	SR
Auburn Univ	AL	12,230	VC
Cornell Univ	NY	41,717	MC
Iowa State Univ	IA	11,831	VC
Kansas State Univ	KS	10,516	VC
Mich State Univ	MI	13,689	VC
Ohio State Univ	OH	15,357	HC
Okla State Univ	OK	10,213	VC
Oregon State Univ	OR	11,055	C
Purdue Univ/West Lafayette	IN	13,458	VC
SUNY/College of Environmental Science and Forestry	NY	15,000	VC
Texas A&M Univ	TX	13,351	HC
Univ of at Calif Davis	CA	15,010	VC
Univ of Calif at Riverside	CA	16,625	C
Univ of Delaware	DE	14,142	HC
Univ of Florida	FL	9,354	HC
Univ of Georgia	GA	11,004	HC
Univ of Idaho	ID	9,310	NC
Univ of Illinois at Urbana-Champaign	IL	15,800	HC+
Univ of Wisc/Madison	WI	13,117	HC
Washington State Univ	WA	12,260	C

ENTREPRENEURIAL STUDIES

School	ST	$IS	SR
American International College	MA	28,710	LC
Antioch College	OH	33,700	C
Baylor Univ	TX	27,555	HC
Boston Univ	MA	42,046	HC+
Bradley Univ	IL	25,280	VC
Canisius College	NY	32,257	VC
Central Mich Univ	MI	12,244	C
Davenport Univ	MI	15,205	NC
Duquesne Univ	PA	29,534	VC
Fairleigh Dickinson Univ/College at Florham	NJ	30,130	C
Fairleigh Dickinson Univ/Metropolitan Campus	NJ	28,590	C
Florida State Univ	FL	9,028	HC
Gallaudet Univ	DC	16,554	
Hawaii Pacific Univ	HI	21,080	C
Hofstra Univ	NY	32,630	VC

ST = STATE $IS = IN-STATE COSTS   SR = SELECTOR RATING

School	ST	$IS	SR
Houston Baptist Univ	TX	18,660	C
Huntington Univ	IN	24,830	C
Indiana Univ Bloomington	IN	13,356	VC
Johnson and Wales Univ/ Charlotte Campus	NC	29,121	LC
Johnson and Wales Univ/ North Miami Campus	FL	30,126	LC
Johnson and Wales Univ/ Providence Campus	RI	28,126	LC
Messiah College	PA	28,910	VC+
Middle Tenn State Univ	TN	8,540	C
Mountain State Univ	WV	11,406	NC
Northern Mich Univ	MI	12,340	VC
Northwood Univ	TX	20,135	LC
Palm Beach Atlantic Univ	FL	23,597	VC
Peirce College	PA	12,760	NC
Quinnipiac Univ	CT	34,640	VC
Robert Morris Univ	PA	22,822	C
St. Edward's Univ	TX	23,560	C
Seton Hill Univ	PA	28,810	C
Southern Adventist Univ	TN	18,500	C
Southwestern College	KS	21,476	C
Suffolk Univ	MA	33,160	C
Syracuse Univ	NY	38,655	HC
Temple Univ	PA	17,438	C
Texas Christian Univ	TX	23,410	VC+
Univ of Arizona	AZ	11,958	VC
Univ of Hartford	CT	34,044	C
Univ of Illinois at Chicago	IL	16,256	VC
Univ of Illinois at Urbana-Champaign	IL	15,800	HC+
Univ of Indianapolis	IN	25,090	C
Univ of Louisiana at Monroe	LA	7,103	C
Univ of Miami	FL	38,397	MC
Univ of N Dak	ND	10,114	VC
Univ of North Texas	TX	7,800	C
Univ of Pennsylvania	PA	41,766	MC
Univ of Pittsburgh at Bradford	PA	17,008	C
Univ of St. Thomas	MN	28,000	VC
Univ of Texas at San Antonio	TX	11,325	LC
Univ of Vermont	VT	18,080	VC
Virginia Polytechnic Inst and State Univ	VA	10,834	VC
Washington State Univ	WA	12,260	C
Washington Univ in St. Louis	MO	42,106	MC
Western Carolina Univ	NC	7,000	C
Wichita State Univ	KS	8,500	C
Wilkes Univ	PA	30,886	C
Xavier Univ	OH	30,490	HC

ENVIRONMENTAL BIOLOGY

School	ST	$IS	SR
Arizona State Univ-Tempe	AZ	11,174	C
Averett Univ	VA	24,920	C
Belmont Univ	TN	24,114	C
Beloit College	WI	32,808	HC
Bethel College	IN	19,680	C
Boston Univ	MA	42,046	HC+
Cal State, Northridge	CA	9,036	LC
CUNY/Queens College	NY	4,356	C
College of Santa Fe	NM	28,978	C
Columbia Univ/Columbia College	NY	42,584	MC
Grand Canyon Univ	AZ	32,000	LC
Greenville College	IL	23,146	C
Heidelberg College	OH	23,242	C
Lock Haven Univ of Pennsylvania	PA	12,098	LC
Mich State Univ	MI	13,689	VC
Montclair State Univ	NJ	16,327	C
Mount Union College	OH	25,840	C
Norfolk State Univ	VA	10,531	LC
Ohio Univ	OH	15,921	C
Plymouth State Univ	NH	12,298	LC
St. Mary's Univ of Minn	MN	23,857	VC
SUNY/College of Environmental Science and Forestry	NY	15,000	VC
Taylor Univ	IN	26,376	VC+
Texas A&M Univ at Galveston	TX	10,000	C+
Unity College	ME	24,320	C
Univ of at Calif Davis	CA	15,010	VC
Univ of Colo at Boulder	CO	13,352	C+
Univ of Dayton	OH	28,826	VC
Univ of La Verne	CA	33,470	C
Univ of Missouri/Rolla	MO	13,332	HC
Univ of North Alabama	AL	8,992	C
Western Carolina Univ	NC	7,000	C
Wingate Univ	NC	23,300	C

ENVIRONMENTAL DESIGN

School	ST	$IS	SR
Art Center College of Design	CA	26,370	SP
Ball State Univ	IN	13,138	C
Brigham Young Univ	UT	9,200	VC
Hampshire College	MA	37,120	HC
Harvard Univ/Harvard College	MA	45,860	MC
Maryland Inst College of Art	MD	34,450	SP
Miami Univ	OH	29,097	HC
Montana State Univ-Bozeman	MT	1,137	C
New York Inst of Technology	NY	28,126	VC
N Car State Univ	NC	11,824	HC
N Dak State Univ	ND	8,500	C
Olivet Nazarene Univ	IL	22,590	C
Otis College of Art and Design	CA	27,546	SP
SUNY/College of Environmental Science and Forestry	NY	15,000	VC
SUNY/Univ at Buffalo	NY	13,694	VC
Syracuse Univ	NY	38,655	HC
Texas A&M Univ	TX	13,351	VC
Univ of at Calif Davis	CA	15,010	VC
Univ of Calif at Irvine	CA	16,475	HC
Univ of Colo at Boulder	CO	13,352	C+
Univ of Houston	TX	7,000	C
Univ of Mass Amherst	MA	15,973	C
Univ of Minn/Twin Cities	MN	13,165	HC
Univ of Nebr at Lincoln	NE	11,401	VC
Univ of New Mexico	NM	11,253	C
Univ of Okla	OK	10,769	VC+
Univ of Pennsylvania	PA	41,766	MC
Univ of PR/Rio Piedras	PR	5,750	

ENVIRONMENTAL EDUCATION

School	ST	$IS	SR
Johnson State College	VT	11,830	LC
Messiah College	PA	28,910	VC+
Ohio State Univ	OH	15,357	HC
Prescott College	AZ	13,445	LC
SUNY/College of Environmental Science and Forestry	NY	15,000	VC
Unity College	ME	24,320	C
Univ of New Hampshire	NH	16,810	VC
Virginia Polytechnic Inst and State Univ	VA	10,834	VC
West Virginia Univ	WV	10,506	C

ENVIRONMENTAL ENGINEERING

School	ST	$IS	SR
Calif Polytechnic State Univ	CA	12,390	VC
Clarkson Univ	NY	34,930	VC
Drexel Univ	PA	27,700	VC
Florida State Univ	FL	9,028	HC
Gannon Univ	PA	26,100	C
Hofstra Univ	NY	32,630	VC
Humboldt State Univ	CA	11,176	C
Johns Hopkins Univ	MD	42,044	MC
Lehigh Univ	PA	42,690	HC+
Louisiana State Univ and A&M College	LA	10,749	VC
Manhattan College	NY	29,000	VC
Marquette Univ	WI	31,066	HC
Mass Inst of Technology	MA	41,800	MC
Mass Maritime Academy	MA	11,571	C
Mercer Univ	GA	27,525	VC+
Mich Tech Univ	MI	14,569	VC
Montana Tech of The Univ of Montana	MT	10,434	C
New Jersey Inst of Technology	NJ	16,396	VC
New Mexico Inst of Mining and Technology	NM	8,510	VC+
New Mexico State Univ	NM	9,250	C
N Car State Univ	NC	11,824	HC
Northern Arizona Univ	AZ	10,353	C
Northwestern Univ	IL	37,595	MC
Old Dominion Univ	VA	11,907	C
Penn State Univ/Univ Park Campus	PA	18,038	HC
Rensselaer Polytechnic Inst	NY	41,288	HC+
Rice Univ	TX	32,290	MC
Roger Williams Univ	RI	30,500	C
San Diego State Univ	CA	12,971	C
Seattle Univ	WA	30,063	VC
S Dak State Univ	SD	9,815	C
Southern Methodist Univ	TX	36,088	VC+
SUNY/College of Environmental Science and Forestry	NY	15,000	VC
SUNY/Univ at Buffalo	NY	13,694	VC
Stevens Inst of Technology	NJ	40,935	HC
Suffolk Univ	MA	33,160	C
Syracuse Univ	NY	38,655	HC
Taylor Univ	IN	26,376	VC+
Tenn Tech Univ	TN	10,044	C
Texas Tech Univ	TX	13,026	VC
Tulane Univ	LA	41,098	MC
United States Air Force Academy	CO		HC+
United States Military Academy	NY		MC
Universidad Politecnica de PR	PR	5,400	
Univ of Calif at Berkeley	CA	18,141	HC+
Univ of Calif at Irvine	CA	16,475	HC
Univ of Calif at Riverside	CA	16,625	C
Univ of Calif at San Diego	CA	16,102	HC
Univ of Central Florida	FL	10,739	VC
Univ of Colo at Boulder	CO	13,352	C+
Univ of Conn	CT	16,628	HC
Univ of Delaware	DE	14,142	HC
Univ of Florida	FL	9,354	HC
Univ of Miami	FL	38,397	MC
Univ of Missouri/Rolla	MO	13,332	HC
Univ of New Hampshire	NH	16,810	VC
Univ of N Car at Chapel Hill	NC	11,129	MC
Univ of Notre Dame	IN	39,552	MC
Univ of Okla	OK	10,769	VC+
Univ of Southern Calif	CA	41,618	MC
Univ of Utah	UT	10,162	VC
Univ of Vermont	VT	18,080	VC
Univ of Wisc/Platteville	WI	9,779	NC
Wentworth Inst of Technology	MA	27,500	C
Wilkes Univ	PA	30,886	C
Worcester Polytechnic Inst	MA	40,450	VC+

ENVIRONMENTAL ENGINEERING TECHNOLOGY

School	ST	$IS	SR
Cornell Univ	NY	41,717	MC
East Carolina Univ	NC	10,000	C
Inter American Univ of PR/ Bayamon Univ College	PR	3,522	
Lake Superior State Univ	MI	12,842	LC
Mesa State College	CO	8,051	C
New York Inst of Technology	NY	28,126	VC
Rochester Inst of Technology	NY	32,070	VC+
Shawnee State Univ	OH	12,237	NC
Southwestern Okla State Univ	OK	4,801	C
Suffolk Univ	MA	33,160	C
Temple Univ	PA	17,438	C
Texas Southern Univ	TX	9,828	C

ENVIRONMENTAL GEOLOGY

School	ST	$IS	SR
Allegheny College	PA	33,500	HC
Samford Univ	AL	20,258	VC
Southern Methodist Univ	TX	36,088	VC+
Taylor Univ	IN	26,376	VC+
Univ of Okla	OK	10,769	VC+
Univ of Pittsburgh at Pittsburgh	PA	18,866	HC
Univ of Wyoming	WY	9,666	C

ENVIRONMENTAL HEALTH SCIENCE

School	ST	$IS	SR
Benedict College	SC	19,114	LC
Boise State Univ	ID	9,438	LC
Cal State, Sacramento	CA	11,122	C+
Cal State, San Bernardino	CA	12,563	LC
CUNY/York College	NY	4,242	NC
Colo State Univ-Fort Collins	CO	10,878	C+
Colo State Univ-Pueblo	CO	7,821	LC
Delaware State Univ	DE	8,130	LC
Dickinson College	PA	40,170	HC+
East Carolina Univ	NC	10,000	C
East Central Univ	OK	6,207	C
East Tenn State Univ	TN	8,497	C
Eastern Kentucky Univ	KY	7,725	C
Illinois State Univ	IL	12,839	C
Indiana State Univ	IN	11,604	C
Indiana Univ of Pennsylvania	PA	11,209	C
Iowa Wesleyan College	IA	22,140	C
Miss Valley State Univ	MS	7,970	C
Missouri Southern State Univ	MO	8,396	NC
New Mexico State Univ	NM	9,250	C
Oakland Univ	MI	11,936	C
Old Dominion Univ	VA	11,907	C
Oregon State Univ	OR	11,055	C
Purdue Univ/West Lafayette	IN	13,458	VC
Salisbury Univ	MD	13,128	VC
Springfield College	MA	25,000	C
Texas Southern Univ	TX	9,828	C
Unity College	ME	24,320	C
Univ of Arkansas at Little Rock	AR	7,230	NC
Univ of at Calif Davis	CA	15,010	VC
Univ of Georgia	GA	11,004	HC
Univ of Mich/Flint	MI	6,398	C
Univ of Missouri/Rolla	MO	13,332	HC
Univ of Southern Maine	ME	12,614	C
Univ of Washington	WA	10,400	VC
Western Carolina Univ	NC	7,000	C
Western Kentucky Univ	KY	10,192	C
Wright State Univ	OH	13,616	LC

ENVIRONMENTAL SCIENCE

School	ST	$IS	SR
Abilene Christian Univ	TX	20,830	C
Adrian College	MI	23,000	C
Alabama A&M Univ	AL	8,890	LC
Alaska Pacific Univ	AK	25,142	C
Albright College	PA	33,920	C
Alfred Univ	NY		VC
Allegheny College	PA	33,500	HC
Alverno College	WI	21,088	C
American Univ	DC	38,719	HC+
Andrews Univ	MI	21,786	C
Antioch College	OH	33,700	C
Appalachian State Univ	NC	8,000	VC
Aquinas College	MI	23,750	C
Arcadia Univ	PA	33,570	VC
Ashland Univ	OH	25,000	C
Assumption College	MA	32,875	C
Auburn Univ	AL	12,230	VC
Aurora Univ	IL	20,645	C
Austin Peay State Univ	TN	7,535	C
Averett Univ	VA	24,920	C
Bard College	NY	41,800	HC+
Barton College	NC	22,316	C
Baylor Univ	TX	27,555	HC
Beloit College	WI	32,808	HC
Benedictine Univ	IL	25,710	C
Berry College	GA	24,342	VC
Bethel Univ	MN	29,840	VC
Boston College	MA	41,608	MC
Boston Univ	MA	42,046	HC+
Bowdoin College	ME	41,660	MC
Bowling Green State Univ	OH	14,964	C
Bradley Univ	IL	25,280	VC
Briar Cliff Univ	IA	23,550	LC
Bridgewater College	VA	27,790	C
Brown Univ	RI	42,015	MC
Bucknell Univ	PA	39,660	MC
Cal State East Bay	CA	10,856	LC
Cal State, Chico	CA	11,395	C
Calif Univ of Pennsylvania	PA	14,217	C
Calvin College	MI	25,735	NC
Canisius College	NY	32,257	VC
Capital Univ	OH	30,444	C
Carroll College	MT	23,324	C+
Carroll College	WI	24,860	C
Case Western Reserve Univ	OH	37,314	MC
Castleton State College	VT	13,158	C
Catawba College	NC	25,000	C
Catholic Univ of America	DC	35,838	VC
Cedar Crest College	PA	30,615	C
Centenary College of Louisiana	LA	24,760	VC
Central College	IA	26,774	VC
Central Methodist Univ	MO	18,000	C
Chapman Univ	CA	37,550	VC
Charleston Southern Univ	SC	17,800	C
Chatham College	PA	27,290	C+
Chestnut Hill College	PA	26,600	LC
Christopher Newport Univ	VA	13,326	VC
CUNY/Hunter College	NY	8,000	C+
CUNY/Medgar Evers College	NY	4,250	NC
CUNY/Queens College	NY	4,356	C
Claflin Univ	SC	16,798	C+
Claremont McKenna College	CA	42,920	MC
Clarion Univ of Pennsylvania	PA	11,844	C
Clark Univ	MA	35,165	VC+
Clarkson Univ	NY	34,930	VC
Cleveland State Univ	OH	10,798	NC
Coe College	IA	27,440	VC
Colby College	ME	41,770	MC
Colgate Univ	NY	41,170	MC
College of St. Rose	NY	25,684	C
College of Santa Fe	NM	28,978	C
Colo College	CO	37,668	HC
Columbia Univ/Barnard College	NY	38,000	VC
Columbia Univ/Columbia College	NY	42,584	MC
Columbia Univ/School of General Studies	NY	41,516	C
Concordia College: Moorhead	MN	22,475	VC
Concordia College-New York	NY	27,740	C
Concordia Univ	OR	24,400	C
Concordia Univ at Austin	TX	23,640	LC
Concordia Univ St.Paul	MN	27,776	C
Conn College	CT	41,975	MC
Cornell College	IA	30,110	VC+
Creighton Univ	NE	29,918	VC+
Curry College	MA	26,100	LC
Dana College	NE	22,390	C
Dartmouth College	NH	39,465	MC
Davis and Elkins College	WV	22,416	C
De Sales Univ	PA	28,580	VC
Defiance College	OH	24,790	C
Delaware Valley College	PA	29,944	C
Delta State Univ	MS	7,709	C
DePaul Univ	IL	29,835	VC
DePauw Univ	IN	32,100	HC
Dickinson College	PA	40,170	HC+
Doane College	NE	22,458	C
Dominican Univ	IL	26,370	C
Dordt College	IA	20,325	VC
Drake Univ	IA	27,632	VC+
Drexel Univ	PA	27,700	VC
Drury Univ	MO	20,117	VC
Duke Univ	NC	41,239	MC
Duquesne Univ	PA	29,534	VC
Earlham College	IN	33,604	HC

School	ST	$IS	SR
East Stroudsburg Univ of Pennsylvania	PA	10,336	C
Eastern Conn State Univ	CT	13,554	C
Eastern Kentucky Univ	KY	7,725	C
Eastern Mennonite Univ	VA	25,450	VC
Eastern Nazarene College	MA	19,500	LC
Edinboro Univ of Pennsylvania	PA	11,809	LC
Elizabethtown College	PA	32,100	VC
Elmhurst College	IL	24,685	C
Elmira College	NY	37,200	VC
Elon Univ	NC	25,371	HC
Emory & Henry College	VA	26,570	C
Fairleigh Dickinson Univ/ Metropolitan Campus	NJ	28,590	C
Ferrum College	VA	24,290	LC
Florida Inst of Technology	FL	29,720	VC
Florida International Univ	FL	9,215	C
Florida Southern College	FL	25,965	C
Florida State Univ	FL	9,028	HC
Franklin and Marshall College	PA	40,590	HC
Franklin Pierce College	NH	31,700	C
Fresno Pacific Univ	CA	25,454	C
Friends Univ	KS	16,250	LC
Frostburg State Univ	MD	12,672	C
Furman Univ	SC	33,264	HC+
Gannon Univ	PA	26,100	C
George Washington Univ	DC	48,820	MC
Georgetown College	KY	24,950	C+
Georgia College and State Univ	GA	11,020	C
Gettysburg College	PA	39,864	HC
Goddard College	VT	21,100	C
Goshen College	IN	22,850	VC
Hamline Univ	MN	27,070	VC
Hampshire College	MA	37,120	HC
Hardin-Simmons Univ	TX	18,641	C
Hartwick College	NY	36,065	C
Harvard Univ/Harvard College	MA	45,860	MC
Hawaii Pacific Univ	HI	21,080	C
Heritage Univ	WA	6,800	NC
Hiram College	OH	28,700	VC
Hobart and William Smith Colleges	NY	41,123	VC
Hood College	MD	30,085	VC
Houghton College	NY	25,980	VC+
Humboldt State Univ	CA	11,176	C
Huntington Univ	IN	24,830	C
Illinois College	IL	21,900	C+
Indiana Univ Bloomington	IN	13,356	VC
Iowa State Univ	IA	11,831	VC
Ithaca College	NY	35,144	VC
Jacksonville Univ	FL	24,040	C
John Brown Univ	AR	20,910	VC
Johns Hopkins Univ	MD	42,044	MC
Johnson State College	VT	11,830	C
Juniata College	PA	33,130	VC
Keene State College	NH	13,836	C
Keuka College	NY	26,050	C
Keystone College	PA	22,810	LC
Knox College	IL	32,385	VC+
Kutztown Univ of Pennsylvania	PA	10,820	C
La Salle Univ	PA	34,950	C
Lake Erie College	OH	27,725	C
Lake Forest College	IL	33,860	VC
Lake Superior State Univ	MI	12,842	LC
Lander Univ	SC	10,600	C
Lawrence Tech Univ	MI	25,475	VC
Lawrence Univ	WI	33,958	HC+
Lehigh Univ	PA	42,690	HC+
Lewis Univ	IL	23,050	C+
Lincoln Memorial Univ	TN	18,144	C
Lincoln Univ	PA	13,658	C+
Linfield College	OR	29,632	VC
Lipscomb Univ	TN	20,967	VC
Louisiana State Univ and A&M College	LA	10,749	VC
Louisiana State Univ in Shreveport	LA	2,900	NC
Louisiana Tech Univ	LA	7,370	C
Lourdes College	OH	15,300	LC
Loyola Marymount Univ	CA	36,321	VC
Loyola Univ Chicago	IL	32,896	VC
Lynchburg College	VA	30,645	C
Mansfield Univ	PA	11,300	C
Marian College	IN	26,160	C
Marietta College	OH	29,327	C
Marist College	NY	30,566	VC
Marshall Univ	WV	9,116	C
Martin Univ	IN	10,300	SP
Marygrove College	MI	19,310	C+
Marymount Univ	VA	25,934	C
Maryville Univ of St. Louis	MO	23,000	VC
Marywood Univ	PA	30,680	C
McDaniel College	MD	31,610	VC
McMurry Univ	TX	18,100	LC
McNeese State Univ	LA	5,270	LC
Mercyhurst College	PA	28,633	VC
Merrimack College	MA	34,380	C
Messiah College	PA	28,910	VC+
Metropolitan State College of Denver	CO	2,338	LC
Miami Univ	OH	29,097	HC
Middle Tenn State Univ	TN	8,540	C
Middlebury College	VT	42,120	MC
Midway College	KY	20,150	C
Midwestern State Univ	TX	9,381	C
Miles College	AL	9,922	NC
Mills College	CA	39,870	C
Minn State Univ, Mankato	MN	10,276	LC
Molloy College	NY	16,510	C
Monmouth College	IL	23,700	C
Montana State Univ-Billings	MT	8,906	C
Montana State Univ-Bozeman	MT	1,137	C
Montana State Univ-Northern	MT	10,000	NC
Montreat College	NC	21,440	C
Mount Marty College	SD	20,590	C
Mount Olive College	NC	16,000	LC
Muhlenberg College	PA	36,030	HC+
Muskingum College	OH	22,970	C
Naropa Univ	CO	26,302	SP
National Univ	CA	8,412	SP
Nazareth College of Rochester	NY	28,175	VC
New College of Florida	FL	10,009	HC+
New England College	NH	31,466	C
New Jersey Inst of Technology	NJ	16,396	VC
New Mexico Highlands Univ	NM	6,272	NC
New Mexico Inst of Mining and Technology	NM	8,510	VC+
New Mexico State Univ	NM	9,250	C
N Car Central Univ	NC	9,000	LC
N Car State Univ	NC	11,824	HC
N Car Wesleyan College	NC	22,670	C
Northern State Univ	SD	8,257	C
Northland College	WI	26,680	C
Northwest Univ	WA	18,854	C
Northwestern Univ	IL	37,595	MC
Norwich Univ	VT	28,212	C
Notre Dame College	OH	20,425	C
Oberlin College	OH	40,904	MC
Ohio State Univ	OH	15,357	HC
Ohio Univ	OH	15,921	C
Ohio Wesleyan Univ	OH	35,830	VC+
Okla State Univ	OK	10,213	VC
Olivet College	MI	19,984	C+
Olivet Nazarene Univ	IL	22,590	C
Oregon Inst of Technology	OR	8,718	C
Oregon State Univ	OR	11,055	C
Pacific Lutheran Univ	WA	28,805	VC
Pfeiffer Univ	NC	21,900	C
Philadelphia Univ	PA	30,006	C
Piedmont College	GA	20,500	C
Pitzer College	CA	41,644	HC
Point Park Univ	PA	24,160	C
Portland State Univ	OR	12,453	C
Prescott College	AZ	13,445	LC
Principia College	IL	27,765	VC+
Ramapo College of New Jersey	NJ	16,630	VC
Richard Stockton College of New Jersey	NJ	14,000	VC
Rider Univ	NJ	32,560	C
Ripon College	WI	27,160	C+
Roanoke College	VA	30,748	VC
Robert Morris Univ	PA	22,822	C
Rochester Inst of Technology	NY	32,070	VC+
Rocky Mountain College	MT	20,805	C
Roger Williams Univ	RI	30,500	C
Rollins College	FL	38,366	VC
Roosevelt Univ	IL	22,605	VC
Rosemont College	PA	29,350	C
Russell Sage College	NY	27,000	C
Rutgers, The State Univ of New Jersey/New Brunswick/Piscataway Campus	NJ	15,810	HC
Rutgers, The State Univ of New Jersey/Newark Campus	NJ	15,640	VC
Sacred Heart Univ	CT	33,404	C
Saginaw Valley State Univ	MI	11,432	C
St. Anselm College	NH	33,810	C
St. Bonaventure Univ	NY	28,785	LC
St. John's Univ	NY	34,370	C
St. Joseph College	CT	32,050	C
St. Joseph's College of Maine	ME	29,185	C
St. Joseph's Univ	PA	37,428	VC
St. Lawrence Univ	NY	40,545	VC
St. Leo Univ	FL	22,140	C+
St. Louis Univ	MO	33,158	VC+
St. Michael's College	VT	33,330	VC
St. Norbert College	WI	28,577	C+
St. Paul's College	VA	16,030	NC
St. Vincent College	PA	26,160	VC
Salem International Univ	WV	18,020	C
Sam Houston State Univ	TX	8,000	C
Samford Univ	AL	20,258	VC
Santa Clara Univ	CA	38,931	VC
Savannah State Univ	GA	7,772	LC
Scripps College	CA	41,000	MC
Shaw Univ	NC	15,488	LC
Shenandoah Univ	VA	27,600	C
Shepherd Univ	WV	10,066	C
Shippensburg Univ of Pennsylvania	PA	11,621	C
Siena College	NY	28,260	VC+
Sierra Nevada College	NV	30,235	C
Simmons College	MA	35,640	VC
Simpson College	IA	26,833	VC
Sonoma State Univ	CA	14,732	C
Southeast Missouri State Univ	MO	10,596	C
Southern Methodist Univ	TX	36,088	VC+
Southwest Minn State Univ	MN	10,975	C
SUNY/College at Brockport	NY	12,747	VC
SUNY/College at Cortland	NY	12,095	C
SUNY/College at Oneonta	NY	12,905	VC
SUNY/College at Plattsburgh	NY	12,362	C
SUNY/College at Purchase	NY	11,989	VC+
SUNY/Maritime College	NY	12,475	C
SUNY/Univ at Binghamton	NY	13,988	HC
Stephen F. Austin State Univ	TX	7,930	C
Stetson Univ	FL	32,725	VC
Suffolk Univ	MA	33,160	C
Sul Ross State Univ	TX	6,600	LC
Susquehanna Univ	PA	33,465	VC
Sweet Briar College	VA	31,460	VC
Syracuse Univ	NY	38,655	HC
Taylor Univ	IN	26,376	VC+
Temple Univ	PA	17,438	C
Texas A&M Univ	TX	13,351	HC
Texas A&M Univ at Corpus Christi	TX	10,280	LC
Texas A&M Univ at Galveston	TX	10,000	C+
Texas Christian Univ	TX	23,410	VC+
Texas State Univ - San Marcos	TX	10,862	C
Thiel College	PA	24,580	C
Thomas Edison State College	NJ	3,780	SP
Towson Univ	MD	13,924	VC
Trinity College	CT	38,040	HC+
Trinity College	DC	24,150	LC
Tri-State Univ-Main Campus	IN	26,200	C
Troy Univ	AL	8,916	C
Tufts Univ	MA	42,018	MC
Tulane Univ	LA	41,098	MC
Tusculum College	TN	21,340	LC
Unity College	ME	24,320	C
Univ of Alabama	AL	9,888	C
Univ of Alaska Fairbanks	AK	10,101	C
Univ of Alaska Southeast	AK	8,050	LC
Univ of Arizona	AZ	11,958	VC
Univ of Arkansas	AR	11,859	VC
Univ of at Calif Davis	CA	15,010	VC
Univ of Calif at Berkeley	CA	18,141	HC+
Univ of Calif at Riverside	CA	16,625	C
Univ of Calif at San Diego	CA	16,102	HC
Univ of Calif at Santa Barbara	CA	11,800	VC
Univ of Central Arkansas	AR	9,984	C
Univ of Chicago	IL	42,369	MC
Univ of Colo at Boulder	CO	13,352	C+
Univ of Conn	CT	16,628	HC
Univ of Delaware	DE	14,142	HC
Univ of Denver	CO	36,376	VC+
Univ of Dubuque	IA	23,390	C
Univ of Evansville	IN	28,320	VC
Univ of Findlay	OH	29,238	C
Univ of Georgia	GA	11,004	HC
Univ of Hawaii at Manoa	HI	10,413	VC
Univ of Indianapolis	IN	25,090	C
Univ of Iowa	IA	12,172	VC
Univ of La Verne	CA	33,470	C
Univ of Maine	ME	13,642	C
Univ of Maine at Farmington	ME	11,515	C
Univ of Maine at Fort Kent	ME	10,832	LC
Univ of Maine at Machias	ME	10,523	C
Univ of Maine at Presque Isle	ME	10,066	LC
Univ of Mary Washington	VA	11,636	HC
Univ of Maryland/Baltimore County	MD	16,642	VC+
Univ of Maryland/College Park	MD	16,036	HC
Univ of Maryland/Eastern Shore	MD	11,210	C
Univ of Maryland/Univ College	MD	5,640	SP
Univ of Mass Amherst	MA	15,973	C+
Univ of Mass Lowell	MA	14,327	VC
Univ of Miami	FL	38,397	MC
Univ of Mich/Dearborn	MI	7,000	C
Univ of Minn/Duluth	MN	13,974	C
Univ of Missouri/Kansas City	MO	15,000	VC
Univ of Montana--Western	MT	8,406	NC
Univ of Nebr at Lincoln	NE	11,401	VC
Univ of Nevada/Las Vegas	NV	11,566	C
Univ of Nevada/Reno	NV	12,155	NC
Univ of New England	ME	31,005	C
Univ of New Hampshire	NH	16,810	VC
Univ of New Haven	CT	31,794	C
Univ of New Mexico	NM	11,253	C
Univ of N Car at Asheville	NC	9,237	VC
Univ of N Car at Chapel Hill	NC	11,129	MC
Univ of N Car at Pembroke	NC	7,940	LC
Univ of N Car at Wilmington	NC	10,107	VC
Univ of Notre Dame	IN	39,552	MC
Univ of Okla	OK	10,769	VC+
Univ of Oregon	OR	13,108	VC
Univ of Pennsylvania	PA	41,766	MC
Univ of Pittsburgh at Pittsburgh	PA	18,866	HC
Univ of Portland	OR	32,300	VC
Univ of Redlands	CA	36,160	VC
Univ of Rhode Island	RI	15,398	C
Univ of Rio Grande	OH	8,728	NC
Univ of Rochester	NY	41,135	MC
Univ of St. Francis	IL	25,430	C
Univ of St. Francis	IN	20,970	C
Univ of St. Thomas	MN	28,000	VC
Univ of St. Thomas	TX	23,810	VC
Univ of San Francisco	CA	37,560	VC
Univ of Scranton	PA	31,100	VC
Univ of South Florida	FL	10,284	VC
Univ of Southern Maine	ME	12,614	C
Univ of Tampa	FL	25,784	C
Univ of Tenn at Chattanooga	TN	7,790	C
Univ of Tenn at Knoxville	TN	11,720	C
Univ of Texas at San Antonio	TX	11,325	LC
Univ of the District of Columbia	DC	2,070	LC
Univ of the Incarnate Word	TX	23,306	C
Univ of the Ozarks	AR	19,250	C
Univ of the Pacific	CA	34,380	VC
Univ of the Sciences in Philadelphia	PA	33,380	VC
Univ of Toledo	OH	15,806	NC
Univ of Vermont	VT	18,080	VC
Univ of Virginia	VA	13,759	MC
Univ of Virginia's College at Wise	VA	11,076	C
Univ of West Alabama	AL	7,611	C
Univ of West Georgia	GA	8,838	C
Univ of Wisc/Green Bay	WI	9,415	VC
Ursinus College	PA	38,950	VC
Utah State Univ	UT	8,002	VC
Valdosta State Univ	GA	8,802	C
Valparaiso Univ	IN	28,970	VC+
Virginia Polytechnic Inst and State Univ	VA	10,834	VC
Walla Walla College	WA	24,489	NC
Washington and Lee Univ	VA	35,880	MC
Washington College	MD	34,990	VC
Washington State Univ	WA	12,260	C
Washington Univ in St. Louis	MO	42,106	MC
Waynesburg College	PA	21,230	C
Weber State Univ	UT	9,635	NC
Webster Univ	MO	24,280	VC
Wesley College	DE	19,905	C
Wesleyan College	GA	19,560	C
West Texas A&M Univ	TX	8,452	C
West Virginia Univ	WV	10,506	C
Western Conn State Univ	CT	12,993	C
Western Washington Univ	WA	11,262	VC
Westfield State College	MA	10,200	C
Westminster College	MO	19,060	VC
Wheaton College	IL	27,760	HC
Wheaton College	MA	40,180	HC+
Whitman College	WA	36,110	HC+
Whitworth College	WA	29,428	VC+
Widener Univ	PA	27,275	C
Willamette Univ	OR	35,416	VC+
William Paterson Univ of New Jersey	NJ	17,810	C+
William Penn Univ	IA	17,685	LC
Wilson College	PA	27,660	C
Youngstown State Univ	OH	12,613	NC

ENVIRONMENTAL STUDIES

School	ST	$IS	SR
Adelphi Univ	NY	27,000	VC
Albertson College of Idaho	ID	21,095	VC
Allegheny College	PA	33,500	HC
American Univ	DC	38,719	HC+
Aquinas College	MI	23,750	C
Bates College	ME	42,100	MC
Boston Univ	MA	42,046	HC+
Brenau Univ Women's College	GA	23,950	VC
Brigham Young Univ	UT	9,200	VC
Cal State East Bay	CA	10,856	LC
Cal State, San Bernardino	CA	12,563	LC
Catawba College	NC	25,000	C
Cazenovia College	NY	26,900	C
Central Mich Univ	MI	12,244	C
Chaminade Univ of Honolulu	HI	23,320	LC
Chatham College	PA	27,290	C+
CUNY/Queens College	NY	4,356	C
Claremont McKenna College	CA	42,920	MC
Colby-Sawyer College	NH	27,850	LC
College of New Rochelle	NY	28,396	C+
College of St. Benedict	MN	30,091	VC
College of Santa Fe	NM	28,978	C

ST = STATE $IS = IN-STATE COSTS   SR = SELECTOR RATING

INDEX OF COLLEGE MAJORS

School	ST	$IS	SR
College of the Holy Cross	MA	40,664	MC
Columbia College	MO	16,900	C
Denison Univ	OH	37,040	HC
Dominican Univ of Calif	CA	36,836	C
Eastern Univ	PA	24,075	C
Eckerd College	FL	35,492	VC
Emory Univ	GA	40,546	MC
Endicott College	MA	30,156	C+
Florida State Univ	FL	9,028	HC
Franklin and Marshall College	PA	40,590	HC
Green Mountain College	VT	32,164	C
Guilford College	NC	28,160	C+
Gustavus Adolphus College	MN	30,920	HC
Hendrix College	AR	27,646	HC+
Hofstra Univ	NY	32,630	VC
Hollins Univ	VA	31,105	C
Illinois Wesleyan Univ	IL	34,050	HC+
Indiana Univ Bloomington	IN	13,356	VC
Indiana Univ South Bend	IN	4,989	LC
Juniata College	PA	33,130	VC
King's College	PA	29,810	C
Lehigh Univ	PA	42,690	HC+
Lewis and Clark College	OR	35,358	VC+
Loyola Univ Chicago	IL	32,896	VC
Lyon College	AR	19,990	VC
Macalester College	MN	36,500	MC
Maharishi Univ of Management	IA	29,450	VC
Marietta College	OH	29,327	C
Maryville Univ	TN	29,224	VC
Maryville Univ of St. Louis	MO	23,000	VC
Meredith College	NC	25,600	C
Messiah College	PA	28,910	VC+
Mich State Univ	MI	13,689	VC
Mills College	CA	39,870	C
Mount Holyoke College	MA	42,148	HC+
Mountain State Univ	WV	11,406	NC
Neumann Univ	PA	25,996	LC
Northeastern Illinois Univ	IL	3,000	NC
Nova Southeastern Univ	FL	24,320	C
Ohio Northern Univ	OH	27,765	VC
Penn State Univ/Altoona	PA	12,635	C
Pennsylvania College of Technology	PA	16,980	LC
Piedmont College	GA	20,500	C
Prescott College	AZ	13,445	LC
Ramapo College of New Jersey	NJ	16,630	VC
Randolph-Macon College	VA	31,250	C
Randolph-Macon Woman's College	VA	31,160	VC+
Roanoke College	VA	30,748	VC
Rocky Mountain College	MT	20,805	VC
St. John's Univ	MN	29,749	VC
St. Lawrence Univ	NY	40,545	VC
St. Norbert College	WI	28,577	C+
St. Olaf College	MN	32,800	HC
Salisbury Univ	MD	13,128	VC
Santa Clara Univ	CA	38,931	VC
Skidmore College	NY	41,779	HC
Southeastern Okla State Univ	OK	6,147	C
Southern New Hampshire Univ	NH	28,764	C
Southwestern Univ	TX	26,767	HC
SUNY/College of Environmental Science and Forestry	NY	15,000	VC
SUNY/Univ at Stony Brook	NY	13,625	HC
Sweet Briar College	VA	31,460	VC
Temple Univ	PA	17,438	C
Texas A&M Univ at Galveston	TX	10,000	C
Thomas Edison State College	NJ	3,780	SP
Univ of Calif at San Diego	CA	16,102	HC
Univ of Calif at Santa Cruz	CA	19,174	VC
Univ of Georgia	GA	11,004	VC
Univ of Hawaii at Manoa	HI	10,413	VC
Univ of Kansas	KS	10,915	VC
Univ of Maryland/Baltimore County	MD	16,642	VC+
Univ of Montana	MT	10,602	C
Univ of Nebr at Lincoln	NE	11,401	VC
Univ of Nebr at Omaha	NE	11,235	C
Univ of New England	ME	31,005	C
Univ of New Hampshire	NH	16,810	VC
Univ of N Car at Chapel Hill	NC	11,129	MC
Univ of Pennsylvania	PA	41,766	MC
Univ of Pittsburgh at Bradford	PA	17,008	C
Univ of Pittsburgh at Johnstown	PA	16,740	LC
Univ of Redlands	CA	36,160	VC
Univ of Rochester	NY	41,135	MC
Univ of St. Thomas	MN	28,000	VC
Univ of Southern Calif	CA	41,618	MC
Univ of the South	TN	34,645	HC
Univ of Tulsa	OK	25,348	HC
Univ of Utah	UT	10,162	VC
Univ of Vermont	VT	18,080	VC
Univ of West Georgia	GA	8,838	C
Vassar College	NY	41,700	MC
Virginia Commonwealth Univ	VA	12,987	C
Virginia Wesleyan College	VA	28,433	C
Warren Wilson College	NC	24,382	VC
Washington Univ in St. Louis	MO	42,106	MC
Wellesley College	MA	41,030	MC
Wells College	NY	23,070	VC
Western Mich Univ	MI	13,299	C
Worcester Polytechnic Inst	MA	40,450	VC+

EQUINE SCIENCE

School	ST	$IS	SR
Averett Univ	VA	24,920	C
Bethany College	WV	21,395	C
Centenary College	NJ	28,870	LC
Colo State Univ-Fort Collins	CO	10,878	C+
Delaware Valley College	PA	29,944	C
Johnson and Wales Univ/Providence Campus	RI	28,126	LC
Lake Erie College	OH	27,725	C
Midway College	KY	20,150	C
Mount Ida College	MA	26,000	C
National American Univ	SD	14,820	NC
N Dak State Univ	ND	8,500	C
Otterbein College	OH	28,986	C
Rocky Mountain College	MT	20,805	C
St. Mary-of-the-Woods College	IN	25,480	C
Salem International Univ	WV	18,020	C
Stephens College	MO	26,930	VC
Sul Ross State Univ	TX	6,600	LC
Truman State Univ	MO	11,242	HC
Univ of Findlay	OH	29,238	C
Univ of Louisville	KY	10,400	VC
Univ of Minn/Crookston	MN	13,157	C
Virginia Intermont College	VA	22,200	LC
William Woods Univ	MO	21,020	C
Wilson College	PA	27,660	C

ESKIMO

School	ST	$IS	SR
Univ of Alaska Fairbanks	AK	10,101	C

ETHICS, POLITICS, AND SOCIAL POLICY

School	ST	$IS	SR
Drake Univ	IA	27,632	VC+
Indiana Univ Bloomington	IN	13,356	VC
Mount Holyoke College	MA	42,148	HC+
Northwestern Univ	IL	37,595	MC
Pine Manor College	MA	25,038	LC
Simon's Rock College of Bard	MA	41,988	VC+
Syracuse Univ	NY	38,655	HC
Univ of Judaism College of A&S	CA	30,010	C
Univ of Mass Amherst	MA	15,973	C+
Univ of Mass Boston	MA	8,024	C
Univ of Northern Colo	CO	10,249	C
Wells College	NY	23,070	VC
Wheeling Jesuit Univ	WV	26,910	C
Yale Univ	CT	41,000	MC

ETHNIC STUDIES

School	ST	$IS	SR
Bethel Univ	MN	29,840	VC
Bowling Green State Univ	OH	14,994	C
Brown Univ	RI	42,015	MC
Cal State East Bay	CA	10,856	LC
Cal State, Chico	CA	11,395	C
Cal State, San Bernardino	CA	12,563	LC
Cal State, Stanislaus	CA	11,283	C
CUNY/City College	NY		C
College of St. Catherine	MN	27,505	VC
Kent State Univ	OH	14,594	C
Metropolitan State Univ	MN	4,682	SP
Mills College	CA	39,870	C
Minn State Univ, Mankato	MN	10,276	LC
New York Univ	NY	43,170	MC
St. Olaf College	MN	32,800	HC
Sonoma State Univ	CA	14,732	C
SUNY/College at Purchase	NY	11,989	VC+
SUNY/Univ at Stony Brook	NY	13,625	HC
Univ of Alaska Fairbanks	AK	10,101	C
Univ of Arizona	AZ	11,958	VC
Univ of Calif at Berkeley	CA	18,141	HC+
Univ of Calif at Riverside	CA	16,625	C
Univ of Calif at San Diego	CA	16,102	HC
Univ of Colo at Boulder	CO	13,352	C+
Univ of Hawaii at Manoa	HI	10,413	VC
Univ of Nebr at Lincoln	NE	11,401	VC
Univ of Oregon	OR	13,108	VC
Univ of Texas at Austin	TX	14,610	HC
Univ of Washington	WA	10,400	VC
Washington Univ in St. Louis	MO	42,106	MC
Wichita State Univ	KS	8,500	C
Yale Univ	CT	41,000	MC

EUROPEAN STUDIES

School	ST	$IS	SR
Amherst College	MA	41,590	MC
Bard College	NY	41,800	HC+
Brandeis Univ	MA	41,551	MC
Canisius College	NY	32,257	VC
Central Mich Univ	MI	12,244	C
Columbia Univ/Barnard College	NY	38,000	MC
Emory & Henry College	VA	26,570	C
George Washington Univ	DC	48,820	MC
Georgetown College	KY	24,950	C+
Hamline Univ	MN	27,070	VC
Harvard Univ/Harvard College	MA	45,860	MC
Hillsdale College	MI	24,160	HC
Hobart and William Smith Colleges	NY	41,123	VC
Huntingdon College	AL	23,090	VC
Loyola Marymount Univ	CA	36,321	VC
Middlebury College	VT	42,120	MC
Millsaps College	MS	28,256	VC+
Mount Holyoke College	MA	42,148	HC+
New York Univ	NY	43,170	MC
Northwestern Univ	IL	37,595	MC
Pitzer College	CA	41,644	HC
Rollins College	FL	38,366	VC
St. Joseph's Univ	PA	37,428	VC
San Diego State Univ	CA	12,971	C
Scripps College	CA	41,000	MC
Seattle Pacific Univ	WA	29,355	C
Simon's Rock College of Bard	MA	41,988	VC+
Suffolk Univ	MA	33,160	C
Syracuse Univ	NY	38,655	HC
Texas State Univ - San Marcos	TX	10,862	C
Univ of Arkansas	AR	11,859	VC
Univ of Calif at Los Angeles	CA	17,681	MC
Univ of Kansas	KS	10,915	VC
Univ of Minn/Morris	MN	15,472	VC
Univ of Nebr at Lincoln	NE	11,401	VC
Univ of New Hampshire	NH	16,810	VC
Univ of New Mexico	NM	11,253	C
Univ of Northern Iowa	IA	11,133	C
Univ of Okla	OK	10,769	VC+
Univ of S Car at Columbia	SC	13,397	VC
Univ of Vermont	VT	18,080	VC
Vanderbilt Univ	TN	41,986	MC
Washington Univ in St. Louis	MO	42,106	MC
Westmont College	CA	36,672	HC

EVOLUTIONARY BIOLOGY

School	ST	$IS	SR
Case Western Reserve Univ	OH	37,314	MC
Cornell Univ	NY	41,717	MC
Dartmouth College	NH	39,465	MC
Florida State Univ	FL	9,028	HC
Ohio State Univ	OH	15,357	HC
Princeton Univ	NJ	40,213	MC
Rutgers, The State Univ of New Jersey/New Brunswick/Piscataway Campus	NJ	15,810	VC
Tulane Univ	LA	41,098	MC
Univ of Arizona	AZ	11,958	VC
Univ of Calif at Santa Barbara	CA	11,800	VC
Univ of Conn	CT	16,628	HC
Univ of Minn/Twin Cities	MN	13,165	VC
Univ of Pittsburgh at Pittsburgh	PA	18,866	HC

EXERCISE SCIENCE

School	ST	$IS	SR
Albertson College of Idaho	ID	21,095	VC
Angelo State Univ	TX	8,340	NC
Appalachian State Univ	NC	8,000	VC
Arkansas State Univ	AR	9,630	C
Asbury College	KY	23,762	VC
Augustana College	SD	24,380	VC
Baldwin-Wallace College	OH	27,256	VC
Barton College	NC	22,316	C
Becker College	MA	24,300	LC
Belhaven College	MS	19,530	NC
Bethel College	IN	19,680	C
Bluefield College	VA	17,230	C+
Boston Univ	MA	42,046	HC+
Bowling Green State Univ	OH	14,994	C
Bridgewater College	VA	27,790	C
Brigham Young Univ	UT	9,200	VC
Bryan College	TN	19,270	C
Calif Baptist Univ	CA	23,780	C
Cal State, Chico	CA	11,395	C
Cal State, Northridge	CA	9,036	VC
Cal State, San Bernardino	CA	12,563	LC
Carroll College	WI	24,860	C
Castleton State College	VT	13,158	C
Cedarville Univ	OH	21,904	VC
Centenary College of Louisiana	LA	24,760	VC
Centra! College	IA	26,774	VC
Central Washington Univ	WA	11,730	C
Chatham College	PA	27,290	C+
CUNY/York College	NY	4,242	NC
Colby-Sawyer College	NH	27,850	LC
College of New Jersey	NJ	18,315	MC
College of St. Scholastica	MN	28,456	C+
Colo State Univ-Fort Collins	CO	10,878	C+
Colo State Univ-Pueblo	CO	7,821	LC
Columbus State Univ	GA	8,664	C
Concordia Univ	CA	26,780	C
Concordia Univ Nebr	NE	20,500	C+
Creighton Univ	NE	29,918	VC+
Drury Univ	MO	20,117	VC
D'Youville College	NY	23,660	C
East Carolina Univ	NC	10,000	C
East Central Univ	OK	6,207	C
Fitchburg State College	MA	11,276	C
Fort Lewis College	CO	11,852	C
George Mason Univ	VA	10,850	VC
Georgetown College	KY	24,950	C+
Georgia Southern Univ	GA	9,762	C
Georgia State Univ	GA	11,444	VC
Gonzaga Univ	WA	30,218	HC
Greensboro College	NC	23,000	C
Guilford College	NC	28,160	C+
Hanover College	IN	28,150	HC
Harding Univ	AR	16,512	VC
Hardin-Simmons Univ	TX	18,641	C
Hendrix College	AR	27,646	HC+
High Point Univ	NC	25,720	C
Hofstra Univ	NY	32,630	VC
Howard Payne Univ	TX	17,115	C
Huntingdon College	AL	23,090	VC
Huntington Univ	IN	24,830	C
Illinois State Univ	IL	12,839	C+
Indiana Univ Bloomington	IN	13,356	VC
Ithaca College	NY	35,144	VC
La Sierra Univ	CA	24,327	C+
Lake Superior State Univ	MI	12,842	LC
Lander Univ	SC	10,600	C
Lasell College	MA	26,250	C
Liberty Univ	VA	19,101	C
Linfield College	OR	29,632	VC
Lipscomb Univ	TN	20,967	VC
Loras College	IA	27,193	C
Louisiana College	LA	13,450	C
Lubbock Christian Univ	TX	16,960	C
Lynchburg College	VA	30,645	C
Malone College	OH	23,040	C
Marquette Univ	WI	35,066	HC
Meredith College	NC	25,600	C
Messiah College	PA	28,910	VC+
Miami Univ	OH	29,097	HC
Milligan College	TN	21,990	VC
Missouri Valley College	MO	18,500	C
Mount Vernon Nazarene Univ	OH	20,810	C
Murray State Univ	KY	8,900	VC
Nebr Wesleyan Univ	NE	23,415	C+
Norfolk State Univ	VA	10,531	LC
N Car Wesleyan College	NC	22,670	C
Northwest Christian College	OR	24,298	C
Northwestern College	MN	25,220	NC
Old Dominion Univ	VA	11,907	C
Palm Beach Atlantic Univ	FL	23,597	VC
Pfeiffer Univ	NC	21,900	C
Purdue Univ/West Lafayette	IN	13,458	VC
Rice Univ	TX	32,290	MC
Ripon College	WI	27,160	C+
Rutgers, The State Univ of New Jersey/New Brunswick/Piscataway Campus	NJ	15,810	HC
Sacred Heart Univ	CT	33,404	C
Saginaw Valley State Univ	MI	11,432	C
St. Louis Univ	MO	33,158	VC+
St. Olaf College	MN	32,800	HC
Salisbury Univ	MD	13,128	VC
Samford Univ	AL	20,258	VC
San Diego State Univ	CA	12,971	C
Schreiner Univ	TX	20,600	C
Seattle Pacific Univ	WA	29,355	C
Shippensburg Univ of Pennsylvania	PA	11,621	C
Skidmore College	NY	41,779	HC
Southern Illinois Univ Edwardsville	IL	11,022	C
Southern Nazarene Univ	OK	14,634	NC
Southwestern Adventist Univ	TX	18,290	LC
Spring Arbor Univ	MI	22,476	C
SUNY/Univ at Buffalo	NY	13,694	VC
Sterling College	KS	19,992	C
Syracuse Univ	NY	38,655	HC
Taylor Univ	IN	26,376	VC+
Texas Christian Univ	TX	23,410	VC+
Texas State Univ - San Marcos	TX	10,862	C
Texas Tech Univ	TX	13,026	VC
Towson Univ	MD	13,924	VC
Transylvania Univ	KY	26,240	VC+
Tulane Univ	LA	41,098	MC
Univ of Arkansas	AR	11,859	VC
Univ of Arkansas at Monticello	AR	7,325	NC
Univ of Central Arkansas	AR	9,984	C
Univ of Colo at Boulder	CO	13,352	C+
Univ of Conn	CT	16,628	HC
Univ of Dayton	OH	28,826	VC
Univ of Evansville	IN	28,320	VC
Univ of Florida	FL	9,354	HC
Univ of Georgia	GA	11,004	HC
Univ of Hawaii at Manoa	HI	10,413	VC
Univ of Illinois at Urbana-Champaign	IL	15,800	HC+

School	ST $IS SR
Univ of Indianapolis	IN 25,090 C
Univ of Mary	ND 15,374 C
Univ of Mary Hardin-Baylor	TX 19,428 C
Univ of Mass Amherst	MA 15,973 C+
Univ of Mass Lowell	MA 14,327 VC
Univ of Memphis	TN 11,153 C
Univ of Miss	MS 9,000 C
Univ of Nebr at Lincoln	NE 11,401 VC
Univ of Nevada/Las Vegas	NV 11,566 C
Univ of New Mexico	NM 11,253 C
Univ of N Car at Chapel Hill	NC 11,129 MC
Univ of N Car at Greensboro	NC 8,993 C
Univ of N Dak	ND 10,114 VC
Univ of Northern Colo	CO 10,249 C
Univ of Puget Sound	WA 35,600 HC
Univ of San Francisco	CA 37,560 VC
Univ of Scranton	PA 31,100 C
Univ of S Car at Columbia	SC 13,397 VC
Univ of Tampa	FL 25,784 C
Univ of Tulsa	OK 25,348 HC
Univ of Utah	UT 10,162 VC
Univ of Vermont	VT 18,080 C
Univ of Wisc/La Crosse	WI 10,045 VC
Univ of Wyoming	WY 9,666 C
Ursinus College	PA 38,950 VC
Valdosta State Univ	GA 8,802 C
Valparaiso Univ	IN 28,970 VC+
Wake Forest Univ	NC 38,290 MC
Warner Southern College	FL 18,000 LC
Washington State Univ	WA 12,260 C
Waynesburg College	PA 21,230 C
West Texas A&M Univ	TX 8,452 C
Western Mich Univ	MI 13,299 C
Westmont College	CA 36,672 HC
Willamette Univ	OR 35,416 VC+
Wilson College	PA 27,660 C
Winona State Univ	MN 11,333 C

EXPERIMENTAL PSYCHOLOGY

School	ST $IS SR
Immaculata Univ	PA 25,350 C
Kent State Univ	OH 14,594 C
Millikin Univ	IL 25,590 C
Moravian College	PA 28,950 VC
Rochester Inst of Technology	NY 32,070 VC+
Tufts Univ	MA 42,018 MC

FAMILY AND COMMUNITY SERVICES

School	ST $IS SR
Central Washington Univ	WA 11,730 C
East Carolina Univ	NC 10,000 C
John Brown Univ	AR 20,910 VC
Kansas State Univ	KS 10,516 VC
Mich State Univ	MI 13,689 VC
Point Loma Nazarene Univ	CA 27,610 VC
Prairie View A&M Univ	TX 11,110 LC
Purdue Univ/West Lafayette	IN 13,458 VC
Union Univ	TN 20,750 VC
Univ of Delaware	DE 14,142 HC
Univ of Northern Iowa	IA 11,133 C
Univ of Oregon	OR 13,108 VC
Univ of Texas at San Antonio	TX 11,325 LC
Youngstown State Univ	OH 12,613 NC

FAMILY/CONSUMER RESOURCE MANAGEMENT

School	ST $IS SR
Arizona State Univ-Tempe	AZ 11,174 C
Bowling Green State Univ	OH 14,994 C
East Central Univ	OK 6,207 C
Iowa State Univ	IA 11,831 VC
Mich State Univ	MI 13,689 VC
Northwest Missouri State Univ	MO 10,000 C
Ohio State Univ at Lima	OH 4,416 NC
Ohio Univ	OH 15,921 C
Seton Hill Univ	PA 28,810 C
Southern Illinois Univ Carbondale	IL 12,391 C
Texas Tech Univ	TX 13,026 VC
Univ of Arizona	AZ 11,958 VC
Univ of Georgia	GA 11,004 HC
Univ of Hawaii at Manoa	HI 10,413 VC
Univ of Missouri/Columbia	MO 13,500 VC
West Virginia Univ	WV 10,506 C

FAMILY/CONSUMER STUDIES

School	ST $IS SR
Alabama A&M Univ	AL 8,890 LC
Alcorn State Univ	MS 8,190 LC
Anderson Univ	IN 25,050 LC
Andrews Univ	MI 21,786 C
Appalachian State Univ	NC 8,000 VC
Baylor Univ	TX 27,555 HC
Bluffton College	OH 26,110 C
Bradley Univ	IL 25,280 VC
Bridgewater College	VA 27,790 C
Brigham Young Univ	UT 9,200 VC
Cal State, Fresno	CA 10,037 LC
Cal State, Northridge	CA 9,036 LC

School	ST $IS SR
Campbell Univ	NC 21,137 VC
Central Mich Univ	MI 12,244 C
Central Washington Univ	WA 11,730 C
CUNY/Queens College	NY 4,356 C
College of St. Catherine	MN 27,505 VC
College of the Ozarks	MO 4,130 VC+
Colo State Univ-Fort Collins	CO 10,878 C+
Concordia College: Moorhead	MN 22,475 VC
Concordia Univ, Ann Arbor	MI 25,153 C+
Cornell Univ	NY 41,717 MC
Cornerstone Univ and Grand Rapids Theological Seminary	MI 21,350 NC
De Sales Univ	PA 28,580 VC
Delta State Univ	MS 7,709 C
Eastern Mich Univ	MI 12,897 C
Fairmont State	WV 8,400 LC
Florida State Univ	FL 9,028 HC
Fontbonne Univ	MO 23,308 C
Framingham State College	MA 11,156 C
Freed-Hardeman Univ	TN 16,370 NC
Gallaudet Univ	DC 16,554
Georgia Southern Univ	GA 9,762 C
Hampshire College	MA 37,120 HC
Henderson State Univ	AR 7,600 C
Idaho State Univ	ID 9,030 C
Illinois State Univ	IL 12,839 C+
Indiana Univ Bloomington	IN 13,356 VC
Indiana Univ of Pennsylvania	PA 11,209 C
Iowa State Univ	IA 11,831 VC
Kansas State Univ	KS 10,516 VC
Kent State Univ	OH 14,594 C
Lamar Univ	TX 6,820 LC
Lambuth Univ	TN 21,700 C+
Liberty Univ	VA 19,101 C
Lipscomb Univ	TN 20,967 VC
Louisiana State Univ and A&M College	LA 10,749 VC
Lubbock Christian Univ	TX 16,960 C
Madonna Univ	MI 16,068 VC
Marywood Univ	PA 30,680 C
McNeese State Univ	LA 5,270 LC
Mercyhurst College	PA 28,633 VC
Meredith College	NC 25,600 C
Miami Univ	OH 29,097 HC
Mich State Univ	MI 13,689 VC
Middle Tenn State Univ	TN 8,540 C
Minn State Univ, Mankato	MN 10,276 LC
Miss College	MS 14,574 VC
Mount Vernon Nazarene Univ	OH 20,810 C
New Mexico State Univ	NM 9,250 C
Nicholls State Univ	LA 6,500 NC
Northwestern State Univ of Louisiana	LA 7,144 C
Oakwood College	AL 14,904 C
Olivet Nazarene Univ	IL 22,590 C
Oregon State Univ	OR 11,055 C
Pittsburg State Univ	KS 8,112 C
St. Joseph College	CT 32,050 C
St. Olaf College	MN 32,800 HC
Samford Univ	AL 20,258 VC
Seattle Pacific Univ	WA 29,355 C
Seton Hill Univ	PA 28,810 C
Shepherd Univ	WV 10,066 C
S Dak State Univ	SD 9,815 C
Southeast Missouri State Univ	MO 10,596 C
Southeastern Louisiana Univ	LA 8,521 LC
Southern Univ and A&M College	LA 8,238 LC
Southern Utah Univ	UT — C
Syracuse Univ	NY 38,655 HC
Tenn State Univ	TN 9,048 LC
Texas State Univ - San Marcos	TX 10,862 C
Texas Tech Univ	TX 13,026 VC
Texas Woman's Univ	TX 7,804 LC
Towson Univ	MD 13,924 VC
Univ of Akron	OH 15,166 NC
Univ of Arizona	AZ 11,958 VC
Univ of Arkansas at Pine Bluff	AR 8,300 C
Univ of Central Arkansas	AR 9,984 C
Univ of Central Okla	OK 8,094 C
Univ of Georgia	GA 11,004 HC
Univ of Houston	TX 7,000 C
Univ of Illinois at Urbana-Champaign	IL 15,800 HC+
Univ of Louisiana at Monroe	LA 7,103 C
Univ of Maryland/College Park	MD 16,036 HC
Univ of Miss	MS 9,000 C
Univ of Nebr at Kearney	NE 9,000 NC
Univ of Nebr at Lincoln	NE 11,401 VC
Univ of New Hampshire	NH 16,810 VC
Univ of New Mexico	NM 11,253 C
Univ of PR/Rio Piedras	PR 5,750
Univ of Rhode Island	RI 15,398 C
Univ of Utah	UT 10,162 VC
Univ of Vermont	VT 18,080 VC
Univ of Wisc/Madison	WI 13,117 HC
Univ of Wisc/Stevens Point	WI 9,384 VC

School	ST $IS SR
Univ of Wisc/Stout	WI 11,164 C
Univ of Wyoming	WY 9,666 C
Villa Julie College	MD 25,222 C
Washington State Univ	WA 12,260 C
Wayne State College	NE 8,033 NC
Weber State Univ	UT 9,635 NC
Western Illinois Univ	IL 13,042 C
Western Mich Univ	MI 13,299 C
Youngstown State Univ	OH 12,613 NC

FAMILY/JUVENILE JUSTICE

School	ST $IS SR
Thiel College	PA 24,580 C
William Woods Univ	MO 21,020 C

FASHION DESIGN AND TECHNOLOGY

School	ST $IS SR
American InterContinental Univ	GA 12,100 NC
Baylor Univ	TX 27,555 HC
Calif College of the Arts	CA 34,325 SP
Cazenovia College	NY 26,900 C
Centenary College	NJ 28,870 LC
College of St. Catherine	MN 27,505 VC
Columbus College of Art and Design	OH 24,500 SP
Dominican Univ	IL 26,370 C
Drexel Univ	PA 27,700 VC
Fashion Inst of Technology/ SUNY	NY 11,600 C+
Florida State Univ	FL 9,028 HC
Framingham State College	MA 11,156 C
Illinois State Univ	IL 12,839 C+
Iowa State Univ	IA 11,831 VC
Kent State Univ	OH 14,594 C
Lasell College	MA 26,250 C
Lindenwood Univ	MO 18,600 VC
Marist College	NY 30,566 VC
Marymount Univ	VA 25,934 C
Mass College of Art	MA 16,650 SP
Moore College of Art and Design	PA 27,200 SP
Mount Ida College	MA 26,000 C
Mount Mary College	WI 22,895 C
Oregon State Univ	OR 11,055 C
Otis College of Art and Design	CA 27,546 SP
Parsons School of Design	NY 32,242 SP
Philadelphia Univ	PA 30,006 C
Pratt Inst	NY 36,156 SP
Savannah College of Art and Design	GA 30,800 SP
School of the Art Inst of Chicago	IL 37,800 SP
Stephens College	MO 26,930 VC
Syracuse Univ	NY 38,655 HC
Texas Woman's Univ	TX 7,804 LC
Univ of Delaware	DE 14,142 HC
Univ of North Texas	TX 7,800 C
Univ of the Incarnate Word	TX 23,306 C
Ursuline College	OH 25,456 C
Virginia Commonwealth Univ	VA 12,987 C
Washington Univ in St. Louis	MO 42,106 MC
Woodbury Univ	CA 30,176 LC
Youngstown State Univ	OH 12,613 NC

FASHION MERCHANDISING

School	ST $IS SR
Albright College	PA 33,920 C
American InterContinental Univ	GA 12,100 NC
Ashland Univ	OH 25,000 C
Auburn Univ	AL 12,230 VC
Baylor Univ	TX 27,555 HC
Bennett College	NC 11,500 C
Brenau Univ Women's College	GA 23,950 VC
Central Mich Univ	MI 12,244 C
Central Washington Univ	WA 11,730 C
College of St. Catherine	MN 27,505 VC
Delaware State Univ	DE 8,130 LC
Delta State Univ	MS 7,709 C
Dominican Univ	IL 26,370 C
Drexel Univ	PA 27,700 VC
Eastern Mich Univ	MI 12,897 C
Fashion Inst of Technology/ SUNY	NY 11,600 C+
Florida State Univ	FL 9,028 HC
Fontbonne Univ	MO 23,308 C
Framingham State College	MA 11,156 C
Georgia Southern Univ	GA 9,762 C
Immaculata Univ	PA 25,350 C
Indiana Univ of Pennsylvania	PA 11,209 C
Iowa State Univ	IA 11,831 VC
Johnson and Wales Univ/ Providence Campus	RI 28,126 LC
Kent State Univ	OH 14,594 C
Laboratory Inst of Merchandising	NY 25,150 SP
Lasell College	MA 26,250 C
Lipscomb Univ	TN 20,967 VC

School	ST $IS SR
Lynn Univ	FL 30,750 C
Marist College	NY 30,566 VC
Mars Hill College	NC 19,000 LC
Marymount Univ	VA 25,934 C
Mercyhurst College	PA 28,633 VC
Meredith College	NC 25,600 C
Miss Univ for Women	MS 6,000 LC
Mount Ida College	MA 26,000 C
Mount Mary College	WI 22,895 C
New Mexico State Univ	NM 9,250 C
Northwood Univ	MI 21,000 LC
Old Dominion Univ	VA 11,907 C
Olivet Nazarene Univ	IL 22,590 C
Philadelphia Univ	PA 30,006 C
Southeast Missouri State Univ	MO 10,596 C
Southern Illinois Univ Carbondale	IL 12,391 C
Southern New Hampshire Univ	NH 28,764 C
SUNY/College at Oneonta	NY 12,905 VC
Stephen F. Austin State Univ	TX 7,930 C
Stephens College	MO 26,930 VC
Tarleton State Univ	TX 8,952 C
Texas A&M Univ at Kingsville	TX 6,800 LC
Texas Christian Univ	TX 23,410 VC+
Texas State Univ - San Marcos	TX 10,862 C
Texas Woman's Univ	TX 7,804 LC
Univ of Bridgeport	CT 29,595 LC
Univ of Central Okla	OK 8,094 C
Univ of Georgia	GA 11,004 HC
Univ of Louisiana at Lafayette	LA 5,830 C
Univ of Rhode Island	RI 15,398 C
Univ of the Incarnate Word	TX 23,306 C
Ursuline College	OH 25,456 C
Utah State Univ	UT 8,002 VC
West Virginia Univ	WV 10,506 C
Woodbury Univ	CA 30,176 LC
Youngstown State Univ	OH 12,613 NC

FIBER/TEXTILES/WEAVING

School	ST $IS SR
Cleveland Inst of Art	OH 34,109 SP
Edinboro Univ of Pennsylvania	PA 11,809 LC
Fashion Inst of Technology/ SUNY	NY 11,600 C+
Florida State Univ	FL 9,028 HC
Kansas City Art Inst	MO 29,542 SP
Maryland Inst College of Art	MD 34,450 SP
Mass College of Art	MA 16,650 SP
Ohio Univ	OH 15,921 C
Savannah College of Art and Design	GA 30,800 SP
School of the Art Inst of Chicago	IL 37,800 SP
Syracuse Univ	NY 38,655 HC
Univ of Georgia	GA 11,004 HC
Univ of Mass Dartmouth	MA 15,985 C
Univ of Mich/Ann Arbor	MI 16,587 HC+
Univ of North Texas	TX 7,800 C
Univ of Oregon	OR 13,108 VC
Univ of Washington	WA 10,400 VC

FILM ARTS

School	ST $IS SR
American Univ	DC 38,719 HC+
Art Center College of Design	CA 26,370 SP
Baldwin-Wallace College	OH 27,256 VC
Ball State Univ	IN 13,138 C
Bard College	NY 41,800 HC+
Bennington College	VT 41,890 HC
Boston College	MA 41,608 MC
Boston Univ	MA 42,046 HC+
Bowling Green State Univ	OH 14,994 C
Burlington College	VT 14,670 SP
Calif College of the Arts	CA 34,325 SP
Calif Inst of the Arts	CA 35,725 SP
Cal State, Fullerton	CA 10,990 C
Cal State, Long Beach	CA 9,512 C
Cal State, Northridge	CA 9,036 LC
Calvin College	MI 25,735 NC
Chapman Univ	CA 37,550 VC
CUNY/Brooklyn College	NY 4,377 C+
CUNY/City College	NY — C
CUNY/College of Staten Island	NY 4,328 NC
CUNY/Hunter College	NY 8,000 C+
CUNY/Queens College	NY 4,356 C
Claremont McKenna College	CA 42,920 MC
Clark Univ	MA 35,165 VC+
College of Santa Fe	NM 28,978 C
Colo College	CO 37,668 HC
Columbia College Chicago	IL 25,125 LC
Columbia Univ/Barnard College	NY 38,000 MC
Columbia Univ/Columbia College	NY 42,584 MC
Columbia Univ/School of General Studies	NY 41,516 C

School	ST	$IS	SR
Cornell Univ	NY	41,717	MC
Dartmouth College	NH	39,465	MC
De Sales Univ	PA	28,580	VC
Denison Univ	OH	37,040	HC
Drexel Univ	PA	27,700	VC
Eastern Mich Univ	MI	12,897	C
Edinboro Univ of Pennsylvania	PA	11,809	LC
Elon Univ	NC	25,371	HC
Emerson College	MA	35,076	HC
Emory Univ	GA	40,546	MC
Florida State Univ	FL	9,028	HC
Fordham Univ	NY	36,000	HC
Georgia State Univ	GA	11,444	VC
Grand Valley State Univ	MI	12,000	VC
Hampshire College	MA	37,120	HC
Hofstra Univ	NY	32,630	VC
Indiana State Univ	IN	11,604	C
Ithaca College	NY	35,144	VC
Keene State College	NH	13,836	C
LIU/C.W. Post Campus	NY	28,282	C
Loyola Univ Chicago	IL	32,896	VC
Mass College of Art	MA	16,650	SP
Middlebury College	VT	42,120	MC
Minneapolis College of Art and Design	MN	31,110	SP
Missouri State Univ	MO	10,748	C+
Montclair State Univ	NJ	16,327	C
Mount Holyoke College	MA	42,148	HC+
New College of Calif	CA	12,842	NC
New York Univ	NY	43,170	MC
N Car School of the Arts	NC	7,401	SP
Oberlin College	OH	40,904	MC
Old Dominion Univ	VA	11,907	C
Oral Roberts Univ	OK	22,650	C
Palm Beach Atlantic Univ	FL	23,597	VC
Penn State Univ/Univ Park Campus	PA	18,038	HC
Pitzer College	CA	41,644	HC
Point Park Univ	PA	24,160	C
Pratt Inst	NY	36,156	SP
Purdue Univ/West Lafayette	IN	13,458	VC
Rhode Island College	RI	11,570	C
Rhode Island School of Design	RI	38,130	SP
Rochester Inst of Technology	NY	32,070	VC+
San Francisco Art Inst	CA	25,640	SP
San Francisco State Univ	CA	13,000	C
San Jose State Univ	CA	11,707	C
Sarah Lawrence College	NY	42,000	HC
Savannah College of Art and Design	GA	30,800	SP
School of the Art Inst of Chicago	IL	37,800	SP
School of Visual Arts	NY	32,580	SP
Southern Adventist Univ	TN	18,500	C
Southern Illinois Univ Carbondale	IL	12,391	C
Southern Methodist Univ	TX	36,088	VC+
Spring Arbor Univ	MI	22,476	C
SUNY/College at Cortland	NY	12,095	C
SUNY/College at Purchase	NY	11,989	VC+
SUNY/Univ at Binghamton	NY	13,988	HC
SUNY/Univ at Stony Brook	NY	13,625	HC
Stephens College	MO	26,930	VC
Suffolk Univ	MA	33,160	C
Syracuse Univ	NY	38,655	HC
Temple Univ	PA	17,438	C
Texas Christian Univ	TX	23,410	VC+
Univ of Calif at Berkeley	CA	18,141	HC+
Univ of Calif at Irvine	CA	16,475	HC
Univ of Calif at Los Angeles	CA	17,681	MC
Univ of Calif at Riverside	CA	16,625	C
Univ of Calif at Santa Barbara	CA	11,800	VC
Univ of Calif at Santa Cruz	CA	19,174	VC
Univ of Central Florida	FL	10,739	VC
Univ of Chicago	IL	42,369	MC
Univ of Colo at Boulder	CO	13,352	C+
Univ of Georgia	GA	11,004	HC
Univ of Hartford	CT	34,044	C
Univ of Illinois at Urbana-Champaign	IL	15,800	HC+
Univ of Iowa	IA	12,172	VC
Univ of Mich/Ann Arbor	MI	16,587	HC+
Univ of Minn/Twin Cities	MN	13,165	HC
Univ of Nebr at Lincoln	NE	11,401	VC
Univ of Nevada/Las Vegas	NV	11,566	C
Univ of N Car at Wilmington	NC	10,107	VC
Univ of North Texas	TX	7,800	C
Univ of Notre Dame	IN	39,552	MC
Univ of Okla	OK	10,769	VC+
Univ of Pittsburgh at Pittsburgh	PA	18,866	HC
Univ of Rochester	NY	41,135	MC
Univ of S Car at Columbia	SC	13,397	VC
Univ of Tenn at Knoxville	TN	11,720	C
Univ of Texas at Austin	TX	14,610	HC
Univ of the Arts	PA	32,330	SP
Univ of Toledo	OH	15,806	NC
Univ of Tulsa	OK	25,348	HC
Univ of Utah	UT	10,162	VC
Univ of Vermont	VT	18,080	VC
Univ of Wisc/Milwaukee	WI	9,427	LC
Vassar College	NY	41,700	MC
Villa Julie College	MD	25,222	C
Washington Univ in St. Louis	MO	42,106	MC
Wayne State Univ	MI	11,805	C
Webster Univ	MO	24,280	VC
Wellesley College	MA	41,030	MC
Wesleyan Univ	CT	42,122	MC
Whitman College	WA	36,110	HC+
Wright State Univ	OH	13,616	LC
Yale Univ	CT	41,000	MC

FINE ARTS

School	ST	$IS	SR
Abilene Christian Univ	TX	20,830	C
Adelphi Univ	NY	27,000	VC
Agnes Scott College	GA	32,070	HC
Alabama State Univ	AL	7,658	C
Albany State Univ	GA	5,770	C
Albertus Magnus College	CT	25,336	C
Alfred Univ	NY		VC
American Univ	DC	38,719	HC+
Amherst College	MA	41,590	MC
Anderson Univ	IN	25,050	LC
Aquinas College	MI	23,750	C
Arcadia Univ	PA	33,570	VC
Arkansas State Univ	AR	9,630	C
Art Academy of Cincinnati	OH	18,100	SP
Art Center College of Design	CA	26,370	SP
Art Inst of Boston at Lesley Univ	MA	28,200	SP
Ashland Univ	OH	25,000	C
Atlanta College of Art	GA	18,630	SP
Auburn Univ Montgomery	AL	9,530	NC
Baker Univ	KS	22,190	C
Ball State Univ	IN	13,138	C
Bellevue Univ	NE	4,440	NC
Bemidji State Univ	MN	11,180	LC
Bennington College	VT	41,890	HC
Bethany College	KS	20,660	LC
Bethany College	WV	21,395	C
Bethel Univ	MN	29,840	VC
Black Hills State Univ	SD	7,800	LC
Bloomfield College	NJ	22,500	LC
Bluefield College	VA	17,230	C+
Boise State Univ	ID	9,438	LC
Bowie State Univ	MD	10,880	C+
Bowling Green State Univ	OH	14,994	C
Brandeis Univ	MA	41,551	MC
Brenau Univ Women's College	GA	23,950	VC
Brigham Young Univ	UT	9,200	VC
Brigham Young Univ/Hawaii	HI	7,740	HC+
Bryn Mawr College	PA	42,780	HC+
Bucknell Univ	PA	39,660	MC
Burlington College	VT	14,670	SP
Caldwell College	NJ	26,450	LC
Calif Inst of the Arts	CA	35,725	SP
Cal State, Chico	CA	11,395	C
Cal State, Fullerton	CA	10,990	C
Cal State, Stanislaus	CA	11,283	C
Capital Univ	OH	30,444	C
Cardinal Stritch Univ	WI	21,910	C
Carnegie Mellon Univ	PA	42,700	MC
Carson-Newman College	TN	16,800	C
Carthage College	WI	26,000	C
Cedar Crest College	PA	30,615	C
Central College	IA	26,774	VC
Central Mich Univ	MI	12,244	C
Central Washington Univ	WA	11,730	C
Centre College	KY	30,810	VC
Charleston Southern Univ	SC	17,800	C
Christopher Newport Univ	VA	13,326	VC
CUNY/City College	NY		C
CUNY/Herbert H. Lehman College	NY	4,000	LC
CUNY/Hunter College	NY	8,000	C+
Clark Univ	MA	35,165	VC+
Clemson Univ	SC	13,366	HC
Coastal Carolina Univ	SC	13,140	C
College for Creative Studies	MI	24,000	SP
College of Mount St. Joseph	OH	24,860	C
College of New Jersey	NJ	18,315	MC
College of Our Lady of the Elms	MA	21,000	C
College of St. Benedict	MN	30,091	VC
College of St. Catherine	MN	27,505	VC
College of St. Elizabeth	NJ	28,495	C
College of the Southwest	NM	12,420	C+
College of Visual Arts	MN	18,040	SP
College of William and Mary	VA	14,147	MC
College of Wooster	OH	31,310	VC+
Columbia Univ	MO	16,900	C
Columbus College of Art and Design	OH	24,500	SP
Concordia Univ Nebr	NE	20,500	C+
Converse College	SC	24,800	VC
Cooper Union for the Advancement of Science and Art	NY	12,450	MC
Corcoran School of Art and Design	DC	32,850	SP
Cornell College	IA	30,110	VC+
Cornell Univ	NY	41,717	MC
Cornerstone Univ and Grand Rapids Theological Seminary	MI	21,350	NC
Cornish College of the Arts	WA	21,200	SP
Creighton Univ	NE	29,918	VC+
Cumberland Univ	TN	18,894	C
Daemen College	NY	24,580	C
Dakota State Univ	SD	7,466	C
Dallas Baptist Univ	TX	17,040	VC
Denison Univ	OH	37,040	HC
DePaul Univ	IL	29,835	VC
Dickinson College	PA	40,170	HC+
Dickinson State Univ	ND	7,847	NC
Dominican Univ	IL	26,370	C
Dordt College	IA	20,325	VC
Dowling College	NY	22,110	LC
Drury Univ	MO	20,117	VC
East Stroudsburg Univ of Pennsylvania	PA	10,336	C
East Tenn State Univ	TN	8,497	C
Eastern Conn State Univ	CT	13,554	C
Eastern Mich Univ	MI	12,897	C
Eastern New Mexico Univ	NM	7,264	C
Edinboro Univ of Pennsylvania	PA	11,809	LC
Elmira College	NY	37,200	VC
Emory Univ	GA	40,546	MC
Endicott College	MA	30,156	C+
Eureka College	IL	19,280	C
Fairfield Univ	CT	39,835	HC
Fairleigh Dickinson Univ/College at Florham	NJ	30,130	C
Fairleigh Dickinson Univ/Metropolitan Campus	NJ	28,590	C
Fisk Univ	TN	19,830	C
Flagler College	FL	13,790	VC+
Florida A&M Univ	FL	8,344	C
Florida Atlantic Univ	FL	11,221	C
Florida Memorial College	FL	6,000	LC
Fontbonne Univ	MO	23,308	C
Fordham Univ	NY	36,000	HC
Fort Hays State Univ	KS	7,638	C
Franklin and Marshall College	PA	40,590	HC
Franklin Pierce College	NH	31,700	C
Freed-Hardeman Univ	TN	16,370	NC
Friends Univ	KS	16,250	LC
George Washington Univ	DC	48,820	MC
Georgetown Univ	DC	43,183	MC
Georgia Southwestern State Univ	GA	6,035	C
Georgia State Univ	GA	11,444	VC
Grand Canyon Univ	AZ	32,000	LC
Grand Valley State Univ	MI	12,000	VC
Green Mountain College	VT	32,164	C
Gustavus Adolphus College	MN	30,920	HC
Hamline Univ	MN	27,070	VC
Hampden-Sydney College	VA	31,148	VC
Hampshire College	MA	37,120	HC
Harding Univ	AR	16,512	VC
Harvard Univ/Harvard College	MA	45,860	MC
Hastings College	NE	22,218	VC
Haverford College	PA	41,600	MC
High Point Univ	NC	25,720	C
Hillsdale College	MI	24,160	HC
Hobart and William Smith Colleges	NY	41,123	VC
Hofstra Univ	NY	32,630	VC
Hope College	MI	28,208	VC+
Humboldt State Univ	CA	11,176	C
Illinois College	IL	21,900	C+
Indiana State Univ	IN	11,604	C
Indiana Univ Bloomington	IN	13,356	VC
Indiana Univ East	IN	4,806	LC
Indiana Univ Northwest	IN	4,902	LC
Indiana Univ of Pennsylvania	PA	11,209	C
Indiana Univ South Bend	IN	4,989	LC
Indiana Univ Southeast	IN	4,880	LC
Indiana Univ-Purdue Univ Fort Wayne	IN	5,067	LC
Indiana Univ-Purdue Univ Indianapolis	IN	10,959	C
Inter American Univ of PR/San German	PR	6,720	C
Iowa State Univ	IA	11,831	VC
Iowa Wesleyan College	IA	22,140	C
Ithaca College	NY	35,144	VC
James Madison Univ	VA	12,010	VC
Jamestown College	ND	14,130	NC
Johnson State College	VT	11,830	LC
Judson College	IL	25,130	C
Kean Univ	NJ	15,880	C
Keene State College	NH	13,836	C
Kendall College of Art and Design of Ferris State Univ	MI	11,870	SP
Kentucky State Univ	KY	10,089	LC
Kentucky Wesleyan College	KY	18,590	C
Kutztown Univ of Pennsylvania	PA	10,820	C
La Salle Univ	PA	34,950	C
La Sierra Univ	CA	24,327	C+
LaGrange College	GA	22,874	C+
Lake Erie College	OH	27,725	C
Lake Superior State Univ	MI	12,842	LC
Lamar Univ	TX	6,820	LC
Lambuth Univ	TN	21,700	C+
Lewis and Clark College	OR	35,358	VC+
Lincoln Memorial Univ	TN	18,144	C
Lock Haven Univ of Pennsylvania	PA	12,098	LC
LIU/Brooklyn Campus	NY	25,000	C
LIU/C.W. Post Campus	NY	28,282	C
Louisiana State Univ and A&M College	LA	10,749	VC
Louisiana State Univ in Shreveport	LA	2,900	NC
Louisiana Tech Univ	LA	7,370	C
Lourdes College	OH	15,300	LC
Loyola College in Maryland	MD	38,898	HC
Loyola Univ Chicago	IL	32,896	VC
Loyola Univ New Orleans	LA	31,050	VC+
Lynn Univ	FL	30,750	C
Madonna Univ	MI	16,068	VC
Maharishi Univ of Management	IA	29,450	VC
Marist College	NY	30,566	VC
Marlboro College	VT	35,980	VC+
Marshall Univ	WV	9,116	C
Martin Univ	IN	10,300	SP
Maryland Inst College of Art	MD	34,450	SP
Marylhurst Univ	OR	14,220	NC
Marymount Manhattan College	NY	30,049	VC
Mass College of Art	MA	16,650	SP
Mass College of Liberal Arts	MA	8,725	LC
McDaniel College	MD	31,610	VC
McNeese State Univ	LA	5,270	LC
Memphis College of Art	TN	24,960	SP
Meredith College	NC	25,600	C
Mesa State College	CO	8,051	C
Metropolitan State College of Denver	CO	2,338	LC
Miami Univ	OH	29,097	HC
Midland Lutheran College	NE	18,600	C
Midwestern State Univ	TX	9,381	LC
Milligan College	TN	21,990	VC
Milwaukee Inst of Art and Design	WI	28,700	SP
Minn State Univ, Moorhead	MN	7,000	LC
Miss Univ for Women	MS	6,000	LC
Miss Valley State Univ	MS	7,970	C
Missouri Southern State Univ	MO	8,396	NC
Missouri Western State Univ	MO	9,534	NC
Montana State Univ-Bozeman	MT	1,137	C
Montana State Univ-Northern	MT	10,000	NC
Montclair State Univ	NJ	16,327	C
Montserrat College of Art	MA	25,929	SP
Moore College of Art and Design	PA	27,200	SP
Morgan State Univ	MD	12,080	C
Mount Mary College	WI	22,895	C
Mount Olive College	NC	16,000	C
Mount St. Mary's Univ	MD	30,930	C
Murray State Univ	KY	8,900	VC
National-Louis Univ	IL	16,915	LC
Nazareth College of Rochester	NY	28,175	VC
New College of Calif	CA	12,842	NC
New College of Florida	FL	10,009	HC+
New England College	NH	31,466	C
New Jersey City Univ	NJ	13,695	LC
New Mexico State Univ	NM	9,250	C
New York Inst of Technology	NY	28,126	VC
New York Univ	NY	43,170	MC
Norfolk State Univ	VA	10,531	LC
North Central College	IL	28,926	VC
Northeastern Illinois Univ	IL	3,000	NC
Northeastern State Univ	OK	5,396	LC
Northern Arizona Univ	AZ	10,353	C
Northern Mich Univ	MI	12,340	LC
Northern State Univ	SD	8,257	C
Northland College	WI	26,680	C+
Northwest Missouri State Univ	MO	10,000	C
Northwestern State Univ of Louisiana	LA	7,144	C
Northwestern Univ	IL	37,595	MC
Notre Dame de Namur Univ	CA	32,790	LC
Oakland City Univ	IN	19,620	NC
Oakland Univ	MI	11,936	C
Oberlin College	OH	40,904	MC
Ohio Northern Univ	OH	27,765	VC
Ohio Univ	OH	15,921	C
Ohio Wesleyan Univ	OH	35,830	VC+
Okla Baptist Univ	OK	17,986	VC
Old Dominion Univ	VA	11,907	C
Olivet College	MI	19,984	C+
Our Lady of the Lake Univ of San Antonio	TX	22,430	LC
Pacific Lutheran Univ	WA	28,805	VC
Pacific Northwest College of Art	OR	17,296	SP
Pacific Union College	CA	24,555	VC+

ST = STATE $IS = IN-STATE COSTS   SR = SELECTOR RATING

ST = STATE   **$IS** = IN-STATE COSTS   **SR** = SELECTOR RATING

Food services technology

School	ST	$IS	SR
Central Washington Univ	WA	11,730	C
Chapman Univ	CA	37,550	VC
Clemson Univ	SC	13,366	HC
College of the Ozarks	MO	4,130	VC+
Cornell Univ	NY	41,717	MC
Delaware Valley College	PA	29,944	C
Dominican Univ	IL	26,370	C
Florida State Univ	FL	9,028	HC
Framingham State College	MA	11,156	C
Georgia Southern Univ	GA	9,762	C
Immaculata Univ	PA	25,350	C
Indiana State Univ	IN	11,604	C
Indiana Univ of Pennsylvania	PA	11,209	C
Iowa State Univ	IA	11,831	VC
Kansas State Univ	KS	10,516	VC
Kent State Univ	OH	14,594	C
Louisiana State Univ and A&M College	LA	10,749	VC
Madonna Univ	MI	16,068	VC
Mich State Univ	MI	13,689	VC
Minn State Univ, Mankato	MN	10,276	LC
Miss State Univ	MS	9,577	C
N Car State Univ	NC	11,824	HC
N Dak State Univ	ND	8,500	C
Northwest Missouri State Univ	MO	10,000	C
Oregon State Univ	OR	11,055	C
Penn State Univ/Univ Park Campus	PA	18,038	HC
Purdue Univ/West Lafayette	IN	13,458	VC
Radford Univ	VA	13,145	C
Rutgers, The State Univ of New Jersey/New Brunswick/Piscataway Campus	NJ	15,810	HC
San Jose State Univ	CA	11,707	C
Seattle Pacific Univ	WA	29,355	C
Simmons College	MA	35,640	VC
S Car State Univ	SC	6,700	LC
S Dak State Univ	SD	9,815	C
Southern Illinois Univ Carbondale	IL	12,391	C
Stephen F. Austin State Univ	TX	7,930	C
Texas A&M Univ at Kingsville	TX	6,800	LC
Texas Tech Univ	TX	13,026	VC
Tuskegee Univ	AL	18,860	LC
Univ of Alabama	AL	9,888	C
Univ of Arkansas	AR	11,859	VC
Univ of at Calif Davis	CA	15,010	VC
Univ of Delaware	DE	14,142	VC
Univ of Florida	FL	9,354	HC
Univ of Georgia	GA	11,004	HC
Univ of Hawaii at Manoa	HI	10,413	VC
Univ of Idaho	ID	9,310	VC
Univ of Illinois at Urbana-Champaign	IL	15,800	HC+
Univ of Kentucky	KY	7,800	VC
Univ of Maine	ME	13,642	C
Univ of Maryland/College Park	MD	16,036	HC
Univ of Mass Amherst	MA	15,973	C+
Univ of Minn/Twin Cities	MN	13,165	HC
Univ of Missouri/Columbia	MO	13,500	VC
Univ of Nebr at Lincoln	NE	11,401	VC
Univ of Rhode Island	RI	15,398	C
Univ of Tenn at Knoxville	TN	11,720	C
Univ of the District of Columbia	DC	2,070	LC
Univ of Vermont	VT	18,080	VC
Univ of Washington	WA	10,400	VC
Univ of Wisc/Madison	WI	13,117	HC
Univ of Wisc/River Falls	WI	9,722	VC
Utah State Univ	UT	8,002	VC
Virginia Polytechnic Inst and State Univ	VA	10,834	VC
Washington State Univ	WA	12,260	VC
Wayne State Univ	MI	11,805	C
Winthrop Univ	SC	11,302	C

FOOD SERVICES TECHNOLOGY

School	ST	$IS	SR
Brigham Young Univ	UT	9,200	VC
Delaware Valley College	PA	29,944	C
Inter American Univ of PR/ Bayamon Univ College	PR	3,522	
Johnson and Wales Univ/ Charlotte Campus	NC	29,121	LC
Johnson and Wales Univ/ North Miami Campus	FL	30,126	LC
Johnson and Wales Univ/ Providence Campus	RI	28,126	LC
Pennsylvania College of Technology	PA	16,980	LC
Univ of Tenn at Knoxville	TN	11,720	C

FOREIGN LANGUAGES EDUCATION

School	ST	$IS	SR
Abilene Christian Univ	TX	20,830	C
Adams State College	CO	8,613	C
Adelphi Univ	NY	27,000	VC

School	ST	$IS	SR
Alabama State Univ	AL	7,658	C
American International College	MA	28,710	LC
Anderson Univ	IN	25,050	LC
Appalachian State Univ	NC	8,000	VC
Arkansas State Univ	AR	9,630	C
Asbury College	KY	23,762	VC
Ashland Univ	OH	25,000	C
Auburn Univ	AL	12,230	VC
Averett Univ	VA	24,920	C
Ball State Univ	IN	13,138	C
Baylor Univ	TX	27,555	HC
Bemidji State Univ	MN	11,180	LC
Bennington College	VT	41,890	HC
Berea College	KY	5,496	VC+
Bethany College	WV	21,395	C
Bethel Univ	MN	29,840	VC
Blue Mountain College	MS	11,086	C
Boston Univ	MA	42,046	HC+
Carroll College	MT	23,324	C+
Carroll College	WI	24,860	C
Carson-Newman College	TN	16,800	C
Carthage College	WI	26,000	C
Cedarville Univ	OH	21,904	VC
Centenary College of Louisiana	LA	24,760	VC
Central Methodist Univ	MO	18,000	C
Central Mich Univ	MI	12,244	C
Central Missouri State Univ	MO	10,000	C
Central Washington Univ	WA	11,730	C
Christopher Newport Univ	VA	13,326	VC
CUNY/Brooklyn College	NY	4,377	C+
CUNY/City College	NY		C
CUNY/Herbert H. Lehman College	NY	4,000	LC
CUNY/Hunter College	NY	8,000	C+
Clarion Univ of Pennsylvania	PA	11,844	C
College of New Jersey	NJ	18,315	MC
College of Notre Dame of Maryland	MD	27,700	C
College of Our Lady of the Elms	MA	21,000	C
College of St. Rose	NY	25,684	C
College of the Ozarks	MO	4,130	VC+
Columbus State Univ	GA	8,664	C
Concordia College: Moorhead	MN	22,475	VC
Conn College	CT	41,975	MC
Converse College	SC	24,800	VC
Cornell College	IA	30,110	VC+
Daemen College	NY	24,580	C
Dana College	NE	22,390	C
Delta State Univ	MS	7,709	C
DePaul Univ	IL	29,835	VC
Dordt College	IA	20,325	VC
East Carolina Univ	NC	10,000	C
East Stroudsburg Univ of Pennsylvania	PA	10,336	C
East Tenn State Univ	TN	8,497	C
East Texas Baptist Univ	TX	16,713	C
Eastern Kentucky Univ	KY	7,725	C
Eastern Mich Univ	MI	12,897	C
Eastern Washington Univ	WA	10,608	C
Edinboro Univ of Pennsylvania	PA	11,809	LC
Elmira College	NY	37,200	VC
Elon Univ	NC	25,371	HC
Emporia State Univ	KS	8,093	C
Erskine College	SC	25,468	VC
Evangel Univ	MO	17,380	C
Fairmont State	WV	8,400	LC
Florida Atlantic Univ	FL	11,221	C
Florida International Univ	FL	9,215	VC
Florida Southern College	FL	25,965	C
Florida State Univ	FL	9,028	HC
Friends Univ	KS	16,250	LC
Gannon Univ	PA	26,100	C
Gardner-Webb Univ	NC	21,500	C
George Mason Univ	VA	10,850	VC
Georgetown Univ	KY	24,950	C+
Georgia Southern Univ	GA	9,762	C
Georgia Southwestern State Univ	GA	6,035	C
Gettysburg College	PA	39,864	HC
Goshen College	IN	22,850	VC
Grace College	IN	22,170	C
Grambling State Univ	LA	6,538	NC
Grand Valley State Univ	MI	12,000	VC
Greensboro College	NC	23,000	C
Gustavus Adolphus College	MN	30,920	HC
Hamline Univ	MN	27,070	VC
Harding Univ	AR	16,512	VC
Hardin-Simmons Univ	TX	18,641	C
Hastings College	NE	22,218	VC
Heidelberg College	OH	23,242	C
Hillsdale College	MI	24,160	HC
Hofstra Univ	NY	32,630	VC
Holy Family Univ	PA	25,740	C
Hood College	MD	30,085	VC
Hope College	MI	28,208	VC+
Illinois College	IL	21,900	C
Immaculata Univ	PA	25,350	C
Indiana State Univ	IN	11,604	C
Indiana Univ of Pennsylvania	PA	11,209	C

School	ST	$IS	SR
Indiana Univ-Purdue Univ Fort Wayne	IN	5,067	LC
Indiana Univ-Purdue Univ Indianapolis	IN	10,959	C
Iona College	NY	30,878	VC
Ithaca College	NY	35,144	VC
Juniata College	PA	33,130	VC
Keene State College	NH	13,836	C
Kennesaw State Univ	GA	12,152	C
King's College	PA	29,810	C
La Roche College	PA	24,724	LC
La Salle Univ	PA	34,950	C
Lamar Univ	TX	6,820	LC
Le Moyne College	NY	29,570	VC
Lenoir-Rhyne College	NC	25,580	C
Lock Haven Univ of Pennsylvania	PA	12,098	LC
LIU/C.W. Post Campus	NY	28,282	C
Loras College	IA	27,193	C
Louisiana Tech Univ	LA	7,370	C
Malone College	OH	23,040	C
Manhattan College	NY	29,000	VC
Mansfield Univ	PA	11,300	C
Marian College of Fond du Lac	WI	21,775	LC
Marshall Univ	WV	9,116	C
McNeese State Univ	LA	5,270	LC
Messiah College	PA	28,910	VC+
Miami Univ	OH	29,097	HC
Millikin Univ	IL	25,590	C
Minn State Univ, Mankato	MN	10,276	LC
Minn State Univ, Moorhead	MN	7,000	LC
Minot State Univ	ND	6,700	LC
Missouri Southern State Univ	MO	8,396	NC
Missouri State Univ	MO	10,748	C+
Missouri Western State Univ	MO	9,534	NC
Monmouth Univ	NJ	28,956	C
Mount Mary College	WI	22,895	C
Mount Vernon Nazarene Univ	OH	20,810	C
Murray State Univ	KY	8,900	VC
Muskingum College	OH	22,970	C
Nazareth College of Rochester	NY	28,175	VC
New York Univ	NY	43,170	MC
Niagara Univ	NY	28,250	C
N Car State Univ	NC	11,824	HC
North Georgia College and State Univ	GA	7,000	C
Northern Arizona Univ	AZ	10,353	C
Northern State Univ	SD	8,257	C
Northwest Nazarene Univ	ID	22,590	VC
Northwestern College of Iowa	IA	22,174	C+
Ohio Wesleyan Univ	OH	35,830	VC+
Okla Baptist Univ	OK	17,986	VC
Okla City Univ	OK	23,965	VC
Old Dominion Univ	VA	11,907	C
Oral Roberts Univ	OK	22,650	C
Ouachita Baptist Univ	AR	21,900	VC
Pittsburg State Univ	KS	8,112	C
Prescott College	AZ	13,445	LC
Providence College	RI	34,580	HC
Purdue Univ/Calumet	IN	10,891	C
Purdue Univ/West Lafayette	IN	13,458	VC
Radford Univ	VA	13,145	C
Rhode Island College	RI	11,570	C
Rider Univ	NJ	32,560	C
Rockhurst Univ	MO	25,440	VC
Rosemont College	PA	29,350	C
Rowan Univ	NJ	16,000	VC
Saginaw Valley State Univ	MI	11,432	C
St. Cloud State Univ	MN	10,010	C
St. Edward's Univ	TX	23,560	C
St. John's Univ	NY	34,370	C
St. Mary-of-the-Woods College	IN	25,480	C
St. Mary's Univ of Minn	MN	23,857	VC
St. Michael's College	VT	33,330	VC
St. Thomas Aquinas College	NY	22,000	LC
St. Xavier Univ	IL	23,160	C
Seton Hill Univ	PA	28,810	C
Shippensburg Univ of Pennsylvania	PA	11,621	C
Slippery Rock Univ of Pennsylvania	PA	10,360	LC
Southeast Missouri State Univ	MO	10,596	C
Southeastern Louisiana Univ	LA	8,521	LC
Southern Conn State Univ	CT	10,310	C
Southern Nazarene Univ	OK	14,634	NC
Southern Univ at New Orleans	LA	1,000	NC
Southern Utah Univ	UT		C
Southwest Minn State Univ	MN	10,975	C
SUNY at Oswego	NY	13,662	VC
SUNY at Potsdam	NY	12,959	C
SUNY/College at Buffalo	NY	11,903	C+
SUNY/College at Cortland	NY	12,095	C
SUNY/College at Fredonia	NY	12,771	VC
SUNY/College at Old Westbury	NY	13,154	C

School	ST	$IS	SR
SUNY/College at Oneonta	NY	12,905	VC
SUNY/Univ at Albany	NY	13,860	VC
SUNY/Univ at New Paltz	NY	12,480	VC
Taylor Univ	IN	26,376	VC+
Temple Univ	PA	17,438	C
Texas Southern Univ	TX	9,828	C
Thomas Edison State College	NJ	3,780	SP
Trinity Univ	TX	30,157	HC+
Turabo Univ	PR	4,110	
Univ of Akron	OH	15,166	NC
Univ of Central Arkansas	AR	9,984	C
Univ of Central Florida	FL	10,739	VC
Univ of Central Okla	OK	8,094	C
Univ of Cincinnati	OH	17,682	C
Univ of Conn	CT	16,628	HC
Univ of Delaware	DE	14,142	HC
Univ of Evansville	IN	28,320	VC
Univ of Findlay	OH	29,238	C
Univ of Georgia	GA	11,004	HC
Univ of Idaho	ID	9,310	NC
Univ of Illinois at Chicago	IL	16,256	VC
Univ of Illinois at Urbana-Champaign	IL	15,800	HC+
Univ of Indianapolis	IN	25,090	C
Univ of Iowa	IA	12,172	VC
Univ of Kentucky	KY	7,800	C
Univ of Louisiana at Lafayette	LA	5,830	C
Univ of Louisiana at Monroe	LA	7,103	C
Univ of Louisville	KY	10,400	C
Univ of Mary Hardin-Baylor	TX	19,428	C
Univ of Maryland/College Park	MD	16,036	HC
Univ of Mich/Flint	MI	6,398	C
Univ of Minn/Duluth	MN	13,974	C
Univ of Miss	MS	9,000	C
Univ of Nebr at Kearney	NE	9,000	NC
Univ of Nebr at Lincoln	NE	11,401	VC
Univ of New Orleans	LA	7,370	C
Univ of North Alabama	AL	8,992	C
Univ of N Car at Chapel Hill	NC	11,129	MC
Univ of N Car at Charlotte	NC	9,101	C
Univ of Northern Iowa	IA	11,133	C
Univ of Okla	OK	10,769	VC+
Univ of PR/Mayaguez	PR	1,250	
Univ of South Florida	FL	10,284	VC
Univ of Southern Miss	MS	10,112	C
Univ of Toledo	OH	15,806	NC
Univ of Vermont	VT	18,080	VC
Univ of Wisc/Eau Claire	WI	9,915	VC
Univ of Wisc/River Falls	WI	9,722	LC
Univ of Wisc/Whitewater	WI	9,274	C
Utah State Univ	UT	8,002	VC
Vassar College	NY	41,700	MC
Virginia Commonwealth Univ	VA	12,987	C
Virginia Polytechnic Inst and State Univ	VA	10,834	VC
Wartburg College	IA	27,315	NC
Washington State Univ	WA	12,260	C
Washington Univ in St. Louis	MO	42,106	MC
Wayne State College	NE	8,033	NC
Weber State Univ	UT	9,635	NC
West Chester Univ of Pennsylvania	PA	12,355	C+
West Texas A&M Univ	TX	8,452	C
West Virginia Univ	WV	10,506	C
Western Carolina Univ	NC	7,000	C
Western State College of Colo	CO	9,942	C
Western Washington Univ	WA	11,262	VC
Whitworth College	WA	29,428	VC+
Winona State Univ	MN	11,333	C
Wittenberg Univ	OH	34,596	VC
Wright State Univ	OH	13,616	LC
Youngstown State Univ	OH	12,613	NC

FORENSIC STUDIES

School	ST	$IS	SR
Albany State Univ	GA	5,770	C+
Alvernia College	PA	26,388	C
Bay Path College	MA	29,362	C
Baylor Univ	TX	27,555	HC
Carlow Univ	PA	24,313	C
Chaminade Univ of Honolulu	HI	23,320	LC
Champlain College	VT	24,605	C
Chatham College	PA	27,290	C+
CUNY/John Jay College of Criminal Justice	NY	5,000	C
College of the Ozarks	MO	4,130	VC+
Columbia College	MO	16,900	C
Defiance College	OH	24,790	C
Eastern Kentucky Univ	KY	7,725	C
Edinboro Univ of Pennsylvania	PA	11,809	LC
Florida Inst of Technology	FL	29,720	VC
Guilford College	NC	28,160	C+
Hilbert College	NY	20,480	LC
Inter American Univ of PR/ Bayamon Univ College	PR	3,522	
King College	TN	23,400	C
Loyola Univ Chicago	IL	32,896	VC
Loyola Univ New Orleans	LA	31,050	VC+

ST = STATE $IS = IN-STATE COSTS   SR = SELECTOR RATING

School	ST	$IS	SR
Mercyhurst College	PA	28,633	VC
Mountain State Univ	WV	11,406	VC
Ohio Univ	OH	15,921	C
Russell Sage College	NY	27,000	C
St. Andrews Presbyterian College	NC	23,530	C
St. Edward's Univ	TX	23,560	C
St. Louis Univ	MO	33,158	VC+
Seton Hill Univ	PA	28,810	C
Simpson College	IA	26,833	VC
Thomas More College	KY	24,470	C
Tri-State Univ-Main Campus	IN	26,200	C
Univ of Central Florida	FL	10,739	VC
Univ of Central Okla	OK	8,094	C
Univ of Findlay	OH	29,238	C
Univ of Miss	MS	9,000	C
Univ of New Haven	CT	31,794	C
Univ of N Dak	ND	10,114	VC
Virginia Commonwealth Univ	VA	12,987	C
Waynesburg College	PA	21,230	C
Western New England College	MA	32,054	C
Youngstown State Univ	OH	12,613	NC

FOREST ENGINEERING

School	ST	$IS	SR
Auburn Univ	AL	12,230	VC
Oregon State Univ	OR	11,055	C
SUNY/College of Environmental Science and Forestry	NY	15,000	VC
Univ of Maine	ME	13,642	C
Univ of Washington	WA	10,400	VC

FORESTRY AND RELATED SCIENCES

School	ST	$IS	SR
Alabama A&M Univ	AL	8,890	LC
Baylor Univ	TX	27,555	HC
Clemson Univ	SC	13,366	HC
College of St. Benedict	MN	30,091	VC
Colo State Univ-Fort Collins	CO	10,878	C+
Eastern Mich Univ	MI	12,897	C
Eastern Oregon Univ	OR	10,400	NC
Elizabethtown College	PA	32,100	VC
High Point Univ	NC	25,720	C
Humboldt State Univ	CA	11,176	C
Iowa State Univ	IA	11,831	VC
Louisiana State Univ and A&M College	LA	10,749	VC
Louisiana Tech Univ	LA	7,370	C
Mich State Univ	MI	13,689	VC
Mich Tech Univ	MI	14,569	VC
N Car State Univ	NC	11,824	HC
Northern Arizona Univ	AZ	10,353	C
Northwest Missouri State Univ	MO	10,000	C
Ohio State Univ	OH	15,357	HC
Okla State Univ	OK	10,213	VC
Oregon State Univ	OR	11,055	C
Penn State Univ/Univ Park Campus	PA	18,038	HC
Purdue Univ/West Lafayette	IN	13,458	VC
St. John's Univ	MN	29,749	VC
Southern Illinois Univ Carbondale	IL	12,391	C
Southern Univ and A&M College	LA	8,238	LC
SUNY/College of Environmental Science and Forestry	NY	15,000	VC
Stephen F. Austin State Univ	TX	7,930	C
Texas A&M Univ	TX	13,351	HC
Thomas Edison State College	NJ	3,780	SP
Univ of Arkansas at Monticello	AR	7,325	NC
Univ of Calif at Berkeley	CA	18,141	VC+
Univ of Florida	FL	9,354	HC
Univ of Georgia	GA	11,004	HC
Univ of Illinois at Urbana-Champaign	IL	15,800	HC+
Univ of Kentucky	KY	7,800	C
Univ of Maine	ME	13,642	C
Univ of Mass Amherst	MA	15,973	C+
Univ of Minn/Twin Cities	MN	13,165	VC
Univ of Montana	MT	10,602	C
Univ of New Hampshire	NH	16,810	VC
Univ of Tenn at Knoxville	TN	11,720	C
Univ of the South	TN	34,645	VC
Univ of Vermont	VT	18,080	VC
Univ of Wisc/Madison	WI	13,117	HC
Univ of Wisc/Stevens Point	WI	9,384	VC
Utah State Univ	UT	8,002	VC
Virginia Polytechnic Inst and State Univ	VA	10,834	VC
Washington State Univ	WA	12,260	C
West Virginia Univ	WV	10,506	C
Western New Mexico Univ	NM	7,233	LC

FORESTRY PRODUCTION AND PROCESSING

School	ST	$IS	SR
Auburn Univ	AL	12,230	VC
Clemson Univ	SC	13,366	HC
Miss State Univ	MS	9,577	C
Oregon State Univ	OR	11,055	C
Penn State Univ/Univ Park Campus	PA	18,038	HC
Stephen F. Austin State Univ	TX	7,930	C
Univ of Idaho	ID	9,310	NC
Univ of Minn/Twin Cities	MN	13,165	HC
Univ of Washington	WA	10,400	VC

FRENCH

School	ST	$IS	SR
Adrian College	MI	23,000	C
Agnes Scott College	GA	32,070	HC
Alabama A&M Univ	AL	8,890	LC
Alabama State Univ	AL	7,658	C
Albany State Univ	GA	5,770	C+
Albion College	MI	26,000	VC
Albright College	PA	33,920	C
Alfred Univ	NY		VC
Allegheny College	PA	33,500	HC
Alma College	MI	28,544	VC
Amherst College	MA	41,590	MC
Anderson Univ	IN	25,050	LC
Andrews Univ	MI	21,786	C
Angelo State Univ	TX	8,340	NC
Appalachian State Univ	NC	8,000	VC
Aquinas College	MI	23,750	C
Arizona State Univ-Tempe	AZ	11,174	C
Arkansas State Univ	AR	9,630	C
Asbury College	KY	23,762	VC
Ashland Univ	OH	25,000	C
Assumption College	MA	32,875	C
Auburn Univ	AL	12,230	VC
Augsburg College	MN	28,300	C
Augusta State Univ	GA	2,920	C
Augustana College	IL	29,862	VC+
Augustana College	SD	24,380	VC
Austin College	TX	27,871	HC
Austin Peay State Univ	TN	7,535	C
Baker Univ	KS	22,190	C
Baldwin-Wallace College	OH	27,256	VC
Ball State Univ	IN	13,138	C
Bard College	NY	41,800	HC+
Barry Univ	FL	24,100	LC
Bates College	ME	42,100	MC
Baylor Univ	TX	27,555	HC
Belmont Univ	TN	24,110	VC
Beloit College	WI	32,808	HC
Benedictine College	KS	21,968	C
Bennington College	VT	41,890	HC
Berea College	KY	5,496	VC+
Berry College	GA	24,342	VC
Bethany College	WV	21,395	C
Birmingham-Southern College	AL	28,494	VC+
Bloomsburg Univ of Pennsylvania	PA	11,602	C
Boston College	MA	41,608	MC
Boston Univ	MA	42,046	HC+
Bowdoin College	ME	41,660	MC
Bowling Green State Univ	OH	14,994	C
Bradley Univ	IL	25,280	VC
Brandeis Univ	MA	41,551	MC
Bridgewater College	VA	27,790	C
Brigham Young Univ	UT	9,200	VC
Bryn Mawr College	PA	42,780	HC+
Bucknell Univ	PA	39,660	MC
Butler Univ	IN	31,944	VC+
Cabrini College	PA	33,340	C
Caldwell College	NJ	26,450	LC
Calif Lutheran Univ	CA	27,800	LC
Cal State East Bay	CA	10,856	LC
Cal State, Chico	CA	11,395	C
Cal State, Fresno	CA	10,037	LC
Cal State, Fullerton	CA	10,990	C
Cal State, Long Beach	CA	9,512	C
Cal State, Los Angeles	CA	5,900	C
Cal State, Northridge	CA	9,036	LC
Cal State, Sacramento	CA	11,122	C+
Cal State, San Bernardino	CA	12,563	LC
Cal State, Stanislaus	CA	11,283	C
Calif Univ of Pennsylvania	PA	14,217	C
Calvin College	MI	25,735	NC
Campbell Univ	NC	21,137	VC
Canisius College	NY	32,257	VC
Capital Univ	OH	30,444	C
Cardinal Stritch Univ	WI	21,910	C
Carleton College	MN	40,467	MC
Carnegie Mellon Univ	PA	32,700	MC
Carroll College	MT	23,324	C+
Carson-Newman College	TN	16,800	C
Carthage College	WI	26,000	C
Case Western Reserve Univ	OH	37,314	MC
Catawba College	NC	25,000	C
Catholic Univ of America	DC	35,838	VC
Cedar Crest College	PA	30,615	C
Centenary College of Louisiana	LA	24,760	VC
Central College	IA	26,774	VC
Central Conn State Univ	CT	13,620	C
Central Methodist Univ	MO	18,000	C
Central Mich Univ	MI	12,244	C
Central Missouri State Univ	MO	10,000	C
Central Washington Univ	WA	11,730	C
Centre College	KY	30,810	VC
Chapman Univ	CA	37,550	VC
Chatham Univ	PA	27,290	C+
Chestnut Hill College	PA	26,600	LC
Christendom College	VA	21,594	VC+
Christopher Newport Univ	VA	13,326	VC
Citadel, The	SC		C+
CUNY/Brooklyn College	NY	4,377	C+
CUNY/City College	NY		C
CUNY/Herbert H. Lehman College	NY	4,000	LC
CUNY/Hunter College	NY	8,000	C
CUNY/Queens College	NY	4,356	C
CUNY/York College	NY	4,242	NC
Claremont McKenna College	CA	42,920	MC
Clarion Univ of Pennsylvania	PA	11,844	C
Clark Univ	MA	35,165	VC+
Clemson Univ	SC	13,366	HC
Cleveland State Univ	OH	10,798	NC
Coe College	IA	27,440	VC
Coker College	SC	21,600	C
Colgate Univ	NY	41,170	MC
College of Charleston	SC	13,616	VC
College of Mount St. Vincent	NY	28,000	C
College of New Rochelle	NY	28,396	C+
College of St. Benedict	MN	30,091	VC
College of St. Catherine	MN	27,505	VC
College of the Holy Cross	MA	40,664	MC
College of William and Mary	VA	14,147	MC
College of Wooster	OH	31,310	VC+
Colo College	CO	37,668	HC
Colo State Univ-Fort Collins	CO	10,878	C+
Columbia College	SC	24,982	LC
Columbia Univ/Barnard College	NY	38,000	MC
Columbia Univ/Columbia College	NY	42,584	MC
Columbia Univ/School of General Studies	NY	41,516	C
Concordia College: Moorhead	MN	22,475	VC
Conn College	CT	41,975	MC
Converse College	SC	24,800	VC
Cornell College	IA	30,110	VC+
Cornell Univ	NY	41,717	MC
Creighton Univ	NE	29,918	VC+
Daemen College	NY	24,580	C
Dartmouth College	NH	39,465	MC
Davidson College	NC	36,825	MC
Delaware State Univ	DE	8,130	LC
Denison Univ	OH	37,040	HC
DePaul Univ	IL	29,835	VC
DePauw Univ	IN	32,100	HC
Dickinson College	PA	40,170	HC+
Dillard Univ	LA	17,500	VC
Doane College	NE	22,458	C
Dominican Univ	IL	26,370	C
Drew Univ/College of Liberal Arts	NJ	39,698	VC
Drury Univ	MO	20,117	VC
Earlham College	IN	33,604	HC
East Carolina Univ	NC	10,000	C
East Stroudsburg Univ of Pennsylvania	PA	10,336	C
Eastern Kentucky Univ	KY	7,725	C
Eastern Mennonite Univ	VA	25,450	VC
Eastern Mich Univ	MI	12,897	C
Eastern Nazarene College	MA	19,500	LC
Eastern Univ	PA	24,075	C
Eastern Washington Univ	WA	10,608	C
Eckerd College	FL	35,492	VC
Edgewood College	WI	22,862	C
Elizabethtown College	PA	32,100	VC
Elmhurst College	IL	24,685	C
Elmira College	NY	37,200	VC
Elon Univ	NC	25,371	HC
Emory Univ	GA	40,546	MC
Fairfield Univ	CT	39,835	HC
Fairmont State	WV	8,400	LC
Fisk Univ	TN	19,830	C
Florida Atlantic Univ	FL	11,221	C
Florida International Univ	FL	9,215	VC
Florida State Univ	FL	9,028	HC
Fordham Univ	NY	36,000	HC
Fort Hays State Univ	KS	7,638	C
Franciscan Univ of Steubenville	OH	20,300	VC
Franklin and Marshall College	PA	40,590	HC
Franklin College	IN		C
Furman Univ	SC	33,264	HC+
Gallaudet Univ	DC	16,554	
Gardner-Webb Univ	NC	21,500	C
George Mason Univ	VA	10,850	VC
George Washington Univ	DC	48,820	MC
Georgetown College	KY	24,950	C+
Georgetown Univ	DC	43,183	MC
Georgia College and State Univ	GA	11,020	C
Georgia Southern Univ	GA	9,762	C
Georgia State Univ	GA	11,444	VC
Georgian Court College	NJ	20,000	LC
Gettysburg College	PA	39,864	HC
Gonzaga Univ	WA	30,218	HC
Gordon College	MA	29,194	C+
Goucher College	MD	36,225	VC
Grace College	IN	22,170	C
Grambling State Univ	LA	6,538	NC
Greensboro College	NC	23,000	C
Grinnell College	IA	34,814	HC+
Grove City College	PA	15,784	HC+
Guilford College	NC	28,160	C+
Gustavus Adolphus College	MN	30,920	HC
Hamilton College	NY	41,660	MC
Hamline Univ	MN	27,070	VC
Hampden-Sydney College	VA	31,148	VC
Hanover College	IN	28,150	HC
Harding Univ	AR	16,512	VC
Hartwick College	NY	36,065	C+
Harvard Univ/Harvard College	MA	45,860	MC
Haverford College	PA	41,600	MC
Hendrix College	AR	27,646	HC+
High Point Univ	NC	25,720	C
Hillsdale College	MI	24,160	HC
Hiram College	OH	28,700	VC
Hobart and William Smith Colleges	NY	41,123	VC
Hofstra Univ	NY	32,630	VC
Hollins Univ	VA	31,105	C
Holy Family Univ	PA	25,740	C
Hood College	MD	30,085	VC
Hope College	MI	28,208	VC+
Houghton College	NY	25,980	VC+
Houston Baptist Univ	TX	18,660	C
Howard Univ	DC	18,481	C+
Humboldt State Univ	CA	11,176	C
Idaho State Univ	ID	9,030	C
Illinois College	IL	21,900	C+
Illinois State Univ	IL	12,839	C+
Illinois Wesleyan Univ	IL	34,050	HC+
Immaculata Univ	PA	25,350	C
Indiana State Univ	IN	11,604	C
Indiana Univ Bloomington	IN	13,356	VC
Indiana Univ Northwest	IN	4,902	LC
Indiana Univ of Pennsylvania	PA	11,209	C
Indiana Univ South Bend	IN	4,989	LC
Indiana Univ Southeast	IN	4,880	LC
Indiana Univ-Purdue Univ Fort Wayne	IN	5,067	LC
Indiana Univ-Purdue Univ Indianapolis	IN	10,959	C
Iona College	NY	30,878	VC
Iowa State Univ	IA	11,831	VC
Ithaca College	NY	35,144	VC
Jacksonville Univ	FL	24,040	C
Jamestown College	ND	14,130	NC
John Carroll Univ	OH	27,658	C+
Johns Hopkins Univ	MD	42,044	MC
Juniata College	PA	33,130	C
Kalamazoo College	MI	32,442	VC+
Keene State College	NH	13,836	C
Kennesaw State Univ	GA	12,152	C
Kent State Univ	OH	14,594	C
Kenyon College	OH	39,500	MC
King College	TN	23,400	C
King's College	PA	29,810	C
Knox College	IL	32,385	VC+
Kutztown Univ of Pennsylvania	PA	10,820	C
La Salle Univ	PA	34,950	C
Lafayette College	PA	39,267	MC
Lake Forest College	IL	33,860	VC
Lamar Univ	TX	6,820	LC
Lambuth Univ	TN	21,700	C+
Lane College	TN	11,220	C+
Lawrence Univ	WI	33,958	HC+
Le Moyne College	NY	29,570	VC
Lebanon Valley College	PA	31,700	VC
Lee Univ	TN	14,780	NC
Lehigh Univ	PA	42,690	HC+
Lenoir-Rhyne College	NC	25,580	C
Lincoln Univ	MO	8,000	NC
Lincoln Univ	PA	13,658	C+
Lindenwood Univ	MO	18,600	VC
Linfield College	OR	29,632	VC
Lipscomb Univ	TN	20,967	VC
Lock Haven Univ of Pennsylvania	PA	12,098	LC
LIU/C.W. Post Campus	NY	28,282	C
Louisiana College	LA	13,450	C
Louisiana State Univ and A&M College	LA	10,749	VC
Louisiana State Univ in Shreveport	LA	2,900	NC
Louisiana Tech Univ	LA	7,370	C
Loyola College in Maryland	MD	38,898	HC
Loyola Marymount Univ	CA	36,321	VC
Loyola Univ Chicago	IL	32,896	VC
Loyola Univ New Orleans	LA	31,050	VC+
Luther College	IA	28,800	VC+
Lycoming College	PA	30,797	C+

ST = STATE   **$IS** = IN-STATE COSTS   **SR** = SELECTOR RATING

School	ST	$IS	SR
Lynchburg College	VA	30,645	C
Macalester College	MN	36,500	MC
Manchester College	IN	23,470	C
Manhattan College	NY	29,000	VC
Manhattanville College	NY	32,500	C+
Mansfield Univ	PA	11,300	C
Marian College	IN	26,160	C
Marist College	NY	30,566	VC
Marlboro College	VT	35,980	VC+
Marquette Univ	WI	31,066	HC
Mary Baldwin College	VA	26,465	C
Marywood Univ	PA	30,680	C
McDaniel College	MD	31,610	C
McMurry Univ	TX	18,100	LC
Mercer Univ	GA	27,525	VC+
Meredith College	NC	25,600	C
Messiah College	PA	28,910	VC+
Methodist College	NC	21,000	C
Miami Univ	OH	29,097	HC
Mich State Univ	MI	13,689	VC
Middle Tenn State Univ	TN	8,540	C
Middlebury College	VT	42,120	MC
Millersville Univ of Pennsylvania	PA	12,113	C
Millikin Univ	IL	25,590	C
Mills College	CA	39,870	C
Millsaps College	MS	28,256	VC+
Minn State Univ, Mankato	MN	10,276	LC
Minn State Univ, Moorhead	MN	7,000	LC
Minot State Univ	ND	6,700	LC
Miss College	MS	14,574	VC
Missouri Southern State Univ	MO	8,396	NC
Missouri State Univ	MO	10,748	C+
Missouri Western State Univ	MO	9,534	NC
Monmouth College	IL	23,700	C
Montana State Univ-Northern	MT	10,000	NC
Montclair State Univ	NJ	16,327	C
Moravian College	PA	28,950	VC
Morehouse College	GA	25,082	C
Mount Holyoke College	MA	42,148	HC+
Mount Mary College	WI	22,895	C
Mount St. Mary's College	CA	32,086	VC
Mount St. Mary's Univ	MD	30,930	C
Mount Union College	OH	25,840	C
Murray State Univ	KY	8,900	VC
Muskingum College	OH	22,970	C
Nazareth College of Rochester	NY	28,175	VC
Nebr Wesleyan Univ	NE	23,415	C+
New York Univ	NY	43,170	MC
Newberry College	SC	23,000	LC
Niagara Univ	NY	28,250	C
Nicholls State Univ	LA	6,500	NC
N Car Agricultural and Technical State Univ	NC	8,000	LC
N Car Central Univ	NC	9,000	LC
N Car State Univ	NC	11,824	HC
North Central College	IL	28,926	VC
N Dak State Univ	ND	8,500	C
North Georgia College and State Univ	GA	7,000	C
Northeastern Illinois Univ	IL	3,900	NC
Northeastern Univ	MA	35,742	HC
Northern Arizona Univ	AZ	10,353	C
Northern Illinois Univ	IL	13,178	C
Northern Kentucky Univ	KY	6,670	NC
Northern Mich Univ	MI	12,340	LC
Northern State Univ	SD	8,257	C
Northwest Missouri State Univ	MO	10,000	C
Northwestern Univ	IL	37,595	MC
Notre Dame de Namur Univ	CA	32,790	LC
Oakland Univ	MI	11,936	C
Oakwood College	AL	14,904	C
Oberlin College	OH	40,904	MC
Occidental College	CA	40,185	MC
Oglethorpe Univ	GA	30,300	VC
Ohio Northern Univ	OH	27,765	VC
Ohio State Univ	OH	15,357	HC
Ohio Univ	OH	15,921	C
Ohio Wesleyan Univ	OH	35,830	VC+
Okla Baptist Univ	OK	17,986	VC
Okla City Univ	OK	23,965	VC
Okla State Univ	OK	10,213	VC
Old Dominion Univ	VA	11,907	C
Oral Roberts Univ	OK	22,650	C
Oregon State Univ	OR	11,055	C
Otterbein College	OH	28,986	C
Ouachita Baptist Univ	AR	21,900	VC
Pacific Lutheran Univ	WA	28,805	VC
Pacific Union College	CA	24,555	VC+
Penn State Univ/Univ Park Campus	PA	18,038	HC
Pepperdine Univ	CA	39,960	HC
Pittsburg State Univ	KS	8,112	C
Pitzer College	CA	41,644	HC
Plymouth State Univ	NH	12,298	LC
Pomona College	CA	40,774	MC
Portland State Univ	OR	12,453	C
Presbyterian College	SC	30,044	VC
Princeton Univ	NJ	40,213	MC
Principia College	IL	27,765	VC+
Providence College	RI	34,580	HC
Purdue Univ/Calumet	IN	10,891	LC
Purdue Univ/West Lafayette	IN	13,458	VC
Queens Univ of Charlotte	NC	24,528	C
Randolph-Macon College	VA	31,250	C
Randolph-Macon Woman's College	VA	31,160	VC+
Regis Univ	CO	31,890	C
Rhode Island College	RI	11,570	C
Rhodes College	TN	32,860	HC
Rider Univ	NJ	32,560	C
Ripon College	WI	27,160	C+
Roanoke College	VA	30,748	VC
Rockford College	IL	28,330	VC
Rockhurst Univ	MO	25,440	VC
Rollins College	FL	38,366	VC
Roosevelt Univ	IL	22,605	VC
Rosemont College	PA	29,350	C
Rutgers, The State Univ of New Jersey/Camden Campus	NJ	15,000	VC
Rutgers, The State Univ of New Jersey/New Brunswick/Piscataway Campus	NJ	15,810	HC
Rutgers, The State Univ of New Jersey/Newark Campus	NJ	15,640	VC
Saginaw Valley State Univ	MI	11,432	C
St. Ambrose Univ	IA	25,495	C
St. Anselm College	NH	33,810	C
St. Augustine's College	NC	14,000	LC
St. Bonaventure Univ	NY	28,785	C
St. Francis Univ	PA	25,880	LC
St. John Fisher College	NY	27,860	C
St. John's Univ	MN	29,749	VC
St. John's Univ	NY	34,370	C
St. Joseph's Univ	PA	37,428	VC
St. Lawrence Univ	NY	40,545	VC
St. Louis Univ	MO	33,158	VC+
St. Mary-of-the-Woods College	IN	25,480	C
St. Mary's College	IN	32,538	VC
St. Mary's College of Calif	CA	37,290	C
St. Mary's Univ of Minn	MN	23,857	VC
St. Mary's Univ of San Antonio	TX	22,444	C
St. Michael's College	VT	33,330	VC
St. Norbert College	WI	28,577	C+
St. Olaf College	MN	32,800	HC
St. Vincent College	PA	26,160	VC
St. Xavier Univ	IL	23,160	C
Salem College	NC	26,226	VC+
Salisbury Univ	MD	13,128	VC
Salve Regina Univ	RI	33,450	C
Sam Houston State Univ	TX	8,000	C
Samford Univ	AL	20,258	VC
San Diego State Univ	CA	12,971	C
San Francisco State Univ	CA	13,000	C
San Jose State Univ	CA	11,707	C
Santa Clara Univ	CA	38,931	VC
Sarah Lawrence College	NY	42,000	HC
Seattle Pacific Univ	WA	29,355	C
Seattle Univ	WA	30,063	VC
Seton Hall Univ	NJ	33,622	VC
Shippensburg Univ of Pennsylvania	PA	11,621	C
Shorter College	GA	19,700	C
Siena College	NY	28,260	VC+
Simmons College	MA	35,640	VC
Simon's Rock College of Bard	MA	41,988	VC+
Simpson College	IA	26,833	VC
Skidmore College	NY	41,779	HC
Slippery Rock Univ of Pennsylvania	PA	10,360	LC
Smith College	MA	41,474	MC
Sonoma State Univ	CA	14,732	C
S Car State Univ	SC	6,700	LC
Southeast Missouri State Univ	MO	10,596	C
Southeastern Louisiana Univ	LA	8,521	LC
Southern Conn State Univ	CT	10,310	C
Southern Illinois Univ Carbondale	IL	12,391	C
Southern Methodist Univ	TX	36,088	VC+
Southern Univ and A&M College	LA	8,238	LC
Southern Utah Univ	UT		C
Southwestern Univ	TX	26,767	HC
Spelman College	GA	24,650	VC
Stanford Univ	CA	41,557	MC
SUNY at Oswego	NY	13,662	VC
SUNY at Potsdam	NY	12,959	C
SUNY/College at Brockport	NY	12,747	VC
SUNY/College at Buffalo	NY	11,903	C+
SUNY/College at Fredonia	NY	12,771	VC
SUNY/College at Geneseo	NY	12,910	HC+
SUNY/College at Oneonta	NY	12,905	VC
SUNY/College at Plattsburgh	NY	12,362	C
SUNY/Univ at Albany	NY	13,860	VC
SUNY/Univ at Binghamton	NY	13,988	VC
SUNY/Univ at Buffalo	NY	13,694	VC
SUNY/Univ at New Paltz	NY	12,480	VC
Stephen F. Austin State Univ	TX	7,930	C
Stetson Univ	FL	32,725	VC
Suffolk Univ	MA	33,160	C
Susquehanna Univ	PA	33,465	VC
Swarthmore College	PA	41,280	MC
Sweet Briar College	VA	31,460	VC
Syracuse Univ	NY	38,655	HC
Taylor Univ	IN	26,376	VC+
Temple Univ	PA	17,438	C
Tenn Tech Univ	TN	10,044	C
Texas A&M Univ	TX	13,351	VC
Texas A&M Univ at Commerce	TX	9,020	C
Texas Southern Univ	TX	9,828	C
Texas State Univ - San Marcos	TX	10,862	C
Texas Tech Univ	TX	13,026	VC
Towson Univ	MD	13,924	VC
Transylvania Univ	KY	26,240	VC+
Trinity College	CT	38,040	HC+
Trinity Univ	TX	30,157	HC+
Truman State Univ	MO	11,242	VC
Tufts Univ	MA	42,018	MC
Tulane Univ	LA	41,098	MC
Union College	NE	18,710	C
Union Univ	TN	20,750	VC
Univ of Akron	OH	15,166	NC
Univ of Alabama	AL	9,888	C
Univ of Alabama at Birmingham	AL	13,716	C
Univ of Arizona	AZ	11,958	VC
Univ of Arkansas	AR	11,859	VC
Univ of Arkansas at Little Rock	AR	7,230	NC
Univ of at Calif Davis	CA	15,010	VC
Univ of Calif at Berkeley	CA	18,141	HC+
Univ of Calif at Irvine	CA	16,475	HC
Univ of Calif at Los Angeles	CA	17,681	MC
Univ of Calif at Riverside	CA	16,625	C
Univ of Calif at Santa Barbara	CA	11,800	VC
Univ of Calif at Santa Cruz	CA	19,174	VC
Univ of Central Arkansas	AR	9,984	C
Univ of Central Florida	FL	10,739	VC
Univ of Central Okla	OK	8,094	C
Univ of Cincinnati	OH	17,682	C
Univ of Colo at Boulder	CO	13,352	C+
Univ of Colo at Denver and Health Sciences Center	CO	5,021	C
Univ of Conn	CT	16,628	HC
Univ of Dallas	TX	27,432	VC+
Univ of Dayton	OH	28,826	VC
Univ of Denver	CO	36,376	VC+
Univ of Evansville	IN	28,320	VC
Univ of Florida	FL	9,354	HC
Univ of Georgia	GA	11,004	HC
Univ of Hawaii at Manoa	HI	10,413	VC
Univ of Houston	TX	7,000	C
Univ of Idaho	ID	9,310	NC
Univ of Illinois at Chicago	IL	16,256	VC
Univ of Illinois at Urbana-Champaign	IL	15,800	HC+
Univ of Indianapolis	IN	25,090	C
Univ of Iowa	IA	12,172	VC
Univ of Kansas	KS	10,915	VC
Univ of Kentucky	KY	7,800	VC
Univ of La Verne	CA	33,470	C
Univ of Louisiana at Lafayette	LA	5,830	C
Univ of Louisiana at Monroe	LA	7,103	C
Univ of Louisville	KY	10,400	VC
Univ of Maine	ME	13,642	C
Univ of Maine at Fort Kent	ME	10,832	LC
Univ of Mary Washington	VA	11,636	HC
Univ of Maryland/Baltimore County	MD	16,642	VC+
Univ of Maryland/College Park	MD	16,036	HC
Univ of Mass Amherst	MA	15,973	C+
Univ of Mass Boston	MA	8,024	C
Univ of Mass Dartmouth	MA	15,985	C
Univ of Miami	FL	38,397	MC
Univ of Mich/Ann Arbor	MI	16,587	HC+
Univ of Mich/Flint	MI	6,398	C
Univ of Minn/Morris	MN	15,472	VC
Univ of Minn/Twin Cities	MN	13,165	HC
Univ of Miss	MS	9,000	C
Univ of Missouri/Columbia	MO	13,500	VC
Univ of Missouri/Kansas City	MO	15,000	VC
Univ of Missouri/St. Louis	MO	14,046	VC
Univ of Montana	MT	10,602	C
Univ of Montevallo	AL	9,630	C
Univ of Nebr at Kearney	NE	9,000	NC
Univ of Nebr at Lincoln	NE	11,401	VC
Univ of Nebr at Omaha	NE	11,235	C
Univ of Nevada/Las Vegas	NV	11,566	C
Univ of Nevada/Reno	NV	12,155	NC
Univ of New Hampshire	NH	16,810	VC
Univ of New Mexico	NM	11,253	C
Univ of New Orleans	LA	7,370	C
Univ of North Alabama	AL	8,992	C
Univ of N Car at Asheville	NC	9,237	VC
Univ of N Car at Charlotte	NC	9,101	C
Univ of N Car at Greensboro	NC	8,993	C
Univ of N Car at Wilmington	NC	10,107	VC
Univ of N Dak	ND	10,114	VC
Univ of North Texas	TX	7,800	C
Univ of Northern Colo	CO	10,249	C
Univ of Northern Iowa	IA	11,133	C
Univ of Notre Dame	IN	39,552	MC
Univ of Okla	OK	10,769	VC+
Univ of Oregon	OR	13,108	VC
Univ of Pennsylvania	PA	41,766	MC
Univ of Pittsburgh at Pittsburgh	PA	18,866	HC
Univ of PR/Mayaguez	PR	1,250	
Univ of Puget Sound	WA	35,600	HC
Univ of Redlands	CA	36,160	VC
Univ of Rhode Island	RI	15,398	C
Univ of Richmond	VA	40,510	MC
Univ of Rochester	NY	41,135	MC
Univ of St. Thomas	MN	28,000	VC
Univ of St. Thomas	TX	23,810	VC
Univ of San Diego	CA	40,620	HC
Univ of San Francisco	CA	37,560	VC
Univ of Scranton	PA	31,100	VC
Univ of S Car at Columbia	SC	13,397	VC
Univ of S Car Upstate	SC	11,957	C
Univ of South Florida	FL	10,284	VC
Univ of Southern Calif	CA	41,618	MC
Univ of Southern Maine	ME	12,614	C
Univ of Tenn at Chattanooga	TN	7,790	C
Univ of Tenn at Knoxville	TN	11,720	C
Univ of Tenn at Martin	TN	8,693	C
Univ of Texas at Arlington	TX	7,195	LC
Univ of Texas at Austin	TX	14,610	HC
Univ of Texas at El Paso	TX	8,764	NC
Univ of Texas at San Antonio	TX	11,325	LC
Univ of the District of Columbia	DC	2,070	LC
Univ of the Pacific	CA	34,380	VC
Univ of the South	TN	34,645	HC
Univ of Toledo	OH	15,806	NC
Univ of Tulsa	OK	25,348	HC
Univ of Utah	UT	10,162	VC
Univ of Vermont	VT	18,080	VC
Univ of Virginia	VA	13,759	MC
Univ of Virginia's College at Wise	VA	11,076	C
Univ of Washington	WA	10,400	VC
Univ of West Georgia	GA	8,838	C
Univ of Wisc/Eau Claire	WI	9,915	VC
Univ of Wisc/Green Bay	WI	9,415	VC
Univ of Wisc/La Crosse	WI	10,045	VC
Univ of Wisc/Madison	WI	13,117	HC
Univ of Wisc/Milwaukee	WI	9,427	LC
Univ of Wisc/Oshkosh	WI	10,426	LC
Univ of Wisc/Parkside	WI	10,181	LC
Univ of Wisc/Stevens Point	WI	9,384	VC
Univ of Wisc/Whitewater	WI	9,274	C
Univ of Wyoming	WY	9,666	C
Ursinus College	PA	38,950	VC
Utah State Univ	UT	8,002	VC
Valdosta State Univ	GA	8,802	C
Valparaiso Univ	IN	28,970	VC+
Vanderbilt Univ	TN	41,986	MC
Villanova Univ	PA	38,672	HC+
Virginia Polytechnic Inst and State Univ	VA	10,834	VC
Virginia Wesleyan College	VA	28,433	C
Wabash College	IN	30,116	VC
Wake Forest Univ	NC	38,290	MC
Walla Walla College	WA	24,489	NC
Walsh Univ	OH	23,440	C
Wartburg College	IA	27,315	NC
Washburn Univ	KS	9,734	NC
Washington and Jefferson College	PA	33,490	VC
Washington and Lee Univ	VA	35,880	MC
Washington College	MD	34,990	VC
Washington State Univ	WA	12,260	C
Washington Univ in St. Louis	MO	42,106	MC
Weber State Univ	UT	9,635	NC
Webster Univ	MO	24,280	VC
Wellesley College	MA	41,030	MC
Wells College	NY	23,070	VC
Wesleyan College	GA	19,560	C
Wesleyan Univ	CT	42,122	MC
West Chester Univ of Pennsylvania	PA	12,355	C+
Western Carolina Univ	NC	7,000	C
Western Illinois Univ	IL	13,042	C
Western Kentucky Univ	KY	10,192	C
Western Mich Univ	MI	13,299	C
Western Washington Univ	WA	11,342	VC
Westminster College	MO	19,060	VC
Westminster College	PA	31,290	C+
Westmont College	CA	36,672	HC
Wheaton College	IL	27,760	HC
Wheaton College	MA	40,180	HC+
Wheeling Jesuit Univ	WV	26,910	C
Whitman College	WA	36,110	HC+
Whittier College	CA	29,108	C
Whitworth College	WA	29,428	VC+
Wichita State Univ	KS	8,500	C

School	ST	$IS	SR
Wilkes Univ	PA	30,886	C
Willamette Univ	OR	35,416	VC+
William Jewell College	MO	24,340	C
Williams College	MA	40,310	HC
Wilson College	PA	27,660	C
Winona State Univ	MN	11,333	C
Winthrop Univ	SC	11,302	C
Wittenberg Univ	OH	34,596	VC
Wofford College	SC	30,935	HC
Wright State Univ	OH	13,616	LC
Xavier Univ	OH	30,490	HC
Xavier Univ of Louisiana	LA	17,600	C
Yale Univ	CT	41,000	MC
Yeshiva Univ	NY	22,000	C
Youngstown State Univ	OH	12,613	NC

FRENCH STUDIES

School	ST	$IS	SR
American Univ	DC	38,719	HC+
Assumption College	MA	32,875	C
Bard College	NY	41,800	HC+
Boston Univ	MA	42,046	HC+
Brown Univ	RI	42,015	MC
Case Western Reserve Univ	OH	37,314	MC
Colby College	ME	41,770	MC
Columbia Univ/School of General Studies	NY	41,516	C
Duke Univ	NC	41,239	MC
Emory Univ	GA	40,546	MC
Fairleigh Dickinson Univ/ College at Florham	NJ	30,130	C
Fairleigh Dickinson Univ/ Metropolitan Campus	NJ	28,590	C
Fordham Univ	NY	36,000	HC
Lewis and Clark College	OR	35,358	VC+
Mass Inst of Technology	MA	41,800	VC
New College of Florida	FL	10,009	HC+
Reed College	OR	41,106	MC
Rice Univ	TX	32,290	MC
St. Joseph's Univ	PA	37,428	VC
Scripps College	CA	41,000	MC
Simon's Rock College of Bard	MA	41,988	VC+
Skidmore College	NY	41,779	HC
Smith College	MA	41,474	MC
S Dak State Univ	SD	9,815	C
SUNY/Univ at Stony Brook	NY	13,625	HC
Univ of Calif at Los Angeles	CA	17,681	MC
Univ of Calif at San Diego	CA	16,102	HC
Univ of New Hampshire	NH	16,810	VC
Univ of S Dak	SD	9,068	C
Univ of the South	TN	34,645	HC
Wartburg College	IA	27,315	NC
Washington State Univ	WA	12,260	C
Wayne State Univ	MI	11,805	C
Wellesley College	MA	41,030	MC
Wesleyan Univ	CT	42,122	MC

FUNERAL HOME SERVICES

School	ST	$IS	SR
Cincinnati College of Mortuary Science	OH	12,000	SP
Gannon Univ	PA	26,100	C
Mount Ida College	MA	26,000	LC
Point Park Univ	PA	24,160	C
St. John's Univ	NY	34,370	C
Southern Illinois Univ Carbondale	IL	12,391	C
Univ of Central Okla	OK	8,094	C
Wayne State Univ	MI	11,805	C

FURNITURE DESIGN

School	ST	$IS	SR
Calif College of the Arts	CA	34,325	SP
Indiana Univ-Purdue Univ Indianapolis	IN	10,959	C
Kendall College of Art and Design of Ferris State Univ	MI	11,870	SP
Minneapolis College of Art and Design	MN	31,110	SP
N Car State Univ	NC	11,824	HC
Rhode Island School of Design	RI	38,130	SP
Rochester Inst of Technology	NY	32,070	VC+
Savannah College of Art and Design	GA	30,800	SP

GENDER STUDIES

School	ST	$IS	SR
American Univ	DC	38,719	HC+
Bates College	ME	42,100	MC
Brown Univ	RI	42,015	MC
Conn College	CT	41,975	MC
Indiana Univ Bloomington	IN	13,356	VC
Kent State Univ	OH	14,594	C
Lawrence Univ	WI	33,958	HC+
Louisiana State Univ and A&M College	LA	10,749	VC
New York Univ	NY	43,170	MC
Northwestern Univ	IL	37,595	MC
Sonoma State Univ	CA	14,732	C
Stonehill College	MA	36,104	HC

School	ST	$IS	SR
Univ of Calif at San Diego	CA	16,102	HC
Univ of Chicago	IL	42,369	MC
Univ of Southern Calif	CA	41,618	MC
Univ of Texas at Dallas	TX	13,244	HC
Univ of Vermont	VT	18,080	VC

GENETICS

School	ST	$IS	SR
Ball State Univ	IN	13,138	C
Cedar Crest College	PA	30,615	C
Cornell Univ	NY	41,717	MC
Dartmouth College	NH	39,465	MC
Florida State Univ	FL	9,028	HC
Iowa State Univ	IA	11,831	VC
Missouri Southern State Univ	MO	8,396	NC
Ohio Wesleyan Univ	OH	35,830	VC+
Rutgers, The State Univ of New Jersey/New Brunswick/Piscataway Campus	NJ	15,810	HC
Texas A&M Univ	TX	13,351	HC
Univ of at Calif Davis	CA	15,010	VC
Univ of Conn	CT	16,628	HC
Univ of Georgia	GA	11,004	HC
Univ of Minn/Twin Cities	MN	13,165	HC
Univ of Rochester	NY	41,135	MC
Univ of Vermont	VT	18,080	VC
Univ of Wisc/Madison	WI	13,117	HC
Washington State Univ	WA	12,260	C
Western Kentucky Univ	KY	10,192	C

GEOCHEMISTRY

School	ST	$IS	SR
Bowdoin College	ME	41,660	MC
Calif Inst of Technology	CA	36,123	MC
Columbia Univ/Columbia College	NY	42,584	MC
Occidental College	CA	40,185	MC
SUNY at Oswego	NY	13,662	VC
SUNY/College at Cortland	NY	12,095	C
SUNY/College at Geneseo	NY	12,910	HC+
Univ of Maine at Farmington	ME	11,515	C
Western Mich Univ	MI	13,299	C

GEODETIC SCIENCE

School	ST	$IS	SR
Univ of Arkansas at Monticello	AR	7,325	NC

GEOENVIRONMENTAL STUDIES

School	ST	$IS	SR
Shippensburg Univ of Pennsylvania	PA	11,621	C
Univ of Calif at Los Angeles	CA	17,681	MC
Univ of N Dak	ND	10,114	VC

GEOGRAPHY

School	ST	$IS	SR
Appalachian State Univ	NC	8,000	VC
Aquinas College	MI	23,750	C
Arizona State Univ-Tempe	AZ	11,174	C
Arkansas State Univ	AR	9,630	C
Auburn Univ	AL	12,230	VC
Augustana College	IL	29,862	VC+
Austin Peay State Univ	TN	7,535	C
Ball State Univ	IN	13,138	C
Baylor Univ	TX	27,555	HC
Bellevue Univ	NE	4,440	NC
Bemidji State Univ	MN	11,180	LC
Bloomsburg Univ of Pennsylvania	PA	11,602	C
Boston Univ	MA	42,046	HC+
Bowling Green State Univ	OH	14,994	C
Bridgewater State College	MA	12,120	C
Brigham Young Univ	UT	9,200	HC
Bucknell Univ	PA	39,660	MC
Calif State Polytechnic Univ, Pomona	CA	18,053	C+
Cal State East Bay	CA	10,856	LC
Cal State, Chico	CA	11,395	C
Cal State, Dominguez Hills	CA	10,220	LC
Cal State, Fresno	CA	10,037	LC
Cal State, Fullerton	CA	10,990	C
Cal State, Long Beach	CA	9,512	C
Cal State, Los Angeles	CA	5,900	C
Cal State, Northridge	CA	9,036	LC
Cal State, Sacramento	CA	11,122	C+
Cal State, San Bernardino	CA	12,563	LC
Cal State, Stanislaus	CA	11,283	C
Calif Univ of Pennsylvania	PA	14,217	C
Calvin College	MI	25,735	NC
Carthage College	WI	26,000	C
Central Conn State Univ	CT	13,620	C
Central Missouri State Univ	MO	10,000	C
Central Washington Univ	WA	11,730	C
Charleston Southern Univ	SC	17,800	C
Cheyney Univ of Pennsylvania	PA	11,497	LC
Chicago State Univ	IL	10,915	C+
CUNY/Herbert H. Lehman College	NY	4,000	LC
CUNY/Hunter College	NY	8,000	C+

School	ST	$IS	SR
Clarion Univ of Pennsylvania	PA	11,844	C
Clark Univ	MA	35,165	VC+
Colgate Univ	NY	41,170	MC
Concord College	WV	9,708	C
Concordia Univ Nebr	NE	20,500	C+
Concordia Univ, River Forest	IL	26,300	C
Dartmouth College	NH	39,465	MC
DePaul Univ	IL	29,835	VC
DePauw Univ	IN	32,100	HC
Dickinson State Univ	ND	7,847	NC
East Carolina Univ	NC	10,000	C
East Stroudsburg Univ of Pennsylvania	PA	10,336	C
East Tenn State Univ	TN	8,497	C
Eastern Illinois Univ	IL	12,569	C
Eastern Kentucky Univ	KY	7,725	C
Eastern Mich Univ	MI	12,897	C
Eastern Washington Univ	WA	10,608	C
Edinboro Univ of Pennsylvania	PA	11,809	LC
Elmhurst College	IL	24,685	C
Emory & Henry College	VA	26,570	C
Excelsior College	NY	995	SP
Fayetteville State Univ	NC	6,000	LC
Fitchburg State College	MA	11,276	C
Florida Atlantic Univ	FL	11,221	C
Florida International Univ	FL	9,215	VC
Florida State Univ	FL	9,028	HC
Framingham State College	MA	11,156	C
Frostburg State Univ	MD	12,672	C
George Mason Univ	VA	10,850	VC
George Washington Univ	DC	48,820	MC
Georgia Southern Univ	GA	9,762	C
Georgia State Univ	GA	11,444	VC
Grand Valley State Univ	MI	12,000	VC
Gustavus Adolphus College	MN	30,920	HC
Hampshire College	MA	37,120	HC
Hofstra Univ	NY	32,630	VC
Humboldt State Univ	CA	11,176	C
Illinois State Univ	IL	12,839	C+
Indiana State Univ	IN	11,604	C
Indiana Univ Bloomington	IN	13,356	VC
Indiana Univ of Pennsylvania	PA	11,209	C
Indiana Univ Southeast	IN	4,880	LC
Indiana Univ-Purdue Univ Indianapolis	IN	10,959	C
Jacksonville State Univ	AL	7,618	LC
Jacksonville Univ	FL	24,040	C
James Madison Univ	VA	12,010	VC
Kansas State Univ	KS	10,516	VC
Keene State College	NH	13,836	C
Kennesaw State Univ	GA	12,152	C
Kutztown Univ of Pennsylvania	PA	10,820	C
Lock Haven Univ of Pennsylvania	PA	12,098	LC
LIU/C.W. Post Campus	NY	28,282	C
Louisiana State Univ and A&M College	LA	10,749	VC
Louisiana State Univ in Shreveport	LA	2,900	NC
Louisiana Tech Univ	LA	7,370	C
Macalester College	MN	36,500	MC
Mansfield Univ	PA	11,300	C
Marshall Univ	WV	9,116	C
Miami Univ	OH	29,097	HC
Mich State Univ	MI	13,689	VC
Middle Tenn State Univ	TN	8,540	C
Middlebury College	VT	42,120	MC
Millersville Univ of Pennsylvania	PA	12,113	C
Minn State Univ, Mankato	MN	10,276	LC
Missouri State Univ	MO	10,748	C+
Montclair State Univ	NJ	16,327	C
Morehead State Univ	KY	9,516	C
Mount Holyoke College	MA	42,148	HC+
Murray State Univ	KY	8,900	VC
New Jersey City Univ	NJ	13,695	LC
New Mexico State Univ	NM	9,250	C
N Car Central Univ	NC	9,000	LC
Northeastern Illinois Univ	IL	3,000	NC
Northeastern State Univ	OK	5,896	LC
Northern Arizona Univ	AZ	10,353	C
Northern Illinois Univ	IL	13,178	C
Northern Kentucky Univ	KY	6,670	NC
Northern Mich Univ	MI	12,340	LC
Northwest Missouri State Univ	MO	10,000	C
Northwestern Univ	IL	37,595	MC
Ohio State Univ	OH	15,357	HC
Ohio Univ	OH	15,921	C
Ohio Wesleyan Univ	OH	35,830	VC+
Okla State Univ	OK	10,213	VC
Old Dominion Univ	VA	11,907	C
Oregon State Univ	OR	11,055	C
Penn State Univ/Univ Park Campus	PA	18,038	HC
Pittsburg State Univ	KS	8,112	C
Plymouth State Univ	NH	12,298	LC
Portland State Univ	OR	12,453	C
Prairie View A&M Univ	TX	11,110	LC
Radford Univ	VA	13,145	C
Rhode Island College	RI	11,570	C

School	ST	$IS	SR
Rowan Univ	NJ	16,000	VC
Rutgers, The State Univ of New Jersey/New Brunswick/Piscataway Campus	NJ	15,810	HC
St. Cloud State Univ	MN	10,010	C
Salem State College	MA	13,161	LC
Salisbury Univ	MD	13,128	VC
Sam Houston State Univ	TX	8,000	C
Samford Univ	AL	20,258	VC
San Diego State Univ	CA	12,971	C
San Francisco State Univ	CA	13,000	C
San Jose State Univ	CA	11,707	C
Shippensburg Univ of Pennsylvania	PA	11,621	C
Slippery Rock Univ of Pennsylvania	PA	10,360	LC
Sonoma State Univ	CA	14,732	C
S Dak State Univ	SD	9,815	C
Southern Conn State Univ	CT	10,310	C
Southern Illinois Univ Carbondale	IL	12,391	C
Southern Illinois Univ Edwardsville	IL	11,022	C
Southern Oregon Univ	OR	12,186	C
SUNY/College at Buffalo	NY	11,903	C+
SUNY/College at Cortland	NY	12,095	C
SUNY/College at Geneseo	NY	12,910	HC+
SUNY/College at Oneonta	NY	12,905	VC
SUNY/College at Plattsburgh	NY	12,362	C
SUNY/Univ at Albany	NY	13,860	VC
SUNY/Univ at Binghamton	NY	13,988	HC
SUNY/Univ at Buffalo	NY	13,694	VC
SUNY/Univ at New Paltz	NY	12,480	VC
Stephen F. Austin State Univ	TX	7,930	C
Stetson Univ	FL	32,725	VC
Syracuse Univ	NY	38,655	HC
Taylor Univ	IN	26,376	VC+
Temple Univ	PA	17,438	C
Texas A&M Univ at Commerce	TX	9,020	C
Texas A&M Univ at Corpus Christi	TX	10,280	LC
Texas A&M Univ at Galveston	TX	10,000	C+
Texas A&M Univ at Kingsville	TX	6,800	LC
Texas Christian Univ	TX	23,410	VC+
Texas State Univ - San Marcos	TX	10,862	C
Texas Tech Univ	TX	13,026	VC
Towson Univ	MD	13,924	VC
United States Air Force Academy	CO		HC+
United States Military Academy	NY		MC
Univ of Akron	OH	15,166	NC
Univ of Alabama	AL	9,888	C
Univ of Alaska Fairbanks	AK	10,101	C
Univ of Arizona	AZ	11,958	VC
Univ of Arkansas	AR	11,859	VC
Univ of at Calif Davis	CA	15,010	VC
Univ of Calif at Berkeley	CA	18,141	HC+
Univ of Calif at Los Angeles	CA	17,681	MC
Univ of Calif at Santa Barbara	CA	11,800	VC
Univ of Central Arkansas	AR	9,984	C
Univ of Central Okla	OK	8,094	C
Univ of Chicago	IL	42,369	MC
Univ of Cincinnati	OH	17,682	C
Univ of Colo at Boulder	CO	13,352	C+
Univ of Colo at Colo Springs	CO	11,517	VC
Univ of Colo at Denver and Health Sciences Center	CO	5,021	C
Univ of Conn	CT	16,628	HC
Univ of Delaware	DE	14,142	HC
Univ of Denver	CO	36,376	VC+
Univ of Florida	FL	9,354	HC
Univ of Georgia	GA	11,004	HC
Univ of Hawaii at Hilo	HI	6,500	C
Univ of Hawaii at Manoa	HI	10,413	VC
Univ of Idaho	ID	9,310	NC
Univ of Illinois at Urbana-Champaign	IL	15,800	HC+
Univ of Iowa	IA	12,172	VC
Univ of Kansas	KS	10,915	VC
Univ of Kentucky	KY	7,800	C
Univ of Louisville	KY	10,400	VC
Univ of Maine at Farmington	ME	11,515	C
Univ of Mary Washington	VA	11,636	HC
Univ of Maryland/Baltimore County	MD	16,642	VC+
Univ of Maryland/College Park	MD	16,036	HC
Univ of Mass Amherst	MA	15,973	C+
Univ of Mass Boston	MA	8,024	C
Univ of Memphis	TN	11,153	C
Univ of Miami	FL	38,397	MC
Univ of Mich/Ann Arbor	MI	16,587	HC+
Univ of Mich/Flint	MI	6,398	C
Univ of Minn/Duluth	MN	13,974	C
Univ of Minn/Twin Cities	MN	13,165	HC

School	ST	$IS	SR
Univ of Missouri/Columbia	MO	13,500	VC
Univ of Missouri/Kansas City	MO	15,000	VC
Univ of Montana	MT	10,602	VC
Univ of Nebr at Kearney	NE	9,000	VC
Univ of Nebr at Lincoln	NE	11,401	VC
Univ of Nebr at Omaha	NE	11,235	C
Univ of Nevada/Reno	NV	12,155	NC
Univ of New Hampshire	NH	16,810	VC
Univ of New Mexico	NM	11,253	C
Univ of New Orleans	LA	7,370	C
Univ of North Alabama	AL	8,992	C
Univ of N Car at Chapel Hill	NC	11,129	MC
Univ of N Car at Charlotte	NC	9,101	C
Univ of N Car at Greensboro	NC	8,993	C
Univ of N Car at Wilmington	NC	10,107	VC
Univ of N Dak	ND	10,114	VC
Univ of North Texas	TX	7,800	C
Univ of Northern Colo	CO	10,249	C
Univ of Northern Iowa	IA	11,133	C
Univ of Okla	OK	10,769	VC+
Univ of Oregon	OR	13,108	VC
Univ of Pittsburgh at Johnstown	PA	16,740	LC
Univ of PR/Rio Piedras	PR	5,750	
Univ of Rhode Island	RI	15,398	C
Univ of St. Thomas	MN	28,000	VC
Univ of South Alabama	AL	8,930	LC
Univ of S Car at Columbia	SC	13,397	VC
Univ of South Florida	FL	10,284	VC
Univ of Southern Calif	CA	41,618	MC
Univ of Southern Maine	ME	12,614	C
Univ of Southern Miss	MS	10,112	C
Univ of Tenn at Knoxville	TN	11,720	C
Univ of Tenn at Martin	TN	8,693	C
Univ of Texas at Austin	TX	14,610	MC
Univ of Texas at Dallas	TX	13,244	HC
Univ of Texas at San Antonio	TX	11,325	LC
Univ of the District of Columbia	DC	2,070	LC
Univ of Toledo	OH	15,806	NC
Univ of Utah	UT	10,162	VC
Univ of Vermont	VT	18,080	VC
Univ of Washington	WA	10,400	VC
Univ of West Georgia	GA	8,838	C
Univ of Wisc/Eau Claire	WI	9,915	VC
Univ of Wisc/La Crosse	WI	10,045	VC
Univ of Wisc/Madison	WI	13,117	VC
Univ of Wisc/Milwaukee	WI	9,427	LC
Univ of Wisc/Oshkosh	WI	10,426	LC
Univ of Wisc/Parkside	WI	10,181	LC
Univ of Wisc/Platteville	WI	9,779	NC
Univ of Wisc/River Falls	WI	9,722	LC
Univ of Wisc/Stevens Point	WI	9,384	VC
Univ of Wisc/Whitewater	WI	9,274	C
Univ of Wyoming	WY	9,666	C
Utah State Univ	UT	8,002	VC
Valparaiso Univ	IN	28,970	VC+
Vassar College	NY	41,700	MC
Villanova Univ	PA	38,672	HC+
Virginia Commonwealth Univ	VA	12,987	C
Virginia Polytechnic Inst and State Univ	VA	10,834	VC
Wayne State College	NE	8,038	NC
Wayne State Univ	MI	11,805	C
Weber State Univ	UT	9,635	NC
West Chester Univ of Pennsylvania	PA	12,355	C+
West Texas A&M Univ	TX	8,452	C
West Virginia Univ	WV	10,506	C
Western Carolina Univ	NC	7,000	C
Western Illinois Univ	IL	13,042	C
Western Kentucky Univ	KY	10,192	C
Western Mich Univ	MI	13,299	C
Western Oregon Univ	OR	10,295	C
Western Washington Univ	WA	11,262	VC
William Paterson Univ of New Jersey	NJ	17,810	C+
Wittenberg Univ	OH	34,596	VC
Worcester State College	MA	12,499	C
Wright State Univ	OH	13,616	LC
Youngstown State Univ	OH	12,613	NC

GEOLOGICAL ENGINEERING

School	ST	$IS	SR
Colo School of Mines	CO	14,893	HC
Columbia Univ/Fu Foundation School of Engineering and Applied Science	NY	42,584	MC
Indiana Univ Bloomington	IN	13,356	VC
Mich Tech Univ	MI	14,569	VC
Montana Tech of The Univ of Montana	MT	10,434	C
Purdue Univ/West Lafayette	IN	13,458	VC
S Dak School of Mines and Technology	SD	7,624	C+
Univ of Alaska Fairbanks	AK	10,101	C
Univ of Arizona	AZ	11,958	VC
Univ of Calif at Los Angeles	CA	17,681	MC
Univ of Idaho	ID	9,310	NC
Univ of Illinois at Urbana-Champaign	IL	15,800	HC+
Univ of Minn/Twin Cities	MN	13,165	HC
Univ of Miss	MS	9,000	C
Univ of Missouri/Rolla	MO	13,332	HC
Univ of Nevada/Reno	NV	12,155	NC
Univ of N Dak	ND	10,114	VC
Univ of Rochester	NY	41,135	MC
Univ of Utah	UT	10,162	VC
Univ of Wisc/Madison	WI	13,117	HC

GEOLOGY

School	ST	$IS	SR
Adams State College	CO	8,613	C
Alfred Univ	NY		VC
Allegheny College	PA	33,500	HC
Amherst College	MA	41,590	MC
Appalachian State Univ	NC	8,000	VC
Arizona State Univ-Tempe	AZ	11,174	C
Arkansas Tech Univ	AR	8,108	VC
Ashland Univ	OH	25,000	C
Auburn Univ	AL	12,230	VC
Augustana College	IL	29,862	VC+
Austin Peay State Univ	TN	7,535	C
Ball State Univ	IN	13,138	C
Bates College	ME	42,100	MC
Baylor Univ	TX	27,555	HC
Beloit College	WI	32,808	HC
Bemidji State Univ	MN	11,180	LQ
Bloomsburg Univ of Pennsylvania	PA	11,602	C
Boise State Univ	ID	9,438	LC
Boston College	MA	41,608	MC
Bowdoin College	ME	41,660	MC
Bowling Green State Univ	OH	14,994	C
Bridgewater State College	MA	12,120	C
Brigham Young Univ	UT	9,200	VC
Brown Univ	RI	42,015	MC
Bryn Mawr College	PA	42,780	HC+
Bucknell Univ	PA	39,660	MC
Calif Inst of Technology	CA	36,123	MC
Calif Lutheran Univ	CA	27,800	LC
Calif State Polytechnic Univ, Pomona	CA	18,053	C+
Cal State East Bay	CA	10,856	LC
Cal State, Bakersfield	CA	6,125	LC
Cal State, Chico	CA	11,395	C
Cal State, Dominguez Hills	CA	10,220	LC
Cal State, Fresno	CA	10,037	LC
Cal State, Fullerton	CA	10,990	C
Cal State, Long Beach	CA	9,512	C
Cal State, Los Angeles	CA	5,900	C
Cal State, Northridge	CA	9,036	LC
Cal State, Sacramento	CA	11,122	C+
Cal State, San Bernardino	CA	12,563	LC
Cal State, Stanislaus	CA	11,283	C
Calif Univ of Pennsylvania	PA	14,217	C
Calvin College	MI	25,735	NC
Carleton College	MN	40,467	MC
Case Western Reserve Univ	OH	37,314	MC
Castleton State College	VT	13,158	C
Centenary College of Louisiana	LA	24,760	VC
Central Mich Univ	MI	12,244	C
Central Missouri State Univ	MO	10,000	C
Central Washington Univ	WA	11,730	C
Charleston Southern Univ	SC	17,800	C
CUNY/Brooklyn College	NY	4,377	C+
CUNY/City College	NY		C
CUNY/Herbert H. Lehman College	NY	4,000	LC
CUNY/Queens College	NY	4,356	C
CUNY/York College	NY	4,242	NC
Clarion Univ of Pennsylvania	PA	11,844	C
Clemson Univ	SC	13,366	HC
Cleveland State Univ	OH	10,798	NC
Colby College	ME	41,770	MC
Colgate Univ	NY	41,170	MC
College of Charleston	SC	13,616	VC
College of William and Mary	VA	14,147	MC
College of Wooster	OH	31,310	VC+
Colo College	CO	37,668	VC
Colo State Univ-Fort Collins	CO	10,878	C+
Columbia Univ/Columbia College	NY	42,584	MC
Columbus State Univ	GA	8,664	C
Cornell College	IA	30,110	VC+
Cornell Univ	NY	41,717	MC
Denison Univ	OH	37,040	HC
DePauw Univ	IN	32,100	HC
Dickinson College	PA	40,170	HC+
Duke Univ	NC	41,239	MC
East Carolina Univ	NC	10,000	C
Eastern Illinois Univ	IL	12,569	C
Eastern Kentucky Univ	KY	7,725	C
Eastern Mich Univ	MI	12,897	C
Eastern New Mexico Univ	NM	7,264	C
Eastern Washington Univ	WA	10,608	C
Edinboro Univ of Pennsylvania	PA	11,809	LC
Elizabeth City State Univ	NC	5,700	LC
Excelsior College	NY	995	SP
Florida Atlantic Univ	FL	11,221	C
Florida International Univ	FL	9,215	VC
Florida State Univ	FL	9,028	HC
Fort Hays State Univ	KS	7,638	C
Fort Lewis College	CO	11,852	C
Franklin and Marshall College	PA	40,590	HC
Furman Univ	SC	33,264	HC+
George Mason Univ	VA	10,850	VC
George Washington Univ	DC	48,820	MC
Georgia Southern Univ	GA	9,762	C
Georgia Southwestern State Univ	GA	6,035	C
Georgia State Univ	GA	11,444	VC
Grand Valley State Univ	MI	12,000	VC
Guilford College	NC	28,160	C+
Gustavus Adolphus College	MN	30,920	HC
Hamilton College	NY	41,660	MC
Hampshire College	MA	37,120	HC
Hanover College	IN	28,150	NC
Hardin-Simmons Univ	TX	18,641	C
Hartwick College	NY	36,065	C+
Harvard Univ/Harvard College	MA	45,860	MC
Haverford College	PA	41,600	MC
Hofstra Univ	NY	32,630	VC
Hope College	MI	28,208	VC+
Humboldt State Univ	CA	11,176	C
Idaho State Univ	ID	9,030	C
Illinois State Univ	IL	12,839	C+
Indiana State Univ	IN	11,604	C
Indiana Univ Bloomington	IN	13,356	VC
Indiana Univ Northwest	IN	4,902	LC
Indiana Univ of Pennsylvania	PA	11,209	C
Indiana Univ-Purdue Univ Fort Wayne	IN	5,067	LC
Indiana Univ-Purdue Univ Indianapolis	IN	10,959	C
Iowa State Univ	IA	11,831	VC
James Madison Univ	VA	12,010	VC
Juniata College	PA	33,130	VC
Kansas State Univ	KS	10,516	VC
Keene State College	NH	13,836	C
Kutztown Univ of Pennsylvania	PA	10,820	C
La Salle Univ	PA	34,950	C
Lafayette College	PA	39,267	MC
Lake Superior State Univ	MI	12,842	LC
Lamar Univ	TX	6,820	LC
Lawrence Univ	WI	33,958	HC+
Lehigh Univ	PA	42,690	HC+
Lock Haven Univ of Pennsylvania	PA	12,098	LC
LIU/C.W. Post Campus	NY	28,282	C
Louisiana State Univ and A&M College	LA	10,749	VC
Louisiana Tech Univ	LA	7,370	C
Macalester College	MN	36,500	MC
Marietta College	OH	29,327	C
Marshall Univ	WV	9,116	C
McNeese State Univ	LA	5,270	LC
Mercyhurst College	PA	28,633	VC
Miami Univ	OH	29,097	HC
Mich State Univ	MI	13,689	VC
Mich Tech Univ	MI	14,569	VC
Middlebury College	VT	42,120	MC
Midwestern State Univ	TX	9,381	LC
Millersville Univ of Pennsylvania	PA	12,113	C
Millsaps College	MS	28,256	VC+
Minot State Univ	ND	6,700	LC
Missouri State Univ	MO	10,748	C+
Morehead State Univ	KY	9,150	C
Mount Holyoke College	MA	42,148	HC+
Mount Union College	OH	25,840	C
Murray State Univ	KY	8,900	VC
Muskingum College	OH	22,970	C
New Jersey City Univ	NJ	13,695	LC
New Mexico State Univ	NM	9,250	C
N Car State Univ	NC	11,824	HC
N Dak State Univ	ND	8,500	C
Northeastern Univ	MA	35,742	HC
Northern Arizona Univ	AZ	10,353	C
Northern Illinois Univ	IL	13,178	C
Northern Kentucky Univ	KY	6,670	NC
Northwest Missouri State Univ	MO	10,000	C
Northwestern Univ	IL	37,595	MC
Norwich Univ	VT	28,212	C
Oberlin College	OH	40,904	MC
Occidental College	CA	40,185	MC
Ohio State Univ	OH	15,357	HC
Ohio Univ	OH	15,921	C
Ohio Wesleyan Univ	OH	35,830	VC+
Okla State Univ	OK	10,213	VC
Old Dominion Univ	VA	11,907	C
Olivet Nazarene Univ	IL	22,590	C
Oregon State Univ	OR	11,055	C
Pomona College	CA	40,774	MC
Portland State Univ	OR	12,453	C
Prescott College	AZ	33,445	LC
Purdue Univ/West Lafayette	IN	13,458	VC
Radford Univ	VA	13,145	C
Rensselaer Polytechnic Inst	NY	41,288	HC+
Rice Univ	TX	32,290	MC
Rocky Mountain College	MT	20,805	C
Rutgers, The State Univ of New Jersey/New Brunswick/Piscataway Campus	NJ	15,810	HC
Rutgers, The State Univ of New Jersey/Newark Campus	NJ	15,640	VC
St. Cloud State Univ	MN	10,010	C
St. Lawrence Univ	NY	40,545	VC
St. Louis Univ	MO	33,158	VC+
St. Norbert College	WI	28,577	C+
Salem State College	MA	13,161	LC
Sam Houston State Univ	TX	8,000	C
San Diego State Univ	CA	12,971	C
San Francisco State Univ	CA	13,000	C
San Jose State Univ	CA	11,707	C
Skidmore College	NY	41,779	HC
Slippery Rock Univ of Pennsylvania	PA	10,360	LC
Smith College	MA	41,474	MC
Sonoma State Univ	CA	14,732	C
S Dak School of Mines and Technology	SD	7,624	C+
Southern Illinois Univ Carbondale	IL	12,391	C
Southern Methodist Univ	TX	36,088	VC+
Southern Oregon Univ	OR	12,186	C
Southern Utah Univ	UT		C
Stanford Univ	CA	41,557	MC
SUNY at Oswego	NY	13,662	VC
SUNY at Potsdam	NY	12,959	C
SUNY/College at Brockport	NY	12,747	VC
SUNY/College at Buffalo	NY	11,903	C+
SUNY/College at Cortland	NY	12,095	C
SUNY/College at Fredonia	NY	12,771	VC
SUNY/College at Geneseo	NY	12,910	HC+
SUNY/College at Oneonta	NY	12,905	VC
SUNY/College at Plattsburgh	NY	12,362	C
SUNY/Univ at Albany	NY	13,860	VC
SUNY/Univ at Binghamton	NY	13,988	HC
SUNY/Univ at Buffalo	NY	13,694	VC
SUNY/Univ at New Paltz	NY	12,480	VC
SUNY/Univ at Stony Brook	NY	13,625	VC
Stephen F. Austin State Univ	TX	7,930	C
Sul Ross State Univ	TX	6,600	LC
Syracuse Univ	NY	38,655	HC
Tarleton State Univ	TX	8,952	C
Temple Univ	PA	17,438	C
Tenn Tech Univ	TN	10,044	C
Texas A&M Univ	TX	13,351	HC
Texas A&M Univ at Commerce	TX	9,020	C
Texas A&M Univ at Corpus Christi	TX	10,280	LC
Texas A&M Univ at Kingsville	TX	6,800	LC
Texas Christian Univ	TX	23,410	VC+
Texas Tech Univ	TX	13,026	VC
Towson Univ	MD	13,924	VC
Tufts Univ	MA	42,018	MC
Tulane Univ	LA	41,098	MC
Union College	NY	41,595	HC
Univ of Akron	OH	15,166	NC
Univ of Alabama	AL	9,888	C
Univ of Alaska Fairbanks	AK	10,101	C
Univ of Arizona	AZ	11,958	VC
Univ of Arkansas	AR	11,859	C
Univ of Arkansas at Little Rock	AR	7,230	NC
Univ of at Calif Davis	CA	15,010	VC
Univ of Calif at Los Angeles	CA	17,681	MC
Univ of Calif at Riverside	CA	16,625	C
Univ of Calif at Santa Barbara	CA	11,800	VC
Univ of Calif at Santa Cruz	CA	19,174	VC
Univ of Cincinnati	OH	17,682	C
Univ of Colo at Boulder	CO	13,352	C+
Univ of Conn	CT	16,628	HC
Univ of Dayton	OH	28,826	VC
Univ of Delaware	DE	14,142	HC
Univ of Florida	FL	9,354	HC
Univ of Georgia	GA	11,004	HC
Univ of Hawaii at Hilo	HI	6,500	C
Univ of Hawaii at Manoa	HI	10,413	VC
Univ of Houston	TX	7,000	C
Univ of Idaho	ID	9,310	NC
Univ of Illinois at Chicago	IL	16,256	VC
Univ of Illinois at Urbana-Champaign	IL	15,800	HC+
Univ of Iowa	IA	12,172	VC
Univ of Kansas	KS	10,915	VC
Univ of Kentucky	KY	7,800	VC
Univ of Louisiana at Lafayette	LA	5,830	C
Univ of Louisiana at Monroe	LA	7,103	C
Univ of Maine at Farmington	ME	11,515	C
Univ of Maryland/College Park	MD	16,036	HC
Univ of Mass Amherst	MA	15,973	C+
Univ of Memphis	TN	11,153	C
Univ of Miami	FL	38,397	MC
Univ of Minn/Duluth	MN	13,974	C
Univ of Minn/Morris	MN	15,472	VC

ST = STATE   **$IS** = IN-STATE COSTS   **SR** = SELECTOR RATING

School	ST	$IS	SR
Univ of Minn/Twin Cities	MN	13,165	HC
Univ of Miss	MS	9,000	C
Univ of Missouri/Columbia	MO	13,500	VC
Univ of Missouri/Kansas City	MO	15,000	VC
Univ of Missouri/Rolla	MO	13,332	HC
Univ of Montana	MT	10,602	C
Univ of Nebr at Lincoln	NE	11,401	VC
Univ of Nebr at Omaha	NE	11,235	C
Univ of Nevada/Las Vegas	NV	11,566	C
Univ of Nevada/Reno	NV	12,155	NC
Univ of New Hampshire	NH	16,810	VC
Univ of New Orleans	LA	7,370	C
Univ of North Alabama	AL	8,992	C
Univ of N Car at Chapel Hill	NC	11,129	MC
Univ of N Car at Charlotte	NC	9,101	C
Univ of N Car at Wilmington	NC	10,107	VC
Univ of N Dak	ND	10,114	VC
Univ of Northern Colo	CO	10,249	C
Univ of Northern Iowa	IA	11,133	C
Univ of Okla	OK	10,769	VC+
Univ of Oregon	OR	13,108	VC
Univ of Pennsylvania	PA	41,766	MC
Univ of Pittsburgh at Johnstown	PA	16,740	LC
Univ of Pittsburgh at Pittsburgh	PA	18,866	HC
Univ of PR/Mayaguez	PR	1,250	
Univ of Puget Sound	WA	35,600	HC
Univ of Rhode Island	RI	15,398	C
Univ of Rochester	NY	41,135	MC
Univ of St. Thomas	MN	28,000	VC
Univ of South Alabama	AL	8,930	LC
Univ of S Car at Columbia	SC	13,397	VC
Univ of South Florida	FL	10,284	VC
Univ of Southern Calif	CA	41,618	MC
Univ of Southern Maine	ME	12,614	C
Univ of Southern Miss	MS	10,112	C
Univ of Tenn at Chattanooga	TN	7,790	C
Univ of Tenn at Knoxville	TN	11,720	C
Univ of Tenn at Martin	TN	8,693	C
Univ of Texas at Arlington	TX	7,195	LC
Univ of Texas at Austin	TX	14,610	HC
Univ of Texas at El Paso	TX	8,764	NC
Univ of Texas at San Antonio	TX	11,325	LC
Univ of the Pacific	CA	34,380	VC
Univ of the South	TN	34,645	HC
Univ of Toledo	OH	15,806	NC
Univ of Tulsa	OK	25,348	HC
Univ of Utah	UT	10,162	VC
Univ of Vermont	VT	18,080	VC
Univ of Washington	WA	10,400	VC
Univ of West Georgia	GA	8,838	C
Univ of Wisc/Eau Claire	WI	9,915	VC
Univ of Wisc/Madison	WI	13,117	HC
Univ of Wisc/Milwaukee	WI	9,427	LC
Univ of Wisc/Oshkosh	WI	10,426	LC
Univ of Wisc/Parkside	WI	10,181	LC
Univ of Wisc/River Falls	WI	9,722	LC
Univ of Wyoming	WY	9,666	C
Utah State Univ	UT	8,002	VC
Valparaiso Univ	IN	28,970	VC+
Vanderbilt Univ	TN	41,986	MC
Vassar College	NY	41,700	MC
Virginia Polytechnic Inst and State Univ	VA	10,834	VC
Washington and Lee Univ	VA	35,880	MC
Washington State Univ	WA	12,260	C
Washington Univ in St. Louis	MO	42,106	MC
Wayne State Univ	MI	11,805	C
Weber State Univ	UT	9,635	NC
Wellesley College	MA	41,030	MC
West Texas A&M Univ	TX	8,452	C
West Virginia Univ	WV	10,506	C
Western Carolina Univ	NC	7,000	C
Western Illinois Univ	IL	13,042	C
Western Kentucky Univ	KY	10,192	C
Western Mich Univ	MI	13,299	C
Western State College of Colo	CO	9,942	C
Western Washington Univ	WA	11,262	VC
Wheaton College	IL	27,760	HC
Whitman College	WA	36,110	HC+
Wichita State Univ	KS	8,500	C
Williams College	MA	40,310	MC
Winona State Univ	MN	11,333	C
Wittenberg Univ	OH	34,596	VC
Wright State Univ	OH	13,616	LC
Yale Univ	CT	41,000	MC
Youngstown State Univ	OH	12,613	NC

GEOPHYSICAL ENGINEERING

School	ST	$IS	SR
Colo School of Mines	CO	14,893	HC
Montana Tech of The Univ of Montana	MT	10,434	C
New Jersey Inst of Technology	NJ	16,396	VC
Univ of Calif at Los Angeles	CA	17,681	MC
Univ of Texas at Austin	TX	14,610	HC

GEOPHYSICS AND SEISMOLOGY

School	ST	$IS	SR
Baylor Univ	TX	27,555	HC
Boise State Univ	ID	9,438	LC
Boston College	MA	41,608	MC
Boston Univ	MA	42,046	HC+
Bowdoin College	ME	41,660	MC
Calif Inst of Technology	CA	36,123	MC
Colgate Univ	NY	41,170	MC
Columbia Univ/Columbia College	NY	42,584	MC
Harvard Univ/Harvard College	MA	45,860	MC
Mich State Univ	MI	13,689	VC
Mich Tech Univ	MI	14,569	VC
Occidental College	CA	40,185	MC
Rice Univ	TX	32,290	MC
St. Louis Univ	MO	33,158	VC+
Southern Methodist Univ	TX	36,088	VC+
Stanford Univ	CA	41,557	MC
SUNY/College at Cortland	NY	12,095	C
SUNY/College at Geneseo	NY	12,910	HC+
Texas A&M Univ	TX	13,351	HC
Texas Tech Univ	TX	13,026	VC
Univ of Calif at Los Angeles	CA	17,681	MC
Univ of Calif at Riverside	CA	16,625	C
Univ of Calif at Santa Barbara	CA	11,800	VC
Univ of Delaware	DE	14,142	HC
Univ of Hawaii at Manoa	HI	10,413	VC
Univ of Houston	TX	7,000	C
Univ of Minn/Twin Cities	MN	13,165	HC
Univ of Missouri/Rolla	MO	13,332	HC
Univ of Nevada/Reno	NV	12,155	NC
Univ of New Orleans	LA	7,370	C
Univ of Okla	OK	10,769	VC+
Univ of S Car at Columbia	SC	13,397	VC
Univ of Texas at Austin	TX	14,610	HC
Univ of Texas at El Paso	TX	8,764	NC
Univ of the Pacific	CA	34,380	VC
Univ of Utah	UT	10,162	VC
Western Mich Univ	MI	13,299	C
Wright State Univ	OH	13,616	LC

GEOSCIENCE

School	ST	$IS	SR
Albion College	MI	26,000	VC
Bradley Univ	IL	25,280	VC
Cal State, Chico	CA	11,395	C
Columbia Univ/School of General Studies	NY	41,516	C
Earlham College	IN	33,604	HC
Hobart and William Smith Colleges	NY	41,123	VC
Indiana Univ of Pennsylvania	PA	11,209	C
Lewis-Clark State College	ID	6,990	C
Mich State Univ	MI	13,689	VC
Miss State Univ	MS	9,577	C
Montclair State Univ	NJ	16,327	C
Northern Illinois Univ	IL	13,178	C
Ohio Univ	OH	15,921	C
Pacific Lutheran Univ	WA	28,805	VC
Penn State Univ/Univ Park Campus	PA	18,038	HC
Princeton Univ	NJ	40,213	MC
Rider Univ	NJ	32,560	C
Rutgers, The State Univ of New Jersey/Newark Campus	NJ	15,640	VC
Stanford Univ	CA	41,557	MC
Texas A&M Univ at Galveston	TX	10,000	C+
Texas Tech Univ	TX	13,026	VC
Towson Univ	MD	13,924	VC
Trinity Univ	TX	30,157	HC+
Univ of Arizona	AZ	11,958	VC
Univ of Chicago	IL	42,369	MC
Univ of Louisiana at Monroe	LA	7,103	C
Univ of Mich/Ann Arbor	MI	16,587	HC+
Univ of Okla	OK	10,769	VC+
Univ of Southern Maine	ME	12,614	C
Univ of Texas at Dallas	TX	13,244	HC
Univ of Tulsa	OK	25,348	HC
Univ of Wisc/Milwaukee	WI	9,427	LC
West Chester Univ of Pennsylvania	PA	12,355	C+
West Virginia Univ	WV	10,506	C

GERMAN

School	ST	$IS	SR
Adrian College	MI	23,000	C
Agnes Scott College	GA	32,070	HC
Albion College	MI	26,000	VC
Alfred Univ	NY		VC
Allegheny College	PA	33,500	HC
Alma College	MI	28,544	VC
Amherst College	MA	41,590	MC
Anderson Univ	IN	25,050	LC
Angelo State Univ	TX	8,340	NC
Aquinas College	MI	23,750	C
Arizona State Univ-Tempe	AZ	11,174	C
Auburn Univ	AL	12,230	VC
Augsburg College	MN	28,300	C
Augustana College	IL	29,862	VC+
Augustana College	SD	24,380	VC
Austin College	TX	27,871	HC
Austin Peay State Univ	TN	7,535	C
Baker Univ	KS	22,190	C
Baldwin-Wallace College	OH	27,256	VC
Ball State Univ	IN	13,138	C
Bard College	NY	41,800	HC+
Bates College	ME	42,100	MC
Baylor Univ	TX	27,555	HC
Beloit College	WI	32,808	HC
Bemidji State Univ	MN	11,180	LC
Berea College	KY	5,496	VC+
Berry College	GA	24,342	VC
Bethany College	WV	21,395	C
Bethel College	KS	21,650	C
Birmingham-Southern College	AL	28,494	VC+
Bloomsburg Univ of Pennsylvania	PA	11,602	C
Boston Univ	MA	42,046	HC+
Bowdoin College	ME	41,660	MC
Bowling Green State Univ	OH	14,994	C
Bradley Univ	IL	25,280	VC
Brandeis Univ	MA	41,551	MC
Brigham Young Univ	UT	9,200	VC
Bryn Mawr College	PA	42,780	HC+
Bucknell Univ	PA	39,660	MC
Butler Univ	IN	31,944	VC+
Calif Lutheran Univ	CA	27,800	LC
Cal State, Chico	CA	11,395	C
Cal State, Fullerton	CA	10,990	C
Cal State, Long Beach	CA	9,512	C
Cal State, Northridge	CA	9,036	LC
Cal State, Sacramento	CA	11,122	C+
Calvin College	MI	25,735	NC
Canisius College	NY	32,257	VC
Carleton College	MN	40,467	MC
Carnegie Mellon Univ	PA	32,700	MC
Carthage College	WI	26,000	C
Case Western Reserve Univ	OH	37,314	MC
Catholic Univ of America	DC	35,838	VC
Centenary College of Louisiana	LA	24,760	VC
Central College	IA	26,774	VC
Central Conn State Univ	CT	13,620	C
Central Mich Univ	MI	12,244	C
Central Missouri State Univ	MO	10,000	C
Central Washington Univ	WA	11,730	C
Centre College	KY	30,810	VC
Christopher Newport Univ	VA	13,326	VC
Citadel, The	SC		C+
CUNY/Brooklyn College	NY	4,377	C+
CUNY/Herbert H. Lehman College	NY	4,000	LC
CUNY/Hunter College	NY	8,000	C+
CUNY/Queens College	NY	4,356	C
Clemson Univ	SC	13,366	HC
Cleveland State Univ	OH	10,798	NC
Coe College	IA	27,440	VC
Colby College	ME	41,770	MC
Colgate Univ	NY	41,170	MC
College of Charleston	SC	13,616	VC
College of St. Benedict	MN	30,091	VC
College of the Holy Cross	MA	40,664	MC
College of William and Mary	VA	14,147	MC
College of Wooster	OH	31,310	VC+
Colo College	CO	37,668	HC
Colo State Univ-Fort Collins	CO	10,878	C+
Columbia Univ/Barnard College	NY	38,000	MC
Columbia Univ/Columbia College	NY	42,584	MC
Columbia Univ/School of General Studies	NY	41,516	C
Concordia College: Moorhead	MN	22,475	VC
Conn College	CT	41,975	MC
Cornell College	IA	30,110	VC+
Cornell Univ	NY	41,717	MC
Creighton Univ	NE	29,918	VC+
Dana College	NE	22,390	C
Dartmouth College	NH	39,465	MC
Davidson College	NC	36,825	MC
Denison Univ	OH	37,040	HC
DePaul Univ	IL	29,835	VC
DePauw Univ	IN	32,100	HC
Dickinson College	PA	40,170	HC+
Doane College	NE	22,458	VC
Dordt College	IA	20,325	VC
Drew Univ/College of Liberal Arts	NJ	39,698	VC
Drury Univ	MO	20,117	VC
Earlham College	IN	33,604	HC
East Carolina Univ	NC	10,000	C
Eastern Mennonite Univ	VA	25,450	VC
Eastern Mich Univ	MI	12,897	C
Eastern Washington Univ	WA	10,608	C
Eckerd College	FL	35,492	VC
Edinboro Univ of Pennsylvania	PA	11,809	LC
Elizabethtown College	PA	32,100	VC
Elmhurst College	IL	24,685	C
Fairfield Univ	CT	39,835	HC
Florida Atlantic Univ	FL	11,221	C
Florida International Univ	FL	9,215	VC
Florida State Univ	FL	9,028	HC
Fordham Univ	NY	36,000	HC
Fort Hays State Univ	KS	7,638	C
Franciscan Univ of Steubenville	OH	20,300	VC
Franklin and Marshall College	PA	40,590	HC
Furman Univ	SC	33,264	HC+
Gallaudet Univ	DC	16,554	
George Washington Univ	DC	48,820	MC
Georgetown College	KY	24,950	C+
Georgetown Univ	DC	43,183	MC
Georgia Southern Univ	GA	9,762	C
Georgia State Univ	GA	11,444	VC
Gettysburg College	PA	39,864	HC
Gonzaga Univ	WA	30,218	HC
Gordon College	MA	29,194	C+
Grace College	IN	22,170	C
Graceland Univ	IA	19,700	C
Grinnell College	IA	34,814	HC+
Guilford College	NC	28,160	C+
Gustavus Adolphus College	MN	30,920	HC
Hamilton College	NY	41,660	MC
Hamline Univ	MN	27,070	VC
Hampden-Sydney College	VA	31,148	VC
Hanover College	IN	28,150	HC
Hartwick College	NY	36,065	C+
Harvard Univ/Harvard College	MA	45,860	MC
Hastings College	NE	22,218	VC
Haverford College	PA	41,600	MC
Heidelberg College	OH	23,242	C
Hendrix College	AR	27,646	HC+
Hillsdale College	MI	24,160	HC
Hiram College	OH	28,700	VC
Hofstra Univ	NY	32,630	VC
Hollins Univ	VA	31,105	C
Hood College	MD	30,085	VC
Hope College	MI	28,208	VC+
Howard Univ	DC	18,481	C+
Humboldt State Univ	CA	11,176	C
Idaho State Univ	ID	9,030	C
Illinois College	IL	21,900	C+
Illinois State Univ	IL	12,839	C+
Illinois Wesleyan Univ	IL	34,050	HC+
Indiana State Univ	IN	11,604	C
Indiana Univ Bloomington	IN	13,356	VC
Indiana Univ of Pennsylvania	PA	11,209	C
Indiana Univ South Bend	IN	4,989	LC
Indiana Univ Southeast	IN	4,880	LC
Indiana Univ-Purdue Univ Fort Wayne	IN	5,067	LC
Indiana Univ-Purdue Univ Indianapolis	IN	10,959	C
Iowa State Univ	IA	11,831	VC
Ithaca College	NY	35,144	VC
Jamestown College	ND	14,130	NC
John Carroll Univ	OH	27,658	C+
Johns Hopkins Univ	MD	42,044	MC
Juniata College	PA	33,130	VC
Kalamazoo College	MI	32,442	VC+
Kenyon College	OH	39,500	MC
Knox College	IL	32,385	VC+
La Salle Univ	PA	34,950	C
Lafayette College	PA	39,267	MC
Lakeland College	WI	22,990	C
Lambuth Univ	TN	21,700	C+
Lawrence Univ	WI	33,958	HC+
Lebanon Valley College	PA	31,700	VC
Lee Univ	TN	14,780	NC
Lehigh Univ	PA	42,690	HC+
Lenoir-Rhyne College	NC	25,580	C
Linfield College	OR	29,632	VC
Lipscomb Univ	TN	20,967	VC
Lock Haven Univ of Pennsylvania	PA	12,098	LC
LIU/C.W. Post Campus	NY	28,282	C
Louisiana State Univ and A&M Univ	LA	10,749	VC
Loyola College in Maryland	MD	38,898	HC
Loyola Univ Chicago	IL	32,896	VC
Loyola Univ New Orleans	LA	31,050	VC+
Luther College	IA	28,800	VC+
Lycoming College	PA	30,797	C+
Manchester College	IN	23,470	C
Manhattanville College	NY	32,500	C+
Mansfield Univ	PA	11,300	C
Marlboro College	VT	35,980	VC+
Marquette Univ	WI	31,066	HC
Mary Baldwin College	VA	26,465	C
McDaniel College	MD	31,610	VC
McMurry Univ	TX	18,100	LC
Mercer Univ	GA	27,525	VC+
Messiah College	PA	28,910	VC+
Miami Univ	OH	29,097	HC
Mich State Univ	MI	13,689	VC
Middle Tenn State Univ	TN	8,540	C
Middlebury College	VT	42,120	HC
Millersville Univ of Pennsylvania	PA	12,113	C
Millikin Univ	IL	25,590	C
Millsaps College	MS	28,256	VC+
Minn State Univ, Mankato	MN	10,276	LC
Minn State Univ, Moorhead	MN	7,000	LC

INDEX OF COLLEGE MAJORS

(German area studies, continued)

School	ST	$IS	SR
Minot State Univ	ND	6,700	LC
Missouri Southern State Univ	MO	8,396	NC
Missouri State Univ	MO	10,748	C+
Moravian College	PA	28,950	VC
Morehouse College	GA	25,082	C
Mount St. Mary's Univ	MD	30,930	C
Mount Union College	OH	25,840	C
Muhlenberg College	PA	36,030	HC+
Murray State Univ	KY	8,900	VC
Muskingum College	OH	22,970	C
Nazareth College of Rochester	NY	28,175	VC
Nebr Wesleyan Univ	NE	23,415	C+
New York Univ	NY	43,170	MC
Newberry College	SC	23,000	LC
North Central College	IL	28,926	VC
Northern Arizona Univ	AZ	10,353	C
Northern Illinois Univ	IL	13,178	C
Northern State Univ	SD	8,257	C
Northwestern Univ	IL	37,595	MC
Oakland Univ	MI	11,936	C
Oberlin College	OH	40,904	MC
Occidental College	CA	40,185	MC
Ohio State Univ	OH	15,357	HC
Ohio Univ	OH	15,921	C
Ohio Wesleyan Univ	OH	35,830	VC+
Okla Baptist Univ	OK	17,986	VC
Okla City Univ	OK	23,965	VC
Okla State Univ	OK	10,213	VC
Old Dominion Univ	VA	11,907	C
Oral Roberts Univ	OK	22,650	C
Oregon State Univ	OR	11,055	C
Pacific Lutheran Univ	WA	28,805	VC
Penn State Univ/Univ Park Campus	PA	18,038	HC
Pepperdine Univ	CA	39,960	HC
Pomona College	CA	40,774	MC
Portland State Univ	OR	12,453	C
Presbyterian College	SC	30,044	VC
Princeton Univ	NJ	40,213	MC
Purdue Univ/Calumet	IN	10,891	LC
Purdue Univ/West Lafayette	IN	13,458	VC
Randolph-Macon College	VA	31,250	C
Randolph-Macon Woman's College	VA	31,160	VC+
Rhodes College	TN	32,860	HC
Rider Univ	NJ	32,560	C
Ripon College	WI	27,160	C+
Rockford College	IL	28,330	VC
Rosemont College	PA	29,350	C
Rutgers, The State Univ of New Jersey/Camden Campus	NJ	15,000	VC
Rutgers, The State Univ of New Jersey/New Brunswick/Piscataway Campus	NJ	15,810	HC
Rutgers, The State Univ of New Jersey/Newark Campus	NJ	15,640	VC
St. Ambrose Univ	IA	25,495	C
St. John's Univ	MN	29,749	VC
St. Joseph's Univ	PA	37,428	VC
St. Lawrence Univ	NY	40,545	VC
St. Mary's Univ of San Antonio	TX	22,444	C
St. Norbert College	WI	28,577	C+
St. Olaf College	MN	32,800	HC
Salem College	NC	26,226	VC+
Sam Houston State Univ	TX	8,000	C
Samford Univ	AL	20,258	VC
San Diego State Univ	CA	12,971	C
San Francisco State Univ	CA	13,000	C
San Jose State Univ	CA	11,707	C
Santa Clara Univ	CA	38,931	VC
Sarah Lawrence College	NY	42,000	HC
Seattle Pacific Univ	WA	29,355	C
Seattle Univ	WA	30,063	VC
Simon's Rock College of Bard	MA	41,988	VC+
Simpson College	IA	26,833	VC
Skidmore College	NY	41,779	HC
Slippery Rock Univ of Pennsylvania	PA	10,360	LC
S Dak State Univ	SD	9,815	C
Southeast Missouri State Univ	MO	10,596	C
Southern Conn State Univ	CT	10,310	C
Southern Illinois Univ Carbondale	IL	12,391	C
Southern Methodist Univ	TX	36,088	VC+
Southern Utah Univ	UT		C
Southwestern Univ	TX	26,767	HC
SUNY at Oswego	NY	13,662	VC
SUNY/Univ at Binghamton	NY	13,988	HC
SUNY/Univ at Buffalo	NY	13,694	VC
SUNY/Univ at New Paltz	NY	12,480	VC
Stetson Univ	FL	32,725	VC
Susquehanna Univ	PA	33,465	VC
Swarthmore College	PA	41,280	MC
Sweet Briar College	VA	31,460	VC
Temple Univ	PA	17,438	C
Tenn Tech Univ	TN	10,044	C
Texas A&M Univ	TX	13,351	LC
Texas A&M Univ at Commerce	TX	9,020	C
Texas State Univ - San Marcos	TX	10,862	C
Texas Tech Univ	TX	13,026	VC
Towson Univ	MD	13,924	VC
Trinity College	CT	38,040	HC+
Trinity Univ	TX	30,157	HC+
Truman State Univ	MO	11,242	HC
Tufts Univ	MA	42,018	MC
Tulane Univ	LA	41,098	MC
Union College	NE	18,710	C
Univ of Akron	OH	15,166	NC
Univ of Alabama	AL	9,888	C
Univ of Arizona	AZ	11,958	VC
Univ of Arkansas	AR	11,859	VC
Univ of at Calif Davis	CA	15,010	VC
Univ of Calif at Berkeley	CA	18,141	HC+
Univ of Calif at Irvine	CA	16,475	HC
Univ of Calif at Los Angeles	CA	17,681	MC
Univ of Calif at Riverside	CA	16,625	C
Univ of Calif at Santa Barbara	CA	11,800	VC
Univ of Central Okla	OK	8,094	C
Univ of Chicago	IL	42,369	MC
Univ of Cincinnati	OH	17,682	C
Univ of Conn	CT	16,628	HC
Univ of Dallas	TX	27,432	VC+
Univ of Dayton	OH	28,826	VC
Univ of Denver	CO	36,376	VC+
Univ of Evansville	IN	28,320	VC
Univ of Florida	FL	9,354	VC
Univ of Georgia	GA	11,004	HC
Univ of Hawaii at Manoa	HI	10,413	VC
Univ of Houston	TX	7,000	C
Univ of Idaho	ID	9,310	NC
Univ of Indianapolis	IN	25,090	C
Univ of Iowa	IA	12,172	VC
Univ of Kansas	KS	10,915	VC
Univ of Kentucky	KY	7,800	C
Univ of La Verne	CA	33,470	C
Univ of Maine	ME	13,642	C
Univ of Mary Washington	VA	11,636	HC
Univ of Maryland/Baltimore County	MD	16,642	VC+
Univ of Mass Amherst	MA	15,973	C+
Univ of Miami	FL	38,397	MC
Univ of Mich/Ann Arbor	MI	16,587	HC+
Univ of Minn/Morris	MN	15,472	VC
Univ of Minn/Twin Cities	MN	13,165	VC
Univ of Miss	MS	9,000	C
Univ of Missouri/Columbia	MO	13,500	VC.
Univ of Missouri/Kansas City	MO	15,000	VC
Univ of Missouri/St. Louis	MO	14,046	VC
Univ of Montana	MT	10,602	C
Univ of Nebr at Kearney	NE	9,000	NC
Univ of Nebr at Lincoln	NE	11,401	VC
Univ of Nebr at Omaha	NE	11,235	C
Univ of Nevada/Las Vegas	NV	11,566	C
Univ of Nevada/Reno	NV	12,155	NC
Univ of New Hampshire	NH	16,810	VC
Univ of New Mexico	NM	11,253	C
Univ of North Alabama	AL	8,992	C
Univ of N Car at Asheville	NC	9,237	VC
Univ of N Car at Chapel Hill	NC	11,129	MC
Univ of N Car at Charlotte	NC	9,101	C
Univ of N Car at Greensboro	NC	8,993	C
Univ of N Dak	ND	10,114	VC
Univ of North Texas	TX	7,800	C
Univ of Northern Colo	CO	10,249	C
Univ of Northern Iowa	IA	11,133	C
Univ of Notre Dame	IN	39,552	MC
Univ of Okla	OK	10,769	VC+
Univ of Oregon	OR	13,108	VC
Univ of Pennsylvania	PA	41,766	MC
Univ of Puget Sound	WA	35,600	HC
Univ of Redlands	CA	36,160	VC
Univ of Rhode Island	RI	15,398	C
Univ of Richmond	VA	40,510	MC
Univ of Rochester	NY	41,135	MC
Univ of St. Thomas	MN	28,000	VC
Univ of Scranton	PA	31,100	VC
Univ of S Car at Columbia	SC	13,397	VC
Univ of S Dak	SD	9,068	C
Univ of South Florida	FL	10,284	VC
Univ of Southern Calif	CA	41,618	MC
Univ of Southern Indiana	IN	12,590	LC
Univ of Tenn at Knoxville	TN	11,720	C
Univ of Texas at Arlington	TX	7,195	LC
Univ of Texas at Austin	TX	14,610	HC
Univ of Texas at El Paso	TX	8,764	NC
Univ of Texas at San Antonio	TX	11,325	LC
Univ of the Pacific	CA	34,380	VC
Univ of the South	TN	34,645	VC
Univ of Toledo	OH	15,806	NC
Univ of Tulsa	OK	25,348	HC
Univ of Utah	UT	10,162	VC
Univ of Vermont	VT	18,080	VC
Univ of Virginia	VA	13,759	MC
Univ of West Georgia	GA	8,838	C
Univ of Wisc/Eau Claire	WI	9,915	VC
Univ of Wisc/Green Bay	WI	9,415	VC
Univ of Wisc/Madison	WI	13,117	HC
Univ of Wisc/Milwaukee	WI	9,427	LC
Univ of Wisc/Oshkosh	WI	10,426	LC
Univ of Wisc/Parkside	WI	10,181	LC
Univ of Wisc/Platteville	WI	9,779	NC
Univ of Wisc/Stevens Point	WI	9,384	C
Univ of Wisc/Whitewater	WI	9,274	C
Univ of Wyoming	WY	9,666	C
Ursinus College	PA	38,950	VC
Utah State Univ	UT	8,002	VC
Valparaiso Univ	IN	28,970	VC+
Vanderbilt Univ	TN	41,986	MC
Villanova Univ	PA	38,672	HC+
Virginia Polytechnic Inst and State Univ	VA	10,834	VC
Virginia Wesleyan College	VA	28,433	C
Wabash College	IN	30,116	VC
Wake Forest Univ	NC	38,290	MC
Walla Walla Univ	WA	24,489	NC
Wartburg College	IA	27,315	VC
Washburn Univ	KS	9,734	NC
Washington and Jefferson College	PA	33,490	VC
Washington and Lee Univ	VA	35,880	MC
Washington College	MD	34,990	VC
Washington State Univ	WA	12,260	C
Washington Univ in St. Louis	MO	42,106	MC
Wayne State Univ	MI	11,805	C
Weber State Univ	UT	9,635	NC
Webster Univ	MO	24,280	VC
Wellesley College	MA	41,030	MC
Wells College	NY	23,070	VC
Wesleyan Univ	CT	42,122	MC
West Chester Univ of Pennsylvania	PA	12,355	C+
Western Carolina Univ	NC	7,000	C
Western Kentucky Univ	KY	10,192	C
Western Mich Univ	MI	13,299	C
Western Washington Univ	WA	11,262	VC
Westminster College	PA	31,290	C+
Wheaton College	IL	27,760	HC
Wheaton College	MA	40,180	HC+
Whitman College	WA	36,110	HC+
Willamette Univ	OR	35,416	VC+
Williams College	MA	40,310	MC
Winona State Univ	MN	11,333	C
Wittenberg Univ	OH	34,596	VC
Wofford College	SC	30,935	HC
Wright State Univ	OH	13,616	LC
Xavier Univ	OH	30,490	HC
Yale Univ	CT	41,000	MC
Youngstown State Univ	OH	12,613	NC

GERMAN AREA STUDIES

School	ST	$IS	SR
American Univ	DC	38,719	HC+
Boston College	MA	41,608	MC
Brown Univ	RI	42,015	MC
Case Western Reserve Univ	OH	37,314	MC
College of the Holy Cross	MA	40,664	MC
Columbia Univ/School of General Studies	NY	41,516	C
Cornell Univ	NY	41,717	MC
Dartmouth College	NH	39,465	MC
Emory Univ	GA	40,546	MC
Fordham Univ	NY	36,000	HC
Guilford College	NC	28,160	C+
Ithaca College	NY	35,144	VC
Lewis and Clark College	OR	35,358	VC+
Macalester College	MN	36,500	MC
Mount Holyoke College	MA	42,148	HC+
Muhlenberg College	PA	36,030	HC+
Pomona College	CA	40,774	MC
Principia College	IL	27,765	VC+
Rice Univ	TX	32,290	MC
St. Louis Univ	MO	33,158	VC+
Scripps College	CA	41,000	MC
Simon's Rock College of Bard	MA	41,988	VC+
Southern Illinois Univ Carbondale	IL	12,391	C
Southern Methodist Univ	TX	36,088	VC+
Stanford Univ	CA	41,557	MC
Suffolk Univ	MA	33,160	C
Swarthmore College	PA	41,280	MC
Sweet Briar College	VA	31,460	VC
Tufts Univ	MA	42,018	MC
Univ of Arizona	AZ	11,958	VC
Univ of Calif at Santa Cruz	CA	19,174	VC
Univ of Colo at Boulder	CO	13,352	C+
Univ of Houston	TX	7,000	VC
Univ of Illinois at Chicago	IL	16,256	VC
Univ of Mass Boston	MA	8,024	C
Univ of N Car at Wilmington	NC	10,107	VC
Univ of the South	TN	34,645	VC
Univ of Wisc/La Crosse	WI	10,045	VC
Wartburg College	IA	27,315	VC
Wellesley College	MA	41,030	MC
Wheaton College	MA	40,180	HC+
Yale Univ	CT	41,000	MC

GERMANIC LANGUAGES AND LITERATURE

School	ST	$IS	SR
Bard College	NY	41,800	HC+
Boston Univ	MA	42,046	HC+
Colby College	ME	41,770	HC+
Columbia Univ/Columbia College	NY	42,584	MC
Duke Univ	NC	41,239	MC
Kent State Univ	OH	14,594	C
New College of Florida	FL	10,009	HC+
New York Univ	NY	43,170	MC
Reed College	OR	41,106	MC
Scripps College	CA	41,000	MC
Simon's Rock College of Bard	MA	41,988	VC+
Smith College	MA	41,474	MC
SUNY/Univ at Stony Brook	NY	13,625	HC
Syracuse Univ	NY	38,655	MC
Temple Univ	PA	17,438	C
Univ of Calif at San Diego	CA	16,102	NC
Univ of Calif at Santa Barbara	CA	11,800	VC
Univ of Colo at Boulder	CO	13,352	C+
Univ of Georgia	GA	11,004	HC
Univ of Illinois at Urbana-Champaign	IL	15,800	HC+
Univ of Kansas	KS	10,915	VC
Univ of Maryland/College Park	MD	16,036	HC
Univ of Washington	WA	10,400	VC
Washington and Lee Univ	VA	35,880	MC
Washington Univ in St. Louis	MO	42,106	MC

GERONTOLOGY

School	ST	$IS	SR
Alfred Univ	NY		VC
Barton College	NC	22,316	C
Bethune-Cookman College	FL	17,922	LC
Cal State, San Bernardino	CA	12,563	LC
Calif Univ of Pennsylvania	PA	14,217	C
Case Western Reserve Univ	OH	37,314	MC
Central Washington Univ	WA	11,730	C
Chestnut Hill College	PA	26,600	LC
CUNY/York College	NY	4,242	NC
College of the Ozarks	MO	4,130	VC+
East Central Univ	OK	6,207	C
Eastern Mich Univ	MI	12,897	C
Indiana Univ Kokomo	IN	4,835	LC
Ithaca College	NY	35,144	VC
Langston Univ	OK	2,308	LC
Madonna Univ	MI	16,068	VC
McKendree College	IL	24,800	VC
Metropolitan College of New York	NY	16,000	C
Missouri State Univ	MO	10,748	C+
Molloy College	NY	16,510	C
Montclair State Univ	NJ	16,527	C
Mount St. Mary's College	CA	32,086	VC
Pontifical Catholic Univ of PR/Ponce	PR	7,310	
Quinnipiac Univ	CT	34,640	VC
St. Mary-of-the-Woods College	IN	25,480	C
San Diego State Univ	CA	12,971	C
Shaw Univ	NC	15,488	LC
Sojourner-Douglass College	MD	4,200	LC
Southeastern Okla State Univ	OK	6,147	C
Springfield College	MA	25,000	C
SUNY/College at Oneonta	NY	12,905	VC
Stephen F. Austin State Univ	TX	7,930	C
Thomas Edison State College	NJ	3,780	SP
Towson Univ	MD	13,924	VC
Univ of Arkansas at Pine Bluff	AR	8,300	C
Univ of Central Arkansas	AR	9,984	C
Univ of Hawaii at Manoa	HI	10,413	VC
Univ of Mass Boston	MA	8,024	C
Univ of Northern Colo	CO	10,249	C
Univ of Scranton	PA	31,100	VC
Univ of South Florida	FL	10,284	VC
Univ of Southern Calif	CA	41,618	MC
Weber State Univ	UT	9,635	NC
Western Mich Univ	MI	13,299	C
Wichita State Univ	KS	8,500	C

GLASS

School	ST	$IS	SR
Alfred Univ	NY		VC
Calif College of the Arts	CA	34,325	SP
Cleveland Inst of Art	OH	34,109	SP
College for Creative Studies	MI	24,000	SP
Mass College of Art	MA	16,650	SP
Rhode Island School of Design	RI	38,130	SP
Rochester Inst of Technology	NY	32,070	VC+

ST = STATE $IS = IN-STATE COSTS   SR = SELECTOR RATING

GRAPHIC AND PRINTING PRODUCTION

School	ST	$IS	SR
Arkansas State Univ	AR	9,630	C
Brenau Univ Women's College	GA	23,950	VC
CUNY/New York City College of Technology	NY	4,269	NC
Rochester Inst of Technology	NY	32,070	VC+
Univ of Wisc/Stout	WI	11,164	C

GRAPHIC ARTS TECHNOLOGY

School	ST	$IS	SR
Andrews Univ	MI	21,786	C
Appalachian State Univ	NC	8,000	NC
Ball State Univ	IN	13,138	C
Bloomfield College	NJ	22,500	LC
Carroll College	WI	24,860	C
Central Missouri State Univ	MO	10,000	C
Central State Univ	OH	9,010	C+
Clemson Univ	SC	13,366	HC
College of the Ozarks	MO	4,130	VC+
Colo Technical Univ	CO	9,500	LC
Emmanuel College	MA	32,000	C
Farmingdale SUNY	NY	13,521	C
Florida State Univ	FL	9,028	HC
Kean Univ	NJ	15,880	C
New York Univ	NY	43,170	MC
Pacific Union College	CA	24,555	VC+
Pennsylvania College of Technology	PA	16,980	LC
Pittsburg State Univ	KS	8,112	C
Purdue Univ/West Lafayette	IN	13,458	VC
Rochester Inst of Technology	NY	32,070	VC+
Southeast Missouri State Univ	MO	10,596	C
Univ of Houston	TX	7,000	C
Univ of Wisc/Stout	WI	11,164	C
Western Mich Univ	MI	13,299	C

GRAPHIC DESIGN

School	ST	$IS	SR
American Univ	DC	38,719	HC+
Anderson Univ	IN	25,050	LC
Andrews Univ	MI	21,786	C
Appalachian State Univ	NC	8,000	NC
Arcadia Univ	PA	33,570	VC
Arizona State Univ-Tempe	AZ	11,174	C
Arkansas State Univ	AR	9,630	C
Art Academy of Cincinnati	OH	18,100	VC
Art Center College of Design	CA	26,370	SP
Art Inst of Atlanta	GA	23,220	SP
Art Inst of Portland	OR	23,040	SP
Atlanta College of Art	GA	18,630	SP
Ball State Univ	IN	13,138	C
Barton College	NC	22,316	C
Becker College	MA	24,300	LC
Bethel College	IN	19,680	C
Boston Univ	MA	42,046	HC+
Bradley Univ	IL	25,280	VC
Brescia Univ	KY	14,240	C
Briar Cliff Univ	IA	23,550	LC
Brigham Young Univ	UT	9,200	VC
Buena Vista Univ	IA	27,742	C
Cabrini College	PA	33,340	C
Calif College of the Arts	CA	34,325	SP
Calif Polytechnic State Univ	CA	12,390	VC
Cal State, Fresno	CA	10,037	LC
Cal State, Fullerton	CA	10,990	C
Cal State, Los Angeles	CA	5,900	C
Cal State, San Bernardino	CA	12,563	LC
Calif Univ of Pennsylvania	PA	14,217	C
Carthage College	WI	26,000	C
Cedarville Univ	OH	21,904	VC
Central Conn State Univ	CT	13,620	C
Central Mich Univ	MI	12,244	C
Champlain College	VT	24,605	C
Chapman Univ	CA	37,550	VC
Cleveland Inst of Art	OH	34,109	SP
Coker College	SC	21,600	C
Colby-Sawyer College	NH	27,850	LC
College for Creative Studies	MI	24,000	SP
College of Mount St. Joseph	OH	24,860	C
College of New Jersey	NJ	18,315	MC
College of Notre Dame of Maryland	MD	27,700	C
College of St. Rose	NY	25,684	C
College of Visual Arts	MN	18,040	SP
Columbus College of Art and Design	OH	24,500	SP
Concordia Univ Wisc	WI	22,660	VC
Cooper Union for the Advancement of Science and Art	NY	12,450	MC
Corcoran School of Art and Design	DC	32,850	SP
Daemen College	NY	24,580	C
Dana College	NE	22,390	C
Defiance College	OH	24,790	C
Dominican Univ	IL	26,370	C
Dordt College	IA	20,325	VC
Drake Univ	IA	27,632	VC+
Drexel Univ	PA	27,700	VC
Eastern Mich Univ	MI	12,897	C
Eastern Washington Univ	WA	10,608	C
Edgewood College	WI	22,862	C
Edinboro Univ of Pennsylvania	PA	11,809	LC
Escuela de Artes Plasticas de PR	PR	2,372	
Fashion Inst of Technology/SUNY	NY	11,600	C+
Flagler College	FL	13,790	VC+
Florida Atlantic Univ	FL	11,221	C
Franklin Pierce College	NH	31,700	C
Gallaudet Univ	DC	16,554	
Grace College	IN	22,170	C
Graceland Univ	IA	19,700	C
Grand Canyon Univ	AZ	32,000	C
Grand View College	IA	21,482	C
Harding Univ	AR	16,512	VC
Hardin-Simmons Univ	TX	18,641	C
Indiana Univ Bloomington	IN	13,356	VC
Iowa State Univ	IA	11,831	VC
John Brown Univ	AR	20,910	VC
Kean Univ	NJ	15,880	C
Keene State College	NH	13,836	C
Kendall College of Art and Design of Ferris State Univ	MI	11,870	SP
Kutztown Univ of Pennsylvania	PA	10,820	C
La Roche College	PA	24,724	LC
La Sierra Univ	CA	24,327	C+
Laguna College of Art and Design	CA	17,600	SP
Limestone College	SC	19,840	C
Louisiana College	LA	13,450	C
Loyola Univ New Orleans	LA	31,050	VC+
Lyndon State College	VT	14,233	LC
Lynn Univ	FL	30,750	C
Madonna Univ	MI	16,068	VC
Maine College of Art	ME	28,820	SP
Marian College	IN	26,160	C
Marietta College	OH	29,327	C
Maryland Inst College of Art	MD	34,450	SP
Marymount Univ	VA	25,934	C
Maryville Univ of St. Louis	MO	23,000	VC
Mass College of Art	MA	16,650	VC
McMurry Univ	TX	18,100	LC
Mercyhurst College	PA	28,633	VC
Miami Univ	OH	29,097	HC
MidAmerica Nazarene Univ	KS	20,584	LC
Middle Tenn State Univ	TN	8,540	C
Milwaukee Inst of Art and Design	WI	28,700	SP
Minneapolis College of Art and Design	MN	31,110	SP
Miss College	MS	14,574	VC
Missouri Southern State Univ	MO	8,396	NC
Missouri Western State Univ	MO	9,534	NC
Montserrat College of Art	MA	25,929	SP
Moore College of Art and Design	PA	27,200	SP
Moravian College	PA	28,950	VC
Morningside College	IA	23,704	C
Mount Ida College	MA	26,000	LC
Mount Mary College	WI	22,895	C
Mount Vernon Nazarene Univ	OH	20,810	C
New Mexico Highlands Univ	NM	6,272	NC
New York Inst of Technology	NY	28,126	VC
Newbury College	MA	25,600	C
Norfolk State Univ	VA	10,531	LC
N Car State Univ	NC	11,824	HC
Northern Kentucky Univ	KY	6,670	NC
Northwest Nazarene Univ	ID	22,590	VC
Northwestern College	MN	25,220	NC
Notre Dame College	OH	20,425	C
Notre Dame de Namur Univ	CA	32,790	LC
Ohio Dominican Univ	OH	25,954	C
Ohio Northern Univ	OH	27,765	VC
Okla City Univ	OK	23,965	VC
Old Dominion Univ	VA	11,907	C
Otis College of Art and Design	CA	27,546	SP
Pacific Northwest College of Art	OR	17,296	SP
Pacific Union College	CA	24,555	VC+
Palm Beach Atlantic Univ	FL	23,597	VC
Park Univ	MO	11,592	C
Parsons School of Design	NY	32,242	SP
Pennsylvania College of Technology	PA	16,980	LC
Philadelphia Univ	PA	30,006	C
Plymouth State Univ	NH	12,298	LC
Purdue Univ/West Lafayette	IN	13,458	VC
Regis College	MA	31,350	LC
Rhode Island School of Design	RI	38,130	SP
Ringling School of Art and Design	FL	31,013	SP
Rivier College	NH	26,600	C
Rochester Inst of Technology	NY	32,070	VC+
Sacred Heart Univ	CT	33,404	C
St. Ambrose Univ	IA	25,495	C
St. Edward's Univ	TX	23,560	C
St. John's Univ	NY	34,370	C
St. Mary-of-the-Woods College	IN	25,480	C
St. Peter's College	NJ	30,160	LC
Sam Houston State Univ	TX	8,000	C
Samford Univ	AL	20,258	VC
Savannah College of Art and Design	GA	30,800	SP
School of Visual Arts	NY	32,580	SP
Schreiner Univ	TX	20,600	C
Seton Hill Univ	PA	28,810	C
Shepherd Univ	WV	10,066	C
S Dak State Univ	SD	9,815	C
South Univ	GA		LC
Southern Adventist Univ	TN	18,500	C
Southern New Hampshire Univ	NH	28,764	C
Southwestern Okla State Univ	OK	4,801	C
Spring Hill College	AL	28,678	C
SUNY at Oswego	NY	13,662	VC
SUNY/College at Fredonia	NY	12,771	VC
Stephens College	MO	26,930	VC
Suffolk Univ	MA	33,160	C
Susquehanna Univ	PA	33,465	VC
Syracuse Univ	NY	38,655	HC
Tabor College	KS	21,614	NC
Texas Christian Univ	TX	23,410	VC+
Union College	NE	18,710	C
Union Univ	TN	20,750	VC
Univ of Bridgeport	CT	29,595	LC
Univ of Central Okla	OK	8,094	C
Univ of Evansville	IN	28,320	VC
Univ of Florida	FL	9,354	HC
Univ of Illinois at Chicago	IL	16,256	VC
Univ of Illinois at Urbana-Champaign	IL	15,800	HC+
Univ of Mass Dartmouth	MA	15,985	C
Univ of Miami	FL	38,397	MC
Univ of Mich/Ann Arbor	MI	16,587	HC+
Univ of Minn/Duluth	MN	13,974	C
Univ of New Haven	CT	31,794	C
Univ of Northern Colo	CO	10,249	C
Univ of Northern Iowa	IA	11,133	C
Univ of Oregon	OR	13,108	VC
Univ of San Francisco	CA	37,560	VC
Univ of S Car Upstate	SC	11,957	C
Univ of Tampa	FL	25,784	C
Univ of Tenn at Knoxville	TN	11,720	C
Univ of the Arts	PA	32,330	SP
Univ of the Pacific	CA	34,380	VC
Univ of Washington	WA	10,400	VC
Upper Iowa Univ	IA	20,130	C
Ursuline College	OH	25,456	C
Viterbo Univ	WI	21,670	C
Walla Walla Univ	WA	24,489	NC
Wartburg College	IA	27,315	NC
Washington Univ in St. Louis	MO	42,106	MC
Wayne State College	NE	8,033	NC
Waynesburg College	PA	21,230	C
Weber State Univ	UT	9,635	NC
West Liberty State College	WV	9,142	LC
West Texas A&M Univ	TX	8,452	C
Western Conn State Univ	CT	12,993	C
Western Mich Univ	MI	13,299	C
Wichita State Univ	KS	8,500	C
William Woods Univ	MO	21,020	C
Winona State Univ	MN	11,333	C
Woodbury Univ	CA	30,176	VC
York College of Pennsylvania	PA	16,550	VC
Youngstown State Univ	OH	12,613	NC

GREEK

School	ST	$IS	SR
Amherst College	MA	41,590	MC
Asbury College	KY	23,762	VC
Brigham Young Univ	UT	9,200	VC
Bryn Mawr College	PA	42,780	HC+
Butler Univ	IN	31,944	VC+
Calvin College	MI	25,735	NC
Carleton College	MN	40,467	MC
CUNY/Brooklyn College	NY	4,377	C+
CUNY/Herbert H. Lehman College	NY	4,000	LC
CUNY/Hunter College	NY	8,000	C+
CUNY/Queens College	NY	4,356	C
Colgate Univ	NY	41,170	MC
Columbia Univ/Barnard College	NY	38,000	MC
Columbia Univ/Columbia College	NY	42,584	MC
Cornell Univ	NY	41,717	MC
Creighton Univ	NE	29,918	VC+
DePauw Univ	IN	32,100	HC
Dickinson College	PA	40,170	HC+
Emory Univ	GA	40,546	MC
Florida State Univ	FL	9,028	HC
Franklin and Marshall College	PA	40,590	HC
Furman Univ	SC	33,264	HC+
Gettysburg College	PA	39,864	HC
Hampden-Sydney College	VA	31,148	VC
Harvard Univ/Harvard College	MA	45,860	MC
Haverford College	PA	41,600	MC
Howard Univ	DC	18,481	C+
Indiana Univ Bloomington	IN	13,356	VC
John Carroll Univ	OH	27,658	C+
Loyola Univ Chicago	IL	32,896	VC
Marlboro College	VT	35,980	VC+
Mercer Univ	GA	27,525	VC+
Miami Univ	OH	29,097	HC
Monmouth College	IL	23,700	C
Mount Holyoke College	MA	42,148	HC+
New York Univ	NY	43,170	MC
Ohio State Univ	OH	15,357	HC
Randolph-Macon College	VA	31,250	C
St. Louis Univ	MO	33,158	VC+
St. Olaf College	MN	32,800	HC
Samford Univ	AL	20,258	VC
Santa Clara Univ	CA	38,931	VC
Sarah Lawrence College	NY	42,000	HC
Smith College	MA	41,474	MC
Swarthmore College	PA	41,280	MC
Temple Univ	PA	17,438	C
Tufts Univ	MA	42,018	MC
Union College	TN	20,750	VC
Univ of at Calif Davis	CA	15,010	VC
Univ of Calif at Berkeley	CA	18,141	HC+
Univ of Calif at Los Angeles	CA	17,681	MC
Univ of Georgia	GA	11,004	HC
Univ of Iowa	IA	12,172	VC
Univ of Mich/Ann Arbor	MI	16,587	HC+
Univ of Minn/Twin Cities	MN	13,165	HC
Univ of Nebr at Lincoln	NE	11,401	VC
Univ of New Hampshire	NH	16,810	VC
Univ of Notre Dame	IN	39,552	MC
Univ of Oregon	OR	13,108	VC
Univ of Richmond	VA	40,510	MC
Univ of Scranton	PA	31,100	VC
Univ of Tenn at Chattanooga	TN	7,790	C
Univ of Texas at Austin	TX	14,610	HC
Univ of the South	TN	34,645	HC
Univ of Vermont	VT	18,080	VC
Wabash College	IN	30,116	HC
Wake Forest Univ	NC	38,290	MC
Wellesley College	MA	41,030	MC
Wheaton College	MA	40,180	HC+

GREEK (CLASSICAL)

School	ST	$IS	SR
Baylor Univ	TX	27,555	HC
Boston Univ	MA	42,046	HC+
College of Wooster	OH	31,310	VC+
Duquesne Univ	PA	29,534	VC
Kenyon College	OH	39,500	MC
New York Univ	NY	43,170	MC
Ohio Univ	OH	15,921	C
Washington Univ in St. Louis	MO	42,106	MC

GREEK (MODERN)

School	ST	$IS	SR
Boston Univ	MA	42,046	HC+
CUNY/Queens College	NY	4,356	C
Univ of Mich/Ann Arbor	MI	16,587	HC+

GUIDANCE EDUCATION

School	ST	$IS	SR
Calif Univ of Pennsylvania	PA	14,217	C
Eastern Washington Univ	WA	10,608	C
McNeese State Univ	LA	5,270	LC
Prescott College	AZ	13,445	LC
St. Cloud State Univ	MN	10,010	C
S Car State Univ	SC	6,700	LC
Texas A&M Univ at Commerce	TX	9,020	C
Univ of Akron	OH	15,166	NC
Univ of Central Arkansas	AR	9,984	C
Univ of Cincinnati	OH	17,682	C
Univ of Nebr at Lincoln	NE	11,401	VC
Univ of Southern Miss	MS	10,112	C
Westminster College	PA	31,290	C+

GUITAR

School	ST	$IS	SR
Ball State Univ	IN	13,138	C
Boston Conservatory	MA	27,500	SP
Central Washington Univ	WA	11,730	C
Indiana Univ Bloomington	IN	13,356	VC
Roosevelt Univ	IL	22,605	VC
Stetson Univ	FL	32,725	VC
Temple Univ	PA	17,438	C
Univ of Miami	FL	38,397	MC

HAWAIIAN

School	ST	$IS	SR
Univ of Hawaii at Manoa	HI	10,413	VC

HAWAIIAN STUDIES

School	ST	$IS	SR
Brigham Young Univ/Hawaii	HI	7,740	HC+
Univ of Hawaii at Hilo	HI	6,500	C

ST = STATE $IS = IN-STATE COSTS   SR = SELECTOR RATING

School	ST	$IS	SR
Univ of Hawaii at Manoa	HI	10,413	VC

HEALTH

School	ST	$IS	SR
Aquinas College	MI	23,750	C
Averett Univ	VA	24,920	C
Becker College	MA	24,300	LC
Boston Univ	MA	42,046	HC+
Cal State, Monterey Bay	CA	10,099	C
Cal State, Northridge	CA	9,036	LC
Cameron Univ	OK	6,314	NC
Chicago State Univ	IL	10,915	C+
Coastal Carolina Univ	SC	13,140	C
College of the Ozarks	MO	4,130	C+
Concordia College: Moorhead	MN	22,475	VC
Concordia Univ Nebr	NE	20,500	C
Eastern Oregon Univ	OR	10,400	NC
Florida Gulf Coast Univ	FL	10,833	C
Georgetown Univ	DC	43,183	MC
Georgia Southern Univ	GA	9,762	C
Graceland Univ	IA	19,700	C
Harding Univ	AR	16,512	VC
Indiana Wesleyan Univ	IN	22,074	C+
International College	FL	9,500	NC
Ithaca College	NY	35,144	VC
Kent State Univ	OH	14,594	C
Lebanon Valley College	PA	31,700	VC
LeTourneau Univ	TX	21,200	C
Luther College	IA	28,800	VC+
Mass College of Pharmacy and Health Sciences	MA	32,020	SP
Miami Univ	OH	29,097	HC
Montana State Univ-Bozeman	MT	1,137	C
Mount Union College	OH	25,840	C
Nebr Methodist College of Nursing and Allied Health	NE	12,950	SP
Nebr Wesleyan Univ	NE	23,415	C+
New Mexico Highlands Univ	NM	6,272	NC
Ohio Northern Univ	OH	27,765	VC
Olivet College	MI	19,984	C+
Oregon State Univ	OR	11,055	C
Prairie View A&M Univ	TX	11,110	LC
Rowan Univ	NJ	16,000	VC
Rust College	MS		C+
Sam Houston State Univ	TX	8,000	C
Samford Univ	AL	20,258	VC
Southeastern Louisiana Univ	LA	8,521	C
Southern Oregon Univ	OR	12,186	C
Southwestern Adventist Univ	TX	18,290	LC
Spring Arbor Univ	MI	22,476	C
SUNY/College at Buffalo	NY	11,903	C+
SUNY/College at Old Westbury	NY	13,154	C
SUNY/Inst of Technology	NY	12,575	VC
Syracuse Univ	NY	38,655	HC
Texas Christian Univ	TX	23,410	VC+
Texas Southern Univ	TX	9,828	C
Texas Tech Univ	TX	13,026	VC
Thomas Edison State College	NJ	3,780	SP
Union College	KY	18,920	C
Union Inst & Univ	OH	8,912	SP
Univ of Houston	TX	7,000	C
Univ of Kansas	KS	10,915	VC
Univ of Louisiana at Monroe	LA	7,103	C
Univ of Louisville	KY	10,400	VC
Univ of N Car at Asheville	NC	9,237	VC
Univ of Pennsylvania	PA	41,766	MC
Univ of Pittsburgh at Pittsburgh	PA	18,866	HC
Univ of Rochester	NY	41,135	MC
Univ of St. Francis	IL	25,430	C
Univ of Southern Calif	CA	41,618	MC
Univ of Texas at San Antonio	TX	11,325	LC
Univ of Texas-Pan American	TX	7,290	C+
Univ of the Cumberlands	KY	18,184	C
Upper Iowa Univ	IA	20,130	C
Voorhees College	SC	11,800	LC
Walla Walla College	WA	24,489	NC
West Chester Univ of Pennsylvania	PA	12,355	C
Western Mich Univ	MI	13,299	C
Worcester State College	MA	12,499	C
Youngstown State Univ	OH	12,613	NC

HEALTH CARE ADMINISTRATION

School	ST	$IS	SR
Alaska Pacific Univ	AK	25,142	C
Appalachian State Univ	NC	8,000	VC
Arcadia Univ	PA	33,570	C
Auburn Univ	AL	12,230	VC
Austin Peay State Univ	TN	7,535	C
Baker College of Flint	MI	7,800	NC
Benedictine Univ	IL	25,710	C
Black Hills State Univ	SD	7,800	LC
Bowling Green State Univ	OH	14,994	C
Cabarrus College of Health Sciences	NC	8,000	SP
Cal State, Long Beach	CA	9,512	C
Cal State, Northridge	CA	9,036	LC
Cal State, San Bernardino	CA	12,563	LC
Calumet College of St. Joseph	IN	9,500	LC
Carroll College	MT	23,324	C+
Central Mich Univ	MI	12,244	C
Chestnut Hill College	PA	26,600	LC
Chicago State Univ	IL	10,915	C+
CUNY/Herbert H. Lehman College	NY	4,000	LC
CUNY/New York City College of Technology	NY	4,269	LC
Clayton College and State Univ	GA	2,445	LC
Cleary College	MI	11,000	LC
College of St. Catherine	MN	27,505	VC
College of St. Scholastica	MN	28,456	C+
Columbia Union College	MD	23,536	LC
Concordia College: Moorhead	MN	22,475	VC
Concordia Univ	OR	24,400	C
Creighton Univ	NE	29,918	VC+
David N. Myers College	OH	9,475	C
Dominican College	NY	26,630	LC
Duquesne Univ	PA	29,534	VC
D'Youville College	NY	23,660	C
Eastern Kentucky Univ	KY	7,725	C
Eastern Mich Univ	MI	12,897	C
Eastern Univ	PA	24,075	C
Eastern Washington Univ	WA	10,608	C
Emporia State Univ	KS	8,093	C
Ferris State Univ	MI	13,698	C
Florida Atlantic Univ	FL	11,221	C
Florida International Univ	FL	9,215	VC
Franklin Univ	OH	6,720	SP
Gwynedd-Mercy College	PA	26,080	C
Hastings College	NE	22,218	VC
Huron Univ	SD	10,700	C
Idaho State Univ	ID	9,030	C
Illinois State Univ	IL	12,839	C+
Indiana Univ Bloomington	IN	13,356	VC
Indiana Univ Kokomo	IN	4,835	LC
Indiana Univ Northwest	IN	4,902	LC
Indiana Univ South Bend	IN	4,989	LC
Indiana Univ-Purdue Univ Fort Wayne	IN	5,067	LC
Indiana Univ-Purdue Univ Indianapolis	IN	10,959	C
International College	FL	9,500	NC
Iona College	NY	30,878	VC
James Madison Univ	VA	12,010	VC
Jamestown College	ND	14,130	NC
Kean Univ	NJ	15,880	C
Kent State Univ	OH	14,594	C
Knoxville College	TN	6,200	LC
Langston Univ	OK	2,308	LC
Lasell College	MA	26,250	C
Lewis Univ	IL	23,050	C+
LIU/C.W. Post Campus	NY	28,282	C
Lourdes College	OH	15,300	LC
Lynn Univ	FL	30,750	C
Mary Baldwin College	VA	26,465	C
Maryville Univ of St. Louis	MO	23,000	C
Marywood Univ	PA	30,680	C
Mercy College of Health Sciences	IA	11,700	SP
Metropolitan State College of Denver	CO	2,338	C
Midwestern State Univ	TX	9,381	LC
Monroe College	NY	15,960	LC
Montana State Univ-Billings	MT	8,906	C
Mount Marty College	SD	20,590	C
Mount Mercy College	IA	23,670	C
Mountain State Univ	WV	11,406	NC
National-Louis Univ	IL	16,915	LC
New York Univ	NY	43,170	MC
Newbury College	MA	25,600	C
Norfolk State Univ	VA	10,531	LC
Northwest Christian College	OR	24,298	C
Ohio Univ	OH	15,921	C
Oregon State Univ	OR	11,055	C
Park Univ	MO	11,592	C
Penn State Univ/Univ Park Campus	PA	18,038	HC
Pennsylvania College of Technology	PA	16,980	LC
Point Park Univ	PA	24,160	C
Presentation College	SD	14,800	LC
Providence College	RI	34,580	HC
Robert Morris Univ	PA	22,822	C
St. Francis College	NY	19,974	LC
St. John's Univ	NY	34,370	C
St. Joseph's College, New York, Brooklyn Campus	NY	12,206	C
St. Joseph's Univ	PA	37,428	VC
St. Leo Univ	FL	22,140	C+
St. Louis Univ	MO	33,158	VC+
St. Peter's College	NJ	30,160	C
Shippensburg Univ of Pennsylvania	PA	11,621	C
Sojourner-Douglass College	MD	4,200	LC
South Univ	GA		LC
Southern Adventist Univ	TN	18,500	C
Southern Illinois Univ Carbondale	IL	12,391	C
Southern Univ at New Orleans	LA	1,000	NC
Southwestern Okla State Univ	OK	4,801	C
Springfield College	MA	25,000	C
SUNY/College at Fredonia	NY	12,771	VC
SUNY/Inst of Technology	NY	12,575	VC
Stonehill College	MA	36,104	HC
Tenn State Univ	TN	9,048	LC
Texas Southern Univ	TX	9,828	C
Texas State Univ - San Marcos	TX	10,862	C
Thomas Edison State College	NJ	3,780	SP
Towson Univ	MD	13,924	VC
Univ of Arizona	AZ	11,958	VC
Univ of Central Arkansas	AR	9,984	C
Univ of Central Florida	FL	10,739	VC
Univ of Colo at Colo Springs	CO	11,517	VC
Univ of Conn	CT	16,628	HC
Univ of Detroit Mercy	MI	27,000	C
Univ of Evansville	IN	28,320	VC
Univ of Great Falls	MT	17,000	C
Univ of Illinois at Urbana-Champaign	IL	15,800	HC+
Univ of La Verne	CA	33,470	C
Univ of Mich/Flint	MI	6,398	C
Univ of Minn/Crookston	MN	13,157	LC
Univ of Nebr at Omaha	NE	11,235	C
Univ of Nevada/Las Vegas	NV	11,566	C
Univ of New England	ME	31,005	C
Univ of New Hampshire	NH	16,810	VC
Univ of N Car at Chapel Hill	NC	11,129	MC
Univ of Pennsylvania	PA	41,766	MC
Univ of Rhode Island	RI	15,398	C
Univ of Scranton	PA	31,100	VC
Univ of S Dak	SD	9,068	C
Univ of Washington	WA	10,400	VC
Univ of Wisc/Eau Claire	WI	9,915	VC
Univ of Wisc/Milwaukee	WI	9,427	LC
Upper Iowa Univ	IA	20,130	C
Ursuline College	OH	25,556	C
Viterbo Univ	WI	21,670	C
Weber State Univ	UT	9,635	NC
West Virginia Univ Inst of Technology	WV	8,788	NC
Western Kentucky Univ	KY	10,192	C
Wichita State Univ	KS	8,500	C
Wilberforce Univ	OH	14,937	LC

HEALTH EDUCATION

School	ST	$IS	SR
Albany State Univ	GA	5,770	C+
Anderson Univ	IN	25,050	LC
Appalachian State Univ	NC	8,000	VC
Arkansas State Univ	AR	9,630	C
Arkansas Tech Univ	AR	8,108	VC
Ashland Univ	OH	25,000	C
Auburn Univ	AL	12,230	VC
Augsburg College	MN	28,300	C
Augusta State Univ	GA	2,920	C
Austin Peay State Univ	TN	7,535	C
Averett Univ	VA	24,920	C
Baldwin-Wallace College	OH	27,256	VC
Ball State Univ	IN	13,138	C
Baylor Univ	TX	27,555	VC
Bemidji State Univ	MN	11,180	LC
Bethel College	KS	21,650	C
Bethel College	TN	16,066	NC
Bethel Univ	MN	29,840	VC
Black Hills State Univ	SD	7,800	LC
Bowling Green State Univ	OH	14,994	C
Brewton-Parker College	GA	14,220	LC
Briar Cliff Univ	IA	23,550	LC
Bridgewater State College	MA	12,120	C
Cal State, Sacramento	CA	11,122	C+
Cal State, San Bernardino	CA	12,563	LC
Cal State, Stanislaus	CA	11,283	C
Carson-Newman College	TN	16,800	C
Central State Univ	OH	9,010	C+
Central Washington Univ	WA	11,730	C
Chadron State College	NE	6,350	NC
Citadel, The	SC		C+
CUNY/Brooklyn College	NY	4,377	C+
CUNY/Herbert H. Lehman College	NY	4,000	LC
CUNY/Hunter College	NY	8,000	C+
College of Mount St. Vincent	NY	28,000	C
College of New Jersey	NJ	18,315	MC
Columbus State Univ	GA	8,664	C
Concordia College: Moorhead	MN	22,475	VC
Curry College	MA	26,100	LC
Daemen College	NY	24,580	C
Dakota State Univ	SD	7,466	C
Defiance College	OH	24,790	C
Delaware State Univ	DE	8,316	LC
Delta State Univ	MS	7,709	C
East Carolina Univ	NC	10,000	C
East Central Univ	OK	6,207	C
East Stroudsburg Univ of Pennsylvania	PA	10,336	C
Eastern Kentucky Univ	KY	7,725	C
Eastern Mich Univ	MI	12,897	C
Eastern Washington Univ	WA	10,608	C
Edinboro Univ of Pennsylvania	PA	11,809	LC
Elon Univ	NC	25,371	HC
Emporia State Univ	KS	8,093	C
Fairmont State	WV	8,400	LC
Fayetteville State Univ	NC	6,000	LC
Florida International Univ	FL	9,215	VC
Florida State Univ	FL	9,028	NC
Franklin College	IN		C
Freed-Hardeman Univ	TN	16,370	NC
Friends Univ	KS	16,250	LC
Gardner-Webb Univ	NC	21,500	C
George Fox Univ	OR	28,490	C
Georgia College and State Univ	GA	11,020	C
Georgia Southern Univ	GA	9,762	C
Gustavus Adolphus College	MN	30,920	HC
Hofstra Univ	NY	32,630	VC
Howard Univ	DC	18,481	C+
Idaho State Univ	ID	9,030	C
Illinois State Univ	IL	12,839	C+
Indiana State Univ	IN	11,604	C
Indiana Univ Bloomington	IN	13,356	VC
Indiana Univ-Purdue Univ Indianapolis	IN	10,959	C
Inter American Univ of PR/San German	PR	6,720	C
Iowa State Univ	IA	11,831	VC
Ithaca College	NY	35,144	VC
Jackson State Univ	MS	8,500	C
Jacksonville State Univ	AL	7,618	LC
Johnson C. Smith Univ	NC	20,000	C
Kennesaw State Univ	GA	12,152	C
Kent State Univ	OH	14,594	C
Knoxville College	TN	6,200	LC
Lamar Univ	TX	6,820	LC
Lenoir-Rhyne College	NC	25,580	C
Lincoln Memorial Univ	TN	18,144	C
Linfield College	OR	29,632	VC
Lipscomb Univ	TN	20,967	VC
LIU/C.W. Post Campus	NY	28,282	C
Louisiana College	LA	13,450	C
Malone College	OH	23,040	C
Manchester College	IN	23,470	C
Manhattan College	NY	29,000	VC
Mayville State Univ	ND	8,667	NC
McNeese State Univ	LA	5,270	C
Miami Univ	OH	29,097	HC
MidAmerica Nazarene Univ	KS	20,584	LC
Middle Tenn State Univ	TN	8,540	C
Minn State Univ, Mankato	MN	10,276	LC
Minn State Univ, Moorhead	MN	7,000	LC
Missouri Southern State Univ	MO	8,396	NC
Missouri State Univ	MO	10,748	C+
Montana State Univ-Billings	MT	8,906	C
Montclair State Univ	NJ	16,327	C
Morehead State Univ	KY	9,150	C
Morgan State Univ	MD	12,080	C
Mountain State Univ	WV	11,406	NC
Murray State Univ	KY	8,900	VC
New Jersey City Univ	NJ	13,695	LC
New York Inst of Technology	NY	28,126	VC
N Car Central Univ	NC	9,000	LC
N Dak State Univ	ND	8,500	C
Northeastern State Univ	OK	5,896	LC
Northern Arizona Univ	AZ	10,353	C
Northern Illinois Univ	IL	13,178	C
Northern Mich Univ	MI	12,340	LC
Northern State Univ	SD	8,257	C
Northwestern State Univ of Louisiana	LA	7,144	C
Ohio Northern Univ	OH	27,765	VC
Okla Panhandle State Univ	OK	7,635	NC
Okla State Univ	OK	10,213	VC
Oral Roberts Univ	OK	22,650	C
Oregon State Univ	OR	11,055	C
Otterbein College	OH	28,986	C
Ouachita Baptist Univ	AR	21,900	VC
Penn State Univ/Univ Park Campus	PA	18,038	HC
Plymouth State Univ	NH	12,298	LC
Portland State Univ	OR	12,453	C
Purdue Univ/West Lafayette	IN	13,458	VC
Rhode Island College	RI	11,570	C
St. Cloud State Univ	MN	10,010	C
St. Mary's College of Calif	CA	37,290	C
Salisbury Univ	MD	13,128	VC
Shepherd Univ	WV	10,066	C
Slippery Rock Univ of Pennsylvania	PA	10,360	LC
S Car State Univ	SC	6,700	LC
S Dak State Univ	SD	9,815	C
Southeastern Louisiana Univ	LA	8,521	LC
Southern Arkansas Univ	AR	6,956	C
Southern Conn State Univ	CT	10,310	C
Southern Illinois Univ Carbondale	IL	12,391	C
Southern Illinois Univ Edwardsville	IL	11,022	C
Southern Methodist Univ	TX	36,088	VC+
Southwest Minn State Univ	MN	10,975	C

ST = STATE $IS = IN-STATE COSTS   SR = SELECTOR RATING

School	ST	$IS	SR
Southwestern Okla State Univ	OK	4,801	C
Springfield College	MA	25,000	C
SUNY/College at Cortland	NY	12,095	C
Tabor College	KS	21,614	NC
Tenn State Univ	TN	9,048	LC
Texas A&M Univ	TX	13,351	C
Texas A&M Univ at Commerce	TX	9,020	C
Texas A&M Univ at Kingsville	TX	6,800	LC
Texas State Univ - San Marcos	TX	10,862	C
Thomas Edison State College	NJ	3,780	SP
Troy Univ	AL	8,916	C
Univ of Akron	OH	15,166	NC
Univ of Alabama at Birmingham	AL	13,716	C
Univ of Arizona	AZ	11,958	VC
Univ of Arkansas at Little Rock	AR	7,230	NC
Univ of Arkansas at Monticello	AR	7,325	NC
Univ of Cincinnati	OH	17,682	C
Univ of Florida	FL	9,354	HC
Univ of Great Falls	MT	17,000	C
Univ of Iowa	IA	12,172	VC
Univ of Kentucky	KY	7,800	C
Univ of Louisiana at Lafayette	LA	5,830	C
Univ of Maine	ME	13,642	C
Univ of Maine at Farmington	ME	11,515	C
Univ of Maine at Presque Isle	ME	10,066	LC
Univ of Maryland/Eastern Shore	MD	11,210	C
Univ of Minn/Duluth	MN	13,974	C
Univ of Missouri/Kansas City	MO	15,000	VC
Univ of Nebr at Kearney	NE	9,000	NC
Univ of Nebr at Lincoln	NE	11,401	VC
Univ of Nevada/Las Vegas	NV	11,566	C
Univ of New Mexico	NM	11,253	C
Univ of N Car at Chapel Hill	NC	11,129	MC
Univ of N Car at Pembroke	NC	7,940	LC
Univ of North Texas	TX	7,800	C
Univ of Northern Iowa	IA	11,133	C
Univ of Rio Grande	OH	8,728	NC
Univ of St. Francis	IN	20,970	C
Univ of St. Thomas	MN	28,000	VC
Univ of South Alabama	AL	8,930	LC
Univ of Southern Calif	CA	41,618	MC
Univ of Southern Miss	MS	10,112	C
Univ of Tenn at Knoxville	TN	11,720	C
Univ of the Cumberlands	KY	18,184	C
Univ of the District of Columbia	DC	2,070	LC
Univ of Toledo	OH	15,806	NC
Univ of Utah	UT	10,162	VC
Univ of Virginia	VA	13,759	MC
Univ of West Florida	FL	8,559	C
Univ of Wisc/La Crosse	WI	10,045	VC
Univ of Wisc/Stevens Point	WI	9,384	VC
Univ of Wyoming	WY	9,666	C
Utah State Univ	UT	8,002	VC
Valdosta State Univ	GA	8,802	C
Valley City State Univ	ND	9,854	LC
Virginia Commonwealth Univ	VA	12,987	C
Wayne State College	NE	8,033	NC
Weber State Univ	UT	9,635	NC
West Chester Univ of Pennsylvania	PA	12,355	C+
West Liberty State College	WV	9,142	LC
Western Conn State Univ	CT	12,993	C
Western Mich Univ	MI	13,299	C
Western Oregon Univ	OR	10,295	C
Western Washington Univ	WA	11,262	VC
William Paterson Univ of New Jersey	NJ	17,810	C+
William Penn Univ	IA	17,685	LC
Winona State Univ	MN	11,333	C
Youngstown State Univ	OH	12,613	NC

HEALTH PSYCHOLOGY

School	ST	$IS	SR
Univ of the Sciences in Philadelphia	PA	33,380	VC

HEALTH SCIENCE

School	ST	$IS	SR
Alcorn State Univ	MS	8,190	LC
Alma College	MI	28,544	VC
American Univ	DC	38,719	HC+
Appalachian State Univ	NC	8,000	VC
Armstrong Atlantic State Univ	GA	7,394	C
Ball State Univ	IN	13,138	C
Baylor Univ	TX	27,555	HC
Benedictine Univ	IL	25,710	C
Boise State Univ	ID	9,438	LC
Boston Univ	MA	42,046	HC+
Bowling Green State Univ	OH	14,994	C
Bradley Univ	IL	25,280	VC

School	ST	$IS	SR
Brigham Young Univ	UT	9,200	VC
Cal State East Bay	CA	10,856	LC
Cal State, Chico	CA	11,395	C
Cal State, Dominguez Hills	CA	10,220	LC
Cal State, Fresno	CA	10,037	LC
Cal State, Fullerton	CA	10,990	C
Cal State, Long Beach	CA	9,512	C
Cal State, Los Angeles	CA	5,900	C
Cal State, San Bernardino	CA	12,563	LC
Carlow Univ	PA	24,313	C
Castleton State College	VT	13,158	C
Chapman Univ	CA	37,550	VC
Chicago State Univ	IL	10,915	C+
CUNY/Brooklyn College	NY	4,377	C+
College of Our Lady of the Elms	MA	21,000	C
College of St. Scholastica	MN	28,456	C+
Columbus State Univ	GA	8,664	C
Daemen College	NY	24,580	C
Dordt College	IA	20,325	VC
Duquesne Univ	PA	29,534	VC
East Tenn State Univ	TN	8,497	C
Eastern Univ	PA	24,075	C
Ferrum College	VA	24,290	LC
Florida Atlantic Univ	FL	11,221	C
Florida Gulf Coast Univ	FL	10,833	C
Florida Hospital College of Health Sciences	FL	11,152	SP
Florida International Univ	FL	9,215	VC
Furman Univ	SC	33,264	HC+
George Mason Univ	VA	10,850	VC
Gettysburg College	PA	39,864	HC
Grand Valley State Univ	MI	12,000	VC
Guilford College	NC	28,160	C+
Hampshire College	MA	37,120	HC
Hardin-Simmons Univ	TX	18,641	C
Hope International Univ	CA	23,700	NC
Idaho State Univ	ID	9,030	C
Ithaca College	NY	35,144	VC
James Madison Univ	VA	12,010	VC
Johnson State College	VT	11,830	C
Kalamazoo College	MI	32,442	VC+
Keene State College	NH	13,836	C
King College	TN	23,400	C
La Sierra Univ	CA	24,327	C+
Lincoln Univ	PA	13,658	C+
Lock Haven Univ of Pennsylvania	PA	12,098	LC
Marietta College	OH	29,327	C
Marymount Univ	VA	25,934	C
Maryville Univ of St. Louis	MO	23,000	VC
Marywood Univ	PA	30,680	C
Middle Tenn State Univ	TN	8,540	C
Midwestern State Univ	TX	9,321	LC
Minn State Univ, Mankato	MN	10,276	LC
Missouri Baptist Univ	MO	19,640	C
New England College	NH	31,466	C
Nicholls State Univ	LA	6,500	NC
Norfolk State Univ	VA	10,531	LC
Northeastern Univ	MA	35,742	HC
Northern Illinois Univ	IL	13,178	C
Nova Southeastern Univ	FL	24,320	C
Oakland Univ	MI	11,936	C
Old Dominion Univ	VA	11,907	C
Oral Roberts Univ	OK	22,650	C
Oregon Inst of Technology	OR	8,718	C
Our Lady of Holy Cross College	LA	8,090	LC
Pennsylvania College of Technology	PA	16,980	LC
Purdue Univ/West Lafayette	IN	13,458	VC
Quinnipiac Univ	CT	34,640	VC
Randolph-Macon Woman's College	VA	31,160	VC+
St. Ambrose Univ	IA	25,495	C
St. Francis College	NY	19,974	LC
St. Mary's College of Calif	CA	37,290	C
San Diego State Univ	CA	12,971	C
San Francisco State Univ	CA	13,000	C
South Univ	GA		LC
Southern Adventist Univ	TN	18,500	C
Southwestern Okla State Univ	OK	4,801	C
SUNY/College at Brockport	NY	12,747	VC
SUNY/College at Cortland	NY	12,095	C
SUNY/Univ at Stony Brook	NY	13,625	HC
Stephen F. Austin State Univ	TX	7,930	C
Stetson Univ	FL	32,725	VC
Syracuse Univ	NY	38,655	HC
Taylor Univ	IN	26,376	VC+
Temple Univ	PA	17,438	C+
Texas A&M Univ at Corpus Christi	TX	10,280	LC
Texas Woman's Univ	TX	7,804	LC
Towson Univ	MD	13,924	VC
Truman State Univ	MO	11,242	HC
Universidad Adventista de las Antillas	PR	7,360	
Univ of Alabama at Birmingham	AL	13,716	C
Univ of Arkansas	AR	11,859	VC
Univ of Arkansas at Little Rock	AR	7,230	NC
Univ of Calif at Santa Cruz	CA	19,174	VC
Univ of Central Arkansas	AR	9,984	C

School	ST	$IS	SR
Univ of Central Florida	FL	10,739	VC
Univ of Findlay	OH	29,238	C
Univ of Florida	FL	9,354	HC
Univ of Hartford	CT	34,044	C
Univ of Maryland/Baltimore County	MD	16,642	VC+
Univ of Miami	FL	38,397	MC
Univ of Mich/Flint	MI	6,398	C
Univ of Minn/Crookston	MN	13,157	LC
Univ of New England	ME	31,005	C
Univ of North Florida	FL	9,908	VC
Univ of Okla	OK	10,769	VC+
Univ of Southern Maine	ME	12,614	C
Univ of Tenn at Knoxville	TN	11,720	C
Univ of Texas at El Paso	TX	8,764	NC
Univ of the Sciences in Philadelphia	PA	33,380	VC
Univ of Wisc/Milwaukee	WI	9,427	LC
Univ of Wyoming	WY	9,666	C
West Chester Univ of Pennsylvania	PA	12,355	C+
Western Baptist College	OR	21,808	C
Western Illinois Univ	IL	13,042	C
William Paterson Univ of New Jersey	NJ	17,810	C+
Worcester State College	MA	12,499	C
Yeshiva Univ	NY	22,000	C
Youngstown State Univ	OH	12,613	NC

HEBREW

School	ST	$IS	SR
CUNY/Brooklyn College	NY	4,377	C+
CUNY/Herbert H. Lehman College	NY	4,000	LC
CUNY/Hunter College	NY	8,000	C+
CUNY/Queens College	NY	4,356	C
Harvard Univ/Harvard College	MA	45,860	MC
Hofstra Univ	NY	32,630	VC
New York Univ	NY	43,170	MC
Ohio State Univ	OH	15,357	HC
SUNY/Univ at Albany	NY	13,860	VC
SUNY/Univ at Binghamton	NY	13,988	HC
Temple Univ	PA	17,438	C
Touro College	NY	17,000	VC
Univ of Calif at Los Angeles	CA	17,681	MC
Univ of Illinois at Urbana-Champaign	IL	15,800	HC+
Univ of Mich/Ann Arbor	MI	16,587	HC+
Univ of Minn/Twin Cities	MN	13,165	HC
Univ of Texas at Austin	TX	14,610	HC
Univ of Wisc/Madison	WI	13,117	HC
Univ of Wisc/Milwaukee	WI	9,427	LC
Washington Univ in St. Louis	MO	42,106	MC
Yeshiva Univ	NY	22,000	C

HISPANIC AMERICAN STUDIES

School	ST	$IS	SR
Arizona State Univ-Tempe	AZ	11,174	C
Boston College	MA	41,608	MC
Boston Univ	MA	42,046	HC+
Brown Univ	RI	42,015	MC
Burlington College	VT	14,670	SP
Cal State, Long Beach	CA	9,512	C
CUNY/Brooklyn College	NY	4,377	C+
CUNY/Hunter College	NY	8,000	C
Columbia Univ/Columbia College	NY	42,584	MC
Columbia Univ/School of General Studies	NY	41,516	C
Conn College	CT	41,975	MC
East Carolina Univ	NC	10,000	C
Hofstra Univ	NY	32,630	VC
Illinois Wesleyan Univ	IL	34,050	HC+
Lewis and Clark College	OR	35,358	VC+
Mills College	CA	39,870	C
Mount St. Mary College	NY	25,250	C
Rice Univ	TX	32,290	MC
Rutgers, The State Univ of New Jersey/New Brunswick/Piscataway Campus	NJ	15,810	VC
St. Olaf College	MN	32,800	HC
Scripps College	CA	41,000	MC
SUNY/College at Oneonta	NY	12,905	VC
SUNY/Univ at Albany	NY	13,860	VC
Univ of Calif at Berkeley	CA	18,141	HC+
Univ of Calif at Los Angeles	CA	17,681	MC
Univ of Mass Boston	MA	8,024	C
Univ of PR/Cayey Univ College	PR	1,250	
Western New Mexico Univ	NM	7,233	LC
Wheaton College	MA	40,180	HC+

HISTORIC PRESERVATION

School	ST	$IS	SR
College of Charleston	SC	13,616	VC
Eastern Mich Univ	MI	12,897	C
Goucher College	MD	36,225	VC
Roger Williams Univ	RI	30,500	C
Salve Regina Univ	RI	33,450	C
Savannah College of Art and Design	GA	30,800	SP

School	ST	$IS	SR
Southeast Missouri State Univ	MO	10,596	C
Univ of Delaware	DE	14,142	HC
Univ of Mary Washington	VA	11,636	HC
Ursuline College	OH	25,456	C

HISTORY

School	ST	$IS	SR
Abilene Christian Univ	TX	20,830	C
Adams State College	CO	8,613	C
Adelphi Univ	NY	27,000	C
Adrian College	MI	23,000	C
Agnes Scott College	GA	32,070	HC
Alabama A&M Univ	AL	8,890	C
Alabama State Univ	AL	7,658	C
Albany State Univ	GA	5,770	C+
Albertson College of Idaho	ID	21,095	VC
Albertus Magnus College	CT	25,336	C
Albion College	MI	26,000	VC
Albright College	PA	33,920	C
Alcorn State Univ	MS	8,190	LC
Alderson-Broaddus College	WV	24,006	C
Alfred Univ	NY		VC
Alice Lloyd College	KY	4,900	C
Allegheny College	PA	33,500	HC
Allen Univ	SC	10,500	NC
Alma College	MI	28,544	VC
Alvernia College	PA	26,388	C
Alverno College	WI	21,088	C
American International College	MA	28,710	LC
American Univ	DC	38,719	HC+
Amherst College	MA	41,590	MC
Anderson Univ	IN	25,050	LC
Andrews Univ	MI	21,786	C
Angelo State Univ	TX	8,340	NC
Anna Maria College	MA	29,815	LC
Appalachian State Univ	NC	8,000	VC
Aquinas College	MI	23,750	C
Arcadia Univ	PA	33,570	VC
Arizona State Univ-Tempe	AZ	11,174	C
Arkansas State Univ	AR	9,630	C
Arkansas Tech Univ	AR	8,108	VC
Armstrong Atlantic State Univ	GA	7,394	C
Asbury College	KY	23,762	VC
Ashland Univ	OH	25,000	C
Assumption College	MA	32,875	C
Atlantic Union College	MA	17,600	LC
Auburn Univ	AL	12,230	VC
Auburn Univ Montgomery	AL	9,530	NC
Augsburg College	MN	28,300	C
Augusta State Univ	GA	2,920	C
Augustana College	IL	29,862	VC+
Augustana College	SD	24,380	VC
Aurora Univ	IL	20,645	C
Austin College	TX	27,871	HC
Austin Peay State Univ	TN	7,535	C
Averett Univ	VA	24,920	C
Avila Univ	MO	22,100	C
Azusa Pacific Univ	CA	28,546	VC
Baker Univ	KS	22,190	C
Baldwin-Wallace College	OH	27,256	VC
Ball State Univ	IN	13,138	C
Bard College	NY	41,800	HC+
Barry Univ	FL	24,100	C
Barton College	NC	22,316	C
Bates College	ME	42,100	MC
Baylor Univ	TX	27,555	HC
Belhaven College	MS	19,350	NC
Bellarmine Univ	KY	27,650	C
Bellevue Univ	NE	4,440	NC
Belmont Abbey College	NC	25,314	C
Belmont Univ	TN	24,110	VC
Beloit College	WI	32,808	HC
Bemidji State Univ	MN	11,180	LC
Benedict College	SC	19,114	LC
Benedictine College	KS	21,968	C
Benedictine Univ	IL	25,710	C
Bennington College	VT	41,890	HC
Bentley College	MA	38,784	HC
Berea College	KY	5,496	VC+
Berry College	GA	24,342	VC
Bethany College	KS	20,660	LC
Bethany College	WV	21,395	C
Bethel College	IN	19,680	C
Bethel College	KS	21,650	C
Bethel College	TN	16,066	NC
Bethel Univ	MN	29,840	VC
Bethune-Cookman College	FL	17,922	LC
Biola Univ	CA	29,372	VC
Birmingham-Southern College	AL	28,494	VC+
Black Hills State Univ	SD	7,800	LC
Blackburn College	IL	13,690	C
Bloomfield College	NJ	22,500	LC
Bloomsburg Univ of Pennsylvania	PA	11,602	C
Blue Mountain College	MS	11,086	C
Bluefield College	VA	17,230	C+
Bluffton College	OH	26,110	C
Boise State Univ	ID	9,438	LC
Boston College	MA	41,608	MC
Boston Univ	MA	42,046	HC+
Bowdoin College	ME	41,660	MC
Bowie State Univ	MD	10,880	C+

ST = STATE $IS = IN-STATE COSTS   SR = SELECTOR RATING

ST = STATE   **$IS** = IN-STATE COSTS   **SR** = SELECTOR RATING

INDEX OF COLLEGE MAJORS

School	ST	$IS	SR
Southwest Baptist Univ	MO	18,300	C
Southwest Minn State Univ	MN	10,975	C
Southwestern Adventist Univ	TX	18,290	LC
Southwestern College	KS	21,476	C
Southwestern Okla State Univ	OK	4,801	C
Southwestern Univ	TX	26,767	HC
Spelman College	GA	24,650	VC
Spring Arbor Univ	MI	22,476	C
Spring Hill College	AL	28,678	C
Springfield College	MA	25,000	C
Stanford Univ	CA	41,557	MC
SUNY at Oswego	NY	13,662	VC
SUNY at Potsdam	NY	12,959	C
SUNY/College at Brockport	NY	12,747	VC
SUNY/College at Buffalo	NY	11,903	C+
SUNY/College at Cortland	NY	12,095	C
SUNY/College at Fredonia	NY	12,771	VC
SUNY/College at Geneseo	NY	12,910	HC+
SUNY/College at Oneonta	NY	12,905	VC
SUNY/College at Plattsburgh	NY	12,362	C
SUNY/College at Purchase	NY	11,989	VC+
SUNY/Empire State College	NY	4,575	SP
SUNY/Univ at Albany	NY	13,860	VC
SUNY/Univ at Binghamton	NY	13,988	HC
SUNY/Univ at Buffalo	NY	13,694	VC
SUNY/Univ at New Paltz	NY	12,480	VC
SUNY/Univ at Stony Brook	NY	13,625	HC
Stephen F. Austin State Univ	TX	7,930	C
Sterling College	KS	19,992	C
Stetson Univ	FL	32,725	VC
Stevens Inst of Technology	NJ	40,935	HC
Stillman College	AL	11,475	LC
Stonehill College	MA	36,104	HC
Suffolk Univ	MA	33,160	C
Sul Ross State Univ	TX	6,600	LC
Susquehanna Univ	PA	33,465	VC
Swarthmore College	PA	41,280	MC
Sweet Briar College	VA	31,460	VC
Syracuse Univ	NY	38,655	HC
Tabor College	KS	21,614	NC
Talladega College	AL	11,240	LC
Tarleton State Univ	TX	8,952	C
Taylor Univ	IN	26,376	VC+
Temple Univ	PA	17,438	C
Tenn State Univ	TN	9,048	LC
Tenn Tech Univ	TN	10,044	C
Tenn Wesleyan College	TN	18,650	C
Texas A&M Univ	TX	13,351	HC
Texas A&M Univ at Commerce	TX	9,020	C
Texas A&M Univ at Corpus Christi	TX	10,280	LC
Texas A&M Univ at Kingsville	TX	6,800	LC
Texas Christian Univ	TX	23,410	VC+
Texas Lutheran Univ	TX	23,530	C
Texas Southern Univ	TX	9,828	C
Texas State Univ - San Marcos	TX	10,862	C
Texas Tech Univ	TX	13,026	VC
Texas Wesleyan Univ	TX	18,700	C
Texas Woman's Univ	TX	7,804	C
Thiel College	PA	24,580	C
Thomas Edison State College	NJ	3,780	SP
Thomas More College	KY	24,470	C
Tougaloo College	MS	15,975	NC
Touro College	NY	17,000	VC
Towson Univ	MD	13,924	VC
Transylvania Univ	KY	26,240	VC+
Trevecca Nazarene Univ	TN	19,594	C
Trinity Christian College	IL	23,645	C
Trinity College	CT	38,040	HC+
Trinity College	DC	24,150	LC
Trinity International Univ	IL	25,686	C
Trinity Univ	TX	30,157	HC+
Troy Univ	AL	8,916	C
Troy Univ Dothan Campus	AL	4,678	C
Troy Univ Montgomery Campus	AL	4,104	NC
Truman State Univ	MO	11,242	HC
Tufts Univ	MA	42,018	MC
Tulane Univ	LA	41,098	MC
Turabo Univ	PR	4,110	
Tusculum College	TN	21,340	LC
Tuskegee Univ	AL	18,860	LC
Union College	KY	18,920	C
Union College	NE	18,710	C
Union College	NY	41,595	HC
Union Univ	TN	20,750	VC
United States Air Force Academy	CO		HC+
United States Military Academy	NY		MC
United States Naval Academy	MD		MC
Universidad Adventista de las Antillas	PR	7,360	
Univ of Akron	OH	15,166	NC
Univ of Alabama	AL	9,888	C
Univ of Alabama at Birmingham	AL	13,716	C
Univ of Alabama in Huntsville	AL	9,516	VC
Univ of Alaska Anchorage	AK	11,275	NC
Univ of Alaska Fairbanks	AK	10,101	C
Univ of Arizona	AZ	11,958	VC
Univ of Arkansas	AR	11,859	VC
Univ of Arkansas at Little Rock	AR	7,230	NC
Univ of Arkansas at Monticello	AR	7,325	NC
Univ of Arkansas at Pine Bluff	AR	8,300	C
Univ of at Calif Davis	CA	15,010	VC
Univ of Calif at Berkeley	CA	18,141	HC+
Univ of Calif at Irvine	CA	16,475	VC
Univ of Calif at Los Angeles	CA	17,681	MC
Univ of Calif at Riverside	CA	16,625	C
Univ of Calif at San Diego	CA	16,102	HC
Univ of Calif at Santa Barbara	CA	11,800	VC
Univ of Calif at Santa Cruz	CA	19,174	VC
Univ of Central Arkansas	AR	9,984	C
Univ of Central Florida	FL	10,739	VC
Univ of Central Okla	OK	8,094	C
Univ of Chicago	IL	42,369	MC
Univ of Cincinnati	OH	17,682	C
Univ of Colo at Boulder	CO	13,352	C+
Univ of Colo at Colo Springs	CO	11,517	VC
Univ of Colo at Denver and Health Sciences Center	CO	5,021	C
Univ of Conn	CT	16,628	HC
Univ of Dallas	TX	27,432	VC+
Univ of Dayton	OH	28,826	VC
Univ of Delaware	DE	14,142	HC
Univ of Denver	CO	36,376	VC+
Univ of Detroit Mercy	MI	27,000	C
Univ of Evansville	IN	28,320	VC
Univ of Findlay	OH	29,238	C
Univ of Florida	FL	9,354	HC
Univ of Georgia	GA	11,004	HC
Univ of Great Falls	MT	17,000	C
Univ of Hartford	CT	34,044	C
Univ of Hawaii at Hilo	HI	6,500	C
Univ of Hawaii at Manoa	HI	10,413	VC
Univ of Houston	TX	7,000	C
Univ of Idaho	ID	9,310	NC
Univ of Illinois at Chicago	IL	16,256	VC
Univ of Illinois at Urbana-Champaign	IL	15,800	HC+
Univ of Indianapolis	IN	25,090	C
Univ of Iowa	IA	12,172	VC
Univ of Kansas	KS	10,915	VC
Univ of Kentucky	KY	7,800	C
Univ of La Verne	CA	33,470	C
Univ of Louisiana at Lafayette	LA	5,830	C
Univ of Louisiana at Monroe	LA	7,103	C
Univ of Louisville	KY	10,400	VC
Univ of Maine	ME	13,642	C
Univ of Maine at Farmington	ME	11,515	C
Univ of Maine at Machias	ME	10,523	C
Univ of Mary Hardin-Baylor	TX	19,428	C
Univ of Mary Washington	VA	11,636	HC
Univ of Maryland/Baltimore County	MD	16,642	VC+
Univ of Maryland/College Park	MD	16,036	HC
Univ of Maryland/Eastern Shore	MD	11,210	C
Univ of Maryland/Univ College	MD	5,640	SP
Univ of Mass Amherst	MA	15,973	C+
Univ of Mass Boston	MA	8,024	C
Univ of Mass Dartmouth	MA	15,985	C
Univ of Mass Lowell	MA	14,327	VC
Univ of Memphis	TN	11,153	C
Univ of Miami	FL	38,397	MC
Univ of Mich/Ann Arbor	MI	16,587	HC+
Univ of Mich/Dearborn	MI	7,000	VC
Univ of Mich/Flint	MI	6,398	C
Univ of Minn/Duluth	MN	13,974	C
Univ of Minn/Morris	MN	15,472	VC
Univ of Minn/Twin Cities	MN	13,165	HC
Univ of Miss	MS	9,000	C
Univ of Missouri/Columbia	MO	13,500	VC
Univ of Missouri/Kansas City	MO	15,000	VC
Univ of Missouri/Rolla	MO	13,332	HC
Univ of Missouri/St. Louis	MO	14,046	VC
Univ of Mobile	AL	16,880	C
Univ of Montana	MT	10,602	C
Univ of Montevallo	AL	9,630	C
Univ of Nebr at Kearney	NE	9,000	NC
Univ of Nebr at Lincoln	NE	11,401	VC
Univ of Nebr at Omaha	NE	11,235	C
Univ of Nevada/Las Vegas	NV	11,566	C
Univ of Nevada/Reno	NV	12,155	NC
Univ of New England	ME	31,005	C
Univ of New Hampshire	NH	16,810	VC
Univ of New Haven	CT	31,794	C
Univ of New Mexico	NM	11,253	C
Univ of New Orleans	LA	7,370	C
Univ of North Alabama	AL	8,992	C
Univ of N Car at Asheville	NC	9,237	VC
Univ of N Car at Chapel Hill	NC	11,129	MC
Univ of N Car at Charlotte	NC	9,101	C
Univ of N Car at Greensboro	NC	8,993	VC
Univ of N Car at Pembroke	NC	7,940	LC
Univ of N Car at Wilmington	NC	10,107	VC
Univ of N Dak	ND	10,114	VC
Univ of North Florida	FL	9,908	VC
Univ of North Texas	TX	7,800	C
Univ of Northern Colo	CO	10,249	C
Univ of Northern Iowa	IA	11,133	C
Univ of Notre Dame	IN	39,552	MC
Univ of Okla	OK	10,769	VC+
Univ of Oregon	OR	13,108	VC
Univ of Pennsylvania	PA	41,766	MC
Univ of Pittsburgh at Bradford	PA	17,008	C
Univ of Pittsburgh at Johnstown	PA	16,740	LC
Univ of Portland	OR	32,300	VC
Univ of PR/Cayey Univ College	PR	1,250	
Univ of PR/Mayaguez	PR	1,250	
Univ of PR/Rio Piedras	PR	5,750	
Univ of Puget Sound	WA	35,600	HC
Univ of Redlands	CA	36,160	VC
Univ of Rhode Island	RI	15,398	C
Univ of Richmond	VA	40,510	MC
Univ of Rio Grande	OH	8,728	NC
Univ of Rochester	NY	41,135	MC
Univ of St. Francis	IL	25,430	C
Univ of St. Francis	IN	20,970	C
Univ of St. Mary	KS	18,900	C
Univ of St. Thomas	MN	28,000	VC
Univ of St. Thomas	TX	23,810	VC
Univ of San Diego	CA	40,620	HC
Univ of San Francisco	CA	37,560	VC
Univ of Science and Arts of Okla	OK	7,650	C
Univ of Scranton	PA	31,100	VC
Univ of Sioux Falls	SD	20,800	C
Univ of South Alabama	AL	8,930	LC
Univ of S Car at Aiken	SC	11,718	LC
Univ of S Car at Columbia	SC	13,397	VC
Univ of S Car Upstate	SC	11,957	C
Univ of S Dak	SD	9,068	C
Univ of South Florida	FL	10,284	VC
Univ of Southern Calif	CA	41,618	MC
Univ of Southern Indiana	IN	12,590	LC
Univ of Southern Maine	ME	12,614	C
Univ of Southern Miss	MS	10,112	C
Univ of Tampa	FL	25,784	C
Univ of Tenn at Chattanooga	TN	7,790	C
Univ of Tenn at Knoxville	TN	11,720	C
Univ of Tenn at Martin	TN	8,693	C
Univ of Texas at Arlington	TX	7,195	LC
Univ of Texas at Austin	TX	14,610	HC
Univ of Texas at Dallas	TX	13,244	HC
Univ of Texas at El Paso	TX	8,764	NC
Univ of Texas at San Antonio	TX	11,325	LC
Univ of Texas-Pan American	TX	7,290	C+
Univ of the Cumberlands	KY	18,184	C
Univ of the District of Columbia	DC	2,070	LC
Univ of the Incarnate Word	TX	23,306	C
Univ of the Ozarks	AR	19,250	C
Univ of the Pacific	CA	34,380	VC
Univ of the South	TN	34,645	HC
Univ of Toledo	OH	15,806	NC
Univ of Tulsa	OK	25,348	HC
Univ of Utah	UT	10,162	VC
Univ of Vermont	VT	18,080	VC
Univ of Virginia	VA	13,759	MC
Univ of Virginia's College at Wise	VA	11,076	C
Univ of Washington	WA	10,400	VC
Univ of West Alabama	AL	7,611	C
Univ of West Florida	FL	8,559	C
Univ of West Georgia	GA	8,838	C
Univ of Wisc/Eau Claire	WI	9,915	VC
Univ of Wisc/Green Bay	WI	9,415	VC
Univ of Wisc/La Crosse	WI	10,045	VC
Univ of Wisc/Madison	WI	13,117	HC
Univ of Wisc/Milwaukee	WI	9,427	C
Univ of Wisc/Oshkosh	WI	10,426	LC
Univ of Wisc/Parkside	WI	10,181	C
Univ of Wisc/Platteville	WI	9,779	NC
Univ of Wisc/River Falls	WI	9,722	C
Univ of Wisc/Stevens Point	WI	9,384	C
Univ of Wisc/Superior	WI	9,610	C+
Univ of Wisc/Whitewater	WI	9,274	C
Univ of Wyoming	WY	9,666	C
Ursinus College	PA	38,950	VC
Ursuline College	OH	25,456	C
Utah State Univ	UT	8,002	VC
Utica College	NY	31,396	C
Valdosta State Univ	GA	8,802	C
Valley City State Univ	ND	9,854	LC
Valparaiso Univ	IN	28,970	VC+
Vanderbilt Univ	TN	41,986	MC
Vanguard Univ of Southern Calif	CA	27,071	C
Vassar College	NY	41,700	MC
Villanova Univ	PA	38,672	HC+
Virginia Commonwealth Univ	VA	12,987	C
Virginia Intermont College	VA	22,200	LC
Virginia Military Inst	VA	12,654	VC-
Virginia Polytechnic Inst and State Univ	VA	10,834	VC
Virginia State Univ	VA	11,318	C
Virginia Union Univ	VA	18,432	LC
Virginia Wesleyan College	VA	28,433	C
Wabash College	IN	30,116	HC
Wagner College	NY	33,300	VC
Wake Forest Univ	NC	38,290	MC
Walla Walla College	WA	24,489	NC
Walsh Univ	OH	23,440	C
Warner Pacific College	OR	21,900	C
Warner Southern College	FL	18,000	LC
Warren Wilson College	NC	24,382	VC
Wartburg College	IA	27,315	NC
Washburn Univ	KS	9,734	NC
Washington and Jefferson College	PA	33,490	VC
Washington and Lee Univ	VA	35,880	MC
Washington College	MD	34,990	VC
Washington State Univ	WA	12,260	C
Washington Univ in St. Louis	MO	42,106	MC
Wayland Baptist Univ	TX	13,484	C
Wayne State College	NE	8,033	NC
Wayne State Univ	MI	11,805	C
Waynesburg College	PA	21,230	C
Weber State Univ	UT	9,635	NC
Webster Univ	MO	24,280	VC
Wellesley College	MA	41,030	MC
Wells College	NY	23,070	VC
Wesley College	DE	19,905	C
Wesleyan College	GA	19,560	C
Wesleyan Univ	CT	42,122	MC
West Chester Univ of Pennsylvania	PA	12,355	C+
West Liberty State College	WV	9,142	LC
West Texas A&M Univ	TX	8,452	C
West Virginia State Univ	WV	8,378	NC
West Virginia Univ	WV	10,506	C
West Virginia Univ Inst of Technology	WV	8,788	NC
West Virginia Wesleyan College	WV	26,880	C
Western Baptist College	OR	21,808	C
Western Carolina Univ	NC	7,000	C
Western Conn State Univ	CT	12,993	C
Western Illinois Univ	IL	13,042	C
Western Kentucky Univ	KY	10,192	C
Western Mich Univ	MI	13,299	C
Western New England College	MA	32,054	C
Western New Mexico Univ	NM	7,233	LC
Western Oregon Univ	OR	10,295	C
Western State College of Colo	CO	9,942	C
Western Washington Univ	WA	11,262	VC
Westfield State College	MA	10,200	C
Westminster College	MO	19,060	VC
Westminster College	PA	31,290	C+
Westminster College	UT	25,656	C
Westmont College	CA	36,672	HC+
Wheaton College	IL	27,760	HC
Wheaton College	MA	40,180	HC+
Wheeling Jesuit Univ	WV	26,910	C
Whitman College	WA	36,110	HC+
Whittier College	CA	29,108	C
Whitworth College	WA	29,428	VC+
Wichita State Univ	KS	8,500	C
Widener Univ	PA	27,275	C
Wiley College	TX	8,100	LC
Wilkes Univ	PA	30,886	C
Willamette Univ	OR	35,416	VC+
William Carey College	MS	11,000	LC
William Jewell College	MO	24,340	C
William Paterson Univ of New Jersey	NJ	17,810	C+
William Penn Univ	IA	17,685	LC
William Tyndale College	MI	13,000	NC
William Woods Univ	MO	21,020	C
Williams Baptist College	AR	13,450	C
Williams College	MA	40,310	MC
Wilmington College	OH	2,806	NC
Wilson College	PA	27,660	C
Wingate Univ	NC	23,300	C
Winona State Univ	MN	11,333	C
Winston-Salem State Univ	NC	8,960	LC
Winthrop Univ	SC	11,302	C
Wisc Lutheran College	WI	23,510	C
Wittenberg Univ	OH	34,596	VC
Wofford College	SC	30,935	HC
Woodbury Univ	CA	30,176	LC
Worcester State College	MA	12,499	C
Wright State Univ	OH	13,616	LC
Xavier Univ	OH	30,490	VC
Xavier Univ of Louisiana	LA	17,600	C
Yale Univ	CT	41,000	MC
Yeshiva Univ	NY	22,000	C
York College	NE	16,330	NC
York College of Pennsylvania	PA	16,550	VC
Youngstown State Univ	OH	12,613	NC

ST = STATE **$IS** = IN-STATE COSTS **SR** = SELECTOR RATING

School	ST	$IS	SR

HISTORY OF PHILOSOPHY

School	ST	$IS	SR
Bard College	NY	41,800	HC+
Colo College	CO	37,668	HC
Univ of Pittsburgh at Pittsburgh	PA	18,866	HC

HISTORY OF SCIENCE

School	ST	$IS	SR
Bard College	NY	41,800	HC+
Case Western Reserve Univ	OH	37,314	MC
Johns Hopkins Univ	MD	42,044	MC
Univ of Pennsylvania	PA	41,766	MC
Univ of Wisc/Madison	WI	13,117	MC
Yale Univ	CT	41,000	MC

HOME ECONOMICS

School	ST	$IS	SR
Ball State Univ	IN	13,138	C
CUNY/Queens College	NY	4,356	C
College of the Ozarks	MO	4,130	VC+
Colo State Univ-Fort Collins	CO	10,878	C+
Florida State Univ	FL	9,028	HC
George Fox Univ	OR	28,490	C
Harding Univ	AR	16,512	VC
Illinois State Univ	IL	12,839	C+
Indiana State Univ	IN	11,604	C
Langston Univ	OK	2,308	LC
Master's College and Seminary	CA	25,850	VC
Montclair State Univ	NJ	16,327	C
Morgan State Univ	MD	12,080	C
Northwest Missouri State Univ	MO	10,000	C
Oakwood College	AL	14,904	C
Oregon State Univ	OR	11,055	C
Point Loma Nazarene Univ	CA	27,610	VC
SUNY/College at Oneonta	NY	12,905	VC
SUNY/College at Plattsburgh	NY	12,362	C
Stephen F. Austin State Univ	TX	7,930	C
Tarleton State Univ	TX	8,952	C
Texas A&M Univ at Kingsville	TX	6,800	LC
Texas Tech Univ	TX	13,026	VC
Univ of Akron	OH	15,166	NC
Univ of Florida	FL	9,354	C
Univ of Maryland/Eastern Shore	MD	11,210	C
Univ of PR/Rio Piedras	PR	5,750	C
Univ of Tenn at Chattanooga	TN	7,790	C
Utah State Univ	UT	8,002	VC
Virginia State Univ	VA	11,318	C
Washington State Univ	WA	12,260	C
Winthrop Univ	SC	11,302	C
Youngstown State Univ	OH	12,613	NC

HOME ECONOMICS EDUCATION

School	ST	$IS	SR
Alabama A&M Univ	AL	8,890	LC
Ashland Univ	OH	25,000	C
Auburn Univ	AL	12,230	VC
Ball State Univ	IN	13,138	C
Baylor Univ	TX	27,555	HC
Berea College	KY	5,496	VC+
Bluffton College	OH	26,110	C
Bradley Univ	IL	25,280	VC
Brigham Young Univ	UT	9,200	VC
Cal State, Northridge	CA	9,036	LC
Carson-Newman College	TN	16,800	C
Central Missouri State Univ	MO	10,000	C
Central Washington Univ	WA	11,730	C
Cheyney Univ of Pennsylvania	PA	11,497	LC
CUNY/Queens College	NY	4,356	C
College of St. Catherine	MN	27,505	VC
Colo State Univ-Fort Collins	CO	10,878	C+
Concordia College: Moorhead	MN	22,475	VC
Concordia Univ Nebr	NE	20,500	C+
Delaware State Univ	DE	8,130	C
East Carolina Univ	NC	10,000	C
East Central Univ	OK	6,207	C
Eastern Kentucky Univ	KY	7,725	C
Eastern New Mexico Univ	NM	7,264	C
Florida International Univ	FL	9,215	VC
Florida State Univ	FL	9,028	HC
Fort Valley State Univ	GA	6,975	C
Gallaudet Univ	DC	16,554	
George Fox Univ	OR	28,490	C
Georgia Southern Univ	GA	9,762	C
Grambling State Univ	LA	6,538	NC
Immaculata Univ	PA	25,350	C
Indiana State Univ	IN	11,604	C
Jacksonville State Univ	AL	7,618	LC
Langston Univ	OK	2,308	LC
Lincoln Univ	MO	8,000	NC
Marshall Univ	WV	9,116	C
Marywood Univ	PA	30,680	C
McNeese State Univ	LA	5,270	LC
Merchurst College	PA	28,633	VC

School	ST	$IS	SR
Missouri State Univ	MO	10,748	C+
Montclair State Univ	NJ	16,327	C
Morehead State Univ	KY	9,150	C
Mount Vernon Nazarene Univ	OH	20,810	C
Murray State Univ	KY	8,900	VC
New Mexico State Univ	NM	9,250	C
N Car Agricultural and Technical State Univ	NC	8,000	LC
N Dak State Univ	ND	8,500	C
Oakwood College	AL	14,904	C
Ouachita Baptist Univ	AR	21,900	VC
Pontifical Catholic Univ of PR/Ponce	PR	7,310	
San Francisco State Univ	CA	13,000	C
Seattle Pacific Univ	WA	29,355	C
Seton Hill Univ	PA	28,810	C
Shepherd Univ	WV	10,066	C
S Car State Univ	SC	6,700	LC
S Dak State Univ	SD	9,815	C
SUNY/College at Oneonta	NY	12,905	VC
Tarleton State Univ	TX	8,952	C
Tenn Tech Univ	TN	10,044	C
Univ of Akron	OH	15,166	NC
Univ of Arizona	AZ	11,958	VC
Univ of Arkansas at Pine Bluff	AR	8,300	C
Univ of Georgia	GA	11,004	HC
Univ of Idaho	ID	9,310	NC
Univ of Louisiana at Lafayette	LA	5,830	C
Univ of Maryland/Eastern Shore	MD	11,210	C
Univ of Minn/Twin Cities	MN	13,165	HC
Univ of Miss	MS	9,000	C
Univ of Montevallo	AL	9,630	C
Univ of Nebr at Lincoln	NE	11,401	VC
Univ of North Alabama	AL	8,992	C
Univ of Southern Miss	MS	10,112	C
Univ of Wisc/Stevens Point	WI	9,384	VC
Univ of Wisc/Stout	WI	11,164	C
Utah State Univ	UT	8,002	VC
Wayne State College	NE	8,033	NC
Western Kentucky Univ	KY	10,192	C
Western Mich Univ	MI	13,299	C
Winthrop Univ	SC	11,302	C
Youngstown State Univ	OH	12,613	NC

HOME FURNISHINGS AND EQUIPMENT MANAGEMENT/ PRODUCTION/SERVICES

School	ST	$IS	SR
Auburn Univ	AL	12,230	VC
Fashion Inst of Technology/ SUNY	NY	11,600	C+
High Point Univ	NC	25,720	C
Univ of North Texas	TX	7,800	C

HORTICULTURE

School	ST	$IS	SR
Alabama A&M Univ	AL	8,890	LC
Andrews Univ	MI	21,786	C
Auburn Univ	AL	12,230	VC
Calif Polytechnic State Univ	CA	12,390	VC
Calif State Polytechnic Univ, Pomona	CA	18,053	C+
Christopher Newport Univ	VA	13,326	VC
Clemson Univ	SC	13,366	VC
College of the Ozarks	MO	4,130	VC+
Colo State Univ-Fort Collins	CO	10,878	C+
Cornell Univ	NY	41,717	MC
Delaware Valley College	PA	29,944	C
Eastern Kentucky Univ	KY	7,725	C
Ferrum College	VA	24,290	LC
Florida A&M Univ	FL	8,344	C
Florida Southern College	FL	25,965	C
Fort Valley State College	GA	6,975	C
Iowa State Univ	IA	11,831	VC
Kansas State Univ	KS	10,516	VC
Kent State Univ	OH	14,594	C
Mich State Univ	MI	13,689	VC
Miss State Univ	MS	9,577	C
Missouri State Univ	MO	10,748	C+
Montana State Univ-Bozeman	MT	1,137	C
Murray State Univ	KY	8,900	VC
New Mexico State Univ	NM	9,250	C
N Car State Univ	NC	11,824	HC
N Dak State Univ	ND	8,500	C
Northwest Missouri State Univ	MO	10,000	C
Okla State Univ	OK	10,213	VC
Oregon State Univ	OR	11,055	C
Penn State Univ/Univ Park Campus	PA	18,038	HC
Purdue Univ/West Lafayette	IN	13,458	VC
Sam Houston State Univ	TX	8,000	C
S Dak State Univ	SD	9,815	C
Southeast Missouri State Univ	MO	10,596	C
Southeastern Louisiana Univ	LA	8,521	LC
Stephen F. Austin State Univ	TX	7,930	C
Tarleton State Univ	TX	8,952	C

School	ST	$IS	SR
Temple Univ	PA	17,438	C
Texas A&M Univ	TX	13,351	HC
Texas Tech Univ	TX	13,026	VC
Thomas Edison State College	NJ	3,780	SP
Tuskegee Univ	AL	18,860	LC
Univ of Arkansas	AR	11,859	VC
Univ of Conn	CT	16,628	HC
Univ of Florida	FL	9,354	HC
Univ of Georgia	GA	11,004	HC
Univ of Idaho	ID	9,310	NC
Univ of Illinois at Urbana-Champaign	IL	15,800	HC+
Univ of Maine	ME	13,642	C
Univ of Maryland/College Park	MD	16,036	HC
Univ of Nebr at Lincoln	NE	11,401	VC
Univ of New Hampshire	NH	16,810	VC
Univ of PR/Mayaguez	PR	1,250	
Univ of Rhode Island	RI	15,398	C
Univ of Vermont	VT	18,080	VC
Univ of Wisc/Madison	WI	13,117	HC
Univ of Wisc/Platteville	WI	9,779	NC
Univ of Wisc/River Falls	WI	9,722	LC
Virginia Polytechnic Inst and State Univ	VA	10,834	VC
Washington State Univ	WA	12,260	C
West Virginia Univ	WV	10,506	C

HOSPICE CARE

School	ST	$IS	SR
Madonna Univ	MI	16,068	VC

HOSPITAL ADMINISTRATION

School	ST	$IS	SR
Ithaca College	NY	35,144	VC
Thomas Edison State College	NJ	3,780	SP

HOSPITALITY MANAGEMENT SERVICES

School	ST	$IS	SR
Appalachian State Univ	NC	8,000	VC
Becker College	MA	24,300	LC
Bowling Green State Univ	OH	14,994	C
Brigham Young Univ/Hawaii	HI	7,740	HC+
Central Conn State Univ	CT	13,620	C
Central Mich Univ	MI	12,244	C
Champlain College	VT	24,605	C
CUNY/New York City College of Technology	NY	4,269	NC
Davis and Elkins College	WV	22,416	C
Delta State Univ	MS	7,709	C
East Carolina Univ	NC	10,000	C
Eastern Mich Univ	MI	12,897	C
Ferris State Univ	MI	13,698	C
Florida Atlantic Univ	FL	11,221	C
Florida International Univ	FL	9,215	VC
Georgia State Univ	GA	11,444	VC
Green Mountain College	VT	32,164	C
Howard Univ	DC	18,481	C+
Husson College	ME	17,410	LC
Indiana Univ-Purdue Univ Fort Wayne	IN	5,067	LC
James Madison Univ	VA	12,010	VC
Johnson and Wales Univ/ Charlotte Campus	NC	29,121	LC
Johnson and Wales Univ/ North Miami Campus	FL	30,126	LC
Johnson and Wales Univ/ Providence Campus	RI	28,126	LC
Johnson State College	VT	11,830	LC
Kendall College	IL	28,800	NC
Lakeland College	WI	22,990	C
Lasell College	MA	26,250	C
Madonna Univ	MI	16,068	VC
Marywood Univ	PA	30,680	C
Metropolitan State College of Denver	CO	2,338	LC
Metropolitan State Univ	MN	4,682	SP
Mich State Univ	MI	13,689	VC
Monroe College	NY	15,960	C
Montclair State Univ	NJ	16,327	C
Morgan State Univ	MD	12,080	C
Mount Ida College	MA	26,000	LC
New York Inst of Technology	NY	28,126	VC
Norfolk State Univ	VA	10,531	C
Northwestern State Univ of Louisiana	LA	7,144	C
Ohio State Univ	OH	15,357	HC
Ohio State Univ at Lima	OH	4,416	NC
Purdue Univ/West Lafayette	IN	13,458	VC
Robert Morris Univ	PA	22,822	C
Rutgers, The State Univ of New Jersey/Camden Campus	NJ	15,000	VC
St. John's Univ	NY	34,370	C
St. Leo Univ	FL	22,140	C+
St. Thomas Univ	FL	23,490	C
Shepherd Univ	WV	10,066	C
Southern New Hampshire Univ	NH	28,764	C
SUNY/College at Buffalo	NY	11,903	C+

School	ST	$IS	SR
Stephen F. Austin State Univ	TX	7,930	C
Syracuse Univ	NY	38,655	HC
Tougaloo College	MS	15,975	NC
Tuskegee Univ	AL	18,860	LC
Univ of Akron	OH	15,166	NC
Univ of Central Florida	FL	10,739	VC
Univ of Denver	CO	36,376	VC+
Univ of Findlay	OH	29,238	C
Univ of Illinois at Urbana-Champaign	IL	15,800	HC+
Univ of Mass Amherst	MA	15,973	C+
Univ of Memphis	TN	11,153	C
Univ of New Hampshire	NH	16,810	VC
Univ of San Francisco	CA	37,560	VC
Univ of Wisc/Stout	WI	11,164	C
Western Carolina Univ	NC	7,000	C
Western Kentucky Univ	KY	10,192	C
Widener Univ	PA	27,275	C
Youngstown State Univ	OH	12,613	NC

HOTEL/MOTEL AND RESTAURANT MANAGEMENT

School	ST	$IS	SR
Ashland Univ	OH	25,000	C
Auburn Univ	AL	12,230	VC
Belmont Univ	TN	24,110	VC
Bethune-Cookman College	FL	17,922	LC
Black Hills State Univ	SD	7,800	LC
Boston Univ	MA	42,046	HC+
Calif State Polytechnic Univ, Pomona	CA	18,053	C+
Central Missouri State Univ	MO	10,000	C
Champlain College	VT	24,605	C
Cheyney Univ of Pennsylvania	PA	11,497	LC
College of the Ozarks	MO	4,130	VC+
Colo State Univ-Fort Collins	CO	10,878	C+
Concord College	WV	9,708	C
Cornell Univ	NY	41,717	MC
Delaware State Univ	DE	8,130	C
Drexel Univ	PA	27,700	VC
East Stroudsburg Univ of Pennsylvania	PA	10,336	C
Endicott College	MA	30,156	C+
Fairleigh Dickinson Univ/ College at Florham	NJ	30,130	C
Fairleigh Dickinson Univ/ Metropolitan Campus	NJ	28,590	C
Florida Southern College	FL	25,965	C
Florida State Univ	FL	9,028	HC
Georgia Southern Univ	GA	9,762	C
Grambling State Univ	LA	6,538	NC
Grand Valley State Univ	MI	12,000	C
Green Mountain College	VT	32,164	C
Indiana Univ of Pennsylvania	PA	11,209	C
Iowa State Univ	IA	11,831	VC
Johnson and Wales Univ/ Charlotte Campus	NC	29,121	LC
Johnson and Wales Univ/ North Miami Campus	FL	30,126	LC
Johnson and Wales Univ/ Providence Campus	RI	28,126	LC
Kansas State Univ	KS	10,516	VC
Kendall College	IL	28,800	NC
Keuka College	NY	26,050	C
Lasell College	MA	26,250	C
Lynn Univ	FL	30,750	C
Mercyhurst College	PA	28,633	VC
Minn State Univ, Moorhead	MN	7,000	LC
Missouri State Univ	MO	10,748	C+
Mountain State Univ	WV	11,406	NC
New Mexico State Univ	NM	9,250	C
New York Univ	NY	43,170	MC
Newbury College	MA	25,600	C
Niagara Univ	NY	28,250	C
N Car Wesleyan College	NC	22,670	C
N Dak State Univ	ND	8,500	C
Northern Arizona Univ	AZ	10,353	C
Northwood Univ	FL	21,040	C
Northwood Univ	MI	21,000	C
Northwood Univ	TX	20,135	LC
Okla State Univ	OK	10,213	VC
Oregon State Univ	OR	11,055	C
Penn State Univ/Univ Park Campus	PA	18,038	HC
Purdue Univ/Calumet	IN	10,891	LC
Purdue Univ/West Lafayette	IN	13,458	VC
Rochester Inst of Technology	NY	32,070	VC+
Roosevelt Univ	IL	22,605	VC
Siena Heights Univ	MI	17,000	LC
S Dak State Univ	SD	9,815	C
Southern New Hampshire Univ	NH	28,764	C
Southwest Minn State Univ	MN	10,975	C
SUNY/College at Plattsburgh	NY	12,362	C
Tenn State Univ	TN	9,048	LC
Texas Tech Univ	TX	13,026	VC
Thomas Edison State College	NJ	3,780	SP
Tiffin Univ	OH	19,490	LC
Univ of Alaska Anchorage	AK	11,275	NC

ST = STATE   **$IS** = IN-STATE COSTS   **SR** = SELECTOR RATING

School	ST	$IS	SR
Univ of Central Okla	OK	8,094	C
Univ of Delaware	DE	14,142	HC
Univ of Houston	TX	7,000	C
Univ of Kentucky	KY	7,800	C
Univ of Louisiana at Lafayette	LA	5,830	C
Univ of Maryland/Eastern Shore	MD	11,210	C
Univ of Minn/Crookston	MN	13,157	LC
Univ of Missouri/Columbia	MO	13,500	C
Univ of Nevada/Las Vegas	NV	11,566	C
Univ of New Hampshire	NH	16,810	C
Univ of New Haven	CT	31,794	C
Univ of New Orleans	LA	7,370	C
Univ of North Texas	TX	7,800	C
Univ of San Francisco	CA	37,560	VC
Univ of S Car at Columbia	SC	13,397	VC
Univ of Southern Miss	MS	10,112	C
Univ of Tenn at Knoxville	TN	11,720	C
Virginia Polytechnic Inst and State Univ	VA	10,834	VC
Virginia State Univ	VA	11,318	C
Washington State Univ	WA	12,260	C
Webber International Univ	FL	17,580	C
Wiley College	TX	8,100	LC
Youngstown State Univ	OH	12,613	NC

HUMAN DEVELOPMENT

School	ST	$IS	SR
Alabama A&M Univ	AL	8,890	LC
Andrews Univ	MI	21,786	C
Anna Maria College	MA	29,815	LC
Auburn Univ	AL	12,230	VC
Bard College	NY	41,800	HC+
Becker College	MA	24,300	LC
Boston College	MA	41,608	MC
Brescia Univ	KY	14,240	C
Brigham Young Univ	UT	9,200	VC
Calif Polytechnic State Univ	CA	12,390	VC
Cal State East Bay	CA	10,856	LC
Cal State, Long Beach	CA	9,512	C
Cal State, San Bernardino	CA	12,563	LC
Cal State, San Marcos	CA	1,800	LC
Colo State Univ-Fort Collins	CO	10,878	C+
Conn College	CT	41,975	MC
Cornell Univ	NY	41,717	MC
Earlham College	IN	33,604	HC
East Tenn State Univ	TN	8,497	C
Eckerd College	FL	35,492	VC
Hellenic College/Holy Cross Greek Orthodox School of Theology	MA	24,975	C
Indiana Univ Bloomington	IN	13,356	VC
Kalamazoo College	MI	32,442	VC+
Kansas State Univ	KS	10,516	VC
Kent State Univ	OH	14,594	C
Lee Univ	TN	14,780	NC
Lynchburg College	VA	30,645	C
Marylhurst Univ	OR	14,220	NC
Messiah College	PA	28,910	VC+
Minn State Univ, Mankato	MN	10,276	LC
Miss Univ for Women	MS	6,000	LC
Mitchell College	CT	26,396	C
Montana State Univ-Bozeman	MT	1,137	C
National-Louis Univ	IL	16,915	LC
Northwestern Univ	IL	37,595	MC
Oakwood College	AL	14,904	C
Ohio State Univ	OH	15,357	HC
Oregon State Univ	OR	11,055	C
Penn State Univ/Altoona	PA	12,635	C
Penn State Univ/Univ Park Campus	PA	18,038	HC
Rivier College	NH	26,600	C
St. Mary's College of Maryland	MD	18,876	VC+
San Diego Christian College	CA	24,172	C
Sonoma State Univ	CA	14,732	C
S Dak State Univ	SD	9,815	C
Southern Christian Univ	AL	9,440	LC
SUNY at Oswego	NY	13,662	VC
SUNY/Empire State College	NY	4,575	SP
SUNY/Univ at Binghamton	NY	13,988	HC
Suffolk Univ	MA	33,160	C
Tarleton State Univ	TX	8,952	C
Tenn Wesleyan College	TN	18,650	C
Texas Tech Univ	TX	13,026	VC
Texas Wesleyan Univ	TX	18,700	C
Univ of Alabama	AL	9,888	C
Univ of Arkansas	AR	11,859	VC
Univ of at Calif Davis	CA	15,010	VC
Univ of Calif at San Diego	CA	16,102	HC
Univ of Conn	CT	16,628	HC
Univ of Delaware	DE	14,142	HC
Univ of Houston	TX	7,000	C
Univ of Illinois at Urbana-Champaign	IL	15,800	HC+
Univ of Memphis	TN	11,153	C
Univ of Missouri/Columbia	MO	13,500	VC
Univ of Nebr at Kearney	NE	9,000	NC
Univ of Nebr at Lincoln	NE	11,401	VC
Univ of New Mexico	NM	11,253	C
Univ of N Car at Greensboro	NC	8,993	C

School	ST	$IS	SR
Univ of Pittsburgh at Bradford	PA	17,008	C
Univ of Rhode Island	RI	15,398	C
Univ of Utah	UT	10,162	VC
Univ of Vermont	VT	18,080	VC
Univ of Wisc/Green Bay	WI	9,415	VC
Utah State Univ	UT	8,002	VC
Vanderbilt Univ	TN	41,986	MC
Virginia Polytechnic Inst and State Univ	VA	10,834	VC
Warner Pacific College	OR	21,900	C
Washington State Univ	WA	12,260	C
Westminster College	UT	25,656	C
Wheelock College	MA	33,075	C

HUMAN ECOLOGY

School	ST	$IS	SR
Burlington College	VT	14,670	SP
Cameron Univ	OK	6,314	NC
College of the Atlantic	ME	33,702	HC
Goddard College	VT	21,100	C
Montclair State Univ	NJ	16,327	C
Ohio State Univ	OH	15,357	HC
Tenn Tech Univ	TN	10,044	C
Unity College	ME	24,320	C
Univ of at Calif Davis	CA	15,010	VC
Univ of Calif at Irvine	CA	16,745	HC
Univ of Nevada/Reno	NV	12,155	NC
Univ of Texas at Austin	TX	14,610	HC
Univ of Wisc/Madison	WI	13,117	HC
Virginia Wesleyan College	VA	28,433	C
Youngstown State Univ	OH	12,613	NC

HUMAN RESOURCES

School	ST	$IS	SR
American International College	MA	28,710	LC
Baldwin-Wallace College	OH	27,256	VC
Barton College	NC	22,316	C
Baylor Univ	TX	27,555	HC
Becker College	MA	24,300	LC
Black Hills State Univ	SD	7,800	LC
Boston College	MA	41,608	MC
Brescia Univ	KY	14,240	C
Briar Cliff Univ	IA	23,550	LC
Cabrini College	PA	33,340	C
Calif State Polytechnic Univ, Pomona	CA	18,053	C+
Cal State, San Bernardino	CA	12,563	LC
Carlow Univ	PA	24,313	C
Central Mich Univ	MI	12,244	C
Central Missouri State Univ	MO	10,000	C
Chestnut Hill College	PA	26,600	LC
Cleary College	MI	11,000	LC
Colo Christian Univ	CO	21,182	VC
Crichton College	TN	15,300	C
Davenport Univ	MI	15,205	NC
De Sales Univ	PA	28,580	VC
Defiance College	OH	24,790	C
Dominican College	NY	26,630	LC
Dominican Univ of Calif	CA	36,836	C
East Texas Baptist Univ	TX	16,713	C
Excelsior College	NY	995	SP
Ferris State Univ	MI	13,698	C
Florida Atlantic Univ	FL	11,221	C
Franklin Univ	OH	6,720	SP
George Fox Univ	OR	28,490	C
George Washington Univ	DC	48,820	MC
Georgia Southern Univ	GA	9,762	C
Golden Gate Univ	CA	12,150	LC
Grand Canyon Univ	AZ	32,000	LC
Gwynedd-Mercy College	PA	26,080	C
Harding Univ	AR	16,512	VC
Hawaii Pacific Univ	HI	21,080	C
Holy Names College	CA	27,980	NC
Huron Univ	SD	10,700	C
Idaho State Univ	ID	9,030	C
Indiana Univ of Pennsylvania	PA	11,209	C
Indiana Univ South Bend	IN	4,989	LC
Indiana Univ-Purdue Univ Indianapolis	IN	10,959	C
Inter American Univ of PR/Bayamon Univ College	PR	3,522	
Ithaca College	NY	35,144	VC
Juniata College	PA	33,130	VC
Kentucky Wesleyan College	KY	18,590	C
Le Moyne College	NY	29,570	VC
Lewis Univ	IL	23,050	C+
Limestone College	SC	19,840	C
Lindenwood Univ	MO	18,600	VC
Lourdes College	OH	15,300	LC
Marietta College	OH	29,327	C
Marquette Univ	WI	31,066	HC
Medaille College	NY	21,000	C
Metropolitan State Univ	MN	4,682	SP
Miami Univ	OH	29,097	HC
Mich State Univ	MI	13,689	VC
Midway College	KY	20,150	C
Mount Olive College	NC	16,000	LC
Niagara Univ	NY	28,250	C
Northeastern Univ	MA	35,742	HC
Notre Dame College	OH	20,425	C
Oakland Univ	MI	11,936	C
Ohio State Univ	OH	15,357	HC
Ohio Valley Univ	WV	17,752	C

School	ST	$IS	SR
Okla Wesleyan Univ	OK	18,950	NC
Our Lady of the Lake Univ of San Antonio	TX	22,430	LC
Park Univ	MO	11,592	C
Peirce College	PA	12,760	NC
Point Park Univ	PA	24,560	C
Rider Univ	NJ	32,560	C
Robert Morris Univ	PA	22,822	C
St. Leo Univ	FL	22,140	C+
St. Louis Univ	MO	33,158	VC+
St. Mary-of-the-Woods College	IN	25,480	C
St. Mary's Univ of Minn	MN	23,857	VC
St. Mary's Univ of San Antonio	TX	22,444	C
Samford Univ	AL	20,258	VC
Seton Hill Univ	PA	28,810	C
Silver Lake College of the Holy Family	WI	18,500	LC
Simpson Univ	CA	22,900	C
Southeast Missouri State Univ	MO	10,596	C
Southern Christian Univ	AL	9,440	LC
Southwestern College	KS	21,476	C
SUNY at Oswego	NY	13,662	VC
Tarleton State Univ	TX	8,952	C
Temple Univ	PA	17,438	C
Thomas Edison State College	NJ	3,780	SP
Trinity International Univ	IL	25,686	C
Univ of Arizona	AZ	11,958	VC
Univ of Central Okla	OK	8,094	C
Univ of Findlay	OH	29,238	C
Univ of Florida	FL	9,354	HC
Univ of Hawaii at Manoa	HI	10,413	VC
Univ of Illinois at Urbana-Champaign	IL	15,800	HC+
Univ of Maryland/College Park	MD	16,036	HC
Univ of Maryland/Univ College	MD	5,640	SP
Univ of Miami	FL	38,397	MC
Univ of Mich/Flint	MI	6,398	C
Univ of Nevada/Las Vegas	NV	11,566	C
Univ of New Mexico	NM	11,253	C
Univ of North Texas	TX	7,800	C
Univ of Okla	OK	10,769	VC+
Univ of PR at Humacao	PR	1,707	
Univ of Scranton	PA	31,100	C
Univ of Texas at San Antonio	TX	11,325	LC
Univ of the Incarnate Word	TX	23,306	C
Univ of Wisc/Oshkosh	WI	10,426	LC
Ursuline College	OH	25,456	C
Valley City State Univ	ND	9,854	LC
Washington Univ in St. Louis	MO	42,106	MC
Weber State Univ	UT	9,635	NC
Western Mich Univ	MI	13,299	C
Wichita State Univ	KS	8,500	C
Winona State Univ	MN	11,333	C
Xavier Univ	OH	30,490	HC
York College	NE	16,330	NC
Youngstown State Univ	OH	12,613	NC

HUMAN SERVICES

School	ST	$IS	SR
Adrian College	MI	23,000	C
Alaska Pacific Univ	AK	25,142	C
Albertus Magnus College	CT	25,336	C
Arkansas Baptist College	AR	5,600	NC
Beacon College	FL	29,560	LC
Bethel College	IN	19,680	C
Bethel College	TN	16,066	NC
Black Hills State Univ	SD	7,800	LC
Boricua College	NY	8,000	C
Burlington College	VT	14,670	SP
Cal State, Dominguez Hills	CA	10,220	LC
Cal State, Fullerton	CA	10,990	C
Cal State, Monterey Bay	CA	10,099	C
Cal State, San Bernardino	CA	12,563	LC
Calumet College of St. Joseph	IN	9,500	LC
Cambridge College	MA	11,055	SP
Cazenovia College	NY	26,900	C
Chestnut Hill College	PA	26,600	LC
CUNY/New York City College of Technology	NY	4,269	NC
Coe College	IA	27,440	VC
College of St. Joseph	VT	20,900	NC
College of St. Mary	NE	23,938	C
Dakota Wesleyan Univ	SD	17,832	C
East Central Univ	OK	6,207	C
Eastern New Mexico Univ	NM	7,264	C
Elmira College	NY	37,200	VC
Elon Univ	NC	25,371	HC
Endicott College	MA	30,156	C+
Fitchburg State College	MA	11,276	C
Florida Gulf Coast Univ	FL	10,833	C
Fontbonne Univ	MO	23,308	C
Friends Univ	KS	16,250	LC
Geneva College	PA	21,850	C
George Washington Univ	DC	48,820	MC
Grace Bible College	MI	18,810	C
Graceland Univ	IA	19,700	C
Grand View College	IA	21,482	C

School	ST	$IS	SR
Hannibal-LaGrange College	MO	16,390	C
Hastings College	NE	22,218	VC
Hawaii Pacific Univ	HI	21,080	C
Henderson State Univ	AR	7,600	C
High Point Univ	NC	25,720	C
Hilbert College	NY	20,480	LC
Holy Names College	CA	27,980	NC
Hope International Univ	CA	23,700	NC
Indiana Inst of Technology	IN	23,430	C
Indiana Univ South Bend	IN	4,989	LC
Indiana Univ-Purdue Univ Fort Wayne	IN	5,067	LC
Kennesaw State Univ	GA	12,152	C
La Roche College	PA	24,724	LC
LaGrange College	GA	22,874	C+
Lake Superior State Univ	MI	12,842	LC
Lasell College	MA	26,250	C
Lenoir-Rhyne College	NC	25,580	C
Lesley Univ	MA	34,950	C
Limestone College	SC	19,840	C
Lincoln Univ	PA	13,658	C+
Lindenwood Univ	MO	18,600	VC
Lindsey Wilson College	KY	16,425	LC
Loyola Univ Chicago	IL	32,896	VC
Lyndon State College	VT	14,233	LC
Lynn Univ	FL	30,750	C
Medaille College	NY	21,000	C
Metropolitan College of New York	NY	16,000	C
Metropolitan State College of Denver	CO	2,338	LC
Millikin Univ	IL	25,590	C
Missouri Baptist Univ	MO	19,640	C
Missouri Valley College	MO	18,500	C
Montreat College	NC	21,440	C
Mount Olive College	NC	16,000	LC
Mount St. Mary College	NY	25,250	C
National-Louis Univ	IL	16,915	LC
N Car Central Univ	NC	9,000	LC
Northeastern Univ	MA	35,742	HC
Northern State Univ	SD	8,257	C
Northwest Christian College	OR	24,298	C
Notre Dame de Namur Univ	CA	32,790	LC
Oglala Lakota College	SD	1,950	NC
Old Dominion Univ	VA	11,907	C
Ottawa Univ	KS	12,000	LC
Park Univ	MO	11,592	C
Pennsylvania College of Technology	PA	16,980	LC
Pfeiffer Univ	NC	21,900	C
Pikeville College	KY	16,500	NC
Quincy Univ	IL	24,920	C
Rockford College	IL	28,330	VC
St. John's Univ	NY	34,370	C
St. Leo Univ	FL	22,140	C+
St. Mary-of-the-Woods College	IN	25,480	C
St. Mary's Univ of Minn	MN	23,857	VC
St. Thomas Univ	FL	23,490	C
Salem International Univ	WV	18,020	C
Seton Hill Univ	PA	28,810	C
Siena Heights Univ	MI	17,000	LC
Simmons College	MA	35,640	VC
Sinte Gleska Univ	SD	2,300	NC
S Car State Univ	SC	6,700	LC
Southern Vermont College	VT	21,322	LC
Southwest Baptist Univ	MO	18,300	C
Springfield College	MA	25,000	C
SUNY/College at Cortland	NY	12,095	C
Suffolk Univ	MA	33,160	C
Tenn Wesleyan College	TN	18,650	C
Texas Southern Univ	TX	9,828	C
Touro College	NY	17,000	VC
Trinity College	DC	24,150	C
Troy Univ	AL	8,916	C
Univ of Alaska Anchorage	AK	11,275	NC
Univ of Bridgeport	CT	29,595	LC
Univ of Detroit Mercy	MI	27,000	C
Univ of Great Falls	MT	17,000	C
Univ of Hartford	CT	34,044	C
Univ of Maine at Machias	ME	10,523	C
Univ of Mass Boston	MA	8,024	C
Univ of New Mexico	NM	11,253	C
Univ of Northern Colo	CO	10,249	C
Univ of Rhode Island	RI	15,398	C
Univ of Scranton	PA	31,100	VC
Univ of Tenn at Chattanooga	TN	7,790	C
Univ of Tenn at Knoxville	TN	11,720	C
Univ of Wisc/Oshkosh	WI	10,426	LC
Upper Iowa Univ	IA	20,130	C
Villanova Univ	PA	38,672	HC+
Washburn Univ	KS	9,734	NC
Wayland Baptist Univ	TX	13,484	C
Waynesburg College	PA	21,230	C
Western New Mexico Univ	NM	7,233	LC
Western Washington Univ	WA	11,262	VC
William Penn Univ	IA	17,685	LC
Wingate Univ	NC	23,300	C
Woodbury College	VT	15,150	LC
York College	NE	16,330	NC

HUMANITIES

School	ST	$IS	SR
Albertus Magnus College	CT	25,336	C

ST = STATE · $IS = IN-STATE COSTS · SR = SELECTOR RATING

School	ST	$IS	SR
Aurora Univ	IL	20,645	C
Belhaven College	MS	19,530	NC
Bennington College	VT	41,890	HC
Biola Univ	CA	29,372	VC
Bluefield State College	WV	3,140	LC
Brigham Young Univ	UT	9,200	VC
Bucknell Univ	PA	39,660	MC
Burlington College	VT	14,670	SP
Cal State, Chico	CA	11,395	C
Cal State, Northridge	CA	9,036	LC
Cal State, San Bernardino	CA	12,563	LC
Chaminade Univ of Honolulu	HI	23,320	LC
Charleston Southern Univ	SC	17,800	C
Clarion Univ of Pennsylvania	PA	11,844	C
Clarkson Univ	NY	34,930	VC
Clearwater Christian College	FL	13,160	LC
Colgate Univ	NY	41,170	MC
College of St. Benedict	MN	30,091	VC
College of St. Mary	NE	23,938	C
College of St. Scholastica	MN	28,456	C+
College of Santa Fe	NM	28,978	C
College of the Southwest	NM	12,420	C+
Concordia College: Moorhead	MN	22,475	VC
Concordia Univ	CA	26,780	C
Concordia Univ	OR	24,400	C
Concordia Univ Wisc	WI	22,660	VC
Defiance College	OH	24,790	C
Dominican College	NY	26,630	LC
Dominican Univ of Calif	CA	36,836	C
Dowling College	NY	22,110	LC
Eastern Washington Univ	WA	10,608	C
Eckerd College	FL	35,492	VC
Edinboro Univ of Pennsylvania	PA	11,809	LC
Fairleigh Dickinson Univ/ College at Florham	NJ	30,130	C
Fairleigh Dickinson Univ/ Metropolitan Campus	NJ	28,590	C
Felician College	NJ	24,300	C
Florida Inst of Technology	FL	29,720	VC
Florida International Univ	FL	9,215	VC
Florida Southern College	FL	25,965	VC
Florida State Univ	FL	9,028	HC
Fort Lewis College	CO	11,852	C
George Washington Univ	DC	48,820	MC
Georgian Court College	NJ	20,000	LC
Hampden-Sydney College	VA	31,148	VC
Hampshire College	MA	37,120	HC
Harvard Univ/Harvard College	MA	45,860	MC
Hawaii Pacific Univ	HI	21,080	C
Hofstra Univ	NY	32,630	VC
Holy Family Univ	PA	25,740	C
Holy Names College	CA	27,980	NC
Houghton College	NY	25,980	VC+
Indiana Univ East	IN	4,806	LC
Indiana Univ Kokomo	IN	4,835	LC
Jacksonville Univ	FL	24,040	C
John Carroll Univ	OH	27,658	C+
Johns Hopkins Univ	MD	42,044	MC
Johnson State College	VT	11,830	C
Juniata College	PA	33,130	VC
Kansas State Univ	KS	10,516	VC
Kent State Univ	OH	14,594	C
Lawrence Tech Univ	MI	25,475	VC
Lees-McRae College	NC	23,000	C
LeMoyne-Owen College	TN	13,150	LC
Lesley Univ	MA	34,950	C
Loyola Marymount Univ	CA	36,321	VC
Lubbock Christian Univ	TX	16,960	C
Lynn Univ	FL	30,750	C
Marshall Univ	WV	9,116	C
Martin Univ	IN	10,300	SP
Mass Inst of Technology	MA	41,800	MC
Medaille College	NY	21,000	C
Messiah College	PA	28,910	VC+
Mich State Univ	MI	13,689	VC
Midwestern State Univ	TX	9,381	LC
Milligan College	TN	21,990	VC
Minn State Univ, Mankato	MN	10,276	LC
Montana State Univ- Northern	MT	10,000	NC
Montclair State Univ	NJ	16,327	C
Mountain State Univ	WV	11,406	NC
New College of Florida	FL	10,009	HC+
New York Univ	NY	43,170	MC
N Dak State Univ	ND	8,500	C
Northwest Christian College	OR	24,298	C
Northwest Missouri State Univ	MO	10,000	C
Notre Dame de Namur Univ	CA	32,790	LC
Nova Southeastern Univ	FL	24,320	C
Oberlin College	OH	40,904	MC
Okla City Univ	OK	23,965	VC
Okla Panhandle State Univ	OK	7,635	NC
Pacific Univ	OR	24,250	C
Pepperdine Univ	CA	39,960	HC
Plymouth State Univ	NH	12,298	LC
Polytechnic Univ/Brooklyn	NY	37,150	VC
Providence College	RI	34,580	HC
Quincy Univ	IL	24,920	C
Rockford College	IL	28,330	VC
Rosemont College	PA	29,350	C
Rutgers, The State Univ of New Jersey/New Brunswick/Piscataway Campus	NJ	15,810	HC
St. John's Univ	MN	29,749	VC
St. Joseph's Univ	PA	37,428	VC
St. Louis Univ	MO	33,158	VC+
St. Martin's Univ	WA	27,555	C
St. Mary-of-the-Woods College	IN	25,480	C
St. Mary's College	IN	32,538	VC
St. Norbert College	WI	28,577	C+
St. Peter's College	NJ	30,160	LC
San Diego State Univ	CA	12,971	C
San Francisco State Univ	CA	13,000	C
Schreiner Univ	TX	20,600	C
Scripps College	CA	41,000	MC
Seattle Univ	WA	30,063	VC
Shawnee State Univ	OH	12,237	NC
Shimer College	IL	26,525	LC
Siena Heights Univ	MI	17,000	LC
Sierra Nevada College	NV	30,235	C
Southern Methodist Univ	TX	36,088	VC
Spalding Univ	KY	18,882	C
Spring Hill College	AL	28,678	C
SUNY/College at Buffalo	NY	11,903	C+
SUNY/College at Old Westbury	NY	13,154	C
SUNY/Maritime College	NY	12,475	C
SUNY/Univ at Stony Brook	NY	13,625	HC
Stephen F. Austin State Univ	TX	7,930	C
Stetson Univ	FL	32,725	VC
Suffolk Univ	MA	33,160	C
Tabor College	KS	21,614	VC
Texas Wesleyan Univ	TX	18,700	C
Thomas Edison State College	NJ	3,780	SP
Thomas More College	KY	24,470	C
Thomas Univ	GA	11,520	NC
Tougaloo College	MS	15,975	NC
Trinity International Univ	IL	25,686	C
Turabo Univ	PR	4,110	
Union College	NY	41,595	HC
United States Air Force Academy	CO		HC+
Universidad Metropolitana	PR	3,330	
Univ of Akron	OH	15,166	NC
Univ of Arizona	AZ	11,958	VC
Univ of Calif at Irvine	CA	16,475	HC
Univ of Central Florida	FL	10,739	VC
Univ of Chicago	IL	42,369	MC
Univ of Colo at Boulder	CO	13,352	C+
Univ of Houston-Downtown	TX	3,326	NC
Univ of Illinois at Urbana- Champaign	IL	15,800	HC+
Univ of Kansas	KS	10,915	VC
Univ of Louisville	KY	10,400	VC
Univ of Maryland/Univ College	MD	5,640	SP
Univ of Mich/Ann Arbor	MI	16,587	HC+
Univ of Mich/Dearborn	MI	7,000	VC
Univ of Minn/Twin Cities	MN	13,165	HC
Univ of New Hampshire	NH	16,810	VC
Univ of Northern Iowa	IA	11,133	C
Univ of Oregon	OR	13,108	VC
Univ of Pennsylvania	PA	41,766	MC
Univ of Pittsburgh at Greensburg	PA	17,640	C
Univ of Pittsburgh at Johnstown	PA	16,740	LC
Univ of Pittsburgh at Pittsburgh	PA	18,866	HC
Univ of PR/Cayey Univ College	PR	1,250	
Univ of Rio Grande	OH	8,728	NC
Univ of San Diego	CA	40,620	VC
Univ of South Florida	FL	10,284	VC
Univ of Tenn at Chattanooga	TN	7,790	C
Univ of Texas at Austin	TX	14,610	HC
Univ of Texas at Dallas	TX	13,244	HC
Univ of Texas at San Antonio	TX	11,325	LC
Univ of Toledo	OH	15,806	NC
Univ of Utah	UT	10,162	VC
Univ of Wisc/Green Bay	WI	9,415	VC
Univ of Wisc/Parkside	WI	10,181	LC
Univ of Wyoming	WY	9,666	C
Ursuline College	OH	25,456	C
Villanova Univ	PA	38,672	HC+
Virginia Wesleyan College	VA	28,433	C
Walla Walla College	WA	24,489	NC
Warren Wilson College	NC	24,382	VC
Washington College	MD	34,990	VC
Washington State Univ	WA	12,260	C
Washington Univ in St. Louis	MO	42,106	MC
Wesleyan College	GA	19,560	C
Western Baptist College	OR	21,808	C
Western New Mexico Univ	NM	7,233	LC
Western Oregon Univ	OR	10,295	C
Widener Univ	PA	27,275	C
Willamette Univ	OR	35,416	VC+
Wofford College	SC	30,935	HC
Worcester Polytechnic Inst	MA	40,450	VC+
Wright State Univ	OH	13,616	LC
Yale Univ	CT	41,000	MC
York College of Pennsylvania	PA	16,550	VC

HUMANITIES AND SOCIAL SCIENCE

School	ST	$IS	SR
Antioch College	OH	33,700	C
Bennington College	VT	41,890	HC
Franciscan Univ of Steubenville	OH	20,300	VC
Lock Haven Univ of Pennsylvania	PA	12,098	LC
Montana Tech of The Univ of Montana	MT	10,434	C
SUNY/Empire State College	NY	4,575	SP
Texas A&M Univ at Galveston	TX	10,000	C+
Univ of Calif at Riverside	CA	16,625	C
Univ of Mass Dartmouth	MA	15,985	C

HYDROGEOLOGY

School	ST	$IS	SR
Rensselaer Polytechnic Inst	NY	41,288	HC+
Western Mich Univ	MI	13,299	C

HYDROLOGY

School	ST	$IS	SR
Indiana Univ Bloomington	IN	13,356	VC
Texas A&M Univ at Galveston	TX	10,000	C+
Univ of Arizona	AZ	11,958	VC
Univ of at Calif Davis	CA	15,010	VC
Univ of Calif at Santa Barbara	CA	11,800	VC
Univ of Nevada/Reno	NV	12,155	NC

IBERIAN STUDIES

School	ST	$IS	SR
Univ of PR/Arecibo	PR	8,327	

ILLUSTRATION

School	ST	$IS	SR
Arcadia Univ	PA	33,570	VC
Art Academy of Cincinnati	OH	18,100	SP
Art Center College of Design	CA	26,370	SP
Art Inst of Boston at Lesley Univ	MA	28,200	SP
Atlanta College of Art	GA	18,630	SP
Bennington College	VT	41,890	HC
Brigham Young Univ	UT	9,200	VC
Calif College of the Arts	CA	34,325	SP
Cal State, Fullerton	CA	10,990	C
Cleveland Inst of Art	OH	34,109	SP
College for Creative Studies	MI	24,000	SP
College of Visual Arts	MN	18,040	SP
Columbus College of Art and Design	OH	24,500	SP
Fashion Inst of Technology/ SUNY	NY	11,600	C+
Indiana Wesleyan Univ	IN	22,074	C+
John Brown Univ	AR	20,910	VC
Kendall College of Art and Design of Ferris State Univ	MI	11,870	SP
Laguna College of Art and Design	CA	17,600	SP
Lawrence Tech Univ	MI	25,475	VC
Lewis Univ	IL	23,050	C+
Maryland Inst College of Art	MD	34,450	SP
Mass College of Art	MA	16,650	SP
Milwaukee Inst of Art and Design	WI	28,700	SP
Minneapolis College of Art and Design	MN	31,110	SP
Montserrat College of Art	MA	25,929	SP
Moore College of Art and Design	PA	27,200	SP
Olivet College	MI	19,984	C+
Otis College of Art and Design	CA	27,546	SP
Pacific Northwest College of Art	OR	17,296	SP
Parsons School of Design	NY	32,242	SP
Rhode Island School of Design	RI	38,130	SP
Ringling School of Art and Design	FL	31,013	SP
Rivier College	NH	26,600	C
Rochester Inst of Technology	NY	32,070	VC+
St. John's Univ	NY	34,370	C
Savannah College of Art and Design	GA	30,800	SP
School of Visual Arts	NY	32,580	SP
Syracuse Univ	NY	38,655	HC
Univ of Bridgeport	CT	29,595	LC
Univ of Findlay	OH	29,238	C
Univ of Georgia	GA	11,004	HC
Univ of Hartford	CT	34,044	C
Univ of Mass Dartmouth	MA	15,985	C
Univ of San Francisco	CA	37,560	VC
Univ of the Arts	PA	32,330	SP
Washington Univ in St. Louis	MO	42,106	MC
Western Conn State Univ	CT	12,993	C

INDUSTRIAL ADMINISTRATION/ MANAGEMENT

School	ST	$IS	SR
Alcorn State Univ	MS	8,190	LC
Aurora Univ	IL	20,645	C
Clarion Univ of Pennsylvania	PA	11,844	C
Clemson Univ	SC	13,366	HC
Colo State Univ-Pueblo	CO	7,821	LC
David N. Myers College	OH	9,475	C
Farmingdale SUNY	NY	13,521	C
Gardner-Webb Univ	NC	21,500	C
Georgia Southern Univ	GA	9,762	C
Grove City College	PA	15,784	HC+
Indiana Univ South Bend	IN	4,989	LC
Inter American Univ of PR/ Bayamon Univ College	PR	3,522	
Lawrence Tech Univ	MI	25,475	VC
LeTourneau Univ	TX	21,200	C
Limestone College	SC	19,840	C
Metropolitan State College of Denver	CO	2,338	LC
Millikin Univ	IL	25,590	C
Missouri State Univ	MO	10,748	C+
Oregon Inst of Technology	OR	8,718	C
Penn State Univ/Univ Park Campus	PA	18,038	HC
Purdue Univ/West Lafayette	IN	13,458	VC
Saginaw Valley State Univ	MI	11,432	C
St. Augustine's College	NC	14,000	LC
San Francisco State Univ	CA	13,000	C
S Dak State Univ	SD	9,815	C
Southeast Missouri State Univ	MO	10,596	C
Southwestern Okla State Univ	OK	4,801	C
Tri-State Univ-Main Campus	IN	26,200	C
Universidad Politecnica de PR	PR	5,400	
Univ of Alabama	AL	9,888	C
Univ of Alabama at Birmingham	AL	13,716	C
Univ of Arkansas at Little Rock	AR	7,230	NC
Univ of Cincinnati	OH	17,682	C
Univ of Houston	TX	7,000	C
Univ of Illinois at Urbana- Champaign	IL	15,800	HC+
Univ of Iowa	IA	12,172	VC
Univ of Mass Lowell	MA	14,327	VC
Univ of Minn/Crookston	MN	13,157	LC
Univ of N Car at Asheville	NC	9,237	VC
Univ of N Car at Chapel Hill	NC	11,129	MC
Univ of N Car at Charlotte	NC	9,101	C
Univ of North Texas	TX	7,800	C
Univ of Wisc/Milwaukee	WI	9,427	LC
Univ of Wisc/Parkside	WI	10,181	LC
Univ of Wisc/Stout	WI	11,164	C
Univ of Wyoming	WY	9,666	C
Washington and Jefferson College	PA	33,490	VC
Wentworth Inst of Technology	MA	27,500	C
West Virginia Univ Inst of Technology	WV	8,788	NC
William Penn Univ	IA	17,685	LC
Youngstown State Univ	OH	12,613	NC

INDUSTRIAL AND ORGANIZATIONAL PSYCHOLOGY

School	ST	$IS	SR
Albertus Magnus College	CT	25,336	C
Averett Univ	VA	24,920	C
CUNY/Baruch College	NY	4,320	VC+
High Point Univ	NC	25,720	C
Ithaca College	NY	35,144	VC
Lincoln Univ	PA	13,658	C+
Marywood Univ	PA	30,680	C
Moravian College	PA	28,950	C
Northwest Missouri State Univ	MO	10,000	C
Ohio State Univ	OH	15,357	HC
Oregon Inst of Technology	OR	8,718	C
Point Loma Nazarene Univ	CA	27,610	VC
St. Joseph's Univ	PA	37,428	VC
Univ of PR/Arecibo	PR	8,327	
Washington Univ in St. Louis	MO	42,106	MC

INDUSTRIAL ARTS EDUCATION

School	ST	$IS	SR
Alabama A&M Univ	AL	8,890	LC
Alcorn State Univ	MS	8,190	LC
Appalachian State Univ	NC	8,900	VC
Auburn Univ	AL	12,230	VC
Ball State Univ	IN	13,138	C

ST = STATE · **$IS** = IN-STATE COSTS · **SR** = SELECTOR RATING

School	ST	$IS	SR
Bemidji State Univ	MN	11,180	LC
Calif Polytechnic State Univ	CA	12,390	VC
Cal State, Los Angeles	CA	5,900	C
Central Missouri State Univ	MO	10,000	C
Central Washington Univ	WA	11,730	C
Chicago State Univ	IL	10,915	C+
Clemson Univ	SC	13,366	HC
Concordia Univ Nebr	NE	20,500	C+
Eastern Kentucky Univ	KY	7,725	C
Eastern Mich Univ	MI	12,897	C
Elizabeth City State Univ	NC	5,700	LC
Fitchburg State College	MA	11,276	C
Florida A&M Univ	FL	8,344	C
Grambling State Univ	LA	6,538	NC
Humboldt State Univ	CA	11,176	C
Indiana State Univ	IN	11,604	C
Iowa State Univ	IA	11,831	VC
Jackson State Univ	MS	8,500	C
Kean Univ	NJ	15,880	C
Langston Univ	OK	2,308	LC
Minn State Univ, Mankato	MN	10,276	VC
Minn State Univ, Moorhead	MN	7,000	LC
Missouri State Univ	MO	10,748	C+
Montana State Univ-Northern	MT	10,000	NC
Morehead State Univ	KY	9,150	C
Murray State Univ	KY	8,900	VC
N Car Agricultural and Technical State Univ	NC	8,000	LC
N Car State Univ	NC	11,824	HC
Northeastern State Univ	OK	5,896	LC
Northern Arizona Univ	AZ	10,353	C
Northern Kentucky Univ	KY	6,670	NC
Northern Mich Univ	MI	12,340	VC
Old Dominion Univ	VA	11,907	C
Penn State Univ/Univ Park Campus	PA	18,038	HC
Purdue Univ/West Lafayette	IN	13,458	VC
Rhode Island College	RI	11,570	C
St. Cloud State Univ	MN	10,010	C
San Francisco State Univ	CA	13,000	C
S Car State Univ	SC	6,700	LC
Southeast Missouri State Univ	MO	10,596	C
Southwestern Okla State Univ	OK	4,801	C
SUNY/College at Buffalo	NY	11,903	C+
Tarleton State Univ	TX	8,952	C
Temple Univ	PA	17,438	C
Texas A&M Univ at Commerce	TX	9,020	C
Univ of Arkansas at Pine Bluff	AR	8,300	C
Univ of Central Okla	OK	8,094	C
Univ of Cincinnati	OH	17,682	C
Univ of Idaho	ID	9,310	NC
Univ of Louisiana at Lafayette	LA	5,830	C
Univ of Maryland/Eastern Shore	MD	11,210	C
Univ of Minn/Twin Cities	MN	13,165	HC
Univ of Montana--Western	MT	8,406	NC
Univ of Nebr at Lincoln	NE	11,401	VC
Univ of Southern Miss	MS	10,112	C
Univ of Wyoming	WY	9,666	C
Utah State Univ	UT	8,002	VC
Wayne State College	NE	8,033	NC
Western Illinois Univ	IL	13,042	C

INDUSTRIAL DESIGN

School	ST	$IS	SR
Arizona State Univ-Tempe	AZ	11,174	C
Art Center College of Design	CA	26,370	SP
Auburn Univ	AL	12,230	VC
Berea College	KY	5,496	VC+
Brigham Young Univ	UT	9,200	VC
Calif College of the Arts	CA	34,325	SP
Cleveland Inst of Art	OH	34,109	SP
College for Creative Studies	MI	24,000	SP
Columbus College of Art and Design	OH	24,500	SP
Escuela de Artes Plasticas de PR	PR	2,372	
Georgia Inst of Technology	GA	11,450	HC+
Kean Univ	NJ	15,880	C
Kendall College of Art and Design of Ferris State Univ	MI	11,870	SP
Mass College of Art	MA	16,650	SP
Metropolitan State College of Denver	CO	2,338	LC
Milwaukee Inst of Art and Design	WI	28,700	SP
N Car State Univ	NC	11,824	HC
Ohio State Univ	OH	15,357	HC
Philadelphia Univ	PA	30,006	C
Pratt Inst	NY	36,156	SP
Purdue Univ/West Lafayette	IN	13,458	VC
Rhode Island School of Design	RI	38,130	SP
Rochester Inst of Technology	NY	32,070	VC+
Savannah College of Art and Design	GA	30,800	SP
Syracuse Univ	NY	38,655	HC
Univ of Bridgeport	CT	29,595	LC
Univ of Illinois at Chicago	IL	16,256	VC
Univ of Illinois at Urbana-Champaign	IL	15,800	HC+
Univ of Kansas	KS	10,915	VC
Univ of Mich/Ann Arbor	MI	16,587	HC+
Univ of the Arts	PA	32,330	SP
Virginia Polytechnic Inst and State Univ	VA	10,834	VC
Wentworth Inst of Technology	MA	27,500	C
Western Mich Univ	MI	13,299	C

INDUSTRIAL ENGINEERING

School	ST	$IS	SR
Arizona State Univ-Tempe	AZ	11,174	C
Bradley Univ	IL	25,280	VC
Calif Polytechnic State Univ	CA	12,390	VC
Calif State Polytechnic Univ, Pomona	CA	18,053	C+
Cal State East Bay	CA	10,856	LC
Cal State, Fresno	CA	10,037	LC
Clemson Univ	SC	13,366	HC
Cleveland State Univ	OH	10,798	NC
Colo State Univ-Pueblo	CO	7,821	LC
Elizabethtown College	PA	32,100	VC
Florida A&M Univ	FL	8,344	C
Florida International Univ	FL	9,215	VC
Florida State Univ	FL	9,028	HC
Georgia Inst of Technology	GA	11,450	HC+
Hofstra Univ	NY	32,630	VC
Indiana Inst of Technology	IN	23,430	C
Inter American Univ of PR/Bayamon Univ College	PR	3,522	
Johns Hopkins Univ	MD	42,044	MC
Kansas State Univ	KS	10,516	VC
Kent State Univ	OH	14,594	C
Kettering Univ	MI	29,338	HC
Lamar Univ	TX	6,820	LC
Lehigh Univ	PA	42,690	HC+
Louisiana State Univ and A&M College	LA	10,749	VC
Louisiana Tech Univ	LA	7,370	C
Mass Maritime Academy	MA	11,571	C
Mercer Univ	GA	27,525	VC+
Milwaukee School of Engineering	WI	29,847	VC+
Miss State Univ	MS	9,577	C
Montana State Univ-Bozeman	MT	1,137	C
New Jersey Inst of Technology	NJ	16,396	VC
New Mexico State Univ	NM	9,250	C
New York Inst of Technology	NY	28,126	VC
N Car Agricultural and Technical State Univ	NC	8,000	LC
N Car State Univ	NC	11,824	HC
N Dak State Univ	ND	8,500	C
Northeastern Univ	MA	35,742	HC
Northern Illinois Univ	IL	13,178	C
Northwestern Univ	IL	37,595	MC
Ohio State Univ	OH	15,357	HC
Ohio Univ	OH	15,921	C
Okla State Univ	OK	10,213	VC
Penn State Univ/Univ Park Campus	PA	18,038	HC
Philadelphia Univ	PA	30,006	C
Purdue Univ/West Lafayette	IN	13,458	VC
Rensselaer Polytechnic Inst	NY	41,288	HC+
Rochester Inst of Technology	NY	32,070	VC+
Rutgers, The State Univ of New Jersey/New Brunswick/Piscataway Campus	NJ	15,810	HC
St. Ambrose Univ	IA	25,495	C
St. Augustine's College	NC	14,000	LC
St. Mary's Univ of San Antonio	TX	22,444	C
San Jose State Univ	CA	11,707	C
S Dak School of Mines and Technology	SD	7,624	C+
Southern Illinois Univ Edwardsville	IL	11,022	C
Stanford Univ	CA	41,557	MC
SUNY/Inst of Technology	NY	12,575	VC
SUNY/Univ at Binghamton	NY	13,988	HC
SUNY/Univ at Buffalo	NY	13,694	VC
Tenn Tech Univ	TN	10,044	C
Texas Tech Univ	TX	13,026	VC
Universidad Politecnica de PR	PR	5,400	
Univ of Alabama	AL	9,888	C
Univ of Alabama in Huntsville	AL	9,516	VC
Univ of Arizona	AZ	11,958	VC
Univ of Arkansas	AR	11,859	VC
Univ of Calif at Berkeley	CA	18,141	HC+
Univ of Houston	TX	7,000	C
Univ of Illinois at Urbana-Champaign	IL	15,800	HC+
Univ of Iowa	IA	12,172	VC
Univ of Louisiana at Lafayette	LA	5,830	C
Univ of Louisville	KY	10,400	VC
Univ of Mass Amherst	MA	15,973	C+
Univ of Memphis	TN	11,153	C
Univ of Miami	FL	38,397	MC
Univ of Mich/Ann Arbor	MI	16,587	HC+
Univ of Mich/Dearborn	MI	7,000	VC
Univ of Minn/Duluth	MN	13,974	C
Univ of Minn/Twin Cities	MN	13,165	HC
Univ of Missouri/Columbia	MO	13,500	VC
Univ of Missouri/Rolla	MO	13,332	HC
Univ of Nebr at Lincoln	NE	11,401	VC
Univ of New Haven	CT	31,794	C
Univ of Okla	OK	10,769	VC+
Univ of Pittsburgh at Pittsburgh	PA	18,866	HC
Univ of PR/Mayaguez	PR	1,250	
Univ of Rhode Island	RI	15,398	C
Univ of San Diego	CA	40,620	HC
Univ of South Florida	FL	10,284	VC
Univ of Southern Calif	CA	41,618	MC
Univ of Tenn at Knoxville	TN	11,720	C
Univ of Toledo	OH	15,806	NC
Univ of Wisc/Madison	WI	13,117	HC
Univ of Wisc/Milwaukee	WI	9,427	LC
Univ of Wisc/Platteville	WI	9,779	NC
Utah State Univ	UT	8,002	VC
Virginia Polytechnic Inst and State Univ	VA	10,834	VC
Western Mich Univ	MI	13,299	C
Western New England College	MA	32,054	C
Wichita State Univ	KS	8,500	C
Worcester Polytechnic Inst	MA	40,450	VC+
Youngstown State Univ	OH	12,613	NC

INDUSTRIAL ENGINEERING TECHNOLOGY

School	ST	$IS	SR
Alabama A&M Univ	AL	8,890	LC
Appalachian State Univ	NC	8,000	VC
Bemidji State Univ	MN	11,180	LC
Berea College	KY	5,496	VC+
Cal State, Chico	CA	11,395	C
Cal State, Fresno	CA	10,037	LC
Cal State, Los Angeles	CA	5,900	C
Calif Univ of Pennsylvania	PA	14,217	C
Caribbean Univ	PR	3,000	
Central Conn State Univ	CT	13,620	C
Central Missouri State Univ	MO	10,000	C
Central Washington Univ	WA	11,730	C
Chadron State College	NE	6,350	NC
Columbia Univ/Fu Foundation School of Engineering and Applied Science	NY	42,584	MC
East Carolina Univ	NC	10,000	C
Eastern Illinois Univ	IL	12,569	C
Elizabeth City State Univ	NC	5,700	C
Farmingdale SUNY	NY	13,521	C
Fitchburg State College	MA	11,276	C
Grand Valley State Univ	MI	12,000	VC
Humboldt State Univ	CA	11,176	C
Illinois State Univ	IL	12,839	C+
Indiana State Univ	IN	11,604	C
Indiana Univ-Purdue Univ Fort Wayne	IN	5,067	LC
Iowa State Univ	IA	11,831	VC
Kean Univ	NJ	15,880	C
Kent State Univ	OH	14,594	C
Lamar Univ	TX	6,820	LC
Langston Univ	OK	2,308	LC
Marquette Univ	WI	31,066	HC
McPherson College	KS	21,010	C
Metropolitan State College of Denver	CO	2,338	LC
Middle Tenn State Univ	TN	8,540	C
Millersville Univ of Pennsylvania	PA	12,113	C
Miss State Univ	MS	9,577	C
Miss Valley State Univ	MS	7,970	C
Morehead State Univ	KY	9,150	C
Morgan State Univ	MD	12,080	C
Northern Kentucky Univ	KY	6,670	NC
Northern Mich Univ	MI	12,340	VC
Northwestern State Univ of Louisiana	LA	7,144	C
Okla Panhandle State Univ	OK	7,635	NC
Oregon State Univ	OR	11,055	C
Prairie View A&M Univ	TX	11,110	LC
Purdue Univ/Calumet	IN	10,891	LC
Purdue Univ/West Lafayette	IN	13,458	VC
Southeast Missouri State Univ	MO	10,596	C
Southeastern Louisiana Univ	LA	8,521	LC
Southern Illinois Univ Carbondale	IL	12,391	C
Southern Polytechnic State Univ	GA	7,640	VC
Southwestern Okla State Univ	OK	4,801	C
SUNY/College at Buffalo	NY	11,903	C+
Sul Ross State Univ	TX	6,600	LC
Tarleton State Univ	TX	8,952	C
Tenn Tech Univ	TN	10,044	C
Texas A&M Univ	TX	13,351	HC
Texas A&M Univ at Kingsville	TX	6,800	LC
Texas Southern Univ	TX	9,828	C
Texas State Univ - San Marcos	TX	10,862	C
Univ of Arkansas at Pine Bluff	AR	8,300	C
Univ of Central Florida	FL	10,739	VC
Univ of Cincinnati	OH	17,682	C
Univ of Dayton	OH	28,826	VC
Univ of Florida	FL	9,354	HC
Univ of Houston	TX	7,000	C
Univ of Illinois at Chicago	IL	16,256	VC
Univ of Mass Lowell	MA	14,327	VC
Univ of Nebr at Lincoln	NE	11,401	VC
Univ of New Haven	CT	31,794	C
Univ of N Dak	ND	10,114	VC
Univ of Northern Iowa	IA	11,133	C
Univ of Rio Grande	OH	8,728	NC
Univ of Southern Maine	ME	12,614	C
Univ of Texas at Arlington	TX	7,195	LC
Univ of Texas at El Paso	TX	8,764	NC
Univ of West Alabama	AL	7,611	C
Univ of Wisc/Platteville	WI	9,779	NC
Univ of Wisc/Stout	WI	11,164	C
Utah State Univ	UT	8,002	VC
Wayne State Univ	MI	11,805	C
West Virginia Univ Inst of Technology	WV	8,788	NC
Western Carolina Univ	NC	7,000	C
Western Illinois Univ	IL	13,042	C
Western Kentucky Univ	KY	10,192	C
Western Mich Univ	MI	13,299	C
William Penn Univ	IA	17,685	LC

INDUSTRIAL HYGIENE

School	ST	$IS	SR
Clarkson Univ	NY	34,930	VC
Oakland Univ	MI	11,936	C
St. Augustine's College	NC	14,000	LC
South Univ	GA		LC
Univ of Central Okla	OK	8,094	C
Univ of North Alabama	AL	8,992	C

INFORMATION SCIENCES AND SYSTEMS

School	ST	$IS	SR
Abilene Christian Univ	TX	20,830	C
Alabama State Univ	AL	7,658	C
Albany State Univ	GA	5,770	C+
Albright College	PA	33,920	C
Alvernia College	PA	26,388	C
Alverno College	WI	21,088	C
American InterContinental Univ	GA	12,100	NC
Andrews Univ	MI	21,786	C
Appalachian State Univ	NC	8,000	VC
Aquinas College	MI	23,750	C
Arizona State Univ-Tempe	AZ	11,174	C
Armstrong Atlantic State Univ	GA	7,394	C
Atlantic Union College	MA	17,600	LC
Auburn Univ Montgomery	AL	9,530	NC
Averett Univ	VA	24,920	C
Avila Univ	MO	22,100	C
Azusa Pacific Univ	CA	28,546	VC
Baker Univ	KS	22,190	C
Baldwin-Wallace College	OH	27,256	VC
Barton College	NC	22,316	C
Baylor Univ	TX	27,555	HC
Belhaven College	MS	19,530	NC
Bellarmine Univ	KY	27,650	C+
Bellevue Univ	NE	4,440	NC
Belmont Abbey College	NC	25,314	C
Bentley College	MA	38,784	HC
Bethune-Cookman College	FL	17,922	LC
Biola Univ	CA	29,372	VC
Bloomfield College	NJ	22,500	LC
Bluffton College	OH	26,110	C
Boise State Univ	ID	9,438	LC
Boston College	MA	41,608	MC
Bowling Green State Univ	OH	14,994	C
Bradley Univ	IL	25,280	VC
Briar Cliff Univ	IA	23,550	LC
Bridgewater College	VA	27,790	C
Brigham Young Univ	UT	9,200	VC
Brigham Young Univ/Hawaii	HI	7,740	HC+
Bryant College	RI	34,330	VC
Cabrini College	PA	33,340	C
Caldwell College	NJ	26,450	LC
Calif Lutheran Univ	CA	27,800	C
Calif State Polytechnic Univ, Pomona	CA	18,053	C+
Cal State, Chico	CA	11,395	C
Cal State, Los Angeles	CA	5,900	C
Cal State, Stanislaus	CA	11,283	C
Calif Univ of Pennsylvania	PA	14,217	C
Calumet College of St. Joseph	IN	9,500	LC
Calvin College	MI	25,735	NC
Campbell Univ	NC	21,137	VC
Campbellsville Univ	KY	21,328	C
Carlow Univ	PA	24,313	C
Carnegie Mellon Univ	PA	32,700	MC
Carroll College	WI	24,860	C

School	ST	$IS	SR
Catawba College	NC	25,000	C
Cedar Crest College	PA	30,615	C
Cedarville Univ	OH	21,904	VC
Central Missouri State Univ	MO	10,000	C
Central Washington Univ	WA	11,730	C
Chaminade Univ of Honolulu	HI	23,320	VC
Champlain College	VT	24,605	C
Chapman Univ	CA	37,550	VC
Chicago State Univ	IL	10,915	C+
Christian Brothers Univ	TN	24,650	VC
Christopher Newport Univ	VA	13,326	VC
CUNY/Baruch College	NY	4,320	VC+
CUNY/Brooklyn College	NY	4,377	C+
CUNY/College of Staten Island	NY	4,328	NC
CUNY/John Jay College of Criminal Justice	NY	5,000	C
CUNY/New York City College of Technology	NY	4,269	NC
CUNY/York College	NY	4,242	NC
Clarion Univ of Pennsylvania	PA	11,844	C
Clarke College	IA	25,390	C
Clarkson Univ	NY	34,930	VC
Clayton College and State Univ	GA	2,445	LC
Cleary College	MI	11,000	C
Clemson Univ	SC	13,366	HC
Cleveland State Univ	OH	10,798	NC
College Misericordia	PA	27,950	C
College of Charleston	SC	13,616	VC
College of Notre Dame of Maryland	MD	27,700	C
College of St. Catherine	MN	27,505	VC
College of St. Rose	NY	25,684	C
College of the Ozarks	MO	4,130	VC+
Colo State Univ-Fort Collins	CO	10,878	C+
Colo State Univ-Pueblo	CO	7,821	C
Colo Technical Univ	CO	9,500	LC
Columbia College	MO	16,900	C
Columbia College	SC	24,982	LC
Columbia Union College	MD	23,536	LC
Concord College	WV	9,708	C
Concordia Univ, Ann Arbor	MI	25,153	C+
Cornell Univ	NY	41,717	MC
Covenant College	GA	26,460	VC+
Culver-Stockton College	MO	20,625	C
Dakota State Univ	SD	7,466	C
Daniel Webster College	NH	24,870	C
Davenport Univ	MI	15,205	NC
David N. Myers College	OH	9,475	C
Defiance College	OH	24,790	C
Delta State Univ	MS	7,709	C
DePaul Univ	IL	29,835	VC
DeVry College of Technology/North Brunswick	NJ	10,500	LC
DeVry/New York	NY	12,000	LC
DeVry Univ/Addison (DuPage County)	IL	10,800	LC
DeVry Univ/Alpharetta	GA	10,675	LC
DeVry Univ/Chicago	IL	10,800	LC
DeVry Univ/Colo Springs	CO	12,000	LC
DeVry Univ/Columbus	OH	11,000	LC
DeVry Univ/Crystal City	VA	12,000	C
DeVry Univ/Dallas	TX	10,700	LC
DeVry Univ/Decatur	GA	10,680	LC
DeVry Univ/Fort Washington	PA	12,000	LC
DeVry Univ/Fremont	CA	13,060	LC
DeVry Univ/Kansas City	MO	10,670	LC
DeVry Univ/Long Beach	CA	12,450	LC
DeVry Univ/Miramar	FL	12,000	LC
DeVry Univ/Orlando	FL	12,000	LC
DeVry Univ/Phoenix	AZ	11,790	LC
DeVry Univ/Pomona	CA	12,450	LC
DeVry Univ/Seattle	WA	12,000	LC
DeVry Univ/Tinley Park	IL	12,000	LC
DeVry Univ/West Hills	CA	12,450	LC
DeVry Univ/Westminster	CO	12,000	LC
Dominican College	NY	26,630	LC
Dominican Univ	IL	26,370	C
Dordt College	IA	20,325	VC
Dowling College	NY	22,110	LC
Drake Univ	IA	27,632	VC+
Drexel Univ	PA	27,700	VC
Drury Univ	MO	20,117	VC
D'Youville College	NY	23,660	C
East Tenn State Univ	TN	8,497	C
East Texas Baptist Univ	TX	16,713	C
Eastern Conn State Univ	CT	13,554	C
Eastern Mich Univ	MI	12,897	C
Eastern New Mexico Univ	NM	7,264	C
Eastern Washington Univ	WA	10,608	C
Edgewood College	WI	22,862	C
Elizabethtown College	PA	32,100	VC
Elmhurst College	IL	24,845	C
Elon Univ	NC	25,371	HC
Emporia State Univ	KS	8,093	C
Excelsior College	NY	995	SP
Fairfield Univ	CT	39,835	HC
Fairleigh Dickinson Univ/Metropolitan Campus	NJ	28,590	C
Ferrum College	VA	24,290	LC
Florida Atlantic Univ	FL	11,221	C
Florida Gulf Coast Univ	FL	10,833	C
Florida Inst of Technology	FL	29,720	VC
Florida International Univ	FL	9,215	VC
Florida Southern College	FL	25,965	C
Florida State Univ	FL	9,028	HC
Fontbonne Univ	MO	23,308	C
Fordham Univ	NY	36,000	HC
Fort Hays State Univ	KS	7,638	C
Fort Lewis College	CO	11,852	C
Fort Valley State Univ	GA	6,975	C
Francis Marion Univ	SC	11,114	C
Franciscan Univ of Steubenville	OH	20,300	VC
Franklin College	IN		
Franklin Pierce College	NH	31,700	C
Freed-Hardeman Univ	TN	16,370	NC
Friends Univ	KS	16,250	LC
Gardner-Webb Univ	NC	21,500	C
George Fox Univ	OR	28,490	C
George Mason Univ	VA	10,850	VC
George Washington Univ	DC	48,820	MC
Georgia College and State Univ	GA	11,020	C
Georgia Southern Univ	GA	9,762	C
Glenville State College	WV	8,778	NC
Goshen College	IN	22,850	VC
Graceland Univ	IA	19,700	C
Grambling State Univ	LA	6,538	NC
Grand View College	IA	21,482	C
Granite State College	NH	4,800	SP
Guilford College	NC	28,160	C+
Gwynedd-Mercy College	PA	26,080	C
Hampton Univ	VA	19,468	C+
Hannibal-LaGrange College	MO	16,390	C
Harding Univ	AR	16,512	VC
Hartwick College	NY	36,065	C+
Haverford College	PA	41,600	MC
Heidelberg College	OH	23,242	C
High Point Univ	NC	25,720	C
Holy Family Univ	PA	25,740	C
Houghton College	NY	25,980	VC+
Houston Baptist Univ	TX	18,660	C
Howard Univ	DC	18,481	C+
Humboldt State Univ	CA	11,176	C
Huntington Univ	IN	24,830	C
Illinois College	IL	21,900	C+
Illinois Inst of Technology	IL	26,465	HC+
Illinois State Univ	IL	12,839	C+
Immaculata Univ	PA	25,350	C
Indiana Inst of Technology	IN	23,430	C
Indiana Univ Bloomington	IN	13,356	VC
Indiana Univ East	IN	4,806	LC
Indiana Univ Kokomo	IN	4,835	LC
Indiana Univ Northwest	IN	4,902	LC
Indiana Univ South Bend	IN	4,989	LC
Indiana Univ-Purdue Univ Fort Wayne	IN	5,067	LC
Indiana Univ-Purdue Univ Indianapolis	IN	10,959	C
Indiana Wesleyan Univ	IN	22,074	C+
International College	FL	9,500	NC
Ithaca College	NY	35,144	VC
Jacksonville Univ	FL	24,040	C
James Madison Univ	VA	12,010	VC
Jamestown College	ND	14,130	VC
Johnson and Wales Univ/Providence Campus	RI	28,126	LC
Johnson State College	VT	11,830	C
Juniata College	PA	33,130	VC
Kansas State Univ	KS	10,516	VC
Kennesaw State Univ	GA	12,152	C
Kent State Univ	OH	14,594	C
Keystone College	PA	22,810	LC
King's College	PA	29,810	C
La Roche College	PA	24,724	LC
La Salle Univ	PA	34,950	C
La Sierra Univ	CA	24,327	C+
Lamar Univ	TX	6,820	LC
Lawrence Tech Univ	MI	25,475	VC
Le Moyne College	NY	29,570	VC
Lehigh Univ	PA	42,690	HC+
Limestone College	SC	19,840	C
Lincoln Memorial Univ	TN	18,144	C
Lincoln Univ	MO	8,000	NC
Lock Haven Univ of Pennsylvania	PA	12,098	LC
LIU/Brooklyn Campus	NY	25,000	C
LIU/C.W. Post Campus	NY	28,282	C
Louisiana State Univ and A&M College	LA	10,749	VC
Loyola Univ New Orleans	LA	31,050	VC+
Lubbock Christian Univ	TX	16,960	C
Madonna Univ	MI	16,068	VC
Manhattan College	NY	29,000	VC
Mansfield Univ	PA	11,300	C
Marian College of Fond du Lac	WI	21,775	LC
Marietta College	OH	29,327	C
Marist College	NY	30,566	VC
Marquette Univ	WI	31,066	HC
Marshall Univ	WV	9,116	C
Marygrove College	MI	19,310	C+
Marymount Manhattan College	NY	30,049	VC
Marymount Univ	VA	25,934	C
Maryville Univ of St. Louis	MO	23,000	VC
Marywood Univ	PA	30,680	C
Master's College and Seminary	CA	25,850	VC
McKendree College	IL	24,800	VC
McMurry Univ	TX	18,100	LC
McNeese State Univ	LA	5,270	LC
Medaille College	NY	21,000	C
Mercy College	NY	20,000	NC
Meredith College	NC	25,600	C
Metropolitan State College of Denver	CO	2,338	LC
Metropolitan State Univ	MN	4,682	SP
Mich State Univ	MI	13,689	VC
Middle Tenn State Univ	TN	8,540	C
Midwestern State Univ	TX	9,381	LC
Milligan College	TN	21,990	VC
Minn State Univ, Mankato	MN	10,276	LC
Miss State Univ	MS	9,577	C
Missouri Baptist Univ	MO	19,640	C
Missouri Southern State Univ	MO	8,396	NC
Missouri State Univ	MO	10,748	C+
Missouri Valley College	MO	18,500	C
Missouri Western State Univ	MO	9,534	NC
Molloy College	NY	16,510	C
Monroe College	NY	15,960	NC
Montana State Univ-Billings	MT	8,906	C
Montclair State Univ	NJ	16,327	C
Morgan State Univ	MD	12,080	C
Mount Aloysius College	PA	20,900	C
Mount Mercy College	IA	23,670	C
Mount Olive College	NC	16,000	LC
Mount St. Mary College	NY	25,250	C
Mount St. Mary's Univ	MD	30,930	C
Mount Union College	OH	25,840	C
Murray State Univ	KY	8,900	VC
National American Univ	SD	14,820	NC
National Univ	CA	8,412	SP
National-Louis Univ	IL	16,915	LC
Nazareth College of Rochester	NY	28,175	VC
Nebr Wesleyan Univ	NE	23,415	C+
New Jersey Inst of Technology	NJ	16,396	VC
New Mexico Inst of Mining and Technology	NM	8,510	VC+
New Mexico State Univ	NM	9,250	C
New York Univ	NY	43,170	MC
Newman Univ	KS	21,106	C
Niagara Univ	NY	28,250	C
Nicholls State Univ	LA	6,500	NC
N Car Wesleyan College	NC	22,670	C
Northeastern State Univ	OK	5,896	NC
Northeastern Univ	MA	35,742	HC
Northern Arizona Univ	AZ	10,353	C
Northern Illinois Univ	IL	13,178	C
Northern Kentucky Univ	KY	6,670	NC
Northern Mich Univ	MI	12,340	LC
Northland College	WI	26,680	C+
Northwest Missouri State Univ	MO	10,000	C
Northwestern College of Iowa	IA	22,174	C+
Northwestern State Univ of Louisiana	LA	7,144	C
Northwestern Univ	IL	37,595	MC
Norwich Univ	VT	28,212	C
Notre Dame College	OH	20,425	C
Notre Dame de Namur Univ	CA	32,790	C
Nova Southeastern Univ	FL	24,320	C
Oakland Univ	MI	11,936	C
Oakwood College	AL	14,904	C
Ohio Dominican Univ	OH	25,954	C
Ohio State Univ	OH	15,357	HC
Okla Baptist Univ	OK	17,986	VC
Okla Christian Univ	OK	18,992	NC
Okla Panhandle State Univ	OK	7,635	NC
Old Dominion Univ	VA	11,907	C
Ottawa Univ	KS	12,000	LC
Our Lady of the Lake Univ of San Antonio	TX	22,430	LC
Pace Univ	NY	30,000	VC
Park Univ	MO	11,592	C
Peirce College	PA	12,760	NC
Pfeiffer Univ	NC	21,900	C
Pittsburg State Univ	KS	8,112	C
Plymouth State Univ	NH	12,248	LC
Point Park Univ	PA	24,160	C
Polytechnic Univ/Brooklyn	NY	37,150	VC
Portland State Univ	OR	12,453	C
Purdue Univ/Calumet	IN	10,891	LC
Purdue Univ/West Lafayette	IN	13,458	VC
Quincy Univ	IL	24,920	C
Radford Univ	VA	13,145	C
Ramapo College of New Jersey	NJ	16,630	C
Regis College	MA	31,350	LC
Rhode Island College	RI	11,570	C
Richard Stockton College of New Jersey	NJ	14,000	VC
Roanoke College	VA	30,748	VC
Robert Morris Univ	PA	22,822	C
Rochester Inst of Technology	NY	32,070	VC+
Roger Williams Univ	RI	30,500	C
Roosevelt Univ	IL	22,605	VC
Rutgers, The State Univ of New Jersey/New Brunswick/Piscataway Campus	NJ	15,810	HC
Rutgers, The State Univ of New Jersey/Newark Campus	NJ	15,640	VC
Saginaw Valley State Univ	MI	11,432	C
St. Augustine's College	NC	14,000	LC
St. Edward's Univ	TX	23,560	C
St. Francis College	NY	19,974	LC
St. John's Univ	NY	34,370	C
St. Joseph's College, New York, Brooklyn Campus	NY	12,206	C
St. Joseph's College, New York, Suffolk Campus	NY	12,000	C
St. Joseph's Univ	PA	37,428	VC
St. Leo Univ	FL	22,140	C+
St. Louis Univ	MO	33,158	VC+
St. Mary-of-the-Woods College	IN	25,480	C
St. Michael's College	VT	33,330	VC
St. Vincent College	PA	26,160	VC
Salem International Univ	WV	18,020	C
Salve Regina Univ	RI	33,450	C
San Diego State Univ	CA	12,971	C
San Francisco State Univ	CA	13,000	C
Santa Clara Univ	CA	38,931	VC
Shepherd Univ	WV	10,066	C
Shippensburg Univ of Pennsylvania	PA	11,621	C
Siena Heights Univ	MI	17,000	LC
Silver Lake College of the Holy Family	WI	18,500	LC
Simpson College	IA	26,833	VC
Slippery Rock Univ of Pennsylvania	PA	10,360	C
Southeastern Okla State Univ	OK	6,147	C
Southeastern Univ	DC	9,000	NC
Southern Adventist Univ	TN	18,500	C
Southern Illinois Univ Carbondale	IL	12,391	C
Southern New Hampshire Univ	NH	28,764	C
Southern Polytechnic State Univ	GA	7,640	VC
Southern Utah Univ	UT		C
Southern Wesleyan Univ	SC	21,675	C
Southwest Baptist Univ	MO	18,300	C
Southwestern Adventist Univ	TX	18,290	C
Southwestern Okla State Univ	OK	4,801	C
Springfield College	MA	25,000	C
SUNY at Oswego	NY	13,662	VC
SUNY/College at Buffalo	NY	11,903	C+
SUNY/College at Old Westbury	NY	13,154	C
SUNY/College of Agriculture and Technology at Cobleskill	NY	12,915	C
SUNY/College of Technology at Alfred	NY	14,000	C
SUNY/Univ at Albany	NY	13,860	VC
SUNY/Univ at Binghamton	NY	13,988	HC
SUNY/Univ at Stony Brook	NY	13,625	HC
Stephen F. Austin State Univ	TX	7,930	C
Stevens Inst of Technology	NJ	40,935	HC
Strayer Univ	DC	8,789	SP
Suffolk Univ	MA	33,160	C
Susquehanna Univ	PA	33,465	VC
Syracuse Univ	NY	38,655	HC
Tarleton State Univ	TX	8,952	C
Temple Univ	PA	17,438	C
Texas Christian Univ	TX	23,410	VC+
Texas Lutheran Univ	TX	23,530	C
Texas State Univ - San Marcos	TX	10,862	C
Texas Wesleyan Univ	TX	18,700	C
Thomas College	ME	23,770	LC
Thomas Edison State College	NJ	3,780	SP
Tiffin Univ	OH	19,490	LC
Towson Univ	MD	13,924	VC
Trevecca Nazarene Univ	TN	19,594	C
Trinity Christian College	IL	23,645	C
Tri-State Univ-Main Campus	IN	26,200	C
Troy Univ	AL	8,916	C
Tulane Univ	LA	41,098	MC
Tusculum College	TN	21,340	LC
Univ of Alabama at Birmingham	AL	13,716	C
Univ of Arkansas at Little Rock	AR	7,230	NC
Univ of Arkansas at Monticello	AR	7,325	NC
Univ of Calif at Irvine	CA	16,475	HC
Univ of Calif at Riverside	CA	16,625	C
Univ of Calif at San Diego	CA	16,102	HC
Univ of Calif at Santa Cruz	CA	19,174	VC
Univ of Central Arkansas	AR	9,984	C

ST = STATE   **$IS** = IN-STATE COSTS   **SR** = SELECTOR RATING

School	ST	$IS	SR
Univ of Charleston	WV	27,600	C
Univ of Cincinnati	OH	17,682	C
Univ of Colo at Boulder	CO	13,352	C+
Univ of Dayton	OH	28,826	VC
Univ of Delaware	DE	14,142	HC
Univ of Denver	CO	36,376	VC+
Univ of Detroit Mercy	MI	27,000	C
Univ of Florida	FL	9,354	HC
Univ of Hartford	CT	34,044	C
Univ of Hawaii at Manoa	HI	10,413	VC
Univ of Houston	TX	7,000	C
Univ of Houston-Downtown	TX	3,326	NC
Univ of Idaho	ID	9,310	NC
Univ of Illinois at Chicago	IL	16,256	VC
Univ of Iowa	IA	12,172	VC
Univ of Kansas	KS	10,915	VC
Univ of Louisiana at Monroe	LA	7,103	C
Univ of Louisville	KY	10,400	VC
Univ of Maine	ME	13,642	C
Univ of Maine at Augusta	ME	5,025	NC
Univ of Mary	ND	15,374	C
Univ of Mary Hardin-Baylor	TX	19,428	C
Univ of Maryland/Baltimore County	MD	16,642	VC+
Univ of Maryland/College Park	MD	16,036	HC
Univ of Maryland/Univ College	MD	5,640	SP
Univ of Mass Lowell	MA	14,327	VC
Univ of Memphis	TN	11,153	C
Univ of Minn/Crookston	MN	13,157	LC
Univ of Missouri/Kansas City	MO	15,000	VC
Univ of Missouri/Rolla	MO	13,332	HC
Univ of Nebr at Kearney	NE	9,000	NC
Univ of Nebr at Lincoln	NE	11,401	VC
Univ of Nebr at Omaha	NE	11,235	C
Univ of Nevada/Reno	NV	12,155	NC
Univ of North Alabama	AL	8,992	C
Univ of N Car at Chapel Hill	NC	11,129	MC
Univ of N Car at Greensboro	NC	8,993	C
Univ of N Dak	ND	10,114	VC
Univ of North Florida	FL	9,908	VC
Univ of North Texas	TX	7,800	C
Univ of Northern Colo	CO	10,249	C
Univ of Northern Iowa	IA	11,133	C
Univ of Okla	OK	10,769	VC+
Univ of PR/Bayamon Univ College Campus	PR	1,600	
Univ of PR/Mayaguez	PR	1,250	
Univ of PR/Rio Piedras	PR	5,750	
Univ of Redlands	CA	36,160	VC
Univ of St. Francis	IL	25,430	C
Univ of St. Mary	KS	18,900	C
Univ of San Francisco	CA	37,560	VC
Univ of Scranton	PA	31,100	VC
Univ of S Car Upstate	SC	11,957	C
Univ of Southern Miss	MS	10,112	C
Univ of Tampa	FL	25,784	C
Univ of Texas at Arlington	TX	7,195	LC
Univ of Texas at San Antonio	TX	11,325	LC
Univ of Texas-Pan American	TX	7,290	C+
Univ of the Cumberlands	KY	18,184	C
Univ of the Incarnate Word	TX	23,306	C
Univ of the Pacific	CA	34,380	VC
Univ of Toledo	OH	15,806	NC
Univ of Tulsa	OK	25,348	HC
Univ of Vermont	VT	18,080	VC
Univ of Virginia's College at Wise	VA	11,076	C
Univ of Washington	WA	10,400	VC
Univ of Wisc/Eau Claire	WI	9,915	VC
Univ of Wisc/Green Bay	WI	9,415	VC
Univ of Wisc/La Crosse	WI	10,045	VC
Univ of Wisc/Madison	WI	13,117	HC
Univ of Wisc/Stevens Point	WI	9,384	VC
Univ of Wisc/Superior	WI	9,610	C+
Utah State Univ	UT	8,002	VC
Valdosta State Univ	GA	8,802	C
Valley City State Univ	ND	9,854	LC
Valparaiso Univ	IN	28,970	VC+
Vermont Technical College	VT	15,751	C
Villa Julie College	MD	25,222	C
Villanova Univ	PA	38,672	HC+
Virginia Commonwealth Univ	VA	12,987	C
Virginia Intermont College	VA	22,200	LC
Viterbo Univ	WI	21,670	C
Walla Walla College	WA	24,489	VC
Warner Southern College	FL	18,000	LC
Wartburg College	IA	27,315	NC
Washburn Univ	KS	9,734	NC
Washington and Jefferson College	PA	33,490	VC
Washington Univ in St. Louis	MO	42,106	MC
Wayne State Univ	MI	11,805	C
Waynesburg College	PA	21,230	C
Weber State Univ	UT	9,635	NC
Webster Univ	MO	24,280	VC
Wentworth Inst of Technology	MA	27,500	C
Wesleyan College	GA	19,560	C

School	ST	$IS	SR
West Liberty State College	WV	9,142	LC
West Texas A&M Univ	TX	8,452	C
Western Carolina Univ	NC	7,000	C
Western New England College	MA	32,054	C
Western Oregon Univ	OR	10,295	C
Westfield State College	MA	10,200	C
Widener Univ	PA	27,275	C
Wilberforce Univ	OH	14,937	LC
Wilkes Univ	PA	30,886	C
William Jewell College	MO	24,340	C
William Woods Univ	MO	21,020	C
Woodbury Univ	CA	30,176	LC
Xavier Univ	OH	30,490	HC
York College of Pennsylvania	PA	16,550	VC
Youngstown State Univ	OH	12,613	NC

INSTITUTIONAL MANAGEMENT

School	ST	$IS	SR
Bowling Green State Univ	OH	14,994	C
Calumet College of St. Joseph	IN	9,500	LC
CUNY/New York City College of Technology	NY	4,269	NC
Felician College	NJ	24,300	C
Goshen College	IN	22,850	VC
La Roche College	PA	24,724	C
Missouri State Univ	MO	10,748	C+
N Dak State Univ	ND	8,500	C
Simpson Univ	CA	22,900	C
Thomas Edison State College	NJ	3,780	SP
Univ of La Verne	CA	33,470	C
Viterbo Univ	WI	21,670	C
Warner Southern College	FL	18,000	LC

INSURANCE

School	ST	$IS	SR
Ball State Univ	IN	13,138	C
Baylor Univ	TX	27,555	HC
Cal State, Sacramento	CA	11,122	C+
Delta State Univ	MS	7,709	C
Ferris State Univ	MI	13,698	C
Howard Univ	DC	18,481	C+
Illinois State Univ	IL	12,839	C+
Indiana State Univ	IN	11,604	C
Inter American Univ of PR/ Fajardo Campus	PR	4,000	
Inter American Univ of PR/ Ponce Regional College	PR	3,700	
Martin Univ	IN	10,300	SP
Miss State Univ	MS	9,577	C
Missouri State Univ	MO	10,748	C+
Olivet College	MI	19,984	C+
Penn State Univ/Univ Park Campus	PA	18,038	HC
Roosevelt Univ	IL	22,605	VC
Thomas Edison State College	NJ	3,780	SP
Troy Univ	AL	8,916	C
Univ of Central Okla	OK	8,094	C
Univ of Florida	FL	9,354	HC
Univ of Hartford	CT	34,044	C
Univ of Illinois at Urbana-Champaign	IL	15,800	HC+
Univ of Louisiana at Monroe	LA	7,103	C
Univ of Miss	MS	9,000	C
Univ of North Texas	TX	7,800	C
Univ of S Car at Columbia	SC	13,397	VC

INSURANCE AND RISK MANAGEMENT

School	ST	$IS	SR
Appalachian State Univ	NC	8,000	VC
Bradley Univ	IL	25,280	VC
Eastern Mich Univ	MI	12,897	C
Excelsior College	NY	995	SP
Florida State Univ	FL	9,028	HC
Gannon Univ	PA	26,100	C
Georgia State Univ	GA	11,444	VC
Illinois Wesleyan Univ	IL	34,050	HC+
Mercyhurst College	PA	28,633	VC
Ohio State Univ	OH	15,357	HC
Roosevelt Univ	IL	22,605	VC
St. John's Univ	NY	34,370	C
Univ of Central Arkansas	AR	9,984	C
Univ of Conn	CT	16,628	HC
Univ of Georgia	GA	11,004	HC
Univ of Memphis	TN	11,153	C
Univ of Pennsylvania	PA	41,766	MC
Univ of Wisc/Madison	WI	13,117	HC
Washington State Univ	WA	12,260	C

INTERDISCIPLINARY STUDIES

School	ST	$IS	SR
Adams State College	CO	8,613	C
Alfred Univ	NY		VC
American Univ	DC	38,719	HC+
Amherst College	MA	41,590	MC
Andrews Univ	MI	21,786	C
Antioch College	OH	33,700	C
Appalachian State Univ	NC	8,000	VC
Aquinas College	MI	23,750	C

School	ST	$IS	SR
Arizona State Univ-Tempe	AZ	11,174	C
Arkansas State Univ	AR	9,630	C
Ashford Univ	IA	20,370	C
Austin College	TX	27,871	HC
Austin Peay State Univ	TN	7,535	C
Averett Univ	VA	24,920	C
Bard College	NY	41,800	HC+
Bates College	ME	42,100	MC
Baylor Univ	TX	27,555	HC
Beloit College	WI	32,808	HC
Bennett College	NC	11,500	C
Bennington College	VT	41,890	HC
Berry College	GA	24,342	VC
Bluefield College	VA	17,230	C+
Boise State Univ	ID	9,438	LC
Boston Univ	MA	42,046	HC+
Bowdoin College	ME	41,660	MC
Bowie State Univ	MD	10,880	C+
Brigham Young Univ/Hawaii	HI	7,740	HC+
Bryn Athyn College of the New Church	PA	14,999	NC
Bucknell Univ	PA	39,660	MC
Calif Baptist Univ	CA	23,780	C
Calif Lutheran Univ	CA	27,800	LC
Cal State, Dominguez Hills	CA	10,220	LC
Cal State, Long Beach	CA	9,512	C
Cal State, Los Angeles	CA	5,900	C
Cal State, Stanislaus	CA	11,283	C
Cambridge Univ	MA	11,055	SP
Cameron Univ	OK	6,314	NC
Cascade College	OR	17,980	NC
Centenary College	NJ	28,870	LC
Centenary College of Louisiana	LA	24,760	VC
Central Methodist Univ	MO	18,000	C
Central Mich Univ	MI	12,244	C
Chatham College	PA	27,290	C
Christopher Newport Univ	VA	13,326	VC
CUNY/New York City College of Technology	NY	4,269	NC
CUNY/Queens College	NY	4,356	C
Claremont McKenna College	CA	42,920	MC
Clarkson Univ	NY	34,930	VC
Clayton College and State Univ	GA	2,445	LC
Coastal Carolina Univ	SC	13,140	C
Coe College	IA	27,440	VC
College Misericordia	PA	27,950	C
College of Notre Dame of Maryland	MD	27,700	C
College of St. Rose	NY	25,684	C
College of Santa Fe	NM	28,978	C
College of the Ozarks	MO	4,130	VC+
College of William and Mary	VA	14,147	MC
College of Wooster	OH	31,310	VC+
Columbia College	MO	16,900	C
Concordia College-New York	NY	27,740	C
Cornerstone Univ and Grand Rapids Theological Seminary	MI	21,350	NC
Covenant College	GA	26,460	VC+
Crichton College	TN	15,300	C
Dallas Baptist Univ	TX	17,040	VC
Dana College	NE	22,390	C
Davidson College	NC	36,825	MC
DePauw Univ	IN	32,100	HC
D'Youville College	NY	23,660	C
East Tenn State Univ	TN	8,497	C
Eastern Mich Univ	MI	12,897	C
Emerson College	MA	35,076	HC
Emmanuel College	MA	32,000	C+
Emory & Henry College	VA	26,570	C
Emory Univ	GA	40,546	MC
Fairleigh Dickinson Univ/ Metropolitan Campus	NJ	28,590	C
Florida Atlantic Univ	FL	11,221	C
Florida Inst of Technology	FL	29,720	VC
Fort Lewis College	CO	11,852	C
Framingham State College	MA	11,156	C
Franklin and Marshall College	PA	40,590	HC
Geneva College	PA	21,850	C
George Mason Univ	VA	10,850	VC
George Washington Univ	DC	48,820	MC
Georgetown Univ	DC	43,183	MC
Georgia State Univ	GA	11,444	VC
Goddard College	VT	21,100	C
Gonzaga Univ	WA	30,218	HC
Goucher College	MD	36,225	VC
Grace Bible College	MI	18,810	C
Haverford College	PA	41,600	MC
Hendrix College	AR	27,646	HC+
Heritage Univ	WA	6,800	NC
Hofstra Univ	NY	32,630	VC
Hollins Univ	VA	31,105	C
Hope International Univ	CA	23,700	NC
Huston-Tillotson Univ	TX	14,232	LC
Illinois State Univ	IL	12,839	C+
Illinois Wesleyan Univ	IL	34,050	HC+
Indiana State Univ	IN	11,604	C
International College	FL	9,500	NC
Ithaca College	NY	35,144	VC
John Brown Univ	AR	20,910	VC
Johns Hopkins Univ	MD	42,044	MC

School	ST	$IS	SR
Judson College	AL	16,522	C
Kalamazoo College	MI	32,442	VC+
King College	TN	23,400	C
Lafayette College	PA	39,267	MC
Lake Erie College	OH	27,725	C
Lambuth Univ	TN	21,700	C+
Lander Univ	SC	10,600	C
Lane College	TN	11,220	C+
Lees-McRae College	NC	23,000	C
LeTourneau Univ	TX	21,200	C
Lewis and Clark College	OR	35,358	VC+
Liberty Univ	VA	19,101	C
Lyndon State College	VT	14,233	LC
Manchester College	IN	23,470	C
Marian College of Fond du Lac	WI	21,775	LC
Marietta College	OH	29,327	C
Marist College	NY	30,566	VC
Marlboro College	VT	35,980	VC+
Marquette Univ	WI	31,066	HC
Marylhurst Univ	OR	14,220	NC
Mass College of Liberal Arts	MA	8,725	LC
McMurry Univ	TX	18,100	LC
Mercy College	NY	20,000	NC
Miami Univ	OH	29,097	HC
Mich State Univ	MI	13,689	VC
Middle Tenn State Univ	TN	8,540	C
Midwestern State Univ	TX	9,381	C
Miss State Univ	MS	9,577	C
Molloy College	NY	16,510	C
Montana State Univ-Northern	MT	10,000	NC
Mount St. Mary College	NY	25,250	C
Mount St. Mary's Univ	MD	30,930	C
Mountain State Univ	WV	11,406	NC
Naropa Univ	CO	26,302	SP
National Univ	CA	8,412	SP
New York Inst of Technology	NY	28,126	VC
Norfolk State Univ	VA	10,531	LC
N Car State Univ	NC	11,824	HC
Northeastern Univ	MA	35,742	HC
Northwest Christian College	OR	24,298	C
Northwest Univ	WA	18,854	C
Northwestern College	MN	25,220	NC
Nyack College	NY	18,540	C
Ohio Dominican Univ	OH	25,954	C
Old Dominion Univ	VA	11,907	C
Piedmont College	GA	20,500	C
Plymouth State Univ	NH	12,298	LC
Prairie View A&M Univ	TX	11,110	LC
Purdue Univ/West Lafayette	IN	13,458	VC
Radford Univ	VA	13,145	C
Rensselaer Polytechnic Inst	NY	41,288	HC+
Rhodes College	TN	32,860	HC
Rochester College	MI	15,636	C+
Russell Sage College	NY	27,000	C
Saginaw Valley State Univ	MI	11,432	C
St. Edward's Univ	TX	23,560	C
St. John Fisher College	NY	27,860	C
St. Lawrence Univ	NY	40,545	VC
St. Olaf College	MN	32,800	HC
St. Peter's College	NJ	30,160	LC
Salisbury Univ	MD	13,128	VC
San Diego Christian College	CA	24,172	C
San Francisco State Univ	CA	13,000	C
Santa Clara Univ	CA	38,931	VC
Shawnee State Univ	OH	12,237	NC
Sheldon Jackson College	AK	17,900	LC
Shippensburg Univ of Pennsylvania	PA	11,621	C
Simon's Rock College of Bard	MA	41,988	VC+
Sonoma State Univ	CA	14,732	C
S Dak School of Mines and Technology	SD	7,624	C+
Southeast Missouri State Univ	MO	10,596	C
Southeastern Univ	FL	17,180	LC
Southern Utah Univ	UT		C
Southwest Minn State Univ	MN	10,975	C
SUNY at Potsdam	NY	12,959	C
SUNY/College at Brockport	NY	12,747	VC
SUNY/College at Fredonia	NY	12,771	VC
SUNY/College at Oneonta	NY	12,905	VC
SUNY/College at Plattsburgh	NY	12,362	C
SUNY/Empire State College	NY	4,575	SP
SUNY/Univ at Binghamton	NY	13,988	VC
SUNY/Univ at Stony Brook	NY	13,625	HC
Stephen F. Austin State Univ	TX	7,930	C
Stonehill College	MA	36,104	HC
Sweet Briar College	VA	31,460	VC
Tarleton State Univ	TX	8,952	C
Temple Univ	PA	17,438	C
Tenn State Univ	TN	9,048	LC
Tenn Wesleyan College	TN	18,650	C
Texas Southern Univ	TX	9,828	C
Texas State Univ - San Marcos	TX	10,862	C
Texas Wesleyan Univ	TX	18,700	C
Texas Woman's Univ	TX	7,804	C
Touro College	NY	17,000	VC

School	ST	$IS	SR
Towson Univ	MD	13,924	VC
Trinity College	CT	38,040	HC+
Truman State Univ	MO	11,242	HC
Unity College	ME	24,320	C
Univ of Alabama	AL	9,888	C
Univ of Alaska Anchorage	AK	11,275	NC
Univ of Alaska Fairbanks	AK	10,101	C
Univ of Arizona	AZ	11,958	VC
Univ of Bridgeport	CT	29,595	LC
Univ of Calif at Berkeley	CA	18,141	HC+
Univ of Calif at Santa Barbara	CA	11,800	VC
Univ of Colo at Denver and Health Sciences Center	CO	5,021	C
Univ of Delaware	DE	14,142	HC
Univ of Evansville	IN	28,320	VC
Univ of Florida	FL	9,354	HC
Univ of Georgia	GA	11,004	HC
Univ of Hartford	CT	34,044	C
Univ of Hawaii at Manoa	HI	10,413	VC
Univ of Houston	TX	7,000	C
Univ of Houston-Downtown	TX	3,326	NC
Univ of Idaho	ID	9,310	NC
Univ of Maine	ME	13,642	C
Univ of Maine at Augusta	ME	5,025	NC
Univ of Maine at Farmington	ME	11,515	C
Univ of Maryland/Baltimore County	MD	16,642	VC+
Univ of Mass Amherst	MA	15,973	C+
Univ of Mass Dartmouth	MA	15,985	C
Univ of Memphis	TN	11,153	C
Univ of Minn/Duluth	MN	13,974	C
Univ of Nebr at Lincoln	NE	11,401	VC
Univ of Nebr at Omaha	NE	11,235	C
Univ of Nevada/Las Vegas	NV	11,566	VC
Univ of New Mexico	NM	11,253	C
Univ of N Car at Chapel Hill	NC	11,129	MC
Univ of N Dak	ND	10,114	VC
Univ of North Texas	TX	7,800	C
Univ of Northern Colo	CO	10,249	C
Univ of Pittsburgh at Pittsburgh	PA	18,866	HC
Univ of Portland	OR	32,300	VC
Univ of PR/Rio Piedras	PR	5,750	C
Univ of Redlands	CA	36,160	VC
Univ of Richmond	VA	40,510	HC
Univ of St. Mary	KS	18,900	C
Univ of S Car at Aiken	SC	11,718	LC
Univ of S Car at Columbia	SC	13,397	VC
Univ of S Car Upstate	SC	11,957	C
Univ of Texas at Arlington	TX	7,195	LC
Univ of Texas at Dallas	TX	13,244	HC
Univ of Texas at El Paso	TX	8,764	NC
Univ of Texas at San Antonio	TX	11,325	LC
Univ of Texas-Pan American	TX	7,290	C+
Univ of Virginia	VA	13,759	MC
Vanderbilt Univ	TN	41,986	MC
Villa Julie College	MD	25,222	C
Virginia Commonwealth Univ	VA	12,987	C
Virginia Intermont College	VA	22,200	LC
Virginia Polytechnic Inst and State Univ	VA	10,834	VC
Virginia State Univ	VA	11,318	C
Virginia Wesleyan College	VA	28,433	C
Washington and Lee Univ	VA	35,880	MC
Washington Univ in St. Louis	MO	42,106	MC
Wayland Baptist Univ	TX	13,484	C
Wayne State College	NE	8,033	NC
Weber State Univ	UT	9,635	NC
Wesleyan College	GA	19,560	C
West Liberty State College	WV	9,142	LC
West Texas A&M Univ	TX	8,452	C
West Virginia Univ	WV	10,506	C
Western Mich Univ	MI	13,299	C
Western Oregon Univ	OR	10,295	C
Westfield State College	MA	10,200	C
Wheaton College	IL	27,760	HC
William Woods Univ	MO	21,020	C
Wisc Lutheran College	WI	23,510	VC
Woodbury College	VT	15,150	LC
Woodbury Univ	CA	30,176	LC
Worcester Polytechnic Inst	MA	40,450	VC+

INTERIOR DESIGN

School	ST	$IS	SR
Adrian College	MI	23,000	C
American InterContinental Univ	GA	12,100	NC
Appalachian State Univ	NC	8,000	VC
Arcadia Univ	PA	33,570	VC
Arizona State Univ-Tempe	AZ	11,174	C
Art Inst of Atlanta	GA	23,220	VC
Art Inst of Portland	OR	23,040	SP
Atlanta College of Art	GA	18,630	SP
Auburn Univ	AL	12,230	VC
Baker College of Flint	MI	7,800	NC
Bay Path College	MA	29,362	C
Baylor Univ	TX	27,555	HC
Becker College	MA	24,300	LC
Bethel College	IN	19,680	C
Boston Architectural Center	MA	6,500	SP
Brenau Univ Women's College	GA	23,950	VC
Calif College of the Arts	CA	34,325	SP
Cal State, Fresno	CA	10,037	LC
Cazenovia College	NY	26,900	C
Central Mich Univ	MI	12,244	C
Central Missouri State Univ	MO	10,000	C
Chaminade Univ of Honolulu	HI	23,320	LC
Cleveland Inst of Art	OH	34,109	SP
College for Creative Studies	MI	24,000	SP
College of Mount St. Joseph	OH	24,860	C
Colo State Univ-Fort Collins	CO	10,878	C+
Columbus College of Art and Design	OH	24,500	SP
Concordia Univ Wisc	WI	22,660	VC
Converse College	SC	24,800	VC
Drexel Univ	PA	27,700	VC
East Carolina Univ	NC	10,000	C
Eastern Kentucky Univ	KY	7,725	C
Eastern Mich Univ	MI	12,897	C
Endicott College	MA	30,156	C+
Fashion Inst of Technology/SUNY	NY	11,600	C+
Florida International Univ	FL	9,215	VC
Florida State Univ	FL	9,028	HC
Georgia Southern Univ	GA	9,762	C
Harding Univ	AR	16,512	VC
High Point Univ	NC	25,720	C
Indiana State Univ	IN	11,604	C
Indiana Univ Bloomington	IN	13,356	VC
Indiana Univ of Pennsylvania	PA	11,209	C
Iowa State Univ	IA	11,831	VC
Kansas State Univ	KS	10,516	VC
Kean Univ	NJ	15,880	C
Kendall College of Art and Design of Ferris State Univ	MI	11,870	SP
Kent State Univ	OH	14,594	C
La Roche College	PA	24,724	LC
Lambuth Univ	TN	21,700	C+
Lawrence Tech Univ	MI	25,475	VC
Louisiana State Univ and A&M College	LA	10,749	VC
Maryland Inst College of Art	MD	34,450	SP
Marymount Univ	VA	25,934	C
Maryville Univ of St. Louis	MO	23,000	VC
Mercyhurst College	PA	28,633	VC
Meredith College	NC	25,600	C
Miami Univ	OH	29,097	HC
Mich State Univ	MI	13,689	VC
Middle Tenn State Univ	TN	8,540	C
Milwaukee Inst of Art and Design	WI	28,700	SP
Minn State Univ, Mankato	MN	10,276	LC
Miss College	MS	14,574	VC
Missouri State Univ	MO	10,748	C+
Moore College of Art and Design	PA	27,200	SP
Mount Ida College	MA	26,000	LC
Mount Mary College	WI	22,895	C
New York Inst of Technology	NY	28,126	VC
Newbury College	MA	25,600	C
N Dak State Univ	ND	8,500	C
Ohio State Univ	OH	15,357	HC
Okla Christian Univ	OK	18,992	NC
Park Univ	MO	11,592	C
Parsons School of Design	NY	32,242	SP
Philadelphia Univ	PA	30,006	C
Pratt Inst	NY	36,156	SP
Purdue Univ/West Lafayette	IN	13,458	VC
Rhode Island School of Design	RI	38,130	SP
Ringling School of Art and Design	FL	31,013	SP
Rochester Inst of Technology	NY	32,070	VC+
Salem College	NC	26,226	VC+
Samford Univ	AL	20,258	VC
San Francisco State Univ	CA	13,000	C
San Jose State Univ	CA	11,707	C
Savannah College of Art and Design	GA	30,800	SP
School of the Art Inst of Chicago	IL	37,800	SP
School of Visual Arts	NY	32,580	SP
S Dak State Univ	SD	9,815	C
Southern Illinois Univ Carbondale	IL	12,391	C
Stephen F. Austin State Univ	TX	7,930	C
Stephens College	MO	26,930	VC
Suffolk Univ	MA	33,160	C
Syracuse Univ	NY	38,655	HC
Texas A&M Univ at Kingsville	TX	6,800	LC
Texas Christian Univ	TX	23,410	VC+
Texas State Univ - San Marcos	TX	10,862	C
Texas Tech Univ	TX	13,026	VC
Univ of Alabama	AL	9,888	C
Univ of Arkansas	AR	11,859	VC
Univ of Bridgeport	CT	29,595	LC
Univ of Central Arkansas	AR	9,984	C
Univ of Central Okla	OK	8,094	C
Univ of Charleston	WV	27,600	C
Univ of Florida	FL	9,354	HC
Univ of Georgia	GA	11,004	HC
Univ of Houston	TX	7,000	C
Univ of Idaho	ID	9,310	NC
Univ of Kansas	KS	10,915	VC
Univ of Louisiana at Lafayette	LA	5,830	C
Univ of Mich/Ann Arbor	MI	16,587	HC+
Univ of Minn/Twin Cities	MN	13,165	HC
Univ of Nebr at Lincoln	NE	11,401	VC
Univ of Nevada/Las Vegas	NV	11,566	C
Univ of Nevada/Reno	NV	12,155	NC
Univ of New Haven	CT	31,794	C
Univ of North Alabama	AL	8,992	C
Univ of North Texas	TX	7,800	C
Univ of Okla	OK	10,769	VC+
Univ of Oregon	OR	13,108	VC
Univ of Tenn at Knoxville	TN	11,720	C
Univ of Texas at Arlington	TX	7,195	LC
Univ of Texas at Austin	TX	14,610	HC
Univ of Texas at San Antonio	TX	11,325	LC
Univ of the Incarnate Word	TX	23,306	C
Univ of Wisc/Madison	WI	13,117	HC
Univ of Wisc/Stevens Point	WI	9,384	HC
Utah State Univ	UT	8,002	VC
Valdosta State Univ	GA	8,802	C
Virginia Commonwealth Univ	VA	12,987	C
Virginia Polytechnic Inst and State Univ	VA	10,834	VC
Washington State Univ	WA	12,260	C
Wentworth Inst of Technology	MA	27,500	C
West Virginia Univ	WV	10,506	C
Western Carolina Univ	NC	7,000	C
Western Mich Univ	MI	13,299	C
Woodbury Univ	CA	30,176	LC

INTERNATIONAL AGRICULTURE

School	ST	$IS	SR
Cornell Univ	NY	41,717	MC
Eastern Mennonite Univ	VA	25,450	VC
Iowa State Univ	IA	11,831	VC
MidAmerica Nazarene Univ	KS	20,584	LC
Tarleton State Univ	TX	8,952	C
Univ of at Calif Davis	CA	15,010	VC
Utah State Univ	UT	8,002	VC

INTERNATIONAL BUSINESS MANAGEMENT

School	ST	$IS	SR
Adams State College	CO	8,613	C
Adrian College	MI	23,000	C
Albertson College of Idaho	ID	21,095	VC
Alma College	MI	28,544	VC
Alverno College	WI	21,088	C
American International College	MA	28,710	LC
American Univ	DC	38,719	HC+
Angelo State Univ	TX	8,340	NC
Aquinas College	MI	23,750	C
Arcadia Univ	PA	33,570	VC
Arkansas State Univ	AR	9,630	C
Assumption College	MA	32,875	C
Auburn Univ	AL	12,230	VC
Augsburg College	MN	28,300	C
Averett Univ	VA	24,920	C
Avila Univ	MO	22,100	C
Baker Univ	KS	22,190	C
Barry Univ	FL	24,100	LC
Bay Path College	MA	29,362	C
Baylor Univ	TX	27,555	HC
Bellarmine Univ	KY	27,650	C+
Belmont Abbey College	NC	25,314	C
Benedictine Univ	IL	25,710	C
Berkeley Colleg/Westchester Campus	NY	26,700	LC
Berkeley College/New York City	NY	16,950	LC
Bethune-Cookman College	FL	17,922	LC
Birmingham-Southern College	AL	28,494	VC+
Blackburn College	IL	13,690	VC
Boston Univ	MA	42,046	HC+
Bowling Green State Univ	OH	14,994	C
Bradley Univ	IL	25,280	VC
Brigham Young Univ/Hawaii	HI	7,740	HC+
Buena Vista Univ	IA	27,742	C
Butler Univ	IN	31,944	VC+
Caldwell College	NJ	26,450	LC
Calif State Polytechnic Univ, Pomona	CA	18,053	C+
Cal State, Fullerton	CA	10,990	C
Cal State, Long Beach	CA	9,512	C
Cal State, Sacramento	CA	11,122	C+
Cal State, San Bernardino	CA	12,563	LC
Campbell Univ	NC	21,137	VC
Canisius College	NY	32,257	VC
Cardinal Stritch Univ	WI	21,910	C
Carlow Univ	PA	24,313	C
Catawba College	NC	25,000	C
Central College	IA	26,774	VC
Central Conn State Univ	CT	13,620	C
Central Mich Univ	MI	12,244	C
Central Washington Univ	WA	11,730	C
Champlain College	VT	24,605	C
Chatham College	PA	27,290	C+
Christopher Newport Univ	VA	13,326	VC
Clarion Univ of Pennsylvania	PA	11,844	C
College of Charleston	SC	13,616	VC
College of New Jersey	NJ	18,315	MC
College of Notre Dame of Maryland	MD	27,700	C
College of Our Lady of the Elms	MA	21,000	C
College of Santa Fe	NM	28,978	C
College of the Ozarks	MO	4,130	VC+
Concordia College: Moorhead	MN	22,475	VC
Cornell College	IA	30,110	VC+
Cornerstone Univ and Grand Rapids Theological Seminary	MI	21,350	NC
Creighton Univ	NE	29,918	VC+
Davenport Univ	MI	15,205	NC
Dickinson College	PA	40,170	HC+
Dominican College	NY	26,630	LC
Dominican Univ	IL	26,370	C
Dominican Univ of Calif	CA	36,836	C
Dowling College	NY	22,110	LC
Drake Univ	IA	27,632	VC+
Drury Univ	MO	20,117	VC
Duquesne Univ	PA	29,534	VC
D'Youville College	NY	23,660	C
Eastern Mennonite Univ	VA	25,450	VC
Eastern Mich Univ	MI	12,897	C
Eckerd College	FL	35,492	VC
Elizabethtown College	PA	32,100	VC
Elmhurst College	IL	24,685	C
Elmira College	NY	37,200	VC
Excelsior College	NY	995	SP
Fairfield Univ	CT	39,835	HC
Ferris State Univ	MI	13,698	C
Florida Atlantic Univ	FL	11,221	C
Florida International Univ	FL	9,215	VC
Florida Southern College	FL	25,965	C
Florida State Univ	FL	9,028	HC
Fordham Univ	NY	36,000	HC
Friends Univ	KS	16,250	LC
Gannon Univ	PA	26,100	C
Gardner-Webb Univ	NC	21,500	C
George Washington Univ	DC	48,820	MC
Georgetown College	KY	24,950	C+
Georgetown Univ	DC	43,183	MC
Georgia College and State Univ	GA	11,020	C
Golden Gate Univ	CA	12,150	LC
Goldey-Beacom College	DE	11,400	C
Graceland Univ	IA	19,700	C
Grand Canyon Univ	AZ	32,000	LC
Grand Valley State Univ	MI	12,000	VC
Grove City College	PA	15,784	HC+
Gustavus Adolphus College	MN	30,920	HC
Gwynedd-Mercy College	PA	26,080	C
Hamline Univ	MN	27,070	VC
Harding Univ	AR	16,512	VC
Hawaii Pacific Univ	HI	21,080	C
High Point Univ	NC	25,720	C
Hillsdale College	MI	24,160	HC
Hofstra Univ	NY	32,630	VC
Howard Univ	DC	18,481	C+
Illinois State Univ	IL	12,839	C+
Illinois Wesleyan Univ	IL	34,050	HC+
Indiana Univ Bloomington	IN	13,356	VC
Indiana Univ of Pennsylvania	PA	11,209	C
Iona College	NY	30,878	VC
Iowa State Univ	IA	11,831	VC
Ithaca College	NY	35,144	VC
Jacksonville Univ	FL	24,040	C
James Madison Univ	VA	12,010	VC
Johnson and Wales Univ/Providence Campus	RI	28,126	LC
Judson College	IL	25,130	C
Juniata College	PA	33,130	VC
King College	TN	23,400	C
King's College	PA	29,810	C
Kutztown Univ of Pennsylvania	PA	10,820	C
La Roche College	PA	24,724	LC
La Sierra Univ	CA	24,327	C+
Lake Erie College	OH	27,725	C
Lakeland College	WI	22,990	C
Lasell College	MA	26,250	C
Lenoir-Rhyne College	NC	25,580	C
Linfield College	OR	29,632	VC
Loras College	IA	27,193	C
Loyola Univ Chicago	IL	32,896	VC
Loyola Univ New Orleans	LA	31,050	VC+
Madonna Univ	MI	16,068	VC
Maine Maritime Academy	ME	14,340	C
Manhattan College	NY	29,000	VC
Mansfield Univ	PA	11,300	C
Marietta College	OH	29,327	C
Marquette Univ	WI	31,066	HC

ST = STATE $IS = IN-STATE COSTS   SR = SELECTOR RATING

School	ST	$IS	SR
Marymount Univ	VA	25,934	C
Marywood Univ	PA	30,680	C
Mass Maritime Academy	MA	11,571	C
Meredith College	NC	25,600	C
Merrimack College	MA	34,380	C
Messiah College	PA	28,910	VC+
Metropolitan State Univ	MN	4,682	SP
MidAmerica Nazarene Univ	KS	20,584	LC
Millikin Univ	IL	25,590	C
Milwaukee School of Engineering	WI	29,847	VC+
Minn State Univ, Mankato	MN	10,276	LC
Minn State Univ, Moorhead	MN	7,000	LC
Minot State Univ	ND	6,700	LC
Missouri Southern State Univ	MO	8,396	NC
Monmouth College	IL	23,700	C
Montclair State Univ	NJ	16,327	C
Moravian College	PA	28,950	VC
Mount Union College	OH	25,840	C
Mount Vernon Nazarene Univ	OH	20,810	C
Muskingum College	OH	22,970	C
Nebr Wesleyan Univ	NE	23,415	C+
Neumann College	PA	25,996	LC
New Mexico State Univ	NM	9,250	C
New York Univ	NY	43,170	MC
Newbury College	MA	25,600	C
North Central College	IL	28,926	VC
North Park Univ	IL	24,050	C
Northeastern Univ	MA	35,742	HC
Northern State Univ	SD	8,257	C
Northwest Missouri State Univ	MO	10,000	C
Northwest Nazarene Univ	ID	22,590	VC
Northwestern College	MN	25,220	NC
Northwood Univ	FL	21,040	C
Northwood Univ	MI	21,000	LC
Northwood Univ	TX	20,135	LC
Notre Dame de Namur Univ	CA	32,790	LC
Ohio Dominican Univ	OH	25,954	C
Ohio Northern Univ	OH	27,765	VC
Ohio State Univ	OH	15,357	HC
Ohio Univ	OH	15,921	C
Ohio Wesleyan Univ	OH	35,830	VC+
Okla State Univ	OK	10,213	VC
Old Dominion Univ	VA	11,907	C
Olivet College	MI	19,984	C+
Oral Roberts Univ	OK	22,650	C
Pace Univ	NY	30,000	VC
Palm Beach Atlantic Univ	FL	23,597	VC
Penn State Univ/Univ Park Campus	PA	18,038	HC
Pepperdine Univ	CA	39,960	HC
Pfeiffer Univ	NC	21,900	C
Philadelphia Univ	PA	30,006	C
Pittsburg State Univ	KS	8,112	C
Quinnipiac Univ	CT	34,640	VC
Ramapo College of New Jersey	NJ	16,630	VC
Regis Univ	CO	31,890	C
Rider Univ	NJ	32,560	C
Rochester Inst of Technology	NY	32,070	VC+
Roger Williams Univ	RI	30,500	C
Rollins College	FL	38,366	VC
Saginaw Valley State Univ	MI	11,432	C
St. Ambrose Univ	IA	25,495	C
St. Augustine's College	NC	14,000	LC
St. Cloud State Univ	MN	10,010	C
St. Edward's Univ	TX	23,560	C
St. Joseph's Univ	PA	37,428	VC
St. Mary's Univ of Minn	MN	23,857	VC
St. Mary's Univ of San Antonio	TX	22,444	C
St. Norbert College	WI	28,577	C+
St. Peter's College	NJ	30,160	LC
St. Thomas Univ	FL	23,490	C
St. Vincent College	PA	26,160	VC
St. Xavier Univ	IL	23,160	C
Salem College	NC	26,226	VC+
San Diego State Univ	CA	12,971	C
San Francisco State Univ	CA	13,000	C
San Jose State Univ	CA	11,707	C
Seattle Univ	WA	30,063	VC
Seton Hill Univ	PA	28,810	C
Simpson College	IA	26,833	VC
Slippery Rock Univ of Pennsylvania	PA	10,360	LC
Southern Adventist Univ	TN	18,500	C
Southern New Hampshire Univ	NH	28,764	C
Spring Hill College	AL	28,678	C
SUNY/College at Brockport	NY	12,747	VC
Stephen F. Austin State Univ	TX	7,930	C
Stetson Univ	FL	32,725	VC
Stonehill College	MA	36,104	HC
Strayer Univ	DC	8,789	SP
Suffolk Univ	MA	33,160	C
Taylor Univ	IN	26,376	VC+
Temple Univ	PA	17,438	C
Texas A&M Univ at Galveston	TX	10,000	C+
Texas Christian Univ	TX	23,410	VC+
Texas Tech Univ	TX	13,026	VC
Texas Wesleyan Univ	TX	18,700	C
Thiel College	PA	24,580	C
Thomas Edison State College	NJ	3,780	SP
Toccoa Falls College	GA	17,125	C
Trinity International Univ	IL	25,686	C
Univ of Akron	OH	15,166	NC
Univ of Arkansas	AR	11,859	VC
Univ of Bridgeport	CT	29,595	LC
Univ of Colo at Boulder	CO	13,352	C+
Univ of Dayton	OH	28,826	VC
Univ of Denver	CO	36,376	VC+
Univ of Evansville	IN	28,320	VC
Univ of Findlay	OH	29,238	C
Univ of Georgia	GA	11,004	HC
Univ of Hawaii at Manoa	HI	10,413	VC
Univ of Indianapolis	IN	25,090	C
Univ of La Verne	CA	33,470	C
Univ of Maryland/College Park	MD	16,036	HC
Univ of Memphis	TN	11,153	C
Univ of Miami	FL	38,397	MC
Univ of Miss	MS	9,000	C
Univ of Nebr at Lincoln	NE	11,401	VC
Univ of Nevada/Las Vegas	NV	11,566	C
Univ of New Haven	CT	31,794	C
Univ of New Mexico	NM	11,253	C
Univ of N Car at Charlotte	NC	9,101	C
Univ of N Car at Greensboro	NC	8,993	C
Univ of Okla	OK	10,769	VC+
Univ of Pennsylvania	PA	41,766	MC
Univ of Portland	OR	32,300	VC
Univ of PR at Humacao	PR	1,707	
Univ of Rio Grande	OH	8,728	NC
Univ of St. Thomas	MN	28,000	VC
Univ of San Francisco	CA	37,560	VC
Univ of Scranton	PA	31,100	VC
Univ of Southern Calif	CA	41,618	MC
Univ of Southern Miss	MS	10,112	C
Univ of Tampa	FL	25,784	C
Univ of Texas at San Antonio	TX	11,325	LC
Univ of Texas-Pan American	TX	7,290	C
Univ of Tulsa	OK	25,348	HC
Univ of Washington	WA	10,400	VC
Univ of Wisc/La Crosse	WI	10,045	VC
Utah State Univ	UT	8,002	VC
Valparaiso Univ	IN	28,970	VC+
Vanguard Univ of Southern Calif	CA	27,071	C
Villanova Univ	PA	38,672	VC+
Wartburg College	IA	27,315	NC
Washington and Jefferson College	PA	33,490	VC
Washington State Univ	WA	12,260	C
Washington Univ in St. Louis	MO	42,106	MC
Waynesburg College	PA	21,230	C
Wesleyan College	GA	19,560	C
Western Carolina Univ	NC	7,000	C
Western New Mexico Univ	NM	7,233	LC
Western Washington Univ	WA	11,262	VC
Westminster College	MO	19,060	VC
Westminster College	PA	31,290	C+
Wheeling Jesuit Univ	WV	26,910	C
Whitworth College	WA	29,428	VC+
Wichita State Univ	KS	8,500	C
Widener Univ	PA	27,275	C
William Jewell College	MO	24,340	C
Xavier Univ	OH	30,490	HC
York College of Pennsylvania	PA	16,550	VC

INTERNATIONAL ECONOMICS

School	ST	$IS	SR
Albertson College of Idaho	ID	21,095	VC
Assumption College	MA	32,875	C
Austin Univ	TX	27,871	VC
Blackburn College	IL	13,690	C
Carthage College	WI	26,000	C
Catholic Univ of America	DC	35,838	VC
College of St. Catherine	MN	27,505	VC
Colo College	CO	37,668	HC
Georgia Southern Univ	GA	9,762	C
Hiram College	OH	28,700	VC
Kent State Univ	OH	14,594	C
La Salle Univ	PA	34,950	C
Lafayette College	PA	39,267	MC
Louisiana State Univ and A&M College	LA	10,749	VC
Middlebury College	VT	42,120	MC
Midwestern State Univ	TX	9,381	LC
Pontifical Catholic Univ of PR/Ponce	PR	7,310	
Southwestern Adventist Univ	TX	18,290	LC
SUNY at Oswego	NY	13,662	VC
Suffolk Univ	MA	33,160	C
Texas Christian Univ	TX	23,410	VC+
Texas Tech Univ	TX	13,026	VC
Univ of Bridgeport	CT	29,595	LC
Univ of Calif at Santa Cruz	CA	19,174	VC
Univ of Puget Sound	WA	35,600	HC
Univ of Vermont	VT	18,080	VC
Univ of West Georgia	GA	8,838	C
Valparaiso Univ	IN	28,970	VC+
Washington Univ in St. Louis	MO	42,106	MC
Youngstown State Univ	OH	12,613	NC

INTERNATIONAL PUBLIC SERVICE

School	ST	$IS	SR
Baylor Univ	TX	27,555	HC
Christopher Newport Univ	VA	13,326	VC
Ohio Univ	OH	15,921	C
Valparaiso Univ	IN	28,970	VC+

INTERNATIONAL RELATIONS

School	ST	$IS	SR
Abilene Christian Univ	TX	20,830	C
Agnes Scott College	GA	32,070	HC
Alverno College	WI	21,088	C
American International College	MA	28,710	LC
Augsburg College	MN	28,300	C
Augustana College	SD	24,380	VC
Beloit College	WI	32,808	HC
Bennington College	VT	41,890	HC
Bethel Univ	MN	29,840	VC
Boston Univ	MA	42,046	HC+
Brigham Young Univ	UT	9,200	VC
Brown Univ	RI	42,015	MC
Bucknell Univ	PA	39,660	MC
Calif Baptist Univ	CA	23,780	C
Cal State, Chico	CA	11,395	C
Cal State, Sacramento	CA	11,122	C+
Canisius College	NY	32,257	VC
Capital Univ	OH	30,444	C
Carleton College	MN	40,467	MC
Carroll College	MT	23,324	C+
Carroll College	WI	24,860	C
Centre College	KY	30,810	VC
Chaminade Univ of Honolulu	HI	23,320	LC
Chatham College	PA	27,290	C+
Christopher Newport Univ	VA	13,326	VC
CUNY/Herbert H. Lehman College	NY	4,000	LC
CUNY/Hunter College	NY	8,000	C+
Claremont McKenna College	CA	42,920	MC
Clark Univ	MA	35,165	VC+
Cleveland State Univ	OH	10,798	NC
Colgate Univ	NY	41,170	MC
College of Notre Dame of Maryland	MD	27,700	C
College of St. Catherine	MN	27,505	VC
College of William and Mary	VA	14,147	MC
College of Wooster	OH	31,310	VC+
Concordia College: Moorhead	MN	22,475	VC
Conn College	CT	41,975	MC
Cornell College	IA	30,110	VC+
Dana College	NE	22,390	C
Dominican Univ	IL	26,370	C
Drake Univ	IA	27,632	VC+
Duquesne Univ	PA	29,534	VC
Eastern Mich Univ	MI	12,897	C
Eastern Washington Univ	WA	10,608	C
Eckerd College	FL	35,492	VC
Edgewood College	WI	22,862	C
Florida International Univ	FL	9,215	VC
Florida State Univ	FL	9,028	HC
George Washington Univ	DC	48,820	MC
Georgetown Univ	DC	43,183	MC
Georgia Inst of Technology	GA	11,450	HC+
Gettysburg College	PA	39,864	HC
Goucher College	MD	36,225	VC
Grand Valley State Univ	MI	12,000	VC
Hamilton College	NY	41,660	MC
Hamline Univ	MN	27,070	VC
Hampshire College	MA	37,120	HC
Hawaii Pacific Univ	HI	21,080	C
Hendrix College	AR	27,646	HC+
Hobart and William Smith Colleges	NY	41,123	VC
Houghton College	NY	25,980	VC+
Illinois College	IL	21,900	C+
Immaculata Univ	PA	25,350	C
Iowa State Univ	IA	11,831	VC
Juniata College	PA	33,130	VC
Kalamazoo College	MI	32,442	VC+
Kent State Univ	OH	14,594	C
Knox College	IL	32,385	VC+
Lafayette College	PA	39,267	MC
Lake Forest College	IL	33,860	VC
Lambuth Univ	TN	21,700	C+
Lawrence Univ	WI	33,958	HC+
Lehigh Univ	PA	42,690	VC+
Lewis and Clark College	OR	35,358	VC+
Lincoln Univ	PA	13,658	C+
Lynchburg College	VA	30,645	C
Marquette Univ	WI	31,066	HC
Marshall Univ	WV	9,116	C
Mary Baldwin College	VA	26,465	C
Maryville College	TN	29,224	VC
McKendree College	IL	24,800	VC
Miami Univ	OH	29,097	HC
Middle Tenn State Univ	TN	8,540	C
Mills College	CA	39,870	C
Morehouse College	GA	25,082	C
Mount Holyoke College	MA	42,148	HC+
Muskingum College	OH	22,970	C
New York Univ	NY	43,170	MC
North Park Univ	IL	24,050	C
Northeastern Univ	MA	35,742	HC
Northern Arizona Univ	AZ	10,353	C
Occidental College	CA	40,185	MC
Ohio Univ	OH	15,921	C
Ohio Wesleyan Univ	OH	35,830	VC+
Oral Roberts Univ	OK	22,650	C
Penn State Univ/Univ Park Campus	PA	18,038	HC
Pitzer College	CA	41,644	HC
Pomona College	CA	40,774	MC
Princeton Univ	NJ	40,213	MC
Principia College	IL	27,765	VC+
Randolph-Macon College	VA	31,250	C
Randolph-Macon Woman's College	VA	31,160	VC+
Regis College	MA	31,350	LC
Roanoke College	VA	30,748	VC
Rockhurst Univ	MO	25,440	VC
Rollins College	FL	38,366	VC
St. Cloud State Univ	MN	10,010	C
St. Edward's Univ	TX	23,560	C
St. Joseph's Univ	PA	37,428	VC
St. Mary's Univ of San Antonio	TX	22,444	C
St. Norbert College	WI	28,577	C
St. Thomas Univ	FL	23,490	C
Salem College	NC	26,226	VC+
Samford Univ	AL	20,258	VC
San Francisco State Univ	CA	13,000	C
Seton Hall Univ	NJ	33,622	VC
Shaw Univ	NC	15,488	LC
Shawnee State Univ	OH	12,237	NC
Simmons College	MA	35,640	VC
Simpson College	IA	26,833	VC
Skidmore College	NY	41,779	HC
Southern Illinois Univ Carbondale	IL	12,391	C
Southwestern Adventist Univ	TX	18,290	LC
Stanford Univ	CA	41,557	MC
SUNY/College at Geneseo	NY	12,910	VC+
SUNY/Univ at New Paltz	NY	12,480	VC
Suffolk Univ	MA	33,160	C
Sweet Briar College	VA	31,460	VC
Syracuse Univ	NY	38,655	HC
Texas Christian Univ	TX	23,410	VC
Texas State Univ - San Marcos	TX	10,862	C
Trinity Univ	TX	30,157	HC+
Tufts Univ	MA	42,018	MC
Univ of Arkansas	AR	11,859	VC
Univ of at Calif Davis	CA	15,010	VC
Univ of Colo at Boulder	CO	13,352	C+
Univ of Delaware	DE	14,142	HC
Univ of Georgia	GA	11,004	HC
Univ of Idaho	ID	9,310	VC
Univ of Indianapolis	IN	25,090	C
Univ of Mary Washington	VA	11,636	HC
Univ of Memphis	TN	11,153	C
Univ of Minn/Twin Cities	MN	13,165	HC
Univ of Nebr at Lincoln	NE	11,401	VC
Univ of Nevada/Reno	NV	12,155	NC
Univ of Northern Colo	CO	10,249	C
Univ of Pennsylvania	PA	41,766	MC
Univ of Redlands	CA	36,160	VC
Univ of San Diego	CA	40,620	HC
Univ of Scranton	PA	31,100	VC
Univ of S Car at Columbia	SC	13,397	VC
Univ of South Florida	FL	10,284	VC
Univ of Southern Calif	CA	41,618	VC
Univ of the Pacific	CA	34,380	VC
Univ of Toledo	OH	15,806	NC
Univ of Virginia	VA	13,759	MC
Univ of Washington	WA	10,400	VC
Univ of Wisc/Madison	WI	13,117	HC
Ursinus College	PA	38,950	VC
Utah State Univ	UT	8,002	VC
Virginia Wesleyan College	VA	28,433	C
Wartburg College	IA	27,315	NC
Washington Univ in St. Louis	MO	42,106	MC
Webster Univ	MO	24,280	VC
Wellesley College	MA	41,030	MC
Wesleyan College	GA	19,560	C
Westminster College	PA	31,290	C+
Wheaton College	MA	40,180	HC+
Widener Univ	PA	27,275	C
William Jewell College	MO	24,340	C
Winona State Univ	MN	11,333	C
Wittenberg Univ	OH	34,596	VC
Wright State Univ	OH	13,616	LC
Xavier Univ	OH	30,490	HC

INTERNATIONAL STUDIES

School	ST	$IS	SR
Adrian College	MI	23,000	C
Albion College	MI	26,000	VC
Allegheny College	PA	33,500	HC
American Univ	DC	38,719	HC+

School	ST	$IS	SR
Aquinas College	MI	23,750	C
Arcadia Univ	PA	33,570	VC
Arkansas Tech Univ	AR	8,108	VC
Ashland Univ	OH	25,000	C
Assumption College	MA	32,875	C
Auburn Univ Montgomery	AL	9,530	NC
Augustana College	SD	24,380	VC
Austin Univ	TX	27,871	HC
Azusa Pacific Univ	CA	28,546	VC
Baker Univ	KS	22,190	C
Baldwin-Wallace College	OH	27,256	VC
Barry Univ	FL	24,100	C
Belhaven College	MS	19,530	NC
Bellarmine Univ	KY	27,650	C+
Benedictine Univ	IL	25,710	C
Bentley College	MA	38,784	HC
Berry College	GA	24,342	VC
Bethany College	WV	21,395	C
Bethel College	IN	19,680	C
Bethune-Cookman College	FL	17,922	LC
Birmingham-Southern College	AL	28,494	VC+
Bowling Green State Univ	OH	14,994	C
Bradley Univ	IL	25,280	VC
Brenau Univ Women's College	GA	23,950	VC
Bridgewater College	VA	27,790	C
Brigham Young Univ/Hawaii	HI	7,740	HC+
Butler Univ	IN	31,944	VC+
Calif Lutheran Univ	CA	27,800	LC
Cal State East Bay	CA	10,856	LC
Cal State, Long Beach	CA	9,512	C
Cal State, Monterey Bay	CA	10,099	C
Calvin College	MI	25,735	NC
Case Western Reserve Univ	OH	37,314	MC
Cedarville Univ	OH	21,904	VC
Centenary College	NJ	28,870	LC
Central College	IA	26,774	VC
Central Conn State Univ	CT	13,620	C
CUNY/City College	NY		C
CUNY/College of Staten Island	NY	4,328	NC
Clark Univ	MA	35,165	VC+
Colby College	ME	41,770	MC
College of New Jersey	NJ	18,315	NC
College of New Rochelle	NY	28,396	C+
College of Our Lady of the Elms	MA	21,000	C
College of St. Elizabeth	NJ	28,495	C
College of William and Mary	VA	14,147	NC
Columbia Univ/Barnard College	NY	38,000	MC
Concordia College-New York	NY	27,740	C
Defiance College	OH	24,790	C
Denison Univ	OH	37,040	HC
DePaul Univ	IL	29,835	VC
Dickinson College	PA	40,170	HC+
Doane College	NE	22,458	C
Dominican Univ of Calif	CA	36,836	C
Drexel Univ	PA	27,700	VC
Drury Univ	MO	20,117	VC
D'Youville College	NY	23,660	C
Earlham College	IN	33,604	HC
Elmira College	NY	37,200	VC
Elon Univ	NC	25,371	HC
Emmanuel College	MA	32,000	C
Emory & Henry College	VA	26,570	C
Emory Univ	GA	40,546	MC
Endicott College	MA	30,156	C+
Evangel Univ	MO	17,380	C
Fairfield Univ	CT	39,835	HC
Fairleigh Dickinson Univ/Metropolitan Campus	NJ	28,590	C
Ferrum College	VA	24,290	LC
Fordham Univ	NY	36,000	HC
Francis Marion Univ	SC	11,114	C
Frostburg State Univ	MD	12,672	C
Gannon Univ	PA	26,100	C
George Fox Univ	OR	28,490	C
Georgia Southern Univ	GA	9,762	C
Gonzaga Univ	WA	30,218	VC
Gordon College	MA	29,194	C+
Graceland Univ	IA	19,700	C
Guilford College	NC	28,160	C+
Hampshire College	MA	37,120	HC
Hanover College	IN	28,150	HC
Harding Univ	AR	16,512	VC
Hawaii Pacific Univ	HI	21,080	C
Heidelberg College	OH	23,242	VC
High Point Univ	NC	25,720	C
Hollins Univ	VA	31,105	C
Hope College	MI	28,208	VC+
Huntingdon College	AL	23,090	VC
Idaho State Univ	ID	9,030	C
Illinois Wesleyan Univ	IL	34,050	HC+
Indiana Univ Bloomington	IN	13,356	VC
Indiana Univ of Pennsylvania	PA	11,209	C
Indiana Univ-Purdue Univ Indianapolis	IN	10,959	C
Iona College	NY	30,878	VC
Jacksonville Univ	FL	24,040	VC
James Madison Univ	VA	12,010	VC
John Brown Univ	AR	20,910	VC
Johns Hopkins Univ	MD	42,044	MC
Juniata College	PA	33,130	VC
Kalamazoo College	MI	32,442	VC+
Kennesaw State Univ	GA	12,152	C
Kenyon College	OH	39,500	MC
La Roche College	PA	24,724	LC
Le Moyne College	NY	29,570	VC
Lees-McRae College	NC	23,000	C
Liberty Univ	VA	19,101	C
Lindenwood Univ	MO	18,600	VC
Lock Haven Univ of Pennsylvania	PA	12,098	LC
LIU/C.W. Post Campus	NY	28,282	C
Loras College	IA	27,193	C
Louisiana State Univ and A&M Univ	LA	10,749	VC
Loyola Univ Chicago	IL	32,896	VC
Lycoming College	PA	30,797	C+
Macalester College	MN	36,500	MC
Manhattanville College	NY	32,500	C+
Mansfield Univ	PA	11,300	C
Marlboro College	VT	35,980	VC+
Mars Hill College	NC	19,000	LC
Marymount Manhattan College	NY	30,049	VC
Meredith College	NC	25,600	C
Methodist College	NC	21,000	C
Miami Univ	OH	29,097	HC
Middlebury College	VT	42,120	MC
Millersville Univ of Pennsylvania	PA	12,113	C
Millikin Univ	IL	25,590	C
Missouri Southern State Univ	MO	8,396	NC
Monmouth College	IL	23,700	C
Mount Mary College	WI	22,895	C
Mount Mercy College	IA	23,670	C
Mount St. Mary College	NY	25,250	C
Mount St. Mary's Univ	MD	30,930	C
Mount Union College	OH	25,840	C
Muhlenberg College	PA	36,030	HC+
Murray State Univ	KY	8,900	C
National Univ	CA	8,412	SP
Nazareth College of Rochester	NY	28,175	VC
Nebr Wesleyan Univ	NE	23,415	C+
New College of Florida	FL	10,009	HC+
Niagara Univ	NY	28,250	C
N Dak State Univ	ND	8,500	C
Northern Kentucky Univ	KY	6,670	NC
Northern Mich Univ	MI	12,340	LC
Northwest Christian College	OR	24,298	C
Northwest Nazarene Univ	ID	22,590	VC
Northwestern Univ	IL	37,595	MC
Norwich Univ	VT	28,212	C
Oakwood College	AL	14,904	C
Oglethorpe Univ	GA	30,300	VC
Ohio Northern Univ	OH	27,765	VC
Ohio State Univ	OH	15,357	HC
Ohio Univ	OH	15,921	C
Old Dominion Univ	VA	11,907	C
Oral Roberts Univ	OK	22,650	C
Otterbein College	OH	28,986	C
Pacific Lutheran Univ	WA	28,805	VC
Pepperdine Univ	CA	39,960	HC
Pittsburg State Univ	KS	8,112	C
Point Park Univ	PA	24,160	C
Portland State Univ	OR	12,453	C
Providence College	RI	34,580	HC
Queens Univ of Charlotte	NC	24,528	C
Ramapo College of New Jersey	NJ	16,630	VC
Randolph-Macon College	VA	31,250	C
Rhodes College	TN	32,860	HC
Ripon College	WI	27,160	C+
Roosevelt Univ	IL	22,605	VC
Russell Sage College	NY	27,000	C
Saginaw Valley State Univ	MI	11,432	C
St. Francis College	NY	19,974	LC
St. Francis Univ	PA	25,880	LC
St. John Fisher College	NY	27,860	VC
St. Joseph College	CT	32,050	C
St. Joseph's College	IN	26,600	C
St. Lawrence Univ	NY	40,545	VC
St. Leo Univ	FL	22,140	C+
St. Mary-of-the-Woods College	IN	25,480	C
St. Mary's Univ of San Antonio	TX	22,444	C
St. Peter's College	NJ	30,160	LC
Salisbury Univ	MD	13,128	VC
Seattle Univ	WA	30,063	VC
Seton Hill Univ	PA	28,810	C
Shaw Univ	NC	15,488	LC
Sonoma State Univ	CA	14,732	C
Southern Adventist Univ	TN	18,500	C
Southern Methodist Univ	TX	36,088	VC+
Southern Nazarene Univ	OK	14,634	NC
Southern Oregon Univ	OR	12,186	C
Southern Polytechnic State Univ	GA	7,640	VC
Southwestern Univ	TX	26,767	HC
Spring Hill College	AL	28,678	C
SUNY at Oswego	NY	13,662	VC
SUNY/College at Brockport	NY	12,747	VC
SUNY/College at Cortland	NY	12,095	C
SUNY/College at Old Westbury	NY	13,154	C
SUNY/College at Oneonta	NY	12,905	VC
SUNY/Univ at Binghamton	NY	13,988	HC
Stetson Univ	FL	32,725	VC
Stonehill College	MA	36,104	HC
Susquehanna Univ	PA	33,465	VC
Tabor College	KS	21,614	NC
Taylor Univ	IN	26,376	VC+
Tenn Wesleyan College	TN	18,650	C
Texas A&M Univ	TX	13,351	NC
Texas Lutheran Univ	TX	23,530	C
Texas State Univ - San Marcos	TX	10,862	C
Texas Wesleyan Univ	TX	18,700	C
Thomas College	ME	23,770	LC
Thomas More College	KY	24,470	C
Tiffin Univ	OH	19,490	LC
Towson Univ	MD	13,924	VC
Trinity College	CT	38,040	HC+
Trinity College	DC	24,150	LC
Union College	NE	18,710	C
United States Air Force Academy	CO		HC+
United States Military Academy	NY		MC
Univ of Alabama	AL	9,888	C
Univ of Alabama at Birmingham	AL	13,716	C
Univ of Arkansas at Little Rock	AR	7,230	NC
Univ of Bridgeport	CT	29,595	LC
Univ of Calif at Irvine	CA	16,475	HC
Univ of Calif at Los Angeles	CA	17,681	MC
Univ of Calif at San Diego	CA	16,102	HC
Univ of Chicago	IL	42,369	MC
Univ of Cincinnati	OH	17,682	C
Univ of Colo at Denver and Health Sciences Center	CO	5,021	C
Univ of Dayton	OH	28,826	VC
Univ of Denver	CO	36,376	VC+
Univ of Evansville	IN	28,320	VC
Univ of Findlay	OH	29,238	C
Univ of Hartford	CT	34,044	C
Univ of Illinois at Urbana-Champaign	IL	15,800	HC+
Univ of Kansas	KS	10,915	VC
Univ of La Verne	CA	33,470	C
Univ of Maine	ME	13,642	C
Univ of Maine at Farmington	ME	11,515	C
Univ of Maine at Presque Isle	ME	10,066	LC
Univ of Memphis	TN	11,153	C
Univ of Miami	FL	38,397	MC
Univ of Mich/Dearborn	MI	7,000	VC
Univ of Minn/Duluth	MN	13,974	C
Univ of Miss	MS	9,000	C
Univ of Missouri/Columbia	MO	13,500	VC
Univ of Nebr at Kearney	NE	9,000	NC
Univ of Nebr at Lincoln	NE	11,401	VC
Univ of Nebr at Omaha	NE	11,235	C
Univ of N Car at Chapel Hill	NC	11,129	MC
Univ of N Car at Charlotte	NC	9,101	C
Univ of N Dak	ND	10,114	VC
Univ of Okla	OK	10,769	VC+
Univ of Oregon	OR	13,108	VC
Univ of Pennsylvania	PA	41,766	MC
Univ of Richmond	VA	40,510	MC
Univ of St. Mary	KS	18,900	C
Univ of St. Thomas	MN	28,000	VC
Univ of St. Thomas	TX	23,810	VC
Univ of South Alabama	AL	8,930	LC
Univ of S Dak	SD	9,068	C
Univ of Southern Miss	MS	10,112	C
Univ of Tampa	FL	25,784	C
Univ of Tenn at Martin	TN	8,693	C
Univ of the Pacific	CA	34,380	VC
Univ of Utah	UT	10,162	VC
Univ of Virginia's College at Wise	VA	11,076	C
Univ of West Georgia	GA	8,838	C
Univ of Wisc/Oshkosh	WI	10,426	LC
Univ of Wisc/Parkside	WI	10,341	LC
Univ of Wisc/Platteville	WI	9,779	NC
Univ of Wisc/Stevens Point	WI	9,384	C
Univ of Wisc/Superior	WI	9,610	C+
Univ of Wisc/Whitewater	WI	9,274	C
Univ of Wyoming	WY	9,666	C
Utica College	NY	31,396	C
Vassar College	NY	41,700	MC
Virginia Commonwealth Univ	VA	12,987	C
Virginia Military Inst	VA	12,654	VC
Virginia Polytechnic Inst and State Univ	VA	10,834	VC
Walsh Univ	OH	23,440	C
Warren Wilson College	NC	24,382	VC
Washington College	MD	34,990	VC
Washington Univ in St. Louis	MO	42,106	MC
Wayne State Univ	MI	11,805	C
Webster Univ	MO	24,280	VC
Wells College	NY	23,070	VC
West Virginia Univ	WV	10,506	C
West Virginia Wesleyan College	WV	26,880	C
Western Mich Univ	MI	13,299	C
Western New England College	MA	32,054	C
Western Oregon Univ	OR	10,295	C
Westminster College	MO	19,060	VC
Wheeling Jesuit Univ	WV	26,910	C
Whittier College	CA	29,108	C
Whitworth College	WA	29,428	VC+
Wilkes Univ	PA	30,886	C
Willamette Univ	OR	35,416	VC+
William Woods Univ	MO	21,020	C
Wilson College	PA	27,660	C

INTERPRETER FOR THE DEAF

School	ST	$IS	SR
Bethel College	IN	19,680	C
Columbia College Chicago	IL	25,125	LC
Gallaudet Univ	DC	16,554	
Gardner-Webb Univ	NC	21,500	C
MacMurray College	IL	20,755	C
Madonna Univ	MI	16,068	VC
Maryville College	TN	29,224	VC
Mount Aloysius College	PA	20,900	LC
Northeastern Univ	MA	35,742	HC
Quincy Univ	IL	24,920	C
Rochester Inst of Technology	NY	32,070	VC+
Univ of Arkansas at Little Rock	AR	7,230	NC
Univ of Rochester	NY	41,135	MC
Virginia Polytechnic Inst and State Univ	VA	10,834	VC
Western Oregon Univ	OR	10,295	C
William Woods Univ	MO	21,020	C

INVESTMENTS AND SECURITIES

School	ST	$IS	SR
Campbell Univ	NC	21,137	VC
Central Mich Univ	MI	12,244	C
CUNY/Baruch College	NY	4,320	VC+
Duquesne Univ	PA	29,534	VC
Univ of Miss	MS	9,000	C

ISLAMIC STUDIES

School	ST	$IS	SR
Brandeis Univ	MA	41,551	MC
Ohio State Univ	OH	15,357	HC
Univ of Calif at Santa Barbara	CA	11,800	VC
Univ of Mich/Ann Arbor	MI	16,587	HC+
Univ of Texas at Austin	TX	14,610	HC
Washington Univ in St. Louis	MO	42,106	MC

ITALIAN

School	ST	$IS	SR
Arizona State Univ-Tempe	AZ	11,174	C
Bard College	NY	41,860	HC+
Bennington College	VT	41,890	HC
Boston College	MA	41,608	MC
Boston Univ	MA	42,046	HC+
Brigham Young Univ	UT	9,200	VC
Bryn Mawr College	PA	42,780	HC+
Central Conn State Univ	CT	13,620	C
CUNY/Brooklyn College	NY	4,377	C+
CUNY/Herbert H. Lehman College	NY	4,000	LC
CUNY/Hunter College	NY	8,000	C+
CUNY/Queens College	NY	4,356	C
College of the Holy Cross	MA	40,664	MC
Columbia Univ/Barnard College	NY	38,000	MC
Columbia Univ/School of General Studies	NY	41,516	C
Conn College	CT	41,975	MC
Cornell Univ	NY	41,717	MC
Dartmouth College	NH	39,465	MC
DePaul Univ	IL	29,835	VC
Dominican Univ	IL	26,370	C
Emory Univ	GA	40,546	MC
Florida Atlantic Univ	FL	11,221	C
Florida State Univ	FL	9,028	HC
Fordham Univ	NY	36,000	HC
Georgetown Univ	DC	43,183	MC
Harvard Univ/Harvard College	MA	45,860	MC
Haverford College	PA	41,600	MC
Hofstra Univ	NY	32,630	VC
Indiana Univ Bloomington	IN	13,356	VC
Iona College	NY	30,878	VC
Johns Hopkins Univ	MD	42,044	MC
La Salle Univ	PA	34,950	C
LIU/C.W. Post Campus	NY	28,282	C
Loyola Univ Chicago	IL	32,896	VC
Marlboro College	VT	35,980	VC+
Middlebury College	VT	42,120	MC
Montclair State Univ	NJ	16,327	C
Mount Holyoke College	MA	42,148	HC+
Nazareth College of Rochester	NY	28,175	VC
New York Univ	NY	43,170	MC
Northwestern Univ	IL	37,595	MC

School	ST	$IS	SR
Ohio State Univ	OH	15,357	HC
Penn State Univ/Univ Park Campus	PA	18,038	HC
Princeton Univ	NJ	40,213	MC
Providence College	RI	34,580	HC
Rutgers, The State Univ of New Jersey/New Brunswick/Piscataway Campus	NJ	15,810	HC
St. John's Univ	NY	34,370	C
San Francisco State Univ	CA	13,000	C
Santa Clara Univ	CA	38,931	VC
Sarah Lawrence College	NY	42,000	MC
Scripps College	CA	41,000	MC
Seton Hall Univ	NJ	33,622	VC
Smith College	MA	41,474	MC
Southern Conn State Univ	CT	10,310	C
Stanford Univ	CA	41,557	MC
SUNY/College at Buffalo	NY	11,903	C+
SUNY/Univ at Albany	NY	13,860	VC
SUNY/Univ at Binghamton	NY	13,988	HC
SUNY/Univ at Buffalo	NY	13,694	VC
Temple Univ	PA	17,438	C
Trinity College	CT	38,040	HC+
Tulane Univ	LA	41,098	MC
Univ of Arizona	AZ	11,958	VC
Univ of at Calif Davis	CA	15,010	VC
Univ of Calif at Berkeley	CA	18,141	HC+
Univ of Calif at Los Angeles	CA	17,681	MC
Univ of Colo at Boulder	CO	13,352	C+
Univ of Delaware	DE	14,142	HC
Univ of Denver	CO	36,376	VC+
Univ of Georgia	GA	11,004	HC
Univ of Illinois at Chicago	IL	16,256	VC
Univ of Illinois at Urbana-Champaign	IL	15,800	HC+
Univ of Iowa	IA	12,172	VC
Univ of Kentucky	KY	7,800	C
Univ of Mass Boston	MA	8,024	C
Univ of Miami	FL	38,397	MC
Univ of Mich/Ann Arbor	MI	16,587	HC+
Univ of Minn/Twin Cities	MN	13,165	HC
Univ of Notre Dame	IN	39,552	MC
Univ of Oregon	OR	13,108	VC
Univ of Pennsylvania	PA	41,766	MC
Univ of Pittsburgh at Pittsburgh	PA	18,866	HC
Univ of Rhode Island	RI	15,398	C
Univ of S Car at Columbia	SC	13,397	VC
Univ of South Florida	FL	10,284	VC
Univ of Southern Calif	CA	41,618	MC
Univ of Tenn at Knoxville	TN	11,720	C
Univ of Texas at Austin	TX	14,610	HC
Univ of Virginia	VA	13,759	HC
Univ of Washington	WA	10,400	VC
Univ of Wisc/Madison	WI	13,117	HC
Univ of Wisc/Milwaukee	WI	9,427	C
Villanova Univ	PA	38,672	HC+
Washington Univ in St. Louis	MO	42,106	MC
Wayne State Univ	MI	11,805	C
Wesleyan Univ	CT	42,122	MC
Yale Univ	CT	41,000	MC
Youngstown State Univ	OH	12,613	NC

ITALIAN STUDIES

School	ST	$IS	SR
Bard College	NY	41,800	HC+
Boston Univ	MA	42,046	HC+
Brown Univ	RI	42,015	MC
Columbia Univ/Columbia College	NY	42,584	MC
Columbia Univ/School of General Studies	NY	41,516	C
Conn College	CT	41,975	MC
Dickinson College	PA	40,170	HC+
Duke Univ	NC	41,239	MC
Emory Univ	GA	40,546	MC
Florida International Univ	FL	9,215	VC
Fordham Univ	NY	36,000	HC
Gonzaga Univ	WA	30,218	HC
Ithaca College	NY	35,144	VC
Purdue Univ/West Lafayette	IN	13,458	VC
Rosemont College	PA	29,350	C
Scripps College	CA	41,000	MC
Southern Methodist Univ	TX	36,088	VC+
SUNY/Univ at Stony Brook	NY	13,625	HC
Sweet Briar College	VA	31,460	VC
Syracuse Univ	NY	38,655	VC
Univ of Calif at Los Angeles	CA	17,681	MC
Univ of Calif at San Diego	CA	16,102	HC
Univ of Calif at Santa Barbara	CA	11,800	VC
Univ of Calif at Santa Cruz	CA	19,174	VC
Univ of Conn	CT	16,628	HC
Univ of Houston	TX	7,000	C
Univ of Maryland/College Park	MD	16,036	HC
Univ of Mass Amherst	MA	15,973	C+
Univ of Pennsylvania	PA	41,766	MC
Univ of Vermont	VT	18,080	VC
Wellesley College	MA	41,030	MC
Wheaton College	MA	40,180	HC+

JAPANESE

School	ST	$IS	SR
Arizona State Univ-Tempe	AZ	11,174	C
Bates College	ME	42,100	HC
Bennington College	VT	41,890	HC
Brigham Young Univ	UT	9,200	VC
Cal State, Fullerton	CA	10,990	C
Cal State, Long Beach	CA	9,512	C
Cal State, Los Angeles	CA	5,900	C
Central Washington Univ	WA	11,730	C
Colgate Univ	NY	41,170	MC
Conn College	CT	41,975	MC
Eastern Mich Univ	MI	12,897	C
Emory Univ	GA	40,546	MC
George Washington Univ	DC	48,820	MC
Georgetown Univ	DC	43,183	MC
Harvard Univ/Harvard College	MA	45,860	MC
Linfield College	OR	29,632	VC
Macalester College	MN	36,500	MC
Middlebury College	VT	42,120	MC
Mount Union College	OH	25,840	C
North Central College	IL	28,926	VC
Oakland Univ	MI	11,936	C
Ohio State Univ	OH	15,357	HC
Pacific Univ	OR	24,250	C
Pomona College	CA	40,774	MC
Portland State Univ	OR	12,453	C
Purdue Univ/West Lafayette	IN	13,458	VC
San Diego State Univ	CA	12,971	C
San Francisco State Univ	CA	13,000	C
Stanford Univ	CA	41,557	MC
Tufts Univ	MA	42,018	MC
Univ of at Calif Davis	CA	15,010	VC
Univ of Calif at Berkeley	CA	18,141	HC+
Univ of Calif at Irvine	CA	16,475	HC
Univ of Calif at Los Angeles	CA	17,681	MC
Univ of Calif at Santa Barbara	CA	11,800	VC
Univ of Chicago	IL	42,369	MC
Univ of Colo at Boulder	CO	13,352	C+
Univ of Findlay	OH	29,238	C
Univ of Hawaii at Manoa	HI	10,413	VC
Univ of Maryland/College Park	MD	16,036	HC
Univ of Mass Amherst	MA	15,973	C+
Univ of Mich/Ann Arbor	MI	16,587	HC+
Univ of Minn/Twin Cities	MN	13,165	HC
Univ of Montana	MT	10,602	C
Univ of Notre Dame	IN	39,552	MC
Univ of Oregon	OR	13,108	VC
Univ of Pittsburgh at Pittsburgh	PA	18,866	HC
Univ of Rochester	NY	41,135	MC
Univ of the Pacific	CA	34,380	VC
Univ of Utah	UT	10,162	VC
Univ of Washington	WA	10,400	VC
Univ of Wisc/Madison	WI	13,117	HC
Vassar College	NY	41,700	MC
Washington Univ in St. Louis	MO	42,106	MC
Wellesley College	MA	41,030	MC
Yale Univ	CT	41,000	MC

JAPANESE STUDIES

School	ST	$IS	SR
Boston Univ	MA	42,046	HC+
Case Western Reserve Univ	OH	37,314	MC
Dillard Univ	LA	17,500	VC
Earlham College	IN	33,604	HC
Gettysburg College	PA	39,864	HC
Madonna Univ	MI	16,068	VC
Salem International Univ	WV	18,020	C
Univ of Alaska Fairbanks	AK	10,101	C
Univ of Calif at San Diego	CA	16,102	HC
Univ of Georgia	GA	11,004	HC
Univ of Hawaii at Hilo	HI	6,500	C
Wellesley College	MA	41,030	MC
Willamette Univ	OR	35,416	VC+
William Jewell College	MO	24,340	C

JAZZ

School	ST	$IS	SR
Bennington College	VT	41,890	HC
Berklee College of Music	MA	37,779	SP
Brigham Young Univ	UT	9,200	VC
DePaul Univ	IL	29,835	VC
Eastman School of Music	NY	35,000	SP
Five Towns College	NY	24,600	SP
Florida State Univ	FL	9,028	HC
Hofstra Univ	NY	32,630	VC
Howard Univ	DC	18,481	C+
Indiana Univ Bloomington	IN	13,356	VC
Ithaca College	NY	35,144	VC
Johnson State College	VT	11,830	LC
Limestone College	SC	19,840	C
Loyola Univ New Orleans	LA	31,050	VC+
Manhattan School of Music	NY	33,000	SP
Mich State Univ	MI	13,689	VC
New England Conservatory of Music	MA	38,750	SP
N Car Central Univ	NC	9,002	LC
Northwestern Univ	IL	37,595	MC
Ohio State Univ	OH	15,357	HC

School	ST	$IS	SR
Roosevelt Univ	IL	22,605	VC
Shenandoah Univ	VA	27,600	C
Temple Univ	PA	17,438	C
Texas State Univ - San Marcos	TX	10,862	C
Univ of Cincinnati	OH	17,682	C
Univ of Denver	CO	36,376	VC+
Univ of Hartford	CT	34,044	C
Univ of Maine at Augusta	ME	5,025	NC
Univ of Miami	FL	38,397	MC
Univ of Mich/Ann Arbor	MI	16,587	HC+
Univ of Minn/Duluth	MN	13,974	C
Univ of N Car at Greensboro	NC	8,993	C
Univ of North Florida	FL	9,908	VC
Univ of North Texas	TX	7,800	C
Univ of Oregon	OR	13,108	VC
Univ of Rochester	NY	41,135	MC
Univ of Southern Calif	CA	41,618	MC
Univ of Washington	WA	10,400	VC
Western Mich Univ	MI	13,299	C

JOURNALISM

School	ST	$IS	SR
Abilene Christian Univ	TX	20,830	C
Adams State College	CO	8,613	C
American Univ	DC	38,719	HC+
Andrews Univ	MI	21,786	C
Angelo State Univ	TX	8,340	NC
Appalachian State Univ	NC	8,000	VC
Arizona State Univ-Tempe	AZ	11,174	C
Arkansas State Univ	AR	9,630	C
Arkansas Tech Univ	AR	8,108	VC
Asbury College	KY	23,762	VC
Ashland Univ	OH	25,000	C
Auburn Univ	AL	12,230	VC
Augustana College	SD	24,380	VC
Averett Univ	VA	24,920	C
Ball State Univ	IN	13,138	C
Baylor Univ	TX	27,555	HC
Bemidji State Univ	MN	11,180	LC
Benedict College	SC	19,114	LC
Benedictine College	KS	21,968	C
Bethany College	WV	21,395	C
Biola Univ	CA	29,372	VC
Boston Univ	MA	42,046	HC+
Bowling Green State Univ	OH	14,994	C
Briar Cliff Univ	IA	23,550	LC
Butler Univ	IN	31,944	VC+
Calif Baptist Univ	CA	23,780	C
Calif Polytechnic State Univ	CA	12,390	VC
Cal State East Bay	CA	10,856	LC
Cal State, Chico	CA	11,395	C
Cal State, Fresno	CA	10,037	LC
Cal State, Fullerton	CA	10,990	C
Cal State, Long Beach	CA	9,512	VC
Cal State, Northridge	CA	9,036	LC
Cal State, Sacramento	CA	11,122	C+
Campbell Univ	NC	21,137	VC
Carnegie Mellon Univ	PA	32,700	MC
Central Mich Univ	MI	12,244	C
Central Missouri State Univ	MO	10,000	C
Central State Univ	OH	9,010	C+
Central Univ of Bayamon	PR	3,335	
Central Washington Univ	WA	11,730	C
Champlain College	VT	24,605	C
Christopher Newport Univ	VA	13,326	VC
CUNY/Baruch College	NY	4,320	VC
CUNY/Brooklyn College	NY	4,377	C+
College of New Jersey	NJ	18,315	MC
College of St. Joseph	VT	20,900	NC
College of the Ozarks	MO	4,130	VC+
Colo State Univ-Fort Collins	CO	10,878	C+
Colo State Univ-Pueblo	CO	7,821	LC
Columbia College Chicago	IL	25,125	LC
Columbia Union College	MD	23,536	LC
Concordia College: Moorhead	MN	22,475	VC
Creighton Univ	NE	29,918	VC+
Delaware State Univ	DE	8,130	LC
Delta State Univ	MS	7,709	C
Dickinson State Univ	ND	7,847	NC
Dominican Univ	IL	26,317	C
Dordt College	IA	20,325	VC
Drake Univ	IA	27,632	VC+
Drury Univ	MO	20,117	VC
Duquesne Univ	PA	29,534	VC
Earlham College	IN	33,604	HC
East Central Univ	OK	6,207	C
Eastern Illinois Univ	IL	12,569	C
Eastern Kentucky Univ	KY	7,725	C
Eastern Mich Univ	MI	12,897	C
Eastern Nazarene College	MA	19,500	LC
Eastern New Mexico Univ	NM	7,264	C
Eastern Washington Univ	WA	10,608	C
Elon Univ	NC	25,371	HC
Emerson College	MA	35,076	HC
Emory & Henry College	VA	26,570	C
Emory Univ	GA	40,546	MC
Evangel Univ	MO	17,380	C
Florida A&M Univ	FL	8,344	C
Florida Atlantic Univ	FL	11,221	C
Florida Southern College	FL	25,965	C
Fordham Univ	NY	36,000	HC
Franklin College	IN		C
George Washington Univ	DC	48,820	MC

School	ST	$IS	SR
Georgia Southern Univ	GA	9,762	C
Georgia State Univ	GA	11,444	VC
Gonzaga Univ	WA	30,218	HC
Grace College	IN	22,170	C
Grand Valley State Univ	MI	12,000	C
Grand View College	IA	21,482	C
Hampshire College	MA	37,120	HC
Harding Univ	AR	16,512	VC
Hawaii Pacific Univ	HI	21,080	C
Hofstra Univ	NY	32,630	VC
Howard Univ	DC	18,481	C+
Humboldt State Univ	CA	11,176	C
Illinois State Univ	IL	12,839	C+
Indiana State Univ	IN	11,604	C
Indiana Univ Bloomington	IN	13,356	VC
Indiana Univ of Pennsylvania	PA	11,209	C
Indiana Univ South Bend	IN	4,989	LC
Indiana Univ Southeast	IN	4,880	LC
Indiana Univ-Purdue Univ Indianapolis	IN	10,959	C
Iowa State Univ	IA	11,831	VC
Ithaca College	NY	35,144	VC
John Brown Univ	AR	20,910	VC
Johnson State College	VT	11,830	LC
Kansas State Univ	KS	10,516	VC
Keene State College	NH	13,836	C
Kent State Univ	OH	14,594	C
Lehigh Univ	PA	42,690	HC+
Lewis Univ	IL	23,050	C+
Lincoln Univ	MO	8,000	NC
Lincoln Univ	PA	13,658	C+
Lipscomb Univ	TN	20,967	VC
Lock Haven Univ of Pennsylvania	PA	12,098	LC
LIU/Brooklyn Campus	NY	25,000	C
LIU/C.W. Post Campus	NY	28,282	C
Loras College	IA	27,193	C
Louisiana College	LA	13,450	C
Louisiana State Univ in Shreveport	LA	2,900	NC
Louisiana Tech Univ	LA	7,370	C
Loyola Univ Chicago	IL	32,896	VC
Lyndon State College	VT	14,233	LC
Madonna Univ	MI	16,068	VC
Mansfield Univ	PA	11,300	C
Marietta College	OH	29,327	C
Marquette Univ	WI	31,066	HC
Marshall Univ	WV	9,116	C
Mercy College	NY	20,000	VC
Mercyhurst College	PA	28,633	VC
Messiah College	PA	28,910	VC+
Metropolitan State College of Denver	CO	2,338	LC
Mich State Univ	MI	13,689	VC
Midland Lutheran College	NE	18,600	C
Minn State Univ, Mankato	MN	10,276	LC
Minn State Univ, Moorhead	MN	7,000	C
Morris College	SC	11,999	LC
Mount Ida College	MA	26,000	LC
Mount Marty College	SD	20,590	C
Mount Vernon Nazarene Univ	OH	20,810	C
Murray State Univ	KY	8,900	VC
Muskingum College	OH	22,970	C
New Mexico State Univ	NM	9,250	C
New York Univ	NY	43,170	MC
Nicholls State Univ	LA	6,500	NC
Norfolk State Univ	VA	10,531	LC
Northeastern State Univ	OK	5,896	LC
Northeastern Univ	MA	35,742	VC
Northern Arizona Univ	AZ	10,353	C
Northern Illinois Univ	IL	13,178	C
Northern Kentucky Univ	KY	6,670	NC
Northwest Missouri State Univ	MO	10,000	C
Northwest Univ	WA	18,854	C
Northwestern State Univ of Louisiana	LA	7,144	C
Northwestern Univ	IL	37,595	MC
Oakland Univ	MI	11,936	C
Ohio Northern Univ	OH	27,765	VC
Ohio State Univ	OH	15,357	HC
Ohio Univ	OH	15,921	C
Ohio Wesleyan Univ	OH	35,830	VC+
Okla Baptist Univ	OK	17,986	VC
Okla Christian Univ	OK	18,992	NC
Okla City Univ	OK	23,965	VC
Okla State Univ	OK	10,213	VC
Old Dominion Univ	VA	11,907	C
Olivet College	MI	19,984	C+
Otterbein College	OH	28,986	C
Pacific Union College	CA	24,555	VC+
Palm Beach Atlantic Univ	FL	23,597	VC
Penn State Univ/Univ Park Campus	PA	18,038	HC
Pepperdine Univ	CA	39,960	HC
Point Loma Nazarene Univ	CA	27,610	VC
Point Park Univ	PA	24,160	VC
Prairie View A&M Univ	TX	11,110	C
Prescott College	AZ	13,445	LC
Purdue Univ/West Lafayette	IN	13,458	VC
Quinnipiac Univ	CT	34,640	VC
Rider Univ	NJ	32,560	C
Roosevelt Univ	IL	22,605	VC
Rowan Univ	NJ	16,000	VC

School	ST	$IS	SR
Rust College	MS		C+
Rutgers, The State Univ of New Jersey/New Brunswick/Piscataway Campus	NJ	15,810	HC
Rutgers, The State Univ of New Jersey/Newark Campus	NJ	15,640	VC
St. Bonaventure Univ	NY	28,785	LC
St. Cloud State Univ	MN	10,010	C
St. John's Univ	NY	34,370	C
St. Joseph's College	IN	26,600	C
St. Mary-of-the-Woods College	IN	25,480	C
St. Michael's College	VT	33,330	VC
Sam Houston State Univ	TX	8,000	C
Samford Univ	AL	20,258	VC
San Diego State Univ	CA	12,971	C
San Francisco State Univ	CA	13,000	C
San Jose State Univ	CA	11,707	C
Seattle Univ	WA	30,063	VC
Seton Hall Univ	NJ	33,622	VC
Seton Hill Univ	PA	28,810	C
Shippensburg Univ of Pennsylvania	PA	11,621	C
Simpson College	IA	26,833	VC
S Dak State Univ	SD	9,815	C
Southeast Missouri State Univ	MO	10,596	C
Southeastern Univ	FL	17,180	LC
Southern Adventist Univ	TN	18,500	C
Southern Arkansas Univ	AR	6,956	C
Southern Conn State Univ	CT	10,310	C
Southern Illinois Univ Carbondale	IL	12,391	C
Southern Methodist Univ	TX	36,088	VC+
Southern Nazarene Univ	OK	14,634	NC
Southern Univ at New Orleans	LA	1,000	NC
Southwestern Adventist Univ	TX	18,290	LC
Spring Hill College	AL	28,678	C
SUNY at Oswego	NY	13,662	VC
SUNY/College at Brockport	NY	12,747	VC
SUNY/College at Buffalo	NY	11,903	C+
SUNY/College at Plattsburgh	NY	12,362	C
SUNY/College at Purchase	NY	11,989	VC+
SUNY/Univ at New Paltz	NY	12,480	VC
Stephen F. Austin State Univ	TX	7,930	C
Suffolk Univ	MA	33,160	C
Syracuse Univ	NY	38,655	HC
Taylor Univ	IN	26,376	VC+
Temple Univ	PA	17,438	C
Tenn Tech Univ	TN	10,044	C
Texas A&M Univ	TX	13,351	HC
Texas A&M Univ at Commerce	TX	9,020	C
Texas Christian Univ	TX	23,410	VC+
Texas State Univ - San Marcos	TX	10,862	C
Texas Tech Univ	TX	13,026	VC
Thomas Edison State College	NJ	3,780	SP
Tougaloo College	MS	15,975	NC
Troy Univ	AL	8,916	C
Truman State Univ	MO	11,242	HC
Union College	NE	18,710	C
Union Univ	TN	20,750	VC
Univ of Alabama	AL	9,888	C
Univ of Alaska Anchorage	AK	11,275	NC
Univ of Alaska Fairbanks	AK	10,101	C
Univ of Arizona	AZ	11,958	VC
Univ of Arkansas	AR	11,859	VC
Univ of Arkansas at Little Rock	AR	7,230	NC
Univ of Arkansas at Monticello	AR	7,325	NC
Univ of Arkansas at Pine Bluff	AR	8,300	C
Univ of Bridgeport	CT	29,595	LC
Univ of Central Arkansas	AR	9,984	C
Univ of Central Florida	FL	10,739	VC
Univ of Central Okla	OK	8,094	C
Univ of Colo at Boulder	CO	13,352	C+
Univ of Conn	CT	16,628	HC
Univ of Dayton	OH	28,826	VC
Univ of Delaware	DE	14,142	HC
Univ of Denver	CO	36,376	VC+
Univ of Florida	FL	9,354	HC
Univ of Georgia	GA	11,004	HC
Univ of Hawaii at Manoa	HI	10,413	VC
Univ of Houston	TX	7,000	C
Univ of Idaho	ID	9,310	NC
Univ of Illinois at Urbana-Champaign	IL	15,800	HC+
Univ of Indianapolis	IN	25,090	C
Univ of Iowa	IA	12,172	VC
Univ of Judaism College of A&S	CA	30,010	C
Univ of Kansas	KS	10,915	VC
Univ of Kentucky	KY	7,800	C
Univ of La Verne	CA	33,470	C
Univ of Maine	ME	13,642	C
Univ of Mary Hardin-Baylor	TX	19,428	C
Univ of Maryland/College Park	MD	16,036	HC
Univ of Mass Amherst	MA	15,973	C+
Univ of Memphis	TN	11,153	C
Univ of Miami	FL	38,397	MC
Univ of Miss	MS	9,000	C
Univ of Missouri/Columbia	MO	13,500	VC
Univ of Montana	MT	10,602	C
Univ of Montevallo	AL	9,630	C
Univ of Nebr at Kearney	NE	9,000	NC
Univ of Nebr at Lincoln	NE	11,401	VC
Univ of Nebr at Omaha	NE	11,235	C
Univ of Nevada/Reno	NV	12,155	NC
Univ of New Mexico	NM	11,253	C
Univ of North Alabama	AL	8,992	C
Univ of N Car at Chapel Hill	NC	11,129	MC
Univ of North Texas	TX	7,800	C
Univ of Northern Colo	CO	10,249	C
Univ of Okla	OK	10,769	VC+
Univ of Oregon	OR	13,108	VC
Univ of Pittsburgh at Johnstown	PA	16,740	LC
Univ of PR/Rio Piedras	PR	5,750	
Univ of Rhode Island	RI	15,398	C
Univ of Richmond	VA	40,510	MC
Univ of St. Francis	IL	25,430	C
Univ of St. Thomas	MN	28,000	VC
Univ of S Car at Columbia	SC	13,397	VC
Univ of S Dak	SD	9,068	C
Univ of Southern Calif	CA	41,618	MC
Univ of Southern Indiana	IN	12,590	LC
Univ of Southern Miss	MS	10,112	C
Univ of Tenn at Knoxville	TN	11,720	C
Univ of Texas at Arlington	TX	7,195	LC
Univ of Texas at Austin	TX	14,610	HC
Univ of Texas at El Paso	TX	8,764	NC
Univ of Texas-Pan American	TX	7,290	C+
Univ of Wisc/Eau Claire	WI	9,915	VC
Univ of Wisc/Madison	WI	13,117	HC
Univ of Wisc/Oshkosh	WI	10,426	LC
Univ of Wisc/River Falls	WI	9,722	LC
Univ of Wisc/Whitewater	WI	9,274	C
Univ of Wyoming	WY	9,666	C
Utah State Univ	UT	8,002	VC
Utica College	NY	31,396	C
Valparaiso Univ	IN	28,970	VC+
Virginia Union Univ	VA	18,432	LC
Virginia Wesleyan College	VA	28,433	C
Wartburg College	IA	27,315	NC
Washington and Lee Univ	VA	35,880	MC
Washington State Univ	WA	12,260	C
Washington Univ in St. Louis	MO	42,106	MC
Wayne State Univ	MI	11,805	C
Weber State Univ	UT	9,635	NC
Webster Univ	MO	24,280	VC
West Virginia Univ	WV	10,506	C
Western Illinois Univ	IL	13,042	C
Western Kentucky Univ	KY	10,192	C
Western Mich Univ	MI	13,299	C
Western Washington Univ	WA	11,262	VC
Whitworth College	WA	29,428	VC+
William Penn Univ	IA	17,685	LC
William Woods Univ	MO	21,020	C
Wingate Univ	NC	23,300	C
Winona State Univ	MN	11,333	C
Youngstown State Univ	OH	12,613	NC

JOURNALISM EDUCATION

School	ST	$IS	SR
Averett Univ	VA	24,920	C
Ball State Univ	IN	13,138	C
Baylor Univ	TX	27,555	HC
Franklin College	IN		C
Grace College	IN	22,170	C
Univ of Nebr at Lincoln	NE	11,401	VC
Wartburg College	IA	27,315	NC

JUDAIC STUDIES

School	ST	$IS	SR
Albert A. List College of Jewish Studies	NY	20,000	HC+
American Univ	DC	38,719	HC+
Baltimore Hebrew Univ	MD	8,900	SP
Bard College	NY	41,800	HC+
Brandeis Univ	MA	41,551	MC
Brown Univ	RI	42,015	MC
CUNY/Brooklyn College	NY	4,377	C+
CUNY/Hunter College	NY	8,000	C+
CUNY/Queens College	NY	4,356	C
DePaul Univ	IL	29,835	VC
Dickinson College	PA	40,170	HC+
Emory Univ	GA	40,546	MC
Florida Atlantic Univ	FL	11,221	C
George Washington Univ	DC	48,820	MC
Hampshire College	MA	37,120	HC
Hofstra Univ	NY	32,630	VC
Indiana Univ Bloomington	IN	13,356	VC
Mount Holyoke College	MA	42,148	HC+
New York Univ	NY	43,170	MC
Oberlin College	OH	40,904	MC
Ohio State Univ	OH	15,357	HC
Purdue Univ/West Lafayette	IN	13,458	VC
Rutgers, The State Univ of New Jersey/New Brunswick/Piscataway Campus	NJ	15,810	HC
Scripps College	CA	41,000	MC
SUNY/Univ at Binghamton	NY	13,988	HC
Touro College	NY	17,000	VC
Trinity College	CT	38,040	HC+
Tufts Univ	MA	42,018	MC
Tulane Univ	LA	41,098	MC
Univ of Arizona	AZ	11,958	VC
Univ of Calif at Los Angeles	CA	17,681	MC
Univ of Calif at San Diego	CA	16,102	HC
Univ of Chicago	IL	42,369	MC
Univ of Cincinnati	OH	17,682	C
Univ of Florida	FL	9,354	HC
Univ of Hartford	CT	34,044	C
Univ of Judaism College of A&S	CA	30,010	C
Univ of Maryland/College Park	MD	16,036	HC
Univ of Mass Amherst	MA	15,973	C+
Univ of Miami	FL	38,397	MC
Univ of Mich/Ann Arbor	MI	16,587	HC+
Univ of Missouri/Kansas City	MO	15,000	VC
Univ of Oregon	OR	13,108	VC
Univ of Pennsylvania	PA	41,766	MC
Univ of Texas at Austin	TX	14,610	HC
Univ of Washington	WA	10,400	VC
Univ of Wisc/Madison	WI	13,117	HC
Vassar College	NY	41,700	MC
Washington Univ in St. Louis	MO	42,106	MC
Wellesley College	MA	41,030	MC
Yale Univ	CT	41,000	MC

KOREAN

School	ST	$IS	SR
Brigham Young Univ	UT	9,200	VC
Univ of Calif at Los Angeles	CA	17,681	MC
Univ of Chicago	IL	42,369	MC
Univ of Hawaii at Manoa	HI	10,413	VC

LABOR STUDIES

School	ST	$IS	SR
Cal State, Dominguez Hills	CA	10,220	LC
CUNY/Queens College	NY	4,356	C
Cleveland State Univ	OH	10,798	NC
Cornell Univ	NY	41,717	MC
Eastern Mich Univ	MI	12,897	C
Hofstra Univ	NY	32,630	VC
Indiana Univ Bloomington	IN	13,356	VC
Indiana Univ Kokomo	IN	4,835	LC
Indiana Univ Northwest	IN	4,902	LC
Indiana Univ South Bend	IN	4,989	LC
Indiana Univ-Purdue Univ Fort Wayne	IN	5,067	LC
Indiana Univ-Purdue Univ Indianapolis	IN	10,959	C
Le Moyne College	NY	29,570	VC
Northern Kentucky Univ	KY	6,670	NC
Penn State Univ/Univ Park Campus	PA	18,038	HC
Rhode Island College	RI	11,570	C
Rutgers, The State Univ of New Jersey/New Brunswick/Piscataway Campus	NJ	15,810	HC
San Francisco State Univ	CA	13,000	C
SUNY/College at Old Westbury	NY	13,154	C
SUNY/Empire State College	NY	4,575	SP
Thomas Edison State College	NJ	3,780	SP
Univ of Illinois at Urbana-Champaign	IL	15,800	HC+
Univ of Mass Boston	MA	8,024	C
Univ of PR/Rio Piedras	PR	5,750	
Wayne State Univ	MI	11,805	C

LAND USE MANAGEMENT AND RECLAMATION

School	ST	$IS	SR
Cal State, Bakersfield	CA	6,125	LC
Central Mich Univ	MI	12,244	C
Eastern Mich Univ	MI	12,897	C
Humboldt State Univ	CA	11,176	C
Metropolitan State College of Denver	CO	2,338	LC
Montana State Univ-Bozeman	MT	1,137	C
Texas A&M Univ at Galveston	TX	10,000	C+
Univ of Louisiana at Lafayette	LA	5,830	C
Univ of Okla	OK	10,769	VC
Univ of Wisc/Platteville	WI	9,779	NC
Univ of Wisc/River Falls	WI	9,722	VC

LANDSCAPE ARCHITECTURE/ DESIGN

School	ST	$IS	SR
Andrews Univ	MI	21,786	C
Arizona State Univ-Tempe	AZ	11,174	C
Auburn Univ	AL	12,230	VC
Augustana College	IL	29,862	VC+
Ball State Univ	IN	13,138	C
Brigham Young Univ	UT	9,200	VC
Calif Polytechnic State Univ	CA	12,390	VC
Calif State Polytechnic Univ, Pomona	CA	18,053	C+
CUNY/City College	NY		C
Clemson Univ	SC	13,366	VC
Colo State Univ-Fort Collins	CO	10,878	C+
Cornell Univ	NY	41,717	MC
Iowa State Univ	IA	11,831	VC
Kansas State Univ	KS	10,516	VC
Louisiana State Univ and A&M College	LA	10,749	VC
Mich State Univ	MI	13,689	VC
Miss State Univ	MS	9,577	C
N Car Agricultural and Technical State Univ	NC	8,000	LC
N Car State Univ	NC	11,824	HC
N Dak State Univ	ND	8,500	C
Ohio State Univ	OH	15,357	HC
Okla State Univ	OK	10,213	VC
Oregon State Univ	OR	11,055	C
Penn State Univ/Univ Park Campus	PA	18,038	HC
Philadelphia Univ	PA	30,006	C
Purdue Univ/West Lafayette	IN	13,458	VC
S Dak State Univ	SD	9,815	C
SUNY/College of Environmental Science and Forestry	NY	15,000	VC
Temple Univ	PA	17,438	C
Texas A&M Univ	TX	13,351	HC
Texas Tech Univ	TX	13,026	VC
Univ of Arizona	AZ	11,958	VC
Univ of Arkansas	AR	11,859	VC
Univ of at Calif Davis	CA	15,010	VC
Univ of Calif at Berkeley	CA	18,141	HC+
Univ of Conn	CT	16,628	HC
Univ of Delaware	DE	14,142	HC
Univ of Florida	FL	9,354	HC
Univ of Georgia	GA	11,004	HC
Univ of Idaho	ID	9,310	NC
Univ of Illinois at Urbana-Champaign	IL	15,800	HC+
Univ of Kentucky	KY	7,800	C
Univ of Maryland/College Park	MD	16,036	HC
Univ of Mass Amherst	MA	15,973	C+
Univ of Mich/Ann Arbor	MI	16,587	HC+
Univ of Minn/Twin Cities	MN	13,165	HC
Univ of Nevada/Las Vegas	NV	11,566	C
Univ of Oregon	OR	13,108	VC
Univ of Rhode Island	RI	15,398	C
Univ of Southern Calif	CA	41,618	MC
Univ of Tenn at Knoxville	TN	11,720	C
Univ of Texas at Arlington	TX	7,195	LC
Univ of Texas at Austin	TX	14,610	HC
Univ of Vermont	VT	18,080	VC
Univ of Washington	WA	10,400	VC
Univ of Wisc/Madison	WI	13,117	HC
Utah State Univ	UT	8,002	VC
Virginia Polytechnic Inst and State Univ	VA	10,834	VC
Washington State Univ	WA	12,260	C
West Virginia Univ	WV	10,506	C

LANGUAGE ARTS

School	ST	$IS	SR
Aquinas College	MI	23,750	C
Catawba College	NC	25,000	C
Central Mich Univ	MI	12,244	C
Central Washington Univ	WA	11,730	C
Christian Brothers Univ	TN	24,650	VC
Doane College	NE	22,458	C
Hiram College	OH	28,700	VC
Kent State Univ	OH	14,594	C
Lake Erie College	OH	27,725	C
LeMoyne-Owen College	TN	13,150	LC
Malone College	OH	23,040	C
Marygrove College	MI	19,310	C+
Miles College	AL	9,922	NC
Nebr Wesleyan Univ	NE	23,415	C+
Ohio Northern Univ	OH	27,765	VC
Samford Univ	AL	20,258	VC
Spring Arbor Univ	MI	22,476	C
Univ of Arizona	AZ	11,958	VC
Univ of Maine at Farmington	ME	11,515	C
Univ of Nebr at Lincoln	NE	11,401	VC
Wells College	NY	23,070	VC
Western Kentucky Univ	KY	10,192	C

LANGUAGES

School	ST	$IS	SR
Adelphi Univ	NY	27,000	VC
Antioch College	OH	33,700	C
Assumption College	MA	32,875	C
Auburn Univ	AL	12,230	VC
Austin Peay State Univ	TN	7,535	C
Baylor Univ	TX	27,555	VC
Bemidji State Univ	MN	11,180	C
Bennington College	VT	41,890	NC
Bethany College	WV	21,395	C
Carnegie Mellon Univ	PA	32,700	MC

ST = STATE $IS = IN-STATE COSTS   SR = SELECTOR RATING

School	ST	$IS	SR
Carson-Newman College	TN	16,800	C
Carthage College	WI	26,000	C
Central College	IA	26,774	VC
CUNY/Brooklyn College	NY	4,377	C+
CUNY/Herbert H. Lehman College	NY	4,000	LC
CUNY/Hunter College	NY	8,000	C+
Clark Atlanta Univ	GA	20,960	LC
Clark Univ	MA	35,165	VC+
College of St. Scholastica	MN	28,456	VC
Columbia College	SC	24,982	LC
Converse College	SC	24,800	VC
Cornell College	IA	30,110	VC+
Cornell Univ	NY	41,717	MC
Davis and Elkins College	WV	22,416	C
Denison Univ	OH	37,040	HC
Dillard Univ	LA	17,500	VC
Dordt College	IA	20,325	VC
Dowling College	NY	22,110	LC
Earlham College	IN	33,604	HC
Eastern Illinois Univ	IL	12,569	C
Elmira College	NY	37,200	VC
Excelsior College	NY	995	SP
Frostburg State Univ	MD	12,672	C
Gannon Univ	PA	26,100	C
Gordon College	MA	29,194	C+
Grand Valley State Univ	MI	12,000	VC
Hamilton College	NY	41,660	MC
Hartwick College	NY	36,065	C+
Ithaca College	NY	35,144	VC
Jackson State Univ	MS	8,500	C
Judson College	AL	16,522	C
Lewis and Clark College	OR	35,358	VC+
LIU/Brooklyn Campus	NY	25,000	C
Louisiana College	LA	13,450	C
McNeese State Univ	LA	5,270	LC
Mercyhurst College	PA	28,633	VC
Miss College	MS	14,574	VC
Miss State Univ	MS	9,577	C
Murray State Univ	KY	8,900	VC
New College of Florida	FL	10,009	HC+
New Mexico State Univ	NM	9,250	C
Newberry College	SC	23,000	LC
Northeastern Univ	MA	35,742	HC
Occidental College	CA	40,185	MC
Pfeiffer Univ	NC	21,900	C
Pomona College	CA	40,774	MC
Portland State Univ	OR	12,453	C
Principia College	IL	27,765	VC+
Purdue Univ/West Lafayette	IN	13,458	VC
Roger Williams Univ	RI	30,500	C
Roosevelt Univ	IL	22,605	VC
St. Cloud State Univ	MN	10,010	C
St. John's Univ	NY	34,370	C
St. Lawrence Univ	NY	40,545	VC
St. Mary-of-the-Woods College	IN	25,480	C
St. Mary's College of Maryland	MD	18,876	VC+
Scripps College	CA	41,000	MC
Southern Illinois Univ Edwardsville	IL	11,022	C
Southern Methodist Univ	TX	36,088	VC+
Southern Oregon Univ	OR	12,186	C
Stonehill College	MA	36,104	HC
Syracuse Univ	NY	38,655	HC
Tenn State Univ	TN	9,048	LC
Texas A&M Univ at Commerce	TX	9,020	C
Trinity College	DC	24,150	LC
United States Military Academy	NY		MC
Univ of Alabama in Huntsville	AL	9,516	VC
Univ of Alaska Anchorage	AK	11,275	NC
Univ of Calif at Riverside	CA	16,625	C
Univ of Central Florida	FL	10,739	VC
Univ of Delaware	DE	14,142	HC
Univ of Denver	CO	36,376	VC+
Univ of Hartford	CT	34,044	C
Univ of Mary Washington	VA	11,636	VC
Univ of Memphis	TN	11,153	C
Univ of Mich/Dearborn	MI	7,000	VC
Univ of Minn/Twin Cities	MN	13,165	VC
Univ of Nebr at Lincoln	NE	11,401	VC
Univ of New Mexico	NM	11,253	C
Univ of Okla	OK	10,769	VC+
Univ of PR/Rio Piedras	PR	5,750	
Univ of South Alabama	AL	8,930	LC
Univ of Southern Miss	MS	10,112	C
Univ of Tenn at Knoxville	TN	11,720	C
Univ of Texas at El Paso	TX	8,764	NC
Vassar College	NY	41,700	MC
Virginia Commonwealth Univ	VA	12,987	C
Virginia Wesleyan College	VA	28,433	C
Washington Univ in St. Louis	MO	42,106	MC
Wilson College	PA	27,660	C
Youngstown State Univ	OH	12,613	NC

LASER ELECTRO-OPTICS TECHNOLOGY

School	ST	$IS	SR
Oregon Inst of Technology	OR	8,718	C

LATIN

School	ST	$IS	SR
Amherst College	MA	41,590	MC
Asbury College	KY	23,762	VC
Austin College	TX	27,871	HC
Baylor Univ	TX	27,555	HC
Boston Univ	MA	42,046	HC+
Bowling Green State Univ	OH	14,994	C
Brigham Young Univ	UT	9,200	VC
Bryn Mawr College	PA	42,780	HC+
Butler Univ	IN	31,944	VC+
Calvin College	MI	25,735	NC
Carleton College	MN	40,467	MC
Catholic Univ of America	DC	35,838	VC
Centenary College of Louisiana	LA	24,760	VC
CUNY/Brooklyn College	NY	4,377	C+
CUNY/Herbert H. Lehman College	NY	4,000	LC
CUNY/Hunter College	NY	8,000	C+
CUNY/Queens College	NY	4,356	C
Colgate Univ	NY	41,170	MC
College of Wooster	OH	31,310	VC+
Columbia Univ/Barnard College	NY	38,000	MC
Columbia Univ/Columbia College	NY	42,584	MC
Concordia College: Moorhead	MN	22,475	VC
Cornell Univ	NY	41,717	MC
Creighton Univ	NE	29,918	VC+
Denison Univ	OH	37,040	HC
DePauw Univ	IN	32,100	HC
Dickinson College	PA	40,170	HC+
Duquesne Univ	PA	29,534	VC
Emory Univ	GA	40,546	MC
Florida State Univ	FL	9,028	HC
Franklin and Marshall College	PA	40,590	HC
Furman Univ	SC	33,264	HC+
Gettysburg College	PA	39,864	HC
Hampden-Sydney College	VA	31,148	VC
Harvard Univ/Harvard College	MA	45,860	MC
Haverford College	PA	41,600	MC
Hope College	MI	28,208	VC+
Indiana Univ Bloomington	IN	13,356	VC
John Carroll Univ	OH	27,658	C+
Kent State Univ	OH	14,594	C
Kenyon College	OH	39,500	MC
Louisiana State Univ and A&M College	LA	10,749	VC
Loyola College in Maryland	MD	38,898	HC
Loyola Univ Chicago	IL	32,896	VC
Marlboro College	VT	35,980	VC+
Mercer Univ	GA	27,525	VC+
Miami Univ	OH	29,097	HC
Mich State Univ	MI	13,689	VC
Missouri State Univ	MO	10,748	C+
Monmouth College	IL	23,700	C
Montclair State Univ	NJ	16,327	C
Mount Holyoke College	MA	42,148	HC+
New York Univ	NY	43,170	MC
Ohio Univ	OH	15,921	C
Purdue Univ/West Lafayette	IN	13,458	VC
Randolph-Macon College	VA	31,250	C
Rutgers, The State Univ of New Jersey/New Brunswick/Piscataway Campus	NJ	15,810	HC
St. Joseph's Univ	PA	37,428	VC
St. Louis Univ	MO	33,158	VC+
St. Olaf College	MN	32,800	HC
Samford Univ	AL	20,258	VC
Sarah Lawrence College	NY	42,000	HC
Seattle Pacific Univ	WA	29,355	C
Smith College	MA	41,474	MC
Southwestern Univ	TX	26,767	HC
SUNY/Univ at Albany	NY	13,860	VC
SUNY/Univ at Binghamton	NY	13,988	HC
Swarthmore College	PA	41,280	MC
Tufts Univ	MA	42,018	MC
Univ of Akron	OH	15,166	NC
Univ of Arizona	AZ	11,958	VC
Univ of at Calif Davis	CA	15,010	VC
Univ of Calif at Berkeley	CA	18,141	HC+
Univ of Calif at Los Angeles	CA	17,681	VC
Univ of Georgia	GA	11,004	HC
Univ of Idaho	ID	9,310	NC
Univ of Iowa	IA	12,172	VC
Univ of Maine	ME	13,642	C
Univ of Mich/Ann Arbor	MI	16,587	HC+
Univ of Minn/Twin Cities	MN	13,165	VC
Univ of Nebr at Lincoln	NE	11,401	VC
Univ of New Hampshire	NH	16,810	VC
Univ of Notre Dame	IN	39,552	MC
Univ of Oregon	OR	13,108	VC
Univ of Richmond	VA	40,510	MC
Univ of St. Thomas	MN	28,000	VC
Univ of Scranton	PA	31,100	VC
Univ of Tenn at Chattanooga	TN	7,790	C
Univ of Texas at Austin	TX	14,610	NC
Univ of the South	TN	34,645	VC
Univ of Vermont	VT	18,080	VC
Univ of Wisc/Madison	WI	13,117	HC
Wabash College	IN	30,116	HC
Wake Forest Univ	NC	38,290	MC
Washington Univ in St. Louis	MO	42,106	MC
Wellesley College	MA	41,030	MC
West Chester Univ of Pennsylvania	PA	12,355	C+
Western Mich Univ	MI	13,299	C
Westminster College	PA	31,290	C+
Wheaton College	MA	40,180	HC+
Wichita State Univ	KS	8,500	C

LATIN AMERICAN STUDIES

School	ST	$IS	SR
Adelphi Univ	NY	27,000	VC
Albright College	PA	33,920	C
American Univ	DC	38,719	HC+
Assumption College	MA	32,875	C
Austin College	TX	27,871	HC
Ball State Univ	IN	13,138	C
Bard College	NY	41,800	HC+
Baylor Univ	TX	27,555	HC
Boston Univ	MA	42,046	HC+
Bowdoin College	ME	41,660	MC
Brandeis Univ	MA	41,551	MC
Brigham Young Univ	UT	9,200	VC
Brown Univ	RI	42,015	MC
Bucknell Univ	PA	39,660	MC
Cal State East Bay	CA	10,856	LC
Cal State, Chico	CA	11,395	C
Cal State, Fullerton	CA	10,990	C
Cal State, Los Angeles	CA	5,900	C
Carleton College	MN	40,467	MC
CUNY/Brooklyn College	NY	4,377	C+
CUNY/City College	NY		C
CUNY/Hunter College	NY	8,000	C+
CUNY/Queens College	NY	4,356	C
Colby College	ME	41,770	MC
Colgate Univ	NY	41,170	MC
College of Charleston	SC	13,616	VC
Columbia Univ/Columbia College	NY	42,584	MC
Columbia Univ/School of General Studies	NY	41,516	C
Conn College	CT	41,975	MC
Cornell College	IA	30,110	VC+
Dartmouth College	NH	39,465	MC
Denison Univ	OH	37,040	HC
DePaul Univ	IL	29,835	VC
Earlham College	IN	33,604	HC
Emory Univ	GA	40,546	MC
Flagler College	FL	13,790	VC+
Florida State Univ	FL	9,028	HC
Fordham Univ	NY	36,000	HC
George Washington Univ	DC	48,820	MC
Hamline Univ	MN	27,070	VC
Hampshire College	MA	37,120	HC
Hanover College	IN	28,150	HC
Hobart and William Smith Colleges	NY	41,123	VC
Hofstra Univ	NY	32,630	VC
Hood College	MD	30,085	VC
Johns Hopkins Univ	MD	42,044	MC
Kent State Univ	OH	14,594	C
Lake Forest College	IL	33,860	VC
Lock Haven Univ of Pennsylvania	PA	12,098	LC
Macalester College	MN	36,500	MC
Middlebury College	VT	42,120	MC
Mount Holyoke College	MA	42,148	HC+
New York Univ	NY	43,170	MC
Notre Dame de Namur Univ	CA	32,790	LC
Oakland Univ	MI	11,936	C
Oberlin College	OH	40,904	MC
Ohio Univ	OH	15,921	C
Penn State Univ/Univ Park Campus	PA	18,038	HC
Pitzer College	CA	41,644	MC
Pomona College	CA	40,774	MC
Rhodes College	TN	32,860	HC
Ripon College	WI	27,160	C+
Rollins College	FL	38,366	VC
Rutgers, The State Univ of New Jersey/New Brunswick/Piscataway Campus	NJ	15,810	HC
St. Edward's Univ	TX	23,560	C
St. Mary's Univ of San Antonio	TX	22,444	C
St. Peter's College	NJ	30,160	LC
Samford Univ	AL	20,258	VC
San Diego State Univ	CA	12,971	C
Scripps College	CA	41,000	MC
Seattle Pacific Univ	WA	29,355	C
Simon's Rock College of Bard	MA	41,988	VC+
Smith College	MA	41,474	MC
Sonoma State Univ	CA	14,732	C
Southern Methodist Univ	TX	36,088	VC+
SUNY/College at Plattsburgh	NY	12,362	C
SUNY/Univ at Albany	NY	13,860	VC
SUNY/Univ at Binghamton	NY	13,988	HC
SUNY/Univ at New Paltz	NY	12,480	VC
Stetson Univ	FL	32,725	VC
Syracuse Univ	NY	38,655	HC
Temple Univ	PA	17,438	C
Texas Christian Univ	TX	23,410	VC+
Texas Tech Univ	TX	13,026	VC
Tulane Univ	LA	41,098	MC
Univ of Arizona	AZ	11,958	VC
Univ of Arkansas	AR	11,859	VC
Univ of Calif at Berkeley	CA	18,141	HC+
Univ of Calif at Los Angeles	CA	17,681	VC
Univ of Calif at Riverside	CA	16,625	C
Univ of Calif at San Diego	CA	16,102	HC
Univ of Calif at Santa Barbara	CA	11,800	VC
Univ of Calif at Santa Cruz	CA	19,174	VC
Univ of Chicago	IL	42,369	MC
Univ of Cincinnati	OH	17,682	C
Univ of Conn	CT	16,628	HC
Univ of Delaware	DE	14,142	HC
Univ of Idaho	ID	9,310	NC
Univ of Illinois at Chicago	IL	16,256	VC
Univ of Illinois at Urbana-Champaign	IL	15,800	HC+
Univ of Kansas	KS	10,915	VC
Univ of Kentucky	KY	7,800	C
Univ of Miami	FL	38,397	MC
Univ of Mich/Ann Arbor	MI	16,587	HC+
Univ of Minn/Morris	MN	15,472	VC
Univ of Nebr at Lincoln	NE	11,401	VC
Univ of Nebr at Omaha	NE	11,235	C
Univ of New Mexico	NM	11,253	C
Univ of N Car at Chapel Hill	NC	11,129	MC
Univ of N Car at Charlotte	NC	9,101	C
Univ of Northern Iowa	IA	11,133	C
Univ of Okla	OK	10,769	VC+
Univ of Pennsylvania	PA	41,766	MC
Univ of Rhode Island	RI	15,398	C
Univ of San Francisco	CA	37,560	VC
Univ of S Car at Columbia	SC	13,397	VC
Univ of Southern Calif	CA	41,618	MC
Univ of Tenn at Knoxville	TN	11,720	C
Univ of Texas at Austin	TX	14,610	NC
Univ of Texas at El Paso	TX	8,764	NC
Univ of Texas-Pan American	TX	7,290	C+
Univ of Vermont	VT	18,080	VC
Univ of Wisc/Eau Claire	WI	9,915	VC
Univ of Wisc/Madison	WI	13,117	HC
Vanderbilt Univ	TN	41,986	MC
Vassar College	NY	41,700	MC
Washington Univ in St. Louis	MO	42,106	MC
Wellesley College	MA	41,030	MC
Wesleyan Univ	CT	42,122	MC
Willamette Univ	OR	35,416	VC+
Yale Univ	CT	41,000	MC

LAW

School	ST	$IS	SR
American Univ	DC	38,719	HC+
Amherst College	MA	41,590	MC
Bay Path College	MA	29,362	C
Becker College	MA	24,300	LC
Chapman Univ	CA	37,550	VC
Christopher Newport Univ	VA	13,326	VC
Claremont McKenna College	CA	42,920	MC
Dickinson College	PA	40,170	HC+
Elizabethtown College	PA	32,100	VC
Hampshire College	MA	37,120	HC
Hood College	MD	30,085	VC
Indiana Univ Bloomington	IN	13,356	VC
Lasell College	MA	26,250	C
Montclair State Univ	NJ	16,327	C
Mount Ida College	MA	26,000	LC
Mountain State Univ	WV	11,406	NC
Oberlin College	OH	40,904	MC
Park Univ	MO	11,592	C
Purdue Univ/West Lafayette	IN	13,458	VC
Ramapo College of New Jersey	NJ	16,630	VC
Regis College	MA	31,350	LC
St. Joseph's Univ	PA	37,428	VC
South Univ	GA		C
Southeastern Univ	DC	9,000	NC
Southern Illinois Univ Carbondale	IL	12,391	C
Texas Wesleyan Univ	TX	18,700	C
Towson Univ	MD	13,924	VC
United States Air Force Academy	CO		HC+
United States Military Academy	NY		MC
Univ of Calif at Berkeley	CA	18,141	HC+
Univ of Calif at Santa Barbara	CA	11,800	VC
Univ of Calif at Santa Cruz	CA	19,174	VC
Univ of Central Florida	FL	10,739	VC
Univ of Chicago	IL	42,369	MC
Univ of Hartford	CT	34,044	C
Univ of Louisiana at Monroe	LA	7,103	C
Univ of Mass Amherst	MA	15,973	C+
Univ of Nebr at Lincoln	NE	11,401	VC
Univ of Pittsburgh at Pittsburgh	PA	18,866	HC
Univ of Wisc/Madison	WI	13,117	HC
Univ of Wisc/Milwaukee	WI	9,427	LC

School	ST	$IS	SR
Univ of Wisc/Superior	WI	9,610	C+
Ursuline College	OH	25,456	C
Webster Univ	MO	24,280	VC
Wilson College	PA	27,660	C
Wingate Univ	NC	23,300	C
Woodbury College	VT	15,150	LC

LAW ENFORCEMENT AND CORRECTIONS

School	ST	$IS	SR
Averett Univ	VA	24,920	C
Calumet College of St. Joseph	IN	9,500	LC
CUNY/John Jay College of Criminal Justice	NY	5,000	C
College of the Ozarks	MO	4,130	VC+
Frostburg State Univ	MD	12,672	C
Lake Erie College	OH	27,725	C
Metropolitan State Univ	MN	4,682	SP
Minn State Univ, Mankato	MN	10,276	LC
Point Park Univ	PA	24,160	C
Portland State Univ	OR	12,453	C
St. Mary's Univ of Minn	MN	23,857	VC
St. Paul's College	VA	16,030	NC
Sam Houston State Univ	TX	8,000	C
Southeast Missouri State Univ	MO	10,596	C
Southern Christian Univ	AL	9,440	LC
Southwest Minn State Univ	MN	10,975	C
Stephen F. Austin State Univ	TX	7,930	C
Tarleton State Univ	TX	8,952	C
Texas State Univ - San Marcos	TX	10,862	C
Tiffin Univ	OH	19,490	LC
Univ of Great Falls	MT	17,000	C
Univ of Indianapolis	IN	25,090	C
Univ of Maine at Augusta	ME	5,025	NC
Univ of New Hampshire	NH	16,810	VC
Univ of New Haven	CT	31,794	C
Univ of San Francisco	CA	37,560	VC
Univ of Virginia's College at Wise	VA	11,076	C
Washburn Univ	KS	9,734	NC
Western Conn State Univ	CT	12,993	C
Western Illinois Univ	IL	13,042	C
Western New Mexico Univ	NM	7,233	LC
Western Oregon Univ	OR	10,295	C
Youngstown State Univ	OH	12,613	NC

LIBERAL ARTS/GENERAL STUDIES

School	ST	$IS	SR
Adelphi Univ	NY	27,000	VC
Alaska Pacific Univ	AK	25,142	C
Albertus Magnus College	CT	25,336	C
Alcorn State Univ	MS	8,190	LC
Alderson-Broaddus College	WV	24,006	C
Alvernia College	PA	26,388	C
American International College	MA	28,710	LC
Angelo State Univ	TX	8,340	NC
Anna Maria College	MA	29,815	LC
Aquinas College	TN	10,660	LC
Arcadia Univ	PA	33,570	VC
Armstrong Atlantic State Univ	GA	7,394	C
Atlantic Union College	MA	17,600	LC
Auburn Univ Montgomery	AL	9,530	NC
Averett Univ	VA	24,920	C
Avila Univ	MO	22,100	C
Azusa Pacific Univ	CA	28,546	VC
Ball State Univ	IN	13,138	C
Barry Univ	FL	24,100	LC
Bay Path College	MA	29,362	C
Beacon College	FL	29,560	LC
Bellarmine Univ	KY	27,650	C+
Belmont Abbey College	NC	25,314	C
Belmont Univ	TN	24,110	VC
Benedictine College	KS	21,968	C
Bennington College	VT	41,890	HC
Bentley College	MA	38,784	HC
Bethel College	IN	19,680	C
Bethel College	TN	16,066	NC
Bethune-Cookman College	FL	17,922	LC
Biola Univ	CA	29,372	VC
Boricua College	NY	8,000	C
Bowling Green State Univ	OH	14,994	C
Brenau Univ Women's College	GA	23,950	VC
Brescia Univ	KY	14,240	C
Brewton-Parker College	GA	14,220	LC
Bridgewater College	VA	27,790	C
Bryan College	TN	19,270	C
Bryant College	RI	34,330	VC
Burlington College	VT	14,670	SP
Cabrini College	PA	33,340	C
Calif Baptist Univ	CA	23,780	C
Calif Lutheran Univ	CA	27,800	LC
Calif State Polytechnic Univ, Pomona	CA	18,053	C+
Cal State East Bay	CA	10,856	LC
Cal State, Bakersfield	CA	6,125	LC
Cal State, Chico	CA	11,395	C
Cal State, Dominguez Hills	CA	10,220	LC
Cal State, Fresno	CA	10,037	LC
Cal State, Fullerton	CA	10,990	C
Cal State, Los Angeles	CA	5,900	C
Cal State, Monterey Bay	CA	10,099	C
Cal State, Northridge	CA	9,036	LC
Cal State, San Bernardino	CA	12,563	LC
Cal State, San Marcos	CA	1,800	LC
Cal State, Stanislaus	CA	11,283	C
Calif Univ of Pennsylvania	PA	14,217	C
Calumet College of St. Joseph	IN	9,500	LC
Cameron Univ	OK	6,314	NC
Carlow Univ	PA	24,313	C
Catholic Univ of America	DC	35,838	VC
Cazenovia College	NY	26,900	C
Cedar Crest College	PA	30,615	C
Centenary College of Louisiana	LA	24,760	VC
Central Washington Univ	WA	11,730	C
Champlain College	VT	24,605	C
Chapman Univ	CA	37,550	VC
Charter Oak State College	CT		SP
Christian Brothers Univ	TN	24,650	VC
City Univ	WA	7,425	NC
CUNY/Medgar Evers College	NY	4,250	NC
CUNY/York College	NY	4,242	NC
Clarion Univ of Pennsylvania	PA	11,844	C
Clarke College	IA	25,390	C
Cleveland State Univ	OH	10,798	NC
College Misericordia	PA	27,950	C
College of Mount St. Vincent	NY	28,000	C
College of Mount St. Joseph	OH	24,860	C
College of New Rochelle - School of New Resources	NY	7,700	SP
College of Notre Dame of Maryland	MD	27,700	C
College of St. Benedict	MN	30,091	VC
College of St. Joseph	VT	20,900	NC
College of St. Mary	NE	23,938	C
College of Visual Arts	MN	18,040	SP
Colo Christian Univ	CO	21,182	VC
Colo College	CO	37,668	HC
Colo State Univ-Fort Collins	CO	10,878	C+
Columbia Union College	MD	23,536	LC
Concordia Univ	CA	26,780	C
Concordia Univ at Austin	TX	23,640	LC
Coppin State College	MD	10,200	LC
Crichton College	TN	15,300	C
Dallas Baptist Univ	TX	17,040	VC
Dana College	NE	22,390	C
De Sales Univ	PA	28,580	VC
Dominican Univ of Calif	CA	36,836	C
Dowling College	NY	22,110	LC
Duquesne Univ	PA	29,534	VC
East Carolina Univ	NC	10,000	C
East Central Univ	OK	6,207	C
East Tenn State Univ	TN	8,497	C
Eastern Conn State Univ	CT	13,554	C
Eastern Mennonite Univ	VA	25,450	VC
Eastern Mich Univ	MI	12,897	C
Eastern Oregon Univ	OR	10,400	VC
Edinboro Univ of Pennsylvania	PA	11,809	LC
Elmhurst College	IL	24,685	C
Emmanuel College	MA	32,000	C+
Emporia State Univ	KS	8,093	C
Endicott College	MA	30,156	C+
Eureka College	IL	19,280	C
Evergreen State College	WA	11,261	C+
Excelsior College	NY	995	SP
Fairleigh Dickinson Univ/ College at Florham	NJ	30,130	C
Fairleigh Dickinson Univ/ Metropolitan Campus	NJ	28,590	C
Faulkner Univ	AL	15,600	C
Ferrum College	VA	24,290	LC
Fitchburg State College	MA	11,276	C
Flagler College	FL	13,790	VC+
Florida Atlantic Univ	FL	11,221	C
Florida Gulf Coast Univ	FL	10,833	C
Florida International Univ	FL	9,215	VC
Fontbonne Univ	MO	23,308	C
Fort Hays State Univ	KS	7,638	C
Francis Marion Univ	SC	11,114	C
Frostburg State Univ	MD	12,672	C
Gannon Univ	PA	26,100	C
George Washington Univ	DC	48,820	MC
Georgetown College	KY	24,950	C+
Georgia College and State Univ	GA	11,020	C
Glenville State College	WV	8,778	NC
Gonzaga Univ	WA	30,218	HC
Graceland Univ	IA	19,700	C
Granite State College	NH	4,800	SP
Green Mountain College	VT	32,164	C
Greenville College	IL	23,146	C
Guilford College	NC	28,160	C+
Hannibal-LaGrange College	MO	16,390	C
Harding Univ	AR	16,512	VC
Haverford College	PA	41,600	MC
Hilbert College	NY	20,480	LC
Hofstra Univ	NY	32,630	VC
Holy Names College	CA	27,980	NC
Hope International Univ	CA	23,700	NC
Houston Baptist Univ	TX	18,660	C
Howard Payne Univ	TX	17,115	C
Humboldt State Univ	CA	11,176	C
Idaho State Univ	ID	9,030	C
Indiana State Univ	IN	11,604	C
Indiana Univ Bloomington	IN	13,356	VC
Indiana Univ East	IN	4,806	LC
Indiana Univ Kokomo	IN	4,835	LC
Indiana Univ Northwest	IN	4,902	LC
Indiana Univ South Bend	IN	4,989	LC
Indiana Univ Southeast	IN	4,880	LC
Indiana Univ-Purdue Univ Fort Wayne	IN	5,067	LC
Indiana Univ-Purdue Univ Indianapolis	IN	10,959	C
Indiana Wesleyan Univ	IN	22,074	C+
Iona College	NY	30,878	VC
Iowa State Univ	IA	11,831	VC
Ithaca College	NY	35,144	VC
James Madison Univ	VA	12,010	VC
Johnson C. Smith Univ	NC	20,000	C
Johnson State College	VT	11,830	LC
Kent State Univ	OH	14,594	C
Kentucky State Univ	KY	10,089	LC
Kutztown Univ of Pennsylvania	PA	10,820	C
La Roche College	PA	24,724	LC
La Sierra Univ	CA	24,327	C+
Lasell College	MA	26,250	C
Lewis Univ	IL	23,050	C+
Lewis-Clark State College	ID	6,990	C
Liberty Univ	VA	19,101	C
Limestone College	SC	19,840	C
Lincoln Univ	MO	8,000	NC
Lincoln Univ	PA	13,658	C+
Lindenwood Univ	MO	18,600	VC
Lindsey Wilson College	KY	16,425	LC
Lock Haven Univ of Pennsylvania	PA	12,098	LC
Longwood Univ	VA	12,426	C
Louisiana State Univ and A&M College	LA	10,749	VC
Louisiana State Univ in Shreveport	LA	2,900	NC
Louisiana Tech Univ	LA	7,370	C
MacMurray College	IL	20,755	C
Madonna Univ	MI	16,068	VC
Malone College	OH	23,040	C
Mansfield Univ	PA	11,300	C
Marymount Manhattan College	NY	30,049	VC
Marymount Univ	VA	25,934	C
Maryville Univ of St. Louis	MO	23,000	C
Master's College and Seminary	CA	25,850	VC
Mayville State Univ	ND	8,667	NC
McNeese State Univ	LA	5,270	LC
Medaille College	NY	21,000	C
Menlo College	CA	33,600	C
Mesa State College	CO	8,051	C
Metropolitan State Univ	MN	4,682	SP
Mich Tech Univ	MI	14,569	VC
Middlebury College	VT	42,120	MC
Midway College	KY	20,150	C
Mills College	CA	39,870	C
Minot State Univ	ND	6,700	LC
Miss State Univ	MS	9,577	C
Missouri Southern State Univ	MO	8,396	NC
Missouri Valley College	MO	18,500	C
Mitchell College	CT	26,396	C
Montana State Univ-Billings	MT	8,906	C
Montana Tech of The Univ of Montana	MT	10,434	C
Montreat College	NC	21,440	C
Morehead State Univ	KY	9,150	C
Morris College	SC	11,999	LC
Mount Ida College	MA	26,000	LC
Mount Olive College	NC	16,000	LC
Mount St. Mary's College	CA	32,086	VC
Murray State Univ	KY	8,900	VC
National Univ	CA	8,412	SP
Neumann College	PA	25,996	LC
New Mexico Inst of Mining and Technology	NM	8,510	VC+
Newman Univ	KS	21,106	C
Niagara Univ	NY	28,250	C
Northern Illinois Univ	IL	13,178	C
Northwest Nazarene Univ	ID	22,590	VC
Northwest Univ	WA	18,854	C
Northwestern State Univ of Louisiana	LA	7,144	C
Norwich Univ	VT	28,212	C
Notre Dame de Namur Univ	CA	32,790	LC
Oakland Univ	MI	11,936	C
Ohio Dominican Univ	OH	25,954	C
Ohio Valley Univ	WV	17,752	C
Okla Christian Univ	OK	18,992	NC
Okla State Univ	OK	10,213	VC
Okla Wesleyan Univ	OK	18,950	NC
Olivet Nazarene Univ	IL	22,590	C
Oral Roberts Univ	OK	22,650	C
Oregon State Univ	OR	11,055	C
Otterbein College	OH	28,986	C
Our Lady of Holy Cross College	LA	8,090	LC
Our Lady of the Lake Univ of San Antonio	TX	22,430	LC
Palm Beach Atlantic Univ	FL	23,597	VC
Park Univ	MO	11,592	C
Penn State Univ/Altoona	PA	12,635	C
Penn State Univ/Univ Park Campus	PA	18,038	HC
Pepperdine Univ	CA	39,960	HC
Pine Manor College	MA	25,038	LC
Pittsburg State Univ	KS	8,112	C
Point Loma Nazarene Univ	CA	27,610	VC
Point Park Univ	PA	24,160	C
Polytechnic Univ/Brooklyn	NY	37,150	VC
Pontifical Catholic Univ of PR/Ponce	PR	7,310	
Portland State Univ	OR	12,453	C
Post Univ	CT	24,875	C
Purdue Univ/West Lafayette	IN	13,458	VC
Quinnipiac Univ	CT	34,640	VC
Radford Univ	VA	13,145	C
Regis College	MA	31,350	LC
Reinhardt College	GA	20,870	C
Richard Stockton College of New Jersey	NJ	14,000	VC
Rider Univ	NJ	32,560	C
Rivier College	NH	26,600	C
Roosevelt Univ	IL	22,605	VC
Rosemont College	PA	29,350	C
Rowan Univ	NJ	16,000	VC
Rutgers, The State Univ of New Jersey/Camden Campus	NJ	15,000	VC
Sacred Heart Univ	CT	33,404	C
St. Andrews Presbyterian College	NC	23,530	C
St. Anselm College	NH	33,810	C
St. Edward's Univ	TX	23,560	C
St. Francis College	NY	19,974	LC
St. John's College	MD	40,451	HC+
St. John's College	NM	38,000	C
St. John's Univ	MN	29,749	VC
St. John's Univ	NY	34,370	C
St. Joseph College	CT	32,050	C
St. Mary-of-the-Woods College	IN	25,480	C
St. Mary's College of Calif	CA	37,290	VC
St. Thomas Univ	FL	23,490	C
St. Vincent College	PA	26,160	VC
Salem International Univ	WV	18,020	C
Samford Univ	AL	20,258	VC
San Diego Christian College	CA	24,172	C
San Francisco State Univ	CA	13,000	C
Santa Clara Univ	CA	38,931	VC
Sarah Lawrence College	NY	42,000	HC
Schreiner Univ	TX	20,600	C
Seattle Pacific Univ	WA	29,355	C
Seattle Univ	WA	30,063	VC
Seton Hall Univ	NJ	33,622	VC
Seton Hill Univ	PA	28,810	C
Shaw Univ	NC	15,488	LC
Sheldon Jackson College	AK	17,900	LC
Shenandoah Univ	VA	27,600	C
Shimer College	IL	26,525	C
Siena Heights Univ	MI	17,000	LC
Simpson Univ	CA	22,900	C
Skidmore College	NY	41,779	HC
Sonoma State Univ	CA	14,732	C
S Dak State Univ	SD	9,815	C
Southeast Missouri State Univ	MO	10,596	C
Southeastern Louisiana Univ	LA	8,521	LC
Southeastern Univ	DC	9,000	NC
Southern Christian Univ	AL	9,440	LC
Southern Illinois Univ Carbondale	IL	12,391	C
Southern Illinois Univ Edwardsville	IL	11,022	C
Southern Methodist Univ	TX	36,088	VC+
Southern New Hampshire Univ	NH	28,764	C
Southern Oregon Univ	OR	12,186	C
Southern Vermont College	VT	21,322	LC
Southwestern College	KS	21,476	C
Spring Hill College	AL	28,678	C
SUNY/College at Purchase	NY	11,989	VC+
SUNY/Empire State College	NY	4,575	SP
SUNY/Inst of Technology	NY	12,575	VC
Stephens College	MO	26,930	VC
Sweet Briar College	VA	31,460	VC
Texas A&M Univ at Galveston	TX	10,000	C+
Texas Christian Univ	TX	23,410	VC+
Texas Southern Univ	TX	9,828	C
Texas Tech Univ	TX	13,026	VC
Thomas Aquinas College	CA	24,400	HC+
Thomas Edison State College	NJ	3,780	SP
Thomas More College	KY	24,470	C
Thomas Univ	GA	11,520	NC
Tiffin Univ	OH	19,490	LC
Touro College	NY	17,000	C
Trinity International Univ	IL	25,686	C

ST = STATE $IS = IN-STATE COSTS SR = SELECTOR RATING

School	ST	$IS	SR
Union Inst & Univ	OH	8,912	SP
Univ of Alaska Southeast	AK	8,050	LC
Univ of Arizona	AZ	11,958	VC
Univ of Arkansas at Little Rock	AR	7,230	NC
Univ of Arkansas at Pine Bluff	AR	8,300	C
Univ of Calif at Riverside	CA	16,625	C
Univ of Central Florida	FL	10,739	VC
Univ of Central Okla	OK	8,094	C
Univ of Charleston	WV	27,600	C
Univ of Detroit Mercy	MI	27,000	C
Univ of Evansville	IN	28,320	C
Univ of Hawaii at Hilo	HI	6,500	C
Univ of Illinois at Urbana-Champaign	IL	15,800	HC+
Univ of Iowa	IA	12,172	VC
Univ of Judaism College of A&S	CA	30,010	C
Univ of La Verne	CA	33,470	C
Univ of Louisiana at Monroe	LA	7,103	C
Univ of Louisville	KY	10,400	VC
Univ of Maine at Augusta	ME	5,025	NC
Univ of Maine at Farmington	ME	11,515	C
Univ of Maine at Fort Kent	ME	10,832	LC
Univ of Maine at Machias	ME	10,523	C
Univ of Maine at Presque Isle	ME	10,066	LC
Univ of Mary	ND	15,374	C
Univ of Maryland/Eastern Shore	MD	11,210	C
Univ of Maryland/Univ College	MD	5,640	SP
Univ of Mass Amherst	MA	15,973	C+
Univ of Mass Lowell	MA	14,327	VC
Univ of Memphis	TN	11,153	C
Univ of Mich/Ann Arbor	MI	16,587	HC+
Univ of Mich/Dearborn	MI	7,000	VC
Univ of Minn/Morris	MN	15,472	VC
Univ of Miss	MS	9,000	C
Univ of Missouri/Columbia	MO	13,500	VC
Univ of Missouri/Kansas City	MO	15,000	VC
Univ of Missouri/St. Louis	MO	14,046	VC
Univ of Mobile	AL	16,880	C
Univ of Montana	MT	10,602	C
Univ of Montana--Western	MT	8,406	NC
Univ of Nebr at Omaha	NE	11,235	C
Univ of Nevada/Reno	NV	12,155	NC
Univ of New England	ME	31,005	C
Univ of New Haven	CT	31,794	C
Univ of N Car at Asheville	NC	9,237	VC
Univ of N Car at Greensboro	NC	8,993	C
Univ of N Dak	ND	10,114	VC
Univ of North Texas	TX	7,800	C
Univ of Northern Iowa	IA	11,133	C
Univ of Notre Dame	IN	39,552	MC
Univ of Okla	OK	10,769	VC+
Univ of Pennsylvania	PA	41,766	MC
Univ of Pittsburgh at Bradford	PA	17,008	C
Univ of Pittsburgh at Pittsburgh	PA	18,866	HC
Univ of PR/Rio Piedras	PR	5,750	
Univ of Redlands	CA	36,160	VC
Univ of St. Francis	IL	25,430	C
Univ of St. Francis	IN	20,970	C
Univ of St. Mary	KS	18,900	C
Univ of St. Thomas	TX	23,810	VC
Univ of San Diego	CA	40,620	HC
Univ of S Car Upstate	SC	11,957	C
Univ of S Dak	SD	9,068	C
Univ of South Florida	FL	10,284	VC
Univ of Southern Calif	CA	41,618	VC
Univ of Tampa	FL	25,784	C
Univ of Texas at Austin	TX	14,610	HC
Univ of Texas-Pan American	TX	7,290	C
Univ of the Ozarks	AR	19,250	C
Univ of the Pacific	CA	34,380	VC
Univ of Virginia's College at Wise	VA	11,076	C
Univ of Washington	WA	10,400	VC
Univ of Wisc/Green Bay	WI	9,415	VC
Univ of Wisc/Oshkosh	WI	10,426	LC
Univ of Wisc/Stevens Point	WI	9,384	VC
Urbana Univ	OH	21,190	C
Utah State Univ	UT	8,002	VC
Valdosta State Univ	GA	8,802	C
Villa Julie College	MD	25,222	C
Villanova Univ	PA	38,672	HC+
Virginia Intermont College	VA	22,200	LC
Virginia Wesleyan College	VA	28,433	C
Viterbo Univ	WI	21,670	C
Warner Pacific College	OR	21,900	C
Washburn Univ	KS	9,734	NC
Washington State Univ	WA	12,260	C
Wayne State Univ	MI	11,805	C
Wesley College	DE	19,905	C
West Chester Univ of Pennsylvania	PA	12,355	C+
West Texas A&M Univ	TX	8,452	C
West Virginia Univ	WV	10,506	C
Western Carolina Univ	NC	7,000	C

School	ST	$IS	SR
Western Kentucky Univ	KY	10,192	C
Western New England College	MA	32,054	C
Westmont College	CA	36,672	HC
Wichita State Univ	KS	8,500	C
Wilberforce Univ	OH	14,937	LC
Wiley College	TX	8,100	LC
Wilkes Univ	PA	30,886	C
William Carey College	MS	11,000	LC
Wilmington College	OH	2,806	NC
Wingate Univ	NC	23,300	C
Winona State Univ	MN	11,333	C
Xavier Univ	OH	30,490	HC
York College	NE	16,330	NC

LIBRARY SCIENCE

School	ST	$IS	SR
Clarion Univ of Pennsylvania	PA	11,844	C
Kent State Univ	OH	14,594	C
Kutztown Univ of Pennsylvania	PA	10,820	C
Northwestern Okla State Univ	OK	6,250	NC
Southern Conn State Univ	CT	10,310	C
Univ of Central Arkansas	AR	9,984	C
Univ of Maine at Augusta	ME	5,025	NC
Univ of Nebr at Omaha	NE	11,235	C

LIFE SCIENCE

School	ST	$IS	SR
Atlantic Union College	MA	17,600	LC
Baylor Univ	TX	27,555	HC
Bowling Green State Univ	OH	14,994	C
Guilford College	NC	28,160	C+
Iowa Wesleyan College	IA	22,140	C
Kansas State Univ	KS	10,516	VC
Lehigh Univ	PA	42,690	HC+
Malone Univ	OH	23,040	C
Minn State Univ, Mankato	MN	10,276	LC
National Univ	CA	8,412	SP
New York Inst of Technology	NY	28,126	VC
Niagara Univ	NY	28,250	C
Northwest Univ	WA	18,854	C
Otterbein College	OH	28,986	C
Suffolk Univ	MA	33,160	C
United States Military Academy	NY		MC
Univ of Missouri/Rolla	MO	13,332	HC
Univ of New Mexico	NM	11,253	C
Wayne State College	NE	8,033	NC

LINGUISTICS

School	ST	$IS	SR
Alabama A&M Univ	AL	8,890	LC
Boston College	MA	41,608	MC
Boston Univ	MA	42,046	HC+
Brandeis Univ	MA	41,551	MC
Brigham Young Univ	UT	9,200	VC
Brown Univ	RI	42,015	MC
Cal State, Fresno	CA	10,037	LC
Cal State, Fullerton	CA	10,990	C
Cal State, Northridge	CA	9,036	LC
Central College	IA	26,774	VC
CUNY/Brooklyn College	NY	4,377	C+
CUNY/Herbert H. Lehman College	NY	4,000	LC
CUNY/Queens College	NY	4,356	C
Cleveland State Univ	OH	10,798	NC
Columbia Univ/Barnard College	NY	38,000	MC
Columbia Univ/Columbia College	NY	42,584	MC
Cornell Univ	NY	41,717	MC
Dartmouth College	NH	39,465	MC
Duke Univ	NC	41,239	MC
Eastern Mich Univ	MI	12,897	C
Emory Univ	GA	40,546	MC
Florida Atlantic Univ	FL	11,221	C
Florida State Univ	FL	9,028	HC
Georgetown Univ	DC	43,183	MC
Georgia Southern Univ	GA	9,762	C
Hampshire College	MA	37,120	HC
Harvard Univ/Harvard College	MA	45,860	MC
Haverford College	PA	41,600	MC
Hofstra Univ	NY	32,630	VC
Indiana Univ Bloomington	IN	13,356	VC
Iowa State Univ	IA	11,831	VC
Lawrence Univ	WI	33,958	HC+
Macalester College	MN	36,500	MC
Marlboro College	VT	35,980	VC+
Mass Inst of Technology	MA	41,800	MC
Miami Univ	OH	29,097	HC
Mich State Univ	MI	13,689	VC
Montclair State Univ	NJ	16,327	C
New York Univ	NY	43,170	MC
Northeastern Univ	MA	35,742	HC
Northwestern Univ	IL	37,595	MC
Oakland Univ	MI	11,936	C
Ohio State Univ	OH	15,357	HC
Ohio Univ	OH	15,921	C
Old Dominion Univ	VA	11,907	C
Pitzer College	CA	41,644	HC

School	ST	$IS	SR
Pomona College	CA	40,774	MC
Purdue Univ/West Lafayette	IN	13,458	VC
Reed College	OR	41,106	MC
Rice Univ	TX	32,290	MC
Rutgers, The State Univ of New Jersey/New Brunswick/Piscataway Campus	NJ	15,810	MC
San Diego State Univ	CA	12,971	C
Southern Illinois Univ Carbondale	IL	12,391	C
Stanford Univ	CA	41,557	MC
SUNY at Oswego	NY	13,662	VC
SUNY/Univ at Albany	NY	13,860	VC
SUNY/Univ at Binghamton	NY	13,988	VC
SUNY/Univ at Buffalo	NY	13,694	VC
SUNY/Univ at Stony Brook	NY	13,625	VC
Swarthmore College	PA	41,280	MC
Syracuse Univ	NY	38,655	HC
Temple Univ	PA	17,438	C
Tulane Univ	LA	41,098	MC
Univ of Alaska Fairbanks	AK	10,101	C
Univ of Arizona	AZ	11,958	VC
Univ of at Calif Davis	CA	15,010	VC
Univ of Calif at Berkeley	CA	18,141	HC+
Univ of Calif at Irvine	CA	16,475	HC
Univ of Calif at Los Angeles	CA	17,681	MC
Univ of Calif at Riverside	CA	16,625	C
Univ of Calif at San Diego	CA	16,102	HC
Univ of Calif at Santa Barbara	CA	11,800	VC
Univ of Calif at Santa Cruz	CA	19,174	VC
Univ of Chicago	IL	42,369	MC
Univ of Cincinnati	OH	17,682	C
Univ of Colo at Boulder	CO	13,352	C+
Univ of Conn	CT	16,628	HC
Univ of Florida	FL	9,354	HC
Univ of Georgia	GA	11,004	HC
Univ of Hawaii at Hilo	HI	6,500	C
Univ of Hawaii at Manoa	HI	10,413	VC
Univ of Illinois at Urbana-Champaign	IL	15,800	HC+
Univ of Iowa	IA	12,172	VC
Univ of Kansas	KS	10,915	VC
Univ of Kentucky	KY	7,800	C
Univ of Louisville	KY	10,400	VC
Univ of Maryland/Baltimore County	MD	16,642	VC+
Univ of Maryland/College Park	MD	16,036	HC
Univ of Mass Amherst	MA	15,973	C+
Univ of Mich/Ann Arbor	MI	16,587	HC+
Univ of Minn/Twin Cities	MN	13,165	HC
Univ of Miss	MS	9,000	C
Univ of Missouri/Columbia	MO	13,500	VC
Univ of New Hampshire	NH	16,810	VC
Univ of New Mexico	NM	11,253	C
Univ of N Car at Chapel Hill	NC	11,129	MC
Univ of Okla	OK	10,769	VC+
Univ of Oregon	OR	13,108	VC
Univ of Pennsylvania	PA	41,766	MC
Univ of Pittsburgh at Pittsburgh	PA	18,866	HC
Univ of Rochester	NY	41,135	MC
Univ of Southern Calif	CA	41,618	MC
Univ of Tenn at Knoxville	TN	11,720	C
Univ of Texas at Austin	TX	14,610	HC
Univ of Texas at El Paso	TX	8,764	NC
Univ of Toledo	OH	15,806	NC
Univ of Utah	UT	10,162	VC
Univ of Wisc/Madison	WI	13,117	HC
Univ of Wisc/Milwaukee	WI	9,427	LC
Washington State Univ	WA	12,260	C
Wayne State Univ	MI	11,805	C
Western Washington Univ	WA	11,262	VC
Yale Univ	CT	41,000	MC

LITERATURE

School	ST	$IS	SR
Alderson-Broaddus College	WV	24,006	C
American Univ	DC	38,719	HC+
Andrews Univ	MI	21,786	C
Aurora Univ	IL	20,645	C
Austin Peay State Univ	TN	7,535	C
Baylor Univ	TX	27,555	HC
Beloit College	WI	32,808	HC
Benedictine Univ	IL	25,710	C
Bennington College	VT	41,890	HC
Brigham Young Univ	UT	9,200	VC
Calif Inst of Technology	CA	36,123	MC
Cal State, San Marcos	CA	1,800	LC
Castleton State College	VT	13,158	C
Central Mich Univ	MI	12,244	C
Claremont McKenna College	CA	42,920	MC
Coe College	IA	27,440	VC
College of the Holy Cross	MA	40,664	MC
Columbia Univ/School of General Studies	NY	41,516	C
Concordia College: Moorhead	MN	22,475	VC
Drexel Univ	PA	27,700	VC
Duke Univ	NC	41,239	MC
Duquesne Univ	PA	29,534	VC
Eastern Mich Univ	MI	12,897	C
Eastern Nazarene College	MA	19,500	LC

School	ST	$IS	SR
Eastern Washington Univ	WA	10,608	C
Emory & Henry College	VA	26,570	C
Fairleigh Dickinson Univ/College at Florham	NJ	30,130	C
George Fox Univ	OR	28,490	C
George Washington Univ	DC	48,820	MC
Gonzaga Univ	WA	30,218	C
Graceland Univ	IA	19,700	C
Hampshire College	MA	37,120	HC
Harvard Univ/Harvard College	MA	45,860	MC
Hawaii Pacific Univ	HI	21,080	C
John Carroll Univ	OH	27,658	C+
Kentucky Christian College	KY	12,680	C
Maharishi Univ of Management	IA	29,450	VC
Mass Inst of Technology	MA	41,800	MC
Middlebury College	VT	42,120	MC
Naropa Univ	CO	26,302	SP
New College of Florida	FL	10,009	HC+
Northwestern College of Iowa	IA	22,174	C+
Ohio Northern Univ	OH	27,765	VC
Old Dominion Univ	VA	11,907	C
Oral Roberts Univ	OK	22,650	C
Pacific Univ	OR	24,250	C
Point Loma Nazarene Univ	CA	27,610	VC
Pomona College	CA	40,774	MC
Ramapo College of New Jersey	NJ	16,630	VC
Rocky Mountain College	MT	20,805	C
Roosevelt Univ	IL	22,605	VC
St. John's Univ	NY	34,370	C
St. Mary's Univ of Minn	MN	23,857	VC
Sarah Lawrence College	NY	42,000	HC
Simon's Rock College of Bard	MA	41,988	VC+
Southeast Missouri State Univ	MO	10,596	C
Southwest Minn State Univ	MN	10,975	C
SUNY/College at Purchase	NY	11,989	VC+
Stevens Inst of Technology	NJ	40,935	HC
Swarthmore College	PA	41,280	MC
Thomas More College of Liberal Arts	NH	17,700	C
Touro College	NY	17,000	VC
Union College	NE	18,710	C
United States Military Academy	NY		MC
Univ of Alaska Southeast	AK	8,050	LC
Univ of Bridgeport	CT	29,595	LC
Univ of Calif at San Diego	CA	16,102	HC
Univ of Calif at Santa Barbara	CA	11,800	VC
Univ of Calif at Santa Cruz	CA	19,174	VC
Univ of Evansville	IN	28,320	C
Univ of Illinois at Chicago	IL	16,256	VC
Univ of Judaism College of A&S	CA	30,010	C
Univ of Mich/Ann Arbor	MI	16,587	HC+
Univ of New Haven	CT	31,794	C
Univ of N Car at Asheville	NC	9,237	VC
Univ of Rhode Island	RI	15,398	C
Univ of St. Thomas	MN	28,000	VC
Univ of Texas at Dallas	TX	13,244	HC
Washington Univ in St. Louis	MO	42,106	MC
Waynesburg College	PA	21,230	C
Webster Univ	MO	24,280	VC
West Chester Univ of Pennsylvania	PA	12,355	C+
Wheaton College	MA	40,180	HC+
Wilberforce Univ	OH	14,937	LC
Williams College	MA	40,310	MC
Yale Univ	CT	41,000	MC

LOGISTICS

School	ST	$IS	SR
Central Mich Univ	MI	12,244	C
Georgia Southern Univ	GA	9,762	C
Inter American Univ of PR/Bayamon Univ College	PR	3,522	
Thomas Edison State College	NJ	3,780	SP
United States Merchant Marine Academy	NY	6,516	HC+
Univ of Illinois at Urbana-Champaign	IL	15,800	HC+
Univ of Maryland/College Park	MD	16,036	HC
Univ of Memphis	TN	11,153	C

LUSO-BRAZILIAN STUDIES

School	ST	$IS	SR
New York Univ	NY	43,170	MC
Smith College	MA	41,474	MC

MANAGEMENT ENGINEERING

School	ST	$IS	SR
Claremont McKenna College	CA	42,920	MC
Pitzer College	CA	41,644	HC
Univ of PR/Bayamon Univ College Campus	PR	1,600	
Western Kentucky Univ	KY	10,192	C

ST = STATE   **$IS** = IN-STATE COSTS   **SR** = SELECTOR RATING

School	ST	$IS	SR
Worcester Polytechnic Inst	MA	40,450	VC+

MANAGEMENT INFORMATION SYSTEMS

School	ST	$IS	SR
Adams State College	CO	8,613	C
Adelphi Univ	NY	27,000	C
Albertus Magnus College	CT	25,336	C
Alderson-Broaddus College	WV	24,006	C
Andrews Univ	MI	21,786	C
Aquinas College	MI	23,750	C
Arkansas State Univ	AR	9,630	C
Ashford Univ	IA	20,370	C
Ashland Univ	OH	25,000	C
Augsburg College	MN	28,300	C
Augustana College	SD	24,380	VC
Aurora Univ	IL	20,645	C
Barry Univ	FL	24,100	LC
Baylor Univ	TX	27,555	HC
Benedictine Univ	IL	25,710	C
Bentley College	MA	38,784	HC
Boston Univ	MA	42,046	HC+
Bowling Green State Univ	OH	14,994	C
Bradley Univ	IL	25,280	VC
Brigham Young Univ	UT	9,200	VC
Cal State, Fullerton	CA	10,990	C
Cal State, Long Beach	CA	9,512	C
Cal State, Northridge	CA	9,036	LC
Cal State, Sacramento	CA	11,122	C+
Cal State, San Bernardino	CA	12,563	LC
Canisius College	NY	32,257	VC
Cedarville Univ	OH	21,904	VC
Central Conn State Univ	CT	13,620	C
Central Mich Univ	MI	12,244	C
Chatham Univ	PA	27,290	C
CUNY/Medgar Evers College	NY	4,250	NC
Claflin Univ	SC	16,798	C+
Clarkson Univ	NY	34,930	VC
Cleveland State Univ	OH	10,798	NC
College of Mount St. Joseph	OH	24,860	C
College of St. Catherine	MN	27,505	VC
College of Santa Fe	NM	28,978	C
Colo Christian Univ	CO	21,182	VC
Colo Technical Univ	CO	9,500	LC
Columbus State Univ	GA	8,664	C
Concordia Univ St.Paul	MN	27,776	C
Creighton Univ	NE	29,918	VC+
Crichton College	TN	15,300	C
Dallas Baptist Univ	TX	17,040	VC
Dana College	NE	22,390	C
Daniel Webster College	NH	24,870	C
De Sales Univ	PA	28,580	VC
Duquesne Univ	PA	29,534	VC
East Carolina Univ	NC	10,000	C
East Central Univ	OK	6,207	C
Eastern Mich Univ	MI	12,897	C
Eastern Univ	PA	24,075	C
Eureka College	IL	19,280	C
Excelsior College	NY	995	SP
Florida Gulf Coast Univ	FL	10,833	C
Florida Inst of Technology	FL	29,720	VC
Florida International Univ	FL	9,215	VC
Florida State Univ	FL	9,028	HC
Fort Hays State Univ	KS	7,638	C
Friends Univ	KS	16,250	LC
Gannon Univ	PA	26,100	C
George Mason Univ	VA	10,850	VC
Georgetown College	KY	24,950	C+
Georgia State Univ	GA	11,444	VC
Goshen College	IN	22,850	VC
Grace College	IN	22,170	C
Greenville College	IL	23,146	C
Grove City College	PA	15,784	HC+
Hofstra Univ	NY	32,630	VC
Humphreys College	CA	7,000	NC
Huron Univ	SD	10,700	C
Indiana State Univ	IN	11,604	C
Indiana Univ Bloomington	IN	13,356	VC
Indiana Univ of Pennsylvania	PA	11,209	C
Inter American Univ of PR/ Aguadilla Campus	PR	3,784	
Inter American Univ of PR/ Bayamon Univ College	PR	3,522	
Inter American Univ of PR/ Fajardo Campus	PR	4,000	
Inter American Univ of PR/ Metropolitan Campus	PR	4,320	
Inter American Univ of PR/ Ponce Regional College	PR	3,700	
Iona College	NY	30,878	VC
Johnson and Wales Univ/ Providence Campus	RI	28,126	LC
Johnson State College	VT	11,830	LC
Juniata College	PA	33,130	VC
Kansas State Univ	KS	10,516	VC
La Salle Univ	PA	34,950	C
Lasell College	MA	26,250	C
Le Moyne College	NY	29,570	VC
LeTourneau Univ	TX	21,200	C
Lewis Univ	IL	23,050	C+
Liberty Univ	VA	19,101	C
Lindenwood Univ	MO	18,600	VC
Loras College	IA	27,193	C
Luther College	IA	28,800	VC+
MacMurray College	IL	20,755	C
Marietta College	OH	29,327	C
Marquette Univ	WI	31,066	HC
McMurry Univ	TX	18,100	LC
Mercyhurst College	PA	28,633	VC
Metropolitan State Univ	MN	4,682	SP
Miami Univ	OH	29,097	NC
Midland Lutheran College	NE	18,600	C
Millikin Univ	IL	25,590	C
Milwaukee School of Engineering	WI	29,847	VC+
Minot State Univ	ND	6,700	LC
Missouri Southern State Univ	MO	8,396	NC
Monmouth Univ	IL	23,700	C
Montclair State Univ	NJ	16,327	C
Morehead State Univ	KY	9,150	C
New Mexico Highlands Univ	NM	6,272	NC
New Mexico State Univ	NM	9,250	C
Newman Univ	KS	21,106	C
Nichols College	MA	28,000	LC
N Dak State Univ	ND	8,500	C
Northeastern Univ	MA	35,742	HC
Northwest Christian College	OR	24,298	C
Northwestern College	MN	25,220	NC
Northwood Univ	FL	21,040	C
Northwood Univ	MI	21,000	C
Northwood Univ	TX	20,135	LC
Oakland Univ	MI	11,936	C
Ohio Dominican Univ	OH	25,954	C
Ohio State Univ	OH	15,357	HC
Okla State Univ	OK	10,213	VC
Old Dominion Univ	VA	11,907	C
Oral Roberts Univ	OK	22,650	C
Oregon Inst of Technology	OR	8,718	C
Ottawa Univ	KS	12,000	LC
Our Lady of the Lake Univ of San Antonio	TX	22,430	LC
Park Univ	MO	11,592	C
Peirce College	PA	12,760	NC
Penn State Erie/The Behrend College	PA	16,256	C
Penn State Univ/Univ Park Campus	PA	18,038	HC
Pennsylvania College of Technology	PA	16,980	LC
Philadelphia Univ	PA	30,006	C
Point Loma Nazarene Univ	CA	27,610	VC
Rensselaer Polytechnic Inst	NY	41,288	HC+
Rivier College	NH	26,600	C
Rochester Inst of Technology	NY	32,070	VC+
Rutgers, The State Univ of New Jersey/New Brunswick/Piscataway Campus	NJ	15,810	HC
St. Francis Univ	PA	25,880	LC
St. Joseph's College	IN	26,600	C
St. Joseph's Univ	PA	37,428	VC
St. Mary's College	IN	32,538	VC
Salisbury Univ	MD	13,128	VC
Santa Clara Univ	CA	38,931	VC
Savannah State Univ	GA	7,772	LC
Schreiner Univ	TX	20,600	C
Seton Hall Univ	NJ	33,622	VC
Seton Hill Univ	PA	28,810	C
Shippensburg Univ of Pennsylvania	PA	11,621	C
Simmons College	MA	35,640	VC
Southeast Missouri State Univ	MO	10,596	C
Southeastern Univ	FL	17,180	LC
Southern Christian Univ	AL	9,440	LC
Southern Illinois Univ Edwardsville	IL	11,022	C
Southern Methodist Univ	TX	36,088	VC+
Southern Nazarene Univ	OK	14,634	NC
Southwestern College	KS	21,476	C
Southwestern Okla State Univ	OK	4,801	C
Spring Arbor Univ	MI	22,476	C
SUNY/College at Old Westbury	NY	13,154	C
Stephen F. Austin State Univ	TX	7,930	C
Syracuse Univ	NY	38,655	HC
Taylor Univ	IN	26,376	VC+
Temple Univ	PA	17,438	C
Texas A&M Univ at Corpus Christi	TX	10,280	LC
Texas Tech Univ	TX	13,026	VC
Texas Wesleyan Univ	TX	18,700	C
Thiel College	PA	24,580	C
Thomas College	ME	23,770	LC
Tri-State Univ-Main Campus	IN	26,200	C
Tusculum College	TN	21,340	LC
Univ of Alabama	AL	9,888	C
Univ of Alabama in Huntsville	AL	9,516	VC
Univ of Alaska Anchorage	AK	11,275	NC
Univ of Arizona	AZ	11,958	VC
Univ of Arkansas at Monticello	AR	7,325	NC
Univ of Bridgeport	CT	29,595	LC
Univ of Central Florida	FL	10,739	VC
Univ of Central Okla	OK	8,094	C
Univ of Conn	CT	16,628	HC
Univ of Dayton	OH	28,826	VC
Univ of Georgia	GA	11,004	HC
Univ of Hartford	CT	34,044	C
Univ of Hawaii at Manoa	HI	10,413	VC
Univ of Houston	TX	7,000	C
Univ of Idaho	ID	9,310	NC
Univ of Illinois at Urbana-Champaign	IL	15,800	HC+
Univ of Indianapolis	IN	25,090	C
Univ of Mary	ND	15,374	C
Univ of Maryland/College Park	MD	16,036	HC
Univ of Mass Dartmouth	MA	15,985	C
Univ of Memphis	TN	11,153	C
Univ of Miami	FL	38,397	MC
Univ of Miss	MS	9,000	C
Univ of Missouri/Rolla	MO	13,332	NC
Univ of Missouri/St. Louis	MO	14,046	VC
Univ of Nebr at Omaha	NE	11,235	C
Univ of Nevada/Las Vegas	NV	11,566	C
Univ of N Car at Charlotte	NC	9,101	C
Univ of N Car at Greensboro	NC	8,993	C
Univ of N Dak	ND	10,114	VC
Univ of North Texas	TX	7,800	C
Univ of Northern Iowa	IA	11,133	C
Univ of Notre Dame	IN	39,552	MC
Univ of Okla	OK	10,769	VC+
Univ of Pennsylvania	PA	41,766	MC
Univ of Rhode Island	RI	15,398	C
Univ of St. Thomas	TX	23,810	VC
Univ of San Francisco	CA	37,560	VC
Univ of South Florida	FL	10,284	VC
Univ of Texas at Austin	TX	14,610	HC
Univ of Texas at El Paso	TX	8,764	VC
Univ of Texas at San Antonio	TX	11,325	LC
Univ of the Sacred Heart	PR	5,590	
Univ of Tulsa	OK	25,348	HC
Univ of Utah	UT	10,162	VC
Univ of West Georgia	GA	8,838	C
Univ of Wisc/Milwaukee	WI	9,427	LC
Univ of Wisc/Oshkosh	WI	10,426	LC
Univ of Wyoming	WY	9,666	C
Upper Iowa Univ	IA	20,130	C
Ursuline College	OH	25,456	C
Utah State Univ	UT	8,002	VC
Villanova Univ	PA	38,672	HC+
Virginia State Univ	VA	11,318	C
Viterbo Univ	WI	21,670	C
Walsh Univ	OH	23,440	C
Washington State Univ	WA	12,260	C
Wayne State Univ	MI	11,805	C
Weber State Univ	UT	9,635	NC
Western Conn State Univ	CT	12,993	C
Western Illinois Univ	IL	13,042	C
Western Kentucky Univ	KY	10,192	C
Western Mich Univ	MI	13,299	C
Western New Mexico Univ	NM	7,233	LC
Westminster College	MO	19,060	VC
Wingate Univ	NC	23,300	C
Winona State Univ	MN	11,333	C
Winston-Salem State Univ	NC	8,960	LC
Worcester Polytechnic Inst	MA	40,450	VC+
Wright State Univ	OH	13,616	LC
Youngstown State Univ	OH	12,613	NC

MANAGEMENT SCIENCE

School	ST	$IS	SR
Abilene Christian Univ	TX	20,830	C
Alfred Univ	NY		VC
Anderson Univ	IN	25,050	LC
Arizona State Univ-Tempe	AZ	11,174	C
Arkansas State Univ	AR	9,630	C
Aurora Univ	IL	20,645	C
Austin Peay State Univ	TN	7,535	C
Averett Univ	VA	24,920	C
Avila Univ	MO	22,100	C
Baldwin-Wallace College	OH	27,256	VC
Ball State Univ	IN	13,138	C
Barry Univ	FL	24,100	LC
Belmont Univ	TN	24,110	VC
Bethel College	TN	16,066	NC
Biola Univ	CA	29,372	VC
Boston College	MA	41,608	MC
Boston Univ	MA	42,046	HC+
Bridgewater State College	MA	12,120	C
Brigham Young Univ	UT	9,200	VC
Caldwell College	NJ	26,450	LC
Calif Baptist Univ	CA	23,780	C
Cal State, Fullerton	CA	10,990	C
Cal State, Monterey Bay	CA	10,099	C
Cal State, San Bernardino	CA	12,563	LC
Calif Univ of Pennsylvania	PA	14,217	C
Cambridge College	MA	11,055	SP
Catholic Univ of America	DC	35,838	VC
Cazenovia College	NY	26,900	C
Central Mich Univ	MI	12,244	C
Central Missouri State Univ	MO	10,000	C
Chaminade Univ of Honolulu	HI	23,320	LC
Champlain College	VT	24,605	C
Chestnut Hill College	PA	26,600	LC
Chicago State Univ	IL	10,915	C+
Christian Brothers Univ	TN	24,650	VC
CUNY/Baruch College	NY	4,320	VC+
CUNY/Herbert H. Lehman College	NY	4,000	LC
Clemson Univ	SC	13,366	NC
Cleveland State Univ	OH	10,798	NC
College of New Jersey	NJ	18,315	MC
College of St. Benedict	MN	30,091	VC
Colo Christian Univ	CO	21,182	VC
Colo Technical Univ	CO	9,500	LC
Columbia Union College	MD	23,536	LC
Concordia Univ Wisc	WI	22,660	VC
Creighton Univ	NE	29,918	VC+
Culver-Stockton College	MO	20,625	C
Cumberland Univ	TN	18,894	C
Davenport Univ	MI	15,205	NC
Davis and Elkins College	WV	22,416	C
Defiance College	OH	24,790	C
Delta State Univ	MS	7,709	C
Drake Univ	IA	27,632	VC+
Duquesne Univ	PA	29,534	VC
East Tenn State Univ	TN	8,497	C
Eastern Mich Univ	MI	12,897	C
Eastern Washington Univ	WA	10,608	C
Eckerd College	FL	35,492	VC
Evangel Univ	MO	17,380	C
Florida Gulf Coast Univ	FL	10,833	C
Florida International Univ	FL	9,215	VC
Florida State Univ	FL	9,028	HC
Franklin Pierce College	NH	31,700	C
Franklin Univ	OH	6,720	SP
Gallaudet Univ	DC	16,554	
George Fox Univ	OR	28,490	C
Georgia College and State Univ	GA	11,020	C
Georgia Inst of Technology	GA	11,450	HC+
Georgia Southern Univ	GA	9,762	C
Goucher College	MD	36,225	VC
Grand Valley State Univ	MI	12,000	VC
Granite State College	NH	4,800	SP
Gwynedd-Mercy College	PA	26,080	C
Hardin-Simmons Univ	TX	18,641	C
Hawaii Pacific Univ	HI	21,080	C
Heidelberg College	OH	23,242	C
Hiram College	OH	28,700	VC
Hood College	MD	30,085	VC
Huron Univ	SD	10,700	C
Idaho State Univ	ID	9,030	C
Illinois State Univ	IL	12,839	C+
Indiana Univ Bloomington	IN	13,356	VC
Indiana Univ Southeast	IN	4,880	LC
Indiana Univ-Purdue Univ Fort Wayne	IN	5,067	LC
Indiana Wesleyan Univ	IN	22,074	C+
Iona College	NY	30,878	VC
Iowa State Univ	IA	11,831	VC
Ithaca College	NY	35,144	VC
Kean Univ	NJ	15,880	C
Keene State College	NH	13,836	C
Kennesaw State Univ	GA	12,152	C
Langston Univ	OK	2,308	LC
Lesley Univ	MA	34,950	C
Louisiana State Univ in Shreveport	LA	2,900	NC
Louisiana Tech Univ	LA	7,370	C
Loyola Univ New Orleans	LA	31,050	VC+
Luther College	IA	28,800	VC+
Lynchburg College	VA	30,645	C
Madonna Univ	MI	16,068	C
Maharishi Univ of Management	IA	29,450	VC
Manhattanville College	NY	32,500	C+
Marian College of Fond du Lac	WI	21,775	LC
Marshall Univ	WV	9,116	C
Marylhurst Univ	OR	14,220	NC
Mass Inst of Technology	MA	41,800	MC
McMurry Univ	TX	18,100	LC
Metropolitan State College of Denver	CO	2,338	LC
Miami Univ	OH	29,097	HC
Midwestern State Univ	TX	9,381	C
Milwaukee School of Engineering	WI	29,847	VC+
Minn State Univ, Mankato	MN	10,276	LC
Minot State Univ	ND	6,700	LC
Missouri Baptist Univ	MO	19,640	C
Missouri Southern State Univ	MO	8,396	NC
Morehead State Univ	KY	9,150	C
National Univ	CA	8,412	SP
National-Louis Univ	IL	16,915	LC
New Jersey Inst of Technology	NJ	16,396	VC
New York Univ	NY	43,170	MC
Newman Univ	KS	21,106	C
Northern Kentucky Univ	KY	6,670	NC
Notre Dame College	OH	20,425	C
Ohio Northern Univ	OH	27,765	VC
Ohio Univ	OH	15,921	C
Okla State Univ	OK	10,213	VC
Old Dominion Univ	VA	11,907	C
Oral Roberts Univ	OK	22,650	C
Palm Beach Atlantic Univ	FL	23,597	VC

School	ST	$IS	SR
Penn State Univ/Univ Park Campus	PA	18,038	HC
Philadelphia Univ	PA	30,006	C
Point Park Univ	PA	24,160	C
Portland State Univ	OR	12,453	C
Post Univ	CT	24,875	C
Purdue Univ/West Lafayette	IN	13,458	VC
Quinnipiac Univ	CT	34,640	VC
Regis College	MA	31,350	LC
Rensselaer Polytechnic Inst	NY	41,288	HC+
Rice Univ	TX	32,290	MC
Richard Stockton College of New Jersey	NJ	14,000	VC
Rider Univ	NJ	32,560	C
Rivier College	NH	26,600	C
Robert Morris Univ	PA	22,822	C
Rochester Inst of Technology	NY	32,070	VC+
Roosevelt Univ	IL	22,605	VC
Rutgers, The State Univ of New Jersey/Camden Campus	NJ	15,000	VC
Rutgers, The State Univ of New Jersey/New Brunswick/Piscataway Campus	NJ	15,810	HC
Rutgers, The State Univ of New Jersey/Newark Campus	NJ	15,640	VC
St. Ambrose Univ	IA	25,495	C
St. Bonaventure Univ	NY	28,785	LC
St. Francis College	NY	19,974	LC
St. Francis Univ	PA	25,880	LC
St. John Fisher College	NY	27,860	C
St. John's Univ	MN	29,749	VC
St. John's Univ	NY	34,370	C
St. Joseph College	CT	32,050	C
St. Leo Univ	FL	22,140	C+
St. Martin's Univ	WA	27,555	C
Salve Regina Univ	RI	33,450	C
San Francisco State Univ	CA	13,000	C
Southern Illinois Univ Carbondale	IL	12,391	C
Southern Methodist Univ	TX	36,088	VC+
Southwestern Adventist Univ	TX	18,290	LC
Southwestern College	KS	21,476	C
Southwestern Okla State Univ	OK	4,801	C
SUNY at Oswego	NY	13,662	VC
SUNY/College at Cortland	NY	12,095	C
SUNY/Empire State College	NY	4,575	SP
Stephen F. Austin State Univ	TX	7,930	C
Stetson Univ	FL	32,725	VC
Suffolk Univ	MA	33,160	C
Tarleton State Univ	TX	8,952	C
Taylor Univ	IN	26,376	VC+
Tenn Tech Univ	TN	10,044	C
Texas A&M Univ	TX	13,351	HC
Texas A&M Univ at Kingsville	TX	6,800	LC
Texas Christian Univ	TX	23,410	VC+
Thomas College	ME	23,770	LC
Thomas Edison State College	NJ	3,780	SP
Touro College	NY	17,000	VC
Tri-State Univ-Main Campus	IN	26,200	C
Troy Univ Montgomery Campus	AL	4,104	NC
Tulane Univ	LA	41,098	MC
Turabo Univ	PR	4,110	
Tusculum College	TN	21,340	LC
Tuskegee Univ	AL	18,860	LC
Union College	NE	18,710	C
Union Univ	TN	20,750	VC
United States Air Force Academy	CO		HC+
United States Coast Guard Academy	CT		HC
United States Military Academy	NY		MC
Universidad Metropolitana	PR	3,330	
Univ of Arizona	AZ	11,958	VC
Univ of Arkansas at Little Rock	AR	7,230	NC
Univ of Bridgeport	CT	29,595	LC
Univ of Calif at Berkeley	CA	18,141	HC+
Univ of Calif at San Diego	CA	16,102	HC
Univ of Central Florida	FL	10,739	VC
Univ of Cincinnati	OH	17,682	C
Univ of Colo at Boulder	CO	13,352	C+
Univ of Dayton	OH	28,826	VC
Univ of Delaware	DE	14,142	HC
Univ of Florida	FL	9,354	HC
Univ of Georgia	GA	11,004	HC
Univ of Great Falls	MT	17,000	C
Univ of Hartford	CT	34,044	C
Univ of Hawaii at Manoa	HI	10,413	VC
Univ of Illinois at Chicago	IL	16,256	VC
Univ of Illinois at Urbana-Champaign	IL	15,800	HC+
Univ of Iowa	IA	12,172	VC
Univ of Louisiana at Lafayette	LA	5,830	C

School	ST	$IS	SR
Univ of Louisiana at Monroe	LA	7,103	C
Univ of Louisville	KY	10,400	VC
Univ of Maryland/College Park	MD	16,036	HC
Univ of Maryland/Univ College	MD	5,640	SP
Univ of Mass Boston	MA	8,024	C
Univ of Memphis	TN	11,153	C
Univ of Minn/Morris	MN	15,472	VC
Univ of Minn/Twin Cities	MN	13,165	HC
Univ of Miss	MS	9,000	C
Univ of Montevallo	AL	9,630	C
Univ of Nebr at Lincoln	NE	11,401	VC
Univ of Nebr at Omaha	NE	11,235	C
Univ of Nevada/Las Vegas	NV	11,566	C
Univ of Nevada/Reno	NV	12,155	NC
Univ of N Dak	ND	10,114	VC
Univ of North Texas	TX	7,800	C
Univ of Northern Colo	CO	10,249	C
Univ of Northern Iowa	IA	11,133	C
Univ of Notre Dame	IN	39,552	MC
Univ of Pittsburgh at Greensburg	PA	17,640	C
Univ of Pittsburgh at Pittsburgh	PA	18,866	HC
Univ of PR/Cayey Univ College	PR	1,250	
Univ of PR/Rio Piedras	PR	5,750	
Univ of S Car at Columbia	SC	13,397	VC
Univ of S Dak	SD	9,068	C
Univ of South Florida	FL	10,284	VC
Univ of Tenn at Knoxville	TN	11,720	C
Univ of Tenn at Martin	TN	8,693	C
Univ of Texas at Arlington	TX	7,195	LC
Univ of Texas at Austin	TX	14,610	HC
Univ of Texas at El Paso	TX	8,764	NC
Univ of Texas at San Antonio	TX	11,325	C
Univ of Texas-Pan American	TX	7,290	C+
Univ of Tulsa	OK	25,348	HC
Univ of West Georgia	GA	8,838	C
Univ of Wisc/Stevens Point	WI	9,384	VC
Univ of Wisc/Stout	WI	11,164	C
Upper Iowa Univ	IA	20,130	C
Virginia Polytechnic Inst and State Univ	VA	10,834	VC
Viterbo Univ	WI	21,670	C
Washington State Univ	WA	12,260	C
Wayne State Univ	MI	11,805	C
Waynesburg College	PA	21,230	C
Webster Univ	MO	24,280	VC
Wesley College	DE	19,905	C
West Liberty State College	WV	9,142	LC
West Texas A&M Univ	TX	8,452	C
Western Carolina Univ	NC	7,000	C
Western Kentucky Univ	KY	10,192	C
Western Mich Univ	MI	13,299	C
Western New England College	MA	32,054	C
Western Washington Univ	WA	11,262	VC
Wheeling Jesuit Univ	WV	26,910	C
Wichita State Univ	KS	8,500	C
Wilberforce Univ	OH	14,937	LC
Wright State Univ	OH	13,616	LC
Xavier Univ	OH	30,490	HC
York College of Pennsylvania	PA	16,550	VC

MANUFACTURING ENGINEERING

School	ST	$IS	SR
Boston Univ	MA	42,046	HC+
Bradley Univ	IL	25,280	VC
Brigham Young Univ	UT	9,200	VC
Calif Polytechnic State Univ	CA	12,390	VC
Calif State Polytechnic Univ, Pomona	CA	18,053	C+
Central State Univ	OH	9,010	C+
Hofstra Univ	NY	32,630	VC
Kansas State Univ	KS	10,516	VC
Miami Univ	OH	29,097	HC
Mich State Univ	MI	13,689	VC
Midwestern State Univ	TX	9,381	LC
New Jersey Inst of Technology	NJ	16,396	VC
New York Inst of Technology	NY	28,126	VC
N Dak State Univ	ND	8,500	C
Northern Kentucky Univ	KY	6,670	NC
Northwestern Univ	IL	37,595	MC
Pennsylvania College of Technology	PA	16,980	LC
Robert Morris Univ	PA	22,822	C
Rochester Inst of Technology	NY	32,070	VC+
St. Cloud State Univ	MN	10,010	C
Seattle Univ	WA	30,063	VC
Southern Illinois Univ Edwardsville	IL	11,022	C
Southern Polytechnic State Univ	GA	7,640	VC
Southwestern Okla State Univ	OK	4,801	C
Tenn Tech Univ	TN	10,044	C

School	ST	$IS	SR
Texas State Univ - San Marcos	TX	10,862	C
Univ of Arkansas at Little Rock	AR	7,230	NC
Univ of Calif at Berkeley	CA	18,141	HC+
Univ of Conn	CT	16,628	HC
Univ of Detroit Mercy	MI	27,000	C
Univ of Miami	FL	38,397	MC
Univ of Mich/Dearborn	MI	7,000	VC
Univ of Missouri/Rolla	MO	13,332	HC
Univ of New Mexico	NM	11,253	C
Univ of Texas-Pan American	TX	7,290	C+
Univ of Wisc/Stout	WI	11,164	C
Washington State Univ	WA	12,260	C
Western Mich Univ	MI	13,299	C
Wichita State Univ	KS	8,500	C
Worcester Polytechnic Inst	MA	40,450	VC+

MANUFACTURING TECHNOLOGY

School	ST	$IS	SR
Alabama State Univ	AL	7,658	C
Arkansas State Univ	AR	9,630	C
Bradley Univ	IL	25,280	VC
Brigham Young Univ	UT	9,200	VC
Central Conn State Univ	CT	13,620	C
Central Mich Univ	MI	12,244	C
Central Missouri State Univ	MO	10,000	C
East Carolina Univ	NC	10,000	C
Eastern Kentucky Univ	KY	7,725	C
Eastern Mich Univ	MI	12,897	C
Fairmont State	WV	8,400	LC
Farmingdale SUNY	NY	13,521	C
Illinois Inst of Technology	IL	26,465	HC+
Indiana State Univ	IN	11,604	C
Indiana Univ-Purdue Univ Indianapolis	IN	10,959	C
Lake Superior State Univ	MI	12,842	LC
Minn State Univ, Mankato	MN	10,276	LC
Missouri Southern State Univ	MO	8,396	NC
Missouri State Univ	MO	10,748	C+
Montana State Univ-Northern	MT	10,000	NC
Nicholls State Univ	LA	6,500	NC
Northern Kentucky Univ	KY	6,670	NC
Northern Mich Univ	MI	12,340	LC
Oregon Inst of Technology	OR	8,718	C
Rochester Inst of Technology	NY	32,070	VC+
S Dak State Univ	SD	9,815	C
Southern Arkansas Univ	AR	6,956	C
Southwestern College	KS	21,476	C
Southwestern Okla State Univ	OK	4,801	C
Texas State Univ - San Marcos	TX	10,862	C
Thomas Edison State College	NJ	3,780	SP
Univ of Akron	OH	15,166	NC
Univ of Dayton	OH	28,826	VC
Univ of Houston	TX	7,000	C
Univ of Memphis	TN	11,153	C
Univ of Nebr at Lincoln	NE	11,401	VC
Univ of Northern Iowa	IA	11,133	C
Univ of Rio Grande	OH	8,728	NC
Wayne State Univ	MI	11,805	C
Weber State Univ	UT	9,635	NC
Western Carolina Univ	NC	7,000	C
Western Illinois Univ	IL	13,042	C
Western Mich Univ	MI	13,299	C
Western Washington Univ	WA	11,262	VC

MARINE BIOLOGY

School	ST	$IS	SR
Alaska Pacific Univ	AK	25,142	C
Auburn Univ	AL	12,230	VC
Barry Univ	FL	24,100	LC
Brown Univ	RI	42,015	MC
Carroll College	WI	24,860	C
College of Charleston	SC	13,616	VC
Dowling College	NY	22,110	LC
Eastern Nazarene College	MA	19,500	LC
Fairleigh Dickinson Univ/College at Florham	NJ	30,130	C
Fairleigh Dickinson Univ/Metropolitan Campus	NJ	28,590	C
Florida Atlantic Univ	FL	11,221	C
Florida Inst of Technology	FL	29,720	VC
Florida International Univ	FL	9,215	VC
Florida State Univ	FL	9,028	HC
Hampshire College	MA	37,120	HC
Missouri Southern State Univ	MO	8,396	NC
Monmouth Univ	NJ	28,956	C
Nova Southeastern Univ	FL	24,320	C
Old Dominion Univ	VA	11,907	C
Roger Williams Univ	RI	30,500	C
St. Paul's College	VA	16,030	NC
San Francisco State Univ	CA	13,000	C
Savannah State Univ	GA	7,772	LC
Southwestern College	KS	21,476	C
Spring Hill College	AL	28,678	C
Stetson Univ	FL	32,725	VC

School	ST	$IS	SR
Texas A&M Univ at Galveston	TX	10,000	C+
Texas State Univ - San Marcos	AL	8,916	C
Troy Univ	AK	8,050	C
Univ of Alaska Southeast	AK	8,050	C
Univ of Calif at Los Angeles	CA	17,681	MC
Univ of Calif at Santa Barbara	CA	11,800	VC
Univ of Calif at Santa Cruz	CA	19,174	VC
Univ of Hawaii at Manoa	HI	10,413	VC
Univ of Maine	ME	13,642	C
Univ of Maine at Machias	ME	10,523	C
Univ of Mass Dartmouth	MA	15,985	C
Univ of New England	ME	31,005	C
Univ of New Haven	CT	31,794	C
Univ of N Car at Wilmington	NC	10,107	VC
Univ of PR at Humacao	PR	1,707	
Univ of West Alabama	AL	7,611	C
Univ of West Florida	FL	8,559	C
Waynesburg College	PA	21,230	C

MARINE ENGINEERING

School	ST	$IS	SR
Calif Maritime Academy	CA	13,490	C
Maine Maritime Academy	ME	14,340	C
Mass Maritime Academy	MA	11,571	C
SUNY/Maritime College	NY	12,475	C
Texas A&M Univ at Galveston	TX	10,000	C+
Thomas Edison State College	NJ	3,780	SP
United States Merchant Marine Academy	NY	6,516	HC+
United States Naval Academy	MD		MC
Univ of New Orleans	LA	7,370	C

MARINE SCIENCE

School	ST	$IS	SR
American Univ	DC	38,719	HC+
Coastal Carolina Univ	SC	13,140	C
East Stroudsburg Univ of Pennsylvania	PA	10,336	C
Eckerd College	FL	35,492	VC
Hawaii Pacific Univ	HI	21,080	C
Jacksonville Univ	FL	24,040	C
Juniata College	PA	33,130	C
Kutztown Univ of Pennsylvania	PA	10,820	C
Old Dominion Univ	VA	11,907	C
Richard Stockton College of New Jersey	NJ	14,000	VC
Rider Univ	NJ	32,560	C
Rutgers, The State Univ of New Jersey/New Brunswick/Piscataway Campus	NJ	15,810	HC
St. Paul's College	VA	16,030	NC
Samford Univ	AL	20,258	VC
SUNY/Maritime College	NY	12,475	C
Suffolk Univ	MA	33,160	C
Texas A&M Univ at Galveston	TX	10,000	C+
United States Coast Guard Academy	CT		HC
Univ of Alabama	AL	9,888	C
Univ of Conn	CT	16,628	HC
Univ of Hawaii at Hilo	HI	6,500	C
Univ of Maine	ME	13,642	C
Univ of Miami	FL	38,397	MC
Univ of New England	ME	31,005	C
Univ of N Car at Wilmington	NC	10,107	VC
Univ of Rhode Island	RI	15,398	C
Univ of San Diego	CA	40,620	HC
Univ of S Car at Columbia	SC	13,397	VC
Univ of Tampa	FL	25,784	C

MARITIME SCIENCE

School	ST	$IS	SR
Calif Maritime Academy	CA	13,490	C
Maine Maritime Academy	ME	14,340	C
SUNY/Maritime College	NY	12,475	C
Texas A&M Univ at Galveston	TX	10,000	C+
United States Merchant Marine Academy	NY	6,516	HC+

MARKETING AND DISTRIBUTION

School	ST	$IS	SR
Alvernia College	PA	26,388	C
Becker College	MA	24,300	LC
Caldwell College	NJ	26,450	LC
Carlow Univ	PA	24,313	C
Central Mich Univ	MI	12,244	C
Clayton College and State Univ	GA	2,445	LC
Duquesne Univ	PA	29,534	VC
Florida Gulf Coast Univ	FL	10,833	C
Franklin Univ	OH	6,720	SP
Georgia College and State Univ	GA	11,020	C
Georgia Southern Univ	GA	9,762	C
Gwynedd-Mercy College	PA	26,080	C

ST = STATE   **$IS** = IN-STATE COSTS   **SR** = SELECTOR RATING

School	ST	$IS	SR
Indiana State Univ	IN	11,604	C
Indiana Univ-Purdue Univ Indianapolis	IN	10,959	C
Inter American Univ of PR/ Arecibo Campus	PR	3,350	
Johnson and Wales Univ/ Charlotte Campus	NC	29,121	LC
Johnson and Wales Univ/ Providence Campus	RI	28,126	LC
Kent State Univ	OH	14,594	C
Metropolitan State Univ	MN	4,682	SP
Mountain State Univ	WV	11,406	NC
Neumann College	PA	25,996	LC
New Mexico Highlands Univ	NM	6,272	NC
New York Inst of Technology	NY	28,126	VC
Newman Univ	KS	21,106	C
Northwest Nazarene Univ	ID	22,590	VC
Ohio State Univ	OH	15,357	HC
Our Lady of Holy Cross College	LA	8,090	LC
Pennsylvania College of Technology	PA	16,980	LC
St. John's Univ	NY	34,370	C
Tarleton State Univ	TX	8,952	C
Taylor Univ	IN	26,376	VC+
Texas Tech Univ	TX	13,026	VC
Thomas Edison State College	NJ	3,780	SP
Union College	NE	18,710	C
Univ of Houston	TX	7,000	C
Univ of Illinois at Urbana-Champaign	IL	15,800	HC+
Univ of La Verne	CA	33,470	C
Univ of Memphis	TN	11,153	C
West Virginia Univ	WV	10,506	C
Western Carolina Univ	NC	7,000	C
Western Kentucky Univ	KY	10,192	C
Youngstown State Univ	OH	12,613	NC

MARKETING AND DISTRIBUTION EDUCATION

School	ST	$IS	SR
Bowling Green State Univ	OH	14,994	C
Central Washington Univ	WA	11,730	C
Dakota State Univ	SD	7,466	C
East Carolina Univ	NC	10,000	C
Eastern Washington Univ	WA	10,608	C
Fayetteville State Univ	NC	6,000	LC
Johnson and Wales Univ/ Providence Campus	RI	28,126	LC
Kent State Univ	OH	14,594	C
N Car State Univ	NC	11,824	HC
Old Dominion Univ	VA	11,907	C
Rider Univ	NJ	32,560	C
Southern New Hampshire Univ	NH	28,764	C
Temple Univ	PA	17,438	C
Univ of Central Okla	OK	8,094	C
Univ of Georgia	GA	11,004	HC
Univ of Idaho	ID	9,310	NC
Univ of N Dak	ND	10,114	VC
Univ of Tenn at Knoxville	TN	11,720	C
Univ of Wisc/Stout	WI	11,164	C
Western Kentucky Univ	KY	10,192	C
Western Mich Univ	MI	13,299	C

MARKETING MANAGEMENT

School	ST	$IS	SR
Ashford Univ	IA	20,370	C
Assumption College	MA	32,875	C
Averett Univ	VA	24,920	C
Baker College of Flint	MI	7,800	NC
Baldwin-Wallace College	OH	27,256	VC
Benedictine Univ	IL	25,710	C
Bentley College	MA	38,784	HC
Berry College	GA	24,342	VC
Biola Univ	CA	29,372	VC
Brigham Young Univ	UT	9,200	VC
Carthage College	WI	26,000	C
Cascade College	OR	17,980	NC
Catawba College	NC	25,000	C
Champlain College	VT	24,605	C
Chatham College	PA	27,290	C+
Christopher Newport Univ	VA	13,326	VC
CUNY/Baruch College	NY	4,320	VC+
Claflin Univ	SC	16,798	C+
Clarke College	IA	25,390	C
Cleary College	MI	11,000	LC
College of St. Joseph	VT	20,900	NC
College of St. Scholastica	MN	28,456	C+
College of the Ozarks	MO	4,130	VC+
Columbia College Chicago	IL	25,125	LC
Concordia Univ St.Paul	MN	27,776	C
Coppin State College	MD	10,200	LC
Cumberland Univ	TN	18,894	C
Davenport Univ	MI	15,205	NC
Drake Univ	IA	27,632	VC+
East Carolina Univ	NC	10,000	C
East Texas Baptist Univ	TX	16,713	C
Edinboro Univ of Pennsylvania	PA	11,809	LC
Emerson College	MA	35,076	HC
Fordham Univ	NY	36,000	HC
George Washington Univ	DC	48,820	MC

School	ST	$IS	SR
Hardin-Simmons Univ	TX	18,641	C
Hawaii Pacific Univ	HI	21,080	C
Hofstra Univ	NY	32,630	VC
Indiana Univ Kokomo	IN	4,835	LC
Iona College	NY	30,878	VC
Ithaca College	NY	35,144	VC
Johnson and Wales Univ/ Charlotte Campus	NC	29,121	LC
Johnson and Wales Univ/ North Miami Campus	FL	30,126	LC
Johnson and Wales Univ/ Providence Campus	RI	28,126	LC
Kent State Univ	OH	14,594	C
King College	TN	23,400	C
La Roche College	PA	24,724	C
La Sierra Univ	CA	24,327	C+
Lakeland College	WI	22,990	C
Le Moyne College	NY	29,570	VC
LeTourneau Univ	TX	21,200	C
Limestone College	SC	19,840	C
Lipscomb Univ	TN	20,967	VC
Lourdes College	OH	15,300	LC
Mary Baldwin College	VA	26,465	C
Metropolitan State Univ	MN	4,682	SP
Mich State Univ	MI	13,689	VC
Monmouth Univ	NJ	28,956	C
Montclair State Univ	NJ	16,327	C
Morehead State Univ	KY	9,150	C
Northwestern College	MN	25,220	NC
Northwood Univ	FL	21,040	C
Northwood Univ	MI	21,000	C
Northwood Univ	TX	20,135	LC
Ohio Univ	OH	15,921	C
Old Dominion Univ	VA	11,907	C
Olivet College	MI	19,984	C+
Oregon State Univ	OR	11,055	C
Our Lady of the Lake Univ of San Antonio	TX	22,430	LC
Palm Beach Atlantic Univ	FL	23,597	VC
Park Univ	MO	11,592	C
Peirce College	PA	12,760	NC
Penn State Erie/The Behrend College	PA	16,256	C
Pennsylvania College of Technology	PA	16,980	LC
Pittsburg State Univ	KS	8,112	C
Plymouth State Univ	NH	12,298	LC
Purdue Univ/West Lafayette	IN	13,458	VC
Rochester College	MI	15,636	C+
Rochester Inst of Technology	NY	32,070	VC+
Saginaw Valley State Univ	MI	11,432	C
St. Edward's Univ	TX	23,560	C
St. Mary's Univ of Minn	MN	23,857	VC
Siena College	NY	28,260	VC+
Southeast Missouri State Univ	MO	10,596	C
Southern New Hampshire Univ	NH	28,764	C
Southern Utah Univ	UT		C
Southwestern College	KS	21,476	C
Spring Hill College	AL	28,678	C
Stephen F. Austin State Univ	TX	7,930	C
Syracuse Univ	NY	38,655	HC
Thomas College	ME	23,770	LC
Troy Univ	AL	8,916	C
Troy Univ Dothan Campus	AL	4,678	C
Troy Univ Montgomery Campus	AL	4,104	NC
Tulane Univ	LA	41,098	MC
Union Univ	TN	20,750	VC
Univ of Arkansas	AR	11,859	VC
Univ of Colo at Boulder	CO	13,352	C+
Univ of Illinois at Urbana-Champaign	IL	15,800	HC+
Univ of Maryland/College Park	MD	16,036	HC
Univ of Maryland/Univ College	MD	5,640	SP
Univ of Mass Amherst	MA	15,973	C+
Univ of Memphis	TN	11,153	C
Univ of Miami	FL	38,397	MC
Univ of North Florida	FL	9,908	VC
Univ of PR/Rio Piedras	PR	5,750	
Univ of Rio Grande	OH	8,728	NC
Univ of St. Thomas	MN	28,000	VC
Univ of S Car Upstate	SC	11,957	C
Univ of Texas at Austin	TX	14,610	HC
Univ of the Sciences in Philadelphia	PA	33,380	VC
Ursuline College	OH	25,456	C
Virginia Polytechnic Inst and State Univ	VA	10,834	VC
Virginia State Univ	VA	11,318	VC
Warner Southern College	FL	18,000	LC
Washington State Univ	WA	12,260	C
Washington Univ in St. Louis	MO	42,106	MC
Weber State Univ	UT	9,635	NC
Western Carolina Univ	NC	7,000	C
Western Conn State Univ	CT	12,993	C
Youngstown State Univ	OH	12,613	NC

MARKETING/RETAILING/ MERCHANDISING

School	ST	$IS	SR
Abilene Christian Univ	TX	20,830	C
Adams State College	CO	8,613	C
Alabama A&M Univ	AL	8,890	LC
Alabama State Univ	AL	7,658	C
Albany State Univ	GA	5,770	C+
Alfred Univ	NY		VC
American International College	MA	28,710	LC
Anderson Univ	IN	25,050	LC
Andrews Univ	MI	21,786	C
Angelo State Univ	TX	8,340	NC
Appalachian State Univ	NC	8,000	VC
Arcadia Univ	PA	33,570	VC
Arizona State Univ-Tempe	AZ	11,174	C
Arkansas State Univ	AR	9,630	C
Ashland Univ	OH	25,000	C
Auburn Univ	AL	12,230	VC
Auburn Univ Montgomery	AL	9,530	NC
Augsburg College	MN	28,300	C
Augusta State Univ	GA	2,920	C
Aurora Univ	IL	20,645	C
Austin Peay State Univ	TN	7,535	C
Avila Univ	MO	22,100	C
Azusa Pacific Univ	CA	28,546	VC
Ball State Univ	IN	13,138	C
Barry Univ	FL	24,100	LC
Bay Path College	MA	29,362	C
Baylor Univ	TX	27,555	HC
Belmont Univ	TN	24,110	VC
Benedictine Univ	IL	25,710	C
Berkeley Colleg/ Westchester Campus	NY	26,700	LC
Berkeley College/New York City	NY	16,950	LC
Bethel Univ	MN	29,840	VC
Black Hills State Univ	SD	7,800	LC
Boise State Univ	ID	9,438	LC
Boston College	MA	41,608	MC
Boston Univ	MA	42,046	HC+
Bowling Green State Univ	OH	14,994	C
Bradley Univ	IL	25,280	VC
Brenau Univ Women's College	GA	23,950	VC
Buena Vista Univ	IA	27,742	C
Butler Univ	IN	31,944	VC+
Cabrini College	PA	33,340	C
Calif Lutheran Univ	CA	27,800	C
Calif State Polytechnic Univ, Pomona	CA	18,053	C+
Cal State East Bay	CA	10,856	LC
Cal State, Fullerton	CA	10,990	C
Cal State, Long Beach	CA	9,512	C
Cal State, Northridge	CA	9,036	LC
Cal State, Sacramento	CA	11,122	C
Canisius College	NY	32,257	VC
Caribbean Univ	PR	3,000	
Carnegie Mellon Univ	PA	32,700	MC
Cedarville Univ	OH	21,904	VC
Central Conn State Univ	CT	13,620	C
Central Mich Univ	MI	12,244	C
Central Missouri State Univ	MO	10,000	C
Central State Univ	OH	9,010	C+
Central Univ of Bayamon	PR	3,335	
Central Washington Univ	WA	11,730	C
Chaminade Univ of Honolulu	HI	23,320	LC
Chestnut Hill College	PA	26,600	LC
Chicago State Univ	IL	10,915	C+
Christian Brothers Univ	TN	24,650	VC
Christopher Newport Univ	VA	13,326	VC
City Univ	WA	7,425	NC
CUNY/Baruch College	NY	4,320	VC+
CUNY/York College	NY	4,242	NC
Clarion Univ of Pennsylvania	PA	11,844	C
Clarkson Univ	NY	34,930	VC
Clemson Univ	SC	13,366	HC
Cleveland State Univ	OH	10,798	NC
Coastal Carolina Univ	SC	13,140	C
College Misericordia	PA	27,950	C
College of New Jersey	NJ	18,315	MC
College of Notre Dame of Maryland	MD	27,700	C
College of Our Lady of the Elms	MA	21,000	C
College of St. Catherine	MN	27,505	VC
College of the Southwest	NM	12,420	C+
Colo State Univ-Fort Collins	CO	10,878	C+
Columbia College	MO	16,900	C
Columbus State Univ	GA	8,664	C
Concord College	WV	9,708	C
Concordia Univ Wisc	WI	22,660	VC
Cornerstone Univ and Grand Rapids Theological Seminary	MI	21,350	NC
Creighton Univ	NE	29,918	VC+
Dallas Baptist Univ	TX	17,040	VC
David N. Myers College	OH	9,475	C
Davis and Elkins College	WV	22,416	C
De Sales Univ	PA	28,580	VC
Defiance College	OH	24,790	C
Delaware State Univ	DE	8,130	LC

School	ST	$IS	SR
Delaware Valley College	PA	29,944	C
Delta State Univ	MS	7,709	C
DePaul Univ	IL	29,835	VC
Dominican College	NY	26,630	LC
Dowling College	NY	22,110	LC
Drexel Univ	PA	27,700	VC
Duquesne Univ	PA	29,534	VC
East Central Univ	OK	6,207	C
East Tenn State Univ	TN	8,497	C
Eastern Illinois Univ	IL	12,569	C
Eastern Kentucky Univ	KY	7,725	C
Eastern Mich Univ	MI	12,897	C
Eastern New Mexico Univ	NM	7,264	C
Eastern Univ	PA	24,075	C
Eastern Washington Univ	WA	10,608	C
Elmhurst College	IL	24,685	C
Elmira College	NY	37,200	VC
Emory Univ	GA	40,546	MC
Emporia State Univ	KS	8,093	C
Evangel Univ	MO	17,380	C
Excelsior College	NY	995	SP
Fairfield Univ	CT	39,835	HC
Fairleigh Dickinson Univ/ College at Florham	NJ	30,130	C
Fairleigh Dickinson Univ/ Metropolitan Campus	NJ	28,590	C
Fairmont State	WV	8,400	LC
Fashion Inst of Technology/ SUNY	NY	11,600	C+
Ferris State Univ	MI	13,698	C
Florida Atlantic Univ	FL	11,221	C
Florida International Univ	FL	9,215	VC
Florida Southern College	FL	25,965	C
Florida State Univ	FL	9,028	HC
Fort Hays State Univ	KS	7,638	C
Fort Valley State Univ	GA	6,975	C
Francis Marion Univ	SC	11,114	C
Franklin Pierce College	NH	31,700	C
Freed-Hardeman Univ	TN	16,370	NC
Gannon Univ	PA	26,100	C
George Mason Univ	VA	10,850	VC
Georgetown College	KY	24,950	C+
Georgetown Univ	DC	43,183	MC
Georgia Southern Univ	GA	9,762	C
Georgia Southwestern State Univ	GA	6,035	C
Georgia State Univ	GA	11,444	VC
Glenville State College	WV	8,778	NC
Goldey-Beacom College	DE	11,440	C
Grambling State Univ	LA	6,538	NC
Grand Canyon Univ	AZ	32,000	LC
Grand Valley State Univ	MI	12,000	VC
Greenville College	IL	23,146	C
Grove City College	PA	15,784	HC+
Hampton Univ	VA	19,468	C+
Harding Univ	AR	16,512	VC
High Point Univ	NC	25,720	C
Hillsdale College	MI	24,160	HC
Holy Family Univ	PA	25,740	C
Howard Univ	DC	18,481	C+
Huron Univ	SD	10,700	C
Husson College	ME	17,410	LC
Huston-Tillotson Univ	TX	14,232	LC
Idaho State Univ	ID	9,030	C
Illinois State Univ	IL	12,839	C+
Indiana State Univ	IN	11,604	C
Indiana Univ Bloomington	IN	13,356	VC
Indiana Univ of Pennsylvania	PA	11,209	C
Indiana Univ South Bend	IN	4,989	LC
Indiana Univ Southeast	IN	4,880	LC
Indiana Univ-Purdue Univ Fort Wayne	IN	5,067	C
Indiana Univ-Purdue Univ Indianapolis	IN	10,959	C
Indiana Wesleyan Univ	IN	22,074	C+
Inter American Univ of PR/ Aguadilla Campus	PR	3,784	
Inter American Univ of PR/ Bayamon Univ College	PR	3,522	
Inter American Univ of PR/ Fajardo Campus	PR	4,000	
Inter American Univ of PR/ Metropolitan Campus	PR	4,320	
Inter American Univ of PR/ Ponce Regional College	PR	3,700	
Inter American Univ of PR/ San German	PR	6,720	
Iona College	NY	30,878	VC
Iowa State Univ	IA	11,831	VC
Ithaca College	NY	35,144	VC
Jackson State Univ	MS	8,500	C
Jacksonville State Univ	AL	7,618	LC
Jacksonville Univ	FL	24,040	C
James Madison Univ	VA	12,010	VC
John Carroll Univ	OH	27,658	C+
Johnson and Wales Univ/ Charlotte Campus	NC	29,121	LC
Johnson and Wales Univ/ North Miami Campus	FL	30,126	LC
Johnson and Wales Univ/ Providence Campus	RI	28,126	LC
Juniata College	PA	33,130	VC
Kansas State Univ	KS	10,516	VC
Kean Univ	NJ	15,880	C
Kennesaw State Univ	GA	12,152	C

INDEX OF COLLEGE MAJORS

School	ST	$IS	SR
Keuka College	NY	26,050	C
King's College	PA	29,810	C
Kutztown Univ of Pennsylvania	PA	10,820	C
La Salle Univ	PA	34,950	C
Laboratory Inst of Merchandising	NY	25,150	SP
Lake Superior State Univ	MI	12,842	LC
Lamar Univ	TX	6,820	LC
Lasell College	MA	26,250	C
Lehigh Univ	PA	42,690	HC+
LeTourneau Univ	TX	21,200	C
Lewis Univ	IL	23,050	C+
Lincoln Univ	MO	8,000	NC
Lindenwood Univ	MO	18,600	VC
LIU/Brooklyn Campus	NY	25,000	C
LIU/C.W. Post Campus	NY	28,282	C
Loras College	IA	27,193	C
Louisiana State Univ and A&M College	LA	10,749	VC
Louisiana State Univ in Shreveport	LA	2,900	NC
Louisiana Tech Univ	LA	7,370	C
Loyola Univ Chicago	IL	32,896	VC
Loyola Univ New Orleans	LA	31,050	VC+
Lynchburg College	VA	30,645	C
Lynn Univ	FL	30,750	C
MacMurray College	IL	20,755	C
Madonna Univ	MI	16,068	VC
Manhattan College	NY	29,000	VC
Mansfield Univ	PA	11,300	C
Marian College of Fond du Lac	WI	21,775	LC
Marietta College	OH	29,327	C
Marquette Univ	WI	31,066	HC
Marshall Univ	WV	9,116	C
Martin Univ	IN	10,300	SP
Marymount Univ	VA	25,934	C
Maryville Univ of St. Louis	MO	23,000	VC
Marywood Univ	PA	30,680	C
McKendree College	IL	24,800	VC
McMurry Univ	TX	18,100	C
McNeese State Univ	LA	5,270	LC
Mercer Univ	GA	27,525	VC+
Mercyhurst College	PA	28,633	VC
Merrimack College	MA	34,380	C
Messiah College	PA	28,910	VC+
Methodist College	NC	21,000	C
Metropolitan State College of Denver	CO	2,338	LC
Miami Univ	OH	29,097	HC
Mich State Univ	MI	13,689	VC
MidAmerica Nazarene Univ	KS	20,584	LC
Middle Tenn State Univ	TN	8,540	C
Midland Lutheran College	NE	18,640	C
Midwestern State Univ	TX	9,381	LC
Millikin Univ	IL	25,590	C
Minn State Univ, Mankato	MN	10,276	LC
Minn State Univ, Moorhead	MN	7,000	LC
Minot State Univ	ND	6,710	LC
Miss College	MS	14,574	VC
Miss State Univ	MS	9,577	C
Missouri Southern State Univ	MO	8,396	NC
Missouri State Univ	MO	10,748	C+
Missouri Western State Univ	MO	9,534	NC
Morehouse College	GA	25,082	C
Morgan State Univ	MD	12,080	C
Mount Ida College	MA	26,000	LC
Mount Mary College	WI	22,895	C
Mount Mercy College	IA	23,670	C
Murray State Univ	KY	8,900	LC
New Mexico Highlands Univ	NM	6,272	NC
New Mexico State Univ	NM	9,250	C
New York Inst of Technology	NY	28,126	VC
New York Univ	NY	43,170	MC
Niagara Univ	NY	28,250	C
Nicholls State Univ	LA	6,500	NC
Nichols College	MA	28,000	LC
North Central College	IL	28,926	VC
North Georgia College and State Univ	GA	7,000	C
North Park Univ	IL	24,050	C
Northeastern Illinois Univ	IL	3,000	NC
Northeastern State Univ	OK	5,896	LC
Northeastern Univ	MA	35,742	HC
Northern Arizona Univ	AZ	10,353	LC
Northern Illinois Univ	IL	13,178	C
Northern Kentucky Univ	KY	6,670	NC
Northern Mich Univ	MI	12,340	LC
Northern State Univ	SD	8,257	C
Northwest Missouri State Univ	MO	10,000	C
Notre Dame College	OH	20,425	C
Notre Dame de Namur Univ	CA	32,790	LC
Oakland Univ	MI	11,936	C
Okla Baptist Univ	OK	17,986	VC
Okla Christian Univ	OK	18,992	NC
Okla State Univ	OK	10,213	VC
Oral Roberts Univ	OK	22,650	C
Oregon State Univ	OR	11,055	C
Pace Univ	NY	30,000	VC
Parsons School of Design	NY	32,242	SP
Penn State Univ/Univ Park Campus	PA	18,038	HC
Peru State College	NE	6,350	NC
Philadelphia Univ	PA	30,006	C
Pontifical Catholic Univ of PR/Ponce	PR	7,310	
Portland State Univ	OR	12,453	C
Post Univ	CT	24,875	C
Prairie View A&M Univ	TX	11,110	LC
Purdue Univ/Calumet	IN	10,891	LC
Quincy Univ	IL	24,920	C
Quinnipiac Univ	CT	34,640	VC
Radford Univ	VA	13,145	C
Regis Univ	CO	31,890	C
Rhode Island College	RI	11,570	C
Rider Univ	NJ	32,560	C
Robert Morris Univ	PA	22,822	C
Roger Williams Univ	RI	30,500	C
Roosevelt Univ	IL	22,605	VC
Rowan Univ	NJ	16,000	VC
Rutgers, The State Univ of New Jersey/Camden Campus	NJ	15,000	VC
Rutgers, The State Univ of New Jersey/New Brunswick/Piscataway Campus	NJ	15,810	HC
Rutgers, The State Univ of New Jersey/Newark Campus	NJ	15,640	VC
St. Ambrose Univ	IA	25,495	C
St. Bonaventure Univ	NY	28,785	C
St. Cloud State Univ	MN	10,010	C
St. Joseph's Univ	PA	37,428	VC
St. Martin's Univ	WA	27,555	C
St. Mary-of-the-Woods College	IN	25,480	C
St. Mary's Univ of San Antonio	TX	22,444	C
St. Peter's College	NJ	30,160	LC
St. Thomas Aquinas College	NY	22,000	LC
St. Thomas Univ	FL	23,490	C
St. Vincent College	PA	26,160	VC
St. Xavier Univ	IL	23,160	C
Sam Houston State Univ	TX	8,000	C
San Diego State Univ	CA	12,971	C
San Francisco State Univ	CA	13,000	C
San Jose State Univ	CA	11,707	C
Santa Clara Univ	CA	38,931	VC
Savannah State Univ	GA	7,772	LC
Seattle Univ	WA	30,063	VC
Seton Hall Univ	NJ	33,622	VC
Seton Hill Univ	PA	28,810	C
Shippensburg Univ of Pennsylvania	PA	11,621	C
Simmons College	MA	35,640	VC
Simpson College	IA	26,833	VC
Slippery Rock Univ of Pennsylvania	PA	10,360	LC
S Car State Univ	SC	6,700	LC
Southeastern Louisiana Univ	LA	8,521	LC
Southeastern Univ	DC	9,000	NC
Southeastern Univ	FL	17,180	LC
Southern Adventist Univ	TN	18,500	C
Southern Conn State Univ	CT	10,310	C
Southern Illinois Univ Carbondale	IL	12,391	C
Southern Methodist Univ	TX	36,088	VC+
Southern Nazarene Univ	OK	14,634	NC
Southern New Hampshire Univ	NH	28,764	C
Southern Oregon Univ	OR	12,186	C
Southern Univ and A&M College	LA	8,238	LC
Southern Utah Univ	UT		C
Southwest Minn State Univ	MN	10,975	C
Southwestern Okla State Univ	OK	4,801	C
SUNY at Oswego	NY	13,662	VC
SUNY/College at Old Westbury	NY	13,154	C
SUNY/Univ at New Paltz	NY	12,480	VC
Stephen F. Austin State Univ	TX	7,930	C
Stetson Univ	FL	32,725	VC
Stonehill College	MA	36,104	VC
Suffolk Univ	MA	33,160	C
Syracuse Univ	NY	38,655	HC
Tabor College	KS	21,614	NC
Tarleton State Univ	TX	8,952	C
Temple Univ	PA	17,438	C
Tenn Tech Univ	TN	10,044	C
Texas A&M Univ	TX	13,351	HC
Texas A&M Univ at Commerce	TX	9,020	C
Texas A&M Univ at Corpus Christi	TX	10,280	LC
Texas A&M Univ at Kingsville	TX	6,800	LC
Texas Christian Univ	TX	23,410	VC+
Texas Southern Univ	TX	9,828	C
Texas State Univ - San Marcos	TX	10,862	C
Texas Wesleyan Univ	TX	18,700	C
Texas Woman's Univ	TX	7,804	LC
Tiffin Univ	OH	19,490	LC
Touro College	NY	17,000	VC
Trevecca Nazarene Univ	TN	19,594	C
Trinity International Univ	IL	25,686	C
Tri-State Univ-Main Campus	IN	26,200	C
Troy Univ	AL	8,916	C
Turabo Univ	PR	4,110	
Tuskegee Univ	AL	18,860	LC
Union Univ	TN	20,750	VC
Univ of Akron	OH	15,166	NC
Univ of Alabama at Birmingham	AL	13,716	C
Univ of Alabama in Huntsville	AL	9,516	VC
Univ of Alaska Anchorage	AK	11,275	NC
Univ of Arizona	AZ	11,958	VC
Univ of Arkansas	AR	11,859	VC
Univ of Arkansas at Little Rock	AR	7,230	NC
Univ of Bridgeport	CT	29,595	LC
Univ of Central Arkansas	AR	9,984	C
Univ of Central Florida	FL	10,739	VC
Univ of Central Okla	OK	8,094	C
Univ of Cincinnati	OH	17,682	C
Univ of Conn	CT	16,628	HC
Univ of Dayton	OH	28,826	VC
Univ of Delaware	DE	14,142	HC
Univ of Denver	CO	36,376	VC+
Univ of Evansville	IN	28,320	VC
Univ of Findlay	OH	29,238	C
Univ of Florida	FL	9,354	HC
Univ of Georgia	GA	11,004	HC
Univ of Great Falls	MT	17,000	C
Univ of Hartford	CT	34,044	C
Univ of Hawaii at Manoa	HI	10,413	VC
Univ of Houston	TX	7,000	C
Univ of Houston-Downtown	TX	3,326	NC
Univ of Idaho	ID	9,310	NC
Univ of Illinois at Chicago	IL	16,256	VC
Univ of Illinois at Urbana-Champaign	IL	15,800	HC+
Univ of Indianapolis	IN	25,090	C
Univ of Iowa	IA	12,172	VC
Univ of Kentucky	KY	7,800	C
Univ of Louisiana at Lafayette	LA	5,830	C
Univ of Louisiana at Monroe	LA	7,103	C
Univ of Louisville	KY	10,400	VC
Univ of Maine at Machias	ME	10,523	C
Univ of Mary Hardin-Baylor	TX	19,428	C
Univ of Mass Dartmouth	MA	15,985	C
Univ of Memphis	TN	11,153	C
Univ of Mich/Flint	MI	6,398	C
Univ of Minn/Twin Cities	MN	13,165	HC
Univ of Miss	MS	9,000	C
Univ of Missouri/Columbia	MO	13,500	VC
Univ of Mobile	AL	16,880	C
Univ of Montana	MT	10,602	C
Univ of Montevallo	AL	9,630	C
Univ of Nebr at Kearney	NE	9,000	NC
Univ of Nebr at Lincoln	NE	11,401	VC
Univ of Nebr at Omaha	NE	11,235	C
Univ of Nevada/Las Vegas	NV	11,566	C
Univ of Nevada/Reno	NV	12,155	NC
Univ of New Haven	CT	31,794	C
Univ of New Mexico	NM	11,253	C
Univ of New Orleans	LA	7,370	C
Univ of North Alabama	AL	8,992	C
Univ of N Car at Charlotte	NC	9,101	C
Univ of N Car at Wilmington	NC	10,107	VC
Univ of N Dak	ND	10,114	VC
Univ of North Texas	TX	7,800	C
Univ of Northern Colo	CO	10,249	C
Univ of Northern Iowa	IA	11,133	C
Univ of Notre Dame	IN	39,552	MC
Univ of Okla	OK	10,769	VC+
Univ of Pennsylvania	PA	41,766	MC
Univ of Pittsburgh at Pittsburgh	PA	18,866	HC
Univ of Portland	OR	32,300	VC
Univ of PR/Arecibo	PR	8,327	
Univ of PR/Bayamon Univ College Campus	PR	1,600	
Univ of PR/Mayaguez	PR	1,250	
Univ of Rhode Island	RI	15,398	C
Univ of St. Francis	IL	25,430	C
Univ of St. Thomas	TX	23,810	VC
Univ of San Francisco	CA	37,560	VC
Univ of Scranton	PA	31,100	VC
Univ of Sioux Falls	SD	20,800	C
Univ of South Alabama	AL	8,930	LC
Univ of S Car at Columbia	SC	13,397	VC
Univ of South Florida	FL	10,284	VC
Univ of Southern Indiana	IN	12,590	LC
Univ of Southern Miss	MS	10,112	C
Univ of Tampa	FL	25,784	C
Univ of Tenn at Knoxville	TN	11,720	C
Univ of Tenn at Martin	TN	8,693	C
Univ of Texas at Arlington	TX	7,195	LC
Univ of Texas at El Paso	TX	8,764	NC
Univ of Texas at San Antonio	TX	11,325	LC
Univ of Texas-Pan American	TX	7,290	C+
Univ of the District of Columbia	DC	2,070	LC
Univ of the Ozarks	AR	19,250	C
Univ of the Sacred Heart	PR	5,590	
Univ of Toledo	OH	15,806	NC
Univ of Tulsa	OK	25,348	HC
Univ of Utah	UT	10,162	VC
Univ of Washington	WA	10,400	VC
Univ of West Florida	FL	8,559	C
Univ of West Georgia	GA	8,838	C
Univ of Wisc/Eau Claire	WI	9,915	VC
Univ of Wisc/La Crosse	WI	10,045	VC
Univ of Wisc/Madison	WI	13,117	HC
Univ of Wisc/Milwaukee	WI	9,427	LC
Univ of Wisc/Oshkosh	WI	10,426	LC
Univ of Wisc/Stout	WI	11,164	C
Univ of Wisc/Whitewater	WI	9,274	C
Univ of Wyoming	WY	9,666	C
Upper Iowa Univ	IA	20,130	C
Utah State Univ	UT	8,002	VC
Valdosta State Univ	GA	8,802	C
Valparaiso Univ	IN	28,970	VC+
Vanguard Univ of Southern Calif	CA	27,071	C
Villanova Univ	PA	38,672	HC+
Virginia Commonwealth Univ	VA	12,987	C
Viterbo Univ	WI	21,670	C
Walsh Univ	OH	23,440	C
Wartburg College	IA	27,315	NC
Washburn Univ	KS	9,734	NC
Washington Univ in St. Louis	MO	42,106	MC
Wayne State Univ	MI	11,805	C
Waynesburg College	PA	21,230	C
Webber International Univ	FL	17,580	LC
Wesley College	DE	19,905	C
West Chester Univ of Pennsylvania	PA	12,355	C+
West Liberty State College	WV	9,142	LC
West Texas A&M Univ	TX	8,452	C
West Virginia State Univ	WV	8,378	NC
West Virginia Wesleyan College	WV	26,880	C
Western Illinois Univ	IL	13,042	C
Western Mich Univ	MI	13,299	C
Western New England College	MA	32,054	C
Western New Mexico Univ	NM	7,233	LC
Western Washington Univ	WA	11,262	VC
Westminster College	PA	31,290	C+
Westminster College	UT	25,656	C
Wheeling Jesuit Univ	WV	26,910	C
Wichita State Univ	KS	8,500	C
Wilberforce Univ	OH	14,937	LC
Wingate Univ	NC	23,300	C
Winona State Univ	MN	11,333	C
Woodbury Univ	CA	30,176	LC
Wright State Univ	OH	13,616	LC
Xavier Univ	OH	30,490	HC
Xavier Univ of Louisiana	LA	17,600	C
Yeshiva Univ	NY	22,000	C
York College of Pennsylvania	PA	16,550	VC
Youngstown State Univ	OH	12,613	NC

MATERIALS ENGINEERING

School	ST	$IS	SR
Alfred Univ	NY		VC
Calif Polytechnic State Univ	CA	12,390	VC
Calif State Polytechnic Univ, Pomona	CA	18,053	C+
Drexel Univ	PA	27,700	VC
Florida State Univ	FL	9,028	HC
Georgia Inst of Technology	GA	11,450	HC+
Iowa State Univ	IA	11,831	VC
Johns Hopkins Univ	MD	42,044	MC
Lehigh Univ	PA	42,690	HC+
Mass Inst of Technology	MA	41,800	MC
Mich State Univ	MI	13,689	VC
Mich Tech Univ	MI	14,569	VC
New Mexico Inst of Mining and Technology	NM	8,510	VC+
Northwestern Univ	IL	37,595	MC
Ohio State Univ	OH	15,357	HC
Purdue Univ/West Lafayette	IN	13,458	VC
Rensselaer Polytechnic Inst	NY	41,288	HC+
San Jose State Univ	CA	11,707	C
Univ of Alabama at Birmingham	AL	13,716	C
Univ of Arizona	AZ	11,958	VC
Univ of at Calif Davis	CA	15,010	VC
Univ of Calif at Berkeley	CA	18,141	HC+
Univ of Calif at Los Angeles	CA	17,681	MC
Univ of Cincinnati	OH	17,682	C
Univ of Florida	FL	9,354	VC
Univ of Illinois at Urbana-Champaign	IL	15,800	HC+
Univ of Kentucky	KY	7,800	C
Univ of Maryland/College Park	MD	16,036	HC

ST = STATE $IS = IN-STATE COSTS   SR = SELECTOR RATING

School	ST	$IS	SR
Univ of Mich/Ann Arbor	MI	16,587	HC+
Univ of Minn/Twin Cities	MN	13,165	HC
Univ of Missouri/Rolla	MO	13,332	HC
Univ of Pennsylvania	PA	41,766	MC
Univ of Pittsburgh at Pittsburgh	PA	18,866	HC
Univ of Tenn at Knoxville	TN	11,720	C
Univ of Utah	UT	10,162	VC
Univ of Wisc/Milwaukee	WI	9,427	LC
Virginia Polytechnic Inst and State Univ	VA	10,834	VC
Washington State Univ	WA	12,260	C
Winona State Univ	MN	11,333	C
Worcester Polytechnic Inst	MA	40,450	VC+
Wright State Univ	OH	13,616	LC
Youngstown State Univ	OH	12,613	NC

MATERIALS SCIENCE

School	ST	$IS	SR
Arizona State Univ-Tempe	AZ	11,174	C
Case Western Reserve Univ	OH	37,314	MC
Columbia Univ/Fu Foundation School of Engineering and Applied Science	NY	42,584	MC
Cornell Univ	NY	41,717	MC
Duke Univ	NC	41,239	MC
Georgia Inst of Technology	GA	11,450	HC+
Johns Hopkins Univ	MD	42,044	MC
Mass Inst of Technology	MA	41,800	MC
N Car State Univ	NC	11,824	HC
Northwestern Univ	IL	37,595	MC
Ohio State Univ	OH	15,357	HC
Penn State Univ/Univ Park Campus	PA	18,038	HC
Rochester Inst of Technology	NY	32,070	VC+
Stanford Univ	CA	41,557	MC
Temple Univ	PA	17,438	C
Univ of Calif at Berkeley	CA	18,141	HC+
Univ of Illinois at Urbana-Champaign	IL	15,800	HC+
Univ of Mass Dartmouth	MA	15,985	C
Univ of Mich/Ann Arbor	MI	16,587	HC+
Univ of Minn/Twin Cities	MN	13,165	HC
Univ of New Haven	CT	31,794	C
Univ of Pittsburgh at Pittsburgh	PA	18,866	HC
Univ of Tenn at Knoxville	TN	11,720	C
Univ of the Ozarks	AR	19,250	C
Univ of Washington	WA	10,400	VC
Univ of Wisc/Madison	WI	13,117	HC

MATHEMATICS

School	ST	$IS	SR
Abilene Christian Univ	TX	20,830	C
Adams State College	CO	8,613	C
Adelphi Univ	NY	27,900	VC
Adrian College	MI	23,000	C
Agnes Scott College	GA	32,070	HC
Alabama A&M Univ	AL	8,890	LC
Alabama State Univ	AL	7,658	C
Albany State Univ	GA	5,770	C+
Albertson College of Idaho	ID	21,095	VC
Albertus Magnus College	CT	25,336	C
Albion College	MI	26,000	VC
Albright College	PA	33,920	C
Alcorn State Univ	MS	8,190	LC
Alderson-Broaddus College	WV	24,006	C
Alfred Univ	NY		VC
Allegheny College	PA	33,500	HC
Allen Univ	SC	10,500	NC
Alma College	MI	28,544	VC
Alvernia College	PA	26,388	C
Alverno College	WI	21,088	C
American International College	MA	28,710	LC
American Univ	DC	38,719	HC+
Amherst College	MA	41,590	MC
Anderson Univ	IN	25,050	LC
Andrews Univ	MI	21,786	C
Angelo State Univ	TX	8,340	NC
Appalachian State Univ	NC	8,000	VC
Aquinas College	MI	23,750	C
Arcadia Univ	PA	33,570	VC
Arizona State Univ-Tempe	AZ	11,174	C
Arkansas State Univ	AR	9,630	C
Arkansas Tech Univ	AR	8,108	VC
Armstrong Atlantic State Univ	GA	7,394	C
Asbury College	KY	23,762	VC
Ashland Univ	OH	25,000	C
Assumption College	MA	32,875	C
Atlantic Union College	MA	17,600	LC
Auburn Univ	AL	12,230	VC
Auburn Univ Montgomery	AL	9,530	NC
Augsburg College	MN	28,300	C
Augusta State Univ	GA	2,920	C
Augustana College	IL	29,862	VC+
Augustana College	SD	24,380	VC
Aurora Univ	IL	20,645	C
Austin College	TX	27,871	HC
Austin Peay State Univ	TN	7,535	C
Averett Univ	VA	24,920	C
Avila Univ	MO	22,100	C
Azusa Pacific Univ	CA	28,546	VC
Baker Univ	KS	22,190	C
Baldwin-Wallace College	OH	27,256	VC
Ball State Univ	IN	13,138	C
Barber-Scotia College	NC	15,000	LC
Bard College	NY	41,800	HC+
Barry Univ	FL	24,100	C
Barton College	NC	22,316	C
Bates College	ME	42,100	MC
Baylor Univ	TX	27,555	HC
Belhaven College	MS	19,530	NC
Bellarmine Univ	KY	27,650	VC
Belmont Univ	TN	24,110	VC
Beloit College	WI	32,808	HC
Bemidji State Univ	MN	11,180	LC
Benedict College	SC	19,114	LC
Benedictine College	KS	21,968	C
Benedictine Univ	IL	25,710	C
Bennett College	NC	11,500	C
Bennington College	VT	41,890	HC
Bentley College	MA	38,784	HC
Berea College	KY	5,496	VC+
Berry College	GA	24,342	VC
Bethany College	KS	20,660	LC
Bethany College	WV	21,395	C
Bethel College	IN	19,680	C
Bethel College	KS	21,650	C
Bethel College	TN	16,066	NC
Bethel Univ	MN	29,840	VC
Bethune-Cookman College	FL	17,922	LC
Biola Univ	CA	29,372	VC
Birmingham-Southern College	AL	28,494	VC+
Black Hills State Univ	SD	7,800	LC
Blackburn College	IL	13,690	C
Bloomsburg Univ of Pennsylvania	PA	11,602	C
Blue Mountain College	MS	11,086	C
Bluefield College	VA	17,230	C+
Bluffton College	OH	26,110	C
Boise State Univ	ID	9,438	LC
Boston College	MA	41,608	MC
Boston Univ	MA	42,046	HC+
Bowdoin College	ME	41,660	MC
Bowie State Univ	MD	10,880	C+
Bowling Green State Univ	OH	14,994	C
Bradley Univ	IL	25,280	VC
Brandeis Univ	MA	41,551	MC
Brescia Univ	KY	14,240	C
Brewton-Parker College	GA	14,220	LC
Briar Cliff Univ	IA	23,550	LC
Bridgewater College	VA	27,790	C
Bridgewater State College	MA	12,120	C
Brigham Young Univ	UT	9,500	C
Brigham Young Univ/Hawaii	HI	7,740	HC+
Brown Univ	RI	42,015	MC
Bryan College	TN	19,270	C
Bryn Mawr College	PA	42,780	HC+
Bucknell Univ	PA	39,660	MC
Buena Vista Univ	IA	27,742	C
Butler Univ	IN	31,944	VC+
Cabrini College	PA	33,340	C
Caldwell College	NJ	26,450	LC
Calif Baptist Univ	CA	23,780	C
Calif Inst of Technology	CA	36,123	MC
Calif Lutheran Univ	CA	27,800	LC
Calif Polytechnic State Univ	CA	12,390	VC
Calif State Polytechnic Univ, Pomona	CA	18,053	C+
Cal State East Bay	CA	10,856	LC
Cal State, Bakersfield	CA	6,125	LC
Cal State, Chico	CA	11,395	C
Cal State, Dominguez Hills	CA	10,220	LC
Cal State, Fresno	CA	10,037	LC
Cal State, Fullerton	CA	10,990	C
Cal State, Long Beach	CA	9,512	C
Cal State, Los Angeles	CA	5,900	C
Cal State, Monterey Bay	CA	10,099	C
Cal State, Northridge	CA	9,036	LC
Cal State, Sacramento	CA	11,122	C+
Cal State, San Bernardino	CA	12,563	LC
Cal State, San Marcos	CA	1,800	LC
Cal State, Stanislaus	CA	11,283	C
Calif Univ of Pennsylvania	PA	14,217	C
Calvin College	MI	25,735	NC
Cameron Univ	OK	6,314	NC
Campbell Univ	NC	21,137	VC
Campbellsville Univ	KY	21,328	C
Canisius College	NY	32,257	VC
Capital Univ	OH	30,444	C
Cardinal Stritch Univ	WI	21,910	C
Caribbean Univ	PR	3,000	
Carleton College	MN	40,467	MC
Carlow Univ	PA	24,313	C
Carnegie Mellon Univ	PA	32,700	MC
Carroll College	MT	23,324	C+
Carroll College	WI	24,860	C
Carthage College	WI	26,000	C
Case Western Reserve Univ	OH	37,314	MC
Castleton State College	VT	13,158	C
Catawba College	NC	25,000	C
Catholic Univ of America	DC	35,838	VC
Cedar Crest College	PA	30,615	C
Cedarville Univ	OH	21,904	VC
Centenary College	NJ	28,870	LC
Centenary College of Louisiana	LA	24,760	VC
Central College	IA	26,774	VC
Central Conn State Univ	CT	13,620	C
Central Methodist Univ	MO	18,000	C
Central Mich Univ	MI	12,244	C
Central Missouri State Univ	MO	10,000	C
Central State Univ	OH	9,010	C+
Central Washington Univ	WA	11,730	C
Centre College	KY	30,810	VC
Chadron State College	NE	6,350	NC
Chapman Univ	CA	37,550	VC
Charleston Southern Univ	SC	17,800	C
Chatham Univ	PA	27,290	C+
Chestnut Hill College	PA	26,600	LC
Cheyney Univ of Pennsylvania	PA	11,497	LC
Chicago State Univ	IL	10,915	C+
Christian Brothers Univ	TN	24,650	VC
Christopher Newport Univ	VA	13,326	VC
Citadel, The	SC		C+
CUNY/Baruch College	NY	4,320	VC+
CUNY/Brooklyn College	NY	4,377	C+
CUNY/City College	NY		C
CUNY/College of Staten Island	NY	4,328	NC
CUNY/Herbert H. Lehman College	NY	4,000	LC
CUNY/Hunter College	NY	8,000	C
CUNY/Medgar Evers College	NY	4,250	NC
CUNY/Queens College	NY	4,356	C
CUNY/York College	NY	4,242	NC
Claflin Univ	SC	16,798	C
Claremont McKenna College	CA	42,920	MC
Clarion Univ of Pennsylvania	PA	11,844	C
Clark Atlanta Univ	GA	20,960	LC
Clark Univ	MA	35,165	VC+
Clarke College	IA	25,390	C
Clarkson Univ	NY	34,930	VC
Clearwater Christian College	FL	13,160	LC
Clemson Univ	SC	13,366	HC
Cleveland State Univ	OH	10,798	NC
Coastal Carolina Univ	SC	13,140	C
Coe College	IA	27,440	VC
Coker College	SC	21,600	C
Colby College	ME	41,770	MC
Colgate Univ	NY	41,170	MC
College Misericordia	PA	27,950	C
College of Charleston	SC	13,616	VC
College of Mount St. Vincent	NY	28,000	C
College of Mount St. Joseph	OH	24,860	C
College of New Jersey	NJ	18,315	MC
College of New Rochelle	NY	28,396	C+
College of Notre Dame of Maryland	MD	27,700	C
College of Our Lady of the Elms	MA	21,000	C
College of St. Benedict	MN	30,091	VC
College of St. Catherine	MN	27,505	VC
College of St. Elizabeth	NJ	28,495	C
College of St. Mary	NE	23,938	C
College of St. Rose	NY	25,684	C
College of St. Scholastica	MN	28,456	C+
College of the Holy Cross	MA	40,664	MC
College of the Ozarks	MO	4,130	VC+
College of the Southwest	NM	12,420	C
College of William and Mary	VA	14,147	MC
College of Wooster	OH	31,310	VC+
Colo College	CO	37,668	HC
Colo School of Mines	CO	14,893	HC
Colo State Univ-Fort Collins	CO	10,878	C+
Colo State Univ-Pueblo	CO	7,821	LC
Columbia College	SC	24,982	C
Columbia Union College	MD	23,536	LC
Columbia Univ/Barnard College	NY	38,000	MC
Columbia Univ/Columbia College	NY	42,584	MC
Columbia Univ/School of General Studies	NY	41,516	C
Columbus State Univ	GA	8,664	C
Concord College	WV	9,708	C
Concordia College: Moorhead	MN	22,475	VC
Concordia College-New York	NY	27,740	C
Concordia Univ Nebr	NE	20,500	C+
Concordia Univ Wisc	WI	22,660	VC
Concordia Univ, Ann Arbor	MI	25,153	C+
Concordia Univ, River Forest	IL	26,300	C
Conn College	CT	41,975	MC
Converse College	SC	24,800	VC
Coppin State College	MD	10,200	LC
Cornell College	IA	30,110	VC+
Cornell Univ	NY	41,717	MC
Covenant College	GA	26,460	VC+
Creighton Univ	NE	29,918	VC+
Culver-Stockton College	MO	20,625	C
Cumberland Univ	TN	18,894	C
Daemen College	NY	24,580	C
Dakota State Univ	SD	7,466	C
Dakota Wesleyan Univ	SD	17,832	C
Dallas Baptist Univ	TX	17,040	VC
Dana College	NE	22,390	C
Dartmouth College	NH	39,465	MC
Davidson College	NC	36,825	MC
Davis and Elkins College	WV	22,416	C
De Sales Univ	PA	28,580	VC
Defiance College	OH	24,790	C
Delaware State Univ	DE	8,130	LC
Delta State Univ	MS	7,709	C
Denison Univ	OH	37,040	HC
DePaul Univ	IL	29,835	VC
DePauw Univ	IN	32,100	HC
Dickinson College	PA	40,170	HC+
Dickinson State Univ	ND	7,847	NC
Dillard Univ	LA	17,500	VC
Doane College	NE	22,458	C
Dominican College	NY	26,630	LC
Dominican Univ	IL	26,370	C
Dordt College	IA	20,325	VC
Dowling College	NY	22,110	LC
Drake Univ	IA	27,632	VC+
Drew Univ/College of Liberal Arts	NJ	39,698	VC
Drexel Univ	PA	27,700	VC
Drury Univ	MO	20,117	VC
Duke Univ	NC	41,239	MC
Duquesne Univ	PA	29,534	VC
D'Youville College	NY	23,660	C
Earlham College	IN	33,604	NC
East Carolina Univ	NC	10,000	C
East Central Univ	OK	6,207	C
East Stroudsburg Univ of Pennsylvania	PA	10,336	C
East Tenn State Univ	TN	8,497	C
East Texas Baptist Univ	TX	16,713	C
Eastern Conn State Univ	CT	13,554	C
Eastern Illinois Univ	IL	12,569	C
Eastern Kentucky Univ	KY	7,725	C
Eastern Mennonite Univ	VA	25,450	VC
Eastern Mich Univ	MI	12,897	C
Eastern Nazarene College	MA	19,500	LC
Eastern New Mexico Univ	NM	7,264	C
Eastern Oregon Univ	OR	10,400	NC
Eastern Univ	PA	24,075	C
Eastern Washington Univ	WA	10,608	C
Eckerd College	FL	35,492	VC
Edgewood College	WI	22,862	C
Edinboro Univ of Pennsylvania	PA	11,809	LC
Edward Waters College	FL	14,374	LC
Elizabeth City State Univ	NC	5,700	LC
Elizabethtown College	PA	32,100	VC
Elmhurst College	IL	24,685	C
Elmira College	NY	37,200	VC
Elon Univ	NC	25,371	HC
Emmanuel College	MA	32,000	C+
Emory & Henry College	VA	26,570	C
Emory Univ	GA	40,546	MC
Emporia State Univ	KS	8,093	C
Erskine College	SC	25,468	VC
Eureka College	IL	19,280	C
Evangel Univ	MO	17,380	C
Excelsior College	NY	995	SP
Fairfield Univ	CT	39,835	HC
Fairleigh Dickinson Univ/ College at Florham	NJ	30,130	C
Fairleigh Dickinson Univ/ Metropolitan Campus	NJ	28,590	C
Fairmont State	WV	8,400	LC
Fayetteville State Univ	NC	6,000	LC
Felician College	NJ	24,300	C
Ferrum College	VA	24,290	LC
Fisk Univ	TN	19,830	C
Fitchburg State College	MA	11,276	C
Florida A&M Univ	FL	8,344	C
Florida Atlantic Univ	FL	11,221	C
Florida International Univ	FL	9,215	VC
Florida Memorial College	FL	6,000	LC
Florida Southern College	FL	25,965	C
Florida State Univ	FL	9,028	HC
Fontbonne Univ	MO	23,308	C
Fordham Univ	NY	36,000	HC
Fort Hays State Univ	KS	7,638	C
Fort Lewis College	CO	11,852	C
Fort Valley State Univ	GA	6,975	C
Framingham State College	MA	11,156	C
Francis Marion Univ	SC	11,114	C
Franciscan Univ of Steubenville	OH	20,300	VC
Franklin and Marshall College	PA	40,590	HC
Franklin College	IN		C
Freed-Hardeman Univ	TN	16,370	NC
Fresno Pacific Univ	CA	25,454	C
Friends Univ	KS	16,250	LC
Frostburg State Univ	MD	12,672	C
Furman Univ	SC	33,264	HC+
Gallaudet Univ	DC	16,554	
Gannon Univ	PA	26,100	C
Gardner-Webb Univ	NC	21,500	C
George Fox Univ	OR	28,490	C
George Mason Univ	VA	10,850	VC

ST = STATE   **$IS** = IN-STATE COSTS   **SR** = SELECTOR RATING

School	ST	$IS	SR
George Washington Univ	DC	48,820	MC
Georgetown College	KY	24,950	C+
Georgetown Univ	DC	43,183	MC
Georgia College and State Univ	GA	11,020	C
Georgia Inst of Technology	GA	11,450	HC+
Georgia Southern Univ	GA	9,762	C
Georgia Southwestern State Univ	GA	6,035	C
Georgia State Univ	GA	11,444	VC
Georgian Court College	NJ	20,000	LC
Gettysburg College	PA	39,864	HC
Gonzaga Univ	WA	30,218	HC
Gordon College	MA	29,194	C+
Goshen College	IN	22,850	VC
Goucher College	MD	36,225	VC
Grace College	IN	22,170	C
Graceland Univ	IA	19,700	C
Grambling State Univ	LA	6,538	NC
Grand Canyon Univ	AZ	32,000	LC
Grand Valley State Univ	MI	12,000	VC
Greensboro College	NC	23,000	C
Greenville College	IL	23,146	C
Grinnell College	IA	34,814	HC+
Grove City College	PA	15,784	HC+
Guilford College	NC	28,160	C+
Gustavus Adolphus College	MN	30,920	HC
Gwynedd-Mercy College	PA	26,080	C
Hamilton College	NY	41,660	MC
Hamline Univ	MN	27,070	VC
Hampden-Sydney College	VA	31,148	VC
Hampshire College	MA	37,120	HC
Hampton Univ	VA	19,468	C+
Hannibal-LaGrange College	MO	16,390	C
Hanover College	IN	28,150	HC
Harding Univ	AR	16,512	VC
Hardin-Simmons Univ	TX	18,641	C
Hartwick College	NY	36,065	C+
Harvard Univ/Harvard College	MA	45,860	MC
Harvey Mudd College	CA	42,352	MC
Hastings College	NE	22,218	VC
Haverford College	PA	41,600	MC
Heidelberg College	OH	23,242	C
Henderson State Univ	AR	7,600	C
Hendrix College	AR	27,646	HC+
Heritage Univ	WA	6,800	NC
High Point Univ	NC	25,720	C
Hillsdale College	MI	24,160	HC
Hiram College	OH	28,700	VC
Hobart and William Smith Colleges	NY	41,123	VC
Hofstra Univ	NY	32,630	VC
Hollins Univ	VA	31,105	C
Holy Family Univ	PA	25,740	C
Hood College	MD	30,085	VC
Hope College	MI	28,208	VC+
Houghton College	NY	25,980	VC
Houston Baptist Univ	TX	18,660	C
Howard Payne Univ	TX	17,115	C
Howard Univ	DC	18,481	C+
Humboldt State Univ	CA	11,176	C
Huntingdon College	AL	23,090	VC
Huntington Univ	IN	24,830	C
Huston-Tillotson Univ	TX	14,232	LC
Idaho State Univ	ID	9,030	C
Illinois College	IL	21,900	C+
Illinois State Univ	IL	12,839	C+
Illinois Wesleyan Univ	IL	34,050	HC+
Immaculata Univ	PA	25,350	C
Indiana State Univ	IN	11,604	C
Indiana Univ Bloomington	IN	13,356	VC
Indiana Univ East	IN	4,806	LC
Indiana Univ Kokomo	IN	4,835	LC
Indiana Univ Northwest	IN	4,902	LC
Indiana Univ of Pennsylvania	PA	11,209	C
Indiana Univ South Bend	IN	4,989	LC
Indiana Univ Southeast	IN	4,880	LC
Indiana Univ-Purdue Univ Fort Wayne	IN	5,067	LC
Indiana Univ-Purdue Univ Indianapolis	IN	10,959	C
Indiana Wesleyan Univ	IN	22,074	C+
Inter American Univ of PR/Bayamon Univ College	PR	3,522	
Inter American Univ of PR/Fajardo Campus	PR	4,000	
Inter American Univ of PR/Metropolitan Campus	PR	4,320	
Inter American Univ of PR/Ponce Regional College	PR	3,700	
Inter American Univ of PR/San German	PR	6,720	
Iona College	NY	30,878	VC
Iowa State Univ	IA	11,831	VC
Iowa Wesleyan College	IA	22,140	C
Ithaca College	NY	35,144	VC
Jackson State Univ	MS	8,500	C
Jacksonville State Univ	AL	7,618	LC
Jacksonville Univ	FL	24,040	C
James Madison Univ	VA	12,010	VC
Jamestown College	ND	14,130	NC
Jarvis Christian College	TX	11,316	NC
John Brown Univ	AR	20,910	VC
John Carroll Univ	OH	27,658	C+
Johns Hopkins Univ	MD	42,044	MC
Johnson C. Smith Univ	NC	20,000	C
Johnson State College	VT	11,830	LC
Judson College	AL	16,522	C
Judson College	IL	25,130	C
Juniata College	PA	33,130	VC
Kalamazoo College	MI	32,442	VC+
Kansas State Univ	KS	10,516	VC
Kansas Wesleyan Univ	KS	21,400	VC
Kean Univ	NJ	15,880	C
Keene State College	NH	13,836	C
Kennesaw State Univ	GA	12,152	C
Kent State Univ	OH	14,594	C
Kentucky Christian College	KY	12,680	C
Kentucky State Univ	KY	10,089	LC
Kenyon College	OH	39,500	MC
King College	TN	23,400	C
King's College	PA	29,810	C
Knox College	IL	32,385	VC+
Kutztown Univ of Pennsylvania	PA	10,820	C
La Roche College	PA	24,724	LC
La Salle Univ	PA	34,950	C
La Sierra Univ	CA	24,327	C+
Lafayette College	PA	39,267	MC
LaGrange College	GA	22,874	C
Lake Erie College	OH	27,725	C
Lake Forest College	IL	33,860	VC
Lake Superior State Univ	MI	12,842	LC
Lakeland College	WI	22,990	C
Lamar Univ	TX	6,820	LC
Lambuth Univ	TN	21,700	C+
Lander Univ	SC	10,600	C
Lane College	TN	11,220	C
Langston Univ	OK	2,308	LC
Lawrence Tech Univ	MI	25,475	VC
Lawrence Univ	WI	33,958	HC+
Le Moyne College	NY	29,570	VC
Lebanon Valley College	PA	31,700	VC
Lee Univ	TN	14,780	NC
Lees-McRae College	NC	23,000	C
Lehigh Univ	PA	42,690	HC+
LeMoyne-Owen College	TN	13,150	LC
Lenoir-Rhyne College	NC	25,580	C
LeTourneau Univ	TX	21,200	C
Lewis and Clark College	OR	35,358	VC+
Lewis Univ	IL	23,050	C+
Lewis-Clark State College	ID	6,990	C
Liberty Univ	VA	19,101	C
Limestone College	SC	19,840	C
Lincoln Memorial Univ	TN	18,144	C
Lincoln Univ	MO	8,000	NC
Lincoln Univ	PA	13,658	C+
Lindenwood Univ	MO	18,600	VC
Linfield College	OR	29,632	VC
Lipscomb Univ	TN	20,967	VC
Livingstone College	NC	17,815	LC
Lock Haven Univ of Pennsylvania	PA	12,098	LC
LIU/Brooklyn Campus	NY	25,000	C
LIU/C.W. Post Campus	NY	28,282	C
Longwood Univ	VA	12,426	C
Loras College	IA	27,193	C
Louisiana College	LA	13,450	C
Louisiana State Univ and A&M College	LA	10,749	VC
Louisiana State Univ in Shreveport	LA	2,900	NC
Louisiana Tech Univ	LA	7,370	C
Loyola College in Maryland	MD	38,898	HC
Loyola Marymount Univ	CA	36,321	VC
Loyola Univ Chicago	IL	32,896	VC
Loyola Univ New Orleans	LA	31,050	VC+
Lubbock Christian Univ	TX	16,960	C
Luther College	IA	28,800	VC+
Lycoming College	PA	30,797	C+
Lynchburg College	VA	30,645	C
Lyndon State College	VT	14,233	LC
Lyon College	AR	19,990	VC
Macalester College	MN	36,500	MC
MacMurray College	IL	20,755	C
Madonna Univ	MI	16,068	VC
Maharishi Univ of Management	IA	29,450	VC
Malone College	OH	23,040	C
Manchester College	IN	23,470	C
Manhattan College	NY	29,000	VC
Manhattanville College	NY	32,500	C+
Mansfield Univ	PA	11,300	C
Marian College	IN	26,160	C
Marian College of Fond du Lac	WI	21,775	LC
Marietta College	OH	29,327	C
Marist College	NY	30,566	VC
Marlboro College	VT	35,980	VC+
Marquette Univ	WI	31,066	HC
Mars Hill College	NC	19,000	LC
Marshall Univ	WV	9,116	C
Martin Univ	IN	10,300	SP
Mary Baldwin College	VA	26,465	C
Marygrove College	MI	19,310	C
Marymount Univ	VA	25,934	C
Maryville Univ of St. Louis	MO	23,000	VC
Marywood Univ	PA	30,680	C
Mass College of Liberal Arts	MA	8,725	LC
Mass Inst of Technology	MA	41,800	MC
Master's College and Seminary	CA	25,850	VC
Mayville State Univ	ND	8,667	NC
McDaniel College	MD	31,610	VC
McKendree College	IL	24,800	VC
McMurry Univ	TX	18,100	LC
McNeese State Univ	LA	5,270	LC
McPherson College	KS	21,010	C
Mercer Univ	GA	27,525	VC+
Mercy College	NY	20,000	NC
Mercyhurst College	PA	28,633	VC
Meredith College	NC	25,600	C
Merrimack College	MA	34,380	C
Mesa State College	CO	8,051	C
Messiah College	PA	28,910	VC+
Methodist College	NC	21,000	C
Metropolitan State College of Denver	CO	2,338	LC
Miami Univ	OH	29,097	HC
Mich State Univ	MI	13,689	VC
Mich Tech Univ	MI	14,569	VC
MidAmerica Nazarene Univ	KS	20,584	LC
Middle Tenn State Univ	TN	8,540	C
Middlebury College	VT	42,120	MC
Midland Lutheran College	NE	18,600	C
Midway College	KY	20,150	C
Midwestern State Univ	TX	9,381	LC
Miles College	AL	9,922	NC
Millersville Univ of Pennsylvania	PA	12,113	C
Milligan College	TN	21,990	C
Millikin Univ	IL	25,590	C
Mills College	CA	39,870	C
Millsaps College	MS	28,256	VC+
Minn State Univ, Mankato	MN	10,276	LC
Minn State Univ, Moorhead	MN	7,000	LC
Minot State Univ	ND	6,700	LC
Miss College	MS	14,574	VC
Miss State Univ	MS	9,577	C
Miss Univ for Women	MS	6,000	LC
Miss Valley State Univ	MS	7,970	C
Missouri Baptist Univ	MO	19,640	C
Missouri Southern State Univ	MO	8,396	NC
Missouri State Univ	MO	10,748	C+
Missouri Valley College	MO	18,500	C
Missouri Western State Univ	MO	9,534	NC
Molloy College	NY	16,510	C
Monmouth College	IL	23,700	C
Monmouth Univ	NJ	28,956	C
Montana State Univ-Billings	MT	8,906	C
Montana State Univ-Bozeman	MT	1,137	C
Montana Tech of The Univ of Montana	MT	10,434	C
Montclair State Univ	NJ	16,327	C
Montreat College	NC	21,440	C
Moravian College	PA	28,950	VC
Morehead State Univ	KY	9,150	C
Morehouse College	GA	25,082	C
Morgan State Univ	MD	12,080	C
Morningside College	IA	23,704	C
Morris College	SC	11,999	LC
Mount Holyoke College	MA	42,148	HC+
Mount Marty College	SD	20,590	C
Mount Mary College	WI	22,845	C
Mount Mercy College	IA	23,670	C
Mount Olive College	NC	16,000	LC
Mount St. Mary College	NY	25,250	C
Mount St. Mary's College	CA	32,086	VC
Mount St. Mary's Univ	MD	30,930	C
Mount Union College	OH	25,840	C
Mount Vernon Nazarene Univ	OH	20,810	C
Muhlenberg College	PA	36,030	HC+
Murray State Univ	KY	8,900	VC
Muskingum College	OH	22,970	C
National Univ	CA	8,412	SP
National-Louis Univ	IL	16,915	LC
Nazareth College of Rochester	NY	28,175	VC
Nebr Wesleyan Univ	NE	23,415	C+
New College of Florida	FL	10,009	HC+
New England College	NH	31,466	C
New Jersey City Univ	NJ	13,695	LC
New Jersey Inst of Technology	NJ	16,396	VC
New Mexico Highlands Univ	NM	6,272	NC
New Mexico Inst of Mining and Technology	NM	8,510	VC
New Mexico State Univ	NM	9,250	C
New York Inst of Technology	NY	28,126	VC
New York Univ	NY	43,170	MC
Newberry College	SC	23,000	LC
Newman Univ	KS	21,106	C
Niagara Univ	NY	28,250	C
Nicholls State Univ	LA	6,500	NC
Nichols College	MA	28,000	LC
Norfolk State Univ	VA	10,531	LC
N Car Agricultural and Technical State Univ	NC	8,000	LC
N Car Central Univ	NC	9,000	LC
N Car State Univ	NC	11,824	HC
N Car Wesleyan College	NC	22,670	C
North Central College	IL	28,926	VC
N Dak State Univ	ND	8,500	C
North Georgia College and State Univ	GA	7,000	C
North Park Univ	IL	24,050	C
Northeastern Illinois Univ	IL	3,000	NC
Northeastern State Univ	OK	5,896	LC
Northeastern Univ	MA	35,742	HC
Northern Arizona Univ	AZ	10,353	C
Northern Illinois Univ	IL	13,178	C
Northern Kentucky Univ	KY	6,670	NC
Northern Mich Univ	MI	12,340	C
Northern State Univ	SD	8,257	C
Northland College	WI	26,680	C
Northwest Missouri State Univ	MO	10,000	C
Northwest Nazarene Univ	ID	22,590	VC
Northwestern College	MN	25,220	NC
Northwestern College of Iowa	IA	22,174	C+
Northwestern Okla State Univ	OK	6,250	NC
Northwestern State Univ of Louisiana	LA	7,144	C
Northwestern Univ	IL	37,595	MC
Norwich Univ	VT	28,212	C
Notre Dame College	OH	20,425	C
Notre Dame de Namur Univ	CA	32,790	LC
Nyack College	NY	18,540	C
Oakland City Univ	IN	19,620	NC
Oakland Univ	MI	11,936	C
Oakwood College	AL	14,904	C
Oberlin College	OH	40,904	MC
Occidental College	CA	40,185	MC
Oglethorpe Univ	GA	30,300	VC
Ohio Dominican Univ	OH	25,954	C
Ohio Northern Univ	OH	27,765	VC
Ohio State Univ	OH	15,357	HC
Ohio Univ	OH	15,921	C
Ohio Wesleyan Univ	OH	35,830	VC+
Okla Baptist Univ	OK	17,986	VC
Okla Christian Univ	OK	18,992	NC
Okla City Univ	OK	23,965	VC
Okla Panhandle State Univ	OK	7,635	NC
Okla State Univ	OK	10,213	VC
Okla Wesleyan Univ	OK	18,950	NC
Old Dominion Univ	VA	11,907	C
Olivet College	MI	19,984	C+
Olivet Nazarene Univ	IL	22,590	C
Oral Roberts Univ	OK	22,650	C
Oregon State Univ	OR	11,055	C
Ottawa Univ	KS	12,000	LC
Otterbein College	OH	28,986	C
Ouachita Baptist Univ	AR	21,900	VC
Our Lady of the Lake Univ of San Antonio	TX	22,430	LC
Pace Univ	NY	30,000	VC
Pacific Lutheran Univ	WA	28,805	VC
Pacific Union College	CA	24,555	VC+
Pacific Univ	OR	24,250	C
Paine College	GA	14,418	LC
Palm Beach Atlantic Univ	FL	23,597	VC
Park Univ	MO	11,592	C
Paul Quinn College	TX	8,300	LC
Penn State Erie/The Behrend College	PA	16,256	C
Penn State Univ/Univ Park Campus	PA	18,038	HC
Pepperdine Univ	CA	39,960	HC
Peru State College	NE	6,350	NC
Pfeiffer Univ	NC	21,900	C
Philander Smith College	AR	13,230	LC
Piedmont College	GA	20,500	C
Pikeville College	KY	16,500	NC
Pittsburg State Univ	KS	8,112	C
Pitzer College	CA	41,644	HC
Plymouth State Univ	NH	12,298	LC
Point Loma Nazarene Univ	CA	27,610	VC
Polytechnic Univ/Brooklyn	NY	37,150	VC
Pomona College	CA	40,774	MC
Pontifical Catholic Univ of PR/Ponce	PR	7,310	
Portland State Univ	OR	12,453	C
Prairie View A&M Univ	TX	11,110	C
Presbyterian College	SC	30,044	VC
Princeton Univ	NJ	40,213	MC
Principia College	IL	27,765	VC+
Providence College	RI	34,580	HC
Purdue Univ/Calumet	IN	10,891	LC
Purdue Univ/West Lafayette	IN	13,458	VC
Queens Univ of Charlotte	NC	24,528	C
Quincy Univ	IL	24,920	C
Quinnipiac Univ	CT	34,640	VC
Radford Univ	VA	13,145	C
Ramapo College of New Jersey	NJ	16,630	VC
Randolph-Macon College	VA	31,250	C
Randolph-Macon Woman's College	VA	31,160	VC+
Reed College	OR	41,106	MC
Regis Univ	CO	31,890	C
Rensselaer Polytechnic Inst	NY	41,288	HC+
Rhode Island College	RI	11,570	C

School	ST	$IS	SR
Rhodes College	TN	32,860	HC
Rice Univ	TX	32,290	MC
Richard Stockton College of New Jersey	NJ	14,000	VC
Rider Univ	NJ	32,560	C
Ripon College	WI	27,160	C+
Rivier College	NH	26,600	C
Roanoke College	VA	30,748	VC
Robert Morris Univ	PA	22,822	C
Roberts Wesleyan College	NY	26,378	C
Rochester Inst of Technology	NY	32,070	VC+
Rockford College	IL	28,330	VC
Rockhurst Univ	MO	25,440	VC
Rocky Mountain College	MT	20,805	C
Roger Williams Univ	RI	30,500	C
Rollins College	FL	38,366	VC
Roosevelt Univ	IL	22,605	VC
Rose-Hulman Inst of Technology	IN	34,557	HC+
Rosemont College	PA	29,350	C
Rowan Univ	NJ	16,000	VC
Russell Sage College	NY	27,000	C
Rust College	MS		C+
Rutgers, The State Univ of New Jersey/Camden Campus	NJ	15,000	VC
Rutgers, The State Univ of New Jersey/New Brunswick/Piscataway Campus	NJ	15,810	HC
Rutgers, The State Univ of New Jersey/Newark Campus	NJ	15,640	VC
Sacred Heart Univ	CT	33,404	C
Saginaw Valley State Univ	MI	11,432	C
St. Ambrose Univ	IA	25,495	C
St. Andrews Presbyterian College	NC	23,530	C
St. Anselm College	NH	33,810	C
St. Augustine's College	NC	14,000	LC
St. Bonaventure Univ	NY	28,785	LC
St. Cloud State Univ	MN	10,010	C
St. Edward's Univ	TX	23,560	C
St. Francis College	NY	19,974	LC
St. Francis Univ	PA	25,880	LC
St. John Fisher College	NY	27,860	C
St. John's Univ	MN	29,749	VC
St. John's Univ	NY	34,370	C
St. Joseph College	CT	32,050	C
St. Joseph's College	IN	26,600	C
St. Joseph's College of Maine	ME	29,185	C
St. Joseph's College, New York, Brooklyn Campus	NY	12,206	C
St. Joseph's College, New York, Suffolk Campus	NY	12,000	C
St. Joseph's Univ	PA	37,428	VC
St. Lawrence Univ	NY	40,545	VC
St. Leo Univ	FL	22,140	C+
St. Louis Univ	MO	33,158	VC+
St. Martin's Univ	WA	27,555	C
St. Mary-of-the-Woods College	IN	25,480	C
St. Mary's College	IN	32,538	VC
St. Mary's College of Calif	CA	37,290	C
St. Mary's College of Maryland	MD	18,876	VC+
St. Mary's Univ of Minn	MN	23,857	VC
St. Mary's Univ of San Antonio	TX	22,444	C
St. Michael's College	VT	33,330	VC
St. Norbert College	WI	28,577	C+
St. Olaf College	MN	32,800	HC
St. Paul's College	VA	16,030	NC
St. Peter's College	NJ	30,160	LC
St. Vincent College	PA	26,160	VC+
St. Xavier Univ	IL	23,160	C
Salem College	NC	26,226	VC+
Salem State College	MA	13,161	LC
Salisbury Univ	MD	13,128	VC
Salve Regina Univ	RI	33,450	C
Sam Houston State Univ	TX	8,000	C
Samford Univ	AL	20,258	VC
San Diego Christian College	CA	24,172	C
San Diego State Univ	CA	12,971	C
San Francisco State Univ	CA	13,000	C
San Jose State Univ	CA	11,707	C
Santa Clara Univ	CA	38,931	VC
Sarah Lawrence College	NY	42,000	HC
Savannah State Univ	GA	7,772	LC
Schreiner Univ	TX	20,600	C
Scripps College	CA	41,000	MC
Seattle Pacific Univ	WA	29,355	C
Seattle Univ	WA	30,063	VC
Seton Hall Univ	NJ	33,622	VC
Seton Hill Univ	PA	28,810	C
Shaw Univ	NC	15,488	LC
Shawnee State Univ	OH	12,237	NC
Shenandoah Univ	VA	27,600	C
Shepherd Univ	WV	10,066	C
Shippensburg Univ of Pennsylvania	PA	11,621	C
Shorter College	GA	19,700	C
Siena College	NY	28,260	VC+
Siena Heights Univ	MI	17,000	LC
Silver Lake College of the Holy Family	WI	18,500	LC
Simmons College	MA	35,640	VC
Simon's Rock College of Bard	MA	41,988	VC+
Simpson College	IA	26,833	VC
Simpson Univ	CA	22,900	C
Skidmore College	NY	41,779	HC
Slippery Rock Univ of Pennsylvania	PA	10,360	LC
Smith College	MA	41,474	MC
Sonoma State Univ	CA	14,732	C
S Car State Univ	SC	6,700	LC
S Dak School of Mines and Technology	SD	7,624	C+
S Dak State Univ	SD	9,815	C
Southeast Missouri State Univ	MO	10,596	C
Southeastern Louisiana Univ	LA	8,521	LC
Southeastern Okla State Univ	OK	6,147	C
Southeastern Univ	FL	17,180	LC
Southern Adventist Univ	TN	18,500	C
Southern Arkansas Univ	AR	6,956	C
Southern Conn State Univ	CT	10,310	C
Southern Illinois Univ Carbondale	IL	12,391	C
Southern Illinois Univ Edwardsville	IL	11,022	C
Southern Methodist Univ	TX	36,088	VC+
Southern Nazarene Univ	OK	14,634	NC
Southern Oregon Univ	OR	12,186	C
Southern Polytechnic State Univ	GA	7,640	VC
Southern Univ and A&M College	LA	8,238	LC
Southern Univ at New Orleans	LA	1,000	NC
Southern Utah Univ	UT		C
Southern Wesleyan Univ	SC	21,675	C
Southwest Baptist Univ	MO	18,300	C
Southwest Minn State Univ	MN	10,975	C
Southwestern Adventist Univ	TX	18,290	LC
Southwestern College	KS	21,476	C
Southwestern Okla State Univ	OK	4,801	C
Southwestern Univ	TX	26,767	HC
Spelman College	GA	24,650	VC
Spring Arbor Univ	MI	22,476	C
Spring Hill College	AL	28,678	C
Springfield College	MA	25,000	C
Stanford Univ	CA	41,557	MC
SUNY at Oswego	NY	13,662	VC
SUNY at Potsdam	NY	12,959	C
SUNY/College at Brockport	NY	12,747	VC
SUNY/College at Buffalo	NY	11,903	C+
SUNY/College at Cortland	NY	12,095	C
SUNY/College at Fredonia	NY	12,771	VC
SUNY/College at Geneseo	NY	12,910	HC+
SUNY/College at Old Westbury	NY	13,154	C
SUNY/College at Oneonta	NY	12,905	VC
SUNY/College at Plattsburgh	NY	12,362	C
SUNY/College at Purchase	NY	11,989	VC+
SUNY/Empire State College	NY	4,575	SP
SUNY/Univ at Albany	NY	13,860	VC
SUNY/Univ at Binghamton	NY	13,988	HC
SUNY/Univ at Buffalo	NY	13,694	VC
SUNY/Univ at New Paltz	NY	12,480	VC
SUNY/Univ at Stony Brook	NY	13,625	HC
Stephen F. Austin State Univ	TX	7,930	C
Sterling College	KS	19,992	C
Stetson Univ	FL	32,725	VC
Stevens Inst of Technology	NJ	40,935	HC
Stillman College	AL	11,475	LC
Stonehill College	MA	36,104	HC
Suffolk Univ	MA	33,160	C
Sul Ross State Univ	TX	6,600	LC
Susquehanna Univ	PA	33,465	VC
Swarthmore College	PA	41,280	MC
Sweet Briar College	VA	31,460	VC
Syracuse Univ	NY	38,655	HC
Tabor College	KS	21,614	NC
Talladega College	AL	11,240	LC
Tarleton State Univ	TX	8,952	C
Taylor Univ	IN	26,376	VC+
Temple Univ	PA	17,438	C
Tenn State Univ	TN	9,048	LC
Tenn Tech Univ	TN	10,044	C
Tenn Wesleyan College	TN	18,650	C
Texas A&M Univ	TX	13,351	HC
Texas A&M Univ at Commerce	TX	9,020	C
Texas A&M Univ at Corpus Christi	TX	10,280	LC
Texas A&M Univ at Kingsville	TX	6,800	LC
Texas Christian Univ	TX	23,410	VC+
Texas Lutheran Univ	TX	23,530	C
Texas Southern Univ	TX	9,828	C
Texas State Univ - San Marcos	TX	10,862	C
Texas Tech Univ	TX	13,026	VC
Texas Wesleyan Univ	TX	18,700	C
Texas Woman's Univ	TX	7,804	LC
Thiel College	PA	24,580	C
Thomas Edison State College	NJ	3,780	SP
Thomas More College	KY	24,470	C
Tougaloo College	MS	15,975	NC
Touro College	NY	17,000	NC
Towson Univ	MD	13,924	VC
Transylvania Univ	KY	26,240	VC+
Trevecca Nazarene Univ	TN	19,594	C
Trinity Christian College	IL	23,645	C
Trinity College	CT	38,040	HC+
Trinity College	DC	24,150	LC
Trinity International Univ	IL	25,686	C
Trinity Univ	TX	30,157	HC+
Tri-State Univ-Main Campus	IN	26,200	C
Troy Univ	AL	8,916	C
Troy Univ Dothan Campus	AL	4,678	C
Troy Univ Montgomery Campus	AL	4,104	NC
Truman State Univ	MO	11,242	HC
Tufts Univ	MA	42,018	MC
Tulane Univ	LA	41,098	MC
Turabo Univ	PR	4,110	
Tuskegee Univ	AL	18,860	LC
Union College	KY	18,920	C
Union College	NE	18,710	C
Union College	NY	41,595	HC
Union Univ	TN	20,750	VC
United States Air Force Academy	CO		HC+
United States Military Academy	NY		MC
United States Naval Academy	MD		MC
Univ of Akron	OH	15,166	NC
Univ of Alabama	AL	9,888	C
Univ of Alabama at Birmingham	AL	13,716	C
Univ of Alabama in Huntsville	AL	9,516	VC
Univ of Alaska Anchorage	AK	11,275	NC
Univ of Alaska Fairbanks	AK	10,101	C
Univ of Alaska Southeast	AK	8,050	LC
Univ of Arizona	AZ	11,958	VC
Univ of Arkansas	AR	11,859	VC
Univ of Arkansas at Little Rock	AR	7,230	NC
Univ of Arkansas at Monticello	AR	7,325	NC
Univ of Arkansas at Pine Bluff	AR	8,300	C
Univ of at Calif Davis	CA	15,010	VC
Univ of Bridgeport	CT	29,595	LC
Univ of Calif at Berkeley	CA	18,141	HC+
Univ of Calif at Irvine	CA	16,475	HC
Univ of Calif at Los Angeles	CA	17,681	MC
Univ of Calif at Riverside	CA	16,625	C
Univ of Calif at San Diego	CA	16,102	HC
Univ of Calif at Santa Barbara	CA	11,800	VC
Univ of Calif at Santa Cruz	CA	19,174	VC
Univ of Central Arkansas	AR	9,984	C
Univ of Central Florida	FL	10,739	VC
Univ of Central Okla	OK	8,094	C
Univ of Chicago	IL	42,369	MC
Univ of Cincinnati	OH	17,682	C
Univ of Colo at Boulder	CO	13,352	C+
Univ of Colo at Colo Springs	CO	11,517	VC
Univ of Colo at Denver and Health Sciences Center	CO	5,021	C
Univ of Conn	CT	16,628	HC
Univ of Dallas	TX	27,432	VC+
Univ of Dayton	OH	28,826	VC
Univ of Delaware	DE	14,142	HC
Univ of Denver	CO	36,376	VC+
Univ of Detroit Mercy	MI	27,000	C
Univ of Evansville	IN	28,320	VC
Univ of Findlay	OH	29,238	C
Univ of Florida	FL	9,354	HC
Univ of Georgia	GA	11,004	HC
Univ of Great Falls	MT	17,000	C
Univ of Hartford	CT	34,044	C
Univ of Hawaii at Hilo	HI	6,500	C
Univ of Hawaii at Manoa	HI	10,413	VC
Univ of Houston	TX	7,000	VC
Univ of Idaho	ID	9,310	NC
Univ of Illinois at Chicago	IL	16,256	VC
Univ of Illinois at Urbana-Champaign	IL	15,800	HC+
Univ of Indianapolis	IN	25,090	C
Univ of Iowa	IA	12,172	VC
Univ of Kansas	KS	10,915	VC
Univ of Kentucky	KY	7,800	C
Univ of La Verne	CA	33,470	C
Univ of Louisiana at Lafayette	LA	5,830	C
Univ of Louisiana at Monroe	LA	7,103	C
Univ of Louisville	KY	10,400	C
Univ of Maine	ME	13,642	C
Univ of Maine at Farmington	ME	11,515	C
Univ of Mary	ND	15,374	C
Univ of Mary Hardin-Baylor	TX	19,428	C
Univ of Mary Washington	VA	11,636	HC
Univ of Maryland/Baltimore County	MD	16,642	VC+
Univ of Maryland/College Park	MD	16,036	HC
Univ of Maryland/Eastern Shore	MD	11,210	C
Univ of Mass Amherst	MA	15,973	C+
Univ of Mass Boston	MA	8,024	C
Univ of Mass Dartmouth	MA	15,985	C
Univ of Mass Lowell	MA	14,327	VC
Univ of Memphis	TN	11,153	C
Univ of Miami	FL	38,397	MC
Univ of Mich/Ann Arbor	MI	16,587	HC+
Univ of Mich/Dearborn	MI	7,000	VC
Univ of Mich/Flint	MI	6,398	C
Univ of Minn/Duluth	MN	13,974	C
Univ of Minn/Morris	MN	15,472	VC
Univ of Minn/Twin Cities	MN	13,165	HC
Univ of Missouri/Columbia	MO	13,500	VC
Univ of Missouri/Kansas City	MO	15,000	VC
Univ of Missouri/Rolla	MO	13,332	HC
Univ of Missouri/St. Louis	MO	14,046	VC
Univ of Mobile	AL	16,880	C
Univ of Montana	MT	10,602	C
Univ of Montevallo	AL	9,630	C
Univ of Nebr at Kearney	NE	9,000	NC
Univ of Nebr at Lincoln	NE	11,401	VC
Univ of Nebr at Omaha	NE	11,235	C
Univ of Nevada/Las Vegas	NV	11,566	C
Univ of Nevada/Reno	NV	12,155	NC
Univ of New England	ME	31,005	C
Univ of New Hampshire	NH	16,810	VC
Univ of New Haven	CT	31,794	C
Univ of New Mexico	NM	11,253	C
Univ of New Orleans	LA	7,370	C
Univ of North Alabama	AL	8,992	C
Univ of N Car at Asheville	NC	9,237	VC
Univ of N Car at Chapel Hill	NC	11,129	MC
Univ of N Car at Charlotte	NC	9,101	C
Univ of N Car at Greensboro	NC	8,993	C
Univ of N Car at Pembroke	NC	7,940	LC
Univ of N Car at Wilmington	NC	10,107	VC
Univ of N Dak	ND	10,114	VC
Univ of North Florida	FL	9,908	VC
Univ of North Texas	TX	7,800	C
Univ of Northern Colo	CO	10,249	C
Univ of Northern Iowa	IA	11,133	C
Univ of Notre Dame	IN	39,552	MC
Univ of Okla	OK	10,769	VC+
Univ of Oregon	OR	13,108	VC
Univ of Pennsylvania	PA	41,766	MC
Univ of Pittsburgh at Bradford	PA	17,008	C
Univ of Pittsburgh at Johnstown	PA	16,740	LC
Univ of Pittsburgh at Pittsburgh	PA	18,866	HC
Univ of Portland	OR	32,300	VC
Univ of PR at Humacao	PR	1,707	
Univ of PR/Cayey Univ College	PR	1,250	
Univ of PR/Mayaguez	PR	1,250	
Univ of Puget Sound	WA	35,600	HC
Univ of Redlands	CA	36,160	VC
Univ of Rhode Island	RI	15,398	C
Univ of Richmond	VA	40,510	MC
Univ of Rio Grande	OH	8,728	NC
Univ of Rochester	NY	41,135	MC
Univ of St. Francis	IL	25,430	C
Univ of St. Mary	KS	18,900	C
Univ of St. Thomas	MN	28,000	VC
Univ of St. Thomas	TX	23,810	VC
Univ of San Diego	CA	40,620	HC
Univ of San Francisco	CA	37,560	VC
Univ of Science and Arts of Okla	OK	7,650	C
Univ of Scranton	PA	31,100	VC
Univ of Sioux Falls	SD	20,800	C
Univ of South Alabama	AL	8,930	LC
Univ of S Car at Columbia	SC	13,397	VC
Univ of S Car Upstate	SC	11,957	C
Univ of S Dak	SD	9,068	C
Univ of South Florida	FL	10,284	VC
Univ of Southern Calif	CA	41,618	MC
Univ of Southern Indiana	IN	12,590	LC
Univ of Southern Maine	ME	12,614	C
Univ of Southern Miss	MS	10,112	C
Univ of Tampa	FL	25,784	C
Univ of Tenn at Chattanooga	TN	7,790	C
Univ of Tenn at Knoxville	TN	11,720	C
Univ of Tenn at Martin	TN	8,693	C
Univ of Texas at Arlington	TX	7,195	C
Univ of Texas at Austin	TX	14,610	VC
Univ of Texas at Dallas	TX	13,244	HC
Univ of Texas at El Paso	TX	8,764	NC
Univ of Texas at San Antonio	TX	11,325	LC

MATHEMATICS EDUCATION

MECHANICAL DESIGN TECHNOLOGY

ST = STATE   **$IS** = IN-STATE COSTS   **SR** = SELECTOR RATING

MECHANICAL ENGINEERING

School	ST	$IS	SR
Alabama A&M Univ	AL	8,890	LC
Alfred Univ	NY		VC
Arizona State Univ-Tempe	AZ	11,174	VC
Auburn Univ	AL	12,230	VC
Baylor Univ	TX	27,555	HC
Bethel College	IN	19,680	VC
Boston Univ	MA	42,046	HC+
Bradley Univ	IL	25,280	VC
Brigham Young Univ	UT	9,200	VC
Bucknell Univ	PA	39,660	MC
Calif Inst of Technology	CA	36,123	MC
Calif Maritime Academy	CA	13,490	VC
Calif Polytechnic State Univ	CA	12,390	VC
Calif State Polytechnic Univ, Pomona	CA	18,053	C+
Cal State, Chico	CA	11,395	C
Cal State, Fresno	CA	10,037	LC
Cal State, Fullerton	CA	10,990	C
Cal State, Long Beach	CA	9,512	C
Cal State, Los Angeles	CA	5,900	C
Cal State, Sacramento	CA	11,122	C+
Calvin College	MI	25,735	NC
Carnegie Mellon Univ	PA	32,700	MC
Case Western Reserve Univ	OH	37,314	MC
Catholic Univ of America	DC	35,838	VC
Cedarville Univ	OH	21,904	VC
Central Mich Univ	MI	12,244	C
Central Washington Univ	WA	11,730	C
Christian Brothers Univ	TN	24,650	VC
CUNY/City College	NY		C
Clarkson Univ	NY	34,930	VC
Clemson Univ	SC	13,366	HC
Cleveland State Univ	OH	10,798	NC
College of New Jersey	NJ	18,315	MC
Colo State Univ-Fort Collins	CO	10,878	C+
Columbia Univ/Fu Foundation School of Engineering and Applied Science	NY	42,584	MC
Cooper Union for the Advancement of Science and Art	NY	12,450	MC
Cornell Univ	NY	41,717	MC
Delaware State Univ	DE	8,130	LC
Dordt College	IA	20,325	VC
Drexel Univ	PA	27,700	VC
Duke Univ	NC	41,239	MC
Fairfield Univ	CT	39,835	HC
Florida A&M Univ	FL	8,344	C
Florida Atlantic Univ	FL	11,221	C
Florida Inst of Technology	FL	29,720	VC
Florida International Univ	FL	9,215	VC
Florida State Univ	FL	9,028	NC
Gannon Univ	PA	26,100	C
George Washington Univ	DC	48,820	MC
Georgia Inst of Technology	GA	11,450	VC+
Gonzaga Univ	WA	30,218	HC
Grove City College	PA	15,784	HC+
Harding Univ	AR	16,512	VC
Henry Cogswell College	WA	16,680	SP
Hofstra Univ	NY	32,630	VC
Howard Univ	DC	18,481	C+
Idaho State Univ	ID	9,030	C
Illinois Inst of Technology	IL	26,465	HC+
Indiana Inst of Technology	IN	23,430	C
Indiana Univ-Purdue Univ Fort Wayne	IN	5,067	LC
Indiana Univ-Purdue Univ Indianapolis	IN	10,959	C
Inter American Univ of PR/Bayamon Univ College	PR	3,522	
Iowa State Univ	IA	11,831	VC
Jacksonville Univ	FL	24,040	VC
Johns Hopkins Univ	MD	42,044	MC
Kansas State Univ	KS	10,516	VC
Kent State Univ	OH	14,594	C
Kettering Univ	MI	29,338	HC
Lafayette College	PA	39,267	MC
Lake Superior State Univ	MI	12,842	LC
Lamar Univ	TX	6,820	LC
Lawrence Tech Univ	MI	25,475	VC
Lehigh Univ	PA	42,690	HC+
LeTourneau Univ	TX	21,200	C
Louisiana State Univ and A&M College	LA	10,749	VC
Louisiana Tech Univ	LA	7,370	C
Loyola Marymount Univ	CA	36,321	VC
Manhattan College	NY	29,000	VC
Marquette Univ	WI	31,066	HC
Mass Inst of Technology	MA	41,800	MC
McNeese State Univ	LA	5,270	LC
Mercer Univ	GA	27,525	VC+
Miami Univ	OH	29,097	HC
Mich State Univ	MI	13,689	VC
Mich Tech Univ	MI	14,569	VC
Milwaukee School of Engineering	WI	29,847	VC+
Minn State Univ, Mankato	MN	10,276	LC
Miss State Univ	MS	9,577	C
Montana State Univ-Bozeman	MT	1,137	C
New Jersey Inst of Technology	NJ	16,396	VC
New Mexico Inst of Mining and Technology	NM	8,510	VC+
New Mexico State Univ	NM	9,250	C
New York Inst of Technology	NY	28,126	VC
N Car Agricultural and Technical State Univ	NC	8,000	LC
N Car State Univ	NC	11,824	HC
N Dak State Univ	ND	8,500	C
Northeastern Univ	MA	35,742	HC
Northern Arizona Univ	AZ	10,353	C
Northern Illinois Univ	IL	13,178	C
Northwestern Univ	IL	37,595	MC
Norwich Univ	VT	28,212	C
Oakland Univ	MI	11,936	C
Ohio Northern Univ	OH	27,765	VC
Ohio State Univ	OH	15,357	HC
Ohio Univ	OH	15,921	C
Okla Christian Univ	OK	18,992	NC
Okla State Univ	OK	10,213	VC
Old Dominion Univ	VA	11,907	C
Oral Roberts Univ	OK	22,650	C
Oregon State Univ	OR	11,055	C
Penn State Univ/Univ Park Campus	PA	18,038	HC
Polytechnic Univ/Brooklyn	NY	37,150	VC
Prairie View A&M Univ	TX	11,110	LC
Princeton Univ	NJ	40,213	MC
Purdue Univ/Calumet	IN	10,891	LC
Purdue Univ/West Lafayette	IN	13,458	VC
Rensselaer Polytechnic Inst	NY	41,288	HC+
Rice Univ	TX	32,290	MC
Rochester Inst of Technology	NY	32,070	VC+
Rose-Hulman Inst of Technology	IN	34,557	HC+
Rutgers, The State Univ of New Jersey/New Brunswick/Piscataway Campus	NJ	15,810	HC
Saginaw Valley State Univ	MI	11,432	C
St. Louis Univ	MO	33,158	VC+
St. Martin's Univ	WA	27,555	C
San Diego State Univ	CA	12,971	C
San Francisco State Univ	CA	13,000	C
San Jose State Univ	CA	11,707	C
Santa Clara Univ	CA	38,931	VC
Savannah State Univ	GA	7,772	LC
Seattle Univ	WA	30,063	VC
S Dak School of Mines and Technology	SD	7,624	C+
S Dak State Univ	SD	9,815	C
Southern Illinois Univ Carbondale	IL	12,391	C
Southern Illinois Univ Edwardsville	IL	11,022	C
Southern Methodist Univ	TX	36,088	VC+
Southern Univ and A&M College	LA	8,238	LC
Stanford Univ	CA	41,557	MC
SUNY/Univ at Binghamton	NY	13,988	VC
SUNY/Univ at Buffalo	NY	13,694	VC
SUNY/Univ at Stony Brook	NY	13,625	HC
Stevens Inst of Technology	NJ	40,935	HC
Syracuse Univ	NY	38,655	HC
Temple Univ	PA	17,438	C
Tenn State Univ	TN	9,048	LC
Tenn Tech Univ	TN	10,044	C
Texas A&M Univ	TX	13,351	HC
Texas A&M Univ at Kingsville	TX	6,800	LC
Texas Tech Univ	TX	13,026	VC
Tri-State Univ-Main Campus	IN	26,200	C
Tufts Univ	MA	42,018	MC
Tulane Univ	LA	41,098	MC
Tuskegee Univ	AL	18,860	LC
Union College	NY	41,595	HC
United States Air Force Academy	CO		HC+
United States Coast Guard Academy	CT		HC
United States Military Academy	NY		MC
United States Naval Academy	MD		MC
Universidad Politecnica de PR	PR	5,400	
Univ of Akron	OH	15,166	VC
Univ of Alabama	AL	9,888	C
Univ of Alabama at Birmingham	AL	13,716	C
Univ of Alabama in Huntsville	AL	9,516	VC
Univ of Alaska Fairbanks	AK	10,101	C
Univ of Arizona	AZ	11,958	VC
Univ of Arkansas	AR	11,859	VC
Univ of at Calif Davis	CA	15,010	VC
Univ of Calif at Berkeley	CA	18,141	HC+
Univ of Calif at Irvine	CA	16,475	HC
Univ of Calif at Los Angeles	CA	17,681	MC
Univ of Calif at Riverside	CA	16,625	C
Univ of Calif at San Diego	CA	16,102	HC
Univ of Calif at Santa Barbara	CA	11,800	VC
Univ of Central Florida	FL	10,739	VC
Univ of Cincinnati	OH	17,682	C
Univ of Colo at Boulder	CO	13,352	C+
Univ of Colo at Denver and Health Sciences Center	CO	5,021	C
Univ of Conn	CT	16,628	HC
Univ of Dayton	OH	28,826	VC
Univ of Delaware	DE	14,142	HC
Univ of Denver	CO	36,376	VC+
Univ of Detroit Mercy	MI	27,000	C
Univ of Evansville	IN	28,320	VC
Univ of Florida	FL	9,354	HC
Univ of Hartford	CT	34,044	C
Univ of Hawaii at Manoa	HI	10,413	VC
Univ of Houston	TX	7,000	C
Univ of Idaho	ID	9,310	NC
Univ of Illinois at Chicago	IL	16,256	VC
Univ of Illinois at Urbana-Champaign	IL	15,800	HC+
Univ of Indianapolis	IN	25,090	C
Univ of Iowa	IA	12,172	VC
Univ of Kansas	KS	10,915	VC
Univ of Kentucky	KY	7,800	C
Univ of Louisiana at Lafayette	LA	5,830	C
Univ of Louisville	KY	10,400	VC
Univ of Maine	ME	13,642	C
Univ of Maryland/Baltimore County	MD	16,642	VC+
Univ of Maryland/College Park	MD	16,036	HC
Univ of Mass Amherst	MA	15,973	C+
Univ of Mass Dartmouth	MA	15,985	C
Univ of Mass Lowell	MA	14,327	VC
Univ of Memphis	TN	11,153	C
Univ of Miami	FL	38,397	MC
Univ of Mich/Ann Arbor	MI	16,587	HC+
Univ of Mich/Dearborn	MI	7,000	C
Univ of Minn/Twin Cities	MN	13,165	HC
Univ of Miss	MS	9,000	C
Univ of Missouri/Columbia	MO	13,500	VC
Univ of Missouri/Kansas City	MO	15,000	VC
Univ of Missouri/Rolla	MO	13,332	HC
Univ of Missouri/St. Louis	MO	14,046	VC
Univ of Nebr at Lincoln	NE	11,401	VC
Univ of Nevada/Las Vegas	NV	11,566	C
Univ of Nevada/Reno	NV	12,155	NC
Univ of New Hampshire	NH	16,810	VC
Univ of New Haven	CT	31,794	C
Univ of New Mexico	NM	11,253	C
Univ of New Orleans	LA	7,370	C
Univ of N Car at Charlotte	NC	9,101	C
Univ of N Dak	ND	10,114	VC
Univ of North Florida	FL	9,908	VC
Univ of Notre Dame	IN	39,552	MC
Univ of Okla	OK	10,769	VC+
Univ of Pennsylvania	PA	41,766	MC
Univ of Pittsburgh at Pittsburgh	PA	18,866	HC
Univ of Portland	OR	32,300	VC
Univ of PR/Mayaguez	PR	1,250	
Univ of Rhode Island	RI	15,398	C
Univ of Rochester	NY	41,135	MC
Univ of St. Thomas	MN	28,000	VC
Univ of South Alabama	AL	8,930	LC
Univ of S Car at Columbia	SC	13,397	VC
Univ of South Florida	FL	10,284	VC
Univ of Southern Calif	CA	41,618	MC
Univ of Tenn at Knoxville	TN	11,720	C
Univ of Texas at Arlington	TX	7,195	LC
Univ of Texas at Austin	TX	14,610	HC
Univ of Texas at El Paso	TX	8,764	NC
Univ of Texas at San Antonio	TX	11,325	LC
Univ of Texas-Pan American	TX	7,290	C+
Univ of the District of Columbia	DC	2,070	LC
Univ of the Pacific	CA	34,380	VC
Univ of Toledo	OH	15,806	NC
Univ of Tulsa	OK	25,348	NC
Univ of Utah	UT	10,162	VC
Univ of Vermont	VT	18,080	VC
Univ of Virginia	VA	13,759	MC
Univ of Wisc/Madison	WI	13,117	HC
Univ of Wisc/Milwaukee	WI	9,427	C
Univ of Wisc/Platteville	WI	9,779	NC
Utah State Univ	UT	8,002	VC
Valparaiso Univ	IN	28,970	VC+
Vanderbilt Univ	TN	41,986	MC
Villanova Univ	PA	38,672	HC+
Virginia Commonwealth Univ	VA	12,987	C
Virginia Military Inst	VA	12,654	VC
Virginia Polytechnic Inst and State Univ	VA	10,834	VC
Washington Univ in St. Louis	MO	42,106	MC
Wayne State Univ	MI	11,805	C
West Texas A&M Univ	TX	8,452	C
West Virginia Univ	WV	10,506	C
West Virginia Univ Inst of Technology	WV	8,788	NC
Western Kentucky Univ	KY	10,192	C
Western Mich Univ	MI	13,299	C
Western New England College	MA	32,054	C
Wichita State Univ	KS	8,500	C
Widener Univ	PA	27,275	C
Wilkes Univ	PA	30,886	C
Worcester Polytechnic Inst	MA	40,450	VC+
Wright State Univ	OH	13,616	LC
Yale Univ	CT	41,000	MC
York College of Pennsylvania	PA	16,550	VC
Youngstown State Univ	OH	12,613	NC

MECHANICAL ENGINEERING TECHNOLOGY

School	ST	$IS	SR
Alabama A&M Univ	AL	8,890	LC
Central Conn State Univ	CT	13,620	C
Central Mich Univ	MI	12,244	C
Cleveland State Univ	OH	10,798	NC
Colo State Univ-Pueblo	CO	7,821	LC
Eastern Washington Univ	WA	10,608	C
Fairleigh Dickinson Univ/Metropolitan Campus	NJ	28,590	C
Fairmont State	WV	8,400	LC
Georgia Southern Univ	GA	9,762	C
Indiana State Univ	IN	11,604	C
Indiana Univ-Purdue Univ Fort Wayne	IN	5,067	LC
Indiana Univ-Purdue Univ Indianapolis	IN	10,959	C
Kent State Univ	OH	14,594	C
Metropolitan State College of Denver	CO	2,338	LC
Mich Tech Univ	MI	14,569	VC
Montana State Univ-Bozeman	MT	1,137	C
Northeastern Univ	MA	35,742	HC
Okla State Univ	OK	10,213	VC
Old Dominion Univ	VA	11,907	C
Oregon Inst of Technology	OR	8,718	C
Penn State Erie/The Behrend College	PA	16,256	C
Pennsylvania College of Technology	PA	16,980	LC
Pittsburg State Univ	KS	8,112	C
Point Park Univ	PA	24,160	C
Purdue Univ/Calumet	IN	10,891	LC
Purdue Univ/West Lafayette	IN	13,458	VC
Rochester Inst of Technology	NY	32,070	VC+
S Car State Univ	SC	6,700	LC
Southern Polytechnic State Univ	GA	7,640	VC
SUNY/College at Buffalo	NY	11,903	C+
SUNY/College of Technology at Alfred	NY	14,000	C
SUNY/Inst of Technology	NY	12,575	VC
Temple Univ	PA	17,438	C
Texas A&M Univ at Corpus Christi	TX	10,280	LC
Texas A&M Univ at Galveston	TX	10,000	C+
Texas Tech Univ	TX	13,026	VC
Thomas Edison State College	NJ	3,780	SP
Univ of Akron	OH	15,166	NC
Univ of Arkansas at Little Rock	AR	7,230	NC
Univ of Cincinnati	OH	17,682	C
Univ of Dayton	OH	28,826	VC
Univ of Hartford	CT	34,044	C
Univ of Houston	TX	7,000	C
Univ of Maine	ME	13,642	C
Univ of N Car at Charlotte	NC	9,101	C
Univ of Pittsburgh at Johnstown	PA	16,740	LC
Univ of Southern Miss	MS	10,112	C
Wayne State Univ	MI	11,805	C
Weber State Univ	UT	9,635	NC
Wentworth Inst of Technology	MA	27,500	C
Youngstown State Univ	OH	12,613	NC

MEDIA ARTS

School	ST	$IS	SR
Art Inst of Portland	OR	23,040	SP
Ashland Univ	OH	25,000	C
Briar Cliff Univ	IA	23,550	LC
Brigham Young Univ	UT	9,200	VC
Brown Univ	RI	42,015	MC
Cal State, Los Angeles	CA	5,900	C
Calumet College of St. Joseph	IN	9,500	C
Calvin College	MI	25,735	NC
Carleton College	MN	40,467	MC
Champlain College	VT	24,605	C
Chatham College	PA	27,290	C+
CUNY/Hunter College	NY	8,000	C+
CUNY/Queens College	NY	4,356	C
Claremont McKenna College	CA	42,920	MC
College of St. Catherine	MN	27,505	VC
College of the Ozarks	MO	4,130	VC+

Medical laboratory science (continued)

School	ST	$IS	SR
Columbus College of Art and Design	OH	24,500	SP
Denison Univ	OH	37,040	HC
East Stroudsburg Univ of Pennsylvania	PA	10,336	C
Edinboro Univ of Pennsylvania	PA	11,809	C
Emerson College	MA	35,076	HC
Gallaudet Univ	DC	16,554	
Goddard College	VT	21,100	C
Greenville College	IL	23,146	C
Hampshire College	MA	37,120	HC
Harding Univ	AR	16,512	VC
Hofstra Univ	NY	32,630	VC
Hollins Univ	VA	31,105	C
Indiana Univ Bloomington	IN	13,356	VC
Indiana Univ of Pennsylvania	PA	11,209	C
Indiana Univ-Purdue Univ Indianapolis	IN	10,959	C
Ithaca College	NY	35,144	VC
James Madison Univ	VA	12,010	VC
Johns Hopkins Univ	MD	42,044	MC
Judson College	IL	25,130	C
Kansas City Art Inst	MO	29,542	SP
Kendall College of Art and Design of Ferris State Univ	MI	11,870	SP
Loras College	IA	27,193	C
Loyola Marymount Univ	CA	36,321	VC
Loyola Univ Chicago	IL	32,896	VC
Maine College of Art	ME	28,820	SP
Maryland Inst College of Art	MD	34,450	SP
Mass College of Art	MA	16,650	SP
Mills College	CA	39,870	C
Montana State Univ-Bozeman	MT	1,137	C
Mount Ida College	MA	26,000	LC
Mount St. Mary College	NY	25,250	C
Mount Union College	OH	25,840	C
New Jersey City Univ	NJ	13,695	LC
New York Univ	NY	43,170	MC
Pitzer College	CA	41,644	HC
Point Park Univ	PA	24,160	C
Pomona College	CA	40,774	MC
Purdue Univ/West Lafayette	IN	13,458	VC
Radford Univ	VA	13,145	C
Rensselaer Polytechnic Inst	NY	41,288	HC+
Robert Morris Univ	PA	22,822	C
Roosevelt Univ	IL	22,605	VC
Sacred Heart Univ	CT	33,404	C
Salve Regina Univ	RI	33,450	C
Savannah College of Art and Design	GA	30,800	SP
Southern Methodist Univ	TX	36,088	VC+
SUNY/College at Fredonia	NY	12,771	VC
SUNY/College at Old Westbury	NY	13,154	C
SUNY/Univ at Buffalo	NY	13,694	VC
Suffolk Univ	MA	33,160	C
Syracuse Univ	NY	38,655	HC
Toccoa Falls College	GA	17,125	C
Towson Univ	MD	13,924	VC
Tulane Univ	LA	41,098	MC
Univ of Arizona	AZ	11,958	VC
Univ of Chicago	IL	42,369	MC
Univ of Hartford	CT	34,044	C
Univ of Illinois at Urbana-Champaign	IL	15,800	HC+
Univ of Maine	ME	13,642	C
Univ of Mich/Ann Arbor	MI	16,587	HC+
Univ of New Mexico	NM	11,253	C
Univ of N Car at Asheville	NC	9,237	VC
Univ of N Car at Greensboro	NC	8,993	C
Univ of San Francisco	CA	37,560	VC
Univ of S Car at Columbia	SC	13,397	VC
Univ of the District of Columbia	DC	2,070	LC
Univ of Utah	UT	10,162	VC
Valdosta State Univ	GA	8,802	C
Vassar College	NY	41,700	MC
Washburn Univ	KS	9,734	NC
Weber State Univ	UT	9,635	NC
Webster Univ	MO	24,280	VC
Western Illinois Univ	IL	13,042	C
Western Mich Univ	MI	13,299	C
Wilkes Univ	PA	30,886	C
Wilmington College	DE	5,594	NC
Wingate Univ	NC	23,300	C

MEDICAL LABORATORY SCIENCE

School	ST	$IS	SR
Eastern Illinois Univ	IL	12,569	C
Idaho State Univ	ID	9,030	C
Marquette Univ	WI	31,066	HC
Mary Baldwin College	VA	26,465	C
Northeastern Univ	MA	35,742	HC
Oakland Univ	MI	11,936	C
Shawnee State Univ	OH	12,237	NC
Univ of Illinois at Chicago	IL	16,256	VC
Univ of Mary	ND	15,374	C
Univ of Mass Dartmouth	MA	15,985	C
Univ of New Hampshire	NH	16,810	VC
Univ of Utah	UT	10,162	VC
Univ of Vermont	VT	18,080	VC

MEDICAL LABORATORY TECHNOLOGY

School	ST	$IS	SR
Alabama A&M Univ	AL	8,890	LC
American International College	MA	28,710	LC
Anderson Univ	IN	25,050	LC
Andrews Univ	MI	21,786	C
Angelo State Univ	TX	8,340	NC
Arkansas Tech Univ	AR	8,108	VC
Asbury College	KY	23,762	VC
Auburn Univ	AL	12,230	VC
Austin Peay State Univ	TN	7,535	C
Avila Univ	MO	22,100	C
Ball State Univ	IN	13,138	C
Baylor Univ	TX	27,555	HC
Bemidji State Univ	MN	11,180	LC
Blackburn College	IL	13,690	C
Bloomsburg Univ of Pennsylvania	PA	11,602	C
Boise State Univ	ID	9,438	LC
Cabrini College	PA	33,340	C
Caldwell Univ	NJ	26,450	LC
Cal State, Northridge	CA	9,036	LC
Cal State, Sacramento	CA	11,122	C+
Calif Univ of Pennsylvania	PA	14,217	C
Campbellsville Univ	KY	21,328	C
Catholic Univ of America	DC	35,838	VC
Cedar Crest College	PA	30,615	C
Central Missouri State Univ	MO	10,000	C
Cheyney Univ of Pennsylvania	PA	11,497	LC
CUNY/Hunter College	NY	8,000	C+
CUNY/York College	NY	4,242	NC
Clemson Univ	SC	13,366	HC
Coe College	IA	27,440	VC
Coker College	SC	21,600	C
College Misericordia	PA	27,950	C
College of Our Lady of the Elms	MA	21,000	C
College of St. Mary	NE	23,938	C
Columbia College	SC	24,982	LC
Concord College	WV	9,708	C
Concordia College: Moorhead	MN	22,475	VC
Concordia Univ Nebr	NE	20,500	C+
Dakota State Univ	SD	7,466	C
Defiance College	OH	24,790	C
DePaul Univ	IL	29,835	VC
Dordt College	IA	20,325	VC
East Central Univ	OK	6,207	C
East Stroudsburg Univ of Pennsylvania	PA	10,336	C
Eastern Mennonite Univ	VA	25,450	VC
Eastern Mich Univ	MI	12,897	C
Eastern New Mexico Univ	NM	7,264	C
Eastern Washington Univ	WA	10,608	C
Edinboro Univ of Pennsylvania	PA	11,809	LC
Elmira College	NY	37,200	VC
Erskine College	SC	25,468	VC
Eureka College	IL	19,280	C
Evangel Univ	MO	17,380	C
Fairleigh Dickinson Univ/College at Florham	NJ	30,130	C
Fairleigh Dickinson Univ/Metropolitan Campus	NJ	28,590	C
Fayetteville State Univ	NC	6,000	LC
Ferrum College	VA	24,290	LC
Florida Atlantic Univ	FL	11,221	C
George Washington Univ	DC	48,820	MC
Graceland Univ	IA	19,700	C
Grand Valley State Univ	MI	12,000	VC
Gwynedd-Mercy College	PA	26,080	C
High Point Univ	NC	25,720	C
Holy Family Univ	PA	25,740	C
Howard Univ	DC	18,481	C+
Huntington Univ	IN	24,830	C
Illinois College	IL	21,900	C+
Illinois State Univ	IL	12,839	C+
Indiana State Univ	IN	11,604	C
Indiana Univ Kokomo	IN	4,835	LC
Indiana Univ-Purdue Univ Indianapolis	IN	10,959	C
Indiana Wesleyan Univ	IN	22,074	C+
Inter American Univ of PR/San German	PR	6,720	
Iona College	NY	30,878	VC
Judson College	IL	25,130	C
Keuka College	NY	26,050	C
King's College	PA	29,810	C
Knoxville College	TN	6,200	LC
Kutztown Univ of Pennsylvania	PA	10,820	C
Lake Superior State Univ	MI	12,842	LC
Lamar Univ	TX	6,820	LC
Langston Univ	OK	2,308	LC
Lebanon Valley College	PA	31,700	VC
Lee Univ	TN	14,780	NC
Lenoir-Rhyne College	NC	25,580	C
Lincoln Memorial Univ	TN	18,144	C
Lock Haven Univ of Pennsylvania	PA	12,098	LC
LIU/C.W. Post Campus	NY	28,282	C
Louisiana College	LA	13,450	C
Louisiana Tech Univ	LA	7,370	C
Madonna Univ	MI	16,068	VC
Malone College	OH	23,040	C
Manchester College	IN	23,470	C
Marian College of Fond du Lac	WI	21,775	LC
Marshall Univ	WV	9,116	C
Mary Baldwin College	VA	26,465	C
Marywood Univ	PA	30,680	C
McKendree College	IL	24,800	VC
McNeese State Univ	LA	5,270	LC
Mercy College	NY	20,000	NC
Mercyhurst College	PA	28,633	VC
Mich State Univ	MI	13,689	VC
Midwestern State Univ	TX	9,381	LC
Minn State Univ, Mankato	MN	10,276	LC
Minn State Univ, Moorhead	MN	7,000	C
Missouri Southern State Univ	MO	8,396	NC
Missouri State Univ	MO	10,748	C+
Missouri Western State Univ	MO	9,534	NC
Monmouth Univ	NJ	28,956	C
Morgan State Univ	MD	12,080	C
Mount Aloysius College	PA	20,900	C
Mount Mercy College	IA	23,670	C
Mount St. Mary College	NY	25,250	C
National-Louis Univ	IL	16,915	LC
New Jersey City Univ	NJ	13,695	LC
N Car State Univ	NC	11,824	HC
North Park Univ	IL	24,050	C
Northeastern State Univ	OK	5,896	LC
Northern Mich Univ	MI	12,340	VC
Northern State Univ	SD	8,257	C
Northwestern College of Iowa	IA	22,174	C+
Northwestern Okla State Univ	OK	6,250	NC
Norwich Univ	VT	28,212	C
Okla Christian Univ	OK	18,992	NC
Oral Roberts Univ	OK	22,650	C
Ouachita Baptist Univ	AR	21,900	VC
Pace Univ	NY	30,000	VC
Pontifical Catholic Univ of PR/Ponce	PR	7,310	
Purdue Univ/Calumet	IN	10,891	LC
Quincy Univ	IL	24,920	C
Rhode Island College	RI	11,570	C
Rutgers, The State Univ of New Jersey/Camden Campus	NJ	15,000	VC
St. Augustine's College	NC	14,000	LC
St. Bonaventure Univ	NY	28,785	LC
St. Francis College	NY	19,974	LC
St. Francis Univ	PA	25,880	LC
St. Peter's College	NJ	30,160	LC
St. Thomas Aquinas College	NY	22,000	LC
Salem College	NC	26,226	VC+
Salem State College	MA	13,161	LC
San Francisco State Univ	CA	13,000	C
Seton Hill Univ	PA	28,810	C
Shorter College	GA	19,700	C
Slippery Rock Univ of Pennsylvania	PA	10,360	LC
Southeastern Okla State Univ	OK	6,147	C
Southern Arkansas Univ	AR	6,956	C
Southern Wesleyan Univ	SC	21,675	C
SUNY/College at Fredonia	NY	12,771	VC
SUNY/College at Plattsburgh	NY	12,362	C
SUNY/Univ at Albany	NY	13,860	VC
Suffolk Univ	MA	33,160	C
Tarleton State Univ	TX	8,952	C
Texas A&M Univ at Kingsville	TX	6,800	LC
Thiel College	PA	24,580	C
Thomas More College	KY	24,470	C
Towson Univ	MD	13,924	VC
Trevecca Nazarene Univ	TN	19,594	C
Union College	NE	18,710	C
Union Univ	TN	20,750	C
Univ of Akron	OH	15,166	NC
Univ of Central Florida	FL	10,739	VC
Univ of Central Okla	OK	8,094	C
Univ of Cincinnati	OH	17,682	C
Univ of Conn	CT	16,628	HC
Univ of Delaware	DE	14,142	HC
Univ of Hartford	CT	34,044	C
Univ of Hawaii at Manoa	HI	10,413	VC
Univ of Idaho	ID	9,310	NC
Univ of Indianapolis	IN	25,090	C
Univ of Iowa	IA	12,172	VC
Univ of Louisville	KY	10,400	VC
Univ of Maine	ME	13,642	C
Univ of Mass Amherst	MA	15,973	C+
Univ of Mich/Flint	MI	6,398	C
Univ of Minn/Twin Cities	MN	13,165	HC
Univ of Miss	MS	9,000	C
Univ of Nebr at Lincoln	NE	11,401	VC
Univ of New Mexico	NM	11,253	C
Univ of N Car at Chapel Hill	NC	11,129	MC
Univ of N Car at Greensboro	NC	8,993	C
Univ of North Texas	TX	7,800	C
Univ of Okla	OK	10,769	VC+
Univ of Pittsburgh at Johnstown	PA	16,740	LC
Univ of Rhode Island	RI	15,398	C
Univ of St. Francis	IN	20,970	C
Univ of Scranton	PA	31,100	VC
Univ of Sioux Falls	SD	20,800	C
Univ of S Car at Columbia	SC	13,397	VC
Univ of Southern Miss	MS	10,112	C
Univ of Tenn at Chattanooga	TN	7,790	C
Univ of Texas at El Paso	TX	8,764	NC
Univ of the Cumberlands	KY	18,184	C
Univ of Vermont	VT	18,080	VC
Univ of Virginia's College at Wise	VA	11,076	C
Univ of Washington	WA	10,400	VC
Univ of West Florida	FL	8,559	C
Univ of Wisc/La Crosse	WI	10,045	VC
Univ of Wisc/Madison	WI	13,117	HC
Univ of Wisc/Oshkosh	WI	10,426	LC
Utah State Univ	UT	8,002	VC
Wartburg College	IA	27,315	VC
Washburn Univ	KS	9,734	NC
Waynesburg College	PA	21,230	C
Wesley College	DE	19,905	C
Western Conn State Univ	CT	12,993	C
Western New Mexico Univ	NM	7,233	LC
Wichita State Univ	KS	8,500	C
William Carey College	MS	11,000	LC
William Jewell College	MO	24,340	C
Winona State Univ	MN	11,333	C
Winthrop Univ	SC	11,302	C
Wright State Univ	OH	13,616	LC
Xavier Univ	OH	30,490	HC
York College of Pennsylvania	PA	16,550	LC
Youngstown State Univ	OH	12,613	NC

MEDICAL PHYSICS

School	ST	$IS	SR
Oakland Univ	MI	11,936	C

MEDICAL RECORDS ADMINISTRATION/SERVICES

School	ST	$IS	SR
College of St. Catherine	MN	27,505	VC
Dakota State Univ	SD	7,466	C
Davenport Univ	MI	15,205	NC
East Carolina Univ	NC	10,000	C
East Central Univ	OK	6,207	C
LIU/C.W. Post Campus	NY	28,282	C
Louisiana Tech Univ	LA	7,370	C
Norfolk State Univ	VA	10,531	LC
Regis Univ	CO	31,890	C
Southwestern Okla State Univ	OK	4,801	C
Tenn State Univ	TN	9,048	LC
Texas State Univ - San Marcos	TX	10,862	C
Univ of Alabama at Birmingham	AL	13,716	C
Western Carolina Univ	NC	7,000	C

MEDICAL SCIENCE

School	ST	$IS	SR
Alderson-Broaddus College	WV	24,006	C
Suffolk Univ	MA	33,160	C
Univ of Arkansas	AR	11,859	VC
Univ of Louisville	KY	10,400	VC
Univ of Wisc/Madison	WI	13,117	HC
Univ of Wisc/Milwaukee	WI	9,427	LC

MEDICAL TECHNOLOGY

School	ST	$IS	SR
Alderson-Broaddus College	WV	24,006	C
Aquinas College	MI	23,750	C
Armstrong Atlantic State Univ	GA	7,394	C
Augustana College	SD	24,380	VC
Averett Univ	VA	24,920	C
Barry Univ	FL	24,100	LC
Bellarmine Univ	KY	27,650	C+
Blue Mountain College	MS	11,086	C
Bradley Univ	IL	25,280	VC
Brescia Univ	KY	14,240	C
Briar Cliff Univ	IA	23,550	LC
Bridgewater College	VA	27,790	C
Catawba College	NC	25,000	C
Central Mich Univ	MI	12,244	C
CUNY/College of Staten Island	NY	4,328	NC
Clarion Univ of Pennsylvania	PA	11,844	C
Cleveland State Univ	OH	10,798	NC
College of St. Rose	NY	25,684	C
College of the Ozarks	MO	4,130	VC+
Colo State Univ-Pueblo	CO	7,821	LC
East Carolina Univ	NC	10,000	C
East Texas Baptist Univ	TX	16,713	C
Edgewood College	WI	22,862	C
Elon Univ	NC	25,371	HC
Gannon Univ	PA	26,100	C
Gardner-Webb Univ	NC	21,500	C

School	ST	$IS	SR
George Mason Univ	VA	10,850	VC
Georgia Southern Univ	GA	9,762	C
Harding Univ	AR	16,512	VC
Hartwick College	NY	36,065	C+
Houghton College	NY	25,980	VC+
Indiana Univ of Pennsylvania	PA	11,209	C
Indiana Univ Southeast	IN	4,880	LC
Indiana Univ-Purdue Univ Fort Wayne	IN	5,067	LC
Inter American Univ of PR/ Fajardo Campus	PR	4,000	
Inter American Univ of PR/ Metropolitan Campus	PR	4,320	
Inter American Univ of PR/ Ponce Regional College	PR	3,700	
Iona College	NY	30,878	VC
Kansas State Univ	KS	10,516	VC
Kean Univ	NJ	15,880	C
King College	TN	23,400	C
Lincoln Univ	MO	8,000	NC
Lindenwood Univ	MO	18,600	VC
Lubbock Christian Univ	TX	16,960	C
Mansfield Univ	PA	11,300	C
Marist College	NY	30,566	VC
Marywood Univ	PA	30,680	C
Miami Univ	OH	29,097	HC
Miss State Univ	MS	9,577	C
Morehead State Univ	KY	9,150	C
Mount Marty College	SD	20,590	C
Mount Vernon Nazarene Univ	OH	20,810	C
Norfolk State Univ	VA	10,531	LC
Oakwood College	AL	14,904	C
Ohio Northern Univ	OH	27,765	VC
Ohio State Univ	OH	15,357	HC
Okla Panhandle State Univ	OK	7,635	NC
Okla State Univ	OK	10,213	VC
Old Dominion Univ	VA	11,907	C
Oregon State Univ	OR	11,055	C
Pittsburg State Univ	KS	8,112	C
Prairie View A&M Univ	TX	11,110	LC
Purdue Univ/West Lafayette	IN	13,458	VC
Radford Univ	VA	13,145	C
Roanoke College	VA	30,748	VC
Roosevelt Univ	IL	22,605	VC
Rutgers, The State Univ of New Jersey/New Brunswick/Piscataway Campus	NJ	15,810	HC
Saginaw Valley State Univ	MI	11,432	C
St. John's Univ	NY	34,370	C
St. Joseph's College	IN	26,600	C
St. Leo Univ	FL	22,140	C+
St. Mary-of-the-Woods College	IN	25,480	C
St. Mary's Univ of Minn	MN	23,857	VC
Salisbury Univ	MD	13,128	VC
Sam Houston State Univ	TX	8,000	C
Seattle Univ	WA	30,063	VC
Southeast Missouri State Univ	MO	10,596	C
Southern Adventist Univ	TN	18,500	C
Southwest Baptist Univ	MO	18,300	C
Southwest Minn State Univ	MN	10,975	C
Southwestern Adventist Univ	TX	18,290	LC
Southwestern Okla State Univ	OK	4,801	C
SUNY/College at Brockport	NY	12,747	VC
SUNY/Univ at Buffalo	NY	13,694	VC
Stetson Univ	FL	32,725	VC
Tenn State Univ	TN	9,048	LC
Texas Southern Univ	TX	9,828	C
Texas Woman's Univ	TX	7,804	C
Thomas Edison State College	NJ	3,780	SP
Tusculum College	TN	21,340	C
Univ of Alabama at Birmingham	AL	13,716	C
Univ of Arizona	AZ	11,958	VC
Univ of Central Arkansas	AR	9,984	C
Univ of Hawaii at Manoa	HI	10,413	VC
Univ of Mary Hardin-Baylor	TX	19,428	C
Univ of Mass Boston	MA	8,024	C
Univ of Mich/Ann Arbor	MI	16,587	HC+
Univ of Miss	MS	9,000	C
Univ of Missouri/Kansas City	MO	15,000	VC
Univ of Montana	MT	10,602	C
Univ of New Orleans	LA	7,370	C
Univ of N Car at Charlotte	NC	9,101	C
Univ of Rio Grande	OH	8,728	NC
Univ of St. Francis	IL	25,430	C
Univ of St. Mary	KS	18,900	C
Univ of S Dak	SD	9,068	C
Univ of South Florida	FL	10,284	VC
Univ of Texas at Arlington	TX	7,195	LC
Univ of Texas at Austin	TX	14,610	HC
Univ of Texas-Pan American	TX	7,290	C+
Univ of the Sacred Heart	PR	5,590	
Univ of the Sciences in Philadelphia	PA	33,380	VC
West Texas A&M Univ	TX	8,452	C
West Virginia Univ	WV	10,506	C
Western Illinois Univ	IL	13,042	C
Western Kentucky Univ	KY	10,192	C
Wilkes Univ	PA	30,886	C
Winston-Salem State Univ	NC	8,960	LC
Youngstown State Univ	OH	12,613	NC

MEDIEVAL STUDIES

School	ST	$IS	SR
Bard College	NY	41,800	HC+
Bates College	ME	42,100	MC
Brown Univ	RI	42,015	MC
Catholic Univ of America	DC	35,838	VC
College of the Holy Cross	MA	40,664	MC
Columbia Univ/Barnard College	NY	38,000	MC
Columbia Univ/Columbia College	NY	42,584	MC
Conn College	CT	41,975	MC
Cornell College	IA	30,110	VC+
Dickinson College	PA	40,170	HC+
Duke Univ	NC	41,239	MC
Emory Univ	GA	40,546	MC
Fordham Univ	NY	36,000	MC
Hanover College	IN	28,150	HC
Mount Holyoke College	MA	42,148	HC+
New College of Florida	FL	10,009	HC+
New York Univ	NY	43,170	MC
Ohio State Univ	OH	15,357	HC
Penn State Univ/Univ Park Campus	PA	18,038	HC
Plymouth State Univ	NH	12,298	LC
Purdue Univ/West Lafayette	IN	13,458	VC
Rice Univ	TX	32,290	MC
Rutgers, The State Univ of New Jersey/New Brunswick/Piscataway Campus	NJ	15,810	HC
Rutgers, The State Univ of New Jersey/Newark Campus	NJ	15,640	VC
St. Olaf College	MN	32,800	HC
Smith College	MA	41,474	MC
Southern Methodist Univ	TX	36,088	VC+
SUNY/Univ at Albany	NY	13,860	VC
SUNY/Univ at Binghamton	NY	13,988	HC
Swarthmore College	PA	41,280	MC
Syracuse Univ	NY	38,655	HC
Tulane Univ	LA	41,090	MC
Univ of at Calif Davis	CA	15,010	VC
Univ of Calif at Santa Barbara	CA	11,800	VC
Univ of Chicago	IL	42,369	MC
Univ of Mich/Ann Arbor	MI	16,587	HC+
Univ of Nebr at Lincoln	NE	11,401	VC
Univ of Notre Dame	IN	39,552	MC
Univ of Tenn at Knoxville	TN	11,720	C
Univ of the South	TN	34,645	VC
Vassar College	NY	41,700	MC
Washington and Lee Univ	VA	35,880	MC
Washington Univ in St. Louis	MO	42,106	MC
Wellesley College	MA	41,030	MC
Wesleyan Univ	CT	42,122	MC

MENTAL HEALTH/HUMAN SERVICES

School	ST	$IS	SR
Calif Univ of Pennsylvania	PA	14,217	C
Franciscan Univ of Steubenville	OH	20,300	VC
Inter American Univ of PR/ Aguadilla Campus	PR	3,784	
Metropolitan College of New York	NY	16,000	C
Morgan State Univ	MD	12,080	C
Northern Kentucky Univ	KY	6,670	NC
Pennsylvania College of Technology	PA	16,560	LC
Sinte Gleska Univ	SD	2,300	NC
Thomas Edison State College	NJ	3,780	SP
Univ of Maine at Augusta	ME	5,025	NC
Univ of the Sciences in Philadelphia	PA	33,380	VC

METAL/JEWELRY

School	ST	$IS	SR
Calif College of the Arts	CA	34,325	SP
Cleveland Inst of Art	OH	34,109	SP
College for Creative Studies	MI	24,000	SP
Edinboro Univ of Pennsylvania	PA	11,809	LC
Hofstra Univ	NY	32,630	VC
Indiana Univ Bloomington	IN	13,356	VC
Kendall College of Art and Design of Ferris State Univ	MI	11,870	SP
Maine College of Art	ME	28,820	SP
Mass College of Art	MA	16,650	SP
Rhode Island School of Design	RI	38,130	SP
Rochester Inst of Technology	NY	32,070	VC+
Savannah College of Art and Design	GA	30,800	SP

School	ST	$IS	SR
Syracuse Univ	NY	38,655	HC
Univ of Georgia	GA	11,004	HC
Univ of Kansas	KS	10,915	VC
Univ of Mass Dartmouth	MA	15,985	C
Univ of Mich/Ann Arbor	MI	16,587	HC+
Univ of North Texas	TX	7,800	C
Univ of Oregon	OR	13,108	VC
Univ of Washington	WA	10,400	VC

METALLURGICAL ENGINEERING

School	ST	$IS	SR
Calif Polytechnic State Univ	CA	12,390	VC
Colo School of Mines	CO	14,893	HC
Columbia Univ/Fu Foundation School of Engineering and Applied Science	NY	42,584	MC
Illinois Inst of Technology	IL	26,465	HC+
Montana Tech of The Univ of Montana	MT	10,434	C
Ohio State Univ	OH	15,357	HC
S Dak School of Mines and Technology	SD	7,624	C+
Univ of Alabama	AL	9,888	C
Univ of Cincinnati	OH	17,682	C
Univ of Idaho	ID	9,310	NC
Univ of Illinois at Urbana-Champaign	IL	15,800	HC+
Univ of Minn/Twin Cities	MN	13,165	VC
Univ of Missouri/Rolla	MO	13,332	HC
Univ of Nevada/Reno	NV	12,155	NC
Univ of Texas at El Paso	TX	8,764	NC
Univ of Utah	UT	10,162	VC

MEXICAN-AMERICAN/ CHICANO STUDIES

School	ST	$IS	SR
Cal State, Dominguez Hills	CA	10,220	C
Cal State, Fresno	CA	10,037	LC
Cal State, Fullerton	CA	10,990	C
Cal State, Los Angeles	CA	5,900	C
Cal State, Northridge	CA	9,036	LC
Concordia Univ at Austin	TX	23,640	C
Metropolitan State College of Denver	CO	2,338	LC
Our Lady of the Lake Univ of San Antonio	TX	22,430	LC
Pitzer College	CA	41,644	HC
San Diego State Univ	CA	12,971	C
Scripps College	CA	41,000	MC
Sonoma State Univ	CA	14,732	C
Southern Methodist Univ	TX	36,088	VC+
Sul Ross State Univ	TX	6,600	LC
Univ of Arizona	AZ	11,958	VC
Univ of at Calif Davis	CA	15,010	VC
Univ of Calif at Riverside	CA	16,625	C
Univ of Calif at Santa Barbara	CA	11,800	VC
Univ of Minn/Twin Cities	MN	13,165	VC
Univ of Northern Colo	CO	10,249	C
Univ of Texas at El Paso	TX	8,764	NC
Univ of Texas at San Antonio	TX	11,325	LC
Univ of Texas-Pan American	TX	7,290	C+
Wayne State Univ	MI	11,805	C

MICROBIOLOGY

School	ST	$IS	SR
Arizona State Univ-Tempe	AZ	11,174	C
Auburn Univ	AL	12,230	VC
Ball State Univ	IN	13,138	C
Bard College	NY	41,800	HC+
Brigham Young Univ	UT	9,200	VC
Calif Polytechnic State Univ	CA	12,390	VC
Calif State Polytechnic Univ, Pomona	CA	18,053	C+
Cal State, Chico	CA	11,395	C
Cal State, Los Angeles	CA	5,900	C
Cal State, Northridge	CA	9,036	LC
Cal State, Sacramento	CA	11,122	C+
Central Mich Univ	MI	12,244	C
Clemson Univ	SC	13,366	HC
Colo State Univ-Fort Collins	CO	10,878	C+
Cornell Univ	NY	41,717	MC
Eastern Kentucky Univ	KY	7,725	C
Eastern Mich Univ	MI	12,897	C
Eastern Washington Univ	WA	10,608	C
Howard Univ	DC	18,481	C+
Idaho State Univ	ID	9,030	C
Indiana Univ Bloomington	IN	13,356	VC
Inter American Univ of PR/ Aguadilla Campus	PR	3,784	
Inter American Univ of PR/ Arecibo Campus	PR	3,350	
Iowa State Univ	IA	11,831	VC
Juniata College	PA	33,130	VC
Kansas State Univ	KS	10,516	VC
Louisiana State Univ and A&M College	LA	10,749	VC
Marlboro College	VT	35,980	VC+
Miami Univ	OH	29,097	HC
Mich State Univ	MI	13,689	VC
Miss State Univ	MS	9,577	C

School	ST	$IS	SR
Miss Univ for Women	MS	6,000	LC
Missouri Southern State Univ	MO	8,396	NC
Montana State Univ-Bozeman	MT	1,137	C
New Mexico State Univ	NM	9,250	C
N Car State Univ	NC	11,824	HC
N Dak State Univ	ND	8,500	C
Northern Arizona Univ	AZ	10,353	C
Northern Mich Univ	MI	12,340	LC
Ohio State Univ	OH	15,357	HC
Ohio Univ	OH	15,921	C
Ohio Wesleyan Univ	OH	35,830	VC+
Okla State Univ	OK	10,213	VC
Oregon State Univ	OR	11,055	C
Penn State Univ/Univ Park Campus	PA	18,038	HC
Purdue Univ/Calumet	IN	10,891	LC
Quinnipiac Univ	CT	34,640	VC
Rutgers, The State Univ of New Jersey/New Brunswick/Piscataway Campus	NJ	15,810	HC
San Diego State Univ	CA	12,971	C
San Francisco State Univ	CA	13,000	C
San Jose State Univ	CA	11,707	C
S Dak State Univ	SD	9,815	C
Southern Illinois Univ Carbondale	IL	12,391	C
SUNY/College of Environmental Science and Forestry	NY	15,000	VC
Texas A&M Univ	TX	13,351	HC
Texas State Univ - San Marcos	TX	10,862	C
Texas Tech Univ	TX	13,026	VC
Univ of Akron	OH	15,166	NC
Univ of Alabama	AL	9,888	C
Univ of Arizona	AZ	11,958	VC
Univ of at Calif Davis	CA	15,010	VC
Univ of Calif at Berkeley	CA	18,141	HC+
Univ of Calif at Los Angeles	CA	17,681	MC
Univ of Calif at San Diego	CA	16,102	HC
Univ of Calif at Santa Barbara	CA	11,800	VC
Univ of Central Florida	FL	10,739	VC
Univ of Florida	FL	9,354	HC
Univ of Georgia	GA	11,004	HC
Univ of Great Falls	MT	17,000	C
Univ of Hawaii at Manoa	HI	10,413	VC
Univ of Houston-Downtown	TX	3,326	NC
Univ of Idaho	ID	9,310	NC
Univ of Illinois at Urbana-Champaign	IL	15,800	HC+
Univ of Iowa	IA	12,172	VC
Univ of Kansas	KS	10,915	VC
Univ of Maine	ME	13,642	C
Univ of Maryland/College Park	MD	16,036	HC
Univ of Mass Amherst	MA	15,973	C+
Univ of Memphis	TN	11,153	C
Univ of Miami	FL	38,397	MC
Univ of Mich/Ann Arbor	MI	16,587	HC+
Univ of Mich/Dearborn	MI	7,000	VC
Univ of Minn/Twin Cities	MN	13,165	VC
Univ of Missouri/Columbia	MO	13,500	VC
Univ of Montana	MT	10,602	C
Univ of New Hampshire	NH	16,810	VC
Univ of Northern Iowa	IA	11,133	C
Univ of Okla	OK	10,769	VC+
Univ of Pittsburgh at Pittsburgh	PA	18,866	HC
Univ of PR at Humacao	PR	1,707	
Univ of PR/Arecibo	PR	8,327	
Univ of PR/Mayaguez	PR	1,250	
Univ of Rhode Island	RI	15,398	C
Univ of Rochester	NY	41,135	MC
Univ of South Florida	FL	10,284	VC
Univ of Tenn at Knoxville	TN	11,720	C
Univ of Texas at Arlington	TX	7,195	LC
Univ of Texas at Austin	TX	14,610	HC
Univ of Texas at El Paso	TX	8,764	NC
Univ of the Sciences in Philadelphia	PA	33,380	VC
Univ of Vermont	VT	18,080	VC
Univ of Washington	WA	10,400	VC
Univ of Wisc/La Crosse	WI	10,045	VC
Univ of Wisc/Madison	WI	13,117	VC
Univ of Wisc/Milwaukee	WI	9,427	LC
Univ of Wisc/Oshkosh	WI	10,426	LC
Univ of Wyoming	WY	9,666	C
Utah State Univ	UT	8,002	VC
Wagner College	NY	33,300	VC
Washington State Univ	WA	12,260	VC
Weber State Univ	UT	9,635	NC
Xavier Univ of Louisiana	LA	17,600	C

MIDDLE EASTERN STUDIES

School	ST	$IS	SR
Brandeis Univ	MA	41,551	MC
Brigham Young Univ	UT	9,200	VC
Brown Univ	RI	42,015	MC
College of the Holy Cross	MA	40,664	MC
Columbia Univ/Barnard College	NY	38,000	MC

School	ST	$IS	SR
Columbia Univ/Columbia College	NY	42,584	MC
Columbia Univ/School of General Studies	NY	41,516	C
Dartmouth College	NH	39,465	MC
Emory & Henry College	VA	26,570	C
Emory Univ	GA	40,546	MC
Fordham Univ	NY	36,000	HC
George Washington Univ	DC	48,820	MC
Hampshire College	MA	37,120	HC
Harvard Univ/Harvard College	MA	45,860	MC
Middlebury College	VT	42,120	MC
New York Univ	NY	43,170	MC
Rutgers, The State Univ of New Jersey/New Brunswick/Piscataway Campus	NJ	15,810	MC
Stevens Inst of Technology	NJ	40,935	HC
Texas State Univ - San Marcos	TX	10,862	C
Tufts Univ	MA	42,018	MC
Univ of Arkansas	AR	11,859	VC
Univ of Calif at Berkeley	CA	18,141	HC+
Univ of Calif at Los Angeles	CA	17,681	MC
Univ of Conn	CT	16,628	HC
Univ of Mass Amherst	MA	15,973	C+
Univ of Mich/Ann Arbor	MI	16,587	HC+
Univ of Minn/Twin Cities	MN	13,165	HC
Univ of Texas at Austin	TX	14,610	HC
Univ of Utah	UT	10,162	VC
Washington Univ in St. Louis	MO	42,106	MC
Wellesley College	MA	41,030	MC

MIDDLE SCHOOL EDUCATION

School	ST	$IS	SR
Abilene Christian Univ	TX	20,830	C
Alabama A&M Univ	AL	8,890	LC
Albany State Univ	GA	5,770	C+
Alice Lloyd College	KY	4,900	C
Alverno College	WI	21,088	C
American International College	MA	28,710	LC
Appalachian State Univ	NC	8,000	VC
Arkansas State Univ	AR	9,630	C
Arkansas Tech Univ	AR	8,108	VC
Armstrong Atlantic State Univ	GA	7,394	C
Asbury College	KY	23,762	VC
Auburn Univ	AL	12,230	VC
Augusta State Univ	GA	2,920	C
Averett Univ	VA	24,920	C
Avila Univ	MO	22,100	C
Baldwin-Wallace College	OH	27,256	VC
Ball State Univ	IN	13,138	C
Barton College	NC	22,316	C
Bellarmine Univ	KY	27,650	C+
Bemidji State Univ	MN	11,180	LC
Bennett College	NC	11,500	C
Berea College	KY	5,496	VC+
Berry College	GA	24,342	VC
Bethany College	KS	20,660	LC
Bluefield College	VA	17,230	C+
Bluefield State College	WV	3,140	LC
Bluffton College	OH	26,110	C
Bowling Green State Univ	OH	14,994	C
Brenau Univ Women's College	GA	23,950	VC
Brewton-Parker College	GA	14,220	LC
Buena Vista Univ	IA	27,742	C
Campbell Univ	NC	21,137	VC
Campbellsville Univ	KY	21,328	C
Canisius College	NY	32,257	VC
Capital Univ	OH	30,444	C
Cardinal Stritch Univ	WI	21,910	C
Caribbean Univ	PR	3,000	
Carson-Newman College	TN	16,800	C
Carthage College	WI	26,000	C
Catawba College	NC	25,000	C
Cedarville Univ	OH	21,904	VC
Central Missouri State Univ	MO	10,000	C
Central Washington Univ	WA	11,730	C
Champlain College	VT	24,605	C
Christopher Newport Univ	VA	13,326	VC
City Univ	WA	7,425	NC
CUNY/Hunter College	NY	8,000	C+
Claflin Univ	SC	16,798	C+
Clark Atlanta Univ	GA	20,960	LC
Clayton College and State Univ	GA	2,445	LC
Coastal Carolina Univ	SC	13,140	C
College of Charleston	SC	13,616	VC
College of Mount St. Joseph	OH	24,860	C
College of Our Lady of the Elms	MA	21,000	C
Columbia College	MO	16,900	C
Columbus State Univ	GA	8,664	C
Concord College	WV	9,708	C
Concordia College: Moorhead	MN	22,475	VC
Concordia Univ Nebr	NE	20,500	C+
Concordia Univ St.Paul	MN	27,776	C
Concordia Univ, River Forest	IL	26,300	C
Cornerstone Univ and Grand Rapids Theological Seminary	MI	21,350	NC
Covenant College	GA	26,460	VC+
Cumberland Univ	TN	18,894	C
Dickinson State Univ	ND	7,847	NC
East Carolina Univ	NC	10,000	C
Eastern Illinois Univ	IL	12,569	C
Eastern Kentucky Univ	KY	7,725	C
Eastern Mich Univ	MI	12,897	C
Eastern Washington Univ	WA	10,608	C
Elizabeth City State Univ	NC	5,700	LC
Elon Univ	NC	25,371	HC
Fairmont State	WV	8,400	LC
Fayetteville State Univ	NC	6,000	LC
Fitchburg State College	MA	11,276	C
Florida Southern College	FL	25,965	C
Fontbonne Univ	MO	23,308	C
Fort Valley State Univ	GA	6,975	C
Freed-Hardeman Univ	TN	16,370	NC
Frostburg State Univ	MD	12,672	C
Gardner-Webb Univ	NC	21,500	C
George Fox Univ	OR	28,490	C
Georgia College and State Univ	GA	11,020	C
Georgia Southern Univ	GA	9,762	C
Georgia Southwestern State Univ	GA	6,035	C
Glenville State College	WV	8,778	NC
Gordon College	MA	29,194	C+
Goshen College	IN	22,850	VC
Grand Valley State Univ	MI	12,000	VC
Greensboro College	NC	23,000	C
Gustavus Adolphus College	MN	30,920	HC
Hardin-Simmons Univ	TX	18,641	C
Harris-Stowe State College	MO	3,200	SP
Heidelberg College	OH	23,242	C
High Point Univ	NC	25,720	C
Hillsdale College	MI	24,160	HC
Humboldt State Univ	CA	11,176	C
Illinois State Univ	IL	12,839	C+
Immaculata Univ	PA	25,350	C
Indiana State Univ	IN	11,604	C
Iona College	NY	30,878	VC
Ithaca College	NY	35,144	VC
John Brown Univ	AR	20,910	VC
Johnson C. Smith Univ	NC	20,000	C
Johnson State College	VT	11,830	LC
Kennesaw State Univ	GA	12,152	C
Kentucky Christian College	KY	12,680	C
Kentucky Wesleyan College	KY	18,590	C
King's College	PA	29,810	C
LaGrange College	GA	22,874	C+
Lake Erie College	OH	27,725	C
Lenoir-Rhyne College	NC	25,580	C
Lesley Univ	MA	34,950	C
Lincoln Memorial Univ	TN	18,144	C
Lubbock Christian Univ	TX	16,960	C
Malone College	OH	23,040	C
Manchester College	IN	23,470	C
Manhattan College	NY	29,000	VC
Marian College of Fond du Lac	WI	21,775	LC
Mars Hill College	NC	19,000	LC
Marshall Univ	WV	9,116	C
Maryville Univ of St. Louis	MO	23,000	VC
McMurry Univ	TX	18,100	LC
Methodist College	NC	21,000	C
Miami Univ	OH	29,097	HC
Midland Lutheran College	NE	18,600	C
Millikin Univ	IL	25,590	C
Missouri Baptist Univ	MO	19,640	C
Missouri Southern State Univ	MO	8,396	NC
Missouri State Univ	MO	10,748	C+
Montana State Univ-Billings	MT	8,906	C
Morehead State Univ	KY	9,150	C
Mount Olive College	NC	16,000	LC
Mount Union College	OH	25,840	C
Mount Vernon Nazarene Univ	OH	20,810	C
Murray State Univ	KY	8,900	VC
Nazareth College of Rochester	NY	28,175	VC
Nebr Wesleyan Univ	NE	23,415	C+
New York Inst of Technology	NY	28,126	VC
Niagara Univ	NY	28,250	C
N Car Central Univ	NC	9,000	LC
N Car State Univ	NC	11,824	HC
N Car Wesleyan College	NC	22,670	C
North Georgia College and State Univ	GA	7,000	C
Northern Kentucky Univ	KY	6,670	NC
Northern State Univ	SD	8,257	C
Northland College	WI	26,680	C+
Northwest Missouri State Univ	MO	10,000	C
Northwest Univ	WA	18,854	C
Northwestern College of Iowa	IA	22,174	C+
Notre Dame College	OH	20,425	C
Oakland City Univ	IN	19,620	NC
Ohio Dominican Univ	OH	25,954	C
Ohio Northern Univ	OH	27,765	VC
Ohio Univ	OH	15,921	C
Ohio Wesleyan Univ	OH	35,830	VC+
Okla Christian Univ	OK	18,992	NC
Okla Wesleyan Univ	OK	18,950	NC
Ouachita Baptist Univ	AR	21,900	VC
Paine College	GA	14,418	LC
Philander Smith College	AR	13,230	LC
Piedmont College	GA	20,500	C
Pikeville College	KY	16,500	NC
Presbyterian College	SC	30,044	VC
Prescott College	AZ	13,445	LC
Rhode Island College	RI	11,570	C
Ripon College	WI	27,160	C+
St. Francis College	NY	19,974	LC
St. John's Univ	NY	34,370	C
St. Joseph's College	IN	26,600	C
St. Leo Univ	FL	22,140	C+
St. Mary-of-the-Woods College	IN	25,480	C
St. Xavier Univ	IL	23,160	C
Schreiner Univ	TX	20,600	C
Shorter College	GA	19,700	C
Southeast Missouri State Univ	MO	10,596	C
Southeastern Louisiana Univ	LA	8,521	LC
Southeastern Univ	FL	17,180	LC
Southern Arkansas Univ	AR	6,956	C
Southern Univ and A&M College	LA	8,238	LC
Southwest Baptist Univ	MO	18,300	C
Spalding Univ	KY	18,882	C
Springfield College	MA	25,000	C
SUNY at Potsdam	NY	12,959	C
SUNY/College at Cortland	NY	12,095	C
SUNY/College at Fredonia	NY	12,771	VC
SUNY/College at Old Westbury	NY	13,154	C
SUNY/Univ at New Paltz	NY	12,480	VC
Syracuse Univ	NY	38,655	HC
Tabor College	KS	21,614	NC
Temple Univ	PA	17,438	C
Texas Christian Univ	TX	23,410	VC+
Texas Tech Univ	TX	13,026	VC
Texas Wesleyan Univ	TX	18,700	C
Thomas More College	KY	24,470	C
Thomas Univ	GA	11,520	NC
Toccoa Falls College	GA	17,125	C
Transylvania Univ	KY	26,240	VC+
Tusculum College	TN	21,340	LC
Union College	KY	18,920	C
Union Univ	TN	20,750	VC
Univ of Arkansas	AR	11,859	VC
Univ of Arkansas at Monticello	AR	7,325	NC
Univ of Arkansas at Pine Bluff	AR	8,300	C
Univ of Central Arkansas	AR	9,984	C
Univ of Cincinnati	OH	17,682	C
Univ of Detroit Mercy	MI	27,000	C
Univ of Findlay	OH	29,238	C
Univ of Georgia	GA	11,004	HC
Univ of Great Falls	MT	17,000	C
Univ of Indianapolis	IN	25,090	C
Univ of Iowa	IA	12,172	VC
Univ of Kansas	KS	10,915	VC
Univ of Kentucky	KY	7,800	C
Univ of Louisville	KY	10,400	VC
Univ of Mary Hardin-Baylor	TX	19,428	C
Univ of Missouri/Columbia	MO	13,500	VC
Univ of Montana--Western	MT	8,406	NC
Univ of Nebr at Kearney	NE	9,000	NC
Univ of Nebr at Lincoln	NE	11,401	VC
Univ of N Car at Chapel Hill	NC	11,129	MC
Univ of N Car at Charlotte	NC	9,101	C
Univ of N Car at Greensboro	NC	8,993	C
Univ of N Car at Pembroke	NC	7,940	LC
Univ of N Car at Wilmington	NC	10,107	VC
Univ of N Dak	ND	10,114	VC
Univ of North Florida	FL	9,908	VC
Univ of Northern Iowa	IA	11,133	C
Univ of San Francisco	CA	37,560	VC
Univ of Sioux Falls	SD	20,800	C
Univ of S Car Upstate	SC	11,957	C
Univ of Southern Indiana	IN	12,590	LC
Univ of Southern Miss	MS	10,112	C
Univ of the Cumberlands	KY	18,184	C
Univ of the Ozarks	AR	19,250	C
Univ of Vermont	VT	18,080	VC
Univ of West Alabama	AL	7,611	C
Univ of West Florida	FL	8,559	C
Univ of West Georgia	GA	8,838	C
Univ of Wisc/Platteville	WI	9,779	NC
Univ of Wisc/Whitewater	WI	9,274	C
Urbana Univ	OH	21,190	C
Ursuline College	OH	25,456	C
Valdosta State Univ	GA	8,802	C
Valparaiso Univ	IN	28,970	VC+
Wagner College	NY	33,300	VC
Walsh Univ	OH	23,440	C
Warren Wilson College	NC	24,382	NC
Washington Univ in St. Louis	MO	42,106	MC
Wesleyan College	GA	19,560	C
West Liberty State College	WV	9,142	LC
Western Carolina Univ	NC	7,000	C
Western Kentucky Univ	KY	10,192	C
Westfield State College	MA	10,200	C
Westminster College	MO	19,060	VC
William Woods Univ	MO	21,020	C
Wingate Univ	NC	23,300	C
Wittenberg Univ	OH	34,596	VC
Xavier Univ	OH	30,490	HC
York College	NE	16,330	NC
Youngstown State Univ	OH	12,613	NC

MILITARY SCIENCE

School	ST	$IS	SR
Austin Peay State Univ	TN	7,535	C
Campbell Univ	NC	21,137	VC
Eastern Mich Univ	MI	12,897	C
Eastern Washington Univ	WA	10,608	C
Elon Univ	NC	25,371	HC
Florida Inst of Technology	FL	29,720	VC
Hawaii Pacific Univ	HI	21,080	C
Norfolk State Univ	VA	10,531	LC
Norwich Univ	VT	28,212	C
Rochester Inst of Technology	NY	32,070	VC+
Rockford College	IL	28,330	VC
United States Air Force Academy	CO		HC+
United States Military Academy	NY		MC

MINING AND MINERAL ENGINEERING

School	ST	$IS	SR
Colo School of Mines	CO	14,893	HC
Columbia Univ/Fu Foundation School of Engineering and Applied Science	NY	42,584	MC
Montana Tech of The Univ of Montana	MT	10,434	C
New Mexico Inst of Mining and Technology	NM	8,510	VC+
Penn State Univ/Univ Park Campus	PA	18,038	HC
S Dak School of Mines and Technology	SD	7,624	C+
Southern Illinois Univ Carbondale	IL	12,391	C
Univ of Alaska Fairbanks	AK	10,101	C
Univ of Arizona	AZ	11,958	VC
Univ of Idaho	ID	9,310	NC
Univ of Kentucky	KY	7,800	C
Univ of Missouri/Rolla	MO	13,332	NC
Univ of Nevada/Reno	NV	12,155	NC
Univ of Utah	UT	10,162	VC
Virginia Polytechnic Inst and State Univ	VA	10,834	C
West Virginia Univ	WV	10,506	C

MINISTRIES

School	ST	$IS	SR
Abilene Christian Univ	TX	20,830	C
American Indian College of the Assemblies of God	AZ	9,405	LC
Asbury College	KY	23,762	VC
Atlantic Union College	MA	17,600	LC
Azusa Pacific Univ	CA	28,546	VC
Bethany College	KS	20,660	VC
Bethel College	IN	19,680	VC
Clearwater Christian College	FL	13,160	LC
College of St. Benedict	MN	30,091	VC
Concordia College: Moorhead	MN	22,475	VC
Concordia Univ Wisc	WI	22,660	VC
Creighton Univ	NE	29,918	VC+
Crichton College	TN	15,300	C
Dakota Wesleyan Univ	SD	17,832	C
East Texas Baptist Univ	TX	16,713	C
Eastern Mennonite Univ	VA	25,450	VC
Eastern Nazarene College	MA	19,500	LC
Freed-Hardeman Univ	TN	16,370	NC
Fresno Pacific Univ	CA	25,454	C
Geneva College	PA	21,850	C
George Fox Univ	OR	28,490	C
Greenville College	IL	23,146	C
Harding Univ	AR	16,512	VC
Hardin-Simmons Univ	TX	18,641	C
Hope International Univ	CA	23,700	NC
Houghton College	NY	25,980	VC+
Huntington Univ	IN	24,830	C
Indiana Wesleyan Univ	IN	22,074	C+
John Brown Univ	AR	20,910	VC
Kentucky Christian College	KY	12,680	C
Lindenwood Univ	MO	18,600	VC
Lubbock Christian Univ	TX	16,960	C
Malone College	OH	23,040	C
Marylhurst Univ	OR	14,220	NC
Messiah College	PA	28,910	VC+
MidAmerica Nazarene Univ	KS	20,584	LC
Missouri Baptist Univ	MO	19,640	C
Mount Olive College	NC	16,000	LC
North Central Univ	MN	16,646	LC
Northwest Christian College	OR	24,298	C
Northwest Nazarene Univ	ID	22,590	VC
Northwest Univ	WA	18,854	C

ST = STATE $IS = IN-STATE COSTS   SR = SELECTOR RATING

School	ST	$IS	SR
Pacific Lutheran Univ	WA	28,805	VC
Pacific Union College	CA	24,555	VC+
Pacific Univ	OR	24,250	C
Paine College	GA	14,418	LC
Palm Beach Atlantic Univ	FL	23,597	VC
Park Univ	MO	11,592	C
Paul Quinn College	TX	8,300	LC
Penn State Univ/Univ Park Campus	PA	18,038	HC
Pepperdine Univ	CA	39,960	HC
Peru State College	NE	6,350	NC
Pfeiffer Univ	NC	21,900	C
Philadelphia Biblical Univ	PA	22,425	C
Philander Smith College	AR	13,230	LC
Piedmont College	GA	20,500	C
Pittsburg State Univ	KS	8,112	C
Pitzer College	CA	41,644	HC
Plymouth State Univ	NH	12,298	LC
Point Loma Nazarene Univ	CA	27,610	VC
Pomona College	CA	40,774	MC
Portland State Univ	OR	12,453	C
Prairie View A&M Univ	TX	11,110	LC
Presbyterian College	SC	30,044	VC
Princeton Univ	NJ	40,213	MC
Principia College	IL	27,765	VC+
Providence College	RI	34,580	HC
Queens Univ of Charlotte	NC	24,528	C
Quincy Univ	IL	24,920	C
Radford Univ	VA	13,145	C
Ramapo College of New Jersey	NJ	16,630	VC
Randolph-Macon College	VA	31,250	C
Randolph-Macon Woman's College	VA	31,160	VC+
Reed College	OR	41,106	MC
Rhode Island College	RI	11,570	C
Rhodes College	TN	32,860	HC
Rice Univ	TX	32,290	MC
Richard Stockton College of New Jersey	NJ	14,000	VC
Rider Univ	NJ	32,560	C
Ripon College	WI	27,160	C
Roanoke College	VA	30,748	VC
Roberts Wesleyan College	NY	26,378	C
Rochester College	MI	15,636	C+
Rockford College	IL	28,330	VC
Roosevelt Univ	IL	22,605	VC
Rowan Univ	NJ	16,000	VC
Rust College	MS		C+
Rutgers, The State Univ of New Jersey/Camden Campus	NJ	15,000	VC
Rutgers, The State Univ of New Jersey/New Brunswick/Piscataway Campus	NJ	15,810	HC
Rutgers, The State Univ of New Jersey/Newark Campus	NJ	15,640	VC
Saginaw Valley State Univ	MI	11,432	C
St. Ambrose Univ	IA	25,495	C
St. Augustine's College	NC	14,000	LC
St. Bonaventure Univ	NY	28,785	LC
St. Cloud State Univ	MN	10,010	C
St. John's Univ	MN	29,749	VC
St. Joseph's College	IN	26,600	C
St. Lawrence Univ	NY	40,545	VC
St. Louis Univ	MO	33,158	VC+
St. Martin's Univ	WA	27,555	C
St. Mary-of-the-Woods College	IN	25,480	C
St. Mary's College	IN	32,538	VC
St. Mary's College of Maryland	MD	18,876	VC+
St. Mary's Univ of San Antonio	TX	22,444	C
St. Michael's College	VT	33,330	VC
St. Norbert College	WI	28,577	C+
St. Olaf College	MN	32,800	HC
St. Vincent College	PA	26,160	VC
St. Xavier Univ	IL	23,160	C
Salem College	NC	26,226	VC+
Salisbury Univ	MD	13,128	VC
Salve Regina Univ	RI	33,450	C
Sam Houston State Univ	TX	8,000	C
Samford Univ	AL	20,258	VC
San Diego Christian College	CA	24,172	C
San Diego State Univ	CA	12,971	C
San Francisco Conservatory of Music	CA	26,200	SP
San Francisco State Univ	CA	13,000	C
San Jose State Univ	CA	11,707	C
Santa Clara Univ	CA	38,931	VC
Sarah Lawrence College	NY	42,000	HC
Savannah State Univ	GA	7,772	LC
Schreiner Univ	TX	20,600	C
Scripps College	CA	41,000	MC
Seattle Pacific Univ	WA	29,355	VC
Seton Hall Univ	NJ	33,622	VC
Seton Hill Univ	PA	28,810	C
Shenandoah Univ	VA	27,600	C
Shepherd Univ	WV	10,066	VC
Shorter College	GA	19,700	C
Siena Heights Univ	MI	17,000	LC
Sierra Nevada College	NV	30,235	C
Silver Lake College of the Holy Family	WI	18,500	LC
Simmons College	MA	35,640	VC
Simpson College	IA	26,833	VC
Simpson Univ	CA	22,900	C
Skidmore College	NY	41,779	HC
Slippery Rock Univ of Pennsylvania	PA	10,360	LC
Smith College	MA	41,474	MC
Sonoma State Univ	CA	14,732	C
S Dak State Univ	SD	9,815	C
Southeast Missouri State Univ	MO	10,596	C
Southeastern Louisiana Univ	LA	8,521	LC
Southeastern Okla State Univ	OK	6,147	C
Southeastern Univ	FL	17,180	LC
Southern Adventist Univ	TN	18,500	C
Southern Illinois Univ Carbondale	IL	12,391	C
Southern Illinois Univ Edwardsville	IL	11,022	C
Southern Nazarene Univ	OK	14,634	NC
Southern Oregon Univ	OR	12,186	C
Southern Univ and A&M College	LA	8,238	LC
Southern Utah Univ	UT		C
Southern Wesleyan Univ	SC	21,675	C
Southwest Baptist Univ	MO	18,300	C
Southwest Minn State Univ	MN	10,975	C
Southwestern Adventist Univ	TX	18,290	LC
Southwestern College	KS	21,476	C
Southwestern Univ	TX	26,767	HC
Spelman College	GA	24,650	VC
Spring Arbor Univ	MI	22,476	C
Stanford Univ	CA	41,557	MC
SUNY at Oswego	NY	13,662	VC
SUNY at Potsdam	NY	12,959	C
SUNY/College at Buffalo	NY	11,903	C+
SUNY/College at Fredonia	NY	12,771	VC
SUNY/College at Geneseo	NY	12,910	HC+
SUNY/College at Oneonta	NY	12,905	VC
SUNY/College at Plattsburgh	NY	12,362	C
SUNY/College of Purchase	NY	11,989	VC+
SUNY/Univ at Albany	NY	13,860	VC
SUNY/Univ at Binghamton	NY	13,988	HC
SUNY/Univ at Buffalo	NY	13,694	VC
SUNY/Univ at New Paltz	NY	12,480	VC
SUNY/Univ at Stony Brook	NY	13,625	HC
Stephen F. Austin State Univ	TX	7,930	C
Sterling College	KS	19,992	C
Stetson Univ	FL	32,725	VC
Stillman College	AL	11,475	LC
Susquehanna Univ	PA	33,465	VC
Swarthmore College	PA	41,280	MC
Sweet Briar College	VA	31,460	VC
Syracuse Univ	NY	38,655	HC
Tabor College	KS	21,614	NC
Tarleton State Univ	TX	8,952	C
Taylor Univ	IN	26,376	VC+
Temple Univ	PA	17,438	C
Tenn State Univ	TN	9,048	LC
Tenn Wesleyan College	TN	18,650	C
Texas A&M Univ at Commerce	TX	9,020	C
Texas A&M Univ at Corpus Christi	TX	10,280	LC
Texas A&M Univ at Kingsville	TX	6,800	LC
Texas Christian Univ	TX	23,410	VC+
Texas Lutheran Univ	TX	23,530	C
Texas Southern Univ	TX	9,828	C
Texas State Univ - San Marcos	TX	10,862	C
Texas Tech Univ	TX	13,026	VC
Texas Wesleyan Univ	TX	18,700	C
Texas Woman's Univ	TX	7,804	LC
Thomas Edison State College	NJ	3,780	SP
Toccoa Falls College	GA	17,125	C
Towson Univ	MD	13,924	VC
Transylvania Univ	KY	26,240	VC+
Trevecca Nazarene Univ	TN	19,594	C
Trinity Christian College	IL	23,645	C
Trinity College	CT	38,040	HC+
Trinity International Univ	IL	25,686	C
Trinity Univ	TX	30,157	HC+
Truman State Univ	MO	11,242	HC
Tufts Univ	MA	42,018	MC
Tulane Univ	LA	41,098	MC
Union College	NE	18,710	C
Union Univ	TN	20,750	VC
Universidad Adventista de las Antillas	PR	7,360	
Univ of Akron	OH	15,166	NC
Univ of Alabama	AL	9,888	C
Univ of Alabama at Birmingham	AL	13,716	C
Univ of Alabama in Huntsville	AL	9,516	VC
Univ of Alaska Anchorage	AK	11,275	NC
Univ of Alaska Fairbanks	AK	10,101	C
Univ of Arizona	AZ	11,958	VC
Univ of Arkansas	AR	11,859	VC
Univ of Arkansas at Little Rock	AR	7,230	NC
Univ of Arkansas at Monticello	AR	7,325	NC
Univ of Arkansas at Pine Bluff	AR	8,300	C
Univ of at Calif Davis	CA	15,010	VC
Univ of Bridgeport	CT	29,595	LC
Univ of Calif at Berkeley	CA	18,141	HC+
Univ of Calif at Irvine	CA	16,475	HC
Univ of Calif at Los Angeles	CA	17,681	MC
Univ of Calif at Riverside	CA	16,625	C
Univ of Calif at San Diego	CA	16,102	HC
Univ of Calif at Santa Barbara	CA	11,800	VC
Univ of Calif at Santa Cruz	CA	19,174	VC
Univ of Central Arkansas	AR	9,984	C
Univ of Central Florida	FL	10,739	VC
Univ of Central Okla	OK	8,094	C
Univ of Chicago	IL	42,369	MC
Univ of Cincinnati	OH	17,682	C
Univ of Colo at Boulder	CO	13,352	C+
Univ of Colo at Denver and Health Sciences Center	CO	5,021	C
Univ of Conn	CT	16,628	HC
Univ of Dayton	OH	28,826	VC
Univ of Delaware	DE	14,142	HC
Univ of Denver	CO	36,376	VC+
Univ of Evansville	IN	28,320	VC
Univ of Florida	FL	9,354	HC
Univ of Georgia	GA	11,004	HC
Univ of Hartford	CT	34,044	C
Univ of Hawaii at Hilo	HI	6,500	C
Univ of Hawaii at Manoa	HI	10,413	VC
Univ of Houston	TX	7,000	C
Univ of Idaho	ID	9,310	NC
Univ of Illinois at Chicago	IL	16,256	VC
Univ of Illinois at Urbana-Champaign	IL	15,800	HC+
Univ of Indianapolis	IN	25,090	C
Univ of Iowa	IA	12,172	VC
Univ of Kentucky	KY	7,800	C
Univ of La Verne	CA	33,470	C
Univ of Louisiana at Lafayette	LA	5,830	C
Univ of Louisiana at Monroe	LA	7,103	C
Univ of Louisville	KY	10,400	VC
Univ of Maine	ME	13,642	C
Univ of Maine at Farmington	ME	11,515	C
Univ of Mary	ND	15,374	C
Univ of Mary Hardin-Baylor	TX	19,428	C
Univ of Mary Washington	VA	11,636	HC
Univ of Maryland/Baltimore County	MD	16,642	VC+
Univ of Maryland/College Park	MD	16,036	HC
Univ of Mass Amherst	MA	15,973	C+
Univ of Mass Boston	MA	8,024	C
Univ of Mass Dartmouth	MA	15,985	C
Univ of Memphis	TN	11,153	C
Univ of Miami	FL	38,397	MC
Univ of Mich/Ann Arbor	MI	16,587	HC+
Univ of Mich/Flint	MI	6,398	C
Univ of Minn/Duluth	MN	13,974	C
Univ of Minn/Morris	MN	15,472	VC
Univ of Minn/Twin Cities	MN	13,165	HC
Univ of Miss	MS	9,000	C
Univ of Missouri/Columbia	MO	13,500	VC
Univ of Missouri/Kansas City	MO	15,000	VC
Univ of Missouri/St. Louis	MO	14,046	VC
Univ of Mobile	AL	16,880	C
Univ of Montana	MT	10,602	C
Univ of Montevallo	AL	9,630	C
Univ of Nebr at Kearney	NE	9,000	NC
Univ of Nebr at Lincoln	NE	11,401	VC
Univ of Nebr at Omaha	NE	11,235	C
Univ of Nevada/Las Vegas	NV	11,566	C
Univ of Nevada/Reno	NV	12,155	NC
Univ of New Hampshire	NH	16,810	VC
Univ of New Haven	CT	31,794	C
Univ of New Mexico	NM	11,253	C
Univ of New Orleans	LA	7,370	C
Univ of N Alabama	AL	8,992	C
Univ of N Car at Asheville	NC	9,237	VC
Univ of N Car at Chapel Hill	NC	11,129	MC
Univ of N Car at Charlotte	NC	9,101	C
Univ of N Car at Greensboro	NC	8,993	C
Univ of N Car at Pembroke	NC	7,940	C
Univ of N Car at Wilmington	NC	10,107	VC
Univ of N Dak	ND	10,114	VC
Univ of North Florida	FL	9,908	VC
Univ of North Texas	TX	7,800	C
Univ of Northern Colo	CO	10,249	C
Univ of Northern Iowa	IA	11,133	C
Univ of Notre Dame	IN	39,552	MC
Univ of Okla	OK	10,769	VC+
Univ of Oregon	OR	13,108	VC
Univ of Pennsylvania	PA	41,766	MC
Univ of Pittsburgh at Pittsburgh	PA	18,866	HC
Univ of Portland	OR	32,300	VC
Univ of PR/Rio Piedras	PR	5,750	
Univ of Puget Sound	WA	35,600	HC
Univ of Redlands	CA	36,160	HC
Univ of Rhode Island	RI	15,398	C
Univ of Richmond	VA	40,510	MC
Univ of Rio Grande	OH	8,728	NC
Univ of Rochester	NY	41,135	MC
Univ of St. Francis	IL	25,430	C
Univ of St. Thomas	MN	28,000	VC
Univ of St. Thomas	TX	23,810	VC
Univ of San Diego	CA	40,620	HC
Univ of Science and Arts of Okla	OK	7,650	C
Univ of Sioux Falls	SD	20,800	C
Univ of South Alabama	AL	8,930	LC
Univ of S Car at Columbia	SC	13,397	VC
Univ of S Dak	SD	9,068	C
Univ of South Florida	FL	10,284	VC
Univ of Southern Calif	CA	41,618	MC
Univ of Southern Maine	ME	12,614	C
Univ of Southern Miss	MS	10,112	C
Univ of Tampa	FL	25,784	C
Univ of Tenn at Chattanooga	TN	7,790	C
Univ of Tenn at Knoxville	TN	11,720	C
Univ of Tenn at Martin	TN	8,693	C
Univ of Texas at Arlington	TX	7,195	C
Univ of Texas at Austin	TX	14,610	HC
Univ of Texas at El Paso	TX	8,764	NC
Univ of Texas at San Antonio	TX	11,325	LC
Univ of Texas-Pan American	TX	7,290	C+
Univ of the Cumberlands	KY	18,184	C
Univ of the District of Columbia	DC	2,070	LC
Univ of the Incarnate Word	TX	23,306	C
Univ of the Ozarks	AR	19,250	C
Univ of the Pacific	CA	34,380	VC
Univ of the South	TN	34,645	NC
Univ of Toledo	OH	15,806	NC
Univ of Tulsa	OK	25,348	NC
Univ of Utah	UT	10,162	VC
Univ of Vermont	VT	18,080	VC
Univ of Virginia	VA	13,759	MC
Univ of West Florida	FL	8,559	C
Univ of West Georgia	GA	8,838	C
Univ of Wisc/Eau Claire	WI	9,915	VC
Univ of Wisc/Green Bay	WI	9,415	VC
Univ of Wisc/La Crosse	WI	10,045	VC
Univ of Wisc/Madison	WI	13,117	HC
Univ of Wisc/Milwaukee	WI	9,427	LC
Univ of Wisc/Oshkosh	WI	10,426	LC
Univ of Wisc/Parkside	WI	10,181	C
Univ of Wisc/Platteville	WI	9,779	NC
Univ of Wisc/River Falls	WI	9,722	LC
Univ of Wisc/Stevens Point	WI	9,384	VC
Univ of Wisc/Superior	WI	9,610	C+
Univ of Wisc/Whitewater	WI	9,274	C
Univ of Wyoming	WY	9,666	C
Utah State Univ	UT	8,002	VC
Valdosta State Univ	GA	8,802	C
Valley City State Univ	ND	9,854	LC
Valparaiso Univ	IN	28,970	VC+
Vanguard Univ of Southern Calif	CA	27,071	C
Vassar College	NY	41,700	MC
Virginia Commonwealth Univ	VA	12,987	C
Virginia Polytechnic Inst and State Univ	VA	10,834	VC
Virginia Union Univ	VA	18,432	LC
Virginia Wesleyan College	VA	28,433	C
Viterbo Univ	WI	21,670	C
Wabash College	IN	30,116	HC
Wagner College	NY	33,300	VC
Wake Forest Univ	NC	38,290	MC
Walla Walla College	WA	24,489	NC
Warner Pacific College	OR	21,900	C
Wartburg College	IA	27,315	NC
Washburn Univ	KS	9,734	NC
Washington and Jefferson College	PA	33,490	VC
Washington and Lee Univ	VA	35,880	MC
Washington College	MD	34,990	VC
Washington State Univ	WA	12,260	C
Washington Univ in St. Louis	MO	42,106	MC
Wayland Baptist Univ	TX	13,484	C
Wayne State College	NE	8,033	NC
Wayne State Univ	MI	11,805	C
Weber State Univ	UT	9,635	NC
Webster Univ	MO	24,280	VC
Wellesley College	MA	41,030	MC
Wells College	NY	23,070	VC
Wesleyan College	GA	19,560	C
Wesleyan Univ	CT	42,122	MC
West Chester Univ of Pennsylvania	PA	12,355	C+
West Liberty State College	WV	9,142	LC
West Texas A&M Univ	TX	8,452	C
West Virginia Univ	WV	10,506	C
West Virginia Wesleyan College	WV	26,880	C
Western Baptist College	OR	21,808	C
Western Carolina Univ	NC	7,000	C

ST = STATE $IS = IN-STATE COSTS   SR = SELECTOR RATING

School	ST	$IS	SR
Western Conn State Univ	CT	12,993	C
Western Illinois Univ	IL	13,042	C
Western Kentucky Univ	KY	10,192	C
Western Mich Univ	MI	13,299	C
Western New Mexico Univ	NM	7,233	LC
Western Oregon Univ	OR	10,295	C
Western State College of Colo	CO	9,942	C
Western Washington Univ	WA	11,262	VC
Westfield State College	MA	10,200	C
Westminster Choir College	NJ	32,670	SP
Westminster College	PA	31,290	C+
Westmont College	CA	36,672	NC
Wheaton College	IL	27,760	HC
Wheaton College	MA	40,180	HC+
Whitman College	WA	36,110	HC+
Whittier College	CA	29,108	C
Whitworth College	WA	29,428	VC+
Wichita State Univ	KS	8,500	C
Wilberforce Univ	OH	14,937	LC
Wiley College	TX	8,100	LC
Wilkes Univ	PA	30,886	C
Willamette Univ	OR	35,416	VC+
William Carey College	MS	11,000	LC
William Jewell College	MO	24,340	C
William Paterson Univ of New Jersey	NJ	17,810	C
William Tyndale College	MI	13,000	NC
Williams Baptist College	AR	13,450	C
Williams College	MA	40,310	MC
Wingate Univ	NC	23,300	C
Winona State Univ	MN	11,333	C
Winthrop Univ	SC	11,302	C
Wisc Lutheran College	WI	23,510	VC
Wittenberg Univ	OH	34,596	VC
Wright State Univ	OH	13,616	LC
Xavier Univ	OH	30,490	HC
Xavier Univ of Louisiana	LA	17,600	C
Yale Univ	CT	41,000	MC
Yeshiva Univ	NY	22,000	C
York College of Pennsylvania	PA	16,550	VC
Youngstown State Univ	OH	12,613	NC

MUSIC BUSINESS MANAGEMENT

School	ST	$IS	SR
Albright College	PA	33,920	C
Anderson Univ	IN	25,050	C
Appalachian State Univ	NC	8,000	VC
Belmont Univ	TN	24,110	VC
Berklee College of Music	MA	37,779	SP
Blackburn College	IL	13,690	C
Bradley Univ	IL	25,280	VC
Butler Univ	IN	31,944	VC+
Central Washington Univ	WA	11,730	C
College of the Ozarks	MO	4,130	VC+
Columbia College Chicago	IL	25,125	LC
DePaul Univ	IL	29,835	VC
DePauw Univ	IN	32,100	VC
Dillard Univ	LA	17,500	VC
Drake Univ	IA	27,632	VC+
Elmhurst College	IL	24,685	C
Five Towns College	NY	24,600	SP
Geneva College	PA	21,850	C
Georgia State Univ	GA	11,444	VC
Greenville College	IL	23,146	C
Grove City College	PA	15,784	HC+
Hardin-Simmons Univ	TX	18,641	C
Hofstra Univ	NY	32,630	VC
Howard Univ	DC	18,481	C+
Huntington Univ	IN	24,830	C
Johnson C. Smith Univ	NC	20,000	C
Johnson State College	VT	11,830	LC
Kentucky Wesleyan College	KY	18,590	C
Lewis Univ	IL	23,050	C+
Loyola Univ New Orleans	LA	31,050	VC+
Mansfield Univ	PA	11,300	C
Marian College of Fond du Lac	WI	21,775	LC
Middle Tenn State Univ	TN	8,540	C
Minn State Univ, Mankato	MN	10,276	LC
Monmouth Univ	NJ	28,956	C
Montreat College	NC	21,440	C
New York Univ	NY	43,170	MC
Northwest Univ	WA	18,854	C
Oakwood College	AL	14,904	C
Ohio Northern Univ	OH	27,765	VC
Peru State College	NE	6,350	NC
Point Loma Nazarene Univ	CA	27,610	VC
Quincy Univ	IL	24,920	C
St. Augustine's College	NC	14,000	LC
St. Joseph's College	IN	26,600	C
St. Mary's Univ of Minn	MN	23,857	VC
S Car State Univ	SC	6,700	LC
S Dak State Univ	SD	9,815	C
Southern Nazarene Univ	OK	14,634	NC
Southern Oregon Univ	OR	12,186	C
SUNY at Potsdam	NY	12,959	C
SUNY/College at Oneonta	NY	12,905	VC
Syracuse Univ	NY	38,655	HC
Trevecca Nazarene Univ	TN	19,594	C
Univ of Evansville	IN	28,320	VC
Univ of Hartford	CT	34,044	C
Univ of Memphis	TN	11,153	C
Univ of New Haven	CT	31,794	C
Univ of St. Thomas	MN	28,000	VC
Univ of Texas at San Antonio	TX	11,325	LC
Univ of the Incarnate Word	TX	23,306	C
Univ of the Pacific	CA	34,380	VC
Wingate Univ	NC	23,300	C
Winston-Salem State Univ	NC	8,960	LC

MUSIC EDUCATION

School	ST	$IS	SR
Abilene Christian Univ	TX	20,830	C
Adams State College	CO	8,613	C
Adelphi Univ	NY	27,000	VC
Alabama A&M Univ	AL	8,890	LC
Alabama State Univ	AL	7,658	C
Albany State Univ	GA	5,770	C+
Alcorn State Univ	MS	8,190	LC
Alderson-Broaddus College	WV	24,006	C
Anderson Univ	IN	25,050	LC
Andrews Univ	MI	21,786	C
Anna Maria College	MA	29,815	LC
Appalachian State Univ	NC	8,000	VC
Aquinas College	MI	23,750	C
Arcadia Univ	PA	33,570	VC
Arizona State Univ-Tempe	AZ	11,174	C
Arkansas State Univ	AR	9,630	C
Arkansas Tech Univ	AR	8,108	VC
Armstrong Atlantic State Univ	GA	7,394	C
Asbury College	KY	23,762	VC
Ashland Univ	OH	25,000	C
Atlantic Union College	MA	17,600	LC
Augsburg College	MN	28,300	C
Augusta State Univ	GA	2,920	C
Augustana College	IL	29,862	VC+
Augustana College	SD	24,380	VC
Azusa Pacific Univ	CA	28,546	VC
Baker Univ	KS	22,190	C
Baldwin-Wallace College	OH	27,256	VC
Ball State Univ	IN	13,138	C
Baylor Univ	TX	27,555	HC
Benedictine College	KS	21,968	C
Bennett College	NC	11,500	C
Berea College	KY	5,496	VC+
Berklee College of Music	MA	37,779	SP
Berry College	GA	24,342	VC
Bethany College	KS	20,660	C
Bethel College	IN	19,680	C
Bethel Univ	MN	29,840	VC
Bethune-Cookman College	FL	17,922	LC
Biola Univ	CA	29,372	VC
Birmingham-Southern College	AL	28,494	VC+
Black Hills State Univ	SD	7,800	LC
Blackburn College	IL	13,690	C
Blue Mountain College	MS	11,086	C
Bluffton College	OH	26,110	C
Boise State Univ	ID	9,438	LC
Boston Conservatory	MA	27,500	SP
Boston Univ	MA	42,046	HC+
Bradley Univ	IL	25,280	VC
Brenau Univ Women's College	GA	23,950	VC
Brewton-Parker College	GA	14,220	LC
Brigham Young Univ	UT	9,200	VC
Bucknell Univ	PA	39,660	MC
Buena Vista Univ	IA	27,742	C
Butler Univ	IN	31,944	VC+
Cal State, Fullerton	CA	10,990	C
Cal State, San Bernardino	CA	12,563	LC
Calvin College	MI	25,735	NC
Carnegie Mellon Univ	PA	32,700	MC
Carroll College	WI	24,860	C
Carson-Newman College	TN	16,800	C
Carthage College	WI	26,000	C
Case Western Reserve Univ	OH	37,314	MC
Catawba College	NC	25,000	C
Catholic Univ of America	DC	35,838	VC
Cedarville Univ	OH	21,904	VC
Centenary College of Louisiana	LA	24,760	VC
Central College	IA	26,774	VC
Central Conn State Univ	CT	13,620	C
Central Methodist Univ	MO	18,000	C
Central Mich Univ	MI	12,244	C
Central Missouri State Univ	MO	10,000	C
Central State Univ	OH	9,010	C+
Central Washington Univ	WA	11,730	C
Chapman Univ	CA	37,550	VC
Charleston Southern Univ	SC	17,800	C
Chicago State Univ	IL	10,915	C+
Christopher Newport Univ	VA	13,326	VC
CUNY/Brooklyn College	NY	4,377	C+
CUNY/Hunter College	NY	8,000	C+
CUNY/Queens College	NY	4,356	C
Claflin Univ	SC	16,798	C+
Clarion Univ of Pennsylvania	PA	11,844	C
Clarke College	IA	25,390	C
Clearwater Christian College	FL	13,160	LC
Cleveland Inst of Music	OH	35,880	SP
Coe College	IA	27,440	VC
Coker College	SC	21,600	C
College of New Jersey	NJ	18,315	MC
College of Notre Dame of Maryland	MD	27,700	C
College of St. Catherine	MN	27,505	VC
College of St. Rose	NY	25,684	C
College of the Ozarks	MO	4,130	VC+
Colo Christian Univ	CO	21,182	VC
Colo State Univ-Pueblo	CO	7,821	LC
Columbia College	SC	24,982	LC
Columbus State Univ	GA	8,664	C
Concord College	WV	9,708	C
Concordia College: Moorhead	MN	22,475	VC
Concordia College-New York	NY	27,740	C
Concordia Univ Nebr	NE	20,500	C+
Concordia Univ St.Paul	MN	27,776	C
Concordia Univ, River Forest	IL	26,300	C
Conn College	CT	41,975	MC
Converse College	SC	24,800	VC
Cornell College	IA	30,110	VC+
Cornerstone Univ and Grand Rapids Theological Seminary	MI	21,350	NC
Culver-Stockton College	MO	20,625	C
Cumberland Univ	TN	18,894	C
Dakota State Univ	SD	7,466	C
Dana College	NE	22,390	C
Delaware State Univ	DE	8,130	LC
Delta State Univ	MS	5,709	C
DePaul Univ	IL	29,835	VC
DePauw Univ	IN	32,100	HC
Dickinson State Univ	ND	7,847	NC
Dordt College	IA	20,325	VC
Dowling College	NY	22,110	LC
Drake Univ	IA	27,632	VC+
Drury Univ	MO	20,117	VC
Duquesne Univ	PA	29,534	VC
East Carolina Univ	NC	10,000	C
East Central Univ	OK	6,207	C
East Texas Baptist Univ	TX	16,713	C
Eastern Kentucky Univ	KY	7,725	C
Eastern Mich Univ	MI	12,897	C
Eastern Nazarene College	MA	19,500	LC
Eastern New Mexico Univ	NM	7,264	C
Eastern Washington Univ	WA	10,608	C
Eastman School of Music	NY	35,000	SP
Edinboro Univ of Pennsylvania	PA	11,809	LC
Elizabethtown College	PA	32,100	VC
Elmhurst College	IL	24,685	C
Elon Univ	NC	25,371	HC
Emporia State Univ	KS	8,093	C
Erskine College	SC	25,468	VC
Eureka College	IL	19,280	C
Evangel Univ	MO	17,380	C
Fairmont State	WV	8,400	LC
Fayetteville State Univ	NC	6,000	LC
Fisk Univ	TN	19,830	C
Five Towns College	NY	24,600	SP
Florida A&M Univ	FL	8,344	C
Florida International Univ	FL	9,215	VC
Florida Southern College	FL	25,965	C
Florida State Univ	FL	9,028	HC
Fort Hays State Univ	KS	7,638	C
Freed-Hardeman Univ	TN	16,370	NC
Fresno Pacific Univ	CA	25,454	C
Friends Univ	KS	16,250	LC
Furman Univ	SC	33,264	HC+
Gardner-Webb Univ	NC	21,500	C
Geneva College	PA	21,850	C
George Fox Univ	OR	28,490	C
Georgetown College	KY	24,950	C+
Georgia College and State Univ	GA	11,020	C
Georgia Southern Univ	GA	9,762	C
Georgia Southwestern State Univ	GA	6,035	C
Gettysburg College	PA	39,864	HC
Glenville State College	WV	8,778	NC
Gonzaga Univ	WA	30,218	HC
Gordon College	MA	29,194	C+
Goshen College	IN	22,850	VC
Grace College	IN	22,170	C
Graceland Univ	IA	19,700	C
Grambling State Univ	LA	6,538	NC
Grand Canyon Univ	AZ	32,000	VC
Grand Valley State Univ	MI	12,000	VC
Grand View College	IA	21,482	C
Greensboro College	NC	23,000	C
Greenville College	IL	23,146	C
Grove City College	PA	15,784	HC+
Gustavus Adolphus College	MN	30,920	HC
Hannibal-LaGrange College	MO	16,390	C
Harding Univ	AR	16,512	VC
Hardin-Simmons Univ	TX	18,641	C
Hartwick College	NY	36,065	C+
Hastings College	NE	22,218	VC
Heidelberg College	OH	23,242	C
Henderson State Univ	AR	7,600	C
Hillsdale College	MI	24,160	HC
Hofstra Univ	NY	32,630	VC
Hope College	MI	28,208	VC+
Hope International Univ	CA	23,700	NC
Houghton College	NY	25,980	VC+
Houston Baptist Univ	TX	18,660	C
Howard Univ	DC	18,481	C+
Humboldt State Univ	CA	11,176	C
Huntingdon College	AL	23,090	VC
Huntington Univ	IN	24,830	C
Idaho State Univ	ID	9,030	C
Illinois State Univ	IL	12,839	C+
Immaculata Univ	PA	25,350	C
Indiana State Univ	IN	11,604	C
Indiana Univ Bloomington	IN	13,356	VC
Indiana Univ of Pennsylvania	PA	11,209	C
Indiana Univ South Bend	IN	4,989	LC
Indiana Univ-Purdue Univ Fort Wayne	IN	5,067	LC
Indiana Wesleyan Univ	IN	22,074	C+
Inter American Univ of PR/ Fajardo Campus	PR	4,000	
Inter American Univ of PR/ Ponce Regional College	PR	3,700	
Inter American Univ of PR/ San German	PR	6,720	
Iowa State Univ	IA	14,831	VC
Iowa Wesleyan College	IA	22,140	C
Ithaca College	NY	35,144	VC
Jackson State Univ	MS	8,500	C
Jacksonville State Univ	AL	7,618	LC
Jacksonville Univ	FL	24,040	C
Jarvis Christian College	TX	11,136	NC
John Brown Univ	AR	20,910	VC
Johnson State College	VT	11,830	LC
Judson College	AL	16,522	C
Judson College	IL	25,130	C
Kansas State Univ	KS	10,516	VC
Kansas Wesleyan Univ	KS	21,400	VC
Kean Univ	NJ	15,880	C
Keene State College	NH	13,836	C
Kennesaw State Univ	GA	12,152	C
Kent State Univ	OH	14,594	C
Kentucky Christian College	KY	12,680	C
Kentucky State Univ	KY	10,936	LC
Kentucky Wesleyan College	KY	18,590	C
Knoxville College	TN	6,200	LC
La Sierra Univ	CA	24,327	C+
Lakeland College	WI	22,990	C
Lamar Univ	TX	6,820	LC
Lambuth Univ	TN	21,700	C+
Lander Univ	SC	10,600	C
Lawrence Univ	WI	33,958	HC+
Lebanon Valley College	PA	31,700	VC
Lee Univ	TN	14,780	NC
Lenoir-Rhyne College	NC	25,580	C
Limestone College	SC	19,840	C
Lincoln Univ	MO	8,000	NC
Lincoln Univ	PA	13,658	C+
Lindenwood Univ	MO	18,600	VC
Lipscomb Univ	TN	20,967	VC
Livingstone College	NC	17,815	LC
LIU/Brooklyn Campus	NY	25,000	C
LIU/C.W. Post Campus	NY	28,282	C
Longwood Univ	VA	12,426	C
Loras College	IA	27,193	C
Louisiana College	LA	13,450	C
Louisiana State Univ and A&M College	LA	10,749	VC
Louisiana Tech Univ	LA	7,370	C
Loyola Univ New Orleans	LA	31,050	VC+
Lubbock Christian Univ	TX	16,960	C
MacMurray College	IL	20,755	C
Madonna Univ	MI	16,068	VC
Malone College	OH	23,040	C
Mansfield Univ	PA	11,300	C
Marian College of Fond du Lac	WI	21,775	LC
Mars Hill College	NC	19,000	LC
Maryville College	TN	29,224	VC
Marywood Univ	PA	30,680	C
McKendree College	IL	24,800	VC
McMurry Univ	TX	18,100	LC
Mercer Univ	GA	27,525	VC+
Mercyhurst College	PA	28,633	VC
Meredith College	NC	25,600	C
Messiah College	PA	28,910	VC+
Methodist College	NC	21,000	C
Metropolitan State College of Denver	CO	2,338	LC
Miami Univ	OH	29,097	HC
Mich State Univ	MI	13,689	VC
MidAmerica Nazarene Univ	KS	20,584	LC
Midland Lutheran College	NE	18,600	C
Midwestern State Univ	TX	9,381	LC
Millersville Univ of Pennsylvania	PA	12,113	C
Milligan College	TN	21,990	VC
Millikin Univ	IL	25,590	C
Minn State Univ, Mankato	MN	10,276	LC
Minn State Univ, Moorhead	MN	7,000	LC
Minot State Univ	ND	6,700	LC
Miss College	MS	14,574	VC
Miss State Univ	MS	9,577	C
Miss Univ for Women	MS	6,000	LC
Miss Valley State Univ	MS	7,970	C
Missouri Baptist Univ	MO	19,640	C
Missouri Southern State Univ	MO	8,396	NC
Missouri State Univ	MO	10,748	C+

School	ST	$IS	SR
Missouri Western State Univ	MO	9,534	NC
Monmouth Univ	NJ	28,956	C
Montana State Univ-Billings	MT	8,906	C
Montana State Univ-Bozeman	MT	1,137	C
Montclair State Univ	NJ	16,327	C
Moravian College	PA	28,950	VC
Morningside College	IA	23,704	C
Mount Mary College	WI	22,895	C
Mount Mercy College	IA	23,670	C
Mount Union College	OH	25,840	C
Mount Vernon Nazarene Univ	OH	20,810	C
Murray State Univ	KY	8,900	VC
Muskingum College	OH	22,970	C
Nazareth College of Rochester	NY	28,175	VC
Nebr Wesleyan Univ	NE	23,415	C+
New Jersey City Univ	NJ	13,695	LC
New Mexico State Univ	NM	9,250	C
New York Univ	NY	43,170	MC
Newberry College	SC	23,000	LC
Nicholls State Univ	LA	6,500	NC
Norfolk State Univ	VA	10,531	C
N Car Agricultural and Technical State Univ	NC	8,000	LC
N Dak State Univ	ND	8,500	C
North Georgia College and State Univ	GA	7,000	C
Northeastern State Univ	OK	5,896	LC
Northern Arizona Univ	AZ	10,353	C
Northern Illinois Univ	IL	13,178	C
Northern Mich Univ	MI	12,340	LC
Northern State Univ	SD	8,257	C
Northland College	WI	26,680	C+
Northwest Missouri State Univ	MO	10,000	C
Northwest Nazarene Univ	ID	22,590	VC
Northwestern College	MN	25,220	NC
Northwestern College of Iowa	IA	22,174	C+
Northwestern Okla State Univ	OK	6,250	NC
Northwestern State Univ of Louisiana	LA	7,144	C
Northwestern Univ	IL	37,595	MC
Nyack College	NY	18,540	C
Oakland City Univ	IN	19,620	NC
Oakland Univ	MI	11,936	C
Oakwood College	AL	14,904	C
Oberlin College	OH	40,904	MC
Ohio Northern Univ	OH	27,765	VC
Ohio State Univ	OH	15,357	HC
Ohio Univ	OH	15,921	C
Ohio Wesleyan Univ	OH	35,830	VC+
Okla Baptist Univ	OK	17,986	VC
Okla Christian Univ	OK	18,992	NC
Okla City Univ	OK	23,965	VC
Okla Panhandle State Univ	OK	7,635	NC
Okla State Univ	OK	10,213	VC
Okla Wesleyan Univ	OK	18,950	NC
Old Dominion Univ	VA	11,907	C
Oral Roberts Univ	OK	22,650	C
Otterbein College	OH	28,986	C
Ouachita Baptist Univ	AR	21,900	VC
Pacific Lutheran Univ	WA	28,805	VC
Palm Beach Atlantic Univ	FL	23,597	VC
Penn State Univ/Univ Park Campus	PA	18,038	HC
Peru State College	NE	6,350	NC
Pfeiffer Univ	NC	21,900	C
Pittsburg State Univ	KS	8,112	C
Plymouth State Univ	NH	12,298	LC
Pontifical Catholic Univ of PR/Ponce	PR	7,310	
Presbyterian College	SC	30,044	VC
Providence College	RI	34,580	HC
Quincy Univ	IL	24,920	C
Rhode Island College	RI	11,570	C
Rider Univ	NJ	32,560	C
Roberts Wesleyan College	NY	26,378	C
Rocky Mountain College	MT	20,805	C
Roosevelt Univ	IL	22,605	VC
Rowan Univ	NJ	16,000	VC
Saginaw Valley State Univ	MI	11,432	C
St. Ambrose Univ	IA	25,495	C
St. Augustine's College	NC	14,000	LC
St. Cloud State Univ	MN	10,010	C
St. Joseph's College	IN	26,600	C
St. Mary-of-the-Woods College	IN	25,480	VC
St. Mary's Univ of Minn	MN	23,857	VC
St. Norbert College	WI	28,577	C+
St. Olaf College	MN	32,800	HC
St. Vincent College	PA	26,160	VC
St. Xavier Univ	IL	23,160	C
Samford Univ	AL	20,258	VC
Schreiner Univ	TX	20,600	C
Seattle Pacific Univ	WA	29,355	C
Seton Hill Univ	PA	28,810	C
Shenandoah Univ	VA	27,600	C
Shepherd Univ	WV	10,066	VC
Shorter College	GA	19,700	C
Siena Heights Univ	MI	17,000	LC

School	ST	$IS	SR
Silver Lake College of the Holy Family	WI	18,500	LC
Simpson College	IA	26,833	VC
Slippery Rock Univ of Pennsylvania	PA	10,360	LC
S Car State Univ	SC	6,700	LC
S Dak State Univ	SD	9,815	C
Southeast Missouri State Univ	MO	10,596	C
Southeastern Louisiana Univ	LA	8,521	LC
Southeastern Okla State Univ	OK	6,147	C
Southeastern Univ	FL	17,180	LC
Southern Adventist Univ	TN	18,500	C
Southern Arkansas Univ	AR	6,956	C
Southern Methodist Univ	TX	36,088	VC+
Southern Nazarene Univ	OK	14,634	NC
Southern Univ and A&M College	LA	8,238	LC
Southern Univ at New Orleans	LA	1,000	NC
Southern Utah Univ	UT		C
Southern Wesleyan Univ	SC	21,675	C
Southwest Baptist Univ	MO	18,300	C
Southwest Minn State Univ	MN	10,975	C
Southwestern College	KS	21,476	C
Southwestern Okla State Univ	OK	4,801	C
Spring Arbor Univ	MI	22,476	C
SUNY at Potsdam	NY	12,959	C
SUNY/College at Fredonia	NY	12,771	VC
Sterling College	KS	19,992	C
Stetson Univ	FL	32,725	VC
Susquehanna Univ	PA	33,465	VC
Syracuse Univ	NY	38,655	HC
Tabor College	KS	21,614	NC
Talladega College	AL	11,240	C
Taylor Univ	IN	26,376	VC+
Temple Univ	PA	17,438	C
Tenn Tech Univ	TN	10,044	C
Tenn Wesleyan College	TN	18,650	C
Texas A&M Univ at Commerce	TX	9,020	C
Texas A&M Univ at Kingsville	TX	6,800	LC
Texas Christian Univ	TX	23,410	VC+
Texas Wesleyan Univ	TX	18,700	C
Toccoa Falls College	GA	17,125	C
Tougaloo College	MS	15,975	NC
Towson Univ	MD	13,924	VC
Trevecca Nazarene Univ	TN	19,594	C
Trinity Christian College	IL	23,645	C
Troy Univ	AL	8,916	C
Union College	NE	18,710	C
Union Univ	TN	20,750	VC
Universidad Adventista de las Antillas	PR	7,360	
Univ of Akron	OH	15,166	NC
Univ of Alabama	AL	9,888	C
Univ of Alaska Anchorage	AK	11,275	NC
Univ of Alaska Fairbanks	AK	10,101	C
Univ of Arizona	AZ	11,958	VC
Univ of Arkansas	AR	11,859	VC
Univ of Arkansas at Monticello	AR	7,325	NC
Univ of Arkansas at Pine Bluff	AR	8,300	C
Univ of Central Arkansas	AR	9,984	C
Univ of Central Florida	FL	10,739	VC
Univ of Central Okla	OK	8,094	C
Univ of Cincinnati	OH	17,682	C
Univ of Colo at Boulder	CO	13,352	C+
Univ of Conn	CT	16,628	HC
Univ of Dayton	OH	28,826	VC
Univ of Delaware	DE	14,142	HC
Univ of Evansville	IN	28,320	VC
Univ of Florida	FL	9,354	HC
Univ of Georgia	GA	11,004	HC
Univ of Hartford	CT	34,044	C
Univ of Idaho	ID	9,310	NC
Univ of Illinois at Urbana-Champaign	IL	15,800	HC+
Univ of Indianapolis	IN	25,090	C
Univ of Iowa	IA	12,172	VC
Univ of Kansas	KS	10,915	VC
Univ of Kentucky	KY	7,800	VC
Univ of Louisiana at Lafayette	LA	5,830	C
Univ of Louisiana at Monroe	LA	7,103	C
Univ of Louisville	KY	10,400	VC
Univ of Maine	ME	13,642	C
Univ of Mary	ND	15,374	C
Univ of Mary Hardin-Baylor	TX	19,428	C
Univ of Maryland/College Park	MD	16,036	HC
Univ of Maryland/Eastern Shore	MD	11,210	C
Univ of Miami	FL	38,397	MC
Univ of Mich/Ann Arbor	MI	16,587	HC+
Univ of Mich/Flint	MI	6,398	C
Univ of Minn/Duluth	MN	13,974	C
Univ of Minn/Twin Cities	MN	13,165	HC
Univ of Missouri/Columbia	MO	13,500	C
Univ of Missouri/Kansas City	MO	15,000	VC

School	ST	$IS	SR
Univ of Missouri/St. Louis	MO	14,046	VC
Univ of Montana	MT	10,602	C
Univ of Montana--Western	MT	8,406	NC
Univ of Montevallo	AL	9,630	C
Univ of Nebr at Kearney	NE	9,000	NC
Univ of Nebr at Lincoln	NE	11,401	VC
Univ of Nevada/Reno	NV	12,155	NC
Univ of New Hampshire	NH	16,810	VC
Univ of New Mexico	NM	11,253	C
Univ of New Orleans	LA	7,370	C
Univ of North Alabama	AL	8,992	C
Univ of N Car at Chapel Hill	NC	11,129	MC
Univ of N Car at Charlotte	NC	9,101	C
Univ of N Car at Greensboro	NC	8,993	C
Univ of N Car at Pembroke	NC	7,940	LC
Univ of N Car at Wilmington	NC	10,107	VC
Univ of N Dak	ND	10,114	VC
Univ of North Florida	FL	9,908	VC
Univ of Northern Colo	CO	10,249	C
Univ of Northern Iowa	IA	11,133	C
Univ of Okla	OK	10,769	VC+
Univ of Oregon	OR	13,108	VC
Univ of Portland	OR	32,300	VC
Univ of Puget Sound	WA	35,600	HC
Univ of Redlands	CA	36,160	VC
Univ of Rhode Island	RI	15,398	C
Univ of Rio Grande	OH	8,728	NC
Univ of Rochester	NY	41,135	MC
Univ of St. Thomas	MN	28,000	VC
Univ of St. Thomas	TX	23,810	VC
Univ of Sioux Falls	SD	20,800	C
Univ of S Car at Aiken	SC	11,718	LC
Univ of S Car at Columbia	SC	13,397	VC
Univ of S Dak	SD	9,068	C
Univ of South Florida	FL	10,284	VC
Univ of Southern Calif	CA	41,618	MC
Univ of Southern Maine	ME	12,614	C
Univ of Southern Miss	MS	10,112	C
Univ of Tenn at Chattanooga	TN	7,790	C
Univ of Tenn at Knoxville	TN	11,720	C
Univ of the Cumberlands	KY	18,184	C
Univ of the Incarnate Word	TX	23,306	C
Univ of the Pacific	CA	34,380	VC
Univ of Toledo	OH	15,806	NC
Univ of Tulsa	OK	25,348	HC
Univ of Vermont	VT	18,080	VC
Univ of Washington	WA	10,400	VC
Univ of West Florida	FL	8,559	C
Univ of West Georgia	GA	8,838	C
Univ of Wisc/Eau Claire	WI	9,915	VC
Univ of Wisc/Milwaukee	WI	9,427	LC
Univ of Wisc/Oshkosh	WI	10,426	LC
Univ of Wisc/River Falls	WI	9,722	LC
Univ of Wisc/Stevens Point	WI	9,384	VC
Univ of Wisc/Superior	WI	9,610	C+
Univ of Wisc/Whitewater	WI	9,274	C
Univ of Wyoming	WY	9,666	C
Utah State Univ	UT	8,002	VC
Valdosta State Univ	GA	8,802	C
Valparaiso Univ	IN	28,970	VC+
VanderCook College of Music	IL	19,430	SP
Virginia Union Univ	VA	18,432	LC
Viterbo Univ	WI	21,670	C
Walla Walla College	WA	24,489	NC
Warner Pacific College	OR	21,900	C
Warner Southern College	FL	18,000	LC
Wartburg College	IA	27,315	NC
Washburn Univ	KS	9,734	NC
Wayland Baptist Univ	TX	13,484	C
Wayne State College	NE	8,033	NC
Weber State Univ	UT	9,635	NC
Webster Univ	MO	24,280	VC
West Chester Univ of Pennsylvania	PA	12,355	C+
West Liberty State College	WV	9,142	LC
West Texas A&M Univ	TX	8,452	C
West Virginia Wesleyan College	WV	26,880	C
Western Carolina Univ	NC	7,000	C
Western Conn State Univ	CT	12,993	C
Western Mich Univ	MI	13,299	C
Western State College of Colo	CO	9,942	C
Western Washington Univ	WA	11,262	VC
Westfield State College	MA	10,200	C
Westminster Choir College	NJ	32,670	SP
Westminster College	PA	31,290	C+
Westmont College	CA	36,672	HC
Wheaton College	IL	27,760	HC
Whitworth College	WA	29,428	VC+
Wichita State Univ	KS	8,500	C
Wiley College	TX	8,100	LC
Wilkes Univ	PA	30,886	C
Willamette Univ	OR	35,416	VC+
William Carey College	MS	11,000	LC
William Jewell College	MO	24,340	C
William Paterson Univ of New Jersey	NJ	17,810	C
Wingate Univ	NC	23,300	C
Winona State Univ	MN	11,333	C
Winston-Salem State Univ	NC	8,960	LC
Winthrop Univ	SC	11,302	C
Wittenberg Univ	OH	34,596	VC

School	ST	$IS	SR
Wright State Univ	OH	13,616	LC
Xavier Univ	OH	30,490	HC
Xavier Univ of Louisiana	LA	17,500	C
York College	NE	16,330	NC
Youngstown State Univ	OH	12,613	NC

MUSIC HISTORY AND APPRECIATION

School	ST	$IS	SR
Baldwin-Wallace College	OH	27,256	VC
Bard College	NY	41,800	HC+
Baylor Univ	TX	27,555	HC
Boston Univ	MA	42,046	HC+
Bucknell Univ	PA	39,660	MC
Cal State, San Bernardino	CA	12,563	LC
Catholic Univ of America	DC	35,838	VC
Central Mich Univ	MI	12,244	C
Florida State Univ	FL	9,028	HC
Hardin-Simmons Univ	TX	18,641	C
Hofstra Univ	NY	32,630	VC
Howard Univ	DC	18,481	C+
Johnson State College	VT	11,830	LC
Kent State Univ	OH	14,594	C
McKendree College	IL	24,800	VC
Nazareth College of Rochester	NY	28,175	VC
New England Conservatory of Music	MA	38,750	SP
Oberlin College	OH	40,904	MC
Ohio State Univ	OH	15,357	HC
Ohio Univ	OH	15,921	C
Rice Univ	TX	32,290	MC
Roosevelt Univ	IL	22,605	VC
Simon's Rock College of Bard	MA	41,988	VC+
Suffolk Univ	MA	33,160	C
Temple Univ	PA	17,438	C
Univ of Calif at Los Angeles	CA	17,681	MC
Univ of Calif at San Diego	CA	16,102	HC
Univ of Cincinnati	OH	17,682	C
Univ of Hartford	CT	34,044	C
Univ of Idaho	ID	9,310	NC
Univ of Illinois at Urbana-Champaign	IL	15,800	HC+
Univ of Kansas	KS	10,915	VC
Univ of Mich/Ann Arbor	MI	16,587	HC+
Univ of Mich/Dearborn	MI	7,000	VC
Univ of New Hampshire	NH	16,810	VC
Univ of North Texas	TX	7,800	C
Univ of the Pacific	CA	34,380	VC
Univ of Washington	WA	10,400	VC
Vanderbilt Univ	TN	41,986	MC
Western Mich Univ	MI	13,299	C
Wright State Univ	OH	13,616	LC
Youngstown State Univ	OH	12,613	NC

MUSIC PERFORMANCE

School	ST	$IS	SR
Adams State College	CO	8,613	C
Anderson Univ	IN	25,050	LC
Andrews Univ	MI	21,786	C
Anna Maria College	MA	29,815	LC
Appalachian State Univ	NC	8,000	VC
Arizona State Univ-Tempe	AZ	11,174	C
Arkansas State Univ	AR	9,630	C
Augustana College	IL	29,862	VC+
Averett Univ	VA	24,920	C
Baldwin-Wallace College	OH	27,256	VC
Ball State Univ	IN	13,138	C
Bard College	NY	41,800	HC+
Barry Univ	FL	24,100	LC
Baylor Univ	TX	27,555	HC
Belmont Univ	TN	24,110	VC
Bennington College	VT	41,890	HC
Berklee College of Music	MA	37,779	SP
Berry College	GA	24,342	VC
Bethel College	IN	19,680	C
Biola Univ	CA	29,372	VC
Blackburn College	IL	13,690	C
Boston Conservatory	MA	27,500	SP
Boston Univ	MA	42,046	HC+
Bradley Univ	IL	25,280	VC
Brenau Univ Women's College	GA	23,950	VC
Brewton-Parker College	GA	14,220	LC
Brigham Young Univ	UT	9,200	VC
Bucknell Univ	PA	39,660	MC
Butler Univ	IN	31,944	VC+
Cal State, Los Angeles	CA	5,900	C
Cal State, San Bernardino	CA	12,563	LC
Cal State, Stanislaus	CA	11,283	C
Catholic Univ of America	DC	35,838	VC
Centenary College of Louisiana	LA	24,760	VC
Central Mich Univ	MI	12,244	C
Chapman Univ	CA	37,550	VC
Christopher Newport Univ	VA	13,326	VC
CUNY/Brooklyn College	NY	4,377	C+
CUNY/Queens College	NY	4,356	C
Clayton College and State Univ	GA	2,445	LC
Colo State Univ-Pueblo	CO	7,821	LC
Columbia College	SC	24,982	LC
Columbus State Univ	GA	8,664	C

School	ST	$IS	SR
Concordia College: Moorhead	MN	22,475	VC
Cornerstone Univ and Grand Rapids Theological Seminary	MI	21,350	NC
Dallas Baptist Univ	TX	17,040	VC
Delta State Univ	MS	7,709	C
DePauw Univ	IN	32,100	HC
Dillard Univ	LA	17,500	VC
Drake Univ	IA	27,632	VC+
Duquesne Univ	PA	29,534	VC
East Carolina Univ	NC	10,000	C
East Texas Baptist Univ	TX	16,713	C
Eastern Mich Univ	MI	12,897	C
Eastern Nazarene College	MA	19,500	LC
Eastern New Mexico Univ	NM	7,264	C
Eastern Washington Univ	WA	10,608	C
Eastman School of Music	NY	35,000	SP
Elon Univ	NC	25,371	HC
Emory & Henry College	VA	26,570	C
Evangel Univ	MO	17,380	C
Five Towns College	NY	24,600	SP
Florida State Univ	FL	9,028	HC
Fort Hays State Univ	KS	7,638	C
Furman Univ	SC	33,264	HC+
George Washington Univ	DC	48,820	MC
Gordon College	MA	29,194	C+
Grove City College	PA	15,784	HC+
Hannibal-LaGrange College	MO	16,390	C
Hardin-Simmons Univ	TX	18,641	C
Hofstra Univ	NY	32,630	VC
Houghton College	NY	25,980	VC+
Houston Baptist Univ	TX	18,660	C
Huntington Univ	IN	24,830	C
Idaho State Univ	ID	9,030	C
Illinois State Univ	IL	12,839	C+
Indiana Univ Bloomington	IN	13,356	VC
Indiana Univ of Pennsylvania	PA	11,209	C
Inter American Univ of PR/ Metropolitan Campus	PR	4,320	
Ithaca College	NY	35,144	VC
Jacksonville Univ	FL	24,040	C
Johnson State College	VT	11,830	C
Keene State College	NH	13,836	C
Kennesaw State Univ	GA	12,152	C
Kent State Univ	OH	14,594	C
Kentucky Christian College	KY	12,680	C
Kentucky State Univ	KY	10,089	LC
La Sierra Univ	CA	24,327	C+
LaGrange College	GA	22,874	C+
Lawrence Univ	WI	33,958	HC+
Lipscomb Univ	TN	20,967	VC
Louisiana Tech Univ	LA	7,370	C
Loyola Univ New Orleans	LA	31,050	VC+
Manhattan School of Music	NY	33,000	SP
Mannes College of Music	NY	31,930	SP
Mansfield Univ	PA	11,300	C
Mars Hill College	NC	19,000	LC
Maryville College	TN	29,224	VC
Marywood Univ	PA	30,680	VC
McMurry Univ	TX	18,100	LC
Meredith College	NC	25,600	C
Methodist College	NC	21,000	C
Metropolitan State College of Denver	CO	2,338	LC
Miami Univ	OH	29,097	HC
Mich State Univ	MI	13,689	VC
MidAmerica Nazarene Univ	KS	20,584	LC
Millikin Univ	IL	25,590	C
Missouri Baptist Univ	MO	19,640	C
Missouri State Univ	MO	10,748	C+
Montana State Univ-Billings	MT	8,906	C
Montclair State Univ	NJ	16,327	C
Montreat College	NC	21,440	C
Mount Union College	OH	25,840	C
Mount Vernon Nazarene Univ	OH	20,810	C
Nazareth College of Rochester	NY	28,175	VC
New England Conservatory of Music	MA	38,750	SP
New York Univ	NY	43,170	MC
Newberry College	SC	23,000	LC
Northwestern College	MN	25,220	NC
Northwestern Univ	IL	37,595	MC
Nyack College	NY	18,540	C
Oakwood College	AL	14,904	C
Oberlin College	OH	40,904	MC
Ohio Northern Univ	OH	27,765	VC
Ohio State Univ	OH	15,357	HC
Old Dominion Univ	VA	11,907	C
Oral Roberts Univ	OK	22,650	C
Otterbein College	OH	28,986	C
Pacific Lutheran Univ	WA	28,805	VC
Palm Beach Atlantic Univ	FL	23,597	VC
Presbyterian College	SC	30,044	VC
Rice Univ	TX	32,290	MC
Rocky Mountain College	MT	20,805	C
Rollins College	FL	38,366	VC
Roosevelt Univ	IL	22,605	VC
St. Mary's Univ of Minn	MN	23,857	VC
St. Olaf College	MN	32,800	HC
St. Vincent College	PA	26,160	VC
Sam Houston State Univ	TX	8,000	C
Samford Univ	AL	20,258	VC
Shenandoah Univ	VA	27,600	C
Shepherd Univ	WV	10,066	C
Simon's Rock College of Bard	MA	41,988	VC+
Simpson College	IA	26,833	VC
Southeast Missouri State Univ	MO	10,596	C
Southern Methodist Univ	TX	36,088	VC+
Southern Nazarene Univ	OK	14,634	NC
SUNY at Potsdam	NY	12,959	C
SUNY/Univ at Binghamton	NY	13,988	HC
SUNY/Univ at Buffalo	NY	13,694	VC
Stetson Univ	FL	32,725	VC
Susquehanna Univ	PA	33,465	VC
Syracuse Univ	NY	38,655	HC
Talladega College	AL	11,240	LC
Temple Univ	PA	17,438	C
Texas Christian Univ	TX	23,410	VC+
Texas State Univ - San Marcos	TX	10,862	C
Texas Tech Univ	TX	13,026	VC
Toccoa Falls College	GA	17,125	C
Tougaloo College	MS	15,975	NC
Trinity Christian College	IL	23,645	C
Truman State Univ	MO	11,242	HC
Union College	NE	18,710	C
Union Univ	TN	20,750	VC
Univ of Alaska Fairbanks	AK	10,101	C
Univ of Arizona	AZ	11,958	VC
Univ of Calif at Santa Barbara	CA	11,800	VC
Univ of Dayton	OH	28,826	VC
Univ of Denver	CO	36,376	VC+
Univ of Evansville	IN	28,320	VC
Univ of Georgia	GA	11,004	HC
Univ of Hartford	CT	34,044	C
Univ of Idaho	ID	9,310	NC
Univ of Illinois at Urbana-Champaign	IL	15,800	HC+
Univ of Indianapolis	IN	25,090	C
Univ of Kansas	KS	10,915	VC
Univ of Kentucky	KY	7,800	C
Univ of Maine	ME	13,642	C
Univ of Mary Hardin-Baylor	TX	19,428	C
Univ of Maryland/College Park	MD	16,036	HC
Univ of Mass Lowell	MA	14,327	VC
Univ of Miami	FL	38,397	MC
Univ of Mich/Ann Arbor	MI	16,587	HC+
Univ of Minn/Duluth	MN	13,974	C
Univ of Missouri/Kansas City	MO	15,000	VC
Univ of Montana	MT	10,602	C
Univ of New Hampshire	NH	16,810	VC
Univ of N Car at Chapel Hill	NC	11,129	MC
Univ of N Car at Charlotte	NC	9,101	C
Univ of N Car at Wilmington	NC	10,107	VC
Univ of N Dak	ND	10,114	VC
Univ of North Florida	FL	9,908	VC
Univ of North Texas	TX	7,800	C
Univ of Northern Iowa	IA	11,133	C
Univ of Oregon	OR	13,108	VC
Univ of Puget Sound	WA	35,600	HC
Univ of S Car at Columbia	SC	13,397	VC
Univ of S Dak	SD	9,068	C
Univ of Southern Calif	CA	41,618	MC
Univ of Southern Maine	ME	12,614	C
Univ of Texas at San Antonio	TX	11,325	LC
Univ of the Arts	PA	32,330	SP
Univ of the Pacific	CA	34,380	VC
Univ of Tulsa	OK	25,348	HC
Univ of Washington	WA	10,400	VC
Univ of Wisc/Superior	WI	9,610	C+
Univ of Wyoming	WY	9,666	C
Valdosta State Univ	GA	8,802	C
Valparaiso Univ	IN	28,970	VC+
Vanderbilt Univ	TN	41,986	MC
Virginia State Univ	VA	11,318	C
Viterbo Univ	WI	21,670	C
Walla Walla College	WA	24,489	NC
Wartburg College	IA	27,315	NC
Washburn Univ	KS	9,734	NC
Washington State Univ	WA	12,260	C
Weber State Univ	UT	9,635	NC
West Chester Univ of Pennsylvania	PA	12,355	C+
Western Conn State Univ	CT	12,993	C
Western Mich Univ	MI	13,299	C
Westminster College	PA	31,290	C+
Wiley College	TX	8,100	LC
Willamette Univ	OR	35,416	VC+
William Carey College	MS	11,000	LC
William Tyndale College	MI	13,000	NC
York College	NE	16,330	NC
Youngstown State Univ	OH	12,613	NC

MUSIC TECHNOLOGY

School	ST	$IS	SR
Brigham Young Univ	UT	9,200	HC
Cal State, San Bernardino	CA	12,563	LC
Cogswell Polytechnical College	CA	13,760	LC
Conn College	CT	41,975	MC
Duquesne Univ	PA	29,534	VC
LaGrange College	GA	22,874	C+
Malone College	OH	23,040	C
New York Univ	NY	43,170	MC
Northwestern Univ	IL	37,595	MC
St. Mary's Univ of Minn	MN	23,857	VC
Stevens Inst of Technology	NJ	40,935	HC
Univ of Calif at San Diego	CA	16,102	HC
Univ of Hartford	CT	34,044	C
Univ of N Car at Asheville	NC	9,237	VC
York College of Pennsylvania	PA	16,550	VC

MUSIC THEORY AND COMPOSITION

School	ST	$IS	SR
Arizona State Univ-Tempe	AZ	11,174	C
Baldwin-Wallace College	OH	27,256	VC
Bard College	NY	41,800	HC+
Baylor Univ	TX	27,555	HC
Bennington College	VT	41,890	VC
Berklee College of Music	MA	37,779	SP
Biola Univ	CA	29,372	VC
Boston Conservatory	MA	37,500	SP
Boston Univ	MA	42,046	HC+
Bradley Univ	IL	25,280	VC
Brigham Young Univ	UT	9,200	HC
Bucknell Univ	PA	39,660	MC
Butler Univ	IN	31,944	VC+
Catholic Univ of America	DC	35,838	VC
Central Mich Univ	MI	12,244	C
Central Washington Univ	WA	11,730	C
Christopher Newport Univ	VA	13,326	VC
CUNY/Brooklyn College	NY	4,377	C+
Clayton College and State Univ	GA	2,445	LC
Colo State Univ-Pueblo	CO	7,821	LC
Cornerstone Univ and Grand Rapids Theological Seminary	MI	21,350	NC
DePauw Univ	IN	32,100	HC
East Carolina Univ	NC	10,000	C
Eastman School of Music	NY	35,000	SP
Emory & Henry College	VA	26,570	C
Five Towns College	NY	24,600	SP
Florida State Univ	FL	9,028	HC
Fort Hays State Univ	KS	7,638	C
Furman Univ	SC	33,264	HC+
Georgia Southern Univ	GA	9,762	C+
Hardin-Simmons Univ	TX	18,641	C
Hofstra Univ	NY	32,630	VC
Houghton College	NY	25,980	VC+
Houston Baptist Univ	TX	18,660	C
Huntington Univ	IN	24,830	C
Illinois Wesleyan Univ	IL	34,050	HC+
Indiana Univ Bloomington	IN	13,356	VC
Indiana Univ South Bend	IN	4,989	LC
Indiana Wesleyan Univ	IN	22,074	C+
Ithaca College	NY	35,144	VC
Jacksonville Univ	FL	24,040	C
Kent State Univ	OH	14,594	C
Lawrence Univ	WI	33,958	HC+
Lehigh Univ	PA	42,690	HC+
Loyola Univ New Orleans	LA	31,050	VC+
Manhattan School of Music	NY	33,000	SP
Mannes College of Music	NY	31,930	SP
Mich State Univ	MI	13,689	VC
Miss College	MS	14,574	VC
Montclair State Univ	NJ	16,327	C
New England Conservatory of Music	MA	38,750	SP
New York Univ	NY	43,170	MC
Newberry College	SC	23,000	LC
Northwestern Univ	IL	37,595	MC
Nyack College	NY	18,540	C
Oberlin College	OH	40,904	MC
Ohio Northern Univ	OH	27,765	VC
Ohio State Univ	OH	15,357	HC
Ohio Univ	OH	15,921	C
Old Dominion Univ	VA	11,907	C
Oral Roberts Univ	OK	22,650	C
Pacific Lutheran Univ	WA	28,805	VC
Palm Beach Atlantic Univ	FL	23,597	VC
Rice Univ	TX	32,290	MC
Roosevelt Univ	IL	22,605	VC
St. Olaf College	MN	32,800	HC
Sam Houston State Univ	TX	8,000	C
Samford Univ	AL	20,258	VC
Shenandoah Univ	VA	27,600	C
Shepherd Univ	WV	10,066	C
Simon's Rock College of Bard	MA	41,988	VC+
Southern Methodist Univ	TX	36,088	VC+
SUNY at Potsdam	NY	12,959	C
Stetson Univ	FL	32,725	VC
Syracuse Univ	NY	38,655	VC
Temple Univ	PA	17,438	C
Texas Christian Univ	TX	23,410	VC+
Texas Tech Univ	TX	13,026	VC
Union College	TN	20,750	VC
Univ of Arizona	AZ	11,958	VC
Univ of Calif at Santa Barbara	CA	11,800	VC
Univ of Cincinnati	OH	17,682	C
Univ of Dayton	OH	28,826	VC
Univ of Delaware	DE	14,142	HC
Univ of Georgia	GA	11,004	HC
Univ of Hartford	CT	34,044	C
Univ of Houston	TX	7,000	C
Univ of Idaho	ID	9,310	NC
Univ of Illinois at Urbana-Champaign	IL	15,800	HC+
Univ of Kansas	KS	10,915	VC
Univ of Mary Hardin-Baylor	TX	19,428	C
Univ of Maryland/College Park	MD	16,036	HC
Univ of Miami	FL	38,397	MC
Univ of Mich/Ann Arbor	MI	16,587	HC+
Univ of Missouri/Kansas City	MO	15,000	VC
Univ of New Hampshire	NH	16,810	VC
Univ of North Texas	TX	7,800	C
Univ of Northern Iowa	IA	11,133	C
Univ of Oregon	OR	13,108	VC
Univ of Rochester	NY	41,135	MC
Univ of Texas at Austin	TX	14,610	HC
Univ of Texas at San Antonio	TX	11,325	LC
Univ of the Arts	PA	32,330	SP
Univ of the Pacific	CA	34,380	VC
Univ of Wyoming	WY	9,666	C
Valparaiso Univ	IN	28,970	VC+
Vanderbilt Univ	TN	41,986	MC
Wartburg College	IA	27,315	NC
Washington State Univ	WA	12,260	C
Washington Univ in St. Louis	MO	42,106	MC
West Chester Univ of Pennsylvania	PA	12,355	C+
West Texas A&M Univ	TX	8,452	C
Western Mich Univ	MI	13,299	C
Westminster Choir College	NJ	32,670	SP
Westminster College	PA	31,290	C+
Willamette Univ	OR	35,416	VC+
Wright State Univ	OH	13,616	LC
Youngstown State Univ	OH	12,613	NC

MUSIC THERAPY

School	ST	$IS	SR
Alverno College	WI	21,088	C
Anna Maria College	MA	29,815	LC
Appalachian State Univ	NC	8,000	VC
Arizona State Univ-Tempe	AZ	11,174	C
Augsburg College	MN	28,300	C
Baldwin-Wallace College	OH	27,256	VC
Berklee College of Music	MA	37,779	SP
Chapman Univ	CA	37,550	VC
Charleston Southern Univ	SC	17,800	C
Duquesne Univ	PA	29,534	VC
East Carolina Univ	NC	10,000	C
Eastern Mich Univ	MI	12,897	C
Elizabethtown College	PA	32,100	VC
Florida State Univ	FL	9,028	HC
Georgia College and State Univ	GA	11,020	C
Howard Univ	DC	18,481	C+
Immaculata Univ	PA	25,350	C
Indiana Univ-Purdue Univ Fort Wayne	IN	5,067	LC
Louisiana College	LA	13,450	C
Loyola Univ New Orleans	LA	31,050	VC+
Mansfield Univ	PA	11,300	C
Marylhurst Univ	OR	14,220	NC
Maryville Univ of St. Louis	MO	23,000	VC
Marywood Univ	PA	30,680	VC
Mich State Univ	MI	13,689	VC
Molloy College	NY	16,510	C
Montclair State Univ	NJ	16,327	C
Nazareth College of Rochester	NY	28,175	VC
Queens Univ of Charlotte	NC	24,528	C
St. Mary-of-the-Woods College	IN	25,480	C
Sam Houston State Univ	TX	8,000	C
Seton Hill Univ	PA	28,810	C
Shenandoah Univ	VA	27,600	C
Southern Methodist Univ	TX	36,088	VC+
Southwestern Okla State Univ	OK	4,801	C
Temple Univ	PA	17,438	C
Texas Woman's Univ	TX	7,804	LC
Univ of Alabama	AL	9,888	C
Univ of Dayton	OH	28,826	VC
Univ of Evansville	IN	28,320	VC
Univ of Georgia	GA	11,004	HC
Univ of Kansas	KS	10,915	VC
Univ of Miami	FL	38,397	MC
Univ of Minn/Twin Cities	MN	13,165	HC
Univ of Missouri/Kansas City	MO	15,000	VC
Univ of N Dak	ND	10,114	VC
Univ of the Incarnate Word	TX	23,306	C
Univ of the Pacific	CA	34,380	VC
Univ of Wisc/Eau Claire	WI	9,915	VC
Univ of Wisc/Oshkosh	WI	10,426	LC
Utah State Univ	UT	8,002	VC
Wartburg College	IA	27,315	NC
West Texas A&M Univ	TX	8,452	C
Western Mich Univ	MI	13,299	C
William Carey College	MS	11,000	LC

MUSICAL THEATER

School	ST	$IS	SR
Adrian College	MI	23,000	C

ST = STATE   **$IS** = IN-STATE COSTS   **SR** = SELECTOR RATING

School	ST	$IS	SR
American Univ	DC	38,719	HC+
Ashland Univ	OH	25,000	C
Baldwin-Wallace College	OH	27,256	VC
Birmingham-Southern College	AL	28,494	VC+
Boston Conservatory	MA	27,500	SP
Brenau Univ Women's College	GA	23,950	VC
Brigham Young Univ	UT	9,200	VC
Cal State, Chico	CA	11,395	C
Catawba College	NC	25,000	C
Catholic Univ of America	DC	35,838	VC
Central Mich Univ	MI	12,244	C
Coastal Carolina Univ	SC	13,140	VC
Coker College	SC	21,600	C
College of Santa Fe	NM	28,978	C
College of the Ozarks	MO	4,130	VC+
Elon Univ	NC	25,371	HC
Emerson College	MA	35,076	HC
Florida State Univ	FL	9,028	HC
Friends Univ	KS	16,250	LC
Howard Univ	DC	18,481	VC
Huntingdon College	AL	23,090	VC
Illinois Wesleyan Univ	IL	34,050	HC+
Ithaca College	NY	35,144	VC
Lees-McRae College	NC	23,000	C
Marietta College	OH	29,327	C
Mars Hill College	NC	19,000	LC
Marywood Univ	PA	30,680	C
Mercyhurst College	PA	28,633	VC
Meredith College	NC	25,600	C
Millikin Univ	IL	25,590	C
Montclair State Univ	NJ	16,327	C
Otterbein College	OH	28,986	C
Ouachita Baptist Univ	AR	21,900	VC
Palm Beach Atlantic Univ	FL	23,597	VC
Roosevelt Univ	IL	22,605	VC
Russell Sage College	NY	27,000	C
Sam Houston State Univ	TX	8,000	C
Samford Univ	AL	20,258	VC
Seton Hill Univ	PA	28,810	C
Shenandoah Univ	VA	27,600	C
Shorter College	GA	19,700	C
SUNY/Univ at Buffalo	NY	13,694	VC
Syracuse Univ	NY	38,655	HC
Univ of Arizona	AZ	11,958	VC
Univ of Hartford	CT	34,044	C
Univ of Hawaii at Manoa	HI	10,413	VC
Univ of Indianapolis	IN	25,090	C
Univ of Miami	FL	38,397	MC
Univ of Mich/Ann Arbor	MI	16,587	HC+
Univ of N Car at Pembroke	NC	7,940	LC
Univ of Northern Colo	CO	10,249	C
Univ of the Arts	PA	32,330	SP
Univ of Tulsa	OK	25,348	HC
Viterbo Univ	WI	21,670	C
Weber State Univ	UT	9,635	NC
Webster Univ	MO	24,280	VC
West Texas A&M Univ	TX	8,452	C
Western Mich Univ	MI	13,299	C
Westminster Choir College	NJ	32,670	SP
Wilkes Univ	PA	30,886	C
Youngstown State Univ	OH	12,613	NC

MUSICOLOGY/ETHNOMUSICOLOGY

School	ST	$IS	SR
Cal State, San Bernardino	CA	12,563	LC

NATIVE AMERICAN STUDIES

School	ST	$IS	SR
Colgate Univ	NY	41,170	MC
College of St. Scholastica	MN	28,456	C+
Creighton Univ	NE	29,918	VC+
Dartmouth College	NH	39,465	MC
Humboldt State Univ	CA	11,176	C
Montana State Univ-Northern	MT	10,000	NC
Univ of Alaska Fairbanks	AK	10,101	C
Univ of at Calif Davis	CA	15,010	VC
Univ of Calif at Berkeley	CA	18,141	HC+
Univ of Calif at Riverside	CA	16,625	C
Univ of Minn/Duluth	MN	13,974	C
Univ of Montana	MT	10,602	C
Univ of New Mexico	NM	11,253	C
Univ of Okla	OK	10,769	VC+
Univ of the Incarnate Word	TX	23,306	C

NATURAL RESOURCE MANAGEMENT

School	ST	$IS	SR
Alaska Pacific Univ	AK	25,142	C
Angelo State Univ	TX	8,340	NC
Ball State Univ	IN	13,138	C
Calif Polytechnic State Univ	CA	12,390	VC
Central Mich Univ	MI	12,244	C
Colo State Univ-Fort Collins	CO	10,878	C+
Cornell Univ	NY	41,717	MC
Delaware State Univ	DE	8,130	LC
Green Mountain College	VT	32,164	C
Humboldt State Univ	CA	11,176	C
Johnson State College	VT	11,830	LC
Kent State Univ	OH	14,594	C
Keystone College	PA	22,810	LC
Mich State Univ	MI	13,689	VC

School	ST	$IS	SR
Montana State Univ-Bozeman	MT	1,137	C
New Mexico Highlands Univ	NM	6,272	NC
N Car State Univ	NC	11,824	HC
N Dak State Univ	ND	8,500	C
Northland College	WI	26,680	C+
Ohio State Univ	OH	15,357	HC
Penn State Univ/Univ Park Campus	PA	18,038	HC
Purdue Univ/West Lafayette	IN	13,458	VC
Rutgers, The State Univ of New Jersey/New Brunswick/Piscataway Campus	NJ	15,810	HC
SUNY/College of Environmental Science and Forestry	NY	15,000	VC
Sterling College	VT	23,286	VC
Sul Ross State Univ	TX	6,600	LC
Texas A&M Univ at Galveston	TX	10,000	C+
Univ of Alaska Fairbanks	AK	10,101	C
Univ of Arizona	AZ	11,958	VC
Univ of Conn	CT	16,628	HC
Univ of Delaware	DE	14,142	HC
Univ of Florida	FL	9,354	HC
Univ of Georgia	GA	11,004	HC
Univ of Hawaii at Manoa	HI	10,413	VC
Univ of Illinois at Urbana-Champaign	IL	15,800	HC+
Univ of Maine	ME	13,642	C
Univ of Maryland/College Park	MD	16,036	HC
Univ of Mass Amherst	MA	15,973	C+
Univ of Mich/Ann Arbor	MI	16,587	HC+
Univ of Minn/Crookston	MN	13,157	LC
Univ of Minn/Twin Cities	MN	13,165	HC
Univ of Nebr at Lincoln	NE	11,401	VC
Univ of Nevada/Reno	NV	12,155	NC
Univ of Northern Colo	CO	10,249	C
Univ of PR/Rio Piedras	PR	5,750	C
Univ of Rhode Island	RI	15,398	C
Univ of Tenn at Martin	TN	8,693	C
Univ of the South	TN	34,645	HC
Univ of Vermont	VT	18,080	VC
Univ of Wyoming	WY	9,666	C
Utah State Univ	UT	8,002	VC
Washington State Univ	WA	12,260	C
West Virginia Univ	WV	10,506	C
Western Carolina Univ	NC	7,000	C

NATURAL SCIENCES

School	ST	$IS	SR
Adelphi Univ	NY	27,000	VC
Avila Univ	MO	22,100	C
Bard College	NY	41,800	HC+
Benedictine College	KS	21,968	C
Bethel College	KS	21,650	C
Cal State, Fresno	CA	10,037	LC
Cal State, Los Angeles	CA	5,900	C
Cameron Univ	OK	6,314	NC
Carthage College	WI	26,000	C
Case Western Reserve Univ	OH	37,314	MC
Castleton State College	VT	13,158	C
Charleston Southern Univ	SC	17,800	C
Christian Brothers Univ	TN	24,650	VC
Clarion Univ of Pennsylvania	PA	11,844	C
Colgate Univ	NY	41,170	MC
College of Mount St. Joseph	OH	24,860	C
College of Our Lady of the Elms	MA	21,000	C
College of St. Benedict	MN	30,091	VC
College of St. Mary	NE	23,938	C
College of St. Scholastica	MN	28,456	C+
Concordia Univ Nebr	NE	20,500	C+
Concordia Univ St.Paul	MN	27,776	C
Concordia Univ, River Forest	IL	26,300	C
Covenant College	GA	26,460	VC+
Daemen College	NY	24,580	C
Dowling College	NY	22,110	LC
Edgewood College	WI	22,862	C
Edinboro Univ of Pennsylvania	PA	11,809	LC
Erskine College	SC	25,468	VC
Fresno Pacific Univ	CA	25,454	C
Gwynedd-Mercy College	PA	26,080	C
Hofstra Univ	NY	32,630	VC
Indiana Univ East	IN	4,806	LC
Indiana Univ of Pennsylvania	PA	11,209	C
Johns Hopkins Univ	MD	42,044	MC
Juniata College	PA	33,130	VC
Keystone College	PA	22,810	LC
LeMoyne-Owen College	TN	13,150	LC
Lesley Univ	MA	34,950	C
Lewis-Clark State College	ID	6,990	C
Loyola Marymount Univ	CA	36,321	VC
Lyndon State College	VT	14,233	LC
Madonna Univ	MI	16,068	VC
Master's College and Seminary	CA	25,850	VC

School	ST	$IS	SR
McMurry Univ	TX	18,100	LC
Mercer Univ	GA	27,525	VC+
Missouri Western State Univ	MO	9,534	NC
Muhlenberg College	PA	36,030	HC+
New College of Florida	FL	10,009	HC+
Northwest Nazarene Univ	ID	22,590	VC
Oakwood College	AL	14,904	C
Our Lady of the Lake Univ of San Antonio	TX	22,430	LC
Pacific Union College	CA	24,555	VC+
Park Univ	MO	11,592	C
Pepperdine Univ	CA	39,960	HC
Purdue Univ/West Lafayette	IN	13,458	VC
Rocky Mountain College	MT	20,805	C
St. Anselm College	NH	33,810	C
St. John's Univ	MN	29,749	VC
St. Mary's College of Maryland	MD	18,876	VC+
St. Norbert College	WI	28,577	C+
St. Peter's College	NJ	30,160	LC
Shawnee State Univ	OH	12,237	NC
Shimer College	IL	26,525	LC
Shorter College	GA	19,700	C
Siena Heights Univ	MI	17,000	LC
Simon's Rock College of Bard	MA	41,988	VC+
Southwestern Okla State Univ	OK	4,801	C
Spalding Univ	KY	18,882	C
Spelman College	GA	24,650	VC
SUNY/College at Geneseo	NY	12,910	HC+
Tabor College	KS	21,614	NC
Taylor Univ	IN	26,376	VC+
Texas A&M Univ at Galveston	TX	10,000	C+
Thomas Edison State College	NJ	3,780	SP
Turabo Univ	PR	4,110	
Universidad Metropolitana	PR	3,330	
Univ of Akron	OH	15,166	NC
Univ of Alabama at Birmingham	AL	13,716	C
Univ of Alaska Anchorage	AK	11,275	NC
Univ of Arizona	AZ	11,958	VC
Univ of Hawaii at Hilo	HI	6,500	C
Univ of Houston-Downtown	TX	3,326	NC
Univ of La Verne	CA	33,470	C
Univ of Nebr at Lincoln	NE	11,401	VC
Univ of New Haven	CT	31,794	C
Univ of Pittsburgh at Greensburg	PA	17,640	C
Univ of Pittsburgh at Pittsburgh	PA	18,866	HC
Univ of PR/Cayey Univ College	PR	1,250	
Univ of Puget Sound	WA	35,600	HC
Univ of Science and Arts of Okla	OK	7,650	C
Univ of Wisc/Stevens Point	WI	9,384	VC
Virginia Wesleyan College	VA	28,433	C
Washington and Lee Univ	VA	35,880	MC
Western Oregon Univ	OR	10,295	C
Worcester State College	MA	12,499	C
Xavier Univ	OH	30,490	MC
York College	NE	16,330	NC

NAVAL ARCHITECTURE AND MARINE ENGINEERING

School	ST	$IS	SR
SUNY/Maritime College	NY	12,475	C
Stevens Inst of Technology	NJ	40,935	HC
Texas A&M Univ at Galveston	TX	10,000	C+
United States Coast Guard Academy	CT		HC
United States Merchant Marine Academy	NY	6,516	HC+
United States Naval Academy	MD		MC
Univ of Mich/Ann Arbor	MI	16,587	HC+
Univ of New Orleans	LA	7,370	C
Univ of Wisc/Madison	WI	13,117	HC
Webb Inst	NY	8,340	MC

NEAR EASTERN STUDIES

School	ST	$IS	SR
Brandeis Univ	MA	41,551	MC
Brigham Young Univ	UT	9,200	VC
Cornell Univ	NY	41,717	MC
Indiana Univ Bloomington	IN	13,356	VC
Johns Hopkins Univ	MD	42,044	MC
Mount Union College	OH	25,840	C
Oberlin College	OH	40,904	MC
Princeton Univ	NJ	40,213	MC
Univ of Arizona	AZ	11,958	VC
Univ of Calif at Berkeley	CA	18,141	HC+
Univ of Calif at Los Angeles	CA	17,681	MC
Univ of Chicago	IL	42,369	MC
Univ of Hawaii at Manoa	HI	10,413	VC
Univ of Mich/Ann Arbor	MI	16,587	HC+
Univ of Washington	WA	10,400	VC
Washington Univ in St. Louis	MO	42,106	MC
Wayne State Univ	MI	11,805	C

School	ST	$IS	SR
Yale Univ	CT	41,000	MC

NEUROSCIENCES

School	ST	$IS	SR
Allegheny College	PA	33,500	MC
Amherst College	MA	41,590	MC
Baldwin-Wallace College	OH	27,256	VC
Bates College	ME	42,100	MC
Baylor Univ	TX	27,555	VC
Boston Univ	MA	42,046	HC+
Bowdoin College	ME	41,660	MC
Bowling Green State Univ	OH	14,994	C
Brandeis Univ	MA	41,551	MC
Brigham Young Univ	UT	9,200	VC
Brown Univ	RI	42,015	MC
Cedar Crest College	PA	30,615	C
Centenary College of Louisiana	LA	24,760	VC
Central Mich Univ	MI	12,244	C
Claremont McKenna College	CA	42,920	MC
Colgate Univ	NY	41,170	MC
Colo College	CO	37,668	HC
Columbia Univ/Columbia College	NY	42,584	MC
Conn College	CT	41,975	MC
Cornell Univ	NY	41,717	MC
Dickinson College	PA	40,170	HC+
Drake Univ	IA	27,632	VC+
Drew Univ/College of Liberal Arts	NJ	39,698	VC
Emory Univ	GA	40,546	MC
Franklin and Marshall College	PA	40,590	HC
Furman Univ	SC	33,264	HC+
Hamilton College	NY	41,660	MC
Johns Hopkins Univ	MD	42,044	MC
Kent State Univ	OH	14,594	C
Kenyon College	OH	39,500	MC
King College	TN	23,400	C
King's College	PA	29,810	C
Lafayette College	PA	39,267	MC
Lawrence Univ	WI	33,958	HC+
Macalester College	MN	36,500	MC
Middlebury College	VT	42,120	MC
Montana State Univ-Bozeman	MT	1,137	C
Mount Holyoke College	MA	42,148	HC+
Muhlenberg College	PA	36,030	HC+
Muskingum College	OH	22,970	C
New York Univ	NY	43,170	MC
Northeastern Univ	MA	35,742	HC
Northwestern Univ	IL	37,595	MC
Oberlin College	OH	40,904	MC
Pitzer College	CA	41,644	HC
Pomona College	CA	40,774	MC
Regis Univ	CO	31,890	C
St. Andrews Presbyterian College	NC	23,530	C
St. Lawrence Univ	NY	40,545	VC
Scripps College	CA	41,000	MC
Skidmore College	NY	41,779	HC
Smith College	MA	41,474	MC
Texas Christian Univ	TX	23,410	VC+
Trinity College	CT	38,040	HC+
Union College	NY	41,595	MC
Univ of Calif at Los Angeles	CA	17,681	MC
Univ of Calif at Riverside	CA	16,625	C
Univ of Pennsylvania	PA	41,766	MC
Univ of Pittsburgh at Pittsburgh	PA	18,866	HC
Univ of Rochester	NY	41,135	MC
Univ of St. Thomas	MN	28,000	VC
Univ of Scranton	PA	31,100	VC
Univ of Southern Calif	CA	41,618	MC
Univ of Texas at Dallas	TX	13,244	HC
Univ of Washington	WA	10,400	VC
Ursinus College	PA	38,950	VC
Vassar College	NY	41,700	MC
Washington and Lee Univ	VA	35,880	MC
Washington State Univ	WA	12,260	C
Washington Univ in St. Louis	MO	42,106	MC
Wellesley College	MA	41,030	MC
Wesleyan Univ	CT	42,122	MC
Westmont College	CA	36,672	HC

NONPROFIT/PUBLIC ORGANIZATION MANAGEMENT

School	ST	$IS	SR
Huntington Univ	IN	24,830	C
Rockhurst Univ	MO	25,440	VC
Southern Adventist Univ	TN	18,500	C
Southwestern College	KS	21,476	C
Univ of S Car Upstate	SC	11,957	C

NORWEGIAN

School	ST	$IS	SR
St. Olaf College	MN	32,800	HC
Univ of N Dak	ND	10,114	VC

NUCLEAR ENGINEERING

School	ST	$IS	SR
Georgia Inst of Technology	GA	11,450	HC+

ST = STATE **$IS** = IN-STATE COSTS **SR** = SELECTOR RATING

School	ST	$IS	SR
Idaho State Univ	ID	9,030	C
Mass Inst of Technology	MA	41,800	MC
N Car State Univ	NC	11,824	HC
Oregon State Univ	OR	11,055	C
Penn State Univ/Univ Park Campus	PA	18,038	HC
Purdue Univ/West Lafayette	IN	13,458	VC
Rensselaer Polytechnic Inst	NY	41,288	HC+
Texas A&M Univ	TX	13,351	HC
United States Military Academy	NY		MC
Univ of Arizona	AZ	11,958	VC
Univ of Calif at Berkeley	CA	18,141	HC+
Univ of Cincinnati	OH	17,682	C
Univ of Florida	FL	9,354	HC
Univ of Illinois at Urbana-Champaign	IL	15,800	HC+
Univ of Mich/Ann Arbor	MI	16,587	HC+
Univ of Missouri/Rolla	MO	13,332	HC
Univ of New Mexico	NM	11,253	C
Univ of Tenn at Knoxville	TN	11,720	C
Univ of Wisc/Madison	WI	13,117	HC

NUCLEAR ENGINEERING TECHNOLOGY

School	ST	$IS	SR
Old Dominion Univ	VA	11,907	C
Thomas Edison State College	NJ	3,780	SP
Univ of Florida	FL	9,354	HC

NUCLEAR MEDICAL TECHNOLOGY

School	ST	$IS	SR
Ashford Univ	IA	20,370	C
Barry Univ	FL	24,100	LC
Benedictine Univ	IL	25,710	C
Cedar Crest College	PA	30,615	C
Edinboro Univ of Pennsylvania	PA	11,809	LC
Ferris State Univ	MI	13,698	C
George Washington Univ	DC	48,820	MC
Indiana Univ Kokomo	IN	4,835	LC
Indiana Univ of Pennsylvania	PA	11,209	C
Indiana Univ-Purdue Univ Indianapolis	IN	10,959	C
Kent State Univ	OH	14,594	C
Mass College of Pharmacy and Health Sciences	MA	32,020	SP
New Jersey City Univ	NJ	13,695	LC
Old Dominion Univ	VA	11,907	C
Roosevelt Univ	IL	22,605	VC
St. Louis Univ	MO	33,158	VC+
St. Mary's Univ of Minn	MN	23,857	VC
SUNY/Univ at Buffalo	NY	13,694	VC
Thomas Edison State College	NJ	3,780	SP
Univ of Alabama at Birmingham	AL	13,716	C
Univ of Central Arkansas	AR	9,984	C
Univ of Cincinnati	OH	17,682	C
Univ of Findlay	OH	29,238	C
Univ of Iowa	IA	12,172	VC
Univ of Nevada/Las Vegas	NV	11,566	C
Univ of St. Francis	IL	25,430	C
Univ of the Incarnate Word	TX	23,306	C
Univ of Vermont	VT	18,080	VC
Univ of Wisc/La Crosse	WI	10,045	VC
Wheeling Jesuit Univ	WV	26,910	C
York College of Pennsylvania	PA	16,550	VC

NUCLEAR TECHNOLOGY

School	ST	$IS	SR
Excelsior College	NY	995	SP
Peru State College	NE	6,350	NC

NURSING

School	ST	$IS	SR
Abilene Christian Univ	TX	20,830	C
Adelphi Univ	NY	27,000	VC
Albany State Univ	GA	5,770	C+
Alcorn State Univ	MS	8,190	LC
Alderson-Broaddus College	WV	24,006	C
Allen College	IA	18,067	SP
Alvernia College	PA	26,388	C
Alverno College	WI	21,088	C
American International College	MA	28,710	LC
Anderson Univ	IN	25,050	LC
Andrews Univ	MI	21,786	C
Angelo State Univ	TX	8,340	NC
Anna Maria College	MA	29,815	LC
Aquinas College	TN	10,660	LC
Arizona State Univ-Tempe	AZ	11,174	C
Arkansas State Univ	AR	9,630	C
Arkansas Tech Univ	AR	8,108	VC
Armstrong Atlantic State Univ	GA	7,394	C
Atlantic Union College	MA	17,600	LC
Auburn Univ	AL	12,230	VC
Auburn Univ Montgomery	AL	9,530	NC
Augustana College	SD	24,380	VC
Aurora Univ	IL	20,645	C
Austin Peay State Univ	TN	7,535	C
Avila Univ	MO	22,100	C
Azusa Pacific Univ	CA	28,546	VC
Ball State Univ	IN	13,138	C
Barry Univ	FL	24,100	LC
Barton College	NC	22,316	C
Baylor Univ	TX	27,555	HC
Bellarmine Univ	KY	27,650	C+
Belmont Univ	TN	24,110	VC
Bemidji State Univ	MN	11,180	LC
Benedictine Univ	IL	25,710	C
Berea College	KY	5,496	VC+
Bethel College	IN	19,680	C
Bethel College	KS	21,650	C
Bethel Univ	MN	29,840	VC
Bethune-Cookman College	FL	17,922	LC
Biola Univ	CA	29,372	VC
Bloomfield College	NJ	22,500	LC
Bloomsburg Univ of Pennsylvania	PA	11,602	C
Bluefield State College	WV	3,140	LC
Boise State Univ	ID	9,438	LC
Boston College	MA	41,608	MC
Bowie State Univ	MD	10,880	C+
Bradley Univ	IL	25,280	VC
Brenau Univ Women's College	GA	23,950	VC
Briar Cliff Univ	IA	23,550	LC
Brigham Young Univ	UT	9,200	VC
Cabarrus College of Health Sciences	NC	8,000	SP
Cal State East Bay	CA	10,856	LC
Cal State, Bakersfield	CA	6,125	LC
Cal State, Chico	CA	11,395	C
Cal State, Dominguez Hills	CA	10,220	LC
Cal State, Fresno	CA	10,037	LC
Cal State, Fullerton	CA	10,990	C
Cal State, Los Angeles	CA	5,900	C
Cal State, Northridge	CA	9,036	LC
Cal State, Sacramento	CA	11,122	C+
Cal State, San Bernardino	CA	12,563	LC
Cal State, Stanislaus	CA	11,283	C
Calif Univ of Pennsylvania	PA	14,217	C
Calvin College	MI	25,735	NC
Capital Univ	OH	30,444	C
Cardinal Stritch Univ	WI	21,910	C
Caribbean Univ	PR	3,000	
Carlow Univ	PA	24,313	C
Carroll College	MT	23,324	C+
Carroll College	WI	24,860	C
Carson-Newman College	TN	16,800	C
Case Western Reserve Univ	OH	37,314	MC
Catholic Univ of America	DC	35,838	VC
Cedar Crest College	PA	30,615	C
Cedarville Univ	OH	21,904	VC
Central Conn State Univ	CT	13,620	C
Central Methodist Univ	MO	18,000	C
Central Missouri State Univ	MO	10,000	C
Central Univ of Bayamon	PR	3,335	
Charleston Southern Univ	SC	17,800	C
Chicago State Univ	IL	10,915	C+
Christopher Newport Univ	VA	13,326	VC
CUNY/College of Staten Island	NY	4,328	NC
CUNY/Herbert H. Lehman College	NY	4,000	LC
CUNY/Hunter College	NY	8,000	C+
CUNY/Medgar Evers College	NY	4,250	NC
CUNY/York College	NY	4,242	NC
Clarion Univ of Pennsylvania	PA	11,844	C
Clarke College	IA	25,390	C
Clarkson College	NE	13,000	C
Clayton College and State Univ	GA	2,445	LC
Clemson Univ	SC	13,366	HC
Cleveland State Univ	OH	10,798	NC
Coe College	IA	27,440	VC
Colby-Sawyer College	NH	27,850	LC
College Misericordia	PA	27,950	C
College of Mount St. Vincent	NY	28,000	C
College of Mount St. Joseph	OH	24,860	C
College of New Jersey	NJ	18,315	MC
College of New Rochelle	NY	28,396	C
College of Notre Dame of Maryland	MD	27,700	C
College of Our Lady of the Elms	MA	21,000	C
College of St. Benedict	MN	30,091	VC
College of St. Catherine	MN	27,505	VC
College of St. Elizabeth	NJ	28,495	C
College of St. Mary	NE	23,938	C
College of St. Scholastica	MN	28,456	C+
Colo State Univ-Pueblo	CO	7,821	LC
Columbia Union College	MD	23,536	LC
Columbus State Univ	GA	8,664	C
Concordia College: Moorhead	MN	22,475	VC
Concordia Univ	OR	24,400	C
Concordia Univ Wisc	WI	22,660	VC
Coppin State College	MD	10,200	LC
Creighton Univ	NE	29,918	VC+
Crichton College	TN	15,300	C
Culver-Stockton College	MO	20,625	C
Cumberland Univ	TN	18,894	C
Curry College	MA	26,100	LC
Daemen College	NY	24,580	C
Davenport Univ	MI	15,205	NC
De Sales Univ	PA	28,580	VC
Deaconess College of Nursing	MO	15,941	SP
Delaware State Univ	DE	8,130	LC
Delta State Univ	MS	7,709	C
Dickinson State Univ	ND	7,847	NC
Dillard Univ	LA	17,500	VC
Dominican College	NY	26,630	LC
Dominican Univ of Calif	CA	36,836	C
Dordt College	IA	20,325	VC
Duquesne Univ	PA	29,534	VC
D'Youville College	NY	23,660	C
East Carolina Univ	NC	10,000	C
East Central Univ	OK	6,207	C
East Stroudsburg Univ of Pennsylvania	PA	10,336	C
East Tenn State Univ	TN	8,497	C
East Texas Baptist Univ	TX	16,713	C
Eastern Kentucky Univ	KY	7,725	C
Eastern Mennonite Univ	VA	25,450	VC
Eastern Mich Univ	MI	12,897	C
Eastern New Mexico Univ	NM	7,264	C
Eastern Oregon Univ	OR	10,400	NC
Eastern Washington Univ	WA	10,608	C
Edgewood College	WI	22,862	C
Edinboro Univ of Pennsylvania	PA	11,809	LC
Elmhurst College	IL	24,685	C
Elmira College	NY	37,200	VC
Emmanuel College	MA	32,000	C+
Emory Univ	GA	40,546	MC
Emporia State Univ	KS	8,093	C
Endicott College	MA	30,156	C+
Excelsior College	NY	995	SP
Fairfield Univ	CT	39,835	HC
Fairleigh Dickinson Univ/Metropolitan Campus	NJ	28,590	C
Fayetteville State Univ	NC	6,000	LC
Felician College	NJ	24,300	C
Ferris State Univ	MI	13,698	C
Fitchburg State College	MA	11,276	C
Florida A&M Univ	FL	8,344	C
Florida Atlantic Univ	FL	11,221	C
Florida Gulf Coast Univ	FL	10,833	C
Florida Hospital College of Health Sciences	FL	11,152	SP
Florida International Univ	FL	9,215	VC
Florida State Univ	FL	9,028	HC
Fort Hays State Univ	KS	7,638	C
Framingham State College	MA	11,156	C
Francis Marion Univ	SC	11,114	C
Franciscan Univ of Steubenville	OH	20,300	VC
Gannon Univ	PA	26,100	C
Gardner-Webb Univ	NC	21,500	C
George Fox Univ	OR	28,490	C
George Mason Univ	VA	10,850	VC
Georgetown Univ	DC	43,183	MC
Georgia College and State Univ	GA	11,020	C
Georgia Southern Univ	GA	9,762	C
Georgia Southwestern State Univ	GA	6,035	C
Georgia State Univ	GA	11,444	VC
Glenville State College	WV	8,778	NC
Gonzaga Univ	WA	30,218	HC
Goshen College	IN	22,850	VC
Graceland Univ	IA	19,700	C
Grambling State Univ	LA	6,538	NC
Grand Canyon Univ	AZ	32,000	LC
Grand Valley State Univ	MI	12,000	VC
Grand View College	IA	21,482	C
Gustavus Adolphus College	MN	30,920	HC
Gwynedd-Mercy College	PA	26,080	C
Hampton Univ	VA	19,468	C+
Hannibal-LaGrange College	MO	16,390	C
Harding Univ	AR	16,512	VC
Hardin-Simmons Univ	TX	18,641	C
Hartwick College	NY	36,065	C+
Hawaii Pacific Univ	HI	21,080	C
Henderson State Univ	AR	7,600	C
Holy Family Univ	PA	25,740	C
Holy Names College	CA	27,980	NC
Hope College	MI	28,208	VC+
Houston Baptist Univ	TX	18,660	C
Howard Univ	DC	18,481	C+
Humboldt State Univ	CA	11,176	C
Huntington Univ	IN	24,830	C
Huron Univ	SD	10,700	C
Husson College	ME	17,410	LC
Idaho State Univ	ID	9,030	C
Illinois State Univ	IL	12,839	C
Illinois Wesleyan Univ	IL	34,050	HC+
Immaculata Univ	PA	25,350	C
Indiana State Univ	IN	11,604	C
Indiana Univ Bloomington	IN	13,356	VC
Indiana Univ East	IN	4,806	LC
Indiana Univ Kokomo	IN	4,835	LC
Indiana Univ Northwest	IN	4,902	LC
Indiana Univ of Pennsylvania	PA	11,209	C
Indiana Univ South Bend	IN	4,989	LC
Indiana Univ Southeast	IN	4,880	LC
Indiana Univ-Purdue Univ Fort Wayne	IN	5,067	LC
Indiana Univ-Purdue Univ Indianapolis	IN	10,959	C
Inter American Univ of PR/Aguadilla Campus	PR	3,784	
Inter American Univ of PR/Arecibo Campus	PR	3,350	
Inter American Univ of PR/Fajardo Campus	PR	4,000	
Inter American Univ of PR/Metropolitan Campus	PR	4,320	
Inter American Univ of PR/Ponce Regional College	PR	3,700	
Inter American Univ of PR/San German	PR	6,720	
Iowa Wesleyan College	IA	22,140	C
Jacksonville State Univ	AL	7,618	LC
Jacksonville Univ	FL	24,040	C
James Madison Univ	VA	12,010	VC
Jamestown College	ND	14,130	NC
Jewish Hospital College of Nursing and Allied Health	MO	12,000	SP
Johnson C. Smith Univ	NC	20,000	C
Judson College	IL	25,130	C
Kansas Wesleyan Univ	KS	21,400	VC
Kean Univ	NJ	15,880	C
Kennesaw State Univ	GA	12,152	C
Kent State Univ	OH	14,594	C
Kentucky State Univ	KY	10,089	LC
Keuka College	NY	26,050	C
King College	TN	23,400	C
Kutztown Univ of Pennsylvania	PA	10,820	C
La Roche College	PA	24,724	LC
La Salle Univ	PA	34,950	C
LaGrange College	GA	22,874	C+
Lake Superior State Univ	MI	12,842	LC
Lamar Univ	TX	6,820	LC
Lander Univ	SC	10,600	C
Langston Univ	OK	2,308	LC
Le Moyne College	NY	29,570	VC
Lenoir-Rhyne College	NC	25,580	C
Lester L. Cox College of Nursing and Health Sciences	MO	12,290	SP
Lewis Univ	IL	23,050	C+
Lewis-Clark State College	ID	6,990	C
Liberty Univ	VA	19,101	C
Lincoln Memorial Univ	TN	18,144	C
Lincoln Univ	MO	8,000	NC
Lipscomb Univ	TN	20,967	VC
LIU/Brooklyn Campus	NY	25,000	C
LIU/C.W. Post Campus	NY	28,282	C
Louisiana College	LA	13,450	C
Lourdes College	OH	15,300	C
Loyola Univ Chicago	IL	32,896	VC
Loyola Univ New Orleans	LA	31,050	VC+
Lubbock Christian Univ	TX	16,960	C
Luther College	IA	28,800	VC+
Lynchburg College	VA	30,645	C
MacMurray College	IL	20,755	C
Madonna Univ	MI	16,068	VC
Malone College	OH	23,040	C
Mansfield Univ	PA	11,300	C
Marian College	IN	26,160	C
Marian College of Fond du Lac	WI	21,775	LC
Marquette Univ	WI	31,066	HC
Marshall Univ	WV	9,116	C
Marymount Univ	VA	25,934	C
Maryville College	TN	29,224	VC
Maryville Univ of St. Louis	MO	23,000	VC
Marywood Univ	PA	30,680	C
Mass College of Pharmacy and Health Sciences	MA	32,020	SP
McKendree College	IL	24,800	VC
McMurry Univ	TX	18,100	LC
McNeese State Univ	LA	5,270	LC
Mercy College	NY	20,000	NC
Mercy College of Health Sciences	IA	11,700	SP
Mesa State College	CO	8,051	C
Messiah College	PA	28,910	VC+
Metropolitan State College of Denver	CO	2,338	LC
Metropolitan State Univ	MN	4,682	SP
Miami Univ	OH	29,097	HC
Mich State Univ	MI	13,689	VC
MidAmerica Nazarene Univ	KS	20,584	LC
Middle Tenn State Univ	TN	8,540	C
Midland Lutheran College	NE	18,600	C
Midway College	KY	20,150	C
Midwestern State Univ	TX	9,381	LC
Millersville Univ of Pennsylvania	PA	12,113	C
Milligan College	TN	21,990	VC
Millikin Univ	IL	25,590	C
Milwaukee School of Engineering	WI	29,847	VC+
Minn State Univ, Mankato	MN	10,276	LC
Minn State Univ, Moorhead	MN	7,000	LC

ST = STATE $IS = IN-STATE COSTS   SR = SELECTOR RATING

School	ST	$IS	SR
Minot State Univ	ND	6,700	LC
Miss College	MS	14,574	VC
Miss Univ for Women	MS	6,000	LC
Missouri Baptist Univ	MO	19,640	C
Missouri Southern State Univ	MO	8,396	NC
Missouri State Univ	MO	10,748	C+
Missouri Western State Univ	MO	9,534	NC
Molloy College	NY	16,510	C
Monmouth Univ	NJ	28,956	C
Montana State Univ-Bozeman	MT	1,137	C
Montana State Univ-Northern	MT	10,000	NC
Moravian College	PA	28,950	VC
Morehead State Univ	KY	9,150	C
Morningside College	IA	23,704	C
Mount Aloysius College	PA	20,900	C
Mount Marty College	SD	20,590	C
Mount Mary College	WI	22,895	C
Mount Mercy College	IA	23,670	C
Mount St. Mary College	NY	25,250	C
Mount St. Mary's College	CA	32,086	VC
Mountain State Univ	WV	11,406	NC
Murray State Univ	KY	8,900	VC
National Univ	CA	8,412	SP
Nazareth College of Rochester	NY	28,175	VC
Nebr Methodist College of Nursing and Allied Health	NE	12,950	SP
Nebr Wesleyan Univ	NE	23,415	C+
Neumann College	PA	25,996	LC
New Jersey City Univ	NJ	13,695	LC
New Mexico State Univ	NM	9,250	C
New York Inst of Technology	NY	28,126	VC
New York Univ	NY	43,170	MC
Newman Univ	KS	21,106	C
Niagara Univ	NY	28,250	C
Nicholls State Univ	LA	6,500	NC
Norfolk State Univ	VA	10,531	LC
N Car Agricultural and Technical State Univ	NC	8,000	LC
N Car Central Univ	NC	9,000	LC
N Dak State Univ	ND	8,500	C
North Georgia College and State Univ	GA	7,000	C
North Park Univ	IL	24,050	C
Northeastern State Univ	OK	5,896	LC
Northeastern Univ	MA	35,742	HC
Northern Arizona Univ	AZ	10,353	C
Northern Illinois Univ	IL	13,178	C
Northern Kentucky Univ	KY	6,670	NC
Northern Mich Univ	MI	12,340	LC
Northwest Nazarene Univ	ID	22,590	C
Northwest Univ	WA	18,854	C
Northwestern Okla State Univ	OK	6,250	NC
Northwestern State Univ of Louisiana	LA	7,144	C
Norwich Univ	VT	28,212	C
Nova Southeastern Univ	FL	24,320	C
Oakland Univ	MI	11,936	C
Oakwood College	AL	14,904	C
Ohio State Univ	OH	15,357	HC
Ohio Univ	OH	15,921	C
Okla Baptist Univ	OK	17,986	VC
Okla City Univ	OK	23,965	VC
Okla Panhandle State Univ	OK	7,635	NC
Old Dominion Univ	VA	11,907	C
Olivet Nazarene Univ	IL	22,590	C
Oral Roberts Univ	OK	22,650	C
Oregon State Univ	OR	11,055	C
Otterbein College	OH	28,986	C
Our Lady of Holy Cross College	LA	8,090	LC
Pace Univ	NY	30,000	VC
Pacific Lutheran Univ	WA	28,805	VC
Pacific Union College	CA	24,555	VC+
Palm Beach Atlantic Univ	FL	23,597	VC
Penn State Univ/Altoona	PA	12,635	C
Penn State Univ/Univ Park Campus	PA	18,038	HC
Pennsylvania College of Technology	PA	16,980	LC
Piedmont College	GA	20,500	C
Pittsburg State Univ	KS	8,112	C
Point Loma Nazarene Univ	CA	27,610	VC
Pontifical Catholic Univ of PR/Ponce	PR	7,310	C
Prairie View A&M Univ	TX	11,110	LC
Presentation College	SD	14,800	LC
Purdue Univ/Calumet	IN	10,891	LC
Purdue Univ/West Lafayette	IN	13,458	VC
Queens Univ of Charlotte	NC	24,528	C
Quincy Univ	IL	24,920	C
Quinnipiac Univ	CT	34,640	VC
Radford Univ	VA	13,145	C
Ramapo College of New Jersey	NJ	16,630	VC
Regis College	MA	31,350	VC
Regis Univ	CO	31,890	C
Research College of Nursing	MO	25,640	SP
Rhode Island College	RI	11,570	C
Richard Stockton College of New Jersey	NJ	14,000	VC
Rivier College	NH	26,600	C
Robert Morris Univ	PA	22,822	C
Roberts Wesleyan College	NY	26,378	C
Rockford College	IL	28,330	VC
Rockhurst Univ	MO	25,440	VC
Russell Sage College	NY	27,000	C
Rutgers, The State Univ of New Jersey/Camden Campus	NJ	15,000	VC
Rutgers, The State Univ of New Jersey/Newark Campus	NJ	15,640	VC
Sacred Heart Univ	CT	33,404	C
Saginaw Valley State Univ	MI	11,432	C
St. Anselm College	NH	33,810	C
St. Francis Univ	PA	25,880	LC
St. John Fisher College	NY	27,860	C
St. John's Univ	MN	29,749	VC
St. Joseph College	CT	32,050	C
St. Joseph's College	IN	26,600	C
St. Joseph's College of Maine	ME	29,185	C
St. Joseph's College, New York, Brooklyn Campus	NY	12,206	C
St. Louis Univ	MO	33,158	VC+
St. Mary's College	IN	32,538	VC
St. Mary's College of Calif	CA	37,290	C
St. Olaf College	MN	32,800	HC
St. Peter's College	NJ	30,160	LC
St. Xavier Univ	IL	23,160	C
Salem State College	MA	13,161	LC
Salisbury Univ	MD	13,128	VC
Salve Regina Univ	RI	33,450	C
Samford Univ	AL	20,258	VC
San Diego State Univ	CA	12,971	C
San Francisco State Univ	CA	13,000	C
San Jose State Univ	CA	11,707	C
Seattle Pacific Univ	WA	29,355	C
Seattle Univ	WA	30,063	VC
Seton Hall Univ	NJ	33,622	VC
Seton Hill Univ	PA	28,810	C
Shawnee State Univ	OH	12,237	NC
Shenandoah Univ	VA	27,600	C
Shepherd Univ	WV	10,066	C
Simmons College	MA	35,640	VC
Slippery Rock Univ of Pennsylvania	PA	10,360	LC
Sonoma State Univ	CA	14,732	C
S Car State Univ	SC	6,700	LC
S Dak State Univ	SD	9,815	C
South Univ	GA		LC
Southeast Missouri State Univ	MO	10,596	C
Southeastern Louisiana Univ	LA	8,521	LC
Southern Adventist Univ	TN	18,500	C
Southern Conn State Univ	CT	10,310	C
Southern Illinois Univ Edwardsville	IL	11,022	C
Southern Nazarene Univ	OK	14,634	NC
Southern Oregon Univ	OR	12,186	C
Southern Univ and A&M College	LA	8,238	LC
Southern Vermont College	VT	21,322	LC
Southwest Baptist Univ	MO	18,300	C
Southwestern Adventist Univ	TX	18,290	LC
Southwestern College	KS	21,476	C
Southwestern Okla State Univ	OK	4,801	C
Spalding Univ	KY	18,882	C
Spring Arbor Univ	MI	22,476	C
Spring Hill College	AL	28,678	C
SUNY/College at Brockport	NY	12,747	VC
SUNY/College at Plattsburgh	NY	12,362	C
SUNY/Inst of Technology	NY	12,575	VC
SUNY/Univ at Binghamton	NY	13,988	HC
SUNY/Univ at Buffalo	NY	13,694	VC
SUNY/Univ at Stony Brook	NY	13,625	HC
Stephen F. Austin State Univ	TX	7,930	C
Tarleton State Univ	TX	8,952	C
Temple Univ	PA	17,438	C
Tenn State Univ	TN	9,048	LC
Tenn Tech Univ	TN	10,044	C
Tenn Wesleyan College	TN	18,650	C
Texas A&M Univ at Corpus Christi	TX	10,280	LC
Texas A&M Univ at Kingsville	TX	6,800	LC
Texas Christian Univ	TX	23,410	VC+
Texas Woman's Univ	TX	7,804	LC
Thomas Edison State College	NJ	3,780	SP
Thomas More College	KY	24,470	C
Thomas Univ	GA	11,520	NC
Towson Univ	MD	13,924	VC
Trinity Christian College	IL	23,645	C
Trinity College of Nursing and Health Sciences	IL	4,620	SP
Troy Univ	AL	8,916	C
Truman State Univ	MO	11,242	HC
Tuskegee Univ	AL	18,860	LC
Union College	NE	18,710	C
Union Univ	TN	20,750	C
Universidad Adventista de las Antillas	PR	7,360	
Universidad Metropolitana	PR	3,330	
Univ of Akron	OH	15,166	NC
Univ of Alabama	AL	9,888	C
Univ of Alabama at Birmingham	AL	13,716	C
Univ of Alabama in Huntsville	AL	9,516	VC
Univ of Alaska Anchorage	AK	11,275	NC
Univ of Arizona	AZ	11,958	VC
Univ of Arkansas	AR	11,859	VC
Univ of Arkansas at Monticello	AR	7,325	NC
Univ of Arkansas at Pine Bluff	AR	8,300	C
Univ of Calif at Los Angeles	CA	17,681	MC
Univ of Central Arkansas	AR	9,984	C
Univ of Central Florida	FL	10,739	VC
Univ of Central Okla	OK	8,094	C
Univ of Charleston	WV	27,600	C
Univ of Cincinnati	OH	17,682	C
Univ of Colo at Colo Springs	CO	11,517	VC
Univ of Conn	CT	16,628	HC
Univ of Delaware	DE	14,142	HC
Univ of Detroit Mercy	MI	27,000	C
Univ of Dubuque	IA	23,390	C
Univ of Evansville	IN	28,320	VC
Univ of Findlay	OH	29,238	C
Univ of Florida	FL	9,354	HC
Univ of Hartford	CT	34,044	C
Univ of Hawaii at Hilo	HI	6,500	C
Univ of Hawaii at Manoa	HI	10,413	VC
Univ of Illinois at Chicago	IL	16,256	VC
Univ of Indianapolis	IN	25,090	C
Univ of Iowa	IA	12,172	VC
Univ of Kansas	KS	10,915	VC
Univ of Kentucky	KY	7,800	C
Univ of Louisiana at Lafayette	LA	5,830	C
Univ of Louisiana at Monroe	LA	7,103	C
Univ of Louisville	KY	10,040	VC
Univ of Maine	ME	13,642	C
Univ of Maine at Fort Kent	ME	10,832	LC
Univ of Mary	ND	15,374	C
Univ of Mary Hardin-Baylor	TX	19,428	C
Univ of Mass Amherst	MA	15,973	C+
Univ of Mass Boston	MA	8,024	C
Univ of Mass Dartmouth	MA	15,985	C
Univ of Mass Lowell	MA	14,327	VC
Univ of Memphis	TN	11,153	C
Univ of Miami	FL	38,397	MC
Univ of Mich/Ann Arbor	MI	16,587	HC+
Univ of Mich/Flint	MI	6,398	C
Univ of Minn/Twin Cities	MN	13,165	HC
Univ of Missouri/Columbia	MO	13,500	C
Univ of Missouri/Kansas City	MO	15,000	C
Univ of Missouri/St. Louis	MO	14,046	C
Univ of Mobile	AL	16,880	C
Univ of Nebr at Kearney	NE	9,000	NC
Univ of Nevada/Las Vegas	NV	11,566	C
Univ of Nevada/Reno	NV	12,155	NC
Univ of New England	ME	31,005	C
Univ of New Hampshire	NH	16,810	VC
Univ of New Mexico	NM	11,253	C
Univ of North Alabama	AL	8,992	C
Univ of N Car at Chapel Hill	NC	11,129	MC
Univ of N Car at Charlotte	NC	9,101	C
Univ of N Car at Greensboro	NC	8,993	C
Univ of N Car at Pembroke	NC	7,940	LC
Univ of N Car at Wilmington	NC	10,107	VC
Univ of N Dak	ND	10,114	VC
Univ of North Florida	FL	9,908	NC
Univ of Northern Colo	CO	10,249	C
Univ of Pennsylvania	PA	41,766	MC
Univ of Pittsburgh at Bradford	PA	17,008	C
Univ of Pittsburgh at Pittsburgh	PA	18,866	HC
Univ of Portland	OR	32,300	VC
Univ of PR at Humacao	PR	1,707	
Univ of PR/Arecibo	PR	8,327	
Univ of PR/Mayaguez	PR	1,250	
Univ of Rhode Island	RI	15,398	C
Univ of Rio Grande	OH	8,728	NC
Univ of Rochester	NY	41,135	MC
Univ of St. Francis	IL	25,430	C
Univ of St. Francis	IN	20,970	C
Univ of San Diego	CA	40,620	HC
Univ of San Francisco	CA	37,560	VC
Univ of Scranton	PA	31,100	VC
Univ of South Alabama	AL	8,930	LC
Univ of S Car at Aiken	SC	11,718	LC
Univ of S Car at Columbia	SC	13,397	VC
Univ of S Car Upstate	SC	11,957	C
Univ of South Florida	FL	10,284	VC
Univ of Southern Indiana	IN	12,590	LC
Univ of Southern Maine	ME	12,614	C
Univ of Southern Miss	MS	10,112	C
Univ of Tampa	FL	25,784	C
Univ of Tenn at Chattanooga	TN	7,790	C
Univ of Tenn at Knoxville	TN	11,720	C
Univ of Tenn at Martin	TN	8,693	C
Univ of Texas at Arlington	TX	7,195	LC
Univ of Texas at Austin	TX	14,610	HC
Univ of Texas at El Paso	TX	8,764	NC
Univ of Texas-Pan American	TX	7,290	C+
Univ of the District of Columbia	DC	2,070	LC
Univ of the Incarnate Word	TX	23,306	C
Univ of the Sacred Heart	PR	5,590	
Univ of Toledo	OH	15,806	NC
Univ of Tulsa	OK	25,348	HC
Univ of Utah	UT	10,162	VC
Univ of Vermont	VT	18,080	VC
Univ of Virginia	VA	13,759	MC
Univ of Virginia's College at Wise	VA	11,076	C
Univ of Washington	WA	10,400	VC
Univ of West Florida	FL	8,559	C
Univ of West Georgia	GA	8,838	C
Univ of Wisc/Eau Claire	WI	9,915	VC
Univ of Wisc/Green Bay	WI	9,415	VC
Univ of Wisc/Madison	WI	13,117	HC
Univ of Wisc/Milwaukee	WI	9,427	C
Univ of Wisc/Oshkosh	WI	10,426	LC
Univ of Wisc/Stevens Point	WI	9,384	C
Univ of Wyoming	WY	9,666	C
Ursuline College	OH	25,456	C
Utica College	NY	31,396	C
Valdosta State Univ	GA	8,802	C
Valparaiso Univ	IN	28,970	VC+
Villa Julie College	MD	25,222	C
Villanova Univ	PA	38,672	HC+
Virginia Commonwealth Univ	VA	12,987	C
Viterbo Univ	WI	21,670	C
Wagner College	NY	33,300	VC
Walla Walla College	WA	24,489	NC
Walsh Univ	OH	23,440	C
Washburn Univ	KS	9,734	NC
Washington State Univ	WA	12,260	C
Wayne State Univ	MI	11,805	C
Waynesburg College	PA	21,230	C
Weber State Univ	UT	9,635	NC
Webster Univ	MO	24,280	VC
Wesley College	DE	19,905	C
West Chester Univ of Pennsylvania	PA	12,355	C+
West Liberty State College	WV	9,142	LC
West Texas A&M Univ	TX	8,452	C
West Virginia Univ	WV	10,506	C
West Virginia Univ Inst of Technology	WV	8,788	NC
West Virginia Wesleyan College	WV	26,880	C
Western Carolina Univ	NC	7,000	C
Western Conn State Univ	CT	12,993	C
Western Kentucky Univ	KY	10,192	C
Western Mich Univ	MI	13,299	C
Westminster College	UT	25,656	C
Wheeling Jesuit Univ	WV	26,910	C
Whitworth College	WA	29,428	VC+
Wichita State Univ	KS	8,500	C
Widener Univ	PA	27,275	C
Wilkes Univ	PA	30,886	C
William Carey College	MS	11,000	C
William Jewell College	MO	24,340	C
William Paterson Univ of New Jersey	NJ	17,810	C+
Wilmington College	DE	5,594	NC
Winona State Univ	MN	11,333	C
Winston-Salem State Univ	NC	8,960	LC
Worcester State College	MA	12,499	C
Wright State Univ	OH	13,616	C
Xavier Univ	OH	30,490	HC
York College of Pennsylvania	PA	16,550	VC
Youngstown State Univ	OH	12,613	NC

NURSING EDUCATION

School	ST	$IS	SR
Indiana Wesleyan Univ	IN	22,074	C+

NURSING HOME ADMINISTRATION

School	ST	$IS	SR
Youngstown State Univ	OH	12,613	NC

NUTRITION

School	ST	$IS	SR
Abilene Christian Univ	TX	20,830	C
Alabama A&M Univ	AL	8,890	LC
Alcorn State Univ	MS	8,190	LC
Andrews Univ	MI	21,786	C
Appalachian State Univ	NC	8,000	VC
Auburn Univ	AL	12,230	VC
Baylor Univ	TX	27,555	HC
Benedictine Univ	IL	25,710	C
Boston Univ	MA	42,046	HC+
Bridgewater College	VA	27,790	C
Brigham Young Univ	UT	9,200	VC
Cal State, Chico	CA	11,395	C

ST = STATE $IS = IN-STATE COSTS   SR = SELECTOR RATING

School	ST	$IS	SR
Case Western Reserve Univ	OH	37,314	MC
CUNY/Hunter College	NY	8,000	C+
College of St. Benedict	MN	30,091	VC
College of St. Catherine	MN	27,505	VC
College of St. Elizabeth	NJ	28,495	C
Colo State Univ-Fort Collins	CO	10,878	C+
Cornell Univ	NY	41,717	MC
Dominican Univ	IL	26,370	C
Drexel Univ	PA	27,700	VC
East Carolina Univ	NC	10,000	C
Edinboro Univ of Pennsylvania	PA	11,809	LC
Florida State Univ	FL	9,028	HC
Fort Valley State Univ	GA	6,975	C
Framingham State College	MA	11,156	C
Georgia Southern Univ	GA	9,762	C
Georgia State Univ	GA	11,444	VC
Hampshire College	MA	37,120	HC
Indiana Univ Bloomington	IN	13,356	VC
Iowa State Univ	IA	11,831	VC
Kansas State Univ	KS	10,516	VC
Kent State Univ	OH	14,594	C
La Salle Univ	PA	34,950	C
Langston Univ	OK	2,308	LC
LIU/C.W. Post Campus	NY	28,282	C
Louisiana State Univ and A&M College	LA	10,749	VC
Madonna Univ	MI	16,068	VC
Meredith College	NC	25,600	C
Mich State Univ	MI	13,689	VC
Middle Tenn State Univ	TN	8,540	C
Missouri State Univ	MO	10,748	C+
New Mexico State Univ	NM	9,250	C
New York Inst of Technology	NY	28,126	VC
New York Univ	NY	43,170	MC
N Car Central Univ	NC	9,000	LC
N Dak State Univ	ND	8,500	C
Northern Illinois Univ	IL	13,178	C
Ohio State Univ	OH	15,357	HC
Ohio Univ	OH	15,921	C
Okla State Univ	OK	10,213	VC
Oregon State Univ	OR	11,055	C
Penn State Univ/Univ Park Campus	PA	18,038	HC
Pepperdine Univ	CA	39,960	HC
Purdue Univ/West Lafayette	IN	13,458	VC
Radford Univ	VA	13,145	C
Rochester Inst of Technology	NY	32,070	VC+
Russell Sage College	NY	27,000	C
Rutgers, The State Univ of New Jersey/New Brunswick/Piscataway Campus	NJ	15,810	HC
St. John's Univ	MN	29,749	VC
St. Joseph College	CT	32,050	C
St. Louis Univ	MO	33,158	VC+
Samford Univ	AL	20,258	VC
San Diego State Univ	CA	12,971	C
Simmons College	MA	35,640	VC
S Car State Univ	SC	6,700	LC
S Dak State Univ	SD	9,815	C
Stephen F. Austin State Univ	TX	7,930	C
Syracuse Univ	NY	38,655	HC
Texas Christian Univ	TX	23,410	VC+
Texas Southern Univ	TX	9,828	C
Texas State Univ - San Marcos	TX	10,862	C
Univ of Arizona	AZ	11,958	VC
Univ of Arkansas	AR	11,859	VC
Univ of at Calif Davis	CA	15,010	VC
Univ of Calif at Berkeley	CA	18,141	HC+
Univ of Central Okla	OK	8,094	C
Univ of Conn	CT	16,628	HC
Univ of Dayton	OH	28,826	VC
Univ of Delaware	DE	14,142	HC
Univ of Georgia	GA	11,004	HC
Univ of Houston	TX	7,000	C
Univ of Illinois at Chicago	IL	16,256	VC
Univ of Illinois at Urbana-Champaign	IL	15,800	HC+
Univ of Maine	ME	13,642	C
Univ of Maryland/College Park	MD	16,036	HC
Univ of Mass Amherst	MA	15,973	C+
Univ of Minn/Twin Cities	MN	13,165	HC
Univ of Missouri/Columbia	MO	13,500	VC
Univ of Nevada/Reno	NV	12,155	NC
Univ of New Hampshire	NH	16,810	VC
Univ of New Mexico	NM	11,253	C
Univ of N Car at Chapel Hill	NC	11,129	MC
Univ of N Car at Greensboro	NC	8,993	C
Univ of Northern Iowa	IA	11,133	C
Univ of PR/Rio Piedras	PR	5,750	
Univ of Rhode Island	RI	15,398	C
Univ of Tenn at Knoxville	TN	11,720	C
Univ of Tenn at Martin	TN	8,693	C
Univ of Texas at Austin	TX	14,610	HC
Univ of the Incarnate Word	TX	23,306	C
Univ of Vermont	VT	18,080	VC
Univ of Wisc/Madison	WI	13,117	HC
Virginia Polytechnic Inst and State Univ	VA	10,834	VC
Viterbo Univ	WI	21,670	C
Washington State Univ	WA	12,260	C
West Virginia Univ	WV	10,506	C
West Virginia Wesleyan College	WV	26,880	C
Western Carolina Univ	NC	7,000	C
Youngstown State Univ	OH	12,613	NC

NUTRITION EDUCATION

School	ST	$IS	SR
Indiana Univ of Pennsylvania	PA	11,209	C
Univ of Cincinnati	OH	17,682	C
Univ of Nebr at Lincoln	NE	11,401	VC

OCCUPATIONAL SAFETY AND HEALTH

School	ST	$IS	SR
Central Missouri State Univ	MO	10,000	C
Howard Payne Univ	TX	17,115	C
Indiana Univ Bloomington	IN	13,356	VC
Madonna Univ	MI	16,068	VC
Millersville Univ of Pennsylvania	PA	12,113	C
Montana Tech of The Univ of Montana	MT	10,434	C
Murray State Univ	KY	8,900	VC
N Car Agricultural and Technical State Univ	NC	8,000	LC
Purdue Univ/West Lafayette	IN	13,458	VC
Southeastern Louisiana Univ	LA	8,521	LC
Southeastern Okla State Univ	OK	6,147	C
Southwest Baptist Univ	MO	18,300	C
Univ of Findlay	OH	29,238	C
Univ of New Haven	CT	31,794	C
Univ of N Dak	ND	10,114	VC

OCCUPATIONAL THERAPY

School	ST	$IS	SR
Alabama State Univ	AL	7,658	C
American International College	MA	28,710	LC
Augustana College	IL	29,862	VC+
Baker College of Flint	MI	7,800	NC
Barry Univ	FL	24,100	LC
Bay Path College	MA	29,362	C
Brenau Univ Women's College	GA	23,950	VC
Cal State, Dominguez Hills	CA	10,220	LC
Calvin College	MI	25,735	NC
CUNY/York College	NY	4,242	NC
Cleveland State Univ	OH	10,798	VC
College Misericordia	PA	27,950	C
College of St. Benedict	MN	30,091	VC
College of St. Catherine	MN	27,505	VC
College of St. Mary	NE	23,938	C
Colo State Univ-Pueblo	CO	7,821	LC
Concordia Univ Wisc	WI	22,660	VC
Dominican College	NY	26,630	LC
Dominican Univ of Calif	CA	36,836	C
D'Youville College	NY	23,660	C
East Carolina Univ	NC	10,000	C
Eastern Kentucky Univ	KY	7,725	C
Eastern Mich Univ	MI	12,897	C
Elizabethtown College	PA	32,100	VC
Florida A&M Univ	FL	8,344	C
Florida Gulf Coast Univ	FL	10,833	C
Florida International Univ	FL	9,215	VC
Gannon Univ	PA	26,100	C
Howard Univ	DC	18,481	C+
Indiana Univ Kokomo	IN	4,835	LC
Ithaca College	NY	35,144	VC
Keuka College	NY	26,050	C
Lamar Univ	TX	6,820	LC
Lenoir-Rhyne College	NC	25,580	C
LIU/Brooklyn Campus	NY	25,000	C
Mount Aloysius College	PA	20,900	LC
Mount Mary College	WI	22,895	C
New York Inst of Technology	NY	28,126	VC
Newman Univ	KS	21,106	C
North Park Univ	IL	24,050	C
Ohio State Univ	OH	15,357	HC
Pennsylvania College of Technology	PA	16,980	LC
Quinnipiac Univ	CT	34,640	VC
Russell Sage College	NY	27,000	C
Saginaw Valley State Univ	MI	11,432	C
St. Francis Univ	PA	25,880	LC
St. John's Univ	MN	29,749	VC
St. Vincent College	PA	26,160	VC
San Jose State Univ	CA	11,707	C
Shawnee State Univ	OH	12,237	NC
Spalding Univ	KY	18,882	C
SUNY/Univ at Buffalo	NY	13,694	VC
Temple Univ	PA	17,438	C
Tenn State Univ	TN	9,048	LC
Touro College	NY	17,000	VC
Towson Univ	MD	13,924	VC
Tuskegee Univ	AL	18,860	LC
Univ of Central Arkansas	AR	9,984	C
Univ of Findlay	OH	29,238	C
Univ of Florida	FL	9,354	HC
Univ of Hartford	CT	34,044	C
Univ of Kansas	KS	10,915	VC
Univ of Louisiana at Monroe	LA	7,103	C
Univ of Mary	ND	15,374	C
Univ of Minn/Twin Cities	MN	13,165	HC
Univ of Missouri/Columbia	MO	13,500	VC
Univ of New Hampshire	NH	16,810	VC
Univ of New Mexico	NM	11,253	C
Univ of Pittsburgh at Pittsburgh	PA	18,866	HC
Univ of PR at Humacao	PR	1,707	
Univ of Scranton	PA	31,100	C
Univ of Southern Calif	CA	41,618	MC
Univ of Southern Indiana	IN	12,590	LC
Univ of Tenn at Chattanooga	TN	7,790	C
Univ of Texas at San Antonio	TX	11,325	LC
Univ of Texas-Pan American	TX	7,290	C+
Univ of the Sciences in Philadelphia	PA	33,380	VC
Univ of Utah	UT	10,162	VC
Univ of Wisc/La Crosse	WI	10,045	VC
Univ of Wisc/Milwaukee	WI	9,427	LC
Wartburg College	IA	27,315	NC
Wayne State Univ	MI	11,805	C
West Virginia Univ	WV	10,506	C
Western Mich Univ	MI	13,299	C
Worcester State College	MA	12,499	C

OCEAN ENGINEERING

School	ST	$IS	SR
Florida Atlantic Univ	FL	11,221	C
Florida Inst of Technology	FL	29,720	VC
Mass Inst of Technology	MA	41,800	MC
Purdue Univ/West Lafayette	IN	13,458	VC
Texas A&M Univ at Galveston	TX	10,000	C+
United States Naval Academy	MD		MC
Univ of Rhode Island	RI	15,398	C
Univ of Washington	WA	10,400	VC
Virginia Polytechnic Inst and State Univ	VA	10,834	VC

OCEANOGRAPHY

School	ST	$IS	SR
Florida Inst of Technology	FL	29,720	VC
Hawaii Pacific Univ	HI	21,080	C
Humboldt State Univ	CA	11,176	C
Maine Maritime Academy	ME	14,340	C
Millersville Univ of Pennsylvania	PA	12,113	C
Old Dominion Univ	VA	11,907	C
Texas A&M Univ at Galveston	TX	10,000	C+
United States Naval Academy	MD		MC
Univ of Mich/Ann Arbor	MI	16,587	HC+
Univ of San Diego	CA	40,620	HC
Univ of Washington	WA	10,400	VC

OFFICE SUPERVISION AND MANAGEMENT

School	ST	$IS	SR
Adams State College	CO	8,613	C
Alabama A&M Univ	AL	8,890	LC
Albany State Univ	GA	5,770	C+
Alcorn State Univ	MS	8,190	LC
Baker College of Flint	MI	7,800	NC
Campbellsville Univ	KY	21,328	C
Central Conn State Univ	CT	13,620	C
Concord College	WV	9,708	C
Concordia College: Moorhead	MN	22,475	VC
David N. Myers College	OH	9,475	C
Eastern Mich Univ	MI	12,897	C
Fayetteville State Univ	NC	6,000	LC
Fort Hays State Univ	KS	7,638	C
Fort Valley State Univ	GA	6,975	C
Georgia State Univ	GA	11,444	VC
Gwynedd-Mercy College	PA	26,080	C
Indiana State Univ	IN	11,604	C
Indiana Univ-Purdue Univ Indianapolis	IN	10,959	C
Inter American Univ of PR/Bayamon Univ College	PR	3,522	
Jackson State Univ	MS	8,500	C
Johnson and Wales Univ/Providence Campus	RI	28,126	LC
Lincoln Univ	MO	8,000	NC
Mayville State Univ	ND	8,667	NC
Middle Tenn State Univ	TN	8,540	C
Miss Valley State Univ	MS	7,970	C
Mount Vernon Nazarene Univ	OH	20,810	C
Northwestern Okla State Univ	OK	6,250	NC
Purdue Univ/West Lafayette	IN	13,458	VC
Rider Univ	NJ	32,560	C
S Car State Univ	SC	6,700	LC
Southeast Missouri State Univ	MO	10,596	C
Southern Nazarene Univ	OK	14,634	NC
Southwestern Adventist Univ	TX	18,290	LC
Stephen F. Austin State Univ	TX	7,930	C
Sul Ross State Univ	TX	6,600	LC
Tabor College	KS	21,614	NC
Tarleton State Univ	TX	8,952	C
Thomas Edison State College	NJ	3,780	SP
Universidad Adventista de las Antillas	PR	7,360	
Univ of Houston-Downtown	TX	3,326	NC
Univ of Idaho	ID	9,310	NC
Univ of S Car at Columbia	SC	13,397	VC
Univ of the Cumberlands	KY	18,184	C
Univ of the District of Columbia	DC	2,070	LC
Univ of Wisc/Whitewater	WI	9,274	C
Valley City State Univ	ND	9,854	LC
Wiley College	TX	8,100	LC
Youngstown State Univ	OH	12,613	NC

OPERA

School	ST	$IS	SR
Boston Conservatory	MA	27,500	SP
Indiana Univ Bloomington	IN	13,356	VC

OPERATIONS MANAGEMENT

School	ST	$IS	SR
Loyola Univ Chicago	IL	32,896	VC
Metropolitan State Univ	MN	4,682	SP
Southwestern College	KS	21,476	C
Thomas Edison State College	NJ	3,780	SP
Univ of Maryland/College Park	MD	16,036	HC
Univ of Memphis	TN	11,153	C
Univ of Wisc/Madison	WI	13,117	HC

OPERATIONS RESEARCH

School	ST	$IS	SR
Boston College	MA	41,608	MC
Boston Univ	MA	42,046	HC+
Calif State Polytechnic Univ, Pomona	CA	18,053	C+
CUNY/Baruch College	NY	4,320	VC+
Columbia Univ/Fu Foundation School of Engineering and Applied Science	NY	42,584	MC
Cornell Univ	NY	41,717	MC
Indiana Univ Bloomington	IN	13,356	VC
Miami Univ	OH	29,097	HC
New York Univ	NY	43,170	MC
Princeton Univ	NJ	40,213	VC
Purdue Univ/West Lafayette	IN	13,458	VC
Seattle Univ	WA	30,063	VC
United States Air Force Academy	CO		HC+
United States Coast Guard Academy	CT		HC
United States Military Academy	NY		MC
Univ of Calif at Berkeley	CA	18,141	HC+
Univ of Dayton	OH	28,826	VC
Univ of Houston	TX	7,000	C
Univ of Illinois at Urbana-Champaign	IL	15,800	HC+
Univ of North Texas	TX	7,800	C
Univ of Pennsylvania	PA	41,766	MC
Univ of Scranton	PA	31,100	VC

OPHTHALMIC TECHNOLOGY

School	ST	$IS	SR
Alderson-Broaddus College	WV	24,006	C

OPTICAL ENGINEERING

School	ST	$IS	SR
Old Dominion Univ	VA	11,907	C
Rose-Hulman Inst of Technology	IN	34,557	HC+
Univ of Alabama in Huntsville	AL	9,516	VC
Univ of Arizona	AZ	11,958	VC

OPTICS

School	ST	$IS	SR
Capitol College	MD	21,250	C
Saginaw Valley State Univ	MI	11,432	C
Univ of Rochester	NY	41,135	MC

OPTOMETRY

School	ST	$IS	SR
Baylor Univ	TX	27,555	HC
Ferris State Univ	MI	13,698	C
Gannon Univ	PA	26,100	C
Oral Roberts Univ	OK	22,650	C
Purdue Univ/Calumet	IN	10,891	C
Univ of Calif at Berkeley	CA	18,141	HC+
Univ of Houston	TX	7,000	C

ORGANIZATIONAL BEHAVIOR

School	ST	$IS	SR
Averett Univ	VA	24,920	C
Baldwin-Wallace College	OH	27,256	VC
Benedictine Univ	IL	25,710	C
Bluffton College	OH	26,110	C
Boston Univ	MA	42,046	HC+
Carroll College	WI	24,860	C
Central Missouri State Univ	MO	10,000	C
Chapman Univ	CA	37,550	C
Claflin Univ	SC	16,798	C+
College of St. Scholastica	MN	28,456	C+
College of Santa Fe	NM	28,978	C
Concordia Univ St.Paul	MN	27,776	C
Franklin Univ	OH	6,720	SP
Hannibal-LaGrange College	MO	16,390	C
Huntington Univ	IN	24,830	C
Huron Univ	SD	10,700	C
Indiana Univ South Bend	IN	4,989	LC
Indiana Univ Southeast	IN	4,880	LC
Ithaca College	NY	35,144	VC
La Salle Univ	PA	34,950	C
Loyola Univ Chicago	IL	32,896	VC
Loyola Univ New Orleans	LA	31,050	VC+
Maryville Univ of St. Louis	MO	23,000	VC
Methodist College	NC	21,000	C
Miami Univ	OH	29,097	HC
Mountain State Univ	WV	11,406	NC
National Univ	CA	8,412	SP
New York Univ	NY	43,170	MC
Northern Kentucky Univ	KY	6,670	NC
Northwestern Univ	IL	37,595	MC
Oral Roberts Univ	OK	22,650	C
Pitzer College	CA	41,644	HC
Purdue Univ/West Lafayette	IN	13,458	VC
Robert Morris Univ	PA	22,822	C
St. Joseph's College, New York, Brooklyn Campus	NY	12,206	C
St. Louis Univ	MO	33,158	VC+
Southern Methodist Univ	TX	36,088	VC+
Spring Hill College	AL	28,678	C
Univ of at Calif Davis	CA	15,010	VC
Univ of Illinois at Urbana-Champaign	IL	15,800	HC+
Univ of Memphis	TN	11,153	C
Univ of North Texas	TX	7,800	C
Univ of San Francisco	CA	37,560	VC
Viterbo Univ	WI	21,670	C
Wilmington College	OH	2,806	NC
Woodbury Univ	CA	30,176	LC

ORGANIZATIONAL LEADERSHIP AND MANAGEMENT

School	ST	$IS	SR
Calif Baptist Univ	CA	23,780	C
Defiance College	OH	24,790	C
Loyola Univ Chicago	IL	32,896	C
Lubbock Christian Univ	TX	16,960	C
National Univ	CA	8,412	SP

PACIFIC AREA STUDIES

School	ST	$IS	SR
Brigham Young Univ/Hawaii	HI	7,740	HC+
Hawaii Pacific Univ	HI	21,080	C
Univ of Hawaii at Manoa	HI	10,413	VC

PAINTING

School	ST	$IS	SR
Andrews Univ	MI	21,786	C
Aquinas College	MI	23,750	C
Atlanta College of Art	GA	18,630	SP
Bard College	NY	41,800	HC+
Barton College	NC	22,316	C
Bennington College	VT	41,890	HC
Birmingham-Southern College	AL	28,494	VC+
Boston Univ	MA	42,046	HC+
Calif College of the Arts	CA	34,325	SP
Cal State, San Bernardino	CA	12,563	LC
Catholic Univ of America	DC	35,838	VC
Cleveland Inst of Art	OH	34,109	SP
College for Creative Studies	MI	24,000	SP
College of Santa Fe	NM	28,978	C
College of Visual Arts	MN	18,040	SP
Edinboro Univ of Pennsylvania	PA	11,809	LC
Escuela de Artes Plasticas de PR	PR	2,372	
Harding Univ	AR	16,512	VC
Hofstra Univ	NY	32,630	VC
Indiana Univ Bloomington	IN	13,356	VC
Indiana Univ-Purdue Univ Indianapolis	IN	10,959	C
Indiana Wesleyan Univ	IN	22,074	C+
Kansas City Art Inst	MO	29,542	SP
Kendall College of Art and Design of Ferris State Univ	MI	11,870	SP
Laguna College of Art and Design	CA	17,600	SP
Lewis Univ	IL	23,050	C+
Maine College of Art	ME	28,820	SP
Maryland Inst College of Art	MD	34,450	SP
Mass College of Art	MA	16,650	SP
McMurry Univ	TX	18,100	LC
Milwaukee Inst of Art and Design	WI	28,700	SP
Minneapolis College of Art and Design	MN	31,110	SP
Montserrat College of Art	MA	25,929	SP
Moore College of Art and Design	PA	27,200	SP
Northwest Nazarene Univ	ID	22,590	VC
Ohio Univ	OH	15,921	C
Otis College of Art and Design	CA	27,546	SP
Pacific Northwest College of Art	OR	17,296	SP
Rhode Island School of Design	RI	38,130	SP
Rochester Inst of Technology	NY	32,070	VC+
San Francisco Art Inst	CA	25,640	C
Savannah College of Art and Design	GA	30,800	SP
School of the Art Inst of Chicago	IL	37,800	SP
Shepherd Univ	WV	10,066	C
Simon's Rock College of Bard	MA	41,988	VC+
SUNY/College at Buffalo	NY	11,903	C+
Syracuse Univ	NY	38,655	HC
Univ of Dallas	TX	27,432	VC+
Univ of Hartford	CT	34,044	C
Univ of Houston	TX	7,000	C
Univ of Illinois at Urbana-Champaign	IL	15,800	HC+
Univ of Kansas	KS	10,915	VC
Univ of Mass Dartmouth	MA	15,985	C
Univ of Miami	FL	38,397	MC
Univ of Mich/Ann Arbor	MI	16,587	HC+
Univ of North Texas	TX	7,800	C
Univ of Oregon	OR	13,108	VC
Univ of San Francisco	CA	37,560	VC
Univ of the Arts	PA	32,330	SP
Univ of Washington	WA	10,400	VC
Virginia Commonwealth Univ	VA	12,987	C
Washington Univ in St. Louis	MO	42,106	MC
Youngstown State Univ	OH	12,613	NC

PALEONTOLOGY

School	ST	$IS	SR
Univ of Calif at Los Angeles	CA	17,681	MC
Univ of Okla	OK	10,769	VC+

PAPER AND PULP SCIENCE

School	ST	$IS	SR
Miami Univ	OH	29,097	HC
N Car State Univ	NC	11,824	HC
SUNY/College of Environmental Science and Forestry	NY	15,000	VC
Univ of Maine	ME	13,642	VC
Univ of Washington	WA	10,400	VC
Univ of Wisc/Stevens Point	WI	9,384	VC
Western Mich Univ	MI	13,299	C

PAPER ENGINEERING

School	ST	$IS	SR
SUNY/College of Environmental Science and Forestry	NY	15,000	VC
Western Mich Univ	MI	13,299	C

PARALEGAL STUDIES

School	ST	$IS	SR
Anna Maria College	MA	29,815	C
Avila Univ	MO	22,100	C
Ball State Univ	IN	13,138	C
Cal State, San Bernardino	CA	12,563	C
Calumet College of St. Joseph	IN	9,500	LC
Central Washington Univ	WA	11,730	C
Champlain College	VT	24,605	C
CUNY/New York City College of Technology	NY	4,269	NC
College of Mount St. Joseph	OH	24,860	C
College of Our Lady of the Elms	MA	21,000	C
College of St. Mary	NE	23,938	C
Concordia Univ Wisc	WI	22,660	VC
Davenport Univ	MI	15,205	NC
David N. Myers College	OH	9,475	C
East Central Univ	OK	6,207	C
Eastern Kentucky Univ	KY	7,725	C
Eastern Mich Univ	MI	12,897	C
Florida Gulf Coast Univ	FL	10,833	C
Franciscan Univ of Steubenville	OH	20,300	VC
Gannon Univ	PA	26,100	C
Hamline Univ	MN	27,070	VC
Hilbert College	NY	20,480	LC
Humphreys College	CA	7,000	NC
Husson College	ME	17,410	LC
International College	FL	9,500	NC
Johnson and Wales Univ/North Miami Campus	FL	30,126	LC
Johnson and Wales Univ/Providence Campus	RI	28,126	LC
Kent State Univ	OH	14,594	C
Lake Erie College	OH	27,725	C
Lake Superior State Univ	MI	12,842	LC
Lasell College	MA	26,250	C
Lock Haven Univ of Pennsylvania	PA	12,098	LC
Marymount Univ	VA	25,934	C
Maryville Univ of St. Louis	MO	23,000	VC
Marywood Univ	PA	30,680	C
Mercy College	NY	20,000	NC
Minn State Univ, Moorhead	MN	7,000	LC
Miss College	MS	14,574	VC
Miss Univ for Women	MS	6,000	LC
Montclair State Univ	NJ	16,327	C
Morehead State Univ	KY	9,150	C
National American Univ	SD	14,820	NC
Nebr Wesleyan Univ	NE	23,415	C+
Newbury College	MA	25,600	C
Nova Southeastern Univ	FL	24,320	C
Peirce College	PA	12,760	NC
Pennsylvania College of Technology	PA	16,980	LC
Point Park Univ	PA	24,160	C
Quinnipiac Univ	CT	34,640	VC
Roger Williams Univ	RI	30,500	C
St. John's Univ	NY	34,370	C
St. Mary-of-the-Woods College	IN	25,480	C
Southern Illinois Univ Carbondale	IL	12,391	C
Suffolk Univ	MA	33,160	C
Texas Wesleyan Univ	TX	18,700	C
Univ of Detroit Mercy	MI	27,000	C
Univ of Great Falls	MT	17,000	C
Univ of La Verne	CA	33,470	C
Univ of Louisville	KY	10,400	VC
Univ of Maryland/Univ College	MD	5,640	SP
Univ of Mass Boston	MA	8,024	C
Univ of Memphis	TN	11,153	C
Univ of Tenn at Chattanooga	TN	7,790	C
Valdosta State Univ	GA	8,802	C
Villa Julie College	MD	25,222	C
Virginia Intermont College	VA	22,200	LC
Wesley College	DE	19,905	C
Western Conn State Univ	CT	12,993	C
William Woods Univ	MO	21,020	C
Winona State Univ	MN	11,333	C
Woodbury College	VT	15,150	LC

PARKS AND RECREATION MANAGEMENT

School	ST	$IS	SR
Alabama State Univ	AL	7,658	C
Arkansas Tech Univ	AR	8,108	VC
Auburn Univ	AL	12,230	VC
Aurora Univ	IL	20,645	C
Ball State Univ	IN	13,138	C
Bemidji State Univ	MN	11,180	VC
Bethany College	KS	20,660	LC
Cal State, Chico	CA	11,395	C
Cal State, Sacramento	CA	11,122	C+
Calif Univ of Pennsylvania	PA	14,217	C
Central Mich Univ	MI	12,244	C
Central Washington Univ	WA	11,730	C
Cheyney Univ of Pennsylvania	PA	11,497	LC
Christopher Newport Univ	VA	13,326	VC
Clemson Univ	SC	13,366	HC
Concord College	WV	9,708	C
Delaware State Univ	DE	8,130	LC
East Carolina Univ	NC	10,000	C
East Stroudsburg Univ of Pennsylvania	PA	10,336	C
Eastern Mich Univ	MI	12,897	C
Eastern Washington Univ	WA	10,608	C
Evangel Univ	MO	17,380	C
Florida International Univ	FL	9,215	VC
Gallaudet Univ	DC	16,554	C
Humboldt State Univ	CA	11,176	VC
Huntington Univ	IN	24,830	C
Illinois State Univ	IL	12,839	C+
Indiana Inst of Technology	IN	23,430	C
Indiana State Univ	IN	11,604	C
Indiana Univ Bloomington	IN	13,356	VC
Johnson and Wales Univ/Charlotte Campus	NC	29,121	LC
Johnson and Wales Univ/North Miami Campus	FL	30,126	LC
Johnson and Wales Univ/Providence Campus	RI	28,126	LC
Kansas State Univ	KS	10,516	VC
Kent State Univ	OH	14,594	C
Lake Superior State Univ	MI	12,842	LC
Marshall Univ	WV	9,116	C
Mich State Univ	MI	13,689	VC
Midland Lutheran College	NE	18,600	C
Minn State Univ, Mankato	MN	10,276	LC
Missouri State Univ	MO	10,748	C+
Missouri Western State Univ	MO	9,534	NC
Montclair State Univ	NJ	16,327	C
Murray State Univ	KY	8,900	VC
N Car State Univ	NC	11,824	HC
Northern Arizona Univ	AZ	10,353	C
Northern Mich Univ	MI	12,340	LC
Northland College	WI	26,680	C+
Ohio Univ	OH	15,921	C
Penn State Univ/Univ Park Campus	PA	18,038	HC
San Diego State Univ	CA	12,971	C
Shorter College	GA	19,700	C
Slippery Rock Univ of Pennsylvania	PA	10,360	LC
S Dak State Univ	SD	9,815	C
Southern Illinois Univ Carbondale	IL	12,391	C
Springfield College	MA	25,000	C
Stephen F. Austin State Univ	TX	7,930	C
Temple Univ	PA	17,438	C
Texas A&M Univ	TX	13,351	HC
Texas Tech Univ	TX	13,026	VC
Unity College	ME	24,320	C
Univ of Arkansas at Pine Bluff	AR	8,300	C
Univ of Delaware	DE	14,142	HC
Univ of Idaho	ID	9,310	NC
Univ of Illinois at Urbana-Champaign	IL	15,800	HC+
Univ of Iowa	IA	12,172	VC
Univ of Maine	ME	13,642	C
Univ of Mary Hardin-Baylor	TX	19,428	C
Univ of Memphis	TN	11,153	C
Univ of Missouri/Columbia	MO	13,500	VC
Univ of N Car at Greensboro	NC	8,993	C
Univ of N Car at Pembroke	NC	7,940	LC
Univ of N Car at Wilmington	NC	10,107	VC
Univ of Southern Miss	MS	10,112	C
Univ of Utah	UT	10,162	VC
Univ of Vermont	VT	18,080	VC
Univ of West Georgia	GA	8,838	C
Univ of Wisc/La Crosse	WI	10,045	VC
Univ of Wyoming	WY	9,666	C
Utah State Univ	UT	8,002	VC
Virginia Polytechnic Inst and State Univ	VA	10,834	VC
Virginia Wesleyan College	VA	28,433	C
Wayne State College	NE	8,033	NC
Wayne State Univ	MI	11,805	C
West Virginia Univ	WV	10,506	C
Western Carolina Univ	NC	7,000	C
Western Illinois Univ	IL	13,042	C
Western Washington Univ	WA	11,262	VC
Wingate Univ	NC	23,300	C
Winona State Univ	MN	11,333	C
York College of Pennsylvania	PA	16,550	VC

PASTORAL STUDIES

School	ST	$IS	SR
Andrews Univ	MI	21,786	C
Brescia Univ	KY	14,240	C
Cedarville Univ	OH	21,904	VC
Clearwater Christian College	FL	13,160	LC
College of Mount St. Joseph	OH	24,860	C
College of St. Benedict	MN	30,091	VC
Concordia Univ Wisc	WI	22,660	VC
Dallas Baptist Univ	TX	17,040	VC
Grace Bible College	MI	18,810	C
Greenville College	IL	23,146	C
Madonna Univ	MI	16,068	VC
Marian College	IN	26,160	C
Morris College	SC	11,999	LC
Newman Univ	KS	21,106	C
North Central Univ	MN	16,646	LC
Northwest Univ	WA	18,854	C
Northwestern College	MN	25,220	NC
Nyack College	NY	18,540	C
Okla Wesleyan Univ	OK	18,950	NC
St. John's Univ	MN	29,749	VC
St. Mary's Univ of Minn	MN	23,857	VC
Simpson Univ	CA	22,900	C
Southeastern Univ	FL	17,180	LC
Southwestern College	KS	21,476	C
Spalding Univ	KY	18,882	C
Tenn Wesleyan College	TN	18,650	C
Toccoa Falls College	GA	17,125	C
Union College	NE	18,710	C
Union Univ	TN	20,750	VC
Universidad Adventista de las Antillas	PR	7,360	
Univ of Mary	ND	15,374	C
Univ of St. Mary	KS	18,900	C
Univ of St. Thomas	TX	23,810	VC
Walsh Univ	OH	23,440	C
Warner Southern College	FL	18,000	C
William Tyndale College	MI	13,000	NC

PEACE STUDIES

School	ST	$IS	SR
Chapman Univ	CA	37,550	VC
Colgate Univ	NY	41,170	MC
College of St. Benedict	MN	30,091	VC

INDEX OF COLLEGE MAJORS

School	ST	$IS	SR
Creighton Univ	NE	29,918	VC+
DePauw Univ	IN	32,100	HC
Earlham College	IN	33,604	HC
Eastern Mennonite Univ	VA	25,450	VC
Goshen College	IN	22,850	VC
Goucher College	MD	36,225	VC
Guilford College	NC	28,160	C+
Hamline Univ	MN	27,070	VC
Hampshire College	MA	37,120	HC
Juniata College	PA	33,130	VC
Kent State Univ	OH	14,594	C
Le Moyne College	NY	29,570	VC
Manchester College	IN	23,470	C
Manhattan College	NY	29,000	VC
Molloy College	NY	16,510	C
Nazareth College of Rochester	NY	28,175	VC
Northland College	WI	26,680	C+
Norwich Univ	VT	28,212	C
Prescott College	AZ	13,445	LC
St. John's Univ	MN	29,749	VC
Salisbury Univ	MD	13,128	VC
San Diego State Univ	CA	12,971	C
Syracuse Univ	NY	38,655	VC
Tufts Univ	MA	42,018	MC
Univ of Calif at Berkeley	CA	18,141	HC+
Univ of Hawaii at Manoa	HI	10,413	VC
Univ of N Car at Chapel Hill	NC	11,129	MC
Univ of St. Thomas	MN	28,000	VC
Univ of Washington	WA	10,400	VC
Wayne State Univ	MI	11,805	C
Wellesley College	MA	41,030	MC
Whitworth College	WA	29,428	VC+

PERCUSSION

School	ST	$IS	SR
Central Washington Univ	WA	11,730	C
Northwestern Univ	IL	37,595	MC
Roosevelt Univ	IL	22,605	VC
Temple Univ	PA	17,438	C
Univ of Miami	FL	38,397	MC
Univ of Mich/Ann Arbor	MI	16,587	HC+
Youngstown State Univ	OH	12,613	NC

PERFORMING ARTS

School	ST	$IS	SR
Adelphi Univ	NY	27,000	VC
Alfred Univ	NY		VC
American Univ	DC	38,719	HC+
Aquinas College	MI	23,750	C
Averett Univ	VA	24,920	C
Baylor Univ	TX	27,555	HC
Bennington College	VT	41,890	HC
Boston Univ	MA	42,046	HC+
Brandeis Univ	MA	41,551	MC
Brigham Young Univ	UT	9,200	VC
Brown Univ	RI	42,015	MC
Butler Univ	IN	31,944	VC+
Carroll College	MT	23,324	C+
Carthage College	WI	26,000	C
Christopher Newport Univ	VA	13,326	VC
CUNY/City College	NY		C
Colby College	ME	41,770	MC
College of Santa Fe	NM	28,978	C
College of the Ozarks	MO	4,130	VC+
Colo State Univ-Fort Collins	CO	10,878	C+
Columbia College	SC	24,982	LC
De Sales Univ	PA	28,580	VC
Dominican Univ	IL	26,370	C
Eastern Conn State Univ	CT	13,554	C
Eastern Kentucky Univ	KY	7,725	C
Eastern Mich Univ	MI	12,897	C
Edgewood College	WI	22,862	C
Emerson College	MA	35,076	HC
Ferrum College	VA	24,290	LC
Fontbonne Univ	MO	23,308	C
Fordham Univ	NY	36,000	VC
Georgetown College	KY	24,950	C+
Georgia Southern Univ	GA	9,762	C
Hampshire College	MA	37,120	HC
Indiana Univ South Bend	IN	4,989	LC
Ithaca College	NY	35,144	VC
Johnson State College	VT	11,830	LC
Lindenwood Univ	MO	18,600	VC
Mars Hill College	NC	19,000	LC
Marywood Univ	PA	30,680	C
Naropa Univ	CO	26,302	SP
Neumann College	PA	25,996	LC
N Car School of the Arts	NC	7,401	SP
N Dak State Univ	ND	8,500	C
Northeastern Univ	MA	35,742	HC
Northern Kentucky Univ	KY	6,670	NC
Northwestern Univ	IL	37,595	MC
Oakland Univ	MI	11,936	C
Old Dominion Univ	VA	11,907	C
Plymouth State Univ	NH	12,298	LC
Roosevelt Univ	IL	22,605	VC
St. Mary's College of Calif	CA	37,290	C
Seton Hill Univ	PA	28,810	C
Shenandoah Univ	VA	27,600	C
Simon's Rock College of Bard	MA	41,988	VC+
Southern Methodist Univ	TX	36,088	VC+
SUNY/College at Geneseo	NY	12,910	HC+
Suffolk Univ	MA	33,160	C
Temple Univ	PA	17,438	C

School	ST	$IS	SR
Texas Tech Univ	TX	13,026	VC
Univ of Arizona	AZ	11,958	VC
Univ of Florida	FL	9,354	HC
Univ of Hartford	CT	34,044	C
Univ of Mary Hardin-Baylor	TX	19,428	C
Univ of Mich/Ann Arbor	MI	16,587	HC+
Univ of Missouri/Kansas City	MO	15,000	VC
Univ of San Francisco	CA	37,560	VC
Univ of Tampa	FL	25,784	C
Univ of Tenn at Martin	TN	8,693	C
Virginia Intermont College	VA	22,200	LC
Washington Univ in St. Louis	MO	42,106	MC
West Texas A&M Univ	TX	8,452	C
Western Kentucky Univ	KY	10,192	C
Youngstown State Univ	OH	12,613	NC

PERSONNEL MANAGEMENT

School	ST	$IS	SR
Arcadia Univ	PA	33,570	VC
Auburn Univ	AL	12,230	VC
Auburn Univ Montgomery	AL	9,530	NC
Ball State Univ	IN	13,138	C
Baylor Univ	TX	27,555	HC
Bellevue Univ	NE	4,440	NC
Bowling Green State Univ	OH	14,994	C
Cal State, Long Beach	CA	9,512	C
CUNY/Baruch College	NY	4,320	VC
Columbia Union College	MD	23,536	LC
Dickinson State Univ	ND	7,847	NC
Eastern Mich Univ	MI	12,897	C
Eastern New Mexico Univ	NM	7,264	C
Eastern Washington Univ	WA	10,608	C
Faulkner Univ	AL	15,600	C
Florida International Univ	FL	9,215	VC
Florida Southern College	FL	25,965	C
Florida State Univ	FL	9,028	HC
Grand Canyon Univ	AZ	32,000	LC
Grand Valley State Univ	MI	12,000	VC
Hawaii Pacific Univ	HI	21,080	C
Ithaca College	NY	35,144	VC
King's College	PA	29,810	C
Lamar Univ	TX	6,820	LC
Loras College	IA	27,193	C
Louisiana Tech Univ	LA	7,370	C
Mansfield Univ	PA	11,300	C
Messiah College	PA	28,910	VC+
Miami Univ	OH	29,097	HC
Mich State Univ	MI	13,689	VC
Murray State Univ	KY	8,900	VC
Nicholls State Univ	LA	6,500	NC
Nichols College	MA	28,000	LC
Northern State Univ	SD	8,257	C
Northwest Missouri State Univ	MO	10,000	C
Oakland Univ	MI	11,936	C
Ohio Univ	OH	15,921	C
Our Lady of the Lake Univ of San Antonio	TX	22,430	LC
Portland State Univ	OR	12,453	C
Rhode Island College	RI	11,570	C
Roosevelt Univ	IL	22,605	VC
Rowan Univ	NJ	16,000	VC
St. Cloud State Univ	MN	10,010	C
San Francisco State Univ	CA	13,000	C
Seton Hall Univ	PA	28,810	C
Silver Lake College of the Holy Family	WI	18,500	LC
Southern Nazarene Univ	OK	14,634	NC
Southern Wesleyan Univ	SC	21,675	C
Tarleton State Univ	TX	8,952	C
Temple Univ	PA	17,438	C
Texas A&M Univ	TX	13,351	VC
Tiffin Univ	OH	19,490	LC
Troy Univ Dothan Campus	AL	4,678	C
Univ of Akron	OH	15,166	NC
Univ of Houston	TX	7,000	C
Univ of Idaho	ID	9,310	VC
Univ of Illinois at Urbana-Champaign	IL	15,800	HC+
Univ of Louisiana at Lafayette	LA	5,830	C
Univ of Montana	MT	10,602	C
Univ of Nebr at Kearney	NE	9,000	NC
Univ of New Mexico	NM	11,253	C
Univ of North Texas	TX	7,800	C
Univ of PR/Rio Piedras	PR	5,750	
Univ of St. Thomas	MN	28,000	VC
Univ of Southern Miss	MS	10,112	C
Univ of Texas at San Antonio	TX	11,325	LC
Univ of the Sacred Heart	PR	5,590	
Univ of Washington	WA	10,400	VC
Univ of Wisc/Whitewater	WI	9,274	C
Utah State Univ	UT	8,002	VC
Washington State Univ	WA	12,260	C
Weber State Univ	UT	9,635	NC
Western Illinois Univ	IL	13,042	C
Wilmington College	DE	5,594	NC
Winona State Univ	MN	11,333	C
Xavier Univ of Louisiana	LA	17,600	C
Youngstown State Univ	OH	12,613	NC

PETROLEUM/NATURAL GAS ENGINEERING

School	ST	$IS	SR
Colo School of Mines	CO	14,893	HC
Louisiana State Univ and A&M College	LA	10,749	VC
Marietta College	OH	29,327	C
Montana Tech of The Univ of Montana	MT	10,434	C
New Mexico Inst of Mining and Technology	NM	8,510	VC+
Nicholls State Univ	LA	6,500	NC
Penn State Univ/Univ Park Campus	PA	18,038	HC
Savannah State Univ	GA	7,772	LC
Stanford Univ	CA	41,557	MC
Texas A&M Univ	TX	13,351	HC
Texas A&M Univ at Kingsville	TX	6,800	LC
Univ of Alaska Fairbanks	AK	10,101	C
Univ of Kansas	KS	10,915	C
Univ of Louisiana at Lafayette	LA	5,830	C
Univ of Missouri/Rolla	MO	13,332	HC
Univ of Okla	OK	10,769	VC+
Univ of Southern Calif	CA	41,618	MC
Univ of Texas at Austin	TX	14,610	HC
Univ of Tulsa	OK	25,348	HC
West Virginia Univ	WV	10,506	C

PHARMACEUTICAL CHEMISTRY

School	ST	$IS	SR
Univ of the Sciences in Philadelphia	PA	33,380	VC

PHARMACEUTICAL SCIENCE

School	ST	$IS	SR
Albany College of Pharmacy	NY	25,090	SP
Univ of the Sciences in Philadelphia	PA	33,380	VC

PHARMACOLOGY

School	ST	$IS	SR
Kent State Univ	OH	14,594	C
SUNY/Univ at Stony Brook	NY	13,625	HC
Univ of the Sciences in Philadelphia	PA	33,380	VC
Wilkes Univ	PA	30,886	C

PHARMACY

School	ST	$IS	SR
Butler Univ	IN	31,944	VC+
Drake Univ	IA	27,632	VC+
Ferris State Univ	MI	13,698	C
Florida A&M Univ	FL	8,344	C
Howard Univ	DC	18,481	C+
Johnson C. Smith Univ	NC	20,000	C
Lamar Univ	TX	6,820	LC
LIU/Brooklyn Campus	NY	25,000	C
Mass College of Pharmacy and Health Sciences	MA	32,020	SP
N Dak State Univ	ND	8,500	C
Northeastern Univ	MA	35,742	HC
Ohio Northern Univ	OH	27,765	VC
Purdue Univ/West Lafayette	IN	13,458	VC
Rutgers, The State Univ of New Jersey/New Brunswick/Piscataway Campus	NJ	15,810	HC
St. John's Univ	NY	34,370	C
S Dak State Univ	SD	9,815	C
SUNY/Univ at Buffalo	NY	13,694	VC
Temple Univ	PA	17,438	C
Univ of Arizona	AZ	11,958	VC
Univ of Calif at Santa Barbara	CA	11,800	VC
Univ of Cincinnati	OH	17,682	C
Univ of Conn	CT	16,628	HC
Univ of Houston	TX	7,000	C
Univ of Iowa	IA	12,712	VC
Univ of Kansas	KS	10,915	VC
Univ of Louisiana at Monroe	LA	7,103	VC
Univ of Mich/Ann Arbor	MI	16,587	HC+
Univ of Minn/Twin Cities	MN	13,165	HC
Univ of Miss	MS	9,000	C
Univ of Montana	MT	10,602	C
Univ of New Mexico	NM	11,253	C
Univ of Rhode Island	RI	15,398	C
Univ of Texas at Austin	TX	14,610	HC
Univ of the Sciences in Philadelphia	PA	33,380	VC
Univ of Toledo	OH	15,806	NC
Washington Univ in St. Louis	MO	42,106	MC
Wayne State Univ	MI	11,805	C
West Virginia Univ	WV	10,506	C

PHILOSOPHY

School	ST	$IS	SR
Adelphi Univ	NY	27,000	VC
Adrian College	MI	23,000	C
Agnes Scott College	GA	32,070	HC

School	ST	$IS	SR
Albertson College of Idaho	ID	21,095	VC
Albertus Magnus College	CT	25,336	C
Albion College	MI	26,000	VC
Albright College	PA	33,920	C
Alfred Univ	NY		VC
Allegheny College	PA	33,500	VC
Alma College	MI	28,544	VC
Alvernia College	PA	26,388	C
Alverno College	WI	21,088	C
American International College	MA	28,710	LC
American Univ	DC	38,719	HC+
Amherst College	MA	41,590	MC
Anderson Univ	IN	25,050	C
Appalachian State Univ	NC	8,000	VC
Aquinas College	MI	23,750	C
Arcadia Univ	PA	33,570	VC
Arizona State Univ-Tempe	AZ	11,174	C
Arkansas State Univ	AR	9,630	C
Asbury College	KY	23,762	VC
Ashland Univ	OH	25,000	C
Assumption College	MA	32,875	C
Auburn Univ	AL	12,230	VC
Augsburg College	MN	28,300	C
Augustana College	IL	29,862	VC+
Augustana College	SD	24,380	VC
Aurora Univ	IL	20,645	C
Austin College	TX	27,871	HC
Austin Peay State Univ	TN	7,535	C
Azusa Pacific Univ	CA	28,546	VC
Baker Univ	KS	22,190	C
Baldwin-Wallace College	OH	27,256	VC
Ball State Univ	IN	13,138	C
Bard College	NY	41,800	HC+
Barry Univ	FL	24,100	LC
Bates College	ME	42,100	MC
Baylor Univ	TX	27,555	HC
Belhaven College	MS	19,530	NC
Bellarmine Univ	KY	27,650	C+
Bellevue Univ	NE	4,440	NC
Belmont Abbey College	NC	25,314	C
Belmont Univ	TN	24,110	VC
Beloit College	WI	32,808	HC
Bemidji State Univ	MN	11,180	LC
Benedict College	SC	19,114	LC
Benedictine College	KS	21,968	C
Benedictine Univ	IL	25,710	C
Bennington College	VT	41,890	HC
Bentley College	MA	38,784	HC
Berea College	KY	5,496	VC+
Berry College	GA	24,342	VC
Bethany College	WV	21,395	C
Bethel College	IN	19,680	C
Bethel Univ	MN	29,840	VC
Biola Univ	CA	29,372	VC
Birmingham-Southern College	AL	28,494	VC+
Bloomfield College	NJ	22,500	LC
Bloomsburg Univ of Pennsylvania	PA	11,602	C
Boise State Univ	ID	9,438	LC
Boston College	MA	41,608	MC
Boston Univ	MA	42,046	HC+
Bowdoin College	ME	41,660	MC
Bowling Green State Univ	OH	14,994	C
Bradley Univ	IL	25,280	VC
Brandeis Univ	MA	41,551	MC
Bridgewater College	VA	27,790	C
Bridgewater State College	MA	12,120	C
Brigham Young Univ	UT	9,200	VC
Brown Univ	RI	42,015	MC
Bryn Mawr College	PA	42,780	HC+
Bucknell Univ	PA	39,660	MC
Buena Vista Univ	IA	27,742	C
Butler Univ	IN	31,944	VC+
Cabrini College	PA	33,340	C
Calif Baptist Univ	CA	23,780	C
Calif Lutheran Univ	CA	27,800	LC
Calif Polytechnic State Univ	CA	12,390	VC
Calif State Polytechnic Univ, Pomona	CA	18,053	C+
Cal State East Bay	CA	10,856	LC
Cal State, Bakersfield	CA	6,125	LC
Cal State, Chico	CA	11,395	C
Cal State, Dominguez Hills	CA	10,220	LC
Cal State, Fresno	CA	10,037	LC
Cal State, Fullerton	CA	10,990	C
Cal State, Long Beach	CA	9,512	C
Cal State, Los Angeles	CA	5,900	C
Cal State, Northridge	CA	9,036	LC
Cal State, Sacramento	CA	11,122	C+
Cal State, San Bernardino	CA	12,563	LC
Cal State, Stanislaus	CA	11,283	C
Calif Univ of Pennsylvania	PA	14,217	C
Calvin College	MI	25,735	NC
Canisius College	NY	32,257	VC
Capital Univ	OH	30,444	C
Carleton College	MN	40,467	MC
Carlow Univ	PA	24,313	C
Carnegie Mellon Univ	PA	32,700	MC
Carroll College	MT	23,324	C+
Carson-Newman College	TN	16,800	C
Carthage College	WI	26,000	C
Case Western Reserve Univ	OH	37,314	MC
Catawba College	NC	25,000	C

ST = STATE   **$IS** = IN-STATE COSTS   **SR** = SELECTOR RATING

School	ST	$IS	SR
Catholic Univ of America	DC	35,838	VC
Cedar Crest College	PA	30,615	C
Cedarville Univ	OH	21,904	VC
Centenary College of Louisiana	LA	24,760	VC
Central College	IA	26,774	VC
Central Conn State Univ	CT	13,620	C
Central Methodist Univ	MO	18,000	C
Central Mich Univ	MI	12,244	C
Central Univ of Bayamon	PR	3,335	
Central Washington Univ	WA	11,730	C
Centre College	KY	30,810	VC
Chapman Univ	CA	37,550	VC
Christendom College	VA	21,594	VC+
Christopher Newport Univ	VA	13,326	VC
CUNY/Baruch College	NY	4,320	VC+
CUNY/Brooklyn College	NY	4,377	C+
CUNY/City College	NY		C
CUNY/College of Staten Island	NY	4,328	NC
CUNY/Herbert H. Lehman College	NY	4,000	LC
CUNY/Hunter College	NY	8,000	C+
CUNY/Queens College	NY	4,356	C
CUNY/York College	NY	4,242	NC
Claremont McKenna College	CA	42,920	MC
Clarion Univ of Pennsylvania	PA	11,844	C
Clark Atlanta Univ	GA	20,960	LC
Clark Univ	MA	35,165	VC+
Clarke College	IA	25,390	C
Clemson Univ	SC	13,366	HC
Cleveland State Univ	OH	10,798	NC
Coastal Carolina Univ	SC	13,140	C
Coe College	IA	27,440	VC
Colby College	ME	41,770	MC
Colgate Univ	NY	41,170	MC
College Misericordia	PA	27,950	C
College of Charleston	SC	13,616	VC
College of Mount St. Vincent	NY	28,000	C
College of New Jersey	NJ	18,315	MC
College of New Rochelle	NY	28,396	C+
College of St. Benedict	MN	30,091	VC
College of St. Catherine	MN	27,505	VC
College of St. Elizabeth	NJ	28,845	C
College of the Holy Cross	MA	40,664	MC
College of the Ozarks	MO	4,130	VC+
College of William and Mary	VA	14,147	MC
College of Wooster	OH	31,310	VC+
Colo College	CO	37,668	HC
Colo State Univ-Fort Collins	CO	10,878	C+
Columbia College	MO	16,900	C
Columbia Univ/Barnard College	NY	38,000	MC
Columbia Univ/Columbia College	NY	42,584	MC
Columbia Univ/School of General Studies	NY	41,516	C
Concordia College: Moorhead	MN	22,475	VC
Conn College	CT	41,955	MC
Cornell College	IA	30,110	VC+
Cornell Univ	NY	41,717	MC
Cornerstone Univ and Grand Rapids Theological Seminary	MI	21,350	NC
Covenant College	GA	26,460	VC+
Creighton Univ	NE	29,918	VC+
Curry College	MA	26,100	LC
Dakota Wesleyan Univ	SD	17,832	C
Dallas Baptist Univ	TX	17,040	VC
Dartmouth College	NH	39,465	MC
Davidson College	NC	36,825	MC
De Sales Univ	PA	28,580	VC
Denison Univ	OH	37,040	HC
DePaul Univ	IL	29,835	VC
DePauw Univ	IN	32,100	HC
Dickinson College	PA	40,170	HC+
Doane College	NE	22,458	C
Dominican Univ	IL	26,370	C
Dordt College	IA	20,325	VC
Dowling College	NY	22,110	LC
Drake Univ	IA	27,632	VC+
Drew Univ/College of Liberal Arts	NJ	39,698	VC
Drury Univ	MO	20,117	VC
Duke Univ	NC	41,239	MC
Duquesne Univ	PA	29,534	C
D'Youville College	NY	23,660	C
Earlham College	IN	33,604	HC
East Carolina Univ	NC	10,000	C
East Stroudsburg Univ of Pennsylvania	PA	10,336	C
East Tenn State Univ	TN	8,497	C
Eastern Illinois Univ	IL	12,569	C
Eastern Kentucky Univ	KY	7,725	C
Eastern Mennonite Univ	VA	25,450	VC
Eastern Mich Univ	MI	12,897	C
Eastern Washington Univ	WA	10,608	C
Eckerd College	FL	35,492	VC
Edinboro Univ of Pennsylvania	PA	11,809	LC
Edward Waters College	FL	14,374	LC
Elizabethtown College	PA	32,100	VC
Elmhurst College	IL	24,685	C
Elmira College	NY	37,200	VC
Elon Univ	NC	25,371	VC
Emory & Henry College	VA	26,570	C
Emory Univ	GA	40,546	MC
Erskine College	SC	25,468	VC
Eureka College	IL	19,280	C
Excelsior College	NY	995	SP
Fairfield Univ	CT	39,835	HC
Fairleigh Dickinson Univ/College at Florham	NJ	30,130	C
Fairleigh Dickinson Univ/Metropolitan Campus	NJ	28,590	C
Felician College	NJ	24,300	C
Ferrum College	VA	24,290	LC
Fisk Univ	TN	19,830	C
Flagler College	FL	13,790	VC+
Florida Atlantic Univ	FL	11,221	C
Florida International Univ	FL	9,215	VC
Florida Memorial College	FL	6,000	LC
Florida State Univ	FL	9,028	HC
Fordham Univ	NY	36,000	HC
Fort Hays State Univ	KS	7,638	C
Fort Lewis College	CO	11,852	C
Franciscan Univ of Steubenville	OH	20,300	VC
Franklin and Marshall College	PA	40,590	HC
Franklin College	IN		C
Fresno Pacific Univ	CA	25,454	C
Frostburg State Univ	MD	12,672	C
Furman Univ	SC	33,264	HC+
Gallaudet Univ	DC	16,554	
Gannon Univ	PA	26,100	C
Geneva College	PA	21,850	C
George Mason Univ	VA	10,850	VC
George Washington Univ	DC	48,820	MC
Georgetown College	KY	24,950	C+
Georgetown Univ	DC	43,183	MC
Georgia Southern Univ	GA	9,762	C
Georgia State Univ	GA	11,444	VC
Gettysburg College	PA	39,864	HC
Gonzaga Univ	WA	30,218	VC
Gordon College	MA	29,194	C+
Goucher College	MD	36,225	VC
Graceland Univ	IA	19,700	C
Grand Valley State Univ	MI	12,000	VC
Green Mountain College	VT	32,164	C
Greenville College	IL	23,146	C
Grinnell College	IA	34,814	HC+
Grove City College	PA	15,784	HC+
Guilford College	NC	28,160	C+
Gustavus Adolphus College	MN	30,920	HC
Hamilton College	NY	41,660	MC
Hamline Univ	MN	27,070	VC
Hampden-Sydney College	VA	31,148	VC
Hampshire College	MA	37,120	HC
Hanover College	IN	28,150	HC
Hardin-Simmons Univ	TX	18,641	C
Hartwick College	NY	36,065	C+
Harvard Univ/Harvard College	MA	45,860	MC
Hastings College	NE	22,218	VC
Haverford College	PA	41,600	MC
Heidelberg College	OH	23,242	C
Hendrix College	AR	27,646	HC+
High Point Univ	NC	25,720	C
Hiram College	OH	28,700	VC
Hobart and William Smith Colleges	NY	41,123	VC
Hofstra Univ	NY	32,630	VC
Hollins Univ	VA	31,105	C
Holy Names College	CA	27,980	NC
Hood College	MD	30,085	VC
Hope College	MI	28,208	VC+
Houghton College	NY	25,980	VC+
Howard Univ	DC	18,481	C+
Humboldt State Univ	CA	11,176	C
Huntington Univ	IN	24,830	C
Idaho State Univ	ID	9,030	C
Illinois College	IL	21,900	C+
Illinois State Univ	IL	12,839	C+
Illinois Wesleyan Univ	IL	34,050	HC+
Indiana State Univ	IN	11,604	C
Indiana Univ Bloomington	IN	13,356	VC
Indiana Univ Northwest	IN	4,902	LC
Indiana Univ of Pennsylvania	PA	11,209	C
Indiana Univ South Bend	IN	4,989	LC
Indiana Univ Southeast	IN	4,880	LC
Indiana Univ-Purdue Univ Fort Wayne	IN	5,067	LC
Indiana Univ-Purdue Univ Indianapolis	IN	10,959	C
Iona College	NY	30,878	VC
Iowa State Univ	IA	11,831	VC
Ithaca College	NY	35,144	VC
Jacksonville Univ	FL	24,040	C
James Madison Univ	VA	12,010	VC
Jamestown College	ND	14,130	NC
John Carroll Univ	OH	27,658	C+
Johns Hopkins Univ	MD	42,044	MC
Juniata College	PA	33,130	VC
Kalamazoo College	MI	32,442	VC+
Kansas State Univ	KS	10,516	VC
Kean Univ	NJ	15,880	C
Kent State Univ	OH	14,594	C
Kentucky Christian College	KY	12,680	C
Kenyon College	OH	39,500	MC
King College	TN	23,400	C
King's College	PA	29,810	C
Knox College	IL	32,385	VC+
Kutztown Univ of Pennsylvania	PA	10,820	C
La Salle Univ	PA	34,950	C
Lafayette College	PA	39,267	MC
Lake Forest College	IL	33,860	VC
Lakeland College	WI	22,990	C
Lawrence Univ	WI	33,958	HC+
Le Moyne College	NY	29,570	VC
Lebanon Valley College	PA	31,700	VC
Lehigh Univ	PA	42,690	HC+
Lenoir-Rhyne College	NC	25,580	C
Lewis and Clark College	OR	35,358	VC+
Lewis Univ	IL	23,050	C
Lincoln Univ	MO	8,000	NC
Lincoln Univ	PA	13,658	C+
Linfield College	OR	29,632	VC
Lock Haven Univ of Pennsylvania	PA	12,098	LC
LIU/Brooklyn Campus	NY	25,000	C
LIU/C.W. Post Campus	NY	28,282	C
Loras College	IA	27,193	C
Louisiana College	LA	13,450	C
Louisiana State Univ and A&M College	LA	10,749	VC
Loyola College in Maryland	MD	38,898	HC
Loyola Marymount Univ	CA	36,321	VC
Loyola Univ Chicago	IL	32,896	VC
Loyola Univ New Orleans	LA	31,050	VC+
Luther College	IA	28,800	VC+
Lycoming College	PA	30,797	C+
Lynchburg College	VA	30,645	C
Macalester College	MN	36,500	MC
MacMurray College	IL	20,755	C
Manchester College	IN	23,470	C
Manhattan College	NY	29,000	VC
Manhattanville College	NY	32,500	C+
Mansfield Univ	PA	11,300	C
Marian College	IN	26,160	C
Marist College	NY	30,566	VC
Marlboro College	VT	35,980	VC+
Marquette Univ	WI	31,066	HC
Mary Baldwin College	VA	26,465	C
Marymount Univ	VA	25,934	C
Mass Inst of Liberal Arts	MA	8,725	LC
Mass Inst of Technology	MA	41,800	MC
McDaniel College	MD	31,610	VC
McKendree College	IL	24,800	VC
McMurry Univ	TX	18,100	LC
McPherson College	KS	21,010	C
Mercer Univ	GA	27,525	VC+
Mercyhurst College	PA	28,633	VC
Merrimack College	MA	34,380	C
Messiah College	PA	28,910	VC+
Metropolitan State College of Denver	CO	2,338	LC
Metropolitan State Univ	MN	4,682	SP
Miami Univ	OH	29,097	HC
Mich State Univ	MI	13,689	VC
Middle Tenn State Univ	TN	8,540	C
Middlebury College	VT	42,120	MC
Millersville Univ of Pennsylvania	PA	12,113	C
Millikin Univ	IL	25,590	C
Mills College	CA	39,870	C
Millsaps College	MS	28,256	VC+
Minn State Univ, Mankato	MN	10,276	LC
Minn State Univ, Moorhead	MN	7,000	LC
Miss State Univ	MS	9,577	C
Missouri State Univ	MO	10,748	C
Missouri Valley College	MO	18,500	C
Molloy College	NY	16,510	C
Monmouth College	IL	23,700	C
Montana State Univ-Bozeman	MT	1,137	C
Montclair State Univ	NJ	16,327	C
Moravian College	PA	28,950	VC
Morehead State Univ	KY	9,150	C
Morehouse College	GA	25,082	C
Morgan State Univ	MD	12,080	C
Morningside College	IA	23,704	C
Mount Holyoke College	MA	42,148	HC+
Mount Mary College	WI	22,895	C
Mount Mercy College	IA	23,670	C
Mount St. Mary's College	CA	32,086	VC
Mount St. Mary's Univ	MD	30,930	C
Mount Union College	OH	25,840	C
Mount Vernon Nazarene Univ	OH	20,810	C
Muhlenberg College	PA	36,030	HC+
Murray State Univ	KY	8,900	VC
Muskingum College	OH	22,970	C
Nazareth College of Rochester	NY	28,175	VC
Nebr Wesleyan Univ	NE	23,415	C+
New College of Florida	FL	10,009	HC+
New England College	NH	31,466	C
New Jersey City Univ	NJ	13,695	LC
New Mexico State Univ	NM	15,211	C
New York Univ	NY	43,170	MC
Newberry College	SC	23,000	LC
Niagara Univ	NY	28,250	C
N Car State Univ	NC	11,824	HC
North Central College	IL	28,926	VC
North Park Univ	IL	24,050	C
Northeastern Illinois Univ	IL	3,000	NC
Northeastern Univ	MA	35,742	HC
Northern Arizona Univ	AZ	10,353	C
Northern Illinois Univ	IL	13,178	C
Northern Kentucky Univ	KY	6,670	NC
Northern Mich Univ	MI	12,340	LC
Northwest Missouri State Univ	MO	10,000	C
Northwest Nazarene Univ	ID	22,590	VC
Northwest Univ	WA	18,854	C
Northwestern College of Iowa	IA	22,174	C+
Northwestern Univ	IL	37,595	MC
Notre Dame de Namur Univ	CA	32,790	LC
Nyack College	NY	18,540	C
Oakland Univ	MI	11,936	C
Oberlin College	OH	40,904	MC
Occidental College	CA	40,185	MC
Oglethorpe Univ	GA	30,300	VC
Ohio Dominican Univ	OH	25,954	C
Ohio Northern Univ	OH	27,765	VC
Ohio State Univ	OH	15,357	HC
Ohio Univ	OH	15,921	C
Ohio Wesleyan Univ	OH	35,830	VC+
Okla City Univ	OK	23,965	VC
Okla State Univ	OK	10,213	VC
Old Dominion Univ	VA	11,907	C
Olivet Nazarene Univ	IL	22,590	C
Oral Roberts Univ	OK	22,650	C
Oregon State Univ	OR	11,055	C
Otterbein College	OH	28,986	C
Ouachita Baptist Univ	AR	21,900	VC
Our Lady of the Lake Univ of San Antonio	TX	22,430	LC
Pacific Lutheran Univ	WA	28,805	VC
Pacific Univ	OR	24,250	C
Paine College	GA	14,418	LC
Palm Beach Atlantic Univ	FL	23,597	VC
Penn State Univ/Univ Park Campus	PA	18,038	HC
Pepperdine Univ	CA	39,960	HC
Piedmont College	GA	20,500	C
Pitzer College	CA	41,644	HC
Plymouth State Univ	NH	12,298	LC
Point Loma Nazarene Univ	CA	27,610	VC
Pomona College	CA	40,774	MC
Pontifical Catholic Univ of PR/Ponce	PR	7,310	
Portland State Univ	OR	12,453	C
Princeton Univ	NJ	40,213	MC
Principia College	IL	27,765	VC+
Providence College	RI	34,580	HC
Purdue Univ/Calumet	IN	10,891	LC
Purdue Univ/West Lafayette	IN	13,458	VC
Queens Univ of Charlotte	NC	24,528	C
Radford Univ	VA	13,145	C
Randolph-Macon College	VA	31,250	C
Randolph-Macon Woman's College	VA	31,160	VC+
Reed College	OR	41,106	MC
Regis Univ	CO	31,890	C
Rensselaer Polytechnic Inst	NY	41,288	HC+
Rhode Island College	RI	11,570	C
Rhodes College	TN	32,860	HC
Rice Univ	TX	32,290	MC
Richard Stockton College of New Jersey	NJ	14,000	VC
Rider Univ	NJ	32,560	C
Ripon College	WI	37,160	C+
Roanoke College	VA	30,748	VC
Rockford College	IL	28,330	VC
Rockhurst Univ	MO	25,440	C
Rocky Mountain College	MT	20,805	C
Roger Williams Univ	RI	30,500	C
Rollins College	FL	38,366	VC
Roosevelt Univ	IL	22,605	VC
Rosemont College	PA	29,350	C
Rutgers, The State Univ of New Jersey/Camden Campus	NJ	15,000	VC
Rutgers, The State Univ of New Jersey/New Brunswick/Piscataway Campus	NJ	15,810	HC
Rutgers, The State Univ of New Jersey/Newark Campus	NJ	15,640	VC
Sacred Heart Univ	CT	33,404	C
St. Ambrose Univ	IA	25,495	C
St. Andrews Presbyterian College	NC	23,530	C
St. Anselm College	NH	33,810	C
St. Bonaventure Univ	NY	28,785	C
St. Cloud State Univ	MN	10,010	C
St. Edward's Univ	TX	23,560	C
St. Francis College	NY	19,974	C
St. Francis Univ	PA	25,880	LC
St. John Fisher College	NY	27,860	C
St. John's Univ	MN	29,749	VC
St. John's Univ	NY	34,370	C
St. Joseph College	CT	32,050	C

ST = STATE $IS = IN-STATE COSTS   SR = SELECTOR RATING

PHILOSOPHY AND RELIGION

PHOTOGRAPHY

School	ST	$IS	SR
Maine College of Art	ME	28,820	SP
Marlboro College	VT	35,980	VC+
Maryland Inst College of Art	MD	34,450	SP
Mass College of Art	MA	16,650	SP
Milwaukee Inst of Art and Design	WI	28,700	SP
Minneapolis College of Art and Design	MN	31,110	SP
Montserrat College of Art	MA	25,929	SP
Morningside College	IA	23,704	C
New Jersey City Univ	NJ	13,695	LC
New York Univ	NY	43,170	MC
Otis College of Art and Design	CA	27,546	SP
Pacific Northwest College of Art	OR	17,296	SP
Pacific Union College	CA	24,555	VC+
Parsons School of Design	NY	32,242	SP
Point Park Univ	PA	24,160	C
Pratt Inst	NY	36,156	SP
Prescott College	AZ	13,445	LC
Purdue Univ/West Lafayette	IN	13,458	VC
Rhode Island College	RI	11,570	C
Rhode Island School of Design	RI	38,130	SP
Ringling School of Art and Design	FL	31,013	SP
Rochester Inst of Technology	NY	32,070	VC+
St. Edward's Univ	TX	23,560	C
St. John's Univ	NY	34,370	C
St. Mary-of-the-Woods College	IN	25,480	C
Salem State College	MA	13,161	LC
Sam Houston State Univ	TX	8,000	C
San Francisco Art Inst	CA	25,640	SP
Savannah College of Art and Design	GA	30,800	SP
School of the Art Inst of Chicago	IL	37,800	SP
School of Visual Arts	NY	32,580	SP
Shepherd Univ	WV	10,066	C
Simon's Rock College of Bard	MA	41,988	VC+
Southern Illinois Univ Carbondale	IL	12,391	C
SUNY/College at Buffalo	NY	11,903	C+
SUNY/Univ at New Paltz	NY	12,480	VC
Syracuse Univ	NY	38,655	HC
Temple Univ	PA	17,438	C
Texas A&M Univ at Commerce	TX	9,020	C
Texas Tech Univ	TX	13,026	VC
Thomas Edison State College	NJ	3,780	SP
Univ of Akron	OH	15,166	NC
Univ of Central Okla	OK	8,094	C
Univ of Dayton	OH	28,826	VC
Univ of Florida	FL	9,354	HC
Univ of Georgia	GA	11,004	HC
Univ of Hartford	CT	34,044	C
Univ of Houston	TX	7,000	C
Univ of Idaho	ID	9,310	NC
Univ of Illinois at Chicago	IL	16,256	VC
Univ of Illinois at Urbana-Champaign	IL	15,800	HC+
Univ of Mass Dartmouth	MA	15,985	C
Univ of Miami	FL	38,397	MC
Univ of Mich/Ann Arbor	MI	16,587	HC+
Univ of North Texas	TX	7,800	C
Univ of Okla	OK	10,769	VC+
Univ of Oregon	OR	13,108	VC
Univ of the Arts	PA	32,330	SP
Univ of Washington	WA	10,400	VC
Univ of Wisc/Eau Claire	WI	9,915	VC
Virginia Commonwealth Univ	VA	12,987	C
Virginia Intermont College	VA	22,200	LC
Washington Univ in St. Louis	MO	42,106	MC
Weber State Univ	UT	9,635	NC
Webster Univ	MO	24,280	VC
Western Conn State Univ	CT	12,993	C
Youngstown State Univ	OH	12,613	NC

PHYSICAL CHEMISTRY

School	ST	$IS	SR
Averett Univ	VA	24,920	C
Centre College	KY	30,810	VC
Union Univ	TN	20,750	VC
Univ of Calif at San Diego	CA	16,102	HC

PHYSICAL EDUCATION

School	ST	$IS	SR
Abilene Christian Univ	TX	20,830	C
Adams State College	CO	8,613	C
Adelphi Univ	NY	27,000	VC
Adrian College	MI	23,000	C
Alabama A&M Univ	AL	8,890	LC
Albany State Univ	GA	5,770	C+
Albertson College of Idaho	ID	21,095	VC
Albion College	MI	26,000	VC
Alcorn State Univ	MS	8,190	LC
Alice Lloyd College	KY	4,900	C
Anderson Univ	IN	25,050	LC
Appalachian State Univ	NC	8,000	VC
Aquinas College	MI	23,750	C
Arkansas State Univ	AR	9,630	C
Armstrong Atlantic State Univ	GA	7,394	C
Asbury College	KY	23,762	VC
Ashland Univ	OH	25,000	C
Auburn Univ	AL	12,230	VC
Augsburg College	MN	28,300	C
Augustana College	IL	29,862	VC+
Augustana College	SD	24,380	VC
Aurora Univ	IL	20,645	C
Averett Univ	VA	24,920	C
Azusa Pacific Univ	CA	28,546	VC
Baker Univ	KS	22,190	C
Baldwin-Wallace College	OH	27,256	VC
Barry Univ	FL	24,100	C
Barton College	NC	22,316	C
Baylor Univ	TX	27,555	HC
Bellevue Univ	NE	4,440	NC
Belmont Univ	TN	24,110	VC
Benedictine College	KS	21,968	C
Berea College	KY	5,496	VC+
Berry College	GA	24,342	VC
Bethany College	KS	20,660	LC
Bethany College	WV	21,395	C
Bethel College	IN	19,680	C
Bethel College	TN	16,066	NC
Bethel Univ	MN	29,840	VC
Bethune-Cookman College	FL	17,922	LC
Biola Univ	CA	29,372	VC
Black Hills State Univ	SD	7,800	LC
Blackburn College	IL	13,690	C
Blue Mountain College	MS	11,086	C
Bluffton College	OH	26,110	C
Boise State Univ	ID	9,438	LC
Boston Univ	MA	42,046	HC+
Bowling Green State Univ	OH	14,994	C
Brewton-Parker College	GA	14,220	LC
Bridgewater College	VA	27,790	C
Bridgewater State College	MA	12,120	C
Bryan College	TN	19,270	C
Calif Baptist Univ	CA	23,780	C
Calif Lutheran Univ	CA	27,800	LC
Calif Polytechnic State Univ	CA	12,390	VC
Cal State, Chico	CA	11,395	C
Cal State, Dominguez Hills	CA	10,220	LC
Cal State, Fullerton	CA	10,990	C
Cal State, Los Angeles	CA	5,900	C
Cal State, Northridge	CA	9,036	LC
Cal State, Stanislaus	CA	11,283	C
Calvin College	MI	25,735	NC
Cameron Univ	OK	6,314	NC
Campbellsville Univ	KY	21,328	C
Canisius College	NY	32,257	VC
Capital Univ	OH	30,444	C
Carroll College	MT	23,324	C
Carroll College	WI	24,860	C
Carthage College	WI	26,000	C
Castleton State College	VT	13,158	C
Catawba College	NC	25,000	C
Cedarville Univ	OH	21,904	VC
Centenary College of Louisiana	LA	24,760	VC
Central Conn State Univ	CT	13,620	C
Central Methodist Univ	MO	18,000	C
Central Mich Univ	MI	12,244	C
Central Missouri State Univ	MO	10,000	C
Central State Univ	OH	9,010	C+
Central Washington Univ	WA	11,730	C
Charleston Southern Univ	SC	17,800	C
Chicago State Univ	IL	10,915	C+
Citadel, The	SC		C+
CUNY/Brooklyn College	NY	4,377	C+
CUNY/Queens College	NY	4,356	C
CUNY/York College	NY	4,242	NC
Claflin Univ	SC	16,798	C+
Clark Atlanta Univ	GA	20,960	LC
Clearwater Christian College	FL	13,160	LC
Cleveland State Univ	OH	10,798	NC
Coastal Carolina Univ	SC	13,140	C
Coe College	IA	27,440	VC
Coker College	SC	21,600	C
College of Charleston	SC	13,616	VC
College of Mount St. Vincent	NY	28,000	C
College of New Jersey	NJ	18,315	MC
College of St. Catherine	MN	27,505	VC
College of the Ozarks	MO	4,130	VC+
Concordia College: Moorhead	MN	22,475	VC
Concordia Univ Nebr	NE	20,500	C+
Concordia Univ St.Paul	MN	27,776	C
Concordia Univ Wisc	WI	22,660	VC
Concordia Univ, Ann Arbor	MI	25,153	C+
Concordia Univ, River Forest	IL	26,300	C
Cornerstone Univ and Grand Rapids Theological Seminary	MI	21,350	NC
Culver-Stockton College	MO	20,625	C
Cumberland Univ	TN	18,894	C
Dakota Wesleyan Univ	SD	17,832	C
Dallas Baptist Univ	TX	17,040	VC
Dana College	NE	22,390	C
Davis and Elkins College	WV	22,416	C
Defiance College	OH	24,790	C
Delaware State Univ	DE	8,130	LC
Denison Univ	OH	37,040	HC
DePauw Univ	IL	29,835	VC
Doane College	NE	22,458	C
Drury Univ	MO	20,117	VC
East Carolina Univ	NC	10,000	C
East Central Univ	OK	6,207	C
East Tenn State Univ	TN	8,497	C
East Texas Baptist Univ	TX	16,713	C
Eastern Conn State Univ	CT	13,554	C
Eastern Illinois Univ	IL	12,569	VC
Eastern Kentucky Univ	KY	7,725	C
Eastern Mennonite Univ	VA	25,450	VC
Eastern Mich Univ	MI	12,897	C
Eastern New Mexico Univ	NM	7,264	C
Eastern Oregon Univ	OR	10,400	NC
Eastern Washington Univ	WA	10,608	C
Edinboro Univ of Pennsylvania	PA	11,809	LC
Edward Waters College	FL	14,374	LC
Elizabeth City State Univ	NC	5,700	LC
Elmhurst College	IL	24,685	C
Elon Univ	NC	25,371	HC
Emory & Henry College	VA	26,570	C
Emporia State Univ	KS	8,093	C
Endicott College	MA	30,156	C+
Erskine College	SC	25,468	VC
Eureka College	IL	19,280	C
Evangel Univ	MO	17,380	C
Faulkner Univ	AL	15,600	C
Ferrum College	VA	24,290	C
Florida Atlantic Univ	FL	11,221	C
Florida International Univ	FL	9,215	VC
Florida Memorial College	FL	6,000	LC
Florida State Univ	FL	9,028	HC
Fort Hays State Univ	KS	7,638	C
Fort Valley State Univ	GA	6,975	C
Franklin College	IN		C
Freed-Hardeman Univ	TN	16,370	NC
Fresno Pacific Univ	CA	25,454	C
Frostburg State Univ	MD	12,672	C
Gallaudet Univ	DC	16,554	
Gardner-Webb Univ	NC	21,500	C
George Fox Univ	OR	28,490	C
George Mason Univ	VA	10,850	VC
Georgia College and State Univ	GA	11,020	C
Georgia State Univ	GA	11,444	VC
Glenville State College	WV	8,778	NC
Gonzaga Univ	WA	30,218	HC
Goshen College	IN	22,850	VC
Grace College	IN	22,170	C
Graceland Univ	IA	19,700	C
Grambling State Univ	LA	6,538	NC
Grand Canyon Univ	AZ	32,000	LC
Greensboro College	NC	23,000	C
Greenville College	IL	23,146	C
Hamline Univ	MN	27,070	VC
Hampton Univ	VA	19,468	C+
Hardin-Simmons Univ	TX	18,641	C
Heidelberg College	OH	23,242	C
Henderson State Univ	AR	7,600	C
High Point Univ	NC	25,720	C
Hillsdale College	MI	24,160	HC
Hofstra Univ	NY	32,630	VC
Houghton College	NY	25,980	VC+
Houston Baptist Univ	TX	18,660	C
Howard Univ	DC	18,481	C+
Humboldt State Univ	CA	11,176	C
Huntingdon College	AL	23,090	NC
Huntington Univ	IN	24,830	C
Huron Univ	SD	10,700	C
Husson College	ME	17,410	C
Huston-Tillotson Univ	TX	14,232	LC
Idaho State Univ	ID	9,030	C
Illinois College	IL	21,900	C+
Illinois State Univ	IL	12,839	C+
Indiana State Univ	IN	11,604	C
Indiana Univ Bloomington	IN	13,356	VC
Indiana Univ of Pennsylvania	PA	11,209	C
Indiana Univ-Purdue Univ Indianapolis	IN	10,959	C
Indiana Wesleyan Univ	IN	22,074	C+
Iowa State Univ	IA	11,831	VC
Iowa Wesleyan College	IA	22,140	C
Ithaca College	NY	35,144	VC
Jacksonville Univ	FL	24,040	C
Jamestown College	ND	14,130	NC
John Brown Univ	AR	20,910	VC
John Carroll Univ	OH	27,658	C
Johnson C. Smith Univ	NC	20,000	C
Johnson State College	VT	11,830	LC
Judson College	IL	25,130	C
Kansas Wesleyan Univ	KS	21,400	VC
Kean Univ	NJ	15,880	C
Keene State College	NH	13,836	C
Kennesaw State Univ	GA	12,152	C
Kent State Univ	OH	14,594	C
Kentucky State Univ	KY	10,089	LC
Kentucky Wesleyan College	KY	18,500	C
King College	TN	23,400	C
Knoxville College	TN	6,200	LC
La Sierra Univ	CA	24,327	C+
Lambuth Univ	TN	21,700	C+
Lander Univ	SC	10,600	C
Lane College	TN	11,220	C+
Langston Univ	OK	2,308	LC
Lee Univ	TN	14,780	NC
Lees-McRae College	NC	23,000	C
LeTourneau Univ	TX	21,200	C
Liberty Univ	VA	19,101	C
Limestone College	SC	19,840	C
Lincoln Univ	MO	8,000	NC
Lincoln Univ	PA	13,658	C+
Lindenwood Univ	MO	18,600	VC
Linfield College	OR	29,632	VC
Lipscomb Univ	TN	20,967	VC
Lock Haven Univ of Pennsylvania	PA	12,098	LC
Longwood Univ	VA	12,426	C
Loras College	IA	27,193	C
Louisiana Tech Univ	LA	7,370	C
Lubbock Christian Univ	TX	16,960	C
Luther College	IA	28,800	VC+
Lyndon State College	VT	14,233	LC
MacMurray College	IL	20,755	C
Malone College	OH	23,040	C
Manhattan College	NY	29,000	VC
Marian College	IN	26,160	C
Mars Hill College	NC	19,000	LC
Maryville College	TN	29,224	VC
Marywood Univ	PA	30,680	C
Master's College and Seminary	CA	25,850	VC
Mayville State Univ	ND	8,667	NC
McDaniel College	MD	31,610	VC
McKendree College	IL	24,800	VC
McMurry Univ	TX	18,100	LC
McPherson College	KS	21,010	C
Messiah College	PA	28,910	VC+
Methodist College	NC	21,000	C
Metropolitan State College of Denver	CO	2,338	LC
Miami Univ	OH	29,097	HC
Mich State Univ	MI	13,689	VC
MidAmerica Nazarene Univ	KS	20,584	LC
Middle Tenn State Univ	TN	8,540	C
Midwestern State Univ	TX	9,381	LC
Millikin Univ	IL	25,590	C
Minn State Univ, Mankato	MN	10,276	LC
Minot State Univ	ND	6,700	LC
Miss State Univ	MS	9,577	C
Miss Valley State Univ	MS	7,970	C
Missouri Southern State Univ	MO	8,396	NC
Missouri State Univ	MO	10,748	C+
Missouri Valley College	MO	18,500	C
Monmouth College	IL	23,700	C
Montana State Univ-Billings	MT	8,906	C
Montana State Univ-Northern	MT	10,000	NC
Montclair State Univ	NJ	16,327	C
Morehead State Univ	KY	9,150	C
Morehouse College	GA	25,082	C
Morgan State Univ	MD	12,080	C
Mount Marty College	SD	20,590	C
Mount Union College	OH	25,840	C
Mount Vernon Nazarene Univ	OH	20,810	C
Muskingum College	OH	22,970	C
Nebr Wesleyan Univ	NE	23,415	C+
New England College	NH	31,466	C
New Mexico State Univ	NM	9,250	C
Newberry College	SC	23,000	LC
N Car Agricultural and Technical State Univ	NC	8,000	LC
N Car Central Univ	NC	9,000	LC
N Dak State Univ	ND	8,500	C
North Georgia College and State Univ	GA	7,000	C
Northeastern Illinois Univ	IL	3,000	NC
Northern Illinois Univ	IL	13,178	C
Northern Kentucky Univ	KY	6,670	NC
Northern Mich Univ	MI	12,340	LC
Northern State Univ	SD	8,257	C
Northwest Missouri State Univ	MO	10,000	C
Northwest Nazarene Univ	ID	22,590	VC
Northwest Univ	WA	18,854	C
Northwestern Univ	MN	25,220	NC
Northwestern College of Iowa	IA	22,174	C+
Northwestern Okla State Univ	OK	6,250	NC
Norwich Univ	VT	28,212	C
Oakwood College	AL	14,904	C
Ohio Northern Univ	OH	27,765	VC
Ohio Wesleyan Univ	OH	35,830	VC+
Okla Baptist Univ	OK	17,986	VC
Okla Christian Univ	OK	18,992	NC
Okla City Univ	OK	23,945	VC
Okla Panhandle State Univ	OK	7,635	NC
Okla State Univ	OK	10,213	VC
Okla Wesleyan Univ	OK	18,950	NC
Old Dominion Univ	VA	11,907	C
Olivet College	MI	19,984	C+
Olivet Nazarene Univ	IL	22,590	C
Oral Roberts Univ	OK	22,650	C
Ottawa Univ	KS	12,000	LC
Otterbein College	OH	28,986	C

School	ST	$IS	SR
Pacific Lutheran Univ	WA	28,805	VC
Pacific Union College	CA	24,555	VC+
Palm Beach Atlantic Univ	FL	23,597	VC
Paul Quinn College	TX	8,300	LC
Pepperdine Univ	CA	39,960	HC
Peru State College	NE	6,350	LC
Pfeiffer Univ	NC	21,900	C
Philander Smith College	AR	13,230	LC
Pittsburg State Univ	KS	8,112	C
Plymouth State Univ	NH	12,298	LC
Point Loma Nazarene Univ	CA	27,610	VC
Pontifical Catholic Univ of PR/Ponce	PR	7,310	
Prairie View A&M Univ	TX	11,110	LC
Purdue Univ/West Lafayette	IN	13,458	VC
Quincy Univ	IL	24,920	C
Radford Univ	VA	13,145	C
Rhode Island College	RI	11,570	C
Roanoke College	VA	30,748	VC
Rockford College	IL	28,330	VC
Rocky Mountain College	MT	20,805	C
Saginaw Valley State Univ	MI	11,432	C
St. Ambrose Univ	IA	25,495	C
St. Andrews Presbyterian College	NC	23,530	C
St. Augustine's College	NC	14,000	LC
St. Bonaventure Univ	NY	28,785	C
St. Edward's Univ	TX	23,560	C
St. Francis College	NY	19,974	LC
St. Joseph's College	IN	26,600	C
St. Joseph's College of Maine	ME	29,185	C
St. Mary's College of Calif	CA	37,290	C
Salisbury Univ	MD	13,128	VC
Sam Houston State Univ	TX	8,000	C
Samford Univ	AL	20,258	VC
San Francisco State Univ	CA	13,000	C
Schreiner Univ	TX	20,600	C
Shaw Univ	NC	15,488	LC
Shepherd Univ	WV	10,066	C
Simpson College	IA	26,833	C
S Car State Univ	SC	6,700	LC
S Dak State Univ	SD	9,815	C
Southeast Missouri State Univ	MO	10,596	C
Southeastern Louisiana Univ	LA	8,521	LC
Southeastern Okla State Univ	OK	6,147	C
Southern Adventist Univ	TN	18,500	C
Southern Conn State Univ	CT	10,310	C
Southern Illinois Univ Carbondale	IL	12,391	C
Southern Methodist Univ	TX	36,088	VC+
Southern Nazarene Univ	OK	14,634	NC
Southern Oregon Univ	OR	12,186	C
Southern Univ at New Orleans	LA	1,000	NC
Southern Utah Univ	UT		C
Southern Wesleyan Univ	SC	21,675	C
Southwest Baptist Univ	MO	18,300	C
Southwest Minn State Univ	MN	10,975	C
Southwestern Adventist Univ	TX	18,290	LC
Southwestern College	KS	21,476	C
Southwestern Okla State Univ	OK	4,801	C
Springfield College	MA	25,000	C
SUNY/College at Brockport	NY	12,747	VC
SUNY/College at Cortland	NY	12,095	C
Stillman College	AL	11,475	LC
Syracuse Univ	NY	38,655	HC
Tabor College	KS	21,614	NC
Tarleton State Univ	TX	8,952	C
Taylor Univ	IN	26,376	VC+
Temple Univ	PA	17,438	C
Tenn Tech Univ	TN	10,044	C
Tenn Wesleyan College	TN	18,650	C
Texas A&M Univ	TX	13,351	HC
Texas A&M Univ at Kingsville	TX	6,800	LC
Texas Christian Univ	TX	23,410	VC+
Texas Southern Univ	TX	9,828	C
Texas Wesleyan Univ	TX	18,700	C
Tougaloo College	MS	15,975	NC
Towson Univ	MD	13,924	VC
Trevecca Nazarene Univ	TN	19,594	C
Trinity International Univ	IL	25,686	C
Tri-State Univ-Main Campus	IN	26,200	C
Troy Univ	AL	8,916	C
Turabo Univ	PR	4,110	C
Tusculum College	TN	21,340	LC
Tuskegee Univ	AL	18,860	LC
Union College	KY	18,920	C
Union College	NE	18,710	C
Union Univ	TN	20,750	NC
Univ of Akron	OH	15,166	NC
Univ of Alabama	AL	9,888	C
Univ of Alabama at Birmingham	AL	13,716	C
Univ of Alaska Anchorage	AK	11,275	NC
Univ of Arizona	AZ	11,958	VC
Univ of Arkansas at Monticello	AR	7,325	NC
Univ of Arkansas at Pine Bluff	AR	8,300	C
Univ of at Calif Davis	CA	15,010	VC
Univ of Central Arkansas	AR	9,984	C
Univ of Central Florida	FL	10,739	VC
Univ of Central Okla	OK	8,094	C
Univ of Charleston	WV	27,600	C
Univ of Dayton	OH	28,826	VC
Univ of Delaware	DE	14,142	HC
Univ of Dubuque	IA	23,390	C
Univ of Evansville	IN	28,320	VC
Univ of Findlay	OH	29,238	C
Univ of Georgia	GA	11,004	HC
Univ of Great Falls	MT	17,000	C
Univ of Hawaii at Manoa	HI	10,413	VC
Univ of Idaho	ID	9,310	NC
Univ of Illinois at Chicago	IL	16,256	VC
Univ of Illinois at Urbana-Champaign	IL	15,800	HC+
Univ of Indianapolis	IN	25,090	C
Univ of Kansas	KS	10,915	VC
Univ of Kentucky	KY	7,800	C
Univ of Louisiana at Monroe	LA	7,103	C
Univ of Louisville	KY	10,400	VC
Univ of Maine	ME	13,642	C
Univ of Maine at Presque Isle	ME	10,066	LC
Univ of Mary	ND	15,374	C
Univ of Mary Hardin-Baylor	TX	19,428	C
Univ of Maryland/College Park	MD	16,036	HC
Univ of Maryland/Eastern Shore	MD	11,210	C
Univ of Mass Boston	MA	8,024	C
Univ of Memphis	TN	11,153	C
Univ of Mich/Ann Arbor	MI	16,587	HC+
Univ of Minn/Duluth	MN	13,974	C
Univ of Minn/Twin Cities	MN	13,165	HC
Univ of Missouri/Kansas City	MO	15,000	VC
Univ of Missouri/St. Louis	MO	14,046	C
Univ of Mobile	AL	16,880	C
Univ of Montana	MT	10,602	C
Univ of Montevallo	AL	9,630	C
Univ of Nebr at Kearney	NE	9,000	NC
Univ of Nebr at Lincoln	NE	11,401	VC
Univ of Nebr at Omaha	NE	11,235	C
Univ of Nevada/Las Vegas	NV	11,566	C
Univ of New Hampshire	NH	16,810	VC
Univ of New Mexico	NM	11,253	C
Univ of New Orleans	LA	7,370	C
Univ of North Alabama	AL	8,992	C
Univ of N Car at Chapel Hill	NC	11,129	MC
Univ of N Car at Pembroke	NC	7,940	LC
Univ of N Car at Wilmington	NC	10,100	VC
Univ of N Dak	ND	10,114	VC
Univ of North Florida	FL	9,908	VC
Univ of North Texas	TX	7,800	C
Univ of Northern Colo	CO	10,249	C
Univ of Northern Iowa	IA	11,133	C
Univ of PR/Arecibo	PR	8,327	C
Univ of Rhode Island	RI	15,398	C
Univ of Rio Grande	OH	8,728	NC
Univ of St. Thomas	MN	28,000	VC
Univ of Science and Arts of Okla	OK	7,650	C
Univ of South Alabama	AL	8,930	LC
Univ of S Car at Columbia	SC	13,397	VC
Univ of S Car Upstate	SC	11,957	C
Univ of S Dak	SD	9,068	C
Univ of South Florida	FL	10,284	VC
Univ of Tenn at Knoxville	TN	11,720	C
Univ of Texas at Arlington	TX	7,195	LC
Univ of the Cumberlands	KY	18,184	C
Univ of the District of Columbia	DC	2,070	LC
Univ of the Incarnate Word	TX	23,306	C
Univ of the Ozarks	AR	19,250	C
Univ of the Pacific	CA	34,380	VC
Univ of the Sacred Heart	PR	5,590	C
Univ of Toledo	OH	15,806	NC
Univ of Vermont	VT	18,080	VC
Univ of Virginia	VA	13,759	MC
Univ of West Alabama	AL	7,611	C
Univ of West Georgia	GA	8,838	C
Univ of Wisc/La Crosse	WI	10,045	VC
Univ of Wisc/Madison	WI	13,117	HC
Univ of Wisc/Oshkosh	WI	10,426	C
Univ of Wisc/Platteville	WI	9,779	NC
Univ of Wisc/River Falls	WI	9,722	C
Univ of Wisc/Stevens Point	WI	9,384	VC
Univ of Wisc/Superior	WI	9,610	C+
Univ of Wisc/Whitewater	WI	9,274	C
Univ of Wyoming	WY	9,065	C
Upper Iowa Univ	IA	20,130	C
Utah State Univ	UT	8,002	VC
Valdosta State Univ	GA	8,802	C
Valley City State Univ	ND	9,854	LC
Valparaiso Univ	IN	28,970	VC+
Vanguard Univ of Southern Calif	CA	27,071	C
Virginia State Univ	VA	11,318	C
Walla Walla College	WA	24,489	NC
Walsh Univ	OH	23,440	C
Warner Pacific College	OR	21,900	C
Warner Southern College	FL	18,000	LC
Wartburg College	IA	27,315	NC
Washburn Univ	KS	9,734	NC
Washington State Univ	WA	12,260	C
Wayland Baptist Univ	TX	13,484	C
Wayne State Univ	MI	11,805	C
Weber State Univ	UT	9,635	NC
Wesley College	DE	19,905	C
West Chester Univ of Pennsylvania	PA	12,355	C+
West Liberty State College	WV	9,142	LC
West Texas A&M Univ	TX	8,452	LC
West Virginia Univ	WV	10,506	C
West Virginia Wesleyan College	WV	26,880	C
Western Baptist College	OR	21,808	C
Western Carolina Univ	NC	7,000	C
Western Illinois Univ	IL	13,042	C
Western Kentucky Univ	KY	10,192	C
Western Mich Univ	MI	13,299	C
Western New Mexico Univ	NM	7,233	LC
Westminster College	MO	19,060	VC
Westmont College	CA	36,672	HC
Whittier College	CA	29,108	C
Wichita State Univ	KS	8,500	C
Wiley College	TX	8,100	LC
William Carey College	MS	11,000	LC
William Paterson Univ of New Jersey	NJ	17,810	C+
William Penn Univ	IA	17,685	C
William Woods Univ	MO	21,020	C
Williams Baptist College	AR	13,450	C
Wilmington College	OH	2,806	NC
Wingate Univ	NC	23,300	C
Winona State Univ	MN	11,333	C
Winston-Salem State Univ	NC	8,960	LC
Winthrop Univ	SC	11,302	C
Wright State Univ	OH	13,616	C
Xavier Univ of Louisiana	LA	17,600	C
Youngstown State Univ	OH	12,613	NC

PHYSICAL FITNESS/MOVEMENT

School	ST	$IS	SR
Adelphi Univ	NY	27,000	VC
Arizona State Univ-Tempe	AZ	11,174	C
Ashland Univ	OH	25,000	C
Auburn Univ	AL	12,230	VC
Augustana College	SD	24,380	VC
Ball State Univ	IN	13,138	C
Baylor Univ	TX	27,555	HC
Bethel College	TN	16,066	VC
Bloomsburg Univ of Pennsylvania	PA	11,602	C
Boston Univ	MA	42,046	HC+
Bowling Green State Univ	OH	14,994	C
Brigham Young Univ/Hawaii	HI	7,740	HC+
Buena Vista Univ	IA	27,742	C
Calif State Polytechnic Univ, Pomona	CA	18,053	C+
Cal State East Bay	CA	10,856	LC
Cal State, Fresno	CA	10,037	LC
Campbell Univ	NC	21,137	VC
Capital Univ	OH	30,444	C
Chapman Univ	CA	37,550	VC
Clarke College	IA	25,390	C
College of St. Catherine	MN	27,505	VC
Concordia Univ Nebr	NE	20,500	C+
Concordia Univ, River Forest	IL	26,300	C
Dallas Baptist Univ	TX	17,040	VC
Defiance College	OH	24,790	C
DePauw Univ	IN	32,100	HC
East Carolina Univ	NC	10,000	C
East Stroudsburg Univ of Pennsylvania	PA	10,336	C
East Texas Baptist Univ	TX	16,713	C
Eastern Nazarene College	MA	19,500	LC
Eureka College	IL	19,280	C
George Washington Univ	DC	48,820	MC
Gordon College	MA	29,194	C+
Grand Canyon Univ	AZ	32,000	LC
High Point Univ	NC	25,720	C
Hope College	MI	28,208	VC+
Houston Baptist Univ	TX	18,660	C
Humboldt State Univ	CA	11,176	C
Indiana Univ Bloomington	IN	13,356	VC
Ithaca College	NY	35,144	VC
James Madison Univ	VA	12,010	VC
Johnson State College	VT	11,830	LC
Kansas State Univ	KS	10,516	VC
Lakeland College	WI	22,990	C
Lasell College	MA	26,250	C
Lewis-Clark State College	ID	6,990	C
Louisiana State Univ and A&M College	LA	10,749	VC
Lubbock Christian Univ	TX	16,960	C
Lynchburg College	VA	30,645	C
Malone College	OH	23,040	C
Marshall Univ	WV	9,116	C
Mesa State College	CO	8,051	C
Metropolitan State College of Denver	CO	2,338	LC
Miami Univ	OH	29,097	HC
Minot State Univ	ND	6,700	LC
Miss Univ for Women	MS	6,000	LC
Missouri Baptist Univ	MO	19,640	C
Mount Union College	OH	25,840	C
New England College	NH	31,466	C
New Mexico Highlands Univ	NM	6,272	NC
New Mexico State Univ	NM	9,250	C
N Dak State Univ	ND	8,500	C
Northeastern Univ	MA	35,742	HC
Northern Illinois Univ	IL	13,178	C
Northern Kentucky Univ	KY	6,670	NC
Northern Mich Univ	MI	12,340	LC
Northern State Univ	SD	8,257	C
Northwestern College of Iowa	IA	22,174	C+
Oakwood College	AL	14,904	C
Occidental College	CA	40,185	MC
Penn State Univ/Univ Park Campus	PA	18,038	HC
St. Augustine's College	NC	14,000	LC
St. Edward's Univ	TX	23,560	C
Sam Houston State Univ	TX	8,000	C
San Diego Christian College	CA	24,172	C
Seattle Pacific Univ	WA	29,355	C
Shenandoah Univ	VA	27,600	C
Shepherd Univ	WV	10,066	C
Sonoma State Univ	CA	14,732	C
Southern Methodist Univ	TX	36,088	VC+
Southwestern Univ	TX	26,767	HC
Spring Arbor Univ	MI	22,476	C
Springfield College	MA	25,000	C
Stephen F. Austin State Univ	TX	7,930	C
Sul Ross State Univ	TX	6,600	LC
Tarleton State Univ	TX	8,952	C
Temple Univ	PA	17,438	C
Texas Christian Univ	TX	23,410	VC+
Texas Southern Univ	TX	9,828	C
Texas Woman's Univ	TX	7,804	LC
Truman State Univ	MO	11,242	NC
Union College	NE	18,710	C
Univ of Central Okla	OK	8,094	C
Univ of Delaware	DE	14,142	HC
Univ of Florida	FL	9,354	HC
Univ of Houston	TX	7,000	C
Univ of La Verne	CA	33,470	C
Univ of Maryland/College Park	MD	16,036	HC
Univ of Mich/Ann Arbor	MI	16,587	HC+
Univ of Nevada/Las Vegas	NV	11,566	C
Univ of New Hampshire	NH	16,810	VC
Univ of N Car at Charlotte	NC	9,101	C
Univ of N Car at Pembroke	NC	7,940	LC
Univ of North Texas	TX	7,800	C
Univ of Northern Colo	CO	10,249	C
Univ of Rio Grande	OH	8,728	NC
Univ of S Car at Aiken	SC	11,718	LC
Univ of Texas at Austin	TX	14,610	HC
Univ of Texas at El Paso	TX	8,764	NC
Univ of Texas at San Antonio	TX	11,325	LC
Univ of Texas-Pan American	TX	7,290	C+
Univ of Toledo	OH	15,806	NC
Univ of Wisc/Eau Claire	WI	9,915	VC
Univ of Wisc/Stevens Point	WI	9,384	VC
Upper Iowa Univ	IA	20,130	C
Urbana Univ	OH	21,190	C
Virginia Polytechnic Inst and State Univ	VA	10,834	VC
West Liberty State College	WV	9,142	LC
Western State College of Colo	CO	9,942	C
Westfield State College	MA	10,200	C
Wheaton College	IL	27,760	HC
Winona State Univ	MN	11,333	C
Youngstown State Univ	OH	12,613	NC

PHYSICAL SCIENCES

School	ST	$IS	SR
Alverno College	WI	21,088	C
Antioch College	OH	33,700	C
Arkansas Tech Univ	AR	8,108	VC
Asbury College	KY	23,762	VC
Auburn Univ Montgomery	AL	9,530	NC
Biola Univ	CA	29,372	VC
Black Hills State Univ	SD	7,800	LC
Bluffton College	OH	26,110	C
Bowling Green State Univ	OH	14,994	C
Brescia Univ	KY	14,240	C
Calif Polytechnic State Univ	CA	12,390	VC
Cal State East Bay	CA	10,856	LC
Cal State, Chico	CA	11,395	C
Cal State, Sacramento	CA	11,122	C+
Cal State, Stanislaus	CA	11,283	C
Calif Univ of Pennsylvania	PA	14,217	C
Central Conn State Univ	CT	13,620	C
Central Mich Univ	MI	12,244	C
Colgate Univ	NY	41,170	MC
Colo State Univ-Fort Collins	CO	10,878	C+
Concordia Univ Nebr	NE	20,500	C+
Concordia Univ, Ann Arbor	MI	25,153	C+
Concordia Univ, River Forest	IL	26,300	C
Doane College	NE	22,458	C
East Stroudsburg Univ of Pennsylvania	PA	10,336	C
Emporia State Univ	KS	8,093	C

ST = STATE $IS = IN-STATE COSTS   SR = SELECTOR RATING

School	ST	$IS	SR
Eureka College	IL	19,280	C
Fort Hays State Univ	KS	7,638	C
Freed-Hardeman Univ	TN	16,370	NC
Harvard Univ/Harvard College	MA	45,860	MC
Indiana Univ Kokomo	IN	4,835	LC
Kansas State Univ	KS	10,516	VC
Keene State College	NH	13,836	C
Le Moyne College	NY	29,570	VC
Lynchburg College	VA	30,645	C
Malone College	OH	23,040	C
Mayville State Univ	ND	8,667	NC
Mesa State College	CO	8,051	C
Mich State Univ	MI	13,689	VC
Minot State Univ	ND	6,700	LC
Miss Univ for Women	MS	6,000	LC
Muhlenberg College	PA	36,030	HC+
Okla Panhandle State Univ	OK	7,635	NC
Olivet Nazarene Univ	IL	22,590	C
Peru State College	NE	6,350	NC
Radford Univ	VA	13,145	C
Ripon College	WI	27,160	C+
St. John's Univ	NY	34,370	C
St. Michael's College	VT	33,330	VC
San Diego State Univ	CA	12,971	C
Shawnee State Univ	OH	12,237	NC
Texas Wesleyan Univ	TX	18,700	C
Trinity College	DC	24,150	LC
Tri-State Univ-Main Campus	IN	26,200	C
Union Univ	TN	20,750	VC
Univ of Arkansas at Monticello	AR	7,325	NC
Univ of Calif at Berkeley	CA	18,141	HC+
Univ of Dayton	OH	28,826	VC
Univ of Great Falls	MT	17,000	C
Univ of Maryland/College Park	MD	16,036	HC
Univ of Mich/Flint	MI	6,398	C
Univ of Pittsburgh at Bradford	PA	17,008	C
Univ of Rio Grande	OH	8,728	NC
Univ of South Florida	FL	10,284	VC
Univ of Wisc/Eau Claire	WI	9,915	VC
Univ of Wisc/Platteville	WI	9,779	NC
Washington State Univ	WA	12,260	C
Washington Univ in St. Louis	MO	42,106	MC
Wayland Baptist Univ	TX	13,484	C
Weber State Univ	UT	9,635	NC
Wesleyan College	GA	19,560	C
Wheaton College	IL	27,760	HC

PHYSICAL THERAPY

School	ST	$IS	SR
American International College	MA	28,710	LC
Armstrong Atlantic State Univ	GA	7,394	C
Baldwin-Wallace College	OH	27,256	VC
Bellarmine Univ	KY	27,650	C+
Boston Univ	MA	42,046	HC+
Bowling Green State Univ	OH	14,994	C
Cal State, Northridge	CA	9,036	LC
Cal State, Sacramento	CA	11,122	C+
Carson-Newman College	TN	16,800	C
CUNY/College of Staten Island	NY	4,328	NC
CUNY/Hunter College	NY	8,000	C+
Clarke College	IA	25,390	C
Cleveland State Univ	OH	10,798	NC
Coe College	IA	27,440	C
College Misericordia	PA	27,950	C
College of St. Benedict	MN	30,091	C
D'Youville College	NY	23,660	C
Florida A&M Univ	FL	8,344	C
Florida Gulf Coast Univ	FL	10,833	C
Gannon Univ	PA	26,100	C
Grand Valley State Univ	MI	12,000	VC
Gustavus Adolphus College	MN	30,920	HC
Howard Univ	DC	18,481	C+
Indiana Univ-Purdue Univ Indianapolis	IN	10,959	C
Ithaca College	NY	35,144	VC
Kent State Univ	OH	14,594	C
King College	TN	23,400	C
Lamar Univ	TX	6,820	LC
Langston Univ	OK	2,308	LC
Lebanon Valley College	PA	31,700	VC
Lewis Univ	IL	23,050	C+
LIU/Brooklyn Campus	NY	25,000	C
Missouri Southern State Univ	MO	8,396	NC
Mount St. Mary College	NY	25,250	C
Nazareth College of Rochester	NY	28,175	VC
New York Inst of Technology	NY	28,126	VC
Newman Univ	KS	21,106	C
North Park Univ	IL	24,050	C
Northeastern Univ	MA	35,742	HC
Oakland Univ	MI	11,936	C
Ohio State Univ	OH	15,357	HC
Ohio Univ	OH	15,921	C
Okla Baptist Univ	OK	17,986	NC
Purdue Univ/Calumet	IN	10,891	LC
Richard Stockton College of New Jersey	NJ	14,000	VC
Russell Sage College	NY	27,000	C
St. Francis Univ	PA	25,880	LC
St. John's Univ	MN	29,749	VC
St. Vincent College	PA	26,160	VC
San Francisco State Univ	CA	13,000	C
Simmons College	MA	35,640	VC
Southern Nazarene Univ	OK	14,634	NC
SUNY/Univ at Buffalo	NY	13,694	VC
Tarleton State Univ	TX	8,952	C
Tenn State Univ	TN	9,048	LC
Thiel College	PA	24,580	C
Touro College	NY	17,000	VC
Trinity International Univ	IL	25,686	C
Truman State Univ	MO	11,242	HC
Univ of Central Arkansas	AR	9,984	C
Univ of Conn	CT	16,628	HC
Univ of Evansville	IN	28,320	VC
Univ of Florida	FL	9,354	HC
Univ of Hartford	CT	34,044	C
Univ of Kentucky	KY	7,800	C
Univ of Mary	ND	15,374	C
Univ of Maryland/Eastern Shore	MD	11,210	C
Univ of Mich/Flint	MI	6,398	C
Univ of Minn/Crookston	MN	13,157	LC
Univ of Minn/Twin Cities	MN	13,165	HC
Univ of Missouri/Columbia	MO	13,500	VC
Univ of N Car at Greensboro	NC	8,993	C
Univ of N Dak	ND	10,114	VC
Univ of Scranton	PA	31,100	VC
Univ of the Sciences in Philadelphia	PA	33,380	C
Univ of Toledo	OH	15,806	NC
Univ of Utah	UT	10,162	VC
Virginia Polytechnic Inst and State Univ	VA	10,834	VC
Walsh Univ	OH	23,440	C
West Virginia Univ	WV	10,506	C
Western State College of Colo	CO	9,942	C
Winona State Univ	MN	11,333	C
Winston-Salem State Univ	NC	8,960	LC

PHYSICAL THERAPY ASSISTANT

School	ST	$IS	SR
Calif Univ of Pennsylvania	PA	14,217	C

PHYSICIAN'S ASSISTANT

School	ST	$IS	SR
Butler Univ	IN	31,944	VC+
CUNY/City College	NY		C
CUNY/College of Staten Island	NY	4,328	NC
Colo State Univ-Pueblo	CO	7,821	LC
Daemen College	NY	24,580	C
De Sales Univ	PA	28,580	VC
D'Youville College	NY	23,660	C
East Carolina Univ	NC	10,000	C
Gannon Univ	PA	26,100	C
Gardner-Webb Univ	NC	21,500	C
George Washington Univ	DC	48,820	MC
Grand Valley State Univ	MI	12,000	VC
Hofstra Univ	NY	32,630	VC
Howard Univ	DC	18,481	C+
Juniata College	PA	33,130	VC
Le Moyne College	NY	29,570	VC
Lenoir-Rhyne College	NC	25,580	C
LIU/Brooklyn Campus	NY	25,000	C
Marietta College	OH	29,327	C
Mars Hill College	NC	19,000	LC
Methodist College	NC	21,000	C
Mountain State Univ	WV	11,406	NC
New York Inst of Technology	NY	28,126	VC
Nova Southeastern Univ	FL	24,320	C
Pace Univ	NY	30,000	VC
Pennsylvania College of Technology	PA	16,980	LC
Philadelphia Univ	PA	30,006	C
Rochester Inst of Technology	NY	32,070	VC+
St. Francis College	NY	19,974	LC
St. Francis Univ	PA	25,880	C
St. John's Univ	NY	34,370	C
St. Vincent College	PA	26,160	VC
Seton Hill Univ	PA	28,810	C
South Univ	GA		C
Southern Illinois Univ Carbondale	IL	12,391	C
SUNY/Univ at Stony Brook	NY	13,625	HC
Union College	NE	18,710	C
Univ of Alabama at Birmingham	AL	13,716	C
Univ of Findlay	OH	29,238	C
Univ of Kentucky	KY	7,800	C
Univ of New Mexico	NM	11,253	C
Univ of Southern Calif	CA	41,618	MC
Univ of Texas-Pan American	TX	7,290	C+
Univ of the Sciences in Philadelphia	PA	33,380	VC
Univ of Wisc/La Crosse	WI	10,045	VC
Univ of Wisc/Madison	WI	13,117	HC
Wagner College	NY	33,300	VC
Wichita State Univ	KS	8,500	C

PHYSICS

School	ST	$IS	SR
Abilene Christian Univ	TX	20,830	C
Adelphi Univ	NY	27,000	VC
Adrian College	MI	23,000	C
Agnes Scott College	GA	32,070	HC
Alabama A&M Univ	AL	8,890	LC
Alabama State Univ	AL	7,658	C
Albion College	MI	26,000	VC
Albright College	PA	33,920	C
Alfred Univ	NY		VC
Allegheny College	PA	33,500	HC
Alma College	MI	28,544	VC
American Univ	DC	38,719	HC+
Amherst College	MA	41,590	MC
Anderson Univ	IN	25,050	LC
Andrews Univ	MI	21,786	C
Angelo State Univ	TX	8,340	NC
Appalachian State Univ	NC	8,000	VC
Arizona State Univ-Tempe	AZ	11,174	C
Arkansas State Univ	AR	9,630	C
Ashland Univ	OH	25,000	C
Auburn Univ	AL	12,230	VC
Augsburg College	MN	28,300	C
Augusta State Univ	GA	2,920	C
Augustana College	IL	29,862	VC+
Augustana College	SD	24,380	VC
Austin College	TX	27,871	HC
Austin Peay State Univ	TN	7,535	C
Azusa Pacific Univ	CA	28,546	VC
Baker Univ	KS	22,190	C
Baldwin-Wallace College	OH	27,256	VC
Ball State Univ	IN	13,138	C
Bard College	NY	41,800	HC+
Bates College	ME	42,100	MC
Baylor Univ	TX	27,555	HC
Belmont Univ	TN	24,110	VC
Beloit College	WI	32,808	HC
Bemidji State Univ	MN	11,180	LC
Benedict College	SC	19,114	LC
Benedictine College	KS	21,968	C
Benedictine Univ	IL	25,710	C
Bennington College	VT	41,890	HC
Berea College	KY	5,496	VC+
Berry College	GA	24,342	VC
Bethany College	WV	21,395	C
Bethel College	IN	19,680	C
Bethel College	KS	21,650	C
Bethel Univ	MN	29,840	VC
Bethune-Cookman College	FL	17,922	LC
Birmingham-Southern College	AL	28,494	VC+
Bloomsburg Univ of Pennsylvania	PA	11,602	C
Boise State Univ	ID	9,438	LC
Boston College	MA	41,608	MC
Boston Univ	MA	42,046	HC+
Bowdoin College	ME	41,660	MC
Bowling Green State Univ	OH	14,994	C
Bradley Univ	IL	25,280	VC
Brandeis Univ	MA	41,551	MC
Bridgewater College	VA	27,790	C
Bridgewater State College	MA	12,120	C
Brigham Young Univ	UT	9,200	VC
Brown Univ	RI	42,015	MC
Bryn Mawr College	PA	42,780	HC+
Bucknell Univ	PA	39,660	MC
Buena Vista Univ	IA	27,742	C
Butler Univ	IN	31,944	VC+
Calif Inst of Technology	CA	36,123	MC
Calif Lutheran Univ	CA	27,800	LC
Calif Polytechnic State Univ	CA	12,390	VC
Calif State Polytechnic Univ, Pomona	CA	18,053	C+
Cal State East Bay	CA	10,856	LC
Cal State, Bakersfield	CA	6,125	LC
Cal State, Chico	CA	11,395	C
Cal State, Dominguez Hills	CA	10,220	LC
Cal State, Fresno	CA	10,037	LC
Cal State, Fullerton	CA	10,990	C
Cal State, Long Beach	CA	9,512	C
Cal State, Los Angeles	CA	5,900	C
Cal State, Northridge	CA	9,036	LC
Cal State, Sacramento	CA	11,122	C
Cal State, San Bernardino	CA	12,563	LC
Cal State, Stanislaus	CA	11,283	C
Calif Univ of Pennsylvania	PA	14,217	C
Calvin College	MI	25,735	NC
Cameron Univ	OK	6,314	NC
Canisius College	NY	32,257	VC
Carleton College	MN	40,467	MC
Carnegie Mellon Univ	PA	42,700	MC
Carthage College	WI	26,000	C
Case Western Reserve Univ	OH	37,314	MC
Catholic Univ of America	DC	35,838	VC
Cedarville Univ	OH	21,904	VC
Centenary College of Louisiana	LA	24,760	VC
Central College	IA	26,774	VC
Central Conn State Univ	CT	13,620	C
Central Methodist Univ	MO	18,000	C
Central Mich Univ	MI	12,244	C
Central Missouri State Univ	MO	10,000	C
Central Washington Univ	WA	11,730	C
Centre College	KY	30,810	VC
Chadron State College	NE	6,350	NC
Chatham College	PA	27,290	C+
Chicago State Univ	IL	10,915	C+
Christian Brothers Univ	TN	24,650	VC
Christopher Newport Univ	VA	13,326	VC
Citadel, The	SC		C+
CUNY/Brooklyn College	NY	4,377	C+
CUNY/City College	NY		C
CUNY/College of Staten Island	NY	4,328	NC
CUNY/Herbert H. Lehman College	NY	4,000	LC
CUNY/Hunter College	NY	8,000	C+
CUNY/Queens College	NY	4,356	C
CUNY/York College	NY	4,242	NC
Claremont McKenna College	CA	42,920	MC
Clarion Univ of Pennsylvania	PA	11,844	C
Clark Atlanta Univ	GA	20,960	LC
Clark Univ	MA	35,165	VC+
Clarkson Univ	NY	34,930	VC
Clemson Univ	SC	13,366	HC
Cleveland State Univ	OH	10,798	NC
Coastal Carolina Univ	SC	13,140	C
Coe College	IA	27,440	VC
Colby College	ME	41,770	MC
Colgate Univ	NY	41,170	MC
College of Charleston	SC	13,616	VC
College of Mount St. Vincent	NY	28,000	C
College of New Jersey	NJ	18,315	MC
College of Notre Dame of Maryland	MD	27,700	C
College of St. Benedict	MN	30,091	VC
College of the Holy Cross	MA	40,664	MC
College of William and Mary	VA	14,147	MC
College of Wooster	OH	31,310	VC+
Colo College	CO	37,668	HC
Colo School of Mines	CO	14,893	HC
Colo State Univ-Fort Collins	CO	10,878	C+
Colo State Univ-Pueblo	CO	7,821	LC
Columbia Univ/Barnard College	NY	38,000	MC
Columbia Univ/Columbia College	NY	42,584	MC
Columbia Univ/School of General Studies	NY	41,516	C
Concordia College: Moorhead	MN	22,475	VC
Conn College	CT	41,975	MC
Cornell College	IA	30,110	VC+
Cornell Univ	NY	41,717	MC
Covenant College	GA	26,460	VC+
Creighton Univ	NE	29,918	VC+
Curry College	MA	26,100	C
Dakota State Univ	SD	7,466	C
Dartmouth College	NH	39,465	MC
Davidson College	NC	36,825	MC
Delaware State Univ	DE	8,130	C
Denison Univ	OH	37,040	HC
DePaul Univ	IL	29,835	VC
DePauw Univ	IN	32,100	HC
Dickinson College	PA	40,170	HC+
Dillard Univ	LA	17,500	VC
Doane College	NE	22,458	C
Dordt College	IA	20,325	VC
Drake Univ	IA	27,632	VC+
Drew Univ/College of Liberal Arts	NJ	39,698	VC
Drexel Univ	PA	27,700	VC
Drury Univ	MO	20,117	VC
Duke Univ	NC	41,239	MC
Duquesne Univ	PA	29,534	VC
Earlham College	IN	33,604	HC
East Carolina Univ	NC	10,000	C
East Central Univ	OK	6,207	C
East Tenn State Univ	TN	8,497	C
Eastern Illinois Univ	IL	12,569	C
Eastern Mich Univ	MI	12,897	C
Eastern Nazarene College	MA	19,500	LC
Eastern New Mexico Univ	NM	7,264	C
Eastern Oregon Univ	OR	10,400	NC
Eastern Washington Univ	WA	10,608	C
Eckerd College	FL	35,492	VC
Edinboro Univ of Pennsylvania	PA	11,809	LC
Elizabeth City State Univ	NC	5,700	LC
Elizabethtown College	PA	32,100	VC
Elmhurst College	IL	24,685	C
Elon Univ	NC	25,371	HC
Emory & Henry College	VA	26,570	C
Emory Univ	GA	40,546	MC
Emporia State Univ	KS	8,093	C
Erskine College	SC	25,468	VC
Excelsior College	NY	995	SP
Fairfield Univ	CT	39,835	HC
Fisk Univ	TN	19,830	C
Florida A&M Univ	FL	8,344	C
Florida Atlantic Univ	FL	11,221	C
Florida Inst of Technology	FL	29,720	VC

INDEX OF COLLEGE MAJORS

School	ST	$IS	SR
Florida International Univ	FL	9,215	VC
Florida State Univ	FL	9,028	HC
Fordham Univ	NY	36,000	HC
Fort Hays State Univ	KS	7,638	C
Fort Lewis College	CO	11,852	C
Francis Marion Univ	SC	11,114	C
Franklin and Marshall College	PA	40,590	HC
Frostburg State Univ	MD	12,672	C
Furman Univ	SC	33,264	HC+
Gallaudet Univ	DC	16,554	
Geneva College	PA	21,850	C
George Mason Univ	VA	10,850	VC
George Washington Univ	DC	48,820	MC
Georgetown College	KY	24,950	C+
Georgetown Univ	DC	43,183	MC
Georgia Inst of Technology	GA	11,450	HC+
Georgia Southern Univ	GA	9,762	C
Georgia State Univ	GA	11,444	VC
Georgian Court College	NJ	20,000	LC
Gettysburg College	PA	39,864	HC
Gonzaga Univ	WA	30,218	HC
Gordon College	MA	29,194	C+
Goshen College	IN	22,850	VC
Goucher College	MD	36,225	VC
Grambling State Univ	LA	6,538	NC
Grand Valley State Univ	MI	12,000	VC
Greenville College	IL	23,146	C
Grinnell College	IA	34,814	HC+
Grove City College	PA	15,784	HC+
Guilford College	NC	28,160	C+
Gustavus Adolphus College	MN	30,920	HC
Hamilton College	NY	41,660	MC
Hamline Univ	MN	27,070	VC
Hampden-Sydney College	VA	31,148	VC
Hampshire College	MA	37,120	HC
Hampton Univ	VA	19,468	C+
Hanover College	IN	28,150	HC
Harding Univ	AR	16,512	VC
Hardin-Simmons Univ	TX	18,641	C
Hartwick College	NY	36,065	C+
Harvard Univ/Harvard College	MA	45,860	MC
Harvey Mudd College	CA	42,352	MC
Hastings College	NE	22,218	VC
Haverford College	PA	41,600	MC
Heidelberg College	OH	23,242	C
Henderson State Univ	AR	7,600	C
Hendrix College	AR	27,646	HC+
Hillsdale College	MI	24,160	HC
Hobart and William Smith Colleges	NY	41,123	VC
Hofstra Univ	NY	32,630	VC
Hollins Univ	VA	31,105	C
Hope College	MI	28,208	VC+
Houghton College	NY	25,980	VC+
Houston Baptist Univ	TX	18,660	C
Howard Univ	DC	18,481	C+
Humboldt State Univ	CA	11,176	C
Idaho State Univ	ID	9,030	C
Illinois College	IL	21,900	C+
Illinois Inst of Technology	IL	26,465	HC+
Illinois State Univ	IL	12,839	C+
Illinois Wesleyan Univ	IL	34,050	HC+
Indiana State Univ	IN	11,604	C
Indiana Univ Bloomington	IN	13,356	VC
Indiana Univ of Pennsylvania	PA	11,209	C
Indiana Univ South Bend	IN	4,989	LC
Indiana Univ-Purdue Univ Fort Wayne	IN	5,067	LC
Indiana Univ-Purdue Univ Indianapolis	IN	10,959	C
Iona College	NY	30,878	VC
Iowa State Univ	IA	11,831	VC
Ithaca College	NY	35,144	VC
Jackson State Univ	MS	8,500	C
Jacksonville State Univ	AL	7,618	LC
Jacksonville Univ	FL	24,040	C
James Madison Univ	VA	12,010	VC
John Carroll Univ	OH	27,658	C+
Johns Hopkins Univ	MD	42,044	MC
Johnson C. Smith Univ	NC	20,000	C
Juniata College	PA	33,130	VC
Kalamazoo College	MI	32,442	VC+
Kansas State Univ	KS	10,516	VC
Kansas Wesleyan Univ	KS	21,400	VC
Kent State Univ	OH	14,594	C
Kentucky Wesleyan College	KY	18,550	C
Kenyon College	OH	39,500	MC
King College	TN	23,400	C
Knox College	IL	32,385	VC+
Kutztown Univ of Pennsylvania	PA	10,820	C
La Sierra Univ	CA	24,327	C+
Lafayette College	PA	39,267	MC
Lake Forest College	IL	33,860	VC
Lamar Univ	TX	6,820	LC
Lane College	TN	11,220	C+
Lawrence Tech Univ	MI	25,475	VC
Lawrence Univ	WI	33,958	HC+
Le Moyne College	NY	29,570	VC
Lebanon Valley College	PA	31,700	VC
Lehigh Univ	PA	42,690	HC+
Lenoir-Rhyne College	NC	25,580	C
Lewis and Clark College	OR	35,358	VC+
Lewis Univ	IL	23,050	C+
Lincoln Univ	MO	8,000	VC
Lincoln Univ	PA	13,658	C+
Linfield College	OR	29,632	VC
Lipscomb Univ	TN	20,967	VC
Lock Haven Univ of Pennsylvania	PA	12,098	LC
LIU/C.W. Post Campus	NY	28,282	C
Longwood Univ	VA	12,426	C
Louisiana State Univ and A&M College	LA	10,749	VC
Louisiana State Univ in Shreveport	LA	2,900	VC
Louisiana Tech Univ	LA	7,370	C
Loyola College in Maryland	MD	38,898	HC
Loyola Marymount Univ	CA	36,321	VC
Loyola Univ Chicago	IL	32,896	VC
Loyola Univ New Orleans	LA	31,050	VC+
Luther College	IA	28,800	VC+
Lycoming College	PA	30,797	C+
Macalester College	MN	36,500	MC
MacMurray College	IL	20,755	C
Manchester College	IN	23,470	C
Manhattan College	NY	29,000	VC
Manhattanville College	NY	32,500	C+
Mansfield Univ	PA	11,300	C
Marietta College	OH	29,327	C
Marlboro College	VT	35,980	VC+
Marquette Univ	WI	31,066	HC
Marshall Univ	WV	9,116	C
Mary Baldwin College	VA	26,465	C
Mass College of Liberal Arts	MA	8,725	LC
Mass Inst of Technology	MA	41,800	MC
McDaniel College	MD	31,610	VC
McMurry Univ	TX	18,100	LC
McNeese State Univ	LA	5,270	LC
McPherson College	KS	21,010	C
Mercer Univ	GA	27,525	VC+
Merrimack College	MA	34,380	C
Messiah College	PA	28,910	VC+
Metropolitan State College of Denver	CO	2,338	LC
Miami Univ	OH	29,097	HC
Mich State Univ	MI	13,689	VC
Mich Tech Univ	MI	14,569	VC
MidAmerica Nazarene Univ	KS	20,584	LC
Middle Tenn State Univ	TN	8,540	C
Middlebury College	VT	42,120	MC
Millersville Univ of Pennsylvania	PA	12,113	C
Millikin Univ	IL	25,590	C
Millsaps College	MS	28,256	VC+
Minn State Univ, Mankato	MN	10,276	LC
Minn State Univ, Moorhead	MN	7,000	LC
Minot State Univ	ND	6,700	LC
Miss College	MS	14,574	VC
Miss State Univ	MS	9,577	C
Missouri Southern State Univ	MO	8,396	NC
Missouri State Univ	MO	10,748	C
Monmouth College	IL	23,700	C
Montana State Univ-Bozeman	MT	1,137	C
Montclair State Univ	NJ	16,327	C
Moravian College	PA	28,950	VC
Morehead State Univ	KY	9,150	C
Morehouse College	GA	25,082	C
Morgan State Univ	MD	12,080	C
Morningside College	IA	23,704	C
Mount Holyoke College	MA	42,148	HC+
Mount Union College	OH	25,840	C
Muhlenberg College	PA	36,030	HC+
Murray State Univ	KY	8,900	C
Muskingum College	OH	22,970	C
Nebr Wesleyan Univ	NE	23,415	C+
New College of Florida	FL	10,009	HC+
New Jersey City Univ	NJ	13,695	LC
New Mexico Highlands Univ	NM	6,272	NC
New Mexico Inst of Mining and Technology	NM	8,510	VC+
New Mexico State Univ	NM	9,250	C
New York Inst of Technology	NY	28,126	VC
New York Univ	NY	43,170	MC
Norfolk State Univ	VA	10,531	LC
N Car Agricultural and Technical State Univ	NC	8,000	LC
N Car Central Univ	NC	9,000	LC
N Car State Univ	NC	11,824	HC
North Central College	IL	28,926	VC
N Dak State Univ	ND	8,500	C
North Georgia College and State Univ	GA	7,000	C
North Park Univ	IL	24,050	C
Northeastern Illinois Univ	IL	3,000	NC
Northeastern Univ	MA	35,742	HC
Northern Arizona Univ	AZ	10,353	C
Northern Illinois Univ	IL	13,178	C
Northern Kentucky Univ	KY	6,670	NC
Northern Mich Univ	MI	12,340	VC
Northwest Missouri State Univ	MO	10,000	C
Northwest Nazarene Univ	ID	22,590	VC
Northwestern Okla State Univ	OK	6,250	NC
Northwestern State Univ of Louisiana	LA	7,144	C
Northwestern Univ	IL	37,595	MC
Norwich Univ	VT	28,212	C
Oakland Univ	MI	11,936	C
Oberlin College	OH	40,904	MC
Occidental College	CA	40,185	MC
Oglethorpe Univ	GA	30,300	VC
Ohio Northern Univ	OH	27,765	VC
Ohio State Univ	OH	15,357	HC
Ohio Univ	OH	15,921	C
Ohio Wesleyan Univ	OH	35,830	VC+
Okla Baptist Univ	OK	17,986	VC
Okla City Univ	OK	23,965	VC
Okla State Univ	OK	10,213	VC
Old Dominion Univ	VA	11,907	C
Oral Roberts Univ	OK	22,650	C
Oregon State Univ	OR	11,055	C
Otterbein College	OH	28,986	C
Ouachita Baptist Univ	AR	21,900	VC
Pace Univ	NY	30,000	VC
Pacific Lutheran Univ	WA	28,805	VC
Pacific Union College	CA	24,555	VC+
Pacific Univ	OR	24,250	C
Penn State Erie/The Behrend College	PA	16,256	C
Penn State Univ/Univ Park Campus	PA	18,038	HC
Pittsburg State Univ	KS	8,112	C
Pitzer College	CA	41,644	HC
Point Loma Nazarene Univ	CA	27,610	VC
Polytechnic Univ/Brooklyn	NY	37,150	VC
Pomona College	CA	40,774	MC
Pontifical Catholic Univ of PR/Ponce	PR	7,310	
Portland State Univ	OR	12,453	C
Prairie View A&M Univ	TX	11,110	LC
Presbyterian College	SC	30,044	VC
Princeton Univ	NJ	40,213	MC
Principia College	IL	27,765	VC+
Purdue Univ/Calumet	IN	10,891	LC
Purdue Univ/West Lafayette	IN	13,458	VC
Ramapo College of New Jersey	NJ	16,630	VC
Randolph-Macon College	VA	31,250	C
Randolph-Macon Woman's College	VA	31,160	VC+
Reed College	OR	41,106	MC
Rensselaer Polytechnic Inst	NY	41,288	HC+
Rhode Island College	RI	11,570	C
Rhodes College	TN	32,860	HC
Rice Univ	TX	32,290	MC
Richard Stockton College of New Jersey	NJ	14,000	VC
Rider Univ	NJ	32,560	C
Ripon College	WI	27,160	C+
Roanoke College	VA	30,748	VC
Roberts Wesleyan College	NY	26,378	C
Rochester Inst of Technology	NY	32,070	VC+
Rockhurst Univ	MO	25,440	VC
Rollins College	FL	38,366	VC
Rose-Hulman Inst of Technology	IN	34,557	HC+
Rowan Univ	NJ	16,000	VC
Rutgers, The State Univ of New Jersey/Camden Campus	NJ	15,000	VC
Rutgers, The State Univ of New Jersey/New Brunswick/Piscataway Campus	NJ	15,810	HC
Rutgers, The State Univ of New Jersey/Newark Campus	NJ	15,640	VC
Saginaw Valley State Univ	MI	11,432	C
St. Ambrose Univ	IA	25,495	C
St. Bonaventure Univ	NY	28,785	LC
St. Cloud State Univ	MN	10,010	C
St. John Fisher College	NY	27,860	C
St. John's Univ	MN	29,749	VC
St. John's Univ	NY	34,370	C
St. Joseph's Univ	PA	37,428	VC
St. Lawrence Univ	NY	40,545	VC
St. Louis Univ	MO	33,158	VC+
St. Mary's College of Calif	CA	37,290	C
St. Mary's College of Maryland	MD	18,876	VC+
St. Mary's Univ of San Antonio	TX	22,444	C
St. Michael's College	VT	33,330	VC
St. Norbert College	WI	28,577	C+
St. Olaf College	MN	32,800	HC
St. Peter's College	NJ	30,160	LC
St. Vincent College	PA	26,160	VC
Salisbury Univ	MD	13,128	VC
Sam Houston State Univ	TX	8,000	C
Samford Univ	AL	20,258	VC
San Diego State Univ	CA	12,971	VC
San Francisco State Univ	CA	13,000	C
San Jose State Univ	CA	11,707	C
Santa Clara Univ	CA	38,931	VC
Savannah State Univ	GA	7,772	LC
Scripps College	CA	41,000	MC
Seattle Pacific Univ	WA	29,355	C
Seattle Univ	WA	30,063	VC
Seton Hall Univ	NJ	33,622	VC
Seton Hill Univ	PA	28,810	C
Shaw Univ	NC	15,488	LC
Shippensburg Univ of Pennsylvania	PA	11,621	C
Siena College	NY	28,260	VC+
Simon's Rock College of Bard	MA	41,988	VC+
Simpson College	IA	26,833	VC
Skidmore College	NY	41,779	HC
Slippery Rock Univ of Pennsylvania	PA	10,360	LC
Smith College	MA	41,474	MC
Sonoma State Univ	CA	14,732	C
S Car State Univ	SC	6,700	LC
S Dak School of Mines and Technology	SD	7,624	C+
S Dak State Univ	SD	9,815	C
Southeast Missouri State Univ	MO	10,596	C
Southeastern Louisiana Univ	LA	8,521	LC
Southeastern Okla State Univ	OK	6,147	C
Southern Adventist Univ	TN	18,500	C
Southern Conn State Univ	CT	10,310	C
Southern Illinois Univ Carbondale	IL	12,391	C
Southern Illinois Univ Edwardsville	IL	11,022	C
Southern Methodist Univ	TX	36,088	VC+
Southern Nazarene Univ	OK	14,634	NC
Southern Oregon Univ	OR	12,186	C
Southern Polytechnic State Univ	GA	7,640	VC
Southern Univ and A&M College	LA	8,238	LC
Southern Univ at New Orleans	LA	1,000	NC
Southwestern Adventist Univ	TX	18,290	LC
Southwestern College	KS	21,476	C
Southwestern Okla State Univ	OK	4,801	C
Southwestern Univ	TX	26,767	HC
Spelman College	GA	24,650	VC
Spring Arbor Univ	MI	22,476	C
Stanford Univ	CA	41,557	MC
SUNY at Oswego	NY	13,662	VC
SUNY at Potsdam	NY	12,959	C
SUNY/College at Brockport	NY	12,747	VC
SUNY/College at Buffalo	NY	11,903	C+
SUNY/College at Cortland	NY	12,095	C
SUNY/College at Fredonia	NY	12,771	VC
SUNY/College at Geneseo	NY	12,910	HC+
SUNY/College at Oneonta	NY	12,905	VC
SUNY/College at Plattsburgh	NY	12,362	C
SUNY/Univ at Albany	NY	13,860	VC
SUNY/Univ at Binghamton	NY	13,988	HC
SUNY/Univ at Buffalo	NY	13,694	VC
SUNY/Univ at New Paltz	NY	12,480	VC
SUNY/Univ at Stony Brook	NY	13,625	HC
Stephen F. Austin State Univ	TX	7,930	C
Stetson Univ	FL	32,725	VC
Stevens Inst of Technology	NJ	40,935	HC
Suffolk Univ	MA	33,160	C
Susquehanna Univ	PA	33,465	VC
Swarthmore College	PA	41,280	MC
Sweet Briar College	VA	31,460	VC
Syracuse Univ	NY	38,655	HC
Talladega College	AL	11,240	LC
Tarleton State Univ	TX	8,952	C
Taylor Univ	IN	26,376	VC+
Temple Univ	PA	17,438	C
Tenn State Univ	TN	9,048	LC
Tenn Tech Univ	TN	10,044	C
Texas A&M Univ	TX	13,351	HC
Texas A&M Univ at Commerce	TX	9,020	C
Texas A&M Univ at Kingsville	TX	6,800	LC
Texas Christian Univ	TX	23,410	VC+
Texas Lutheran Univ	TX	23,530	C
Texas Southern Univ	TX	9,828	C
Texas State Univ - San Marcos	TX	10,862	C
Texas Tech Univ	TX	13,026	VC
Thiel College	PA	24,580	C
Thomas More College	KY	24,470	C
Tougaloo College	MS	15,975	NC
Touro College	NY	17,000	VC
Towson Univ	MD	13,924	VC
Transylvania Univ	KY	26,240	VC+
Trevecca Nazarene Univ	TN	19,594	C
Trinity College	CT	38,040	HC+
Trinity Univ	TX	30,157	HC+
Truman State Univ	MO	11,242	HC
Tufts Univ	MA	42,018	MC
Tulane Univ	LA	41,098	MC
Tuskegee Univ	AL	18,860	LC
Union College	NE	18,710	C
Union College	NY	41,595	HC
Union Univ	TN	20,750	C

ST = STATE $IS = IN-STATE COSTS   SR = SELECTOR RATING

School	ST	$IS	SR
United States Air Force Academy	CO		HC+
United States Military Academy	NY		MC
United States Naval Academy	MD		MC
Univ of Akron	OH	15,166	NC
Univ of Alabama	AL	9,888	C
Univ of Alabama at Birmingham	AL	13,716	C
Univ of Alabama in Huntsville	AL	9,516	VC
Univ of Alaska Fairbanks	AK	10,101	C
Univ of Arizona	AZ	11,958	VC
Univ of Arkansas	AR	11,859	VC
Univ of Arkansas at Little Rock	AR	7,230	NC
Univ of Arkansas at Pine Bluff	AR	8,300	C
Univ of at Calif Davis	CA	15,010	VC
Univ of Calif at Berkeley	CA	18,141	HC+
Univ of Calif at Irvine	CA	16,475	HC
Univ of Calif at Los Angeles	CA	17,681	MC
Univ of Calif at Riverside	CA	16,625	C
Univ of Calif at San Diego	CA	16,102	HC
Univ of Calif at Santa Barbara	CA	11,800	VC
Univ of Calif at Santa Cruz	CA	19,174	VC
Univ of Central Arkansas	AR	9,984	C
Univ of Central Florida	FL	10,739	VC
Univ of Chicago	IL	42,369	MC
Univ of Cincinnati	OH	17,682	C
Univ of Colo at Boulder	CO	13,352	C+
Univ of Colo at Colo Springs	CO	11,517	VC
Univ of Colo at Denver and Health Sciences Center	CO	5,021	C
Univ of Conn	CT	16,628	HC
Univ of Dallas	TX	27,432	VC+
Univ of Dayton	OH	28,826	VC
Univ of Delaware	DE	14,142	HC
Univ of Denver	CO	36,376	VC+
Univ of Evansville	IN	28,320	VC
Univ of Florida	FL	9,354	VC
Univ of Georgia	GA	11,004	HC
Univ of Hartford	CT	34,044	C
Univ of Hawaii at Hilo	HI	6,500	C
Univ of Hawaii at Manoa	HI	10,413	VC
Univ of Houston	TX	7,000	C
Univ of Houston-Downtown	TX	3,326	NC
Univ of Idaho	ID	9,310	NC
Univ of Illinois at Chicago	IL	16,256	VC
Univ of Illinois at Urbana-Champaign	IL	15,800	HC+
Univ of Indianapolis	IN	25,090	C
Univ of Iowa	IA	12,172	VC
Univ of Kansas	KS	10,915	VC
Univ of Kentucky	KY	7,800	VC
Univ of La Verne	CA	33,470	C
Univ of Louisiana at Lafayette	LA	5,830	VC
Univ of Louisville	KY	10,400	VC
Univ of Maine	ME	13,642	C
Univ of Mary Washington	VA	11,636	HC
Univ of Maryland/Baltimore County	MD	16,642	VC+
Univ of Maryland/College Park	MD	16,036	HC
Univ of Mass Amherst	MA	15,973	C+
Univ of Mass Boston	MA	8,024	C
Univ of Mass Dartmouth	MA	15,985	C
Univ of Mass Lowell	MA	14,327	C
Univ of Memphis	TN	11,153	C
Univ of Miami	FL	38,397	MC
Univ of Mich/Ann Arbor	MI	16,587	HC+
Univ of Mich/Dearborn	MI	7,000	VC
Univ of Mich/Flint	MI	6,398	C
Univ of Minn/Duluth	MN	13,974	C
Univ of Minn/Morris	MN	15,472	VC
Univ of Minn/Twin Cities	MN	13,165	HC
Univ of Miss	MS	9,000	VC
Univ of Missouri/Columbia	MO	13,500	VC
Univ of Missouri/Kansas City	MO	15,000	VC
Univ of Missouri/Rolla	MO	13,332	HC
Univ of Missouri/St. Louis	MO	14,046	VC
Univ of Montana	MT	10,602	C
Univ of Nebr at Kearney	NE	9,000	NC
Univ of Nebr at Lincoln	NE	11,401	VC
Univ of Nebr at Omaha	NE	11,235	C
Univ of Nevada/Las Vegas	NV	11,566	C
Univ of Nevada/Reno	NV	12,155	NC
Univ of New Hampshire	NH	16,810	VC
Univ of New Mexico	NM	11,253	C
Univ of New Orleans	LA	7,370	C
Univ of North Alabama	AL	8,992	C
Univ of N Car at Asheville	NC	9,237	VC
Univ of N Car at Chapel Hill	NC	11,129	MC
Univ of N Car at Charlotte	NC	9,101	C
Univ of N Car at Greensboro	NC	8,993	C
Univ of N Car at Pembroke	NC	7,940	LC
Univ of N Car at Wilmington	NC	10,107	VC
Univ of N Dak	ND	10,114	VC
Univ of North Florida	FL	9,908	VC
Univ of North Texas	TX	7,800	C
Univ of Northern Colo	CO	10,249	C
Univ of Northern Iowa	IA	11,133	C
Univ of Notre Dame	IN	39,552	MC
Univ of Okla	OK	10,769	VC+
Univ of Oregon	OR	13,108	VC
Univ of Pennsylvania	PA	41,766	MC
Univ of Pittsburgh at Pittsburgh	PA	18,866	NC
Univ of Portland	OR	32,300	VC
Univ of PR at Humacao	PR	1,707	
Univ of PR/Mayaguez	PR	1,250	
Univ of Puget Sound	WA	35,600	HC
Univ of Redlands	CA	36,160	VC
Univ of Rhode Island	RI	15,398	C
Univ of Richmond	VA	40,510	MC
Univ of Rochester	NY	41,135	MC
Univ of St. Thomas	MN	28,000	VC
Univ of San Diego	CA	40,620	HC
Univ of San Francisco	CA	37,560	VC
Univ of Science and Arts of Okla	OK	7,650	C
Univ of Scranton	PA	31,100	C
Univ of South Alabama	AL	8,930	LC
Univ of S Car at Columbia	SC	13,397	VC
Univ of S Dak	SD	9,068	C
Univ of South Florida	FL	10,284	VC
Univ of Southern Calif	CA	41,618	MC
Univ of Southern Maine	ME	12,614	C
Univ of Southern Miss	MS	10,112	C
Univ of Tenn at Chattanooga	TN	7,790	C
Univ of Tenn at Knoxville	TN	11,720	C
Univ of Texas at Arlington	TX	7,195	LC
Univ of Texas at Austin	TX	14,610	HC
Univ of Texas at Dallas	TX	13,244	VC
Univ of Texas at El Paso	TX	8,764	NC
Univ of Texas at San Antonio	TX	11,325	LC
Univ of Texas-Pan American	TX	7,290	C+
Univ of the Cumberlands	KY	18,184	C
Univ of the District of Columbia	DC	2,070	LC
Univ of the Pacific	CA	34,380	VC
Univ of the South	TN	34,645	VC
Univ of Toledo	OH	15,806	NC
Univ of Tulsa	OK	25,348	HC
Univ of Utah	UT	10,162	VC
Univ of Vermont	VT	18,080	VC
Univ of Virginia	VA	13,759	MC
Univ of Washington	WA	10,400	VC
Univ of West Alabama	AL	7,611	C
Univ of West Florida	FL	8,559	C
Univ of West Georgia	GA	8,838	C
Univ of Wisc/Eau Claire	WI	9,915	VC
Univ of Wisc/La Crosse	WI	10,045	VC
Univ of Wisc/Madison	WI	13,117	HC
Univ of Wisc/Milwaukee	WI	9,427	LC
Univ of Wisc/Oshkosh	WI	10,426	LC
Univ of Wisc/Parkside	WI	10,181	LC
Univ of Wisc/Platteville	WI	9,779	VC
Univ of Wisc/River Falls	WI	9,722	LC
Univ of Wisc/Stevens Point	WI	9,384	VC
Univ of Wisc/Whitewater	WI	9,274	C
Univ of Wyoming	WY	9,666	C
Ursinus College	PA	38,950	VC
Utah State Univ	UT	8,002	VC
Utica College	NY	31,396	C
Valdosta State Univ	GA	8,802	C
Valparaiso Univ	IN	28,970	VC+
Vanderbilt Univ	TN	41,986	MC
Vassar College	NY	41,700	MC
Villanova Univ	PA	38,672	HC+
Virginia Commonwealth Univ	VA	12,987	C
Virginia Military Inst	VA	12,654	C
Virginia Polytechnic Inst and State Univ	VA	10,834	VC
Virginia State Univ	VA	11,318	C
Wabash College	IN	30,116	HC
Wagner College	NY	33,300	VC
Wake Forest Univ	NC	38,290	MC
Walla Walla College	WA	24,489	NC
Wartburg College	IA	27,315	NC
Washburn Univ	KS	9,734	NC
Washington and Jefferson College	PA	33,490	VC
Washington and Lee Univ	VA	35,880	MC
Washington College	MD	34,990	VC
Washington State Univ	WA	12,260	C
Washington Univ in St. Louis	MO	42,106	MC
Wayne State Univ	MI	11,805	C
Weber State Univ	UT	9,635	NC
Wellesley College	MA	41,030	MC
Wells College	NY	23,070	VC
Wesleyan College	GA	19,560	C
Wesleyan Univ	CT	42,122	MC
West Chester Univ of Pennsylvania	PA	12,355	C+
West Texas A&M Univ	TX	8,452	C
West Virginia Univ	WV	10,506	C
West Virginia Univ Inst of Technology	WV	8,788	NC
West Virginia Wesleyan College	WV	26,880	C
Western Illinois Univ	IL	13,042	C
Western Kentucky Univ	KY	10,192	C
Western Mich Univ	MI	13,299	C
Western Washington Univ	WA	11,262	VC
Westminster College	MO	19,060	VC
Westminster College	PA	31,290	C+
Westminster College	UT	25,656	C
Westmont College	CA	36,672	HC
Wheaton College	IL	27,760	HC
Wheaton College	MA	40,180	HC+
Wheeling Jesuit Univ	WV	26,910	C
Whitman College	WA	36,110	HC+
Whittier College	CA	29,108	C
Whitworth College	WA	29,428	VC+
Wichita State Univ	KS	8,500	C
Widener Univ	PA	27,275	C
Wiley College	TX	8,100	LC
Willamette Univ	OR	35,416	VC+
William Jewell College	MO	24,340	C
Williams College	MA	40,310	MC
Winona State Univ	MN	11,333	C
Wittenberg Univ	OH	34,596	VC
Wofford College	SC	30,935	HC
Worcester Polytechnic Inst	MA	40,450	VC+
Wright State Univ	OH	13,616	C
Xavier Univ	OH	30,490	HC
Xavier Univ of Louisiana	LA	17,600	C
Yale Univ	CT	41,000	MC
Youngstown State Univ	OH	12,613	C

PHYSIOLOGY

School	ST	$IS	SR
Boston Univ	MA	42,046	HC+
Brigham Young Univ	UT	9,200	VC
Cal State, Long Beach	CA	9,512	C
Florida State Univ	FL	9,028	HC
Hampshire College	MA	37,120	HC
Marquette Univ	WI	31,066	HC
Mich State Univ	MI	13,689	VC
Northern Mich Univ	MI	12,340	LC
Okla State Univ	OK	10,213	VC
Rutgers, The State Univ of New Jersey/New Brunswick/Piscataway Campus	NJ	15,810	HC
San Francisco State Univ	CA	13,000	C
Southern Illinois Univ Carbondale	IL	12,391	C
Texas State Univ - San Marcos	TX	10,862	C
Univ of Arizona	AZ	11,958	VC
Univ of at Calif Davis	CA	15,010	VC
Univ of Calif at Los Angeles	CA	17,681	MC
Univ of Calif at San Diego	CA	16,102	HC
Univ of Calif at Santa Barbara	CA	11,800	VC
Univ of Conn	CT	16,628	HC
Univ of Great Falls	MT	17,000	C
Univ of Illinois at Urbana-Champaign	IL	15,800	HC+
Univ of Minn/Twin Cities	MN	13,165	HC
Univ of Oregon	OR	13,108	VC

PIANO/ORGAN

School	ST	$IS	SR
Ball State Univ	IN	13,138	C
Blue Mountain College	MS	11,086	C
Boston Conservatory	MA	27,500	SP
Catholic Univ of America	DC	35,838	VC
Central Mich Univ	MI	12,244	C
Central Washington Univ	WA	11,730	C
Columbia College	SC	24,982	LC
East Central Univ	OK	6,207	C
East Texas Baptist Univ	TX	16,713	C
Eastern Mich Univ	MI	12,897	C
Florida State Univ	FL	9,028	HC
Furman Univ	SC	33,264	HC+
Grand Canyon Univ	AZ	32,000	LC
Hannibal-LaGrange College	MO	16,390	C
Hardin-Simmons Univ	TX	18,641	C
Illinois Wesleyan Univ	IL	34,050	HC+
Indiana Univ Bloomington	IN	13,356	VC
Indiana Univ South Bend	IN	4,989	LC
Jackson State Univ	MS	8,500	C
Loyola Univ New Orleans	LA	31,050	VC+
Manhattan School of Music	NY	33,000	SP
McMurry Univ	TX	18,100	LC
Miss College	MS	14,574	VC
Northwestern Univ	IL	37,595	MC
Nyack College	NY	18,540	C
Okla City Univ	OK	23,965	VC
Pacific Lutheran Univ	WA	28,805	VC
Palm Beach Atlantic Univ	FL	23,597	VC
Rider Univ	NJ	32,560	C
Roosevelt Univ	IL	22,605	VC
Samford Univ	AL	20,258	VC
Shenandoah Univ	VA	27,600	C
Shorter College	GA	19,700	C
Southern Methodist Univ	TX	36,088	VC+
Southern Nazarene Univ	OK	14,634	NC
Stetson Univ	FL	32,725	VC
Temple Univ	PA	17,438	C
Texas Christian Univ	TX	23,410	VC
Union Univ	TN	20,750	VC
Univ of Cincinnati	OH	17,682	C
Univ of Miami	FL	38,397	MC
Univ of Mich/Ann Arbor	MI	16,587	HC+
Univ of Tulsa	OK	25,348	HC
Weber State Univ	UT	9,635	NC
Westminster Choir College	NJ	32,670	SP
Youngstown State Univ	OH	12,613	NC

PLANETARY AND SPACE SCIENCE

School	ST	$IS	SR
Boston Univ	MA	42,046	HC+
Calif Inst of Technology	CA	36,123	MC
Florida Inst of Technology	FL	29,720	VC
Juniata College	PA	33,130	VC
Virginia Polytechnic Inst and State Univ	VA	10,834	VC

PLANT GENETICS

School	ST	$IS	SR
Brigham Young Univ	UT	9,200	VC
Purdue Univ/West Lafayette	IN	13,458	VC
SUNY/College of Environmental Science and Forestry	NY	15,000	VC
Univ of Calif at Berkeley	CA	18,141	HC+
Washington State Univ	WA	12,260	C

PLANT PATHOLOGY

School	ST	$IS	SR
Iowa State Univ	IA	11,831	VC
Kansas State Univ	KS	10,516	VC
Mich State Univ	MI	13,689	VC
Oregon State Univ	OR	11,055	C
Univ of Delaware	DE	14,142	HC
Univ of Wisc/Madison	WI	13,117	HC
Washington State Univ	WA	12,260	C

PLANT PHYSIOLOGY

School	ST	$IS	SR
Brigham Young Univ	UT	9,200	VC
Calif State Polytechnic Univ, Pomona	CA	18,053	C+
Ohio State Univ	OH	15,357	HC
SUNY/College of Environmental Science and Forestry	NY	15,000	VC
Univ of Illinois at Urbana-Champaign	IL	15,800	HC+

PLANT PROTECTION (PEST MANAGEMENT)

School	ST	$IS	SR
Iowa State Univ	IA	11,831	VC
Miss State Univ	MS	9,577	C
N Dak State Univ	ND	8,500	C
Purdue Univ/West Lafayette	IN	13,458	VC
Texas Tech Univ	TX	13,026	VC
Univ of Arkansas	AR	11,859	VC
Univ of Hawaii at Manoa	HI	10,413	VC
Univ of Minn/Crookston	MN	13,157	LC
Univ of Nebr at Lincoln	NE	11,401	VC
Washington State Univ	WA	12,260	C
West Texas A&M Univ	TX	8,452	C

PLANT SCIENCE

School	ST	$IS	SR
Alcorn State Univ	MS	8,190	LC
Arizona State Univ-Tempe	AZ	11,174	C
Arkansas State Univ	AR	9,630	C
Brigham Young Univ	UT	9,200	VC
Cal State, Fresno	CA	10,037	LC
Cornell Univ	NY	41,717	MC
Florida State Univ	FL	9,028	HC
Fort Valley State Univ	GA	6,975	C
Iowa State Univ	IA	11,831	VC
Louisiana State Univ and A&M College	LA	10,749	VC
Middle Tenn State Univ	TN	8,540	C
Montana State Univ-Bozeman	MT	1,137	C
N Dak State Univ	ND	8,500	C
Ohio State Univ	OH	15,357	HC
Ohio Univ	OH	15,921	C
Okla State Univ	OK	10,213	VC
Penn State Univ/Univ Park Campus	PA	18,038	HC
Purdue Univ/West Lafayette	IN	13,458	VC
Rutgers, The State Univ of New Jersey/New Brunswick/Piscataway Campus	NJ	15,810	HC
Southeast Missouri State Univ	MO	10,596	C
Southern Illinois Univ Carbondale	IL	12,391	C
SUNY/College of Agriculture and Technology at Cobleskill	NY	12,915	C
SUNY/College of Environmental Science and Forestry	NY	15,000	VC
Tarleton State Univ	TX	8,952	C
Tenn Tech Univ	TN	10,044	C
Texas A&M Univ at Kingsville	TX	6,800	LC

ST = STATE $IS = IN-STATE COSTS   SR = SELECTOR RATING

School	ST	$IS	SR
Univ of Arizona	AZ	11,958	VC
Univ of at Calif Davis	CA	15,010	VC
Univ of Calif at Los Angeles	CA	17,681	MC
Univ of Delaware	DE	14,142	HC
Univ of Florida	FL	9,354	HC
Univ of Georgia	GA	11,004	HC
Univ of Hawaii at Manoa	HI	10,413	VC
Univ of Mass Amherst	MA	15,973	C+
Univ of Minn/Crookston	MN	13,157	LC
Univ of Missouri/Columbia	MO	13,500	VC
Univ of New Hampshire	NH	16,810	VC
Univ of Tenn at Knoxville	TN	11,720	C
Univ of Tenn at Martin	TN	8,693	C
Univ of Vermont	VT	18,080	VC
Utah State Univ	UT	8,002	VC
Washington Univ in St. Louis	MO	42,106	MC
West Texas A&M Univ	TX	8,452	C
West Virginia Univ	WV	10,506	C

PLASTICS ENGINEERING

School	ST	$IS	SR
Ferris State Univ	MI	13,698	C
Kent State Univ	OH	14,594	C
Pennsylvania College of Technology	PA	16,980	LC
Univ of Illinois at Urbana-Champaign	IL	15,800	HC+
Univ of Mass Lowell	MA	14,327	VC
Univ of Missouri/Rolla	MO	13,332	C

PLASTICS TECHNOLOGY

School	ST	$IS	SR
Eastern Mich Univ	MI	12,897	C
Kent State Univ	OH	14,594	C
Penn State Erie/The Behrend College	PA	16,256	C
Pennsylvania College of Technology	PA	16,980	LC
Shawnee State Univ	OH	12,237	NC

PLAYWRITING/SCREENWRITING

School	ST	$IS	SR
Bennington College	VT	41,890	HC
Metropolitan State Univ	MN	4,682	SP

POLISH

School	ST	$IS	SR
Univ of Illinois at Chicago	IL	16,256	VC
Univ of Pittsburgh at Pittsburgh	PA	18,866	HC
Univ of Wisc/Madison	WI	13,117	HC

POLITICAL SCIENCE/GOVERNMENT

School	ST	$IS	SR
Abilene Christian Univ	TX	20,830	C
Adams State College	CO	8,613	C
Adelphi Univ	NY	27,000	VC
Adrian College	MI	23,000	C
Agnes Scott College	GA	32,070	HC
Alabama A&M Univ	AL	8,890	C
Alabama State Univ	AL	7,658	C
Albany State Univ	GA	5,770	C+
Albertson College of Idaho	ID	21,095	VC
Albertus Magnus College	CT	25,336	C
Albion College	MI	26,000	VC
Albright College	PA	33,920	C
Alcorn State Univ	MS	8,190	LC
Alderson-Broaddus College	WV	24,006	C
Alfred Univ	NY		VC
Allegheny College	PA	33,500	HC
Allen Univ	SC	10,500	NC
Alma College	MI	28,544	VC
Alvernia College	PA	26,388	C
American International College	MA	28,710	LC
American Univ	DC	38,719	HC+
Amherst College	MA	41,590	MC
Anderson Univ	IN	25,050	LC
Andrews Univ	MI	21,786	C
Angelo State Univ	TX	8,340	NC
Anna Maria College	MA	29,815	LC
Aquinas College	MI	23,750	C
Arcadia Univ	PA	33,570	VC
Arizona State Univ-Tempe	AZ	11,174	C
Arkansas State Univ	AR	9,630	C
Armstrong Atlantic State Univ	GA	7,394	C
Ashland Univ	OH	25,000	VC
Assumption College	MA	32,875	C
Auburn Univ	AL	12,230	VC
Auburn Univ Montgomery	AL	9,530	NC
Augsburg College	MN	28,300	C
Augusta State Univ	GA	2,920	C
Augustana College	IL	29,862	VC+
Augustana College	SD	24,380	VC
Aurora Univ	IL	20,645	C
Austin College	TX	27,871	HC
Austin Peay State Univ	TN	7,535	C
Averett Univ	VA	24,920	C
Avila Univ	MO	22,100	C
Azusa Pacific Univ	CA	28,546	VC
Baker Univ	KS	22,190	C
Baldwin-Wallace College	OH	27,256	VC
Ball State Univ	IN	13,138	C
Barber-Scotia College	NC	15,000	LC
Bard College	NY	41,800	HC+
Barry Univ	FL	24,100	LC
Barton College	NC	22,316	C
Bates College	ME	42,100	MC
Baylor Univ	TX	27,555	HC
Belhaven College	MS	19,530	NC
Bellarmine Univ	KY	27,650	C+
Bellevue Univ	NE	4,440	NC
Belmont Abbey College	NC	25,314	C
Belmont Univ	TN	24,110	VC
Beloit College	WI	32,808	HC
Bemidji State Univ	MN	11,180	LC
Benedict College	SC	19,114	LC
Benedictine College	KS	21,968	C
Benedictine Univ	IL	25,710	C
Bennett College	NC	11,500	C
Bennington College	VT	41,890	HC
Berea College	KY	5,496	VC+
Berry College	GA	24,342	VC
Bethany College	WV	21,395	C
Bethel Univ	MN	29,840	VC
Bethune-Cookman College	FL	17,922	LC
Birmingham-Southern College	AL	28,494	VC+
Black Hills State Univ	SD	7,800	LC
Blackburn College	IL	13,690	C
Bloomfield College	NJ	22,500	C
Bloomsburg Univ of Pennsylvania	PA	11,602	C
Boise State Univ	ID	9,438	LC
Boston College	MA	41,608	MC
Boston Univ	MA	42,046	HC+
Bowdoin College	ME	41,660	MC
Bowie State Univ	MD	10,880	C+
Bowling Green State Univ	OH	14,994	C
Bradley Univ	IL	25,280	VC
Brandeis Univ	MA	41,551	MC
Brenau Univ Women's College	GA	23,950	VC
Brewton-Parker College	GA	14,220	LC
Briar Cliff Univ	IA	23,550	LC
Bridgewater College	VA	27,790	C
Bridgewater State College	MA	12,120	C
Brigham Young Univ	UT	9,090	VC
Brigham Young Univ/Hawaii	HI	7,740	HC+
Brown Univ	RI	42,015	MC
Bryn Mawr College	PA	42,780	HC+
Bucknell Univ	PA	39,660	MC
Buena Vista Univ	IA	27,742	C
Butler Univ	IN	31,944	VC+
Cabrini College	PA	33,340	C
Caldwell College	NJ	26,450	LC
Calif Baptist Univ	CA	23,780	C
Calif Inst of Technology	CA	36,123	MC
Calif Lutheran Univ	CA	27,800	C
Calif Polytechnic State Univ	CA	12,390	VC
Calif State Polytechnic Univ, Pomona	CA	18,053	C+
Cal State East Bay	CA	10,856	LC
Cal State, Bakersfield	CA	6,125	LC
Cal State, Chico	CA	11,395	C
Cal State, Dominguez Hills	CA	10,220	LC
Cal State, Fresno	CA	10,037	LC
Cal State, Fullerton	CA	10,990	C
Cal State, Long Beach	CA	9,512	C
Cal State, Los Angeles	CA	5,900	C
Cal State, Northridge	CA	9,036	LC
Cal State, San Bernardino	CA	12,563	LC
Cal State, San Marcos	CA	1,800	LC
Cal State, Stanislaus	CA	11,283	C
Calif Univ of Pennsylvania	PA	14,217	C
Calvin College	MI	25,735	NC
Cameron Univ	OK	6,314	NC
Campbell Univ	NC	21,137	VC
Campbellsville Univ	KY	21,328	C
Canisius College	NY	32,257	VC
Capital Univ	OH	30,444	C
Carleton College	MN	40,467	MC
Carlow Univ	PA	24,313	C
Carnegie Mellon Univ	PA	32,700	MC
Carroll College	MT	23,324	C+
Carroll College	WI	24,860	C
Carthage College	WI	26,000	C
Case Western Reserve Univ	OH	37,314	MC
Catawba College	NC	25,000	C
Catholic Univ of America	DC	35,838	VC
Cedar Crest College	PA	30,615	C
Cedarville Univ	OH	21,904	VC
Centenary College	NJ	28,870	LC
Centenary College of Louisiana	LA	24,760	VC
Central College	IA	26,774	VC
Central Conn State Univ	CT	13,620	C
Central Methodist Univ	MO	18,000	C
Central Mich Univ	MI	12,244	C
Central Missouri State Univ	MO	10,000	C
Central State Univ	OH	9,010	C+
Central Washington Univ	WA	11,730	C
Centre College	KY	30,810	VC
Chadron State College	NE	6,350	NC
Chapman Univ	CA	37,550	VC
Charleston Southern Univ	SC	17,800	C
Chatham College	PA	27,290	C+
Chestnut Hill College	PA	26,600	LC
Cheyney Univ of Pennsylvania	PA	11,497	LC
Chicago State Univ	IL	10,915	C+
Christendom College	VA	21,594	VC+
Christopher Newport Univ	VA	13,326	VC
Citadel, The	SC		C+
CUNY/Baruch College	NY	4,320	VC+
CUNY/Brooklyn College	NY	4,377	C+
CUNY/City College	NY		C
CUNY/College of Staten Island	NY	4,328	NC
CUNY/Herbert H. Lehman College	NY	4,000	LC
CUNY/Hunter College	NY	8,000	C+
CUNY/John Jay College of Criminal Justice	NY	5,000	C
CUNY/Queens College	NY	4,356	C
CUNY/York College	NY	4,242	NC
Claremont McKenna College	CA	42,920	MC
Clarion Univ of Pennsylvania	PA	11,844	C
Clark Atlanta Univ	GA	20,960	LC
Clark Univ	MA	35,165	VC+
Clarke College	IA	25,390	C
Clarkson Univ	NY	34,930	VC
Clemson Univ	SC	13,366	HC
Cleveland State Univ	OH	10,798	NC
Coastal Carolina Univ	SC	13,140	C
Coe College	IA	27,440	VC
Coker College	SC	21,600	C
Colby College	ME	41,770	MC
Colgate Univ	NY	41,170	MC
College of Charleston	SC	13,616	VC
College of New Jersey	NJ	18,315	MC
College of New Rochelle	NY	28,396	C+
College of Notre Dame of Maryland	MD	27,700	C
College of St. Benedict	MN	30,091	VC
College of St. Catherine	MN	27,505	VC
College of St. Rose	NY	25,684	C
College of Santa Fe	NM	28,978	C
College of the Holy Cross	MA	40,664	MC
College of the Ozarks	MO	4,130	VC+
College of William and Mary	VA	14,147	MC
College of Wooster	OH	31,310	VC+
Colo College	CO	37,668	HC
Colo State Univ-Fort Collins	CO	10,878	C+
Colo State Univ-Pueblo	CO	7,821	LC
Columbia College	MO	16,900	C
Columbia College	SC	24,982	LC
Columbia Univ/Barnard College	NY	38,000	MC
Columbia Univ/Columbia College	NY	42,584	MC
Columbia Univ/School of General Studies	NY	41,516	C
Columbus State Univ	GA	8,664	C
Concord College	WV	9,708	C
Concordia College: Moorhead	MN	22,475	VC
Concordia Univ	CA	26,780	C
Concordia Univ, River Forest	IL	26,300	C
Conn College	CT	41,975	MC
Converse College	SC	24,800	VC
Cornell College	IA	30,110	VC+
Cornell Univ	NY	41,717	MC
Cornerstone Univ and Grand Rapids Theological Seminary	MI	21,350	NC
Creighton Univ	NE	29,918	VC+
Cumberland Univ	TN	18,894	C
Daemen College	NY	24,580	C
Dartmouth College	NH	39,465	MC
Davidson College	NC	36,825	MC
Davis and Elkins College	WV	22,416	C
De Sales Univ	PA	28,580	VC
Delaware State Univ	DE	8,130	LC
Delta State Univ	MS	7,709	C
Denison Univ	OH	37,040	HC
DePaul Univ	IL	29,835	VC
DePauw Univ	IN	32,100	HC
Dickinson College	PA	40,170	HC+
Dickinson State Univ	ND	7,847	NC
Dillard Univ	LA	17,500	VC
Doane College	NE	22,458	VC
Dominican Univ	IL	26,370	C
Dominican Univ of Calif	CA	36,836	C
Dordt College	IA	20,325	VC
Dowling College	NY	22,110	LC
Drake Univ	IA	27,632	VC+
Drew Univ/College of Liberal Arts	NJ	39,698	VC
Drexel Univ	PA	27,700	VC
Drury Univ	MO	20,117	VC
Duke Univ	NC	41,239	MC
Duquesne Univ	PA	29,534	VC
Earlham College	IN	33,604	HC
East Carolina Univ	NC	10,000	C
East Central Univ	OK	6,207	C
East Stroudsburg Univ of Pennsylvania	PA	10,336	NC
East Tenn State Univ	TN	8,497	C
Eastern Conn State Univ	CT	13,554	C
Eastern Illinois Univ	IL	12,569	C
Eastern Kentucky Univ	KY	7,725	C
Eastern Mich Univ	MI	12,897	C
Eastern New Mexico Univ	NM	7,264	C
Eastern Univ	PA	24,075	C
Eastern Washington Univ	WA	10,608	C
Eckerd College	FL	35,492	VC
Edgewood College	WI	22,862	C
Edinboro Univ of Pennsylvania	PA	11,809	LC
Edward Waters College	FL	14,374	LC
Elizabeth City State Univ	NC	5,700	C
Elizabethtown College	PA	32,100	VC
Elmhurst College	IL	24,685	C
Elmira College	NY	37,200	VC
Elon Univ	NC	25,371	HC
Emmanuel College	MA	32,000	C+
Emory & Henry College	VA	26,570	C
Emory Univ	GA	40,546	MC
Emporia State Univ	KS	8,093	C
Eugene Lang College New School for Liberal Arts	NY	38,800	C+
Eureka College	IL	19,280	C
Evangel Univ	MO	17,380	C
Excelsior College	NY	995	SP
Fairfield Univ	CT	39,835	HC
Fairleigh Dickinson Univ/College at Florham	NJ	30,130	C
Fairleigh Dickinson Univ/Metropolitan Campus	NJ	28,590	C
Fairmont State	WV	8,400	LC
Fayetteville State Univ	NC	6,000	LC
Ferrum College	VA	24,290	LC
Fisk Univ	TN	19,830	C
Fitchburg State College	MA	11,276	C
Flagler College	FL	13,790	VC+
Florida A&M Univ	FL	8,344	C
Florida Atlantic Univ	FL	11,221	C
Florida Gulf Coast Univ	FL	10,833	C
Florida International Univ	FL	9,215	VC
Florida Memorial College	FL	6,000	LC
Florida Southern College	FL	25,965	C
Florida State Univ	FL	9,028	HC
Fordham Univ	NY	36,000	HC
Fort Hays State Univ	KS	7,638	C
Fort Lewis College	CO	11,852	C
Fort Valley State Univ	GA	6,975	C
Framingham State College	MA	11,156	C
Francis Marion Univ	SC	11,114	C
Franciscan Univ of Steubenville	OH	20,300	VC
Franklin and Marshall College	PA	40,590	HC
Franklin College	IN		C
Franklin Pierce College	NH	31,700	C
Friends Univ	KS	16,250	LC
Frostburg State Univ	MD	12,672	C
Furman Univ	SC	33,264	HC+
Gallaudet Univ	DC	16,554	
Gannon Univ	PA	26,100	C
Geneva College	PA	21,850	C
George Fox Univ	OR	28,490	C
George Mason Univ	VA	10,850	VC
George Washington Univ	DC	48,820	MC
Georgetown College	KY	24,950	C+
Georgetown Univ	DC	43,183	MC
Georgia College and State Univ	GA	11,020	C
Georgia Southern Univ	GA	9,762	C
Georgia Southwestern State Univ	GA	6,035	C
Georgia State Univ	GA	11,444	VC
Gettysburg College	PA	39,864	HC
Gonzaga Univ	WA	30,218	HC
Gordon College	MA	29,194	C
Goucher College	MD	36,225	VC
Grambling State Univ	LA	6,538	NC
Grand Valley State Univ	MI	12,000	VC
Grand View College	IA	21,482	C
Greensboro College	NC	23,000	C
Greenville College	IL	23,146	C
Grinnell College	IA	34,814	HC+
Grove City College	PA	15,784	HC+
Guilford College	NC	28,160	C+
Gustavus Adolphus College	MN	30,920	HC
Hamilton College	NY	41,660	MC
Hamline Univ	MN	27,070	VC
Hampden-Sydney College	VA	31,148	VC
Hampshire College	MA	37,120	HC
Hampton Univ	VA	19,468	C+
Hanover College	IN	28,150	VC
Harding Univ	AR	16,512	VC
Hardin-Simmons Univ	TX	18,641	C
Hartwick College	NY	36,065	C+
Harvard Univ/Harvard College	MA	45,860	MC
Hastings College	NE	22,218	VC
Haverford College	PA	41,600	MC
Hawaii Pacific Univ	HI	21,080	C
Heidelberg College	OH	23,242	C
Henderson State Univ	AR	7,600	C
Hendrix College	AR	27,646	HC+
High Point Univ	NC	25,720	C
Hilbert College	NY	20,480	LC

ST = STATE   **$IS** = IN-STATE COSTS   **SR** = SELECTOR RATING

School	ST	$IS	SR
Hillsdale College	MI	24,160	HC
Hiram College	OH	28,700	VC
Hobart and William Smith Colleges	NY	41,123	VC
Hofstra Univ	NY	32,630	VC
Hollins Univ	VA	31,105	C
Hood College	MD	30,085	VC
Hope College	MI	28,208	VC+
Houghton College	NY	25,980	VC+
Houston Baptist Univ	TX	18,660	C
Howard Payne Univ	TX	17,115	C
Howard Univ	DC	18,481	C+
Humboldt State Univ	CA	11,176	C
Huntingdon College	AL	23,090	VC
Huston-Tillotson Univ	TX	14,232	LC
Idaho State Univ	ID	9,030	C
Illinois College	IL	21,900	C+
Illinois Inst of Technology	IL	26,465	HC+
Illinois State Univ	IL	12,839	C+
Illinois Wesleyan Univ	IL	34,050	HC+
Indiana State Univ	IN	11,604	C
Indiana Univ Bloomington	IN	13,356	VC
Indiana Univ Northwest	IN	4,902	LC
Indiana Univ of Pennsylvania	PA	11,209	C
Indiana Univ South Bend	IN	4,989	LC
Indiana Univ Southeast	IN	4,880	LC
Indiana Univ-Purdue Univ Fort Wayne	IN	5,067	LC
Indiana Univ-Purdue Univ Indianapolis	IN	10,959	C
Indiana Wesleyan Univ	IN	22,074	C+
Inter American Univ of PR/Fajardo Campus	PR	4,000	
Inter American Univ of PR/Metropolitan Campus	PR	4,320	
Inter American Univ of PR/Ponce Regional College	PR	3,700	
Inter American Univ of PR/San German	PR	6,720	
Iona College	NY	30,878	VC
Iowa State Univ	IA	11,831	VC
Ithaca College	NY	35,144	VC
Jackson State Univ	MS	8,500	C
Jacksonville State Univ	AL	7,618	LC
Jacksonville Univ	FL	24,040	C
James Madison Univ	VA	12,010	VC
Jamestown College	ND	14,130	NC
John Brown Univ	AR	20,910	VC
John Carroll Univ	OH	27,658	C+
Johns Hopkins Univ	MD	42,044	MC
Johnson C. Smith Univ	NC	20,000	C
Johnson State College	VT	11,830	C
Judson College	IL	25,130	C
Juniata College	PA	33,130	VC
Kalamazoo College	MI	32,442	VC+
Kansas State Univ	KS	10,516	VC
Kean Univ	NJ	15,880	C
Kennesaw State Univ	GA	12,152	C
Kent State Univ	OH	14,594	C
Kentucky State Univ	KY	10,089	LC
Kentucky Wesleyan College	KY	18,590	C
Kenyon College	OH	39,500	MC
Keuka College	NY	26,050	C
King College	TN	23,400	C
King's College	PA	29,810	C
Knox College	IL	32,385	VC+
Knoxville College	TN	6,200	LC
Kutztown Univ of Pennsylvania	PA	10,820	C
La Salle Univ	PA	34,950	C
La Sierra Univ	CA	24,327	C+
Lafayette College	PA	39,267	MC
LaGrange College	GA	22,874	C+
Lake Forest College	IL	33,860	VC
Lake Superior State Univ	MI	12,842	LC
Lamar Univ	TX	6,820	LC
Lambuth Univ	TN	21,700	C+
Lander Univ	SC	10,600	C
Lawrence Univ	WI	33,958	HC+
Le Moyne College	NY	29,570	VC
Lebanon Valley College	PA	31,700	VC
Lehigh Univ	PA	42,690	HC+
LeMoyne-Owen College	TN	13,150	LC
Lenoir-Rhyne College	NC	25,580	C
Lewis and Clark College	OR	35,358	VC+
Lewis Univ	IL	23,050	VC
Liberty Univ	VA	19,101	C
Lincoln Univ	MO	8,000	NC
Lincoln Univ	PA	13,658	C
Lindenwood Univ	MO	18,600	VC
Linfield College	OR	29,632	VC
Lipscomb Univ	TN	20,967	VC
Livingstone College	NC	17,815	LC
Lock Haven Univ of Pennsylvania	PA	12,098	LC
LIU/Brooklyn Campus	NY	25,000	C
LIU/C.W. Post Campus	NY	28,282	C
Longwood Univ	VA	12,426	C
Loras College	IA	27,193	C
Louisiana State Univ and A&M College	LA	10,749	VC
Louisiana State Univ in Shreveport	LA	2,900	NC
Louisiana Tech Univ	LA	7,370	C
Loyola College in Maryland	MD	38,898	HC
Loyola Marymount Univ	CA	36,321	VC
Loyola Univ Chicago	IL	32,896	VC
Loyola Univ New Orleans	LA	31,050	VC+
Luther College	IA	28,800	VC+
Lycoming College	PA	30,797	C+
Lynchburg College	VA	30,645	C
Lynn Univ	FL	30,750	C
Lyon College	AR	19,990	VC
Macalester College	MN	36,500	MC
MacMurray College	IL	20,755	C
Malone College	OH	23,040	C
Manchester College	IN	23,470	C
Manhattan College	NY	29,000	VC
Manhattanville College	NY	32,500	C+
Mansfield Univ	PA	11,300	C
Marian College	IN	26,160	C
Marietta College	OH	29,327	C
Marist College	NY	30,566	VC
Marlboro College	VT	35,980	VC+
Marquette Univ	WI	31,066	HC
Mars Hill College	NC	19,000	LC
Marshall Univ	WV	9,116	C
Martin Univ	IN	10,300	SP
Mary Baldwin College	VA	26,465	C
Marygrove College	MI	19,310	C+
Marymount Manhattan College	NY	30,049	VC
Marymount Univ	VA	25,934	C
Maryville College	TN	29,224	VC
Mass Inst of Technology	MA	41,800	MC
Master's College and Seminary	CA	25,850	VC
McDaniel College	MD	31,610	VC
McKendree College	IL	24,800	VC
McMurry Univ	TX	18,100	LC
Medaille College	NY	21,000	C
Mercer Univ	GA	27,525	VC+
Mercy College	NY	20,000	NC
Mercyhurst College	PA	28,633	VC
Meredith College	NC	25,600	C
Merrimack College	MA	34,380	C
Mesa State College	CO	8,051	C
Messiah College	PA	28,910	VC+
Methodist College	NC	21,000	C
Metropolitan State College of Denver	CO	2,338	LC
Miami Univ	OH	29,097	HC
Mich State Univ	MI	13,689	VC
Middle Tenn State Univ	TN	8,540	C
Middlebury College	VT	42,120	MC
Midwestern State Univ	TX	9,381	LC
Miles College	AL	9,922	NC
Millersville Univ of Pennsylvania	PA	12,113	C
Millikin Univ	IL	25,590	C
Mills College	CA	39,870	C
Millsaps College	MS	28,256	VC+
Minn State Univ, Mankato	MN	10,276	LC
Minn State Univ, Moorhead	MN	7,000	LC
Miss College	MS	14,574	VC
Miss State Univ	MS	9,577	C
Miss Univ for Women	MS	6,000	LC
Miss Valley State Univ	MS	7,970	C
Missouri Southern State Univ	MO	8,396	NC
Missouri State Univ	MO	10,748	C
Missouri Valley College	MO	18,500	C
Missouri Western State Univ	MO	9,534	NC
Molloy College	NY	16,510	C
Monmouth College	IL	23,700	C
Monmouth Univ	NJ	28,956	C
Montana State Univ-Bozeman	MT	1,137	C
Montclair State Univ	NJ	16,327	C
Moravian College	PA	28,950	VC
Morehead State Univ	KY	9,150	C
Morehouse College	GA	25,082	C
Morgan State Univ	MD	12,080	C
Morningside College	IA	23,704	C
Morris College	SC	11,999	LC
Mount Holyoke College	MA	42,148	HC+
Mount Mercy College	IA	23,670	C
Mount St. Mary College	NY	25,250	C
Mount St. Mary's College	CA	32,086	VC
Mount St. Mary's Univ	MD	30,930	C
Mount Union College	OH	25,840	C
Muhlenberg College	PA	36,030	HC+
Murray State Univ	KY	8,900	VC
Muskingum College	OH	22,970	C
Nazareth College of Rochester	NY	28,175	VC
Nebr Wesleyan Univ	NE	23,415	C+
Neumann College	PA	25,996	LC
New College of Calif	CA	12,842	NC
New College of Florida	FL	10,009	HC+
New England College	NH	31,466	C
New Jersey City Univ	NJ	13,695	LC
New Mexico Highlands Univ	NM	6,272	NC
New Mexico State Univ	NM	9,250	C
New York Inst of Technology	NY	28,126	VC
New York Univ	NY	43,170	MC
Newberry College	SC	23,000	LC
Niagara Univ	NY	28,250	C
Nicholls State Univ	LA	6,500	NC
Norfolk State Univ	VA	10,531	LC
N Car Agricultural and Technical State Univ	NC	8,000	LC
N Car Central Univ	NC	9,000	LC
N Car State Univ	NC	11,824	HC
N Car Wesleyan College	NC	22,670	C
North Central College	IL	28,926	VC
N Dak State Univ	ND	8,500	C
North Georgia College and State Univ	GA	7,000	C
North Park Univ	IL	24,050	C
Northeastern Illinois Univ	IL	3,000	NC
Northeastern State Univ	OK	5,896	LC
Northeastern Univ	MA	35,742	HC
Northern Arizona Univ	AZ	10,353	C
Northern Illinois Univ	IL	13,178	C
Northern Kentucky Univ	KY	6,670	NC
Northern Mich Univ	MI	12,340	LC
Northern State Univ	SD	8,257	C
Northwest Missouri State Univ	MO	10,000	C
Northwest Nazarene Univ	ID	22,590	VC
Northwestern College of Iowa	IA	22,174	C+
Northwestern Okla State Univ	OK	6,250	NC
Northwestern State Univ of Louisiana	LA	7,144	C
Northwestern Univ	IL	37,595	MC
Norwich Univ	VT	28,212	C
Notre Dame College	OH	20,425	C
Notre Dame de Namur Univ	CA	32,790	LC
Oakland Univ	MI	11,936	C
Oberlin College	OH	40,904	MC
Occidental College	CA	40,185	MC
Oglethorpe Univ	GA	30,300	VC
Ohio Dominican Univ	OH	25,954	C
Ohio Northern Univ	OH	27,765	VC
Ohio State Univ	OH	15,357	HC
Ohio Univ	OH	15,921	C
Ohio Wesleyan Univ	OH	35,830	VC+
Okla Baptist Univ	OK	17,986	VC
Okla City Univ	OK	23,965	VC
Okla State Univ	OK	10,213	VC
Okla Wesleyan Univ	OK	18,950	NC
Old Dominion Univ	VA	11,907	C
Olivet Nazarene Univ	IL	22,590	C
Oral Roberts Univ	OK	22,650	C
Oregon State Univ	OR	11,055	C
Ottawa Univ	KS	12,000	LC
Otterbein College	OH	28,986	C
Ouachita Baptist Univ	AR	21,900	VC
Our Lady of the Lake Univ of San Antonio	TX	22,430	LC
Pace Univ	NY	30,000	VC
Pacific Lutheran Univ	WA	28,805	VC
Pacific Univ	OR	24,250	C
Palm Beach Atlantic Univ	FL	23,597	VC
Park Univ	MO	11,592	C
Penn State Erie/The Behrend College	PA	16,256	C
Penn State Univ/Univ Park Campus	PA	18,038	HC
Pepperdine Univ	CA	39,960	HC
Pfeiffer Univ	NC	21,900	C
Philander Smith College	AR	13,230	LC
Piedmont College	GA	20,500	C
Pikeville College	KY	16,500	NC
Pittsburg State Univ	KS	8,112	C
Pitzer College	CA	41,644	HC
Plymouth State Univ	NH	12,298	LC
Point Loma Nazarene Univ	CA	27,610	VC
Point Park Univ	PA	24,160	C
Pomona College	CA	40,774	MC
Pontifical Catholic Univ of PR/Ponce	PR	7,310	
Portland State Univ	OR	12,453	C
Prairie View A&M Univ	TX	11,110	LC
Presbyterian College	SC	30,044	VC
Princeton Univ	NJ	40,213	MC
Principia College	IL	27,765	VC+
Providence College	RI	34,580	HC
Purdue Univ/Calumet	IN	10,891	LC
Purdue Univ/West Lafayette	IN	13,458	VC
Queens Univ of Charlotte	NC	24,528	C
Quincy Univ	IL	24,920	C
Quinnipiac Univ	CT	34,640	VC
Radford Univ	VA	13,145	C
Ramapo College of New Jersey	NJ	16,630	VC
Randolph-Macon College	VA	31,250	C
Randolph-Macon Woman's College	VA	31,160	VC+
Reed College	OR	41,106	MC
Regis College	MA	31,350	LC
Regis Univ	CO	31,890	C
Rhode Island College	RI	11,570	C
Rhodes College	TN	32,860	HC
Rice Univ	TX	32,290	MC
Richard Stockton College of New Jersey	NJ	14,000	VC
Rider Univ	NJ	32,560	C
Ripon College	WI	27,160	C+
Rivier College	NH	26,600	C
Roanoke College	VA	30,748	VC
Rockford College	IL	28,330	VC
Rockhurst Univ	MO	25,440	VC
Rocky Mountain College	MT	20,805	C
Roger Williams Univ	RI	30,500	C
Rollins College	FL	38,366	VC
Roosevelt Univ	IL	22,605	VC
Rosemont College	PA	29,350	C
Rowan Univ	NJ	16,000	VC
Russell Sage College	NY	27,000	C
Rust College	MS		C+
Rutgers, The State Univ of New Jersey/Camden Campus	NJ	15,000	VC
Rutgers, The State Univ of New Jersey/New Brunswick/Piscataway Campus	NJ	15,810	HC
Rutgers, The State Univ of New Jersey/Newark Campus	NJ	15,640	VC
Sacred Heart Univ	CT	33,404	C
Saginaw Valley State Univ	MI	11,432	C
St. Ambrose Univ	IA	25,495	C
St. Andrews Presbyterian College	NC	23,530	C
St. Anselm College	NH	33,810	C
St. Augustine's College	NC	14,000	LC
St. Bonaventure Univ	NY	28,785	LC
St. Cloud State Univ	MN	10,010	C
St. Edward's Univ	TX	23,560	C
St. Francis College	NY	19,974	LC
St. Francis Univ	PA	25,880	LC
St. John Fisher College	NY	27,860	C
St. John's Univ	MN	29,749	VC
St. John's Univ	NY	34,370	C
St. Joseph's College	IN	26,600	C
St. Joseph's Univ	PA	37,428	VC
St. Lawrence Univ	NY	40,545	VC
St. Leo Univ	FL	22,140	C+
St. Louis Univ	MO	33,158	VC+
St. Martin's Univ	WA	27,555	C
St. Mary-of-the-Woods College	IN	25,480	C
St. Mary's College	IN	32,538	VC
St. Mary's College of Calif	CA	37,290	C
St. Mary's College of Maryland	MD	18,876	VC+
St. Mary's Univ of Minn	MN	23,857	VC
St. Mary's Univ of San Antonio	TX	22,444	C
St. Michael's College	VT	33,330	VC
St. Norbert College	WI	28,577	C+
St. Olaf College	MN	32,800	HC
St. Paul's College	VA	16,030	NC
St. Peter's College	NJ	30,160	LC
St. Thomas Univ	FL	23,490	C
St. Vincent College	PA	26,160	VC
St. Xavier Univ	IL	23,160	C
Salisbury Univ	MD	13,128	VC
Salve Regina Univ	RI	33,450	C
Sam Houston State Univ	TX	8,000	C
Samford Univ	AL	20,258	VC
San Diego State Univ	CA	12,971	C
San Francisco State Univ	CA	13,000	C
San Jose State Univ	CA	11,707	C
Santa Clara Univ	CA	38,931	VC
Sarah Lawrence College	NY	42,000	HC
Savannah State Univ	GA	7,772	LC
Schreiner Univ	TX	20,600	C
Scripps College	CA	41,000	MC
Seattle Pacific Univ	WA	29,355	C
Seattle Univ	WA	30,063	VC
Seton Hall Univ	NJ	33,622	VC
Seton Hill Univ	PA	28,810	C
Shaw Univ	NC	15,488	LC
Shenandoah Univ	VA	27,600	C
Shepherd Univ	WV	10,066	C
Shippensburg Univ of Pennsylvania	PA	11,621	C
Siena College	NY	28,260	VC+
Simmons College	MA	35,640	VC
Simon's Rock College of Bard	MA	41,988	VC+
Simpson College	IA	26,833	VC
Skidmore College	NY	41,779	HC
Slippery Rock Univ of Pennsylvania	PA	10,360	LC
Smith College	MA	41,474	MC
Sonoma State Univ	CA	14,732	C
S Car State Univ	SC	6,700	LC
S Dak State Univ	SD	9,815	C
Southeast Missouri State Univ	MO	10,596	C
Southeastern Louisiana Univ	LA	8,521	LC
Southeastern Okla State Univ	OK	6,147	C
Southern Arkansas Univ	AR	6,956	C
Southern Conn State Univ	CT	10,310	C
Southern Illinois Univ Carbondale	IL	12,391	C
Southern Illinois Univ Edwardsville	IL	11,022	C
Southern Methodist Univ	TX	36,088	VC+
Southern Nazarene Univ	OK	14,634	NC
Southern New Hampshire Univ	NH	28,764	C

ST = STATE   **$IS** = IN-STATE COSTS   **SR** = SELECTOR RATING

INDEX OF COLLEGE MAJORS

School	ST	$IS	SR
Southern Oregon Univ	OR	12,186	C
Southern Univ and A&M College	LA	8,238	LC
Southern Univ at New Orleans	LA	1,000	NC
Southern Utah Univ	UT		C
Southwest Baptist Univ	MO	18,300	C
Southwest Minn State Univ	MN	10,975	C
Southwestern Okla State Univ	OK	4,801	C
Southwestern Univ	TX	26,767	HC
Spelman College	GA	24,650	VC
Spring Hill College	AL	28,678	C
Springfield College	MA	25,000	C
Stanford Univ	CA	41,557	MC
SUNY at Oswego	NY	13,662	VC
SUNY at Potsdam	NY	12,959	C
SUNY/College at Brockport	NY	12,747	VC
SUNY/College at Buffalo	NY	11,903	C+
SUNY/College at Cortland	NY	12,095	C
SUNY/College at Fredonia	NY	12,771	VC
SUNY/College at Geneseo	NY	12,910	HC+
SUNY/College at Old Westbury	NY	13,154	C
SUNY/College at Oneonta	NY	12,905	VC
SUNY/College at Plattsburgh	NY	12,362	C
SUNY/College at Purchase	NY	11,989	VC+
SUNY/Univ at Albany	NY	13,860	VC
SUNY/Univ at Binghamton	NY	13,988	HC
SUNY/Univ at Buffalo	NY	13,694	VC
SUNY/Univ at New Paltz	NY	12,480	VC
SUNY/Univ at Stony Brook	NY	13,625	HC
Stephen F. Austin State Univ	TX	7,930	C
Stetson Univ	FL	32,725	VC
Stonehill College	MA	36,104	HC
Suffolk Univ	MA	33,160	C
Sul Ross State Univ	TX	6,600	LC
Susquehanna Univ	PA	33,465	VC
Swarthmore College	PA	41,280	MC
Sweet Briar College	VA	31,460	VC
Syracuse Univ	NY	38,655	HC
Tarleton State Univ	TX	8,952	C
Taylor Univ	IN	26,376	VC+
Temple Univ	PA	17,438	C
Tenn State Univ	TN	9,048	LC
Tenn Tech Univ	TN	10,044	C
Texas A&M Univ	TX	13,351	HC
Texas A&M Univ at Commerce	TX	9,020	C
Texas A&M Univ at Corpus Christi	TX	10,280	LC
Texas A&M Univ at Kingsville	TX	6,800	LC
Texas Christian Univ	TX	23,410	VC+
Texas Lutheran Univ	TX	23,530	C
Texas Southern Univ	TX	9,828	C
Texas State Univ - San Marcos	TX	10,862	C
Texas Tech Univ	TX	13,026	VC
Texas Wesleyan Univ	TX	18,700	C
Texas Woman's Univ	TX	7,804	LC
Thiel College	PA	24,580	C
Thomas Edison State College	NJ	3,780	SP
Thomas More College	KY	24,470	C
Thomas More College of Liberal Arts	NH	17,700	C
Tougaloo College	MS	15,975	NC
Touro College	NY	17,000	VC
Towson Univ	MD	13,924	VC
Transylvania Univ	KY	26,240	VC+
Trevecca Nazarene Univ	TN	19,594	C
Trinity College	CT	38,040	HC+
Trinity College	DC	24,150	LC
Trinity Univ	TX	30,157	HC+
Troy Univ	AL	8,916	C
Troy Univ Montgomery Campus	AL	4,104	NC
Truman State Univ	MO	11,242	HC
Tufts Univ	MA	42,018	MC
Tulane Univ	LA	41,098	MC
Tuskegee Univ	AL	18,860	LC
Union College	KY	18,920	C
Union College	NY	41,595	HC
Union Univ	TN	20,750	VC
United States Air Force Academy	CO		HC+
United States Coast Guard Academy	CT		HC
United States Military Academy	NY		MC
United States Naval Academy	MD		MC
Univ of Akron	OH	15,166	NC
Univ of Alabama	AL	9,888	C
Univ of Alabama at Birmingham	AL	13,716	C
Univ of Alabama in Huntsville	AL	9,516	VC
Univ of Alaska Anchorage	AK	11,275	NC
Univ of Alaska Fairbanks	AK	10,101	C
Univ of Alaska Southeast	AK	8,050	LC
Univ of Arizona	AZ	11,958	VC
Univ of Arkansas	AR	11,859	VC
Univ of Arkansas at Little Rock	AR	7,230	NC
Univ of Arkansas at Monticello	AR	7,325	NC
Univ of Arkansas at Pine Bluff	AR	8,300	C
Univ of at Calif Davis	CA	15,010	VC
Univ of Calif at Berkeley	CA	18,141	HC+
Univ of Calif at Irvine	CA	16,475	HC
Univ of Calif at Los Angeles	CA	17,681	MC
Univ of Calif at Riverside	CA	16,625	C
Univ of Calif at San Diego	CA	16,102	HC
Univ of Calif at Santa Barbara	CA	11,800	VC
Univ of Calif at Santa Cruz	CA	19,174	VC
Univ of Central Arkansas	AR	9,984	C
Univ of Central Florida	FL	10,739	VC
Univ of Central Okla	OK	8,094	C
Univ of Charleston	WV	27,600	C
Univ of Chicago	IL	42,369	MC
Univ of Cincinnati	OH	17,982	C
Univ of Colo at Boulder	CO	13,352	C+
Univ of Colo at Colo Springs	CO	11,517	VC
Univ of Colo at Denver and Health Sciences Center	CO	5,021	C
Univ of Conn	CT	16,628	HC
Univ of Dallas	TX	27,432	VC+
Univ of Dayton	OH	28,826	VC
Univ of Delaware	DE	14,142	HC
Univ of Denver	CO	36,374	VC+
Univ of Detroit Mercy	MI	27,000	C
Univ of Evansville	IN	28,320	VC
Univ of Findlay	OH	29,238	C
Univ of Florida	FL	9,354	HC
Univ of Georgia	GA	11,004	HC
Univ of Great Falls	MT	17,000	C
Univ of Hartford	CT	34,044	C
Univ of Hawaii at Hilo	HI	6,500	C
Univ of Hawaii at Manoa	HI	10,413	VC
Univ of Houston	TX	7,000	C
Univ of Idaho	ID	9,310	NC
Univ of Illinois at Chicago	IL	16,256	VC
Univ of Illinois at Urbana-Champaign	IL	15,800	HC+
Univ of Indianapolis	IN	25,090	C
Univ of Iowa	IA	12,172	VC
Univ of Judaism College of A&S	CA	30,010	C
Univ of Kansas	KS	10,915	VC
Univ of Kentucky	KY	7,800	C
Univ of La Verne	CA	33,470	C
Univ of Louisiana at Lafayette	LA	5,830	C
Univ of Louisiana at Monroe	LA	7,103	C
Univ of Louisville	KY	10,400	C
Univ of Maine	ME	13,642	C
Univ of Maine at Farmington	ME	11,515	C
Univ of Mary Hardin-Baylor	TX	19,428	C
Univ of Mary Washington	VA	11,636	HC
Univ of Maryland/Baltimore County	MD	16,642	VC+
Univ of Maryland/College Park	MD	16,036	HC
Univ of Mass Amherst	MA	15,973	C+
Univ of Mass Boston	MA	8,024	C
Univ of Mass Dartmouth	MA	15,985	C
Univ of Mass Lowell	MA	14,327	VC
Univ of Memphis	TN	11,153	C
Univ of Miami	FL	38,397	MC
Univ of Mich/Ann Arbor	MI	16,587	HC+
Univ of Mich/Dearborn	MI	7,000	VC
Univ of Mich/Flint	MI	6,398	C
Univ of Minn/Duluth	MN	13,974	C
Univ of Minn/Morris	MN	15,472	VC
Univ of Minn/Twin Cities	MN	13,165	HC
Univ of Miss	MS	9,000	C
Univ of Missouri/Columbia	MO	13,500	VC
Univ of Missouri/Kansas City	MO	15,000	VC
Univ of Missouri/St. Louis	MO	14,046	VC
Univ of Montana	MT	10,602	C
Univ of Montevallo	AL	9,630	C
Univ of Nebr at Kearney	NE	9,000	NC
Univ of Nebr at Lincoln	NE	11,401	VC
Univ of Nebr at Omaha	NE	11,235	C
Univ of Nevada/Las Vegas	NV	11,566	C
Univ of Nevada/Reno	NV	12,155	NC
Univ of New England	ME	31,005	C
Univ of New Hampshire	NH	16,810	VC
Univ of New Haven	CT	31,794	C
Univ of New Mexico	NM	11,253	C
Univ of New Orleans	LA	7,370	C
Univ of North Alabama	AL	8,992	C
Univ of N Car at Asheville	NC	9,237	VC
Univ of N Car at Chapel Hill	NC	11,129	MC
Univ of N Car at Charlotte	NC	9,101	C
Univ of N Car at Greensboro	NC	8,993	C
Univ of N Car at Pembroke	NC	7,940	LC
Univ of N Car at Wilmington	NC	10,114	VC
Univ of N Dak	ND	10,114	VC
Univ of North Florida	FL	9,908	VC
Univ of North Texas	TX	7,800	C
Univ of Northern Colo	CO	10,249	C
Univ of Northern Iowa	IA	11,133	C
Univ of Notre Dame	IN	39,552	MC
Univ of Okla	OK	10,769	VC+
Univ of Oregon	OR	13,108	VC
Univ of Pennsylvania	PA	41,766	MC
Univ of Pittsburgh at Bradford	PA	17,008	C
Univ of Pittsburgh at Greensburg	PA	17,640	C
Univ of Pittsburgh at Johnstown	PA	16,740	C
Univ of Pittsburgh at Pittsburgh	PA	18,866	NC
Univ of Portland	OR	32,300	VC
Univ of PR/Mayaguez	PR	1,250	
Univ of PR/Rio Piedras	PR	5,750	
Univ of Puget Sound	WA	35,600	HC
Univ of Redlands	CA	36,160	VC
Univ of Rhode Island	RI	15,398	C
Univ of Richmond	VA	40,510	MC
Univ of Rio Grande	OH	8,728	NC
Univ of Rochester	NY	41,135	MC
Univ of St. Francis	IL	25,430	C
Univ of St. Mary	KS	18,900	C
Univ of St. Thomas	MN	28,000	C
Univ of St. Thomas	TX	23,810	VC
Univ of San Diego	CA	40,620	HC
Univ of San Francisco	CA	37,560	VC
Univ of Science and Arts of Okla	OK	7,650	C
Univ of Scranton	PA	31,100	VC
Univ of Sioux Falls	SD	20,800	C
Univ of South Alabama	AL	8,930	LC
Univ of S Car at Aiken	SC	11,718	LC
Univ of S Car at Columbia	SC	13,397	VC
Univ of S Car Upstate	SC	11,957	C
Univ of S Dak	SD	9,068	C
Univ of South Florida	FL	10,284	VC
Univ of Southern Calif	CA	41,618	MC
Univ of Southern Indiana	IN	12,590	LC
Univ of Southern Maine	ME	12,614	C
Univ of Southern Miss	MS	10,112	C
Univ of Tampa	FL	25,784	C
Univ of Tenn at Chattanooga	TN	7,790	C
Univ of Tenn at Knoxville	TN	11,720	C
Univ of Tenn at Martin	TN	8,693	C
Univ of Texas at Arlington	TX	7,195	LC
Univ of Texas at Austin	TX	14,610	HC
Univ of Texas at Dallas	TX	13,244	NC
Univ of Texas at El Paso	TX	8,764	NC
Univ of Texas at San Antonio	TX	11,325	LC
Univ of Texas-Pan American	TX	7,290	C+
Univ of the Cumberlands	KY	18,184	C
Univ of the District of Columbia	DC	2,070	LC
Univ of the Incarnate Word	TX	23,306	C
Univ of the Ozarks	AR	19,250	C
Univ of the Pacific	CA	34,380	VC
Univ of the South	TN	34,645	HC
Univ of Toledo	OH	15,806	NC
Univ of Tulsa	OK	25,348	HC
Univ of Utah	UT	10,162	VC
Univ of Vermont	VT	18,080	VC
Univ of Virginia	VA	13,759	MC
Univ of Virginia's College at Wise	VA	11,076	C
Univ of Washington	WA	10,400	VC
Univ of West Florida	FL	8,559	C
Univ of West Georgia	GA	8,838	C
Univ of Wisc/Eau Claire	WI	9,915	VC
Univ of Wisc/Green Bay	WI	9,415	VC
Univ of Wisc/La Crosse	WI	10,045	VC
Univ of Wisc/Madison	WI	13,117	HC
Univ of Wisc/Milwaukee	WI	9,427	LC
Univ of Wisc/Oshkosh	WI	10,426	LC
Univ of Wisc/Parkside	WI	10,181	LC
Univ of Wisc/Platteville	WI	9,779	NC
Univ of Wisc/River Falls	WI	9,722	LC
Univ of Wisc/Stevens Point	WI	9,384	VC
Univ of Wisc/Superior	WI	9,610	C+
Univ of Wisc/Whitewater	WI	9,274	C
Univ of Wyoming	WY	9,666	C
Ursinus College	PA	38,950	VC
Utah State Univ	UT	8,002	VC
Utica College	NY	31,396	C
Valdosta State Univ	GA	8,802	C
Valparaiso Univ	IN	28,970	VC+
Vanderbilt Univ	TN	41,986	MC
Vanguard Univ of Southern Calif	CA	27,071	C
Vassar College	NY	41,700	MC
Villanova Univ	PA	38,672	HC+
Virginia Commonwealth Univ	VA	12,987	C
Virginia Intermont College	VA	22,200	LC
Virginia Polytechnic Inst and State Univ	VA	10,834	VC
Virginia State Univ	VA	11,318	C
Virginia Union Univ	VA	18,432	LC
Virginia Wesleyan College	VA	28,433	C
Wabash College	IN	30,116	HC
Wagner College	NY	33,300	VC
Wake Forest Univ	NC	38,290	MC
Walsh Univ	OH	23,440	C
Wartburg College	IA	27,315	NC
Washburn Univ	KS	9,734	NC
Washington and Jefferson College	PA	33,490	VC
Washington and Lee Univ	VA	35,880	MC
Washington College	MD	34,990	VC
Washington State Univ	WA	12,260	C
Washington Univ in St. Louis	MO	42,106	MC
Wayland Baptist Univ	TX	13,484	C
Wayne State College	NE	8,033	NC
Wayne State Univ	MI	11,805	C
Waynesburg College	PA	21,230	C
Weber State Univ	UT	9,635	NC
Webster Univ	MO	24,280	VC
Wellesley College	MA	41,030	MC
Wells College	NY	23,070	VC
Wesley College	DE	19,905	C
Wesleyan College	GA	19,560	C
Wesleyan Univ	CT	42,122	MC
West Chester Univ of Pennsylvania	PA	12,355	C+
West Liberty State College	WV	9,142	LC
West Texas A&M Univ	TX	8,452	C
West Virginia State Univ	WV	8,378	NC
West Virginia Univ	WV	10,506	C
West Virginia Wesleyan College	WV	26,880	C
Western Carolina Univ	NC	7,000	C
Western Conn State Univ	CT	12,993	C
Western Illinois Univ	IL	13,042	C
Western Kentucky Univ	KY	10,192	C
Western Mich Univ	MI	13,299	C
Western New England College	MA	32,054	C
Western Oregon Univ	OR	10,295	C
Western State College of Colo	CO	9,942	C
Western Washington Univ	WA	11,262	VC
Westfield State College	MA	10,200	C
Westminster College	MO	19,060	VC
Westminster College	PA	31,290	C+
Westmont College	CA	36,672	VC
Wheaton College	IL	27,760	HC
Wheaton College	MA	40,180	HC+
Wheeling Jesuit Univ	WV	26,910	C
Whitman College	WA	36,110	HC+
Whittier College	CA	29,108	C
Whitworth College	WA	29,428	VC+
Wichita State Univ	KS	8,500	C
Widener Univ	PA	27,275	C
Wilberforce Univ	OH	14,937	LC
Wilkes Univ	PA	30,886	C
Willamette Univ	OR	35,416	VC+
William Jewell College	MO	24,340	C
William Paterson Univ of New Jersey	NJ	17,810	C+
William Penn Univ	IA	17,685	LC
William Woods Univ	MO	21,020	C
Williams College	MA	40,310	MC
Wilson College	PA	27,660	C
Winona State Univ	MN	11,333	C
Winston-Salem State Univ	NC	8,960	LC
Winthrop Univ	SC	11,302	C
Wisc Lutheran College	WI	23,510	VC
Wittenberg Univ	OH	34,596	VC
Wofford College	SC	30,935	VC
Woodbury Univ	CA	30,176	LC
Wright State Univ	OH	13,616	LC
Xavier Univ	OH	30,490	VC
Xavier Univ of Louisiana	LA	17,600	C
Yale Univ	CT	41,000	MC
Yeshiva Univ	NY	22,000	C
York College of Pennsylvania	PA	16,550	VC
Youngstown State Univ	OH	12,613	NC

POLYMER SCIENCE

School	ST	$IS	SR
Case Western Reserve Univ	OH	37,314	MC
Eastern Mich Univ	MI	12,897	C
Georgia Inst of Technology	GA	11,450	HC+
Pennsylvania College of Technology	PA	16,980	LC
Rochester Inst of Technology	NY	32,070	VC+
SUNY/College of Environmental Science and Forestry	NY	15,000	VC
Univ of at Calif Davis	CA	15,010	VC
Univ of Missouri/Rolla	MO	13,332	HC
Univ of Southern Miss	MS	10,112	C

PORTUGUESE

School	ST	$IS	SR
Brigham Young Univ	UT	9,200	VC
Brown Univ	RI	42,015	MC
Florida International Univ	FL	9,215	VC
Georgetown Univ	DC	43,183	MC
Harvard Univ/Harvard College	MA	45,860	MC
Indiana Univ Bloomington	IN	13,356	VC
New York Univ	NY	43,170	MC
Ohio State Univ	OH	15,357	HC

School	ST	$IS	SR
Princeton Univ	NJ	40,213	MC
Rutgers, The State Univ of New Jersey/New Brunswick/Piscataway Campus	NJ	15,810	HC
Rutgers, The State Univ of New Jersey/Newark Campus	NJ	15,640	VC
Tulane Univ	LA	41,098	MC
Univ of Arizona	AZ	11,958	VC
Univ of Calif at Los Angeles	CA	17,681	MC
Univ of Calif at Santa Barbara	CA	11,800	VC
Univ of Florida	FL	9,354	HC
Univ of Illinois at Urbana-Champaign	IL	15,800	HC+
Univ of Iowa	IA	12,172	VC
Univ of Mass Amherst	MA	15,973	C+
Univ of Mass Dartmouth	MA	15,985	C
Univ of New Mexico	NM	11,253	C
Univ of Texas at Austin	TX	14,610	HC
Univ of Wisc/Madison	WI	13,117	HC
Yale Univ	CT	41,000	MC

POULTRY SCIENCE

School	ST	$IS	SR
Auburn Univ	AL	12,230	VC
Louisiana State Univ and A&M College	LA	10,749	VC
Miss State Univ	MS	9,577	C
N Car State Univ	NC	11,824	HC
Oregon State Univ	OR	11,055	C
Penn State Univ/Univ Park Campus	PA	18,038	HC
Stephen F. Austin State Univ	TX	7,930	C
Texas A&M Univ	TX	13,351	HC
Univ of Arkansas	AR	11,859	VC
Univ of Georgia	GA	11,004	HC
Univ of Maryland/Eastern Shore	MD	11,210	C
Univ of Wisc/Madison	WI	13,117	HC
Virginia Polytechnic Inst and State Univ	VA	10,834	VC

PREALLIED HEALTH

School	ST	$IS	SR
Juniata College	PA	33,130	C
La Salle Univ	PA	34,950	C
Univ of N Dak	ND	10,114	VC

PREDENTISTRY

School	ST	$IS	SR
Abilene Christian Univ	TX	20,830	C
Adams State College	CO	8,613	C
Albertus Magnus College	CT	25,336	C
Albion College	MI	26,000	VC
American International College	MA	28,710	LC
Arcadia Univ	PA	33,570	VC
Ashland Univ	OH	25,000	C
Auburn Univ	AL	12,230	VC
Austin Peay State Univ	TN	7,535	C
Averett Univ	VA	24,920	C
Baldwin-Wallace College	OH	27,256	VC
Ball State Univ	IN	13,138	C
Bard College	NY	41,800	HC+
Barry Univ	FL	24,100	LC
Baylor Univ	TX	27,555	HC
Bellarmine Univ	KY	27,650	C+
Beloit College	WI	32,808	HC
Bemidji State Univ	MN	11,180	LC
Bethany College	KS	20,660	LC
Bethany College	WV	21,395	C
Bethel College	IN	19,680	C
Boise State Univ	ID	9,438	LC
Brigham Young Univ/Hawaii	HI	7,740	HC+
Calif Lutheran Univ	CA	27,800	LC
Calvin College	MI	25,735	NC
Capital Univ	OH	30,444	C
Cardinal Stritch Univ	WI	21,910	C
Carroll College	MT	23,324	C+
Central Mich Univ	MI	12,244	C
Central Missouri State Univ	MO	10,000	C
Chadron State College	NE	6,350	NC
Chicago State Univ	IL	10,915	C+
Christopher Newport Univ	VA	13,326	VC
Citadel, The	SC		C
CUNY/City College	NY		C
CUNY/Herbert H. Lehman College	NY	4,000	LC
CUNY/Hunter College	NY	8,000	C+
Clark Univ	MA	35,165	VC+
Clemson Univ	SC	13,366	HC
Coastal Carolina Univ	SC	13,140	C
Coe College	IA	27,440	VC
College of Charleston	SC	13,616	VC
College of Notre Dame of Maryland	MD	27,700	C
College of Our Lady of the Elms	MA	21,000	C
College of St. Benedict	MN	30,091	VC
Colo State Univ-Pueblo	CO	7,821	LC
Columbia Union College	MD	23,536	LC
Concord College	WV	9,708	C

School	ST	$IS	SR
Concordia College: Moorhead	MN	22,475	VC
Concordia Univ Nebr	NE	20,500	C+
Concordia Univ, Ann Arbor	MI	25,153	C+
Converse College	SC	24,800	VC
Coppin State College	MD	10,200	LC
Cornerstone Univ and Grand Rapids Theological Seminary	MI	21,350	NC
Dakota Wesleyan Univ	SD	17,832	C
Davis and Elkins College	WV	22,416	C
Delta State Univ	MS	7,709	C
Dordt College	IA	20,325	VC
Drexel Univ	PA	27,700	VC
Drury Univ	MO	20,117	VC
Eastern Mich Univ	MI	12,897	C
Eastern Washington Univ	WA	10,608	C
Eckerd College	FL	35,492	VC
Edinboro Univ of Pennsylvania	PA	11,809	LC
Elmira College	NY	37,200	VC
Florida A&M Univ	FL	8,344	C
Florida State Univ	FL	9,028	HC
Freed-Hardeman Univ	TN	16,370	NC
Gannon Univ	PA	26,100	C
George Fox Univ	OR	28,490	C
Gettysburg College	PA	39,864	HC
Goshen College	IN	22,850	VC
Grace College	IN	22,170	C
Graceland Univ	IA	19,700	C
Grand Valley State Univ	MI	12,000	VC
Grove City College	PA	15,784	HC+
Gustavus Adolphus College	MN	30,920	HC
Hamline Univ	MN	27,070	VC
Harding Univ	AR	16,512	VC
Hardin-Simmons Univ	TX	18,641	C
Heidelberg College	OH	23,242	C
Hillsdale College	MI	24,160	HC
Hofstra Univ	NY	32,630	VC
Howard Univ	DC	18,481	C+
Humboldt State Univ	CA	11,176	C
Indiana Univ South Bend	IN	4,989	LC
Indiana Univ-Purdue Univ Fort Wayne	IN	5,067	LC
Indiana Univ-Purdue Univ Indianapolis	IN	10,959	C
Iona College	NY	30,878	VC
Iowa Wesleyan College	IA	22,140	C
Ithaca College	NY	35,144	VC
Johnson C. Smith Univ	NC	20,000	C
Judson College	IL	25,130	C
Juniata College	PA	33,130	VC
Kent State Univ	OH	14,594	C
Kentucky Wesleyan College	KY	18,590	C
Keuka College	NY	26,050	C
King's College	PA	29,810	C
La Salle Univ	PA	34,950	C
LaGrange College	GA	22,874	C+
Lake Superior State Univ	MI	12,842	LC
Lamar Univ	TX	6,820	LC
Le Moyne College	NY	29,570	VC
Lehigh Univ	PA	42,690	HC+
Lewis Univ	IL	23,050	C+
Lincoln Memorial Univ	TN	18,144	C
Lipscomb Univ	TN	20,967	VC
Livingstone College	NC	17,815	LC
LIU/Brooklyn Campus	NY	25,000	C
LIU/C.W. Post Campus	NY	28,282	C
Louisiana College	LA	13,450	C
MacMurray College	IL	20,755	C
Manhattan College	NY	29,000	VC
Mars Hill College	NC	19,000	LC
Maryville College	TN	29,224	VC
Mercer Univ	GA	27,525	VC+
Mercyhurst College	PA	28,633	VC
Merrimack College	MA	34,380	C
Methodist College	NC	21,000	C
Midland Lutheran College	NE	18,600	C
Midwestern State Univ	TX	9,381	LC
Minn State Univ, Mankato	MN	10,276	LC
Minn State Univ, Moorhead	MN	7,000	LC
Missouri Southern State Univ	MO	8,396	NC
Missouri State Univ	MO	10,748	C+
Montclair State Univ	NJ	16,327	C
Mount Mary College	WI	22,895	C
Murray State Univ	KY	8,900	VC
New York Univ	NY	43,170	MC
Newman Univ	KS	21,106	C
Niagara Univ	NY	28,250	C
N Car State Univ	NC	11,824	HC
North Central College	IL	28,926	VC
North Georgia College and State Univ	GA	7,000	C
North Park Univ	IL	24,050	C
Northern Arizona Univ	AZ	10,353	C
Northern Kentucky Univ	KY	6,670	NC
Northern Mich Univ	MI	12,340	LC
Northern State Univ	SD	8,257	C
Northwest Missouri State Univ	MO	10,000	C
Northwestern College of Iowa	IA	22,174	C+
Notre Dame de Namur Univ	CA	32,790	LC
Ohio Univ	OH	15,921	C
Ohio Wesleyan Univ	OH	35,830	VC+

School	ST	$IS	SR
Okla Baptist Univ	OK	17,986	VC
Okla Wesleyan Univ	OK	18,950	NC
Olivet College	MI	19,984	C+
Oral Roberts Univ	OK	22,650	C
Ouachita Baptist Univ	AR	21,900	VC
Purdue Univ/West Lafayette	IN	13,458	VC
Quinnipiac Univ	CT	34,640	VC
Rivier College	NH	26,600	C
Rochester Inst of Technology	NY	32,070	VC+
Rockford College	IL	28,330	VC
Roosevelt Univ	IL	22,605	VC
Rosemont College	PA	29,350	C
St. Anselm College	NH	33,810	C
St. Cloud State Univ	MN	10,010	C
St. Edward's Univ	TX	23,560	VC
St. John's Univ	MN	29,749	VC
St. John's Univ	NY	34,370	C
St. Joseph's College	IN	26,600	C
St. Martin's Univ	WA	27,555	C
St. Mary-of-the-Woods College	IN	25,480	C
St. Mary's Univ of San Antonio	TX	22,444	C
St. Michael's College	VT	33,330	VC
St. Peter's College	NJ	30,160	LC
St. Thomas Univ	FL	23,490	C
St. Vincent College	PA	26,160	VC
St. Xavier Univ	IL	23,160	C
Savannah State Univ	GA	7,772	C
Seton Hill Univ	PA	28,810	C
Southeast Missouri State Univ	MO	10,596	C
Southern Nazarene Univ	OK	14,634	NC
Spring Hill College	AL	28,678	C
Springfield College	MA	25,000	C
SUNY/College at Fredonia	NY	12,771	VC
SUNY/College at Oneonta	NY	12,905	VC
SUNY/College of Environmental Science and Forestry	NY	15,000	VC
SUNY/Univ at Albany	NY	13,860	VC
Syracuse Univ	NY	38,655	HC
Tarleton State Univ	TX	8,952	C
Temple Univ	PA	17,438	C
Texas A&M Univ at Commerce	TX	9,020	C
Texas A&M Univ at Kingsville	TX	6,800	LC
Thiel College	PA	24,580	C
Touro College	NY	17,000	VC
Trinity Christian College	IL	23,645	C
Truman State Univ	MO	11,242	HC
Union Univ	TN	20,750	VC
Univ of Akron	OH	15,166	NC
Univ of Arkansas	AR	11,859	VC
Univ of Arkansas at Pine Bluff	AR	8,300	C
Univ of Bridgeport	CT	29,595	LC
Univ of Central Arkansas	AR	9,984	C
Univ of Cincinnati	OH	17,682	C
Univ of Dayton	OH	28,826	VC
Univ of Detroit Mercy	MI	27,000	C
Univ of Evansville	IN	28,320	VC
Univ of Great Falls	MT	17,000	C
Univ of Hartford	CT	34,044	C
Univ of Iowa	IA	12,172	VC
Univ of Mass Amherst	MA	15,973	C+
Univ of Miami	FL	38,397	MC
Univ of Minn/Crookston	MN	13,157	LC
Univ of Minn/Twin Cities	MN	13,165	HC
Univ of Missouri/Rolla	MO	13,332	HC
Univ of Nebr at Kearney	NE	9,000	NC
Univ of Nebr at Lincoln	NE	11,401	VC
Univ of New Haven	CT	31,794	C
Univ of N Car at Greensboro	NC	8,993	C
Univ of North Florida	FL	9,908	VC
Univ of Notre Dame	IN	39,552	MC
Univ of Rio Grande	OH	8,728	NC
Univ of St. Francis	IL	25,430	C
Univ of St. Francis	IN	20,970	C
Univ of Southern Indiana	IN	12,590	LC
Univ of Southern Miss	MS	10,112	C
Univ of Tenn at Knoxville	TN	11,720	C
Univ of Tenn at Martin	TN	8,693	C
Univ of West Alabama	AL	7,611	C
Univ of West Florida	FL	8,559	C
Univ of Wisc/Milwaukee	WI	9,427	LC
Utah State Univ	UT	8,002	VC
Virginia Polytechnic Inst and State Univ	VA	10,834	VC
Walsh Univ	OH	23,440	C
Washington State Univ	WA	12,260	C
Washington Univ in St. Louis	MO	42,106	MC
Waynesburg College	PA	21,230	C
West Chester Univ of Pennsylvania	PA	12,355	C+
West Liberty State College	WV	9,142	LC
West Texas A&M Univ	TX	8,452	C
Western Carolina Univ	NC	7,000	C
Western Mich Univ	MI	13,299	C
Western New Mexico Univ	NM	7,233	LC
Western State College of Colo	CO	9,942	C

School	ST	$IS	SR
Westminster College	PA	31,290	C+
Whitworth College	WA	29,428	VC+
Widener Univ	PA	27,275	C
Wilkes Univ	PA	30,886	C
Wilmington College	OH	2,806	NC
Wingate Univ	NC	23,300	C
Winona State Univ	MN	11,333	C
Wittenberg Univ	OH	34,596	VC
Wright State Univ	OH	13,616	LC
Xavier Univ of Louisiana	LA	17,600	C
Youngstown State Univ	OH	12,613	NC

PREENGINEERING

School	ST	$IS	SR
Adams State College	CO	8,613	C
Alice Lloyd College	KY	4,900	C
Augustana College	IL	29,862	VC+
Baldwin-Wallace College	OH	27,256	VC
Barry Univ	FL	24,100	LC
Bellarmine Univ	KY	27,650	C+
Bethel College	TN	16,066	NC
Campbell Univ	NC	21,137	VC
Canisius College	NY	32,257	VC
CUNY/Hunter College	NY	8,000	C+
Coe College	IA	27,440	VC
College of Notre Dame of Maryland	MD	27,700	C
College of St. Benedict	MN	30,091	VC
College of the Ozarks	MO	4,130	VC+
Colo State Univ-Pueblo	CO	7,821	LC
Concordia College: Moorhead	MN	22,475	VC
Coppin State College	MD	10,200	LC
DePauw Univ	IN	32,100	HC
Eastern Mich Univ	MI	12,897	C
Edgewood College	WI	22,862	C
Freed-Hardeman Univ	TN	16,370	NC
Furman Univ	SC	33,264	HC+
Goshen College	IN	22,850	VC
Harvard Univ/Harvard College	MA	45,860	MC
Heidelberg College	OH	23,242	C
Indiana Univ South Bend	IN	4,989	LC
Iowa Wesleyan College	IA	22,140	C
Johnson C. Smith Univ	NC	20,000	C
Judson College	IL	25,130	C
Juniata College	PA	33,130	C
Kentucky Wesleyan College	KY	18,590	C
Lewis Univ	IL	23,050	C+
Lincoln Univ	PA	13,658	C+
Lipscomb Univ	TN	20,967	VC
LIU/C.W. Post Campus	NY	28,282	C
MacMurray College	IL	20,755	C
Mansfield Univ	PA	11,300	C
Maryville College	TN	29,224	VC
Midwestern State Univ	TX	9,381	LC
Minn State Univ, Mankato	MN	10,276	LC
Newman Univ	KS	21,106	C
Niagara Univ	NY	28,250	C
North Central College	IL	28,926	VC
North Georgia College and State Univ	GA	7,000	C
Northern Kentucky Univ	KY	6,670	NC
Northwest Missouri State Univ	MO	10,000	C
Oral Roberts Univ	OK	22,650	C
Peru State College	NE	6,350	NC
Pfeiffer Univ	NC	21,900	C
Providence College	RI	34,580	VC
Purdue Univ/West Lafayette	IN	13,458	VC
Richard Stockton College of New Jersey	NJ	14,000	VC
Rockford College	IL	28,330	VC
St. Edward's Univ	TX	23,560	C
St. John's Univ	MN	29,749	VC
St. John's Univ	NY	34,370	C
St. Mary's College of Calif	CA	37,290	VC
St. Michael's College	VT	33,330	VC
Scripps College	CA	41,000	MC
Shaw Univ	NC	15,488	LC
Southeast Missouri State Univ	MO	10,596	C
Southern Nazarene Univ	OK	14,634	NC
Stephen F. Austin State Univ	TX	7,930	C
Texas A&M Univ at Commerce	TX	9,020	C
Thiel College	PA	24,580	C
Truman State Univ	MO	11,242	HC
Union Univ	TN	20,750	VC
Univ of Arkansas at Pine Bluff	AR	8,300	C
Univ of Central Arkansas	AR	9,984	C
Univ of Georgia	GA	11,004	HC
Univ of Rio Grande	OH	8,728	NC
West Liberty State College	WV	9,142	LC
West Texas A&M Univ	TX	8,452	C
Western Carolina Univ	NC	7,000	C
Western State College of Colo	CO	9,942	C
Wilberforce Univ	OH	14,937	LC
Wingate Univ	NC	23,300	C
Yeshiva Univ	NY	22,000	C
Youngstown State Univ	OH	12,613	NC

ST = STATE $IS = IN-STATE COSTS   SR = SELECTOR RATING

PRELAW

School	ST	$IS	SR
Abilene Christian Univ	TX	20,830	C
Adams State College	CO	8,613	C
Albertus Magnus College	CT	25,336	C
American International College	MA	28,710	LC
Arcadia Univ	PA	33,570	VC
Ashland Univ	OH	25,000	C
Austin Peay State Univ	TN	7,535	C
Averett Univ	VA	24,920	C
Baldwin-Wallace College	OH	27,256	VC
Ball State Univ	IN	13,138	C
Bard College	NY	41,800	HC+
Barry Univ	FL	24,100	LC
Bellarmine Univ	KY	27,650	C+
Beloit College	WI	32,808	HC
Bemidji State Univ	MN	11,180	LC
Bethany College	KS	20,660	LC
Bethany College	WV	21,395	C
Bethel College	IN	19,680	C
Black Hills State Univ	SD	7,800	LC
Calif Lutheran Univ	CA	27,800	LC
Calvin College	MI	25,735	NC
Campbell Univ	NC	21,137	VC
Capital Univ	OH	30,444	C
Cardinal Stritch Univ	WI	21,910	C
Carroll College	MT	23,324	C+
Catawba College	NC	25,000	C
Cedar Crest College	PA	30,615	C
Cedarville Univ	OH	21,904	NC
Central Missouri State Univ	MO	10,000	C
Central Washington Univ	WA	11,730	C
Chadron State College	NE	6,350	NC
Chicago State Univ	IL	10,915	C+
Christopher Newport Univ	VA	13,326	VC
CUNY/City College	NY		C
CUNY/Herbert H. Lehman College	NY	4,000	LC
CUNY/Hunter College	NY	8,000	LC
Clark Univ	MA	35,165	VC+
Clearwater Christian College	FL	13,160	LC
Clemson Univ	SC	13,366	HC
Coastal Carolina Univ	SC	13,140	C
Coe College	IA	27,440	VC
College of Notre Dame of Maryland	MD	27,700	C
College of Our Lady of the Elms	MA	21,000	C
College of St. Benedict	MN	30,091	VC
College of St. Elizabeth	NJ	28,495	C
College of the Ozarks	MO	4,130	VC+
Colo State Univ-Pueblo	CO	7,821	LC
Columbia Union College	MD	23,536	LC
Concord College	WV	9,708	C
Concordia College: Moorhead	MN	22,475	VC
Concordia Univ Nebr	NE	20,500	C+
Concordia Univ, River Forest	IL	26,300	C
Converse College	SC	24,800	VC
Cornerstone Univ and Grand Rapids Theological Seminary	MI	21,350	NC
Creighton Univ	NE	29,918	VC+
Davis and Elkins College	WV	22,416	C
Dordt College	IA	20,325	VC
Drexel Univ	PA	27,700	VC
Drury Univ	MO	20,117	VC
East Central Univ	OK	6,207	C
Eastern Mich Univ	MI	12,897	C
Eastern Washington Univ	WA	10,608	C
Eckerd College	FL	35,492	VC
Edgewood College	WI	22,862	C
Edinboro Univ of Pennsylvania	PA	11,809	LC
Elmira College	NY	37,200	C
Eugene Lang College New School for Liberal Arts	NY	38,800	C+
Faulkner Univ	AL	15,600	C
Florida State Univ	FL	9,028	HC
Fontbonne Univ	MO	23,308	C
Fresno Pacific Univ	CA	25,454	C
Gannon Univ	PA	26,100	C
George Fox Univ	OR	28,490	C
Gettysburg College	PA	39,864	HC
Grace College	IN	22,170	C
Grambling State Univ	LA	6,538	NC
Grand Valley State Univ	MI	12,000	VC
Grove City College	PA	15,784	HC+
Gustavus Adolphus College	MN	30,920	HC
Hamline Univ	MN	27,070	VC
Hardin-Simmons Univ	TX	18,641	C
Heidelberg College	OH	23,242	C
Hillsdale College	MI	24,160	HC
Holy Family Univ	PA	25,740	C
Humboldt State Univ	CA	11,176	C
Huntington Univ	IN	24,830	C
Illinois College	IL	21,900	C+
Immaculata Univ	PA	25,350	C
Indiana Univ of Pennsylvania	PA	11,209	C
Indiana Univ South Bend	IN	4,989	LC
Indiana Univ-Purdue Univ Fort Wayne	IN	5,067	LC
Indiana Univ-Purdue Univ Indianapolis	IN	10,959	C
Indiana Wesleyan Univ	IN	22,074	C+
Iowa Wesleyan College	IA	22,140	C
Ithaca College	NY	35,144	VC
Johnson C. Smith Univ	NC	20,000	C
Johnson State College	VT	11,830	LC
Judson College	IL	25,130	C
Juniata College	PA	33,130	VC
Kansas Wesleyan Univ	KS	21,400	VC
Kentucky Wesleyan College	KY	18,590	C
Keuka College	NY	26,050	C
King's College	PA	29,810	C
La Salle Univ	PA	34,950	C
Lafayette College	PA	39,267	MC
LaGrange College	GA	22,874	C+
Lake Superior State Univ	MI	12,842	LC
Lamar Univ	TX	6,820	LC
Le Moyne College	NY	29,570	VC
Lenoir-Rhyne College	NC	25,580	C
LeTourneau Univ	TX	21,200	C
Lewis Univ	IL	23,050	C+
Limestone College	SC	19,840	C
Lincoln Memorial Univ	TN	18,144	C
Lindenwood Univ	MO	18,600	VC
Lipscomb Univ	TN	20,967	VC
LIU/Brooklyn Campus	NY	25,000	C
LIU/C.W. Post Campus	NY	28,282	C
Louisiana College	LA	13,450	C
Lynn Univ	FL	30,750	C
MacMurray College	IL	20,755	C
Manchester College	IN	23,470	C
Manhattan College	NY	29,000	VC
Mansfield Univ	PA	11,300	C
Marlboro College	VT	35,980	VC+
Mars Hill College	NC	19,000	LC
Maryville College	TN	29,224	VC
Mercer Univ	GA	27,525	VC+
Mercyhurst College	PA	28,633	VC
Merrimack College	MA	34,380	C
Methodist College	NC	21,000	C
Metropolitan College of New York	NY	16,000	C
Miami Univ	OH	29,097	HC
Mich State Univ	MI	13,689	VC
Middle Tenn State Univ	TN	8,540	C
Midland Lutheran College	NE	18,600	C
Midwestern State Univ	TX	9,381	C
Minn State Univ, Mankato	MN	10,276	LC
Minn State Univ, Moorhead	MN	7,000	LC
Monmouth Univ	NJ	28,956	C
Mount Aloysius College	PA	20,900	LC
Mount Mary College	WI	22,895	C
Mount St. Mary College	NY	25,250	C
Murray State Univ	KY	8,900	VC
National Univ	CA	8,412	SP
New York Inst of Technology	NY	28,126	VC
Newbury College	MA	25,600	C
Newman Univ	KS	21,106	C
Niagara Univ	NY	28,250	C
N Car State Univ	NC	11,824	HC
North Central Univ	IL	28,926	VC
North Georgia College and State Univ	GA	7,000	C
North Park Univ	IL	24,050	C
Northern Arizona Univ	AZ	10,353	C
Northern Kentucky Univ	KY	6,670	NC
Northern Mich Univ	MI	12,340	LC
Northern State Univ	SD	8,257	C
Northwest Missouri State Univ	MO	10,000	C
Northwestern College of Iowa	IA	22,174	C+
Notre Dame de Namur Univ	CA	32,790	LC
Nova Southeastern Univ	FL	24,320	C
Oakland City Univ	IN	19,620	NC
Ohio Univ	OH	15,921	C
Ohio Wesleyan Univ	OH	35,830	VC+
Okla Baptist Univ	OK	17,986	VC
Okla Christian Univ	OK	18,992	NC
Okla City Univ	OK	23,965	VC
Okla State Univ	OK	10,213	VC
Okla Wesleyan Univ	OK	18,950	NC
Olivet College	MI	19,984	C+
Oral Roberts Univ	OK	22,650	C
Ouachita Baptist Univ	AR	21,900	VC
Palm Beach Atlantic Univ	FL	23,597	VC
Penn State Univ/Univ Park Campus	PA	18,038	HC
Peru State College	NE	6,350	NC
Pfeiffer Univ	NC	21,900	C
Purdue Univ/West Lafayette	IN	13,458	VC
Quinnipiac Univ	CT	34,640	VC
Regis Univ	CO	31,890	C
Rensselaer Polytechnic Inst	NY	41,288	HC+
Rhode Island College	RI	11,570	C
Rider Univ	NJ	32,560	C
Rivier College	NH	26,600	C
Roberts Wesleyan College	NY	26,378	C
Rochester Inst of Technology	NY	32,070	VC+
Rockford College	IL	28,330	VC
Roger Williams Univ	RI	30,500	C
Roosevelt Univ	IL	22,605	VC
Rosemont College	PA	29,350	C
St. Anselm College	NH	33,810	C
St. Augustine's College	NC	14,000	LC
St. Bonaventure Univ	NY	28,785	LC
St. Cloud State Univ	MN	10,010	C
St. Edward's Univ	TX	23,560	C
St. John's Univ	MN	29,749	VC
St. John's Univ	NY	34,370	C
St. Joseph's College	IN	26,600	C
St. Martin's Univ	WA	27,555	C
St. Mary-of-the-Woods College	IN	25,480	C
St. Mary's Univ of San Antonio	TX	22,444	C
St. Michael's College	VT	33,330	VC
St. Peter's College	NJ	30,160	LC
St. Thomas Aquinas College	NY	22,000	LC
St. Thomas Univ	FL	23,490	C
St. Vincent College	PA	26,160	VC
St. Xavier Univ	IL	23,160	C
Schreiner Univ	TX	20,600	C
Scripps College	CA	41,000	MC
Seton Hill Univ	PA	28,810	C
Shawnee State Univ	OH	12,237	NC
Simmons College	MA	35,640	VC
Southeast Missouri State Univ	MO	10,596	C
Southern Nazarene Univ	OK	14,634	NC
Southern Oregon Univ	OR	12,186	C
Springfield College	MA	25,000	C
SUNY/College at Oneonta	NY	12,905	VC
SUNY/College of Environmental Science and Forestry	NY	15,000	VC
SUNY/Univ at Albany	NY	13,860	VC
Stephen F. Austin State Univ	TX	7,930	C
Stephens College	MO	26,930	VC
Stetson Univ	FL	32,725	VC
Stillman College	AL	11,475	LC
Syracuse Univ	NY	38,655	HC
Tarleton State Univ	TX	8,952	C
Temple Univ	PA	17,438	C
Texas A&M Univ at Commerce	TX	9,020	C
Texas A&M Univ at Kingsville	TX	6,800	LC
Thiel College	PA	24,580	C
Toccoa Falls College	GA	17,125	C
Touro College	NY	17,000	VC
Trinity Christian College	IL	23,645	C
Trinity College	DC	24,150	LC
Truman State Univ	MO	11,242	HC
Union Univ	TN	20,750	VC
Univ of Akron	OH	15,166	NC
Univ of Arkansas	AR	11,859	VC
Univ of Bridgeport	CT	29,555	LC
Univ of Cincinnati	OH	17,682	C
Univ of Dayton	OH	28,826	VC
Univ of Detroit Mercy	MI	27,000	C
Univ of Evansville	IN	28,320	VC
Univ of Findlay	OH	29,238	C
Univ of Great Falls	MT	17,000	C
Univ of Illinois at Urbana-Champaign	IL	15,800	HC+
Univ of Iowa	IA	12,172	VC
Univ of Louisiana at Monroe	LA	7,103	C
Univ of Mary	ND	15,374	C
Univ of Mass Amherst	MA	15,973	C+
Univ of Miami	FL	38,397	MC
Univ of Minn/Morris	MN	15,472	VC
Univ of Minn/Twin Cities	MN	13,165	HC
Univ of Missouri/Rolla	MO	13,332	HC
Univ of Nebr at Kearney	NE	9,000	NC
Univ of Nebr at Lincoln	NE	11,401	VC
Univ of N Car at Greensboro	NC	8,993	C
Univ of North Florida	FL	9,908	VC
Univ of Rio Grande	OH	8,728	NC
Univ of Sioux Falls	SD	20,800	C
Univ of Southern Indiana	IN	12,590	LC
Univ of Southern Miss	MS	10,112	C
Univ of Tenn at Martin	TN	8,693	C
Univ of the Incarnate Word	TX	23,306	C
Univ of Tulsa	OK	25,348	HC
Univ of West Alabama	AL	7,611	C
Univ of West Florida	FL	8,559	C
Univ of Wisc/Milwaukee	WI	9,427	LC
Univ of Wisc/River Falls	WI	9,722	LC
Univ of Wisc/Whitewater	WI	9,274	C
Urbana Univ	OH	21,190	C
Ursuline College	OH	25,456	C
Utah State Univ	UT	8,002	VC
Vassar College	NY	41,700	MC
Virginia Polytechnic Inst and State Univ	VA	10,834	VC
Walsh Univ	OH	23,440	C
Waynesburg College	PA	21,230	C
Webber International Univ	FL	17,580	LC
West Chester Univ of Pennsylvania	PA	12,355	C+
West Liberty State College	WV	9,142	LC
West Texas A&M Univ	TX	8,452	C
Western Carolina Univ	NC	7,000	C
Western Mich Univ	MI	13,299	C
Western State College of Colo	CO	9,942	C
Westminster College	PA	31,290	C+
Whitworth College	WA	29,428	VC+
Widener Univ	PA	27,275	C
Wilberforce Univ	OH	14,937	LC
Wilkes Univ	PA	30,886	C
Wilmington College	OH	2,806	NC
Wingate Univ	NC	23,300	C
Winona State Univ	MN	11,333	C
Wittenberg Univ	OH	34,596	VC
Wright State Univ	OH	13,616	LC
Xavier Univ of Louisiana	LA	17,600	C
York College of Pennsylvania	PA	16,550	VC
Youngstown State Univ	OH	12,613	NC

PREMEDICINE

School	ST	$IS	SR
Abilene Christian Univ	TX	20,830	C
Adams State College	CO	8,613	C
Albertus Magnus College	CT	25,336	C
Albion College	MI	26,000	VC
American International College	MA	28,710	LC
Arcadia Univ	PA	33,570	VC
Ashland Univ	OH	25,000	C
Auburn Univ	AL	12,230	VC
Augustana College	IL	29,862	VC+
Austin Peay State Univ	TN	7,535	C
Averett Univ	VA	24,920	C
Avila Univ	MO	22,100	C
Azusa Pacific Univ	CA	28,546	VC
Baldwin-Wallace College	OH	27,256	VC
Ball State Univ	IN	13,138	C
Bard College	NY	41,800	HC+
Barry Univ	FL	24,100	LC
Baylor Univ	TX	27,555	HC
Bellarmine Univ	KY	27,650	C+
Beloit College	WI	32,808	HC
Bemidji State Univ	MN	11,180	LC
Bennington College	VT	41,890	HC
Bethany College	KS	20,660	LC
Bethany College	WV	21,395	C
Bethel College	IN	19,680	C
Bluffton College	OH	26,110	C
Boise State Univ	ID	9,438	LC
Brigham Young Univ/Hawaii	HI	7,740	HC+
Calif Lutheran Univ	CA	27,800	LC
Cal State, San Bernardino	CA	12,563	LC
Calvin College	MI	25,735	NC
Capital Univ	OH	30,444	C
Cardinal Stritch Univ	WI	21,910	C
Carroll College	MT	23,324	C+
Central Mich Univ	MI	12,244	C
Central Missouri State Univ	MO	10,000	C
Central Univ of Bayamon	PR	3,335	
Chadron State College	NE	6,350	NC
Chicago State Univ	IL	10,915	C+
Christopher Newport Univ	VA	13,326	VC
Citadel, The	SC		C+
CUNY/City College	NY		C
CUNY/Herbert H. Lehman College	NY	4,000	LC
CUNY/Hunter College	NY	8,000	C+
Clark Univ	MA	35,165	VC+
Clearwater Christian College	FL	13,160	LC
Clemson Univ	SC	13,366	HC
Cleveland State Univ	OH	10,798	NC
Coastal Carolina Univ	SC	13,140	C
Coe College	IA	27,440	VC
College of Charleston	SC	13,616	VC
College of Notre Dame of Maryland	MD	27,700	C
College of Our Lady of the Elms	MA	21,000	C
College of St. Benedict	MN	30,091	VC
College of St. Elizabeth	NJ	28,495	C
College of the Ozarks	MO	4,130	VC+
Colo State Univ-Pueblo	CO	7,821	LC
Columbia Union College	MD	23,536	LC
Concord College	WV	9,708	C
Concordia College: Moorhead	MN	22,475	VC
Concordia Univ	OR	24,400	C
Concordia Univ Nebr	NE	20,500	C+
Concordia Univ, Ann Arbor	MI	25,153	C+
Concordia Univ, River Forest	IL	26,300	C
Converse College	SC	24,800	VC
Cornerstone Univ and Grand Rapids Theological Seminary	MI	21,350	NC
Dakota State Univ	SD	7,466	C
Dakota Wesleyan Univ	SD	17,832	C
Davis and Elkins College	WV	22,416	C
Delta State Univ	MS	7,709	C
Dominican Univ of Calif	CA	36,836	C
Dordt College	IA	20,325	VC
Drexel Univ	PA	27,700	VC
Drury Univ	MO	20,117	VC
East Stroudsburg Univ of Pennsylvania	PA	10,336	C

ST = STATE $IS = IN-STATE COSTS   SR = SELECTOR RATING

School	ST	$IS	SR
Eastern Mich Univ	MI	12,897	C
Eastern Washington Univ	WA	10,608	C
Eckerd College	FL	35,492	VC
Edinboro Univ of Pennsylvania	PA	11,809	LC
Elizabethtown College	PA	32,100	VC
Elmira College	NY	37,200	VC
Florida A&M Univ	FL	8,344	C
Florida Inst of Technology	FL	29,720	VC
Florida State Univ	FL	9,028	C
Freed-Hardeman Univ	TN	16,370	NC
Fresno Pacific Univ	CA	25,454	C
Friends Univ	KS	16,250	LC
Gannon Univ	PA	26,100	C
George Fox Univ	OR	28,490	C
George Washington Univ	DC	48,820	MC
Gettysburg College	PA	39,864	HC
Goshen College	IN	22,850	VC
Grace College	IN	22,170	C
Graceland Univ	IA	19,700	C
Grambling State Univ	LA	6,538	NC
Grand Valley State Univ	MI	12,000	VC
Grove City College	PA	15,784	HC+
Gustavus Adolphus College	MN	30,920	VC
Hamline Univ	MN	27,070	VC
Hampshire College	MA	37,120	HC
Harding Univ	AR	16,512	VC
Hardin-Simmons Univ	TX	18,641	C
Hawaii Pacific Univ	HI	21,080	C
Heidelberg College	OH	23,242	C
Hillsdale College	MI	24,160	HC
Hofstra Univ	NY	32,630	VC
Holy Family Univ	PA	25,740	C
Howard Univ	DC	18,481	C+
Humboldt State Univ	CA	11,176	C
Huntington Univ	IN	24,830	C
Immaculata Univ	PA	25,350	C
Indiana Univ of Pennsylvania	PA	11,209	C
Indiana Univ South Bend	IN	4,989	LC
Indiana Univ-Purdue Univ Fort Wayne	IN	5,067	LC
Indiana Univ-Purdue Univ Indianapolis	IN	10,959	C
Indiana Wesleyan Univ	IN	22,074	C+
Inter American Univ of PR/ San German	PR	6,720	C
Iona College	NY	30,878	VC
Iowa Wesleyan College	IA	22,140	C
Ithaca College	NY	35,144	VC
Jackson State Univ	MS	8,500	C
Jarvis Christian College	TX	11,136	NC
Johnson C. Smith Univ	NC	20,000	C
Johnson State College	VT	11,830	LC
Judson College	IL	25,130	C
Juniata College	PA	33,130	C
Kent State Univ	OH	14,594	C
Kentucky Wesleyan College	KY	18,590	C
Keuka College	NY	26,050	C
King's College	PA	29,810	C
La Salle Univ	PA	34,950	C
LaGrange College	GA	22,874	C+
Lake Superior State Univ	MI	12,842	LC
Lamar Univ	TX	6,820	LC
Le Moyne College	NY	29,570	VC
Lehigh Univ	PA	42,690	HC+
Lenoir-Rhyne College	NC	25,580	C
LeTourneau Univ	TX	21,200	C
Lewis Univ	IL	23,050	C+
Lincoln Memorial Univ	TN	18,144	C
Lipscomb Univ	TN	20,967	VC
Livingstone College	NC	17,815	LC
LIU/Brooklyn Campus	NY	25,000	C
LIU/C.W. Post Campus	NY	28,282	C
Louisiana College	LA	13,450	C
MacMurray College	IL	20,755	C
Manhattan College	NY	29,000	VC
Mansfield Univ	PA	11,300	C
Marlboro College	VT	35,980	VC+
Marquette Univ	WI	31,066	HC
Mars Hill College	NC	19,000	MC
Marymount Manhattan College	NY	30,049	VC
Maryville College	TN	29,224	VC
Mass College of Pharmacy and Health Sciences	MA	32,020	SP
Mercer Univ	GA	27,525	VC+
Mercyhurst College	PA	28,633	VC
Merrimack College	MA	34,380	C
Miami Univ	OH	29,097	HC
Midland Lutheran College	NE	18,600	C
Midwestern State Univ	TX	9,381	LC
Milligan College	TN	21,990	VC
Minn State Univ, Mankato	MN	10,276	LC
Minn State Univ, Moorhead	MN	7,000	LC
Missouri Southern State Univ	MO	8,396	NC
Monmouth Univ	NJ	28,956	C
Montclair State Univ	NJ	16,327	C
Mount Mary College	WI	22,895	C
Mount St. Mary College	NY	25,250	C
Murray State Univ	KY	8,900	VC
New York Univ	NY	43,170	MC
Newman Univ	KS	21,106	C
Niagara Univ	NY	28,250	C
N Car State Univ	NC	11,824	HC
N Car Wesleyan College	NC	22,670	C
North Central College	IL	28,926	VC
North Georgia College and State Univ	GA	7,000	C
North Park Univ	IL	24,050	C
Northern Arizona Univ	AZ	10,353	C
Northern Kentucky Univ	KY	6,670	NC
Northern Mich Univ	MI	12,340	LC
Northern State Univ	SD	8,257	C
Northwest Missouri State Univ	MO	10,000	C
Northwest Nazarene Univ	ID	22,590	VC
Northwestern College of Iowa	IA	22,174	C+
Northwestern Univ	IL	37,595	MC
Notre Dame de Namur Univ	CA	32,790	LC
Oakland City Univ	IN	19,620	NC
Ohio Univ	OH	15,921	C
Ohio Wesleyan Univ	OH	35,830	VC+
Okla Baptist Univ	OK	17,986	VC
Okla Christian Univ	OK	18,992	NC
Okla City Univ	OK	23,965	VC
Okla State Univ	OK	10,213	VC
Okla Wesleyan Univ	OK	18,950	NC
Olivet College	MI	19,984	C+
Oral Roberts Univ	OK	22,650	C
Ouachita Baptist Univ	AR	21,900	VC
Penn State Univ/Univ Park Campus	PA	18,038	HC
Peru State College	NE	6,350	NC
Pfeiffer Univ	NC	21,900	C
Philadelphia Univ	PA	30,006	C
Purdue Univ/West Lafayette	IN	13,458	VC
Quinnipiac Univ	CT	34,640	VC
Rensselaer Polytechnic Inst	NY	41,288	HC+
Rider Univ	NJ	32,560	C
Rivier College	NH	26,600	C
Roberts Wesleyan College	NY	26,378	C
Rochester Inst of Technology	NY	32,070	VC+
Rockford College	IL	28,330	VC
Roger Williams Univ	RI	30,500	C
Roosevelt Univ	IL	22,605	VC
Rosemont College	PA	29,350	C
St. Anselm College	NH	33,810	C
St. Augustine's College	NC	14,000	LC
St. Bonaventure Univ	NY	28,785	LC
St. Cloud State Univ	MN	10,010	C
St. Edward's Univ	TX	23,560	C
St. John's Univ	MN	29,749	VC
St. John's Univ	NY	34,370	C
St. Joseph's College	IN	26,600	C
St. Martin's Univ	WA	27,555	C
St. Mary-of-the-Woods College	IN	25,480	C
St. Mary's Univ of San Antonio	TX	22,444	C
St. Peter's College	NJ	30,160	LC
St. Thomas Aquinas College	NY	22,000	LC
St. Thomas Univ	FL	23,490	C
St. Vincent College	PA	26,160	VC
St. Xavier Univ	IL	23,160	C
Sarah Lawrence College	NY	42,000	HC
Seton Hill Univ	PA	28,810	C
Shawnee State Univ	OH	12,237	NC
Siena Heights Univ	MI	17,000	LC
Simmons College	MA	35,640	VC
Simon's Rock College of Bard	MA	41,988	VC+
Southeast Missouri State Univ	MO	10,596	C
Southern Nazarene Univ	OK	14,634	NC
Southern Oregon Univ	OR	12,186	C
Spring Hill College	AL	28,678	C
Springfield College	MA	25,000	C
SUNY/College at Fredonia	NY	12,771	VC
SUNY/College at Oneonta	NY	12,905	VC
SUNY/College of Environmental Science and Forestry	NY	15,000	VC
SUNY/Univ at Albany	NY	13,860	VC
SUNY/Univ at New Paltz	NY	12,480	VC
Stephen F. Austin State Univ	TX	7,930	C
Stillman College	AL	11,475	LC
Syracuse Univ	NY	38,655	HC
Tarleton State Univ	TX	8,952	C
Taylor Univ	IN	26,376	VC+
Temple Univ	PA	17,438	C
Texas A&M Univ at Commerce	TX	9,020	C
Texas A&M Univ at Kingsville	TX	6,800	LC
Thiel College	PA	24,580	C
Touro College	NY	17,000	VC
Trinity Christian College	IL	23,645	C
Trinity College	DC	24,150	LC
Trinity International Univ	IL	25,686	C
Tri-State Univ-Main Campus	IN	26,200	C
Truman State Univ	MO	11,242	HC
Tusculum College	TN	21,340	LC
Union Univ	TN	20,750	VC
Univ of Akron	OH	15,166	NC
Univ of Arkansas	AR	11,859	VC
Univ of Arkansas at Pine Bluff	AR	8,300	C
Univ of Bridgeport	CT	29,595	LC
Univ of Central Arkansas	AR	9,984	C
Univ of Cincinnati	OH	17,682	C
Univ of Dayton	OH	28,826	VC
Univ of Detroit Mercy	MI	27,000	C
Univ of Evansville	IN	28,320	VC
Univ of Findlay	OH	29,238	C
Univ of Georgia	GA	11,004	HC
Univ of Great Falls	MT	17,000	C
Univ of Hartford	CT	34,044	C
Univ of Iowa	IA	12,172	VC
Univ of Judaism College of A&S	CA	30,010	C
Univ of Mary	ND	15,374	C
Univ of Mass Amherst	MA	15,973	C+
Univ of Miami	FL	38,397	MC
Univ of Minn/Crookston	MN	13,157	LC
Univ of Minn/Morris	MN	15,472	VC
Univ of Minn/Twin Cities	MN	13,165	HC
Univ of Missouri/Rolla	MO	13,332	HC
Univ of Nebr at Kearney	NE	9,000	NC
Univ of Nebr at Lincoln	NE	11,401	VC
Univ of New Haven	CT	31,794	C
Univ of New Orleans	LA	7,370	C
Univ of N Car at Greensboro	NC	8,993	C
Univ of Notre Dame	IN	39,552	MC
Univ of PR/Mayaguez	PR	1,250	C
Univ of Rio Grande	OH	8,728	NC
Univ of St. Francis	IL	25,430	C
Univ of St. Francis	IN	20,970	C
Univ of Sioux Falls	SD	20,800	C
Univ of Southern Indiana	IN	12,590	LC
Univ of Southern Miss	MS	10,112	C
Univ of Tenn at Knoxville	TN	11,720	C
Univ of Tenn at Martin	TN	8,693	C
Univ of Tulsa	OK	25,348	HC
Univ of West Alabama	AL	7,611	C
Univ of West Florida	FL	8,559	C
Univ of Wisc/Milwaukee	WI	9,427	LC
Univ of Wisc/River Falls	WI	9,722	LC
Urbana Univ	OH	21,190	C
Ursuline College	OH	25,456	C
Utah State Univ	UT	8,002	VC
Vanguard Univ of Southern Calif	CA	27,071	C
Vassar College	NY	41,700	MC
Virginia Intermont College	VA	22,200	C
Virginia Polytechnic Inst and State Univ	VA	10,834	VC
Walsh Univ	OH	23,440	C
Washington State Univ	WA	12,260	C
Washington Univ in St. Louis	MO	42,106	MC
Waynesburg College	PA	21,230	C
West Chester Univ of Pennsylvania	PA	12,355	C+
West Liberty State College	WV	9,142	LC
West Texas A&M Univ	TX	8,452	C
Western Carolina Univ	NC	7,000	C
Western Mich Univ	MI	13,299	C
Western New Mexico Univ	NM	7,233	LC
Westminster College	PA	31,290	C+
Whitworth College	WA	29,428	VC+
Widener Univ	PA	27,275	C
Wilkes Univ	PA	30,886	C
Wilmington College	OH	2,806	NC
Wingate Univ	NC	23,300	C
Winona State Univ	MN	11,333	C
Wittenberg Univ	OH	34,596	VC
Wright State Univ	OH	13,616	LC
Xavier Univ of Louisiana	LA	17,600	C
York College of Pennsylvania	PA	16,550	VC
Youngstown State Univ	OH	12,613	NC

PREOPTOMETRY

School	ST	$IS	SR
Adams State College	CO	8,613	C
Arcadia Univ	PA	33,570	VC
Ashland Univ	OH	25,000	C
Auburn Univ	AL	12,230	VC
Cardinal Stritch Univ	WI	21,910	C
Carroll College	MT	23,324	C+
Central Mich Univ	MI	12,244	C
Colo State Univ-Pueblo	CO	7,821	LC
Eastern Mich Univ	MI	12,897	C
Florida State Univ	FL	9,028	HC
Freed-Hardeman Univ	TN	16,370	NC
Gannon Univ	PA	26,100	C
Hofstra Univ	NY	32,630	VC
Indiana Univ South Bend	IN	4,989	LC
Indiana Univ-Purdue Univ Indianapolis	IN	10,959	C
Iowa Wesleyan College	IA	22,140	C
Juniata College	PA	33,130	C
Le Moyne College	NY	29,570	VC
Lehigh Univ	PA	42,690	HC+
Lewis Univ	IL	23,050	C+
Lipscomb Univ	TN	20,967	VC
Louisiana College	LA	13,450	C
Missouri Southern State Univ	MO	8,396	NC
Newman Univ	KS	21,106	C
Southeast Missouri State Univ	MO	10,596	C
Stephen F. Austin State Univ	TX	7,930	C
Trinity Christian College	IL	23,645	C
Truman State Univ	MO	11,242	HC
Univ of Arkansas	AR	11,859	VC
Univ of Central Arkansas	AR	9,984	C
Univ of Evansville	IN	28,320	VC
Univ of Hartford	CT	34,044	C
Univ of Tenn at Martin	TN	8,693	C
Western Carolina Univ	NC	7,000	C
Youngstown State Univ	OH	12,613	NC

PREOSTEOPATHY

School	ST	$IS	SR
Central Mich Univ	MI	12,244	C
Colo State Univ-Pueblo	CO	7,821	LC
Gannon Univ	PA	26,100	C
Hofstra Univ	NY	32,630	VC
Indiana Univ-Purdue Univ Indianapolis	IN	10,959	C
Mercyhurst College	PA	28,633	VC
Minn State Univ, Mankato	MN	10,276	LC
New York Inst of Technology	NY	28,126	VC
Youngstown State Univ	OH	12,613	NC

PREPHARMACY

School	ST	$IS	SR
Adams State College	CO	8,613	C
Alice Lloyd College	KY	4,900	C
Austin Peay State Univ	TN	7,535	C
Ball State Univ	IN	13,138	C
Barry Univ	FL	24,100	LC
Bellarmine Univ	KY	27,650	C+
Calvin College	MI	25,735	NC
Campbell Univ	NC	21,137	VC
Carroll College	MT	23,324	C+
Central Mich Univ	MI	12,244	C
Clemson Univ	SC	13,366	HC
College of Notre Dame of Maryland	MD	27,700	C
College of St. Benedict	MN	30,091	VC
College of the Ozarks	MO	4,130	VC+
Colo State Univ-Pueblo	CO	7,821	LC
Concord College	WV	9,708	C
Coppin State College	MD	10,200	LC
Eastern Mich Univ	MI	12,897	C
Florida State Univ	FL	9,028	HC
Freed-Hardeman Univ	TN	16,370	NC
Gannon Univ	PA	26,100	C
Goshen College	IN	22,850	VC
Huntingdon College	AL	23,090	VC
Indiana Univ South Bend	IN	4,989	LC
Indiana Univ-Purdue Univ Indianapolis	IN	10,959	C
Iona College	NY	30,878	VC
Juniata College	PA	33,130	C
Kent State Univ	OH	14,594	C
Le Moyne College	NY	29,570	VC
Lewis Univ	IL	23,050	C+
Lipscomb Univ	TN	20,967	VC
LIU/C.W. Post Campus	NY	28,282	C
Mars Hill College	NC	19,000	LC
Mercer Univ	GA	27,525	VC+
Mercyhurst College	PA	28,633	VC
Midwestern State Univ	TX	9,381	LC
Minn State Univ, Mankato	MN	10,276	LC
Minn State Univ, Moorhead	MN	7,000	LC
Missouri Southern State Univ	MO	8,396	NC
Montclair State Univ	NJ	16,327	C
Newman Univ	KS	21,106	C
North Georgia College and State Univ	GA	7,000	C
Northern Kentucky Univ	KY	6,670	NC
Northwest Missouri State Univ	MO	10,000	C
Notre Dame de Namur Univ	CA	32,790	LC
Ohio Univ	OH	15,921	C
Peru State College	NE	6,350	NC
Purdue Univ/West Lafayette	IN	13,458	VC
Roberts Wesleyan College	NY	26,378	C
Rockford College	IL	28,330	VC
Roosevelt Univ	IL	22,605	VC
St. John's Univ	MN	29,749	VC
St. Joseph's College of Maine	ME	29,185	C
St. Martin's Univ	WA	27,555	C
St. Vincent College	PA	26,160	VC
St. Xavier Univ	IL	23,160	C
Southeast Missouri State Univ	MO	10,596	C
Southern Nazarene Univ	OK	14,634	NC
SUNY/College of Environmental Science and Forestry	NY	15,000	VC
Stephen F. Austin State Univ	TX	7,930	C
Tarleton State Univ	TX	8,952	C
Texas A&M Univ at Commerce	TX	9,020	C
Texas A&M Univ at Kingsville	TX	6,800	LC
Thiel College	PA	24,580	C

ST = STATE $IS = IN-STATE COSTS   SR = SELECTOR RATING

School	ST	$IS	SR
Truman State Univ	MO	11,242	HC
Union Univ	TN	20,750	NC
Univ of Akron	OH	15,166	NC
Univ of Arkansas	AR	11,859	VC
Univ of Arkansas at Pine Bluff	AR	8,300	C
Univ of Central Arkansas	AR	9,984	C
Univ of Evansville	IN	28,320	VC
Univ of Florida	FL	9,354	HC
Univ of Houston	TX	7,000	C
Univ of Miami	FL	38,397	MC
Univ of Minn/Crookston	MN	13,157	LC
Univ of Minn/Twin Cities	MN	13,165	HC
Univ of Nebr at Lincoln	NE	11,401	VC
Univ of N Car at Greensboro	NC	8,993	C
Univ of Tenn at Martin	TN	8,693	C
Univ of the Pacific	CA	34,380	VC
Univ of Wisc/River Falls	WI	9,722	C
Washington Univ in St. Louis	MO	42,106	MC
West Liberty State College	WV	9,142	LC
West Texas A&M Univ	TX	8,452	C
Western Carolina Univ	NC	7,000	C
Western New Mexico Univ	NM	7,233	LC
Wilkes Univ	PA	30,886	C
Wingate Univ	NC	23,300	C
Xavier Univ	OH	30,490	HC
Youngstown State Univ	OH	12,613	NC

PREPHYSICAL THERAPY

School	ST	$IS	SR
Walsh Univ	OH	23,440	C
Waynesburg College	PA	21,230	C

PREPODIATRY

School	ST	$IS	SR
Colo State Univ-Pueblo	CO	7,821	LC
Gannon Univ	PA	26,100	C
Hofstra Univ	NY	32,630	VC
Juniata College	PA	33,130	VC
Le Moyne College	NY	29,570	VC
Minn State Univ, Mankato	MN	10,276	LC
Univ of Arkansas	AR	11,859	VC
Wilkes Univ	PA	30,886	C

PREVENTIVE/WELLNESS HEALTH CARE

School	ST	$IS	SR
Central Mich Univ	MI	12,244	C
Oakland Univ	MI	11,936	C
Southeast Missouri State Univ	MO	10,596	C
Univ of New England	ME	31,005	C

PREVETERINARY SCIENCE

School	ST	$IS	SR
Adams State College	CO	8,613	C
Alabama A&M Univ	AL	8,890	C
Albertus Magnus College	CT	25,336	C
Andrews Univ	MI	21,786	C
Arcadia Univ	PA	33,570	VC
Ashland Univ	OH	25,000	C
Auburn Univ	AL	12,230	VC
Bellarmine Univ	KY	27,650	C+
Beloit College	WI	32,808	HC
Calvin College	MI	25,735	NC
Cardinal Stritch Univ	WI	21,910	C
Carroll College	MT	23,324	C+
Clemson Univ	SC	13,366	NC
College of St. Benedict	MN	30,091	VC
College of the Ozarks	MO	4,130	VC+
Colo State Univ-Pueblo	CO	7,821	LC
Concordia College: Moorhead	MN	22,475	VC
Cornerstone Univ and Grand Rapids Theological Seminary	MI	21,350	NC
Drury Univ	MO	20,117	VC
Eastern Washington Univ	WA	10,608	C
Edinboro Univ of Pennsylvania	PA	11,809	LC
Florida State Univ	FL	9,028	HC
Freed-Hardeman Univ	TN	16,370	NC
Gannon Univ	PA	26,100	C
George Fox Univ	OR	28,490	C
Goshen College	IN	22,850	VC
Graceland Univ	IA	19,700	C
Hillsdale College	MI	24,160	HC
Hofstra Univ	NY	32,630	VC
Indiana Univ South Bend	IN	4,989	LC
Indiana Univ-Purdue Univ Indianapolis	IN	10,959	C
Iona College	NY	30,878	VC
Iowa Wesleyan College	IA	22,140	C
Juniata College	PA	33,130	VC
Keuka College	NY	26,050	C
Le Moyne College	NY	29,570	VC
LeTourneau Univ	TX	21,200	C
Lewis Univ	IL	23,050	C+
Louisiana College	LA	13,450	C
MacMurray College	IL	20,755	C
Mars Hill College	NC	19,000	LC
Mercyhurst College	PA	28,633	VC
Midwestern State Univ	TX	9,381	LC

School	ST	$IS	SR
Minn State Univ, Mankato	MN	10,276	LC
Minn State Univ, Moorhead	MN	7,000	LC
Missouri Southern State Univ	MO	8,396	NC
Mount St. Mary College	NY	25,250	C
Newman Univ	KS	21,106	C
N Car State Univ	NC	11,824	HC
North Central College	IL	28,926	VC
N Dak State Univ	ND	8,500	C
North Georgia College and State Univ	GA	7,000	C
Northern Kentucky Univ	KY	6,670	NC
Northern Mich Univ	MI	12,340	LC
Northwest Missouri State Univ	MO	10,000	C
Notre Dame de Namur Univ	CA	32,790	LC
Ohio Wesleyan Univ	OH	35,830	VC+
Okla State Univ	OK	10,213	VC
Olivet College	MI	19,984	C
Peru State College	NE	6,350	NC
Purdue Univ/West Lafayette	IN	13,458	VC
Rivier College	NH	26,600	C
Roberts Wesleyan College	NY	26,378	C
Rochester Inst of Technology	NY	32,070	VC+
Rockford College	IL	28,330	VC
Roger Williams Univ	RI	30,500	C
Roosevelt Univ	IL	22,605	VC
St. John's Univ	MN	29,749	VC
St. Martin's Univ	WA	27,555	C
St. Mary-of-the-Woods College	IN	25,480	C
St. Vincent College	PA	26,160	VC
Seton Hill Univ	PA	28,810	C
Southeast Missouri State Univ	MO	10,596	C
Spring Hill College	AL	28,678	C
Stephen F. Austin State Univ	TX	7,930	C
Syracuse Univ	NY	38,655	HC
Tarleton State Univ	TX	8,952	C
Texas A&M Univ at Kingsville	TX	6,800	LC
Thiel College	PA	24,580	C
Truman State Univ	MO	11,242	HC
Univ of Akron	OH	15,166	NC
Univ of Central Arkansas	AR	9,984	C
Univ of Evansville	IN	28,320	VC
Univ of Findlay	OH	29,238	C
Univ of Georgia	GA	11,004	HC
Univ of Illinois at Urbana-Champaign	IL	15,800	HC+
Univ of Maryland/College Park	MD	16,036	HC
Univ of Mass Amherst	MA	15,973	C+
Univ of Miami	FL	38,397	MC
Univ of Minn/Crookston	MN	13,157	LC
Univ of Minn/Twin Cities	MN	13,165	HC
Univ of New Hampshire	NH	16,810	VC
Univ of New Haven	CT	31,794	C
Univ of New Orleans	LA	7,370	C
Univ of N Car at Greensboro	NC	8,993	C
Univ of Rio Grande	OH	8,728	NC
Univ of St. Francis	IL	25,430	C
Univ of Tenn at Knoxville	TN	11,720	C
Virginia Intermont College	VA	22,200	LC
Walsh Univ	OH	23,440	C
Washington Univ in St. Louis	MO	42,106	MC
Waynesburg College	PA	21,230	C
West Texas A&M Univ	TX	8,452	C
Western Carolina Univ	NC	7,000	C
Wilkes Univ	PA	30,886	C
Wilmington College	OH	2,806	NC
Wingate Univ	NC	23,300	C
Winona State Univ	MN	11,333	C
Youngstown State Univ	OH	12,613	NC

PRINTING TECHNOLOGY

School	ST	$IS	SR
Georgia Southern Univ	GA	9,762	C
Missouri State Univ	MO	10,748	C+
Pennsylvania College of Technology	PA	16,980	LC
Rochester Inst of Technology	NY	32,070	VC+

PRINTMAKING

School	ST	$IS	SR
Aquinas College	MI	23,750	C
Atlanta College of Art	GA	18,630	SP
Bennington College	VT	41,890	HC
Birmingham-Southern College	AL	28,494	VC+
Bradley Univ	IL	25,280	VC
Calif College of the Arts	CA	34,325	SP
Cal State, Fullerton	CA	10,990	C
Cal State, San Bernardino	CA	12,563	LC
Cleveland Inst of Art	OH	34,109	SP
College for Creative Studies	MI	24,000	VC
College of Visual Arts	MN	18,040	SP
Drake Univ	IA	27,632	VC+
Edinboro Univ of Pennsylvania	PA	11,809	LC
Howard Univ	DC	18,481	C+

School	ST	$IS	SR
Indiana Univ Bloomington	IN	13,356	VC
Indiana Univ-Purdue Univ Indianapolis	IN	10,959	C
Indiana Wesleyan Univ	IN	22,074	C+
Kansas City Art Inst	MO	29,542	SP
Kendall College of Art and Design of Ferris State Univ	MI	11,870	SP
Maine College of Art	ME	28,820	SP
Maryland Inst College of Art	MD	34,450	SP
Mass College of Art	MA	16,650	SP
Milwaukee Inst of Art and Design	WI	28,700	SP
Minneapolis College of Art and Design	MN	31,110	SP
Montserrat College of Art	MA	25,929	SP
Ohio Univ	OH	15,921	C
Pacific Northwest College of Art	OR	17,296	SP
Rhode Island School of Design	RI	38,130	SP
San Francisco Art Inst	CA	25,640	SP
School of the Art Inst of Chicago	IL	37,800	SP
Shepherd Univ	WV	10,066	C
SUNY/College at Buffalo	NY	11,903	C+
Syracuse Univ	NY	38,655	HC
Texas A&M Univ at Commerce	TX	9,020	C
Univ of Dallas	TX	27,432	VC+
Univ of Georgia	GA	11,004	HC
Univ of Hartford	CT	34,044	C
Univ of Houston	TX	7,000	C
Univ of Kansas	KS	10,915	VC
Univ of Miami	FL	38,397	MC
Univ of Mich/Ann Arbor	MI	16,587	HC+
Univ of North Texas	TX	7,800	C
Univ of Oregon	OR	13,108	VC
Univ of the Arts	PA	32,330	SP
Univ of Washington	WA	10,400	VC
Washington Univ in St. Louis	MO	42,106	MC
Youngstown State Univ	OH	12,613	NC

PSYCHOBIOLOGY

School	ST	$IS	SR
Albright College	PA	33,920	C
Arcadia Univ	PA	33,570	VC
Averett Univ	VA	24,920	C
Centre College	KY	30,810	VC
Earlham College	IN	33,604	HC
Florida Atlantic Univ	FL	11,221	C
Hamilton College	NY	41,660	MC
Hiram College	OH	28,700	VC
La Sierra Univ	CA	24,327	C+
Lebanon Valley College	PA	31,700	VC
Lincoln Univ	PA	13,658	C+
Mount Holyoke College	MA	42,148	HC+
Occidental College	CA	40,185	MC
Quinnipiac Univ	CT	34,640	VC
Ripon College	WI	27,160	C+
Simmons College	MA	35,640	VC
SUNY/Univ at Binghamton	NY	13,988	HC
Swarthmore College	PA	41,280	MC
Univ of Calif at Los Angeles	CA	17,681	MC
Univ of Calif at Santa Cruz	CA	19,174	VC
Univ of Evansville	IN	28,320	VC
Univ of Miami	FL	38,397	MC
Univ of New England	ME	31,005	C
Univ of Pennsylvania	PA	41,766	MC
Univ of Southern Calif	CA	41,618	MC
Wheaton College	MA	40,180	HC+
Wilson College	PA	27,660	C

PSYCHOLOGY

School	ST	$IS	SR
Abilene Christian Univ	TX	20,830	C
Adams State College	CO	8,613	C
Adelphi Univ	NY	27,000	VC
Adrian College	MI	23,000	C
Agnes Scott College	GA	32,070	HC
Alabama A&M Univ	AL	8,890	C
Alabama State Univ	AL	7,658	C
Alaska Pacific Univ	AK	25,142	C
Albany State Univ	GA	5,770	C+
Albertson College of Idaho	ID	21,095	VC
Albertus Magnus College	CT	25,336	C
Albion College	MI	26,000	VC
Albright College	PA	33,920	C
Alcorn State Univ	MS	8,190	LC
Alderson-Broaddus College	WV	24,006	C
Alfred Univ	NY		C
Allegheny College	PA	33,500	HC
Alma College	MI	28,544	VC
Alvernia College	PA	26,388	C
Alverno College	WI	21,088	C
American International College	MA	28,710	LC
American Univ	DC	38,719	HC+
Amherst College	MA	41,990	MC
Anderson Univ	IN	25,050	LC
Andrews Univ	MI	21,786	C
Angelo State Univ	TX	8,340	NC
Anna Maria College	MA	29,815	LC
Appalachian State Univ	NC	8,000	VC
Aquinas College	MI	23,750	C

School	ST	$IS	SR
Arcadia Univ	PA	33,570	VC
Arizona State Univ-Tempe	AZ	11,174	C
Arkansas State Univ	AR	9,630	C
Arkansas Tech Univ	AR	8,108	VC
Armstrong Atlantic State Univ	GA	7,394	C
Asbury College	KY	23,762	VC
Ashford Univ	IA	20,370	C
Ashland Univ	OH	25,000	C
Assumption College	MA	32,875	C
Atlantic Union College	MA	17,600	LC
Auburn Univ	AL	12,230	VC
Auburn Univ Montgomery	AL	9,530	NC
Augsburg College	MN	28,300	C
Augusta State Univ	GA	2,920	C
Augustana College	IL	29,862	VC+
Augustana College	SD	24,380	VC
Aurora Univ	IL	20,645	C
Austin College	TX	27,871	HC
Austin Peay State Univ	TN	7,535	C
Averett Univ	VA	24,920	C
Avila Univ	MO	22,100	C
Azusa Pacific Univ	CA	28,546	VC
Baker Univ	KS	22,190	C
Baldwin-Wallace College	OH	27,256	VC
Ball State Univ	IN	13,138	C
Barry Univ	FL	24,100	LC
Barton College	NC	22,316	C
Bates College	ME	42,100	MC
Bay Path College	MA	29,362	C
Baylor Univ	TX	27,555	HC
Becker College	MA	24,300	LC
Belhaven College	MS	19,530	NC
Bellarmine Univ	KY	27,650	C+
Bellevue Univ	NE	4,440	NC
Belmont Abbey College	NC	25,314	C
Belmont Univ	TN	24,110	VC
Beloit College	WI	32,808	HC
Bemidji State Univ	MN	11,180	LC
Benedictine College	KS	21,968	C
Benedictine Univ	IL	25,710	C
Bennett College	NC	11,500	C
Bennington College	VT	41,890	HC
Berea College	KY	5,496	VC+
Berry College	GA	24,342	VC
Bethany College	KS	20,660	LC
Bethany College	WV	21,395	C
Bethel College	IN	19,680	C
Bethel College	KS	21,650	C
Bethel College	TN	16,066	NC
Bethel Univ	MN	29,840	VC
Bethune-Cookman College	FL	17,922	LC
Biola Univ	CA	29,372	VC
Birmingham-Southern College	AL	28,494	VC+
Black Hills State Univ	SD	7,800	C
Blackburn College	IL	13,690	C
Bloomfield College	NJ	22,500	C
Bloomsburg Univ of Pennsylvania	PA	11,602	C
Blue Mountain College	MS	11,086	C
Bluefield College	VA	17,230	C+
Bluffton College	OH	26,110	C
Boise State Univ	ID	9,438	LC
Boston College	MA	41,608	MC
Boston Univ	MA	42,046	HC+
Bowdoin College	ME	41,660	MC
Bowie State Univ	MD	10,880	C+
Bowling Green State Univ	OH	14,994	C
Bradley Univ	IL	25,280	VC
Brandeis Univ	MA	41,551	MC
Brenau Univ Women's College	GA	23,950	VC
Brescia Univ	KY	14,240	C
Brewton-Parker College	GA	14,220	LC
Briar Cliff Univ	IA	23,550	LC
Bridgewater College	VA	27,790	C
Bridgewater State College	MA	12,120	C
Brigham Young Univ	UT	9,200	VC
Brigham Young Univ/Hawaii	HI	7,740	HC+
Brown Univ	RI	42,015	MC
Bryan College	TN	19,270	C
Bryn Mawr College	PA	42,780	HC+
Bucknell Univ	PA	39,660	MC
Buena Vista Univ	IA	27,742	C
Burlington College	VT	14,670	SP
Butler Univ	IN	31,944	VC+
Cabrini College	PA	33,340	C
Caldwell College	NJ	26,450	LC
Calif Baptist Univ	CA	23,780	C
Calif Lutheran Univ	CA	27,800	C
Calif Polytechnic State Univ	CA	12,390	VC
Calif State Polytechnic Univ, Pomona	CA	18,053	C+
Cal State East Bay	CA	10,856	LC
Cal State, Bakersfield	CA	6,125	LC
Cal State, Chico	CA	11,395	C
Cal State, Dominguez Hills	CA	10,220	LC
Cal State, Fresno	CA	10,037	LC
Cal State, Fullerton	CA	10,990	C
Cal State, Long Beach	CA	9,512	C
Cal State, Los Angeles	CA	5,900	C
Cal State, Northridge	CA	9,036	LC
Cal State, Sacramento	CA	11,122	C+
Cal State, San Bernardino	CA	12,563	LC
Cal State, San Marcos	CA	1,800	LC

ST = STATE $IS = IN-STATE COSTS   SR = SELECTOR RATING

School	ST	$IS	SR
Cal State, Stanislaus	CA	11,283	C
Calif Univ of Pennsylvania	PA	14,217	C
Calumet College of St. Joseph	IN	9,500	LC
Calvin College	MI	25,735	NC
Cambridge College	MA	11,055	SP
Cameron Univ	OK	6,314	NC
Campbell Univ	NC	21,137	VC
Campbellsville Univ	KY	21,328	C
Canisius College	NY	32,257	VC
Capital Univ	OH	30,444	C
Cardinal Stritch Univ	WI	21,910	C
Carleton College	MN	40,467	MC
Carlos Albizu Univ	FL	11,109	C
Carlow Univ	PA	24,313	C
Carnegie Mellon Univ	PA	32,700	MC
Carroll College	MT	23,324	C+
Carroll College	WI	24,860	C
Carson-Newman College	TN	16,800	C
Carthage College	WI	26,000	C
Cascade College	OR	17,980	NC
Case Western Reserve Univ	OH	37,314	MC
Castleton State College	VT	13,158	C
Catawba College	NC	25,000	C
Catholic Univ of America	DC	35,838	VC
Cazenovia College	NY	26,900	C
Cedar Crest College	PA	30,615	C
Cedarville Univ	OH	21,904	VC
Centenary College	NJ	28,870	LC
Centenary College of Louisiana	LA	24,760	VC
Central College	IA	26,774	VC
Central Conn State Univ	CT	13,620	C
Central Methodist Univ	MO	18,000	C
Central Mich Univ	MI	12,244	C
Central Missouri State Univ	MO	10,000	C
Central State Univ	OH	9,010	C+
Central Univ of Bayamon	PR	3,335	
Central Washington Univ	WA	11,730	C
Centre College	KY	30,810	VC
Chadron State College	NE	6,350	NC
Chaminade Univ of Honolulu	HI	23,320	LC
Champlain College	VT	24,605	C
Chapman Univ	CA	37,550	VC
Charleston Southern Univ	SC	17,800	C
Chatham College	PA	27,290	C+
Chestnut Hill College	PA	26,600	LC
Cheyney Univ of Pennsylvania	PA	11,497	LC
Chicago State Univ	IL	10,915	C+
Christian Brothers Univ	TN	24,650	VC
Christopher Newport Univ	VA	13,326	VC
Citadel, The	SC		C+
CUNY/Baruch College	NY	4,320	C
CUNY/Brooklyn College	NY	4,377	C+
CUNY/City College	NY		C
CUNY/College of Staten Island	NY	4,328	NC
CUNY/Herbert H. Lehman College	NY	4,000	LC
CUNY/Hunter College	NY	8,000	C+
CUNY/Medgar Evers College	NY	4,250	NC
CUNY/Queens College	NY	4,356	C
CUNY/York College	NY	4,242	NC
Claremont McKenna College	CA	42,920	MC
Clarion Univ of Pennsylvania	PA	11,844	C
Clark Atlanta Univ	GA	20,960	LC
Clark Univ	MA	35,165	VC+
Clarke College	IA	25,390	C
Clarkson Univ	NY	34,930	VC
Clearwater Christian College	FL	13,160	LC
Clemson Univ	SC	13,366	HC
Cleveland State Univ	OH	10,798	NC
Coastal Carolina Univ	SC	13,140	C
Coe College	IA	27,440	VC
Coker College	SC	21,600	C
Colby College	ME	41,770	MC
Colby-Sawyer College	NH	27,852	LC
Colgate Univ	NY	41,170	MC
College Misericordia	PA	27,950	C
College of Charleston	SC	13,616	VC
College of Mount St. Vincent	NY	28,000	C
College of Mount St. Joseph	OH	24,860	C
College of New Jersey	NJ	18,315	MC
College of New Rochelle	NY	28,396	C+
College of Notre Dame of Maryland	MD	27,700	C
College of Our Lady of the Elms	MA	21,000	C
College of St. Benedict	MN	30,091	VC
College of St. Catherine	MN	27,505	VC
College of St. Elizabeth	NJ	28,495	C
College of St. Joseph	VT	20,900	NC
College of St. Mary	NE	23,938	C
College of St. Rose	NY	25,684	C
College of St. Scholastica	MN	28,456	C+
College of Santa Fe	NM	28,978	C
College of the Holy Cross	MA	40,664	MC
College of the Ozarks	MO	4,130	VC+
College of the Southwest	NM	12,420	C+
College of William and Mary	VA	14,147	MC
College of Wooster	OH	31,310	VC+
Colo Christian Univ	CO	21,182	VC
Colo College	CO	37,668	HC
Colo State Univ-Fort Collins	CO	10,878	C+
Colo State Univ-Pueblo	CO	7,821	LC
Columbia College	MO	16,900	C
Columbia College	SC	24,982	LC
Columbia Union College	MD	23,536	LC
Columbia Univ/Barnard College	NY	38,000	MC
Columbia Univ/Columbia College	NY	42,584	MC
Columbia Univ/School of General Studies	NY	41,516	C
Columbus State Univ	GA	8,664	C
Concord College	WV	9,708	C
Concordia College: Moorhead	MN	22,475	VC
Concordia Univ	CA	26,780	VC
Concordia Univ	OR	24,400	C
Concordia Univ Nebr	NE	20,500	C+
Concordia Univ St.Paul	MN	27,776	C
Concordia Univ Wisc	WI	22,660	VC
Concordia Univ, Ann Arbor	MI	25,153	C+
Concordia Univ, River Forest	IL	26,300	C
Conn College	CT	41,975	MC
Converse College	SC	24,800	VC
Coppin State College	MD	10,200	LC
Cornell College	IA	30,110	VC+
Cornell Univ	NY	41,717	MC
Cornerstone Univ and Grand Rapids Theological Seminary	MI	21,350	NC
Covenant College	GA	26,460	VC+
Creighton Univ	NE	29,918	VC+
Crichton College	TN	15,300	C
Culver-Stockton College	MO	20,625	C
Cumberland Univ	TN	18,894	C
Curry College	MA	26,100	LC
Daemen College	NY	24,580	C
Dakota Wesleyan Univ	SD	17,832	C
Dallas Baptist Univ	TX	17,040	VC
Dana College	NE	22,390	C
Dartmouth College	NH	39,465	MC
Davidson College	NC	36,825	MC
Davis and Elkins College	WV	22,416	C
De Sales Univ	PA	28,580	VC
Defiance College	OH	24,790	C
Delaware State Univ	DE	8,130	LC
Delta State Univ	MS	7,709	C
Denison Univ	OH	37,040	HC
DePaul Univ	IL	29,835	VC
DePauw Univ	IN	32,100	HC
Dickinson College	PA	40,170	HC+
Dillard Univ	LA	17,500	VC
Doane College	NE	22,458	C
Dominican College	NY	26,630	LC
Dominican Univ	IL	26,370	C
Dominican Univ of Calif	CA	36,836	C
Dordt College	IA	20,325	VC
Dowling College	NY	22,110	LC
Drake Univ	IA	27,632	VC+
Drew Univ/College of Liberal Arts	NJ	39,698	VC
Drexel Univ	PA	27,700	VC
Drury Univ	MO	20,117	VC
Duke Univ	NC	41,239	MC
Duquesne Univ	PA	29,534	VC
D'Youville College	NY	23,660	C
Earlham College	IN	33,604	HC
East Carolina Univ	NC	10,000	C
East Central Univ	OK	6,207	C
East Stroudsburg Univ of Pennsylvania	PA	10,336	C
East Tenn State Univ	TN	8,497	C
East Texas Baptist Univ	TX	16,713	C
Eastern Conn State Univ	CT	13,554	C
Eastern Illinois Univ	IL	12,569	C
Eastern Kentucky Univ	KY	7,725	C
Eastern Mennonite Univ	VA	25,450	VC
Eastern Mich Univ	MI	12,897	C
Eastern Nazarene College	MA	19,500	LC
Eastern New Mexico Univ	NM	7,264	C
Eastern Oregon Univ	OR	10,400	NC
Eastern Univ	PA	24,075	C
Eastern Washington Univ	WA	10,608	C
Eckerd College	FL	35,492	VC
Edgewood College	WI	22,862	C
Edinboro Univ of Pennsylvania	PA	11,809	C
Edward Waters College	FL	14,374	LC
Elizabeth City State Univ	NC	5,700	LC
Elizabethtown College	PA	32,100	VC
Elmhurst College	IL	24,685	C
Elmira College	NY	37,200	VC
Elon Univ	NC	25,371	HC
Emmanuel College	MA	32,000	C+
Emory & Henry College	VA	26,570	C
Emory Univ	GA	40,546	MC
Emporia State Univ	KS	8,093	C
Endicott College	MA	30,156	C+
Erskine College	SC	25,468	VC
Eugene Lang College New School for Liberal Arts	NY	38,800	C+
Eureka College	IL	19,280	C
Evangel Univ	MO	17,380	C
Excelsior College	NY	995	SP
Fairfield Univ	CT	39,835	HC
Fairleigh Dickinson Univ/College at Florham	NJ	30,130	C
Fairleigh Dickinson Univ/Metropolitan Campus	NJ	28,590	C
Fairmont State	WV	8,400	LC
Fayetteville State Univ	NC	6,000	LC
Felician College	NJ	24,300	C
Ferrum College	VA	24,290	LC
Fisk Univ	TN	19,830	C
Fitchburg State College	MA	11,276	C
Flagler College	FL	13,790	VC+
Florida A&M Univ	FL	8,344	C
Florida Atlantic Univ	FL	11,221	C
Florida Inst of Technology	FL	29,720	VC
Florida International Univ	FL	9,215	VC
Florida Memorial College	FL	6,000	LC
Florida Southern College	FL	25,965	C
Florida State Univ	FL	9,028	HC
Fordham Univ	NY	36,000	HC
Fort Hays State Univ	KS	7,638	C
Fort Lewis College	CO	11,852	C
Fort Valley State Univ	GA	6,975	C
Framingham State College	MA	11,156	C
Francis Marion Univ	SC	11,114	C
Franciscan Univ of Steubenville	OH	20,300	VC
Franklin and Marshall College	PA	40,590	HC
Franklin College	IN		C
Franklin Pierce College	NH	31,700	C
Freed-Hardeman Univ	TN	16,370	NC
Fresno Pacific Univ	CA	25,454	C
Friends Univ	KS	16,250	LC
Frostburg State Univ	MD	12,672	C
Furman Univ	SC	33,264	HC+
Gallaudet Univ	DC	16,554	
Gannon Univ	PA	26,100	C
Gardner-Webb Univ	NC	21,500	C
Geneva College	PA	21,850	C
George Fox Univ	OR	28,490	C
George Mason Univ	VA	10,850	VC
George Washington Univ	DC	48,820	MC
Georgetown College	KY	24,950	C+
Georgetown Univ	DC	43,183	MC
Georgia College and State Univ	GA	11,020	C
Georgia Southern Univ	GA	9,762	C
Georgia Southwestern State Univ	GA	6,035	C
Georgia State Univ	GA	11,444	VC
Georgian Court College	NJ	20,000	LC
Gettysburg College	PA	39,864	HC
Gonzaga Univ	WA	30,218	HC
Gordon College	MA	29,194	C+
Goshen College	IN	22,850	VC
Goucher College	MD	36,225	VC
Grace College	IN	22,170	C
Graceland Univ	IA	19,700	C
Grambling State Univ	LA	6,538	NC
Grand Canyon Univ	AZ	32,000	LC
Grand Valley State Univ	MI	12,000	VC
Grand View College	IA	21,482	C
Green Mountain College	VT	32,164	C
Greensboro College	NC	23,000	C
Greenville College	IL	23,146	C
Grinnell College	IA	34,814	HC+
Grove City College	PA	15,784	HC+
Guilford College	NC	28,160	C+
Gustavus Adolphus College	MN	30,920	HC
Gwynedd-Mercy College	PA	26,080	C
Hamilton College	NY	41,660	MC
Hamline Univ	MN	27,070	VC
Hampden-Sydney College	VA	31,148	VC
Hampshire College	MA	37,120	HC
Hampton Univ	VA	19,468	C+
Hannibal-LaGrange College	MO	16,390	C
Hanover College	IN	28,150	HC
Harding Univ	AR	16,512	VC
Hardin-Simmons Univ	TX	18,641	VC
Hartwick College	NY	36,065	C+
Harvard Univ/Harvard College	MA	45,860	MC
Hastings College	NE	22,218	VC
Haverford College	PA	41,600	MC
Hawaii Pacific Univ	HI	21,080	C
Heidelberg College	OH	23,242	C
Henderson State Univ	AR	7,600	C
Hendrix College	AR	27,646	HC+
Heritage Univ	WA	6,800	NC
High Point Univ	NC	25,720	C
Hilbert College	NY	20,480	LC
Hillsdale College	MI	24,160	HC
Hiram College	OH	28,700	VC
Hobart and William Smith Colleges	NY	41,123	VC
Hofstra Univ	NY	32,630	VC
Hollins Univ	VA	31,105	C
Holy Family Univ	PA	25,740	C
Holy Names College	CA	27,980	NC
Hood College	MD	30,085	VC
Hope College	MI	28,208	VC+
Hope International Univ	CA	23,700	NC
Houghton College	NY	25,980	VC+
Houston Baptist Univ	TX	18,660	C
Howard Payne Univ	TX	17,115	C
Howard Univ	DC	18,481	C+
Humboldt State Univ	CA	11,176	C
Huntingdon College	AL	23,090	VC
Huntington Univ	IN	24,830	C
Husson College	ME	17,410	LC
Huston-Tillotson Univ	TX	14,232	LC
Idaho State Univ	ID	9,030	C
Illinois College	IL	21,900	C+
Illinois Inst of Technology	IL	26,465	HC+
Illinois State Univ	IL	12,839	C+
Illinois Wesleyan Univ	IL	34,050	HC+
Immaculata Univ	PA	25,350	C
Indiana Inst of Technology	IN	23,430	C
Indiana State Univ	IN	11,604	C
Indiana Univ Bloomington	IN	13,356	VC
Indiana Univ Kokomo	IN	4,835	LC
Indiana Univ Northwest	IN	4,902	LC
Indiana Univ of Pennsylvania	PA	11,209	C
Indiana Univ South Bend	IN	4,989	LC
Indiana Univ Southeast	IN	4,880	LC
Indiana Univ-Purdue Univ Fort Wayne	IN	5,067	LC
Indiana Univ-Purdue Univ Indianapolis	IN	10,959	C
Indiana Wesleyan Univ	IN	22,074	C+
Inter American Univ of PR/Fajardo Campus	PR	4,000	
Inter American Univ of PR/Metropolitan Campus	PR	4,320	
Inter American Univ of PR/Ponce Regional College	PR	3,700	
Inter American Univ of PR/San German	PR	6,720	
Iona College	NY	30,878	VC
Iowa State Univ	IA	11,831	VC
Iowa Wesleyan College	IA	22,140	C
Ithaca College	NY	35,144	VC
Jackson State Univ	MS	8,500	C
Jacksonville State Univ	AL	7,618	LC
Jacksonville Univ	FL	24,040	C
James Madison Univ	VA	12,010	VC
Jamestown College	ND	14,130	NC
John Brown Univ	AR	20,910	VC
John Carroll Univ	OH	27,658	C+
Johns Hopkins Univ	MD	42,044	MC
Johnson C. Smith Univ	NC	20,000	C
Johnson State College	VT	11,830	LC
Judson College	AL	16,522	C
Judson College	IL	25,130	C
Juniata College	PA	33,130	VC
Kalamazoo College	MI	32,442	VC+
Kansas State Univ	KS	10,516	VC
Kansas Wesleyan Univ	KS	21,400	VC
Kean Univ	NJ	15,880	C
Keene State College	NH	13,836	C
Kennesaw State Univ	GA	12,152	C
Kent State Univ	OH	14,594	C
Kentucky Christian College	KY	12,680	C
Kentucky State Univ	KY	10,089	LC
Kentucky Wesleyan College	KY	18,590	C
Kenyon College	OH	39,500	MC
Keuka College	NY	26,050	C
King College	TN	23,400	C
King's College	PA	29,810	C
Knox College	IL	32,385	VC+
Knoxville College	TN	6,200	LC
Kutztown Univ of Pennsylvania	PA	10,820	C
La Roche College	PA	24,724	LC
La Salle Univ	PA	34,950	C
La Sierra Univ	CA	24,327	C+
Lafayette College	PA	39,267	MC
LaGrange College	GA	22,874	C+
Lake Erie College	OH	27,725	C
Lake Forest College	IL	33,860	VC
Lake Superior State Univ	MI	12,842	LC
Lakeland College	WI	22,990	C
Lamar Univ	TX	6,820	LC
Lambuth Univ	TN	21,700	C+
Lander Univ	SC	10,600	C
Langston Univ	OK	2,308	LC
Lasell College	MA	26,250	C
Lawrence Tech Univ	MI	25,475	VC
Lawrence Univ	WI	33,958	HC+
Le Moyne College	NY	29,570	VC
Lebanon Valley College	PA	31,700	VC
Lee Univ	TN	14,780	NC
Lees-McRae College	NC	23,000	C
Lehigh Univ	PA	42,690	HC+
Lenoir-Rhyne College	NC	25,580	C
Lesley Univ	MA	34,950	C
LeTourneau Univ	TX	21,200	C
Lewis and Clark College	OR	35,358	VC+
Lewis Univ	IL	23,050	C+
Lewis-Clark State College	ID	6,990	C
Liberty Univ	VA	19,101	C
Limestone College	SC	19,840	C
Lincoln Memorial Univ	TN	18,144	C
Lincoln Univ	MO	8,000	NC
Lincoln Univ	PA	13,658	C+

ST = STATE $IS = IN-STATE COSTS   SR = SELECTOR RATING

ST = STATE **$IS** = IN-STATE COSTS **SR** = SELECTOR RATING

School	ST	$IS	SR
Southwestern Univ	TX	26,767	HC
Spalding Univ	KY	18,882	C
Spelman College	GA	24,650	VC
Spring Arbor Univ	MI	22,476	C
Spring Hill College	AL	28,678	C
Springfield College	MA	25,000	C
Stanford Univ	CA	41,557	MC
SUNY at Oswego	NY	13,662	VC
SUNY at Potsdam	NY	12,959	C
SUNY/College at Brockport	NY	12,747	VC
SUNY/College at Buffalo	NY	11,903	C+
SUNY/College at Cortland	NY	12,095	C
SUNY/College at Fredonia	NY	12,771	VC
SUNY/College at Geneseo	NY	12,910	HC+
SUNY/College at Old Westbury	NY	13,154	C
SUNY/College at Oneonta	NY	12,905	VC
SUNY/College at Purchase	NY	11,989	VC+
SUNY/Inst of Technology	NY	12,575	VC
SUNY/Univ at Albany	NY	13,860	VC
SUNY/Univ at Binghamton	NY	13,988	HC
SUNY/Univ at Buffalo	NY	13,694	VC
SUNY/Univ at New Paltz	NY	12,480	VC
SUNY/Univ at Stony Brook	NY	13,625	VC
Stephen F. Austin State Univ	TX	7,930	C
Stetson Univ	FL	32,725	VC
Stonehill College	MA	36,104	HC
Suffolk Univ	MA	33,160	C
Sul Ross State Univ	TX	6,600	LC
Susquehanna Univ	PA	33,465	VC
Swarthmore College	PA	41,280	MC
Sweet Briar College	VA	31,460	VC
Syracuse Univ	NY	38,655	HC
Tabor College	KS	21,614	NC
Talladega College	AL	11,240	LC
Taylor Univ	IN	26,376	VC+
Temple Univ	PA	17,438	C
Tenn State Univ	TN	9,048	LC
Tenn Tech Univ	TN	10,044	C
Tenn Wesleyan College	TN	18,650	C
Texas A&M Univ	TX	13,351	HC
Texas A&M Univ at Commerce	TX	9,020	C
Texas A&M Univ at Corpus Christi	TX	10,280	LC
Texas A&M Univ at Kingsville	TX	6,800	LC
Texas Christian Univ	TX	23,410	VC+
Texas Lutheran Univ	TX	23,530	C
Texas Southern Univ	TX	9,828	C
Texas State Univ - San Marcos	TX	10,862	C
Texas Tech Univ	TX	13,026	VC
Texas Wesleyan Univ	TX	18,700	C
Texas Woman's Univ	TX	7,804	LC
Thiel College	PA	24,580	C
Thomas College	ME	23,770	LC
Thomas Edison State College	NJ	3,780	SP
Thomas More College	KY	24,470	C
Thomas Univ	GA	11,520	NC
Tougaloo College	MS	15,975	NC
Touro College	NY	17,000	VC
Towson Univ	MD	13,924	VC
Transylvania Univ	KY	26,240	VC+
Trevecca Nazarene Univ	TN	19,594	C
Trinity Christian College	IL	23,645	C
Trinity College	CT	38,040	HC+
Trinity College	DC	24,150	LC
Trinity International Univ	IL	25,686	C
Trinity Univ	TX	30,157	HC+
Tri-State Univ-Main Campus	IN	26,200	C
Troy Univ	AL	8,916	C
Troy Univ Dothan Campus	AL	4,678	C
Troy Univ Montgomery Campus	AL	4,104	NC
Truman State Univ	MO	11,242	HC
Tufts Univ	MA	42,018	MC
Tulane Univ	LA	41,098	MC
Turabo Univ	PR	4,110	
Tusculum College	TN	21,340	LC
Tuskegee Univ	AL	18,860	LC
Union College	KY	18,920	C
Union College	NE	18,710	C
Union College	NY	41,595	HC
Union Inst & Univ	OH	8,912	SP
Union Univ	TN	20,750	VC
United States Air Force Academy	CO		HC+
Universidad Metropolitana	PR	3,330	
Univ of Akron	OH	15,166	NC
Univ of Alabama	AL	9,888	C
Univ of Alabama at Birmingham	AL	13,716	C
Univ of Alabama in Huntsville	AL	9,516	VC
Univ of Alaska Anchorage	AK	11,275	NC
Univ of Alaska Fairbanks	AK	10,101	C
Univ of Arizona	AZ	11,958	VC
Univ of Arkansas	AR	11,859	VC
Univ of Arkansas at Little Rock	AR	7,230	NC
Univ of Arkansas at Monticello	AR	7,325	NC
Univ of Arkansas at Pine Bluff	AR	8,300	C
Univ of at Calif Davis	CA	15,010	VC
Univ of Bridgeport	CT	29,595	LC
Univ of Calif at Berkeley	CA	18,141	HC+
Univ of Calif at Irvine	CA	16,475	HC
Univ of Calif at Los Angeles	CA	17,681	MC
Univ of Calif at Riverside	CA	16,625	C
Univ of Calif at San Diego	CA	16,102	HC
Univ of Calif at Santa Barbara	CA	11,800	VC
Univ of Calif at Santa Cruz	CA	19,174	VC
Univ of Central Arkansas	AR	9,984	C
Univ of Central Florida	FL	10,739	VC
Univ of Central Okla	OK	8,094	C
Univ of Charleston	WV	27,600	C
Univ of Chicago	IL	42,369	MC
Univ of Cincinnati	OH	17,682	C
Univ of Colo at Boulder	CO	13,352	C+
Univ of Colo at Colo Springs	CO	11,517	VC
Univ of Colo at Denver and Health Sciences Center	CO	5,021	C
Univ of Conn	CT	16,628	HC
Univ of Dallas	TX	27,432	VC+
Univ of Dayton	OH	28,826	VC
Univ of Delaware	DE	14,142	HC
Univ of Denver	CO	36,376	VC+
Univ of Detroit Mercy	MI	27,000	C
Univ of Dubuque	IA	23,390	C
Univ of Evansville	IN	28,320	VC
Univ of Findlay	OH	29,238	C
Univ of Florida	FL	9,354	HC
Univ of Georgia	GA	11,004	HC
Univ of Great Falls	MT	17,000	C
Univ of Hartford	CT	34,044	C
Univ of Hawaii at Hilo	HI	6,500	C
Univ of Hawaii at Manoa	HI	10,413	VC
Univ of Houston	TX	7,000	C
Univ of Idaho	ID	9,310	NC
Univ of Illinois at Chicago	IL	16,256	VC
Univ of Illinois at Urbana-Champaign	IL	15,800	HC+
Univ of Indianapolis	IN	25,090	C
Univ of Iowa	IA	12,172	VC
Univ of Judaism College of A&S	CA	30,010	C
Univ of Kansas	KS	10,915	VC
Univ of Kentucky	KY	7,800	C
Univ of La Verne	CA	33,470	C
Univ of Louisiana at Lafayette	LA	5,830	C
Univ of Louisiana at Monroe	LA	7,103	C
Univ of Louisville	KY	10,400	VC
Univ of Maine	ME	13,642	C
Univ of Maine at Farmington	ME	11,515	C
Univ of Mary	ND	15,374	C
Univ of Mary Hardin-Baylor	TX	19,428	C
Univ of Mary Washington	VA	11,636	HC
Univ of Maryland/Baltimore County	MD	16,642	VC+
Univ of Maryland/College Park	MD	16,036	HC
Univ of Maryland/Univ College	MD	5,640	SP
Univ of Mass Amherst	MA	15,973	C+
Univ of Mass Boston	MA	8,024	C
Univ of Mass Dartmouth	MA	15,985	C
Univ of Mass Lowell	MA	14,327	VC
Univ of Memphis	TN	11,153	C
Univ of Miami	FL	38,397	MC
Univ of Mich/Ann Arbor	MI	16,587	HC+
Univ of Mich/Dearborn	MI	7,000	VC
Univ of Mich/Flint	MI	6,398	C
Univ of Minn/Duluth	MN	13,974	C
Univ of Minn/Morris	MN	15,472	VC
Univ of Minn/Twin Cities	MN	13,165	HC
Univ of Miss	MS	9,000	C
Univ of Missouri/Columbia	MO	13,500	VC
Univ of Missouri/Kansas City	MO	15,000	VC
Univ of Missouri/Rolla	MO	13,332	HC
Univ of Missouri/St. Louis	MO	14,046	VC
Univ of Mobile	AL	16,880	C
Univ of Montana	MT	10,602	C
Univ of Montevallo	AL	9,630	C
Univ of Nebr at Kearney	NE	9,000	NC
Univ of Nebr at Lincoln	NE	11,401	VC
Univ of Nebr at Omaha	NE	11,235	C
Univ of Nevada/Las Vegas	NV	11,566	C
Univ of Nevada/Reno	NV	12,155	NC
Univ of New England	ME	31,005	C
Univ of New Hampshire	NH	16,810	VC
Univ of New Haven	CT	31,794	C
Univ of New Mexico	NM	11,253	C
Univ of New Orleans	LA	7,370	C
Univ of North Alabama	AL	8,992	C
Univ of N Car at Asheville	NC	9,237	VC
Univ of N Car at Chapel Hill	NC	11,129	MC
Univ of N Car at Charlotte	NC	9,101	C
Univ of N Car at Greensboro	NC	8,993	C
Univ of N Car at Pembroke	NC	7,940	LC
Univ of N Car at Wilmington	NC	10,107	VC
Univ of N Dak	ND	10,114	VC
Univ of North Florida	FL	9,908	VC
Univ of North Texas	TX	7,800	C
Univ of Northern Colo	CO	10,249	C
Univ of Northern Iowa	IA	11,133	C
Univ of Notre Dame	IN	39,552	MC
Univ of Okla	OK	10,769	VC+
Univ of Oregon	OR	13,108	VC
Univ of Pennsylvania	PA	41,766	MC
Univ of Pittsburgh at Bradford	PA	17,008	C
Univ of Pittsburgh at Greensburg	PA	17,640	C
Univ of Pittsburgh at Johnstown	PA	16,740	LC
Univ of Pittsburgh at Pittsburgh	PA	18,866	HC
Univ of Portland	OR	32,300	VC
Univ of PR/Cayey Univ College	PR	1,250	
Univ of PR/Mayaguez	PR	1,250	
Univ of PR/Rio Piedras	PR	5,750	
Univ of Puget Sound	WA	35,600	HC
Univ of Redlands	CA	36,160	VC
Univ of Rhode Island	RI	15,398	C
Univ of Richmond	VA	40,510	MC
Univ of Rio Grande	OH	8,728	NC
Univ of Rochester	NY	41,135	MC
Univ of St. Francis	IL	25,430	C
Univ of St. Francis	IN	20,970	C
Univ of St. Mary	KS	18,900	C
Univ of St. Thomas	MN	28,000	VC
Univ of St. Thomas	TX	23,810	VC
Univ of San Diego	CA	40,620	HC
Univ of San Francisco	CA	37,560	VC
Univ of Science and Arts of Okla	OK	7,650	C
Univ of Scranton	PA	31,100	VC
Univ of Sioux Falls	SD	20,800	C
Univ of South Alabama	AL	8,930	LC
Univ of S Car at Aiken	SC	11,718	LC
Univ of S Car at Columbia	SC	13,397	VC
Univ of S Car Upstate	SC	11,957	C
Univ of S Dak	SD	9,068	C
Univ of South Florida	FL	10,284	VC
Univ of Southern Calif	CA	41,618	MC
Univ of Southern Indiana	IN	12,590	LC
Univ of Southern Maine	ME	12,614	C
Univ of Southern Miss	MS	10,112	C
Univ of Tampa	FL	25,784	C
Univ of Tenn at Chattanooga	TN	7,790	C
Univ of Tenn at Knoxville	TN	11,720	C
Univ of Tenn at Martin	TN	8,693	C
Univ of Texas at Arlington	TX	7,195	LC
Univ of Texas at Austin	TX	14,610	HC
Univ of Texas at Dallas	TX	13,244	HC
Univ of Texas at El Paso	TX	8,764	NC
Univ of Texas at San Antonio	TX	11,325	LC
Univ of Texas-Pan American	TX	7,290	C+
Univ of the Cumberlands	KY	18,184	C
Univ of the District of Columbia	DC	2,070	LC
Univ of the Incarnate Word	TX	23,306	C
Univ of the Ozarks	AR	19,250	C
Univ of the Pacific	CA	34,380	VC
Univ of the Sacred Heart	PR	5,590	
Univ of the Sciences in Philadelphia	PA	33,380	VC
Univ of the South	TN	34,645	HC
Univ of Toledo	OH	15,806	NC
Univ of Tulsa	OK	25,348	HC
Univ of Utah	UT	10,162	VC
Univ of Vermont	VT	18,080	VC
Univ of Virginia	VA	13,759	MC
Univ of Virginia's College at Wise	VA	11,076	C
Univ of Washington	WA	10,400	VC
Univ of West Alabama	AL	7,611	C
Univ of West Florida	FL	8,559	C
Univ of West Georgia	GA	8,838	C
Univ of Wisc/Eau Claire	WI	9,915	VC
Univ of Wisc/Green Bay	WI	9,415	VC
Univ of Wisc/La Crosse	WI	10,045	VC
Univ of Wisc/Madison	WI	13,117	HC
Univ of Wisc/Milwaukee	WI	9,427	C
Univ of Wisc/Oshkosh	WI	10,426	LC
Univ of Wisc/Parkside	WI	10,181	LC
Univ of Wisc/Platteville	WI	9,779	NC
Univ of Wisc/River Falls	WI	9,722	C
Univ of Wisc/Stevens Point	WI	9,384	VC
Univ of Wisc/Stout	WI	11,164	C
Univ of Wisc/Superior	WI	9,610	C
Univ of Wisc/Whitewater	WI	9,274	C
Univ of Wyoming	WY	9,666	C
Upper Iowa Univ	IA	20,130	C
Urbana Univ	OH	21,190	C
Ursinus College	PA	38,950	VC
Ursuline College	OH	25,456	C
Utah State Univ	UT	8,002	VC
Utica College	NY	31,396	C
Valdosta State Univ	GA	8,802	C
Valparaiso Univ	IN	28,970	VC+
Vanderbilt Univ	TN	41,986	MC
Vanguard Univ of Southern Calif	CA	27,071	C
Vassar College	NY	41,700	MC
Villa Julie College	MD	25,222	C
Villanova Univ	PA	38,672	HC+
Virginia Commonwealth Univ	VA	12,987	C
Virginia Intermont College	VA	22,200	LC
Virginia Military Inst	VA	12,654	VC
Virginia Polytechnic Inst and State Univ	VA	10,834	VC
Virginia State Univ	VA	11,318	C
Virginia Union Univ	VA	18,432	LC
Virginia Wesleyan College	VA	28,433	C
Viterbo Univ	WI	21,670	C
Wabash College	IN	30,116	HC
Wagner College	NY	33,300	VC
Wake Forest Univ	NC	38,290	MC
Walla Walla College	WA	24,489	NC
Walsh Univ	OH	23,440	C
Warner Southern College	FL	18,000	LC
Warren Wilson College	NC	24,382	VC
Wartburg College	IA	27,915	NC
Washburn Univ	KS	9,734	NC
Washington and Jefferson College	PA	33,490	VC
Washington and Lee Univ	VA	35,880	MC
Washington College	MD	34,990	VC
Washington State Univ	WA	12,260	C
Washington Univ in St. Louis	MO	42,106	MC
Wayland Baptist Univ	TX	13,484	C
Wayne State College	NE	8,033	NC
Wayne State Univ	MI	11,805	C
Waynesburg College	PA	21,230	C
Weber State Univ	UT	9,635	NC
Webster Univ	MO	24,280	VC
Wellesley College	MA	41,030	MC
Wells College	NY	23,070	VC
Wesley College	DE	19,905	C
Wesleyan College	GA	19,560	C
Wesleyan Univ	CT	42,122	MC
West Chester Univ of Pennsylvania	PA	12,355	C+
West Liberty State College	WV	9,142	LC
West Texas A&M Univ	TX	8,452	C
West Virginia State Univ	WV	8,378	NC
West Virginia Univ	WV	10,506	C
West Virginia Wesleyan College	WV	26,880	C
Western Baptist College	OR	21,808	C
Western Carolina Univ	NC	7,000	C
Western Conn State Univ	CT	12,993	C
Western Illinois Univ	IL	13,042	C
Western Kentucky Univ	KY	10,192	C
Western Mich Univ	MI	13,299	C
Western New England College	MA	32,054	C
Western New Mexico Univ	NM	7,233	LC
Western Oregon Univ	OR	10,295	C
Western State College of Colo	CO	9,942	C
Western Washington Univ	WA	11,262	VC
Westfield State College	MA	10,200	C
Westminster College	MO	19,060	VC
Westminster College	PA	31,290	C+
Westminster College	UT	25,656	C
Westmont College	CA	36,672	HC
Wheaton College	IL	27,760	HC
Wheaton College	MA	40,180	HC+
Wheeling Jesuit Univ	WV	26,910	C
Whitman College	WA	36,110	HC+
Whittier College	CA	29,108	C
Whitworth College	WA	29,428	VC+
Wichita State Univ	KS	8,500	C
Widener Univ	PA	27,275	C
Wilberforce Univ	OH	14,937	LC
Wilkes Univ	PA	30,886	C
Willamette Univ	OR	35,416	VC+
William Carey College	MS	11,000	LC
William Jewell College	MO	24,340	C
William Paterson Univ of New Jersey	NJ	17,810	C+
William Penn Univ	IA	17,685	LC
William Tyndale College	MI	13,000	NC
William Woods Univ	MO	21,020	C
Williams Baptist College	AR	13,450	C
Williams College	MA	40,310	MC
Wilmington College	OH	2,806	NC
Wilson College	PA	27,660	C
Wingate Univ	NC	23,300	C
Winona State Univ	MN	11,333	C
Winston-Salem State Univ	NC	8,960	LC
Winthrop Univ	SC	11,302	C
Wisc Lutheran College	WI	23,510	VC
Wittenberg Univ	OH	34,596	VC
Wofford College	SC	30,935	HC
Woodbury Univ	CA	30,176	LC
Worcester State College	MA	12,499	C
Wright State Univ	OH	13,616	LC
Xavier Univ	OH	30,440	HC
Xavier Univ of Louisiana	LA	17,600	C
Yale Univ	CT	41,000	MC
Yeshiva Univ	NY	22,000	C
York College	NE	16,330	NC

ST = STATE   **$IS** = IN-STATE COSTS   **SR** = SELECTOR RATING

INDEX OF COLLEGE MAJORS

School	ST	$IS	SR
York College of Pennsylvania	PA	16,550	VC
Youngstown State Univ	OH	12,613	NC

PSYCHOLOGY EDUCATION

School	ST	$IS	SR
Eastern Mich Univ	MI	12,897	C
Marymount Univ	VA	25,934	C
Pittsburg State Univ	KS	8,112	C
Rocky Mountain College	MT	20,805	C
St. Vincent College	PA	26,160	VC
Shenandoah Univ	VA	27,600	C
Univ of Delaware	DE	14,142	HC
Univ of Rio Grande	OH	8,728	NC
York College	NE	16,330	NC

PUBLIC ADMINISTRATION

School	ST	$IS	SR
Alfred Univ	NY		VC
American International College	MA	28,710	LC
Auburn Univ	AL	12,230	VC
Augustana College	IL	29,862	VC+
Austin Peay State Univ	TN	7,535	C
Baylor Univ	TX	27,555	HC
Blackburn College	IL	13,690	C
Bowling Green State Univ	OH	14,994	C
Brown Univ	RI	42,015	MC
Buena Vista Univ	IA	27,742	C
Cal State, Bakersfield	CA	6,125	C
Cal State, Chico	CA	11,395	C
Cal State, Dominguez Hills	CA	10,220	LC
Cal State, Fresno	CA	10,037	LC
Cal State, Fullerton	CA	10,990	C
Cal State, Sacramento	CA	11,122	C+
Cal State, San Bernardino	CA	12,563	LC
Carlow Univ	PA	24,313	C
Carnegie Mellon Univ	PA	32,700	MC
Carroll College	MT	23,324	C+
Catawba College	NC	25,000	C
Cedarville Univ	OH	21,904	VC
Central Methodist Univ	MO	18,000	C
Central State Univ	OH	9,010	C+
Central Washington Univ	WA	11,730	C
Christopher Newport Univ	VA	13,326	VC
CUNY/John Jay College of Criminal Justice	NY	5,000	C
CUNY/Medgar Evers College	NY	4,250	NC
College of Santa Fe	NM	28,978	C
David N. Myers College	OH	9,475	C
Doane College	NE	22,458	C
Eastern Mich Univ	MI	12,897	C
Edgewood College	WI	22,862	C
Elon Univ	NC	25,371	HC
Evangel Univ	MO	17,380	C
Fayetteville State Univ	NC	6,000	LC
Florida A&M Univ	FL	8,344	C
Florida Atlantic Univ	FL	11,221	C
Florida International Univ	FL	9,215	VC
Florida Memorial College	FL	6,000	LC
George Mason Univ	VA	10,850	VC
Grambling State Univ	LA	6,538	NC
Grand Valley State Univ	MI	12,000	VC
Harding Univ	AR	16,512	VC
Hawaii Pacific Univ	HI	21,080	C
Heidelberg College	OH	23,242	C
Henderson State Univ	AR	7,600	C
Heritage Univ	WA	6,800	NC
Huntingdon College	AL	23,090	VC
Indiana Univ Bloomington	IN	13,356	VC
Indiana Univ Northwest	IN	4,902	LC
Indiana Univ South Bend	IN	4,989	LC
Indiana Univ-Purdue Univ Fort Wayne	IN	5,067	LC
Inter American Univ of PR/ Fajardo Campus	PR	4,000	
Inter American Univ of PR/ Ponce Regional College	PR	3,700	
Inter American Univ of PR/ San German	PR	6,720	
James Madison Univ	VA	12,010	VC
John Carroll Univ	OH	27,658	C+
Juniata College	PA	33,130	VC
Kean Univ	NJ	15,880	C
Kent State Univ	OH	14,594	C
Kentucky State Univ	KY	10,089	LC
Kentucky Wesleyan College	KY	18,590	C
Kutztown Univ of Pennsylvania	PA	10,820	C
La Salle Univ	PA	34,950	C
Lakeland College	WI	22,990	C
Lamar Univ	TX	6,820	LC
LeTourneau Univ	TX	21,200	C
Lewis Univ	IL	23,050	C+
Lincoln Univ	MO	8,000	NC
Lindenwood Univ	MO	18,600	VC
LIU/C.W. Post Campus	NY	28,282	C
Louisiana College	LA	13,450	C
Metropolitan State Univ	MN	4,682	SP
Miami Univ	OH	29,097	HC
Mich State Univ	MI	13,689	VC
Middle Tenn State Univ	TN	8,540	C
Mills College	CA	39,870	C
Miss Valley State Univ	MS	7,970	C
Missouri State Univ	MO	10,748	C+

School	ST	$IS	SR
Missouri Valley College	MO	18,500	C
Mountain State Univ	WV	11,406	NC
New College of Florida	FL	10,009	HC+
Norfolk State Univ	VA	10,531	LC
Northern Arizona Univ	AZ	10,353	C
Northern Kentucky Univ	KY	6,670	NC
Northern Mich Univ	MI	12,340	LC
Northland College	WI	26,680	C+
Northwest Missouri State Univ	MO	10,000	C
Oakland Univ	MI	11,936	C
Ohio Univ	OH	15,921	VC
Park Univ	MO	11,592	C
Penn State Univ/Univ Park Campus	PA	18,038	HC
Plymouth State Univ	NH	12,298	LC
Point Park Univ	PA	24,160	C
Pontifical Catholic Univ of PR/Ponce	PR	7,310	
Rhode Island College	RI	11,570	C
Roosevelt Univ	IL	22,605	VC
Saginaw Valley State Univ	MI	11,432	C
St. Ambrose Univ	IA	25,495	C
St. Cloud State Univ	MN	10,010	C
St. Francis Univ	PA	25,880	LC
St. John's Univ	NY	34,370	C
St. Joseph's Univ	PA	37,428	VC
St. Mary's Univ of Minn	MN	23,857	VC
Samford Univ	AL	20,258	VC
San Diego State Univ	CA	12,971	C
Seattle Univ	WA	30,063	VC
Shaw Univ	NC	15,488	LC
Shenandoah Univ	VA	27,600	C
Shippensburg Univ of Pennsylvania	PA	11,621	C
Siena Heights Univ	MI	17,000	LC
Silver Lake College of the Holy Family	WI	18,500	LC
Slippery Rock Univ of Pennsylvania	PA	10,360	LC
Sojourner-Douglass College	MD	4,200	LC
Southeastern Univ	DC	9,000	NC
Southeastern Univ	FL	17,180	LC
Southern Adventist Univ	TN	18,500	C
Southwest Minn State Univ	MN	10,975	C
Stephen F. Austin State Univ	TX	7,930	C
Stonehill College	MA	36,104	HC
Suffolk Univ	MA	33,160	C
Talladega College	AL	11,240	LC
Texas A&M Univ at Kingsville	TX	6,800	LC
Texas State Univ - San Marcos	TX	10,862	C
Thomas Edison State College	NJ	3,780	SP
Turabo Univ	PR	4,110	
Union Inst & Univ	OH	8,912	SP
Univ of Akron	OH	15,166	NC
Univ of Alaska Southeast	AK	8,050	LC
Univ of Arizona	AZ	11,958	VC
Univ of Arkansas	AR	11,859	VC
Univ of Central Arkansas	AR	9,984	C
Univ of Central Florida	FL	10,739	VC
Univ of Central Okla	OK	8,094	C
Univ of Kansas	KS	10,915	VC
Univ of La Verne	CA	33,470	C
Univ of Maine	ME	13,642	C
Univ of Maine at Augusta	ME	5,025	NC
Univ of Mich/Flint	MI	6,398	C
Univ of Miss	MS	9,000	C
Univ of Nebr at Omaha	NE	11,235	C
Univ of Nevada/Las Vegas	NV	11,566	C
Univ of N Dak	ND	10,114	VC
Univ of Northern Iowa	IA	11,133	C
Univ of Oregon	OR	13,108	VC
Univ of Pennsylvania	PA	41,766	MC
Univ of Pittsburgh at Pittsburgh	PA	18,866	HC
Univ of San Francisco	CA	37,560	VC
Univ of Tenn at Knoxville	TN	11,720	C
Univ of Tenn at Martin	TN	8,693	C
Univ of Texas at Dallas	TX	13,244	HC
Univ of the District of Columbia	DC	2,070	LC
Univ of Wisc/Green Bay	WI	9,415	VC
Univ of Wisc/La Crosse	WI	10,045	VC
Univ of Wisc/Stevens Point	WI	9,384	VC
Univ of Wisc/Superior	WI	9,610	C
Univ of Wisc/Whitewater	WI	9,274	C
Virginia Intermont College	VA	22,200	LC
Virginia State Univ	VA	11,318	C
Wagner College	NY	33,300	VC
Washburn Univ	KS	9,734	NC
Washington State Univ	WA	12,260	C
West Chester Univ of Pennsylvania	PA	12,355	C+
West Texas A&M Univ	TX	8,452	C
West Virginia Univ Inst of Technology	WV	8,788	NC
Western Mich Univ	MI	13,299	C
Western New Mexico Univ	NM	7,233	LC
Western Oregon Univ	OR	10,295	C
Winona State Univ	MN	11,333	C
Winston-Salem State Univ	NC	8,960	LC
Youngstown State Univ	OH	12,613	NC

PUBLIC AFFAIRS

School	ST	$IS	SR
Albion College	MI	26,000	VC
Chatham College	PA	27,290	C+
CUNY/Baruch College	NY	4,320	VC+
Columbia College	SC	24,982	LC
Cornell Univ	NY	41,717	MC
Dickinson College	PA	40,170	HC+
Duke Univ	NC	41,239	MC
Emory & Henry College	VA	26,570	C
Florida Gulf Coast Univ	FL	10,833	C
Georgia Inst of Technology	GA	11,450	HC+
Hamilton College	NY	41,660	MC
Huntingdon College	AL	23,090	VC
Indiana Univ Bloomington	IN	13,356	VC
Indiana Univ Kokomo	IN	4,835	LC
Indiana Univ South Bend	IN	4,989	LC
Indiana Univ-Purdue Univ Indianapolis	IN	10,959	C
Meredith College	NC	25,600	C
Mills College	CA	39,870	C
Muskingum College	OH	22,970	C
Olivet Nazarene Univ	IL	22,590	C
Pomona College	CA	40,774	MC
Rice Univ	TX	32,290	MC
Rochester Inst of Technology	NY	32,070	VC+
St. Mary's College of Maryland	MD	18,876	VC+
St. Vincent College	PA	26,160	VC
Southern Methodist Univ	TX	36,088	VC+
Southern New Hampshire Univ	NH	28,764	C
Syracuse Univ	NY	38,655	HC
Texas Southern Univ	TX	9,828	C
Trinity College	CT	38,040	HC+
Univ of Calif at Santa Barbara	CA	11,800	VC
Univ of Chicago	IL	42,369	MC
Univ of Denver	CO	36,376	VC+
Univ of N Car at Chapel Hill	NC	11,129	MC
Univ of Okla	OK	10,769	VC+
Vanderbilt Univ	TN	41,986	MC
Virginia Polytechnic Inst and State Univ	VA	10,834	VC
Washington and Lee Univ	VA	35,880	MC
Washington State Univ	WA	12,260	C
Wayne State Univ	MI	11,805	C
Wells College	NY	23,070	VC

PUBLIC HEALTH

School	ST	$IS	SR
Andrews Univ	MI	21,786	C
Benedict College	SC	19,114	LC
Case Western Reserve Univ	OH	37,314	MC
Central Mich Univ	MI	12,244	C
Central Washington Univ	WA	11,730	C
CUNY/Hunter College	NY	8,000	C
Dillard Univ	LA	17,500	VC
East Tenn State Univ	TN	8,497	C
Edinboro Univ of Pennsylvania	PA	11,809	LC
Indiana Univ Bloomington	IN	13,356	VC
Indiana Univ-Purdue Univ Indianapolis	IN	10,959	C
Ithaca College	NY	35,144	VC
Kent State Univ	OH	14,594	C
Minn State Univ, Mankato	MN	10,276	C
New Jersey City Univ	NJ	13,695	LC
Penn State Univ/Univ Park Campus	PA	18,038	HC
Richard Stockton College of New Jersey	NJ	14,000	VC
Russell Sage College	NY	27,000	C
Rutgers, The State Univ of New Jersey/New Brunswick/Piscataway Campus	NJ	15,810	HC
St. Cloud State Univ	MN	10,010	C
San Francisco State Univ	CA	13,000	C
Southern Conn State Univ	CT	10,310	C
Univ of Calif at Berkeley	CA	18,141	HC+
Univ of Illinois at Urbana-Champaign	IL	15,800	HC+
Univ of N Car at Chapel Hill	NC	11,129	MC
Univ of N Car at Greensboro	NC	8,993	C
Univ of Rochester	NY	41,135	MC
Univ of the Cumberlands	KY	18,184	C
Univ of Utah	UT	10,162	VC
Univ of Wisc/Eau Claire	WI	9,915	VC
Utah State Univ	UT	8,002	VC
West Chester Univ of Pennsylvania	PA	12,355	C+
Western Kentucky Univ	KY	10,192	C
Western New Mexico Univ	NM	7,233	LC
Winona State Univ	MN	11,333	C

PUBLIC HISTORY/ARCHIVES

School	ST	$IS	SR
St. Andrews Presbyterian College	NC	23,530	C

PUBLIC RELATIONS

School	ST	$IS	SR
American Univ	DC	38,719	HC+
Andrews Univ	MI	21,786	C
Appalachian State Univ	NC	8,000	VC
Auburn Univ	AL	12,230	VC
Baldwin-Wallace College	OH	27,256	VC
Barry Univ	FL	24,100	LC
Belmont Univ	TN	24,110	VC
Boston Univ	MA	42,046	HC+
Brigham Young Univ	UT	9,200	VC
Cal State, Fullerton	CA	10,990	C
Capital Univ	OH	30,444	C
Cardinal Stritch Univ	WI	21,910	C
Carroll College	MT	23,324	C+
Central Mich Univ	MI	12,244	C
Central Missouri State Univ	MO	10,000	C
Central Washington Univ	WA	11,730	C
Champlain College	VT	24,605	C
Chapman Univ	CA	37,550	VC
Coe College	IA	27,440	VC
College of the Ozarks	MO	4,130	VC+
Concordia College: Moorhead	MN	22,475	VC
Drake Univ	IA	27,632	VC+
Drury Univ	MO	20,117	VC
East Central Univ	OK	6,207	C
Eastern Kentucky Univ	KY	7,725	C
Emerson College	MA	35,076	HC
Ferris State Univ	MI	13,698	C
Florida Southern College	FL	25,965	C
Florida State Univ	FL	9,028	HC
Freed-Hardeman Univ	TN	16,370	NC
George Washington Univ	DC	48,820	MC
Georgia Southern Univ	GA	9,762	C
Gonzaga Univ	WA	30,218	HC
Greenville College	IL	23,146	C
Gwynedd-Mercy College	PA	26,080	C
Hardin-Simmons Univ	TX	18,641	C
Hawaii Pacific Univ	HI	21,080	C
Heidelberg College	OH	23,242	C
Hofstra Univ	NY	32,630	VC
Huntington Univ	IN	24,830	C
Illinois State Univ	IL	12,839	C+
Indiana Univ South Bend	IN	4,989	LC
Ithaca College	NY	35,144	VC
John Brown Univ	AR	20,910	VC
Kent State Univ	OH	14,594	C
Lewis Univ	IL	23,050	C+
LIU/C.W. Post Campus	NY	28,282	C
Loras College	IA	27,193	C
Mansfield Univ	PA	11,300	C
Marietta College	OH	29,327	C
Marquette Univ	WI	31,066	HC
McKendree College	IL	24,800	VC
Mercyhurst College	PA	28,633	VC
Middle Tenn State Univ	TN	8,540	C
Minn State Univ, Moorhead	MN	7,000	LC
Montana State Univ-Billings	MT	8,906	C
Montclair State Univ	NJ	16,327	C
Mount Mary College	WI	22,895	C
Mount St. Mary College	NY	25,250	C
Murray State Univ	KY	8,900	VC
Northeastern Univ	MA	35,742	HC
Northern Mich Univ	MI	12,340	LC
Northwest Missouri State Univ	MO	10,000	C
Northwestern Okla State Univ	OK	6,250	NC
Ohio Dominican Univ	OH	25,954	C
Ohio Northern Univ	OH	27,765	VC
Otterbein College	OH	28,986	C
Pacific Union College	CA	24,555	VC+
Park Univ	MO	11,592	C
Pepperdine Univ	CA	39,960	HC
Pontifical Catholic Univ of PR/Ponce	PR	7,310	
Purdue Univ/Calumet	IN	10,891	LC
Purdue Univ/West Lafayette	IN	13,458	VC
Quinnipiac Univ	CT	34,640	VC
Regis College	MA	31,350	LC
Rider Univ	NJ	32,560	C
Roosevelt Univ	IL	22,605	VC
St. Mary's Univ of Minn	MN	23,857	VC
Shorter College	GA	19,700	C
Southeast Missouri State Univ	MO	10,596	C
Southeastern Univ	FL	17,180	LC
Southern Adventist Univ	TN	18,500	C
Southern Methodist Univ	TX	36,088	VC+
SUNY at Oswego	NY	13,662	VC
Stephens College	MO	26,930	VC
Suffolk Univ	MA	33,160	C
Syracuse Univ	NY	38,655	HC
Texas Christian Univ	TX	23,410	VC+
Texas State Univ - San Marcos	TX	10,862	C
Texas Tech Univ	TX	13,026	VC
Union College	NE	18,710	C
Union Univ	TN	20,750	VC
Univ of Alabama	AL	9,888	C
Univ of Central Florida	FL	10,739	VC
Univ of Central Okla	OK	8,094	C
Univ of Dayton	OH	28,826	VC
Univ of Florida	FL	9,354	HC

ST = STATE   **$IS** = IN-STATE COSTS   **SR** = SELECTOR RATING

School	ST	$IS	SR
Univ of Georgia	GA	11,004	HC
Univ of Indianapolis	IN	25,090	C
Univ of Louisiana at Lafayette	LA	5,830	C
Univ of Miami	FL	38,397	MC
Univ of North Alabama	AL	8,992	C
Univ of Northern Colo	CO	10,249	C
Univ of Northern Iowa	IA	11,133	C
Univ of Okla	OK	10,769	VC+
Univ of Pittsburgh at Bradford	PA	17,008	C
Univ of Rio Grande	OH	8,728	NC
Univ of S Car at Columbia	SC	13,397	C
Univ of Southern Calif	CA	41,618	MC
Univ of Texas at Austin	TX	14,610	HC
Univ of Wisc/Whitewater	WI	9,274	C
Ursuline College	OH	25,456	C
Utica College	NY	31,396	C
Valparaiso Univ	IN	28,970	VC+
Wartburg College	IA	27,315	NC
Washington State Univ	WA	12,260	C
Wayne State Univ	MI	11,805	C
Weber State Univ	UT	9,635	NC
Webster Univ	MO	24,280	VC
West Texas A&M Univ	TX	8,452	C
West Virginia Univ	WV	10,506	C
West Virginia Wesleyan College	WV	26,880	C
Western Kentucky Univ	KY	10,192	C
Western Mich Univ	MI	13,299	C
Westminster College	PA	31,290	C+
William Penn Univ	IA	17,685	LC
Wingate Univ	NC	23,300	C
Winthrop Univ	SC	11,302	C
Xavier Univ	OH	30,490	HC
Youngstown State Univ	OH	12,613	NC

PUBLISHING

School	ST	$IS	SR
Benedictine Univ	IL	25,710	C
Emerson College	MA	35,076	HC
Hofstra Univ	NY	32,630	VC
Rochester Inst of Technology	NY	32,070	VC+
Syracuse Univ	NY	38,655	HC
Texas Christian Univ	TX	23,410	VC+
Texas Tech Univ	TX	13,026	VC
West Texas A&M Univ	TX	8,452	C

PUERTO RICAN STUDIES

School	ST	$IS	SR
Rutgers, The State Univ of New Jersey/Newark Campus	NJ	15,640	VC

PURCHASING/INVENTORY MANAGEMENT

School	ST	$IS	SR
Arizona State Univ-Tempe	AZ	11,174	C
Central Mich Univ	MI	12,244	C
Duquesne Univ	PA	29,534	VC
Kennesaw State Univ	GA	12,152	C
Miami Univ	OH	29,097	HC
St. Joseph's Univ	PA	37,428	VC
Southwestern College	KS	21,476	C
Syracuse Univ	NY	38,655	HC
Thomas Edison State College	NJ	3,780	SP
Univ of Houston-Downtown	TX	3,326	NC
Univ of Illinois at Urbana-Champaign	IL	15,800	HC+
Weber State Univ	UT	9,635	NC

QUANTITATIVE METHODS

School	ST	$IS	SR
CUNY/City College	NY		C
Clarion Univ of Pennsylvania	PA	11,844	C
James Madison Univ	VA	12,010	VC
Simon's Rock College of Bard	MA	41,988	VC+
Univ of Cincinnati	OH	17,682	C
Univ of Houston	TX	7,000	C
Univ of Houston-Downtown	TX	3,326	NC
Univ of Washington	WA	10,400	VC
Whitworth College	WA	29,428	VC+

RADIATION THERAPY

School	ST	$IS	SR
Benedictine Univ	IL	25,710	C
Gwynedd-Mercy College	PA	26,080	C
Indiana Univ Kokomo	IN	4,835	LC
Indiana Univ-Purdue Univ Indianapolis	IN	10,959	C
Kent State Univ	OH	14,594	C
Texas State Univ - San Marcos	TX	10,862	C
Thomas Edison State College	NJ	3,780	SP
Univ of Mich/Flint	MI	6,398	C
Univ of St. Francis	IL	25,430	C
Univ of Vermont	VT	18,080	VC
Univ of Wisc/La Crosse	WI	10,045	VC
Wayne State Univ	MI	11,805	C

RADIO/TELEVISION TECHNOLOGY

School	ST	$IS	SR
Arkansas State Univ	AR	9,630	C
CUNY/Brooklyn College	NY	4,377	C
Columbia College Chicago	IL	25,125	LC
De Sales Univ	PA	28,580	VC
Emerson College	MA	35,076	HC
Hardin-Simmons Univ	TX	18,641	C
Hofstra Univ	NY	32,630	VC
Kent State Univ	OH	14,594	C
Lewis Univ	IL	23,050	C+
Lyndon State College	VT	14,233	LC
Marietta College	OH	29,327	C
Mount Ida College	MA	26,000	LC
New York Univ	NY	43,170	MC
Northern Kentucky Univ	KY	6,670	NC
Northwestern Univ	IL	37,595	MC
Pacific Union College	CA	24,555	VC+
St. John's Univ	NY	34,370	C
Southeast Missouri State Univ	MO	10,596	C
Southern Illinois Univ Carbondale	IL	12,391	C
Texas Christian Univ	TX	23,410	VC+
Univ of Arkansas at Little Rock	AR	7,230	NC
Univ of Houston	TX	7,000	C
Univ of Miss	MS	9,000	C
Univ of Montana	MT	10,602	C
Univ of North Texas	TX	7,800	C
Univ of Southern Miss	MS	10,112	C
Valparaiso Univ	IN	28,970	VC+

RADIOGRAPH MEDICAL TECHNOLOGY

School	ST	$IS	SR
Alderson-Broaddus College	WV	24,006	C
Averett Univ	VA	24,920	C
Clarkson College	NE	13,000	C
College Misericordia	PA	27,950	C
Howard Univ	DC	18,481	C+
Indiana Univ Kokomo	IN	4,835	LC
La Roche College	PA	24,724	LC
Missouri State Univ	MO	10,748	C+
Ohio State Univ	OH	15,357	HC
Oregon Inst of Technology	OR	8,718	C
Pennsylvania College of Technology	PA	16,980	LC
Univ of St. Francis	IL	25,430	C
Weber State Univ	UT	9,635	NC

RADIOLOGICAL SCIENCE

School	ST	$IS	SR
Arkansas State Univ	AR	9,630	C
Armstrong Atlantic State Univ	GA	7,394	C
Florida Hospital College of Health Sciences	FL	11,152	SP
George Washington Univ	DC	48,820	MC
Idaho State Univ	ID	9,030	C
Indiana Univ Kokomo	IN	4,835	LC
Indiana Univ Northwest	IN	4,902	LC
Jewish Hospital College of Nursing and Allied Health	MO	12,000	SP
Manhattan College	NY	29,000	VC
Midwestern State Univ	TX	9,381	LC
Northwestern State Univ of Louisiana	LA	7,144	C
Pennsylvania College of Technology	PA	16,980	LC
Purdue Univ/West Lafayette	IN	13,458	VC
Quinnipiac Univ	CT	34,640	VC
St. Francis College	NY	19,974	LC
Suffolk Univ	MA	33,160	C
Univ of Alabama at Birmingham	AL	13,716	C
Univ of Central Arkansas	AR	9,984	C
Univ of Central Florida	FL	10,739	VC
Univ of Charleston	WV	27,600	C
Univ of Missouri/Columbia	MO	13,500	VC
Univ of New Mexico	NM	11,253	C
Univ of N Car at Chapel Hill	NC	11,129	MC
Univ of Pittsburgh at Bradford	PA	17,008	C
Univ of South Alabama	AL	8,930	LC

RADIOLOGICAL TECHNOLOGY

School	ST	$IS	SR
Austin Peay State Univ	TN	7,535	C
Averett Univ	VA	24,920	C
Avila Univ	MO	22,100	C
Bloomsburg Univ of Pennsylvania	PA	11,602	C
Boise State Univ	ID	9,438	LC
Briar Cliff Univ	IA	23,550	LC
Cal State, Northridge	CA	9,036	LC
Champlain College	VT	24,605	C
Clarion Univ of Pennsylvania	PA	11,844	C
Clarkson College	NE	13,000	C
Concordia Univ Wisc	WI	22,660	VC
Fairleigh Dickinson Univ/ College at Florham	NJ	30,130	C

RANGE/FARM MANAGEMENT

School	ST	$IS	SR
Colo State Univ-Fort Collins	CO	10,878	C+
Eastern Oregon Univ	OR	10,400	NC
Lake Erie College	OH	27,725	C
Montana State Univ-Bozeman	MT	1,137	C
New Mexico State Univ	NM	9,250	C
N Dak State Univ	ND	8,500	C
Oregon State Univ	OR	11,055	C
S Dak State Univ	SD	9,815	C
Stephen F. Austin State Univ	TX	7,930	C
Tarleton State Univ	TX	8,952	C
Texas A&M Univ	TX	13,351	HC
Texas A&M Univ at Kingsville	TX	6,800	LC
Texas Christian Univ	TX	23,410	VC+
Texas Tech Univ	TX	13,026	VC
Univ of Arizona	AZ	11,958	VC
Univ of at Calif Davis	CA	15,010	VC
Univ of Idaho	ID	9,310	NC
Univ of Illinois at Urbana-Champaign	IL	15,800	HC+
Univ of Nebr at Lincoln	NE	11,401	VC
Univ of Wyoming	WY	9,666	C
Utah State Univ	UT	8,002	VC
Washington State Univ	WA	12,260	C

READING EDUCATION

School	ST	$IS	SR
Baylor Univ	TX	27,555	HC
Calif Univ of Pennsylvania	PA	14,217	C
Defiance College	OH	24,790	C
Eastern Mich Univ	MI	12,897	C
Florida State Univ	FL	9,028	HC
Hardin-Simmons Univ	TX	18,641	C
Houston Baptist Univ	TX	18,660	C
Jarvis Christian College	TX	11,136	NC
Kent State Univ	OH	14,594	C
Missouri Southern State Univ	MO	8,396	NC
Muskingum College	OH	22,970	C
S Car State Univ	SC	6,700	LC
Texas Wesleyan Univ	TX	18,700	C
Univ of Great Falls	MT	17,000	C
Univ of Louisiana at Monroe	LA	7,103	C
Univ of Mary Hardin-Baylor	TX	19,428	C
Univ of Nebr at Lincoln	NE	11,401	VC
Univ of North Texas	TX	7,800	C
Univ of Rio Grande	OH	8,728	NC
West Texas A&M Univ	TX	8,452	C
Wingate Univ	NC	23,300	C

REAL ESTATE

School	ST	$IS	SR
Angelo State Univ	TX	8,340	NC
Ball State Univ	IN	13,138	C
Baylor Univ	TX	27,555	HC
Calif State Polytechnic Univ, Pomona	CA	18,053	C+
Cal State, Sacramento	CA	11,122	C+
Christopher Newport Univ	VA	13,326	VC
CUNY/Baruch College	NY	4,320	VC+
Clarion Univ of Pennsylvania	PA	11,844	C
David N. Myers College	OH	9,475	C
Eastern Mich Univ	MI	12,897	C
Florida Atlantic Univ	FL	11,221	C
Florida International Univ	FL	9,215	VC
Georgia State Univ	GA	11,444	VC
Indiana Univ Bloomington	IN	13,356	VC
La Roche College	PA	24,724	LC
Marylhurst Univ	OR	14,220	NC
Miss State Univ	MS	9,577	C
Morehead State Univ	KY	9,150	C
New York Univ	NY	43,170	MC
Ohio State Univ	OH	15,357	HC
Peirce College	PA	12,760	NC

RECREATION AND LEISURE SERVICES

School	ST	$IS	SR
Arizona State Univ-Tempe	AZ	11,174	C
Asbury College	KY	23,762	VC
Austin Peay State Univ	TN	7,535	C
Bowling Green State Univ	OH	14,994	C
Brigham Young Univ	UT	9,200	VC
Calif Polytechnic State Univ	CA	12,390	VC
Cal State East Bay	CA	10,856	LC
Cal State, Dominguez Hills	CA	10,220	LC
Cal State, Northridge	CA	9,036	LC
Calvin College	MI	25,735	NC
Catawba College	NC	25,000	C
Central Missouri State Univ	MO	10,000	C
Central Washington Univ	WA	11,730	C
Chicago State Univ	IL	10,915	C+
Christopher Newport Univ	VA	13,326	VC
Colo State Univ-Pueblo	CO	7,821	LC
Cumberland Univ	TN	18,894	C
East Central Univ	OK	6,207	C
Eastern Conn State Univ	CT	13,554	C
Eastern Mich Univ	MI	12,897	C
Eastern Washington Univ	WA	10,608	C
Emporia State Univ	KS	8,093	C
Ferrum College	VA	24,290	LC
Florida State Univ	FL	9,028	HC
Franklin College	IN		C
Frostburg State Univ	MD	12,672	C
Gallaudet Univ	DC	16,554	
Georgia Southern Univ	GA	9,762	C
Gordon College	MA	29,194	C+
Graceland Univ	IA	19,700	C
Grambling State Univ	LA	6,538	NC
Green Mountain College	VT	32,164	C
Greenville College	IL	23,146	C
Hannibal-LaGrange College	MO	16,390	C
Henderson State Univ	AR	7,600	C
High Point Univ	NC	25,720	C
Houghton College	NY	25,980	VC+
Indiana State Univ	IN	11,604	C
Indiana Univ Bloomington	IN	13,356	VC
Ithaca College	NY	35,144	VC
James Madison Univ	VA	12,010	VC
Johnson and Wales Univ/ North Miami Campus	FL	30,126	LC
Johnson and Wales Univ/ Providence Campus	RI	28,126	LC
Kean Univ	NJ	15,880	C
Kent State Univ	OH	14,594	C
Lyndon State College	VT	14,233	LC
Mars Hill College	NC	19,000	LC
Maryville College	TN	29,224	VC
Metropolitan State College of Denver	CO	2,338	LC
Middle Tenn State Univ	TN	8,540	C
Missouri State Univ	MO	10,748	C+
Montclair State Univ	NJ	16,327	C
Morris College	SC	11,999	LC
Mount Olive College	NC	16,000	LC
Mountain State Univ	WV	11,406	NC
Murray State Univ	KY	8,900	VC
New England College	NH	31,466	C
New York Univ	NY	43,170	MC
N Car State Univ	NC	11,824	HC
N Dak State Univ	ND	8,500	C
North Georgia College and State Univ	GA	7,000	C
Northwest Missouri State Univ	MO	10,000	C
Northwest Nazarene Univ	ID	22,590	VC

School	ST	$IS	SR
Fairleigh Dickinson Univ/ Metropolitan Campus	NJ	28,590	C
Fort Hays State Univ	KS	7,638	C
Friends Univ	KS	16,250	LC
Jamestown College	ND	14,130	NC
Kent State Univ	OH	14,594	C
LIU/C.W. Post Campus	NY	28,282	C
Marian College of Fond du Lac	WI	21,775	LC
Mass College of Pharmacy and Health Sciences	MA	32,020	SP
McNeese State Univ	LA	5,270	LC
Minot State Univ	ND	6,700	LC
Mount Marty College	SD	20,590	C
N Dak State Univ	ND	8,500	C
Presentation College	SD	14,800	LC
Rhode Island College	RI	11,570	C
Southern Illinois Univ Carbondale	IL	12,391	C
Univ of Hartford	CT	34,044	C
Univ of Louisiana at Monroe	LA	7,103	C
Univ of Mary	ND	15,374	C
Univ of Nevada/Las Vegas	NV	11,566	C
William Carey College	MS	11,000	LC

School	ST	$IS	SR
Penn State Univ/Univ Park Campus	PA	18,038	HC
St. John's Univ	NY	34,370	C
San Diego State Univ	CA	12,971	C
San Francisco State Univ	CA	13,000	C
Southern Methodist Univ	TX	36,088	VC+
Temple Univ	PA	17,438	C
Texas A&M Univ at Kingsville	TX	6,800	LC
Texas Christian Univ	TX	23,410	VC+
Thomas Edison State College	NJ	3,780	SP
Univ of Cincinnati	OH	17,682	C
Univ of Conn	CT	16,628	HC
Univ of Denver	CO	36,376	VC+
Univ of Georgia	GA	11,004	HC
Univ of Illinois at Urbana-Champaign	IL	15,800	HC+
Univ of Memphis	TN	11,153	C
Univ of Miss	MS	9,000	C
Univ of Missouri/Columbia	MO	13,500	VC
Univ of Nebr at Omaha	NE	11,235	C
Univ of Nevada/Las Vegas	NV	11,566	C
Univ of North Texas	TX	7,800	C
Univ of Northern Iowa	IA	11,133	C
Univ of Okla	OK	10,769	VC+
Univ of Pennsylvania	PA	41,766	MC
Univ of St. Thomas	MN	28,000	VC
Univ of S Car at Columbia	SC	13,397	VC
Univ of Texas at Arlington	TX	7,195	VC
Univ of West Georgia	GA	8,838	C
Univ of Wisc/Madison	WI	13,117	HC
Univ of Wisc/Milwaukee	WI	9,427	LC
Washington State Univ	WA	12,260	C

School	ST	$IS	SR
Ohio Univ	OH	15,921	C
Okla State Univ	OK	10,213	VC
Old Dominion Univ	VA	11,907	C
Oral Roberts Univ	OK	22,650	C
Pacific Lutheran Univ	WA	28,805	VC
Pittsburg State Univ	KS	8,112	C
Plymouth State Univ	NH	12,298	LC
Purdue Univ/West Lafayette	IN	13,458	VC
Radford Univ	VA	13,145	C
St. Joseph's College, New York, Suffolk Campus	NY	12,000	C
St. Thomas Aquinas College	NY	22,000	LC
Shaw Univ	NC	15,488	LC
Shepherd Univ	WV	10,066	C
Southeast Missouri State Univ	MO	10,596	C
Southeastern Okla State Univ	OK	6,147	C
Southern Conn State Univ	CT	10,310	C
Southern Illinois Univ Carbondale	IL	12,391	C
Southern Wesleyan Univ	SC	21,675	C
Southwest Baptist Univ	MO	18,300	C
SUNY/College at Brockport	NY	12,747	VC
Taylor Univ	IN	26,376	VC+
Texas A&M Univ at Galveston	TX	10,000	C+
Thomas Edison State College	NJ	3,780	SP
Tougaloo College	MS	15,975	NC
Tri-State Univ-Main Campus	IN	26,200	C
Univ of Delaware	DE	14,142	HC
Univ of Florida	FL	9,354	HC
Univ of Georgia	GA	11,004	HC
Univ of Hawaii at Manoa	HI	10,413	VC
Univ of Illinois at Urbana-Champaign	IL	15,800	HC+
Univ of Iowa	IA	12,172	VC
Univ of Maine at Machias	ME	10,523	C
Univ of Maine at Presque Isle	ME	10,066	LC
Univ of Memphis	TN	11,153	C
Univ of Mich/Ann Arbor	MI	16,587	HC+
Univ of Minn/Twin Cities	MN	13,165	HC
Univ of Miss	MS	9,000	C
Univ of Nebr at Omaha	NE	11,235	C
Univ of New Hampshire	NH	16,810	VC
Univ of New Mexico	NM	11,253	C
Univ of N Dak	ND	10,114	VC
Univ of North Texas	TX	7,800	C
Univ of Northern Colo	CO	10,249	C
Univ of Northern Iowa	IA	11,133	C
Univ of South Alabama	AL	8,930	LC
Univ of S Dak	SD	9,068	C
Univ of Tenn at Chattanooga	TN	7,790	C
Univ of Toledo	OH	15,806	NC
Univ of Wisc/Milwaukee	WI	9,427	LC
Upper Iowa Univ	IA	20,130	C
Virginia Commonwealth Univ	VA	12,987	C
Voorhees College	SC	11,800	LC
Wartburg College	IA	27,315	NC
West Virginia Univ	WV	10,506	C
Western Kentucky Univ	KY	10,192	C
Western Mich Univ	MI	13,299	C
Western State College of Colo	CO	9,942	C
William Penn Univ	IA	17,685	LC
Winona State Univ	MN	11,333	C

RECREATION EDUCATION

School	ST	$IS	SR
Alcorn State Univ	MS	8,190	LC
Alderson-Broaddus College	WV	24,006	C
Baylor Univ	TX	27,555	HC
Benedict College	SC	19,114	LC
Campbellsville Univ	KY	21,328	C
College of the Ozarks	MO	4,130	VC+
Eastern Washington Univ	WA	10,608	V
Georgia College and State Univ	GA	11,020	C
Georgia Southwestern State Univ	GA	6,035	C
Howard Univ	DC	18,481	C+
Johnson State College	VT	11,830	LC
Knoxville College	TN	6,200	LC
Lyndon State College	VT	14,233	LC
Northwest Missouri State Univ	MO	10,000	C
Oral Roberts Univ	OK	22,650	C
Plymouth State Univ	NH	12,298	LC
Prescott College	AZ	13,445	LC
St. Mary's College of Calif	CA	37,290	C
San Francisco State Univ	CA	13,000	C
Southern Adventist Univ	TN	18,500	C
Southern Univ at New Orleans	LA	1,000	NC
SUNY/College at Cortland	NY	12,095	C
Sterling College	VT	23,286	VC
Univ of Arkansas	AR	11,859	VC
Univ of Conn	CT	16,628	HC
Univ of Idaho	ID	9,310	NC
Univ of Maine	ME	13,642	C

School	ST	$IS	SR
Univ of Minn/Duluth	MN	13,974	C
Univ of Nevada/Las Vegas	NV	11,566	C
Univ of New Hampshire	NH	16,810	VC
Univ of Tenn at Knoxville	TN	11,720	C
Warren Wilson College	NC	24,382	VC
Washington State Univ	WA	12,260	C

RECREATION THERAPY

School	ST	$IS	SR
Ashland Univ	OH	25,000	C
Cal State, Northridge	CA	9,036	LC
Catawba College	NC	25,000	C
Central Mich Univ	MI	12,244	C
East Carolina Univ	NC	10,000	C
Eastern Mich Univ	MI	12,897	C
Eastern Washington Univ	WA	10,608	C
Gallaudet Univ	DC	16,554	
Georgia Southern Univ	GA	9,762	C
Green Mountain College	VT	32,164	C
Hampton Univ	VA	19,468	C+
Indiana Inst of Technology	IN	23,430	C
Ithaca College	NY	35,144	VC
Lake Superior State Univ	MI	12,842	LC
Lincoln Univ	PA	13,658	C+
Longwood Univ	VA	12,426	C
Mercy College	NY	20,000	NC
Messiah College	PA	28,910	VC+
Ohio Univ	OH	15,921	C
Shaw Univ	NC	15,488	LC
Shepherd Univ	WV	10,066	C
Southern Univ and A&M College	LA	8,238	LC
Springfield College	MA	25,000	C
Univ of Southern Maine	ME	12,614	C
Univ of Wisc/La Crosse	WI	10,045	VC
Utica College	NY	31,396	C
West Virginia State Univ	WV	8,378	NC
Western Carolina Univ	NC	7,000	C
Winston-Salem State Univ	NC	8,960	LC

RECREATIONAL FACILITIES MANAGEMENT

School	ST	$IS	SR
Alaska Pacific Univ	AK	25,142	C
Appalachian State Univ	NC	8,000	VC
Ashland Univ	OH	25,000	C
Barber-Scotia College	NC	15,000	LC
Bluffton College	OH	26,110	C
Cal State, Fresno	CA	10,037	LC
Carroll College	WI	24,860	C
Central Methodist Univ	MO	18,000	C
College of St. Joseph	VT	20,900	NC
Colo State Univ-Fort Collins	CO	10,878	C+
Culver-Stockton College	MO	20,625	C
East Carolina Univ	NC	10,000	C
Eastern Mennonite Univ	VA	25,450	VC
Elmhurst College	IL	24,685	C
Florida State Univ	FL	9,028	HC
Georgia Southern Univ	GA	9,762	C
Graceland Univ	IA	19,700	C
Green Mountain College	VT	32,164	C
Indiana Wesleyan Univ	IN	22,074	C+
Inter American Univ of PR/Aguadilla Campus	PR	3,784	
Johnson and Wales Univ/Providence Campus	RI	28,126	LC
Johnson State College	VT	11,830	LC
Keystone College	PA	22,810	LC
Lynn Univ	FL	30,750	C
Malone College	OH	23,040	C
Missouri Valley College	MO	18,500	C
New Mexico State Univ	NM	9,250	C
Savannah State Univ	GA	7,772	LC
Shorter College	GA	19,700	C
Sierra Nevada College	NV	30,235	C
Southwestern Okla State Univ	OK	4,801	C
SUNY at Oswego	NY	13,662	VC
Texas State Univ - San Marcos	TX	10,862	C
Tri-State Univ-Main Campus	IN	26,200	C
Union College	KY	18,920	C
Univ of Central Okla	OK	8,094	C
Univ of Minn/Twin Cities	MN	13,165	HC
Univ of Miss	MS	9,000	C
Univ of Nebr at Lincoln	NE	11,401	VC
Univ of Nevada/Las Vegas	NV	11,566	C
Univ of N Car at Chapel Hill	NC	11,129	MC
Univ of St. Francis	IL	25,430	C

REHABILITATION THERAPY

School	ST	$IS	SR
Arkansas Tech Univ	AR	8,108	VC
Assumption College	MA	32,875	C
Boston Univ	MA	42,046	HC+
Cal State, Los Angeles	CA	5,900	C
Clarion Univ of Pennsylvania	PA	11,844	C
College of St. Catherine	MN	27,505	VC
East Carolina Univ	NC	10,000	C
East Central Univ	OK	6,207	C
Emporia State Univ	KS	8,093	C
Florida International Univ	FL	9,215	VC
Florida State Univ	FL	9,028	HC

School	ST	$IS	SR
Hilbert College	NY	20,480	LC
Indiana Univ of Pennsylvania	PA	11,209	C
Ithaca College	NY	35,144	VC
Kean Univ	NJ	15,880	C
Montana State Univ-Billings	MT	8,906	C
Northeastern Univ	MA	35,742	HC
Penn State Univ/Univ Park Campus	PA	18,038	HC
Shaw Univ	NC	15,488	LC
Southern Illinois Univ Carbondale	IL	12,391	C
Southern Univ and A&M College	LA	8,238	LC
Springfield College	MA	25,000	C
Stephen F. Austin State Univ	TX	7,930	C
Stetson Univ	FL	32,725	VC
Thomas Univ	GA	11,520	NC
Troy Univ	AL	8,916	C
Univ of Arkansas at Pine Bluff	AR	8,300	C
Univ of Florida	FL	9,354	HC
Univ of Illinois at Urbana-Champaign	IL	15,800	HC+
Univ of Maine at Farmington	ME	11,515	C
Univ of Maryland/Eastern Shore	MD	11,210	C
Univ of N Dak	ND	10,114	VC
Univ of North Texas	TX	7,800	C
Univ of Northern Colo	CO	10,249	C
Univ of Pittsburgh at Pittsburgh	PA	18,866	HC
Univ of Tenn at Chattanooga	TN	7,790	C
Univ of Texas-Pan American	TX	7,290	C+
Univ of Wisc/Stout	WI	11,164	C
Wilberforce Univ	OH	14,937	LC
Wright State Univ	OH	13,616	LC

RELIGION

School	ST	$IS	SR
Abilene Christian Univ	TX	20,830	C
Adrian College	MI	23,000	C
Agnes Scott College	GA	32,070	HC
Albertson College of Idaho	ID	21,095	VC
Albertus Magnus College	CT	25,336	C
Albion College	MI	26,000	VC
Albright College	PA	33,920	C
Allegheny College	PA	33,500	HC
Alma College	MI	28,544	VC
Alverno College	WI	21,088	C
Amherst College	MA	41,590	MC
Anderson Univ	IN	25,050	LC
Andrews Univ	MI	21,786	C
Appalachian State Univ	NC	8,000	VC
Arizona State Univ-Tempe	AZ	11,174	C
Arkansas Baptist College	AR	5,600	NC
Ashford Univ	IA	20,370	C
Ashland Univ	OH	25,000	C
Atlantic Union College	MA	17,600	LC
Augsburg College	MN	28,300	C
Augustana College	IL	29,862	VC+
Augustana College	SD	24,380	VC
Aurora Univ	IL	20,645	C
Austin College	TX	27,871	HC
Averett Univ	VA	24,920	C
Azusa Pacific Univ	CA	28,546	VC
Baker Univ	KS	22,596	C
Baldwin-Wallace College	OH	27,256	VC
Ball State Univ	IN	13,138	C
Bard College	NY	41,800	HC+
Barton College	NC	22,316	C
Bates College	ME	42,100	MC
Baylor Univ	TX	27,555	HC
Belmont Univ	TN	24,110	VC
Beloit College	WI	32,808	HC
Benedict College	SC	19,114	LC
Benedictine College	KS	21,968	C
Berea College	KY	5,496	VC+
Berry College	GA	24,342	VC
Bethany College	WV	21,395	C
Bethel College	IN	19,680	C
Bethel College	KS	21,650	C
Bethel Univ	MN	29,840	VC
Bethune-Cookman College	FL	17,922	LC
Birmingham-Southern College	AL	28,494	VC+
Bloomfield College	NJ	22,500	LC
Bluefield College	VA	17,230	C+
Bluffton College	OH	26,110	C
Boston Univ	MA	42,046	HC+
Bowdoin College	ME	41,660	MC
Bradley Univ	IL	25,280	VC
Brescia Univ	KY	14,240	C
Brewton-Parker College	GA	14,220	LC
Bridgewater College	VA	27,790	C
Bryan College	TN	19,270	C
Bryn Athyn College of the New Church	PA	14,999	NC
Bryn Mawr College	PA	42,780	HC+
Bucknell Univ	PA	39,660	MC
Buena Vista Univ	IA	27,742	C
Butler Univ	IN	31,944	VC+

School	ST	$IS	SR
Cabrini College	PA	33,340	C
Calif Lutheran Univ	CA	27,800	LC
Cal State, Bakersfield	CA	6,125	LC
Cal State, Chico	CA	11,395	C
Cal State, Fullerton	CA	10,990	C
Cal State, Long Beach	CA	9,512	C
Calumet College of St. Joseph	IN	9,500	LC
Calvin College	MI	25,735	NC
Campbell Univ	NC	21,137	VC
Canisius College	NY	32,257	VC
Capital Univ	OH	30,444	C
Cardinal Stritch Univ	WI	21,910	C
Carleton College	MN	40,467	MC
Carroll College	MT	23,324	C+
Carroll College	WI	24,860	C
Carson-Newman College	TN	16,800	C
Carthage College	WI	26,000	C
Case Western Reserve Univ	OH	37,314	MC
Catawba College	NC	25,000	C
Catholic Univ of America	DC	35,838	VC
Centenary College of Louisiana	LA	24,760	VC
Central College	IA	26,774	VC
Central Methodist Univ	MO	18,000	C
Central Mich Univ	MI	12,244	C
Central Univ of Bayamon	PR	3,335	
Centre College	KY	30,810	VC
Chaminade Univ of Honolulu	HI	23,320	LC
Chapman Univ	CA	37,550	VC
Charleston Southern Univ	SC	17,800	C
Christian Brothers Univ	TN	24,650	VC
Christopher Newport Univ	VA	13,326	VC
CUNY/Brooklyn College	NY	4,377	C+
CUNY/Hunter College	NY	8,000	C+
CUNY/Queens College	NY	4,356	C
Claremont McKenna College	CA	42,920	MC
Clark Atlanta Univ	GA	20,960	LC
Clarke College	IA	25,390	C
Cleveland State Univ	OH	10,798	NC
Coe College	IA	27,440	VC
Colby College	ME	41,770	MC
Colgate Univ	NY	41,170	MC
College of Charleston	SC	13,616	VC
College of Mount St. Vincent	NY	28,000	C
College of Mount St. Joseph	OH	24,860	C
College of New Rochelle	NY	28,396	C+
College of Notre Dame of Maryland	MD	27,700	C
College of Our Lady of the Elms	MA	21,000	C
College of St. Rose	NY	25,684	C
College of St. Scholastica	MN	28,456	C+
College of Santa Fe	NM	28,978	C
College of the Holy Cross	MA	40,664	MC
College of the Ozarks	MO	4,130	VC+
College of William and Mary	VA	14,147	MC
College of Wooster	OH	31,310	VC+
Colo College	CO	37,668	HC
Columbia College	SC	24,982	LC
Columbia Union College	MD	23,536	C
Columbia Univ/Barnard College	NY	38,000	MC
Columbia Univ/Columbia College	NY	42,584	MC
Columbia Univ/School of General Studies	NY	41,516	C
Concordia College: Moorhead	MN	22,475	VC
Concordia College-New York	NY	27,740	C
Concordia Univ St.Paul	MN	27,776	C
Concordia Univ Wisc	WI	22,660	C
Concordia Univ, Ann Arbor	MI	25,153	C+
Concordia Univ, River Forest	IL	26,300	C
Conn College	CT	41,975	MC
Converse College	SC	24,800	C
Cornell College	IA	30,110	VC+
Cornell Univ	NY	41,717	MC
Cornerstone Univ and Grand Rapids Theological Seminary	MI	21,350	NC
Covenant College	GA	26,460	VC+
Culver-Stockton College	MO	20,625	C
Daemen College	NY	24,580	C
Dakota Wesleyan Univ	SD	17,832	C
Dana College	NE	22,390	C
Dartmouth College	NH	39,465	MC
Davidson College	NC	36,825	MC
Davis and Elkins College	WV	22,416	C
Defiance College	OH	24,790	C
Denison Univ	OH	37,040	HC
DePaul Univ	IL	29,835	VC
DePauw Univ	IN	32,100	HC
Dickinson College	PA	40,170	HC+
Doane College	NE	22,458	C
Dominican Univ	IL	26,370	C
Dominican Univ of Calif	CA	36,836	C
Dordt College	IA	20,325	VC
Drake Univ	IA	27,632	VC+

School	ST	$IS	SR
Drew Univ/College of Liberal Arts	NJ	39,698	VC
Duke Univ	NC	41,239	MC
Earlham College	IN	33,604	HC
East Texas Baptist Univ	TX	16,713	C
Eastern Mennonite Univ	VA	25,450	VC
Eastern Nazarene College	MA	19,500	LC
Eastern New Mexico Univ	NM	7,264	C
Eckerd College	FL	35,492	VC
Edgewood College	WI	22,862	C
Edward Waters College	FL	14,374	LC
Elizabethtown College	PA	32,100	VC
Elmhurst College	IL	24,685	C
Elon Univ	NC	25,371	VC
Emmanuel College	MA	32,000	C+
Emory & Henry College	VA	26,570	C
Emory Univ	GA	40,546	MC
Erskine College	SC	25,468	VC
Eureka College	IL	19,280	C
Evangel Univ	MO	17,380	C
Fairfield Univ	CT	39,835	HC
Felician College	NJ	24,300	C
Ferrum College	VA	24,290	LC
Fisk Univ	TN	19,830	C
Flagler College	FL	13,790	VC
Florida International Univ	FL	9,215	VC
Florida Memorial College	FL	6,000	LC
Florida Southern College	FL	25,965	C
Florida State Univ	FL	9,028	HC
Fordham Univ	NY	36,000	HC
Franciscan Univ of Steubenville	OH	20,300	VC
Franklin and Marshall College	PA	40,590	HC
Franklin College	IN		C
Fresno Pacific Univ	CA	25,454	C
Friends Univ	KS	16,250	LC
Furman Univ	SC	33,264	HC+
Gallaudet Univ	DC	16,554	
Gardner-Webb Univ	NC	21,500	C
George Fox Univ	OR	28,490	C
George Mason Univ	VA	10,850	VC
George Washington Univ	DC	48,820	MC
Georgetown College	KY	24,950	C+
Georgetown Univ	DC	43,183	MC
Georgian Court College	NJ	20,000	C
Gettysburg College	PA	39,864	HC
Gonzaga Univ	WA	30,218	HC
Goshen College	IN	22,850	VC
Goucher College	MD	36,225	VC
Grace Bible College	MI	18,810	C
Grace College	IN	22,170	C
Graceland Univ	IA	19,700	C
Greensboro College	NC	23,000	C
Greenville College	IL	23,146	C
Grinnell College	IA	34,814	HC+
Grove City College	PA	15,784	HC+
Guilford College	NC	28,160	C+
Gustavus Adolphus College	MN	30,920	HC
Hamilton College	NY	41,660	MC
Hamline Univ	MN	27,000	VC
Hampden-Sydney College	VA	31,148	VC
Hampshire College	MA	37,120	HC
Harding Univ	AR	16,512	VC
Hartwick College	NY	36,065	C+
Harvard Univ/Harvard College	MA	45,860	MC
Hastings College	NE	22,218	VC
Haverford College	PA	41,600	MC
Heidelberg College	OH	23,242	C
Hellenic College/Holy Cross Greek Orthodox School of Theology	MA	24,975	C
Hendrix College	AR	27,646	HC+
High Point Univ	NC	25,720	C
Hillsdale College	MI	24,160	HC
Hiram College	OH	28,700	VC
Hobart and William Smith Colleges	NY	41,123	VC
Hollins Univ	VA	31,105	C
Holy Family Univ	PA	25,740	C
Holy Names College	CA	27,980	NC
Hood College	MD	30,085	VC
Hope College	MI	28,208	VC+
Houghton College	NY	25,980	VC+
Humboldt State Univ	CA	11,176	VC
Huntingdon College	AL	23,090	VC
Illinois College	IL	21,900	C
Illinois Wesleyan Univ	IL	34,050	HC+
Indiana Univ Bloomington	IN	13,356	VC
Indiana Univ of Pennsylvania	PA	11,209	C
Indiana Univ-Purdue Univ Indianapolis	IN	10,959	C
Indiana Wesleyan Univ	IN	22,074	C+
Iona College	NY	30,878	VC
Iowa State Univ	IA	11,831	VC
Iowa Wesleyan College	IA	22,140	C
James Madison Univ	VA	12,010	VC
Jamestown College	ND	14,130	NC
Jarvis Christian College	TX	11,136	NC
John Carroll Univ	OH	27,658	C+
Judson College	AL	16,522	C
Kalamazoo College	MI	32,442	VC+
Kansas Wesleyan Univ	KS	21,400	VC
Kenyon College	OH	39,500	MC
La Roche College	PA	24,724	LC
La Salle Univ	PA	34,950	C
La Sierra Univ	CA	24,327	C+
Lafayette College	PA	39,267	MC
LaGrange College	GA	22,874	C+
Lakeland College	WI	22,990	C
Lambuth Univ	TN	21,700	C+
Lane College	TN	11,220	C+
Lawrence Univ	WI	33,958	HC+
Le Moyne College	NY	29,570	VC
Lebanon Valley College	PA	31,700	VC
Lees-McRae College	NC	23,000	C
Lehigh Univ	PA	42,690	HC+
Lewis and Clark College	OR	35,358	VC+
Lewis Univ	IL	23,050	C+
Liberty Univ	VA	19,101	C
Lincoln Univ	PA	13,658	C+
Lindenwood Univ	MO	18,600	VC
Linfield College	OR	29,632	VC
Loras College	IA	27,193	C
Louisiana College	LA	13,450	C
Lourdes College	OH	15,300	LC
Loyola Univ Chicago	IL	32,896	VC
Loyola Univ New Orleans	LA	31,050	VC+
Luther College	IA	28,800	VC+
Lycoming College	PA	30,797	C+
Lynchburg College	VA	30,645	C
Lyon College	AR	19,990	VC
Macalester College	MN	36,500	MC
MacMurray College	IL	20,755	C
Madonna Univ	MI	16,068	VC
Manchester College	IN	23,470	C
Manhattan College	NY	29,000	VC
Manhattanville College	NY	32,500	C+
Mars Hill College	NC	19,000	LC
Martin Univ	IN	10,300	SP
Mary Baldwin College	VA	26,465	C
Marygrove College	MI	19,310	C
Marylhurst Univ	OR	14,220	NC
Maryville College	TN	29,224	VC
Marywood Univ	PA	30,680	C
McDaniel College	MD	31,610	VC
McKendree College	IL	24,800	VC
McMurry Univ	TX	18,100	LC
McPherson College	KS	21,010	C
Mercer Univ	GA	27,525	VC+
Mercyhurst College	PA	28,633	VC
Meredith College	NC	25,600	C
Merrimack College	MA	34,380	C
Messiah College	PA	28,910	VC+
Methodist College	NC	21,000	C
Miami Univ	OH	29,097	HC
Mich State Univ	MI	13,689	VC
Middlebury College	VT	42,120	MC
Midland Lutheran College	NE	18,600	C
Millikin Univ	IL	25,590	C
Millsaps College	MS	28,256	VC+
Missouri Baptist Univ	MO	19,640	C
Missouri State Univ	MO	10,748	C
Missouri Valley College	MO	18,500	C
Monmouth Univ	IL	23,700	C
Montclair State Univ	NJ	16,327	C
Montreat College	NC	21,440	C
Moravian College	PA	28,950	VC
Morehouse College	GA	25,082	C
Morgan State Univ	MD	12,080	C
Morningside College	IA	23,704	C
Mount Holyoke College	MA	42,148	HC+
Mount Marty College	SD	20,590	C
Mount Mercy College	IA	23,670	C
Mount Olive College	NC	16,600	LC
Mount St. Mary's College	CA	32,086	VC
Mount Union College	OH	25,840	C
Mount Vernon Nazarene Univ	OH	20,810	C
Muhlenberg College	PA	36,030	HC+
Muskingum College	OH	22,970	C
Naropa Univ	CO	26,302	SP
Nazareth College of Rochester	NY	28,175	VC
Nebr Wesleyan Univ	NE	23,415	C+
New College of Florida	FL	10,009	HC+
New York Univ	NY	43,170	MC
Newberry College	SC	23,000	LC
Niagara Univ	NY	28,250	C
N Car State Univ	NC	11,824	HC
N Car Wesleyan College	NC	22,670	C
North Central College	IL	28,926	VC
North Central Univ	MN	16,646	LC
North Park Univ	IL	24,050	C
Northern Arizona Univ	AZ	10,353	C
Northland College	WI	26,680	C+
Northwest Nazarene Univ	ID	22,590	VC
Northwest Univ	WA	18,854	C
Northwestern College of Iowa	IA	22,174	C+
Northwestern Univ	IL	37,595	MC
Notre Dame de Namur Univ	CA	32,790	LC
Nyack College	NY	18,540	C
Oakland City Univ	IN	19,620	NC
Oakwood Univ	AL	14,904	C
Oberlin College	OH	40,904	MC
Occidental College	CA	40,185	MC
Ohio Northern Univ	OH	27,765	VC
Ohio Valley Univ	WV	17,752	C
Ohio Wesleyan Univ	OH	35,830	VC+
Okla Baptist Univ	OK	17,986	VC
Okla City Univ	OK	23,965	VC
Okla Wesleyan Univ	OK	18,950	NC
Olivet Nazarene Univ	IL	22,590	VC
Oral Roberts Univ	OK	22,650	C
Ottawa Univ	KS	12,000	LC
Otterbein College	OH	28,986	C
Ouachita Baptist Univ	AR	21,900	VC
Our Lady of the Lake Univ of San Antonio	TX	22,430	LC
Pacific Lutheran Univ	WA	28,805	VC
Pacific Union College	CA	24,555	VC+
Paul Quinn College	TX	8,300	LC
Penn State Univ/Univ Park Campus	PA	18,038	HC
Pepperdine Univ	CA	39,960	HC
Pfeiffer Univ	NC	21,900	C
Piedmont College	GA	20,500	C
Pikeville College	KY	16,500	NC
Point Loma Nazarene Univ	CA	27,610	VC
Pomona College	CA	40,774	MC
Pontifical Catholic Univ of PR/Ponce	PR	7,310	
Presbyterian College	SC	30,044	VC
Princeton Univ	NJ	40,213	MC
Principia College	IL	27,765	VC+
Purdue Univ/West Lafayette	IN	13,458	VC
Queens Univ of Charlotte	NC	24,528	C
Radford Univ	VA	13,145	C
Randolph-Macon College	VA	31,250	C
Randolph-Macon Woman's College	VA	31,160	VC+
Reed College	OR	41,106	MC
Regis Univ	CO	31,890	C
Rhodes College	TN	32,860	HC
Rice Univ	TX	32,290	MC
Richard Stockton College of New Jersey	NJ	14,000	C
Ripon College	WI	27,160	C+
Roanoke College	VA	30,748	VC
Rockford College	IL	28,330	VC
Rocky Mountain College	MT	20,805	C
Rollins College	FL	38,366	VC
Rosemont College	PA	29,350	C
Rutgers, The State Univ of New Jersey/Camden Campus	NJ	15,000	C
Rutgers, The State Univ of New Jersey/New Brunswick/Piscataway Campus	NJ	15,810	HC
Sacred Heart Univ	CT	33,404	C
St. Andrews Presbyterian College	NC	23,530	C
St. Edward's Univ	TX	23,560	C
St. Francis College	NY	19,974	C
St. Francis Univ	PA	25,880	LC
St. John Fisher College	NY	27,860	C
St. Joseph College	CT	32,050	C
St. Joseph's College	IN	26,600	C
St. Joseph's College	PA	37,428	VC
St. Lawrence Univ	NY	40,545	VC
St. Leo Univ	FL	22,140	C+
St. Martin's Univ	WA	27,555	C
St. Mary's College	IN	32,538	VC
St. Mary's College of Calif	CA	37,290	C
St. Mary's College of Maryland	MD	18,876	VC+
St. Michael's College	VT	33,330	VC
St. Norbert College	WI	28,577	C+
St. Olaf College	MN	32,800	HC
St. Thomas Aquinas College	NY	22,000	LC
St. Thomas Univ	FL	23,490	VC
St. Xavier Univ	IL	23,160	C
Salem College	NC	26,226	VC+
Salve Regina Univ	RI	33,450	C
Samford Univ	AL	20,258	VC
San Diego State Univ	CA	12,971	VC
San Jose State Univ	CA	11,707	VC
Santa Clara Univ	CA	38,931	VC
Sarah Lawrence College	NY	42,000	HC
Schreiner Univ	TX	20,600	C
Scripps College	CA	41,000	MC
Seattle Pacific Univ	WA	29,355	C
Seattle Univ	WA	30,063	VC
Seton Hall Univ	NJ	33,622	VC
Seton Hill Univ	PA	28,810	C
Shaw Univ	NC	15,488	LC
Shenandoah Univ	VA	27,600	C
Shorter College	GA	19,700	C
Siena College	NY	28,260	VC+
Siena Heights Univ	MI	17,000	LC
Silver Lake College of the Holy Family	WI	18,500	LC
Simpson College	IA	26,833	VC
Simpson Univ	CA	22,900	C
Skidmore College	NY	41,779	HC
Smith College	MA	41,474	MC
Southeastern Univ	FL	17,180	LC
Southern Methodist Univ	TX	36,088	VC+
Southern Nazarene Univ	OK	14,634	NC
Southern Wesleyan Univ	SC	21,675	C
Southwest Baptist Univ	MO	18,300	C
Southwestern Adventist Univ	TX	18,290	LC
Southwestern Univ	TX	26,767	HC
Spelman College	GA	24,650	VC
Stanford Univ	CA	41,557	MC
SUNY/College at Old Westbury	NY	13,154	C
SUNY/Univ at Albany	NY	13,860	VC
SUNY/Univ at Stony Brook	NY	13,625	HC
Stetson Univ	FL	32,725	VC
Stillman College	AL	11,475	LC
Stonehill College	MA	36,104	HC
Susquehanna Univ	PA	33,465	VC
Swarthmore College	PA	41,280	MC
Sweet Briar College	VA	31,460	VC
Syracuse Univ	NY	38,655	HC
Tabor College	KS	21,614	NC
Temple Univ	PA	17,438	C
Texas A&M Univ at Commerce	TX	9,020	C
Texas Christian Univ	TX	23,410	VC+
Texas Wesleyan Univ	TX	18,700	C
Thiel College	PA	24,580	C
Thomas Edison State College	NJ	3,780	SP
Tougaloo College	MS	15,975	NC
Towson Univ	MD	13,924	VC
Transylvania Univ	KY	26,240	VC+
Trevecca Nazarene Univ	TN	19,594	C
Trinity College	CT	38,040	HC+
Trinity Univ	TX	30,157	HC+
Truman State Univ	MO	11,242	HC
Tufts Univ	MA	42,018	MC
Tulane Univ	LA	41,098	MC
Union College	KY	18,920	C
Union College	NE	18,710	C
Union Univ	TN	20,750	VC
Universidad Adventista de las Antillas	PR	7,360	
Univ of Alabama	AL	9,888	C
Univ of Arizona	AZ	11,958	VC
Univ of at Calif Davis	CA	15,010	VC
Univ of Bridgeport	CT	29,595	LC
Univ of Calif at Berkeley	CA	18,311	HC+
Univ of Calif at Los Angeles	CA	17,681	MC
Univ of Calif at Riverside	CA	16,625	C
Univ of Calif at San Diego	CA	16,102	HC
Univ of Calif at Santa Barbara	CA	11,800	VC
Univ of Calif at Santa Cruz	CA	19,174	VC
Univ of Central Arkansas	AR	9,984	C
Univ of Chicago	IL	42,369	MC
Univ of Colo at Boulder	CO	13,352	C+
Univ of Dayton	OH	28,826	VC
Univ of Denver	CO	36,376	VC+
Univ of Detroit Mercy	MI	27,000	C
Univ of Dubuque	IA	23,390	C
Univ of Findlay	OH	29,238	C
Univ of Florida	FL	9,354	HC
Univ of Georgia	GA	11,004	HC
Univ of Great Falls	MT	17,000	C
Univ of Hawaii at Manoa	HI	10,413	VC
Univ of Illinois at Urbana-Champaign	IL	15,800	HC+
Univ of Indianapolis	IN	25,090	C
Univ of Iowa	IA	12,172	VC
Univ of Kansas	KS	10,915	VC
Univ of La Verne	CA	33,470	C
Univ of Mary Hardin-Baylor	TX	19,428	C
Univ of Mary Washington	VA	11,636	MC
Univ of Miami	FL	38,397	MC
Univ of Mich/Ann Arbor	MI	16,587	HC+
Univ of Missouri/Columbia	MO	13,500	VC
Univ of Mobile	AL	16,880	C
Univ of Nebr at Lincoln	NE	11,401	VC
Univ of New Mexico	NM	11,253	C
Univ of N Car at Chapel Hill	NC	11,129	MC
Univ of N Car at Charlotte	NC	9,101	C
Univ of N Car at Pembroke	NC	7,940	LC
Univ of N Car at Wilmington	NC	10,107	VC
Univ of N Dak	ND	10,114	VC
Univ of Northern Iowa	IA	11,133	C
Univ of Okla	OK	10,769	VC+
Univ of Oregon	OR	13,108	VC
Univ of Pennsylvania	PA	41,766	MC
Univ of Pittsburgh at Pittsburgh	PA	18,866	HC
Univ of Puget Sound	WA	35,600	HC
Univ of Redlands	CA	36,160	VC
Univ of Richmond	VA	40,510	MC
Univ of Rochester	NY	41,135	MC
Univ of St. Francis	IN	20,970	C
Univ of San Diego	CA	40,620	HC
Univ of San Francisco	CA	37,560	VC
Univ of Sioux Falls	SD	20,800	C
Univ of S Car at Columbia	SC	13,397	VC
Univ of South Florida	FL	10,284	VC
Univ of Southern Calif	CA	41,618	MC
Univ of Tenn at Knoxville	TN	11,720	C
Univ of Texas at Austin	TX	14,610	HC
Univ of the Cumberlands	KY	18,184	C
Univ of the Incarnate Word	TX	23,306	C
Univ of the Ozarks	AR	19,250	C
Univ of the Pacific	CA	34,380	VC
Univ of the South	TN	34,645	HC
Univ of Tulsa	OK	25,348	HC
Univ of Vermont	VT	18,080	VC
Univ of Virginia	VA	13,759	VC

ST = STATE $IS = IN-STATE COSTS   SR = SELECTOR RATING

School	ST	$IS	SR
Univ of Washington	WA	10,400	VC
Univ of West Florida	FL	8,559	C
Univ of Wisc/Eau Claire	WI	9,915	VC
Univ of Wisc/Madison	WI	13,117	HC
Univ of Wisc/Milwaukee	WI	9,427	LC
Univ of Wisc/Oshkosh	WI	10,426	LC
Ursinus College	PA	38,950	VC
Ursuline College	OH	25,456	C
Valparaiso Univ	IN	28,970	VC+
Vanderbilt Univ	TN	41,986	MC
Vassar College	NY	41,700	MC
Villanova Univ	PA	38,672	HC+
Virginia Commonwealth Univ	VA	12,987	C
Virginia Intermont College	VA	22,200	LC
Virginia Union Univ	VA	18,432	LC
Virginia Wesleyan College	VA	28,433	C
Viterbo Univ	WI	21,670	C
Wabash College	IN	30,116	HC
Wake Forest Univ	NC	38,290	MC
Walla Walla College	WA	24,489	NC
Wartburg College	IA	27,315	NC
Washburn Univ	KS	9,734	NC
Washington and Lee Univ	VA	35,880	MC
Washington State Univ	WA	12,260	C
Washington Univ in St. Louis	MO	42,106	MC
Wayland Baptist Univ	TX	13,484	C
Webster Univ	MO	24,280	VC
Wellesley College	MA	41,030	MC
Wells College	NY	23,070	VC
Wesleyan College	GA	19,560	C
Wesleyan Univ	CT	42,122	MC
West Chester Univ of Pennsylvania	PA	12,355	C+
West Virginia Wesleyan College	WV	26,880	C
Western Kentucky Univ	KY	10,192	C
Western Mich Univ	MI	13,299	C
Westminster College	MO	19,060	VC
Westminster College	PA	31,290	C+
Westmont College	CA	36,672	HC
Wheaton College	IL	27,760	HC
Wheaton College	MA	40,180	HC+
Wheeling Jesuit Univ	WV	26,910	C
Whitman College	WA	36,110	HC+
Whittier College	CA	29,108	C
Whitworth College	WA	29,428	VC+
Wiley College	TX	8,100	LC
Willamette Univ	OR	35,416	VC+
William Carey College	MS	11,000	LC
William Jewell College	MO	24,340	C
Williams Baptist College	AR	13,450	C
Williams College	MA	40,310	MC
Wilmington College	OH	2,806	VC
Wilson College	PA	27,660	C
Wingate Univ	NC	23,300	C
Winthrop Univ	SC	11,302	C
Wittenberg Univ	OH	34,596	VC
Wofford College	SC	30,935	HC
Wright State Univ	OH	13,616	LC
Yale Univ	CT	41,000	MC
Yeshiva Univ	NY	22,000	C
Youngstown State Univ	OH	12,613	NC

RELIGIOUS EDUCATION

School	ST	$IS	SR
Andrews Univ	MI	21,786	C
Baylor Univ	TX	27,555	HC
Brown Univ	RI	42,015	MC
Campbellsville Univ	KY	21,328	C
Clearwater Christian College	FL	13,160	LC
College of Mount St. Joseph	OH	24,860	C
Concordia Univ St.Paul	MN	27,776	C
Cornerstone Univ and Grand Rapids Theological Seminary	MI	21,350	NC
Dallas Baptist Univ	TX	17,040	VC
Franciscan Univ of Steubenville	OH	20,300	VC
Georgia State Univ	GA	11,444	VC
Grace Bible College	MI	18,810	C
Huntington College	AL	23,090	VC
Kansas Wesleyan Univ	KS	21,400	VC
La Roche College	PA	24,724	LC
Lee Univ	TN	14,780	NC
Lenoir-Rhyne Univ	NC	25,580	C
Louisiana College	LA	13,450	C
Loyola Univ New Orleans	LA	31,050	VC+
Marian College	IN	26,160	C
Mercyhurst College	PA	28,633	VC
Missouri Baptist Univ	MO	19,640	C
Morris College	SC	11,999	C
Mount Vernon Nazarene Univ	OH	20,810	C
Muskingum College	OH	22,970	C
North Central Univ	MN	16,646	LC
Northwest Univ	WA	18,854	C
Nyack College	NY	18,540	C
Oakwood College	AL	14,004	C
Okla Christian Univ	OK	18,992	NC
Oral Roberts Univ	OK	22,650	C
Pfeiffer Univ	NC	21,900	C
Point Loma Nazarene Univ	CA	27,610	VC

School	ST	$IS	SR
Presbyterian College	SC	30,044	VC
Quincy Univ	IL	24,920	C
St. Edward's Univ	TX	23,560	C
St. Mary-of-the-Woods College	IN	25,480	C
St. Mary's Univ of Minn	MN	23,857	VC
St. Vincent College	PA	26,160	VC
Seattle Pacific Univ	WA	29,355	C
Simpson Univ	CA	22,900	C
Southern Adventist Univ	TN	18,500	C
Southern Nazarene Univ	OK	14,634	NC
Southwest Baptist Univ	MO	18,300	C
Sterling College	KS	19,992	C
Tenn Wesleyan College	TN	18,650	C
Thiel College	PA	24,580	C
Trinity Bible College	ND		
Union College	NE	18,710	C
Univ of N Car at Greensboro	NC	8,993	C
Vanguard Univ of Southern Calif	CA	27,071	C
Wayland Baptist Univ	TX	13,484	C
West Virginia Wesleyan College	WV	26,880	C
Williams Baptist College	AR	13,450	C

RELIGIOUS MUSIC

School	ST	$IS	SR
Alderson-Broaddus College	WV	24,006	C
Aquinas College	MI	23,750	C
Averett Univ	VA	24,920	C
Baylor Univ	TX	27,555	HC
Belhaven College	MS	19,530	NC
Bethel College	IN	19,680	C
Campbellsville Univ	KY	21,328	C
Cedarville Univ	OH	21,904	VC
Centenary College of Louisiana	LA	24,760	VC
Charleston Southern Univ	SC	17,800	C
Clearwater Christian College	FL	13,160	LC
College of the Ozarks	MO	4,130	VC+
Columbia College	SC	24,982	LC
Concordia College-New York	NY	27,740	C
Concordia Univ at Austin	TX	23,640	LC
Concordia Univ St.Paul	MN	27,776	C
Concordia Univ Wisc	WI	22,660	VC
Concordia Univ, Ann Arbor	MI	25,153	C+
East Texas Baptist Univ	TX	16,713	C
Eastern Nazarene College	MA	19,500	LC
Evangel Univ	MO	17,380	C
Furman Univ	SC	33,264	HC+
Gardner-Webb Univ	NC	21,500	C
Georgetown College	KY	24,950	C+
Grand Canyon Univ	AZ	32,000	LC
Grove City College	PA	15,784	HC+
Hannibal-LaGrange College	MO	16,390	C
Hardin-Simmons Univ	TX	18,641	C
Houston Baptist Univ	TX	18,660	C
Huntington Univ	IN	24,830	C
Indiana Wesleyan Univ	IN	22,074	C+
Johnson C. Smith Univ	NC	20,000	C
Kentucky Christian College	KY	12,680	C
LaGrange College	GA	22,874	C+
Lenoir-Rhyne College	NC	25,580	C
Louisiana College	LA	13,450	C
Madonna Univ	MI	16,068	VC
Malone College	OH	23,040	C
Marywood Univ	PA	30,680	C
McKendree College	IL	24,890	C
Milligan College	TN	21,990	VC
Miss College	MS	14,574	VC
Missouri Baptist Univ	MO	19,640	C
North Central Univ	MN	16,646	C
Northwest Univ	WA	18,854	C
Northwestern College of Iowa	IA	22,174	C+
Nyack College	NY	18,540	C
Okla Wesleyan Univ	OK	18,950	NC
Oral Roberts Univ	OK	22,650	C
Palm Beach Atlantic Univ	FL	23,597	VC
Pfeiffer Univ	NC	21,900	C
Presbyterian College	SC	30,044	VC
St. Olaf College	MN	32,800	HC
Samford Univ	AL	20,258	VC
Seton Hill Univ	PA	28,810	C
Shenandoah Univ	VA	27,600	C
Shorter College	GA	19,700	C
Southeastern Univ	FL	17,180	LC
Southwest Baptist Univ	MO	18,300	C
Susquehanna Univ	PA	33,465	VC
Tenn Wesleyan College	TN	18,650	C
Texas Christian Univ	TX	23,410	VC+
Toccoa Falls College	GA	17,125	C
Trevecca Nazarene Univ	TN	19,594	C
Union Univ	TN	20,750	VC
Univ of the Cumberlands	KY	18,184	C
Valparaiso Univ	IN	28,970	VC+
Warner Pacific College	OR	21,900	C
Warner Southern College	FL	18,000	LC
Wartburg College	IA	27,315	NC
Wayland Baptist Univ	TX	13,484	C
Westminster College	PA	31,290	C+
William Carey College	MS	11,000	LC
William Tyndale College	MI	13,000	NC

School	ST	$IS	SR
Williams Baptist College	AR	13,450	C

RESPIRATORY THERAPY

School	ST	$IS	SR
Armstrong Atlantic State Univ	GA	7,394	C
Bellarmine Univ	KY	27,650	C+
Boise State Univ	ID	9,438	LC
College of St. Catherine	MN	27,505	VC
Columbia Union College	MD	23,536	LC
Dakota State Univ	SD	7,466	C
Gannon Univ	PA	26,100	C
Georgia State Univ	GA	11,444	VC
Gwynedd-Mercy College	PA	26,080	C
Indiana Univ Kokomo	IN	4,835	LC
Indiana Univ of Pennsylvania	PA	11,209	C
Indiana Univ-Purdue Univ Indianapolis	IN	10,959	C
La Roche College	PA	24,724	LC
Midwestern State Univ	TX	9,381	LC
Missouri State Univ	MO	10,748	C+
Mountain State Univ	WV	11,406	NC
Nebr Methodist College of Nursing and Allied Health	NE	12,950	SP
N Dak State Univ	ND	8,500	C
Ohio State Univ	OH	15,357	HC
Point Park Univ	PA	24,160	C
Salisbury Univ	MD	13,128	VC
Shenandoah Univ	VA	27,600	C
Southern Illinois Univ Carbondale	IL	12,391	C
SUNY/Univ at Stony Brook	NY	13,625	HC
Tenn State Univ	TN	9,048	LC
Texas Southern Univ	TX	9,828	C
Texas State Univ - San Marcos	TX	10,862	C
Thomas Edison State College	NJ	3,780	SP
Univ of Alabama at Birmingham	AL	13,716	C
Univ of Central Florida	FL	10,739	VC
Univ of Hartford	CT	34,044	C
Univ of Indianapolis	IN	25,090	C
Univ of Kansas	KS	10,915	VC
Univ of Mary	ND	15,374	C
Univ of Missouri/Columbia	MO	13,500	VC
Univ of South Alabama	AL	8,930	LC
Univ of the Ozarks	AR	19,250	C
Weber State Univ	UT	9,635	NC
Wheeling Jesuit Univ	WV	26,910	C
York College of Pennsylvania	PA	16,550	VC
Youngstown State Univ	OH	12,613	NC

RETAILING

School	ST	$IS	SR
Central Mich Univ	MI	12,244	C
David N. Myers College	OH	9,475	C
East Central Univ	OK	6,207	C
Johnson and Wales Univ/ Providence Campus	RI	28,126	LC
Montclair State Univ	NJ	16,327	C
Mount Ida College	MA	26,000	LC
New Jersey City Univ	NJ	13,695	LC
Purdue Univ/West Lafayette	IN	13,458	VC
Siena Heights Univ	MI	17,000	LC
Southern New Hampshire Univ	NH	28,764	C
Syracuse Univ	NY	38,655	HC
Texas Tech Univ	TX	13,026	VC
Thomas Edison State College	NJ	3,780	SP
Univ of Arizona	AZ	11,958	VC
Univ of Memphis	TN	11,153	C
Univ of Minn/Twin Cities	MN	13,165	HC
Univ of S Car at Columbia	SC	13,397	VC
Univ of Tenn at Knoxville	TN	11,720	C
Univ of Wisc/Madison	WI	13,117	HC
Univ of Wisc/Stout	WI	11,164	C
Youngstown State Univ	OH	12,613	NC

ROMANCE LANGUAGES AND LITERATURE

School	ST	$IS	SR
Boston College	MA	41,608	MC
Bowdoin College	ME	41,660	MC
Bryn Mawr College	PA	42,780	HC+
Cameron Univ	OK	6,314	NC
Carleton College	MN	40,467	MC
CUNY/City College	NY		C
Clark Univ	MA	35,165	VC+
Colo College	CO	37,668	HC
Dartmouth College	NH	39,465	MC
DePauw Univ	IN	32,100	HC
Dowling College	NY	22,110	C
Haverford College	PA	41,600	MC
Johns Hopkins Univ	MD	42,044	MC
Manhattanville College	NY	32,500	C+
Mount Holyoke College	MA	42,148	HC+
New York Univ	NY	43,170	MC
Oberlin College	OH	40,904	MC
Olivet Nazarene Univ	IL	22,590	C
Point Loma Nazarene Univ	CA	27,610	VC

School	ST	$IS	SR
Williams Baptist College	AR	13,450	C

RUSSIAN

School	ST	$IS	SR
Amherst College	MA	41,590	MC
Arizona State Univ-Tempe	AZ	11,174	C
Bard College	NY	41,800	HC+
Bates College	ME	42,100	MC
Baylor Univ	TX	27,555	HC
Beloit College	WI	32,808	HC
Bowdoin College	ME	41,660	MC
Bowling Green State Univ	OH	14,994	C
Brandeis Univ	MA	41,551	MC
Brigham Young Univ	UT	9,200	VC
Bryn Mawr College	PA	42,780	HC+
Bucknell Univ	PA	39,660	MC
Carleton College	MN	40,467	MC
Central Washington Univ	WA	11,730	C
CUNY/Brooklyn College	NY	4,377	C+
CUNY/Herbert H. Lehman College	NY	4,000	LC
CUNY/Hunter College	NY	8,000	C+
CUNY/Queens College	NY	4,356	C
Colgate Univ	NY	41,170	MC
College of the Holy Cross	MA	40,664	MC
Colo College	CO	37,668	HC
Columbia Univ/Barnard College	NY	38,000	MC
Columbia Univ/Columbia College	NY	42,584	MC
Cornell College	IA	30,110	C+
Cornell Univ	NY	41,717	MC
Dartmouth College	NH	39,465	MC
Dickinson College	PA	40,170	HC+
Eckerd College	FL	35,492	VC
Ferrum College	VA	24,290	LC
Florida State Univ	FL	9,028	HC
Gallaudet Univ	DC	16,554	
George Washington Univ	DC	48,820	MC
Georgetown Univ	DC	43,183	MC
Goucher College	MD	36,225	VC
Grinnell College	IA	34,814	VC+
Gustavus Adolphus College	MN	30,920	HC
Harvard Univ/Harvard College	MA	45,860	MC
Haverford College	PA	41,600	MC
Hofstra Univ	NY	32,630	VC
Howard Univ	DC	18,481	C+
Indiana Univ of Pennsylvania	PA	11,209	C
Iowa State Univ	IA	11,831	VC
Juniata College	PA	33,130	VC
La Salle Univ	PA	34,950	C
Lawrence Univ	WI	33,958	HC+
Loyola Univ New Orleans	LA	31,050	VC+
Macalester College	MN	36,500	MC
Marlboro College	VT	35,980	VC+
Miami Univ	OH	29,097	HC
Mich State Univ	MI	13,689	VC
Middlebury College	VT	42,120	MC
Mount Holyoke College	MA	42,148	HC+
New York Univ	NY	43,170	MC
Northern Illinois Univ	IL	13,178	VC
Oakland Univ	MI	11,936	C
Oberlin College	OH	40,904	MC
Ohio State Univ	OH	15,357	HC
Ohio Univ	OH	15,921	C
Okla State Univ	OK	10,213	VC
Penn State Univ/Univ Park Campus	PA	18,038	HC
Pomona College	CA	40,774	MC
Portland State Univ	OR	12,453	C
Purdue Univ/West Lafayette	IN	13,458	VC
Rider Univ	NJ	32,560	C

RURAL ECONOMICS

School	ST	$IS	SR
Georgia Southern Univ	GA	9,762	C
Univ of Alaska Fairbanks	AK	10,101	C
Univ of Idaho	ID	9,310	NC

RURAL SOCIOLOGY

School	ST	$IS	SR
Auburn Univ	AL	12,230	VC
Cornell Univ	NY	41,717	MC
S Dak State Univ	SD	9,815	C
Univ of Wisc/Madison	WI	13,117	HC

St. Thomas Aquinas College	ST	$IS	SR
St. Thomas Aquinas College	NY	22,000	LC
Univ of Chicago	IL	42,369	MC
Univ of Georgia	GA	11,004	HC
Univ of Maine	ME	13,642	C
Univ of Maryland/College Park	MD	16,036	HC
Univ of Mich/Ann Arbor	MI	16,587	HC+
Univ of Nevada/Las Vegas	NV	11,566	C
Univ of N Car at Chapel Hill	NC	11,129	MC
Univ of Notre Dame	IN	39,552	MC
Univ of Oregon	OR	13,108	VC
Univ of Pennsylvania	PA	41,766	MC
Univ of PR/Rio Piedras	PR	5,750	
Washington and Lee Univ	VA	35,880	MC
Washington Univ in St. Louis	MO	42,106	MC
Wesleyan Univ	CT	42,122	MC
Wheeling Jesuit Univ	WV	26,910	C

School	ST	$IS	SR
Rutgers, The State Univ of New Jersey/New Brunswick/Piscataway Campus	NJ	15,810	HC
St. Olaf College	MN	32,800	HC
San Diego State Univ	CA	12,971	C
San Francisco State Univ	CA	13,000	C
Sarah Lawrence College	NY	42,000	HC
Seattle Pacific Univ	WA	29,355	C
Smith College	MA	41,474	MC
Southern Illinois Univ Carbondale	IL	12,391	C
Southern Methodist Univ	TX	36,088	VC+
SUNY/Univ at Albany	NY	13,860	VC
Swarthmore College	PA	41,280	MC
Syracuse Univ	NY	38,655	HC
Temple Univ	PA	17,438	C
Texas A&M Univ	TX	13,351	HC
Trinity College	CT	38,040	HC+
Trinity Univ	TX	30,157	HC+
Truman State Univ	MO	11,242	HC
Tufts Univ	MA	42,018	MC
Tulane Univ	LA	41,098	MC
Univ of Akron	OH	15,166	NC
Univ of Alabama	AL	9,888	C
Univ of Arizona	AZ	11,958	VC
Univ of Arkansas	AR	11,859	VC
Univ of at Calif Davis	CA	15,010	VC
Univ of Calif at Riverside	CA	16,625	C
Univ of Chicago	IL	42,369	MC
Univ of Florida	FL	9,354	HC
Univ of Georgia	GA	11,004	HC
Univ of Hawaii at Manoa	HI	10,413	VC
Univ of Illinois at Chicago	IL	16,256	VC
Univ of Iowa	IA	12,172	VC
Univ of Kentucky	KY	7,800	C
Univ of Maryland/Baltimore County	MD	16,642	VC+
Univ of Maryland/College Park	MD	16,036	HC
Univ of Mass Boston	MA	8,024	C
Univ of Mich/Ann Arbor	MI	16,587	HC+
Univ of Minn/Twin Cities	MN	13,165	VC
Univ of Missouri/Columbia	MO	13,500	VC
Univ of Montana	MT	10,602	C
Univ of Nebr at Lincoln	NE	11,401	VC
Univ of New Hampshire	NH	16,810	VC
Univ of New Mexico	NM	11,253	C
Univ of N Car at Chapel Hill	NC	11,129	MC
Univ of Notre Dame	IN	39,552	MC
Univ of Okla	OK	10,769	VC+
Univ of Oregon	OR	13,108	VC
Univ of Pennsylvania	PA	41,766	MC
Univ of Pittsburgh at Pittsburgh	PA	18,866	HC
Univ of Rochester	NY	41,135	MC
Univ of St. Thomas	MN	28,000	VC
Univ of S Car at Columbia	SC	13,397	VC
Univ of South Florida	FL	10,284	VC
Univ of Southern Calif	CA	41,618	MC
Univ of Tenn at Knoxville	TN	11,720	C
Univ of Texas at Arlington	TX	7,195	LC
Univ of Texas at Austin	TX	14,610	VC
Univ of the South	TN	34,645	HC
Univ of Utah	UT	10,162	VC
Univ of Vermont	VT	18,080	VC
Univ of Wisc/Madison	WI	13,117	HC
Univ of Wisc/Milwaukee	WI	9,427	C
Univ of Wyoming	WY	9,666	C
Vanderbilt Univ	TN	41,986	MC
Washington State Univ	WA	12,260	C
Washington Univ in St. Louis	MO	42,106	MC
Wayne State Univ	MI	11,805	C
Wellesley College	MA	41,030	MC
Wesleyan Univ	CT	42,122	MC
West Chester Univ of Pennsylvania	PA	12,355	C+
Wheaton College	MA	40,180	HC+
Williams College	MA	40,310	MC
Wittenberg Univ	OH	34,596	VC
Yale Univ	CT	41,000	MC

RUSSIAN AND SLAVIC STUDIES

School	ST	$IS	SR
American Univ	DC	38,719	HC+
Augsburg College	MN	28,300	C
Bard College	NY	41,800	HC+
Baylor Univ	TX	27,555	HC
Boston College	MA	41,608	VC
Brown Univ	RI	42,015	MC
Cal State, Fullerton	CA	10,990	C
Colgate Univ	NY	41,170	MC
College of the Holy Cross	MA	40,664	MC
College of Wooster	OH	31,310	VC+
Columbia Univ/Columbia College	NY	42,584	MC
Concordia College: Moorhead	MN	22,475	VC
Conn College	CT	41,975	MC
Cornell Univ	NY	41,717	MC
Dartmouth College	NH	39,465	MC
DePauw Univ	IN	32,100	HC
Dickinson College	PA	40,170	HC+
Emory Univ	GA	40,546	MC

School	ST	$IS	SR
Florida State Univ	FL	9,028	HC
George Mason Univ	VA	10,850	VC
Hamilton College	NY	41,660	MC
Harvard Univ/Harvard College	MA	45,860	MC
Hobart and William Smith Colleges	NY	41,123	VC
Indiana Univ Bloomington	IN	13,356	VC
Kent State Univ	OH	14,594	C
Lafayette College	PA	39,267	MC
Lehigh Univ	PA	42,690	HC+
Macalester College	MN	36,500	MC
Middlebury College	VT	42,120	MC
Muhlenberg College	PA	36,030	HC+
Oakland Univ	MI	11,936	C
Randolph-Macon Woman's College	VA	31,160	VC+
Rhodes College	TN	32,860	HC
Rice Univ	TX	32,290	MC
Rutgers, The State Univ of New Jersey/New Brunswick/Piscataway Campus	NJ	15,810	HC
St. Louis Univ	MO	33,158	VC+
St. Olaf College	MN	32,800	HC
San Diego State Univ	CA	12,971	C
Sarah Lawrence College	NY	42,000	HC
Simon's Rock College of Bard	MA	41,988	VC+
Smith College	MA	41,474	MC
Southern Methodist Univ	TX	36,088	VC+
SUNY/Univ at Albany	NY	13,860	VC
Stetson Univ	FL	32,725	VC
Syracuse Univ	NY	38,655	VC
Texas State Univ - San Marcos	TX	10,862	C
Texas Tech Univ	TX	13,026	VC
Tufts Univ	MA	42,018	MC
Tulane Univ	LA	41,098	VC
Union College	NY	41,595	HC
Univ of Alaska Fairbanks	AK	10,101	C
Univ of Calif at Los Angeles	CA	17,681	MC
Univ of Calif at San Diego	CA	16,102	HC
Univ of Calif at Santa Cruz	CA	19,174	VC
Univ of Colo at Boulder	CO	13,352	C+
Univ of Denver	CO	36,374	VC+
Univ of Houston	TX	7,000	C
Univ of Illinois at Urbana-Champaign	IL	15,800	HC+
Univ of Iowa	IA	12,172	VC
Univ of Kansas	KS	10,915	VC
Univ of Maryland/College Park	MD	16,036	HC
Univ of Mass Amherst	MA	15,973	C+
Univ of Mich/Ann Arbor	MI	16,587	HC+
Univ of Minn/Twin Cities	MN	13,165	VC
Univ of N Car at Chapel Hill	NC	11,129	MC
Univ of Northern Iowa	IA	11,133	C
Univ of Okla	OK	10,769	VC+
Univ of St. Thomas	MN	28,000	VC
Univ of Tenn at Knoxville	TN	11,720	C
Univ of Texas at Austin	TX	14,610	VC
Univ of the South	TN	34,645	HC
Univ of Tulsa	OK	25,348	HC
Univ of Vermont	VT	18,080	VC
Univ of Washington	WA	10,400	VC
Washington Univ in St. Louis	MO	42,106	MC
Wesleyan Univ	CT	42,122	MC
Wheaton College	MA	40,180	HC+

RUSSIAN LANGUAGES AND LITERATURE

School	ST	$IS	SR
Emory Univ	GA	40,546	MC
Kent State Univ	OH	14,594	C
New College of Florida	FL	10,009	HC+
Ouachita Baptist Univ	AR	21,900	VC
Reed College	OR	41,106	MC
SUNY/Univ at Stony Brook	NY	13,625	HC
Univ of Calif at Los Angeles	CA	17,681	MC
Univ of Illinois at Urbana-Champaign	IL	15,800	HC+
Washington and Lee Univ	VA	35,880	MC
Wellesley College	MA	41,030	MC

SAFETY AND SECURITY TECHNOLOGY

School	ST	$IS	SR
Farmingdale SUNY	NY	13,521	C
Indiana Univ of Pennsylvania	PA	11,209	C
Lewis Univ	IL	23,050	C+
Madonna Univ	MI	16,068	C
Marshall Univ	WV	9,116	C
Univ of Wisc/Whitewater	WI	9,274	C
Youngstown State Univ	OH	12,613	NC

SAFETY MANAGEMENT

School	ST	$IS	SR
Central Missouri State Univ	MO	10,000	C
CUNY/John Jay College of Criminal Justice	NY	5,000	C
Franklin Univ	OH	6,720	SP
Illinois State Univ	IL	12,839	C+
Indiana State Univ	IN	11,604	C
Keene State College	NH	13,836	C
S Dak State Univ	SD	9,815	C
Southern Christian Univ	AL	9,440	LC
Univ of Maine at Fort Kent	ME	10,832	LC

SAFETY SCIENCE

School	ST	$IS	SR
Central Washington Univ	WA	11,730	C
Embry-Riddle Aeronautical Univ	AZ	30,280	C+
Embry-Riddle Aeronautical Univ	FL	30,280	C+
Kent State Univ	OH	14,594	C
Virginia Commonwealth Univ	VA	12,987	C

SANSKRIT AND INDIAN STUDIES

School	ST	$IS	SR
Harvard Univ/Harvard College	MA	45,860	MC

SCANDINAVIAN LANGUAGES

School	ST	$IS	SR
Augsburg College	MN	28,300	C
Augustana College	IL	29,862	VC+
Gustavus Adolphus College	MN	30,920	HC
Pacific Lutheran Univ	WA	28,805	VC
Univ of Calif at Berkeley	CA	18,141	HC+
Univ of Calif at Los Angeles	CA	17,681	MC
Univ of Minn/Twin Cities	MN	13,165	VC
Univ of Texas at Austin	TX	14,610	HC
Univ of Washington	WA	10,400	VC

SCANDINAVIAN STUDIES

School	ST	$IS	SR
Augsburg College	MN	28,300	C
Concordia College: Moorhead	MN	22,475	VC
Luther College	IA	28,800	VC+
Minn State Univ, Mankato	MN	10,276	LC
Pacific Lutheran Univ	WA	28,805	VC
Univ of Mich/Ann Arbor	MI	16,587	HC+
Univ of Wisc/Madison	WI	13,117	HC

SCHOOL PSYCHOLOGY

School	ST	$IS	SR
Calif Univ of Pennsylvania	PA	14,217	C
Crichton College	TN	15,300	C
Eastern Mich Univ	MI	12,897	C
Idaho State Univ	ID	9,030	C
Kent State Univ	OH	14,594	C
Southwestern Okla State Univ	OK	4,801	C

SCIENCE

School	ST	$IS	SR
Alfred Univ	NY		VC
Alvernia College	PA	26,388	C
Alverno College	WI	21,088	C
American International College	MA	28,710	LC
Arcadia Univ	PA	33,570	VC
Bennington College	VT	41,890	HC
Brandeis Univ	MA	41,551	MC
Buena Vista Univ	IA	27,742	C
Caribbean Univ	PR	3,000	
Cascade College	OR	17,980	NC
Cheyney Univ of Pennsylvania	PA	11,497	LC
Clarkson Univ	NY	34,930	VC
Coe College	IA	27,440	VC
Colo Christian Univ	CO	21,182	VC
Concordia Univ, Ann Arbor	MI	25,153	C+
Drexel Univ	PA	27,700	VC
East Stroudsburg Univ of Pennsylvania	PA	10,336	C
Eastern Nazarene College	MA	19,500	LC
Elizabethtown College	PA	32,100	VC
Fairleigh Dickinson Univ/Metropolitan Campus	NJ	28,590	C
Ferrum College	VA	24,290	LC
Fordham Univ	NY	36,000	HC
Fort Hays State Univ	KS	7,638	C
Frostburg State Univ	MD	12,672	C
Gannon Univ	PA	26,100	C
Grace College	IN	22,170	C
Graceland Univ	IA	19,700	C
Grinnell College	IA	34,814	HC+
Hampshire College	MA	37,120	HC
Hawaii Pacific Univ	HI	21,080	C
Heritage Univ	WA	6,800	NC
Houghton College	NY	25,980	VC+
Indiana Wesleyan Univ	IN	22,074	C+
John Brown Univ	AR	20,910	VC
Johnson C. Smith Univ	NC	20,000	C
Kentucky Christian College	KY	12,680	C
King's College	PA	29,810	C
La Salle Univ	PA	34,950	C
Le Moyne College	NY	29,570	VC
Lee Univ	TN	14,780	NC
LeMoyne-Owen College	TN	13,150	LC
Lincoln Univ	PA	13,658	C+
Linfield College	OR	29,632	VC
Loras College	IA	27,193	C
Lyndon State College	VT	14,233	LC
Madonna Univ	MI	16,068	VC
Malone College	OH	23,040	C
Marygrove College	MI	19,310	C+
Marylhurst Univ	OR	14,220	NC
Maryville Univ of St. Louis	MO	23,000	VC
Mayville State Univ	ND	8,667	NC
Middle Tenn State Univ	TN	8,540	C
Miss State Univ	MS	9,577	C
Missouri Baptist Univ	MO	19,640	C
Montana Tech of The Univ of Montana	MT	10,434	C
Mount Aloysius College	PA	20,900	LC
Mount St. Mary College	NY	25,250	C
National-Louis Univ	IL	16,915	LC
Northwest Missouri State Univ	MO	10,000	C
Okla City Univ	OK	23,965	VC
Okla Wesleyan Univ	OK	18,950	NC
Oregon State Univ	OR	11,055	C
Penn State Erie/The Behrend College	PA	16,256	C
Penn State Univ/Altoona	PA	12,635	C
Penn State Univ/Univ Park Campus	PA	18,038	HC
Piedmont College	GA	20,500	C
Pitzer College	CA	41,644	HC
Pomona College	CA	40,774	MC
Purdue Univ/West Lafayette	IN	13,458	VC
Rockford College	IL	28,330	VC
Rutgers, The State Univ of New Jersey/Camden Campus	NJ	15,000	VC
Samford Univ	AL	20,258	VC
San Francisco State Univ	CA	13,000	C
Santa Clara Univ	CA	38,931	VC
Seattle Univ	WA	30,063	VC
Sierra Nevada College	NV	30,235	C
Simon's Rock College of Bard	MA	41,988	VC+
Southern Oregon Univ	OR	12,186	C
SUNY/Empire State College	NY	4,575	SP
Trevecca Nazarene Univ	TN	19,594	C
Troy Univ Dothan Campus	AL	4,678	C
Union College	NE	18,710	C
Union College	NY	41,595	HC
United States Air Force Academy	CO		HC+
United States Naval Academy	MD		MC
Univ of Alaska Fairbanks	AK	10,101	C
Univ of Denver	CO	36,374	VC+
Univ of Findlay	OH	29,238	C
Univ of Great Falls	MT	17,000	C
Univ of Mass Amherst	MA	15,973	C+
Univ of Mich/Dearborn	MI	7,000	VC
Univ of Mich/Flint	MI	6,398	C
Univ of Northern Iowa	IA	11,133	VC
Univ of Oregon	OR	13,108	VC
Univ of St. Francis	IN	20,970	C
Univ of Texas at El Paso	TX	8,764	NC
Univ of Wisc/Parkside	WI	10,181	LC
Univ of Wisc/River Falls	WI	9,722	LC
Univ of Wisc/Stout	WI	11,164	C
Univ of Wyoming	WY	9,666	C
Upper Iowa Univ	IA	20,130	C
Urbana Univ	OH	21,190	C
Valley City State Univ	ND	9,854	LC
Villanova Univ	PA	38,672	HC+
Virginia Commonwealth Univ	VA	12,987	C
Walsh Univ	OH	23,440	C
Washburn Univ	KS	9,734	NC
Washington State Univ	WA	12,260	C
Wayland Baptist Univ	TX	13,484	C
West Virginia Univ	WV	10,506	C
Western New Mexico Univ	NM	7,233	LC
Wheeling Jesuit Univ	WV	26,910	C
Wilberforce Univ	OH	14,937	LC
Willamette Univ	OR	35,416	VC+
William Woods Univ	MO	21,020	C
Youngstown State Univ	OH	12,613	NC

SCIENCE AND MANAGEMENT

School	ST	$IS	SR
Philadelphia Univ	PA	30,006	C
Pitzer College	CA	41,644	HC
Scripps College	CA	41,000	MC
Texas A&M Univ at Galveston	TX	10,000	C+

SCIENCE AND SOCIETY

School	ST	$IS	SR
Butler Univ	IN	31,944	VC+
Northwestern Univ	IL	37,595	MC
Rutgers, The State Univ of New Jersey/Newark Campus	NJ	15,640	VC

SCIENCE EDUCATION

School	ST	$IS	SR
Abilene Christian Univ	TX	20,830	C
Adams State College	CO	8,613	C
Adelphi Univ	NY	27,000	VC

ST = STATE　　**$IS** = IN-STATE COSTS　　**SR** = SELECTOR RATING

INDEX OF COLLEGE MAJORS

School	ST	$IS	SR
Alabama A&M Univ	AL	8,890	LC
Albany State Univ	GA	5,770	C+
Alcorn State Univ	MS	8,190	LC
Alfred Univ	NY		VC
Alverno College	WI	21,088	C
American International College	MA	28,710	LC
Anderson Univ	IN	25,050	LC
Andrews Univ	MI	21,786	C
Appalachian State Univ	NC	8,000	VC
Arkansas State Univ	AR	9,630	C
Asbury College	KY	23,762	VC
Ashford Univ	IA	20,370	C
Ashland Univ	OH	25,000	C
Auburn Univ	AL	12,230	VC
Averett Univ	VA	24,920	C
Baldwin-Wallace College	OH	27,256	VC
Ball State Univ	IN	13,138	C
Baylor Univ	TX	27,555	HC
Belmont Univ	TN	24,110	VC
Bemidji State Univ	MN	11,180	LC
Bennett College	NC	11,500	C
Bethany College	KS	20,660	LC
Bethany College	WV	21,395	C
Bethel College	IN	19,680	C
Bethel Univ	MN	29,840	VC
Bethune-Cookman College	FL	17,922	LC
Black Hills State Univ	SD	7,800	LC
Bloomsburg Univ of Pennsylvania	PA	11,602	C
Blue Mountain College	MS	11,086	C
Boston Univ	MA	42,046	HC+
Bowie State Univ	MD	10,880	C+
Brewton-Parker College	GA	14,220	LC
Brigham Young Univ	UT	9,200	VC
Brigham Young Univ/Hawaii	HI	7,740	HC+
Bryan College	TN	19,270	C
Buena Vista Univ	IA	27,742	C
Cal State, Long Beach	CA	9,512	C
Caribbean Univ	PR	3,000	
Carroll College	WI	24,860	C
Carson-Newman College	TN	16,800	C
Catawba College	NC	25,000	C
Cedar Crest College	PA	30,615	C
Cedarville Univ	OH	21,904	VC
Central Methodist Univ	MO	18,000	C
Central Missouri State Univ	MO	10,000	C
Central Univ of Bayamon	PR	3,335	
Central Washington Univ	WA	11,730	C
Chadron State College	NE	6,350	NC
Charleston Southern Univ	SC	17,800	C
Christopher Newport Univ	VA	13,326	VC
CUNY/Brooklyn College	NY	4,377	C+
CUNY/Herbert H. Lehman College	NY	4,000	LC
CUNY/Hunter College	NY	8,000	C+
Coker College	SC	21,600	C
Colby-Sawyer College	NH	27,850	LC
College of New Jersey	NJ	18,315	MC
College of Notre Dame of Maryland	MD	27,700	C
College of Our Lady of the Elms	MA	21,000	C
College of St. Rose	NY	25,684	C
Concord College	WV	9,708	C
Concordia College: Moorhead	MN	22,475	VC
Concordia Univ Nebr	NE	20,500	C+
Concordia Univ St.Paul	MN	27,776	C
Concordia Univ, River Forest	IL	26,300	C
Conn College	CT	41,975	MC
Converse College	SC	24,800	VC
Cornell College	IA	30,110	VC+
Cornerstone Univ and Grand Rapids Theological Seminary	MI	21,350	NC
Crichton College	TN	15,300	C
Daemen College	NY	24,580	C
Dana College	NE	22,390	C
Defiance College	OH	24,790	C
Delaware State Univ	DE	8,130	LC
Delta State Univ	MS	7,709	C
Dickinson State Univ	ND	7,847	NC
Dominican College	NY	26,630	LC
East Carolina Univ	NC	10,000	C
East Central Univ	OK	6,207	C
East Texas Baptist Univ	TX	16,713	C
Eastern Mich Univ	MI	12,897	C
Eastern Nazarene College	MA	19,500	LC
Eastern Washington Univ	WA	10,608	C
Edgewood College	WI	22,862	C
Edinboro Univ of Pennsylvania	PA	11,809	LC
Elmira College	NY	37,200	VC
Elon Univ	NC	25,371	HC
Eureka College	IL	19,280	C
Evangel Univ	MO	17,380	C
Fairmont State	WV	8,400	LC
Florida A&M Univ	FL	8,344	C
Florida Inst of Technology	FL	29,720	VC
Florida International Univ	FL	9,215	VC
Florida Southern College	FL	25,965	C
Florida State Univ	FL	9,028	HC
Franklin College	IN		C
Freed-Hardeman Univ	TN	16,370	NC
Fresno Pacific Univ	CA	25,454	C
Friends Univ	KS	16,250	LC
George Fox Univ	OR	28,490	C
Georgia Southern Univ	GA	9,762	C
Georgia Southwestern State Univ	GA	6,035	C
Gettysburg College	PA	39,864	VC
Glenville State College	WV	8,778	NC
Goshen College	IN	22,850	VC
Grace College	IN	22,170	C
Grambling State Univ	LA	6,538	LC
Grand Canyon Univ	AZ	32,000	LC
Grand Valley State Univ	MI	12,000	VC
Greensboro College	NC	23,000	C
Grove City College	PA	15,784	HC+
Gustavus Adolphus College	MN	30,920	HC
Gwynedd-Mercy College	PA	26,080	C
Hamline Univ	MN	27,070	VC
Hardin-Simmons Univ	TX	18,641	C
Hastings College	NE	22,218	VC
Heidelberg College	OH	23,242	C
Heritage Univ	WA	6,800	NC
Hillsdale College	MI	24,160	HC
Hofstra Univ	NY	32,630	VC
Holy Family Univ	PA	25,740	C
Hood College	MD	30,085	VC
Hope College	MI	28,208	VC+
Houghton College	NY	25,980	VC+
Humboldt State Univ	CA	11,176	C
Huntington Univ	IN	24,830	C
Huron Univ	SD	10,700	C
Illinois College	IL	21,900	C+
Immaculata Univ	PA	25,350	C
Indiana State Univ	IN	11,604	C
Indiana Univ Bloomington	IN	13,356	VC
Indiana Univ of Pennsylvania	PA	11,209	C
Indiana Univ South Bend	IN	4,989	LC
Indiana Univ-Purdue Univ Fort Wayne	IN	5,067	LC
Indiana Univ-Purdue Univ Indianapolis	IN	10,959	C
Indiana Wesleyan Univ	IN	22,074	C+
Inter American Univ of PR/San German	PR	6,720	
Iona College	NY	30,878	VC
Iowa Wesleyan College	IA	22,140	C
John Brown Univ	AR	20,910	VC
Johnson State College	VT	11,830	LC
Judson College	AL	16,522	C
Judson College	IL	25,130	C
Juniata College	PA	33,130	VC
Keene State College	NH	13,836	C
Kennesaw State Univ	GA	12,152	C
Kent State Univ	OH	14,594	C
King's College	PA	29,810	C
Knoxville College	TN	6,200	LC
La Roche College	PA	24,724	LC
La Salle Univ	PA	34,950	C
Lamar Univ	TX	6,820	LC
Langston Univ	OK	2,308	LC
Le Moyne College	NY	29,570	VC
Lenoir-Rhyne College	NC	25,580	C
LeTourneau Univ	TX	21,200	C
Limestone College	SC	19,840	C
Lincoln Memorial Univ	TN	18,144	C
Lindenwood Univ	MO	18,600	VC
Livingstone College	NC	17,815	LC
Lock Haven Univ of Pennsylvania	PA	12,098	LC
LIU/Brooklyn Campus	NY	25,000	C
LIU/C.W. Post Campus	NY	28,282	C
Loras College	IA	27,193	C
Louisiana College	LA	13,450	C
Lubbock Christian Univ	TX	16,960	C
Lyndon State College	VT	14,233	LC
MacMurray College	IL	20,755	C
Malone College	OH	23,040	C
Manhattan College	NY	29,000	VC
Mansfield Univ	PA	11,300	C
Marian College of Fond du Lac	WI	21,775	LC
Mars Hill College	NC	19,000	LC
Maryville College	TN	29,224	VC
Marywood Univ	PA	30,680	C
Mayville State Univ	ND	8,667	NC
McNeese State Univ	LA	5,270	LC
Mercyhurst College	PA	28,633	VC
Messiah College	PA	28,910	VC+
Miami Univ	OH	29,097	HC
MidAmerica Nazarene Univ	KS	20,584	LC
Midland Lutheran College	NE	18,600	C
Miles College	AL	9,922	NC
Millikin Univ	IL	25,590	C
Minn State Univ, Mankato	MN	10,276	LC
Minn State Univ, Moorhead	MN	7,000	LC
Minot State Univ	ND	6,700	LC
Miss Valley State Univ	MS	7,970	C
Missouri Southern State Univ	MO	8,396	NC
Missouri State Univ	MO	10,748	C+
Monmouth Univ	NJ	28,956	C
Montana State Univ-Billings	MT	8,906	C
Montana State Univ-Northern	MT	10,000	NC
Morningside College	IA	23,704	C
Morris College	SC	11,999	LC
Mount Mary College	WI	22,895	C
Mount Vernon Nazarene Univ	OH	20,810	C
Muskingum College	OH	22,970	C
Nazareth College of Rochester	NY	28,175	VC
Nebr Wesleyan Univ	NE	23,415	C+
New Mexico Highlands Univ	NM	6,272	NC
New York Inst of Technology	NY	28,126	VC
New York Univ	NY	43,170	MC
Niagara Univ	NY	28,250	C
N Car State Univ	NC	11,824	HC
North Georgia College and State Univ	GA	7,000	C
Northeastern State Univ	OK	5,896	LC
Northern Arizona Univ	AZ	10,353	C
Northern Kentucky Univ	KY	6,670	NC
Northern Mich Univ	MI	12,340	LC
Northern State Univ	SD	8,257	C
Northwest Missouri State Univ	MO	10,000	C
Northwest Nazarene Univ	ID	22,590	VC
Northwestern College of Iowa	IA	22,174	C+
Northwestern Okla State Univ	OK	6,250	NC
Oakland City Univ	IN	19,620	NC
Oakwood College	AL	14,904	C
Ohio Univ	OH	15,921	C
Ohio Wesleyan Univ	OH	35,830	VC+
Okla Baptist Univ	OK	17,986	VC
Okla Christian Univ	OK	18,992	NC
Okla City Univ	OK	23,965	VC
Okla Panhandle State Univ	OK	7,635	NC
Old Dominion Univ	VA	11,907	C
Oral Roberts Univ	OK	22,650	C
Ouachita Baptist Univ	AR	21,900	VC
Palm Beach Atlantic Univ	FL	23,597	VC
Peru State College	NE	6,350	NC
Pfeiffer Univ	NC	21,900	C
Pittsburg State Univ	KS	8,112	C
Plymouth State Univ	NH	12,298	LC
Pontifical Catholic Univ of PR/Ponce	PR	7,310	
Purdue Univ/Calumet	IN	10,891	C
Purdue Univ/West Lafayette	IN	13,458	VC
Quincy Univ	IL	24,920	C
Rhode Island College	RI	11,570	C
Rider Univ	NJ	32,560	C
Rocky Mountain College	MT	20,805	C
Rowan Univ	NJ	16,000	VC
Rust College	MS		C+
Saginaw Valley State Univ	MI	11,432	C
St. Augustine's College	NC	14,000	LC
St. Cloud State Univ	MN	10,010	C
St. Edward's Univ	TX	23,560	C
St. John Fisher College	NY	27,860	C
St. John's Univ	NY	34,370	C
St. Mary-of-the-Woods College	IN	25,480	C
St. Mary's Univ of Minn	MN	23,857	VC
St. Mary's Univ of San Antonio	TX	22,444	C
St. Michael's College	VT	33,330	VC
St. Thomas Aquinas College	NY	22,000	C
St. Vincent College	PA	26,160	VC
St. Xavier Univ	IL	23,160	C
Salem State College	MA	13,161	C
Schreiner Univ	TX	20,600	C
Seattle Pacific Univ	WA	29,355	C
Seton Hill Univ	PA	28,810	C
Shaw Univ	NC	15,488	LC
Sheldon Jackson College	AK	17,900	LC
Shepherd Univ	WV	10,066	C
Shippensburg Univ of Pennsylvania	PA	11,621	C
Slippery Rock Univ of Pennsylvania	PA	10,360	LC
Southeast Missouri State Univ	MO	10,596	C
Southeastern Louisiana Univ	LA	8,521	LC
Southeastern Okla State Univ	OK	6,147	C
Southern Arkansas Univ	AR	6,956	C
Southern Conn State Univ	CT	10,310	C
Southern Illinois Univ Edwardsville	IL	11,022	C
Southern Univ at New Orleans	LA	1,000	NC
Southern Utah Univ	UT		C
Southwest Minn State Univ	MN	10,975	C
Southwestern College	KS	21,476	C
Southwestern Okla State Univ	OK	4,801	C
Springfield College	MA	25,000	C
SUNY at Potsdam	NY	12,959	C
SUNY/College at Buffalo	NY	11,903	C+
SUNY/College at Fredonia	NY	12,771	VC
SUNY/College at Old Westbury	NY	13,154	C
SUNY/College at Oneonta	NY	12,905	VC
SUNY/College at Plattsburgh	NY	12,362	C
SUNY/College of Environmental Science and Forestry	NY	15,000	VC
SUNY/Univ at Albany	NY	13,860	VC
SUNY/Univ at New Paltz	NY	12,480	VC
Suffolk Univ	MA	33,160	C
Syracuse Univ	NY	38,655	HC
Tabor College	KS	21,614	NC
Taylor Univ	IN	26,376	VC+
Temple Univ	PA	17,438	C
Texas A&M Univ at Commerce	TX	9,020	C
Texas Christian Univ	TX	23,410	VC+
Texas Tech Univ	TX	13,026	VC
Tougaloo College	MS	15,975	NC
Trevecca Nazarene Univ	TN	19,594	C
Tri-State Univ-Main Campus	IN	26,200	C
Troy Univ	AL	8,916	C
Troy Univ Dothan Campus	AL	4,678	C
Turabo Univ	PR	4,110	
Univ of Akron	OH	15,166	NC
Univ of Arizona	AZ	11,958	VC
Univ of Arkansas at Pine Bluff	AR	8,300	C
Univ of Calif at San Diego	CA	16,102	HC
Univ of Central Arkansas	AR	9,984	C
Univ of Central Florida	FL	10,739	VC
Univ of Central Okla	OK	8,094	C
Univ of Charleston	WV	27,600	C
Univ of Cincinnati	OH	17,682	C
Univ of Conn	CT	16,628	HC
Univ of Delaware	DE	14,142	VC
Univ of Evansville	IN	28,320	VC
Univ of Georgia	GA	11,004	HC
Univ of Great Falls	MT	17,000	C
Univ of Idaho	ID	9,310	NC
Univ of Illinois at Chicago	IL	16,256	VC
Univ of Illinois at Urbana-Champaign	IL	15,800	HC+
Univ of Indianapolis	IN	25,090	C
Univ of Iowa	IA	12,172	VC
Univ of Kentucky	KY	7,800	C
Univ of Louisiana at Lafayette	LA	5,830	C
Univ of Louisiana at Monroe	LA	7,103	C
Univ of Louisville	KY	10,400	VC
Univ of Mary	ND	15,374	C
Univ of Mary Hardin-Baylor	TX	19,428	C
Univ of Maryland/College Park	MD	16,036	HC
Univ of Maryland/Eastern Shore	MD	11,210	C
Univ of Mich/Dearborn	MI	7,000	VC
Univ of Minn/Duluth	MN	13,974	C
Univ of Minn/Twin Cities	MN	13,165	VC
Univ of Miss	MS	9,000	C
Univ of Montana	MT	10,602	C
Univ of Montana--Western	MT	8,406	NC
Univ of Nebr at Kearney	NE	9,000	C
Univ of Nebr at Lincoln	NE	11,401	VC
Univ of New Hampshire	NH	16,810	VC
Univ of New Orleans	LA	7,370	C
Univ of North Alabama	AL	8,992	C
Univ of N Car at Charlotte	NC	9,101	C
Univ of N Car at Pembroke	NC	7,940	LC
Univ of N Dak	ND	10,114	VC
Univ of North Florida	FL	9,908	VC
Univ of Northern Colo	CO	10,249	C
Univ of Northern Iowa	IA	11,133	C
Univ of Notre Dame	IN	39,552	MC
Univ of Okla	OK	10,769	VC+
Univ of Pittsburgh at Johnstown	PA	16,740	LC
Univ of Rio Grande	OH	8,728	NC
Univ of St. Francis	IN	20,970	C
Univ of St. Thomas	MN	28,000	C
Univ of Scranton	PA	31,100	VC
Univ of Sioux Falls	SD	20,800	C
Univ of South Florida	FL	10,284	VC
Univ of Southern Indiana	IN	12,590	C
Univ of Southern Miss	MS	10,112	C
Univ of the Cumberlands	KY	18,184	C
Univ of Toledo	OH	15,806	NC
Univ of Vermont	VT	18,080	VC
Univ of West Alabama	AL	7,611	C
Univ of Wisc/Eau Claire	WI	9,915	VC
Univ of Wisc/La Crosse	WI	10,045	VC
Univ of Wisc/Oshkosh	WI	10,426	C
Univ of Wisc/Superior	WI	9,610	C+
Univ of Wisc/Whitewater	WI	9,274	C
Utah State Univ	UT	8,002	VC
Vanguard Univ of Southern Calif	CA	27,071	C
Virginia Polytechnic Inst and State Univ	VA	10,834	VC
Viterbo Univ	WI	21,670	C
Warner Southern College	FL	18,000	C
Wartburg College	IA	27,315	NC
Washington State Univ	WA	12,260	C
Washington Univ in St. Louis	MO	42,106	MC
Wayne State College	NE	8,033	NC
Wayne State Univ	MI	11,805	C

ST = STATE $IS = IN-STATE COSTS   SR = SELECTOR RATING

School	ST	$IS	SR
Weber State Univ	UT	9,635	NC
West Liberty State College	WV	9,142	LC
West Texas A&M Univ	TX	8,452	C
Western Carolina Univ	NC	7,000	C
Western New Mexico Univ	NM	7,233	LC
Western State College of Colo	CO	9,942	C
Western Washington Univ	WA	11,262	VC
Westfield State College	MA	10,200	C
Wheaton College	IL	27,760	HC
Whitworth College	WA	29,428	VC+
Widener Univ	PA	27,275	C
William Penn Univ	IA	17,685	LC
Wingate Univ	NC	23,300	C
Winona State Univ	MN	11,333	C
Wittenberg Univ	OH	34,596	VC
Wright State Univ	OH	13,616	LC
Xavier Univ	OH	30,490	HC
Xavier Univ of Louisiana	LA	17,600	C
York College	NE	16,330	NC
York College of Pennsylvania	PA	16,550	LC
Youngstown State Univ	OH	12,613	NC

SCIENCE TECHNOLOGY

School	ST	$IS	SR
Claremont McKenna College	CA	42,920	MC
Colby College	ME	41,770	MC
Cornell Univ	NY	41,717	MC
James Madison Univ	VA	12,010	VC
Lehigh Univ	PA	42,690	HC+
Marshall Univ	WV	9,116	C
Mass Inst of Technology	MA	41,800	MC
Olivet Nazarene Univ	IL	22,590	C
Rensselaer Polytechnic Inst	NY	41,288	HC+
St. John Fisher College	NY	27,860	C
Scripps College	CA	41,000	MC
Stevens Inst of Technology	NJ	40,935	HC
Wesleyan Univ	CT	42,122	MC

SCIENTIFIC/MEDICAL MARKETING

School	ST	$IS	SR
Carlow Univ	PA	24,313	C

SCULPTURE

School	ST	$IS	SR
Aquinas College	MI	23,750	C
Atlanta College of Art	GA	18,630	SP
Bard College	NY	41,800	HC+
Bennington College	VT	41,890	HC
Birmingham-Southern College	AL	28,494	VC+
Boston Univ	MA	42,046	HC+
Bradley Univ	IL	25,280	VC
Calif College of the Arts	CA	34,325	SP
Cal State, Fullerton	CA	10,990	C
Cal State, San Bernardino	CA	12,563	LC
Catholic Univ of America	DC	35,838	VC
Cleveland Inst of Art	OH	34,109	SP
College for Creative Studies	MI	24,000	SP
College of Santa Fe	NM	28,978	C
College of Visual Arts	MN	18,040	SP
Edinboro Univ of Pennsylvania	PA	11,809	C
Escuela de Artes Plasticas de PR	PR	2,372	
Indiana Univ-Purdue Univ Indianapolis	IN	10,959	C
Kansas City Art Inst	MO	29,542	SP
Kendall College of Art and Design of Ferris State Univ	MI	11,870	SP
Maine Inst of Art	ME	28,820	SP
Maryland Inst College of Art	MD	34,450	SP
Mass College of Art	MA	16,650	SP
Milwaukee Inst of Art and Design	WI	28,700	SP
Minneapolis College of Art and Design	MN	31,110	SP
Montserrat College of Art	MA	25,929	SP
Moore College of Art and Design	PA	27,200	SP
Northwest Nazarene Univ	ID	22,590	VC
Pacific Northwest College of Art	OR	17,296	SP
Rhode Island School of Design	RI	38,130	SP
Rochester Inst of Technology	NY	32,070	VC+
San Francisco Art Inst	CA	25,640	SP
School of the Art Inst of Chicago	IL	37,800	SP
Shepherd Univ	WV	10,066	C
SUNY/College at Buffalo	NY	11,903	C+
Syracuse Univ	NY	38,655	HC
Univ of Dallas	TX	27,432	VC+
Univ of Georgia	GA	11,004	HC
Univ of Hartford	CT	34,044	C
Univ of Houston	TX	7,000	C
Univ of Illinois at Urbana-Champaign	IL	15,800	HC+
Univ of Kansas	KS	10,915	VC
Univ of Mass Dartmouth	MA	15,985	C

School	ST	$IS	SR
Univ of Miami	FL	38,397	MC
Univ of Mich/Ann Arbor	MI	16,587	HC+
Univ of North Texas	TX	7,800	C
Univ of Oregon	OR	13,108	VC
Univ of the Arts	PA	32,330	SP
Univ of Washington	WA	10,400	VC
Virginia Commonwealth Univ	VA	12,987	C
Washington Univ in St. Louis	MO	42,106	MC

SECONDARY EDUCATION

School	ST	$IS	SR
Abilene Christian Univ	TX	20,830	C
Adams State College	CO	8,613	C
Adelphi Univ	NY	27,000	VC
Adrian College	MI	23,000	C
Alabama A&M Univ	AL	8,890	LC
Alabama State Univ	AL	7,658	C
Albright College	PA	33,920	C
Alderson-Broaddus College	WV	24,006	C
Alfred Univ	NY		VC
Alice Lloyd College	KY	4,900	C
Alma College	MI	28,544	VC
Alvernia College	PA	26,388	C
Alverno College	WI	21,088	C
American International College	MA	28,710	LC
American Univ	DC	38,719	HC+
Andrews Univ	MI	21,786	C
Appalachian State Univ	NC	8,000	VC
Arcadia Univ	PA	33,570	VC
Arizona State Univ-Tempe	AZ	11,174	C
Arkansas Tech Univ	AR	8,108	VC
Armstrong Atlantic State Univ	GA	7,394	C
Asbury College	KY	23,762	VC
Ashland Univ	OH	25,000	C
Auburn Univ	AL	12,230	VC
Auburn Univ Montgomery	AL	9,530	NC
Augsburg College	MN	28,300	C
Augustana College	IL	29,862	VC+
Augustana College	SD	24,380	VC
Averett Univ	VA	24,920	C
Ball State Univ	IN	13,138	C
Baylor Univ	TX	27,555	HC
Bellarmine Univ	KY	27,650	C+
Bemidji State Univ	MN	11,180	LC
Benedictine College	KS	21,968	C
Bennett College	NC	11,500	C
Berea College	KY	5,496	VC+
Bethany College	KS	20,660	LC
Bethany College	WV	21,395	C
Bethel College	IN	19,680	C
Bethel Univ	MN	29,840	VC
Birmingham-Southern College	AL	28,494	VC+
Black Hills State Univ	SD	7,800	LC
Blackburn College	IL	13,690	C
Bloomsburg Univ of Pennsylvania	PA	11,602	C
Blue Mountain College	MS	11,086	C
Bluefield College	VA	17,230	C+
Boise State Univ	ID	9,438	LC
Boston College	MA	41,608	MC
Bradley Univ	IL	25,280	VC
Brewton-Parker College	GA	14,220	LC
Briar Cliff Univ	IA	23,550	LC
Bucknell Univ	PA	39,660	MC
Buena Vista Univ	IA	27,742	C
Butler Univ	IN	31,944	VC+
Calif Univ of Pennsylvania	PA	14,217	C
Calumet College of St. Joseph	IN	9,500	LC
Calvin College	MI	25,735	NC
Canisius College	NY	32,257	VC
Capital Univ	OH	30,444	C
Cardinal Stritch Univ	WI	21,910	C
Caribbean Univ	PR	3,000	
Carlow Univ	PA	24,313	C
Carroll College	MT	23,324	C+
Carson-Newman College	TN	16,800	C
Carthage College	WI	26,000	C
Catholic Univ of America	DC	35,838	VC
Cedar Crest College	PA	30,615	C
Centenary College	NJ	28,870	LC
Central College	IA	26,774	VC
Central Missouri State Univ	MO	10,000	C
Central State Univ	OH	9,010	C+
Central Univ of Bayamon	PR	3,335	
Central Washington Univ	WA	11,730	C
Chadron State College	NE	6,350	NC
Chaminade Univ of Honolulu	HI	23,320	LC
Champlain College	VT	24,605	C
Cheyney Univ of Pennsylvania	PA	11,497	LC
Chicago State Univ	IL	10,915	C+
Christopher Newport Univ	VA	13,326	VC
Citadel, The	SC		C+
CUNY/Brooklyn Campus	NY	4,377	C+
CUNY/City College	NY		C
CUNY/Herbert H. Lehman College	NY	4,000	LC
CUNY/Hunter College	NY	8,000	C+

School	ST	$IS	SR
Clarion Univ of Pennsylvania	PA	11,844	C
Clarke College	IA	25,390	C
Clearwater Christian College	FL	13,160	LC
Clemson Univ	SC	13,366	HC
Cleveland State Univ	OH	10,798	NC
Coe College	IA	27,440	VC
College Misericordia	PA	27,950	C
College of Notre Dame of Maryland	MD	27,700	C
College of Our Lady of the Elms	MA	21,000	C
College of St. Joseph	VT	20,900	NC
College of Santa Fe	NM	28,978	C
College of the Ozarks	MO	4,130	VC+
College of the Southwest	NM	12,420	C+
Colo Christian Univ	CO	21,182	VC
Columbia College	MO	16,900	C
Columbus State Univ	GA	8,664	C
Concord College	WV	9,708	C
Concordia College: Moorhead	MN	22,475	VC
Concordia Univ	OR	24,400	C
Concordia Univ at Austin	TX	23,640	LC
Concordia Univ Nebr	NE	20,500	C+
Concordia Univ St.Paul	MN	27,776	C
Concordia Univ Wisc	WI	22,660	VC
Concordia Univ, Ann Arbor	MI	25,153	C+
Concordia Univ, River Forest	IL	26,300	C
Converse College	SC	24,800	VC
Cornell College	IA	30,110	VC+
Cornerstone Univ and Grand Rapids Theological Seminary	MI	21,350	NC
Creighton Univ	NE	29,918	VC+
Crichton College	TN	15,300	C
Cumberland Univ	TN	18,894	C
Dakota State Univ	SD	7,466	C
Dakota Wesleyan Univ	SD	17,832	C
Dana College	NE	22,390	C
Davis and Elkins College	WV	22,416	C
Defiance College	OH	24,790	C
Delaware Valley College	PA	29,944	C
Delta State Univ	MS	7,709	C
DePaul Univ	IL	29,835	VC
Dickinson State Univ	ND	7,847	NC
Dillard Univ	LA	17,500	VC
Dominican College	NY	26,630	LC
Dordt College	IA	20,325	VC
Dowling College	NY	22,110	LC
Drake Univ	IA	27,632	VC+
Drury Univ	MO	20,117	VC
Duquesne Univ	PA	29,534	VC
East Stroudsburg Univ of Pennsylvania	PA	10,336	C
East Texas Baptist Univ	TX	16,713	C
Eastern Illinois Univ	IL	12,569	C
Eastern Kentucky Univ	KY	7,725	C
Eastern Mennonite Univ	VA	25,450	VC
Eastern Mich Univ	MI	12,897	C
Eastern Univ	PA	24,075	C
Eastern Washington Univ	WA	10,608	C
Edinboro Univ of Pennsylvania	PA	11,809	LC
Elizabethtown College	PA	32,100	VC
Elmhurst College	IL	24,685	C
Elmira College	NY	37,200	VC
Elon Univ	NC	25,371	HC
Emmanuel College	MA	32,000	C+
Emporia State Univ	KS	8,093	C
Eureka College	IL	19,280	C
Evangel Univ	MO	17,380	C
Fairmont State	WV	8,400	LC
Faulkner Univ	AL	15,600	C
Fayetteville State Univ	NC	6,000	LC
Fitchburg State College	MA	11,276	C
Flagler College	FL	13,790	VC+
Florida Gulf Coast Univ	FL	10,833	C
Florida Memorial Univ	FL	6,000	LC
Florida Southern College	FL	25,965	C
Fort Valley State Univ	GA	6,975	C
Franklin College	IN		C
Franklin Pierce College	NH	31,700	C
Freed-Hardeman Univ	TN	16,370	NC
Friends Univ	KS	16,250	LC
Gallaudet Univ	DC	16,554	
Gannon Univ	PA	26,100	C
Gardner-Webb Univ	NC	21,500	C
George Fox Univ	OR	28,490	C
Georgia Southwestern State Univ	GA	6,035	C
Gettysburg College	PA	39,864	HC
Glenville State College	WV	8,778	NC
Gordon College	MA	29,194	C+
Goshen College	IN	22,850	VC
Grace Bible College	MI	18,810	C
Grand Canyon Univ	AZ	32,000	LC
Grand Valley State Univ	MI	12,000	VC
Grand View College	IA	21,482	C
Green Mountain College	VT	32,164	C
Greensboro College	NC	23,000	C
Grove City College	PA	15,784	HC+
Gustavus Adolphus College	MN	30,920	HC
Gwynedd-Mercy College	PA	26,080	C

School	ST	$IS	SR
Hamline Univ	MN	27,070	VC
Hannibal-LaGrange College	MO	16,390	C
Harding Univ	AR	16,512	VC
Hardin-Simmons Univ	TX	18,641	C
Hastings College	NE	22,218	VC
Heidelberg College	OH	23,242	C
Heritage Univ	WA	6,800	NC
High Point Univ	NC	25,720	C
Hillsdale College	MI	24,160	HC
Hofstra Univ	NY	32,630	VC
Holy Family Univ	PA	25,740	C
Hood College	MD	30,085	VC
Hope College	MI	28,208	VC+
Hope International Univ	CA	23,700	NC
Houghton College	NY	25,980	VC+
Houston Baptist Univ	TX	18,660	C
Howard Payne Univ	TX	17,115	C
Howard Univ	DC	18,481	C+
Humboldt State Univ	CA	11,176	C
Huron Univ	SD	10,700	C
Idaho State Univ	ID	9,030	C
Illinois College	IL	21,900	C+
Immaculata Univ	PA	25,350	C
Indiana State Univ	IN	11,604	C
Indiana Univ East	IN	4,806	LC
Indiana Univ Northwest	IN	4,902	LC
Indiana Univ South Bend	IN	4,989	LC
Indiana Univ Southeast	IN	4,880	LC
Indiana Univ-Purdue Univ Fort Wayne	IN	5,067	LC
Indiana Univ-Purdue Univ Indianapolis	IN	10,959	C
Indiana Wesleyan Univ	IN	22,074	C+
Inter American Univ of PR/ Aguadilla Campus	PR	3,784	
Inter American Univ of PR/ Arecibo Campus	PR	3,350	
Inter American Univ of PR/ Barranquitas Regional College	PR	3,350	
Inter American Univ of PR/ Fajardo Campus	PR	4,000	
Inter American Univ of PR/ Metropolitan Campus	PR	4,320	
Inter American Univ of PR/ Ponce Regional College	PR	3,700	
Inter American Univ of PR/ San German	PR	6,720	
Iona College	NY	30,878	VC
Iowa State Univ	IA	11,831	VC
Iowa Wesleyan College	IA	22,140	C
Ithaca College	NY	35,144	VC
Jacksonville State Univ	AL	7,618	LC
Jarvis Christian College	TX	11,136	NC
John Brown Univ	AR	20,910	VC
John Carroll Univ	OH	27,658	C+
Johnson C. Smith Univ	NC	20,000	C
Johnson State College	VT	11,830	LC
Judson College	IL	25,130	C
Juniata College	PA	33,130	VC
Kansas State Univ	KS	10,516	VC
Kansas Wesleyan Univ	KS	21,400	VC
Keene State College	NH	13,836	C
Kent State Univ	OH	14,594	C
Kentucky State Univ	KY	10,089	LC
Kentucky Wesleyan College	KY	18,590	C
Keuka College	NY	26,050	C
King College	TN	23,400	C
King's College	PA	29,810	C
Knox College	IL	32,385	VC+
Kutztown Univ of Pennsylvania	PA	10,820	C
La Salle Univ	PA	34,950	C
La Sierra Univ	CA	24,327	C+
Lake Superior State Univ	MI	12,842	LC
Lakeland College	WI	22,990	C
Lamar Univ	TX	6,820	LC
Lambuth Univ	TN	21,700	C+
Lasell College	MA	26,250	C
Lawrence Univ	WI	33,958	HC+
Le Moyne College	NY	29,570	VC
Lenoir-Rhyne College	NC	25,580	C
LeTourneau Univ	TX	21,200	C
Lewis Univ	IL	23,050	C+
Lewis-Clark State College	ID	6,990	C
Lincoln Memorial Univ	TN	18,144	C
Lincoln Univ	PA	13,658	C
Lindenwood Univ	MO	18,600	VC
Lindsey Wilson College	KY	16,425	LC
Livingstone College	NC	17,815	LC
Lock Haven Univ of Pennsylvania	PA	12,098	LC
LIU/Brooklyn Campus	NY	25,000	C
LIU/C.W. Post Campus	NY	28,282	C
Loras College	IA	27,193	C
Louisiana College	LA	13,450	C
Louisiana State Univ and A&M College	LA	10,749	VC
Louisiana State Univ in Shreveport	LA	2,900	NC
Louisiana Tech Univ	LA	7,370	C
Loyola Univ Chicago	IL	32,896	VC
Lubbock Christian Univ	TX	16,960	C
Lynn Univ	FL	30,750	C
MacMurray College	IL	20,755	C
Madonna Univ	MI	16,068	VC

ST = STATE $IS = IN-STATE COSTS   SR = SELECTOR RATING

School	ST	$IS	SR
Malone College	OH	23,040	C
Manchester College	IN	23,470	C
Manhattan College	NY	29,000	VC
Mansfield Univ	PA	11,300	C
Marian College of Fond du Lac	WI	21,775	LC
Marquette Univ	WI	31,066	HC
Maryville College	TN	29,224	C
Maryville Univ of St. Louis	MO	23,000	VC
Marywood Univ	PA	30,680	C
Master's College and Seminary	CA	25,850	VC
Mayville State Univ	ND	8,667	NC
McMurry Univ	TX	18,100	LC
McPherson College	KS	21,010	C
Mercer Univ	GA	27,525	VC+
Mercyhurst College	PA	28,633	VC
Merrimack College	MA	34,380	C
Methodist College	NC	21,000	C
Miami Univ	OH	29,007	HC
Midland Lutheran College	NE	18,600	C
Miles College	AL	9,922	NC
Millikin Univ	IL	25,590	C
Minn State Univ, Mankato	MN	10,276	LC
Minn State Univ, Moorhead	MN	7,000	LC
Miss State Univ	MS	9,577	C
Missouri Southern State Univ	MO	8,396	NC
Missouri State Univ	MO	10,748	C+
Missouri Western State Univ	MO	9,534	NC
Molloy College	NY	16,510	C
Monmouth College	IL	23,700	C
Monmouth Univ	NJ	28,956	C
Montana State Univ-Billings	MT	8,906	C
Montana State Univ-Bozeman	MT	1,137	C
Montana State Univ-Northern	MT	10,000	NC
Moravian College	PA	28,950	VC
Mount Marty College	SD	20,590	C
Mount Mary College	WI	22,895	C
Mount Mercy College	IA	23,670	C
Mount Olive College	NC	16,000	LC
Mount St. Mary College	NY	25,250	C
Mount St. Mary's College	CA	32,086	VC
Mount St. Mary's Univ	MD	30,930	C
Mount Vernon Nazarene Univ	OH	20,810	C
Murray State Univ	KY	8,900	VC
Muskingum College	OH	22,970	C
New England College	NH	31,466	C
New Jersey City Univ	NJ	13,695	LC
New Mexico State Univ	NM	9,250	C
New York Inst of Technology	NY	28,126	VC
New York Univ	NY	43,170	MC
Newman Univ	KS	21,106	C
Niagara Univ	NY	28,250	C
Nicholls State Univ	LA	6,500	NC
N Car State Univ	NC	11,824	HC
North Central College	IL	28,926	VC
N Dak State Univ	ND	8,500	C
North Georgia College and State Univ	GA	7,000	C
North Park Univ	IL	24,050	C
Northeastern Illinois Univ	IL	3,000	NC
Northeastern State Univ	OK	5,896	LC
Northern Arizona Univ	AZ	10,353	C
Northern Kentucky Univ	KY	6,670	NC
Northern Mich Univ	MI	12,340	LC
Northern State Univ	SD	8,257	C
Northland College	WI	26,680	C+
Northwest Missouri State Univ	MO	10,000	C
Northwest Univ	WA	18,854	C
Northwestern College of Iowa	IA	22,174	C+
Northwestern Okla State Univ	OK	6,250	NC
Northwestern State Univ of Louisiana	LA	7,144	C
Northwestern Univ	IL	37,595	MC
Notre Dame College	OH	20,425	C
Nyack College	NY	18,540	C
Oakland City Univ	IN	19,620	NC
Ohio Univ	OH	15,921	C
Ohio Valley Univ	WV	17,752	C
Okla Baptist Univ	OK	17,986	VC
Okla State Univ	OK	10,213	VC
Okla Wesleyan Univ	OK	18,950	NC
Old Dominion Univ	VA	11,907	C
Olivet College	MI	19,984	C+
Ouachita Baptist Univ	AR	21,900	VC
Our Lady of Holy Cross College	LA	8,090	LC
Paine College	GA	14,148	LC
Palm Beach Atlantic Univ	FL	23,597	VC
Paul Quinn College	TX	8,300	LC
Penn State Univ/Univ Park Campus	PA	18,038	HC
Pepperdine Univ	CA	39,960	HC
Peru State College	NE	6,350	NC
Pfeiffer Univ	NC	21,900	C
Pikeville College	KY	16,500	NC
Point Park Univ	PA	24,160	C

School	ST	$IS	SR
Pontifical Catholic Univ of PR/Ponce	PR	7,310	
Presbyterian College	SC	30,044	VC
Prescott College	AZ	13,445	LC
Providence College	RI	34,580	HC
Purdue Univ/Calumet	IN	10,891	LC
Purdue Univ/West Lafayette	IN	13,458	VC
Quincy Univ	IL	24,920	C
Rhode Island College	RI	11,570	C
Rider Univ	NJ	32,560	C
Ripon College	WI	27,160	C+
Rivier College	NH	26,600	C
Rockhurst Univ	MO	25,440	VC
Roger Williams Univ	RI	30,500	C
Roosevelt Univ	IL	22,605	VC
Rosemont College	PA	29,350	C
Rust College	MS		C+
St. Ambrose Univ	IA	25,495	C
St. Anselm College	NH	33,810	C
St. Cloud State Univ	MN	10,010	C
St. Francis College	NY	19,974	LC
St. Francis Univ	PA	25,880	LC
St. John Fisher College	NY	27,860	C
St. John's Univ	NY	34,370	C
St. Joseph's College	IN	26,600	C
St. Joseph's College, New York, Brooklyn Campus	NY	12,206	C
St. Joseph's College, New York, Suffolk Campus	NY	12,000	C
St. Joseph's Univ	PA	37,428	VC
St. Mary-of-the-Woods College	IN	25,480	C
St. Mary's Univ of San Antonio	TX	22,444	C
St. Michael's College	VT	33,330	VC
St. Paul's College	VA	16,030	NC
St. Peter's College	NJ	30,160	LC
St. Thomas Aquinas College	NY	22,000	LC
St. Thomas Univ	FL	23,490	C
St. Xavier Univ	IL	23,160	C
Salem International Univ	WV	18,020	C
Salem State College	MA	13,161	LC
Salve Regina Univ	RI	33,450	C
Samford Univ	AL	20,258	VC
San Francisco State Univ	CA	13,000	C
Schreiner Univ	TX	20,600	C
Seton Hall Univ	NJ	33,622	NC
Seton Hill Univ	PA	28,810	C
Shaw Univ	NC	15,488	LC
Sheldon Jackson College	AK	17,900	LC
Shepherd Univ	WV	10,066	C
Shippensburg Univ of Pennsylvania	PA	11,621	C
Silver Lake College of the Holy Family	WI	18,500	LC
Simmons College	MA	35,640	VC
Simpson Univ	CA	22,900	C
Slippery Rock Univ of Pennsylvania	PA	10,360	LC
S Dak State Univ	SD	9,815	C
Southeast Missouri State Univ	MO	10,596	C
Southeastern Okla State Univ	OK	6,147	C
Southeastern Univ	FL	17,180	LC
Southern Conn State Univ	CT	10,310	C
Southern Nazarene Univ	OK	14,634	NC
Southern New Hampshire Univ	NH	28,764	C
Southern Univ and A&M College	LA	8,238	LC
Southern Univ at New Orleans	LA	1,000	NC
Southwestern Adventist Univ	TX	18,290	LC
Southwestern Okla State Univ	OK	4,801	C
Spring Hill College	AL	28,678	C
Springfield College	MA	25,000	C
SUNY at Oswego	NY	13,662	VC
SUNY at Potsdam	NY	12,959	C
SUNY/College at Buffalo	NY	11,903	C+
SUNY/College at Cortland	NY	12,095	C
SUNY/College at Fredonia	NY	12,771	VC
SUNY/College at Old Westbury	NY	13,154	C
SUNY/College at Oneonta	NY	12,905	VC
SUNY/College at Plattsburgh	NY	12,362	C
SUNY/Univ at Albany	NY	13,860	VC
SUNY/Univ at New Paltz	NY	12,480	VC
Stetson Univ	FL	32,725	VC
Syracuse Univ	NY	38,655	HC
Tabor College	KS	21,614	NC
Temple Univ	PA	17,438	C
Tenn Tech Univ	TN	10,044	C
Texas A&M Univ	TX	13,351	HC
Texas A&M Univ at Commerce	TX	9,020	C
Texas A&M Univ at Kingsville	TX	6,800	LC
Texas Christian Univ	TX	23,410	VC+
Texas Wesleyan Univ	TX	18,700	C
Thiel College	PA	24,580	C
Thomas More College	KY	24,470	C

School	ST	$IS	SR
Thomas Univ	GA	11,520	NC
Toccoa Falls College	GA	17,125	C
Trinity International Univ	IL	25,686	C
Tri-State Univ-Main Campus	IN	26,200	C
Troy Univ	AL	8,916	C
Troy Univ Dothan Campus	AL	4,678	C
Turabo Univ	PR	4,110	
Tuskegee Univ	AL	18,860	LC
Union College	KY	18,920	C
Union College	NE	18,710	C
Union Univ	TN	20,750	VC
Universidad Adventista de las Antillas	PR	7,360	
Universidad Metropolitana	PR	3,330	
Univ of Akron	OH	15,166	NC
Univ of Alabama	AL	9,888	C
Univ of Alabama at Birmingham	AL	13,716	C
Univ of Alaska Anchorage	AK	11,275	NC
Univ of Arizona	AZ	11,958	VC
Univ of Central Arkansas	AR	9,984	C
Univ of Cincinnati	OH	17,682	C
Univ of Dayton	OH	28,826	VC
Univ of Delaware	DE	14,142	HC
Univ of Detroit Mercy	MI	27,000	C
Univ of Findlay	OH	29,238	C
Univ of Great Falls	MT	17,000	C
Univ of Hartford	CT	34,044	C
Univ of Hawaii at Manoa	HI	10,413	C
Univ of Houston-Downtown	TX	3,326	NC
Univ of Idaho	ID	9,310	NC
Univ of Illinois at Chicago	IL	16,256	VC
Univ of Illinois at Urbana-Champaign	IL	15,800	HC+
Univ of Indianapolis	IN	25,090	C
Univ of Iowa	IA	12,172	VC
Univ of Kentucky	KY	7,800	C
Univ of Louisiana at Lafayette	LA	5,830	C
Univ of Louisville	KY	10,400	VC
Univ of Maine	ME	13,642	C
Univ of Maine at Farmington	ME	11,515	C
Univ of Maine at Presque Isle	ME	10,066	LC
Univ of Mary Hardin-Baylor	TX	19,428	C
Univ of Maryland/College Park	MD	16,036	HC
Univ of Maryland/Eastern Shore	MD	11,210	C
Univ of Mass Amherst	MA	15,973	C+
Univ of Miami	FL	38,397	MC
Univ of Mich/Ann Arbor	MI	16,587	HC+
Univ of Mich/Dearborn	MI	7,000	VC
Univ of Mich/Flint	MI	6,398	C
Univ of Minn/Morris	MN	15,472	VC
Univ of Missouri/Columbia	MO	13,500	VC
Univ of Missouri/Kansas City	MO	15,000	VC
Univ of Missouri/Rolla	MO	13,332	HC
Univ of Missouri/St. Louis	MO	14,046	VC
Univ of Mobile	AL	16,880	C
Univ of Montana	MT	10,602	C
Univ of Montana--Western	MT	8,406	NC
Univ of Nebr at Kearney	NE	9,000	NC
Univ of Nebr at Lincoln	NE	11,401	VC
Univ of Nebr at Omaha	NE	11,235	C
Univ of Nevada/Las Vegas	NV	11,566	C
Univ of Nevada/Reno	NV	12,155	NC
Univ of New Orleans	LA	7,370	C
Univ of North Alabama	AL	8,992	C
Univ of N Car at Chapel Hill	NC	11,129	MC
Univ of N Car at Wilmington	NC	10,107	VC
Univ of North Florida	FL	9,908	VC
Univ of Pittsburgh at Johnstown	PA	16,740	LC
Univ of Portland	OR	32,300	VC
Univ of PR/Cayey Univ College	PR	1,250	
Univ of PR/Rio Piedras	PR	5,750	
Univ of Rhode Island	RI	15,398	C
Univ of Rio Grande	OH	8,728	NC
Univ of St. Francis	IL	25,430	C
Univ of St. Francis	IN	20,970	C
Univ of St. Thomas	MN	28,000	VC
Univ of San Diego	CA	40,620	HC
Univ of San Francisco	CA	37,560	VC
Univ of Scranton	PA	31,100	VC
Univ of Sioux Falls	SD	20,800	C
Univ of South Alabama	AL	8,930	LC
Univ of S Car at Aiken	SC	11,718	LC
Univ of S Car at Columbia	SC	13,397	VC
Univ of S Car Upstate	SC	11,957	C
Univ of S Dak	SD	9,068	C
Univ of Southern Indiana	IN	12,590	LC
Univ of Southern Miss	MS	10,112	C
Univ of Tampa	FL	25,784	C
Univ of Tenn at Chattanooga	TN	7,790	C
Univ of Tenn at Martin	TN	8,693	C
Univ of Texas-Pan American	TX	7,290	C+
Univ of the Incarnate Word	TX	23,306	C
Univ of Toledo	OH	15,806	NC
Univ of Vermont	VT	18,080	C

School	ST	$IS	SR
Univ of West Alabama	AL	7,611	C
Univ of West Florida	FL	8,559	C
Univ of Wisc/Eau Claire	WI	9,915	VC
Univ of Wisc/La Crosse	WI	10,045	VC
Univ of Wisc/Madison	WI	13,117	HC
Univ of Wisc/Oshkosh	WI	10,426	LC
Univ of Wisc/Platteville	WI	9,779	NC
Univ of Wisc/River Falls	WI	9,722	C
Univ of Wisc/Superior	WI	9,610	C+
Univ of Wisc/Whitewater	WI	9,274	C
Univ of Wyoming	WY	9,666	C
Urbana Univ	OH	21,190	C
Ursinus College	PA	38,950	VC
Ursuline College	OH	25,456	C
Utah State Univ	UT	8,002	VC
Valdosta State Univ	GA	8,802	C
Valparaiso Univ	IN	28,970	VC+
Vanderbilt Univ	TN	41,986	MC
Vanguard Univ of Southern Calif	CA	27,071	C
Villanova Univ	PA	38,672	HC+
Virginia Intermont College	VA	22,200	LC
Virginia Polytechnic Inst and State Univ	VA	10,834	VC
Virginia Union Univ	VA	18,432	LC
Virginia Wesleyan College	VA	28,433	C
Wagner College	NY	33,300	VC
Walsh Univ	OH	23,440	C
Wartburg College	IA	27,315	NC
Washburn Univ	KS	9,734	NC
Washington State Univ	WA	12,260	C
Washington Univ in St. Louis	MO	42,106	MC
Weber State Univ	UT	9,635	NC
Wesley College	DE	19,905	C
West Chester Univ of Pennsylvania	PA	12,355	C+
West Liberty State College	WV	9,142	LC
West Virginia State Univ	WV	8,378	NC
West Virginia Wesleyan College	WV	26,880	C
Western Carolina Univ	NC	7,000	C
Western Conn State Univ	CT	12,993	C
Western Mich Univ	MI	13,299	C
Western New England College	MA	32,054	C
Western New Mexico Univ	NM	7,233	LC
Western State College of Colo	CO	9,942	C
Western Washington Univ	WA	11,262	VC
Westfield State College	MA	10,200	C
Westminster College	MO	19,660	VC
Westminster College	PA	31,290	C+
Westminster College	UT	25,656	C
Wheaton College	IL	27,760	HC
Whitworth College	WA	29,428	VC+
Wichita State Univ	KS	8,500	C
Wiley College	TX	8,100	C
William Jewell College	MO	24,340	C
William Penn Univ	IA	17,685	LC
Williams Baptist College	AR	13,450	C
Wilmington College	OH	2,806	NC
Winona State Univ	MN	11,333	C
Winthrop Univ	SC	11,302	C
Wittenberg Univ	OH	34,596	VC
Wright State Univ	OH	13,616	LC
Xavier Univ of Louisiana	LA	17,600	C
York College	NE	16,330	NC
York College of Pennsylvania	PA	16,550	VC
Youngstown State Univ	OH	12,613	NC

SECRETARIAL STUDIES/ OFFICE MANAGEMENT

School	ST	$IS	SR
Bennett College	NC	11,500	C
Caribbean Univ	PR	3,000	
David N. Myers College	OH	9,475	C
Delta State Univ	MS	7,709	C
Eastern Mich Univ	MI	12,897	C
Inter American Univ of PR/ Aguadilla Campus	PR	3,784	
Inter American Univ of PR/ Barranquitas Regional College	PR	3,350	
Inter American Univ of PR/ Bayamon Univ College	PR	3,522	
Inter American Univ of PR/ Fajardo Campus	PR	4,000	
Inter American Univ of PR/ Metropolitan Campus	PR	4,320	
Inter American Univ of PR/ Ponce Regional College	PR	3,700	
Inter American Univ of PR/ San German	PR	6,720	
Johnson and Wales Univ/ Providence Campus	RI	28,126	LC
Kent State Univ	OH	14,594	C
Southeastern Okla State Univ	OK	6,147	C
Southern Univ at New Orleans	LA	1,000	NC
Turabo Univ	PR	4,110	
Univ of PR at Humacao	PR	1,707	
Univ of PR/Arecibo	PR	8,327	

ST = STATE $IS = IN-STATE COSTS   SR = SELECTOR RATING

School	ST	$IS	SR
Univ of PR/Cayey Univ College	PR	1,250	
Univ of PR/Rio Piedras	PR	5,750	
Univ of the Sacred Heart	PR	5,590	
Youngstown State Univ	OH	12,613	NC

SLAVIC LANGUAGES

School	ST	$IS	SR
Columbia Univ/School of General Studies	NY	41,516	C
Duke Univ	NC	41,239	MC
Northwestern Univ	IL	37,595	MC
Princeton Univ	NJ	40,213	MC
St. Olaf College	MN	32,800	HC
Stanford Univ	CA	41,557	MC
Univ of Calif at Berkeley	CA	18,141	HC+
Univ of Calif at Los Angeles	CA	17,681	MC
Univ of Calif at Santa Barbara	CA	11,800	VC
Univ of Chicago	IL	42,369	MC
Univ of Kansas	KS	10,915	VC
Univ of Pennsylvania	PA	41,766	MC
Univ of Texas at Austin	TX	14,610	NC
Univ of Virginia	VA	13,759	MC
Univ of Washington	WA	10,400	VC
Wayne State Univ	MI	11,805	C

SMALL BUSINESS MANAGEMENT

School	ST	$IS	SR
Adams State College	CO	8,613	C
Cal State, San Bernardino	CA	12,563	LC
Carroll College	WI	24,860	C
Concord College	WV	9,708	C
Concordia Univ	CA	26,780	C
Ferris State Univ	MI	13,698	C
Florida Atlantic Univ	FL	11,221	C
Florida State Univ	FL	9,028	HC
Hawaii Pacific Univ	HI	21,080	C
Johnson and Wales Univ/ Providence Campus	RI	28,126	LC
Johnson State College	VT	11,830	LC
Mount Ida College	MA	26,000	LC
Rowan Univ	NJ	16,000	VC
Thomas Edison State College	NJ	3,780	SP
Tusculum College	TN	21,340	LC
Union College	NE	18,710	C
Univ of Colo at Boulder	CO	13,352	C+
Univ of Montana	MT	10,602	C
Univ of North Texas	TX	7,800	C
Waynesburg College	PA	21,230	C

SOCIAL FOUNDATIONS

School	ST	$IS	SR
Eastern Mich Univ	MI	12,897	C
Southern Christian Univ	AL	9,440	LC

SOCIAL PSYCHOLOGY

School	ST	$IS	SR
Bard College	NY	41,800	HC+
Bennington College	VT	41,890	VC
Clarion Univ of Pennsylvania	PA	11,844	C
Florida Atlantic Univ	FL	11,221	C
Our Lady of Holy Cross College	LA	8,090	LC
Park Univ	MO	11,592	C

SOCIAL SCIENCE

School	ST	$IS	SR
Abilene Christian Univ	TX	20,830	C
Adelphi Univ	NY	27,000	VC
Alverno College	WI	21,088	C
Anna Maria College	MA	29,815	LC
Aquinas College	MI	23,750	C
Ashford Univ	IA	20,370	C
Ashland Univ	OH	25,000	C
Averett Univ	VA	24,920	C
Azusa Pacific Univ	CA	28,546	VC
Bard College	NY	41,800	HC+
Bellevue Univ	NE	4,440	NC
Bemidji State Univ	MN	11,180	LC
Benedict College	SC	19,114	LC
Benedictine College	KS	21,968	C
Benedictine Univ	IL	25,710	C
Bennington College	VT	41,890	VC
Berry College	GA	24,342	VC
Bethany College	KS	20,660	LC
Bethel College	IN	19,680	C
Biola Univ	CA	29,372	VC
Black Hills State Univ	SD	7,800	LC
Blue Mountain College	MS	11,086	C
Bluefield State College	WV	3,140	LC
Bluffton College	OH	26,110	C
Boise State Univ	ID	9,438	LC
Bowling Green State Univ	OH	14,994	C
Brewton-Parker College	GA	14,220	LC
Buena Vista Univ	IA	27,742	C
Calif Baptist Univ	CA	23,780	C
Calif Inst of Technology	CA	36,123	MC
Calif Lutheran Univ	CA	27,800	LC
Calif Polytechnic State Univ	CA	12,390	VC
Calif State Polytechnic Univ, Pomona	CA	18,053	C+

School	ST	$IS	SR
Cal State, Chico	CA	11,395	C
Cal State, Los Angeles	CA	5,900	C
Cal State, Monterey Bay	CA	10,099	C
Cal State, Sacramento	CA	11,122	C+
Cal State, San Bernardino	CA	12,563	LC
Cal State, San Marcos	CA	1,800	LC
Cal State, Stanislaus	CA	11,283	C
Calif Univ of Pennsylvania	PA	14,217	C
Cardinal Stritch Univ	WI	21,910	C
Caribbean Univ	PR	3,000	
Carnegie Mellon Univ	PA	32,700	MC
Carroll College	MT	23,324	C+
Carson-Newman Univ	TN	16,800	C
Carthage College	WI	26,000	C
Castleton State College	VT	13,158	C
Cazenovia College	NY	26,900	C
Central Mich Univ	MI	12,244	C
Central Washington Univ	WA	11,730	C
Chadron State College	NE	6,350	NC
Chapman Univ	CA	37,550	VC
Charleston Southern Univ	SC	17,800	C
Cheyney Univ of Pennsylvania	PA	11,497	LC
CUNY/Hunter College	NY	8,000	C+
Clarion Univ of Pennsylvania	PA	11,844	C
Clarkson Univ	NY	34,930	VC
Cleveland State Univ	OH	10,798	NC
Colgate Univ	NY	41,170	MC
College of St. Benedict	MN	30,091	VC
Colo Christian Univ	CO	21,182	VC
Colo State Univ-Pueblo	CO	7,821	C
Concord College	WV	9,708	C
Concordia Univ Wisc	WI	22,660	VC
Concordia Univ, River Forest	IL	26,300	C
Coppin State College	MD	10,200	LC
Cumberland Univ	TN	18,894	C
Daniel Webster College	NH	24,870	C
Dartmouth College	NH	39,465	MC
David N. Myers College	OH	9,475	C
Delta State Univ	MS	7,709	C
DePaul Univ	IL	29,835	VC
Dominican College	NY	26,630	LC
Dominican Univ	IL	26,370	C
Dordt College	IA	20,325	VC
Dowling College	NY	22,110	LC
Eastern Conn State Univ	CT	13,554	C
Eastern Mennonite Univ	VA	25,450	VC
Eastern Mich Univ	MI	12,897	C
Eastern Washington Univ	WA	10,608	C
Edinboro Univ of Pennsylvania	PA	11,809	LC
Elizabeth City State Univ	NC	5,700	LC
Emporia State Univ	KS	8,093	C
Eugene Lang College New School for Liberal Arts	NY	38,800	C+
Eureka College	IL	19,280	C
Evangel Univ	MO	17,380	C
Fayetteville State Univ	NC	6,000	LC
Florida A&M Univ	FL	8,344	C
Florida Atlantic Univ	FL	11,221	C
Florida Southern College	FL	25,965	C
Florida State Univ	FL	9,028	HC
Fordham Univ	NY	36,000	HC
Fresno Pacific Univ	CA	25,454	C
Frostburg State Univ	MD	12,672	C
Gannon Univ	PA	26,100	C
Gardner-Webb Univ	NC	21,500	C
Goddard College	VT	21,100	C
Graceland Univ	IA	19,700	C
Grand Canyon Univ	AZ	32,000	LC
Grand Valley State Univ	MI	12,000	VC
Gustavus Adolphus College	MN	30,920	HC
Hamline Univ	MN	27,070	VC
Harding Univ	AR	16,512	VC
Harvard Univ/Harvard College	MA	45,860	MC
Hastings College	NE	22,218	VC
Hawaii Pacific Univ	HI	21,080	C
Heidelberg College	OH	23,242	C
Hillsdale College	MI	24,160	HC
Hofstra Univ	NY	32,630	VC
Hope International Univ	CA	23,700	NC
Humboldt State Univ	CA	11,176	C
Illinois State Univ	IL	12,839	C+
Immaculata Univ	PA	25,350	C
Indiana Univ Kokomo	IN	4,835	LC
Indiana Univ of Pennsylvania	PA	11,209	C
Indiana Univ-Purdue Univ Fort Wayne	IN	5,067	LC
Iona College	NY	30,878	VC
James Madison Univ	VA	12,010	VC
Johns Hopkins Univ	MD	42,044	MC
Johnson C. Smith Univ	NC	20,000	C
Juniata College	PA	33,130	VC
Kansas State Univ	KS	10,516	VC
Keene State College	NH	13,836	C
Lake Erie College	OH	27,725	C
Lake Superior State Univ	MI	12,842	LC
Lamar Univ	TX	6,820	LC
Langston Univ	OK	2,308	LC
Lee Univ	TN	14,780	NC
LeMoyne-Owen College	TN	13,150	LC
Lesley Univ	MA	34,950	C

School	ST	$IS	SR
Lewis-Clark State College	ID	6,990	C
Liberty Univ	VA	19,101	C
Lincoln Memorial Univ	TN	18,144	C
Lindsey Wilson College	KY	16,425	LC
Lock Haven Univ of Pennsylvania	PA	12,098	LC
LIU/Brooklyn Campus	NY	25,000	C
Loyola Univ New Orleans	LA	31,050	VC+
Lyndon State College	VT	14,233	LC
Madonna Univ	MI	16,068	VC
Mansfield Univ	PA	11,300	C
Marlboro College	VT	35,980	VC+
Marygrove College	MI	19,310	C+
Marylhurst Univ	OR	14,220	NC
Maryville College	TN	29,224	VC
Marywood Univ	PA	30,680	C
Mayville State Univ	ND	8,667	NC
McKendree College	IL	24,800	VC
Medaille College	NY	21,000	C
Mercer Univ	GA	27,525	VC+
Mesa State College	CO	8,051	C
Metropolitan State Univ	MN	4,682	SP
Miami Univ	OH	29,097	HC
Mich State Univ	MI	13,689	VC
Mich Tech Univ	MI	14,569	VC
Midland Lutheran College	NE	18,600	C
Millikin Univ	IL	25,590	C
Minn State Univ, Moorhead	MN	7,000	LC
Minot State Univ	ND	6,700	LC
Miss Univ for Women	MS	6,000	LC
Missouri Baptist Univ	MO	19,640	C
Missouri Southern State Univ	MO	8,396	NC
Missouri State Univ	MO	10,748	C+
Montana State Univ- Northern	MT	10,000	NC
Moravian College	PA	28,950	VC
Morehead State Univ	KY	9,150	C
Mount Marty College	SD	20,590	C
Mount St. Mary College	NY	25,250	C
Mount St. Mary's College	CA	32,086	VC
Mount Union College	OH	25,840	C
Muskingum College	OH	22,970	C
National-Louis Univ	IL	16,915	LC
Nazareth College of Rochester	NY	28,175	VC
New College of Calif	CA	12,842	NC
New College of Florida	FL	10,009	HC+
New York Univ	NY	43,170	MC
Niagara Univ	NY	28,250	C
N Car State Univ	NC	11,824	HC
North Central College	IL	28,926	VC
N Dak State Univ	ND	8,500	C
North Georgia College and State Univ	GA	7,000	C
Northeastern State Univ	OK	5,896	LC
Northern Kentucky Univ	KY	6,670	NC
Northern State Univ	SD	8,257	C
Northwest Christian College	OR	24,298	C
Northwest Missouri State Univ	MO	10,000	C
Northwestern College	MN	25,220	NC
Northwestern Okla State Univ	OK	6,250	NC
Notre Dame de Namur Univ	CA	32,790	LC
Nyack College	NY	18,540	C
Ohio Wesleyan Univ	OH	35,830	VC+
Okla Baptist Univ	OK	17,986	VC
Olivet Nazarene Univ	IL	22,590	C
Our Lady of Holy Cross College	LA	8,090	LC
Pace Univ	NY	30,000	VC
Pepperdine Univ	CA	39,960	HC
Peru State College	NE	6,350	NC
Piedmont College	GA	20,500	C
Pikeville College	KY	16,500	NC
Pittsburg State Univ	KS	8,112	C
Plymouth State Univ	NH	12,298	LC
Point Loma Nazarene Univ	CA	27,610	VC
Polytechnic Univ/Brooklyn	NY	37,150	VC
Pontifical Catholic Univ of PR/Ponce	PR	7,310	
Providence College	RI	34,580	HC
Quinnipiac Univ	CT	34,640	VC
Radford Univ	VA	13,145	C
Ramapo College of New Jersey	NJ	16,630	VC
Rhode Island College	RI	11,570	C
Robert Morris Univ	PA	22,822	C
Rockford College	IL	28,330	VC
Roger Williams Univ	RI	30,500	C
Roosevelt Univ	IL	22,605	VC
Rosemont College	PA	29,350	C
St. Bonaventure Univ	NY	28,785	LC
St. Cloud State Univ	MN	10,010	C
St. John's Univ	MN	29,749	VC
St. John's Univ	NY	34,370	C
St. Joseph's College, New York, Brooklyn Campus	NY	12,206	C
St. Joseph's College, New York, Suffolk Campus	NY	12,000	C
St. Joseph's Univ	PA	37,428	VC
St. Mary-of-the-Woods College	IN	25,480	C
St. Mary's Univ of Minn	MN	23,857	VC
St. Paul's College	VA	16,030	NC

School	ST	$IS	SR
St. Peter's College	NJ	30,160	LC
St. Thomas Aquinas College	NY	22,000	LC
St. Xavier Univ	IL	23,160	C
Samford Univ	AL	20,258	VC
San Diego State Univ	CA	12,971	C
San Jose State Univ	CA	11,707	C
Seton Hall Univ	NJ	33,622	VC
Shawnee State Univ	OH	12,237	NC
Shimer College	IL	26,525	LC
Shorter College	GA	19,700	C
Siena Heights Univ	MI	17,000	LC
Silver Lake College of the Holy Family	WI	18,500	LC
Simpson Univ	CA	22,900	C
Skidmore College	NY	41,779	HC
Slippery Rock Univ of Pennsylvania	PA	10,360	LC
Southeastern Okla State Univ	OK	6,147	C
Southern Illinois Univ Carbondale	IL	12,391	C
Southern Methodist Univ	TX	36,088	VC+
Southern Nazarene Univ	OK	14,634	NC
Southern New Hampshire Univ	NH	28,764	C
Southern Oregon Univ	OR	12,186	C
Southern Wesleyan Univ	SC	21,675	C
Southwestern Adventist Univ	TX	18,290	LC
Spalding Univ	KY	18,882	C
Spring Arbor Univ	MI	22,476	C
Spring Hill College	AL	28,678	C
SUNY/Univ at Buffalo	NY	13,694	VC
SUNY/Univ at New Paltz	NY	12,480	VC
SUNY/Univ at Stony Brook	NY	13,625	HC
Stetson Univ	FL	32,725	VC
Suffolk Univ	MA	33,160	C
Sul Ross State Univ	TX	6,600	LC
Syracuse Univ	NY	38,655	HC
Tabor College	KS	21,614	NC
Temple Univ	PA	17,438	C
Texas Wesleyan Univ	TX	18,700	C
Thomas Edison State College	NJ	3,780	SP
Thomas Univ	GA	11,520	NC
Touro College	NY	17,000	VC
Towson Univ	MD	13,924	VC
Trevecca Nazarene Univ	TN	19,594	C
Trinity International Univ	IL	25,686	C
Tri-State Univ-Main Campus	IN	26,200	C
Troy Univ	AL	8,916	C
Troy Univ Dothan Campus	AL	4,678	C
Troy Univ Montgomery Campus	AL	4,104	NC
Turabo Univ	PR	4,710	
Union College	NE	18,710	C
Union College	NY	41,595	HC
Union Inst & Univ	OH	8,912	SP
United States Air Force Academy	CO		HC+
Universidad Metropolitana	PR	3,330	
Univ of Akron	OH	15,166	NC
Univ of Alaska Southeast	AK	8,050	LC
Univ of Arizona	AZ	11,958	VC
Univ of at Calif Davis	CA	15,010	VC
Univ of Bridgeport	CT	29,595	LC
Univ of Calif at Berkeley	CA	18,141	HC+
Univ of Calif at Irvine	CA	16,475	HC
Univ of Central Florida	FL	10,739	VC
Univ of Chicago	IL	42,369	MC
Univ of Cincinnati	OH	17,682	C
Univ of Denver	CO	36,376	VC+
Univ of Great Falls	MT	17,000	C
Univ of Houston	TX	7,000	C
Univ of Houston-Downtown	TX	3,326	NC
Univ of Indianapolis	IN	25,090	C
Univ of Iowa	IA	12,172	VC
Univ of La Verne	CA	33,470	C
Univ of Maine at Augusta	ME	5,025	NC
Univ of Maine at Fort Kent	ME	10,832	LC
Univ of Mary	ND	15,374	C
Univ of Maryland/Univ College	MD	5,640	SP
Univ of Mich/Ann Arbor	MI	16,587	HC+
Univ of Mich/Dearborn	MI	7,000	VC
Univ of Mich/Flint	MI	6,398	C
Univ of Minn/Morris	MN	15,472	VC
Univ of Missouri/Columbia	MO	13,500	VC
Univ of Montana--Western	MT	8,406	NC
Univ of Montevallo	AL	9,630	C
Univ of Nebr at Kearney	NE	9,000	NC
Univ of Nevada/Las Vegas	NV	11,566	C
Univ of N Dak	ND	10,114	VC
Univ of North Texas	TX	7,800	C
Univ of Northern Colo	CO	10,249	C
Univ of Northern Iowa	IA	11,133	C
Univ of Pittsburgh at Bradford	PA	17,008	C
Univ of Pittsburgh at Greensburg	PA	17,640	C
Univ of Pittsburgh at Johnstown	PA	16,740	LC
Univ of Pittsburgh at Pittsburgh	PA	18,866	HC

ST = STATE $IS = IN-STATE COSTS   SR = SELECTOR RATING

School	ST	$IS	SR
Univ of PR/Mayaguez	PR	1,250	
Univ of PR/Rio Piedras	PR	5,750	
Univ of St. Thomas	MN	28,000	VC
Univ of South Florida	FL	10,284	VC
Univ of Southern Calif	CA	41,618	MC
Univ of Southern Miss	MS	10,112	C
Univ of Tampa	FL	25,784	C
Univ of the Ozarks	AR	19,250	C
Univ of the Pacific	CA	34,380	VC
Univ of the South	TN	34,645	HC
Univ of Utah	UT	10,162	VC
Univ of Virginia's College at Wise	VA	11,076	C
Univ of West Alabama	AL	7,611	C
Univ of West Florida	FL	8,559	C
Univ of Wisc/Eau Claire	WI	9,915	VC
Univ of Wisc/Platteville	WI	9,779	NC
Univ of Wisc/Stevens Point	WI	9,384	VC
Univ of Wyoming	WY	9,666	C
Upper Iowa Univ	IA	20,130	C
Valley City State Univ	ND	9,854	LC
Virginia Wesleyan College	VA	28,433	C
Warner Pacific College	OR	21,900	C
Washington State Univ	WA	12,260	C
Washington Univ in St. Louis	MO	42,106	MC
Wayland Baptist Univ	TX	13,484	C
Wayne State College	NE	8,033	NC
Waynesburg College	PA	21,230	C
Webster Univ	MO	24,280	VC
Wesleyan College	GA	19,560	C
West Liberty State College	WV	9,142	LC
West Texas A&M Univ	TX	8,452	C
West Virginia Wesleyan College	WV	26,880	C
Western Baptist College	OR	21,808	C
Western Carolina Univ	NC	7,000	C
Western Conn State Univ	CT	12,993	C
Western New Mexico Univ	NM	7,233	LC
Western Oregon Univ	OR	10,295	C
Westminster College	PA	31,290	C+
Westminster College	UT	25,656	C
Westmont College	CA	36,672	HC
Wheaton College	IL	27,760	HC
Wilberforce Univ	OH	14,937	LC
Wiley College	TX	8,100	LC
William Carey College	MS	11,000	LC
William Tyndale College	MI	13,000	NC
Wilmington College	OH	2,806	NC
Winona State Univ	MN	11,333	C
Wisc Lutheran College	WI	23,510	VC
Worcester Polytechnic Inst	MA	40,450	VC+
Youngstown State Univ	OH	12,613	NC

SOCIAL SCIENCE EDUCATION

School	ST	$IS	SR
Appalachian State Univ	NC	8,000	VC
Arkansas State Univ	AR	9,630	C
Armstrong Atlantic State Univ	GA	7,394	C
Auburn Univ	AL	12,230	VC
Averett Univ	VA	24,920	C
Baylor Univ	TX	27,555	HC
Bethune-Cookman College	FL	17,922	LC
Blackburn College	IL	13,690	C
Blue Mountain College	MS	11,086	C
Brigham Young Univ	UT	9,200	VC
Brigham Young Univ/Hawaii	HI	7,740	HC+
Central Methodist Univ	MO	18,000	C
Coker College	SC	21,600	C
College of St. Scholastica	MN	28,456	C+
Dana College	NE	22,390	C
Delta State Univ	MS	7,709	C
Eastern Illinois Univ	IL	12,569	C
Eastern Mich Univ	MI	12,897	C
Eastern Nazarene College	MA	19,500	LC
Eastern Washington Univ	WA	10,608	C
Elon Univ	NC	25,371	HC
Fayetteville State Univ	NC	6,000	LC
Florida State Univ	FL	9,028	HC
Fresno Pacific Univ	CA	25,454	C
Friends Univ	KS	16,250	LC
Georgia Southern Univ	GA	9,762	C
Georgia Southwestern State Univ	GA	6,035	C
Hope International Univ	CA	23,700	NC
Humboldt State Univ	CA	11,176	C
Indiana Univ of Pennsylvania	PA	11,209	C
Jackson State Univ	MS	8,500	C
Lincoln Univ	MO	8,000	NC
Marian College of Fond du Lac	WI	21,775	LC
Mercyhurst College	PA	28,633	VC
Miles College	AL	9,922	NC
Miss Valley State Univ	MS	7,970	C
Missouri Southern State Univ	MO	8,396	NC
Montana State Univ-Billings	MT	8,906	C
Montana State Univ-Northern	MT	10,000	NC
Nebr Wesleyan Univ	NE	23,415	C+
N Car Agricultural and Technical State Univ	NC	8,000	LC
North Georgia College and State Univ	GA	7,000	C
Northwest Nazarene Univ	ID	22,590	VC
Oakwood College	AL	14,904	C
Palm Beach Atlantic Univ	FL	23,597	VC
Rocky Mountain College	MT	20,805	C
Rust College	MS		C+
St. Mary's Univ of Minn	MN	23,857	VC
Schreiner Univ	TX	20,600	C
Seattle Pacific Univ	WA	29,355	C
Seton Hill Univ	PA	28,810	C
Sheldon Jackson College	AK	17,900	LC
Southern Utah Univ	UT		C
Southwest Baptist Univ	MO	18,300	C
Southwestern Okla State Univ	OK	4,801	C
SUNY/College at Oneonta	NY	12,905	VC
Stetson Univ	FL	32,725	VC
Tri-State Univ-Main Campus	IN	26,200	C
Troy Univ	AL	8,916	C
Troy Univ Dothan Campus	AL	4,678	C
Turabo Univ	PR	4,110	
Union College	NE	18,710	C
Univ of Arkansas at Pine Bluff	AR	8,300	C
Univ of Central Florida	FL	10,739	VC
Univ of Georgia	GA	11,004	HC
Univ of Mary	ND	15,374	C
Univ of Maryland/Eastern Shore	MD	11,210	C
Univ of Miss	MS	9,000	C
Univ of North Alabama	AL	8,992	C
Univ of Northern Colo	CO	10,249	C
Univ of Pittsburgh at Johnstown	PA	16,740	LC
Univ of Rio Grande	OH	8,728	NC
Univ of Utah	UT	10,162	VC
Univ of Wisc/Milwaukee	WI	9,427	LC
Univ of Wisc/Oshkosh	WI	10,426	LC
Warner Southern College	FL	18,000	C
Washington Univ in St. Louis	MO	42,106	MC
Weber State Univ	UT	9,635	NC
Western Carolina Univ	NC	7,000	C
Westmont College	CA	36,672	HC
Wiley College	TX	8,100	LC
York College	NE	16,330	NC
Youngstown State Univ	OH	12,613	NC

SOCIAL STUDIES

School	ST	$IS	SR
Alvernia College	PA	26,388	C
Andrews Univ	MI	21,786	C
Aquinas College	MI	23,750	C
Barton College	NC	22,316	C
Bluefield College	VA	17,230	C+
Brescia Univ	KY	14,240	C
Caldwell College	NJ	26,450	LC
Carlow Univ	PA	24,313	C
Central Mich Univ	MI	12,244	C
Chaminade Univ of Honolulu	HI	23,320	LC
Cleveland State Univ	OH	10,798	NC
College of St. Catherine	MN	27,505	VC
Concordia Univ, Ann Arbor	MI	25,153	C+
DePaul Univ	IL	29,835	VC
East Stroudsburg Univ of Pennsylvania	PA	10,336	C
Eastern Nazarene College	MA	19,500	LC
Eastern New Mexico Univ	NM	7,264	C
Elizabethtown College	PA	32,100	VC
Erskine College	SC	25,468	VC
Ferrum College	VA	24,290	LC
Grand Canyon Univ	AZ	32,000	LC
Harvard Univ/Harvard College	MA	45,860	MC
Hiram College	OH	28,700	VC
Indiana Wesleyan Univ	IN	22,074	C+
Ithaca College	NY	35,144	VC
Methodist College	NC	21,000	C
Minn State Univ, Mankato	MN	10,276	C
Miss College	MS	14,574	VC
Missouri Southern State Univ	MO	8,396	NC
Mount St. Mary's Univ	MD	30,930	C
New York Inst of Technology	NY	28,126	VC
Ohio Northern Univ	OH	27,765	VC
Ohio Univ	OH	15,921	C
Okla Panhandle State Univ	OK	7,635	NC
Okla Wesleyan Univ	OK	18,950	NC
Olivet College	MI	19,984	C+
Our Lady of the Lake Univ of San Antonio	TX	22,430	LC
Pacific Union College	CA	24,555	VC+
Pfeiffer Univ	NC	21,900	C
St. Francis College	NY	19,974	LC
St. John's Univ	NY	34,370	C
S Car State Univ	SC	6,700	LC
Southern Illinois Univ Carbondale	IL	12,391	C
Southwestern Adventist Univ	TX	18,290	LC
Spring Arbor Univ	MI	22,476	C
Univ of Arizona	AZ	11,958	VC
Univ of N Car at Greensboro	NC	8,993	C
Univ of St. Thomas	MN	28,000	VC
Univ of Wisc/River Falls	WI	9,722	LC
Univ of Wisc/Superior	WI	9,610	C+
Utica College	NY	31,396	C
Vassar College	NY	41,700	MC
Virginia Wesleyan College	VA	28,433	C
Viterbo Univ	WI	21,670	C
Washington State Univ	WA	12,260	C
Wayland Baptist Univ	TX	13,484	C
Western Kentucky Univ	KY	10,192	C
Youngstown State Univ	OH	12,613	NC

SOCIAL STUDIES EDUCATION

School	ST	$IS	SR
Adams State College	CO	8,613	C
Adelphi Univ	NY	27,000	VC
Alabama State Univ	AL	7,658	C
Alfred Univ	NY		VC
Alice Lloyd College	KY	4,900	C
Anderson Univ	IN	25,050	LC
Andrews Univ	MI	21,786	C
Asbury College	KY	23,762	VC
Augustana College	SD	24,380	VC
Averett Univ	VA	24,920	C
Ball State Univ	IN	13,138	C
Baylor Univ	TX	27,555	HC
Bethel College	IN	19,680	C
Bloomsburg Univ of Pennsylvania	PA	11,602	C
Boston Univ	MA	42,046	HC+
Brewton-Parker College	GA	14,220	LC
Catawba College	NC	25,000	C
Cedarville Univ	OH	21,904	VC
Centenary College of Louisiana	LA	24,760	VC
Central Mich Univ	MI	12,244	C
Central Missouri State Univ	MO	10,000	C
Central Washington Univ	WA	11,730	C
CUNY/Brooklyn College	NY	4,377	C+
CUNY/City College	NY		C
Clearwater Christian College	FL	13,160	LC
Colby-Sawyer College	NH	27,850	LC
College of New Jersey	NJ	18,315	MC
College of St. Rose	NY	25,684	C
College of the Ozarks	MO	4,130	VC+
Concordia College: Moorhead	MN	22,475	VC
Concordia College-New York	NY	27,740	C
Concordia Univ St.Paul	MN	27,776	C
Daemen College	NY	24,580	C
Dana College	NE	22,390	C
Defiance College	OH	24,790	C
Delta State Univ	MS	7,709	C
East Carolina Univ	NC	10,000	C
East Texas Baptist Univ	TX	16,713	C
Edgewood College	WI	22,862	C
Edinboro Univ of Pennsylvania	PA	11,809	LC
Florida International Univ	FL	9,215	VC
Franklin College	IN		C
George Fox Univ	OR	28,490	C
Green Mountain College	VT	32,164	C
Greensboro College	NC	23,000	C
Gwynedd-Mercy College	PA	26,080	C
Hardin-Simmons Univ	TX	18,641	C
Heritage Univ	WA	6,800	NC
Hofstra Univ	NY	32,630	VC
Huntington Univ	IN	24,830	C
Indiana State Univ	IN	11,604	C
Indiana Univ Bloomington	IN	13,356	VC
Indiana Univ South Bend	IN	4,989	LC
Indiana Univ Southeast	IN	4,880	LC
Indiana Univ-Purdue Univ Indianapolis	IN	10,959	C
Indiana Wesleyan Univ	IN	22,074	C+
Ithaca College	NY	35,144	VC
Johnson C. Smith Univ	NC	20,000	C
Judson College	AL	16,522	C
Juniata College	PA	33,130	VC
Kennesaw State Univ	GA	12,152	C
Kent State Univ	OH	14,594	C
Kentucky State Univ	KY	10,089	LC
La Salle Univ	PA	34,950	C
Le Moyne College	NY	29,570	VC
Limestone College	SC	19,840	C
Louisiana College	LA	13,450	C
Malone College	OH	23,040	C
Mansfield Univ	PA	11,300	C
Mars Hill College	NC	19,000	LC
Marygrove College	MI	19,310	C+
Messiah College	PA	28,910	VC+
MidAmerica Nazarene Univ	KS	20,584	LC
Millersville Univ of Pennsylvania	PA	12,113	C
Minn State Univ, Moorhead	MN	7,000	LC
Missouri Southern State Univ	MO	8,396	NC
Missouri Valley College	MO	18,500	C
Montana State Univ-Billings	MT	8,906	C
Morningside College	IA	23,704	C
Morris College	SC	11,999	LC
Mount Vernon Nazarene Univ	OH	20,810	C
Nazareth College of Rochester	NY	28,175	VC
New York Univ	NY	43,170	MC
Niagara Univ	NY	28,250	C
N Car State Univ	NC	11,824	HC
Northwestern College	MN	25,220	NC
Notre Dame de Namur Univ	CA	32,790	LC
Okla Christian Univ	OK	18,992	NC
Okla Panhandle State Univ	OK	7,635	NC
Okla Wesleyan Univ	OK	18,950	NC
Old Dominion Univ	VA	11,907	C
Oral Roberts Univ	OK	22,650	C
Pittsburg State Univ	KS	8,112	C
Pontifical Catholic Univ of PR/Ponce	PR	7,310	
Presbyterian College	SC	30,044	VC
Providence College	RI	34,580	HC
Purdue Univ/West Lafayette	IN	13,458	VC
Rider Univ	NJ	32,560	C
Rivier College	NH	26,600	C
Rocky Mountain College	MT	20,805	C
Saginaw Valley State Univ	MI	11,432	C
St. Augustine's College	NC	14,000	LC
St. Edward's Univ	TX	23,560	C
St. John Fisher College	NY	27,860	C
St. John's Univ	NY	34,370	C
St. Martin's Univ	WA	27,555	C
St. Olaf College	MN	32,800	HC
St. Thomas Univ	FL	23,490	C
Shaw Univ	NC	15,488	LC
Shepherd Univ	WV	10,066	C
Shippensburg Univ of Pennsylvania	PA	11,621	C
Southeast Missouri State Univ	MO	10,596	C
Southeastern Louisiana Univ	LA	8,521	LC
Southeastern Okla State Univ	OK	6,147	C
Southern New Hampshire Univ	NH	28,764	C
Southern Univ at New Orleans	LA	1,000	NC
Southern Utah Univ	UT		C
SUNY at Potsdam	NY	12,959	C
SUNY/College at Old Westbury	NY	13,154	C
SUNY/College at Plattsburgh	NY	12,362	C
SUNY/Univ at Albany	NY	13,860	VC
Syracuse Univ	NY	38,655	HC
Taylor Univ	IN	26,376	VC+
Temple Univ	PA	17,438	C
Texas Christian Univ	TX	23,410	VC+
Univ of Central Okla	OK	8,094	C
Univ of Charleston	WV	27,600	C
Univ of Conn	CT	16,628	HC
Univ of Evansville	IN	28,320	VC
Univ of Great Falls	MT	17,000	C
Univ of Indianapolis	IN	25,090	C
Univ of Kentucky	KY	7,800	C
Univ of Louisiana at Lafayette	LA	5,830	C
Univ of Louisiana at Monroe	LA	7,103	C
Univ of Mary	ND	15,374	C
Univ of Mary Hardin-Baylor	TX	19,428	C
Univ of Maryland/College Park	MD	16,036	HC
Univ of Mich/Dearborn	MI	7,000	VC
Univ of Minn/Duluth	MN	13,974	C
Univ of Minn/Twin Cities	MN	13,165	HC
Univ of New Mexico	NM	11,253	C
Univ of N Car at Chapel Hill	NC	11,129	MC
Univ of N Car at Charlotte	NC	9,101	C
Univ of N Car at Pembroke	NC	7,940	C
Univ of N Dak	ND	10,114	VC
Univ of Okla	OK	10,769	VC+
Univ of Rio Grande	OH	8,728	NC
Univ of St. Francis	IN	20,970	C
Univ of S Car Upstate	SC	11,957	C
Univ of South Florida	FL	10,284	VC
Univ of the Cumberlands	KY	18,184	C
Univ of Vermont	VT	18,080	VC
Univ of Wisc/La Crosse	WI	10,045	VC
Univ of Wisc/Whitewater	WI	9,274	C
Virginia Wesleyan College	VA	28,433	C
Wartburg College	IA	27,315	NC
Washington State Univ	WA	12,260	C
Washington Univ in St. Louis	MO	42,106	MC
Wesley College	DE	19,905	C
West Chester Univ of Pennsylvania	PA	12,355	C+
West Texas A&M Univ	TX	8,452	C
Whitworth Univ	WA	29,428	VC+
Xavier Univ of Louisiana	LA	17,600	C
York College of Pennsylvania	PA	16,550	VC
Youngstown State Univ	OH	12,613	NC

SOCIAL WORK

School	ST	$IS	SR
Abilene Christian Univ	TX	20,830	C
Adams State College	CO	8,613	C
Adelphi Univ	NY	27,000	VC
Alabama A&M Univ	AL	8,890	LC

School	ST	$IS	SR
Alabama State Univ	AL	7,658	C
Albany State Univ	GA	5,770	C+
Alvernia College	PA	26,388	C
Anderson Univ	IN	25,050	LC
Andrews Univ	MI	21,786	C
Anna Maria College	MA	29,815	LC
Appalachian State Univ	NC	8,000	VC
Arizona State Univ-Tempe	AZ	11,174	C
Arkansas State Univ	AR	9,630	C
Asbury College	KY	23,762	VC
Ashland Univ	OH	25,000	C
Atlantic Union College	MA	17,600	LC
Auburn Univ	AL	12,230	VC
Augsburg College	MN	28,300	C
Augustana College	SD	24,380	VC
Aurora Univ	IL	20,645	C
Austin Peay State Univ	TN	7,535	C
Avila Univ	MO	22,100	C
Azusa Pacific Univ	CA	28,546	VC
Ball State Univ	IN	13,138	C
Barton College	NC	22,316	C
Baylor Univ	TX	27,555	HC
Belhaven College	MS	19,530	NC
Belmont Univ	TN	24,110	VC
Bemidji State Univ	MN	11,180	LC
Benedict College	SC	19,114	LC
Bennett College	NC	11,500	C
Bethany College	KS	20,660	LC
Bethany College	WV	21,395	C
Bethel College	KS	21,650	C
Bethel Univ	MN	29,840	VC
Bloomsburg Univ of Pennsylvania	PA	11,602	C
Bluffton College	OH	26,110	C
Boise State Univ	ID	9,438	LC
Bowie State Univ	MD	10,880	C+
Bradley Univ	IL	25,280	VC
Brescia Univ	KY	14,240	C
Briar Cliff Univ	IA	23,550	LC
Bridgewater State College	MA	12,120	C
Brigham Young Univ	UT	9,200	VC
Brigham Young Univ/Hawaii	HI	7,740	HC+
Buena Vista Univ	IA	27,742	C
Cabrini College	PA	33,340	C
Cal State, Chico	CA	11,395	C
Cal State, Fresno	CA	10,037	LC
Cal State, Los Angeles	CA	5,900	C
Cal State, Sacramento	CA	11,122	C+
Cal State, San Bernardino	CA	12,563	LC
Calif Univ of Pennsylvania	PA	14,217	C
Calvin College	MI	25,735	NC
Campbell Univ	NC	21,137	VC
Campbellsville Univ	KY	21,328	C
Capital Univ	OH	30,444	C
Caribbean Univ	PR	3,000	
Carlow Univ	PA	24,313	C
Carthage College	WI	26,000	C
Castleton State College	VT	13,158	C
Catholic Univ of America	DC	35,838	VC
Cedar Crest College	PA	30,615	C
Cedarville Univ	OH	21,904	VC
Central Conn State Univ	CT	13,620	C
Central Mich Univ	MI	12,244	C
Central Missouri State Univ	MO	10,000	C
Central State Univ	OH	9,010	C
Central Univ of Bayamon	PR	3,335	
Central Washington Univ	WA	11,730	C
Chadron State College	NE	6,350	NC
Champlain College	VT	24,605	C
Chatham College	PA	27,290	C+
Christopher Newport Univ	VA	13,326	VC
CUNY/College of Staten Island	NY	4,328	NC
CUNY/Herbert H. Lehman College	NY	4,000	LC
CUNY/York College	NY	4,242	NC
Clark Atlanta Univ	GA	20,960	LC
Clarke College	IA	25,390	C
Cleveland State Univ	OH	10,798	NC
Coker College	SC	21,600	C
College Misericordia	PA	27,950	C
College of Mount St. Joseph	OH	24,860	C
College of New Rochelle	NY	28,396	C+
College of Our Lady of the Elms	MA	21,000	C
College of St. Benedict	MN	30,091	VC
College of St. Catherine	MN	27,505	VC
College of St. Rose	NY	25,684	C
College of St. Scholastica	MN	28,456	C+
College of the Ozarks	MO	4,130	VC+
Colo State Univ-Fort Collins	CO	10,878	C+
Colo State Univ-Pueblo	CO	7,821	LC
Columbia College	MO	16,900	C
Columbia College	SC	24,982	LC
Concord College	WV	9,708	C
Concordia College: Moorhead	MN	22,475	VC
Concordia College-New York	NY	27,740	C
Concordia Univ	OR	24,404	C
Concordia Univ Wisc	WI	22,660	VC
Concordia Univ, River Forest	IL	26,300	C
Coppin State College	MD	10,200	LC
Cornerstone Univ and Grand Rapids Theological Seminary	MI	21,350	NC
Creighton Univ	NE	29,918	VC+
Daemen College	NY	24,580	C
Dana College	NE	22,390	C
De Sales Univ	PA	28,580	VC
Defiance College	OH	24,790	C
Delaware State Univ	DE	8,130	LC
Delta State Univ	MS	7,709	C
Dickinson State Univ	ND	7,847	NC
Dominican College	NY	26,630	LC
Dordt College	IA	20,325	VC
East Carolina Univ	NC	10,000	C
East Central Univ	OK	6,207	C
East Tenn State Univ	TN	8,497	C
Eastern Conn State Univ	CT	13,554	C
Eastern Kentucky Univ	KY	7,725	C
Eastern Mennonite Univ	VA	25,450	VC
Eastern Mich Univ	MI	12,897	C
Eastern Nazarene College	MA	19,500	LC
Eastern Univ	PA	24,075	C
Eastern Washington Univ	WA	10,608	C
Edinboro Univ of Pennsylvania	PA	11,809	LC
Elizabeth City State Univ	NC	5,700	LC
Elizabethtown College	PA	32,100	VC
Evangel Univ	MO	17,380	C
Ferris State Univ	MI	13,698	C
Ferrum College	VA	24,290	LC
Florida A&M Univ	FL	8,344	C
Florida Atlantic Univ	FL	11,221	C
Florida Gulf Coast Univ	FL	10,833	C
Florida International Univ	FL	9,215	VC
Florida State Univ	FL	9,028	HC
Fordham Univ	NY	36,000	HC
Fort Hays State Univ	KS	7,638	C
Fort Valley State Univ	GA	6,975	C
Franciscan Univ of Steubenville	OH	20,300	VC
Franklin Pierce College	NH	31,700	C
Freed-Hardeman Univ	TN	16,370	NC
Fresno Pacific Univ	CA	25,454	VC
Frostburg State Univ	MD	12,672	C
Gallaudet Univ	DC	16,554	
Gannon Univ	PA	26,100	C
George Fox Univ	OR	28,490	C
George Mason Univ	VA	10,850	VC
Georgia Southern Univ	GA	9,762	C
Georgia State Univ	GA	11,444	VC
Georgian Court College	NJ	20,000	LC
Gordon College	MA	29,194	C+
Goshen College	IN	22,850	VC
Grace College	IN	22,170	C
Grambling State Univ	LA	6,538	NC
Grand Valley State Univ	MI	12,000	VC
Greenville College	IL	23,146	C
Gwynedd-Mercy College	PA	26,080	C
Harding Univ	AR	16,512	VC
Hardin-Simmons Univ	TX	18,641	C
Hawaii Pacific Univ	HI	21,080	C
Heritage Univ	WA	6,800	NC
Holy Family Univ	PA	25,740	C
Hood College	MD	30,085	VC
Hope College	MI	28,208	VC+
Howard Payne Univ	TX	17,115	C
Humboldt State Univ	CA	11,176	C
Huntington Univ	IN	24,830	C
Idaho State Univ	ID	9,030	C
Illinois State Univ	IL	12,839	C+
Indiana State Univ	IN	11,604	C
Indiana Univ Bloomington	IN	13,356	VC
Indiana Univ East	IN	4,806	LC
Indiana Univ South Bend	IN	4,989	LC
Indiana Univ-Purdue Univ Indianapolis	IN	10,959	C
Indiana Wesleyan Univ	IN	22,074	C+
Inter American Univ of PR/ Arecibo Campus	PR	3,350	
Inter American Univ of PR/ Fajardo Campus	PR	4,000	
Inter American Univ of PR/ Metropolitan Campus	PR	4,320	
Inter American Univ of PR/ Ponce Regional College	PR	3,700	
Iona College	NY	30,878	VC
Jackson State Univ	MS	8,500	C
Jacksonville State Univ	AL	7,618	LC
James Madison Univ	VA	12,010	VC
Johnson C. Smith Univ	NC	20,000	C
Juniata College	PA	33,130	VC
Kansas State Univ	KS	10,516	VC
Kean Univ	NJ	15,880	C
Kentucky Christian College	KY	12,680	C
Kentucky State Univ	KY	10,089	LC
Keuka College	NY	26,050	C
Kutztown Univ of Pennsylvania	PA	10,820	C
La Salle Univ	PA	34,950	C
La Sierra Univ	CA	24,327	C+
LaGrange College	GA	22,874	C+
Lamar Univ	TX	6,820	LC
LeMoyne-Owen College	TN	13,150	LC
Lewis Univ	IL	23,050	C+
Lewis-Clark State College	ID	6,990	C
Limestone College	SC	19,840	C
Lincoln Memorial Univ	TN	18,144	C
Lindenwood Univ	MO	18,600	VC
Livingstone College	NC	17,815	LC
Lock Haven Univ of Pennsylvania	PA	12,098	LC
LIU/Brooklyn Campus	NY	25,000	C
LIU/C.W. Post Campus	NY	28,282	C
Longwood Univ	VA	12,426	C
Loras College	IA	27,193	C
Louisiana College	LA	13,450	C
Lourdes College	OH	15,300	LC
Loyola Univ Chicago	IL	32,896	VC
Lubbock Christian Univ	TX	16,960	C
Luther College	IA	28,800	VC+
MacMurray College	IL	20,755	C
Madonna Univ	MI	16,068	VC
Malone College	OH	23,040	C
Manchester College	IN	23,470	C
Mansfield Univ	PA	11,300	C
Marian College of Fond du Lac	WI	21,775	LC
Marist College	NY	30,566	VC
Mars Hill College	NC	19,000	LC
Marshall Univ	WV	9,116	C
Mary Baldwin College	VA	26,465	C
Marygrove College	MI	19,310	C+
Marywood Univ	PA	30,680	C
McDaniel College	MD	31,610	VC
McKendree College	IL	24,800	VC
Mercy College	NY	20,000	NC
Mercyhurst College	PA	28,633	VC
Meredith College	NC	25,600	C
Messiah College	PA	28,910	VC+
Methodist College	NC	21,000	C
Metropolitan College of New York	NY	16,000	C
Metropolitan State Univ of Denver	CO	2,338	LC
Metropolitan State Univ	MN	4,682	SP
Miami Univ	OH	29,097	HC
Mich State Univ	MI	13,689	VC
Middle Tenn State Univ	TN	8,540	C
Midwestern State Univ	TX	9,381	LC
Miles College	AL	9,922	NC
Millersville Univ of Pennsylvania	PA	12,113	C
Minn State Univ, Mankato	MN	10,276	LC
Minn State Univ, Moorhead	MN	7,000	C
Minot State Univ	ND	6,700	LC
Miss College	MS	14,574	VC
Miss State Univ	MS	9,577	C
Miss Valley State Univ	MS	7,970	C
Missouri State Univ	MO	10,748	C+
Missouri Western State Univ	MO	9,534	NC
Molloy College	NY	16,510	C
Monmouth Univ	NJ	28,956	C
Morehead State Univ	KY	9,150	C
Morgan State Univ	MD	12,080	C
Mount Mary College	WI	22,895	C
Mount Mercy College	IA	23,670	C
Mount St. Mary College	NY	25,250	C
Mount Vernon Nazarene Univ	OH	20,810	C
Mountain State Univ	WV	11,406	NC
Murray State Univ	KY	8,900	NC
Nazareth College of Rochester	NY	28,175	VC
Nebr Wesleyan Univ	NE	23,415	C+
New Mexico Highlands Univ	NM	6,272	NC
New Mexico State Univ	NM	9,250	C
New York Univ	NY	43,170	MC
Niagara Univ	NY	28,250	C
N Car Agricultural and Technical State Univ	NC	8,000	LC
N Car Central Univ	NC	9,000	LC
N Car State Univ	NC	11,824	HC
Northeastern Illinois Univ	IL	3,000	NC
Northeastern State Univ	OK	5,896	C
Northern Arizona Univ	AZ	10,353	C
Northern Kentucky Univ	KY	6,670	NC
Northern Mich Univ	MI	12,340	VC
Northwest Nazarene Univ	ID	22,590	VC
Northwestern College of Iowa	IA	22,174	C+
Northwestern Okla State Univ	OK	6,250	NC
Northwestern State Univ of Louisiana	LA	7,144	C
Nyack College	NY	18,540	C
Oakwood College	AL	14,904	C
Oglethorpe Univ	GA	30,300	VC
Ohio Dominican Univ	OH	25,954	C
Ohio State Univ	OH	15,357	HC
Ohio Univ	OH	15,921	C
Okla Baptist Univ	OK	17,986	VC
Olivet Nazarene Univ	IL	22,590	C
Oral Roberts Univ	OK	22,650	C
Our Lady of the Lake Univ of San Antonio	TX	22,430	LC
Pacific Lutheran Univ	WA	28,805	VC
Pacific Union College	CA	24,555	VC+
Pacific Univ	OR	24,250	C
Park Univ	MO	11,592	C
Philadelphia Biblical Univ	PA	22,425	C
Philander Smith College	AR	13,230	LC
Pittsburg State Univ	KS	8,112	C
Plymouth State Univ	NH	12,298	LC
Point Loma Nazarene Univ	CA	27,610	VC
Pontifical Catholic Univ of PR/Ponce	PR	7,310	
Prairie View A&M Univ	TX	11,110	LC
Prescott College	AZ	13,445	LC
Presentation College	SD	14,800	LC
Providence College	RI	34,580	HC
Quincy Univ	IL	24,920	C
Radford Univ	VA	13,145	C
Ramapo College of New Jersey	NJ	16,630	VC
Regis College	MA	31,350	LC
Rhode Island College	RI	11,570	C
Richard Stockton College of New Jersey	NJ	14,000	VC
Roberts Wesleyan College	NY	26,378	C
Rockford College	IL	28,330	VC
Rust College	MS		C+
Rutgers, The State Univ of New Jersey/Camden Campus	NJ	15,000	VC
Rutgers, The State Univ of New Jersey/New Brunswick/Piscataway Campus	NJ	15,810	HC
Rutgers, The State Univ of New Jersey/Newark Campus	NJ	15,640	VC
Sacred Heart Univ	CT	33,404	C
Saginaw Valley State Univ	MI	11,432	C
St. Cloud State Univ	MN	10,010	C
St. Edward's Univ	TX	23,560	C
St. Francis Univ	PA	25,880	LC
St. John's Univ	MN	29,749	VC
St. Joseph College	CT	32,050	C
St. Joseph's College	IN	26,600	C
St. Leo Univ	FL	22,140	C+
St. Louis Univ	MO	33,158	VC+
St. Mary-of-the-Woods College	IN	25,480	C
St. Mary's College	IN	32,538	VC
St. Olaf College	MN	32,800	HC
Salem State College	MA	13,161	LC
Salisbury Univ	MD	13,128	VC
Salve Regina Univ	RI	33,450	C
San Diego State Univ	CA	12,971	C
San Francisco State Univ	CA	13,000	C
San Jose State Univ	CA	11,707	C
Savannah State Univ	GA	7,772	LC
Seattle Univ	WA	30,063	VC
Seton Hall Univ	NJ	33,622	VC
Seton Hill Univ	PA	28,810	C
Shaw Univ	NC	15,488	LC
Shepherd Univ	WV	10,066	C
Shippensburg Univ of Pennsylvania	PA	11,621	C
Siena College	NY	28,260	VC+
Siena Heights Univ	MI	17,000	LC
Skidmore College	NY	41,779	HC
Slippery Rock Univ of Pennsylvania	PA	10,360	C
Sojourner-Douglass College	MD	4,200	LC
S Car State Univ	SC	6,700	LC
Southeast Missouri State Univ	MO	10,596	C
Southeastern Louisiana Univ	LA	8,521	LC
Southeastern Univ	FL	17,180	LC
Southern Adventist Univ	TN	18,500	C
Southern Conn State Univ	CT	10,310	C
Southern Illinois Univ Carbondale	IL	12,391	C
Southern Illinois Univ Edwardsville	IL	11,022	C
Southern Univ and A&M College	LA	8,238	LC
Southern Univ at New Orleans	LA	1,000	NC
Southwest Minn State Univ	MN	10,975	C
Southwestern Adventist Univ	TX	18,290	LC
Southwestern Okla State Univ	OK	4,801	C
Spalding Univ	KY	18,882	C
Spring Arbor Univ	MI	22,476	C
SUNY/College at Brockport	NY	12,747	VC
SUNY/College at Buffalo	NY	11,903	C+
SUNY/College at Fredonia	NY	12,771	VC
SUNY/College at Plattsburgh	NY	12,362	C
SUNY/Univ at Albany	NY	13,860	VC
SUNY/Univ at Stony Brook	NY	13,625	HC
Stephen F. Austin State Univ	TX	7,930	C
Syracuse Univ	NY	38,655	HC
Talladega College	AL	11,240	LC
Tarleton State Univ	TX	8,952	C
Taylor Univ	IN	26,376	VC+
Temple Univ	PA	17,438	C
Tenn State Univ	TN	9,048	LC
Texas A&M Univ at Commerce	TX	9,020	C
Texas Christian Univ	TX	23,410	VC+
Texas Southern Univ	TX	9,828	C

INDEX OF COLLEGE MAJORS

School	ST	$IS	SR
Texas State Univ - San Marcos	TX	10,862	C
Texas Tech Univ	TX	13,026	VC
Texas Woman's Univ	TX	7,804	C
Thomas Edison State College	NJ	3,780	SP
Thomas Univ	GA	11,520	NC
Trevecca Nazarene Univ	TN	19,594	C
Trinity Christian College	IL	23,645	C
Troy Univ	AL	8,916	C
Tuskegee Univ	AL	18,860	LC
Union College	NE	18,710	C
Union Inst & Univ	OH	8,912	SP
Union Univ	TN	20,750	VC
Univ of Akron	OH	15,166	NC
Univ of Alabama	AL	9,888	C
Univ of Alabama at Birmingham	AL	13,716	C
Univ of Alaska Anchorage	AK	11,275	NC
Univ of Alaska Fairbanks	AK	10,101	C
Univ of Arkansas	AR	11,859	VC
Univ of Arkansas at Monticello	AR	7,325	NC
Univ of Arkansas at Pine Bluff	AR	8,300	C
Univ of Calif at Berkeley	CA	18,141	HC+
Univ of Central Florida	FL	10,739	VC
Univ of Cincinnati	OH	17,682	VC
Univ of Detroit Mercy	MI	27,000	C
Univ of Findlay	OH	29,238	C
Univ of Georgia	GA	11,004	HC
Univ of Hawaii at Manoa	HI	10,413	VC
Univ of Illinois at Chicago	IL	16,256	VC
Univ of Indianapolis	IN	25,090	C
Univ of Iowa	IA	12,172	VC
Univ of Kansas	KS	10,915	VC
Univ of Kentucky	KY	7,800	C
Univ of Louisiana at Monroe	LA	7,103	C
Univ of Maine	ME	13,642	C
Univ of Maine at Presque Isle	ME	10,066	LC
Univ of Mary	ND	15,374	C
Univ of Mary Hardin-Baylor	TX	19,428	C
Univ of Maryland/Baltimore County	MD	16,642	VC+
Univ of Memphis	TN	11,153	C
Univ of Mich/Flint	MI	6,398	C
Univ of Miss	MS	9,000	C
Univ of Missouri/Columbia	MO	13,500	VC
Univ of Missouri/St. Louis	MO	14,046	VC
Univ of Montana	MT	10,602	C
Univ of Montevallo	AL	9,630	C
Univ of Nebr at Kearney	NE	9,000	NC
Univ of Nebr at Omaha	NE	11,235	C
Univ of Nevada/Las Vegas	NV	11,566	C
Univ of Nevada/Reno	NV	12,155	NC
Univ of New Hampshire	NH	16,810	VC
Univ of North Alabama	AL	8,992	C
Univ of N Car at Charlotte	NC	9,101	C
Univ of N Car at Greensboro	NC	8,993	C
Univ of N Car at Pembroke	NC	7,940	LC
Univ of N Car at Wilmington	NC	10,107	VC
Univ of N Dak	ND	10,114	VC
Univ of North Texas	TX	7,800	C
Univ of Northern Iowa	IA	11,133	C
Univ of Okla	OK	10,769	VC+
Univ of Pittsburgh at Pittsburgh	PA	18,866	HC
Univ of Portland	OR	32,300	VC
Univ of PR at Humacao	PR	1,707	
Univ of PR/Rio Piedras	PR	5,750	
Univ of Rio Grande	OH	8,728	NC
Univ of St. Francis	IL	25,430	C
Univ of St. Francis	IN	20,970	C
Univ of St. Thomas	MN	28,000	VC
Univ of Sioux Falls	SD	20,800	C
Univ of S Dak	SD	9,068	C
Univ of South Florida	FL	10,284	VC
Univ of Southern Indiana	IN	12,590	LC
Univ of Southern Maine	ME	12,614	C
Univ of Southern Miss	MS	10,112	C
Univ of Tenn at Chattanooga	TN	7,790	C
Univ of Tenn at Knoxville	TN	11,720	NC
Univ of Tenn at Martin	TN	8,693	C
Univ of Texas at Arlington	TX	7,195	LC
Univ of Texas at Austin	TX	14,610	HC
Univ of Texas at El Paso	TX	8,764	NC
Univ of Texas-Pan American	TX	7,290	C+
Univ of the Cumberlands	KY	18,184	C
Univ of the District of Columbia	DC	2,070	LC
Univ of the Sacred Heart	PR	5,590	
Univ of Toledo	OH	15,806	NC
Univ of Vermont	VT	18,080	VC
Univ of Washington	WA	10,400	VC
Univ of West Florida	FL	8,559	C
Univ of Wisc/Eau Claire	WI	9,915	VC
Univ of Wisc/Green Bay	WI	9,415	VC
Univ of Wisc/Madison	WI	13,117	HC
Univ of Wisc/Milwaukee	WI	9,427	LC
Univ of Wisc/Oshkosh	WI	10,426	LC
Univ of Wisc/River Falls	WI	9,722	LC
Univ of Wisc/Superior	WI	9,610	C
Univ of Wisc/Whitewater	WI	9,274	C
Univ of Wyoming	WY	9,666	VC
Ursuline College	OH	25,456	C
Utah State Univ	UT	8,002	VC
Valparaiso Univ	IN	28,970	VC+
Virginia Commonwealth Univ	VA	12,987	C
Virginia Intermont College	VA	22,200	LC
Virginia State Univ	VA	11,318	LC
Virginia Union Univ	VA	18,432	LC
Virginia Wesleyan College	VA	28,433	C
Viterbo Univ	WI	21,670	C
Walla Walla College	WA	24,489	NC
Warner Southern College	FL	18,000	LC
Warren Wilson College	NC	24,382	VC
Wartburg College	IA	27,315	NC
Washburn Univ	KS	9,734	NC
Washington State Univ	WA	12,260	C
Wayne State Univ	MI	11,805	C
Weber State Univ	UT	9,635	NC
West Chester Univ of Pennsylvania	PA	12,355	C+
West Texas A&M Univ	TX	8,452	C
West Virginia State Univ	WV	8,378	NC
West Virginia Univ	WV	10,506	C
Western Carolina Univ	NC	7,000	C
Western Conn State Univ	CT	12,993	C
Western Illinois Univ	IL	13,042	C
Western Kentucky Univ	KY	10,192	C
Western Mich Univ	MI	13,299	C
Western New England College	MA	32,054	C
Western New Mexico Univ	NM	7,233	C
Westfield State College	MA	10,200	C
Wheelock College	MA	33,075	C
Whittier College	CA	29,108	C
Wichita State Univ	KS	8,500	C
Widener Univ	PA	27,275	C
Wilberforce Univ	OH	14,937	LC
William Woods Univ	MO	21,020	C
Wilmington College	OH	2,806	NC
Winona State Univ	MN	11,333	C
Winthrop Univ	SC	11,302	C
Wright State Univ	OH	13,616	LC
Xavier Univ	OH	30,490	HC
Youngstown State Univ	OH	12,613	NC

SOCIOLOGY

School	ST	$IS	SR
Abilene Christian Univ	TX	20,830	C
Adams State College	CO	8,613	C
Adelphi Univ	NY	27,000	VC
Adrian College	MI	23,000	C
Agnes Scott College	GA	32,070	HC
Alabama A&M Univ	AL	8,890	LC
Alabama State Univ	AL	7,658	C
Albany State Univ	GA	5,770	C+
Albertus Magnus College	CT	25,336	C
Albion College	MI	26,000	VC
Albright College	PA	33,920	C
Alcorn State Univ	MS	8,190	LC
Alfred Univ	NY		VC
Allen Univ	SC	10,500	NC
Alma College	MI	28,544	VC
American International College	MA	28,710	LC
American Univ	DC	38,719	HC+
Amherst College	MA	41,590	MC
Anderson Univ	IN	25,050	LC
Andrews Univ	MI	21,786	C
Angelo State Univ	TX	8,340	NC
Appalachian State Univ	NC	8,000	VC
Aquinas College	MI	23,750	C
Arcadia Univ	PA	33,570	VC
Arizona State Univ-Tempe	AZ	11,174	C
Arkansas State Univ	AR	9,630	C
Arkansas Tech Univ	AR	8,108	LC
Asbury College	KY	23,762	VC
Ashland Univ	OH	25,000	C
Assumption College	MA	32,875	C
Auburn Univ	AL	12,230	VC
Auburn Univ Montgomery	AL	9,530	NC
Augsburg College	MN	28,300	C
Augusta State Univ	GA	2,920	C
Augustana College	IL	29,862	VC+
Augustana College	SD	24,380	VC
Aurora Univ	IL	20,645	C
Austin College	TX	27,871	HC
Austin Peay State Univ	TN	7,535	C
Averett Univ	VA	24,920	C
Avila Univ	MO	22,100	C
Azusa Pacific Univ	CA	28,546	VC
Baker Univ	KS	22,190	C
Baldwin-Wallace College	OH	27,256	VC
Ball State Univ	IN	13,138	C
Barber-Scotia College	NC	15,000	LC
Bard College	NY	41,800	HC+
Barry Univ	FL	24,100	LC
Bates College	ME	42,100	MC
Baylor Univ	TX	27,555	NC
Bellarmine Univ	KY	27,650	C+
Bellevue Univ	NE	4,440	NC
Belmont Abbey College	NC	25,314	C
Beloit College	WI	32,808	HC
Bemidji State Univ	MN	11,180	LC
Benedict College	SC	19,114	LC
Benedictine College	KS	21,968	C
Benedictine Univ	IL	25,710	C
Bennett College	NC	11,500	C
Bennington College	VT	41,890	HC
Berea College	KY	5,496	VC+
Berry College	GA	24,342	VC
Bethel College	IN	19,680	C
Bethel College	TN	16,066	NC
Bethune-Cookman College	FL	17,922	LC
Biola Univ	CA	29,372	VC
Birmingham-Southern College	AL	28,494	VC+
Black Hills State Univ	SD	7,800	LC
Bloomfield College	NJ	22,500	LC
Bloomsburg Univ of Pennsylvania	PA	11,602	C
Bluffton College	OH	26,110	C
Boise State Univ	ID	9,438	LC
Boston College	MA	41,608	MC
Boston Univ	MA	42,046	HC+
Bowdoin College	ME	41,660	MC
Bowie State Univ	MD	10,880	C+
Bowling Green State Univ	OH	14,994	C
Bradley Univ	IL	25,280	VC
Brandeis Univ	MA	41,551	MC
Brewton-Parker College	GA	14,220	LC
Briar Cliff Univ	IA	23,550	LC
Bridgewater College	VA	27,790	C
Bridgewater State College	MA	12,120	C
Brigham Young Univ	UT	9,200	VC
Brown Univ	RI	42,015	MC
Bryn Mawr College	PA	42,780	HC+
Bucknell Univ	PA	39,660	MC
Butler Univ	IN	31,944	VC+
Cabrini College	PA	33,340	C
Caldwell College	NJ	26,450	LC
Calif Baptist Univ	CA	23,780	C
Calif Lutheran Univ	CA	27,800	LC
Calif State Polytechnic Univ, Pomona	CA	18,053	C+
Cal State East Bay	CA	10,856	LC
Cal State, Bakersfield	CA	6,125	LC
Cal State, Chico	CA	11,395	C
Cal State, Dominguez Hills	CA	10,220	LC
Cal State, Fresno	CA	10,037	LC
Cal State, Fullerton	CA	10,990	C
Cal State, Long Beach	CA	9,512	C
Cal State, Los Angeles	CA	5,900	C
Cal State, Northridge	CA	9,036	LC
Cal State, Sacramento	CA	11,122	C+
Cal State, San Bernardino	CA	12,563	LC
Cal State, San Marcos	CA	1,800	LC
Cal State, Stanislaus	CA	11,283	C
Calvin College	MI	25,735	NC
Cameron Univ	OK	6,314	NC
Campbellsville Univ	KY	21,328	C
Canisius College	NY	32,257	VC
Capital Univ	OH	30,444	C
Cardinal Stritch Univ	WI	21,910	C
Carleton College	MN	40,467	MC
Carlow Univ	PA	24,313	C
Carroll College	MT	23,324	C+
Carroll College	WI	24,860	C
Carson-Newman College	TN	16,800	VC
Carthage College	WI	26,000	C
Case Western Reserve Univ	OH	37,314	MC
Castleton State College	VT	13,158	C
Catawba College	NC	25,000	C
Catholic Univ of America	DC	35,838	VC
Cedar Crest College	PA	30,615	C
Cedarville Univ	OH	21,904	VC
Centenary College	NJ	28,870	LC
Centenary College of Louisiana	LA	24,760	VC
Central College	IA	26,774	VC
Central Conn State Univ	CT	13,620	C
Central Methodist Univ	MO	18,000	C
Central Mich Univ	MI	12,244	VC
Central Missouri State Univ	MO	10,000	C
Central State Univ	OH	9,010	C+
Central Univ of Bayamon	PR	3,335	
Central Washington Univ	WA	11,730	C
Centre College	KY	30,810	VC
Chadron State College	NE	6,350	NC
Chapman Univ	CA	37,550	VC
Charleston Southern Univ	SC	17,800	C
Chestnut Hill College	PA	26,600	LC
Chicago State Univ	IL	10,915	C+
Christopher Newport Univ	VA	13,326	VC
CUNY/Baruch College	NY	4,320	VC+
CUNY/Brooklyn College	NY	4,377	C+
CUNY/City College	NY		C
CUNY/College of Staten Island	NY	4,328	NC
CUNY/Herbert H. Lehman College	NY	4,000	LC
CUNY/Hunter College	NY	8,000	C
CUNY/Queens College	NY	4,356	C
CUNY/York College	NY	4,242	NC
Claflin Univ	SC	16,798	C+
Clarion Univ of Pennsylvania	PA	11,844	C
Clark Atlanta Univ	GA	20,960	LC
Clark Univ	MA	35,165	VC+
Clarke College	IA	25,390	C
Clarkson Univ	NY	34,930	VC
Clemson Univ	SC	13,366	NC
Cleveland State Univ	OH	10,798	NC
Coastal Carolina Univ	SC	13,140	C
Coe College	IA	27,440	VC
Coker College	SC	21,600	C
Colby College	ME	41,770	MC
Colgate Univ	NY	41,170	MC
College of Charleston	SC	13,616	VC
College of Mount St. Vincent	NY	28,000	C
College of Mount St. Joseph	OH	24,860	C
College of New Jersey	NJ	18,315	MC
College of New Rochelle	NY	28,396	C+
College of Our Lady of the Elms	MA	21,000	C
College of St. Benedict	MN	30,091	VC
College of St. Catherine	MN	27,505	VC
College of St. Elizabeth	NJ	28,495	C
College of St. Rose	NY	25,684	C
College of the Holy Cross	MA	40,664	MC
College of the Ozarks	MO	4,130	VC+
College of the Southwest	NM	12,420	C+
College of William and Mary	VA	14,147	MC
College of Wooster	OH	31,310	VC+
Colo College	CO	37,668	HC
Colo State Univ-Fort Collins	CO	10,878	C+
Colo State Univ-Pueblo	CO	7,821	LC
Columbia College	MO	16,900	C
Columbia College	SC	24,982	LC
Columbia Univ/Barnard College	NY	38,000	MC
Columbia Univ/Columbia College	NY	42,584	MC
Columbia Univ/School of General Studies	NY	41,516	C
Columbus State Univ	GA	8,664	C
Concord College	WV	9,708	C
Concordia College: Moorhead	MN	22,475	VC
Concordia Univ St.Paul	MN	27,776	C
Concordia Univ, River Forest	IL	26,300	C
Conn College	CT	41,975	MC
Cornell College	IA	30,110	VC+
Cornell Univ	NY	41,717	MC
Cornerstone Univ and Grand Rapids Theological Seminary	MI	21,350	NC
Covenant College	GA	26,460	VC+
Creighton Univ	NE	29,918	VC+
Cumberland Univ	TN	18,894	C
Curry College	MA	26,100	LC
Dakota Wesleyan Univ	SD	17,832	C
Dallas Baptist Univ	TX	17,040	VC
Dana College	NE	22,390	C
Dartmouth College	NH	39,465	MC
Davidson College	NC	36,825	MC
Davis and Elkins College	WV	22,416	C
Delaware State Univ	DE	8,130	LC
Delta State Univ	MS	7,709	C
Denison Univ	OH	37,040	MC
DePaul Univ	IL	29,835	VC
DePauw Univ	IN	32,100	HC
Dickinson College	PA	40,170	HC+
Dickinson State Univ	ND	7,847	NC
Dillard Univ	LA	17,500	VC
Doane College	NE	22,458	C
Dominican Univ	IL	26,370	C
Dordt College	IA	20,325	VC
Dowling College	NY	22,110	LC
Drake Univ	IA	27,632	VC+
Drew Univ/College of Liberal Arts	NJ	39,698	VC
Drexel Univ	PA	27,700	VC
Drury Univ	MO	20,117	VC
Duke Univ	NC	41,239	MC
Duquesne Univ	PA	29,534	VC
D'Youville College	NY	23,660	C
Earlham College	IN	33,604	HC
East Carolina Univ	NC	10,000	C
East Central Univ	OK	6,207	C
East Stroudsburg Univ of Pennsylvania	PA	10,336	C
East Tenn State Univ	TN	8,497	C
East Texas Baptist Univ	TX	16,713	C
Eastern Conn State Univ	CT	13,554	C
Eastern Illinois Univ	IL	12,569	C
Eastern Kentucky Univ	KY	7,725	C
Eastern Mennonite Univ	VA	25,450	VC
Eastern Mich Univ	MI	12,897	VC
Eastern Nazarene College	MA	19,500	LC
Eastern New Mexico Univ	NM	7,264	C
Eastern Oregon Univ	OR	10,400	NC
Eastern Univ	PA	24,075	C
Eastern Washington Univ	WA	10,608	C
Eckerd College	FL	35,492	VC
Edgewood College	WI	22,862	C
Edinboro Univ of Pennsylvania	PA	11,809	LC
Edward Waters College	FL	14,374	LC
Elizabeth City State Univ	NC	5,700	LC
Elizabethtown College	PA	32,100	VC
Elmhurst College	IL	24,685	C
Elmira College	NY	37,200	VC

ST = STATE $IS = IN-STATE COSTS   SR = SELECTOR RATING

School	ST	$IS	SR
Elon Univ	NC	25,371	HC
Emmanuel College	MA	32,000	C+
Emory & Henry College	VA	26,570	C
Emory Univ	GA	40,546	MC
Emporia State Univ	KS	8,093	C
Eugene Lang College New School for Liberal Arts	NY	38,800	C+
Eureka College	IL	19,280	C
Evangel Univ	MO	17,380	C
Excelsior College	NY	995	SP
Fairfield Univ	CT	39,835	HC
Fairleigh Dickinson Univ/College at Florham	NJ	30,130	C
Fairleigh Dickinson Univ/Metropolitan Campus	NJ	28,590	C
Fairmont State	WV	8,400	C
Fayetteville State Univ	NC	6,000	LC
Fisk Univ	TN	19,830	C
Fitchburg State College	MA	11,276	C
Flagler College	FL	13,790	VC+
Florida A&M Univ	FL	8,344	C
Florida Atlantic Univ	FL	11,221	C
Florida Gulf Coast Univ	FL	10,833	C
Florida International Univ	FL	9,215	VC
Florida Memorial College	FL	6,000	LC
Florida Southern College	FL	25,965	C
Florida State Univ	FL	9,028	HC
Fordham Univ	NY	36,000	HC
Fort Hays State Univ	KS	7,638	C
Fort Lewis College	CO	11,852	C
Fort Valley State Univ	GA	6,975	C
Framingham State College	MA	11,156	C
Francis Marion Univ	SC	11,114	C
Franciscan Univ of Steubenville	OH	20,300	VC
Franklin and Marshall College	PA	40,590	HC
Franklin College	IN		C
Frostburg State Univ	MD	12,672	C
Furman Univ	SC	33,264	HC+
Gardner-Webb Univ	NC	21,500	C
Geneva College	PA	21,850	C
George Fox Univ	OR	28,490	C
George Mason Univ	VA	10,850	VC
George Washington Univ	DC	48,820	MC
Georgetown College	KY	24,950	C+
Georgetown Univ	DC	43,183	MC
Georgia College and State Univ	GA	11,020	C
Georgia Southern Univ	GA	9,762	C
Georgia Southwestern State Univ	GA	6,035	C
Georgia State Univ	GA	11,444	C
Georgian Court College	NJ	20,000	LC
Gettysburg College	PA	39,864	HC
Gonzaga Univ	WA	30,218	HC
Gordon College	MA	29,194	C+
Goshen College	IN	22,850	VC
Goucher College	MD	36,225	VC
Grace College	IN	22,170	C
Graceland Univ	IA	19,700	C
Grambling State Univ	LA	6,538	NC
Grand Canyon Univ	AZ	32,000	LC
Grand Valley State Univ	MI	12,000	VC
Green Mountain College	VT	32,164	C
Greensboro College	NC	23,000	C
Greenville College	IL	23,146	C
Grinnell College	IA	34,814	HC+
Guilford College	NC	28,160	C
Gustavus Adolphus College	MN	30,920	HC
Gwynedd-Mercy College	PA	26,080	C
Hamilton Univ	NY	41,660	MC
Hamline Univ	MN	27,070	VC
Hampshire College	MA	37,120	HC
Hampton Univ	VA	19,468	C+
Hannibal-LaGrange College	MO	16,390	C
Hanover College	IN	28,150	HC
Harding Univ	AR	16,512	VC
Hardin-Simmons Univ	TX	18,641	C
Hartwick College	NY	36,065	C+
Harvard Univ/Harvard College	MA	45,860	MC
Hastings College	NE	22,218	VC
Haverford College	PA	41,600	MC
Hawaii Pacific Univ	HI	21,080	C
Henderson State Univ	AR	7,600	C
Hendrix College	AR	27,646	HC+
Heritage Univ	WA	6,800	NC
High Point Univ	NC	25,720	C
Hillsdale College	MI	24,160	HC
Hiram College	OH	28,700	VC
Hobart and William Smith Colleges	NY	41,123	VC
Hofstra Univ	NY	32,630	VC
Hollins Univ	VA	31,105	C
Holy Family Univ	PA	25,740	C
Holy Names College	CA	27,980	NC
Hood College	MD	30,085	VC
Hope College	MI	28,208	VC+
Houghton College	NY	25,980	VC+
Houston Baptist Univ	TX	18,660	C
Howard Payne Univ	TX	17,115	C
Howard Univ	DC	18,481	C
Humboldt State Univ	CA	11,176	C
Huntington Univ	IN	24,830	C
Huston-Tillotson Univ	TX	14,232	LC
Idaho State Univ	ID	9,030	C
Illinois College	IL	21,900	C+
Illinois State Univ	IL	12,839	C+
Illinois Wesleyan Univ	IL	34,050	HC+
Immaculata Univ	PA	25,350	C
Indiana State Univ	IN	11,604	C
Indiana Univ Bloomington	IN	13,356	VC
Indiana Univ Kokomo	IN	4,835	LC
Indiana Univ Northwest	IN	4,902	LC
Indiana Univ of Pennsylvania	PA	11,209	C
Indiana Univ South Bend	IN	4,989	LC
Indiana Univ Southeast	IN	4,880	LC
Indiana Univ-Purdue Univ Fort Wayne	IN	5,067	LC
Indiana Univ-Purdue Univ Indianapolis	IN	10,959	C
Indiana Wesleyan Univ	IN	22,074	C+
Inter American Univ of PR/Fajardo Campus	PR	4,000	
Inter American Univ of PR/Metropolitan Campus	PR	4,320	
Inter American Univ of PR/Ponce Regional College	PR	3,700	
Inter American Univ of PR/San German	PR	6,720	
Iona College	NY	30,878	VC
Iowa State Univ	IA	11,831	VC
Iowa Wesleyan College	IA	22,140	C
Ithaca College	NY	35,144	VC
Jackson State Univ	MS	8,500	C
Jacksonville State Univ	AL	7,618	LC
Jacksonville Univ	FL	24,040	C
James Madison Univ	VA	12,010	VC
Jarvis Christian College	TX	11,136	NC
John Carroll Univ	OH	27,658	C+
Johns Hopkins Univ	MD	42,044	MC
Johnson C. Smith Univ	NC	20,000	C
Johnson State College	VT	11,830	LC
Judson College	IL	25,130	C
Juniata College	PA	33,130	VC
Kalamazoo College	MI	32,442	VC+
Kansas State Univ	KS	10,516	VC
Kansas Wesleyan Univ	KS	21,400	VC
Kean Univ	NJ	15,880	C
Keene State College	NH	13,836	C
Kennesaw State Univ	GA	12,152	C
Kent State Univ	OH	14,594	C
Kentucky State Univ	KY	10,089	LC
Kentucky Wesleyan College	KY	18,590	C
Kenyon College	OH	39,500	MC
Keuka College	NY	26,050	C
King's College	PA	29,810	C
Knox College	IL	32,385	VC+
Knoxville College	TN	6,200	LC
Kutztown Univ of Pennsylvania	PA	10,820	C
La Roche College	PA	24,724	LC
La Salle Univ	PA	34,950	C
La Sierra Univ	CA	24,327	C+
Lafayette College	PA	39,267	MC
Lake Forest College	IL	33,860	VC
Lake Superior State Univ	MI	12,842	LC
Lakeland College	WI	22,990	C
Lamar Univ	TX	6,820	LC
Lambuth Univ	TN	21,700	C
Lander Univ	SC	10,600	C
Lane College	TN	11,220	C+
Langston Univ	OK	2,308	LC
Lasell College	MA	26,250	C
Le Moyne College	NY	29,570	VC
Lebanon Valley College	PA	31,700	VC
Lee Univ	TN	14,780	NC
Lees-McRae College	NC	23,000	C
Lehigh Univ	PA	42,690	HC+
LeMoyne-Owen College	TN	13,150	LC
Lenoir-Rhyne College	NC	25,580	C
Lewis and Clark College	OR	35,358	VC+
Lewis Univ	IL	23,050	C+
Lincoln Univ	MO	8,000	NC
Lincoln Univ	PA	13,658	C+
Lindenwood Univ	MO	18,600	VC
Linfield College	OR	29,632	VC
Livingstone College	NC	17,815	LC
Lock Haven Univ of Pennsylvania	PA	12,098	LC
LIU/Brooklyn Campus	NY	25,000	C
Longwood Univ	VA	12,426	C
Loras College	IA	27,193	C
Louisiana College	LA	13,450	C
Louisiana State Univ and A&M College	LA	10,749	VC
Louisiana State Univ in Shreveport	LA	2,900	NC
Louisiana Tech Univ	LA	7,370	C
Lourdes College	OH	15,300	LC
Loyola College in Maryland	MD	38,898	HC
Loyola Marymount Univ	CA	36,321	VC
Loyola Univ Chicago	IL	32,896	VC
Loyola Univ New Orleans	LA	31,050	VC+
Luther College	IA	28,800	VC+
Lycoming College	PA	30,797	C+
Lynchburg College	VA	30,645	C
Lynn Univ	FL	30,750	C
Macalester College	MN	36,500	MC
Madonna Univ	MI	16,068	VC
Manchester College	IN	23,470	C
Manhattan College	NY	29,000	VC
Manhattanville College	NY	32,500	C+
Mansfield Univ	PA	11,300	C
Marian College	IN	26,160	C
Marian College of Fond du Lac	WI	21,775	LC
Marlboro College	VT	35,980	VC+
Marquette Univ	WI	31,066	HC
Mars Hill College	NC	19,000	LC
Marshall Univ	WV	9,116	C
Martin Univ	IN	10,300	SP
Mary Baldwin College	VA	26,465	C
Marylhurst Univ	OR	14,220	NC
Marymount Manhattan College	NY	30,049	VC
Marymount Univ	VA	25,934	C
Maryville College	TN	29,224	VC
Maryville Univ of St. Louis	MO	23,000	VC
Marywood Univ	PA	30,680	C
Mass College of Liberal Arts	MA	8,725	LC
McDaniel College	MD	31,610	VC
McKendree College	IL	24,800	VC
McMurry Univ	TX	18,100	LC
McNeese State Univ	LA	5,270	LC
McPherson College	KS	21,010	C
Mercer Univ	GA	27,525	VC+
Mercy College	NY	20,000	NC
Mercyhurst College	PA	28,633	VC
Meredith College	NC	25,600	C
Merrimack College	MA	34,380	C
Mesa State College	CO	8,051	C
Messiah College	PA	28,910	VC+
Methodist College	NC	21,000	C
Metropolitan State College of Denver	CO	2,338	LC
Miami Univ	OH	29,097	HC
Mich State Univ	MI	13,689	VC
MidAmerica Nazarene Univ	KS	20,584	LC
Middle Tenn State Univ	TN	8,540	C
Middlebury College	VT	42,190	MC
Midland Lutheran College	NE	18,600	C
Midwestern State Univ	TX	9,381	LC
Millersville Univ of Pennsylvania	PA	12,113	C
Milligan College	TN	21,990	VC
Millikin Univ	IL	25,590	C
Mills College	CA	39,870	C
Millsaps College	MS	28,256	VC+
Minn State Univ, Mankato	MN	10,276	LC
Minn State Univ, Moorhead	MN	7,000	LC
Minot State Univ	ND	6,700	LC
Miss College	MS	14,574	VC
Miss State Univ	MS	9,577	C
Miss Valley State Univ	MS	7,970	C
Missouri Southern State Univ	MO	8,396	NC
Missouri State Univ	MO	10,748	C+
Missouri Valley College	MO	18,500	C
Molloy College	NY	16,510	C
Monmouth College	IL	23,700	C
Montana State Univ-Billings	MT	8,906	C
Montana State Univ-Bozeman	MT	1,137	C
Montclair State Univ	NJ	16,327	C
Moravian College	PA	28,950	VC
Morehead State Univ	KY	9,150	C
Morehouse College	GA	25,082	C
Morgan State Univ	MD	12,080	C
Morris College	SC	11,999	LC
Mount Holyoke College	MA	42,148	HC+
Mount Mercy College	IA	23,670	C
Mount St. Mary College	NY	25,250	C
Mount St. Mary's College	CA	32,086	VC
Mount St. Mary's Univ	MD	30,930	C
Mount Union College	OH	25,840	C
Mount Vernon Nazarene Univ	OH	20,810	C
Muhlenberg College	PA	36,030	HC+
Murray State Univ	KY	9,900	VC
Muskingum College	OH	22,970	C
National Univ	CA	8,412	SP
Nazareth College of Rochester	NY	28,175	VC
Nebr Wesleyan Univ	NE	23,415	C+
New College of Florida	FL	10,009	HC+
New England College	NH	31,466	C
New Jersey City Univ	NJ	13,695	LC
New Mexico Highlands Univ	NM	6,272	NC
New Mexico State Univ	NM	9,250	C
New York Inst of Technology	NY	28,126	VC
New York Univ	NY	43,170	MC
Newberry College	SC	23,000	C
Newman Univ	KS	21,106	C
Niagara Univ	NY	28,252	C
Nicholls State Univ	LA	6,500	NC
Norfolk State Univ	VA	10,531	VC
N Car Agricultural and Technical State Univ	NC	8,000	LC
N Car Central Univ	NC	9,000	LC
N Car State Univ	NC	11,824	HC
N Car Wesleyan College	NC	22,670	C
North Central College	IL	28,926	VC
N Dak State Univ	ND	8,500	C
North Georgia College and State Univ	GA	7,000	C
North Park Univ	IL	24,050	C
Northeastern Illinois Univ	IL	3,000	NC
Northeastern State Univ	OK	5,896	LC
Northeastern Univ	MA	35,742	HC
Northern Arizona Univ	AZ	10,353	C
Northern Illinois Univ	IL	13,178	C
Northern Kentucky Univ	KY	6,670	NC
Northern Mich Univ	MI	12,340	LC
Northern State Univ	SD	8,257	C
Northland College	WI	26,680	C+
Northwest Missouri State Univ	MO	10,000	C
Northwestern College of Iowa	IA	22,174	C+
Northwestern Okla State Univ	OK	6,250	NC
Northwestern State Univ of Louisiana	LA	7,144	C
Northwestern Univ	IL	37,595	MC
Notre Dame de Namur Univ	CA	32,790	LC
Oakland Univ	MI	11,936	C
Oberlin College	OH	40,904	MC
Occidental College	CA	40,185	MC
Oglala Lakota College	SD	1,950	NC
Oglethorpe Univ	GA	30,300	VC
Ohio Dominican Univ	OH	25,954	C
Ohio Northern Univ	OH	27,765	VC
Ohio State Univ	OH	15,357	HC
Ohio Univ	OH	15,921	C
Ohio Wesleyan Univ	OH	35,830	VC+
Okla Baptist Univ	OK	17,986	VC
Okla City Univ	OK	23,965	VC
Okla State Univ	OK	10,213	VC
Oklahoma Wesleyan Univ	OK	18,950	NC
Old Dominion Univ	VA	11,907	C
Olivet College	MI	19,984	C+
Olivet Nazarene Univ	IL	22,590	C
Oregon State Univ	OR	11,055	C
Ottawa Univ	KS	12,000	C
Otterbein College	OH	28,986	C
Ouachita Baptist Univ	AR	21,900	VC
Our Lady of the Lake Univ of San Antonio	TX	22,430	LC
Pace Univ	NY	30,000	VC
Pacific Lutheran Univ	WA	28,805	VC
Pacific Univ	OR	24,250	C
Paine College	GA	14,418	LC
Park Univ	MO	11,592	C
Paul Quinn College	TX	8,300	LC
Penn State Univ/Univ Park Campus	PA	18,038	HC
Pepperdine Univ	CA	39,960	HC
Peru State College	NE	6,350	NC
Pfeiffer Univ	NC	21,900	C
Philander Smith College	AR	13,230	LC
Piedmont College	GA	20,500	C
Pikeville College	KY	16,500	NC
Pittsburg State Univ	KS	8,112	C
Pitzer College	CA	41,644	HC
Point Loma Nazarene Univ	CA	27,610	VC
Pomona College	CA	40,774	MC
Pontifical Catholic Univ of PR/Ponce	PR	7,310	
Portland State Univ	OR	12,453	C
Post Univ	CT	24,875	C
Prairie View A&M Univ	TX	11,110	LC
Presbyterian College	SC	30,044	VC
Prescott College	AZ	13,445	LC
Princeton Univ	NJ	40,324	MC
Principia College	IL	27,765	VC+
Providence College	RI	34,580	HC
Purdue Univ/Calumet	IN	10,891	LC
Purdue Univ/West Lafayette	IN	13,458	VC
Quinnipiac Univ	CT	34,640	VC
Radford Univ	VA	13,145	C
Ramapo College of New Jersey	NJ	16,630	VC
Randolph-Macon College	VA	31,250	C
Randolph-Macon Woman's College	VA	31,160	VC+
Reed College	OR	41,106	MC
Regis College	MA	31,350	LC
Regis Univ	CO	31,890	C
Rhode Island College	RI	11,570	C
Rhodes College	TN	32,860	HC
Rice Univ	TX	32,290	MC
Rider Univ	NJ	32,560	C
Ripon College	WI	21,760	C+
Rivier College	NH	26,600	C
Roanoke College	VA	30,748	VC
Roberts Wesleyan College	NY	26,378	C
Rockford College	IL	28,330	VC
Rockhurst Univ	MO	25,440	VC
Rocky Mountain College	MT	20,805	C
Rollins College	FL	38,366	VC
Roosevelt Univ	IL	22,605	VC
Rosemont College	PA	29,350	C
Rowan Univ	NJ	16,000	VC
Russell Sage College	NY	27,000	C
Rust College	MS		C+
Rutgers, The State Univ of New Jersey/Camden Campus	NJ	15,000	VC

ST = STATE   **$IS** = IN-STATE COSTS   **SR** = SELECTOR RATING

School	ST	$IS	SR
Rutgers, The State Univ of New Jersey/New Brunswick/Piscataway Campus	NJ	15,810	HC
Rutgers, The State Univ of New Jersey/Newark Campus	NJ	15,640	HC
Sacred Heart Univ	CT	33,404	C
Saginaw Valley State Univ	MI	11,432	C
St. Ambrose Univ	IA	25,495	C
St. Anselm College	NH	33,810	C
St. Augustine's College	NC	14,000	LC
St. Bonaventure Univ	NY	28,785	LC
St. Cloud State Univ	MN	10,010	C
St. Edward's Univ	TX	23,560	C
St. Francis College	NY	19,974	LC
St. Francis Univ	PA	25,880	LC
St. John Fisher College	NY	27,860	C
St. John's Univ	MN	29,749	VC
St. John's Univ	NY	34,370	C
St. Joseph College	CT	32,050	C
St. Joseph's College	IN	26,600	C
St. Joseph's College of Maine	ME	29,185	C
St. Joseph's Univ	PA	37,428	VC
St. Lawrence Univ	NY	40,545	VC
St. Leo Univ	FL	22,140	C+
St. Louis Univ	MO	33,158	VC+
St. Mary's College	IN	32,538	VC
St. Mary's College of Maryland	MD	18,876	VC+
St. Mary's Univ of Minn	MN	23,857	VC
St. Mary's Univ of San Antonio	TX	22,444	C
St. Michael's College	VT	33,330	VC
St. Norbert College	WI	28,577	C+
St. Olaf College	MN	32,800	HC
St. Paul's College	VA	16,030	NC
St. Peter's College	NJ	30,160	LC
St. Vincent College	PA	26,160	VC
St. Xavier Univ	IL	23,160	C
Salem College	NC	26,226	VC+
Salem State College	MA	13,161	LC
Salisbury Univ	MD	13,128	VC
Salve Regina Univ	RI	33,450	C
Sam Houston State Univ	TX	8,000	C
Samford Univ	AL	20,258	VC
San Diego State Univ	CA	12,971	C
San Francisco State Univ	CA	13,000	C
San Jose State Univ	CA	11,707	C
Santa Clara Univ	CA	38,931	VC
Sarah Lawrence College	NY	42,000	HC
Savannah State Univ	GA	7,772	LC
Seattle Pacific Univ	WA	29,355	C
Seattle Univ	WA	30,063	VC
Seton Hall Univ	NJ	33,622	VC
Seton Hill Univ	PA	28,810	C
Shaw Univ	NC	15,488	LC
Shawnee State Univ	OH	12,237	NC
Shenandoah Univ	VA	27,600	C
Shepherd Univ	WV	10,066	C
Shippensburg Univ of Pennsylvania	PA	11,621	C
Shorter College	GA	19,700	C
Siena College	NY	28,260	VC+
Simmons College	MA	35,640	VC
Simpson College	IA	26,833	VC
Skidmore College	NY	41,779	HC
Slippery Rock Univ of Pennsylvania	PA	10,360	LC
Smith College	MA	41,474	MC
Sonoma State Univ	CA	14,732	C
S Car State Univ	SC	6,700	LC
S Dak State Univ	SD	9,815	C
Southeast Missouri State Univ	MO	10,596	C
Southeastern Louisiana Univ	LA	8,521	LC
Southeastern Okla State Univ	OK	6,147	C
Southern Arkansas Univ	AR	6,956	C
Southern Conn State Univ	CT	10,310	C
Southern Illinois Univ Carbondale	IL	12,391	C
Southern Illinois Univ Edwardsville	IL	11,022	C
Southern Methodist Univ	TX	36,088	VC+
Southern Nazarene Univ	OK	14,634	NC
Southern Oregon Univ	OR	12,186	C
Southern Univ and A&M College	LA	8,238	LC
Southern Univ at New Orleans	LA	1,000	NC
Southern Utah Univ	UT		C
Southwest Baptist Univ	MO	18,300	C
Southwest Minn State Univ	MN	10,975	C
Southwestern Univ	TX	26,767	HC
Spelman College	GA	24,650	VC
Spring Arbor Univ	MI	22,476	C
Spring Hill College	AL	28,678	C
Springfield College	MA	25,000	C
Stanford Univ	CA	41,557	MC
SUNY at Oswego	NY	13,662	VC
SUNY at Potsdam	NY	12,959	C
SUNY/College at Brockport	NY	12,747	VC
SUNY/College at Buffalo	NY	11,903	C+

School	ST	$IS	SR
SUNY/College at Cortland	NY	12,095	C
SUNY/College at Fredonia	NY	12,771	VC
SUNY/College at Geneseo	NY	12,910	HC+
SUNY/College at Old Westbury	NY	13,154	C
SUNY/College at Oneonta	NY	12,905	VC
SUNY/College at Plattsburgh	NY	12,362	C
SUNY/College at Purchase	NY	11,989	VC+
SUNY/Empire State College	NY	4,575	SP
SUNY/Inst of Technology	NY	12,575	VC
SUNY/Univ at Albany	NY	13,860	VC
SUNY/Univ at Binghamton	NY	13,988	HC
SUNY/Univ at Buffalo	NY	13,694	VC
SUNY/Univ at New Paltz	NY	12,480	VC
SUNY/Univ at Stony Brook	NY	13,625	HC
Stephen F. Austin State Univ	TX	7,930	C
Stetson Univ	FL	32,725	VC
Stonehill College	MA	36,104	HC
Suffolk Univ	MA	33,160	C
Susquehanna Univ	PA	33,465	VC
Swarthmore College	PA	41,280	MC
Sweet Briar College	VA	31,460	VC
Syracuse Univ	NY	38,655	HC
Tabor College	KS	21,614	NC
Talladega College	AL	11,240	LC
Tarleton State Univ	TX	8,952	C
Taylor Univ	IN	26,376	VC+
Temple Univ	PA	17,438	C
Tenn State Univ	TN	9,048	LC
Tenn Tech Univ	TN	10,044	C
Texas A&M Univ	TX	13,351	HC
Texas A&M Univ at Commerce	TX	9,020	C
Texas A&M Univ at Corpus Christi	TX	10,280	LC
Texas A&M Univ at Kingsville	TX	6,800	LC
Texas Christian Univ	TX	23,410	VC+
Texas Lutheran Univ	TX	23,530	C
Texas Southern Univ	TX	9,828	C
Texas State Univ - San Marcos	TX	10,862	C
Texas Tech Univ	TX	13,026	VC
Texas Woman's Univ	TX	7,804	LC
Thiel College	PA	24,580	C
Thomas Edison State College	NJ	3,780	SP
Thomas More College	KY	24,470	C
Tougaloo College	MS	15,975	NC
Touro College	NY	17,000	VC
Towson Univ	MD	13,924	VC
Transylvania Univ	KY	26,240	VC+
Trinity Christian College	IL	23,645	C
Trinity College	CT	38,040	HC+
Trinity College	DC	24,150	LC
Trinity Univ	TX	30,157	HC+
Troy Univ Dothan Campus	AL	4,678	C
Truman State Univ	MO	11,242	HC
Tufts Univ	MA	42,018	MC
Tulane Univ	LA	41,098	MC
Turabo Univ	PR	4,110	
Tuskegee Univ	AL	18,860	LC
Union College	KY	18,920	C
Union College	NY	41,595	HC
Union Univ	TN	20,750	VC
Universidad Metropolitana	PR	3,330	
Univ of Akron	OH	15,166	NC
Univ of Alabama at Birmingham	AL	13,716	C
Univ of Alabama in Huntsville	AL	9,516	VC
Univ of Alaska Anchorage	AK	11,275	NC
Univ of Alaska Fairbanks	AK	10,101	C
Univ of Arizona	AZ	11,958	VC
Univ of Arkansas	AR	11,859	VC
Univ of Arkansas at Little Rock	AR	7,230	NC
Univ of Arkansas at Pine Bluff	AR	8,300	C
Univ of at Calif Davis	CA	15,010	VC
Univ of Calif at Berkeley	CA	18,141	HC+
Univ of Calif at Irvine	CA	16,475	HC
Univ of Calif at Los Angeles	CA	17,681	MC
Univ of Calif at Riverside	CA	16,625	C
Univ of Calif at San Diego	CA	16,102	HC
Univ of Calif at Santa Barbara	CA	11,800	VC
Univ of Calif at Santa Cruz	CA	19,174	VC
Univ of Central Arkansas	AR	9,984	C
Univ of Central Florida	FL	10,739	VC
Univ of Central Okla	OK	8,094	C
Univ of Chicago	IL	42,369	MC
Univ of Cincinnati	OH	17,682	C
Univ of Colo at Boulder	CO	13,352	C+
Univ of Colo at Colo Springs	CO	11,517	VC
Univ of Colo at Denver and Health Sciences Center	CO	5,021	C
Univ of Conn	CT	16,628	HC
Univ of Dayton	OH	28,826	VC
Univ of Delaware	DE	14,142	HC
Univ of Denver	CO	36,376	VC+
Univ of Detroit Mercy	MI	27,009	C
Univ of Dubuque	IA	23,390	C

School	ST	$IS	SR
Univ of Evansville	IN	28,320	VC
Univ of Findlay	OH	29,238	C
Univ of Florida	FL	9,354	HC
Univ of Georgia	GA	11,004	HC
Univ of Great Falls	MT	17,000	C
Univ of Hartford	CT	34,044	C
Univ of Hawaii at Hilo	HI	6,500	C
Univ of Hawaii at Manoa	HI	10,413	VC
Univ of Houston	TX	7,000	C
Univ of Idaho	ID	9,310	NC
Univ of Illinois at Chicago	IL	16,256	VC
Univ of Illinois at Urbana-Champaign	IL	15,800	HC+
Univ of Indianapolis	IN	25,090	C
Univ of Iowa	IA	12,172	VC
Univ of Kansas	KS	10,915	VC
Univ of Kentucky	KY	7,800	C
Univ of La Verne	CA	33,470	C
Univ of Louisiana at Lafayette	LA	5,830	C
Univ of Louisiana at Monroe	LA	7,103	C
Univ of Louisville	KY	10,400	VC
Univ of Maine	ME	13,642	C
Univ of Maine at Farmington	ME	11,515	C
Univ of Mary Hardin-Baylor	TX	19,428	C
Univ of Mary Washington	VA	11,636	HC
Univ of Maryland/Baltimore County	MD	16,642	VC+
Univ of Maryland/College Park	MD	16,036	HC
Univ of Maryland/Eastern Shore	MD	11,210	C
Univ of Mass Amherst	MA	15,973	C+
Univ of Mass Boston	MA	8,024	C
Univ of Mass Dartmouth	MA	15,985	C
Univ of Mass Lowell	MA	14,327	VC
Univ of Memphis	TN	11,153	C
Univ of Miami	FL	38,397	MC
Univ of Mich/Ann Arbor	MI	16,587	HC+
Univ of Mich/Dearborn	MI	7,000	VC
Univ of Mich/Flint	MI	6,398	C
Univ of Minn/Duluth	MN	13,974	C
Univ of Minn/Morris	MN	15,472	VC
Univ of Minn/Twin Cities	MN	13,165	HC
Univ of Miss	MS	9,000	C
Univ of Missouri/Columbia	MO	13,500	VC
Univ of Missouri/Kansas City	MO	15,000	VC
Univ of Missouri/St. Louis	MO	14,046	VC
Univ of Mobile	AL	16,880	C
Univ of Montana	MT	10,602	C
Univ of Montevallo	AL	9,630	C
Univ of Nebr at Kearney	NE	9,000	NC
Univ of Nebr at Lincoln	NE	11,401	VC
Univ of Nebr at Omaha	NE	11,235	C
Univ of Nevada/Las Vegas	NV	11,566	C
Univ of Nevada/Reno	NV	12,155	NC
Univ of New England	ME	31,005	C
Univ of New Hampshire	NH	16,810	VC
Univ of New Mexico	NM	11,253	C
Univ of New Orleans	LA	7,370	C
Univ of North Alabama	AL	8,992	C
Univ of N Car at Asheville	NC	9,237	VC
Univ of N Car at Chapel Hill	NC	11,129	MC
Univ of N Car at Charlotte	NC	9,101	C
Univ of N Car at Greensboro	NC	8,993	C
Univ of N Car at Pembroke	NC	7,940	VC
Univ of N Car at Wilmington	NC	10,107	VC
Univ of N Dak	ND	10,114	VC
Univ of North Florida	FL	9,908	VC
Univ of North Texas	TX	7,800	C
Univ of Northern Colo	CO	10,249	C
Univ of Northern Iowa	IA	11,133	C
Univ of Notre Dame	IN	39,552	MC
Univ of Okla	OK	10,769	VC+
Univ of Oregon	OR	13,108	VC
Univ of Pennsylvania	PA	41,766	MC
Univ of Pittsburgh at Bradford	PA	17,008	C
Univ of Pittsburgh at Johnstown	PA	16,740	LC
Univ of Pittsburgh at Pittsburgh	PA	18,866	HC
Univ of Portland	OR	32,300	VC
Univ of PR/Mayaguez	PR	1,250	
Univ of PR/Rio Piedras	PR	5,750	
Univ of Puget Sound	WA	35,600	HC
Univ of Redlands	CA	36,160	VC
Univ of Rhode Island	RI	15,398	C
Univ of Richmond	VA	40,510	MC
Univ of Rio Grande	OH	8,728	NC
Univ of St. Mary	KS	18,900	C
Univ of St. Thomas	MN	28,900	VC
Univ of San Diego	CA	40,620	HC
Univ of San Francisco	CA	37,560	VC
Univ of Science and Arts of Okla	OK	7,650	C
Univ of Scranton	PA	31,100	VC
Univ of Sioux Falls	SD	20,800	C
Univ of S Car at Aiken	SC	11,718	LC
Univ of S Car at Columbia	SC	13,397	VC
Univ of S Car Upstate	SC	11,957	C
Univ of S Dak	SD	9,068	C

School	ST	$IS	SR
Univ of South Florida	FL	10,284	VC
Univ of Southern Calif	CA	41,618	MC
Univ of Southern Indiana	IN	12,590	LC
Univ of Southern Maine	ME	12,614	C
Univ of Southern Miss	MS	10,112	C
Univ of Tampa	FL	25,784	C
Univ of Tenn at Chattanooga	TN	7,790	C
Univ of Tenn at Knoxville	TN	11,720	C
Univ of Tenn at Martin	TN	8,693	C
Univ of Texas at Arlington	TX	7,195	LC
Univ of Texas at Austin	TX	14,610	HC
Univ of Texas at Dallas	TX	13,244	NC
Univ of Texas at El Paso	TX	8,764	NC
Univ of Texas at San Antonio	TX	11,325	LC
Univ of Texas-Pan American	TX	7,290	C+
Univ of the District of Columbia	DC	2,070	LC
Univ of the Incarnate Word	TX	23,306	C
Univ of the Ozarks	AR	19,250	C
Univ of the Pacific	CA	34,380	VC
Univ of Toledo	OH	15,806	NC
Univ of Tulsa	OK	25,348	HC
Univ of Utah	UT	10,162	VC
Univ of Vermont	VT	18,080	VC
Univ of Virginia	VA	13,759	MC
Univ of Washington	WA	10,400	VC
Univ of West Alabama	AL	7,611	C
Univ of West Georgia	GA	8,838	C
Univ of Wisc/Eau Claire	WI	9,915	VC
Univ of Wisc/La Crosse	WI	10,045	VC
Univ of Wisc/Madison	WI	13,117	HC
Univ of Wisc/Milwaukee	WI	9,427	C
Univ of Wisc/Oshkosh	WI	10,426	LC
Univ of Wisc/Parkside	WI	10,181	LC
Univ of Wisc/River Falls	WI	9,722	C
Univ of Wisc/Stevens Point	WI	9,384	VC
Univ of Wisc/Superior	WI	9,610	C+
Univ of Wisc/Whitewater	WI	9,274	C
Univ of Wyoming	WY	9,666	C
Upper Iowa Univ	IA	20,130	C
Urbana Univ	OH	21,190	C
Ursinus College	PA	38,950	VC
Ursuline College	OH	25,456	C
Utah State Univ	UT	8,002	VC
Utica College	NY	31,396	C
Valdosta State Univ	GA	8,802	C
Valparaiso Univ	IN	28,970	VC+
Vanderbilt Univ	TN	41,986	MC
Vanguard Univ of Southern Calif	CA	27,071	C
Vassar College	NY	41,700	MC
Villanova Univ	PA	38,672	HC+
Virginia Commonwealth Univ	VA	12,987	C
Virginia Polytechnic Inst and State Univ	VA	10,834	VC
Virginia State Univ	VA	11,318	C
Virginia Union Univ	VA	18,432	LC
Virginia Wesleyan College	VA	28,433	C
Viterbo Univ	WI	21,670	C
Voorhees College	SC	11,800	C
Wagner College	NY	33,300	VC
Wake Forest Univ	NC	38,290	MC
Walla Walla College	WA	24,489	NC
Walsh Univ	OH	23,440	C
Warner Pacific College	OR	21,900	C
Warren Wilson College	NC	24,382	VC
Wartburg College	IA	27,315	NC
Washburn Univ	KS	9,734	NC
Washington and Jefferson College	PA	33,490	VC
Washington and Lee Univ	VA	35,880	MC
Washington College	MD	34,990	VC
Washington State Univ	WA	12,260	C
Wayne State College	NE	8,033	NC
Wayne State Univ	MI	11,805	C
Waynesburg College	PA	21,230	C
Weber State Univ	UT	9,635	NC
Webster Univ	MO	24,280	VC
Wellesley College	MA	41,030	MC
Wells College	NY	23,070	VC
Wesleyan Univ	CT	42,122	MC
West Chester Univ of Pennsylvania	PA	12,355	C+
West Liberty State College	WV	9,142	LC
West Texas A&M Univ	TX	8,452	C
West Virginia State Univ	WV	8,378	NC
West Virginia Univ	WV	10,506	C
West Virginia Wesleyan College	WV	26,880	C
Western Carolina Univ	NC	7,000	C
Western Conn State Univ	CT	12,993	C
Western Illinois Univ	IL	13,042	C
Western Kentucky Univ	KY	10,192	C
Western Mich Univ	MI	13,299	C
Western New England College	MA	32,054	C
Western New Mexico Univ	NM	7,233	LC
Western Oregon Univ	OR	10,295	C
Western State College of Colo	CO	9,942	C
Western Washington Univ	WA	11,262	VC
Westfield State College	MA	10,200	C

ST = STATE **$IS** = IN-STATE COSTS **SR** = SELECTOR RATING

School	ST	$IS	SR
Westminster College	MO	19,060	VC
Westminster College	PA	31,290	C+
Westminster College	UT	25,656	C
Westmont College	CA	36,672	HC
Wheaton College	IL	27,760	HC
Wheaton College	MA	40,180	HC+
Whitman College	WA	36,110	HC+
Whittier College	CA	29,108	C
Whitworth College	WA	29,428	VC+
Wichita State Univ	KS	8,500	C
Widener Univ	PA	27,275	C
Wilberforce Univ	OH	14,937	LC
Wiley College	TX	8,100	LC
Wilkes Univ	PA	30,886	C
Willamette Univ	OR	35,416	VC+
William Paterson Univ of New Jersey	NJ	17,810	C+
William Penn Univ	IA	17,685	LC
Williams College	MA	40,310	MC
Wilmington College	OH	2,806	NC
Wilson College	PA	27,660	C
Wingate Univ	NC	23,300	C
Winona State Univ	MN	11,333	C
Winston-Salem State Univ	NC	8,960	LC
Winthrop Univ	SC	11,302	C
Wittenberg Univ	OH	34,596	VC
Wofford College	SC	30,935	HC
Worcester State College	MA	12,499	C
Wright State Univ	OH	13,616	LC
Xavier Univ	OH	30,490	HC
Xavier Univ of Louisiana	LA	17,600	C
Yale Univ	CT	41,000	MC
Yeshiva Univ	NY	22,000	C
York College of Pennsylvania	PA	16,550	VC
Youngstown State Univ	OH	12,613	NC

SOFTWARE ENGINEERING

School	ST	$IS	SR
Allegheny College	PA	33,500	HC
Central Washington Univ	WA	11,730	C
Champlain College	VT	24,605	C
Clarkson Univ	NY	34,930	VC
Embry-Riddle Aeronautical Univ	AZ	30,280	C+
Embry-Riddle Aeronautical Univ	FL	30,280	C
Fairfield Univ	CT	39,835	HC
Limestone College	SC	19,840	C
Mich Tech Univ	MI	14,569	VC
Milwaukee School of Engineering	WI	29,847	VC+
Monmouth Univ	NJ	28,956	C
National Univ	CA	8,412	SP
Rochester Inst of Technology	NY	32,070	VC+
Rose-Hulman Inst of Technology	IN	34,557	HC+
S Dak State Univ	SD	9,815	C
Southern Polytechnic State Univ	GA	7,640	VC
Univ of Minn/Crookston	MN	13,157	LC
Univ of Texas at Dallas	TX	13,244	HC
Univ of Wisc/Platteville	WI	9,779	NC
Vermont Technical College	VT	15,751	C

SOIL SCIENCE

School	ST	$IS	SR
Alabama A&M Univ	AL	8,890	LC
Auburn Univ	AL	12,230	VC
Baylor Univ	TX	27,555	HC
Calif Polytechnic State Univ	CA	12,390	VC
Clemson Univ	SC	13,366	HC
Cornell Univ	NY	41,717	MC
Eastern Oregon Univ	OR	10,400	NC
Huntingdon College	AL	23,090	VC
Mich State Univ	MI	13,689	VC
New Mexico State Univ	NM	9,250	C
N Car State Univ	NC	11,824	HC
N Dak State Univ	ND	8,500	C
Oregon State Univ	OR	11,055	C
Penn State Univ/Univ Park Campus	PA	18,038	HC
Purdue Univ/West Lafayette	IN	13,458	VC
Southeast Missouri State Univ	MO	10,596	C
SUNY/College of Environmental Science and Forestry	NY	15,000	VC
Tenn Tech Univ	TN	10,044	C
Texas A&M Univ at Kingsville	TX	6,800	LC
Univ of Arizona	AZ	11,958	VC
Univ of at Calif Davis	CA	15,010	VC
Univ of Delaware	DE	14,142	HC
Univ of Florida	FL	9,354	HC
Univ of Hawaii at Manoa	HI	10,413	VC
Univ of Idaho	ID	9,310	NC
Univ of Mass Amherst	MA	15,973	C+
Univ of Missouri/Columbia	MO	13,500	VC
Univ of Nebr at Lincoln	NE	11,401	VC
Univ of New Hampshire	NH	16,810	VC
Univ of Tenn at Knoxville	TN	11,720	C
Univ of Wisc/Madison	WI	13,117	HC
Univ of Wisc/Platteville	WI	9,779	NC
Univ of Wisc/River Falls	WI	9,722	LC

School	ST	$IS	SR
Univ of Wisc/Stevens Point	WI	9,384	VC
Utah State Univ	UT	8,002	VC
Virginia Polytechnic Inst and State Univ	VA	10,834	VC
Washington State Univ	WA	12,260	C
West Texas A&M Univ	TX	8,452	C

SOUTH ASIAN STUDIES

School	ST	$IS	SR
Brown Univ	RI	42,015	MC
Oakland Univ	MI	11,936	C
Syracuse Univ	NY	38,655	HC
Univ of Calif at Berkeley	CA	18,141	HC+
Univ of Calif at Los Angeles	CA	17,681	VC
Univ of Calif at Santa Cruz	CA	19,174	VC
Univ of Chicago	IL	42,369	MC
Univ of Minn/Twin Cities	MN	13,165	HC
Univ of Pennsylvania	PA	41,766	MC
Univ of Washington	WA	10,400	VC
Washington Univ in St. Louis	MO	42,106	MC

SOUTHWEST AMERICAN STUDIES

School	ST	$IS	SR
College of Santa Fe	NM	28,978	C
Colo College	CO	37,668	HC
Fort Lewis College	CO	11,852	C
Southern Methodist Univ	TX	36,088	VC+

SPANISH

School	ST	$IS	SR
Abilene Christian Univ	TX	20,830	C
Adams State College	CO	8,613	C
Adrian College	MI	23,000	C
Agnes Scott College	GA	32,070	HC
Alabama State Univ	AL	7,658	C
Albany State Univ	GA	5,770	C+
Albertson College of Idaho	ID	21,095	VC
Albion College	MI	26,000	VC
Albright College	PA	33,920	C
Alfred Univ	NY		VC
Allegheny College	PA	33,500	HC
Alma College	MI	28,544	VC
American International College	MA	28,710	LC
Amherst College	MA	41,590	MC
Anderson Univ	IN	25,050	LC
Andrews Univ	MI	21,786	C
Angelo State Univ	TX	8,340	NC
Appalachian State Univ	NC	8,000	VC
Aquinas College	MI	23,750	C
Arizona State Univ-Tempe	AZ	11,174	C
Arkansas State Univ	AR	9,630	C
Armstrong Atlantic State Univ	GA	7,394	C
Asbury College	KY	23,762	VC
Ashland Univ	OH	25,000	C
Assumption College	MA	32,875	C
Auburn Univ	AL	12,230	VC
Augsburg College	MN	28,300	C
Augusta State Univ	GA	2,920	C
Augustana College	IL	29,862	VC+
Augustana College	SD	24,380	VC
Austin College	TX	27,871	HC
Austin Peay State Univ	TN	7,535	C
Azusa Pacific Univ	CA	28,546	VC
Baker Univ	KS	22,190	C
Baldwin-Wallace College	OH	27,256	VC
Ball State Univ	IN	13,138	C
Bard College	NY	41,800	HC+
Barry Univ	FL	24,100	LC
Bates College	ME	42,100	MC
Baylor Univ	TX	27,555	HC
Beloit College	WI	32,808	HC
Bemidji State Univ	MN	11,180	LC
Benedictine College	KS	21,968	C
Benedictine Univ	IL	25,710	C
Bennington College	VT	41,890	HC
Berea College	KY	5,496	VC+
Berry College	GA	24,342	VC
Bethany College	WV	21,395	C
Bethel College	KS	21,650	C
Bethel Univ	MN	29,840	VC
Biola Univ	CA	29,372	VC
Birmingham-Southern College	AL	28,494	VC+
Black Hills State Univ	SD	7,800	LC
Blackburn College	IL	13,690	C
Bloomsburg Univ of Pennsylvania	PA	11,602	C
Blue Mountain College	MS	11,086	C
Bluffton College	OH	26,110	C
Boston Univ	MA	42,046	HC+
Bowdoin College	ME	41,660	MC
Bowling Green State Univ	OH	14,994	C
Bradley Univ	IL	25,280	VC
Brandeis Univ	MA	41,551	MC
Briar Cliff Univ	IA	23,550	LC
Bridgewater College	VA	27,790	C
Bridgewater State College	MA	12,120	C
Brigham Young Univ	UT	9,200	VC
Bryan College	TN	19,270	C
Bryn Mawr College	PA	42,780	HC+
Bucknell Univ	PA	39,660	MC

School	ST	$IS	SR
Buena Vista Univ	IA	27,742	C
Butler Univ	IN	31,944	VC+
Cabrini College	PA	33,340	C
Caldwell College	NJ	26,450	LC
Calif Lutheran Univ	CA	27,800	LC
Calif State Polytechnic Univ, Pomona	CA	18,053	C+
Cal State East Bay	CA	10,856	LC
Cal State, Bakersfield	CA	6,125	LC
Cal State, Chico	CA	11,395	C
Cal State, Dominguez Hills	CA	10,220	LC
Cal State, Fresno	CA	10,037	LC
Cal State, Fullerton	CA	10,990	C
Cal State, Long Beach	CA	9,512	C
Cal State, Los Angeles	CA	5,900	C
Cal State, Northridge	CA	9,036	LC
Cal State, Sacramento	CA	11,122	C+
Cal State, San Bernardino	CA	12,563	LC
Cal State, San Marcos	CA	1,800	LC
Cal State, Stanislaus	CA	11,283	C
Calif Univ of Pennsylvania	PA	14,217	C
Calvin College	MI	25,735	NC
Campbell Univ	NC	21,137	VC
Canisius College	NY	32,257	VC
Capital Univ	OH	30,444	C
Cardinal Stritch Univ	WI	21,910	C
Carleton College	MN	40,467	MC
Carlow Univ	PA	24,313	C
Carnegie Mellon Univ	PA	32,700	MC
Carroll College	MT	23,324	C+
Carroll College	WI	24,860	C
Carson-Newman College	TN	16,800	C
Carthage College	WI	26,000	C
Case Western Reserve Univ	OH	37,314	MC
Castleton State College	VT	13,158	C
Catawba College	NC	25,000	C
Catholic Univ of America	DC	35,838	VC
Cedar Crest College	PA	30,615	C
Cedarville Univ	OH	21,904	VC
Centenary College of Louisiana	LA	24,760	VC
Central College	IA	26,774	VC
Central Conn State Univ	CT	13,620	C
Central Methodist Univ	MO	18,000	C
Central Mich Univ	MI	12,244	C
Central Missouri State Univ	MO	10,000	C
Central Univ of Bayamon	PR	3,335	
Central Washington Univ	WA	11,730	C
Centre College	KY	30,810	VC
Chapman Univ	CA	37,550	VC
Charleston Southern Univ	SC	17,800	C
Chatham Univ	PA	27,290	C+
Chestnut Hill College	PA	26,600	LC
Chicago State Univ	IL	10,915	C+
Christopher Newport Univ	VA	13,326	VC
Citadel, The	SC		C+
CUNY/Baruch College	NY	4,320	VC+
CUNY/Brooklyn College	NY	4,377	C+
CUNY/City College	NY		C
CUNY/College of Staten Island	NY	4,328	NC
CUNY/Herbert H. Lehman College	NY	4,000	LC
CUNY/Hunter College	NY	8,000	C+
CUNY/Queens College	NY	4,356	C
CUNY/York College	NY	4,242	NC
Claremont McKenna College	CA	42,920	MC
Clarion Univ of Pennsylvania	PA	11,844	C
Clark Univ	MA	35,165	VC+
Clarke College	IA	25,390	C
Clemson Univ	SC	13,366	HC
Cleveland State Univ	OH	10,798	NC
Coastal Carolina Univ	SC	13,140	C
Coe College	IA	27,440	VC
Coker College	SC	21,600	C
Colby College	ME	41,770	MC
Colgate Univ	NY	41,170	MC
College of Charleston	SC	13,616	VC
College of Mount St. Vincent	NY	28,000	C
College of New Jersey	NJ	18,315	MC
College of New Rochelle	NY	28,396	C+
College of Our Lady of the Elms	MA	21,000	C
College of St. Benedict	MN	30,091	VC
College of St. Catherine	MN	27,505	VC
College of St. Elizabeth	NJ	28,495	C
College of St. Rose	NY	25,684	C
College of the Holy Cross	MA	40,664	MC
College of the Ozarks	MO	4,130	VC+
College of William and Mary	VA	14,147	MC
College of Wooster	OH	31,310	VC+
Colo College	CO	37,668	HC
Colo State Univ-Fort Collins	CO	10,878	C+
Colo State Univ-Pueblo	CO	7,821	LC
Columbia Univ	SC	24,982	LC
Columbia Univ/Barnard College	NY	38,000	MC
Columbia Univ/Columbia College	NY	42,584	MC
Columbia Univ/School of General Studies	NY	41,516	C

School	ST	$IS	SR
Concordia College: Moorhead	MN	22,475	VC
Concordia Univ at Austin	TX	23,640	LC
Concordia Univ Wisc	WI	22,660	VC
Converse College	SC	24,800	VC
Cornell College	IA	30,110	VC+
Cornell Univ	NY	41,717	MC
Creighton Univ	NE	29,918	VC+
Daemen College	NY	24,580	C
Dana College	NE	22,390	C
Dartmouth College	NH	39,465	MC
Davidson College	NC	36,825	MC
De Sales Univ	PA	28,580	VC
Delaware State Univ	DE	8,130	LC
Denison Univ	OH	37,040	HC
DePaul Univ	IL	29,835	VC
DePauw Univ	IN	32,100	HC
Dickinson College	PA	40,170	HC+
Dickinson State Univ	ND	7,847	NC
Dillard Univ	LA	17,500	VC
Doane College	NE	22,458	C
Dominican College	NY	26,630	LC
Dominican Univ	IL	26,370	C
Dordt College	IA	20,325	VC
Drew Univ/College of Liberal Arts	NJ	39,698	VC
Drury Univ	MO	20,117	VC
Duke Univ	NC	41,239	MC
Duquesne Univ	PA	29,534	VC
Earlham College	IN	33,604	HC
East Stroudsburg Univ of Pennsylvania	PA	10,336	C
East Texas Baptist Univ	TX	16,713	C
Eastern Conn State Univ	CT	13,554	C
Eastern Kentucky Univ	KY	7,725	C
Eastern Mennonite Univ	VA	25,450	VC
Eastern Mich Univ	MI	12,897	C
Eastern Nazarene College	MA	19,500	LC
Eastern New Mexico Univ	NM	7,264	C
Eastern Univ	PA	24,075	C
Eastern Washington Univ	WA	10,608	C
Eckerd College	FL	35,492	VC
Edgewood College	WI	22,862	C
Edinboro Univ of Pennsylvania	PA	11,809	LC
Elizabethtown College	PA	32,100	VC
Elmhurst College	IL	24,685	C
Elmira College	NY	37,200	VC
Elon Univ	NC	25,371	HC
Emmanuel College	MA	32,000	C+
Emory Univ	GA	40,546	MC
Endicott College	MA	30,156	C+
Evangel Univ	MO	17,380	C
Fairfield Univ	CT	39,835	HC
Fayetteville State Univ	NC	6,000	LC
Ferrum College	VA	24,290	LC
Fisk Univ	TN	19,830	C
Flagler College	FL	13,790	VC+
Florida Atlantic Univ	FL	11,221	C
Florida International Univ	FL	9,215	VC
Florida Southern College	FL	25,965	C
Florida State Univ	FL	9,028	HC
Fordham Univ	NY	36,000	HC
Fort Hays State Univ	KS	7,638	C
Fort Lewis College	CO	11,852	C
Framingham State College	MA	11,156	C
Francis Marion Univ	SC	11,114	C
Franciscan Univ of Steubenville	OH	20,300	VC
Franklin and Marshall College	PA	40,590	HC
Franklin College	IN		C
Fresno Pacific Univ	CA	25,454	C
Friends Univ	KS	16,250	LC
Furman Univ	SC	33,264	HC+
Gallaudet Univ	DC	16,554	
Gardner-Webb Univ	NC	21,500	C
Geneva College	PA	21,850	C
George Fox Univ	OR	28,490	C
George Mason Univ	VA	10,850	VC
George Washington Univ	DC	48,820	MC
Georgetown College	KY	24,950	C+
Georgetown Univ	DC	43,183	MC
Georgia College and State Univ	GA	11,020	C
Georgia Southern Univ	GA	9,762	C
Georgia State Univ	GA	11,444	VC
Georgian Court College	NJ	20,000	LC
Gettysburg College	PA	39,864	HC
Gonzaga Univ	WA	30,218	HC
Gordon College	MA	29,194	C+
Goshen College	IN	22,850	VC
Goucher College	MD	36,225	VC
Grace College	IN	22,170	C
Graceland Univ	IA	19,700	C
Grambling State Univ	LA	6,538	NC
Grand Canyon Univ	AZ	32,000	C
Greensboro College	NC	23,000	C
Greenville College	IL	23,146	C
Grinnell College	IA	34,814	HC+
Grove City College	PA	15,784	HC+
Guilford College	NC	28,160	C+
Gustavus Adolphus College	MN	30,920	HC
Hamilton College	NY	41,660	MC
Hamline Univ	MN	27,070	VC
Hampden-Sydney College	VA	31,148	VC

ST = STATE   **$IS** = IN-STATE COSTS   **SR** = SELECTOR RATING

INDEX OF COLLEGE MAJORS

School	ST	$IS	SR
Hanover College	IN	28,150	HC
Harding Univ	AR	16,512	VC
Hardin-Simmons Univ	TX	18,641	C
Hartwick College	NY	36,065	C+
Harvard Univ/Harvard College	MA	45,860	MC
Hastings College	NE	22,218	VC
Haverford College	PA	41,600	MC
Heidelberg College	OH	23,242	C
Henderson State Univ	AR	7,600	C
Hendrix College	AR	27,646	HC+
Heritage Univ	WA	6,800	NC
High Point Univ	NC	25,720	C
Hillsdale College	MI	24,160	HC
Hiram College	OH	28,700	VC
Hofstra Univ	NY	32,630	VC
Hollins Univ	VA	31,105	C
Holy Family Univ	PA	25,740	C
Hood College	MD	30,085	VC
Hope College	MI	28,208	VC+
Hope International Univ	CA	23,700	NC
Houghton College	NY	25,980	VC+
Houston Baptist Univ	TX	18,660	C
Howard Payne Univ	TX	17,115	C
Howard Univ	DC	18,481	C+
Humboldt State Univ	CA	11,176	C
Idaho State Univ	ID	9,030	C
Illinois College	IL	21,900	C+
Illinois State Univ	IL	12,839	C+
Illinois Wesleyan Univ	IL	34,050	HC+
Immaculata Univ	PA	25,350	C
Indiana State Univ	IN	11,604	C
Indiana Univ Bloomington	IN	13,356	VC
Indiana Univ Northwest	IN	4,902	LC
Indiana Univ of Pennsylvania	PA	11,209	C
Indiana Univ South Bend	IN	4,989	LC
Indiana Univ Southeast	IN	4,880	LC
Indiana Univ-Purdue Univ Fort Wayne	IN	5,067	LC
Indiana Univ-Purdue Univ Indianapolis	IN	10,959	C
Indiana Wesleyan Univ	IN	22,074	C+
Inter American Univ of PR/ Fajardo Campus	PR	4,000	
Inter American Univ of PR/ Metropolitan Campus	PR	4,320	
Inter American Univ of PR/ Ponce Regional College	PR	3,700	
Inter American Univ of PR/ San German	PR	6,720	
Iona College	NY	30,878	VC
Iowa State Univ	IA	11,831	VC
Ithaca College	NY	35,144	VC
Jacksonville Univ	FL	24,040	C
Jamestown College	ND	14,130	NC
John Brown Univ	AR	20,910	VC
John Carroll Univ	OH	27,658	C+
Johns Hopkins Univ	MD	42,044	MC
Johnson C. Smith Univ	NC	20,000	C
Juniata College	PA	33,130	VC
Kalamazoo College	MI	32,442	VC+
Kansas Wesleyan Univ	KS	21,400	VC
Kean Univ	NJ	15,880	C
Keene State College	NH	13,836	C
Kennesaw State Univ	GA	12,152	C
Kent State Univ	OH	14,594	C
Kentucky Wesleyan College	KY	18,590	C
Kenyon College	OH	39,500	MC
King College	TN	23,400	C
King's College	PA	29,810	C
Knox College	IL	32,385	VC+
Kutztown Univ of Pennsylvania	PA	10,820	C
La Salle Univ	PA	34,950	C
La Sierra Univ	CA	24,327	C+
Lafayette College	PA	39,267	MC
LaGrange College	GA	22,874	C+
Lake Forest College	IL	33,860	VC
Lakeland College	WI	22,990	C
Lamar Univ	TX	6,820	LC
Lambuth Univ	TN	21,700	C+
Lander Univ	SC	10,600	C
Lawrence Univ	WI	33,958	HC+
Le Moyne College	NY	29,570	VC
Lebanon Valley College	PA	31,700	VC
Lee Univ	TN	14,760	NC
Lehigh Univ	PA	42,690	HC+
Lenoir-Rhyne College	NC	25,580	C
Liberty Univ	VA	19,101	C
Lincoln Univ	MO	8,000	NC
Lincoln Univ	PA	13,658	C+
Lindenwood Univ	MO	18,600	VC
Linfield College	OR	29,632	VC
Lipscomb Univ	TN	20,967	VC
Lock Haven Univ of Pennsylvania	PA	12,098	LC
LIU/C.W. Post Campus	NY	28,282	C
Loras College	IA	27,193	C
Louisiana State Univ and A&M College	LA	10,749	VC
Louisiana State Univ in Shreveport	LA	2,900	NC
Louisiana Tech Univ	LA	7,370	C
Loyola College in Maryland	MD	38,898	HC
Loyola Marymount Univ	CA	36,321	VC
Loyola Univ Chicago	IL	32,896	VC
Loyola Univ New Orleans	LA	31,050	VC+
Luther College	IA	28,800	VC+
Lycoming College	PA	30,797	C+
Lynchburg College	VA	30,645	C
Lyon College	AR	19,990	VC
Macalester College	MN	36,500	MC
MacMurray College	IL	20,755	C
Madonna Univ	MI	16,068	VC
Malone College	OH	23,040	C
Manchester College	IN	23,470	C
Manhattan College	NY	29,000	VC
Manhattanville College	NY	32,500	VC
Mansfield Univ	PA	11,300	C
Marian College	IN	26,160	C
Marian College of Fond du Lac	WI	21,775	LC
Marietta College	OH	29,327	C
Marist College	NY	30,566	VC
Marlboro College	VT	35,980	VC+
Marquette Univ	WI	31,066	VC
Mars Hill College	NC	19,000	LC
Martin Univ	IN	10,300	SP
Mary Baldwin College	VA	26,465	C
Maryville College	TN	29,224	VC
Marywood Univ	PA	30,680	C
McDaniel College	MD	31,610	VC
McMurry Univ	TX	18,100	LC
McPherson College	KS	21,010	C
Mercer Univ	GA	27,525	VC+
Meredith College	NC	25,600	C
Messiah College	PA	28,910	VC+
Methodist College	NC	21,000	C
Metropolitan State College of Denver	CO	2,338	LC
Miami Univ	OH	29,097	HC
Mich State Univ	MI	13,689	VC
MidAmerica Nazarene Univ	KS	20,584	LC
Middle Tenn State Univ	TN	8,540	C
Middlebury College	VT	42,120	MC
Midwestern State Univ	TX	9,381	LC
Millersville Univ of Pennsylvania	PA	12,113	C
Millikin Univ	IL	25,590	C
Millsaps College	MS	28,256	VC+
Minn State Univ, Mankato	MN	10,276	LC
Minn State Univ, Moorhead	MN	7,000	LC
Minot State Univ	ND	6,700	LC
Miss College	MS	14,574	VC
Miss Univ for Women	MS	6,000	LC
Missouri Southern State Univ	MO	8,396	NC
Missouri State Univ	MO	10,748	C+
Missouri Western State Univ	MO	9,534	NC
Molloy College	NY	16,510	C
Monmouth College	IL	23,700	C
Montclair State Univ	NJ	16,327	C
Moravian College	PA	28,950	VC
Morehouse College	GA	25,082	C
Morningside College	IA	23,704	C
Mount Holyoke College	MA	42,148	HC+
Mount Mary College	WI	22,895	C
Mount St. Mary's College	CA	32,086	VC
Mount St. Mary's Univ	MD	30,930	C
Mount Union College	OH	25,840	C
Mount Vernon Nazarene Univ	OH	20,810	C
Muhlenberg College	PA	36,030	HC+
Murray State Univ	KY	8,900	VC
Muskingum College	OH	22,970	C
Nazareth College of Rochester	NY	28,175	VC
Nebr Wesleyan Univ	NE	23,415	C+
New College of Calif	CA	12,842	NC
New Jersey City Univ	NJ	13,695	LC
New Mexico Highlands Univ	NM	6,272	NC
New York Univ	NY	43,170	MC
Newberry College	SC	23,000	LC
Niagara Univ	NY	28,250	C
N Car Central Univ	NC	9,000	LC
N Car State Univ	NC	11,824	HC
North Central College	IL	28,926	VC
N Dak State Univ	ND	8,500	C
North Georgia College and State Univ	GA	7,000	C
North Park Univ	IL	24,050	C
Northeastern Illinois Univ	IL	3,000	NC
Northeastern State Univ	OK	5,896	LC
Northeastern Univ	MA	35,742	HC
Northern Arizona Univ	AZ	10,353	C
Northern Illinois Univ	IL	13,178	C
Northern Kentucky Univ	KY	6,670	NC
Northern Mich Univ	MI	12,340	LC
Northern State Univ	SD	8,257	C
Northwest Missouri State Univ	MO	10,000	C
Northwest Nazarene Univ	ID	22,590	VC
Northwestern College of Iowa	IA	22,174	C+
Northwestern Univ	IL	37,595	MC
Oakland Univ	MI	11,936	C
Oakwood College	AL	14,904	C
Oberlin College	OH	40,904	MC
Occidental College	CA	40,185	MC
Oglethorpe Univ	GA	30,300	VC
Ohio Northern Univ	OH	27,765	VC
Ohio State Univ	OH	15,357	HC
Ohio Univ	OH	15,921	C
Ohio Wesleyan Univ	OH	35,830	VC+
Okla Baptist Univ	OK	17,986	VC
Okla Christian Univ	OK	18,992	NC
Okla City Univ	OK	23,965	VC
Okla State Univ	OK	10,213	VC
Old Dominion Univ	VA	11,907	C
Oral Roberts Univ	OK	22,650	C
Oregon State Univ	OR	11,055	C
Otterbein College	OH	28,986	C
Ouachita Baptist Univ	AR	21,900	VC
Our Lady of the Lake Univ of San Antonio	TX	22,430	LC
Pace Univ	NY	30,000	VC
Pacific Lutheran Univ	WA	28,805	VC
Pacific Union College	CA	24,555	VC+
Pacific Univ	OR	24,250	C
Park Univ	MO	11,592	C
Penn State Univ/Univ Park Campus	PA	18,038	HC
Pepperdine Univ	CA	39,960	HC
Piedmont College	GA	20,500	C
Pittsburg State Univ	KS	8,112	C
Pitzer College	CA	41,644	HC
Plymouth State Univ	NH	12,298	LC
Point Loma Nazarene Univ	CA	27,610	VC
Pomona College	CA	40,774	MC
Pontifical Catholic Univ of PR/Ponce	PR	7,310	
Portland State Univ	OR	12,453	C
Prairie View A&M Univ	TX	11,110	LC
Presbyterian College	SC	30,044	VC
Prescott College	AZ	13,445	LC
Princeton Univ	NJ	40,213	MC
Principia College	IL	27,765	VC+
Providence College	RI	34,580	VC
Purdue Univ/Calumet	IN	10,891	LC
Purdue Univ/West Lafayette	IN	12,120	MC
Queens Univ of Charlotte	NC	24,528	C
Quinnipiac Univ	CT	34,640	VC
Randolph-Macon College	VA	31,250	C
Randolph-Macon Woman's College	VA	31,160	VC+
Regis College	MA	31,350	C
Regis Univ	CO	31,890	C
Rhode Island College	RI	11,570	C
Rhodes College	TN	32,860	HC
Rider Univ	NJ	32,560	C
Ripon College	WI	27,160	C+
Roanoke College	VA	30,748	VC
Rockford College	IL	28,330	VC
Rockhurst Univ	MO	25,440	VC
Rollins College	FL	38,366	VC
Roosevelt Univ	IL	22,605	VC
Rosemont College	PA	29,350	C
Rowan Univ	NJ	16,000	VC
Russell Sage College	NY	27,000	C
Rutgers, The State Univ of New Jersey/Camden Campus	NJ	15,000	C
Rutgers, The State Univ of New Jersey/New Brunswick/Piscataway Campus	NJ	15,810	HC
Rutgers, The State Univ of New Jersey/Newark Campus	NJ	15,640	VC
Sacred Heart Univ	CT	33,404	C
Saginaw Valley State Univ	MI	11,432	C
St. Ambrose Univ	IA	25,495	C
St. Anselm College	NH	33,810	C
St. Augustine's College	NC	14,000	LC
St. Bonaventure Univ	NY	28,785	C
St. Edward's Univ	TX	23,560	C
St. Francis College	NY	19,974	LC
St. Francis Univ	PA	25,880	C
St. John Fisher College	NY	27,860	C
St. John's Univ	MN	29,749	VC
St. John's Univ	NY	34,370	C
St. Joseph College	CT	32,050	C
St. Joseph's College, New York, Brooklyn Campus	NY	12,206	C
St. Joseph's Univ	PA	37,428	VC
St. Lawrence Univ	NY	40,545	VC
St. Louis Univ	MO	33,158	VC+
St. Mary-of-the-Woods College	IN	25,480	C
St. Mary's College	IN	32,538	VC
St. Mary's College of Calif	CA	37,290	C
St. Mary's Univ of Minn	MN	23,857	VC
St. Mary's Univ of San Antonio	TX	22,444	C
St. Michael's College	VT	33,330	VC
St. Norbert College	WI	28,577	C+
St. Olaf College	MN	32,800	HC
St. Peter's College	NJ	30,160	LC
St. Thomas Aquinas College	NY	22,000	LC
St. Vincent College	PA	26,160	VC
St. Xavier Univ	IL	23,160	C
Salem College	NC	26,226	VC+
Salisbury Univ	MD	13,128	VC
Salve Regina Univ	RI	33,450	C
Sam Houston State Univ	TX	8,000	C
Samford Univ	AL	20,258	VC
San Diego State Univ	CA	12,971	C
San Jose State Univ	CA	11,707	C
Santa Clara Univ	CA	38,931	VC
Sarah Lawrence College	NY	42,000	HC
Seattle Pacific Univ	WA	29,355	C
Seattle Univ	WA	30,063	VC
Seton Hall Univ	NJ	33,622	VC
Seton Hill Univ	PA	28,810	C
Shenandoah Univ	VA	27,600	C
Shippensburg Univ of Pennsylvania	PA	11,621	C
Shorter College	GA	19,700	C
Siena College	NY	28,260	VC+
Siena Heights Univ	MI	17,000	LC
Simmons College	MA	35,640	VC
Simon's Rock College of Bard	MA	41,988	VC+
Simpson College	IA	26,833	VC
Skidmore College	NY	41,779	HC
Slippery Rock Univ of Pennsylvania	PA	10,360	LC
Smith College	MA	41,474	MC
Sonoma State Univ	CA	14,732	C
S Car State Univ	SC	6,700	LC
S Dak State Univ	SD	9,815	C
Southeast Missouri State Univ	MO	10,596	C
Southeastern Louisiana Univ	LA	8,521	LC
Southern Arkansas Univ	AR	6,956	C
Southern Conn State Univ	CT	10,310	C
Southern Illinois Univ Carbondale	IL	12,391	C
Southern Methodist Univ	TX	36,088	VC+
Southern Nazarene Univ	OK	14,634	NC
Southern Oregon Univ	OR	12,186	C
Southern Univ and A&M College	LA	8,238	LC
Southern Univ at New Orleans	LA	1,000	NC
Southern Utah Univ	UT		C
Southwest Baptist Univ	MO	18,300	C
Southwest Minn State Univ	MN	10,975	C
Southwestern Univ	TX	26,767	HC
Spelman College	GA	24,650	VC
Spring Arbor Univ	MI	22,476	C
Spring Hill College	AL	28,678	C
Stanford Univ	CA	41,557	MC
SUNY at Oswego	NY	13,662	VC
SUNY at Potsdam	NY	12,959	C
SUNY/College at Brockport	NY	12,747	VC
SUNY/College at Buffalo	NY	11,903	C+
SUNY/College at Fredonia	NY	12,771	VC
SUNY/College at Geneseo	NY	12,910	HC+
SUNY/College at Old Westbury	NY	13,154	C
SUNY/College at Oneonta	NY	12,905	VC
SUNY/College at Plattsburgh	NY	12,362	C
SUNY/Univ at Albany	NY	13,860	VC
SUNY/Univ at Binghamton	NY	13,988	VC
SUNY/Univ at Buffalo	NY	13,694	VC
SUNY/Univ at New Paltz	NY	12,480	VC
Stephen F. Austin State Univ	TX	7,930	C
Stetson Univ	FL	32,725	VC
Suffolk Univ	MA	33,160	C
Sul Ross State Univ	TX	6,600	LC
Susquehanna Univ	PA	33,465	VC
Swarthmore College	PA	41,280	MC
Sweet Briar College	VA	31,460	VC
Syracuse Univ	NY	38,655	HC
Tarleton State Univ	TX	8,952	C
Taylor Univ	IN	26,376	VC+
Temple Univ	PA	17,438	C
Tenn Tech Univ	TN	10,044	C
Texas A&M Univ	TX	13,351	HC
Texas A&M Univ at Commerce	TX	9,020	C
Texas A&M Univ at Corpus Christi	TX	10,280	LC
Texas A&M Univ at Kingsville	TX	6,800	LC
Texas Christian Univ	TX	23,410	VC+
Texas Lutheran Univ	TX	23,530	C
Texas Southern Univ	TX	9,828	C
Texas State Univ - San Marcos	TX	10,862	C
Texas Tech Univ	TX	13,026	VC
Texas Wesleyan Univ	TX	18,700	C
Thiel College	PA	24,580	C
Towson Univ	MD	13,924	VC
Transylvania Univ	KY	26,240	VC+
Trinity Christian College	IL	23,645	C
Trinity College	CT	38,040	HC+
Trinity College	DC	24,150	LC
Trinity Univ	TX	30,157	HC+
Truman State Univ	MO	11,242	HC
Tufts Univ	MA	42,018	MC
Tulane Univ	LA	41,098	MC
Turabo Univ	PR	4,110	
Union College	NE	18,710	C
Union Univ	TN	20,750	C
Universidad Adventista de las Antillas	PR	7,360	

ST = STATE   **$IS** = IN-STATE COSTS   **SR** = SELECTOR RATING

School	ST	$IS	SR
Univ of Akron	OH	15,166	NC
Univ of Alabama	AL	9,888	C
Univ of Alabama at Birmingham	AL	13,716	C
Univ of Arizona	AZ	11,958	VC
Univ of Arkansas	AR	11,859	VC
Univ of Arkansas at Little Rock	AR	7,230	NC
Univ of at Calif Davis	CA	15,010	VC
Univ of Calif at Berkeley	CA	18,141	HC+
Univ of Calif at Irvine	CA	16,475	VC
Univ of Calif at Los Angeles	CA	17,681	MC
Univ of Calif at Riverside	CA	16,625	C
Univ of Calif at Santa Barbara	CA	11,800	VC
Univ of Central Arkansas	AR	9,984	C
Univ of Central Florida	FL	10,739	VC
Univ of Central Okla	OK	8,094	C
Univ of Cincinnati	OH	17,682	VC
Univ of Colo at Boulder	CO	13,352	C+
Univ of Colo at Colo Springs	CO	11,517	VC
Univ of Colo at Denver and Health Sciences Center	CO	5,021	C
Univ of Conn	CT	16,628	HC
Univ of Dallas	TX	27,432	VC+
Univ of Dayton	OH	28,826	VC
Univ of Denver	CO	36,376	VC+
Univ of Evansville	IN	28,320	VC
Univ of Findlay	OH	29,238	C
Univ of Florida	FL	9,354	HC
Univ of Georgia	GA	11,004	HC
Univ of Hawaii at Manoa	HI	10,413	VC
Univ of Houston	TX	7,000	C
Univ of Idaho	ID	9,310	NC
Univ of Illinois at Chicago	IL	16,256	VC
Univ of Illinois at Urbana-Champaign	IL	15,800	HC+
Univ of Indianapolis	IN	25,090	C
Univ of Iowa	IA	12,172	VC
Univ of Kansas	KS	10,915	VC
Univ of Kentucky	KY	7,800	C
Univ of La Verne	CA	33,470	C
Univ of Louisiana at Lafayette	LA	5,830	C
Univ of Louisiana at Monroe	LA	7,103	C
Univ of Louisville	KY	10,400	VC
Univ of Maine	ME	13,642	C
Univ of Mary Hardin-Baylor	TX	19,428	C
Univ of Mary Washington	VA	11,636	HC
Univ of Maryland/Baltimore County	MD	16,642	VC+
Univ of Maryland/College Park	MD	16,036	HC
Univ of Mass Amherst	MA	15,973	C+
Univ of Mass Boston	MA	8,024	C
Univ of Mass Dartmouth	MA	15,985	C
Univ of Miami	FL	38,397	MC
Univ of Mich/Ann Arbor	MI	16,587	HC+
Univ of Mich/Flint	MI	6,398	C
Univ of Minn/Duluth	MN	13,974	C
Univ of Minn/Morris	MN	15,472	VC
Univ of Minn/Twin Cities	MN	13,165	NC
Univ of Miss	MS	9,000	C
Univ of Missouri/Columbia	MO	13,500	VC
Univ of Missouri/Kansas City	MO	15,000	VC
Univ of Missouri/St. Louis	MO	14,046	VC
Univ of Montana	MT	10,602	C
Univ of Montevallo	AL	9,630	C
Univ of Nebr at Kearney	NE	9,000	NC
Univ of Nebr at Lincoln	NE	11,401	VC
Univ of Nebr at Omaha	NE	11,235	C
Univ of Nevada/Las Vegas	NV	11,566	C
Univ of Nevada/Reno	NV	12,155	NC
Univ of New Hampshire	NH	16,810	VC
Univ of New Mexico	NM	11,253	C
Univ of New Orleans	LA	7,370	C
Univ of North Alabama	AL	8,992	C
Univ of N Car at Asheville	NC	9,237	VC
Univ of N Car at Charlotte	NC	9,101	C
Univ of N Car at Greensboro	NC	8,993	C
Univ of N Car at Pembroke	NC	7,940	LC
Univ of N Car at Wilmington	NC	10,107	VC
Univ of N Dak	ND	10,114	VC
Univ of North Florida	FL	9,908	VC
Univ of North Texas	TX	7,800	C
Univ of Northern Colo	CO	10,249	C
Univ of Northern Iowa	IA	11,133	C
Univ of Notre Dame	IN	39,552	MC
Univ of Okla	OK	10,769	VC+
Univ of Oregon	OR	13,108	VC
Univ of Pennsylvania	PA	41,766	MC
Univ of Pittsburgh at Pittsburgh	PA	18,866	HC
Univ of Portland	OR	32,300	VC
Univ of Puget Sound	WA	35,600	VC
Univ of Redlands	CA	36,160	VC
Univ of Rhode Island	RI	15,398	C
Univ of Richmond	VA	40,510	MC
Univ of Rochester	NY	41,155	MC
Univ of St. Thomas	MN	28,000	VC
Univ of St. Thomas	TX	23,810	VC
Univ of San Diego	CA	40,620	HC
Univ of San Francisco	CA	37,560	VC
Univ of Scranton	PA	31,100	VC
Univ of S Car at Columbia	SC	13,397	VC
Univ of S Car Upstate	SC	11,957	C
Univ of S Dak	SD	9,068	C
Univ of South Florida	FL	10,284	VC
Univ of Southern Calif	CA	41,618	MC
Univ of Southern Indiana	IN	12,590	VC
Univ of Tampa	FL	25,784	C
Univ of Tenn at Chattanooga	TN	7,790	C
Univ of Tenn at Knoxville	TN	11,720	C
Univ of Tenn at Martin	TN	8,693	C
Univ of Texas at Arlington	TX	7,195	VC
Univ of Texas at Austin	TX	14,610	HC
Univ of Texas at El Paso	TX	8,764	NC
Univ of Texas at San Antonio	TX	11,325	LC
Univ of Texas-Pan American	TX	7,290	C+
Univ of the District of Columbia	DC	2,070	LC
Univ of the Incarnate Word	TX	23,306	C
Univ of the Pacific	CA	34,380	VC
Univ of the South	TN	34,645	HC
Univ of Toledo	OH	15,806	NC
Univ of Tulsa	OK	25,348	HC
Univ of Utah	UT	10,162	VC
Univ of Vermont	VT	18,080	VC
Univ of Virginia	VA	13,759	MC
Univ of Virginia's College at Wise	VA	11,076	C
Univ of Washington	WA	10,400	VC
Univ of West Georgia	GA	8,838	C
Univ of Wisc/Eau Claire	WI	9,915	VC
Univ of Wisc/Green Bay	WI	9,415	VC
Univ of Wisc/La Crosse	WI	10,045	VC
Univ of Wisc/Madison	WI	13,117	HC
Univ of Wisc/Milwaukee	WI	9,427	VC
Univ of Wisc/Oshkosh	WI	10,426	LC
Univ of Wisc/Parkside	WI	10,181	LC
Univ of Wisc/Platteville	WI	9,779	NC
Univ of Wisc/Stevens Point	WI	9,384	VC
Univ of Wisc/Whitewater	WI	9,274	C
Univ of Wyoming	WY	9,666	C
Ursinus College	PA	38,950	VC
Utah State Univ	UT	8,002	VC
Valdosta State Univ	GA	8,802	C
Valley City State Univ	ND	9,854	LC
Valparaiso Univ	IN	28,970	VC+
Vanderbilt Univ	TN	41,986	MC
Vanguard Univ of Southern Calif	CA	27,071	C
Villanova Univ	PA	38,672	HC+
Virginia Polytechnic Inst and State Univ	VA	10,834	VC
Virginia Wesleyan College	VA	28,433	C
Viterbo Univ	WI	21,670	C
Wabash College	IN	30,116	HC
Wake Forest Univ	NC	38,290	MC
Walla Walla College	WA	24,489	NC
Walsh Univ	OH	23,440	VC
Warren Wilson College	NC	24,382	VC
Wartburg College	IA	27,315	NC
Washburn Univ	KS	9,734	NC
Washington and Jefferson College	PA	33,490	VC
Washington and Lee Univ	VA	35,880	MC
Washington College	MD	34,990	VC
Washington State Univ	WA	12,260	C
Washington Univ in St. Louis	MO	42,106	MC
Wayland Baptist Univ	TX	13,484	C
Wayne State College	NE	8,033	NC
Wayne State Univ	MI	11,805	C
Weber State Univ	UT	9,635	NC
Webster Univ	MO	24,280	VC
Wellesley College	MA	41,030	MC
Wells College	NY	23,070	VC
Wesleyan College	GA	19,560	C
Wesleyan Univ	CT	42,122	MC
West Chester Univ of Pennsylvania	PA	12,355	C+
West Texas A&M Univ	TX	8,452	C
Western Carolina Univ	NC	7,000	C
Western Conn State Univ	CT	12,993	C
Western Illinois Univ	IL	13,042	C
Western Kentucky Univ	KY	10,192	C
Western Mich Univ	MI	13,299	C
Western New Mexico Univ	NM	7,233	LC
Western Oregon Univ	OR	10,295	C
Western State College of Colo	CO	9,942	C
Western Washington Univ	WA	11,262	VC
Westminster College	MO	19,060	VC
Westminster College	PA	31,290	C
Westmont College	CA	36,672	HC
Wheaton College	IL	27,760	HC
Wheeling Jesuit Univ	WV	26,910	C
Whitman College	WA	36,110	HC+
Whittier College	CA	29,108	C
Whitworth College	WA	29,428	VC+
Wichita State Univ	KS	8,500	C
Wilkes Univ	PA	30,886	C
Willamette Univ	OR	35,416	VC+
William Carey College	MS	11,000	LC
William Jewell College	MO	24,340	C
William Paterson Univ of New Jersey	NJ	17,810	C+
Williams College	MA	40,310	MC
Wilmington College	OH	2,806	NC
Wilson College	PA	27,660	VC
Wingate Univ	NC	23,300	C
Winona State Univ	MN	11,333	C
Winston-Salem State Univ	NC	8,960	LC
Winthrop Univ	SC	11,302	C
Wisc Lutheran College	WI	23,510	VC
Wittenberg Univ	OH	34,596	VC
Wofford College	SC	30,935	NC
Worcester State College	MA	12,499	C
Wright State Univ	OH	13,616	LC
Xavier Univ	OH	30,490	VC
Xavier Univ of Louisiana	LA	17,600	C
Yale Univ	CT	41,000	MC
York College of Pennsylvania	PA	16,550	VC
Youngstown State Univ	OH	12,613	NC

SPANISH STUDIES

School	ST	$IS	SR
American Univ	DC	38,719	HC+
Assumption College	MA	32,875	C
Bard College	NY	41,800	HC+
Barton College	NC	22,316	C
Cal State, San Bernardino	CA	12,563	LC
Dartmouth College	NH	39,465	MC
Fairleigh Dickinson Univ/College at Florham	NJ	30,130	C
Fairleigh Dickinson Univ/Metropolitan Campus	NJ	28,590	C
Fordham Univ	NY	36,000	HC
Hobart and William Smith Colleges	NY	41,123	VC
Holy Names College	CA	27,980	NC
Mass Inst of Technology	MA	41,800	MC
Montana State Univ-Billings	MT	8,906	C
New College of Florida	FL	10,009	HC+
Reed College	OR	41,106	MC
SUNY/Univ at Stony Brook	NY	13,625	HC
Sweet Briar College	VA	31,460	VC
Univ of Calif at San Diego	CA	16,102	HC
Vassar College	NY	41,700	MC
Washington State Univ	WA	12,260	C

SPECIAL EDUCATION

School	ST	$IS	SR
Alabama A&M Univ	AL	8,890	LC
Alabama State Univ	AL	7,658	C
Albany State Univ	GA	5,770	C+
Albright College	PA	33,920	C
Alcorn State Univ	MS	8,190	LC
American International College	MA	28,710	LC
Appalachian State Univ	NC	8,000	VC
Aquinas College	MI	23,750	C
Arcadia Univ	PA	33,570	VC
Arizona State Univ-Tempe	AZ	11,174	C
Arkansas State Univ	AR	9,630	C
Armstrong Atlantic State Univ	GA	7,394	C
Auburn Univ	AL	12,230	VC
Augusta State Univ	GA	2,920	C
Augustana College	SD	24,380	VC
Austin Peay State Univ	TN	7,535	C
Avila Univ	MO	22,100	C
Ball State Univ	IN	13,138	C
Baylor Univ	TX	27,555	HC
Bellarmine Univ	KY	27,650	C+
Benedictine College	KS	21,968	C
Benedictine Univ	IL	25,710	C
Bennett College	NC	11,500	C
Bethany College	WV	21,395	C
Black Hills State Univ	SD	7,800	VC
Bloomsburg Univ of Pennsylvania	PA	11,602	C
Boston College	MA	41,608	MC
Boston Univ	MA	42,046	HC+
Bowling Green State Univ	OH	14,994	C
Bradley Univ	IL	25,280	VC
Brenau Univ Women's College	GA	23,950	VC
Brescia Univ	KY	14,240	C
Bridgewater State College	MA	12,120	C
Brigham Young Univ	UT	9,200	VC
Brigham Young Univ/Hawaii	HI	7,740	HC+
Buena Vista Univ	IA	27,742	C
Cabrini College	PA	33,340	C
Cal State, Long Beach	CA	9,512	C
Calif Univ of Pennsylvania	PA	14,217	C
Calvin College	MI	25,735	NC
Canisius College	NY	32,257	VC
Cardinal Stritch Univ	WI	21,910	C
Caribbean Univ	PR	3,000	
Carlow Univ	PA	24,313	C
Cedarville Univ	OH	21,904	VC
Central Mich Univ	MI	12,244	C
Central Missouri State Univ	MO	10,000	C
Central State Univ	OH	9,010	C+
Central Washington Univ	WA	11,730	C
Cheyney Univ of Pennsylvania	PA	11,497	LC
CUNY/City College	NY		C
CUNY/Medgar Evers College	NY	4,250	NC
Clarion Univ of Pennsylvania	PA	11,844	C
Clarke College	IA	25,390	C
Clearwater Christian College	FL	13,160	LC
Clemson Univ	SC	13,366	HC
Cleveland State Univ	OH	10,798	NC
Coastal Carolina Univ	SC	13,140	C
College Misericordia	PA	27,950	C
College of Charleston	SC	13,616	VC
College of Mount St. Vincent	NY	28,000	C
College of Mount St. Joseph	OH	24,860	C
College of New Jersey	NJ	18,315	MC
College of Notre Dame of Maryland	MD	27,700	C
College of Our Lady of the Elms	MA	21,000	C
College of St. Elizabeth	NJ	28,495	C
College of St. Joseph	VT	20,900	NC
College of St. Mary	NE	23,938	C
College of St. Rose	NY	25,684	C
College of the Southwest	NM	12,420	C+
Columbia College	SC	24,982	LC
Columbus State Univ	GA	8,664	C
Concord College	WV	9,708	C
Concordia Univ Nebr	NE	20,500	C+
Coppin State College	MD	10,200	LC
Creighton Univ	NE	29,918	VC+
Cumberland Univ	TN	18,894	C
Curry College	MA	26,100	C
Daemen College	NY	24,580	C
Dana College	NE	22,390	C
Delaware State Univ	DE	8,130	LC
Delta State Univ	MS	7,709	C
Dillard Univ	LA	17,500	VC
Doane College	NE	22,458	C
Dominican College	NY	26,630	LC
Dowling College	NY	22,110	LC
D'Youville College	NY	23,660	C
East Carolina Univ	NC	10,000	C
East Central Univ	OK	6,207	C
East Stroudsburg Univ of Pennsylvania	PA	10,336	C
East Tenn State Univ	TN	8,497	C
Eastern Illinois Univ	IL	12,569	C
Eastern Kentucky Univ	KY	7,725	C
Eastern Mennonite Univ	VA	25,450	VC
Eastern Mich Univ	MI	12,897	C
Eastern New Mexico Univ	NM	7,264	C
Eastern Univ	PA	24,075	C
Edinboro Univ of Pennsylvania	PA	11,809	LC
Elizabeth City State Univ	NC	5,700	LC
Elmhurst College	IL	24,685	C
Elon Univ	NC	25,371	HC
Erskine College	SC	25,468	VC
Evangel Univ	MO	17,380	C
Felician College	NJ	24,300	C
Fitchburg State College	MA	11,276	C
Florida Atlantic Univ	FL	11,221	C
Florida Gulf Coast Univ	FL	10,833	C
Florida International Univ	FL	9,215	VC
Florida Southern College	FL	25,965	C
Fontbonne Univ	MO	23,308	C
Freed-Hardeman Univ	TN	16,370	NC
Gannon Univ	PA	26,100	C
Georgia College and State Univ	GA	11,020	C
Georgia Southern Univ	GA	9,762	C
Georgia Southwestern State Univ	GA	6,035	C
Georgian Court College	NJ	20,000	LC
Glenville State College	WV	8,778	NC
Gonzaga Univ	WA	30,218	HC
Gordon College	MA	29,194	C+
Goucher College	MD	36,225	VC
Grace College	IN	22,170	C
Grambling State Univ	LA	6,538	NC
Grand Canyon Univ	AZ	32,000	LC
Green Mountain College	VT	32,164	C
Greensboro College	NC	23,000	C
Greenville College	IL	23,146	C
Gwynedd-Mercy College	PA	26,080	C
Hastings College	NE	22,218	VC
High Point Univ	NC	25,720	C
Holy Family Univ	PA	25,740	C
Hood College	MD	30,085	VC
Hope College	MI	28,208	VC+
Houston Baptist Univ	TX	18,660	C
Idaho State Univ	ID	9,030	C
Illinois State Univ	IL	12,839	C+
Indiana State Univ	IN	11,604	C
Indiana Univ Bloomington	IN	13,356	VC
Indiana Univ of Pennsylvania	PA	11,209	C
Indiana Univ South Bend	IN	4,989	LC
Indiana Univ Southeast	IN	4,880	LC
Indiana Wesleyan Univ	IN	22,074	C+
Inter American Univ of PR/Arecibo Campus	PR	3,350	
Inter American Univ of PR/Fajardo Campus	PR	4,000	

ST = STATE $IS = IN-STATE COSTS   SR = SELECTOR RATING

School	ST	$IS	SR
Inter American Univ of PR/ Metropolitan Campus	PR	4,320	
Inter American Univ of PR/ Ponce Regional College	PR	3,700	
Inter American Univ of PR/ San German	PR	6,720	
Jackson State Univ	MS	8,500	C
Jacksonville State Univ	AL	7,618	LC
Jarvis Christian College	TX	11,136	NC
Juniata College	PA	33,130	VC
Kansas Wesleyan Univ	KS	21,400	VC
Kean Univ	NJ	15,880	C
Keene State College	NH	13,836	C
Kent State Univ	OH	14,594	C
King's College	PA	29,810	C
Kutztown Univ of Pennsylvania	PA	10,820	C
La Salle Univ	PA	34,950	C
Lamar Univ	TX	6,820	LC
Lambuth Univ	TN	21,700	C+
Lander Univ	SC	10,600	C
LeMoyne-Owen College	TN	13,150	C
Lesley Univ	MA	34,950	C
Lewis Univ	IL	23,050	C
Lincoln Univ	MO	8,000	NC
Lincoln Univ	PA	13,658	C+
Lipscomb Univ	TN	20,967	VC
Lock Haven Univ of Pennsylvania	PA	12,098	LC
LIU/Brooklyn Campus	NY	25,000	C
Longwood Univ	VA	12,426	C
Loras College	IA	27,193	C
Louisiana College	LA	13,450	C
Louisiana Tech Univ	LA	7,370	C
Loyola Univ Chicago	IL	32,896	VC
MacMurray College	IL	20,755	C
Malone College	OH	23,040	C
Manhattan College	NY	29,000	VC
Mansfield Univ	PA	11,300	C
Marian College	IN	26,160	C
Marist College	NY	30,566	VC
Marygrove College	MI	19,310	C+
Marywood Univ	PA	30,680	C
McNeese State Univ	LA	5,270	LC
McPherson College	KS	21,010	C
Mercer Univ	GA	27,525	VC+
Mercy College	NY	20,000	NC
Mercyhurst College	PA	28,633	VC
Methodist College	NC	21,000	C
Miami Univ	OH	29,097	HC
Mich State Univ	MI	13,689	VC
Middle Tenn State Univ	TN	8,540	C
Millersville Univ of Pennsylvania	PA	12,113	C
Minn State Univ, Moorhead	MN	7,000	LC
Miss College	MS	14,574	NC
Miss State Univ	MS	9,577	C
Missouri Southern State Univ	MO	8,396	NC
Missouri State Univ	MO	10,748	C+
Molloy College	NY	16,510	C
Monmouth Univ	NJ	28,956	C
Montana State Univ-Billings	MT	8,906	C
Morehead State Univ	KY	9,150	C
Morningside College	IA	23,704	C
Mount Marty College	SD	20,590	C
Mount Vernon Nazarene Univ	OH	20,810	C
Murray State Univ	KY	8,900	VC
Muskingum College	OH	22,970	C
Nazareth College of Rochester	NY	28,175	VC
Nebr Wesleyan Univ	NE	23,415	C+
New England College	NH	31,466	C
New Jersey City Univ	NJ	13,695	LC
New Mexico Highlands Univ	NM	6,272	NC
New Mexico State Univ	NM	9,250	C
New York Univ	NY	43,170	MC
Niagara Univ	NY	28,250	C
Nicholls State Univ	LA	6,500	NC
N Car Agricultural and Technical State Univ	NC	8,000	LC
North Georgia College and State Univ	GA	7,000	C
Northeastern Illinois Univ	IL	3,000	NC
Northeastern State Univ	OK	5,896	LC
Northern Arizona Univ	AZ	10,353	C
Northern Illinois Univ	IL	13,178	C
Northern State Univ	SD	8,257	C
Northwest Missouri State Univ	MO	10,000	C
Northwest Univ	WA	18,854	C
Northwestern College of Iowa	IA	22,174	C+
Northwestern Okla State Univ	OK	6,250	NC
Ohio Dominican Univ	OH	25,954	C
Okla Christian Univ	OK	18,992	NC
Oral Roberts Univ	OK	22,650	C
Our Lady of the Lake Univ of San Antonio	TX	22,430	LC
Penn State Univ/Univ Park Campus	PA	18,038	HC
Peru State College	NE	6,350	NC
Pfeiffer Univ	NC	21,900	C
Piedmont College	GA	20,500	C

School	ST	$IS	SR
Pontifical Catholic Univ of PR/Ponce	PR	7,310	
Presbyterian College	SC	30,044	VC
Prescott College	AZ	13,445	LC
Providence College	RI	34,580	VC
Purdue Univ/West Lafayette	IN	13,458	VC
Quincy Univ	IL	24,920	C
Rhode Island College	RI	11,570	C
Saginaw Valley State Univ	MI	11,432	C
St. John Fisher College	NY	27,860	C
St. John's Univ	NY	34,370	C
St. Joseph College	CT	32,050	C
St. Joseph's College, New York, Brooklyn Campus	NY	12,206	C
St. Joseph's Univ	PA	37,428	VC
St. Martin's Univ	WA	27,555	C
St. Mary-of-the-Woods College	IN	25,480	C
St. Thomas Aquinas College	NY	22,000	LC
Salve Regina Univ	RI	33,450	C
San Francisco State Univ	CA	13,000	C
Seattle Pacific Univ	WA	29,355	C
Seton Hall Univ	NJ	33,622	VC
Seton Hill Univ	PA	28,810	C
Shaw Univ	NC	15,488	LC
Shawnee State Univ	OH	12,237	NC
Silver Lake College of the Holy Family	WI	18,500	LC
Simmons College	MA	35,640	VC
Slippery Rock Univ of Pennsylvania	PA	10,360	LC
S Car State Univ	SC	6,700	LC
Southeastern Louisiana Univ	LA	8,521	LC
Southern Conn State Univ	CT	10,310	C
Southern Illinois Univ Carbondale	IL	12,391	C
Southern Illinois Univ Edwardsville	IL	11,022	C
Southern New Hampshire Univ	NH	28,764	C
Southern Univ and A&M College	LA	8,238	LC
Southern Utah Univ	UT		C
Southern Wesleyan Univ	SC	21,675	C
Southwestern Okla State Univ	OK	4,801	C
Spring Arbor Univ	MI	22,476	C
SUNY/College at Buffalo	NY	11,903	C
SUNY/College at Geneseo	NY	12,910	HC+
SUNY/College at Old Westbury	NY	13,154	C
SUNY/College at Plattsburgh	NY	12,362	C
Syracuse Univ	NY	38,655	HC
Tabor College	KS	21,614	NC
Tenn State Univ	TN	9,048	LC
Tenn Tech Univ	TN	10,044	C
Texas State Univ - San Marcos	TX	10,862	C
Tougaloo College	MS	15,975	NC
Touro College	NY	17,000	VC
Towson Univ	MD	13,924	VC
Trinity Christian College	IL	23,645	C
Troy Univ Dothan Campus	AL	4,678	C
Turabo Univ	PR	4,110	
Tusculum College	TN	21,340	LC
Tuskegee Univ	AL	18,860	LC
Union College	KY	18,920	C
Union Univ	TN	20,750	VC
Univ of Akron	OH	15,166	NC
Univ of Alabama	AL	9,888	C
Univ of Alabama at Birmingham	AL	13,716	C
Univ of Arizona	AZ	11,958	VC
Univ of Arkansas	AR	11,859	VC
Univ of Arkansas at Pine Bluff	AR	8,300	C
Univ of Central Arkansas	AR	9,984	C
Univ of Central Florida	FL	10,739	VC
Univ of Central Okla	OK	8,094	C
Univ of Cincinnati	OH	17,682	C
Univ of Conn	CT	16,628	HC
Univ of Dayton	OH	28,826	VC
Univ of Delaware	DE	14,142	HC
Univ of Detroit Mercy	MI	27,000	C
Univ of Evansville	IN	28,320	VC
Univ of Georgia	GA	11,004	HC
Univ of Great Falls	MT	17,000	C
Univ of Hartford	CT	34,044	C
Univ of Idaho	ID	9,310	NC
Univ of Kentucky	KY	7,800	C
Univ of Louisiana at Lafayette	LA	5,830	C
Univ of Maine at Farmington	ME	11,515	C
Univ of Mary	ND	15,374	C
Univ of Mary Hardin-Baylor	TX	19,428	C
Univ of Maryland/College Park	MD	16,036	HC
Univ of Memphis	TN	11,153	C
Univ of Miami	FL	38,397	MC
Univ of Miss	MS	9,000	C
Univ of Missouri/St. Louis	MO	14,046	VC
Univ of Nebr at Kearney	NE	10,900	NC

School	ST	$IS	SR
Univ of Nebr at Lincoln	NE	11,401	VC
Univ of Nevada/Las Vegas	NV	11,566	C
Univ of Nevada/Reno	NV	12,155	NC
Univ of New Mexico	NM	11,253	C
Univ of N Car at Greensboro	NC	8,993	C
Univ of N Car at Pembroke	NC	7,940	LC
Univ of N Car at Wilmington	NC	10,107	VC
Univ of North Florida	FL	9,908	VC
Univ of Northern Colo	CO	10,249	C
Univ of Northern Iowa	IA	11,133	C
Univ of Okla	OK	10,769	VC+
Univ of PR/Cayey Univ. College	PR	1,250	
Univ of PR/Rio Piedras	PR	5,750	
Univ of St. Francis	IL	25,430	C
Univ of St. Francis	IN	20,970	C
Univ of Scranton	PA	31,100	VC
Univ of South Alabama	AL	8,930	LC
Univ of S Car at Aiken	SC	11,718	LC
Univ of S Car Upstate	SC	11,957	C
Univ of S Dak	SD	9,068	C
Univ of South Florida	FL	10,284	VC
Univ of Southern Indiana	IN	12,590	C
Univ of Tenn at Chattanooga	TN	7,790	C
Univ of Tenn at Knoxville	TN	11,720	C
Univ of Tenn at Martin	TN	8,693	C
Univ of the Cumberlands	KY	18,184	C
Univ of Toledo	OH	15,806	NC
Univ of Utah	UT	10,162	VC
Univ of Vermont	VT	18,080	VC
Univ of West Alabama	AL	7,611	C
Univ of West Georgia	GA	8,838	C
Univ of Wisc/Eau Claire	WI	9,915	VC
Univ of Wisc/Oshkosh	WI	10,426	LC
Univ of Wisc/Whitewater	WI	9,274	C
Univ of Wyoming	WY	9,666	C
Ursuline College	OH	25,456	C
Utah State Univ	UT	8,002	VC
Valdosta State Univ	GA	8,802	C
Vanderbilt Univ	TN	41,986	MC
Virginia Union Univ	VA	18,432	LC
Walla Walla College	WA	24,489	NC
Walsh Univ	OH	23,440	C
Wayne State College	NE	8,033	NC
Wayne State Univ	MI	11,805	C
Waynesburg College	PA	21,230	C
West Chester Univ of Pennsylvania	PA	12,355	C+
West Liberty State College	WV	9,142	LC
West Texas A&M Univ	TX	8,452	C
Western Carolina Univ	NC	7,000	C
Western Illinois Univ	IL	13,042	C
Western Mich Univ	MI	13,299	C
Western New Mexico Univ	NM	7,233	LC
Westfield State College	MA	10,200	C
Wheelock College	MA	33,075	C
Wichita State Univ	KS	8,500	C
Wiley College	TX	8,100	LC
William Paterson Univ of New Jersey	NJ	17,810	C+
William Penn Univ	IA	17,685	LC
William Woods Univ	MO	21,020	C
Winona State Univ	MN	11,333	C
Winston-Salem State Univ	NC	8,960	LC
Winthrop Univ	SC	11,302	C
Wittenberg Univ	OH	34,596	VC
Wright State Univ	OH	13,616	LC
Xavier Univ	OH	30,490	HC
York College	NE	16,330	NC
York College of Pennsylvania	PA	16,550	VC
Youngstown State Univ	OH	12,613	NC

SPECIFIC LEARNING DISABILITIES

School	ST	$IS	SR
Baldwin-Wallace College	OH	27,256	VC
Barton College	NC	22,316	C
Florida International Univ	FL	9,215	VC
Florida State Univ	FL	9,028	HC
Northwest Missouri State Univ	MO	10,000	C
Palm Beach Atlantic Univ	FL	23,597	VC
Univ of South Florida	FL	10,284	VC
Youngstown State Univ	OH	12,613	NC

SPEECH CORRECTION

School	ST	$IS	SR
Columbia College	SC	24,982	LC
East Texas Baptist Univ	TX	16,713	C
Ithaca College	NY	35,144	VC
Lewis Univ	IL	23,050	C+
MidAmerica Nazarene Univ	KS	20,584	LC
New York Univ	NY	43,170	MC
Western Carolina Univ	NC	7,000	C

SPEECH PATHOLOGY/ AUDIOLOGY

School	ST	$IS	SR
Abilene Christian Univ	TX	20,830	VC
Adelphi Univ	NY	27,000	VC
Alabama A&M Univ	AL	8,890	LC
Andrews Univ	MI	21,786	C

School	ST	$IS	SR
Arizona State Univ-Tempe	AZ	11,174	C
Arkansas State Univ	AR	9,630	C
Armstrong Atlantic State Univ	GA	7,394	C
Auburn Univ	AL	12,230	VC
Augustana College	IL	29,862	VC+
Augustana College	SD	24,380	VC
Ball State Univ	IN	13,138	C
Baylor Univ	TX	27,555	HC
Berea College	KY	5,496	VC+
Biola Univ	CA	29,372	VC
Bloomsburg Univ of Pennsylvania	PA	11,602	C
Boston Univ	MA	42,046	HC+
Bowling Green State Univ	OH	14,994	C
Brescia Univ	KY	14,240	C
Brigham Young Univ	UT	9,200	VC
Butler Univ	IN	31,944	VC+
Cal State East Bay	CA	10,856	LC
Cal State, Chico	CA	11,395	C
Cal State, Fresno	CA	10,037	LC
Cal State, Fullerton	CA	10,990	C
Cal State, Los Angeles	CA	5,900	C
Cal State, Northridge	CA	9,036	LC
Cal State, Sacramento	CA	11,122	C+
Calvin College	MI	25,735	NC
Case Western Reserve Univ	OH	37,314	MC
Central Mich Univ	MI	12,244	C
Central Missouri State Univ	MO	10,000	C
CUNY/Brooklyn College	NY	4,377	C+
CUNY/Herbert H. Lehman College	NY	4,000	LC
Clarion Univ of Pennsylvania	PA	11,844	C
Clemson Univ	SC	13,366	HC
College of Our Lady of the Elms	MA	21,000	C
College of St. Rose	NY	25,684	C
Colo State Univ-Pueblo	CO	7,821	LC
Delta State Univ	MS	7,709	C
East Carolina Univ	NC	10,000	C
East Stroudsburg Univ of Pennsylvania	PA	10,336	C
Eastern Illinois Univ	IL	12,569	C
Eastern Mich Univ	MI	12,897	C
Eastern New Mexico Univ	NM	7,264	C
Eastern Washington Univ	WA	10,608	C
Edinboro Univ of Pennsylvania	PA	11,809	LC
Elmhurst College	IL	24,685	C
Elmira College	NY	37,200	VC
Emerson College	MA	35,076	HC
Florida State Univ	FL	9,028	HC
Fontbonne Univ	MO	23,308	C
Fort Hays State Univ	KS	7,638	C
Geneva College	PA	21,850	C
George Washington Univ	DC	48,820	MC
Georgia Southern Univ	GA	9,762	C
Grambling State Univ	LA	6,538	NC
Hampton Univ	VA	19,468	C+
Harding Univ	AR	16,512	VC
Hardin-Simmons Univ	TX	18,641	C
Hofstra Univ	NY	32,630	VC
Howard Univ	DC	18,481	C+
Idaho State Univ	ID	9,030	C
Illinois State Univ	IL	12,839	C+
Indiana State Univ	IN	11,604	C
Indiana Univ Bloomington	IN	13,356	VC
Indiana Univ of Pennsylvania	PA	11,209	C
Indiana Univ-Purdue Univ Fort Wayne	IN	5,067	LC
Iona College	NY	30,878	VC
Ithaca College	NY	35,144	VC
James Madison Univ	VA	12,010	VC
Kean Univ	NJ	15,880	C
Kent State Univ	OH	14,594	C
Kutztown Univ of Pennsylvania	PA	10,820	C
La Salle Univ	PA	34,950	C
Lamar Univ	TX	6,820	LC
LIU/C.W. Post Campus	NY	28,282	C
Louisiana State Univ and A&M College	LA	10,749	VC
Louisiana Tech Univ	LA	7,370	C
Loyola College in Maryland	MD	38,898	HC
Marquette Univ	WI	31,066	HC
Marymount Manhattan College	NY	30,049	VC
Marywood Univ	PA	30,680	C
Miami Univ	OH	29,097	HC
Mich State Univ	MI	13,689	VC
Minn State Univ, Mankato	MN	10,276	C
Minn State Univ, Moorhead	MN	7,000	LC
Minot State Univ	ND	6,700	LC
Miss Univ for Women	MS	6,000	LC
Missouri State Univ	MO	10,748	C
Molloy College	NY	16,510	C
Mount St. Mary College	NY	25,250	C
Murray State Univ	KY	8,900	VC
Nazareth College of Rochester	NY	28,175	VC
New Mexico State Univ	NM	9,250	C
New York Univ	NY	43,170	MC
Nicholls State Univ	LA	6,500	NC

ST = STATE   **$IS** = IN-STATE COSTS   **SR** = SELECTOR RATING

School	ST	$IS	SR
N Car State Univ	NC	11,824	HC
Northeastern Univ	MA	35,742	HC
Northern Arizona Univ	AZ	10,353	C
Northern Illinois Univ	IL	13,178	C
Northern Mich Univ	MI	12,340	LC
Northern State Univ	SD	8,257	C
Northwestern Univ	IL	37,595	HC
Ohio State Univ	OH	15,357	HC
Ohio Univ	OH	15,921	C
Okla State Univ	OK	10,213	VC
Old Dominion Univ	VA	11,907	C
Ouachita Baptist Univ	AR	21,900	VC
Our Lady of the Lake Univ of San Antonio	TX	22,430	LC
Penn State Univ/Univ Park Campus	PA	18,038	HC
Purdue Univ/West Lafayette	IN	13,458	VC
Radford Univ	VA	13,145	C
Richard Stockton College of New Jersey	NJ	14,000	VC
Rockhurst Univ	MO	25,440	VC
St. Cloud State Univ	MN	10,010	C
St. John's Univ	NY	34,370	C
St. Louis Univ	MO	33,158	VC+
St. Xavier Univ	IL	23,160	C
San Diego State Univ	CA	12,971	C
San Francisco State Univ	CA	13,000	C
San Jose State Univ	CA	11,707	C
Shaw Univ	NC	15,488	LC
S Car State Univ	SC	6,700	LC
Southeast Missouri State Univ	MO	10,596	C
Southeastern Louisiana Univ	LA	8,521	LC
Southern Illinois Univ Carbondale	IL	12,391	C
Southern Illinois Univ Edwardsville	IL	11,022	C
Southern Methodist Univ	TX	36,088	VC+
Southern Univ and A&M College	LA	8,238	LC
SUNY/College at Buffalo	NY	11,903	C+
SUNY/College at Cortland	NY	12,095	C
SUNY/College at Fredonia	NY	12,771	VC
SUNY/College at Geneseo	NY	12,910	HC+
SUNY/Univ at Buffalo	NY	13,694	VC
SUNY/Univ at New Paltz	NY	12,480	VC
Syracuse Univ	NY	38,655	HC
Tenn State Univ	TN	9,048	LC
Texas A&M Univ at Kingsville	TX	6,800	LC
Texas Christian Univ	TX	23,410	VC+
Texas State Univ - San Marcos	TX	10,862	C
Thiel College	PA	24,580	C
Towson Univ	MD	13,924	VC
Truman State Univ	MO	11,242	HC
Univ of Akron	OH	15,166	NC
Univ of Arizona	AZ	11,958	VC
Univ of Arkansas	AR	11,859	VC
Univ of Arkansas at Little Rock	AR	7,230	NC
Univ of Central Arkansas	AR	9,984	C
Univ of Central Florida	FL	10,739	VC
Univ of Central Okla	OK	8,094	C
Univ of Cincinnati	OH	17,682	C
Univ of Colo at Boulder	CO	13,352	C+
Univ of Florida	FL	9,354	HC
Univ of Georgia	GA	11,004	HC
Univ of Hawaii at Manoa	HI	10,413	VC
Univ of Iowa	IA	12,172	VC
Univ of Kansas	KS	10,915	VC
Univ of Louisiana at Lafayette	LA	5,830	C
Univ of Maine	ME	13,642	C
Univ of Maryland/College Park	MD	16,036	HC
Univ of Mass Amherst	MA	15,973	C+
Univ of Minn/Duluth	MN	13,974	C
Univ of Minn/Twin Cities	MN	13,165	HC
Univ of Miss	MS	9,000	C
Univ of Montevallo	AL	9,630	C
Univ of Nebr at Lincoln	NE	11,401	VC
Univ of Nevada/Reno	NV	12,155	NC
Univ of New Hampshire	NH	16,810	VC
Univ of New Mexico	NM	11,253	C
Univ of N Car at Greensboro	NC	8,993	C
Univ of North Texas	TX	7,800	C
Univ of Northern Colo	CO	10,249	C
Univ of Northern Iowa	IA	11,133	C
Univ of Oregon	OR	13,106	VC
Univ of Rhode Island	RI	15,398	C
Univ of Science and Arts of Okla	OK	7,650	C
Univ of South Alabama	AL	8,930	LC
Univ of S Dak	SD	9,068	C
Univ of Southern Miss	MS	10,112	C
Univ of Tenn at Knoxville	TN	11,720	C
Univ of Texas at Austin	TX	14,610	HC
Univ of Texas at Dallas	TX	13,244	HC
Univ of Texas-Pan American	TX	7,290	C+
Univ of the District of Columbia	DC	2,070	LC
Univ of the Pacific	CA	34,380	VC
Univ of Toledo	OH	15,806	NC
Univ of Tulsa	OK	25,348	HC
Univ of Utah	UT	10,162	VC
Univ of Vermont	VT	18,080	VC
Univ of Virginia	VA	13,759	MC
Univ of Washington	WA	10,400	VC
Univ of West Georgia	GA	8,838	C
Univ of Wisc/Eau Claire	WI	9,915	VC
Univ of Wisc/Madison	WI	13,117	HC
Univ of Wisc/Milwaukee	WI	9,427	LC
Univ of Wisc/Oshkosh	WI	10,426	LC
Univ of Wisc/River Falls	WI	9,722	LC
Univ of Wisc/Stevens Point	WI	9,384	VC
Univ of Wyoming	WY	9,666	C
Utah State Univ	UT	8,002	VC
Valdosta State Univ	GA	8,802	C
Washington State Univ	WA	12,260	C
Wayne State Univ	MI	11,805	C
West Chester Univ of Pennsylvania	PA	12,355	C+
West Liberty State College	WV	9,142	LC
West Texas A&M Univ	TX	8,452	C
West Virginia Univ	WV	10,506	C
Western Illinois Univ	IL	13,042	C
Western Kentucky Univ	KY	10,192	C
Western Mich Univ	MI	13,299	C
Western Washington Univ	WA	11,262	VC
Wichita State Univ	KS	8,500	C
Winthrop Univ	SC	11,302	C
Worcester State College	MA	12,499	C
Xavier Univ of Louisiana	LA	17,600	C

SPEECH THERAPY

School	ST	$IS	SR
Baylor Univ	TX	27,555	HC
Cal State, Fresno	CA	10,037	LC
Cleveland State Univ	OH	10,798	NC
College Misericordia	PA	27,950	C
Idaho State Univ	ID	9,030	C
Ithaca College	NY	35,144	VC
Southern Univ and A&M College	LA	8,238	LC
Stephen F. Austin State Univ	TX	7,930	C
Univ of Miss	MS	9,000	C

SPEECH/DEBATE/RHETORIC

School	ST	$IS	SR
Abilene Christian Univ	TX	20,830	C
Adams State College	CO	8,613	C
Albany State Univ	GA	5,770	C+
Albion College	MI	26,000	VC
Arkansas State Univ	AR	9,630	C
Arkansas Tech Univ	AR	8,108	VC
Ashland Univ	OH	25,000	C
Auburn Univ	AL	12,230	VC
Augsburg College	MN	28,300	C
Augustana College	IL	29,862	VC+
Austin Peay State Univ	TN	7,535	C
Ball State Univ	IN	13,138	C
Bates College	ME	42,100	MC
Baylor Univ	TX	27,555	HC
Beloit College	WI	32,808	HC
Berea College	KY	5,496	VC+
Bethel Univ	MN	29,840	VC
Black Hills State Univ	SD	7,800	LC
Bloomsburg Univ of Pennsylvania	PA	11,602	C
Blue Mountain College	MS	11,086	C
Brewton-Parker College	GA	14,220	LC
Buena Vista Univ	IA	27,742	C
Butler Univ	IN	31,944	VC+
Calif Baptist Univ	CA	23,780	C
Cal State East Bay	CA	10,856	LC
Cal State, Fresno	CA	10,037	LC
Cal State, Fullerton	CA	10,990	C
Cal State, Los Angeles	CA	5,900	C
Cal State, Northridge	CA	9,036	LC
Calif Univ of Pennsylvania	PA	14,217	C
Capital Univ	OH	30,444	C
Central Mich Univ	MI	12,244	C
Central Missouri State Univ	MO	10,000	C
Central Washington Univ	WA	11,730	C
Chadron State College	NE	6,350	NC
Charleston Southern Univ	SC	17,800	C
Chicago State Univ	IL	10,915	C+
CUNY/Herbert H. Lehman College	NY	4,000	LC
CUNY/York College	NY	4,242	NC
Clarion Univ of Pennsylvania	PA	11,844	C
Clark Atlanta Univ	GA	20,960	LC
College of St. Catherine	MN	27,505	VC
College of William and Mary	VA	14,147	MC
Colo State Univ-Fort Collins	CO	10,878	C+
Concordia College: Moorhead	MN	22,475	VC
Concordia Univ Nebr	NE	20,500	C
Concordia Univ Wisc	WI	22,660	VC
Cornerstone Univ and Grand Rapids Theological Seminary	MI	21,350	NC
Creighton Univ	NE	29,918	VC+
Denison Univ	OH	37,040	HC
Dickinson State Univ	ND	7,847	NC
Doane College	NE	22,458	C
Dordt College	IA	20,325	VC
Dowling College	NY	22,110	LC
Drake Univ	IA	27,632	VC+
Drury Univ	MO	20,117	VC
East Central Univ	OK	6,207	C
East Tenn State Univ	TN	8,497	C
East Texas Baptist Univ	TX	16,713	C
Eastern Kentucky Univ	KY	7,725	C
Eastern Mich Univ	MI	12,897	C
Eastern Nazarene College	MA	19,500	LC
Eastern New Mexico Univ	NM	7,264	C
Eastern Washington Univ	WA	10,608	C
Edinboro Univ of Pennsylvania	PA	11,809	LC
Emerson College	MA	35,076	HC
Evangel Univ	MO	17,380	C
Fairmont State	WV	8,400	LC
Fayetteville State Univ	NC	6,000	LC
Fisk Univ	TN	19,830	C
Florida State Univ	FL	9,028	HC
Freed-Hardeman Univ	TN	16,370	NC
Geneva College	PA	21,850	C
Georgia College and State Univ	GA	11,020	C
Georgia State Univ	GA	11,444	VC
Gonzaga Univ	WA	30,218	HC
Graceland Univ	IA	19,700	C
Grand Canyon Univ	AZ	32,000	LC
Greenville College	IL	23,146	C
Gustavus Adolphus College	MN	30,920	HC
Hannibal-LaGrange College	MO	16,390	C
Hardin-Simmons Univ	TX	18,641	C
Hastings College	NE	22,218	VC+
Hillsdale College	MI	24,160	HC
Hofstra Univ	NY	32,630	VC
Humboldt State Univ	CA	11,176	C
Huntingdon College	AL	23,090	VC
Idaho State Univ	ID	9,030	C
Illinois College	IL	21,900	C+
Illinois State Univ	IL	12,839	C+
Indiana Univ Bloomington	IN	13,356	VC
Indiana Univ South Bend	IN	4,989	LC
Indiana Univ-Purdue Univ Fort Wayne	IN	5,067	LC
Iona College	NY	30,878	VC
Iowa State Univ	IA	11,831	VC
Ithaca College	NY	35,144	VC
Jackson State Univ	MS	8,500	C
James Madison Univ	VA	12,010	VC
Kansas Wesleyan Univ	KS	21,400	C
Kent State Univ	OH	14,594	C
Kutztown Univ of Pennsylvania	PA	10,820	C
Lamar Univ	TX	6,820	LC
Lander Univ	SC	10,600	C
Langston Univ	OK	2,308	LC
Lock Haven Univ of Pennsylvania	PA	12,098	LC
LIU/Brooklyn Campus	NY	25,000	C
Loras College	IA	27,193	C
Louisiana College	LA	13,450	C
Louisiana State Univ and A&M College	LA	10,749	VC
Louisiana State Univ in Shreveport	LA	2,900	NC
Louisiana Tech Univ	LA	7,370	C
Luther College	IA	28,800	VC+
Madonna Univ	MI	16,068	VC
Mansfield Univ	PA	11,300	C
Marietta College	OH	29,327	C
McKendree College	IL	24,800	VC
McNeese State Univ	LA	5,270	LC
McPherson College	KS	21,010	C
Metropolitan State College of Denver	CO	2,338	LC
Miami Univ	OH	29,097	HC
Minn State Univ, Mankato	MN	10,276	C
Minn State Univ, Moorhead	MN	7,000	LC
Miss Valley State Univ	MS	7,970	C
Missouri Southern State Univ	MO	8,396	NC
Missouri State Univ	MO	10,748	C+
Missouri Valley College	MO	18,500	C
Missouri Western State Univ	MO	9,534	NC
Montclair State Univ	NJ	16,327	C
Morehead State Univ	KY	9,150	C
Morgan State Univ	MD	12,080	C
Mount Mercy College	IA	23,670	C
Murray State Univ	KY	8,900	C
Muskingum College	OH	22,970	C
Nazareth College of Rochester	NY	28,175	VC
New York Univ	NY	43,170	MC
N Car Agricultural and Technical State Univ	NC	8,000	LC
North Central College	IL	28,926	VC
Northeastern Illinois Univ	IL	3,000	NC
Northeastern State Univ	OK	5,896	LC
Northern Arizona Univ	AZ	10,353	C
Northern Kentucky Univ	KY	6,670	NC
Northern Mich Univ	MI	12,340	LC
Northwest Missouri State Univ	MO	10,000	C
Northwestern Okla State Univ	OK	6,250	NC
Ohio Univ	OH	15,921	C
Okla Baptist Univ	OK	17,986	VC
Okla City Univ	OK	23,965	VC
Olivet Nazarene Univ	IL	22,590	C
Oral Roberts Univ	OK	22,650	C
Oregon State Univ	OR	11,055	C
Otterbein College	OH	28,986	C
Ouachita Baptist Univ	AR	21,900	VC
Palm Beach Atlantic Univ	FL	23,597	VC
Penn State Univ/Univ Park Campus	PA	18,038	HC
Pepperdine Univ	CA	39,960	HC
Point Loma Nazarene Univ	CA	27,610	VC
Portland State Univ	OR	12,453	C
Prairie View A&M Univ	TX	11,110	LC
Radford Univ	VA	13,145	C
Rowan Univ	NJ	16,000	VC
St. Ambrose Univ	IA	25,495	C
St. Cloud State Univ	MN	10,010	C
St. John's Univ	NY	34,370	C
St. Joseph's College, New York, Brooklyn Campus	NY	12,206	C
St. Joseph's College, New York, Suffolk Campus	NY	12,000	C
St. Mary's Univ of San Antonio	TX	22,444	C
St. Norbert College	WI	28,577	C+
Sam Houston State Univ	TX	8,000	C
San Francisco State Univ	CA	13,000	C
San Jose State Univ	CA	11,707	C
Shippensburg Univ of Pennsylvania	PA	11,621	C
Simpson College	IA	26,833	VC
Southeastern Okla State Univ	OK	6,147	C
Southern Illinois Univ Carbondale	IL	12,391	C
Southern Illinois Univ Edwardsville	IL	11,022	C
Southern Nazarene Univ	OK	14,634	NC
Southern Univ at New Orleans	LA	1,000	NC
Southwestern Adventist Univ	TX	18,290	LC
SUNY at Potsdam	NY	12,959	C
SUNY/College at Oneonta	NY	12,905	VC
SUNY/Univ at Binghamton	NY	13,988	HC
SUNY/Univ at New Paltz	NY	12,480	VC
Stephen F. Austin State Univ	TX	7,930	C
Suffolk Univ	MA	33,160	C
Syracuse Univ	NY	38,655	HC
Tarleton State Univ	TX	8,952	C
Temple Univ	PA	17,438	C
Tenn State Univ	TN	9,048	LC
Texas A&M Univ	TX	13,351	HC
Texas A&M Univ at Corpus Christi	TX	10,280	LC
Texas Christian Univ	TX	23,410	VC+
Thomas More College	KY	24,470	C
Touro College	NY	17,000	VC
Trinity Univ	TX	30,157	HC+
Truman State Univ	MO	11,242	HC
Univ of Akron	OH	15,166	NC
Univ of Alaska Southeast	AK	8,050	LC
Univ of Arkansas at Monticello	AR	7,325	NC
Univ of Arkansas at Pine Bluff	AR	8,300	C
Univ of at Calif Davis	CA	15,010	VC
Univ of Calif at Berkeley	CA	18,141	HC+
Univ of Central Arkansas	AR	9,984	C
Univ of Central Okla	OK	8,094	C
Univ of Dubuque	IA	23,390	C
Univ of Florida	FL	9,354	HC
Univ of Georgia	GA	11,004	HC
Univ of Hawaii at Manoa	HI	10,413	VC
Univ of Houston	TX	7,000	C
Univ of Illinois at Chicago	IL	16,256	VC
Univ of Illinois at Urbana-Champaign	IL	15,800	HC+
Univ of Indianapolis	IN	25,090	C
Univ of Iowa	IA	12,172	VC
Univ of Kansas	KS	10,915	VC
Univ of La Verne	CA	33,470	C
Univ of Louisiana at Monroe	LA	7,103	C
Univ of Maine	ME	13,642	C
Univ of Mich/Ann Arbor	MI	16,587	HC+
Univ of Minn/Morris	MN	15,472	VC
Univ of Minn/Twin Cities	MN	13,165	HC
Univ of Missouri/Kansas City	MO	15,000	VC
Univ of Nebr at Kearney	NE	9,000	NC
Univ of Nebr at Lincoln	NE	11,401	VC
Univ of Nebr at Omaha	NE	11,235	C
Univ of Nevada/Reno	NV	12,155	NC
Univ of N Car at Chapel Hill	NC	11,133	MC
Univ of N Car at Wilmington	NC	10,107	VC
Univ of Northern Iowa	IA	11,133	C
Univ of Rhode Island	RI	15,398	C
Univ of Richmond	VA	40,510	MC
Univ of Sioux Falls	SD	20,800	C
Univ of S Car at Columbia	SC	13,397	VC
Univ of South Florida	FL	10,284	VC
Univ of Southern Indiana	IN	12,590	LC
Univ of Southern Miss	MS	10,112	C

INDEX OF COLLEGE MAJORS

School	ST	$IS	SR
Univ of Tenn at Knoxville	TN	11,720	C
Univ of Texas at Arlington	TX	7,195	LC
Univ of Texas at Austin	TX	14,610	NC
Univ of Texas at El Paso	TX	8,764	NC
Univ of Washington	WA	10,400	VC
Univ of Wisc/La Crosse	WI	10,045	VC
Univ of Wisc/Oshkosh	WI	10,426	LC
Univ of Wisc/Platteville	WI	9,779	NC
Univ of Wisc/River Falls	WI	9,722	LC
Univ of Wisc/Superior	WI	9,610	C+
Univ of Wisc/Whitewater	WI	9,274	C
Valdosta State Univ	GA	8,802	C
Wabash College	IN	30,116	HC
Walla Walla College	WA	24,489	NC
Washburn Univ	KS	9,734	NC
Wayne State College	NE	8,033	NC
West Chester Univ of Pennsylvania	PA	12,355	C+
West Texas A&M Univ	TX	8,452	C
West Virginia Univ	WV	10,506	C
West Virginia Wesleyan College	WV	26,880	C
Western Carolina Univ	NC	7,000	C
Western Oregon Univ	OR	10,295	C
Whitman College	WA	36,110	HC+
Whitworth College	WA	29,428	VC+
Willamette Univ	OR	35,416	VC+
Winona State Univ	MN	11,333	C
Winthrop Univ	SC	11,302	C
Yeshiva Univ	NY	22,000	C
York College of Pennsylvania	PA	16,550	VC
Youngstown State Univ	OH	12,613	NC

SPORTS AND WELLNESS STUDIES

School	ST	$IS	SR
Nova Southeastern Univ	FL	24,320	C

SPORTS MANAGEMENT

School	ST	$IS	SR
Adams State College	CO	8,613	C
Albertson College of Idaho	ID	21,095	VC
Alvernia College	PA	26,388	C
Anderson Univ	IN	25,050	C
Arkansas State Univ	AR	9,630	C
Ashford Univ	IA	20,370	C
Averett Univ	VA	24,920	C
Baldwin-Wallace College	OH	27,256	VC
Ball State Univ	IN	13,138	C
Barry Univ	FL	24,100	LC
Barton College	NC	22,316	C
Becker College	MA	24,300	C
Belmont Abbey College	NC	25,314	C
Bethel College	IN	19,680	C
Bluffton College	OH	26,110	C
Bowling Green State Univ	OH	14,994	C
Buena Vista Univ	IA	27,742	C
Calif Univ of Pennsylvania	PA	14,217	C
Campbell Univ	NC	21,137	VC
Catawba College	NC	25,000	C
Cedarville Univ	OH	21,904	VC
Claflin Univ	SC	16,798	C+
Coastal Carolina Univ	SC	13,140	C
Colby-Sawyer College	NH	27,850	LC
College Misericordia	PA	27,950	C
College of St. Joseph	VT	20,900	NC
Concordia Univ Nebr	NE	20,500	C+
Coppin State College	MD	10,200	LC
Dakota Wesleyan Univ	SD	17,832	C
Daniel Webster College	NH	24,870	C
De Sales Univ	PA	28,580	VC
Defiance College	OH	24,790	C
Delaware Valley College	PA	29,944	C
Dowling College	NY	22,110	LC
Drury Univ	MO	20,117	VC
Eastern Conn State Univ	CT	13,554	C
Edinboro Univ of Pennsylvania	PA	11,809	LC
Elon Univ	NC	25,371	HC
Endicott College	MA	30,156	C+
Erskine College	SC	25,468	VC
Faulkner Univ	AL	15,600	C
Ferrum College	VA	24,290	LC
Flagler College	FL	13,790	VC+
Florida State Univ	FL	9,028	HC
Fontbonne Univ	MO	23,308	C
Franklin Pierce College	NH	31,700	C
Fresno Pacific Univ	CA	25,454	C
Gardner-Webb Univ	NC	21,500	C
George Mason Univ	VA	10,850	VC
Georgia Southern Univ	GA	9,762	VC
Guilford College	NC	28,160	C+
Gwynedd-Mercy College	PA	26,080	C
Hampton Univ	VA	19,468	C+
Harding Univ	AR	16,512	VC
Heidelberg College	OH	23,242	C
High Point Univ	NC	25,720	C
Huron Univ	SD	10,700	C
Husson College	ME	17,410	LC
Indiana Inst of Technology	IN	23,430	C
Indiana State Univ	IN	11,164	C
Indiana Univ Bloomington	IN	13,356	VC
Iowa Wesleyan College	IA	22,140	C
Ithaca College	NY	35,144	VC
Johnson and Wales Univ/ Charlotte Campus	NC	29,121	LC
Johnson and Wales Univ/ North Miami Campus	FL	30,126	LC
Johnson and Wales Univ/ Providence Campus	RI	28,126	LC
Judson College	IL	25,130	C
Kennesaw State Univ	GA	12,152	C
Kentucky Wesleyan College	KY	18,590	C
King College	TN	23,400	C
Lasell College	MA	26,250	C
Lewis Univ	IL	23,050	C+
Liberty Univ	VA	19,101	C
Limestone College	SC	19,840	C
Lindenwood Univ	MO	18,600	VC
Livingstone College	NC	17,815	LC
Loras College	IA	27,193	C
Loyola Univ Chicago	IL	32,896	VC
Lubbock Christian Univ	TX	16,960	C
Lynchburg College	VA	30,645	C
Lyndon State College	VT	14,233	LC
Lynn Univ	FL	30,750	C
MacMurray College	IL	20,755	C
Malone College	OH	23,040	C
Marian College	IN	26,160	C
Marian College of Fond du Lac	WI	21,775	C
Medaille College	NY	21,000	C
Methodist College	NC	21,000	C
Miami Univ	OH	29,097	HC
MidAmerica Nazarene Univ	KS	20,584	LC
Midway College	KY	20,150	C
Miss Univ for Women	MS	6,000	LC
Missouri Baptist Univ	MO	19,640	C
Mitchell College	CT	26,396	C
Mount St. Mary's Univ	MD	30,930	C
Mount Union College	OH	25,840	C
Mount Vernon Nazarene Univ	OH	20,810	C
Mountain State Univ	WV	11,406	NC
Nebr Wesleyan Univ	NE	23,415	C+
Neumann College	PA	25,996	LC
New England College	NH	31,466	C
New York Univ	NY	43,170	MC
Nichols College	MA	28,000	LC
N Dak State Univ	ND	8,500	C
Northwood Univ	FL	21,040	C
Northwood Univ	MI	21,000	C
Northwood Univ	TX	20,135	LC
Nova Southeastern Univ	FL	24,320	C
Ohio Dominican Univ	OH	25,954	C
Ohio Northern Univ	OH	27,765	VC
Ohio Univ	OH	15,921	C
Old Dominion Univ	VA	11,907	C
Palm Beach Atlantic Univ	FL	23,597	VC
Peru State College	NE	6,350	NC
Pfeiffer Univ	NC	21,900	C
Piedmont College	GA	20,500	C
Point Park Univ	PA	24,160	C
Principia College	IL	27,765	VC+
Quincy Univ	IL	24,920	C
Robert Morris Univ	PA	22,822	C
Rochester College	MI	15,636	C+
Sacred Heart Univ	CT	33,404	C
St. Ambrose Univ	IA	25,495	C
St. John Fisher College	NY	27,860	C
St. John's Univ	NY	34,370	C
St. Leo Univ	FL	22,140	C+
St. Thomas Univ	FL	23,490	C
Salem International Univ	WV	18,020	C
Seton Hall Univ	NJ	33,622	VC
Shawnee State Univ	OH	12,237	NC
Shepherd Univ	WV	10,066	C
Simpson College	IA	26,833	VC
Southeast Missouri State Univ	MO	10,596	C
Southeastern Univ	FL	17,180	LC
Southern Nazarene Univ	OK	14,634	NC
Southern New Hampshire Univ	NH	28,764	C
Southwest Baptist Univ	MO	18,300	C
Southwestern College	KS	21,476	C
Springfield College	MA	25,000	C
SUNY/College at Fredonia	NY	12,771	VC
Stetson Univ	FL	32,725	VC
Syracuse Univ	NY	38,655	HC
Taylor Univ	IN	26,376	VC+
Temple Univ	PA	17,438	C
Thomas College	ME	23,770	LC
Towson Univ	MD	13,924	VC
Trinity International Univ	IL	25,686	C
Tri-State Univ-Main Campus	IN	26,200	C
Troy Univ	AL	8,916	C
Tusculum College	TN	21,340	LC
Union College	KY	18,920	C
Union Univ	TN	20,750	VC
Univ of Charleston	WV	27,600	C
Univ of Dayton	OH	28,826	VC
Univ of Evansville	IN	28,320	VC
Univ of Houston	TX	7,000	C
Univ of Idaho	ID	9,310	NC
Univ of Indianapolis	IN	25,090	C
Univ of Louisville	KY	10,400	VC
Univ of Mary Hardin-Baylor	TX	19,428	C
Univ of Mass Amherst	MA	15,973	C+
Univ of Miami	FL	38,397	MC
Univ of Mich/Ann Arbor	MI	16,587	HC+
Univ of Minn/Crookston	MN	13,157	LC
Univ of New England	ME	31,005	C
Univ of New Haven	CT	31,794	C
Univ of Pittsburgh at Bradford	PA	17,008	C
Univ of St. Mary	KS	18,900	C
Univ of S Car at Columbia	SC	13,397	VC
Univ of Tenn at Knoxville	TN	11,720	C
Univ of the Incarnate Word	TX	23,306	C
Univ of Tulsa	OK	25,348	HC
Urbana Univ	OH	21,190	C
Valparaiso Univ	IN	28,970	VC+
Virginia Commonwealth Univ	VA	12,987	C
Virginia Intermont College	VA	22,200	C
Warner Southern College	FL	18,000	LC
Washington State Univ	WA	12,260	C
Wayne State College	NE	8,033	NC
Webber International Univ	FL	17,580	LC
West Virginia Univ	WV	10,506	C
Western Carolina Univ	NC	7,000	C
Western New England College	MA	32,054	C
Wichita State Univ	KS	8,500	C
William Penn Univ	IA	17,685	LC
Wilmington College	DE	5,594	NC
Wilmington College	OH	2,806	NC
Wingate Univ	NC	23,300	C
Winston-Salem State Univ	NC	8,960	LC
Winthrop Univ	SC	11,302	C
Xavier Univ	OH	30,490	HC
York College of Pennsylvania	PA	16,550	VC

SPORTS MARKETING

School	ST	$IS	SR
Baylor Univ	TX	27,555	HC

SPORTS MEDIA

School	ST	$IS	SR
College of the Southwest	NM	12,420	C+
Ithaca College	NY	35,144	VC

SPORTS MEDICINE

School	ST	$IS	SR
Averett Univ	VA	24,920	C
Avila Univ	MO	22,100	C
Briar Cliff Univ	IA	23,550	LC
Cabrini College	PA	33,340	C
Calif Lutheran Univ	CA	27,800	LC
Campbellsville Univ	KY	21,328	C
Capital Univ	OH	30,444	C
Central Mich Univ	MI	12,244	C
Concordia Univ Wisc	WI	22,660	VC
De Sales Univ	PA	28,580	VC
Eastern Mich Univ	MI	12,897	C
Eastern Nazarene College	MA	19,500	LC
Elon Univ	NC	25,371	HC
Florida State Univ	FL	9,028	HC
Gannon Univ	PA	26,100	C
Georgia Southern Univ	GA	9,762	VC
High Point Univ	NC	25,720	C
Hope International Univ	CA	23,700	NC
Ithaca College	NY	35,144	VC
John Brown Univ	AR	20,910	VC
Johnson State College	VT	11,830	LC
King's College	PA	29,810	C
Lander Univ	SC	10,600	C
Lees-McRae College	NC	23,000	C
Lynchburg College	VA	30,645	C
Mercyhurst College	PA	28,633	VC
Merrimack College	MA	34,380	C
Missouri Baptist Univ	MO	19,640	C
Norwich Univ	VT	28,212	C
Ohio Univ	OH	15,921	C
Pepperdine Univ	CA	39,960	HC
Samford Univ	AL	20,258	VC
Southeast Missouri State Univ	MO	10,596	C
Towson Univ	MD	13,924	VC
Trinity International Univ	IL	25,686	C
Tusculum College	TN	21,340	LC
Union Univ	TN	20,750	VC
Univ of Charleston	WV	27,600	C
Univ of Detroit Mercy	MI	27,000	C
Univ of Evansville	IN	28,320	VC
Univ of Kansas	KS	10,915	VC
Univ of Nevada/Las Vegas	NV	11,566	C
Univ of Pittsburgh at Bradford	PA	17,008	C
Univ of Southern Maine	ME	12,614	C
Urbana Univ	OH	21,190	C
Valdosta State Univ	GA	8,802	C
Wingate Univ	NC	23,300	C

SPORTS STUDIES

School	ST	$IS	SR
Ithaca College	NY	35,144	VC
Univ of Georgia	GA	11,004	HC

STATISTICS

School	ST	$IS	SR
American Univ	DC	38,719	HC+
Appalachian State Univ	NC	8,000	VC
Bowling Green State Univ	OH	14,994	C
Brigham Young Univ	UT	9,200	VC
Brown Univ	RI	42,015	MC
Calif Polytechnic State Univ	CA	12,390	VC
Cal State East Bay	CA	10,856	LC
Cal State, Long Beach	CA	9,512	C
Carnegie Mellon Univ	PA	32,700	MC
Case Western Reserve Univ	OH	37,314	MC
Central Mich Univ	MI	12,244	C
CUNY/Baruch College	NY	4,320	VC+
CUNY/Hunter College	NY	8,000	C+
College of New Jersey	NJ	18,315	MC
Colo State Univ-Fort Collins	CO	10,878	C+
Columbia Univ/Barnard College	NY	38,000	MC
Columbia Univ/Columbia College	NY	42,584	MC
Columbia Univ/School of General Studies	NY	41,516	C
Cornell Univ	NY	41,717	MC
Eastern Kentucky Univ	KY	7,725	C
Eastern Mich Univ	MI	12,897	C
Eastern New Mexico Univ	NM	7,264	C
Florida International Univ	FL	9,215	VC
Florida State Univ	FL	9,028	HC
George Washington Univ	DC	48,820	MC
Georgia State Univ	GA	11,444	VC
Harvard Univ/Harvard College	MA	45,860	MC
Indiana Univ Bloomington	IN	13,356	VC
Iowa State Univ	IA	11,831	VC
James Madison Univ	VA	12,010	VC
Kansas State Univ	KS	10,516	VC
Lehigh Univ	PA	42,690	HC+
Loyola Univ Chicago	IL	32,896	VC
Luther College	IA	28,800	VC+
Marquette Univ	WI	31,066	HC
Miami Univ	OH	29,097	HC
Mich State Univ	MI	13,689	VC
Mount Holyoke College	MA	42,148	VC
New York Univ	NY	43,170	MC
N Car State Univ	NC	11,824	HC
N Dak State Univ	ND	8,500	C
Northwest Missouri State Univ	MO	10,000	C
Northwestern Univ	IL	37,595	MC
Oakland Univ	MI	11,936	C
Ohio Northern Univ	OH	27,765	VC
Okla State Univ	OK	10,213	VC
Penn State Univ/Univ Park Campus	PA	18,038	HC
Purdue Univ/West Lafayette	IN	13,458	VC
Rice Univ	TX	32,290	MC
Rochester Inst of Technology	NY	32,070	VC+
Roosevelt Univ	IL	22,605	VC
Rutgers, The State Univ of New Jersey/New Brunswick/Piscataway Campus	NJ	15,810	HC
St. Cloud State Univ	MN	10,010	C
San Diego State Univ	CA	12,971	C
San Francisco State Univ	CA	13,000	C
San Jose State Univ	CA	11,707	C
Southern Methodist Univ	TX	36,088	VC+
SUNY/College at Oneonta	NY	12,905	VC
SUNY/Univ at Buffalo	NY	13,694	VC
Syracuse Univ	NY	38,655	HC
Temple Univ	PA	17,438	C
Univ of Akron	OH	15,166	NC
Univ of Alaska Fairbanks	AK	10,101	C
Univ of at Calif Davis	CA	15,010	VC
Univ of Calif at Berkeley	CA	18,141	HC+
Univ of Calif at Los Angeles	CA	17,681	MC
Univ of Calif at Riverside	CA	16,625	C
Univ of Calif at Santa Barbara	CA	11,800	VC
Univ of Central Florida	FL	10,739	VC
Univ of Chicago	IL	42,369	MC
Univ of Conn	CT	16,628	HC
Univ of Denver	CO	36,376	VC+
Univ of Florida	FL	9,354	HC
Univ of Georgia	GA	11,004	HC
Univ of Houston	TX	7,000	C
Univ of Illinois at Chicago	IL	16,256	VC
Univ of Illinois at Urbana-Champaign	IL	15,800	HC+
Univ of Iowa	IA	12,172	VC
Univ of Louisiana at Lafayette	LA	5,830	C
Univ of Maryland/Baltimore County	MD	16,642	VC+
Univ of Mich/Ann Arbor	MI	16,587	HC+
Univ of Minn/Morris	MN	15,472	VC
Univ of Minn/Twin Cities	MN	13,165	HC
Univ of Missouri/Columbia	MO	13,500	VC
Univ of Missouri/Rolla	MO	13,332	HC
Univ of Nebr at Kearney	NE	9,000	NC
Univ of New Mexico	NM	11,253	C
Univ of N Car at Wilmington	NC	10,107	VC
Univ of North Florida	FL	9,908	VC
Univ of Northern Colo	CO	10,249	C
Univ of Pennsylvania	PA	41,766	MC

School	ST	$IS	SR
Univ of Pittsburgh at Pittsburgh	PA	18,866	HC
Univ of Rhode Island	RI	15,398	C
Univ of Rochester	NY	41,135	MC
Univ of S Car at Columbia	SC	13,397	VC
Univ of Southern Miss	MS	10,112	C
Univ of Tenn at Knoxville	TN	11,720	C
Univ of Texas at Dallas	TX	13,244	HC
Univ of Texas at El Paso	TX	8,764	NC
Univ of Vermont	VT	18,080	VC
Univ of Virginia	VA	13,759	MC
Univ of Washington	WA	10,400	VC
Univ of West Florida	FL	8,559	C
Univ of Wisc/Eau Claire	WI	9,915	VC
Univ of Wisc/Madison	WI	13,117	MC
Univ of Wyoming	WY	9,666	C
Utah State Univ	UT	8,002	VC
Virginia Polytechnic Inst and State Univ	VA	10,834	VC
Washington Univ in St. Louis	MO	42,106	MC
Western Mich Univ	MI	13,299	C
Winona State Univ	MN	11,333	C
Xavier Univ of Louisiana	LA	17,600	C

STRINGS

School	ST	$IS	SR
Central Washington Univ	WA	11,730	C
Florida State Univ	FL	9,028	HC
Hardin-Simmons Univ	TX	18,641	C
Manhattan School of Music	NY	33,000	SP
Northwestern Univ	IL	37,595	MC
Roosevelt Univ	IL	22,605	VC
Temple Univ	PA	17,438	C
Univ of Mich/Ann Arbor	MI	16,587	HC+

STUDIO ART

School	ST	$IS	SR
Allegheny College	PA	33,500	HC
American Univ	DC	38,719	HC+
Angelo State Univ	TX	8,340	NC
Anna Maria College	MA	29,815	LC
Appalachian State Univ	NC	8,000	VC
Augsburg College	MN	28,300	C
Augusta State Univ	GA	2,920	C
Augustana College	IL	29,862	VC+
Baker Univ	KS	22,190	C
Baldwin-Wallace College	OH	27,256	VC
Barton College	NC	22,316	C
Baylor Univ	TX	27,555	VC
Beloit College	WI	32,808	HC
Benedict College	SC	19,114	LC
Benedictine Univ	IL	25,710	C
Bennington College	VT	41,890	HC
Berry College	GA	24,342	VC
Birmingham-Southern College	AL	28,494	VC+
Bloomsburg Univ of Pennsylvania	PA	11,602	C
Boston College	MA	41,608	MC
Bradley Univ	IL	25,280	VC
Brenau Univ Women's College	GA	23,950	VC
Brigham Young Univ	UT	9,200	VC
Caldwell College	NJ	26,450	LC
Cal State, Fullerton	CA	10,990	C
Carleton College	MN	40,467	MC
Carthage College	WI	26,000	C
Cazenovia College	NY	26,900	C
Central Missouri State Univ	MO	10,000	C
Central Washington Univ	WA	11,730	C
Chapman Univ	CA	37,550	VC
CUNY/Queens College	NY	4,356	C
CUNY/York College	NY	4,242	NC
Clark Univ	MA	35,165	VC+
Clarke College	IA	25,390	C
Cleveland Inst of Art	OH	34,109	SP
Coastal Carolina Univ	SC	13,140	C
Colgate Univ	NY	41,170	MC
College of Charleston	SC	13,616	VC
College of Notre Dame of Maryland	MD	27,700	C
College of St. Rose	NY	25,684	C
College of Santa Fe	NM	28,978	C
College of the Holy Cross	MA	40,664	MC
College of the Ozarks	MO	4,130	VC+
Colo College	CO	37,668	HC
Columbia College	SC	24,982	LC
Concordia College: Moorhead	MN	22,475	VC
Concordia Univ Nebr	NE	20,500	C+
Concordia Univ St.Paul	MN	27,776	C
Denison Univ	OH	37,040	HC
DePauw Univ	IN	32,100	HC
Drake Univ	IA	27,632	VC+
Duquesne Univ	PA	29,534	VC
East Carolina Univ	NC	10,000	VC
Eastern Conn State Univ	CT	13,554	C
Eastern Univ	PA	24,075	C
Eastern Washington Univ	WA	10,608	C
Emmanuel College	MA	32,000	C
Florida State Univ	FL	9,028	HC
Framingham State College	MA	11,156	C
Franklin and Marshall College	PA	40,590	HC
Gallaudet Univ	DC	16,554	
George Mason Univ	VA	10,850	VC
Georgia State Univ	GA	11,444	VC
Gettysburg College	PA	39,864	HC
Graceland Univ	IA	19,700	C
Grand Canyon Univ	AZ	32,000	LC
Hamilton College	NY	41,660	MC
Henderson State Univ	AR	7,600	C
Hobart and William Smith Colleges	NY	41,123	VC
Hollins Univ	VA	31,105	C
Indiana State Univ	IN	11,604	C
Indiana Univ Bloomington	IN	13,356	VC
Indiana Univ of Pennsylvania	PA	11,209	C
Indiana Wesleyan Univ	IN	22,074	C+
Ithaca College	NY	35,144	VC
Jacksonville Univ	FL	24,040	C
Johnson State College	VT	11,830	LC
Juniata College	PA	33,130	VC
Kansas Wesleyan Univ	KS	21,400	VC
Kean Univ	NJ	15,880	C
Kentucky State Univ	KY	10,089	LC
Kenyon College	OH	39,500	MC
Knox College	IL	32,385	VC+
Lawrence Univ	WI	33,958	HC+
Lewis and Clark College	OR	35,358	VC+
Lewis Univ	IL	23,050	C+
Limestone College	SC	19,840	C
Lincoln Univ	PA	13,658	C
Lindenwood Univ	MO	18,600	VC
Loras College	IA	27,193	C
Louisiana College	LA	13,450	C
Loyola Marymount Univ	CA	36,321	VC
Loyola Univ New Orleans	LA	31,050	VC+
Lycoming College	PA	30,797	C+
Mansfield Univ	PA	11,300	C
Marian College	IN	26,160	C
Marietta College	OH	29,327	C
Mary Baldwin College	VA	26,465	C
Maryville Univ of St. Louis	MO	23,000	VC
Marywood Univ	PA	30,680	C
Mass College of Art	MA	16,650	SP
Mercyhurst College	PA	28,633	VC
Messiah College	PA	28,910	VC+
Mich State Univ	MI	13,689	VC
Middle Tenn State Univ	TN	8,540	C
Middlebury College	VT	42,120	MC
Mills College	CA	39,870	C
Minneapolis College of Art and Design	MN	31,110	SP
Montclair State Univ	NJ	16,327	C
Moravian College	PA	28,950	VC
Mount Holyoke College	MA	42,148	HC+
Nebr Wesleyan Univ	NE	23,415	C+
New York Univ	NY	43,170	MC
Northern Illinois Univ	IL	13,178	C
Northwestern College	MN	25,220	NC
Notre Dame College	OH	20,425	C
Oakland Univ	MI	11,936	C
Old Dominion Univ	VA	11,907	C
Oral Roberts Univ	OK	22,650	C
Parsons School of Design	NY	32,242	SP
Pomona College	CA	40,774	MC
Principia College	IL	27,765	VC+
Providence College	RI	34,580	HC
Randolph-Macon College	VA	31,250	C
Rivier College	NH	26,600	C
Rochester Inst of Technology	NY	32,070	VC+
Rollins College	FL	38,366	VC
St. Lawrence Univ	NY	40,545	VC
St. Louis Univ	MO	33,158	VC+
St. Olaf College	MN	32,800	HC
St. Vincent College	PA	26,160	VC
Salem College	NC	26,226	VC+
Salve Regina Univ	RI	33,450	C
Santa Clara Univ	CA	38,931	VC
Scripps College	CA	41,000	MC
Seton Hill Univ	PA	28,810	C
Silver Lake College of the Holy Family	WI	18,500	LC
Simon's Rock College of Bard	MA	41,988	VC+
Smith College	MA	41,474	MC
Southern Conn State Univ	CT	10,310	C
Southern Methodist Univ	TX	36,088	VC+
Spring Hill College	AL	28,678	C
SUNY at Potsdam	NY	12,959	C
SUNY/College at Brockport	NY	12,747	VC
SUNY/College at Geneseo	NY	12,910	HC+
SUNY/Univ at Binghamton	NY	13,988	HC
SUNY/Univ at Buffalo	NY	13,694	VC
SUNY/Univ at Stony Brook	NY	13,625	HC
Sweet Briar College	VA	31,460	VC
Texas Christian Univ	TX	23,410	VC+
Texas State Univ - San Marcos	TX	10,862	C
Texas Tech Univ	TX	13,026	VC
Transylvania Univ	KY	26,240	VC+
Trinity Christian College	IL	23,645	C
Trinity College	CT	38,040	HC+
Troy Univ	AL	8,916	C
Tulane Univ	LA	41,098	MC
Union College	NE	18,710	C
Union College	NY	41,595	HC
Univ of Arizona	AZ	11,958	VC
Univ of at Calif Davis	CA	15,010	VC
Univ of Calif at Irvine	CA	16,475	HC
Univ of Calif at San Diego	CA	16,102	HC
Univ of Evansville	IN	28,320	VC
Univ of Findlay	OH	29,238	C
Univ of Georgia	GA	11,004	MC
Univ of Houston	TX	7,000	C
Univ of Idaho	ID	9,310	NC
Univ of Illinois at Chicago	IL	16,256	VC
Univ of Indianapolis	IN	25,090	C
Univ of Maine	ME	13,642	C
Univ of Mary Washington	VA	11,636	VC
Univ of Maryland/College Park	MD	16,036	HC
Univ of Mass Amherst	MA	15,973	C+
Univ of Miami	FL	38,397	MC
Univ of Minn/Morris	MN	15,472	VC
Univ of Minn/Twin Cities	MN	13,165	VC
Univ of Missouri/Kansas City	MO	15,000	VC
Univ of Missouri/St. Louis	MO	14,046	VC
Univ of Montevallo	AL	9,630	C
Univ of New Hampshire	NH	16,810	VC
Univ of New Mexico	NM	11,253	C
Univ of N Car at Chapel Hill	NC	11,129	MC
Univ of N Car at Wilmington	NC	10,107	VC
Univ of Northern Iowa	IA	11,133	C
Univ of Notre Dame	IN	39,552	MC
Univ of Pittsburgh at Pittsburgh	PA	18,866	HC
Univ of Redlands	CA	36,160	VC
Univ of Richmond	VA	40,510	MC
Univ of Rochester	NY	41,135	MC
Univ of St. Thomas	TX	23,810	VC
Univ of S Car at Columbia	SC	13,397	VC
Univ of S Car Upstate	SC	11,957	C
Univ of Southern Calif	CA	41,618	MC
Univ of Tenn at Knoxville	TN	11,720	C
Univ of Texas at Arlington	TX	7,195	LC
Univ of Texas at Austin	TX	14,610	VC
Univ of the Pacific	CA	34,380	VC
Univ of Washington	WA	10,400	VC
Univ of West Florida	FL	8,559	C
Univ of Wisc/Superior	WI	9,610	C+
Viterbo Univ	WI	21,670	C
Washington and Lee Univ	VA	35,880	VC
Washington Univ in St. Louis	MO	42,106	MC
Wellesley College	MA	41,030	MC
Wesleyan College	GA	19,560	C
Wesleyan Univ	CT	42,122	MC
West Chester Univ of Pennsylvania	PA	12,355	C+
West Texas A&M Univ	TX	8,452	C
Western Carolina Univ	NC	7,000	C
Western Conn State Univ	CT	12,993	C
Wheaton College	MA	40,180	HC+
Wichita State Univ	KS	8,500	C
Willamette Univ	OR	35,416	VC+
William Paterson Univ of New Jersey	NJ	17,810	C+
William Woods Univ	MO	21,020	C
Youngstown State Univ	OH	12,613	NC

SUPPLY CHAIN MANAGEMENT

School	ST	$IS	SR
Lehigh Univ	PA	42,690	HC+
Robert Morris Univ	PA	22,822	C
Texas Christian Univ	TX	23,410	VC+
Univ of Maryland/College Park	MD	16,036	HC

SURVEY AND MAPPING TECHNOLOGY

School	ST	$IS	SR
East Tenn State Univ	TN	8,497	C
Metropolitan State College of Denver	CO	2,338	LC
Pennsylvania College of Technology	PA	16,980	LC
Southern Polytechnic State Univ	GA	7,640	VC
SUNY/College of Environmental Science and Forestry	NY	15,000	C
SUNY/College of Technology at Alfred	NY	14,000	C
Thomas Edison State College	NJ	3,780	SP
Univ of Akron	OH	15,166	NC
Univ of Alaska Anchorage	AK	11,275	NC

SURVEYING ENGINEERING

School	ST	$IS	SR
Cal State, Fresno	CA	10,037	LC
Ferris State Univ	MI	13,698	C
Metropolitan State College of Denver	CO	2,338	LC
Mich Tech Univ	MI	14,569	VC
New Mexico State Univ	NM	9,250	C
Oregon Inst of Technology	OR	8,718	C
Pennsylvania College of Technology	PA	16,980	LC
Purdue Univ/West Lafayette	IN	13,458	VC
Universidad Metropolitana	PR	3,330	
Universidad Politecnica de PR	PR	5,400	
Univ of Arkansas at Little Rock	AR	7,230	NC
Univ of Maine	ME	13,642	C
Univ of PR/Mayaguez	PR	1,250	

SYSTEMS ANALYSIS

School	ST	$IS	SR
George Washington Univ	DC	48,820	MC
Johnson and Wales Univ/ Providence Campus	RI	28,126	LC
Rochester Inst of Technology	NY	32,070	VC+
Univ of Miami	FL	38,397	MC

SYSTEMS ENGINEERING

School	ST	$IS	SR
Case Western Reserve Univ	OH	37,314	MC
George Mason Univ	VA	10,850	VC
Huron Univ	SD	10,700	C
Oakland Univ	MI	11,936	C
Point Park Univ	PA	24,160	C
Purdue Univ/West Lafayette	IN	13,458	VC
SUNY/Univ at Binghamton	NY	13,988	HC
Stevens Inst of Technology	NJ	40,935	HC
Texas A&M Univ at Galveston	TX	10,000	C+
United States Military Academy	NY		MC
United States Naval Academy	MD		MC
Univ of Arizona	AZ	11,958	VC
Univ of Missouri/Rolla	MO	13,332	HC
Univ of Pennsylvania	PA	41,766	MC
Univ of Virginia	VA	13,759	MC
Washington Univ in St. Louis	MO	42,106	MC
West Virginia Univ	WV	10,506	C
Wright State Univ	OH	13,616	LC
Youngstown State Univ	OH	12,613	NC

SYSTEMS SCIENCE

School	ST	$IS	SR
Johnson and Wales Univ/ Providence Campus	RI	28,126	LC
Kent State Univ	OH	14,594	C
Stanford Univ	CA	41,557	MC
Washington Univ in St. Louis	MO	42,106	MC
Worcester Polytechnic Inst	MA	40,450	VC+

TEACHING ENGLISH AS A SECOND/FOREIGN LANGUAGE (TESOL/TEFOL)

School	ST	$IS	SR
Abilene Christian Univ	TX	20,830	C
Andrews Univ	MI	21,786	C
Brigham Young Univ/Hawaii	HI	7,740	HC+
Caribbean Univ	PR	3,000	
Carroll College	MT	23,324	C+
College of Our Lady of the Elms	MA	21,000	C
Eastern Mich Univ	MI	12,897	C
Hawaii Pacific Univ	HI	21,080	C
Houston Baptist Univ	TX	18,660	C
Howard Payne Univ	TX	17,115	C
Inter American Univ of PR/ Arecibo Campus	PR	3,350	
Inter American Univ of PR/ San German	PR	6,720	
Kent State Univ	OH	14,594	C
LIU/Brooklyn Campus	NY	25,000	C
Mercy College	NY	20,000	NC
Missouri Southern State Univ	MO	8,396	NC
Nyack College	NY	18,540	C
Okla Christian Univ	OK	18,992	NC
Pontifical Catholic Univ of PR/Ponce	PR	7,310	
San Jose State Univ	CA	11,707	C
SUNY at Oswego	NY	13,662	VC
Temple Univ	PA	17,438	C
Texas Wesleyan Univ	TX	18,700	C
Union Univ	TN	20,750	VC
Univ of Louisville	KY	10,400	VC
Univ of Minn/Twin Cities	MN	13,165	VC
Univ of Nebr at Kearney	NE	9,000	NC
Univ of New Mexico	NM	11,253	C
Univ of Northern Iowa	IA	11,133	C
Univ of PR/Mayaguez	PR	1,250	
Univ of Utah	UT	10,162	VC

TECHNICAL AND BUSINESS WRITING

School	ST	$IS	SR
Carlow Univ	PA	24,313	C
Cedarville Univ	OH	21,904	C
Champlain College	VT	24,605	C
Clarkson Univ	NY	34,930	VC
College of Santa Fe	NM	28,978	C
Colo State Univ-Fort Collins	CO	10,878	C+
Illinois Inst of Technology	IL	26,465	HC+
King College	TN	23,400	C

ST = STATE **$IS** = IN-STATE COSTS **SR** = SELECTOR RATING

INDEX OF COLLEGE MAJORS

School	ST	$IS	SR
Lawrence Tech Univ	MI	25,475	VC
Madonna Univ	MI	16,068	VC
Metropolitan State Univ	MN	4,682	SP
Mich Tech Univ	MI	14,569	VC
Milwaukee School of Engineering	WI	29,847	VC+
Missouri State Univ	MO	10,748	C+
Mount Mary College	WI	22,895	C
New Jersey Inst of Technology	NJ	16,396	VC
New Mexico Inst of Mining and Technology	NM	8,510	VC+
New York Inst of Technology	NY	28,126	VC
New York Univ	NY	43,170	MC
Ohio Dominican Univ	OH	25,954	C
Pennsylvania College of Technology	PA	16,980	LC
Polytechnic Univ/Brooklyn	NY	37,150	VC
Southern Polytechnic State Univ	GA	7,640	VC
Tenn Tech Univ	TN	10,044	C
Univ of Arkansas at Little Rock	AR	7,230	NC
Univ of Findlay	OH	29,238	C
Univ of Hartford	CT	34,044	C
Univ of Houston-Downtown	TX	3,326	NC
Univ of Mass Dartmouth	MA	15,985	C
Univ of Missouri/Rolla	MO	13,332	HC
Univ of Montana--Western	MT	8,406	NC
Univ of New Mexico	NM	11,253	C
Univ of Washington	WA	10,400	VC
Valparaiso Univ	IN	28,970	VC+
Wheeling Jesuit Univ	WV	26,910	C
Worcester Polytechnic Inst	MA	40,450	VC+
Youngstown State Univ	OH	12,613	NC

TECHNICAL EDUCATION

School	ST	$IS	SR
Ball State Univ	IN	13,138	C
Brigham Young Univ	UT	9,200	VC
Central Conn State Univ	CT	13,620	C
CUNY/New York City College of Technology	NY	4,269	NC
College of New Jersey	NJ	18,315	MC
College of St. Rose	NY	25,684	C
Eastern Kentucky Univ	KY	7,725	C
Elizabeth City State Univ	NC	5,700	LC
Ferris State Univ	MI	13,698	C
Fort Hays State Univ	KS	7,638	C
Georgia Southern Univ	GA	9,762	C
Kean Univ	NJ	15,880	C
Millersville Univ of Pennsylvania	PA	12,113	C
Miss State Univ	MS	9,577	C
Montana State Univ-Bozeman	MT	1,137	C
New York Inst of Technology	NY	28,126	VC
Norfolk State Univ	VA	10,531	LC
N Car State Univ	NC	11,824	HC
Ohio State Univ	OH	15,357	HC
Okla State Univ	OK	10,213	VC
Pittsburg State Univ	KS	8,112	C
Rochester College	MI	15,636	C+
Southwestern Okla State Univ	OK	4,801	C
Tuskegee Univ	AL	18,860	LC
Univ of Akron	OH	15,166	NC
Univ of Nebr at Lincoln	NE	11,401	VC
Univ of Northern Iowa	IA	11,133	C
Univ of Southern Maine	ME	12,614	C
Univ of Wisc/Platteville	WI	9,779	NC
Univ of Wisc/Stout	WI	11,164	C
Valley City State Univ	ND	9,854	LC
Wayne State Univ	MI	11,805	C
Western Illinois Univ	IL	13,042	C
Western Kentucky Univ	KY	10,192	C

TECHNOLOGICAL MANAGEMENT

School	ST	$IS	SR
Arkansas State Univ	AR	9,630	C
Clayton College and State Univ	GA	2,445	LC
Colo Technical Univ	CO	9,500	LC
DeVry Univ/Addison (DuPage County)	IL	10,800	LC
DeVry Univ/Alpharetta	GA	10,675	LC
DeVry Univ/Chicago	IL	10,800	LC
DeVry Univ/Colo Springs	CO	12,000	LC
DeVry Univ/Columbus	OH	11,000	LC
DeVry Univ/Crystal City	VA	12,000	C
DeVry Univ/Dallas	TX	10,700	LC
DeVry Univ/Decatur	GA	10,680	LC
DeVry Univ/Fort Washington	PA	12,000	LC
DeVry Univ/Fremont	CA	13,060	LC
DeVry Univ/Kansas City	MO	10,670	LC
DeVry Univ/Long Beach	CA	12,450	LC
DeVry Univ/Miramar	FL	12,000	LC
DeVry Univ/Orlando	FL	12,000	LC
DeVry Univ/Phoenix	AZ	11,790	LC
DeVry Univ/Pomona	CA	12,450	LC
DeVry Univ/Seattle	WA	12,000	LC

School	ST	$IS	SR
DeVry Univ/Tinley Park	IL	12,000	LC
DeVry Univ/West Hills	CA	12,450	LC
DeVry Univ/Westminster	CO	12,000	LC
Excelsior College	NY	995	SP
Franklin Univ	OH	6,720	SP
Golden Gate Univ	CA	12,150	LC
Johnson and Wales Univ/Providence Campus	RI	28,126	LC
Lawrence Tech Univ	MI	25,475	VC
Murray State Univ	KY	8,900	VC
New Jersey Inst of Technology	NJ	16,396	VC
New York Inst of Technology	NY	28,126	VC
Northern Illinois Univ	IL	13,178	C
Ohio Northern Univ	OH	27,765	VC
Pennsylvania College of Technology	PA	16,980	LC
Pittsburg State Univ	KS	8,112	C
Southern Illinois Univ Carbondale	IL	12,391	C
Southern Univ at New Orleans	LA	1,000	NC
SUNY at Oswego	NY	13,662	VC
SUNY/College of Agriculture and Technology at Cobleskill	NY	12,915	C
Troy Univ	AL	8,916	C
Troy Univ Dothan Campus	AL	4,678	C
Univ of Alaska Anchorage	AK	11,275	NC
Univ of Alaska Fairbanks	AK	10,101	C
Univ of Findlay	OH	29,238	C
Washburn Univ	KS	9,734	NC
Wayne State College	NE	8,033	NC
Wentworth Inst of Technology	MA	27,500	C

TECHNOLOGY AND PUBLIC AFFAIRS

School	ST	$IS	SR
Cameron Univ	OK	6,314	NC
Georgia Inst of Technology	GA	11,450	HC+
New Jersey Inst of Technology	NJ	16,396	VC
Pomona College	CA	40,774	MC
Univ of Georgia	GA	11,004	VC
Vassar College	NY	41,700	MC
Washington Univ in St. Louis	MO	42,106	MC
Western Kentucky Univ	KY	10,192	C
Worcester Polytechnic Inst	MA	40,450	VC+

TELECOMMUNICATIONS

School	ST	$IS	SR
Alabama A&M Univ	AL	8,890	LC
Ball State Univ	IN	13,138	C
Baylor Univ	TX	27,555	HC
Bowling Green State Univ	OH	14,994	C
Butler Univ	IN	31,944	VC+
Cal State, Monterey Bay	CA	10,099	C
Capitol College	MD	21,250	C
Champlain College	VT	24,605	C
CUNY/New York City College of Technology	NY	4,269	NC
Colo Technical Univ	CO	9,500	LC
Concordia Univ Wisc	WI	22,660	VC
DeVry College of Technology/North Brunswick	NJ	10,500	LC
DeVry/New York	NY	12,000	LC
DeVry Univ/Addison (DuPage County)	IL	10,800	LC
DeVry Univ/Alpharetta	GA	10,675	LC
DeVry Univ/Chicago	IL	10,800	LC
DeVry Univ/Colo Springs	CO	12,000	LC
DeVry Univ/Columbus	OH	11,000	LC
DeVry Univ/Crystal City	VA	12,000	C
DeVry Univ/Dallas	TX	10,700	LC
DeVry Univ/Decatur	GA	10,680	LC
DeVry Univ/Fort Washington	PA	12,000	LC
DeVry Univ/Fremont	CA	13,060	LC
DeVry Univ/Kansas City	MO	10,670	LC
DeVry Univ/Long Beach	CA	12,450	LC
DeVry Univ/Miramar	FL	12,000	LC
DeVry Univ/Orlando	FL	12,000	LC
DeVry Univ/Phoenix	AZ	11,790	LC
DeVry Univ/Pomona	CA	12,450	LC
DeVry Univ/Seattle	WA	12,000	LC
DeVry Univ/Tinley Park	IL	12,000	LC
DeVry Univ/West Hills	CA	12,450	LC
Eastern Mich Univ	MI	12,897	C
Fort Hays State Univ	KS	7,638	C
George Fox Univ	OR	28,490	C
Illinois State Univ	IL	12,839	C+
Indiana Univ Bloomington	IN	13,356	VC
Indiana Univ-Purdue Univ Fort Wayne	IN	5,067	NC
Ithaca College	NY	35,144	VC
Kent State Univ	OH	14,594	C
Kutztown Univ of Pennsylvania	PA	10,820	C
Marywood Univ	PA	30,680	C
Miami Univ	OH	29,097	HC
Mich State Univ	MI	13,689	VC

School	ST	$IS	SR
Morgan State Univ	MD	12,080	C
Murray State Univ	KY	8,900	VC
New York Inst of Technology	NY	28,126	VC
Northern Arizona Univ	AZ	10,353	C
Ohio Univ	OH	15,921	C
Okla Baptist Univ	OK	17,986	VC
Pepperdine Univ	CA	39,960	HC
Purdue Univ/West Lafayette	IN	13,458	VC
Rochester Inst of Technology	NY	32,070	VC+
Roosevelt Univ	IL	22,605	VC
St. John's Univ	NY	34,370	C
Southern Methodist Univ	TX	36,088	VC+
SUNY/Inst of Technology	NY	12,575	VC
Syracuse Univ	NY	38,655	HC
Temple Univ	PA	17,438	C
Texas Tech Univ	TX	13,026	VC
Univ of Alabama	AL	9,888	C
Univ of Colo at Boulder	CO	13,352	C+
Univ of Florida	FL	9,354	HC
Univ of Georgia	GA	11,004	VC
Univ of Idaho	ID	9,310	HC
Univ of Kentucky	KY	7,800	C
Univ of Louisiana at Lafayette	LA	5,830	C
Univ of Miami	FL	38,397	MC
Univ of Nebr at Kearney	NE	9,000	NC
Univ of Northern Colo	CO	10,249	C
Univ of PR/Arecibo	PR	8,327	
Univ of Texas at Dallas	TX	13,244	VC
Univ of the Sacred Heart	PR	5,590	
Univ of Wisc/Stout	WI	11,164	C
Western Mich Univ	MI	13,299	C
Youngstown State Univ	OH	12,613	NC

TEXTILE ENGINEERING

School	ST	$IS	SR
Auburn Univ	AL	12,230	VC
Georgia Inst of Technology	GA	11,450	HC+
N Car State Univ	NC	11,824	HC
Philadelphia Univ	PA	30,006	C
Univ of Kansas	KS	10,915	VC

TEXTILE TECHNOLOGY

School	ST	$IS	SR
Auburn Univ	AL	12,230	VC
Clemson Univ	SC	13,366	HC
Fashion Inst of Technology/SUNY	NY	11,600	C+
Mich State Univ	MI	13,689	VC
Philadelphia Univ	PA	30,006	C
Univ of Mass Dartmouth	MA	15,985	C
Univ of Wisc/Madison	WI	13,117	HC

TEXTILES AND CLOTHING

School	ST	$IS	SR
Albright College	PA	33,920	C
Auburn Univ	AL	12,230	VC
Calif College of the Arts	CA	34,325	SP
Central Missouri State Univ	MO	10,000	C
College for Creative Studies	MI	24,000	SP
Cornell Univ	NY	41,717	MC
Fashion Inst of Technology/SUNY	NY	11,600	C+
Framingham State College	MA	11,156	C
Georgia Inst of Technology	GA	11,450	HC+
Indiana State Univ	IN	11,604	C
Indiana Univ Bloomington	IN	13,356	VC
Iowa State Univ	IA	11,831	VC
Kansas State Univ	KS	10,516	VC
Lipscomb Univ	TN	20,967	VC
Louisiana State Univ and A&M Univ	LA	10,749	VC
Middle Tenn State Univ	TN	8,540	C
Moore College of Art and Design	PA	27,200	SP
N Car State Univ	NC	11,824	HC
N Dak State Univ	ND	8,500	C
Northern Illinois Univ	IL	13,178	C
Northwest Missouri State Univ	MO	10,000	C
Oregon State Univ	OR	11,055	C
Rhode Island School of Design	RI	38,130	SP
Syracuse Univ	NY	38,655	HC
Univ of at Calif Davis	CA	15,010	VC
Univ of Delaware	DE	14,142	HC
Univ of Idaho	ID	9,310	HC
Univ of Illinois at Urbana-Champaign	IL	15,800	HC+
Univ of Kentucky	KY	7,800	C
Univ of Minn/Twin Cities	MN	13,165	HC
Univ of Missouri/Columbia	MO	13,500	VC
Univ of Nebr at Lincoln	NE	11,401	VC
Univ of Rhode Island	RI	15,398	C
Univ of Tenn at Knoxville	TN	11,720	C
Univ of Texas at Austin	TX	14,610	HC
Univ of Wisc/Madison	WI	13,117	HC
Western Kentucky Univ	KY	10,192	C
Western Mich Univ	MI	13,299	C

THEATER DESIGN

School	ST	$IS	SR
Adelphi Univ	NY	27,000	VC

School	ST	$IS	SR
Arcadia Univ	PA	33,570	VC
Baylor Univ	TX	27,555	HC
Bennington College	VT	41,890	HC
Boston Univ	MA	42,046	HC+
Central Mich Univ	MI	12,244	C
Central Missouri State Univ	MO	10,000	C
College of Santa Fe	NM	28,978	C
College of the Ozarks	MO	4,130	VC+
Cornish College of the Arts	WA	21,200	SP
Creighton Univ	NE	29,918	VC+
DePaul Univ	IL	29,835	VC
Emerson College	MA	35,076	HC
Florida State Univ	FL	9,028	HC
Hofstra Univ	NY	32,630	VC
Huntington Univ	IN	24,830	C
Ithaca College	NY	35,144	VC
Johnson State College	VT	11,830	LC
Keene State College	NH	13,836	C
Mich Tech Univ	MI	14,569	VC
Montclair State Univ	NJ	16,327	C
N Car School of the Arts	NC	7,401	SP
Pace Univ	NY	30,000	VC
Purdue Univ/West Lafayette	IN	13,458	VC
Roosevelt Univ	IL	22,605	VC
St. Mary's Univ of Minn	MN	23,857	VC
Seton Hill Univ	PA	28,810	C
Shenandoah Univ	VA	27,600	C
SUNY/College at Purchase	NY	11,989	VC+
Stephens College	MO	26,930	VC
Syracuse Univ	NY	38,655	HC
Texas Tech Univ	TX	13,026	VC
Towson Univ	MD	13,924	VC
Univ of Arizona	AZ	11,958	VC
Univ of Cincinnati	OH	17,682	C
Univ of Conn	CT	16,628	HC
Univ of Evansville	IN	28,320	VC
Univ of Florida	FL	9,354	HC
Univ of Kansas	KS	10,915	VC
Univ of Maryland/Baltimore County	MD	16,642	VC+
Univ of Miami	FL	38,397	MC
Univ of Northern Iowa	IA	11,133	C
Univ of Southern Calif	CA	41,618	MC
Vanderbilt Univ	TN	41,986	MC
Washburn Univ	KS	9,734	VC
Webster Univ	MO	24,280	VC
Western Mich Univ	MI	13,299	C
Wright State Univ	OH	13,616	LC

THEATER MANAGEMENT

School	ST	$IS	SR
Barry Univ	FL	24,100	LC
Benedictine College	KS	21,968	C
Boston Univ	MA	42,046	HC+
Catawba College	NC	25,000	C
CUNY/Brooklyn College	NY	4,377	C+
College of St. Scholastica	MN	28,456	C+
College of Santa Fe	NM	28,978	C
Emerson College	MA	35,076	HC
Hofstra Univ	NY	32,630	VC
Ithaca College	NY	35,144	VC
Johnson State College	VT	11,830	LC
Roosevelt Univ	IL	22,605	VC
St. Mary's Univ of Minn	MN	23,857	VC
Salisbury Univ	MD	13,128	VC
Seton Hill Univ	PA	28,810	C
Syracuse Univ	NY	38,655	HC
Trinity College	CT	38,040	HC+
Univ of Delaware	DE	14,142	HC
Univ of Evansville	IN	28,320	VC
Univ of Hartford	CT	34,044	C
Univ of Miami	FL	38,397	MC
Univ of Portland	OR	32,300	VC
Univ of Southern Calif	CA	41,618	MC
Univ of Texas at El Paso	TX	8,764	NC
Viterbo Univ	WI	21,670	C
Yale Univ	CT	41,000	MC

THEOLOGICAL STUDIES

School	ST	$IS	SR
Alvernia College	PA	26,388	C
Andrews Univ	MI	21,786	C
Aquinas College	MI	23,750	C
Assumption College	MA	32,875	C
Atlantic Union College	MA	17,600	LC
Avila Univ	MO	22,100	C
Barry Univ	FL	24,100	LC
Bellarmine Univ	KY	27,650	C+
Belmont Abbey College	NC	25,314	C
Boston College	MA	41,608	MC
Brewton-Parker College	GA	14,220	LC
Briar Cliff Univ	IA	23,550	LC
Caldwell College	NJ	26,450	LC
Calif Baptist Univ	CA	23,780	C
Calumet College of St. Joseph	IN	9,500	LC
Carlow Univ	PA	24,313	C
Christendom College	VA	21,594	VC+
College of St. Benedict	MN	30,091	VC
College of St. Catherine	MN	27,505	VC
College of St. Elizabeth	NJ	28,495	C
Colo Christian Univ	CO	21,182	VC
Concordia Univ	CA	26,780	C
Concordia Univ	OR	24,400	C
Concordia Univ Nebr	NE	20,500	C+
Concordia Univ St.Paul	MN	27,776	C

ST = STATE   **$IS** = IN-STATE COSTS   **SR** = SELECTOR RATING

School	ST $IS	SR
Concordia Univ Wisc	WI 22,660	VC
Concordia Univ, River Forest	IL 26,300	C
Creighton Univ	NE 29,918	VC+
De Sales Univ	PA 28,580	VC
Duquesne Univ	PA 29,534	VC
Eastern Mennonite Univ	VA 25,450	VC
Eastern Univ	PA 24,075	C
Fordham Univ	NY 36,000	HC
Franciscan Univ of Steubenville	OH 20,300	VC
Gannon Univ	PA 26,100	C
Hanover College	IN 28,150	HC
Hardin-Simmons Univ	TX 18,641	C
Immaculata Univ	PA 25,350	C
John Brown Univ	AR 20,910	VC
Juniata College	PA 33,130	VC
King's College	PA 29,810	C
Lenoir-Rhyne College	NC 25,580	C
Livingstone College	NC 17,815	LC
Loyola College in Maryland	MD 38,898	HC
Loyola Marymount Univ	CA 36,321	VC
Loyola Univ Chicago	IL 32,896	VC
Malone College	OH 23,040	C
Marian College	IN 26,160	C
Marquette Univ	WI 31,066	HC
Marymount Univ	VA 25,934	C
Minn State Univ, Mankato	MN 10,276	LC
Molloy College	NY 16,510	C
Mount Mary College	WI 22,895	C
Mount St. Mary's Univ	MD 30,930	VC
Newman Univ	KS 21,106	C
Northwest Univ	WA 18,854	C
Notre Dame College	OH 20,425	C
Ohio Univ	OH 15,921	C
Ouachita Baptist Univ	AR 21,900	VC
Pacific Union College	CA 24,555	VC+
Pontifical Catholic Univ of PR/Ponce	PR 7,310	
Providence College	RI 34,580	HC
Roanoke College	VA 30,748	VC
Rockhurst Univ	MO 25,440	VC
St. Ambrose Univ	IA 25,495	C
St. Anselm College	NH 33,810	C
St. Bonaventure Univ	NY 28,785	LC
St. John's Univ	MN 29,749	VC
St. John's Univ	NY 34,370	C
St. Joseph's College of Maine	ME 29,185	C
St. Louis Univ	MO 33,158	VC+
St. Mary-of-the-Woods College	IN 25,480	C
St. Mary's Univ of Minn	MN 23,857	VC
St. Mary's Univ of San Antonio	TX 22,444	C
St. Peter's College	NJ 30,160	LC
St. Vincent College	PA 26,160	VC
Seattle Pacific Univ	WA 29,355	C
Southern Adventist Univ	TN 18,500	C
Southwestern Adventist Univ	TX 18,290	LC
Spring Hill College	AL 28,678	C
Sterling College	KS 19,992	C
Texas Lutheran Univ	TX 23,530	C
Thomas More College	KY 24,470	C
Trinity Christian College	IL 23,645	C
Union College	NE 18,710	C
Universidad Adventista de las Antillas	PR 7,360	
Univ of Arizona	AZ 11,958	VC
Univ of Dallas	TX 27,432	VC+
Univ of Evansville	IN 28,320	VC
Univ of Great Falls	MT 17,000	C
Univ of Mary	ND 15,374	C
Univ of Notre Dame	IN 39,552	MC
Univ of Portland	OR 32,300	VC
Univ of St. Francis	IL 25,430	C
Univ of St. Mary	KS 18,900	C
Univ of St. Thomas	MN 28,000	VC
Univ of St. Thomas	TX 23,810	VC
Univ of San Francisco	CA 37,560	VC
Univ of Scranton	PA 31,100	VC
Valparaiso Univ	IN 28,970	VC+
Villanova Univ	PA 38,672	HC+
Walla Walla College	WA 24,489	NC
Walsh Univ	OH 23,440	C
William Tyndale College	MI 13,000	NC
Wisc Lutheran College	WI 23,510	VC
Xavier Univ	OH 30,490	HC
Xavier Univ of Louisiana	LA 17,600	C

THERAPEUTIC RIDING

School	ST $IS	SR
St. Andrews Presbyterian College	NC 23,530	C
Univ of N Car at Wilmington	NC 10,107	VC

THIRD WORLD STUDIES

School	ST $IS	SR
Pitzer College	CA 41,644	RC
Univ of Calif at San Diego	CA 16,102	HC
Univ of the South	TN 34,645	HC

TOURISM

School	ST $IS	SR
Brigham Young Univ	UT 9,200	VC
Brigham Young Univ/Hawaii	HI 7,740	HC+
Cal State, Dominguez Hills	CA 10,220	LC
Cal State, Fullerton	CA 10,990	C
Central Missouri State Univ	MO 10,000	C
Central Washington Univ	WA 11,730	C
Champlain College	VT 24,605	C
Coastal Carolina Univ	SC 13,140	C
Dowling College	NY 22,110	LC
Eastern Mich Univ	MI 12,897	C
Florida International Univ	FL 9,215	VC
George Washington Univ	DC 48,820	MC
Georgia Southern Univ	GA 9,762	C
Hawaii Pacific Univ	HI 21,080	C
Indiana Univ Bloomington	IN 13,356	VC
Indiana Univ-Purdue Univ Indianapolis	IN 10,959	C
James Madison Univ	VA 12,010	VC
Johnson and Wales Univ/ Charlotte Campus	NC 29,121	LC
Johnson and Wales Univ/ North Miami Campus	FL 30,126	LC
Johnson and Wales Univ/ Providence Campus	RI 28,126	LC
Johnson State College	VT 11,830	LC
Lasell College	MA 26,250	C
Lynn Univ	FL 30,750	C
Mansfield Univ	PA 11,300	C
Mich State Univ	MI 13,689	VC
Montclair State Univ	NJ 16,327	C
National American Univ	SD 14,820	NC
New Mexico State Univ	NM 9,250	C
Niagara Univ	NY 28,250	C
Rochester Inst of Technology	NY 32,070	VC+
St. Thomas Univ	FL 23,490	C
Seton Hill Univ	PA 28,810	C
Sojourner-Douglass College	MD 4,200	LC
Southern New Hampshire Univ	NH 28,764	C
Temple Univ	PA 17,438	C
Univ of Colo at Boulder	CO 13,352	C+
Univ of Hawaii at Manoa	HI 10,413	VC
Univ of Missouri/Columbia	MO 13,500	VC
Univ of Nebr at Kearney	NE 9,000	NC
Univ of New Hampshire	NH 16,810	VC
Univ of New Haven	CT 31,794	C
Univ of New Orleans	LA 7,370	C
Univ of N Car at Greensboro	NC 8,993	C
Univ of Tenn at Knoxville	TN 11,720	C
Univ of Texas at San Antonio	TX 11,325	LC
Univ of the Sacred Heart	PR 5,590	
Virginia Polytechnic Inst and State Univ	VA 10,834	VC
West Liberty State College	WV 9,142	LC
West Virginia Univ	WV 10,506	C
Western Mich Univ	MI 13,299	C

TOXICOLOGY

School	ST $IS	SR
Ashland Univ	OH 25,000	C
CUNY/John Jay College of Criminal Justice	NY 5,000	C
College of St. Elizabeth	NJ 28,495	C
Northeastern Univ	MA 35,742	HC
St. John's Univ	NY 34,370	C
Univ of at Calif Davis	CA 15,010	VC
Univ of Louisiana at Monroe	LA 7,103	C
Univ of the Sciences in Philadelphia	PA 33,380	VC
Univ of Wisc/Madison	WI 13,117	HC
Xavier Univ of Louisiana	LA 17,600	C

TOY DESIGN

School	ST $IS	SR
Fashion Inst of Technology/ SUNY	NY 11,600	C+
Otis College of Art and Design	CA 27,546	SP

TRADE AND INDUSTRIAL EDUCATION

School	ST $IS	SR
Alabama A&M Univ	AL 8,890	LC
Central Mich Univ	MI 12,244	C
Kent State Univ	OH 14,594	C
Missouri Southern State Univ	MO 8,396	NC
New York Inst of Technology	NY 28,126	VC
SUNY at Oswego	NY 13,662	VC
Univ of Houston	TX 7,000	C
Univ of Nebr at Lincoln	NE 11,401	VC
Univ of Nevada/Las Vegas	NV 11,566	VC
Univ of Wyoming	WY 9,666	C
Valdosta State Univ	GA 8,802	C
Virginia State Univ	VA 11,318	C

TRADE AND INDUSTRIAL SUPERVISION AND MANAGEMENT

School	ST $IS	SR
Metropolitan State Univ	MN 4,682	SP
Minn State Univ, Moorhead	MN 7,000	LC
Miss State Univ	MS 9,577	C
Washington State Univ	WA 12,260	C
Washington Univ in St. Louis	MO 42,106	MC

TRANSPORTATION AND TRAVEL MARKETING

School	ST $IS	SR
Johnson and Wales Univ/ Providence Campus	RI 28,126	LC
Northwood Univ	FL 21,040	C
Northwood Univ	MI 21,000	C
Northwood Univ	TX 20,135	LC

TRANSPORTATION ENGINEERING

School	ST $IS	SR
Purdue Univ/West Lafayette	IN 13,458	VC
Texas A&M Univ at Galveston	TX 10,000	C+

TRANSPORTATION MANAGEMENT

School	ST $IS	SR
Arkansas State Univ	AR 9,630	C
Auburn Univ	AL 12,230	VC
Calif Maritime Academy	CA 13,490	C
Dowling College	NY 22,110	LC
Elmhurst College	IL 24,685	C
Embry-Riddle Aeronautical Univ	FL 30,280	C
Florida International Univ	FL 9,215	VC
Florida Memorial College	FL 6,000	LC
Iowa State Univ	IA 11,831	VC
Mass Maritime Academy	MA 11,571	C
Niagara Univ	NY 28,250	C
Ohio State Univ	OH 15,357	HC
Penn State Univ/Univ Park Campus	PA 18,038	HC
Robert Morris Univ	PA 22,822	C
St. John's Univ	NY 34,370	C
San Francisco State Univ	CA 13,000	C
Southern Univ at New Orleans	LA 1,000	NC
SUNY/Maritime College	NY 12,475	C
Texas A&M Univ at Galveston	TX 10,000	C+
Thomas Edison State College	NJ 3,780	SP
United States Merchant Marine Academy	NY 6,516	HC+
Univ of Alaska Anchorage	AK 11,275	NC
Univ of Arkansas	AR 11,859	VC
Univ of Maryland/College Park	MD 16,036	HC
Univ of North Florida	FL 9,908	VC
Univ of Pennsylvania	PA 41,766	MC
Univ of Tenn at Knoxville	TN 11,720	C

TRANSPORTATION TECHNOLOGY

School	ST $IS	SR
Maine Maritime Academy	ME 14,340	C
Pennsylvania College of Technology	PA 16,980	LC
United States Merchant Marine Academy	NY 6,516	HC+

ULTRASOUND TECHNOLOGY

School	ST $IS	SR
Barry Univ	FL 24,100	LC
Mountain State Univ	WV 11,406	NC
Newman Univ	KS 21,106	C
Oregon Inst of Technology	OR 8,718	C
Rochester Inst of Technology	NY 32,070	VC
Seattle Univ	WA 30,063	VC

URBAN DESIGN

School	ST $IS	SR
Arizona State Univ-Tempe	AZ 11,174	C
New York Univ	NY 43,170	MC
Oregon State Univ	OR 11,055	C
SUNY/Univ at Albany	NY 13,860	VC

URBAN PLANNING TECHNOLOGY

School	ST $IS	SR
Arizona State Univ-Tempe	AZ 11,174	C
Ball State Univ	IN 13,138	C
Eastern Mich Univ	MI 12,897	C
Florida Atlantic Univ	FL 11,221	C
Mich State Univ	MI 13,689	VC
Missouri State Univ	MO 10,748	C+
Univ of Nevada/Las Vegas	NV 11,566	C
Univ of Utah	UT 10,162	VC

URBAN STUDIES

School	ST $IS	SR
Adams State College	CO 8,613	C
Albertus Magnus College	CT 25,336	C
Augsburg College	MN 28,300	C
Baylor Univ	TX 27,555	HC
Bellevue Univ	NE 4,440	NC
Boston Univ	MA 42,046	HC+
Brown Univ	RI 42,015	MC
Bryn Mawr College	PA 42,780	HC+
Butler Univ	IN 31,944	VC+
Calif State Polytechnic Univ, Pomona	CA 18,053	C+
Cal State, Northridge	CA 9,036	LC
Calumet College of St. Joseph	IN 9,500	LC
Canisius College	NY 32,257	VC
Carnegie Mellon Univ	PA 32,700	MC
CUNY/City College	NY	C
CUNY/Hunter College	NY 8,000	C+
CUNY/Queens College	NY 4,356	C
Cleveland State Univ	OH 10,798	NC
College of Charleston	SC 13,616	VC
College of Mount St. Vincent	NY 28,000	C
College of Wooster	OH 31,310	VC+
Columbia Univ/Barnard College	NY 38,000	MC
Columbia Univ/Columbia College	NY 42,584	MC
Columbia Univ/School of General Studies	NY 41,516	C
Conn College	CT 41,975	MC
Cornell Univ	NY 41,717	MC
DePaul Univ	IL 29,835	VC
Dillard Univ	LA 17,500	VC
Eastern Univ	PA 24,075	C
Eastern Washington Univ	WA 10,608	C
Elmhurst College	IL 24,685	C
Eugene Lang College New School for Liberal Arts	NY 38,800	C+
Florida International Univ	FL 9,215	VC
Fordham Univ	NY 36,000	HC
Furman Univ	SC 33,264	HC+
Georgia State Univ	GA 11,444	VC
Hamline Univ	MN 27,070	VC
Hampshire College	MA 37,120	HC
Haverford College	PA 41,600	MC
Hobart and William Smith Colleges	NY 41,123	VC
Indiana Univ Bloomington	IN 13,356	VC
Jackson State Univ	MS 8,500	C
Langston Univ	OK 2,308	LC
Lehigh Univ	PA 42,690	HC+
Lipscomb Univ	TN 20,967	VC
Loyola Marymount Univ	CA 36,321	VC
Macalester College	MN 36,500	MC
Manhattan College	NY 29,000	C
Mass Inst of Technology	MA 41,800	MC
Metropolitan State College of Denver	CO 2,338	LC
Miami Univ	OH 29,097	HC
MidAmerica Nazarene Univ	KS 20,584	LC
Minn State Univ, Mankato	MN 10,276	LC
Morehouse College	GA 25,082	C
Mount Mercy College	IA 23,670	C
New College of Florida	FL 10,009	HC+
New York Univ	NY 43,170	MC
Northwestern Univ	IL 37,595	MC
Occidental College	CA 40,185	MC
Ohio Univ	OH 15,921	C
Purdue Univ/West Lafayette	IN 13,458	VC
Rhodes College	TN 32,860	HC
Rockford College	IL 28,330	VC
Roosevelt Univ	IL 22,605	VC
Rutgers, The State Univ of New Jersey/Camden Campus	NJ 15,000	C
Rutgers, The State Univ of New Jersey/New Brunswick/Piscataway Campus	NJ 15,810	HC
St. Augustine's College	NC 14,000	LC
St. Cloud State Univ	MN 10,010	C
St. Louis Univ	MO 33,158	VC+
St. Peter's College	NJ 30,160	LC
San Diego State Univ	CA 12,971	C
San Francisco State Univ	CA 13,000	C
Stanford Univ	CA 41,557	MC
SUNY/College at Buffalo	NY 11,903	C+
Temple Univ	PA 17,438	C
Trinity Univ	TX 30,157	HC+
Univ of Calif at Berkeley	CA 18,141	HC+
Univ of Calif at San Diego	CA 16,102	HC
Univ of Cincinnati	OH 17,682	C
Univ of Conn	CT 16,628	HC
Univ of Mich/Flint	MI 6,398	C
Univ of Minn/Duluth	MN 13,974	C
Univ of Minn/Twin Cities	MN 13,165	HC
Univ of Missouri/Kansas City	MO 15,000	VC
Univ of New Orleans	LA 7,370	C
Univ of Pennsylvania	PA 41,766	MC
Univ of Pittsburgh at Pittsburgh	PA 18,866	HC

ST = STATE $IS = IN-STATE COSTS   SR = SELECTOR RATING

School	ST	$IS	SR
Univ of Richmond	VA	40,510	MC
Univ of San Diego	CA	40,620	MC
Univ of Tampa	FL	25,784	C
Univ of Tenn at Knoxville	TN	11,720	C
Univ of Texas at Austin	TX	14,610	HC
Univ of the District of Columbia	DC	2,070	LC
Univ of the Sacred Heart	PR	5,590	
Univ of Utah	UT	10,162	VC
Univ of Wisc/Green Bay	WI	9,415	VC
Univ of Wisc/Oshkosh	WI	10,426	LC
Vanderbilt Univ	TN	41,986	MC
Vassar College	NY	41,700	MC
Virginia Commonwealth Univ	VA	12,987	C
Virginia Polytechnic Inst and State Univ	VA	10,834	VC
Washington Univ in St. Louis	MO	42,106	MC
Wayne State Univ	MI	11,805	C
Westfield State College	MA	10,200	C
Worcester State College	MA	12,499	C
Wright State Univ	OH	13,616	LC

VETERINARY SCIENCE

School	ST	$IS	SR
Becker College	MA	24,300	LC
Fort Valley State Univ	GA	6,975	C
Lincoln Memorial Univ	TN	18,144	C
Medaille College	NY	21,000	C
Mercy College	NY	20,000	VC
Mich State Univ	MI	13,689	VC
Mount Ida College	MA	26,000	LC
Murray State Univ	KY	8,900	VC
National American Univ	SD	14,820	NC
Newberry College	SC	23,000	LC
N Dak State Univ	ND	8,508	C
Purdue Univ/West Lafayette	IN	13,458	VC
Quinnipiac Univ	CT	34,640	VC
Tuskegee Univ	AL	18,860	LC
Univ of Arizona	AZ	11,958	VC
Univ of Idaho	ID	9,310	NC
Univ of Maryland/College Park	MD	16,036	HC
Univ of Nebr at Lincoln	NE	11,401	VC
Univ of Wyoming	WY	9,666	C
Utah State Univ	UT	8,002	VC
Washington State Univ	WA	12,260	VC
West Virginia Univ	WV	10,506	VC
Wilson College	PA	27,660	C

VICTORIAN STUDIES

School	ST	$IS	SR
Vassar College	NY	41,700	MC

VIDEO

School	ST	$IS	SR
American InterContinental Univ	GA	12,100	VC
Art Inst of Atlanta	GA	23,220	SP
Atlanta College of Art	GA	18,630	SP
Bennington College	VT	41,890	HC
Bethel College	IN	19,680	C
CUNY/City College	NY		C
Drexel Univ	PA	27,700	VC
Fairleigh Dickinson Univ/College at Florham	NJ	30,130	C
Five Towns College	NY	24,600	SP
Hampshire College	MA	37,120	HC
Hofstra Univ	NY	32,630	VC
Ithaca College	NY	35,144	VC
Kansas City Art Inst	MO	29,542	SP
Madonna Univ	MI	16,068	VC
Maryland Inst College of Art	MD	34,450	SP
Minneapolis College of Art and Design	MN	31,110	SP
Point Park Univ	PA	24,160	C
Rochester Inst of Technology	NY	32,070	VC+
San Francisco Art Inst	CA	25,640	SP
School of the Art Inst of Chicago	IL	37,800	SP
School of Visual Arts	NY	32,580	SP
Southeast Missouri State Univ	MO	10,596	C
Southern Methodist Univ	TX	36,088	VC+
Syracuse Univ	NY	38,655	HC
Univ of Hartford	CT	34,044	C
Univ of Miami	FL	38,397	MC
Univ of Okla	OK	10,769	VC+
Univ of Pennsylvania	PA	41,766	MC
Webster Univ	MO	24,280	VC
Wilmington College	DE	5,594	NC

VISUAL AND PERFORMING ARTS

School	ST	$IS	SR
Adelphi Univ	NY	27,000	VC
Albion College	MI	26,000	VC
Alverno College	WI	21,088	C
Andrews Univ	MI	21,786	VC
Antioch College	OH	33,700	C
Armstrong Atlantic State Univ	GA	7,394	C
Ashford Univ	IA	20,370	C
Assumption College	MA	32,875	C
Bennett College	NC	11,500	C
Bennington College	VT	41,890	HC
Bowdoin College	ME	41,660	MC
Bradley Univ	IL	25,280	VC
Brigham Young Univ	UT	9,200	VC
Brown Univ	RI	42,015	MC
Cabrini College	PA	33,340	C
Calif Baptist Univ	CA	23,780	C
Calif College of the Arts	CA	34,325	SP
Cal State, Monterey Bay	CA	10,099	C
Cal State, San Marcos	CA	1,800	LC
Central Mich Univ	MI	12,244	C
Central Washington Univ	WA	11,730	C
Chatham Univ	PA	27,290	C+
CUNY/Brooklyn College	NY	4,377	C+
Clark Univ	MA	35,165	VC+
Columbia Univ/Columbia College	NY	42,584	MC
Columbia Univ/School of General Studies	NY	41,516	C
Columbus State Univ	GA	8,664	C
Curry College	MA	26,100	LC
Dowling College	NY	22,110	LC
Duke Univ	NC	41,239	MC
Eastern Conn State Univ	CT	13,554	C
Eckerd College	FL	35,492	VC
Erskine College	SC	25,468	VC
Fairfield Univ	CT	39,835	VC
Fayetteville State Univ	NC	6,000	LC
Florida Atlantic Univ	FL	11,221	C
Fordham Univ	NY	36,000	HC
Goddard College	VT	21,100	C
Grand View Univ	IA	21,482	C
Green Mountain College	VT	32,164	C
Haverford College	PA	41,600	MC
Hendrix College	AR	27,646	HC+
Hofstra Univ	NY	32,630	VC
Illinois Wesleyan Univ	IL	34,050	HC+
Indiana Univ Bloomington	IN	13,356	VC
Inter American Univ of PR/Bayamon Univ College	PR	3,522	
Inter American Univ of PR/Fajardo Campus	PR	4,000	
Inter American Univ of PR/Ponce Regional College	PR	3,700	
Ithaca College	NY	35,144	VC
Johnson State College	VT	11,830	LC
Kent State Univ	OH	14,594	C
Keystone College	PA	22,810	LC
King College	TN	23,400	C
Kutztown Univ of Pennsylvania	PA	10,820	C
Lambuth Univ	TN	21,700	C+
Lander Univ	SC	10,600	C
Lesley Univ	MA	34,950	C
Lipscomb Univ	TN	20,967	VC
Longwood Univ	VA	12,426	C
Loras College	IA	27,193	C
Loyola Univ New Orleans	LA	31,050	VC+
McNeese State Univ	LA	5,270	LC
Medaille College	NY	21,000	C
Mount Mercy College	IA	23,670	C
Naropa Univ	CO	26,302	SP
New England Conservatory of Music	MA	38,750	SP
Notre Dame College	OH	20,425	C
Ohio Univ	OH	15,921	C
Oregon State Univ	OR	11,055	C
Otterbein College	OH	28,986	C
Presbyterian College	SC	30,044	VC
Ramapo College of New Jersey	NJ	16,630	VC
Rice Univ	TX	32,290	MC
Roger Williams Univ	RI	30,500	C
Rutgers, The State Univ of New Jersey/New Brunswick/Piscataway Campus	NJ	15,810	HC
Rutgers, The State Univ of New Jersey/Newark Campus	NJ	15,640	VC
St. Andrews Presbyterian College	NC	23,530	C
St. Augustine's College	NC	14,000	LC
St. Bonaventure Univ	NY	28,785	LC
St. Lawrence Univ	NY	40,545	VC
St. Peter's College	NJ	30,160	LC
St. Vincent College	PA	26,160	VC
Sarah Lawrence College	NY	42,000	HC
School of the Art Inst of Chicago	IL	37,800	SP
Schreiner Univ	TX	20,600	C
Seattle Pacific Univ	WA	29,355	C
Shaw Univ	NC	15,488	LC
Siena College	NY	28,260	VC+
Simon's Rock College of Bard	MA	41,988	VC+
Sonoma State Univ	CA	14,732	C
Southern Oregon Univ	OR	12,186	C
Spring Arbor Univ	MI	22,476	C
SUNY/College at Old Westbury	NY	13,154	C
SUNY/College at Purchase	NY	11,989	VC+
SUNY/Univ at New Paltz	NY	12,480	VC
Taylor Univ	IN	26,376	VC+
Texas Tech Univ	TX	13,026	VC
Univ of Arkansas at Little Rock	AR	7,230	NC
Univ of Calif at San Diego	CA	16,102	NC
Univ of Chicago	IL	42,369	MC
Univ of Conn	CT	16,628	HC
Univ of Florida	FL	9,354	HC
Univ of Hartford	CT	34,044	C
Univ of Maine at Farmington	ME	11,515	C
Univ of Maryland/Baltimore County	MD	16,642	VC+
Univ of N Dak	ND	10,114	VC
Univ of North Texas	TX	7,800	C
Univ of Northern Colo	CO	10,249	C
Univ of Pennsylvania	PA	41,766	MC
Univ of St. Francis	IL	25,430	C
Univ of San Francisco	CA	37,560	VC
Univ of Texas at Austin	TX	14,610	HC
Univ of Texas at Dallas	TX	13,244	HC
Univ of the Sacred Heart	PR	5,590	
Univ of Utah	UT	10,162	VC
Univ of Wisc/Platteville	WI	9,779	NC
Virginia State Univ	VA	11,318	C
Washington State Univ	WA	12,260	VC
Washington Univ in St. Louis	MO	42,106	MC
Weber State Univ	UT	9,635	NC
Wells College	NY	23,070	VC
West Virginia Univ	WV	10,506	C
Western Kentucky Univ	KY	10,192	C
Wichita State Univ	KS	8,500	C

VISUAL DESIGN

School	ST	$IS	SR
Cazenovia College	NY	26,900	C
Villa Julie College	MD	25,222	C

VISUAL EFFECTS

School	ST	$IS	SR
Savannah College of Art and Design	GA	30,800	SP

VOCATIONAL EDUCATION

School	ST	$IS	SR
Auburn Univ	AL	12,230	VC
Cal State, Los Angeles	CA	5,900	C
Cal State, San Bernardino	CA	12,563	LC
Central Conn State Univ	CT	13,620	C
Chicago State Univ	IL	10,915	C+
CUNY/New York City College of Technology	NY	4,269	NC
College of New Jersey	NJ	18,315	MC
College of the Ozarks	MO	4,130	VC
Florida International Univ	FL	9,215	VC
Indiana Univ of Pennsylvania	PA	11,209	C
Louisiana State Univ and A&M College	LA	10,749	VC
Martin Univ	IN	10,300	SP
N Car State Univ	NC	11,824	HC
Pennsylvania College of Technology	PA	16,980	LC
Pittsburg State Univ	KS	8,112	C
San Diego State Univ	CA	12,971	C
San Francisco State Univ	CA	13,000	C
S Dak State Univ	SD	9,815	C
Southern Illinois Univ Carbondale	IL	12,391	C
SUNY at Oswego	NY	13,662	VC
Univ of Arkansas	AR	11,859	VC
Univ of Central Florida	FL	10,739	VC
Univ of Georgia	GA	11,004	HC
Univ of Idaho	ID	9,310	NC
Univ of Illinois at Urbana-Champaign	IL	15,800	HC+
Univ of North Texas	TX	7,800	C
Univ of Toledo	OH	15,806	NC
Univ of Wisc/Stout	WI	11,164	C
Valley City State Univ	ND	9,854	LC
Wayland Baptist Univ	TX	13,484	C
Western Kentucky Univ	KY	10,192	C
Western Mich Univ	MI	13,299	C
Western New Mexico Univ	NM	7,233	LC
Youngstown State Univ	OH	12,613	NC

VOICE

School	ST	$IS	SR
Ball State Univ	IN	13,138	C
Bennington College	VT	41,890	HC
Calvin College	MI	25,735	NC
Catholic Univ of America	DC	35,838	VC
Central Mich Univ	MI	12,244	C
Central Washington Univ	WA	11,730	C
East Central Univ	OK	6,207	C
East Texas Baptist Univ	TX	16,713	C
Florida State Univ	FL	9,028	HC
Grand Canyon Univ	AZ	32,000	LC
Hardin-Simmons Univ	TX	18,641	C
Illinois Wesleyan Univ	IL	34,050	HC+
Indiana Univ Bloomington	IN	13,356	VC
Indiana Univ South Bend	IN	4,989	LC
Manhattan School of Music	NY	33,000	SP
Mannes College of Music	NY	31,930	SP
McMurry Univ	TX	18,100	LC
Miss College	MS	14,574	VC
New York Univ	NY	43,170	MC
Northwestern Univ	IL	37,595	MC
Nyack College	NY	18,540	C
Ohio Univ	OH	15,921	C
Pacific Lutheran Univ	WA	28,805	VC
Palm Beach Atlantic Univ	FL	23,597	VC
Rider Univ	NJ	32,560	C
Roosevelt Univ	IL	22,605	VC
Samford Univ	AL	20,258	VC
Shorter College	GA	19,700	C
Southeast Missouri State Univ	MO	10,596	C
Southern Nazarene Univ	OK	14,634	NC
Stetson Univ	FL	32,725	VC
Temple Univ	PA	17,438	C
Union Univ	TN	20,750	VC
Univ of Cincinnati	OH	17,682	C
Univ of Illinois at Urbana-Champaign	IL	15,800	HC+
Univ of Kansas	KS	10,915	C
Univ of Miami	FL	38,397	MC
Univ of Mich/Ann Arbor	MI	16,587	HC+
Univ of New Hampshire	NH	16,810	C
Univ of Tulsa	OK	25,348	HC
Weber State Univ	UT	9,635	NC
Westminster Choir College	NJ	32,670	SP
York College	NE	16,330	NC
Youngstown State Univ	OH	12,613	NC

WATER AND WASTEWATER TECHNOLOGY

School	ST	$IS	SR
Texas State Univ - San Marcos	TX	10,862	C
Wright State Univ	OH	13,616	LC

WATER RESOURCES

School	ST	$IS	SR
Central State Univ	OH	9,010	C+
Colo State Univ-Fort Collins	CO	10,878	C+
Heidelberg College	OH	23,242	C
Northern Mich Univ	MI	12,340	LC
SUNY/College at Brockport	NY	12,747	VC
SUNY/College at Oneonta	NY	12,905	VC
Tarleton State Univ	TX	8,952	C
Texas A&M Univ at Galveston	TX	10,000	C+
Univ of Arizona	AZ	11,958	VC
Univ of Georgia	GA	11,004	HC
Univ of Nebr at Lincoln	NE	11,401	VC
Univ of New Hampshire	NH	16,810	C
Univ of Rhode Island	RI	15,398	C
Univ of Wisc/Stevens Point	WI	9,384	VC
Univ of Wyoming	WY	9,666	C

WEB SERVICES

School	ST	$IS	SR
Champlain College	VT	24,605	C
Indiana Inst of Technology	IN	23,430	C
Johnson and Wales Univ/Providence Campus	RI	28,126	LC
Limestone College	SC	19,840	C
Maharishi Univ of Management	IA	29,450	VC
Mercyhurst College	PA	28,633	VC
Southern Adventist Univ	TN	18,500	C
Southern Wesleyan Univ	SC	21,675	C
SUNY/College of Technology at Alfred	NY	14,000	C
Thiel College	PA	24,580	C
Univ of Wisc/Stevens Point	WI	9,384	VC

WEB TECHNOLOGY

School	ST	$IS	SR
Bethel College	IN	19,680	C
Cabrini College	PA	33,340	C
Cogswell Polytechnical College	CA	13,760	LC
Davenport Univ	MI	15,205	NC
Duquesne Univ	PA	29,534	VC
Illinois Inst of Technology	IL	26,465	HC+
Mercyhurst College	PA	28,633	VC
Strayer Univ	DC	8,789	SP
Tenn Tech Univ	TN	10,044	C
Univ of St. Francis	IL	25,430	C

WELDING ENGINEERING

School	ST	$IS	SR
LeTourneau Univ	TX	21,200	C
Ohio State Univ	OH	15,357	HC
Pennsylvania College of Technology	PA	16,980	LC

WESTERN CIVILIZATION/CULTURE

School	ST	$IS	SR
Bowling Green State Univ	OH	14,994	C
St. John's College	MD	40,451	HC+

WESTERN EUROPEAN STUDIES

School	ST	$IS	SR
Denison Univ	OH	37,040	HC

School	ST $IS	SR
St. John's College	MD 40,451	HC+
Washington Univ in St. Louis	MO 42,106	MC

WILDLIFE BIOLOGY

School	ST $IS	SR
Auburn Univ	AL 12,230	VC
Baker Univ	KS 22,190	C
Ball State Univ	IN 13,138	C
Colo State Univ-Fort Collins	CO 10,878	C+
Humboldt State Univ	CA 11,176	C
Kansas State Univ	KS 10,516	VC
Murray State Univ	KY 8,900	VC
New Mexico State Univ	NM 9,250	C
Ohio Univ	OH 15,921	C
Oregon State Univ	OR 11,055	C
Penn State Univ/Univ Park Campus	PA 18,038	HC
Tarleton State Univ	TX 8,952	C
Texas State Univ - San Marcos	TX 10,862	C
Unity College	ME 24,320	C
Univ of Alaska Fairbanks	AK 10,101	C
Univ of Arizona	AZ 11,958	VC
Univ of at Calif Davis	CA 15,010	VC
Univ of Florida	FL 9,354	HC
Univ of Illinois at Urbana-Champaign	IL 15,800	HC+
Univ of Minn/Twin Cities	MN 13,165	HC
Univ of Montana	MT 10,602	C
Univ of Vermont	VT 18,080	VC
Univ of Wisc/Madison	WI 13,117	HC
Univ of Wisc/Stevens Point	WI 9,384	VC
Washington State Univ	WA 12,260	C
West Texas A&M Univ	TX 8,452	C

WILDLIFE MANAGEMENT

School	ST $IS	SR
Arkansas State Univ	AR 9,630	C
Brigham Young Univ	UT 9,200	C
Delaware Valley College	PA 29,944	C
Eastern Kentucky Univ	KY 7,725	C
Eastern New Mexico Univ	NM 7,264	C
Frostburg State Univ	MD 12,672	C
Lake Superior State Univ	MI 12,842	C
Lincoln Memorial Univ	TN 18,144	C
Louisiana Tech Univ	LA 7,370	C
McNeese State Univ	LA 5,270	LC
Mich State Univ	MI 13,689	VC
Mich Tech Univ	MI 14,569	VC
Miss State Univ	MS 9,577	C
Missouri State Univ	MO 10,748	C+
Northwest Missouri State Univ	MO 10,000	C
Peru State College	NE 6,350	NC
Purdue Univ/West Lafayette	IN 13,458	VC
SUNY/College of Agriculture and Technology at Cobleskill	NY 12,915	C
Sterling College	VT 23,286	VC
Sul Ross State Univ	TX 6,600	LC
Tenn Tech Univ	TN 10,044	C
Texas A&M Univ at Commerce	TX 9,020	C
Texas Tech Univ	TX 13,026	VC
Univ of Alaska Fairbanks	AK 10,101	C
Univ of Arkansas at Monticello	AR 7,325	NC
Univ of Georgia	GA 11,004	HC
Univ of Idaho	ID 9,310	NC
Univ of Illinois at Urbana-Champaign	IL 15,800	HC+
Univ of Maine	ME 13,642	C
Univ of Mass Amherst	MA 15,973	C
Univ of New Hampshire	NH 16,810	VC
Univ of PR at Humacao	PR 1,707	
Univ of Rhode Island	RI 15,398	C
Univ of Wyoming	WY 9,666	C
Utah State Univ	UT 8,002	VC
Washington State Univ	WA 12,260	C

WINDS

School	ST $IS	SR
Florida State Univ	FL 9,028	HC
Miss College	MS 14,574	VC
Northwestern Univ	IL 37,595	MC
Roosevelt Univ	IL 22,605	VC
Stetson Univ	FL 32,725	VC
Temple Univ	PA 17,438	VC
Univ of Mich/Ann Arbor	MI 16,587	HC+
Youngstown State Univ	OH 12,613	NC

WOMEN'S STUDIES

School	ST $IS	SR
Agnes Scott College	GA 32,070	HC
Albright College	PA 33,920	C
Allegheny College	PA 33,500	HC
American Univ	DC 38,719	HC+
Amherst College	MA 41,590	MC
Arizona State Univ-Tempe	AZ 11,174	C
Augsburg College	MN 28,300	C
Bates College	ME 42,100	MC
Beloit College	WI 32,808	HC
Berea College	KY 5,496	VC+
Bowdoin College	ME 41,660	MC

School	ST $IS	SR
Bowling Green State Univ	OH 14,994	C
Brown Univ	RI 42,015	MC
Bucknell Univ	PA 39,660	MC
Cal State, Fresno	CA 10,037	LC
Cal State, Fullerton	CA 10,990	C
Cal State, Long Beach	CA 9,512	C
Cal State, Northridge	CA 9,036	LC
Cal State, San Marcos	CA 1,800	LC
Carleton College	MN 40,467	MC
Case Western Reserve Univ	OH 37,314	MC
Central Mich Univ	MI 12,244	C
Chatham College	PA 27,290	C+
CUNY/Brooklyn College	NY 4,377	C+
CUNY/College of Staten Island	NY 4,328	NC
CUNY/Hunter College	NY 8,000	C+
CUNY/Queens College	NY 4,356	C
Coe College	IA 27,440	VC
Colby College	ME 41,770	MC
Colgate Univ	NY 41,170	MC
College of New Jersey	NJ 18,315	MC
College of New Rochelle	NY 28,396	C+
College of St. Catherine	MN 27,505	VC
College of Wooster	OH 31,310	VC+
Colo College	CO 37,668	HC
Columbia Univ/Barnard College	NY 38,000	MC
Columbia Univ/Columbia College	NY 42,584	MC
Columbia Univ/School of General Studies	NY 41,516	C
Cornell College	IA 30,110	VC+
Cornell Univ	NY 41,717	MC
Dartmouth College	NH 39,465	MC
Denison Univ	OH 37,040	HC
DePaul Univ	IL 29,835	VC
DePauw Univ	IN 32,100	HC
Dickinson College	PA 40,170	HC+
Drew Univ/College of Liberal Arts	NJ 39,698	VC
Duke Univ	NC 41,239	MC
Earlham College	IN 33,604	HC
East Carolina Univ	NC 10,000	C
Eastern Mich Univ	MI 12,897	C
Eckerd College	FL 35,492	VC
Emory Univ	GA 40,546	MC
Eugene Lang College New School for Liberal Arts	NY 38,800	C+
Florida International Univ	FL 9,215	VC
Florida State Univ	FL 9,028	HC
Fordham Univ	NY 36,000	HC
Georgia State Univ	GA 11,444	VC
Gettysburg College	PA 39,864	HC
Goddard College	VT 21,100	C
Goucher College	MD 36,225	VC
Guilford College	NC 28,160	C+
Gustavus Adolphus College	MN 30,920	HC
Hamilton College	NY 41,660	MC
Hamline Univ	MN 27,070	VC
Hampshire College	MA 37,120	HC
Harvard Univ/Harvard College	MA 45,860	MC
Hobart and William Smith Colleges	NY 41,123	VC
Hollins Univ	VA 31,105	C
Illinois Wesleyan Univ	IL 34,050	HC+
Indiana Univ South Bend	IN 4,989	LC
Indiana Univ-Purdue Univ Fort Wayne	IN 5,067	LC
Knox College	IL 32,385	VC+
Louisiana State Univ and A&M College	LA 10,749	VC
Macalester College	MN 36,500	MC
Metropolitan State Univ	MN 4,682	SP
Miami Univ	OH 29,097	HC
Mich State Univ	MI 13,689	VC
Middlebury College	VT 42,120	MC
Mills College	CA 39,870	C
Minn State Univ, Mankato	MN 10,276	LC
Montclair State Univ	NJ 16,327	C
Mount Holyoke College	MA 42,148	HC+
Nebr Wesleyan Univ	NE 23,415	C+
New College of Florida	FL 10,009	HC+
New England College	NH 31,466	C
New Mexico State Univ	NM 9,250	C
Oakland Univ	MI 11,936	C
Oberlin College	OH 40,904	MC
Occidental College	CA 40,185	MC
Ohio State Univ	OH 15,357	HC
Ohio Wesleyan Univ	OH 35,830	VC+
Old Dominion Univ	VA 11,907	C
Pacific Lutheran Univ	WA 28,805	VC
Penn State Univ/Univ Park Campus	PA 18,038	HC
Pitzer College	CA 41,644	HC
Pomona College	CA 40,774	MC
Portland State Univ	OR 12,453	C
Purdue Univ/West Lafayette	IN 13,458	VC
Randolph-Macon College	VA 31,250	C
Rhode Island College	RI 11,570	C
Rice Univ	TX 32,290	MC
Roosevelt Univ	IL 22,605	VC
Rosemont College	PA 29,350	C

School	ST $IS	SR
Rutgers, The State Univ of New Jersey/New Brunswick/Piscataway Campus	NJ 15,810	HC
Rutgers, The State Univ of New Jersey/Newark Campus	NJ 15,640	VC
St. Joseph College	CT 32,050	C
St. Louis Univ	MO 33,158	VC+
St. Olaf College	MN 32,800	HC
San Diego State Univ	CA 12,971	C
San Francisco State Univ	CA 13,000	C
Santa Clara Univ	CA 38,931	VC
Sarah Lawrence College	NY 42,000	HC
Scripps College	CA 41,000	MC
Simmons College	MA 35,640	VC
Skidmore College	NY 41,779	HC
Smith College	MA 41,474	MC
Sonoma State Univ	CA 14,732	C
Southwestern Univ	TX 26,767	HC
Spelman College	GA 24,650	VC
Stanford Univ	CA 41,557	MC
SUNY at Oswego	NY 13,662	VC
SUNY/College at Brockport	NY 12,747	VC
SUNY/College at Purchase	NY 11,989	VC+
SUNY/Univ at Albany	NY 13,860	VC
SUNY/Univ at Buffalo	NY 13,694	VC
SUNY/Univ at New Paltz	NY 12,480	VC
SUNY/Univ at Stony Brook	NY 13,625	HC
Suffolk Univ	MA 33,160	C
Syracuse Univ	NY 38,655	HC
Temple Univ	PA 17,438	C
Towson Univ	MD 13,924	VC
Trinity College	CT 38,040	HC+
Tufts Univ	MA 42,018	MC
Tulane Univ	LA 41,098	MC
Union College	NY 41,595	HC
Univ of Arizona	AZ 11,958	VC
Univ of at Calif Davis	CA 15,010	VC
Univ of Calif at Berkeley	CA 18,141	HC+
Univ of Calif at Irvine	CA 16,475	HC
Univ of Calif at Los Angeles	CA 17,681	MC
Univ of Calif at Riverside	CA 16,625	C
Univ of Calif at Santa Barbara	CA 11,800	VC
Univ of Calif at Santa Cruz	CA 19,174	VC
Univ of Colo at Boulder	CO 13,352	C+
Univ of Conn	CT 16,628	HC
Univ of Delaware	DE 14,142	HC
Univ of Denver	CO 36,376	VC+
Univ of Georgia	GA 11,004	HC
Univ of Hawaii at Manoa	HI 10,413	VC
Univ of Illinois at Urbana-Champaign	IL 15,800	HC+
Univ of Kansas	KS 10,915	VC
Univ of Louisville	KY 10,400	VC
Univ of Maine	ME 13,642	C
Univ of Maine at Farmington	ME 11,515	C
Univ of Maryland/College Park	MD 16,036	HC
Univ of Mass Amherst	MA 15,973	C+
Univ of Mass Boston	MA 8,024	C
Univ of Miami	FL 38,397	MC
Univ of Mich/Ann Arbor	MI 16,587	HC+
Univ of Minn/Duluth	MN 13,974	C
Univ of Minn/Morris	MN 15,472	VC
Univ of Minn/Twin Cities	MN 13,165	HC
Univ of Montana	MT 10,602	C
Univ of Nebr at Lincoln	NE 11,401	VC
Univ of Nebr at Omaha	NE 11,235	C
Univ of Nevada/Las Vegas	NV 11,566	C
Univ of New Hampshire	NH 16,810	VC
Univ of N Car at Asheville	NC 9,237	VC
Univ of N Car at Chapel Hill	NC 11,129	MC
Univ of N Car at Greensboro	NC 8,993	C
Univ of Okla	OK 10,769	VC+
Univ of Oregon	OR 13,108	VC
Univ of Pennsylvania	PA 41,766	MC
Univ of Rhode Island	RI 15,398	C
Univ of Richmond	VA 40,510	MC
Univ of Rochester	NY 41,135	MC
Univ of St. Thomas	MN 28,000	VC
Univ of S Car at Columbia	SC 13,397	VC
Univ of Southern Calif	CA 41,618	MC
Univ of Southern Maine	ME 12,614	C
Univ of Tenn at Chattanooga	TN 7,790	C
Univ of Tenn at Knoxville	TN 11,720	C
Univ of Toledo	OH 15,806	NC
Univ of Utah	UT 10,162	VC
Univ of Washington	WA 10,400	VC
Univ of Wisc/Madison	WI 13,117	HC
Univ of Wisc/Whitewater	WI 9,274	C
Univ of Wyoming	WY 9,666	C
Vassar College	NY 41,700	MC
Virginia Wesleyan College	VA 28,433	C
Warren Wilson College	NC 24,382	VC
Washington State Univ	WA 12,260	C
Washington Univ in St. Louis	MO 42,106	MC
Wayne State Univ	MI 11,805	C
Wellesley College	MA 41,030	MC
Wells College	NY 23,070	VC
Wesleyan Univ	CT 42,122	MC

School	ST $IS	SR
West Chester Univ of Pennsylvania	PA 12,355	C+
Western Mich Univ	MI 13,299	C
Wheaton College	MA 40,180	HC+
Whitworth College	WA 29,428	VC+
Wichita State Univ	KS 8,500	C
Willamette Univ	OR 35,416	VC+
Williams College	MA 40,310	MC
Yale Univ	CT 41,000	MC

WOOD SCIENCE

School	ST $IS	SR
N Car State Univ	NC 11,824	VC
Pittsburg State Univ	KS 8,112	C
Purdue Univ/West Lafayette	IN 13,458	VC
SUNY/College of Environmental Science and Forestry	NY 15,000	VC
Univ of Maine	ME 13,642	C
Univ of Washington	WA 10,400	VC

WOODWORKING

School	ST $IS	SR
Edinboro Univ of Pennsylvania	PA 11,809	LC
Kendall College of Art and Design of Ferris State Univ	MI 11,870	SP
Rochester Inst of Technology	NY 32,070	VC+
Univ of Rio Grande	OH 8,728	NC

YOUTH MINISTRY

School	ST $IS	SR
Andrews Univ	MI 21,786	C
Benedictine College	KS 21,968	C
Bethel College	IN 19,680	C
Bethel Univ	MN 29,840	VC
Charleston Southern Univ	SC 17,800	C
Colo Christian Univ	CO 21,182	VC
Concordia Univ	OR 24,400	C
Cornerstone Univ and Grand Rapids Theological Seminary	MI 21,350	NC
Crichton College	TN 15,300	C
Dakota Wesleyan Univ	SD 17,832	C
Dordt College	IA 20,325	VC
Eastern Univ	PA 24,075	C
Gordon College	MA 29,194	C+
Grace Bible College	MI 18,810	C
Grace College	IN 22,170	C
Greenville College	IL 23,146	C
Hardin-Simmons Univ	TX 18,641	C
Hope International Univ	CA 23,700	NC
Huntington Univ	IN 24,830	C
John Brown Univ	AR 20,910	VC
Judson College	IL 25,130	C
Kentucky Christian College	KY 12,680	C
King College	TN 23,400	C
Lubbock Christian Univ	TX 16,960	C
MacMurray College	IL 20,755	C
Malone College	OH 23,040	C
MidAmerica Nazarene Univ	KS 20,584	LC
Mount Vernon Nazarene Univ	OH 20,810	C
Northwest Univ	WA 18,854	C
Northwestern College	MN 25,220	NC
Northwestern College of Iowa	IA 22,174	C+
Nyack College	NY 18,540	C
Ohio Northern Univ	OH 27,765	VC
Okla Christian Univ	OK 18,992	NC
Okla Wesleyan Univ	OK 18,950	NC
Rochester College	MI 15,636	C+
St. Mary's Univ of Minn	MN 23,857	VC
Simpson Univ	CA 22,900	C
Southeastern Univ	FL 17,180	LC
Spring Arbor Univ	MI 22,476	C
Toccoa Falls College	GA 17,125	C
Trinity International Univ	IL 25,686	C
Union Univ	TN 20,750	VC
Univ of Indianapolis	IN 25,090	C
Washington State Univ	WA 12,260	C
William Tyndale College	MI 13,000	NC
York College	NE 16,330	NC

ZOOLOGY

School	ST $IS	SR
Alabama A&M Univ	AL 8,890	LC
Andrews Univ	MI 21,786	C
Auburn Univ	AL 12,230	VC
Ball State Univ	IN 13,138	C
Bethel College	TN 16,066	NC
Calif State Polytechnic Univ, Pomona	CA 18,053	C+
Cal State, Long Beach	CA 9,512	C
Colo State Univ-Fort Collins	CO 10,878	C+
Delaware Valley College	PA 29,944	C
Eastern Mich Univ	MI 12,897	C
Eastern Washington Univ	WA 10,608	C
Florida State Univ	FL 9,028	HC
Fort Valley State Univ	GA 6,975	C
Friends Univ	KS 16,250	LC
Howard Univ	DC 18,481	C+
Humboldt State Univ	CA 11,176	C

School	ST	$IS	SR	School	ST	$IS	SR	School	ST	$IS	SR	School	ST	$IS	SR
Idaho State Univ	ID	9,030	C	Ohio State Univ	OH	15,357	HC	Texas State Univ - San				Univ of Montana	MT	10,602	C
Juniata College	PA	33,130	VC	Ohio Wesleyan Univ	OH	35,830	VC+	Marcos	TX	10,862	C	Univ of New Hampshire	NH	16,810	VC
Kent State Univ	OH	14,594	C	Okla State Univ	OK	10,213	VC	Texas Tech Univ	TX	13,026	VC	Univ of Okla	OK	10,769	VC+
Kentucky Wesleyan College	KY	18,590	C	Olivet Nazarene Univ	IL	22,590	C	Univ of Akron	OH	15,166	NC	Univ of Rhode Island	RI	15,398	C
Malone College	OH	23,040	C	Oregon State Univ	OR	11,055	C	Univ of at Calif Davis	CA	15,010	VC	Univ of Vermont	VT	18,080	VC
Mars Hill College	NC	19,000	LC	Rutgers, The State Univ of				Univ of Calif at Santa				Univ of Washington	WA	10,400	VC
Miami Univ	OH	29,097	HC	New Jersey/Newark				Barbara	CA	11,800	VC	Univ of Wisc/Madison	WI	13,117	HC
Mich State Univ	MI	13,689	VC	Campus	NJ	15,640	VC	Univ of Florida	FL	9,354	HC	Univ of Wisc/Milwaukee	WI	9,427	LC
N Car State Univ	NC	11,824	HC	San Francisco State Univ	CA	13,000	C	Univ of Georgia	GA	11,004	HC	Univ of Wyoming	WY	9,666	C
N Dak State Univ	ND	8,500	C	San Jose State Univ	CA	11,707	C	Univ of Hawaii at Manoa	HI	10,413	VC	Washington State Univ	WA	12,260	C
Northern Arizona Univ	AZ	10,353	C	Southern Illinois Univ				Univ of Idaho	ID	9,310	NC	Weber State Univ	UT	9,635	NC
Northern Mich Univ	MI	12,340	LC	Carbondale	IL	12,391	C	Univ of Kentucky	KY	7,800	C	Western New Mexico Univ	NM	7,233	LC
Northwest Missouri State				SUNY at Oswego	NY	13,662	VC	Univ of Maine	ME	13,642	C				
Univ	MO	10,000	C	Texas A&M Univ	TX	13,351	HC	Univ of Mich/Ann Arbor	MI	16,587	HC+				

ST = STATE   **$IS** = IN-STATE COSTS   **SR** = SELECTOR RATING

PART IV

A CLOSE LOOK AT

THE COLLEGES

This section will help you understand the college Profiles that are at the heart of this directory, so you can get the most out of them.

The College Admissions Selector explains Barron's unique system of comparing every school's degree of admissions competitiveness. Colleges are rated from Most Competitive to Less Competitive, and more.

Explanations of the ratings are followed by an in-depth look at the college capsule and essay.

Next comes the Profiles—some 1700 four-year accredited colleges and universities in the United States—followed by encapsulated descriptions of about fifty religious schools. Universities outside the boundaries of this country are profiled here, too, including Canadian, European, and more.

COLLEGE ADMISSIONS SELECTOR

This index groups all the colleges listed in this book according to degree of admissions competitiveness. The *Selector* is not a rating of colleges by academic standards or quality of education; it is rather an attempt to describe, in general terms, the situation a prospective student will meet when applying for admission.

THE CRITERIA USED

The factors used in determining the category for each college were: median entrance examination scores for the 2005–2006 freshman class (the SAT I score used was derived by averaging the median verbal reasoning and the median mathematics reasoning scores; the ACT score used was the median composite score); percentages of 2005–2006 freshmen scoring 500 and above and 600 and above on both the verbal reasoning and mathematics reasoning sections of the SAT I; percentages of 2005–2006 freshmen scoring 21 and above and 27 and above on the ACT; percentage of 2005–2006 freshmen who ranked in the upper fifth and the upper two-fifths of their high school graduating classes; minimum class rank and grade point average required for admission (if any); and percentage of applicants to the 2005–2006 freshman class who were accepted. The *Selector* cannot and does not take into account all the other factors that each college considers when making admissions decisions. Colleges place varying degrees of emphasis on the factors that comprise each of these categories.

IMPORTANT NOTE: At press time, median SAT scores were only available for classes admitted based on the SAT I, which had only verbal and math sections.

USING THE SELECTOR

To use the *Selector* effectively, the prospective student's records should be compared realistically with the freshmen enrolled by the colleges in each category, as shown by the SAT I or ACT scores, the quality of high school record emphasized by the colleges in each category, and the kinds of risks that the applicant wishes to take.

The student should also be aware of what importance a particular school places on various nonacademic factors; when available, this information is presented in the profile of the school. If a student has unusual qualifications that may compensate for exam scores or high school record, the student should examine admissions policies of the colleges in the next higher category than the one that encompasses his or her score and consider those colleges that give major consideration to factors other than exam scores and high school grades. The "safety" college should usually be chosen from the next lower category, where the student can be reasonably sure that his or her scores and high school record will fall above the median scores and records of the freshmen enrolled in the college.

The listing within each category is alphabetical and not in any qualitative order. State-supported institutions have been classified according to the requirements for state residents, but standards for admission of out-of-state students are usually higher. Colleges that are experimenting with the admission of students of higher potential but lower achievement may appear in a less competitive category because of this fact.

A WORD OF CAUTION

The *Selector* is intended primarily for preliminary screening, to eliminate the majority of colleges that are not suitable for a particular student. Be sure to examine the admissions policies spelled out in the *Admissions* section of each profile. And remember that many colleges have to reject *qualified* students; the *Selector* will tell you what your chances are, not which college will accept you.

MOST COMPETITIVE

Even superior students will encounter a great deal of competition for admission to the colleges in this category. In general, these colleges require high school rank in the top 10% to 20% and grade averages of A to B+. Median freshman test scores at these colleges are generally between 655 and 800 on the SAT I and 29 and above on the ACT. In addition, many of these colleges admit only a small percentage of those who apply—usually fewer than one third.

Amherst College, MA
Bates College, ME
Boston College, MA
Bowdoin College, ME
Brandeis University, MA
Brown University, RI
Bucknell University, PA
California Institute of Technology, CA
Carleton College, MN
Carnegie Mellon University, PA
Case Western Reserve University, OH
Claremont McKenna College, CA
Colby College, ME
Colgate University, NY
College of New Jersey, The, NJ
College of the Holy Cross, MA
College of William and Mary, VA
Columbia University/Barnard College, NY
Columbia University/Columbia College, NY
Columbia University/Fu Foundation School of Engineering and
   Applied Science, NY
Connecticut College, CT
Cooper Union for the Advancement of Science and Art, NY
Cornell University, NY
Dartmouth College, NH
Davidson College, NC
Duke University, NC
Emory University, GA
George Washington University, DC
Georgetown University, DC
Hamilton College, NY

Harvard University/Harvard College, MA
Harvey Mudd College, CA
Haverford College, PA
Johns Hopkins University, MD
Kenyon College, OH
Lafayette College, PA
Macalester College, MN
Massachusetts Institute of Technology, MA
Middlebury College, VT
New York University, NY
Northwestern University, IL
Oberlin College, OH
Occidental College, CA
Pomona College, CA
Princeton University, NJ
Reed College, OR
Rice University, TX
Scripps College, CA
Smith College, MA
Stanford University, CA
Swarthmore College, PA
Tufts University, MA
Tulane University, LA
United States Military Academy, NY
United States Naval Academy, MD
University of California at Los Angeles, CA
University of Chicago, IL
University of Miami, FL
University of North Carolina at Chapel Hill, NC
University of Notre Dame, IN
University of Pennsylvania, PA

University of Richmond, VA
University of Rochester, NY
University of Southern California, CA
University of Virginia, VA
Vanderbilt University, TN
Vassar College, NY
Wake Forest University, NC

Washington and Lee University, VA
Washington University in Saint Louis, MO
Webb Institute, NY
Wellesley College, MA
Wesleyan University, CT
Williams College, MA
Yale University, CT

HIGHLY COMPETITIVE

Colleges in this group generally look for students with grade averages of B+ to B and accept most of their students from the top 20% to 35% of the high school class. Median freshman test scores at these colleges generally range from 620 to 654 on the SAT I and 27 or 28 on the ACT. These schools generally accept between one third and one half of their applicants.

To provide for finer distinctions within this admissions category, a plus (+) symbol has been placed before some entries. These are colleges with median freshman scores of 645 or more on the SAT I or 28 or more on the ACT (depending on which test the college prefers), and colleges that accept fewer than one quarter of their applicants.

Agnes Scott College, GA
+Albert A. List College of Jewish Studies, NY
Allegheny College, PA
+American University, DC
Austin College, TX
Babson College, MA
+Bard College, NY
Baylor University, TX
Beloit College, WI
Bennington College, VT
Bentley College, MA
+Boston University, MA
+Brigham Young University/Hawaii, HI
+Bryn Mawr College, PA
Clemson University, SC
College of the Atlantic, ME
Colorado College, CO
Colorado School of Mines, CO
Denison University, OH
DePauw University, IN
+Dickinson College, PA
Earlham College, IN
Elon University, NC
Emerson College, MA
Fairfield University, CT
Florida State University, FL
Fordham University, NY
Franklin and Marshall College, PA
+Furman University, SC
+Georgia Institute of Technology, GA
Gettysburg College, PA
Gonzaga University, WA
+Grinnell College, IA
+Grove City College, PA
Gustavus Adolphus College, MN
Hampshire College, MA
Hanover College, IN
+Hendrix College, AR
Hillsdale College, MI
+Illinois Institute of Technology, IL
+Illinois Wesleyan University, IL
Kettering University, MI
+Lawrence University, WI
+Lehigh University, PA
Loyola College in Maryland, MD
Marquette University, WI
Miami University, OH
+Mount Holyoke College, MA
+Muhlenberg College, PA
+New College of Florida, FL
North Carolina State University, NC
Northeastern University, MA
Ohio State University, OH
Penn State University/University Park Campus, PA
Pepperdine University, CA
Pitzer College, CA

Providence College, RI
+Rensselaer Polytechnic Institute, NY
Rhodes College, TN
+Rose-Hulman Institute of Technology, IN
Rutgers, The State University of New Jersey/New Brunswick/
   Piscataway Campus, NJ
+Saint John's College, MD
Saint Olaf College, MN
Sarah Lawrence College, NY
Skidmore College, NY
Southwestern University, TX
+State University of New York/College at Geneseo, NY
State University of New York/University at Binghamton, NY
State University of New York/University at Stony Brook, NY
Stevens Institute of Technology, NJ
Stonehill College, MA
Syracuse University, NY
Texas A&M University, TX
+Thomas Aquinas College, CA
+Trinity College, CT
+Trinity University, TX
Truman State University, MO
Union College, NY
+United States Air Force Academy, CO
United States Coast Guard Academy, CT
+United States Merchant Marine Academy, NY
+University of California at Berkeley, CA
University of California at Irvine, CA
University of California at San Diego, CA
University of Connecticut, CT
University of Delaware, DE
University of Florida, FL
University of Georgia, GA
+University of Illinois at Urbana-Champaign, IL
University of Mary Washington, VA
University of Maryland/College Park, MD
+University of Michigan/Ann Arbor, MI
University of Minnesota/Twin Cities, MN
University of Missouri/Rolla, MO
University of Pittsburgh at Pittsburgh, PA
University of Puget Sound, WA
University of San Diego, CA
University of Texas at Austin, TX
University of Texas at Dallas, TX
University of the South, TN
University of Tulsa, OK
University of Wisconsin/Madison, WI
+Villanova University, PA
Wabash College, IN
Westmont College, CA
Wheaton College, IL
+Wheaton College, MA
+Whitman College, WA
Wofford College, SC
Xavier University, OH

VERY COMPETITIVE

The colleges in this category generally admit students whose averages are no less than B- and who rank in the top 35% to 50% of their graduating class. They generally report median freshman test scores in the 573 to 619 range on the SAT I and from 24 to 26 on the ACT. These schools generally accept between one half and three quarters of their applicants.

The plus (+) has been placed before colleges with median freshman scores of 610 or above on the SAT I or 26 or better on the ACT (depending on which test the college prefers), and colleges that accept fewer than one third of their applicants.

Adelphi University, NY
Albertson College of Idaho, ID
Albion College, MI
Alfred University, NY
Alma College, MI
Appalachian State University, NC
Arcadia University, PA
Arkansas Tech University, AR
Asbury College, KY
Auburn University, AL
+Augustana College, IL
Augustana College, SD
Azusa Pacific University, CA
Baldwin-Wallace College, OH
Belmont University, TN
+Berea College, KY
Berry College, GA
Bethel University, MN
Biola University, CA
+Birmingham-Southern College, AL
Bradley University, IL
Brenau University Women's College, GA
Brigham Young University, UT
Bryant College, RI
+Butler University, IN
California Polytechnic State University, CA
Campbell University, NC
Canisius College, NY
Catholic University of America, DC
Cedarville University, OH
Centenary College of Louisiana, LA
Central College, IA
Centre College, KY
Chapman University, CA
+Christendom College, VA
Christian Brothers University, TN
Christopher Newport University, VA
+City University of New York/Baruch College, NY
+Clark University, MA
Clarkson University, NY
Coe College, IA
College of Charleston, SC
College of Saint Benedict, MN
College of Saint Catherine, MN
+College of the Ozarks, MO
+College of Wooster, OH
Colorado Christian University, CO
Concordia College: Moorhead, MN
Concordia University Wisconsin, WI
Converse College, SC
+Cornell College, IA
+Covenant College, GA
+Creighton University, NE
Dallas Baptist University, TX
De Sales University, PA
DePaul University, IL
Dillard University, LA
Dordt College, IA
+Drake University, IA
Drew University/College of Liberal Arts, NJ
Drexel University, PA
Drury University, MO
Duquesne University, PA
Eastern Mennonite University, VA
Eckerd College, FL
Elizabethtown College, PA
Elmira College, NY

Erskine College, SC
+Flagler College, FL
Florida Institute of Technology, FL
Florida International University, FL
Franciscan University of Steubenville, OH
George Mason University, VA
Georgia State University, GA
Goshen College, IN
Goucher College, MD
Grand Valley State University, MI
Hamline University, MN
Hampden-Sydney College, VA
Harding University, AR
Hastings College, NE
Hiram College, OH
Hobart and William Smith Colleges, NY
Hofstra University, NY
Hood College, MD
+Hope College, MI
+Houghton College, NY
Huntingdon College, AL
Indiana University Bloomington, IN
Iona College, NY
Iowa State University, IA
Ithaca College, NY
James Madison University, VA
John Brown University, AR
Juniata College, PA
+Kalamazoo College, MI
Kansas State University, KS
Kansas Wesleyan University, KS
+Knox College, IL
Lake Forest College, IL
Lawrence Technological University, MI
Le Moyne College, NY
Lebanon Valley College, PA
+Lewis and Clark College, OR
Lindenwood University, MO
Linfield College, OR
Lipscomb University, TN
Louisiana State University and Agricultural and Mechanical College, LA
Loyola Marymount University, CA
Loyola University Chicago, IL
+Loyola University New Orleans, LA
+Luther College, IA
Lyon College, AR
Madonna University, MI
Maharishi University of Management, IA
Manhattan College, NY
Marist College, NY
+Marlboro College, VT
Marymount Manhattan College, NY
Maryville College, TN
Maryville University of Saint Louis, MO
Master's College and Seminary, The, CA
McDaniel College, MD
McKendree College, IL
+Mercer University, GA
Mercyhurst College, PA
+Messiah College, PA
Michigan State University, MI
Michigan Technological University, MI
Milligan College, TN
+Millsaps College, MS
+Milwaukee School of Engineering, WI
Mississippi College, MS

Moravian College, PA
Mount Saint Mary's College, CA
Murray State University, KY
Nazareth College of Rochester, NY
New Jersey Institute of Technology, NJ
+New Mexico Institute of Mining and Technology, NM
New York Institute of Technology, NY
North Central College, IL
Northwest Nazarene University, ID
Oglethorpe University, GA
Ohio Northern University, OH
+Ohio Wesleyan University, OH
Oklahoma Baptist University, OK
Oklahoma City University, OK
Oklahoma State University, OK
Ouachita Baptist University, AR
Pace University, NY
Pacific Lutheran University, WA
+Pacific Union College, CA
Palm Beach Atlantic University, FL
Point Loma Nazarene University, CA
Polytechnic University, Brooklyn, NY
Presbyterian College, SC
+Principia College, IL
Purdue University/West Lafayette, IN
Quinnipiac University, CT
Ramapo College of New Jersey, NJ
+Randolph-Macon Woman's College, VA
Richard Stockton College of New Jersey, NJ
Roanoke College, VA
+Rochester Institute of Technology, NY
Rockford College, IL
Rockhurst University, MO
Rollins College, FL
Roosevelt University, IL
Rowan University, NJ
Rutgers, The State University of New Jersey/
    Camden Campus, NJ
Rutgers, The State University of New Jersey/
    Newark Campus, NJ
Saint John's University, MN
Saint Joseph's University, PA
Saint Lawrence University, NY
+Saint Louis University, MO
Saint Mary's College, IN
+Saint Mary's College of Maryland, MD
Saint Mary's University of Minnesota, MN
Saint Michael's College, VT
Saint Vincent College, PA
+Salem College, NC
Salisbury University, MD
Samford University, AL
Santa Clara University, CA
Seattle University, WA
Seton Hall University, NJ
+Siena College, NY
Simmons College, MA
+Simon's Rock College of Bard, MA
Simpson College, IA
+Southern Methodist University, TX
Southern Polytechnic State University, GA
Spelman College, GA
State University of New York at Oswego, NY
State University of New York/College at Brockport, NY
State University of New York/College at Fredonia, NY
State University of New York/College at Oneonta, NY
+State University of New York/College at Purchase, NY
State University of New York/College of Environmental Science
    and Forestry, NY
State University of New York/Institute of Technology, NY
State University of New York/University at Albany, NY
State University of New York/University at Buffalo, NY
State University of New York/University at New Paltz, NY
Stephens College, MO
Sterling College, VT
Stetson University, FL
Susquehanna University, PA

Sweet Briar College, VA
+Taylor University, IN
+Texas Christian University, TX
Texas Tech University, TX
Touro College, NY
Towson University, MD
+Transylvania University, KY
Union University, TN
University of Alabama in Huntsville, AL
University of Arizona, AZ
University of Arkansas, AR
University of California at Davis, CA
University of California at Santa Barbara, CA
University of California at Santa Cruz, CA
University of Central Florida, FL
University of Colorado at Colorado Springs, CO
+University of Dallas, TX
University of Dayton, OH
+University of Denver, CO
University of Evansville, IN
University of Hawaii at Manoa, HI
University of Illinois at Chicago, IL
University of Iowa, IA
University of Kansas, KS
University of Louisville, KY
+University of Maryland/Baltimore County, MD
University of Massachusetts Lowell, MA
University of Michigan/Dearborn, MI
University of Minnesota/Morris, MN
University of Missouri/Columbia, MO
University of Missouri/Kansas City, MO
University of Missouri/St. Louis, MO
University of Nebraska at Lincoln, NE
University of New Hampshire, NH
University of North Carolina at Asheville, NC
University of North Carolina at Wilmington, NC
University of North Dakota, ND
University of North Florida, FL
+University of Oklahoma, OK
University of Oregon, OR
University of Portland, OR
University of Redlands, CA
University of Saint Thomas, MN
University of Saint Thomas, TX
University of San Francisco, CA
University of Scranton, PA
University of South Carolina at Columbia, SC
University of South Florida, FL
University of the Pacific, CA
University of the Sciences in Philadelphia, PA
University of Utah, UT
University of Vermont, VT
University of Washington, WA
University of Wisconsin/Eau Claire, WI
University of Wisconsin/Green Bay, WI
University of Wisconsin/La Crosse, WI
University of Wisconsin/Stevens Point, WI
Ursinus College, PA
Utah State University, UT
+Valparaiso University, IN
Virginia Military Institute, VA
Virginia Polytechnic Institute and State University, VA
Wagner College, NY
Warren Wilson College, NC
Washington and Jefferson College, PA
Washington College, MD
Webster University, MO
Wells College, NY
Western Washington University, WA
Westminster College, MO
+Whitworth College, WA
+Willamette University, OR
Wisconsin Lutheran College, WI
Wittenberg University, OH
+Worcester Polytechnic Institute, MA
York College of Pennsylvania, PA

COMPETITIVE

This category is a very broad one, covering colleges that generally have median freshman test scores between 500 and 572 on the SAT I and between 21 and 23 on the ACT. Some of these colleges require that students have high school averages of B- or better, although others state a minimum of C+ or C. Generally, these colleges prefer students in the top 50% to 65% of the graduating class and accept between 75% and 85% of their applicants.

Colleges with a plus (+) are those with median freshman SAT I scores of 563 or more or median freshman ACT scores of 24 or more (depending on which test the colleges prefers), and those that admit fewer than half of their applicants.

Abilene Christian University, TX
Adams State College, CO
Adrian College, MI
Alabama State University, AL
Alaska Pacific University, AK
+Albany State University, GA
Albertus Magnus College, CT
Albright College, PA
Alderson-Broaddus College, WV
Alice Lloyd College, KY
Alvernia College, PA
Alverno College, WI
Andrews University, MI
Antioch College, OH
Aquinas College, MI
Arizona State University-Tempe, AZ
Arkansas State University, AR
Armstrong Atlantic State University, GA
Ashford University, IA
Ashland University, OH
Assumption College, MA
Augsburg College, MN
Augusta State University, GA
Aurora University, IL
Austin Peay State University, TN
Averett University, VA
Avila University, MO
Baker University, KS
Ball State University, IN
Barton College, NC
Bay Path College, MA
+Bellarmine University, KY
Belmont Abbey College, NC
Benedictine College, KS
Benedictine University, IL
Bennett College, NC
Bethany College, WV
Bethel College, IN
Bethel College, KS
Blackburn College, IL
Bloomsburg University of Pennsylvania, PA
Blue Mountain College, MS
+Bluefield College, VA
Bluffton College, OH
Boricua College, NY
+Bowie State University, MD
Bowling Green State University, OH
Brescia University, KY
Bridgewater College, VA
Bridgewater State College, MA
Bryan College, TN
Buena Vista University, IA
Cabrini College, PA
California Baptist University, CA
California Maritime Academy, CA
+California State Polytechnic University, Pomona, CA
California State University, Chico, CA
California State University, Fullerton, CA
California State University, Long Beach, CA
California State University, Los Angeles, CA
California State University, Monterey Bay, CA
+California State University, Sacramento, CA
California State University, Stanislaus, CA
California University of Pennsylvania, PA
Campbellsville University, KY
Capital University, OH
Capitol College, MD
Cardinal Stritch University, WI
Carlos Albizu University, FL
Carlow University, PA

+Carroll College, MT
Carroll College, WI
Carson-Newman College, TN
Carthage College, WI
Castleton State College, VT
Catawba College, NC
Cazenovia College, NY
Cedar Crest College, PA
Central Connecticut State University, CT
Central Methodist University, MO
Central Michigan University, MI
Central Missouri State University, MO
+Central State University, OH
Central Washington University, WA
Champlain College, VT
Charleston Southern University, SC
+Chatham College, PA
+Chicago State University, IL
+Citadel, The, SC
+City University of New York/Brooklyn College, NY
City University of New York/City College, NY
+City University of New York/Hunter College, NY
City University of New York/John Jay College of Criminal Justice, NY
City University of New York/Queens College, NY
+Claflin University, SC
Clarion University of Pennsylvania, PA
Clarke College, IA
Clarkson College, NE
Coastal Carolina University, SC
Coker College, SC
College Misericordia, PA
College of Mount Saint Vincent, NY
College of Mount St. Joseph, OH
+College of New Rochelle, NY
College of Notre Dame of Maryland, MD
College of Our Lady of the Elms, MA
College of Saint Elizabeth, NJ
College of Saint Mary, NE
College of Saint Rose, NY
+College of Saint Scholastica, MN
College of Santa Fe, NM
+College of the Southwest, NM
+Colorado State University-Fort Collins, CO
Columbia College, MO
Columbia University/School of General Studies, NY
Columbus State University, GA
Concord College, WV
Concordia College-New York, NY
Concordia University, CA
Concordia University, OR
+Concordia University Nebraska, NE
Concordia University St.Paul, MN
+Concordia University, Ann Arbor, MI
Concordia University, River Forest, IL
Crichton College, TN
Culver-Stockton College, MO
Cumberland University, TN
Daemen College, NY
Dakota State University, SD
Dakota Wesleyan University, SD
Dana College, NE
Daniel Webster College, NH
David N. Myers College, OH
Davis and Elkins College, WV
Defiance College, OH
Delaware Valley College, PA
Delta State University, MS
DeVry University/Crystal City, VA
Doane College, NE

Dominican University, IL
Dominican University of California, CA
D'Youville College, NY
East Carolina University, NC
East Central University, OK
East Stroudsburg University of Pennsylvania, PA
East Tennessee State University, TN
East Texas Baptist University, TX
Eastern Connecticut State University, CT
Eastern Illinois University, IL
Eastern Kentucky University, KY
Eastern Michigan University, MI
Eastern New Mexico University, NM
Eastern University, PA
Eastern Washington University, WA
Edgewood College, WI
Elmhurst College, IL
+Embry-Riddle Aeronautical University, AZ
Embry-Riddle Aeronautical University, FL
+Emmanuel College, MA
Emory & Henry College, VA
Emporia State University, KS
+Endicott College, MA
+Eugene Lang College New School for Liberal Arts, NY
Eureka College, IL
Evangel University, MO
+Evergreen State College, WA
Fairleigh Dickinson University/College at Florham, NJ
Fairleigh Dickinson University/Metropolitan Campus, NJ
Farmingdale State University of New York, NY
+Fashion Institute of Technology/State University of New York, NY
Faulkner University, AL
Felician College, NJ
Ferris State University, MI
Fisk University, TN
Fitchburg State College, MA
Florida Agricultural and Mechanical University, FL
Florida Atlantic University, FL
Florida Gulf Coast University, FL
Florida Southern College, FL
Fontbonne University, MO
Fort Hays State University, KS
Fort Lewis College, CO
Fort Valley State University, GA
Framingham State College, MA
Francis Marion University, SC
Franklin College, IN
Franklin Pierce College, NH
Fresno Pacific University, CA
Frostburg State University, MD
Gannon University, PA
Gardner-Webb University, NC
Geneva College, PA
George Fox University, OR
+Georgetown College, KY
Georgia College and State University, GA
Georgia Southern University, GA
Georgia Southwestern State University, GA
Goddard College, VT
Goldey-Beacom College, DE
+Gordon College, MA
Grace Bible College, MI
Grace College, IN
Graceland University, IA
Grand View College, IA
Green Mountain College, VT
Greensboro College, NC
Greenville College, IL
+Guilford College, NC
Gwynedd-Mercy College, PA
+Hampton University, VA
Hannibal-LaGrange College, MO
Hardin-Simmons University, TX
+Hartwick College, NY
Hawaii Pacific University, HI
Heidelberg College, OH
Hellenic College/Holy Cross Greek Orthodox School of
    Theology, MA
Henderson State University, AR
High Point University, NC
Hollins University, VA
Holy Family University, PA

Houston Baptist University, TX
Howard Payne University, TX
+Howard University, DC
Humboldt State University, CA
Huntington University, IN
Huron University, SD
Idaho State University, ID
+Illinois College, IL
+Illinois State University, IL
Immaculata University, PA
Indiana Institute of Technology, IN
Indiana State University, IN
Indiana University of Pennsylvania, PA
Indiana University-Purdue University Indianapolis, IN
+Indiana Wesleyan University, IN
Iowa Wesleyan College, IA
Jackson State University, MS
Jacksonville University, FL
+John Carroll University, OH
Johnson C. Smith University, NC
Judson College, AL
Judson College, IL
Kean University, NJ
Keene State College, NH
Kennesaw State University, GA
Kent State University, OH
Kentucky Christian College, KY
Kentucky Wesleyan College, KY
Keuka College, NY
King College, TN
King's College, PA
Kutztown University of Pennsylvania, PA
La Salle University, PA
+La Sierra University, CA
+LaGrange College, GA
Lake Erie College, OH
Lakeland College, WI
+Lambuth University, TN
Lander University, SC
+Lane College, TN
Lasell College, MA
Lees-McRae College, NC
Lenoir-Rhyne College, NC
Lesley University, MA
LeTourneau University, TX
+Lewis University, IL
Lewis-Clark State College, ID
Liberty University, VA
Limestone College, SC
Lincoln Memorial University, TN
+Lincoln University, PA
Long Island University/Brooklyn Campus, NY
Long Island University/C.W. Post Campus, NY
Longwood University, VA
Loras College, IA
Louisiana College, LA
Louisiana Tech University, LA
Lubbock Christian University, TX
+Lycoming College, PA
Lynchburg College, VA
Lynn University, FL
MacMurray College, IL
Maine Maritime Academy, ME
Malone College, OH
Manchester College, IN
+Manhattanville College, NY
Mansfield University, PA
Marian College, IN
Marietta College, OH
Marshall University, WV
Mary Baldwin College, VA
+Marygrove College, MI
Marymount University, VA
Marywood University, PA
Massachusetts Maritime Academy, MA
McPherson College, KS
Medaille College, NY
Menlo College, CA
Meredith College, NC
Merrimack College, MA
Mesa State College, CO
Methodist College, NC

Metropolitan College of New York, NY
Middle Tennessee State University, TN
Midland Lutheran College, NE
Midway College, KY
Millersville University of Pennsylvania, PA
Millikin University, IL
Mills College, CA
Mississippi State University, MS
Mississippi Valley State University, MS
Missouri Baptist University, MO
+Missouri State University, MO
Missouri Valley College, MO
Mitchell College, CT
Molloy College, NY
Monmouth College, IL
Monmouth University, NJ
Montana State University-Billings, MT
Montana State University-Bozeman, MT
Montana Tech of The University of Montana, MT
Montclair State University, NJ
Montreat College, NC
Morehead State University, KY
Morehouse College, GA
Morgan State University, MD
Morningside College, IA
Mount Marty College, SD
Mount Mary College, WI
Mount Mercy College, IA
Mount Saint Mary College, NY
Mount Saint Mary's University, MD
Mount Union College, OH
Mount Vernon Nazarene University, OH
Muskingum College, OH
+Nebraska Wesleyan University, NE
New England College, NH
New Mexico State University, NM
Newbury College, MA
Newman University, KS
Niagara University, NY
North Carolina Wesleyan College, NC
North Dakota State University, ND
North Georgia College and State University, GA
North Park University, IL
Northeastern Illinois University, IL
Northern Arizona University, AZ
Northern Illinois University, IL
Northern State University, SD
+Northland College, WI
Northwest Christian College, OR
Northwest Missouri State University, MO
Northwest University, WA
+Northwestern College of Iowa, IA
Northwestern State University of Louisiana, LA
Northwood University, FL
Norwich University, VT
Notre Dame College, OH
Nova Southeastern University, FL
Nyack College, NY
Oakland University, MI
Oakwood College, AL
Ohio Dominican University, OH
Ohio University, OH
Ohio Valley University, WV
Old Dominion University, VA
+Olivet College, MI
Olivet Nazarene University, IL
Oral Roberts University, OK
Oregon Institute of Technology, OR
Oregon State University, OR
Otterbein College, OH
Pacific University, OR
Park University, MO
Penn State Erie/The Behrend College, PA
Penn State University/Altoona, PA
Pfeiffer University, NC
Philadelphia Biblical University, PA
Philadelphia University, PA
Piedmont College, GA
Pittsburg State University, KS
Point Park University, PA
Portland State University, OR
Post University, CT

Queens University of Charlotte, NC
Quincy University, IL
Radford University, VA
Randolph-Macon College, VA
Regis University, CO
Reinhardt College, GA
Rhode Island College, RI
Rider University, NJ
+Ripon College, WI
Rivier College, NH
Robert Morris University, PA
Roberts Wesleyan College, NY
+Rochester College, MI
Rocky Mountain College, MT
Roger Williams University, RI
Rosemont College, PA
Russell Sage College, NY
+Rust College, MS
Sacred Heart University, CT
Saginaw Valley State University, MI
Saint Ambrose University, IA
Saint Andrews Presbyterian College, NC
Saint Anselm College, NH
Saint Cloud State University, MN
Saint Edward's University, TX
Saint John Fisher College, NY
Saint John's College, NM
Saint John's University, NY
Saint Joseph College, CT
Saint Joseph's College, IN
Saint Joseph's College of Maine, ME
Saint Joseph's College, New York, Brooklyn Campus, NY
Saint Joseph's College, New York, Suffolk Campus, NY
+Saint Leo University, FL
Saint Martin's University, WA
Saint Mary-of-the-Woods College, IN
Saint Mary's College of California, CA
Saint Mary's University of San Antonio, TX
+Saint Norbert College, WI
Saint Thomas University, FL
Saint Xavier University, IL
Salem International University, WV
Salve Regina University, RI
Sam Houston State University, TX
San Diego Christian College, CA
San Diego State University, CA
San Francisco State University, CA
San Jose State University, CA
Schreiner University, TX
Seattle Pacific University, WA
Seton Hill University, PA
Shenandoah University, VA
Shepherd University, WV
Shippensburg University of Pennsylvania, PA
Shorter College, GA
Sierra Nevada College, NV
Simpson University, CA
Sonoma State University, CA
+South Dakota School of Mines and Technology, SD
South Dakota State University, SD
Southeast Missouri State University, MO
Southeastern Oklahoma State University, OK
Southern Adventist University, TN
Southern Arkansas University, AR
Southern Connecticut State University, CT
Southern Illinois University Carbondale, IL
Southern Illinois University Edwardsville, IL
Southern New Hampshire University, NH
Southern Oregon University, OR
Southern Utah University, UT
Southern Wesleyan University, SC
Southwest Baptist University, MO
Southwest Minnesota State University, MN
Southwestern College, KS
Southwestern Oklahoma State University, OK
Spalding University, KY
Spring Arbor University, MI
Spring Hill College, AL
Springfield College, MA
State University of New York at Potsdam, NY
+State University of New York/College at Buffalo, NY
State University of New York/College at Cortland, NY

State University of New York/College at Old Westbury, NY
State University of New York/College at Plattsburgh, NY
State University of New York/College of Agriculture and
    Technology at Cobleskill, NY
State University of New York/College of Technology at Alfred, NY
State University of New York/Maritime College, NY
Stephen F. Austin State University, TX
Sterling College, KS
Suffolk University, MA
Tarleton State University, TX
Temple University, PA
Tennessee Technological University, TN
Tennessee Wesleyan College, TN
Texas A&M University at Commerce, TX
+Texas A&M University at Galveston, TX
Texas Lutheran University, TX
Texas Southern University, TX
Texas State University - San Marcos, TX
Texas Wesleyan University, TX
Thiel College, PA
Thomas More College, KY
Thomas More College of Liberal Arts, NH
Toccoa Falls College, GA
Trevecca Nazarene University, TN
Trinity Christian College, IL
Trinity International University, IL
Tri-State University-Main Campus, IN
Troy University, AL
Troy University Dothan Campus, AL
Union College, KY
Union College, NE
Unity College, ME
University of Alabama, AL
University of Alabama at Birmingham, AL
University of Alaska Fairbanks, AK
University of Arkansas at Pine Bluff, AR
University of California at Riverside, CA
University of Central Arkansas, AR
University of Central Oklahoma, OK
University of Charleston, WV
University of Cincinnati, OH
+University of Colorado at Boulder, CO
University of Colorado at Denver and Health Sciences Center, CO
University of Detroit Mercy, MI
University of Dubuque, IA
University of Findlay, OH
University of Great Falls, MT
University of Hartford, CT
University of Hawaii at Hilo, HI
University of Houston, TX
University of Indianapolis, IN
University of Judaism College of Arts and Sciences, CA
University of Kentucky, KY
University of La Verne, CA
University of Louisiana at Lafayette, LA
University of Louisiana at Monroe, LA
University of Maine, ME
University of Maine at Farmington, ME
University of Maine at Machias, ME
University of Mary, ND
University of Mary Hardin-Baylor, TX
University of Maryland/Eastern Shore, MD
+University of Massachusetts Amherst, MA
University of Massachusetts Boston, MA
University of Massachusetts Dartmouth, MA
University of Memphis, TN
University of Michigan/Flint, MI
University of Minnesota/Duluth, MN
University of Mississippi, MS
University of Mobile, AL
University of Montana, MT
University of Montevallo, AL
University of Nebraska at Omaha, NE
University of Nevada/Las Vegas, NV
University of New England, ME
University of New Haven, CT
University of New Mexico, NM
University of New Orleans, LA
University of North Alabama, AL
University of North Carolina at Charlotte, NC
University of North Carolina at Greensboro, NC
University of North Texas, TX
University of Northern Colorado, CO

University of Northern Iowa, IA
University of Pittsburgh at Bradford, PA
University of Pittsburgh at Greensburg, PA
University of Rhode Island, RI
University of Saint Francis, IL
University of Saint Francis, IN
University of Saint Mary, KS
University of Science and Arts of Oklahoma, OK
University of Sioux Falls, SD
University of South Carolina Upstate, SC
University of South Dakota, SD
University of Southern Maine, ME
University of Southern Mississippi, MS
University of Tampa, FL
University of Tennessee at Chattanooga, TN
University of Tennessee at Knoxville, TN
University of Tennessee at Martin, TN
+University of Texas-Pan American, TX
University of the Cumberlands, KY
University of the Incarnate Word, TX
University of the Ozarks, AR
University of Virginia's College at Wise, VA
University of West Alabama, AL
University of West Florida, FL
University of West Georgia, GA
University of Wisconsin/Stout, WI
+University of Wisconsin/Superior, WI
University of Wisconsin/Whitewater, WI
University of Wyoming, WY
Upper Iowa University, IA
Urbana University, OH
Ursuline College, OH
Utica College, NY
Valdosta State University, GA
Vanguard University of Southern California, CA
Vermont Technical College, VT
Villa Julie College, MD
Virginia Commonwealth University, VA
Virginia State University, VA
Virginia Wesleyan College, VA
Viterbo University, WI
Walsh University, OH
Warner Pacific College, OR
Washington State University, WA
Wayland Baptist University, TX
Wayne State University, MI
Waynesburg College, PA
Wentworth Institute of Technology, MA
Wesley College, DE
Wesleyan College, GA
+West Chester University of Pennsylvania, PA
West Texas A&M University, TX
West Virginia University, WV
West Virginia Wesleyan College, WV
Western Baptist College, OR
Western Carolina University, NC
Western Connecticut State University, CT
Western Illinois University, IL
Western Kentucky University, KY
Western Michigan University, MI
Western New England College, MA
Western Oregon University, OR
Western State College of Colorado, CO
Westfield State College, MA
+Westminster College, PA
Westminster College, UT
Wheeling Jesuit University, WV
Wheelock College, MA
Whittier College, CA
Wichita State University, KS
Widener University, PA
Wilkes University, PA
William Jewell College, MO
+William Paterson University of New Jersey, NJ
William Woods University, MO
Williams Baptist College, AR
Wilson College, PA
Wingate University, NC
Winona State University, MN
Winthrop University, SC
Worcester State College, MA
Xavier University of Louisiana, LA
Yeshiva University, NY

LESS COMPETITIVE

Included in this category are colleges with median freshman test scores generally below 500 on the SAT I and below 21 on the ACT; some colleges that require entrance examinations but do not report median scores; and colleges that admit students with averages generally below C who rank in the top 65% of the graduating class. These colleges usually admit 85% or more of their applicants.

Alabama Agricultural and Mechanical University, AL
Alcorn State University, MS
American Indian College of the Assemblies of God, AZ
American International College, MA
Anderson University, IN
Anna Maria College, MA
Aquinas College, TN
Atlantic Union College, MA
Barber-Scotia College, NC
Barry University, FL
Beacon College, FL
Becker College, MA
Bemidji State University, MN
Benedict College, SC
Berkeley College of New York City, NY
Berkeley College-Westchester Campus, NY
Bethany College, KS
Bethune-Cookman College, FL
Black Hills State University, SD
Bloomfield College, NJ
Bluefield State College, WV
Boise State University, ID
Brewton-Parker College, GA
Briar Cliff University, IA
Caldwell College, NJ
California Lutheran University, CA
California State University, Bakersfield, CA
California State University, Dominguez Hills, CA
California State University, East Bay, CA
California State University, Fresno, CA
California State University, Northridge, CA
California State University, San Bernardino, CA
California State University, San Marcos, CA
Calumet College of St. Joseph, IN
Centenary College, NJ
Chaminade University of Honolulu, HI
Chestnut Hill College, PA
Cheyney University of Pennsylvania, PA
City University of New York/Herbert H. Lehman College, NY
Clark Atlanta University, GA
Clayton College and State University, GA
Clearwater Christian College, FL
Cleary College, MI
Cogswell Polytechnical College, CA
Colby-Sawyer College, NH
Colorado State University-Pueblo, CO
Colorado Technical University, CO
Columbia College, SC
Columbia College Chicago, IL
Columbia Union College, MD
Concordia University at Austin, TX
Coppin State College, MD
Curry College, MA
Delaware State University, DE
DeVry College of Technology/North Brunswick, NJ
DeVry Institute of Technology/New York, NY
DeVry University/Addison (DuPage County), IL
DeVry University/Alpharetta, GA
DeVry University/Chicago, IL
DeVry University/Colorado Springs, CO
DeVry University/Columbus, OH
DeVry University/Dallas, TX
DeVry University/Decatur, GA
DeVry University/Fort Washington, PA
DeVry University/Fremont, CA
DeVry University/Kansas City, MO
DeVry University/Long Beach, CA
DeVry University/Miramar, FL
DeVry University/Orlando, FL
DeVry University/Phoenix, AZ

DeVry University/Pomona, CA
DeVry University/Seattle, WA
DeVry University/Tinley Park, IL
DeVry University/West Hills, CA
DeVry University/Westminster, CO
Dominican College, NY
Dowling College, NY
Eastern Nazarene College, MA
East-West University, IL
Edinboro University of Pennsylvania, PA
Edward Waters College, FL
Elizabeth City State University, NC
Fairmont State, WV
Fayetteville State University, NC
Ferrum College, VA
Florida Memorial College, FL
Friends University, KS
Georgian Court College, NJ
Golden Gate University, CA
Grand Canyon University, AZ
Hesser College, NH
Hilbert College, NY
Husson College, ME
Huston-Tillotson University, TX
Indiana University East, IN
Indiana University Kokomo, IN
Indiana University Northwest, IN
Indiana University South Bend, IN
Indiana University Southeast, IN
Indiana University-Purdue University Fort Wayne, IN
Jacksonville State University, AL
Johnson and Wales University/Charlotte Campus, NC
Johnson and Wales University/Denver Campus, CO
Johnson and Wales University/North Miami Campus, FL
Johnson and Wales University/Providence Campus, RI
Johnson State College, VT
Kentucky State University, KY
Keystone College, PA
Knoxville College, TN
La Roche College, PA
Lake Superior State University, MI
Lamar University, TX
Langston University, OK
LeMoyne-Owen College, TN
Lindsey Wilson College, KY
Livingstone College, NC
Lock Haven University of Pennsylvania, PA
Lourdes College, OH
Lyndon State College, VT
Marian College of Fond du Lac, WI
Mars Hill College, NC
Massachusetts College of Liberal Arts, MA
McMurry University, TX
McNeese State University, LA
Metropolitan State College of Denver, CO
MidAmerica Nazarene University, KS
Midwestern State University, TX
Minnesota State University, Mankato, MN
Minnesota State University, Moorhead, MN
Minot State University, ND
Mississippi University for Women, MS
Monroe College, NY
Morris College, SC
Mount Aloysius College, PA
Mount Ida College, MA
Mount Olive College, NC
National-Louis University, IL
Neumann College, PA
New Jersey City University, NJ
Newberry College, SC

Nichols College, MA
Norfolk State University, VA
North Carolina Agricultural and Technical State University, NC
North Carolina Central University, NC
North Central University, MN
Northeastern State University, OK
Northern Michigan University, MI
Northwood University, MI
Northwood University, TX
Notre Dame de Namur University, CA
Ottawa University, KS
Our Lady of Holy Cross College, LA
Our Lady of the Lake University of San Antonio, TX
Paine College, GA
Paul Quinn College, TX
Pennsylvania College of Technology, PA
Philander Smith College, AR
Pine Manor College, MA
Plymouth State University, NH
Prairie View A&M University, TX
Prescott College, AZ
Presentation College, SD
Purdue University/Calumet, IN
Regis College, MA
Saint Augustine's College, NC
Saint Bonaventure University, NY
Saint Francis College, NY
Saint Francis University, PA
Saint Peter's College, NJ
Saint Thomas Aquinas College, NY
Salem State College, MA
Savannah State University, GA
Shaw University, NC
Sheldon Jackson College, AK
Shimer College, IL
Siena Heights University, MI
Silver Lake College of the Holy Family, WI
Slippery Rock University of Pennsylvania, PA
Sojourner-Douglass College, MD
South Carolina State University, SC
South University, GA
Southeastern Louisiana University, LA
Southeastern University, FL
Southern Christian University, AL
Southern University and A&M College, LA
Southern Vermont College, VT

Southwestern Adventist University, TX
Stillman College, AL
Sul Ross State University, TX
Talladega College, AL
Tennessee State University, TN
Texas A&M University at Corpus Christi, TX
Texas A&M University at Kingsville, TX
Texas Woman's University, TX
Thomas College, ME
Tiffin University, OH
Trinity College, DC
Tusculum College, TN
Tuskegee University, AL
University of Alaska Southeast, AK
University of Bridgeport, CT
University of Maine at Fort Kent, ME
University of Maine at Presque Isle, ME
University of Minnesota/Crookston, MN
University of North Carolina at Pembroke, NC
University of Pittsburgh at Johnstown, PA
University of South Alabama, AL
University of South Carolina at Aiken, SC
University of Southern Indiana, IN
University of Texas at Arlington, TX
University of Texas at San Antonio, TX
University of the District of Columbia, DC
University of Wisconsin/Milwaukee, WI
University of Wisconsin/Oshkosh, WI
University of Wisconsin/Parkside, WI
University of Wisconsin/River Falls, WI
Valley City State University, ND
Virginia Intermont College, VA
Virginia Union University, VA
Voorhees College, SC
Warner Southern College, FL
Webber International University, FL
West Liberty State College, WV
Western New Mexico University, NM
Wilberforce University, OH
Wiley College, TX
William Carey College, MS
William Penn University, IA
Winston-Salem State University, NC
Woodbury College, VT
Woodbury University, CA
Wright State University, OH

NONCOMPETITIVE

The colleges in this category generally only require evidence of graduation from an accredited high school (although they may also require completion of a certain number of high school units). Some require that entrance examinations be taken for placement purposes only, or only by graduates of unaccredited high schools or only by out-of-state students. In some cases, insufficient capacity may compel a college in this category to limit the number of students that are accepted; generally, however, if a college accepts 98% or more of its applicants, it automatically falls in this category. Colleges are also rated Noncompetitive if they admit all state residents, but have some requirements for nonresidents.

Allen University, SC
American InterContinental University, GA
Angelo State University, TX
Arkansas Baptist College, AR
Auburn University Montgomery, AL
Baker College of Flint, MI
Belhaven College, MS
Bellevue University, NE
Bethel College, TN
Bryn Athyn College of the New Church, PA
Calvin College, MI
Cameron University, OK
Cascade College, OR
Chadron State College, NE
City University, WA
City University of New York/College of Staten Island, NY
City University of New York/Medgar Evers College, NY
City University of New York/New York City College of Technology, NY
City University of New York/York College, NY
Cleveland State University, OH
College of Saint Joseph, VT
Concordia College, AL
Cornerstone University and Grand Rapids Theological Seminary, MI
Davenport University, MI
Dickinson State University, ND
Eastern Oregon University, OR
Freed-Hardeman University, TN
Glenville State College, WV
Grambling State University, LA
Heritage University, WA
Holy Names College, CA
Hope International University, CA
Humphreys College, CA
International College, FL
Jamestown College, ND
Jarvis Christian College, TX
Kendall College, IL
Lee University, TN
Lincoln University, MO
Louisiana State University in Shreveport, LA
Marylhurst University, OR
Mayville State University, ND
Mercy College, NY
Miles College, AL
Missouri Southern State University, MO
Missouri Western State University, MO
Montana State University-Northern, MT
Mountain State University, WV
National American University, SD
New College of California, CA
New Mexico Highlands University, NM

Nicholls State University, LA
Northern Kentucky University, KY
Northwestern College, MN
Northwestern Oklahoma State University, OK
Oakland City University, IN
Oglala Lakota College, SD
Ohio State University at Lima, OH
Ohio State University at Mansfield, OH
Ohio State University at Marion, OH
Ohio State University at Newark, OH
Oklahoma Christian University, OK
Oklahoma Panhandle State University, OK
Oklahoma Wesleyan University, OK
Peirce College, PA
Peru State College, NE
Pikeville College, KY
Saint Gregory's University, OK
Saint Paul's College, VA
Shawnee State University, OH
Sinte Gleska University, SD
Southeastern University, DC
Southern Nazarene University, OK
Southern University at New Orleans, LA
Tabor College, KS
Thomas University, GA
Tougaloo College, MS
Troy University Montgomery Campus, AL
University of Akron, OH
University of Alaska Anchorage, AK
University of Arkansas at Little Rock, AR
University of Arkansas at Monticello, AR
University of Houston-Downtown, TX
University of Idaho, ID
University of Maine at Augusta, ME
University of Montana—Western, MT
University of Nebraska at Kearney, NE
University of Nevada/Reno, NV
University of Rio Grande, OH
University of Texas at El Paso, TX
University of Toledo, OH
University of Wisconsin/Platteville, WI
Walla Walla College, WA
Wartburg College, IA
Washburn University, KS
Wayne State College, NE
Weber State University, UT
West Virginia State University, WV
West Virginia University Institute of Technology, WV
William Tyndale College, MI
Wilmington College, DE
Wilmington College, OH
York College, NE
Youngstown State University, OH

SPECIAL

Listed here are colleges whose programs of study are specialized; professional schools of art, music, nursing, and other disciplines. In general, the admissions requirements are not based primarily on academic criteria, but on evidence of talent or special interest in the field. Many other colleges and universities offer special-interest programs *in addition* to regular academic curricula, but such institutions have been given a regular competitive rating based on academic criteria. Schools oriented toward working adults have also been assigned this rating.

Albany College of Pharmacy, NY
Allen College, IA
Art Academy of Cincinnati, OH
Art Center College of Design, CA
Art Institute of Atlanta, GA
Art Institute of Boston at Lesley University, MA
Art Institute of Portland, OR
Atlanta College of Art, GA
Baltimore Hebrew University, MD
Benjamin Franklin Institute of Technology, MA
Berklee College of Music, MA
Boston Architectural Center, MA
Boston Conservatory, MA
Burlington College, VT
Cabarrus College of Health Sciences, NC
California College of the Arts, CA
California Institute of the Arts, CA
Cambridge College, MA
Charter Oak State College, CT
Cincinnati College of Mortuary Science, OH
Cleveland Institute of Art, OH
Cleveland Institute of Music, OH
College for Creative Studies, MI
College of New Rochelle - School of New Resources, NY
College of Visual Arts, MN
Columbus College of Art and Design, OH
Corcoran School of Art and Design, DC
Cornish College of the Arts, WA
Curtis Institute of Music, PA
Deaconess College of Nursing, MO
Eastman School of Music, NY
Excelsior College, NY
Five Towns College, NY
Florida Hospital College of Health Sciences, FL
Franklin University, OH
Gallaudet University, DC
Granite State College, NH
Harris-Stowe State College, MO
Henry Cogswell College, WA
Jewish Hospital College of Nursing and Allied Health, MO
Juilliard School, NY
Kansas City Art Institute, MO
Kendall College of Art and Design of Ferris State University, MI
Laboratory Institute of Merchandising, NY

Laguna College of Art and Design, CA
Lester L. Cox College of Nursing and Health Sciences, MO
Maine College of Art, ME
Manhattan School of Music, NY
Mannes College of Music, NY
Martin University, IN
Maryland Institute College of Art, MD
Massachusetts College of Art, MA
Massachusetts College of Pharmacy and Health Sciences, MA
Memphis College of Art, TN
Mercy College of Health Sciences, IA
Metropolitan State University, MN
Milwaukee Institute of Art and Design, WI
Minneapolis College of Art and Design, MN
Montserrat College of Art, MA
Moore College of Art and Design, PA
NAES College of Eastern Illinios University, IL
Naropa University, CO
National University, CA
Nebraska Methodist College of Nursing and Allied Health, NE
New England Conservatory of Music, MA
North Carolina School of the Arts, NC
Otis College of Art and Design, CA
Pacific Northwest College of Art, OR
Parsons School of Design, NY
Pratt Institute, NY
Research College of Nursing, MO
Rhode Island School of Design, RI
Ringling School of Art and Design, FL
San Francisco Art Institute, CA
San Francisco Conservatory of Music, CA
Savannah College of Art and Design, GA
School of the Art Institute of Chicago, IL
School of Visual Arts, NY
State University of New York/Empire State College, NY
Strayer University, DC
Thomas Edison State College, NJ
Trinity College of Nursing and Health Sciences, IL
Union Institute & University, OH
University of Maryland/University College, MD
University of the Arts, PA
VanderCook College of Music, IL
Vaughn College of Aeronautics and Technology, NY
Westminster Choir College, NJ

THE BASICS

Some 1700 U.S. colleges and universities, public and private college systems, and Canadian and other foreign universities are described in detail in the Profiles that follow.

The Choice of Schools

Colleges and universities in this country may achieve recognition from a number of professional organizations, but we have based our choice of U.S. colleges on accreditation from the U.S. regional accrediting associations.

Accreditation amounts to a stamp of approval given to a college. The accreditation process evaluates institutions and programs to determine whether they meet established standards of educational quality. The regional associations listed below supervise an aspect of the accrediting procedure—the study of a detailed report submitted by the institution applying for accreditation, and then an inspection visit by members of the accrediting agency. The six agencies are associated with the Commission on Recognition of Postsecondary Accreditation (CORPA). They include:

Middle States Association of Colleges and Schools
New England Association of Schools and Colleges
North Central Association of Colleges and Schools
Northwest Commission on Colleges and Universities
Southern Association of Colleges and Schools
Western Association of Schools and Colleges

Getting accreditation for the first time can take a school several years. To acknowledge that schools have begun this process, the agencies accord them candidate status. Most candidates eventually are awarded full accreditation.

The U.S. schools included in this book are fully accredited or are candidates for that status. If the latter is the case, it is indicated below the address of the school. Because the U.S. regional accrediting bodies do not officially accredit Canadian colleges and universities, and because there is no equivalent accrediting system in Canada, we have chosen to include only the larger, English-language Canadian schools—those with total full-time undergraduate enrollment of more than 10,000. It should be understood that size in no way relates to quality; there are many excellent Canadian colleges and universities with fewer than 10,000 students.

Four-Year Colleges Only

This book presents Profiles for all accredited four-year colleges that grant bachelor's degrees and admit freshmen with no previous college experience. Most of these colleges also accept transfer students. Profiles of upper-division schools, which offer only the junior or senior year of undergraduate study, are not included, nor are junior or community colleges.

Consistent Entries

Each Profile of a U.S. college is organized in the same way; the only Profiles that vary are those of Canada, schools abroad, and religious schools. The following discussion applies to the U.S. college Profiles, but refers to the other Profiles as well.

Every Profile begins with a capsule and is followed by separate sections covering the campus environment, student life, programs of study, admissions, financial aid, information for international students, computers, graduates, and the admissions contact. These categories are always introduced in the same sequence, so you can find data and compare specific points easily. The following commentary will help you evaluate and interpret the information given for each college.

Data Collection

Barron's *Profiles of American Colleges* was first published in 1964. Since then, it has been revised almost every year; comprehensive revisions are undertaken every two years. Such frequent updating is necessary because so much information about colleges—particularly enrollment figures, costs, programs of study, and admissions standards—changes rapidly.

The facts in the capsule portion of each Profile in this edition were gathered in the fall of 2005 and apply to the 2005–2006 academic year. Figures on tuition and room-and-board costs generally change soon after the book is published. For the most up-to-date information on such items, you should always check with the colleges. Other information—such as the basic nature of the school, its campus, and the educational goals of its students—changes less rapidly. A few new programs of study might be added or new services made available, but the basic educational offerings generally will remain constant.

THE CAPSULE

The capsule of each Profile provides basic information about the college at a glance. An explanation of the standard capsule is shown in the accompanying box.

All toll-free phone numbers are presumed to be out-of-state or both in-state and out-of-state, unless noted.

A former name is given if the name has been changed recently. To use the map code to the right of the college name, turn to the appropriate college-locator map at the beginning of each chapter. Wherever "n/av" is used in the capsule, it means the information was not available. The abbreviation "n/app" means not applicable.

Full-time, Part-time, Graduate

Enrollment figures are the clearest indication of the size of a college, and show whether or not it is coeducational and what the

---

COMPLETE NAME OF SCHOOL
(Former Name, if any)
City, State, Zip Code
(Accreditation Status, if a candidate)

MAP CODE

Fax and Phone Numbers

Full-time: Full-time undergraduate enrollment
Part-time: Part-time undergraduate enrollment
Graduate: Graduate enrollment
Year: Semesters, quarters, summer sessions
Application Deadline: Fall admission deadline

Faculty: Number of full-time faculty; AAUP category of school, salary-level symbol
Ph.D.s: Percentage of faculty holding Ph.D.
Student/Faculty: Full-time student/full-time faculty ratio
Tuition: Yearly tuition and fees (out-of-state if different)
Room & Board: Yearly room-and-board costs

Freshman Class: Number of students who applied, number accepted, number enrolled
SAT: Median Verbal, Median Math*

ACT: Median composite ACT

IMPORTANT NOTE: At press time, median SAT scores were only available for classes admitted based on the SAT I, which had only verbal and math sections.

ADMISSIONS SELECTOR RATING

male-female ratio is. Graduate enrollment is presented to give a better idea of the size of the entire student body; some schools have far more graduate students enrolled than undergraduates.

Year

Some of the more innovative college calendars include the 4-1-4, 3-2-3, 3-3-1, and 1-3-1-4-3 terms. College administrators sometimes utilize various intersessions or interims—special short terms—for projects, independent study, short courses, or travel programs. The early semester calendar, which allows students to finish spring semesters earlier than those of the traditional semester calendar, gives students a head start on finding summer jobs. A modified semester (4-1-4) system provides a January or winter term, approximately four weeks long, for special projects that usually earn the same credit as one semester-long course. The trimester calendar divides the year into three equal parts; students may attend college during all three but generally take a vacation during any one. The quarter calendar divides the year into four equal parts; students usually attend for three quarters each year. The capsule also indicates schools that offer a summer session.

Application Deadline

Indicated here is the deadline for applications for admission to the fall semester. If there are no specific deadlines, it will say "open." Application deadlines for admission to other semesters are, where available, given in the admissions section of the profile.

Faculty

The first number given refers to the number of full-time faculty members at the college or university.

The Roman numeral and symbol that follow represent the salary level of faculty at the entire institution as compared with faculty salaries nationally. This information is based on the salary report* published by the American Association of University Professors (AAUP). The Roman numeral refers to the AAUP category to which the particular college or university is assigned. (This allows for comparison of faculty salaries at the same types of schools.) Category I includes "institutions that offer the doctorate degree, and that conferred in the most recent three years an annual average of fifteen or more earned doctorates covering a minimum of three nonrelated disciplines." Category IIA includes "institutions awarding degrees above the baccalaureate, but not included in Category I." Category IIB includes "institutions awarding only the baccalaureate or equivalent degree." Category III includes "institutions with academic ranks, mostly two-year institutions." Category IV includes "institutions without academic ranks." (With the exception of a few liberal arts colleges, this category includes mostly two-year institutions.)

The symbol that follows the Roman numeral indicates into which percentile range the average salary of professors, associate professors, assistant professors, and instructors at the school falls, as compared with other schools in the same AAUP category. The symbols used in this book represent the following:

++$	95th percentile and above
+$	80th–94.9th percentile
av$	60th–79.9th percentile
–$	40th–59.9th percentile
––$	39.9th percentile and below

If the school is not a member of AAUP, nothing will appear.

Ph.D.s

The figure here indicates the percentage of full-time faculty who have Ph.D.s or the highest terminal degree.

*Source: Annual Report on the Economic Status of the Profession published in the March-April 2005 issue of *Academe:* Bulletin of the AAUP, 1012 Fourteenth St. N.W., Suite 500, Washington, D.C. 20005.

Student/Faculty

Student/faculty ratios may be deceptive because the faculties of many large universities include scholars and scientists who do little or no teaching. Nearly every college has some large lecture classes, usually in required or popular subjects, and many small classes in advanced or specialized fields. Here, the ratio reflects full-time students and full-time faculty, and some colleges utilize the services of a large part-time faculty. Additionally, some institutions factor in an FTE component in determining this ratio. We do not, and thus the Student/Faculty ratio that we report may differ somewhat from what the college reports. In general, a student/faculty ratio of 10 to 1 is very good.

If the faculty and student body are both mostly part-time, the entry will say "n/app."

Tuition

It is important to remember that tuition costs change continually and that in many cases, these changes are substantial. Particularly heavy increases have occurred recently and will continue to occur. On the other hand, some smaller colleges are being encouraged to lower tuitions, in order to make higher education more affordable. Students are therefore urged to contact individual colleges for the most current tuition figures.

The figure given here includes tuition and student fees for the school's standard academic year. If costs differ for state residents and out-of-state residents, the figure for nonresidents is given in parentheses. Where tuition costs are listed per credit hour (p/c), per course (p/course), or per unit (p/unit), student fees are not included. In some university systems, tuition is the same for all schools. However, student fees, and therefore the total tuition figure, may vary from school to school.

Room and Board

It is suggested that students check with individual schools for the most current room-and-board figures because, like tuition figures, they increase continually. The room-and-board figures given here represent the annual cost of a double room and all meals. The word "none" indicates that the college does not charge for room and board; "n/app" indicates that room and board are not provided.

Freshman Class

The numbers apply to the number of students who applied, were accepted, and enrolled in the 2005–2006 freshman class or in a recent class.

SAT, ACT

Whenever available, the median SAT I scores—both Verbal and Mathematics—and the median ACT composite score for the 2005–2006 freshman class are given. If the school has not reported median SAT I or ACT scores, the capsule indicates whether the SAT or ACT is required. Note: Test scores are reported for mainstream students.

At press time, median SAT scores were only available for classes admitted based on the SAT I exam, which had only two section (Verbal and Math). This should provide a basis for estimating similar scores on the new SAT, which also includes a writing section and essay.

Admissions Selector Rating

The College Admissions Selector Rating indicates the degree of competitiveness of admission to the college.

THE GENERAL DESCRIPTION

The Introductory Paragraph

This paragraph indicates, in general, what types of programs the college offers, when it was founded, whether it is public or private, and its religious affiliation. Baccalaureate program accreditation and information on the size of the school's library collection are also provided.

In evaluating the size of the collection, keep in mind the difference between college and university libraries: A university's graduate and professional schools require many specialized books that would be of no value to an undergraduate. For a university, a ratio of one undergraduate to 500 books generally means an outstanding library, one to 200 an adequate library, one to 100 an inferior library. For a college, a ratio of one to 400 is outstanding, one to 300 superior, one to 200 adequate, one to 50 inferior.

These figures are somewhat arbitrary, because a large university with many professional schools or campuses requires more books than a smaller university. Furthermore, a recently founded college would be expected to have fewer books than an older school, since it has not inherited from the past what might be a great quantity of outdated and useless books. Most libraries can make up for deficiencies through interlibrary loans.

The ratio of students to the number of subscriptions to periodicals is less meaningful, and again, a university requires more periodicals than a college. But for a university, subscription to more than 15,000 periodicals is outstanding, and 6000 is generally more than adequate. For a college, 1500 subscriptions is exceptional, 700 very good, and 400 adequate. Subscription to fewer than 200 periodicals generally implies an inferior library with a very tight budget. Microform items are assuming greater importance within a library's holdings, and this information is included when available. Services of a Learning Resource Center and special facilities, such as a museum, radio or TV station, and Internet access are also described in this paragraph.

This paragraph also provides information on the campus: its size, the type of area in which it is located, and its proximity to a large city.

At most institutions, the existence of classrooms, administrative offices, and dining facilities may be taken for granted, and they generally are not mentioned in the entries unless they have been recently constructed or are considered exceptional.

Student Life

This section, with subdivisions that detail housing, campus activities, sports, facilities for disabled students, services offered to students, and campus safety concentrates on the everyday life of students.

The introductory paragraph, which includes various characteristics of the student body, gives an idea of the mix of attitudes and backgrounds. It includes, where available, percentages of students from out-of-state and from private or public high schools. It also indicates what percentage of the students belong to minority groups and what percentages are Protestant, Catholic, and Jewish. Finally, it tells the average age of all enrolled freshmen and of all undergraduates, and gives data on the freshman dropout rate and the percentage of freshmen who remain to graduate.

Housing. Availability of on-campus housing is described here. If you plan to live on campus, note the type, quantity, and capacity of the dormitory accommodations. Some colleges provide dormitory rooms for freshmen, but require upperclass students to make their own arrangements to live in fraternity or sorority houses, off-campus apartments, or rented rooms in private houses. Some small colleges require all students who do not live with parents or other relatives to live on campus. And some colleges have no residence halls.

This paragraph tells whether special housing is available and whether campus housing is single-sex or coed. It gives the percentage of those who live on campus and those who remain on campus on weekends. Finally, it states if alcohol is not permitted on campus and whether students may keep cars on campus.

Activities. Campus organizations play a vital part in students' social lives. This subsection lists types of activities, including student government, special interest or academic clubs, fraternities and sororities, and cultural and popular campus events sponsored at the college.

Sports. Sports are important on campus, so we indicate the extent of the athletic program by giving the number of intercollegiate and intramural sports offered for men and for women. We have also included the athletic and recreation facilities and campus stadium seating capacity.

Disabled Students. The colleges' own estimates of how accessible their campuses are to the physically disabled are provided. This information should be considered along with the specific kinds of special facilities available. If a Profile does not include a subsection on the disabled, the college did not provide the information.

Services. Services that may be available to students—free or for a fee—include counseling, tutoring, remedial instruction, and reader service for the blind.

Safety. This section lists the safety and security measures that are in place on the campus. These vary among schools, but may include 24-hour foot and vehicle patrol, self-defense education, security escort services, shuttle buses, informal discussions, pamphlets/posters/films, emergency telephones, and lighted pathways/sidewalks.

Programs of Study

Listed here are the bachelor's degrees granted, strongest and most popular majors, and whether associate, master's, and doctoral degrees are awarded. Major areas of study have been included under broader general areas (shown in capital letters in the profiles) for quicker reference; however, the general areas do not necessarily correspond to the academic divisions of the college or university but are more career-oriented.

Required. Wherever possible, information on specific required courses and distribution requirements is supplied, in addition to the number of credits or hours required for graduation. If the college requires students to maintain a certain grade point average (GPA) or pass comprehensive exams to graduate, that also is given.

Special. Special programs are described here. Students at almost every college now have the opportunity to study abroad, either through their college or through other institutions. Internships with businesses, schools, hospitals, and public agencies permit students to gain work experience as they learn. The pass/fail grading option, now quite prevalent, allows students to take courses in unfamiliar areas without threatening their academic average. Many schools offer students the opportunity to earn a combined B.A.-B.S. degree, pursue a general studies (no major) degree, or design their own major. Frequently students may take advantage of a cooperative program offered by two or more universities. Such a program might be referred to, for instance, as a 3-2 engineering program; a student in this program would spend three years at one institution and two at another. The number of national honor societies represented on campus is included. Schools also may conduct honors programs for qualified students, either university-wide or in specific major fields, and these also are listed.

Faculty/Classroom. The percentage of male and female faculty is mentioned here if provided by the college, along with the percentage of introductory courses taught by graduate students (if any). The average class size in an introductory lecture, laboratory, and regular class offering may also be indicated.

Admissions

The admissions section gives detailed information on standards so you can evaluate your chances for acceptance. Where the SAT I or ACT scores of the 2005–2006 freshman class are broken down, you may compare your own scores. Because the role of standardized tests in the admissions process has been subject to criticism, more colleges are considering other factors such as recommendations from high school officials, leadership record, special talents, extracurricular activities, and advanced placement or honors courses completed. A few schools may consider education of parents, ability to pay for college, and relationship to alumni. Some give preference to state residents; others seek a geographically diverse student body.

If a college indicates that it follows an open admissions policy, it is noncompetitive and generally accepts all applicants who meet certain basic requirements, such as graduation from an accredited high school. If a college has rolling admissions, it decides on each application as soon as possible if the applicant's file is complete and does not specify a notification deadline. As a general rule, it is best to submit applications as early as possible.

Some colleges offer special admissions programs for nontraditional applicants. Early admissions programs allow students to begin college either during the summer before their freshman year or during what would have been their last year of high school; in the latter case, a high school diploma is not required. These programs are designed for students who are emotionally and educationally prepared for college at an earlier age than usual.

Deferred admissions plans permit students to spend a year at another activity, such as working or traveling, before beginning college. Students who take advantage of this option can relax during the year off, because they already have been accepted at a college and have a space reserved. During the year off from study, many students become clearer about their educational goals, and they perform better when they do begin study.

Early decision plans allow students to be notified by their first-choice school during the first term of the senior year. This plan may eliminate the anxiety of deciding whether or not to send a deposit to a second-choice college that offers admission before the first-choice college responds.

Requirements. This subsection specifies the minimum high school class rank and GPA, if any, required by the college for freshman applicants. It indicates what standardized tests (if any) are required, specifically the SAT or ACT, or for Puerto Rican schools, the CEEB (the Spanish-language version of the SAT). Additional requirements are given such as whether an essay, interview, or audition is necessary, and if AP*/CLEP credit is given. If a college accepts applications on computer disk or on-line, those facts are so noted and described. Other factors used by the school in the admissions decision are also listed.

Procedure. This subsection indicates when you should take entrance exams, the application deadlines for various sessions, the application fee, and when students are notified of the admissions decision. Some schools note that their application deadlines are open; this can mean either that they will consider applications until a class is filled, or that applications are considered right up until registration for the term in which the student wishes to enroll. If a waiting list is an active part of the admissions procedure, the college may indicate the number of applicants placed on that list and the number of wait-listed applicants accepted.

Transfer. Nearly every college admits some transfer students. These students may have earned associate degrees at two-year colleges and want to continue their education at a four-year college or wish to attend a different school. One important thing to consider when transferring is how many credits earned at one school will be accepted at another, so entire semesters won't be spent making up lost work. Because most schools require students to spend a specified number of hours in residence to earn a degree, it is best not to wait too long to transfer if you decide to do so.

Visiting. Some colleges hold special orientation programs for prospective students to give them a better idea of what the school is like. Many also will provide guides for informal visits, often allowing students to spend a night in the residence halls. You should make arrangements with the college before visiting.

Financial Aid

This paragraph in each Profile describes the availability of financial aid. It includes the percentage of freshmen and continuing students who receive aid, the average freshman award, and average and maximum amounts for various types of need-based and non-need-based financial aid. Aid application deadlines and required forms are also indicated.

International Students

This section begins by telling how many of the school's students come from outside the United States. It tells which English proficiency exam, if any, applicants must take. Any necessary college entrance exams, including SAT Subject tests, are listed.

Computers

This section details the scope of computerized facilities that are available for academic use. Limitations (if any) on student use of computer facilities are outlined. It also gives information on the required or recommended ownership of a PC.

Graduates

This section gives the number of graduates in the 2004–2005 class, the most popular majors and percentage of graduates earning degrees in those fields, and the percentages of graduates in the 2004 class who enrolled in graduate school or found employment within 6 months of graduation.

Admissions Contact

This is the name or title of the person to whom all correspondence regarding your application should be sent. Internet addresses are included here, along with the availability of a video of the campus.

---

* Advanced Placement and AP are registered trademarks owned by the College Entrance Examination Board. No endorsement of this product is implied or given.

PROFILES OF

AMERICAN

COLLEGES

ALABAMA

POPULATION
DENSITY
• 25,000 and over

0 20 40 60 80 100
Miles

ALABAMA AGRICULTURAL AND MECHANICAL UNIVERSITY

C-1

Normal, AL 35762

(256) 372-5245
(800) 553-0816; Fax: (256) 372-9747

Full-time: 2000 men, 2000 women	Faculty: 150; IIA, --$
Part-time: 175 men, 200 women	Ph.D.s: 70%
Graduate: 375 men, 800 women	Student/Faculty: 27 to 1
Year: semesters, summer session	Tuition: $4420 ($8320)
Application Deadline: July 15	Room & Board: $4700
Freshman Class: n/av	
SAT or ACT: required	LESS COMPETITIVE

Alabama Agricultural and Mechanical University, founded in 1875, is a public land-grant institution offering undergraduate and graduate studies in agriculture, home economics, arts and sciences, business, education, engineering, and technology. Most figures in above capsule and in this profile are approximate. There are 5 undergraduate schools and 1 graduate school. In addition to regional accreditation, A&M has baccalaureate program accreditation with ABET, ADA, AHEA, CSWE, FIDER, and NCATE. The library contains 253,620 volumes, 48,300 microform items, and 3010 audio/video tapes/CDs/DVDs, and subscribes to 2070 periodicals including electronic. Computerized library services include the card catalog, interlibrary loans, and database searching. Special learning facilities include a learning resource center, art gallery, radio station, TV station, and State Black Archives. The 2001-acre campus is in a suburban area 90 miles north of Birmingham and 95 miles south of Nashville. Including any residence halls, there are 55 buildings.

Student Life: 70% of undergraduates are from Alabama. Others are from 42 states, 29 foreign countries, and Canada. 90% are from public schools. 90% are African American. Most are Protestant. The average age of freshmen is 18; all undergraduates, 20. 30% do not continue beyond their first year; 60% remain to graduate.

Housing: 3100 students can be accommodated in college housing, which includes single-sex dorms. On-campus housing is guaranteed for all 4 years. 60% of students live on campus; of those, 60% remain on campus on weekends. Alcohol is not permitted. All students may keep cars.

Activities: 7% of men belong to 4 national fraternities; 9% of women belong to 4 national sororities. There are 109 groups on campus, including band, cheerleading, choir, chorus, computers, dance, debate, drama, drill team, ethnic, forensics, honors, international, jazz band, marching band, newspaper, orchestra, pep band, political, professional, radio and TV, religious, social, student government, symphony, and yearbook. Popular campus events include Magic City Classic, Women's Week, and Men's Week.

Sports: There are 7 intercollegiate sports for men and 7 for women, and 7 intramural sports for men and 7 for women. Facilities include a 7000-seat gym, an Olympic-size pool, track and playing fields, and a 21,000-seat stadium/health education complex.

Disabled Students: 95% of the campus is accessible. Wheelchair ramps, elevators, special parking, specially equipped rest rooms, and lowered drinking fountains are available.

Services: Counseling and information services are available, as is tutoring in most subjects. There is a reader service for the blind.

Campus Safety and Security: Measures include 24-hour foot and vehicle patrol, self-defense education, security escort services, and informal discussions. There are pamphlets/posters/films and lighted pathways/sidewalks.

Programs of Study: A&M confers B.A., B.S., B.S.C.E., B.S.E.E., B.S.E.T., B.S.M.E., and B.S.W. degrees. Associate, master's, and doctoral degrees are also awarded. Bachelor's degrees are awarded in AGRICULTURE (agricultural business management, agricultural economics, agronomy, animal science, forestry and related sciences, horticulture, and soil science), BIOLOGICAL SCIENCE (biology/biological science, nutrition, and zoology), BUSINESS (accounting, banking and finance, business administration and management, marketing/retailing/merchandising, and office supervision and management), COMMUNICATIONS AND THE ARTS (art, dramatic arts, English, French, linguistics, and telecommunications), COMPUTER AND PHYSICAL SCIENCE (chemistry, computer science, mathematics, and physics), EDUCATION (agricultural, art, early childhood, elementary, home economics, industrial arts, middle school, music, physical, science, secondary, special, and trade and industrial), ENGINEERING AND ENVIRONMENTAL DESIGN (city/community/regional planning, civil engineering, civil engineering technology, drafting and design technology, electrical/electronics engineering, electrical/electronics engineering technology, environmental science, industrial engineering technology, mechanical engineering, and mechanical engineering technology), HEALTH PROFESSIONS (medical laboratory technology, preveterinary science, and speech pathology/audiology), SOCIAL SCIENCE (economics, family/consumer studies, food science, history, human development, political science/government, psychology, social work, and sociology). Physics, food science, and teacher education are the strongest academically. Business administration, education, and computer science are the largest.

Required: All students are required to take at least 52 hours of general studies, including phys ed, music, and art, and to maintain a minimum GPA of 2.0. Students must complete a total of 120 to 126 credit hours, with 30 to 36 in the major. A comprehensive exam is required for some majors.

Special: Co-op programs with Georgia Institute of Technology and Tuskegee University, cross-registration with the University of Alabama in Huntsville, Oakwood College, Calhoun Community College, and Athens State College, internships with various government agencies, dual majors, and work-study programs are available. There is a 3-2 engineering degree program with Georgia Institute of Technology. There are 5 national honor societies, a freshman honors program, and 5 departmental honors programs.

Faculty/Classroom: 70% of faculty are male; 30%, female. 50% teach undergraduates, 30% do research, and 30% do both. No introductory courses are taught by graduate students. The average class size in an introductory lecture is 90; in a laboratory, 20; and in a regular course, 30.

Requirements: The SAT or ACT is required. Applicants must have 4 years each of English, math, science, social studies, and history. An interview is recommended. The GED is accepted. A GPA of 2.0 is required. AP and CLEP credits are accepted. Important factors in the admissions decision are advanced placement or honor courses, leadership record, and recommendations by school officials.

Procedure: Freshmen are admitted to all sessions. There are early decision, early admissions, and deferred admissions plans. Applications should be filed by July 15 for fall entry, December 1 for spring entry, and May 15 for summer entry, along with a $10 fee. Notification is sent on a rolling basis. Applications are accepted on-line.

Transfer: Transfer students must have a minimum GPA of 2.0 and have earned at least 12 semester credit hours. 30 of 128 credits required for the bachelor's degree must be completed at A&M.

Visiting: There are regularly scheduled orientations for prospective students, consisting of sessions in June, July, and November. There are guides for informal visits and visitors may stay overnight. To schedule a visit, contact Antonio Boyle, Director of Admissions at (256) 851-5248.

Financial Aid: The college's own financial statement and the CSS/Profile, FAFSA, FFS, or SFS are required. Check with the school for current application deadlines.

International Students: The school actively recruits these students. They must score satisfactorily on the written TOEFL.

Computers: All students may access the system. There are no time limits. The fee is $50. It is strongly recommended that all students have a personal computer.

Admissions Contact: Antonio Boyle, Director of Admissions. A video is available. E-mail: *aboyle@asnaam.aamu.edu* Web: *www.aamu.edu*

ALABAMA STATE UNIVERSITY   C-4

Montgomery, AL 36101-0271

(334) 229-4291
(800) 253-5037; Fax: (334) 229-4984

Full-time: 1598 men, 2360 women	**Faculty:** 226
Part-time: 179 men, 348 women	**Ph.D.s:** 60%
Graduate: 260 men, 724 women	**Student/Faculty:** 18 to 1
Year: semesters, summer session	**Tuition:** $4158 ($8166)
Application Deadline: July 30	**Room & Board:** $3500
Freshman Class: 6202 applied, 4154 accepted, 1213 enrolled	
SAT or ACT: recommended	**COMPETITIVE**

Alabama State University, founded in 1867, is a state-assisted institution offering undergraduate programs in liberal arts and sciences, business administration, education, music, social work, aerospace studies, and health science. There are 6 undergraduate schools and 1 graduate school. In addition to regional accreditation, ASU has baccalaureate program accreditation with ACBSP, ACOTE, CAAHEP CSWE, NASDTEC, NASM, and NCATE. The library contains 413,298 volumes, 2,645,183 microform items, and 42,798 audio/video tapes/CDs/DVDs, and subscribes to 2025 periodicals including electronic. Computerized library services include the card catalog, interlibrary loans, database searching, and Internet access. Special learning facilities include a learning resource center, art gallery, and radio station. The 172-acre campus is in an urban area 91 miles south of Birmingham. Including any residence halls, there are 64 buildings.

Student Life: 66% of undergraduates are from Alabama. Students are from 25 states, 14 foreign countries, and Canada. 96% are African American. The average age of freshmen is 19; all undergraduates, 23. 36% do not continue beyond their first year; 21% remain to graduate.

Housing: 2330 students can be accommodated in college housing, which includes single-sex dorms and on-campus apartments. In addition, there are honors houses. On-campus housing is available on a first-come, first-served basis. 55% of students commute. Alcohol is not permitted. All students may keep cars.

Activities: 8% of men belong to 4 national fraternities; 6% of women belong to 4 national sororities. There are 50 groups on campus, including art, band, cheerleading, choir, chorus, dance, debate, drama, drum and bugle corps, honors, international, jazz band, marching band, musical theater, newspaper, orchestra, pep band, political, professional, radio and TV, social service, student government, symphony, and yearbook. Popular campus events include Founders Day, Fall Convocation, and Honors Day Program.

Sports: There are 8 intercollegiate sports for men and 9 for women, and 6 intramural sports for men and 5 for women. Facilities include an 8000-seat acadome, a stadium, a gym, 12 tennis courts, a swimming pool, an 8-lane indoor track, and 2 weight rooms.

Disabled Students: 80% of the campus is accessible. Wheelchair ramps, elevators, special parking, specially equipped rest rooms, special class scheduling, lowered drinking fountains, lowered telephones, and semiautomatic doors are available.

Services: Counseling and information services are available, as is tutoring in some subjects, including math and English. There is remedial math, reading, and writing.

Campus Safety and Security: Measures include 24-hour foot and vehicle patrol, self-defense education, security escort services, and informal discussions. There are pamphlets/posters/films, emergency telephones, lighted pathways/sidewalks, and a campus police department with 22 officers.

Programs of Study: ASU confers B.A., B.S., B.M.E., B.S.Ed., and B.S.W. degrees. Master's and doctoral degrees are also awarded. Bachelor's degrees are awarded in BIOLOGICAL SCIENCE (biology/biological science), BUSINESS (accounting, banking and finance, business administration and management, business economics, and marketing/retailing/merchandising), COMMUNICATIONS AND THE ARTS (art, broadcasting, communications, dramatic arts, English, fine arts, French, music, and Spanish), COMPUTER AND PHYSICAL SCIENCE (chemistry, information sciences and systems, mathematics, and physics), EDUCATION (art, business, early childhood, elementary, English, foreign languages, music, secondary, social studies, and special), ENGINEERING AND ENVIRONMENTAL DESIGN (engineering and manufacturing technology), HEALTH PROFESSIONS (occupational therapy), SOCIAL SCIENCE (criminal justice, history, parks and recreation management, political science/government, psychology, social work, and sociology).

Business and education are the strongest academically. Computer information systems and elementary education are the largest.

Required: All students must complete a 42-hour core curriculum and pass an English proficiency exam and a senior comprehensive exam. A total of 120 semester hours, with at least 27 in the major, and a minimum GPA of 2.0 are required for graduation.

Special: Cooperative programs are offered in all majors, including engineering and math with Auburn University and marine biology with Dauphin Island Sea Laboratory. The Division of Aerospace Studies, in conjunction with the AFROTC curriculum, offers programs leading to a commission in the U.S. Air Force. There is a 3-2 engineering program with Auburn University, and cross enrollment is possible. Internships, dual majors, a general studies degree, work study, nondegree study, and credit for military experience are available. There are 16 national honor societies, a freshman honors program, and 9 departmental honors programs.

Faculty/Classroom: 48% of faculty are male; 52%, female. All teach undergraduates. No introductory courses are taught by graduate students. The average class size in an introductory lecture is 40; in a laboratory, 40; and in a regular course, 40.

Admissions: 67% of the 2005-2006 applicants were accepted. 4 freshmen graduated first in their class.

Requirements: The SAT or ACT is recommended. In addition, applicants should be high school graduates with at least 3 units of English and 8 units combined in math, natural sciences, social sciences, and foreign languages. An interview is recommended. A GPA of 2.0 is required. AP and CLEP credits are accepted.

Procedure: Freshmen are admitted fall, spring, and summer. Entrance exams should be taken in the fall of the senior year. There are early decision, early admissions, deferred admissions and rolling admissions plans. Applications should be filed by July 30 for fall entry, December 1 for spring entry, and May 30 for summer entry. Notification is sent on a rolling basis. Applications are accepted on-line.

Transfer: 166 transfer students enrolled in 2004-2005. A minimum college GPA of 2.0 is required. An interview is recommended. No more than 64 semester hours are accepted for credit from 2-year colleges. 30 of 120 credits required for the bachelor's degree must be completed at ASU.

Visiting: There are regularly scheduled orientations for prospective students, including visits for spring, January 5 to 7, and fall, July 6 to 11, and August 17 to 22. There are guides for informal visits. To schedule a visit, contact the Office of Admissions and Recruitment.

Financial Aid: In 2005-2006, 85% of all full-time freshmen and 78% of continuing full-time students received some form of financial aid. 72% of full-time freshmen and 65% of continuing full-time students received need-based aid. The average freshman award was $9674. 14% of undergraduates work part time. Average annual earnings from campus work are $1984. The average financial indebtedness of the 2005 graduate was $21,150. ASU is a member of CSS. The FAFSA is required. The deadline for filing freshman financial aid applications for fall entry is May 1.

International Students: There are 13 international students enrolled. They must score satisfactorily on the written TOEFL or complete ESL Level 109. They must also take the SAT or the ACT.

Computers: All students may access the system 24 hours a day.

Graduates: From July 1, 2004 to June 30, 2005, 520 bachelor's degrees were awarded. The most popular majors were computer information systems (12%), elementary education (10%), and criminal justice (9%). 88 companies recruited on campus in 2004-2005.

Admissions Contact: Danielle Kennedy-Lamar, Director of Admissions. A video is available. E-mail: *dlamar@alasu.edu* Web: *www.alasu.edu*

AUBURN UNIVERSITY SYSTEM

The Auburn University System, established in 1856, is a public system in Alabama. It is governed by a board of trustees, whose chief administrator is the president. The primary goal of the system is service through its instruction, research, and extension divisions. The main priorities are to provide a high-quality undergraduate degree at minimal cost, to expand and diversify overall research effort, and to disseminate and apply knowledge for Alabama residents use through extension and public service programs. The total enrollment of both campuses is usually about 28,000, with 1500 faculty members. Altogether there are 172 baccalaureate, 74 master's, and 39 doctoral programs offered in Auburn University System. There is a 4-year campus located in Auburn and Montgomery. Profiles of the 4-year campuses are included in this section.

AUBURN UNIVERSITY   D-3

Auburn, AL 36849-5145   (334) 844-4080; (800) 282-8769

Full-time: 8987 men, 8791 women	Faculty: 1028; I, -$
Part-time: 933 men, 543 women	Ph.D.s: 93%
Graduate: 1958 men, 2121 women	Student/Faculty: 17 to 1
Year: semesters, summer session	Tuition: $5278 ($14,878)
Application Deadline: August 1	Room & Board: $6952
Freshman Class: 14,249 applied, 11,616 accepted, 4197 enrolled	
SAT Verbal/Math: 550/560*	ACT: 24 **VERY COMPETITIVE**

Auburn University, founded in 1856, is a state-supported land grant institution offering undergraduate, first professional, and graduate degrees in agriculture, business, education, engineering, liberal arts, sciences and math, veterinary medicine, architecture/design and construction, forestry, human sciences, nursing, and pharmacy. There are 12 undergraduate schools and 1 graduate school. In addition to regional accreditation, Auburn has baccalaureate program accreditation with AACSB, AAFCS, ABET, ACEJMC, ACPE, ACS, ADA, AHEA, APA, ASLA, AVMA, CAA, CACREP, CADE, CSAB, CSWE, FIDER, NAAB, NASAD, NASM, NAST, NASPA, NCATE, NLN, and SAF. The 3 libraries contain 2,938,859 volumes, 2,670,252 microform items, and 14,760 audio/video tapes/CDs/DVDs, and subscribe to 30,355 periodicals including electronic. Computerized library services include the card catalog, interlibrary loans, database searching, and Internet access. Special learning facilities include a learning resource center, art gallery, radio station, TV station, and a nuclear science center, arboretum, electron microscope laboratory, and a museum of fine arts. The 1875-acre campus is in a small town 110 miles southwest of Atlanta, Georgia. Including any residence halls, there are 307 buildings.

Student Life: 66% of undergraduates are from Alabama. Others are from 48 states, 55 foreign countries, and Canada. 87% are from public schools. 86% are white. The average age of freshmen is 18; all undergraduates, 20. 15% do not continue beyond their first year; 62% remain to graduate.

Housing: 3080 students can be accommodated in college housing, which includes single-sex and coed dorms, on-campus apartments, married-student housing, and fraternity houses. In addition, there are honors houses. On-campus housing is available on a first-come, first-served basis. 84% of students commute. Alcohol is not permitted. All students may keep cars.

Activities: 20% of men and about 1% of women belong to 31 national fraternities; 32% of women belong to 18 national sororities. There are 300 groups on campus, including art, band, cheerleading, chess, choir, chorale, chorus, computers, dance, drama, drill team, ethnic, film, gay, honors, international, jazz band, literary magazine, marching band, musical theater, newspaper, opera, orchestra, pep band, photography, political, professional, radio and TV, religious, social, social service, student government, symphony, and yearbook. Popular campus events include Hey Day, ODK Cake Race, and pep rallies.

Sports: There are 10 intercollegiate sports for men and 12 for women, and 14 intramural sports for men and 14 for women. Facilities include a stadium, a coliseum, an athletic complex, a women's sports center, a track, a park, a student activities center, intramural field houses, racquetball, tennis, and basketball courts, a swim center, a fitness/weight room, and an aerobics-cardio theater.

Disabled Students: 80% of the campus is accessible. Wheelchair ramps, elevators, special parking, specially equipped rest rooms, special class scheduling, lowered drinking fountains, special housing, and elevators with Braille controls, wheelchair lifts, and an assistive technology lab are available.

Services: Counseling and information services are available, as is tutoring in every subject. There is a reader service for the blind.

Campus Safety and Security: Measures include 24-hour foot and vehicle patrol, self-defense education, security escort services, and shuttle buses. There are informal discussions, pamphlets/posters/films, emergency telephones, and lighted pathways/sidewalks.

Programs of Study: Auburn confers B.A., B.S., B.A.E., B.Arch, B.B.E., B.C.E., B.Che.E., B.E.E., B.F.A., B.Int. Arch., B.Int.Design, B.I.S.E., B.M.H.E., B.M.E., B.Mus.Ed., B.Sw.E., B.T.E., and B.T.M.T. degrees. Master's and doctoral degrees are also awarded. Bachelor's degrees are awarded in AGRICULTURE (agricultural business management, agriculture, animal science, fishing and fisheries, forest engineering, forestry production and processing, horticulture, poultry science, and soil science), BIOLOGICAL SCIENCE (biochemistry, biology/biological science, botany, entomology, marine biology, microbiology, molecular biology, nutrition, wildlife biology, and zoology), BUSINESS (accounting, banking and finance, business administration and management, business economics, fashion merchandising, hotel/motel and restaurant management, international business management, marketing/retailing/merchandising, personnel management, and transportation management), COMMUNICATIONS AND THE ARTS (communications, design, dramatic arts, English, French, German, industrial design, journalism, languages, public relations, Spanish, and speech/debate/rhetoric), COMPUTER AND PHYSICAL SCIENCE (applied mathematics, chemistry, computer science, geology, mathematics, and physics), EDUCATION (business, early childhood, elementary, English, foreign languages, health, home economics, industrial arts, mathematics, middle school, physical, science, secondary, social science, special, and vocational), ENGINEERING AND ENVIRONMENTAL DESIGN (aeronautical engineering, agricultural engineering, architecture, aviation administration/management, chemical engineering, civil engineering, computer engineering, construction management, electrical/electronics engineering, environmental science, interior design, landscape architecture/design, mechanical engineering, textile engineering, and textile technology), HEALTH PROFESSIONS (health care administration, medical laboratory technology, nursing, predentistry, premedicine, preoptometry, preveterinary science, and speech pathology/audiology), SOCIAL SCIENCE (anthropology, criminology, economics, food science, geography, history, home furnishings and equipment management/production/services, human development, parks and recreation management, philosophy, physical fitness/movement, political science/government, psychology, public administration, rural sociology, social work, sociology, and textiles and clothing). Engineering, business, and architecture are the strongest academically. Business, engineering, and education are the largest.

Required: All students must complete the core curriculum of 8 semester hours in science, 6 semester hours each in English composition, English literature, history, and social science, and 3 each in math, philosophy, and fine arts. Students must choose a curriculum and complete its requirements and those of the college or school with at least a 2.0 average. Total number of credit hours is at least 120; some majors require more.

Special: Opportunities are available for co-op programs, internships, work-study, and dual majors on a program-by-program basis; students should contact their advisers for specific information. A 3-2 degree is offered in conjunction with several area institutions. Other options available to students include study abroad in 30 countries, credit by exam, nondegree study, and pass/fail grading on select courses. There are 82 national honor societies, including Phi Beta Kappa, and a freshman honors program.

Faculty/Classroom: 68% of faculty are male; 32%, female. 89% teach undergraduates. Graduate students teach 21% of introductory courses. The average class size in an introductory lecture is 43; in a laboratory, 21; and in a regular course, 36.

Admissions: 82% of the 2005-2006 applicants were accepted. The SAT scores for the 2005-2006 freshman class were: Verbal--22% below 500, 51% between 500 and 599, 24% between 600 and 700, and 3% above 700; Math--13% below 500, 49% between 500 and 599, 33% between 600 and 700, and 5% above 700. The ACT scores were 17% below 21, 31% between 21 and 23, 26% between 24 and 26, 12% between 27 and 28, and 14% above 28. 43% of the current freshmen were in the top fifth of their class; 74% were in the top two fifths. There were 24 National Merit finalists and 3 semifinalists. 3 freshmen graduated first in their class.

Requirements: The SAT or ACT is required. In addition, favorable consideration for admission will be given to accredited secondary school graduates whose college ability test scores and high school grades give promise of the greatest level of success in college courses. Secondary school students planning to apply for admission are required to complete 4 years of English, 3 years each of social studies and math, and 2 years of science. Aplicants of a mature age who are not high school graduates may be considered for admission if their educational attainments are shown through testing to be equivalent to those of high school graduate. The test include the USAFI General Education Development Test, the American College Test, nad/or other tests recommended by the Admissions Committee. The Committee will consider applicants from nonaccredited high schools on an individual basis. AP and CLEP credits are accepted. Important factors in the admissions decision are advanced placement or honor courses, evidence of special talent, and parents or siblings attending the school.

Procedure: Freshmen are admitted to all sessions. Entrance exams should be taken in the spring of the junior year. There are early decision, early admissions, and deferred admissions and rolling admissions plans. Early decision applications should be filed by November 1; regular applications, by August 1 for fall entry, December 10 for spring entry, and May 1 for summer entry, along with a $25 fee. Notification is sent on a rolling basis. A waiting list is an active part of the admissions procedure. Applications are accepted on-line.

Transfer: 1928 transfer students enrolled in 2004-2005. Transfer applicants must provide official transcripts from each college attended. A satisfactory citizenship record, a minimum 2.5 GPA on all college work and eligibility to re-enter the institution last attended are required for transfer admission. All transfer students who have attempted 32 semester hours of college work have earned a cumulative 2.5 GPA in at least 20 semester hours of standard academic courses, in addition to the overall 2.5 cumulative average. These 20 semester hours must include at least 1 course in each of the following areas: English (college-level composition or literature), and natural science with a lab. 30 of 120 credits required for the bachelor's degree must be completed at Auburn.

Visiting: There are regularly scheduled orientations for prospective students, including War Eagle Days held in the fall and spring semesters offering students and their families the opportunity to meet with representatives from admissions office, financial aid, housing and residence life, various academic departments, and current students. There are guides for informal visits and visitors may sit in on classes. To schedule a visit, contact the Admissions Office at *admissions@auburn.edu*.

Financial Aid: In 2005-2006, 52% of all full-time freshmen and 55% of continuing full-time students received some form of financial aid. 24% of full-time freshmen and 30% of continuing full-time students received need-based aid. The average freshman award was $7286. Need-based scholarships or need-based grants averaged $4417; need-based self-help aid (loans and jobs) averaged $3222; non-need-based athletic scholarships averaged $13,084; and other non-need-based awards and non-need-based scholarships averaged $3047. 15% of undergraduates work part time. Average annual earnings from campus work are $3733. The average financial indebtedness of the 2005 graduate was $19,423. Auburn is a member of CSS. The FAFSA and the college's own financial statement are required. The deadline for filing freshman financial aid applications for fall entry is March 1.

International Students: There are 144 international students enrolled. The school actively recruits these students. Satisfactory scores are required on the written TOEFL and the SAT or the ACT.

Computers: Wireless access is available. All students may access the system 24 hours a day. There are no time limits and no fees.

Graduates: From July 1, 2004 to June 30, 2005, 3919 bachelor's degrees were awarded. The most popular majors were business (26%), engineering (15%), and education (9%). In an average class, 2% graduate in 3 years or less, 34% graduate in 4 years or less, 57% graduate in 5 years or less, and 62% graduate in 6 years or less. Of the 2004 graduating class, 35% were enrolled in graduate school within 6 months of graduation.

Admissions Contact: Doyle Bickers, Director of Admissions. A video is available. E-mail: *admissions@auburn.edu* Web: *www.auburn.edu*

AUBURN UNIVERSITY MONTGOMERY   C-4

Montgomery, AL 36124-4023
(334) 244-3611
(800) 227-2649; Fax: (334) 244-3795

Full-time: 980 men, 1722 women	Faculty: 186; IIA, -$
Part-time: 538 men, 1060 women	Ph.Ds: n/av
Graduate: 254 men, 574 women	Student/Faculty: 15 to 1
Year: semesters, summer session	Tuition: $4640 ($13,460)
Application Deadline: open	Room & Board: $4890
Freshman Class: 814 applied, 798 accepted, 758 enrolled	
SAT or ACT: required	NONCOMPETITIVE

Auburn University Montgomery, founded in 1967, is a public institution. There are 5 undergraduate and 4 graduate schools. In addition to regional accreditation, AUM has baccalaureate program accreditation with AACSB and NCATE. The library contains 338,238 volumes, 2,969,181 microform items, and 25,427 audio/video tapes/CDs/DVDs, and subscribes to 2278 periodicals including electronic. Computerized library services include the card catalog, interlibrary loans, database searching, and Internet access. Special learning facilities include a learning resource center, art gallery, a graphic arts center, and a mass communication lab. The 500-acre campus is in an urban area 7 miles east of downtown Montgomery. Including any residence halls, there are 50 buildings.

Student Life: 95% of undergraduates are from Alabama. Others are from 34 states, 21 foreign countries, and Canada. 60% are white; 34% African American. The average age of freshmen is 20; all undergraduates, 25.

Housing: 923 students can be accommodated in college housing, which includes single-sex and coed on-campus apartments and married-student housing. On-campus housing is available on a first-come, first-served basis. 90% of students commute. Alcohol is not permitted. All students may keep cars.

Activities: 4% of men belong to 5 national fraternities; 4% of women belong to 7 national sororities. There are 67 groups on campus, including campus activities board, cheerleading, computers, drama, ethnic, honors, international, literary magazine, professional, social service, student government, and yearbook. Popular campus events include AUM Fest and Mardi Gras Parade.

Sports: There are 4 intercollegiate sports for men and 3 for women, and 9 intramural sports for men and 7 for women. Facilities include a multipurpose gym-auditorium, an indoor jogging and walking track, baseball and soccer fields, and tennis courts.

Disabled Students: 95% of the campus is accessible. Wheelchair ramps, elevators, special parking, specially equipped rest rooms, special class scheduling, lowered drinking fountains, lowered telephones, and special housing are available.

Services: Counseling and information services are available, as is tutoring in every subject. There is a reader service for the blind, and remedial math, reading, and writing. Help with study skills is also available.

Campus Safety and Security: Measures include 24-hour foot and vehicle patrol, security escort services, informal discussions, and pamphlets/posters/films. There are emergency telephones and lighted pathways/sidewalks.

Programs of Study: AUM confers B.A., B.S., B.L.A., B.S.B.A., and B.S.N. degrees. Master's and doctoral degrees are also awarded. Bachelor's degrees are awarded in BIOLOGICAL SCIENCE (biology/biological science), BUSINESS (accounting, banking and finance, business administration and management, business economics, marketing/retailing/merchandising, and personnel management), COMMUNICATIONS AND THE ARTS (communications, English, and fine arts), COMPUTER AND PHYSICAL SCIENCE (information sciences and systems, mathematics, and physical sciences), EDUCATION (elementary and secondary), HEALTH PROFESSIONS (nursing), SOCIAL SCIENCE (criminal justice, history, international studies, liberal arts/general studies, political science/government, psychology, and sociology). Education and liberal arts are the strongest academically. Elementary education, general business, and biology are the largest.

Required: To graduate, students must complete a minimum of 120 credit hours with a minimum GPA of 2.0 in the major and overall. All students must fulfill English composition requirements and liberal education program requirements.

Special: AUM offers co-op programs in all majors, cross-registration with Alabama State University, Huntingdon College, and Faulkner University, and study abroad in England and other countries. There are 13 national honor societies, a freshman honors program, and 9 departmental honors programs.

Faculty/Classroom: 53% of faculty are male; 47%, female. The average class size in a laboratory is 22 and in a regular course, 20.

Admissions: 98% of the 2005-2006 applicants were accepted. The ACT scores for the 2005-2006 freshman class were: 65% below 21, 19% between 21 and 23, 10% between 24 and 26, 2% between 27 and 28, and 2% above 28.

Requirements: The SAT or ACT is required. In addition, high school preparation should include English, math, social studies, science, and foreign language. The GED may be used for admission. A GPA of 2.3 is required. AP and CLEP credits are accepted.

Procedure: Freshmen are admitted to all sessions. Entrance exams should be taken in the junior year. There are deferred admissions and rolling admissions plans. Application deadlines are open. Application fee is $25. Applications are accepted on-line.

Transfer: Applicants for transfer must have a C average and be in good standing at their last school. 30 of 120 credits required for the bachelor's degree must be completed at AUM.

Visiting: There are regularly scheduled orientations for prospective students, including meetings with faculty, staff, advising, and registration. There are guides for informal visits and visitors may sit in on classes. To schedule a visit, contact the Office of Enrollment Services at (334) 244-3668 or *vsamuel@mail.aum.edu*.

Financial Aid: In a recent year, 83% of all full-time freshmen received some form of financial aid. 72% of full-time freshmen received need-based aid. The average freshman award was $5503. Need-based scholarships or need-based grants averaged $3425; need-based self-help aid (loans and jobs) averaged $2560; and other non-need-based awards and non-need-based scholarships averaged $3377. 79% of undergraduates work part time. Average annual earnings from campus work are $3882. The FAFSA and the college's own financial statement are required. The priority date for freshman financial aid applications for fall entry is March 1.

International Students: There are 2 international students enrolled. The school actively recruits these students. A satisfactory score is required on the written TOEFL. Applicants must also take SAT or ACT.

Computers: All students may access the system from 7 A.M. to 1 A.M. There are no time limits and no fees. It is strongly recommended that all students have a personal computer.

Graduates: From July 1, 2004 to June 30, 2005, 621 bachelor's degrees were awarded. The most popular majors were management information systems (33%), elementary education (25%), and professional services/public administration (10%). 99 companies recruited on campus in 2004-2005.

Admissions Contact: Lynn Bacon, Director/University Registrar. A video is available. E-mail: *auminfo@mail.aum.edu*
Web: *www.aum.edu*

BIRMINGHAM-SOUTHERN COLLEGE   C-2

Birmingham, AL 35254

(205) 226-4696
(800) 523-5793; Fax: (205) 226-3074

Full-time: 564 men, 730 women	**Faculty:** 101; IIB, av$
Part-time: 13 men, 17 women	**Ph.D.s:** 94%
Graduate: 37 men, 50 women	**Student/Faculty:** 13 to 1
Year: 4-1-4, summer session	**Tuition:** $21,450
Application Deadline: January 15	**Room & Board:** $7044
Freshman Class: 2209 applied, 1393 accepted, 316 enrolled	
SAT Verbal/Math: 600/580*	**ACT: 26 VERY COMPETITIVE+**

Birmingham-Southern College, founded in 1856, is a private liberal arts college affiliated with the United Methodist Church. There are 2 graduate schools. In addition to regional accreditation, BSC has baccalaureate program accreditation with AACSB, NASM, NCATE, and SACS. The library contains 277,000 volumes, 175,038 microform items, and 29,000 audio/video tapes/CDs/DVDs, and subscribes to 1215 periodicals including electronic. Computerized library services include the card catalog, interlibrary loans, database searching, Internet access, and laptop Internet portals. Special learning facilities include a learning resource center, art gallery, planetarium, an environmental center, and an outdoor educational center. The 192-acre campus is in an urban area 3 miles west of downtown Birmingham. Including any residence halls, there are 28 buildings.

Student Life: 75% of undergraduates are from Alabama. Stuents are from 33 states, 8 foreign countries, and Canada. 65% are from public schools. 88% are white. 85% are Protestant. 12% Catholic. The average age of freshmen is 18; all undergraduates, 24. 16% do not continue beyond their first year; 75% remain to graduate.

Housing: 1321 students can be accommodated in college housing, which includes single-sex dorms, on-campus apartments, married-student housing, fraternity houses, and sorority houses. On-campus housing is guaranteed for all 4 years. 85% of students live on campus; of those, 70% remain on campus on weekends. All students may keep cars.

Activities: 54% of men belong to 6 national fraternities; 60% of women belong to 7 national sororities. There are 78 groups on campus, including art, choir, chorale, chorus, computers, dance, drama, ethnic, gay, honors, international, jazz band, literary magazine, musical theater, newspaper, opera, orchestra, pep band, political, professional, religious, social, social service, student government, symphony, and yearbook. Popular campus events include Southern Comfort, Honors Day, and Entertainment Fest.

Sports: There are 6 intercollegiate sports for men and 8 for women, and 17 intramural sports for men and 17 for women. Facilities include a coliseum, a baseball field, racquetball and tennis courts, 2 soccer fields, a weight room, an intramural athletic field, an indoor pool, a game room, an indoor jogging track, 3 gyms, and an aerobics studio.

Disabled Students: 80% of the campus is accessible. Wheelchair ramps, elevators, special parking, specially equipped rest rooms, special class scheduling, lowered drinking fountains, lowered telephones, and special housing are available.

Services: Counseling and information services are available, as is tutoring in some subjects, including math, English, computer science, and other subjects as requested. Tutoring is arranged on an individual basis; assistance in finding teachers is provided upon request.

Campus Safety and Security: Measures include 24-hour foot and vehicle patrol, self-defense education, security escort services, and shuttle buses. There are informal discussions, pamphlets/posters/films, emergency telephones, and lighted pathways/sidewalks.

Programs of Study: BSC confers B.A., B.S., B.F.A., B.Mus., and B.Mus.Ed. degrees. Master's degrees are also awarded. Bachelor's degrees are awarded in BIOLOGICAL SCIENCE (biology/biological science), BUSINESS (accounting, business administration and management, and international business management), COMMUNICATIONS AND THE ARTS (art history and appreciation, dance, dramatic arts, English, French, German, music, musical theater, painting, photography, printmaking, sculpture, Spanish, and studio art), COMPUTER AND PHYSICAL SCIENCE (chemistry, computer science, mathematics, and physics), EDUCATION (art, collaborative, dance, education services, music, and secondary), SOCIAL SCIENCE (Asian/Oriental studies, economics, history, international studies, philosophy, political science/government, psychology, religion, and sociology). Biology, English, and psychology are the strongest academically. Business administration, accounting, and education are the largest.

Required: All students must complete 32 regular units with courses in English composition and literature, lab sciences, math, fine arts, foreign language, social sciences, history, and philosophy or religion as well as 4 (January) interim projects. A total of 128 credits with a GPA of at least 2.0 is required to graduate.

Special: Co-op programs are offered in nursing, engineering, and environmental studies. There is cross-registration with the University of Alabama at Birmingham, Miles College, the University of Montevallo, and Samford University. Student-designed, dual, and interdisciplinary majors, a Washington semester, internships, work-study programs, and study abroad are offered. There is a 3-2 nursing program with Vanderbilt University and a 3-2 environmental studies program wih Duke University. A 3-2 engineering degree is offered with the University of Alabama at Birmingham, Auburn University, Columbia University, and Washington University at St. Louis. There are 22 national honor societies, including Phi Beta Kappa, a freshman honors program, and 6 departmental honors programs.

Faculty/Classroom: 59% of faculty are male; 41%, female. 95% teach undergraduates and 80% both teach and do research. No introductory courses are taught by graduate students. The average class size in an introductory lecture is 17 and in a laboratory, 20.

Admissions: 63% of the 2005-2006 applicants were accepted. The SAT scores for the 2005-2006 freshman class were: Verbal--15% below 500, 35% between 500 and 599, 40% between 600 and 700, and 10% above 700; Math--13% below 500, 40% between 500 and 599, 38% between 600 and 700, and 10% above 700. The ACT scores were 8% below 21, 22% between 21 and 23, 26% between 24 and 26, 15% between 27 and 28, and 28% above 28. 61% of the current freshmen were in the top fifth of their class; 85% were in the top two fifths. There were 3 National Merit finalists and 5 semifinalists. 23 freshmen graduated first in their class.

Requirements: A satisfactory score on the SAT or ACT is required. Applicants should have graduated from an accredited secondary school with 4 courses each in English, math, science, and social studies and a recommended 2 in foreign language. The GED is also accepted. An essay is required and an interview is recommended. Fine arts majors are advised to submit a portfolio or arrange an audition. BSC requires applicants to be in the upper 50% of their class. A GPA of 2.0 is required. AP and CLEP credits are accepted. Important factors in the admissions decision are advanced placement or honor courses, leadership record, and recommendations by school officials.

Procedure: Freshmen are admitted fall, spring, and summer. Entrance exams should be taken in the spring of the junior year. There are early admissions and deferred admissions plans. There is a rolling admissions plan. Applications should be filed by January 15 for fall entry, December 15 for winter entry, January 15 for spring entry, and May 1 for summer entry. The fall 2005 application fee was $25. Notification is sent on a rolling basis. Applications are accepted on-line.

Transfer: 42 transfer students enrolled in 2004-2005. Transfer applicants must have a minimum GPA of 2.0 and leave their former school in good standing. An essay and a school recommendation are required. An interview is recommended. 72 of 144 credits required for the bachelor's degree must be completed at BSC.

Visiting: There are regularly scheduled orientations for prospective students, including Preview Days, Scholarship Days, and individual visits. There are guides for informal visits and visitors may sit in on classes and stay overnight. To schedule a visit, contact the Office of Admission at admission@bsc.edu.

Financial Aid: In 2005-2006, 98% of all full-time students received some form of financial aid. 42% of all full-time students received need-based aid. The average freshman award was $12,158. Need-based scholarships or need-based grants averaged $3475 ($4050 maximum); need-based self-help aid (loans and jobs) averaged $4125 ($8125 maximum); non-need-based athletic scholarships averaged $15,420 ($28,060 maximum); and other non-need-based awards and non-need-based scholarships averaged $8180 ($32,040 maximum). 20% of undergraduates work part time. Average annual earnings from campus work are $750. The average financial indebtedness of the 2005 graduate was $17,972. The FAFSA is required. The priority date for freshman financial aid applications for fall entry is March 1.

International Students: There are 35 international students enrolled. The school actively recruits these students. They must achieve a satisfactory score on the TOEFL. A satisfactory score on the SAT or ACT is required instead of the TOEFL for students whose primary language is English.

Computers: Connectivity for student-owned machines is available in all residence halls, sororities, and fraternities. Lab facilities include 9 computer classroom labs, 5 small departmental labs, as well as computers in essentially all science labs. There are 58 classrooms with ceiling- mounted computer/video projectors and computers. A fractional DS3 line provides Internet access to all members of the college community. All students may access the system 24 hours a day. There are no time limits. The fee is $320. It is strongly recommended that all students have a personal computer.

Graduates: From July 1, 2004 to June 30, 2005, 297 bachelor's degrees were awarded. The most popular majors were business administration (17%), education (11%), and English (8%). In an average class, 1% graduate in 3 years or less, 69% graduate in 4 years or less, 77% graduate in 5 years or less, and 79% graduate in 6 years or less. Of the 2004 graduating class, 48% were enrolled in graduate school within 6 months of graduation and 42% were employed.

Admissions Contact: Sheri S. Salmon, Dean of Enrollment Management. A video is available. E-mail: ssalmon@bsc.edu Web: www.bsc.edu

CONCORDIA COLLEGE   B-4

Selma, AL 36701   **(334) 874-5700; Fax: (334) 874-5755**

Full-time: 170 men, 540 women	Faculty: 17
Part-time: 15 men, 150 women	Ph.D.s: 47%
Graduate: none	Student/Faculty: 41 to 1
Year: semesters	Tuition: $6500
Application Deadline: see profile	Room & Board: $4000
Freshman Class: n/av	
SAT or ACT: not required	NONCOMPETITIVE

Concordia College, founded in 1922, is a historically black institution, where the Christian faith as taught from the Holy Scriptures and subscribed to by the Lutheran Church-Missouri Synod is the foundation and guide for all programs, activities, and relationships. Figures in the above capsule and in this profile are approximate. The library contains 50,000 volumes, 4500 microform items, and 2100 audio/video tapes/CDs/DVDs, and subscribes to 170 periodicals including electronic. Computerized library services include the card catalog, interlibrary loans, and database searching. Special learning facilities include a learning resource center. The 22-acre campus is in a small town 50 miles west of Montgomery. Including any residence halls, there are 13 buildings.

Student Life: 91% of undergraduates are from Alabama. Others are from 12 states and 6 foreign countries. 93% are African American. 57% are Baptist; 17% claim no religious affiliation. The average age of freshmen is 18.

Housing: 350 students can be accommodated in college housing, which includes single-sex dorms. On-campus housing is guaranteed for all 4 years. 79% of students commute. Alcohol is not permitted. All students may keep cars.

Activities: There are no fraternities or sororities. There are 11 groups on campus, including cheerleading, choir, drama, international, religious, and student government. Popular campus events include Spiritual Enrichment Week.

Sports: There are 3 intercollegiate sports for men and 2 for women, and 3 intramural sports for men and 2 for women. Facilities include a gym, a swimming pool, a health and fitness center, and a game room.

Disabled Students: 80% of the campus is accessible. Wheelchair ramps, elevators, special parking, specially equipped rest rooms, lowered drinking fountains, and lowered telephones are available.

Services: Counseling and information services are available, as is tutoring in most subjects. There is remedial math, reading, and writing.

Campus Safety and Security: Measures include informal discussions, lighted pathways/sidewalks, security guards, security gates, and 24-hour foot patrol.

Programs of Study: CC confers B.A. and B.S. degrees. Associate degrees are also awarded. Bachelor's degrees are awarded in BUSINESS (business administration and management), EDUCATION (early childhood and elementary). Education is the strongest academically and has the largest enrollment.

Required: To graduate, students must complete 126 to 137 credit hours, depending on the major, with a minium 2.0 GPA and pass a comprehensive exam. General education requirements include 18 hours of humanities, 12 of social sciences, 9 of math, 6 of religion, 3 each of computer science and health/phys ed, and 1 of orientation to college.

Special: CC offers internships, a Lutheran teacher diploma program, and cross-registration with other schools in the Concordia University system. There is 1 national honor society and a freshman honors program.

Faculty/Classroom: 59% of faculty are male; 41%, female. All teach undergraduates. The average class size in an introductory lecture is 25; in a laboratory, 15; and in a regular course, 30.

Admissions: In a recent year, 5% of the current freshmen were in the top fifth of their class; 18% were in the top two fifths. 4 freshmen graduated first in their class.

Requirements: The ACT is required. A GPA of 2.0 is required. AP and CLEP credits are accepted. Important factors in the admissions decision are advanced placement or honor courses, evidence of special talent, and leadership record.

Procedure: Freshmen are admitted fall and spring. Entrance exams should be taken at the beginning of fall and spring semesters. There is a deferred admissions plan. Check with the school for current application deadlines and fee.The college accepts all applicants.

Transfer: Courses completed with a passing grade of C or better at an accredited postsecondary institution is accepted for transfer, but only work at Concordia is included in the cumultive GPA. 36 of 126 credits required for the bachelor's degree must be completed at CC.

Visiting: There are regularly scheduled orientations for prospective students. There are guides for informal visits and visitors may sit in on classes and stay overnight. To schedule a visit, contact, Director of Enrollment Management at (334) 874-5700 ext. 171 or *epickens@concordiaselma.edu.*

Financial Aid: In a recent year, all full-time freshmen received some form of financial aid.15% of undergraduates work part time.The FAFSA is required. Check with the school for current deadlines.

International Students: International students must take the TOEFL and also take the college's own entrance exam.

Computers: All students may access the system. There are no time limits.

Graduates: In a recent year, 35 bachelor's degrees were awarded. The most popular majors were business administration (38%) and education (22%).

Admissions Contact: Evelyn Pickens, Director of Enrollment Management. A video is available. E-mail: *epickens@concordiaselma.edu* Web: *www.concordiaselma.edu*

FAULKNER UNIVERSITY   C-4

Montgomery, AL 36109-3398   **(334) 386-7200**
                                        (800) 879-9816; Fax: (334) 386-7137

Full-time: 587 men, 1011 women	Faculty: 60
Part-time: 171 men, 456 women	Ph.D.s: 63%
Graduate: 154 men, 130 women	Student/Faculty: 27 to 1
Year: semesters, summer session	Tuition: $10,400
Application Deadline: open	Room & Board: $5200
Freshman Class: 420 applied, 311 accepted, 205 enrolled	
SAT Verbal/Math: 527/525*	ACT: 22 COMPETITIVE

Faulkner University, founded in 1942, is a private, multicampus university affiliated with the Church of Christ, offering undergraduate programs in Bible studies, business, education, and liberal arts and sciences. There are 4 undergraduate and 2 graduate schools. The 2 libraries contain 220,610 volumes, 170,939 microform items, and 1447 audio/video tapes/CDs/DVDs, and subscribe to 3323 periodicals including electronic. Computerized library services include the card catalog, interlibrary loans, and database searching. Special learning facilities include a learning resource center and stellar observatory. The 92-acre campus is in an urban area. Including any residence halls, there are 20 buildings.

Student Life: 88% of undergraduates are from Alabama. Others are from 26 states and 6 foreign countries. 91% are from public schools. 56% are white; 42% African American. 93% are Protestant; 18% claim no religious affiliation. The average age of freshmen is 18; all undergraduates, 28. 45% do not continue beyond their first year; 25% remain to graduate.

Housing: 416 students can be accommodated in college housing, which includes single-sex dorms and on-campus apartments. On-campus housing is available on a first-come, first-served basis. Priority is given to out-of-town students. 82% of students commute. Alcohol is not permitted. All students may keep cars.

Activities: There are 4 local fraternities and 4 local sororities. There are 12 groups on campus, including cheerleading, chorus, drama, honors, literary magazine, musical theater, newspaper, religious, social, social service, student government, and yearbook. Popular campus events include the Annual Bible Lectureship, Jamboree, and Fall Visitation Weekend.

Sports: There are 3 intercollegiate sports for men and 3 for women, and 6 intramural sports for men and 6 for women. Facilities include a gym, a weight room, baseball and softball fields, and lighted tennis courts.

Disabled Students: All of the campus is accessible. Wheelchair ramps, elevators, special parking, specially equipped rest rooms, and special housing, are available. Special needs are met.

Services: Counseling and information services are available, as is tutoring in some subjects, including basic math, English, and reading comprehension. There is remedial math, reading, and writing.

Campus Safety and Security: Measures include 24-hour foot and vehicle patrol, informal discussions, pamphlets/posters/films, and lighted pathways/sidewalks.

Programs of Study: Faulkner confers B.A. and B.S. degrees. Associate, master's, and doctoral degrees are also awarded. Bachelor's degrees are awarded in BIOLOGICAL SCIENCE (biology/biological science), BUSINESS (business administration and management, business data processing, personnel management, and sports management), COMMUNICATIONS AND THE ARTS (English), EDUCATION (elementary, physical, and secondary), SOCIAL SCIENCE (biblical studies, liberal arts/general studies, and prelaw). Business, criminal justice and education are the largest.

Required: Students must complete a 52-semester-hour core curriculum, including courses in Bible, history, social science, English composition, literature, art/music appreciation, speech communication, physical and natural science, math, computer literacy, and phys ed. B.A. students must take 2 semesters of foreign language. At least 120 semester hours with a minimum GPA of 2.0 are required to graduate.

Special: A second bachelor's degree in a separate major may be completed with a minimum of 24 semester hours earned beyond the first degree. Cross-registration with Auburn University at Montgomery and Huntingdon College, dual majors, credit for life/military/work experience, and nondegree study are offered. Internships in education, psychology, criminal justice, Bible, and sports management are available, as are accelerated degree programs in some majors. There are 6 national honor societies and a freshman honors program. All departments have honors programs.

Faculty/Classroom: 62% of faculty are male; 38%, female. 68% teach undergraduates and 8% both teach and do research. No introductory courses are taught by graduate students. The average class size in an introductory lecture is 27; in a laboratory, 15; and in a regular course, 20.

Admissions: 74% of the 2005-2006 applicants were accepted. The SAT scores for the 2005-2006 freshman class were: Verbal--37% below 500, 44% between 500 and 599, 12% between 600 and 700, and 7% above 700; Math--32% below 500, 46% between 500 and 599, 21% between 600 and 700, and 1% above 700. The ACT scores were 36% below 21, 32% between 21 and 23, 16% between 24 and 26, 8% between 27 and 28, and 8% above 28. 22% of the current freshmen were in the top fifth of their class; 39% were in the top two fifths. There were 2 National Merit semifinalists. 5 freshmen graduated first in their class.

Requirements: The ACT is required and the SAT is recommended. Candidates must be graduates of an accredited secondary school, or have the GED equivalent, with a minimum of 15 academic units, including 3 in English. A GPA of 2.0 is required. AP and CLEP credits are accepted.

Procedure: Freshmen are admitted to all sessions. There is a rolling admissions plan. Application deadlines are open. Application fee is $10. Notification is sent on a rolling basis. Applications are accepted on-line.

Transfer: 69 transfer students enrolled in 2004-2005. Applicants must be in good academic standing from another accredited college. 30 of 120 credits required for the bachelor's degree must be completed at Faulkner.

Visiting: There are regularly scheduled orientations for prospective students. There are guides for informal visits and visitors may sit in on classes and stay overnight. To schedule a visit, contact the Admissions Office at *admissions@faulkner.edu.*

Financial Aid: In a recent year, 95% of all full-time students received some form of financial aid. 80% of full-time freshmen and 77% of continuing full-time students received need-based aid. The average freshman award was $6500. Need-based scholarships or need-based grants averaged $4000 ($6000 maximum); need-based self-help aid (loans and jobs) averaged $4500 ($5000 maximum); and non-need-based athletic scholarships averaged $5500 ($14,000 maximum). 59% of undergraduates work part time. Average annual earnings from campus work are $1200. The average financial indebtedness of a recent graduate was $15,500. Faulkner is a member of CSS. The FAFSA, FFS, and the college's own financial statement are required. The deadline for filing freshman financial aid applications for fall entry is May 1.

International Students: There are 6 international students enrolled. They must take the TOEFL and also take the ACT, scoring 17.

Computers: All students may access the system. There are no time limits and no fees. It is strongly recommended that all students have a personal computer.

Graduates: From July 1, 2004 to June 30, 2005, 583 bachelor's degrees were awarded. The most popular majors were business administration (57%), management of human resources (19%), and criminal justice (15%). In an average class, 13% graduate in 4 years or less, 18% graduate in 5 years or less, and 46% graduate in 6 years or less.

Admissions Contact: Keith Mock, Director of Admissions.
E-mail: *kmock@faulkner.edu*

HUNTINGDON COLLEGE C-4
Montgomery, AL 36106-2148

(334) 833-4497
(800) 763-0313; Fax: (334) 833-4347

Full-time: 400 men, 400 women	**Faculty:** 46; IIB, --$
Part-time: 10 men, 25 women	**Ph.Ds:** 80%
Graduate: none	**Student/Faculty:** 13 to 1
Year: 4-1-4, summer session	**Tuition:** $15,990
Application Deadline: open	**Room & Board:** $7100
Freshman Class: n/av	
SAT or ACT: required	**VERY COMPETITIVE**

Huntingdon College, founded in 1854, is a private liberal arts institution related to the United Methodist Church. Some figures in the above capsule and in this profile are approximate. In addition to regional accreditation, Huntingdon has baccalaureate program accreditation with NASM. The library contains 102,074 volumes, 47,443 microform items, and 1517 audio/video tapes/CDs/DVDs, and subscribes to 391 periodicals including electronic. Computerized library services include interlibrary loans and database searching. Special learning facilities include a learning resource center, art gallery, and recital hall and theater. The 58-acre campus is in a suburban area 90 miles south of Birmingham. Including any residence halls, there are 18 buildings.

Student Life: 66% of undergraduates are from Alabama. Others are from 24 states, 12 foreign countries, and Canada. 75% are from public schools. 86% are white. 78% are Protestant; 12% claim no religious affiliation; 10% Catholic. The average age of freshmen is 18; all undergraduates, 20. 27% do not continue beyond their first year; 48% remain to graduate.

Housing: 656 students can be accommodated in college housing, which includes coed dorms. On-campus housing is guaranteed for all 4 years. 72% of students live on campus; of those, 80% remain on campus on weekends. Alcohol is not permitted. All students may keep cars.

Activities: 29% of men belong to 2 national fraternities; 32% of women belong to 3 national sororities. There are 50 groups on campus, including art, cheerleading, choir, chorale, chorus, computers, dance, drama, ethnic, forensics, gay, honors, international, jazz band, literary magazine, musical theater, newspaper, opera, photography, political, professional, religious, social, social service, student government, and yearbook. Popular campus events include Stallworth Lecture Series, Performing Arts Series, and Madrigal Dinner.

Sports: There are 6 intercollegiate sports for men and 6 for women, and 16 intramural sports for men and 16 for women. Facilities include a student center with a 1500-seat gym for volleyball, basketball, and badminton, a swimming pool, weight and training rooms, ping-pong tables, pool tables, video games, 2 dance studios, and sports medicine facilities. There are also outdoor tennis courts, softball, baseball, and soccer fields, and an outdoor volleyball court.

Disabled Students: 80% of the campus is accessible. Wheelchair ramps, elevators, special parking, specially equipped rest rooms, special class scheduling, lowered drinking fountains, and lowered telephones are available.

Services: Counseling and information services are available, as is tutoring in most subjects. There is also a reading and writing lab.

Campus Safety and Security: Measures include 24-hour foot and vehicle patrol, self-defense education, security escort services, and informal discussions. There are pamphlets/posters/films, emergency telephones, lighted pathways/sidewalks, controlled access to residence halls, and weather alert broadcasts.

Programs of Study: Huntingdon confers the B.A. degree. Associate degrees are also awarded. Bachelor's degrees are awarded in AGRICULTURE (soil science), BIOLOGICAL SCIENCE (biology/biological science), BUSINESS (accounting and business administration and management), COMMUNICATIONS AND THE ARTS (art, arts administration/management, communications, dance, dramatic arts, English, music, musical theater, and speech/debate/rhetoric), COMPUTER AND PHYSICAL SCIENCE (chemistry, computer science, digital arts/technology, and mathematics), EDUCATION (art, athletic training, dance, music, and physical), ENGINEERING AND ENVIRONMENTAL DESIGN (computer graphics), HEALTH PROFESSIONS (exercise science and prepharmacy), SOCIAL SCIENCE (American studies, European studies, history, international studies, political science/government, psychology, public administration, public affairs, religion, and religious education). Biology, chemistry, and psychology are the strongest academically. Biology, business, education are the largest.

Required: Huntingdon's core curriculum includes a 12-hour liberal arts symposium, a 3-hour rhetoric seminar, up to 9 hours of foreign languages, and a 3-hour senior capstone course. Additionally, students take 9 hours each of aesthetic expression and science and technology, and 12 hours of social and self-awareness. Students must maintain a minimum GPA of 2.0 over 124 credits for the B.A. Major requirements range from 30 to 42 hours.

Special: The Huntingdon plan includes an opportunity for travel/study experiences offered as part of regular educational costs, hands-on learning experiences in every program of study, dual majors, internships, and co-op programs in business and computer science. The public affairs trisubject major combines politics with 2 other areas, including history, philosophy, psychology, and communications. Cross-registration is available with Auburn University Montgomery, Faulkner University, and the Marine Environmental Sciences Consortium in Dauphin Island. There are 14 national honor societies and 13 departmental honors programs.

Faculty/Classroom: 67% of faculty are male; 33%, female. The average class size in an introductory lecture is 16; in a laboratory, 13; and in a regular course, 13.

Requirements: The SAT or ACT is required. In addition, applicants should have completed 4 years of high school English, 3 credits each in math and history, 2 credits of science, 2 credits of foreign language, and 2 credits in humanities. An interview is recommended. A portfolio or audition may be required. A GPA of 2.25 is required. AP and CLEP credits are accepted. Important factors in the admissions decision are evidence of special talent, leadership record, and advanced placement or honor courses.

Procedure: Freshmen are admitted fall and spring. Entrance exams should be taken in the spring of the junior year. There is an early admissions plan. Application deadlines are open. Application fee is $20. Applications are accepted on-line.

Transfer: High school and college transcripts are required. An interview is recommended. 31 of 124 credits required for the bachelor's degree must be completed at Huntingdon.

Visiting: There are regularly scheduled orientations for prospective students, consisting of class visitation, a campus tour, a meeting with an admissions counselor, and student panel, financial aid, and faculty presentations. There are guides for informal visits and visitors may sit in on classes and stay overnight. To schedule a visit, contact the Office of Admission.

Financial Aid: The FAFSA and the college's own financial statement are required. Check with the school for current deadlines.

International Students: The school actively recruits these students. They must score satisfactorily on the written TOEFL.

Computers: All students may access the system 24 hours a day, 7 days a week.

Graduates: In an average class, 1% graduate in 3 years or less, 45% graduate in 4 years or less, 66% graduate in 5 years or less, and 70% graduate in 6 years or less.

Admissions Contact: Laura Duncan, Director of Admission.

E-mail: *admiss@huntingdon.edu* Web: *www.huntingdon.edu*

JACKSONVILLE STATE UNIVERSITY D-2
Jacksonville, AL 36265

(256) 782-5400
(800) 231-5291; Fax: (256) 782-5121

Full-time: 2537 men, 3276 women	**Faculty:** 305; IIA, --$
Part-time: 595 men, 877 women	**Ph.D.s:** 70%
Graduate: 617 men, 1208 women	**Student/Faculty:** 19 to 1
Year: semesters, summer session	**Tuition:** $4040 ($8080)
Application Deadline: open	**Room & Board:** $3570
Freshman Class: 2839 applied, 2499 accepted, 1151 enrolled	
SAT or ACT: required	**LESS COMPETITIVE**

Jacksonville State University, founded in 1883, is a public institution offering programs in business, arts and sciences, criminal justice, education, and nursing. There are 4 undergraduate schools and 1 graduate school. Some figures in the above capsule and in this profile are approximate. In addition to regional accreditation, JSU has baccalaureate program accreditation with AACSB, ABET, ADA, CSWE, NASAD, NASM, NCATE, and NLN. The library contains 684,342 volumes, 1,404,194 microform items, and 34,323 audio/video tapes/CDs/DVDs, and subscribes to 14,295 periodicals including electronic. Computerized library services include the card catalog, interlibrary loans, database searching, and Internet access. Special learning facilities include a learning resource center, planetarium, radio station, TV station, and stellar observatory. The 318-acre campus is in a small town 75 miles east of Birmingham. Including any residence halls, there are 58 buildings.

Student Life: 84% of undergraduates are from Alabama. Others are from 47 states, 73 foreign countries, and Canada. 95% are from public schools. 72% are white; 22% African American. The average age of freshmen is 19; all undergraduates, 24. 31% do not continue beyond their first year; 62% remain to graduate.

Housing: 1737 students can be accommodated in college housing, which includes single-sex and coed dorms, on-campus apartments, off-campus apartments, married-student housing, and fraternity houses. In addition, there are honors houses, language houses, and special-interest houses. There iss an international house available for students on Rotary Club International Scholarships. On-campus housing is available on a first-come, first-served basis. 80% of students commute. Alcohol is not permitted. All students may keep cars.

Activities: 10% of men belong to 9 national fraternities; 10% of women belong to 8 national sororities. There are 100 groups on campus, including art, band, cheerleading, chess, choir, chorale, chorus, computers, dance, drama, drill team, drum and bugle corps, ethnic, honors, international, jazz band, marching band, musical theater, newspaper, opera, orchestra, pep band, political, professional, radio and TV, religious, social, social service, student government, symphony, and yearbook. Popular campus events include Visitation Day and Parents Day.

Sports: There are 7 intercollegiate sports for men and 8 for women, and 15 intramural sports for men and 15 for women. Facilities include a 15,000-seat football stadium, indoor and outdoor courts, athletic fields, a 5000-seat indoor gym, an indoor pool, a weight room, and a fitness center.

Disabled Students: 85% of the campus is accessible. Wheelchair ramps, elevators, special parking, specially equipped rest rooms, lowered drinking fountains, and lowered telephones are available.

Services: Counseling and information services are available, as is tutoring in most subjects. There is remedial math, reading, and writing.

Campus Safety and Security: Measures include 24-hour foot and vehicle patrol, security escort services, informal discussions, and pamphlets/posters/films. There are emergency telephones and lighted pathways/sidewalks.

Programs of Study: JSU confers B.A., B.S., B.F.A., B.S.Ed., and B.S.W. degrees. Master's degrees are also awarded. Bachelor's degrees are awarded in BIOLOGICAL SCIENCE (biology/biological science), BUSINESS (accounting, banking and finance, and marketing/retailing/merchandising), COMMUNICATIONS AND THE ARTS (communications, dramatic arts, English, and music), COMPUTER AND PHYSICAL SCIENCE (chemistry, computer science, mathematics, and physics), EDUCATION (early childhood, elementary, health, home economics, music, secondary, and special), HEALTH PROFESSIONS (nursing), SOCIAL SCIENCE (criminal justice, economics, geography, history,

political science/government, psychology, social work, and sociology). Elementary education, criminal justice, and nursing are the strongest academically.

Required: All students are required to complete a core curriculum of 46 semester hours, including 15 hours in fine arts and humanities, 8 each in communications and natural sciences, 6 each in analysis and social sciences, and 3 in wellness. English competency and courses in computer literacy are required. A total of 128 semester hours, with at least 52 hours in courses numbered 300 or above and a minimum GPA of 2.0, are required to graduate. At least 32 semester hours must be completed in residence at JSU with no more than 12 hours in correspondence work.

Special: Co-op programs with major area employees are available. JSU has cross-registration with the Marine Environmental Sciences Consortium and internships in education, political science, communication, journalism, and criminal justice. Work-study programs, dual majors in most programs, and credit for military experience are offered. There are 13 national honor societies and 1 departmental honors program.

Faculty/Classroom: 51% of faculty are male; 49%, female. 68% teach undergraduates. No introductory courses are taught by graduate students. The average class size in a laboratory is 25 and in a regular course, 25.

Admissions: 88% of the 2005-2006 applicants were accepted. The SAT scores for the 2005-2006 freshman class were: Verbal--62% below 500, 29% between 500 and 599, 8% between 600 and 700, and 1% above 700; Math--64% below 500, 30% between 500 and 599, and 6% between 600 and 700. The ACT scores were 63% below 21, 18% between 21 and 23, 13% between 24 and 26, 4% between 27 and 28, and 2% above 28. 9% of the current freshmen were in the top fifth of their class; 24% were in the top two fifths.

Requirements: The SAT or ACT is required. In addition, applicants should be graduates of an accredited high school; the GED is also accepted. 19 on the ACT or a satisfactory score on the SAT is required for unconditional admission; 16 to 18 on the ACT or a minium satisfactory score on the SAT is required for conditional admission. AP and CLEP credits are accepted.

Procedure: Freshmen are admitted to all sessions. There is a rolling admissions plan. Application deadlines are open. Applications are accepted on-line.

Transfer: 726 transfer students enrolled in 2004-2005. Transfer applicants must be eligible to return to the last institution attended. 32 of 128 credits required for the bachelor's degree must be completed at JSU.

Visiting: There are regularly scheduled orientations for prospective students, consisting of 2-day orientations scheduled during the summer. There are guides for informal visits. To schedule a visit, contact Tracy Phillips at (800) 231-5291 ext. 6 or *phillips@jsucc.jsu.edu.*

Financial Aid: 55% of undergraduates work part time. The FAFSA is required. The deadline for filing freshman financial aid applications for fall entry is March 15.

International Students: There are 174 international students enrolled. They must score satisfactorily on the written TOEFL. The SAT or ACT may be substituted with satisfactory scores.

Computers: All students may access the system during specific lab hours. There are no time limits and no fees.

Graduates: From July 1, 2004 to June 30, 2005, 1154 bachelor's degrees were awarded. The most popular majors were elementary education (13%), criminal justice (7%), and nursing (6%). 84 companies recruited on campus in 2004-2005.

Admissions Contact: Martha Mitchell, Director of Admissions.

E-mail: *info@jsucc.jsu.edu* Web: *www.jsu.edu*

JUDSON COLLEGE B-3
Marion, AL 36756

(334) 683-5110
(800) 447-9472; Fax: (334) 683-5147

Full-time: 4 men, 253 women	**Faculty:** 29
Part-time: 10 men, 64 women	**Ph.D.s:** 70%
Graduate: none	**Student/Faculty:** 9 to 1
Year: semesters, summer session	**Tuition:** $10,004
Application Deadline: open	**Room & Board:** $6518
Freshman Class: 280 applied, 214 accepted, 79 enrolled	
SAT or ACT: required	**COMPETITIVE**

Judson College, founded in 1838, is a private women's liberal arts college affiliated with the Alabama Baptist Convention. In addition to regional accreditation, Judson has baccalaureate program accreditation with NASM. The library contains 56,338 volumes, 2035 microform items, and 7303 audio/video tapes/CDs/DVDs, and subscribes to 429 periodicals including electronic. Computerized library services include the card catalog, interlibrary loans, database searching, and Internet access. Special learning facilities include a learning resource center and the Alabama Women's Hall of Fame. The 80-acre campus is in a small town 27 miles west of Selma. Including any residence halls, there are 18 buildings.

Student Life: 71% of undergraduates are from Alabama. Others are from 23 states and 3 foreign countries. 73% are from public schools. 82% are white; 15% African American. Most are Protestant. The average age of freshmen is 19; all undergraduates, 25. 36% do not continue beyond their first year; 40% remain to graduate.

Housing: 264 students can be accommodated in college housing, which includes single-sex dorms. On-campus housing is guaranteed for all 4 years. 57% of students live on campus; of those, 33% remain on campus on weekends. Alcohol is not permitted. All students may keep cars.

Activities: There are no fraternities. There are 28 groups on campus, including art, band, cheerleading, choir, chorale, chorus, computers, dance, drama, environmental, honors, literary magazine, marching band, musical theater, newspaper, orchestra, photography, political, professional, religious, social, social service, student government, woodwind ensemble, and yearbook. Popular campus events include Winter Ball, Junior-Sophomore Dance, and Hockey Day.

Sports: Facilities include an indoor swimming pool, riding stables and a riding arena, tennis courts, a wellness center, a gym, an aerobics room, a weight training facility, a hockey field, and a game room.

Disabled Students: 75% of the campus is accessible. Elevators, special parking, specially equipped rest rooms, lowered drinking fountains, and lowered telephones are available.

Services: Counseling and information services are available, as is tutoring in most subjects. There is remedial math and writing.

Campus Safety and Security: Measures include 24-hour foot and vehicle patrol, self-defense education, informal discussions, and lighted pathways/sidewalks.

Programs of Study: Judson confers B.A. and B.S. degrees. Bachelor's degrees are awarded in BIOLOGICAL SCIENCE (biology/biological science), BUSINESS (business administration and management), COMMUNICATIONS AND THE ARTS (applied music, art, English, and languages), COMPUTER AND PHYSICAL SCIENCE (chemistry and mathematics), EDUCATION (elementary, English, mathematics, music, science, and social studies), SOCIAL SCIENCE (criminal justice, history, interdisciplinary studies, psychology, and religion). Biology, education, and psychology are the strongest academically. Biology, elementary education, and business are the largest.

Required: All students are required to complete courses in women's studies, English, history, multicultural studies, speech, religion, social science, math, science, humanities, computer literacy, and health/phys ed. A total of 128 credit hours, with a minimum GPA of 2.0, (2.5 for education majors) is required to graduate. To graduate, all students must complete a minimum of 30 hours in the major with a minimum GPA of 2.0. B.A. students must also complete at least 6 hours of foreign languages at the 200-level or above; B.S. students must complete at least 12 hours of math or science electives in addition to the core competency. A passing score is required on the English Proficiency Usage Test.

Special: Cross-registration with the Marion Military Institute is available for ROTC students. B.A.-B.S. degrees are offered in criminal justice, math, business, biology, psychology, and chemistry. Study abroad in 7 countries, dual majors, an accelerated degree program, an interdisciplinary major, a 3-2 engineering degree with the University of Alabama, work-study programs, and internships are offered. There are preprofessional programs in health, engineering, and law. The Distance Learning program offers credit for prior learning experience and provides individually paced instruction leading to a baccalaureate degree. There are 7 national honor societies and 17 departmental honors programs.

Faculty/Classroom: 51% of faculty are male; 49%, female. All teach undergraduates. The average class size in an introductory lecture is 14; in a laboratory, 8; and in a regular course, 6.

Admissions: 76% of the 2005-2006 applicants were accepted. The SAT scores for the 2005-2006 freshman class were: Verbal--29% below 500, 43% between 500 and 599, 14% between 600 and 700, and 14% above 700; Math--43% below 500, 29% between 500 and 599, and 29% between 600 and 700. The ACT scores were 40% below 21, 27% between 21 and 23, 17% between 24 and 26, 7% between 27 and 28, and 9% above 28. 24% of the current freshmen were in the top fifth of their class; 56% were in the top two fifths. 2 freshmen graduated first in their class.

Requirements: The SAT or ACT is required. Applicants should have completed 17 high school credits, including 4 in English. Non-high school graduates must provide the GED equivalent. An interview is required. A GPA of 2.0 is required. AP and CLEP credits are accepted. Important factors in the admissions decision are advanced placement and honor courses, evidence of special talent, and leadership record.

Procedure: Freshmen are admitted fall, winter, and summer. Entrance exams should be taken in the spring of the junior year. There are early admissions, rolling admissions and deferred admissions plans. Application deadlines are open. The fall 2005 application fee was $30. Applications are accepted on-line.

Transfer: 8 transfer students enrolled in 2004-2005. Transfer students must have a minimum GPA of 2.0 and be eligible to return to the school from which they transfer. 32 of 128 credits required for the bachelor's degree must be completed at Judson.

Visiting: There are regularly scheduled orientations for prospective students, consisting of 2 college Preview Days, 1 in June and 1 in August. There are guides for informal visits and visitors may sit in on classes and stay overnight. To schedule a visit, contact Admissions at *admissions@future.judson.edu*.

Financial Aid: In 2005-2006, 84% of all full-time freshmen and 78% of continuing full-time students received some form of financial aid. 73% of full-time freshmen and 69% of continuing full-time students received need-based aid. The average freshman award was $11,477. Need-based scholarships or need-based grants averaged $7376; need-based self-help aid (loans and jobs) averaged $4101; and other non-need-based awards and non-need-based scholarships averaged $5903. 49% of undergraduates work part time. Average annual earnings from campus work are $1000. The average financial indebtedness of the 2005 graduate was $15,690. The FAFSA, the state aid form, and the college's own financial statement are required. The deadline for filing freshman financial aid applications for fall entry is March 15.

International Students: They must score satisfactorily on the written TOEFL and also take the college's own test.

Computers: All students may access the system 8 A.M. to 1 A.M. Monday to Friday, Saturday, 12 P.M. to 5 P.M., Sunday, 5 P.M. to 1 A.M. There are no time limits and no fees.

Graduates: From July 1, 2004 to June 30, 2005, 72 bachelor's degrees were awarded. The most popular majors were biology (18%), psychology (15%), and history (15%). In an average class, 19% graduate in 3 years or less, 83% graduate in 4 years or less, 86% graduate in 5 years or less, and 88% graduate in 6 years or less. 10 companies recruited on campus in 2004-2005. Of the 2004 graduating class, 21% were enrolled in graduate school within 6 months of graduation and 73% were employed.

Admissions Contact: Michael Scotto, Director of Admissions. E-mail: *admissions@future.judson.edu* Web: *home.judson.edu*

MILES COLLEGE   C-2
Birmingham, AL 35208

(205) 929-1656
(800) 445-0708; Fax: (205) 929-1668

Full-time: 730 men, 890 women	**Faculty:** 92
Part-time: 30 men, 66 women	**Ph.D.s:** 38%
Graduate: none	**Student/Faculty:** 18 to 1
Year: semesters, summer session	**Tuition:** $5826
Application Deadline: open	**Room & Board:** $4096
Freshman Class: 700 accepted, 409 enrolled	
SAT or ACT: recommended	NONCOMPETITIVE

Miles College, founded in 1908, is a private institution affiliated with and controlled by the Christian Methodist Episcopal Church. The college offers undergraduate programs in the liberal arts and sciences, business, and education. There are 5 undergraduate schools. The library contains 180,000 volumes and 850 microform items, and subscribes to 250 periodicals including electronic. Computerized library services include interlibrary loans, database searching, and Internet access. Special learning facilities include a learning resource center, art gallery, an Afro-American materials center, and a media center. The 35-acre campus is in an urban area 7 miles from downtown Birmingham. Including any residence halls, there are 19 buildings.

Student Life: 90% of undergraduates are from Alabama. Others are from 37 states. 98% are African American. The average age of freshmen is 18; all undergraduates, 22. 15% do not continue beyond their first year; 80% remain to graduate.

Housing: 750 students can be accommodated in college housing, which includes single-sex dormitories and off-campus apartments. On-campus housing is available on a first-come, first-served basis. Priority is given to out-of-town students. 57% of students commute. Alcohol is not permitted. All students may keep cars.

Activities: 7% of men belong to 2 local and 5 national fraternities; 12% of women belong to 2 local and 5 national sororities. There are 12 groups on campus, including cheerleading, choir, drama, ethnic, honors, newspaper, professional, religious, and student government. Popular campus events include Senior Class Day, Spring Cultural and Arts Festival, and Honors Day.

Sports: There are 6 intercollegiate sports for men and 4 for women. Facilities include a 2000-seat football field, a 1500-seat gym, a weight room, and a baseball field.

Disabled Students: Wheelchair ramps, elevators, special parking, specially equipped rest rooms, special class scheduling, and lowered drinking fountains are available.

Services: Counseling and information services are available, as is tutoring in every subject. There is remedial math, reading, and writing. Miles offers a Student Support Services Program for students with an academically challenged developmental background.

Campus Safety and Security: Measures include 24-hour foot and vehicle patrol.

Programs of Study: Miles confers B.A., B.S., and B.S.W. degrees. Bachelor's degrees are awarded in BIOLOGICAL SCIENCE (biology/

biological science), BUSINESS (accounting and business administration and management), COMMUNICATIONS AND THE ARTS (communications, English, and language arts), COMPUTER AND PHYSICAL SCIENCE (chemistry, computer science, and mathematics), EDUCATION (early childhood, elementary, mathematics, science, secondary, and social science), ENGINEERING AND ENVIRONMENTAL DESIGN (environmental science), SOCIAL SCIENCE (criminal justice, history, political science/government, and social work). Business is the strongest academically. Early childhood and elementary education are the largest.

Required: To graduate, all students must complete a minimum of 51 hours of general education requirements, including the 33-hour freshman studies program. A minimum of 124 credit hours is required for a bachelor's degree, with a minimum GPA of 2.0 in the major. All students must pass English proficiency and exit exams.

Special: Miles offers co-op programs in all majors, internships, federal work-study, and cross-registration with the University of Alabama at Birmingham and other area colleges and universities. There are cooperative programs in allied health sciences with the University of Alabama at Birmingham, and in engineering, physics, veterinary medicine, and Asian studies. There is 1 national honor society and a freshman honors program.

Faculty/Classroom: 49% of faculty are male; 51%, female. All teach undergraduates. The average class size in an introductory lecture is 20 and in a regular course, 12.

Requirements: The SAT or ACT is recommended. The ACT Optional Writing test is also recommended. Students should be graduates of an accredited high school or hold a GED. A personal interview is recommended. A GPA of 2.0 is required.

Procedure: Freshmen are admitted to all sessions. Application deadlines are open. Application fee is $25.

Transfer: 420 transfer students enrolled in 2004-2005. To qualify for admission as a transfer, students must be in good standing at the last institution attended and submit official transcripts. 32 of 124 credits required for the bachelor's degree must be completed at Miles.

Visiting: There are guides for informal visits and visitors may sit in on classes. To schedule a visit, contact Admissions at 205-929-1000.

Financial Aid: In 2005-2006, 98% of all full-time students received some form of financial aid. 98% of all full-time students received need-based aid. Need-based scholarships or need-based grants averaged $3313; and need-based self-help aid (loans and jobs) averaged $3627. Average annual earnings from campus work are $800. The average financial indebtedness of the 2005 graduate was $20,000. Miles is a member of CSS. The FAFSA is required. The deadline for filing freshman financial aid applications for fall entry is April 15.

International Students: They must score satisfactorily on the written TOEFL or take the MELAB and also take the SAT or the ACT.

Computers: Wireless access is available. Wireless access is available in the learning resource center. Computers are located in labs throughout the campus. All students may access the system. There are no time limits and no fees.

Graduates: From July 1, 2004 to June 30, 2005, 183 bachelor's degrees were awarded. The most popular majors were business administration management (16%), social work (11%), and communications (11%). In an average class, 16% graduate in 4 years or less, 24% graduate in 5 years or less, and 23% graduate in 6 years or less. 40 companies recruited on campus in 2004-2005. Of the 2004 graduating class, 17% were enrolled in graduate school within 6 months of graduation and 48% were employed.

Admissions Contact: Christopher Robertson, Director of Admissions. A video is available. E-mail: *crobertson@miles.edu*
Web: *www.miles.edu*

OAKWOOD COLLEGE
C-1

Huntsville, AL 35896

(256) 726-7000
(800) 824-5312; Fax: (256) 726-7154

Full-time: 675 men, 900 women	**Faculty:** 96; IIB, --$
Part-time: 100 men, 100 women	**Ph.D.s:** 54%
Graduate: none	**Student/Faculty:** 16 to 1
Year: semesters, summer session	**Tuition:** $9420
Application Deadline: open	**Room & Board:** $5484
Freshman Class: n/av	
SAT or ACT: recommended	**COMPETITIVE**

Oakwood College, founded in 1896, is a private, historically black, Seventh-day Adventist institution offering undergraduate programs in business and education, humanities, natural sciences and math, religion and theology, and social sciences. Some figures in the above capsule and in this profile are approximate. In addition to regional accreditation, Oakwood has baccalaureate program accreditation with ACBSP, ADA, CSWE, and NCATE. The library contains 125,373 volumes, 2140 microform items, and 4816 audio/video tapes/CDs/DVDs, and subscribes to 630 periodicals including electronic. Computerized library services include the card catalog and database searching. Special learning facilities include a learning resource center, radio station, and a black history mu-

seum. The 105-acre campus is in a suburban area 5 miles northwest of Huntsville. Including any residence halls, there are 30 buildings.

Student Life: 79% of undergraduates are from out of state, mostly the South. Students are from 39 states, 22 foreign countries, and Canada. 52% are from public schools. 79% are African American; 12% foreign nationals. The average age of freshmen is 19; all undergraduates, 23. 27% do not continue beyond their first year.

Housing: 1173 students can be accommodated in college housing, which includes single-sex dorms and married-student housing. On-campus housing is available on a first-come, first-served basis. Priority is given to out-of-town students. 71% of students live on campus; of those, 98% remain on campus on weekends. Alcohol is not permitted. Upperclassmen may keep cars.

Activities: There are no fraternities or sororities. There are 20 groups on campus, including band, choir, chorale, drama, honors, international, newspaper, professional, radio and TV, religious, student government, and yearbook. Popular campus events include Convocations, the Arts and Lecture Series, and Centennial.

Sports: There are 4 intramural sports for men and 3 for women. Facilities include a gym, a skating rink, an Olympic-size pool, tennis courts, playing fields, racquetball courts, and a weight room.

Disabled Students: 80% of the campus is accessible. Wheelchair ramps, elevators, special parking, and specially equipped rest rooms are available.

Services: Counseling and information services are available, as is tutoring in most subjects. There is remedial math, reading, and writing. Testing, counseling, and developmental guidance services are available through the counseling center.

Campus Safety and Security: Measures include 24-hour foot and vehicle patrol, security escort services, informal discussions, pamphlets/posters/films, and lighted pathways/sidewalks.

Programs of Study: Oakwood confers B.A., B.S., B.B.A., B.M., and B.S.W. degrees. Associate degrees are also awarded. Bachelor's degrees are awarded in BIOLOGICAL SCIENCE (biochemistry and biology/biological science), BUSINESS (accounting and business administration and management), COMMUNICATIONS AND THE ARTS (communications, English, French, music, music business management, music performance, and Spanish), COMPUTER AND PHYSICAL SCIENCE (chemistry, computer mathematics, computer science, information sciences and systems, mathematics, and natural sciences), EDUCATION (business, elementary, English, home economics, mathematics, music, physical, science, and social science), HEALTH PROFESSIONS (medical technology and nursing), SOCIAL SCIENCE (dietetics, family/consumer studies, history, home economics, human development, international studies, ministries, physical fitness/movement, psychology, religion, religious education, and social work). Biochemistry, chemistry, and nursing are the strongest academically. Business and biology are the largest.

Required: To graduate, students must complete 128 semester hours, including 30 in the major and 40 in upper-division courses, with a GPA of 2.0. Regular chapel attendance is required. All students must complete a liberal arts core and must meet English oral and written proficiency requirements.

Special: Students may cross-register with Alabama A&M, Athens State, or the University of Alabama at Huntsville. The college offers a student missionary abroad program as well as a study abroad program through the Adventist College Consortium. Internships, work-study, dual majors, independent study, life experience credit, and pass/fail options are also available. A second bachelor's degree is offered to students completing at least 160 semester credits. There is 1 national honor society and 2 departmental honors program.

Faculty/Classroom: 51% of faculty are male; 49%, female. All teach undergraduates. The average class size in an introductory lecture is 30; in a laboratory, 30; and in a regular course, 40.

Requirements: The SAT or ACT is recommended. In addition, applicants should be high school graduates with a minimum GPA of 2.0 and at least 11 academic units, distributed as follows: 4 in English, 2 each in math, science, and social studies, and 1 in typing. The GED is accepted. Two character references are required. Students with GPAs between 1.7 and 2.0 may be admitted on probation. Applicants admitted without test scores must take the ACT during freshman orientation. A GPA of 2.0 is required. AP and CLEP credits are accepted. Important factors in the admissions decision are recommendations by school officials, ability to finance college education, and leadership record.

Procedure: Freshmen are admitted to all sessions. Entrance exams should be taken before high school graduation. There is an early decision plan. Application deadlines are open. Check with the school or current application fee.

Transfer: Applicants must submit a college transcript and a statement of honorable dismissal. Grades of C minus or better transfer for credit. 32 of 128 credits required for the bachelor's degree must be completed at Oakwood.

Visiting: There are guides for informal visits and visitors may sit in on classes and stay overnight. To schedule a visit, contact Fred Pullins, Enrollment Management at (256) 726-7030.

Financial Aid: Oakwood is a member of CSS. The FAFSA, the college's own financial statement, and the student and parent federal income tax returns are required.

International Students: They must score satisfactorily on the written TOEFL and also take the college's own test and the SAT or ACT. Students may take the ACT on campus prior to registration.

Computers: There are no time limits. Fees vary.

Admissions Contact: Fred Pullins, Enrollment Management Director. E-mail: *admission@oakwood.edu* Web: *www.oakwood.edu*

SAMFORD UNIVERSITY   C-2
Birmingham, AL 35229
                                        (205) 726-3673
                        (800) 888-7218; Fax: (205) 726-2171

Full-time: 944 men, 1708 women	**Faculty:** 184; IIA, av$
Part-time: 63 men, 141 women	**Ph.Ds:** 82%
Graduate: 767 men, 793 women	**Student/Faculty:** 14 to 1
Year: 4-1-4, summer session	**Tuition:** $14,642
Application Deadline: August 1	**Room & Board:** $5616
Freshman Class: 2025 applied, 1,792 accepted, 696 enrolled	
SAT Verbal/Math: 570/570*	**ACT:** 25 **VERY COMPETITIVE**

Samford University, founded in 1841, is a private, liberal arts school and maintains a close relationship with the Alabama Baptist Convention. There are 5 undergraduate and 8 graduate schools. In addition to regional accreditation, Samford has baccalaureate program accreditation with AACSB, CAAHEP, CCNE, FIDER, NASM, and NCATE. The 6 libraries contain 446,272 volumes, 1,318,119 microform items, and 15,181 audio/video tapes/CDs/DVDs, and subscribe to 3522 periodicals including electronic. Computerized library services include the card catalog, interlibrary loans, and database searching. Special learning facilities include a learning resource center, art gallery, planetarium, radio station, TV station, a global center, a drug information center, and a conservatory. The 180-acre campus is in a suburban area 4 miles south of Birmingham. Including any residence halls, there are 62 buildings.

Student Life: 55% of undergraduates are from out of state, mostly the South. Students are from 44 states, 15 foreign countries, and Canada. 57% are from public schools. 89% are white. 76% are Protestant; 15% Islamic and other. The average age of freshmen is 18; all undergraduates, 21. 16% do not continue beyond their first year; 84% remain to graduate.

Housing: 1860 students can be accommodated in college housing, which includes single-sex dormitories, fraternity houses, ans a university-owned facility for study in England. On-campus housing is available on a first-come, first-served basis. 65% of students live on campus. Alcohol is not permitted. All students may keep cars.

Activities: 29% of men belong to 6 national fraternities; 34% of women belong to 7 national sororities. There are 106 groups on campus, including band, cheerleading, choir, chorale, chorus, computers, dance, debate, drama, drill team, ethnic, honors, international, jazz band, literary magazine, marching band, musical theater, newspaper, opera, orchestra, pep band, political, professional, radio and TV, religious, social, social service, student government, and symphony. Popular campus events include Step Sing, Spring Fling, and Family Weekend.

Sports: There are 8 intercollegiate sports for men and 9 for women, and 16 intramural sports for men and 16 for women. Facilities include a 6700-seat stadium, a 4000-seat gym, intramural fields, tennis and racquetball courts, practice fields, baseball, soccer, and softball fields, and a swimming pool.

Disabled Students: 99% of the campus is accessible. Wheelchair ramps, elevators, special parking, specially equipped rest rooms, special class scheduling, lowered drinking fountains, lowered telephones, and special housing are available.

Services: Counseling and information services are available, as is tutoring in most subjects. There is a reader service for the blind.

Campus Safety and Security: Measures include 24-hour foot and vehicle patrol, self-defense education, security escort services, and shuttle buses. There are informal discussions, pamphlets/posters/films, emergency telephones, and lighted pathways/sidewalks.

Programs of Study: Samford confers B.A., B.S., B.G.S., B.M., B.S.B.A., B.S.E., and B.S.N. degrees. Associate, master's, and doctoral degrees are also awarded. Bachelor's degrees are awarded in BIOLOGICAL SCIENCE (biochemistry, biology/biological science, marine science, and nutrition), BUSINESS (accounting and human resources), COMMUNICATIONS AND THE ARTS (art, classics, communications, English, English literature, French, German, graphic design, Greek, journalism, language arts, Latin, music, music performance, music theory and composition, musical theater, piano/organ, Spanish, and voice), COMPUTER AND PHYSICAL SCIENCE (chemistry, computer science, environmental geology, mathematics, physics, and science), EDUCATION (athletic training, early childhood, elementary, music, physical, and secondary), ENGINEERING AND ENVIRONMENTAL DESIGN (engineering physics, environmental science, and interior design), HEALTH PROFESSIONS (exercise science, health, nursing, and sports medicine), SOCIAL SCIENCE (Asian/Oriental studies, community ser-

vices, counseling/psychology, family/consumer studies, geography, history, international relations, Latin American studies, liberal arts/general studies, philosophy, political science/government, psychology, public administration, religion, religious music, social science, and sociology). Teacher education, business, and nursing are the strongest academically. Law, pharmacy, and education are the largest.

Required: All students must receive an overall GPA of at least 2.0 and take at least 128 credits, including 30 semester hours in their major. Distribution requirements include 8 semester hours in cultural perspectives, 8 semester hours in communication arts, 4 hours in Biblical perspectives, and 2 hours in phys ed. Students also must demonstrate writing proficiency. 50% of credits must be in the degree field, with 15 credits in the major field.

Special: A 3-2 engineering degree is available with Auburn, Washington (St. Louis), and Mercer Universities and the University of Alabama. The School of Arts and Sciences offers an interdisciplinary core curriculum with team teaching. Cross-registration with Birmingham-Southern College, the University of Alabama at Birmingham, the University of Montevallo, and Miles College, study abroad in England and 16 other countries, additional major options, internships, credit for life experience, and pass/fail options are also offered. Accelerated degree programs are possible in some majors. There are 28 national honor societies, a freshman honors program, and 17 departmental honors programs.

Faculty/Classroom: 53% of faculty are male; 47%, female. 70% teach undergraduates. No introductory courses are taught by graduate students. The average class size in an introductory lecture is 21; in a laboratory, 25; and in a regular course, 21.

Admissions: 65% of the 2005-2006 applicants were accepted. The SAT scores for the 2005-2006 freshman class were: Verbal--17% below 500, 44% between 500 and 599, 34% between 600 and 700, and 5% above 700; Math--14% below 500, 51% between 500 and 599, 31% between 600 and 700, and 4% above 700. The ACT scores were 9% below 21, 31% between 21 and 23, 23% between 24 and 26, 16% between 27 and 28, and 21% above 28. 56% of the current freshmen were in the top fifth of their class; 81% were in the top two fifths. There were 7 National Merit finalists and 2 semifinalists. 27 freshmen graduated first in their class.

Requirements: The SAT or ACT is required. In addition, applicants need 18 academic credits and 16 Carnegie units, including 4 in English, 3 each in math and science, and 2 each in social studies and history. 2 units in foreign language are recommended. An essay is required and an interview suggested. The GED is accepted. AP and CLEP credits are accepted. Important factors in the admissions decision are advanced placement or honor courses, leadership record, and recommendations by school officials.

Procedure: Freshmen are admitted fall, spring, and summer. Entrance exams should be taken in the junior year. There are early admissions, deferred admissions, and rolling admissions plans. Applications should be filed by August 1 for fall entry. Notification is sent on a rolling basis. Applications are accepted on-line. The fall 2005 application fee was $35.

Transfer: 110 transfer students enrolled in 2004-2005. A minimum of 15 credits in the major field must be earned at Samford. 64 of 128 credits required for the bachelor's degree must be completed at Samford.

Visiting: There are regularly scheduled orientations for prospective students, consisting of a 2-day program during which students stay on campus, take placement tests, meet advisers, and register for classes. There are guides for informal visits and visitors may sit in on classes and stay overnight. To schedule a visit, contact the Admissions Office.

Financial Aid: 49% of undergraduates work part time. Average annual earnings from campus work are $1600. The average financial indebtedness of the 2005 graduate was $15,959. The FAFSA is required. The deadline for freshman financial aid applications for fall entry is March 1.

International Students: There are 8 international students enrolled. They must score satisfactorily on the written TOEFL or on the electronic version and also take the SAT or the ACT.

Computers: Wireless access is available. There are 6 computer labs available for general academic and student use. Near semester's end, hours of operation may be extended. PCs include Dell and Power Mac. There is a voice/data connection for every resident student. All students may access the system. There are no time limits and no fees.

Graduates: From July 1, 2004 to June 30, 2005, 627 bachelor's degrees were awarded. The most popular majors were business and marketing (18%), health professions and related sciences (13%), and social science and history (10%). In an average class, 51% graduate in 4 years or less, 67% graduate in 5 years or less, and 71% graduate in 6 years or less. 164 companies recruited on campus in 2004-2005.

Admissions Contact: Phil Kimrey, Dean of Admission and Financial Aid. E-mail: *admiss@samford.edu* Web: *www.samford.edu*

SOUTHERN CHRISTIAN UNIVERSITY   C-4

Montgomery, AL 36117-3553   (334) 387-3877, ext. 213
(800) 351-4040; Fax: (334) 387-3878

Full-time: 180 men, 150 women	Faculty: 50
Part-time: 6 men, 6 women	Ph.D.s: 63%
Graduate: 200 men, 125 women	Student/Faculty: 7 to 1
Year: semesters, summer session	Tuition: $10,000
Application Deadline: open	Room & Board: n/app
Freshman Class: n/av	
SAT or ACT: n/av	LESS COMPETITIVE

Southern Christian University, founded in 1967 and affiliated with the Church of Christ, merges traditional and on-line education; 90% of its students access SCU programs via Distance Learning. There is 1 undergraduate school and 2 graduate schools. Figures in the above capsule and in this profile are approximate. The library contains 73,000 volumes, 500 microform items, and 800 audio/video tapes/CDs/DVDs, and subscribes to 1200 periodicals including electronic. Computerized library services include the card catalog, interlibrary loans, database searching, and Internet access. Special learning facilities include a learning resource center. The 9-acre campus is in an urban area in Montgomery. There is one building.

Student Life: 65% of undergraduates are from out of state. Others are from 50 states and 3 foreign countries. 68% are white; 30% African American. Most are Protestant. The average age of freshmen is 28; all undergraduates, 35.

Housing: There are no residence halls. Alcohol is not permitted. All students may keep cars.

Activities: There are no fraternities or sororities. There are some groups and organizations on campus, including student government.

Disabled Students: All classrooms and the learning resource center are accessible.

Programs of Study: SCU confers B.A. and B.S. degrees. Master's and doctoral degrees are also awarded. Bachelor's degrees are awarded in BUSINESS (human resources and management information systems), EDUCATION (social foundations), SOCIAL SCIENCE (biblical studies, human development, law enforcement and corrections, liberal arts/general studies, ministries, and safety management). Human and social development, management communication, and ministry/Bible are the largest.

Required: Students must complete at least 128 credit hours, with 36 in the major and a minimum GPA of 2.0.

Faculty/Classroom: 77% of faculty are male; 23%, female. No introductory courses are taught by graduate students.

Requirements: CLEP credit is accepted.

Procedure: Freshmen are admitted to all sessions. Application deadlines are open. Applications are accepted on-line. Check with the school for current application fee.

Transfer: Unconditional admission requires a 2.0 GPA on prior course work; below 2.0, students are admitted on a conditional basis. 32 of 128 credits required for the bachelor's degree must be completed at SCU.

Financial Aid: The FAFSA and the college's own financial statement are required.

International Students: 4 international students were enrolled in a recent year. They must take the TOEFL and also take the SAT or the ACT.

Computers: All students may access the system. All students are required to have personal computers.

Graduates: In a recent year, 95 bachelor's degrees were awarded. The most popular majors were ministry/Bible (41%), human development (34%), and management communication (23%). Of a recent graduating class, 50% were enrolled in graduate school within 6 months of graduation and 90% were employed.

Admissions Contact: Rick Johnson, Director of Enrollment Management. E-mail: *rickkjohnson@southernchristian.edu*
Web: *www.southernchristian.edu*

SPRING HILL COLLEGE   A-5

Mobile, AL 36608   (251) 380-3030
(800) 742-6704; Fax: (251) 460-2186

Full-time: 430 men, 744 women	Faculty: 72; IIA, --$
Part-time: 34 men, 91 women	Ph.D.s: 85%
Graduate: 65 men, 133 women	Student/Faculty: 16 to 1
Year: semesters, summer session	Tuition: $20,948
Application Deadline: July 1	Room & Board: $7730
Freshman Class: 1190 applied, 953 accepted, 275 enrolled	
SAT Verbal/Math: 540/540*	ACT: 23 COMPETITIVE

Spring Hill College, founded in 1830, is a private Catholic liberal arts and sciences college. There are 4 graduate schools. In addition to regional accreditation, Spring Hill has baccalaureate program accreditation with ACBSP and CCNE. The 2 libraries contain 176,693 volumes, 307,991 microform items, and 591 audio/video tapes/CDs/DVDs, and subscribe to 547 periodicals including electronic. Computerized library services include the card catalog, interlibrary loans, database searching, Internet access, and laptop Internet portals. Special learning facilities include a learning resource center and a theater. The 450-acre campus is in a suburban area in Mobile. Including any residence halls, there are 33 buildings.

Student Life: 54% of undergraduates are from out of state, mostly the South. Students are from 36 states and 8 foreign countries. 75% are white; 16% African American. 52% are Catholic; 26% claim no religious affiliation; 22% Protestant. The average age of freshmen is 18; all undergraduates, 22. 19% do not continue beyond their first year; 59% remain to graduate.

Housing: 916 students can be accommodated in college housing, which includes single-sex and coed dorms and on-campus apartments. On-campus housing is guaranteed for all 4 years. 72% of students live on campus; of those, 90% remain on campus on weekends. All students may keep cars.

Activities: 14% of men belong to 2 national fraternities; 23% of women belong to 4 national sororities. There are 32 groups on campus, including art, cheerleading, chorale, computers, dance, drama, drill team, ethnic, honors, international, literary magazine, newspaper, photography, political, professional, religious, social, social service, student government, and yearbook. Popular campus events include Mardi Gras, Fall Formal, and band parties.

Sports: There are 7 intercollegiate sports for men and 8 for women, and 8 intramural sports for men and 8 for women. Facilities include an 18-hole golf course, tennis and basketball courts, an outdoor sand volleyball area, and baseball, softball, football, rugby, and soccer fields. A recreation center houses the intercollegiate basketball arena, 2 basketball courts, 2 racquetball courts, a cardiovascular exercise room, an indoor pool, and a running track.

Disabled Students: 90% of the campus is accessible. Wheelchair ramps, elevators, special parking, specially equipped rest rooms, special class scheduling, lowered drinking fountains, lowered telephones, and special housing are available.

Services: Counseling and information services are available, as is tutoring in some subjects, including English, theology, math, languages, philosophy, economics, biology, chemistry, psychology, history, and accounting. There is remedial math, reading, and writing.

Campus Safety and Security: Measures include 24-hour foot and vehicle patrol, self-defense education, security escort services, and informal discussions. There are pamphlets/posters/films, emergency telephones, and lighted pathways/sidewalks.

Programs of Study: Spring Hill confers B.A., B.S., and B.S.N. degrees. Associate and master's degrees are also awarded. Bachelor's degrees are awarded in BIOLOGICAL SCIENCE (biochemistry, biology/biological science, and marine biology), BUSINESS (accounting, banking and finance, business administration and management, international business management, marketing management, and organizational behavior), COMMUNICATIONS AND THE ARTS (arts administration/management, communications, creative writing, dramatic arts, English, graphic design, journalism, Spanish, and studio art), COMPUTER AND PHYSICAL SCIENCE (chemistry, computer science, and mathematics), EDUCATION (early childhood, elementary, and secondary), ENGINEERING AND ENVIRONMENTAL DESIGN (engineering), HEALTH PROFESSIONS (art therapy, nursing, predentistry, premedicine, and preveterinary science), SOCIAL SCIENCE (economics, history, humanities, international studies, liberal arts/general studies, philosophy, political science/government, psychology, social science, sociology, and theological studies). Theology, English, and business are the strongest academically. Business administration, biology, and nursing are the largest.

Required: All students must take core curriculum courses in English composition and literature, history, philosophy, theology, math, science, social science, fine art, and foreign language. Students must also take 1 cultural diversity course and at least 3 writing-enriched courses (including 1 in the major) beyond the required 4 core curriculum English courses. Graduation requirements include completion of a minimum of 128 semester hours with a minimum GPA of 2.0 and 30 to 36 upper-division semester hours in the major with a minimum GPA of 2.0.

Special: SHC offers 3-2 engineering programs with the University of Alabama-Birmingham, Auburn University, the University of Florida, Marquette University, and Texas A & M University. It also offers 3-3 occupational therapy and physical therapy programs with Rockhurst University and Nova Southeastern University. The college is a member of the Marine Environmental Sciences Consortium and offers marine biology courses at the Dauphin Island Sea Lab. Several study-abroad options are available. Internships are also available in many majors. An accelerated degree program is offered in organizational leadership, and most majors may be completed in 3 years by taking summer courses. Also available are dual majors, student-designed majors, a Washington semester, and pass/fail options. There are 8 national honor societies and a freshman honors program.

Faculty/Classroom: 56% of faculty are male; 44%, female. All teach undergraduates. No introductory courses are taught by graduate stu-

dents. The average class size in an introductory lecture is 23; in a laboratory, 20; and in a regular course, 16.

Admissions: 80% of the 2005-2006 applicants were accepted. The SAT scores for the 2005-2006 freshman class were: Verbal--30% below 500, 41% between 500 and 599, 25% between 600 and 700, and 4% above 700; Math--39% below 500, 30% between 500 and 599, 28% between 600 and 700, and 3% above 700. The ACT scores were 24% below 21, 32% between 21 and 23, 23% between 24 and 26, 15% between 27 and 28, and 6% above 28. 31% of the current freshmen were in the top fifth of their class; 51% were in the top two fifths. 5 freshmen graduated first in their class.

Requirements: The SAT or ACT is required; the ACT is preferred. Applicants should have completed at least 16 high school units, including 4 in English, 3 each in math, science, and social studies, and 3 in other academic areas. The GED equivalent is accepted. An essay and an interview are strongly recommended. Spring Hill requires applicants to be in the upper 50% of their class. A GPA of 2.5 is required. AP and CLEP credits are accepted. Important factors in the admissions decision are recommendations by school officials, leadership record, and personality/intangible qualities.

Procedure: Freshmen are admitted fall, spring, and summer. Entrance exams should be taken in spring of the junior year or fall of the senior year. There is a deferred admissions plan. There is a rolling admissions plan. Applications should be filed by July 1 for fall entry and December 15 for spring entry, along with a $25 fee. Notification is sent on a rolling basis. Applications are accepted on-line.

Transfer: 35 transfer students enrolled in 2005-2006. Transfer applicants must have at least 20 semester hours of college credit, a minimum cumulative GPA of 2.5, good academic standing at the last college or university attended, and satisfactory recommendations. 32 of 128 credits required for the bachelor's degree must be completed at Spring Hill.

Visiting: There are regularly scheduled orientations for prospective students, including a campus tour, faculty appointment, attending a class, lunch with a student, and an interview with an admission counselor. There are guides for informal visits and visitors may sit in on classes and stay overnight. To schedule a visit, contact the Office of Admissions.

Financial Aid: In 2005-2006, 97% of all full-time students received some form of financial aid. 70% of full-time freshmen and 64% of continuing full-time students received need-based aid. The average freshman award was $21,652. Need-based scholarships or need-based grants averaged $11,354 ($25,230 maximum); need-based self-help aid (loans and jobs) averaged $4630 ($12,988 maximum); non-need-based athletic scholarships averaged $3926 ($28,678 maximum); and other non-need-based awards and non-need-based scholarships averaged $8690 ($25,000 maximum). 31% of undergraduates work part time. Average annual earnings from campus work are $1452. The average financial indebtedness of the 2005 graduate was $16,646. Spring Hill is a member of CSS. The FAFSA, the state aid form, and the college's own financial statement are required. The priority date for freshman financial aid applications for fall entry is March 1.

International Students: There are 12 international students enrolled. The school actively recruits these students. They must take the TOEFL achieving a satisfactory score, or take the MELAB. They must also take either the ACT (preferred) or the SAT if their first language is English.

Computers: Wireless access is available. Students are served by a network of Windows-based and Mac computers, and the college intranet is connected to the Internet. Computer labs contain 161 computers. In addition to its 4 computer labs/classrooms, the library contains 25 general-use computer workstations. Residence halls are wired for students' personal computers and also contain 6 computers available to all students. A laptop classroom in the main classroom building also provides computer access. All students may access the system. Students may access the system from residence halls anytime. Computer labs are open Monday to Thursday, 8 A.M. to midnight; Friday, 8 A.M. to 10 P.M.; Saturday, 10 A.M. to 5 P.M.; Sunday noon to midnight. There are no time limits and no fees.

Graduates: From July 1, 2004 to June 30, 2005, 212 bachelor's degrees were awarded. The most popular majors were business administration (20%), biology (12%), and communication arts (11%). In an average class, 1% graduate in 3 years or less, 48% graduate in 4 years or less, 58% graduate in 5 years or less, and 59% graduate in 6 years or less. 15 companies recruited on campus in 2004-2005. Of the 2004 graduating class, 34% were enrolled in graduate school within 6 months of graduation and 69% were employed.

Admissions Contact: Florence Hines, Vice President of Enrollment Management. E-mail: *admit@shc.edu* Web: *http://www.shc.edu/admission*

STILLMAN COLLEGE   B-3

Tuscaloosa, AL 35403-9990   (205)366-8837
(800) 841-5722; Fax: (205) 366-8817

Full-time: 645 men, 785 women	**Faculty:** 52
Part-time: 25 men, 25 women	**Ph.D.s:** 70%
Graduate: none	**Student/Faculty:** 27 to 1
Year: semesters, summer session	**Tuition:** $7450
Application Deadline: n/av	**Room & Board:** $4025
Freshman Class: n/av	
SAT or ACT: required	**LESS COMPETITIVE**

Stillman College, founded in 1876, is a small, private liberal arts institution affiliated with the Presbyterian Church (U.S.A.). Figures in the above capsule and in this profile are approximate. The library contains 113,120 volumes, 7240 microform items, and 3550 audio/video tapes/CDs/DVDs, and subscribes to 360 periodicals including electronic. Computerized library services include the card catalog, interlibrary loans, and database searching. Special learning facilities include a learning resource center, art gallery, and radio station. The 100-acre campus is in a small town 60 miles from Birmingham and 105 miles from Montgomery. Including any residence halls, there are 26 buildings.

Student Life: 70% of undergraduates are from Alabama. Others are from 27 states and 8 foreign countries. 95% are from public schools. 98% are African American. Most are Protestant. The average age of freshmen is 19.

Housing: 750 students can be accommodated in college housing, which includes single-sex dorms and off-campus apartments. On-campus housing is available on a first-come, first-served basis. 50% of students live on campus. Alcohol is not permitted. All students may keep cars.

Activities: 10% of men belong to 4 national fraternities; 20% of women belong to 4 national sororities. There are 19 groups on campus, including art, band, cheerleading, choir, chorus, dance, debate, drama, honors, international, jazz band, marching band, newspaper, pep band, radio and TV, religious, social, social service, student government, and yearbook. Popular campus events include "S" Day, Founder's Day, and Coffee House.

Sports: There are 6 intercollegiate sports for men and 6 for women. Facilities include a college center, tennis courts, a stress center, bowling lanes, billiards, a swimming pool, a gym, a football field, and a weight room.

Disabled Students: Wheelchair ramps, elevators, special parking, and specially equipped rest rooms are available.

Services: Counseling and information services are available, as is tutoring in some subjects, including reading, writing, math, physics, and chemistry. There is remedial math, reading, and writing.

Campus Safety and Security: Measures include 24-hour foot and vehicle patrol, self-defense education, security escort services, and informal discussions. There are pamphlets/posters/films and lighted pathways/sidewalks.

Programs of Study: Stillman confers B.A. and B.S. degrees. Bachelor's degrees are awarded in BIOLOGICAL SCIENCE (biology/biological science), BUSINESS (business administration and management), COMMUNICATIONS AND THE ARTS (art, English, and music), COMPUTER AND PHYSICAL SCIENCE (computer science and mathematics), EDUCATION (elementary and physical), HEALTH PROFESSIONS (premedicine), SOCIAL SCIENCE (history, prelaw, and religion).

Required: To graduate, students must complete a minimum of 124 credit hours, with at least 30 in the major, and maintain a minimum GPA of 2.0 overall and in the major. The 53-credit-hour general education core includes courses in religion, logic, English composition, public speaking, African heritage, African American experience, history, social science, physical and life sciences, math, computer literacy, health, and phys ed. All students must submit a senior thesis and take a senior departmental exam.

Special: Stillman offers local, national, and international opportunites for cooperative education and internships. Cross-registration is possible with the University of Alabama at Birmingham, with which there also are cooperative degree programs in nursing and allied health. Federal work-study is available on and off campus, and students may earn credit for prior learning experiences. There are 3 national honor societies.

Faculty/Classroom: 40% of faculty are male; 60%, female. All teach undergraduates. The average class size in an introductory lecture is 40; in a laboratory, 40; and in a regular course, 35.

Requirements: The SAT or ACT is required. In addition, applicants should be high school graduates or have earned the GED. Secondary preparation should include 4 units of English and 1 unit each of math, science, and history. All applicants must have an interview. Music majors must audition. A GPA of 2.0 is required. AP and CLEP credits are accepted.

Procedure: Freshmen are admitted to all sessions. Check with the school for application deadlines. There is a rolling admissions plan. Notification is sent on a rolling basis. The fall 2005 application fee was $25.

Transfer: Transfer applicants should present at least a C average in previous college work and must plan to spend at least a year in residence. 64 of 124 credits required for the bachelor's degree must be completed at Stillman.

Visiting: There are regularly scheduled orientations for prospective students. To schedule a visit, contact the director of recruitment.

Financial Aid: The CSS/Profile, FAFSA, FFS or SFS and the college's own financial statement are required. Check with the school for application deadlines.

International Students: The school actively recruits these students. They must take the SAT or the ACT.

Computers: All students may access the system 8 A.M. to 9 P.M. Monday through Saturday. Students may access the system 69 hours per week. There are no fees.

Admissions Contact: Mrs. Hatter, Director of Admissions.
E-mail: *mbonner@www.stillman.edu* Web: *www.stillman.edu*

TALLADEGA COLLEGE	C-2
Talladega, AL 35160	**(256) 761-6416; (800) 633-2440**
Full-time: 250 men, 400 women	**Faculty:** 40
Part-time: 10 men, 20 women	**Ph.D.s:** 60%
Graduate: none	**Student/Faculty:** 16 to 1
Year: semesters	**Tuition:** $7000
Application Deadline: open	**Room & Board:** $4240
Freshman Class: n/av	
SAT or ACT: required	**LESS COMPETITIVE**

Talladega College, founded in 1867, is a private liberal arts institution offering emphases on business, sciences, and social work. Figures given in above capsule and in this profile are approximate. In addition to regional accreditation, Dega has baccalaureate program accreditation with CSWE. The library contains 87,960 volumes and 350 audio/video tapes/CDs/DVDs, and subscribes to 330 periodicals including electronic. Computerized library services include the card catalog and interlibrary loans. Special learning facilities include a learning resource center, art gallery science drop-in center, curriculum and writing labs, and financial computer lab. The 130-acre campus is in a small town 55 miles east of Birmingham and 115 miles west of Atlanta. Including any residence halls, there are 42 buildings.

Student Life: 60% of undergraduates are from Alabama. Others are from 29 states and 2 foreign countries. 99% are African American. Most are Protestant. The average age of freshmen is 18; all undergraduates, 20. 22% do not continue beyond their first year; 45% remain to graduate.

Housing: 580 students can be accommodated in college housing, which includes single-sex dorms and on-campus apartments. In addition, there are honors houses. On-campus housing is guaranteed for all 4 years. 70% of students live on campus; of those, 90% remain on campus on weekends. Alcohol is not permitted. All students may keep cars.

Activities: 14% of men belong to 4 national fraternities; 40% of women belong to 4 national sororities. There are 23 groups on campus, including art, cheerleading, choir, chorus, computers, dance, drama, honors, jazz band, newspaper, professional, social, student government, and yearbook. Popular campus events include Spring Concert, Carnival, and Coronation.

Sports: There are 4 intercollegiate sports for men and 4 for women, and 8 intramural sports for men and 3 for women. Facilities include a swimming pool, a 150-seat gym, lounges, game rooms, tennis courts, and a baseball field.

Disabled Students: 50% of the campus is accessible. Wheelchair ramps, elevators, special parking, and specially equipped rest rooms are available.

Services: Counseling and information services are available, as is tutoring in every subject. There is remedial math, reading, and writing.

Campus Safety and Security: Measures include 24-hour foot and vehicle patrol, security escort services, informal discussions, pamphlets/posters/films, lighted pathways/sidewalks.

Programs of Study: Dega confers the B.A. degree. Bachelor's degrees are awarded in BIOLOGICAL SCIENCE (biology/biological science), BUSINESS (accounting, banking and finance, and business administration and management), COMMUNICATIONS AND THE ARTS (English and music performance), COMPUTER AND PHYSICAL SCIENCE (chemistry, computer science, mathematics, and physics), EDUCATION (music), SOCIAL SCIENCE (economics, history, psychology, public administration, social work, and sociology). Business, biology, and chemistry are the strongest academically. Biology is the largest.

Required: To graduate, students must maintain a minimum GPA of 2.5 while taking 124 to 127 total semester hours, including 60 in the major and completion of a core curriculum. Distribution requirements at the freshman level include 8 semester hours in natural sciences, 6 each in communications, social sciences, and humanities, 2 in phys ed, and 1 in freshman orientation; additional hours in these subjects vary by major at the sophomore level.

Special: Talladega offers co-op programs with other schools through individual departments, a 3-2 engineering degree with Auburn University, internships involving historic preservation work, work-study plans with Adopt-a-Family and Adult Literacy, and B.A.-B.S. degrees in biology, business administration, chemistry, and computer science. There are dual majors available in law, nursing, engineering, and allied health. There are 4 national honor societies.

Faculty/Classroom: 60% of faculty are male; 40%, female. All teach undergraduates and 25% both teach and do research. The average class size in an introductory lecture is 30; in a laboratory, 20; and in a regular course, 18.

Requirements: The SAT or ACT is required. In addition, applicants must be graduates of an accredited secondary school with 22 academic units, including 4 in English, 3 in social studies, and 2 each in math, science, health/phys ed, and electives. The GED is considered. An essay and interview are recommended. An audition is required for music majors. A GPA of 2.5 is required. CLEP credit is accepted. Important factors in the admissions decision are advanced placement or honor courses, recommendations by school officials, and recommendations by alumni.

Procedure: Freshmen are admitted fall and spring. Entrance exams should be taken in the junior year. There is a deferred admissions plan. Application deadlines are open. Applications are accepted on-line. Check with the school for current application fee.

Transfer: Applicants must have a cumulative GPA of 2.0 in college work. The SAT or ACT is recommended. 60 of 124 credits required for the bachelor's degree must be completed at Dega.

Visiting: There are guides for informal visits and visitors may sit in on classes and stay overnight. To schedule a visit, contact the Admissions Office.

Financial Aid: The CSS/Profile, FAFSA, FFS, or SFS and the college's own financial statement are required. Check with the school for current deadlines.

International Students: The school actively recruits these students. They must take the TOEFL or the college's own test and also take the SAT or the ACT.

Computers: All students may access the system from 8 A.M. to 4:30 P.M. and 7 P.M. to 10 P.M. daily. There are no time limits and no fees.

Admissions Contact: Admissions Office.
E-mail: *admissions@talladega.edu* Web: *www.talladega.edu*

TROY UNIVERSITY

The Troy University, established in 1887, is a private University in Alabama. It is governed by a board of trustees, whose chief administrator is chancellor. The primary goal of the system is to provide an academic, cultural, and social environment conducive to the development of students as well as productive, individual members of society. The main priorities are the preprofessional and professional preparation of students in the arts and sciences, fine arts, business, education, communication, applied science, nursing, and allied health sciences. The total enrollment of all 12 campuses is usually about 14,000, with 650 faculty members. Profiles of the 4-year campuses are included in this section.

TROY UNIVERSITY (Formerly Troy State University)	C-4
Troy, AL 36082	**(334) 670-3179**
	(800) 551-9716; Fax: (334) 670-3733
Full-time: 2736 men, 3619 women	**Faculty:** 298; IIA, --$
Part-time: 4430 men, 3083 women	**Ph.D.s:** 56%
Graduate: 2381 men, 4792 women	**Student/Faculty:** 21 to 1
Year: semesters, summer session	**Tuition:** $4104 ($8108)
Application Deadline: open	**Room & Board:** $4812
Freshman Class: n/av	
SAT or ACT: required	**COMPETITIVE**

Troy University in Troy, founded in 1887, is a public institution. International in scope Troy University provides a variety of educational programs at the undergraduate, and graduate levels for a diverse student body. Academic programs are offered in traditional, nontraditional and emerging electronic formats. There are 5 undergraduate and 5 graduate schools. In addition to regional accreditation, TSU has baccalaureate program accreditation with ACBSP, CSWE, NASM, NCATE, NLN, and CAAHEP. The 2 libraries contain 443,415 volumes, 1,578,145 microform items, and 16,473 audio/video tapes/CDs/DVDs, and subscribe to 1446 periodicals including electronic. Computerized library services include the card catalog, interlibrary loans, database searching, Internet access, and laptop Internet portals. Special learning facilities include a learning resource center, art gallery, radio station, TV station, and arboretum. The 512-acre campus is in a rural area Troy Campus is 50 miles south of Montgomery, Phenix City is 5 miles south of Phenix City, AL. Univer. Including any residence halls, there are 87 buildings.

Student Life: 60% of undergraduates are from out of state, mostly the South. Others are from 49 states, 55 foreign countries, and Canada.

54% are white; 31% African American. The average age of freshmen is 26; all undergraduates, 29. 51% of freshmen remain to graduate.

Housing: 1525 students can be accommodated in college housing, which includes single-sex and coed dorms, on-campus apartments, off-campus apartments, married-student housing, fraternity houses, and sorority houses. In addition, there are honors houses and special-interest houses. On-campus housing is guaranteed for all 4 years. 71% of students commute. Alcohol is not permitted. All students may keep cars.

Activities: 16% of men belong to 12 national fraternities; 17% of women belong to 9 national sororities. There are 125 groups on campus, including art, band, cheerleading, choir, chorale, chorus, computers, dance, debate, drama, drill team, ethnic, film, forensics, honors, international, jazz band, literary magazine, marching band, musical theater, newspaper, opera, orchestra, pep band, photography, political, professional, radio and TV, religious, social, social service, student government, symphony, and yearbook. Popular campus events include Greek Week, SGA Martin Luther King Celebration and ISCO Festival.

Sports: There are 7 intercollegiate sports for men and 9 for women, and 11 intramural sports for men and 11 for women. Facilities include a 150-seat auditorium, a 3,000-square-foot weight training center, a 2,250-seat Pace-Riddle baseball stadium, 9-hole golf course, a 30,000-seat Movie Gallery Veteran's Stadium, and 2 football practice fields. Other nearby facilities include a softball and soccer/track complex. The 4,000-seat Trojan Arena is home to both basketball teams and the volleyball team. Also, available for student use is the Natatorium with an indoor swimming pool, the recreational gym with an outdoor swimming pool and fitness centers, and intramural fields.

Disabled Students: 95% of the campus is accessible. Wheelchair ramps, elevators, special parking, specially equipped rest rooms, special class scheduling, lowered drinking fountains, lowered telephones, and graded inclines, and specially equipped apartments are available.

Services: Counseling and information services are available, as is tutoring in most subjects. There is a reader service for the blind, and remedial math, reading, and writing.

Campus Safety and Security: Measures include 24-hour foot and vehicle patrol, self-defense education, security escort services, and pamphlets/posters/films. There are lighted pathways/sidewalks.

Programs of Study: Troy confers B.A., B.S., B.A.B.A., B.A.Ed., B.Applied Sc., B.F.A., B.M.Ed., B.S.B.A., B.S.Ed., and B.S.N. degrees. Associate and master's degrees are also awarded. Bachelor's degrees are awarded in BIOLOGICAL SCIENCE (biology/biological science, and marine biology), BUSINESS (accounting, banking and finance, business administration and management, insurance, marketing management, marketing/retailing/merchandising, and sports management), COMMUNICATIONS AND THE ARTS (art, art history and appreciation, broadcasting, communications, design, dramatic arts, English, journalism, and studio art), COMPUTER AND PHYSICAL SCIENCE (chemistry, computer science, information sciences and systems, and mathematics), EDUCATION (art, athletic training, collaborative, early childhood, elementary, English, health, mathematics, music, physical, science, secondary, and social science), ENGINEERING AND ENVIRONMENTAL DESIGN (environmental science, and technological management), HEALTH PROFESSIONS (nursing, and rehabilitation therapy), SOCIAL SCIENCE (criminal justice, history, human services, political science/government, psychology, social science, and social work). Business and education are the strongest academically. Business is the largest.

Required: All students must maintain a minimum GPA of 2.0 while taking 120 to 140 semester credit hours, 54 of which must be in their major field. Distribution requirements include 48 hours of general studies, covering such subjects as English, math, history, science, and fine arts.

Special: Cross-registration with the Marine Biological Consortium, internships in education, journalism, and nursing, study abroad in 2 countries, work-study programs at the university, and student-designed majors in public relations, advertising, and other fields are offered. Credit for life experience and nondegree study are also offered. There are 22 national honor societies, including Phi Beta Kappa, a freshman honors program, and 14 departmental honors programs.

Faculty/Classroom: 52% of faculty are male; 48%, female. All teach undergraduates.

Requirements: The SAT or ACT is required. In addition, with a recommended composite score for the ACT. Applicants must have earned at least 15 Carnegie units, with 11 in academic courses and 3 to 4 in English. An interview is recommended, along with a portfolio or audition for some programs. The GED is accepted. A GPA of 2.0 is required. AP and CLEP credits are accepted. Important factors in the admissions decision are ability to finance college education, evidence of special talent, and extracurricular activities record.

Procedure: Freshmen are admitted fall, spring, and summer. Entrance exams should be taken in the fall of the senior year. Application deadlines are open. Applications are accepted on-line.

Transfer: Transfer applicants need 20 semester hours attempted at their previous institution, with a GPA of at least 2.0.

Visiting: There are regularly scheduled orientations for prospective students, including a campus tour, classroom visitation, academic consulta-

tion, and interviews. There are guides for informal visits and visitors may sit in on classes. To schedule a visit, contact the Office of Enrollment Services.

Financial Aid: 9% of undergraduates work part time. Average annual earnings from campus work are $3214. The FAFSA and the college's own financial statement are required. The deadline for filing freshman financial aid applications for fall entry is May 1.

International Students: There are 350 international students enrolled. The school actively recruits these students. They must score satisfactorily on the written TOEFL. And also take International English Language Testing System (IELTS) and also take the SAT or the ACT.

Computers: Wireless access is available. PCs are located in the library and computer labs as well as the Trojan Center. All students may access the system 7 days a week. There are no time limits and no fees.

Graduates: From July 1, 2004 to June 30, 2005, 1791 bachelor's degrees were awarded. The most popular majors were business (27%), criminal justice (12%), and psychology (8%). In an average class, 33% graduate in 4 years or less, 47% graduate in 5 years or less, and 51% graduate in 6 years or less.

Admissions Contact: Buddy Starling, Dean of Enrollment Services. A video is available. E-mail: *bstar@trojan.troyst.edu* Web: *www.troyst.edu*

TROY UNIVERSITY DOTHAN CAMPUS D-5
(Formerly Troy State University Dothan)

Dothan, AL 36304   (334) 983-6556; Fax: (334) 983-6322

Full-time: 238 men, 499 women	**Faculty:** 54; IIA, --$
Part-time: 235 men, 497 women	**Ph.D.s:** 78%
Graduate: 96 men, 295 women	**Student/Faculty:** 14 to 1
Year: semesters, summer session	**Tuition:** $4678 ($8682)
Application Deadline: open	**Room & Board:** n/app
Freshman Class: 140 applied, 136 accepted, 101 enrolled	
SAT or ACT: 21	**COMPETITIVE**

Troy University Dothan Campus, founded in 1965, is a public liberal arts school. With a permanent campus established in Dothan in 1977, the university serves the tri-state region (Alabama, Georgia, and Florida). It continues to offer degree completion studies for the military at Fort Rucker. There are 3 undergraduate and 3 graduate schools. In addition to regional accreditation, Troy Dothan has baccalaureate program accreditation with ACBSP and NCATE. The library contains 103,223 volumes, 290,051 microform items, and 1599 audio/video tapes/CDs/DVDs, and subscribes to 403 periodicals including electronic. Computerized library services include the card catalog, interlibrary loans, database searching, and Internet access. Special learning facilities include a learning resource center. The 250-acre campus is in an urban area 90 miles southeast of Montgomery. There are 3 buildings.

Student Life: Almost all students are from the South. Students are from 10 states. 73% are white; 20% African American. The average age of freshmen is 26; all undergraduates, 29. 52% do not continue beyond their first year; 23% remain to graduate.

Housing: There are no residence halls. All students commute. Alcohol is not permitted. All students may keep cars.

Activities: There are no fraternities or sororities. There are 15 groups on campus, including band, computers, ethnic, honors, literary magazine, professional, religious, social, and student government. Popular campus events include Spring Picnic, Heritage Week, and Black History Program.

Sports: There is no sports program at Troy Dothan.

Disabled Students: All of the campus is accessible. Wheelchair ramps, elevators, special parking, specially equipped rest rooms, lowered drinking fountains, and lowered telephones are available.

Services: Counseling and information services are available, as is tutoring in most subjects. There is remedial math and writing.

Campus Safety and Security: Measures include 24-hour foot and vehicle patrol, pamphlets/posters/films, and lighted pathways/sidewalks.

Programs of Study: Troy Dothan confers B.A., B.S., B.A.Ed., B.A.S., and B.S.Ed degrees. Associate and master's degrees are also awarded. Bachelor's degrees are awarded in BIOLOGICAL SCIENCE (biology/biological science), BUSINESS (accounting, banking and finance, business administration and management, business economics, marketing management, and personnel management), COMMUNICATIONS AND THE ARTS (English), COMPUTER AND PHYSICAL SCIENCE (chemistry, computer science, mathematics, and science), EDUCATION (early childhood, elementary, English, mathematics, science, secondary, social science, and special), ENGINEERING AND ENVIRONMENTAL DESIGN (technological management), SOCIAL SCIENCE (criminal justice, history, psychology, social science, and sociology). Computer information systems and psychology are the strongest academically. Accounting, elementary education, and criminal justice are the largest.

Required: All students must take a minimum of 120 semester hours, including 30 in their major, and must maintain an overall GPA of at least 2.0. Distribution requirements include English composition I and II, 6 hours each of literature, history, and social science, 3 hours each of music and art, microcomputing and speech, math, biology, philosophy, and science.

Special: Internships in the accounting and education programs, nondegree study, and pass/fail options are available. There are 4 national honor societies.

Faculty/Classroom: 54% of faculty are male; 46%, female. All teach undergraduates. No introductory courses are taught by graduate students. The average class size in a laboratory is 15 and in a regular course, 14.

Admissions: 97% of the 2005-2006 applicants were accepted. The ACT scores for the 2005-2006 freshman class were: 45% below 21, 27% between 21 and 23, 25% between 24 and 26, and 2% between 27 and 28.

Requirements: The SAT or ACT is required. In addition, applicants must be graduates of an accredited high school. Beginning freshmen under age 21 must have a minimum ACT score of 18 or a satisfactory SAT score. The GED is accepted. A GPA of 2.0 is required. AP and CLEP credits are accepted. Important factors in the admissions decision are leadership record, advanced placement or honor courses, and ability to finance college education.

Procedure: Freshmen are admitted fall, spring, and summer. Entrance exams should be taken during the junior year of high school. There is a rolling admissions plan. Application deadlines are open. The application fee is $30. Applications are accepted on-line.

Transfer: 376 transfer students enrolled in 2004-2005. Transfer applicants receive unconditional acceptance if their GPA is 2.0 or above. 30 of 120 credits required for the bachelor's degree must be completed at Troy Dothan.

Visiting: There are regularly scheduled orientations for prospective students, including review of program and services, introduction of department deans, and meetings with advisers. There are guides for informal visits and visitors may sit in on classes. To schedule a visit, contact Inga Oberst at (334) 983-6556 ext. 217 or *ioberst@troy.edu.*

Financial Aid: In 2005-2006, 10% of all full-time freshmen and 60% of continuing full-time students received some form of financial aid. 4% of full-time freshmen and 40% of continuing full-time students received need-based aid. Need-based scholarships or need-based grants averaged $3021 ($4050 maximum); and need-based self-help aid (loans and jobs) averaged $4591 ($8500 maximum). 1% of undergraduates work part time. Average annual earnings from campus work are $2140. The average financial indebtedness of the 2005 graduate was $22,352. The FAFSA and the college's own financial statement are required. The priority date for freshman financial aid applications for fall entry is March 1. The deadline for filing freshman financial aid applications for fall entry is July 1.

International Students: They must score satisfactorily on the TOEFL.

Computers: Wireless access is available. All students may access the system between 8 A.M. and 9 P.M., Monday through Thursday and 8:00 A.M. to 12:00 P.M. Friday. There are no time limits and no fees.

Graduates: From July 1, 2004 to June 30, 2005, 254 bachelor's degrees were awarded. The most popular majors were computer information system (14%), accounting (13%), and psychology (9%). In an average class, 21% graduate in 4 years or less. 56 companies recruited on campus in 2004-2005. Of the 2004 graduating class, 90% were employed within 6 months of graduation.

Admissions Contact: Andrew Rivers, Enrollment Services. E-mail: *ariversjr@troy.edu* Web: *http://dothan.troy.edu*

TROY UNIVERSITY MONTGOMERY CAMPUS C-4
(Formerly Troy State University Montgomery)

Montgomery, AL 36103-4419
(334) 241-9506
(800) 355-TSUM; Fax: (334) 241-9714

Full-time: 349 men, 879 women	**Faculty:** 44
Part-time: 661 men, 1772 women	**Ph.D.s:** n/av
Graduate: 136 men, 458 women	**Student/Faculty:** 28 to 1
Year: semesters, summer session	**Tuition:** $4104 ($8108)
Application Deadline: open	**Room & Board:** n/app
Freshman Class: n/av	
SAT or ACT: not required	**NONCOMPETITIVE**

Troy University Montgomery campus, founded in 1965 as a branch of the Troy University is a public evening commuter institution offering undergraduate and graduate degrees in arts and sciences, education, and business. There are 3 undergraduate schools and 1 graduate school. In addition to regional accreditation, Troy Montgomery has baccalaureate program accreditation with ACBSP and NCATE. The library contains 27,808 volumes, 87,915 microform items, and 9396 audio/video tapes/CDs/DVDs, and subscribes to 502 periodicals including electronic. Computerized library services include the card catalog, interlibrary loans, database searching, and Internet access. Special learning facilities include a learning resource center, planetarium, radio station, TV station, and the Rosa L. Parks Library and Museum. The 6-acre campus is in an urban area in downtown Montgomery. There are 9 buildings.

Student Life: 99% of undergraduates are from Alabama. 52% are African American; 44% white. The average age of all undergraduates is 28.

Housing: There are no residence halls. All students commute. Alcohol is not permitted.

Activities: There are no fraternities or sororities. There are 7 groups on campus, including honors, professional, social service, and student government. Popular campus events include Golf Classic.

Sports: There is no sports program at Troy Montgomery.

Disabled Students: 95% of the campus is accessible. Wheelchair ramps, elevators, special parking, specially equipped rest rooms, lowered drinking fountains, and lowered telephones are available.

Services: Counseling and information services are available, as is tutoring in some subjects. There is a reader service for the blind, and remedial math, reading, and writing. Tutors may be provided for students upon request.

Campus Safety and Security: Measures include security escort services, informal discussions, pamphlets/posters/films, and lighted pathways/sidewalks. There are foot and vehicle patrols during class hours.

Programs of Study: Troy Montgomery confers B.A. and B.S. degrees. Associate and master's degrees are also awarded. Bachelor's degrees are awarded in BUSINESS (accounting, banking and finance, business administration and management, management science, and marketing management), COMMUNICATIONS AND THE ARTS (English), COMPUTER AND PHYSICAL SCIENCE (computer science and mathematics), SOCIAL SCIENCE (history, political science/government, psychology, and social science). Computer and information science are the strongest academically. Resources management is the largest.

Required: Students must complete a minimum of 120 semester hours, with 36 hours within Troy University in the major area, and maintain a minimum GPA of 2.0. At least half of the required total hours must be composed of traditional credits, excluding credit by correspondence or by exam.

Special: Troy University - Montgomery Campus offers an external degree program in professional studies for those unable to attend regularly scheduled classes because of handicap, work, or family restrictions. Credit may be granted for military service and experiential learning. Guided independent study/research, accelerated degree programs, nondegree study, and pass/fail options are possible. Flexible schedules and televised courses are available to meet the needs of adult students. Cross-registration with Alabama State University is offered. There are 2 national honor societies.

Faculty/Classroom: No introductory courses are taught by graduate students.

Requirements: Graduates from accredited secondary schools should have 15 Carnegie units, with 3 or more in English and 11 others in academic courses. Graduates from nonaccredited secondary schools may be admitted if they meet the same requirements and are deemed capable of performing satisfactorily. The GED is accepted. Other applicants may be admitted as unclassified, nondegree-seeking students. For students under 21, the high school GPA and SAT or ACT scores are used in a formula to determine admissions eligibility; those applicants not having a test score may be admitted with conditional status. For students over 21, requirements include a minimum high school GPA of 2.0. Applicants with a lower GPA may be admitted conditionally.

Procedure: Freshmen are admitted to all sessions. Entrance exams should be taken by the fall of the senior year. There is a rolling admissions plan. Application deadlines are open. Application fee is $20. Applications are accepted on-line.

Transfer: Transfer students must submit college transcripts from each college attended. Those with fewer than 15 quarter hours (or 9 semester hours) of credit are required to submit a high school transcript as well. Applicants should have a college GPA of at least 2.0 and be in good standing; others may be admitted conditionally.

Visiting: There are guides for informal visits and visitors may sit in on classes.

Computers: Students taking computer and information science courses may access the system 7 days a week.

Graduates: From July 1, 2004 to June 30, 2005, 294 bachelor's degrees were awarded.

Admissions Contact: Larry Hawkins, Director of Enrollment Management. E-mail: *admit@troy.edu* Web: *Montgomery.troy.edu*

TUSKEGEE UNIVERSITY — D-4

Tuskegee, AL 36088
(334) 727-8500
(800) 622-6531; Fax: (334) 724-4402

Full-time: 1000 men, 1300 women	**Faculty:** 231
Part-time: 50 men, 50 women	**Ph.D.s:** 70%
Graduate: 150 men, 225 women	**Student/Faculty:** 10 to 1
Year: semesters, summer session	**Tuition:** $12,400
Application Deadline: open	**Room & Board:** $6460
Freshman Class: n/av	
SAT or ACT : required	**LESS COMPETITIVE**

Tuskegee University, founded in 1881 by Booker T. Washington, is an independent professional and technical institution offering degree programs in liberal arts and sciences, agriculture, architecture, business, education, engineering, and health professions. Some information in this profile is approximate. There are 5 undergraduate and 4 graduate schools. In addition to regional accreditation, Tuskegee has baccalaureate program accreditation with ABET, CSWE, NAAB, NCATE, and NLN. The 3 libraries contain 293,660 volumes and 300 microform items, and subscribe to 1150 periodicals including electronic. Computerized library services include the card catalog, interlibrary loans, and database searching. Special learning facilities include a learning resource center the Carver Museum, a child development center, and special engineering labs. The 5200-acre campus is in a rural area 40 miles east of Montgomery. Including any residence halls, there are 150 buildings.
Student Life: 70% of undergraduates are from out of state, mostly the South. Students are from 41 states, 31 foreign countries, and Canada. 90% are from public schools. 90% are African American. The average age of freshmen is 18; all undergraduates, 22. 29% do not continue beyond their first year; 51% remain to graduate.
Housing: 2300 students can be accommodated in college housing, which includes single-sex dorms, on-campus apartments, and married-student housing. In addition, there are honors houses. On-campus housing is guaranteed for the freshman year only. 60% of students live on campus. Alcohol is not permitted. All students may keep cars.
Activities: 4% of men belong to 6 local and 4 national fraternities; 4% of women belong to 5 local and 4 national sororities. There are 60 groups on campus, including band, cheerleading, choir, chorus, drama, honors, international, jazz band, marching band, newspaper, orchestra, religious, social service, and student government. Popular campus events include Spring Pageant, Campus All-Star Challenge, and Student Leadership Retreat.
Sports: There are 5 intercollegiate sports for men and 5 for women, and 7 intramural sports for men and 6 for women. Facilities include a 10,000-seat stadium, a 5000-seat arena, a student center, tennis courts, a rifle range, playing fields, and an Olympic-size natatorium.
Disabled Students: Wheelchair ramps, elevators, special parking, specially equipped rest rooms, special class scheduling, lowered drinking fountains, and lowered telephones are available.
Services: Counseling and information services are available, as is tutoring in some subjects. There is a reader service for the blind.
Campus Safety and Security: Measures include 24-hour foot and vehicle patrol, security escort services, informal discussions, and lighted pathways/sidewalks.
Programs of Study: Tuskegee confers B.A., B.S., and B.S.N. degrees. Master's and doctoral degrees are also awarded. Bachelor's degrees are awarded in AGRICULTURE (animal science and horticulture), BIOLOGICAL SCIENCE (biology/biological science), BUSINESS (accounting, banking and finance, business administration and management, business economics, hospitality management services, management science, and marketing/retailing/merchandising), COMMUNICATIONS AND THE ARTS (English), COMPUTER AND PHYSICAL SCIENCE (chemistry, computer science, mathematics, and physics), EDUCATION (early childhood, elementary, physical, secondary, special, and technical), ENGINEERING AND ENVIRONMENTAL DESIGN (chemical engineering, construction management, electrical/electronics engineering, and mechanical engineering), HEALTH PROFESSIONS (nursing, occupational therapy, and veterinary science), SOCIAL SCIENCE (dietetics, food science, history, political science/government, psychology, social work, and sociology). Engineering, biology, and veterinary science are the largest.
Required: All students must complete a general education curriculum, including courses in history, sociology, philosophy, art, English, humanities, political science, math, natural sciences, and phys ed. A minimum of 124 semester credits with a GPA of 2.0 is required for graduation.
Special: Cooperative programs, internships, work-study programs, dual majors, nondegree study, and a B.A.-B.S. degree are offered. There are 17 national honor societies, a freshman honors program, and 9 departmental honors programs.
Faculty/Classroom: 70% of faculty are male; 30%, female. No introductory courses are taught by graduate students.
Requirements: The SAT or ACT is required with the SAT preferred. A GPA of 2.5 is recommended. Applicants should be graduates of an accredited secondary school or hold the GED. They should have completed 4 units of English, 3 each of social science and math, and 1 each of physical science and biological science. SAT Subject tests in mathematics (level I or II) and 1 other subject are recommended. An essay is required. A GPA of 2.0 is required. AP and CLEP credits are accepted.
Procedure: Freshmen are admitted to all sessions. Students entering the college of Nursing and Allied Health and Veterinary Medicine are admitted in the fall only. There is an early admissions plan. The priority deadlines for fall admission is March 30; October 30, Spring; April 30, Summer, Applications will be considered until 4 weeks prior to the registration period for any semester. The application fee is $25.
Transfer: Applicants must be in good standing at all previously attended institutions and have completed 12 or more semester hours with a GPA of 2.0. 44 of 124 credits required for the bachelor's degree must be completed at Tuskegee.
Visiting: Visitors may sit in on classes and stay overnight. To schedule a visit, contact the Office of Admissions.
Financial Aid: Tuskegee is a member of CSS. The CSS/Profile and federal tax returns are required.
International Students: They must take the TOEFL and also take the SAT or the ACT.
Computers: All students may access the system. There are no time limits and no fees.
Graduates: 472 bachelor's degrees were awarded. The most popular majors were engineering (13%), veterinary medicine (12%), and biiology (11%). In an average class, 25% graduate in 4 years or less, 6% graduate in 5 years or less, and 20% graduate in 6 years or less.
Admissions Contact: Monette Evans, Vice President/Director for Admissions and Enrollment Management.
E-mail: *admi@acd.tuskegee.edu* Web: *www.tuskegee.edu*

UNIVERSITY OF ALABAMA SYSTEM

The University of Alabama System, established in 1969, is a public system in Alabama. It is governed by a board of trustees, whose chief administrator is the chancellor. The primary goal of the system is to serve all the people of the state through teaching, research, and service. The total enrollment is approximately 44,000. There are 4-year campuses located in Tuscaloosa, Birmingham, and Huntsville. Profiles of the 4-year campuses are included in this section.

UNIVERSITY OF ALABAMA — B-3

Tuscaloosa, AL 35487
(205) 348-5666
(800) 933-BAMA; Fax: (205) 348-9046

Full-time: 7421 men, 8411 women	**Faculty:** 688; I, --$
Part-time: 797 men, 924 women	**Ph.D.s:** 90%
Graduate: 1892 men, 2390 women	**Student/Faculty:** 23 to 1
Year: semesters, summer session	**Tuition:** $4864 ($13,516)
Application Deadline: April 1	**Room & Board:** $5024
Freshman Class: 10,538 applied, 7759 accepted, 3739 enrolled	
SAT Verbal/Math: 550/550*	**ACT:** 23 **COMPETITIVE**

The University of Alabama, the state of Alabama's first public university, is a senior comprehensive doctoral level institution. The university was established by constitutional provision under statutory mandates and authorizations. It's mission is to advance the intellectual and social condition of the people of the state through quality programs of teaching, research and service. There are 9 undergraduate and 11 graduate schools. In addition to regional accreditation, UA has baccalaureate program accreditation with AACSB, AAFCS, ABET, ACEJMC, ADA, CAAHEP, CCNE, CSWE, FIDER, NASAD, NASD, NASM, NAST, and NCATE. The 10 libraries contain 2.5 million volumes, 4 million microform items, and 526,856 audio/video tapes/CDs/DVDs, and subscribe to 23,222 periodicals including electronic. Computerized library services include the card catalog, interlibrary loans, database searching, and Internet access. Special learning facilities include a learning resource center, art gallery, natural history museum, radio station, TV station, special collections department, map library, observatory, specialized computer labs, and archeological site. The 1000-acre campus is in a suburban area 50 miles southwest of Birmingham. Including any residence halls, there are 216 buildings.
Student Life: 80% of undergraduates are from Alabama. Others are from 50 states, 79 foreign countries, and Canada. 89% are from public schools. 81% are white; 12% African American. 56% are Protestant; 32% claim no religious affiliation; 8% Catholic. The average age of freshmen is 19; all undergraduates, 22. 14% do not continue beyond their first year; 63% remain to graduate.
Housing: Approximately 5800 students can be accommodated in university housing, which includes single-sex and coed dormitories, on-campus apartments, married-student housing, fraternity houses, and sorority houses. In addition, there are honors houses, language houses, and special-interest houses. On-campus housing is guaranteed for the freshman year only and is available on a first-come, first-served basis. 70% of students commute. All students may keep cars.

Activities: 19% of men belong to 1 local and 26 national fraternities; 26% of women belong to 1 local and 20 national sororities. There are 391 groups on campus, including academic, art, band, cheerleading, chess, choir, chorale, chorus, computers, dance, debate, drama, drill team, ethnic, film, forensics, gay, honors, international, jazz band, leadership, literary magazine, marching band, musical theater, newspaper, opera, orchestra, pep band, photography, political, professional, radio and TV, religious service, social service, student government, symphony, and yearbook. Popular campus events include Honors Week, Get on Board Day, and Family Weekend.

Sports: There are 9 intercollegiate sports for men and 12 for women, and 17 intramural sports for men and 16 for women. Facilities include an 83,000-seat football stadium, a 15,000-seat basketball arena, a track and field facility, a 6,100-seat baseball stadium, a 1,600-foot softball stadium, an indoor football practice facility, lighted varsity and public tennis courts, an aquatic complex with Olympic-size and standard pools, a weight-lifting facility, a soccer field, racquetball, basketball, and volleyball courts, weight and exercise rooms, an indoor/outdoor pool, and an 18-hole golf course with clubhouse and driving range.

Disabled Students: 90% of the campus is accessible. Wheelchair ramps, elevators, special parking, specially equipped rest rooms, special class scheduling, lowered drinking fountains, lowered telephones, special housing, automatic doors, TDD, adaptive technology, and areas of rescue assistance are available.

Services: Counseling and information services are available, as is tutoring in some subjects, including statistics math, chemistry, physics, computer science, accounting, finance, economics, and foreign languages. There is a reader service for the blind, and remedial math, reading, and writing. The University of Alabama has a center for teaching and learning, a writing lab, a career center, computer-based self-tutoring, and a math computer lab. Many departments and colleges offer tutorial services or tutorial references.

Campus Safety and Security: Measures include 24-hour foot and vehicle patrol, self-defense education, security escort services, and informal discussions. There are pamphlets/posters/films, emergency telephones, lighted pathways/sidewalks, community-oriented police service (COPS), UA Police Bike Patrol, educational awareness for personal safety, alcohol awareness, child seat installations, and domestic violence awareness programs.

Programs of Study: UA confers B.A., B.S., B.A.Com., B.F.A., B.M., B.S.A.E., B.S.C.B.A., B.S.C.E., B.S.Che.E., B.S.Chem., B.S.C.S., B.S.Ed., B.S.E.E., B.S.Geo., B.S.H.E.S., B.S.I.E., B.S.M.E., B.S.Met., B.S. Micr., B.S.N., and B.S.W. degrees. Master's and doctoral degrees are also awarded. Bachelor's degrees are awarded in BIOLOGICAL SCIENCE (biology/biological science, marine science, and microbiology), BUSINESS (accounting and management information systems), COMMUNICATIONS AND THE ARTS (advertising, art history and appreciation, classics, communications, dance, English, French, German, journalism, music, public relations, Russian, Spanish, and telecommunications), COMPUTER AND PHYSICAL SCIENCE (chemistry, computer science, geology, mathematics, and physics), EDUCATION (athletic training, early childhood, elementary, music, physical, secondary, and special), ENGINEERING AND ENVIRONMENTAL DESIGN (aerospace studies, chemical engineering, civil engineering, electrical/electronics engineering, environmental science, industrial administration/management, industrial engineering, interior design, mechanical engineering, and metallurgical engineering), HEALTH PROFESSIONS (music therapy and nursing), SOCIAL SCIENCE (American studies, anthropology, clothing and textiles management/production/services, criminal justice, economics, food science, geography, history, human development, interdisciplinary studies, international studies, philosophy, political science/government, psychology, religion, and social work). Advertising, accounting, and engineering are the strongest academically. Business, elementary education, and nursing are the largest.

Required: To graduate, all students must complete a minimum of 120 semester hours, including at least 27 in the major, with a minimum GPA of 2.0. Core curriculum requirements include 12 hours each of humanities/fine arts and history/social science, 11 of natural science/math, 6 of computer studies or a foreign language, 6 of English composition, and 6 of upper-level courses with a writing component.

Special: UA offers cross-registration with Stillman College and Shelton State Community College, internships, international study programs, a Washington semester, a 3-week May-June interim term, exchange study within the United States, work-study, co-op programs, accelerated programs, B.A.-B.S. degrees, dual majors, student-designed majors, interdisciplinary majors in the New College arts and sciences program, credit for life experiences, nondegree study, and pass/fail options. There are 27 national honor societies, including Phi Beta Kappa, a freshman honors program, and 17 departmental honors programs.

Faculty/Classroom: 60% of faculty are male; 40%, female. 71% teach undergraduates, 5% do research, and 4% do both. Graduate students teach 28% of introductory courses. The average class size in an introductory lecture is 52; in a laboratory, 19; and in a regular course, 26.

Admissions: 74% of the 2005-2006 applicants were accepted. The SAT scores for the 2005-2006 freshman class were: Verbal--24% below 500, 39% between 500 and 599, 28% between 600 and 700, and 8% above 700; Math--23% below 500, 42% between 500 and 599, 26% between 600 and 700, and 9% above 700. The ACT scores were 26% below 21, 30% between 21 and 23, 20% between 24 and 26, 11% between 27 and 28, and 13% above 28. 39% of the current freshmen were in the top fifth of their class; 64% were in the top two fifths. There were 72 National Merit finalists. 58 freshmen graduated first in their class.

Requirements: The SAT or ACT is required. The ACT Optional Writing test is also required for some programs. In addition, a minimum GPA of 2.0 is required; admission is based on a sliding scale of test scores and high school GPA. The GED is accepted. High school preparation should include 4 units each of English and social studies, 3 each of math and science, 1 of foreign language, and 5 of academic electives. Students with a 3.0 cumulative GPA and satisfactory ACT or SAT scores will generally be admitted. A GPA of 2.0 is required. AP and CLEP credits are accepted. Important factors in the admissions decision are advanced placement or honor courses, evidence of special talent, and leadership record.

Procedure: Freshmen are admitted fall, spring, and summer. Entrance exams should be taken in the spring of the junior year. There is an early admissions plan. Applications should be filed by April 1 for fall entry and February 1 for summer entry, along with a $35 fee. Notification is sent on a rolling basis. Applications are accepted on-line.

Transfer: 1734 transfer students enrolled in 2004-2005. Applicants need an overall minimum GPA of 2.0 with at least 24 semester hours earned. Those with fewer than 24 hours must meet freshman standards. 30 of a minimum 120 credits required for the bachelor's degree must be completed at UA.

Visiting: There are regularly scheduled orientations for prospective students, consisting of a campus tour followed by meetings with admissions counselors and faculty and staff. Customized visits to suit student and parent needs are possible. University Day (4 times a year) offers tours and information sessions. There are guides for informal visits and visitors may sit in on classes and stay overnight. To schedule a visit, contact the Office of Undergraduate Admissions at *tour@ua.edu*.

Financial Aid: In 2005-2006, 72% of all full-time freshmen and 73% of continuing full-time students received some form of financial aid. 30% of full-time freshmen and 33% of continuing full-time students received need-based aid. The average freshman award was $8732. Need-based scholarships or need-based grants averaged $3476 ($6750 maximum); need-based self-help aid (loans and jobs) averaged $3347 ($8735 maximum); non-need-based athletic scholarships averaged $12,829 ($22,116 maximum); and other non-need-based awards and non-need-based scholarships averaged $6795 ($28,242 maximum). Average annual earnings from campus work are $3110. The average financial indebtedness of the 2005 graduate was $18,989. The FAFSA is required. The priority date for freshman financial aid applications for fall entry is March 1.

International Students: There are 298 international students enrolled. The school actively recruits these students. They must score 500 on the written TOEFL or 173 on the electronic version and earn a proficiency certificate from the university's English Language Institute. The SAT or ACT is required for U.S. high school graduates or for scholarship consideration.

Computers: Wireless access is available. There are over 70 labs and 1,500 public computers, but most students bring their own. All residence halls and labs have wired Internet access and many buildings provide public wireless access. All students may access the system 24 hours a day. There are no time limits and no fees. It is recommended that students in Law School have personal computers.

Graduates: In a recent year, 2892 bachelor's degrees were awarded. The most popular majors were marketing (7%), finance (7%), and management (7%). In an average class, 1% graduate in 3 years or less, 35% graduate in 4 years or less, 57% graduate in 5 years or less, and 63% graduate in 6 years or less. 596 companies recruited on campus in 2004-2005.

Admissions Contact: Mary K. Spiegel, Director of Undergraduarte Admissions. A video is available. E-mail: *admissions@ua.edu* Web: *http://gobama.ua.edu*

UNIVERSITY OF ALABAMA AT BIRMINGHAM   C-2
Birmingham, AL 35294

(205) 934-8221
(800) 421-8743; Fax: (205) 975-7114

Full-time: 3124 men, 4935 women	**Faculty:** 777; I, --$
Part-time: 1366 men, 2045 women	**Ph.Ds:** 86%
Graduate: 1552 men, 2583 women	**Student/Faculty:** 10 to 1
Year: semesters, summer session	**Tuition:** $4792 ($10,732)
Application Deadline: March 1	**Room & Board:** $8924
Freshman Class: 4255 applied, 3731 accepted, 1587 enrolled	
ACT: 22	**COMPETITIVE**

The University of Alabama at Birmingham, founded in 1969, is a public institution offering degrees in the arts and humanities, business, education, engineering, natural sciences and math, health-related professions, and social and behavorial sciences. There are 9 undergraduate and 13 graduate schools. In addition to regional accreditation, UAB has baccalaureate program accreditation with AACSB, ABET, CAHEA, CSWE, NASAD, NASM, NCATE, and NLN. The 2 libraries contain 1,224,842 volumes, 1,293,397 microform items, and 76,079 audio/video tapes/CDs/DVDs, and subscribe to 3538 periodicals including electronic. Computerized library services include the card catalog, interlibrary loans, database searching, Internet access, and laptop Internet portals. Special learning facilities include an art gallery, radio station, and Reynolds Historical Library, and Alabama Museum of the Health Sciences. The 180-acre campus is in an urban area in Birmingham. Including any residence halls, there are 110 buildings.

Student Life: 94% of undergraduates are from Alabama. Others are from 46 states, 73 foreign countries, and Canada. 92% are from public schools. 61% are white; 26% African American. The average age of freshmen is 19; all undergraduates, 24. 23% do not continue beyond their first year; 38% remain to graduate.

Housing: 1665 students can be accommodated in college housing, which includes single-sex and coed dormitories, on-campus apartments, and married-student housing. On-campus housing is available on a first-come, first-served basis. 86% of students commute. Alcohol is not permitted. All students may keep cars.

Activities: 6% of men belong to 9 national fraternities; 6% of women belong to 8 national sororities. There are 150 groups on campus, including band, cheerleading, chess, choir, chorale, chorus, dance, drama, ethnic, honors, international, jazz band, literary magazine, marching band, musical theater, newspaper, opera, orchestra, pep band, political, professional, radio and TV, religious, social, social service, and student government. Popular campus events include Springfest and Madrigal Feaste.

Sports: There are 6 intercollegiate sports for men and 9 for women, and 11 intramural sports for men and 11 for women. Facilities include 11 tennis courts; 3 enclosed, lighted fields; a quarter-mile running track; and a phys ed complex, which includes 2 gyms, 3 basketball courts, 4 volleyball courts, 6 racquetball/handball courts, 2 wallyball courts, a squash court, fitness weight areas, 2 cardio-fitness rooms with equipment, an indoor track, an indoor heated swimming pool, and equipment.

Disabled Students: 80% of the campus is accessible. Wheelchair ramps, elevators, special parking, specially equipped rest rooms, lowered drinking fountains, and lowered telephones are available.

Services: Counseling and information services are available, as is tutoring in most subjects. There is a reader service for the blind, and remedial math, reading, and writing.

Campus Safety and Security: Measures include 24-hour foot and vehicle patrol, self-defense education, security escort services, and shuttle buses. There are informal discussions, pamphlets/posters/films, emergency telephones, lighted pathways/sidewalks, and a bike and mounted patrol, and a campus watch program.

Programs of Study: UAB confers B.A., B.S., B.F.A., B.S.B.M.E., B.S.C.E., B.S.E.E., B.S.M.E., B.S.Mt.E., B.S.N., and B.S.S.W. degrees. Master's and doctoral degrees are also awarded. Bachelor's degrees are awarded in BIOLOGICAL SCIENCE (biology/biological science), BUSINESS (accounting, banking and finance, business administration and management, and marketing/retailing/merchandising), COMMUNICATIONS AND THE ARTS (art, communications, dramatic arts, English, French, music, and Spanish), COMPUTER AND PHYSICAL SCIENCE (chemistry, computer science, information sciences and systems, mathematics, natural sciences, and physics), EDUCATION (early childhood, elementary, health, physical, secondary, and special), ENGINEERING AND ENVIRONMENTAL DESIGN (biomedical engineering, civil engineering, electrical/electronics engineering, industrial administration/management, materials engineering, and mechanical engineering), HEALTH PROFESSIONS (cytotechnology, health science, medical records administration/services, medical technology, nuclear medical technology, nursing, physician's assistant, radiological science, and respiratory therapy), SOCIAL SCIENCE (African American studies, anthropology, criminal justice, economics, history, international studies, philosophy, political science/government, psychology, social work, and sociology). Biology, psychology, and communication studies are the largest.

Required: All students must complete a core curriculum that includes courses in math, computers, English, history, science, and technology, social sciences, philosophy, fine arts, foreign language or culture, and literature. To receive a bachelor's degree, students must complete 128 semester hours for most programs, with a GPA of at least 2.0.

Special: UAB offers student-designed majors, cross-registration with the Birmingham Area Consortium for Higher Education, internships, study abroad in 17 countries, work-study programs, nondegree study, pass/fail options, and credit by exam and for life experience. Cooperative education programs in the student's area of interest provide full-time or part-time work. There are 28 national honor societies, a freshman honors program, and 100 departmental honors programs.

Faculty/Classroom: 62% of faculty are male; 38%, female.

Admissions: 88% of the 2005-2006 applicants were accepted. The ACT scores for the 2005-2006 freshman class were: 30% below 21, 28%

between 21 and 23, 21% between 24 and 26, 10% between 27 and 28, and 11% above 28. 42% of the current freshmen were in the top fifth of their class; 67% were in the top two fifths. 42 freshmen graduated first in their class.

Requirements: The SAT or ACT is required. In addition, applicants should have completed 12 Carnegie units, including 4 in English and 2 each in math, science, and social studies. The GED is accepted if the student's score on the test is at least 52. A GPA of 2.0 is required. AP and CLEP credits are accepted.

Procedure: Freshmen are admitted to all sessions. Entrance exams should be taken by the beginning of the senior year. There is a deferred admissions plan. Applications should be filed by March 1 for fall entry, December 1 for spring entry, and April 15 for summer entry. Notification is sent on a rolling basis. Applications are accepted on-line.

Transfer: 975 transfer students enrolled in 2004-2005. Applicants should have earned at least 24 semester hours at an accredited institution with a minimum GPA of 2.0. College transcripts and statements of good standing from prior colleges are required of all transfer students. 64 of 128 credits required for the bachelor's degree must be completed at UAB.

Visiting: There are regularly scheduled orientations for prospective students, including a question-and-answer session, academic advising, sessions for parents, and presentations on student life, financial aid, housing, and student development. There are guides for informal visits and visitors may sit in on classes. To schedule a visit, contact Yolanda Tait at (205) 934-8142.

Financial Aid: The FAFSA and the college's own financial statement are required. The priority date for freshman financial aid applications for fall entry is April 1.

International Students: There are 232 international students enrolled. They must score 500 on the written TOEFL and also take the SAT or the ACT.

Computers: Wireless access is available. Students are given a Blazer ID that gives them free access to the university networks (including wireless) and computer labs. All students may access the system. There are no time limits and no fees.

Graduates: From July 1, 2004 to June 30, 2005, 1622 bachelor's degrees were awarded. The most popular majors were nursing (10%), psychology (8%), and accounting (6%). In an average class, 15% graduate in 4 years or less, 31% graduate in 5 years or less, and 38% graduate in 6 years or less. 60 companies recruited on campus in 2004-2005.

Admissions Contact: Office of Undergraduate Admissions.
E-mail: *undergradadmit@uab.edu* Web: *www.uab.edu*

UNIVERSITY OF ALABAMA IN HUNTSVILLE   C-1

Huntsville, AL 35899

(256) 824-6070
(800) UAH-CALL; Fax: (256) 824-6073

Full-time: 1975 men, 1900 women	**Faculty:** 277; I, --$
Part-time: 800 men, 800 women	**Ph.D.s:** 87%
Graduate: 925 men, 650 women	**Student/Faculty:** 14 to 1
Year: semesters, summer session	**Tuition:** $4516 ($9518)
Application Deadline: August 15	**Room & Board:** $5000
Freshman Class: n/av	
SAT or ACT: required	**VERY COMPETITIVE**

The University of Alabama in Huntsville, founded in 1950 and part of the University of Alabama system, is a public institution offering programs in liberal arts and sciences, business, nursing, and engineering. There are 5 undergraduate schools and 1 graduate school. In addition to regional accreditation, UAH has baccalaureate program accreditation with AACSB, ABET, CCNE, CSAB, NASM, and NLN. The library contains 326,399 volumes, 579,663 microform items, and 2677 audio/video tapes/CDs/DVDs, and subscribes to 1169 periodicals including electronic. Computerized library services include the card catalog, interlibrary loans, and database searching. Special learning facilities include an art gallery and radio station. The 376-acre campus is in a suburban area 100 miles north of Birmingham and 90 miles south of Nashville. Including any residence halls, there are 34 buildings.

Student Life: 86% of undergraduates are from Alabama. Others are from 45 states, 55 foreign countries, and Canada. 85% are from public schools. 74% are white; 14% African American. 71% are Protestant; 13% Catholic; 7% claim no religious affiliation. The average age of freshmen is 18; all undergraduates, 21. 24% do not continue beyond their first year; 44% remain to graduate.

Housing: 1042 students can be accommodated in college housing, which includes coed dormitories, on-campus apartments, and married-student housing. In addition, there are suites for fraternities and sororities. On-campus housing is available on a first-come, first-served basis. 83% of students commute. Alcohol is not permitted. All students may keep cars.

Activities: 7% of men belong to 6 national fraternities; 6% of women belong to 4 national sororities. There are 110 groups on campus, including art, cheerleading, chess, choir, chorale, chorus, computers, dance, drama, ethnic, film, gay, honors, international, jazz band, literary magazine, newspaper, pep band, photography, political, professional, radio and TV, religious, social, social service, student government, and symphony. Popular campus events include FallFest, SpringFest, and Frosh Mosh.

Sports: There are 8 intercollegiate sports for men and 8 for women, and 16 intramural sports for men and 16 for women. Facilities include a 2800-seat gym, a swimming pool, racquetball and tennis courts, soccer fields, softball diamonds, and a fitness center with cardio equipment, indoor track, weight room, fitness classes, aquatics, sand volleyball, and sports nutrition center.

Disabled Students: 98% of the campus is accessible. Wheelchair ramps, elevators, special parking, specially equipped rest rooms, special class scheduling, lowered drinking fountains, special housing, and a swimming pool lift are available.

Services: Counseling and information services are available, as is tutoring in most subjects. There is a reader service for the blind, and remedial math, reading, and writing. Study skills classes are also offered.

Campus Safety and Security: Measures include 24-hour foot and vehicle patrol, security escort services, informal discussions, and pamphlets/posters/films. There are lighted pathways/sidewalks and and card-controlled dorm access.

Programs of Study: UAH confers B.A., B.S., B.S.B.A., B.S.E., and B.S.N. degrees. Master's and doctoral degrees are also awarded. Bachelor's degrees are awarded in BIOLOGICAL SCIENCE (biology/biological science), BUSINESS (accounting, banking and finance, business administration and management, management information systems, and marketing/retailing/merchandising), COMMUNICATIONS AND THE ARTS (communications, English, fine arts, languages, and music), COMPUTER AND PHYSICAL SCIENCE (chemistry, computer science, mathematics, and physics), EDUCATION (education), ENGINEERING AND ENVIRONMENTAL DESIGN (chemical engineering, civil engineering, computer engineering, electrical/electronics engineering, industrial engineering, mechanical engineering, and optical engineering), HEALTH PROFESSIONS (nursing), SOCIAL SCIENCE (history, philosophy, political science/government, psychology, and sociology). Engineering, nursing, and computer science are the largest.

Required: All students must earn a minimum GPA of 2.0 over 128 to 137 credit hours, including 21 to 36 in their major. The core curriculum includes courses in English composition, literature, world history, foreign language and communications, fine arts, math, science, and social sciences.

Special: UAH offers co-op programs in all majors, cross-registration with Alabama Agricultural and Mechanical University, Athens State University, and Calhoun Community College, and internships in administrative science, communications, education, and political science. A 3-2 engineering degree is available with Oakwood College. Dual majors, B.A.-B.S. degrees in math and biology, nondegree study, and a pass/fail option are also offered. There are 23 national honor societies and a freshman honors program.

Faculty/Classroom: 64% of faculty are male; 36%, female. All both teach and do research. Graduate students teach 5% of introductory courses. The average class size in an introductory lecture is 29; in a laboratory, 14; and in a regular course, 23.

Admissions: 88% of recent applicants were accepted. The SAT scores for the recent freshman class were: Verbal--17% below 500, 46% between 500 and 599, 31% between 600 and 700, and 5% above 700; Math--18% below 500, 45% between 500 and 599, 32% between 600 and 700, and 5% above 700. The ACT scores were 14% below 21, 25% between 21 and 23, 31% between 24 and 26, 15% between 27 and 28, and 15% above 28. 53% of recent freshmen were in the top fifth of their class; 83% were in the top two fifths.

Requirements: The SAT or ACT is required. A sliding scale with the GPA determines the minimum test score needed. The GED is accepted. Students should present a minimum of 20 Carnegie units, including 4 years of English and social studies, and 3 each of math and science. AP and CLEP credits are accepted.

Procedure: Freshmen are admitted fall, spring, and summer. Entrance exams should be taken during the junior year. There are early admissions, deferred admissions, and rolling admissions plans. Applications should be filed by July 1 for fall entry, along with a $30 fee. Notification is sent on a rolling basis. Applications are accepted on-line.

Transfer: 641 transfer students enrolled in a recent year. Applicants need a minimum GPA of 2.0, in 18 hours of credit from an accredited college or university. 32 of 128 credits required for the bachelor's degree must be completed at UAH.

Visiting: There are regularly scheduled orientations for prospective students, including new student orientation, held prior to the beginning of each semester or during the first week of classes. There are guides for informal visits and visitors may sit in on classes and stay overnight. To schedule a visit, contact Ann Lee, Recruiting Coordinator at (256) 824-7142 or leev@uah.edu.

Financial Aid: In a recent year, 82% of all full-time freshmen and 68% of continuing full-time students received some form of financial aid. 41% of full-time freshmen and 47% of continuing full-time students received

need-based aid. The average freshman award was $3633. Need-based scholarships or need-based grants averaged $3386 ($15,500 maximum); need-based self-help aid (loans and jobs) averaged $4219 ($14,625 maximum); and non-need-based athletic scholarships averaged $6157. 10% of undergraduates work part time. Average annual earnings from campus work are $4115. The average financial indebtedness of the a recent graduate was $17,058. The FAFSA is required. The deadline for filing freshman financial aid applications for fall entry is May 1.

International Students: The school actively recruits these students. They must score satisfactorily on the TOEFL, take the college's own test, and take the SAT or the ACT.

Computers: All students may access the system 24 hours a day. There are no time limits and no fees.

Graduates: 807 bachelor's degrees were awarded. The most popular majors were nursing (18%), management information systems (12%), and mechanical engineering (7%). In an average class, 13% graduate in 4 years or less, 36% graduate in 5 years or less, and 44% graduate in 6 years or less. 296 companies recruited on campus in a recent year.

Admissions Contact: Scott Verzyl, Associate Vice President for Enrollment Svc, Reg. And Dir of Adm. E-mail: *admitme@email.uah.edu* Web: *www.uah.edu*

UNIVERSITY OF MOBILE A-5

Mobile, AL 36613-2842
(251) 442-2249
(800) 946-7267; Fax: (251) 675-6329

Full-time: 476 men, 797 women	**Faculty:** 91
Part-time: 61 men, 215 women	**Ph.D.s:** 70%
Graduate: 48 men, 161 women	**Student/Faculty:** 14 to 1
Year: semesters, summer session	**Tuition:** $10,490
Application Deadline: September 10	**Room & Board:** $6390
Freshman Class: 504 applied, 266 accepted, 264 enrolled	
ACT: 22	**COMPETITIVE**

University of Mobile, founded in 1961, is a private liberal arts institution affiliated with the Southern Baptists. There are 6 undergraduate and 4 graduate schools. In addition to regional accreditation, Mobile has baccalaureate program accreditation with ACBSP, NASM, and NLN. The library contains 71,136 volumes, 221 microform items, and 3000 audio/video tapes/CDs/DVDs, and subscribes to 525 periodicals including electronic. Computerized library services include the card catalog, interlibrary loans, database searching, and Internet access. Special learning facilities include a learning resource center, art gallery, and a forest learning center. The 830-acre campus is in a suburban area 10 miles northwest of Mobile. Including any residence halls, there are 52 buildings.

Student Life: 81% of undergraduates are from Alabama. Students are from 33 states, 27 foreign countries, and Canada. 86% are from public schools. 69% are white; 24% African American. 84% are Protestant; 9% Catholic; 6% claim no religious affiliation. The average age of freshmen is 18; all undergraduates, 27. 45% do not continue beyond their first year; 46% remain to graduate.

Housing: 499 students can be accommodated in college housing, which includes single-sex dorms. On-campus housing is guaranteed for the freshman year only and is available on a first-come, first-served basis. 80% of students commute. Alcohol is not permitted. All students may keep cars.

Activities: There are no fraternities or sororities. There are 52 groups on campus, including art, band, cheerleading, choir, chorale, chorus, computers, dance, drama, drum and bugle corps, ethnic, honors, international, musical theater, newspaper, opera, orchestra, pep band, political, professional, religious, social, social service, student government, and symphony. Popular campus events include College Preview Day, Upper Room Dinner Theater, and Starlight Pageant.

Sports: There are 6 intercollegiate sports for men and 7 for women, and 7 intramural sports for men and 6 for women. Facilities include an 800-seat gym, a tennis complex with 10 courts, a swimming pool, a track, baseball, softball, and soccer fields, and a golf driving range with 2 putting greens.

Disabled Students: All of the campus is accessible. Wheelchair ramps, elevators, special parking, specially equipped rest rooms, special class scheduling, lowered drinking fountains, and lowered telephones are available.

Services: Counseling and information services are available, as is tutoring in some subjects, including writing, English, and math. There is remedial math, reading, and writing.

Campus Safety and Security: Measures include 24-hour foot and vehicle patrol, self-defense education, informal discussions, and pamphlets/posters/films. There are emergency telephones and lighted pathways/sidewalks. A professional campus security service is available 24 hours a day.

Programs of Study: Mobile confers B.A., B.S., BBA, B.M., and B.S.N. degrees. Associate and master's degrees are also awarded. Bachelor's degrees are awarded in BIOLOGICAL SCIENCE (biology/biological science), BUSINESS (accounting, business administration and management, and marketing/retailing/merchandising), COMMUNICATIONS AND THE ARTS (communications, English, and music), COMPUTER AND PHYSICAL SCIENCE (computer science and mathematics), EDUCATION (early childhood, elementary, physical, and secondary), HEALTH PROFESSIONS (nursing), SOCIAL SCIENCE (economics, history, liberal arts/general studies, psychology, religion, and sociology). Education and nursing are the strongest academically. Business administration, elementary education, and nursing are the largest.

Required: All students are required to complete 128 credit hours, with at least 30 in their major field, and earn a minimum GPA of 2.0. Distribution requirements include 12 hours in English, 8 hours in lab science, 6 hours each in religion and history, 6 hours from the following subjects: business, computer science, economics, political science, psychology, and sociology, 4 hours in health/phys ed and recreation, 3 hours each in speech and math, and 3 hours in art, music, or philosophy. Computer literacy must be demonstrated. Chapel attendance is also required.

Special: A variety of internships and work-study programs, B.A.-B.S. degrees, accelerated degree program, and dual majors are available, as is a 3-2 engineering degree with Auburn University and the University of South Alabama. There are 11 national honor societies, a freshman honors program, and 7 departmental honors programs.

Faculty/Classroom: 47% of faculty are male; 53%, female. All teach undergraduates. No introductory courses are taught by graduate students. The average class size in an introductory lecture is 25; in a laboratory, 16; and in a regular course, 20.

Admissions: 53% of the 2005-2006 applicants were accepted. The ACT scores for the 2005-2006 freshman class were: 49% below 21, 21% between 21 and 23, 15% between 24 and 26, 7% between 27 and 28, and 8% above 28. 42% of the current freshmen were in the top fifth of their class; 70% were in the top two fifths.

Requirements: The ACT is required. In addition, applicants must have 22 Carnegie units and a minimum composite score of 19 on the ACT. An essay, portfolio, and interview are recommended. The GED is accepted. The ACT is not required of applicants over age 30. A GPA of 2.0 is required. AP and CLEP credits are accepted. Important factors in the admissions decision are advanced placement or honor courses, ability to finance college education, and leadership record.

Procedure: Freshmen are admitted fall, spring, and summer. Entrance exams should be taken in August before the junior year. There are early decision, deferred admissions, and rolling admissions plans. Early decision applications should be filed by October 31; regular applications, by September 10 for fall entry, January 24 for spring entry, and May 1 for summer entry. Notification of early decision is sent November 1; regular decision, on a rolling basis. The fall 2005 application fee was $30. Applications are accepted on-line.

Transfer: 160 transfer students enrolled in 2004-2005. Transfer students need to have earned a minimum GPA of 2.0 for previous college work. If fewer than 30 semester hours are accepted, a minimum score of 19 on the ACT and a high school transcript, or GED, are required. 35 of 128 credits required for the bachelor's degree must be completed at Mobile.

Visiting: There are regularly scheduled orientations for prospective students, including financial aid seminars, academic seminars, faculty advising, campus tours, and admissions counseling. There are guides for informal visits and visitors may sit in on classes and stay overnight. To schedule a visit, contact Kris Nelson, Director of Admissions at (251) 442-2249.

Financial Aid: In a recent year, 98% of all full-time freshmen and 97% of continuing full-time students received some form of financial aid. 36% of full-time freshmen and 32% of continuing full-time students received need-based aid. The average freshman award was $6500. Need-based scholarships or need-based grants averaged $4283 ($12,374 maximum); need-based self-help aid (loans and jobs) averaged $1545 ($10,500 maximum); and non-need-based athletic scholarships averaged $5823 ($16,220 maximum). 15% of undergraduates work part time. Average annual earnings from campus work are $1545. The average financial indebtedness of the recent year's graduate was $8683. The FAFSA and the college's own financial statement are required.

International Students: There were 31 international students enrolled in a recent year. The school actively recruits these students. A satisfactory score is required on the written TOEFL. Students must also take the ACT, scoring satisfactorily.

Computers: All students may access the system 8 A.M. to 9 P.M. Monday through Friday and a half day Saturday. There are no time limits. The fee is $60 per semester. It is strongly recommended that all students have a personal computer.

Graduates: From July 1, 2004 to June 30, 2005, 258 bachelor's degrees were awarded. The most popular majors were education (30%), interdisciplinary studies (28%), and religion (10%). 35 companies recruited on campus in 2004-2005.

Admissions Contact: Kris Nelson, Director of Admissions.
E-mail: *brianb@mail.umobile.edukrisn@mail.umobile.edu*
Web: *www.umobile.edu*

UNIVERSITY OF MONTEVALLO   C-3
Montevallo, AL 35115-6000   (205) 665-6030
                               (800) 292-4349; Fax: (205) 665-6032

Full-time: 751 men, 1590 women	**Faculty:** 140; IIA, --$
Part-time: 66 men, 164 women	**Ph.Ds:** 81%
Graduate: 83 men, 268 women	**Student/Faculty:** 17 to 1
Year: semesters, summer session	**Tuition:** $5664 ($11,124)
Application Deadline: August 1	**Room & Board:** $3966
Freshman Class: 1426 applied, 1054 accepted, 496 enrolled	
SAT: not required	**ACT:** required **COMPETITIVE**

The University of Montevallo, founded in 1896, is a public, liberal arts institution offering courses in business, fine arts, music, preprofessional training, and teacher preparation. There are 4 undergraduate schools and 1 graduate school. In addition to regional accreditation, UM has baccalaureate program accreditation with AACSB, ADA, AHEA, CSWE, NASAD, NASM, and NCATE. The library contains 258,169 volumes, 795,344 microform items, and 4175 audio/video tapes/CDs/DVDs, and subscribes to 813 periodicals including electronic. Computerized library services include the card catalog, interlibrary loans, and database searching. Special learning facilities include a learning resource center, art gallery, TV station, and a university theater. The 160-acre campus is in a small town 35 miles south of Birmingham. Including any residence halls, there are 37 buildings.

Student Life: 96% of undergraduates are from Alabama. Others are from 26 states, 23 foreign countries, and Canada. 94% are from public schools. 82% are white; 13% African American. The average age of freshmen is 19; all undergraduates, 21. 27% do not continue beyond their first year; 42% remain to graduate.

Housing: 1276 students can be accommodated in college housing, which includes single-sex and coed dormitories and on-campus apartments. On-campus housing is available on a first-come, first-served basis. 68% of students commute. All students may keep cars.

Activities: 20% of men belong to 7 national fraternities; 16% of women belong to 7 national sororities. There are 74 groups on campus, including art, cheerleading, choir, chorus, dance, debate, drama, ethnic, forensics, gay, honors, international, jazz band, literary magazine, musical theater, newspaper, pep band, photography, political, professional, radio and TV, religious, social, social service, and student government. Popular campus events include College Night, Springfest, and Honors Day.

Sports: There are 4 intercollegiate sports for men and 6 for women, and 7 intramural sports for men and 4 for women. Facilities include a 90,000 square foot Student Activity Center with six lane collegiate-competition-size pool; a 6,000 square foot weight training and cardio-conditioning theatre, and a 3,500 seat arena.

Disabled Students: 90% of the campus is accessible. Wheelchair ramps, elevators, special parking, specially equipped rest rooms, special class scheduling, lowered drinking fountains, and lowered telephones are available.

Services: Counseling and information services are available, as is tutoring in some subjects, including study skills. There is a reader service for the blind, and remedial math, reading, and writing, and a speech and hearing center.

Campus Safety and Security: Measures include 24-hour foot and vehicle patrol, security escort services, informal discussions, and pamphlets/posters/films. There are lighted pathways/sidewalks, campus lighting, and electronic access into residence halls.

Programs of Study: UM confers B.A., B.S., B.B.A., B.F.A., B.M., and B.M.E. degrees. Master's degrees are also awarded. Bachelor's degrees are awarded in BIOLOGICAL SCIENCE (biology/biological science), BUSINESS (accounting, banking and finance, business administration and management, management science, and marketing/retailing/merchandising), COMMUNICATIONS AND THE ARTS (art, communications, dramatic arts, English, French, journalism, music, Spanish, and studio art), COMPUTER AND PHYSICAL SCIENCE (chemistry and mathematics), EDUCATION (art, early childhood, education of the deaf and hearing impaired, elementary, home economics, music, and physical), HEALTH PROFESSIONS (speech pathology/audiology), SOCIAL SCIENCE (history, political science/government, psychology, social science, social work, and sociology). Elementary/early childhood education, business, and art are the largest.

Required: To graduate, students must complete a minimum of 130 semester hours with an overall 2.0 GPA while meeting core, major, and minor requirements. Core requirements include 12 hours of writing reinforcement courses (usually met with literature and major/minor courses), 7 hours of sciences (2 branches), 6 hours each of foundations in writing, world literature, world civilizations, and institutions and issues courses, 4 hours of health/phys ed, and 3 hours each of oral communications, math, computer science, fine arts, and human behavior and inquiry courses.

Special: A 3-2 engineering degree is offered with Auburn University and the University of Alabama at Birmingham. Internships, study abroad, work-study, an accelerated degree plan, B.A.-B.S. degrees, dual degrees, and pass/fail options are available. There are 22 national honor societies and a freshman honors program.

Faculty/Classroom: 49% of faculty are male; 51%, female. 99% teach undergraduates. No introductory courses are taught by graduate students. The average class size in an introductory lecture is 27; in a laboratory, 24; and in a regular course, 24.

Admissions: 74% of the 2005-2006 applicants were accepted.

Requirements: The SAT or ACT is required, the ACT is preferred. In addition, applicants must be high school graduates with a minimum of 16 academic credits, including 4 units each of English, social studies, and academic electives and 2 each of math and science. 1 year each of algebra and plane geometry is recommended. The GED is accepted with a minimum standard score average of 50. A GPA of 2.0 is required. AP and CLEP credits are accepted. Important factors in the admissions decision are advanced placement or honor courses, evidence of special talent, and geographic diversity.

Procedure: Freshmen are admitted to all sessions. Entrance exams should be taken in April or June of the junior year or October of the senior year. There are early admissions, deferred admissions, and rolling admissions plans. Applications should be filed by August 1 for fall entry, December 1 for spring entry, and May 1 for summer entry. Notification is sent on a rolling basis. Applications are accepted on-line. The fall 2005 application fee was $25.

Transfer: 284 transfer students enrolled in a recent year. Applicants need a minimum GPA of 2.0 on previous college study attempted. 30 of 130 credits required for the bachelor's degree must be completed at UM.

Visiting: There are regularly scheduled orientations for prospective students, consisting of 1 day of preregistration in July and 2 days of orientation in August, including on-site visits, mentor groups, play activities, and career and learning style assessments. There are guides for informal visits and visitors may sit in on classes and stay overnight. To schedule a visit, contact the Office of Admissions.

Financial Aid: In 2005-2006, 59% of all full-time freshmen and 57% of continuing full-time students received some form of financial aid. 39% of full-time freshmen and 42% of continuing full-time students received need-based aid. The average freshman award was $6143. Need-based scholarships or need-based grants averaged $4511; need-based self-help aid (loans and jobs) averaged $1817; non-need-based athletic scholarships averaged $8338; and other non-need-based awards and non-need-based scholarships averaged $3774. The average financial indebtedness of the 2005 graduate was $11,550. The FAFSA is required. The priority date for freshman financial aid applications for fall entry is April 15.

International Students: They must score satisfactorily on the written TOEFL and take the SAT or ACT.

Computers: Wireless access is available. Wired access to the college's network for student's personally owned PCs is available to all students living in residence halls. Wireless access to the college's network for student's personally owned computers is available in 72% of the administrative and academic buildings on campus including, but not limited to, the library, Student Union Building, cafeteria, and most buildings where classes are held. The university maintains a lab consisting of 55 PC and 6 Macintosh computers available for all students located in the library. Additional computer labs are located across the campus and are primarily focused for use by students involved with studies in a particular department or college. All students may access the system. Network access in the residence halls is available whenever those buildings are open. Computer lab access hours are posted and availablility is determined by those departments. There are no time limits and no fees.

Graduates: From July 1, 2004 to June 30, 2005, 462 bachelor's degrees were awarded. The most popular majors were business/marketing (19%), social sciences and history (13%), and education (10%). In an average class, 28% graduate in 4 years or less, 41% graduate in 5 years or less, and 43% graduate in 6 years or less. 80 companies recruited on campus in 2004-2005.

Admissions Contact: Lynn Gurganus, Director of Admissions.
E-mail: *admissions@montevallo.edu* Web: *www.montevallo.edu*

UNIVERSITY OF NORTH ALABAMA   B-1

Florence, AL 35632-0001
(256) 765-4608
(800) TALKUNA; Fax: (256) 765-4960

Full-time: 1955 men, 2489 women	Faculty: 209; IIA, --$
Part-time: 347 men, 626 women	Ph.D.s: 74%
Graduate: 444 men, 554 women	Student/Faculty: 21 to 1
Year: semesters, summer session	Tuition: $4282 ($7930)
Application Deadline: July 1	Room & Board: $4710
Freshman Class: 1942 applied, 1704 accepted, 934 enrolled	
SAT: required	ACT: 21* COMPETITIVE

The University of North Alabama, founded in 1872, is a public institution offering degree programs in arts and sciences, business, education, and nursing. There are 4 undergraduate and 3 graduate schools. In addition to regional accreditation, UNA has baccalaureate program accred-

itation with AACSB, ACBSP, CSWE, NASAD, NASM, NCATE, and NLN. The 2 libraries contain 358,393 volumes, 1,006,142 microform items, and 9898 audio/video tapes/CDs/DVDs, and subscribe to 3126 periodicals including electronic. Computerized library services include the card catalog, interlibrary loans, database searching, and Internet access. Special learning facilities include a learning resource center, art gallery, planetarium, and radio station. The 125-acre campus is in an urban area 116 miles north of Birmingham. Including any residence halls, there are 68 buildings.

Student Life: 76% of undergraduates are from Alabama. Students are from 34 states, 38 foreign countries, and Canada. 89% are from public schools. 73% are white; 10% African American. The average age of freshmen is 20; all undergraduates, 23. 32% do not continue beyond their first year; 55% remain to graduate.

Housing: 1300 students can be accommodated in college housing, which includes single-sex and coed dorms, on-campus apartments, off-campus apartments, married-student housing, fraternity houses, and sorority houses. There is an international house. On-campus housing is available on a first-come, first-served basis. 81% of students commute. Alcohol is not permitted. All students may keep cars.

Activities: 9% of men belong to 6 national fraternities; 8% of women belong to 6 national sororities. There are 91 groups on campus, including band, cheerleading, choir, chorus, computers, debate, drama, drill team, ethnic, film, honors, international, jazz band, literary magazine, marching band, musical theater, newspaper, pep band, photography, political, professional, radio and TV, religious, social, social service, student government, and yearbook. Popular campus events include Spring Fling and George Lindsey Film Festival.

Sports: There are 6 intercollegiate sports for men and 6 for women, and 19 intramural sports for men and 19 for women. Facilities include a 13,500-seat football stadium, a 4000-seat gym, a baseball field, an outdoor track, an indoor swimming pool, and tennis courts.

Disabled Students: 96% of the campus is accessible. Wheelchair ramps, elevators, special parking, specially equipped rest rooms, special class scheduling, lowered drinking fountains, and lowered telephones are available.

Services: Counseling and information services are available, as is tutoring in some subjects, including math, English, history, biology, chemistry, accounting, finance, and economics. There is a reader service for the blind, remedial math and writing, and an academic resource center that features computer-assisted tutoring and faculty mentoring.

Campus Safety and Security: Measures include 24-hour foot and vehicle patrol, shuttle buses, informal discussions, and pamphlets/posters/films. There are emergency telephones and lighted pathways/sidewalks.

Programs of Study: UNA confers B.A., B.S., B.A.M., B.B.A., B.F.A., B.G.S., B.M.M.Ed., B.S.Ed., B.S.M., B.S.N., and B.S.W. degrees. Master's degrees are also awarded. Bachelor's degrees are awarded in BIOLOGICAL SCIENCE (biology/biological science and environmental biology), BUSINESS (accounting, banking and finance, business economics, and marketing/retailing/merchandising), COMMUNICATIONS AND THE ARTS (art, communications, dramatic arts, English, French, German, journalism, music, public relations, and Spanish), COMPUTER AND PHYSICAL SCIENCE (chemistry, computer science, geology, information sciences and systems, mathematics, and physics), EDUCATION (art, business, early childhood, elementary, foreign languages, home economics, music, physical, science, secondary, and social science), ENGINEERING AND ENVIRONMENTAL DESIGN (interior design), HEALTH PROFESSIONS (industrial hygiene and nursing), SOCIAL SCIENCE (criminal justice, geography, history, political science/government, psychology, social work, and sociology). Physical sciences, biological sciences, and math are the strongest academically. Management, accounting, and marketing are the largest.

Required: Students must complete a core curriculum, which includes 12 semester hours in history, social and behavioral sciences, humanities, and fine arts, 11 in natural sciences and math, and 6 in language composition. Total number of hours in majors vary. Passing grades in 1 writing emphasis and 1 computer course also are needed. A minimum of 128 semester hours and a minimum GPA of 2.0 are required to graduate.

Special: UNA offers cooperative programs in all majors, work-study programs, various B.A.-B.S. degrees, dual majors, and a general studies degree. Nondegree study is possible. There are 13 national honor societies, including Phi Beta Kappa, a freshman honors program, and 2 departmental honors programs.

Faculty/Classroom: 59% of faculty are male; 41%, female. All teach undergraduates. No introductory courses are taught by graduate students.

Admissions: 88% of the 2005-2006 applicants were accepted. The ACT scores for the 2005-2006 freshman class were: 49% below 21, 22% between 21 and 23, 19% between 24 and 26, 6% between 27 and 28, and 4% above 28. 40% of the current freshmen were in the top fifth of their class; 76% were in the top two fifths.

Requirements: The SAT or ACT is required. In addition, applicants should be graduates of an accredited high school or have earned a GED. A GPA of 2.0 is required. AP and CLEP credits are accepted.

Procedure: Freshmen are admitted fall, spring, and summer. Entrance exams should be taken in the senior year. There is a deferred admissions plan and a rolling admissions plan. Applications should be filed by July 1 for fall entry, December 1 for spring entry, and May 25 for summer entry. The fall 2005 application fee was $25. Notification is sent on a rolling basis. Applications are accepted on-line.

Transfer: 594 transfer students enrolled in 2004-2005. Applicants should be eligible to return to the school last attended. 30 of 128 credits required for the bachelor's degree must be completed at UNA.

Visiting: There are regularly scheduled orientations for prospective students, including orientation programs conducted each summer prior to the fall semester. There are guides for informal visits.

Financial Aid: In a recent year, 51% of all full-time freshmen and 54% of continuing full-time students received some form of financial aid. 50% of full-time freshmen and 45% of continuing full-time students received need-based aid. Need-based scholarships or need-based grants averaged $2098; need-based self-help aid (loans and jobs) averaged $3033; and non-need-based athletic scholarships averaged $6961. 8% of undergraduates work part time. Average annual earnings from campus work are $2250. The FAFSA is required. The deadline for filing freshman financial aid applications for fall entry is April 1.

International Students: There were 158 international students enrolled in a recent year.The school actively recruits these students. They must take the TOEFL.

Computers: All students may access the system. There are no time limits and no fees. It is strongly recommended that all students have a personal computer.

Graduates: From July 1, 2004 to June 30, 2005, 819 bachelor's degrees were awarded. The most popular majors were business (29%), education (16%), and nursing (12%). In an average class, 12% graduate in 4 years or less, 28% graduate in 5 years or less, and 36% graduate in 6 years or less. 100 companies recruited on campus in 2004-2005.

Admissions Contact: Kim Mauldin, Director of Admissions. A video is available. E-mail: *admissions@una.edu* Web: *http://www.una.edu*

UNIVERSITY OF SOUTH ALABAMA
Mobile, AL 36688

A-5

(334) 460-6141
(800) 872-5247; Fax: (334) 460-7023

Full-time: 2996 men, 4499 women	Faculty: 720; IIA, -$
Part-time: 1023 men, 1626 women	Ph.Ds: 77%
Graduate: 858 men, 2120 women	Student/Faculty: 10 to 1
Year: semesters, summer session	Tuition: $4502 ($8312)
Application Deadline: August 10	Room & Board: $4428
Freshman Class: 2627 applied, 2269 accepted, 1258 enrolled	
ACT: 22	SAT: not required
	LESS COMPETITIVE

The University of South Alabama, a state-supported institution established in 1963, offers undergraduate and graduate degrees in the allied health professions, arts and sciences, business and management studies, education, engineering, nursing, computer and information sciences, and medicine. There are 9 undergraduate and 9 graduate schools. In addition to regional accreditation, USA has baccalaureate program accreditation with AACSB, ABET, ACOTE, AHEA, APTA, ARC-PA, ASLHA, CAAHEP, CAHEA, CCNE, CSAB, JRCERT, LCME, NAACLS, NASAD, NASM, NCATE, AND NLN. The 2 libraries contain 548,847 volumes and 1,502,658 microform items, and subscribe to 5215 periodicals including electronic. Computerized library services include the card catalog, interlibrary loans, and database searching. Special learning facilities include a learning resource center, art gallery, radio station, TV station, and the Dauphin Island Sea Lab. The 1224-acre campus is in a suburban area 150 miles east of New Orleans. Including any residence halls, there are 114 buildings.

Student Life: 77% of undergraduates are from Alabama. Others are from 45 states, 102 foreign countries, and Canada. 68% are white; 17% African American. The average age of all undergraduates is 24. 30% do not continue beyond their first year.

Housing: 1966 students can be accommodated in college housing, which includes coed dorms, on-campus apartments, married-student housing, fraternity houses, and sorority houses. On-campus housing is available on a first-come, first-served basis. 88% of students commute. Alcohol is not permitted. All students may keep cars.

Activities: 10% of men belong to 12 national fraternities; 7% of women belong to 8 national sororities. There are 130 groups on campus, including art, band, cheerleading, chess, choir, chorale, chorus, dance, debate, drama, ethnic, film, gay, honors, international, jazz band, literary magazine, musical theater, newspaper, opera, orchestra, pep band, political, professional, radio and TV, religious, social, social service, student government, and symphony. Popular campus events include Club South, Greek Week, and Chi Omega Songfest.

Sports: There are 7 intercollegiate sports for men and 8 for women, and 13 intramural sports for men and 12 for women. Facilities include a 10,000-seat arena; a 49,000-square-foot student recreation center, including 6 handball courts, fitness rooms, 2 basketball/volleyball courts,

and an indoor track; several intramural fields; and an outdoor swimming pool.

Disabled Students: 90% of the campus is accessible. Wheelchair ramps, elevators, special parking, specially equipped rest rooms, lowered drinking fountains, and lowered telephones are available.

Services: Counseling and information services are available, as is tutoring in some subjects. There is a reader service for the blind, and remedial math, reading, and writing.

Campus Safety and Security: Measures include 24-hour foot and vehicle patrol, self-defense education, security escort services, and informal discussions. There are pamphlets/posters/films, emergency telephones, and lighted pathways/sidewalks.

Programs of Study: USA confers B.A., B.S., B.F.A., B.Mus., B.S.B.A., B.S.Cardioresp.Sc., B.S.C.E., B.S.Ch.E., B.S.C.L.S., B.S.Comp.Eng., B.S.Ed., B.S.E.E., B.S.M.E., B.S.N., B.S.Preprof.Hlth.Sc., B.S.R.S., and B.S.Sp.Hear.Sc. degrees. Master's and doctoral degrees are also awarded. Bachelor's degrees are awarded in BIOLOGICAL SCIENCE (biology/biological science), BUSINESS (accounting, banking and finance, business administration and management, business economics, electronic business, marketing/retailing/merchandising, and recreation and leisure services), COMMUNICATIONS AND THE ARTS (communications, dramatic arts, English, fine arts, languages, and music), COMPUTER AND PHYSICAL SCIENCE (atmospheric sciences and meteorology, chemistry, computer science, geology, mathematics, and physics), EDUCATION (early childhood, education, elementary, health, physical, secondary, and special), ENGINEERING AND ENVIRONMENTAL DESIGN (chemical engineering, civil engineering, computer engineering, electrical/electronics engineering, and mechanical engineering), HEALTH PROFESSIONS (biomedical science, clinical science, nursing, radiological science, respiratory therapy, and speech pathology/audiology), SOCIAL SCIENCE (anthropology, criminal justice, geography, history, international studies, philosophy, political science/government, psychology, and sociology). Business administration, nursing, and elementary education are the largest.

Required: General education requirements consist of 12 hours in written composition, 12 hours in humanities and fine arts, at least 12 hours in history and the social and behavioral sciences and 11 hours in natural science and math. A minimum of 128 semester hours, with a minimum GPA of 2.0, are required for graduation.

Special: USA offers co-op programs in most majors, federal work-study, internships, study abroad in 4 countries, dual majors, an adult degree program, and a personalized studies program. There are 43 national honor societies, and a freshman honors program.

Faculty/Classroom: 64% of faculty are male; 36%, female. No introductory courses are taught by graduate students. The average class size in an introductory lecture is 76; in a laboratory, 31; and in a regular course, 32.

Admissions: 86% of the 2005-2006 applicants were accepted.

Requirements: The ACT is required. In addition, applicants should be high school graduates or have a GED certificate. AP and CLEP credits are accepted.

Procedure: Freshmen are admitted to all sessions. Entrance exams should be taken during the junior year or early in the senior year. There is an early admissions and a rolling admissions plan. Applications should be filed by August 10 for fall entry, December 15 for spring entry, and May 20 for summer entry. The fall 2005 application fee was $ 25. Notification is sent on a rolling basis.

Transfer: 1077 transfer students enrolled in 2004-2005. Transfer applicants must have at least a 2.0 GPA on all college work attempted for regular admission. 32 of 128 credits required for the bachelor's degree must be completed at USA.

Visiting: There are regularly scheduled orientations for prospective students, including 3 Saturday visiting days in November, February, and April. There are guides for informal visits and visitors may sit in on classes. To schedule a visit, contact Melissa Haab, Director of Admissions.

Financial Aid: In a recent year, 65% of all full-time students received some form of financial aid. 65% of all full-time students received need-based aid. The average freshman award was $10,000. 35% of undergraduates work part time. Average annual earnings from campus work are $4000. The average financial indebtedness of a recent graduate was $11,000. The FAFSA and the college's own financial statement are required. The deadline for filing freshman financial aid applications for fall entry is May 1.

International Students: There are 723 international students enrolled. The school actively recruits these students. They must score satisfactorily on the TOEFL and also take the college's own test.

Computers: All students may access the system at various times. All students are required to have personal computers. Students enrolled in the entry-level programming sequence are required to have laptops.

Graduates: From July 1, 2004 to June 30, 2005, 1365 bachelor's degrees were awarded. The most popular majors were nursing (16%), elementary education (10%), and communication/marketing (5%). In an average class, 14% graduate in 4 years or less, 27% graduate in 5 years or less, and 34% graduate in 6 years or less. 283 companies recruited on campus in 2004-2005. Of the 2004 graduating class, 67% were employed within 6 months of graduation.

Admissions Contact: Melissa Haab, Director of Admissions.
E-mail: *admiss@.usouthal.edu* Web: *www.southalabama.edu*

UNIVERSITY OF WEST ALABAMA   A-3
Livingston, AL 35470   (205) 652-3578
                                        (888) 636-8800; Fax: (205) 652-3522

Full-time: 675 men, 800 women	**Faculty:** 87; IIA, --$
Part-time: 50 men, 100 women	**Ph.D.s:** 65%
Graduate: 75 men, 250 women	**Student/Faculty:** 17 to 1
Year: semesters, summer session	**Tuition:** $4326 ($8164)
Application Deadline: open	**Room & Board:** $3285
Freshman Class: n/av	
SATor ACT: required	**COMPETITIVE**

University of West Alabama, founded in 1835, is a state-controlled institution offering programs in liberal arts and sciences, business and commerce, general studies, and education. There are 5 undergraduate schools and 1 graduate school. Most figures in the above capsule and in this profile are approximate. In addition to regional accreditation, UWA has baccalaureate program accreditation with NCATE and NLN. The 2 libraries contain 135,000 volumes, 500,000 microform items, and 7500 audio/video tapes/CDs/DVDs, and subscribe to 700 periodicals including electronic. Computerized library services include interlibrary loans and database searching. Special learning facilities include a learning resource center, art gallery, and TV station. The 600-acre campus is in a small town 35 miles east of Meridian, Mississippi. Including any residence halls, there are 36 buildings.

Student Life: 80% of undergraduates are from Alabama. Others are from 21 states, 9 foreign countries, and Canada. 88% are from public schools. 61% are white; 37% African American. The average age of freshmen is 18; all undergraduates, 22. 39% do not continue beyond their first year.

Housing: 903 students can be accommodated in college housing, which includes single-sex dorms, on-campus apartments, and married-student housing. In addition, there are honors houses. On-campus housing is guaranteed for all 4 years. Alcohol is not permitted. All students may keep cars.

Activities: 10% of men belong to 6 national fraternities; 6% of women belong to 4 national sororities. There are 30 groups on campus, including band, cheerleading, choir, chorus, drama, drill team, ethnic, honors, international, jazz band, marching band, newspaper, pep band, photography, political, professional, radio and TV, religious, social, student government, symphony, and yearbook. Popular campus events include Springfest and Club Luie.

Sports: There are 5 intercollegiate sports for men and 5 for women, and 8 intramural sports for men and 8 for women. Facilities include an 800-seat gym, a 7500-seat football stadium, a baseball field, tennis and racquetball courts, a pool, weight rooms, a lake, and hiking trails.

Disabled Students: 95% of the campus is accessible. Wheelchair ramps, elevators, special parking, specially equipped rest rooms, special class scheduling, and lowered drinking fountains are available.

Services: Counseling and information services are available, as is tutoring in most subjects. There is remedial math, reading, and writing.

Campus Safety and Security: Measures include 24-hour foot and vehicle patrol, informal discussions, pamphlets/posters/films, and lighted pathways/sidewalks.

Programs of Study: UWA confers B.A., B.S., B.B.A., and B.T. degrees. Associate and master's degrees are also awarded. Bachelor's degrees are awarded in BIOLOGICAL SCIENCE (biology/biological science and marine biology), BUSINESS (accounting and business administration and management), COMMUNICATIONS AND THE ARTS (English), COMPUTER AND PHYSICAL SCIENCE (chemistry, computer science, mathematics, and physics), EDUCATION (athletic training, early childhood, elementary, middle school, physical, science, secondary, and special), ENGINEERING AND ENVIRONMENTAL DESIGN (environmental science and industrial engineering technology), HEALTH PROFESSIONS (predentistry and premedicine), SOCIAL SCIENCE (history, prelaw, psychology, social science, and sociology). English, business, and sciences are the strongest academically. Education and business are the largest.

Required: To graduate, all students must complete at least 120 semester hours with a minimum GPA of 2.0.

Special: There is a 3-2 engineering program with Auburn University and the University of Alabama at Birmingham. The 2-year technical division offers programs leading to a possible B.T. degree. B.A.-B.S. degrees, a co-op program in environmental science, and an accelerated degree are available. Nondegree study is possible. There are 5 national honor societies, a freshman honors program, and 4 departmental honors programs.

Faculty/Classroom: 60% of faculty are male; 40%, female. 90% teach undergraduates. Graduate students teach 4% of introductory courses. The average class size in an introductory lecture is 30; in a laboratory, 18; and in a regular course, 15.

Requirements: The SAT or ACT is required. In addition, applicants should have completed 15 high school credits or the GED equivalent. AP and CLEP credits are accepted.

Procedure: Freshmen are admitted to all sessions. Entrance exams should be taken during the junior or senior year. There are early admissions and deferred admissions plans. Application deadlines are open. Applications are accepted on-line. Check with the school for current application fee.

Transfer: Transfer applicants must have maintained a minimum GPA of 2.0 in all previous college courses. 30 of 120 credits required for the bachelor's degree must be completed at UWA.

Visiting: There are regularly scheduled orientations for prospective students. There are guides for informal visits and visitors may sit in on classes and stay overnight. To schedule a visit, contact the Admissions Office.

Financial Aid: The CSS/Profile, FAFSA, FFS, or SFS is required. Check with the school for current deadlines.

International Students: They must score satisfactorily on the written TOEFL and also take the SAT or the ACT.

Computers: All students may access the system. There are no time limits. The fee is $20. It is strongly recommended that all students have a personal computer.

Graduates: In an average class, 17% graduate in 3 years or less, 28% graduate in 4 years or less, 33% graduate in 5 years or less, and 37% graduate in 6 years or less.

Admissions Contact: Richard Hester, Director of Admissions. A video is available. E-mail: *rhester@uwa.edu* Web: *www.uwa.edu*

Map labels: A B C D E F (columns); 1 2 3 4 (rows)

Fairbanks •
Eielson •
Fort Richardson •
Anchorage • Spenard
Juneau •
Sitka •
Ketchikan •

0 20 40 60 80 100
Miles

POPULATION
DENSITY

• 5000 and over

ALASKA

ALASKA PACIFIC UNIVERSITY   D-3
Anchorage, AK 99508-4672

(907) 564-8248
(800) 252-7528; Fax: (907) 564-8317

Full-time: 126 men, 210 women	**Faculty:** 38
Part-time: 48 men, 196 women	**Ph.D.s:** 68%
Graduate: 82 men, 138 women	**Student/Faculty:** 9 to 1
Year: 4-1-4, summer session	**Tuition:** $18,342
Application Deadline: February 1	**Room & Board:** $6800
Freshman Class: 122 applied, 54 accepted, 52 enrolled	
SAT Verbal/Math: 520/490*	**ACT:** 21 **COMPETITIVE**

Alaska Pacific University, founded in 1957, is a private institution offering undergraduate programs in business administration, elementary and middle school education, environmental science and outdoor studies, liberal studies, and psychology. Adult Degree Completion Programs are offered in Organizational Management, Accounting Information for Management, Human Services, and Health Service Administration. The library contains 760,423 volumes, 559,496 microform items, and 1032 audio/video tapes/CDs/DVDs, and subscribes to 3430 periodicals including electronic. Computerized library services include the card catalog, interlibrary loans, and Internet access. Special learning facilities include a learning resource center, art gallery, radio station, TV station, and an Alaskana Collection located in the Consortium Library. The 170-acre campus is in a suburban area in midtown Anchorage. Including any residence halls, there are 7 buildings.

Student Life: 69% of undergraduates are from Alaska. Students are from 40 states and 2 foreign countries. 66% are white; 19% Native American/Eskimo. The average age of freshmen is 21; all undergraduates, 30. 49% do not continue beyond their first year; 30% remain to graduate.

Housing: 120 students can be accommodated in college housing, which includes coed dorms and on-campus apartments. In addition, there are special-interest houses. On-campus housing is guaranteed for the freshman year only, is available on a first-come, first-served basis, and is available on a lottery system for upperclassmen. 78% of students commute. Alcohol is not permitted. All students may keep cars.

Activities: There are no fraternities or sororities. There are 18 groups on campus, including art, band, chorus, departmental, drama, ethnic, in-

ternational, newspaper, photography, professional, religious, social service, student government, and student in free enterprise. Popular campus events include Earth Day, Spring Honors Convocation, and Fall Academic Convocation.

Sports: There are 2 intramural sports for men and 2 for women. Facilities include a 300-seat sports center, an indoor swimming pool, cross-country skiing and running trails, a climbing wall, a soccer field, a lake for boating, and a weight/exercise room.

Disabled Students: 75% of the campus is accessible. Wheelchair ramps, elevators, special parking, specially equipped rest rooms, lowered drinking fountains, and lowered telephones are available.

Services: Counseling and information services are available, as is tutoring in most subjects, including math, writing, and other subjects as needed. There is remedial math and writing.

Campus Safety and Security: Measures include informal discussions, pamphlets/posters/films, emergency telephones, and lighted pathways/sidewalks. Safety signs are posted as needed.

Programs of Study: APU confers B.A. and B.S. degrees. Associate and master's degrees are also awarded. Bachelor's degrees are awarded in AGRICULTURE (natural resource management), BIOLOGICAL SCIENCE (marine biology), BUSINESS (business administration and management and recreational facilities management), EDUCATION (elementary), ENGINEERING AND ENVIRONMENTAL DESIGN (environmental science), HEALTH PROFESSIONS (health care administration), SOCIAL SCIENCE (human services, liberal arts/general studies, and psychology). Outdoor Studies, education (K-8), and environmental science are the largest.

Required: All students must complete 4 semester hours each in an Orientation to Active Learning class, a lab science, a course in social/behavioral science, and a course in ethics or religion; 2 courses in humanities; a sophomore seminar in major; and a world language course which includes American Sign Language. Courses to meet writing, speech, and quantitative skills competencies are also required, as well as a 3-semester-hour practicum, portfolio, and senior project.

Special: The internship program is very strong. The Degree Completion Program for working adults leads to a B.A. in organizational management, accounting information for management, human services, or health services administration. All general university requirements apply to these programs. There are 2 national honor societies and 2 departmental honors programs.

Faculty/Classroom: 61% of faculty are male; 39%, female. 88% teach undergraduates. No introductory courses are taught by graduate students. The average class size in an introductory lecture is 12; in a laboratory, 9; and in a regular course, 9.

Admissions: 44% of the 2005-2006 applicants were accepted. The SAT scores for the 2005-2006 freshman class were: Verbal--40% below 500, 48% between 500 and 599, and 12% between 600 and 700; Math--52% below 500, 32% between 500 and 599, 12% between 600 and 700, and 4% above 700. The ACT scores were 39% below 21, 22% between 21 and 23, 28% between 24 and 26, 6% between 27 and 28, and 6% above 28. 39% of the current freshmen were in the top fifth of their class; 61% were in the top two fifths.

Requirements: A satisfactory score is required on the SAT or on the ACT. Two teacher recommendations and an essay are required. A GED is acceptable in lieu of a high school transcript. A GPA of 2.5 is required. AP and CLEP credits are accepted. Important factors in the admissions decision are advanced placement or honor courses, leadership record, and recommendations by school officials.

Procedure: Freshmen are admitted to all sessions. Entrance exams should be taken before January of the senior year. There are early decision, early admissions, and rolling admissions plans. Early decision applications should be filed by December 1; regular applications, by February 1 for fall entry, open for spring entry, and open for summer entry. The fall 2005 apllication fee was $25. Notification of early decision is sent December 15; regular decision, March 15. Applications are accepted on-line.

Transfer: 85 transfer students enrolled in 2005-2006. Transfer applicants must have a 2.0 cumulative GPA. 32 of 128 credits required for the bachelor's degree must be completed at APU.

Visiting: There are guides for informal visits and visitors may sit in on classes and stay overnight. To schedule a visit, contact the Admissions Office at *admissions@alaskapacific.edu.*

Financial Aid: In 2005-2006, 90% of all full-time freshmen and 83% of continuing full-time students received some form of financial aid. 67% of full-time freshmen and 60% of continuing full-time students received need-based aid. The average freshman award was $20,775. Need-based scholarships or need-based grants averaged $6725 ($14,475 maximum); need-based self-help aid (loans and jobs) averaged $5324 ($8300 maximum); non-need-based athletic scholarships averaged $8590 ($19,640 maximum); and average first-time freshman total institutional award averaged $8200. 18% of undergraduates work part time. Average annual earnings from campus work are $1326. The average financial indebtedness of the 2005 graduate was $17,775. APU is a member of CSS. The FAFSA is required. The recommended deadline for filing freshman financial aid applications for fall entry is April 15.

International Students: There are 2 international students enrolled. Satisfactory scores are required on the written TOEFL and the SAT or the ACT.

Computers: All students are required to have a university email address; all dorms are wired for Internet as are all computer labs and the academic support system. All students may access the system. There are no time limits and no fees.

Graduates: From July 1, 2004 to June 30, 2005, 90 bachelor's degrees were awarded. The most popular majors were outdoor studies (23%), education (K-8) (21%), and environmental science (16%). In an average class, 17% graduate in 4 years or less, 31% graduate in 5 years or less, and 36% graduate in 6 years or less.

Admissions Contact: Michael Warner, Director of Admissions.
E-mail: *admissions@alaskapacific.edu*
Web: *http://www.alaskapacific.edu*

SHELDON JACKSON COLLEGE   F-3
Sitka, AK 99835
(907) 747-5221
(800) 478-4556; Fax: (907) 747-6366

Full-time: 175 men and women	Faculty: 17
Part-time: 75 men and women	Ph.D.s: 71%
Graduate: none	Student/Faculty: 10 to 1
Year: semesters	Tuition: $10,600
Application Deadline: open	Room & Board: $7300
Freshman Class: n/av	
SAT or ACT: recommended	LESS COMPETITIVE

Sheldon Jackson College, founded in 1878, is a private liberal arts college, offering emphases in natural and aquatic resources, outdoor recreation, fisheries, marine biology, business, elementary and secondary education, and interdisciplinary studies. Most figures in this profile are approximate. In addition to regional accreditation, Sheldon Jackson College has baccalaureate program accreditation with NASDTEC. The library contains 80,000 volumes, and subscribes to 500 periodicals including electronic. Computerized library services include the card catalog, interlibrary loans, and database searching. Special learning facilities include a learning resource center, natural history museum, state-

owned museum, and salmon hatchery. The 345-acre campus is in a small town in southeast Alaska. Including any residence halls, there are 23 buildings.

Student Life: 70% of undergraduates are from out of state, mostly the Northwest. Students are from 35 states and 4 foreign countries. 99% are from public schools. 70% are white; 26% Native American/Eskimo. The average age of freshmen is 20; all undergraduates, 24. 18% do not continue beyond their first year; 21% remain to graduate.

Housing: 240 students can be accommodated in college housing, which includes single-sex dorms, on-campus apartments, and married-student housing. On-campus housing is guaranteed for the freshman year only and is available on a first-come, first-served basis. 75% of students live on campus; of those, All remain on campus on weekends. Alcohol is not permitted. All students may keep cars.

Activities: There are no fraternities or sororities. There are 14 groups on campus, including art, choir, chorus, computers, drama, ethnic, musical theater, outdoor, photography, political, religious, social, social service, and student government. Popular campus events include Alaska Day, Gathering of the People (Alaska native dances and dinner), and Spring Expo.

Sports: There are 5 intramural sports for men and 5 for women. Facilities include a 2-court gym, a 25-meter pool, a weight room, 2 racquetball courts, a wilderness center, a student center, sea kayaks, and a climbing wall.

Disabled Students: Wheelchair ramps, elevators, special parking, specially equipped rest rooms, and special class scheduling are available.

Services: Counseling and information services are available, as is tutoring in most subjects. There is remedial math, reading, and writing.

Campus Safety and Security: Measures include self-defense education, informal discussions, pamphlets/posters/films, lighted pathways/sidewalks, and a security officer.

Programs of Study: Sheldon Jackson College confers B.A. and B.S. degrees. Associate degrees are also awarded. Bachelor's degrees are awarded in EDUCATION (elementary, mathematics, science, secondary, and social science), SOCIAL SCIENCE (interdisciplinary studies and liberal arts/general studies). Environmental science/education is the strongest academically and has the largest enrollment.

Required: All students must complete a core curriculum in writing, math, speech, science, fine arts, computer competence, and multicultural awareness. A minimum GPA of 2.0 and a major of more than 30 credits out of a total of at least 120 credits are required for graduation.

Special: Business and education internships are required. Work-study programs with the U.S. Forest and Park Services, child care centers, and the Alaska Native Museum, combined B.A.-B.S. degrees, student-designed majors, a general studies degree, and a dual major in natural and aquatic resources are available. Nondegree study is possible.

Faculty/Classroom: 59% of faculty are male; 41%, female. All teach undergraduates. The average class size in an introductory lecture is 32; in a laboratory, 11; and in a regular course, 13.

Requirements: The SAT or ACT is recommended. The GED is accepted. A GPA of 2.0 is required. AP and CLEP credits are accepted.

Procedure: Freshmen are admitted fall and spring. Application deadlines are open. Application fee is $25. Applications are accepted on-line.

Transfer: The college follows a nonselective admissions policy for transfer applicants with a 2.0 GPA. 30 of 120 credits required for the bachelor's degree must be completed at Sheldon Jackson College.

Visiting: There are regularly scheduled orientations for prospective students, including campus tour visits to classrooms and meetings with financial aid counselors. There are guides for informal visits and visitors may sit in on classes and stay overnight. To schedule a visit, contact the Admissions Office.

Financial Aid: The FAFSA is required. Check with the school for current deadlines.

International Students: They must score satisfactorily on the TOEFL.

Computers: All students may access the system. There are no time limits. The fee is $370 per year. It is strongly recommended that all students have a personal computer.

Graduates: In an average class, 40% graduate in 4 years or less, 50% graduate in 5 years or less, and 60% graduate in 6 years or less.

Admissions Contact: Elizabeth Lower, Director of Admissions.
E-mail: *elower@sj-alaska.edu* Web: *http://www.sj-alaska.edu*

UNIVERSITY OF ALASKA SYSTEM

The University of Alaska is the only public institution of higher learning in the state of Alaska. It is a statewide system consisting of three multimission main campuses located in Anchorage, Fairbanks, and Juneau, with extended satellite colleges and sites throughout Alaska. Four year undergraduate programs are offered by each institution. The university was established at Fairbanks in 1917 as the Alaska Agricultural College and School of Mines; in 1935 it was renamed the University of Alaska. The university now includes full-service universities in Fairbanks, Anchorage, and Juneau; lower division college centers in Bethel, Dillington,

Ketkikan, Kodiak, Kotzebue, Nome, Palmer, Sitka, and Soldotna; a community college at Valdez; and vocational, rural education, and extension sites through the state. The university is governed by an eleven-member Board of Regents. The board is an autonomous organization and the highest authority in the administration of the university, governed by the Alaska Statutes, which provides for the appointment of the regents by the governor for overlapping terms of eight years. Since 1975, students have been represented on the board; they are appointed for two-year terms. For more information, visit *www.alaska.edu*.

UNIVERSITY OF ALASKA ANCHORAGE   D-3

Anchorage, AK 99508   (907) 786-1480; Fax: (907) 786-4888

Full-time: 2466 men, 3716 women	**Faculty:** IIA, -$
Part-time: 1206 men, 2473 women	**Ph.D.s:** 63%
Graduate: 277 men, 503 women	**Student/Faculty:** n/av
Year: semesters, summer session	**Tuition:** $3465 ($9561)
Application Deadline: July 1	**Room & Board:** $7810
Freshman Class: 2564 applied, 2073 accepted, 1079 enrolled	
SAT or ACT: required	**NONCOMPETITIVE**

The University of Alaska Anchorage, founded in 1954, is a public institution and a major unit of the University of Alaska statewide system. Its baccalaureate programs are administered through the Colleges of Arts and Sciences, Business and Public Policy, Health, Education, and Social Welfare, and the School of Engineering, and the Community and Technical College. Tuition is based on the level of course work and number of credits taken; fees also vary by credits. There are 5 undergraduate and 5 graduate schools. In addition to regional accreditation, UAA has baccalaureate program accreditation with AACSB, ABET, ACEJMC, ADA, CAHEA, CSWE, NASAD, NASDTEC, and NLN. The library contains 676,750 volumes, 574,010 microform items, and 7080 audio/video tapes/CDs/DVDs, and subscribes to 3480 periodicals including electronic. Computerized library services include interlibrary loans and database searching. Special learning facilities include a learning resource center, art gallery, radio station, TV station, a dental clinic, a welding lab, an auto-diesel garage, a theater, photography labs, and a student art museum show case. The 428-acre campus is in an urban area. Including any residence halls, there are 27 buildings.
Student Life: 94% of undergraduates are from Alaska. Others are from 49 states, 41 foreign countries, and Canada. 69% are white; 10% Native American/Eskimo. The average age of freshmen is 20; all undergraduates, 31. 33% do not continue beyond their first year.
Housing: 388 students can be accommodated in college housing, which includes coed dorms and on-campus apartments. In addition, there are floors for Alaska natives studing engineering, nursing students, honors students, under age 20, healthy livestyle, quiet lifestyle, and language and cultures. On-campus housing is available on a first-come, first-served basis. Priority is given to out-of-town students. 94% of students commute. Alcohol is not permitted. All students may keep cars.
Activities: There are no fraternities or sororities. There are 75 groups on campus, including art, band, cheerleading, chess, choir, chorus, computers, dance, debate, drama, ethnic, film, gay, honors, international, jazz band, literary magazine, newspaper, orchestra, photography, political, professional, radio and TV, religious, social, social service, student government, and yearbook. Popular campus events include Great Alaska Shoot-Out, Northern Lights Invitational, and Student Showcase.
Sports: There are 6 intercollegiate sports for men and 4 for women, and 10 intramural sports for men and 10 for women. Facilities include an ice rink, an indoor jogging track, a gym, a swimming/diving pool, a weight room, and racquetball/squash courts.
Disabled Students: All of the campus is accessible. Wheelchair ramps, elevators, special parking, specially equipped rest rooms, lowered drinking fountains, lowered telephones, and special housing are available.
Services: Counseling and information services are available, as is tutoring in most subjects. There is a reader service for the blind, and remedial math, reading, and writing. Sign language, interpreters, and note takers are available.
Campus Safety and Security: Measures include 24-hour foot and vehicle patrol, self-defense education, security escort services, and informal discussions. There are pamphlets/posters/films, emergency telephones, and lighted pathways/sidewalks.
Programs of Study: UAA confers B.A., B.S., B.B.A., B.Ed., B.F.A., B.Mus., and B.S.W. degrees. Associate and master's degrees are also awarded. Bachelor's degrees are awarded in BIOLOGICAL SCIENCE (biology/biological science), BUSINESS (accounting, banking and finance, business administration and management, hotel/motel and restaurant management, management information systems, marketing/retailing/merchandising, and transportation management), COMMUNICATIONS AND THE ARTS (art, communications, dramatic arts, English, fine arts, journalism, languages, and music), COMPUTER AND PHYSICAL SCIENCE (chemistry, computer science, mathematics, and natural sciences), EDUCATION (elementary, music, physical, and secondary), ENGINEERING AND ENVIRONMENTAL DESIGN (aeronautical technology, civil engineering, survey and mapping technology, and

technological management), HEALTH PROFESSIONS (nursing), SOCIAL SCIENCE (anthropology, criminal justice, economics, history, human services, interdisciplinary studies, political science/government, psychology, social work, and sociology). Education, nursing, and social sciences are the strongest academically. Elementary education, accounting, and nursing are the largest.
Required: General education requirements include 7 credits in natural science, 6 each in written communications, humanities, and social sciences, and 3 each in oral communication, quantitative skills, and fine arts. A total of 120 to 132 credits, with 48 upper-division courses, and a minimum GPA of 2.0 are required to graduate.
Special: UAA participates in the National Student Exchange Program and offers study abroad. UAA also offers B.A.-B.S. degrees, student-designed and dual majors, internships, pass/fail options, a 3-2 electrical engineering degree, a general studies degree, nondegree study, and credit for life experience. The Community and Technical College provides educational and vocational courses for career development. There are 2 national honor societies and 3 departmental honors programs.
Faculty/Classroom: 51% of faculty are male; 49%, female. The average class size in an introductory lecture is 50; in a laboratory, 20; and in a regular course, 35.
Admissions: 81% of the 2005-2006 applicants were accepted.
Requirements: The SAT or ACT is required. In addition, applicants should be graduates of an accredited secondary school or have a high school or GED certificate. A GPA of 2.5 is required. AP and CLEP credits are accepted.
Procedure: Freshmen are admitted to all sessions. Entrance exams should be taken by May of the senior year. There are deferred admissions and rolling admissions plans. Early decision applications should be filed by July 1. The college accepts all applicants. Notification is sent on a rolling basis. Applications are accepted on-line. The fall 2005 application fee was $40.
Transfer: 478 transfer students enrolled in 2004-2005. Applicants must meet admission requirements and must have a minimum GPA of 2.0 and at least 30 credit hours earned at an accredited postsecondary institution. 24 of 120 credits required for the bachelor's degree must be completed at UAA.
Visiting: There are regularly scheduled orientations for prospective students, consisting of registration orientation, application process, campus tours, student appointments, and classes. There are guides for informal visits and visitors may sit in on classes. To schedule a visit, contact the Office of Admissions.
Financial Aid: In 2004-2005, 32% of all full-time freshmen and 40% of continuing full-time students received some form of financial aid. At least 23% of full-time freshmen and at least 34% of continuing full-time students received need-based aid. The average freshman award was $8007. Need-based scholarships or need-based grants averaged $3906; need-based self-help aid (loans and jobs) averaged $6435; and other non-need-based awards and non-need-based scholarships averaged $2755. The average financial indebtedness of the 2004 graduate was $15,621. UAA is a member of CSS. The FAFSA and the college's own financial statement are required. The priority date for freshman financial aid applications for fall entry is April 1.
International Students: They must score satisfactorily on the written TOEFL and also take the SAT or the ACT.
Computers: All students may access the system. There are no time limits and no fees.
Graduates: From July 1, 2003 to June 30, 2004, 768 bachelor's degrees were awarded. The most popular majors were business/marketing (21%), health professions and related sciences (17%), and English (6%).
Admissions Contact: Enrollment Services. A video is available.
E-mail: *enroll@uaa.alaska.edu* Web: *www.uaa.alaska.edu*

UNIVERSITY OF ALASKA FAIRBANKS   D-2

Fairbanks, AK 99775-7480   (907) 474-7500
(800) 478-1823; Fax: (907) 474-5379

Full-time: 1690 men, 1772 women	**Faculty:** 288; I, --$
Part-time: 1236 men, 2438 women	**Ph.D.s:** n/av
Graduate: 531 men, 563 women	**Student/Faculty:** 12 to 1
Year: semesters, summer session	**Tuition:** $4521 ($12,903)
Application Deadline: August 1	**Room & Board:** $5580
Freshman Class: 1777 applied, 1383 accepted, 1000 enrolled	
SAT Verbal/Math: 530/510*	**ACT:** 20 **COMPETITIVE**

The University of Alaska Fairbanks, founded in 1917 is the nation's northernmost Land, Sea, and Space Grant university and international research center. The institution advances and disseminates knowledge through teaching, research, and public service with an emphasis on Alaska and circumpolar regions. There are 8 undergraduate and 8 graduate schools. In addition to regional accreditation, UAF has baccalaureate program accreditation with AACSB, ABET, ACEJMC, ACS, CAAHEP, CSAB, CSWE, NASDTEC, NASM, NCATE, and SAF. The 3 libraries contain 1,035,638 volumes, 151,948 microform items, and 34,787 audio/video tapes/CDs/DVDs, and subscribe to 24,179 periodicals including electronic. Computerized library services include the card catalog, interlibrary loans, database searching, Internet access, and laptop Internet portals. Special learning facilities include a learning resource center, art gallery, natural history museum, radio station and TV station. Several research institutes and labs for study in the physical and natural sciences are associated with the university. The 2250-acre campus is in a small town 4 miles northwest of Fairbanks. Including any residence halls, there are 175 buildings.

Student Life: 87% of undergraduates are from Alaska. Students are from 48 states, 18 foreign countries, and Canada. 62% are white; 19% Native American/Eskimo. The average age of freshmen is 18; all undergraduates, 22. 31% do not continue beyond their first year.

Housing: 1554 students can be accommodated in college housing, which includes coed dorms, on-campus apartments, and married-student housing. In addition, there are honors floors and first year experience residence. On-campus housing is available on a first-come, first-served basis. 71% of students commute. All students may keep cars.

Activities: There is 1 national fraternity and 1 national sorority. There are 90 groups on campus, including art, band, cheerleading, chess, choir, chorus, computers, dance, drama, ethnic, film, gay, honors, international, jazz band, literary magazine, musical theater, newspaper, orchestra, pep band, photography, political, professional, radio and TV, religious, social, student government, and symphony. Popular campus events include All-Campus Day, Alcohol Awareness Week, and Meltdown (spring event).

Sports: There are 4 intercollegiate sports for men and 4 for women, and 21 intramural sports for men and 21 for women. Facilities include a 4500-seat arena, a 2000-seat gym, a 1500-seat skating rink, 2 racquetball courts, 2 weight rooms, 4 basketball courts, an Olympic-size swimming pool, a small-bore rifle range, and a lighted 30-mile ski trail.

Disabled Students: 90% of the campus is accessible. Wheelchair ramps, elevators, special parking, specially equipped rest rooms, special class scheduling, lowered drinking fountains, lowered telephones, special housing, a shuttle bus, and a swimming pool equipped with hydraulic lifts are available.

Services: Counseling and information services are available, as is tutoring in some subjects, including chemistry, calculus, languages, biology, math, physics, geology, and English. There is a reader service for the blind, and remedial math, reading, and writing.

Campus Safety and Security: Measures include 24-hour foot and vehicle patrol, self-defense education, security escort services, and shuttle buses. There are informal discussions, pamphlets/posters/films, emergency telephones, lighted pathways/sidewalks, a 24-hour dorm lockup, a 24-hour crisis line, evening patrols inside dorms, residence hall check-in, and security escort service.

Programs of Study: UAF confers B.A., B.S., B.B.A., B.A.S., B.F.A., B.M., and B.T. degrees. Associate, master's, and doctoral degrees are also awarded. Bachelor's degrees are awarded in AGRICULTURE (fishing and fisheries, natural resource management, and wildlife management), BIOLOGICAL SCIENCE (biology/biological science and wildlife biology), BUSINESS (accounting, business administration and management, and business economics), COMMUNICATIONS AND THE ARTS (art, communications, dramatic arts, English, Eskimo, journalism, linguistics, modern language, music, and music performance), COMPUTER AND PHYSICAL SCIENCE (applied physics, chemistry, computer science, earth science, geology, mathematics, physics, science, and statistics), EDUCATION (elementary and music), ENGINEERING AND ENVIRONMENTAL DESIGN (civil engineering, electrical/electronics engineering, environmental science, geological engineering, mechanical engineering, mining and mineral engineering, petroleum/natural gas engineering, and technological management), SOCIAL SCIENCE (anthropology, area studies, criminal justice, ethnic studies, geography, history, interdisciplinary studies, Japanese studies, Native American studies, philosophy, political science/government, psychology, rural economics, Russian and Slavic studies, social work, and sociology). Engineering, fisheries, and biology are the strongest academically. Biological sciences, business administration, and elementary education are the largest.

Required: All students must complete core courses in English and oral communication, library skills, humanities, social science, natural science, and math. A minimum of 120 credit hours, with 27 to 30 in the major, and a 2.0 GPA are required for graduation. Courses in English and speech communication are required.

Special: The university's College of Rural and Community Development offers satellite education programs to Alaska residents to reach students at remote sites. Study abroad is offered in 8 countries, and B.A.-B.S. degrees are available in 8 majors (anthropology, biological sciences, chemistry, physics, interdisciplinary studies, math, psychology, and sociology). Internships are offered through the Rural Alaska Honors Institute. Student-designed majors, credit/no credit options, nondegree study, and credit for life, military, and work experience are also available. There are 10 national honor societies and a freshman honors program.

Faculty/Classroom: 58% of faculty are male; 42%, female. The average class size in a regular course is 14.

Admissions: 78% of the 2005-2006 applicants were accepted. The SAT scores for the 2005-2006 freshman class were: Verbal--38% below 500, 35% between 500 and 599, 21% between 600 and 700, and 6% above 700; Math--41% below 500, 40% between 500 and 599, 17% between 600 and 700, and 2% above 700. The ACT scores were 53% below 21, 19% between 21 and 23, 18% between 24 and 26, 4% between 27 and 28, and 4% above 28. 26% of the current freshmen were in the top fifth of their class; 50% were in the top two fifths. 2 freshmen graduated first in their class.

Requirements: The SAT or ACT is required. In addition, applicants should be graduates of an accredited secondary school with 16 academic credits, including 4 in English and 3 each in math, natural or physical sciences, and social sciences, with a minimum GPA of 2.5 in these courses. The GED or its equivalent is accepted. A GPA of 2.0 is required. AP and CLEP credits are accepted.

Procedure: Freshmen are admitted to all sessions. There is an early admissions and a rolling admissions plan. Applications should be filed by August 1 for fall entry and December 1 for spring entry, along with a $40 fee. Notification is sent on a rolling basis. Applications are accepted online.

Transfer: 430 transfer students enrolled in 2004-2005. A GPA of 2.0 in all previous college work and an honorable dismissal from all schools attended are required. Applicants with fewer than 30 semester hours of transferable credit also must have a high school GPA of 2.0 and ACT or SAT scores. 30 of 120 credits required for the bachelor's degree must be completed at UAF.

Visiting: There are regularly scheduled orientations for prospective students. There are guides for informal visits and visitors may sit in on classes and stay overnight. To schedule a visit, contact the Admissions Counseling Office.

Financial Aid: In 2005-2006, 67% of all full-time freshmen and 50% of continuing full-time students received some form of financial aid. 35% of full-time freshmen and 23% of continuing full-time students received need-based aid. Need-based scholarships or need-based grants averaged $3768; and need-based self-help aid (loans and jobs) averaged $7670. 8% of undergraduates work part time. Average annual earnings from campus work are $6630. The average financial indebtedness of the 2005 graduate was $23,994. The FAFSA is required. The deadline for filing freshman financial aid applications for fall entry is May 15.

International Students: There are 199 international students enrolled. They must score satisfactorily on the written TOEFL and also take the SAT or the ACT.

Computers: Wireless access is available. All students may access the system 24 hours per day. There are no time limits and no fees.

Graduates: From July 1, 2004 to June 30, 2005, 432 bachelor's degrees were awarded. The most popular majors were biological sciences (7%), business administration (7%), and psychology (6%). In an average class, 7% graduate in 4 years or less, 18% graduate in 5 years or less, and 23% graduate in 6 years or less.

Admissions Contact: Nancy Dix, Director of Admissions. A video is available. E-mail: *admissions@uaf.edu* Web: *www.uaf.edu*

UNIVERSITY OF ALASKA SOUTHEAST F-3

Juneau, AK 99801 (907) 465-6457
(877) 465-4827; Fax: (907) 465-6365

Full-time: 255 men, 315 women	**Faculty:** 60; IIA, --$
Part-time: 585 men, 855 women	**Ph.D.s:** 52%
Graduate: 45 men, 55 women	**Student/Faculty:** 50 to 1
Year: semesters, summer session	**Tuition:** $2600 ($7500)
Application Deadline: open	**Room & Board:** $5450
Freshman Class: n/av	
SAT or ACT: recommended	**LESS COMPETITIVE**

The University of Alaska Southeast, a multicampus institution founded in 1972, is part of the University of Alaska statewide system, with baccalaureate programs offered in business and public administration, education, and liberal arts and science. Figures in the above capsule and in this profile are approximate. There are 3 undergraduate and 2 graduate schools. The library contains 250,000 volumes, 250,000 microform items, and 1850 audio/video tapes/CDs/DVDs, and subscribes to 1500 periodicals including electronic. Computerized library services include the card catalog, interlibrary loans, and database searching. Special learning facilities include a learning resource center and media and educational technology classrooms. The 198-acre campus is in a suburban area 10 miles north of Juneau. Including any residence halls, there are 18 buildings.

Student Life: 75% of undergraduates are from Alaska. Students are from 37 states, 12 foreign countries, and Canada. 95% are from public schools. 70% are white; 17% Native American/Eskimo. The average age of freshmen is 18; all undergraduates, 24.

Housing: 250 students can be accommodated in college housing, which includes single-sex dorms, on-campus apartments, and married-student housing. On-campus housing is available on a first-come, first-served basis. Priority is given to out-of-town students. 90% of students commute. All students may keep cars.

Activities: There are no fraternities or sororities. There are 16 groups on campus, including choir, ethnic, gay, honors, literary magazine, newspaper, political, professional, religious, and student government. Popular campus events include Ski Day, whale-watching, and Eagle Preserve field trips.

Sports: There are 3 intramural sports for men and 3 for women. Facilities include a community gym and pool, an activity center, and access to health club facilities.

Disabled Students: 95% of the campus is accessible. Wheelchair ramps, elevators, special parking, specially equipped rest rooms, lowered drinking fountains, and lowered telephones are available.

Services: Counseling and information services are available, as is tutoring in most subjects. There is a reader service for the blind, and remedial math, reading, and writing.

Campus Safety and Security: Measures include shuttle buses, informal discussions, pamphlets/posters/films, and emergency telephones. There are lighted pathways/sidewalks and late-night security at student housing.

Programs of Study: UAS confers B.A., B.S., B.B.A., B.Ed., and B.L.A. degrees. Associate and master's degrees are also awarded. Bachelor's degrees are awarded in BIOLOGICAL SCIENCE (biology/biological science and marine biology), BUSINESS (accounting and business administration and management), COMMUNICATIONS AND THE ARTS (art, communications, literature, and speech/debate/rhetoric), COMPUTER AND PHYSICAL SCIENCE (mathematics), EDUCATION (elementary), ENGINEERING AND ENVIRONMENTAL DESIGN (environmental science), SOCIAL SCIENCE (liberal arts/general studies, political science/government, public administration, and social science). Accounting, marine biology, and environmental science are the strongest academically. Liberal arts is the largest.

Required: All students are required to complete general education courses, including 15 credits in humanities and social science, 10 in math and natural sciences, 6 in written communication skills, and 3 in speech. A total of 120 semester credits, with at least 36 in the major, and a minimum GPA of 2.0 are required in order to graduate. In the liberal arts program, a portfolio is required.

Special: UAS offers cross-registration through the National Student Exchange, and internships with federal and state agencies. Study abroad, work-study, dual and student-designed majors, credit/no credit options, and credit for military experience are also available. The School of Career and Continuing Education offers courses and certificate programs in technological skills.

Faculty/Classroom: 98% teach undergraduates. No introductory courses are taught by graduate students. The average class size in an introductory lecture is 20 and in a laboratory, 12.

Requirements: The SAT or ACT is recommended. Applicants should be graduates of an accredited secondary school or have the GED. A GPA of 2.0 is required. AP and CLEP credits are accepted.

Procedure: Freshmen are admitted fall and spring. There are early admissions, deferred admissions and rolling admissions plans. Application deadlines are open. The fall 2005 application fee was $35.

Transfer: A minimum GPA of 2.0 from an accredited institution is required. 30 of 120 credits required for the bachelor's degree must be completed at UAS.

Visiting: There are regularly scheduled orientations for prospective students. There are guides for informal visits and visitors may sit in on classes. To schedule a visit, contact Greg Wagner.

Financial Aid: UAS is a member of CSS. The FAFSA and the college's own financial statement are required. Check with the school for application deadlines.

International Students: They must score satisfactorily on the written TOEFL and also take the SAT or the ACT.

Computers: All students may access the system. There are no time limits and no fees.

Admissions Contact: Greg Wagner, Director of Admissions.
E-mail: *jyuas@alaska.edu* Web: *http://www.jun.alaska.edu*

ARIZONA

POPULATION DENSITY
●10,000 and over

0 20 40 60 80 100
Miles

AMERICAN INDIAN COLLEGE OF THE ASSEMBLIES OF GOD
C-4

Phoenix, AZ 85021

(602) 944-3335 x 235
(800) 933-3828; Fax: (602) 943-8299

Full-time: 35 men, 30 women
Part-time: 5 men, 10 women
Graduate: none
Year: semesters
Application Deadline: open
Freshman Class: n/av
SAT or ACT: required

Faculty: 5
Ph.D.s: 10%
Student/Faculty: 12 to 1
Tuition: $5555
Room & Board: $3850

LESS COMPETITIVE

American Indian College of the Assemblies of God, founded in 1957, is a Christian college with a specific mission of preparing American Indians for leadership in churches, education, and the community. Some figures in the above capsule and in this profile are approximate. The library contains 20,000 volumes and 35 audio/video tapes/CDs/DVDs, and subscribes to 102 periodicals including electronic. Computerized library services include the card catalog and Internet access. Special learning facilities include a learning resource center and a student-led chapel. The 10-acre campus is in an urban area in north Phoenix, just east of I17 and the Metrocenter area. Including any residence halls, there are 9 buildings.

Student Life: 72% of undergraduates are from Arizona. Others are from 10 states and 1 foreign country 85% are from public schools. 67% are Native American/Eskimo; 18% white. Most are Protestant. The average age of freshmen is 23; all undergraduates, 26.

Housing: 80 students can be accommodated in college housing, which includes single-sex dorms and off-campus apartments. 52% of students live on campus; of those, All remain on campus on weekends. Alcohol is not permitted. All students may keep cars.

Activities: There are no fraternities or sororities. There are some groups and organizations on campus, including band, cheerleading, drama, ethnic, religious, student government, and yearbook. Popular campus events include missions conventions and College Days.

Sports: There is no sports program at AIC. Facilities include a full-size gym with a locker room and a weight room.

Disabled Students: All of the campus is accessible. Wheelchair ramps, special parking, specially equipped rest rooms, and lowered drinking fountains are available.

Services: Counseling and information services are available, as is tutoring in most subjects. There is remedial math, reading, and writing.

Campus Safety and Security: Measures include informal discussions, pamphlets/posters/films, lighted pathways/sidewalks, and night security.

Programs of Study: AIC confers the B.A. degree. Associate degrees are also awarded. Bachelor's degrees are awarded in EDUCATION (elementary), SOCIAL SCIENCE (ministries).

Required: To graduate, all students must maintain a GPA of 2.0 and complete 128 total credits. Students must complete courses in history, science, math, computer, and bible studies. A comprehensive bible exam is required.

Special: Internships and dual majors are available.

Faculty/Classroom: 65% of faculty are male; 35%, female. All teach undergraduates and 1% both teach and do research. The average class size in an introductory lecture is 11; in a laboratory, 6; and in a regular course, 6.

Admissions: 71% of recent applicants were accepted. The ACT scores for a recent freshman class were: 100% below 21.

Requirements: The SAT or ACT is required. In addition, transcripts from high school and any other secondary schools attended are required along with a pastor's reference form. Applicants are required to take placement tests with satisfactory results. A 2.0 GPA is required and the GED is accepted. AP and CLEP credits are accepted. Important factors in the admissions decision are advanced placement or honor courses, evidence of special talent, and extracurricular activities record.

Procedure: Freshmen are admitted to all sessions. Entrance exams should be taken prior to acceptance. There are early decision, early admissions, and deferred admissions plans. Application deadlines are open. 1 early decision candidates was accepted in a recent year.

Transfer: 31 transfer students enrolled in a recent year. Official transcripts from high school and each college attended, plus a pastor's reference form are required. Students must demonstrate proficiency in English, writing, math, and reading. 30 of 128 credits required for the bachelor's degree must be completed at AIC.

Visiting: There are regularly scheduled orientations for prospective students, consisting of College Days in the fall and spring semesters that include class visits, overnight stays in dorms, and meals in the cafeteria for 2 days. There are guides for informal visits and visitors may sit in on classes and stay overnight. To schedule a visit, contact Admissions at aicadm@aicag.edu.

Financial Aid: In a recent year, 88% of all full-time freshmen and 96% of continuing full-time students received some form of financial aid. 88% of full-time freshmen and 90% of continuing full-time students received need-based aid. The average freshman award was $4924. 34% of undergraduates work part time. Average annual earnings from campus work are $1489. The average financial indebtedness of a recent graduate was $6772. The FAFSA is required. Check with the school for current deadlines.

International Students: There was 1 international students enrolled in a recent year. They must score satisfactorily on the written TOEFL and also take the SAT or the ACT.

Computers: All students may access the system. There are no time limits and no fees. It is strongly recommended that all students have a personal computer.

Graduates: In an average class, 35% graduate in 6 years or less.

Admissions Contact: Steve Clindaniel, Admissions Director.
E-mail: aicadm@aicag.edu Web: www.aicag.edu

ARIZONA BOARD OF REGENTS

The Arizona Board of Regents, established in 1945, is a private system in Arizona. It is governed by a board of regents, whose chief administrator is executive director and chief executive officer. The primary goal of the system is teaching, research, and service. The main priorities are to provide strong undergraduate instruction programs; to conduct extensive research and graduate instruction programs; and to ensure access for qualified Arizona residents, especially underrepresented ethnic minorities. The total enrollment is usually about 95,000 with 3500 faculty members. Altogether there are some 325 baccalaureate, 250 master's, and 140 doctoral programs offered in Arizona Board of Regents. Profiles of the 4-year campuses are included in this section.

ARIZONA STATE UNIVERSITY - MAIN
(See Arizona State University-Tempe)

ARIZONA STATE UNIVERSITY-TEMPE   C-4

Tempe, AZ 85287-0112   (480) 965-7788

Full-time: 15,881 men, 16,984 women	**Faculty:** 1314; I, -$
Part-time: 4055 men, 4336 women	**Ph.D.s:** 84%
Graduate: 5056 men, 5300 women	**Student/Faculty:** 25 to 1
Year: semesters, summer session	**Tuition:** $4406 ($15,095)
Application Deadline: open	**Room & Board:** $6768
Freshman Class: 19,914 applied, 18,126 accepted, 7706 enrolled	
SAT Verbal/Math: 549/559*	**ACT:** 23 **COMPETITIVE**

Arizona State University-Tempe, formerly Arizona State University-Main, founded in 1885, is a publicly funded institution offering undergraduate programs in the arts and sciences, business, education, engineering, nursing, public programs, architecture and environmental design, social work, and fine arts. There are 11 undergraduate and 11 graduate schools. In addition to regional accreditation, ASU - Tempe has baccalaureate program accreditation with AACSB, ABET, ACCE, ACEJMC, ADA, APA, CAA, CACREP, CCNE, CCTE, CSAB, CSWE, FIDER, NAAB, NAIT, NASAD, NASM, and NRPA. The 5 libraries contain 3,593,677 volumes, 6,010,180 microform items, and 1,269,023 audio/video tapes/CDs/DVDs, and subscribe to 32,001 periodicals including electronic. Computerized library services include the card catalog, interlibrary loans, database searching, and Internet access. Special learning facilities include a learning resource center, art gallery, planetarium, radio station, and TV station. The 814-acre campus is in a suburban area 10 miles east of Phoenix. Including any residence halls, there are 75 buildings.

Student Life: 73% of undergraduates are from Arizona. Others are from 50 states, 104 foreign countries, and Canada. 69% are white; 13% Hispanic. The average age of freshmen is 18; all undergraduates, 22. 23% do not continue beyond their first year; 55% remain to graduate.

Housing: 6000 students can be accommodated in college housing, which includes coed dorms, on-campus apartments, and fraternity houses. In addition, there are honors houses, special-interest houses and a residence for freshmen. On-campus housing is available on a first-come, first-served basis. 83% of students commute. All students may keep cars.

Activities: 6% of men belong to 25 national fraternities; 6% of women belong to 21 national sororities. There are 502 groups on campus, including academic, adult reentry, art, band, cheerleading, chess, choir, chorus, computers, dance, drama, ethnic, film, gay, honors, international, jazz band, literary magazine, marching band, musical theater, newspaper, opera, orchestra, photography, political, professional, radio and TV, religious, social, social service, student government, student leadership, and symphony. Popular campus events include World Fest international food and cultural festival and Insight Bowl.

Sports: There are 10 intercollegiate sports for men and 11 for women, and 35 intramural sports for men and 35 for women. Facilities include 4 stadiums (including football and baseball), a tennis center, an aquatic complex, a golf course, 2 activity centers, a student recreation complex, and a track.

Disabled Students: 99% of the campus is accessible. Wheelchair ramps, elevators, special parking, specially equipped rest rooms, special class scheduling, lowered drinking fountains, lowered telephones, flashing alarms for the deaf, braille maps, modified residence hall rooms, and an adaptive exercise program and facility are available.

Services: Counseling and information services are available, as is tutoring in most subjects, including 125 different courses. There is a reader service for the blind, and remedial math, reading, and writing. There is also on-line tutoring and graduate test preparation.

Campus Safety and Security: Measures include 24-hour foot and vehicle patrol, self-defense education, security escort services, and shuttle buses. There are informal discussions, pamphlets/posters/films, emergency telephones, and lighted pathways/sidewalks.

Programs of Study: ASU-Tempe confers B.A., B.S., B.A.E., B.F.A., B.I.S., B.L.S., B.Mus., B.S.D., B.S.E., B.S.L.A., B.S.N., B.S.P., and B.S.W. degrees. Master's and doctoral degrees are also awarded. Bachelor's degrees are awarded in AGRICULTURE (plant science), BIOLOGICAL SCIENCE (biochemistry, biology/biological science, environmental biology, microbiology, and molecular biology), BUSINESS (accounting, banking and finance, management science, marketing/retailing/merchandising, purchasing/inventory management, and recreation and leisure services), COMMUNICATIONS AND THE ARTS (art, Chinese, communications, dance, dramatic arts, English, French, German, graphic design, industrial design, Italian, Japanese, journalism, music, music performance, music theory and composition, Russian, and Spanish), COMPUTER AND PHYSICAL SCIENCE (chemistry, computer science, geology, information sciences and systems, mathematics, and physics), EDUCATION (early childhood, elementary, music, secondary, and special), ENGINEERING AND ENVIRONMENTAL DESIGN (aeronautical engineering, architecture, bioengineering, chemical engineering, civil engineering, computer engineering, construction engineering, electrical/electronics engineering, engineering, industrial engineering, interior design, landscape architecture/design, materials science, mechanical engineering, urban design, and urban planning technology), HEALTH PROFESSIONS (clinical science, music therapy, nursing, and speech pathology/audiology), SOCIAL SCIENCE (African American studies, American Indian studies, anthropology, criminal justice, economics, family/consumer resource management, geography, Hispanic American studies, history, interdisciplinary studies, philosophy, physical fitness/movement, political science/government, psychology, religion, social work, sociology, and women's studies). Engineering, architecture, and computer science are the strongest academically. Business, psychology, and communication are the largest.

Required: To graduate, students must have a minimum GPA of 2.0 and a total of at least 120 credit hours, including 50 hours of upper-level work. The number of hours in the major varies by degree program. All students must take English composition and fulfill the general studies requirement of 35 hours in the areas of numeracy, literacy and critical inquiry, humanities and fine arts, social and behavioral sciences, natural sciences, global awareness, and historical awareness.

Special: ASU Tempe offers internships in many disciplines, study abroad in 45 countries, and a variety of interdisciplinary undergraduate programs. Students may participate in educational programs supported by several institutes and centers, such as the National Center for Electron Microscopy, the American Indian Institute, and the Center for Medieval and Renaissance Studies. Also available are continuing education programs and a summer math and science program for high school students. There are 14 national honor societies, including Phi Beta Kappa, and a freshman honors program.

Faculty/Classroom: 61% of faculty are male; 39%, female. The average class size in an introductory lecture is 43 and in a laboratory, 24.

Admissions: 91% of the 2005-2006 applicants were accepted. The SAT scores for the 2005-2006 freshman class were: Verbal--28% below 500, 43% between 500 and 599, 23% between 600 and 700, and 6% above 700; Math--23% below 500, 42% between 500 and 599, 28% between 600 and 700, and 7% above 700. The ACT scores were 27% below 21, 27% between 21 and 23, 24% between 24 and 26, 11% between 27 and 28, and 11% above 28. 45% of the current freshmen were in the top fifth of their class; 73% were in the top two fifths. There were 152 National Merit finalists.

Requirements: The SAT or ACT is required. The ACT Optional Writing test is also recommended. Graduation from an accredited secondary school must include 4 years each of English and math, 3 years of lab science, 2 years each of social science (including American history) and the same foreign language, and 1 year of fine arts. The GED, minimum score 50, is also accepted. ASU-Tempe requires applicants to be in the upper 25% of their class. A GPA of 3.0 is required. AP and CLEP credits are accepted.

Procedure: Freshmen are admitted to all sessions. Entrance exams should be taken late in the junior year. There is a rolling admissions plan. Application deadlines are open. The priority date is February1. Notification is sent on a rolling basis. The fee is $50 for nonresidents, $25 for residents. Applications are accepted on-line.

Transfer: 3744 transfer students enrolled in 2004-2005. Applicants with fewer than 36 transferable hours must meet the requirements for freshman admission. A minimum GPA of 2.0 is required for in-state applicants; 2.5 for out-of-state applicants. 30 of 120 credits required for the bachelor's degree must be completed at ASU- Tempe.

Visiting: There are regularly scheduled orientations for prospective students. There are guides for informal visits and visitors may sit in on classes. To schedule a visit, contact Undergraduate Admissions at (480) 727-7013 or asuvisit@asu.edu.

Financial Aid: In 2005-2006, 60% of all full-time freshmen and 55% of continuing full-time students received some form of financial aid. 38% of full-time freshmen and 42% of continuing full-time students received need-based aid. The average freshman award was $7790. Need-based scholarships or need-based grants averaged $5946; need-based self-help aid (loans and jobs) averaged $2761; and non-need-based athletic scholarships averaged $5463. The average financial indebtedness of the 2005 graduate was $17,016. The FAFSA is required. The priority date for freshman financial aid applications for fall entry is March 1.

International Students: There are 984 international students enrolled. They must take the TOEFL or and also take the SATor the ACT.

Computers: Wireless access is available. All students may access the system. 1 site is open 24 hours per day. There are no time limits and no fees.

Graduates: From July 1, 2004 to June 30, 2005, 7498 bachelor's degrees were awarded. The most popular majors were interdisciplinary studies (10%), communication (6%), and psychology (5%). In an average class, 2% graduate in 3 years or less, 27% graduate in 4 years or less, 50% graduate in 5 years or less, and 55% graduate in 6 years or less. 928 companies recruited on campus in 2004-2005.

Admissions Contact: Martha Byrd, Dean Undergraduate Admissions. E-mail: ugrading@asu.edu Web: www.asu.edu

DEVRY UNIVERSITY/PHOENIX — C-4

Phoenix, AZ 85021-2995

(602) 870-9201
(800) 528-0250; Fax: (602) 331-1494

Full-time: 1175 men, 325 women	**Faculty:** n/av
Part-time: 375 men, 125 women	**Ph.D.s:** n/av
Graduate: none	**Student/Faculty:** n/av
Year: semesters, summer session	**Tuition:** $11,790
Application Deadline: open	**Room & Board:** n/app
Freshman Class: n/av	
SAT or ACT: n/av	**LESS COMPETITIVE**

DeVry University/Phoenix is a private institution opened in 1967; there are 66 other DeVry University locations in the United States and Canada. Most figures in this profile are approximate. The school offers a hands-on technology-based curriculum in business administration, computer information systems, electronics, technical management, information technology, computer engineering technology, and telecommunications. In addition to regional accreditation, DeVry has baccalaureate program accreditation with ABET. The library contains 22,500 volumes, and subscribes to 7230 periodicals including electronic. Computerized library services include database searching. Special learning facilities include a learning resource center and electronics and other labs. The 18-acre campus is in a suburban area in Phoenix. There is one building.
Student Life: 63% are white; 17% Hispanic. The average age of all undergraduates is 25.
Housing: There are no residence halls. Allof students commute. Housing referrals may be obtaines through the Student Housing Office. There are private apartments, student plan housing, and private rooms. Alcohol is not permitted. All students may keep cars.
Activities: There are no fraternities or sororities. There are 13 groups on campus, including ethnic, honors, professional, radio and TV, religious, social, and yearbook. Popular campus events include Thanksgiving Dinner, Ethnic Day, and Cinco de Mayo.
Sports: There is 1 intramural sports for men and 1 for women. Facilities include a game room. Students can obtain free passes for a fitness center.
Disabled Students: All of the campus is accessible. Wheelchair ramps, elevators, special parking, specially equipped rest rooms, special class scheduling, lowered drinking fountains, and lowered telephones are available.
Services: Counseling and information services are available, as is tutoring in every subject.
Campus Safety and Security: Measures include security escort services, informal discussions, pamphlets/posters/films, and emergency telephones. There are lighted pathways/sidewalks and a security guard service Monday through Friday 8 A.M. to 11 P.M. and from 12 noon to 6 P.M. on Sunday. The building is guarded during hours of closure by a motion-detector system.
Programs of Study: DeVry confers the B.S. degree. Associate and master's degrees are also awarded. Bachelor's degrees are awarded in BIOLOGICAL SCIENCE (bioinformatics), BUSINESS (business administration and management), COMMUNICATIONS AND THE ARTS (telecommunications), COMPUTER AND PHYSICAL SCIENCE (information sciences and systems), ENGINEERING AND ENVIRONMENTAL DESIGN (biomedical engineering, computer engineering, electrical/electronics engineering technology, and technological management). Computer information systems and electronics engineering technology are the largest.
Required: To graduate, students must achieve a GPA of at least 2.0 and satisfactorily complete all curriculum requirements. Course requirements vary according to program. All first-semester students take courses in business organization, computer applications, algebra, psychology, and student success strategies.
Special: Accelerated degrees, co-op programs, nondegree study, distance learning, and evening and weekend classes are possible. There is 1 national honor society.
Faculty/Classroom: All teach undergraduates.
Requirements: Admissions requirements include graduation from a secondary school; the GED is also accepted. Applicants must pass the DeVry entrance exam or present satisfactory ACT or SAT scores. An interview is required. CLEP credit is accepted.
Procedure: Freshmen are admitted fall, spring, and summer. There are early admissions and deferred admissions plans. Application deadlines are open. The fall 2005 application fee was $50. Applications are accepted on-line.
Transfer: Applicants must present passing grades in all completed college course work, demonstrate language skills proficiency with at least 24 completed semester hours, and evidence math proficiency by appropriate college-level credits. 25 of 48 credits required for the bachelor's degree must be completed at DeVry.
Visiting: There are regularly scheduled orientations for prospective students. There are guides for informal visits and visitors may sit in on classes. To schedule a visit, contact the Director of Admissions.

Financial Aid: In a recent year, 49% of all full-time freshmen and 75% of continuing full-time students received some form of financial aid. 48% of full-time freshmen and 73% of continuing full-time students received need-based aid. The average freshman award was $6765. Need-based scholarships or need-based grants averaged $3997; need-based self-help aid (loans and jobs) averaged $4108; and other non-need-based awards and non-need-based scholarships averaged $9288. The FAFSA is required. Check with the school for current deadlines.
International Students: They must score satisfactorily on the TOEFL and also take DeVry's computerized placement test, achieving a minimum score that varies by program.
Computers: Students in the computer information systems program may access the system during published lab hours. There are no time limits and no fees. Students in the information technology program have DeVry-issued laptop computers.
Graduates: 892 bachelor's degrees were awarded. The most popular majors were computer information systems (49%), business (28%), and electronics engineering technology (23%).
Admissions Contact: Director of Admissions.
E-mail: *admissions@phx.devry.edu* Web: *www.phx.devry.edu*

EMBRY-RIDDLE AERONAUTICAL UNIVERSITY — C-3

Prescott, AZ 86301-3720

(928) 777-6692
(800) 442-ERAU; Fax: (9928) 777-6606

Full-time: 1212 men, 254 women	**Faculty:** 101; IIB, av$
Part-time: 160 men, 27 women	**Ph.D.s:** 62%
Graduate: 25 men, 7 women	**Student/Faculty:** 15 to 1
Year: semesters, summer session	**Tuition:** $23,550
Application Deadline: open	**Room & Board:** $6730
Freshman Class: 1163 applied, 1041 accepted, 359 enrolled	
SAT Verbal/Math: 560/590*	**ACT:** 24 **COMPETITIVE+**

Embry-Riddle Aeronautical University, founded in 1926, is a private institution offering undergraduate programs in aviation, engineering, business, and professional training on 2 campuses: the Prescott campus, founded in 1978, and the Daytona Beach, Florida, campus. Graduate programs are also offered at both campuses. There are 3 undergraduate schools and 1 graduate school. In addition to regional accreditation, ERAU has baccalaureate program accreditation with ABET and CAA. The library contains 40,438 volumes, 206,861 microform items, and 8662 audio/video tapes/CDs/DVDs, and subscribes to 572 periodicals including electronic. Computerized library services include the card catalog, interlibrary loans, database searching, and Internet access. Special learning facilities include a learning resource center, radio station, 4 wind tunnels, an aviation safety center, and an aircraft structures lab. The Flight Training Center at Ernest A. Love Field offers a simulator lab and flight operations center. The 539-acre campus is in a rural area 100 miles north of Phoenix. Including any residence halls, there are 91 buildings.
Student Life: 22% of undergraduates are from Arizona. Others are from 48 states, 25 foreign countries, and Canada. 70% are white. The average age of freshmen is 18; all undergraduates, 21. 22% do not continue beyond their first year; 54% remain to graduate.
Housing: 849 students can be accommodated in college housing, which includes coed dorms and on-campus apartments. On-campus housing is guaranteed for the freshman year only and is available on a first-come, first-served basis. 52% of students commute. Alcohol is not permitted. All students may keep cars.
Activities: 10% of men belong to 4 national fraternities; 14% of women belong to 1 national sorority. There are 75 groups on campus, including ethnic, gay, honors, international, jazz band, literary magazine, newspaper, political, professional, radio and TV, religious, social, social service, and student government. Popular campus events include Octoberwest, Spring Fling, and Hawaii Luau Club.
Sports: There are 2 intercollegiate sports for men and 1 for women, and 19 intramural sports for men and 19 for women. Facilities include an activity center with 3 basketball courts and 3 volleyball courts, a gym/weight room, a multipurpose athletic playing field, a game room, a swimming pool complex, and a fitness facility.
Disabled Students: 20% of the campus is accessible. Wheelchair ramps, special parking, specially equipped rest rooms, special class scheduling, lowered drinking fountains, lowered telephones, special housing, and pneumatic doors are available.
Services: Counseling and information services are available, as is tutoring in most subjects. There is remedial math, reading, and writing.
Campus Safety and Security: Measures include 24-hour foot and vehicle patrol, self-defense education, security escort services, and shuttle buses. There are informal discussions, pamphlets/posters/films, emergency telephones, and lighted pathways/sidewalks.
Programs of Study: ERAU confers the B.S. degree. Master's degrees are also awarded. Bachelor's degrees are awarded in COMMUNICATIONS AND THE ARTS (communications), COMPUTER AND PHYSICAL SCIENCE (atmospheric sciences and meteorology, computer science, and software engineering), ENGINEERING AND ENVIRON-

MENTAL DESIGN (aeronautical engineering, aeronautical science, aerospace studies, aviation administration/management, aviation maintenance management, computer engineering, electrical/electronics engineering, and engineering physics), SOCIAL SCIENCE (safety science). Aerospace engineering is the strongest academically. Aeronautical science is the largest.

Required: All students must complete 36 credits of general education requirements, including courses in communication skills, technical report writing, humanities/social sciences, math, physical science, economics, and computer science. A total of 120 to 136 credit hours with a minimum GPA of 2.0 is required to graduate.

Special: Cooperative and work-study programs, nondegree study, internships in all majors, and study abroad in 21 countries are offered. Flight training may be taken in conjunction with aeronautical science and other degree programs. Credit is given for life and military experience. There are 4 national honor societies and a freshman honors program.

Faculty/Classroom: 77% of faculty are male; 23%, female. All teach undergraduates. No introductory courses are taught by graduate students. The average class size in an introductory lecture is 23; in a laboratory, 16; and in a regular course, 23.

Admissions: 90% of the 2005-2006 applicants were accepted. The SAT scores for the 2005-2006 freshman class were: Verbal--23% below 500, 40% between 500 and 599, 31% between 600 and 700, and 6% above 700; Math--15% below 500, 37% between 500 and 599, 39% between 600 and 700, and 9% above 700. The ACT scores were 18% below 21, 26% between 21 and 23, 21% between 24 and 26, 18% between 27 and 28, and 17% above 28. 42% of the current freshmen were in the top fifth of their class; 71% were in the top two fifths. 39 freshmen graduated first in their class.

Requirements: The SAT or ACT is required. In addition, applicants must be graduates of an accredited secondary school or have a GED equivalent. All admissions items are processed at Daytona Beach headquarters. AP and CLEP credits are accepted. Important factors in the admissions decision are advanced placement or honor courses, recommendations by school officials, and evidence of special talent.

Procedure: Freshmen are admitted to all sessions. Entrance exams should be taken during the fall of the senior year. There is a deferred admissions plan. There is a rolling admissions plan. Application deadlines are open. The application fee is $50. Notification is sent on a rolling basis. Applications are accepted on-line.

Transfer: 102 transfer students enrolled in 2004-2005. Applicants must have a minimum GPA of 2.0 in at least 12 credit hours earned. 30 of 120 to 136 credits required for the bachelor's degree must be completed at ERAU.

Visiting: There are regularly scheduled orientations for prospective students. There are guides for informal visits. To schedule a visit, contact Bill Thompson at (928) 777-6600 or *pradmit@erau.edu*.

Financial Aid: In 2005-2006, 99% of all full-time freshmen and 74% of continuing full-time students received some form of financial aid. 59% of full-time freshmen and 82% of continuing full-time students received need-based aid. The average freshman award was $22,820. Need-based scholarships or need-based grants averaged $3614 ($8100 maximum); need-based self-help aid (loans and jobs) averaged $3436 ($5000 maximum); and other non-need-based awards and non-need-based scholarships averaged $9949 ($27,486 maximum). 36% of undergraduates work part time. Average annual earnings from campus work are $1833. The average financial indebtedness of the 2005 graduate was $49,532. The FAFSA is required. The deadline for filing freshman financial aid applications for fall entry is April 15.

International Students: There are 41 international students enrolled. The school actively recruits these students. A satisfactory score on the TOEFL is required.

Computers: All students may access the system. There are no time limits and no fees. A PC is highly recommended for computer science students.

Graduates: From July 1, 2004 to June 30, 2005, 315 bachelor's degrees were awarded. The most popular majors were aeronautical science (40%), aerospace engineering (28%), and global securities and intelligence studies (8%). In an average class, 5% graduate in 3 years or less, 30% graduate in 4 years or less, 51% graduate in 5 years or less, and 57% graduate in 6 years or less. 21 companies recruited on campus in 2004-2005. Of the 2004 graduating class, 17% were enrolled in graduate school within 6 months of graduation and 83% were employed.

Admissions Contact: Bill Thompson, Director of Admissions.
E-mail: *pradmit@erau.edu* Web: *www.embryriddle.edu*

GRAND CANYON UNIVERSITY

C-4

Phoenix, AZ 85061-1097

(602) 589-2855
(800) 800-9776, ext. 2855; Fax: (602) 589-2580

Full-time: 450 men, 880 women	**Faculty:** n/av
Part-time: 130 men, 155 women	**Ph.D.s:** 80%
Graduate: 570 men, 1935 women	**Student/Faculty:** n/av
Year: semesters, summer session	**Tuition:** $22,000
Application Deadline: open	**Room & Board:** $10,000
Freshman Class: n/av	
SAT or ACT: required	**LESS COMPETITIVE**

Grand Canyon University, founded in 1949, is a small, private, nonsectarian liberal arts institution. Figures in the above capsule and in this profile are approximate. There are 5 undergraduate and 2 graduate schools. In addition to regional accreditation, GCU has baccalaureate program accreditation with NLN. The library contains 166,000 volumes, 97,324 microform items, and 4100 audio/video tapes/CDs/DVDs, and subscribes to 700 periodicals including electronic. Computerized library services include the card catalog, interlibrary loans, and database searching. Special learning facilities include an art gallery. The 90-acre campus is in a suburban area in Phoenix. Including any residence halls, there are 32 buildings.

Student Life: 81% of undergraduates are from Arizona. Students are from 43 states, 6 foreign countries, and Canada. 77% are white; 10% Hispanic. 87% are Protestant; 9% Catholic. The average age of freshmen is 19; all undergraduates, 25.

Housing: 600 students can be accommodated in college housing, which includes single-sex dorms and on-campus apartments. On-campus housing is available on a first-come, first-served basis. 52% of students live on campus; of those, 90% remain on campus on weekends. Alcohol is not permitted. All students may keep cars.

Activities: There are no fraternities or sororities. There are many groups and organizations on campus, including art, band, cheerleading, choir, chorale, chorus, computers, drama, ethnic, honors, international, jazz band, literary magazine, musical theater, newspaper, opera, orchestra, pep band, photography, political, professional, religious, social service, student government, and yearbook. Popular campus events include Spiritual Emphasis Week, Harvest Festival, and Spring Formal.

Sports: There are 5 intercollegiate sports for men and 4 for women, and 4 intramural sports for men and 4 for women. Facilities include a baseball field, a 500-seat gym, a 1750-seat gym, a 3000-seat stadium, 6 tennis courts, a weight room, and a swimming pool.

Disabled Students: All of the campus is accessible. Wheelchair ramps, elevators, special parking, and specially equipped rest rooms are available.

Services: Counseling and information services are available, as is tutoring in most subjects. There is a reader service for the blind and remedial reading and writing. Tutors are also trained in test-taking techniques, study skills, and time management.

Campus Safety and Security: Measures include 24-hour foot and vehicle patrol, self-defense education, security escort services, and informal discussions. There are emergency telephones, lighted pathways/sidewalks, and a university safety committee that provides controlled after-hours access to residence halls.

Programs of Study: GCU confers B.A., B.S., B.B.A., B.L.S., B.M., and B.S.N. degrees. Master's degrees are also awarded. Bachelor's degrees are awarded in BIOLOGICAL SCIENCE (biology/biological science and environmental biology), BUSINESS (accounting, banking and finance, business administration and management, human resources, international business management, marketing/retailing/merchandising, and personnel management), COMMUNICATIONS AND THE ARTS (applied music, communications, dramatic art, English, fine arts, graphic design, music, piano/organ, Spanish, speech/debate/rhetoric, studio art, and voice), COMPUTER AND PHYSICAL SCIENCE (chemistry, computer science, and mathematics), EDUCATION (art, business, elementary, music, physical, science, secondary, and special), HEALTH PROFESSIONS (nursing), SOCIAL SCIENCE (Christian studies, criminal justice, economics, history, physical fitness/movement, psychology, religious music, social science, social studies, and sociology). Natural sciences, elementary education, and nursing are the strongest academically and have the largest enrollments.

Required: All students are required to complete 39 hours of general studies, including 3 hours each in Old Testament history and New Testament history, 6 each in English and humanities, 9 in social studies, 10 in science, and 2 in phys ed. Chapel attendance is required. A writing proficiency exam along with a total of 128 semester hours, with a minimum GPA of 2.0, are required to graduate.

Special: Co-op programs with several schools in the Christian College Coalition are available. Internships are offered for most majors through organizations, corporations, and agencies in the Phoenix area. Dual majors, study abroad in 5 countries, and a Washington semester are possible. A 3-2 engineering degree with Arizona State University is available. There is 1 national honor society, including Phi Beta Kappa, a freshman honors program, and 1 departmental honors program.

Faculty/Classroom: 50% of faculty are male; 50%, female. All teach undergraduates. The average class size in an introductory lecture is 25; in a laboratory, 10; and in a regular course, 25.

Requirements: The SAT or ACT is required. In addition, applicants should be graduates of an accredited high school or have a GED. A GPA of 2.14 is required. AP and CLEP credits are accepted. Important factors in the admissions decision are evidence of special talent, extracurricular activities record, and leadership record.

Procedure: Freshmen are admitted to all sessions. Entrance exams should be taken during the junior or senior year of high school. There are early admissions and rolling admissions plans. Application deadlines are open. Application fee is $50.

Transfer: Transfer applicants must have a minimum GPA of 2.0 and a minimum of 24 transferable hours. 30 of 128 credits required for the bachelor's degree must be completed at GCU.

Visiting: There are regularly scheduled orientations for prospective students, including High School Preview Days in February and Transfer Preview Days in March. There are guides for informal visits and visitors may sit in on classes and stay overnight. To schedule a visit, contact the Admission Office.

Financial Aid: The The FAFSA is recommended. Check with the school for current application deadlines.

International Students: The school actively recruits these students. They must score satisfactorily on the written TOEFL and the SAT or the ACT is required of students with English as their first language, with a 50 national percentile score or higher required.

Computers: Wireless access is available. Students have wireless access in the dorms, apartments, and the student labs (PC lab and library) if they have their own systems. The labs are the only place where there are free PCs to use. There are about 50 PCs in the PC Lab and about 15 in the library. These PCs are free for any students use, but they need to know their Ids to log in. All students may access the system usually from morning until midnight. There are no time limits. The fee is $85 per semester.

Admissions Contact: April Chapman, Director of Admissions. A video is available. E-mail: *admiss@grand-canyon.edu*
Web: *www.grand-canyon.edu*

NORTHERN ARIZONA UNIVERSITY	C-2
Flagstaff, AZ 86011	**(928) 523-5511**
	(888) MORE-NAU; Fax: (928) 523-6023

Full-time: 4537 men, 6724 women		Faculty: 723; I, --$	
Part-time: 746 men, 1245 women		Ph.D.s: 83%	
Graduate: 1608 men, 3919 women		Student/Faculty: 16 to 1	
Year: semesters, summer session		Tuition: $4393 ($13,023)	
Application Deadline: March 1		Room & Board: $5960	
Freshman Class: 6308 accepted, 2279 enrolled			
SAT Verbal/Math: 524/520*		ACT: 22	**COMPETITIVE**

Northern Arizona University, founded in 1899, is a public institution offering undergraduate and graduate degrees in a full range of disciplines from liberal arts and sciences to professional and career-related fields. There are 6 undergraduate and 6 graduate schools. In addition to regional accreditation, NAU has baccalaureate program accreditation with AACSB, ABET, ADA, AHEA, APTA, CAPTE, NASM, NCATE, NLN, NRPA, and SAF. The library contains 1.4 million volumes, 373,000 microform items, and 28,000 audio/video tapes/CDs/DVDs, and subscribes to 20,000 periodicals including electronic. Computerized library services include the card catalog, interlibrary loans, database searching, and Internet access. Special learning facilities include a learning resource center, art gallery, radio station, TV station, an observatory, research centers, and the Institute for Human Development. The 738-acre campus is in a rural area 140 miles north of Phoenix. Including any residence halls, there are 102 buildings.

Student Life: 84% of undergraduates are from Arizona. Others are from 48 states, 37 foreign countries, and Canada. 73% are white; 12% Hispanic. The average age of freshmen is 19; all undergraduates, 24. 31% do not continue beyond their first year; 69% remain to graduate.

Housing: 6106 students can be accommodated in college housing, which includes single-sex and coed dormitories, on-campus apartments, married-student housing, fraternity houses, and sorority houses. In addition, there are honors houses. On-campus housing is guaranteed for the freshman year only and is available on a first-come, first-served basis. 63% of students commute. Alcohol is not permitted. All students may keep cars.

Activities: 3% of men belong to 15 national fraternities; 6% of women belong to 8 national sororities. There are 107 groups on campus, including art, band, cheerleading, chess, choir, chorale, chorus, computers, dance, debate, drama, ethnic, film, forensics, gay, honors, international, jazz band, marching band, musical theater, newspaper, opera, orchestra, pep band, photography, political, professional, radio and TV, religious, social, social service, student government, symphony, and yearbook. Popular campus events include Martin Luther King Jr. Day and Luminario Lighting.

Sports: There are 5 intercollegiate sports for men and 8 for women, and 32 intramural sports for men and 32 for women. Facilities include the Skydome for football, basketball, and indoor track and field, 3 recreation centers with basketball and racquetball courts and weight rooms, a 50-meter indoor swimming pool with diving facilities, and numerous outdoor grass fields for soccer, rugby, and lacrosse.

Disabled Students: 90% of the campus is accessible. Wheelchair ramps, elevators, special parking, specially equipped rest rooms, special class scheduling, lowered drinking fountains, and lowered telephones are available.

Services: Counseling and information services are available, as is tutoring in most subjects. There is a reader service for the blind, and remedial math, reading, and writing. Most counseling and tutoring is done by volunteers and student interns.

Campus Safety and Security: Measures include 24-hour foot and vehicle patrol, self-defense education, security escort services, and shuttle buses. There are informal discussions, pamphlets/posters/films, emergency telephones, and lighted pathways/sidewalks.

Programs of Study: NAU confers B.A., B.S., B.A.I.L.S., B.A.S., B.F.A., B.G.S., B.Mus., B.Mus.Ed., B.S.A.C.C.Y., B.S.B.A., B.S.C.S.E., B.S.D.H., B.S.E., B.S.Ed., B.S.F., B.S.J., B.S.N., and B.S.W. degrees. Master's and doctoral degrees are also awarded. Bachelor's degrees are awarded in AGRICULTURE (forestry and related sciences), BIOLOGICAL SCIENCE (biology/biological science, botany, microbiology, and zoology), BUSINESS (accounting, banking and finance, business administration and management, business economics, hotel/motel and restaurant management, and marketing/retailing/merchandising), COMMUNICATIONS AND THE ARTS (advertising, art history and appreciation, arts administration/management, broadcasting, communications, design, dramatic arts, English, fine arts, French, German, journalism, music, Spanish, speech/debate/rhetoric, and telecommunications), COMPUTER AND PHYSICAL SCIENCE (chemistry, computer science, geology, information sciences and systems, mathematics, and physics), EDUCATION (art, early childhood, elementary, foreign languages, health, industrial arts, music, science, secondary, and special), ENGINEERING AND ENVIRONMENTAL DESIGN (civil engineering, computer engineering, electrical/electronics engineering, engineering, environmental engineering, and mechanical engineering), HEALTH PROFESSIONS (nursing, predentistry, premedicine, and speech pathology/audiology), SOCIAL SCIENCE (anthropology, criminal justice, economics, geography, history, international relations, parks and recreation management, philosophy, political science/government, prelaw, psychology, public administration, religion, social work, and sociology). Nursing, engineering, and forestry are the strongest academically. Education, hotel/restaurant management, and psychology are the largest.

Required: To graduate, students must have at least 120 credit hours, including at least 30 units of upper-division courses (36 for B.A.I.L.S.). Students must maintain a minimum GPA of 2.0 and complete 35 units of liberal studies requirements and 6 to 7 units of university requirements. The liberal studies program includes 7 units of foundation requirements (English composition and math), 25 units of distribution requirements (asthetic and humanistic inquiry, cultural understanding, lab science, science and applied science, social and political worlds, and liberal studies elective), and 6 to 7 units of university requirements (junior-level writing requirements and senior capstone).

Special: NAU offers co-op programs in business and hotel/restaurant management, cross-registration with many universities through the National Student Exchange, and internships in most majors. Legislative internships are offered through the Arizona State Senate and House of Representatives. Students may study abroad in 19 countries. Work-study programs are available in numerous fields, including engineering, business, park services, and arts management. Accelerated degrees in more than 50 majors, a general studies degree, dual majors, nondegree study, and pass/fail options are possible. There are 7 national honor societies and a freshman honors program.

Faculty/Classroom: 51% of faculty are male; 49%, female. All both teach and do research. The average class size in a laboratory is 22 and in a regular course, 35.

Admissions: The SAT scores for the 2005-2006 freshman class were: Verbal--34% below 500, 45% between 500 and 599, 20% between 600 and 700, and 2% above 700; Math--34% below 500, 44% between 500 and 599, 20% between 600 and 700, and 2% above 700. The ACT scores were 39% below 21, 29% between 21 and 23, 20% between 24 and 26, 8% between 27 and 28, and 4% above 28.

Requirements: The SAT or ACT is required. In addition, students must have a minimum GPA of 3.0 or rank in the top 25% of their class, or have a satisfactory SAT ot ACT scores. Requirements include a grade of C or better in each class of 4 years of English and math, 3 years of lab science, 2 years of foreign language, and 1 year each of American history, social science, and fine arts. Consult the college catalog for details on these requirements. A GPA of 2.5 is required. AP and CLEP credits are accepted.

Procedure: Freshmen are admitted fall, spring, and summer. There is a rolling admissions plan. Entrance exams should be taken before the last semester of the senior year. Applications should be filed by March

1 for fall entry, October 1 for spring entry, and May 15 for summer entry. Notification is sent on a rolling basis. The fall 2005 application fee was $25.

Transfer: 1266 transfer students enrolled in a recent year. Transfer students with fewer than 24 transferrable credits are admitted based on their high school record. Requirements for in-state residents differ from nonresidents. Contact the school for specific requirements. A minimum of 30 of 120 credits required for the bachelor's degree must be completed at NAU.

Visiting: There are regularly scheduled orientations for prospective students, including 8 2-day orientation/registration sessions for new students held mid-June through mid-July, and a 4-day program held the week before the fall and spring semesters. There are guides for informal visits and visitors may sit in on classes and stay overnight. To schedule a visit, contact the Office of Undergraduate Admissions.

Financial Aid: In a recent year, 75% of all full-time freshmen and 68% of continuing full-time students received some form of financial aid. 57% of full-time freshmen received need-based aid. The average freshman award was $5168. Need-based scholarships or need-based grants averaged $5168; need-based self-help aid (loans and jobs) averaged $5026; and non-need-based athletic scholarships averaged $9768. 65% of undergraduates worked part time. Average annual earnings from campus work were $1447. The average financial indebtedness a recent graduate was $16,319. The FAFSA is required. The deadline for filing freshman financial aid applications for fall entry is April 15.

International Students: There are 254 international students enrolled. The school actively recruits these students. They must score satisfactorily on the written TOEFL or on the electronic version or take the MELAB.

Computers: Wireless access is available. All students may access the system. There are no time limits and no fees. It is strongly recommended that all students have a personal computer.

Graduates: From July 1, 2004 to June 30, 2005, 2864 bachelor's degrees were awarded. The most popular majors were elementary education (24%), business administration (19%), and communications (6%). In an average class, 1% graduate in 3 years or less, 2% graduate in 4 years or less, 25% graduate in 5 years or less, and 48% graduate in 6 years or less.

Admissions Contact: Christopher Lynch, Director of Admissions. A video is available. E-mail: *undergraduate.admissions@nau.edu* Web: *www.nau.edu*

PRESCOTT COLLEGE   C-3

Prescott, AZ 86305   (928) 350-2100
(800) 628-6364; Fax: (928) 776-5243

Full-time: 248 men, 437 women	**Faculty:** 50
Part-time: 32 men, 35 women	**Ph.Ds:** 39%
Graduate: 84 men, 167 women	**Student/Faculty:** 14 to 1
Year: semesters, summer session	**Tuition:** $13,445
Application Deadline: August 15	**Room & Board:** n/app
Freshman Class: 147 applied, 129 accepted, 54 enrolled	
SAT or ACT: required	**LESS COMPETITIVE**

Prescott College, founded in 1966, is a private commuter institution offering a nontraditional undergraduate program in the liberal arts. The curriculum is organized into multidisciplinary courses that allow students to pursue individual areas of competency. Evaluations of a student's work are conducted through a portfolio/contract system and an ongoing series of student self-evaluations. Tution fees in the above capsule are approximate. There are 3 undergraduate schools and 1 graduate school. The library contains 22,417 volumes, 125 microform items, and 1304 audio/video tapes/CDs/DVDs, and subscribes to 270 periodicals including electronic. Computerized library services include the card catalog, interlibrary loans, and database searching. Special learning facilities include a learning resource center, art gallery, a greenhouse, weather station, and recycling center. The 4-acre campus is in a small town 100 miles north of Phoenix. There are 16 buildings.

Student Life: 33% of undergraduates are from Arizona. Others are from 43 states, 5 foreign countries, and Canada. 89% are white. The average age of freshmen is 20; all undergraduates, 29. 32% do not continue beyond their first year; 46% remain to graduate.

Housing: There are no residence halls. All of students commute. Alcohol is not permitted. All students may keep cars.

Activities: There are no fraternities or sororities. There are 10 groups on campus, including Amnesty International, agriculture/garden, art, arts and activision, dance, drama, environmental, gay, indigenous rights, literary magazine, martial arts, newspaper, photography, political, social, social service, student government and student union. Popular campus events include Earth Day, Southwest Writers Series, and Student-Directed Days.

Sports: There is no sports program at Prescott. There are no sports facilities on campus, but students have access to the local community pool, weight room, gym, and city league sports.

Disabled Students: 60% of the campus is accessible. Wheelchair ramps, special parking, and specially equipped rest rooms are available.

Services: There is remedial math and writing. There is a learning specialist on staff, and untimed tests are available.

Campus Safety and Security: Measures include self-defense education, informal discussions, pamphlets/posters/films, and emergency telephones.

Programs of Study: Prescott confers the B.A. degree. Master's and doctoral degrees are also awarded. Bachelor's degrees are awarded in AGRICULTURE (environmental studies), BIOLOGICAL SCIENCE (biology/biological science), COMMUNICATIONS AND THE ARTS (communications, English, fine arts, journalism, photography, and Spanish), COMPUTER AND PHYSICAL SCIENCE (earth science and geology), EDUCATION (art, early childhood, education, elementary, environmental, foreign languages, guidance, middle school, recreation, secondary, and special), ENGINEERING AND ENVIRONMENTAL DESIGN (environmental science), SOCIAL SCIENCE (anthropology, community services, criminal justice, economics, peace studies, psychology, social work, and sociology). Environmental studies is the strongest academically. Education is the largest.

Required: Prescott does not specify any formal graduation requirements. Students may design an individual program of studies within 4 multidisciplinary areas: environmental studies, adventure education, arts and letters, and integrative studies. Each student is required to submit a graduation proposal at the end of the junior year to the Graduation Review Committee.

Special: Student-coordinated internships, study abroad in almost any country, dual majors, a general studies degree, pass/fail options, and credit for life experience are offered. All majors are student-designed.

Faculty/Classroom: 61% of faculty are male; 39%, female. All teach undergraduates. The average class size in an introductory lecture is 12; in a laboratory, 12; and in a regular course, 12.

Admissions: 88% of the 2005-2006 applicants were accepted.

Requirements: The SAT or ACT is required. In addition, a high school diploma is required; the GED is accepted. The school requires essays, transcripts, and letters of recommendation. Students may also submit portfolios and writing samples. Important factors in the admissions decision are extracurricular activities record, personality/intangible qualities, and leadership record.

Procedure: Freshmen are admitted fall and spring. There are early decision and deferred admissions plans. There is a rolling admissions plan. Early decision applications should be filed by December 1; regular applications, by August 15 for fall entry, along with a $25 fee. Notification of early decision is sent December 1; regular decision, on a rolling basis.

Transfer: 76 transfer students enrolled in 2004-2005. Transfer applicants must meet the same requirements as entering freshmen and must also submit official college transcripts and an essay or personal statement. Students who successfully completed 2 years of college work (60 semester hours or 90 quarter credits) need not submit high school transcripts. There is a 2-year residency requirement. 90 of 186 credits required for the bachelor's degree must be completed at Prescott.

Visiting: There are regularly scheduled orientations for prospective students, including a college video, a campus tour, and an interview with an admissions counselor. There are guides for informal visits and visitors may sit in on classes. To schedule a visit, contact the Admissions Office.

Financial Aid: In 2005-2006, 56% of all full-time freshmen received some form of financial aid. At least 20% of full-time freshmen received need-based aid. The average freshman award was $7974. Need-based scholarships or need-based grants averaged $4627; and need-based self-help aid (loans and jobs) averaged $3347. 17% of undergraduates work part time. Average annual earnings from campus work are $1780. The average financial indebtedness of the 2005 graduate was $18,235. The FAFSA is required. The priority date for freshman financial aid applications for fall entry is April 1.

International Students: They must score satisfactorily on the written TOEFL.

Computers: All students may access the system 100 hours per week. There are no time limits and no fees.

Graduates: From July 1, 2004 to June 30, 2005, 264 bachelor's degrees were awarded. The most popular majors were education (37%), natural resources/environmental science (13%), and psychology (10%). In an average class, 23% graduate in 4 years or less, 41% graduate in 5 years or less, and 46% graduate in 6 years or less.

Admissions Contact: Shari Sterling, Director of Admissions. E-mail: *admissions@prescott.edu* Web: *www.prescott.edu*

UNIVERSITY OF ARIZONA

Tucson, AZ 85721

(520) 621-3237; Fax: (520) 621-9799

D-4

Full-time: 11,300 men, 12,825 women	**Faculty:** 1495; I, av$
Part-time: 1750 men, 1925 women	**Ph.D.s:** 94%
Graduate: 3175 men, 3275 women	**Student/Faculty:** 16 to 1
Year: semesters, summer session	**Tuition:** $4498 ($13,682)
Application Deadline: April 1	**Room & Board:** $6810
Freshman Class: n/a	
SAT or ACT: required	**VERY COMPETITIVE**

The University of Arizona, founded in 1885, is a public land-grant institution controlled by the state of Arizona. Enrollment figures in the above capsule are approximate. Undergraduate programs are offered in agriculture, architecture, arts and sciences, business and public administration, education, engineering and mines, and nursing, pharmacy, and other health-related professions. There are 13 undergraduate and 5 graduate schools. In addition to regional accreditation, UA has baccalaureate program accreditation with AACSB, ABET, ACPE, ADA, ASLA, NAAB, NASAD, NASM, NCATE, and NLN. The 7 libraries contain 4,918,178 volumes, 5,992,439 microform items, and 55,173 audio/video tapes/CDs/DVDs, and subscribe to 26,711 periodicals including electronic. Computerized library services include the card catalog, interlibrary loans, and database searching. Special learning facilities include a learning resource center, art gallery, natural history museum, planetarium, radio station, TV station, the Ansel Adams Center for creative photography, and the Integrated Learning Center. The 357-acre campus is in an urban area in Tucson. Including any residence halls, there are 172 buildings.

Student Life: 72% of undergraduates are from Arizona. Others are from 49 states, 131 foreign countries, and Canada. 90% are from public schools. 65% are white; 13% Hispanic. The average age of freshmen is 19; all undergraduates, 21. 23% do not continue beyond their first year; 55% remain to graduate.

Housing: 4600 students can be accommodated in college housing, which includes single-sex and coed dorms, on-campus apartments, off-campus apartments, fraternity houses, and sorority houses. In addition, there are honors houses and special-interest houses. On-campus housing is available on a first-come, first-served basis. Alcohol is not permitted. All students may keep cars.

Activities: 7% of men belong to 24 national fraternities; 11% of women belong to 21 national sororities. There are 375 groups on campus, including art, band, cheerleading, chess, choir, chorale, chorus, computers, dance, drama, drill team, ethnic, film, gay, honors, international, jazz band, literary magazine, marching band, musical theater, newspaper, orchestra, pep band, photography, political, professional, radio and TV, religious, social, social service, student government, and yearbook. Popular campus events include the Spring Fling carnival.

Sports: There are 8 intercollegiate sports for men and 10 for women, and 27 intramural sports for men and 26 for women. Facilities include an athletic center, a 53,000-seat stadium, a 13,500-seat arena, and a student recreation facility with a weight room, a waveless swimming pool, two gyms, aerobics facilities, treadmills, stairclimbers, stationary bicycles, and racquetball, squash, and handball courts. Hiking, backpacking, and skiing trails as well as facilities for kayaking, caving, and scuba diving are available.

Disabled Students: 95% of the campus is accessible. Wheelchair ramps, elevators, special parking, specially equipped rest rooms, lowered drinking fountains, lowered telephones, physical therapy, counseling, interpreters, note taking, equipment maintenance, and an adaptive athletics program are available.

Services: Counseling and information services are available, as is tutoring in most subjects. There is a reader service for the blind.

Campus Safety and Security: Measures include 24-hour foot and vehicle patrol, self-defense education, security escort services, and shuttle buses. There are emergency telephones and lighted pathways/sidewalks.

Programs of Study: UA confers B.A., B.S., B.Arch., B.F.A., B.L.A., B.M., B.S.B.A., B.S.H.S., B.S.N., and B.S.P.A. degrees. Master's and doctoral degrees are also awarded. Bachelor's degrees are awarded in AGRICULTURE (agricultural economics, animal science, natural resource management, plant science, range/farm management, and soil science), BIOLOGICAL SCIENCE (biochemistry, biology/biological science, ecology, evolutionary biology, microbiology, molecular biology, nutrition, physiology, and wildlife biology), BUSINESS (accounting, banking and finance, business administration and management, business economics, entrepreneurial studies, human resources, management information systems, management science, marketing/retailing/merchandising, and retailing), COMMUNICATIONS AND THE ARTS (art history and appreciation, classics, communications, creative writing, dance, dramatic arts, English, fine arts, French, German, Italian, journalism, language arts, Latin, linguistics, media arts, music, music performance, music theory and composition, musical theater, performing arts, Portuguese, Russian, Spanish, studio art, and theater design), COMPUTER AND PHYSICAL SCIENCE (applied science, astronomy, atmospheric sciences and meteorology, chemistry, computer science, earth science, geology, geoscience, hydrology, mathematics, natural sciences, and physics), EDUCATION (agricultural, art, drama, early childhood, elementary, health, home economics, music, physical, science, secondary, and special), ENGINEERING AND ENVIRONMENTAL DESIGN (aeronautical engineering, aerospace studies, agricultural engineering technology, architecture, bioengineering, chemical engineering, city/community/regional planning, civil engineering, computer engineering, electrical/electronics engineering, engineering, engineering physics, environmental science, geological engineering, industrial engineering, landscape architecture/design, materials engineering, mechanical engineering, mining and mineral engineering, nuclear engineering, optical engineering, and systems engineering), HEALTH PROFESSIONS (health care administration, medical technology, nursing, pharmacy, speech pathology/audiology, and veterinary science), SOCIAL SCIENCE (anthropology, child care/child and family studies, criminal justice, East Asian studies, economics, ethnic studies, family/consumer resource management, family/consumer studies, geography, German area studies, history, humanities, interdisciplinary studies, Judaic studies, Latin American studies, liberal arts/general studies, Mexican-American/Chicano studies, Near Eastern studies, philosophy, political science/government, psychology, public administration, religion, social science, social studies, sociology, theological studies, water resources, and women's studies). Sciences, social sciences, and management information systems are the strongest academically. Social sciences and business are the largest.

Required: All students must complete a core curriculum of courses in natural sciences, traditions and cultures, individuals and societies, math, English, art, and a foreign language. A total of 125 credits, with a minimum GPA of 2.0, is required to graduate.

Special: Co-op programs are available in almost all majors. B.A.-B.S. degrees, dual majors, interdisciplinary degrees such as engineering-math and theater arts-education, a 3-2 arts and sciences-business degree, and student-designed majors are offered. Internships in almost all disciplines, a Washington semester, study abroad in numerous countries, work-study programs on campus, a general studies degree, and pass/fail options are offered. Nondegree study is possible.

Faculty/Classroom: 67% of faculty are male; 33%, female. 62% teach undergraduates and 94% do research. Graduate students teach 42% of introductory courses. The average class size in an introductory lecture is 45; in a laboratory, 22; and in a regular course, 34.

Admissions: 85% of recent applicants were accepted. The SAT scores for a recent freshman class were: Verbal--26% below 500, 44% between 500 and 599, 26% between 600 and 700, and 4% above 700; Math--23% below 500, 41% between 500 and 599, 31% between 600 and 700, and 5% above 700. The ACT scores were 23% below 21, 25% between 21 and 23, 28% between 24 and 26, 12% between 27 and 28, and 12% above 28. 56% of recent freshmen were in the top fifth of their class; 82% were in the top two fifths.

Requirements: The SAT or ACT is required. In addition, applicants should have completed 4 years each in high school English and math, 3 in science, 2 of a foreign language, and 1 each in history, fine arts, and social studies. A GED may be considered in place of a high school diploma. Some fine arts programs require auditions prior to admission. A GPA of 3.0 is required. AP and CLEP credits are accepted. Important factors in the admissions decision are advanced placement or honor courses, leadership record, and extracurricular activities record.

Procedure: Freshmen are admitted to all sessions. Entrance exams should be taken from March of the junior year through December of the senior year. There is an early admissions plan. Applications should be filed by April 1 for fall entry, November 1 for spring entry, and April 1 for summer entry The fall 2005 application fee was $50. Notification is sent on a rolling basis. Applications are accepted on-line.

Transfer: 1845 transfer students enrolled in a recent year. Resident transfer applicants must have a minimum GPA of 2.0; nonresidents, 2.5. Some university divisions have higher requirements. Admission is competitive for out-of-state students. 30 of 125 credits required for the bachelor's degree must be completed at UA.

Visiting: There are regularly scheduled orientations for prospective students, consisting of an admissions presentation and tour. There are guides for informal visits and visitors may sit in on classes. To schedule a visit, contact the Tour Desk at (520) 621-3641 or visitua@arizona.edu.

Financial Aid: UA is a member of CSS. The FAFSA is required. The priority date for freshman financial aid applications for fall is March 1.

International Students: There were 2732 international students enrolled in a recent year. The school actively recruits these students. They must score satisfactorily on the TOEFL or take the Comprehensive English Language Test. The SAT or ACT is required only if the applicant is a graduate of a U.S. high school.

Computers: All students may access the system 18 hours a day. There are no fees.

Graduates: In a recent year 5352 bachelor's degrees were awarded. The most popular majors were business/marketing (17%), social sciences and history (11%), and communications/commun. technology (9%).

Admissions Contact: Lori Goldman, Director of Admissions. A video is available. E-mail: appinfo@arizona.edu Web: www.arizona.edu

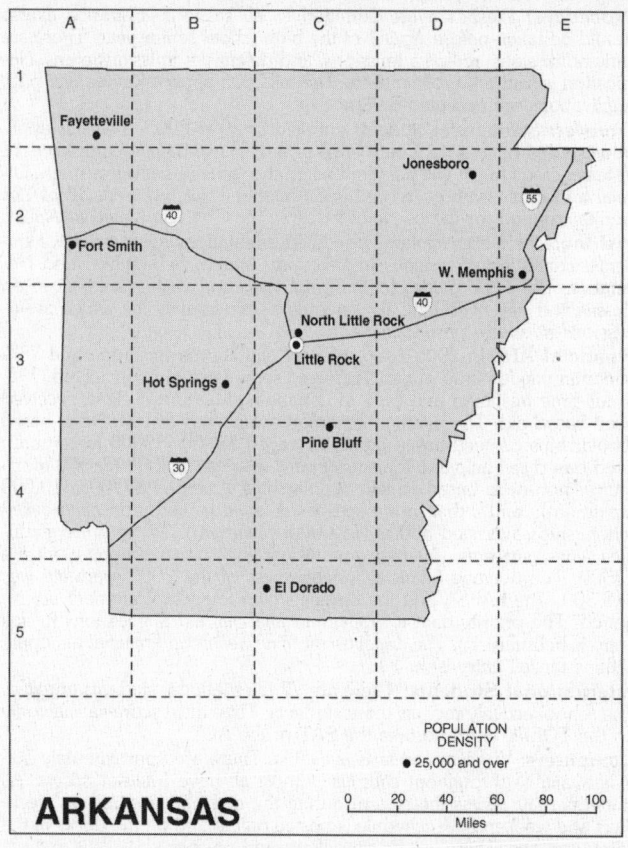

ARKANSAS

POPULATION
DENSITY
● 25,000 and over

0   20   40   60   80   100
Miles

ARKANSAS BAPTIST COLLEGE   C-3
Little Rock, AR 72202-6099

(501) 374-7856, ext. 19
Fax: (501) 375-9257

Full-time: 360 men and women	**Faculty:** n/av
Part-time: none	**Ph.D.s:** n/av
Graduate: none	**Student/Faculty:** 23 to 1
Year: semesters, summer session	**Tuition:** $2600
Application Deadline: see profile	**Room & Board:** $3000
Freshman Class: n/av	
SAT or ACT: not required	**NONCOMPETITIVE**

Arkansas Baptist College, founded in 1884, is a private liberal arts institution affiliated with American Baptist Churches, U.S.A. Figures in the above capsule and in this profile are approximate. The library contains 32,000 volumes, 10,000 microform items, and 2000 audio/video tapes/CDs/DVDs, and subscribes to 75 periodicals including electronic. Computerized library services include the card catalog, interlibrary loans, database searching, and Internet access. The campus is in an urban area in downtown Little Rock. Including any residence halls, there are 9 buildings.

Student Life: 90% of undergraduates are from Arkansas. All are African American. Most are Protestant. The average age of freshmen is 18; all undergraduates, 22.

Housing: 160 students can be accommodated in college housing, which includes single-sex dorms. On-campus housing is guaranteed for all 4 years. 50% of students live on campus; of those, 30% remain on campus on weekends. Alcohol is not permitted. All students may keep cars.

Activities: 10% of men belong to 3 local fraternities; 10% of women belong to 2 local sororities. There are 5 groups on campus, including cheerleading, computers, religious, social, and student government. Popular campus events include Ms. ABC and Mr. ABC Pageants.

Sports: There are 2 intercollegiate sports for men and 2 for women. Facilities include a gym.

Disabled Students: 40% of the campus is accessible. Wheelchair ramps and special parking are available.

Services: There is remedial math, reading, and writing.

Campus Safety and Security: Measures include 24-hour foot and vehicle patrol, informal discussions, and lighted pathways/sidewalks.

Programs of Study: ABC confers B.A. and B.S. degrees. Associate degrees are also awarded. Bachelor's degrees are awarded in BUSINESS (accounting and business administration and management), COMPUTER AND PHYSICAL SCIENCE (computer science), EDUCATION (elementary), SOCIAL SCIENCE (human services and religion). Business administration is the strongest academically and is the largest.

Required: Students must complete a minimim of 124 credit hours, with 45 in upper-division courses, and must maintain a minimum GPA of 2.0 overall and in the major. Required courses include the Old Testament, theology, humanities, liberal arts, and art or music appreciation.

Special: The college offers a co-op program with Ouachita Baptist University, work-study programs, combined B.A.-B.S. degrees, dual majors, and 1 general studies degree.

Admissions: All of the applicants were accepted in a recent year.

Requirements: For unconditional admission, applicants must be graduates of an accredited high school or have a GED. Others may be admitted conditionally. A GPA of 2.0 is required. Important factors in the admissions decision are ability to finance college education, evidence of special talent, and parents or siblings attending the school.

Procedure: Freshmen are admitted fall, spring, and summer. Entrance exams should be taken during the registration/orientation period of each semester. The college accepts all applicants. Check with the school for current application deadlines. The fall 2005 application fee was $25.

Transfer: 50 transfer students enrolled in a recent year. For unconditional admission, transfer applicants must have a cumulative GPA of 2.0 and not have been suspended from the previously attended institution. Others may be admitted conditionally. 124 of 124 credits required for the bachelor's degree must be completed at ABC.

Visiting: There are regularly scheduled orientations for prospective students, tour of campus. There are guides for informal visits and visitors may sit in on classes. To schedule a visit, contact the Admissions and Enrollment Office at (501) 244-5160.

Financial Aid: In a recent year, 90% of all full-time students received need-based aid. The average freshman award was $2025. 15% of undergraduates work part time. Average annual earnings from campus work are $816. The average financial indebtedness of a recent graduate was $5600. The FAFSA is required. Check with the school for current deadlines.

International Students: They must score satisfactorily on the written TOEFL and also take the college's own entrance exam.

Computers: All students may access the system.

Graduates: In a recent year, 15 bachelor's degrees were awarded. The most popular majors were business administration (20%), human resources (10%), and teacher education (10%). Of a recent graduating class, 5% were enrolled in graduate school within 6 months of graduation and 30% were employed.

Admissions Contact: Freddie M. Fox, Registrar.
Web: *www.arbaptcol.edu*

ARKANSAS STATE UNIVERSITY   D-2
State University, AR 72467

(870) 972-3024
(800) 382-3030; Fax: (870) 910-8094

Full-time: 2996 men, 4198 women	**Faculty:** 414; IIA, --$
Part-time: 720 men, 1224 women	**Ph.D.s:** 66%
Graduate: 443 men, 833 women	**Student/Faculty:** 17 to 1
Year: semesters, summer session	**Tuition:** $5440 ($12,145)
Application Deadline: Open	**Room & Board:** $4190
Freshman Class: 3488 applied, 2259 accepted, 1584 enrolled	
ACT: 21	**SAT:** required **COMPETITIVE**

Arkansas State University, founded in 1909 and part of the Arkansas State University System, is a state-supported institution offering undergraduate and graduate degrees in agriculture, humanities and social sciences, business, communications, education, engineering, sciences and math, fine arts, nursing, and health professions. There are 11 undergraduate schools and 1 graduate school. In addition to regional accreditation, ASU has baccalaureate program accreditation with AACSB, ABET, ACEJMC, ASLA, CAAHEP, CACREP, CAPTE, CSAB, CSWE, NAACLS, NASAD, NASM, NASPAA, NCATE, and NLN. The library contains 595,791 volumes, 584,730 microform items, and 16,910 audio/video tapes/CDs/DVDs, and subscribes to 1691 periodicals including electronic. Computerized library services include the card catalog, interlibrary loans, and database searching. Special learning facilities include a learning resource center, art gallery, natural history museum, radio station, TV station, facilities for agriculture and environmental ecotoxicology research, the Arkansas Biosciences Institute, the Fowler Center for Performing Arts, distance learning, the Hemingway-Pfeiffer Museum and Educational Center,a geographic information system facility, an electron microscope lab, and the Delta Studies Center. The 2008-acre campus is in a small town 70 miles west of Memphis, Tennessee. Including any residence halls, there are 100 buildings.

Student Life: 89% of undergraduates are from Arkansas. Others are from 41 states, 49 foreign countries, and Canada. 93% are from public schools. 79% are white; 16% African American. The average age of freshmen is 19; all undergraduates, 24. 33% do not continue beyond their first year; 35% remain to graduate.

Housing: 2280 students can be accommodated in college housing, which includes single-sex dormitories, on-campus apartments, married-student housing, and fraternity houses. In addition, there is an honors wing and a first-experience wing. On-campus housing is available on a first-come, first-served basis. 80% of students commute. Alcohol is not permitted. All students may keep cars.

Activities: 12% of men belong to 12 national fraternities; 8% of women belong to 9 national sororities. There are 216 groups on campus, including academic, art, cheerleading, choir, computers, dance, debate, drama, drill team, ethnic, forensics, gay, honors, international, jazz band, marching band, musical theater, newspaper, pep band, photography, political, professional, radio and TV, religious, social, social service, student government, symphony, and yearbook. Popular campus events include Springfest, Convocation of Scholars Week, and International Night.

Sports: There are 7 intercollegiate sports for men and 9 for women, and 13 intramural sports for men and 13 for women. Facilities include a 10,529-seat convocation center, a 30,964-seat football stadium, a 1000-seat baseball complex, a 500-seat track facility, and a 500-seat soccer field.

Disabled Students: 95% of the campus is accessible. Wheelchair ramps, elevators, special parking, specially equipped rest rooms, special class scheduling, lowered drinking fountains, lowered telephones, and automatic doors are available.

Services: Counseling and information services are available, as is tutoring in some subjects. There is a reader service for the blind, and remedial math, reading, and writing. Tutoring is available in basic courses.

Campus Safety and Security: Measures include 24-hour foot and vehicle patrol, security escort services, pamphlets/posters/films, and emergency telephones. There are lighted pathways/sidewalks.

Programs of Study: ASU confers B.A., B.S., B.F.A., B.M.E., B.S.A., B.S.E., B.S.N., B.S.E.N., B.S.R.S., and B.S.W. degrees. Associate, master's, and doctoral degrees are also awarded. Bachelor's degrees are awarded in AGRICULTURE (agricultural business management, agriculture, animal science, plant science, and wildlife management), BIOLOGICAL SCIENCE (biology/biological science), BUSINESS (accounting, banking and finance, business administration and management, business economics, business systems analysis, international business management, management information systems, management science, marketing/retailing/merchandising, sports management, and transportation management), COMMUNICATIONS AND THE ARTS (art, English, fine arts, French, graphic design, journalism, music, music performance, radio/television technology, Spanish, and speech/debate/rhetoric), COMPUTER AND PHYSICAL SCIENCE (chemistry, computer science, digital arts/technology, mathematics, and physics), EDUCATION (agricultural, art, athletic training, business, early childhood, English, foreign languages, health, mathematics, middle school, music, physical, science, social science, and special), ENGINEERING AND ENVIRONMENTAL DESIGN (engineering, graphic and printing production, manufacturing technology, and technological management), HEALTH PROFESSIONS (clinical science, exercise science, nursing, radiological science, and speech pathology/audiology), SOCIAL SCIENCE (criminology, economics, geography, history, interdisciplinary studies, philosophy, political science/government, psychology, social work, and sociology). Early childhood education, engineering, and nursing are the strongest academically. Nursing, early childhood education, and biological sciences are the largest.

Required: All students must complete a 46 to 49 credit distribution of general education courses. A total of at least 124 credits, with a minimum GPA of 2.0, is required to graduate. All students must take a state-administered comprehensive exam.

Special: An interdisciplinary studies degree, co-op programs, study abroad in 13 countries, and work-study programs are offered. Dual majors and internships are available in many areas. Nondegree study is possible. There are 13 national honor societies and a freshman honors program.

Faculty/Classroom: 53% of faculty are male; 47%, female. 92% teach undergraduates, 22% do research, and 19% do both. Graduate students teach 3% of introductory courses. The average class size in an introductory lecture is 28; in a laboratory, 22; and in a regular course, 27.

Admissions: 65% of the 2005-2006 applicants were accepted. The ACT scores for the 2005-2006 freshman class were: 44% below 21, 25% between 21 and 23, 19% between 24 and 26, 9% between 27 and 28, and 4% above 28.

Requirements: SAT, ACT, ASSET, or COMPASS scores are required, with ACT scores recommended. Applicants should have completed 16 academic high school units, including 4 each in English and math, 3 in

social studies, 3 in science (must be labs), and 2 in 1 foreign language. The university places those applicants scoring low on the ACT in developmental or remedial courses. A high school transcript is also required. A GPA of 2.0 is required. AP and CLEP credits are accepted.

Procedure: Freshmen are admitted to all sessions. Entrance exams should be taken before April 1 of the high school senior year. There are early admissions, rolling admissions, and deferred admissions plans. Notification is sent on a rolling basis. The fall 2005 application fee was $15. Applications are accepted on-line.

Transfer: 860 transfer students enrolled in 2004-2005. Transfer applicants should have a minimum GPA of 2.0. Those having completed 12 or fewer credit hours will be admitted on the same basis as freshmen. Official transcripts from every institution attended are required. 32 of 124 credits required for the bachelor's degree must be completed at ASU.

Visiting: There are regularly scheduled orientations for prospective students, consisting of sessions in February, March, September, and November. There are guides for informal visits and visitors may sit in on classes and stay overnight. To schedule a visit, contact the Office of Admissions at *admissions@astate.edu*.

Financial Aid: In 2005-2006, 85% of all full-time freshmen and 78% of continuing full-time students received some form of financial aid. 79% of full-time freshmen and 66% of continuing full-time students received need-based aid. The average freshman award was $6100. Need-based scholarships or need-based grants averaged $5900 ($9000 maximum); need-based self-help aid (loans and jobs) averaged $3300 ($8500 maximum); non-need-based athletic scholarships averaged $7700 ($10,000 maximum); and other non-need-based awards and non-need-based scholarships averaged $5000 ($12,000 maximum). 7% of undergraduates work part time. Average annual earnings from campus work are $3500. The average financial indebtedness of the 2005 graduate was $18,500. The FAFSA and the college's own financial statement are required. The priority date for freshman financial aid applications for fall entry is February 15. The deadline for filing freshman financial aid applications for fall entry is July 1.

International Students: There are 77 international students enrolled. The school actively recruits these students. They must score satisfactorily on the TOEFL and also take the SAT or the ACT.

Computers: Wireless access is available. There are approximately 500 PCs available throughout campus. Almost all have Internet access. All students may access the system during the day and evening on weekdays and weekends. A schedule is posted online and on the doors of the computer labs. There are no time limits and no fees.

Graduates: From July 1, 2004 to June 30, 2005, 1555 bachelor's degrees were awarded. The most popular majors were early childhood education (8%), nursing (6%), and management (5%). In an average class, 1% graduate in 3 years or less, 20% graduate in 4 years or less, 36% graduate in 5 years or less, and 39% graduate in 6 years or less. 97 companies recruited on campus in 2004-2005.

Admissions Contact: Vacant, Director of Admissions. A video is available. E-mail: *admissions@astate.edu*
Web: *www.astate.edu/admissions.htm*

ARKANSAS TECH UNIVERSITY — B-2

Russellville, AR 72801-2222

(479) 968-0343
(800) 582-6953; Fax: (479) 964-0522

Full-time: 2569 men, 2796 women	**Faculty:** IIB, --$
Part-time: 379 men, 584 women	**Ph.D.s:** 68%
Graduate: 169 men, 345 women	**Student/Faculty:** 21 to 1
Year: semesters, summer session	**Tuition:** $3818 ($7250)
Application Deadline: open	**Room & Board:** $4290
Freshman Class: 3459 applied, 1673 accepted, 1529 enrolled	
ACT: 22	**SAT:** recommended

VERY COMPETITIVE

Arkansas Tech University, founded in 1909, is a state-supported institution offering undergraduate instruction in the liberal and fine arts, business, education, physical and life sciences, information technology, systems science, and other technical fields. Graduate instruction is offered in education, liberal arts, instructional technology, information technology, and fisheries and wildlife. There are 7 undergraduate schools and 1 graduate school. In addition to regional accreditation, Tech has baccalaureate program accreditation with AACSB, ABET, ACS, CAHEA, NASM, NCATE, NLN, and NRPA. The library contains 281,445 volumes, 884,359 microform items, and 8005 audio/video tapes/CDs/DVDs, and subscribes to 1038 periodicals including electronic. Computerized library services include the card catalog, interlibrary loans, database searching, and Internet access. Special learning facilities include a learning resource center, art gallery, natural history museum, radio station, TV station, an energy center, and a library with distance learning classrooms, satellite downlink, and 400 data drops for laptop computers. The 516-acre campus is in a small town 75 miles west of Little Rock. Including any residence halls, there are 50 buildings.

Student Life: 96% of undergraduates are from Arkansas. Others are from 38 states, 32 foreign countries, and Canada. 88% are white. The average age of freshmen is 19; all undergraduates, 23. 34% do not continue beyond their first year; 36% remain to graduate.

Housing: 1587 students can be accommodated in college housing, which includes single-sex and coed dorms and on-campus apartments. 69% of students commute. Alcohol is not permitted. All students may keep cars.

Activities: 5% of men belong to 4 national fraternities; 4% of women belong to 3 national sororities. There are 111 groups on campus, including art, band, cheerleading, chess, choir, chorale, chorus, computers, dance, debate, drama, drill team, ethnic, film, honors, international, jazz band, literary magazine, marching band, musical theater, newspaper, opera, orchestra, pep band, photography, political, professional, radio and TV, religious, social, social service, student government, symphony, and yearbook. Popular campus events include Greek Week, Family Day, and Spring Fling.

Sports: There are 4 intercollegiate sports for men and 5 for women, and 28 intramural sports for men and 28 for women. Facilities include a coliseum, fields, an Olympic-size indoor pool, racquetball courts, and a 10,000-seat stadium. The Student Activities Building is the hub of indoor recreational activities.

Disabled Students: All of the campus is accessible. Wheelchair ramps, elevators, special parking, specially equipped rest rooms, special class scheduling, lowered drinking fountains, lowered telephones, and special housing are available.

Services: Counseling and information services are available, as is tutoring in most subjects. There is a reader service for the blind, and remedial math, reading, and writing.

Campus Safety and Security: Measures include 24-hour foot and vehicle patrol, self-defense education, security escort services, and informal discussions. There are pamphlets/posters/films and lighted pathways/sidewalks.

Programs of Study: Tech confers B.A., B.S., B.F.A., B.M.E., B.S.B.A., B.S.E.E., B.S.E.G., B.S.M.E., and B.S.N. degrees. Associate and master's degrees are also awarded. Bachelor's degrees are awarded in AGRICULTURE (agricultural business management), BIOLOGICAL SCIENCE (biology/biological science), BUSINESS (accounting), COMMUNICATIONS AND THE ARTS (art, creative writing, English, journalism, music, and speech/debate/rhetoric), COMPUTER AND PHYSICAL SCIENCE (chemistry, computer science, geology, mathematics, and physical sciences), EDUCATION (art, business, health, middle school, music, and secondary), ENGINEERING AND ENVIRONMENTAL DESIGN (emergency/disaster science), HEALTH PROFESSIONS (medical laboratory technology, nursing, and rehabilitation therapy), SOCIAL SCIENCE (economics, history, international studies, parks and recreation management, psychology, and sociology). Elementary education, management marketing, and computer science are the strongest academically.

Required: Students must complete at least 124 semester hours, including 40 hours of upper-level courses to fulfill a major, and maintain a minimum GPA of 2.0. General education requirements include 12 hours of social studies, 8 to 12 of science, 6 of communications, 3 each of math, fine arts, and the humanities, and 2 of phys ed or military science. Activity credits are limited to 4 semester hours.

Special: Special academic features include internships and work-study programs, as well as study abroad, accelerated programs, B.A.-B.S. degrees, dual majors, and student-designed majors. Independent study is available to seniors. Off-campus courses and on-line telecourses are also offered. There are 3 national honor societies and a freshman honors program.

Faculty/Classroom: 58% of faculty are male; 42%, female.

Admissions: 48% of the 2005-2006 applicants were accepted.

Requirements: The ACT is required and the SAT is recommended. In addition, applicants must be graduates of a secondary school on the Arkansas preparatory track. Academic ability must be demonstrated by one of the following: a high school GPA of at least 2.0 on a 4.0 scale; a satisfactory ACT score, attainment of Freshman Placement test score standards; or completion of 6 semester hours with a cumulative average of C or better in summer sessions or as a part-time student in regular sessions, with at least 3 of the hours being in English, math, social studies, or science. AP and CLEP credits are accepted.

Procedure: Freshmen are admitted to all sessions. Entrance exams should be taken no later than the second semester of the senior year of high school. There is a rolling admissions plan. Application deadlines are open. Notification is sent on a rolling basis. Applications are accepted on-line.

Transfer: 676 transfer students enrolled in a recent year. Transfers are accepted for second-semester freshman, sophomore, and junior classes. A C average is required; no D grades are accepted. 30 of 124 credits required for the bachelor's degree must be completed at Tech.

Visiting: There are regularly scheduled orientations for prospective students, including the opportunity to visit with or attend presentations by faculty in each academic discipline. There are guides for informal visits and visitors may sit in on classes. To schedule a visit, contact the Admissions Office.

Financial Aid: In 2005-2006, 62% of all full-time freshmen and 64% of continuing full-time students received some form of financial aid. 49% of full-time freshmen and 48% of continuing full-time students received need-based aid. The average freshman award was $3393. The average financial indebtedness of the 2005 graduate was $17,064. The FAFSA and the college's own financial statement are required. The deadline for filing freshman financial aid applications for fall entry is May 1.

International Students: There are 202 international students enrolled. The school actively recruits these students. A satisfactory score is required on the TOEFL as well as on the SAT or ACT.

Computers: More than 700 general-use PCs are available on campus with wireless access in most areas for personal PCs. All students may access the system. There are no time limits and no fees.

Graduates: From July 1, 2004 to June 30, 2005, 783 bachelor's degrees were awarded. The most popular majors were management marketing (10%), nursing (7%), and early childhood education (7%). In an average class, 18% graduate in 4 years or less, 31% graduate in 5 years or less, and 36% graduate in 6 years or less.

Admissions Contact: Shauna Donnell, Director of Enrollment Management. A video is available. E-mail: *tech.enroll@atu.edu* Web: *www.atu.edu*

HARDING UNIVERSITY   C-2

Searcy, AR 72149-0001 (501) 279-4407
(800) 477-4407; Fax: (501) 279-4129

Full-time: 1773 men, 2106 women	**Faculty:** 226
Part-time: 100 men, 113 women	**Ph.D.s:** 61%
Graduate: 347 men, 1305 women	**Student/Faculty:** 17 to 1
Year: semesters, summer session	**Tuition:** $11,200
Application Deadline: June 1	**Room & Board:** $5312
Freshman Class: 1658 applied, 1020 accepted	
SAT Verbal/Math: 560/550*	**ACT:** 23 **VERY COMPETITIVE**

Harding University, founded in 1924, is a private Christian institution comprised of the Colleges of Arts and Humanities, Sciences, Bible and Religion, Business, Education, and Nursing. There are 6 undergraduate and 5 graduate schools. In addition to regional accreditation, Harding has baccalaureate program accreditation with ACBSP, CSWE, NASM, NCATE, and NLN. The library contains 440,200 volumes, 251,046 microform items, and 8238 audio/video tapes/CDs/DVDs, and subscribes to 15,237 periodicals including electronic. Computerized library services include the card catalog, interlibrary loans, database searching, Internet access, and laptop Internet portals. Special learning facilities include a learning resource center, art gallery, natural history museum, radio station, and TV station. The 200-acre campus is in a small town 50 miles northeast of Little Rock. Including any residence halls, there are 50 buildings.

Student Life: 72% of undergraduates are from out of state, mostly the Southwest. Students are from 49 states, 45 foreign countries, and Canada. 73% are from public schools. 87% are white. Most are Protestant. The average age of freshmen is 18; all undergraduates, 21. 17% do not continue beyond their first year; 60% remain to graduate.

Housing: 2914 students can be accommodated in college housing, which includes single-sex dorms, on-campus apartments, off-campus apartments, and married-student housing. On-campus housing is guaranteed for all 4 years. 75% of students live on campus; of those, 80% remain on campus on weekends. Alcohol is not permitted. All students may keep cars.

Activities: 50% of men belong to 15 local fraternities; 39% of women belong to 15 local sororities. There are 103 groups on campus, including art, band, cheerleading, choir, chorale, chorus, computers, debate, drama, drill team, ethnic, film, forensics, honors, international, jazz band, literary magazine, marching band, musical theater, newspaper, orchestra, pep band, photography, political, professional, radio and TV, religious, social, social service, student government, symphony, and yearbook. Popular campus events include Spring Sing, Bison Daze, and Parents Weekend.

Sports: There are 7 intercollegiate sports for men and 7 for women, and 11 intramural sports for men and 8 for women. Facilities include baseball and softball fields, racquetball, handball, and tennis courts, a football stadium, an indoor and outdoor track, a golf practice range, a gymnastics room, 2 weight rooms, an Olympic-size swimming pool, and 2 gyms. Harding owns a 2000-acre camp in the Ozark Mountains with horses, 25 rustic cabins, streams, and hiking trails.

Disabled Students: 95% of the campus is accessible. Wheelchair ramps, elevators, special parking, specially equipped rest rooms, special class scheduling, lowered drinking fountains, lowered telephones, and special housing are available.

Services: Counseling and information services are available, as is tutoring in every subject. There is a reader service for the blind, and remedial math, reading, and writing.

Campus Safety and Security: Measures include 24-hour foot and vehicle patrol, self-defense education, security escort services, and informal

discussions. There are pamphlets/posters/films, emergency telephones, and lighted pathways/sidewalks.

Programs of Study: Harding confers B.A., B.S., B.B.A., B.F.A, B.M.E., B.Mus., B.S.M.T., B.S.N., and B.S.W. degrees. Master's degrees are also awarded. Bachelor's degrees are awarded in BIOLOGICAL SCIENCE (biochemistry and biology/biological science), BUSINESS (accounting, business administration and management, business economics, human resources, international business management, marketing/retailing/merchandising, and sports management), COMMUNICATIONS AND THE ARTS (advertising, art, broadcasting, communications, design, dramatic arts, English, fine arts, French, graphic design, journalism, media arts, music, painting, and Spanish), COMPUTER AND PHYSICAL SCIENCE (chemistry, computer science, information sciences and systems, mathematics, and physics), EDUCATION (athletic training, early childhood, elementary, foreign languages, music, and secondary), ENGINEERING AND ENVIRONMENTAL DESIGN (computer engineering, electrical/electronics engineering, interior design, and mechanical engineering), HEALTH PROFESSIONS (exercise science, health, medical technology, nursing, predentistry, premedicine, and speech pathology/audiology), SOCIAL SCIENCE (American studies, child care/child and family studies, criminal justice, dietetics, economics, history, home economics, international studies, liberal arts/general studies, ministries, political science/government, psychology, public administration, religion, social science, social work, and sociology). Business, premedicine, and nursing are the strongest academically. Business, nursing, and education are the largest.

Required: All students must complete 54 hours of general education courses, including religion, English composition, history, speech communications, social sciences, biology, physical science, math, Western literature, music and art appreciation, and phys ed. A total of 128 semester hours, with a minimum GPA of 2.0, is required to graduate.

Special: The Harding campus in Florence, Italy, and programs in Greece, England, Latin America, France, Switzerland, and Australia offer international studies. Internships are given in in social work, teaching, nursing, and international missions. Co-op programs in all majors, work-study programs, dual majors, a general studies degree, nondegree study, and pass/fail options are available. A 3-2 engineering degree is offered with the University of Missouri, Georgia Institute of Technology, and the University of Southern California. There are 3 national honor societies, a freshman honors program, and 13 departmental honors programs.

Faculty/Classroom: 60% of faculty are male; 46%, female. All teach undergraduates and 20% do research. No introductory courses are taught by graduate students. The average class size in an introductory lecture is 35; in a laboratory, 19; and in a regular course, 24.

Admissions: 62% of the 2005-2006 applicants were accepted. The SAT scores for the 2005-2006 freshman class were: Verbal--24% below 500, 39% between 500 and 599, 25% between 600 and 700, and 12% above 700; Math--28% below 500, 35% between 500 and 599, 27% between 600 and 700, and 10% above 700. The ACT scores were 26% below 21, 25% between 21 and 23, 24% between 24 and 26, 10% between 27 and 28, and 14% above 28. 55% of the current freshmen were in the top fifth of their class; 80% were in the top two fifths. There were 24 National Merit finalists and 20 semifinalists. 41 freshmen graduated first in their class.

Requirements: The SAT or ACT is required. A lower GPA can be offset by higher test scores. Applicants should be graduates of an accredited secondary school and have completed 15 high school hours, including 4 in English, 3 each in math, and social studies, 3 in art, history, or music, and 2 in a science. An interview is highly recommended. Harding requires applicants to be in the upper 50% of their class. A GPA of 3.0 is required. AP and CLEP credits are accepted. Important factors in the admissions decision are leadership record, recommendations by school officials, and advanced placement or honor courses.

Procedure: Freshmen are admitted to all sessions. Entrance exams should be taken in the junior year or early in the senior year. There are early admissions, deferred admissions, and rolling admissions plan. Applications should be filed by June 1 for fall entry and November 1 for spring entry. Notification is sent on a rolling basis. A waiting list is an active part of the admissions procedure. Applications are accepted on-line. The fall 2005 application fee was $35.

Transfer: 249 transfer students enrolled in 2004-2005. Applicants with a minimum GPA of 2.0 and at least 14 semester hours earned are considered for admission. An interview is highly recommended. 32 of 128 credits required for the bachelor's degree must be completed at Harding.

Visiting: There are regularly scheduled orientations for prospective students. There are guides for informal visits and visitors may sit in on classes and stay overnight. To schedule a visit, contact the Admissions Office.

Financial Aid: In a recent year, 93% of all full-time freshmen and 91% of continuing full-time students received some form of financial aid. 52% of full-time freshmen and 57% of continuing full-time students received need-based aid. The average freshman award was $8687. Need-based scholarships or need-based grants averaged $5828 ($13,500 maximum); need-based self-help aid (loans and jobs) averaged $3879 ($14,500 maximum); and non-need-based athletic scholarships averaged $7000 ($14,000 maximum). 33% of undergraduates work part time. Average

annual earnings from campus work are $866. The average financial indebtedness of a recent graduate was $19,711. The CSS/Profile or FFS is required. The deadline for filing freshman financial aid applications for fall entry is April 1.

International Students: The school actively recruits these students. They must score satisfactorily on the written TOEFL and also take the SAT or the ACT.

Computers: Wireless access is available. All students may access the system. The fee is $200 per semester. It is strongly recommended that all students have a personal computer.

Admissions Contact: Glen Dillard, Director of Enrollment Management. A video is available. E-mail: gdillard@harding.edu
Web: www.harding.edu

HENDERSON STATE UNIVERSITY   B-4
Arkadelphia, AR 71999-0001

(870) 230-5028
Fax: (870) 230-5066

Full-time: 1200 men, 1550 women	**Faculty:** 168; IIA, --$
Part-time: 125 men, 200 women	**Ph.D.s:** 71%
Graduate: 125 men, 300 women	**Student/Faculty:** 16 to 1
Year: semesters, summer session	**Tuition:** $4000 ($7500)
Application Deadline: open	**Room & Board:** $3600
Freshman Class: n/av	**ACT:** required COMPETITIVE

Henderson State University began in 1890 as Arkadelphia Methodist College, an affiliate of the Methodist Church. In 1929 it became a state institution offering liberal arts courses. There are 3 undergraduate schools and 1 graduate school. Figures in the above capsule and in this profile are approximate. In addition to regional accreditation, HSU has baccalaureate program accreditation with AACSB, NASM, NCATE, and NLN. The library contains 636,952 volumes, 213,922 microform items, and 18,983 audio/video tapes/CDs/DVDs, and subscribes to 1519 periodicals including electronic. Computerized library services include the card catalog, interlibrary loans, database searching, and Internet access. Special learning facilities include an art gallery, planetarium, radio station, and TV station. The 157-acre campus is in a small town 60 miles southwest of Little Rock. Including any residence halls, there are 32 buildings.

Student Life: 77% of undergraduates are from Arkansas. Others are from 24 states, 28 foreign countries, and Canada. 80% are white; 15% African American. The average age of freshmen is 18; all undergraduates, 23.

Housing: 878 students can be accommodated in college housing, which includes single-sex and coed dorms and off-campus apartments. In addition, there are honors houses and apartments on campus that are managed by an outside group. On-campus housing is available on a first-come, first-served basis. 71% of students commute. Alcohol is not permitted. All students may keep cars.

Activities: There are 8 national fraternities and 8 national sororities. There are 70 groups on campus, including art, band, cheerleading, choir, chorale, chorus, dance, drama, ethnic, gay, honors, international, jazz band, marching band, musical theater, newspaper, pep band, political, professional, radio and TV, religious, social, social service, student government, and yearbook. Popular campus events include Spring Fling, orientation and Family Day.

Sports: There are 5 intercollegiate sports for men and 6 for women, and 5 intramural sports for men and 5 for women. Facilities include a 9600-seat football stadium, a gym, an auxiliary gym, a weight room, an intramural practice field for football, a swimming pool, 6 tennis courts, baseball and softball fields, and a track.

Disabled Students: 72% of the campus is accessible. Wheelchair ramps, elevators, special parking, specially equipped rest rooms, special class scheduling, lowered drinking fountains, and lowered telephones are available.

Services: Counseling and information services are available, as is tutoring in most subjects. There is a reader service for the blind and remedial math and reading.

Campus Safety and Security: Measures include 24-hour foot and vehicle patrol, informal discussions, and lighted pathways/sidewalks.

Programs of Study: HSU confers B.A., B.S., B.B.A., B.F.A., B.M., B.S.E., and B.S.N. degrees. Associate and master's degrees are also awarded. Bachelor's degrees are awarded in BIOLOGICAL SCIENCE (biology/biological science), BUSINESS (accounting, business administration and management, and recreation and leisure services), COMMUNICATIONS AND THE ARTS (communications, dramatic arts, English, music, Spanish, and studio art), COMPUTER AND PHYSICAL SCIENCE (chemistry, computer science, mathematics, and physics), EDUCATION (athletic training, business, elementary, music, and physical), ENGINEERING AND ENVIRONMENTAL DESIGN (aviation administration/management), HEALTH PROFESSIONS (nursing), SOCIAL SCIENCE (family/consumer studies, history, human services, political science/government, psychology, public administration, and sociology). Elementary education, business administration, and nursing are the largest.

Required: All students must complete a total of 124 credit hours, including 30 in the major, with a minimum GPA of 2.0. Core requirements include 12 semester hours in social science, 11 in natural science, 9 in English, 6 in humanities, 3 each in non-Western culture, math, and oral communication, and 2 in phys ed or military science. Students must take the comprehensive Rising Junior Examination.

Special: HSU offers co-op programs and cross-registration with Ouachita Baptist University, internships in business, psychology, political science, recreation, and education, work-study programs, credit for military experience, nondegree study, and pass/fail options. There are 11 national honor societies and a freshman honors program.

Faculty/Classroom: 62% of faculty are male; 38%, female. All teach undergraduates and 30% both teach and do research. Graduate students teach 1% of introductory courses. The average class size in an introductory lecture is 50; in a laboratory, 20; and in a regular course, 30.

Admissions: The SAT scores for a recent freshman class were: Verbal--35% below 500, 35% between 500 and 599, and 30% between 600 and 700; Math--40% below 500, 40% between 500 and 599, and 20% between 600 and 700. The ACT scores were 41% below 21, 22% between 21 and 23, 22% between 24 and 26, and 5% above 28. 37% of recent freshmen were in the top fifth of their class; 64% were in the top two fifths.

Requirements: The ACT is required. In addition, applicants need at least 15 academic credits or 15 Carnegie units. Students with a predicted GPA of 1.5 or below will be admitted conditionally. 4 units of English, 3 of history, civics, or American government, 2 each of natural science, math, and foreign language, and a half unit of computer science are recommended. HSU requires applicants to be in the upper 50% of their class. A GPA of 3.13 is required. AP and CLEP credits are accepted.

Procedure: Freshmen are admitted fall, spring, and summer. Entrance exams should be taken during the senior year. Application deadlines are open. Check with the school for application fee. Applications are accepted on-line.

Transfer: Applicants with a cumulative GPA below 2.0 will be admitted conditionally. The entire academic record is considered. 30 of 124 credits required for the bachelor's degree must be completed at HSU.

Visiting: There are regularly scheduled orientations for prospective students. There are guides for informal visits and visitors may stay overnight. To schedule a visit, contact Vikita Hardwrick at buckg@hsu.edu.

Financial Aid: The FAFSA or FFS is required. Check with the school for current deadlines.

International Students: There were 110 international students enrolled in a recent year. The school actively recruits these students. They must score satisfactorily on the TOEFL or take the MELAB. They must also take the ACT or SAT.

Computers: All students may access the system. There are no time limits and no fees.

Graduates: In a recent year, 402 bachelor's degrees were awarded. The most popular majors were education (19%), business administration (19%), and psychology (8%). In an average class, 1% graduate in 3 years or less, 17% graduate in 4 years or less, 22% graduate in 5 years or less, and 27% graduate in 6 years or less. 100 companies recruited on campus in a recent year.

Admissions Contact: Vikita Hardwrick, Director of University Relations/Admissions. E-mail: hardwrv@hsu.edu
Web: www.hsu.edu/dept/ura/index.html

HENDRIX COLLEGE
C-3
Conway, AR 72032
(501) 450-1362
(800) 277-9017; Fax: (501) 450-3843

Full-time: 441 men, 560 women	Faculty: 85; IIB, av$
Part-time: 10 men, 11 women	Ph.D.s: 100%
Graduate: 5 men, 4 women	Student/Faculty: 12 to 1
Year: semesters	Tuition: $21,636
Application Deadline: open	Room & Board: $6010
Freshman Class: 1086 applied, 896 accepted, 281 enrolled	
SAT Verbal/Math: 636/611*	ACT: 28

HIGHLY COMPETITIVE+

Hendrix College, founded in 1876, is a private (not for profit) liberal arts college affiliated with the United Methodist Church. In addition to regional accreditation, Hendrix has baccalaureate program accreditation with NASM and NCATE. The library contains 218,390 volumes, 186,042 microform items, and 1899 audio/video tapes/CDs/DVDs, and subscribes to 9178 periodicals including electronic. Computerized library services include the card catalog, interlibrary loans, database searching, and Internet access. Special learning facilities include an art gallery, radio station, and a writing lab. The 65-acre campus is in a suburban area 25 miles northwest of Little Rock. Including any residence halls, there are 39 buildings.

Student Life: 55% of undergraduates are from Arkansas. Others are from 34 states and 4 foreign countries. 72% are white. 43% are Protestant; 42% claim no religious affiliation; 10% Catholic. The average age

of freshmen is 18; all undergraduates, 20. 19% do not continue beyond their first year; 81% remain to graduate.

Housing: 901 students can be accommodated in college housing, which includes single-sex and coed dorms, on-campus apartments, and off-campus apartments. In addition, there are language houses. On-campus housing is guaranteed for all 4 years. 85% of students live on campus; of those, 80% remain on campus on weekends. All students may keep cars.

Activities: There are no fraternities or sororities. There are 75 groups on campus, including art, band, cheerleading, choir, chorale, chorus, dance, debate, drama, ethnic, gay, honors, international, jazz band, literary magazine, musical theater, newspaper, opera, orchestra, pep band, photography, political, professional, radio and TV, religious, social, social service, student government, and yearbook. Popular campus events include Candlelight Carol Service, Basketball Homecoming, and Kampus Kitty Week.

Sports: There are 8 intercollegiate sports for men and 9 for women, and 20 intramural sports for men and 20 for women. Facilities include a 1,100 seat gym, a free weight room, and a pool; an indoor activity center with racquetball courts, a wallyball court, tennis courts, and a fitness center; outdoor tennis courts, baseball, softball, and soccer fields; a nature fitness trail, and a jogging track.

Disabled Students: 95% of the campus is accessible. Wheelchair ramps, elevators, special parking, specially equipped rest rooms, and push-button door openers are available.

Services: Counseling and information services are available, as is tutoring in some subjects, including math, biology, writing, chemistry, foreign languanges, accounting, physics, and psychology.

Campus Safety and Security: Measures include 24-hour foot and vehicle patrol, self-defense education, security escort services, and informal discussions. There are pamphlets/posters/films, emergency telephones, and lighted pathways/sidewalks.

Programs of Study: Hendrix confers the B.A. degree. Master's degrees are also awarded. Bachelor's degrees are awarded in AGRICULTURE (environmental studies), BIOLOGICAL SCIENCE (biology/biological science), BUSINESS (accounting and business economics), COMMUNICATIONS AND THE ARTS (art, dramatic arts, English, French, German, music, Spanish, and visual and performing arts), COMPUTER AND PHYSICAL SCIENCE (chemistry, computer science, mathematics, and physics), EDUCATION (elementary), HEALTH PROFESSIONS (exercise science), SOCIAL SCIENCE (American studies, economics, history, interdisciplinary studies, international relations, philosophy, philosophy and religion, political science/government, psychology, religion, and sociology). Psychology, biology and religion are the strongest academically. Psychology, biology, and English are the largest.

Required: To graduate, students must complete a total of 32 courses with a minimum 2.0 GPA. General education requirements consist of 3 components: (1) Collegiate Center, (2) Learning Domains, and (3) Capacities. The Collegiate Center includes Journeys (first year common course), 1 course from Explorations, and 1 course from Challenges of the Contemporary World. Students must also take 7 courses across 6 distinct Learning Domains and meet basic skill standards in 4 Capacities sections (writing skills, foreign language, quantitative skills, and physical activity).

Special: Internships and work-study may be arranged in all fields. The college offers 3-2 engineering programs with Columbia, Vanderbilt, and Washington Universities. Also available are a Washington semester, study abroad, dual majors, and student-designed interdisciplinary studies. Students can pursue minors in all academic departments, as well as gender studies and cultural anthropology. There are 6 national honor societies, including Phi Beta Kappa.

Faculty/Classroom: 60% of faculty are male; 40%, female. All teach undergraduates, 78% do research, and 78% do both. No introductory courses are taught by graduate students. The average class size in an introductory lecture is 19; in a laboratory, 16; and in a regular course, 16.

Admissions: 83% of the 2005-2006 applicants were accepted. The SAT scores for the 2005-2006 freshman class were: Verbal--7% below 500, 20% between 500 and 599, 48% between 600 and 700, and 25% above 700; Math--8% below 500, 33% between 500 and 599, 45% between 600 and 700, and 14% above 700. The ACT scores were 2% below 21, 10% between 21 and 23, 28% between 24 and 26, 17% between 27 and 28, and 43% above 28. 61% of the current freshmen were in the top fifth of their class; 87% were in the top two fifths. There were 11 National Merit finalists and 3 semifinalists. 17 freshmen graduated first in their class.

Requirements: The SAT or ACT is required. In addition, Hendrix recommends that applicants have completed 4 high school units in English, 3 to 4 each in math and social studies, 2 to 3 in science, and 2 in a foreign language. The GED is accepted. AP and CLEP credits are accepted. Important factors in the admissions decision are extracurricular activities record, advanced placement or honor courses, and leadership record.

Procedure: Freshmen are admitted fall and spring. Entrance exams should be taken during the junior and senior years. There is a deferred admissions plan. Application deadlines are open. Application fee is $40.

10 applicants were on the 2005 waiting list; 2 were admitted. Applications are accepted on-line.

Transfer: 14 transfer students enrolled in 2004-2005. Official transcripts and a Dean of Students Affairs form from all colleges previously attended must be submitted. 16 of 32 credits required for the bachelor's degree must be completed at Hendrix.

Visiting: There are regularly scheduled orientations for prospective students, including attending a class, visits with students and faculty, a campus tour, and a luncheon with speakers. Students may also stay overnight in a residence hall. There are guides for informal visits and visitors may sit in on classes and stay overnight. To schedule a visit, contact the Office of Admission at adm@hendrix.edu.

Financial Aid: In 2005-2006, 97% of all full-time freshmen and 96% of continuing full-time students received some form of financial aid. 56% of full-time freshmen and 54% of continuing full-time students received need-based aid. The average freshman award was $18,143. Need-based scholarships or need-based grants averaged $2527 ($14,600 maximum); need-based self-help aid (loans and jobs) averaged $3578 ($10,125 maximum); and other non-need-based awards and non-need-based scholarships averaged $12,129 ($27,646 maximum). 47% of undergraduates work part time. Average annual earnings from campus work are $1086. The average financial indebtedness of the 2005 graduate was $16,122. The FAFSA and the college's own financial statement are required. The deadline for filing freshman financial aid applications for fall entry is February 15.

International Students: There are 14 international students enrolled. The school actively recruits these students. They must take the TOEFL.

Computers: Wireless access is available. All students may access the system 24 hours a day, 7 days a week. There are no time limits and no fees.

Graduates: From July 1, 2004 to June 30, 2005, 202 bachelor's degrees were awarded. The most popular majors were psychology (16%), biology (14%), and history (11%). In an average class, 2% graduate in 3 years or less, 55% graduate in 4 years or less, 58% graduate in 5 years or less, and 61% graduate in 6 years or less. 55 companies recruited on campus in 2004-2005. Of the 2004 graduating class, 60% were enrolled in graduate school within 6 months of graduation and 52% were employed.

Admissions Contact: Karen Foust, Vice President for Enrollment.
E-mail: adm@hendrix.edu Web: www.hendrix.edu

JOHN BROWN UNIVERSITY   A-1
Siloam Springs, AR 72761

(479) 524-7150
(877) JBU-INFO; Fax: (479) 524-4196

Full-time: 775 men, 806 women	**Faculty:** 76; IIB, --$
Part-time: 34 men, 44 women	**Ph.D.s:** 73%
Graduate: 101 men, 144 women	**Student/Faculty:** 21 to 1
Year: semesters, summer session	**Tuition:** $15,280
Application Deadline: May 1	**Room & Board:** $5630
Freshman Class: 874 applied, 545 accepted, 262 enrolled	
SAT Verbal/Math: 590/580*	**ACT:** 25 **VERY COMPETITIVE**

John Brown University, founded in 1919, is a private, nondenominational Christian institution offering undergraduate programs in arts and literature, Bible studies, business, communication, engineering and technology, general studies, health and sports performance, music, natural science, social studies, and teacher education. In addition to regional accreditation, JBU has baccalaureate program accreditation with ABET, ACCE, IACBE and NCATE. The library contains 95,000 volumes, 30,000 microform items, and 3000 audio/video tapes/CDs/DVDs, and subscribes to 450 periodicals including electronic. Computerized library services include interlibrary loans and database searching. Special learning facilities include a learning resource center, art gallery, radio station, TV station, and wellness assessment laboratory. The 200-acre campus is in a small town 80 miles east of Tulsa, Oklahoma. Including any residence halls, there are 16 buildings.

Student Life: 58% of undergraduates are from out of state, mostly the Southwest. Students are from 43 states, 40 foreign countries, and Canada. 88% are white; 10% foreign nationals. Most are Protestant. The average age of freshmen is 19; all undergraduates, 21. 24% do not continue beyond their first year; 45% remain to graduate.

Housing: 1001 students can be accommodated in college housing, which includes single-sex and coed dorms, on-campus apartments, off-campus apartments, and married-student housing. On-campus housing is guaranteed for all 4 years. 70% of students live on campus; of those, 65% remain on campus on weekends. Alcohol is not permitted. All students may keep cars.

Activities: There are no fraternities or sororities. There are many groups and organizations on campus, including band, cheerleading, choir, chorale, chorus, drama, ethnic, honors, newspaper, pep band, photography, radio and TV, religious, and student government. Popular campus events include Christmas Candlelight Service, Spiritual Emphasis Week, and the Toilet Paper game.

Sports: There are 3 intercollegiate sports for men and 5 for women, and 6 intramural sports for men and 5 for women. Facilities include a 1500-seat gym, soccer and softball fields, a baseball diamond, a training room, and a swimming pool. The Lifetime Health Complex includes an indoor track, 4 racquetball courts, a Nautilus fitness center, an aerobics room, tennis courts, a rugby pitch, and a 3-court recreation center.

Disabled Students: 80% of the campus is accessible. Wheelchair ramps, elevators, special parking, specially equipped rest rooms, special class scheduling, lowered drinking fountains, lowered telephones, and special housing are available.

Services: Counseling and information services are available, as is tutoring in most subjects. There is remedial math, reading, and writing.

Campus Safety and Security: Measures include 24-hour foot and vehicle patrol, security escort services, informal discussions, and pamphlets/posters/films. There are lighted pathways/sidewalks.

Programs of Study: JBU confers B.A., B.S., B.Mus.Ed., and B.S.E. degrees. Associate and master's degrees are also awarded. Bachelor's degrees are awarded in BIOLOGICAL SCIENCE (biochemistry and biology/biological science), BUSINESS (accounting and business administration and management), COMMUNICATIONS AND THE ARTS (broadcasting, design, English, graphic design, illustration, journalism, music, public relations, and Spanish), COMPUTER AND PHYSICAL SCIENCE (chemistry, computer science, digital arts/technology, mathematics, and science), EDUCATION (early childhood, elementary, middle school, music, physical, science, and secondary), ENGINEERING AND ENVIRONMENTAL DESIGN (construction management, electrical/electronics engineering, engineering, and environmental science), HEALTH PROFESSIONS (community health work and sports medicine), SOCIAL SCIENCE (biblical studies, crosscultural studies, family and community services, history, interdisciplinary studies, international studies, ministries, political science/government, psychology, theological studies, and youth ministry). Engineering, teacher education, and business are the strongest academically. Business, broadcasting, and psychology are the largest.

Required: All students must complete 25 hours of lower-level core courses, 19 to 22 of elective courses in wellness, natural science, mathematics, philosophy, arts, social studies, and global studies; and 8 hours in upper-level core courses. A total of 142 to 145 credit hours with a minimum GPA of 2.25 (2.5 in profession education, teaching and other state-required courses) is required in order to graduate. Students must complete an exit assessment before graduation.

Special: Internships or field experiences are available in most majors. Study abroad in 15 countries, a Washington semester, work-study, and accelerated degree programs in Business Information Systems and Organizational Management, are offered. There is 1 national honor society, a freshman honors program, and there are honors programs in all major fields of study.

Faculty/Classroom: 78% of faculty are male; 22%, female. 57% teach undergraduates and 43% both teach and do research. The average class size in an introductory lecture is 22; in a laboratory, 20; and in a regular course, 19.

Admissions: 62% of the 2005-2006 applicants were accepted. The SAT scores for the 2005-2006 freshman class were: Verbal--14% below 500, 40% between 500 and 599, 37% between 600 and 700, and 9% above 700; Math--20% below 500, 40% between 500 and 599, 34% between 600 and 700, and 6% above 700. The ACT scores were 14% below 21, 26% between 21 and 23, 28% between 24 and 26, 13% between 27 and 28, and 19% above 28. 54% of the current freshmen were in the top fifth of their class; 81% were in the top two fifths. 9 freshmen graduated first in their class.

Requirements: The SAT or ACT is recommended. In addition, applicants should have completed 14 high school units, including 4 in English, 3 in math, 2 each in science and social studies and 1 in history or foreign language. Two references are required: one from a high school counselor or teacher, the other from a pastor or church leader. An essay and an interview are recommended. Applicants 21 years of age or older may be admitted without ACT or SAT scores. JBU requires applicants to be in the upper 50% of their class. A GPA of 2.5 is required. AP and CLEP credits are accepted. Important factors in the admissions decision are advanced placement or honor courses, leadership record, and evidence of special talent.

Procedure: Freshmen are admitted fall and spring. Entrance exams should be taken during the spring of the junior year or fall of the senior year. There is a rolling admissions plans. Early decision applications should be filed by May 1, along with a $25 fee. Notification is sent on a rolling basis. Applications are accepted on-line.

Transfer: 38 transfer students enrolled in 2004-2005. Transfer applicants must have completed at least 12 units of college work, with at least 9 transferable, and a minimum 2.5 GPA. 39 of 142 to 145 credits required for the bachelor's degree must be completed at JBU.

Visiting: There are regularly scheduled orientations for prospective students, including campus tours, consultations with faculty and coaches, and examination of financial aid opportunities. There are guides for informal visits and visitors may sit in on classes and stay overnight. To schedule a visit, contact the Admissions Office.

Financial Aid: In 2005-2006, 94% of all full-time freshmen and 90% of continuing full-time students received some form of financial aid. 78% of full-time freshmen and 71% of continuing full-time students received need-based aid. In a recent year the average freshman award was $10,060. Average annual earnings from campus work are $1400. The average financial indebtedness of the 2005 graduate was $19,125. The CSS/Profile, FAFSA, or FFS is required. The priority date for freshman financial aid applications for fall entry is March 1.

International Students: They must score satisfactorily on the written TOEFL or on the electronic version.

Computers: Wireless access is available. Labs are available and all residents halls are wired for access and have computer labs. All students may access the system from 7:30 A.M. to 12 A.M. Monday through Thursday, 7:30 A.M. to 5 P.M. on Friday, 12 P.M. to 5 P.M. on Saturday and 3 P.M. to 11 P.M. on Sunday. There are no time limits and no fees.

Graduates: From July 1, 2004 to June 30, 2005, 501 bachelor's degrees were awarded. The most popular majors were business administration (10%), digital media (10%), and graphic design (9%). In an average class, 1% graduate in 3 years or less, 42% graduate in 4 years or less, 57% graduate in 5 years or less, and 58% graduate in 6 years or less. 62 companies recruited on campus in 2004-2005. Of the 2004 graduating class, 28% were enrolled in graduate school within 6 months of graduation and 96% were employed.

Admissions Contact: Don Crandall, Vice President for Enrollment. A video is available. E-mail: *jbuinfo@jbu.edu* Web: *www.jbu.edu*

LYON COLLEGE — C-2

Batesville, AR 72503-2317

(870) 698-4250

(800) 423-2542; Fax: (870) 793-1791

Full-time: 229 men, 229 women	**Faculty:** 44; IIB, -$
Part-time: 9 men, 21 women	**Ph.D.s:** 91%
Graduate: none	**Student/Faculty:** 10 to 1
Year: semesters, summer session	**Tuition:** $13,905
Application Deadline: August	**Room & Board:** $6085
Freshman Class: 470 applied, 337 accepted, 111 enrolled	
SAT Verbal/Math: 590/585*	**ACT:** 25 **VERY COMPETITIVE**

Lyon College, founded in 1872, is a selective, private, residential, liberal arts college affiliated with the Presbyterian Church (U.S.A.). In addition to regional accreditation, Lyon has baccalaureate program accreditation with NCATE. The library contains 199,686 volumes, 2928 microform items, and 6901 audio/video tapes/CDs/DVDs, and subscribes to 23,502 periodicals including electronic. Computerized library services include the card catalog, interlibrary loans, database searching, Internet access, and laptop Internet portals. Special learning facilities include a learning resource center, art gallery, a language lab, and a computer lab. The 136-acre campus is in a small town 90 miles north of Little Rock. Including any residence halls, there are 30 buildings.

Student Life: 80% of undergraduates are from Arkansas. Students are from 22 states, 14 foreign countries, and Canada. 86% are white. 61% are Protestant; 21% claim no religious affiliation; 8% Catholic. The average age of freshmen is 18; all undergraduates, 21. 25% do not continue beyond their first year; 56% remain to graduate.

Housing: 421 students can be accommodated in college housing, which includes single-sex and coed dorms, on-campus apartments, and freshman-only housing. On-campus housing is guaranteed for all 4 years. 76% of students live on campus; of those, 75% remain on campus on weekends. All students may keep cars.

Activities: 10% of men belong to 3 national fraternities; 13% of women belong to 2 national sororities. There are 44 groups on campus, including art, bagpipe band, cheerleading, choir, drama, ethnic, honors, international, literary magazine, newspaper, orchestra, political, professional, religious, social, social service, student government, and yearbook. Popular campus events include Arkansas Scottish Festival, Service Day, and Baccalaureate and Commencement.

Sports: There are 6 intercollegiate sports for men and 6 for women, and 14 intramural sports for men and 14 for women. Facilities include an 1100-seat gym, softball, baseball, and soccer fields, a cross-country trail, an indoor swimming pool, 6 tennis courts, an indoor baseball practice facility, and a weight room.

Disabled Students: 80% of the campus is accessible. Wheelchair ramps, elevators, special parking, specially equipped rest rooms, and special housing are available.

Services: Counseling and information services are available, as is tutoring in some subjects, including foreign language and chemistry. There is remedial math and writing. Writing and math labs are available.

Campus Safety and Security: Measures include 24-hour foot and vehicle patrol, security escort services, informal discussions, and pamphlets/posters/films. There are lighted pathways/sidewalks.

Programs of Study: Lyon confers B.A. and B.S. degrees. Bachelor's degrees are awarded in AGRICULTURE (environmental studies), BIOLOGICAL SCIENCE (biology/biological science), BUSINESS (accounting and business administration and management), COMMUNICATIONS AND THE ARTS (art, dramatic arts, English, music, and Spanish), COMPUTER AND PHYSICAL SCIENCE (chemistry, computer science, and mathematics), SOCIAL SCIENCE (economics, history, political science/government, psychology, and religion). Business administration, biology, and psychology are the largest.

Required: All students are required to demonstrate proficiency in English composition, math, and foreign language; meet distribution requirements in social sciences, arts and literature, natural science and math, and religion and philosophy; take the 2-semester Western Tradition course sequence; complete the freshman orientation program; and take 1 semester of phys ed in each of the 4 years. The core curriculum requires 31 to 49 credit hours. A total of 120 credits, with a minimum GPA of 2.0, is required to graduate.

Special: Internships are offered, as is cross-registration (for certain courses) with the University of Arkansas Community College at Batesville. A 2-2 engineering program is offered with the University of Missouri in Rolla, and a 3-2 program is offered with the University of Arkansas at Fayetteville. Work-study courses, study abroad in 3 countries, dual majors, student-designed majors, pass/fail options, a Washington semester, and credit for military experience are available. There are 14 national honor societies.

Faculty/Classroom: 77% of faculty are male; 23%, female. 100% both teach and do research. The average class size in an introductory lecture is 19; in a laboratory, 13; and in a regular course, 12.

Admissions: 72% of the 2005-2006 applicants were accepted. The SAT scores for the 2005-2006 freshman class were: Verbal--25% below 500, 25% between 500 and 599, 20% between 600 and 700, and 30% above 700; Math--15% below 500, 40% between 500 and 599, and 45% between 600 and 700. The ACT scores were 5% below 21, 23% between 21 and 23, 34% between 24 and 26, 17% between 27 and 28, and 22% above 28. There were 4 National Merit finalists. 11 freshmen graduated first in their class.

Requirements: The SAT or ACT is required. In addition, applicants should have completed a minimum of 16 high school units, including 4 in English, 3 each in science, math, and social sciences, and 2 in a foreign language. A letter of recommendation and an admission interview are recommended. AP credits are accepted.

Procedure: Freshmen are admitted fall and spring. Entrance exams should be taken in the spring of junior year and the fall of senior year. There are early admissions, rolling admissions, and deferred admissions plans. The fall 2005 application fee was $25. Applications should be filed by August for fall entry and January for spring entry. Notification is sent on a rolling basis. Applications are accepted on-line.

Transfer: 47 transfer students enrolled in 2004-2005. Transfer applicants with 24 or more semester hours must submit a transcript and statement of good standing from each institution attended. Students with fewer than 24 semester hours must submit their final high school transcript and ACT or SAT scores. 24 of 120 credits required for the bachelor's degree must be completed at Lyon.

Visiting: There are regularly scheduled orientations for prospective students, consisting of a campus tour, admission and financial aid orientation, and information sessions with faculty and students. There are guides for informal visits and visitors may sit in on classes and stay overnight. To schedule a visit, contact the Admission Office at *admissions@lyon.edu.*

Financial Aid: In 2005-2006, All of all full-time freshmen and continuing full-time students received some form of financial aid. 63% of full-time freshmen and 70% of continuing full-time students received need-based aid. The average freshman award was $13,235. Need-based scholarships or need-based grants averaged $10,531; need-based self-help aid (loans and jobs) averaged $4392; non-need-based athletic scholarships averaged $4957; and other non-need-based awards and non-need-based scholarships averaged $11,096. 14% of undergraduates work part time. Average annual earnings from campus work are $1625. The average financial indebtedness of the 2005 graduate was $15,956. The FAFSA is required. The priority date for freshman financial aid applications for fall entry is March 1.

International Students: There are 17 international students enrolled. Satisfactory score is required on the written TOEFL and the SAT or the ACT.

Computers: Wireless access is available. All students may access the system. There are no time limits. The fee is $240.

Graduates: From July 1, 2004 to June 30, 2005, 112 bachelor's degrees were awarded. The most popular majors were biology (20%), business administration (17%), and psychology (15%). In an average class, 53% graduate in 4 years or less, 65% graduate in 5 years or less, and 68% graduate in 6 years or less. 33 companies recruited on campus in 2004-2005. Of the 2004 graduating class, 14% were enrolled in graduate school within 6 months of graduation and 80% were employed.

Admissions Contact: Denny Bardos, Vice President for Enrollment Services. A video is available. E-mail: *admissions@lyon.edu* Web: *www.lyon.edu*

OUACHITA BAPTIST UNIVERSITY   B-4

Arkadelphia, AR 71998-0001

(870) 245-5110
(800) 342-5628; Fax: (870) 245-5500

Full-time: 675 men, 800 women	**Faculty:** 111; IIB, -$
Part-time: 25 men, 20 women	**Ph.D.s:** 76%
Graduate: none	**Student/Faculty:** 13 to 1
Year: semesters, summer session	**Tuition:** $16,990
Application Deadline: open	**Room & Board:** 5000
Freshman Class: n/av	
SAT or ACT: required	**VERY COMPETITIVE**

Ouachita Baptist University, founded in 1886, is a private liberal arts institution affiliated with the Arkansas Baptist State Convention. Some information in the above capsule and in this profile is approximate. There are 7 undergraduate schools. In addition to regional accreditation, Ouachita has baccalaureate program accreditation with NASM and NCATE. The 2 libraries contain 117,517 volumes, 205,614 microform items, and 3159 audio/video tapes/CDs/DVDs, and subscribe to 1067 periodicals including electronic. Computerized library services include the card catalog, interlibrary loans, and database searching. Special learning facilities include a learning resource center, art gallery, and planetarium. The 60-acre campus is in a small town 65 miles southwest of Little Rock. Including any residence halls, there are 33 buildings.

Student Life: 53% of undergraduates are from Arkansas. Others are from 32 states and 62 foreign countries. 95% are from public schools. 90% are white. Most are Protestant. The average age of freshmen is 18; all undergraduates, 21. 25% do not continue beyond their first year.

Housing: 1352 students can be accommodated in college housing, which includes single-sex dorms, on-campus apartments, off-campus apartments, and married-student housing. On-campus housing is guaranteed for the freshman year only and is available on a first-come, first-served basis. 90% of students live on campus; of those, 60% remain on campus on weekends. Alcohol is not permitted. All students may keep cars.

Activities: 30% of men belong to 5 local fraternities; 30% of women belong to 5 local sororities. There are 30 groups on campus, including band, cheerleading, choir, chorale, chorus, computers, debate, drama, drill team, ethnic, film, honors, international, jazz band, marching band, musical theater, newspaper, opera, orchestra, pep band, photography, political, professional, religious, social, social service, student government, and yearbook. Popular campus events include International Student Fair, Tiger Tunes, and Tiger Traks.

Sports: There are 9 intercollegiate sports for men and 5 for women, and 4 intramural sports for men and 3 for women. Facilities include a 6000-seat football stadium, an athletic complex featuring a 2500-seat basketball arena, a swimming pool, a weight room, and tennis, racquetball, and volleyball courts.

Disabled Students: 95% of the campus is accessible. Wheelchair ramps, elevators, special parking, specially equipped rest rooms, and special class scheduling are available.

Services: Counseling and information services are available, as is tutoring in most subjects. There is a reader service for the blind, and remedial math, reading, and writing.

Campus Safety and Security: Measures include 24-hour foot and vehicle patrol, informal discussions, pamphlets/posters/films, emergency telephones and lighted pathways/sidewalks.

Programs of Study: Ouachita confers B.A., B.S., B.M., B.M.E., and B.S.E. degrees. Associate degrees are also awarded. Bachelor's degrees are awarded in BIOLOGICAL SCIENCE (biology/biological science), BUSINESS (accounting, business administration and management, and business economics), COMMUNICATIONS AND THE ARTS (communications, dramatic arts, English, French, music, musical theater, Russian languages and literature, Spanish, and speech/debate/rhetoric), COMPUTER AND PHYSICAL SCIENCE (chemistry, computer science, mathematics, and physics), EDUCATION (art, business, early childhood, elementary, foreign languages, health, home economics, middle school, music, science, and secondary), HEALTH PROFESSIONS (medical laboratory technology, predentistry, premedicine, and speech pathology/audiology), SOCIAL SCIENCE (biblical studies, dietetics, economics, history, ministries, philosophy, political science/government, prelaw, psychology, religion, sociology, and theological studies). Education, business, and religion are the largest.

Required: All students must fulfill 44 semester hours of general education courses, including 2 semesters of 1 foreign language, 7 chapel credits, and 2 semester hours of phys ed. A total of 128 semester hours, with a minimum GPA of 2.0, is required for graduation.

Special: Ouachita offers cross-registration with Henderson State University, a Washington semester for political science majors, internships and co-op programs for business majors, B.A.-B.S. degrees, dual majors, pass/fail options, and nondegree study. Study-abroad opportunities are available in Germany, England, France, Italy, Russia, Japan, China, Hong Kong, Kazakhstan, Austria, Israel, Belize, and Morocco. There is a freshman honors program.

Faculty/Classroom: 73% of faculty are male; 27%, female. All teach undergraduates. The average class size in an introductory lecture is 30; in a laboratory, 11; and in a regular course, 13.

Admissions: 80% of recent applicants were accepted. The SAT scores for a recent freshman class were: Verbal--29% below 500, 39% between 500 and 599, 24% between 600 and 700, and 8% above 700; Math--26% below 500, 45% between 500 and 599, 22% between 600 and 700, and 7% above 700. The ACT scores were 23% below 21, 27% between 21 and 23, 26% between 24 and 26, 13% between 27 and 28, and 11% above 28. 53% of recent freshmen were in the top fifth of their class; 80% were in the top two fifths.

Requirements: The SAT or ACT is required. In addition, applicants should have completed 19 high school units, including 4 in English, 3 in social science, and 2 each in natural science and math; 2 in a foreign language and 1/2 in computer science are also recommended. A GPA of 2.75 is required. AP and CLEP credits are accepted.

Procedure: Freshmen are admitted to all sessions. Entrance exams should be taken in the junior year. There are early decision, early admissions, deferred admissions and rolling admissions plans. Application deadlines are open. Application fee is $50. 10 early decision candidates were accepted for a recent class.

Transfer: Applicants must be eligible to return to their previous school. 60 of 128 credits required for the bachelor's degree must be completed at Ouachita.

Visiting: There are regularly scheduled orientations for prospective students, including a campus tour, a question-and-answer session, and meetings with professors and students. There are guides for informal visits and visitors may sit in on classes and stay overnight. To schedule a visit, contact the Admissions Counseling Office at jonesr@obu.edu.

Financial Aid: In a recent year, 97% of all full-time freshmen and 94% of continuing full-time students received some form of financial aid. 32% of full-time freshmen and 35% of continuing full-time students received need-based aid. The average freshman award was $12,418. Need-based scholarships or need-based grants averaged $3630 ($7650 maximum); need-based self-help aid (loans and jobs) averaged $3815 ($14,000 maximum); non-need-based athletic scholarships averaged $8326 ($19,460 maximum); and other non-need-based awards and non-need-based scholarships averaged $4098 ($10,000 maximum). 52% of undergraduates work part time. The FAFSA and the college's own financial statement are required.

International Students: The school actively recruits these students. They must score satisfactorily on the written TOEFL and also take the SAT or the ACT.

Computers: All students may access the system. There are no time limits and no fees.

Graduates: In an average class, 30% graduate in 4 years or less, 45% graduate in 5 years or less, and 50% graduate in 6 years or less.

Admissions Contact: David Goodman, Director of Admissions Counseling. E-mail: admissions@alpha.obu.edu Web: www.obu.edu

PHILANDER SMITH COLLEGE   C-3

Little Rock, AR 72202

(501) 370-5221
(800) 446-6772; Fax: (501) 370-5225

Full-time: 232 men, 438 women	**Faculty:** 32
Part-time: 32 men, 83 women	**Ph.D.s:** 20%
Graduate: none	**Student/Faculty:** 21 to 1
Year: semesters, summer session	**Tuition:** $8080
Application Deadline: July 15	**Room & Board:** $5150
Freshman Class: 126 enrolled	
ACT: required	**LESS COMPETITIVE**

Philander Smith College, founded in 1877, is affiliated with the United Methodist Church. The college offers undergraduate degrees in education, humanities, natural and physical sciences, business, and social science. In addition to regional accreditation, PSC has baccalaureate program accreditation with ACBSP, CSWE, and NCATE. The library contains 83,000 volumes, 170 microform items, and 60 audio/video tapes/CDs/DVDs, and subscribes to 370 periodicals including electronic. Computerized library services include interlibrary loans, database searching, Internet access, and laptop Internet portals. The 25-acre campus is in an urban area in Little Rock. There are 14 buildings.

Student Life: 77% of undergraduates are from Arkansas. Students are from 28 states and 9 foreign countries. 97% are African American. The average age of freshmen is 18; all undergraduates, 24. 49% do not continue beyond their first year; 20% remain to graduate.

Housing: 256 students can be accommodated in college housing, which includes coed dorms. 67% of students commute. All students may keep cars.

Activities: 4% of men belong to 4 local and 4 national fraternities; 2% of women belong to 4 local sororities. There are 20 groups on campus, including cheerleading, choir, dance, honors, opera, pep band, political, professional, religious, social, social service, and student government.

Sports: Facilities include a gym with racquetball court and weight rooms.

Disabled Students: 90% of the campus is accessible. Wheelchair ramps, elevators, and special parking are available.

Services: Counseling and information services are available, as is tutoring in every subject. There is remedial math, reading, and writing.

Campus Safety and Security: Measures include 24-hour foot and vehicle patrol, security escort services, informal discussions, and pamphlets/posters/films. There are lighted pathways/sidewalks.

Programs of Study: PSC confers B.A., B.S., B.B.A., and B.S.W. degrees. Bachelor's degrees are awarded in BIOLOGICAL SCIENCE (biology/biological science), BUSINESS (business administration and management), COMMUNICATIONS AND THE ARTS (music), COMPUTER AND PHYSICAL SCIENCE (chemistry, computer science, and mathematics), EDUCATION (business, Christian, early childhood, education administration, middle school, and physical), SOCIAL SCIENCE (philosophy and religion, political science/government, psychology, social work, and sociology). Biology is the strongest academically. Business administration is the largest.

Required: To graduate, all students must complete at least 124 credit hours with a minimum 2.0 GPA and satisfy general education requirements, which include courses in speech, English composition, literature, philosophy and religion, physical and life science, math, computing, psychology, political science or sociology, economics, U.S. history, phys ed, and health.

Special: Internships in science, business administration, and other fields are available. There are 2 national honor societies and a freshman honors program.

Faculty/Classroom: 48% of faculty are male; 52%, female. All teach undergraduates. The average class size in an introductory lecture is 30; in a laboratory, 15; and in a regular course, 20.

Requirements: The ACT is required. In addition, the SAT is accepted. Applicants must be graduates of an accredited secondary school or have a GED certificate. A GPA of 2.0 is required for unconditional admission. Students should have completed 16 academic credits, including 4 units of English, 2 of math, and 2 from 2 of the following: foreign language, science, or social studies. A GPA of 2.0 is required. CLEP credit is accepted.

Procedure: Freshmen are admitted fall, spring, and summer. There are early admissions and deferred admissions plans. Applications should be filed by July 15 for fall entry, along with a $25 fee. Notification of early decision is sent January 15. Applications are accepted on-line.

Transfer: 170 transfer students enrolled in 2004-2005. A 2.0 GPA is required. 22 of 124 credits required for the bachelor's degree must be completed at PSC.

Visiting: There are regularly scheduled orientations for prospective students including a presentation with handouts and questions and answers and a campus tour. There are guides for informal visits and visitors may sit in on classes. To schedule a visit, contact *tstarr@philander.edu*.

Financial Aid: In 2005-2006, 95% of all full-time freshmen and 93% of continuing full-time students received some form of financial aid. The FAFSA and the college's own financial statement are required. The priority date for freshman financial aid applications for fall entry is March 15.

International Students: There are 10 international students enrolled. They must score satisfactorily on the written TOEFL or on the electronic version or take IELP, or present an ESL certificate, they must also take the ACT.

Computers: Wireless access is available. There are approximately 250 PC in 10 labs with full Internet access. All students may access the system. There are no time limits and no fees.

Graduates: From July 1, 2004 to June 30, 2005, 111 bachelor's degrees were awarded. The most popular majors were organizational management (30%) and business administration (26%). In an average class, 6% graduate in 4 years or less, 8% graduate in 5 years or less, and 20% graduate in 6 years or less. 75 companies recruited on campus in 2004-2005.

Admissions Contact: Arnella Hayes, Director of Admissions. A video is available. E-mail: *admarnella@philander.edu*
Web: *www.philander.edu*

SOUTHERN ARKANSAS UNIVERSITY
Magnolia, AR 71754

B-5

(870) 235-4040
(800) 332-SAUM; Fax: (870) 235-4931

Full-time: 1108 men, 1300 women	**Faculty:** 138; IIB, --$
Part-time: 124 men, 344 women	**Ph.D.s:** 58%
Graduate: 47 men, 186 women	**Student/Faculty:** 17 to 1
Year: semesters, summer session	**Tuition:** $3496 ($5186)
Application Deadline: open	**Room & Board:** $3460
Freshman Class: 1356 applied, 1107 accepted, 572 enrolled	
ACT: required	**COMPETITIVE**

Southern Arkansas University, founded in 1909, is a state-supported liberal arts institution offering degrees in business administration, education, liberal and performing arts, and science and technology. There are 4 undergraduate schools and 1 graduate school. In addition to regional accreditation, SAU has baccalaureate program accreditation with CSWE, NASAD, NASM, NCATE, and NLN. The library contains 150,341 volumes, 669,721 microform items, and 12,214 audio/video tapes/CDs/DVDs, and subscribes to 725 periodicals including electronic. Computerized library services include the card catalog, interlibrary loans, database searching, and Internet access. Special learning facilities include a learning resource center, art gallery, radio station, biological field station, and university farm. The 781-acre campus is in a small town. Including any residence halls, there are 27 buildings.

Student Life: 71% of undergraduates are from Arkansas. Others are from 22 states, 40 foreign countries, and Canada. 97% are from public schools. 69% are white; 24% African American. The average age of freshmen is 18; all undergraduates, 28. 32% do not continue beyond their first year.

Housing: 1043 students can be accommodated in college housing, which includes single-sex and coed dorms. In addition, there are honors houses and an Internation house. On-campus housing is guaranteed for all 4 years. 66% of students commute. Alcohol is not permitted. All students may keep cars.

Activities: 6% of men belong to 7 national fraternities; 5% of women belong to 7 national sororities. There are 80 groups on campus, including art, band, cheerleading, choir, chorale, computers, dance, drama, drill team, ethnic, honors, international, jazz band, literary magazine, marching band, musical theater, newspaper, pep band, photography, political, professional, radio and TV, religious, social, and student government. Popular campus events include Spring Fling and Celebration of Lights (Christmas).

Sports: There are 8 intercollegiate sports for men and 8 for women, and 7 intramural sports for men and 7 for women. Facilities include a 6500-seat stadium, a 1450-seat gym, 10 lighted tennis courts, baseball and softball fields, a track, an indoor pool, a dance studio, a multipurpose building with basketball and volleyball courts, and a wellness center.

Disabled Students: 95% of the campus is accessible. Wheelchair ramps, elevators, special parking, specially equipped rest rooms, special class scheduling, lowered drinking fountains, lowered telephones, and automatic doors are available.

Services: Counseling and information services are available, as is tutoring in most subjects. There is remedial math, reading, and writing and supplemental instruction in courses with high drop/failure rates.

Campus Safety and Security: Measures include 24-hour foot and vehicle patrol, security escort services, informal discussions, and pamphlets/posters/films. There are emergency telephones and lighted pathways/sidewalks.

Programs of Study: SAU confers B.A., B.S., B.A.S., B.B.A., B.M.E., B.S.E., and B.S.W. degrees. Associate and master's degrees are also awarded. Bachelor's degrees are awarded in AGRICULTURE (agricultural business management and agriculture), BIOLOGICAL SCIENCE (biology/biological science), BUSINESS (accounting and business administration and management), COMMUNICATIONS AND THE ARTS (art, broadcasting, communications, English, journalism, and Spanish), COMPUTER AND PHYSICAL SCIENCE (chemistry, computer science, and mathematics), EDUCATION (agricultural, art, business, elementary, health, middle school, music, and science), ENGINEERING AND ENVIRONMENTAL DESIGN (manufacturing technology), HEALTH PROFESSIONS (medical laboratory technology), SOCIAL SCIENCE (community services, history, political science/government, psychology, and sociology). Accounting and physical science are the strongest academically. Business administration and health education/kinesiology are the largest.

Required: All students must complete 43 semester hours of general education courses, including 18 in humanities, 12 in social sciences, 4 each in biological and physical science, 3 in math, and 2 to 3 in physical and health education. A minimum of 124 total semester hours, with a minimum GPA of 2.0, is required to graduate.

Special: Work-study programs at SAU, business and Spanish internships, study abroad in Russia and Mexico, and a general studies degree are offered. There is 1 national honor society, a freshman honors program, and 6 departmental honors programs.

Faculty/Classroom: 56% of faculty are male; 44%, female. 97% teach undergraduates, 10% do research, and 10% do both. No introductory courses are taught by graduate students. The average class size in an introductory lecture is 23; in a laboratory, 18; and in a regular course, 20.

Admissions: 82% of the 2005-2006 applicants were accepted. The ACT scores for the 2005-2006 freshman class were: 54% below 21, 21% between 21 and 23, 15% between 24 and 26, 7% between 27 and 28, and 3% above 28.

Requirements: The ACT is required, with a minimum composite of 19. Applicants should have completed 4 high school units in English, 3 each in math and social studies, and 2 each in natural science and a foreign language. The GED is accepted. AP and CLEP credits are accepted.

Procedure: Freshmen are admitted to all sessions. Entrance exams should be taken in the fall prior to enrollment. There are deferred admissions and rolling admissions plans. Application deadlines are open. Applications are accepted on-line.

Transfer: 184 transfer students enrolled in 2004-2005. Applicants must be eligible to return to their previous school and meet GPA requirements. Those with fewer than 24 credit hours must submit ACT or SAT scores and a high school transcript or GED. 30 of 124 credits required for the bachelor's degree must be completed at SAU.

Visiting: There are regularly scheduled orientations for prospective students. There are guides for informal visits and visitors may sit in on classes and stay overnight. To schedule a visit, contact the Admissions Office.

Financial Aid: In 2005-2006, 85% of all full-time freshmen received some form of financial aid. 49% of undergraduates work part time. The FAFSA is required. The priority date for freshman financial aid applications for fall entry is July 1.

International Students: There are 149 international students enrolled. The school actively recruits these students. They must score satisfactorily on the written TOEFL or on the electronic version and also take the ACT.

Computers: All students may access the system. There are no time limits and no fees.

Graduates: From July 1, 2004 to June 30, 2005, 399 bachelor's degrees were awarded. The most popular majors were business administration (27%), early childhood education (10%), and criminal justice (7%). In an average class, 2% graduate in 3 years or less, 14% graduate in 4 years or less, 11% graduate in 5 years or less, and 35% graduate in 6 years or less.

Admissions Contact: Sarah Jennings, Dean of Enrollment Services. E-mail: *sejennings@saumag.edu* Web: *www.saumag.edu*

UNIVERSITY OF ARKANSAS SYSTEM

The University of Arkansas System, established in 1871, is a system in Arkansas. It is governed by a board of trustees, whose chief administrator is president. The primary goal of the system is teaching, research, and public service. The total enrollment of all 5 campuses is usually about 32,000; there were 2334 faculty members. Altogether there are 236 baccalaureate, 112 master's, and 30 doctoral programs offered in University of Arkansas System. Profiles of the 4-year campuses are included in this section.

UNIVERSITY OF ARKANSAS
A-1

Fayetteville, AR 72701

(479) 575-5346
(800) 377-8632; Fax: (479) 575-7515

Full-time: 5919 men, 5824 women	Faculty: 763; I, --$
Part-time: 1333 men, 1205 women	Ph.D.s: 90%
Graduate: 1817 men, 1723 women	Student/Faculty: 15 to 1
Year: semesters, summer session	Tuition: $5494 ($13,222)
Application Deadline: August 15	Room & Board: $6365
Freshman Class: 6041 applied, 5283 accepted, 2752 enrolled	
SAT Verbal/Math: 570/570*	ACT: 24 VERY COMPETITIVE

The University of Arkansas, founded in 1871, is a land-grant institution offering undergraduate and graduate programs in liberal arts and sciences, agricultural, food, social and natural sciences, life sciences, business administration, engineering, architecture, education, law, and human environmental sciences. There are 8 undergraduate and 2 graduate schools. In addition to regional accreditation, U of A has baccalaureate program accreditation with AACSB, ABET, ACEJMC, ADA, ASLA, CSWE, FIDER, NAAB, NASM, NCATE, and NLN. The 4 libraries contain 1,727,892 volumes, 5,472,437 microform items, and 79,558 audio/video tapes/CDs/DVDs, and subscribe to 18,131 periodicals including electronic. Computerized library services include the card catalog, interlibrary loans, database searching, and Internet access. Special learning facilities include a planetarium, radio station, TV station, and numerous research centers. The 345-acre campus is in an urban area 190 miles northwest of Little Rock. Including any residence halls, there are 130 buildings.

Student Life: 81% of undergraduates are from Arkansas. Others are from 49 states, 100 foreign countries, and Canada. 85% are from public schools. 80% are white. The average age of freshmen is 18; all undergraduates, 22. 19% do not continue beyond their first year; 56% remain to graduate.

Housing: 4000 students can be accommodated in college housing, which includes single-sex and coed dorms, on-campus apartments, married-student housing, fraternity houses, and sorority houses. In addition, there are honors, special interest floors, apartments with dependent children, and a First-year Experience Program area. On-campus housing is available on a first-come, first-served basis. 70% of students commute. All students may keep cars.

Activities: 20% of men belong to 15 national fraternities; 19% of women belong to 10 national sororities. There are 215 groups on campus, including art, band, cheerleading, chess, choir, chorale, chorus, computers, dance, debate, drama, drill team, ethnic, film, gay, honors, international, jazz band, literary magazine, marching band, musical theater, newspaper, opera, orchestra, pep band, photography, political,

professional, radio and TV, religious, social, social service, student government, symphony, and yearbook. Popular campus events include Academic Festival, Native American Pow Wow, and Martin Luther King Jr. Event.

Sports: There are 7 intercollegiate sports for men and 11 for women, and 48 intramural sports for men and 48 for women. Facilities include a 72,000-seat stadium, a 20,000-seat basketball arena, a 3300-seat baseball stadium, a 9000-seat volleyball arena, a 1500-seat soccer stadium, 4 gyms, indoor and outdoor jogging tracks, 2 dance studios, 10 racquetball courts, a fitness and weight training center, a swimming pool, an outdoor recreation center, 20 outdoor and 6 indoor tennis courts, 10 multipurpose playing fields, an indoor practice football field, a 3000-seat indoor running track, a 1500-seat softball stadium, and a gym/weight training and conditioning facility.

Disabled Students: All of the campus is accessible. Wheelchair ramps, elevators, special parking, specially equipped rest rooms, special class scheduling, lowered drinking fountains, lowered telephones, and automatic doors on entrances to buildings are available.

Services: Counseling and information services are available, as is tutoring in some subjects. There is a reader service for the blind, and remedial math, reading, and writing. a math resource center, a writing center, Student Support Services and individual colleges have labs and other facilities.

Campus Safety and Security: Measures include 24-hour foot and vehicle patrol, self-defense education, security escort services, and shuttle buses. There are informal discussions, pamphlets/posters/films, emergency telephones, lighted pathways/sidewalks, crime prevention lectures, a rape defense program, property engraving, bicycle patrol, and electronic card access in residence halls.

Programs of Study: U of A confers B.A., B.S., B.Arch., B.I.D., B.L.A., B.M., B.S.A., B.S.B.A., B.S.B.A.E., B.S.C.E., B.S.Ch.E., B.S.C.S.E., B.S.E., B.S.E.E., B.S.E.M., B.S.H.E.S., B.S.I.B., B.S.I.M., B.S.M.E., B.S.N., and B.S.P.A. degrees. Master's and doctoral degrees are also awarded. Bachelor's degrees are awarded in AGRICULTURE (agricultural business management, agricultural economics, animal science, horticulture, plant protection (pest management), and poultry science), BIOLOGICAL SCIENCE (biology/biological science and nutrition), BUSINESS (accounting, apparel and accessories marketing, banking and finance, business administration and management, business economics, international business management, marketing management, marketing/retailing/merchandising, and transportation management), COMMUNICATIONS AND THE ARTS (art, classics, communications, dramatic arts, English, French, German, journalism, music, Russian, and Spanish), COMPUTER AND PHYSICAL SCIENCE (chemistry, computer science, earth science, geology, mathematics, and physics), EDUCATION (agricultural, early childhood, elementary, middle school, music, recreation, special, and vocational), ENGINEERING AND ENVIRONMENTAL DESIGN (agricultural engineering, architecture, bioengineering, chemical engineering, civil engineering, computer engineering, electrical/electronics engineering, environmental science, industrial engineering, interior design, landscape architecture/design, and mechanical engineering), HEALTH PROFESSIONS (exercise science, health science, medical science, nursing, predentistry, premedicine, preoptometry, prepharmacy, prepodiatry, and speech pathology/audiology), SOCIAL SCIENCE (African American studies, American studies, anthropology, criminal justice, economics, European studies, food science, geography, history, human development, international relations, Latin American studies, Middle Eastern studies, philosophy, political science/government, prelaw, psychology, public administration, social work, and sociology). Business, chemical and electrical engineering, and computer science are the strongest academically. Marketing management, finance, and journalism are the largest.

Required: To graduate, all students must complete 35 hours of general education courses, including 9 in social sciences, 8 in science, 6 in English, and 3 each in fine arts, math, humanities, and history/government. No more than 25% of the minimum total of 124 hours may be D or below.

Special: Co-op programs and internships are available, as well as dual majors and B.A.-B.S. degrees in many majors, and study abroad in 47 countries. There are 3-2 engineering degrees with several universities, a combined medical/dental degree, and a 6-year B.S./J.D. degree for highly qualified students. Non-degree study is possible. There are 36 national honor societies, including Phi Beta Kappa, a freshman honors program, and 84 departmental honors programs.

Faculty/Classroom: 68% of faculty are male; 32%, female. 96% teach undergraduates. Graduate students teach 39% of introductory courses. The average class size in an introductory lecture is 37; in a laboratory, 14; and in a regular course, 25.

Admissions: 87% of the 2005-2006 applicants were accepted. The SAT scores for the 2005-2006 freshman class were: Verbal--20% below 500, 39% between 500 and 599, 32% between 600 and 700, and 9% above 700; Math--18% below 500, 40% between 500 and 599, 33% between 600 and 700, and 9% above 700. The ACT scores were 15% below 21, 28% between 21 and 23, 27% between 24 and 26, 11% between 27 and 28, and 19% above 28. 52% of the current freshmen were in the top fifth of their class; 79% were in the top two fifths. There were 51 National Merit finalists and 7 semifinalists. 126 freshmen graduated first in their class.

Requirements: The SAT or ACT is required. U of A recommends 4 years of English and math and 3 years each of social science and natural science. AP and honors level courses will enhance the applicant's opportunity for admission. A GPA of 3.0 is required. AP and CLEP credits are accepted. Important factors in the admissions decision are advanced placement or honor courses, leadership record, and evidence of special talent.

Procedure: Freshmen are admitted fall, spring, and summer. Entrance exams should be taken in the junior year or in October or December of the senior year. There are early admissions, deferred admissions, and rolling admissions plans. Early decision applications should be filed by February 15; regular applications, by August 15 for fall entry and January 1 for spring entry. Notification of early decision is sent December 15; regular decision, on a rolling basis. Applications are accepted on-line. The fall 2005 application fee was $40.

Transfer: 1240 transfer students enrolled in 2004-2005. Applicants must present a GPA of 2.0 on all college course work attempted and be in good standing at the last institution attended. Those with fewer than 24 transferable semester credits must meet the requirements of entering freshmen. 30 of 124 credits required for the bachelor's degree must be completed at U of A.

Visiting: There are regularly scheduled orientations for prospective students, consisting of individual or group campus tours, meetings with an academic adviser, residence hall tours, and a meeting with an admissions counselor. Appointments are recommended, but not required. There are guides for informal visits and visitors may sit in on classes. To schedule a visit, contact the Admissions Office at 1 (800) 377-UofA.

Financial Aid: In 2004-2005, 71% of all full-time freshmen and 70% of continuing full-time students received some form of financial aid. 71% of full-time freshmen and 67% of continuing full-time students received need-based aid. The average freshman award was $9174. Need-based scholarships or need-based grants averaged $4003 ($8150 maximum); need-based self-help aid (loans and jobs) averaged $3243 ($8625 maximum); non-need-based athletic scholarships averaged $9031 ($12,241 maximum); and other non-need-based awards and non-need-based scholarships averaged $5860 ($19,525 maximum). 12% of undergraduates work part time. Average annual earnings from campus work are $1160. The average financial indebtedness of the 2005 graduate was $18,734. The FAFSA is required. The deadline for filing freshman financial aid applications for fall entry is March 1.

International Students: There are 888 international students enrolled. The school actively recruits these students. They must score satisfactorily on the written TOEFL or on the electronic version and also take the SAT or ACT. Electrical engineering and computer systems engineering require a satisfactory score on the SAT on the ACT and on the TSE. Check with the school for details.

Computers: Wireless access is available. There are 7 general access computer labs with a total of 165 PCs. Wireless Internet is available in designated areas. All students may access the system 24 hours daily. There are no time limits and no fees.

Graduates: From July 1, 2004 to June 30, 2005, 3414 bachelor's degrees were awarded. The most popular majors were marketing (7%), finance (5%), and journalism (5%). In an average class, 33% graduate in 4 years or less, 50% graduate in 5 years or less, and 56% graduate in 6 years or less. 210 companies recruited on campus in 2004-2005. Of the 2004 graduating class, 35% were enrolled in graduate school within 6 months of graduation and 25% were employed.

Admissions Contact: Dawn Medley, Director. A video is available. Web: *http://www.uark.edu*

UNIVERSITY OF ARKANSAS AT LITTLE ROCK   C-3
Little Rock, AR 72204-1099   **(501) 569-3492**
                                        (800) 482-8892; Fax: (501) 569-8956

Full-time: 2150 men, 3300 women	**Faculty:** IIA, -$
Part-time: 1350 men, 2400 women	**Ph.D.s:** 45%
Graduate: 500 men, 1250 women	**Student/Faculty:** n/av
Year: semesters, summer session	**Tuition:** $4230 ($11,100)
Application Deadline: open	**Room & Board:** $3000
Freshman Class: n/av	
SAT or ACT: required	**NONCOMPETITIVE**

The University of Arkansas at Little Rock began in 1927 as Little Rock Junior College, took the name of Little Rock University in 1957, and joined the University of Arkansas system in 1969. There are 5 undergraduate and 2 graduate schools. Some figures in the capsule and in the profile are approximate. In addition to regional accreditation, UALR has baccalaureate program accreditation with AACSB, ABET, ACEJMC, ASLA, CSWE, NASAD, NASM, NCATE, and NLN. The library contains 394,780 volumes, 691,612 microform items, and 8300 audio/video tapes/CDs/DVDs, and subscribes to 2626 periodicals including electronic. Computerized library services include the card catalog, interlibrary

loans, and database searching. Special learning facilities include a learning resource center, art gallery, planetarium, radio station, TV station, and a speech and hearing clinic. The 150-acre campus is in an urban area in Little Rock. Including any residence halls, there are 38 buildings.

Student Life: 93% of undergraduates are from Arkansas. Others are from 44 states, 62 foreign countries, and Canada. 70% are white; 24% African American. The average age of freshmen is 19; all undergraduates, 26. 41% do not continue beyond their first year.

Housing: 306 students can be accommodated in college housing, which includes coed dorms and on-campus apartments. On-campus housing is available on a first-come, first-served basis. 97% of students commute. Alcohol is not permitted. All students may keep cars.

Activities: 5% of men belong to 6 national fraternities; 3% of women belong to 6 national sororities. There are 75 groups on campus, including cheerleading, chess, chorale, dance, drama, honors, jazz band, literary magazine, musical theater, newspaper, opera, pep band, political, professional, radio and TV, religious, social service, and student government. Popular campus events include International Week, Sunshine Days, and Art Spree.

Sports: There are 6 intercollegiate sports for men and 7 for women, and 18 intramural sports for men and 18 for women. Facilities include a 2000-seat gym, a swimming pool, tennis courts, baseball and intramural fields, a horseshoe pit, a bowling alley, a fitness and weight room, an indoor jogging track, basketball, volleyball, and racquetball courts, a steam room, and a sauna.

Disabled Students: 85% of the campus is accessible. Wheelchair ramps, elevators, special parking, specially equipped rest rooms, special class scheduling, lowered drinking fountains, and study rooms are available.

Services: Counseling and information services are available, as is tutoring in every subject. There is a reader service for the blind, and remedial math, reading, and writing. Also available are a braille dictionary, typewriter, reading machine, and interpreters.

Campus Safety and Security: Measures include 24-hour foot and vehicle patrol, self-defense education, security escort services, and informal discussions. There are emergency telephones, lighted pathways/sidewalks, emergency phones, and a student patrol crime prevention unit.

Programs of Study: UALR confers B.A., B.S., B.B.A., and B.S.W. degrees. Associate, master's, and doctoral degrees are also awarded. Bachelor's degrees are awarded in BIOLOGICAL SCIENCE (biology/biological science), BUSINESS (accounting, banking and finance, business administration and management, management science, and marketing/retailing/merchandising), COMMUNICATIONS AND THE ARTS (advertising, art, art history and appreciation, dramatic arts, English, French, journalism, music, radio/television technology, Spanish, technical and business writing, and visual and performing arts), COMPUTER AND PHYSICAL SCIENCE (chemistry, computer science, geology, information sciences and systems, mathematics, and physics), EDUCATION (early childhood, education of the deaf and hearing impaired, elementary, and health), ENGINEERING AND ENVIRONMENTAL DESIGN (computer technology, construction technology, electrical/electronics engineering technology, industrial administration/management, manufacturing engineering, mechanical engineering technology, and surveying engineering), HEALTH PROFESSIONS (environmental health science, health science, and speech pathology/audiology), SOCIAL SCIENCE (criminal justice, economics, history, international studies, interpreter for the deaf, liberal arts/general studies, philosophy, political science/government, psychology, and sociology). Psychology, biology, and liberal arts are the largest.

Required: All students must complete a minimum of 124 credit hours, including 45 at the upper level, while maintaining a GPA of 2.0. A minimum 44-hour core curriculum must be completed, and distribution requirements include freshman composition, speech and history, 3 hours of math, and 2 hours of leisure science. Each student must complete a major and a minor or a double major. There also is an exam in written English. Language proficiency is required for the B.A. degree.

Special: Study abroad in Mexico, France, Spain, and Austria is available; UALR has exchange relationships with more than 30 countries. In addition, internships, work-study programs with the university, cross-registration with the University of Arkansas Medical School, B.A.-B.S. degrees, a general studies degree, student-designed majors, nondegree study, and pass/fail options are offered. There are 3 national honor societies, including Phi Beta Kappa, a freshman honors program, and 5 departmental honors programs.

Faculty/Classroom: 53% of faculty are male; 47%, female.

Requirements: The SAT or ACT is required. In addition, 2 or more of the following criteria must be met: a high school GPA of at least 2.5 or a passing GED test score; an ACT composite score of at least 21 or a satisfactory combined verbal/math SAT score taken within the past 5 years; completion of a college preparatory core in high school that includes 4 units of English, 3 each of math and social studies, and 2 each of natural science and a single foreign language. Students with test subscores below the state minimum requirement will be placed in the appropriate development courses. A GPA of 2.5 is required. AP and CLEP credits are accepted.

Procedure: Freshmen are admitted to all sessions. Entrance exams should be taken during the fall of the senior year. There are early admissions, deferred admissions and rolling admissions plans. Application deadlines are open. Check with the school for current application fee.

Transfer: 939 transfer students enrolled in recent year. Applicants must have a minimum college GPA of 2.0. They must submit official transcripts from each college previously attended. Students who have 12 or fewer acceptable transfer credits must meet all the admission requirements for entering freshmen. 30 of 124 credits required for the bachelor's degree must be completed at UALR.

Visiting: There are regularly scheduled orientations for prospective students, which take place before each semester and at which attendance is required. There are guides for informal visits and visitors may sit in on classes. To schedule a visit, contact the Admissions Office.

Financial Aid: The FAFSA is required. Check with the school for current deadlines.

International Students: They must score satisfactorily on the written TOEFL and also take the college's own test, Test of Written English (TWE), with a score of at least 4 points.

Computers: All students may access the system 24 hours daily. There are no time limits and no fees.

Admissions Contact: John Noah, Director.
Web: *www.ualr.edu/~adminfo/*

UNIVERSITY OF ARKANSAS AT MONTICELLO   C-4
Monticello, AR 71656-3596   (870) 460-1026
(800) 844-1826; Fax: (870) 460-1933

Full-time: 949 men, 1274 women	**Faculty:** n/av
Part-time: 215 men, 473 women	**Ph.D.s:** 60%
Graduate: 16 men, 32 women	**Student/Faculty:** 19 to 1
Year: semesters, summer session	**Tuition:** $3905 ($7655)
Application Deadline: open	**Room & Board:** $3420
Freshman Class: n/av	
SAT or ACT: required	**NONCOMPETITIVE**

The University of Arkansas at Monticello was established in 1909 as the Fourth District Agricultural School. Made part of the public University of Arkansas System in 1971, UAM offers liberal arts undergraduate courses and graduate programs. There are 13 undergraduate and 2 graduate schools. In addition to regional accreditation, UAM has baccalaureate program accreditation with CSWE, NASM, NCATE, NLN, and SAF. The library contains 146,000 volumes, 221,000 microform items, and 640 audio/video tapes/CDs/DVDs, and subscribes to 1140 periodicals including electronic. Computerized library services include the card catalog, interlibrary loans, and database searching. Special learning facilities include a learning resource center, natural history museum, planetarium, a university forest, and a university farm. The 1556-acre campus is in a small town 90 miles south of Little Rock. Including any residence halls, there are 37 buildings.

Student Life: 90% of undergraduates are from Arkansas. Others are from 27 states, 4 foreign countries, and Canada. 99% are from public schools. 68% are white; 29% African American. The average age of freshmen is 22; all undergraduates, 24. 57% do not continue beyond their first year; 26% remain to graduate.

Housing: 800 students can be accommodated in college housing, which includes single-sex dorms, on-campus apartments, and married-student housing. On-campus housing is guaranteed for all 4 years. 82% of students commute. Alcohol is not permitted. All students may keep cars.

Activities: 5% of men belong to 8 national fraternities; 3% of women belong to 5 national sororities. There are 63 groups on campus, including art, band, cheerleading, chess, choir, chorus, debate, ethnic, honors, jazz band, literary magazine, marching band, musical theater, newspaper, political, religious, social, social service, student government, and yearbook. Popular campus events include Forestry Festival, Special Olympics, and Greek Week.

Sports: There are 5 intercollegiate sports for men and 5 for women, and 20 intramural sports for men and 20 for women. Facilities include a 4000-seat stadium, a 2500-seat gym, a swimming pool, baseball and softball fields, tennis and racquetball courts, and facilities for numerous intramural sports.

Disabled Students: All of the campus is accessible. Wheelchair ramps, elevators, special parking, specially equipped rest rooms, special class scheduling, lowered drinking fountains, lowered telephones, extended test times, books on tape, note takers, quiet test facilities, and word processing assistance are available.

Services: Counseling and information services are available, as is tutoring in some subjects, including general education. There is a reader service for the blind, and remedial math, reading, and writing.

Campus Safety and Security: Measures include 24-hour foot and vehicle patrol, informal discussions, pamphlets/posters/films, and emergency telephones. There are lighted pathways/sidewalks.

Programs of Study: UAM confers B.A., B.S., B.B.A., B.S.N., and B.S.W degrees. Associate and master's degrees are also awarded. Bachelor's degrees are awarded in AGRICULTURE (agriculture, forestry and related sciences, and wildlife management), BIOLOGICAL SCIENCE (biology/biological science), BUSINESS (accounting, business administration and management, and management information systems), COMMUNICATIONS AND THE ARTS (art, English, journalism, music, and speech/debate/rhetoric), COMPUTER AND PHYSICAL SCIENCE (chemistry, geodetic science, information sciences and systems, mathematics, and physical sciences), EDUCATION (early childhood, health, middle school, music, and physical), HEALTH PROFESSIONS (exercise science and nursing), SOCIAL SCIENCE (criminal justice, history, political science/government, psychology, and social work). Forestry and sciences are the strongest academically. Nursing, business administration, and P-4 early childhood special education are the largest.

Required: All students are required to complete 124 total semester hours, approximately 30 within their major, and maintain a minimum GPA of 2.0 (2.75 in education). Distribution requirements include 11 hours in basic sciences, 6 hours each in composition and humanities, and 3 hours each in fine arts, speech, U.S. history or government, psychology or sociology, social science, and math.

Special: A general studies degree, cross-registration within the University of Arkansas system, credit for military experience, dual majors, and nondegree study are available. There is 1 national honor society.

Faculty/Classroom: 65% of faculty are male; 35%, female. All teach undergraduates and 11% do research. No introductory courses are taught by graduate students. The average class size in an introductory lecture is 27; in a laboratory, 15; and in a regular course, 20.

Requirements: The SAT or ACT is required. In addition, a high school diploma or GED is required. The Arkansas high school core curriculum is recommended. State law requires proof of immunization. AP and CLEP credits are accepted.

Procedure: Freshmen are admitted to all sessions. Entrance exams should be taken by December of the senior year. There is an early admissions plan and a rolling admissions plan. Application deadlines are open. Applications are accepted on-line.

Transfer: 282 transfer students enrolled in 2004-2005. Transfer students must be in good academic standing at the previous college. ACT or SAT test scores are required only if the student has not successfully completed Freshman Composition I and College Math. 30 of 124 credits required for the bachelor's degree must be completed at UAM.

Visiting: There are regularly scheduled orientations for prospective students, including a review of admission requirements and financial aid opportunities and a visit to academic departments and faculty in the field of interest. There are guides for informal visits and visitors may sit in on classes and stay overnight. To schedule a visit, contact the Office of Admissions.

Financial Aid: In 2005-2006, 87% of all full-time freshmen and 81% of continuing full-time students received some form of financial aid. 65% of full-time freshmen and 59% of continuing full-time students received need-based aid. The average freshman award was $5806. 13% of undergraduates work part time. Average annual earnings from campus work are $1476. The average financial indebtedness of the 2005 graduate was $11,000. UAM is a member of CSS. The FAFSA is required. The deadline for filing freshman financial aid applications for fall entry is June 1.

International Students: There are 18 international students enrolled. They must take the TOEFL and also take the SAT or the ACT.

Computers: All students may access the system. There are no time limits and no fees. It is strongly recommended that all students have a personal computer.

Graduates: From July 1, 2004 to June 30, 2005, 307 bachelor's degrees were awarded. The most popular majors were business administration (19%), computer information systems (11%), and nursing (10%). In an average class, 11% graduate in 4 years or less, 21% graduate in 5 years or less, and 26% graduate in 6 years or less.

Admissions Contact: Mary Whiting, Director of Admissions. A video is available. E-mail: *whitingm@uamont.edu* Web: *www.uamont.edu*

UNIVERSITY OF ARKANSAS AT PINE BLUFF   C-4
Pine Bluff, AR 71601-2799   (870) 575-8492
(800) 264-6585; Fax: (870) 543-8014

Full-time: 1250 men, 1500 women	**Faculty:** 171; IIB, --$
Part-time: 125 men, 200 women	**Ph.D.s:** 57%
Graduate: 25 men, 70 women	**Student/Faculty:** 16 to 1
Year: semesters, summer session	**Tuition:** $3300 ($6600)
Application Deadline: see profile	**Room & Board:** $5000
Freshman Class: n/av	
SAT or ACT: required	**COMPETITIVE**

The University of Arkansas at Pine Bluff, established in 1873, is a historically black land-grant institution providing a liberal arts education as part of the public University of Arkansas system. There are 5 undergraduate schools and 1 graduate school. Figures in the above capsule and in this profile are approximate. In addition to regional accreditation, UAPB has baccalaureate program accreditation with AHEA, CSWE, NASM, NCATE, and NLN. The library contains 271,547 volumes, 119,205 microform items, and 4299 audio/video tapes/CDs/DVDs, and subscribes to 1050 periodicals including electronic. Computerized library services include the card catalog, interlibrary loans, and database searching. Special learning facilities include a learning resource center, art gallery, radio station, and TV station. The 318-acre campus is in a small town 40 miles southeast of Little Rock and approximately 142 miles southwest of Memphis. Including any residence halls, there are 49 buildings.

Student Life: 80% of undergraduates are from Arkansas. Others are from 28 states, 17 foreign countries, and Canada. 94% are African American. The average age of freshmen is 18; all undergraduates, 23% do not continue beyond their first year.

Housing: 1099 students can be accommodated in college housing, which includes single-sex dorms. On-campus housing is guaranteed for all 4 years. 65% of students commute. Alcohol is not permitted. All students may keep cars.

Activities: There are 4 local and 4 national fraternities and 4 local and 4 national sororities. There are 65 groups on campus, including art, band, cheerleading, choir, computers, drama, drill team, honors, jazz band, marching band, newspaper, orchestra, photography, political, professional, radio and TV, religious, social, social service, student government, and yearbook. Popular campus events include Founders Day, Spring Emphasis, and Unity Fest.

Sports: There are 7 intercollegiate sports for men and 8 for women, and 20 intramural sports for men and 19 for women. Facilities include a phys ed complex that provides activities such as flag football, basketball, volleyball, softball, tennis, handball, racquetball, track and field, and badminton. There is also a swimming pool and a 6000-seat football stadium.

Disabled Students: 98% of the campus is accessible. Wheelchair ramps, elevators, special parking, specially equipped rest rooms, special class scheduling, lowered drinking fountains, and lowered telephones are available.

Services: Counseling and information services are available, as is tutoring in most subjects. There is a reader service for the blind, and remedial math, reading, and writing.

Campus Safety and Security: Measures include 24-hour foot and vehicle patrol, self-defense education, security escort services, and informal discussions. There are pamphlets/posters/films, emergency telephones, lighted pathways/sidewalks, and a department of public safety and security on campus.

Programs of Study: UAPB confers B.A. and B.S. degrees. Associate and master's degrees are also awarded. Bachelor's degrees are awarded in AGRICULTURE (agriculture, conservation and regulation, and fishing and fisheries), BIOLOGICAL SCIENCE (biology/biological science), BUSINESS (accounting and business administration and management), COMMUNICATIONS AND THE ARTS (art, English, journalism, music, and speech/debate/rhetoric), COMPUTER AND PHYSICAL SCIENCE (applied mathematics, chemistry, computer science, mathematics, and physics), EDUCATION (agricultural, art, business, early childhood, English, home economics, industrial arts, mathematics, middle school, music, physical, science, social science, and special), ENGINEERING AND ENVIRONMENTAL DESIGN (industrial engineering technology and preengineering), HEALTH PROFESSIONS (nursing, predentistry, premedicine, prepharmacy, and rehabilitation therapy), SOCIAL SCIENCE (criminal justice, family/consumer studies, gerontology, history, liberal arts/general studies, parks and recreation management, political science/government, psychology, social work, and sociology). Business administration, biology and computer science are the strongest academically and are the largest.

Required: All students must complete at least 124 hours of credit, including 30 hours in their major, while earning an overall 2.0 GPA (2.5 for teacher education majors) and a C or better in all major courses. Distribution requirements include English, math, social and natural science, and phys ed courses. Students must pass a comprehensive exam in their major.

Special: The university offers formal co-op education and work-study programs, concurrent registration with members of the University of Arkansas system, internships, B.A.-B.S. degrees, and dual and student-designed majors. Also offered are credit for military experience, nondegree study, individualized programs of study for honors college students, and study abroad. There are 4 national honor societies, a freshman honors program, and 6 departmental honors programs.

Faculty/Classroom: 54% of faculty are male; 46%, female. The average class size in a laboratory is 20 and in a regular course, 21.

Requirements: The SAT or ACT is required. The ACT is preferred. Applicants must have earned 15 credits, including 4 units of English and 3 each in social studies, math, and science. The GED is accepted. Students not meeting these requirements may apply for conditional admission. A GPA of 2.0 is required. AP and CLEP credits are accepted.

Procedure: Freshmen are admitted fall, spring, and summer. Entrance exams should be taken during the junior or senior year. There are early

admissions, deferred admissions and rolling admissions plans. Notification is sent on a rolling basis. Check with the school for current application deadline and fee.

Transfer: Transfer students must have a minimum GPA of 2.0. Applicants with fewer than 60 semester hours of college credit must submit an application, ACT or SAT scores, and all college transcripts. 30 of 124 credits required for the bachelor's degree must be completed at UAPB.

Visiting: There are regularly scheduled orientations for prospective students. There are guides for informal visits and visitors may sit in on classes and stay overnight. To schedule a visit, contact the Director of Recruitment at (501) 575-8961 or (800) 525-5272.

Financial Aid: UAPB is a member of CSS. The FAFSA is required.

International Students: They must score satisfactorily on the written TOEFL and also take the SAT/ ACT. The ACT, with a minimum score of 19, is preferred. SAT scores may be used.

Computers: All students may access the system 7 A.M. to 11 P.M. Monday through Friday, and during special weekend hours. There are no time limits. There is a $15 laboratory fee.

Graduates: In an average class, 1% graduate in 3 years or less, 9% graduate in 4 years or less, 20% graduate in 5 years or less, and 26% graduate in 6 years or less.

Admissions Contact: Erica Fulton, Director of Admissions and Academic Records. E-mail: *fulton_e@4500.uabb.edu* Web: *www.uapb.edu*

UNIVERSITY OF CENTRAL ARKANSAS   C-3

Conway, AR 72035-0001	(501) 450-3128; (800) 243-8245
Full-time: 3812 men, 5315 women	Faculty: IIA, --$
Part-time: 318 men, 524 women	Ph.D.s: 60%
Graduate: 586 men, 820 women	Student/Faculty: n/av
Year: semesters, summer session	Tuition: $5664 ($10,164)
Application Deadline: August 1	Room & Board: $4320
Freshman Class: 5830 applied, 3966 accepted, 2503 enrolled	
SAT Verbal/Math: 490/515*	ACT: 23 COMPETITIVE

The University of Central Arkansas, established in 1907, is a comprehensive public institution offering undergraduate and graduate degrees in liberal arts, business, health-related sciences, and education. There are 7 undergraduate schools and 1 graduate school. In addition to regional accreditation, UCA has baccalaureate program accreditation with AACSB, ADA, APTA, CAHEA, NASAD, NASM, NCATE, and NLN. The library contains 434,099 volumes, 909,589 microform items, and 2500 audio/video tapes/CDs/DVDs, and subscribes to 15,298 periodicals including electronic. Computerized library services include the card catalog, interlibrary loans, database searching, Internet access, and laptop Internet portals. Special learning facilities include a learning resource center, art gallery, planetarium, radio station, and TV station. The 262-acre campus is in a small town 29 miles north of Little Rock. Including any residence halls, there are 53 buildings.

Student Life: 93% of undergraduates are from Arkansas. Others are from 42 states, 55 foreign countries, and Canada. 96% are from public schools. 74% are white; 16% African American. The average age of freshmen is 19; all undergraduates, 23. 30% do not continue beyond their first year; 37% remain to graduate.

Housing: 3860 students can be accommodated in college housing, which includes single-sex and coed dorms, on-campus apartments, off-campus apartments, and married-student housing. In addition, there are honors houses and an international students' residence hall. On-campus housing is guaranteed for all 4 years and is available on a first-come, first-served basis. 75% of students commute. Alcohol is not permitted. All students may keep cars.

Activities: 10% of men belong to 12 national fraternities; 10% of women belong to 7 national sororities. There are 95 groups on campus, including art, band, cheerleading, choir, chorale, chorus, dance, drama, ethnic, gay, honors, international, jazz band, literary magazine, marching band, musical theater, newspaper, orchestra, pep band, photography, political, professional, radio and TV, religious, social, social service, student government, symphony, and yearbook. Popular campus events include Bear Facts Day.

Sports: There are 6 intercollegiate sports for men and 7 for women, and 18 intramural sports for men and 18 for women. Facilities include a gym, a swimming pool, a fitness center, racquetball and tennis courts, a track, and soccer fields.

Disabled Students: 98% of the campus is accessible. Wheelchair ramps, elevators, special parking, specially equipped rest rooms, special class scheduling, lowered drinking fountains, lowered telephones, and special dorm rooms are available.

Services: Counseling and information services are available, as is tutoring in some subjects. There is a reader service for the blind, and remedial math, reading, and writing.

Campus Safety and Security: Measures include 24-hour foot and vehicle patrol, security escort services, informal discussions, and pamphlets/posters/films. There are emergency telephones, lighted pathways/sidewalks, and security checkpoints.

Programs of Study: UCA confers B.A., B.S., B.B.A., B.M., B.M.E., and B.S.E. degrees. Associate, master's, and doctoral degrees are also awarded. Bachelor's degrees are awarded in BIOLOGICAL SCIENCE (biology/biological science), BUSINESS (accounting, banking and finance, business administration and management, business economics, insurance and risk management, and marketing/retailing/merchandising), COMMUNICATIONS AND THE ARTS (communications, English, French, journalism, music, Spanish, and speech/debate/rhetoric), COMPUTER AND PHYSICAL SCIENCE (chemistry, computer science, information sciences and systems, mathematics, and physics), EDUCATION (art, athletic training, early childhood, education of the exceptional child, elementary, foreign languages, guidance, library science, middle school, music, physical, science, secondary, and special), ENGINEERING AND ENVIRONMENTAL DESIGN (environmental science, interior design, and preengineering), HEALTH PROFESSIONS (exercise science, health care administration, health science, medical technology, nuclear medical technology, nursing, occupational therapy, physical therapy, predentistry, premedicine, preoptometry, prepharmacy, preveterinary science, radiological science, and speech pathology/audiology), SOCIAL SCIENCE (dietetics, economics, family/consumer studies, geography, gerontology, history, philosophy, political science/government, psychology, public administration, religion, and sociology). Business, health-related sciences, and education are the strongest academically. Business and health-related sciences are the largest.

Required: All students must earn a minimum of 124 semester hours, including 40 in upper-division courses. Distribution requirements include 7 hours in science, and 6 hours each in the humanities and social sciences. A minimum GPA of 2.25 is needed for the B.B.A., 2.5 for most education programs. Minimum requirements also include 2 semester hours in phys ed.

Special: Study abroad, work-study programs, a B.S.-B.A. degree, a 3-2 engineering degree with Arkansas State University, dual majors, nondegree study, and pass/fail options are available. Co-op programs in business, computer science, and health sciences and internships in education are also possible. There are 18 national honor societies, a freshman honors program, and 25 departmental honors programs.

Faculty/Classroom: 48% of faculty are male; 52%, female. No introductory courses are taught by graduate students. The average class size in a laboratory is 20 and in a regular course, 34.

Admissions: 68% of the 2005-2006 applicants were accepted. The SAT scores for the 2005-2006 freshman class were: Verbal--57% below 500, 33% between 500 and 599, and 10% between 600 and 700; Math--38% below 500, 38% between 500 and 599, and 24% between 600 and 700. The ACT scores were 32% below 21, 20% between 21 and 23, 20% between 24 and 26, 15% between 27 and 28, and 13% above 28. 40% of the current freshmen were in the top fifth of their class; 67% were in the top two fifths.

Requirements: The SAT or ACT is required. The GED is accepted. UCA requires applicants to be in the upper 33% of their class. A GPA of 3.0 is required. AP and CLEP credits are accepted. Important factors in the admissions decision are advanced placement or honor courses, evidence of special talent, and recommendations by school officials.

Procedure: Freshmen are admitted to all sessions. Applications should be filed by August 1 for fall entry and December 15 for spring entry. There is a rolling admissions plan. Notification is sent on a rolling basis.

Transfer: 1082 transfer students enrolled in 2004-2005. Applicants need, on UCA's scale, a minimum cumulative GPA of 2.0. 24 of 124 credits required for the bachelor's degree must be completed at UCA.

Visiting: There are regularly scheduled orientations for prospective students, including tours at 11 A.M. and 2 P.M.; departments and dormitories may be visited. There are also special visitation days that include a campus tour, departmental session, lunch, parents' session, optional residence hall tour, and classroom visit or planetarium show. Visitors may sit in on classes. To schedule a visit, contact the Admissions Office.

Financial Aid: 10% of undergraduates work part time. The FAFSA is required. The deadline for filing freshman financial aid applications for fall entry is April 15.

International Students: The school actively recruits these students. They must score satisfactorily on the written TOEFL or on the electronic version.

Computers: Wireless access is available. All students may access the system. There are no time limits and no fees. It is strongly recommended that all students have a personal computer.

Graduates: From July 1, 2004 to June 30, 2005, 1198 bachelor's degrees were awarded. The most popular majors were family and consumer sciences (8%), health sciences (6%), and computer information systems (6%).

Admissions Contact: Director of Admissions.
E-mail: *admissions@uca.edu* Web: *http://www.uca.edu*

Full-time: 282 men, 306 women	**Faculty:** 44; IIB, --$
Part-time: 13 men, 27 women	**Ph.D.s:** 82%
Graduate: none	**Student/Faculty:** 13 to 1
Year: semesters, summer session	**Tuition:** $14,170
Application Deadline: April 1	**Room & Board:** $5080
Freshman Class: 632 applied, 530 accepted, 170 enrolled	
SAT Verbal/Math: 545/520*	**ACT:** 22 **COMPETITIVE**

The University of the Ozarks, founded in 1834, is a private, comprehensive liberal arts institution affiliated with the Presbyterian Church (U.S.A.). There are 4 undergraduate schools. In addition to regional accreditation, Ozarks has baccalaureate program accreditation with IACBE and NCATE. The library contains 69,960 volumes, 6927 microform items, and 2955 audio/video tapes/CDs/DVDs, and subscribes to 611 periodicals including electronic. Computerized library services include the card catalog, interlibrary loans, database searching, and Internet access. Special learning facilities include a learning resource center, art gallery, radio station, TV station, and the Jones Learning Center for students with diagnosed learning disabilities. The 35-acre campus is in a small town 100 miles northwest of Little Rock. Including any residence halls, there are 16 buildings.

Student Life: 54% of undergraduates are from Arkansas. Others are from 19 states, 220 foreign countries, and Canada. 92% are from public schools. 69% are white; 14% foreign nationals. 55% are Protestant; 28% claim no religious affiliation; 15% Catholic. The average age of freshmen is 19; all undergraduates, 21. 36% do not continue beyond their first year.

Housing: 550 students can be accommodated in college housing, which includes single-sex and coed dorms. On-campus housing is guaranteed for the freshman year only and is available on a first-come, first-served basis. Priority is given to out-of-town students. 64% of students live on campus; of those, 51% remain on campus on weekends. Alcohol is not permitted. All students may keep cars.

Activities: There are no fraternities or sororities. There are 30 groups on campus, including art, cheerleading, choir, chorale, chorus, dance, debate, drama, film, forensics, honors, international, literary magazine, newspaper, political, professional, radio and TV, religious, social, social service, and student government. Popular campus events include International Fair and Banquet, Family Weekend, and Freshman Matriculation Ceremony.

Sports: There are 5 intercollegiate sports for men and 5 for women, and 6 intramural sports for men and 5 for women. Facilities include a sports complex housing racquetball courts, a pool, and a 2200-seat basketball arena. In addition, there are softball, soccer, and baseball fields, tennis courts, and a 700-seat soccer stadium.

Disabled Students: 90% of the campus is accessible. Elevators, special parking, specially equipped rest rooms, special class scheduling, and lowered drinking fountains are available.

Services: Counseling and information services are available, as is tutoring in every subject. There is remedial math, reading, and writing.

Campus Safety and Security: Measures include 24-hour foot and vehicle patrol, informal discussions, emergency telephones, and lighted pathways/sidewalks.

Programs of Study: Ozarks confers B.A., B.S., and B.G.S. degrees. Bachelor's degrees are awarded in BIOLOGICAL SCIENCE (biology/biological science), BUSINESS (accounting, business administration and management, and marketing/retailing/merchandising), COMMUNICATIONS AND THE ARTS (art, communications, dramatic arts, English, and music), COMPUTER AND PHYSICAL SCIENCE (chemistry and mathematics), EDUCATION (business, early childhood, middle school, and physical), ENGINEERING AND ENVIRONMENTAL DESIGN (environmental science and materials science), HEALTH PROFESSIONS (respiratory therapy), SOCIAL SCIENCE (economics, history, liberal arts/general studies, political science/government, psychology, religion, social science, and sociology). Chemistry, English, and business are the strongest academically. Business and biology are the largest.

Required: Students are required to earn 124 hours, with 30 to 54 in the major, and maintain a minimum GPA of 2.0. Distribution requirements include 9 hours in civic awareness and social science, 7 to 10 hours in math and science, 4 hours in phys ed and wellness, 3 hours in literature, fine arts, and religion, and up to 6 hours in global awareness.

Special: Internships, study abroad in 8 countries including Japan, numerous work-study programs, dual majors, a general studies degree, and a 3-2 engineering degree with the University of Arkansas are available. There are 3 national honor societies.

Faculty/Classroom: 67% of faculty are male; 33%, female. All teach undergraduates. The average class size in an introductory lecture is 17; in a laboratory, 20; and in a regular course, 12.

Admissions: 84% of the 2005-2006 applicants were accepted. The SAT scores for the 2005-2006 freshman class were: Verbal--10% below

500, 75% between 500 and 599, 10% between 600 and 700, and 5% above 700; Math--52% below 500, 29% between 500 and 599, 18% between 600 and 700, and 1% above 700. The ACT scores were 34% below 21, 37% between 21 and 23, 16% between 24 and 26, 7% between 27 and 28, and 6% above 28. 31% of the current freshmen were in the top fifth of their class; 66% were in the top two fifths. There was 1 National Merit finalist and 4 semifinalists. 7 freshmen graduated first in their class.

Requirements: The SAT or ACT is required with a satisfactory score. An interview is recommended. The GED is accepted. A GPA of 2.0 is required. AP and CLEP credits are accepted. Important factors in the admissions decision are personality/intangible qualities, advanced placement or honor courses, and evidence of special talent.

Procedure: Freshmen are admitted to all sessions. Entrance exams should be taken as early as possible. There is a deferred admissions plan and a rolling admissions plan. Applications should be filed by April 1 for fall entry and December 1 for spring entry. Notification is sent on a rolling basis. Applications are accepted on-line. The fall 2005 application fee was $10.

Transfer: 34 transfer students enrolled in 2004-2005. A GPA of 2.0 and college transcripts are required. Applicants with a GPA of less than 2.0 or fewer than 30 hours of college work must furnish high school transcripts and ACT or SAT results. 30 of 124 credits required for the bachelor's degree must be completed at Ozarks.

Visiting: There are regularly scheduled orientations for prospective students, including a campus tour and meetings with faculty and students, admissions, and financial aid. In most cases, prospective students may meet with the president and coaches as requested. There are guides for informal visits and visitors may sit in on classes and stay overnight. To schedule a visit, contact the Admissions Office at *admiss@ozarks.edu.*

Financial Aid: In a recent year, 82% of all full-time freshmen and 92% of continuing full-time students received some form of financial aid. 48% of full-time freshmen and 50% of continuing full-time students received need-based aid. The average recent freshman award was $11,000. Need-based scholarships or need-based grants averaged $10,400 ($20,000 maximum); need-based self-help aid (loans and jobs) averaged $5349 ($7300 maximum); and other non-need-based awards and non-need-based scholarships averaged $11,237. 43% of undergraduates work part time. Average annual earnings from campus work are $1700. The average financial indebtedness of a recent graduate was $13,900. The FAFSA is required. The priority date for freshman financial aid applications for fall entry is February 15.

International Students: There are 101 international students enrolled. The school actively recruits these students. They must take the TOEFL and also take the MELAB, the Comprehensive English Language Test, or the college's own test.

Computers: There are 11 labs containing 150 computers. All students may access the system. There are no time limits. The fee is $100. It is strongly recommended that all students have a personal computer.

Graduates: From July 1, 2004 to June 30, 2005, 118 bachelor's degrees were awarded. The most popular majors were business administration/management (21%), marketing (13%), and political science (10%). In an average class, 32% graduate in 4 years, 16% graduate in 5 years, and 3% graduate in 6 years. 50 companies recruited on campus in a recent year. Of the 2004 graduating class, 11% were enrolled in graduate school within 6 months of graduation and 68% were employed.

Admissions Contact: Jim Decker, Associate Director of Admissions. E-mail: *jdecker@ozarks.edu.* Web: *www.ozarks.edu*

WILLIAMS BAPTIST COLLEGE   D-1
Walnut Ridge, AR 72476

(870) 759-4121
(800) 722-4434; Fax: (870) 886-3924

Full-time: 213 men, 279 women	Faculty: 29
Part-time: 46 men, 72 women	Ph.D.s: n/av
Graduate: none	Student/Faculty: 17 to 1
Year: semesters, summer session	Tuition: $9250
Application Deadline: open	Room & Board: $4200
Freshman Class: 479 applied, 310 accepted, 130 enrolled	
ACT: 21	COMPETITIVE

Williams Baptist College, founded in 1941, is a private liberal arts institution providing undergraduate education in business, education, humanities, natural sciences, religion, and social sciences. WBC is affiliated with the Southern Baptist Church and is sponsored by the Arkansas Baptist Convention. In addition to regional accreditation, WBC has baccalaureate program accreditation with NCATE. The library contains 68,964 volumes and 18,626 microform items, and subscribes to 152 periodicals including electronic. Computerized library services include the card catalog, interlibrary loans, database searching, and Internet access. Special learning facilities include a learning resource center, art gallery, and an education curriculum lab. The 180-acre campus is in a rural area 100 miles northwest of Memphis, Tennessee, and 125 miles north of Little Rock. Including any residence halls, there are 40 buildings.

Student Life: 86% of undergraduates are from Arkansas. Others are from 13 states and 3 foreign countries. 94% are from public schools. 93% are white. Most are Protestant. The average age of freshmen is 18; all undergraduates, 24. 40% do not continue beyond their first year.

Housing: 419 students can be accommodated in college housing, which includes single-sex dorms, on-campus apartments, and married-student housing. On-campus housing is guaranteed for all 4 years. 63% of students live on campus; of those, 35% remain on campus on weekends. Alcohol is not permitted. All students may keep cars.

Activities: There are 32 groups on campus, including art, cheerleading, chess, choir, chorale, chorus, drama, honors, international, magazine, pep band, professional, religious, social, symphony, and yearbook.

Sports: There are 4 intercollegiate sports for men and 3 for women, and 4 intramural sports for men and 4 for women. Facilities include a gym, a weight room, racquetball and tennis courts, and a track.

Disabled Students: 90% of the campus is accessible. Wheelchair ramps, elevators, special parking, specially equipped rest rooms, special class scheduling, and lowered drinking fountains are available.

Services: Counseling services are available, as is tutoring. There is a reader service for the blind, and remedial classes.

Campus Safety and Security: Measures include lighted pathways/sidewalks and vehicle and foot patrols.

Programs of Study: WBC confers B.A., B.S., B.F.A., B.S.B.A., and B.S.Ed. degrees. Associate degrees are also awarded. Bachelor's degrees are awarded in BIOLOGICAL SCIENCE (biology/biological science), BUSINESS (business administration and management), COMMUNICATIONS AND THE ARTS (art, English, and music), COMPUTER AND PHYSICAL SCIENCE (computer science), EDUCATION (elementary, physical, and secondary), SOCIAL SCIENCE (counseling/psychology, history, psychology, religion, religious education, and religious music). Education and religion are the largest.

Required: To graduate, all students must follow a core curriculum including humanities, social science and religion, natural science and math, and physical activity. Chapel attendance is mandatory. A total of 128 credits, with 36 to 64 hours in the major, and a minimum GPA of 2.0 are required to graduate.

Special: WBC offers study abroad, a Washington semester through the American Studies Program, and a general studies major. There are 9 national honor societies.

Faculty/Classroom: 48% of faculty are male; 52%, female. All teach and do research. The average class size in an introductory lecture is 21; in a laboratory, 23; and in a regular course, 9.

Admissions: 65% of the 2005-2006 applicants were accepted. The ACT scores for the 2005-2006 freshman class were: 45% below 21, 23% between 21 and 23, 23% between 24 and 26, 4% between 27 and 28, and 5% above 28.

Requirements: The ACT is required. In addition, applicants must be graduates of an accredited secondary school. A minimum of 16 academic credits is required and should include at least 12 in the areas of English, math, social science, and natural science. A GPA of 2.5 is required. AP and CLEP credits are accepted.

Procedure: Freshmen are admitted to all sessions. There is a rolling admissions plan. Application deadlines are open. Application fee is $20. Applications are accepted on-line.

Transfer: 66 transfer students enrolled in a recent year. Transfer students must have a GPA of 2.0 for unconditional admission. 32 of 128 credits required for the bachelor's degree must be completed at WBC.

Visiting: There are regularly scheduled orientations for prospective students.

Financial Aid: In 2005-2006, 100% of all full-time freshmen and 99% of continuing full-time students received some form of financial aid. 65% of full-time freshmen and 67% of continuing full-time students received need-based aid. The average freshman award was $9520. Need-based scholarships or need-based grants averaged $3148 ($4650 maximum); need-based self-help aid (loans and jobs) averaged $2803 ($4544 maximum); non-need-based athletic scholarships averaged $4310 ($15,100 maximum); and other non-need-based awards and non-need-based scholarships averaged $3433 ($14,450 maximum). 42% of undergraduates work part time. Average annual earnings from campus work are $1377. The average financial indebtedness of the 2005 graduate was $14,768. The FAFSA is required. The priority date for freshman financial aid applications for fall entry is February 1. The deadline for filing freshman financial aid applications for fall entry is May 1.

International Students: There were 6 international students enrolled in a recent year. A satisfactory score is required on the written TOEFL, the ACT, and the college's own interest inventory test.

Computers: Wireless access is available. All students may access the system. There are no time limits. The fee is $125.

Graduates: From July 1, 2004 to June 30, 2005, 128 bachelor's degrees were awarded. The most popular majors were psychology (20%), business (15%), and elementary education (13%). In an average class, 24% graduate in 4 years or less, 42% graduate in 5 years or less, and 46% graduate in 6 years or less.

Admissions Contact: Angela Flippo, Director of Admissions. A video is available. E-mail: *admissions@wbclab.edu* Web: *www.wbcoll.edu*

CALIFORNIA

Programs of Study: Art Center confers B.S. and B.F.A. degrees. Master's degrees are also awarded. Bachelor's degrees are awarded in COMMUNICATIONS AND THE ARTS (advertising, design, film arts, fine arts, graphic design, illustration, industrial design, and photography), ENGINEERING AND ENVIRONMENTAL DESIGN (environmental design). Illustration, graphic design, and industrial design are the largest.

Required: To graduate, students must complete a total of 135 credit hours, with 90 in the major, and 45 units of liberal arts and sciences. Course requirements vary by the program. A minimum GPA of 2.5 and a core curriculum of English Composition and Introduction to Modernism are also required.

Special: The college offers cross-registration with Occidental College, the California Institute of Technology, and the Southern California Institute of Architecture, internships, and nondegree study.

Faculty/Classroom: 74% of faculty are male; 26%, female. 99% teach undergraduates. No introductory courses are taught by graduate students. The average class size in an introductory lecture is 22 and in a regular course, 30.

Admissions: 74% of the 2005-2006 applicants were accepted.

Requirements: The SAT or ACT is required. The ACT Optional Writing test is also required. In addition, applicants must be graduates of an accredited secondary school or have a GED. Official transcripts and a portfolio must be submitted. An interview is recommended. A GPA of 2.5 is required. AP credits are accepted. Important factors in the admissions decision are evidence of special talent, advanced placement or honor courses, and extracurricular activities record.

Procedure: Freshmen are admitted fall, spring, and summer. Entrance exams should be taken in the senior year. Application deadlines are open. Application fee is $45.

Transfer: 486 transfer students enrolled in a recent year. Transfer applicants must have a minimum 2.5 GPA and provide official transcripts from all colleges attended. Up to 60 units of liberal arts and studio credits may be transferred. Portfolios are required, and interviews are recommended. Up to 32 of the 45 liberal arts and science units required for graduation may be transferred. There is a 4-semester residency requirement. 75 of 135 credits required for the bachelor's degree must be completed at Art Center.

Visiting: There are regularly scheduled orientations for prospective students. There are guides for informal visits. To schedule a visit, contact Admissions.

Financial Aid: In 2005-2006, 73% of all full-time freshmen and 76% of continuing full-time students received some form of financial aid. 70% of full-time freshmen and 74% of continuing full-time students received need-based aid. The average freshman award was $12,000. Need-based scholarships or need-based grants averaged $7000 ($10,000 maximum); and need-based self-help aid (loans and jobs) averaged $5500 ($8600 maximum). 30% of undergraduates work part time. Average annual earnings from campus work are $1500. The average financial indebtedness of the 2005 graduate was $70,000. Art Center is a member of CSS. The FAFSA is required. The deadline for filing freshman financial aid applications for fall entry is March 1.

International Students: There are 244 international students enrolled. The school actively recruits these students. They must take the TOEFL and also take the college's own test.

Computers: There are no time limits and no fees. It is strongly recommended that all students have a personal computer. A Mac is recommended.

Graduates: From July 1, 2004 to June 30, 2005, 413 bachelor's degrees were awarded. The most popular majors were illustration (20%), graphic design (19%), and product design (16%). In an average class, 70% graduate in 4 years or less, and 77% graduate in 5 years or less. 200 companies recruited on campus in 2004-2005. Of the 2004 graduating class, 94% were employed within 6 months of graduation.

Admissions Contact: Kit Baron, Vice President of Student Services. A video is available. E-mail: *admissions@artcenter.edu*
Web: *www.artcenter.edu*

ART CENTER COLLEGE OF DESIGN C-5

Pasadena, CA 91103 (626) 396-2373; Fax: (626) 795-0578

Full-time: 778 men, 526 women	**Faculty:** n/av
Part-time: 123 men, 85 women	**Ph.Ds:** n/av
Graduate: 73 men, 57 women	**Student/Faculty:** 12 to 1
Year: trimesters, summer session	**Tuition:** $26,370
Application Deadline: open	**Room & Board:** n/app
Freshman Class: 1079 applied, 796 accepted, 588 enrolled	
SAT or ACT: required	**SPECIAL**

Art Center College of Design, founded in 1930, is a private institution offering programs in fine arts and design. In addition to regional accreditation, Art Center has baccalaureate program accreditation with NASAD. The library contains 64,000 volumes, 60,000 microform items, and 4000 audio/video tapes/CDs/DVDs, and subscribes to 400 periodicals including electronic. Computerized library services include the card catalog, database searching, and Internet access. Special learning facilities include an art gallery. The 175-acre campus is in a suburban area 10 miles northwest of Los Angeles. There is one building.

Student Life: 63% of undergraduates are from California. Others are from 46 states, 34 foreign countries, and Canada. 45% are Asian American; 42% white; 21% foreign nationals; 10% Hispanic. The average age of freshmen is 23; all undergraduates, 24. 5% do not continue beyond their first year; 89% remain to graduate.

Housing: There are no residence halls. All of students commute. Alcohol is not permitted. All students may keep cars.

Activities: There are no fraternities or sororities. There are 12 groups on campus, including ethnic, gay, international, religious, social, and student government.

Sports: There is no sports program at Art Center. Students have access to athletic facilities at Occidental College and California Institute of Technology.

Disabled Students: All of the campus is accessible. Wheelchair ramps, elevators, special parking, specially equipped rest rooms, lowered drinking fountains, and lowered telephones are available.

Services: Counseling and information services are available, as is tutoring in some subjects, including some art classes.

Campus Safety and Security: Measures include 24-hour foot and vehicle patrol, emergency telephones, and lighted pathways/sidewalks.

ART INSTITUTE OF SOUTHERN CALIFORNIA
(See Laguna College of Art and Design)

AZUSA PACIFIC UNIVERSITY   D-5
Azusa, CA 91702-7000

(626) 812-3016
(800) TALK-APU; Fax: (626) 812-3096

Full-time: 1477 men, 2470 women | **Faculty:** 333; IIA, -$
Part-time: 201 men, 454 women | **Ph.D.s:** 70%
Graduate: 1377 men, 2348 women | **Student/Faculty:** 12 to 1
Year: semesters, summer session | **Tuition:** $22,210
Application Deadline: February 15 | **Room & Board:** $6336
Freshman Class: 3127 applied, 2151 accepted, 881 enrolled
SAT Verbal/Math: 555/550* | **ACT:** 24 | **VERY COMPETITIVE**

Azusa Pacific University, founded in 1899, is a private, interdenominational Christian institution offering undergraduate and graduate programs in the liberal arts and emphasizing spiritual growth. There are 6 undergraduate and 6 graduate schools. In addition to regional accreditation, APU has baccalaureate program accreditation with CSWE and NLN. The 2 libraries contain 185,708 volumes, 691,829 microform items, and 17,706 audio/video tapes/CDs/DVDs, and subscribe to 14,031 periodicals including electronic. Computerized library services include the card catalog, interlibrary loans, database searching, and Internet access. Special learning facilities include a learning resource center, art gallery, radio station, and TV station. The 60-acre campus is in an urban area 26 miles east of Los Angeles. Including any residence halls, there are 67 buildings.

Student Life: 79% of undergraduates are from California. Others are from 47 states, 50 foreign countries, and Canada. 72% are white; 12% Hispanic. Most are Catholic. The average age of freshmen is 18; all undergraduates, 22. 18% do not continue beyond their first year; 64% remain to graduate.

Housing: 2807 students can be accommodated in college housing, which includes single-sex and coed dorms, on-campus apartments, and off-campus apartments. On-campus housing is available on a first-come, first-served basis and is available on a lottery system for upperclassmen. 64% of students commute. Alcohol is not permitted. All students may keep cars.

Activities: There are no fraternities or sororities. There are 32 groups on campus, including art, band, cheerleading, choir, chorale, chorus, computers, drama, ethnic, honors, international, jazz band, newspaper, orchestra, pep band, photography, political, religious, social, student government, and yearbook. Popular campus events include Missions Week, Mega Weekend-Homecoming/Dinner Rally, and Night of Champions.

Sports: There are 7 intercollegiate sports for men and 7 for women, and 6 intramural sports for men and 6 for women. Facilities include an all-weather track, a 3000-seat football stadium, a baseball field, a 1200-seat gym, a residence hall lounge, and a recreation room.

Disabled Students: All of the campus is accessible. Wheelchair ramps, elevators, special parking, specially equipped rest rooms, lowered drinking fountains, and lowered telephones are available.

Services: Counseling and information services are available, as is tutoring in most subjects. There is remedial math, reading, and writing.

Campus Safety and Security: Measures include 24-hour foot and vehicle patrol, security escort services, shuttle buses, and informal discussions. There are pamphlets/posters/films, emergency telephones, and lighted pathways/sidewalks.

Programs of Study: APU confers B.A. and B.S. degrees. Master's and doctoral degrees are also awarded. Bachelor's degrees are awarded in BIOLOGICAL SCIENCE (biochemistry and biology/biological science), BUSINESS (accounting, business administration and management, and marketing/retailing/merchandising), COMMUNICATIONS AND THE ARTS (communications, English, music, and Spanish), COMPUTER AND PHYSICAL SCIENCE (chemistry, computer science, information sciences and systems, mathematics, and physics), EDUCATION (art, music, and physical), HEALTH PROFESSIONS (nursing and premedicine), SOCIAL SCIENCE (biblical studies, history, international studies, liberal arts/general studies, ministries, philosophy, political science/government, psychology, religion, social science, social work, and sociology). Nursing, education, and religion are the strongest academically. Liberal studies is the largest.

Required: All students must take 126 semester units and earn a minimum GPA of 2.0. 18 units of Bible courses, 120 hours of community ministry, and 2 units of health are required. General education requirements include courses in public speaking, fine arts, religion and philosophy, English, algebra, foreign language, and phys ed. Heritage and Institution, Identity and Relationships, and Nature are also required courses.

Special: Internships in ministerial and American studies, study abroad in Japan, Latin America, Taiwan, England, Australia, China, Tanzania, Italy, Israel, France, Lithuania, Spain, and Uganda, and a Washington semester are available. In addition, work-study with the university, a B.A.-B.S. degree, dual majors in all programs, and a 3-2 engineering degree are offered. APU awards credit for life experience and allows non-degree study. There are 2 national honor societies and a freshman honors program.

Faculty/Classroom: 56% of faculty are male; 44%, female. No introductory courses are taught by graduate students. The average class size in an introductory lecture is 40 and in a regular course, 35.

Admissions: 69% of the 2005-2006 applicants were accepted. The SAT scores for the 2005-2006 freshman class were: Verbal--19% below 500, 52% between 500 and 599, 25% between 600 and 700, and 4% above 700; Math--22% below 500, 47% between 500 and 599, 28% between 600 and 700, and 3% above 700. The ACT scores were 16% below 21, 34% between 21 and 23, 25% between 24 and 26, 12% between 27 and 28, and 13% above 28. 60% of the current freshmen were in the top fifth of their class; 86% were in the top two fifths.

Requirements: The SAT or ACT is required, but no minimum score is necessary. An essay is required. A portfolio and an interview are recommended for certain programs. The GED is accepted. A GPA of 2.5 is required. AP and CLEP credits are accepted. Important factors in the admissions decision are personality/intangible qualities, evidence of special talent, and advanced placement or honor courses.

Procedure: Freshmen are admitted to all sessions. Entrance exams should be taken prior to enrollment. There are early action, early admissions, and deferred admissions plans. Early action applications should be filed by December 1; regular applications, by February 15 for fall entry and November 1 for spring entry for priority considerations, along with a $45 fee. Notification of early action is sent January 15; regular decision, on a rolling basis beginning April 1. 383 applicants were on the 2005 waiting list; 56 were admitted. Applications are accepted on-line.

Transfer: 473 transfer students enrolled in a recent year. Applicants must have a minimum GPA of 2.0 on previous college work. The SAT or ACT is not required if 30 or more semester units have been completed. An associate degree and an interview are recommended. 30 of 126 credits required for the bachelor's degree must be completed at APU.

Visiting: There are regularly scheduled orientations for prospective students, including Seniors Only Day in November, and a brother/sister weekend in February that is open to both juniors and seniors. There are guides for informal visits and visitors may sit in on classes and stay overnight. To schedule a visit, contact the Admissions Office at (626) 815-6000, ext. 3016.

Financial Aid: The average freshman award was $9499. 20% of undergraduates work part time. The average financial indebtedness of the 2005 graduate was $19,487. The FAFSA and the college's own financial statement are required. The deadline for filing freshman financial aid applications for fall entry is July 1.

International Students: There are 80 international students enrolled. The school actively recruits these students. They must score satisfactorily on the TOEFL.

Computers: Wireless access is available. All students may access the system Monday through Friday 8 A.M. to 11 P.M., Saturday 8:30 A.M. to 8 P.M., and Sunday 1 P.M. to 6 P.M. There are no time limits and no fees. It is recommended that students in Human Development (degree completion program) have personal computers.

Graduates: From July 1, 2004 to June 30, 2005, 1103 bachelor's degrees were awarded. The most popular majors were liberal arts (9%), communication studies (7%), and nursing (6%). In an average class, 52% graduate in 4 years or less, 63% graduate in 5 years or less, and 64% graduate in 6 years or less.

Admissions Contact: David Burke, Director of Undergraduate Admissions. A video is available. E-mail: admissions@apu.edu
Web: http://www.apu.edu

BIOLA UNIVERSITY   D-5
La Mirada, CA 90639-0001

(562) 903-4752
(800) OK-BIOLA; Fax: (562) 903-4709

Full-time: 1306 men, 2006 women | **Faculty:** 133; IIA, -$
Part-time: 155 men, 196 women | **Ph.D.s:** 78%
Graduate: 1164 men, 720 women | **Student/Faculty:** 25 to 1
Year: 4-1-4, summer session | **Tuition:** $22,602
Application Deadline: December 1 | **Room & Board:** $6770
Freshman Class: 2077 applied, 1709 accepted, 779 enrolled
SAT Verbal/Math: 563/555* | **ACT:** 24 | **VERY COMPETITIVE**

Biola University, founded in 1908, is a private, interdenominational Christian institution offering undergraduate and graduate degrees in arts and sciences, psychology, theology, intercultural studies, and business. There are 6 undergraduate and 6 graduate schools. In addition to regional accreditation, Biola has baccalaureate program accreditation with ACBSP, APA, ATS, NASAD, NASM, and NLN. The library contains 279,560 volumes, 570,437 microform items, and 14,347 audio/video tapes/CDs/DVDs, and subscribes to 13,123 periodicals including electronic. Computerized library services include the card catalog, interlibrary loans, database searching, and Internet access. Special learning facilities include a learning resource center, art gallery, radio station, TV station, film studio a 3-D art facility, MIDI lab for music composition majors, electronic piano lab, listening lab with music archives, physical science labs, and scanning electron microscope. The 95-acre campus is in a suburban area 22 miles southeast of Los Angeles. Including any residence halls, there are 39 buildings.

Student Life: 75% of undergraduates are from California. Students are from Canada. 75% are from public schools. 64% are white; 12% Asian American. Most are Protestant. The average age of freshmen is 18; all undergraduates, 20. 17% do not continue beyond their first year; 60% remain to graduate.

Housing: 2307 students can be accommodated in college housing, which includes single-sex and coed dorms, on-campus apartments, and off-campus apartments. On-campus housing is guaranteed for the freshman year only and is available on a first-come, first-served basis. 65% of students live on campus; of those, 73% remain on campus on weekends. Alcohol is not permitted. All students may keep cars.

Activities: There are no fraternities or sororities. There are 52 groups on campus, including band, cheerleading, chess, chorale, dance, debate, drama, ethnic, film, forensics, gospel choir, honors, international, jazz band, ministries, missionary, musical theater, newspaper, orchestra, political, professional, radio and TV, religious, social, social service, student government, symphony, and yearbook. Popular campus events include Multicultural Week, Christmas Celebration, and Harvest Festival.

Sports: There are 7 intercollegiate sports for men and 8 for women, and 5 intramural sports for men and 5 for women. Facilities include a gym-swimming complex, a 450-seat auditorium, athletic fields, including one for soccer, a quarter-mile track, a baseball diamond, tennis, sand volleyball, and basketball courts, and a fitness center.

Disabled Students: 88% of the campus is accessible. Wheelchair ramps, elevators, special parking, specially equipped rest rooms, special class scheduling, lowered drinking fountains, and lowered telephones are available.

Services: Counseling and information services are available, as is tutoring in most subjects. There is a reader service for the blind. A Writing Center is available to all students.

Campus Safety and Security: Measures include 24-hour foot and vehicle patrol, self-defense education, security escort services, and informal discussions. There are pamphlets/posters/films, emergency telephones, lighted pathways/sidewalks, and a bike patrol.

Programs of Study: Biola confers B.A., B.S., and B.M. degrees. Master's and doctoral degrees are also awarded. Bachelor's degrees are awarded in BIOLOGICAL SCIENCE (biochemistry and biology/biological science), BUSINESS (accounting, business administration and management, management science, and marketing management), COMMUNICATIONS AND THE ARTS (art, broadcasting, communications, English, journalism, music, music performance, music theory and composition, and Spanish), COMPUTER AND PHYSICAL SCIENCE (applied mathematics, computer science, information sciences and systems, mathematics, and physical sciences), EDUCATION (Christian, mathematics, music, and physical), HEALTH PROFESSIONS (nursing and speech pathology/audiology), SOCIAL SCIENCE (anthropology, biblical studies, crosscultural studies, history, humanities, liberal arts/general studies, philosophy, psychology, social science, and sociology). Business administration, biological science, and chemistry are the strongest academically. Business, psychology, and liberal studies are the largest.

Required: To graduate, students must pass a writing competency exam, complete 30 units of biblical studies and theology, and fulfill the general education and phys ed requirements. At least 130 semester hours must be completed, with 30 hours in the major and 24 of these in upper-division work. Other requirements vary by major. A minimum 2.0 GPA is required.

Special: Cross-registration with the Au Sable Institute of Environmental Studies is possible. Biola offers internships, summer travel tours, study abroad in 11 countries, and an American studies program in Washington D.C., sponsored by the Christian College Coalition. Special programs include L.A. Film Studies, a semester in Hollywood working in the film industry; Biola Baja, a 3-week program at Vermillion Sea Field, Baja; a family studies course at Focus on the Family Institute in Colorado Springs; a China studies program at Fudan University in Shanghai, China; and a development theory studies program in Honduras. Also available are on- and off-campus work-study programs, a B.A.-B.S. degree, a 3-2 engineering degree with the University of Southern California, dual majors, and nondegree study. There are several preprofessional programs available, including prelaw, prephysical therapy, and prechiropractic. A 3-1 program with Los Angeles College of Chiropractic is offered. Students can also attend a semester at Martha's Vineyard with the Contemporary Music Center and explore the many areas of the Christian music industry. There are 2 national honor societies, a freshman honors program, and 7 departmental honors programs.

Faculty/Classroom: 72% of faculty are male; 28%, female. 76% teach undergraduates. No introductory courses are taught by graduate students. The average class size in an introductory lecture is 35 and in a laboratory, 15.

Admissions: 82% of the 2005-2006 applicants were accepted. The SAT scores for the 2005-2006 freshman class were: Verbal--19% below 500, 41% between 500 and 599, 30% between 600 and 700, and 10%

above 700; Math--21% below 500, 43% between 500 and 599, 30% between 600 and 700, and 6% above 700. The ACT scores were 25% below 21, 21% between 21 and 23, 25% between 24 and 26, 14% between 27 and 28, and 15% above 28. 69% of the current freshmen were in the top fifth of their class; 91% were in the top two fifths.

Requirements: The SAT or ACT is required. Applicants need not be graduates of an accredited secondary school. The GED is accepted. Students should have completed 15 academic credits, including 4 years of English and foreign language, 3 years of math, and 2 each of social studies and science. All students must be evangelical Christians who can demonstrate Christian character, leadership ability, and the aptitude for possible success in college. Applicants must submit 2 personal references: 1 from their pastor or someone on the pastoral staff, and 1 from the school last attended, or from an employer if they have been out of school for a year and have been working. An essay and an interview are required. A GPA of 3.0 is required. AP and CLEP credits are accepted. Important factors in the admissions decision are personality/intangible qualities, recommendations by school officials, and leadership record.

Procedure: Freshmen are admitted to all sessions. There are deferred admissions and rolling admissions plans. Applications should be filed by December 1 for fall entry and January 15 for spring entry, along with a $45 fee. Notification of early decision is sent December 24; regular decision, on a rolling basis. Applications are accepted on-line.

Transfer: 280 transfer students enrolled in 2004-2005. Applicants with fewer than 27 credit hours must submit both college transcripts and SAT scores. All students must provide high school transcripts. A minimum 2.0 GPA and an interview are required. 30 of 130 credits required for the bachelor's degree must be completed at Biola.

Visiting: There are regularly scheduled orientations for prospective students, including class visits; orientation with the departments of admissions, financial aid, and student affairs; chapel; a sporting event; and a Disneyland or Knott's Berry Farm visit. There are guides for informal visits and visitors may sit in on classes and stay overnight. To schedule a visit, contact the Admissions Office.

Financial Aid: In 2005-2006, 80% of all full-time freshmen and 77% of continuing full-time students received some form of financial aid. 81% of full-time freshmen and 80% of continuing full-time students received need-based aid. The average freshman award was $17,410. Need-based scholarships or need-based grants averaged $2655 ($6000 maximum); need-based self-help aid (loans and jobs) averaged $4920 ($5625 maximum); non-need-based athletic scholarships averaged $2121 ($20,932 maximum); and other non-need-based awards and non-need-based scholarships averaged $2779 ($7000 maximum). 34% of undergraduates work part time. Average annual earnings from campus work are $2235. The average financial indebtedness of the 2005 graduate was $28,007. Biola is a member of CSS. The FAFSA, the college's own financial statement, and California residents should submit the Cal Grant GPA verification form. The deadline for filing freshman financial aid applications for fall entry is May 15.

International Students: There are 339 international students enrolled. The school actively recruits these students. They must score satisfactorily on the written TOEFL or on the electronic version and also take the SAT or the ACT.

Computers: All students may access the system every day. There are no time limits and no fees.

Graduates: From July 1, 2004 to June 30, 2005, 776 bachelor's degrees were awarded. The most popular majors were business administration (7%), psychology (7%), and liberal studies (6%). In an average class, 2% graduate in 3 years or less, 50% graduate in 4 years or less, 67% graduate in 5 years or less, and 69% graduate in 6 years or less. 90 companies recruited on campus in 2004-2005. Of a recent graduating class, 45% were employed within 6 months of graduation.

Admissions Contact: Gregory G. Vaughan, Director of Enrollment Management. E-mail: *admissions@biola.edu* Web: *www.biola.edu*

CALIFORNIA BAPTIST UNIVERSITY   D-5
Riverside, CA 92504-3297

(951) 343-4212
(877) 228-8866; Fax: (951) 343-4525

Full-time: 692 men, 1284 women	Faculty: 90
Part-time: 153 men, 286 women	Ph.D.s: 64%
Graduate: 164 men, 526 women	Student/Faculty: 22 to 1
Year: semesters, summer session	Tuition: $17,470
Application Deadline: open	Room & Board: $6310
Freshman Class: 1072 applied, 764 accepted, 439 enrolled	
SAT Verbal/Math: 500/500*	ACT: 21 COMPETITIVE

California Baptist University, founded in 1950, is a private institution supported by the California Southern Baptist Convention and offering degree programs in the arts and sciences, business, education, and religious studies. There are 7 undergraduate and 7 graduate schools. In addition to regional accreditation, CBU has baccalaureate program accreditation with ACBSP and NASM. The library contains 104,415 volumes, 53,752 microform items, and 4666 audio/video tapes/CDs/DVDs, and subscribes to 360 periodicals including electronic. Computerized library services include the card catalog, interlibrary loans, database searching, and Internet access. Special learning facilities include a learning resource center and art gallery. The 90-acre campus is in a suburban area 60 miles east of Los Angeles. Including any residence halls, there are 61 buildings.

Student Life: 95% of undergraduates are from California. Others are from 34 states, 22 foreign countries, and Canada. 80% are from public schools. 59% are white; 16% Hispanic. 88% are Protestant; 6% Catholic; 6% claim no religious affiliation. The average age of freshmen is 19; all undergraduates, 24. 13% do not continue beyond their first year; 63% remain to graduate.

Housing: 1200 students can be accommodated in college housing, which includes single-sex dorms, on-campus apartments, off-campus apartments, and married-student housing. On-campus housing is guaranteed for all 4 years. 50% of students live on campus; of those, 45% remain on campus on weekends. Alcohol is not permitted. All students may keep cars.

Activities: There are no fraternities or sororities. There are 31 groups on campus, including art, band, choir, chorale, chorus, computers, debate, drama, ethnic, forensics, honors, international, jazz band, musical theater, newspaper, orchestra, pep band, political, professional, religious, social, social service, student government, symphony, and yearbook. Popular campus events include Campus Day, Twirp Week, and Octoberfest.

Sports: There are 6 intercollegiate sports for men and 6 for women, and 9 intramural sports for men and 9 for women. Facilities include a 950-seat gym, baseball, soccer, and softball fields, tennis and sand volleyball courts, an Olympic swimming facility, fitness center, and activity center.

Disabled Students: 95% of the campus is accessible. Wheelchair ramps, elevators, special parking, specially equipped rest rooms, and lowered drinking fountains are available.

Services: Counseling and information services are available, as is tutoring in most subjects. There is remedial math, reading, and writing.

Campus Safety and Security: Measures include 24-hour foot and vehicle patrol, self-defense education, security escort services, and informal discussions. There are pamphlets/posters/films, emergency telephones, and lighted pathways/sidewalks.

Programs of Study: CBU confers B.A., B.S., and B.B.A. degrees. Master's degrees are also awarded. Bachelor's degrees are awarded in BIOLOGICAL SCIENCE (biology/biological science), BUSINESS (business administration and management, management science, and organizational leadership and management), COMMUNICATIONS AND THE ARTS (English, journalism, music, speech/debate/rhetoric, and visual and performing arts), COMPUTER AND PHYSICAL SCIENCE (mathematics), EDUCATION (physical), HEALTH PROFESSIONS (exercise science), SOCIAL SCIENCE (behavioral science, Christian studies, criminal justice, history, interdisciplinary studies, international relations, liberal arts/general studies, philosophy, political science/government, psychology, social science, sociology, and theological studies). Liberal studies (education) is the strongest academically. Business, psychology, and kinesiology are the largest.

Required: All students must be proficient in English and complete courses in arts, interdisciplinary and multicultural studies, humanities, natural sciences, Christian studies, and social sciences. A total of 124 units, with a minimum GPA of 2.0, is required to graduate.

Special: CBU offers an accelerated program in several disciplines. Study abroad, internships, work-study programs, a Washington semester, B.A.-B.S. degrees, dual majors, and credit for military/work experience are available. There are 2 national honor societies, a freshman honors program, and honors programs in all departments.

Faculty/Classroom: 59% of faculty are male; 41%, female. 92% teach undergraduates. No introductory courses are taught by graduate students. The average class size in an introductory lecture is 38; in a laboratory, 21; and in a regular course, 21.

Admissions: 71% of the 2005-2006 applicants were accepted. The SAT scores for the 2005-2006 freshman class were: Verbal--47% below 500, 41% between 500 and 599, 11% between 600 and 700, and 1% above 700; Math--47% below 500, 40% between 500 and 599, and 13% between 600 and 700. The ACT scores were 46% below 21, 34% between 21 and 23, 18% between 24 and 26, and 2% between 27 and 28. 43% of the current freshmen were in the top fifth of their class; 32% were in the top two fifths. 2 freshmen graduated first in their class.

Requirements: The SAT or ACT is required. In addition, applicants should be graduates of an accredited high school or have a GED. An essay and interview are recommended, and 2 references, preferably from a church leader and an official of an academic institution, are required. A GPA of 2.5 is required. AP and CLEP credits are accepted. Important factors in the admissions decision are recommendations by school officials, leadership record, and advanced placement or honor courses.

Procedure: Freshmen are admitted fall and spring. Entrance exams should be taken during the junior year. There is a deferred admissions plan and a rolling admissions plan. Early decision applications should be filed by December 15; regular applications, open. Notification is sent on a rolling basis. Application fee is $45. Applications are accepted on-line.

Transfer: 204 transfer students enrolled in 2004-2005. Applicants must have a minimum GPA of 2.0, if they are transferring at least 30 transferable semester units. Only courses with a grade of C- or better may transfer. If transferring less than 30 units, students high school GPA must be at least 2.5 and they must submit SAT or ACT scores. 36 of 124 credits required for the bachelor's degree must be completed at CBU.

Visiting: There are regularly scheduled orientations for prospective students, consisting of a welcome, orientation, academic fair, and tours. There are guides for informal visits and visitors may sit in on classes and stay overnight. To schedule a visit, contact the Admissions Office.

Financial Aid: The FAFSA is required. The priority date for freshman financial aid applications for fall entry is March 2.

International Students: There are 38 international students enrolled. The school actively recruits these students. They must take the TOEFL or take the SAT or the ACT, scoring satisfactorily.

Computers: Wireless access is available. There are 154 computers in computer labs and library as well as ports available in all student housing. All students may access the system during open lab and library hours and anytime from ports in student housing. There are no time limits and no fees. It is recommended that students in music majors have personal computers. Macintosh is recommended.

Graduates: From July 1, 2004 to June 30, 2005, 508 bachelor's degrees were awarded. The most popular majors were liberal studies (education) (31%), psychology/behavioral science (17%), and business (16%). In an average class, 9% graduate in 3 years or less, 49% graduate in 4 years or less, 54% graduate in 5 years or less, and 56% graduate in 6 years or less. 57 companies recruited on campus in 2004-2005.

Admissions Contact: Allen Johnson, Director, Undergraduate Admissions. E-mail: *admissions@calbaptist.edu* Web: *www.calbaptist.edu*

CALIFORNIA COLLEGE OF THE ARTS   B-3

San Francisco, CA 94107   (415) 703-9535
                                     (800) 447-1ART; Fax: (415) 703-9539

Full-time: 507 men, 720 women	**Faculty:** 136
Part-time: 37 men, 48 women	**Ph.D.s:** 64%
Graduate: 112 men, 192 women	**Student/Faculty:** 9 to 1
Year: semesters, summer session	**Tuition:** $26,095
Application Deadline: February 1	**Room & Board:** $8230
Freshman Class: 785 applied, 616 accepted, 181 enrolled	
SAT Verbal/Math: 547/507*	**ACT:** 22 SPECIAL

California College of the Arts, formerly California College of Arts and Crafts, established in 1907, is a private professional arts institution offering programs in fine arts, design, and architecture studies. In addition to regional accreditation, CCA has baccalaureate program accreditation with FIDER, NAAB, and NASAD. The 2 libraries contain 39,000 volumes, 50 microform items, and 520 audio/video tapes/CDs/DVDs, and subscribe to 340 periodicals including electronic. Computerized library services include the card catalog, interlibrary loans, and database searching. Special learning facilities include a learning resource center and art gallery. The 4-acre campus is in an urban area. Including any residence halls, there are 15 buildings.

Student Life: 65% of undergraduates are from California. Others are from 40 states, 21 foreign countries, and Canada. 73% are from public schools. 56% are white; 11% Asian American. The average age of freshmen is 18; all undergraduates, 24. 21% do not continue beyond their first year; 79% remain to graduate.

Housing: 275 students can be accommodated in college housing, which includes coed dorms and on-campus apartments, and an off-campus residence hall. On-campus housing is guaranteed for the freshman year only, is available on a first-come, first-served basis, and is available on a lottery system for upperclassmen. Priority is given to out-of-town students. 83% of students commute. Alcohol is not permitted. No one may keep cars.

Activities: There are no fraternities or sororities. There are 18 groups on campus, including art, ethnic, gay, honors, international, newspaper, professional, and student government. Popular campus events include All-College Honors, Holiday and Spring Fair, and Student Gala.

Sports: There is no sports program at CCA.

Disabled Students: 80% of the campus is accessible. Wheelchair ramps, elevators, special parking, specially equipped rest rooms, special class scheduling, lowered drinking fountains, and lowered telephones are available.

Services: Counseling and information services are available, as is tutoring in some subjects, including humanities and sciences.

Campus Safety and Security: Measures include self-defense education, security escort services, shuttle buses, and informal discussions. There are pamphlets/posters/films, emergency telephones, and lighted pathways/sidewalks.

Programs of Study: CCA confers B.A., B.Arch, and B.F.A. degrees. Master's degrees are also awarded. Bachelor's degrees are awarded in COMMUNICATIONS AND THE ARTS (art, ceramic art and design, creative writing, film arts, glass, graphic design, illustration, industrial design, metal/jewelry, painting, photography, printmaking, sculpture, and visual and performing arts), ENGINEERING AND ENVIRONMENTAL DESIGN (architecture, furniture design, and interior design), SOCIAL SCIENCE (fashion design and technology and textiles and clothing). Design, painting, and architecture are the largest.

Required: Students must successfully complete 126 credits for the B.F.A. and B.A. with 57 in the major, and 162 for the B.Arch., with 96 in the major. Distribution requirements are 51 credits in humanities and science, plus 75 in studio work for fine arts majors and 111 in studio work for architecture majors. All students must complete the core curriculum and maintain a minimum GPA of 2.0.

Special: Co-op programs in design are available. Cross-registration is permitted with Mills and Holy Names colleges in Oakland and with the University of San Francisco in San Francisco. Opportunities are provided for internships, study abroad in 11 countries, student-designed majors, and nondegree study. The Association of Independent Colleges of Art and Design Mobility Program is also possible.

Faculty/Classroom: 54% of faculty are male; 46%, female. 91% teach undergraduates. No introductory courses are taught by graduate students. The average class size in an introductory lecture is 15 and in a regular course, 15.

Admissions: 78% of the 2005-2006 applicants were accepted. The SAT scores for the 2005-2006 freshman class were: Verbal--27% below 500, 38% between 500 and 599, 30% between 600 and 700, and 5% above 700; Math--27% below 500, 46% between 500 and 599, 24% between 600 and 700, and 3% above 700. The ACT scores were 10% below 21, 65% between 21 and 23, 25% between 24 and 26, and 9% between 27 and 28. 36% of the current freshmen were in the top fifth of their class; 86% were in the top two fifths.

Requirements: The SAT or ACT is recommended. In addition, graduation from an accredited secondary school is required; a GED will be accepted. An essay, portfolio, and letters of recommendation are required. An interview is strongly recommended. A GPA of 2.0 is required. AP credits are accepted. Important factors in the admissions decision are evidence of special talent, recommendations by school officials, and extracurricular activities record.

Procedure: Freshmen are admitted fall and spring. There is a rolling admissions plan. Applications should be filed by February 1 for fall entry and October 1 for spring entry, along with a $50 fee. Notification is sent on a rolling basis. Applications are accepted on-line.

Transfer: 195 transfer students enrolled in 2004-2005. Applicants must submit a portfolio. 30 of 126 credits required for the bachelor's degree must be completed at CCA.

Visiting: There are regularly scheduled orientations for prospective students, including fall and spring open houses and orientation for admitted students a week prior to start of the semester. There are guides for informal visits and visitors may sit in on classes. To schedule a visit, contact the Office of Enrollment Services at (415) 703-9523.

Financial Aid: In 2005-2006, 57% of all full-time freshmen and 65% of continuing full-time students received some form of financial aid. 53% of full-time freshmen and 63% of continuing full-time students received need-based aid. The average freshman award was $16,935. Need-based scholarships or need-based grants averaged $12,663; need-based self-help aid (loans and jobs) averaged $4551; and other non-need-based awards and non-need-based scholarships averaged $5431. All of undergraduates work part time. Average annual earnings from campus work are $1500. The average financial indebtedness of the 2005 graduate was $28,549. The FAFSA and the college's own financial statement are required. The deadline for filing freshman financial aid applications for fall entry is March 1.

International Students: There are 91 international students enrolled. The school actively recruits these students. They must score satisfactorily on the TOEFL.

Computers: Wireless access is available. All students may access the system. There are no time limits and no fees.

Graduates: From July 1, 2004 to June 30, 2005, 258 bachelor's degrees were awarded. The most popular majors were painting/drawing (14%) and individualized major (9%). In an average class, 22% graduate in 4 years, 22% graduate in 5 years, and 7% graduate in 6 years. 5 companies recruited on campus in 2004-2005.

Admissions Contact: Sheri Sivin McKenzie, Vice President for Enrollment Management. E-mail: *smckenzie@cca.edu* Web: *www.cca.edu*

CALIFORNIA INSTITUTE OF TECHNOLOGY   C-5

Pasadena, CA 91125	(626) 395-6341; Fax: (626) 683-3026
Full-time: 614 men, 282 women	Faculty: 295
Part-time: none	Ph.D.s: 100%
Graduate: 920 men, 356 women	Student/Faculty: 3 to 1
Year: quarters	Tuition: $27,309
Application Deadline: January 1	Room & Board: $8814
Freshman Class: n/av	
SAT or ACT: required	MOST COMPETITIVE

California Institute of Technology, founded in 1891, is a private institution offering programs in engineering, science, and math. Some information in this profile is approximate. In addition to regional accreditation, Caltech has baccalaureate program accreditation with ABET and ACS. The 16 libraries contain 705,350 volumes, 613,155 microform items, and 920 audio/video tapes/CDs/DVDs, and subscribe to 3901 periodicals including electronic. Computerized library services include the card catalog, interlibrary loans, database searching, and Internet access. Special learning facilities include a learning resource center. The 124-acre campus is in a suburban area 12 miles northeast of Los Angeles. Including any residence halls, there are 103 buildings.

Student Life: 65% of undergraduates are from out of state, mostly the West. Students are from 48 states, 24 foreign countries, and Canada. 80% are from public schools. 51% are white; 31% Asian American. The average age of freshmen is 18; all undergraduates, 20. 5% do not continue beyond their first year; 89% remain to graduate.

Housing: 820 students can be accommodated in college housing, which includes coed dorms, off-campus apartments, and married-student housing. On-campus housing is guaranteed for all 4 years. 90% of students live on campus. Alcohol is not permitted. All students may keep cars.

Activities: There are no fraternities or sororities. There are 85 groups on campus, including art, band, cheerleading, chess, choir, chorale, chorus, computers, dance, drama, ethnic, film, gay, honors, international, jazz band, literary magazine, musical theater, newspaper, opera, orchestra, pep band, photography, political, professional, religious, social, social service, student government, symphony, and yearbook. Popular campus events include Ditch Day, International Day, and Pre-Frosh Weekend.

Sports: There are 10 intercollegiate sports for men and 8 for women, and 16 intramural sports for men and 13 for women. Facilities include 2 Olympic-size swimming pools, a 300-seat gym, a 440-meter track, a football field, 4 baseball fields, and 8 tennis courts. Another athletic facility includes a gym, a 4000-square-foot exercise room with equipment, and racquetball courts.

Disabled Students: 98% of the campus is accessible. Wheelchair ramps, elevators, special parking, specially equipped rest rooms, and lowered telephones are available.

Services: Counseling and information services are available, as is tutoring in every subject. There is a reader service for the blind.

Campus Safety and Security: Measures include 24-hour foot and vehicle patrol, self-defense education, security escort services, and informal discussions. There are pamphlets/posters/films, emergency telephones, and lighted pathways/sidewalks.

Programs of Study: Caltech confers the B.S. degree. Master's and doctoral degrees are also awarded. Bachelor's degrees are awarded in BIOLOGICAL SCIENCE (biology/biological science), COMMUNICATIONS AND THE ARTS (literature), COMPUTER AND PHYSICAL SCIENCE (astronomy, chemistry, geochemistry, geology, geophysics and seismology, mathematics, physics, and planetary and space science), ENGINEERING AND ENVIRONMENTAL DESIGN (aeronautical engineering, chemical engineering, civil engineering, electrical/electronics engineering, engineering, engineering and applied science, and mechanical engineering), SOCIAL SCIENCE (economics, history, political science/government, and social science). Engineering, applied science, and electrical engineering are the largest.

Required: All students must complete 108 units in humanities and social science, 90 each in math and physics, 21 in chemistry, 9 in biology, 6 in lab, and 9 in additional science courses, and 3 terms of phys ed. A total of 780 quarter units, including 516 in the major, and a minimum GPA of 1.9 are required to graduate.

Special: Caltech offers cross-registration with Scripps College, Occidental College, and Art Center College of Design, various work-study programs, including those with NASA's Jet Propulsion Laboratory, dual majors in any major, and independent studies degrees with faculty-approved student-designed majors. A 3-2 engineering degree is possible with several institutions. Pass/fail options are available for freshmen. A summer undergraduate research fellowship program is offered. Study abroad is available at University College in London, Cambridge University, and University of Copenhagen in Denmark.

Faculty/Classroom: 85% of faculty are male; 15%, female. All both teach and do research. No introductory courses are taught by graduate students. The average class size in an introductory lecture is 150 and in a regular course, 12.

Admissions: 17% of recent applicants were accepted. The SAT scores for a recent freshman class were: Verbal--1% below 500, 5% between 500 and 599, 17% between 600 and 700, and 77% above 700; Math--4% between 600 and 700, and 96% above 700. 99% of the current freshmen were in the top fifth of their class; 100% were in the top two fifths.

Requirements: The SAT or ACT is required. In addition, SAT Subject Tests in writing, math level II, and one in physics, biology, or chemistry are required. Applicants should have completed 4 years of high school math, 3 of English, 1 each of chemistry and history, and 5 units from other concentrations. Important factors in the admissions decision are advanced placement or honor courses, recommendations by school officials, and evidence of special talent.

Procedure: Freshmen are admitted in the fall. Entrance exams should be taken through December of the senior year. There are early decision, early admissions, and deferred admissions plans. Early decision applications should be filed by November 1; regular applications, by January 1 for fall entry, along with a $50 fee. Notification of early decision is sent December 31; regular decision, April 1. 151 early decision candidates were accepted for a recent class. A waiting list is an active part of the admissions procedure. Applications are accepted on-line.

Transfer: 23 transfer students enrolled in a recent year. Transfers, admitted only into sophomore and junior classes, need a minimum GPA of 3.0. Applicants must have completed 1 year (2 years for juniors) of calculus and calculus-based physics, and must take Caltech's entrance exams in math and physics. Chemistry or chemical engineering majors also should have completed 1 year of chemistry and must take an additional entrance exam. 216 of 780 credits required for the bachelor's degree must be completed at Caltech.

Visiting: There are regularly scheduled orientations for prospective students, including a 1:30 video screening, and a 2 P.M. student-led tour followed by an information session with an admissions counselor. There are guides for informal visits and visitors may sit in on classes. To schedule a visit, contact the Admissions Office.

Financial Aid: In a recent year, 60% of all full-time freshmen and 58% of continuing full-time students received some form of financial aid. 51% of continuing full-time students received need-based aid. The average freshman award was $21,687. The average financial indebtedness of a recent graduate was $10,244. Caltech is a member of CSS. The CSS/Profile or FAFSA is required. Check with the school for current deadlines.

International Students: There were 92 international students enrolled in a recent year. They must take the SAT or the ACT as well as SAT: Subject tests in math level IIC, writing, and chemistry, physics, or biology.

Computers: All students may access the system any time. There are no time limits and no fees. It is strongly recommended that all students have a personal computer.

Graduates: From July 1, 2004 to June 30, 2005, 217 bachelor's degrees were awarded. The most popular majors were engineering and applied science (50%), physical sciences (33%), and biology (9%). In an average class, 89% graduate in 6 years or less. 85 companies recruited on campus in a recent year. Of a recent graduating class, 45% were enrolled in graduate school within 6 months of graduation and 30% were employed.

Admissions Contact: Dan Langdale, Director of Admissions.
E-mail: *ugadmissions@caltech.edu* Web: *www.admissions.caltech.edu*

CALIFORNIA INSTITUTE OF THE ARTS   C-5

Valencia, CA 91355

(661) 255-1050
(800) 545-ARTS; Fax: (661) 253-7710

Full-time: 457 men, 355 women	**Faculty:** n/av
Part-time: 6 men, 3 women	**Ph.D.s:** n/av
Graduate: 244 men, 262 women	**Student/Faculty:** n/av
Year: semesters	**Tuition:** $28,025
Application Deadline: January 5	**Room & Board:** $7700
Freshman Class: 2979 applied, 923 accepted, 484 enrolled	
SAT or ACT: nor required	**SPECIAL**

California Institute of the Arts, founded in 1961, is a private institution offering undergraduate and graduate programs in art, dance, film and video, music, and theater, and graduate majors in directing, integrated media, and writing. There are 6 undergraduate and 6 graduate schools. In addition to regional accreditation, Cal-Arts has baccalaureate program accreditation with NASAD, NASD, NASM, and NAST. The library contains 94,839 volumes, 7160 microform items, and 27,256 audio/video tapes/CDs/DVDs, and subscribes to 309 periodicals including electronic. Computerized library services include the card catalog, interlibrary loans, database searching, and Internet access. Special learning facilities include an art gallery, radio station, TV station, movie theater, sound stages, scenery construction shops, and slide and film libraries. The 60-acre campus is in a suburban area 30 miles north of Los Angeles. Including any residence halls, there are 3 buildings.

Student Life: 61% of undergraduates are from out of state, mostly the Northeast. Others are from 50 states, 33 foreign countries, and Canada. 67% are white; 14% foreign nationals; 12% Hispanic; 11% Asian American. The average age of freshmen is 19; all undergraduates, 22. 79% do not continue beyond their first year; 92% remain to graduate.

Housing: 450 students can be accommodated in college housing, which includes coed dorms and on-campus apartments. On-campus housing is available on a first-come, first-served basis and is available on a lottery system for upperclassmen. Priority is given to out-of-town students. 53% of students live on campus. All students may keep cars.

Activities: There are no fraternities or sororities. There are 21 groups on campus, including art, chess, dance, drama, ethnic, film, gay, international, jazz band, literary magazine, newspaper, opera, orchestra, photography, political, radio and TV, student government, and symphony.

Popular campus events include music festivals, theater productions, and poetry readings.

Sports: There is no sports program at Cal-Arts. Facilities include tennis courts, sand volleyball courts, and a swimming pool.

Disabled Students: 95% of the campus is accessible. Wheelchair ramps, elevators, special parking, specially equipped rest rooms, special class scheduling, lowered drinking fountains, lowered telephones, and special housing are available.

Services: Counseling and information services are available, as is tutoring in some subjects, including ESL. There is a reader service for the blind. All computerized media systems are used in the 6 major departments, and other subjects, which vary each year.

Campus Safety and Security: Measures include 24-hour foot and vehicle patrol, security escort services, informal discussions, and pamphlets/posters/films. There are lighted pathways/sidewalks.

Programs of Study: Cal-Arts confers the B.F.A. degree. Master's degrees are also awarded. Bachelor's degrees are awarded in COMMUNICATIONS AND THE ARTS (dance, dramatic arts, film arts, fine arts, and music). Art, music, and acting are the strongest academically. Art, film/video, and theater are the largest.

Required: To graduate, all students must complete a total of 120 credit hours, with 48 in critical studies and 72 in the major, and must satisfy all curriculum and degree requirements of the particular school.

Special: Cal Arts offers internships with local and national companies, student-designed majors, interdisciplinary studies, study abroad in 6 countries, and a cooperative education program.

Faculty/Classroom: 62% of faculty are male; 38%, female. No introductory courses are taught by graduate students. The average class size in an introductory lecture is 15 and in a regular course, 8.

Admissions: 31% of the 2005-2006 applicants were accepted.

Requirements: Applicants must be graduates of an accredited secondary school or have a GED certificate. They must submit an official transcript and an essay. Portfolios and auditions are required and an interview is recommended for some programs. AP credits are accepted. Important factors in the admissions decision are evidence of special talent and advanced placement or honor courses.

Procedure: Freshmen are admitted fall and spring. Applications should be filed by January 5 for fall entry and November 15 for spring entry, along with a $65 fee. Notification is sent April 1. A waiting list is an active part of the admissions procedure.

Transfer: 42 transfer students enrolled in 2004-2005. Applicants must submit official college and high school transcripts. An audition or a portfolio is required. Depending on the program, at least 1 or 2 years, including the final semester, must be completed in residence.

Visiting: There are regularly scheduled orientations for prospective students, including tours held Monday through Friday at 12 P.M. throughout the academic year. Visitors may sit in on classes. To schedule a visit, contact the Office of Admissions at *admiss@calarts.edu*.

Financial Aid: In 2005-2006, 77% of all full-time freshmen and 84% of continuing full-time students received some form of financial aid. 62% of full-time freshmen and 72% of continuing full-time students received need-based aid. The average freshman award was $13,008. Need-based scholarships or need-based grants averaged $8044 ($30,260 maximum); and need-based self-help aid (loans and jobs) averaged $4528 ($10,625 maximum). 29% of undergraduates work part time. Average annual earnings from campus work are $1341. The average financial indebtedness of the 2005 graduate was $34,602. Cal-Arts is a member of CSS. The FAFSA is required. The priority date for freshman financial aid applications for fall entry is March 2.

International Students: There are 63 international students enrolled. A satisfactory score is required on the written TOEFL.

Computers: Wireless access is available. Students may access the system through 6 airports across campus and in the main library. All students may access the system. There are no time limits and no fees. It is recommended that students in graphic design have personal computers.

Graduates: From July 1, 2004 to June 30, 2005, 175 bachelor's degrees were awarded. The most popular majors were animation (15%), acting (12%), and music performance (10%). In an average class, 66% graduate in 6 years or less. 25 companies recruited on campus in 2004-2005.

Admissions Contact: Carol Kim, Dean of Enrollment Services.
E-mail: *admiss@calarts.edu* Web: *www.calarts.edu*

CALIFORNIA LUTHERAN UNIVERSITY   C-5
Thousand Oaks, CA 91360-2700   (805) 493-3135
(877) 258-3678; Fax: (805) 493-3114

Full-time: 745 men, 970 women	**Faculty:** 100; IIA, av$
Part-time: 105 men, 100 women	**Ph.D.s:** 94%
Graduate: 295 men, 710 women	**Student/Faculty:** 17 to 1
Year: semesters, summer session	**Tuition:** $20,500
Application Deadline: see profile	**Room & Board:** $7300
Freshman Class: n/av	
SAT or ACT: required	**LESS COMPETITIVE**

California Lutheran University, founded in 1959, is a private, nonprofit liberal arts institution affiliated with the Evangelical Lutheran Church of America. The comprehensive university offers undergraduate programs in arts and sciences, business, and education. Figures in this capsule and in this profile are approximate. There are 3 undergraduate and 4 graduate schools. The library contains 114,280 volumes, 18,080 microform items, and 1140 audio/video tapes/CDs/DVDs, and subscribes to 610 periodicals including electronic. Computerized library services include the card catalog, interlibrary loans, and database searching. Special learning facilities include a learning resource center, art gallery, radio station, TV station, and a state-of-the-art science center. The 290-acre campus is in a suburban area 45 miles north of downtown Los Angeles in Ventura County, 50 miles south of Santa Barbara. Including any residence halls, there are 41 buildings.

Student Life: 67% of undergraduates are from California. Others are from 35 states, 33 foreign countries, and Canada. 70% are from public schools. 67% are white; 12% Hispanic. 48% are Protestant; 26% claim no religious affiliation; 21% Catholic. The average age of freshmen is 18; all undergraduates, 20. 18% do not continue beyond their first year; 60% remain to graduate.

Housing: 1300 students can be accommodated in college housing, which includes coed dorms and on-campus apartments. In addition, there are honors houses, a quiet hall, graduate housing, and senior singles. On-campus housing is guaranteed for all 4 years. 82% of students live on campus; of those, 75% remain on campus on weekends. Alcohol is not permitted. All students may keep cars.

Activities: There are no fraternities or sororities. There are 36 groups on campus, including art, band, cheerleading, choir, chorale, chorus, computers, dance, debate, drama, drum and bugle corps, environmental, ethnic, film, forensics, gay, honors, international, jazz band, literary magazine, marching band, musical theater, newspaper, orchestra, pep band, photography, political, professional, radio and TV, religious, social, social service, student alumni, student government, symphony, and yearbook. Popular campus events include Santa Lucia, Scandinavian Day, and the Pulitzer Prize Symposium.

Sports: There are 11 intercollegiate sports for men and 10 for women, and 10 intramural sports for men and 10 for women. Facilities include a 400-seat gym, 2 fields, a swimming pool, tennis courts, and a 2000-seat stadium.

Disabled Students: 75% of the campus is accessible. Wheelchair ramps, elevators, special parking, specially equipped rest rooms, lowered drinking fountains, and lowered telephones are available.

Services: Counseling and information services are available, as is tutoring in every subject, including The learning resources and writing centers offer help with study and writing skills. There is remedial math, reading, and writing. A student support services program helps low-income first-generation students adapt to the academic and social life of the campus.

Campus Safety and Security: Measures include 24-hour foot and vehicle patrol, security escort services, shuttle buses, and informal discussions. There are pamphlets/posters/films, emergency telephones, and lighted pathways/sidewalks. All residence halls are equipped with security systems.

Programs of Study: CLU confers B.A. and B.S. degrees. Master's and doctoral degrees are also awarded. Bachelor's degrees are awarded in BIOLOGICAL SCIENCE (biochemistry and biology/biological science), BUSINESS (accounting, business administration and management, and marketing/retailing/merchandising), COMMUNICATIONS AND THE ARTS (art, communications, dramatic arts, English, French, German, multimedia, music, and Spanish), COMPUTER AND PHYSICAL SCIENCE (chemistry, computer science, geology, information sciences and systems, mathematics, and physics), EDUCATION (education and physical), HEALTH PROFESSIONS (predentistry, premedicine, and sports medicine), SOCIAL SCIENCE (criminal justice, economics, history, interdisciplinary studies, international studies, liberal arts/general studies, philosophy, political science/government, prelaw, psychology, religion, social science, and sociology). Biology, accounting, and humanities are the strongest academically. Business, psychology, and communication arts are the largest.

Required: To graduate, all students must complete a core curriculum including 16 to 20 units in social science, 8 each in religion, foreign language, and science, 7 in English, 4 to 6 in creative arts, 4 in math, and 3 in phys ed. Students must also fulfill content requirements of a freshman cluster and take 2 writing-intensive courses, global studies, gender

and ethnic studies, and a senior level capstone course. Also needed are a total of 124 units, 40 of which must be upper division with 32 hours in the major for a B.A. and a minimum of 36 hours for a B.S. The final 30 credits before graduation must be completed at CLU. Students must have a minimum 2.0 GPA, with 2.25 in the major.

Special: CLU offers co-op programs, cross-registration with Wagner College, internships, a Washington semester, and study abroad in 20 countries. Also available are work-study, accelerated degrees in business, computer science, and accounting, a general studies degree, and dual and student-designed interdisciplinary degree majors. A 3-2 engineering degree with Washington University of St. Louis, credit for experiential learning, special student status for nondegree study, pass/fail options, continuing education, English as a second language, and an adult degree evening program are also offered. There are 6 national honor societies and a freshman honors program.

Faculty/Classroom: 56% of faculty are male; 44%, female. 94% teach undergraduates. No introductory courses are taught by graduate students. The average class size in an introductory lecture is 35; in a laboratory, 17; and in a regular course, 22.

Requirements: The SAT or ACT is required. Applicants must be graduates of an accredited secondary school and have completed a minimum of 4 years of English, 2 years each of math, foreign language, and social studies, and 1 of lab science. The GED is accepted. An essay is required and an interview is recommended. AP and CLEP credits are accepted. Important factors in the admissions decision are advanced placement or honor courses, recommendations by school officials, and evidence of special talent.

Procedure: Freshmen are admitted fall and spring. Entrance exams should be taken in the fall. There are early decision, deferred admissions, and rolling admissions plans. Check with the school for application deadlines. The application fee is $45. A waiting list is an active part of the admissions procedure. Applications are accepted on-line.

Transfer: 182 transfer students enrolled in a recent year. Transfers must have a minimum 2.25 GPA and at least 24 credit hours earned. An application is required. An interview is recommended. Applicants must be in good standing at the previous college and may submit a recommendation from a college professor in lieu of a high school recommendation. 32 of 124 credits required for the bachelor's degree must be completed at CLU.

Visiting: There are regularly scheduled orientations for prospective students, including an admission and financial aid interview, a tour, visits with faculty or coaches, and lunch. There are guides for informal visits and visitors may sit in on classes and stay overnight. To schedule a visit, contact the Admission Office.

Financial Aid: In a recent year, 90% of all full-time freshmen and 85% of continuing full-time students received some form of financial aid. The average freshman award was $16,729. 45% of undergraduates worked part time. Average annual earnings from campus work were $1000. The FAFSA is required. Check with the school for application deadlines.

International Students: The school actively recruits these students. They must score satisfactorily on the written TOEFL, take the college's own test, and also take the SAT or the ACT.

Computers: All students may access the system any time. There are no time limits and no fees.

Admissions Contact: Matt Warden, Dean of Admission.
E-mail: *dcalkins@clunet.edu* Web: *www.clunet.edu*

CALIFORNIA MARITIME ACADEMY   B-3
Vallejo, CA 94590-0644   (707) 654-1330
(800) 561-1945; Fax: (707) 654-1336

Full-time: 494 men, 140 women	**Faculty:** 49; IIB, +$
Part-time: 30 men, 75 women	**Ph.D.s:** 31%
Graduate: none	**Student/Faculty:** 12 to 1
Year: semesters, summer session	**Tuition:** $6220 ($13,870)
Application Deadline: see profile	**Room & Board:** $7270
Freshman Class: n/av	
SAT or ACT: required	**COMPETITIVE**

California Maritime Academy, founded in 1929, is a public college that awards undergraduate degrees in marine transportation, business, engineering, and technology. In addition to regional accreditation, Cal Maritime has baccalaureate program accreditation with ABET. The library contains 30,000 volumes and 15,000 microform items, and subscribes to 300 periodicals including electronic. Computerized library services include the card catalog, interlibrary loans, database searching, and Internet access. Special learning facilities include a learning resource center, training ship, navigation, steam plant, and diesel engine simulators, and fluid dynamics lab with wind tunnels and a miniature jet turbine engine. The 67-acre campus is in a suburban area 30 miles northeast of San Francisco. Including any residence halls, there are 27 buildings.

Student Life: 80% of undergraduates are from California. Others are from 19 states and 14 foreign countries. 70% are from public schools. 55% are white; 13% Asian American. The average age of freshmen is 19; all undergraduates, 22. 7% do not continue beyond their first year.

Housing: 457 students can be accommodated in college housing, which includes single-sex and coed dorms. In addition, there are 24-hour quiet residences. On-campus housing is guaranteed for all 4 years. 65% of students live on campus; of those, 30% remain on campus on weekends. Alcohol is not permitted. All students may keep cars.

Activities: There are no fraternities or sororities. There are 26 groups on campus, including auto shop, drill team, engineering, ethnic, international, photography, professional, religious, social, social service, surf club, and student government. Popular campus events include movie nights, cave exploring, and cafe night.

Sports: There are 7 intercollegiate sports for men and 5 for women, and 10 intramural sports for men and 8 for women. Facilities include a gym, a weight room, physical therapy and exercise rooms, a 25-meter pool, tennis and racquetball courts, and a sports field.

Disabled Students: 70% of the campus is accessible. Wheelchair ramps, special parking, specially equipped rest rooms, lowered drinking fountains, and lowered telephones are available.

Services: Counseling and information services are available, as is tutoring in some subjects, including math, English, engineering, and science. There is remedial math, reading, and writing.

Campus Safety and Security: Measures include 24-hour foot and vehicle patrol, self-defense education, security escort services, and informal discussions. There are pamphlets/posters/films, lighted pathways/sidewalks, and and surveillance cameras.

Programs of Study: Cal Maritime confers the B.S degree. Bachelor's degrees are awarded in BUSINESS (business administration and management and transportation management), ENGINEERING AND ENVIRONMENTAL DESIGN (engineering technology, marine engineering, maritime science, and mechanical engineering). Mechanical engineering is the strongest academically. Marine transportation is the largest.

Required: Graduation requirements for all students include a minimum 2.0 GPA and completion of English composition, American government, U.S. history, algebra and trigonometry, computer science, and survival swimming courses. All students must participate in at least one 2-month training cruise. A total of 129 to 187 credits is required for graduation.

Special: The academy has simulator training and requires a 2-month session aboard the academy's ship. Lab time is a major part of each program. Industry internships are available during the summer. Dual majors and co-op programs are available, as is cross-registration with other Cal State institutions. There are B.A.- B.S. degrees in mechanical engineering, business, marine transportation, facilities engineering, global studies, and marine engineering.

Faculty/Classroom: 85% of faculty are male; 15%, female. All teach undergraduates. The average class size in an introductory lecture is 20; in a laboratory, 9; and in a regular course, 20.

Requirements: The SAT or ACT is required. In addition, secondary school courses must include 4 years of English, 3 each of math and electives, 2 of language, and 1 each of lab science, history, and a visual or performing art. A GPA of 2.0 is required. AP and CLEP credits are accepted. Important factors in the admissions decision are leadership record, advanced placement or honor courses, and evidence of special talent.

Procedure: Freshmen are admitted in the fall. Entrance exams should be taken by December of the senior year. There is a rolling admissions plan. Early decision applications should be filed by November. The fall 2005 application fee was $55. Notification is sent on a rolling basis. Applications are accepted on-line.

Transfer: 50 transfer students enrolled in 2004-2005. Applicants must have a 2.0 GPA, provide SAT or ACT scores, and be in good standing at the last institution attended.

Visiting: There are regularly scheduled orientations for prospective students. There are guides for informal visits. To schedule a visit, contact the Admissions Office.

Financial Aid: 80% of undergraduates work part time. Average annual earnings from campus work are $700. The FAFSA is required. Check with the school for current deadlines.

International Students: There are 20 international students enrolled. They must score satisfactorily on the TOEFL or take the SAT or ACT.

Computers: All students may access the system. There are no time limits and no fees.

Graduates: In an average class, 2% graduate in 3 years, 49% graduate in 4 years, 8% graduate in 5 years, and 3% graduate in 6 years. 30 companies recruited on campus in 2004-2005. Of the 2004 graduating class, 1% were enrolled in graduate school within 6 months of graduation and 10% were employed.

Admissions Contact: Chris Krzak, Director of Admissions and Outreach. E-mail: *admission@csum.edu* Web: *www.csum.edu*

CALIFORNIA POLYTECHNIC STATE UNIVERSITY   B-4
San Luis Obispo, CA 93407-0005
(805) 756-2311
Fax: (805) 756-5400

Full-time: 9320 men, 7201 women	**Faculty:** 726; IIA, +$
Part-time: 511 men, 353 women	**Ph.Ds:** 72%
Graduate: 467 men, 496 women	**Student/Faculty:** 23 to 1
Year: quarters, summer session	**Tuition:** $4245 ($14,415)
Application Deadline: November 30	**Room & Board:** $8145
Freshman Class: 23,691 applied, 10,551 accepted, 3372 enrolled	
SAT Verbal/Math: 575/590*	**ACT:** 25 **VERY COMPETITIVE**

California Polytechnic State University, founded in 1901, is a public institution that is part of the California State University system. It offers programs in agriculture, architecture and environmental design, business, education, engineering, liberal arts, sciences and math, and pre-professional studies. There are 6 undergraduate and 19 graduate schools. In addition to regional accreditation, Cal Poly has baccalaureate program accreditation with AACSB, ABET, ACCE, ADA, AHEA, ASLA, CSAB, NAAB, NRPA, and SAF. The library contains 1,206,340 volumes, 2,055,543 microform items, and 37,256 audio/video tapes/CDs/DVDs, and subscribes to 3198 periodicals including electronic. Computerized library services include the card catalog, interlibrary loans, and database searching. Special learning facilities include a learning resource center, art gallery, radio station, and TV station. The 6000-acre campus is in a suburban area 200 miles from both San Francisco and Los Angeles. Including any residence halls, there are 130 buildings.

Student Life: 94% of undergraduates are from California. Students are from 48 states, 41 foreign countries, and Canada. 68% are white; 12% Asian American; 11% Hispanic. The average age of freshmen is 19; all undergraduates, 21. 9% do not continue beyond their first year; 69% remain to graduate.

Housing: 2783 students can be accommodated in college housing, which includes single-sex and coed dorms. In addition, there are special-interest houses, living/learning centers with an academis theme, and shared, department-style housing.. On-campus housing is available on a first-come, first-served basis. 81% of students commute. Alcohol is not permitted. All students may keep cars.

Activities: There are 1 local and 26 national fraternities and 8 national sororities. There are 400 groups on campus, including art, band, cheerleading, chess, choir, chorale, chorus, computers, dance, drama, ethnic, film, gay, honors, international, jazz band, literary magazine, marching band, musical theater, newspaper, orchestra, pep band, photography, political, professional, radio and TV, religious, social, social service, student government, and symphony. Popular campus events include Rose Float, Week of Welcome (WOW), and Civil Rights Awareness Week.

Sports: There are 9 intercollegiate sports for men and 8 for women, and 19 intramural sports for men and 19 for women. Facilities include an indoor/outdoor swimming pool, volleyball, tennis, basketball, and racquetball courts, weight rooms, playing fields, and a track.

Disabled Students: 95% of the campus is accessible. Wheelchair ramps, elevators, special parking, specially equipped rest rooms, and lowered telephones are available.

Services: Counseling and information services are available, as is tutoring in most subjects. There is a reader service for the blind, a writing skills lab, and a test office. Psychological and career services are available.

Campus Safety and Security: Measures include 24-hour foot and vehicle patrol, security escort services, pamphlets/posters/films, and emergency telephones. There are lighted pathways/sidewalks.

Programs of Study: Cal Poly confers B.A., B.S., and B.Arch. degrees. Master's degrees are also awarded. Bachelor's degrees are awarded in AGRICULTURE (agricultural business management, agriculture, dairy science, horticulture, natural resource management, and soil science), BIOLOGICAL SCIENCE (biochemistry, biology/biological science, ecology, and microbiology), BUSINESS (business administration and management and recreation and leisure services), COMMUNICATIONS AND THE ARTS (English, graphic design, and journalism), COMPUTER AND PHYSICAL SCIENCE (chemistry, computer science, mathematics, physical sciences, physics, and statistics), EDUCATION (industrial arts, and physical), ENGINEERING AND ENVIRONMENTAL DESIGN (aeronautical engineering, agricultural engineering, architecture, architectural engineering, city/community/regional planning, civil engineering, computer engineering, construction management, electrical/electronics engineering, engineering, environmental engineering, industrial engineering, landscape architecture/design, manufacturing engineering, materials engineering, mechanical engineering, and metallurgical engineering), SOCIAL SCIENCE (economics, food science, history, human development, philosophy, political science/government, psychology, and social science). Agricultural management, architecture, and business administration are the largest.

Required: Students must have a minimum 2.0 GPA and complete general education and breadth requirements, including the following: 18 units each of physical and life sciences, social sciences, and literature and the arts; 14 units of English; and 5 units of psychology and health. Math, philosophy, history, computer literacy courses and a senior project are required. 186 to 263 quarter units are needed to graduate.

Special: Cal Poly offers work-study programs, co-op programs in numerous majors, cross-registration, study abroad in 11 countries, dual majors, and internships in many majors. Credit for military experience and pass/fail options are available, as is an external degree cross-registration program.

Faculty/Classroom: 67% of faculty are male; 33%, female.

Admissions: 45% of the 2005-2006 applicants were accepted. The SAT scores for the 2005-2006 freshman class were: Verbal--9% below 500, 47% between 500 and 599, 37% between 600 and 700, and 7% above 700; Math--4% below 500, 31% between 500 and 599, 49% between 600 and 700, and 15% above 700. The ACT scores were 7% below 21, 20% between 21 and 23, 33% between 24 and 26, 21% between 27 and 28, and 19% above 28. 67% of the current freshmen were in the top fifth of their class; 92% were in the top two fifths.

Requirements: The SAT or ACT is required. In addition, applicants must be graduates of an accredited high school or have a GED. 15 academic credits are required including 4 years of English, 3 each of math and science (1 lab), 2 of social sciences and a foreign language, and 1 each of history, visual and performing arts, and electives. A GPA of 2.0 is required. AP and CLEP credits are accepted. Important factors in the admissions decision are advanced placement or honor courses, extracurricular activities record, and evidence of special talent.

Procedure: Freshmen are admitted fall and summer. Entrance exams should be taken by January 15. There are early decision and early admissions plans. Early decision applications should be filed by October 31; regular applications, by November 30 for fall entry and February 28 for summer entry, along with a $55 fee. Notification of early decision is sent December 15; regular decision, March 1. Applications are accepted on-line.

Transfer: 868 transfer students enrolled in 2004-2005. Applicants must meet general education and breadth requirements, and submit college transcripts with a minimum GPA of 2.0. 50 of 186 to 263 credits required for the bachelor's degree must be completed at Cal Poly.

Visiting: There are regularly scheduled orientations for prospective students, held on Mondays and Wednesdays at 10 A.M. and 2 P.M. There are guides for informal visits and visitors may stay overnight. To schedule a visit, contact the Admissions Office at (805) 756-2792.

Financial Aid: In 2005-2006, 31% of all full-time freshmen and 34% of continuing full-time students received some form of financial aid. At least 25% of full-time freshmen and at least 27% of continuing full-time students received need-based aid. The average freshman award was $6588. Need-based scholarships or need-based grants averaged $1459; and need-based self-help aid (loans and jobs) averaged $2731. The average financial indebtedness of the 2005 graduate was $13,788. The FAFSA and the college's own financial statement are required. The priority date for freshman financial aid applications for fall entry is March 1. The deadline for filing freshman financial aid applications for fall entry is June 30.

International Students: The school actively recruits these students. A satisfactory score on the written TOEFL is required.

Computers: All students may access the system. There are no time limits and no fees. It is strongly recommended that all students have a personal computer.

Graduates: From July 1, 2004 to June 30, 2005, 3410 bachelor's degrees were awarded. The most popular majors were engineering (20%), business (18%), and agriculture (15%). In an average class, 15% graduate in 4 years or less, 47% graduate in 5 years or less, and 59% graduate in 6 years or less.

Admissions Contact: James L. Maraviglia, Director of Admissions. E-mail: *admissions@calpoly.edu* Web: *www.calpoly.edu*

CALIFORNIA STATE POLYTECHNIC UNIVERSITY, POMONA

D-5

Pomona, CA 91768-4019	(909) 869-3427; Fax: (909) 869-4529
Full-time: 8476 men, 6506 women	Faculty: 659; IIA, +$
Part-time: 1796 men, 1196 women	Ph.D.s: 74%
Graduate: 837 men, 1074 women	Student/Faculty: 23 to 1
Year: quarters, summer session	Tuition: $3012 ($10,500)
Application Deadline: November 1	Room & Board: $7506
Freshman Class: 17,252 applied, 4121 accepted, 2793 enrolled	
SAT Verbal/Math: 480/520*	ACT: 20 COMPETITIVE+

California State Polytechnic University, Pomona, an occupationally oriented institution founded in 1938, is part of the state-supported university system. It offers undergraduate and graduate programs in agriculture, liberal arts and sciences, business, engineering, and technical and professional training. Tuition figures in the above capsule are approximate. There are 8 undergraduate and 7 graduate schools. In addition to regional accreditation, Cal Poly Pomona has baccalaureate program accreditation with AACSB, ABET, ADA, ASLA, CSAB, and NAAB. The library contains 755,671 volumes, 1,828,685 microform items, and 11,188 audio/video tapes/CDs/DVDs, and subscribes to 5153 periodicals

including electronic. Computerized library services include the card catalog, interlibrary loans, database searching, and Internet access. Special learning facilities include a learning resource center, art gallery, TV station, and an interactive TV studio. The 1438-acre campus is in a suburban area 30 miles east of Los Angeles. Including any residence halls, there are 80 buildings.

Student Life: 98% of undergraduates are from California. Others are from 49 states, 54 foreign countries, and Canada. 84% are from public schools. 31% are Asian American; 28% Hispanic; 24% white. The average age of freshmen is 18; all undergraduates, 22. 15% do not continue beyond their first year; 46% remain to graduate.

Housing: 1800 students can be accommodated in college housing, which includes coed dorms. In addition, there are special-interest houses and a center for regenerative studies. On-campus housing is available on a first-come, first-served basis. 91% of students commute. All students may keep cars.

Activities: 1% of men belong to 6 local and 11 national fraternities; 1% of women belong to 3 local and 4 national sororities. There are 220 groups on campus, including art, band, cheerleading, choir, chorale, chorus, computers, ethnic, film, gay, honors, international, literary magazine, musical theater, newspaper, pep band, photography, political, professional, religious, social, social service, student government, and yearbook. Popular campus events include Rose Float, Broncofest, and Founder's Day.

Sports: There are 6 intercollegiate sports for men and 6 for women. Facilities include a 5000-seat stadium, tennis and racquetball courts, basketball and volleyball courts, soccer, baseball, and softball fields, a track, a swimming pool, gymnastics and weight rooms, a horse arena, and dance studios.

Disabled Students: 96% of the campus is accessible. Wheelchair ramps, elevators, special parking, specially equipped rest rooms, special class scheduling, lowered drinking fountains, lowered telephones, and specialized tram, van, and shuttle transportation are available.

Services: Counseling and information services are available, as is tutoring in most subjects. There is a reader service for the blind and remedial math and writing.

Campus Safety and Security: Measures include 24-hour foot and vehicle patrol, self-defense education, security escort services, and shuttle buses. There are informal discussions, pamphlets/posters/films, emergency telephones, lighted pathways/sidewalks, vehicle assists, and crime prevention programs.

Programs of Study: Cal Poly Pomona confers B.A., B.S., Barch., and B.F.A. degrees. Master's degrees are also awarded. Bachelor's degrees are awarded in AGRICULTURE (agricultural business management, agriculture, agronomy, animal science, and horticulture), BIOLOGICAL SCIENCE (biology/biological science, biotechnology, botany, microbiology, plant physiology, and zoology), BUSINESS (accounting, apparel and accessories marketing, banking and finance, business administration and management, hotel/motel and restaurant management, human resources, international business management, marketing/retailing/merchandising, operations research, and real estate), COMMUNICATIONS AND THE ARTS (art, communications, dramatic arts, English, music, and Spanish), COMPUTER AND PHYSICAL SCIENCE (chemistry, computer science, geology, information sciences and systems, mathematics, and physics), ENGINEERING AND ENVIRONMENTAL DESIGN (aeronautical engineering, architecture, chemical engineering, civil engineering, computer technology, construction technology, electrical/electronics engineering, engineering technology, industrial engineering, landscape architecture/design, manufacturing engineering, materials engineering, and mechanical engineering), SOCIAL SCIENCE (anthropology, behavioral science, economics, food science, geography, history, liberal arts/general studies, philosophy, physical fitness/movement, political science/government, psychology, social science, sociology, and urban studies). Engineering, architecture, and business are the strongest academically. Computer information systems, electrical engineering, and mechanical engineering are the largest.

Required: All students must complete general education requirements, including courses in written and oral communications, critical thinking, math, humanities, natural sciences, and social sciences, and must pass a graduation writing test. A total of 180 (B.A.) to 246 (B.S.) quarter units with a minimum GPA of 2.0 is required to graduate.

Special: Cross-registration is possible with any California State University school. Internships and co-op programs are available in agriculture, business, environmental design, engineering, science, political science, behavioral science, and phys ed. An international study program in 17 countries, work-study programs, B.A.-B.S. degrees, a liberal studies degree, credit for military experience, an external degree program, and credit/no credit options are offered. Nondegree study is possible. There are 30 national honor societies and a freshman honors program.

Faculty/Classroom: 61% of faculty are male; 39%, female. The average class size in a regular course is 30.

Admissions: 24% of the 2005-2006 applicants were accepted. The SAT scores for the 2005-2006 freshman class were: Verbal--50% below 500, 37% between 500 and 599, 12% between 600 and 700, and 1%

above 700; Math--32% below 500, 39% between 500 and 599, 25% between 600 and 700, and 4% above 700. The ACT scores were 51% below 21, 25% between 21 and 23, 14% between 24 and 26, 6% between 27 and 28, and 4% above 28.

Requirements: The SAT or ACT is recommended. In addition, applicants must be graduates of an accredited secondary school or have a GED equivalent. Secondary school courses must include 4 years of high school English, 3 each of math and electives, 2 of foreign language, and 1 each of science, history, and art. A GPA of 2.0 is required. AP and CLEP credits are accepted.

Procedure: Freshmen are admitted to all sessions. Entrance exams should be taken during the fall of the senior year. There is a deferred admissions and a rolling admissions plan. Applications should be filed by November 1 for fall entry, June 1 for winter entry, August 1 for spring entry, and February 1 for summer entry, along with a $55 fee. Notification is sent on a rolling basis. Applications are accepted on-line.

Transfer: 1496 transfer students enrolled in 2004-2005. Applicants must have completed 56 semester or 84 quarter units including college preparatory subjects. A 2.0 GPA (2.4 for nonresidents) is required. 50 of 180 to 246 quarter units required for the bachelor's degree must be completed at Cal Poly Pomona.

Visiting: There are regularly scheduled orientations for prospective students, consisting of tours of the campus led by current undergraduate students and a 90 minute walking tour. There are guides for informal visits and visitors may sit in on classes and stay overnight. To schedule a visit, contact Visitor Services at (909) 869-3529.

Financial Aid: In 2005-2006, 41% of all full-time freshmen and 54% of continuing full-time students received some form of financial aid. 48% of full-time freshmen and 52% of continuing full-time students received need-based aid. The average freshman award was $7625. Average annual earnings from campus work are $2000. The average financial indebtedness of the 2005 graduate was $11,258. The FAFSA is required. The deadline for filing freshman financial aid applications for fall entry is March 2.

International Students: There are 602 international students enrolled. Satisfactory scores are required on the written TOEFL and the SAT or the ACT.

Computers: All students may access the system 24 hours per day. There are no time limits and no fees. It is recommended that students in environmental design have PCs.

Graduates: From July 1, 2004 to June 30, 2005, 3292 bachelor's degrees were awarded. In a recent year, the most popular majors were marketing management (8%), management/human resources (7%), and computer information systems (6%). In an average class, 9% graduate in 4 years or less, 31% graduate in 5 years or less, and 46% graduate in 6 years or less. 230 companies recruited on campus in 2004-2005.

Admissions Contact: Dr. George R. Bradshaw, Director of Admissions and Outreach. A video is available.
E-mail: *grbradshaw@csupomona.edu* Web: *www.csupomona.edu*

CALIFORNIA STATE UNIVERSITY SYSTEM

The California State University system, established in 1961, is a public system in California. It is governed by a board of trustees, whose chief administrator is the chancellor. A primary goal of the system is teaching. The main priorities are to emphasize quality in instruction; to provide an environment in which scholarship, research, creative, artistic, and professional activity are valued and supported; and to stress the importance of the liberal arts and sciences. The total enrollment of all 23 campuses is usually about 400,000; there were 21,000 faculty members. Altogether there are more than 1150 baccalaureate, 750 master's, and 26 joint doctoral programs offered in the California State University system. 4-year campuses are located in Bakersfield, Chico, Dominguez Hills, East Bay, Fresno, Fullerton, Humboldt, Long Beach, Los Angeles, Northridge, Pomona, Sacramento, San Bernadino, San Diego, San Francisco, San Jose, San Luis Obispo, Sonoma, and the Maritime Academy at Vallejo. Profiles of the 4-year campuses are included in this section.

CALIFORNIA STATE UNIVERSITY, BAKERSFIELD   C-4

Bakersfield, CA 93311-1099

(661) 664-2160
(800) 788-2782; Fax: (661) 664-3389

Full-time: 1440 men, 2700 women	**Faculty:** 234; IIA, +$
Part-time: 395 men, 705 women	**Ph.D.s:** 50%
Graduate: 570 men, 1260 women	**Student/Faculty:** 14 to 1
Year: quarters, summer session	**Tuition:** $1975 ($9350)
Application Deadline: open	**Room & Board:** $4150
Freshman Class: n/av	
SAT or ACT: required	**LESS COMPETITIVE**

California State University/Bakersfield, founded in 1965, is part of the California State University System. It offers graduate and undergraduate programs in liberal arts and sciences, business, public administration, education, health fields, preengineering, and preprofessional training. Figures given in the above capsule and in this profile are approximate. There are 3 undergraduate and 10 graduate schools. In addition to regional accreditation, Cal State Bakersfield has baccalaureate program accreditation with AACSB, NCATE, and NLN. The library contains 339,900 volumes, 603,300 microform items, and 5180 audio/video tapes/CDs/DVDs, and subscribes to 2700 periodicals including electronic. Computerized library services include the card catalog, interlibrary loans, and database searching. Special learning facilities include a learning resource center, art gallery, natural history museum, geological data sample repository, archeological information center, an instructional television network, applied research center, and animal care and treatment facility. The 375-acre campus is in an urban area in southwest Bakersfield. Including any residence halls, there are 30 buildings.

Student Life: 98% of undergraduates are from California. Others are from 25 states, 50 foreign countries, and Canada. 98% are from public schools. 51% are white; 25% Hispanic. The average age of freshmen is 19; all undergraduates, 25. 15% do not continue beyond their first year.

Housing: 330 students can be accommodated in college housing, which includes single-sex and coed dorms. On-campus housing is guaranteed for all 4 years. 98% of students commute. Alcohol is not permitted. All students may keep cars.

Activities: 2% of men belong to 3 national fraternities; 2% of women belong to 4 national sororities. There are 74 groups on campus, including art, band, cheerleading, chess, choir, chorale, computers, dance, drama, ethnic, film, gay, honors, international, jazz band, literary magazine, musical theater, newspaper, opera, orchestra, pep band, photography, political, professional, radio and TV, religious, social, social service, student government, and symphony. Popular campus events include Cinco de Mayo, Open Campus, and Jazz Festival.

Sports: There are 7 intercollegiate sports for men and 6 for women, and 12 intramural sports for men and 12 for women. Facilities include a 4000-seat gymn, a wrestling sport center, an aquatic center, tennis and racquetball courts, and softball and soccer fields.

Disabled Students: Wheelchair ramps, elevators, special parking, specially equipped rest rooms, special class scheduling, lowered drinking fountains, and lowered telephones are available.

Services: Counseling and information services are available, as is tutoring in most subjects, as well as in study skills. There is a reader service for the blind, and remedial math, reading, and writing.

Campus Safety and Security: Measures include 24-hour foot and vehicle patrol, self-defense education, security escort services, and informal discussions. There are pamphlets/posters/films, emergency telephones, and lighted pathways/sidewalks.

Programs of Study: Cal State Bakersfield confers B.A. and B.S. degrees. Master's degrees are also awarded. Bachelor's degrees are awarded in BIOLOGICAL SCIENCE (biology/biological science), BUSINESS (business administration and management), COMMUNICATIONS AND THE ARTS (art, communications, dramatic arts, English, music, and Spanish), COMPUTER AND PHYSICAL SCIENCE (chemistry, computer science, geology, mathematics, and physics), ENGINEERING AND ENVIRONMENTAL DESIGN (land use management and reclamation), HEALTH PROFESSIONS (clinical science and nursing), SOCIAL SCIENCE (anthropology, child psychology/development, criminal justice, economics, history, liberal arts/general studies, philosophy, political science/government, psychology, public administration, religion, and sociology). Business, education, and public administration are the strongest academically. Business is the largest.

Required: All students must complete 72 quarter units of general education requirements in basic skills, Western civilization, non-Western culture, philosophy, fine arts, literature, technology, and physical, social, and life sciences. They must also take a comprehensive writing examination or complete an upper-division writing course with a grade of C or better, demonstrate understanding of American history and government institutions, and complete a senior seminar. A total of 186 quarter units with a minimum GPA of 2.0 is required in order to graduate.

Special: Cal State Bakersfield offers co-op programs in education and business administration, cross-registration through the National Student Exchange Program, study abroad at 36 universities in 16 countries, a 3-2 engineering degree with California Polytechnic State University/San Luis Obispo, and student-designed majors. Credit for life experience, pass/fail options, and nondegree study are available. Students may also earn credits as interns and participate in work-study programs on and off campus. There is a freshman honors program.

Faculty/Classroom: 62% of faculty are male; 38%, female. All both teach and do research. No introductory courses are taught by graduate students. The average class size in an introductory lecture is 40; in a laboratory, 24; and in a regular course, 30.

Requirements: The SAT or ACT is required, if the GPA is below 3.0. (3.6 for nonresidents). Admission is based on an eligibility index that weights the GPA and standardized test scores. Applicants must be graduates of an accredited secondary school or GED equivalent, and have a total of 15 academic units, including 4 years of English, 3 of math, 2 of foreign language, 1 each of lab science, U.S. history/government, and visual and performing arts, and 3 of electives. Cal State Bakersfield requires applicants to be in the upper 33% of their class. A GPA of 2.0 is required. AP and CLEP credits are accepted.

Procedure: Freshmen are admitted fall, winter, and spring. Entrance exams should be taken by December of the senior year. There are early decision, early admissions, deferred admissions, and rolling admissions plans. Application deadlines are open. Application fee is $55.

Transfer: A 2.0 GPA (2.4 for nonresidents) is required in a minimum of 56 semester or 84 quarter units earned, including English and math. 45 of 186 credits required for the bachelor's degree must be completed at Cal State Bakersfield.

Visiting: There are regularly scheduled orientations for prospective students, consisting of a day-long orientation that includes meetings with faculty advisers and school deans. There are guides for informal visits and visitors may sit in on classes. To schedule a visit, contact the Office of Outreach Services at (805) 664-3138.

Financial Aid: Cal State Bakersfield is a member of CSS. The FAFSA is required. Check with the school for application deadlines.

International Students: The school actively recruits these students. They must score satisfactorily on the written TOEFL and also the SAT or ACT is required if the GPA is below 3.0.

Computers: All students may access the system. There are no time limits and no fees.

Admissions Contact: Dr. Homer Montalvo, Dean of Admissions. E-mail: *hmontalvo@csubak.edu*

CALIFORNIA STATE UNIVERSITY, CHICO — B-2

Chico, CA 95929-0722

(530) 898-4428
(800) 542-4426; Fax: (530) 898-6456

Full-time: 6164 men, 6915 women	Faculty: 499; IIA, +$
Part-time: 638 men, 809 women	Ph.Ds: 65%
Graduate: 342 men, 508 women	Student/Faculty: 26 to 1
Year: semesters, summer session	Tuition: $3402 ($13,572)
Application Deadline: November 30	Room & Board: $7993
Freshman Class: 12,457 applied, 10,881 accepted, 2335 enrolled	
SAT Verbal/Math: 520/550*	ACT: 22	COMPETITIVE

California State University/Chico, founded in 1887, is a public institution offering undergraduate programs in behavioral and social sciences, business, communication and education, engineering, computer science and technology, humanities and fine arts, natural sciences, agriculture, and nursing. The university offers web-based classes. There are 7 undergraduate schools and 1 graduate school. In addition to regional accreditation, CSU has baccalaureate program accreditation with AACSB, ABET, ACCE, ADA, CSAB, CSWE, NASAD, NASM, NLN, and NRPA. The library contains 948,564 volumes, 1,140,465 microform items, and 22,968 audio/video tapes/CDs/DVDs, and subscribes to 20,404 periodicals including electronic. Computerized library services include the card catalog, interlibrary loans, and database searching. Special learning facilities include a learning resource center, art gallery, planetarium, radio station, instructional media center, university farm, biological field station, anthropology museum, media preparation lab, computer graphics lab, and recording arts studio. The 130-acre campus is in a small town 100 miles north of Sacramento. Including any residence halls, there are 72 buildings.

Student Life: 99% of undergraduates are from California. Students are from 44 states, 48 foreign countries, and Canada. 94% are from public schools. 73% are white; 12% Hispanic. The average age of freshmen is 18; all undergraduates, 22. 15% do not continue beyond their first year; 51% remain to graduate.

Housing: 1700 students can be accommodated in college housing, which includes coed dorms, on-campus apartments, off-campus apartments, fraternity houses, and sorority houses. In addition, there are honors houses, language houses, special-interest houses, and thematic housing for minorities in engineering and science, math, and business. Theme floors include community service, recreational sports, leadership, and adventure outings. In-campus housing is available on a first-come, first-served basis. 87% of students commute. Alcohol is not permitted. All students may keep cars.

Activities: 7% of men belong to 4 local and 14 national fraternities; 6% of women belong to 8 local and 10 national sororities. There are 200 groups on campus, including art, band, cheerleading, chess, choir, chorale, chorus, computers, dance, debate, drama, drill team, ethnic, film, forensics, gay, honors, international, jazz band, literary magazine, musical theater, newspaper, opera, orchestra, pep band, political, professional, radio and TV, religious, social, social service, student government, symphony, and yearbook. Popular campus events include International Festival, Greek Week, and Fun Without Alcohol Fair.

Sports: There are 6 intercollegiate sports for men and 7 for women, and 17 intramural sports for men and 16 for women. Facilities include 2 gyms, athletic training rooms, a dance studio, swimming and diving pools, a par course, putting greens and sand trap, handball /racquetball courts, baseball/softball fields, an all-weather track, a soccer stadium, a 7500-seat football stadium, and a residence hall sports center.

Disabled Students: 95% of the campus is accessible. Wheelchair ramps, elevators, special parking, specially equipped rest rooms, special class scheduling, lowered drinking fountains, lowered telephones, special housing, sign language interpreters, on-campus transportation, Braille signage, books on tape, adaptive computer lab, and disability support services are available.

Services: Counseling and information services are available, as is tutoring in every subject. There is a reader service for the blind, and remedial math, reading, and writing. student learning center offers a tutorial program, study skills development, and learning assistance workshops.

Campus Safety and Security: Measures include 24-hour foot and vehicle patrol, self-defense education, security escort services, and shuttle buses. There are informal discussions, pamphlets/posters/films, emergency telephones, lighted pathways/sidewalks, a victim awareness program, and crime prevention workshops.

Programs of Study: CSU confers B.A., B.S., and B.F.A. degrees. Master's degrees are also awarded. Bachelor's degrees are awarded in AGRICULTURE (agricultural business management and agriculture), BIOLOGICAL SCIENCE (biology/biological science, microbiology, and nutrition), BUSINESS (business administration and management), COMMUNICATIONS AND THE ARTS (art, communications, dramatic arts, English, fine arts, French, German, journalism, music, musical theater, and Spanish), COMPUTER AND PHYSICAL SCIENCE (chemistry, computer science, geology, geoscience, information sciences and systems, mathematics, physical sciences, and physics), EDUCATION (physical), ENGINEERING AND ENVIRONMENTAL DESIGN (civil engineering, computer engineering, construction management, electrical/electronics engineering, environmental science, industrial engineering technology, and mechanical engineering), HEALTH PROFESSIONS (exercise science, health science, nursing, and speech pathology/audiology), SOCIAL SCIENCE (American studies, anthropology, Asian/Oriental studies, child psychology/development, economics, ethnic studies, geography, history, humanities, international relations, Latin American studies, liberal arts/general studies, parks and recreation management, philosophy, political science/government, psychology, public administration, religion, social science, social work, and sociology). Nursing, accounting, and biology are the strongest academically. Business administration, liberal studies, and communications are the largest.

Required: Graduation requirements for all students include the completion of arts/fine arts, computer literacy, humanities, philosophy, sciences, social sciences, math, writing proficiency, ethnic studies, non-Western studies, U.S. history, U.S. Constitution, and U.S./California government courses. Also required are a 48-unit general education program, a 2.0 minimum GPA, 124 to 132 total credit hours, and 24 to 115 hours in the major.

Special: The university offers co-op programs and cross-registration as part of the National Student Exchange. Internships, distance learning, teacher certification, study abroad in 16 countries, work-study, student-designed majors, independent study, credit for experience, nondegree study, and pass/fail options are available. There are 4 national honor societies, a freshman honors program, and 28 departmental honors programs.

Faculty/Classroom: 58% of faculty are male; 42%, female. All teach undergraduates. Graduate students teach 2% of introductory courses. The average class size in an introductory lecture is 25; in a laboratory, 21; and in a regular course, 22.

Admissions: 87% of the 2005-2006 applicants were accepted. The SAT scores for the 2005-2006 freshman class were: Verbal--35% below 500, 49% between 500 and 599, 15% between 600 and 700, and 1% above 700; Math--29% below 500, 48% between 500 and 599, 21% between 600 and 700, and 2% above 700. The ACT scores were 35% below 21, 36% between 21 and 23, 21% between 24 and 26, 6% between 27 and 28, and 2% above 28.

Requirements: The SAT or ACT is required. In addition, an index combining GPA and SAT and ACT scores is used to determine eligibility for admission. Applicants must be graduates of secondary school or have a GED and have completed 4 years of English, 3 years each of math and college preparatory electives, 2 years of a foreign language and social studies, and 1 year academic electives art and/or music. Applicants are accepted on-line at *www.csumentor.edu*. A GPA of 2.0 is required. AP and CLEP credits are accepted.

Procedure: Freshmen are admitted fall and spring. Entrance exams should be taken in fall of the senior year. There is a first-time deferred admissions plan and a rolling admissions plan. Early decision applications is October1 to November 30; regular applications, by November 30 for fall entry, along with a $55 fee. Notification of regular decision is sent March 1. Applications are accepted on-line.

Transfer: 1386 transfer students enrolled in 2004-2005. Transfer students who are California residents must have a minimum 2.0 GPA, and nonresidents need 2.4. A minimum of 56 transferable credit hours are needed, and students must have made up any missing college preparatory subjects and provide a statement of good standing and transcripts from prior institutions. 30 of 124 credits required for the bachelor's degree must be completed at CSU.

Visiting: There are guides for informal visits and visitors may sit in on classes. To schedule a visit, contact University Outreach.

Financial Aid: In 2005-2006, 37% of all full-time freshmen and 42% of continuing full-time students received some form of financial aid. At least 26% of full-time freshmen and 30% of continuing full-time students received need-based aid. The average freshman award was $6032. Need-based scholarships or need-based grants averaged $5735; need-based self-help aid (loans and jobs) averaged $3533; non-need-based athletic scholarships averaged $3634; and other non-need-based awards and non-need-based institutional scholarships averaged $1465. The FAFSA and Scholarship application form are required. The priority date for freshman financial aid applications for fall entry is March 2.

International Students: The school actively recruits these students. A satisfactory score is required on the written TOEFL.

Computers: All students may access the system. There are no time limits and no fees. It is strongly recommended that all students have a personal computer. A Power Mac 7100 (500MB hard drive or better) or a PC is recommended.

Graduates: From July 1, 2004 to June 30, 2005, 2724 bachelor's degrees were awarded. The most popular majors were business/marketing (16%), liberal studies/general studies (12%), and social sciences (9%). In an average class, 16% graduate in 4 years or less, 42% graduate in 5 years or less, and 51% graduate in 6 years or less. 282 companies recruited on campus in 2004-2005.

Admissions Contact: John Swiney, Director of Admissions. E-mail: *info@csuchico.edu* Web: *http://www.csuchico.edu*

CALIFORNIA STATE UNIVERSITY, DOMINGUEZ HILLS C-5

Carson, CA 90747-0005 (310) 243-3696

Full-time: 1475 men, 3150 women	Faculty: 290; IIA, +$
Part-time: 800 men, 2275 women	Ph.D.s: 80%
Graduate: 1475 men, 3350 women	Student/Faculty: 16 to 1
Year: semesters, summer session	Tuition: $2520 ($10,170)
Application Deadline: April 1	Room & Board: $7700
Freshman Class: n/av	
SAT or ACT: required	LESS COMPETITIVE

California State University, Dominguez Hills, founded in 1960 as part of the state-supported university system, offers graduate and undergraduate programs in liberal arts and sciences, business, fine arts, health sciences, and technology to a primarily commuter student body. Some figures in above capsule and in this profile are approximate. There are 4 undergraduate and 4 graduate schools. In addition to regional accreditation, CSU Dominguez Hills has baccalaureate program accreditation with CAHEA, NASAD, NASM, NCATE, and NLN. The library contains 396,520 volumes, 569,630 microform items, and 17,130 audio/video tapes/CDs/DVDs, and subscribes to 4740 periodicals including electronic. Computerized library services include the card catalog and database searching. Special learning facilities include a learning resource center, art gallery, planetarium, and TV station. The 350-acre campus is in an urban area 10 miles south of Los Angeles. There are 40 buildings.

Student Life: 98% of undergraduates are from California. Others are from 29 states, 79 foreign countries, and Canada. 98% are from public schools. 30% are African American; 30% Hispanic; 20% white; 10% Asian American. The average age of freshmen is 19; all undergraduates, 29. 30% do not continue beyond their first year; 30% remain to graduate.

Housing: There are no residence halls. 710 students can be accommodated in college housing, which includes single-sex and coed on-campus apartments. On-campus housing is guaranteed for all 4 years. 96% of students commute. All students may keep cars.

Activities: There are 4 national fraternities and 1 local and 2 national sororities. There are 69 groups on campus, including art, band, cheerleading, choir, chorale, computers, dance, drama, drill team, ethnic, gay, honors, international, jazz band, literary magazine, musical theater, newspaper, orchestra, photography, political, professional, radio and TV, religious, social, social service, student government, symphony, and yearbook. Popular campus events include .

Sports: There are 4 intercollegiate sports for men and 4 for women. Facilities include the Olympic Velodrome (bicycle racing stadium), a gym, tennis courts, a baseball field, a track, a weight room, a swimming pool, and a soccer field.

Disabled Students: Wheelchair ramps, elevators, special parking, specially equipped rest rooms, lowered drinking fountains, and lowered telephones are available.

Services: Counseling and information services are available, as is tutoring in most subjects. There is a reader service for the blind, and remedial math, reading, and writing.

Campus Safety and Security: Measures include 24-hour foot and vehicle patrol, security escort services, informal discussions, and pamphlets/posters/films. There are emergency telephones and lighted pathways/sidewalks.

Programs of Study: CSU Dominguez Hills confers B.A. and B.S. degrees. Master's degrees are also awarded. Bachelor's degrees are award-

ed in BIOLOGICAL SCIENCE (biology/biological science), BUSINESS (business administration and management, labor studies, recreation and leisure services, and tourism), COMMUNICATIONS AND THE ARTS (art, communications, dramatic arts, English, music, and Spanish), COMPUTER AND PHYSICAL SCIENCE (chemistry, computer science, digital arts/technology, geology, mathematics, and physics), EDUCATION (physical), HEALTH PROFESSIONS (clinical science, health science, nursing, and occupational therapy), SOCIAL SCIENCE (African studies, anthropology, behavioral science, economics, geography, history, human services, interdisciplinary studies, liberal arts/general studies, Mexican-American/Chicano studies, philosophy, political science/government, psychology, public administration, and sociology). Liberal studies is the strongest academically. Business administration is the largest.

Required: To graduate, students must complete 120 to 132 semester units, including 54 to 60 units in general education, 40 units in upper-division courses, and specific courses or proficiency tests in U.S. history and politics, math, and writing. A minimum GPA of 2.0 must be maintained.

Special: Cross-registration is offered with 7 other California State University schools. Study abroad in 15 countries, co-op programs in all majors, on-campus work-study, internships, B.A.-B.S. degrees, dual and student-designed majors, credit for life experience, and pass/fail options are available. A B.A. in interdisciplinary studies, in which an accelerated degree is possible, and in liberal studies is offered. Many majors have evening programs. There are 2 national honor societies, a freshman honors program, and 13 departmental honors programs.

Faculty/Classroom: 50% of faculty are male; 50%, female. 95% teach undergraduates. The average class size in an introductory lecture is 45; in a laboratory, 19; and in a regular course, 32.

Requirements: The SAT or ACT is required. Except of those with a GPA of at least 3.0 (3.6 for nonresidents). Students must be high school graduates with a GPA of at least 2.0 and 15 academic units, including 4 in English, 3 in math, 2 in foreign language, and 1 each in U.S. history, lab science, and visual and performing arts. The GED is accepted. CSU Dominguez Hills requires applicants to be in the upper 33% of their class. AP and CLEP credits are accepted.

Procedure: Freshmen are admitted fall and spring. Entrance exams should be taken prior to submitting an application. There are early decision and early admissions plans. Regular applications shoyld be filed by January 1 for fall entry. Check with the school for current application fee. Notification is sent on a rolling basis. Applications are accepted online.

Transfer: Applicants should have a college GPA of at least 2.0 (2.4 for nonresidents) and submit SAT or ACT scores if transferring fewer than 56 semester or 84 quarter units. 30 of 120 credits required for the bachelor's degree must be completed at CSU Dominguez Hills.

Visiting: There are regularly scheduled orientations for prospective students. There are guides for informal visits and visitors may sit in on classes. To schedule a visit, contact the Outreach Office for group visits at (310) 516-3699 or the Information and Services Center for individual visits at (310) 516-3696.

Financial Aid: The FAFSA is required. Check with ther school for current deadlines.

International Students: The school actively recruits these students. They must score satisfactory on the written TOEFL and also take the SAT or the ACT.

Computers: All students may access the system. There are no time limits and no fees. It is strongly recommended that all students have a personal computer.

Admissions Contact: Information and Services Center. Web: *www.csudh.edu*

CALIFORNIA STATE UNIVERSITY EAST BAY B-3
(Formerly California State University Hayward)

Hayward, CA 94542-3095 (510) 885-2784

Full-time: 2750 men, 4650 women	Faculty: 370; IIA, ++$
Part-time: 750 men, 1275 women	Ph.D.s: 90%
Graduate: 1475 men, 2600 women	Student/Faculty: 20 to 1
Year: quarters, summer session	Tuition: $2916 ($11,000)
Application Deadline: August 31	Room & Board: $7940
Freshman Class: n/av	
SAT or ACT: recommended	LESS COMPETITIVE

California State University, East Bay, formerly California State University, Hayward, founded in 1957, is part of the California State University system. The institution offers degree programs in the arts, sciences, business and economics, and education to a primarily commuter student body. Some information in the above capsule and in this profile is approximate. There are 4 undergraduate and 4 graduate schools. In addition to regional accreditation, Cal State, East Bay has baccalaureate program accreditation with AACSB, NASAD, NASM, NCATE, and NLN. The library contains 850,000 volumes, 700,000 microform items, and 26,000 audio/video tapes/CDs/DVDs, and subscribes to 2000 periodicals including electronic. Computerized library services include the card catalog, interlibrary loans, and database searching. Special learning facilities include a learning resource center, art gallery, natural history museum, radio station, TV station, marine biology lab, and geology summer field camp. The 342-acre campus is in a suburban area 20 miles southeast of San Francisco in the Hayward Hills. Including any residence halls, there are 17 buildings.

Student Life: 90% of undergraduates are from California. 85% are from public schools. 50% are white; 25% Asian American; 10% African American; 10% Hispanic. The average age of freshmen is 20; all undergraduates, 25. 15% do not continue beyond their first year; 60% remain to graduate.

Housing: 400 students can be accommodated in college housing, which includes coed on-campus apartments. On-campus housing is guaranteed for the freshman year only and is available on a first-come, first-served basis. 94% of students commute. All students may keep cars.

Activities: 1% of men belong to 4 national fraternities; 1% of women belong to 3 national sororities. There are 90 groups on campus, including art, cheerleading, chorale, chorus, computers, dance, drama, ethnic, film, gay, honors, international, jazz band, literary magazine, musical theater, newspaper, opera, orchestra, pep band, photography, political, professional, radio and TV, religious, social, social service, student government, symphony, and yearbook. Popular campus events include Science Fair and several leadership conferences.

Sports: There are 4 intercollegiate sports for men and 7 for women. Facilities include tennis and racquetball courts, 2 swimming pools, a track, a football field, a martial arts facility, a gymnastics center, a dance studio, baseball and softball diamonds, a 9000-seat stadium, a 5000-seat gym, and a 500-seat theater.

Disabled Students: 90% of the campus is accessible. Wheelchair ramps, elevators, special parking, specially equipped rest rooms, lowered drinking fountains, and lowered telephones are available. The Disabled Student Services Center provides scribe, interpretive, and translation services.

Services: Counseling and information services are available, as is tutoring in most subjects. There is a reader service for the blind, and remedial math, reading, and writing.

Campus Safety and Security: Measures include 24-hour foot and vehicle patrol, self-defense education, security escort services, and shuttle buses. There are informal discussions, pamphlets/posters/films, emergency telephones, and lighted pathways/sidewalks.

Programs of Study: Cal State, East Bay confers B.A. and B.S. degrees. Master's degrees are also awarded. Bachelor's degrees are awarded in AGRICULTURE (environmental studies), BIOLOGICAL SCIENCE (biochemistry and biology/biological science), BUSINESS (accounting, business administration and management, marketing/retailing/merchandising, and recreation and leisure services), COMMUNICATIONS AND THE ARTS (advertising, art, arts administration/management, broadcasting, communications, dramatic arts, English, French, journalism, music, Spanish, and speech/debate/rhetoric), COMPUTER AND PHYSICAL SCIENCE (chemistry, computer science, geology, mathematics, physical sciences, physics, and statistics), ENGINEERING AND ENVIRONMENTAL DESIGN (engineering, environmental science, and industrial engineering), HEALTH PROFESSIONS (health science, nursing, and speech pathology/audiology), SOCIAL SCIENCE (anthropology, criminal justice, economics, ethnic studies, geography, history, human development, international studies, Latin American studies, liberal arts/general studies, philosophy, physical fitness/movement, political science/government, psychology, and sociology). Business administration, liberal studies, and computer science are the strongest academically. Business administration and liberal studies are the largest.

Required: In order to graduate, students must fulfill the university writing skills requirement, have a 2.0 minimum GPA, and complete 186 quarter units, including 72 in distribution requirements. The number of hours in the major varies by program from 56 to 153 quarter units.

Special: Cal State, East Bay offers cross-registration with local community colleges, other CSU campuses, and the University of California/Berkeley. Internships, study abroad in 15 countries, work-study programs, and student-designed majors are also available. The PACE program provides degree opportunities in liberal studies and in human development to working adults. There is 1 national honor society, a freshman honors program, and 1 departmental honors program.

Requirements: The SAT or ACT is recommended. All students must meet the eligibility index, a combination of the high school GPA and SAT or ACT scores. Applicants must be graduates of an accredited secondary school or have a GED certificate. Secondary school courses must include 4 years of English, 3 of math, 2 each of foreign language, history, and science, and 1 each of art, dance, drama/theater, or music, and electives. A GPA of 2.0 is required. AP and CLEP credits are accepted. Important factors in the admissions decision are advanced placement or honor courses, leadership record, and evidence of special talent.

Procedure: Freshmen are admitted to all sessions. There are early decision, early admissions, and deferred admissions plans. Applications

should be filed by August 31 for fall entry, November 30 for winter entry, February 28 for spring entry, and May 31 for summer entry. Notification is sent on a rolling basis. Applications are accepted on-line. Check with the school for current application fee.

Transfer: Applicants must have a minimum 2.0 GPA (2.45 for nonresidents), be in good standing at the last college attended, and either meet freshman admission requirements or have completed at least 56 transferable semester (84 quarter) units. 45 of 186 credits required for the bachelor's degree must be completed at Cal State, East Bay.

Visiting: There are regularly scheduled orientations for prospective students. There are guides for informal visits. To schedule a visit, contact Enrollment Services at (510) 885-2556.

Financial Aid: In a recent year, 43% of all full-time freshmen and 42% of continuing full-time students received some form of financial aid. 43% of full-time freshmen and 42% of continuing full-time students received need-based aid. The average freshman award was $6918. Need-based scholarships or need-based grants averaged $6494, and need-based self-help aid (loans and jobs) averaged $2413. CSUH is a member of CSS. The FAFSA is required. Check with the school for current deadlines.

International Students: They must score satisfactorily on the TOEFL. Graduates of a U.S. high school must also take the SAT or ACT.

Computers: All students may access the system on a 24-hour basis from home and 16 hours per day on campus. There are no time limits and no fees.

Admissions Contact: Admissions. E-mail: *askes@csueastbay.edu* Web: *www.csueastbay.edu*

CALIFORNIA STATE UNIVERSITY, FRESNO   C-3

Fresno, CA 93740-8027	(559) 278-2261; Fax: (559) 278-4812
Full-time: 5850 men, 8450 women	**Faculty:** 681; IIA, +$
Part-time: 1975 men, 2300 women	**Ph.D.s:** n/av
Graduate: 1350 men, 2400 women	**Student/Faculty:** 21 to 1
Year: semesters, summer session	**Tuition:** $3037 ($9200)
Application Deadline: see profile	**Room & Board:** 7000
Freshman Class: n/av	
SAT or ACT: see profile	**LESS COMPETITIVE**

California State University, Fresno, founded in 1911, is part of the state-supported university system. The school offers undergraduate and graduate programs in agriculture and technology, liberal arts and sciences, business administration, education, engineering, health fields, and pre-professional training. There are 8 undergraduate and 8 graduate schools. Figures in the above capsule and in the profile are approximate. In addition to regional accreditation, Fresno State has baccalaureate program accreditation with AACSB, ABET, ACCE, ACEJMC, ADA, AHEA, APTA, ASLA, CSWE, FIDER, NASM, NCATE, NLN, and NRPA. The library contains 977,198 volumes, 1,207,118 microform items, and 71,482 audio/video tapes/CDs/DVDs, and subscribes to 2559 periodicals including electronic. Computerized library services include the card catalog, interlibrary loans, and database searching. Special learning facilities include a learning resource center, art gallery, planetarium, radio station, and various farm lab units. The 327-acre campus is in a suburban area 300 miles southeast of San Francisco. Including any residence halls, there are 47 buildings.

Student Life: 96% of undergraduates are from California. Others are from 48 states, 89 foreign countries, and Canada. 99% are from public schools. 36% are white; 26% Hispanic; 14% Asian American. The average age of freshmen is 18; all undergraduates, 23. 20% do not continue beyond their first year; 55% remain to graduate.

Housing: 1100 students can be accommodated in college housing, which includes single-sex and coed dorms. In addition, there are special-interest houses. On-campus housing is available on a first-come, first-served basis. 94% of students commute. Alcohol is not permitted. All students may keep cars.

Activities: 3% of men belong to 4 local and 15 national fraternities; 3% of women belong to 4 local and 9 national sororities. There are 270 groups on campus, including art, band, cheerleading, chess, choir, chorale, chorus, computers, dance, drama, drill team, ethnic, film, gay, honors, international, jazz band, marching band, musical theater, newspaper, orchestra, pep band, photography, political, professional, radio and TV, religious, social, social service, and student government. Popular campus events include Vintage Days, International Week, and Black History Month.

Sports: There are 10 intercollegiate sports for men and 12 for women, and 4 intramural sports for men and 4 for women. Facilities include 2 gyms, an indoor/outdoor swimming pool, 12 tennis courts, 6 indoor handball/racquetball courts, and 2 putting greens and driving areas. There are sports clubs in cycling, fencing, judo, karate, rodeo, and rugby. The campus stadium seats 41,031, the baseball stadium seats 6,575, and the softball stadium seats 5,467. There is also a 10,800-square-foot strength and conditioning center.

Disabled Students: All of the campus is accessible. Wheelchair ramps, elevators, special parking, specially equipped rest rooms, special class scheduling, lowered drinking fountains, and lowered telephones are available.

Services: Counseling and information services are available, as is tutoring in most subjects. There is a reader service for the blind, and remedial math, reading, and writing.

Campus Safety and Security: Measures include 24-hour foot and vehicle patrol, self-defense education, security escort services, and informal discussions. There are pamphlets/posters/films, emergency telephones, lighted pathways/sidewalks, closed circuit television cameras, and bicycle safety patrols.

Programs of Study: Fresno State confers B.A. and B.S. degrees. Master's and doctoral degrees are also awarded. Bachelor's degrees are awarded in AGRICULTURE (agricultural business management, animal science, and plant science), BIOLOGICAL SCIENCE (biology/biological science), BUSINESS (business administration and management and recreational facilities management), COMMUNICATIONS AND THE ARTS (art, communications, dramatic arts, English, French, graphic design, journalism, linguistics, music, Spanish, and speech/debate/rhetoric), COMPUTER AND PHYSICAL SCIENCE (chemistry, computer science, geology, mathematics, natural sciences, and physics), EDUCATION (agricultural), ENGINEERING AND ENVIRONMENTAL DESIGN (civil engineering, computer engineering, construction management, electrical/electronics engineering, industrial engineering, industrial engineering technology, interior design, mechanical engineering, and surveying engineering), HEALTH PROFESSIONS (health science, nursing, speech pathology/audiology, and speech therapy), SOCIAL SCIENCE (African American studies, anthropology, child psychology/development, criminology, economics, family/consumer studies, food science, geography, history, liberal arts/general studies, Mexican-American/Chicano studies, philosophy, physical fitness/movement, political science/government, psychology, public administration, social work, sociology, and women's studies). Business and liberal arts are the largest.

Required: All students must complete general education requirements. A minimum of 124 to 137 semester units, with a GPA of 2.0, is required to graduate. The number of required hours in the major varies.

Special: Study abroad in 17 countries, including London, New Zealand, China, and the South Pacific, co-op programs, internships, work-study programs, B.A.-B.S. degrees, dual majors, and student-designed majors are offered. A liberal studies major, credit for military experience, pass/fail options, and nondegree study are available. There are 22 national honor societies, a freshman honors program, and 2 departmental honors programs.

Faculty/Classroom: 57% of faculty are male; 43%, female. 100% both teach and do research. The average class size in an introductory lecture is 28; in a laboratory, 20; and in a regular course, 26.

Admissions: The SAT scores for the 2005-2006 freshman class were: Verbal--62% below 500, 28% between 500 and 599, 9% between 600 and 700, and 1% above 700; Math--54% below 500, 34% between 500 and 599, 11% between 600 and 700, and 1% above 700. The ACT scores were 68% below 21, 17% between 21 and 23, 10% between 24 and 26, 3% between 27 and 28, and 2% above 28.

Requirements: The SAT or ACT is required. In addition, only students with a GPA below 3.0 are required to submit the SAT I or ACT scores. Applicants must be graduates of an accredited secondary school or have a GED. Secondary school courses must include 15 academic credits: 4 years of high school English, 3 each of math and electives, 2 of a foreign language, and 1 each of science, history/government, and visual/performing arts. A GPA of 2.0 is required. AP and CLEP credits are accepted.

Procedure: Freshmen are admitted fall and spring. Entrance exams should be taken as early as possible, by the first semester of the senior year. Applications should be filed by May 15 for fall entry and October 15 for spring entry. Notification is sent on a rolling basis. Applications are accepted on-line.

Transfer: 1993 transfer students enrolled in a recent year. Transfer applicants must have a minimum GPA of 2.0 and 56 transferable semester units earned, including English and math. 30 of 124 credits required for the bachelor's degree must be completed at Fresno State.

Visiting: There are regularly scheduled orientations for prospective students, including 1- and 2-day overnight programs for entering students. There are guides for informal visits and visitors may stay overnight. To schedule a visit, contact Orientation and Transition Services or University Outreach Services at (559) 278-7533 or (559) 278-2048.

Financial Aid: Fresno State is a member of CSS. The FAFSA is required. Check with the school for current deadlines.

International Students: The school actively recruits these students. They must score satisfactorily on the written TOEFL and also take the SAT or the ACT.

Computers: All students may access the system anytime. There are no time limits and no fees. All students are required to have personal computers.

Graduates: In a recent year, 2922 bachelor's degrees were awarded. The most popular majors were liberal studies (23%), business administration (16%), and criminology (5%). In an average class, 11% graduate

in 4 years or less, 31% graduate in 5 years or less, and 40% graduate in 6 years or less. 259 companies recruited on campus in a recent year.

Admissions Contact: Vivian Franco, Director of Admissions.
E-mail: *vivian-franco@csufresno.edu* Web: *www.csufresno.edu*

CALIFORNIA STATE UNIVERSITY, FULLERTON   D-5

Fullerton, CA 92834 (714) 278-2370

Full-time: 8918 men, 12,269 women	**Faculty:** 719; IIA, +$
Part-time: 3475 men, 4800 women	**Ph.D.s:** 84%
Graduate: 1942 men, 3636 women	**Student/Faculty:** 29 to 1
Year: semesters, summer session	**Tuition:** $2990 ($13,160)
Application Deadline: November 30	**Room & Board:** $8000
Freshman Class: 25,525 applied, 16,304 accepted, 3943 enrolled	
SAT Verbal/Math: 480/500*	**ACT:** 20 **COMPETITIVE**

California State University, Fullerton, founded in 1957, is part of the California State University system. The school offers programs in the arts, business and economics, communications, engineering and computer science, education, human development and community services, humanities and social science, and natural science and math. There are 8 undergraduate and 8 graduate schools. In addition to regional accreditation, Cal State Fullerton has baccalaureate program accreditation with AACSB, ABET, ACEJMC, NASAD, NASM, NCATE, and NLN. The library contains 1,189,727 volumes, 1,144,177 microform items, and 15,790 audio/video tapes/CDs/DVDs, and subscribes to 3690 periodicals including electronic. Computerized library services include the card catalog, interlibrary loans, database searching, Internet access, and laptop Internet portals. Special learning facilities include a learning resource center, art gallery, TV station, an arboretum, an herbarium, a center for economic education, a developmental research center, a foreign language lab, an institute for economic and environmental studies, an institute for molecular biology and nutrition, a phonetic research lab, a social science research center, and a sport and movement institute. The 236-acre campus is in a suburban area 30 miles east of Los Angeles. Including any residence halls, there are 27 buildings.

Student Life: 98% of undergraduates are from California. Others are from 39 states, 51 foreign countries, and Canada. 32% are white; 27% Hispanic; 22% Asian American. The average age of freshmen is 18; all undergraduates, 23. 19% do not continue beyond their first year; 60% remain to graduate.

Housing: 836 students can be accommodated in college housing, which includes coed on-campus apartments and fraternity houses. On-campus housing is available on a first-come, first-served basis. 98% of students commute. All students may keep cars.

Activities: There are 5 local and 13 national fraternities and 1 local and 8 national sororities. There are 250 groups on campus, including art, band, cheerleading, choir, chorus, computers, dance, debate, drama, ethnic, film, forensics, gay, honors, international, jazz band, literary magazine, musical theater, newspaper, opera, orchestra, pep band, photography, political, professional, radio and TV, religious, social, social service, and student government.

Sports: There are 7 intercollegiate sports for men and 9 for women, and 15 intramural sports for men and 11 for women. Facilities include a gym, a swimming pool, tennis and racquetball courts, baseball/softball, track, and soccer fields, a bowling alley, and a stadium.

Disabled Students: All of the campus is accessible. Wheelchair ramps, elevators, special parking, specially equipped rest rooms, lowered drinking fountains, lowered telephones, and automatic doors are available.

Services: Counseling and information services are available, as is tutoring in most subjects, including English and math. There is a reader service for the blind, and remedial math, reading, and writing.

Campus Safety and Security: Measures include 24-hour foot and vehicle patrol, self-defense education, security escort services, and shuttle buses. There are pamphlets/posters/films, emergency telephones, and lighted pathways/sidewalks.

Programs of Study: Cal State Fullerton confers B.A., B.S., B.F.A., and B.M. degrees. Master's degrees are also awarded. Bachelor's degrees are awarded in BIOLOGICAL SCIENCE (biochemistry and biology/biological science), BUSINESS (accounting, banking and finance, business administration and management, business economics, international business management, management information systems, management science, marketing/retailing/merchandising, and tourism), COMMUNICATIONS AND THE ARTS (advertising, animation, art history and appreciation, broadcasting, ceramic art and design, communications, comparative literature, crafts, dance, dramatic arts, drawing, English, film arts, fine arts, French, German, graphic design, illustration, Japanese, journalism, linguistics, music, photography, printmaking, public relations, sculpture, Spanish, speech/debate/rhetoric, and studio art), COMPUTER AND PHYSICAL SCIENCE (chemistry, computer science, geology, mathematics, and physics), EDUCATION (art, music, and physical), ENGINEERING AND ENVIRONMENTAL DESIGN (civil engineering, electrical/electronics engineering, engineering and applied science, and mechanical engineering), HEALTH PROFESSIONS (health science, nursing, and speech pathology/audiology), SOCIAL SCIENCE (African

American studies, American studies, anthropology, Asian/American studies, child psychology/development, criminal justice, economics, geography, history, human services, Latin American studies, liberal arts/general studies, Mexican-American/Chicano studies, philosophy, political science/government, psychology, public administration, religion, Russian and Slavic studies, sociology, and women's studies). Business administration, communications, and child and adolescent studies are the largest.

Required: Graduation requirements for all students include the completion of a minimum of 51 units of general education courses, a 2.0 GPA, and an upper-division writing course designated by the major department. 120 to 135 credit hours must be completed for graduation, and students must pass a writing proficiency exam.

Special: The university offers cross-registration with other schools in the California State University system, the University of California, and California Community Colleges, internships and co-op programs in 45 academic areas, study abroad in 18 countries, and work-study programs both on and off campus. A B.A.-B.S. degree in chemistry, dual majors, and pass/fail options are also available. There are 16 national honor societies, a freshman honors program, and 24 departmental honors programs.

Faculty/Classroom: 58% of faculty are male; 42%, female. All both teach and do research. No introductory courses are taught by graduate students. The average class size in an introductory lecture is 50; in a laboratory, 24; and in a regular course, 25.

Admissions: 64% of the 2005-2006 applicants were accepted. The SAT scores for the 2005-2006 freshman class were: Verbal--56% below 500, 35% between 500 and 599, and 9% between 600 and 700; Math--46% below 500, 39% between 500 and 599, 15% between 600 and 700, and 1% above 700. The ACT scores were 60% below 21, 23% between 21 and 23, 12% between 24 and 26, 4% between 27 and 28, and 1% above 28.

Requirements: The SAT or ACT is required. In addition, applicants must be graduates of an accredited secondary school or have a GED certificate. Secondary school courses must include 4 years of English, 3 of math, 2 each of a foreign language, science, and history, and 1 of visual or performing arts. Admission is based on the Qualifiable Eligibility Index, a combination of the high school GPA and either the SAT or ACT score. Auditions are required for music majors. A GPA of 2.0 is required. AP and CLEP credits are accepted.

Procedure: Freshmen are admitted fall and spring. Entrance exams should be taken during the senior year of high school. Applications should be filed by November 30 for fall entry, along with a $55 fee. There is a rolling admissions plan. Notification is sent on a rolling basis. Applications are accepted on-line.

Transfer: 6616 transfer students enrolled in 2004-2005. Applicants must have a minimum 2.0 GPA. The SAT or ACT is required for students with fewer than 56 transferable units earned. Students with 56 transferable units or more must have 30 units of general education completed with a C or better, including English composition, math, speech, and critical thinking. 30 of 120 credits required for the bachelor's degree must be completed at Cal State Fullerton.

Visiting: There are regularly scheduled orientations for prospective students. There are guides for informal visits. To schedule a visit, contact New Student Orientation at (714) 278-3120.

Financial Aid: In 2005-2006, 39% of all full-time freshmen and 36% of continuing full-time students received some form of financial aid. 30% of full-time freshmen and 29% of continuing full-time students received need-based aid. Need-based scholarships or need-based grants averaged $6122; need-based self-help aid (loans and jobs) averaged $2728; non-need-based athletic scholarships averaged $6289; and other non-need-based awards and non-need-based scholarships averaged $3123. The FAFSA is required. The priority date for freshman financial aid applications for fall entry is March 2.

International Students: There are 864 international students enrolled. They must take the TOEFL.

Computers: Wireless access is available. All students may access the system 24 hours a day. There are no time limits and no fees.

Graduates: From July 1, 2004 to June 30, 2005, 5761 bachelor's degrees were awarded. The most popular majors were business administration (24%), communications (10%), and child and adolescent studies (8%). In an average class, 13% graduate in 4 years or less, 38% graduate in 5 years or less, and 49% graduate in 6 years or less.

Admissions Contact: Director of Admissions.
Web: *www.fullerton.edu*

CALIFORNIA STATE UNIVERSITY, HAYWARD
(See California State University, East Bay)

CALIFORNIA STATE UNIVERSITY, LONG BEACH   D-5
Long Beach, CA 90840-0106

(562) 985-4141
Fax: (562) 985-4973

Full-time: 8715 men, 13,810 women	**Faculty:** 1108; IIA, +$
Part-time: 2595 men, 3394 women	**Ph.D.s:** 88%
Graduate: 2221 men, 3812 women	**Student/Faculty:** 20 to 1
Year: semesters, summer session	**Tuition:** $2864 ($13,034)
Application Deadline: November 30	**Room & Board:** $6648
Freshman Class: 38,879 applied, 21,037 accepted, 4383 enrolled	
SAT or ACT: required	**COMPETITIVE**

California State University, Long Beach, founded in 1949, is a nonprofit institution that is part of the California State University system. The commuter university offers undergraduate programs through the Colleges of Health and Human Services, Liberal Arts, Natural Sciences and Math, Business Administration, Engineering, the Arts, and Education. There are 7 undergraduate and 7 graduate schools. In addition to regional accreditation, CSULB has baccalaureate program accreditation with AACSB, ABET, ACEJMC, AHEA, APTA, CSWE, FIDER, NASAD, NASM, NLN, and NRPA. The library contains 1,445,244 volumes, 1,499,734 microform items, and 29,766 audio/video tapes/CDs/DVDs, and subscribes to 26,478 periodicals including electronic. Computerized library services include the card catalog, interlibrary loans, database searching, and Internet access. Special learning facilities include a learning resource center, art gallery, radio station, and TV station. The 322-acre campus is in a suburban area 25 miles southeast of Los Angeles. Including any residence halls, there are 84 buildings.

Student Life: 95% of undergraduates are from California. Others are from Canada. 90% are from public schools. 34% are white; 24% Hispanic; 21% Asian American. The average age of freshmen is 18; all undergraduates, 22. 15% do not continue beyond their first year; 45% remain to graduate.

Housing: 1962 students can be accommodated in college housing, which includes single-sex and coed dorms. On-campus housing is available on a first-come, first-served basis. 95% of students commute. All students may keep cars.

Activities: 4% of men belong to 17 national fraternities; 4% of women belong to 14 national sororities. There are 150 groups on campus, including art, band, cheerleading, choir, chorale, chorus, computers, dance, drama, drill team, ethnic, film, gay, honors, international, jazz band, literary magazine, musical theater, newspaper, opera, orchestra, pep band, photography, political, professional, radio and TV, religious, social, social service, student government, and symphony. Popular campus events include the Kaleidoscope Spring Festival and Engineering Day, Blues Festival, and Odyssey Theme Year.

Sports: There are 10 intercollegiate sports for men and 9 for women, and 14 intramural sports for men and 12 for women. Facilities include the Long Beach Arena (seats 11,500 for basketball), a baseball field (seats 1500), the Pyramid Sports Arena (seats 5000) and an indoor gym (seats 2000).

Disabled Students: 99% of the campus is accessible. Wheelchair ramps, elevators, special parking, specially equipped rest rooms, special class scheduling, lowered drinking fountains, and lowered telephones are available. The university also offers registration and mobility assistance, adaptive equipment, counseling, community referrals, and services to the learning-disabled.

Services: Counseling and information services are available, as is tutoring in most subjects. There is a reader service for the blind, and remedial math, reading, and writing.

Campus Safety and Security: Measures include 24-hour foot and vehicle patrol, security escort services, shuttle buses, and informal discussions. There are pamphlets/posters/films, emergency telephones, and lighted pathways/sidewalks.

Programs of Study: CSULB confers B.A., B.S., B.F.A., B.M., and B.Voc.Ed. degrees. Master's degrees are also awarded. Bachelor's degrees are awarded in BIOLOGICAL SCIENCE (biochemistry, biology/biological science, botany, cell biology, ecology, physiology, and zoology), BUSINESS (accounting, banking and finance, business administration and management, international business management, management information systems, marketing/retailing/merchandising, and personnel management), COMMUNICATIONS AND THE ARTS (art, communications, comparative literature, dance, design, dramatic arts, English, film arts, French, German, Japanese, journalism, music, and Spanish), COMPUTER AND PHYSICAL SCIENCE (applied mathematics, chemistry, computer science, earth science, geology, mathematics, physics, and statistics), EDUCATION (elementary, mathematics, science, and special), ENGINEERING AND ENVIRONMENTAL DESIGN (aerospace studies, chemical engineering, civil engineering, computer engineering, electrical/electronics engineering, engineering technology, and mechanical engineering), HEALTH PROFESSIONS (health care administration, and health science), SOCIAL SCIENCE (African American studies, anthropology, Asian/Oriental studies, economics, geography, Hispanic American studies, history, human development, interdisciplinary studies, international studies, philosophy, political science/

government, psychology, religion, sociology, and women's studies). Art, biological sciences, and music are the strongest academically. Business administration, psychology, and liberal studies are the largest.

Required: Graduation requirements for all students include the completion of 51 units in general education (45 for engineering majors), 40 units of upper-division course work, and 30 units in residence at the university. Students must have a minimum 2.0 GPA and a total of 124 to 140 credit hours, depending on the major. Required courses include University 100: "The University in Your Future."

Special: The university offers cross-registration with California State University, Dominguez Hills for courses not offered at CSULB. Internships, study abroad in 22 countries, dual majors in engineering, a 3-2 engineering degree, student-designed majors, and pass/fail options are also available. There are 23 national honor societies, including Phi Beta Kappa, and a freshman honors program.

Faculty/Classroom: 52% of faculty are male; 48%, female. All teach undergraduates, 60% do research, and 60% do both. Graduate students teach 3% of introductory courses. The average class size in an introductory lecture is 68; in a laboratory, 24; and in a regular course, 26.

Admissions: 54% of the 2005-2006 applicants were accepted. The SAT scores for the 2005-2006 freshman class were: Verbal--48% below 500, 39% between 500 and 599, 12% between 600 and 700, and 1% above 700; Math--38% below 500, 43% between 500 and 599, 17% between 600 and 700, and 2% above 700. There were 13 National Merit finalists and 2 semifinalists. 53 freshmen graduated first in their class.

Requirements: The SAT or ACT is required. In addition, applicants must be graduates of an accredited secondary school and have completed 4 years of English, 3 years each of math and electives, 2 years of foreign language, and 1 year each of lab science, U.S. history or U.S. history and government, and 1 visual and performing arts. Students are admitted on the basis of the eligibility index, which is computed from the secondary school GPA and the SAT or ACT scores. California residents with a minimum 3.0 GPA are automatically admissible. A portfolio is required for art and design students. An audition is required for dance, music, and theater students. A GPA of 2.0 is required. AP and CLEP credits are accepted.

Procedure: Freshmen are admitted fall and spring. Entrance exams should be taken during the fall semester of the senior year. There is a rolling admissions plan. Applications should be filed by November 30 for fall entry and August 31 for spring entry. The fall 2005 application fee was $55. Notification is sent on a rolling basis. Applications are accepted on-line.

Transfer: 2886 transfer students enrolled in 2004-2005. Upper-division students must have completed a minimum of 60 semester units, and have a minimum 2.0 GPA, lower division students must meet the same requirements as entering freshmen. 30 of 120 to 140 credits required for the bachelor's degree must be completed at CSULB.

Visiting: There are regularly scheduled orientations for prospective students, consisting of Student Orientation, Advising, and Registration (SOAR) sessions. Students may participate in SOAR I, which consists of advising and registration, or SOAR II, which involves a campus tour and an orientation to activities. There are guides for informal visits. To schedule a visit, contact the Office of School Relations at (562) 985-5358.

Financial Aid: CSULB is a member of CSS. The FAFSA is required. The deadline for filing freshman financial aid applications for fall entry is March 2.

International Students: The school actively recruits these students. They must score satisfactorily on the written TOEFL.

Computers: All students may access the system during open lab hours, which vary across campus. There are no time limits and no fees.

Graduates: From July 1, 2004 to June 30, 2005, 4703 bachelor's degrees were awarded. The most popular majors were business (22%), liberal arts (9%), and visual and performing arts (9%). In an average class, 10% graduate in 4 years or less, and 48% graduate in 6 years or less.

Admissions Contact: Thomas Enders, Assistant Vice President, Enrollment Services. Web: *www.csulb.edu*

CALIFORNIA STATE UNIVERSITY, LOS ANGELES   C-5

Los Angeles, CA 90032   (323) 343-3940; Fax: (323) 343-3945

Full-time: 3900 men, 6550 women	**Faculty:** 565; IIA, +$
Part-time: 1550 men, 2400 women	**Ph.Ds:** n/av
Graduate: 2175 men, 4050 women	**Student/Faculty:** 19 to 1
Year: quarters, summer session	**Tuition:** $2500 ($9300)
Application Deadline: June 15	**Room & Board:** $3400
Freshman Class: n/av	
SAT or ACT: required	**COMPETITIVE**

California State University, Los Angeles, founded in 1947 as part of the state system, offers undergraduate and graduate programs in liberal arts and sciences, business education, engineering, health science, and professional training. There are 6 undergraduate schools. Figures in the above capsule and in the profile are approximate. In addition to regional accreditation, Cal State, LA has baccalaureate program accreditation with AACSB, ABET, ACS, ADA, ASHA, CACREP, COA, CORE, CSWE, NASAD, NASM, NASPAA, NCATE, and NLN. The library contains 1,127,398 volumes, 1,080,781 microform items, and 5498 audio/video tapes/CDs/DVDs, and subscribes to 2110 periodicals including electronic. Computerized library services include the card catalog, interlibrary loans, database searching, and Internet access. Special learning facilities include a learning resource center, art gallery, and TV station. The 173-acre campus is in an urban area 5 miles east of downtown Los Angeles. Including any residence halls, there are 22 buildings.

Student Life: 95% of undergraduates are from California. Others are from Canada. 52% are Hispanic; 22% Asian American; 16% white. The average age of freshmen is 18; all undergraduates, 25.

Housing: 1006 students can be accommodated in college housing, which includes single-sex and coed on-campus apartments. In addition, there are special-interest houses and an international house. On-campus housing is available on a first-come, first-served basis. 60% of students live on campus. All students may keep cars.

Activities: There are 8 national fraternities and 2 local and 6 national sororities. There are 115 groups on campus, including band, chess, choir, chorale, chorus, computers, dance, drama, ethnic, forensics, gay, honors, international, jazz band, literary magazine, musical theater, newspaper, opera, orchestra, political, professional, radio and TV, religious, social, social service, student government, symphony, and yearbook. Popular campus events include Christmas Toy and Food Drive, Earth Week, and Career Day.

Sports: There are 6 intercollegiate sports for men and 6 for women, and 9 intramural sports for men and 7 for women. Facilities include a 4800-seat stadium, a 5500-seat gym, a swimming pool, tennis and racquetball courts, a track, and athletic fields.

Disabled Students: 95% of the campus is accessible. Wheelchair ramps, elevators, special parking, specially equipped rest rooms, and lowered telephones are available.

Services: Counseling and information services are available, as is tutoring in most subjects. There is a reader service for the blind, and remedial math, reading, and writing.

Campus Safety and Security: Measures include 24-hour foot and vehicle patrol, self-defense education, security escort services, and shuttle buses. There are informal discussions, pamphlets/posters/films, emergency telephones, and lighted pathways/sidewalks.

Programs of Study: Cal State, LA confers B.A., B.S., B.M., and B.Voc.Ed. degrees. Master's and doctoral degrees are also awarded. Bachelor's degrees are awarded in BIOLOGICAL SCIENCE (biochemistry, biology/biological science, and microbiology), BUSINESS (business administration and management), COMMUNICATIONS AND THE ARTS (dramatic arts, English, French, graphic design, Japanese, media arts, music, music performance, Spanish, and speech/debate/rhetoric), COMPUTER AND PHYSICAL SCIENCE (chemistry, computer science, geology, information sciences and systems, mathematics, natural sciences, and physics), EDUCATION (industrial arts, physical, and vocational), ENGINEERING AND ENVIRONMENTAL DESIGN (civil engineering, electrical/electronics engineering, engineering, industrial engineering technology, and mechanical engineering), HEALTH PROFESSIONS (health science, nursing, rehabilitation therapy, and speech pathology/audiology), SOCIAL SCIENCE (African American studies, anthropology, child psychology/development, criminal justice, dietetics, economics, fire protection, geography, history, interdisciplinary studies, Latin American studies, liberal arts/general studies, Mexican-American/Chicano studies, philosophy, political science/government, psychology, social science, social work, and sociology). Child development, computer information systems, and criminal justice are the largest.

Required: To graduate, students must complete 186 to 203 quarter units, with a minimum 2.0 GPA, and must demonstrate skills in math and oral and written communications. General education requirements include 72 quarter units in the social sciences, natural sciences, and humanities.

Special: Cross-registration is offered with other California State University schools. The school, as part of the state university system, is part of the California Desert Studies Consortium, which provides a field facility in the Mojave Desert to develop desert studies educational programs. It is also part of the Ocean Studies Institute, which facilitates marine educational and research activities. Students may design their own majors. Internships, study-abroad in 18 countries, work-study programs, B.A.-B.S. degrees, dual majors, pass/fail options, and credit for life experience are available. An accelerated degree program in nursing is offered. There are 21 national honor societies, including Phi Beta Kappa, a freshman honors program, and 5 departmental honors programs.

Faculty/Classroom: 55% of faculty are male; 45%, female. All teach undergraduates. No introductory courses are taught by graduate students. The average class size in an introductory lecture is 40; in a laboratory, 8; and in a regular course, 40.

Admissions: 56% of recent applicants were accepted.

Requirements: The SAT or ACT is required. In addition, applicants should be graduates of accredited secondary schools or have a GED equivalent. 15 academic credits are required, including 4 years of English, 3 of math, 2 of the same foreign language, 1 each of biological and physical science with lab, 1 each of U.S. history and social science, and 1 year in electives and the visual and performing arts. A GPA of 2.0 is required. AP and CLEP credits are accepted.

Procedure: Freshmen are admitted to all sessions. Entrance exams should be taken during the junior year or senior year. Applications should be filed by June 15 for fall entry, October 1 for winter entry, February 1 for spring entry, and April 1 for summer entry, along with a $55 fee. Notification is sent on a rolling basis. Applications are accepted on-line.

Transfer: 1592 transfer students enrolled in a recent year. Applicants must have 56 semester units (84 quarter units), a 2.0 GPA (2.4 GPA for nonresidents), and have completed the CSU graduation requirements in English compostion, speech communication, critical thinking, and quantitative reasoning. 45 of 186 credits required for the bachelor's degree must be completed at Cal State, LA.

Visiting: There are guides for informal visits.

Financial Aid: The CSS/Profile or FAFSA and the SAAC (in-state) are required. Check with the school for current deadlines.

International Students: They must score satisfactorily on the TOEFL and also take the SAT or the ACT.

Computers: All students may access the system 24 hours a day. There is a 2-hour limit in the open access labs during peak demand periods. There are no fees.

Graduates: In a recent year, 2899 bachelor's degrees were awarded. The most popular majors were child development (12%), computer information systems (8%), and psychology (7%). 376 companies recruited on campus in a recent year.

Admissions Contact: Joan Woosley, Director of Admission and University Registrar. E-mail: *imedina@cslanet.calstatela.edu*

CALIFORNIA STATE UNIVERSITY, MONTEREY BAY   B-3

Seaside, CA 93955   (831) 582-5100; Fax: (831) 582-5110

Full-time: 1332 men, 1724 women	**Faculty:** 106; IIA, av$
Part-time: 128 men, 223 women	**Ph.D.s:** 74%
Graduate: 119 men, 247 women	**Student/Faculty:** 29 to 1
Year: semesters, summer session	**Tuition:** $2999 ($13,169)
Application Deadline: March 15	**Room & Board:** $7100
Freshman Class: 6409 applied, 3801 accepted, 624 enrolled	
SAT Verbal/Math: 490/490*	**ACT:** 20 **COMPETITIVE**

California State University, Monterey Bay, founded in 1994, is a public institution with 13 undergraduate divisions, including arts and sciences, communications, education and professional training, and science and technology. There are 4 undergraduate and 4 graduate schools. The library contains 50,000 volumes and 1250 audio/video tapes/CDs/DVDs, and subscribes to 10,000 periodicals including electronic. Computerized library services include interlibrary loans, database searching, and Internet access. Special learning facilities include a learning resource center. The 1397-acre campus is in a suburban area 90 miles south of San Francisco. Including any residence halls, there are 58 buildings.

Student Life: 96% of undergraduates are from California. Others are from 39 states, 29 foreign countries, and Canada. 92% are from public schools. 48% are white; 28% Hispanic. The average age of freshmen is 19; all undergraduates, 23. 25% do not continue beyond their first year; 40% remain to graduate.

Housing: 2450 students can be accommodated in college housing, which includes single-sex and coed dorms, on-campus apartments, and married-student housing. On-campus housing is guaranteed for the freshman year only and is available on a first-come, first-served basis. 62% of students live on campus; of those, 60% remain on campus on weekends. All students may keep cars.

Activities: 2% of men belong to 4 local fraternities; 1% of women belong to 4 local sororities. There are 50 groups on campus, including cheerleading, choir, chorus, computers, dance, disabilities, drama, disabilities, ethnic, gay, international, musical theater, photography, political, professional, religious, social, social service, student government, and yearbook. Popular campus events include Capstone Festival, Diversity Days, and Spring Formal.

Sports: There are 4 intercollegiate sports for men and 5 for women, and 5 intramural sports for men and 5 for women. Facilities include 3 racquetball courts, a 2500-square-foot fitness room, saunas, and a 10,000-square-foot gym with facilities for basketball, volleyball, badminton, indoor soccer, aerobics, and dance. There is also a soccer complex, an aquatic center, a disc golf course, a stadium track, and a baseball field.

Disabled Students: All of the campus is accessible. Wheelchair ramps, elevators, special parking, specially equipped rest rooms, special class scheduling, lowered drinking fountains, lowered telephones, and special housing are available. Any official campus program can accommodate, with notice.

Services: Counseling and information services are available, as is tutoring in some subjects, including computer skills and others by demand. There is a reader service for the blind, and remedial math, reading, and writing.

Campus Safety and Security: Measures include 24-hour foot and vehicle patrol, self-defense education, security escort services, and shuttle buses. There are informal discussions, pamphlets/posters/films, emergency telephones, and lighted pathways/sidewalks.

Programs of Study: CSUMB confers B.A. and B.S. degrees. Master's degrees are also awarded. Bachelor's degrees are awarded in BUSINESS (business administration and management and management science), COMMUNICATIONS AND THE ARTS (communications technology, music, telecommunications, and visual and performing arts), COMPUTER AND PHYSICAL SCIENCE (computer science, earth science, and mathematics), EDUCATION (education), HEALTH PROFESSIONS (health), SOCIAL SCIENCE (behavioral science, human services, international studies, liberal arts/general studies, and social science). Computer science and technology, liberal studies, and business administration are the strongest academically. Business administraion, liberal studies, and human communication are the largest.

Required: To graduate, students must complete 120 to 132 credit hours, including general education requirements and at least 24 hours in the major. Courses in physical education, technology, foreign language, and service learning are also required.

Special: Study abroad in 18 countries, internships, work-study programs, and an integrated studies major are available.

Faculty/Classroom: 48% of faculty are male; 52%, female. All teach undergraduates. The average class size in an introductory lecture is 23; in a laboratory, 17; and in a regular course, 22.

Admissions: 59% of the 2005-2006 applicants were accepted. The SAT scores for the 2005-2006 freshman class were: Verbal--51% below 500, 37% between 500 and 599, 11% between 600 and 700, and 1% above 700; Math--51% below 500, 38% between 500 and 599, 11% between 600 and 700, and 1% above 700. The ACT scores were 54% below 21, 22% between 21 and 23, 20% between 24 and 26, 2% between 27 and 28, and 2% above 28.

Requirements: The SAT or ACT is required. The ACT Optional Writing test is also required for some programs. A GPA of 2.0 is required. AP and CLEP credits are accepted.

Procedure: Freshmen are admitted fall and spring. Entrance exams should be taken March, April, or May of each year. Applications should be filed by March 15 for fall entry and November 30 for spring entry, along with a $55 fee. Notification is sent November 30. Applications are accepted on-line.

Transfer: 472 transfer students enrolled in 2004-2005. Transfer requirements include a college GPA of 2.0 (residents) or 2.4 (non-residents) and 60 transferrable baccalaureate semester units, including 30 units of general education courses. 30 credits of 120 to 132 credits required for the bachelor's degree must be completed at CSUMB.

Visiting: There are regularly scheduled orientations for prospective students, including onsite academic advising and registration, campus tours, and campus fair. There are guides for informal visits and visitors may sit in on classes and stay overnight.

Financial Aid: In a recent year, 53% of all full-time freshmen and 47% of continuing full-time students received some form of financial aid. 51% of full-time freshmen and 49% of continuing full-time students received need-based aid. The average freshman award was $6558. Need-based scholarships or need-based grants averaged $6041 ($12,147 maximum); need-based self-help aid (loans and jobs) averaged $4075 ($15,952 maximum); non-need-based athletic scholarships averaged $1575 ($2000 maximum); and other non-need-based awards and non-need-based scholarships averaged $1918 ($2473 maximum). Average annual earnings from campus work are $3000. The average financial indebtedness of a recent year's graduate was $7400. The FAFSA and the state aid form are required. The priority date for freshman financial aid applications for fall entry is March 2.

International Students: There are 16 international students enrolled. They must score satisfactorily on the TOEFL and also take the SAT or the ACT.

Computers: Wireless access is available. Multiple computer labs (both Mac and PC) available for student use. All students may use the network with student ID, and wireless access is available in and around campus bulidings. All students may access the system. There are no time limits and no fees. It is strongly recommended that all students have a personal computer.

Graduates: From July 1, 2004 to June 30, 2005, 582 bachelor's degrees were awarded. The most popular majors were liberal studies (24%), human communication (10%), and telecommunication (10%). In an average class, 1% graduate in 3 years or less, 10% graduate in 4 years or less, 23% graduate in 5 years or less, and 37% graduate in 6 years or less.

Admissions Contact: Campus Service Center, One-Stop-Shop. A video is available. E-mail: *onestop@csumb.edu*
Web: *http://onestop.csumb.edu*

CALIFORNIA STATE UNIVERSITY, NORTHRIDGE   C-5

Northridge, CA 91330　　　(818) 677-3700; Fax: (818) 677-3766

Full-time: 8125 men, 11,475 women	**Faculty:** 865; IIA, +$
Part-time: 2425 men, 3450 women	**Ph.D.s:** 84%
Graduate: 2500 men, 5000 women	**Student/Faculty:** 23 to 1
Year: semesters, summer session	**Tuition:** $3036 ($8700)
Application Deadline: see profile	**Room & Board:** $6000
Freshman Class: n/av	
SAT or ACT: required	**LESS COMPETITIVE**

California State University, Northridge, founded in 1958, is part of the state-supported university system offering degree programs in the liberal arts and sciences, business administration, education, engineering, music, health fields, and fine arts. There are 8 undergraduate schools and 1 graduate school. Figures in the above capsule and in this profile are approximate. In addition to regional accreditation, CSUN has baccalaureate program accreditation with AACSB, ABET, ACEJMC, AHEA, APTA, CAHEA, CSAB, NASAD, NASM, NCATE, and NRPA. The library contains 1,274,351 volumes, 3,128,169 microform items, and 17,677 audio/video tapes/CDs/DVDs, and subscribes to 16,973 periodicals including electronic. Computerized library services include the card catalog, interlibrary loans, and database searching. Special learning facilities include a learning resource center, art gallery, planetarium, radio station, TV station, observatory, anthropological museum, botanical gardens, urban archives center, Natural Center on Deafness, and Center for the Study of Cancer and Development Biology. The 353-acre campus is in a suburban area 25 miles north of Los Angeles. Including any residence halls, there are 76 buildings.

Student Life: 93% of undergraduates are from California. Others are from 46 states and Canada. 93% are from public schools. 32% are white; 23% Hispanic. The average age of freshmen is 18; all undergraduates, 24.

Housing: 2400 students can be accommodated in college housing, which includes coed on-campus apartments and an international house. On-campus housing is guaranteed for all 4 years and is available on a first-come, first-served basis. All students may keep cars.

Activities: There are 5 local and 13 national fraternities and 6 local and 8 national sororities. There are 181 groups on campus, including art, band, cheerleading, choir, chorale, chorus, computers, dance, drama, ethnic, film, gay, honors, international, jazz band, literary magazine, marching band, musical theater, newspaper, opera, orchestra, photography, political, professional, radio and TV, religious, social, social service, student government, symphony, and yearbook. Popular campus events include International Student Days, Campus Community Day, and Welcome Week.

Sports: There are 8 intercollegiate sports for men and 10 for women, and 9 intramural sports for men and 9 for women. Facilities include 2 gyms, 2 swimming pools, softball and soccer fields, handball, racquetball, and tennis courts, a baseball field, and a track.

Disabled Students: 98% of the campus is accessible. Wheelchair ramps, elevators, special parking, specially equipped rest rooms, special class scheduling, lowered drinking fountains, lowered telephones, and electric doors are available.

Services: Counseling and information services are available, as is tutoring in some subjects, including English and math. There is a reader service for the blind, and remedial math, reading, and writing. Student tutors are available for other selected subjects as well.

Campus Safety and Security: Measures include 24-hour foot and vehicle patrol, security escort services, shuttle buses, and informal discussions. There are pamphlets/posters/films, emergency telephones, and lighted pathways/sidewalks.

Programs of Study: CSUN confers B.A., B.S., and B.M. degrees. Master's degrees are also awarded. Bachelor's degrees are awarded in BIOLOGICAL SCIENCE (biochemistry, biology/biological science, environmental biology, and microbiology), BUSINESS (accounting, banking and finance, business administration and management, management information systems, marketing/retailing/merchandising, and recreation and leisure services), COMMUNICATIONS AND THE ARTS (art, dance, dramatic arts, English, film arts, French, German, journalism, linguistics, music, Spanish, and speech/debate/rhetoric), COMPUTER AND PHYSICAL SCIENCE (astrophysics, chemistry, computer science, earth science, geology, mathematics, physics, and radiological technology), EDUCATION (business, education of the deaf and hearing impaired, home economics, and physical), ENGINEERING AND ENVIRONMENTAL DESIGN (engineering), HEALTH PROFESSIONS (biomedical science, exercise science, health, health care administration, medical laboratory technology, nursing, physical therapy, recreation therapy, and speech pathology/audiology), SOCIAL SCIENCE (African American studies, anthropology, Asian/American studies, child psychology/development, criminology, economics, family/consumer studies, geography, history, humanities, liberal arts/general studies, Mexican-American/Chicano studies, philosophy, political science/government, psychology, sociology, urban studies, and women's studies). Liberal studies is the strongest academically. Business administration and economics, social and behavioral sciences, and arts, media and communication are the largest.

Required: All students must complete 52 units of general education requirements in 6 areas, including courses in American history, U.S. Constitution, state and local government, English, math, logic, and oral and written communication. A total of 124 semester units for the B.A., 128 to 132 for the B.S., and 132 for the B.M., with a minimum GPA of 2.0, is required to graduate. At least 30 semester units must be completed in residence.

Special: Cross-registration is offered through the Intra System Visitor Program. Study abroad in 16 countries, internships, university work-study programs, dual majors, student-designed majors, credit for military experience, and pass/fail options for elective courses are offered. There are 4 national honor societies, a freshman honors program, and 5 departmental honors programs.

Faculty/Classroom: 60% of faculty are male; 40%, female. All teach undergraduates. Graduate students teach 12% of introductory courses. The average class size in an introductory lecture is 33 and in a laboratory, 20.

Admissions: 76% of recent applicants were accepted. The SAT scores for a recent freshman class were: Verbal--65% below 500, 27% between 500 and 599, 7% between 600 and 700, and 1% above 700; Math--61% below 500, 28% between 500 and 599, 11% between 600 and 700, and 1% above 700.

Requirements: The SAT or ACT is required. For students with a GPA below 3.0 (3.6 for nonresidents). Applicants should have completed 4 years of high school English, 3 each of math and academic electives, 2 of foreign language, and 1 each of lab science, U.S. history/government, and visual/performing arts. CSUN requires applicants to be in the upper 33% of their class. A GPA of 2.0 is required. AP and CLEP credits are accepted. Important factors in the admissions decision are recommendations by school officials, evidence of special talent, and leadership record.

Procedure: Freshmen are admitted fall and spring. Entrance exams should be taken by December of the senior year. There is an early decision plan. Check with the school for current application deadlines and fee. Notification is sent on a rolling basis. Applications are accepted online.

Transfer: A GPA of 2.0 (2.4 for nonresidents) is required in a minimum of 56 transferable semester units. Basic courses in writing, math, speech, and logic must be completed with a grade of C or better. 30 of 124 credits required for the bachelor's degree must be completed at CSUN.

Visiting: There are regularly scheduled orientations for prospective students, held in June and July for fall entrance and in November for spring entrance. There are guides for informal visits and visitors may sit in on classes and stay overnight. To schedule a visit, contact Student Outreach and Recruitment at (818) 677-2879 or *jason.roberts@csun.edu*.

Financial Aid: CSUN is a member of CSS. The SAAC is required.

International Students: They must score satisfactorily on the written TOEFL.

Computers: All students may access the system 24 hours a day, 7 days a week.

Graduates: In a recent year, 6142 bachelor's degrees were awarded. The most popular majors were business administration (18%), liberal studies (9%), and psychology (8%). In an average class, 3% graduate in 4 years or less, 15% graduate in 5 years or less, and 25% graduate in 6 years or less. 400 companies recruited on campus in a recent year.

Admissions Contact: Eric Forbes, Registrar and Director of Operations, Admissions, and Records. Web: *http://www.csun.edu/index.html*

CALIFORNIA STATE UNIVERSITY, SACRAMENTO   B-3

Sacramento, CA 95819-6048　　　(916) 278-7362
(800) 722-4748; Fax: (916) 278-5603

Full-time: 7505 men, 10,360 women	**Faculty:** 604; IIA, +$
Part-time: 2308 men, 2855 women	**Ph.D.s:** n/av
Graduate: 1554 men, 3350 women	**Student/Faculty:** 30 to 1
Year: semesters, summer session	**Tuition:** $3624 ($13,794)
Application Deadline: November 30	**Room & Board:** $7498
Freshman Class: 15,982 applied, 7586 accepted, 2520 enrolled	
SAT Verbal/Math: 480/500*	**ACT:** 19　　**COMPETITIVE+**

California State University/Sacramento, founded in 1947, is part of the state-supported university system. The school offers graduate and undergraduate programs in the liberal arts and sciences, business administration, education, engineering, music, health and human services, natural sciences, math, and social sciences. There are 8 undergraduate and 7 graduate schools. In addition to regional accreditation, Sac State has baccalaureate program accreditation with AACSB, ABET, ACBSP, ACCE, ADA, AHEA, APTA, ASLA, CSWE, FIDER, NASAD, NASM, NCATE, NLN, NRPA, and TEAC. The library contains 1,309,619 volumes, 2,317,502 microform items, and 53,515 audio/video tapes/CDs/DVDs, and subscribes to 3761 periodicals including electronic. Computerized library services include the card catalog, interlibrary loans, database searching, and Internet access. Special learning facilities include a learning resource center, art gallery, radio station, TV station, an aquatic center, and an anthropology museum. The 300-acre campus is in a suburban area 90 miles northeast of San Francisco. Including any residence halls, there are 51 buildings.

Student Life: 99% of undergraduates are from California. Others are from 37 states, 36 foreign countries, and Canada. 96% are from public schools. 44% are white; 18% Asian American; 14% Hispanic. The average age of freshmen is 18; all undergraduates, 23. 18% do not continue beyond their first year; 45% remain to graduate.

Housing: 1100 students can be accommodated in college housing, which includes coed dorms. On-campus housing is available on a first-come, first-served basis. 95% of students commute. All students may keep cars.

Activities: 7% of men belong to 3 local and 18 national fraternities; 5% of women belong to 1 local and 20 national sororities. There are 230 groups on campus, including art, band, cheerleading, chess, choir, chorale, chorus, computers, dance, debate, drama, ethnic, film, gay, honors, international, jazz band, marching band, musical theater, newspaper, opera, orchestra, pep band, photography, political, professional, radio and TV, religious, social, social service, student government, and symphony. Popular campus events include Greek Week, Festival of New American Music, and River City Days.

Sports: There are 9 intercollegiate sports for men and 11 for women, and 13 intramural sports for men and 13 for women. Facilities include a 17,000-seat stadium, 2 gyms, 2 swimming pools, an all-weather outdoor track, 16 tennis courts, baseball, softball, and soccer fields, and an aquatic center, with sailing, wind-surfing, rowing, and canoeing.

Disabled Students: 90% of the campus is accessible. Wheelchair ramps, elevators, special parking, specially equipped rest rooms, special class scheduling, lowered drinking fountains, and lowered telephones are available.

Services: Counseling and information services are available, as is tutoring in most subjects. There is a reader service for the blind, and remedial math, reading, and writing.

Campus Safety and Security: Measures include 24-hour foot and vehicle patrol, self-defense education, security escort services, and shuttle buses. There are informal discussions, pamphlets/posters/films, emergency telephones, and lighted pathways/sidewalks.

Programs of Study: Sac State confers B.A., B.S., B.M., and B.V.E degrees. Master's and doctoral degrees are also awarded. Bachelor's degrees are awarded in BIOLOGICAL SCIENCE (biology/biological science and microbiology), BUSINESS (accounting, banking and finance, business administration and management, insurance, international business management, management information systems, marketing/retailing/merchandising, and real estate), COMMUNICATIONS AND THE ARTS (communications, dramatic arts, English, French, German, journalism, music, and Spanish), COMPUTER AND PHYSICAL SCIENCE (chemistry, computer science, geology, mathematics, physical sciences, and physics), EDUCATION (business, early childhood, and health), ENGINEERING AND ENVIRONMENTAL DESIGN (civil engineering, computer engineering, electrical/electronics engineering, engineering technology, and mechanical engineering), HEALTH PROFESSIONS (environmental health science, medical laboratory technology, nursing, physical therapy, and speech pathology/audiology), SOCIAL SCIENCE (anthropology, criminal justice, economics, geography, history, international relations, parks and recreation management, philosophy, psychology, public administration, social science, social work, and sociology). Nursing, criminal justice, and business administration are the strongest academically. Business administration, communications, and criminal justice are the largest.

Required: In order to graduate, students must complete a minimum of 120 semester hours, including 30 to 86 hours in the major, with a minimum 2.0 GPA. Students must complete 51 units in general education requirements and take proficiency exams in writing and a foreign language. Distribution requirements include 15 units in the individual and society; 12 each in arts and humanities and physical universe/life forms, 9 in English language communciation, and 3 in understanding personal development. A course in race and ethnicity in American society is required.

Special: The university offers cross-registration with other California State University schools, co-op programs in many academic programs, internships, a Washington semester, study abroad in 12 countries, and dual and student-designed majors. A joint Ph.D. program in public history is available with the university of California at Santa Barbara. There are 3 national honor societies, including Phi Beta Kappa, a freshman honors program, and 26 departmental honors programs.

Faculty/Classroom: 53% of faculty are male; 47%, female. All both teach and do research. The average class size in an introductory lecture is 38; in a laboratory, 19; and in a regular course, 34.

Admissions: 47% of the 2005-2006 applicants were accepted. The SAT scores for the 2005-2006 freshman class were: Verbal--58% below 500, 33% between 500 and 599, and 9% between 600 and 700; Math--50% below 500, 37% between 500 and 599, 13% between 600 and 700, and 1% above 700. The ACT scores were 63% below 21, 25% between 21 and 23, 10% between 24 and 26, and 3% between 27 and 28.

Requirements: The SAT or ACT is required of applicants with a high school GPA below 3.0. Applicants should have completed 4 years of high school English, 3 years of math, 2 years of a foreign language, 1 year each of lab science, history, and visual/performing arts and 3 years of college preparatory electives. A GPA of 2.0 is required. AP and CLEP credits are accepted.

Procedure: Freshmen are admitted fall and spring. Entrance exams should be taken before December of the senior year. There is a deferred admissions and a rolling admissions plan. Applications should be filed by November 30 for fall entry. Notification is sent on a rolling basis. Applications are accepted on-line. The fall 2005 application fee was $55.

Transfer: 3303 transfer students enrolled in 2004-2005. Applicants must have a 2.0 GPA and 56 transferable semester units, including 30 units of specific general education courses to include oral and written communication, critical thinking, and math. 30 of 120 credits required for the bachelor's degree must be completed at Sac State.

Visiting: There are regularly scheduled orientations for prospective students. There are guides for informal visits and visitors may sit in on classes. To schedule a visit, contact the University Outreach Services Office.

Financial Aid: In 2005-2006, 50% of all full-time freshmen and 47% of continuing full-time students received some form of financial aid. 50% of full-time freshmen and 75% of continuing full-time students received need-based aid. The average freshman award was $8153. Need-based scholarships or need-based grants averaged $2219 ($7774 maximum); need-based self-help aid (loans and jobs) averaged $3907 ($7600 maximum); and other non-need-based awards and non-need-based scholarships averaged $6077 ($12,549 maximum). 75% of undergraduates work part time. Average annual earnings from campus work are $1678. The average financial indebtedness of the 2005 graduate was $17,288. Sac State is a member of CSS. The FAFSA and SAAC are required. The deadline for filing freshman financial aid applications for fall entry is March 2.

International Students: There are 201 international students enrolled. The school actively recruits these students. They must score satisfactorily on the written TOEFL or on the electronic version and also take the SAT or the ACT.

Computers: Wireless access is available. All students may access the system. There are no fees. It is strongly recommended that all students have a personal computer.

Graduates: From July 1, 2004 to June 30, 2005, 5861 bachelor's degrees were awarded. The most popular majors were business management (15%), criminal justice (6%), and nursing (6%). In an average class, 1% graduate in 3 years or less, 17% graduate in 4 years or less, 33% graduate in 5 years or less, and 42% graduate in 6 years or less. Of the 2004 graduating class, 19% were enrolled in graduate school within 6 months of graduation.

Admissions Contact: Emiliano Diaz, Director of University Outreach Services. E-mail: *outreach@csus.edu* Web: *http://www.csus.edu/admr/*

CALIFORNIA STATE UNIVERSITY, SAN BERNARDINO D-5

San Bernardino, CA 92407-2397

(909) 537-5188
Fax: (909) 537-7034

Full-time: 3529 men, 6846 women	**Faculty:** IIA, +$
Part-time: 759 men, 1330 women	**Ph.D.s:** n/av
Graduate: 1339 men, 2628 women	**Student/Faculty:** 22 to 1
Year: quarters, summer session	**Tuition:** $6677
Application Deadline: open	**Room & Board:** $5886
Freshman Class: n/av	
SAT Verbal/Math: 455/468*	**ACT:** 19 **LESS COMPETITIVE**

California State University, San Bernardino, founded in 1965, is a public, comprehensive regional university offering programs in business and public administration, natural sciences, education, arts and letters, and social and behavioral sciences. There are 5 undergraduate and 19 graduate schools. In addition to regional accreditation, CSUSB has baccalaureate program accreditation with AACSB, ADA, CSAB, CSWE, NASAD, and NLN. Computerized library services include the card catalog, interlibrary loans, and database searching. Special learning facilities include a learning resource center, art gallery, and radio station. The 430-acre campus is in a suburban area 60 miles east of Los Angeles. Including any residence halls, there are 45 buildings.

Student Life: 34% are white; 32% Hispanic; 11% African American. The average age of freshmen is 18; all undergraduates, 22. 19% do not continue beyond their first year; 81% remain to graduate.

Housing: College housing includes single-sex and coed dorms, on-campus apartments, and 1 all-women dorm. On-campus housing is available on a first-come, first-served basis. 90% of students commute. All students may keep cars.

Activities: 4% of men belong to 1 local and 8 national fraternities; 3% of women belong to 6 national sororities. There are 80 groups on campus, including art, cheerleading, choir, chorale, chorus, computers, dance, drama, ethnic, gay, honors, international, jazz band, musical theater, newspaper, orchestra, political, professional, radio and TV, religious, social, social service, and student government. Popular campus events include Dia de los Muertos, California Indian Cultural Awareness Conference, and Around the World.

Sports: There are 4 intercollegiate sports for men and 7 for women. Facilities include an arena for basketball and volleyball, baseball, softball, and soccer fields, tennis courts, swimming pools for water polo and recreational swimming, and a gym for recreational workouts.

Disabled Students: 95% of the campus is accessible. Wheelchair ramps, elevators, special parking, specially equipped rest rooms, lowered drinking fountains, lowered telephones, student assistants, cart service, and special equipment such as TSS, phonic ear, and VisualTek are available.

Services: Counseling and information services are available, as is tutoring in most subjects. There is a reader service for the blind and remedial math and writing.

Campus Safety and Security: Measures include 24-hour foot and vehicle patrol, self-defense education, security escort services, and emergency telephones. There are lighted pathways/sidewalks and e-mail and web site alerts.

Programs of Study: CSUSB confers B.A., B.S., and B.V.E. degrees. Master's degrees are also awarded. Bachelor's degrees are awarded in AGRICULTURE (environmental studies), BIOLOGICAL SCIENCE (biochemistry and biology/biological science), BUSINESS (accounting, banking and finance, business administration and management, business economics, human resources, international business management, management information systems, management science, and small business management), COMMUNICATIONS AND THE ARTS (art, art history and appreciation, ceramic art and design, communications, dance, dramatic arts, English, French, graphic design, music, music history and appreciation, music performance, music technology, musicology/ethnomusicology, painting, photography, printmaking, sculpture, and Spanish), COMPUTER AND PHYSICAL SCIENCE (applied physics, chemistry, computer science, geology, mathematics, and physics), EDUCATION (bilingual/bicultural, health, music, and vocational), HEALTH PROFESSIONS (environmental health science, exercise science, health care administration, health science, nursing, and premedicine), SOCIAL SCIENCE (American studies, anthropology, child psychology/development, criminal justice, economics, ethnic studies, food science, geography, gerontology, history, human development, human services, humanities, liberal arts/general studies, paralegal studies, philosophy, political science/government, psychology, public administration, social science, social work, sociology, and Spanish studies). Liberal studies, nursing, and psychology are the largest.

Required: To graduate, students must complete 180 to 198 quarter hours, including 60 in upper-division courses and requirements for the major, with a minimum GPA of 2.0. The 82-credit general education program includes courses in basic skills, natural sciences, humanities, social and behavioral sciences, lifelong understanding, upper-division writing, multicultural/gender studies, and electives. Students must also demonstrate an understanding of the U.S. Constitution, American history, and California government.

Special: The university offers cross-registration with other CSU campuses and with the University of California in Riverdale, and study abroad in 18 countries. Also available are internships, accelerated study, campus and community work-study programs, B.A.-B.S. degrees, dual and student-designed majors, credit for vocational education and military experience, and nondegree study. There are 3 national honor societies, including Phi Beta Kappa, and a freshman honors program.

Faculty/Classroom: The average class size in an introductory lecture is 40; in a laboratory, 18; and in a regular course, 24.

Admissions: The SAT scores for the 2005-2006 freshman class were: Verbal--70% below 500, 24% between 500 and 599, and 6% between 600 and 700; Math--65% below 500, 28% between 500 and 599, and 7% between 600 and 700. The ACT scores were 71% below 21, 17% between 21 and 23, 8% between 24 and 26, 2% between 27 and 28, and 1% above 28.

Requirements: The SAT or ACT is required for some programs. In addition, applicants must be graduates of an accredited secondary school. Preparatory work should include 4 years of English, 3 of math, 2 of foreign language, 1 each of U.S. history/government, lab science, and visual and performing arts, and 3 of electives. Admission is based on an eligibility index that weighs the high school GPA and the SAT or ACT score. Students with GPAs of 3.0 or better (3.6 for nonresidents) are exempt from test score requirements. AP and CLEP credits are accepted. Important factors in the admissions decision are advanced placement or honor courses, recommendations by school officials, and leadership record.

Procedure: Freshmen are admitted to all sessions. Entrance exams should be taken prior to applying.There is a rolling admissions plan. Application deadlines are open. The fall 2005 application fee was $55. Notification is sent on a roling basis. Applications are accepted on-line.

Transfer: 1610 transfer students enrolled in 2004-2005. Applicants must have a minimum college GPA of 2.0 (2.4 for nonresidents) and be in good standing at the previously attended institution. Those with fewer than 56 transferable semester units must submit ACT or SAT scores. 45 of 180 credits required for the bachelor's degree must be completed at CSUSB.

Visiting: There are regularly scheduled orientations for prospective students, including sessions on admissions requirements, financial aid information, and campus (student) life information. There are guides for informal visits and visitors may sit in on classes and stay overnight. To schedule a visit, contact the Outreach Services Office.

Financial Aid: The FAFSA is required. The deadline for filing freshman financial aid applications for fall entry is March 2.

International Students: There are 370 international students enrolled. The school actively recruits these students. A satisfactory score is required on the written TOEFL.

Computers: All students may access the system. There are no time limits and no fees.

Graduates: In a recent year, 2331 bachelor's degrees were awarded. The most popular majors were business administration (23%), liberal studies (22%), and social science/history (10%).

Admissions Contact: Olivia Rosas, Director. A video is available.
E-mail: *www.moreinfo@mail.csusb,edu*
Web: *http://enrollment.csusb.edu*

CALIFORNIA STATE UNIVERSITY, SAN MARCOS   D-5

San Marcos, CA 92096-0001   (760) 750-4848
   Fax: (760) 750-3248

Full-time: 5750 men and women	**Faculty:** 170; IIA, av$
Part-time: none	**Ph.D.s:** 92%
Graduate: 750 men and women	**Student/Faculty:** n/av
Year: semesters, summer session	**Tuition:** $1800 ($10,000)
Application Deadline: see profile	**Room & Board:** n/app
Freshman Class: n/av	
SAT or ACT: recommended	**LESS COMPETITIVE**

California State University, San Marcos, founded in 1989, is a public commuter institution that is part of the California State University system. There are 2 undergraduate and 3 graduate schools. Figures in the above capsule and in this profile are approximate. In addition to regional accreditation, Cal State, San Marcos has baccalaureate program accreditation with NCATE. The library contains 148,114 volumes, 755,260 microform items, and 5668 audio/video tapes/CDs/DVDs, and subscribes to 1871 periodicals including electronic. Computerized library services include the card catalog, interlibrary loans, and database searching. Special learning facilities include a learning resource center. The 304-acre campus is in a suburban area 32 miles northeast of San Diego. There are 8 buildings.

Student Life: 98% of undergraduates are from California. Others are from Canada. 55% are white; 18% Hispanic. The average age of freshmen is 19; all undergraduates, 25.

Housing: There are no residence halls. All of students commute. Alcohol is not permitted.

Activities: 3% of men belong to 2 national fraternities; 2% of women belong to 2 national sororities. There are 35 groups on campus, including computers, ethnic, gay, honors, international, political, professional, religious, social, student government, and yearbook. Popular campus events include Admissions Day, San Marcos Grand Festival, and Preview Day.

Sports: There are 3 intercollegiate sports for men and 3 for women, and 5 intramural sports for men and 5 for women. Facilities include an Olympic-quality track.

Disabled Students: All of the campus is accessible. Wheelchair ramps, elevators, special parking, specially equipped rest rooms, special class scheduling, lowered drinking fountains, and lowered telephones are available.

Services: There is a reader service for the blind, and remedial math, reading, and writing, a writing center, and math, accounting, and computer labs.

Campus Safety and Security: Measures include 24-hour foot and vehicle patrol, security escort services, informal discussions, and pamphlets/posters/films. There are emergency telephones and lighted pathways/sidewalks.

Programs of Study: Cal State, San Marcos confers B.A. and B.S. degrees. Master's degrees are also awarded. Bachelor's degrees are awarded in BIOLOGICAL SCIENCE (biology/biological science), BUSINESS (business administration and management), COMMUNICATIONS AND THE ARTS (communications, creative writing, literature, Spanish, and visual and performing arts), COMPUTER AND PHYSICAL SCIENCE (chemistry, computer science, and mathematics), SOCIAL SCIENCE (economics, history, human development, liberal arts/general studies, political science/government, psychology, social science, sociology, and women's studies). Business administration, psychology, and liberal studies are the largest.

Required: To graduate, students must attain foreign language proficiency at the intermediate level, demonstrate computer competency, fulfill a writing requirement, and maintain a GPA of 2.0. The number of credits required for graduation varies from 124 to 132 depending on the major.

Special: There is cross-registration with other CSU campuses. Internships, study abroad in 16 countries, and work-study programs are available.

Faculty/Classroom: 53% of faculty are male; 47%, female. Graduate students teach 5% of introductory courses. The average class size in an introductory lecture is 25; in a laboratory, 25; and in a regular course, 25.

Requirements: The SAT or ACT is recommended. A GPA of 2.0 is required. AP and CLEP credits are accepted.

Procedure: Freshmen are admitted fall and spring. Check with the school for current application deadlines and fee. Applications are accepted on-line.

Transfer: Requirements include 56 units completed and a 2.0 GPA for California residents, 2.4 for nonresidents. 30 of 124 credits required for the bachelor's degree must be completed at Cal State, San Marcos.

Visiting: There are regularly scheduled orientations for prospective students, including workshops and a campus tour. There are guides for informal visits and visitors may sit in on classes. To schedule a visit, contact the Office of Admissions.

Financial Aid: Cal State, San Marcos is a member of CSS. The FAFSA is required. Check with the school for current deadlines.

International Students: The school actively recruits these students. They must score satisfactorily on the written TOEFL.

Computers: All students may access the system. There are no time limits and no fees. It is strongly recommended that all students have a personal computer.

Admissions Contact: Cherine Heckman, Director of Admissions. A video is available. E-mail: *apply@csusm.edu* Web: *www.csusm.edu*

CALIFORNIA STATE UNIVERSITY, STANISLAUS B-3
Turlock, CA 95382

(209) 667-3070
(800) 300-7420; Fax: (209) 667-3788

Full-time: 1542 men, 2958 women	Faculty: 285; IIA, av$
Part-time: 657 men, 1326 women	Ph.Ds: 56%
Graduate: 495 men, 1159 women	Student/Faculty: 16 to 1
Year: 4-1-4, summer session	Tuition: $3030 ($13,200)
Application Deadline: July 1	Room & Board: $8253
Freshman Class: 4292 applied, 2778 accepted, 870 enrolled	
SAT Verbal/Math: 469/479*	ACT: 19	COMPETITIVE

California State University, Stanislaus, founded in 1957, is a state-supported institution offering undergraduate and graduate programs in liberal and fine arts, business, health science, and teacher preparation. There are 3 undergraduate schools and 1 graduate school. In addition to regional accreditation, CSU Stanislaus has baccalaureate program accreditation with AACSB, ABA, ACS, CCNE, CCTC, CSWE, NASAD, NASM, NASPAA, NAST, and NCATE. The library contains 363,479 volumes, 1,259,689 microform items, and 4288 audio/video tapes/CDs/DVDs, and subscribes to 1398 periodicals including electronic. Computerized library services include the card catalog, interlibrary loans, database searching, Internet access, and laptop Internet portals. Special learning facilities include a learning resource center, art gallery, radio station, laser lab, marine sciences station, greenhouse, art gallery, main stage theater, recital hall, observatory, art complex, and distance learning studios. The 228-acre campus is in a suburban area in the San Joaquin Valley, about 100 miles south of San Francisco. Including any residence halls, there are 26 buildings.

Student Life: 94% of undergraduates are from California. Others are from 21 states, 46 foreign countries, and Canada. 95% are from public schools. 43% are white; 27% Hispanic; 11% Asian American. The average age of freshmen is 18; all undergraduates, 25. 18% do not continue beyond their first year; 50% remain to graduate.

Housing: 650 students can be accommodated in college housing, which includes coed dorms and on-campus apartments. On-campus housing is available on a first-come, first-served basis. 90% of students commute. All students may keep cars.

Activities: 3% of men belong to 1 local and 4 national fraternities; 3% of women belong to 5 local and 3 national sororities. There are 64 groups on campus, including art, band, cheerleading, choir, chorale, chorus, computers, dance, drama, ethnic, gay, honors, international, jazz band, newspaper, opera, orchestra, photography, political, professional, radio and TV, religious, social, social service, student government, and symphony. Popular campus events include Warrior Day, College Day, and Wellness Day.

Sports: There are 6 intercollegiate sports for men and 6 for women, and 9 intramural sports for men and 9 for women. Facilities include a field house, a 2300-seat gym, softball and baseball diamonds, a soccer field, tennis courts, an all-weather track, a swimming pool, and a weight room.

Disabled Students: 99% of the campus is accessible. Wheelchair ramps, elevators, special parking, specially equipped rest rooms, lowered drinking fountains, lowered telephones, special housing, tutors, cart service, and note taking are available.

Services: Counseling and information services are available, as is tutoring in most subjects. There is a reader service for the blind, and remedial math, reading, and writing.

Campus Safety and Security: Measures include 24-hour foot and vehicle patrol, self-defense education, security escort services, and shuttle buses. There are informal discussions, pamphlets/posters/films, emergency telephones, lighted pathways/sidewalks, and CPR and first-aid training.

Programs of Study: CSU Stanislaus confers B.A., B.S., B.F.A., and B.M. degrees. Master's degrees are also awarded. Bachelor's degrees are awarded in AGRICULTURE (agriculture), BIOLOGICAL SCIENCE (biology/biological science), BUSINESS (business administration and management), COMMUNICATIONS AND THE ARTS (art, art history and appreciation, communications, dramatic arts, English, fine arts, French, music, music performance, and Spanish), COMPUTER AND PHYSICAL SCIENCE (applied physics, chemistry, computer science, geology, information sciences and systems, mathematics, physical sciences, and physics), EDUCATION (health and physical), HEALTH PROFESSIONS (nursing), SOCIAL SCIENCE (anthropology, child psychology/development, cognitive science, criminal justice, developmental psychology, economics, ethnic studies, geography, history, interdisciplinary studies, liberal arts/general studies, philosophy, political science/government, psychology, social science, and sociology). Liberal studies, business administration, and psychology are the largest.

Required: To graduate, students must complete at least 120 semester units, including 51 in the general education program and 40 in upper-division courses, with a minimum GPA of 2.0. Distribution requirements consist of 12 units of social, economic, and political institutions and human behavior; 9 each of communication skills, natural sciences and math, and humanities; and 3 of individual resources for modern living.

Special: Numerous co-op programs and internships are offered. Cross-registration with the Higher Education Consortium of Central California, study abroad, work-study programs, nondegree study, an accelerated degree program, B.A.-B.S. degrees, dual majors, student-designed majors, and pass/fail options are also available. There are 10 national honor societies, including Phi Beta Kappa, and a freshman honors program. All majors have honors programs.

Faculty/Classroom: 53% of faculty are male; 47%, female. All teach undergraduates.

Admissions: 65% of the 2005-2006 applicants were accepted. The SAT scores for the 2005-2006 freshman class were: Verbal--45% below 500, 47% between 500 and 599, 8% between 600 and 700, and 1% above 700; Math--42% below 500, 49% between 500 and 599, 8% between 600 and 700, and 1% above 700. The ACT scores were 61% below 21, 24% between 21 and 23, 11% between 24 and 26, 4% between 27 and 28, and 1% above 28.

Requirements: The SAT or ACT is required for some programs. Admission is based on an eligibility index that weights GPA and the SAT or ACT scores. Applicants with a GPA of 3.0 (3.4 for nonresidents) are exempt from test score requirements. Applicants should be graduates of an accredited secondary school. Preparatory course work should include 4 years of English, 3 of math, 2 each of foreign language, history/social sciences, and lab science, 1 of visual and performing arts, and 1 academic elective. A GPA of 3.0 is required. AP and CLEP credits are accepted. Important factors in the admissions decision are advanced placement or honor courses, evidence of special talent, and geographic diversity.

Procedure: Freshmen are admitted to all sessions. Entrance exams should be taken in fall of the senior year. There is a rolling admissions plan. Applications should be filed by July 1 for fall entry, November 30 for winter entry, January 15 for spring entry, and May 1 for summer entry, along with a $55 fee. Notification is sent on a rolling basis. Applications are accepted on-line.

Transfer: 878 transfer students enrolled in 2004-2005. Applicants must have a college GPA of 2.0 (2.4 for nonresidents) and have completed their lower-division general education English and math courses. Those with fewer than 60 transferable semester credits must meet freshman entrance requirements. 30 of a minimum of 120 credits required for the bachelor's degree must be completed at CSU Stanislaus.

Visiting: There are regularly scheduled orientations for prospective students. There are guides for informal visits and visitors may sit in on classes with prior approval. To schedule a visit, contact University Outreach.

Financial Aid: In 2005-2006, 61% of all full-time freshmen and 48% of continuing full-time students received some form of financial aid. 53% of full-time freshmen and 42% of continuing full-time students received need-based aid. The average freshman award was $7816. Need-based scholarships or need-based grants averaged $4361; need-based self-help aid (loans and jobs) averaged $3132; non-need-based athletic scholarships averaged $2094; and other non-need-based awards and non-need-based scholarships averaged $1501. 7% of undergraduates work part time. The average financial indebtedness of the 2005 graduate was $15,500. The FAFSA and the SAAC for California residents are required. The deadline for filing freshman financial aid applications for fall entry is March 2.

International Students: There are 64 international students enrolled.They must take the TOEFL and also take the SAT, ACT, or EPT/ELM if the high school GPA is under 3.0.

Computers: Wireless access is available. All students may access the system. There are no time limits and no fees.

Graduates: From July 1, 2004 to June 30, 2005, 1454 bachelor's degrees were awarded. The most popular majors were liberal studies (24%), business administration (16%), and psychology (8%). In an average class, 21% graduate in 4 years or less, 42% graduate in 5 years or less, and 52% graduate in 6 years or less. 46 companies recruited on campus in 2004-2005.

Admissions Contact: Lisa Bernardo, Director of Admissions and Records. A video is available. E-mail: *outreach_help_desk@csustan.edu* Web: *http://www.csustan.edu*

CHAPMAN UNIVERSITY   D-5

Orange, CA 92866

(714) 997-6711
(888) CUAPPLY; Fax: (714) 997-6713

Full-time: 1375 men, 1875 women	**Faculty:** 199; IIA, +$
Part-time: 100 men, 100 women	**Ph.D.s:** 90%
Graduate: 400 men, 800 women	**Student/Faculty:** 16 to 1
Year: 4-1-4, summer session	**Tuition:** $28,050
Application Deadline: January 31	**Room & Board:** $9500
Freshman Class: 3908 applied, 2040 accepted, 859 enrolled	
SAT or ACT: required	**VERY COMPETITIVE**

Chapman University, founded in 1861, is an independent institution affiliated with the Disciples of Christ Christian Church, offering degree programs in liberal and fine arts, business, education, and the health sciences. There are 7 undergraduate and 8 graduate schools. Some figures in this profile are approximate. In addition to regional accreditation, Chapman has baccalaureate program accreditation with AACSB, APTA, and NASM. The library contains 178,986 volumes, 423,569 microform items, and 5421 audio/video tapes/CDs/DVDs, and subscribes to 1196 periodicals including electronic. Computerized library services include the card catalog, interlibrary loans, database searching, and Internet access. Special learning facilities include a learning resource center, art gallery, radio station, TV station, and a food science sensory lab. The 60-acre campus is in a suburban area 35 miles southeast of Los Angeles. Including any residence halls, there are 25 buildings.

Student Life: 74% of undergraduates are from California. Others are from 48 states, 37 foreign countries, and Canada. 62% are from public schools. 65% are white. 26% are Protestant; 23% claim no religious affiliation; 22% Catholic. The average age of freshmen is 19; all undergraduates, 22. 13% do not continue beyond their first year.

Housing: 1450 students can be accommodated in college housing, which includes coed dormitories, on-campus apartments, and married-student housing. In addition, there are special-interest houses and women's communities. On-campus housing is guaranteed for the freshman year only, is available on a first-come, first-served basis, and is available on a lottery system for upperclassmen. Priority is given to out-of-town students. 57% of students commute. All students may keep cars.

Activities: 14% of men belong to 5 national fraternities; 17% of women belong to 5 national sororities. There are 60 groups on campus, including art, band, cheerleading, choir, chorale, chorus, community service, dance, debate, drama, ethnic, film, forensics, gay, honors, international, jazz band, literary magazine, newspaper, opera, orchestra, pep band, photography, political, professional, radio and TV, religious, social, social service, student government, symphony, and yearbook. Popular campus events include lunchtime concerts, Spring Sizzle, and All University Formal.

Sports: There are 10 intercollegiate sports for men and 10 for women, and 10 intramural sports for men and 10 for women. Facilities include a gym, a weight room, 3 practice fields, and 4 tennis courts. Baseball and softball fields, a track, and a pool are available for student use nearby in the city of Orange.

Disabled Students: 75% of the campus is accessible. Wheelchair ramps, elevators, special parking, specially equipped rest rooms, special class scheduling, lowered drinking fountains, lowered telephones, and special housing are available.

Services: Counseling and information services are available, as is tutoring in most subjects, including math, sciences, business, and English. There is a reader service for the blind, and remedial math, reading, and writing. In addition, there are note takers, readers, and tapes for deaf, blind, and international students; special study skills workshops; and help for the learning disabled.

Campus Safety and Security: Measures include 24-hour foot and vehicle patrol, self-defense education, security escort services, and informal discussions. There are pamphlets/posters/films, emergency telephones, lighted pathways/sidewalks, and rape awareness and victim assistance programs.

Programs of Study: Chapman confers B.A., B.S., B.F.A., B.M., and B.S.B.A. degrees. Master's and doctoral degrees are also awarded. Bachelor's degrees are awarded in BIOLOGICAL SCIENCE (biology/

biological science), BUSINESS (accounting, business administration and management, and organizational behavior), COMMUNICATIONS AND THE ARTS (art, art history and appreciation, communications, creative writing, dance, dramatic arts, English, film arts, French, graphic design, music, music performance, public relations, Spanish, and studio art), COMPUTER AND PHYSICAL SCIENCE (chemistry, computer science, information sciences and systems, and mathematics), EDUCATION (athletic training, and music), ENGINEERING AND ENVIRONMENTAL DESIGN (environmental science), HEALTH PROFESSIONS (health science and music therapy), SOCIAL SCIENCE (economics, food science, history, law, liberal arts/general studies, peace studies, philosophy, physical fitness/movement, political science/government, psychology, religion, social science, and sociology). Business is the strongest academically. Business, communications, and film and television are the largest.

Required: Students in the B.A., B.F.A., B.S., and B.S.B.A. programs must complete a total of 124 credits with at least a 2.0 GPA. In addition, students must meet requirements in basic subjects such as writing, oral communication, freshman seminar, math, and phys ed through course work, advanced credit, or exam. General education requirements include 10 credits in natural sciences and 9 each in humanities and social sciences. Also required are 6 credits each of cultural heritage/human diversity and foreign language, and a junior writing proficiency exam.

Special: Cooperative and internship programs are available. Students may study abroad for a semester or spend a semester in Washington, D.C. Dual and student-designed majors are possible. A general studies degree, B.A.-B.S. degrees, nondegree study options, and pass/fail options are also permitted. A 3-2 engineering degree with the University of California, Irvine, is possible. There is 1 national honor society and a freshman honors program.

Faculty/Classroom: 60% of faculty are male; 40%, female. 96% teach undergraduates. No introductory courses are taught by graduate students. The average class size in an introductory lecture is 23; in a laboratory, 17; and in a regular course, 21.

Admissions: 52% of the 2005-2006 applicants were accepted. The SAT scores for a recent freshman class were: Verbal--6% below 500, 51% between 500 and 599, 36% between 600 and 700, and 7% above 700; Math--5% below 500, 50% between 500 and 599, 40% between 600 and 700, and 5% above 700. 41% of recent freshmen were in the top fifth of their class; 83% were in the top two fifths.

Requirements: The SAT or ACT is required. In addition, applicants should be graduates of accredited high schools or have earned the GED. Secondary preparation should include 4 years of English, 3 each of math and social science or electives, and 2 each of science and a foreign language. Prospective art or music majors should show some preparation in those fields. A personal essay is required. An on-campus interview is recommended. A GPA of 2.75 is required. AP and CLEP credits are accepted. Important factors in the admissions decision are advanced placement or honor courses, evidence of special talent, and leadership record.

Procedure: Freshmen are admitted fall and spring. Entrance exams should be taken by fall of the senior year. There is an early admissions plan. Early action applications should be filed by November 30, regular applications by January 31 for fall entry, along with a $55 fee. 153 applicants were on the 2005 waiting list in a recent year. Applications are accepted on-line.

Transfer: 304 transfer students enrolled in a recent year. Transfer applicants should have completed at least 12 credits of transferable college work with a 2.25 minimum GPA. High school records and SAT or ACT scores should be submitted if fewer than 30 transferable credits have been completed. 24 of 124 credits required for the bachelor's degree must be completed at Chapman.

Visiting: There are regularly scheduled orientations for prospective students, consisting of Fall and Spring Campus Exploration Day events. Weekday appointments and campus tours are also available. There are guides for informal visits and visitors may sit in on classes. To schedule a visit, contact the Office of Admissions.

Financial Aid: In a recent year, 90% of all full-time freshmen and 86% of continuing full-time students received some form of financial aid. 64% of full-time freshmen and 61% of continuing full-time students received need-based aid. The average freshman award was $23,422. Need-based scholarships or need-based grants averaged $16,363 ($34,050 maximum); need-based self-help aid (loans and jobs) averaged $4433 ($10,625 maximum); and other non-need-based awards and non-need-based scholarships averaged $14,271 ($37,200 maximum). 60% of undergraduates work part time. Average annual earnings from campus work are $1695. The average financial indebtedness of a recent graduate was $18,574. Chapman is a member of CSS. The FAFSA and the state aid form are required. Check with the school for current deadlines.

International Students: There were 88 international students enrolled in a recent year. The school actively recruits these students. They must score satisfactorily on the TOEFL and also take the SAT or the ACT.

Computers: All students may access the system 8 A.M. to 11 P.M. There are no time limits and no fees. It is strongly recommended that all students have a personal computer.

Graduates: In a recent year, 695 bachelor's degrees were awarded. The most popular majors were business administration (16%), film and television (13%), and liberal studies (8%). In an average class, 49% graduate in 4 years or less, and 59% graduate in 6 years or less. 80 companies recruited on campus in a recent year. Of a recent graduating class, 40% were enrolled in graduate school within 6 months of graduation and 93% were employed.

Admissions Contact: Mike Drummy, Assistant Vice President of Enrollment Services and Chief Admiss. E-mail: *admit@chapman.edu* Web: *www.chapman.edu*

CHRISTIAN HERITAGE COLLEGE
(See San Diego Christian College)

CLAREMONT COLLEGES, THE

Established in 1925, this prestigious group of seven private colleges is a consortium of higher education institutions. It is comprised of five undergraduate liberal arts colleges: Claremont McKenna, Harvey Mudd, Pitzer, Pomona, and Scripps; and two graduate institutions: Claremont Graduate University and Keck Graduate Institute of Applied Life Sciences. Collectively, the seven institutions serve nearly 6,200 students from 50 states and more than 80 foreign countries. 2500 courses are taught each year by 700 professors, often with class sizes under 20. Six contiguous campuses with 175 buildings are spread over 350 acres of land with the seventh campus located nearby. Each institution is independent, with its own faculty, student body, administration, curricular emphasis, and distinctive style. However, each is enriched by the presence of the others. The consortium offers students a variety of intellectual, cultural, and social activities in facilities and shared academic resources. Claremont University Consortium (CUC) is the central coordinating and support organization for The Claremont Colleges. Some of the 28 services include campus safety, libraries, health and counseling services, ethnic student centers, an interfaith office of chaplains, a centralized bookstore, food services, information technology, human resources, real estate, risk management, and employee benefits. In the words of the founding father, Dr. Robert J. Bernard, "This pioneering enterprise has given national leadership in demonstrating how the advantages of small colleges and the advantages of a university can be combined to build a notable center of learning."

CLAREMONT McKENNA COLLEGE   D-5

Claremont, CA 91711-6425	**(909) 621-8088; Fax: (909) 621-8516**
Full-time: 615 men, 523 women	Faculty: 134; IIB, ++$
Part-time: 2 men	Ph.D.s: 96%
Graduate: none	Student/Faculty: 8 to 1
Year: semesters	Tuition: $30,800
Application Deadline: January 1	Room & Board: $12,120
Freshman Class: 3734 applied, 786 accepted, 271 enrolled	
SAT Verbal/Math: 700/700*	ACT: 31 MOST COMPETITIVE

Claremont McKenna College, founded in 1946, is a liberal arts college with a curricular emphasis on economics, government, international relations, and public affairs. In addition to regional accreditation, CMC has baccalaureate program accreditation with WASC. The 5 libraries contain 2,476,503 volumes, 1,455,319 microform items, and 10,861 audio/video tapes/CDs/DVDs, and subscribe to 15,995 periodicals including electronic. Computerized library services include the card catalog, interlibrary loans, database searching, and laptop Internet portals. Special learning facilities include a learning resource center, art gallery, radio station, and 11 research institutes. The 50-acre campus is in a small town 35 miles east of downtown Los Angeles. Including any residence halls, there are 31 buildings.

Student Life: 50% of undergraduates are from out of state, mostly the Northwest. Students are from 40 states, 27 foreign countries, and Canada. 73% are from public schools. 56% are white; 15% Asian American; 12% Hispanic. 31% claim no religious affiliation; 30% are Protestant; 19% Catholic; 8% Jewish. The average age of freshmen is 18; all undergraduates, 20. 3% do not continue beyond their first year; 86% remain to graduate.

Housing: 989 students can be accommodated in college housing, which includes coed dorms and on-campus apartments. On-campus housing is guaranteed for all 4 years. 96% of students live on campus; of those, 80% remain on campus on weekends. All students may keep cars.

Activities: There are no fraternities or sororities. There are 185 groups on campus, including art, band, cheerleading, choir, chorale, chorus, computers, dance, debate, drama, ethnic, film, forensics, gay, honors, international, jazz band, literary magazine, musical theater, newspaper, orchestra, photography, political, professional, radio and TV, religious, social, social service, student government, symphony, and yearbook. Popular campus events include International Festival, Madrigal Dinners, and Monte Carlo Night.

Sports: There are 10 intercollegiate sports for men and 10 for women, and 10 intramural sports for men and 9 for women. Facilities include

basketball courts, a weight room, a fitness center, a track and football field, an aquatic center, tennis courts, baseball, softball, lacrosse, and soccer fields, an archery range, and squash and volleyball courts.

Disabled Students: 90% of the campus is accessible. Wheelchair ramps, elevators, special parking, specially equipped rest rooms, special class scheduling, and special housing, are available. The campus complies with ADA requirements and reasonably accommodates students with physical disabilities as necessary to meet their access needs.

Services: Counseling and information services are available, as is tutoring in most subjects. The Writing Center offers writing help and specialized workshops.

Campus Safety and Security: Measures include 24-hour foot and vehicle patrol, self-defense education, security escort services, and informal discussions. There are pamphlets/posters/films, emergency telephones, and lighted pathways/sidewalks.

Programs of Study: CMC confers the B.A. degree. Bachelor's degrees are awarded in AGRICULTURE (environmental studies), BIOLOGICAL SCIENCE (biochemistry, biology/biological science, ecology, molecular biology, and neurosciences), BUSINESS (management engineering), COMMUNICATIONS AND THE ARTS (English literature, film arts, French, literature, media arts, and Spanish), COMPUTER AND PHYSICAL SCIENCE (chemistry, mathematics, physics, and science technology), ENGINEERING AND ENVIRONMENTAL DESIGN (environmental science), SOCIAL SCIENCE (American studies, Asian/Oriental studies, economics, history, interdisciplinary studies, international relations, law, philosophy, political science/government, psychology, and religion). Economics, government, and international relations are strongest academically and have the largest enrollments.

Required: All students must complete 32 courses (128 semester hours) with a C average. Required courses include a minimum of 3 semesters each of social science and phys ed; 2 each of sciences and humanities; 1 each of English, calculus, and civilization; and foreign language proficiency equal to 3 college semesters. A thesis is required of all students. At least 16 courses must be taken in residence.

Special: CMC students may cross-register at any of the Claremont Colleges and may participate in exchange programs with Haverford, Spelman, or Colby Colleges. Students may study abroad in 39 countries or spend a semester in Washington, D.C. Part-time and full-time internships and dual and student-designed majors are available. There is a 3-2 economics-engineering program with Harvey Mudd College and a 3-2 management-engineering program. A multidisciplinary program in leadership studies and an interdisciplinary program in legal studies are offered. There are limited pass/fail options. There are 5 national honor societies, including Phi Beta Kappa.

Faculty/Classroom: 63% of faculty are male; 37%, female. All both teach and do research. The average class size in a laboratory is 18 and in a regular course, 17.

Admissions: 21% of the 2005-2006 applicants were accepted. The SAT scores for the 2005-2006 freshman class were: Verbal--12% between 500 and 599, 38% between 600 and 700, and 50% above 700; Math--7% between 500 and 599, 40% between 600 and 700, and 53% above 700. The ACT scores were 2% between 21 and 23, 10% between 24 and 26, 19% between 27 and 28, and 69% above 28. 96% of the current freshmen were in the top fifth of their class. There were 22 National Merit finalists. 16 freshmen graduated first in their class.

Requirements: The SAT is required. The ACT Optional Writing test is also required. In addition, applicants must be graduates of an accredited high school or have earned the GED. Secondary preparation must include 4 years of English, 3 years (preferably 4) of math, at least 3 years of a foreign language , 2 years (preferably 3) of science, and 1 year of history. A personal essay is required, and an interview is optional. AP credits are accepted. Important factors in the admissions decision are advanced placement or honor courses, leadership record, and extracurricular activities record.

Procedure: Freshmen are admitted fall and spring. Entrance exams should be taken during the junior year or between October and January of the senior year. There is an early decision plan. Early decision applications should be filed by November 15; regular applications, by January 1 for fall entry and November 1 for spring entry. Notification of early decision is sent December 15; regular decision, April 1. 76 early decision candidates were accepted for the 2005-2006 class. 412 applicants were on the 2005 waiting list; 24 were admitted. Applications are accepted on-line.

Transfer: 38 transfer students enrolled in 2004-2005. Applicants must submit SAT or ACT scores, high school and college transcripts, essays, a college report form, midsemester grades, and recommendations from a college professor or counselor. 64 of 128 credits required for the bachelor's degree must be completed at CMC.

Visiting: There are regularly scheduled orientations for prospective students, including a campus tour, faculty presentations, student discussions, and admissions and financial aid workshops. There are guides for informal visits and visitors may sit in on classes and stay overnight. To schedule a visit, contact the Admissions Office at *admission@claremontmckenna.edu.*

Financial Aid: In 2005-2006, 64% of all full-time freshmen and 66% of continuing full-time students received some form of financial aid. 47% of full-time freshmen and 51% of continuing full-time students received need-based aid. The average freshman award was $25,115. Need-based scholarships or need-based grants averaged $22,364 ($37,570 maximum); and need-based self-help aid (loans and jobs) averaged $3087 ($5200 maximum). 52% of undergraduates work part time. Average annual earnings from campus work are $2139. The average financial indebtedness of the 2005 graduate is $10,769. The CSS/Profile or FAFSA is required. The deadline for filing freshman financial aid applications for fall entry is February 1.

International Students: There are 33 international students enrolled. The school actively recruits these students. They must achieve a satisfactory score on the TOEFL and also take the SAT.

Computers: Wireless access is available. Poppa Lab hosts 32 PC and 3 Mac workstations, and is open 24 hours a day with support staff typically available between 8 A.M. and midnight. It provides students with high-capacity balck-and-white and color laser printing. South Lab, also open 24 hours a day, hosts 14 PC workstations, as well as a high-capacity black-and-white printer. Bauer Technology Classroom is open evenings as a student lab, with 16 PC workstations. It offers students the opportunity to work collectively on group projects and is staffed by technology assistants selected to provide advanced drop-in support on more complex software packages and technical tasks. All students may access the system. There are no time limits and no fees.

Graduates: From July 1, 2004 to June 30, 2005, 286 bachelor's degrees were awarded. The most popular majors were economics (29%), government (22%), and psychology (15%). In an average class, 86% graduate in 4 years or less, and 88% graduate in 5 years or less. 129 companies recruited on campus in 2004-2005. Of the 2004 graduating class, 20% were enrolled in graduate school within 6 months of graduation and 60% were employed.

Admissions Contact: Richard C. Vos, Vice President, Dean of Admission and Financial Aid. E-mail: *admission@claremontmckenna.edu* Web: *www.mckennna.edu*

COGSWELL POLYTECHNICAL COLLEGE   B-3

Sunnyvale, CA 94089   (408) 541-0100, ext. 152
(800)-264-7955 (COGSWLL); Fax: (408) 747-0764

Full-time: 200 men and women	**Faculty:** 10
Part-time: 300 men and women	**Ph.D.s:** 35%
Graduate: none	**Student/Faculty:** 20 to 1
Year: trimesters, summer session	**Tuition:** $13,760
Application Deadline: open	**Room & Board:** n/app
Freshman Class: n/av	
SAT or ACT: not required	**LESS COMPETITIVE**

Cogswell Polytechnical College, founded in 1887, is a small, independent engineering and arts college. Figures in the above capsule and in this profile are approximate. The library contains 13,000 volumes, 250 microform items, and 200 audio/video tapes/CDs/DVDs, and subscribes to 125 periodicals including electronic. Computerized library services include the card catalog and database searching. Special learning facilities include an art gallery, commercial studio, and video postproduction company. The 4-acre campus is in a suburban area 40 miles south of San Francisco in California's Silicon Valley. There is one building.

Student Life: 70% of undergraduates are from California. 65% are from public schools. The average age of freshmen is 19; all undergraduates, 28. 10% do not continue beyond their first year; 70% remain to graduate.

Housing: There are no residence halls. Arrangements can be made to accommodate students in private houses or at nearby corporate apartments. Alcohol is not permitted. All students may keep cars.

Activities: There are no fraternities or sororities. There are 7 groups on campus, including art, computers, honors, international, jazz band, professional, and student government. Popular campus events include Founders Day, club competitions, and ski trips.

Sports: There is no sports program at Cogswell College. Facilities include a game room, a student lounge, and access to community athletic facilities.

Disabled Students: Wheelchair ramps, special parking, specially equipped rest rooms, special class scheduling, lowered drinking fountains, and lowered telephones are available.

Services: Counseling and information services are available, as is tutoring in every subject. There is remedial writing.

Campus Safety and Security: Measures include pamphlets/posters/films, lighted pathways/sidewalks, an emergency evacuation plan, and maps in the classrooms.

Programs of Study: Cogswell College confers B.A.C.V.I. (Computer and Video Imaging), B.S.E.E., B.S.F.S. (Fire Science), and B.S.S.W.E. (Software Engineering) degrees. Bachelor's degrees are awarded in COMMUNICATIONS AND THE ARTS (animation, audio technology, and music technology), COMPUTER AND PHYSICAL SCIENCE (computer programming, digital arts/technology, and web technology), ENGI-

NEERING AND ENVIRONMENTAL DESIGN (computer engineering, computer graphics, and electrical/electronics engineering), SOCIAL SCIENCE (fire control and safety technology and fire protection). Engineering and animation are the strongest academically. Computer video imaging is the largest.

Required: To graduate, students must complete a total of 120 to 128 credits with 18 to 27 in the major and have a 2.0 GPA. 45 to 56 credits in general education core courses are required, depending on the major, and include courses in English, math, natural sciences, social sciences, and humanities.

Special: Cogswell offers various internships and work-study programs. The college administers the Open Learning for the Fire Service (OLFS) program for Arizona, California, and Nevada, through which nonresident students can earn a B.S. in fire science. Nondegree study and pass/fail options are possible. There is a freshman honors program.

Faculty/Classroom: 65% of faculty are male; 35%, female. The average class size in an introductory lecture is 15; in a laboratory, 8; and in a regular course, 25.

Requirements: Applicants must be high school graduates or have the GED. Secondary preparation must include 3 years of English, 2 to 3 of math, including algebra, geometry, and trigonometry, and 1 year of science. Cogswell requires a personal essay and recommends a personal interview. A portfolio is required for computer and video imaging programs. A GPA of 2.7 is required. AP and CLEP credits are accepted. Important factors in the admissions decision are advanced placement or honor courses, recommendations by school officials, and ability to finance college education.

Procedure: Freshmen are admitted to all sessions. There are early decision and early admissions plans. Application deadlines are open. The application fee is $55.

Transfer: Applicants must have completed at least 12 college credits with a 2.2 GPA. An interview is recommended. 27 of 120 credits required for the bachelor's degree must be completed at Cogswell College.

Visiting: Visitors may sit in on classes. To schedule a visit, contact the dean of marketing and recruiting.

Financial Aid: Cogswell College is a member of CSS. The FAFSA and the college's own financial statement are required.

International Students: The school actively recruits these students. They must score satisfactorily on the written TOEFL.

Computers: All students may access the system during school hours. There are no time limits and no fees. It is strongly recommended that all students have a personal computer.

Admissions Contact: Patricia DelRio, Director of Admissions. E-mail: *admin@cogswell.edu* Web: *www.cogswell.edu*

CONCORDIA UNIVERSITY   D-5

Irvine, CA 92612-3299   (949) 854-8002 ext. 1170
(800) 229-1200; Fax: (949) 854-6894

Full-time: 480 men, 827 women	**Faculty:** 77
Part-time: 20 men, 30 women	**Ph.D.s:** 62%
Graduate: 207 men, 440 women	**Student/Faculty:** 17 to 1
Year: semesters	**Tuition:** $19,930
Application Deadline: May 1	**Room & Board:** $6850
Freshman Class: 998 applied, 696 accepted, 265 enrolled	
SAT Verbal/Math: 520/530*	**ACT:** 22 **COMPETITIVE**

Concordia University, founded in 1972, is a private liberal arts college affiliated with the Lutheran Church-Missouri Synod. There are 5 undergraduate and 4 graduate schools. In addition to regional accreditation, Concordia Irvine has baccalaureate program accreditation with WASC. The library contains 85,553 volumes, 53,175 microform items, and 3693 audio/video tapes/CDs/DVDs, and subscribes to 9763 periodicals including electronic. Computerized library services include the card catalog, interlibrary loans, database searching, and Internet access. Special learning facilities include a learning resource center, art gallery, and radio station. The 70-acre campus is in a suburban area 40 miles south of Los Angeles. Including any residence halls, there are 24 buildings.

Student Life: 83% of undergraduates are from California. Others are from 35 states, 12 foreign countries, and Canada. 69% are white; 13% Hispanic. 11% nondenominational; 14% are Catholic; 10% Protestant. The average age of freshmen is 18; all undergraduates, 22. 22% do not continue beyond their first year; 78% remain to graduate.

Housing: 1128 students can be accommodated in college housing, which includes single-sex dorms. On-campus housing is guaranteed for all 4 years. 64% of students live on campus. All students may keep cars.

Activities: There are no fraternities or sororities. There are 19 groups on campus, including art, choir, chorale, chorus, dance, debate, drama, ethnic, literary magazine, newspaper, radio and TV, religious, social, social service, student government, and yearbook. Popular campus events include Closing Banquet, Christmas Dance, and Octoberfest.

Sports: There are 7 intercollegiate sports for men and 8 for women, and 6 intramural sports for men and 6 for women. Facilities include a 1800-seat gym, a soccer field, a baseball/softball diamond, volleyball, tennis, and racquetball courts, a track field, a weight room, a dance room, team rooms, and locker rooms.

Disabled Students: 90% of the campus is accessible. Wheelchair ramps, elevators, special parking, and specially equipped rest rooms are available.

Services: Counseling and information services are available, as is tutoring in some subjects, including math, chemistry, critical thinking, Spanish, biology, and calculus.

Campus Safety and Security: Measures include 24-hour foot and vehicle patrol, security escort services, informal discussions, and pamphlets/posters/films. There are lighted pathways/sidewalks.

Programs of Study: Concordia Irvine confers the B.A. degree. Associate and master's degrees are also awarded. Bachelor's degrees are awarded in BIOLOGICAL SCIENCE (biology/biological science), BUSINESS (business administration and management and small business management), COMMUNICATIONS AND THE ARTS (art, communications, dramatic arts, English, and music), COMPUTER AND PHYSICAL SCIENCE (chemistry and mathematics), EDUCATION (Christian and early childhood), HEALTH PROFESSIONS (exercise science), SOCIAL SCIENCE (behavioral science, history, humanities, liberal arts/general studies, political science/government, psychology, and theological studies). Business administration, education, and social science are the strongest academically.

Required: All students must complete 49 semester hours of general education requirements, including courses in humanities and fine arts, math and science, social science, religion, and exercise and sport science. A total of 128 credits, including 36 to 45 in the major, is required to graduate. A GPA of 2.0 in major and program course work must be maintained.

Special: Cross-registration is possible with 9 Concordia University institutions nationwide. Internships, an accelerated degree program in the liberal arts major with an emphasis on business and teacher education, and dual and student-designed majors are available. There are 4 national honor societies, a freshman honors program, and 2 departmental honors programs.

Faculty/Classroom: 60% of faculty are male; 40%, female. 84% teach undergraduates. No introductory courses are taught by graduate students.

Admissions: 70% of the 2005-2006 applicants were accepted. The SAT scores for the 2005-2006 freshman class were: Verbal--36% below 500, 49% between 500 and 599, 13% between 600 and 700, and 2% above 700; Math--35% below 500, 46% between 500 and 599, 18% between 600 and 700, and 1% above 700. The ACT scores were 31% below 21, 33% between 21 and 23, 25% between 24 and 26, 7% between 27 and 28, and 5% above 28. 38% of the current freshmen were in the top fifth of their class; 76% were in the top two fifths.

Requirements: The SAT or ACT is required. In addition, applicants should be high school graduates with 4 years of English, 3 each of math and science, and 2 each of social studies and a foreign language. The GED is accepted. A school reference is also required. Concordia Irvine requires applicants to be in the upper 50% of their class. A GPA of 2.8 is required. AP and CLEP credits are accepted. Important factors in the admissions decision are leadership record, extracurricular activities record, and evidence of special talent.

Procedure: Freshmen are admitted fall and spring. Entrance exams should be taken by the fall of the senior year. There is a deferred admissions plan. Applications should be filed by May 1 for fall entry and December 1 for spring entry. The fall 2000 application fee was $50. Notification is sent on a rolling basis. Applications are accepted on-line.

Transfer: 132 transfer students enrolled in 2004-2005. A GPA of 2.3 is required in a minimum of 24 semester or 36 quarter units completed. An academic reference is required, as are official high school transcripts. 32 of 128 credits required for the bachelor's degree must be completed at Concordia Irvine.

Visiting: There are regularly scheduled orientations for prospective students. There are guides for informal visits and visitors may sit in on classes and stay overnight. To schedule a visit, contact the Admission Office at (949) 854-8002, ext. 1106 or admission@cui.edu.

Financial Aid: In 2005-2006, 98% of all full-time freshmen and 93% of continuing full-time students received some form of financial aid. 68% of full-time freshmen and 59% of continuing full-time students received need-based aid. The average freshman award was $19,857. Need-based scholarships or need-based grants averaged $10,657; need-based self-help aid (loans and jobs) averaged $3189; non-need-based athletic scholarships averaged $8250; and other non-need-based awards and non-need-based scholarships averaged $6333. 25% of undergraduates work part time. Average annual earnings from campus work are $2000. The average financial indebtedness of the 2005 graduate was $19,200. The FAFSA and the college's own financial statement are required. The deadline for filing freshman financial aid applications for fall entry is March 2.

International Students: There are 81 international students enrolled. The school actively recruits these students. They must score satisfactorily on the written TOEFL or on the electronic version.

Computers: All students may access the system. There are no time limits and no fees.

Graduates: From July 1, 2004 to June 30, 2005, 334 bachelor's degrees were awarded. The most popular majors were liberal studies (17%), business administration (17%), and applied liberal arts (12%). In an average class, 5% graduate in 3 years, 86% graduate in 4 years, 8% graduate in 5 years, and 2% graduate in 6 years. Of the 2004 graduating class, 43% were enrolled in graduate school within 6 months of graduation and 59% were employed.

Admissions Contact: Lori McDonald, Director of Enrollment Services. E-mail: lori.mcdonald@cui.edu Web: www.cui.edu

DEVRY UNIVERSITY/FREMONT   B-3
Fremont, CA 94555   (510) 574-1200
                                        (888) 201-9941; Fax: (510) 742-0868

Full-time: 1000 men, 270 women	**Faculty:** n/av
Part-time: 275 men, 110 women	**Ph.D.s:** n/av
Graduate: none	**Student/Faculty:** n/av
Year: semesters, summer session	**Tuition:** $13,060
Application Deadline: open	**Room & Board:** n/app
Freshman Class: n/av	
SAT or ACT: n/av	**LESS COMPETITIVE**

DeVry University/Fremont, founded in 1998, is a private institution offering hands-on programs in electronics, business administration, computer information systems, telecommunications management, computer engineering technology, and technical management. The school is 1 of 67 DeVry University locations throughout the United States and Canada. Some figures in the above capsule and in this profile are approximate. In addition to regional accreditation, DeVry has baccalaureate program accreditation with ABET. The library contains 27,000 volumes and 3000 audio/video tapes/CDs/DVDs, and subscribes to 60 periodicals including electronic. Computerized library services include the card catalog, interlibrary loans, and database searching. Special learning facilities include a learning resource center and electronic labs. The 17-acre campus is in a suburban area. There is one building.

Student Life: 36% are Asian American; 23% white; 17% Hispanic. The average age of all undergraduates is 24.

Housing: There are no residence halls. Housing referrals can be obtained through the Student Housing Office. There are private apartments, student plan housing, and private rooms. All of students commute. Alcohol is not permitted. All students may keep cars.

Activities: There are no fraternities or sororities. There are 6 groups on campus, including chess, ethnic, professional, and religious. Popular campus events include Thanksgiving Dinner, Summer BBQ, and Book Fair.

Sports: There is no sports program at DeVry.

Disabled Students: 90% of the campus is accessible. Wheelchair ramps, elevators, special parking, specially equipped rest rooms, and lowered drinking fountains are available.

Services: Counseling and information services are available, as is tutoring in every subject.

Campus Safety and Security: Measures include 24-hour foot and vehicle patrol, self-defense education, security escort services, and informal discussions. There are pamphlets/posters/films, emergency telephones, and lighted pathways/sidewalks.

Programs of Study: DeVry confers the B.S. degree. Associate and master's degrees are also awarded. Bachelor's degrees are awarded in BIOLOGICAL SCIENCE (bioinformatics), BUSINESS (business administration and management), COMMUNICATIONS AND THE ARTS (telecommunications), COMPUTER AND PHYSICAL SCIENCE (information sciences and systems), ENGINEERING AND ENVIRONMENTAL DESIGN (biomedical engineering, computer engineering, electrical/electronics engineering technology, and technological management). Electronics, telecommunications, and computer information systems are the largest.

Required: To graduate, students must achieve a cumulative GPA of at least 2.0 and satisfactorily complete all curriculum requirements. Course requirements vary according to program. All first-semester students take courses in business organization, computer applications, algebra, psychology, and student success strategies.

Special: Accelerated degrees, co-op programs, nondegree study, and evening and weekend classes are possible.

Faculty/Classroom: All teach undergraduates.

Requirements: Admissions requirements include graduation from a secondary school; the GED is also accepted. Applicants must pass the DeVry entrance exam or present satisfactory ACT or SAT scores. An interview is required. CLEP credit is accepted.

Procedure: Freshmen are admitted fall, spring, and summer. There are early admissions and deferred admissions plans. Application deadlines are open. The fall 2005 application fee was $50. Applications are accepted on-line.

Transfer: Applicants must present passing grades in all completed college course work, demonstrate language skills proficiency in at least 24

completed semester hours, and present evidence of math proficiency by appropriate college-level credits. 25 of 48 credits required for the bachelor's degree must be completed at DeVry.

Visiting: There are regularly scheduled orientations for prospective students. There are guides for informal visits and visitors may sit in on classes. To schedule a visit, contact the New Student Coordinator.

Financial Aid: In a recent year, 59% of all full-time freshmen and 80% of continuing full-time students received some form of financial aid. At least 58% of full-time freshmen and 78% of continuing full-time students received need-based aid. The average freshman award was $8061. Need-based scholarships or need-based grants averaged $5933; need-based self-help aid (loans and jobs) averaged $4577; and institutional non-need-based awards and non-need-based scholarships averaged $10,077. The FAFSA is required. Check with the school for current deadlines.

International Students: They must score satisfactorily on the TOEFL and also take the college's own entrance exam.

Computers: All students may access the system. Students may access the system during lab hours. There are no fees. It is strongly recommended that all students have a personal computer. Students in the Information Technology program have DeVry-issued laptop computers.

Graduates: In a recent year bachelor's degrees were awarded. The most popular majors were computer information systems (65%), business (18%), and electronics engineering technology (17%).

Admissions Contact: Mark Martin, Director of Admissions. Web: *www.fre.devry.edu*

DEVRY UNIVERSITY/LONG BEACH C-5

Long Beach, CA 90806-2449 (562) 427-4162
(800) 597-0444; Fax: (562) 997-5371

Full-time: 880 men, 300 women	**Faculty:** n/av
Part-time: 550 men, 200 women	**Ph.D.s:** n/av
Graduate: none	**Student/Faculty:** n/av
Year: semesters, summer session	**Tuition:** $12,450
Application Deadline: open	**Room & Board:** n/app
Freshman Class: n/av	
SAT or ACT: n/av	**LESS COMPETITIVE**

DeVry University/Long Beach is 1 of 67 DeVry University locations in the United States and Canada. The school offers programs in business administration, computer information systems, electronics, telecommunications management, technical management, information technology, and computer engineering technology. There is 1 undergraduate school. Some figures in the above capsule and in this profile are approximate. In addition to regional accreditation, DeVry has baccalaureate program accreditation with ABET. The library contains 13,251 volumes and 2069 audio/video tapes/CDs/DVDs, and subscribes to 76 periodicals including electronic. Computerized library services include the card catalog, interlibrary loans, and database searching. Special learning facilities include a learning resource center and electronics and other labs. The 11-acre campus is in an urban area midway between Los Angeles and Orange County. There is one building.

Student Life: 33% are Hispanic; 27% Asian American; 19% white; 13% African American. The average age of all undergraduates is 24.

Housing: There are no residence halls. Housing referrals may be obrained through the Student Housing Office. There are private apartments, student-plan housing, and private rooms. All of students commute. Alcohol is not permitted. All students may keep cars.

Activities: There are no fraternities or sororities. There are 13 groups on campus, including ethnic and professional. Popular campus events include Welcome BBQ, Cleo's Cafe, and Winter Formal.

Sports: There is 1 intramural sport for men and 1 for women.

Disabled Students: 90% of the campus is accessible. Wheelchair ramps, elevators, special parking, specially equipped rest rooms, lowered drinking fountains, and lowered telephones are available.

Services: Counseling and information services are available, as is tutoring in every subject.

Campus Safety and Security: Measures include security escort services, informal discussions, pamphlets/posters/films, emergency telephones, and lighted pathways/sidewalks. A DeVry employee patrols the building from 4 P.M. to midnight, and a guard service patrols the lot from 6:30 A.M. to midnight.

Programs of Study: DeVry confers the B.S. degree. Associate and master's degrees are also awarded. Bachelor's degrees are awarded in BIOLOGICAL SCIENCE (bioinformatics), BUSINESS (business administration and management), COMMUNICATIONS AND THE ARTS (telecommunications), COMPUTER AND PHYSICAL SCIENCE (information sciences and systems), ENGINEERING AND ENVIRONMENTAL DESIGN (computer engineering, electrical/electronics engineering technology, and technological management). Computer information systems, telecommunications, and business are the largest.

Required: To graduate, students must achieve a cumulative GPA of at least 2.0 and satisfactorily complete all curriculum requirements. Course

requirements vary according to program. All first-semester students take courses in business organization, computer applications, algebra, psychology, and student success strategies.

Special: Evening and weekend classes, co-op programs, distance learning, and nondegree study are possible. There is 1 national honor society.

Faculty/Classroom: All teach undergraduates.

Requirements: Admissions requirements include graduation from a secondary school; the GED is also accepted. Applicants must pass the DeVry entrance exam or present satisfactory ACT or SAT scores. An interview is required. CLEP credit is accepted.

Procedure: Freshmen are admitted fall, spring, and summer. There are early admissions and deferred admissions plans. Application deadlines are open. The fall 2005 application fee was $50. Applications are accepted on-line.

Transfer: Applicants must present passing grades in all completed college course work, demonstrate language skills proficiency with at least 24 completed semester hours, and evidence math proficiency by appropriate college-level credits. 25 of 48 credits required for the bachelor's degree must be completed at DeVry.

Visiting: There are regularly scheduled orientations for prospective students. There are guides for informal visits and visitors may sit in on classes. To schedule a visit, contact the New Student Coordinator.

Financial Aid: In a recent year, 49% of all full-time freshmen and 73% of continuing full-time students received some form of financial aid. At least 48% of full-time freshmen and 71% of continuing full-time students received need-based aid. The average freshman award was $7322. Need-based scholarships or need-based grants averaged $4637; need-based self-help aid (loans and jobs) averaged $4038; and institutional non-need-based awards and non-need-based scholarships averaged $12,342. DeVry is a member of CSS. The FAFSA is required. Check with the school for current deadlines.

International Students: They must score satisfactorily on the TOEFL and also take the college's own entrance exam.

Computers: Computer information systems students may access the system during published lab hours. There are no fees.

Graduates: In a recent year, 530 bachelor's degrees were awarded. The most popular majors were computer information systems (66%), business (22%), and electronics engineering technology (11%).

Admissions Contact: Alex Kotoyantz, Director of Admissions. E-mail: *cblas@socal.devry.edu* Web: *www.lb.devry.edu*

DEVRY UNIVERSITY/POMONA D-5

Pomona, CA 91768-2642 (909) 622-9800
(800) 882-7536; Fax: (909) 623-4165

Full-time: 1150 men, 350 women	**Faculty:** n/av
Part-time: 650 men, 250 women	**Ph.D.s:** n/av
Graduate: none	**Student/Faculty:** n/av
Year: semesters, summer session	**Tuition:** $12,450
Application Deadline: open	**Room & Board:** n/app
Freshman Class: n/av	
SAT or ACT: n/av	**LESS COMPETITIVE**

DeVry University/Pomona is 1 of 67 DeVry University locations in the United States and Canada. The school offers programs in business administration, computer information systems, electronics, telecommunications management, technical management, information technology, and computer engineering technology. There is 1 undergraduate school. Some figures in the above capsule and in this profile are approximate. In addition to regional accreditation, DeVry has baccalaureate program accreditation with ABET. The library contains 15,580 volumes and 875 audio/video tapes/CDs/DVDs, and subscribes to 90 periodicals including electronic. Computerized library services include the card catalog, interlibrary loans, and database searching. Special learning facilities include a learning resource center and electronics and other labs. The 11-acre campus is in an urban area 30 miles east of Los Angeles. There is one building.

Student Life: 40% are Hispanic; 26% Asian American; 21% white. The average age of all undergraduates is 24.

Housing: There are no residence halls. Housing referrals may be obtained through the Student Housing Office. There are private apartments, student-run housing, and private rooms. All of students commute. Alcohol is not permitted. All students may keep cars.

Activities: There are no fraternities or sororities. There are 14 groups on campus, including computers, ethnic, honors, professional, and social. Popular campus events include Welcome Barbecue, Winter Formal, and Part-time Jobs Fair.

Sports: There is 1 intramural sport for men and 1 for women.

Disabled Students: 90% of the campus is accessible. Wheelchair ramps, elevators, special parking, specially equipped rest rooms, lowered drinking fountains, and lowered telephones are available.

Services: Counseling and information services are available, as is tutoring in every subject.

Campus Safety and Security: Measures include security escort services, informal discussions, pamphlets/posters/films, emergency telephones, and lighted pathways/sidewalks. A DeVry employee patrols the building from 4 P.M. to midnight, and a guard service patrols the lot from 6:30 A.M. to midnight.

Programs of Study: DeVry confers the B.S. degree. Associate and master's degrees are also awarded. Bachelor's degrees are awarded in BUSINESS (business administration and management), COMMUNICATIONS AND THE ARTS (telecommunications), COMPUTER AND PHYSICAL SCIENCE (computer programming and information sciences and systems), ENGINEERING AND ENVIRONMENTAL DESIGN (biomedical engineering, computer engineering, electrical/electronics engineering technology, and technological management). Computer information systems and telecommunications are the largest.

Required: To graduate, students must achieve a cumulative GPA of at least 2.0 and satisfactorily complete all curriculum requirements. Course requirements vary according to program. All first-semester students take courses in business organization, computer applications, algebra, psychology, and student success strategies.

Special: Evening and weekend classes, nondegree study, distance learning, and co-op programs in all majors are possible. There are 5 national honor societies.

Faculty/Classroom: All teach undergraduates.

Requirements: Admissions requirements include graduation from a secondary school; the GED is also accepted. Applicants must pass the DeVry entrance exam or present satisfactory ACT or SAT scores. An interview is required. CLEP credit is accepted.

Procedure: Freshmen are admitted fall, spring, and summer. There are early admissions and deferred admissions plans. Application deadlines are open. The fall 2005 application fee was $50. Applications are accepted on-line.

Transfer: Applicants must present passing grades in all completed college course work, demonstrate language skills proficiency with at least 24 completed semester hours, and evidence math proficiency by appropriate college-level credits. A minimum 2.0 GPA is required. 25 of 48 credits required for the bachelor's degree must be completed at DeVry.

Visiting: There are regularly scheduled orientations for prospective students. There are guides for informal visits and visitors may sit in on classes. To schedule a visit, contact the New Student Coordinators.

Financial Aid: In a recent year, 53% of all full-time freshmen and 76% of continuing full-time students received some form of financial aid. At least 52% of full-time freshmen and 74% of continuing full-time students received need-based aid. The average freshman award was $6813. Need-based scholarships or need-based grants averaged $4377; need-based self-help aid (loans and jobs) averaged $3814; and institutional non-need-based awards and non-need-based scholarships averaged $11,356. DeVry is a member of CSS. The FAFSA is required. Check with the school for current deadlines.

International Students: They must score satisfactorily on the TOEFL and also take the college's own entrance exam.

Computers: Computer information systems students may access the system during published lab hours. There are no time limits and no fees.

Graduates: In a recent year, 651 bachelor's degrees were awarded. The most popular majors were computer information systems (65%), business (25%), and electronics engineering technology (10%).

Admissions Contact: Jere Thrasher, Director of Admissions. Web: www.pom.devry.edu

---

DEVRY UNIVERSITY/WEST HILLS
West Hills, CA 91304-3200

C-5

(818) 932-3001
(888) 610-0800; Fax: (818) 868-4165

Full-time: 490 men, 160 women	Faculty: n/av
Part-time: 370 men, 150 women	Ph.D.s: n/av
Graduate: none	Student/Faculty: n/av
Year: semesters, summer session	Tuition: $12,450
Application Deadline: open	Room & Board: n/app
Freshman Class: n/av	
SAT or ACT: n/av	LESS COMPETITIVE

DeVry University/West Hills, founded in 1999, is a private institution offering hands-on programs in electronics, business administration, computer information systems, telecommunications management, information technology, computer engineering technology, and technical management. The school is 1 of 67 DeVry University locations throughout the United States and Canada. Some figures in the above capsule and in this profile are approximate. The library contains 14,728 volumes and 411 audio/video tapes/CDs/DVDs, and subscribes to 130 periodicals including electronic. Computerized library services include the card catalog, interlibrary loans, and database searching. Special learning facilities include a learning resource center and electronics and other labs. The 15-acre campus is in a suburban area in the San Fernando Valley. There is one building.

Student Life: 32% are white; 26% Asian American; 26% Hispanic. The average age of all undergraduates is 24.

Housing: All students commute. Housing referrals may be obtained through the Student Housing Office. There are private apartments, stu-

dent-plan housing, and private rooms. Alcohol is not permitted. All students may keep cars.

Activities: There are no fraternities or sororities. There are 10 groups on campus, including computers, ethnic, international, professional, religious, and social. Popular campus events include Welcome BBQ, Cosmic Bowling, and Winter Formal.

Sports: There are 3 intramural sports for men and 3 for women.

Disabled Students: All of the campus is accessible. Wheelchair ramps, elevators, special parking, specially equipped rest rooms, lowered drinking fountains, and lowered telephones are available.

Services: Counseling and information services are available, as is tutoring in every subject.

Campus Safety and Security: Measures include emergency telephones and lighted pathways/sidewalks.

Programs of Study: DeVry confers the B.S. degree. Associate and master's degrees are also awarded. Bachelor's degrees are awarded in BUSINESS (business administration and management), COMMUNICATIONS AND THE ARTS (telecommunications), COMPUTER AND PHYSICAL SCIENCE (information sciences and systems), ENGINEERING AND ENVIRONMENTAL DESIGN (biomedical engineering, computer engineering, electrical/electronics engineering technology, and technological management). Computer information systems and business are the largest.

Required: To graduate, students must achieve a cumulative GPA of at least 2.0 and satisfactorily complete all curriculum requirements. Course requirements vary according to program. All first-semester students take courses in business organization, computer applications, algebra, psychology, and student success strategies.

Special: Co-op programs, nondegree study, distance learning, and evening and weekend classes are possible.

Faculty/Classroom: All teach undergraduates.

Requirements: Admissions requirements include graduation from a secondary school; the GED is also accepted. Applicants must pass the DeVry entrance exam or present satisfactory ACT or SAT scores. An interview is required. CLEP credit is accepted.

Procedure: Freshmen are admitted fall, spring, and summer. There are early admissions and deferred admissions plans. Application deadlines are open. The fall 2005 application fee was $50. Applications are accepted on-line.

Transfer: Applicants must present passing grades in all completed college course work, demonstrate language skills proficiency in at least 24 completed semester hours, and present evidence of math proficiency by appropriate college-level credits. 25 of 48 credits required for the bachelor's degree must be completed at DeVry.

Visiting: There are regularly scheduled orientations for prospective students. There are guides for informal visits and visitors may sit in on classes. To schedule a visit, contact the New Student Coordinator.

Financial Aid: In a recent year, 45% of all full-time freshmen and 74% of continuing full-time students received some form of financial aid. At least 44% of full-time freshmen and 72% of continuing full-time students received need-based aid. The average freshman award was $6485. Need-based scholarships or need-based grants averaged $4699; need-based self-help aid (loans and jobs) averaged $3568; and institutional non-need-based awards and non-need-based scholarships averaged $10,824. The FAFSA is required. Check with the school for current deadlines.

International Students: They must score satisfactorily on the TOEFL and also take the college's own entrance exam.

Computers: Computer information students may access the system during published lab hours.There are no fees.

Graduates: In a recent year 2005, 217 bachelor's degrees were awarded. The most popular majors were business (64%), electronics engineering technology (21%), and computer information systems (15%).

Admissions Contact: Dewey McGuirk, Director of Admissions. E-mail: admissions@devry.edu Web: www.wh.devry.edu

---

DOMINICAN UNIVERSITY OF CALIFORNIA
San Rafael, CA 94901-2298

B-3

(415) 485-3204
(888) 323-6763; Fax: (415) 485-3214

Full-time: 256 men, 841 women	Faculty: 60
Part-time: 73 men, 221 women	Ph.D.s: 83%
Graduate: 123 men, 423 women	Student/Faculty: 18 to 1
Year: semesters, summer session	Tuition: $26,350
Application Deadline: March 2	Room & Board: $10,486
Freshman Class: 2581 applied, 1361 accepted, 227 enrolled	
SAT Verbal/Math: 500/500*	ACT: 21* COMPETITIVE

Dominican University of California, founded in 1890, is an independent, international, learner-centered university of Catholic heritage. There are 5 undergraduate and 4 graduate schools. In addition to regional accreditation, Dominican has baccalaureate program accreditation with AOTA, CCTE, CCNE, and NLN. The library contains 92,536 volumes, 3500 microform items, and 1640 audio/video tapes/CDs/DVDs, and subscribes to 597 periodicals including electronic. Computerized library services include the card catalog, interlibrary loans, database searching, Internet access, and laptop Internet portals. Special learning facilities include a learning resource center, art gallery, radio station, and a music library, and art history slide and print collection. The 80-acre campus is in a suburban area 11 miles north of San Francisco. Including any residence halls, there are 21 buildings.

Student Life: 91% of undergraduates are from California. Students are from 22 states and 17 foreign countries. 48% are from public schools. 43% are white; 17% Asian American; 15% Hispanic. 33% are Catholic; 14% Protestant; 7% claim no religious affiliation. The average age of freshmen is 18; all undergraduates, 28. 26% do not continue beyond their first year; 53% remain to graduate.

Housing: 550 students can be accommodated in college housing, which includes coed dorms. On-campus housing is available on a first-come, first-served basis and is available on a lottery system for upperclassmen. 54% of students commute. All students may keep cars.

Activities: There are no fraternities or sororities. There are 23 groups on campus, including art, cheerleading, choir, computers, drama, ethnic, film, gay, honors, international, jazz band, literary magazine, newspaper, orchestra, radio and TV, religious, social service and student government. Popular campus events include Shield Day (welcoming the freshman class) and student congregation.

Sports: There are 4 intercollegiate sports for men and 6 for women, and 5 intramural sports for men and 5 for women. Facilities include a gym, a fitness center, a 6-lane swimming pool, 2 full-sized baketball courts, a multipurpose room for dance and exercise classes, tennis courts, a soccer field, and a sand volleyball court.

Disabled Students: 50% of the campus is accessible. Wheelchair ramps, elevators, special parking, specially equipped rest rooms, special class scheduling, and lowered drinking fountains are available.

Services: Counseling and information services are available, as is tutoring in most subjects, including writing, math, chemistry, economics, time management, study skills, anatomy, physiology, algbra, and physics. There is a reader service for the blind and remedial math and writing.

Campus Safety and Security: Measures include 24-hour foot and vehicle patrol, security escort services, informal discussions, and emergency telephones. There are lighted pathways/sidewalks.

Programs of Study: Dominican confers B.A., B.S., B.F.A., and B.S.N. degrees. Master's degrees are also awarded. Bachelor's degrees are awarded in AGRICULTURE (environmental studies), BIOLOGICAL SCIENCE (biology/biological science), BUSINESS (business administration and management, electronic business, human resources, and international business management), COMMUNICATIONS AND THE ARTS (art, art history and appreciation, communications, creative writing, English literature, and music), COMPUTER AND PHYSICAL SCIENCE (digital arts/technology), HEALTH PROFESSIONS (nursing, occupational therapy, and premedicine), SOCIAL SCIENCE (history, humanities, international studies, liberal arts/general studies, political science/government, psychology, and religion). Biology, psychology, and nursing are the strongest academically. Nursing, psychology, and business management are the largest.

Required: All students must complete 124 credit hours including at least 24 in upper-division work, with a minimum 2.0 GPA. Core requirements include a cultural heritage colloquium of 9 units; 6 units each in religion and first-year interdisciplinary studies, 3 to 4 units of natural science and math and quantitative reasoning, social science, moral philosophy and ethics, and creativity and performing arts, and 1 unit of information and research. A senior thesis, project, recital, or comprehensive exam is required.

Special: There is a semester interchange program with colleges in Michigan, Florida, or New York. Dominican also offers study abroad, dual majors for students with a 3.0 GPA or better, B.A.-B.S. degrees, student-designed majors, internships, pass/fail options outside of major and general education courses, and an evening/weekend bachelor's degree program. There are 3 national honor societies and a freshman honors program.

Faculty/Classroom: 36% of faculty are male; 64%, female. 82% teach undergraduates. No introductory courses are taught by graduate students. The average class size in an introductory lecture is 16; in a laboratory, 13; and in a regular course, 16.

Admissions: 53% of the 2005-2006 applicants were accepted. The SAT scores for the 2005-2006 freshman class were: Verbal--45% below 500, 36% between 500 and 599, 17% between 600 and 700, and 2% above 700; Math--46% below 500, 41% between 500 and 599, 11% between 600 and 700, and 2% above 700. The ACT scores were 40% below 21, 35% between 21 and 23, 14% between 24 and 26, 9% between 27 and 28, and 5% above 28. 22% of the current freshmen were in the top fifth of their class; 40% were in the top two fifths.

Requirements: The SAT is required. In addition, applicants must be graduates of an accredited high school or have earned the GED. Secondary preparation must include 4 years of English, 2 each of math and a foreign language, and 1 each of lab science and history. An essay and a recommendation are required. An interview and a visit to the campus

are highly recommended. Prospective music majors are encouraged to schedule an audition. A GPA of 2.0 is required. AP and CLEP credits are accepted. Important factors in the admissions decision are recommendations by school officials, extracurricular activities record, and evidence of special talent.

Procedure: Freshmen are admitted fall and spring. Entrance exams should be taken in the late fall or early spring of the senior year. There is a rolling admissions and a deferred admissions plan. Applications should be filed by March 2 for fall entry, December 15 for spring entry, and May 1 for summer entry, along with a $40 fee. Notification is sent on a rolling basis. Applications are accepted on-line.

Transfer: 93 transfer students enrolled in 2004-2005. Applicants must have a 2.0 GPA at an accredited college. They must also submit official high school and college transcripts and a letter of recommendation from a professor, academic dean, or counselor. 30 of 124 credits required for the bachelor's degree must be completed at Dominican.

Visiting: There are regularly scheduled orientations for prospective students, including financial aid conferences, math and writing placement testing, meeting with the prospective academic adviser, and a campus tour. There are guides for informal visits and visitors may sit in on classes and stay overnight. To schedule a visit, contact the Admissions Office at (415) 457-4440 or *enroll@dominican.edu*.

Financial Aid: In 2005-2006, 98% of all full-time freshmen and 85% of continuing full-time students received some form of financial aid. 70% of full-time freshmen and 72% of continuing full-time students received need-based aid. The average freshman award was $20,852. Need-based scholarships or need-based grants averaged $14,006 ($28,922 maximum); need-based self-help aid (loans and jobs) averaged $4646 ($7375 maximum); non-need-based athletic scholarships averaged $2567 ($6000 maximum); and other non-need-based awards and non-need-based scholarships averaged $7660 ($15,500 maximum). 17% of undergraduates work part time. Average annual earnings from campus work are $2254. The average financial indebtedness of the 2005 graduate was $19,092. Dominican is a member of CSS. The FAFSA and the college's own financial statement are required. The deadline for filing freshman financial aid applications for fall entry is March 2.

International Students: There are 30 international students enrolled. The school actively recruits these students. They must score satisfactorily on the written TOEFL or on the electronic version and also take the SAT or the ACT.

Computers: All students may access the system. There is a 2-hour time limit only when other students are waiting. There are no fees.

Graduates: From July 1, 2004 to June 30, 2005, 203 bachelor's degrees were awarded. The most popular majors were nursing (27%), psychology (15%), and business (11%). In an average class, 44% graduate in 4 years or less, 46% graduate in 5 years or less, and 51% graduate in 6 years or less.

Admissions Contact: Art Criss, Director of Admissions (Day Program). E-mail: *enroll@dominican.edu* Web: *www.dominican.edu*

FRESNO PACIFIC UNIVERSITY C-3
Fresno, CA 93702
(559) 453-2039
(800) 660-6089; Fax: (559) 453-2007

Full-time: 445 men, 857 women	**Faculty:** 53
Part-time: 63 men, 88 women	**Ph.D.s:** 63%
Graduate: 257 men, 551 women	**Student/Faculty:** 25 to 1
Year: varies by program, summer session	**Tuition:** $19,664
	Room & Board: $5790
Application Deadline: July 31	
Freshman Class: 636 applied, 424 accepted, 229 enrolled	
SAT Verbal/Math: 500/510*	**ACT:** 21 **COMPETITIVE**

Fresno Pacific University, founded in 1944, is a private Christian liberal arts college affiliated with the Mennonite Brethren. There are 3 undergraduate and 4 graduate schools. The library contains 165,112 volumes, 312,157 microform items, and 10,415 audio/video tapes/CDs/DVDs, and subscribes to 10,334 periodicals including electronic. Computerized library services include the card catalog, interlibrary loans, database searching, and Internet access. Special learning facilities include a learning resource center, the Center for Mennonite Brethren Studies, the Center for Conflict Studies and Peacemaking, and the Center for Degree Completion. The 42-acre campus is in a suburban area 150 miles southeast of San Francisco. Including any residence halls, there are 18 buildings.

Student Life: 97% of undergraduates are from California. Others are from 14 states, 12 foreign countries, and Canada. 86% are from public schools. 62% are white; 20% Hispanic. 89% are Protestant; 7% Catholic. The average age of freshmen is 21; all undergraduates, 22. 18% do not continue beyond their first year; 54% remain to graduate.

Housing: 574 students can be accommodated in college housing, which includes single-sex dorms and on-campus apartments. In addition, there are special-interest houses. On-campus housing is available on a first-come, first-served basis and is available on a lottery system for upperclassmen. Priority is given to out-of-town students. 53% of students live on campus; of those, 32% remain on campus on weekends. Alcohol is not permitted. All students may keep cars.

Activities: There are no fraternities or sororities. There are 15 groups on campus, including art, choir, chorale, chorus, dance, drama, ethnic, honors, international, jazz band, newspaper, pep band, professional, religious, social, social service, student government, and yearbook. Popular campus events include Carol Sing, Winter Ball, and Junior/Senior Banquet.

Sports: There are 6 intercollegiate sports for men and 6 for women, and 9 intramural sports for men and 9 for women. Facilities include a gym, 3 soccer fields, swimming pool, track and field facility, weight room, 2 racquetball courts, and 7 tennis courts.

Disabled Students: All of the campus is accessible. Wheelchair ramps, elevators, special parking, specially equipped rest rooms, lowered drinking fountains, lowered telephones, and special housing are available.

Services: Counseling and information services are available, as is tutoring in every subject. There is a reader service for the blind, remedial math, reading, and writing, and audio books.

Campus Safety and Security: Measures include 24-hour foot and vehicle patrol, self-defense education, security escort services, and shuttle buses. There are informal discussions, pamphlets/posters/films, emergency telephones, lighted pathways/sidewalks, and 24-hour CCTV monitored in real-time closed-circuit security cameras, which create a virtual perimeter patrol of the campus.

Programs of Study: FPU confers the B.A. degree. Associate and master's degrees are also awarded. Bachelor's degrees are awarded in BIOLOGICAL SCIENCE (biology/biological science), BUSINESS (accounting, business administration and management, and sports management), COMMUNICATIONS AND THE ARTS (English, music, and Spanish), COMPUTER AND PHYSICAL SCIENCE (chemistry, mathematics, and natural sciences), EDUCATION (English, mathematics, music, physical, science, and social science), ENGINEERING AND ENVIRONMENTAL DESIGN (environmental science), HEALTH PROFESSIONS (premedicine), SOCIAL SCIENCE (history, ministries, missions, philosophy, prelaw, psychology, religion, social science, and social work). Business, education, and religion are the strongest academically. Business, education, and psychology are the largest.

Required: Students must complete 124 semester units, 40 of which are in upper division courses, with at least a 2.0 GPA. General education requirements include a biblical studies/world civilization series, 2 courses each in humanities, natural sciences, social sciences, and phys ed and math. Students are required to attend College Hour, a twice-weekly program of lectures, films, and concerts. Students are encouraged to volunteer 2 hours of community service per week. Several majors require internships.

Special: Accelerated degrees and internships are available, as is a 1-semester cooperative program with the University of California, Davis. Cross-registration is possible with San Joaquin College of Law and California State University, Fresno. A B.A. in management and organizational development is offered to working adults. Other off-campus learning opportunities include programs in American studies in Washington, D.C., urban studies in Chicago, and study abroad in Israel, Japan, Costa Rica, and Brethren Colleges in England, Spain, France, Germany, or China. A summer semester in Mexico is offered. There is 1 national honor society and a freshman honors program.

Faculty/Classroom: 62% of faculty are male; 38%, female. 54% teach undergraduates. No introductory courses are taught by graduate students. The average class size in a laboratory is 14 and in a regular course, 18.

Admissions: 67% of the 2005-2006 applicants were accepted. The SAT scores for the 2005-2006 freshman class were: Verbal--50% below 500, 36% between 500 and 599, 12% between 600 and 700, and 2% above 700; Math--46% below 500, 38% between 500 and 599, 15% between 600 and 700, and 1% above 700. The ACT scores were 51% below 21, 26% between 21 and 23, 13% between 24 and 26, 6% between 27 and 28, and 4% above 28.

Requirements: The SAT or ACT is required. In addition, applicants should be graduates of an accredited high school or have the GED. Required secondary preparation includes 4 years of college prep English, 2 years of social studies, algebra 1 and 2, and geometry, and at least 1 year of a lab science. The college recommends that applicants also take courses in art, music, and 2 years of the same foreign language, all with a grade of C or better. An essay is required, and an audition is recommended for prospective music majors. A GPA of 3.1 is required. AP and CLEP credits are accepted. Important factors in the admissions decision are recommendations by school officials, advanced placement or honor courses, and extracurricular activities record.

Procedure: Freshmen are admitted fall and spring. Entrance exams should be taken during the fall of the senior year. There is a rolling admissions plan. Early decision applications should be filed by January 31; regular applications, by July 31 for fall entry and December 5 for spring entry, along with a $40 fee. Notification is sent on a rolling basis. Applications are accepted on-line.

Transfer: 168 transfer students enrolled in 2004-2005. Applicants should have completed at least 24 transferable units of college work with a 2.4 GPA. Those with fewer credits may apply any time but must meet freshman admission requirements. The SAT or ACT scores are recommended. 30 of 124 credits required for the bachelor's degree must be completed at FPU.

Visiting: There are regularly scheduled orientations for prospective students. There are guides for informal visits and visitors may sit in on classes and stay overnight. To schedule a visit, contact Suzana Dobric, Undergraduate College Admissions at *ugadmis@fresno.edu*.

Financial Aid: In 2005-2006, 93% of all full-time freshmen and 79% of continuing full-time students received some form of financial aid. 67% of full-time freshmen and 63% of continuing full-time students received need-based aid. The average freshman award was $13,776. The average financial indebtedness of the 2005 graduate was $16,414. The FAFSA and the college's own financial statement are required. The deadline for filing freshman financial aid applications for fall entry is May 1.

International Students: There are 51 international students enrolled. The school actively recruits these students. They must score satisfactorily on the written TOEFL.

Computers: Wireless access is available. All students have access to the network and the Internet from their residence hall rooms, and there are 4 PC labs spread out on campus with approximately 20 PCs each. There is wireless access as well as 20 laptops at each of the 3 regional centers. All students may access the system any time (24 hours/day). There are no time limits and no fees. It is strongly recommended that all students have a personal computer.

Graduates: From July 1, 2004 to June 30, 2005, 389 bachelor's degrees were awarded. The most popular majors were business (38%), liberal studies (28%), and psychology (12%). In an average class, 80% graduate in 4 years or less, 83% graduate in 5 years or less, and 85% graduate in 6 years or less. Of the 2004 graduating class, 41% were enrolled in graduate school within 6 months of graduation.

Admissions Contact: Suzana Dobric, Undergraduate College Admission. A video is available. E-mail: *ugadmis@fresno.edu*
Web: *www.fresno.edu*

GOLDEN GATE UNIVERSITY
San Francisco, CA 94105-2968 B-3
(415) 442-7800
(800) 448-4968; Fax: (415) 442-7807

Full-time: 58 men, 77 women	**Faculty:** n/av
Part-time: 206 men, 226 women	**Ph.D.s:** n/av
Graduate: 1543 men, 1781 women	**Student/Faculty:** n/av
Year: trimesters, summer session	**Tuition:** $12,150
Application Deadline: see profile	**Room & Board:** n/app
Freshman Class: n/av	
SAT or ACT: not required	**LESS COMPETITIVE**

Golden Gate University, founded in 1901, is a private, independent, commuter institution offering undergraduate and graduate degrees in business administration, accounting, human and social sciences, and special programs. There are 3 undergraduate and 4 graduate schools. The 2 libraries contain 300,000 volumes, and subscribe to 2500 periodicals including electronic. Computerized library services include interlibrary loans and database searching. Special learning facilities include a learning resource center and an English as a Second Language center. The 1-acre campus is in an urban area in San Francisco. There are 2 buildings.

Student Life: 51% are white; 19% Asian American; 18% foreign nationals; 10% African American; 10% Hispanic. The average age of freshmen is 21; all undergraduates, 37. 12% do not continue beyond their first year.

Housing: There are no residence halls. All students commute. Alcohol is not permitted.

Activities: There are no fraternities or sororities. There are 5 groups on campus, including ethnic, international, newspaper, professional, and social. Popular campus events include Commencement Ball and other social functions.

Sports: There is no sports program at Golden Gate.

Disabled Students: All of the campus is accessible. Wheelchair ramps, elevators, special parking, and specially equipped rest rooms are available.

Services: Counseling and information services are available, as is tutoring in some subjects. There is remedial math, reading, and writing.

Campus Safety and Security: Measures include security escort services, informal discussions, and pamphlets/posters/films.

Programs of Study: Golden Gate confers B.S. and B.B.A. degrees. Master's and doctoral degrees are also awarded. Bachelor's degrees are awarded in BUSINESS (accounting, banking and finance, human resources, and international business management), ENGINEERING AND ENVIRONMENTAL DESIGN (technological management). Accounting, finance, and information systems are the strongest academically. Finance, accounting, and management are the largest.

Required: A total of 123 trimester hours, with 21 to 33 in the major, are required to graduate. A minimum GPA of 2.0 is also required.

Special: The university offers cooperative programs, cross-registration with the San Francisco Consortium, internships, an accelerated degree program, dual majors, credit for military experience, nondegree study, and credit/no credit options. Also available are weekend classes and 10-week terms.

Faculty/Classroom: All teach undergraduates. No introductory courses are taught by graduate students. The average class size in an introductory lecture is 25; in a laboratory, 15; and in a regular course, 20.

Requirements: Applicants must be graduates of an accredited secondary school or have a GED. A GPA of 3.0 is required. AP and CLEP credits are accepted.

Procedure: Freshmen are admitted fall, spring, and summer. There is a rolling admissions plan. Notification is sent on a rolling basis. Applications are accepted on-line. Check with school for current deadlines and fee.

Transfer: At least 24 transferable units and a 2.0 overall GPA are required. A minimum of 30 units out of 123, including 21 in the major, must be completed at GGU.

Visiting: Visitors may sit in on classes. To schedule a visit, contact Student Affairs Office at (415) 442-7299 or *studentaffairs@ggu.edu*.

Financial Aid: The FAFSA is required. Check with the school for current deadlines.

International Students: The school actively recruits these students. A satisfactory score is required on the written TOEFL.

Computers: All students may access the system at designated hours. There are no time limits and no fees.

Admissions Contact: Office of Admissions and Student Affairs.
E-mail: *info@ggu.edu* Web: *www.ggu.edu*

HARVEY MUDD COLLEGE   D-5

Claremont, CA 91711	(909) 621-8011; Fax: (909) 607-7046
Full-time: 514 men, 237 women	Faculty: 77; IIB, ++$
Part-time: none	Ph.D.s: 100%
Graduate: none	Student/Faculty: 10 to 1
Year: semesters	Tuition: $31,940
Application Deadline: January 15	Room & Board: $10,412
Freshman Class: 1899 applied, 683 accepted, 195 enrolled	
SAT Verbal/Math: 720/760*	MOST COMPETITIVE

Harvey Mudd College, founded in 1955, is one of the Claremont Colleges. It is a private college specializing in engineering and physical science education within a liberal arts tradition. There are 5 undergraduate and 2 graduate schools. In addition to regional accreditation, Harvey Mudd has baccalaureate program accreditation with ABET and ACS. Computerized library services include the card catalog, interlibrary loans, database searching, and Internet access. Special learning facilities include an art gallery, planetarium, and radio station. The 30-acre campus is in a suburban area 35 miles east of Los Angeles. Including any residence halls, there are 20 buildings.

Student Life: 56% of undergraduates are from out of state, mostly the Northwest. Students are from 45 states, 16 foreign countries, and Canada. 80% are from public schools. 67% are white; 21% Asian American. The average age of freshmen is 18; all undergraduates, 20. 3% do not continue beyond their first year.

Housing: 632 students can be accommodated in college housing, which includes single-sex and coed dorms and on-campus apartments. On-campus housing is guaranteed for the freshman year only, is available on a first-come, first-served basis, and is available on a lottery system for upperclassmen. 98% of students live on campus; of those, 96% remain on campus on weekends. All students may keep cars.

Activities: There are no fraternities or sororities. There are 74 groups on campus, including art, band, chess, choir, chorale, chorus, computers, dance, drama, ethnic, gay, international, jazz band, literary magazine, musical theater, newspaper, orchestra, pep band, photography, political, professional, radio and TV, religious, social, social service, student government, symphony, and yearbook. Popular campus events include 5-class competition relay races, Wednesday night lecture/dinner series, and film nights.

Sports: There are 10 intercollegiate sports for men and 10 for women, and 6 intramural sports for men and 6 for women. Facilities include an athletic facility housing 2 gym floors, a weight room, a 400-meter track, a swimming pool, 9 tennis courts, and sports fields. The campus recreation facility houses a full-size gym floor, an aerobic/dance room, and a fitness room with treadmills, steppers, exercycles, and weight equipment.

Disabled Students: 99% of the campus is accessible. Wheelchair ramps, elevators, special parking, specially equipped rest rooms, special class scheduling, and lowered drinking fountains are available.

Services: Counseling and information services are available, as is tutoring in most subjects. Support is offered on a case-by-case basis.

Campus Safety and Security: Measures include 24-hour foot and vehicle patrol, self-defense education, security escort services, and informal discussions. There are pamphlets/posters/films, emergency telephones, lighted pathways/sidewalks, and a biweekly electronic newsletter on campus security issues.

Programs of Study: Harvey Mudd confers the B.S. degree. Bachelor's degrees are awarded in BIOLOGICAL SCIENCE (biology/biological science), COMPUTER AND PHYSICAL SCIENCE (chemistry, computer science, mathematics, and physics), ENGINEERING AND ENVIRONMENTAL DESIGN (engineering). Physics and chemistry are the strongest academically. Engineering and computer science are the largest.

Required: To graduate, all students must have a 2.0 GPA and complete a total of 128 hours, including 45 hours in a common core. This consists of 4 semesters of math, 3 semesters of physics, 2 semesters of chemistry, and courses in biology, programming, and system engineering, plus 2 electives chosen from core offerings. Another 37 hours are required in humanities and social sciences, including literature, psychology, philosophy, history, and institutions, and 46 in the major and electives. All students take 3 semesters of noncredit phys ed courses. A senior research or corporate clinic project is required.

Special: Students may cross-register at any of the other Claremont Colleges. Internships are available for engineering and math majors. Study abroad, a Washington semester, work-study, computer science/math, math/biology, and biology/chemistry majors, and student-designed majors are available. A 3-2 engineering degree with Claremont McKenna College or Scripps College is possible. A corporate clinic project is required. Some courses may be audited. The first semester for freshmen is taken on a pass/fail basis; thereafter, only 1 noncore and nonmajor course per semester may be taken on that basis. There is 1 national honor society and 7 departmental honors programs.

Faculty/Classroom: 65% of faculty are male; 35%, female. All both teach and do research. The average class size in an introductory lecture is 20; in a laboratory, 10; and in a regular course, 15.

Admissions: 36% of the 2005-2006 applicants were accepted. 90% of the current freshmen were in the top fifth of their class. There were 51 National Merit finalists. 33 freshmen graduated first in their class.

Requirements: The SAT is required. In addition, applicants must be graduates of an accredited secondary school and have completed 4 years each of English and math (including algebra, demonstrative and analytic geometry, trigonometry, and calculus) and 1 year each of physics and chemistry. The college strongly recommends that applicants take 2 years of a foreign language and 1 year each of history and biology. SAT Subject tests in math level 2 and 1 other subject are required. Letters of recommendation are required from the student's counselor; a math or science teacher; and an English, social science, or foreign language teacher. Applicants must submit 2 personal essays and are encouraged to seek an interview. AP credits are accepted. Important factors in the admissions decision are advanced placement or honor courses, recommendations by school officials, and leadership record.

Procedure: Freshmen are admitted in the fall. Entrance exams should be taken by January of the senior year. There are early decision and deferred admissions plans. Early decision applications should be filed by November 15; regular applications, by January 15 for fall entry, along with a $50 fee. Notification of early decision is sent December 15; regular decision, April 1. 43 early decision candidates were accepted for the 2005-2006 class. 236 applicants were on the 2005 waiting list. Applications are accepted on-line.

Transfer: 7 transfer students enrolled in 2004-2005. Applicants must submit SAT Subject Test scores, transcripts, course descriptions, and references from a college math, science, or engineering teacher and from a counselor. An interview is recommended. Students must have completed courses in calculus, physics, chemistry, and English composition. 64 of 128 credits required for the bachelor's degree must be completed at Harvey Mudd.

Visiting: There are regularly scheduled orientations for prospective students, including tours and interviews conducted Monday through Friday and Saturday mornings in the fall. There are guides for informal visits and visitors may sit in on classes and stay overnight. To schedule a visit, contact the Admission Office.

Financial Aid: In 2005-2006, 87% of all full-time freshmen and 79% of continuing full-time students received some form of financial aid. 59% of full-time freshmen and 53% of continuing full-time students received need-based aid. The average freshman award was $24,824. 27% of undergraduates work part time. Average annual earnings from campus work are $924. The average financial indebtedness of the 2005 graduate was $16,055. The CSS/Profile or FAFSA is required. The deadline for filing freshman financial aid applications for fall entry is February 1.

International Students: There were 21 international students enrolled in a recent year. They must take the SAT and SAT Subject tests in math and 1 other subject. Students whose first language is not English are encouraged to submit TOEFL scores.

Computers: All students may access the system 24 hours a day. There are no time limits and no fees. It is strongly recommended that all students have a personal computer.

Graduates: From July 1, 2004 to June 30, 2005, 152 bachelor's degrees were awarded. The most popular majors were engineering (41%), computer science (14%), and mathematics (12%). In an average class, 77% graduate in 4 years or less, 82% graduate in 5 years or less, and 88% graduate in 6 years or less. 36 companies recruited on campus in

2004-2005. Of the 2004 graduating class, 43% were enrolled in graduate school within 6 months of graduation and 43% were employed.

Admissions Contact: Youlonda Copeland-Morgan, Vice President, Dean of Admissions and Financial Aid. E-mail: *admission@hmc.edu* Web: *www.hmc.edu*

HOLY NAMES UNIVERSITY · B-3
Oakland, CA 94619

(510) 436-1321
(800) 430-1321; Fax: (510) 436-1325

Full-time: 100 men, 300 women	**Faculty:** 22
Part-time: 25 men, 175 women	**Ph.D.s:** 90%
Graduate: 60 men, 290 women	**Student/Faculty:** 18 to 1
Year: semesters, summer session	**Tuition:** $21,000
Application Deadline: August 1	**Room & Board:** $8000
Freshman Class: n/av	
SAT or ACT: required	**NONCOMPETITIVE**

Holy Names University, founded in 1868, is an independent college affiliated with the Roman Catholic Church. It offers education in the liberal arts and preparation for some professions. Figures in the above capsule and in this profile are approximate. In addition to regional accreditation, Holy Names has baccalaureate program accreditation with NASM and NLN. The library contains 111,472 volumes, 50,931 microform items, and 5142 audio/video tapes/CDs/DVDs, and subscribes to 190 periodicals including electronic. Computerized library services include database searching and Internet access. Special learning facilities include a learning resource center, art gallery, performing arts center, 400-seat theater, and black box theater. The 60-acre campus is in an urban area 20 miles east of San Francisco. Including any residence halls, there are 15 buildings.

Student Life: 96% of undergraduates are from California. Others are from 14 states, 12 foreign countries, and Canada. 62% are from public schools. 31% are white; 30% African American ; 13% Hispanic. The average age of freshmen is 18; all undergraduates, 32. 38% do not continue beyond their first year; 46% remain to graduate.

Housing: 351 students can be accommodated in college housing, which includes coed dorms. On-campus housing is guaranteed for all 4 years. 67% of students commute. All students may keep cars.

Activities: There are no fraternities or sororities. There are 10 groups on campus, including choir, chorale, computers, drama, ethnic, gay, honors, international, orchestra, religious, social service, and student government. Popular campus events include Humanistic Studies Days and Founders Day.

Sports: There are 4 intercollegiate sports for men and 4 for women. Facilities include a gym, a pool, a fitness center, locker rooms and training rooms, and an outdoor fitness course.

Disabled Students: 60% of the campus is accessible. Elevators, special parking, specially equipped rest rooms, lowered drinking fountains, lowered telephones, a learning disability program, and special accomodations based on student need and eligibility are available.

Services: Counseling and information services are available, as is tutoring in most subjects. There is remedial math and writing. Note takers and extended time for tests may be arranged.

Campus Safety and Security: Measures include self-defense education, security escort services, informal discussions, and lighted pathways/sidewalks. There is a 24-hour manned entrance gate and a nighttime foot patrol.

Programs of Study: Holy Names confers B.A., B.S., B.Mus., and B.S.N. degrees. Master's degrees are also awarded. Bachelor's degrees are awarded in BIOLOGICAL SCIENCE (biology/biological science), BUSINESS (business administration and management and human resources), COMMUNICATIONS AND THE ARTS (communications, English, English as a second/foreign language, and music), COMPUTER AND PHYSICAL SCIENCE (computer science), HEALTH PROFESSIONS (nursing), SOCIAL SCIENCE (history, human services, humanities, liberal arts/general studies, philosophy, psychology, religion, sociology, and Spanish studies). Business administration, nursing, and psychology are the largest.

Required: Students must have a 2.0 GPA and complete at least 120 hours with 24 to 36 in the major and 20 upper-division hours taken outside the major field. Students must complete a core curriculum, including foundation courses in critical thinking and communication, and courses in disciplinary studies, integrative studies across cultures, and writing across the curriculum. In some cases these requirements may be satisfied by secondary record, advanced placement, or challenge test. All students must take multidisciplinary courses in humanistic studies and a senior colloquium.

Special: Students may cross-register for 1 course per semester at any of 9 members of the Regional Association of East Bay Colleges and Universities. Internships, study abroad, and cooperative exchange programs with Central College in Iowa, Anna Maria College in Massachusetts, the Center for Bilingual Multicultural Studies in Mexico, and Kansai University of Foreign Studies in Japan are available. Dual and student-designed majors, and interdisciplinary majors, including business administration

and communication and business administration and philosophy are offered. Accelerated degrees are available in all B.A. programs. A weekend college for adults, limited nondegree study, and pass/fail options are available. There are 10 national honor societies and 1 departmental honors program.

Faculty/Classroom: 36% of faculty are male; 64%, female. 61% teach undergraduates. No introductory courses are taught by graduate students. The average class size in an introductory lecture is 22; in a laboratory, 13; and in a regular course, 15.

Admissions: 98% of recent applicants were accepted. The SAT scores for a recent freshman class were: Verbal--58% below 500, 35% between 500 and 599, and 7% between 600 and 700; Math--58% below 500, 35% between 500 and 599, and 7% between 600 and 700. 30% of recent freshmen were in the top fifth of their class; 74% were in the top two fifths.

Requirements: The SAT or ACT is required. In addition, applicants must be graduates of an accredited secondary school or have earned the GED. Secondary preparation should include at least 4 years of English, 3 years of math, 2 years of a single foreign language, 1 year each of lab science and U.S. history, 1 additional year of advanced courses in math, lab science, or foreign language, and 3 other 1-year college preparatory electives. In addition, the college requires a personal essay. Music auditions are required for scholarship applicants and recommended for others. AP and CLEP credits are accepted. Important factors in the admissions decision are advanced placement or honor courses, leadership record, and recommendations by school officials.

Procedure: Freshmen are admitted fall and spring. Entrance exams should be taken during the fall of the senior year. There is a deferred admissions plan. Priority applications should be filed by March 2 for fall entry and December 1 for spring entry, along with a $50 fee. Notification is sent on a rolling basis.

Transfer: 97 transfer students enrolled in a recent year. Applicants must have at least a 2.2 GPA in college work or a minimum of 30 transferable units. They must submit college records, a letter of recommendation from a college teacher or counselor, and a personal statement of their educational goals. 24 of 120 credits required for the bachelor's degree must be completed at Holy Names.

Visiting: There are guides for informal visits and visitors may sit in on classes and stay overnight. To schedule a visit, contact the Admissions Office at (510) 436-1351.

Financial Aid: In a recent year, 79% of all full-time freshmen and 65% of continuing full-time students received some form of financial aid. 74% of full-time freshmen and 65% of continuing full-time students received need-based aid. The average freshman award was $22,883. Need-based scholarships or need-based grants averaged $9918 ($9918 maximum); need-based self-help aid (loans and jobs) averaged $2625 ($2625 maximum); non-need-based athletic scholarships averaged $7715 ($19,970 maximum); and other non-need-based awards and non-need-based scholarships averaged $9370 ($19,970 maximum). 25% of undergraduates work part- time. Average annual earnings from campus work are $2000. The average financial indebtedness of a recent graduate was $21,000. The FAFSA is required. The priority date for freshman financial aid applications for fall entry is March 2. The deadline for filing freshman financial aid applications for fall entry is August 1.

International Students: There were 16 international students enrolled in a recent year. The school actively recruits these students. They must score satisfactorily on the TOEFL or take the MELAB.

Computers: All students may access the system 8 A.M. to 10 P.M. daily in the labs. Network access is available 24 hours a day. There are no time limits and no fees.

Graduates: In a recent year, 113 bachelor's degrees were awarded. The most popular majors were nursing (27%), business and marketing (22%), and liberal studies (10%). In an average class, 30% graduate in 4 years or less, 41% graduate in 5 years or less, and 46% graduate in 6 years or less. 14 companies recruited on campus in a recent year.

Admissions Contact: Jeffrey Miller, Vice President for Enrollment Management. E-mail: *admissions@hnu.edu* Web: *www.hnu.edu*

HOPE INTERNATIONAL UNIVERSITY · D-5
Fullerton, CA 92831

(714) 879-3901, ext. 2215
(800) 762-1294; Fax: (714) 524-0231

Full-time: 300 men, 400 women	**Faculty:** 29
Part-time: 40 men, 100 women	**Ph.D.s:** 48%
Graduate: 80 men, 80 women	**Student/Faculty:** 24 to 1
Year: 4-1-4, summer session	**Tuition:** $17,700
Application Deadline: see profile	**Room & Board:** $6000
Freshman Class: n/av	
SAT or ACT: required	**NONCOMPETITIVE**

Hope International University, founded in 1928, is a small, private liberal arts institution affiliated with the Independent Christian Church/Churches of Christ. Some figures given in the above capsule and in this profile are approximate. There are 2 undergraduate schools and 1 graduate school. The library contains 65,000 volumes, 100 microform items, and 3300 audio/video tapes/CDs/DVDs, and subscribes to 300 periodicals including electronic. Computerized library services include the card catalog and database searching. Special learning facilities include a learning resource center and a 1000-seat theater. The 15-acre campus is in an urban area 45 miles southeast of Los Angeles. Including any residence halls, there are 9 buildings.

Student Life: 53% of undergraduates are from California. Others are from 25 states, 27 foreign countries, and Canada. 88% are from public schools. 61% are white; 20% foreign nationals. Most are Protestant. The average age of freshmen is 18; all undergraduates, 21. 19% do not continue beyond their first year; 48% remain to graduate.

Housing: 450 students can be accommodated in college housing, which includes single-sex dorms. On-campus housing is guaranteed for all 4 years. 52% of students live on campus; of those, 75% remain on campus on weekends. Alcohol is not permitted. All students may keep cars.

Activities: There are no fraternities or sororities. There are 17 groups on campus, including band, cheerleading, choir, chorale, chorus, drama, international, literary magazine, newspaper, orchestra, religious, social service, student government, and yearbook. Popular campus events include Sadie Hawkins, Spring Formal, and Service on Saturday (community outreach).

Sports: There are 4 intercollegiate sports for men and 5 for women, and 10 intramural sports for men and 8 for women. Facilities include a swimming pool and game rooms.

Disabled Students: 95% of the campus is accessible. Elevators, special parking, and specially equipped rest rooms are available. Priority is given to disabled students for first-floor housing.

Services: Counseling and information services are available, as is tutoring in most subjects. There is a reader service for the blind, and remedial math, reading, and writing.

Campus Safety and Security: Measures include 24-hour foot and vehicle patrol, security escort services, and lighted pathways/sidewalks.

Programs of Study: Hope confers B.A., B.S., B.M., and B.M.E. degrees. Associate and master's degrees are also awarded. Bachelor's degrees are awarded in BUSINESS (business administration and management), COMMUNICATIONS AND THE ARTS (music and Spanish), EDUCATION (education, music, secondary, and social science), HEALTH PROFESSIONS (health science and sports medicine), SOCIAL SCIENCE (biblical studies, child psychology/development, crosscultural studies, human services, interdisciplinary studies, liberal arts/general studies, ministries, psychology, social science, and youth ministry). Education, business, and church ministry are the largest.

Required: Regular attendance at convocation and Christian service is required. To graduate, students must complete at least 124 credit units with 36 to 51 in the major, and demonstrate 80% or better competency on the university placement test. A minimum GPA of 2.0 must be maintained. Distribution requirements include 18 credits in biblical studies and 55 in general education courses.

Special: Hope International offers co-op programs and cross-registration with California State University, Fullerton. Internships, study abroad in 3 countries, work-study programs, dual and student-designed majors, nondegree study, pass/fail options, and credit for life, military, and work experience are also offered. There is a freshman honors program.

Faculty/Classroom: 69% of faculty are male; 31%, female. 83% teach undergraduates. No introductory courses are taught by graduate students. The average class size in an introductory lecture is 33; in a laboratory, 20; and in a regular course, 30.

Requirements: The SAT or ACT is required. In addition, applicants must be high school graduates with a GPA of 2.5. The GED is accepted. A personal essay and references from a church leader and an academic counselor are required. AP and CLEP credits are accepted.

Procedure: Freshmen are admitted fall and spring. Entrance exams should be taken before enrolling. There are early admissions and deferred admissions plans Check with the school for current application deadlines and fee. The college accepts all applicants. Notification is sent on a rolling basis.

Transfer: Transfer students must submit copies of college transcripts and SAT scores if fewer than 30 college units have been completed. A minimum GPA of 2.0 is required. 30 of 124 credits required for the bachelor's degree must be completed at Hope.

Visiting: There are regularly scheduled orientations for prospective students. There are guides for informal visits and visitors may sit in on classes and stay overnight. To schedule a visit, contact the Admissions Office.

Financial Aid: The FAFSA and the college's own financial statement are required. Check with the school for current deadlines.

International Students: The school actively recruits these students. They must score satisfactorily on the written TOEFL and also take the college's own entrance exam.

Computers: All students may access the system at any time. There are no time limits and no fees. It is strongly recommended that all students have a personal computer.

Graduates: In an average class, 42% graduate in 4 years or less, 54% graduate in 5 years or less, and 56% graduate in 6 years or less.

Admissions Contact: Kaylene Carr, Director of Admissions. A video is available. E-mail: *twinston@hiu.edu* Web: *www.hiu.ed*

HUMBOLDT STATE UNIVERSITY — A-1
Arcata, CA 95521-8299

(707) 826-4402
(866) 850-9556; Fax: (707) 826-6194

Full-time: 2613 men, 3140 women	**Faculty:** 276; IIA, +$
Part-time: 314 men, 328 women	**Ph.D.s:** 80%
Graduate: 427 men, 640 women	**Student/Faculty:** 21 to 1
Year: semesters, summer session	**Tuition:** $3180 ($11,316)
Application Deadline: June 1	**Room & Board:** $7996
Freshman Class: 7206 applied, 861 enrolled	
SAT Verbal/Math: 530/510*	**ACT:** 22 **COMPETITIVE**

Humboldt State University, founded in 1913, is a liberal arts institution and the northernmost campus of the California State University system. There are 3 undergraduate schools and 1 graduate school. In addition to regional accreditation, Humboldt has baccalaureate program accreditation with ABET, CSWE, NASAD, NASM, NAST, NLN, and SAF. The library contains 594,735 volumes, 603,251 microform items, and 25,000 audio/video tapes/CDs/DVDs, and subscribes to 7750 periodicals including electronic. Computerized library services include the card catalog, interlibrary loans, database searching, Internet access, and laptop Internet portals. Special learning facilities include a learning resource center, art gallery, natural history museum, radio station, observatory, greenhouse, solar hydrogen project, wildlife sanctuaries, the Center for Appropriate Technology, child development lab, ceramics lab, jewelry lab, marine lab, fish hatchery, and wildlife care center. The 161-acre campus is in a small town 275 miles north of San Francisco. Including any residence halls, there are 93 buildings.

Student Life: 84% of undergraduates are from California. Others are from 49 states, 22 foreign countries, and Canada. 95% are from public schools. 58% are white. The average age of freshmen is 19; all undergraduates, 24. 24% do not continue beyond their first year.

Housing: 1376 students can be accommodated in college housing, which includes single-sex and coed dormitories and on-campus apartments. In addition, there are special-interest houses and living learning houses. On-campus housing is available on a first-come, first-served basis. 82% of students commute. All students may keep cars.

Activities: There are 2 national fraternities and 4 local sororities. There are 178 groups on campus, including art, band, cheerleading, chorale, chorus, computers, dance, debate, drama, environmental, ethnic, film, gay, honors, international, jazz band, literary magazine, marching band, musical theater, newspaper, opera, orchestra, pep band, photography, political, professional, radio and TV, religious, social, social service, student government, and symphony. Popular campus events include Native American Motivation Day, Asian Pacific Heritage Week, and Black Liberation Month.

Sports: There are 5 intercollegiate sports for men and 7 for women, and 4 intramural sports for men and 4 for women. Facilities include a 7000-seat stadium, all-weather track, swimming pool, tennis and racquetball courts, playing fields, 2 gyms, student recreation center with exercise equipment weight room, and rock-climbing wall.

Disabled Students: 60% of the campus is accessible. Wheelchair ramps, elevators, special parking, specially equipped rest rooms, special class scheduling, lowered drinking fountains, lowered telephones, wheelchair-accessible transportation, and a study center are available.

Services: Counseling and information services are available, as is tutoring in every subject. There is a reader service for the blind, and remedial math, reading, and writing.

Campus Safety and Security: Measures include 24-hour foot and vehicle patrol, self-defense education, security escort services, and informal discussions. There are pamphlets/posters/films, emergency telephones, lighted pathways/sidewalks, and emergency transportation services.

Programs of Study: Humboldt confers B.A. and B.S. degrees. Master's degrees are also awarded. Bachelor's degrees are awarded in AGRICULTURE (fishing and fisheries, forestry and related sciences, and natural resource management), BIOLOGICAL SCIENCE (biology/biological science, botany, wildlife biology, and zoology), BUSINESS (business administration and management and business economics), COMMUNICATIONS AND THE ARTS (art, communications, dramatic arts, English, fine arts, French, German, journalism, music, Spanish, and speech/debate/rhetoric), COMPUTER AND PHYSICAL SCIENCE (chemistry, geology, information sciences and systems, mathematics, oceanography, and physics), EDUCATION (business, elementary, English, industrial arts, mathematics, middle school, music, physical, science, secondary, and social science), ENGINEERING AND ENVIRONMENTAL DESIGN (environmental engineering, environmental science, industrial engineering technology, and land use management and reclamation), HEALTH PROFESSIONS (nursing, predentistry, and premedicine), SOCIAL SCIENCE (anthropology, child psychology/development, geography, history, liberal arts/general studies, Native American studies, parks and recreation management, philosophy, physical fitness/movement, political science/government, prelaw, psychology, religion, social science, social work, and sociology). Environmental resources engineering, natural resources, and performing arts are the strongest academically. Biological sciences is the largest.

Required: To graduate, students must complete 120 to 132 semester credits, including 48 in general education courses and at least 24 to 36 in the major, including up to 40 units in electives, with a minimum overall GPA of 2.0. Requirements include freshman reading and composition, diversity and common ground coursework, U.S. history coursework as required by the California legislature.

Special: HSU offers campus work-study programs and co-op programs with a variety of public and private agencies, including the areas of fisheries, biology, geology, botany, engineering, soil science, hydrology, and range and soil conservation. Internships and study abroad in 25 countries, with semesters in London, China, and Greece are also offered. Dual majors, student-designed majors, credit for life and military experience, and credit/no credit grading options are also available. There are 5 national honor societies and 6 departmental honors programs.

Faculty/Classroom: 53% of faculty are male; 47%, female. The average class size in an introductory lecture is 33; in a laboratory, 21; and in a regular course, 24.

Admissions: The SAT scores for the 2005-2006 freshman class were: Verbal--37% below 500, 39% between 500 and 599, 21% between 600 and 700, and 3% above 700; Math--41% below 500, 43% between 500 and 599, 15% between 600 and 700, and 1% above 700. The ACT scores were 41% below 21, 24% between 21 and 23, 22% between 24 and 26, 8% between 27 and 28, and 5% above 28.

Requirements: The SAT or ACT is recommended. Applicants must be high school graduates with a minimum GPA of 2.0 and 15 academic credits, to include 4 years in English, 3 years in college prep math, 2 years each in foreign language, social science, and lab science, including 1 year physical and 1 year life science, and 1 year each of U.S. history/government and visual and performing arts. The GED is accepted. HSU uses an eligibility index that combines GPA and ACT or SAT scores for admission. Requirements are higher for out-of-state applicants. Contact the Office of Admissions for further information. A GPA of 2.0 is required. AP and CLEP credits are accepted.

Procedure: Freshmen are admitted fall and spring. Entrance exams should be taken prior to admission. There are early decision and rolling admissions plans. Applications should be filed by June 1 for fall entry and December for spring entry, along with a $55 fee. Notification is sent on a rolling basis. Applications are accepted on-line.

Transfer: 1070 transfer students enrolled in 2004-2005. Applicants must have a minimum college GPA of 2.0 (2.4 for nonresidents). To enter, students need 30 general education units with a grade of C or better, including courses in written and speech communication, critical thinking, and math. Students with fewer than 56 transferable semester units must meet freshman requirements. 30 of 120 credits required for the bachelor's degree must be completed at Humboldt.

Visiting: There are regularly scheduled orientations for prospective students, including Preview Day in the spring and mandatory summer orientation for new students, which provides peer and academic counseling, registration, and a variety of social activities. There are guides for informal visits and visitors may sit in on classes and stay overnight. To schedule a visit, contact the Office of Admissions.

Financial Aid: The FAFSA is required. The deadline for filing freshman financial aid applications for fall entry is March 2.

International Students: There are 43 international students enrolled. The school actively recruits these students. They must score satisfactorily on the written TOEFL.

Computers: Wireless access is available. Humboldt offers 12 computer labs with a total of 190 PCs and 102 Macs that are available 7 days a week for student use. Five areas of campus are covered by wireless hotspots. All students may access the system 24 hours a day. There are no time limits and no fees. It is strongly recommended that all students have a personal computer.

Graduates: From July 1, 2004 to June 30, 2005, 1431 bachelor's degrees were awarded. The most popular majors were liberal studies (11%), art (7%), and psychology (7%). In an average class, 12% graduate in 4 years or less, 33% graduate in 5 years or less, and 41% graduate in 6 years or less.

Admissions Contact: Rebecca Kalal, Assistant Director, Admissions. A video is available. E-mail: hsuinfo@.humboldt.edu
Web: www.humboldt.edu

HUMPHREYS COLLEGE
B-3

Stockton, CA 95207 (209) 478-0800; Fax: (209) 478-8721

Full-time: 260 men, 400 women	Faculty: 22
Part-time: 30 men, 70 women	Ph.D.s: 46%
Graduate: 40 men, 20 women	Student/Faculty: 30 to 1
Year: quarters, summer session	Tuition: $7000
Application Deadline: open	Room & Board: n/app
Freshman Class: n/av	
SAT or ACT: not required	NONCOMPETITIVE

Humphreys College, founded in 1896, is an independent institution offering undergraduate degrees in business management, accounting, paralegal studies, computer management, law, early childhood education, and liberal arts to a primarily commuter student body.Some information in this capsule and profile is approximate. The 2 libraries contain 21,000 volumes and 1000 audio/video tapes/CDs/DVDs, and subscribe to 110 periodicals including electronic. Computerized library services include the card catalog and database searching. The 10-acre campus is in a suburban area 40 miles south of Sacramento. Including any residence halls, there are 9 buildings.

Student Life: 97% of undergraduates are from California. Students are from 4 states and 5 foreign countries. 97% are from public schools. 70% are white; 17% Hispanic. The average age of freshmen is 23; all undergraduates, 25. 20% do not continue beyond their first year; 50% remain to graduate.

Housing: 64 students can be accommodated in college housing, which includes single-sex on-campus apartments and married-student housing. On-campus housing is available on a first-come, first-served basis. Priority is given to out-of-town students. 90% of students commute. Alcohol is not permitted. All students may keep cars.

Activities: There are no fraternities or sororities. There are 4 groups on campus, including professional and student government. Popular campus events include a Halloween party, a Christmas dinner, and a quarterly Hot Dog Day barbecue.

Sports: There is no sports program at Humphreys. Facilities include a swimming pool, a basketball court, a tennis court, and sports fields.

Disabled Students: All of the campus is accessible. Wheelchair ramps, special parking, specially equipped rest rooms, special class scheduling, lowered drinking fountains, and lowered telephones are available.

Services: Counseling and information services are available, as is tutoring in some subjects, including accounting. There is remedial math and writing.

Campus Safety and Security: Measures include 24-hour foot and vehicle patrol, security escort services, and lighted pathways/sidewalks.

Programs of Study: Humphreys confers the B.S. degree. Associate and doctoral degrees are also awarded. Bachelor's degrees are awarded in BUSINESS (accounting, business administration and management, court reporting, and management information systems), EDUCATION (early childhood), SOCIAL SCIENCE (community services and paralegal studies). Paralegal studies is the largest.

Required: To graduate, students must complete a total of 180 quarter units, including 56 in the major and 72 in general education courses, with a minimum GPA of 2.0.

Special: Local internship positions are available for students of paralegal studies and business administration. Dual majors in business studies are possible.

Faculty/Classroom: 51% of faculty are male; 49%, female. All teach undergraduates. No introductory courses are taught by graduate students. The average class size in an introductory lecture is 17.

Requirements: Applicants must be graduates of an accredited secondary school or have earned a GED. AP and CLEP credits are accepted.

Procedure: Freshmen are admitted to all sessions. Entrance exams should be taken at any time. There is a deferred admissions plan and a rolling admissions plan. Application deadlines are open. Check with the school for current fee.

Transfer: Applicants must submit official transcripts and have a GPA of at least 2.0. 36 of 180 credits required for the bachelor's degree must be completed at Humphreys.

Visiting: There are regularly scheduled orientations for prospective students, including a campus tour, classroom visits, and meetings with admissions, financial aid, and academic advisers. There are guides for informal visits and visitors may sit in on classes. To schedule a visit, contact Santa Lopez in Admissions.

Financial Aid: 64% of undergraduates work part time. Average annual earnings from campus work are $1200. Humphreys is a member of CSS. The FAFSA is required. Check with the school for current deadlines.

International Students: They must score satisfactorily on the written TOEFL or take the MELAB.

Computers: All students may access the system when a lab aide or instructor is present or with an instructor's permission. There are no time limits and no fees.

Graduates: In a recent year, 48 bachelor's degrees were awarded.

Admissions Contact: Santa Lopez, Director of Admissions.
Web: www.humphreys.edu

LA SIERRA UNIVERSITY
Riverside, CA 92515-8247

D-5

(951) 785-2176
(800) 874-5587; Fax: (951) 785-2901

Full-time: 597 men, 857 women	**Faculty:** n/av
Part-time: 81 men, 103 women	**Ph.Ds:** n/av
Graduate: 143 men, 160 women	**Student/Faculty:** n/av
Year: quarters, summer session	**Tuition:** $19,083
Application Deadline: February 1	**Room & Board:** $5244
Freshman Class: 1389 applied, 533 accepted, 388 enrolled	
SAT Verbal/Math: 480/490*	**ACT:** 19	COMPETITIVE+

La Sierra University, founded originally as La Sierra Academy in 1922, is a Seventh-day Adventist, private university, offering undergraduate and graduate programs in applied and liberal arts and sciences, business and management, religion, and education. Some figures in this profile are approximate. There are 5 undergraduate and 4 graduate schools. In addition to regional accreditation, La Sierra has baccalaureate program accreditation with ABET. The library contains 230,000 volumes and 285,000 microform items, and subscribes to 1500 periodicals including electronic. Computerized library services include the card catalog, interlibrary loans, and database searching. Special learning facilities include a learning resource center, art gallery, natural history museum, radio station, observatory, missionary museum, and arboretum. The 300-acre campus is in a suburban area 40 miles east of Los Angeles. Including any residence halls, there are 48 buildings.

Student Life: 71% of undergraduates are from California. Students are from 34 states, 58 foreign countries, and Canada. 39% are from public schools. 35% are white; 31% Asian American; 19% Hispanic. 90% are Protestant; 12% claim no religious affiliation. The average age of freshmen is 19; all undergraduates, 22.

Housing: 650 students can be accommodated in college housing, which includes single-sex dorms, on-campus apartments, off-campus apartments, and married-student housing. In addition, there are honors houses. On-campus housing is available on a first-come, first-served basis. 56% of students commute. Alcohol is not permitted. All students may keep cars.

Activities: There are no fraternities or sororities. There are 30 groups on campus, including band, choir, chorus, computers, drama, ethnic, international, literary magazine, newspaper, orchestra, professional, religious, social service, student government, and yearbook. Popular campus events include University Experience, Academic Expo, and Community Service Day.

Sports: There are 3 intercollegiate sports for men and 2 for women, and 9 intramural sports for men and 9 for women. Facilities include a gym, soccer and flag football fields, a running track, a swimming pool, and a fitness center.

Disabled Students: 99% of the campus is accessible. Wheelchair ramps, elevators, special parking, specially equipped rest rooms, and special class scheduling are available.

Services: Counseling and information services are available, as is tutoring in most subjects. There is a reader service for the blind, and remedial math, reading, and writing, and a learning support center.

Campus Safety and Security: Measures include 24-hour foot and vehicle patrol, security escort services, informal discussions, and lighted pathways/sidewalks.

Programs of Study: La Sierra confers B.A., B.S., B.B.A., B.F.A., B.Mus., and B.S.W. degrees. Associate, master's, and doctoral degrees are also awarded. Bachelor's degrees are awarded in BIOLOGICAL SCIENCE (biochemistry, biology/biological science, biometrics and biostatistics, and biophysics), BUSINESS (accounting, banking and finance, business administration and management, electronic business, international business management, and marketing management), COMMUNICATIONS AND THE ARTS (art, communications, English, English as a second/foreign language, fine arts, graphic design, music, music performance, and Spanish), COMPUTER AND PHYSICAL SCIENCE (chemistry, computer science, information sciences and systems, mathematics, and physics), EDUCATION (elementary, music, physical, and secondary), HEALTH PROFESSIONS (exercise science, and health science), SOCIAL SCIENCE (history, liberal arts/general studies, political science/government, psychobiology, psychology, religion, social work, and sociology). English and history are the strongest academically. Biology, psychology, and business are the largest.

Required: To graduate, students must complete 190 units, at least 60 of which must be upper-division, with a GPA of 2.0. All students must complete a University Studies curriculum consisting of a 29-unit core curriculum and the distribution requirements, and 15 clock hours of community service per year.

Special: Cross-registration with Walla Walla College is necessary for engineering students. Study abroad is available in 3 countries through the Adventist Colleges Abroad Consortium. Liberal studies students work with an adviser to design their own major. There is a freshman honors program.

Faculty/Classroom: All teach undergraduates, 70% do research, and 70% do both. Graduate students teach 1% of introductory courses. The average class size in an introductory lecture is 30; in a laboratory, 21; and in a regular course, 20.

Admissions: 38% of the 2005-2006 applicants were accepted. The SAT scores for the 2005-2006 freshman class were: Verbal--58% below 500, 32% between 500 and 599, 9% between 600 and 700, and 1% above 700; Math--53% below 500, 34% between 500 and 599, 11% between 600 and 700, and 2% above 700. The ACT scores were 67% below 21, 16% between 21 and 23, 7% between 24 and 26, 7% between 27 and 28, and 3% above 28. 32% of the current freshmen were in the top fifth of their class; 60% were in the top two fifths.

Requirements: The SAT or ACT is required. In addition, prospective students should have a high school diploma or equivalent. Completion of college preparatory work is required. A recommendation is also required. A GPA of 2.5 is required. AP and CLEP credits are accepted. Important factors in the admissions decision are recommendations by school officials, leadership record, and evidence of special talent.

Procedure: Freshmen are admitted to all sessions. Entrance exams should be taken during the senior year. There is a deferred admissions plan and a rolling admissions plan. Applications should be filed by August 15 for fall entry, December 1 for winter entry, March 1 for spring entry, and May 1 for summer entry. The fall 2005 application fee was $30. Notification is sent on a rolling basis.

Transfer: 228 transfer students enrolled in 2004-2005. Transcripts from all previous colleges are required. 36 of 190 credits required for the bachelor's degree must be completed at La Sierra.

Visiting: There are regularly scheduled orientations for prospective students, including a tour and meetings with faculty and administrators. There are guides for informal visits and visitors may sit in on classes and stay overnight. To schedule a visit, contact Recruitment/Admissions at (951) 785-2422.

Financial Aid: In 2005-2006, 93% of all full-time freshmen and 97% of continuing full-time students received some form of financial aid. 75% of full-time freshmen and 69% of continuing full-time students received need-based aid. The average freshman award was $13,182. Need-based scholarships or need-based grants averaged $9686; need-based self-help aid (loans and jobs) averaged $1831; and other non-need-based awards and non-need-based scholarships averaged $1665. La Sierra is a member of CSS. The FAFSA is required. Check with the school for current deadlines.

International Students: The school actively recruits these students. Satisfactory scores are required on the written TOEFL or the MELAB. Students must also take take the SAT or the ACT.

Computers: All students may access the system 24 hours a day. There are no time limits and no fees.

Admissions Contact: Gene Edelbach, Vice President, Enrollment Services. E-mail: admissions@lasierra.edu Web: www.lasierra.edu

LAGUNA COLLEGE OF ART AND DESIGN
(Formerly Art Institute of Southern California)

D-5

Laguna Beach, CA 92651

(949) 376-6000
(800) 255-0762; Fax: (949) 376-6009

Full-time: 100 men, 60 women	**Faculty:** 8
Part-time: 20 men, 30 women	**Ph.D.s:** 85%
Graduate: none	**Student/Faculty:** 20 to 1
Year: semesters, summer session	**Tuition:** $17,600
Application Deadline: February 2	**Room & Board:** n/app
Freshman Class: n/av	
SAT or ACT: required	SPECIAL

Laguna College of Art and Desighn, Formerly Art Institute, Southern California, founded in 1961, is a nonprofit, independent, institution offering full- and part-time undergraduate art programs leading to the Bachelor of Fine Arts. In addition to regional accreditation, AISC has baccalaureate program accreditation with NASAD. The library contains 15,000 volumes and 300 audio/video tapes/CDs/DVDs, and subscribes to 90 periodicals including electronic. Computerized library services include the card catalog and interlibrary loans. Special learning facilities include a learning resource center and art gallery. The 9-acre campus is in a small town 47 miles southeast of Los Angeles. There are 11 buildings.

Student Life: 60% of undergraduates are from California. Others are from 33 states, 13 foreign countries, and Canada. 85% are from public schools. 66% are white; 13% foreign nationals; 11% Asian American. The average age of freshmen is 19; all undergraduates, 23. 15% do not continue beyond their first year; 60% remain to graduate.

Housing: There are no residence halls. 100% of students commute. The college will asssist in the location of of campus housing. Alcohol is not permitted. All students may keep cars.

Activities: There are no fraternities or sororities. There are 2 groups on campus, including art and student government.

Sports: There is no sports program at Laguna.

Disabled Students: 90% of the campus is accessible. Special parking, specially equipped rest rooms, special class scheduling, and lowered drinking fountains are available.

Services: There is remedial reading and writing.

Campus Safety and Security: Measures include security escort services and and night security.

Programs of Study: Laguna confers the B.F.A. degree. Bachelor's degrees are awarded in COMMUNICATIONS AND THE ARTS (animation, drawing, graphic design, illustration, and painting).

Required: All students must complete 122 credit hours, with approximately 55 in the major, including studio electives. General education requirements include 30 hours in liberal arts and 15 in art history. 22 hours of studio foundation courses are required, in which students explore all artistic medium.

Special: Internships are possible, and work-study is available on campus. Students may petition the registrar if they wish to attempt more than 15 semester units.

Faculty/Classroom: 65% of faculty are male; 35%, female. All teach undergraduates. The average class size in an introductory lecture is 15 and in a regular course, 12.

Requirements: The SAT or ACT is required, for applicants currently in high school. Students must be high school graduates or hold an equivalent GED. A personal essay and letter of recommendation are required, as is a personal or telephone interview, and a 10-piece portfolio. A GPA of 2.5 is required. AP and CLEP credits are accepted. Important factors in the admissions decision are evidence of special talent, recommendations by school officials, and ability to finance college education.

Procedure: Freshmen are admitted fall and spring. There is a deferred admissions plan. Regular applications should be filed by February 2 for the fall entry, by January 2 for spring entry, along with a $45 fee. Notification is sent within 3 weeks of completion of all requirements. Applications are accepted on-line (no fee).

Transfer: In addition to freshman requirements, transfer students must submit all prior college transcripts. 45 of 122 credits required for the bachelor's degree must be completed at AISC.

Visiting: There are regularly scheduled orientations for prospective students, consisting of national portfolio days and open house. There are guides for informal visits and visitors may sit in on classes. To schedule a visit, contact the Admissions Office.

Financial Aid: Laguna is a member of CSS. The CSS/Profile, FAFSA, or FFS as well as SAAC for California grants is required.

International Students: The school actively recruits these students. They must score satisfactorily on the TOEFL or and also take the college's own test.

Computers: All students may access the system. There are no time limits and no fees. It is strongly recommended that all students have a personal computer.

Admissions Contact: Anthony Padilla, Vice President of Enrollment. A video is available. E-mail: *admissions@lagunacollege.edu* Web: *http://www.aisc.edu*

LOYOLA MARYMOUNT UNIVERSITY   C-5

Los Angeles, CA 90045   (310) 338-2750
(800) LMU-INFO; Fax: (310) 338-2797

Full-time: 2100 men, 3200 women	**Faculty:** 419; IIA, ++$
Part-time: 90 men, 100 women	**Ph.D.s:** 86%
Graduate: 630 men, 1180 women	**Student/Faculty:** 13 to 1
Year: semesters, summer session	**Tuition:** $27,162
Application Deadline: January 15	**Room & Board:** $9159
Freshman Class: n/av	
SAT: required	**ACT:** recommended
	VERY COMPETITIVE

Loyola Marymount University, a private institution founded in 1911 and affiliated with the Roman Catholic Church, offers programs in liberal arts, business administration, fine arts, science, engineering, and law. There are 5 undergraduate schools and 1 graduate school. Some figures in the above capsule and in this profile are approximate. In addition to regional accreditation, LMU has baccalaureate program accreditation with AACSB, ABET, NASAD, NASDTEC, NCATE, and ACS. The 2 libraries contain 943,637 volumes, 1,560,619 microform items, and 20,880 audio/video tapes/CDs/DVDs, and subscribe to 10,086 periodicals including electronic. Computerized library services include the card catalog, interlibrary loans, database searching, and Internet access. Special learning facilities include a learning resource center, art gallery, radio station, the Burns Fine Arts Center, and the Little Theatre. The 128-acre campus is in a suburban area 15 miles southwest of downtown Los Angeles on a mesa overlooking Marina del Rey. Including any residence halls, there are 40 buildings.

Student Life: 76% of undergraduates are from California. Others are from 50 states, 72 foreign countries, and Canada. 51% are white; 17% Hispanic; 13% Asian American. 53% are Catholic; 25% Christian, Buddhist, and other. The average age of freshmen is 18; all undergraduates, 20. 13% do not continue beyond their first year; 72% remain to graduate.

Housing: 2897 students can be accommodated in college housing, which includes single-sex and coed dorms and on-campus apartments.

In addition, there are honors houses and special-interest houses. On-campus housing is available on a lottery system for upperclassmen. 54% of students live on campus; of those, 50% remain on campus on weekends. All students may keep cars.

Activities: 14% of men belong to 5 national fraternities; 6% of women belong to 7 national sororities. There are 120 groups on campus, including art, cheerleading, chess, choir, chorale, chorus, computers, dance, drama, ethnic, film, gay, honors, international, literary magazine, newspaper, orchestra, pep band, political, professional, radio and TV, religious, social, social service, student government, and yearbook. Popular campus events include Cinco de Mayo, Special Games (disabled children), and the ASLMU Formal Dance.

Sports: There are 8 intercollegiate sports for men and 9 for women, and 6 intramural sports for men and 6 for women. Facilities include an athletic pavilion, a 4166-seat gym, a swimming pool, tennis, handball, and racquetball courts, a baseball stadium, a floating crew shell house, soccer, rugby, and football fields, and a recreation center.

Disabled Students: 95% of the campus is accessible. Wheelchair ramps, elevators, special parking, specially equipped rest rooms, special class scheduling, lowered drinking fountains, and lowered telephones are available. Special arrangements are possible for placement tests and registration. Hearing aid equipment is provided for disabled students in the library are available.

Services: Counseling and information services are available, as is tutoring in most subjects. There is a reader service for the blind, and remedial math, reading, and writing. There is an extensive learning resource center with full-time specialists in reading, writing, and study skills as well as a peer tutoring staff and computer-aided instruction. Note takers and special equipment and materials are available.

Campus Safety and Security: Measures include 24-hour foot and vehicle patrol, security escort services, informal discussions, emergency telephones, and lighted pathways/sidewalks.

Programs of Study: LMU confers B.A., B.S., B.B.A., B.S.A., and B.S.E. degrees. Master's degrees are also awarded. Bachelor's degrees are awarded in BIOLOGICAL SCIENCE (biochemistry and biology/biological science), BUSINESS (accounting and business administration and management), COMMUNICATIONS AND THE ARTS (art history and appreciation, classics, communications, dance, dramatic arts, English, French, media arts, music, Spanish, and studio art), COMPUTER AND PHYSICAL SCIENCE (chemistry, computer science, mathematics, natural sciences, and physics), ENGINEERING AND ENVIRONMENTAL DESIGN (civil engineering, computer graphics, electrical/electronics engineering, engineering physics, environmental science, and mechanical engineering), SOCIAL SCIENCE (African American studies, Asian/Oriental studies, classical/ancient civilization, economics, European studies, history, humanities, philosophy, political science/government, psychology, sociology, theological studies, and urban studies). Communication arts, political science, and engineering are the strongest academically. Psychology, communication studies, and business administration are the largest.

Required: The core curriculum required for all students in the liberal arts college includes 6 hours each of communication skills, history, science/technology, philosophy, and theology, and 3 hours of fine arts, literature/psychology, and social studies. A minimum 2.0 GPA is required, as are at least 120 semester credits, with at least 40 hours in the major. The last 30 semester hours of academic work and at least 12 hours of the major must be completed at LMU.

Special: LMU offers internships and volunteer work experience with local firms, study abroad in Europe, Mexico, Japan, and China, a Washington semester, dual majors, work-study, student-designed and individualized studies majors, accelerated degree programs in all majors, a general studies degree, nondegree study, and pass/fail options for electives. There are 2 national honor societies and a freshman honors program.

Faculty/Classroom: 60% of faculty are male; 40%, female. All both teach and do research. No introductory courses are taught by graduate students. The average class size in an introductory lecture is 19 and in a regular course, 19.

Admissions: 59% of recent applicants were accepted. The SAT scores for a recent freshman class were: Verbal--13% below 500, 51% between 500 and 599, 32% between 600 and 700, and 4% above 700; Math--13% below 500, 46% between 500 and 599; 36% between 600 and 700, and 5% above 700.

Requirements: The SAT is required and the ACT is recommended. In addition, prospective students must be graduates of an accredited secondary school and have completed 4 years of English, 3 each of a foreign language, math, and social studies, 2 of science, and 1 of an academic elective. A recommendation from an official of a previous school and essays are required. An interview is recommended. A GPA of 2.9 is required. AP credits are accepted. Important factors in the admissions decision are recommendations by school officials, advanced placement or honor courses, and evidence of special talent.

Procedure: Freshmen are admitted fall and spring. Entrance exams should be taken during the spring of the junior year or fall of the senior year. There is a deferred admissions plan. Applications should be filed by January 15 for fall entry and December 1 for spring entry, along with a $50 fee. Notification is sent on a rolling basis. A waiting list is an active part of the admissions procedure. Applications are accepted on-line.

Transfer: 193 transfer students enrolled in a recent year. Applicants must have a minimum 2.75 GPA and at least 30 credit hours earned. No minimum credit hours are necessary for students who meet freshman requirements. The SAT and an interview are recommended. 30 of 120 credits required for the bachelor's degree must be completed at LMU.

Visiting: There are regularly scheduled orientations for prospective students, consisting of an open house in the fall. There are guides for informal visits and visitors may sit in on classes. To schedule a visit, contact the Admissions Office.

Financial Aid: The CSS/Profile or FAFSA is required. The deadline for filing freshman financial aid applications for fall entry is March 2.

International Students: There are 250 international students enrolled. They must score satisfactorily on the written TOEFL.

Computers: All students may access the system. Labs are available more than 60 hours per week. Students may access the system 2 hours for remote access. There are no fees. It is strongly recommended that all students have a personal computer.

Graduates: In a recent year, 1188 bachelor's degrees were awarded. The most popular majors were business administration (25%), psychology (7%), and communication studies (7%). In an average class, 1% graduate in 3 years or less, 57% graduate in 4 years or less, 69% graduate in 5 years or less, and 73% graduate in 6 years or less. 112 companies recruited on campus in a recent year.

Admissions Contact: Matthew Fissinger, Director of Undergraduate Admissions. A video is available. E-mail: admissions@lmu.edu
Web: www.lmu.edu

MASTER'S COLLEGE AND SEMINARY, THE   C-5

Santa Clarita, CA 91321-1200   (661) 259-3540 ext 3369
(800) 568-6248; Fax: (661) 288-1037

Full-time: 453 men, 508 women	**Faculty:** 76; IIA, --$
Part-time: 120 men, 79 women	**Ph.D.s:** 82%
Graduate: 351 men, 47 women	**Student/Faculty:** 13 to 1
Year: semesters, summer session	**Tuition:** $19,230
Application Deadline: March 2	**Room & Board:** $6620
Freshman Class: 654 applied, 551 accepted, 331 enrolled	
SAT Verbal/Math: 576/556*	**ACT:** 24 **VERY COMPETITIVE**

The Master's College, founded in 1927, is a private, nondenominational Christian liberal arts institution. The library contains 134,181 volumes, 31,307 microform items, and 7620 audio/video tapes/CDs/DVDs, and subscribes to 12,112 periodicals including electronic. Computerized library services include the card catalog, interlibrary loans, database searching, and Internet access. Special learning facilities include a learning resource center. The 110-acre campus is in a rural area 35 miles north of Los Angeles. Including any residence halls, there are 27 buildings.

Student Life: 72% of undergraduates are from California. Others are from 43 states, 25 foreign countries, and Canada. 46% are from public schools. 83% are white. Most are Protestant. The average age of freshmen is 19; all undergraduates, 20. 17% do not continue beyond their first year; 57% remain to graduate.

Housing: 805 students can be accommodated in college housing, which includes single-sex dorm and off-campus apartments. In addition, there are special-interest houses. On-campus housing is guaranteed for the freshman year only and is available on a first-come, first-served basis. 78% of students live on campus; of those, 95% remain on campus on weekends. Alcohol is not permitted. All students may keep cars.

Activities: There are no fraternities or sororities. There are 15 groups on campus, including band, choir, chorale, drama, film, jazz band, musical theater, opera, orchestra, pep band, radio and TV, religious, social service, and student government. Popular campus events include College View Weekend, Community Day, and Mission Conference.

Sports: There are 5 intercollegiate sports for men and 5 for women, and 7 intramural sports for men and 7 for women. Facilities include a gym, a sports field, tennis and volleyball courts, an intramural field, a swimming pool, and a fitness center.

Disabled Students: All of the campus is accessible. Wheelchair ramps, special parking, specially equipped rest rooms, lowered drinking fountains, and lowered telephones are available.

Services: Counseling and information services are available, as is tutoring in most subjects. There is remedial math.

Campus Safety and Security: Measures include 24-hour foot and vehicle patrol, shuttle buses, and lighted pathways/sidewalks.

Programs of Study: TMC confers B.A., B.S., and B.Th. degrees. Master's degrees are also awarded. Bachelor's degrees are awarded in BIOLOGICAL SCIENCE (biology/biological science), BUSINESS (business administration and management), COMMUNICATIONS AND THE ARTS (communications, English, and music), COMPUTER AND PHYSICAL SCIENCE (information sciences and systems, mathematics, and

natural sciences), EDUCATION (elementary, physical, and secondary), SOCIAL SCIENCE (biblical studies, history, home economics, liberal arts/general studies, and political science/government). Biological sciences, biblical studies, and business administration are the strongest academically. Biblical studies, education, and business administration are the largest.

Required: Students must complete at least 122 semester hours, including 78 distributed as follows: 24 hours in Biblical studies, 18 in social sciences, 9 in English, 7 in natural science, 6 in cross-cultural studies, and 3 each in communication, business, logical reasoning, and fine arts. Students must complete at least 40 semester hours in upper-division courses and at least 40 in the major and must maintain a minimum GPA of 2.0.

Special: Students may cross-register with the Coalition of Christian Colleges and Universities and may participate in a co-op program with the College of the Canyons. Internships are offered with local churches, radio stations, and newspapers. A Washington semester, study abroad, dual majors in music plus a second discipline, and a general studies degree are available. The Master's Institute, a 1-year certificate Bible program, is also offered.

Faculty/Classroom: 82% of faculty are male; 18%, female. All teach undergraduates. No introductory courses are taught by graduate students. The average class size in an introductory lecture is 36; in a laboratory, 14; and in a regular course, 11.

Admissions: 84% of the 2005-2006 applicants were accepted. The SAT scores for the 2005-2006 freshman class were: Verbal--19% below 500, 47% between 500 and 599, 25% between 600 and 700, and 9% above 700; Math--26% below 500, 38% between 500 and 599, 32% between 600 and 700, and 5% above 700. The ACT scores were 31% below 21, 16% between 21 and 23, 27% between 24 and 26, 8% between 27 and 28, and 19% above 28. 49% of the current freshmen were in the top fifth of their class; 65% were in the top two fifths. 5 freshmen graduated first in their class.

Requirements: The SAT or ACT is required. In addition, applicants must have completed 4 years of English, 3 each of math and science, 2 of history, and 8 units of electives. A GPA of 2.5 is required. AP and CLEP credits are accepted. Important factors in the admissions decision are personality/intangible qualities, recommendations by school officials, and leadership record.

Procedure: Freshmen are admitted fall and spring. Entrance exams should be taken in the fall. There are early admissions and deferred admissions plans. Early decision applications should be filed by November 15; regular applications, by March 2 for fall entry, deadlines are open for spring entry. There is a $55 fee. Notification of early decision is sent December 22; regular decision, on a rolling basis beginning April 1. Applications are accepted on-line.

Transfer: 129 transfer students enrolled in 2004-2005. Applicants must meet freshman requirements. A maximum of 70 units can be transferred from a junior college; 94 units from a 4-year college. 28 of 122 credits required for the bachelor's degree must be completed at TMC.

Visiting: There are regularly scheduled orientations for prospective students, including class visitation, meetings with faculty, interviews, athletic events, an overnight stay, and college activities. There are guides for informal visits and visitors may sit in on classes and stay overnight. To schedule a visit, contact the Enrollment Office at (800) 568-6428, ext. 3363 or visit@masters.edu.

Financial Aid: In 2005-2006, 92% of all full-time freshmen and 85% of continuing full-time students received some form of financial aid. 66% of full-time freshmen and 69% of continuing full-time students received need-based aid. The average freshman award was $15,645. 19% of undergraduates work part time. Average annual earnings from campus work are $2450. The average financial indebtedness of the 2005 graduate was $13,900. TMC is a member of CSS. The FAFSA and the college's own financial statement are required. The priority date for freshman financial aid applications for fall entry is March 2.

International Students: There are 27 international students enrolled. They must take the TOEFL.

Computers: Wireless access is available. The Master's College has a policy requiring all students to possess a laptop computer. All students have continuous access to the campus wireless network. All students may access the system. There are no time limits and no fees. All students in all academic programs are required to have personal computers.

Graduates: From July 1, 2004 to June 30, 2005, 300 bachelor's degrees were awarded. The most popular majors were biblical studies (27%), business (17%), and education (10%). In an average class, 4% graduate in 3 years or less, 43% graduate in 4 years or less, 56% graduate in 5 years or less, and 58% graduate in 6 years or less. Of the 2004 graduating class, 10% were enrolled in graduate school within 6 months of graduation.

Admissions Contact: Hollie Gorsh, Director of Admissions. A video is available. E-mail: admissions@masters.edu
Web: http://www.masters.edu

MENLO COLLEGE

B-3

Atherton, CA 94027

(650) 543-3753
(800) 55-MENLO; Fax: (650) 543-4476

Full-time: 430 men, 279 women	Faculty: 23
Part-time: 28 men, 32 women	Ph.D.s: 65%
Graduate: none	Student/Faculty: 31 to 1
Year: semesters, summer session	Tuition: $24,000
Application Deadline: open	Room & Board: $9600
Freshman Class: 565 accepted, 195 enrolled	
SAT Verbal/Math: 520/530*	ACT: 21 COMPETITIVE

Menlo College, founded in 1927, is a private college offering programs in management, liberal arts, and mass communication. The library contains 65,000 volumes, 313 microform items, and 600 audio/video tapes/CDs/DVDs, and subscribes to 1200 periodicals including electronic. Computerized library services include the card catalog, interlibrary loans, database searching, Internet access, and laptop Internet portals. Special learning facilities include a learning resource center, radio station, TV station, a newspaper production facility, live/learn center, and the Russell Center for International Learning. The 62-acre campus is in a suburban area 30 miles south of San Francisco. Including any residence halls, there are 23 buildings.

Student Life: 60% of undergraduates are from California. Others are from 23 states, 21 foreign countries, and Canada. 60% are from public schools. 36% are white; 15% Hispanic; 13% Asian American; 10% foreign nationals. The average age of freshmen is 18; all undergraduates, 23. 62% do not continue beyond their first year; 43% remain to graduate.

Housing: 400 students can be accommodated in college housing, which includes single-sex and coed dorms and on-campus apartments. In addition, there are special-interest houses. On-campus housing is guaranteed for all 4 years. 62% of students live on campus; of those, 65% remain on campus on weekends. All students may keep cars.

Activities: There are no fraternities or sororities. There are 75 groups on campus, including animation, art, bagpipe band, cheerleading, chess, choir, chorus, computers, debate, drama, ethnic, film, gay, honors, international, newspaper, opera, pep band, political, professional, radio and TV, religious, social, social service, and student government. Popular campus events include Management Day, Luau, and Celebration of the Goddess.

Sports: There are 8 intercollegiate sports for men and 6 for women, and 4 intramural sports for men and 4 for women. Facilities include 2 swimming pools, a soccer field, tennis courts, a track, a 600-seat gym, a fitness center, a weight facility, and a baseball diamond. The campus stadium seats 1000, the largest auditorium/arena, 220.

Disabled Students: 95% of the campus is accessible. Wheelchair ramps, elevators, special parking, specially equipped rest rooms, lowered drinking fountains, lowered telephones, and special housing are available.

Services: Counseling and information services are available, as is tutoring in every subject. There is a reader service for the blind, and remedial math, reading, and writing.

Campus Safety and Security: Measures include 24-hour foot and vehicle patrol, informal discussions, pamphlets/posters/films, and lighted pathways/sidewalks.

Programs of Study: Menlo confers B.A. and B.S. degrees. Associate degrees are also awarded. Bachelor's degrees are awarded in BUSINESS (business administration and management), COMMUNICATIONS AND THE ARTS (communications), SOCIAL SCIENCE (liberal arts/general studies). Management is the strongest academically and the largest.

Required: All students must complete 59 units in the general education curriculum, including 9 units each of English, math, management, and economics, 7 of science, 6 of diversity, 4 of quantitative skills, and 3 each of American institutions and computer competency. A total of 124 units, including 21 to 30 in the major and 18 in a concentration, and a minimum 2.0 GPA are required to graduate.

Special: Students may earn up to 12 credits through internships. Menlo also offers study abroad in Spain, China, and Chile, dual and student-designed majors, B.A.-B.S. degrees, and an accelerated degree program in management. There are 2 national honor societies, and 1 departmental honors program.

Faculty/Classroom: 60% of faculty are male; 40%, female. All teach undergraduates. The average class size in an introductory lecture is 23; in a laboratory, 20; and in a regular course, 16.

Admissions: The SAT scores for the 2005-2006 freshman class were: Verbal--61% below 500, 35% between 500 and 599, and 4% between 600 and 700; Math--62% below 500, 32% between 500 and 599, 4% between 600 and 700, and 2% above 700. The ACT scores were 59% below 21, 31% between 21 and 23, 6% between 24 and 26, and 4% above 28.

Requirements: The SAT or ACT is required. In addition, a personal essay and letter of recommendation should be submitted. The GED is ac-

cepted. A GPA of 2.5 is required. AP and CLEP credits are accepted. Important factors in the admissions decision are advanced placement or honor courses, evidence of special talent, and leadership record.

Procedure: Freshmen are admitted fall and spring. Entrance exams should be taken during the junior or senior year. There are early decision, deferred admissions, and rolling admissions plans. Application deadlines are open. Notification of early action is sent January 1; regular decision, on a rolling basis. Application fee is $40. 35 early decision candidates were accepted for a recent class. Applications are accepted online.

Transfer: 95 transfer students enrolled in 2004-2005. Transfer applicants must show potential for success indicated by a 2.5 GPA at the college level. Those with fewer than 24 credits must meet freshman requirements. 30 of 124 credits required for the bachelor's degree must be completed at Menlo.

Visiting: There are regularly scheduled orientations for prospective students, including a fall preview with an introduction to college life and college decision making. The spring visit for accepted students provides an in-depth view of Menlo. There are guides for informal visits and visitors may sit in on classes and stay overnight. To schedule a visit, contact the Office of Admissions.

Financial Aid: In 2005-2006, 88% of all full-time freshmen and 93% of continuing full-time students received some form of financial aid. 60% of all full-time students received need-based aid. The average freshman award was $22,754. Need-based scholarships or need-based grants averaged $9566 ($15,950 maximum); need-based self-help aid (loans and jobs) averaged $3032 ($3625 maximum); other non-need-based awards and non-need-based scholarships averaged $14,117 ($37,800 maximum); and other awards averaged $4021 ($15,600 maximum). 60% of undergraduates work part time. Average annual earnings from campus work are $1300. The average financial indebtedness of the 2005 graduate was $21,905. The FAFSA is required. The priority date for freshman financial aid applications for fall entry is March 2.

International Students: There are 84 international students enrolled. The school actively recruits these students. A satisfactory score is required on the written TOEFL. Applicants must also take the SAT or ACT if English is their first language.

Computers: All students may access the system 8 A.M. to 11 P.M. daily. There are no time limits and no fees.

Graduates: From July 1, 2004 to June 30, 2005, 128 bachelor's degrees were awarded. The most popular majors were management (73%), mass communication (15%), and liberal arts (13%).

Admissions Contact: Sara Sato, Director of Admissions.
E-mail: ssargent@menlo.edu Web: www.menlo.edu

MILLS COLLEGE

B-3

Oakland, CA 94613

(510) 430-2135
(800) 87-MILLS; Fax: (510) 430-3314

Full-time: 849 women	Faculty: 90; II A, +$
Part-time: 32 women	Ph.D.s: 91%
Graduate: 95 men, 396 women	Student/Faculty: 9 to 1
Year: semesters	Tuition: $29,990
Application Deadline: February 1	Room & Board: $9880
Freshman Class: 783 applied, 604 accepted, 207 enrolled	
SAT Verbal/Math: 529/555*	ACT: 23 COMPETITIVE

Mills College, founded in 1852, is a private women's college offering instruction in liberal and fine arts, sciences, and teacher preparation. Graduate programs are coeducational. The library contains 230,082 volumes, 28,253 microform items, and 9328 audio/video tapes/CDs/DVDs, and subscribes to 700 periodicals including electronic. Computerized library services include the card catalog, interlibrary loans, database searching, and Internet access. Special learning facilities include an art gallery, a children's school, a small book press, an electronic/computer music studio, a botanical garden, and a computer learning studio. The 135-acre campus is in an urban area 12 miles east of San Francisco. Including any residence halls, there are 84 buildings.

Student Life: 77% of undergraduates are from California. Others are from 38 states, 13 foreign countries, and Canada. 80% are from public schools. 55% are white; 11% African American; 11% Asian American; 11% Hispanic. The average age of freshmen is 19; all undergraduates, 22. 23% do not continue beyond their first year; 67% remain to graduate.

Housing: 503 students can be accommodated in college housing, which includes single-sex and coed dorms, on-campus apartments, and married-student housing. Married student housing is offered on an equal basis to domestic partners of lesbian and gay students, and a student co-op house is available for juniors and seniors. In addition, there are language houses and special-interest houses. On-campus housing is guaranteed for all 4 years. 52% of students live on campus; of those, 75% remain on campus on weekends. All students may keep cars.

Activities: There are no fraternities or sororities. There are 40 groups on campus, including art, band, choir, chorale, chorus, dance, drama, ethnic, gay, honors, international, literary magazine, newspaper, political, professional, religious, social, social service, student government, and yearbook. Popular campus events include Black and White Ball, Fine Arts Festival, and Writer's Harvest.

Sports: Facilities include an 872-seat gym, a weight room/fitness center, athletic fields, an aquatic center, and 6 tennis courts.

Disabled Students: 90% of the campus is accessible. Wheelchair ramps, elevators, special parking, specially equipped rest rooms, special class scheduling, lowered telephones, and special housing are available.

Services: Counseling and information services are available, as is tutoring in every subject. There is a reader service for the blind.

Campus Safety and Security: Measures include 24-hour foot and vehicle patrol, self-defense education, security escort services, and shuttle buses. There are informal discussions, pamphlets/posters/films, emergency telephones, and lighted pathways/sidewalks.

Programs of Study: Mills confers the B.A. degree. Master's and doctoral degrees are also awarded. Bachelor's degrees are awarded in AGRICULTURE (environmental studies), BIOLOGICAL SCIENCE (biochemistry and biology/biological science), BUSINESS (business economics), COMMUNICATIONS AND THE ARTS (art history and appreciation, comparative literature, creative writing, dance, English, French, media arts, modern language, music, and studio art), COMPUTER AND PHYSICAL SCIENCE (chemistry, computer science, and mathematics), ENGINEERING AND ENVIRONMENTAL DESIGN (environmental science), SOCIAL SCIENCE (American studies, anthropology, biopsychology, child psychology/development, economics, ethnic studies, Hispanic American studies, history, international relations, liberal arts/general studies, philosophy, political science/government, psychology, public administration, public affairs, sociology, and women's studies). Art, biology, and political, legal, and economic analysis are the strongest academically. English and psychology are the largest.

Required: To graduate, all students must fulfill general education requirements, earn a total of 34 semester course credits, with 10 to 17 in the major, and maintain a minimum GPA of 2.0. Required courses include English, a second-semester writing course, a quantitative and computational reasoning course, and an information literacy and technology course.

Special: There is cross-registration with the University of California/Berkeley and California State University, among others. Mills offers co-op programs, internships, study abroad, a Washington semester, work-study programs, dual, student-designed, and interdisciplinary majors, including political, legal, and economic analysis. Accelerated degree programs, including 3-2 engineering, a 4+1 M.B.A., and 4+1 interdisciplinary computer science, a general studies degree, credit by exam, and pass/fail options are also offered. There is 1 national honor society, Phi Beta Kappa.

Faculty/Classroom: 41% of faculty are male; 59%, female. All both teach and do research. No introductory courses are taught by graduate students. The average class size in a laboratory is 15 and in a regular course, 12.

Admissions: 77% of the 2005-2006 applicants were accepted. The SAT scores for the 2005-2006 freshman class were: Verbal--19% below 500, 35% between 500 and 599, 29% between 600 and 700, and 17% above 700; Math--27% below 500, 46% between 500 and 599, 24% between 600 and 700, and 3% above 700. 81% of the current freshmen were in the top fifth of their class; 94% were in the top two fifths.

Requirements: The SAT or ACT is required. In addition, SAT Subject tests are recommended. Applicants should graduate from an accredited secondary school or have a GED. An essay is required; an interview, recommended. Mills requires applicants to be in the upper 50% of their class. A GPA of 3.0 is required. AP credits are accepted. Important factors in the admissions decision are advanced placement or honor courses, personality/intangible qualities, and recommendations by school officials.

Procedure: Freshmen are admitted fall and spring. Entrance exams should be taken at least 1 month prior to application. There is a deferred admissions plan. Early decision applications should be filed by November 15; regular applications, by February 1 for fall entry and November 1 for spring entry, along with a $40 fee. Notification of early decision is sent December 20; regular decision, March 30. Applications are accepted on-line.

Transfer: 128 transfer students enrolled in 2004-2005. Transfer applicants with fewer than 24 transferable semester hours should take the SAT or ACT. 12 of 34 credits required for the bachelor's degree must be completed at Mills.

Visiting: There are regularly scheduled orientations for prospective students, consisting of class visits, campus tours, lunch with faculty, financial aid workshops, an admissions interview, and an overnight stay. There are guides for informal visits. To schedule a visit, contact the Admission Office at admission@mills.edu.

Financial Aid: The FAFSA and the college's own financial statement are required. The priority date for freshman financial aid applications for fall entry is February 15.

International Students: There are 49 international students enrolled. The school actively recruits these students. They must score satisfactorily on the TOEFL.

Computers: Internet access is available remotely or on campus via 200 public computers. Wireless access is also available in all residence and administrative buildings. All students may access the system 24 hours a day, year-round. There are no time limits. The fee is $150. It is recommended that students in computer science and book arts have personal computers. A Mac is recommended.

Graduates: From July 1, 2004 to June 30, 2005, 182 bachelor's degrees were awarded. The most popular majors were English (14%), political science (9%), and psychology (7%). 25 companies recruited on campus in 2004-2005.

Admissions Contact: Julie Richardson, Vice President for Enrollment Management. A video is available. E-mail: admission@mills.edu Web: www.mills.edu

MOUNT SAINT MARY'S COLLEGE   C-5

Los Angeles, CA 90049

(310) 954-4250
(800) 999-9893; Fax: (310) 954-4259

Full-time: 20 men, 900 women	Faculty: 74; IIB, -$
Part-time: 2 men, 30 women	Ph.D.s: 51%
Graduate: 70 men, 340 women	Student/Faculty: 12 to 1
Year: semesters	Tuition: $23,594
Application Deadline: February 15	Room & Board: $8492
Freshman Class: n/av	
SATor ACT: required	**VERY COMPETITIVE**

Mount Saint Mary's College, founded in 1925 and affiliated with the Catholic Church, is a private, primarily women's institution that offers programs in the liberal arts and sciences. Some figures in the above capsule and in this profile are approximate. In addition to regional accreditation, The Mount has baccalaureate program accreditation with NASM and NLN. The library contains 132,000 volumes, 320 microform items, and 2520 audio/video tapes/CDs/DVDs, and subscribes to 690 periodicals including electronic. Computerized library services include the card catalog, interlibrary loans, and database searching. Special learning facilities include a learning resource center and art gallery. The 72-acre campus is in an urban area 10 miles west of Los Angeles. Including any residence halls, there are 26 buildings.

Student Life: 89% of undergraduates are from California. Others are from 19 states and 1 foreign country. 74% are from public schools. 44% are Hispanic; 20% Asian American; 18% white. 71% are claim no religious affiliation; 23% Catholic. The average age of freshmen is 18; all undergraduates, 23.

Housing: 482 students can be accommodated in college housing, which includes single-sex dorms. On-campus housing is guaranteed for all 4 years. 56% of students live on campus. All students may keep cars.

Activities: 66% of women belong to 2 local and 1 national sorority. There are no fraternities. There are 29 groups on campus, including art, choir, chorale, chorus, computers, dance, departmental, drama, ethnic, honors, musical theater, newspaper, political, professional, religious, social, social service, student government, and yearbook. Popular campus events include Mary's Day (honors and awards), Horizon's Day, and Spring Sing.

Sports: There are 4 intramural sports for women. Facilities include a pool, tennis courts, exercise and weight rooms, and cardiovascular equipment.

Disabled Students: Wheelchair ramps, elevators, and special parking are available.

Services: Counseling and information services are available, as is tutoring in most subjects. A peer tutoring program is available.

Campus Safety and Security: Measures include 24-hour foot and vehicle patrol, self-defense education, shuttle buses, and informal discussions. There are pamphlets/posters/films and lighted pathways/sidewalks.

Programs of Study: The Mount confers B.A., B.S., and B.A.M. degrees. Associate and master's degrees are also awarded. Bachelor's degrees are awarded in BIOLOGICAL SCIENCE (biochemistry and biology/biological science), BUSINESS (business administration and management), COMMUNICATIONS AND THE ARTS (art, English, French, music, and Spanish), COMPUTER AND PHYSICAL SCIENCE (chemistry and mathematics), EDUCATION (elementary and secondary), HEALTH PROFESSIONS (nursing), SOCIAL SCIENCE (American studies, child psychology/development, gerontology, history, liberal arts/general studies, philosophy, political science/government, psychology, religion, social science, and sociology). Premedicine is the strongest academically. Nursing and biological science are the largest.

Required: Requirements for graduation include completion of 59 units of distribution requirements and 124 total credit hours, with the number of hours in the major varying by department. English courses and a minimum 2.0 GPA are required.

Special: The Mount offers cross-registration with UCLA, internships within the business department, study abroad in Spain, England, and France, a Washington semester through American University, dual and student-designed majors, credit for prior experiences, and pass/fail options. There are 11 national honor societies, a freshman honors program, and 9 departmental honors programs.

Faculty/Classroom: 25% of faculty are male; 75%, female. No introductory courses are taught by graduate students. The average class size in an introductory lecture is 20; in a laboratory, 20; and in a regular course, 19.

Admissions: The SAT scores for a recent freshman class were: Verbal--43% below 500, 46% between 500 and 599, and 11% between 600 and 700; Math--43% below 500, 48% between 500 and 599, and 9% between 600 and 700.

Requirements: The SAT or ACT is required. In addition, applicants must be graduates of an accredited secondary school or have earned the GED, with 16 academic credits and 16 Carnegie units, including 4 years of English literature and composition, 2 or 3 years each of math, science, and social studies, and 1 or 2 years of history. An essay is required, and an interview is recommended. A GPA of 3.25 is required. AP and CLEP credits are accepted. Important factors in the admissions decision are recommendations by school officials, recommendations by alumni, and advanced placement or honor courses.

Procedure: Freshmen are admitted in the fall. Entrance exams should be taken at the end of the junior year or the beginning of the senior year. Applications should be filed by February 15 for fall entry and November 1 for spring entry, along with a $40 fee ($20 online) Notification is sent on a rolling basis.

Transfer: 76 transfer students enrolled in a reecent year. Transfer students must have a minimum 2.25 GPA with at least 24 completed credit hours. 30 of 124 credits required for the bachelor's degree must be completed at The Mount.

Visiting: There are regularly scheduled orientations for prospective students, including workshops, student panels, tours, class visits, and faculty presentations. There are guides for informal visits and visitors may sit in on classes. To schedule a visit, contact the Admissions Office.

Financial Aid: In a recent year, 96% of all full-time freshmen and 92% of continuing full-time students received some form of financial aid. The average freshman award was $14,500. 45% of undergraduates work part time. Average annual earnings from campus work are $1800. The Mount is a member of CSS. The FAFSA is required.

International Students: They must score satisfactorily on the written TOEFL.

Computers: All students may access the system during regular working hours, 4 nights per week, and from 3 P.M. to 11 P.M. on Sunday. There are no time limits and no fees.

Graduates: The most popular majors were nursing (32%), liberal studies (11%), and business (9%). In an average class, 66% graduate in 5 years or less.

Admissions Contact: Dean Kilgour, Dean of Admissions.
E-mail: *admissions@msmc.la.edu* Web: *www.msmc.la.edu*

NATIONAL UNIVERSITY — D-5
La Jolla, CA 92037

	800-NAT-UNIV
	(800) NAT-UNIV; Fax: (858) 642-8709
Full-time: 626 men, 974 women	Faculty: 208
Part-time: 2014 men, 2206 women	Ph.Ds: 86%
Graduate: 7611 men, 12,253 women	Student/Faculty: 8 to 1
Year: see profile	Tuition: $8412
Application Deadline: open	Room & Board: n/app
Freshman Class: n/av	
SAT or ACT: not required	SPECIAL

National University is a private institution that makes lifelong learning opportunities accessible to nontraditional learners in 11 major cities. Courses are offered in an accelerated 1 course per month format. National also offers more than 30 degrees and 300 courses on-line. There are 6 undergraduate and 6 graduate schools. In addition to regional accreditation, National has baccalaureate program accreditation with CCNE, CCTC, and IACBE. The library contains 250,916 volumes, 2.6 million microform items, and 7459 audio/video tapes/CDs/DVDs, and subscribes to 14,111 periodicals including electronic. Computerized library services include the card catalog, interlibrary loans, database searching, Internet access, and laptop Internet portals. Special learning facilities include a learning resource center and TV station. The 880,228-square-foot campus is in an urban area 3 miles northeast of downtown San Diego.

Student Life: 94% of undergraduates are from California. Others are from 47 states, 76 foreign countries, and Canada. 55% are white; 17% Hispanic; 10% African American. The average age of freshmen is 29; all undergraduates, 32. 71% of freshmen remain to graduate.

Housing: There are no residence halls. All of students commute. Alcohol is not permitted. All students may keep cars.

Activities: There are no fraternities or sororities. There is 1 group on campus, radio and TV.

Sports: There is no sports program at National.

Disabled Students: All of the campus is accessible. Wheelchair ramps, elevators, special parking, specially equipped rest rooms, special class scheduling, lowered drinking fountains, and lowered telephones are available.

Services: There is remedial math, reading, and writing.

Campus Safety and Security: Measures include 24-hour foot and vehicle patrol and lighted pathways/sidewalks.

Programs of Study: National confers B.A., B.S., B.B.A., and B.S.N. degrees. Associate and master's degrees are also awarded. Bachelor's degrees are awarded in BIOLOGICAL SCIENCE (life science), BUSINESS (accounting, banking and finance, management science, organizational behavior, and organizational leadership and management), COMMUNICATIONS AND THE ARTS (design, English, and multimedia), COMPUTER AND PHYSICAL SCIENCE (computer science, earth science, information sciences and systems, mathematics, and software engineering), ENGINEERING AND ENVIRONMENTAL DESIGN (construction engineering, construction management, and environmental science), HEALTH PROFESSIONS (allied health and nursing), SOCIAL SCIENCE (behavioral science, criminal justice, early childhood studies, history, interdisciplinary studies, international studies, liberal arts/general studies, prelaw, psychology, and sociology). Criminal justice, psychology, and interdisciplinary studies have the largest enrollments.

Required: To graduate, students must complete 180 quarter units, including 36 upper-division quarter units with a minimum GPA of 2.0. A minimum of 45 quarter units in the major and 70.5 in the core curriculum are required.

Special: Cross-registration with California Community Colleges is possible. National offers all degree programs in an accelerated format of 1 course per month. There are 3 national honor societies.

Faculty/Classroom: 67% of faculty are male; 33%, female. All both teach and do research. No introductory courses are taught by graduate students. The average class size in an introductory lecture is 18 and in a regular course, 18.

Requirements: Graduation from an accredited secondary school or satisfactory scores on the GED are required for admission. AP and CLEP credits are accepted.

Procedure: Freshmen are admitted to all sessions. There is a deferred admissions plan and a rolling admissions plan. Application deadlines are open. Application fee is $60. Notification is sent on a weekly basis. Applications are accepted on-line.

Transfer: 4754 transfer students enrolled in 2004-2005. Transfer applicants must have a minimum GPA of 2.0. Transcripts from all previous institutions attended must be submitted and an interview is required. 45 of 180 quarter units required for the bachelor's degree must be completed at National.

Visiting: There are guides for informal visits and visitors may sit in on classes. To schedule a visit, contact Megan Magee at *advisor@nu.edu*.

Financial Aid: In 2005-2006, 80% of all full-time freshmen received some form of financial aid, including need-based aid. Need-based scholarships or need-based grants averaged $3412 ($6825 maximum); need-based self-help aid (loans and jobs) averaged $3825 ($4720 maximum); and other non-need-based awards and non-need-based scholarships averaged $1600 (maximum). The FAFSA is required. Thereis a rolling deadline for filing freshman financial aid applications for fall entry.

International Students: There are 25 international students enrolled. The school actively recruits these students. They must take the TOEFL or the MELAB.

Computers: Wireless access is available. 2500 computers are available to all students. Computer equipment and network access for student use is provided in the computer center, labs, and library. All students may access the system Monday through Friday, 8 A.M. to 9 P.M., and Saturday, 8 A.M. to 2 P.M. There are no time limits and no fees.

Graduates: From July 1, 2004 to June 30, 2005, 1015 bachelor's degrees were awarded. The most popular majors were business administration (21%), psychology (9%), and criminal justice (9%). In an average class, 71% graduate in 3 years or less.

Admissions Contact: Megan Magee, Associate Regional Dean - San Diego. E-mail: *advisor@nu.edu* Web: *www.nu.edu*

NEW COLLEGE OF CALIFORNIA — B-3
San Francisco, CA 94110

	(415) 437-3460
	(888) 437-3460; Fax: (415) 437-3470
Full-time: 311 men, 331 women	Faculty: 16
Part-time: 3 men, 4 women	Ph.Ds: 20%
Graduate: 153 men, 362 women	Student/Faculty: 11 to 1
Year: semesters, summer session	Tuition: $12,842
Application Deadline: August	Room & Board: n/app
Freshman Class: 72 accepted, 50 enrolled	
SAT or ACT: not required	NONCOMPETITIVE

New College of California, founded in 1971, is a private college offering a liberal arts program. Some figures in the above capsule and in this profile are approximate. The library contains 30,000 volumes. Computerized library services include the card catalog, interlibrary loans, and database searching. Special learning facilities include a learning resource center, a video-editing lab, and a theater. The 2-acre campus is in an urban area in the mission district of San Francisco. There are 3 buildings.

Student Life: 70% of undergraduates are from California. Students are from 10 states, 5 foreign countries, and Canada. 80% are from public schools. 61% are white; 16% African American; 10% Hispanic. The average age of freshmen is 25; all undergraduates, 28. 30% do not continue beyond their first year; 70% remain to graduate.

Housing: There are no residence halls. All of students commute. Alcohol is not permitted.

Activities: There are no fraternities or sororities. There are 10 groups on campus, including band, drama, ethnic, film, gay, literary magazine, newspaper, political, professional, social, social service, and student government. Popular campus events include an arts and social change showcase, movie nights, and acoustic band nights.

Sports: There is 1 intercollegiate sport for men.

Disabled Students: 60% of the campus is accessible. Wheelchair ramps, specially equipped rest rooms, and special class scheduling are available.

Services: There is remedial math, reading, and writing.

Campus Safety and Security: Measures include front-desk security in all buildings.

Programs of Study: New College confers the B.A. degree. Master's degrees are also awarded. Bachelor's degrees are awarded in COMMUNICATIONS AND THE ARTS (dramatic arts, English, film arts, fine arts, music, and Spanish), SOCIAL SCIENCE (anthropology, political science/government, psychology, and social science). Humanities and is the strongest academically, and has the largest enrollment.

Required: To graduate, students must complete at least 120 credit hours, including 30 in the major. Requirements include 6 units of core humanities and 3 units each of arts, literature or writing, social sciences, scientific reasoning, quantitative reasoning, research methods, a practicum, and a senior project. A minimum GPA of 2.0 is required.

Special: Internships include a required 3-unit practicum on or off campus. New College offers work-study programs, independent study, study abroad in Mexico and Nepal, an accelerated degree program, student-designed majors, and pass/fail options. Students can earn up to 30 units of credit for prior life, military, and work experience.

Faculty/Classroom: 60% of faculty are male; 40%, female. 80% teach undergraduates. The average class size in an introductory lecture is 12; in a laboratory, 10; and in a regular course, 12.

Requirements: New College requires graduation from an accredited secondary school; the GED is also accepted. An essay is required. AP and CLEP credits are accepted.

Procedure: Freshmen are admitted fall, spring, and summer. There are a deferred admissions and rolling admissions plan. Applications should be filed by late August for fall entry, mid January for spring entry, and early June for summer entry, along with a $50 fee. The college accepts all applicants. Notification is sent on a rolling basis.

Transfer: 318 transfer students enrolled in 2004-2005. Students can transfer into the 4-year B.A. Humanities program with up to 90 units from other accredited institutions of higher education. For entrance into B.A. completion programs, at least 54 transferable units (68-72 preferred) are required. 30 of 120 credits required for the bachelor's degree must be completed at New College.

Visiting: There are regularly scheduled orientations for prospective students, consisting of monthly open houses. There are guides for informal visits and visitors may sit in on classes. To schedule a visit, contact the Administration Director at (415) 437-3458.

Financial Aid: New College is a member of CSS. The FAFSA and the college's own financial statement are required. Check with the school for current application deadlines.

International Students: They must score satisfactorily on the written TOEFL.

Computers: All students may access the system. There are no time limits and no fees.

Graduates: Of a recent graduating class, 30% were enrolled in graduate school within 6 months of graduation and 75% were employed.

Admissions Contact: Violetta Babich, Student Service Counselor. E-mail: *admissions@newcollege.edu* Web: *www.newcollege.edu*

NOTRE DAME DE NAMUR UNIVERSITY B-3
Belmont, CA 94002-1908

	(650) 508-3600
	(800) 263-0545; Fax: (650) 508-3426
Full-time: 246 men, 385 women	**Faculty:** 44; IIA, -$
Part-time: 85 men, 174 women	**Ph.D.s:** 75%
Graduate: 154 men, 544 women	**Student/Faculty:** 14 to 1
Year: semesters, summer session	**Tuition:** $22,720
Application Deadline: see profile	**Room & Board:** $10,070
Freshman Class: 643 applied, 617 accepted, 145 enrolled	
SAT Verbal/Math: 480/490*	**ACT:** 19 **LESS COMPETITIVE**

The College of Notre Dame, founded in 1851, is an independent liberal arts institution affiliated with the Roman Catholic Church. Figures in above capsule are approximate. In addition to regional accreditation, NDNU has baccalaureate program accreditation with NASM and

NCATE. The library contains 100,000 volumes, 70,000 microform items, and 8000 audio/video tapes/CDs/DVDs, and subscribes to 750 periodicals including electronic. Computerized library services include the card catalog, interlibrary loans, and database searching. Special learning facilities include an art gallery and the Archives of Modern Christian Art. The 80-acre campus is in a suburban area 25 miles south of San Francisco. Including any residence halls, there are 23 buildings.

Student Life: 80% of undergraduates are from California. Others are from 23 states, 18 foreign countries, and Canada. 70% are from public schools. 38% are white; 25% Asian American; 17% foreign nationals; 13% Hispanic. 55% are Catholic; 30% claim no religious affiliation. The average age of freshmen is 18; all undergraduates, 24. 19% do not continue beyond their first year; 60% remain to graduate.

Housing: 300 students can be accommodated in college housing, which includes coed dorms and on-campus apartments. On-campus housing is guaranteed for all 4 years. 63% of students commute. All students may keep cars.

Activities: There are no fraternities or sororities. There are 27 groups on campus, including art, band, cheerleading, choir, chorale, chorus, computers, dance, drama, ethnic, gay, honors, international, jazz band, literary magazine, musical theater, newspaper, orchestra, photography, political, professional, religious, social, social service, student government, symphony, and yearbook. Popular campus events include Honors Day, Ralston Concert Series, and Fiesta Latina.

Sports: There are 5 intercollegiate sports for men and 6 for women, and 2 intramural sports for men and 2 for women. Facilities include a gym, a recreation center, tennis courts, a soccer field, a weight room, a swimming pool, a par course, an arcade, and pool and Ping Pong tables.

Disabled Students: 90% of the campus is accessible. Wheelchair ramps, special parking, specially equipped rest rooms, and special class scheduling are available.

Services: Counseling and information services are available, as is tutoring in every subject. There is remedial math, reading, and writing.

Campus Safety and Security: Measures include 24-hour foot and vehicle patrol, security escort services, informal discussions, and pamphlets/posters/films. There are lighted pathways/sidewalks.

Programs of Study: NDNU confers B.A., B.S., B.F.A., and B.Mus. degrees. Associate and master's degrees are also awarded. Bachelor's degrees are awarded in BIOLOGICAL SCIENCE (biochemistry and biology/biological science), BUSINESS (accounting, banking and finance, business administration and management, business economics, international business management, and marketing/retailing/merchandising), COMMUNICATIONS AND THE ARTS (art, communications, dramatic arts, English, fine arts, French, graphic design, and music), COMPUTER AND PHYSICAL SCIENCE (computer science, information sciences and systems, and mathematics), EDUCATION (social studies), HEALTH PROFESSIONS (predentistry, premedicine, prepharmacy, and preveterinary science), SOCIAL SCIENCE (history, human services, humanities, Latin American studies, liberal arts/general studies, philosophy, political science/government, prelaw, psychology, religion, social science, and sociology). Biology, premedicine, and English are the strongest academically. Business administration, liberal studies, and psychology are the largest.

Required: All students must complete general education requirements, 3 units of career development, and a writing proficiency exam. American history is required for those students who have not completed this course in an American high school. A total of 124 semester units with an overall GPA of 2.0 is required to graduate.

Special: The college offers a Washington semester through Trinity College as well as an exchange program with Emmanuel College in Boston. Internships, accelerated degree programs in business administration and human service, B.A.-B.S. degrees in biology and biochemistry, a 3-2 engineering degree with Boston University, dual and student-designed majors, a general studies degree, credit for military experience, and pass/fail options are offered. Study abroad is available in 7 countries. Nondegree study is possible. There are 3 national honor societies and a freshman honors program.

Faculty/Classroom: 46% of faculty are male; 54%, female. 71% teach undergraduates. No introductory courses are taught by graduate students. The average class size in an introductory lecture is 25; in a laboratory, 10; and in a regular course, 15.

Admissions: 96% of the 2005-2006 applicants were accepted. The SAT scores for the 2005-2006 freshman class were: Verbal--58% below 500, 29% between 500 and 599, 12% between 600 and 700, and 1% above 700; Math--51% below 500, 37% between 500 and 599, 11% between 600 and 700, and 1% above 700. The ACT scores were 63% below 21, 10% between 21 and 23, 17% between 24 and 26, and 10% between 27 and 28. 30% of the current freshmen were in the top fifth of their class; 56% were in the top two fifths.

Requirements: The SAT or ACT is required. The average GPA is a 3.0. Applicants should have completed 13 Carnegie units, including 4 years of high school English, 2 each of math, history/social studies, foreign language, and 1 of lab science. In addition, students should have 1 year in 3 of these areas beyond the basic requirements. An essay is required. An audition is required for music programs. A GPA of 2.0 is required. AP and CLEP credits are accepted. Important factors in the admissions decision are advanced placement or honor courses, evidence of special talent, and leadership record.

Procedure: Freshmen are admitted to all sessions. Entrance exams should be taken by the December test date of the senior year. There are early admissions and deferred admissions plans. There is a rolling admissions plan. Notification is sent on a rolling basis, starting December 1. Check with ths school for current application deadlines and fee.

Transfer: 115 transfer students enrolled in 2004-2005. Transfer applicants must have a 2.0 GPA to be considered for admission. 30 of 124 credits required for the bachelor's degree must be completed at NDNU.

Visiting: There are regularly scheduled orientations for prospective students, consisting of tours and information on student life, financial aid, and academics. There are guides for informal visits and visitors may sit in on classes and stay overnight. To schedule a visit, contact the Admission Office.

Financial Aid: In 2005-2006, 88% of all full-time freshmen received some form of financial aid. 76% of full-time freshmen received need-based aid. The average freshman award was $19,212. NDNU is a member of CSS. The FAFSA and the college's own financial statement are required. Check with the school for current deadlines.

International Students: The school actively recruits these students. A satisfactory score on the TOEFL is required.

Computers: All students may access the system 7 days a week. There are no time limits and no fees.

Graduates: In an average class, 56% graduate in 4 years or less.

Admissions Contact: Katy Murphy, Dean of Enrollment.
E-mail: *admissions@ndnu.edu* Web: *www.ndnu.edu*

OCCIDENTAL COLLEGE   C-5
Los Angeles, CA 90041

(323) 259-2700
(800) 825-5262; Fax: (323) 341-4875

Full-time: 777 men, 1017 women	Faculty: 145; IIB, +$
Part-time: 12 men, 13 women	Ph.D.s: 97%
Graduate: 10 men, 10 women	Student/Faculty: 12 to 1
Year: semesters, summer session	Tuition: $31,513
Application Deadline: January 10	Room & Board: $8672
Freshman Class: 5121 applied, 2086 accepted, 436 enrolled	
SAT Verbal/Math: 640/650*	ACT: 29 MOST COMPETITIVE

Occidental College, founded in 1887, is a private nonsectarian school of liberal arts and sciences. The library contains 486,241 volumes, 416,081 microform items, and 17,892 audio/video tapes/CDs/DVDs, and subscribes to 1434 periodicals including electronic. Computerized library services include the card catalog, interlibrary loans, database searching, and Internet access. Special learning facilities include a learning resource center, art gallery, radio station, theater, art studio, ornithology collection, physics, plasma, and optic labs, green house, and geology collection. The 120-acre campus is in an urban area in Los Angeles. Including any residence halls, there are 44 buildings.

Student Life: 51% of undergraduates are from California. Others are from 45 states, 26 foreign countries, and Canada. 59% are from public schools. 62% are white; 16% Hispanic; 14% Asian American. 35% are Protestant; 30% claim no religious affiliation; 19% Catholic; 11% Jewish. The average age of freshmen is 18; all undergraduates, 20. 8% do not continue beyond their first year; 84% remain to graduate.

Housing: 1320 students can be accommodated in college housing, which includes single-sex and coed dormitories and fraternity houses. In addition, there are special-interest houses, women's center, and multicultural hall. On-campus housing is guaranteed for the freshman year only and is available on a lottery system for upperclassmen. 70% of students live on campus; of those, 60% remain on campus on weekends. All students may keep cars.

Activities: 6% of men belong to 3 national fraternities; 13% of women belong to 2 local and 2 national sororities. There are 109 groups on campus, including art, cheerleading, chess, choir, chorale, dance, debate, drama, ethnic, film, forensics, gay, honors, international, investment, jazz band, literary magazine, musical theater, newspaper, orchestra, photography, political, professional, radio and TV, religious, social, social service, student government, symphony, and yearbook. Popular campus events include Da Getaway, Black History Month, and Taste of Oxy.

Sports: There are 9 intercollegiate sports for men and 9 for women, and 4 intramural sports for men and 4 for women. Facilities include soccer, baseball, and softball fields, an all-weather track, football field, tennis courts, an outdoor pool, a dance studio, a sports medicine center, 2 gyms, and a fitness center.

Disabled Students: 80% of the campus is accessible. Wheelchair ramps, elevators, special parking, specially equipped rest rooms, lowered drinking fountains, and lowered telephones are available.

Services: Counseling and information services are available, as is tutoring in most subjects. Peer and faculty advisers are available through the Center for Academic Excellence.

Campus Safety and Security: Measures include 24-hour foot and vehicle patrol, security escort services, shuttle buses, and informal discussions. There are pamphlets/posters/films, emergency telephones, lighted pathways/sidewalks, residence halls are always locked and a whistle alert program is available.

Programs of Study: Oxy confers the A.B. degree. Master's degrees are also awarded. Bachelor's degrees are awarded in BIOLOGICAL SCIENCE (biochemistry and biology/biological science), COMMUNICATIONS AND THE ARTS (art history and appreciation, comparative literature, dramatic arts, French, German, languages, music, and Spanish), COMPUTER AND PHYSICAL SCIENCE (chemistry, geochemistry, geology, geophysics and seismology, mathematics, and physics), SOCIAL SCIENCE (American studies, anthropology, Asian/Oriental studies, cognitive science, economics, history, international relations, philosophy, physical fitness/movement, political science/government, psychobiology, psychology, religion, sociology, urban studies, and women's studies). Social sciences, biology, and chemistry are the strongest academically. Social sciences, English, and diplomacy and world affairs are the largest.

Required: To graduate, students must complete 32 courses of 4 semester hours each and maintain a minimum GPA of 2.0. In addition, all students must fulfill core course requirements in foreign language, fine arts, writing proficiency; 12 units are required in science and math and cultural studies. To graduate, all students must complete a comprehensive exam; some majors require a thesis.

Special: Cross-registration is permitted with the California Institute of Technology and the Art Center College of Design. Students may study abroad in 41 countries in Europe, Asia, Africa, and Latin America. Opportunities are provided for internships, a Washington semester, a U.N. semester in New York City, dual and student-designed majors, a 3-2 engineering degree with the California Institute of Technology, a 3-3 law program with Columbia, a 4-2 biotech program with Keck, and an exchange program with Spelman and Morehouse. There are 8 national honor societies, including Phi Beta Kappa.

Faculty/Classroom: 54% of faculty are male; 46%, female. All both teach and do research. No introductory courses are taught by graduate students. The average class size in an introductory lecture is 21; in a laboratory, 16; and in a regular course, 20.

Admissions: 41% of the 2005-2006 applicants were accepted. The SAT scores for the 2005-2006 freshman class were: Verbal--3% below 500, 20% between 500 and 599, 55% between 600 and 700, and 22% above 700; Math--2% below 500, 18% between 500 and 599, 56% between 600 and 700, and 24% above 700. 80% of the current freshmen were in the top fifth of their class; 96% were in the top two fifths. 9 freshmen graduated first in their class.

Requirements: The SAT or ACT is required. In addition, applicants should be high school graduates of high academic standing with 4 years of English, 4 of math, 3 each of foreign language and science, and 2 each of social studies and history. The GED is accepted. An essay is required and an interview is recommended. AP credits are accepted. Important factors in the admissions decision are extracurricular activities record, advanced placement or honor courses, and recommendations by school officials.

Procedure: Freshmen are admitted in the fall. Entrance exams should be taken no later than December of the senior year. There are early decision and deferred admissions plans. Early decision applications should be filed by November 15; regular applications, by January 10 for fall entry, along with a $50 fee. Notification of early decision is sent December 15; regular decision, April 1. 47 early decision candidates were accepted for the 2005-2006 class. 234 applicants were on the 2005 waiting list; 24 were admitted. Applications are accepted on-line.

Transfer: 53 transfer students enrolled in 2004-2005. Students must have at least a B average (3.0 GPA) in all courses submitted for transfer credit. The SAT or ACT is required. The application deadline is March 15 for the fall, October 15 for the spring. 64 of 128 credits required for the bachelor's degree must be completed at Oxy.

Visiting: There are regularly scheduled orientations for prospective students, including campus tours Monday through Friday at 10:30 A.M. and 3 P.M., followed by information sessions with an admission officer at 11:30 A.M. and 4 P.M. There are guides for informal visits and visitors may sit in on classes and stay overnight. To schedule a visit, contact the Office of Admission .

Financial Aid: In 2005-2006, 78% of all full-time freshmen and 73% of continuing full-time students received some form of financial aid. 48% of full-time freshmen and 56% of continuing full-time students received need-based aid. The average freshman award was $23,949. 42% of undergraduates work part time. The average financial indebtedness of the 2005 graduate was $15,943. The CSS/Profile or FAFSA and non-custodial parent's statement and business farm supplement are required. The deadline for filing freshman financial aid applications for fall entry is February 1.

International Students: There are 64 international students enrolled. The school actively recruits these students. They must score satisfactorily on the written TOEFL or on the electronic version and also take the SAT or the ACT.

Computers: Wireless access is available. The entire campus is wireless. In addition, students have access to 300 PCs in resdience halls, the library, and the computer center. All students are provided with an email account and Internet access. All students may access the system at any time. There are no time limits and no fees.

Graduates: From July 1, 2004 to June 30, 2005, 438 bachelor's degrees were awarded. The most popular majors were psychology (11%), diplomacy and world affairs (9%), and English (9%). In an average class, 75% graduate in 4 years or less, 80% graduate in 5 years or less, and 84% graduate in 6 years or less. Of the 2004 graduating class, 28% were enrolled in graduate school within 6 months of graduation.

Admissions Contact: Vince Cuseo, Director of Admission.
E-mail: *admission@oxy.edu* Web: *www.oxy.edu*

OTIS COLLEGE OF ART AND DESIGN

C-2

Los Angeles, CA 90045

(310) 665-6820
(800) 527-6847; Fax: (310) 665-6821

Full-time: 355 men, 655 women	**Faculty:** 38
Part-time: 10 men, 15 women	**Ph.D.s:** 71%
Graduate: 15 men, 35 women	**Student/Faculty:** 27 to 1
Year: semesters, summer session	**Tuition:** $27,546
Application Deadline: open	**Room & Board:** n/app
Freshman Class: n/av	
SAT or ACT: required	**SPECIAL**

Otis College of Art and Design, founded in 1918, is a private college offering undergraduate programs in fine arts, ceramics, graphic design and illustration, environmental design, fashion design, toy design, and digital media design and graduate programs in fine arts and writing. As part of their instruction, students work directly with professional artists, designers, critics, and writers. Enrollment figures in the above capsule are approximate. There are 3 undergraduate schools and 1 graduate school. In addition to regional accreditation, Otis has baccalaureate program accreditation with NASAD. The library contains 42,000 volumes and 2500 audio/video tapes/CDs/DVDs, and subscribes to 150 periodicals including electronic. Computerized library services include the card catalog and database searching. Special learning facilities include an art gallery and a photographic darkroom, printmaking studios, a fine books press room, a woodworking studio, a digital imaging room, a metalworking shop, and multiuse studios. The 5-acre campus is in an urban area on the west side of Los Angeles. There are 3 buildings.

Student Life: 72% of undergraduates are from California. Students are from 50 states, 32 foreign countries, and Canada. 75% are from public schools. 33% are white; 30% Asian American; 12% foreign nationals; 12% Hispanic. The average age of all undergraduates is 22. 31% do not continue beyond their first year.

Housing: There are no residence halls. All students commute. Alcohol is not permitted. All students may keep cars.

Activities: There are no fraternities or sororities. There are some groups and organizations on campus, including literary magazine, newspaper, and student government. Popular campus events include gallery openings, a yearly fashion design show, and a student leadership retreat.

Sports: There is no sports program at Otis.

Disabled Students: All of the campus is accessible. Wheelchair ramps, elevators, special parking, specially equipped rest rooms, lowered drinking fountains, and lowered telephones are available.

Services: Counseling and information services are available, as is tutoring in most subjects. There is remedial math, reading, and writing.

Campus Safety and Security: Measures include 24-hour foot and vehicle patrol, self-defense education, security escort services, and informal discussions. There are pamphlets/posters/films, emergency telephones, and lighted pathways/sidewalks.

Programs of Study: Otis confers the B.F.A. degree. Master's degrees are also awarded. Bachelor's degrees are awarded in COMMUNICATIONS AND THE ARTS (advertising, design, graphic design, illustration, painting, photography, and toy design), COMPUTER AND PHYSICAL SCIENCE (digital arts/technology), ENGINEERING AND ENVIRONMENTAL DESIGN (environmental design), SOCIAL SCIENCE (fashion design and technology). Graphic design and digital media are the strongest academically. Digital media design, communication arts (graphic design and illustration), and fashion design are the largest.

Required: The Bachelor of Fine Arts is awarded to students in good academic standing who have successfully completed no less than 130 credits, of which a minimum of 30 are in the liberal arts, and 12 in the history of art and design. Graduation requirements include course work in computer literacy, English, humanities, math, biological or physical sciences, and social science.

Special: Study abroad is available in London, Paris, and Stockholm. Internships and independent study are also available. There is a freshman honors program.

Faculty/Classroom: 45% of faculty are male; 55%, female. All teach undergraduates.

Requirements: The SAT or ACT is required. In addition, applicants must be graduates of an accredited secondary school or have a GED

certificate, and submit a portfolio. Interviews are recommended for students, and essays are required. Applicants must have 4 units of English, 3 of math, 2 each of science (1 lab) and history, and 1 of social studies. A GPA of 2.5 is required. AP credits are accepted.

Procedure: Freshmen are admitted fall and spring. Entrance exams should be taken in the fall. There is a rolling admissions plan. Early decision application should be filed by February 15; application deadlines are open for regular decision. Application fee is $50. Applications are accepted on-line.

Transfer: 170 transfer students enrolled in a recent year. Transfer students must have a minimum 2.5 GPA and submit high school and college transcripts, an essay, and a statement of good standing from prior institutions. A portfolio is required. An interview is recommended. 62 of 130 credits required for the bachelor's degree must be completed at Otis.

Visiting: There are regularly scheduled orientations for prospective students, including a campus tour and departmental, portfolio, and financial aid presentations. There are guides for informal visits and visitors may sit in on classes. To schedule a visit, contact the Admissions Office.

Financial Aid: In a recent year, 72% of all full-time freshmen and 74% of continuing full-time students received some form of financial aid. 64% of full-time freshmen and 63% of continuing full-time students received need-based aid. The average freshman award was $9899. Need-based scholarships or need-based grants averaged $7927; need-based self-help aid (loans and jobs) averaged $2340; and other non-need-based awards and non-need-based scholarships averaged $3558. The average financial indebtedness of the recent year's graduate was $25,700. The FAFSA and the state aid form are required. The priority date for freshman financial aid applications for fall entry is February 15.

International Students: The school actively recruits these students. A satisfactory score is required on the written TOEFL. Students must also take the SAT or ACT. Students from countries where English is the official language should take the ACT or SAT, not the TOEFL.

Computers: All students may access the system. There are no time limits and no fees. It is strongly recommended that all students have a PC.

Graduates: In a recent year, 163 bachelor's degrees were awarded. In an average class, 35% graduate in 4 years or less, 3% graduate in 5 years or less, and 2% graduate in 6 years or less.

Admissions Contact: Marc D. Meredith, Dean of Admissions.
E-mail: *admissions@otis.edu* Web: *http://www.otis.edu*

PACIFIC UNION COLLEGE

B-2

Angwin, CA 94508-9707

(707) 965-6336
(800) 862-7080; Fax: (707) 965-6432

Full-time: 613 men, 677 women	**Faculty:** 80
Part-time: 51 men, 81 women	**Ph.D.s:** 56%
Graduate: 2 women	**Student/Faculty:** 16 to 1
Year: quarters, summer session	**Tuition:** $19,125
Application Deadline: open	**Room & Board:** $5430
Freshman Class: 2173 applied, 628 accepted, 347 enrolled	
SAT Verbal/Math: 585/525*	**ACT:** 23 **VERY COMPETITIVE+**

Pacific Union College, founded in 1888, is a private college affiliated with the Seventh-day Adventist Church, offering programs in liberal arts, religion, business, health science, and teacher preparation, among others. In addition to regional accreditation, PUC has baccalaureate program accreditation with CAADE, CCTC, IACBE, CSWE, NASM, and NLN. The library contains 144,069 volumes, 125,268 microform items, and 6267 audio/video tapes/CDs/DVDs, and subscribes to 805 periodicals including electronic. Computerized library services include the card catalog, interlibrary loans, database searching, Internet access, and laptop Internet portals. Special learning facilities include a learning resource center, art gallery, natural history museum, radio station, video production studio, an observatory, and a marin field station. The 1500-acre campus is in a rural area 70 miles north of San Francisco. Including any residence halls, there are 60 buildings.

Student Life: 80% of undergraduates are from California. Others are from 37 states, 18 foreign countries, and Canada. 44% are white; 23% Asian American; 12% Hispanic. Most are claim no religious affiliation. The average age of freshmen is 19; all undergraduates, 21.

Housing: 1344 students can be accommodated in college housing, which includes single-sex dorms and married-student housing. On-campus housing is guaranteed for the freshman year only. 80% of students live on campus. Alcohol is not permitted. All students may keep cars.

Activities: There are no fraternities or sororities. There are 50 groups on campus, including academic interest groups, art, band, campus ministries, chess, choir, chorale, computers, drama, ethnic, film, honors, jazz band, literary magazine, newspaper, orchestra, photography, political, radio and TV, religious, social, student government, symphony, and yearbook. Popular campus events include picnic and ski days, All-College Get-Acquainted Party, and Fall Festival.

Sports: There are 3 intercollegiate sports for men and 3 for women, and 6 intramural sports for men and 6 for women. Facilities include a

gym, a pool, a stadium, lighted tennis courts, and 3 athletic fields for softball, soccer, volleyball, flagball, and track and field.

Disabled Students: 95% of the campus is accessible. Wheelchair ramps, elevators, special parking, specially equipped rest rooms, and special class scheduling are available.

Services: Counseling and information services are available, as is tutoring in most subjects. There is a reader service for the blind and remedial math and writing.

Campus Safety and Security: Measures include 24-hour foot and vehicle patrol, self-defense education, security escort services, and informal discussions. There are pamphlets/posters/films, emergency telephones, lighted pathways/sidewalks, and a safety committee.

Programs of Study: PUC confers B.A., B.S., B.B.A., B.Mus., B.S.Med.Tech., and B.S.W. degrees. Associate and master's degrees are also awarded. Bachelor's degrees are awarded in BIOLOGICAL SCIENCE (biology/biological science and biophysics), BUSINESS (business administration and management), COMMUNICATIONS AND THE ARTS (communications, English, fine arts, French, graphic design, journalism, music, photography, public relations, radio/television technology, and Spanish), COMPUTER AND PHYSICAL SCIENCE (applied mathematics, chemistry, computer science, mathematics, natural sciences, and physics), EDUCATION (early childhood and physical), ENGINEERING AND ENVIRONMENTAL DESIGN (airline piloting and navigation, electrical/electronics engineering technology, and graphic arts technology), HEALTH PROFESSIONS (nursing), SOCIAL SCIENCE (history, psychology, religion, social studies, social work, and theological studies). Sciences and behavioral science are the strongest academically. Nursing and business administration are the largest.

Required: To graduate, a student must complete a minimum of 192 quarter hours, including 60 in upper-level courses. The student must maintain a minimum GPA of 2.0. A general education core curriculum includes courses in history, scientific revolutions, statistics, English, and Great Books.The required total hours in the major and the general education requirements vary according to the major. A religion course is required, as is a thesis in some programs.

Special: Students may study abroad in Austria, Spain, France, Argentina, and Italy, earn B.A.-B.S. degrees, take dual majors, and pursue a major in interdisciplinary studies. Internships (social work, education, and ministerial field experiences) and accelerated degree programs in business management, early childhood education, and achieving California teaching credentials are also offered. The college offers nondegree study and credit for life, military, and work experience. There are 5 national honor societies, and a freshman honors program.

Faculty/Classroom: 61% of faculty are male; 39%, female. All teach undergraduates. The average class size in an introductory lecture is 19; in a laboratory, 18; and in a regular course, 17.

Admissions: 29% of the 2005-2006 applicants were accepted. The SAT scores for the 2005-2006 freshman class were: Verbal--42% below 500, 36% between 500 and 599, 19% between 600 and 700, and 3% above 700; Math--42% below 500, 36% between 500 and 599, 19% between 600 and 700, and 3% above 700. The ACT scores were 42% below 21, 23% between 21 and 23, 23% between 24 and 26, 6% between 27 and 28, and 5% above 28. 28% of the current freshmen were in the top fifth of their class; 52% were in the top two fifths.

Requirements: The SAT or ACT is recommended. Scores are used only for advising purposes. Candidates for admission should have completed 4 years of English, 2 of math, and 1 each of science and history. A GPA of 2.3 is required. AP and CLEP credits are accepted. Important factors in the admissions decision are recommendations by school officials, leadership record, and advanced placement or honor courses.

Procedure: Freshmen are admitted to all sessions. Entrance exams should be taken in the junior or senior year. There is a rolling admissions plan. Application deadlines are open. Application fee is $30. Applications are accepted on-line.

Transfer: Admission requirements are the same as for nontransfer students. 36 of 192 credits required for the bachelor's degree must be completed at PUC.

Visiting: There are regularly scheduled orientations for prospective students. There are guides for informal visits and visitors may sit in on classes and stay overnight. To schedule a visit, contact the Admissions Office at (707) 965-6425.

Financial Aid: In 2005-2006, 100% of all full-time freshmen and 99% of continuing full-time students received some form of financial aid. 95% of full-time freshmen and 64% of continuing full-time students received need-based aid. The average freshman award was $15,899. 80% of undergraduates work part time. Average annual earnings from campus work are $1500. The average financial indebtedness of the 2005 graduate was $13,000. The FAFSA and the college's own financial statement are required. The deadline for filing freshman financial aid applications for fall entry is March 2.

International Students: There are 58 international students enrolled. Satisfactory scores are required on the written TOEFL and the SAT or the ACT.

Computers: Wireless access is available. All dorms have an Ethernet port available. Wireless access is available in public areas such as dorm lobbies, dining commons, and the campus center. Labs providing Internet connectivity total approximately 175 computers. All students may access the system at any time. There are no time limits and no fees. It is strongly recommended that all students have a personal computer.

Graduates: From July 1, 2004 to June 30, 2005, 260 bachelor's degrees were awarded. The most popular majors were nursing (33%), business (16%), and childhood education (11%). In an average class, 12% graduate in 4 years or less, 19% graduate in 5 years or less, and 24% graduate in 6 years or less.

Admissions Contact: Sean Kootsey, Director of Enrollment Services. A video is available. E-mail: *enroll@puc.edu* Web: *www.puc.edu*

PEPPERDINE UNIVERSITY

C-5

Malibu, CA 90263-4392

(310) 506-4392; Fax: (310) 506-4861

Full-time: 1107 men, 1544 women	**Faculty:** 192; IIA, ++$
Part-time: 280 men, 270 women	**Ph.D.s:** 100%
Graduate: 1781 men, 2188 women	**Student/Faculty:** 14 to 1
Year: semesters, summer session	**Tuition:** $30,860
Application Deadline: January 15	**Room & Board:** $9100
Freshman Class: 6447 applied, 1756 accepted, 727 enrolled	
SAT or ACT: required	**HIGHLY COMPETITIVE**

Pepperdine University, founded in 1937, is a private liberal arts university affiliated with the Church of Christ. In addition to regional accreditation, Pepperdine has baccalaureate program accreditation with AACSB and NCATE. The library contains 312,846 volumes, 546,788 microform items, and 5351 audio/video tapes/CDs/DVDs, and subscribes to 9288 periodicals including electronic. Computerized library services include the card catalog, interlibrary loans, database searching, and Internet access. Special learning facilities include an art gallery, radio station, TV station, writing center, and Japanese tea ceremony room. The 830-acre campus is in a suburban area 35 miles northwest of Los Angeles, overlooking the Pacific Ocean. Including any residence halls, there are 76 buildings.

Student Life: 50% of undergraduates are from out of state, mostly the Southwest. Others are from 50 states, 60 foreign countries, and Canada. 65% are from public schools. 54% are white; 12% Asian American; 12% Hispanic. Most are Catholic. The average age of freshmen is 18; all undergraduates, 20. 11% do not continue beyond their first year; 80% remain to graduate.

Housing: 2106 students can be accommodated in college housing, which includes single-sex dorms, on-campus apartments, off-campus apartments, and married-student housing. On-campus housing is guaranteed for all 4 years. 62% of students live on campus; of those, 55% remain on campus on weekends. Alcohol is not permitted. All students may keep cars.

Activities: 24% of men belong to 6 national fraternities; 29% of women belong to 8 national sororities. There are 64 groups on campus, including art, band, cheerleading, chess, choir, chorale, computers, cycling, dance, debate, drama, ethnic, honors, international, jazz band, literary magazine, musical theater, newspaper, opera, orchestra, pep band, photography, political, professional, radio and TV, religious, social, social service, student government, symphony, and yearbook. Popular campus events include Midnight Madness, Songfest, and Parents Weekend.

Sports: There are 7 intercollegiate sports for men and 8 for women, and 11 intramural sports for men and 11 for women. Facilities include a field house, a pool, a weight room, basketball, racquetball, and tennis courts, playing fields, an all-weather track, an aerobics room, and a whirlpool/hot tub.

Disabled Students: 90% of the campus is accessible. Wheelchair ramps, elevators, special parking, specially equipped rest rooms, special class scheduling, lowered drinking fountains, lowered telephones, and special housing are available.

Services: Counseling and information services are available, as is tutoring in most subjects.

Campus Safety and Security: Measures include 24-hour foot and vehicle patrol, self-defense education, security escort services, and shuttle buses. There are informal discussions, pamphlets/posters/films, emergency telephones, lighted pathways/sidewalks, and guarded entrances to campus, security cameras, a late-night escort service, and a campus crimewatch program.

Programs of Study: Pepperdine confers B.A., B.S., and B.S.M. degrees. Master's and doctoral degrees are also awarded. Bachelor's degrees are awarded in BIOLOGICAL SCIENCE (biology/biological science and nutrition), BUSINESS (accounting, business administration and management, and international business management), COMMUNICATIONS AND THE ARTS (advertising, art, communications, dramatic arts, English, French, German, journalism, music, public relations, Spanish, speech/debate/rhetoric, and telecommunications), COMPUTER AND PHYSICAL SCIENCE (chemistry, computer science, mathematics, and natural sciences), EDUCATION (elementary, physical, and secondary), ENGINEERING AND ENVIRONMENTAL DESIGN (engineering), HEALTH PROFESSIONS (sports medicine), SOCIAL SCIENCE (economics, history, humanities, international studies, liberal arts/general studies, philosophy, political science/government, psychology, religion, social science, and sociology). Natural sciences (premedical), sports medicine, and political science are the strongest academically. Communication and business are the largest.

Required: To graduate, students must complete 128 units, including 64 units of general education requirements. 2 years of a broad liberal arts core curriculum are needed. Courses are required in English, religion, Western heritage, non-Western heritage, American heritage, behavioral science, foreign language, lab science, math, speech and rhetoric, freshman seminar, and phys ed. Students must take at least 40 upper-division units and complete a 28-unit residency requirement. Pepperdine requires a minimum GPA of 2.0 for graduation.

Special: Students may earn 1 to 4 units for an internship, available in most majors, participate in a Washington or a Sacramento semester, and study abroad in 8 countries. The school offers a 3-2 engineering degree with Washington University in St. Louis, the University of Southern California, and Boston University. There are dual majors in any discipline, student-designed contract majors, federal work-study programs, nondegree study, and pass/fail options. There are 16 national honor societies, and 3 departmental honors programs.

Faculty/Classroom: All teach undergraduates and 100% both teach and do research. No introductory courses are taught by graduate students. The average class size in an introductory lecture is 18; in a laboratory, 15; and in a regular course, 17.

Admissions: 27% of the 2005-2006 applicants were accepted. The SAT scores for the 2005-2006 freshman class were: Verbal--11% below 500, 37% between 500 and 599, 42% between 600 and 700, and 10% above 700; Math--6% below 500, 36% between 500 and 599, 45% between 600 and 700, and 13% above 700.

Requirements: The SAT or ACT is required. In addition, it is strongly recommended that candidates for admission present a college preparatory program that includes 4 years of English, 3 of math, 2 each of foreign language and science, and courses in speech communication, humanities, and social science. AP and CLEP credits are accepted. Important factors in the admissions decision are advanced placement or honor courses, recommendations by school officials, and evidence of special talent.

Procedure: Freshmen are admitted fall and spring. Entrance exams should be taken in the fall. There is a deferred admissions plan. Early decision applications should be filed by November 15; regular applications, by January 15 for fall entry and October 15 for spring entry, along with a $65 fee. Notification of early decision is sent December 15; regular decision, April 1. 331 applicants were on the 2005 waiting list; 65 were admitted.

Transfer: 71 transfer students enrolled in 2004-2005. Transfer applicants should have a minimum GPA of 3.0 from an accredited college. SAT or ACT scores are required for applicants who have completed fewer than 30 transferable semester hours at an accredited college. 28 of 128 credits required for the bachelor's degree must be completed at Pepperdine.

Visiting: There are regularly scheduled orientations for prospective students, including tours of the campus, meetings with faculty and current students, and sessions on admission and financial aid; interviews may be arranged on the hour with admission counselors. There are guides for informal visits and visitors may sit in on classes and stay overnight. To schedule a visit, contact the Admissions Office.

Financial Aid: In 2005-2006, 79% of all full-time freshmen and 70% of continuing full-time students received some form of financial aid. 55% of full-time freshmen received need-based aid. The average freshman award was $27,105. Need-based scholarships or need-based grants averaged $19,996; need-based self-help aid (loans and jobs) averaged $7720; non-need-based athletic scholarships averaged $25,477; and other non-need-based awards and non-need-based scholarships averaged $21,569. 97% of undergraduates work part time. Average annual earnings from campus work are $3000. The average financial indebtedness of the 2005 graduate was $29,148. The FAFSA, the college's own financial statement and the the federal income tax form, the state scholarship/grant form (California residents), and W-2 wage statement are required. The deadline for filing freshman financial aid applications for fall entry is February 15.

International Students: There are 196 international students enrolled. The school actively recruits these students. Satisfactory scores are required on the written TOEFL, the college's own test, and the SAT.

Computers: Wireless access is available. Students may access the system with permission from the faculty. Word processing labs are open to all students. There are no time limits and no fees.

Graduates: From July 1, 2004 to June 30, 2005, 700 bachelor's degrees were awarded. The most popular majors were business administration (15%), psychology (8%), and political science (6%). In an average class, 3% graduate in 3 years or less, 70% graduate in 4 years or less, 78% graduate in 5 years or less, and 78% graduate in 6 years or less. 70 companies recruited on campus in 2004-2005.

Admissions Contact: Paul A. Long, Dean of Admission and Enrollment Management. A video is available.
E-mail: *admission-seaver@pepperdine.edu* Web: *www.pepperdine.edu*

PITZER COLLEGE
D-5

Claremont, CA 91711-6101

(909) 621-8129
(800) PITZER-1; Fax: (909) 621-8770

Full-time: 376 men, 535 women	**Faculty:** 68; IIB, +$
Part-time: 17 men, 35 women	**Ph.D.s:** 96%
Graduate: none	**Student/Faculty:** 13 to 1
Year: semesters, summer session	**Tuition:** $33,012
Application Deadline: January 1	**Room & Board:** $8632
Freshman Class: 3251 applied, 1276 accepted, 239 enrolled	
SAT Verbal/Math: 625/610*	**HIGHLY COMPETITIVE**

Pitzer College, founded in 1963, is a private liberal arts college emphasizing the social and behavioral sciences. It is one of the Claremont Colleges. There are 5 undergraduate and 2 graduate schools. The library contains 2.5 million volumes, 1.2 million microform items, and 17,000 audio/video tapes/CDs/DVDs, and subscribes to 12,000 periodicals including electronic. Computerized library services include the card catalog, interlibrary loans, database searching, Internet access, and laptop Internet portals. Special learning facilities include an art gallery, radio station, TV station, a social science lab, and an arboretum. The 30-acre campus is in a suburban area 35 miles east of Los Angeles. Including any residence halls, there are 13 buildings.

Student Life: 58% of undergraduates are from California. Students are from 40 states, 7 foreign countries, and Canada. 42% are white; 15% Hispanic; 10% Asian American. The average age of freshmen is 18. 12% do not continue beyond their first year; 70% remain to graduate.

Housing: 601 students can be accommodated in college housing, which includes coed dorms and off-campus apartments. In addition, there is a quiet hall, involvement tower, A-1 food co-op, substance-free, and all female floor. On-campus housing is guaranteed for the freshman year only. 73% of students live on campus. All students may keep cars.

Activities: There are no fraternities or sororities. There are 27 groups on campus, including art, band, chess, choir, chorale, chorus, computers, dance, debate, drama, ethnic, film, gay, honors, international, jazz band, literary magazine, newspaper, orchestra, photography, political, professional, radio and TV, religious, social, social service, and student government. Popular campus events include the Kohoutek Festival, Atherton dinners, and Marquis Library Firesides.

Sports: There are 10 intercollegiate sports for men and 9 for women. Facilities include 3 gyms, 5 swimming pools, 20 tennis courts, numerous playing fields, and lighted volleyball courts. The campus stadium seats 1200. There are also shared intercollegiate sports with Pomona College. The Gold Student Center features a fitness room, lap pool, Frisbee field, and basketball and volleyball courts.

Disabled Students: 95% of the campus is accessible. Wheelchair ramps, elevators, special parking, specially equipped rest rooms, lowered drinking fountains, lowered telephones, and special housing are available.

Services: Counseling and information services are available, as is tutoring in every subject and tutoring software and programs for the learning disabled. There is a reader service for the blind and remedial writing.

Campus Safety and Security: Measures include 24-hour foot and vehicle patrol, self-defense education, security escort services, and informal discussions. There are pamphlets/posters/films, emergency telephones, and lighted pathways/sidewalks.

Programs of Study: Pitzer confers the B.A. degree. Bachelor's degrees are awarded in BIOLOGICAL SCIENCE (biochemistry, biology/biological science, and neurosciences), BUSINESS (management engineering and organizational behavior), COMMUNICATIONS AND THE ARTS (art, classics, dance, dramatic arts, English, film arts, French, linguistics, media arts, music, and Spanish), COMPUTER AND PHYSICAL SCIENCE (chemistry, mathematics, physics, science, and science and management), ENGINEERING AND ENVIRONMENTAL DESIGN (environmental science), SOCIAL SCIENCE (African American studies, American studies, anthropology, Asian/American studies, Asian/Oriental studies, Caribbean studies, economics, European studies, history, international relations, Latin American studies, Mexican-American/Chicano studies, philosophy, political science/government, psychology, sociology, Third World studies, and women's studies). Social and behavioral sciences are the strongest academically and the largest.

Required: Students must complete a total of 32 courses with a 2.0 GPA. Although requirements vary according to major, most students take introductory or preparatory courses in their first 2 years and courses in or related to their major in the last 2 years. All students must fulfill educational objectives in the following areas: interdisciplinary and intercultural exploration; social responsibility and the ethical implications of knowledge and action; breadth of knowledge, and written expression. More than 10 courses are required in the major.

Special: Students may cross-register at any of the other Claremont Colleges, or study abroad in 60 countries in Africa, Asia, Europe, Latin

America, North America, or Oceania. There are co-op programs, work-study, internships, dual majors, student-designed majors, an extensive first-year seminar program, and interdisciplinary study offered in science and technology, and international or intercultural studies. Joint advanced degrees are offered in math, business administration, and public policy, as is a 7-year B.A./D.O. program with the College of Western Health Sciences. There are independent study and limited pass/fail options. There is 1 national honor society and 18 departmental honors programs.

Faculty/Classroom: 58% of faculty are male; 42%, female. All both teach and do research. The average class size in an introductory lecture is 30; in a laboratory, 50; and in a regular course, 18.

Admissions: 39% of the 2005-2006 applicants were accepted. The SAT scores for the 2005-2006 freshman class were: Verbal--5% below 500, 27% between 500 and 599, 50% between 600 and 700, and 18% above 700; Math--5% below 500, 35% between 500 and 599, 49% between 600 and 700, and 11% above 700. 45% of the current freshmen were in the top fifth of their class; 92% were in the top two fifths.

Requirements: The SAT or ACT is recommended. In addition, applicants must be graduates of an accredited secondary school or have earned the GED. Secondary school courses must include 4 years of English courses requiring extensive writing, and 3 years each of social and behavioral sciences including history, lab science, foreign language, and math. A personal essay is required and a personal interview is recommended. Starting in fall of 2004, Pitzer implemented a 3-year trial that exempts students in the top 10% of their class, or those with an unweighted GPA in academic subjects of 3.5, from submitting ACT or SAT scores. Students without these qualifications must submit either ACT, SAT, 2 SAT Subject Tests, 2 AP test scores over 4 (1 in English, 1 in math or science), 2 IB exams (1 in English, 1 in math) or a higher-level math course, or a recent graded writing sample from a humanities or social science course and a graded advanced math exam, both including teacher's comments and grades. AP credits are accepted. Important factors in the admissions decision are advanced placement or honor courses, leadership record, and evidence of special talent.

Procedure: Freshmen are admitted fall and spring. Entrance exams should be taken by January 1. There is a deferred admissions plan. Early decision applications should be filed by December 1; regular applications, by January 1 for fall entry and October 15 for spring entry. Notification is sent April 1. 704 applicants were on the 2005 waiting list. Applications are accepted on-line. The fall 2005 application fee was $50.

Transfer: 25 transfer students enrolled in 2004-2005. No more than 2 years of previous credits may be transferred. 64 of 128 credits required for the bachelor's degree must be completed at Pitzer.

Visiting: There are regularly scheduled orientations for prospective students. There are guides for informal visits and visitors may sit in on classes and stay overnight. To schedule a visit, contact the Office of Admissions at (909) 621-8889.

Financial Aid: In 2005-2006, 46% of all full-time freshmen and 45% of continuing full-time students received some form of financial aid. 39% of full-time freshmen and 40% of continuing full-time students received need-based aid. The average freshman award was $28,858. Need-based scholarships or need-based grants averaged $28,858; need-based self-help aid (loans and jobs) averaged $5179; and other non-need-based awards and non-need-based scholarships averaged $5000. 60% of undergraduates work part time. Average annual earnings from campus work are $2300. The average financial indebtedness of the 2005 graduate was $20,900. The CSS/Profile or FAFSA is required. The deadline for filing freshman financial aid applications for fall entry is February 1.

International Students: There are 20 international students enrolled. The school actively recruits these students. They must score satisfactorily on the written TOEFL or on the electronic version.

Computers: Wireless access is available. All dorm rooms are hardwired; there are student computer labs. All students may access the system. There are no time limits and no fees.

Graduates: From July 1, 2004 to June 30, 2005, 266 bachelor's degrees were awarded. The most popular majors were psychology (15%), sociology (14%), and art/art history (10%). In an average class, 1% graduate in 3 years or less, 61% graduate in 4 years or less, 7% graduate in 5 years or less, and 2% graduate in 6 years or less. 25 companies recruited on campus in 2004-2005.

Admissions Contact: Arnaldo Rodriguez, Vice President, Admission and Financial Aid. E-mail: *admission@pitzer.edu* Web: *www.pitzer.edu*

POINT LOMA NAZARENE UNIVERSITY   D-5

San Diego, CA 92106-2899   (619) 849-2565
(800) 733-7770; Fax: (619) 849-2601

Full-time: 908 men, 1374 women	**Faculty:** 115; IIB, +$
Part-time: 33 men, 45 women	**Ph.D.s:** 61%
Graduate: 364 men, 721 women	**Student/Faculty:** 20 to 1
Year: semesters, summer session	**Tuition:** $20,730
Application Deadline: March 1	**Room & Board:** $6880
Freshman Class: 1216 accepted, 563 enrolled	
SAT Verbal/Math: 570/580*	**ACT:** 25 **VERY COMPETITIVE**

Point Loma Nazarene University, founded in 1902, is a private liberal arts university affiliated with the Church of the Nazarene. Figures in the above capsule and in this profile are approximate. In addition to regional accreditation, PLNU has baccalaureate program accreditation with ACB-SP and NLN. The library contains 145,000 volumes, 35,000 microform items, and 10,000 audio/video tapes/CDs/DVDs, and subscribes to 625 periodicals including electronic. Computerized library services include the card catalog, interlibrary loans, and database searching. Special learning facilities include a learning resource center, radio station, and a laboratory preschool. The 90-acre campus is in a suburban area 5 miles southwest of San Diego. Including any residence halls, there are 42 buildings.

Student Life: 77% of undergraduates are from California. Students are from 36 states, 14 foreign countries, and Canada. 82% are from public schools. 84% are white. Most are Protestant. The average age of freshmen is 18; all undergraduates, 20. 21% do not continue beyond their first year; 89% remain to graduate.

Housing: 1460 students can be accommodated in college housing, which includes single-sex dorms, on-campus apartments, off-campus apartments, and married-student housing. On-campus housing is available on a first-come, first-served basis and is available on a lottery system for upperclassmen. 67% of students live on campus. Alcohol is not permitted. Upperclassmen may keep cars.

Activities: There are 3 local fraternities and 2 local and 1 national sorority. There are 41 groups on campus, including art, band, cheerleading, choir, chorale, computers, debate, drama, ethnic, forensics, honors, international, jazz band, literary magazine, newspaper, opera, orchestra, pep band, political, professional, radio and TV, religious, social, social service, student government, and yearbook. Popular campus events include Spiritual Emphasis Week and Christmas Messiah Concert.

Sports: There are 7 intercollegiate sports for men and 5 for women, and 18 intramural sports for men and 17 for women. Facilities include a gym, baseball and soccer fields, a track, tennis courts, dormitory lounges, and table tennis and pool tables.

Disabled Students: 75% of the campus is accessible. Wheelchair ramps, elevators, special parking, specially equipped rest rooms, special class scheduling, lowered drinking fountains, and lowered telephones are available.

Services: Counseling and information services are available, as is tutoring in most subjects. There is a reader service for the blind, and remedial math, reading, and writing.

Campus Safety and Security: Measures include 24-hour foot and vehicle patrol, self-defense education, security escort services, and shuttle buses. There are informal discussions, pamphlets/posters/films, emergency telephones, and lighted pathways/sidewalks.

Programs of Study: PLNU confers B.A., B.S., and B.S.N. degrees. Master's degrees are also awarded. Bachelor's degrees are awarded in BIOLOGICAL SCIENCE (biology/biological science), BUSINESS (accounting, business administration and management, and management information systems), COMMUNICATIONS AND THE ARTS (art, communications, dramatic arts, journalism, literature, music, music business management, romance languages and literature, Spanish, and speech/debate/rhetoric), COMPUTER AND PHYSICAL SCIENCE (chemistry, computer science, mathematics, and physics), EDUCATION (physical), ENGINEERING AND ENVIRONMENTAL DESIGN (engineering physics), HEALTH PROFESSIONS (nursing), SOCIAL SCIENCE (child psychology/development, dietetics, economics, family and community services, history, home economics, industrial and organizational psychology, liberal arts/general studies, philosophy, political science/government, psychology, religion, religious education, social science, social work, and sociology). Biology, chemistry, and art are the strongest academically. Liberal studies and business are the largest.

Required: To graduate, students must complete a minimum of 128 semester units. At least 24 upper-division semester units are needed for the major. A minimum GPA of 2.0 is required. Students must complete the general education requirements, though B.S.N. candidates need not take a foreign language. General education requirements include 9 courses in cultural studies, 5 in the sciences, 4 in cognitive studies, and 3 in religious studies. Students must demonstrate proficiency in writing and math.

Special: PLNU offers internships in the church, in state and national governments, in journalism, in small business, and in the film industry. Students may study abroad in several world capitals and in Russia, the

Middle East, and Costa Rica. There are Washington and United Nations semester programs. Various dual or interdepartmental majors are offered, including biology-chemistry, graphic communications, human environmental science-business, and church music-youth ministries. There are preprofessional programs in medicine/dentistry, law, and engineering. A general studies degree in liberal studies is available, as is credit for life, military, and work experience for nursing students. PLNU also offers nondegree study and credit/no credit options. There is 1 national honor society, a freshman honors program, and 1 departmental honors program.

Faculty/Classroom: 55% of faculty are male; 45%, female. 95% teach undergraduates and 10% both teach and do research. No introductory courses are taught by graduate students. The average class size in an introductory lecture is 75; in a laboratory, 18; and in a regular course, 25.

Admissions: The SAT scores for the 2005-2006 freshman class were: Verbal--16% below 500, 43% between 500 and 599, 34% between 600 and 700, and 78% above 700; Math--15% below 500, 43% between 500 and 599, 34% between 600 and 700, and 8% above 700. 24 freshmen graduated first in their class.

Requirements: The SAT or ACT is required. In addition, candidates for admission should have completed 4 years of English, 2 years each of foreign language and math, and 1 year each of history and science. A GPA of 2.8 is required. AP and CLEP credits are accepted on a limited basis. Important factors in the admissions decision are personality/intangible qualities, leadership record, and advanced placement or honor courses.

Procedure: Freshmen are admitted fall and spring. Entrance exams should be taken in the junior year or early in the senior year. There are early admissions and deferred admissions plans. Applications should be filed by March 1 for fall entry, along with a $50 fee. Notification is sent on a rolling basis. Applications are accepted on-line.

Transfer: 140 transfer students enrolled in 2004-2005. Transfer students must have a C average in all college work and present transcripts, including certificates of honorable dismissal. Credits submitted from non-accredited schools will be evaluated individually. Advanced standing is provisional for at least one term, in which the student must maintain at least a C average. 24 of 128 credits required for the bachelor's degree must be completed at PLNU.

Visiting: There are regularly scheduled orientations for prospective students, including campus tours and appointments with major advisers. There are guides for informal visits and visitors may sit in on classes and stay overnight. To schedule a visit, contact the Admissions Office at (619) 221-2273 or admissions@ptloma.edu.

Financial Aid: PLNU is a member of CSS. The CSS/Profile or FAFSA and the college's own financial statement are required. Check with the school for current deadlines.

International Students: There are 19 international students enrolled. A satisfactory score is required on the written TOEFL. Students must also take the SAT.

Computers: All students may access the system when computer labs are open. There are no time limits and no fees. It is recommended that students in business administration have PC.

Admissions Contact: Scott Shoemaker, Dean of Admissions. A video is available. E-mail: admissions@ptloma.edu
Web: www.ptloma.edu/admissions

POMONA COLLEGE — D-5

Claremont, CA 91711	(909) 621-8134; Fax: (909) 621-8952
Full-time: 780 men, 750 women	**Faculty:** 155; IIB, ++$
Part-time: 20 men, 15 women	**Ph.D.s:** 100%
Graduate: none	**Student/Faculty:** 10 to 1
Year: semesters	**Tuition:** $29,923
Application Deadline: January 2	**Room & Board:** $10,851
Freshman Class: n/av	
SAT Verbal/Math: 730/720*	**MOST COMPETITIVE**

Pomona College, the oldest and largest of the Claremont Colleges, (a consortium of colleges) is an independent, national liberal arts and sciences institution founded in 1887. There are 5 undergraduate and 2 graduate schools. Enrollment figures in the above capsule are approximate. The 3 libraries contain 2,022,481 volumes, 1,382,687 microform items, and 777 audio/video tapes/CDs/DVDs, and subscribe to 6624 periodicals including electronic. Computerized library services include the card catalog, interlibrary loans, and database searching. Special learning facilities include an art gallery, radio station, observatory, and modern languages and international relations center. The 140-acre campus is in a suburban area 35 miles east of Los Angeles, and 20 miles east of Pasadena. Including any residence halls, there are 47 buildings.

Student Life: 61% of undergraduates are from out of state, mostly the Northwest. Students are from 49 states, 31 foreign countries, and Canada. 61% are from public schools. 59% are white; 13% Asian American; 9% Hispanic. The average age of freshmen is 18; all undergraduates, 20. 1% do not continue beyond their first year; 94% remain to graduate.

Housing: 1335 students can be accommodated in college housing, which includes coed dorms and on-campus apartments. In addition, there are language houses. On-campus housing is guaranteed for all 4 years. 97% of students live on campus; of those, 95% remain on campus on weekends. All students may keep cars.

Activities: 6% of men and about 4% of women belong to 6 local fraternities. There are no sororities. There are 280 groups on campus, including art, band, chess, choir, chorus, dance, debate, drama, ethnic, film, gay, honors, international, jazz band, literary magazine, musical theater, newspaper, orchestra, pep band, photography, political, professional, radio and TV, religious, social, social service, student government, symphony, and yearbook.

Sports: There are 10 intercollegiate sports for men and 10 for women, and 13 intramural sports for men and 13 for women. Facilities include an all-weather track, 2 swimming pools, a weight room, a fitness center, a dance studio, various playing fields, and courts for tennis, squash, racquetball, basketball, volleyball, and badminton.

Disabled Students: 80% of the campus is accessible. Wheelchair ramps, elevators, special parking, specially equipped rest rooms, special class scheduling, lowered drinking fountains and lowered telephones are available.

Services: Counseling and information services are available, as is tutoring in most subjects. There is a reader service for the blind.

Campus Safety and Security: Measures include 24-hour foot and vehicle patrol, self-defense education, security escort services, and informal discussions. There are pamphlets/posters/films, emergency telephones, and lighted pathways/sidewalks.

Programs of Study: Pomona confers the B.A. degree. Bachelor's degrees are awarded in BIOLOGICAL SCIENCE (biology/biological science, molecular biology, and neurosciences), COMMUNICATIONS AND THE ARTS (art history and appreciation, Chinese, classics, dramatic arts, English, fine arts, French, German, Japanese, languages, linguistics, literature, media arts, music, Russian, Spanish, and studio art), COMPUTER AND PHYSICAL SCIENCE (chemistry, computer science, geology, mathematics, physics, and science), ENGINEERING AND ENVIRONMENTAL DESIGN (technology and public affairs), SOCIAL SCIENCE (African American studies, American studies, anthropology, Asian/Oriental studies, economics, German area studies, history, international relations, Latin American studies, philosophy, political science/government, psychology, public affairs, religion, sociology, and women's studies). Social sciences and sciences are the largest.

Required: Students must pass 1 course in each of the following categories: read literature critically, use and understand scientific method, use and understand formal reasoning, understand and analyze data, analyze creative art critically, perform or produce creative art, explore and understand human behavior, explore and understand historical culture, compare and contrast contemporary culture, and think critically about values and rationality. In all, 32 semester courses must be completed with a 6.0 GPA on a 12.0 scale.

Special: Students may cross-register at any of the Claremont Colleges, study abroad in 22 countries, and spend a semester in Washington, D.C. Dual and student-designed majors, internships, and independent study are possible. A 3-2 engineering program is offered with California Institute of Technology or Washington University in St. Louis. Students may study for 1 semester at Colby, Smith, Spelman, or Swarthmore Colleges. There are pass/fail options. There are 9 national honor societies, including Phi Beta Kappa.

Faculty/Classroom: 58% of faculty are male; 42%, female. All teach undergraduates do research. The average class size in an introductory lecture is 30; in a laboratory, 14; and in a regular course, 14.

Requirements: The SAT or ACT is required. Although applicants need not be graduates of accredited high schools (some may be admitted after the junior year), most are, or have earned the GED. Secondary preparation must include 4 years of English, 3 years each of math and foreign languages, and 2 years each of lab and social sciences. An essay is required and an interview is strongly recommended. AP credits are accepted. Important factors in the admissions decision are recommendations by school officials, leadership record, and recommendations by alumni.

Procedure: Freshmen are admitted in the fall. Entrance exams should be taken before December of the senior year. There are early decision, early admissions, and deferred admissions plans. Early Decision 1 applications should be filed by November 15; Early Decision 2, by December 28; regular applications, by January 2 for fall entry. Notification of early decision is sent December 15; regular decision, April 10. A waiting list is an active part of the admissions procedure. Applications are accepted on-line.

Transfer: Applicants must have completed at least 1 year (24 semester hours) of college-level courses at the time of enrollment. 16 of 32 credits required for the bachelor's degree must be completed at Pomona.

Visiting: There are regularly scheduled orientations for prospective students, including interviews, information sessions, and tours. There are guides for informal visits and visitors may sit in on classes and stay overnight. To schedule a visit, contact the Admissions Office.

Financial Aid: Pomona is a member of CSS. The CSS/Profile or FAFSA and tax returns are required. The deadline for filing freshman financial aid applications for fall entry is February 1.

International Students: The school actively recruits these students. They must score satisfactorily on the TOEFL and also take the SAT or the ACT.

Computers: All students may access the system. There are no time limits and no fees.

Admissions Contact: Bruce J. Poch, Vice President and Dean of Admissions. E-mail: *admissions@pomona.edu* Web: *www.pomona.edu*

SAINT MARY'S COLLEGE OF CALIFORNIA   B-3
Moraga, CA 94575-4800

(925) 631-4224
(800) 800-4SMC; Fax: (925) 376-7193

Full-time: 968 men, 1546 women	**Faculty:** 197; IIA, +$
Part-time: 252 men, 525 women	**Ph.D.s:** 90%
Graduate: 343 men, 798 women	**Student/Faculty:** 13 to 1
Year: 4-1-4	**Tuition:** $27,280
Application Deadline: January 15	**Room & Board:** $10,010
Freshman Class: 3381 applied, 2861 accepted, 675 enrolled	
SAT Verbal/Math: 540/540*	**ACT:** 23 **COMPETITIVE**

Saint Mary's College of California, founded in 1863, is a private, independent, liberal arts college affiliated with the Roman Catholic Church. The school offers undergraduate and graduate programs in liberal arts, nursing, economics and business administration, education, and pre-professional studies. There are 5 undergraduate and 5 graduate schools. In addition to regional accreditation, SMC has baccalaureate program accreditation with NLN. The library contains 210,516 volumes, 484,760 microform items, and 11,062 audio/video tapes/CDs/DVDs, and subscribes to 1042 periodicals including electronic. Computerized library services include the card catalog, interlibrary loans, database searching, and Internet access. Special learning facilities include an art gallery, radio station, and TV station. The 420-acre campus is in a suburban area 20 miles east of San Francisco. Including any residence halls, there are 58 buildings.

Student Life: 86% of undergraduates are from California. Others are from 25 states, 14 foreign countries, and Canada. 58% are from public schools. 51% are white; 16% Hispanic. 55% are Catholic; 19% claim no religious affiliation. The average age of freshmen is 18; all undergraduates, 20. 12% do not continue beyond their first year; 70% remain to graduate.

Housing: 1585 students can be accommodated in college housing, which includes single-sex and coed dormitories and on-campus apartments. On-campus housing is guaranteed for the freshman year only and is available on a lottery system for upperclassmen. 63% of students live on campus; of those, 68% remain on campus on weekends. All students may keep cars.

Activities: There are no fraternities or sororities. There are 42 groups on campus, including art, cheerleading, choir, chorus, dance, drama, ethnic, gay, honors, international, jazz band, literary magazine, musical theater, newspaper, pep band, political, professional, radio and TV, religious, social, social service, student government, and yearbook. Popular campus events include Welcome Back Dance, OASIS, and St. Mary's Day Off.

Sports: There are 7 intercollegiate sports for men and 8 for women, and 9 intramural sports for men and 9 for women. Facilities include a gym, football and baseball fields, a swimming pool, lighted tennis courts, a soccer field and rugby pitch, a weight room, and a workout facility.

Disabled Students: 90% of the campus is accessible. Wheelchair ramps, elevators, special parking, specially equipped rest rooms, special class scheduling, lowered drinking fountains, and lowered telephones are available.

Services: Counseling and information services are available, as is tutoring in most subjects. Tutoring is available in 1-on-1 sessions or group workshops. Readers, note takers, and other services are provided to learning or physically disabled students.

Campus Safety and Security: Measures include 24-hour foot and vehicle patrol, security escort services, informal discussions, and pamphlets/posters/films. There are emergency telephones and lighted pathways/sidewalks.

Programs of Study: SMC confers B.A., B.S., and B.S.N. degrees. Master's and doctoral degrees are also awarded. Bachelor's degrees are awarded in BIOLOGICAL SCIENCE (biology/biological science), BUSINESS (accounting and business administration and management), COMMUNICATIONS AND THE ARTS (art, classical languages, communications, English, French, performing arts, and Spanish), COMPUTER AND PHYSICAL SCIENCE (chemistry, mathematics, and physics), EDUCATION (health, physical, and recreation), ENGINEERING AND ENVIRONMENTAL DESIGN (preengineering), HEALTH PROFESSIONS (health science and nursing), SOCIAL SCIENCE (anthropology, economics, history, liberal arts/general studies, philosophy, political science/government, psychology, and religion). Business administration, communications, and psychology are the largest.

Required: To graduate, students must complete 36 course credits, including 17 at the upper-division level, with a GPA of 2.0 overall and in the major. Specific requirements include 4 Great Books seminars and 2 courses each in religious studies, humanities, math/science, and social sciences. All students must demonstrate competence in written English.

Special: Saint Mary's College and Samuel Merritt College confer the B.S.N. degree to students completing the Intercollegiate Nursing Program. The college offers seminars in all fields, dual and student-designed majors, study abroad in 10 countries, a Washington semester, cross-registration with the Regional Association of East Bay Colleges and Universities, and an integral liberal arts degree. There are 3-2 engineering programs with Washington University, the University of Southern California, and Boston University.

Faculty/Classroom: 52% of faculty are male; 48%, female. All both teach and do research. No introductory courses are taught by graduate students. The average class size in an introductory lecture is 25; in a laboratory, 16; and in a regular course, 20.

Admissions: 85% of the 2005-2006 applicants were accepted. The SAT scores for the 2005-2006 freshman class were: Verbal--26% below 500, 46% between 500 and 599, 25% between 600 and 700, and 3% above 700; Math--26% below 500, 45% between 500 and 599, 26% between 600 and 700, and 3% above 700. The ACT scores were 29% below 21, 28% between 21 and 23, 19% between 24 and 26, 11% between 27 and 28, and 13% above 28.

Requirements: The SAT or ACT is required. In addition, candidates should be graduates of an accredited secondary school, with 16 academic units, including 4 in English and 1 each in algebra, advanced algebra, geometry, and U.S. history. It is recommended that the remaining units be made up of foreign language, lab science, and additional academic electives in the student's areas of strength. The GED is accepted. An essay is required. AP and CLEP credits are accepted. Important factors in the admissions decision are recommendations by school officials, advanced placement or honor courses, and parents or siblings attending the school.

Procedure: Freshmen are admitted to all sessions. Entrance exams should be taken by December of the senior year. There is a deferred admissions plan. Applications should be filed by January 15 for fall entry, December 1 for winter entry, and January 1 for spring entry. Notification of early decision is sent January 1; regular decision, April 1. 115 applicants were on the 2005 waiting list; 40 were admitted. Applications are accepted on-line. The fall 2005 application fee was $55.

Transfer: 159 transfer students enrolled in 2004-2005. Applicants must have a GPA of 2.3 and a minimum of 23 transferable academic semester units. 9 of 36 course credits required for the bachelor's degree must be completed at SMC.

Visiting: There are regularly scheduled orientations for prospective students. There are guides for informal visits and visitors may sit in on classes and stay overnight. To schedule a visit, contact the Admissions Office at (925) 631-4106.

Financial Aid: In 2005-2006, 73% of all full-time freshmen and 74% of continuing full-time students received some form of financial aid. 60% of full-time freshmen and 61% of continuing full-time students received need-based aid. The average freshman award was $20,109. Need-based scholarships or need-based grants averaged $16,812 ($26,718 maximum); need-based self-help aid (loans and jobs) averaged $4233 ($8625 maximum); non-need-based athletic scholarships averaged $18,698 ($37,290 maximum); and other non-need-based awards and non-need-based scholarships averaged $12,554 ($27,130 maximum). 55% of undergraduates work part time. Average annual earnings from campus work are $1925. The average financial indebtedness of the 2005 graduate was $21,892. The FAFSA and California GPA verification form for residents only are required. The deadline for filing freshman financial aid applications for fall entry is March 2.

International Students: There are 60 international students enrolled. The school actively recruits these students. They must score satisfactorily on the written TOEFL or on the electronic version. Nonnative English speakers who submit a satisfactory score on the TOEFL may be admitted as full-time undergraduates. Others may be accepted conditionally and enrolled in the college's Intensive English Program.

Computers: Wireless access is available. All students may access the system. There are no time limits and no fees.

Graduates: From July 1, 2004 to June 30, 2005, 700 bachelor's degrees were awarded. The most popular majors were business administration (27%), psychology (12%), and social sciences (12%). In an average class, 58% graduate in 4 years or less, 65% graduate in 5 years or less, and 66% graduate in 6 years or less. 74 companies recruited on campus in 2004-2005. Of the 2004 graduating class, 14% were enrolled in graduate school within 6 months of graduation and 64% were employed.

Admissions Contact: Dorothy Jones, Dean of Admissions. A video is available. E-mail: *smcadmit@stmarys-ca.edu* Web: *http://www.stmarys-ca.edu*

SAN DIEGO CHRISTIAN COLLEGE
(Formerly Christian Heritage College)

D-5

El Cajon, CA 92019-1157

(619) 588-7747
(800) 676-2242; Fax: (619) 590-1739

Full-time: 500 men and women	**Faculty:** 30
Part-time: 100 men and women	**Ph.D.s:** 50%
Graduate: none	**Student/Faculty:** 17 to 1
Year: semesters, summer session	**Tuition:** $16,992
Application Deadline: open	**Room & Board:** $7180
Freshman Class: n/av	
SAT or ACT: required	**ACT:** n/av **COMPETITIVE**

San Diego Christian College, formerly Christian Heritage College, is a small, private institution founded in 1970 by the Scott Memorial Baptist Church of San Diego, with which it is still affiliated. It offers programs in the liberal arts, business, and education. Some information in this capsule and profile is approximate. The library contains 70,000 volumes, 80 microform items, and 3820 audio/video tapes/CDs/DVDs, and subscribes to 250 periodicals including electronic. Computerized library services include database searching. Special learning facilities include the nearby Institute for Creation Research. The 32-acre campus is in a suburban area 15 miles east of San Diego. Including any residence halls, there are 14 buildings.

Student Life: 80% of undergraduates are from California. 75% are from public schools. 70% are white; 10% African American; 10% Hispanic. Most are Protestant. The average age of freshmen is 18; all undergraduates, 21. 40% do not continue beyond their first year; 30% remain to graduate.

Housing: 200 students can be accommodated in college housing, which includes single-sex dorms and off-campus apartments. In addition, there are language houses. On-campus housing is guaranteed for all 4 years and is available on a first-come, first-served basis. 50% of students live on campus; of those, 30% remain on campus on weekends. Alcohol is not permitted. All students may keep cars.

Activities: There are no fraternities or sororities. There are 16 groups on campus, including art, cheerleading, choir, chorale, chorus, computers, drama, honors, international, musical theater, newspaper, pep band, political, religious, social, student government, and yearbook. Popular campus events include spring, winter, and Valentine's Day banquets, and the Missions Conference.

Sports: There are 3 intercollegiate sports for men and 4 for women, and 5 intramural sports for men and 4 for women. Facilities include a swimming pool, a gym, outdoor courts for tennis, volleyball, and basketball, and soccer and softball fields.

Disabled Students: 90% of the campus is accessible. Wheelchair ramps, elevators, and special parking are available.

Services: Counseling and information services are available, as is tutoring in some subjects.

Campus Safety and Security: Measures include 24-hour foot and vehicle patrol, lighted pathways/sidewalks, and a fenced campus.

Programs of Study: SDCC confers B.A. and B.S. degrees. Associate degrees are also awarded. Bachelor's degrees are awarded in BIOLOGICAL SCIENCE (biology/biological science), BUSINESS (business administration and management), COMMUNICATIONS AND THE ARTS (communications, English, and music), COMPUTER AND PHYSICAL SCIENCE (mathematics), EDUCATION (education), ENGINEERING AND ENVIRONMENTAL DESIGN (aviation administration/management), SOCIAL SCIENCE (biblical studies, history, human development, interdisciplinary studies, liberal arts/general studies, physical fitness/movement, and psychology). Counseling psychology, education, and business are the strongest academically. Business, education, and human development are the largest.

Required: The required credits for graduation vary by degree program and major. All students must take 46 to 52 credits in sciences and math, social science, and humanities; 20 credits in personal Christian development and biblical studies; and the balance in major field requirements and electives. A 2.0 GPA is required for graduation.

Special: Students attend chapel 3 times each week, participate in an annual Bible conference, and complete a student ministry assignment each semester. Independent study for 1 to 3 credits can be arranged. There are internships in psychology, pastoral studies, and education.

Faculty/Classroom: 60% of faculty are male; 40%, female. All teach undergraduates. The average class size in an introductory lecture is 40; in a laboratory, 15; and in a regular course, 16.

Requirements: The SAT or ACT is required, the ACT is preferred. Applicants must have a high school diploma or the GED, or have successfully completed the California State High School Proficiency Exam. Secondary preparation should include 4 units of English, 3 each of math, natural science, and social studies, and 2 of a single foreign language. A personal essay is also required. In addition, applicants must meet certain spiritual requirements. SDCC requires applicants to be in the upper 50% of their class. A GPA of 2.25 is required. AP and CLEP credits are accepted. Important factors in the admissions decision are recommendations by school officials, leadership record, and extracurricular activities record.

Procedure: Freshmen are admitted fall and spring. Entrance exams should be taken during the junior year. Application deadlines are open. Check with the school for current application fee.

Transfer: 30 of 124 credits required for the bachelor's degree must be completed at SDCC.

Visiting: There are regularly scheduled orientations for prospective students, including a campus tour, cafeteria meal, and class and chapel attendance. There are guides for informal visits and visitors may sit in on classes and stay overnight. To schedule a visit, contact the Admissions Office.

Financial Aid: 70% of undergraduates work part time. SDCC is a member of CSS. The FAFSA and the college's own financial statement are required. Check with the school for current deadlines.

International Students: The school actively recruits these students. They must take the college's own test and also take the SAT or the ACT, scoring satisfactorily.

Computers: All students may access the system. There are no time limits and no fees.

Graduates: In an average class, 1% graduate in 3 years or less, 78% graduate in 4 years or less, 97% graduate in 5 years or less, and 99% graduate in 6 years or less.

Admissions Contact: Misty Chappelle, Director of Admissions.
E-mail: *chcadm@adm.sdcc.edu* Web: *www.sdcc.edu*

SAN DIEGO STATE UNIVERSITY

D-5

San Diego, CA 92182-7455   (619) 594-6336; Fax: (619) 594-1250

Full-time: 8956 men, 12,826 women	**Faculty:** IIA, +$
Part-time: 2008 men, 2900 women	**Ph.D.s:** 93%
Graduate: 2176 men, 3643 women	**Student/Faculty:** n/av
Year: semesters, summer session	**Tuition:** $3122 ($13,292)
Application Deadline: November 30	**Room & Board:** $9849
Freshman Class: 36,718 applied, 16,266 accepted, 4105 enrolled	
SAT Verbal/Math: 530/550*	**ACT:** 22 **COMPETITIVE**

San Diego State University, founded in 1897, is a public liberal arts university that is part of the California State University system. There are 8 undergraduate schools. In addition to regional accreditation, SDSU has baccalaureate program accreditation with ACEJMC, ADA, ASLA, CSWE, FIDER, NASAD, NASM, NCATE, NLN, and NRPA. The library contains 1,342,735 volumes, 4,262,210 microform items, and 12,616 audio/video tapes/CDs/DVDs, and subscribes to 8245 periodicals including electronic. Computerized library services include the card catalog, interlibrary loans, and database searching. Special learning facilities include a learning resource center, art gallery, planetarium, radio station, TV station, theater, and recital hall. The 282-acre campus is in an urban area 8 miles east of downtown San Diego. Including any residence halls, there are 56 buildings.

Student Life: 95% of undergraduates are from California. Others are from 49 states, 82 foreign countries, and Canada. 45% are white; 22% Hispanic; 16% Asian American. The average age of freshmen is 18; all undergraduates, 23. 16% do not continue beyond their first year; 46% remain to graduate.

Housing: 3087 students can be accommodated in college housing, which includes coed dorms, on-campus apartments, fraternity houses, and sorority houses. In addition, there are honors houses, special-interest houses and international housing. On-campus housing is available on a first-come, first-served basis. 87% of students commute. All students may keep cars.

Activities: 10% of men belong to 15 national fraternities; 8% of women belong to 9 national sororities. There are 300 groups on campus, including art, band, cheerleading, choir, chorale, chorus, dance, drama, drill team, ethnic, film, gay, honors, international, jazz band, literary magazine, marching band, musical theater, newspaper, opera, orchestra, pep band, political, professional, radio and TV, religious, social, social service, student government, and symphony. Popular campus events include Ethnic Pride and PowWow.

Sports: There are 6 intercollegiate sports for men and 11 for women, and 7 intramural sports for men and 7 for women. Facilities include a gym, basketball, racquetball, tennis, and volleyball courts, a swimming pool, a track, soccer, softball, baseball, and football fields, an aquatic center, a weight room, bowling and gymnastic equipment, a cardio room, and a 30-foot climbing wall.

Disabled Students: 95% of the campus is accessible. Wheelchair ramps, elevators, special parking, specially equipped rest rooms, special class scheduling, lowered drinking fountains, lowered telephones, orientation, counseling, transportation, books on tape, sign language interpreters, testing assistance, support equipment for loan, special computers, and note-taking services are available.

Services: Counseling and information services are available, as is tutoring in most subjects. There is a reader service for the blind, and remedial math, reading, and writing.

Campus Safety and Security: Measures include 24-hour foot and vehicle patrol, self-defense education, security escort services, and informal discussions. There are pamphlets/posters/films, emergency telephones, and lighted pathways/sidewalks.

Programs of Study: SDSU confers B.A., B.S., and B.M. degrees. Master's and doctoral degrees are also awarded. Bachelor's degrees are awarded in BIOLOGICAL SCIENCE (biology/biological science, microbiology, and nutrition), BUSINESS (accounting, banking and finance, business administration and management, international business management, marketing/retailing/merchandising, and real estate), COMMUNICATIONS AND THE ARTS (broadcasting, classics, communications, comparative literature, dance, dramatic arts, English, fine arts, French, German, Japanese, journalism, linguistics, music, Russian, and Spanish), COMPUTER AND PHYSICAL SCIENCE (astronomy, chemistry, computer science, geology, information sciences and systems, mathematics, physical sciences, physics, and statistics), EDUCATION (vocational), ENGINEERING AND ENVIRONMENTAL DESIGN (aeronautical engineering, civil engineering, computer engineering, electrical/electronics engineering, environmental engineering, and mechanical engineering), HEALTH PROFESSIONS (exercise science, health science, nursing, and speech pathology/audiology), SOCIAL SCIENCE (African studies, American studies, anthropology, Asian/Oriental studies, child psychology/development, criminal justice, economics, European studies, geography, gerontology, history, humanities, Latin American studies, Mexican-American/Chicano studies, parks and recreation management, peace studies, philosophy, political science/government, psychology, public administration, religion, Russian and Slavic studies, social science, social work, sociology, urban studies, and women's studies). Business administration is the strongest academically and has the largest enrollment.

Required: To graduate, students must complete 124 to 133 credit hours, including 49 general education units. The number of hours in the major varies by program. A 2.0 or higher GPA must be maintained, depending on the major. Students must demonstrate math and writing competency and fulfill requirements in upper-division writing and in American Institutions. History majors must complete a senior thesis.

Special: Students may study abroad in London and Paris and receive credit for life, military, and work experience. Cross-registration with the University of California, community colleges, and California State University, internships, dual majors, an interdisciplinary major, a political science internship in Sacramento or Washington, D.C., an off-campus public administration program, and a prelaw program in cooperation with California Western School of Law are available. There are 30 national honor societies, including Phi Beta Kappa, a freshman honors program, and 24 departmental honors programs.

Faculty/Classroom: 53% of faculty are male; 47%, female. Graduate students teach 13% of introductory courses. The average class size in an introductory lecture is 32 and in a regular course, 29.

Admissions: 44% of the 2005-2006 applicants were accepted. The SAT scores for the 2005-2006 freshman class were: Verbal--33% below 500, 49% between 500 and 599, 18% between 600 and 700, and 1% above 700; Math--24% below 500, 48% between 500 and 599, 27% between 600 and 700, and 1% above 700. The ACT scores were 31% below 21, 32% between 21 and 23, 27% between 24 and 26, 7% between 27 and 28, and 4% above 28.

Requirements: The SAT or ACT is required. In addition, applicants must have a qualifying CSU eligibility index, based on a combination of GPA and standardized test scores. Candidates for admission should have completed 4 years of English, 3 of math, 2 each of science and a foreign language, 1 each of social studies, U.S. history, and visual and performing arts, and 1 of electives. A GPA of 2.5 is required.

Procedure: Freshmen are admitted fall and spring. Entrance exams should be taken by October of the senior year. Applications should be filed by November 30 for fall entry and August 31 for spring entry. The Fall 2005 application fee was $55. Notification is sent in March. Applications are accepted on-line.

Transfer: 3813 transfer students enrolled in fall 2005. A minimum 2.0 GPA is required. Students with fewer than 56 transferable semester units must complete the regular admission procedure. Any number of units are accepted from a 4-year institution, but a maximum of 70 units may transfer from a 2-year institution. 30 of 124 to 133 credits required for the bachelor's degree must be completed at SDSU.

Visiting: There are regularly scheduled orientations for prospective students, including tours that can be scheduled with SDSU ambassadors. Visitors may stay overnight. To schedule a visit, contact Housing and Residential Life at (619) 594-6868.

Financial Aid: In 2005-2006, 79% of all full-time freshmen and 57% of continuing full-time students received some form of financial aid. At least 47% of full-time freshmen and at least 43% of continuing full-time students received need-based aid. The average freshman award was $6100. Need-based scholarships or need-based grants averaged $5600; need-based self-help aid (loans and jobs) averaged $2400; non-need-based athletic scholarships averaged $9900; and other non-need-based awards and non-need-based scholarships averaged $2500. The average financial indebtedness of the 2005 graduate was $14,500. SDSU is a member of CSS. The FAFSA and the state aid form are required.

International Students: There were 840 international students enrolled in a recent year. They must achieve a satisfactory score on the TOEFL and also take the college's own test and the SAT or the ACT.

Computers: All students may access the system. There are no time limits and no fees.

Graduates: From July 1, 2004 to June 30, 2005, 6325 bachelor's degrees were awarded. The most popular majors were business/marketing (18%), social sciences (11%), and liberal arts/general studies (10%). In an average class, 14% graduate in 4 years or less, 42% graduate in 5 years or less, and 53% graduate in 6 years or less.

Admissions Contact: Kathleen Deaver, Director of Admissions.
E-mail: *arweb.sdsu.edu/es/admissions* Web: *www.csumentor.edu*

SAN FRANCISCO ART INSTITUTE
San Francisco, CA 94133

B-3

(415) 749-4500
(800) 345-SFAI; Fax: (415) 749-4592

Full-time: 225 men, 200 women	**Faculty:** 35
Part-time: 40 men, 40 women	**Ph.D.s:** 99%
Graduate: 50 men, 80 women	**Student/Faculty:** 12 to 1
Year: semesters, summer session	**Tuition:** $25,640
Application Deadline: February 15	**Room & Board:** n/app
Freshman Class: n/av	
SAT or ACT: required	**SPECIAL**

San Francisco Art Institute, founded in 1871, is a private, commuter college devoted solely to the fine arts. Some figures in the above capsule and in this profile are approximate. In addition to regional accreditation, SFAI has baccalaureate program accreditation with NASAD. The library contains 22,000 volumes and 1500 audio/video tapes/CDs/DVDs, and subscribes to 210 periodicals including electronic. Special learning facilities include a learning resource center and art gallery. The 3-acre campus is in an urban area. There is one building.

Student Life: 66% are white; 11% foreign nationals. The average age of freshmen is 26; all undergraduates, 26. 12% do not continue beyond their first year; 15% remain to graduate.

Housing: There are no residence halls. All students commute. Alcohol is not permitted.

Activities: There are no fraternities or sororities. There are 7 groups on campus, including art, ethnic, gay, international, newspaper, and student government. Popular campus events include visiting artist lectures, symposia, and graduate open studios.

Sports: There is no sports program at SFAI.

Disabled Students: 70% of the campus is accessible. Wheelchair ramps, elevators, special parking, specially equipped rest rooms, and special class scheduling are available.

Services: Counseling and information services are available, as is tutoring in most subjects. There is remedial math, reading, and writing.

Campus Safety and Security: Measures include 24-hour foot and vehicle patrol, emergency telephones, and and video security cameras.

Programs of Study: SFAI confers the B.F.A. degree. Master's degrees are also awarded. Bachelor's degrees are awarded in COMMUNICATIONS AND THE ARTS (film arts, fine arts, painting, photography, printmaking, sculpture, and video). Painting and photography are the largest.

Required: Students are required to complete at least 120 credit hours, 36 of which must be in the major. 6 liberal arts units, 24 studio units, and 15 art history units must be completed, as well as 33 units in the Letters and Science Program. SFAI requires a minimum GPA of 2.0.

Special: Students may participate in off-campus internships for credit. There are study-abroad opportunities in 9 countries. There is an interdisciplinary program in which studio curricula are chosen that best support specific artistic direction. The institute offers dual majors in all subjects, nondegree study, work-study with SFAI, and pass/fail options in the senior year.

Faculty/Classroom: 52% of faculty are male; 48%, female. 96% teach undergraduates. No introductory courses are taught by graduate students. The average class size in an introductory lecture is 100; in a laboratory, 17; and in a regular course, 17.

Requirements: The SAT or ACT is required. A GPA of 2.5 is required. AP and CLEP credits are accepted. Important factors in the admissions decision are evidence of special talent, recommendations by school officials, and recommendations by alumni.

Procedure: Freshmen are admitted to all sessions. There is a deferred admissions plan. Priority applications should be filed by February 15 for fall entry. Notification is sent on a rolling basis.

Transfer: Transfer students must have satisfactory prior college performance and a portfolio appropriate to their level of experience. College transcripts and an essay are required. 30 of 120 credits required for the bachelor's degree must be completed at SFAI.

Visiting: There are guides for informal visits and visitors may sit in on classes. To schedule a visit, contact the Office of Admissions.

Financial Aid: The FAFSA is required. The recommended date for filing freshman financial aid applications for fall entry is March 1.

International Students: The school actively recruits these students. They must score satisfactorily on the written TOEFL.

Computers: All students may access the system. Students registered in CDM classes may access the system from 9 A.M. to 10 P.M. There are no time limits.

Admissions Contact: Mark Takiguchi, Director of Admissions. E-mail: *admissions@sfai.edu* Web: *www.sfai.edu*

SAN FRANCISCO CONSERVATORY OF MUSIC — B-3

San Francisco, CA 94122	(415) 759-3431; Fax: (415) 759-3499
Full-time: 60 men, 75 women	**Faculty:** 24
Part-time: 5 men, 5 women	**Ph.D.s:** 21%
Graduate: 50 men, 80 women	**Student/Faculty:** 6 to 1
Year: semesters	**Tuition:** $26,200
Application Deadline: January 15	**Room & Board:** n/app
Freshman Class: n/av	
SAT or ACT: required	**SPECIAL**

San Francisco Conservatory of Music, founded in 1917, is a private institution offering undergraduate, graduate, and nondegree programs in music. There is 1 graduate school. Some figures in the above profile and in this capsule are approximate. In addition to regional accreditation, SFCM has baccalaureate program accreditation with NASM. The library contains 44,782 volumes and 15,538 audio/video tapes/CDs/DVDs, and subscribes to 72 periodicals including electronic. Computerized library services include the card catalog, interlibrary loans, and database searching. The 5-acre campus is in an urban area in a residential neighborhood of San Francisco. There are 3 buildings.

Programs of Study: SFCM confers the B.Mus. degree. Master's degrees are also awarded. Bachelor's degrees are awarded in COMMUNICATIONS AND THE ARTS (music). Voice, piano, and violin are the largest.

Required: Students must complete 130 credit hours, 100 of which must be music related, and the remainder in general education courses, including courses in fine arts, English, history, and humanities . Specific required courses and total number of hours in the major vary by instrument. Students must also pass the senior recital and maintain a minimum GPA of 2.0.

Special: Work-study programs and accelerated degree programs are available.

Faculty/Classroom: 67% of faculty are male; 33%, female. All teach undergraduates. No introductory courses are taught by graduate students. The average class size in an introductory lecture is 15 and in a regular course, 7.

Requirements: The SAT or ACT is required. In addition, all applicants must have reached a high level of musical proficiency. An audition is required. A GPA of 2.5 is required. AP and CLEP credits are accepted. Important factors in the admissions decision are evidence of special talent, personality/intangible qualities, and extracurricular activities record.

Procedure: Freshmen are admitted fall and spring. Entrance exams should be taken by the late fall or early spring. There is an early admissions plan. Applications should be filed by January 15 for fall entry and October 1 for spring entry, along with a $100 fee.

Transfer: Transfer students must demonstrate a high level of musical proficiency, submit 2 letters of recommendation, and have a good academic record. An audition is required. 30 of 130 credits required for the bachelor's degree must be completed at SFCM.

Visiting: There are guides for informal visits and visitors may sit in on classes. To schedule a visit, contact Alex Brose in the Admissions Office.

Financial Aid: 85% of undergraduates work part time. Average annual earnings from campus work are $1700. The FAFSA and the college's own financial statement are required. Check with the school for current deadlines.

International Students: They must score satisfactorily on the TOEFL and also take the SAT or the ACT.

Computers: All students may access the system when the building is open. There are no time limits and no fees.

Graduates: In an average class, 61% graduate in 4 years or less, 64% graduate in 5 years or less, and 64% graduate in 6 years or less.

Admissions Contact: Alex Brose, Admissions Office. E-mail: *admit@sfcm.edu* Web: *www.sfcm.edu*

SAN FRANCISCO STATE UNIVERSITY — B-3

San Francisco, CA 94132	(415) 338-2355; Fax: (415) 338-0903
Full-time: 21,000 men and women	**Faculty:** 977; IIA, ++$
Part-time: none	**Ph.D.s:** n/av
Graduate: 7500 men and women	**Student/Faculty:** 21 to 1
Year: semesters, summer session	**Tuition:** $3000 ($11,000)
Application Deadline: see profile	**Room & Board:** $10,000
Freshman Class: n/av	
SAT or ACT: required	**COMPETITIVE**

San Francisco State University, founded in 1899, is a public liberal arts institution offering graduate and undergraduate programs as part of the California State University system. There are 8 undergraduate and 8 graduate schools. Figures in the above capsule and in this profile are approximate. In addition to regional accreditation, San Francisco State has baccalaureate program accreditation with AACSB, ACEJMC, ADA, AHEA, NASM, and NLN. The library contains 780,230 volumes, 2,209,455 microform items, and 72,245 audio/video tapes/CDs/DVDs, and subscribes to 5679 periodicals including electronic. Computerized library services include the card catalog, interlibrary loans, database searching, and Internet access. Special learning facilities include a learning resource center, art gallery, natural history museum, planetarium, radio station, TV station, field campus, Labor Archives and Research Center, Media Access Center, and anthropology museum. The 130-acre campus is in an urban area in San Francisco. Including any residence halls, there are 23 buildings.

Student Life: Most undergraduaties are from California. Others are from 17 states, 12 foreign countries, and Canada. 48% are white; 28% Asian American; 10% Hispanic. The average age of all undergraduates is 24. 17% do not continue beyond their first year; 62% remain to graduate.

Housing: College housing includes coed dorms. On-campus housing is available on a first-come, first-served basis. 95% of students commute. Alcohol is not permitted. All students may keep cars.

Activities: There are 12 national fraternities and 4 local and 8 national sororities. There are 200 groups on campus, including art, band, cheerleading, choir, chorale, chorus, dance, debate, drama, ethnic, film, gay, honors, jazz band, literary magazine, musical theater, newspaper, opera, orchestra, pep band, political, professional, radio and TV, social service, student government, symphony, and yearbook. Popular campus events include Activities Fair and Crafts Festival, Morrison Artists' Series Chamber Music Program, and the Alexander String Quartet.

Sports: There are 8 intercollegiate sports for men and 7 for women, and 10 intramural sports for men and 10 for women. Facilities include a 6500-seat stadium, 2 gyms, an indoor pool, a weight room, a training room, wrestling and gymnastics areas, an all-weather track, 14 tennis courts, softball and baseball fields, and auxiliary practice fields.

Disabled Students: Wheelchair ramps, elevators, special parking, specially equipped rest rooms, lowered drinking fountains, lowered telephones, and readers, interpreters, an equipment loan, on-campus transportation, and priority registration are available.

Services: Counseling and information services are available, as is tutoring in every subject.

Campus Safety and Security: Measures include 24-hour foot and vehicle patrol, self-defense education, security escort services, and shuttle buses. There are informal discussions, pamphlets/posters/films, emergency telephones, and lighted pathways/sidewalks.

Programs of Study: San Francisco State confers B.A., B.S., B.M., and B.Voc.Ed. degrees. Associate, master's, and doctoral degrees are also awarded. Bachelor's degrees are awarded in BIOLOGICAL SCIENCE (biochemistry, biology/biological science, botany, cell biology, ecology, marine biology, microbiology, physiology, and zoology), BUSINESS (accounting, banking and finance, business administration and management, international business management, labor studies, management science, marketing/retailing/merchandising, personnel management, real estate, and transportation management), COMMUNICATIONS AND THE ARTS (broadcasting, Chinese, classics, comparative literature, dance, dramatic arts, English, film arts, fine arts, French, German, Italian, Japanese, journalism, music, Russian, and speech/debate/rhetoric), COMPUTER AND PHYSICAL SCIENCE (applied mathematics, chemistry, computer science, geology, information sciences and systems, mathematics, physics, science, and statistics), EDUCATION (early childhood, elementary, home economics, industrial arts, physical, recreation, secondary, special, and vocational), ENGINEERING AND ENVIRONMENTAL DESIGN (civil engineering, electrical/electronics engineering, engineering, industrial administration/management, interior design, and mechanical engineering), HEALTH PROFESSIONS (allied health, clinical science, health science, medical laboratory technology, nursing, physical therapy, public health, and speech pathology/audiology), SOCIAL SCIENCE (African American studies, American studies, anthropology, clothing and textiles management/production/services, dietetics, economics, geography, history, humanities, interdisciplinary studies, international relations, liberal arts/general studies, philosophy, political science/government, psychology, social work, sociology, urban studies, and women's studies).

Required: To graduate, students must complete 124 to 132 credits with a minimum GPA of 2.0. The required general education core includes 27 credits in arts and sciences, 12 in basic skills subjects, and 9 in upper-division courses. English composition and U.S. history and government competency requirements may be fulfilled by either exam or course work.

Special: Students may cross-register with the California College of Podiatric Medicine, the City College of San Francisco, Cogswell College of Engineering, and several other area universities. Study abroad in numerous countries, a Washington semester, campus work-study, a general studies degree, dual and student-designed majors, credit for life experience, nondegree study, and pass/fail options are also offered. There is a chapter of Phi Beta Kappa and a freshman honors program.

Faculty/Classroom: 61% of faculty are male; 39%, female. No introductory courses are taught by graduate students.

Admissions: 66% of recent applicants were accepted. The ACT scores for a recent freshman class were: 33% below 21, 46% between 21 and 23, 20% between 24 and 26, and 2% above 28.

Requirements: The SAT or ACT is required. In addition, applicants should be graduates of an accredited secondary school with a minimum GPA of 2.0. The GED is accepted. High school courses should include 4 years of English, 3 of math, 2 of foreign language, and 1 each of U.S. history or government, lab science, and visual and performing arts. A GPA of 2.0 is required. AP and CLEP credits are accepted.

Procedure: Freshmen are admitted fall and spring. Notification is sent on a rolling basis. Applications are accepted on-line. Check with the school for current application deadlines and fee.

Transfer: Applicants must have a college GPA of 2.0 (2.4 for nonresidents). Those with fewer than 56 transferable semester credits must meet freshman entrance requirements. 30 of 124 credits required for the bachelor's degree must be completed at San Francisco State.

Visiting: There are regularly scheduled orientations for prospective students. There are guides for informal visits and visitors may sit in on classes. To schedule a visit, contact Student Outreach Services.

Financial Aid: In a recent year, need-based scholarships or need-based grants averaged $4652; and need-based self-help aid (loans and jobs) averaged $1855. The average financial indebtedness of a recent graduate was $15,265. San Francisco State is a member of CSS. The CSS/Profile or FFS is required.

International Students: They must score satisfactorily on the written TOEFL.

Computers: All students may access the system 24 hours daily. There are no time limits and no fees.

Graduates: In a recent year, 7344 bachelor's degrees were awarded. The most popular majors were business/marketing (25%), social sciences/history (10%), and visual and performing arts (9%). 33 companies recruited on campus in a recent year.

Admissions Contact: Student Outreach Services.
E-mail: *outreach@sfsu.edu* Web: *www.sfsu.edu*

SAN JOSE STATE UNIVERSITY   B-3

San Jose, CA 95192	**(408) 924-2000; Fax: (408) 924-2050**
Full-time: 7000 men, 7600 women	Faculty: 868; IIA, +$
Part-time: 3450 men, 3400 women	Ph.D.s: 84%
Graduate: 2000 men, 3550 women	Student/Faculty: 17 to 1
Year: semesters, summer session	Tuition: $3292 ($8000)
Application Deadline: April 1	Room & Board: $8415
Freshman Class: n/av	
SAT or ACT: required	**COMPETITIVE**

San Jose State University, founded in 1857 and part of the California State University system, is a public institution offering undergraduate and graduate programs in applied arts and science, social science, and social work to a primarily commuter student body. There are 8 undergraduate and 8 graduate schools. Some figures in the above capsule and in this profile are approximate. In addition to regional accreditation, SJSU has baccalaureate program accreditation with AACSB, ABET, ACEJMC, ADA, ASLA, NASAD, NASM, NCATE, and NLN. The 2 libraries contain 1,101,995 volumes, 1,621,426 microform items, and 37,146 audio/video tapes/CDs/DVDs, and subscribe to 2504 periodicals including electronic. Computerized library services include the card catalog, interlibrary loans, and database searching. Special learning facilities include a learning resource center, art gallery, radio station, and TV station. The 104-acre campus is in an urban area in the center of San Jose. Including any residence halls, there are 55 buildings.

Student Life: Most undergraduates are from California. Others are from 40 states, 114 foreign countries, and Canada. 89% are from public schools. 36% are Asian American; 30% white; 14% Hispanic. The average age of freshmen is 20; all undergraduates, 25.

Housing: 2014 students can be accommodated in college housing, which includes coed dorms, on-campus apartments, fraternity houses,

and sorority houses. In addition, there are special-interest houses and an international students center. On-campus housing is available on a first-come, first-served basis. Alcohol is not permitted. All students may keep cars.

Activities: 8% of men belong to 6 local and 15 national fraternities; 4% of women belong to 3 local and 9 national sororities. There are 175 groups on campus, including art, band, cheerleading, choir, chorale, chorus, dance, drama, ethnic, film, gay, international, literary magazine, marching band, musical theater, newspaper, photography, political, radio and TV, social, student government, and symphony. Popular campus events include International Food Bazaar, Welcome Day, and National Collegiate Alcohol Awareness Week.

Sports: There are 6 intercollegiate sports for men and 10 for women, and 17 intramural sports for men and 13 for women. Facilities include a gym, a pool, a track, a football field, and a recreation center with racquetball courts and a bowling alley.

Disabled Students: 95% of the campus is accessible. Wheelchair ramps, elevators, special parking, specially equipped rest rooms, special class scheduling, lowered drinking fountains, lowered telephones, and preadmission assistance are available.

Services: Counseling and information services are available, as is tutoring in most subjects. There is a reader service for the blind. There are also test accommodations, sign-language interpreters, liaisons to faculty, and note takers.

Campus Safety and Security: Measures include 24-hour foot and vehicle patrol, self-defense education, security escort services, and shuttle buses. There are informal discussions, pamphlets/posters/films, emergency telephones, lighted pathways/sidewalks, and and a canine patrol.

Programs of Study: SJSU confers B.A., B.S., B.F.A., and B.Mus. degrees. Master's degrees are also awarded. Bachelor's degrees are awarded in BIOLOGICAL SCIENCE (biochemistry, biology/biological science, botany, microbiology, and zoology), BUSINESS (accounting, banking and finance, business administration and management, international business management, and marketing/retailing/merchandising), COMMUNICATIONS AND THE ARTS (advertising, broadcasting, dance, design, dramatic arts, English, film arts, fine arts, French, German, journalism, music, Spanish, and speech/debate/rhetoric), COMPUTER AND PHYSICAL SCIENCE (chemistry, computer science, geology, mathematics, physics, and statistics), EDUCATION (early childhood and teaching English as a second/foreign language (TESOL/TEFOL)), ENGINEERING AND ENVIRONMENTAL DESIGN (aeronautical engineering, chemical engineering, civil engineering, computer engineering, electrical/electronics engineering, engineering, industrial engineering, interior design, materials engineering, and mechanical engineering), HEALTH PROFESSIONS (nursing, occupational therapy, and speech pathology/audiology), SOCIAL SCIENCE (anthropology, criminal justice, economics, food science, geography, history, philosophy, political science/government, psychology, religion, social science, social work, and sociology). Accounting is the strongest academically. Accounting, electrical engineering, and management are the largest.

Required: Students must complete 39 units of core general education, including 12 units of upper-division courses in residence and 6 units of American history and institutions. A minimum of 124 credits, with at least 24 in the major, a minimum GPA of 2.0, and the successful completion of writing, English, and entry-level math tests are required to graduate.

Special: SJSU has opportunities for cooperative programs in business, science, engineering, arts, and the humanities, work-study with many employers, internships (some required, some optional), study abroad in 16 countries, field experiences, and student teaching. An accelerated program is offered in nursing, and the B.A.-B.S. degree and dual majors are available in various areas of study. A general studies degree, student-designed majors, nondegree study, and credit/no-credit options are possible. There are 3 national honor societies and 18 departmental honors programs.

Faculty/Classroom: 66% of faculty are male; 34%, female. The average class size in an introductory lecture is 30; in a laboratory, 20; and in a regular course, 25.

Requirements: The SAT or ACT is required. In addition, scores are used to calculate an eligibility index rating, which determines qualification for admission. Graduation from an accredited secondary school is required; the GED is accepted. Applicants must have completed 4 years of English, 3 each of math and electives, 2 of a foreign language, and 1 each of history, science, and art. AP and CLEP credits are accepted. Important factors in the admissions decision are personality/intangible qualities, recommendations by alumni, and recommendations by school officials.

Procedure: Freshmen are admitted fall and spring. Entrance exams should be taken prior to the fall semester. There are early admissions and deferred admissions plans. There is a rolling admissions plan. The priority application period for fall entry is October 1 to November 30, for spring entry, August 1 to August 31. The application deadlines for regular applications is April 1 for fall, November 1 for Spring. Check with the school for current application fee.

Transfer: 2779 transfer students enrolled in 2004-2005. Applicants must have a minimum GPA of 2.0. The student's rating in the eligibility index is also considered in determining qualification for transfer. 30 of 124 credits required for the bachelor's degree must be completed at SJSU.

Visiting: There are regularly scheduled orientations for prospective students. There are guides for informal visits and visitors may sit in on classes. To schedule a visit, contact the Office of Relations with Schools at (408) 924-2564.

Financial Aid: SJSU is a member of CSS. The FAFSA is required. The deadline for filing freshman financial aid applications for fall entry is March 1.

International Students: The school actively recruits these students. They must score satisfactorily on the written TOEFL and also take the SAT or the ACT.

Computers: All students may access the system 9 A.M. to 8 P.M. Monday through Friday and 9 A.M. to 5 P.M. Saturday. There are no time limits and no fees.

Graduates: In an average class, 9% graduate in 4 years or less, 39% graduate in 5 years or less, and 70% graduate in 6 years or less.

Admissions Contact: John Bradbury, Director of Admissions. E-mail: *contact@anrnet.sjsu.edu*

SANTA CLARA UNIVERSITY   B-3

Santa Clara, CA 95053	(408) 554-4700; Fax: (408) 554-5255
Full-time: 1995 men, 2530 women	Faculty: 364; IIA, ++$
Part-time: 57 men, 56 women	Ph.D.s: 92%
Graduate: 1966 men, 1493 women	Student/Faculty: 12 to 1
Year: quarters, summer session	Tuition: $28,899
Application Deadline: January 15	Room & Board: $10,032
Freshman Class: 8904 applied, 5419 accepted, 1198 enrolled	
SAT Verbal/Math: 619/598*	ACT: 25 VERY COMPETITIVE

Santa Clara University, founded in 1851 by Jesuit priests, is a private institution offering undergraduate and graduate degrees in arts and sciences, engineering, business law, education, and counseling. There are 3 undergraduate and 5 graduate schools. In addition to regional accreditation, Santa Clara University has baccalaureate program accreditation with AACSB, ABET, and NASM. The 2 libraries contain 944,029 volumes, 1,880,611 microform items, and 15,497 audio/video tapes/CDs/DVDs, and subscribe to 8757 periodicals including electronic. Computerized library services include the card catalog, interlibrary loans, database searching, Internet access, and laptop Internet portals. Special learning facilities include a learning resource center, art gallery, planetarium, radio station, TV station, and a California Mission (archeology lab). The 106-acre campus is in a suburban area 46 miles south of San Francisco. Including any residence halls, there are 51 buildings.

Student Life: 65% of undergraduates are from California. Others are from 36 states, 11 foreign countries, and Canada. 49% are from public schools. 57% are white; 18% Asian American; 13% Hispanic. 45% are Catholic; 32% claim no religious affiliation; 12% Protestant. The average age of freshmen is 19; all undergraduates, 20. 6% do not continue beyond their first year; 85% remain to graduate.

Housing: 2300 students can be accommodated in college housing, which includes coed dorms, on-campus apartments, and off-campus apartments (graduate only). On-campus housing is guaranteed for the freshman year only, is available on a first-come, first-served basis, and is available on a lottery system for upperclassmen. Priority is given to out-of-town students. 54% of students commute. All students may keep cars.

Activities: There are no fraternities or sororities. There are 85 groups on campus, including art, cheerleading, choir, chorale, chorus, computers, dance, debate, drama, ethnic, film, forensics, gay, gospel choir, honors, international, jazz band, literary magazine, major-specific, musical theater, newspaper, opera, orchestra, pep band, photography, political, professional, radio and TV, religious, social, social service, student government, symphony, and yearbook. Popular campus events include Bronco Bust (Spirit Week), Special Olympics, and Cinco de Mayo.

Sports: There are 9 intercollegiate sports for men and 10 for women, and 8 intramural sports for men and 8 for women. Facilities include an activities center with a basketball pavilion, volleyball courts, a swimming pool, a weight-training section, and a sauna. There also is a 6800-seat stadium with practice fields nearby, and several fields for general recreation and intramurals.

Disabled Students: All of the campus is accessible. Wheelchair ramps, elevators, special parking, specially equipped rest rooms, special class scheduling, lowered drinking fountains, lowered telephones, and a TTY phone system are available. Residence halls have been restructured to allow disabled students to open all doors with a remote control. Scribes and note takers are also available.

Services: Counseling and information services are available, as is tutoring in most subjects.

Campus Safety and Security: Measures include 24-hour foot and vehicle patrol, security escort services, informal discussions, and pamphlets/posters/films. There are emergency telephones and lighted pathways/sidewalks.

Programs of Study: Santa Clara University confers B.A., B.S., B.S.C., and B.S.Ch. degrees. Master's and doctoral degrees are also awarded. Bachelor's degrees are awarded in AGRICULTURE (environmental studies), BIOLOGICAL SCIENCE (biology/biological science), BUSINESS (accounting, banking and finance, business administration and management, business economics, management information systems, and marketing/retailing/merchandising), COMMUNICATIONS AND THE ARTS (art history and appreciation, classical languages, classics, communications, dramatic arts, English, French, German, Greek, Italian, music, Spanish, and studio art), COMPUTER AND PHYSICAL SCIENCE (chemistry, computer science, information sciences and systems, mathematics, physics, and science), ENGINEERING AND ENVIRONMENTAL DESIGN (civil engineering, computer engineering, electrical/electronics engineering, engineering, engineering physics, environmental science, and mechanical engineering), SOCIAL SCIENCE (anthropology, classical/ancient civilization, economics, history, interdisciplinary studies, liberal arts/general studies, philosophy, political science/government, psychology, religion, sociology, and women's studies). Social sciences and engineering are the strongest academically. Social sciences and business are the largest.

Required: All students are required to maintain a GPA of at least 2.0 in both major and minor subjects. Students must take 175 quarter units for most bachelor's degrees. Core requirements include composition and literature, Western culture, foreign language, social sciences, math and natural sciences, technology, ethics, religious studies, United States, and World Cultures/Societies. The total number of hours in the major varies.

Special: Study abroad in 26 countries at 75 sites is offered, as are international internship and volunteer opportunities. A co-op program in engineering, dual majors, internships in business, government, and non-profit agencies, a general studies degree, student-designed majors, work-study, a Washington semester, and pass/fail options also are available. Minors are offered in environmental, retail, international studies, and international business. There are 21 national honor societies, including Phi Beta Kappa, a freshman honors program, and 4 departmental honors programs.

Faculty/Classroom: 61% of faculty are male; 39%, female. 70% teach undergraduates and 100% both teach and do research. No introductory courses are taught by graduate students. The average class size in an introductory lecture is 30; in a laboratory, 16; and in a regular course, 22.

Admissions: 61% of the 2005-2006 applicants were accepted. The SAT scores for the 2005-2006 freshman class were: Verbal--7% below 500, 38% between 500 and 599, 41% between 600 and 700, and 14% above 700; Math--4% below 500, 33% between 500 and 599, 47% between 600 and 700, and 16% above 700. The ACT scores were 18% above 28. 42 freshmen graduated first in their class.

Requirements: The SAT or ACT is required. In addition, applicants should have 18 academic units, including 4 years each of English and math, 3 each of foreign language and science, 1 or 2 of which are a lab, 1 each in social studies and history, and 2 in electives. An essay is required. An audition is recommended for theater arts majors. The GED is not accepted. AP credits are accepted. Important factors in the admissions decision are extracurricular activities record, advanced placement or honor courses, and recommendations by school officials.

Procedure: Freshmen are admitted fall, winter, and spring. Entrance exams should be taken by February 1. There are early decision, deferred admissions, and rolling admissions plans. Early decision applications should be filed by November 15; regular applications, by January 15 for fall entry, along with a $55 fee. Notification of early decision is sent December 20; regular decision, on a rolling basis. 1200 early decision candidates were accepted for the 2005-2006 class. 505 applicants were on the 2005 waiting list; 351 were admitted. Applications are accepted online.

Transfer: 242 transfer students enrolled in 2004-2005. Transfer students need a minimum GPA of 3.0. 87 of 175 credits required for the bachelor's degree must be completed at Santa Clara University.

Visiting: There are regularly scheduled orientations for prospective students, including an open house in October, with overviews of academic programs and student activities, and preview weekend in April for accepted students. There are guides for informal visits and visitors may sit in on classes and stay overnight. To schedule a visit, contact the Undergraduate Admissions Office.

Financial Aid: In 2005-2006, 37% of all full-time freshmen and 43% of continuing full-time students received some form of financial aid. 38% of full-time freshmen and 40% of continuing full-time students received need-based aid. The average freshman award was $17,578. Need-based scholarships or need-based grants averaged $14,253; need-based self-help aid (loans and jobs) averaged $5022; non-need-based athletic scholarships averaged $19,722; and other non-need-based awards and non-need-based scholarships averaged $10,595. 57% of undergraduates work part time. Average annual earnings from campus work are $1324. The average financial indebtedness of the 2005 graduate was $17,620. The CSS/Profile or FAFSA is required. The priority date for freshman financial aid applications for fall entry is February 1.

International Students: There are 120 international students enrolled. Satisfactory scores are required on the written TOEFL and the SAT or the ACT.

Computers: Wireless access is available. PCs are concentrated in 6 general-purpose computing labs and 21 discipline or college specific labs and are loaded with software for word processing, spreadsheet, database, presentation, programming, and discipline-specific use. There are more than 800 campus computer or kiosks. High-speed Ethernet access is available in residence hall rooms. Access to the network is monitored. Students may use their own computers to access the network. Wireless access is available in libraries, some classrooms, and campus common areas. All students may access the system. There are no time limits and no fees.

Graduates: From July 1, 2004 to June 30, 2005, 1233 bachelor's degrees were awarded. The most popular majors were business/marketing (32%), social studies and history (13%), and engineering/engineering technologies (11%). In an average class, 78% graduate in 4 years, 86% graduate in 5 years, and 84% graduate in 6 years. 230 companies recruited on campus in 2004-2005. Of the 2004 graduating class, 14% were enrolled in graduate school within 6 months of graduation and 71% were employed.

Admissions Contact: Sandra Hayes, Dean of Admissions. A video is available. E-mail: *ugadmissions@scu.edu* Web: *www.scu.edu*

SCRIPPS COLLEGE   D-5
Claremont, CA 91711-3948

	(909) 621-8149
	(800) 770-1333; Fax: (909) 607-7508
Full-time: 872 women	**Faculty:** 63; IIB, ++$
Part-time: 6 women	**Ph.D.s:** 97%
Graduate: none	**Student/Faculty:** 14 to 1
Year: semesters	**Tuition:** $31,500
Application Deadline: January 1	**Room & Board:** $9500
Freshman Class: 1836 applied, 847 accepted, 234 enrolled	
SAT Verbal/Math: 690/670*	**ACT:** 30 **MOST COMPETITIVE**

Scripps College, founded in 1926, is a private liberal arts institution for women. A member of the Claremont Colleges, Scripps emphasizes a challenging core curriculum based on interdisciplinary humanistic studies. In addition to regional accreditation, Scripps has baccalaureate program accreditation with WASC. The 4 libraries contain 2,476,503 volumes, 1,455,319 microform items, and 10,861 audio/video tapes/CDs/DVDs, and subscribe to 15,995 periodicals including electronic. Computerized library services include the card catalog, interlibrary loans, database searching, and laptop Internet portals. Special learning facilities include an art gallery, radio station, TV station, humanities museum, and biological field station. The 30-acre campus is in a suburban area 35 miles east of Los Angeles. Including any residence halls, there are 27 buildings.

Student Life: 58% of undergraduates are from out of state, mostly the Northwest. Others are from 47 states, 18 foreign countries, and Canada. 60% are from public schools. 58% are white; 13% Asian American. The average age of freshmen is 18; all undergraduates, 20. 12% do not continue beyond their first year; 76% remain to graduate.

Housing: 784 students can be accommodated in college housing, which includes single-sex dorms, on-campus apartments, and foreign language corridors. On-campus housing is guaranteed for all 4 years. 96% of students live on campus; of those, 80% remain on campus on weekends. All students may keep cars.

Activities: There are no fraternities. There are 200 groups on campus, including art, choir, chorale, chorus, computers, dance, debate, drama, ethnic, film, gay, honors, international, literary magazine, musical theater, newspaper, orchestra, photography, political, professional, radio and TV, religious, social, social service, student government, symphony, and yearbook. Popular campus events include Break Away Series, Scripps Outdoor Adventure Program, and Freshman Mugging.

Sports: Facilities include 2 gyms, tennis court, 3 swimming pools, a climbing wall, a workout room, an outdoor track, and fields for baseball, softball, and soccer.

Disabled Students: 70% of the campus is accessible. Wheelchair ramps, elevators, special parking, specially equipped rest rooms, special class scheduling, lowered drinking fountains, and special housing are available.

Services: Counseling and information services are available, as is tutoring in every subject. There is a reader service for the blind.

Campus Safety and Security: Measures include 24-hour foot and vehicle patrol, self-defense education, security escort services, and informal discussions. There are pamphlets/posters/films, emergency telephones, and lighted pathways/sidewalks.

Programs of Study: Scripps confers the B.A. degree. Bachelor's degrees are awarded in BIOLOGICAL SCIENCE (biology/biological science, molecular biology, and neurosciences), COMMUNICATIONS AND THE ARTS (art history and appreciation, classical languages, dance, dramatic arts, English, Germanic languages and literature, Italian, languages, music, and studio art), COMPUTER AND PHYSICAL SCI-

ENCE (chemistry, computer science, mathematics, physics, science and management, and science technology), ENGINEERING AND ENVIRONMENTAL DESIGN (engineering, environmental science, and pre-engineering), SOCIAL SCIENCE (African American studies, American studies, anthropology, Asian/American studies, Asian/Oriental studies, classical/ancient civilization, economics, European studies, French studies, German area studies, Hispanic American studies, history, humanities, Italian studies, Judaic studies, Latin American studies, Mexican-American/Chicano studies, philosophy, political science/government, prelaw, psychology, religion, and women's studies). English, studio art, and biology are the strongest academically. Social science, politics, and international relations are the largest.

Required: To graduate, students must complete a total of 128 credits, or 32 courses with a minimum C average. Core requirements include the 3-semester humanities core, 2 additional courses in humanities, and 1 course each in fine arts, letters, natural sciences, social sciences, and math. All students must also fulfill language and thesis requirements.

Special: Students may cross-register with any of the other Claremont Colleges. Scripps also offers internships, work-study programs, study abroad in 25 countries, a Washington semester, and student-designed, dual, and interdisciplinary majors, including organizational studies and science, technology, and society. Many courses are offered as seminars. There are 3-2 accelerated degree programs in the arts and business administration. A 3-2 engineering program (B.A.-B.S.) is offered with Harvey Mudd College, Washington University in St. Louis, USC, UC Berkeley, and Columbia, Stanford, and Boston Universities. There are 3 national honor societies, including Phi Beta Kappa, and 16 departmental honors programs.

Faculty/Classroom: 42% of faculty are male; 58%, female. 100% both teach and do research. The average class size in an introductory lecture is 30; in a laboratory, 20; and in a regular course, 16.

Admissions: 46% of the 2005-2006 applicants were accepted. The SAT scores for the 2005-2006 freshman class were: Verbal--1% below 500, 5% between 500 and 599, 51% between 600 and 700, and 43% above 700; Math--1% below 500, 11% between 500 and 599, 59% between 600 and 700, and 29% above 700. The ACT scores were 4% between 21 and 23, 17% between 24 and 26, 30% between 27 and 28, and 49% above 28. 87% of the current freshmen were in the top fifth of their class; 99% were in the top two fifths. There were 17 National Merit finalists and 8 semifinalists. 8 freshmen graduated first in their class.

Requirements: The SAT or ACT is required. In addition, applicants must have completed 4 units each of high school English and math, 3 each of lab science and social studies, and either 3 of a single foreign language or 2 each of 2 languages. SAT: Subject tests and an interview are recommended. An essay and a graded writing assignment from the junior or senior year are required. Scripps requires applicants to be in the upper 25% of their class. A GPA of 3.5 is required. AP and CLEP credits are accepted. Important factors in the admissions decision are advanced placement or honor courses, evidence of special talent, and leadership record.

Procedure: Freshmen are admitted fall and spring. Entrance exams should be taken by December of the senior year. There are early decision and deferred admissions plans. Early decision applications should be filed by November 1; regular applications, by January 1 for fall entry and November 15 for spring entry, along with a $50 fee. Notification of early decision is sent December 15; regular decision, April 1. 49 early decision candidates were accepted for the 2005-2006 class. 428 applicants were on the 2005 waiting list; 1 was admitted.

Transfer: 18 transfer students enrolled in a recent year. A cumulative college GPA of 3.0 is required. 64 of 128 credits required for the bachelor's degree must be completed at Scripps.

Visiting: There are guides for informal visits and visitors may sit in on classes and stay overnight. To schedule a visit, contact the Admission Office at *admission@scrippscollege.edu*.

Financial Aid: In 2005-2006, 64% of all full-time freshmen and 61% of continuing full-time students received some form of financial aid. 43% of all full-time students received need-based aid. The average freshman award was $26,229. Need-based scholarships or need-based grants averaged $22,305 ($37,771 maximum); need-based self-help aid (loans and jobs) averaged $3878 ($5425 maximum); and other non-need-based awards and non-need-based scholarships averaged $13,626 ($42,100 maximum). Average annual earnings from campus work are $1800. The average financial indebtedness of the 2005 graduate was $12,907. Scripps is a member of CSS. The CSS/Profile or FAFSA is required. The priority date for freshman financial aid applications for fall entry is February 1.

International Students: There are 10 international students enrolled. The school actively recruits these students. They must take the TOEFL.

Computers: Wireless access is available. All students may access the system. There are no time limits and no fees.

Graduates: From July 1, 2004 to June 30, 2005, 181 bachelor's degrees were awarded. The most popular majors were psychology (12%), English (9%), and studio art (9%). In an average class, 2% graduate in

3 years or less, 74% graduate in 4 years or less, 83% graduate in 5 years or less, and 84% graduate in 6 years or less. 214 companies recruited on campus in 2004-2005. Of the 2004 graduating class, 22% were enrolled in graduate school within 6 months of graduation and 62% were employed.

Admissions Contact: Patricia F. Goldsmith, Vice President and Dean of Admissions, Financial Aid. E-mail: *admission@scrippscollege.edu* Web: *www.scrippscol.edu*

SIMPSON UNIVERSITY (Formerly Simpson College) — B-3

Redding, CA 96003
(530) 224-5600
(800) 598-2493; Fax: (530) 226-4861

Full-time: 321 men, 575 women	**Faculty:** 40
Part-time: 6 men, 22 women	**Ph.Ds:** 60%
Graduate: 62 men, 108 women	**Student/Faculty:** 22 to 1
Year: semesters, summer session	**Tuition:** $17,000
Application Deadline: open	**Room & Board:** $5900
Freshman Class: 784 applied, 743 accepted, 186 enrolled	
SAT Verbal/Math: 520/500*	**ACT:** 21 COMPETITIVE

Simpson University, formerly Simpson College, founded in 1921, is a private Christian liberal arts college. An official institution of the Christian and Missionary Alliance, the student population represents more than 25 evangelical denominations. In addition to regional accreditation, Simpson has baccalaureate program accreditation with WASC. The library contains 90,000 volumes, 225,000 microform items, and 2240 audio/video tapes/CDs/DVDs, and subscribes to 350 periodicals including electronic. Computerized library services include the card catalog, interlibrary loans, database searching, and Internet access. Special learning facilities include a learning resource center. The 92-acre campus is in a suburban area in the northeast city limits of Redding. Including any residence halls, there are 11 buildings.

Student Life: 86% of undergraduates are from California. Students are from 24 states, 6 foreign countries, and Canada. 86% are white. Most are Protestant. The average age of freshmen is 18; all undergraduates, 25. 40% do not continue beyond their first year; 60% remain to graduate.

Housing: 590 students can be accommodated in college housing, which includes single-sex dorms, off-campus apartments, and married-student housing. On-campus housing is guaranteed for all 4 years. 66% of students live on campus; of those, 90% remain on campus on weekends. Alcohol is not permitted. All students may keep cars.

Activities: There are no fraternities or sororities. There are 17 groups on campus, including art, cheerleading, choir, chorale, drama, ethnic, jazz band, literary magazine, newspaper, pep band, photography, professional, religious, social, social service, student government, and yearbook. Popular campus events include Spring and Winter Banquet, Missions Emphasis Week, and Multicultural Appreciation Day.

Sports: There are 3 intercollegiate sports for men and 3 for women, and 4 intramural sports for men and 4 for women. Facilities include a soccer field, a 1450-seat gym, weight and training rooms, softball field, and outdoor volleyball and basketball courts. Students have access to nearby facilities for swimming, boating, mountain climbing, and skiing.

Disabled Students: 95% of the campus is accessible. Wheelchair ramps, elevators, special parking, specially equipped rest rooms, lowered drinking fountains, lowered telephones, and special housing are available.

Services: Counseling and information services are available, as is tutoring in every subject.

Campus Safety and Security: Measures include 24-hour foot and vehicle patrol, security escort services, informal discussions, and emergency telephones. There are lighted pathways/sidewalks, an emergency whistle program, local police patrols, and monthly campus safety meetings.

Programs of Study: Simpson confers the B.A. degree. Associate and master's degrees are also awarded. Bachelor's degrees are awarded in BUSINESS (accounting, business administration and management, human resources, and institutional management), COMMUNICATIONS AND THE ARTS (communications, English, and music), COMPUTER AND PHYSICAL SCIENCE (mathematics), EDUCATION (elementary and secondary), SOCIAL SCIENCE (biblical studies, history, liberal arts/general studies, ministries, missions, pastoral studies, psychology, religion, religious education, social science, and youth ministry). Psychology, education, and human resources are the largest.

Required: Students must complete at least 124 credits, with a minimum of 36-upper division credits and at least 30 major credits (of which 24 must be upper division). A minimum grade point average of 2.0 must be maintained. Foundational studies requirements include 24 credits in Biblical Christianity and its foundations and 48 credits in human expression, human history and behavior, and global environment. Additionally, graduation requirements include the completion of an application for degree and recommendation by the undergraduate faculty.

Special: Off-Campus educational programs are offered through the China Studies Program, Contemporary Music Program in Martha's Vineyard, Latin American Studies Program, Los Angeles Film Studies Center, Middle East Studies Program, Oxford Honors Program, and the Russian Studies Program. Students may study abroad in a variety of countries. Internships are available in Christian education, pastoral studies, youth ministries business, and psychology. Work-study programs in elementary education and with the federal government are also available. There is also a 1-year, non-degree certificate program in Bible and contemporary church music. An accelerated degree program in business and human resources management, liberal arts, psychology, organizational leadership, and Christian ministry leadership are also available for students with 60 college credits and 5 years of full-time experience. There is 1 national honor society.

Faculty/Classroom: 80% of faculty are male; 20%, female. All teach undergraduates. The average class size in an introductory lecture is 25; in a laboratory, 13; and in a regular course, 14.

Admissions: 95% of the 2005-2006 applicants were accepted. The SAT scores for the 2005-2006 freshman class were: Verbal--43% below 500, 45% between 500 and 599, 11% between 600 and 700, and 1% above 700; Math--49% below 500, 43% between 500 and 599, 7% between 600 and 700, and 1% above 700. The ACT scores were 47% below 21, 22% between 21 and 23, 13% between 24 and 26, 13% between 27 and 28, and 5% above 28. 35% of the current freshmen were in the top fifth of their class; 60% were in the top two fifths. 1 freshman graduated first in the class.

Requirements: The SAT or ACT is required. In addition, applicants must be graduates of an accredited high school or have a GED. It is recommended that applicants have completed 4 years of high school English, 3 each of math, science, and social studies/history, and 2 of a foreign language. A GPA of 2.0 is required. AP and CLEP credits are accepted. Important factors in the admissions decision are leadership record, personality/intangible qualities, and recommendations by school officials.

Procedure: Freshmen are admitted to all sessions. Entrance exams should be taken during the junior year or in the fall of the senior year. There is a deferred admissions plan and a rolling admissions plan. Application deadlines are open. Application fee is $20. Notification is sent on a rolling basis. Applications are accepted on-line.

Transfer: 101 transfer students enrolled in a recent year. Transfer applicants with at least 30 semester college credits need not submit SAT or ACT scores. 30 of 124 credits required for the bachelor's degree must be completed at Simpson.

Visiting: There are regularly scheduled orientations for prospective students, consisting of College Days weekend, offered each spring. There are guides for informal visits and visitors may sit in on classes and stay overnight. To schedule a visit, contact Sarah Kriz, visit coordinator at the Admissions Office.

Financial Aid: In 2005-2006, 85% of all full-time students received some form of financial aid. 77% of full-time freshmen and 81% of continuing full-time students received need-based aid. The average freshman award was $10,975. Need-based scholarships or need-based grants averaged $4600; need-based self-help aid (loans and jobs) averaged $3750; and other non-need-based awards and non-need-based scholarships averaged $2625. Simpson is a member of CSS. The FAFSA and the college's own financial statement are required. The priority date for freshman financial aid applications for fall entry is March 2.

International Students: There were 5 international students enrolled in a recent year. A satisfactory score is required on the written TOEFL. Students must also take the SAT or the ACT.

Computers: All students may access the system. Students may access the system only during hours of operation of the specific facility. There are no fees. It is strongly recommended that all students have a PC.

Graduates: In a recent year, 296 bachelor's degrees were awarded. The most popular majors were liberal arts (25%), psychology (20%), and human resources management (18%). In an average class, 1% graduate in 3 years or less, 4% graduate in 4 years or less, 36% graduate in 5 years or less, and 45% graduate in 6 years or less.

Admissions Contact: Ron Cushman, Director of Enrollment. E-mail: *admissions@simpsonca.edu* Web: *www.simpsonca.edu*

SONOMA STATE UNIVERSITY — B-3

Rohnert Park, CA 94928
(707) 664-2778; Fax: (707) 664-2060

Full-time: 2200 men, 3850 women	**Faculty:** 246; IIA, +$
Part-time: 400 men, 550 women	**Ph.Ds:** 95%
Graduate: 400 men, 975 women	**Student/Faculty:** 24 to 1
Year: semesters, summer session	**Tuition:** $3616 ($8400)
Application Deadline: November	**Room & Board:** $7500
Freshman Class: n/av	
SAT or ACT: required	COMPETITIVE

Sonoma State University, founded in 1960 and part of the California State University system, offers undergraduate programs in business and economics, natural sciences, social sciences, and arts and humanities, and graduate programs in education, counseling, business, and other fields. There are 4 undergraduate schools and 1 graduate school. Figures in the above capsule and in this profile are approximate. In addition to regional accreditation, Sonoma State has baccalaureate program accreditation with NASAD, NASM, NLN, and ACS. The library contains 706,537 volumes, 1,669,872 microform items, and 27,895 audio/video tapes/CDs/DVDs, and subscribes to 1085 periodicals including electronic. Computerized library services include the card catalog, interlibrary loans, and database searching. Special learning facilities include a learning resource center, art gallery, radio station, observatory, and natural preserve. The 275-acre campus is in a suburban area 45 miles north of San Francisco. Including any residence halls, there are 62 buildings.

Student Life: 97% of undergraduates are from California. Others are from 39 states, 36 foreign countries, and Canada. 93% are from public schools. 64% are white; 10% Hispanic. The average age of freshmen is 18; all undergraduates, 23. 20% do not continue beyond their first year; 50% remain to graduate.

Housing: 2341 students can be accommodated in college housing, which includes single-sex and coed dormitories and on-campus apartments. In addition, there are special-interest houses, and women-in-science, substance-free, and intensive houses. On-campus housing is guaranteed for the freshman year only and is available on a first-come, first-served basis. 62% of students commute. All students may keep cars.

Activities: 6% of men belong to 5 national fraternities; 5% of women belong to 4 national sororities. There are 100 groups on campus, including art, cheerleading, chess, choir, chorale, chorus, computers, dance, drama, ethnic, gay, honors, international, jazz band, literary magazine, musical theater, newspaper, orchestra, pep band, political, professional, radio and TV, religious, social, social service, student government, and video. Popular campus events include Science Night, Parents Day, and Unity Through Diversity Week.

Sports: There are 4 intercollegiate sports for men and 7 for women, and 10 intramural sports for men and 10 for women. Facilities include a 5000-seat stadium, a 3000-seat gym, a field house, tennis courts, a pool, a 500-seat auditorium, and various playing fields.

Disabled Students: All of the campus is accessible. Wheelchair ramps, elevators, special parking, specially equipped rest rooms, special class scheduling, lowered drinking fountains, and lowered telephones are available. A reading machine, phonic listening devices, PC and mainframe access, and interpreters are also available.

Services: Counseling and information services are available, as is tutoring in most subjects. There is a reader service for the blind, and remedial math, reading, and writing. Learning disability assessment is also available.

Campus Safety and Security: Measures include 24-hour foot and vehicle patrol, self-defense education, security escort services, and pamphlets/posters/films. There are emergency telephones and lighted pathways/sidewalks.

Programs of Study: Sonoma State confers B.A., B.S., and B.F.A. degrees. Master's degrees are also awarded. Bachelor's degrees are awarded in BIOLOGICAL SCIENCE (biology/biological science), BUSINESS (business administration and management), COMMUNICATIONS AND THE ARTS (art, communications, English, fine arts, French, music, Spanish, and visual and performing arts), COMPUTER AND PHYSICAL SCIENCE (chemistry, computer science, geology, mathematics, and physics), ENGINEERING AND ENVIRONMENTAL DESIGN (environmental science), HEALTH PROFESSIONS (nursing), SOCIAL SCIENCE (African American studies, American Indian studies, anthropology, criminal justice, economics, ethnic studies, gender studies, geography, history, human development, interdisciplinary studies, international studies, Latin American studies, liberal arts/general studies, Mexican-American/Chicano studies, philosophy, physical fitness/movement, political science/government, psychology, sociology, and women's studies). Liberal arts, physics, and math are the strongest academically. Business, psychology, and liberal studies are the largest.

Required: Undergraduate students must complete 120 to 132 units, depending on the degree program, consisting of 48 to 51 units of general education, a concentration of study in a specific major, and electives. General education programs require experience in oral and written communications, critical thinking, natural science and math, arts and humanities, social sciences, and personal integration. All students must take an ethnic studies course and the equivalent of courses in U.S. government, U.S. history, and California government.

Special: Students may cross-register at Mills College, Oakland, and University of California, Berkeley. Study-abroad programs are available in 17 countries. Community service internships, work-study, nondegree study through Open University, and pass/fail grading options are available. B.A. and B.S. options in biology, chemistry, environmental studies, geology, interdisciplinary studies, math, and physics are offered. The Hutchins School B.A. in liberal studies offers small seminar classes and an interdisciplinary curriculum. Distance learning programs in nursing are available at 3 off-site centers. There are 6 national honor societies and 5 departmental honors programs.

Faculty/Classroom: 58% of faculty are male; 42%, female. 99% teach undergraduates. Graduate students teach 1% of introductory courses. The average class size in an introductory lecture is 45; in a laboratory, 20; and in a regular course, 26.

Admissions: 84% of recent applicants were accepted. The SAT scores for a recent freshman class were: Verbal--39% below 500, 44% between 500 and 599, 15% between 600 and 700, and 2% above 700; Math--37% below 500, 47% between 500 and 599, 15% between 600 and 700, and 1% above 700. The ACT scores were 39% below 21, 35% between 21 and 23, 21% between 24 and 26, 3% between 27 and 28, and 2% above 28.

Requirements: The SAT or ACT is required unless the applicant has a 3.0 GPA. In addition, applicants should be graduates of accredited high schools or have earned the GED. Secondary school preparation should include 4 years each of arts and humanities, 3 each of English, math, social science, and academic electives, and 1 each of music, history, and a lab science. A GPA of 2.0 is required. AP and CLEP credits are accepted. Geographic diversity is an important factor in the admission decision.

Procedure: Freshmen are admitted fall and spring. Applications should be filed by November for fall entry and August for spring entry. Notification is sent on a rolling basis. Applications are accepted on-line. Check with the school for the current application fee.

Transfer: 646 transfer students enrolled in a recent year. Applicants must have a minimum 2.0 GPA. The maximum number of transferable credits is 70. 30 of 120 credits required for the bachelor's degree must be completed at Sonoma State.

Visiting: There are regularly scheduled orientations for prospective students, consisting of programs in the spring and summer. There are guides for informal visits and visitors may sit in on classes. To schedule a visit, contact the Admissions Development Office at (707) 664-3032.

Financial Aid: In a recent year, 66% of all full-time freshmen received some form of financial aid. 36% of full-time freshmen received need-based aid. The average freshman award was $12,548. Need-based scholarships or need-based grants averaged $5858; need-based self-help aid (loans and jobs) averaged $2865; and other non-need-based awards and non-need-based scholarships averaged $2120. 5% of undergraduates work part time. Average annual earnings from campus work are $1919. The average financial indebtedness of a recent graduate was $7848. The FAFSA is required. Check with the school for current deadlines.

International Students: There were 101 international students enrolled in a recent year. The school actively recruits these students. They must score satisfactorily on the TOEFL.

Computers: All students may access the system. There are no time limits and no fees. It is strongly recommended that all students have a personal computer.

Graduates: In a recent year, 1372 bachelor's degrees were awarded. The most popular majors were business administration (16%), psychology (11%), and liberal studies (10%). In an average class, 2% graduate in 3 years or less, 20% graduate in 4 years or less, 42% graduate in 5 years or less, and 49% graduate in 6 years or less. 275 companies recruited on campus in a recent year.

Admissions Contact: Gustavo Flores, Admissions Office. A video is available. E-mail: *gustavo.flores@sonoma.edu* Web: *www.sonoma.edu*

STANFORD UNIVERSITY
B-3

Stanford, CA 94305   (650) 725-3770; Fax: (650) 725-2846

Full-time: 3436 men, 3079 women	**Faculty:** 1010; I, ++$
Part-time: 27 men, 34 women	**Ph.D.s:** 99%
Graduate: 7470 men, 4996 women	**Student/Faculty:** 6 to 1
Year: trimesters, summer session	**Tuition:** $31,625
Application Deadline: December 15	**Room & Board:** $9932

Freshman Class: 20,192 applied, 2426 accepted, 1633 enrolled
SAT or ACT: required   **MOST COMPETITIVE**

Stanford University, founded in 1885, is a private research-intensive university offering a broad curriculum in undergraduate liberal arts, graduate education, and professional training. There are 3 undergraduate and 7 graduate schools. In addition to regional accreditation, Stanford has baccalaureate program accreditation with AACSB and ABET. The 19 libraries contain 82 million volumes, 58 million microform items, and 1,534,751 audio/video tapes/CDs/DVDs, and subscribe to 82,717 periodicals including electronic. Computerized library services include interlibrary loans, database searching, Internet access, and laptop Internet portals. Special learning facilities include a learning resource center, art gallery, radio station, TV station, an art museum, a biological preserve, and a linear accelerator. The 8180-acre campus is in a suburban area 30 miles south of San Francisco. Including any residence halls, there are 678 buildings.

Student Life: 56% of undergraduates are from out of state, mostly the Middle Atlantic. Students are from 50 states, 87 foreign countries, and Canada. 62% are from public schools. 41% are white; 24% Asian American; 11% Hispanic; 10% African American. The average age of freshmen is 18; all undergraduates, 20. 3% do not continue beyond their first year; 94% remain to graduate.

Housing: 10,290 students can be accommodated in college housing, which includes single-sex and coed dormitories, on-campus apartments, off-campus apartments, married-student housing, fraternity houses, and sorority houses. In addition, there are language houses, special-interest houses, and ethnic theme houses. On-campus housing is guaranteed for all 4 years. 99% of students live on campus; of those, 95% remain on campus on weekends. Upperclassmen may keep cars.

Activities: 13% of men belong to 15 national fraternities; 13% of women belong to 11 national sororities. There are 640 groups on campus, including art, band, cheerleading, chess, choir, chorale, computers, dance, debate, drama, ethnic, film, gay, honors, international, jazz band, literary magazine, marching band, musical theater, newspaper, orchestra, pep band, photography, political, professional, radio and TV, religious, social, social service, student government, symphony, and yearbook. Popular campus events include the Big Game, Full Moon on the Quad, and Pow Wow.

Sports: There are 15 intercollegiate sports for men and 19 for women, and 37 intramural sports for men and 37 for women. Facilities include athletic fields, gyms, swimming pools, volleyball courts, lighted tennis courts, dance studios, an 18-hole golf course, a sailing facility, a rowing facility, handball, racquetball, and squash courts, a baseball diamond, a football stadium, a softball stadium, and field hockey, lacrosse, and soccer fields.

Disabled Students: 92% of the campus is accessible. Wheelchair ramps, elevators, special parking, specially equipped rest rooms, special class scheduling, lowered drinking fountains, and lowered telephonesare available. Stanford has a Diversity and Access Office and an Office of Accessible Education to provide help.

Services: Counseling and information services are available, as is tutoring in most subjects. There is a reader service for the blind. Services also include a writing center and assistance for students with learning disabilities.

Campus Safety and Security: Measures include 24-hour foot and vehicle patrol, self-defense education, security escort services, and shuttle buses. There are informal discussions, pamphlets/posters/films, emergency telephones, and lighted pathways/sidewalks.

Programs of Study: Stanford confers A.B., B.S., and B.A.S. degrees. Master's and doctoral degrees are also awarded. Bachelor's degrees are awarded in BIOLOGICAL SCIENCE (biology/biological science), COMMUNICATIONS AND THE ARTS (art, Chinese, classics, communications, comparative literature, dramatic arts, English, fine arts, French, Italian, Japanese, linguistics, music, Slavic languages, and Spanish), COMPUTER AND PHYSICAL SCIENCE (chemistry, computer science, earth science, geology, geophysics and seismology, geoscience, mathematics, and physics), ENGINEERING AND ENVIRONMENTAL DESIGN (aeronautical science, chemical engineering, civil engineering, electrical/electronics engineering, engineering, industrial engineering, materials science, mechanical engineering, and petroleum/natural gas engineering), SOCIAL SCIENCE (African American studies, American studies, anthropology, archeology, crosscultural studies, East Asian studies, economics, German area studies, history, international relations, philosophy, political science/government, psychology, religion, sociology, systems science, urban studies, and women's studies). Biology, economics, and computer science are the largest.

Required: To graduate, students must complete 180 units, including requirements for the major, a writing requirement, and 1 year of a foreign language. General education requirements include 1 year of Introduction to the Humanities, 5 courses in disciplinary breadth, which includes engineering and applied sciences, humanities, math, natural sciences, and social sciences; and 2 courses in education for citizenship, which includes ethical reasoning, the global community, American cultures, and gender studies.

Special: Internships, study abroad, a Washington semester, student-designed majors, dual majors, a B.A.-B.S. degree, pass/no credit options, and numerous research opportunities are offered. There is a chapter of Phi Beta Kappa.

Faculty/Classroom: 76% of faculty are male; 24%, female. All both teach and do research. Graduate students teach 5% of introductory courses.

Admissions: 12% of the 2005-2006 applicants were accepted. The SAT scores for the 2005-2006 freshman class were: Verbal-5% between 500 and 599, 27% between 600 and 700, and 67% above 700; Math-3% between 500 and 599, 23% between 600 and 700, and 74% above 700. 96% of the current freshmen were in the top fifth of their class; 99% were in the top two fifths; 89% were in the top 10 percent.

Requirements: The SAT or ACT is required, the SAT is preferred. The SAT writing test is used for admission; the ACT writing test is required. The university recommends that applicants have strong preparation in high school English, math, a foreign language, science, and social studies. SAT Subject tests are strongly recommended. AP credits are accepted. Important factors in the admissions decision are advanced placement or honor courses, personality/intangible qualities, and recommendations by school officials.

Procedure: Freshmen are admitted in the fall. Entrance exams should be taken before December of the application year. There are early action and deferred admissions plans. Early action applications should be filed by November 1; regular applications, by December 15 for fall entry,

along with a $75 fee. A waiting list is an active part of the admissions procedure.Applications are accepted on-line.

Transfer: 81 transfer students enrolled in a recent year. Transfer students must complete 1 full year of academic work prior to enrollment. There is only fall quarter enrollment for transfer students. The application deadline is March 15. 90 of 180 credits required for the bachelor's degree must be completed at Stanford.

Visiting: There are regularly scheduled orientations for prospective students, including group information sessions and campus tours. There are guides for informal visits and visitors may sit in on classes. To schedule a visit, contact the Office of Undergraduate Admission at 650-723-2091.

Financial Aid: In 2005-2006, 76% of continuing full-time students received some form of financial aid. The average freshman award was $28,453. Need-based scholarships or need-based grants averaged $24,449; and need-based self-help aid (loans and jobs) averaged $3831. The average financial indebtedness of the 2005 graduate was $15,172. The CSS/Profile or FAFSA is required. The priority date for freshman financial aid applications for fall entry is February 1.

International Students: There are 403 international students enrolled. The school actively recruits these students. They must take the SAT or ACT. SAT Subject tests are strongly recommended.

Computers: Wireless access is available. Services include e-mail; individual, departmental and course web pages; a distributed file system; off-campus access to the Internet; and a variety of computer servers. Computer labs are available in all residences and libraries, as well as in many departments. All students may access the system. There are no time limits and no fees.

Graduates: From July 1, 2004 to June 30, 2005, 1788 bachelor's degrees were awarded. The most popular majors were biology/human biology (16%), economics (8%), and computer science (8%). In an average class, 94% graduate in 6 years or less. 325 companies recruited on campus in 2004-2005.

Admissions Contact: Richard H. Shaw, Dean of Admission. A video is available. E-mail: *rmamlet@stanford.edu* Web: *www.stanford.edu*

THOMAS AQUINAS COLLEGE C-5
Santa Paula, CA 93060

(805) 634-9797
(800) 634-9797; Fax: (805) 525-9342

Full-time: 176 men, 183 women	Faculty: 29
Part-time: none	Ph.D.s: 62%
Graduate: none	Student/Faculty: 12 to 1
Year: semesters	Tuition: $16,600
Application Deadline: open	Room & Board: $5800
Freshman Class: 196 applied, 159 accepted, 102 enrolled	
SAT Verbal/Math: 680/610	ACT: 26

HIGHLY COMPETITIVE+

Thomas Aquinas College, founded in 1969 and affiliated with the Roman Catholic Church, is a small, private, liberal arts college offering an integrated studies curriculum based on the Great Books. All classes are conducted as conversations directed by teachers using the Socratic method. In addition to regional accreditation, TAC has baccalaureate program accreditation with AALE. The library contains 58,000 volumes, 220 microform items, and 7920 audio/video tapes/CDs/DVDs, and subscribes to 60 periodicals including electronic. Computerized library services include the card catalog, interlibrary loans, database searching, and Internet access. Special learning facilities include a learning resource center and art gallery. The 170-acre campus is in a rural area 60 miles northwest of Los Angeles. Including any residence halls, there are 22 buildings.

Student Life: 64% of undergraduates are from out of state, mostly the Midwest. Students are from 41 states, 9 foreign countries, and Canada. 16% are from public schools. 82% are white. Most are Catholic. The average age of freshmen is 19; all undergraduates, 20. 13% do not continue beyond their first year; 77% remain to graduate.

Housing: 398 students can be accommodated in college housing, which includes single-sex dorms. On-campus housing is guaranteed for all 4 years. 99% of students live on campus; of those, 95% remain on campus on weekends. Alcohol is not permitted. All students may keep cars.

Activities: There are no fraternities or sororities. There are some groups and organizations on campus, including choir, drama, literary magazine, orchestra, and religious. Popular campus events include St. Thomas Aquinas Day, President's Day, and concerts, dances, and formal dinners.

Sports: There are 4 intramural sports for men and 2 for women. Facilities include tennis, basketball, and volleyball courts, a soccer field, a swimming area, a weight-lifting room, and a softball field.

Disabled Students: All of the campus is accessible. Wheelchair ramps, elevators, special parking, specially equipped rest rooms, lowered drinking fountains, lowered telephones, and special housing are available.

Services: All students may be tutored by the full-time teaching faculty.

Campus Safety and Security: Measures include lighted pathways/sidewalks, a security guard, and a campus gate.

Programs of Study: TAC confers the B.A. degree. Bachelor's degrees are awarded in SOCIAL SCIENCE (liberal arts/general studies).

Required: The entire curriculum is required of all students: this includes 4 years each of philosophy, theology, math, science, and seminar (which covers modern philosophy, literature, history, and social science), 2 years of language, and 1 year of music. Seniors are required to write a thesis. A total of 146 semester hours, with a minimum GPA of 2.0, is required to graduate.

Faculty/Classroom: 91% of faculty are male; 9%, female. All teach undergraduates. The average class size in an introductory lecture is 17; in a laboratory, 17; and in a regular course, 17.

Admissions: 81% of the 2005-2006 applicants were accepted. The SAT scores for the 2005-2006 freshman class were: Verbal--1% below 500, 11% between 500 and 599, 48% between 600 and 700, and 40% above 700; Math--3% below 500, 42% between 500 and 599, 44% between 600 and 700, and 11% above 700. The ACT scores were 13% below 21, 38% between 24 and 26, 13% between 27 and 28, and 38% above 28.

Requirements: The SAT or ACT is required. In addition, candidates for admission should have completed 4 years of English, 3 years of math, and 2 years each of a foreign language, history, and science. Important factors in the admissions decision are personality/intangible qualities, advanced placement or honor courses, and recommendations by school officials.

Procedure: Freshmen are admitted in the fall. Entrance exams should be taken by February. There is a deferred admissions plan. There is a rolling admissions plan. Application deadlines are open.

Transfer: Transfers are not accepted.

Visiting: There are regularly scheduled orientations for prospective students, including hosting of prospective students by current students. Visits are for up to 5 days and consist of observing classes and attending lectures, concerts, and meals. There are guides for informal visits and visitors may sit in on classes and stay overnight. To schedule a visit, contact the Admissions Office at (800) 634-9797, ext. 360 or *admissions@thomasaquinas.edu.*

Financial Aid: In 2005-2006, 78% of all full-time freshmen and 69% of continuing full-time students received some form of financial aid. 75% of full-time freshmen and 63% of continuing full-time students received need-based aid. The average freshman award was $15,962. Need-based scholarships or need-based grants averaged $10,157 ($17,074 maximum), and need-based self-help aid (loans and jobs) averaged $4980 ($6680 maximum). 60% of undergraduates work part time. Average annual earnings from campus work are $3180. The average financial indebtedness of the 2005 graduate was $14,000. TAC is a member of CSS. The FAFSA, the college's own financial statement, and parent and student federal tax returns are required. The deadline for filing freshman financial aid applications for fall entry is July 1.

International Students: There are 25 international students enrolled. They must achieve a satisfactory score on the TOEFL and also take the SAT or the ACT.

Computers: College e-mail access is available in the library through the college PCs and laptop ports and in the career center through a college PC. All students may access the system whenever available, or during library hours. There are no time limits and no fees.

Graduates: From July 1, 2004 to June 30, 2005, 63 bachelor's degrees were awarded. The most popular major was liberal arts (100%). In an average class, 69% graduate in 4 years, 74% graduate in 5 years, and 73% graduate in 6 years. 7 companies recruited on campus in 2004-2005. Of the 2004 graduating class, 15% were enrolled in graduate school within 6 months of graduation and 70% were employed.

Admissions Contact: Johnathan P. Daly, Director of Admission. A video is available. E-mail: *admissions@thomasaquinas.edu* Web: *thomasaquinas.edu*

UNIVERSITY OF CALIFORNIA SYSTEM

The University of California System, established in 1868, is a public system in California. It is governed by a board of regents, whose chief administrator is the president. The primary goal of the system is teaching, research, and public service. The total enrollment of all 9 campuses is usually about 163,000; there were 7050 faculty members. Altogether there are some 565 baccalaureate, 250 master's, and 200 doctoral programs offered in University of California System. 4-year campuses are located in Berkeley,, Davis,, Irvine,, Los Angeles,, Riverside,, San Diego,, and Santa Barbara, and. Profiles of the 4-year campuses are included in this section.

UNIVERSITY OF CALIFORNIA AT BERKELEY   B-3

Berkeley, CA 94720-5800   (510) 642-2316; Fax: (510) 642-7333

Full-time: 9989 men, 11,782 women	**Faculty:** 1496; I, +$
Part-time: 546 men, 563 women	**Ph.D s:** 99%
Graduate: 5385 men, 4549 women	**Student/Faculty:** 15 to 1
Year: semesters, summer session	**Tuition:** $6512 ($24,332)
Application Deadline: November 30	**Room & Board:** $11,629
Freshman Class: 36,784 applied, 9024 accepted, 3671 enrolled	
SAT Verbal/Math: 653/691*	**HIGHLY COMPETITIVE+**

The University of California at Berkeley, founded in 1868, is a public institution offering a wide variety of programs in the social and physical sciences, liberal arts, and professional fields. It is the oldest campus of the University of California system. There are 7 undergraduate and 14 graduate schools. In addition to regional accreditation, Cal has baccalaureate program accreditation with AACSB, ABET, ADA, ASLA, CSWE, NAAB, and SAF. The 35 libraries contain 9,812,900 volumes, 6,708,400 microform items, and 121,400 audio/video tapes/CDs/DVDs, and subscribe to 79,390 periodicals including electronic. Computerized library services include the card catalog, interlibrary loans, and database searching. Special learning facilities include a learning resource center, art gallery, natural history museum, radio station, TV station, a botanical garden, an anthropology museum, a hall of science, the University Art Museum and Pacific Film Archive, a seismographic station, an herbaria, the Hall for the Performing Arts, an observatory, and many off-campus facilities. The 1232-acre campus is in an urban area 10 miles east of San Francisco. Including any residence halls, there are 100 buildings.

Student Life: 89% of undergraduates are from California. Students are from 46 states, 79 foreign countries, and Canada. 85% are from public schools. 43% are Asian American; 31% white; 11% Hispanic. The average age of freshmen is 19; all undergraduates, 21. 3% do not continue beyond their first year; 87% remain to graduate.

Housing: 8000 students can be accommodated in college housing, which includes single-sex and coed dorms, off-campus apartments, married-student housing, fraternity houses, and sorority houses. In addition, there are honors houses, language houses, special-interest houses, substance-free housing, an international house, theme housing, and co-ops. On-campus housing is guaranteed for the freshman year only and is available on a lottery system for upperclassmen. All students may keep cars.

Activities: 11% of men belong to 14 local and 38 national fraternities; 10% of women belong to 7 local and 13 national sororities. There are more than 400 groups on campus, including art, band, cheerleading, chess, choir, chorale, chorus, computers, dance, debate, drama, ethnic, film, forensics, gay, honors, international, jazz band, literary magazine, marching band, musical theater, newspaper, orchestra, pep band, photography, political, professional, radio and TV, religious, social, social service, student government, symphony, and yearbook. Popular campus events include The Big Game, Cal Performances, and E-Week.

Sports: There are 13 intercollegiate sports for men and 13 for women, and 14 intramural sports for men and 14 for women. Facilities include a football stadium, a track stadium, a basketball pavilion, 4 gyms, a martial arts room, 7 swimming pools, 3 weight rooms, squash, racquetball, handball, volleyball, and tennis courts, and baseball and softball fields.

Disabled Students: 95% of the campus is accessible. Wheelchair ramps, elevators, special parking, specially equipped rest rooms, special class scheduling, lowered drinking fountains, and lowered telephones are available.

Services: Counseling and information services are available, as is tutoring in most subjects. There is a reader service for the blind, a workshop in study strategy and note taking, counseling, an athletic study center, and a disabled students program.

Campus Safety and Security: Measures include 24-hour foot and vehicle patrol, self-defense education, security escort services, and shuttle buses. There are informal discussions, pamphlets/posters/films, emergency telephones, lighted pathways/sidewalks, a rape prevention peer education program, and an earthquake emergency preparedness program.

Programs of Study: Cal confers A.B. and B.S. degrees. Master's and doctoral degrees are also awarded. Bachelor's degrees are awarded in AGRICULTURE (conservation and regulation and forestry and related sciences), BIOLOGICAL SCIENCE (biology/biological science, microbiology, molecular biology, nutrition, and plant genetics), BUSINESS (business administration and management, management science, and operations research), COMMUNICATIONS AND THE ARTS (art, art history and appreciation, Chinese, classical languages, communications, comparative literature, dance, dramatic arts, Dutch, English, film arts, French, German, Greek, Italian, Japanese, Latin, linguistics, music, Scandinavian languages, Slavic languages, Spanish, and speech/debate/rhetoric), COMPUTER AND PHYSICAL SCIENCE (applied mathematics, astrophysics, chemistry, computer science, earth science, mathematics, physical sciences, physics, and statistics), ENGINEERING AND ENVIRONMENTAL DESIGN (architecture, bioengineering, chemical engineering, civil engineering, computer engineering, electrical/electronics engineering, engineering and applied science, engineering physics, environmental engineering, environmental science, industrial engineering, landscape architecture/design, manufacturing engineering, materials engineering, materials science, mechanical engineering, and nuclear engineering), HEALTH PROFESSIONS (optometry and public health), SOCIAL SCIENCE (African American studies, American studies, anthropology, Asian/American studies, Asian/Oriental studies, Celtic studies, classical/ancient civilization, cognitive science, economics, ethnic studies, geography, Hispanic American studies, history, interdisciplinary studies, Latin American studies, law, Middle Eastern studies, Native American studies, Near Eastern studies, peace studies, philosophy, political science/government, psychology, religion, social science, social work, sociology, South Asian studies, urban studies, and women's studies). Electrical engineering and computer science, political science, and English are the largest.

Required: All undergraduate students are required to satisfy the general university requirements of English and writing proficiency, and integrative and comparative courses in American history, institutions, and cultures. Students must complete 120 units with a minimum GPA of 2.0.

Special: Co-op programs, cross-registration with many area schools, internships, work-study programs, and study abroad in 33 countries are available. Interdisciplinary majors are also available. Students may double-major, earn dual degrees, design their own majors, study independently, and choose pass/fail options. Students have opportunities for independent or team research. There are 6 national honor societies, including Phi Beta Kappa.

Faculty/Classroom: 73% of faculty are male; 27%, female. All teach undergraduates and 80% do research. The average class size in a regular course is 38.

Admissions: 25% of the 2005-2006 applicants were accepted. The SAT scores for the 2005-2006 freshman class were: Verbal--8% below 500, 21% between 500 and 599, 41% between 600 and 700, and 30% above 700; Math--4% below 500, 15% between 500 and 599, 35% between 600 and 700, and 46% above 700. All of the current freshmen were in the top fifth of their class.

Requirements: The SAT or ACT is required. In addition, 2 SAT subject tests. Also required are 4 years of English, 3 of math (4 recommended), 2 each of history/social sciences, lab science (3 recommended), foreign language (3 recommended), and college preparatory electives. A GPA of 2.8 is required for California residents; non-residents, 3.4 GPA. AP credits are accepted. Important factors in the admissions decision are advanced placement or honor courses, evidence of special talent, and leadership record.

Procedure: Freshmen are admitted in the fall. Entrance exams should be taken no later than December test dates in the senior year. There is a deferred admissions plan. Applications should be filed by November 30 for fall entry, along with a $60 fee ($70 for international applicants). Notification is sent March 30. Applications are accepted on-line.

Transfer: 1737 transfer students enrolled in 2004-2005. A minimum GPA of 2.4 generally is required for in-state students and 2.8 for out-of-state students. Admission is competitive, so meeting the minimum does not guarantee admission. Students must have completed at least 60 transferable semester units and no more than 80 to 90 semester units (depending upon the specific college). They must complete all lower-division courses for their intended major prior to admission. 24 of 120 credits required for the bachelor's degree must be completed at Cal.

Visiting: There are regularly scheduled orientations for prospective students, 1 1/2 hour, student-led walking tours are usually followed by an admissions information presentation; self-guided tours are also available. There are guides for informal visits and visitors may sit in on classes. To schedule a visit, contact Visitor Services at (510) 642-5215 or *www.berkeley.edu/visitors/.*

Financial Aid: In 2005-2006, 47% of all full-time freshmen and 50% of continuing full-time students received some form of financial aid. 44% of full-time freshmen and 47% of continuing full-time students received need-based aid. The average freshman award was $15,425. Need-based scholarships or need-based grants averaged $11,096; need-based self-help aid (loans and jobs) averaged $5991; non-need-based athletic scholarships averaged $13,167; and other non-need-based awards and non-need-based scholarships averaged $2393. 27% of undergraduates work part time. Average annual earnings from campus work are $1936. The average financial indebtedness of the 2005 graduate was $13,277. The FAFSA is required. The deadline for filing freshman financial aid applications for fall entry is March 2.

International Students: There are 736 international students enrolled. A satisfactory score is required on the written TOEFL; the IELTS may be substituted. Students must also take the SAT Subject and Reasoning or ACT Assessment plus Writing Test and 2 different SAT: Subject Tests (if Math, must be level 2).

Computers: Wireless access is available. All students must have a college email address. There are more than 15 computer labs and classrooms, and more than 600 computers available on campus. All students may access the system. There are no time limits and no fees. It is strongly recommended that all students have a PC.

Graduates: From July 1, 2004 to June 30, 2005, 6767 bachelor's degrees were awarded. The most popular majors were molecular biology

(8%), political science (7%), and economics (6%). In an average class, 3% graduate in 3 years or less, 61% graduate in 4 years or less, 84% graduate in 5 years or less, and 87% graduate in 6 years or less. 625 companies recruited on campus in 2004-2005.

Admissions Contact: Walter A. Robinson, Director, Undergraduate Admission. E-mail: *ouars@uclink.berkeley.edu* Web: *www.berkeley.edu*

UNIVERSITY OF CALIFORNIA AT DAVIS   B-2

Davis, CA 95616-8507	(530) 752-2971; Fax: (530) 752-1280
Total Enrollment 27115	Faculty: I, +$
Year: quarters, summer session	Ph.D.s: n/av
Application Deadline: n/av	Student/Faculty: n/av
	Tuition: $5860 ($20,100)
	Room & Board: $9150
Freshman Class: n/av	
SAT or ACT: required	VERY COMPETITIVE

University of California at Davis, founded in 1905, is a public, comprehensive institution offering programs in arts and science, agricultural and environmental sciences, and engineering. Figures in the above capsule and profile are approximate. There are 3 undergraduate and 5 graduate schools. In addition to regional accreditation, UCD has baccalaureate program accreditation with ABET, ADA, and ASLA. The 5 libraries contain 3,180,865 volumes, 3,948,731 microform items, and 14,047 audio/video tapes/CDs/DVDs, and subscribe to 44,232 periodicals including electronic. Computerized library services include the card catalog and database searching. Special learning facilities include a learning resource center, art gallery, radio station, experimental farms, a 150-acre arboretum, a raptor center, an equestrian center, a primate research center, and the Crocker Nuclear Laboratory. The 5980-acre campus is in a suburban area 15 miles west of Sacramento and 72 miles northeast of San Francisco. Including any residence halls, there are 1083 buildings.

Student Life: 96% of undergraduates are from California. Others are from 47 states, 113 foreign countries, and Canada. 90% are from public schools. 45% are white; 35% Asian American; 10% Hispanic. The average age of freshmen is 18; all undergraduates, 21. 1% do not continue beyond their first year; 76% remain to graduate.

Housing: 6062 students can be accommodated in college housing, which includes single-sex and coed dormitories, on-campus apartments, off-campus apartments, and married-student housing. In addition, there are honors houses, language houses, and special-interest houses. On-campus housing is guaranteed for the freshman year only. 81% of students commute. Alcohol is not permitted. All students may keep cars.

Activities: 9% of men belong to 28 national fraternities; 9% of women belong to 20 national sororities. There are 320 groups on campus, including art, band, cheerleading, chess, choir, chorus, computers, dance, drama, ethnic, film, gay, honors, international, jazz band, literary magazine, marching band, musical theater, newspaper, orchestra, pep band, photography, political, professional, radio and TV, religious, social, social service, student government, symphony, and yearbook. Popular campus events include Picnic Day, Whole Earth Festival, and Asian Pacific Cultural Week.

Sports: There are 11 intercollegiate sports for men and 9 for women, and 18 intramural sports for men and 18 for women. Facilities include a football stadium, tennis and basketball courts, equestrian trails, a track field, baseball, soccer, and softball fields, a recreation hall, 2 gyms, 2 swimming pools, bowling alleys, weight-training facilities, and an outdoor roller hockey rink.

Disabled Students: 99% of the campus is accessible. Wheelchair ramps, elevators, special parking, specially equipped rest rooms, special class scheduling, lowered drinking fountains, lowered telephones, and lowered automatic teller machines are available.

Services: Counseling and information services are available, as is tutoring in most subjects. There is a reader service for the blind and remedial math and writing.

Campus Safety and Security: Measures include 24-hour foot and vehicle patrol, self-defense education, security escort services, and shuttle buses. There are informal discussions, pamphlets/posters/films, emergency telephones, and lighted pathways/sidewalks, and There is also a rape prevention program, a crime prevention unit, a bike patrol unit, and a K-9 program.

Programs of Study: UCD confers B.S., A.B., and B.A.S. degrees. Master's and doctoral degrees are also awarded. Bachelor's degrees are awarded in AGRICULTURE (agricultural business management, agricultural economics, animal science, international agriculture, plant science, range/farm management, and soil science), BIOLOGICAL SCIENCE (avian sciences, bacteriology, biochemistry, biology/biological science, botany, ecology, entomology, environmental biology, genetics, microbiology, nutrition, physiology, toxicology, wildlife biology, and zoology), BUSINESS (organizational behavior), COMMUNICATIONS AND THE ARTS (art history and appreciation, Chinese, communications, comparative literature, design, dramatic arts, English, fine arts, French, German, Greek, Italian, Japanese, Latin, linguistics, music, Russian, Spanish, speech/debate/rhetoric, and studio art), COMPUTER AND PHYSICAL SCIENCE (atmospheric sciences and meteorology, chemistry, computer science, geology, hydrology, mathematics, physics, polymer science, and statistics), EDUCATION (physical), ENGINEERING AND ENVIRON-MENTAL DESIGN (aeronautical engineering, agricultural engineering, bioengineering, chemical engineering, civil engineering, computer engineering, electrical/electronics engineering, environmental design, environmental science, landscape architecture/design, materials engineering, and mechanical engineering), HEALTH PROFESSIONS (community health work and environmental health science), SOCIAL SCIENCE (African studies, American studies, anthropology, behavioral science, classical/ancient civilization, dietetics, East Asian studies, economics, food science, geography, history, human development, human ecology, international relations, medieval studies, Mexican-American/Chicano studies, Native American studies, philosophy, political science/government, psychology, religion, social science, sociology, textiles and clothing, and women's studies). Agricultural, biological, and biotechnical sciences are the strongest academically. Biological science, biochemistry, and psychology are the largest.

Required: General education requirements vary by college but are based on 3 components: topical breadth, social-cultural diversity, and writing experience. A minimum of 180 quarter units with a minimum GPA of 2.0 are required for graduation, as is proficiency in English composition and an American History and Institutions requirement.

Special: There are credit and noncredit internship programs. Study abroad in more than 32 countries and a Washington semester are offered. Students may participate in college work-study, federal work-study, and California work-study programs. Several A.B.-B.S. degrees are offered. Students may design their own majors, take dual majors, and elect pass/fail options. Interdisciplinary majors are offered in African American and African studies, American Studies, Chicana/Chicano (Mexican American) studies, comparative literature, East Asian studies, exercise science, international relations, linguistics, medieval studies, Native American studies, religious studies, and women's studies. There are 24 national honor societies, including Phi Beta Kappa, a freshman honors program, and 3 departmental honors programs.

Faculty/Classroom: The average class size in a laboratory is 21 and in a regular course, 56.

Requirements: The SAT or ACT is required. In addition, candidates for admission should have completed 4 units of English, 3 of math, and 2 each of foreign language, history/social science, lab science, and college preparatory electives, for a total of 15 units. SAT: Subject tests are required in writing, math, and 1 other subject chosen from English literature, foreign language, science, or social studies. A GPA of 3.3 is required. AP credits are accepted. Important factors in the admissions decision are advanced placement or honor courses, evidence of special talent, and leadership record.

Procedure: Freshmen are admitted fall, winter, and spring. Entrance exams should be taken no later than December of the senior year. There is a deferred admissions plan. Applications are accepted on-line. Check with the school for application deadlines.

Transfer: 2251 transfer students enrolled in a recent year. Junior-level transfers have priority. Requirements vary by college, discipline, and major.

Visiting: There are regularly scheduled orientations for prospective students, including weekend tours of the campus, weekday tours by appointment, and drop-in counseling with staff and faculty. The campus also offers a 1-day preview for prospective students and their families. There are guides for informal visits and visitors may sit in on classes and stay overnight. To schedule a visit, contact UCDavis Visitor Services at (530) 752-8111.

Financial Aid: UCD is a member of CSS. The CSS/Profile or FFS is required. Check with the school for application deadlines.

International Students: They must score satisfactorily on the written TOEFL. Students must take SAT: Subject tests in writing, math, and 1 other subject.

Computers: All students may access the system. There are no time limits and no fees. It is strongly recommended that all students have a personal computer.

Graduates: In a recent year, 5166 bachelor's degrees were awarded. In an average class, 1% graduate in 3 years or less, 28% graduate in 4 years or less, 65% graduate in 5 years or less, and 75% graduate in 6 years or less. Of a recent graduating class, 38% were enrolled in graduate school within 6 months of graduation and 79% were employed.

Admissions Contact: Admissions Officer.
E-mail: *freshmanadmission@ucdavis.edu* Web: *http://why.ucdavis.edu*

UNIVERSITY OF CALIFORNIA AT IRVINE   D-5

Irvine, CA 92697-1075	(949) 824-6703; Fax: (949) 824-2711
Full-time: 8850 men, 9575 women	**Faculty:** I, +$
Part-time: 450 men, 325 women	**Ph.D.s:** 98%
Graduate: 2075 men, 1325 women	**Student/Faculty:** n/av
Year: quarters, summer session	**Tuition:** $7475 ($25,295)
Application Deadline: November 30	**Room & Board:** $9000
Freshman Class: n/av	
SAT or ACT: required	**HIGHLY COMPETITIVE**

The University of California, Irvine, founded in 1965, is a public research university and part of the University of California System. Some figures in this profile are approximate. There are 8 undergraduate and 3 graduate schools. In addition to regional accreditation, UCI has baccalaureate program accreditation with AACSB and ABET. The 3 libraries contain 2,560,259 volumes, 2,584,114 microform items, and 101,335 audio/video tapes/CDs/DVDs, and subscribe to 28,416 periodicals including electronic. Computerized library services include the card catalog, interlibrary loans, and database searching. Special learning facilities include a learning resource center, art gallery, planetarium, radio station, freshwater marsh reserve, arboretum, laser institute, and numerous research centers. The 1489-acre campus is in a suburban area 40 miles south of Los Angeles. Including any residence halls, there are 418 buildings.

Student Life: 98% of undergraduates are from California. Others are from 49 states, 59 foreign countries, and Canada. 88% are from public schools. 51% are Asian American; 24% white; 11% Hispanic. The average age of freshmen is 18; all undergraduates, 21. 8% do not continue beyond their first year.

Housing: 4645 students can be accommodated in college housing, which includes single-sex and coed dorms, on-campus apartments, and married-student housing. In addition, there are honors houses, language houses, special-interest houses, academic theme houses, an 80 space recreational vehicle park (vehicles not included), and houses for lease to fraternities and sororities. On-campus housing is guaranteed for the freshman year only, is available on a first-come, first-served basis, and is available on a lottery system for upperclassmen. 74% of students commute. Alcohol is not permitted. All students may keep cars.

Activities: 8% of men belong to 12 national fraternities; 8% of women belong to 9 national sororities. There are 275 groups on campus, including art, band, cheerleading, choir, chorale, chorus, computers, dance, drama, ethnic, film, gay, honors, international, jazz band, literary magazine, musical theater, newspaper, opera, orchestra, pep band, political, professional, radio and TV, religious, social, social service, student government, symphony, and yearbook. Popular campus events include Celebrate UCI, Rainbow Festival, and Engineering Week.

Sports: There are 11 intercollegiate sports for men and 9 for women, and 23 intramural sports for men and 20 for women. Facilities include a 2500-seat track stadium, a 5000-seat events center, a 1000-seat soccer field, a 500-seat tennis stadium, baseball and other fields, a swimming pool, 6 indoor handball/racquetball/squash courts, and an activities hall with areas for badminton, basketball, volleyball, combatives, fencing, and weight training. A sailing and crew base is located in nearby Newport Beach.

Disabled Students: 99% of the campus is accessible. Wheelchair ramps, elevators, special parking, specially equipped rest rooms, special class scheduling, lowered drinking fountains, lowered telephones, special housing, automatic doors, and transportation on and off campus are available.

Services: Counseling and information services are available, as is tutoring in most subjects. There is a reader service for the blind, and remedial math, reading, and writing.

Campus Safety and Security: Measures include 24-hour foot and vehicle patrol, self-defense education, security escort services, and shuttle buses. There are informal discussions, pamphlets/posters/films, emergency telephones, and lighted pathways/sidewalks.

Programs of Study: UCI confers B.A., B.S., B.F.A., and B.Mus. degrees. Master's and doctoral degrees are also awarded. Bachelor's degrees are awarded in BIOLOGICAL SCIENCE (biology/biological science and ecology), COMMUNICATIONS AND THE ARTS (art history and appreciation, Chinese, classics, comparative literature, dance, dramatic arts, English, film arts, French, German, Japanese, linguistics, music, Spanish, and studio art), COMPUTER AND PHYSICAL SCIENCE (chemistry, information sciences and systems, mathematics, and physics), ENGINEERING AND ENVIRONMENTAL DESIGN (aeronautical engineering, chemical engineering, civil engineering, computer engineering, electrical/electronics engineering, engineering, environmental design, environmental engineering, and mechanical engineering), SOCIAL SCIENCE (anthropology, classical/ancient civilization, criminology, crosscultural studies, East Asian studies, economics, history, human ecology, humanities, international studies, philosophy, political science/government, psychology, social science, sociology, and women's studies). Biological sciences, political science, and economics are the strongest academically. Biological sciences, social ecology, and economics are the largest.

Required: To graduate, students must maintain a GPA of at least 2.0, earn 180 quarter units, and fulfill requirements in English composition and in American history and institutions. Under distribution requirements, 3 courses each must be completed in writing beyond the introductory level, natural sciences, social and behavioral sciences, humanistic inquiry, and math and symbolic systems, and 1 course each in multicultural studies and global issues.

Special: Students may study abroad in Spain, England, India, Kenya, Sweden, and Egypt. UCI also offers internships, a Washington semester, work-study programs with the university, B.A.-B.S. degrees, dual majors, and pass/fail options. There are 3 national honor societies, including Phi Beta Kappa, a freshman honors program, and 14 departmental honors programs.

Faculty/Classroom: 67% of faculty are male; 33%, female. All both teach and do research. The average class size in an introductory lecture is 250; in a laboratory, 24; and in a regular course, 37.

Admissions: 54% of recent applicants were accepted. The SAT scores for a recent freshman class were: Verbal--13% below 500, 48% between 500 and 599, 34% between 600 and 700, and 5% above 700; Math--5% below 500, 32% between 500 and 599, 47% between 600 and 700, and 16% above 700. All of a current freshmen class were in the top fifth of their class.

Requirements: The SAT or ACT is required. Required minimum scores are determined by an eligibility index. In addition, SAT: Subject tests in writing, math, and a third chosen from science, social science, foreign language, or English literature are required. Applicants need 15 academic credits, including 4 years of English, 3 in math, and 2 each in foreign language, history/social science, lab science, and electives. An additional year each in foreign language, math, and science is recommended. An essay also is needed. The GED is accepted. AP credits are accepted.

Procedure: Freshmen are admitted in the fall. Entrance exams should be taken no later than December of the senior year. Applications should be filed by November 30 for fall entry, along with a $60 application fee. Notification is sent in late March. Applications are accepted on-line.

Transfer: 1447 transfer students enrolled in 2004-2005. Applicants must have completed 60 transferable units, including 2 semesters of English composition and 1 semester of math. Some majors require completion of prerequisites. California Community College transfers receive preference. 36 of 180 credits required for the bachelor's degree must be completed at UCI.

Visiting: There are regularly scheduled orientations for prospective students. There are guides for informal visits and visitors may sit in on classes and stay overnight. To schedule a visit, contact the Office of Admissions and Relations with Schools and Colleges.

Financial Aid: Average annual earnings from campus work are $1640. UCI is a member of CSS. The FAFSA and GPA verification form to state agency are required. The priority date for freshman financial aid applications for fall entry is March 2. The deadline for filing freshman financial aid applications for fall entry is May 1.

International Students: They must score satisfactorily on the TOEFL and also take the SAT or the ACT. Students must take SAT: Subject tests in SAT Subject tests in writing and math, and a third in an area of the student's choice.

Computers: All students may access the system 24 hours a day. Students may access the system 2-hour sessions. There are no fees.

Graduates: From July 1, 2004 to June 30, 2005, 3630 bachelor's degrees were awarded. The most popular majors were social sciences and history (30%), biological/life sciences (14%), and psychology (11%). In an average class, 37% graduate in 4 years or less, 70% graduate in 5 years or less, and 76% graduate in 6 years or less.

Admissions Contact: Marguerite Bonous-Hammarth, Director, Admissions. Web: *www.uci.edu*

UNIVERSITY OF CALIFORNIA AT LOS ANGELES   C-5

Los Angeles, CA 90095	(310) 825-3101; Fax: (310) 206-1206
Full-time: 10,326 men, 13,524 women	Faculty: 1859; I, +$
Part-time: 467 men, 494 women	Ph.D.s: 98%
Graduate: 5531 men, 5383 women	Student/Faculty: 13 to 1
Year: quarters, summer session	Tuition: $7062 ($24,882)
Application Deadline: November 30	Room & Board: $10,619
Freshman Class: 42,227 applied, 11,361 accepted, 4422 enrolled	
SAT Verbal/Math: 630/670*	ACT: 27 MOST COMPETITIVE

University of California at Los Angeles (UCLA), founded in 1919, is a public institution offering undergraduate and graduate degrees. Its disciplines include arts and sciences, engineering, applied science, health sciences, law, management, and theater, film, and television. There are 5 undergraduate and 12 graduate schools. In addition to regional accreditation, UCLA has baccalaureate program accreditation with AACSB, ABET, ADA, CSWE, NAAB, and NLN. The 13 libraries contain 7,988,925 volumes, 6,961,130 microform items, and 5,065,965 audio/video tapes/CDs/DVDs, and subscribe to 78,171 periodicals including electronic. Computerized library services include the card catalog, interlibrary loans, database searching, and Internet access. Special learning fa-

cilities include a learning resource center, art gallery, natural history museum, planetarium, and radio station. The 419-acre campus is in an urban area in Los Angeles. Including any residence halls, there are more than 300 buildings.

Student Life: 92% of undergraduates are from California. Others are from 49 states, 100 foreign countries, and Canada. 81% are from public schools. 38% are Asian American; 34% white; 15% Hispanic. The average age of freshmen is 18; all undergraduates, 21. 3% do not continue beyond their first year; 88% remain to graduate.

Housing: 12,782 students can be accommodated in college housing, which includes coed dormitories, off-campus apartments, married-student housing, and sorority houses. On-campus housing is guaranteed for the freshman year only and is available on a lottery system for upperclassmen. 73% of students commute. Alcohol is not permitted.

Activities: 14% of men belong to 4 local and 23 national fraternities; 11% of women belong to 4 local and 14 national sororities. There are 700 groups on campus, including art, band, cheerleading, choir, chorale, chorus, computers, dance, debate, drama, ethnic, film, forensics, gay, honors, international, jazz band, literary magazine, marching band, musical theater, newspaper, opera, orchestra, pep band, photography, political, professional, radio and TV, religious, social, social service, student government, symphony, and yearbook.

Sports: There are 10 intercollegiate sports for men and 12 for women, and 21 intramural sports for men and 19 for women. Facilities include a pavilion, a stadium, a tennis center, and a recreation and sports center.

Disabled Students: All of the campus is accessible. Wheelchair ramps, elevators, special parking, specially equipped rest rooms, special class scheduling, lowered drinking fountains, and lowered telephones are available.

Services: Counseling and information services are available, as is tutoring in most subjects. There is a reader service for the blind, and remedial math, reading, and writing.

Campus Safety and Security: Measures include 24-hour foot and vehicle patrol, self-defense education, security escort services, and shuttle buses. There are informal discussions, pamphlets/posters/films, emergency telephones, and lighted pathways/sidewalks.

Programs of Study: UCLA confers B.A., B.S., and B.A.S degrees. Master's and doctoral degrees are also awarded. Bachelor's degrees are awarded in AGRICULTURE (plant science), BIOLOGICAL SCIENCE (biochemistry, biology/biological science, biophysics, ecology, marine biology, microbiology, molecular biology, neurosciences, and physiology), BUSINESS (business economics), COMMUNICATIONS AND THE ARTS (African languages, American literature, Arabic, art, art history and appreciation, Chinese, communications, comparative literature, design, dramatic arts, English, film arts, French, German, Greek, Hebrew, Italian, Japanese, Korean, Latin, linguistics, music, music history and appreciation, Portuguese, Russian languages and literature, Scandinavian languages, Slavic languages, and Spanish), COMPUTER AND PHYSICAL SCIENCE (applied mathematics, astrophysics, atmospheric sciences and meteorology, chemistry, computer science, cybernetics, earth science, geoenvironmental studies, geology, geophysics and seismology, mathematics, paleontology, physics, and statistics), ENGINEERING AND ENVIRONMENTAL DESIGN (aeronautical engineering, aerospace studies, bioengineering, chemical engineering, civil engineering, computer engineering, electrical/electronics engineering, geological engineering, geophysical engineering, materials engineering, and mechanical engineering), HEALTH PROFESSIONS (nursing), SOCIAL SCIENCE (African American studies, American Indian studies, American studies, anthropology, Asian/American studies, classical/ancient civilization, cognitive science, East Asian studies, economics, European studies, French studies, geography, Hispanic American studies, history, international studies, Italian studies, Judaic studies, Latin American studies, Middle Eastern studies, Near Eastern studies, philosophy, political science/government, psychobiology, psychology, religion, Russian and Slavic studies, sociology, South Asian studies, and women's studies). Economics, psychology, and political science are the largest.

Required: Students must complete a minimum of 180 quarter units and maintain a minimum GPA of 2.0 in all courses. All students must demonstrate a proficiency in English composition, or take specific courses to achieve this proficiency, and must also meet course requirements in American history and institutions. Other requirements vary by major and college or school.

Special: Opportunities are provided for internships, work-study programs, study abroad in 33 countries, B.A.-B.S. degrees, student-designed majors, dual majors, and interdisciplinary majors, including chemistry and materials science, Chicana and Chicano studies, and math and engineering. There is a Washington, D.C. program for 20 to 30 students selected each fall and spring. There are 4 national honor societies, including Phi Beta Kappa, a freshman honors program, and all departments in Letters and Science have honors programs.

Faculty/Classroom: 68% of faculty are male; 32%, female. All both teach and do research.

Admissions: 27% of the 2005-2006 applicants were accepted. The SAT scores for the 2005-2006 freshman class were: Verbal--8% below

500, 30% between 500 and 599, 44% between 600 and 700, and 18% above 700; Math--5% below 500, 20% between 500 and 599, 40% between 600 and 700, and 34% above 700. The ACT scores were 18% below 21, 23% between 18 and 23, between 24 and 29, 47%, and 30 and above, 29%.

Requirements: The SAT or ACT is required. The ACT Optional Writing test is also required. In addition, graduation from an accredited secondary school is required. Applicants must submit a challenging academic program, including honors and AP-level courses in English, math, a language other than English, science, and history and social science; most students complete at least 42 semester courses in these areas. All applicants must take the ACT Assessment plus the new ACT Writing Test or the new SAT Reasoning Test (critical reading, mathematics, and writing). In addition, all applicants must take two SAT Subject Tests in two different subject areas. (If a Math SAT Subject Test is chosen by the applicant, he/she must take the Math Level 2). An essay is required, and a portfolio and audition are required for all art, theater, and film and television majors. A GPA of 3.3 is required. AP credits are accepted. Important factors in the admissions decision are advanced placement or honor courses, evidence of special talent, and leadership record.

Procedure: Freshmen are admitted in the fall. Entrance exams should be taken preferably in the junior year, but no later than December of the senior year. Applications should be filed by November 30 for fall entry. Notification is sent March 15. Applications are accepted on-line. The fall 2005 application fee was $60 for domestic; $70 for international applicants.

Transfer: 3066 transfer students enrolled in 2004-2005. For minimum requirements, transfer students must have earned 90 quarter units at the previous college and have completed preparatory courses for the selected major. Most students selected present a GPA of 3.0 or better. 68 of 180 quarter units required for the bachelor's degree must be completed at UCLA.

Visiting: There are regularly scheduled orientations for prospective students, including campus tours by current UCLA students, offered weekdays at 10:15 A.M. and 2:15 P.M. Reservations are required. Visitors may sit in on classes. To schedule a visit, contact Tours in Undergraduate Admissions at (310) 825-8764.

Financial Aid: In 2005-2006, 57% of all full-time freshmen and 60% of continuing full-time students received some form of financial aid. 48% of full-time freshmen and 51% of continuing full-time students received need-based aid. The average freshman award was $14,143. Need-based scholarships or need-based grants averaged $11,316; need-based self-help aid (loans and jobs) averaged $4382; non-need-based athletic scholarships averaged $10,672; and other non-need-based awards and non-need-based scholarships averaged $6778. The average financial indebtedness of the 2005 graduate was $13,894. The FAFSA and the college's own financial statement are required. The deadline for filing freshman financial aid applications for fall entry is March 2.

International Students: There are 530 international students enrolled. They must score satisfactorily on the written TOEFL or on the electronic version and also take IELTS. They must also take the SAT or ACT. Students must take SAT: Subject tests in English, history, math, science, and languages.

Computers: Wireless access is available. All students may access the system 24 hours a day, 7 days a week. Students may access the system varies by individual department. There are no fees.

Graduates: From July 1, 2004 to June 30, 2005, 7336 bachelor's degrees were awarded. The most popular majors were political science (9%), psychology (9%), and sociology (8%). In an average class, 3% graduate in 3 years or less, 57% graduate in 4 years or less, 84% graduate in 5 years or less, and 87% graduate in 6 years or less. 396 companies recruited on campus in 2004-2005.

Admissions Contact: Director of Undergraduate Admissions and Relations with Schools. E-mail: ugadm@saonet.ucla.edu
Web: http://www.admissions.ucla.edu

UNIVERSITY OF CALIFORNIA AT RIVERSIDE D-5

Riverside, CA 92521   (951) 827-3411; Fax: (951) 827-6344

Full-time: 6607 men, 7521 women	**Faculty:** 709; I, av$
Part-time: 247 men, 196 women	**Ph.D.s:** 98%
Graduate: 1043 men, 1008 women	**Student/Faculty:** 20 to 1
Year: quarters, summer session	**Tuition:** $7250 ($25,070)
Application Deadline: November 30	**Room & Board:** $9375
Freshman Class: 19,060 applied, 14,474 accepted, 2988 enrolled	
SAT Verbal/Math: 517/557*	**ACT:** 21 **COMPETITIVE**

The University of California at Riverside, founded in 1954, is a public research university with undergraduate and graduate programs in engineering, humanities, arts, social sciences, natural and agricultural sciences, health sciences, education, and business. There are 3 undergraduate and 6 graduate schools. In addition to regional accreditation, UCR has baccalaureate program accreditation with ABET and ACS. The 5 libraries contain 2,368,843 volumes, 2,121,062 microform items, and 23,613 audio/video tapes/CDs/DVDs, and subscribe to 28,151 periodicals including electronic. Computerized library services include the card catalog, interlibrary loans, database searching, Internet access, and laptop Internet portals. Special learning facilities include a learning resource center, art gallery, radio station, a museum of photography, botanical gardens, and various research centers. The 1200-acre campus is in a suburban area 50 miles east of Los Angeles. Including any residence halls, there are 486 buildings.

Student Life: 99% of undergraduates are from California. Others are from 28 states, 49 foreign countries, and Canada. 83% are from public schools. 42% are Asian American; 24% Hispanic; 24% white. The average age of freshmen is 18; all undergraduates, 20. 15% do not continue beyond their first year; 66% remain to graduate.

Housing: 4257 students can be accommodated in college housing, which includes coed dorms, on-campus apartments, off-campus apartments, married-student housing, and fraternity houses. In addition, there are honors houses, special-interest houses and an international village. On-campus housing is guaranteed for the freshman year only, is available on a first-come, first-served basis, and is available on a lottery system for upperclassmen. 73% of students commute. All students may keep cars.

Activities: 4% of men belong to 7 local and 15 national fraternities; 4% of women belong to 9 local and 12 national sororities. There are 252 groups on campus, including art, bagpipe band, band, cheerleading, chess, choir, chorale, chorus, computers, dance, debate, drama, ethnic, film, gay, honors, international, jazz band, literary magazine, musical theater, newspaper, orchestra, pep band, photography, political, professional, radio and TV, religious, social, social service, and student government. Popular campus events include block party, spring splash, and nooner series.

Sports: There are 8 intercollegiate sports for men and 9 for women, and 12 intramural sports for men and 12 for women. Facilities include a heated Olympic-size pool, an 80,000 square-foot student recreation center with a weight room/fitness center, 4 indoor multi-use courts, 4 racquetball courts, 1 squash court, 3 fitness studios, 10 tennis courts, a roller hockey rink, a challenge ropes course, and a jogging trail.

Disabled Students: 90% of the campus is accessible. Wheelchair ramps, elevators, special parking, specially equipped rest rooms, special class scheduling, lowered drinking fountains, lowered telephones, and automatic doors are available.

Services: Counseling and information services are available, as is tutoring in most subjects, including individual and group tutoring. There is a reader service for the blind, and remedial math, reading, and writing. There are also study skills classes and preparation sessions for graduate and professional school entrance exams.

Campus Safety and Security: Measures include 24-hour foot and vehicle patrol, self-defense education, security escort services, and shuttle buses. There are informal discussions, pamphlets/posters/films, emergency telephones, lighted pathways/sidewalks, and a ride-along program.

Programs of Study: UCR confers B.A. and B.S. degrees. Master's and doctoral degrees are also awarded. Bachelor's degrees are awarded in BIOLOGICAL SCIENCE (biochemistry, biology/biological science, botany, cell biology, entomology, and neurosciences), BUSINESS (business administration and management and business economics), COMMUNICATIONS AND THE ARTS (art, art history and appreciation, classics, comparative literature, creative writing, dance, dramatic arts, English, film arts, French, German, languages, linguistics, music, Russian, and Spanish), COMPUTER AND PHYSICAL SCIENCE (chemistry, computer science, geology, geophysics and seismology, information sciences and systems, mathematics, physics, and statistics), ENGINEERING AND ENVIRONMENTAL DESIGN (bioengineering, chemical engineering, computer engineering, electrical/electronics engineering, environmental engineering, environmental science, and mechanical engineering), SOCIAL SCIENCE (African American studies, anthropology, Asian/American studies, Asian/Oriental studies, classical/ancient civilization, economics, ethnic studies, history, humanities and social science, Latin American studies, liberal arts/general studies, Mexican-American/Chicano studies, Native American studies, philosophy, political science/government, psychology, religion, sociology, and women's studies). Engineering is the strongest academically. Business administration, biology, and psychology are the largest.

Required: Students must demonstrate proficiency in English and a knowledge of American history and institutions. A total of 180 quarter credit hours with a minimum GPA of 2.0 is required to graduate. The number of hours in the major varies. All students must complete a 1-year sequence in English composition, in computers, math, or statistics, and in concepts/issues of ethnicity. There are breadth requirements in humanities, social sciences, and natural sciences/math for all students; the number of units/courses in each group depends on the student's college and major. A thesis is required for honors program students.

Special: Internships, work-study programs with various agencies and employers on and off campus, study abroad in 35 countries, and a semester in Washington are available. An accelerated M.D. degree in biomedical science is offered in conjunction with UCLA. Student-designed majors, dual majors, opportunities for undergraduate research, and pass/fail options in elective subjects are possible. Grants are available for research, fieldwork, or other creative activity. Academic internships and co-op programs are offered in all majors. There are 9 national honor societies, including Phi Beta Kappa, a freshman honors program, and 7 departmental honors programs.

Faculty/Classroom: 68% of faculty are male; 32%, female. All teach undergraduates, 74% do research, and 74% do both. No introductory courses are taught by graduate students. The average class size in an introductory lecture is 25; in a laboratory, 20; and in a regular course, 22.

Admissions: 76% of the 2005-2006 applicants were accepted. The SAT scores for the 2005-2006 freshman class were: Verbal--42% below 500, 39% between 500 and 599, 16% between 600 and 700, and 3% above 700; Math--26% below 500, 38% between 500 and 599, 29% between 600 and 700, and 7% above 700. The ACT scores were 46% below 21, 30% between 21 and 23, 15% between 24 and 26, 5% between 27 and 28, and 4% above 28. All of the current freshmen were in the top fifth of their class.

Requirements: The SAT or ACT is required. The ACT Optional Writing Test is also required. The minimum GPA varies depending on SAT or ACT scores. Candidates for admission should have completed 4 years of English, 3 of math, 2 of foreign language, history, and science, of 1 visual/performing arts, and electives. SAT Subject Tests in 2 different areas: history/social sciences, English literature, math (level 2), science, or languages are required. A GPA of 2.8 is required. AP credits are accepted. Advanced placement or honor courses are an important factor in the admissions decision.

Procedure: Freshmen are admitted in the fall. Entrance exams should be taken no later than December of the senior year. Applications should be filed by November 30 for fall entry. Notification is sent March 1. Applications are accepted on-line. The fall 2005 application fee was $60.

Transfer: 877 transfer students enrolled in 2004-2005. Applicants need a minimum college GPA of 2.4 and must complete a 7-course pattern. Some majors require additional course completion and a higher GPA. 35 of 180 credits required for the bachelor's degree must be completed at UCR.

Visiting: There are regularly scheduled orientations for prospective students, including Preview Day in October, Discover Days, and Chancellor's receptions in the spring. Tours are available throughout the year on weekdays and some Saturdays. There are guides for informal visits and visitors may sit in on classes and stay overnight. To schedule a visit, contact the Office of Relations with Schools at (951) 827-5045 or *discover@ucr.edu.*

Financial Aid: In 2005-2006, 80% of all full-time freshmen and 70% of continuing full-time students received some form of financial aid. 62% of full-time freshmen and 60% of continuing full-time students received need-based aid. The average freshman award was $15,112. Need-based scholarships or need-based grants averaged $11,026 ($35,621 maximum); need-based self-help aid (loans and jobs) averaged $5749 ($27,577 maximum); non-need-based athletic scholarships averaged $12,364 ($35,011 maximum); and other non-need-based awards and non-need-based scholarships averaged $2611 ($22,536 maximum). The average financial indebtedness of the 2005 graduate was $14,814. The FAFSA is required. The deadline for filing freshman financial aid applications for fall entry is March 2.

International Students: There are 235 international students enrolled. They must take the TOEFL or IELT and also take the SAT or ACT. Students must also take SAT Subject Tests in 2 different areas: history/social sciences, English (literature), math (level 2), science, or languages.

Computers: Wireless access is available. Students with laptop computers can access an extensive wireless network in every major building and in approximately 80% of outdoor areas on campus. There are also 7 public student computer labs featuring 220 workstations, with both Windows and Mac computers. The Department of Engineering also operates computer labs for use by students in their department. Engineering students have access to a total of 14 computer labs with 593 workstations. The UCR library also offers 188 workstations for students. All students may access the system. There are no time limits and no fees. It is strongly recommended that all students have a personal computer. It is recommended that students in the UCR/UCLA Thomas Haider Program in Biomedical Sciences own a computer.

Graduates: From July 1, 2004 to June 30, 2005, 3080 bachelor's degrees were awarded. The most popular majors were business administration (23%), psychology (8%), and liberal studies (7%). In an average class, 37% graduate in 4 years or less, 60% graduate in 5 years or less, and 66% graduate in 6 years or less. 284 companies recruited on campus in 2004-2005.

Admissions Contact: LaRae Lundgren, Director of Undergraduate Admissions. E-mail: *discover@ucr.edu* Web: *http://www.my.ucr.edu*

UNIVERSITY OF CALIFORNIA AT SAN DIEGO   D-5
La Jolla, CA 92093   (858) 534-4831

Full-time: 9733 men, 10,606 women	**Faculty:** 946; I, +$
Part-time: none	**Ph.D.s:** 98%
Graduate: 2134 men, 1425 women	**Student/Faculty:** 22 to 1
Year: quarters, summer session	**Tuition:** $6681 ($23,985)
Application Deadline: November 30	**Room & Board:** $9421
Freshman Class: 41,330 applied, 17,269 accepted, 33,874 enrolled	
SAT Verbal/Math: 598/644*	**ACT:** 26 **HIGHLY COMPETITIVE**

University of California at San Diego, founded in 1960, is a public liberal arts institution. There are 6 undergraduate and 5 graduate schools. In addition to regional accreditation, UCSD has baccalaureate program accreditation with ABET. The 10 libraries contain 2,616,776 volumes, 2,880,645 microform items, and 87,625 audio/video tapes/CDs/DVDs, and subscribe to 24,986 periodicals including electronic. Computerized library services include the card catalog, interlibrary loans, database searching, and Internet access. Special learning facilities include an art gallery, radio station, TV station, aquarium-museum, supercomputer center, and theater. The 1976-acre campus is in a suburban area 12 miles north of downtown San Diego. Including any residence halls, there are 501 buildings.

Student Life: 95% of undergraduates are from California. Others are from 70 foreign countries and Canada. 88% are from public schools. 41% are Asian American; 34% white; 10% Hispanic. The average age of freshmen is 18; all undergraduates, 21. 7% do not continue beyond their first year; 93% remain to graduate.

Housing: 6352 students can be accommodated in college housing, which includes coed dorms, on-campus apartments, off-campus apartments, and married-student housing. In addition, there are language houses and special-interest houses. On-campus housing is available on a lottery system for upperclassmen. 64% of students commute. All students may keep cars.

Activities: 10% of men belong to 14 national fraternities; 10% of women belong to 19 national sororities. There are 450 groups on campus, including academic, art, band, cheerleading, chess, choir, chorale, chorus, computers, dance, debate, drama, enterprise, ethnic, film, gay, honors, international, jazz band, literary magazine, musical theater, newspaper, opera, orchestra, pep band, photography, political, professional, radio and TV, religious, social, social service, student government, symphony, and yearbook. Popular campus events include Fall Festival on the Green, Spring Sun God Festival, and Asian Pacific Awareness Week.

Sports: There are 12 intercollegiate sports for men and 12 for women, and 27 intramural sports for men and 23 for women. Facilities include a 9-lane, all-weather track, soccer and softball fields, an athletic training facility, 2 pools, a spa, a weight room, tennis courts, playing fields, and a golf driving range. An 188,000-square-foot recreation complex features a 5000-seat arena, 8 handball/racquetball courts, 2 squash courts, a 12,000-square-foot weight-training facility, a climbing wall, and basketball, volleyball, and badminton courts.

Disabled Students: 95% of the campus is accessible. Wheelchair ramps, elevators, special parking, specially equipped rest rooms, special class scheduling, lowered drinking fountains, lowered telephones, special accommodations, and administrative support services are available.

Services: Counseling and information services are available, as is tutoring in most subjects. There is a reader service for the blind.

Campus Safety and Security: Measures include 24-hour foot and vehicle patrol, self-defense education, security escort services, and shuttle buses. There are informal discussions, pamphlets/posters/films, emergency telephones, lighted pathways/sidewalks, a student safety awareness program, peer educators, and an on-campus police department.

Programs of Study: UCSD confers B.A. and B.S. degrees. Master's and doctoral degrees are also awarded. Bachelor's degrees are awarded in AGRICULTURE (animal science and environmental studies), BIOLOGICAL SCIENCE (biochemistry, bioinformatics, biology/biological science, biophysics, biotechnology, ecology, microbiology, molecular biology, and physiology), BUSINESS (management science), COMMUNICATIONS AND THE ARTS (art history and appreciation, Chinese, classics, communications, dance, dramatic arts, English literature, Germanic languages and literature, linguistics, literature, music, music history and appreciation, music technology, studio art, and visual and performing arts), COMPUTER AND PHYSICAL SCIENCE (applied mathematics, applied physics, chemistry, computer science, earth science, information sciences and systems, mathematics, physical chemistry, and physics), EDUCATION (mathematics and science), ENGINEERING AND ENVIRONMENTAL DESIGN (aerospace studies, bioengineering, chemical engineering, computer engineering, electrical/electronics engineering, engineering, engineering physics, environmental engineering, environmental science, and mechanical engineering), SOCIAL SCIENCE (anthropology, cognitive science, economics, ethnic studies, French studies, gender studies, history, human development, international studies, Italian studies, Japanese studies, Judaic studies, Latin American studies, philosophy, political science/government, psychology, religion, Russian and Slavic studies, sociology, Spanish studies, Third World studies, and urban studies). Sciences, engineering, and the arts are the strongest academically. Biology, economics, and psychology are the largest.

Required: Graduation requirements vary by undergraduate college but students must complete 180 to 184 total quarter units or 45 to 46 courses, with a minimum of 60 credit hours or 12 to 22 courses in the major. Students must maintain a minimum GPA of 2.0.

Special: Internships in many fields, work-study, study abroad in more than 30 countries, and a Washington semester are offered. B.A.-B.S. degrees, an accelerated degree, dual majors, student-designed majors, and exchange programs with Dartmouth College, Spelman College, and Morehouse College are available. Nondegree study, credit for military experience, and pass/fail options are possible. There are 2 national honor societies, including Phi Beta Kappa, a freshman honors program, and 14 departmental honors programs.

Faculty/Classroom: 73% of faculty are male; 27%, female. 98% teach undergraduates and 100% do research. Graduate students teach 2% of introductory courses. The average class size in an introductory lecture is 300; in a laboratory, 40; and in a regular course, 100.

Admissions: 42% of the 2005-2006 applicants were accepted. The SAT scores for the 2005-2006 freshman class were: Verbal--12% below 500, 37% between 500 and 599, 39% between 600 and 700, and 10% above 700; Math--1% below 500, 23% between 500 and 599, 47% between 600 and 700, and 25% above 700. The ACT scores were 3% below 21, 25% between 21 and 23, 20% between 24 and 26, 33% between 27 and 28, and 19% above 28. All of the current freshmen were in the top fifth of their class.

Requirements: The SAT or ACT is required. In addition, the SAT Reasoning Test with critical reading, math, and writing, or ACT Assesment plus Writing, and 2 SAT Subject Tests in two different areas: history/social science, literature, math (Level 2 only), science or language other than English, are required. Tests must be taken by December of senior year. A GPA of 2.8 is required. AP credits are accepted. Important factors in the admissions decision are advanced placement or honor courses, leadership record, and extracurricular activities record.

Procedure: Freshmen are admitted in the fall. Entrance exams should be taken by December of the senior year. Applications should be filed by November 30 for fall entry, along with a $55 fee. Notification is sent March 30. Applications are accepted on-line.

Transfer: 1325 transfer students enrolled in 2004-2005. California residents should have a competitive GPA; average 2004 GPA was 3.42. Transfers should have completed 90 quarter units. Preference is given to applicants from state community colleges. 36 of 180 credits required for the bachelor's degree must be completed at UCSD.

Visiting: There are regularly scheduled orientations for prospective students. There are guides for informal visits and visitors may sit in on classes. To schedule a visit, contact Campus Tours at (858) 822-1455 or *campustours@ucsd.edu*.

Financial Aid: In 2005-2006, 50% of all full-time freshmen and 46% of continuing full-time students received some form of financial aid. 47% of full-time freshmen and 42% of continuing full-time students received need-based aid. The average freshman award was $10,426. Need-based scholarships or need-based grants averaged $7109; need-based self-help aid (loans and jobs) averaged $4609; and other non-need-based awards and non-need-based scholarships averaged $2413. 75% of undergraduates work part time. Average annual earnings from campus work are $1878. The average financial indebtedness of the 2005 graduate was $13,800. UCSD is a member of CSS. The FAFSA, and the state aid form are required. The priority date for freshman financial aid applications for fall entry is March 2. The deadline for filing freshman financial aid applications for fall entry is May 1.

International Students: There are 400 international students enrolled. They must take the TOEFL and also take the SAT or the ACT as well as the SAT Subject tests in writing, math I or II, and either English literature, foreign language, science, or social studies.

Computers: All students may access the system 24 hours every day. There are no time limits and no fees. It is strongly recommended that all students have a personal computer.

Graduates: The most popular majors were engineering (20%), biology (17%), and economics (9%). In an average class, 1% graduate in 3 years or less, 52% graduate in 4 years or less, 88% graduate in 5 years or less, and 96% graduate in 6 years or less. 600 companies recruited on campus in 2004-2005. Of the 2004 graduating class, 33% were enrolled in graduate school within 6 months of graduation and 65% were employed.

Admissions Contact: Mae Brown, Assistant Vice Chancellor, Admissions and Enrollment. E-mail: *admissionsinfo@ucsd.edu* Web: *http://admissions.ucsd.edu/*

UNIVERSITY OF CALIFORNIA AT SANTA BARBARA C-5

Santa Barbara, CA 93106 (805) 893-2881; Fax: (805) 893-2676

Full-time: 7785 men, 9210 women	**Faculty:** 792; I, +$
Part-time: 390 men, 345 women	**Ph.D.s:** 100%
Graduate: 1460 men, 1190 women	**Student/Faculty:** 21 to 1
Year: quarters, summer session	**Tuition:** $3900 ($14,950)
Application Deadline: see profile	**Room & Board:** $7900
Freshman Class: n/av	
SAT: required	**ACT:** recommended

VERY COMPETITIVE

The University of California at Santa Barbara, founded in 1909, is a public liberal arts institution offering programs in creative studies, engineering, and letters and science. There are 3 undergraduate schools and 1 graduate school. Figures in the above capsule and profile are approximate. In addition to regional accreditation, UCSB has baccalaureate program accreditation with ABET and CSAB. The library contains 2,674,331 volumes, 3,669,358 microform items, and 103,495 audio/video tapes/CDs/DVDs, and subscribes to 18,898 periodicals including electronic. Computerized library services include the card catalog, interlibrary loans, and database searching. Special learning facilities include a learning resource center, art gallery, radio station, language and learning lab, and numerous national and multicampus research institutes. The 813-acre campus is in a suburban area 10 miles west of Santa Barbara. Including any residence halls, there are 300 buildings.

Student Life: 94% of undergraduates are from California. Others are from 48 states, 45 foreign countries, and Canada. 86% are from public schools. 56% are white; 15% Hispanic; 14% Asian American. The average age of freshmen is 18; all undergraduates, 21. 12% do not continue beyond their first year; 67% remain to graduate.

Housing: 4069 students can be accommodated in college housing, which includes coed dormitories, on-campus apartments, off-campus apartments, married-student housing, and special interest floor. On-campus housing is available on a first-come, first-served basis. 79% of students commute. All students may keep cars.

Activities: 15% of men belong to 2 local and 20 national fraternities; 16% of women belong to 4 local and 14 national sororities. There are 300 groups on campus, including band, cheerleading, chess, choir, chorale, chorus, computers, dance, drama, ethnic, film, gay, honors, international, jazz band, literary magazine, newspaper, pep band, photography, political, professional, radio and TV, religious, social, social service, student government, and yearbook. Popular campus events include Club Day, Activities Fair, and UCEN Cultural Festival.

Sports: There are 11 intercollegiate sports for men and 10 for women, and 18 intramural sports for men and 18 for women. Facilities include a football stadium, a track, 24 tennis courts, an aquatics complex plus a campus swimming pool, 2 gyms, a gymnastics area, a weight room, a Nautilus facility, a wellness institute, an aerobics studio, outdoor basketball courts, softball and baseball fields, a ropes course and climbing wall, and a sailing center.

Disabled Students: 98% of the campus is accessible. Wheelchair ramps, elevators, special parking, specially equipped rest rooms, special class scheduling, lowered drinking fountains, and lowered telephones are available.

Services: Counseling and information services are available, as is tutoring in most subjects. There is a reader service for the blind and remedial reading and writing.

Campus Safety and Security: Measures include 24-hour foot and vehicle patrol, self-defense education, security escort services, and emergency telephones. There are lighted pathways/sidewalks.

Programs of Study: UCSB confers B.A., B.S., B.F.A., and B.M. degrees. Master's and doctoral degrees are also awarded. Bachelor's degrees are awarded in BIOLOGICAL SCIENCE (biochemistry, biology/biological science, cell biology, evolutionary biology, marine biology, microbiology, physiology, and zoology), BUSINESS (business economics), COMMUNICATIONS AND THE ARTS (art, art history and appreciation, Chinese, classics, communications, comparative literature, dance, dramatic arts, English, film arts, French, German, Germanic languages and literature, Japanese, linguistics, literature, music, music performance, music theory and composition, Portuguese, Slavic languages, and Spanish), COMPUTER AND PHYSICAL SCIENCE (chemistry, computer science, geology, geophysics and seismology, hydrology, mathematics, physics, and statistics), ENGINEERING AND ENVIRONMENTAL DESIGN (chemical engineering, electrical/electronics engineering, environmental science, and mechanical engineering), HEALTH PROFESSIONS (pharmacy), SOCIAL SCIENCE (African American studies, anthropology, Asian/American studies, Asian/Oriental studies, biopsychology, economics, geography, history, interdisciplinary studies, Islamic studies, Italian studies, Latin American studies, law, medieval studies, Mexican-American/Chicano studies, philosophy, political science/government, psychology, public affairs, religion, sociology, and women's studies). Business economics, political science, and biological science are the largest.

Required: Graduation requirements vary by college. Generally, students will take one third of their distribution in the major subject, one third in general education courses, and one third in elective courses. General subject requirements include courses in English, foreign language, science/math/technology, social sciences, civilization and thought, literature, and the arts; specific subject requirements include 6 writing-intensive courses and 1 course each in non-Western culture, quantitative relationships, and ethnic studies. To graduate, students must earn at least 180 quarter units, with a minimum GPA of 2.0, and have completed the American History and Institutions requirement.

Special: A Washington semester, internships, study abroad in 32 countries, work-study programs, student-designed majors, the B.A.-B.S. degree, and an accelerated degree program in electrical engineering are offered. There are 6 national honor societies, including Phi Beta Kappa, and a freshman honors program.

Faculty/Classroom: 69% of faculty are male; 31%, female. All both teach and do research. The average class size in an introductory lecture is 60; in a laboratory, 24; and in a regular course, 30.

Requirements: The SAT is required and the ACT is recommended, as well as SAT: Subject tests in writing, math, and 1 other choice. Candidates for admission must have completed 4 years of English, 3 of math, and 2 each of foreign language, lab science, history/social science, and college-preparatory electives. An additional year each in foreign language, math, and science is recommended. AP and CLEP credits are accepted.

Procedure: Freshmen are admitted in the fall. Entrance exams should be taken by November of the senior year. Check with the school for application deadlines. Applications are accepted on-line. The fall 2005 application fee was $40.

Transfer: California residents should have a minimum 2.0 GPA in transferable course work; nonresidents, a 2.8 GPA. Students with fewer than 12 quarter or semester units of transferable course work must provide standardized test scores. 35 of 180 credits required for the bachelor's degree must be completed at UCSB.

Visiting: There are regularly scheduled orientations for prospective students, consisting of a campus film, an information session, and a walking tour of the campus led by a student guide. There are guides for informal visits and visitors may sit in on classes and stay overnight. To schedule a visit, contact the Office of Relations with Schools at (805) 893-2485.

Financial Aid: UCSB is a member of CSS. The FAFSA is required. Check with the school for application deadlines.

International Students: They must score satisfactorily on the written TOEFL and also take the SAT or the ACT. Students must take SAT: Subject tests in in writing, math, and 1 other choice.

Computers: All students may access the system at any time, if students have their own computer and modem.

Admissions Contact: Undergraduate Admissions Office.
E-mail: *appinfo@sa.ucsb.edu* Web: *www.ucsb.edu*

UNIVERSITY OF CALIFORNIA AT SANTA CRUZ   B-3

Santa Cruz, CA 95064   (831) 459-4008; Fax: (831) 459-4452

Full-time: 6046 men, 7093 women	**Faculty:** 537; I, av$
Part-time: 236 men, 250 women	**Ph.D:** 98%
Graduate: 691 men, 696 women	**Student/Faculty:** 24 to 1
Year: quarters, summer session	**Tuition:** $7603 ($24,907)
Application Deadline: November 30	**Room & Board:** $11,571
Freshman Class: 23,015 applied, 17,347 accepted, 3000 enrolled	
SAT Verbal/Math: 572/577*	**ACT:** 23 **VERY COMPETITIVE**

University of California, Santa Cruz, opened in 1965, is a public institution with a small-college setting and the academic resources of a major university, offering programs in the arts, engineering, humanities, physical and biological sciences, and social sciences. There are 10 undergraduate schools and 1 graduate school. In addition to regional accreditation, UCSC has baccalaureate program accreditation with ABET. The 10 libraries contain 1.53 million volumes, 845,646 microform items, and 65,425 audio/video tapes/CDs/DVDs, and subscribe to 21,924 periodicals including electronic. Computerized library services include the card catalog, interlibrary loans, database searching, and Internet access. Special learning facilities include a learning resource center, art gallery, natural history museum, radio station, TV station, agroecology program farm, arboretum, Long Marine Lab, and Lick Observatory on Mt. Hamilton. The 2000-acre campus is in a small town 30 miles southwest of San Jose and 75 miles south of San Francisco. Including any residence halls, there are 471 buildings.

Student Life: 96% of undergraduates are from California. Others are from 49 states, 22 foreign countries, and Canada. 80% are from public schools. 52% are white; 19% Asian American; 15% Hispanic. The average age of freshmen is 19; all undergraduates, 21. 11% do not continue beyond their first year; 68% remain to graduate.

Housing: 6000 students can be accommodated in college housing, which includes single-sex and coed dormitories, on-campus apartments, off-campus apartments, and married-student housing. In addition, there are language houses, special-interest houses, and multicultural residence

halls. On-campus housing is available on a lottery system for upperclassmen. 55% of students commute. Alcohol is not permitted in the housing areas. Upperclassmen may keep cars.

Activities: 1% of men belong to 4 national fraternities; 1% of women belong to 3 local and 3 national sororities. There are 100 groups on campus, including art, band, cheerleading, chess, choir, chorale, chorus, computers, dance, debate, drama, ethnic, film, gay, honors, international, jazz band, literary magazine, musical theater, newspaper, opera, orchestra, photography, political, professional, radio and TV, religious, social, social service, student government, symphony, and yearbook. Popular campus events include Multicultural Festival and Martin Luther King, Jr. Convocation.

Sports: There are 15 intercollegiate sports for men and 17 for women, and 10 intramural sports for men and 11 for women. Facilities include a 50-meter pool, 2 playing fields, a weight room, an all-weather jogging track, fully equipped gyms, a fitness course, racquetball, tennis, and basketball courts, and a 12,000-square-foot fitness center.

Disabled Students: 90% of the campus is accessible. Wheelchair ramps, elevators, special parking, specially equipped rest rooms, special class scheduling, lowered drinking fountains, lowered telephones, and wheelchair lift-equipped transportation are available.

Services: Counseling and information services are available, as is tutoring in most subjects, including writing. There is a reader service for the blind. A learning center helps SAA/EOP students with math and writing skills. There is also a program to help any student who is having trouble with certain courses.

Campus Safety and Security: Measures include 24-hour foot and vehicle patrol, self-defense education, security escort services, and shuttle buses. There are informal discussions, pamphlets/posters/films, emergency telephones, lighted pathways/sidewalks, a rape prevention program, seminars for residential staff, and guards at each entrance from 8 P.M. until dawn.

Programs of Study: UCSC confers B.A., B.S., and B.M. degrees. Master's and doctoral degrees are also awarded. Bachelor's degrees are awarded in AGRICULTURE (environmental studies), BIOLOGICAL SCIENCE (biochemistry, bioinformatics, biology/biological science, and marine biology), BUSINESS (business economics and international economics), COMMUNICATIONS AND THE ARTS (art, art history and appreciation, classical languages, dramatic arts, film arts, French, linguistics, literature, and music), COMPUTER AND PHYSICAL SCIENCE (chemistry, computer science, earth science, geology, information sciences and systems, mathematics, and physics), ENGINEERING AND ENVIRONMENTAL DESIGN (computer engineering), HEALTH PROFESSIONS (health science), SOCIAL SCIENCE (American studies, anthropology, community services, economics, German area studies, history, Italian studies, Latin American studies, law, philosophy, political science/government, psychobiology, psychology, religion, Russian and Slavic studies, sociology, South Asian studies, and women's studies). Psychology, business management economics, and art are the largest.

Required: To graduate, all students must complete 36 full-credit courses (180 quarter units) with a minimum GPA of 2.0. Courses are required in arts, English, history, writing-intensive, U.S. ethnic minorities/non-Western society, humanities, math, sciences, and social sciences. They must satisfy university requirements in U.S. history and institutions and in English composition, the residence requirement, the core course, and a comprehensive exam or equivalent body of work, or a senior thesis. Particular college requirements and those of an approved major vary. All students must also satisfy each of the UCSC general education requirements with a course graded C or better.

Special: Cross-registration is possible with other University of California campuses, Hampshire College, the University of New Hampshire, and the University of New Mexico. UCSC also offers work-study, a Washington semester, internships in many arenas, study abroad in 34 countries, student-designed majors, dual majors, and a B.A.-B.S. degree in earth sciences, chemistry, and computer science. There is a chapter of Phi Beta Kappa and a freshman honors program.

Faculty/Classroom: 59% of faculty are male; 41%, female. All both teach and do research. Graduate students teach 1% of introductory courses. The average class size in an introductory lecture is 100.

Admissions: 75% of the 2005-2006 applicants were accepted. The SAT scores for the 2005-2006 freshman class were: Verbal--18% below 500, 38% between 500 and 599, 35% between 600 and 700, and 9% above 700; Math--14% below 500, 40% between 500 and 599, 38% between 600 and 700, and 8% above 700. All of the current freshmen were in the top fifth of their class; All were in the top two fifths.

Requirements: The SAT or ACT is required. The ACT Optional Writing test is also required. In addition, applicants must be graduates of an accredited secondary school or have a GED certificate. They should have completed 15 academic credits, including 4 years of English, 3 of math, and 2 each of foreign language, history, lab science, visual or performing arts, and college preparatory electives. Auditions are required for music majors, and portfolios are required for art majors. All students must submit a personal statement. Nonresidents must meet additional requirements. A GPA of 2.8 is required. AP credits are accepted. Important factors in the admissions decision are advanced placement or honor courses, evidence of special talent, and extracurricular activities record.

Procedure: Freshmen are admitted fall and winter. Entrance exams should be taken by December of the senior year. Applications should be filed by November 30 for fall entry, along with a $65 fee. Notification is sent March. Applications are accepted on-line.

Transfer: 894 transfer students enrolled in 2004-2005. Applicants should have completed 84 quarter credits, with a GPA of 2.4 required for California residents and 2.8 for nonresidents, and all subject areas must be completed. No senior transfers are accepted. 35 of 180 credits required for the bachelor's degree must be completed at UCSC.

Visiting: There are guides for informal visits and visitors may sit in on classes. To schedule a visit, contact the Office of Admissions.

Financial Aid: In 2005-2006, 60% of continuing full-time students received some form of financial aid. The FAFSA is required. The deadline for filing freshman financial aid applications for fall entry is March 2.

International Students: There are 128 international students enrolled. They must score satisfactorily on the written TOEFL or on the electronic version and also take the SAT or the ACT. Students must also take 2 SAT Subjects tests.

Computers: Wireless access is available. Students have access to high-speed Internet in their rooms and at any one of 15 open-access computer labs throughout campus. All students may access the system. There are no time limits and no fees. It is strongly recommended that all students have a personal computer.

Graduates: From July 1, 2004 to June 30, 2005, 2991 bachelor's degrees were awarded. In an average class, 1% graduate in 3 years or less, 48% graduate in 4 years or less, and 68% graduate in 6 years or less.

Admissions Contact: Kevin M. Browne, Executive Director of Admissions and University Registrar. E-mail: *admissions@ucsc.edu* Web: *admissions.ucsc.edu*

UNIVERSITY OF JUDAISM COLLEGE OF ARTS AND SCIENCES   C-5

Bel Air, CA 90077

(310) 476-9777, ext. 261
(888) UJ FOR ME; Fax: (310) 471-3657

Full-time: 40 men, 60 women	**Faculty:** 10
Part-time: 4 men, 4 women	**Ph.D.s:** 100%
Graduate: 60 men, 70 women	**Student/Faculty:** 10 to 1
Year: semesters	**Tuition:** $19,300
Application Deadline: January 1	**Room & Board:** $10,710
Freshman Class: n/av	
SAT or ACT: required	**COMPETITIVE**

The College of Arts and Sciences at the University of Judaism is distinguished by its core curriculum integrating the study of Western and Jewish civilizations. It prepares students for careers and graduate studies in law, business, psychology, education, and other fields. There is 1 undergraduate and 3 graduate schools. Enrollment figures in the above capsule and some information in this profile are approximate. The library contains 105,000 volumes and subscribes to 400 periodicals including electronic. Computerized library services include the card catalog and interlibrary loans. Special learning facilities include a learning resource center, art gallery, and radio station. The 28-acre campus is in a suburban area. Including any residence halls, there are 9 buildings.

Student Life: 71% of undergraduates are from California. Others are from 22 states and 2 foreign countries. 80% are from public schools. 81% are white; 10% Hispanic. Most are Jewish. The average age of freshmen is 18; all undergraduates, 23. 5% do not continue beyond their first year; 90% remain to graduate.

Housing: 192 students can be accommodated in college housing, which includes coed dorms, on-campus apartments, and married-student housing. On-campus housing is guaranteed for all 4 years. 85% of students live on campus; of those, 80% remain on campus on weekends. All students may keep cars.

Activities: There are no fraternities or sororities. There are many groups and organizations on campus, including art, chorus, dance, drama, literary magazine, newspaper, political, radio and TV, religious, social, social service, student government, and yearbook.

Sports: Facilities include a weight room, basketball and volleyball courts, and a soccer field.

Disabled Students: All of the campus is accessible. Elevators, special parking, specially equipped rest rooms, lowered drinking fountains, lowered telephones, and specially equipped dormitory rooms are available.

Services: Counseling and information services are available, as is tutoring in most subjects. There is remedial math and writing.

Campus Safety and Security: Measures include 24-hour foot and vehicle patrol, self-defense education, informal discussions, and pamphlets/posters/films. There are lighted pathways/sidewalks.

Programs of Study: UJ confers the B.A. degree. Master's degrees are also awarded. Bachelor's degrees are awarded in BUSINESS (business administration and management), COMMUNICATIONS AND THE ARTS (journalism and literature), HEALTH PROFESSIONS (premedi-

cine), SOCIAL SCIENCE (ethics, politics, and social policy, Judaic studies, liberal arts/general studies, political science/government, and psychology).

Required: All students must complete a core curriculum combining the study of Jewish and Western civilizations, as well as courses in communications and foreign language, and 1 in computer science. There are distribution requirements in math, natural and behavioral sciences, and fine arts. Other requirements vary according to the major, with at least 32 to 36 upper-division credits needed. A total of 127 semester units, with a minimum GPA of 2.0, is required to graduate.

Special: There is a 5-year joint business management program with University of Judaism's Lieber School of Graduate Studies. Student-designed and dual majors are available. Internships in all available majors, study abroad, work-study programs, accelerated degree programs, and pass/fail options are offered. Students may apply for independent study projects.

Faculty/Classroom: 75% of faculty are male; 25%, female. All teach undergraduates and all both teach and do research. No introductory courses are taught by graduate students. The average class size in an introductory lecture is 13; in a laboratory, 6; and in a regular course, 9.

Requirements: The SAT or ACT is required. In addition, applicants must be graduates of an accredited secondary school or have the GED. A visit and an interview are recommended for all students. Two recommendations from teachers, an autobiographical essay, and a secondary school report/recommendation from an academic counselor also are required. Students scoring below the minimum verbal on the SAT or earning below a 3.2 GPA are occasionally admitted if their essay, recommendations, and grades in English and other humanities courses are exceptionally strong. A GPA of 3.2 is required. AP credits are accepted.

Procedure: Freshmen are admitted fall and spring. Entrance exams should be taken no later than November of the year prior to enrollment. There are early decision and deferred admissions plans. Early decision applications should be filed by November 15; regular applications, by January 1 for fall entry and November 1 for spring entry. Notification of early decision is sent December 15; regular decision, on a rolling basis. Check with the school for current application fee.

Transfer: Previous college work should be at the B level to transfer. Students with fewer than 60 college credits should also have a minimum 3.0 high school GPA, a satisfactory minimum score on the SAT or 23 on the ACT, 2 recommendations, and an autobiographical essay. The SAT or ACT requirement is waived if the applicant has 60 or more transferable credits. A visit and an interview are recommended. 34 of 127 credits required for the bachelor's degree must be completed at UJ.

Visiting: There are regularly scheduled orientations for prospective students, including meetings with admissions representatives and campus tours. There are guides for informal visits and visitors may sit in on classes and stay overnight. To schedule a visit, contact Amnon Finkelstein, Dean of Admissions at (310) 476-9777, ext. 252 or *finaid@uj.edu*.

Financial Aid: 78% of undergraduates work part time. UJ is a member of CSS. The FAFSA, the college's own financial statement, and the tax returns and W2s are required. Check with the school for current deadlines.

International Students: They must score satisfactorily on the TOEFL and also take the SAT or the ACT, scoring satisfactorily.

Computers: All students may access the system. There are no time limits and no fees.

Graduates: In an average class, 75% graduate in 4 years or less, and 25% graduate in 5 years or less.

Admissions Contact: Dr. Amnon Finkelstein, Dean of Admissions. E-mail: *afinkelstein@uj.edu* Web: *www.uj.edu*

UNIVERSITY OF LA VERNE   D-5

La Verne, CA 91750-4443

(909) 392-2800
(800) 876-4858; Fax: (909) 392-2714

Full-time: 548 men, 1035 women	**Faculty:** 187; I, --$
Part-time: 43 men, 59 women	**Ph.D.s:** 82%
Graduate: 764 men, 1551 women	**Student/Faculty:** 8 to 1
Year: 4-1-4, summer session	**Tuition:** $24,260
Application Deadline: February 1	**Room & Board:** $9210
Freshman Class: 1638 applied, 1008 accepted, 339 enrolled	
SAT Verbal/Math: 510/510*	**ACT:** 21 **COMPETITIVE**

The University of La Verne, founded in 1891, is an independent, liberal arts university offering associates, bachelor's, and doctorate degrees. There are 3 undergraduate and 4 graduate schools. In addition to regional accreditation, ULV has baccalaureate program accreditation with CAAHEP. The library contains 248,000 volumes, and subscribes to 17,500 periodicals including electronic. Computerized library services include the card catalog, interlibrary loans, database searching, Internet access, and laptop Internet portals. Special learning facilities include a learning resource center, art gallery, natural history museum, radio station, TV station, a theater, and an archeology lab. The 26-acre campus is in a suburban area 35 miles east of Los Angeles. Including any residence halls, there are 26 buildings.

Student Life: 95% of undergraduates are from California. Students are from 18 states and 6 foreign countries. 39% are white; 30% Hispanic. 33% are Catholic; 32% Protestant; 8% claim no religious affiliation. The average age of freshmen is 18; all undergraduates, 20. 11% do not continue beyond their first year.

Housing: 540 students can be accommodated in college housing, which includes single-sex and coed dorms. In addition, there are special-interest houses, a diversity floor, and a health and well-being floor. On-campus housing is available on a first-come, first-served basis and is available on a lottery system for upperclassmen. Priority is given to out-of-town students. 68% of students commute. Alcohol is not permitted. All students may keep cars.

Activities: 9% of men belong to 1 local and 2 national fraternities; 16% of women belong to 2 local and 3 national sororities. There are 40 groups on campus, including art, cheerleading, choir, chorale, chorus, computers, dance, debate, departmental, drama, environmental, ethnic, forensics, gay, honors, international, jazz band, literary magazine, musical theater, newspaper, photography, political, professional, radio and TV, religious, social, social service, student government, and yearbook. Popular campus events include Cinco de Mayo, International Week, and Commuter Day.

Sports: There are 11 intercollegiate sports for men and 9 for women, and 6 intramural sports for men and 6 for women. Facilities include a football stadium, 2 gyms, a pool, a weight and fitness center, tennis courts, an outdoor track, and soccer and other playing fields.

Disabled Students: 95% of the campus is accessible. Wheelchair ramps, elevators, special parking, specially equipped rest rooms, and lowered telephones are available.

Services: Counseling and information services are available, as is tutoring in most subjects. There is a reader service for the blind, and remedial math, reading, and writing. Students may use the computerized Learning Enhancement Center or schedule tutoring free of charge.

Campus Safety and Security: Measures include 24-hour foot and vehicle patrol, security escort services, informal discussions, and pamphlets/posters/films. There are emergency telephones and lighted pathways/sidewalks.

Programs of Study: ULV confers B.A. and B.S. degrees. Associate, master's, and doctoral degrees are also awarded. Bachelor's degrees are awarded in BIOLOGICAL SCIENCE (biology/biological science and environmental biology), BUSINESS (accounting, business administration and management, business economics, electronic business, institutional management, international business management, and marketing and distribution), COMMUNICATIONS AND THE ARTS (art, art history and appreciation, broadcasting, communications, comparative literature, dramatic arts, English, French, German, journalism, music, Spanish, and speech/debate/rhetoric), COMPUTER AND PHYSICAL SCIENCE (chemistry, computer science, mathematics, natural sciences, and physics), EDUCATION (athletic training and education), ENGINEERING AND ENVIRONMENTAL DESIGN (computer engineering and environmental science), HEALTH PROFESSIONS (health care administration), SOCIAL SCIENCE (anthropology, behavioral science, child psychology/development, criminology, history, international studies, liberal arts/general studies, paralegal studies, philosophy, physical fitness/movement, political science/government, psychology, public administration, religion, social science, and sociology). Natural science, education, and psychology are the strongest academically. Business, liberal studies, and psychology are the largest.

Required: To graduate, students must complete a minimum of 128 credit hours, with a minimum GPA of 2.0. 32 hours in the major are required, and 6 in general education. Required core courses include Values and Critical Thinking, Service Learning, International/Intercultural Experience, and Interdisciplinary (The Human Condition, and Toward a Sustainable Planet. Students) must cmplete at least 24 hours in their major and a senior project.

Special: Internships, study abroad in 19 countries, work-study programs, B.A.-B.S. degrees, dual majors, and nondegree study are available. Pass/fail options are also available. There are 9 national honor societies and a freshman honors program.

Faculty/Classroom: 52% of faculty are male; 46%, female. 88% teach undergraduates. No introductory courses are taught by graduate students. The average class size in an introductory lecture is 12; in a laboratory, 10; and in a regular course, 14.

Admissions: 62% of the 2005-2006 applicants were accepted. The SAT scores for the 2005-2006 freshman class were: Verbal--45% below 500, 42% between 500 and 599, 13% between 600 and 700, and 1% above 700; Math--39% below 500, 46% between 500 and 599, and 15% between 600 and 700. The ACT scores were 45% below 21, 31% between 21 and 23, 21% between 24 and 26, and 3% between 27 and 28. 57% of the current freshmen were in the top fifth of their class; 87% were in the top two fifths. 3 freshmen graduated first in their class.

Requirements: The SAT or ACT is required. In addition, applicants must be graduates of an accredited secondary school. An essay is required, and an interview is recommended. AP and CLEP credits are accepted. Important factors in the admissions decision are advanced place-

ment or honor courses, recommendations by school officials, and extracurricular activities record.

Procedure: Freshmen are admitted fall and spring. Entrance exams should be taken in the junior or senior year. There are deferred admissions and rolling admissions plans. Applications should be filed by February 1 for fall entry and December 1 for spring entry, along with a $50 fee. Notification is sent on a rolling basis. Applications are accepted online.

Transfer: 142 transfer students enrolled in 2004-2005. Applicants must demonstrate academic ability at all previous colleges attended. Students with fewer than 32 transferable semester credits must submit SAT or ACT scores and a high school transcript. 32 of 128 credits required for the bachelor's degree must be completed at ULV.

Visiting: There are regularly scheduled orientations for prospective students, including campus tours, faculty and student panels, class, and meals. There are guides for informal visits and visitors may sit in on classes and stay overnight. To schedule a visit, contact the Admissions Office.

Financial Aid: In 2005-2006, 85% of all full-time freshmen and 83% of continuing full-time students received some form of financial aid. 70% of full-time freshmen and 75% of continuing full-time students received need-based aid. The average freshman award was $18,403. Need-based scholarships or need-based grants averaged $9243; need-based self-help aid (loans and jobs) averaged $6200; and other non-need-based awards and non-need-based scholarships averaged $8988. The FAFSA and Cal Grant Application are required. The deadline for filing freshman financial aid applications for fall entry is March 2.

International Students: In a recent year, there were 30 international students enrolled. The school actively recruits these students. They must score satisfactorily on the written TOEFL or on the electronic version or take the MELAB or the college's own test. International applicants must demonstrate English proficiency by presenting either a satisfactory TOEFL score, and a satisfactory SAT verbal score, a grade of 3.0 on ULV's own test, or 30 transferable college credits, including the equivalent of English 110.

Computers: Wireless access is available. All students may access the system 24 hours, 7 days a week. There are no time limits and no fees.

Graduates: From July 1, 2004 to June 30, 2005, 312 bachelor's degrees were awarded. The most popular majors were business administration (24%), social sciences (14%), and liberal studies (13%). In an average class, 38% graduate in 4 years or less, 44% graduate in 5 years or less, and 52% graduate in 6 years or less.

Admissions Contact: Ana Liza V. Zell, Director of Admissions. E-mail: *admissions@ulv.edu* Web: *www.ulv.edu*

UNIVERSITY OF REDLANDS D-5
Redlands, CA 92373-0999

(909) 335-4074
(800) 455-5064; Fax: (909) 335-4089

Full-time: 968 men, 1370 women	**Faculty:** 163; IIA, av$
Part-time: 10 men, 14 women	**Ph.D.s:** 86%
Graduate: 28 men, 64 women	**Student/Faculty:** 14 to 1
Year: 4-1-4	**Tuition:** $27,164
Application Deadline: February 1	**Room & Board:** $8996
Freshman Class: 3752 applied, 2421 accepted, 719 enrolled	
SAT Verbal/Math: 579/581*	**ACT:** 24 **VERY COMPETITIVE**

University of Redlands, founded in 1907, is a private institution that offers programs in liberal and fine arts, business, and teacher preparation. There are 2 undergraduate and 4 graduate schools. The library contains 421,219 volumes, 317,465 microform items, and 6091 audio/video tapes/CDs/DVDs, and subscribes to 12,800 periodicals including electronic. Computerized library services include the card catalog, interlibrary loans, database searching, and Internet access. Special learning facilities include an art gallery, a radio station, a language lab, a computer center, and a geographic information systems lab. The 160-acre campus is in a suburban area 60 miles east of Los Angeles. Including any residence halls, there are 86 buildings.

Student Life: 71% of undergraduates are from California. Others are from 45 states, 8 foreign countries, and Canada. 60% are white; 12% Hispanic. The average age of freshmen is 18; all undergraduates, 20. 15% do not continue beyond their first year; 60% remain to graduate.

Housing: 1621 students can be accommodated in college housing, which includes single-sex and coed dorms, on-campus apartments, off-campus apartments, fraternity houses, and sorority houses. In addition, there are honors houses and special-interest houses. On-campus housing is guaranteed for all 4 years. 70% of students live on campus. All students may keep cars.

Activities: 3% of men belong to 6 local fraternities; 6% of women belong to 5 local sororities. There are 105 groups on campus, including art, band, cheerleading, chess, choir, chorale, chorus, dance, debate, drama, drill team, ethnic, film, gay, honors, international, jazz band, literary magazine, musical theater, newspaper, opera, orchestra, pep band, photography, political, professional, radio and TV, religious, social, social service, student government, symphony, and yearbook. Popular campus events include Mayfest, Multicultural Festival, and Feast of Lights.

Sports: There are 10 intercollegiate sports for men and 10 for women, and 7 intramural sports for men and 7 for women. Facilities include a fitness center, an aquatic center, a football stadium, tennis courts, and baseball, softball, soccer, and lacrosse fields.

Disabled Students: 25% of the campus is accessible. Wheelchair ramps, elevators, special parking, specially equipped rest rooms, special class scheduling, lowered drinking fountains, and lowered telephones are available.

Services: Counseling and information services are available, as is tutoring in every subject. There is a reader service for the blind.

Campus Safety and Security: Measures include 24-hour foot and vehicle patrol, self-defense education, security escort services, and shuttle buses. There are informal discussions, pamphlets/posters/films, emergency telephones, lighted pathways/sidewalks, and safety whistles.

Programs of Study: Redlands confers B.A., B.S., and B.Mus. degrees. Master's degrees are also awarded. Bachelor's degrees are awarded in AGRICULTURE (environmental studies), BIOLOGICAL SCIENCE (biochemistry and biology/biological science), BUSINESS (accounting and business administration and management), COMMUNICATIONS AND THE ARTS (art, creative writing, dramatic arts, English, English literature, French, German, music, Spanish, and studio art), COMPUTER AND PHYSICAL SCIENCE (chemistry, computer science, information sciences and systems, mathematics, and physics), EDUCATION (music), ENGINEERING AND ENVIRONMENTAL DESIGN (environmental science), SOCIAL SCIENCE (anthropology, Asian/Oriental studies, economics, history, interdisciplinary studies, international relations, liberal arts/general studies, philosophy, political science/government, psychology, religion, and sociology). Liberal arts is the strongest academically. Business is the largest.

Required: Requirements for graduation vary according to the degree and major. Students must complete at least 128 units with at least 32 in residence, and maintain a minimum GPA of 2.0. Students pursuing a B.S. degree must fulfill an additional field requirement or a minor. A comprehensive exam is required for some programs. A liberal arts core curriculum, first-year seminar, community service, and participation in 2 May terms are required.

Special: Cross-registration with sister colleges, various internships, and study abroad in 50 countries are offered. A Washington semester, a Sacramento program, various work-study programs, B.A.-B.S. degrees, a liberal studies degree, dual majors, and accelerated degree programs are available. Students may pursue nondegree study, take advantage of pass/fail options, and receive credit for life or work experience. At the Johnston Center for Integrative studies, students design their own majors and courses of study. There are 4 national honor societies, including Phi Beta Kappa, a freshman honors program, and 23 departmental honors programs.

Faculty/Classroom: 48% of faculty are male; 52%, female. All teach undergraduates. No introductory courses are taught by graduate students. The average class size in an introductory lecture is 20; in a laboratory, 10; and in a regular course, 12.

Admissions: 65% of the 2005-2006 applicants were accepted. The SAT scores for the 2005-2006 freshman class were: Verbal--9% below 500, 51% between 500 and 599, 34% between 600 and 700, and 6% above 700; Math--8% below 500, 49% between 500 and 599, 38% between 600 and 700, and 5% above 700. The ACT scores were 18% below 21, 29% between 21 and 23, 29% between 24 and 26, 13% between 27 and 28, and 11% above 28. There were 4 National Merit finalists.

Requirements: The SAT or ACT is required. In addition, applicants should complete at least 16 credits in academic areas, including 4 years of English, 3 years of math, up to and including Algebra II, and 2 to 3 years of foreign language, sciences, and social studies. AP and CLEP credits are accepted. Important factors in the admissions decision are advanced placement or honor courses, leadership record, and personality/intangible qualities.

Procedure: Freshmen are admitted fall and spring. Entrance exams should be taken prior to application. There are deferred admissions and rolling admissions plans. Applications should be filed by February 1 for fall entry and November 15 for spring entry. Notification is sent on a rolling basis. 25 applicants were on the 2005 waiting list; 3 were admitted. Applications are accepted on-line.

Transfer: 90 transfer students enrolled in 2004-2005. The SAT or the ACT may be required of transfer applicants, depending on how many units are accepted. 32 of 128 credits required for the bachelor's degree must be completed at Redlands.

Visiting: There are regularly scheduled orientations for prospective students, including campus tours at 10 A.M., 1 P.M., and 4 P.M., on weekdays and 11 A.M. and 1 P.M. on Saturdays during the school year. Visits may include interviews with counselors, department heads, and coaches. There are guides for informal visits and visitors may sit in on classes and stay overnight. To schedule a visit, contact the Admissions office at (909) 793-2121, ext. 4074 or *admissions@redlands.edu*.

Financial Aid: In 2005-2006, 90% of all full-time freshmen and 91% of continuing full-time students received some form of financial aid. 79% of full-time freshmen and 81% of continuing full-time students received need-based aid. The average freshman award was $24,949. Need-based scholarships or need-based grants averaged $11,668 ($19,600 maximum); need-based self-help aid (loans and jobs) averaged $4218 ($5000 maximum); other non-need-based awards and non-need-based scholarships averaged $10,547 ($9517 maximum); and non-need-based loans (outside loans, parent loans, unsubsidized loans) averaged $9518 ($36,000 maximum). 51% of undergraduates work part time. Average annual earnings from campus work are $1245. The average financial indebtedness of the 2005 graduate was $18,100. The FAFSA, the college's own financial statement and the the GPA verification form for California residents are required. The priority date for freshman financial aid applications for fall entry is December 15. The deadline for filing freshman financial aid applications for fall entry is February 1.

International Students: There are 22 international students enrolled. The school actively recruits these students. Satisfactory scores are required on the written TOEFL and the SAT or the ACT.

Computers: Wireless access is available. Housed within the Fletcher Jones Center are labs/classrooms, a hands-on lab, and a faculty technology center. All labs/classrooms are available when not being used for class. All students may access the system. There are no time limits and no fees.

Graduates: From July 1, 2004 to June 30, 2005, 508 bachelor's degrees were awarded. The most popular majors were liberal studies (24%), business administration (14%), and psychology (7%). In an average class, 52% graduate in 4 years or less, 58% graduate in 5 years or less, and 60% graduate in 6 years or less. Of the 2004 graduating class, 50% were employed within 6 months of graduation.

Admissions Contact: Paul M. Driscoll, Dean of Admissions. E-mail: *admissions@uor.edu* Web: *www.redlands.edu*

UNIVERSITY OF SAN DIEGO   D-5
San Diego, CA 92110   **(619) 260-4506**
                              (800) 248-4873; Fax: (619) 260-6836

Full-time: 4801 men and women	**Faculty:** 314; I, av$
Part-time: 169 men and women	**Ph.D.s:** 97%
Graduate: 1150 men, 1300 women	**Student/Faculty:** 15 to 1
Year: 4-1-4, summer session	**Tuition:** $30,620
Application Deadline: January 5	**Room & Board:** $10,000
Freshman Class: 7273 applied, 3709 accepted, 1064 enrolled	
SAT or ACT: required	**HIGHLY COMPETITIVE**

The University of San Diego, founded in 1949, is a private, Catholic liberal arts university. There are 4 undergraduate and 5 graduate schools. Some information in this profile is approximate. In addition to regional accreditation, USD has baccalaureate program accreditation with AACSB and ABET. The 2 libraries contain 714,082 volumes, 839,992 microform items, and 8624 audio/video tapes/CDs/DVDs, and subscribe to 10,451 periodicals including electronic. Computerized library services include the card catalog, interlibrary loans, and database searching. Special learning facilities include a learning resource center, art gallery, TV station, a media center, and child development center. The 180-acre campus is in an urban area 10 miles north of downtown San Diego. Including any residence halls, there are 101 buildings.

Student Life: 60% of undergraduates are from California. Others are from 50 states, 63 foreign countries, and Canada. 57% are from public schools. 68% are white; 16% Hispanic. 55% are Catholic; 10% Protestant. The average age of freshmen is 18; all undergraduates, 21. 14% do not continue beyond their first year; 72% remain to graduate.

Housing: 1900 students can be accommodated in college housing, which includes single-sex and coed dorms and on-campus apartments. In addition, there are honors houses and special-interest houses. On-campus housing is guaranteed for all 4 years. 52% of students live on campus; of those, 70% remain on campus on weekends. All students may keep cars.

Activities: 14% of men belong to 4 national fraternities; 19% of women belong to 4 national sororities. There are 60 groups on campus, including academic, art, cheerleading, choir, chorus, dance, drama, ethnic, gay, honors, international, jazz band, newspaper, opera, orchestra, political, professional, religious, social, social service, student government, and yearbook. Popular campus events include Walk on Water Contest, Orientation week, and sponsored concerts and events.

Sports: There are 8 intercollegiate sports for men and 8 for women, and 15 intramural sports for men and 15 for women. Facilities include a sports center, a stadium, tennis courts, a swimming pool, soccer, baseball, and softball fields, and the Mission Bay Aquatic Center.

Disabled Students: 80% of the campus is accessible. Wheelchair ramps, elevators, special parking, specially equipped rest rooms, lowered drinking fountains are available. Individual needs can be accommodated.

Services: Counseling and information services are available, as is tutoring in most subjects.

Campus Safety and Security: Measures include 24-hour foot and vehicle patrol, self-defense education, security escort services, and shuttle buses. There are informal discussions, pamphlets/posters/films, emergency telephones, and lighted pathways/sidewalks.

Programs of Study: USD confers B.A., B.A./B.S., B.Acc., B.B.A., and B.S.N. degrees. Master's and doctoral degrees are also awarded. Bachelor's degrees are awarded in BIOLOGICAL SCIENCE (biology/biological science and marine science), BUSINESS (accounting, business administration and management, and business economics), COMMUNICATIONS AND THE ARTS (communications, English, fine arts, French, music, and Spanish), COMPUTER AND PHYSICAL SCIENCE (chemistry, computer science, mathematics, oceanography, and physics), EDUCATION (elementary and secondary), ENGINEERING AND ENVIRONMENTAL DESIGN (electrical/electronics engineering, and industrial engineering), HEALTH PROFESSIONS (nursing), SOCIAL SCIENCE (anthropology, economics, history, humanities, international relations, liberal arts/general studies, philosophy, political science/government, psychology, religion, sociology, and urban studies). Business administration and communication studies are the largest.

Required: All students must take 124 credit hours, including 36 to 72 in their major, while maintaining a minimum GPA of 2.0. Distribution requirements include 9 units each of religious studies and humanities and fine arts, 6 each of philosophy, natural sciences, and social sciences, 3 or 4 of math, 3 of composition and literature, as well as 3 semesters of foreign language.

Special: A B.A.-B.S. degree is offered in electrical, industrial, and mechanical engineering. Internships in all disciplines, study abroad in 9 countries and work-study programs on campus are available. There are 15 national honor societies, including Phi Beta Kappa, and a freshman honors program.

Faculty/Classroom: 57% of faculty are male; 43%, female. 90% teach undergraduates, 50% do research, and 50% do both. No introductory courses are taught by graduate students. The average class size in an introductory lecture is 25; in a laboratory, 15; and in a regular course, 22.

Requirements: The SAT is required. Admission is highly selective. Applicants should present a well-balanced secondary school program of college preparatory courses in English, foreign language, math, laboratory science, history, and social science. Both the content of the academic program as well as the quality of performance is considered. In addition, SAT/ACT results are used to broaden understanding of the applicant's potential. Participation in extracurricular activities at the school and in the community or church is taken into consideration in the admission decision. AP and CLEP credits are accepted. Important factors in the admissions decision are recommendations by school officials, extracurricular activities record, and advanced placement or honor courses.

Procedure: Freshmen are admitted fall, spring, and summer. Entrance exams should be taken before December 30 for early action and before March 1 for regular consideration. There is an early admissions plan. Applications should be filed by January 5 for fall entry and October 1 for spring entry, along with a $55 fee. Notification is sent beginning April 15. 97 applicants were on the 2003 waiting list; 8 were admitted. Applications are accepted on-line.

Transfer: 341 transfer students enrolled in a recent year. Transfer students must have a minimum GPA of 3.0 and have earned 24 credit hours. 30 of 124 credits required for the bachelor's degree must be completed at USD.

Visiting: There are regularly scheduled orientations for prospective students, including tours and information sessions offered by the Admissions Office Monday through Friday 10 A.M. and 2 P.M., and Saturday from November through April at 10 A.M. and noon. There are guides for informal visits and visitors may sit in on classes. To schedule a visit, contact the Admissions Office.

Financial Aid: In a recent year, 74% of all full-time freshmen and 71% of continuing full-time students received some form of financial aid. 55% of full-time freshmen and 64% of continuing full-time students received need-based aid. The average freshman award was $17,508. Need-based scholarships or need-based grants averaged $17,508; need-based self-help aid (loans and jobs) averaged $3507; non-need-based athletic scholarships averaged $15,398; and other non-need-based awards and non-need-based scholarships averaged $6268. 21% of undergraduates work part time. Average annual earnings from campus work are $18,000. The average financial indebtedness of a recent graduate was $25,631. The FAFSA is required. Check with the school for current deadlines.

International Students: There were 125 international students enrolled in a recent year. The school actively recruits these students. They must score satisfactorily on the TOEFL and also take the SAT or the ACT and SAT Subject tests in writing.

Computers: All students may access the system. There are no time limits and no fees. It is strongly recommended that all students have a personal computer.

Graduates: In a recent year, 1176 bachelor's degrees were awarded. The most popular majors were business administration (34%), communication (12%), and psychology (7%). In an average class, 59% graduate in 4 years or less, 70% graduate in 5 years or less, and 68% graduate in 6 years or less. 115 companies recruited on campus in a recent year. Of a recent graduating class, 36% were enrolled in graduate school within 6 months of graduation and 96% were employed.

Admissions Contact: Stephen Pultz, Director of Admissions. E-mail: *admissions@sandiego.edu* Web: *www.sandiego.edu*

UNIVERSITY OF SAN FRANCISCO B-3

San Francisco, CA 94117-1080 (415) 422-6563
(800) CALLUSF; Fax: (415) 422-2217

Full-time: 1710 men, 3017 women	**Faculty:** 270; I, +$
Part-time: 102 men, 138 women	**Ph.D.s:** 93%
Graduate: 1342 men, 1962 women	**Student/Faculty:** 17 to 1
Year: 4-1-4, summer session	**Tuition:** $26,840
Application Deadline: see profile	**Room & Board:** $10,720
Freshman Class: 6090 applied, 4376 accepted, 934 enrolled	
SAT or ACT: required	**VERY COMPETITIVE**

The University of San Francisco, founded in 1855, is a private Roman Catholic institution run by the Jesuit Fathers and offering degree programs in the arts and sciences, business, education, nursing, and law. There are 5 undergraduate and 6 graduate schools. In addition to regional accreditation, USF has baccalaureate program accreditation with AACSB, ACS, APA, CSAB, and NLN. The 2 libraries contain 915,000 volumes, 900,000 microform items, and 6000 audio/video tapes/CDs/DVDs, and subscribe to 2500 periodicals including electronic. Computerized library services include the card catalog, interlibrary loans, and database searching. Special learning facilities include a learning resource center, art gallery, radio station, rare book room, the Institute for Chinese-Western Cultural History, and the Center for Pacific Rim Studies. The 55-acre campus is in an urban area in the heart of the city. Including any residence halls, there are 17 buildings.

Student Life: 69% of undergraduates are from California. Students are from 49 states, 53 foreign countries, and Canada. 44% are from public schools. 39% are white; 25% Asian American; 13% Hispanic. 48% are Catholic; 33% Buddhist, Hindu, or Muslim; 9% claim no religious affiliation; 8% Protestant. The average age of freshmen is 18; all undergraduates, 21. 20% do not continue beyond their first year; 67% remain to graduate.

Housing: 2250 students can be accommodated in college housing, which includes single-sex and coed dorms, on-campus apartments, and off-campus apartments. In addition, there are special-interest houses, a multicultural floor, an academic interest floor, a freshman experiences floor, and a quiet floor. On-campus housing is guaranteed for the freshman year only. 64% of students live on campus. Alcohol is not permitted. All students may keep cars.

Activities: 1% of men belong to 2 local and 1 national fraternity; 2% of women belong to 4 local and 2 national sororities. There are 75 groups on campus, including cheerleading, choir, chorale, chorus, computers, drama, ethnic, honors, international, literary magazine, musical theater, newspaper, orchestra, pep band, political, professional, radio and TV, religious, social, social service, and student government. Popular campus events include Founders Day and International Week.

Sports: There are 7 intercollegiate sports for men and 7 for women, and 8 intramural sports for men and 8 for women. Facilities include a 600-seat soccer stadium, a recreation center with a 50-meter swimming pool, a multipurpose gym, a weight room, a dance and aerobics room, a martial arts room, and 5 racquetball/handball courts.

Disabled Students: 95% of the campus is accessible. Wheelchair ramps, elevators, special parking, specially equipped rest rooms, lowered drinking fountains, and exam accommodations are available.

Services: Counseling and information services are available, as is tutoring in every subject. There is a reader service for the blind. There is a full-time counselor for learning-disabled students, as well as a learning and writing center for students in need of academic assistance.

Campus Safety and Security: Measures include 24-hour foot and vehicle patrol, self-defense education, security escort services, and shuttle buses. There are informal discussions, pamphlets/posters/films, emergency telephones, and lighted pathways/sidewalks.

Programs of Study: USF confers B.A., B.S., B.Arch., B.F.A., B.P.A., B.S.B.A., and B.S.N. degrees. Master's and doctoral degrees are also awarded. Bachelor's degrees are awarded in BIOLOGICAL SCIENCE (biology/biological science), BUSINESS (accounting, banking and finance, business administration and management, hospitality management services, hotel/motel and restaurant management, international business management, management information systems, marketing/retailing/merchandising, and organizational behavior), COMMUNICATIONS AND THE ARTS (art history and appreciation, arts administration/management, communications, drawing, English, fine arts, French, graphic design, illustration, media arts, painting, performing arts, Spanish, and visual and performing arts), COMPUTER AND PHYSICAL SCIENCE (chemistry, computer science, information sciences and systems, mathematics, and physics), EDUCATION (athletic training, elementary, middle school, and secondary), ENGINEERING AND ENVIRONMEN-

TAL DESIGN (architecture and environmental science), HEALTH PRO-FESSIONS (exercise science and nursing), SOCIAL SCIENCE (economics, history, Latin American studies, law enforcement and corrections, philosophy, political science/government, psychology, public administration, religion, sociology, and theological studies). Sciences and business are the strongest academically. Communications, nursing, and psychology are the largest.

Required: All students must maintain a GPA of at least 2.0 and take 128 credit hours, including 58 in upper-division courses. 36 to 58 hours are required in the major. The current general education requirements include 9 units each of basic skills and history/social science, 6 each of philosophy, religious studies, cultural perspectives, natural science, and literature and fine arts, and 3 of ethics.

Special: Cross-registration with the San Francisco Consortium, internships with local business, social services, and research opportunities are available. Study abroad in Europe and Japan, work-study programs both on and off campus, and with social service agencies, a B.A.-B.S. degree in exercise and sports science, dual majors in liberal arts and education, 3-2 engineering degrees with the University of Southern California, student-designed majors, nondegree study, and limited pass/fail options are also available. The College of Professional Studies is a degree completion program for working adults. There are 5 national honor societies, a freshman honors program, and 1 departmental honors program.

Faculty/Classroom: 60% of faculty are male; 40%, female. 90% teach undergraduates, 75% do research, and 90% do both. No introductory courses are taught by graduate students. The average class size in an introductory lecture is 28; in a laboratory, 13; and in a regular course, 20.

Admissions: 72% of the 2005-2006 applicants were accepted. 18% of the current freshmen were in the top fifth of their class; 80% were in the top two fifths. 2 freshmen graduated first in their class.

Requirements: The SAT or ACT is required. In addition, applicants are required to have 20 academic units, based on 6 years of academic electives, 4 of English, 3 each of math and social studies, and 2 each of foreign language and lab science. An essay is required. The GED is accepted. A GPA of 3.0 is required. AP and CLEP credits are accepted. Important factors in the admissions decision are extracurricular activities record, evidence of special talent, and leadership record.

Procedure: Freshmen are admitted fall and spring. Entrance exams should be taken during the first half of the senior year. There are early admissions, deferred admissions and rolling admissions plans. Notification is sent on a rolling basis. Applications are accepted on-line. Check with the school for current application deadlines.

Transfer: 359 transfer students enrolled in a recent year. Applicants need a minimum GPA of 2.0, or 2.8 if they have earned fewer than 24 semester units. 45 of 128 credits required for the bachelor's degree must be completed at USF.

Visiting: There are regularly scheduled orientations for prospective students, including a tour of campus, academic buildings, library, residence halls, recreation centers, and a group information session hosted by an admissions staff member. There are guides for informal visits and visitors may sit in on classes and stay overnight. To schedule a visit, contact the Office of Admissions.

Financial Aid: In a recent year, 71% of all full-time freshmen and 57% of continuing full-time students received some form of financial aid. 62% of full-time freshmen and 57% of continuing full-time students received need-based aid. The average freshman award was $19,976. 29% of undergraduates worked part time. Average annual earnings from campus work were $2900. The average financial indebtedness of a recent graduate was $19,958. The FAFSA is required. Check with the school for current application deadlines.

International Students: In a recent year, there were 347 international students enrolled. The school actively recruits these students. They must score satisfactorily on the written TOEFL or on the electronic version and also take the SAT. Students must take SAT Writing test for placement only.

Computers: All students may access the system. There are no time limits and no fees.

Graduates: In a recent year, 1192 bachelor's degrees were awarded. The most popular majors were communication (10%), business administration (9%), and psychology (8%). In an average class, 1% graduate in 3 years or less, 47% graduate in 4 years or less, 63% graduate in 5 years or less, and 67% graduate in 6 years or less. 110 companies recruited on campus in a recent year. Of a recent graduating class, 15% were enrolled in graduate school within 6 months of graduation and 70% were employed.

Admissions Contact: Thomas Matos, Director of Admissions.
E-mail: *admissions@usfca.edu* Web: *http://www.usfca.edu/*

UNIVERSITY OF SOUTHERN CALIFORNIA C-5

Los Angeles, CA 90089- (213) 740-1111; Fax: (213) 740-6364

Full-time: 7870 men, 8202 women	**Faculty:** 1489; I, +$
Part-time: 420 men, 405 women	**Ph.D.s:** 88%
Graduate: 8572 men, 6367 women	**Student/Faculty:** 11 to 1
Year: semesters, summer session	**Tuition:** $32,008
Application Deadline: January 10	**Room & Board:** $9610
Freshman Class: 31,634 applied, 8418 accepted, 2741 enrolled	
SAT Verbal/Math: 668/690*	**ACT:** 30 **MOST COMPETITIVE**

University of Southern California, founded in 1880, is a private institution offering undergraduate and graduate programs in liberal arts, fine arts, education, business, law, dentistry, engineering, communications, health professions, and more. There are 15 undergraduate and 18 graduate schools. In addition to regional accreditation, USC has baccalaureate program accreditation with AACSB, ABET, ACEJMC, ACPE, ACS, ADA, AOTA, APTA, CAHEA, CSAB, CSWE, NAAB, NASM, NASPAA, and NLN. The 21 libraries contain 3,921,189 volumes, 6,187,918 microform items, and 70,534 audio/video tapes/CDs/DVDs, and subscribe to 34,100 periodicals including electronic. Computerized library services include the card catalog, interlibrary loans, database searching, and Internet access. Special learning facilities include a learning resource center, art gallery, natural history museum, radio station, TV station, labs, state-of-the-art cinema/film-making facilities, wind tunnel, and marine science center. The 155-acre campus is in an urban area 3 miles south of the Los Angeles Civic Center. Including any residence halls, there are 166 buildings.

Student Life: 61% of undergraduates are from California. Others are from 50 states, 116 foreign countries, and Canada. 64% are from public schools. 47% are white; 21% Asian American; 13% Hispanic. The average age of freshmen is 18; all undergraduates, 21. 5% do not continue beyond their first year; 83% remain to graduate.

Housing: 6600 students can be accommodated in college housing, which includes coed dorms, on-campus apartments, off-campus apartments, married-student housing, fraternity houses, and sorority houses. In addition, there are special-interest houses. On-campus housing is guaranteed for the freshman year only, is available on a first-come, first-served basis, and is available on a lottery system for upperclassmen. 62% of students commute. All students may keep cars.

Activities: 16% of men belong to 7 local and 23 national fraternities; 20% of women belong to 11 local and 13 national sororities. There are more than 600 groups on campus, including art, band, cheerleading, chess, choir, chorale, chorus, computers, dance, debate, drama, drill team, ethnic, film, forensics, gay, honors, international, jazz band, literary magazine, marching band, musical theater, newspaper, opera, orchestra, pep band, photography, political, professional, radio and TV, religious, social, social service, student government, symphony, and yearbook. Popular campus events include Springfest, International Food and Cultural Fair, and Spectrum concert series.

Sports: There are 9 intercollegiate sports for men and 10 for women, and 26 intramural sports for men and 23 for women. Facilities include a student athletic center, a track, a gym, 2 Olympic pools, and tennis, swimming, and baseball stadiums.

Disabled Students: 97% of the campus is accessible. Wheelchair ramps, elevators, special parking, specially equipped rest rooms, special housing, and shuttle service for students with temporary disabilities are available.

Services: Counseling and information services are available, as is tutoring in every subject. There is a reader service for the blind. Accommodations are made for students with disabilities.

Campus Safety and Security: Measures include 24-hour foot and vehicle patrol, self-defense education, security escort services, and shuttle buses. There are informal discussions, pamphlets/posters/films, emergency telephones, lighted pathways/sidewalks, and and the safety department responds to calls for service on and off campus (off campus areas are agreed upon with the LAPD).

Programs of Study: USC confers B.A., B.S., B.Arch., B.F.A., B. Land. Arch., and B.M. degrees. Master's and doctoral degrees are also awarded. Bachelor's degrees are awarded in AGRICULTURE (environmental studies), BIOLOGICAL SCIENCE (biology/biological science, biophysics, and neurosciences), BUSINESS (accounting, business administration and management, and international business management), COMMUNICATIONS AND THE ARTS (American literature, art history and appreciation, broadcasting, classics, communications, comparative literature, creative writing, East Asian languages and literature, English, English literature, fine arts, French, German, Italian, jazz, journalism, linguistics, music, music performance, public relations, Russian, Spanish, studio art, theater design, and theater management), COMPUTER AND PHYSICAL SCIENCE (astronomy, chemistry, computer science, geology, mathematics, and physics), EDUCATION (health and music), ENGINEERING AND ENVIRONMENTAL DESIGN (aeronautical engineering, aerospace studies, architecture, biomedical engineering, chemical engineering, civil engineering, computer engineering, electrical/electronics engineering, environmental engineering, industrial engineering, landscape architecture/design, mechanical engineering, and petroleum/natural gas engineering), HEALTH PROFESSIONS (dental hygiene, health, occupational therapy, and physician's assistant), SOCIAL SCIENCE (African American studies, American studies, anthropology, Asian/American studies, East Asian studies, economics, gender studies, geography, gerontology, history, international relations, Latin American studies, liberal arts/general studies, philosophy, political science/government, psychobiology, psychology, religion, social science, sociology, and women's studies). Business, engineering, and communications are the largest.

Required: All students must satisfy requirements in foreign language, freshman writing, and general education and take 1 multicultural course. Graduation requirements include a minimum of 128 credit hours and a minimum GPA of 2.0.

Special: Cross-registration is permitted with Hebrew Union College and Howard University. Internships in various majors, a Washington semester, work-study programs, study abroad in 28 countries, dual majors, a general studies degree, student-designed majors, a 3-2 engineering degree, and pass/fail options are available. Students are encouraged to pursue interdisciplinary study linking core art and science disciplines to professional programs. There are 41 national honor societies, including Phi Beta Kappa, and a freshman honors program.

Faculty/Classroom: 70% of faculty are male; 30%, female. 100% do research. No introductory courses are taught by graduate students. The average class size in an introductory lecture is 30; in a laboratory, 24; and in a regular course, 28.

Admissions: 27% of the 2005-2006 applicants were accepted. The SAT scores for the 2005-2006 freshman class were: Verbal--1% below 500, 13% between 500 and 599, 51% between 600 and 700, and 35% above 700; Math--7% between 500 and 599, 43% between 600 and 700, and 50% above 700. The ACT scores were 3% between 21 and 23, 12% between 24 and 26, 18% between 27 and 28, and 67% above 28. There were 158 National Merit finalists.

Requirements: The SAT or ACT is required. In addition, 3 SAT Subject Tests are recommended. Graduation form an accredited secondary school is required. Applicants must have completed at least 13 year-long courses in English, humanities, math, natural sciences, social sciences, and foreign languages, plus 3 additional year-long courses in those areas or in computer science and with some exceptions, theater, fine arts, journalism, music or speech. AP credits are accepted. Important factors in the admissions decision are advanced placement or honor courses, recommendations by school officials, and evidence of special talent.

Procedure: Freshmen are admitted fall and spring. Entrance exams should be taken by November of the senior year for scholarship applicants; by December for all others. Applications should be filed by January 10 for fall entry, along with a $65 fee. Notification is sent April 1. Applications are accepted on-line.

Transfer: 1423 transfer students enrolled in 2004-2005. Transfer applicants must submit 30 units of transferable work with a strong GPA in a rigorous selection of courses. SAT or ACT scores are considered if 30 units have not been completed by the time of application. 64 of 128 credits required for the bachelor's degree must be completed at USC.

Visiting: There are regularly scheduled orientations for prospective students. There are guides for informal visits and visitors may sit in on classes and stay overnight. To schedule a visit, contact the Admission Office at (213) 740-6616.

Financial Aid: In 2004-2005, 67% of all full-time freshmen and 63% of continuing full-time students received some form of financial aid. 42% of full-time freshmen and 44% of continuing full-time students received need-based aid. The average freshman award was $21,957. Need-based scholarships or need-based grants averaged $18,919; need-based self-help aid (loans and jobs) averaged $5278; non-need-based athletic scholarships averaged $28,715; and other non-need-based awards and non-need-based scholarships averaged $12,134. 108% of undergraduates work part time. The average financial indebtedness of the 2005 graduate was $19,131. The CSS/Profile or FAFSA and tax forms are required. The priority date for freshman financial aid applications for fall entry is January 20. The deadline for filing freshman financial aid applications for fall entry is January 20.

International Students: There are 1384 international students enrolled. The school actively recruits these students. Undergraduate students who meet or exceed the required score on the verbal portion of the SAT are exempted from providing TOEFL scores. Upon arrival, students with low TOEFL scores are required to take our local English proficiency examination and the SAT.

Computers: Wireless access is available. All students may access the system. There are no time limits and no fees.

Graduates: From July 1, 2004 to June 30, 2005, 3975 bachelor's degrees were awarded. The most popular majors were business administration (18%), Communications (6%), and Political Science (6%). In an average class, 2% graduate in 3 years or less, 66% graduate in 4 years or less, 81% graduate in 5 years or less, and 83% graduate in 6 years or less. More than 600 companies recruited on campus in 2004-2005.

Admissions Contact: Katherine Harrington, Dean of Admission and Financial Aid. A video is available. Web: *www.usc.edu*

UNIVERSITY OF THE PACIFIC
B-3

Stockton, CA 95211-0197

(209) 946-2211

(800) 959-2867; Fax: (209) 946-2413

Full-time: 1469 men, 1888 women	**Faculty:** 235; IIA, +$
Part-time: 35 men, 65 women	**Ph.D.s:** 95%
Graduate: 1294 men, 1445 women	**Student/Faculty:** 14 to 1
Year: semesters, summer session	**Tuition:** $26,088
Application Deadline: January 15	**Room & Board:** $8292
Freshman Class: 5869 applied, 3304 accepted, 800 enrolled	
SAT Verbal/Math: 580/610*	**ACT:** 25 VERY COMPETITIVE

The University of the Pacific, founded in 1851, is a private nonreligious institution. It offers undergraduate and graduate programs in arts and sciences, and professional programs in pharmacy, law, and dentistry. There are 8 undergraduate schools and 1 graduate school. In addition to regional accreditation, Pacific has baccalaureate program accreditation with AACSB, ABET, ACS, CAAHEP, NASAD, NASM, and NCATE, ACS, and CAAHEP. The 2 libraries contain 364,040 volumes, 691,873 microform items, and 10,561 audio/video tapes/CDs/DVDs, and subscribe to 1285 periodicals including electronic. Computerized library services include the card catalog, interlibrary loans, database searching, and Internet access. Special learning facilities include a learning resource center, art gallery, radio station, and the Brubeck Institute. The 175-acre campus is in a suburban area 80 miles east of San Francisco and 40 miles south of Sacramento. Including any residence halls, there are 85 buildings.

Student Life: 87% of undergraduates are from California. Others are from Canada. 44% are white; 24% Asian American; 10% Hispanic. The average age of freshmen is 18; all undergraduates, 20. 13% do not continue beyond their first year; 65% remain to graduate.

Housing: 2226 students can be accommodated in college housing, which includes coed dorms, on-campus apartments, off-campus apartments, married-student housing, fraternity houses, and sorority houses. In addition, there are honors houses special-interest houses, and intercultural, wellness, pharmacy, and learning involvement theme house. On-campus housing is guaranteed for the freshman year only, is available on a first-come, first-served basis, and is available on a lottery system for upperclassmen. Priority is given to out-of-town students. 58% of students live on campus. Alcohol is not permitted. All students may keep cars.

Activities: 19% of men belong to 1 local and 7 national fraternities; 18% of women belong to 1 local and 6 national sororities. There are 100 groups on campus, including art, band, cheerleading, choir, chorale, chorus, club sports, computers, dance, debate, drama, ethnic, forensics, gay, honors, international, jazz band, literary magazine, musical theater, newspaper, opera, orchestra, pep band, photography, political, professional, radio and TV, religious, social, social service, student government, and symphony. Popular campus events include Alumni Weekend, Pacific Boardwalk Carnival, and Cultural Diversity Week.

Sports: There are 7 intercollegiate sports for men and 9 for women, and 30 intramural sports for men and 30 for women. Facilities include a 6000-seat sports arena, an Olympic-size pool, tennis courts, a softball field, and a fitness center.

Disabled Students: 90% of the campus is accessible. Wheelchair ramps, elevators, special parking, specially equipped rest rooms, special class scheduling, lowered drinking fountains, and lowered telephones are available.

Services: Counseling and information services are available, as is tutoring in every subject. There is a reader service for the blind, and remedial math, reading, and writing.

Campus Safety and Security: Measures include 24-hour foot and vehicle patrol, security escort services, informal discussions, and pamphlets/posters/films. There are emergency telephones and lighted pathways/sidewalks.

Programs of Study: Pacific confers B.A., B.S., B.F.A., B.M., B.S.B.A., B.S.B.E., B.S.C.E., B.S.E.E., B.S.E.M., B.S.E.P., and B.S.M.E. degrees. Master's and doctoral degrees are also awarded. Bachelor's degrees are awarded in BIOLOGICAL SCIENCE (biochemistry, and biology/biological science), BUSINESS (business administration and management), COMMUNICATIONS AND THE ARTS (art, communications, dramatic arts, English, French, German, graphic design, Japanese, music, music business management, music history and appreciation, music performance, music theory and composition, Spanish, and studio art), COMPUTER AND PHYSICAL SCIENCE (applied mathematics, chemistry, computer science, geology, geophysics and seismology, information sciences and systems, mathematics, and physics), EDUCATION (education, music, and physical), ENGINEERING AND ENVIRONMENTAL DESIGN (civil engineering, computer engineering, electrical/electronics engineering, engineering management, engineering physics, environmental science, and mechanical engineering), HEALTH PROFESSIONS (music therapy, prepharmacy, and speech pathology/audiology), SOCIAL SCIENCE (economics, history, international relations, international studies, liberal arts/general studies, philosophy, political science/government, psychology, religion, social science, and sociology). Natural sciences and the professions are the strongest academically. Arts and sciences, pharmacy, and business are the largest.

Required: Students must complete at least 124 credit hours to graduate. The required general education program consists of 3 "mentor seminars" and 6 to 9 other courses chosen from categories such as the Individual and Society, the Human Heritage, and the Natural World and Formal Systems of Thought.

Special: The engineering school requires and guarantees a co-op program for specialized training in the field. Internships for credit or pay in all majors, more than 230 study-abroad programs in more than 80 countries, a Washington semester, and more than 20 work-study programs also are available. Student-designed majors, B.A./B.S. degrees, dual majors in most disciplines, and pass/fail options are possible. There are 18 national honor societies, a freshman honors program, and 42 departmental honors programs.

Faculty/Classroom: 64% of faculty are male; 36%, female. All teach undergraduates. No introductory courses are taught by graduate students. The average class size in a regular course is 19.

Admissions: 56% of the 2005-2006 applicants were accepted. The SAT scores for the 2005-2006 freshman class were: Verbal--14% below 500, 41% between 500 and 599, 40% between 600 and 700, and 5% above 700; Math--9% below 500, 35% between 500 and 599, 43% between 600 and 700, and 14% above 700. The ACT scores were 9% below 21, 25% between 21 and 23, 28% between 24 and 26, 20% between 27 and 28, and 19% above 28. 66% of the current freshmen were in the top fifth of their class; 85% were in the top two fifths.

Requirements: The SAT or ACT is required. In addition, applicants must have 16 academic credits, including a recommended 4 years of high school English, 3 of math, 2 in the same foreign language, 2 of lab science, 1 of U.S history or government, 1 of fine or performing arts, and 4 additional academic courses. An essay is required; an interview is recommended. An audition is necessary for music students. The GED is accepted plus one year of math and science for science and health related majors. A GPA of 2.5 is required. AP and CLEP credits are accepted. Important factors in the admissions decision are advanced placement or honor courses, leadership record, and extracurricular activities record.

Procedure: Freshmen are admitted fall and spring. Entrance exams should be taken in the spring of the junior year or fall of the senior year. There are early decision, early admissions, and deferred admissions plans. There is a rolling admissions plan. Early decision applications should be filed by November 15; regular applications, by January 15 for fall entry and November 15 for spring entry. Notification of early decision is sent January 15; regular decision, on a rolling basis. A waiting list is an active part of the admissions procedure. The fall 2005 admission fee was $60. Applications are accepted on-line.

Transfer: 229 transfer students enrolled in 2004-2005. Applicants should have a minimum GPA of 2.5 and at least 16 credit hours. The SAT or ACT and high school transcripts are required if fewer than 30 units of college work have been completed. 32 of 124 credits required for the bachelor's degree must be completed at Pacific.

Visiting: There are regularly scheduled orientations for prospective students, including a tour, appointments with faculty, admissions, financial aid personnel, and class visits. There are guides for informal visits and visitors may sit in on classes and stay overnight. To schedule a visit, contact Admissions at *admissions@pacific.edu.*

Financial Aid: In 2005-2006, 91% of all full-time freshmen and 87% of continuing full-time students received some form of financial aid. 67% of full-time freshmen and 69% of continuing full-time students received need-based aid. The average freshman award was $19,845. Need-based scholarships or need-based grants averaged $13,779 ($26,222 maximum); need-based self-help aid (loans and jobs) averaged $4740 ($11,625 maximum); non-need-based athletic scholarships averaged $15,376 ($38,320 maximum); and other non-need-based awards and non-need-based scholarships averaged $8180 ($23,092 maximum). 36% of undergraduates work part time. Average annual earnings from campus work are $1300. Pacific is a member of CSS. The FAFSA is required. The deadline for filing freshman financial aid applications for fall entry is February 15.

International Students: There are 78 international students enrolled. The school actively recruits these students. They must score satisfactorily on the TOEFL. The SAT or ACT is required if the student has attended a U.S.-style high school.

Computers: Wireless access is available. All students may access the system any time. There are no time limits and no fees. It is recommended that students in pharmacy have personal computers.

Graduates: From July 1, 2004 to June 30, 2005, 686 bachelor's degrees were awarded. The most popular majors were pharmacy (18%), business (13%), and engineering (8%). In an average class, 1% graduate in 3 years or less, 43% graduate in 4 years or less, 58% graduate in 5 years or less, and 65% graduate in 6 years or less.

Admissions Contact: Marc McGee, Director of Admissions.
E-mail: *admissions@pacific.edu* Web: *www.pacific.edu*

VANGUARD UNIVERSITY OF SOUTHERN CALIFORNIA   D-5

Costa Mesa, CA 92626

(714) 556-3610
(800) 722-6279; Fax: (714) 966-5471

Full-time: 514 men, 981 women	**Faculty:** 72; IIB, av$
Part-time: 135 men, 184 women	**Ph.D.s:** 74%
Graduate: 149 men, 197 women	**Student/Faculty:** 21 to 1
Year: semesters, summer session	**Tuition:** $20,315
Application Deadline: December 1	**Room & Board:** $6756
Freshman Class: 903 applied, 775 accepted, 403 enrolled	
SAT Verbal/Math: 509/502*	**ACT:** 21 COMPETITIVE

Vanguard University of Southern California, founded in 1920, is a private Christian comprehensive university of liberal arts and profesional studies affiliated with the Assemblies of God. The library contains 175,877 volumes, 20,562 microform items, and 6503 audio/video tapes/CDs/DVDs, and subscribes to 10,000 periodicals including electronic. Computerized library services include the card catalog, interlibrary loans, database searching, and Internet access. Special learning facilities include a learning resource center. The 38-acre campus is in a suburban area 40 miles southeast of Los Angeles and 5 miles north of Newport Beach. Including any residence halls, there are 25 buildings.

Student Life: 80% of undergraduates are from California. Students are from 39 states, 18 foreign countries, and Canada. 75% are from public schools. 70% are white; 16% Hispanic. Most are Protestant. The average age of freshmen is 18; all undergraduates, 20. 24% do not continue beyond their first year; 42% remain to graduate.

Housing: 1048 students can be accommodated in college housing, which includes single-sex dorms, on-campus apartments, off-campus apartments, and married-student housing. On-campus housing is guaranteed for the freshman year only, is available on a first-come, first-served basis, and is available on a lottery system for upperclassmen. Priority is given to out-of-town students. 74% of students live on campus; of those, 75% remain on campus on weekends. Alcohol is not permitted. All students may keep cars.

Activities: There are no fraternities or sororities. There are 30 groups on campus, including art, band, chess, choir, chorale, chorus, dance, debate, drama, ethnic, film, forensics, gay, international, jazz band, musical theater, newspaper, orchestra, pep band, photography, political, professional, radio and TV, religious, social, social service, student government, student ministries and yearbook. Popular campus events include Harvest Party, International Missions Week, and Christmas Party.

Sports: There are 6 intercollegiate sports for men and 7 for women. Facilities include a gym, baseball, softball, and soccer fields, a weight room, and contracted off-campus tennis courts and track course.

Disabled Students: 95% of the campus is accessible. Wheelchair ramps, elevators, special parking, specially equipped rest rooms, special class scheduling, and special housing are available.

Services: Counseling and information services are available, as is tutoring in most subjects.

Campus Safety and Security: Measures include 24-hour foot and vehicle patrol, security escort services, pamphlets/posters/films, and emergency telephones. There are lighted pathways/sidewalks and room and vehicle unlocks.

Programs of Study: VU confers B.A. and B.S. degrees. Master's degrees are also awarded. Bachelor's degrees are awarded in BIOLOGICAL SCIENCE (biology/biological science), BUSINESS (accounting, business administration and management, international business management, and marketing/retailing/merchandising), COMMUNICATIONS AND THE ARTS (communications, dramatic arts, English, music, and Spanish), COMPUTER AND PHYSICAL SCIENCE (chemistry and mathematics), EDUCATION (elementary, physical, science, and secondary), HEALTH PROFESSIONS (premedicine), SOCIAL SCIENCE (anthropology, biblical studies, history, ministries, political science/government, psychology, religious education, and sociology). Religion, social sciences, and natural sciences are the strongest academically. Business, liberal studies, and religion are the largest.

Required: Students must complete a minimum of 124 credits, with 40 to 70 in the major. General education requirements include 16 credits in religion, 15 in humanities and fine arts, 12 in social science, 7 in natural sciences and math, and 2 in phys ed. VU requires a minimum GPA of 2.0.

Special: Study abroad in Costa Rica, Australia, China, England, Egypt, and Russia, internships, a Washington semester, a general studies degree, work-study, accelerated degree programs in business, psychology, and religion, and pass/fail options are available. 3 summer sessions are offered.

Faculty/Classroom: 60% of faculty are male; 40%, female. 84% teach undergraduates. No introductory courses are taught by graduate students. The average class size in an introductory lecture is 40; in a laboratory, 12; and in a regular course, 19.

Admissions: 86% of the 2005-2006 applicants were accepted. The SAT scores for the 2005-2006 freshman class were: Verbal--36% below

500, 42% between 500 and 599, 19% between 600 and 700, and 3% above 700; Math--41% below 500, 41% between 500 and 599, 16% between 600 and 700, and 2% above 700. 48% of the current freshmen were in the top fifth of their class; 76% were in the top two fifths. There was 1 National Merit finalist. 5 freshmen graduated first in their class.

Requirements: The SAT or ACT is required. In addition, high school courses should include 4 years of English, 3 of social studies, and 2 of math and science. Applicants are required to write application essays and submit 2 references, 1 academic and 1 from a pastor/minister. A GPA of 2.8 is required. AP and CLEP credits are accepted. Important factors in the admissions decision are leadership record, advanced placement or honor courses, and evidence of special talent.

Procedure: Freshmen are admitted fall and spring. Entrance exams should be taken in the junior year. There is a rolling admissions plan. Applications should be filed by December 1 for fall entry, along with a $45 fee. Notification is sent on a rolling basis beginning January 15. A waiting list is an active part of the admissions procedure. Applications are accepted on-line.

Transfer: 130 transfer students enrolled in 2004-2005. Transfer applicants must submit college transcripts and have a minimum college GPA of 2.0. 24 of 124 credits required for the bachelor's degree must be completed at VU.

Visiting: There are regularly scheduled orientations for prospective students, consisting of fall and spring university visit days with schedules for students and parents. There are guides for informal visits and visitors may sit in on classes and stay overnight. To schedule a visit, contact Undergraduate Admissions at admissions@vanguard.edu.

Financial Aid: In 2005-2006, 92% of all full-time freshmen and 94% of continuing full-time students received some form of financial aid. 73% of full-time freshmen and 70% of continuing full-time students received need-based aid. The average freshman award was $18,887, with $5062 ($16,650 maximum) from need-based scholarships or grants,$1832 ($7865 maixmum) from need-based self-help aid (loans and jobs), $774 ($27,356 maximum) from non-need-based athletic scholarships and $11,219 ($31,590 maximum) from other non-need-based awards and non-need-based scholarships. 15% of undergraduates work part time. Average annual earnings from campus work are $3025. The average financial indebtedness of the 2005 graduate was $18,834. The FAFSA and state scholarship/grant forms are required. The deadline for filing freshman financial aid applications for fall entry is March 2.

International Students: There are 18 international students enrolled. They must take the TOEFL.

Computers: Wireless access is available. There are 175 computers in labs, 90% wireless coverage and 2 to 3 ports per dorm room. Access is included in tuition. All students may access the system 24 hours a day 7 days a week. There are no time limits and no fees.

Graduates: From July 1, 2004 to June 30, 2005, 546 bachelor's degrees were awarded. The most popular majors were business (30%), psychology (18%), and religion (13%). In an average class, 42% graduate in 4 years or less, 43% graduate in 5 years or less, and 45% graduate in 6 years or less. 30 companies recruited on campus in 2004-2005.

Admissions Contact: Jennifer Purga, Director of Admissions. A video is available. E-mail: admissions@vanguard.edu
Web: www.vanguard.edu/admissions

WESTMONT COLLEGE C-5
Santa Barbara, CA 93108
(805) 565-6005
(800) 777-9011; Fax: (805) 565-6234

Full-time: 524 men, 830 women	**Faculty:** 87; IIB, +$
Part-time: none	**Ph.D.s:** 95%
Graduate: none	**Student/Faculty:** 16 to 1
Year: semesters, summer session	**Tuition:** $27,806
Application Deadline: February 15	**Room & Board:** $8866

Freshman Class: 1813 applied, 1231 accepted, 333 enrolled
SAT Verbal/Math: 620/610*   **HIGHLY COMPETITIVE**

Westmont College, founded in 1937, is a selective, nondenominational Christian college devoted to the intellectual and spiritual development of students through a rigorous liberal arts curriculum. The library contains 162,274 volumes, 20,687 microform items, and 7926 audio/video tapes/CDs/DVDs, and subscribes to 3211 periodicals including electronic. Computerized library services include the card catalog, interlibrary loans, database searching, and Internet access. Special learning facilities include a learning resource center, art gallery, radio station, observatory, science center with a premedical center, physiology lab, and a fitness center. The 111-acre campus is in a suburban area 90 miles north of Los Angeles. Including any residence halls, there are 30 buildings.

Student Life: 68% of undergraduates are from California. Others are from 38 states, 10 foreign countries, and Canada. 70% are from public schools. 78% are white; 11% Hispanic. Most are Protestant. The average age of freshmen is 18; all undergraduates, 20. 9% do not continue beyond their first year; 70% remain to graduate.

Housing: 1113 students can be accommodated in college housing, which includes single-sex and coed dormitories and off-campus apart-

ments. On-campus housing is guaranteed for all 4 years. 85% of students live on campus; of those, 65% remain on campus on weekends. Alcohol is not permitted. Upperclassmen may keep cars.

Activities: There are no fraternities or sororities. There are 50 groups on campus, including art, band, chess, choir, chorale, chorus, computers, dance, debate, drama, ethnic, film, honors, international, jazz band, leadership, literary magazine, musical theater, newspaper, opera, orchestra, pep band, photography, political, professional, radio and TV, religious, social, social service, student government, symphony, and yearbook. Popular campus events include Community Service Day, Multicultural Fellowship Week, and theatrical and musical productions.

Sports: There are 6 intercollegiate sports for men and 6 for women, and 10 intramural sports for men and 10 for women. Facilities include a 2133-seat gym, a soccer/baseball field, a swimming pool, a fitness room, a dance studio, a track, and volleyball, tennis, basketball, and racquetball courts.

Disabled Students: 60% of the campus is accessible. Wheelchair ramps, elevators, special parking, specially equipped rest rooms, special class scheduling, lowered drinking fountains, lowered telephones, and special housing are available.

Services: Counseling and information services are available, as is tutoring in every subject. There is a reader service for the blind and remedial math. A writers' corner supervised by tutors is available.

Campus Safety and Security: Measures include 24-hour foot and vehicle patrol, self-defense education, security escort services, and shuttle buses. There are informal discussions, pamphlets/posters/films, emergency telephones, and lighted pathways/sidewalks.

Programs of Study: Westmont confers B.A. and B.S. degrees. Bachelor's degrees are awarded in BIOLOGICAL SCIENCE (biology/biological science and neurosciences), BUSINESS (business economics), COMMUNICATIONS AND THE ARTS (art, communications, dramatic arts, English, French, modern language, music, and Spanish), COMPUTER AND PHYSICAL SCIENCE (chemistry, computer science, mathematics, and physics), EDUCATION (art, English, mathematics, music, physical, and social science), ENGINEERING AND ENVIRONMENTAL DESIGN (engineering physics), HEALTH PROFESSIONS (exercise science), SOCIAL SCIENCE (European studies, history, liberal arts/general studies, philosophy, political science/government, psychology, religion, social science, and sociology). Biology, communication studies, and economics/business are the largest.

Required: Of the 124 semester unite required for graduation, the college's general education requirements include 20 semester units of Common Context courses and 32 semester units of Common Inquiries courses. In addition, students must complete Common skills courses and courses relating to Competent and Compassionate Action. Courses in religions studies and phys ed are required as are courses in the history of Western civilization and English composition. Math proficiency is also required.There are distribution requirements in social sciences, humanities, and natural sciences. The total number of hours in the major varies from 36 to 66. A GPA of 2.0 must be maintained.

Special: Westmont offers cross-registration with 12 Christian colleges in the Christian College Consortium, internships in local businesses and social agencies, study abroad in 11 countries, and semesters in Washington, D.C., San Francisco, and Los Angeles. B.A.-B.S. degrees, student-designed majors, work-study programs, a 3-2 engineering program with several California universities, University of Washington, and Boston University, and pass/fail options also are available. There are also preprofessional programs in dentistry, law, medicine, ministry/missions, optometry, pharmacology, physical therapy, and veterinary medicine. There are 7 national honor societies, a freshman honors program, and 9 departmental honors programs.

Faculty/Classroom: 69% of faculty are male; 31%, female. All both teach and do research. The average class size in an introductory lecture is 30; in a laboratory, 15; and in a regular course, 20.

Admissions: 68% of the 2005-2006 applicants were accepted. The SAT scores for the 2005-2006 freshman class were: Verbal--6% below 500, 34% between 500 and 599, 43% between 600 and 700, and 17% above 700; Math--7% below 500, 37% between 500 and 599, 40% between 600 and 700, and 16% above 700. The ACT scores were 4% below 21, 14% between 21 and 23, 34% between 24 and 26, 25% between 27 and 28, and 23% above 28. 70% of the current freshmen were in the top fifth of their class; 92% were in the top two fifths. There were 10 National Merit finalists. 21 freshmen graduated first in their class.

Requirements: The SAT or ACT is required. The ACT Optional Writing test is also required. In addition, applicants need 16 academic credits, including 4 years of high school English, 3 of math, 2 each of a foreign language, social science, and physical science, and 1 each of history and biological science. Interviews are recommended. Essays are required. The GED is accepted. AP and CLEP credits are accepted. Important factors in the admissions decision are advanced placement or honor courses, leadership record, and extracurricular activities record.

Procedure: Freshmen are admitted fall and spring. Entrance exams should be taken during the spring of the junior year or the beginning of the senior year. There is an early admissions plan. Early decision applications should be filed by November 1; regular applications, by February 15 for fall entry and November 1 for spring entry. Notification of early decision is sent December 20; regular decision, April 1. A waiting list is an active part of the admissions procedure. Applications are accepted on-line. The fall 2005 application fee was $40.

Transfer: 60 transfer students enrolled in 2004-2005. Transfer students from 2-year colleges should have a minimum GPA of 2.8, and those students from 4-year colleges or universities, a 2.5. The college will not accept more than 64 transferable units from a community college; there is no maximum number of transferable units from a 4-year college. High school transcripts and test scores are required if the student has fewer than 24 transferable units. 32 of 124 credits required for the bachelor's degree must be completed at Westmont.

Visiting: There are regularly scheduled orientations for prospective students, consisting of meeting faculty and administrators and attending classes, academic seminars, student/parent panels, academic open houses, admission and financial aid sessions, student led small groups, campus tours, and various cultural events. There are guides for informal visits and visitors may sit in on classes and stay overnight. To schedule a visit, contact Admissions/Campus Visit Coordinator.

Financial Aid: In 2005-2006, 84% of all full-time freshmen and 85% of continuing full-time students received some form of financial aid. 83% of full-time freshmen and 84% of continuing full-time students received need-based aid. The average freshman award was $16,502. 54% of undergraduates work part time. Average annual earnings from campus work are $909. The average financial indebtedness of the 2005 graduate was $16,999. The FAFSA is required. The deadline for filing freshman financial aid applications for fall entry is March 2.

International Students: There are 11 international students enrolled. They must score satisfactorily on the written TOEFL or on the electronic version and also take the SAT or the ACT.

Computers: Wireless access is available. High-speed Internet access is available in all dorms. All students may access the system. There are no time limits and no fees. It is strongly recommended that all students have a personal computer.

Graduates: From July 1, 2004 to June 30, 2005, 308 bachelor's degrees were awarded. The most popular majors were communication studies (13%), biology (13%), and English (12%). In an average class, 4% graduate in 3 years or less, 65% graduate in 4 years or less, 71% graduate in 5 years or less, and 72% graduate in 6 years or less. 50 companies recruited on campus in 2004-2005. Of the 2004 graduating class, 48% were enrolled in graduate school within 6 months of graduation and 85% were employed.

Admissions Contact: Joyce M. Luy, Director of Admissions.
E-mail: *admissions@westmont.edu* Web: *http://www.westmont.edu*

WHITTIER COLLEGE	**D-5**
Whittier, CA 90608	**(562) 907-4238; Fax: (562) 907-4870**
Full-time: 525 men, 700 women	**Faculty:** 96; IIB, ++$
Part-time: 30 men, 15 women	**Ph.D.s:** 88%
Graduate: 350 men, 500 women	**Student/Faculty:** 13 to 1
Year: 4-1-4, summer session	**Tuition:** $27,906
Application Deadline: see profile	**Room & Board:** $8054
Freshman Class: n/av	
SAT or ACT: required	**COMPETITIVE**

Whittier College, founded in 1887 by the Society of Friends, is an independent, liberal arts institution with no religious affiliation. There are 2 graduate schools. Some information in the above capsule and in this profile is approximate. In addition to regional accreditation, Whittier has baccalaureate program accreditation with CSWE. The 2 libraries contain 225,337 volumes, 33,729 microform items, and 4650 audio/video tapes/CDs/DVDs, and subscribe to 700 periodicals including electronic. Computerized library services include the card catalog, interlibrary loans, and database searching. Special learning facilities include a learning resource center, art gallery, radio station, Fairchild Aerial Photography Collection, performing arts center, and writing center. The 95-acre campus is in a suburban area 18 miles southeast of Los Angeles, in the foothills of the San Gabriel Mountains. Including any residence halls, there are 50 buildings.

Student Life: 73% of undergraduates are from California. Others are from 27 states, 20 foreign countries, and Canada. 69% are from public schools. 50% are white; 30% Hispanic; 10% Asian American. The average age of freshmen is 18; all undergraduates, 21. 26% do not continue beyond their first year; 54% remain to graduate.

Housing: 813 students can be accommodated in college housing, which includes coed dorms. In addition, there are special-interest houses a multi-cultural community residence hall, and a substance-free living environment residence hall. On-campus housing is guaranteed for all 4 years. 60% of students live on campus; of those, 75% remain on campus on weekends. All students may keep cars.

Activities: 15% of men belong to 4 local fraternities; 15% of women belong to 5 local sororities. There are 54 groups on campus, including art, band, cheerleading, choir, chorale, chorus, computers, dance, dra-

ma, ethnic, film, gay, honors, international, jazz band, literary magazine, musical theater, newspaper, photography, political, professional, radio and TV, religious, social, social service, student government, and yearbook. Popular campus events include the Spring Sing (annual talent show), Hawaiian Islander Club Luau, and Asian Night.

Sports: There are 11 intercollegiate sports for men and 10 for women, and 10 intramural sports for men and 10 for women. Facilities include a 7000-seat stadium, a 2000-seat gym, 3 playing fields, an athletics center, an aquatics center, a fitness center, and tennis courts.

Disabled Students: 75% of the campus is accessible. Wheelchair ramps, elevators, special parking, specially equipped rest rooms, special class scheduling, lowered drinking fountains, and lowered telephones are available.

Services: Counseling and information services are available, as is tutoring in every subject.

Campus Safety and Security: Measures include 24-hour foot and vehicle patrol, self-defense education, security escort services, and informal discussions. There are pamphlets/posters/films, emergency telephones, and lighted pathways/sidewalks.

Programs of Study: Whittier confers the B.A. degree. Master's and doctoral degrees are also awarded. Bachelor's degrees are awarded in BIOLOGICAL SCIENCE (biochemistry and biology/biological science), BUSINESS (business administration and management), COMMUNICATIONS AND THE ARTS (art, dramatic arts, English, French, music, and Spanish), COMPUTER AND PHYSICAL SCIENCE (chemistry, earth science, mathematics, and physics), EDUCATION (physical), SOCIAL SCIENCE (child psychology/development, economics, history, international studies, philosophy, political science/government, psychology, religion, social work, and sociology). Business administration, political science, and English are the largest.

Required: All students must take a total of 120 credits, including at least 30 in the major field, with a minimum GPA of 2.0. Distribution requirements include 3 credits in college writing, 6 in paired courses from European and North American civilizations, Asian, African, and Latin American civilizations, or contemporary society and the individual, 8 in natural sciences, and 3 each in humanities, math, and fine arts.

Special: Internships are possible in business, counseling, teaching, and other areas. Study abroad is offered in 5 countries, with additional opportunities with 36 universities overseas through the University of Miami consortium. A Washington semester in January is optional. The Whittier Scholars Program offers self-designed interdisciplinary curricula. Nondegree study and pass/fail options are available. Whittier offers a 3-2 engineering program with University of Southern California, Dartmouth College, and Columbia, Washington, Case Western Reserve, and Colorado State universities. There are 10 national honor societies.

Faculty/Classroom: 60% of faculty are male; 40%, female. All teach undergraduates. No introductory courses are taught by graduate students. The average class size in an introductory lecture is 20; in a laboratory, 24; and in a regular course, 22.

Requirements: The SAT or ACT is required, the SAT is preferred. The college recommends that applicants have 4 years of high school English, 3 years each of history, math, science, and 2 years of a foreign language. An essay is required. An interview is recommended. A GPA of 2.0 is required. AP credits are accepted. Important factors in the admissions decision are advanced placement or honor courses, recommendations by school officials, and leadership record.

Procedure: Freshmen are admitted in the fall. Entrance exams should be taken during the junior year or fall of the senior year. There is a deferred admissions plan. Notification of early decision is sent December 29; regular decision, on a rolling basis. Applications are accepted on-line. The application fee is $50 (free on-line). Check with the school for current application deadlines.

Transfer: Transfer applicants are considered on a case-by-case basis, but a minimum GPA of 2.5 is recommended in academic course work. The SAT or the ACT is required for students with fewer than 30 academic units. The GED is accepted for transfer applicants with at least 30 academic units. 30 of 120 credits required for the bachelor's degree must be completed at Whittier.

Visiting: There are regularly scheduled orientations for prospective students, consisting of an interview with an admission officer and a campus tour. Customized visits can be arranged to include faculty, coaches, extracurricular activities, class visits, and residence hall tours. There are guides for informal visits and visitors may sit in on classes and stay overnight. To schedule a visit, contact the Office of Admissions.

Financial Aid: 64% of undergraduates work part time. Whittier is a member of CSS. The CSS/Profile or FAFSA is required. Check with the school for current deadlines.

International Students: The school actively recruits these students. They must score satisfactorily on the TOEFL and also take the SAT or the ACT.

Computers: All students may access the system 24 hours daily. There are no time limits and no fees.

Graduates: In an average class, 51% graduate in 4 years or less, 57% graduate in 5 years or less, and 58% graduate in 6 years or less.

Admissions Contact: Urmi Kar, Dean of Enrollment.
E-mail: *admission@whittier.edu* Web: *www.whittier.edu*

WOODBURY UNIVERSITY   C-5
Burbank, CA 91510-7846

| | (818) 767-0888 |
| | (800) 784-9663; Fax: (818) 767-7520 |

Full-time: 1026 men and women	**Faculty:** 35; IIA, av$
Part-time: 242 men and women	**Ph.D.s:** n/av
Graduate: 168 men and women	**Student/Faculty:** 29 to 1
Year: semesters, summer session	**Tuition:** $22,368
Application Deadline: open	**Room & Board:** $7808
Freshman Class: 311 accepted, 128 enrolled	
SAT Verbal/Math: 464/465*	**ACT:** 19 **LESS COMPETITIVE**

Woodbury University, founded in 1884, is a private institution that emphasizes business and professional design education. There are 3 undergraduate and 2 graduate schools. In addition to regional accreditation, Woodbury has baccalaureate program accreditation with ACBSP, FIDER, and NAAB. The library contains 68,075 volumes, 93,993 microform items, and 1639 audio/video tapes/CDs/DVDs, and subscribes to 568 periodicals including electronic. Computerized library services include the card catalog, interlibrary loans, and database searching. Special learning facilities include a learning resource center, art gallery, and architecture gallery. The 23-acre campus is in a suburban area 17 miles north of Los Angeles. Including any residence halls, there are 22 buildings.

Student Life: Students are from 38 foreign countries and Canada. 39% are white; 35% Hispanic; 12% Asian American. The average age of freshmen is 18; all undergraduates, 21. 17% do not continue beyond their first year; 50% remain to graduate.

Housing: 210 students can be accommodated in college housing, which includes single-sex and coed dorms, off-campus apartments, and nonsmoking suites. On-campus housing is available on a first-come, first-served basis. 80% of students commute. Alcohol is not permitted. All students may keep cars.

Activities: 5% of men belong to 1 local and 1 national fraternity; 6% of women belong to 2 local and 1 national sorority. There are 30 groups on campus, including art, drama, ethnic, film, international, newspaper, professional, religious, social, social service, and student government. Popular campus events include Black History Dinner, Founders Week, and Winter Formal.

Sports: There are 4 intramural sports for men and 4 for women. Facilities include basketball and volleyball courts, weight training and aerobics rooms, an outdoor swimming pool, a quarter-mile track, and a field for soccer and other sports.

Disabled Students: 95% of the campus is accessible. Wheelchair ramps, elevators, special parking, specially equipped rest rooms, special class scheduling, and special housing are available.

Services: Counseling and information services are available, as is tutoring in some subjects, including accounting, physics, structures, economics, and math. There is remedial math, reading, and writing. Books on tape are available for the blind.

Campus Safety and Security: Measures include 24-hour foot and vehicle patrol, self-defense education, security escort services, and informal discussions. There are pamphlets/posters/films, emergency telephones, and lighted pathways/sidewalks.

Programs of Study: Woodbury confers B.A., B.S., B.Arch., and B.F.A. degrees. Master's degrees are also awarded. Bachelor's degrees are awarded in BUSINESS (accounting, business administration and management, fashion merchandising, marketing/retailing/merchandising, and organizational behavior), COMMUNICATIONS AND THE ARTS (animation, communications, and graphic design), COMPUTER AND PHYSICAL SCIENCE (information sciences and systems), ENGINEERING AND ENVIRONMENTAL DESIGN (architecture and interior design), SOCIAL SCIENCE (fashion design and technology, history, interdisciplinary studies, political science/government, and psychology). Business and architecture are the strongest academically and have the largest enrollments.

Required: To graduate with a B.S., students must complete 126 semester units, including 61 to 66 in the major; with a B.A., 120 including 45-54 in the major; with a B.F.A., 128 including 68 in the major; with a

B.Arch., 160 semester units, including 98 in the major. All students must maintain a minimum GPA of 2.0 and take freshman composition, computer literacy, and public speaking courses. Course work in behavioral and social sciences, fine arts and humanities, physical and biological sciences, and math are also part of the curriculum.

Special: Internships or verified work experience is required for all majors with the exception of organizational leadership and interdisciplinary studies. Concurrent registration with area institutions, work-study programs, study abroad in France and Spain, dual majors, and pass/fail options also are offered. .

Faculty/Classroom: 66% of faculty are male; 34%, female. 89% teach undergraduates, 3% do research, and 3% do both. No introductory courses are taught by graduate students. The average class size in an introductory lecture is 30; in a laboratory, 16; and in a regular course, 25.

Admissions: The SAT scores for the 2005-2006 freshman class were: Verbal--68% below 500, 24% between 500 and 599, 7% between 600 and 700, and 1% above 700; Math--57% below 500, 30% between 500 and 599, 12% between 600 and 700, and 1% above 700. 48% of the current freshmen were in the top fifth of their class; 100% were in the top two fifths.

Requirements: The SAT is required. In addition, application form, essay, 2 academic references, official high school transcripts, and official SAT or ACT scores are required for all applicants. A GPA of 2.0 is required. AP and CLEP credits are accepted. Important factors in the admissions decision are advanced placement or honor courses, evidence of special talent, and recommendations by school officials.

Procedure: Freshmen are admitted fall, spring, and summer. Entrance exams should be taken prior to application (SAT or ACT). There are deferred admissions and rolling admissions plans. Application deadlines are open. Application fee is $35. Notification is sent on a rolling basis. Applications are accepted on-line.

Transfer: 136 transfer students enrolled in 2004-2005. Applicants are required to have maintained a minimum GPA of 2.0 and to take the SAT or ACT if they have completed fewer than 30 semester units. The priority application deadline for fall entry is April 15. 45 credits of the 120-128 credits required for the bachelor's degree (160 credits for Architecture) must be completed at Woodbury.

Visiting: There are regularly scheduled orientations for prospective students, consisting of meeting with admissions counselors, the president, faculty members, students, financial aid counselors, and student services staff. There are guides for informal visits and visitors may sit in on classes and stay overnight. To schedule a visit, contact the Admissions Office.

Financial Aid: In 2005-2006, 94% of all full-time freshmen and 93% of continuing full-time students received some form of financial aid. 94% of full-time freshmen and 90% of continuing full-time students received need-based aid. The average freshman award was $17,819. Need-based scholarships or need-based grants averaged $15,604; need-based self-help aid (loans and jobs) averaged $2722; and other non-need-based awards and non-need-based scholarships averaged $11,084. 11% of undergraduates work part time. Average annual earnings from campus work are $1200. The average financial indebtedness of the 2005 graduate was $20,134. Woodbury is a member of CSS. The FAFSA and the college's own financial statement are required. The deadline for filing freshman financial aid applications for fall entry is February 15.

International Students: There are 76 international students enrolled. The school actively recruits these students. A satisfactory score is required on the written TOEFL.

Computers: Wireless access is available. All full-time freshmen are provided with a multimedia notebook computer that allows them access to the Internet and Web. Many PCs are available throughout campus. All students may access the system Because students have their own computers, there is 24-hour access. There are no time limits. There is a $100 technology free per academic year. It is strongly recommended that all students have a personal computer. Recommended make or model is major specific.

Graduates: From July 1, 2004 to June 30, 2005, 255 bachelor's degrees were awarded. In an average class, 36% graduate in 4 years or less, 48% graduate in 5 years or less, and 57% graduate in 6 years or less.

Admissions Contact: Mauro Diaz, Director of Admissions.
E-mail: *info@woodbury.edu* Web: *www.woodbury.edu*

COLORADO

POPULATION DENSITY | 0 20 40 60 80 100

● 50,000 and over | Miles

ADAMS STATE COLLEGE
C-4

Alamosa, CO 81102

(719) 587-7712

(800) 824-6494; Fax: (719) 587-7522

Full-time: 852 men, 924 women	Faculty: 104; IIB, --$
Part-time: 180 men, 382 women	Ph.D.s: 90%
Graduate: 667 men, 2473 women	Student/Faculty: 17 to 1
Year: semesters, summer session	Tuition: $2853 ($9123)
Application Deadline: August 1	Room & Board: $5760
Freshman Class: 1765 applied, 1066 accepted, 512 enrolled	
SAT Verbal/Math: 490/510	ACT: 19 COMPETITIVE

Adams State College, founded in 1921, is a public liberal arts college awarding undergraduate and graduate degrees, with teacher education, biology, and business as the most popular programs. There is 1 graduate school. In addition to regional accreditation, Adams State has baccalaureate program accreditation with AACSB, CACREP, NASM, and TEAC. The library contains 180,579 volumes, 745,580 microform items, and 2381 audio/video tapes/CDs/DVDs, and subscribes to 22,601 periodicals including electronic. Computerized library services include the card catalog, interlibrary loans, database searching, Internet access, and laptop Internet portals. Special learning facilities include a learning resource center, art gallery, natural history museum, planetarium, radio station, geology museum, cross-cultural center, counseling lab andnursing lab. The 90-acre campus is in a small town 220 miles south of Denver and 200 miles north of Albuquerque, New Mexico. Including any residence halls, there are 55 buildings.

Student Life: 82% of undergraduates are from Colorado. Others are from 42 states, 3 foreign countries, and Canada. 59% are white; 29% Hispanic. The average age of freshmen is 19; all undergraduates, 25. 42% do not continue beyond their first year; 37% remain to graduate.

Housing: 912 students can be accommodated in college housing, which includes single-sex and coed dorms, on-campus apartments, and married-student housing. In addition, there is freshman interest-group housing, a pledge lerning community (pledge to stay drug and alcohol free), an outdoor adventure community, and housing for "making the grade" (must maintain a 3.5 GPA). On-campus housing is guaranteed for the freshman year only, is available on a first-come, first-served basis, and is available on a lottery system for upperclassmen. 69% of students commute. Alcohol is not permitted. All students may keep cars.

Activities: There are no fraternities or sororities. There are 50 groups on campus, including band, cheerleading, chess, choir, chorale, computers, drama, ethnic, gay, honors, international, jazz band, literary magazine, marching band, musical theater, pep band, photography, political, professional, radio and TV, religious, social service, and student government. Popular campus events include Spud Bowl, Grizzly Days, and Comedians.

Sports: There are 7 intercollegiate sports for men and 8 for women, and 5 intramural sports for men and 5 for women. Facilities include a multipurpose gym, a multipurpose field house, a swimming pool, outdoor handball, racquetball, and tennis courts, indoor and outdoor tracks, a varsity softball field, an intramural softball field, a soccer field, a football practice field, a weight room, free weights and weight machines, an 1800-square-foot climbing wall, an aerobics studio, a cardiovascular area, and game facilities.

Disabled Students: 95% of the campus is accessible. Wheelchair ramps, elevators, special parking, specially equipped rest rooms, special class scheduling, lowered drinking fountains, and lowered telephones are available.

Services: Counseling and information services are available, as is tutoring in every subject. There is a reader service for the blind, and remedial math, reading, and writing. Interpreters and tapes for the blind are also available.

Campus Safety and Security: Measures include 24-hour foot and vehicle patrol, security escort services, informal discussions, and pamphlets/posters/films. There are emergency telephones, lighted pathways/sidewalks, and formal safety seminars.

Programs of Study: Adams State confers B.A. and B.S. degrees. Associate and master's degrees are also awarded. Bachelor's degrees are awarded in BIOLOGICAL SCIENCE (biology/biological science and ecology), BUSINESS (accounting, banking and finance, business administration and management, business economics, international business management, management information systems, marketing/retailing/merchandising, office supervision and management, small business management, and sports management), COMMUNICATIONS AND THE ARTS (advertising, art, dramatic arts, English, journalism, music, music performance, Spanish, and speech/debate/rhetoric), COMPUTER AND PHYSICAL SCIENCE (chemistry, computer science, earth science, geology, and mathematics), EDUCATION (art, athletic training, business, elementary, English, foreign languages, mathematics, music, physical, science, secondary, and social studies), ENGINEERING AND ENVIRONMENTAL DESIGN (preengineering), HEALTH PROFESSIONS (allied health, predentistry, premedicine, preoptometry, prepharmacy, and preveterinary science), SOCIAL SCIENCE (criminology, history, interdisciplinary studies, political science/government, prelaw, psychology, social work, sociology, and urban studies). Biology and allied health sciences are the strongest academically. Business and education are the largest.

Required: All students must maintain a GPA of at least 2.0 and complete 120 credit hours, including 24 in the major. General education requirements total 38 hours; students are also required to pass both a technology proficiency exam and a writing assessment.

Special: Cross-registration through the State Colleges of Colorado consortium is available. Work-study programs with the college, dual majors, a general studies degree, and student-designed majors are possible. Nondegree study is offered.

Faculty/Classroom: 36% of faculty are male; 64%, female. All teach undergraduates. No introductory courses are taught by graduate students. The average class size in an introductory lecture is 32; in a laboratory, 9; and in a regular course, 14.

Admissions: 60% of the 2005-2006 applicants were accepted. The SAT scores for the 2005-2006 freshman class were: Verbal--57% below 500, 31% between 500 and 599, 9% between 600 and 700, and 3% above 700; Math--47% below 500, 43% between 500 and 599, and 10% between 600 and 700. The ACT scores were 67% below 21, 18% between 21 and 23, 11% between 24 and 26, 2% between 27 and 28, and 2% above 28. 11% of the current freshmen were in the top fifth of their class; 35% were in the top two fifths. 1 freshman graduated first in the class.

Requirements: The SAT or ACT is recommended. In addition, applicants are required to have at least 15 academic credits with 4 in English, 3 in social science, 2 each in math, lab science, and foreign language, and 1/2 in computer applications recommended. The GED is accepted. A GPA of 2.5 is required. AP and CLEP credits are accepted.

Procedure: Freshmen are admitted fall, spring, and summer. Entrance exams should be taken during the junior year. There is a deferred admissions plan. There is a rolling admissions plan. Applications should be filed by August 1 for fall entry and December 1 for spring entry, along with a $20 fee. Notification is sent on a rolling basis. Applications are accepted on-line.

Transfer: 157 transfer students enrolled in 2004-2005. Applicants must have a minimum GPA of 2.0. If they have fewer than 12 credits, the SAT or ACT test scores and official high school transcripts are also required. 30 of 120 credits required for the bachelor's degree must be completed at Adams State.

Visiting: There are regularly scheduled orientations for prospective students, including a meeting with academic faculty, a campus tour, information on financial aid and housing, and a free ticket to an athletic event (when applicable). There are guides for informal visits and visitors may sit in on classes and stay overnight. To schedule a visit, contact the Admissions Office.

Financial Aid: In 2005-2006, 88% of all full-time freshmen and 67% of continuing full-time students received some form of financial aid. 64% of full-time freshmen and 49% of continuing full-time students received need-based aid. The average freshman award was $7956. Need-based scholarships or need-based grants averaged $4040 ($11,171 maximum); need-based self-help aid (loans and jobs) averaged $3033 ($7575 maximum); non-need-based athletic scholarships averaged $3311 ($12,480 maximum); and other non-need-based awards and non-need-based scholarships averaged $4262 ($17,979 maximum). 37% of undergraduates work part time. Average annual earnings from campus work are $1938. The average financial indebtedness of the 2005 graduate was $15,332. The FAFSA is required. The priority date for freshman financial aid applications for fall entry is March 15. The deadline for filing freshman financial aid applications for fall entry is April 15.

International Students: There are 4 international students enrolled. Satisfactory scores are required on the TOEFL and the ACT.

Computers: Wireless access is available. There are 326 Internet-capable terminals across the campus in both labs and classrooms. All residence halls have either wired or wireless access to the Internet. All students may access the system 24 hours a day, 7 days a week. There are no time limits. The fee is $112 per semester.

Graduates: From July 1, 2004 to June 30, 2005, 286 bachelor's degrees were awarded. The most popular majors were liberal arts (26%), business (24%), and social sciences (11%). In an average class, 17% graduate in 4 years or less, 29% graduate in 5 years or less, and 37% graduate in 6 years or less. 85 companies recruited on campus in 2004-2005.

Admissions Contact: Eric Carpio, Director of Admissions. A video is available. E-mail: *ascadmit@adams.edu* Web: *www.adams.edu*

COLORADO CHRISTIAN UNIVERSITY — C-2
Lakewood, CO 80226-7499
(303) 963-3410
(800) 44 FAITH; Fax: (303) 963-3401

Full-time: 425 men, 700 women	**Faculty:** n/av
Part-time: 175 men, 175 women	**Ph.D.s:** 85%
Graduate: 50 men, 75 women	**Student/Faculty:** 28 to 1
Year: semesters, summer session	**Tuition:** $16590
Application Deadline: see profile	**Room & Board:** $6300
Freshman Class: 1185 applied, 877 accepted, 324 enrolled	
SAT or ACT: required	**VERY COMPETITIVE**

Colorado Christian University, founded in 1914, is a private, Christian interdenominational institution offering undergraduate and graduate programs in the arts and sciences, biblical studies, music and education. There are 4 undergraduate and 3 graduate schools. Some figures in the above capsule and in this profile are approximate. The library contains 53,532 volumes, 281,234 microform items, and 3917 audio/video tapes/CDs/DVDs, and subscribes to 415 periodicals including electronic. Computerized library services include the card catalog, interlibrary loans, database searching, and Internet access. Special learning facilities include a learning resource center and art gallery. The 29-acre campus is in a suburban area 10 miles west of Denver. Including any residence halls, there are 21 buildings.

Student Life: 59% of undergraduates are from Colorado. Others are from 44 states, 16 foreign countries, and Canada. 81% are white. Most are Protestant. The average age of freshmen is 19; all undergraduates, 20. 33% do not continue beyond their first year.

Housing: 732 students can be accommodated in college housing, which includes single-sex dorms, on-campus apartments, off-campus apartments, and married-student housing. In addition, there are special-interest houses. On-campus housing is guaranteed for the freshman year only, is available on a first-come, first-served basis, and is available on a lottery system for upperclassmen. Priority is given to out-of-town students. 65% of students live on campus; of those, 38% remain on campus on weekends. Alcohol is not permitted. All students may keep cars.

Activities: There are no fraternities or sororities. There are 21 groups on campus, including band, cheerleading, choir, chorus, computers, drama, honors, international, jazz band, literary magazine, musical theater, newspaper, orchestra, photography, professional, religious, social, social service, student government, symphony, and yearbook. Popular campus events include Preview Days, Spring Retreat, and New Student Retreat.

Sports: There are 5 intercollegiate sports for men and 5 for women, and 6 intramural sports for men and 6 for women. Facilities include a gym and soccer and practice fields.

Disabled Students: 85% of the campus is accessible. Wheelchair ramps, special parking, specially equipped rest rooms, special class scheduling, lowered drinking fountains, lowered telephones, and special housing are available.

Services: Counseling and information services are available, as is tutoring in every subject. There is remedial math, reading, and writing.

Campus Safety and Security: Measures include 24-hour foot and vehicle patrol, security escort services, emergency telephones, and lighted pathways/sidewalks.

Programs of Study: CCU confers B.A., B.S., and B.M. degrees. Associate and master's degrees are also awarded. Bachelor's degrees are awarded in BIOLOGICAL SCIENCE (biology/biological science), BUSINESS (accounting, business administration and management, human resources, management information systems, and management science), COMMUNICATIONS AND THE ARTS (art, communications, English, and music), COMPUTER AND PHYSICAL SCIENCE (computer management and science), EDUCATION (elementary, music, and secondary), SOCIAL SCIENCE (biblical studies, history, liberal arts/general studies, psychology, social science, theological studies, and youth ministry). Science, biology, and education are the strongest academically. Human resources management, computer/information technology, and liberal arts are the largest.

Required: To graduate, students must complete at least 128 semester hours, including the 48-hour general education requirement and courses specified for the major, with a minimum cumulative GPA of 2.0; 2.5 in the major. The university requires 4 semesters of Christian service and regular chapel attendance. All students must complete 12 credits in biblical studies.

Special: The school offers an ROTC program in cooperation with CU Boulder, cross-registration with the Focus on the Family Institute, internships, study abroad in 7 countries, a Washington semester, and work-study programs. Accelerated degree programs are available in Christian leadership, organizational management, and management of information systems. Dual and student-designed majors, nondegree study, pass/fail options, and credit for life, military, and work experience are also available. There are 2 national honor societies, a freshman honors program, and 1 departmental honors program.

Faculty/Classroom: 65% of faculty are male; 35%, female. No introductory courses are taught by graduate students. The average class size in an introductory lecture is 25; in a laboratory, 18; and in a regular course, 30.

Admissions: 74% of recent applicants were accepted. The SAT scores for a recent freshman class were: Verbal--18% below 500, 47% between 500 and 599, 25% between 600 and 700, and 10% above 700; Math--31% below 500, 40% between 500 and 599, 25% between 600 and 700, and 4% above 700. The ACT scores were 24% below 21, 25% between 21 and 23, 28% between 24 and 26, 15% between 27 and 28, and 8% above 28. 53% of a recent freshmen were in the top fifth of their class; 80% were in the top two fifths. There was 1 National Merit finalist.

Requirements: The SAT or ACT is required. In addition, applicants must be graduates of an accredited secondary school. The GED is accepted. An essay is required. A campus visit is recommended. A GPA of 2.8 is required. AP and CLEP credits are accepted.

Procedure: Freshmen are admitted to all sessions. There is a deferred admissions plan and a rolling admissions plan priority applications should be filed by March 1 for fall entry, along with a $50 fee. Notification is sent on a rolling basis. Applications are accepted on-line ($30 application fee).

Transfer: Applicants for transfer should have completed 12 college credits with a minimum GPA of 2.0. 30 of 128 credits required for the bachelor's degree must be completed at CCU.

Visiting: There are regularly scheduled orientations for prospective students. There are guides for informal visits and visitors may sit in on classes and stay overnight. To schedule a visit, contact the Office of Admissions at *admission@ccu.edu*.

Financial Aid: In a recent year, 64% of all full-time students received some form of financial aid. 59% of full-time freshmen and 56% of continuing full-time students received need-based aid. The average freshman award was $9712. Need-based scholarships or need-based grants averaged $7355; need-based self-help aid (loans and jobs) averaged $3105; non-need-based athletic scholarships averaged $6616; and other non-need-based awards and non-need-based scholarships averaged $15,070. 5% of undergraduates work part time. Average annual earnings from campus work are $1720. The average financial indebtedness of a recent graduate was $20,390. The FAFSA is required. The priority deadline for filing freshman financial aid applications for fall entry is March 1.

International Students: There were 13 international students enrolled in a recent year. The school actively recruits these students. They must score satisfactorily on the written TOEFL and also take the college's own test and the SAT or the ACT.

Computers: All students may access the system.

Graduates: In a recent year, 463 bachelor's degrees were awarded. The most popular majors were business/marketing (69%), liberal arts (9%), and philosophy/religion/theology (5%). In an average class, 31% graduate in 4 years or less, and 6% graduate in 5 years or less.

Admissions Contact: Waynette Moreland, Director of Admission Operations. A video is available. E-mail: *wmoreland@ccu.edu* Web: *www.ccu.edu*

COLORADO COLLEGE D-3
Colorado Springs, CO 80903
(719) 389-6344
(800) 542-7214; Fax: (719) 389-6816

Full-time: 893 men, 1035 women	Faculty: IIB
Part-time: none	Ph.D.s: 93%
Graduate: 9 men, 27 women	Student/Faculty: n/av
Year: see profile, summer session	Tuition: $30,048
Application Deadline: December 20	Room & Board: $7620
Freshman Class: 4089 applied, 1535 accepted, 476 enrolled	
SAT or ACT: required	**HIGHLY COMPETITIVE**

Colorado College, founded in 1874, is an independent liberal arts and sciences institution. The academic year is based on the Block Plan, under which students take only 1 course during each of the 8 3-1/2-week-long blocks of study; there is also a 9-week 3-block summer session. The library contains 579,362 volumes, 122,707 microform items, and 2189 audio/video tapes/CDs/DVDs, and subscribes to 2328 periodicals including electronic. Computerized library services include the card catalog, interlibrary loans, and database searching. Special learning facilities include a learning resource center, art gallery, radio station, an electronic music studio, a telescope dome, multimedia computer lab, the Colorado College Press, an herbarium, a Fourier transform nuclear magnetic resonance spectrometer, a scanning electronic microscope and transmission electronic microscope, and an environmental service van equipped for field research. The 90-acre campus is in a suburban area 70 miles south of Denver. Including any residence halls, there are 52 buildings.
Student Life: 98% of undergraduates are from out of state, mostly the West. Students are from 49 states, 25 foreign countries, and Canada. 70% are from public schools. 79% are white. The average age of freshmen is 18; all undergraduates, 20. 83% of freshmen remain to graduate.
Housing: 1476 students can be accommodated in college housing, which includes single-sex and coed dorms and on-campus apartments. In addition, there are language houses and special-interest houses. On-campus housing is guaranteed for all 4 years. 75% of students live on campus. Upperclassmen may keep cars.
Activities: There are 3 national fraternities and 3 national sororities. There are 80 groups on campus, including art, band, chess, choir, chorale, chorus, computers, dance, drama, ethnic, film, forensics, gay, honors, international, jazz band, literary magazine, musical theater, newspaper, orchestra, photography, political, professional, radio and TV, religious, social, social service, student government, symphony, and yearbook. Popular campus events include an afternoon and evening concert, an annual arts and crafts sale, and Division I men's ice hockey games.
Sports: There are 9 intercollegiate sports for men and 9 for women, and 17 intramural sports for men and 17 for women. Facilities include a sports center with 2 gyms, weight and exercise rooms, squash, tennis, and racquetball courts, a pool, an ice rink, and playing fields.
Disabled Students: 80% of the campus is accessible. Wheelchair ramps, elevators, special parking, specially equipped rest rooms, lowered drinking fountains, and lowered telephones are available.
Services: Counseling and information services are available, as is tutoring in most subjects. There is a writing center.
Campus Safety and Security: Measures include 24-hour foot and vehicle patrol, self-defense education, security escort services, and shuttle buses. There are informal discussions, pamphlets/posters/films, emergency telephones, and lighted pathways/sidewalks.
Programs of Study: CC confers the B.A. degree. Master's degrees are also awarded. Bachelor's degrees are awarded in BIOLOGICAL SCIENCE (biochemistry, biology/biological science, and neurosciences), BUSINESS (international economics), COMMUNICATIONS AND THE ARTS (art history and appreciation, classics, comparative literature, creative writing, dance, dramatic arts, English, film arts, French, German, music, romance languages and literature, Russian, Spanish, and studio art), COMPUTER AND PHYSICAL SCIENCE (chemistry, computer mathematics, geology, mathematics, and physics), ENGINEERING AND ENVIRONMENTAL DESIGN (environmental science), SOCIAL SCIENCE (anthropology, Asian/Oriental studies, economics, history, history of philosophy, liberal arts/general studies, philosophy, political science/government, psychology, religion, sociology, Southwest American studies, and women's studies). Biology, English, and psychology are the largest.
Required: Students must complete 32 units, with at least 9 units outside the division of the major, 18 outside the major department, and 4 in Alternative Perspectives. At least 3 courses in each division are required. Students must take 3 units of natural science with 1 lab science, 3 of social science, and 3 of humanities. Major requirements vary from 8 to 14 units. Students must earn a 2.0 GPA and achieve intermediate-level proficiency in a foreign language. Most majors offer (if not require) a comprehensive exam or a thesis.
Special: CC offers co-op programs with Columbia University School of Law, study abroad in several countries, and 3-2 engineering degrees. There are 3 national honor societies, including Phi Beta Kappa, and 100 departmental honors programs.

Faculty/Classroom: 62% of faculty are male; 38%, female. All both teach and do research. No introductory courses are taught by graduate students. The average class size in an introductory lecture is 20; in a laboratory, 17; and in a regular course, 14.
Admissions: 38% of the 2005-2006 applicants were accepted.
Requirements: The SAT or ACT is required. In addition, applicants should have completed at least 16 (18 to 20 recommended) high school academic credits. The GED is accepted. An essay is required. AP credits are accepted. Important factors in the admissions decision are advanced placement or honor courses, extracurricular activities record, and evidence of special talent.
Procedure: Freshmen are admitted fall and spring. Entrance exams should be taken by the fall of the senior year. There are early decision and deferred admissions plans. Early decision applications should be filed by November 15; regular applications, by January 15 for fall entry and November 1 for spring entry, along with a $50 fee. Notification of early decision is sent December 20; regular decision, April 1. 546 early decision candidates were accepted for a recent year's class. 770 applicants were on the 2005 waiting list; 18 were admitted. Applications are accepted on-line.
Transfer: 28 transfer students enrolled in 2004-2005. Transfer candidates who are not submitting 3 semesters or 4 quarters of college work must submit their high school record. A letter of recommendation from a professor or teacher and a dean's form are required, as well as an application essay. 16 of 32 units (1 unit = 4 semester hours) required for the bachelor's degree must be completed at CC.
Visiting: There are regularly scheduled orientations for prospective students, including a class visit, an information session with an admissions director, and a student-led tour. There are guides for informal visits and visitors may sit in on classes and stay overnight. To schedule a visit, contact the Admissions Office.
Financial Aid: In 2005-2006, 49% of all full-time freshmen and 44% of continuing full-time students received some form of financial aid. At least 48% of full-time freshmen and 40% of continuing full-time students received need-based aid. The average freshman award was $28,058. Need-based scholarships or need-based grants averaged $24,621; need-based self-help aid (loans and jobs) averaged $4162; institutional non-need-based athletic scholarships averaged $31,711; and other institutional non-need-based awards and non-need-based scholarships averaged $9053. The average financial indebtedness of a recent graduate was $13,850. CC is a member of CSS. The CSS/Profile or FAFSA, non-custodial (divorced/separated) parents' statement, parent and student tax returns, and parent W-2 forms are required. The deadline for filing freshman financial aid applications for fall entry is February 15.
International Students: The school actively recruits these students. Satisfactory scores are required on the written TOEFL and the SAT or the ACT.
Computers: All students may access the system. There are no time limits and no fees. It is strongly recommended that all students have a personal computer.
Graduates: From July 1, 2004 to June 30, 2005, 479 bachelor's degrees were awarded. The most popular majors were social sciences (28%), biological/life sciences (12%), and visual and performing arts (9%). In an average class, 77% graduate in 4 years or less, 82% graduate in 5 years or less, and 83% graduate in 6 years or less.
Admissions Contact: Dean of Admission and Financial Aid. A video is available. E-mail: admission@coloradocollege.edu
Web: www.coloradocollege.edu

COLORADO SCHOOL OF MINES C-2
Golden, CO 80401-1842
(303) 273-3220
(888) 446-9489; Fax: (303) 273-3509

Full-time: 2278 men, 621 women	Faculty: 180; I, av$
Part-time: 156 men, 43 women	Ph.D.s: 75%
Graduate: 546 men, 205 women	Student/Faculty: 16 to 1
Year: semesters, summer session	Tuition: $8143 ($20,725)
Application Deadline: June 1	Room & Board: $6750
Freshman Class: 2937 applied, 2556 accepted, 816 enrolled	
SAT Verbal/Math: 595/660*	ACT: 27 **HIGHLY COMPETITIVE**

The Colorado School of Mines, founded in 1874, is a public institution offering programs in math, science, economics, and engineering. There is 1 undergraduate and 1 graduate school. In addition to regional accreditation, Mines has baccalaureate program accreditation with ABET. The library contains 356,000 volumes and 236,000 microform items, and subscribes to 2700 periodicals including electronic. Computerized library services include the card catalog, interlibrary loans, database searching, and Internet access. Special learning facilities include a geology museum. The 373-acre campus is in a small town 20 miles west of Denver. Including any residence halls, there are 40 buildings.
Student Life: 80% of undergraduates are from Colorado. Others are from 49 states, 52 foreign countries, and Canada. 90% are from public schools. 82% are white. 52% are Protestant; 21% Catholic; 20% claim no religious affiliation. The average age of freshmen is 18; all undergrad-

uates, 20. 16% do not continue beyond their first year; 67% remain to graduate.

Housing: 855 students can be accommodated in college housing, which includes single-sex and coed dormitories, on-campus apartments, married-student housing, fraternity houses, and sorority houses. On-campus housing is guaranteed for the freshman year only and is available on a first-come, first-served basis. All students may keep cars.

Activities: 19% of men belong to 7 national fraternities; 19% of women belong to 3 national sororities. There are 95 groups on campus, including band, cheerleading, choir, chorus, computers, drama, ethnic, honors, international, literary magazine, marching band, musical theater, newspaper, political, professional, religious, social, social service, student government, and yearbook. Popular campus events include International Day, Winter Carnival, and Parents Day.

Sports: There are 9 intercollegiate sports for men and 7 for women, and 20 intramural sports for men and 20 for women. Facilities include a 10,000-seat stadium, a recreation center, a gym, numerous intramural fields, tennis courts, and a field house.

Disabled Students: All of the campus is accessible. Wheelchair ramps, elevators, special parking, specially equipped rest rooms, special class scheduling, lowered drinking fountains, lowered telephones, and special housing are available.

Services: Counseling and information services are available, as is tutoring in most subjects. There is a reader service for the blind and remedial math and writing.

Campus Safety and Security: Measures include 24-hour foot and vehicle patrol, self-defense education, informal discussions, and pamphlets/posters/films. There are emergency telephones and lighted pathways/sidewalks.

Programs of Study: Mines confers the B.S. degree. Master's and doctoral degrees are also awarded. Bachelor's degrees are awarded in COMPUTER AND PHYSICAL SCIENCE (chemistry, mathematics, and physics), ENGINEERING AND ENVIRONMENTAL DESIGN (chemical engineering, engineering, geological engineering, geophysical engineering, metallurgical engineering, mining and mineral engineering, and petroleum/natural gas engineering), SOCIAL SCIENCE (economics). Chemical engineering, geological engineering, and geophysical engineering are the strongest academically. General engineering, chemical engineering, and mathematical and computing sciences are the largest.

Required: Students must complete 138 to 148 credit hours, with 35 to 40 hours in the major and a GPA of 2.0. Required courses include humanities, calculus, physics, computer science, chemistry, and phys ed.

Special: Co-op programs, internships in the humanities, accelerated degree programs in all majors, dual majors, study abroad in 10 countries, and non-degree study are offered. There is 1 national honor society, a freshman honors program, and 3 departmental honors programs.

Faculty/Classroom: 80% of faculty are male; 20%, female. 93% teach undergraduates, 50% do research, and 50% do both. No introductory courses are taught by graduate students. The average class size in an introductory lecture is 100; in a laboratory, 22; and in a regular course, 29.

Admissions: 87% of the 2005-2006 applicants were accepted. The SAT scores for the 2005-2006 freshman class were: Verbal--10% below 500, 38% between 500 and 599, 41% between 600 and 700, and 11% above 700; Math--2% below 500, 17% between 500 and 599, 56% between 600 and 700, and 25% above 700. The ACT scores were 1% below 21, 11% between 21 and 23, 27% between 24 and 26, 22% between 27 and 28, and 39% above 28. 80% of the current freshmen were in the top fifth of their class; all were in the top two fifths. 65 freshmen graduated first in their class.

Requirements: The SAT or ACT is required. In addition, applicants must be graduates of an accredited secondary school. The GED is accepted. Students should have completed 16 high school academic credits, including 4 credits each of English and math, 3 of science, 2 of social studies, and 3 academic electives. Mines recommends applicants be in the upper 33% of their class. AP credits are accepted. Important factors in the admissions decision are advanced placement or honor courses, leadership record, and recommendations by school officials.

Procedure: Freshmen are admitted to all sessions. Entrance exams should be taken by late in the junior year or early in the senior year. There are deferred admissions and rolling admissions plans. Applications should be filed by June 1 for fall entry, December 1 for spring entry, and June 10 for summer entry, along with a $45 fee. Notification is sent on a rolling basis. Applications are accepted on-line.

Transfer: 94 transfer students enrolled in 2004-2005. Transfer applicants must have a minimum GPA of 2.75. 30 of 138 to 148 credits required for the bachelor's degree must be completed at Mines.

Visiting: There are regularly scheduled orientations for prospective students, including a half day-long visitation program twice each fall where students may visit departments and talk with faculty. Sessions in admissions and financial aid also are given. There are guides for informal visits and visitors may sit in on classes. To schedule a visit, contact the Admissions Office at (303) 273-3226 / (888) 446-9489.

Financial Aid: In a recent year, 85% of all full-time students received some form of financial aid. 74% of all full-time students received need-

based aid. The average freshman award was $12,900. 70% of undergraduates worked part time. Average annual earnings from campus work were $750. The average financial indebtedness of the 2005 graduate was $17,500. Mines is a member of CSS. The FAFSA is required. The priority date for freshman financial aid applications for fall entry is March 1.

International Students: There are 86 international students enrolled. The school actively recruits these students. They must score satisfactorily on the written TOEFL and also take the Comprehensive English Language Test.

Computers: Wireless access is available. Several hundred PCs are located around campus for student use. All residence hall rooms are wired for direct access to the campus network and the Internet. Many buildings, but not all, have wireless access. All students may access the system 24 hours through dial-in access and direct network connection. Computer labs are open 7 A.M. to midnight Monday to Thursday, 7 A.M. to 6 P.M. on Friday, 9 A.M. to 5:30 P.M. on Saturday, and 9 A.M. to midnight on Sunday. There are no time limits and no fees.

Graduates: From July 1, 2004 to June 30, 2005, 505 bachelor's degrees were awarded. The most popular majors were general engineering (42%), mathematics and computer science (15%), and chemical engineering (10%). In an average class, 1% graduate in 3 years or less, 37% graduate in 4 years or less, 64% graduate in 5 years or less, and 67% graduate in 6 years or less. 267 companies recruited on campus in 2004-2005. Of the 2004 graduating class, 20% were enrolled in graduate school within 6 months of graduation and 95% were employed.

Admissions Contact: Bill Young, Director of Enrollment Management. E-mail: admit@mines.edu Web: www.mines.edu

COLORADO STATE UNIVERSITY-FORT COLLINS   C-1

Fort Collins, CO 80523-0015 (970) 491-6909
Fax: (970) 491-7799

Full-time: 9069 men, 9922 women	Faculty: 851; I, -$
Part-time: 959 men, 770 women	Ph.D.s: 99%
Graduate: 1912 men, 2315 women	Student/Faculty: 22 to 1
Year: semesters, summer session	Tuition: $4562 ($15,524)
Application Deadline: July 1	Room & Board: $6316
Freshman Class: 10,770 applied, 9516 accepted, 3893 enrolled	
SAT Verbal/Math: 550/560*	ACT: 24 COMPETITIVE+

Colorado State University, founded in 1870 and part of the Colorado State University system, is a public, land-grant institution, offering 66 undergraduate majors in 51 departments within 8 colleges. There are 8 undergraduate schools and 1 graduate school. In addition to regional accreditation, Colorado State has baccalaureate program accreditation with AACSB, ABET, ACCE, ACEJMC, ADA, ASLA, CSWE, FIDER, NASM, NCATE, NRPA, and SAF. The 4 libraries contain 2,014,059 volumes, 2,511,097 microform items, and 15,139 audio/video tapes/CDs/DVDs, and subscribe to 25,678 periodicals including electronic. Computerized library services include the card catalog, interlibrary loans, database searching, Internet access, and laptop Internet portals. Special learning facilities include a learning resource center, art gallery, radio station, TV station, and , an environmental learning center, and a plant environmental research center. The 666-acre campus is in a suburban area in Fort Collins, 65 miles north of Denver. Including any residence halls, there are 149 buildings.

Student Life: 82% of undergraduates are from Colorado. Others are from 50 states, 85 foreign countries, and Canada. 80% are white. The average age of freshmen is 18; all undergraduates, 21. 18% do not continue beyond their first year; 63% remain to graduate.

Housing: 4550 students can be accommodated in college housing, which includes coed dormitories, on-campus apartments, married-student housing, fraternity houses, and sorority houses. On-campus housing is guaranteed for the freshman year only and is available on a first-come, first-served basis. 70% of students commute. All students may keep cars.

Activities: 8% of men belong to 20 national fraternities; 9% of women belong to 15 national sororities. There are 178 groups on campus, including art, band, cheerleading, chess, choir, chorale, chorus, computers, dance, debate, drama, drill team, ethnic, film, forensics, gay, honors, international, jazz band, literary magazine, marching band, musical theater, newspaper, opera, orchestra, pep band, photography, political, professional, radio and TV, religious, social, social service, student government, symphony, and yearbook. Popular campus events include Centertainment, International Poster Exhibition, and Summer Outdoor Theater.

Sports: There are 5 intercollegiate sports for men and 9 for women, and 18 intramural sports for men and 18 for women. Facilities include a 9,000-seat arena, indoor and outdoor tracks, a football stadium, a baseball diamond, intramural fields, indoor swimming pools, a comprehensive student recreation center, and an obstacle course for personal development.

Disabled Students: 90% of the campus is accessible. Wheelchair ramps, elevators, special parking, specially equipped rest rooms, special

class scheduling, lowered drinking fountains, lowered telephones, special housing, and , an advocacy office for disabled students, telecommunication devices for the deaf, and special transportation are available.

Services: Counseling and information services are available, as is tutoring in most subjects. There is a reader service for the blind. There are interpreters and note takers available.

Campus Safety and Security: Measures include 24-hour foot and vehicle patrol, self-defense education, security escort services, and shuttle buses. There are informal discussions, pamphlets/posters/films, emergency telephones, lighted pathways/sidewalks, and , lectures by campus police on a variety of safety issues, a crime victim support unit, and a bike patrol.

Programs of Study: Colorado State confers B.A., B.S., B.F.A., and B.M. degrees. Master's and doctoral degrees are also awarded. Bachelor's degrees are awarded in AGRICULTURE (agricultural business management, agricultural economics, agronomy, animal science, equine science, fishing and fisheries, forestry and related sciences, horticulture, natural resource management, and range/farm management), BIOLOGICAL SCIENCE (biochemistry, biology/biological science, botany, microbiology, nutrition, wildlife biology, and zoology), BUSINESS (accounting, apparel and accessories marketing, banking and finance, business administration and management, hotel/motel and restaurant management, marketing/retailing/merchandising, and recreational facilities management), COMMUNICATIONS AND THE ARTS (art, English, French, German, journalism, music, performing arts, Spanish, speech/debate/rhetoric, and technical and business writing), COMPUTER AND PHYSICAL SCIENCE (chemistry, computer science, geology, information sciences and systems, mathematics, physical sciences, physics, and statistics), EDUCATION (agricultural, and home economics), ENGINEERING AND ENVIRONMENTAL DESIGN (agricultural engineering, chemical engineering, civil engineering, construction management, electrical/electronics engineering, engineering and applied science, interior design, landscape architecture/design, and mechanical engineering), HEALTH PROFESSIONS (environmental health science, and exercise science), SOCIAL SCIENCE (anthropology, economics, family/consumer studies, history, home economics, human development, liberal arts/general studies, philosophy, political science/government, psychology, social work, sociology, and water resources). Engineering and applied science, chemistry, and microbiology are the strongest academically. Business, psychology, and excersise and sport science are the largest.

Required: To graduate, students must complete at least 120 credit hours, 27 of them in the major, with a minimum GPA of 2.0. Students must complete the All University Core described in the catalog.

Special: Colorado State offers co-op programs with Metropolitan State College and Universidad Autonoma in Mexico and participates in cross-registration with Aims Community College. Study abroad in more than 30 countries, a semester at sea, work-study programs, internships, B.A.-B.S. degrees, and pass/fail options are available. Teaching certification students receive a bachelor's degree in their chosen subject and also complete a certification sequence through the School of Education. There are 43 national honor societies, including Phi Beta Kappa, a freshman honors program.

Faculty/Classroom: 72% of faculty are male; 28%, female. 100% both teach and do research. Graduate students teach 10% of introductory courses. The average class size in an introductory lecture is 46; in a laboratory, 22; and in a regular course, 32.

Admissions: 88% of the 2005-2006 applicants were accepted. The SAT scores for the 2005-2006 freshman class were: Verbal--24% below 500, 45% between 500 and 599, 27% between 600 and 700, and 4% above 700; Math--20% below 500, 45% between 500 and 599, 32% between 600 and 700, and 3% above 700. The ACT scores were 16% below 21, 32% between 21 and 23, 29% between 24 and 26, 12% between 27 and 28, and 11% above 28. 34% of the current freshmen were in the top fifth of their class; 66% were in the top two fifths. There were 9 National Merit finalists and 2 semifinalists. 116 freshmen graduated first in their class.

Requirements: The SAT or ACT is required. In addition, the average freshman has a composite SAT score of 1114 and an ACT composite of 24. Graduation from secondary school is required, but the GED is accepted. Students should have complete at least 18 high school credits, 15 of which are academic credits, including 4 years of English, 3 of math algebra I, geometry, algebra II, 2 of natural science, 2 of social science, plus 1 additional year of natural or social science, and 2 years of the same foreign language. Additionally an essay is recommended. AP and CLEP credits are accepted. Important factors in the admissions decision are advanced placement or honor courses, leadership record, and recommendations by school officials.

Procedure: Freshmen are admitted to all sessions. Entrance exams should be taken during the junior year or early fall of the senior year. Applications should be filed by July 1 for fall entry and December 1 for spring entry, along with a $50 fee. Notification is sent on a rolling basis. Applications are accepted on-line.

Transfer: 1436 transfer students enrolled in 2004-2005. Applicants must have a minimum cumulative 2.0 GPA. However, at least 13 semester credits and a 2.7 cumulative GPA are required to be considered

strong candidates for admission. Admission is subject to satisfactory completion of current courses and submission of current courses and submission of a final, complete, official transcript. Students holding an associate degree from an accredited Colorado institution are guaranteed admission providing that it is the last institution attended and that a cumulative 2.0 GPA has been achieved from all institutions attended. Specific majors may require prerequisites and enrollment may be limited. 32 of 120 credits required for the bachelor's degree must be completed at Colorado State.

Visiting: There are regularly scheduled orientations for prospective students, including Visit Days, which provide information about admissions, financial aid, and housing. A presentation on admissions, financial aid, and student life is offered each weekday, followed by a campus tour guided by student volunteers. The presentations start at 9:15 A.M. and 1:15 P.M. There are guides for informal visits and visitors may sit in on classes. To schedule a visit, contact Andrea Moss in the Office of Admissions at (970) 491-6393.

Financial Aid: In 2005-2006, 64% of all full-time freshmen and 63% of continuing full-time students received some form of financial aid. 36% of full-time freshmen and 40% of continuing full-time students received need-based aid. The average freshman award was $9809. 49% of undergraduates work part time. Average annual earnings from campus work are $3130. The average financial indebtedness of the 2005 graduate was $16,887. The FAFSA is required. The deadline for filing freshman financial aid applications for fall entry is March 1.

International Students: There are 244 international students enrolled. The school actively recruits these students. They must score satisfactorily on the written TOEFL or on the electronic versionScores from other English language proficiency exams may be considered in lieu of the TOEFL. and also take only the English proficiency test (either the TOEFL or the IELTS).

Computers: Wireless access is available. Students can change personal information; view billing, reocrds, and grades; access Web and e-mail; take online courses; and register for courses. There are approximately 2700 PCs in 90 labs, classrooms, dorms, and student centers. All students may access the system 24 hours a day. There are no time limits and no fees.

Graduates: From July 1, 2004 to June 30, 2005, 4281 bachelor's degrees were awarded. The most popular majors were business administration (16%), psychology (4%), and human development and family studies (4%). In an average class, 34% graduate in 4 years or less, 58% graduate in 5 years or less, and 63% graduate in 6 years or less. 149 companies recruited on campus in 2004-2005.

Admissions Contact: Mary Ontiveros, Admissions Counselor. A video is available. E-mail: *admissions@vines.colostate.edu* Web: *www.colostate.edu/depts/admission/*

COLORADO STATE UNIVERSITY-PUEBLO   D-3
Pueblo, CO 81001-4901   **(719) 549-2462**
                              (877) 872-9653; Fax: (719) 549-2419

Full-time: 1500 men, 1850 women	**Faculty:** 159; IIA, --$
Part-time: 775 men, 1200 women	**Ph.D.s:** 70%
Graduate: 50 men, 100 women	**Student/Faculty:** 21 to 1
Year: semesters, summer session	**Tuition:** $4116 ($14,758)
Application Deadline: August 1	**Room & Board:** $7452
Freshman Class: n/av	
SAT or ACT: required	**LESS COMPETITIVE**

Colorado State University-Pueblo, formerly the University of Southern Colorado, founded in 1933, is part of the Colorado State University System. The public institution offers undergraduate programs in humanities and social sciences, business administration, nursing, applied science, technology, engineering, and education. There are 5 undergraduate and 3 graduate schools. Some figures in the capsule and in this profile are approximate. In addition to regional accreditation, USC has baccalaureate program accreditation with ABET, CSWE, NASM, NLN, and ACS. The library contains 180,000 volumes, 10,000 microform items, and 16,862 audio/video tapes/CDs/DVDs, and subscribes to 1327 periodicals including electronic. Computerized library services include the card catalog, interlibrary loans, and database searching. Special learning facilities include a learning resource center, art gallery, radio station, TV station, and nature center. The 275-acre campus is in an urban area 100 miles south of Denver. Including any residence halls, there are 15 buildings.

Student Life: 87% of undergraduates are from Colorado. Students are from 41 states, 32 foreign countries, and Canada. 59% are white; 26% Hispanic. The average age of freshmen is 19; all undergraduates, 26. 39% do not continue beyond their first year; 27% remain to graduate.

Housing: 652 students can be accommodated in college housing, which includes coed dorms and on-campus apartments. On-campus housing is guaranteed for the freshman year only and is available on a first-come, first-served basis. 81% of students commute. Alcohol is not permitted. All students may keep cars.

Activities: 1% of men belong to 2 national fraternities; 1% of women belong to 1 local sorority. There are 68 groups on campus, including art, cheerleading, choir, chorale, computers, drama, ethnic, gay, honors, international, jazz band, literary magazine, newspaper, pep band, political, professional, radio and TV, religious, social, social service, student government, and symphony. Popular campus events include the Town and Gown series, Teacher Career Fair, and departmental lecture series.

Sports: There are 5 intercollegiate sports for men and 5 for women, and 5 intramural sports for men and 3 for women. Facilities include an arena with an indoor swimming pool, a weight room, a rock climbing wall, and racquetball, basketball, and volleyball courts; a sports complex with tennis courts, and baseball, softball, and soccer fields; bike trails; a rope course; and a nature center.

Disabled Students: All of the campus is accessible. Wheelchair ramps, elevators, special parking, specially equipped rest rooms, special class scheduling, lowered drinking fountains, and lowered telephones are available.

Services: Counseling and information services are available, as is tutoring in most subjects. Remedial math and English are available on-campus from a local community college.

Campus Safety and Security: Measures include 24-hour foot and vehicle patrol, self-defense education, security escort services, and informal discussions. There are pamphlets/posters/films, emergency telephones, and lighted pathways/sidewalks.

Programs of Study: Colorado State-Pueblo confers B.A., B.S., B.S.B.A., B.S.C.E.T., B.S.E.E.T., B.S.I.En., B.S.M.E.T., B.S.N., and B.S.W. degrees. Master's degrees are also awarded. Bachelor's degrees are awarded in BIOLOGICAL SCIENCE (biochemistry, biology/biological science, and biotechnology), BUSINESS (accounting, business administration and management, and recreation and leisure services), COMMUNICATIONS AND THE ARTS (art, broadcasting, communications, English, journalism, music performance, music theory and composition, and Spanish), COMPUTER AND PHYSICAL SCIENCE (chemistry, information sciences and systems, mathematics, and physics), EDUCATION (music), ENGINEERING AND ENVIRONMENTAL DESIGN (automotive technology, civil engineering technology, electrical/electronics engineering technology, industrial administration/management, industrial engineering, mechanical engineering technology, and preengineering), HEALTH PROFESSIONS (chiropractic, environmental health science, exercise science, medical technology, nursing, occupational therapy, physician's assistant, predentistry, premedicine, preoptometry, preosteopathy, prepharmacy, prepodiatry, preveterinary science, and speech pathology/audiology), SOCIAL SCIENCE (criminology, economics, history, political science/government, prelaw, psychology, social science, social work, and sociology). Business, engineering technology, and nursing are the strongest academically. Accounting, biology, and management are the largest.

Required: To graduate, all students must complete at least 120 semester hours, including 40 in upper-division courses and 30 to 48 in the major, with a minimum GPA of 2.0. General education requirements include a 14-credit skills component of courses in communication, computer literacy, and quantitative skills, as well as a 19-credit knowledge component of courses in humanities, social sciences, and science and technology. Other requirements vary with the major.

Special: Colorado State-Pueblo offers co-op programs, internships, study abroad in 8 countries, and on-campus work-study programs. Also available are 5-year combined B.S.B.A./M.B.A. degrees, a 3-2 engineering degree with Colorado State University, dual majors, nondegree study, and preprofessional programs in forestry, physical therapy, and wildlife management. USC is a member of the National Student Exchange. There are 10 national honor societies, including Phi Beta Kappa, a freshman honors program, and 10 departmental honors programs.

Faculty/Classroom: 60% of faculty are male; 39%, female. 99% teach undergraduates, 10% do research, and 4% do both. No introductory courses are taught by graduate students. The average class size in an introductory lecture is 70; in a laboratory, 24; and in a regular course, 22.

Requirements: The SAT or ACT is required. In addition, applicants must be graduates of an accredited secondary school or have a GED certificate with a minimum score of 45. USC computes a CCHE admission index, comprised of the high school GPA and SAT or ACT scores. Students scoring below 80 will still be considered by an admissions committee. Academic preparation should consist of 4 years of English, 3 of math including algebra and geometry, 2 of natural science including physical science, 3 of social studies including American government, and 2 of a foreign language. AP and CLEP credits are accepted. Important factors in the admissions decision are advanced placement or honor courses, leadership record, and recommendations by school officials.

Procedure: Freshmen are admitted to all sessions. Entrance exams should be taken during spring of the junior year or fall of the senior year. Applications should be filed by August 1 for fall entry and January 2 for spring entry, along with a $25 fee. Notification is sent on a rolling basis.

Transfer: A minimum GPA of 2.0 and official transcripts of previous college work are required. Applicants with fewer than 30 credit hours must submit ACT or SAT scores and high school transcripts. 30 of 120 credits required for the bachelor's degree must be completed at USC.

Visiting: There are regularly scheduled orientations for prospective students, including a tour, lunch, and mini-sessions on financial aid, athletics, scholarships, and student services. There are guides for informal visits and visitors may sit in on classes. To schedule a visit, contact the Admissions Office at (719) 549-2461.

Financial Aid: The FAFSA is required. Check with the school for current deadlines.

International Students: The school actively recruits these students. They must score satisfactorily on the TOEFL or take the MELAB.

Computers: All students may access the system 24 hours a day. There are no time limits. The fee is $2 per credit hour.

Admissions Contact: Pam Anastassiou, Director of Admissions and Records. E-mail: *info@colostate-pueblo.edu*
Web: *www.colostate-pueblo.edu*

COLORADO TECHNICAL UNIVERSITY D-3

Colorado Springs, CO 80907-3896
(719) 590-6810
Fax: (719) 590-3740

Full-time: 325 men, 100 women	**Faculty:** 30
Part-time: 525 men, 250 women	**Ph.D.s:** 50%
Graduate: 500 men, 200 women	**Student/Faculty:** 14 to 1
Year: quarters, summer session	**Tuition:** $10,000
Application Deadline: open	**Room & Board:** n/app
Freshman Class: n/av	
SAT or ACT: recommended	**LESS COMPETITIVE**

Colorado Technical University, founded in 1965, is a private commuter institution offering programs with technical and management emphasis in computer science, electronic engineering technology, management, computer engineering, and electrical engineering. A large percentage of the students are working adults who have transferred from other colleges. There are branch campuses in Denver, Kansas City, and Sioux Falls, South Dakota. There are 3 undergraduate and 3 graduate schools. Figures in the above capsule and in this profile are approximate. In addition to regional accreditation, Colorado Tech has baccalaureate program accreditation with ABET and CAAHEP. The library contains 33,000 volumes, 15,000 microform items, and 400 audio/video tapes/CDs/DVDs, and subscribes to 362 periodicals including electronic. Computerized library services include the card catalog, interlibrary loans, and database searching. Special learning facilities include a learning resource center. The 5-acre campus is in a suburban area in Colorado Springs. There are 2 buildings.

Student Life: Most students are from Colorado. Others are from 14 foreign countries. 76% are white; 11% African American.

Housing: There are no residence halls. Alcohol is not permitted.

Activities: There are no fraternities or sororities. There are 6 groups on campus, including computers, honors, international, professional, and student government. Popular campus events include a summer picnic.

Sports: There is no sports program at Colorado Tech. Facilities include a high-tech workout facility.

Disabled Students: All of the campus is accessible. Wheelchair ramps, special parking, specially equipped rest rooms, and lowered drinking fountains are available.

Services: Counseling and information services are available, as is tutoring in most subjects, including including English, math and computer science. Taped tutorials are offered as well. There is remedial math and writing. Upon entry to Colorado Tech, students are assigned a counselor/mentor who can assist them throughout their academic career.

Campus Safety and Security: Measures include informal discussions, pamphlets/posters/films, emergency telephones, lighted pathways/sidewalks, and a security service.

Programs of Study: Colorado Tech confers the B.S. degree. Associate, master's, and doctoral degrees are also awarded. Bachelor's degrees are awarded in BUSINESS (business administration and management, management information systems, and management science), COMMUNICATIONS AND THE ARTS (telecommunications), COMPUTER AND PHYSICAL SCIENCE (computer science and information sciences and systems), ENGINEERING AND ENVIRONMENTAL DESIGN (computer engineering, electrical/electronics engineering, electrical/electronics engineering technology, graphic arts technology, and technological management), SOCIAL SCIENCE (criminal justice). Engineering, computer science, and engineering technology are the strongest academically.

Required: All students must complete a core of general education courses, including math, engineering science, English, and humanities/social sciences. An average of 180 quarter hours, with a cumulative GPA of 2.0, is required to graduate, as is a course in career development.

Special: Internships are possible with several local technology companies. Work-study programs are available with social services, the public library, and the university. Nondegree study, co-op programs, study abroad in London, and credit for life, military, and work experience are possible.

Faculty/Classroom: 67% of faculty are male; 33%, female. All teach undergraduates. No introductory courses are taught by graduate students. The average class size in an introductory lecture is 19 and in a laboratory, 19.

Requirements: The SAT or ACT is recommended. Applicants should be graduates of an accredited high school. The GED is accepted. An essay is required for scholarships. An interview is recommended. Students without transfer of credit or an ACT or SAT test report must pass Colorado Tech's entrance exams in math and English. AP and CLEP credits are accepted. Important factors in the admissions decision are ability to finance college education, personality/intangible qualities, and recommendations by school officials.

Procedure: Freshmen are admitted to all sessions. Entrance exams should be taken prior to the student's desired entry date. There are early admissions and deferred admissions plans. Application deadlines are open. Check with the school for current application fee.

Transfer: 800 transfer students enrolled in a recent year. Most new students are transfers. They must meet the same criteria as entering freshmen. The university uses placement tests in math and English for acceptance and placement. 45 of 180 credits required for the bachelor's degree must be completed at Colorado Tech.

Visiting: There are regularly scheduled orientations for prospective students, consisting of a tour and an admissions overview program. There are guides for informal visits and visitors may sit in on classes. To schedule a visit, contact the Admissions Director.

Financial Aid: In a recent year, 20% of all full-time freshmen and 33% of continuing full-time students received some form of financial aid. 50% of full-time freshmen and 60% of continuing full-time students received need-based aid. The average freshman award was $7000. Need-based scholarships or need-based grants averaged $3000 ($4050 maximum), and need-based self-help aid (loans and jobs) averaged $4000 ($6625 maximum). 2% of undergraduates work part time. Average annual earnings from campus work are $1500. The average financial indebtedness of a recent graduate was $30,000. The FAFSA and the state aid form are required. Check with the school for current deadlines.

International Students: There were 14 international students enrolled in a recent year. They must score satisfactorily on the written TOEFL and also take or provide satisfactory evidence of completion of ELS or college-level English. They must take the SAT, ACT, or the college's own entrance exam.

Computers: All students may access the system 8 A.M. to 9 P.M. Monday through Thursday and 8 A.M. to 5 P.M. Friday and Saturday. There are no time limits and no fees.

Graduates: In a recent year, 147 bachelor's degrees were awarded. The most popular majors were information technology/information technology (33%), management (26%), and computer science (15%). 72 companies recruited on campus in a recent year.

Admissions Contact: Rob Dillman, Vice President of Admissions. A video is available. E-mail: *rdillman@coloradotech.edu* Web: *http://www.coloradotech.edu*

DEVRY UNIVERSITY/COLORADO SPRINGS — D-3

Colorado Springs, CO 80910-3124

(719) 632-3000
Fax: (719) 632-1909

Full-time: 125 men, 50 women	Faculty: n/av
Part-time: 100 men, 45 women	Ph.D.s: n/av
Graduate: none	Student/Faculty: n/av
Year: semesters, summer session	Tuition: $12,000
Application Deadline: open	Room & Board: n/app
Freshman Class: n/av	
SAT or ACT: n/av	LESS COMPETITIVE

DeVry University/Colorado Springs, founded in 2001, is 1 of 67 DeVry University locations throughout the United States and Canada. The private institution offers career-oriented degree programs with hands-on training in various fields of business and technology. Figures in the above capsule and in this profile are approximate. The library contains 1800 volumes and 20 audio/video tapes/CDs/DVDs, and subscribes to 20 periodicals including electronic. Computerized library services include the card catalog, interlibrary loans, and database searching. Special learning facilities include a learning resource center and electronics and other labs.

Student Life: 60% are white; 14% African American. The average age of all undergraduates is 27.

Housing: There are no residence halls. All students commute. Alcohol is not permitted. All students may keep cars.

Activities: There are no fraternities or sororities. There is 1 professional group on campus. Popular campus events include various food events.

Sports: There is no sports program at DeVry.

Disabled Students: 90% of the campus is accessible. Wheelchair ramps, elevators, special parking, specially equipped rest rooms, and lowered telephones are available.

Services: Counseling and information services are available, as is tutoring in every subject.

Campus Safety and Security: Measures include 24-hour foot and vehicle patrol, security escort services, informal discussions, and pamphlets/posters/films. There are emergency telephones and full-time security personnel.

Programs of Study: DeVry confers the B.S. degree. Associate and master's degrees are also awarded. Bachelor's degrees are awarded in BUSINESS (business administration and management), COMMUNICATIONS AND THE ARTS (telecommunications), COMPUTER AND PHYSICAL SCIENCE (information sciences and systems), ENGINEERING AND ENVIRONMENTAL DESIGN (technological management). Computer information systems and business administration are the largest.

Required: To graduate, students must achieve a GPA of at least 2.0 and satisfactorily complete all curriculum requirements. Course requirements vary according to program. All first-semester students take courses in business organization, algebra, psychology, and student success strategies.

Special: Accelerated degree programs are offered in computer information systems and business administration. Co-op programs, nondegree study, distance learning, and evening and weekend classes are possible.

Faculty/Classroom: All teach undergraduates.

Requirements: Admissions requirements include graduation from a secondary school; the GED is also accepted. Applicants must pass the DeVry entrance exam or present satisfactory ACT or SAT scores. An interview is also required. CLEP credit is accepted.

Procedure: Freshmen are admitted to all sessions. There are early admissions and deferred admissions plans. Application deadlines are open. Check with the school for current application fee. Applications are accepted on-line.

Transfer: Applicants must submit official transcripts from all previous colleges attended indicating passing grades in all completed course work, demonstrate language skills proficiency in at least 24 completed semester hours, and present evidence of math proficiency by appropriate college-level credits. A minimum GPA of 2.0 is required. 25 of 48 credits required for the bachelor's degree must be completed at DeVry.

Visiting: There are regularly scheduled orientations for prospective students. There are guides for informal visits and visitors may sit in on classes. To schedule a visit, contact New Student Coordinator.

Financial Aid: In a recent year, 62% of all full-time freshmen and 73% of continuing full-time students received some form of financial aid. 62% of full-time freshmen and 73% of continuing full-time students received need-based aid. The average freshman award was $7137. Need-based scholarships or need-based grants averaged $4149; need-based self-help aid (loans and jobs) averaged $4172; and other non-need-based awards and non-need-based scholarships averaged $8712. The FAFSA is required.

International Students: International students must take the TOEFL and also take the college's own entrance exam.

Graduates: In a recent year, 2 bachelor's degrees were awarded. The most popular major was computer information systems.

Admissions Contact: Pam Smith, Director of Admissions. E-mail: *admitcs@cs.devry.edu* Web: *www.cs.devry.edu*

DEVRY UNIVERSITY/WESTMINSTER — C-2

Westminster, CO 80234-2010

(303) 280-7600
(888) 212-1857; Fax: (303) 280-7606

Full-time: 350 men, 110 women	Faculty: n/av
Part-time: 150 men, 70 women	Ph.D.s: n/av
Graduate: none	Student/Faculty: n/av
Year: semesters, summer session	Tuition: $12,000
Application Deadline: open	Room & Board: n/app
Freshman Class: n/av	
SAT or ACT: n/av	LESS COMPETITIVE

DeVry University/Westminster, founded in 2001, is a private institution offering hands-on programs in electronics, business administration, computer information systems, information technology, and computer engineering technology. The school is 1 of 67 DeVry University locations throughout the United States and Canada. Figures in the above capsule and in this profile are approximate. The library contains 500 volumes and 150 audio/video tapes/CDs/DVDs, and subscribes to 50 periodicals including electronic. Computerized library services include the card catalog, interlibrary loans, and database searching. Special learning facilities include a learning resource center and electronics and other labs.

Student Life: 58% are white. The average age of all undergraduates is 24.

Housing: All students commute. All students may keep cars.

Activities: There are no fraternities or sororities. There are 3 groups on campus, including professional and yearbook. Popular campus events include BBQ and other food events.

Sports: There is no sports program at DeVry University/Westminster.

Disabled Students: 90% of the campus is accessible. Wheelchair ramps, elevators, special parking, specially equipped rest rooms, and lowered telephones are available.

Services: Counseling and information services are available, as is tutoring in every subject.

Campus Safety and Security: Measures include security escort services, informal discussions, pamphlets/posters/films, and emergency telephones. There are lighted pathways/sidewalks.

Programs of Study: DeVry University/Westminster confers the B.S. degree. Associate degrees are also awarded. Bachelor's degrees are awarded in BIOLOGICAL SCIENCE (bioinformatics), BUSINESS (business administration and management), COMPUTER AND PHYSICAL SCIENCE (information sciences and systems), ENGINEERING AND ENVIRONMENTAL DESIGN (biomedical engineering, computer engineering, electrical/electronics engineering technology, and technological management). Electronics is the largest.

Required: To graduate, students must achieve a GPA of 2.0 and satisfactorily complete all curriculum requirements. Course requirements vary according to program. All first-semester students take courses in business organization, computer applications, algebra, psychology, and student success strategies.

Special: Accelerated degrees, co-op programs, nondegree study, distance learning, and evening and weekend classes are possible.

Faculty/Classroom: All teach undergraduates.

Requirements: Admissions requirements include graduation from a secondary school; the GED is also accepted. Applicants must pass the DeVry entrance exam or present satisfactory ACT or SAT scores. An interview is required. CLEP credit is accepted.

Procedure: Freshmen are admitted fall, spring, and summer. There are early admissions and deferred admissions plans. Application deadlines are open. Check with the school for current application fee. Applications are accepted on-line.

Transfer: Applicants must present passing grades in all completed college course work, demonstrate language proficiency in at least 24 completed semester hours, and present evidence of math proficiency by appropriate college-level credits. 25 of 48 credits required for the bachelor's degree must be completed at DeVry University/Westminster.

Visiting: There are regularly scheduled orientations for prospective students. There are guides for informal visits and visitors may sit in on classes. To schedule a visit, contact Dean of Admissions.

Financial Aid: In a recent year, 59% of all full-time freshmen and 67% of continuing full-time students received some form of financial aid. 58% of full-time freshmen and 66% of continuing full-time students received need-based aid. The average freshman award was $5618. Need-based scholarships or need-based grants averaged $3687; need-based self-help aid (loans and jobs) averaged $3764; and other non-need-based awards and non-need-based scholarships averaged $12,266. The FAFSA is required.

International Students: International students must take the TOEFL and also take the college's own entrance exam.

Admissions Contact: Pam Smith, Dean of Admissions.
E-mail: *Denver-admissions@den.devry.edu* Web: *www.den.devry.edu*

FORT LEWIS COLLEGE   B-4

Durango, CO 81301	**(970) 247-7184; Fax: (970) 247-7179**
Full-time: 1884 men, 1753 women	Faculty: 177; IIB, --$
Part-time: 157 men, 152 women	Ph.Ds: 78%
Graduate: none	Student/Faculty: 22 to 1
Year: trimesters, summer session	Tuition: $5692 ($13,700)
Application Deadline: August 1	Room & Board: $6160
Freshman Class: 2765 applied, 2042 accepted, 910 enrolled	
SAT Verbal/Math: 510/503*	ACT: 21 COMPETITIVE

Fort Lewis College, founded in 1911, is a public institution with undergraduate programs in arts and sciences, business, and education. There are 4 undergraduate schools. In addition to regional accreditation, FLC has baccalaureate program accreditation with AACSB, NASM, and TEAC. The library contains 194,889 volumes, 344,100 microform items, and 5004 audio/video tapes/CDs/DVDs, and subscribes to 452 periodicals including electronic. Computerized library services include the card catalog, interlibrary loans, database searching, Internet access, and laptop Internet portals. Special learning facilities include a learning resource center, art gallery, radio station, and a center for Southwest Studies. The 600-acre campus is in a small town 350 miles southwest of Denver and 250 miles northwest of Albuquerque, New Mexico. Including any residence halls, there are 46 buildings.

Student Life: 71% of undergraduates are from Colorado. Others are from 45 states, 13 foreign countries, and Canada. 99% are from public schools. 66% are white; 18% Native American/Eskimo. The average age of freshmen is 18; all undergraduates, 22. 42% do not continue beyond their first year; 58% remain to graduate.

Housing: 1460 students can be accommodated in college housing, which includes single-sex and coed dorms, on-campus apartments, and married-student housing. In addition, there is a Hispanic center, a Native American center, and an environmental center. On-campus housing is guaranteed for the freshman year only and is available on a first-come, first-served basis. 67% of students commute. Alcohol is not permitted. All students may keep cars.

Activities: There are no fraternities or sororities. There are 60 groups on campus, including art, band, cheerleading, chess, choir, chorale, chorus, computers, dance, drama, drill team, ethnic, gay, honors, international, jazz band, literary magazine, musical theater, newspaper, orchestra, political, professional, radio and TV, religious, social, social service, student government, and symphony. Popular campus events include Weekend Wipeout and Hozhoni Days.

Sports: There are 5 intercollegiate sports for men and 5 for women, and 16 intramural sports for men and 16 for women. Facilities include a field house, outdoor sports complex, indoor swimming pool, and a student life center, which includes a 3-court gym, racquetball court, aerobic/dance studio, track, climbing wall, and a cardio/weight area.

Disabled Students: All of the campus is accessible. Wheelchair ramps, elevators, special parking, specially equipped rest rooms, special class scheduling, lowered drinking fountains, lowered telephones, special housing, and workstations modified for individual needs are available.

Services: Counseling and information services are available, as is tutoring in most subjects. There is a reader service for the blind, and remedial math, reading, and writing.

Campus Safety and Security: Measures include 24-hour foot and vehicle patrol, self-defense education, security escort services, and shuttle buses. There are informal discussions, pamphlets/posters/films, emergency telephones, and lighted pathways/sidewalks.

Programs of Study: FLC confers B.A. and B.S. degrees. Associate degrees are also awarded. Bachelor's degrees are awarded in BIOLOGICAL SCIENCE (biology/biological science), BUSINESS (accounting and business administration and management), COMMUNICATIONS AND THE ARTS (art, dramatic arts, English, music, and Spanish), COMPUTER AND PHYSICAL SCIENCE (chemistry, geology, information sciences and systems, mathematics, and physics), HEALTH PROFESSIONS (exercise science), SOCIAL SCIENCE (anthropology, economics, history, humanities, interdisciplinary studies, philosophy, political science/government, psychology, sociology, and Southwest American studies). Business, chemistry, and geology are the strongest academically. Business is the largest.

Required: To graduate, students must complete 120 semester hours with 30 to 40 hours in the major, 50 credits outside the major, and a minimum GPA of 2.0 overall and within the major. A total of 32 to 44 hours in general distribution courses is required.

Special: The college offers cooperative programs in most majors, numerous internships, a Washington semester for political science majors, study abroad in 32 countries, student-designed majors, a general studies degree, non-degree study, pass/fail option, and B.A.-B.S. degrees. There are 3-2 engineering degrees with 4 universities and a preforestry degree with Colorado State and Northern Arizona Universities. There are 16 national honor societies and a freshman honors program.

Faculty/Classroom: 52% of faculty are male; 48%, female. All teach undergraduates. The average class size in an introductory lecture is 23; in a laboratory, 16; and in a regular course, 22.

Admissions: 74% of the 2005-2006 applicants were accepted. The SAT scores for the 2005-2006 freshman class were: Verbal--42% below 500, 45% between 500 and 599, 11% between 600 and 700, and 2% above 700; Math--47% below 500, 39% between 500 and 599, 12% between 600 and 700, and 2% above 700. The ACT scores were 51% below 21, 30% between 21 and 23, 14% between 24 and 26, 4% between 27 and 28, and 3% above 28. 14% of the current freshmen were in the top fifth of their class; 38% were in the top two fifths. 5 freshmen graduated first in their class.

Requirements: A satisfactory score on the SAT or ACT is required. Applicants must be graduates of an accredited secondary school or have a GED certificate. An interview is recommended. A GPA of 2.0 is required. AP and CLEP credits are accepted.

Procedure: Freshmen are admitted to all sessions. Entrance exams should be taken in the spring of the junior year in high school. There is a rolling admissions plan. Applications should be filed by August 1 for fall entry, December 1 for winter entry, and April 1 for summer entry. Notification is sent on a rolling basis. Applications are accepted on-line.

Transfer: 279 transfer students enrolled in 2004-2005. Applicants for transfer should have completed a minimum of 12 credit hours and have a GPA of 2.0. Courses completed with a grade of C- or better may transfer. An interview is recommended. 30 of 120 credits required for the bachelor's degree must be completed at FLC.

Visiting: There are regularly scheduled orientations for prospective students. There are guides for informal visits and visitors may sit in on classes and stay overnight. To schedule a visit, contact the Office of Admission at *admission@fortlewis.edu.*

Financial Aid: In 2005-2006, 45% of all full-time freshmen received some form of financial aid. 26% of full-time freshmen received need-based aid. Need-based scholarships or need-based grants averaged $3192; need-based self-help aid (loans and jobs) averaged $2507; and non-need-based athletic scholarships averaged $1400. The average financial indebtedness of the 2005 graduate was $16,966. FLC is a member of CSS. The FAFSA is required. The deadline for filing freshman financial aid applications for fall entry is February 15.

International Students: There are 52 international students enrolled. They must score satisfacatorily on the written TOEFL.

Computers: All students may access the system. There are no time limits and no fees.

Graduates: From July 1, 2004 to June 30, 2005, 698 bachelor's degrees were awarded. The most popular majors were business/marketing (19%), English (education) (10%), and interdisciplinary studies (9%). In an average class, 1% graduate in 3 years or less, 11% graduate in 4 years or less, 26% graduate in 5 years or less, and 30% graduate in 6 years or less. 65 companies recruited on campus in 2004-2005. Of the 2004 graduating class, 21% were enrolled in graduate school within 6 months of graduation and 77% were employed.

Admissions Contact: Gretchen Foster, Director, Admission and Development. A video is available. E-mail: *admission@fortlewis.edu* Web: *www.fortlewis.edu*

JOHNSON AND WALES UNIVERSITY/DENVER CAMPUS

Denver, CO 80220	(877) 598-3368; Fax: (303) 256-9333
Full-time: 768 men, 753 women	Faculty: 47
Part-time: 14 men, 9 women	Ph.Ds: 23%
Graduate: none	Student/Faculty: 32 to 1
Year: quarters, summer session	Tuition: $20,826
Application Deadline: see profile	Room & Board: $7300
Freshman Class: 2754 accepted, 511 enrolled	
SATor ACT : required for some programs	LESS COMPETITIVE

Johnson & Wales University/Denver Campus, founded in 2000, offers degree programs in its College of Business, College of Culinary Arts, Hospitality College, and School of Education. There are 4 undergraduate schools. The library contains 29,000 volumes and 1200 audio/video tapes/CDs/DVDs, and subscribes to 215 periodicals including electronic. Computerized library services include interlibrary loans, database searching, Internet access, and laptop Internet portals. Special learning facilities include a learning resource center. The 26-acre campus is in a suburban area. Including any residence halls, there are 19 buildings.

Student Life: 55% of undergraduates are from out of state, mostly the West. Students are from 47 states, 27 foreign countries, and Canada. 69% are white; 11% Hispanic. The average age of freshmen is 19; all undergraduates, 20.

Housing: 683 students can be accommodated in college housing, which includes coed dorms. Housing is available to freshmen on a first-deposited, first-contract-received basis. On-campus housing is available on a lottery system for upperclassmen. 78% of students live on campus. Alcohol is not permitted. All students may keep cars.

Activities: There are 2 national fraternities and 2 national sororities. There are some groups and organizations on campus, including chorale, dance, international, literary magazine, professional, social, student government, and yearbook.

Sports: There are 3 intercollegiate sports for men and 2 for women, and 5 intramural sports for men and 5 for women. Facilities include a gym, a weight room, a cardio room, a sand volleyball pit, and an outdoor basketball court.

Disabled Students: All of the campus is accessible. Wheelchair ramps, elevators, special parking, specially equipped rest rooms, special class scheduling, lowered drinking fountains, and lowered telephones are available.

Services: Counseling and information services are available, as is tutoring in every subject.

Campus Safety and Security: Measures include 24-hour foot and vehicle patrol, security escort services, shuttle buses, and informal discussions. There are pamphlets/posters/films and emergency telephones.

Programs of Study: J&W confers the B.S. degree. Associate degrees are also awarded. Culinary, sports entertainment event management, and food service management are the largest.

Required: To graduate, students must complete 180 quarter credit hours, including at least 36 in the major, with a minimum GPA of 2.0. Required classes include English, math, history, economics, science, psychology, sociology, and professional development.

Special: The university offers co-op programs, accelerated degree programs, dual majors, study abroad, and worldwide work-study opportunities in business, hospitality, technology, and culinary arts, Most majors require 11-week internships. There is a freshman honors program.

Faculty/Classroom: 56% of faculty are male; 44%, female. All teach undergraduates.

Requirements: The SAT or ACT is required for some programs. In addition, although SAT and ACT scores are required only for students applying for honors admissions, students who have taken these tests are encouraged to submit their scores. A GPA of 2.0 is required. AP and CLEP credits are accepted. Important factors in the admissions decision are advanced placement or honor courses, extracurricular activities record, and recommendations by school officials.

Procedure: Freshmen are admitted to all sessions. There is a deferred admissions and a rolling admissions plan. Application deadlines are open. Notification is sent on a rolling basis. Applications are accepted on-line.

Transfer: 124 transfer students enrolled in 2004-2005. Applicants are required to submit official high school and college transcripts and must have earned a minimum college GPA of 2.0. 45 of 180 quarter credit hours required for the bachelor's degree must be completed at J&W.

Visiting: There are guides for informal visits and visitors may sit in on classes and stay overnight. To schedule a visit, contact the Admissions Office.

Financial Aid: In 2005-2006, 77% of all full-time freshmen and 73% of continuing full-time students received some form of financial aid. 59% of full-time freshmen and 51% of continuing full-time students received need-based aid. Need-based scholarships or need-based grants averaged $5180; need-based self-help aid (loans and jobs) averaged $7166; and other non-need-based awards and non-need-based scholarships averaged $5015. The average financial indebtedness of the 2005 graduate was $14,798. J&W is a member of CSS. The FAFSA and the college's own financial statement are required.

International Students: There are 50 international students enrolled. The school actively recruits these students. A satisfactory score is required on the written TOEFL.

Computers: Wireless access is available. Computers and printers are available for students to use in the Achievement Center. All students may access the system. There are no fees.

Graduates: From July 1, 2004 to June 30, 2005, 424 bachelor's degrees were awarded. The most popular majors were culinary (56%), business (29%), and food and service management (10%).

Admissions Contact: Dave McKlveen, Director of Admissions. A video is available. E-mail: *admissions.den@jwu.edu* Web: *www.jwu.edu*

MESA STATE COLLEGE

Grand Junction, CO 81501	A-2
	(970) 248-1698
	(800) 982-MESA; Fax: (970) 248-1973
Full-time: 1750 men, 2250 women	Faculty: 204; IIB, --$
Part-time: 500 men, 825 women	Ph.Ds: 72%
Graduate: 25 men, 25 women	Student/Faculty: 20 to 1
Year: semesters, summer session	Tuition: $5480 ($10,266)
Application Deadline: see profile	Room & Board: $6498
Freshman Class: n/av	
SAT or ACT: required	COMPETITIVE

Mesa State College, founded in 1925, is a public institution offering undergraduate programs in liberal arts, sciences, business, and preprofessional areas. There are 3 undergraduate schools and 1 graduate school. Most figures in the above capsule and in this profile are approximate. In addition to regional accreditation, Mesa State has baccalaureate program accreditation with CAHEA and NLN. The library contains 189,000 volumes, 803,012 microform items, and 25,578 audio/video tapes/CDs/DVDs, and subscribes to 1035 periodicals including electronic. Computerized library services include the card catalog, interlibrary loans, and database searching. Special learning facilities include a learning resource center, art gallery, radio station, and TV studio. The 42-acre campus is in a small town 250 miles west of Denver. Including any residence halls, there are 26 buildings.

Student Life: 90% of undergraduates are from Colorado. Others are from 30 states, 43 foreign countries, and Canada. 86% are white. The average age of freshmen is 20; all undergraduates, 25. 39% do not continue beyond their first year; 53% remain to graduate.

Housing: 918 students can be accommodated in college housing, which includes coed dorms and on-campus apartments. On-campus housing is available on a first-come, first-served basis. 81% of students commute. Alcohol is not permitted. All students may keep cars.

Activities: There are no fraternities or sororities. There are 50 groups on campus, including art, cheerleading, choir, chorus, computers, dance, ethnic, honors, international, jazz band, literary magazine, musical theater, newspaper, outdoors, political, professional, radio and TV, religious, social, social service, and student government. Popular campus events include Unity Fest, spring series, and art shows.

Sports: There are 4 intercollegiate sports for men and 7 for women, and 18 intramural sports for men and 18 for women. Facilities include a weight room, tennis courts, a swimming pool, and a recreation center with climbing walls, racquetball courts, an elevated running track, and workout facilities.

Disabled Students: 98% of the campus is accessible. Wheelchair ramps, elevators, special parking, specially equipped rest rooms, special class scheduling, lowered drinking fountains, and lowered telephones are available.

Services: Counseling and information services are available, as is tutoring in every subject, except accounting. There is a reader service for the blind, and remedial math, reading, and writing.

Campus Safety and Security: Measures include 24-hour foot and vehicle patrol, self-defense education, security escort services, and informal discussions. There are pamphlets/posters/films, lighted pathways/

sidewalks, a crime watch program, an emergency contact service, and first-aid and CPR courses.

Programs of Study: Mesa State confers B.A., B.S., B.B.A., and B.S.N. degrees. Associate and master's degrees are also awarded. Bachelor's degrees are awarded in BIOLOGICAL SCIENCE (biology/biological science), BUSINESS (accounting, and business administration and management), COMMUNICATIONS AND THE ARTS (communications, English, and fine arts), COMPUTER AND PHYSICAL SCIENCE (computer science, mathematics, and physical sciences), ENGINEERING AND ENVIRONMENTAL DESIGN (environmental engineering technology), HEALTH PROFESSIONS (nursing), SOCIAL SCIENCE (history, liberal arts/general studies, physical fitness/movement, political science/government, psychology, social science, and sociology). Nursing and allied health, natural science, and math are the strongest academically. Business, natural science, and math are the largest.

Required: To graduate, students must complete a minimum of 123 credits, with 40 hours in upper-level courses in the emphasis area and a minimum GPA of 2.0. All students must take English 111 and 112 as well as 33 hours of general education courses and 3 hours of phys ed. A comprehensive exam is required.

Special: Mesa State offers internships in many of its programs, including one in the state legislature, a Washington semester, work-study programs, student-designed majors in selected studies, and the B.A.-B.S. degree in several majors. Nondegree study for students over 20 years of age and credit for life, military, and work experience are available. There are 10 national honor societies, a freshman honors program, and 5 departmental honors programs.

Faculty/Classroom: 62% of faculty are male; 38%, female. All teach undergraduates. No introductory courses are taught by graduate students. The average class size in an introductory lecture is 30; in a laboratory, 20; and in a regular course, 30.

Requirements: The SAT or ACT is required with a satisfactory minimum score on the SAT or on the ACT. In addition applicants must be graduates of an accredited secondary school or hold the GED. The college prefers that students complete 4 years of high school English, 3 each of math, science, and social studies, 2 of foreign language, and 1 of history. An essay, an interview, and an audition for some classes are recommended. Mesa State requires applicants to be in the upper 75% of their class. A GPA of 2.6 is required. AP and CLEP credits are accepted. Important factors in the admissions decision are recommendations by school officials, personality/intangible qualities, and evidence of special talent.

Procedure: Freshmen are admitted to all sessions. Entrance exams should be taken late in the junior year or early in the senior year. There is a deferred admissions plan. Notification is sent on a rolling basis. Applications are accepted on-line. Check with the school for current application deadlines and fee.

Transfer: Applicants must have a minimum GPA of 2.0 with 30 semester hours; otherwise, they must meet the criteria for entering freshmen.

Visiting: There are regularly scheduled orientations for prospective students, including advising sessions. There are guides for informal visits and visitors may sit in on classes. To schedule a visit, contact the Admissions Office.

Financial Aid: The FAFSA is required. The priority deadline for filing freshman financial aid applications for fall entry is March 1.

International Students: They must score satisfactorily on the written TOEFL and also take the MELAB or the Comprehensive English Language Test, the SAT or the ACT.

Computers: All students may access the system. There are no time limits. The fee is $27 per semester. It is strongly recommended that all students have a personal computer.

Admissions Contact: Tyre Bush, Director of Admissions and Recruitment. A video is available. E-mail: tbush@mesastate.edu
Web: www.mesastate.edu

METROPOLITAN STATE COLLEGE OF DENVER C-2

Denver, CO 80217-3362   (303) 556-3058; Fax: (303) 556-6345

Full-time: 4550 men, 5825 women	Faculty: 446
Part-time: 3325 men, 4775 women	Ph.D.s: n/av
Graduate: none	Student/Faculty: 23 to 1
Year: semesters, summer session	Tuition: $2338 ($8186)
Application Deadline: August 12	Room & Board: n/app
Freshman Class: n/av	
SAT or ACT: required	LESS COMPETITIVE

Metropolitan State College of Denver, founded in 1963, is a public commuter institution offering degree programs in the liberal arts and sciences, business, and professional studies, as well as individualized degree programs. There are 3 undergraduate schools. Most figures in the above capsule and in this profile are approximate. In addition to regional accreditation, Metro State has baccalaureate program accreditation with ABET, CSWE, NASM, NCATE, NLN, and NRPA. The library contains 692,677 volumes, 1,053,419 microform items, and 16,975 audio/video tapes/CDs/DVDs, and subscribes to 4150 periodicals including electron-

ic. Computerized library services include the card catalog, interlibrary loans, and database searching. Special learning facilities include a learning resource center, art gallery, radio station, world indoor airport, a writing center, and student support services. The 175-acre campus is in an urban area in Denver. There are 38 buildings.

Student Life: 99% of undergraduates are from Colorado. Others are from 40 states, 66 foreign countries, and Canada. 96% are from public schools. 71% are white; 12% Hispanic. The average age of freshmen is 22; all undergraduates, 26. 38% do not continue beyond their first year.

Housing: There are no residence halls. All students commute. All students may keep cars.

Activities: There are no fraternities or sororities. There are 100 groups on campus, including art, band, cheerleading, chess, choir, chorale, chorus, computers, debate, drama, ethnic, gay, honors, international, jazz band, literary magazine, musical theater, newspaper, orchestra, political, professional, radio and TV, religious, social, social service, student government, and symphony. Popular campus events include Club Day, World Friendship Festival, and Family Night.

Sports: There are 5 intercollegiate sports for men and 5 for women, and 10 intramural sports for men and 6 for women. Facilities include playing fields, volleyball, basketball, badminton, racquetball, handball, squash, and tennis courts, a swimming pool, a dance studio, a weight room, a fitness center and green room, a 3500-seat events center, an auxiliary gym, and a three-quarter-mile jogging path.

Disabled Students: 90% of the campus is accessible. Wheelchair ramps, elevators, special parking, specially equipped rest rooms, special class scheduling, lowered drinking fountains, lowered telephones, telephones, tapes, and classroom aids for the hearing impaired, an adaptive computer lab, testing accommodations, sign-language and oral interpreters, priority registration, and a resource and referral library are available.

Services: Counseling and information services are available, as is tutoring in most subjects. ESL services and an adult learning services office are available.

Campus Safety and Security: Measures include 24-hour foot and vehicle patrol, self-defense education, security escort services, and shuttle buses. There are informal discussions, pamphlets/posters/films, emergency telephones, lighted pathways/sidewalks, bicycle registration, and date/acquaintance rape education seminars.

Programs of Study: Metro State confers B.A., B.S., and B.F.A. degrees. Bachelor's degrees are awarded in BIOLOGICAL SCIENCE (biology/biological science), BUSINESS (accounting, banking and finance, hospitality management services, management science, marketing/retailing/merchandising, and recreation and leisure services), COMMUNICATIONS AND THE ARTS (art, communications, English, fine arts, industrial design, journalism, modern language, music performance, Spanish, and speech/debate/rhetoric), COMPUTER AND PHYSICAL SCIENCE (atmospheric sciences and meteorology, chemistry, computer management, computer science, information sciences and systems, mathematics, and physics), EDUCATION (music and physical), ENGINEERING AND ENVIRONMENTAL DESIGN (airline piloting and navigation, aviation administration/management, aviation computer technology, civil engineering technology, electrical/electronics engineering technology, environmental science, industrial administration/management, industrial engineering technology, land use management and reclamation, mechanical engineering technology, survey and mapping technology, and surveying engineering), HEALTH PROFESSIONS (health care administration, and nursing), SOCIAL SCIENCE (African American studies, anthropology, behavioral science, criminal justice, economics, history, human services, Mexican-American/Chicano studies, philosophy, physical fitness/movement, political science/government, psychology, social work, sociology, and urban studies). Criminal justice, psychology, and computer information systems are the largest.

Required: To graduate, students must complete at least 120 credit hours, 40 of which must be upper division, and 30 in the major, with a minimum overall GPA of 2.0. There are 3 levels of general studies requirements, totaling 33 hours and including a multicultural requirement and a senior experience.

Special: Metro State offers co-op and service-learning programs in most majors, and cross-registration with a consortium of state colleges and the University of Colorado at Denver. Internships, study abroad, work-study programs, dual majors, student-designed majors, nondegree study, and pass/fail options are available. There are 9 national honor societies, a freshman honors program, and 10 departmental honors programs.

Faculty/Classroom: 56% of faculty are male; 44%, female. All teach undergraduates. The average class size in an introductory lecture is 25; in a laboratory, 14; and in a regular course, 19.

Requirements: The SAT or ACT is required. In addition, applicants should be graduates of an accredited secondary school, with 15 Carnegie units. The GED is accepted. AP and CLEP credits are accepted. Important factors in the admissions decision are recommendations by school officials, extracurricular activities record, and evidence of special talent.

Procedure: Freshmen are admitted to all sessions. Entrance exams should be taken prior to application. Notification is sent on a rolling basis. Applications are accepted on-line. Check with the school for current application deadlines and fee.

Transfer: Applicants must have a 2.0 GPA and be in good standing at their previous school. Some probationary transfers are considered. 30 of 120 credits required for the bachelor's degree must be completed at Metro State.

Visiting: There are regularly scheduled orientations for prospective students, including class scheduling and registration, college services and resources, transfer of credit, academic advising, choice of major, career counseling, and assessment testing if needed. There are guides for informal visits and visitors may sit in on classes. To schedule a visit, contact the Office of Admissions.

Financial Aid: Metro State is a member of CSS. The FAFSA is required. Check with the school for current deadlines.

International Students: They must score satisfactorily on the written TOEFL. The SAT or ACT is required if the applicant is under 20 and has graduated from a U.S. high school.

Computers: All students may access the system. Labs are open 96 hours a week, and 64 call-up lines are available 24 hours a day. There are no time limits. The fee is $4 to $21 depending upon the number of credits a student is taking.

Graduates: In an average class, 4% graduate in 4 years or less, 13% graduate in 5 years or less, and 20% graduate in 6 years or less.

Admissions Contact: Office of Admissions. A video is available. Web: *www.mscd.edu or gopher://mscdgopher*

NAROPA UNIVERSITY   C-2
Boulder, CO 80302-6697

(303) 546-5295
(800) 772-6951; Fax: (303) 546-3572

Full-time: 166 men, 234 women	Faculty: 29; IIA, --$
Part-time: 22 men, 29 women	Ph.D.s: 27%
Graduate: 211 men, 531 women	Student/Faculty: 14 to 1
Year: semesters, summer session	Tuition: $19,066
Application Deadline: January 15	Room & Board: $7236
Freshman Class: 122 applied, 103 accepted, 39 enrolled	
SAT Verbal/Math: 582/547*	ACT: 24	SPECIAL

Naropa University, founded in 1974, is a private nonprofit, nonsectarian Buddhist-inspired, experiential liberal arts institution. It offers undergraduate and graduate degrees in the arts, social sciences, and the humanities. The library contains 27,376 volumes and 2336 audio/video tapes/CDs/DVDs, and subscribes to 62 periodicals including electronic. Computerized library services include the card catalog, interlibrary loans, database searching, and Internet access. Special learning facilities include an art gallery, 2 meditation halls, a writing center, a volunteer center, a community arts center, and a career center. The 12-acre campus is in an urban area in Boulder. Including any residence halls, there are 19 buildings.

Student Life: 73% of undergraduates are from out of state, mostly the West. Students are from 46 states, 8 foreign countries, and Canada. 69% are white. The average age of freshmen is 22; all undergraduates, 24. 18% do not continue beyond their first year; 32% remain to graduate.

Housing: 70 students can be accommodated in college housing, which includes coed on-campus apartments. On-campus housing is guaranteed for the freshman year only, is available on a first-come, first-served basis, and is available on a lottery system for upperclassmen. 96% of students commute. Alcohol is not permitted. All students may keep cars.

Activities: There are no fraternities or sororities. There are 20 groups on campus, including chorus, dance, drama, environmental, ethnic, gay, international, literary magazine, newspaper, political, professional, religious, social, social service, and student government. Popular campus events include African dance and drumming, Gay Pride Week, and cultural festivals.

Sports: There is 1 intramural sport for men and 1 for women.

Disabled Students: 85% of the campus is accessible. Wheelchair ramps, elevators, special parking, specially equipped rest rooms, special class scheduling, lowered drinking fountains, and lowered telephones are available.

Services: Counseling and information services are available, as is tutoring in some subjects, including writing. There is a reader service for the blind.

Campus Safety and Security: Measures include self-defense education, security escort services, informal discussions, and pamphlets/posters/films. There are lighted pathways/sidewalks and evening foot and vehicle patrol.

Programs of Study: Naropa confers B.A. and B.F.A. degrees. Master's degrees are also awarded. Bachelor's degrees are awarded in COMMUNICATIONS AND THE ARTS (literature, music, performing arts, and visual and performing arts), EDUCATION (early childhood), ENGINEERING AND ENVIRONMENTAL DESIGN (environmental science), SOCIAL SCIENCE (East Asian studies, interdisciplinary studies, psychology, and religion). Psychology, writing and literature, and interdisciplinary studies are the largest.

Required: Students must complete 120 credits, 27 to 37 in the major, with a 2.0 average GPA. An extensive core curriculum includes courses in contemplative practices, world wisdom studies, cultural and historical studies, artistic process, scientific inquiry, diversity, humanities, and civic engagement. A writing proficiency exam is required.

Special: Cross-registration with the University of Colorado, work-study programs, internships, dual majors, and student-designed majors are available, as well as study abroad in Bali, Nepal, India, and the Czech Republic. Volunteer opportunities are also available.

Faculty/Classroom: 41% of faculty are male; 59%, female. 34% teach undergraduates. No introductory courses are taught by graduate students. The average class size in a regular course is 14.

Admissions: 84% of the 2005-2006 applicants were accepted. The SAT scores for the 2005-2006 freshman class were: Verbal--10% below 500, 60% between 500 and 599, 15% between 600 and 700, and 15% above 700; Math--10% below 500, 75% between 500 and 599, and 15% between 600 and 700. The ACT scores were 14% below 21, 43% between 21 and 23, 14% between 24 and 26, 14% between 27 and 28, and 14% above 28.

Requirements: The SAT or ACT is required for some programs. The ACT Optional Writing test is also required for some programs. In addition, a high school transcript, an interview, 2 recommendations, and an essay are required. The GED is accepted. AP and CLEP credits are accepted. Important factors in the admissions decision are personality/intangible qualities, recommendations by school officials, and evidence of special talent.

Procedure: Freshmen are admitted fall and spring. There are deferred admissions and rolling admissions plans. Applications should be filed by January 15 for fall entry and October 15 for spring entry, along with a $50 fee. Notification is sent on a rolling basis. Applications are accepted on-line.

Transfer: 102 transfer students enrolled in 2004-2005. Requirements for transfer students are unique to each academic department. 60 of 120 credits required for the bachelor's degree must be completed at Naropa.

Visiting: There are regularly scheduled orientations for prospective students, including daily tours, class visitation, meetings with counselors and 2 Preview Weekends (fall and spring). There are guides for informal visits and visitors may sit in on classes. To schedule a visit, contact the Visitation Coordinator at (303) 546-3548.

Financial Aid: In 2005-2006, 54% of all full-time freshmen and 63% of continuing full-time students received some form of financial aid. 60% of full-time freshmen and 63% of continuing full-time students received need-based aid. The average freshman award was $14,615. Need-based scholarships or need-based grants averaged $12,267 ($17,550 maximum); and need-based self-help aid (loans and jobs) averaged $5415 ($12,375 maximum). 24% of undergraduates work part time. Average annual earnings from campus work are $2046. The average financial indebtedness of the 2005 graduate was $21,203. The FAFSA is required. The priority date for freshman financial aid applications for fall entry is March 1.

International Students: There are 13 international students enrolled. They must score satisfactorily on the written TOEFL or on the electronic version.

Computers: Wireless access is available. 80% of the campus is covered in a wireless network that is available for any currently enrolled students. In addition, the school also offers 2 public-use PCs in the dorms, 6 PCs in the lab at the Nalanda campus, 14 PCs at the Paramita campus, and a total of 59 PCs at the Arapahoe computer lab. All students may access the system. There are no time limits and no fees. It is strongly recommended that all students have a personal computer.

Graduates: From July 1, 2004 to June 30, 2005, 108 bachelor's degrees were awarded. The most popular majors were psychology (44%), interdisciplinary (22%), and performing arts (9%). In an average class, 4% graduate in 3 years or less, and 31% graduate in 6 years or less.

Admissions Contact: Susan Boyle, Assistant Vice President of Admissions and Marketing. E-mail: *admissions@naropa.edu* Web: *www.naropa.edu*

REGIS UNIVERSITY   C-2
Denver, CO 80221-1099

(303) 458-4900
(800) 388-2366; Fax: (303) 964-5534

Full-time: 574 men, 976 women	Faculty: 68
Part-time: none	Ph.D.s: 95%
Graduate: none	Student/Faculty: 15 to 1
Year: semesters, summer session	Tuition: $23,700
Application Deadline: open	Room & Board: $8190
Freshman Class: 1600 applied, 1493 accepted, 402 enrolled	
SAT Verbal/Math: 530/530*	ACT: 23	COMPETITIVE

Regis University, founded in 1877, is a private, Roman Catholic liberal arts institution operated by the Jesuits. There are 3 undergraduate schools. In addition to regional accreditation, Regis has baccalaureate program accreditation with CAHEA, NCATE, and NLN. The library contains 425,000 volumes, 140,000 microform items, and 110,000 audio/

video tapes/CDs/DVDs, and subscribes to 4000 periodicals including electronic. Computerized library services include the card catalog, interlibrary loans, and database searching. Special learning facilities include a learning resource center and radio station. The 90-acre campus is in a suburban area in north Denver. Including any residence halls, there are 12 buildings.

Student Life: 57% of undergraduates are from Colorado. Students are from 40 states, 23 foreign countries, and Canada. 77% are white. 56% are Catholic; 55% Buddhist, Latter-Day Saints, and unknown; 9% Protestant. The average age of freshmen is 18; all undergraduates, 21. 50% of freshmen remain to graduate.

Housing: 600 students can be accommodated in college housing, which includes coed dorms. On-campus housing is guaranteed for all 4 years and is available on a first-come, first-served basis. 63% of students commute. All students may keep cars.

Activities: There are no fraternities or sororities. There are 30 groups on campus, including cheerleading, choir, chorus, dance, ethnic, forensics, gay, honors, international, literary magazine, newspaper, political, professional, radio and TV, religious, social, social service, student government, and yearbook. Popular campus events include Mistletoe Madness, Ranger Week, and Hall Olympics.

Sports: There are 6 intercollegiate sports for men and 6 for women, and 8 intramural sports for men and 8 for women. Facilities include a 2800-seat gym, a pool, tennis courts, and playing fields.

Disabled Students: 80% of the campus is accessible. Wheelchair ramps, elevators, special parking, specially equipped rest rooms, special class scheduling, lowered drinking fountains, and lowered telephones are available.

Services: Counseling and information services are available, as is tutoring in every subject. There is a reader service for the blind.

Campus Safety and Security: Measures include 24-hour foot and vehicle patrol, self-defense education, security escort services, and pamphlets/posters/films. There are emergency telephones and lighted pathways/sidewalks.

Programs of Study: Regis confers B.A., B.S., and B.S.N. degrees. Master's degrees are also awarded. Bachelor's degrees are awarded in BIOLOGICAL SCIENCE (biochemistry, biology/biological science, and neurosciences), BUSINESS (accounting, business administration and management, business economics, international business management, and marketing/retailing/merchandising), COMMUNICATIONS AND THE ARTS (communications, English, French, and Spanish), COMPUTER AND PHYSICAL SCIENCE (chemistry, computer science, and mathematics), ENGINEERING AND ENVIRONMENTAL DESIGN (engineering), HEALTH PROFESSIONS (medical records administration/services, and nursing), SOCIAL SCIENCE (economics, history, philosophy, political science/government, prelaw, psychology, religion, and sociology). Business is the largest.

Required: Students must complete 128 credit hours with a minimum GPA of 2.0. Required courses include 58 credit hours in the core curriculum, of which 12 are seminars, 7 to 8 are math and natural science, 6 are in literature/humanities, social science, religious studies, and philosophy, and 3 each are in economics, communication arts, and fine arts.

Special: Cross-registration is possible with Denver University and Metropolitan State. Internships, study abroad, and work-study programs with Regis are available. The college offers B.A.-B.S. degrees, dual majors, student-designed majors, a 3-2 engineering degree with Washington University, and pass/fail options. There is 1 national honor society and a freshman honors program.

Faculty/Classroom: 57% of faculty are male; 43%, female. All both teach and do research. The average class size in an introductory lecture is 30; in a laboratory, 15; and in a regular course, 30.

Admissions: 93% of the 2005-2006 applicants were accepted. The SATscores for the 2005-2006 freshman class were: Verbal--37% below 500, 37% between 500 and 599, 21% between 600 and 700, and 5% above 700; Math--36% below 500, 43% between 500 and 599, 18% between 600 and 700, and 3% above 700. The ACT scores were 24% below 21, 29% between 21 and 23, 26% between 24 and 26, 7% between 27 and 28, and 14% above 28. 48% of the current freshmen were in the top fifth of their class; 74% were in the top two fifths. 25 freshmen graduated first in their class.

Requirements: The SAT or ACT is required. In addition, applicants should be graduates of an accredited secondary school. The GED is accepted. Students should have completed 16 high school academic credits, including 4 years of English, 3 each of math, science, and history, 2 of a foreign language, and 1 to 2 of social studies. A recommendation from the high school counselor and an essay are required. An interview is recommended. Applications are accepted on-line or on computer disk. A GPA of 2.3 is required. AP and CLEP credits are accepted. Important factors in the admissions decision are recommendations by school officials, leadership record, and extracurricular activities record.

Procedure: Freshmen are admitted fall and spring. Entrance exams should be taken in the fall. There is a deferred admissions plan and a rolling admissions plan. Application deadlines are open. Notification is sent on a rolling basis. Application fee is $40.

Transfer: 70 transfer students enrolled in 2004-2005. Applicants must have a GPA of 2.5. All previous college work is considered. The college reviews each applicant individually. 30 of 128 credits required for the bachelor's degree must be completed at Regis.

Visiting: There are guides for informal visits and visitors may sit in on classes and stay overnight. To schedule a visit, contact the Admissions Office.

Financial Aid: In 2005-2006, 90% of all full-time students received some form of financial aid. 63% of full-time freshmen and 65% of continuing full-time students received need-based aid. Need-based scholarships or need-based grants averaged $10,000 (full tuition maximum); and need-based self-help aid (loans and jobs) averaged $5025. The FAFSA and the college's own financial statement are required. Check with the school for current deadlines.

International Students: The school actively recruits these students. A satisfactory score is required on the written TOEFL or the MELAB, and the ELS/ALA.

Computers: All students may access the system. There are no time limits and no fees. It is strongly recommended that all students have a PC.

Admissions Contact: Vic Davolt, Director of Admissions. A video is available. E-mail: *regisadm@regis.edu*

UNITED STATES AIR FORCE ACADEMY D-3
USAFA, CO 80840-5025 (719) 333-2520
(800) 443-9266; Fax: (719) 333-3012

Full-time: 3450 men, 700 women	**Faculty:** 577; IIB, +$
Part-time: none	**Ph.D.s:** 57%
Graduate: none	**Student/Faculty:** 8 to 1
Year: semesters, summer session	**Tuition:** see profile
Application Deadline: see profile	**Room & Board:** n/app
Freshman Class: n/av	
SAT or ACT: required	**HIGHLY COMPETITIVE+**

The United States Air Force Academy, the newest of the United States service academies, was founded in 1954 and is a public institution. Graduates receive the B.S. degree and a second lieutenant's commission in the regular Air Force. All graduates are obligated to serve at least 5 years of active duty miltary service. Tuition, room, board, medical, and dental expenses are paid by the U.S. government. Each cadet receives a monthly salary from which to pay for uniforms, supplies, and personal expenses. Entering freshmen are required to deposit $2,500 to defray the initial costs of uniforms and personal expenses incurred upon entry. Students who are unable to submit the full deposit will receive a reduced monthly cash allotment until prescribed levels are reached. Figures in the above capsule and in this profile are approximate. In addition to regional accreditation, USAFA has baccalaureate program accreditation with ABET and CSAB. The 3 libraries contain 688,801 volumes, 621,792 microform items, and 4860 audio/video tapes/CDs/DVDs, and subscribe to 2106 periodicals including electronic. Computerized library services include the card catalog, interlibrary loans, and database searching. Special learning facilities include a learning resource center, art gallery, planetarium, radio station, TV station, field engineering and readiness lab, and aeronautics lab/aeronautical research center. The 18,000-acre campus is in a suburban area 70 miles south of downtown Denver and 8 miles north of downtown Colorado Springs. Including any residence halls, there are 13 buildings.

Student Life: 95% of undergraduates are from out of state. Others are from 50 states and 26 foreign countries. 81% are white. 63% are Protestant; 30% Catholic; 12% claim no religious affiliation; 6% Buddhist, Muslim, and other. The average age of freshmen is 18; all undergraduates, 20. 18% do not continue beyond their first year; 71% remain to graduate.

Housing: 4400 students can be accommodated in college housing, which includes coed dorms. On-campus housing is guaranteed for all 4 years. All students live on campus. Alcohol is not permitted. Upperclassmen may keep cars.

Activities: There are no fraternities or sororities. There are 87 groups on campus, including band, chamber music, cheerleading, chess, choir, chorale, chorus, computers, drama, drill team, drum and bugle corps, ethnic, film, forensics, honors, literary magazine, marching band, musical theater, newspaper, pep band, photography, professional, radio and TV, religious, show choir, social, social service, student government, and yearbook. Popular campus events include Acceptance Parade, Christmas "Messiah" program, and Graduation Week.

Sports: There are 17 intercollegiate sports for men and 10 for women, and 13 intramural sports for men and 12 for women. Facilities include a 47,000-seat stadium, a cadet gym, a field house, 143 acres of athletic facilities and recreational areas, 3 basketball gyms, 4 indoor tennis courts, an Olympic-size swimming pool, a water polo pool, 3 squash and 19 racquetball/handball courts, and 2 weight training rooms.

Disabled Students: Wheelchair ramps, elevators, special parking, specially equipped rest rooms, and lowered drinking fountains are available.

Services: Counseling and information services are available, as is tutoring in every subject, including studying techniques and English as a second language. There is remedial math, reading, and writing.

Campus Safety and Security: Measures include 24-hour foot and vehicle patrol, self-defense education, security escort services, and informal discussions. There are pamphlets/posters/films, emergency telephones, and lighted pathways/sidewalks.

Programs of Study: USAFA confers the B.S. degree. Bachelor's degrees are awarded in BIOLOGICAL SCIENCE (biology/biological science), BUSINESS (management science and operations research), COMMUNICATIONS AND THE ARTS (English), COMPUTER AND PHYSICAL SCIENCE (atmospheric sciences and meteorology, chemistry, computer science, mathematics, physics, and science), ENGINEERING AND ENVIRONMENTAL DESIGN (aeronautical engineering, aerospace studies, civil engineering, computer engineering, electrical/electronics engineering, engineering, engineering and applied science, engineering mechanics, environmental engineering, mechanical engineering, and military science), SOCIAL SCIENCE (behavioral science, economics, geography, history, humanities, international studies, law, political science/government, psychology, and social science). Engineering and basic sciences are the strongest academically. Engineering, management, social sciences are the largest.

Required: Cadets must complete the requirements for the core curriculum and for an academic major. They must be proficient in phys ed and military training, and demonstrate an aptitude for commissioned service and leadership. A total of 145 to 161 semester hours is required, with a minimum GPA of 2.0, to graduate. The required curriculum includes 9 hours of military arts and sciences, 6 hours of phys ed, and 1 hour of aviation.

Special: All cadets receive orientation flights in Air Force aircraft and take aviation science courses. A semester exchange program is available with the French Air Force Academy and U.S. Army, Naval, and Coast Guard academies. Freshman classes start in June, and basic cadet training must be completed before academics begin in August. Work-study programs are available, and dual majors are possible in all areas. There is an interdisciplinary space operations major. There are 2 national honor societies.

Faculty/Classroom: 85% of faculty are male; 15%, female. All teach undergraduates and 10% do research. The average class size in an introductory lecture is 17; in a laboratory, 17; and in a regular course, 17.

Admissions: 15% of recent applicants were accepted. The SAT scores for a recent freshman class were: Verbal--2% below 500, 32% between 500 and 599, 51% between 600 and 700, and 15% above 700; Math--1% below 500, 20% between 500 and 599, 54% between 600 and 700, and 25% above 700. 80% of recent freshmen were in the top fifth of their class; 85% were in the top two fifths.

Requirements: The SAT or ACT is required. In addition, candidates must be U.S. citizens between 17 and 22 years of age, unmarried and with no dependents, and nominated from a legal source. Students should have completed 4 years each of English, math, and lab sciences, and 2 years each of social sciences and foreign languages. A computer course is recommended. A personal interview is required, as is an essay and a drug and alcohol abuse certificate. A GPA of 2.0 is required. AP credits are accepted. Important factors in the admissions decision are advanced placement or honor courses, leadership record, and personality/intangible qualities.

Procedure: Freshmen are admitted in the summer. Entrance exams should be taken in the spring of the junior year. Check with the school for current application deadlines.

Transfer: All students must enter as freshmen and attend 4 years. All 145 credits required for the bachelor's degree must be completed at USAFA.

Visiting: There are regularly scheduled orientations for prospective students, consisting of a 2-day orientation held in March and April. Students are given briefings by the superintendent, the commandant of cadets, the dean of cadets, and the director of athletics. Students stay overnight in the dormitories and shadow their escort cadets the second day, attending classes, training, and meals. There is also a daily tour. There are guides for informal visits. To schedule a visit, contact the Director of Admissions.

International Students: There were 48 international students enrolled in a recent year. They must take the SAT or the ACT.

Computers: All students may access the system 24 hours per day. There are no time limits and no fees. All students are required to have personal computers.

Graduates: In an average class, 71% graduate in 4 years or less, and 77% graduate in 5 years or less. Of a recent graduating class, 3% were enrolled in graduate school within 6 months of graduation and 100% were employed.

Admissions Contact: Rolland Stoneman, Associate Director, Admissions/Selections. Web: *www.usafa.edu/rr/*

UNIVERSITY OF COLORADO SYSTEM

The University of Colorado System, established in 1876, is a private system in Colorado. It is governed by a board of regents, whose chief administrator is president. The primary goal of the system is comprehensive research. The main priorities are research, teaching, and public service. The total enrollment of all 4 campuses is usually about 42,000; with 4500 faculty members. Profiles of the 4-year campuses are included in this section.

UNIVERSITY OF COLORADO AT BOULDER   C-2

Boulder, CO 80309-0552   (303) 492-6301; Fax: (303) 492-7115

Full-time: 12,326 men, 11,120 women	Faculty: 1182; I, -$
Part-time: 982 men, 777 women	Ph.D.s: 91%
Graduate: 3029 men, 1897 women	Student/Faculty: 20 to 1
Year: semesters, summer session	Tuition: $5372 ($23,826)
Application Deadline: January 15	Room & Board: $7980
Freshman Class: 17,111 applied, 15,003 accepted, 5047 enrolled	
SAT Verbal/Math: 570/600*	ACT: 25 COMPETITIVE+

The University of Colorado at Boulder, established in 1876, is a public institution offering undergraduate and graduate programs in arts and sciences, business, engineering, architecture and planning, music, education, and journalism. There are 7 undergraduate and 3 graduate schools. In addition to regional accreditation, CU-Boulder has baccalaureate program accreditation with AACSB, ABET, ACEJMC, NASM, and NCATE. The 8 libraries contain 3,484,982 volumes, 6,756,506 microform items, and 444,169 audio/video tapes/CDs/DVDs, and subscribe to 20,677 periodicals including electronic. Computerized library services include the card catalog, interlibrary loans, database searching, Internet access, and laptop Internet portals. Special learning facilities include a learning resource center, art gallery, natural history museum, planetarium, radio station, TV station, and an interactive foreign language video center, a mountain research station, an integrated teaching and learning lab in engineering, and multi-disciplinary IT center in its own building in the center of campus. The 600-acre campus is in a suburban area 30 miles northwest of Denver. Including any residence halls, there are more than 200 buildings.

Student Life: 67% of undergraduates are from Colorado. Others are from 50 states, 100 foreign countries, and Canada. 79% are white. The average age of freshmen is 19; all undergraduates, 21. 17% do not continue beyond their first year; 83% remain to graduate.

Housing: 5744 students can be accommodated in college housing, which includes coed dorms, on-campus apartments, off-campus apartments, married-student housing, fraternity houses, and sorority houses. In addition, there are honors houses, special-interest houses, and 8 residential academic programs that include housing. On-campus housing is guaranteed for the freshman year only and is available on a first-come, first-served basis. 77% of students commute. All students may keep cars.

Activities: 7% of men belong to 1 local and 16 national fraternities; 8% of women belong to 3 local and 13 national sororities. There are approximately 300 groups on campus, including art, band, cheerleading, chess, choir, chorale, chorus, computers, dance, drama, drill team, environmental, ethnic, film, gay, honors, international, jazz band, literary magazine, marching band, musical theater, newspaper, opera, orchestra, pep band, photography, political, professional, radio and TV, religious, social, social service, special interest, student government, symphony, and yearbook. Popular campus events include World Affairs Conference, International Women's Week, and Trivia Bowl.

Sports: There are 7 intercollegiate sports for men and 8 for women, and 13 intramural sports for men and 13 for women. Facilities include a 52,000-seat stadium and an 8700-seat events center, a recreation center that includes an 8-lane swimming pool, diving pool, ice rink, handball and racquetball courts, basketball and squash courts, outdoor tennis courts, weight-training rooms, an indoor running track, and an indoor climbing wall.

Disabled Students: 77% of the campus is accessible. Wheelchair ramps, elevators, special parking, specially equipped rest rooms, special class scheduling, lowered drinking fountains, lowered telephones, and assisted classroom listening devices, and TTY, TDD, and TT phone support systems are available.

Services: Counseling and information services are available, as is tutoring in most subjects, including a learning disabilities program, and an interpreter for the deaf (curricular and non-curricular). There is a reader service for the blind and remedial writing. There is also a Multicultural Center for Counseling and Community Development, which includes counselors for individuals and groups.

Campus Safety and Security: Measures include 24-hour foot and vehicle patrol, self-defense education, security escort services, and shuttle buses. There are informal discussions, pamphlets/posters/films, emergency telephones, and lighted pathways/sidewalks. Campus police are academy-trained and commissioned officers of the Boulder police force.

Programs of Study: CU-Boulder confers B.A., B.S., B.Env.D., B.F.A., B.Mus., and B.Mus.Ed. degrees. Master's and doctoral degrees are also awarded. Bachelor's degrees are awarded in BIOLOGICAL SCIENCE (biochemistry, cell biology, environmental biology, and molecular biology), BUSINESS (accounting, banking and finance, business administration and management, international business management, management science, marketing management, small business management, and tourism), COMMUNICATIONS AND THE ARTS (advertising, art history and appreciation, broadcasting, Chinese, classics, communications, dance, dramatic arts, English, film arts, fine arts, French, Germanic languages and literature, Italian, Japanese, journalism, linguistics, music, Spanish, and telecommunications), COMPUTER AND PHYSICAL SCIENCE (applied mathematics, astronomy, chemistry, computer science, geology, information sciences and systems, mathematics, and physics), EDUCATION (music), ENGINEERING AND ENVIRONMENTAL DESIGN (aeronautical engineering, architectural engineering, chemical engineering, civil engineering, computer engineering, electrical/electronics engineering, engineering, engineering physics, environmental design, environmental engineering, environmental science, and mechanical engineering), HEALTH PROFESSIONS (exercise science and speech pathology/audiology), SOCIAL SCIENCE (anthropology, Asian/Oriental studies, economics, ethnic studies, geography, German area studies, history, humanities, international relations, philosophy, political science/government, psychology, religion, Russian and Slavic studies, sociology, and women's studies). Physics, pyschology, and geography are the strongest academically. Psychology, integrative physiology, and English are the largest.

Required: For graduation, students must complete at least 120 credits, including a minimum of 30 in the major. A GPA of at least 2.0 is required. Other requirements vary by undergraduate college and program.

Special: Sewall, Farrand, and other residential programs for freshmen and sophomores offer a small liberal arts college atmosphere while taking advantage of the resources of a major university. A residential program in Baker Hall Village offers courses in the environmental sciences. Student-designed and dual majors, internships, 5-year B.A.- M.A. degrees, and cooperative programs in business and engineering are available. Study abroad in more than 60 countries, work-study programs in federal labs, internships, a 3-2 engineering degree, and cross registration with other University of Colorado campuses are offered. There are 15 national honor societies, including Phi Beta Kappa, a freshman honors program, and 47 departmental honors programs.

Faculty/Classroom: 61% of faculty are male; 39%, female. 100% both teach and do research. Graduate students teach 19% of introductory courses. The average class size in an introductory lecture is 45; in a laboratory, 19; and in a regular course, 26.

Admissions: 88% of the 2005-2006 applicants were accepted. The SAT scores for the 2005-2006 freshman class were: Verbal--14% below 500, 46% between 500 and 599, 35% between 600 and 700, and 5% above 700; Math--10% below 500, 39% between 500 and 599, 44% between 600 and 700, and 7% above 700. The ACT scores were 9% below 21, 24% between 21 and 23, 33% between 24 and 26, 17% between 27 and 28, and 17% above 28. 44% of the current freshmen were in the top fifth of their class; 78% were in the top two fifths. There were 7 National Merit finalists. 150 freshmen graduated first in their class.

Requirements: The SAT or ACT is required. In addition, applicants must have completed 16 credits of high school work as identified by the University of Colorado minimum Academic Preparation Standards. Students are asked to write a personal statement. Interviews are not used in the decision-making process. Auditions are required for consideration to the College of Music. Portfolios are discouraged. Students with a GED are considered on an individual basis. A GPA of 2.0 is required. AP and CLEP credits are accepted. Important factors in the admissions decision are advanced placement or honor courses, geographic diversity, and leadership record.

Procedure: Freshmen are admitted to all sessions. Entrance exams should be taken no later than December of the senior year. There are deferred admissions and rolling admissionsplans. Applications should be filed by January 15 for fall entry, October 1 for spring entry, and January 15 for summer entry, along with a $50 fee. Notification of regular decision is sent November 1. 59 applicants were on the 2005 waiting list; 3 were admitted. Applications are accepted on-line.

Transfer: 1219 transfer students enrolled in 2004-2005. All applicants must submit official high school and college transcripts. Students who have completed fewer than 30 semester hours must also submit SAT or ACT results. 30 of 120 credits required for the bachelor's degree must be completed at CU-Boulder.

Visiting: There are regularly scheduled orientations for prospective students, including advising, placement testing, registration, social and campus orientation, and meetings with college deans and faculty. Parents are invited. There are guides for informal visits and visitors may sit in on classes. To schedule a visit, contact the Admissions/Campus Visit Programs at *http://www.colorado.edu/visit.*

Financial Aid: In 2005-2006, 81% of all full-time freshmen and 69% of continuing full-time students received some form of financial aid. 46% of full-time freshmen and 34% of continuing full-time students received need-based aid. Need-based scholarships or need-based grants averaged $3635 ($28,095 maximum); need-based self-help aid (loans and

jobs) averaged $4030 ($32,153 maximum); non-need-based athletic scholarships averaged $14,220 ($26,502 maximum); and other non-need-based awards and non-need-based scholarships averaged $2793 ($36,307 maximum). 24% of undergraduates work part time. Average annual earnings from campus work are $1806. The average financial indebtedness of the 2005 graduate was $17,225. The FAFSA and tax returns are required. The deadline for filing freshman financial aid applications for fall entry is March 1.

International Students: There are 330 international students enrolled. Satisfactory scores are required on the written TOEFL and the MELAB. Other tests or verification of proficiency will be considered on an individual basis.

Computers: Wireless access is available. There are PC labs and kiosks throughout campus. Labs have either PC or Macintosh computers and a variety of other hardware and software and high-speed access to the Internet for Web surfing and e-mail. Kiosks are meant to be a place quick e-mail checks and Web surfing. All students may access the system 24 hours a day. There are no time limits and no fees. It is strongly recommended that all students have a personal computer.

Graduates: From July 1, 2004 to June 30, 2005, 5124 bachelor's degrees were awarded. The most popular majors were psychology (8%), finance (5%), and communication (5%). In an average class, 38% graduate in 4 years or less, 61% graduate in 5 years or less, and 66% graduate in 6 years or less. 400 companies recruited on campus in 2004-2005.

Admissions Contact: Kevin MacLennan, Interim Director of Admissions. Web: *www.colorado.edu/admissions/apply.html*

UNIVERSITY OF COLORADO AT COLORADO SPRINGS
D-3

Colorado Springs, CO 80918   (719) 262-3383; (800) 990-8227

Full-time: 1841 men, 2965 women	**Faculty:** n/av
Part-time: 537 men, 776 women	**Ph.D.s:** 64%
Graduate: 592 men, 856 women	**Student/Faculty:** n/av
Year: semesters, summer session	**Tuition:** $4732 ($16,202)
Application Deadline: July 1	**Room & Board:** $6785
Freshman Class: 2915 applied, 1953 accepted, 911 enrolled	
SAT Verbal/Math: 531/540*	**ACT:** 23 **VERY COMPETITIVE**

The University of Colorado at Colorado Springs, established in 1965, is a public institution, with programs in liberal arts, business, engineering, education, and nursing. There are 4 undergraduate and 5 graduate schools. In addition to regional accreditation, UCCS has baccalaureate program accreditation with AACSB, ABET, CSAB, NCATE, and NLN. The library contains 669,757 volumes, 432,872 microform items, and 5979 audio/video tapes/CDs/DVDs, and subscribes to 2247 periodicals including electronic. Computerized library services include the card catalog, interlibrary loans, database searching, and Internet access. Special learning facilities include a learning resource center, art gallery, and a center for excellence in oral communication, a math learning center, a science learning center, a writing center, and a language technology center. The 504-acre campus is in an urban area 70 miles south of Denver. Including any residence halls, there are 24 buildings.

Student Life: 92% of undergraduates are from Colorado. Others are from 48 states, 35 foreign countries, and Canada. 76% are white. The average age of freshmen is 18; all undergraduates, 28. 35% do not continue beyond their first year; 40% remain to graduate.

Housing: 900 students can be accommodated in college housing, which includes single-sex and coed dormitories and on-campus apartments. On-campus housing is available on a first-come, first-served basis. 88% of students commute. All students may keep cars.

Activities: 1% of men and about 1% of women belong to 1 national fraternity 1% of women belong to 1 local sorority. There are 50 groups on campus, including art, choir, computers, dance, drama, ethnic, film, gay, honors, international, literary magazine, newspaper, photography, political, professional, radio and TV, religious, social, and student government. Popular campus events include Winter Holiday Festival and Comedy Night.

Sports: There are 5 intercollegiate sports for men and 5 for women, and 13 intramural sports for men and 12 for women. Facilities include a gym, softball and soccer fields, a multipurpose field, tennis and volleyball courts, and a fitness center.

Disabled Students: 95% of the campus is accessible. Wheelchair ramps, elevators, special parking, specially equipped rest rooms, lowered drinking fountains, and lowered telephones are available.

Services: Counseling and information services are available, as is tutoring in most subjects. There is a reader service for the blind.

Campus Safety and Security: Measures include 24-hour foot and vehicle patrol, self-defense education, security escort services, and shuttle buses. There are informal discussions, pamphlets/posters/films, emergency telephones, and lighted pathways/sidewalks.

Programs of Study: UCCS confers B.A. and B.S. degrees. Master's and doctoral degrees are also awarded. Bachelor's degrees are awarded in BIOLOGICAL SCIENCE (biology/biological science), BUSINESS

(business administration and management), COMMUNICATIONS AND THE ARTS (communications, English, fine arts, and Spanish), COMPUTER AND PHYSICAL SCIENCE (chemistry, computer science, mathematics, and physics), ENGINEERING AND ENVIRONMENTAL DESIGN (electrical/electronics engineering), HEALTH PROFESSIONS (health care administration and nursing), SOCIAL SCIENCE (anthropology, economics, geography, history, philosophy, political science/government, psychology, and sociology). Business, engineering, and psychology are the strongest academically.

Required: To graduate, students must complete 124 credit hours, with at least 30 of them in the major, with a minimum GPA of 2.0. All students must take English and a computer literacy course. Other requirements vary with the program.

Special: The university offers work-study, dual majors, nondegree study, and pass/fail options. There are 3 national honor societies, including Phi Beta Kappa.

Faculty/Classroom: 51% of faculty are male; 49%, female. 93% teach undergraduates, 80% do research, and 80% do both. Graduate students teach 1% of introductory courses. The average class size in an introductory lecture is 32; in a laboratory, 45; and in a regular course, 22.

Admissions: 67% of the 2005-2006 applicants were accepted. The SAT scores for the 2005-2006 freshman class were: Verbal--29% below 500, 47% between 500 and 599, 19% between 600 and 700, and 5% above 700; Math--28% below 500, 41% between 500 and 599, 29% between 600 and 700, and 2% above 700. The ACT scores were 24% below 21, 21% between 21 and 23, 38% between 24 and 26, 9% between 27 and 28, and 8% above 28. 34% of the current freshmen were in the top fifth of their class; 65% were in the top two fifths.

Requirements: The SAT or ACT is required. Applicants must be graduates of an accredited secondary school. The GED is accepted. Secondary school courses must include 15 high school credits, including 4 years of English, 3 years each of math and science, 2 years each of foreign language and social studies, and 1 academic elective. AP and CLEP credits are accepted. Important factors in the admissions decision are advanced placement or honor courses, evidence of special talent, and recommendations by school officials.

Procedure: Freshmen are admitted to all sessions. Entrance exams should be taken during the senior year. There are deferred admissions and rolling admissions plans. Early decision applications should be filed by April 1; regular applications, by July 1 for fall entry, December 1 for spring entry, and May 1 for summer entry, along with a $50 fee. Notification is sent on a rolling basis. Applications are accepted on-line.

Transfer: 723 transfer students enrolled in 2004-2005. Applicants must have a minimum GPA of 2.5 and a minimum of 12 credit hours earned. 30 of 124 credits required for the bachelor's degree must be completed at UCCS.

Visiting: There are regularly scheduled orientations for prospective students. There are guides for informal visits and visitors may sit in on classes. To schedule a visit, contact the Marketing Office at (719) 262-3084.

Financial Aid: In 2005-2006, 67% of all full-time freshmen and 63% of continuing full-time students received some form of financial aid. 49% of full-time freshmen and 55% of continuing full-time students received need-based aid. The average freshman award was $5621. Need-based scholarships or need-based grants averaged $3926 ($15,618 maximum); need-based self-help aid (loans and jobs) averaged $2859 ($8934 maximum); non-need-based athletic scholarships averaged $1810 ($6500 maximum); and other non-need-based awards and non-need-based scholarships averaged $3053 ($29,632 maximum). 10% of undergraduates work part time. Average annual earnings from campus work are $3440. The average financial indebtedness of the 2005 graduate was $11,347. The FAFSA is required. The deadline for filing freshman financial aid applications for fall entry is April 1.

International Students: There are 55 international students enrolled. They must score satisfactorily on the written TOEFL and also take the SAT or the ACT.

Computers: All students may access the system 8 A.M. to 10 P.M. daily. There are no time limits and no fees. It is strongly recommended that all students have a personal computer.

Graduates: From July 1, 2004 to June 30, 2005, 1579 bachelor's degrees were awarded. The most popular majors were business (17%), psychology (14%), and communications (13%). In an average class, 12% graduate in 4 years or less, 20% graduate in 5 years or less, and 29% graduate in 6 years or less. 120 companies recruited on campus in a recent year.

Admissions Contact: Admissions Office. E-mail: admrec@uccs.edu Web: www.uccs.edu

UNIVERSITY OF COLORADO AT DENVER AND HEALTH SCIENCES CENTER (Formerly University of Colorado at Denver) — C-2

Denver, CO 80217-3364	**(303) 556-3287; Fax: (303) 556-4838**
Full-time: 2390 men, 2762 women	**Faculty:** 443; IIA, av$
Part-time: 2050 men, 2719 women	**Ph.D.s:** 87%
Graduate: 2677 men, 4012 women	**Student/Faculty:** 12 to 1
Year: semesters, summer session	**Tuition:** $5021 ($16,191)
Application Deadline: July 22	**Room & Board:** n/app
Freshman Class: 2291 applied, 1639 accepted, 729 enrolled	
SAT Verbal/Math: 539/540*	**ACT:** 22 COMPETITIVE

The University of Colorado at Denver and Health Sciences Center, formerly known as the University of Colorado at Denver and established in 1912, is a public 2 campus system. The downtown Denver campus is a commuter institution with programs in the liberal arts and sciences, business, engineering and applied sciences, music, architecture and planning, and education. The health and sciences center is a commuter institution with programs in medicine, nursing, pharmacy, and dentistry. There are 4 undergraduate and 7 graduate schools. In addition to regional accreditation, UCDHSC has baccalaureate program accreditation with AACSB, ABET, ACS, CACREP, NAAB, NASM, and NCATE. The library contains 705,088 volumes, 1,768,209 microform items, and 10,598 audio/video tapes/CDs/DVDs, and subscribes to 3544 periodicals including electronic. Computerized library services include the card catalog, interlibrary loans, database searching, Internet access, and laptop Internet portals. Special learning facilities include a learning resource center, art gallery, and a writing center. The campus is in an urban area in downtown Denver.

Student Life: 94% of undergraduates are from Colorado. Others are from 49 states, 52 foreign countries, and Canada. 90% are from public schools. 61% are white. The average age of freshmen is 20; all undergraduates, 24. 28% do not continue beyond their first year; 39% remain to graduate.

Housing: There are no residence halls. All of students commute. Alcohol is not permitted. All students may keep cars.

Activities: There are no fraternities or sororities. There are 60 groups on campus, including art, chorale, computers, dance, drama, ethnic, gay, honors, international, jazz band, musical theater, newspaper, political, professional, radio and TV, religious, social, social service, and student government. Popular campus events include Fall Festival.

Sports: Facilities include a phys ed building with a pool including a diving well, a weight room, squash, racquetball/handball, and tennis courts and a basketball half-court, a dance studio, 3 gym arenas, a fitness center and a green room, a 400-meter track, a football/rugby/lacrosse field, softball fields, a baseball field, a soccer field, and a sand volleyball court.

Disabled Students: All of the campus is accessible. Wheelchair ramps, elevators, special parking, specially equipped rest rooms, special class scheduling, lowered drinking fountains, lowered telephones, a transit system, and an adaptive computer lab are available.

Services: Counseling and information services are available, as is tutoring in most subjects. There is a reader service for the blind. There are ESL classes and study skills courses.

Campus Safety and Security: Measures include 24-hour foot and vehicle patrol, self-defense education, security escort services, and shuttle buses. There are informal discussions, pamphlets/posters/films, emergency telephones, lighted pathways/sidewalks, crime prevention programs, and emergency response.

Programs of Study: UCDHSC confers B.A., B.S., and B.F.A degrees. Master's and doctoral degrees are also awarded. Bachelor's degrees are awarded in BIOLOGICAL SCIENCE (biology/biological science), BUSINESS (business administration and management), COMMUNICATIONS AND THE ARTS (communications, creative writing, dramatic arts, English, fine arts, French, music, and Spanish), COMPUTER AND PHYSICAL SCIENCE (chemistry, computer science, mathematics, and physics), ENGINEERING AND ENVIRONMENTAL DESIGN (civil engineering, electrical/electronics engineering, and mechanical engineering), SOCIAL SCIENCE (anthropology, economics, geography, history, interdisciplinary studies, international studies, philosophy, political science/government, psychology, and sociology). Business, engineering, and psychology are the strongest academically. Business administration, biology, and psychology are the largest.

Required: To graduate, students must complete 120 credit hours with a minimum GPA of 2.0. All students must complete the core curriculum courses in addition to the requirements for the major.

Special: Cross-registration is possible with Metropolitan State College, Community College of Denver, and Red Rocks Commmunity College. Concurrent enrollment with any University of Colorado campus is possible. Cooperative programs, 1-semester internships, study abroad in 12 countries, work-study programs, an accelerated degree program in Liberal Arts and Arts and Media, and B.A.-B.S. degrees are available. The university offers dual majors, a general studies degree, nondegree study, and pass/fail options. There are small individualized classes, peer advocates, and workshops. There are 8 national honor societies.

Faculty/Classroom: 59% of faculty are male; 41%, female. The average class size in an introductory lecture is 24; in a laboratory, 16; and in a regular course, 24.

Admissions: 72% of the 2005-2006 applicants were accepted. The SAT scores for the 2005-2006 freshman class were: Verbal--34% below 500, 42% between 500 and 599, 20% between 600 and 700, and 4% above 700; Math--37% below 500, 42% between 500 and 599, 16% between 600 and 700, and 5% above 700. 17% of the current freshmen were in the top fifth of their class; 43% were in the top two fifths.

Requirements: The SAT or ACT is required. Preference for admission is given to applicants who rank in the top 30% of their high school graduating class and present a composite score of 21 or higher on the ACT or a satisfactory score on the SAT. UCDHSC requires applicants to be in the upper 30% of their class. A GPA of 2.5 is required. AP and CLEP credits are accepted. Important factors in the admissions decision are advanced placement or honor courses, evidence of special talent, and extracurricular activities record.

Procedure: Freshmen are admitted fall, spring, and summer. Entrance exams should be taken in the junior or senior year of high school. There is a deferred admissions plan and a rolling admissions. Applications should be filed by July 22 for fall entry, December 1 for spring entry, and May 3 for summer entry, along with a $50 fee. Notification is sent on a rolling basis. Applications are accepted on-line.

Transfer: 1039 transfer students enrolled in 2004-2005. Applicants for transfer must have earned at least 12 credit hours for admission to liberal arts and sciences and music programs, and 24 credit hours for admission to business and engineering. A minimum GPA of 2.4 is required, or 2.0 if transferring from Colorado School of Mines, Colorado State University, or the University of Colorado at Boulder and Colorado Springs. 30 of 120 credits required for the bachelor's degree must be completed at UCDHSC.

Visiting: There are regularly scheduled orientations for prospective students, including a mini-lecture, a tour of campus, and financial aid and academic advising. There are guides for informal visits and visitors may sit in on classes. To schedule a visit, contact the Office of Admissions at (303) 556-2704.

Financial Aid: In 2005-2006, 42% of all full-time freshmen and 45% of continuing full-time students received some form of financial aid. 35% of full-time freshmen and 31% of continuing full-time students received need-based aid. The average freshman award was $5362. Need-based scholarships or need-based grants averaged $4296; need-based self-help aid (loans and jobs) averaged $2751; and other non-need-based awards and non-need-based scholarships averaged $1733. The average financial indebtedness of the 2005 graduate was $16,933. The FAFSA, the college's own financial statement and tax returns are required. The priority date for freshman financial aid applications for fall entry is April 1.

International Students: There are 585 international students enrolled. The school actively recruits these students. They must score satisfactorily on the written TOEFL or on the electronic version. The SAT or ACT is required for undergraduate engineering students only.

Computers: Wireless access is available. All students may access the system any time. There are no time limits and no fees.

Graduates: From July 1, 2004 to June 30, 2005, 1352 bachelor's degrees were awarded. The most popular majors were business administration (27%), communications (9%), and economics (7%). In an average class, 15% graduate in 4 years or less, 15% graduate in 5 years or less, and 9% graduate in 6 years or less. 256 companies recruited on campus in 2004-2005.

Admissions Contact: Barbara Edwards, Director of Admissions.
E-mail: *admissions@cudenver.edu*
Web: *www.cudenver.edu/Admissions/default.htm*

UNIVERSITY OF DENVER   C-2
Denver, CO 80208

	(303) 871-2036
	(800) 525-9495; Fax: (303) 871-3301

Full-time: 2119 men, 2364 women	**Faculty:** 346; I, -$
Part-time: 69 men, 59 women	**Ph.D.s:** 93%
Graduate: 2718 men, 3337 women	**Student/Faculty:** 13 to 1
Year: quarters, summer session	**Tuition:** $28,410
Application Deadline: January 15	**Room & Board:** $7965
Freshman Class: n/av	
SAT Verbal/Math: 580/585*	**ACT:** 26 **VERY COMPETITIVE+**

The University of Denver, established in 1864, is a private institution offering degrees in arts and sciences, fine arts, music, business, engineering, and education. There are 7 undergraduate and 6 graduate schools. In addition to regional accreditation, DU has baccalaureate program accreditation with AACSB, ABET, ACS, CSWE, NASAD, and NASM. The 3 libraries contain 2.7 million volumes, 1 million microform items, and 1736 audio/video tapes/CDs/DVDs, and subscribe to 6000 periodicals including electronic. Computerized library services include the card catalog, interlibrary loans, and database searching. Special learning facilities include a learning resource center, art gallery, radio station, a high-altitude research field station, an observatory, and elementary, middle, and high schools. The 125-acre campus is in an urban area 8 miles south of downtown Denver in a residential neighborhood. Including any residence halls, there are 104 buildings.

Student Life: 56% of undergraduates are from out of state, mostly the West. Students are from 50 states, 94 foreign countries, and Canada. 77% are white. The average age of freshmen is 18; all undergraduates, 20. 13% do not continue beyond their first year.

Housing: 2100 students can be accommodated in college housing, which includes single-sex and coed dormitories, on-campus apartments, married-student housing, fraternity houses, and sorority houses. Housing is guaranteed for freshman and sophomore years. 57% of students commute. All students may keep cars.

Activities: 13% of men belong to 7 national fraternities; 12% of women belong to 5 national sororities. There are 120 groups on campus, including art, band, cheerleading, chess, choir, chorale, chorus, computers, dance, drama, ethnic, film, gay, honors, international, jazz band, literary magazine, musical theater, newspaper, opera, orchestra, pep band, photography, political, professional, radio and TV, religious, social, social service, student government, symphony, and yearbook. Popular campus events include Winter Carnival, May Days and Festival of Nations Celebration.

Sports: There are 9 intercollegiate sports for men and 10 for women, and 33 intramural sports for men and 32 for women. Facilities include a sports and wellness center housing 2 ice arenas, a gym, a multipurpose field house, an Olympic-size swimming pool, a fitness center, racquetball courts, studios for yoga, dance, and karate, a 25-foot climbing wall, a health clinic, a soccer field, a lacrosse stadium, and a tennis pavilion.

Disabled Students: Wheelchair ramps, elevators, special parking, specially equipped rest rooms, special class scheduling, lowered drinking fountains, and lowered telephones are available.

Services: Counseling and information services are available, as is tutoring in most subjects. There is a reader service for the blind and remedial math and writing.

Campus Safety and Security: Measures include 24-hour foot and vehicle patrol, security escort services, shuttle buses, and informal discussions. There are pamphlets/posters/films, emergency telephones, lighted pathways/sidewalks, and a bicycle patrol.

Programs of Study: DU confers B.A., B.S., B.F.A., B.M., B.S.Acc., B.S.A.T., B.S.B.A., B.S.Ch., B.S.Comp.E., B.S.E., B.S.E.E., and B.S.M.E. degrees. Master's and doctoral degrees are also awarded. Bachelor's degrees are awarded in AGRICULTURE (animal science), BIOLOGICAL SCIENCE (biochemistry and biology/biological science), BUSINESS (accounting, banking and finance, business administration and management, business economics, hospitality management services, international business management, marketing/retailing/merchandising, and real estate), COMMUNICATIONS AND THE ARTS (art, art history and appreciation, communications, dramatic arts, English, French, German, Italian, jazz, journalism, languages, music, music performance, and Spanish), COMPUTER AND PHYSICAL SCIENCE (astronomy, chemistry, computer science, digital arts/technology, information sciences and systems, mathematics, physics, science, and statistics), ENGINEERING AND ENVIRONMENTAL DESIGN (computer engineering, construction management, electrical/electronics engineering, environmental science, and mechanical engineering), SOCIAL SCIENCE (anthropology, Asian/Oriental studies, cognitive science, economics, geography, history, international studies, philosophy, political science/government, psychology, public affairs, religion, Russian and Slavic studies, social science, sociology, and women's studies).

Required: For graduation, students must complete 183 to 204 quarter hours, including 42 to 135 in the major, with a minimum GPA of 2.0. All students must take 12 quarter hours each of English, natural sciences, arts and humanities, and social sciences, 8 of math and computer science, and 4 of oral communication. The language proficiency requirement applies to all students in programs leading to the B.A., B.S., and B.S.Ch. degrees.

Special: DU offers co-op programs, study abroad in more than 45 countries, internships, a Washington quarter, work-study programs, accelerated degree programs, and dual majors. Nondegree study and pass/fail options are also available. There are 13 national honor societies, including Phi Beta Kappa, a freshman honors program, and 13 departmental honors programs.

Faculty/Classroom: 61% of faculty are male; 39%, female. Graduate students teach 5% of introductory courses. The average class size in an introductory lecture is 40; in a laboratory, 16; and in a regular course, 20.

Admissions: 61% of the current freshmen were in the top fifth of their class; 84% were in the top two fifths.

Requirements: The SAT or ACT is required. In addition, applicants must be graduates of an accredited secondary school. The GED is accepted. DU recommends that applicants have 15 to 20 high school academic credits, including 4 in English, 3 to 4 in math, and 2 to 4 each in foreign language, social science, and natural sciences (2 with lab).

Course work in the arts is encouraged. An essay is required of all students. A Hyde interview is required of all applicants. An audition is required for music applicants. Admission to the B.F.A. program is by portfolio review. AP and CLEP credits are accepted. Important factors in the admissions decision are advanced placement or honor courses, personality/intangible qualities, and evidence of special talent.

Procedure: Freshmen are admitted to all sessions. Entrance exams should be taken by January of the senior year. There are early decision, early admissions, and deferred admissions plans. There is a rolling admissions plan. Early action applications should be filed by November 1; regular applications, by January 15 for fall entry, December 1 for winter entry, February 15 for spring entry, and May 1 for summer entry. Notification of early action is sent January 15; regular decision, March 15. 1157 early action candidates were accepted for the 2005-2006 class. A waiting list is an active part of the admissions procedure. Applications are accepted on-line.

Transfer: Applicants must submit a transcript from all colleges attended. Those students with fewer than 30 semester hours of college credit must submit a high school record as well. A minimum GPA of 2.0 is required, but a GPA of 3.0 is recommended. Transfer applicants are required to complete the Hyde Interview. 45 of 183 credits required for the bachelor's degree must be completed at DU.

Visiting: There are regularly scheduled orientations for prospective students, including an information session and campus tour. As part of the visit, additional options may include visiting with a professor, having lunch with a student, or other activities that are part of the overall university experience. Additional visit programs, held on selected dates throughout the year, offer an opportunity to further explore the DU campus. Visitors may sit in on classes and stay overnight. To schedule a visit, contact the Office of Undergraduate Admission Appointment Desk.

Financial Aid: 26% of undergraduates work part time. Average annual earnings from campus work are $1400. The FAFSA is required. The deadline for filing freshman financial aid applications for fall entry is March 1.

International Students: There are 179 international students enrolled. The school actively recruits these students. They must take the TOEFL, the IELTS, Intensive English Language Program, and also take the SAT or the ACT.

Computers: Logging into the system requires DU ID and passcode using IVPN software, which is provided free to members of the university community. All students may access the system 24 hours a day. There are no time limits and no fees. All students are required to have personal computers. Minimum specifications are required such as operating system, software, and virus and antispyware protection. Laptop PCs are required. (no specific make or model).

Graduates: In an average class, 2% graduate in 3 years or less, 56% graduate in 4 years or less, 68% graduate in 5 years or less, and 71% graduate in 6 years or less.

Admissions Contact: The Office of Undergraduate Admission. E-mail: admission@du.edu Web: www.du.edu

UNIVERSITY OF NORTHERN COLORADO D-1

Greeley, CO 80639 (970) 351-2881
(888) 700-4UNC; Fax: (970) 351-2984

Full-time: 3817 men, 5868 women	Faculty: 439; I, --$
Part-time: 424 men, 702 women	Ph.D.s: 77%
Graduate: 634 men, 1711 women	Student/Faculty: 22 to 1
Year: semesters, summer session	Tuition: $3837 ($12,381)
Application Deadline: August 1	Room & Board: $6412
Freshman Class: 7318 applied, 6025 accepted, 2494 enrolled	
SAT Verbal/Math: 530/520*	ACT: 22 COMPETITIVE

The University of Northern Colorado, founded in 1890, is a state-supported public institution offering undergraduate and graduate programs in liberal arts and sciences, business, education, health and human sciences, and performing and visual arts. Enrollment figures in the above capsule are for fall 2004. There are 5 undergraduate schools and 1 graduate school. In addition to regional accreditation, UNC has baccalaureate program accreditation with AACSB, ADA, NASM, NCATE, and NLN. The 2 libraries contain 1,035,973 volumes, 2,047,315 microform items, and 31,695 audio/video tapes/CDs/DVDs, and subscribe to 2713 periodicals including electronic. Computerized library services include the card catalog, interlibrary loans, database searching, Internet access, and laptop Internet portals. Special learning facilities include a learning resource center, art gallery, radio station, and more than 30 partner schools. The 240-acre campus is in a suburban area 50 miles north of Denver. Including any residence halls, there are 61 buildings.

Student Life: 90% of undergraduates are from Colorado. Others are from 46 states, 50 foreign countries, and Canada. 92% are from public schools. 80% are white. The average age of freshmen is 18; all undergraduates, 21. 28% do not continue beyond their first year; 45% remain to graduate.

Housing: 3101 students can be accommodated in college housing, which includes single-sex and coed dorms, on-campus apartments, mar-

ried-student housing, and sorority houses. There are also off-campus houses, graduate women's houses, and special-interest floors. On-campus housing is guaranteed for the freshman year only, is available on a first-come, first-served basis, and is available on a lottery system for upperclassmen. 68% of students commute. All students may keep cars.

Activities: 6% of men belong to 10 national fraternities; 4% of women belong to 8 national sororities. There are 118 groups on campus, including art, band, cheerleading, chess, choir, chorale, chorus, computers, dance, drama, drill team, ethnic, film, gay, honors, international, jazz band, literary magazine, marching band, musical theater, newspaper, opera, orchestra, pep band, photography, political, professional, radio and TV, religious, social, social service, student government, and symphony. Popular campus events include Hawaiian Luau, Academic Excellence Week, and International Dinner.

Sports: There are 7 intercollegiate sports for men and 9 for women, and 12 intramural sports for men and 11 for women. Facilities include a stadium and a recreation center with 5 gyms, 3 racquetball courts, a weight room and aerobics room, and an indoor track.

Disabled Students: All of the campus is accessible. Wheelchair ramps, elevators, special parking, specially equipped rest rooms, special class scheduling, lowered drinking fountains, lowered telephones, and academic support services such as note taking, transportation, interpreters, adaptive computer instruction, and library assistance are available.

Services: Counseling and information services are available, as is tutoring in most subjects. There is a reader service for the blind, and remedial math, reading, and writing.

Campus Safety and Security: Measures include 24-hour foot and vehicle patrol, security escort services, shuttle buses, and pamphlets/posters/films. There are emergency telephones and lighted pathways/sidewalks.

Programs of Study: UNC confers B.A., B.S., B.A.S., B.A.T., B.M., and B.M.E. degrees. Master's and doctoral degrees are also awarded. Bachelor's degrees are awarded in AGRICULTURE (natural resource management), BIOLOGICAL SCIENCE (biochemistry and biology/biological science), BUSINESS (accounting, business administration and management, management science, marketing/retailing/merchandising, and recreation and leisure services), COMMUNICATIONS AND THE ARTS (advertising, art, communications, dance, dramatic arts, English, fine arts, French, German, graphic design, journalism, music, musical theater, public relations, Spanish, telecommunications, and visual and performing arts), COMPUTER AND PHYSICAL SCIENCE (atmospheric sciences and meteorology, chemistry, computer science, earth science, geology, information sciences and systems, mathematics, physics, and statistics), EDUCATION (music, physical, science, social science, and special), HEALTH PROFESSIONS (allied health, community health work, exercise science, nursing, rehabilitation therapy, and speech pathology/audiology), SOCIAL SCIENCE (African American studies, criminal justice, dietetics, economics, ethics, politics, and social policy, geography, gerontology, history, human services, interdisciplinary studies, international relations, Mexican-American/Chicano studies, philosophy, physical fitness/movement, political science/government, psychology, social science, and sociology). Business, music, and nursing are the strongest academically. Business, interdisciplinary studies, and sport and exercise science are the largest.

Required: Students must earn a minimum of 120 semester hours (some majors require additional hours) with a minimum GPA of 2.0. All students must complete 40 semester hours in required general education courses and meet all degree requirements in the major.

Special: UNC offers internships and co-op programs in many majors and study abroad in England, Australia, Spain, France, and Germany or through the International Student Exchange Program. Dual majors, student-designed majors, credit by exam, and pass/fail options are also available. There are 10 national honor societies and a freshman honors program.

Faculty/Classroom: 50% of faculty are male; 50%, female. All both teach and do research. Graduate students teach 17% of introductory courses. The average class size in an introductory lecture is 41; in a laboratory, 23; and in a regular course, 28.

Admissions: 82% of the 2005-2006 applicants were accepted. The SAT scores for the 2005-2006 freshman class were: Verbal--33% below 500, 47% between 500 and 599, 18% between 600 and 700, and 2% above 700; Math--35% below 500, 46% between 500 and 599, 16% between 600 and 700, and 3% above 700. The ACT scores were 33% below 21, 34% between 21 and 23, 22% between 24 and 26, 7% between 27 and 28, and 4% above 28. 23% of the current freshmen were in the top fifth of their class; 47% were in the top two fifths. 27 freshmen graduated first in their class.

Requirements: The SAT or ACT is required. In addition, admission standards are set by the Colorado Commission on Higher Education, but each applicant is evaluated on an individual basis. Graduation from an accredited high school is required. A GPA of 2.9 is required. AP and CLEP credits are accepted. Important factors in the admissions decision are recommendations by school officials, evidence of special talent, and advanced placement or honor courses.

Procedure: Freshmen are admitted fall, spring, and summer. Entrance exams should be taken as early as possible. There is a deferred admissions and a rolling admissions plan. Applications should be filed by August 1 for fall entry, December 20 for spring entry, and May 1 for summer entry, along with a $40 fee. Notification is sent on a rolling basis. Applications are accepted on-line.

Transfer: 953 transfer students enrolled in 2004-2005. Transfer students who have completed 12 or fewer hours of college must meet the same criteria for admission as entering freshmen. Transfers with 13 or more semester hours must have a minimum 2.4 GPA. 30 of 120 credits required for the bachelor's degree must be completed at UNC.

Visiting: There are regularly scheduled orientations for prospective students, including academic advising, registration, tours, and special activities. There are guides for informal visits and visitors may sit in on classes. To schedule a visit, contact the UNC Visitors Center at (970) 351-2097 or www.unco.edu/admissions/tourform.html.

Financial Aid: In 2005-2006, 80% of all full-time freshmen and 74% of continuing full-time students received some form of financial aid. 59% of full-time freshmen and 60% of continuing full-time students received need-based aid. The average freshman award was $7300. Need-based scholarships or need-based grants averaged $3818 ($20,005 maximum); need-based self-help aid (loans and jobs) averaged $6921 ($20,324 maximum); non-need-based athletic scholarships averaged $5188 ($10,749 maximum); and other non-need-based awards and non-need-based scholarships averaged $2805 ($13,130 maximum). 20% of undergraduates work part time. Average annual earnings from campus work are $1946. The FAFSA is required. The deadline for filing freshman financial aid applications for fall entry is March 1.

International Students: There are 27 international students enrolled. They must score satisfactorily on the TOEFL or take the MELAB and also take the SAT or the ACT.

Computers: Wireless access is available. UNC has 19 computer labs containing 565 computers with Internet access. High-tech classrooms and 36 smart classrooms offer varying degrees of Internet access. All students may access the system. There are no time limits. The fee is $4.50 per credit hour.

Graduates: From July 1, 2004 to June 30, 2005, 2047 bachelor's degrees were awarded. The most popular majors were special education (24%), sport and exercise science (17%), and professional psychology (15%). In an average class, 1% graduate in 3 years or less, 26% graduate in 4 years or less, 43% graduate in 5 years or less, and 47% graduate in 6 years or less. 469 companies recruited on campus in 2004-2005. Of the 2004 graduating class, 12% were enrolled in graduate school within 6 months of graduation and 81% were employed.

Admissions Contact: Gary Gullickson, Director of Admissions. A video is available. E-mail: unc@mail.unco.edu Web: http://www.unco.edu

---

WESTERN STATE COLLEGE OF COLORADO
B-3

Gunnison, CO 81231

(970) 943-2119
(800) 876-5309; Fax: (970) 943-2212

Full-time: 2000 men and women	Faculty: 107; IIB, --$
Part-time: n/av	Ph.D.s: 85%
Graduate: none	Student/Faculty: 20 to 1
Year: semesters, summer session	Tuition: $3138 ($11,754)
Application Deadline: see profile	Room & Board: $6804
Freshman Class: 1509 applied, 1309 accepted, 480 enrolled	
SAT Verbal/Math: 520/505*	ACT: 21 COMPETITIVE

Western State College of Colorado, founded in 1901, is a public institution offering undergraduate programs in liberal arts and sciences, business, recreation, and education. Some figures in this capsule and in this profile are approximate. There are 8 undergraduate schools. In addition to regional accreditation, Western has baccalaureate program accreditation with NASM. The library contains 156,000 volumes, 1 million microform items, and 5000 audio/video tapes/CDs/DVDs, and subscribes to 650 periodicals including electronic. Computerized library services include the card catalog, interlibrary loans, and database searching. Special learning facilities include a learning resource center, art gallery, radio station, TV station, and botanical gardens. The 228-acre campus is in a rural area 210 miles southwest of Denver. Including any residence halls, there are 30 buildings.

Student Life: 76% of undergraduates are from Colorado. Students are from 49 states, 12 foreign countries, and Canada. 85% are from public schools. 90% are white. 66% claim no religious affiliation; 8% Protestant. The average age of freshmen is 18; all undergraduates, 21. 41% do not continue beyond their first year; 35% remain to graduate.

Housing: 1200 students can be accommodated in college housing, which includes single-sex and coed dorms, on-campus apartments, and married-student housing. In addition, there are special-interest houses, and theme floors on art, science, and outdoor pursuits. On-campus housing is guaranteed for the freshman year only and is available on a first-come, first-served basis. 55% of students commute. All students may keep cars.

Activities: 3% of men belong to 1 local and 2 national fraternities; 2% of women belong to 2 local and 1 national sorority here are 60 groups on campus, including art, band, cheerleading, choir, chorale, chorus, dance, drama, ethnic, gay, honors, international, jazz band, literary magazine, marching band, musical theater, opera, orchestra, outdoor/wilderness, pep band, photography, political, professional, radio and TV, religious, social, social service, student government, symphony, and yearbook. Popular campus events include Parents Weekend, Spring Carnival, and weekly entertainment programs.

Sports: There are 6 intercollegiate sports for men and 5 for women, and 10 intramural sports for men and 10 for women. Facilities include a fitness center, 2 gyms, a 5000-seat football stadium, an all-weather track, a number of playing fields, a weight room, an indoor swimming pool, a par course, a games/pool area with a bowling alley, and racquetball, tennis, and volleyball courts.

Disabled Students: 75% of the campus is accessible. Wheelchair ramps, elevators, special parking, specially equipped rest rooms, lowered drinking fountains, lowered telephones, and an audio device to increase telephone volume are available.

Services: Counseling and information services are available, as is tutoring in most subjects. There is a reader service for the blind and remedial math and writing.

Campus Safety and Security: Measures include security escort services, informal discussions, pamphlets/posters/films, and emergency telephones. There are lighted pathways/sidewalks and van shuttle service during special events to prevent students' drinking and driving.

Programs of Study: Western confers B.A. and B.F.A. degrees. Bachelor's degrees are awarded in BIOLOGICAL SCIENCE (biology/biological science), BUSINESS (accounting, business administration and management, and recreation and leisure services), COMMUNICATIONS AND THE ARTS (art, communications, dramatic arts, English, fine arts, music, and Spanish), COMPUTER AND PHYSICAL SCIENCE (chemistry, computer science, geology, and mathematics), EDUCATION (art, elementary, foreign languages, music, science, and secondary), ENGINEERING AND ENVIRONMENTAL DESIGN (preengineering), HEALTH PROFESSIONS (physical therapy and predentistry), SOCIAL SCIENCE (anthropology, economics, history, physical fitness/movement, political science/government, prelaw, psychology, and sociology). Business, biological sciences, and communications are the strongest academically. Kinesiology and education are the largest.

Required: For graduation, students must complete 120 credit hours with a minimum GPA of 2.0. There are liberal arts requirements of 27 credits in human relationships, natural sciences, and creative arts, as well as competencies in written expression, oral communication, and math.

Special: The Department of Business and Accounting offers a co-op program. Students may cross-register with Mesa, Adams, and Metro State colleges. Study abroad, internships, work-study programs, an accelerated degree program in teacher education, dual and student-designed majors, and credit for military and work experience are available. There are 9 national honor societies, a freshman honors program, and 2 departmental honors programs.

Faculty/Classroom: 58% of faculty are male; 42%, female. All both teach and do research. The average class size in an introductory lecture is 22; in a laboratory, 15; and in a regular course, 19.

Admissions: 87% of the 2005-2006 applicants were accepted. The SAT scores for the 2005-2006 freshman class were: Verbal--41% below 500, 41% between 500 and 599, 17% between 600 and 700, and 1% above 700; Math--43% below 500, 45% between 500 and 599, and 12% between 600 and 700. The ACT scores were 49% below 21, 27% between 21 and 23, 15% between 24 and 26, 7% between 27 and 28, and 2% above 28. 19% of the current freshmen were in the top fifth of their class; 43% were in the top two fifths. 14 freshmen graduated first in their class.

Requirements: The SAT or ACT is required. In addition, an essay and an interview are recommended. Applicants must be graduates of an accredited secondary school. Western recommends that in high school students complete 4 years of English, 3 of math, and 2 each of natural and social science. Coursework in a foreign language and computer science is strongly recommended. Western requires applicants to be in the upper 67% of their class. A GPA of 2.5 is required. AP and CLEP credits are accepted. Important factors in the admissions decision are advanced placement or honor courses, leadership record, and extracurricular activities record.

Procedure: Freshmen are admitted to all sessions. Entrance exams should be taken during spring of junior year or fall of senior year. There are a deferred admissions and rolling admissions plans. Notification is sent on a rolling basis. Applications are accepted on-line. Check with the school for current application deadlines.

Transfer: Applicants for transfer must have a minimum GPA of 2.0 and may be asked to submit SAT or ACT test scores. 30 of 120 credits required for the bachelor's degree must be completed at Western.

Visiting: There are regularly scheduled orientations for prospective students. There are guides for informal visits and visitors may sit in on classes. To schedule a visit, contact the Admissions Office at (800) 876-5309.

Financial Aid: In a recent year, 80% of all full-time freshmen and 85% of continuing full-time students received some form of financial aid. 65% of full-time freshmen and 70% of continuing full-time students received need-based aid. The average freshman award was $4000. Need-based scholarships or need-based grants averaged $500 ($4000 maximum); need-based self-help aid (loans and jobs) averaged $3000 ($5000 maximum); non-need-based athletic scholarships averaged $450 ($5000 maximum); and other non-need-based awards and non-need-based scholarships averaged $500 ($3000 maximum). 35% of undergraduates worked part time. Average annual earnings from campus work were $1500. The average financial indebtedness of a recent graduate was $12,000. The FAFSA is required. Check with the school for current application deadlines.

International Students: In a recent year, there were 38 international students enrolled. They must score satisfactorily on the written TOEFL or on the electronic version.

Computers: All students may access the system at all times. There are no time limits. The fee is $25 per year.

Graduates: In a recent year, 441 bachelor's degrees were awarded. The most popular majors were business/accounting (20%), biology (10%), and history (9%). 15 companies recruited on campus in a recent year. Of a recent graduating class, 4% were enrolled in graduate school within 6 months of graduation and 95% were employed.

Admissions Contact: Tonya Van Hee, Assistant Director. A video is available. E-mail: *tvanhee@western.edu* Web: *www.western.edu*

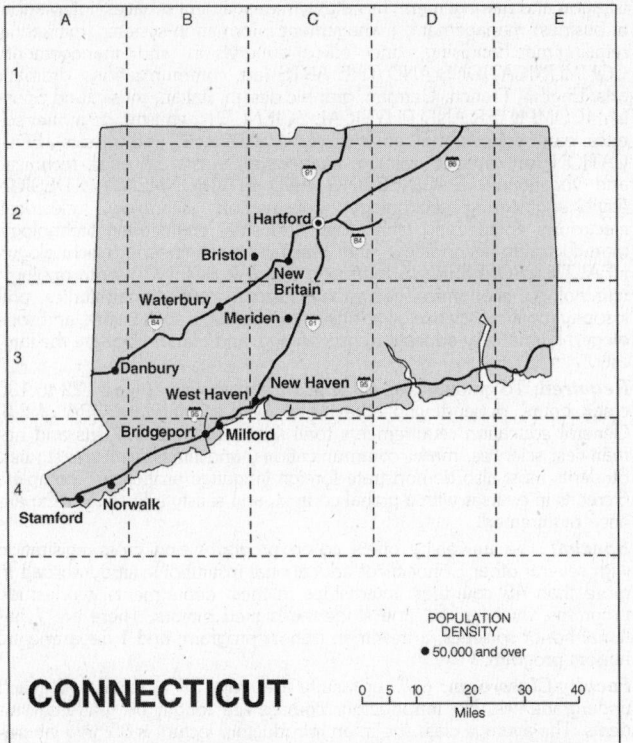

POPULATION DENSITY
● 50,000 and over

CONNECTICUT

0 5 10   20   30   40
Miles

ALBERTUS MAGNUS COLLEGE — C-3
New Haven, CT 06511-1189
(203) 773-8501
(800) 578-9160; Fax: (203) 773-9539

Full-time: 545 men, 1268 women	Faculty: 37; IIB, -$
Part-time: 25 men, 54 women	Ph.D.s: 90%
Graduate: 207 men, 246 women	Student/Faculty: 49 to 1
Year: semesters, summer session	Tuition: $17,408
Application Deadline: open	Room & Board: $7928
Freshman Class: 444 applied, 377 accepted, 128 enrolled	
SAT Verbal/Math: 460/496*	**COMPETITIVE**

Albertus Magnus College, founded in 1925, is a private college affiliated with the Roman Catholic Church and sponsored by the Dominican Sisters of St. Mary of the Springs. The college offers undergraduate and graduate degrees in the liberal arts and sciences and in business. In addition to regional accreditation, Albertus Magnus has baccalaureate program accreditation with IACBE. The library contains 125,000 volumes, 7500 microform items, and 2000 audio/video tapes/CDs/DVDs, and subscribes to 780 periodicals including electronic. Computerized library services include the card catalog, interlibrary loans, database searching, and Internet access. Special learning facilities include a learning resource center, art gallery, theater, and academic skill center. The 55-acre campus is in a suburban area 80 miles from New York City. Including any residence halls, there are 17 buildings.

Student Life: 94% of undergraduates are from Connecticut. Others are from 10 states and 6 foreign countries. 50% are from public schools. 66% are white; 20% African American. Most are Catholic. The average age of freshmen is 19; all undergraduates, 22. 19% do not continue beyond their first year; 80% remain to graduate.

Housing: 320 students can be accommodated in college housing, which includes single-sex and coed dorms. Residence halls are mainly converted mansions, each housing 15 to 65 students. On-campus housing is guaranteed for all 4 years. 60% of students live on campus; of those, 70% remain on campus on weekends. All students may keep cars.

Activities: There are no fraternities or sororities. There are 20 groups on campus, including art, computers, dance, debate, drama, ethnic, film, honors, international, literary magazine, musical theater, photography, political, professional, religious, social, social service, student government, and yearbook. Popular campus events include Fall Candlelight Ceremony, Christmas events, and Laurel Day.

Sports: There are 5 intercollegiate sports for men and 7 for women. Facilities include an Olympic-size pool, a gym, indoor and outdoor tracks, racquetball and volleyball courts, weight and dance rooms, 4 tennis courts, a game room, and soccer and softball fields.

Disabled Students: All of the campus is accessible. Wheelchair ramps, elevators, special parking, specially equipped rest rooms, special class scheduling, lowered drinking fountains, and lowered telephones are available.

Services: Counseling and information services are available, as is tutoring in every subject. There is remedial math, reading, and writing.

Campus Safety and Security: Measures include 24-hour foot and vehicle patrol, security escort services, shuttle buses, and informal discussions. There are pamphlets/posters/films and lighted pathways/sidewalks.

Programs of Study: Albertus Magnus confers B.A., B.S., and B.F.A. degrees. Associate and master's degrees are also awarded. Bachelor's degrees are awarded in BIOLOGICAL SCIENCE (biology/biological science), BUSINESS (accounting, business administration and management, and management information systems), COMMUNICATIONS AND THE ARTS (communications, dramatic arts, English, and fine arts), COMPUTER AND PHYSICAL SCIENCE (mathematics), EDUCATION (education), HEALTH PROFESSIONS (art therapy, predentistry, premedicine, and preveterinary science), SOCIAL SCIENCE (criminology, history, human services, humanities, industrial and organizational psychology, liberal arts/general studies, philosophy, political science/government, prelaw, psychology, religion, sociology, and urban studies). Liberal arts, business, and computer technology are the strongest academically. Business/economics, sociology, and psychology are the largest.

Required: To graduate, all students must complete at least 120 credit hours, including 60 outside the major and at least 30 in the major. General education requirements, including 6 credits each in English and humanities and 3 each in fine arts, math, science, and senior humanities, must be fulfilled. Distribution requirements include 3 credits each of history, social science, philosophy, religion, and literature. Service learning or career explorations are also required. A minimum 2.0 GPA is required.

Special: The college offers junior-and senior-year internships allowing up to 12 credits, study abroad, a Washington semester, work-study programs, and accelerated degree programs in business and information technology, psychology, criminal justice, communications, English, humanities, and general studies. Also available are dual and student-designed majors, nondegree study, pass/fail options, independent study, and preprofessional programs. Students may take accelerated degree programs in the evening or take weekend courses. The college also offers a teacher certification program, including placement for the student teaching. There are 5 national honor societies, a freshman honors program, and 12 departmental honors programs.

Faculty/Classroom: 49% of faculty are male; 51%, female. All both teach and do research. No introductory courses are taught by graduate students. The average class size in an introductory lecture is 20; in a laboratory, 10; and in a regular course, 15.

Admissions: 85% of the 2005-2006 applicants were accepted. The SAT scores for the 2005-2006 freshman class were: Verbal--62% below 500, 30% between 500 and 599, 7% between 600 and 700, and 1% above 700; Math--70% below 500, 21% between 500 and 599, 8% between 600 and 700, and 1% above 700. 22% of the current freshmen were in the top fifth of their class; 46% were in the top two fifths. In a recent year, there were 7 National Merit semifinalists and 4 freshmen graduated first in their class.

Requirements: The SAT is required. In addition, applicants must be graduates of an accredited secondary school or have a GED certificate and have completed 16 academic credits, including 4 years of English, 2 or 3 years each of foreign language, math, and science, 2 years of history, and 1 year of social studies. High school transcripts, rank, and 2 letters of recommendation are required. An interview is recommended. Albertus Magnus requires applicants to be in the upper 50% of their class. A GPA of 2.5 is required. AP and CLEP credits are accepted. Important factors in the admissions decision are advanced placement or honor courses, recommendations by school officials, and leadership record.

Procedure: Freshmen are admitted to all sessions. Entrance exams should be taken between April of the junior year and November of the senior year. There is a deferred admissions plan. Application deadlines are open. The fall 2005 application fee was $35. Notification is sent on a rolling basis beginning December 15. Applications are accepted online.

Transfer: 27 transfer students enrolled in 2004-2005. Transfer students must present a minimum 2.0 overall GPA and a 2.0 GPA for all transferable, compatible course work. 30 of 120 credits required for the bachelor's degree must be completed at Albertus Magnus.

Visiting: There are regularly scheduled orientations for prospective students, consisting of registration, a general introduction, a financial aid/major introduction, lunch, a campus tour, and an interview. There are guides for informal visits and visitors may sit in on classes and stay overnight. To schedule a visit, contact the Admissions Office.

Financial Aid: 10% of undergraduates work part time. Average annual earnings from campus work are $1000. The CSS/Profile or FAFSA and the college's own financial statement are required. The deadline for filing freshman financial aid applications for fall entry is March 15.

International Students: The school actively recruits these students. They must score 550 on the written TOEFL.

Computers: Wireless access is available in residence hall rooms, the library, the cyber-café, and several stations throughout the academic buildings besides the labs and classrooms when not being used for class. All students may access the system 9 A.M. to 10 P.M. There are no time limits and no fees. It is strongly recommended that all students have a personal computer.

Graduates: From July 1, 2004 to June 30, 2005, 760 bachelor's degrees were awarded. The most popular majors were management (63%), psychology (5%), and sociology (4%). In an average class, 53% graduate in 4 years and, and 60% graduate in 5 years or less. 24 companies recruited on campus in 2004-2005. Of the 2004 graduating class, 25% were enrolled in graduate school within 6 months of graduation and 70% were employed.

Admissions Contact: Richard Lolatte, Dean of Admissions and Financial Aid. E-mail: *admissions@albertus.edu* Web: *www.albertus.edu*

CENTRAL CONNECTICUT STATE UNIVERSITY   C-2

New Britain, CT 06050

(860) 832-2278
(888) 733-2278; Fax: (860) 832-2522

Full-time: 3648 men, 3797 women	Faculty: 394; IIA, av$
Part-time: 1124 men, 1109 women	Ph.D.s: 77%
Graduate: 929 men, 1708 women	Student/Faculty: 19 to 1
Year: semesters, summer session	Tuition: $6164 ($14,102)
Application Deadline: May 1	Room & Board: $7456
Freshman Class: 5549 applied, 3421 accepted, 1334 enrolled	
SAT Verbal/Math: 516/516*	COMPETITIVE

Central Connecticut State University, founded in 1849, offers degree programs in liberal arts, engineering technology, business, and education. It is part of the Connecticut State University system. There are 4 undergraduate schools and 1 graduate school. In addition to regional accreditation, CCSU has baccalaureate program accreditation with ABET, ACS, CSAB, CSWE, NAIT, NCATE and NLN. The library contains 665,605 volumes, 554,168 microform items, and 7259 audio/video tapes/CDs/DVDs, and subscribes to 2772 periodicals including electronic. Computerized library services include the card catalog, interlibrary loans, and database searching. Special learning facilities include a learning resource center, art gallery, planetarium, radio station, TV station, and writing and math centers. The 294-acre campus is in a suburban area 10 miles west of Hartford. Including any residence halls, there are 39 buildings.

Student Life: 93% of undergraduates are from Connecticut. Others are from 26 states, 54 foreign countries, and Canada. 74% are white. 56% are claim no religious affiliation; 30% are Catholic. The average age of freshmen is 18; all undergraduates, 21. 24% do not continue beyond their first year; 43% remain to graduate.

Housing: 1900 students can be accommodated in college housing, which includes single-sex and coed dorms. On-campus housing is guaranteed for all 4 years. 79% of students commute. All students may keep cars.

Activities: 1% of men belong to 2 national fraternities; 1% of women belong to 1 national sorority. There are 100 groups on campus, including art, band, cheerleading, choir, chorale, chorus, computers, dance, drama, ethnic, gay, honors, international, jazz band, literary magazine, marching band, newspaper, pep band, photography, political, professional, radio and TV, religious, social, social service, student government, symphony, and yearbook. Popular campus events include Winter and Spring Weekends, First Week, and Vance Lectures.

Sports: There are 7 intercollegiate sports for men and 8 for women, and 8 intramural sports for men and 8 for women. Facilities include a 3800-seat gym, 8 tennis courts, a 6000-seat football stadium, a 37,000-square-foot air-supported recreation facility, a natatorium, weight training rooms, and softball, baseball, touch football, and soccer fields.

Disabled Students: 90% of the campus is accessible. Wheelchair ramps, elevators, special parking, specially equipped rest rooms, special class scheduling, lowered drinking fountains, lowered telephones, and personal care attendants who serve as roommates for physically disabled resident students are available.

Services: Counseling and information services are available, as is tutoring in some subjects. There is a reader service for the blind, and remedial math, reading, and writing.

Campus Safety and Security: Measures include 24-hour foot and vehicle patrol, self-defense education, security escort services, and shuttle buses. There are informal discussions, pamphlets/posters/films, emergency telephones, and lighted pathways/sidewalks.

Programs of Study: CCSU confers B.A., B.S., B.F.A., B.S.Ed., and B.S.N. degrees. Master's and doctoral degrees are also awarded. Bachelor's degrees are awarded in BIOLOGICAL SCIENCE (biology/biological science), BUSINESS (accounting, banking and finance, business administration and management, hospitality management services, international business management, management information systems, marketing/retailing/merchandising, and office supervision and management), COMMUNICATIONS AND THE ARTS (art, communications, dramatic arts, English, French, German, graphic design, Italian, music, and Spanish), COMPUTER AND PHYSICAL SCIENCE (chemistry, computer science, earth science, mathematics, physical sciences, and physics), EDUCATION (art, athletic training, elementary, music, physical, technical, and vocational), ENGINEERING AND ENVIRONMENTAL DESIGN (civil engineering technology, construction technology, electrical/electronics engineering technology, industrial engineering technology, manufacturing technology, and mechanical engineering technology), HEALTH PROFESSIONS (nursing), SOCIAL SCIENCE (anthropology, criminology, economics, geography, history, international studies, philosophy, political science/government, psychology, social work, and sociology). Elementary education, psychology, and criminology are the largest.

Required: To graduate, all students must complete at least 122 to 130 credit hours, depending on the major, with a minimum GPA of 2.0. General education requirements total 44 to 46 credits in arts and humanities, sciences, math, communications, and fitness/wellness studies. Students must also demonstrate foreign language proficiency, complete 6 credits in courses with a global context, and satisfy a First-Year Experience requirement.

Special: The university offers co-op programs and cross-registration with several other Connecticut educational institutions, study abroad in more than 45 countries, internships in most departments, work-study programs, dual majors, and student-designed majors. There are 7 national honor societies, a freshman honors program, and 1 departmental honors program.

Faculty/Classroom: 61% of faculty are male; 39%, female. All teach undergraduates. No introductory courses are taught by graduate students. The average class size in an introductory lecture is 35; in a laboratory, 20; and in a regular course, 25.

Admissions: 62% of the 2005-2006 applicants were accepted. The SAT scores for the 2005-2006 freshman class were: Verbal--39% below 500, 49% between 500 and 599, 12% between 600 and 700, and 1% above 700; Math--38% below 500, 47% between 500 and 599, 13% between 600 and 700, and 1% above 700.

Requirements: The SAT is required. The ACT Optional Writing test is also required. In addition, applicants must be graduates of an accredited secondary school or have earned a GED. An interview is recommended. CCSU also recommends that applicants have 14 academic credits: 4 in English, 3 each in math and a foreign language, and 2 each in science and social sciences, including 1 in U.S. history. AP and CLEP credits are accepted. Important factors in the admissions decision are extracurricular activities record, recommendations by school officials, and advanced placement or honor courses.

Procedure: Freshmen are admitted fall and spring. Entrance exams should be taken in May of the junior year or November of the senior year. There is a deferred admissions plan. Applications should be filed by May 1 for fall entry and November 1 for spring entry. The fall application fee was $40. Notification is sent December 1.

Transfer: 722 transfer students enrolled in 2004-2005. Applicants must have a minimum of 12 transferable credits and a GPA of 2.0 and must submit official transcripts from previous schools attended. 45 of 122 credits required for the bachelor's degree must be completed at CCSU.

Visiting: There are regularly scheduled orientations for prospective students, including a fall open house in October and daily and select Saturday visits throughout the fall and spring. There are guides for informal visits and visitors may sit in on classes. To schedule a visit, contact the Admissions Office at *admissions@ccsu.edu*.

Financial Aid: In a recent year, 46% of all full-time freshmen and 67% of continuing full-time students received some form of financial aid. 44% of full-time freshmen and 64% of continuing full-time students received need-based aid. The average freshman award was $4730. Need-based scholarships or need-based grants averaged $3583 ($6000 maximum); need-based self-help aid (loans and jobs) averaged $2373 ($4000 maximum); non-need-based athletic scholarships averaged $10,949 ($19,000 maximum); and other non-need-based awards and non-need-based scholarships averaged $1914 ($2700 maximum). 40% of undergraduates work part time. Average annual earnings from campus work are $1000. The average financial indebtedness of a recent graduate was $13,500. CCSU is a member of CSS. The FAFSA and federal income tax returns are required. The priority date for freshman financial aid applications for fall entry is March 1. The deadline for filing freshman financial aid applications for fall entry is September 1.

International Students: There were 158 international students enrolled in a recent year. The school actively recruits these students. They must score satisfactorily on the written TOEFL.

Computers: All students may access the system 8:30 A.M. to 12 P.M., Monday to Thursday; 8:30 A.M. to 6 P.M., Friday; 9 A.M. to 6 P.M., Saturday; and 1 P.M. to 10 P.M., Sunday. There are no time limits and no fees.

Graduates: From July 1, 2004 to June 30, 2005, 1530 bachelor's degrees were awarded. The most popular majors were elementary education (7%), psychology (6%), and marketing (6%). In an average class, 43% graduate in 6 years or less. 63 companies recruited on campus in a recent year.

Admissions Contact: Richard Bishop, Interim Director of Recruitment and Admissions. E-mail: *admissions@ccsu.edu* Web: *www.ccsu.edu*

CHARTER OAK STATE COLLEGE   C-2
New Britain, CT 06053-2142

(860) 832-3800
Fax: (860) 832-3999

Full-time: none	**Faculty:** n/av
Part-time: 754 men, 1148 women	**Ph.D.s:** 54%
Graduate: none	**Student/Faculty:** n/av
Year: , summer session	**Tuition:** $940 ($1140)
Application Deadline: open	**Room & Board:** n/app
Freshman Class: n/av	
SAT or ACT: n/av	**SPECIAL**

Charter Oak State College, founded in 1973, is a public liberal arts institution offering degree programs for adult students who cannot complete a college degree by conventional means because of family, job, or financial considerations. Credits may be earned by transfer, testing, portfolio review, contract learning, or by taking Charter Oak's online and video courses. Matriculation and admission fees are $995 in state ($1245 out of state) for the first year and $430 in state ($630 out of state) for continuing students. Charter Oak course tuition is $160 per credit in state ($227 out of state) plus a $30 registration fee. 3-credit courses run for 8 or 15 weeks. Computerized library services include interlibrary loans and database searching. The campus is in a suburban area The offices are in a suburban area 7 miles south of Hartford. There is one building.

Student Life: 56% of undergraduates are from out of state, mostly the Northeast. Others are from 50 states, 2 foreign countries, and Canada. 69% are white; 10% African American. The average age of all undergraduates is 41.

Housing: There are no residence halls.

Disabled Students: All of the campus is accessible. Wheelchair ramps, elevators, special parking, specially equipped rest rooms, and lowered drinking fountains are available. The program is a distance-learning one that does not require students to come to the facility. They can obtain services by phone, fax, and e-mail.

Services: Counseling and information services are available, as is tutoring in some subjects, including writing, math, and psychology. Tutoring is available online.

Programs of Study: Charter Oak confers B.A. and B.S. degrees. Associate degrees are also awarded. Bachelor's degrees are awarded in SOCIAL SCIENCE (liberal arts/general studies).

Required: All baccalaureate students must complete 120 total credits, at least 60 of which must be in liberal arts for the B.S. and 90 for the B.A.; 36 credits must be in the field of concentration.

Special: Student-designed concentrations and accelerated degree programs are available in all majors. There is 1 national honor society.

Faculty/Classroom: 55% of faculty are male; 45%, female. The average class size in a laboratory is 13.

Requirements: In addition, charter Oak State College requires applicants to have earned at least 9 college credits. AP and CLEP credits are accepted.

Procedure: Freshmen are admitted to all sessions. There is a rolling admissions plan. Application deadlines are open. Application fee is $60. Applications are accepted on-line.

Transfer: Most students who enroll in Charter Oak State College have attended college previously.

Financial Aid: The average financial indebtedness of a recent graduate was $4828. The FAFSA and the college's own financial statement are required. The deadline for filing freshman financial aid applications for fall entry is June 30.

Computers: Since Charter Oak is a distance education college, PCs are strongly recommended.

Graduates: From July 1, 2004 to June 30, 2005, 437 bachelor's degrees were awarded.

Admissions Contact: Lori Gagne Pendleton, Director of Admissions. E-mail: *info@charteroak.edu* Web: *www.charteroak.edu*

CONNECTICUT COLLEGE   E-3
New London, CT 06320-4196

(860) 439-2200
Fax: (860) 439-4301

Full-time: 729 men, 1079 women	**Faculty:** 162; IIB, +$
Part-time: 22 men, 57 women	**Ph.D.s:** 91%
Graduate: 3 men, 8 women	**Student/Faculty:** 11 to 1
Year: semesters	**Tuition:** and Room and Board
Application Deadline: January 1	$41,975
	Room & Board: Null
Freshman Class: 4183 applied, 1477 accepted, 492 enrolled	
SAT Verbal/Math: 670/660*	**ACT:** 27 **MOST COMPETITVE**

Connecticut College, founded in 1911, is a private institution offering degree programs in the liberal arts and sciences. Tuition and room and board are combined in a comprehensive fee of $41,975 per year. The 2 libraries contain 652,509 volumes and 151,979 microform items, and subscribe to 3458 periodicals including electronic. Computerized library services include the card catalog, interlibrary loans, database searching, and Internet access. Special learning facilities include an art gallery, radio station, and an observatory, and an arboretum. The 702-acre campus is in a small town midway between Boston and New York City. Including any residence halls, there are 51 buildings.

Student Life: 82% of undergraduates are from out of state, mostly the Northeast. Students are from 42 states, 41 foreign countries, and Canada. 49% are from public schools. 73% are white. 27% are Protestant; 26% Catholic; 17% claim no religious affiliation; 14% Jewish; 7% Buddhist, Moslem, Hindu, and others. The average age of freshmen is 18; all undergraduates, 20. 8% do not continue beyond their first year; 87% remain to graduate.

Housing: 1750 students can be accommodated in college housing, which includes coed dormitories and on-campus apartments. In addition, there are language houses and special-interest houses. On-campus housing is guaranteed for all 4 years. 99% of students live on campus. All students may keep cars.

Activities: There are no fraternities or sororities. There are 55 groups on campus, including a capella art, band, chess, choir, chorale, chorus, computers, dance, drama, ethnic, film, gay, honors, international, jazz band, literary magazine, newspaper, opera, orchestra, photography, political, radio and TV, religious, social, social service, student government, symphony, and yearbook. Popular campus events include Eclipse Weekend, Harvestfest, and Floralia.

Sports: There are 12 intercollegiate sports for men and 14 for women, and 12 intramural sports for men and 10 for women. Facilities include an 800-seat gym, playing fields, an ice rink, a boathouse, a weight training room, an indoor pool, a dance studio, 12 tennis courts, and courts for squash, racquetball, badminton, basketball, and volleyball. There is also a track and field facility with an all-weather, 8-lane, 400-meter track, facilities for all field events, and a game field.

Disabled Students: 25% of the campus is accessible. Wheelchair ramps, elevators, special parking, specially equipped rest rooms, special class scheduling, lowered drinking fountains, and lowered telephones are available.

Services: Counseling and information services are available, as is tutoring in most subjects.

Campus Safety and Security: Measures include 24-hour foot and vehicle patrol, security escort services, informal discussions, and pamphlets/posters/films. There are emergency telephones, lighted pathways/sidewalks, and an electronic access system in student residences.

Programs of Study: Connecticut College confers the B.A. degree. Master's degrees are also awarded. Bachelor's degrees are awarded in BIOLOGICAL SCIENCE (biochemistry, biology/biological science, botany, and neurosciences), COMMUNICATIONS AND THE ARTS (art, art history and appreciation, Chinese, classics, comparative literature, dance, dramatic arts, English, French, German, Italian, Japanese, music, and music technology), COMPUTER AND PHYSICAL SCIENCE (astrophysics, chemistry, mathematics, and physics), EDUCATION (foreign languages, music, and science), ENGINEERING AND ENVIRONMENTAL DESIGN (architecture, engineering physics, and environmental science), SOCIAL SCIENCE (African studies, American studies, anthropology, East Asian studies, economics, gender studies, Hispanic American studies, history, human development, international relations, Italian studies, Latin American studies, medieval studies, philosophy, political science/government, psychology, religion, Russian and Slavic studies, sociology, and urban studies). Government, history, and psychology are the largest.

Required: To graduate, students must complete at least 128 credit hours with a minimum GPA of 2.0. Distribution requirements cover 7 courses from 7 academic areas, plus a foreign language and 2 writing-intensive courses.

Special: Cross-registration with 12 area colleges, internships in government, human services, and other fields, a Washington semester at American University, dual majors, student-designed majors, a 3-2 engineering degree with Washington University in St. Louis and Boston University, nondegree study, and satisfactory/unsatisfactory options are available.

One third of the junior class studies abroad. An international studies certificate program is available, which combines competency in a foreign language, an internship, and study abroad. There are also certificate programs in museum studies, community action and public policy, conservation biology and environmental studies, arts and technology, and education. There are 5 national honor societies, including Phi Beta Kappa, and all departments have honors programs.

Faculty/Classroom: 55% of faculty are male; 45%, female. All teach undergraduates. No introductory courses are taught by graduate students. The average class size in an introductory lecture is 27; in a laboratory, 15; and in a regular course, 20.

Admissions: 35% of the 2005-2006 applicants were accepted. The SAT scores for the 2005-2006 freshman class were: Verbal--2% below 500, 10% between 500 and 599, 58% between 600 and 700, and 30% above 700; Math--13% between 500 and 599, 62% between 600 and 700, and 25% above 700.

Requirements: Any 2 SAT Subject tests or the ACT is required. In addition, applicants must be graduates of an accredited secondary school. An essay is required and an interview is recommended. AP credits are accepted. Important factors in the admissions decision are advanced placement or honor courses, leadership record, and evidence of special talent.

Procedure: Freshmen are admitted fall and spring. Entrance exams should be taken by January of the senior year. There are early decision, early admissions, and deferred admissions plans. Early decision applications should be filed by November 15; regular applications, by January 1 for fall entry and December 1 for spring entry, along with a $55 fee. Notification of early decision is sent December 15; regular decision, April 1. 214 early decision candidates were accepted for the 2005-2006 class. 403 applicants were on the 2005 waiting list; 80 were admitted. Applications are accepted on-line.

Transfer: 10 transfer students enrolled in 2005-2006. Applicants must have a minimum college GPA of 3.0 and be in good standing at the previous school attended. SAT or ACT scores are required and an interview is recommended. 64 of 128 credits required for the bachelor's degree must be completed at Connecticut College.

Visiting: There are regularly scheduled orientations for prospective students, including an introduction to the college, student perspectives, academic programs, a luncheon for parents and students, tours, and a reception. There are guides for informal visits and visitors may sit in on classes and stay overnight. To schedule a visit, contact the Admissions Office.

Financial Aid: In 2005-2006, 41% of all full-time freshmen received some form of financial aid. 35% of full-time freshmen received need-based aid. The average freshman award was $25,759. The average financial indebtedness of the 2005 graduate was $22,524. Connecticut College is a member of CSS. The CSS/Profile or FAFSA and parent and student tax forms, including noncustodial parent's statement or business supplement when applicable are required. The deadline for filing freshman financial aid applications for fall entry is January 15.

International Students: In a recent year were 150 international students enrolled. The school actively recruits these students. They must score satisfactorily on the written TOEFL or on the electronic version or take APIEL, IELTS, MELAB, ELPT or equivalent. Students must take the SAT and Subject tests in any 2 subjects.

Computers: Wireless access is available. The campus has 36 wireless access points in academic buildings and all residence halls. All students may access the system 24 hours a day. There are no time limits and no fees. It is strongly recommended that all students have a personal computer.

Graduates: From July 1, 2004 to June 30, 2005, 419 bachelor's degrees were awarded. The most popular majors were economics (9%), English (9%), and government/international relations (8%). In an average class, 84% graduate in 4 years or less, 87% graduate in 5 years or less, and 87% graduate in 6 years or less.

Admissions Contact: Martha Merrill, Dean of Admissions.
E-mail: *admission@conncoll.edu*
Web: *www.connecticutcollege.edu/admissions*

CONNECTICUT STATE UNIVERSITY SYSTEM

The Connecticut State University System, established in 1983, is a public system in Connecticut. It is governed by a board of trustees, whose chief administrator is president. The primary goal of the system is teaching. The main priorities are access, with emphasis on a multi-cultural experience; quality, within a context of curriculum diversity and a range of delivery systems; and public service, including linkages with schools, state government, and private enterprise. Profiles of the 4-year campuses are included in this section.

EASTERN CONNECTICUT STATE UNIVERSITY   D-2

Willimantic, CT 06226	**(860) 465-5286; Fax: (860) 465-4382**
Full-time: 1693 men, 2058 women	**Faculty:** 188; IIA, av$
Part-time: 403 men, 591 women	**Ph.D.s:** 92%
Graduate: 98 men, 270 women	**Student/Faculty:** 20 to 1
Year: semesters, summer session	**Tuition:** $5964 ($13,903)
Application Deadline: May 1	**Room & Board:** $7590
Freshman Class: n/av	
SAT Verbal/Math: 514/507*	**COMPETITIVE**

Eastern Connecticut State University, founded in 1889, is the state's public liberal arts university. There are 3 undergraduate schools and 1 graduate school. The library contains 331,451 volumes, 828,029 microform items, and 3858 audio/video tapes/CDs/DVDs, and subscribes to 3185 periodicals including electronic. Computerized library services include the card catalog, interlibrary loans, database searching, Internet access, and laptop Internet portals. Special learning facilities include a learning resource center, art gallery, planetarium, radio station, and TV station. The 177-acre campus is in a suburban area 29 miles east of Hartford and 90 miles southwest of Boston. Including any residence halls, there are 47 buildings.

Student Life: 92% of undergraduates are from Connecticut. Others are from 28 states, 31 foreign countries, and Canada. 82% are white. The average age of freshmen is 19; all undergraduates, 26. 22% do not continue beyond their first year; 42% remain to graduate.

Housing: 2467 students can be accommodated in college housing, which includes single-sex and coed dorms and on-campus apartments. In addition, there are special-interest houses. On-campus housing is available on a first-come, first-served basis and is available on a lottery system for upperclassmen. Priority is given to out-of-town students. 62% of students live on campus. Alcohol is not permitted. Upperclassmen may keep cars.

Activities: There are no fraternities or sororities. There are 57 groups on campus, including art, band, cheerleading, choir, chorale, chorus, computers, dance, drama, ethnic, gay, honors, international, jazz band, literary magazine, musical theater, newspaper, orchestra, photography, political, professional, radio and TV, religious, social, social service, student government, and yearbook. Popular campus events include Spring Weekend, Parents Day, and International Festival.

Sports: There are 7 intercollegiate sports for men and 10 for women, and 20 intramural sports for men and 16 for women. Facilities include a 2800-seat field house, a 6-lane swimming pool, a soccer field, a baseball complex, a softball stadium, a 400 meter 8-lane track, field hockey/lacrosse field, intramural field, and tennis, basketball, racquetball, and squash courts.

Disabled Students: 93% of the campus is accessible. Wheelchair ramps, elevators, special parking, specially equipped rest rooms, special class scheduling, lowered drinking fountains, lowered telephones, and special housing are available.

Services: Counseling and information services are available, as is tutoring in most subjects. There is a reader service for the blind, and remedial math, reading, and writing.

Campus Safety and Security: Measures include 24-hour foot and vehicle patrol, self-defense education, security escort services, and shuttle buses. There are informal discussions, pamphlets/posters/films, emergency telephones, and lighted pathways/sidewalks.

Programs of Study: Eastern confers B.A., B.S. and B.G.S. degrees. Associate and master's degrees are also awarded. Bachelor's degrees are awarded in BIOLOGICAL SCIENCE (biochemistry and biology/biological science), BUSINESS (accounting, business administration and management, recreation and leisure services, and sports management), COMMUNICATIONS AND THE ARTS (communications, English, fine arts, performing arts, Spanish, studio art, and visual and performing arts), COMPUTER AND PHYSICAL SCIENCE (computer science, information sciences and systems, and mathematics), EDUCATION (early childhood, elementary, and physical), ENGINEERING AND ENVIRONMENTAL DESIGN (environmental science), SOCIAL SCIENCE (American studies, economics, history, liberal arts/general studies, political science/government, psychology, social science, social work, and sociology). Biology, Spanish, and math are the strongest academically. Psychology, business administration, and sociology and applied social relations are the largest.

Required: To graduate, students must complete 120 credit hours, including 30 to 48 hours in the major, with a GPA of 2.0. General education requirements include 12 credits in interdisciplinary studies, 9 in social sciences, 7 in natural sciences, and 3 each in math, fine arts, literature, writing, health and phys ed, and computer literacy. .

Special: Eastern offers co-op programs in all majors, cross-registration with the University of Connecticut, internships, study abroad in 22 countries, a Washington semester, work-study programs, accelerated degree programs, dual majors, a general studies degree, nondegree study, pass/fail options, and credit for military experience. In addition to the B.S. certification programs for early childhood and elementary education, teacher certification is available for middle school and secondary education studies. There are 5 national honor societies, a freshman honors program, and 4 departmental honors programs.

Faculty/Classroom: 59% of faculty are male; 41%, female. All teach undergraduates. No introductory courses are taught by graduate students. The average class size in a laboratory is 18 and in a regular course, 24.

Requirements: The SAT or ACT is required. In addition, applicants must be graduates of an accredited secondary school or have a GED. They should have completed 13 high school academic credits, including 4 years of English, 3 of math, and 2 each of foreign language, social studies, and science (including 1 of lab science). An interview is recommended. Eastern requires applicants to be in the upper 50% of their class. A GPA of 2.5 is required. AP and CLEP credits are accepted. Important factors in the admissions decision are recommendations by school officials, advanced placement or honor courses, and leadership record.

Procedure: Freshmen are admitted fall and spring. Entrance exams should be taken in November or December of the senior year. There are deferred admissions and rolling admissions plans. Applications should be filed by May 1 for fall entry and rolling for spring entry, along with a $40 fee. Notification of early decision is sent November 1; regular decision, on a rolling basis. 20 applicants on the 2005 waiting list were admitted.

Transfer: 274 transfer students enrolled in 2004-2005. Applicants should have completed a minimum of 12 credit hours with a GPA of 2.5. Official college and high school transcripts are required. 30 of 120 credits required for the bachelor's degree must be completed at Eastern.

Visiting: There are regularly scheduled orientations for prospective students, including small group discussions, a tour of the campus, and a personal interview. There are guides for informal visits and visitors may sit in on classes. To schedule a visit, contact the Office of Admissions at www.admissions@easternct.edu.

Financial Aid: Average annual earnings from campus work are $2500. Eastern is a member of CSS. The FAFSA is required. The deadline for filing freshman financial aid applications for fall entry is March 15.

International Students: There are 141 international students enrolled. The school actively recruits these students. Satisfactory scores are required on the written TOEFL and the SAT or the ACT.

Computers: Wireless access is available in selected areas. All students may access the system. There are no time limits and no fees.

Graduates: From July 1, 2004 to June 30, 2005, 859 bachelor's degrees were awarded. The most popular majors were psychology (14%), business/business information systems (10%), and sociology (9%). In an average class, 1% graduate in 3 years or less, 25% graduate in 4 years or less, 38% graduate in 5 years or less, and 42% graduate in 6 years or less. 150 companies recruited on campus in 2004-2005. Of the 2004 graduating class, 35% were enrolled in graduate school within 6 months of graduation and 95% were employed.

Admissions Contact: A video is available.
E-mail: admissions@ecsu.ctstateu.edu Web: ecsu.ctstateu.edu

FAIRFIELD UNIVERSITY   B-4

Fairfield, CT 06824-5195	**(203) 254-4100; Fax: (203) 254-4199**
Full-time: 1491 men, 1994 women	**Faculty:** 209; IIA, +$
Part-time: 242 men, 346 women	**Ph.D.s:** 94%
Graduate: 377 men, 723 women	**Student/Faculty:** 17 to 1
Year: semesters, summer session	**Tuition:** $30,235
Application Deadline: January 15	**Room & Board:** $9600
Freshman Class: 6895 applied, 5130 accepted, 940 enrolled	
SAT Verbal/Math: 587/601*	**ACT: 26 HIGHLY COMPETITIVE**

Fairfield University, founded by the Jesuits in 1942, is a private, Roman Catholic Jesuit institution. There are 5 undergraduate and 5 graduate schools. In addition to regional accreditation, Fairfield has baccalaureate program accreditation with AACSB, AAMFT, ABET, ACS, NLN, and GACREP. The library contains 333,251 volumes, 994,169 microform items, and 15,115 audio/video tapes/CDs/DVDs, and subscribes to 17,760 periodicals including electronic. Computerized library services include the card catalog, interlibrary loans, and database searching. Special learning facilities include an art gallery, radio station, TV station, a media center, a 750-seat concert hall/theater, and a rehearsal and improvisation theater. The 200-acre campus is in a suburban area 60 miles northeast of New York City. Including any residence halls, there are 34 buildings.

Student Life: Others are from 38 states, 41 foreign countries, and Canada. 54% are from public schools. 90% are white. 80% are Catholic; 18% Protestant. The average age of freshmen is 18; all undergraduates, 20. 9% do not continue beyond their first year; 80% remain to graduate.

Housing: 2516 students can be accommodated in college housing, which includes coed dorms and on-campus apartments. In addition, there are special-interest houses and a substance-free floor. On-campus housing is guaranteed for all 4 years. 80% of students live on campus; of those, 90% remain on campus on weekends. Upperclassmen may keep cars.

Activities: There are no fraternities or sororities. There are 100 groups on campus, including art, band, cheerleading, chorale, computers, dance, debate, drama, ethnic, film, gay, honors, international, jazz band, literary magazine, musical theater, newspaper, orchestra, pep band, political, professional, radio and TV, religious, social, social service, student government, and yearbook. Popular campus events include Dogwood Festival, Martin Luther King Week, and Harvest Weekend.

Sports: There are 8 intercollegiate sports for men and 11 for women, and 15 intramural sports for men and 15 for women. Facilities include a gym, a 25-meter swimming pool, weight rooms, indoor and outdoor tennis courts, racquetball and volleyball courts, indoor and outdoor tracks, a sauna, a whirlpool, and fitness equipment.

Disabled Students: All of the campus is accessible. Wheelchair ramps, elevators, special parking, specially equipped rest rooms, special class scheduling, lowered drinking fountains, lowered telephones, special housing, and accommodations for seeing-eye dogs and a library computer station for physically challenged students are available.

Services: Counseling and information services are available, as is tutoring in every subject. There is a reader service for the blind.

Campus Safety and Security: Measures include 24-hour foot and vehicle patrol, self-defense education, security escort services, and shuttle buses. There are informal discussions, pamphlets/posters/films, emergency telephones, lighted pathways/sidewalks, EMT security officers, and a bike patrol.

Programs of Study: Fairfield confers B.A. and B.S. degrees. Associate and master's degrees are also awarded. Bachelor's degrees are awarded in BIOLOGICAL SCIENCE (biology/biological science), BUSINESS (accounting, banking and finance, business administration and management, international business management, and marketing/retailing/merchandising), COMMUNICATIONS AND THE ARTS (communications, English, fine arts, French, German, Spanish, and visual and performing arts), COMPUTER AND PHYSICAL SCIENCE (chemistry, computer science, information sciences and systems, mathematics, physics, and software engineering), ENGINEERING AND ENVIRONMENTAL DESIGN (computer engineering, electrical/electronics engineering, and mechanical engineering), HEALTH PROFESSIONS (nursing), SOCIAL SCIENCE (American studies, economics, history, international studies, philosophy, political science/government, psychology, religion, and sociology). Finance and biology are the strongest academically. Finance, psychology, and communications are the largest.

Required: To graduate, students must complete 120 credits, 60 of them in general education core requirements, with a minimum GPA of 2.0. Distribution requirements include 15 credits in philosophy, religious studies, and ethics, 15 credits in English and fine arts, 12 credits in math and natural sciences, 12 credits in history and social sciences, and 6 credits in foreign languages. First-year students are required to take a course in multiculturalism.

Special: Fairfield participates in CIEE and offers study abroad in 6 countries, a Washington semester, a federal work-study program, B.A.-B.S. degrees in economics, international studies, and psychology, student-designed majors, and dual majors in all subjects. A 3-2 engineering degree is offered with the University of Connecticut, Rensselaer Polytechnic Institute, Columbia University, and Stevens Institute of Technology. A general studies degree and credit for life, military, and work experience are available through the School of Continuing Education. Internships, both credit and noncredit, are offered at area corporations, publications, banks, and other businesses. Minors include women's studies, marine science, black studies, environmental studies, jazz, classical studies, Russian and Eastern studies, biochemistry, and Judaic studies. There are 14 national honor societies, including Phi Beta Kappa, a freshman honors program, and a university-wide honors program.

Faculty/Classroom: 52% of faculty are male; 48%, female. All both teach and do research. No introductory courses are taught by graduate students. The average class size in an introductory lecture is 29; in a laboratory, 13; and in a regular course, 23.

Admissions: 74% of the 2005-2006 applicants were accepted. The SAT scores for the 2005-2006 freshman class were: Verbal--6% below 500, 49% between 500 and 599, 36% between 600 and 700, and 5% above 700; Math--4% below 500, 41% between 500 and 599, 44% between 600 and 700, and 7% above 700. 57% of the current freshmen were in the top fifth of their class; 93% were in the top two fifths. There were 8 National Merit semifinalists.

Requirements: The SAT is required. In addition, applicants must be graduates of an accredited secondary school. A B average is required. Students should have completed 15 academic credits, including 4 credits of English, 3 to 4 credits each of history, math, and lab science, and 2 to 4 credits of a foreign language. The school recommends SAT Subject tests in language and math, and, for nursing and science majors, in the sciences. An interview is recommended. Fairfield requires applicants to be in the upper 30% of their class. A GPA of 3.0 is required. AP and CLEP credits are accepted. Important factors in the admissions decision are advanced placement or honor courses, leadership record, and evidence of special talent.

Procedure: Freshmen are admitted in the fall. Entrance exams should be taken in the spring of the junior year or fall of the senior year. There are early admissions and deferred admissions plans. Early action applications should be filed by November 15; regular applications, by January 15 for fall entry. Notification of early action is sent before December 25; regular decision, April 1. 135 early decision candidates were accepted for the 2005-2006 class. 918 applicants were on the 2005 waiting list; 64 were admitted. The fall 2005 application fee was $55. Applications are accepted on-line.

Transfer: 74 transfer students enrolled in 2004-2005. The SAT and a college GPA of 2.5 are required (2.8 in business). 60 of 120 credits required for the bachelor's degree must be completed at Fairfield.

Visiting: There are regularly scheduled orientations for prospective students, consisting of a summer orientation the third week in June and a fall program 2 days before classes begin. There are guides for informal visits and visitors may sit in on classes and stay overnight. To schedule a visit, contact the Admissions Office.

Financial Aid: In 2005-2006, 73% of all full-time freshmen and 68% of continuing full-time students received some form of financial aid. 51% of full-time freshmen and 45% of continuing full-time students received need-based aid. The average freshman award was $17,929. Need-based scholarships or need-based grants averaged $13,151 ($20,000 maximum); need-based self-help aid (loans and jobs) averaged $4271 ($6125 maximum); non-need-based athletic scholarships averaged $18,332 ($39,330 maximum); and other non-need-based awards and non-need-based scholarships averaged $11,803 ($27,930 maximum). 13% of undergraduates work part time. Average annual earnings from campus work are $1016. The average financial indebtedness of the 2005 graduate was $25,081. Fairfield is a member of CSS. The CSS/Profile or FAFSA, parent and student tax returns, and a verification statement from first-time applicants are required. The deadline for filing freshman financial aid applications for fall entry is February 15.

International Students: There are 32 international students enrolled. The school actively recruits these students. They must score satisfactorily on the TOEFL and also take the SAT or the ACT.

Computers: All students may access the system daily until midnight. There are no time limits and no fees. It is strongly recommended that all students have a personal computer.

Graduates: From July 1, 2004 to June 30, 2005, 850 bachelor's degrees were awarded. The most popular majors were marketing (12%), communications (10%), and nursing (10%). In an average class, 78% graduate in 4 years or less, 80% graduate in 5 years or less, and 81% graduate in 6 years or less. 117 companies recruited on campus in 2004-2005. Of the 2004 graduating class, 20% were enrolled in graduate school within 6 months of graduation and 60% were employed.

Admissions Contact: Karen Pellegrino, Director. A video is available. E-mail: *admis@mail.fairfield.edu* Web: *www.fairfield.edu*

MITCHELL COLLEGE
New London, CT 06320

(800) 443-2811
(800) 443-2811; Fax: (860) 444-1209

Full-time: 500 men and women	**Faculty:** 24
Part-time: 150 men and women	**Ph.D.s:** 55%
Graduate: none	**Student/Faculty:** 26 to 1
Year: semesters, summer session	**Tuition:** $18,128
Application Deadline: open	**Room & Board:** $8268
Freshman Class: n/av	
SAT or ACT: required	**COMPETITIVE**

Mitchell College, founded in 1938, is a private institution offering associate and bachelor degree programs in the liberal arts and professional areas. Some information in this capsule and profile is approximate. The 2 libraries contain 45,000 volumes, 38,928 microform items, and 50 audio/video tapes/CDs/DVDs, and subscribe to 90 periodicals including electronic. Computerized library services include the card catalog, interlibrary loans, and database searching. Special learning facilities include a learning resource center. The 65-acre campus is in a suburban area on the shore of the Thames River where it meets Long Island Sound. Including any residence halls, there are 19 buildings.

Student Life: 54% of undergraduates are from Connecticut. Others are from 28 states, 18 foreign countries, and Canada. 50% are from public schools. 60% are white; 10% African American. 44% are Catholic; 31% claim no religious affiliation; 16% Protestant; 7% Jewish. The average age of freshmen is 18; all undergraduates, 20. 35% do not continue beyond their first year; 65% remain to graduate.

Housing: 450 students can be accommodated in college housing, which includes single-sex and coed dorms. On-campus housing is guaranteed for all 4 years. 85% of students live on campus; of those, 68% remain on campus on weekends. Alcohol is not permitted. All students may keep cars.

Activities: There are no fraternities or sororities. There are 35 groups on campus, including art, cheerleading, choir, chorus, computers, dance, drama, ethnic, gay, honors, international, newspaper, professional, religious, social, social service, student government, and yearbook.

Sports: There are 9 intercollegiate sports for men and 9 for women, and 15 intramural sports for men and 15 for women. Facilities include

a basketball court, a fitness center, 2 beaches, natural and groomed trails, woods, tennis courts, and athletic fields for all varsity teams.

Disabled Students: 50% of the campus is accessible. Wheelchair ramps, elevators, special parking, specially equipped rest rooms, and special class scheduling are available.

Services: Counseling and information services are available, as is tutoring in every subject. There is a reader service for the blind.

Campus Safety and Security: Measures include 24-hour foot and vehicle patrol, security escort services, shuttle buses, and informal discussions. There are emergency telephones and lighted pathways/sidewalks.

Programs of Study: Mitchell College confers B.A. and B.S. degrees. Associate degrees are also awarded. Bachelor's degrees are awarded in BUSINESS (business administration and management and sports management), EDUCATION (early childhood), SOCIAL SCIENCE (criminal justice, human development, liberal arts/general studies, and psychology). Early childhood education is the strongest academically. Business administration and liberal and professional studies are the largest.

Required: To graduate, students must complete 120 credits with a minimum GPA of 2.0; 2.67 for early childhood education. A first-year seminar and a course in computer systems is required. A capstone is required in human development.

Special: Numerous internships are available through department heads. Work-study programs and B.A.-B.S. degrees are available. Student-designed majors are possible in liberal and professional studies. There are 2 national honor societies, including Phi Beta Kappa, and 1 departmental honors program.

Faculty/Classroom: 46% of faculty are male; 54%, female. All teach undergraduates. The average class size in an introductory lecture is 12; in a laboratory, 10; and in a regular course, 12.

Requirements: The SAT or ACT is required. The GED is accepted. A recommendation and a personal statement are required. A GPA of 2.0 is required. AP and CLEP credits are accepted. Important factors in the admissions decision are extracurricular activities record, recommendations by school officials, and personality/intangible qualities.

Procedure: Freshmen are admitted fall and spring. Entrance exams should be taken during summer orientation. There are early decision and deferred admissions plans. There is a rolling admissions plan. Application deadlines are open. Chek with the school for current application fee. 35 early decision candidates were accepted for a recent class. Applications are accepted on-line.

Transfer: 45 transfer students enrolled in a recent year. Applicants must submit college transcripts and a letter of good standing, in addition to fulfilling regular application requirements. 30 of 120 credits required for the bachelor's degree must be completed at Mitchell College.

Visiting: There are regularly scheduled orientations for prospective students, including a student-guided tour and an interview with an admissions counselor. There are guides for informal visits and visitors may sit in on classes. To schedule a visit, contact the Admissions Office at *admissions@mitchell.edu*.

Financial Aid: The FAFSA is required. The deadline for filing freshman financial aid applications for fall entry is March 1.

International Students: There were 12 international students enrooled in a recent year. The school actively recruits these students. They must score satisfactorily on the TOEFL and also take the APIEL and the SAT or the ACT.

Computers: All students may access the system at all times. There are no time limits and no fees. It is strongly recommended that all students have a personal computer.

Graduates: In an average class, 60% graduate in 4 years or less.

Admissions Contact: Kathleen Neal, Director of Admissions. A video is available. E-mail: *neal_k@mitchell.edu* Web: *www.mitchell.edu*

POST UNIVERSITY
B-3
(Formerly Teikyo Post University)
Waterbury, CT 06723-2540

(203) 596-4520
(800) 345-2562; Fax: (203) 756-5810

Full-time: 300 men, 364 women	**Faculty:** 33
Part-time: 135 men, 302 women	**Ph.D.s:** 61%
Graduate: none	**Student/Faculty:** 20 to 1
Year: semesters, summer session	**Tuition:** $17,500
Application Deadline: open	**Room & Board:** $7375
Freshman Class: 1115 applied, 734 accepted, 204 enrolled	
SAT or ACT: recommended	**COMPETITIVE**

Post University, founded in 1890, is a private institution offering liberal arts and business programs. There are 2 undergraduate schools. The library contains 85,000 volumes, 75,158 microform items, and 1027 audio/video tapes/CDs/DVDs, and subscribes to 427 periodicals including electronic. Computerized library services include the card catalog, interlibrary loans, and database searching. Special learning facilities include a learning resource center and a tutorial center. The 70-acre campus is in an urban area 1 mile west of Waterbury. Including any residence halls, there are 13 buildings.

Student Life: 83% of undergraduates are from Connecticut. Others are from 12 states, 20 foreign countries, and Canada. 75% are from public schools. 63% are white; 17% African American. The average age of freshmen is 19; all undergraduates, 26. 23% do not continue beyond their first year; 39% remain to graduate.

Housing: 424 students can be accommodated in college housing, which includes coed dormitories and off-campus apartments. On-campus housing is guaranteed for all 4 years. 58% of students live on campus; of those, 60% remain on campus on weekends. All students may keep cars.

Activities: There are no fraternities or sororities. There are 30 groups on campus, including cheerleading, chorale, chorus, computers, drama, ethnic, gay, honors, international, literary magazine, musical theater, social, social service, student government, and yearbook. Popular campus events include dances, concerts, and international food festivals.

Sports: There are 5 intercollegiate sports for men and 5 for women, and 4 intramural sports for men and 4 for women. Facilities include a soccer field, a fitness center, a weight room, a racquetball court, a swimming pool, and tennis courts.

Disabled Students: 70% of the campus is accessible. Wheelchair ramps, elevators, special parking, specially equipped rest rooms, and special class scheduling are available.

Services: Counseling and information services are available, as is tutoring in most subjects. There is a reader service for the blind, and remedial math, reading, and writing.

Campus Safety and Security: Measures include 24-hour foot and vehicle patrol, self-defense education, security escort services, and shuttle buses. There are informal discussions, pamphlets/posters/films, and lighted pathways/sidewalks.

Programs of Study: TPU confers B.A. and B.S. degrees. Associate degrees are also awarded. Bachelor's degrees are awarded in BUSINESS (accounting, banking and finance, business administration and management, management science, and marketing/retailing/merchandising), COMMUNICATIONS AND THE ARTS (English), SOCIAL SCIENCE (criminal justice, history, liberal arts/general studies, psychology, and sociology). Biology is the strongest academically. Management and general studies are the largest.

Required: To graduate, all students must maintain a minimum GPA of 2.0, earn a total of 120 credits, including at least 33 in the major, and take a computer course.

Special: Co-op programs in all majors, cross-registration with Naugatuck Valley Community College, study abroad in England, the Netherlands, and Japan, internships with area businesses, general studies degrees, accelerated degree programs, B.A.-B.S. degrees, and credit for life experience are available. There are 2 national honor societies and 1 departmental honors program.

Faculty/Classroom: 57% of faculty are male; 43%, female. All teach undergraduates. The average class size in an introductory lecture is 20; in a laboratory, 15; and in a regular course, 35.

Admissions: 66% of the 2005-2006 applicants were accepted.

Requirements: The SAT or ACT is recommended. Applicants must be graduates of an accredited secondary school, with 4 years of English and at least 16 total academic credits. The GED is accepted. TPU requires applicants to be in the upper 50% of their class. A GPA of 2.0 is required. AP and CLEP credits are accepted. Important factors in the admissions decision are personality/intangible qualities, extracurricular activities record, and recommendations by school officials.

Procedure: Freshmen are admitted to all sessions. There are early decision, early admissions, rolling admissions, and deferred admissions plans. Early decision applications should be filed by November 1; regular applications are open for fall entry. The application fee is $40. Notification of early decision is sent December 15; regular decision, on a rolling basis. Applications are accepted on-line.

Transfer: 68 transfer students enrolled in 2004-2005. Applicants must have a minimum college GPA of 2.0, submit an official college transcript, and have an interview. The SAT is recommended. 30 of 120 credits required for the bachelor's degree must be completed at TPU.

Visiting: There are regularly scheduled orientations for prospective students, including tours, interviews with admissions counselors, and meetings with faculty and students. There are guides for informal visits and visitors may sit in on classes and stay overnight. To schedule a visit, contact the Admissions Office at (203) 596-4620.

Financial Aid: In 2005-2006, 94% of all full-time freshmen and 90% of continuing full-time students received some form of financial aid. 87% of full-time freshmen and 85% of continuing full-time students received need-based aid. The average freshman award was $18,500. 62% of undergraduates work part time. Average annual earnings from campus work are $1005. The average financial indebtedness of the 2005 graduate was $19,875. The FAFSA, the college's own financial statement and the parent and student federal tax returns are required. The priority date for filing freshman financial aid applications for fall entry is May 1. The deadline for filing freshman financial aid applications for fall entry is rolling.

International Students: There are 65 international students enrolled. The school actively recruits these students. They must score satisfactorily on the written TOEFL.

Computers: All students may access the system. There are no time limits and no fees. It is strongly recommended that all students have a personal computer.

Graduates: From July 1, 2004 to June 30, 2005, 204 bachelor's degrees were awarded. The most popular majors were management (27%), general studies (15%), and marketing (10%). In an average class, 36% graduate in 4 years or less, 31% graduate in 5 years or less, and 5% graduate in 6 years or less. 43 companies recruited on campus in 2004-2005. Of the 2004 graduating class, 10% were enrolled in graduate school within 6 months of graduation and 75% were employed.

Admissions Contact: Aline Rossiter, Dean of Admissions. A video is available. E-mail: *tpuadmis@teikyopost.edu* Web: *http://teikopost.edu*

QUINNIPIAC UNIVERSITY C-3
Hamden, CT 06518
(203) 582-8600
(800) 462-1944; Fax: (203) 582-8906

Full-time: 2039 men, 3247 women	**Faculty:** 225; IIA, ++$
Part-time: 159 men, 261 women	**Ph.D.s:** 82%
Graduate: 612 men, 975 women	**Student/Faculty:** 23 to 1
Year: semesters, summer session	**Tuition:** $24,340
Application Deadline: February 1	**Room & Board:** $10,300
Freshman Class: 11,397 applied, 6011 accepted, 1361 enrolled	
SAT Verbal/Math: 547/564*	**ACT:** 25 **VERY COMPETITIVE**

Quinnipiac University, founded in 1929, is a private institution offering undergraduate and graduate degrees in health sciences, business, communications, liberal arts, education, and law. There are 4 undergraduate and 5 graduate schools. In addition to regional accreditation, Quinnipiac has baccalaureate program accreditation with AACSB, ABA, ACOTE, APTA, CAHEA and NLN. The 2 libraries contain 304,875 volumes, 9100 microform items, and 1890 audio/video tapes/CDs/DVDs, and subscribe to 3900 periodicals including electronic. Computerized library services include interlibrary loans, database searching, Internet access, and laptop Internet portals. Special learning facilities include a learning resource center, radio station, TV station, a critical care nursing lab, and an exhibit on the Irish famine. The 500-acre campus is in a suburban area 8 miles north of New Haven and 35 miles south of Hartford. Including any residence halls, there are 35 buildings.

Student Life: 72% of undergraduates are from out of state, mostly the Middle Atlantic. Students are from 26 states, 12 foreign countries, and Canada. 75% are from public schools. 88% are white. 58% are Catholic; 20% Protestant; 12% claim no religious affiliation; 8% Jewish. The average age of freshmen is 19; all undergraduates, 21. 12% do not continue beyond their first year; 70% remain to graduate.

Housing: 3450 students can be accommodated in college housing, which includes coed dorms, on-campus apartments, and off-campus apartments. In addition, there is wellness housing. 75% of students live on campus; of those, 70% remain on campus on weekends. Upperclassmen may keep cars.

Activities: 5% of men belong to 1 local and 1 national fraternity; 6% of women belong to 1 local sorority and 2 national sororities. There are 75 groups on campus, including cheerleading, chorale, dance, drama, ethnic, film, gay, honors, international, literary magazine, musical theater, newspaper, pep band, political, professional, radio and TV, religious, social, social service, student government, and yearbook. Popular campus events include May Weekend, Parents Weekend, and holiday party.

Sports: There are 9 intercollegiate sports for men and 10 for women, and 6 intramural sports for men and 6 for women. Facilities include more than 20 acres of playing fields, a 1500-seat gym, 2 basketball courts, a weight-training room, a steam room, and a state-of-the-art fitness facility with a large multipurpose room for indoor tennis, basketball, volleyball, and aerobics, and a suspended indoor track.

Disabled Students: All of the campus is accessible. Wheelchair ramps, elevators, special parking, specially equipped rest rooms, special class scheduling, lowered drinking fountains, lowered telephones, and special housing are available.

Services: Counseling and information services are available, as is tutoring in most subjects, including all freshman-level courses and others by request. Special workshops on work study skills, library resources, and time management are available.

Campus Safety and Security: Measures include 24-hour foot and vehicle patrol, self-defense education, security escort services, and shuttle buses. There are informal discussions, pamphlets/posters/films, emergency telephones, lighted pathways/sidewalks, perimeter security in the form of contract security officers at all entrances, and vehicle and occupant check-in identification.

Programs of Study: Quinnipiac confers B.A., B.S., and B.H.S. degrees. Master's and doctoral degrees are also awarded. Bachelor's degrees are awarded in BIOLOGICAL SCIENCE (biochemistry, biology/biological science, biotechnology, and microbiology), BUSINESS (accounting, banking and finance, business administration and management, business economics, entrepreneurial studies, international business management, management science, and marketing/retailing/

merchandising), COMMUNICATIONS AND THE ARTS (advertising, communications, English, journalism, public relations, and Spanish), COMPUTER AND PHYSICAL SCIENCE (chemistry, computer science, digital arts/technology, and mathematics), HEALTH PROFESSIONS (health science, nursing, occupational therapy, predentistry, premedicine, radiological science, and veterinary science), SOCIAL SCIENCE (criminal justice, economics, gerontology, history, liberal arts/general studies, paralegal studies, political science/government, prelaw, psychobiology, psychology, social science, and sociology). Psychology and physical therapy are the strongest academically. Mass communications, physical therapy, and accounting are the largest.

Required: All students must complete 46 semester hours of the core curriculum, which includes competency in English and math. Courses in fine arts, social sciences, humanities, and physical and biological sciences are also part of the core. To graduate, students must maintain a GPA of 2.0 over 120 total semester hours. The foundation of the core curriculum is 3 university seminars that explore the community, with an individual, national, and global focus.

Special: Internships in all majors, study abroad in more than 25 countries, a Washington semester with American University, work-study programs, dual and student-designed majors, B.A.-B.S. degrees, credit for life experience, and nondegree study are available. A 6 1/2-year freshman entry-level doctorate in physical therapy and a 5 1/2-year freshman entry-level master's in occupational therapy are offered, as well as a 6-year B.S. in Health Sciences/M.H.S. in a physician assistant master's program, and a 5-year master of arts in education for those interested in teaching at the elementary, middle, or high school level. There are 8 national honor societies, a freshman honors program, and 9 departmental honors programs.

Faculty/Classroom: 58% of faculty are male; 42%, female. 85% teach undergraduates, 58% do research, and 53% do both. No introductory courses are taught by graduate students. The average class size in an introductory lecture is 24; in a laboratory, 15; and in a regular course, 22.

Admissions: 53% of the 2005-2006 applicants were accepted. The SAT scores for the 2005-2006 freshman class were: Verbal--19% below 500, 58% between 500 and 599, 21% between 600 and 700, and 2% above 700; Math--14% below 500, 55% between 500 and 599, 29% between 600 and 700, and 2% above 700. The ACT scores were 6% below 21, 29% between 21 and 23, 34% between 24 and 26, 25% between 27 and 28, and 6% above 28. 44% of the current freshmen were in the top fifth of their class; 80% were in the top two fifths. 35 freshmen graduated first in their class.

Requirements: The SAT or ACT is required. All students must have completed 16 academic credits, including 4 in English, 3 in math, 2 each in science and social studies, and 5 in electives. The GED is accepted. An interview is recommended, and an essay is required. Quinnipiac requires applicants to be in the upper 40% of their class. A GPA of 2.8 is required. AP and CLEP credits are accepted. Important factors in the admissions decision are advanced placement or honor courses, extracurricular activities record, and ability to finance college education.

Procedure: Freshmen are admitted fall and spring. Entrance exams should be taken in the junior year and early in the senior year. There is a deferred admissions plan. There is a rolling admissions plan. Applications should be filed by February 1 for fall entry and December 15 for spring entry, along with a $45 fee. Notification is sent December 15. 1800 applicants were on the 2005 waiting list; 150 were admitted. Applications are accepted on-line.

Transfer: 195 transfer students enrolled in 2004-2005. Transfer students must have a minimum college GPA of 2.5 (some programs require a minimum of 3.0) and must submit SAT scores and high school or college transcripts if they have not received an associate degree prior to enrollment. An interview is recommended. 45 of 120 credits required for the bachelor's degree must be completed at Quinnipiac.

Visiting: There are regularly scheduled orientations for prospective students, consisting of interviews, a group information session, student-guided tours, financial aid sessions, an opportunity to speak with faculty, and open houses. There are guides for informal visits and visitors may sit in on classes. To schedule a visit, contact the Admissions Office.

Financial Aid: In 2005-2006, 70% of all full-time students received some form of financial aid. 55% of all full-time students received need-based aid. The average freshman award was $14,000. 28% of undergraduates work part time. Average annual earnings from campus work are $2000. The average financial indebtedness of the 2005 graduate was $18,500. The FAFSA is required. The deadline for filing freshman financial aid applications for fall entry is March 1.

International Students: There are 60 international students enrolled. A satisfactory score on the TOEFL is required. The SAT or the ACT is required only if English is the student's native language.

Computers: Wireless access is available. All students must purchase a university-recommended laptop when they enter Quinnipiac for classroom and residence hall use. All students may access the system 24 hours a day. There are no time limits and no fees.

Graduates: From July 1, 2004 to June 30, 2005, 1110 bachelor's degrees were awarded. The most popular majors were mass communica-

tions (11%), occupational therapy (10%), and physical therapy (9%). In an average class, 60% graduate in 4 years or less, 64% graduate in 5 years or less, and 69% graduate in 6 years or less. 75 companies recruited on campus in 2004-2005. Of the 2004 graduating class, 15% were enrolled in graduate school within 6 months of graduation and 88% were employed.

Admissions Contact: Joan Isaac Mohr, Dean of Admissions. A video is available. E-mail: *admissions@quinnipiac.edu* Web: *www.quinnipiac.edu*

SACRED HEART UNIVERSITY   B-4

Fairfield, CT 06825	(203) 371-7880; Fax: (203) 365-7607
Full-time: 1309 men, 1935 women	Faculty: 169; IIA, av$
Part-time: 277 men, 583 women	Ph.D.s: 80%
Graduate: 453 men, 1003 women	Student/Faculty: 19 to 1
Year: semesters, summer session	Tuition: $23,750
Application Deadline: open	Room & Board: $9654
Freshman Class: 5856 applied, 3731 accepted, 886 enrolled	
SAT Verbal/Math: 530/540*	COMPETITIVE

Sacred Heart University, founded in 1963, is a private Catholic institution that offers majors within health sciences, liberal arts and sciences, business, education, and information technology. There are 4 undergraduate and 3 graduate schools. In addition to regional accreditation, SHU has baccalaureate program accreditation with APTA, CSWE, and NLN. The library contains 131,237 volumes, 255,731 microform items, and 1646 audio/video tapes/CDs/DVDs, and subscribes to 15,100 periodicals including electronic. Computerized library services include the card catalog, interlibrary loans, database searching, Internet access, and laptop Internet portals. Special learning facilities include a learning resource center, art gallery, radio station, and center for performing arts. The 65-acre campus is in a suburban area in southwestern Connecticut, 55 miles northeast of New York City. Including any residence halls, there are 23 buildings.

Student Life: 56% of undergraduates are from out of state, mostly the Northeast. Students are from 31 states, 40 foreign countries, and Canada. 68% are from public schools. 86% are white. 72% are Catholic; 16% Protestant; 7% claim no religious affiliation. The average age of freshmen is 18; all undergraduates, 20. 15% do not continue beyond their first year; 80% remain to graduate.

Housing: 2200 students can be accommodated in college housing, which includes coed dorms, on-campus apartments, and off-campus apartments. In addition, there are honors floors and wellness floors. On-campus housing is guaranteed for all 4 years. 68% of students live on campus; of those, 75% remain on campus on weekends. Alcohol is not permitted. Upperclassmen may keep cars.

Activities: 5% of men belong to 4 local fraternities; 5% of women belong to 6 local sororities. There are 85 groups on campus, including art, band, cheerleading, choir, chorale, chorus, computers, dance, debate, drama, drill team, ethnic, film, gay, honors, international, jazz band, literary magazine, marching band, musical theater, newspaper, orchestra, pep band, photography, political, professional, radio and TV, religious, social, social service, student government, and yearbook. Popular campus events include Harvest Weekend, Black History Month, and Latino Month.

Sports: There are 15 intercollegiate sports for men and 17 for women, and 10 intramural sports for men and 10 for women. Facilities include a health and recreation center with 4 multipurpose athletic courts, seating for 2200, and a fitness center. There is a field turf football field, an all-weather track, 6 championship tennis courts, and a softball field.

Disabled Students: 90% of the campus is accessible. Wheelchair ramps, elevators, special parking, specially equipped rest rooms, special class scheduling, lowered drinking fountains, lowered telephones, and room nameplates are available.

Services: Counseling and information services are available, as is tutoring in every subject. There is a reader service for the blind, and remedial math, reading, and writing.

Campus Safety and Security: Measures include 24-hour foot and vehicle patrol, self-defense education, security escort services, and shuttle buses. There are informal discussions, pamphlets/posters/films, emergency telephones, and lighted pathways/sidewalks. All campus-owned residence halls have sprinklers and alarms and are designated nonsmoking.

Programs of Study: SHU confers B.A. and B.S. degrees. Associate, master's, and doctoral degrees are also awarded. Bachelor's degrees are awarded in BIOLOGICAL SCIENCE (biology/biological science), BUSINESS (accounting, banking and finance, business administration and management, business economics, and sports management), COMMUNICATIONS AND THE ARTS (art, communications technology, English, graphic design, media arts, and Spanish), COMPUTER AND PHYSICAL SCIENCE (chemistry, computer science, and mathematics), ENGINEERING AND ENVIRONMENTAL DESIGN (environmental science), HEALTH PROFESSIONS (exercise science and nursing), SOCIAL SCIENCE (criminal justice, history, liberal arts/general studies, philosophy, political science/government, psychology, religion, social work, and sociology). Business, finance, and biology are the strongest academically. Psychology, business and health science are the largest.

Required: All students must complete 120 credit hours, including 30 to 58 in the major, while maintaining a minimum 2.0 GPA. Distribution requirements include an 18-credit required core consisting of freshman writing, oral communication, college math, and literature and civilizations, and a 30- to 32-credit elective core consisting of 9 credits of social science, 9 of philosophy and religious studies, 6 of arts and humanities, and 6 of science and math. B.S. candidates need an additional course each of math and science; B.A. candidates, an additional 6 credits of foreign language.

Special: SHU offers co-op programs in all majors, paid and unpaid internships at area corporations, including Fortune 500 companies, hospitals, newspapers, and social service agencies, study abroad worldwide, legislative internships, and on-campus work-study. There are 12 national honor societies, a freshman honors program, and 1 departmental honors program.

Faculty/Classroom: 52% of faculty are male; 48%, female. 96% teach undergraduates and 80% do research. No introductory courses are taught by graduate students. The average class size in an introductory lecture is 20; in a laboratory, 10; and in a regular course, 20.

Admissions: 64% of the 2005-2006 applicants were accepted. The SAT scores for the 2005-2006 freshman class were: Verbal--30% below 500, 54% between 500 and 599, 15% between 600 and 700, and 1% above 700; Math--21% below 500, 59% between 500 and 599, 19% between 600 and 700, and 1% above 700. 33% of the current freshmen were in the top fifth of their class; 65% were in the top two fifths. 71 freshmen graduated first in their class.

Requirements: The SAT or ACT is required. In addition, a writing component is required for those taking the ACT. A completed application, essay, and 1 letter of recommendation are required. An interview is required for early decision candidates and recommended for all other candidates. Required are 4 years of English and 3 years of math, science, history, and language, with 4 years preferred. SHU requires applicants to be in the upper 50% of their class. A GPA of 3.0 is required. AP and CLEP credits are accepted. Important factors in the admissions decision are advanced placement or honor courses, leadership record, and recommendations by school officials.

Procedure: Freshmen are admitted fall and spring. Entrance exams should be taken in May of the junior year and/or November of the senior year. There are early decision, early admissions, and deferred admissions plans. There is a rolling admissions plan. Early decision applications should be filed by October or December; regular applications are open for fall entry. The fee is $50. Notification of early decision is sent October 15; regular decision, on a rolling basis. 166 early decision candidates were accepted for the 2005-2006 class. Applications are accepted on-line.

Transfer: 190 transfer students enrolled in 2004-2005. A minimum GPA of 2.7 is required. 30 of 120 credits required for the bachelor's degree must be completed at SHU.

Visiting: There are regularly scheduled orientations for prospective students, including Monday-Friday tours and interviews, weekend tours, interviews and information sessions, and open house programs during the academic year and summer. There are guides for informal visits and visitors may sit in on classes and stay overnight. To schedule a visit, contact the Office of Undergraduate Admissions at *enroll@scaredheart.edu*.

Financial Aid: In 2005-2006, 84% of all full-time freshmen and 80% of continuing full-time students received some form of financial aid. 60% of full-time freshmen and 68% of continuing full-time students received need-based aid. The average freshman award was $13,922. Need-based scholarships or need-based grants averaged $9266 ($11,500 maximum); need-based self-help aid (loans and jobs) averaged $5636 ($6625 maximum); and non-need-based athletic scholarships averaged $16,934 ($34,789 maximum). 28% of undergraduates work part time. Average annual earnings from campus work are $1157. The average financial indebtedness of the 2005 graduate was $19,926. SHU is a member of CSS. The CSS/Profile or FAFSA is required. The priority date for freshman financial aid applications for fall entry is February 15.

International Students: There are 97 international students enrolled. The school actively recruits these students. They must score satisfactorily on the TOEFL and also take the SAT or the ACT.

Computers: Wireless access is available. Access to the university's network and the Internet is seamless throughout the campus. The entire campus, including all the dorms and all outside areas, is located within the university's wireless footprint. All students may access the system 24 hours a day. There are no time limits and no fees. All students are required to have personal computers. An IBM ThinkPad is recommended.

Graduates: From July 1, 2004 to June 30, 2005, 794 bachelor's degrees were awarded. The most popular majors were business/finance (35%), psychology (16%), and health professions (nursing, exercise science, athletic training) (9%). In an average class, 2% graduate in 3 years or less, 55% graduate in 4 years or less, 61% graduate in 5 years or less, and 63% graduate in 6 years or less. 152 companies recruited on campus in 2004-2005. Of the 2004 graduating class, 46% were enrolled in

graduate school within 6 months of graduation and 52% were employed.

Admissions Contact: Karen N. Guastelle, Dean of Undergraduate Admissions. A video is available. E-mail: *enroll@sacredheart.edu* Web: *www.sacredheart.edu*

SAINT JOSEPH COLLEGE   C-2
West Hartford, CT 06117   (860) 231-5216
(866) 442-8752; Fax: (860) 233-5695

Full-time: 2 men, 869 women	**Faculty:** 73; IIA, av$
Part-time: 9 men, 279 women	**Ph.D.s:** 81%
Graduate: 76 men, 623 women	**Student/Faculty:** 12 to 1
Year: semesters, summer session	**Tuition:** $22,825
Application Deadline: rolling	**Room & Board:** $9225
Freshman Class: 923 applied, 751 accepted, 207 enrolled	
SAT Verbal/Math: 500/490*	**COMPETITIVE**

Saint Joseph College, founded in 1932 and affiliated with the Roman Catholic Church, is a private primarily women's college offering a liberal arts education with preprofessional programs in nursing, education, and business at the undergraduate level. The Prime Time Program and the graduate school offer coed studies. In addition to regional accreditation, SJC has baccalaureate program accreditation with ADA, CSWE, and NLN. The library contains 120,500 volumes, 72,185 microform items, and 3627 audio/video tapes/CDs/DVDs, and subscribes to 469 periodicals including electronic. Computerized library services include the card catalog, interlibrary loans, database searching, and Internet access. Special learning facilities include a learning resource center, art gallery, academic resources center, and 2 lab schools: the Gengras Center for Exceptional Children and the School for Young Children. The 84-acre campus is in a suburban area 3 miles west of Hartford. Including any residence halls, there are 13 buildings.

Student Life: 91% of undergraduates are from Connecticut. Students are from 7 states and 1 foreign country. 88% are from public schools. 69% are white; 13% African American. The average age of freshmen is 18; all undergraduates, 21. 20% do not continue beyond their first year; 65% remain to graduate.

Housing: 410 students can be accommodated in college housing, which includes single-sex dorms. Priority for on-campus housing is given to out-of-town students. 52% of students commute. Alcohol is not permitted. All students may keep cars.

Activities: There are no fraternities or sororities. There are 19 groups on campus, including art, cheerleading, choir, chorale, chorus, dance, drama, ethnic, gay, honors, international, literary magazine, musical theater, political, professional, religious, social, social service, student government, and yearbook. Popular campus events include Convocation, Cultural Awareness Day, and Symposium Day.

Sports: There are 8 intercollegiate sports for women and 8 intramural sports for women. Facilities include indoor and outdoor tracks, a gym, an exercise room, tennis courts, a dance studio, a pool, and a softball diamond.

Disabled Students: 75% of the campus is accessible. Wheelchair ramps, elevators, special parking, specially equipped rest rooms, special class scheduling, lowered drinking fountains, and lowered telephones are available. Other needs are met on a case-by-case basis.

Services: Counseling and information services are available, as is tutoring in most subjects, including ESL. There is remedial math, reading, and writing. Other services are arranged as needed through the Academic Resource Center.

Campus Safety and Security: Measures include 24-hour foot and vehicle patrol, self-defense education, security escort services, and shuttle buses. There are informal discussions, pamphlets/posters/films, emergency telephones, and lighted pathways/sidewalks.

Programs of Study: SJC confers B.A., B.S., and B.S.N. degrees. Master's degrees are also awarded. Bachelor's degrees are awarded in BIOLOGICAL SCIENCE (biology/biological science and nutrition), BUSINESS (management science), COMMUNICATIONS AND THE ARTS (art history and appreciation, English, and Spanish), COMPUTER AND PHYSICAL SCIENCE (chemistry and mathematics), EDUCATION (special), ENGINEERING AND ENVIRONMENTAL DESIGN (environmental science), HEALTH PROFESSIONS (nursing), SOCIAL SCIENCE (American studies, child psychology/development, dietetics, economics, family/consumer studies, history, international studies, liberal arts/general studies, philosophy, psychology, religion, social work, sociology, and women's studies). Psychology, education, and sciences are the strongest academically. Education, psychology, and nursing are the largest.

Required: All students must maintain a minimum GPA of 2.0, pass a written or oral comprehensive exam, and take 120 total credit hours, including a minimum of 30 in the major, and liberal arts requirements of 12 credits in 4 core areas, plus 6 credits in religion, 9 in humanities, 9 in social studies, 7 to 8 in natural science/math, and 1 in phys ed, and an information technology course.

Special: The college offers cross-registration through the Greater Hartford consortium, numerous internships, study abroad in Great Britain, Europe, and Japan, a dual major in biology and chemistry, and student-designed majors. Credit for life experience, nondegree study, and pass/fail options are available. There is 1 national honor society and a freshman honors program.

Faculty/Classroom: 42% of faculty are male; 58%, female. 92% teach undergraduates. No introductory courses are taught by graduate students. The average class size in an introductory lecture is 30; in a laboratory, 20; and in a regular course, 20.

Admissions: 81% of the 2005-2006 applicants were accepted. The SAT scores for the 2005-2006 freshman class were: Verbal--48% below 500, 39% between 500 and 599, 12% between 600 and 700, and 1% above 700; Math--54% below 500, 38% between 500 and 599, 7% between 600 and 700, and 1% above 700. 34% of the current freshmen were in the top fifth of their class; 68% were in the top two fifths.

Requirements: The SAT or ACT is required. In addition, applicants need 16 academic credits distributed among English, foreign language, history, math, science, and social studies. The GED is accepted, and an interview is recommended. A GPA of 2.5 is required. AP and CLEP credits are accepted. Important factors in the admissions decision are advanced placement or honor courses, recommendations by school officials, and evidence of special talent.

Procedure: Freshmen are admitted fall and spring. There are early decision, early admissions, and deferred admissions plans. There is a rolling admission plan. Early decision applications should be filed by November 15; regular applications, by rolling for fall entry and rolling for spring entry, along with a $35 fee. Notification of early decision is sent by December 15; regular decision, on a rolling basis. Applications are accepted on-line.

Transfer: 109 transfer students enrolled in 2004-2005. SJC accepts transfers up to the beginning of the junior year. Applicants need a minimum college GPA of 2.7. 45 of 120 credits required for the bachelor's degree must be completed at SJC.

Visiting: There are regularly scheduled orientations for prospective students, including open houses, preview days, overnights, individual appointments, and campus tours. There are guides for informal visits and visitors may sit in on classes and stay overnight. To schedule a visit, contact Alan Chesterton, Associate Vice President for Admission and Enrollment Services.

Financial Aid: In 2005-2006, all full-time freshmen and 92% of continuing full-time students received some form of financial aid. 78% of full-time freshmen and 77% of continuing full-time students received need-based aid. The average freshman award was $23,956. Need-based scholarships or need-based grants averaged $5690 ($20,300 maximum); need-based self-help aid (loans and jobs) averaged $3465 ($6425 maximum); and other non-need-based awards and non-need-based scholarships averaged $8261 ($13,500 maximum). 32% of undergraduates work part time. Average annual earnings from campus work are $1332. The average financial indebtedness of the 2005 graduate was $23,709. SJC is a member of CSS. The FAFSA is required. The deadline for filing freshman financial aid applications for fall entry is February 15.

International Students: There is 1 international students enrolled. They must score satisfactorily on the written TOEFL.

Computers: Wireless access is available. There are 150 PCs throughout campus, including the Network Center, the library, science labs, nursing labs, and the Student Center. All students may access the system any time. There are no time limits and no fees.

Graduates: From July 1, 2004 to June 30, 2005, 229 bachelor's degrees were awarded. In an average class, 58% graduate in 4 years, 15% graduate in 5 years, and 6% graduate in 6 years. 140 companies recruited on campus in 2004-2005. Of the 2004 graduating class, 21% were enrolled in graduate school within 6 months of graduation and 79% were employed.

Admissions Contact: Alan Chesterton, Associate Vice President for Admission and Enrollment Services. A video is available.
E-mail: admissions@sjc.edu Web: www.sjc.edu

SOUTHERN CONNECTICUT STATE UNIVERSITY   C-3

New Haven, CT 06515   (203) 392-5649; Fax: (203) 392-5727

Full-time: 2475 men, 3800 women	**Faculty:** 328; IIA,
Part-time: 900 men, 1200 women	**Ph.D.s:** 83%
Graduate: 1000 men, 2925 women	**Student/Faculty:** 17 to 1
Year: semesters, summer session	**Tuition:** $5813 (13,572)
Application Deadline: May 1	**Room & Board:** $7696
Freshman Class: n/av	
SAT or ACT: required	**COMPETITIVE**

Southern Connecticut State University, founded in 1893, provides undergraduate and graduate liberal arts programs in the arts, business, education, professional studies, and the sciences. It is part of the Connecticut State University system. Some figures given in this profile are approximate. There are 5 undergraduate and 6 graduate schools. In addition to regional accreditation, SCSU has baccalaureate program accreditation with CSWE and NLN. The library contains 495,660 volumes, 753,033 microform items, and 4689 audio/video tapes/CDs/DVDs, and subscribes to 3549 periodicals including electronic. Computerized library services include the card catalog, interlibrary loans, and database searching. Special learning facilities include a learning resource center, art gallery, planetarium, radio station, and TV station. The 168-acre campus is in an urban area 35 miles south of Hartford and 90 miles from New York City. Including any residence halls, there are 28 buildings.

Student Life: 92% of undergraduates are from Connecticut. Others are from 20 states, 36 foreign countries, and Canada. 90% are from public schools. 77% are white. 64% are Catholic; 18% Protestant. The average age of freshmen is 19; all undergraduates, 22. 25% do not continue beyond their first year; 48% remain to graduate.

Housing: 2100 students can be accommodated in college housing, which includes single-sex dorms and on-campus apartments. On-campus housing is guaranteed for all 4 years. 72% of students commute. Upperclassmen may keep cars.

Activities: 1% of men belong to 3 local and 3 national fraternities; 1% of women belong to 1 local and 2 national sororities. There are 70 groups on campus, including art, band, cheerleading, choir, chorale, chorus, computers, dance, drama, drill team, ethnic, gay, honors, international, jazz band, literary magazine, marching band, musical theater, newspaper, pep band, photography, political, professional, radio and TV, religious, social, social service, student government, and yearbook. Popular campus events include Springfest, Parents Day, and Octoberfest.

Sports: There are 9 intercollegiate sports for men and 8 for women. Facilities include a 6000-seat artificial-surface playing complex for football, soccer, field hockey, and track; field house and gym facilities for basketball, gymnastics, badminton, tennis, track and field, volleyball, and indoor baseball; and an 8-lane swimming pool.

Disabled Students: 80% of the campus is accessible. Wheelchair ramps, elevators, special parking, specially equipped rest rooms, special class scheduling, lowered drinking fountains, lowered telephones, and special computer facilities are available.

Services: Counseling and information services are available, as is tutoring in every subject. There is a reader service for the blind, and remedial math, reading, and writing.

Campus Safety and Security: Measures include 24-hour foot and vehicle patrol, self-defense education, security escort services, and shuttle buses. There are informal discussions, pamphlets/posters/films, emergency telephones, and lighted pathways/sidewalks. Campus security is provided by a campus-based police force.

Programs of Study: SCSU confers B.A., B.S., B.S.Bus.Adm., and B.S.Ed. degrees. Associate and master's degrees are also awarded. Bachelor's degrees are awarded in BIOLOGICAL SCIENCE (biochemistry and biology/biological science), BUSINESS (accounting, banking and finance, business administration and management, business economics, marketing/retailing/merchandising, and recreation and leisure services), COMMUNICATIONS AND THE ARTS (art history and appreciation, communications, dramatic arts, English, fine arts, French, German, Italian, journalism, Spanish, and studio art), COMPUTER AND PHYSICAL SCIENCE (chemistry, computer science, earth science, mathematics, and physics), EDUCATION (art, early childhood, elementary, foreign languages, health, library science, physical, science, secondary, and special), HEALTH PROFESSIONS (nursing and public health), SOCIAL SCIENCE (economics, geography, history, philosophy, political science/government, psychology, social work, and sociology). Psychology, communications, and elementary education are the largest.

Required: All students must complete distribution requirements that include 6 credits each in English composition and speech, natural sciences, and social sciences, 3 credits each in American politics, fine arts, foreign languages, math, literature, philosophy, and Western civilization, and 1 credit each in phys ed and health. Students must take 122 total credits, with a minimum of 30 hours in the major field, and maintain a minimum overall GPA of 2.0.

Special: SCSU offer co-op programs in all academic majors, internships in many departments, study abroad in a variety of countries, a combined B.A.-B.S. degree, dual majors, a general studies degree, student-designed majors in liberal studies, and pass/fail options. There are 2 national honor societies, a freshman honors program, and 1 departmental honors program.

Faculty/Classroom: 61% of faculty are male; 39%, female. 96% teach undergraduates. No introductory courses are taught by graduate students. The average class size in an introductory lecture is 30; in a laboratory, 25; and in a regular course, 22.

Requirements: A satisfactory score on the SAT, or on the ACT is needed. In addition, applicants should be in the upper 50% of their high school class and should graduate with 4 years in English, 3 in math, and 2 each in natural sciences and social sciences, including American history. The GED is accepted. 2 years of foreign language are recommended. An essay also is needed. A GPA of 2.5 is required. AP and CLEP credits are accepted. Important factors in the admissions decision are advanced placement or honor courses, recommendations by school officials, and leadership record.

Procedure: Freshmen are admitted fall and spring. There are early decision and early admissions plans. Recommended application filing dates are May 1 for fall entry, December 1, Spring. The application fee is $50.
Transfer: Transfer applicants must have a minimum of 6 college credits with a grade of C or better and an overall GPA of 2.0. The SAT is required for applicants with fewer than 24 college credits. 30 of 122 credits required for the bachelor's degree must be completed at SCSU.
Visiting: There are regularly scheduled orientations for prospective students. Visitors may sit in on classes. To schedule a visit, contact Admissions Office.
Financial Aid: SCSU is a member of CSS. The FAFSA and the college's own financial statement are required. Check with the school for current deadlines.
International Students: They must score satisfactorily on the written TOEFL and also take the SAT or the ACT, scoring satisfactorily.
Computers: All students may access the system 17 hours a day. There are no time limits and no fees.
Graduates: In an average class, 13% graduate in 4 years or less, 29% graduate in 5 years or less, and 34% graduate in 6 years or less.
Admissions Contact: Heather Stearns, Assistant Director of Admissions.

TEIKYO POST UNIVERSITY
(See Post University)

TRINITY COLLEGE
C-2
Hartford, CT 06106   (860) 297-2180; Fax: (860) 297-2287
Full-time: 1000 men, 1000 women   **Faculty:** 187; IIB, ++$
Part-time: 75 men, 110 women   **Ph.D.s:** 90%
Graduate: 90 men, 70 women   **Student/Faculty:** 11 to 1
Year: semesters   **Tuition:** $31,990
Application Deadline: January 1   **Room & Board:** $8590
Freshman Class: 5510 applied, 1993 accepted, 550 enrolled
SAT or ACT: required   **HIGHLY COMPETITIVE+**

Founded in 1823, Trinity College in Hartford is an independent, nonsectarian liberal arts college of the highest quality. Its rigorous curriculum is firmly grounded in the traditional liberal arts disciplines and marked by an array of interdisciplinary studies, exceptional offerings in science and engineering, and distinctive educational connections with Connecticut's capital city and cities around the world. Some figures in the above capsule and in this profile are approximate. In addition to regional accreditation, Trinity has baccalaureate program accreditation with ABET. The library contains 992,817 volumes, 399,394 microform items, and 225,477 audio/video tapes/CDs/DVDs, and subscribes to 2438 periodicals including electronic. Computerized library services include the card catalog, interlibrary loans, database searching, and Internet access. Special learning facilities include an art gallery, radio station, TV station, and Connecticut Public Television and Radio. The 100-acre campus is in an urban area southwest of downtown Hartford. Including any residence halls, there are 78 buildings.
Student Life: 79% of undergraduates are from out of state, mostly the Northeast. Students are from 44 states, 28 foreign countries, and Canada. 43% are from public schools. 79% are white. 32% are Protestant; 28% Catholic; 25% claim no religious affiliation; 8% Jewish; 7% miscellaneous. The average age of freshmen is 18; all undergraduates, 20. 8% do not continue beyond their first year; 84% remain to graduate.
Housing: 1861 students can be accommodated in college housing, which includes coed dorms, on-campus apartments, and fraternity houses. In addition, there are special-interest houses. On-campus housing is guaranteed for all 4 years. 93% of students live on campus; of those, 70% remain on campus on weekends. Upperclassmen may keep cars.
Activities: 20% of men and about 16% of women belong to 3 local and 4 national fraternities. There are no sororities. There are 112 groups on campus, including art, bagpipe band, band, cheerleading, chess, choir, chorale, chorus, dance, debate, drama, ethnic, film, gay, honors, international, jazz band, literary magazine, musical theater, newspaper, pep band, photography, political, professional, radio and TV, religious, social, social service, student government, and yearbook. Popular campus events include Human Rights Lecture Series, Black History Month, and Latino Heritage Week.
Sports: There are 15 intercollegiate sports for men and 13 for women, and 14 intramural sports for men and 14 for women. Facilities include a pool, outdoor and indoor tracks, playing fields, a weight room, a fitness center, and tennis, squash, and basketball courts.
Disabled Students: 60% of the campus is accessible. Wheelchair ramps, elevators, special parking, specially equipped rest rooms, special class scheduling, lowered drinking fountains, and lowered telephones are available.
Services: Counseling and information services are available, as is tutoring in every subject. There is a reader service for the blind. The writing center offers instruction in all forms of writing, and the math center provides individual tutoring on topics related to math and other courses involving quantitative reasoning.

Campus Safety and Security: Measures include 24-hour foot and vehicle patrol, self-defense education, security escort services, and shuttle buses. There are informal discussions, pamphlets/posters/films, emergency telephones, and lighted pathways/sidewalks.
Programs of Study: Trinity confers B.A. and B.S. degrees. Master's degrees are also awarded. Bachelor's degrees are awarded in BIOLOGICAL SCIENCE (biochemistry, biology/biological science, and neurosciences), COMMUNICATIONS AND THE ARTS (art history and appreciation, classics, comparative literature, dance, dramatic arts, English, fine arts, French, German, Italian, modern language, music, Russian, Spanish, studio art, and theater management), COMPUTER AND PHYSICAL SCIENCE (chemistry, computer science, mathematics, and physics), EDUCATION (education), ENGINEERING AND ENVIRONMENTAL DESIGN (engineering and environmental science), SOCIAL SCIENCE (American studies, anthropology, classical/ancient civilization, economics, history, interdisciplinary studies, international studies, Judaic studies, philosophy, political science/government, psychology, public affairs, religion, sociology, and women's studies). Political science, economics, and English are the largest.
Required: All students must complete 36 course credits, including 10 to 15 in the major and 1 from each of 5 distribution areas: arts, humanities, natural sciences, numerical and symbolic reasoning, and social sciences. Students must maintain at least a C average overall.
Special: Trinity offers special freshman programs for exceptional students, including interdisciplinary programs in the sciences and the humanities. There is an intensive study program under which students can devote a semester to 1 subject. Cross-registration through such programs as the Hartford Consortium and the Twelve-College Exchange Program, hundreds of internships (some with Connecticut Public Radio and TV on campus), study abroad virtually worldwide, including San Francisco, Rome, South Africa, Trinidad, Russia, and Nepal, a Washington semester, dual majors in all disciplines, student-designed majors, nondegree study, and pass/fail options also are offered. A 5-year advanced degree in electrical or mechanical engineering with Rensselaer Polytechnic Institute also is available. There are 4 national honor societies, including Phi Beta Kappa.
Faculty/Classroom: 60% of faculty are male; 40%, female. All both teach and do research. No introductory courses are taught by graduate students. The average class size in an introductory lecture is 21; in a laboratory, 15; and in a regular course, 13.
Admissions: 36% of the recent applicants were accepted. The SAT scores for a recent freshman class were: Verbal--3% below 500, 26% between 500 and 599, 54% between 600 and 700, and 15% above 700; Math--4% below 500, 22% between 500 and 599, 55% between 600 and 700, and 20% above 700. The ACT scores were 5% below 21, 12% between 21 and 23, 23% between 24 and 26, 25% between 27 and 28, and 35% above 28. 73% of the recent freshmen were in the top fifth of their class; 91% were in the top two fifths.
Requirements: The SAT or ACT is required along with the SAT: Subject test in writing or SAT: Subject tests in writing and 2 additional SAT Subject tests. Trinity strongly emphasizes individual character and personal qualities in admission. Consequently, an interview and essay are recommended. The college requires 4 years of English, 2 years each in foreign language and algebra, and 1 year each in geometry, history, and lab science. AP credits are accepted. Important factors in the admissions decision are advanced placement or honor courses, extracurricular activities record, and evidence of special talent.
Procedure: Freshmen are admitted in the fall. Entrance exams should be taken in the fall of the senior year. There are early decision and deferred admissions plans. Early decision applications should be filed by November 15; regular applications, by January 1 for fall entry. Notification of early decision is sent mid December; regular decision, early April. The application fee is $60. 271 early decision candidates were accepted for a recent class. 364 applicants were on the 2005 waiting list; 7 were admitted. Applications are accepted on-line.
Transfer: 21 transfer students enrolled in a recent year. Transfer applicants must take the SAT or ACT. A minimum college GPA of 3.0 is recommended. 18 of 36 credits required for the bachelor's degree must be completed at Trinity.
Visiting: There are regularly scheduled orientations for prospective students. There are guides for informal visits and visitors may sit in on classes and stay overnight. To schedule a visit, contact the Admissions Office at admissions.office@trincoll.edu.
Financial Aid: In a recent year, 36% of all full-time freshmen and 45% of continuing full-time students received some form of financial aid. 35% of full-time freshmen and 41% of continuing full-time students received need-based aid. The average freshman award was $23,630. Need-based scholarships or need-based grants averaged $21,694 ($39,740 maximum); need-based self-help aid (loans and jobs) averaged $3800 ($8325 maximum); and other non-need-based awards and non-need-based scholarships averaged $6088 ($10,461 maximum). 30% of undergraduates work part time. Average annual earnings from campus work are $1624. The average financial indebtedness of a recent graduate was $13,792. Trinity is a member of CSS. The CSS/Profile or FAFSA is re-

quired. The deadline for filing freshman financial aid applications for fall entry is March 1.

International Students: The school actively recruits these students. They must score satisfactorily on the written TOEFL and also take the SAT or the ACT.

Computers: All students may access the system 24 hours daily. There are no time limits and no fees. It is strongly recommended that all students have a personal computer.

Graduates: In a recent year, 553 bachelor's degrees were awarded. The most popular majors were political science (16%), economics (12%), and history (10%). In an average class, 82% graduate in 4 years or less, 89% graduate in 5 years or less, and 90% graduate in 6 years or less.

Admissions Contact: Larry R. Dow, Dean of Admissions/Financial Aid. E-mail: admissions.office@mail.trincoll.edu
Web: http://www.trincoll.edu

UNITED STATES COAST GUARD ACADEMY   E-3
New London, CT 06320-8103   (860) 444-8500
                                     (800) 883-8724; Fax: (860) 701-6700

Full-time: 752 men, 300 women	**Faculty:** 112
Part-time: none	**Ph.D.s:** 30%
Graduate: none	**Student/Faculty:** 9 to 1
Year: semesters, summer session	**Tuition:** see profile
Application Deadline: March 1	**Room & Board:** n/app
Freshman Class: 1202 applied, 420 accepted, 307 enrolled	
SAT Verbal/Math: 630/650*	**ACT:** 27 HIGHLY COMPETITIVE

The U.S. Coast Guard Academy, founded in 1876, is an Armed Forces Service Academy for men and women. Appointments are made solely on the basis of an annual nationwide competition. Except for an entrance fee of $3,000, the federal government covers all cadet expenses by providing a monthly allowance of $600 plus a daily food allowance. In addition to regional accreditation, USCGA has baccalaureate program accreditation with ABET. The library contains 150,000 volumes, 60,000 microform items, and 1500 audio/video tapes/CDs/DVDs, and subscribes to 850 periodicals including electronic. Computerized library services include the card catalog, interlibrary loans, and database searching. Special learning facilities include the Coast Guard Museum, a $5 million ship's bridge simulator, and the Leadership Development Center for the Coast Guard. The 110-acre campus is in a suburban area 45 miles southeast of Hartford. Including any residence halls, there are 25 buildings.

Student Life: 93% of undergraduates are from out of state, mostly the Northeast. Students are from 50 states and 14 foreign countries. 79% are white. 33% are Catholic; 30% claim no religious affiliation; 29% Protestant. The average age of freshmen is 18; all undergraduates, 21. 21% do not continue beyond their first year; 67% remain to graduate.

Housing: 1000 students can be accommodated in college housing, which includes coed dorms. On-campus housing is guaranteed for all 4 years. All students live on campus. Alcohol is not permitted. Upperclassmen may keep cars.

Activities: There are no fraternities or sororities. There are many groups and organizations on campus, including bagpipe band, band, cheerleading, choir, chorale, chorus, dance, debate, drama, drill team, drum and bugle corps, ethnic, international, jazz band, marching band, musical theater, newspaper, pep band, political, professional, religious, social, social service, student government, and yearbook. Popular campus events include Coast Guard Day and Hispanic Heritage and Black History months.

Sports: There are 13 intercollegiate sports for men and 11 for women, and 13 intramural sports for men and 13 for women. Facilities include a field house with 3 basketball courts, a 6-lane swimming pool, 5 racquetball courts, and facilities for track meets, tennis matches, and baseball and softball games; an additional athletic facility with wrestling and weight rooms, basketball courts, gymnastics areas, a swimming pool, and saunas; a 4500-seat stadium; and practice and playing fields, outdoor tennis courts, and rowing and seamanship-sailing centers.

Disabled Students: 24% of the campus is accessible. Wheelchair ramps, elevators, special parking, and specially equipped rest rooms are available.

Services: Counseling and information services are available, as is tutoring in every subject.

Campus Safety and Security: Measures include 24-hour foot and vehicle patrol, self-defense education, and lighted pathways/sidewalks.

Programs of Study: USCGA confers the B.S. degree. Bachelor's degrees are awarded in BIOLOGICAL SCIENCE (marine science), BUSINESS (management science and operations research), ENGINEERING AND ENVIRONMENTAL DESIGN (civil engineering, electrical/electronics engineering, mechanical engineering, and naval architecture and marine engineering), SOCIAL SCIENCE (political science/government). Political science/government is the largest.

Required: To graduate, cadets must pass at least 37 courses, of which 25 are core; accumulate a minimum of 126 credit hours, with at least 90

credits of C or better, exclusive of phys ed; complete the academic requirements for one of the approved majors and attain a minimum GPA of 2.0 in all required upper-division courses in the major; successfully complete all professional development and phys ed requirements; and maintain a high sense of integrity.

Special: Cross-registration with Connecticut College, summer cruises to foreign ports, 6-week internships with various government agencies and some engineering and science organizations, and a 1-semester exchange program with the 3 other military academies are available. All graduates are commissioned in the U.S. Coast Guard. There are 2 national honor societies, a freshman honors program, and 3 departmental honors programs.

Faculty/Classroom: 90% of faculty are male; 10%, female. The average class size in an introductory lecture is 28; in a laboratory, 18; and in a regular course, 20.

Admissions: 35% of the 2005-2006 applicants were accepted. The SAT scores for the 2005-2006 freshman class were: Verbal--1% below 500, 29% between 500 and 599, 53% between 600 and 700, and 17% above 700; Math--10% between 500 and 599, 70% between 600 and 700, and 20% above 700. The ACT scores were 14% between 18 and 23, 63% between 24 and 29, and 23% between 30 and 36. 80% of the current freshmen were in the top fifth of their class; 95% were in the top two fifths. 14 freshmen graduated first in their class.

Requirements: The SAT or ACT is required. The ACT Optional Writing test is also required. In addition, applicants must have reached the age of 17 but not the age of 23 by July 1 of the year of admission, be citizens of the United States, and be single at the time of appointment and remain single while attending the academy. Required secondary school courses include 4 years each of English and math.

Procedure: Freshmen are admitted in the fall. Entrance exams should be taken by January 31. There are early admissions and rolling admissions plans. Early action applications should be filed by November 1; regular applications, by March 1 for fall entry. Notification of early action is sent December 15; regular decision, on a rolling basis. 409 applicants were on the 2005 waiting list; 204 were admitted. Applications are accepted on-line.

Transfer: All transfer students must meet the same standards as incoming freshmen and must begin as freshmen no matter how many semesters or years of college they have completed.

Visiting: There are regularly scheduled orientations for prospective students, including an admissions briefing and tour of the academy every Monday, Wednesday, and Friday from 1 P.M. To schedule a visit, contact Admissions Receptionist. All 126 credits required for the bachelor's degree must be completed at USCGA.

International Students: Satisfactory scores are required on the written TOEFL and the SAT or the ACT.

Computers: All students may access the system 24 hours a day. There are no time limits and no fees. All students are required to have PCs.

Admissions Contact: Susan D. Bibeau, Director of Admissions. A video is available. E-mail: admissions@exmail.uscga.edu
Web: www.cga.edu

UNIVERSITY OF BRIDGEPORT   B-4
Bridgeport, CT 06604   (203) 576-4552
                                      (800) EXCEL-UB; Fax: (203) 576-4941

Full-time: 502 men, 745 women	**Faculty:** 67; IIA, -$
Part-time: 105 men, 324 women	**Ph.D.s:** 85%
Graduate: 903 men, 1047 women	**Student/Faculty:** 19 to 1
Year: semesters, summer session	**Tuition:** $20,595
Application Deadline: April 1	**Room & Board:** $9000
Freshman Class: 2332 applied, 1709 accepted, 365 enrolled	
SAT Verbal/Math: 430/440*	**ACT:** 18 LESS COMPETITIVE

The University of Bridgeport, founded in 1927, is a private, independent, nonsectarian university offering programs in the arts, humanities, and social sciences, business, engineering and design, natural sciences, human services, dental hygiene, chiropractic and naturopathic medicine, and teacher preparation. There are 7 undergraduate and 7 graduate schools. In addition to regional accreditation, UB has baccalaureate program accreditation with ABET, ADA, and NASAD. The library contains 275,000 volumes, 1 million microform items, and 5000 audio/video tapes/CDs/DVDs, and subscribes to 1700 periodicals including electronic. Computerized library services include interlibrary loans and database searching. Special learning facilities include a learning resource center and art gallery. The 86-acre campus is in an urban area 60 miles northeast of New York City. Including any residence halls, there are 30 buildings.

Student Life: 52% of undergraduates are from Connecticut. Others are from 39 states, 64 foreign countries, and Canada. 89% are from public schools. 33% are African American; 31% white; 14% Hispanic; 13% foreign nationals. 69% claim no religious affiliation; 14% Catholic. The average age of freshmen is 19; all undergraduates, 24. 32% do not continue beyond their first year; 50% remain to graduate.

Housing: 1078 students can be accommodated in college housing, which includes coed dorms. In addition, there are special-interest houses and alcohol- and tobaco-free buildings. On-campus housing is guaranteed for all 4 years. 54% of students commute. All students may keep cars.

Activities: 1% of men belong to 2 local fraternities; 2% of women belong to 1 local sorority. There are 44 groups on campus, including art, cheerleading, computers, debate, ethnic, honors, international, literary magazine, newspaper, photography, political, professional, radio and TV, religious, social, social service, student government, and yearbook. Popular campus events include International Festival, Winter Prelude, and Wisteria Ball.

Sports: There are 4 intercollegiate sports for men and 6 for women, and 8 intramural sports for men and 8 for women. Facilities include a gym, athletic fields, tennis and racquetball courts, and a recreation center with an indoor pool.

Disabled Students: 80% of the campus is accessible. Wheelchair ramps, elevators, special parking, specially equipped rest rooms, and special class scheduling are available.

Services: Counseling and information services are available, as is tutoring in every subject. There is a reader service for the blind, and remedial math, reading, and writing.

Campus Safety and Security: Measures include 24-hour foot and vehicle patrol, security escort services, informal discussions, and pamphlets/posters/films. There are emergency telephones, lighted pathways/sidewalks, and campus security systems.

Programs of Study: UB confers B.A., B.S., B.F.A., and B.M. degrees. Associate, master's, and doctoral degrees are also awarded. Bachelor's degrees are awarded in BIOLOGICAL SCIENCE (biology/biological science), BUSINESS (accounting, banking and finance, business administration and management, fashion merchandising, international business management, international economics, management information systems, management science, and marketing/retailing/merchandising), COMMUNICATIONS AND THE ARTS (communications, English, graphic design, illustration, industrial design, journalism, literature, and music), COMPUTER AND PHYSICAL SCIENCE (computer science and mathematics), ENGINEERING AND ENVIRONMENTAL DESIGN (computer engineering and interior design), HEALTH PROFESSIONS (dental hygiene, predentistry, and premedicine), SOCIAL SCIENCE (human services, interdisciplinary studies, international studies, prelaw, psychology, religion, and social science). Computer science/engineering, business, and dental hygiene are the strongest academically. Dental hygiene, psychology, and computer science/engineering are the largest.

Required: All students are required to complete at least 120 credit hours, including at least 30 in the major field. A minimum GPA of 2.0 is necessary. Distribution requirements cover 33 core credits and are composed of skills, heritage, and capstone sections, including 3 hours each in English composition and quantitative skills, and 24 semester hours consisting of 6 hours each in humanities, natural science, and social science and 3 each in integrated studies and fine arts.

Special: UB offers co-op programs with several local institutions, cross-registration with Sacred Heart and Fairfield Universities, internships in many degree programs, study abroad in England, Switzerland, or Spain, a Washington semester, and work-study programs. In addition, a general studies accelerated degree program, dual majors, student-designed majors, and B.A.-B.S. degrees are available. Credit for life experience, non-degree study, and pass/fail options are offered. There are 11 national honor societies and 1 departmental honors program.

Faculty/Classroom: 74% of faculty are male; 26%, female. All both teach and do research. No introductory courses are taught by graduate students. The average class size in an introductory lecture is 14; in a laboratory, 10; and in a regular course, 14.

Admissions: 73% of the 2005-2006 applicants were accepted. The SAT scores for the 2005-2006 freshman class were: Verbal--78% below 500, 19% between 500 and 599, and 3% between 600 and 700; Math--77% below 500, 17% between 500 and 599, 5% between 600 and 700, and 1% above 700. 19% of the current freshmen were in the top fifth of their class; 40% were in the top two fifths. 1 freshman graduated first in the class.

Requirements: The SAT or ACT is required. In addition, applicants are required to have 16 academic credits or Carnegie units, including 4 units of English, 3 of math, 2 in social studies, 2 in a lab science, and 5 electives. A portfolio is required for B.F.A. students and an audition for B.M. candidates. UB requires applicants to be in the upper 40% of their class. A GPA of 2.0 is required. AP and CLEP credits are accepted. Important factors in the admissions decision are advanced placement or honor courses, extracurricular activities record, and recommendations by school officials.

Procedure: Freshmen are admitted fall and spring. Entrance exams should be taken during the senior year. There are early decision, early admissions, and deferred admissions plans. There is a rolling admissions plan. Applications should be filed by April 1 for fall entry and December 1 for spring entry. The fall 2005 application fee was $25. Notification is sent on a rolling basis. Applications are accepted on-line.

Transfer: 174 transfer students enrolled in 2004-2005. Transfer applicants need a minimum GPA of 2.5 and at least 12 earned credit hours. The SAT or ACT and an interview are recommended. 30 of 120 credits required for the bachelor's degree must be completed at UB.

Visiting: There are regularly scheduled orientations for prospective students. There are guides for informal visits and visitors may sit in on classes and stay overnight. To schedule a visit, contact the Admissions Office.

Financial Aid: UB is a member of CSS. The FAFSA and the college's own financial statement are required. The deadline for filing freshman financial aid applications for fall entry is April 15.

International Students: There are 201 international students enrolled. The school actively recruits these students. They must take the TOEFL, or the MELAB, the Comprehensive English Language Test, or the college's own test, achieving a satisfactory score. They must also take the SAT.

Computers: All students may access the system 8 A.M. to 11 P.M. daily. UBnet is available 24 hours a day from dorm rooms or dial-ups. There are no time limits and no fees.

Graduates: From July 1, 2004 to June 30, 2005, 176 bachelor's degrees were awarded. The most popular majors were elective studies (24%), business administration (8%), and human services (6%). In an average class, 40% graduate in 4 years or less, 45% graduate in 5 years or less, and 50% graduate in 6 years or less. Of the 2004 graduating class, 10% were enrolled in graduate school within 6 months of graduation and 60% were employed.

Admissions Contact: Audrey Ashton-Savage, Vice President, Enrollment Management. A video is available.
E-mail: *admit@bridgeport.edu* Web: *www.bridgeport.edu*

UNIVERSITY OF CONNECTICUT   D-2

Storrs, CT 06269-3088   (860) 486-3137; Fax: (860) 486-1476

Full-time: 7207 men, 8089 women	**Faculty:** 975; I, av$
Part-time: 449 men, 367 women	**Ph.Ds:** 93%
Graduate: 2922 men, 3258 women	**Student/Faculty:** 17 to 1
Year: semesters, summer session	**Tuition:** $8362 ($21,562)
Application Deadline: February 1	**Room & Board:** $8266

Freshman Class: 18,608 applied, 9498 accepted, 3260 enrolled
SAT Verbal/Math: 585/604*   **HIGHLY COMPETITIVE**

The University of Connecticut, founded in 1881, is a public, land-grant, sea-grant, multicampus research institution offering degree programs in liberal arts and sciences and professional studies. There are 9 undergraduate and 5 graduate schools. In addition to regional accreditation, UConn has baccalaureate program accreditation with AACSB, ABET, ACPE, ADA, APTA, ASLA, CAAHEP, CCNE, CSAB, NAACLS, NASAD, NASM, NAST, NCATE, and NLN. The library contains 2,334,581 volumes, 2,602,161 microform items, and 5067 audio/video tapes/CDs/DVDs, and subscribes to 35,263 periodicals including electronic. Computerized library services include the card catalog, interlibrary loans, database searching, and Internet access. Special learning facilities include a learning resource center, art gallery, natural history museum, planetarium, radio station, and TV station. The 4104-acre campus is in a rural area 25 miles east of Hartford. Including any residence halls, there are 350 buildings.

Student Life: 77% of undergraduates are from Connecticut. Students are from 50 states, 53 foreign countries, and Canada. 87% are from public schools. 72% are white. The average age of freshmen is 18; all undergraduates, 20. 8% do not continue beyond their first year; 72% remain to graduate.

Housing: 11,062 students can be accommodated in college housing, which includes single-sex and coed dorms, on-campus apartments, off-campus apartments, married-student housing, fraternity houses, and sorority houses. In addition, there are honors houses, language houses, special-interest houses, engineering, substance-free, older-student, and freshman year experience housing. On-campus housing is guaranteed for the freshman year only. 72% of students live on campus; of those, 70% remain on campus on weekends. Upperclassmen may keep cars.

Activities: 8% of men belong to 18 national fraternities; 7% of women belong to 9 national sororities. There are 303 groups on campus, including art, band, cheerleading, chess, choir, chorale, chorus, computers, dance, debate, drama, drill team, ethnic, film, gay, honors, international, jazz band, literary magazine, marching band, musical theater, newspaper, opera, orchestra, pep band, photography, political, professional, radio and TV, religious, social, social service, student government, symphony, and yearbook. Popular campus events include Spring Weekend, "UConn Do It" campus clean-up day, and Winter Weekend.

Sports: There are 11 intercollegiate sports for men and 13 for women, and 29 intramural sports for men and 28 for women. Facilities include a sports center, a field house, a 16,000-seat football stadium, a 10,000-seat basketball stadium, and a student, faculty, and staff workout center.

Disabled Students: 80% of the campus is accessible. Wheelchair ramps, elevators, special parking, specially equipped rest rooms, special class scheduling, lowered drinking fountains, lowered telephones, special housing, a tactile map, and 4 specially equipped transportation vans are available.

Services: Counseling and information services are available, as is tutoring in most subjects. There is a reader service for the blind. Also available are a Braille printer, a Kurzweil reading machine and Mac computer with voice synthesizer, a machine to enlarge printed material, a talking calculator, and a TDD.

Campus Safety and Security: Measures include 24-hour foot and vehicle patrol, self-defense education, security escort services, and shuttle buses. There are informal discussions, pamphlets/posters/films, emergency telephones, and lighted pathways/sidewalks.

Programs of Study: UConn confers B.A., B.S., B.F.A., B.G.S., B.Mus., B.S.E., B.S.N., and B.S.Pharm. degrees. Associate, master's, and doctoral degrees are also awarded. Bachelor's degrees are awarded in AGRICULTURE (agricultural economics, agriculture, agronomy, animal science, horticulture, and natural resource management), BIOLOGICAL SCIENCE (biology/biological science, biophysics, evolutionary biology, genetics, marine science, molecular biology, nutrition, and physiology), BUSINESS (accounting, banking and finance, business administration and management, insurance and risk management, management information systems, marketing/retailing/merchandising, and real estate), COMMUNICATIONS AND THE ARTS (art, art history and appreciation, classics, communications, dramatic arts, English, French, German, journalism, linguistics, music, Spanish, theater design, and visual and performing arts), COMPUTER AND PHYSICAL SCIENCE (chemistry, computer science, geology, mathematics, physics, and statistics), EDUCATION (agricultural, athletic training, education, elementary, English, foreign languages, mathematics, music, recreation, science, social studies, and special), ENGINEERING AND ENVIRONMENTAL DESIGN (biomedical engineering, chemical engineering, civil engineering, computer engineering, electrical/electronics engineering, environmental engineering, environmental science, landscape architecture/design, manufacturing engineering, materials engineering, and mechanical engineering), HEALTH PROFESSIONS (cytotechnology, exercise science, health care administration, medical laboratory technology, nursing, pharmacy, and physical therapy), SOCIAL SCIENCE (anthropology, dietetics, economics, geography, history, human development, Italian studies, Latin American studies, Middle Eastern studies, philosophy, political science/government, psychology, sociology, urban studies, and women's studies). Psychology, political science, and nursing are the largest.

Required: To graduate, students must complete 120 credits with a GPA of 2.0. There are general education requirements in foreign language, expository writing, math, literature and the arts, culture and modern society, philosophical and ethical analysis, social scientific and comparative analysis, and science and technology. Students must complete a course that provides hands-on experience in a major computer application.

Special: UConn offers co-op programs in most majors, internships, study abroad in 28 countries, dual majors, general studies degrees, student-designed majors, work-study programs, nondegree study, and pass/fail options. There are 30 national honor societies, including Phi Beta Kappa, and a freshman honors program.

Faculty/Classroom: 62% of faculty are male; 38%, female. 77% teach undergraduates and 3% do research. Graduate students teach 34% of introductory courses. The average class size in an introductory lecture is 46; in a laboratory, 17; and in a regular course, 39.

Admissions: 51% of the 2005-2006 applicants were accepted. The SAT scores for the 2005-2006 freshman class were: Verbal--10% below 500, 45% between 500 and 599, 38% between 600 and 700, and 7% above 700; Math--7% below 500, 38% between 500 and 599, 44% between 600 and 700, and 11% above 700. 60% of the current freshmen were in the top fifth of their class; 94% were in the top two fifths. There were 2 National Merit semifinalists. 49 freshmen graduated first in their class.

Requirements: The SAT or ACT is required. In addition, applicants must be graduates of an approved secondary school and should rank in the upper range of their class. The GED is accepted. Students must complete 16 high school academic units, including 4 years of English, 3 of math, 2 each of foreign language, science, and social studies, and 3 of electives. An essay is required. An audition is required for music and theater students and a portfolio for art students. AP credits are accepted. Important factors in the admissions decision are advanced placement or honor courses, evidence of special talent, and leadership record.

Procedure: Freshmen are admitted fall and spring. Entrance exams should be taken in the spring of the junior year or fall of the senior year. There are deferred admissions and rolling admissions plans. Applications should be filed by February 1 for fall entry and October 15 for spring entry, along with a $70 fee. Notification is sent on a rolling basis. 3287 applicants were on the 2005 waiting list; 325 were admitted. Applications are accepted on-line.

Transfer: 636 transfer students enrolled in 2004-2005. Applicants should have a minimum GPA of 2.5 and submit official transcripts from all colleges previously attended, the high school transcript, and SAT or ACT scores as needed. An associate degree or a minimum of 54 credit hours is recommended. 30 of 120 credits required for the bachelor's degree must be completed at UConn.

Visiting: There are regularly scheduled orientations for prospective students, including daily tours and information sessions. Visitors may sit in on classes. To schedule a visit, contact the Lodewick Visitors Center at (860) 486-4900 or tours@lvc.pr.uconn.edu.

Financial Aid: In 2005-2006, 86% of all full-time freshmen and 74% of continuing full-time students received some form of financial aid. 74% of full-time freshmen and 73% of continuing full-time students received need-based aid. The average freshman award was $9035. Need-based scholarships or need-based grants averaged $6393 ($16,600 maximum); need-based self-help aid (loans and jobs) averaged $3641 ($4289 maximum); and non-need-based athletic scholarships averaged $15,072 ($29,266 maximum). 48% of undergraduates work part time. Average annual earnings from campus work are $1800. The average financial indebtedness of the 2005 graduate was $19,410. The FAFSA is required. The priority date for freshman financial aid applications for fall entry is March 1.

International Students: There are 147 international students enrolled. The school actively recruits these students. A satisfactory score is required on the written TOEFL. Students must also take the SAT or the ACT.

Computers: All students may access the system 24 hours weekdays; 8 A.M. to 12 P.M. weekends. There are no time limits and no fees.

Graduates: From July 1, 2004 to June 30, 2005, 3816 bachelor's degrees were awarded. The most popular majors were psychology (8%), human development and family studies (6%), and political science (6%). In an average class, 50% graduate in 4 years or less, 69% graduate in 5 years or less, and 72% graduate in 6 years or less. 200 companies recruited on campus in 2004-2005. Of the 2004 graduating class, 27% were enrolled in graduate school within 6 months of graduation and 81% were employed.

Admissions Contact: Lee H. Melvin, Director of Admissions. E-mail: beahusky@uconnvm.uconn.edu Web: www.uconn.edu

UNIVERSITY OF HARTFORD   C-2
West Hartford, CT 06117   (860) 243-4296
                    (800) 947-4303; Fax: (860) 768-4961

Full-time: 2345 men, 2312 women	**Faculty:** 325; IIA, av$
Part-time: 368 men, 567 women	**Ph.D.s:** 79%
Graduate: 643 men, 1025 women	**Student/Faculty:** 14 to 1
Year: semesters, summer session	**Tuition:** $24,596
Application Deadline: open	**Room & Board:** $9448
Freshman Class: 12,745 applied, 8312 accepted, 1469 enrolled	
SAT Verbal/Math: 530/540*	**ACT:** 23 COMPETITIVE

The University of Hartford, founded in 1877, is an independent, nonsectarian institution offering extensive undergraduate and graduate programs ranging from liberal arts to business. There are 7 undergraduate and 6 graduate schools. In addition to regional accreditation, University of Hartford has baccalaureate program accreditation with AACSB, ABET, APTA, CAHEA, NASAD, NASM, NCATE, and NLN. The 3 libraries contain 606,154 volumes and 383,367 microform items, and subscribe to 3903 periodicals including electronic. Computerized library services include the card catalog, interlibrary loans, database searching, Internet access, and laptop Internet portals. Special learning facilities include a learning resource center, art gallery, radio station, TV station, and the Museum of American Political Life. The 320-acre campus is in a suburban area 4 miles northwest of Hartford. Including any residence halls, there are 32 buildings.

Student Life: 61% of undergraduates are from out of state, mostly the Northeast. Students are from 47 states, 50 foreign countries, and Canada. 82% are from public schools. 79% are white; 12% African American. 70% claim no religious affiliation; 17% Catholic; 7% Protestant; 6% Jewish. The average age of freshmen is 18; all undergraduates, 22. 24% do not continue beyond their first year; 55% remain to graduate.

Housing: 3472 students can be accommodated in college housing, which includes coed dorms and on-campus apartments. In addition, there are honors houses, special-interest houses, the Residential College for the Arts, and the International Residence College. On-campus housing is guaranteed for all 4 years. 62% of students live on campus; of those, 85% remain on campus on weekends. All students may keep cars.

Activities: 17% of men belong to 7 national fraternities; 21% of women belong to 7 national sororities. There are 45 groups on campus, including art, band, cheerleading, choir, chorale, chorus, computers, drama, ethnic, gay, honors, international, jazz band, literary magazine, musical theater, newspaper, opera, orchestra, pep band, political, professional, radio and TV, religious, social, social service, student government, and symphony. Popular campus events include Welcome Weekend, Spring Weekend, and Winter Carnival.

Sports: There are 9 intercollegiate sports for men and 9 for women, and 15 intramural sports for men and 15 for women. Facilities include playing fields, a 25-meter outdoor pool, tennis courts, golf practice cages, a fitness trail, and a sports center with a 4600-seat multipurpose court, an 8-lane swimming pool, a weight room, racquetball courts, a squash court, and saunas.

Disabled Students: Wheelchair ramps, elevators, special parking, specially equipped rest rooms, lowered drinking fountains, lowered telephones, and special housing are available.

Services: Counseling and information services are available, as is tutoring in most subjects. There is a reader service for the blind, and remedial math, reading, and writing. The health education office offers peer counseling and workshops on health-related topics. Professional counseling is available.

Campus Safety and Security: Measures include 24-hour foot and vehicle patrol, self-defense education, security escort services, and shuttle buses. There are informal discussions, pamphlets/posters/films, emergency telephones, lighted pathways/sidewalks, and a bicycle patrol.

Programs of Study: University of Hartford confers B.A., B.S., B.F.A., B.Mus., B.S.A.E.T., B.S.B.A., B.S.C.E., B.S.Comp.E., B.S.Ed., B.S.E.E., B.S.M.E., and B.S.N. degrees. Associate, master's, and doctoral degrees are also awarded. Bachelor's degrees are awarded in BIOLOGICAL SCIENCE (biology/biological science), BUSINESS (accounting, banking and finance, business administration and management, entrepreneurial studies, insurance, management information systems, management science, and marketing/retailing/merchandising), COMMUNICATIONS AND THE ARTS (art history and appreciation, audio technology, ceramic art and design, communications, dance, design, dramatic arts, drawing, English, film arts, illustration, jazz, languages, media arts, music, music business management, music history and appreciation, music performance, music technology, music theory and composition, musical theater, painting, performing arts, photography, printmaking, sculpture, technical and business writing, theater management, video, and visual and performing arts), COMPUTER AND PHYSICAL SCIENCE (chemistry, computer science, information sciences and systems, mathematics, physics, and radiological technology), EDUCATION (early childhood, elementary, music, secondary, and special), ENGINEERING AND ENVIRONMENTAL DESIGN (architectural engineering, biomedical engineering, chemical engineering technology, civil engineering, computer engineering, electrical/electronics engineering, electrical/electronics engineering technology, engineering, engineering technology, mechanical engineering, and mechanical engineering technology), HEALTH PROFESSIONS (health science, medical laboratory technology, nursing, occupational therapy, physical therapy, predentistry, premedicine, preoptometry, and respiratory therapy), SOCIAL SCIENCE (criminal justice, economics, history, human services, interdisciplinary studies, international studies, Judaic studies, law, philosophy, political science/government, psychology, and sociology). Music, engineering, and physical therapy are the strongest academically. Communication, psychology, and architechial engineering technology are the largest.

Required: To graduate, students must complete at least 120 credit hours, fulfill the university's core curriculum requirements, and maintain an overall GPA of 2.0. Specific core and course requirements vary with the major.

Special: Cross-registration with the Greater Hartford Consortium, internships in all majors, study abroad, a Washington semester, work-study programs, credit for life experience, nondegree study, and pass/fail options are available. In addition, students may pursue accelerated degrees, B.A.-B.S. degrees, dual majors, or their own individually designed majors. There are interdisciplinary majors in acoustics and music and in experimental studio combining performing, literary, and visual arts. Also available are preprofessional programs in biology/preoptometry with the New England College of Optometry, predentistry with the New York University School of Dentistry, prechiropractic with the New York Chiropractic College, preosteopathic with the University of New England College of Octeopathic Medicine, and prepodiatry with the New York College of Podiatric Medicine. There are 19 national honor societies, a freshman honors program, and 7 departmental honors programs.

Faculty/Classroom: 64% of faculty are male; 36%, female. All teach undergraduates and 97% do research. No introductory courses are taught by graduate students. The average class size in an introductory lecture is 43; in a laboratory, 22; and in a regular course, 23.

Admissions: 65% of the 2005-2006 applicants were accepted. The SAT scores for the 2005-2006 freshman class were: Verbal--30% below 500, 49% between 500 and 599, 19% between 600 and 700, and 2% above 700; Math--25% below 500, 48% between 500 and 599, 24% between 600 and 700, and 3% above 700. 33% of the current freshmen were in the top fifth of their class; 64% were in the top two fifths.

Requirements: The SAT is required. In addition, applicants should have 16 academic high school credits and 16 Carnegie units, including 4 units in English, 3 in math (3.5 for B.S. candidates), and 2 each in foreign language, science, and social studies. A portfolio and an audition are required for B.F.A. and B.Mus. candidates, respectively. A personal statement is required, and an interview is recommended for all students. AP and CLEP credits are accepted. Important factors in the admissions decision are advanced placement or honor courses, recommendations by school officials, and leadership record.

Procedure: Freshmen are admitted fall and spring. Entrance exams should be taken in the spring of the junior year or the fall of the senior year. There are early admissions and deferred admissions plans. There is a rolling admissions plan. Application deadlines are open. The fall 2005 application fee was $35. Notification is sent on a rolling basis. Applications are accepted on-line.

Transfer: 232 transfer students enrolled in 2004-2005. Transfer students must have a minimum college GPA of 2.25, with 2.5 recommended, and must submit SAT or ACT scores if they have fewer than 30 transferable college-level credits. An interview is also recommended. 30 of 120 credits required for the bachelor's degree must be completed at University of Hartford.

Visiting: There are regularly scheduled orientations for prospective students. There are guides for informal visits and visitors may sit in on classes and stay overnight. To schedule a visit, contact the Office of Admissions.

Financial Aid: In 2005-2006, 97% of all full-time freshmen and 95% of continuing full-time students received some form of financial aid. 74% of full-time freshmen and 78% of continuing full-time students received need-based aid. The average freshman award was $14,471. Need-based scholarships or need-based grants averaged $11,833; need-based self-help aid (loans and jobs) averaged $5955; non-need-based athletic scholarships averaged $30,192; and other non-need-based awards and non-need-based scholarships averaged $6557. 20% of undergraduates work part time. Average annual earnings from campus work are $2561. The average financial indebtedness of the 2005 graduate was $25,553. The FAFSA is required. The priority date for freshman financial aid applications for fall entry is February 1.

International Students: There are 136 international students enrolled. The school actively recruits these students. They must take the TOEFL. The SAT or ACT is recommended.

Computers: Wireless access is available. There is access at the main library and there are PC connections in each dorm room. All students may access the system. There are no time limits and no fees. It is strongly recommended that all students have a personal computer.

Graduates: From July 1, 2004 to June 30, 2005, 934 bachelor's degrees were awarded. The most popular majors were communications (10%), psychology (5%), and management (5%). In an average class, 42% graduate in 4 years or less, and 53% graduate in either 5 or 6 years. 316 companies recruited on campus in 2004-2005. Of the 2004 graduating class, 21% were enrolled in graduate school within 6 months of graduation and 87% were employed.

Admissions Contact: Richard A. Zeiser, Dean of Admissions.
E-mail: *admission@hartford.edu* Web: *www.hartford.edu*

UNIVERSITY OF NEW HAVEN   C-3
West Haven, CT 06516   (203) 932-7319
(800) DIAL-UNH; Fax: (203) 931-6093

Full-time: 1075 men, 925 women	**Faculty:** IIA, +$
Part-time: 350 men, 275 women	**Ph.D.s:** 92%
Graduate: 850 men, 925 women	**Student/Faculty:** 11 to 1
Year: 4-1-4, summer session	**Tuition:** $22,380
Application Deadline: open	**Room & Board:** $9414
Freshman Class: n/av	
SAT or ACT: required	**COMPETITIVE**

The University of New Haven, founded in 1920, is a private institution offering undergraduate programs in arts and sciences, business, engineering, public safety and professional studies, and hotel, restaurant, and tourism administration. There are 5 undergraduate schools and 1 graduate school. Some figures in the above capsule and in this profile are approximate. In addition to regional accreditation, UNH has baccalaureate program accreditation with ABET. The library contains 383,969 volumes, 511,144 microform items, and 1066 audio/video tapes/CDs/DVDs, and subscribes to 1321 periodicals including electronic. Computerized library services include the card catalog, interlibrary loans, database searching, and Internet access. Special learning facilities include a learning resource center, art gallery, radio station, and TV station. The 78-acre campus is in a suburban area 5 miles west of New Haven. Including any residence halls, there are 31 buildings.

Student Life: 63% of undergraduates are from Connecticut. Others are from 30 states, 58 foreign countries, and Canada. 85% are from public schools. 72% are white; 11% African American. The average age of freshmen is 18; all undergraduates, 20. 22% do not continue beyond their first year; 40% remain to graduate.

Housing: 1300 students can be accommodated in college housing, which includes coed dorms and on-campus apartments. On-campus housing is available on a first-come, first-served basis and is available on a lottery system for upperclassmen. Priority is given to out-of-town students. 73% of students live on campus; of those, 70% remain on campus on weekends. All students may keep cars.

Activities: 4% of men belong to 2 local and 1 national fraternity; 4% of women belong to 3 local and 1 national sorority. There are 50 groups on campus, including cheerleading, chorus, dance, drama, ethnic, forensics, gay, honors, international, jazz band, newspaper, pep band, photography, political, professional, radio and TV, religious, social, social service, student government, and yearbook. Popular campus events include Family Day, Snow Ball Formal, and Spring Weekend.

Sports: There are 9 intercollegiate sports for men and 10 for women, and 10 intramural sports for men and 9 for women. Facilities include baseball, softball, and intramural playing fields; tennis courts; a gym with basketball courts, weight training room, racquetball court, and gymnastics area; and a stadium for football, soccer, and lacrosse.

Disabled Students: 82% of the campus is accessible. Wheelchair ramps, elevators, special parking, specially equipped rest rooms, special class scheduling, lowered drinking fountains, lowered telephones, and special door handles are available.

Services: Counseling and information services are available, as is tutoring in most subjects. There is remedial math, reading, and writing.

Campus Safety and Security: Measures include 24-hour foot and vehicle patrol, security escort services, informal discussions, and pamphlets/posters/films. There are emergency telephones, lighted pathways/sidewalks, and required programs during orientation for new students.

Programs of Study: UNH confers B.A. and B.S. degrees. Associate and master's degrees are also awarded. Bachelor's degrees are awarded in BIOLOGICAL SCIENCE (biology/biological science, biotechnology, and marine biology), BUSINESS (accounting, banking and finance, business administration and management, business economics, hotel/motel and restaurant management, international business management, marketing/retailing/merchandising, sports management, and tourism), COMMUNICATIONS AND THE ARTS (art, audio technology, communications, creative writing, English, graphic design, literature, music, and music business management), COMPUTER AND PHYSICAL SCIENCE (applied mathematics, chemistry, computer management, computer science, mathematics, and natural sciences), ENGINEERING AND ENVIRONMENTAL DESIGN (aviation administration/management, chemical engineering, civil engineering, computer engineering, electrical/electronics engineering, engineering, environmental science, fire protection engineering, industrial engineering, industrial engineering technology, interior design, materials science, mechanical engineering, and occupational safety and health), HEALTH PROFESSIONS (dental hygiene, predentistry, premedicine, and preveterinary science), SOCIAL SCIENCE (clinical psychology, community psychology, corrections, criminal justice, dietetics, fire control and safety technology, fire science, forensic studies, history, law enforcement and corrections, liberal arts/general studies, political science/government, and psychology). Criminal justice, business administration, and fire protection are the strongest academically. Business and marketing, criminal justice, and engineering are the largest.

Required: To graduate, all students must maintain a GPA of 2.0, pass a writing proficiency exam, and complete a total of 120 to 136 credits, depending on the major. Students must complete the Freshman Experience Seminar and take at least 34 credits from the university core curriculum, including a total of 19 in lab science, social sciences, history, literature or philosophy, and art, music, or theater, 6 in communication skills, and 3 each in quantitative skills, computers, and scientific methodology.

Special: UNH offers co-op programs in most majors, internships, work-study programs, student-designed majors in the School of Professional Studies, interdisciplinary majors including biomedical computing, B.A.-B.S. degrees, a 5-year B.S.-M.S. program in environmental science, and nondegree study. Study-abroad programs are available. There are 5 national honor societies, and a freshman honors program.

Faculty/Classroom: 72% of faculty are male; 28%, female. 90% teach undergraduates. No introductory courses are taught by graduate students. The average class size in an introductory lecture is 20; in a laboratory, 15; and in a regular course, 20.

Admissions: 67% of the recent applicants were accepted. The SAT scores for the recent freshman class were: Verbal--44% below 500, 40% between 500 and 599, 15% between 600 and 700, and 1% above 700; Math--43% below 500, 39% between 500 and 599, 16% between 600 and 700, and 2% above 700. 29% of the recent freshmen were in the top fifth of their class; 56% were in the top two fifths.

Requirements: The SAT or ACT is required, the SAT is preferred, with a satisfactory minimum combined score. The GED is accepted. In addition, applicants should be graduates of an accredited secondary school. An interview is recommended. A letter of recommendation is required along with a personal essay. A GPA of 2.0 is required. AP and CLEP credits are accepted.

Procedure: Freshmen are admitted fall and spring. Entrance exams should be taken in the fall or winter of the senior year. There is a deferred admissions plan. Application deadlines are open. The applicatioin fee is $50. Applications are accepted on-line ($25 fee).

Transfer: 158 transfer students enrolled in a recent year. Applicant should have a minimum college GPA of 2.0 and should submit all official transcripts. An interview is recommended, and the SAT is required for students with fewer than 30 college credits. 30 of 120 credits required for the bachelor's degree must be completed at UNH.

Visiting: There are regularly scheduled orientations for prospective students, including daily information sessions, Open House, Accepted Student Days, and Junior Open House. There are guides for informal visits and visitors may sit in on classes and stay overnight. To schedule a visit, contact the Admissions Office at adminfo@newhaven.edu.

Financial Aid: UNH is a member of CSS. The FAFSA, the college's own financial statement, and the student's and parents' 1040 tax form are required. Check with the school for current deadlines.

International Students: There were 93 international students enrolled in a recent year. The school actively recruits these students. They must score satisfactorily on the TOEFL. English-speaking students may submit the SAT or ACT scores instead.

Computers: All students may access the system 24 hours a day.

Graduates: In an average class, 40% graduate in 6 years or less.

Admissions Contact: Jane Sangeloty, Director of Undergraduate Admissions. E-mail: adminfo@newhaven.edu. Web: http://www.newhaven.edu

---

WESLEYAN UNIVERSITY — C-3

Middletown, CT 06459-4890
(860) 685-3000
Fax: (860) 685-3001

Full-time: 1326 men, 1411 women	**Faculty:** 325; IIA, ++$
Part-time: 9 men, 5 women	**Ph.Ds:** 91%
Graduate: 180 men, 263 women	**Student/Faculty:** 8 to 1
Year: semesters	**Tuition:** $33,190
Application Deadline: January 1	**Room & Board:** $8932
Freshman Class: 6879 applied, 1902 accepted, 717 enrolled	
SAT Verbal/Math: 700/700*	**ACT:** 31 **MOST COMPETITIVE**

Wesleyan University, founded in 1831, is an independent institution offering programs in the liberal arts and sciences. The 3 libraries contain 1,324,647 volumes, 292,687 microform items, and 49,017 audio/video tapes/CDs/DVDs, and subscribe to 6793 periodicals including electronic. Computerized library services include the card catalog, interlibrary loans, database searching, Internet access, and laptop Internet portals. Special learning facilities include a learning resource center, art gallery, radio station, and an observatory. The 170-acre campus is in a suburban area 15 miles south of Hartford and 2 hours from both Boston and New York City. Including any residence halls, there are 90 buildings.

Student Life: 91% of undergraduates are from out of state, mostly the Northeast. Students are from 47 states, 46 foreign countries, and Canada. 56% are from public schools. 67% are white. The average age of freshmen is 18; all undergraduates, 20.

Housing: 2600 students can be accommodated in college housing, which includes single-sex and coed dorms, on-campus apartments, off-campus apartments, married-student housing, and fraternity houses. In addition, there are language houses and special-interest houses. On-campus housing is guaranteed for all 4 years. 98% of students live on campus; of those, 99% remain on campus on weekends. All students may keep cars.

Activities: 2% of men belong to 2 local and 5 national fraternities; 1% of women belong to 2 local sororities. There are 190 groups on campus, including art, band, cheerleading, chess, choir, chorale, chorus, computers, dance, debate, drama, ethnic, film, gay, honors, international, jazz band, literary magazine, musical theater, newspaper, opera, orchestra, pep band, photography, political, professional, radio and TV, religious, social, social service, student government, symphony, and yearbook. Popular campus events include Fall Ball and Spring Fling.

Sports: There are 15 intercollegiate sports for men and 14 for women, and 16 intramural sports for men and 16 for women. Facilities include a 5000-seat stadium, a 3000-seat gym, a 50-meter Olympic-size pool, a 400-meter outdoor track, a 200-meter indoor track, a hockey arena, a strength and fitness center, 16 tennis courts, 14 squash courts, 4 soccer fields, 2 football practice fields, 2 rugby pitches, a boathouse, and field hockey, ultimate Frisbee, baseball, and softball fields.

Disabled Students: 25% of the campus is accessible. Wheelchair ramps, elevators, special parking, specially equipped rest rooms, special class scheduling, lowered drinking fountains, and lowered telephones are available.

Services: Counseling and information services are available, as is tutoring in most subjects. There is remedial math and writing.

Campus Safety and Security: Measures include 24-hour foot and vehicle patrol, self-defense education, security escort services, and shuttle buses. There are informal discussions, pamphlets/posters/films, emergency telephones, and lighted pathways/sidewalks.

Programs of Study: Wesleyan confers the B.A. degree. Master's and doctoral degrees are also awarded. Bachelor's degrees are awarded in BIOLOGICAL SCIENCE (biochemistry, biology/biological science, molecular biology, and neurosciences), COMMUNICATIONS AND THE ARTS (art history and appreciation, classics, dance, dramatic arts, English, film arts, French, German, Italian, music, romance languages and literature, Russian, Spanish, and studio art), COMPUTER AND PHYSICAL SCIENCE (astronomy, chemistry, computer science, earth science, mathematics, physics, and science technology), SOCIAL SCIENCE (African American studies, American studies, anthropology, archeology, Asian/Oriental studies, classical/ancient civilization, economics, French studies, history, Latin American studies, medieval studies, philosophy, political science/government, psychology, religion, Russian and Slavic studies, sociology, and women's studies). Sciences, economics, and history are the strongest academically. English, government, and history are the largest.

Required: To graduate, all students must complete 128 credit hours. Distribution requirements include 3 courses each in humanities and arts, social and behavioral sciences, and natural science and math. A minimum academic average of 74 must be maintained, with at least 6 semesters of full-time residency.

Special: Wesleyan offers exchange programs with 11 northeastern colleges, cross-registration with 2 area colleges, study abroad in 41 countries on 6 continents, internships, a Washington semester, dual and student-designed majors, and pass/fail options. 3-2 engineering programs with Cal Tech and Columbia University are also available. There are 2 national honor societies, including Phi Beta Kappa, and 40 departmental honors programs.

Faculty/Classroom: 61% of faculty are male; 39%, female. All both teach and do research. No introductory courses are taught by graduate students. The average class size in an introductory lecture is 40; in a laboratory, 15; and in a regular course, 24.

Admissions: 28% of the 2005-2006 applicants were accepted. The SAT scores for the 2005-2006 freshman class were: Verbal--2% below 500, 10% between 500 and 599, 33% between 600 and 700, and 55% above 700; Math--8% between 500 and 599, 38% between 600 and 700, and 54% above 700. The ACT scores were 1% below 21, 2% between 21 and 23, 11% between 24 and 26, 15% between 27 and 28, and 70% above 28. 88% of the current freshmen were in the top fifth of their class. There were 72 National Merit semifinalists in a recent year.

Requirements: The SAT or ACT is required as are 2 SAT Subject Tests. In addition, applicants should have 20 academic credits, including 4 years each of English, foreign language, math, science, and social studies. An essay is necessary. AP credits are accepted. Important factors in the admissions decision are advanced placement or honor courses, recommendations by school officials, and leadership record.

Procedure: Freshmen are admitted in the fall. Entrance exams should be taken in the spring of the junior year or the fall of the senior year. There are early decision and deferred admissions plans. Early decision applications should be filed by November 15; regular applications, by January 1 for fall entry. Notification of early decision is sent December 15; regular decision, The fall 2005 application fee was $55. April 1. 278 early decision candidates were accepted for the 2005-2006 class. A waiting list is an active part of the admissions procedure. Applications are accepted on-line.

Transfer: 64 transfer students enrolled in 2004-2005. Applicants need a strong academic record and either SAT or ACT scores. An interview is recommended.

Visiting: There are regularly scheduled orientations for prospective students, including hour-long campus tours and group information sessions. There are guides for informal visits and visitors may sit in on classes and stay overnight. To schedule a visit, contact the Admissions Office.

Financial Aid: In 2005-2006, 42% of all full-time freshmen and 50% of continuing full-time students received some form of financial aid, including need-based aid. The average freshman award was $28,280. Need-based scholarships or need-based grants averaged $23,568, and need-based self-help aid (loans and jobs) averaged $4587. 89% of undergraduates work part time. Average annual earnings from campus work are $1350. The average financial indebtedness of the 2005 graduate was $22,395. Wesleyan is a member of CSS. The CSS/Profile and FAFSA are required. The deadline for filing freshman financial aid applications for fall entry is February 1.

International Students: The school actively recruits these students. They must take the TOEFL or the IELTS, and also take the SAT or the ACT. Students must also take SAT Subject Tests.

Computers: Wireless access is available. All students may access the system. There are no time limits and no fees. It is strongly recommended that all students have a personal computer.

Graduates: From July 1, 2004 to June 30, 2005, 725 bachelor's degrees were awarded. The most popular majors were government (10%), psychology (9%), and English (9%). In an average class, 83% graduate in 4 years or less, 89% graduate in 5 years or less, and 90% graduate in 6 years or less. 60 companies recruited on campus in 2004-2005. Of the 2004 graduating class, 24% were enrolled in graduate school within 6 months of graduation and 58% were employed.

Admissions Contact: Nancy Hargrave-Meislahn, Dean of Admissions and Financial Aid. E-mail: *admissions@wesleyan.edu* Web: *www.wesleyan.edu*

WESTERN CONNECTICUT STATE UNIVERSITY   A-3

Danbury, CT 06810-6855

(203) 837-9000
(877) 837-9278; Fax: (203) 837-8276

Full-time: 1826 men, 2176 women	Faculty: 197; IIA, +$
Part-time: 472 men, 721 women	Ph.D.s: 80%
Graduate: 234 men, 478 women	Student/Faculty: 20 to 1
Year: semesters, summer session	Tuition: $5800 ($13,739)
Application Deadline: open	Room & Board: $7193
Freshman Class: 3603 applied, 2029 accepted, 774 enrolled	
SAT Verbal/Math: 504/494*	COMPETITIVE

Western Connecticut State University, founded in 1903, is a public institution offering programs in business, arts and sciences, and professional studies. It is part of the Connecticut State University system. There are 3 undergraduate schools and 1 graduate school. In addition to regional accreditation, West Conn has baccalaureate program accreditation with CSWE and NLN. The 2 libraries contain 182,915 volumes, 471,099 microform items, and 8654 audio/video tapes/CDs/DVDs, and subscribe to 1273 periodicals including electronic. Computerized library services include the card catalog, interlibrary loans, and database searching. Special learning facilities include a learning resource center, art gallery, radio station, an observatory, electron microscope, and photography studio. The 346-acre campus is in a suburban area 65 miles north of New York City. Including any residence halls, there are 19 buildings.

Student Life: 90% of undergraduates are from Connecticut. Others are from 20 states, 21 foreign countries, and Canada. 91% are from public schools. 77% are white. The average age of freshmen is 18; all undergraduates, 21. 30% do not continue beyond their first year.

Housing: 1609 students can be accommodated in college housing, which includes single-sex and coed dorms and on-campus apartments. On-campus housing is guaranteed for all 4 years. 70% of students commute. All students may keep cars.

Activities: 3% of men belong to 3 national fraternities; 2% of women belong to 3 local and 2 national sororities. There are 50 groups on campus, including art, band, cheerleading, chess, choir, chorale, chorus, computers, dance, drama, ethnic, film, gay, honors, international, jazz band, literary magazine, musical theater, newspaper, opera, orchestra, photography, political, professional, radio and TV, religious, social, social service, student government, and yearbook. Popular campus events include West Fest, Midnight Breakfast, and Student Leadership Banquet.

Sports: There are 5 intercollegiate sports for men and 8 for women, and 6 intramural sports for men and 5 for women. Facilities include 2 gyms, a weight training area, 4 tennis courts, 5 playing fields, an indoor swimming pool, and a field house with an indoor running track.

Disabled Students: 95% of the campus is accessible. Wheelchair ramps, elevators, special parking, specially equipped rest rooms, special class scheduling, lowered drinking fountains, and lowered telephones are available.

Services: Counseling and information services are available, as is tutoring in some subjects. There is a reader service for the blind, remedial math, reading, and writing, and a computer science clinic.

Campus Safety and Security: Measures include 24-hour foot and vehicle patrol, security escort services, shuttle buses, and informal discussions. There are pamphlets/posters/films, emergency telephones, and lighted pathways/sidewalks.

Programs of Study: West Conn confers B.A., B.S., B.B.A., and B. Music degrees. Associate, master's, and doctoral degrees are also awarded. Bachelor's degrees are awarded in BIOLOGICAL SCIENCE (biology/biological science), BUSINESS (accounting, banking and finance, business administration and management, management information systems, and marketing management), COMMUNICATIONS AND THE ARTS (art, communications, dramatic arts, English, graphic design, illustration, music, music performance, photography, Spanish, and studio art), COMPUTER AND PHYSICAL SCIENCE (atmospheric sciences and meteorology, chemistry, computer mathematics, computer science, earth science, and mathematics), EDUCATION (elementary, health, music, and secondary), ENGINEERING AND ENVIRONMENTAL DESIGN (environmental science), HEALTH PROFESSIONS (community health work, medical laboratory technology, and nursing), SOCIAL SCIENCE (American studies, anthropology, criminal justice, economics, history, law enforcement and corrections, paralegal studies, political science/government, psychology, social science, social work, and sociology). Education, business, justice and law administration are the strongest academically and are the largest.

Required: To graduate, students must complete 122 credit hours, with a minimum GPA of 2.0 or higher for some programs. All students must also fulfill the general education distribution requirements, including phys ed, and the foreign language requirement.

Special: The university offers co-op programs with local corporations and the New England Regional Student Program. Student-designed majors, dual majors, study abroad, and pass/fail options are available. Non-degree study is offered at the University Center for Adult Education. There are 7 national honor societies, a freshman honors program, and 2 departmental honors programs.

Faculty/Classroom: 57% of faculty are male; 43%, female. All teach undergraduates, 25% do research, and 25% do both. No introductory courses are taught by graduate students. The average class size in an introductory lecture is 38; in a laboratory, 17; and in a regular course, 23.

Admissions: 56% of the 2005-2006 applicants were accepted. The SAT scores for the 2005-2006 freshman class were: Verbal--50% below 500, 37% between 500 and 599, 12% between 600 and 700, and 1% above 700; Math--53% below 500, 38% between 500 and 599, 8% between 600 and 700, and 1% above 700. 11% of the current freshmen were in the top fifth of their class; 37% were in the top two fifths.

Requirements: The SAT is required, the ACTis accepted in lieu of SAT scores. Applicants must be graduates of an accredited secondary school. The GED is accepted. Students should have completed 13 high school academic credits, including 4 in English, 3 in math, 2 to 3 in foreign language, 2 in science, and 1 each in history and social studies. Additional credits in art, music, and computer science are highly recommended. An essay and an interview are recommended. A GPA of 2.5 is required. AP and CLEP credits are accepted. Important factors in the admissions decision are advanced placement or honor courses, evidence of special talent, and recommendations by school officials.

Procedure: Freshmen are admitted fall and spring. Entrance exams should be taken by December of the senior year. There is a deferred admissions plan, and a rolling admissions plan. Application deadlines are open. Notification is sent Decemeber 15. Application fee is $40. Applications are accepted on-line.

Transfer: 308 transfer students enrolled in a recent year. Transfers must have a minimum of 12 college credits. Applicants must have a cumulative GPA of 2.0 for all college course work. A higher GPA is requied for some programs. 30 of 122 credits required for the bachelor's degree must be completed at West Conn.

Visiting: There are regularly scheduled orientations for prospective students, including campus tours on weekdays when classes are in session. There is an Open House on a Sunday in early November. There are guides for informal visits and visitors may sit in on classes. To schedule a visit, contact the Office of Admissions.

Financial Aid: In a recent year, 58% of all full-time freshmen and 55% of continuing full-time students received some form of financial aid. 44% of full-time freshmen and 40% of continuing full-time students received need-based aid. The average freshman award was $4680. Need-based scholarships or need-based grants averaged $2325 ($8998 maximum); need-based self-help aid (loans and jobs) averaged $995 ($15,000 maximum); and other non-need-based awards and non-need-based scholarships averaged $1360 ($16,904 maximum). 93% of undergraduates work part time. Average annual earnings from campus work are $1722. The average financial indebtedness of the 2005 graduate was $8403. West Conn is a member of CSS. The FAFSA and the college's own financial statement are required. The deadline for filing freshman financial aid applications for fall entry is March 15.

International Students: International students must score satisfactorily on the TOEFL and also take the SAT.

Computers: All students may access the system at any time. There are no time limits and no fees.

Graduates: From July 1, 2004 to June 30, 2005, 683 bachelor's degrees were awarded. The most popular majors were business (26%), education (11%), and justice and law (7%). In an average class, 1% graduate in 3 years or less, 19% graduate in 4 years or less, 36% graduate in 5 years or less, and 41% graduate in 6 years or less. 108 companies recruited on campus in a recent year. Of a recent graduating class, 24% were enrolled in graduate school within 6 months of graduation and 92% were employed.

Admissions Contact: William Hawkins, Director of University Admissions/Enrollment Planning. A video is available.
Web: *www.wcsu.edu/admissions*

YALE UNIVERSITY   C-3
New Haven, CT 06520-8234

	(203) 432-9316
	Fax: (203) 432-9392
Full-time: 2644 men, 2598 women	**Faculty:** I, ++$
Part-time: 15 men, 11 women	**Ph.Ds:** 85%
Graduate: 2311 men, 2430 women	**Student/Faculty:** n/av
Year: semesters, summer session	**Tuition:** $31,460
Application Deadline: December 31	**Room & Board:** $9540
Freshman Class: 19,451 applied, 1880 accepted, 1321 enrolled	
SAT Verbal/Math: 750/750*	**ACT:** 32 **MOST COMPETITIVE**

Yale University, founded in 1701, is a private liberal arts institution. In addition to regional accreditation, Yale has baccalaureate program accreditation with AACSB, ABET, AMA, APA, ATS, CAAHEP, CAHEA, CCNE, LCME, NAAB, NASM, NLN, and SAF. The 43 libraries contain 10.9 million volumes, 6.5 million microform items, and 15,554 audio/video tapes/CDs/DVDs, and subscribe to 69,664 periodicals including electronic. Computerized library services include the card catalog, interlibrary loans, and database searching. Special learning facilities include an art gallery, natural history museum, planetarium, radio station, Beinecke Rare Books and Manuscript Library, Marsh Botanical Gardens and Yale Natural Preserves, and several research centers. The 200-acre campus is in an urban area 75 miles northeast of New York City. Including any residence halls, there are 200 buildings.

Student Life: 91% of undergraduates are from out of state, mostly the Middle Atlantic. Students are from 49 states, 74 foreign countries, and Canada. 60% are from public schools. 51% are white; 14% Asian American. The average age of freshmen is 18; all undergraduates, 20. 2% do not continue beyond their first year; 96% remain to graduate.

Housing: 4690 students can be accommodated in college housing, which includes coed dorms and on-campus apartments. Students are randomly assigned to one of 12 residential colleges where they live, eat, socialize, and pursue various academic and extra curricular activities. On-campus housing is guaranteed for the freshman year only and is available on a lottery system for upperclassmen. 87% of students live on campus. All students may keep cars.

Activities: There are 300 groups on campus, including art, band, cheerleading, chess, choir, chorale, chorus, computers, dance, debate, drama, ethnic, film, gay, honors, international, jazz band, literary magazine, marching band, musical theater, newspaper, opera, orchestra, pep band, photography, political, professional, radio and TV, religious, social, social service, student government, symphony, and yearbook. Popular campus events include Communiversity Day, fall and spring concerts, and the East/West Film Festival.

Sports: There are 16 intercollegiate sports for men and 18 for women, and 25 intramural sports for men and 21 for women. Facilities include the 71,000-seat Yale Bowl, a sports complex, a gym, a swimming pool, a skating rink, a sailing center, an equestrian center, and golf courses.

Disabled Students: Wheelchair ramps, elevators, special parking, specially equipped rest rooms, special class scheduling, lowered drinking fountains, lowered telephones, and a door-to-door lift-van service are available.

Services: Counseling and information services are available, as is tutoring in every subject. There is a reader service for the blind.

Campus Safety and Security: Measures include 24-hour foot and vehicle patrol, self-defense education, security escort services, and shuttle buses. There are informal discussions, pamphlets/posters/films, emergency telephones, and lighted pathways/sidewalks.

Programs of Study: Yale confers B.A., B.S., and B.L.S. degrees. Master's and doctoral degrees are also awarded. Bachelor's degrees are awarded in BIOLOGICAL SCIENCE (biochemistry, biology/biological science, and biophysics), COMMUNICATIONS AND THE ARTS (art, art history and appreciation, Chinese, classics, dramatic arts, English, film arts, French, German, Italian, Japanese, linguistics, literature, music, Portuguese, Russian, Spanish, and theater management), COMPUTER AND PHYSICAL SCIENCE (applied mathematics, astronomy, chemistry, computer science, geology, mathematics, and physics), ENGINEERING AND ENVIRONMENTAL DESIGN (architecture, biomedical engineering, chemical engineering, electrical/electronics engineering, engineering, engineering and applied science, and mechanical engineering), SOCIAL SCIENCE (African American studies, American studies, anthropology, archeology, classical/ancient civilization, East Asian studies, Eastern European studies, economics, ethics, politics, and social policy, ethnic studies, German area studies, history, history of science, humanities, Judaic studies, Latin American studies, Near Eastern studies, philosophy, political science/government, psychology, religion, sociology, and women's studies). History, political science, and economics are the largest.

Required: To graduate, students must complete 36 semester courses, including at least 3 courses in each of 4 distributional groups and at least 12 courses from outside the distributional group that includes their major. Foreign language proficiency must be demonstrated.

Special: The university offers study abroad in several countries including England, Russia, Germany, and Japan, and cooperates with other study-abroad opportunities. It also offers an accelerated degree program, B.A.-B.S. degrees, dual majors, and student-designed majors. Directed Studies, a special freshman program in the humanities, affords outstanding students the opportunity to survey the Western cultural tradition. Programs in the residential colleges allow students with special interests to pursue them in a more informal atmosphere. There is a chapter of Phi Beta Kappa.

Faculty/Classroom: 66% of faculty are male; 34%, female.

Admissions: 10% of the 2005-2006 applicants were accepted. The SAT scores for the 2005-2006 freshman class were: Verbal--2% between 500 and 599, 24% between 600 and 700, and 74% above 700; Math--2% between 500 and 599, 26% between 600 and 700, and 72% above 700.

Requirements: The SAT or ACT is required. The ACT Optional Writing test is also required. In addition, only those applicants submitting SAT scores must also take any 3 SAT: Subject tests. Most successful applicants rank in the top 10% of their high school class. All students must have completed a rigorous high school program encompassing all academic disciplines. 2 essays are required, and an interview is recommended. AP credits are accepted. Important factors in the admissions decision are advanced placement or honor courses, leadership record, and extra-curricular activities record.

Procedure: Freshmen are admitted in the fall. Entrance exams should be taken at any time up to and including the January test date in the year of application. There are early action and deferred admissions plans. Early action applications should be filed by November 1; regular applications, by December 31 for fall entry. Notification of early action is sent December 15; regular decision, April 1. 1239 applicants were on the 2004 waiting list; 8 were admitted. Applications are accepted on-line.

Transfer: 21 transfer students enrolled in 2004-2005. Applicants must take either the SAT or ACT and have 1 full year of credit. An essay and 3 letters of recommendation are required. 18 of 36 term courses required for the bachelor's degree must be completed at Yale.

Visiting: There are regularly scheduled orientations for prospective students. There are guides for informal visits and visitors may sit in on classes and stay overnight. To schedule a visit, contact the Admissions Office.

Financial Aid: In 2005-2006, 44% of all full-time freshmen and 41% of continuing full-time students received some form of financial aid. 44% of full-time freshmen and 41% of continuing full-time students received need-based aid. The average freshman award was $27,683. Need-based scholarships or need-based grants averaged $25,415; and need-based self-help aid (loans and jobs) averaged $2454. The average financial indebtedness of the 2005 graduate was $14,882. Yale is a member of CSS. The CSS/Profile or FAFSA and student and parent tax returns, as well as the CSS Divorced/Separated Parents Statement and Business/Farm Supplement, if applicable, are required. The deadline for filing freshman financial aid applications for fall entry is March 1.

International Students: In a recent year, there were 463 international students enrolled. The school actively recruits these students. A satisfactory score is required on the written TOEFL. Students must also take the SAT and 3 SAT: Subject tests, or the ACT.

Computers: All students may access the system 24 hours a day. There are no time limits and no fees. It is strongly recommended that all students have a personal computer.

Graduates: From July 1, 2004 to June 30, 2005, 1339 bachelor's degrees were awarded. The most popular majors were social studies and history (37%), biological/life science (9%), and english (8%). Of a recent graduating class, 31% were enrolled in graduate school within 6 months of graduation and 64% were employed.

Admissions Contact: Dan O'Neill, Assistant Director of Admissions. E-mail: *daniel.j.oneill@yale.edu* Web: *www.yale.edu/admit*

A B C D E

DELAWARE

POPULATION DENSITY
● 10,000 and over

0 5 10 15 20 25
Miles

Wilmington
Manor
Wilmington
Newark
95
Dover

DELAWARE STATE UNIVERSITY   B-3
Dover, DE 19901   (302) 739-4917

Full-time: 975 men, 1305 women   **Faculty:** 184; IIA, av$
Part-time: 245 men, 405 women   **Ph.D.s:** 74%
Graduate: 85 men, 175 women   **Student/Faculty:** 12 to 1
Year: semesters, summer session   **Tuition:** $3430 $7180
Application Deadline: see profile   **Room & Board:** $4700
Freshman Class: n/av
SAT or ACT: required   **LESS COMPETITIVE**

Delaware State University, founded in 1891, is a publicly assisted institution offering programs in agricultural and technical fields, business, engineering, liberal and fine arts, health science, professional training, and teacher preparation. Figures in above capsule and this profile are approximate. There are 4 undergraduate schools and 1 graduate school. In addition to regional accreditation, DSU has baccalaureate program accreditation with ACBSP and NCATE. The library contains 201,550 volumes, 76,096 microform items, and 13,652 audio/video tapes/CDs/DVDs, and subscribes to 3058 periodicals including electronic. Computerized library services include the card catalog, interlibrary loans, and database searching. Special learning facilities include a learning resource center, art gallery, planetarium, and radio station. The 400-acre campus is in a suburban area 45 miles south of Wilmington. Including any residence halls, there are 31 buildings.
Student Life: 56% of undergraduates are from Delaware. Others are from 29 states, 40 foreign countries, and Canada. 90% are from public schools. 64% are African American; 32% white. Most claim no religious affiliation. The average age of freshmen is 18; all undergraduates, 21. 32% do not continue beyond their first year; 28% remain to graduate.
Housing: 1334 students can be accommodated in college housing, which includes single-sex dormitories. In addition, there are honors houses and an honors dormitory. On-campus housing is available on a first-come, first-served basis. 54% of students commute. Alcohol is not permitted. All students may keep cars.
Activities: 50% of men belong to 4 national fraternities; 50% of women belong to 4 national sororities. There are 53 groups on campus, including cheerleading, choir, drama, ethnic, honors, international, jazz band, marching band, newspaper, pep band, radio and TV, religious, social service, student government, and yearbook. Popular campus events include Parent's Day, Annual Career Fair, and Annual Pride Day.

Sports: There are 8 intercollegiate sports for men and 7 for women, and 20 intramural sports for men and 20 for women. Facilities include an indoor swimming pool, a dance studio, racquetball and handball courts, 2 gyms, a football stadium, a baseball field, and outdoor track, and tennis courts.
Disabled Students: Wheelchair ramps, elevators, special parking and specially equipped rest rooms are available. The Office of Disabilities Services provides assistance to students with all types of disabilities.
Services: Counseling and information services are available, as is tutoring in every subject. There is remedial math, reading, and writing. A university tutoring program is available with a tutoring lab and tutorial service available in residence halls. A supplemental instruction program is available for challenging courses.
Campus Safety and Security: Measures include 24-hour foot and vehicle patrol, shuttle buses, informal discussions, and pamphlets/posters/films. There are emergency telephones and lighted pathways/sidewalks.
Programs of Study: DSU confers B.A., B.S., B.S.W., and B.Tech. degrees. Master's degrees are also awarded. Bachelor's degrees are awarded in AGRICULTURE (agricultural business management, fish and game management, and natural resource management), BIOLOGICAL SCIENCE (biology/biological science and botany), BUSINESS (accounting, business administration and management, fashion merchandising, hotel/motel and restaurant management, and marketing/retailing/merchandising), COMMUNICATIONS AND THE ARTS (English, French, journalism, music, and Spanish), COMPUTER AND PHYSICAL SCIENCE (chemistry, computer science, mathematics, and physics), EDUCATION (agricultural, art, business, early childhood, elementary, health, home economics, music, physical, science, and special), ENGINEERING AND ENVIRONMENTAL DESIGN (chemical engineering, civil engineering, electrical/electronics engineering, and mechanical engineering), HEALTH PROFESSIONS (community health work, environmental health science, and nursing), SOCIAL SCIENCE (economics, history, parks and recreation management, political science/government, psychology, social work, and sociology). Education is the strongest academically. Business administration, education, and English and mass communications are the largest.
Required: 52 hours of general education requirements must be completed, distributed as follows: 16 hours of core courses, 3 hours of arts and humanities, 6 hours of foreign languages, 6 hours of literature, 6 hours of math, 6 hours of natural sciences, and a minimum 3-hour Senior Capstone Experience course. A total of 121 credit hours and a minimum GPA of 2.0 are required.
Special: The university offers accelerated degrees, combined B.A.-B.S. degrees, student-designed majors, and a 3-2 engineering program with the University of Delaware. Work-study is available on campus. There are assisted internships in airway science and nursing, and co-op programs in business, education, home economics, social work, and agriculture. There are 6 national honor societies, including Phi Beta Kappa, and a freshman honors program.
Faculty/Classroom: 61% of faculty are male; 39%, female. No introductory courses are taught by graduate students. The average class size in a regular course is 16.
Admissions: In a recent year, 6 freshmen graduated first in their class.
Requirements: The SAT or ACT is required. In addition, applicants should graduate from an accredited secondary school or have a GED. 16 academic credits are required, including 4 units of English and 3 of math, of which 2 must be in algebra and 1 must be in geometry, 3 of science courses with a lab, 2 of history and/or social studies, and 4 of electives, including foreign language or computer science courses. A GPA of 2.0 is required. CLEP credit is accepted. Important factors in the admissions decision are extracurricular activities record, advanced placement or honor courses, and recommendations by school officials.
Procedure: Freshmen are admitted fall and spring. Entrance exams should be taken in December or January of the senior year. There are early admissions and roling admissions plans. Check with the school for application deadlines. The application fee is $10. Notification is sent on a rolling basis.
Transfer: 145 transfer students enrolled in a recent year. Applicants must submit a statement of honorable withdrawal and high school and college transcripts. 30 of 121 credits required for the bachelor's degree must be completed at DSU.
Visiting: There are regularly scheduled orientations for prospective students, including a High School Day Program. There are guides for informal visits. To schedule a visit, contact Jethro Williams.
Financial Aid: DSU is a member of CSS. The CSS/Profile or FFS is required. Check with the school for current application deadlines.
International Students: They must score satisfactorily on the written TOEFL and also take the SAT or the ACT.
Computers: All students may access the system 24 hours a day. There are no time limits and no fees.

Graduates: In a recent year, 405 bachelor's degrees were awarded. The most popular majors were business administration (17%), education (14%), and accounting and finance (10%). In an average class, 10% graduate in 4 years or less, 24% graduate in 5 years or less, and 28% graduate in 6 years or less. Of a recent graduating class, 13% were enrolled in graduate school within 6 months of graduation and 62% were employed.

Admissions Contact: Jethro Williams, Admissions Director. E-mail: *jwilliam@dsc.edu* Web: *www.dsc.edu*

GOLDEY-BEACOM COLLEGE — B-1

Wilmington, DE 19808

(302) 998-8814
(800) 833-4877; Fax: (302) 996-5408

Full-time: 305 men, 445 women	Faculty: 24
Part-time: 235 men, 345 women	Ph.D.s: 49%
Graduate: 75 men, 75 women	Student/Faculty: 30 to 1
Year: semesters, summer session	Tuition: $8050
Application Deadline: open	Room & Board: $3500
Freshman Class: n/av	
SAT: required	COMPETITIVE

Goldey-Beacom College, founded in 1886, is a private business college that provides undergraduate training and education for careers in business, industry, and government. There is 1 graduate school. Figures in the above capsule and profile are approximate. In addition to regional accreditation, Goldey-Beacom College has baccalaureate program accreditation with AACSB and ACBSP. The library contains 48,000 volumes, 27,283 microform items, and 693 audio/video tapes/CDs/DVDs, and subscribes to 800 periodicals including electronic. Computerized library services include interlibrary loans and database searching. Special learning facilities include a learning resource center. The 28-acre campus is in a suburban area 10 miles west of Wilmington. Including any residence halls, there are 8 buildings.

Student Life: 60% of undergraduates are from Delaware. Others are from 22 states, 50 foreign countries, and Canada. 75% are from public schools. 81% are white; 10% African American. The average age of freshmen is 19; all undergraduates, 21. 30% do not continue beyond their first year; 70% remain to graduate.

Housing: 300 students can be accommodated in college housing, which includes coed on-campus apartments. In addition, there are special-interest houses. On-campus housing is guaranteed for all 4 years. 80% of students commute. All students may keep cars.

Activities: 10% of men belong to 2 national fraternities; 10% of women belong to 2 national sororities. There are 23 groups on campus, including cheerleading, chorus, computers, drama, ethnic, honors, international, literary magazine, newspaper, professional, religious, social service, and student government. Popular campus events include Goldey-Beacom Follies, Spring Fest, and International Night.

Sports: Facilities include soccer and softball fields, and tennis, basketball, and handball courts.

Disabled Students: All of the campus is accessible. Wheelchair ramps, elevators, special parking, specially equipped rest rooms, lowered drinking fountains, and lowered telephones are available.

Services: Counseling and information services are available, as is tutoring in most subjects. There is a reader service for the blind, and remedial math, reading, and writing, and computer-based tutorials.

Campus Safety and Security: Measures include 24-hour foot and vehicle patrol, self-defense education, informal discussions, and pamphlets/posters/films. There are lighted pathways/sidewalks and security from 6 P.M. to 6 A.M. on the small campus.

Programs of Study: Goldey-Beacom College confers the B.S. degree. Associate and master's degrees are also awarded. Bachelor's degrees are awarded in BUSINESS (accounting, banking and finance, international business management, and marketing/retailing/merchandising), COMPUTER AND PHYSICAL SCIENCE (computer programming). Accounting and computer science are the strongest academically. Accounting and management are the largest.

Required: To graduate, students must complete a minimum of 136 credit hours with an overall GPA of 2.0. Students must also fulfill the college's core requirements in English, math, and computer science.

Special: Co-op programs in all majors, an accelerated degree program, a 5-year advanced business degree, dual majors, internships, study abroad, and work-study programs are available. There is 1 national honor society, a freshman honors program, and 3 departmental honors program.

Faculty/Classroom: 66% of faculty are male; 34%, female. All teach undergraduates. No introductory courses are taught by graduate students. The average class size in an introductory lecture is 35 and in a regular course, 25.

Requirements: The SAT is required. In addition, applicants must be high school graduates or have a GED. A GPA of 2.0 is required. AP and CLEP credits are accepted. Important factors in the admissions decision are leadership record, evidence of special talent, and recommendations by school officials.

Procedure: Freshmen are admitted to all sessions. There are early admissions, deferred admissions and rolling admissions plans. Application deadlines are open. Application fee is $30.

Transfer: 67 transfer students enrolled in a recent year. Transfer applicants must submit high school and college transcripts. 65 of 136 credits required for the bachelor's degree must be completed at Goldey-Beacom College.

Visiting: There are regularly scheduled orientations for prospective students, including an open house. There are guides for informal visits and visitors may sit in on classes and stay overnight. To schedule a visit, contact the Admissions Office.

Financial Aid: In a recent year, 70% of all full-time freshmen received some form of financial aid. 80% of full-time freshmen and 60% of continuing full-time students received need-based aid. The average freshman award was $4180. 90% of undergraduates worked part time. Average annual earnings from campus work were $1200. Goldey-Beacom College is a member of CSS. The FAFSA is required. Check with the school for application deadlines.

International Students: The school actively recruits these students. They must score satisfactorily on the written TOEFL.

Computers: There are no fees.

Graduates: In a recent year, 180 bachelor's degrees were awarded. The most popular majors were management (33%) and accounting (17%). In an average class, 30% graduate in 3 years or less, 40% graduate in 4 years or less, 20% graduate in 5 years or less, and 10% graduate in 6 years or less. 70 companies recruited on campus in a recent year. Of a recent year graduating class, all were employed within 6 months of graduation.

Admissions Contact: Director of Admissions and Associate Dean. A video is available. Web: *www.goldey.gbc.edu*

UNIVERSITY OF DELAWARE — A-1

Newark, DE 19716-6210

(302) 831-8123; Fax: (302) 831-6905

Full-time: 6266 men, 8633 women	Faculty: 1126; I, av$
Part-time: 927 men, 1113 women	Ph.D.s: 75%
Graduate: 1665 men, 1769 women	Student/Faculty: 13 to 1
Year: 4-1-4, summer session	Tuition: $7318 ($17,474)
Application Deadline: January 15	Room & Board: $6824
Freshman Class: 21,617 applied, 10,256 accepted, 3522 enrolled	
SAT Verbal/Math: 590/610*	ACT: 27 HIGHLY COMPETITIVE

The University of Delaware, founded in 1743 and chartered in 1833, is a privately controlled, state-assisted institution, offering programs in agricultural and natural resources, liberal arts and sciences, business, education, human services, health and nursing sciences, and engineering. There are 6 undergraduate and 7 graduate schools. In addition to regional accreditation, Delaware has baccalaureate program accreditation with AACSB, ABET, ADA, APTA, CAHEA, NASDTEC, NASM, NCATE, and NLN. The 5 libraries contain 3,019,990 volumes, 3,346,374 microform items, and 16,461 audio/video tapes/CDs/DVDs, and subscribe to 12,496 periodicals including electronic. Computerized library services include the card catalog, interlibrary loans, database searching, and Internet access. Special learning facilities include a learning resource center, art gallery, radio station, TV station, a preschool lab, development ice skating science center, computer-controlled greenhouse, nursing practice labs, physical therapy clinic, 400-acre agricultural research complex, exercise physiology biomechanics labs, foreign language media center, and composite materials center. The 1000-acre campus is in a small town 12 miles southwest of Wilmington; centered on the east coast between New York City and Washington, D.C. Including any residence halls, there are 400 buildings.

Student Life: 59% of undergraduates are from out of state, mostly the Middle Atlantic. Students are from 50 states, 100 foreign countries, and Canada. 79% are from public schools. 84% are white. 34% are Catholic; 30% claim no religious affiliation; 23% Protestant; 10% Jewish. The average age of freshmen is 18; all undergraduates, 20. 11% do not continue beyond their first year; 76% remain to graduate.

Housing: 7100 students can be accommodated in college housing, which includes single-sex and coed dormitories, on-campus apartments, married-student housing, fraternity houses, and sorority houses. In addition, there are honors houses, language houses, special-interest houses alcohol/smoke-free residence halls, and suite. On-campus housing is guaranteed for all 4 years. 50% of students live on campus; of those, 75% remain on campus on weekends. All students may keep cars.

Activities: 13% of men belong to 1 local and 17 national fraternities; 13% of women belong to 2 local and 14 national sororities. There are 203 groups on campus, including band, choir, chorale, chorus, dance, drama, ethnic, film, jazz band, literary magazine, marching band, music ensembles, musical theater, newspaper, opera, orchestra, pep band, radio and TV, and student government. Popular campus events include Greek Week, Convocation Commencement, and Parents and Family Day.

Sports: There are 11 intercollegiate sports for men and 12 for women, and 15 intramural sports for men and 15 for women. Facilities include

a 23,000-seat football stadium, 3 multipurpose gyms, 6 outdoor multipurpose fields, 8 outdoor basketball courts, 2 squash courts, 15 racquetball courts, 21 outdoor tennis courts, indoor and outdoor pools, a universal weight room, a 6000-seat basketball arena, a rock climbing wall, a high-ropes challenge course, 4 student fitness centers, a strength and conditioning room with free weights, outdoor and indoor tracks, softball, baseball, lacrosse, and soccer fields, 2 ice arenas, an outdoor hockey rink, and 4 wallyball courts.

Disabled Students: 95% of the campus is accessible. Wheelchair ramps, elevators, special parking, specially equipped rest rooms, special class scheduling, lowered drinking fountains, lowered telephones, and special housing are available.

Services: Counseling and information services are available, as is tutoring in every subject. There is a reader service for the blind, and remedial math, reading, and writing. There is also a writing center, a math center, and an academic services center for assistance with academic self-management development, critical thinking, and problem solving and for individual assistance for learning-disabled students.

Campus Safety and Security: Measures include 24-hour foot and vehicle patrol, self-defense education, security escort services, and shuttle buses. There are informal discussions, pamphlets/posters/films, emergency telephones, lighted pathways/sidewalks, ongoing student-awareness programs in the residence halls, community policing, and keycard access to residence halls.

Programs of Study: Delaware confers B.A., B.S., B.A. Liberal Studies, B.A.S., B.C.E., B.Ch.E., B.C.P.E., B.E.E., B.E.N.E., B.F.A., B.M.E., B.Mus., B.S.Acc., B.S.Ag., B.S.A.T., B.S.B.A., B.S.Ed., B.S.N., and B.S.P.E. degrees. Associate, master's, and doctoral degrees are also awarded. Bachelor's degrees are awarded in AGRICULTURE (agricultural business management, agricultural economics, agriculture, animal science, natural resource management, plant science, and soil science), BIOLOGICAL SCIENCE (biochemistry, biology/biological science, biotechnology, entomology, nutrition, and plant pathology), BUSINESS (accounting, banking and finance, business administration and management, hotel/motel and restaurant management, management science, marketing/retailing/merchandising, and recreation and leisure services), COMMUNICATIONS AND THE ARTS (art, art history and appreciation, communications, comparative literature, English, fine arts, historic preservation, Italian, journalism, languages, music, music theory and composition, and theater management), COMPUTER AND PHYSICAL SCIENCE (astronomy, chemistry, computer science, geology, geophysics and seismology, information sciences and systems, mathematics, and physics), EDUCATION (agricultural, athletic training, early childhood, education, elementary, English, foreign languages, mathematics, music, physical, psychology, science, secondary, and special), ENGINEERING AND ENVIRONMENTAL DESIGN (bioengineering, chemical engineering, civil engineering, computer engineering, electrical/electronics engineering, engineering technology, environmental engineering, environmental science, landscape architecture/design, and mechanical engineering), HEALTH PROFESSIONS (medical laboratory technology and nursing), SOCIAL SCIENCE (anthropology, community services, consumer services, criminal justice, dietetics, economics, family and community services, fashion design and technology, food science, geography, history, human development, interdisciplinary studies, international relations, Latin American studies, parks and recreation management, philosophy, physical fitness/movement, political science/government, psychology, sociology, textiles and clothing, and women's studies). Engineering, all sciences, and business are the strongest academically. Biological sciences, elementary teacher education, and engineering are the largest.

Required: For graduation, students must complete at least 120 credits with a minimum GPA of 2.0. All students must take freshman English and 3 credits of course work with multicultural or multiethnic content. Most majors require more than 120 credits. Most degree programs require that half of the courses be in the major field of study.

Special: Students may participate in cooperative programs, internships, study abroad in 25 countries, a Washington semester, and work-study programs. The university offers accelerated degree programs, B.A.-B.S. degrees, dual majors, 68 minors, student-designed majors (Bachelor of Arts in Liberal Studies), and pass/fail options. There are 4-1 degree programs in engineering, and hotel and restaurant management. Nondegree study is available through the Division of Continuing Education. There is an extensive undergraduate research program. Students may earn an enriched degree through the University Honors Program. There are 37 national honor societies, including Phi Beta Kappa and a freshman honors program.

Faculty/Classroom: 61% of faculty are male; 39%, female. All teach undergraduates. The average class size in a laboratory is 18 and in a regular course, 35.

Admissions: 47% of the 2005-2006 applicants were accepted. The SAT scores for the 2005-2006 freshman class were: Verbal--13% below 500, 45% between 500 and 599, 35% between 600 and 700, and 7% above 700; Math--10% below 500, 35% between 500 and 599, 44% between 600 and 700, and 11% above 700. The ACT scores were 5% below 21, 14% between 21 and 23, 33% between 24 and 26, 27% be-

tween 27 and 28, and 21% above 28. 69% of the current freshmen were in the top fifth of their class; 92% were in the top two fifths.

Requirements: The SAT or ACT is required. The ACT Optional Writing Test is also required. In addition, applicants should be graduates of an accredited secondary school. The GED is accepted. Students should have completed a minimum of 18 high school academic units, including 4 units of English, 3 units math, 3 units of science with 2 lab units, 2 units each of foreign language, history, and social studies, and 2 units of academic course electives. SAT subject tests are recommended, especially for honors program applicants. A writing sample and at least 1 letter of recommendation are required for all applicants. AP credits are accepted. Important factors in the admissions decision are advanced placement or honor courses, recommendations by school officials, and personality/intangible qualities.

Procedure: Freshmen are admitted fall and spring. Entrance exams should be taken at the end of the junior year or the beginning of the senior year. There are early decision, early admissions, and deferred admissions plans. Early decision applications should be filed by November 15; regular applications, by January 15 for fall entry and December 15 for spring entry, along with a $60 fee. Notification of early decision is sent December 15; regular decision, mid-March. 596 early decision candidates were accepted for the 2005-2006 class. 3176 applicants were on the 2005 waiting list; 142 were admitted. Applications are accepted online.

Transfer: 490 transfer students enrolled in 2004-2005. Applicants for transfer should have completed at least 24 credits with a minimum GPA of 2.5 for most majors; some majors require a GPA of 3.0 or better and/or specific course work. All transfer students must submit high school and college transcripts, an essay, and a statement of good standing from prior institution (s). In some cases, an interview and standardized test scores are required. 30 of 120 credits required for the bachelor's degree must be completed at Delaware.

Visiting: There are regularly scheduled orientations for prospective students, consisting of a 30-minute admissions information session and a 90-minute walking tour of campus. There are guides for informal visits and visitors may sit in on classes. To schedule a visit, contact the Admissions Office.

Financial Aid: In 2005-2006, 40% of all full-time freshmen and 38% of continuing full-time students received some form of financial aid. At least 31% of full-time freshmen and at least 28% of continuing full-time students received need-based aid. The average freshman award was $10,400. Need-based scholarships or need-based grants averaged $6600; need-based self-help aid (loans and jobs) averaged $4750; non-need-based athletic scholarships averaged $13,200; and institutional awards and scholarships averaged $4500. 20% of undergraduates work part time. Average annual earnings from campus work are $1000. The average financial indebtedness of the 2005 graduate was $15,200. The FAFSA is required. The priority date for freshman financial aid applications for fall entry is February 1. The deadline for filing freshman financial aid applications for fall entry is March 15.

International Students: In a recent year there were 140 international students enrolled. The school actively recruits these students. They must score satisfactorily on the written TOEFL or on the electronic version and also take the ELPT.

Computers: All students may access the system 24 hours a day. There are no time limits and no fees.

Graduates: From July 1, 2004 to June 30, 2005, 3602 bachelor's degrees were awarded. The most popular majors were business/marketing (17%), social sciences (14%), and education (12%). In an average class, 62% graduate in 4 years or less, 75% graduate in 5 years or less, and 76% graduate in 6 years or less. 500 companies recruited on campus in 2004-2005. Of the 2004 graduating class, 20% were enrolled in graduate school within 6 months of graduation and 79% were employed.

Admissions Contact: Lou Hirsh, Director of Admissions.
E-mail: *admissions@udel.edu* Web: *www.udel.edu*

WESLEY COLLEGE   B-3
Dover, DE 19901-3875   (302) 736-2400
(800) 937-5398; Fax: (302) 736-2301

Full-time: 600 men, 670 women	**Faculty:** 57; IIB, -$
Part-time: 140 men, 195 women	**Ph.D.s:** 75%
Graduate: 20 men, 105 women	**Student/Faculty:** 22 to 1
Year: semesters, summer session	**Tuition:** $13,720
Application Deadline: open	**Room & Board:** $6210
Freshman Class: n/av	
SAT: required	**COMPETITIVE**

Wesley College, founded in 1873, is a private liberal arts institution affiliated with the United Methodist Church. Figures in the above capsule and profile are approximate. In addition to regional accreditation, Wesley has baccalaureate program accreditation with ABA, NCATE, and NLN. The library contains 100,842 volumes, 172,548 microform items, and 940 audio/video tapes/CDs/DVDs, and subscribes to 232 periodicals including electronic. Computerized library services include interlibrary loans, database searching, and Internet access. Special learning facilities include a learning resource center. The 26-acre campus is in a small town 75 miles south of Philadelphia. Including any residence halls, there are 20 buildings.

Student Life: 60% of undergraduates are from out of state, mostly the Middle Atlantic. Students are from 18 states and 9 foreign countries. 85% are from public schools. 78% are white; 17% African American. 61% are Protestant; 35% Catholic. The average age of freshmen is 18; all undergraduates, 20. 23% do not continue beyond their first year; 53% remain to graduate.

Housing: 778 students can be accommodated in college housing, which includes single-sex and coed dormitories and on-campus apartments. In addition, there are honors houses. On-campus housing is guaranteed for all 4 years. 62% of students live on campus; of those, 30% remain on campus on weekends. Alcohol is not permitted. All students may keep cars.

Activities: 15% of men belong to 3 national fraternities; 15% of women belong to 3 local sororities. There are 30 groups on campus, including band, cheerleading, choir, chorale, chorus, drama, ethnic, honors, international, jazz band, literary magazine, newspaper, photography, political, professional, religious, social, social service, student government, and yearbook. Popular campus events include Family Day, International Fair, and Spring Fling.

Sports: There are 8 intercollegiate sports for men and 8 for women, and 4 intramural sports for men and 4 for women. Facilities include a swimming pool, tennis courts, a football stadium, athletic fields, a gym, a game room, and an exercise room.

Disabled Students: 65% of the campus is accessible. Wheelchair ramps, elevators, special parking, specially equipped rest rooms, special class scheduling, and lowered drinking fountains, are available.

Services: Counseling and information services are available, as is tutoring in every subject. There is remedial math, reading, and writing.

Campus Safety and Security: Measures include 24-hour foot and vehicle patrol, security escort services, informal discussions, and pamphlets/posters/films. There are emergency telephones and lighted pathways/sidewalks.

Programs of Study: Wesley confers B.A. and B.S. degrees. Associate and master's degrees are also awarded. Bachelor's degrees are awarded in BIOLOGICAL SCIENCE (biology/biological science), BUSINESS (accounting, business administration and management, management science, and marketing/retailing/merchandising), COMMUNICATIONS AND THE ARTS (communications and English), EDUCATION (elementary, English, physical, secondary, and social studies), ENGINEERING AND ENVIRONMENTAL DESIGN (environmental science), HEALTH PROFESSIONS (medical laboratory technology and nursing), SOCIAL SCIENCE (American studies, history, liberal arts/general studies, paralegal studies, political science/government, and psychology). Education, psychology, and business are the strongest academically and have the largest enrollments.

Required: For graduation, students must complete 124 credit hours, with at least 15 hours in the major and a minimum GPA of 2.0. 50 hours of core courses, including English, religion, science, math, American culture, non-American culture, and phys ed are required.

Special: Wesley offers internships in business and industry, environmental science, medical technology, and government agencies. Study abroad in 5 countries, work-study programs, dual majors, pass/fail options, and credit for life, military, and work experience are available. There are 2 national honor societies and 1 departmental honors program.

Faculty/Classroom: 58% of faculty are male; 42%, female. All teach undergraduates, 3% do research, and 3% do both. No introductory courses are taught by graduate students. The average class size in an introductory lecture is 20; in a laboratory, 12; and in a regular course, 20.

Admissions: In a recent year, 5 freshmen graduated first in their class.

Requirements: The SAT is required. In addition, applicants must be graduates of an accredited secondary school; the GED is accepted. Students should have completed 12 academic credits or 16 Carnegie units, including 4 units of English and 2 units each of math, history, science, and social studies. An interview is recommended. Wesley requires applicants to be in the upper 80% of their class. A GPA of 2.2 is required. AP and CLEP credits are accepted. Important factors in the admissions decision are recommendations by school officials, extracurricular activities record, and leadership record.

Procedure: Freshmen are admitted fall and winter. Entrance exams should be taken in the junior year. There are early decision, deferred admissions and rolling admissions plans. Application deadlines are open. Application fee is $20. Applications are accepted on-line

Transfer: 30 transfer students enrolled in a recent year. Applicants must have a minimum GPA of 2.0 and a satisfactorily SAT score. 36 of 124 credits required for the bachelor's degree must be completed at Wesley.

Visiting: There are regularly scheduled orientations for prospective students. There are guides for informal visits and visitors may sit in on classes and stay overnight. To schedule a visit, contact the Office of Admissions at (800) WESLEYU.

Financial Aid: The FAFSA or SFS, and the college's own financial statement are required. Check with the school for application deadlines.

International Students: In a recent year, there were 20 international students enrolled. The school actively recruits these students. They must score satisfactorily on the written TOEFL and also take the SAT.

Computers: All students may access the system 24 hours a day, 7 days a week. There are no time limits and no fees. It is strongly recommended that all students have a personal computer.

Graduates: In a recent year, 214 bachelor's degrees were awarded. The most popular majors were education (16%), psychology (14%), and management (12%). In an average class, 1% graduate in 3 years or less, 48% graduate in 4 years or less, 50% graduate in 5 years or less, 53% graduate in 6 years or less. 30 companies recruited on campus in a recent year. Of a recent graduating class, 16% were enrolled in graduate school within 6 months of graduation and 62% were employed.

Admissions Contact: Arthur Jacobs, Director of Admissions. A video is available. E-mail: *jacobsar@wesley.edu* Web: *www.wesley.edu*

WILMINGTON COLLEGE
New Castle, DE 19720

B-1

(302) 328-9407
(877) 967-5464; Fax: (302) 328-5902

Full-time: 715 men, 1305 women	Faculty: 41; IIA, -$
Part-time: 570 men, 1395 women	Ph.Ds: 55%
Graduate: 730 men, 1725 women	Student/Faculty: 49 to 1
Year: semesters, summer session	Tuition: $5605
Application Deadline: open	Room & Board: n/app
Freshman Class: n/av	
SAT or ACT: not required	NONCOMPETITIVE

Wilmington College, founded in 1967, is a private, liberal arts commuter college offering admission to students from varied academic backgrounds. There are 6 undergraduate and 7 graduate schools. Figures in the above capsule and profile are approximate. In addition to regional accreditation, Wilmington has baccalaureate program accreditation with NASDTEC and NLN. The library contains 191,885 volumes, 93,545 microform items, and 2611 audio/video tapes/CDs/DVDs, and subscribes to 468 periodicals including electronic. Computerized library services include the card catalog, interlibrary loans, database searching, and Internet access. Special learning facilities include a learning resource center, radio station, and TV station. The 18-acre campus is in an urban area 7 miles south of Wilmington. There are 18 buildings.

Student Life: 87% of undergraduates are from Delaware. Others are from 12 states, 5 foreign countries, and Canada. 85% are from public schools. 45% are white; 12% African American. The average age of freshmen is 27; all undergraduates, 30. 8% do not continue beyond their first year; 76% remain to graduate.

Housing: There are no residence halls. All students commute. Alcohol is not permitted. All students may keep cars.

Activities: There is 1 national fraternity. There are 11 groups on campus, including cheerleading, film, honors, newspaper, photography, radio and TV, student government, and yearbook.

Sports: There are 4 intercollegiate sports for men and 5 for women. Facilities include a 1000-seat gym and a recreation room.

Disabled Students: All of the campus is accessible. Wheelchair ramps, elevators, special parking, specially equipped rest rooms, lowered drinking fountains, and lowered telephones are available.

Services: Counseling and information services are available, as is tutoring in some subjects, including math and English. There is remedial math and reading. Staff members also are available to assist students with study skills such as test taking, reading, concentration development, and time management.

Campus Safety and Security: Measures include 24-hour foot and vehicle patrol, security escort services, emergency telephones, and lighted pathways/sidewalks.

Programs of Study: Wilmington confers B.A., B.S., and B.S.N. degrees. Associate, master's, and doctoral degrees are also awarded. Bachelor's degrees are awarded in BUSINESS (accounting, banking and finance, business administration and management, personnel management, and sports management), COMMUNICATIONS AND THE ARTS (communications technology, media arts, multimedia, and video), EDUCATION (early childhood and elementary), ENGINEERING AND ENVIRONMENTAL DESIGN (aeronautical science and aviation administration/management), HEALTH PROFESSIONS (nursing), SOCIAL SCIENCE (behavioral science and criminal justice). Nursing and elementary education are the strongest academically. Business, nursing, and elementary education are the largest.

Required: To graduate, students must complete a total of 120 hours with a minimum GPA of 2.0. 54 hours are required in the major. The 36-hour general studies core requirement includes 12 hours of social science, 9 each of English and humanities, and 3 each of math and science. At least 45 credit hours of upper-division course work are required, as is demonstrated competence in verbal and written communication and computational skills. At least 3 credits must be taken in computer operations. Nursing students must also submit official transcripts verifying graduation from a diploma or associate degree nursing program. Candidates for the B.S.N. degree must possess an R.N. license.

Special: The school offers practicums for education students, co-op programs, work-study programs with area employers, internships, a general studies degree, an accelerated degree program, dual majors, pass/fail options, credit for life experience, and by-challenge exam. There is 1 national honor society and 2 departmental honors programs.

Faculty/Classroom: 70% of faculty are male; 30%, female. 66% teach undergraduates. The average class size in an introductory lecture is 25; in a laboratory, 10; and in a regular course, 17.

Requirements: Graduation from an accredited secondary school or satisfactory scores on the GED are required for admission. An interview may be required of some students, and an essay is recommended. A GPA of 2.0 is required. AP and CLEP credits are accepted.

Procedure: Freshmen are admitted to all sessions. There are deferred admissions and rollings admissions plans. Application deadlines are open. Application fee is $25.

Transfer: 2736 transfer students enrolled in a recent year. Applicants must have a 2.0 GPA; those with a lower GPA must have an interview. Some applicants may be required to submit SAT or ACT scores. Those with fewer than 15 semester credits must submit high school transcripts. No more than 75 semester credits will be accepted for transfer credit. 45 of 120 credits required for the bachelor's degree must be completed at Wilmington.

Visiting: There are guides for informal visits and visitors may sit in on classes. To schedule a visit, contact the Admissions Office.

Financial Aid: In a recent year, 33% of all full-time freshmen received some form of financial aid. 10% of full-time freshmen received need-based aid. The average freshman award was $5034. The FAFSA is required. Check with the school for application deadlines.

International Students: In a recent year there were 40 international students enrolled. They must score satisfactorily on the written TOEFL or they may submit a transcript of successful completion of at least 12 credit hours from a U.S. institution of higher education.

Computers: Only students matriculated in communications technology majors may access the system during designated class/lab time. There are no time limits and no fees.

Graduates: 128 companies recruited on campus in a recent year.

Admissions Contact: Andrey Mattern, Manager of Admissions. E-mail: *apara@wilmcoll.edu* Web: *www.wilmcoll.edu*

DISTRICT of COLUMBIA

0 1 2 3
Miles

Potomac River

66
95
695
295

AMERICAN UNIVERSITY
A-2
Washington, DC 20016-8001

(202) 885-6000
Fax: (202) 885-1025

Full-time: 2114 men, 3510 women   **Faculty:** 441; I, av$

Part-time: 133 men, 164 women   **Ph.D.s:** 96%

Graduate: 2092 men, 3266 women   **Student/Faculty:** 13 to 1

Year: semesters, summer session   **Tuition:** $28,019

Application Deadline: January 15   **Room & Board:** $10,700

Freshman Class: 13,596 applied, 6975 accepted, 1288 enrolled

SAT Verbal/Math: 640/630*   **ACT:** 28

HIGHLY COMPETITIVE+

American University, founded in 1893, is a private liberal arts institution affiliated with the United Methodist Church. There are 5 undergraduate and 6 graduate schools. In addition to regional accreditation, AU has baccalaureate program accreditation with AACSB, ACEJMC, NCS, NASDTEC, NASM, and NCATE. The library contains 1 million volumes, 1.1 million microform items, and 60,870 audio/video tapes/CDs/DVDs, and subscribes to 17,400 periodicals including electronic. Computerized library services include the card catalog, interlibrary loans, database searching, Internet access, and laptop Internet portals. Special learning facilities include a learning resource center, art gallery, radio station, TV station, language resource center, art and dance studios, graphic design and multimedia design and development labs, national center for health fitness, audiotechnology lab, broadcast newsroom, journalism center, and spectroscopy, laser physics, computational physics, and neural computing labs. The 84-acre campus is in an urban area 5 miles northwest of downtown Washington D.C. Including any residence halls, there are 37 buildings.

Student Life: 87% of undergraduates are from out of state, mostly the Middle Atlantic. Students are from 50 states, 106 foreign countries, and Canada. 67% are white; 10% African American; 10% foreign nationals. The average age of freshmen is 18; all undergraduates, 20. 11% do not continue beyond their first year; 70% remain to graduate.

Housing: 4000 students can be accommodated in college housing, which includes single-sex and coed dormitories and off-campus apartments. In addition, there is an international-intercultural hall, honors floors, and special-interest floors, including a community service floor. All dorms are smoke-free. On-campus housing is guaranteed for all 4 years. 65% of students live on campus. Alcohol is not permitted. Upperclassmen may keep cars.

Activities: 14% of men belong to 10 national fraternities; 16% of women belong to 13 national sororities. There are 180 groups on campus, including art, band, cheerleading, chess, choir, chorale, chorus, computers, dance, debate, drama, ethnic, film, forensics, gay, honors, international, jazz band, literary magazine, musical theater, newspaper, orchestra, pep band, photography, political, professional, radio and TV, religious, social, social service, student government, symphony, and

yearbook. Popular campus events include Family Weekend, Founders Day Ball, and Campus Beautification Day.

Sports: There are 9 intercollegiate sports for men and 10 for women, and 16 intramural sports for men and 17 for women. Facilities include a 6000-seat gym, 2 swimming pools, hockey and soccer fields, a softball diamond, an all-purpose field, cardiovascular and strength training equipment, weight rooms, courts for tennis, basketball, and volleyball, an aerobics studio, an indoor jogging track, and an outdoor, 6-lane tartan track.

Disabled Students: 95% of the campus is accessible. Wheelchair ramps, elevators, special parking, specially equipped rest rooms, special class scheduling, lowered drinking fountains, lowered telephones, special housing, and a university shuttle equipped to accommodate students in wheelchairs are available.

Services: Counseling and information services are available, as is tutoring in every subject. There is a reader service for the blind, and remedial math, reading, and writing. A math and statistics tutoring lab, a writing center, and a foreign language resource center are available.

Campus Safety and Security: Measures include 24-hour foot and vehicle patrol, self-defense education, security escort services, and shuttle buses. There are informal discussions, pamphlets/posters/films, emergency telephones, lighted pathways/sidewalks, safety orientation programs, alarms and closed-circuit cameras, and posted crime alerts.

Programs of Study: AU confers B.A., B.S., B.F.A., and B.S.B.A. degrees. Associate, master's, and doctoral degrees are also awarded. Bachelor's degrees are awarded in AGRICULTURE (environmental studies), BIOLOGICAL SCIENCE (biochemistry, biology/biological science, and marine science), BUSINESS (business administration and management and international business management), COMMUNICATIONS AND THE ARTS (art history and appreciation, audio technology, communications, dramatic arts, film arts, fine arts, graphic design, journalism, literature, multimedia, music, musical theater, performing arts, public relations, and studio art), COMPUTER AND PHYSICAL SCIENCE (applied mathematics, chemistry, computer science, mathematics, physics, and statistics), EDUCATION (elementary and secondary), ENGINEERING AND ENVIRONMENTAL DESIGN (environmental science), HEALTH PROFESSIONS (health science), SOCIAL SCIENCE (American studies, anthropology, area studies, criminal justice, economics, French studies, gender studies, German area studies, history, interdisciplinary studies, international studies, Judaic studies, Latin American studies, law, philosophy, political science/government, psychology, Russian and Slavic studies, sociology, Spanish studies, and women's studies). Political science, international studies, and business administration are the strongest academically and are the largest.

Required: To graduate, students must complete 120 credit hours with a minimum GPA of 2.0. In addition, students must complete 30 credit hours of general education requirements in 5 curricular areas and fulfill the school's competency requirements in English composition and math by either passing an exam or taking a course in each area. Many majors require internships, selecting a minor, or senior seminars.

Special: AU offers co-op programs and internships in all majors, study abroad in more than 50 countries, and a Washington semester program. Work-study is available on campus and with local community service agencies. Dual majors, interdisciplinary programs, student-designed majors, 3-2 engineering degrees, and B.A.-B.S. degrees are also available. Combined bachelor's/master's programs are available in most majors. Cross-registration may be arranged through the Consortium of Universities of the Washington Metropolitan Area. Credit for life experience, non-degree study, and pass/fail options are available. There are preprofessional programs in dentistry, engineering, law, medicine, optometry, osteopathy, pharmacy, and veterinary medicine. There are 12 national honor societies, including Phi Beta Kappa, a freshman honors program, and 27 departmental honors programs.

Faculty/Classroom: 56% of faculty are male; 44%, female. No introductory courses are taught by graduate students. The average class size in an introductory lecture is 29 and in a regular course, 26.

Admissions: 51% of the 2005-2006 applicants were accepted. The SAT scores for the 2005-2006 freshman class were: Verbal--1% below 500, 20% between 500 and 599, 58% between 600 and 700, and 21% above 700; Math--1% below 500, 29% between 500 and 599, 59% between 600 and 700, and 11% above 700. The ACT scores were 7% between 21 and 23, 28% between 24 and 26, 26% between 27 and 28, and 39% above 28. 78% of the current freshmen were in the top fifth of their class; 97% were in the top two fifths. There were 11 National Merit finalists. 31 freshmen graduated first in their class.

Requirements: The SAT or ACT is required. The ACT Optional Writing test is also required. In addition, students must have graduated from an accredited secondary school with at least 16 Carnegie units, including at least 4 units in English, 3 units in college preparatory math (including the equivalent of 2 units in algebra), 3 units in social sciences/history, 2 units in foreign language(s), and 2 units in natural or lab science. Applicants who have satisfactory scores on the GED may also apply. All students must submit an essay and 2 letters of recommendation. Interviews are recommended. A GPA of 2.0 is required. AP and CLEP credits are accepted. Important factors in the admissions decision are advanced placement or honor courses, recommendations by school officials, and extracurricular activities record.

Procedure: Freshmen are admitted to all sessions. Entrance exams should be taken in the spring of the junior year or the fall of the senior year. There are early decision and deferred admissions plans. Early decision applications should be filed by November 15; regular applications, by January 15 for fall entry, December 1 for spring entry, and April 1 for summer entry, along with a $45 fee. Notification of early decision is sent December 31; regular decision, April 1. 251 early decision candidates were accepted for the 2005-2006 class. Applications are accepted online.

Transfer: 413 transfer students enrolled in 2004-2005. Transfer applicants must be in good academic and social standing at the school previously attended and have a minimum cumulative GPA of 2.5 from all institutions attended to be considered competitive for admission. 45 of 120 credits required for the bachelor's degree must be completed at AU.

Visiting: There are regularly scheduled orientations for prospective students, including student-led daily tours and information sessions, open houses, and overnight programs. There are guides for informal visits and visitors may sit in on classes and stay overnight. To schedule a visit, contact the Admissions Office.

Financial Aid: In 2005-2006, 82% of all full-time freshmen and 65% of continuing full-time students received some form of financial aid. 50% of full-time freshmen and 44% of continuing full-time students received need-based aid. Need-based scholarships or need-based grants averaged $17,056; need-based self-help aid (loans and jobs) averaged $11,443; and non-need-based athletic scholarships averaged $16,875. 18% of undergraduates work part time. Average annual earnings from campus work are $1544. The average financial indebtedness of the 2005 graduate was $19,132. The FAFSA and the college's own financial statement are required. The deadline for filing freshman financial aid applications for fall entry is February 15.

International Students: The school actively recruits these students. They must score satisfactorily on the written TOEFL or on the electronic version and also take the college's own test, or take the SAT and score satisfactorily on the critical reading section, or the IELTS and score 6.5 or higher.

Computers: Wireless access is available with the appropriate wireless Ethernet adapter, as is access to the campus data network and the Internet, with the appropriate Ethernet network port or network card. An Internet connection fire wall is required. All students may access the system. There are no time limits and no fees. It is strongly recommended that all students have a personal computer.

Graduates: From July 1, 2004 to June 30, 2005, 1419 bachelor's degrees were awarded. The most popular majors were international studies (20%), business administration (17%), and political science/government (9%). In an average class, 2% graduate in 3 years or less, 61% graduate in 4 years or less, 68% graduate in 5 years or less, and 70% graduate in 6 years or less. 240 companies recruited on campus in 2004-2005. Of the 2004 graduating class, 71% were enrolled in graduate school within 6 months of graduation and 63% were employed.

Admissions Contact: Dr. Sharon Alston, Director of Admissions. E-mail: *afa@american.edu* Web: *admissions@american.edu*

CATHOLIC UNIVERSITY OF AMERICA   C-2
Washington, DC 20064

(202) 319-5305
(800) 673-2772; Fax: (202) 319-6171

Full-time: 1251 men, 1551 women	**Faculty:** 242; I, --$
Part-time: 83 men, 168 women	**Ph.D.s:** 98%
Graduate: 1490 men, 1587 women	**Student/Faculty:** 12 to 1
Year: semesters, summer session	**Tuition:** $26,000
Application Deadline: February 15	**Room & Board:** $9838
Freshman Class: 3152 applied, 2561 accepted, 792 enrolled	
SAT Verbal/Math: 580/570*	**ACT:** 24 **VERY COMPETITIVE**

Catholic University of America, founded in 1887 and affiliated with the Roman Catholic Church, offers undergraduate programs through the schools of arts and sciences, engineering, architecture, nursing, philosophy, the Benjamin T. Rome School of Music, and the Metropolitan College. There are 7 undergraduate and 11 graduate schools. In addition to regional accreditation, CUA has baccalaureate program accreditation with ABET, ACPE, APA, CSWE, NAAB, NASM, NCATE, and NLN. The 3 libraries contain 1,595,284 volumes, 1,160,516 microform items, and 40,697 audio/video tapes/CDs/DVDs, and subscribe to 10,448 periodicals including electronic. Computerized library services include the card catalog, interlibrary loans, database searching, Internet access, and laptop Internet portals. Special learning facilities include a learning resource center, art gallery, radio station, an archeology lab, a rare book collection, and electronic/computer classrooms. The 193-acre campus is in an urban area in Washington, D.C. Including any residence halls, there are 52 buildings.

Student Life: 93% of undergraduates are from out of state, mostly the Middle Atlantic. Students are from 50 states, 34 foreign countries, and Canada. 67% are white. Most are Catholic. The average age of freshmen is 18; all undergraduates, 22. 18% do not continue beyond their first year; 73% remain to graduate.

Housing: 2101 students can be accommodated in college housing, which includes single-sex and coed dorms and on-campus apartments. In addition, there are honors houses, special-interest houses, and residential colleges for freshmen and upperclassmen. On-campus housing is available on a first-come, first-served basis and is available on a lottery system for upperclassmen. 95% of students live on campus. Upperclassmen may keep cars.

Activities: 1% of men belong to 2 national fraternities. There is 1 local and 1 national sorority. There are 128 groups on campus, including art, cheerleading, choir, chorale, chorus, computers, dance, debate, drama, ethnic, film, gay, honors, international, jazz band, literary magazine, musical theater, newspaper, opera, orchestra, pep band, political, professional, radio and TV, religious, social, social service, student government, symphony, and yearbook. Popular campus events include Family Weekend, Beaux Arts Ball, and Mistletoe Ball.

Sports: There are 10 intercollegiate sports for men and 11 for women, and 9 intramural sports for men and 9 for women. Facilities include an athletic center that houses 4 basketball and 5 handball/racquetball courts, a 6-lane, 25-meter swimming pool, tennis plaza, weight-training room, aerobics room, men's and women's saunas, adjoining playing fields, 2 dance studios, an indoor jogging track, and 3 volleyball courts.

Disabled Students: 78% of the campus is accessible. Wheelchair ramps, elevators, special parking, specially equipped rest rooms, special class scheduling, lowered drinking fountains, lowered telephones, special housing, and accessible classrooms, theater, and student/conference center are available.

Services: Counseling and information services are available, as is tutoring in most subjects. There is a reader service for the blind, and remedial math, reading, and writing. Taped books/scanned books, assistive technology (AT) including reading software and screen readers, test accommodations, and sign language interpreters are available.

Campus Safety and Security: Measures include 24-hour foot and vehicle patrol, self-defense education, security escort services, and shuttle buses. There are informal discussions, pamphlets/posters/films, emergency telephones, lighted pathways/sidewalks, fixed security posts, emergency whistles, watch captains in every building, and an access control system.

Programs of Study: CUA confers B.A., B.S., B.A.G.S., B. Arch., B.B.E., B.C.E., B.E.E., B.M., B.M.E., B.S. Arch., and B.S.N. degrees. Master's and doctoral degrees are also awarded. Bachelor's degrees are awarded in BIOLOGICAL SCIENCE (biochemistry and biology/biological science), BUSINESS (accounting, banking and finance, business administration and management, international economics, and management science), COMMUNICATIONS AND THE ARTS (art, art history and appreciation, classics, communications, dramatic arts, English, French, German, Latin, music, music history and appreciation, music performance, music theory and composition, musical theater, painting, piano/organ, sculpture, Spanish, and voice), COMPUTER AND PHYSICAL SCIENCE (chemistry, computer science, elementary particle physics, mathematics, and physics), EDUCATION (art, drama, early childhood, education, elementary, English, mathematics, music, and secondary), ENGINEERING AND ENVIRONMENTAL DESIGN (architecture, biomedical engineering, civil engineering, electrical/electronics engineering, engineering, environmental science, and mechanical engineering), HEALTH PROFESSIONS (medical laboratory technology and nursing), SOCIAL SCIENCE (anthropology, economics, history, liberal arts/general studies, medieval studies, philosophy, political science/government, psychology, religion, social work, and sociology). Politics is the strongest academically. Architecture is the largest.

Required: To graduate, students must complete 120 credit hours, including 36 to 42 hours in the major, with a minimum GPA of 2.0. Courses must meet distribution requirements in theology and religious studies, philosophy, English composition, humanities, language and literature, math and natural science, and social and behavioral sciences. A comprehensive exam is required in most majors.

Special: Cross-registration is available with the Consortium of Universities of the Washington Metropolitan Area. Opportunities are also provided for internships, accelerated degree programs, dual majors, B.A./B.S. degrees, work-study, pass/fail options, and study abroad in 13 countries. There are 15 national honor societies, including Phi Beta Kappa and a freshman honors program.

Faculty/Classroom: 62% of faculty are male; 38%, female. 68% teach undergraduates and all do research. The average class size in an introductory lecture is 21; in a laboratory, 20; and in a regular course, 19.

Admissions: 81% of the 2005-2006 applicants were accepted. The SAT scores for the 2005-2006 freshman class were: Verbal--14% below 500, 43% between 500 and 599, 35% between 600 and 700, and 8%

above 700; Math--18% below 500, 46% between 500 and 599, 31% between 600 and 700, and 5% above 700. The ACT scores were 20% below 21, 22% between 21 and 23, 27% between 24 and 26, 18% between 27 and 28, and 13% above 28. 44% of the current freshmen were in the top fifth of their class; 73% were in the top two fifths. 4 freshmen graduated first in their class.

Requirements: The SAT or ACT is required. In addition, applicants must be graduates of an accredited secondary school. Students should present 17 academic credits, including 4 each in English and social studies, 3 each in math and science, 2 in foreign languages, and 1 in fine arts or humanities. An essay is required. An audition is required for music applicants, and a portfolio for architecture applicants is recommended. A GPA of 3.0 is required. AP credits are accepted. Important factors in the admissions decision are extracurricular activities record, leadership record, and advanced placement or honor courses.

Procedure: Freshmen are admitted fall and spring. Entrance exams should be taken by February of the senior year of high school. There are early action and deferred admissions plans. Early action applications should be filed by November 15; regular applications, by February 15 for fall entry, along with a $55 fee. Notification of early action is sent December 15; regular decision, March 15. Applications are accepted online.

Transfer: 99 transfer students enrolled in 2004-2005. Applicants must submit high school and college transcripts and SAT or ACT scores. A letter of recommendation and an essay are required. Terms of admission are finalized by the dean of the appropriate school. 30 of 120 credits required for the bachelor's degree must be completed at CUA.

Visiting: There are regularly scheduled orientations for prospective students, including an information session with an admissions counselor and a guided campus tour. There are guides for informal visits and visitors may sit in on classes and stay overnight. To schedule a visit, contact the Office of Admissions.

Financial Aid: In 2005-2006, 98% of all full-time freshmen and 93% of continuing full-time students received some form of financial aid. 57% of full-time freshmen and 49% of continuing full-time students received need-based aid. CUA is a member of CSS. The FAFSA is required. The priority date for freshman financial aid applications for fall entry is January 15. The deadline for filing freshman financial aid applications for fall entry is February 1.

International Students: There are 66 international students enrolled. The school actively recruits these students. They must take the TOEFL.

Computers: Wireless access is available. There are 500 PCs located around campus for student use. All students may access the system 24 hours a day, 7 days a week. There are no time limits and no fees. It is strongly recommended that all students have a personal computer. A Dell or Gateway is recommended.

Graduates: From July 1, 2004 to June 30, 2005, 563 bachelor's degrees were awarded. The most popular majors were architecture and planning (12%), politics (9%), and media studies and psychology (9%). In an average class, 59% graduate in 4 years or less, 67% graduate in 5 years or less, and 73% graduate in 6 years or less. 100 companies recruited on campus in 2004-2005. Of the 2004 graduating class, 41% were enrolled in graduate school within 6 months of graduation and 88% were employed.

Admissions Contact: Christine Mica, Director of University Admissions. A video is available. E-mail: *cua-admissions@cua.edu* Web: *http://admissions.cua.edu/*

CORCORAN SCHOOL OF ART AND DESIGN C-3
(Formerly Corcoran School of Art)

Washington, DC 20006 (202) 639-1814
(888) CORCORAN; Fax: (202) 639-1830

Full-time: 121 men, 220 women	**Faculty:** 34
Part-time: 17 men, 35 women	**Ph.D.s:** 41%
Graduate: 9 men, 61 women	**Student/Faculty:** 10 to 1
Year: semesters, summer session	**Tuition:** $22,800
Application Deadline: open	**Room & Board:** $10,050
Freshman Class: n/av	
SAT or ACT: required	**SPECIAL**

Established in 1890, the Corcoran college of Art and Design is a private professional art college offering undergraduate programs in fine art, design, and photography. In addition to regional accreditation, Corcoran has baccalaureate program accreditation with NASAD. The library contains 19,000 volumes, and subscribes to 130 periodicals including electronic. Computerized library services include interlibrary loans, Internet access, and laptop Internet portals. Special learning facilities include a learning resource center and art gallery. The 7-acre campus is in an urban area in Washington, D.C. Including any residence halls, there are 3 buildings.

Student Life: 73% of undergraduates are from out of state, mostly the Middle Atlantic. Students are from 24 states, 32 foreign countries, and Canada. 75% are from public schools. 64% are white; 21% foreign nationals; 10% Asian American. The average age of freshmen is 18; all un-

dergraduates, 22. 3% do not continue beyond their first year; 60% remain to graduate.

Housing: 110 students can be accommodated in college housing, which includes coed off-campus apartments. On-campus housing is guaranteed for the freshman year only and is available on a first-come, first-served basis. 73% of students commute. Alcohol is not permitted. No one may keep cars.

Activities: There are no fraternities or sororities. There are 4 groups on campus, including art, literary magazine, newspaper, and student government. Popular campus events include New York trip, Off-the-Walls Art Sale, and juried art exhibits.

Sports: There is no sports program at Corcoran.

Disabled Students: 70% of the campus is accessible. Wheelchair ramps, elevators, special parking, specially equipped rest rooms, lowered drinking fountains, and lowered telephones are available.

Services: Counseling and information services are available, as is tutoring in most subjects, including art history, writing, humanities, and general academic subjects. There is remedial writing.

Campus Safety and Security: Measures include 24-hour foot and vehicle patrol, informal discussions, pamphlets/posters/films, and lighted pathways/sidewalks.

Programs of Study: Corcoran confers the B.F.A. degree. Associate and master's degrees are also awarded. Bachelor's degrees are awarded in COMMUNICATIONS AND THE ARTS (fine arts, graphic design, and photography), EDUCATION (art). Fine arts is the largest.

Required: Students must complete 126 credits, with 65 to 70 of these in the major, and 23 in the core curriculum, and must maintain a minimum GPA of 2.0. Course distribution must involve the disciplines of art history, humanities, liberal arts, and writing. Curricula will include courses in drawing, design, idea resources, and media. Seniors must present thesis exhibitions.

Special: Cooperative programs are permitted with the ACE and AICA art college consortiums. Opportunities are provided for internships in graphic design and photography, credit by exam, work-study programs with the Corcoran Gallery of Art, and nondegree study. A B.F.A./M.A.T. degree is offered.

Faculty/Classroom: 45% of faculty are male; 55%, female. All teach undergraduates. The average class size in an introductory lecture is 23; in a laboratory, 10; and in a regular course, 10.

Requirements: The SAT or ACT is required. Applicants must have graduated from an approved secondary school; a GED will be accepted. A portfolio is required, and an interview is recommended. A GPA of 2.5 is required. AP and CLEP credits are accepted. Important factors in the admissions decision are evidence of special talent, personality/intangible qualities, and advanced placement or honor courses.

Procedure: Freshmen are admitted fall and spring. Entrance exams should be taken prior to January 30 of the senior year. There is a deferred admissions and a rolling admissions plan. Application deadlines are open. Application fee is $40. Applications are accepted on-line.

Transfer: 54 transfer students enrolled in 2004-2005. A review of studio art transcripts will be considered for the level of entry of transfer students. A portfolio review will be the final determining factor. 48 of 126 credits required for the bachelor's degree must be completed at Corcoran.

Visiting: There are regularly scheduled orientations for prospective students, including an introduction to staff, faculty, and the city, and an overview of activities and housing. There are guides for informal visits and visitors may sit in on classes. To schedule a visit, contact the Admissions Department.

Financial Aid: 12% of undergraduates work part time. Average annual earnings from campus work are $1849. Corcoran is a member of CSS. The FAFSA and the college's own financial statement are required. The priority date for freshman financial aid applications for fall entry is April 15. The deadline for filing freshman financial aid applications for fall entry is May 1.

International Students: There are 23 international students enrolled. The school actively recruits these students. They must score satisfactorily on the written TOEFL or on the electronic version and also take the SAT or the ACT.

Computers: Wireless access is available. All students may access the system. Students may access the system during lab hours in Computer Graphics. There are no fees. It is recommended that students in Graphic Design in the sophomore year have personal computers. A Macintosh is recommended.

Graduates: From July 1, 2004 to June 30, 2005, 75 bachelor's degrees were awarded.

Admissions Contact: Elizabeth S. Paladino, Director of Admissions. E-mail: *admissions@corcoran.org* Web: *www.corcoran.edu*

GALLAUDET UNIVERSITY   C-3
Washington, DC 20002-3695

(202) 651-5114 (TTY) or (202) 651-5750 (
(800) 995-0550 (TTY/V); Fax: (202) 651-5744

Full-time: 485 men, 575 women	**Faculty:** 300; IIA, +$
Part-time: 105 men, 105 women	**Ph.D.s:** 66%
Graduate: 100 men, 335 women	**Student/Faculty:** 4 to 1
Year: semesters, summer session	**Tuition:** $9000
Application Deadline: open	**Room & Board:** $7570
Freshman Class: n/av	
SAT or ACT: not required	**SPECIAL**

Gallaudet University, founded in 1864 as a university designed exclusively for deaf and hard-of-hearing students, offers programs in liberal and fine arts, teacher preparation, and professional training. Figures in above capsule and in this profile are approximate. There are 4 undergraduate and 4 graduate schools. In addition to regional accreditation, Gallaudet has baccalaureate program accreditation with CSWE and NCATE. The library contains 215,500 volumes, 371,000 microform items, and 4530 audio/video tapes/CDs/DVDs, and subscribes to 1415 periodicals including electronic. Computerized library services include the card catalog, interlibrary loans, and database searching. Special learning facilities include a learning resource center, TV station, a child development center, national and international centers on deafness, and a research institute on deafness. The 99-acre campus is in an urban area in Washington, D.C. Including any residence halls, there are 30 buildings.

Student Life: 95% of undergraduates are from out of state, mostly the Northeast. Students are from 50 states and Canada. 74% are white; 14% foreign nationals.

Housing: College housing includes single-sex and coed dormitories. On-campus housing is guaranteed for the freshman year only and is available on a first-come, first-served basis. 51% of students live on campus; of those, 51% remain on campus on weekends. Alcohol is not permitted. All students may keep cars.

Activities: 15% of men belong to 1 local and 3 national fraternities; 20% of women belong to 2 local and 3 national sororities. There are 32 groups on campus, including art, cheerleading, computers, dance, drama, ethnic, gay, honors, international, literary magazine, newspaper, political, religious, social, social service, student government, and yearbook. Popular campus events include rock festival, drama productions, and lecture series.

Sports: There are 9 intercollegiate sports for men and 8 for women, and 12 intramural sports for men and 12 for women. Facilities include a field house, a gym, a swimming pool, tennis and racquetball courts, weight training rooms, playing fields, and bowling alleys.

Disabled Students: Wheelchair ramps, elevators, special parking, specially equipped rest rooms, special class scheduling, lowered drinking fountains, lowered telephones, and phones with TTY are available. Sign language skills are required of all faculty and professional staff.

Services: Counseling and information services are available, as is tutoring in every subject, including the tutorial, English, and writing centers. There is remedial math, reading, and writing. An information-on-deafness center is also available.

Campus Safety and Security: Measures include 24-hour foot and vehicle patrol, security escort services, shuttle buses, and informal discussions. There are pamphlets/posters/films and lighted pathways/sidewalks.

Programs of Study: Gallaudet confers B.A. and B.S. degrees. Associate, master's, and doctoral degrees are also awarded. Bachelor's degrees are awarded in BIOLOGICAL SCIENCE (biology/biological science), BUSINESS (accounting, business administration and management, entrepreneurial studies, management science, and recreation and leisure services), COMMUNICATIONS AND THE ARTS (apparel design, art history and appreciation, communications, dramatic arts, English, French, German, graphic design, media arts, Russian, Spanish, and studio art), COMPUTER AND PHYSICAL SCIENCE (chemical technology, chemistry, computer science, mathematics, and physics), EDUCATION (art, early childhood, elementary, home economics, physical, and secondary), ENGINEERING AND ENVIRONMENTAL DESIGN (engineering technology), HEALTH PROFESSIONS (recreation therapy), SOCIAL SCIENCE (child care/child and family studies, economics, family/consumer studies, history, interpreter for the deaf, parks and recreation management, philosophy, political science/government, psychology, religion, and social work).

Required: The core curriculum requires 12 hours each of social science and English, 9 of literature and humanities, 8 of lab science, 5 of communication arts, 4 of phys ed, and 3 of philosophy, plus demonstrated proficiency in a foreign language. A total of 124 credits, with 30 to 60 in the major, and a minimum 2.0 GPA are required for graduation.

Special: Gallaudet offers co-op programs with Oberlin College in Ohio and Western Maryland College, cross-registration with the Consortium of Universities of the Washington Metropolitan Area, and a 3-2 engineering degree with George Washington University. Internships, study abroad,

dual majors, work-study programs, and B.A.-B.S. degrees are available. There is a chapter of Phi Beta Kappa and a freshman honors program.

Faculty/Classroom: No introductory courses are taught by graduate students.

Requirements: Applicants must submit a recent audiogram and results of the most recent edition of the Stanford Achievement Test. SAT or ACT scores may be submitted. High school transcripts, letters of recommendation, and writing samples are also required. The GED is accepted. AP and CLEP credits are accepted. Important factors in the admissions decision are advanced placement or honor courses, recommendations by school officials, and leadership record.

Procedure: Freshmen are admitted fall and spring. Entrance exams should be taken in October or November of the senior year. There are a deferred admissions and rolling admissions plans. Application deadlines are open. Application fee is $35.

Transfer: Deaf and hard-of-hearing transfer applicants must submit a recent audiogram, official college transcripts from all schools attended, and at least 2 letters of recommendation. Students should have completed 12 or more credit hours with at least a 2.0 GPA; those who do not meet these requirements must submit recent SAT or ACT scores and a final high school transcript.

Visiting: There are regularly scheduled orientations for prospective students, including a tour of campus, classroom observations, and interviews with selected offices and programs. There are guides for informal visits and visitors may sit in on classes. To schedule a visit, contact the Gallaudet University Visitor's Center at (202) 651-5050.

Financial Aid: The FAFSA and the college's own financial statement are required. Check with the school for current application deadlines.

International Students: They must take the TOEFL, or the MELAB, or the Comprehensive English Language Test, or the college's own test. They must also take the college's own entrance exam and the most recent edition of the Stanford Achievement Test; SAT or ACT scores may be submitted.

Computers: All students may access the system 24 hours a day. There are no time limits and no fees.

Admissions Contact: Director of Admissions.
E-mail: *admission@gallua.gallaudet.edu*

GEORGE WASHINGTON UNIVERSITY   B-3
Washington, DC 20052

(202) 994-6040
(800) 447-3765; Fax: (202) 994-0325

Full-time: 4230 men, 5511 women	**Faculty:** I, av$
Part-time: 501 men, 519 women	**Ph.D.s:** 73%
Graduate: 6115 men, 7223 women	**Student/Faculty:** n/av
Year: semesters, summer session	**Tuition:** $37,820
Application Deadline: January 15	**Room & Board:** $11,000
Freshman Class: 19,406 applied, 7275 accepted, 2411 enrolled	
SAT Verbal/Math: 650/650*	**ACT:** 28 **MOST COMPETITIVE**

George Washington University, founded in 1821, is a private institution providing degree programs in arts and sciences, business, engineering, international affairs, health sciences, education, law, and public health. There are 7 undergraduate and 9 graduate schools. In addition to regional accreditation, GW has baccalaureate program accreditation with AACSB, ABET, CAHEA, CSAB, NASAD, NASM, and NCATE. The 3 libraries contain 2,104,962 volumes, 2,771,235 microform items, and 206,826 audio/video tapes/CDs/DVDs, and subscribe to 1098 periodicals including electronic. Computerized library services include the card catalog, interlibrary loans, and database searching. Special learning facilities include a learning resource center, art gallery, radio station, and TV station. The 37-acre campus is in an urban area 3 blocks west of the White House. Including any residence halls, there are 123 buildings.

Student Life: 98% of undergraduates are from out of state, mostly the Middle Atlantic. Others are from 50 states, 137 foreign countries, and Canada. 70% are from public schools. 65% are white. The average age of freshmen is 19; all undergraduates, 20. 9% do not continue beyond their first year; 78% remain to graduate.

Housing: 7015 students can be accommodated in college housing, which includes coed dorms, on-campus apartments, fraternity houses, and sorority houses. In addition, there are special-interest houses and sorority floors. On-campus housing is available on a lottery system for upperclassmen. 67% of students live on campus. All students may keep cars.

Activities: 16% of men belong to 11 national fraternities; 13% of women belong to 7 national sororities. There are 257 groups on campus, including art, band, cheerleading, chess, choir, chorale, chorus, computers, dance, debate, drama, ethnic, film, folk life, forensics, gay, geology, honors, international, jazz band, literary magazine, marching band, musical theater, newspaper, opera, orchestra, pep band, photography, political, professional, radio and TV, religious, social, social service, and student government. Popular campus events include a yearly benefit auction, Spring Fling, and Fall Fest.

Sports: There are 9 intercollegiate sports for men and 8 for women, and 16 intramural sports for men and 16 for women. Facilities include

a 5000-seat gym with 2 auxiliary gyms, an AAU swimming pool, weight rooms, a jogging track, squash and racquetball courts, and soccer and baseball fields.

Disabled Students: 95% of the campus is accessible. Wheelchair ramps, elevators, special parking, specially equipped rest rooms, special class scheduling, lowered drinking fountains, and lowered telephones are available.

Services: Counseling and information services are available, as is tutoring in every subject. There is a reader service for the blind.

Campus Safety and Security: Measures include 24-hour foot and vehicle patrol, self-defense education, security escort services, and informal discussions. There are pamphlets/posters/films, emergency telephones, lighted pathways/sidewalks, and a bike patrol.

Programs of Study: GW confers B.A., B.S., B.Accy., B.B.A., B.Mus., B.S.C.E., B.S.C.Eng., B.S.C.S., B.S.E.E., B.S.H.S., B.S.M.E., and B.S.S.A. degrees. Associate, master's, and doctoral degrees are also awarded. Bachelor's degrees are awarded in BIOLOGICAL SCIENCE (biology/biological science), BUSINESS (accounting, banking and finance, business administration and management, business economics, human resources, international business management, marketing management, and tourism), COMMUNICATIONS AND THE ARTS (art history and appreciation, broadcasting, Chinese, classics, communications, dance, dramatic arts, English, fine arts, French, German, Japanese, journalism, literature, multimedia, music, music performance, public relations, Russian, and Spanish), COMPUTER AND PHYSICAL SCIENCE (applied mathematics, chemistry, computer science, geology, information sciences and systems, mathematics, physics, statistics, and systems analysis), ENGINEERING AND ENVIRONMENTAL DESIGN (civil engineering, computer engineering, electrical/electronics engineering, engineering, environmental science, and mechanical engineering), HEALTH PROFESSIONS (clinical science, emergency medical technologies, medical laboratory technology, nuclear medical technology, physician's assistant, premedicine, radiological science, and speech pathology/audiology), SOCIAL SCIENCE (American studies, anthropology, archeology, criminal justice, East Asian studies, economics, European studies, geography, history, human services, humanities, interdisciplinary studies, international relations, Judaic studies, Latin American studies, liberal arts/general studies, Middle Eastern studies, philosophy, physical fitness/movement, political science/government, psychology, religion, and sociology). Political communication, international affairs, and biological sciences are the strongest academically. Psychology, political science, and international affairs are the largest.

Required: Students must complete 120 semester hours with a minimum GPA of 2.0 for most majors. Arts and sciences majors must meet general curriculum requirements that include literacy, quantitative and logical reasoning, natural sciences, social and behavioral sciences, creative and performing arts, literature, Western civilization, and foreign languages or culture. Other specific course requirements vary with the different divisions of the university.

Special: Cross-registration is available through the Consortium of Colleges and Universities. There are co-op programs in education, business, engineering, arts and sciences, and international affairs, and internships throughout the Washington metropolitan area. Study abroad in locations throughout the world, work-study programs, dual majors, student-designed majors, and a 3-2 engineering degree program with 8 colleges are also available. Nondegree study, a general studies degree, credit by exam, and pass/fail options are possible. There are 12 national honor societies, including Phi Beta Kappa, a freshman honors program, and 21 departmental honors programs.

Faculty/Classroom: 61% of faculty are male; 39%, female. Graduate students teach 2% of introductory courses. The average class size in an introductory lecture is 32 and in a regular course, 22.

Admissions: 37% of the 2005-2006 applicants were accepted. The SAT scores for the 2005-2006 freshman class were: Verbal--3% below 500, 20% between 500 and 599, 51% between 600 and 700, and 25% above 700; Math--1% below 500, 19% between 500 and 599, 56% between 600 and 700, and 23% above 700. 83% of the current freshmen were in the top fifth of their class; 97% were in the top two fifths.

Requirements: The SAT or ACT is required. In addition, students must have successfully completed a strong academic program in high school. SAT: Subject tests are strongly recommended. An essay, 1 teacher recommendation, and 1 counselor recommendation are required. An interview is encouraged. AP and CLEP credits are accepted. Important factors in the admissions decision are advanced placement or honor courses, recommendations by school officials, and leadership record.

Procedure: Freshmen are admitted to all sessions. Entrance exams should be taken in the junior year and the fall semester of the senior year. There are early decision and deferred admissions plans. Early decision applications should be filed by December 1; regular applications, by January 15 for fall entry. Notification of early decision is sent December 15; regular decision, March 15. The fall 2005 application fee was $60. A waiting list is an active part of the admissions procedure. Applications are accepted on-line.

Transfer: 383 transfer students enrolled in 2004-2005. In addition to a record of high marks and exam scores, applicants must submit official transcripts of all postsecondary work. Minimum GPA requirements vary from 2.5 to 3.0, depending on the major. The SAT or ACT is required, and an interview is encouraged. 30 of 120 credits required for the bachelor's degree must be completed at GW.

Visiting: There are regularly scheduled orientations for prospective students, including group information sessions and campus tours. Class visitation, lunch with current students, and other activities can be arranged, if requested in advance. There are guides for informal visits and visitors may sit in on classes and stay overnight. To schedule a visit, contact the University Visitor Center at (202) 994-6602.

Financial Aid: In 2005-2006, 39% of all full-time freshmen and 38% of continuing full-time students received some form of financial aid. 38% of full-time freshmen and 37% of continuing full-time students received need-based aid. The average freshman award was $31,381. Need-based scholarships or need-based grants averaged $19,024; need-based self-help aid (loans and jobs) averaged $6284; non-need-based athletic scholarships averaged $18,796; and other non-need-based awards and non-need-based scholarships averaged $13,836. The average financial indebtedness of the 2005 graduate was $27,041. GW is a member of CSS. The CSS/Profile or FAFSA is required. The priority date for freshman financial aid applications for fall entry is February 1.

International Students: The school actively recruits these students. A satisfactory score is required on the written TOEFL Students must also take the college's own test and also take the SAT or the ACT.

Computers: All students may access the system at any time. There are no time limits and no fees. It is strongly recommended that all students have a PC. An IBM, Mac Dell, or Compaq is recommended.

Graduates: In a recent year, 2007 bachelor's degrees were awarded. The most popular majors were social sciences and history (33%), business/marketing (16%), and psychology (8%). In an average class, 69% graduate in 4 years or less, 74% graduate in 5 years or less, and 75% graduate in 6 years or less.

Admissions Contact: Dr. Kathryn M. Napper, Director of Admissions. E-mail: *gwadm@gwu.edu* Web: *www.gwu.edu*

GEORGETOWN UNIVERSITY   B-3

Washington, DC 20057   (202) 687-3600; Fax: (202) 687-5084

Full-time: 3007 men, 3497 women	**Faculty:** 659; I, +$
Part-time: 93 men, 122 women	**Ph.D.s:** 92%
Graduate: 3504 men, 3429 women	**Student/Faculty:** 10 to 1
Year: semesters, summer session	**Tuition:** $32,024
Application Deadline: January 10	**Room & Board:** $11,159
Freshman Class: 15,285 applied, 3286 accepted, 1551 enrolled	
SAT or ACT: required	**MOST COMPETITIVE**

Georgetown University, founded in 1789, is a private institution affiliated with the Roman Catholic Church and offers programs in arts and sciences, business administration, foreign service, languages and linguistics, and nursing. There are 4 undergraduate and 3 graduate schools. In addition to regional accreditation, Georgetown has baccalaureate program accreditation with AACSB and CCNE. The 6 libraries contain 2,407,125 volumes, 3,847,029 microform items, and 33,270 audio/video tapes/CDs/DVDs, and subscribe to 28,173 periodicals including electronic. Computerized library services include the card catalog, interlibrary loans, database searching, Internet access, and laptop Internet portals. Special learning facilities include a learning resource center, art gallery, planetarium, radio station, and TV station. The 104-acre campus is in an urban area 1.5 miles northwest of downtown Washington D.C. Including any residence halls, there are 64 buildings.

Student Life: 98% of undergraduates are from out of state, mostly the Middle Atlantic. Students are from 50 states, 86 foreign countries, and Canada. 51% are from public schools. 65% are white; 10% Native American/Eskimo; 52% are Catholic; 24% Protestant; 12% claim no religious affiliation; 7% Hindu, Buddhist, Islamic, unspecified. The average age of freshmen is 18; all undergraduates, 20. 2% do not continue beyond their first year; 93% remain to graduate.

Housing: 5053 students can be accommodated in college housing, which includes coed dormitories and on-campus apartments. Special interest floors are available in some residence halls. On-campus housing is available on a lottery system for upperclassmen. 72% of students live on campus; of those, 95% remain on campus on weekends. No one may keep cars.

Activities: There are no fraternities or sororities. There are 143 groups on campus, including art, band, cheerleading, chess, choir, chorale, chorus, computers, dance, debate, drama, ethnic, film, gay, honors, international, jazz band, literary magazine, musical theater, newspaper, orchestra, pep band, photography, political, professional, radio and TV, religious, social, social service, student government, symphony, and yearbook. Popular campus events include GU Day and Career Week.

Sports: There are 13 intercollegiate sports for men and 14 for women, and 21 intramural sports for men and 21 for women. Facilities include a 5000-seat gym for basketball and volleyball, along with sports medicine and training room facilities, a 2,500-seat multi-sport field for football and lacrosse, and a 4-level sports and recreation facilty that houses a swimming pool, basketball courts, aerobics rooms, a weight area, cardio-vascular equipment, a wellness center, locker rooms, and racquetball courts.

Disabled Students: 94% of the campus is accessible. Wheelchair ramps, elevators, special parking, specially equipped rest rooms, special class scheduling, lowered drinking fountains, lowered telephones, special housing, and a special map of the campus with accessibility routes, a tactile map of the campus for visually disabled students, and a paratransit vehicle for mobility on the main campus are available.

Services: Counseling and information services are available, as is tutoring in some subjects, including accounting, finance, biological sciences, math, Spanish, French, and Arabic. There is a reader service for the blind.

Campus Safety and Security: Measures include 24-hour foot and vehicle patrol, security escort services, shuttle buses, and informal discussions. There are pamphlets/posters/films, emergency telephones, lighted pathways/sidewalks, laptop computer registration, bicycle registration, and off-campus security assesments.

Programs of Study: Georgetown confers A.B., B.S., B.A.L.S., B.S.B.A., B.S.F.S., and B.S.N. degrees. Master's and doctoral degrees are also awarded. Bachelor's degrees are awarded in BIOLOGICAL SCIENCE (biochemistry and biology/biological science), BUSINESS (accounting, banking and finance, business administration and management, international business management, and marketing/retailing/merchandising), COMMUNICATIONS AND THE ARTS (Arabic, Chinese, classics, comparative literature, English, fine arts, French, German, Italian, Japanese, linguistics, Portuguese, Russian, and Spanish), COMPUTER AND PHYSICAL SCIENCE (chemistry, computer science, mathematics, and physics), HEALTH PROFESSIONS (health and nursing), SOCIAL SCIENCE (American studies, anthropology, economics, history, interdisciplinary studies, international relations, philosophy, political science/government, psychology, religion, and sociology). International affairs, government, and English are the largest.

Required: Students must complete 120 credits and maintain a minimum GPA of 2.0. A core of liberal arts courses is required, consisting of 2 courses each in philosophy and theology. Additional requirements are specific to undergraduate school as well as major concentration.

Special: Cross-registration is available with a consortium of universities in the Washington metropolitian area. Opportunities are provided for internships, study abroad in 35 countries, work-study programs, student-designed majors, and dual majors. A liberal studies degree, B.A. and B.S. degrees, non-degree study, credit by examination, and pass/fail options are also offered. There are 16 national honor societies, including Phi Beta Kappa, a freshman honors program, and 16 departmental honors programs.

Faculty/Classroom: 65% of faculty are male; 35%, female. All both teach and do research. The average class size in an introductory lecture is 32; in a laboratory, 14; and in a regular course, 28.

Admissions: 21% of the 2005-2006 applicants were accepted. 95% of the current freshmen were in the top fifth of their class; 99% were in the top two fifths.

Requirements: The SAT or ACT is required. In addition, graduation from an accredited secondary school is required, including 4 years of English, a minimum of 2 each of a foreign language, math, and social studies, and 1 of natural science. An additional 2 years each of math and science is required for students intending to major in math, science, nursing, or business. SAT subject tests are strongly recommended. AP credits are accepted. Important factors in the admissions decision are evidence of special talent and leadership record.

Procedure: Freshmen are admitted in the fall. Entrance exams should be taken in the junior year and again at the beginning of the senior year. There are early action and deferred admissions plans. Early action applications should be filed by November 1; regular applications, by January 10 for fall entry, along with a $60 fee. Notification of early action is sent December 15; regular decision, April 1. 1832 applicants were on the 2005 waiting list; 65 were admitted.

Transfer: 181 transfer students enrolled in 2004-2005. Transfer students must have successfully completed a minimum of 12 credit hours with a minimum GPA of 3.0. Either the SAT or the ACT is required. An interview is recommended. Transfers must complete their last 2 years at Georgetown. 60 of 120 credits required for the bachelor's degree must be completed at Georgetown.

Visiting: There are regularly scheduled orientations for prospective students, throughout the year, including a question and answer period led by an admissions officer, followed by a campus tour led by a student guide. There are guides for informal visits and visitors may sit in on classes. To schedule a visit, contact the Office of Undergraduate Admissions at (202) 687-3600.

Financial Aid: In 2005-2006, 45% of all full-time freshmen and 44% of continuing full-time students received some form of financial aid. 42% of all full-time students received need-based aid. Need-based scholarships or need-based grants averaged $23,000; need-based self-help aid (loans and jobs) averaged $3800; and non-need-based athletic scholarships averaged $18,000. Average annual earnings from campus work

are $3000. The average financial indebtedness of the 2005 graduate was $23,724. Georgetown is a member of CSS. The CSS/Profile or FAFSA, non-custodial profile, business/farm supplement, and tax returns are required. The deadline for filing freshman financial aid applications for fall entry is February 1.

International Students: There are 442 international students enrolled. The school actively recruits these students. They must score satisfactorily on the written TOEFL or on the electronic version and also take the SAT or the ACT. Students must take SAT: Subject tests in 3 of the students choice.

Computers: Wireless access is available. There is a campuswide wired network in all of the dorms. One network jack per dorm resident in their room is guaranteed. The campus wireless network is available in all identified "common areas" of the university where individuals congregate and work collaboratively and in select locations to facilitate teaching, research, and learning. There are 11 computer labs and print stations across campus open to students, containing a variety of Windows and Apple computers. All students may access the system. There are no time limits and no fees.

Graduates: From July 1, 2004 to June 30, 2005, 1679 bachelor's degrees were awarded. The most popular majors were international affairs (20%), government (10%), and English (9%). In an average class, 1% graduate in 3 years or less, 90% graduate in 4 years or less, 93% graduate in 5 years or less, and 93% graduate in 6 years or less. 121 companies recruited on campus in 2004-2005. Of the 2004 graduating class, 21% were enrolled in graduate school within 6 months of graduation and 66% were employed.

Admissions Contact: Charles A. Deacon, Dean of Admissions. Web: *www.georgetown.edu/undergrad/admissions/*

HOWARD UNIVERSITY   C-3
Washington, DC 20059
(202) 806-2700
(800) 822-6363; Fax: (202) 806-2740

Full-time: 2228 men, 4538 women	**Faculty:** 669; I, --$
Part-time: 147 men, 251 women	**Ph.D.s:** 78%
Graduate: 1457 men, 2409 women	**Student/Faculty:** 10 to 1
Year: semesters, summer session	**Tuition:** $12,295
Application Deadline: February 2	**Room & Board:** $6186
Freshman Class: 9542 applied, 4227 accepted, 1410 enrolled	
SAT or ACT: required	**COMPETITIVE+**

Howard University, founded in 1867, is a private, nonsectarian institution and the largest predominantly black university in the United States. There are 6 undergraduate and 11 graduate schools. In addition to regional accreditation, Howard has baccalaureate program accreditation with AACSB, ABA, ABET, ACEJMC, ACPE, ADA, AHEA, AOTA, APTA, ASLA, ATS, CAHEA, CSAB, CSWE, NAAB, NAACLS, NASAD, NASDTEC, NASM, NCATE, and NLN. The 8 libraries contain 2 million volumes and 3.4 million microform items, and subscribe to 26,280 periodicals including electronic. Computerized library services include the card catalog, interlibrary loans, database searching, Internet access, and laptop Internet portals. Special learning facilities include a learning resource center, art gallery, radio station, TV station, and history and culture research centers. The 256-acre campus is in an urban area in Washington, D.C. and Silver Spring and Beltsville, Maryland. Including all residence halls, there are 116 buildings.

Student Life: 86% of undergraduates are from out of state, mostly the Middle Atlantic. Students are from 50 states, 61 foreign countries, and Canada. 78% are from public schools. 86% are African American. The average age of freshmen is 18; all undergraduates, 21. 11% do not continue beyond their first year; 63% remain to graduate.

Housing: 4748 students can be accommodated in college housing, which includes coed dorms, on-campus apartments, off-campus apartments, and married-student housing. On-campus housing is guaranteed for the freshman year only, is available on a first-come, first-served basis, and is available on a lottery system for upperclassmen. Priority is given to out-of-town students. 55% of students commute. All students may keep cars.

Activities: There are 4 national fraternities; 1% of women belong to 4 national sororities. There are 150 groups on campus, including art, bagpipe band, band, cheerleading, chess, choir, chorale, chorus, computers, dance, debate, drama, drill team, drum and bugle corps, film, gay, honors, international, jazz band, literary magazine, marching band, musical theater, newspaper, orchestra, pep band, political, professional, radio and TV, religious, social, social service, student government, and yearbook. Popular campus events include Spring Festival, Opening Convocation, and Charter Day.

Sports: There are 15 intercollegiate sports for men and 15 for women, and 5 intramural sports for men and 5 for women. Facilities include a sports center, a gym, and practice fields.

Disabled Students: All of the campus is accessible. Wheelchair ramps, elevators, special parking, specially equipped rest rooms, special class scheduling, lowered drinking fountains, and lowered telephones are available.

Services: Counseling and information services are available, as is tutoring in most subjects. There is a reader service for the blind, and remedial math, reading, and writing.

Campus Safety and Security: Measures include 24-hour foot and vehicle patrol, security escort services, shuttle buses, and informal discussions. There are pamphlets/posters/films, emergency telephones, and lighted pathways/sidewalks.

Programs of Study: Howard confers B.A., B.S., B.Arch., B.B.A., B.F.A., B.M., B.M.E., B.S.C.E., B.S.Ch.E., B.S.C.L.S., B.S. Comp.Eng., B.S. Comp. Sci., B.S.E.E., B.S.M.E., B.S.N., B.S.N.S., B.S.O.T., B.S. in P.A., B.S.P.T., and B.S. in R.T.T. degrees. Master's and doctoral degrees are also awarded. Bachelor's degrees are awarded in BIOLOGICAL SCIENCE (biology/biological science, microbiology, and zoology), BUSINESS (accounting, banking and finance, business administration and management, hospitality management services, insurance, international business management, and marketing/retailing/merchandising), COMMUNICATIONS AND THE ARTS (art history and appreciation, classics, communications, dance, design, dramatic arts, English, French, German, Greek, jazz, journalism, music, music business management, music history and appreciation, musical theater, photography, printmaking, Russian, and Spanish), COMPUTER AND PHYSICAL SCIENCE (chemistry, computer science, information sciences and systems, mathematics, and physics), EDUCATION (art, early childhood, elementary, health, music, physical, recreation, and secondary), ENGINEERING AND ENVIRONMENTAL DESIGN (architecture, chemical engineering, civil engineering, electrical/electronics engineering, and mechanical engineering), HEALTH PROFESSIONS (medical laboratory technology, music therapy, nursing, occupational therapy, pharmacy, physical therapy, physician's assistant, predentistry, premedicine, radiograph medical technology, and speech pathology/audiology), SOCIAL SCIENCE (African American studies, African studies, anthropology, criminal justice, dietetics, economics, history, philosophy, political science/government, psychology, and sociology). Psychology, business, and engineering are the strongest academically. Accounting, finance, and electrical engineering are the largest.

Required: To graduate, students must complete 121 to 171 credit hours, including 21 to 78 in a major and 12 to 39 in a minor, with a minimum GPA of 2.0. General requirements include 4 courses in phys ed, 2 in freshman English, 1 in writing and in Afro-American studies; 1 year of college-level math; demonstrated proficiency in a foreign language; and successful completion of a comprehensive exam in the major.

Special: Cross-registration is available with the Consortium of Universities in the Washington Metropolitan Area. Opportunities are also provided for internships, work-study, and co-op programs, study abroad in 5 countries in Europe and Africa, B.A.-B.S. degrees in engineering and business, student-designed majors, pass/fail options, and accelerated degree programs in medicine and dentistry. There are 15 national honor societies, including Phi Beta Kappa, a freshman honors program, and 15 departmental honors programs.

Faculty/Classroom: 68% of faculty are male; 32%, female. The average class size in an introductory lecture is 40; in a laboratory, 20; and in a regular course, 20.

Admissions: 44% of the 2005-2006 applicants were accepted. 46% of the current freshmen were in the top fifth of their class; 75% were in the top two fifths. 15 freshmen graduated first in their class in a recent year.

Requirements: The SAT or ACT is required. In addition, graduation from an accredited secondary school is required. The GED is accepted. Students must have a minimum of 14 academic credits, including 4 in English, 3 in math, and 2 each in foreign language, science, and social science. Students must submit letters of recommendation from 2 high school teachers and 1 high school counselor. Other requirements vary by college. Engineering majors must take the SAT Subject Test in math I. Art majors must submit a portfolio. A GPA of 2.0 is required. AP credits are accepted. Important factors in the admissions decision are advanced placement or honor courses, recommendations by school officials, and personality/intangible qualities.

Procedure: Freshmen are admitted fall, spring, and summer. Entrance exams should be taken in the fall of the senior year. There are early admissions and deferred admissions plan. There is a rolling admissions plan. Applications should be filed by February 2 for fall entry, November 1 for spring entry, and April 1 for summer entry, along with a $45 fee. Notification of early decision is sent December 24; regular decision, on a rolling basis.

Transfer: 331 transfer students enrolled in a recent year. All applicants must submit 2 official transcripts from each college or university attended. Students transferring to the School of Business must have successfully completed 18 semester hours or 23 quarter hours of courses, with a minimum GPA of 2.5. For many other majors, the requirement is 12 semester hours or 18 quarter hours, with a minimum GPA of 2.0. Applicants to the College of Arts and Sciences need 3 credits each in English composition and college-level algebra. 30 of 121 credits required for the bachelor's degree must be completed at Howard.

Visiting: There are regularly scheduled orientations for prospective students, including an admissions interview, classroom and dorm visits, and visits to other university facilities. There are guides for informal visits and visitors may sit in on classes and stay overnight. To schedule a visit, contact the Office of Enrollment Management/Recruitment at (202) 806-2900 or www.howard.edu/enrollmentmanagement.

Financial Aid: In 2005-2006, 71% of all full-time freshmen and 75% of continuing full-time students received some form of financial aid. 63% of full-time freshmen and 82% of continuing full-time students received need-based aid. The average freshman award was $16,313. Need-based scholarships or need-based grants averaged $4134; need-based self-help aid (loans and jobs) averaged $3603; other non-need-based awards and non-need-based scholarships averaged $147; and other awards averaged $13,329. 9% of undergraduates work part time. Average annual earnings from campus work are $3700. The average financial indebtedness of the 2005 graduate was $17,548. Howard is a member of CSS. The FAFSA is required. The priority date for freshman financial aid applications for fall entry is February 2.

International Students: There were 668 international students enrolled in a recent year. They must achieve a satisfactory score on the TOEFL and also take the SAT or the ACT.

Computers: All students may access the system. Facilities are open 24 hours a day. There are no time limits and no fees. It is strongly recommended that all students have a personal computer.

Graduates: In a recent year, 1187 bachelor's degrees were awarded. The most popular majors were biology (8%), psychology (7%), and marketing (6%). In an average class, 58% graduate in 4 years or less, 91% graduate in 5 years or less, and 99% graduate in 6 years or less. 300 companies recruited on campus in a recent year. Of a recent graduating class, 35% were enrolled in graduate school within 6 months of graduation and 40% were employed.

Admissions Contact: Linda Sanders-Hawkins, Acting Director, Office of Enrollment Management. A video is available.
E-mail: admission@howard.edu Web: www.howard.edu

SOUTHEASTERN UNIVERSITY   D-4

Washington, DC 20024   (202) 478-8210; Fax: (202)488-3172

Full-time: 51 men, 75 women	**Faculty:** 13
Part-time: 106 men, 281 women	**Ph.D.s:** 62%
Graduate: 184 men, 285 women	**Student/Faculty:** 11 to 1
Year: quarters, summer session	**Tuition:** $9000
Application Deadline: open	**Room & Board:** n/app
Freshman Class: 197 accepted, 197 enrolled	
SAT or ACT: recommended	**NONCOMPETITIVE**

Southeastern University, founded as Washington School for Accountancy in 1879, is a private, commuter college offering programs in business administration, accounting, computer information systems, finance, banking, and marketing to a student body comprised primarily of working adults. There is 1 undergraduate school. Figures in the above capsule and in this profile are approximate. The library contains 40,000 volumes, and subscribes to 1200 periodicals including electronic. Computerized library services include the card catalog and database searching. Special learning facilities include a learning resource center. The 3-acre campus is in an urban area in a residential part of southwest Washington, D.C. There is 1 building.

Student Life: 56% of undergraduates are from the District of Columbia. Others are from 4 states, 40 foreign countries, and Canada. 58% are African American; 35% foreign nationals. The average age of freshmen is 29; all undergraduates, 30. 4% do not continue beyond their first year; 70% remain to graduate.

Housing: There are no residence halls. Referral listings of long-and short term housing are available. Alcohol is not permitted. No one may keep cars.

Activities: 10% of men belong to 1 local fraternity; 10% of women belong to 2 local sororities. There are some groups and organizations on campus, including chess, computers, ethnic, honors, newspaper, and student government. Popular campus events include Annual Awards Ceremony, a chess tournament, and International Week.

Sports: There is no sports program at Southeastern.

Disabled Students: All of the campus is accessible. Wheelchair ramps, special parking, specially equipped rest rooms, special class scheduling, and lowered telephones are available.

Services: Counseling and information services are available, as is tutoring in most subjects. There is remedial math, reading, and writing. There are also individualized learning programs for students in upper-level courses.

Campus Safety and Security: Measures include 24-hour foot and vehicle patrol, security escort services, shuttle buses, and lighted pathways/sidewalks.

Programs of Study: Southeastern confers the B.S. degree. Associate and master's degrees are also awarded. Bachelor's degrees are awarded in BUSINESS (accounting, banking and finance, business administration and management, and marketing/retailing/merchandising), COMPUTER AND PHYSICAL SCIENCE (information sciences and systems), SOCIAL SCIENCE (law, liberal arts/general studies, and public administration).

Business and computer science are the strongest academically. Business and computer science/information systems are the largest.

Required: To graduate, students must complete 120 credit hours, maintaining a 2.0 GPA, including the general studies core curriculum, which consists of 30 hours in the fields of English, information systems, math, humanities, and social science. Also required are 24 hours in the general studies electives, 27 hours of major requirements, 27 hours in the professional core, 6 hours of professional electives, and 6 hours of general electives. All students must take an orientation course and a computer course.

Special: Southeastern offers extensive co-op programs, internships, work-study, accelerated degree programs, B.A.-B.S.degrees, dual majors, and credit by exam and for life/military/work experience. The Add-a-Degree program allows any student with a bachelor's degree to add a second area of expertise, add professional qualifications, or prepare for graduate study by completing necessary foundation courses. There is 1 national honor society, Phi Beta Kappa, and 4 departmental honors programs.

Faculty/Classroom: 81% of faculty are male; 19%, female. All teach undergraduates. No introductory courses are taught by graduate students. The average class size in an introductory lecture is 25.

Requirements: The SAT or ACT is recommended. In addition, students must be graduates of an accredited secondary school or have a GED and must pass Southeastern's placement test for regular admission. A GPA of 2.0 is required. CLEP credit is accepted. Important factors in the admissions decision are ability to finance college education, personality/intangible qualities, and leadership record.

Procedure: Freshmen are admitted to all sessions. There is a rolling admissions plan. Application deadlines are open. The fall 2005 application fee was $45. Notification is sent on a rolling basis.

Transfer: All transfer applicants must submit transcripts. Up to 60 credits, with a grade of C or better, may be transferred. 60 of 120 credits required for the bachelor's degree must be completed at Southeastern.

Visiting: To schedule a visit, contact Ronald Burleson at (202) 474-8210 or rburleson@admin.seu.edu.

Financial Aid: Need-based scholarships or need-based grants averaged $2626 ($4000 maximum). 79% of undergraduates work part time. The FAFSA, the college's own financial statement and the are required. The priority date for freshman financial aid applications for fall entry is September 1. The deadline for filing freshman financial aid applications for fall entry is August 15.

International Students: Students must take the TOEFL. Those with low scores are required to take 2 English courses or must enroll in the university's Language Institute.

Computers: Wireless access is available. All students may access the system. There are no time limits and no fees.

Graduates: In a recent year, the most popular majors were management (40%), information systems (23%), and liberal studies (20%). In an average class, 15% graduate in 3 years or less, 20% graduate in 4 years or less, and 40% graduate in 5 or 6 years or less. Of the 2004 graduating class, 40% were enrolled in graduate school within 6 months of graduation and 55% were employed.

Admissions Contact: Ronald Burleson, Director of Admissions. E-mail: rburleson@admin.seu.edu

STRAYER UNIVERSITY
C-3

Washington, DC 20005

(202) 408-2400
(888) 4-STRAYER; Fax: (202) 289-1831

Full-time: 1240 men, 1270 women	**Faculty:** 117
Part-time: 3825 men, 5460 women	**Ph.D.s:** 51%
Graduate: 1070 men, 1170 women	**Student/Faculty:** 22 to 1
Year: quarters, summer session	**Tuition:** $8800
Application Deadline: open	**Room & Board:** n/app
Freshman Class: n/av	
SAT or ACT: recommended	**SPECIAL**

Strayer University, founded in 1892, is an independent commuter institution with 17 campuses in Washington, D.C., Maryland, and Virginia, as well as a distance learning program via the Internet. All programs are computer or business related. Figures in the above capsule and this profile are approximate. The library contains 35,000 volumes and 2813 audio/video tapes/CDs/DVDs, and subscribes to 550 periodicals including electronic. Computerized library services include the card catalog, interlibrary loans, and database searching. Special learning facilities include a learning resource center. The campus is in an urban area. 2 of the campuses are located in Washington D.C., and 6 campuses are in suburban Virgin. There are 13 buildings.

Student Life: 97% of undergraduates are from District of Columbia. Others are from 26 states, 124 foreign countries, and Canada. 42% are African American; 32% white. The average age of all undergraduates is 33.

Housing: There are no residence halls. All of students commute. Alcohol is not permitted. All students may keep cars.

Activities: There are no fraternities or sororities. There are 13 groups on campus, including computers, debate, ethnic, honors, international, newspaper, professional, and religious.

Sports: The sports program is an athletic club, which uses intercollegiate athletic participation to promote education and student development.

Disabled Students: All of the campus is accessible. Wheelchair ramps, elevators, special parking, specially equipped rest rooms, lowered drinking fountains, and lowered telephones are available.

Services: Counseling and information services are available, as is tutoring in some subjects, including accounting, computer information systems, English, and math at the introductory course level. There is remedial reading and writing.

Campus Safety and Security: Measures include security escort services, informal discussions, pamphlets/posters/films, and lighted pathways/sidewalks. There are security guards at all the urban campuses and during evening hours at other campuses, crime seminars held regularly for students and employees, and a campus crime awareness booklet is published annually or available via the school's website.

Programs of Study: Strayer confers the B.S. degree. Associate and master's degrees are also awarded. Bachelor's degrees are awarded in BUSINESS (accounting, business administration and management, and international business management), COMPUTER AND PHYSICAL SCIENCE (information sciences and systems and web technology), SOCIAL SCIENCE (economics). Computer information systems, business administration, and accounting are the strongest academically. Computer information systems and business administration are the largest.

Required: To graduate, students must complete 180 quarter hours, including 54 in the major, with a minimum GPA of 2.0. There is a core general studies component to each undergraduate degree, as well as a general business component.

Special: Strayer offers co-op programs in all majors, dual majors, internships with area businesses, accelerated diploma programs in computer information systems and accounting, and credit for military and work experience. There are 2 national honor societies.

Faculty/Classroom: 71% of faculty are male; 29%, female. All teach undergraduates. No introductory courses are taught by graduate students.

Requirements: The SAT or ACT is recommended. Applicants must either submit satisfactory SAT scores or take Stayer's placement tests. Students must have earned a high school diploma or a GED. AP and CLEP credits are accepted.

Procedure: Freshmen are admitted to all sessions. Entrance exams should be taken by the beginning of the first quarter of attendance. There are deferred admissions and rolling admissions plans. Application deadlines are open. Applications are accepted on-line. The fall 2005 application fee was $35.

Transfer: Requirements are the same as for freshmen. 54 of 180 credits required for the bachelor's degree must be completed at Strayer.

Visiting: There are regularly scheduled orientations for prospective students. Scheduled orientations for prospective students rotate among the campuses. There are guides for informal visits. To schedule a visit, contact the Campus Manager.

Financial Aid: The FAFSA is required. Check with the school for current application deadlines.

International Students: The school actively recruits these students. They must score satisfactorily on the written TOEFL or on the electronic version.

Computers: All students may access the system. There are no time limits and no fees.

Admissions Contact: Melvin Menns, Washington Campus Manager. E-mail: info45@strayer.edu Web: www.strayer.edu

TRINITY COLLEGE
C-2

Washington, DC 20017

(202) 884-9400
(800) 492-6882; Fax: (202) 884-9403

Full-time: 10 men, 560 women	**Faculty:** 48; IIB, -$
Part-time: 20 men, 435 women	**Ph.D.s:** 98%
Graduate: 100 men, 535 women	**Student/Faculty:** 12 to 1
Year: semesters	**Tuition:** $16,915
Application Deadline: open	**Room & Board:** $7300
Freshman Class: n/av	
SAT or ACT: recommended	**LESS COMPETITIVE**

Trinity College, founded in 1897, is a private, women's liberal arts college affiliated with the Roman Catholic Church. The school year consists of traditional semesters plus 1-week courses during January and May. There are 2 undergraduate and 2 graduate schools. Figures in the above capsule and this profile are approximate. In addition to regional accreditation, Trinity has baccalaureate program accreditation with NASDTEC. The library contains 215,338 volumes, 6826 microform items, and 13,797 audio/video tapes/CDs/DVDs, and subscribes to 509 periodicals including electronic. Computerized library services include the card catalog, interlibrary loans, and database searching. Special learning facilities include a learning resource center, art gallery, computer center, writing center, and career and counseling center. The 26-acre campus is in an urban area 2 1/2 miles north of the U.S. Capitol. Including any residence halls, there are 7 buildings.

Student Life: 50% of undergraduates are from out of state, mostly the Middle Atlantic. Students are from 24 states and 22 foreign countries. 60% are from public schools. 67% are African American. 61% are Protestant; 23% Catholic; 13% claim no religious affiliation. The average age of freshmen is 18; all undergraduates, 22. 30% do not continue beyond their first year; 50% remain to graduate.

Housing: 250 students can be accommodated in college housing, which includes single-sex dormitories. On-campus housing is guaranteed for all 4 years. 78% of students commute. All students may keep cars.

Activities: There are no fraternities. There are 23 groups on campus, including choir, chorale, computers, dance, drama, ethnic, Future Female Attorneys of America, gay, honors, international, literary magazine, newspaper, photography, political, professional, psychology, religious, social, social service, student government, and yearbook. Popular campus events include Founders Day, Class Days, and Junior Ring Day.

Sports: Facilities include 2 athletic fields for soccer and field hockey, a fitness center, 6 tennis courts, an outdoor sand volleyball court, and a state-of-the-art sports center with pool, weight room, and basketball court.

Disabled Students: 80% of the campus is accessible. Wheelchair ramps, elevators, special parking, specially equipped rest rooms, and lowered telephones are available.

Services: Counseling and information services are available, as is tutoring in every subject. There is a reader service for the blind. and signing for hearing-impaired students.

Campus Safety and Security: Measures include 24-hour foot and vehicle patrol, self-defense education, security escort services, and shuttle buses. There are informal discussions, pamphlets/posters/films, emergency telephones, and lighted pathways/sidewalks.

Programs of Study: Trinity confers B.A. and B.S. degrees. Master's degrees are also awarded. Bachelor's degrees are awarded in BIOLOGICAL SCIENCE (biochemistry and biology/biological science), BUSINESS (business administration and management and business economics), COMMUNICATIONS AND THE ARTS (communications, English, languages, and Spanish), COMPUTER AND PHYSICAL SCIENCE (chemistry, computer science, mathematics, and physical sciences), EDUCATION (elementary), ENGINEERING AND ENVIRONMENTAL DESIGN (engineering and environmental science), HEALTH PROFESSIONS (premedicine), SOCIAL SCIENCE (criminal justice, economics, history, human services, international studies, political science/government, prelaw, psychology, and sociology). English, history, and political science are the strongest academically. Psychology, business administration, and communication are the largest.

Required: To graduate, students must complete a total of 128 credit hours with a minimum GPA of 2.0. Between 42 and 50 hours are required in the major. All students must take the courses required in the Foundation for Leadership curriculum and must complete a senior seminar.

Special: Cross-registration is offered through the Consortium of Universities of the Washington Area. Trinity offers internships in all majors and minors, as well as work-study programs. Students may study in France, Italy, and various other countries by arrangement with their faculty adviser. B.A.-B.S. degrees, a 5-year accelerated degree in teaching, a 3-2 engineering degree with George Washington University, dual and student-designed majors, a general studies degree, credit for life experience, nondegree study, and pass/fail options are also available. There are 2 national honor societies, including Phi Beta Kappa, and a freshman honors program.

Faculty/Classroom: 35% of faculty are male; 65%, female. 72% teach undergraduates. No introductory courses are taught by graduate students. The average class size in an introductory lecture is 16; in a laboratory, 16; and in a regular course, 13.

Requirements: The SAT or ACT is recommended. Graduation from an accredited secondary school or satisfactory scores on the GED are required for admission. A total of 16 academic credits is required, including 4 years of English and 3 to 4 years each of a foreign language, history, math, and science. AP examinations and SAT: Subject tests are recommended. An interview and an essay or graded writing sample are required. A GPA of 2.0 is required. AP and CLEP credits are accepted. Important factors in the admissions decision are leadership record, extracurricular activities record, and recommendations by school officials.

Procedure: Freshmen are admitted fall, spring, and summer. Entrance exams should be taken in the junior year. There are early admissions, deferred admissions and rolling admissions plans. Application deadlines are open. Application fee is $35.

Transfer: 28 transfer students enrolled in a recent year. Transfer applicants must have a GPA of 2.5. An interview is recommended, an essay is required. 45 of 128 credits required for the bachelor's degree must be completed at Trinity.

Visiting: There are regularly scheduled orientations for prospective students, consisting of a full-day program, including an overview of the college, the curriculum, financing, and student life. There are guides for informal visits and visitors may sit in on classes and stay overnight. To schedule a visit, contact the Office of Admissions.

Financial Aid: In a recent year, 84% of all full-time freshmen and 87% of continuing full-time students received some form of financial aid. 83% of full-time freshmen and 82% of continuing full-time students received need-based aid. The average freshman award was $14,537. Need-based scholarships or need-based grants averaged $6771; need-based self-help aid (loans and jobs) averaged $5828; and other non-need-based awards and non-need-based scholarships averaged $10,558. 8% of undergraduates worked part time. Average annual earnings from campus work were $1000. The average financial indebtedness of a recent graduate was $24,093. Trinity is a member of CSS. The FAFSA is required. Check with the school for current application deadlines.

International Students: In a recent year there were 38 international students enrolled. The school actively recruits these students. They must score satisfactorily on the written TOEFL.

Computers: All students may access the system. There are no time limits and no fees. It is strongly recommended that all students have a personal computer.

Graduates: In a recent year, the most popular majors were psychology (29%), business administration (25%), and communication (14%).

Admissions Contact: Renee Orlick, Director of Admissions.
E-mail: *admissions@trinitydc.edu* Web: *www.trinitydc.edu*

UNIVERSITY OF THE DISTRICT OF COLUMBIA   C-2

Washington, DC 20008	**(202) 274-6069; Fax: (202) 274-6341**
Full-time: 790 men, 1115 women	**Faculty:** 343
Part-time: 1065 men, 2045 women	**Ph.D.s:** 52%
Graduate: 90 men, 160 women	**Student/Faculty:** 6 to 1
Year: semesters, summer session	**Tuition:** $2175 ($4675)
Application Deadline: open	**Room & Board:** n/app
Freshman Class: n/av	
SAT: not required	**ACT:** required
	LESS COMPETITIVE

The University of the District of Columbia, founded in 1977, is a publicly funded, land-grant commuter institution offering programs in liberal arts, business, education, and technical fields. Some figures given in above capsule and in this profile are approximate. There are 5 undergraduate schools and 1 graduate school. In addition to regional accreditation, UDC has baccalaureate program accreditation with ABET, CAHEA, CSWE, NASDTEC, NASM, and NLN. The 4 libraries contain 470,330 volumes, 623,991 microform items, and 21,207 audio/video tapes/CDs/DVDs, and subscribe to 2787 periodicals including electronic. Computerized library services include database searching. Special learning facilities include a learning resource center, art gallery, radio station, TV station, and early childhood learning center. The 22-acre campus is in a suburban area in northwest Washington, D.C. There are 26 buildings.

Student Life: 87% of undergraduates are from District of Columbia. Others are from 49 states and 55 foreign countries. 85% are from public schools. 72% are African American. The average age of freshmen is 18; all undergraduates, 27. 35% do not continue beyond their first year; 65% remain to graduate.

Housing: There are no residence halls. All students commute. Alcohol is not permitted.

Activities: 2% of men belong to 7 national fraternities; 2% of women belong to 5 national sororities. There are 139 groups on campus, including art, band, cheerleading, chess, choir, chorale, computers, dance, drama, drum and bugle corps, ethnic, film, honors, international, jazz band, marching band, newspaper, orchestra, pep band, photography, political, professional, radio and TV, religious, social, social service, student government, and yearbook. Popular campus events include the Cross-Cultural Extended Family Program and International Multicultural Recognition Day.

Sports: There are 6 intercollegiate sports for men and 6 for women, and 8 intramural sports for men and 6 for women. Facilities include a 3000-seat gym, a swimming pool, a weight room, and racquetball and tennis courts.

Disabled Students: All of the campus is accessible. Wheelchair ramps, elevators, special parking, specially equipped rest rooms, lowered drinking fountains, and lowered telephones are available.

Services: Counseling and information services are available, as is tutoring in every subject. There is a reader service for the blind and remedial math and reading.

Campus Safety and Security: Measures include 24-hour foot and vehicle patrol, emergency telephones, and lighted pathways/sidewalks.

Programs of Study: UDC confers B.A. and B.S. degrees. Associate and master's degrees are also awarded. Bachelor's degrees are awarded in BIOLOGICAL SCIENCE (biology/biological science), BUSINESS (accounting, banking and finance, business administration and management, marketing/retailing/merchandising, and office supervision and management), COMMUNICATIONS AND THE ARTS (dramatic arts, English, fine arts, French, media arts, music, and Spanish), COMPUTER AND PHYSICAL SCIENCE (chemistry, computer science, mathematics, and physics), EDUCATION (early childhood, elementary, health, and physical), ENGINEERING AND ENVIRONMENTAL DESIGN (architecture, aviation administration/management, civil engineering, construction engineering, electrical/electronics engineering, electromechanical technology, environmental science, and mechanical engineering), HEALTH PROFESSIONS (nursing, and speech pathology/audiology), SOCIAL SCIENCE (criminal justice, economics, fire science, food science, geography, history, philosophy, political science/government, psychology, public administration, social work, sociology, and urban studies). Business is the strongest academically. Fine arts is the largest.

Required: To graduate, students must complete 120 to 130 semester hours with a minimum GPA of 2.0. All students must take 6 hours each of English composition, literature and advanced writing, foreign language, social science, math, and natural sciences, 4 of personal and community health, and 3 each of philosophy and fine arts.

Special: Cross-registration may be arranged through the Consortium of Universities of the Washington Metropolitan Area. Co-op programs with the federal government, internships, study abroad in 4 countries, work-study programs, and B.A.-B.S. degrees in administration of justice, chemistry, and physics are offered. Nondegree study and credit for life experience are also available. There are 4 national honor societies and a freshman honors program.

Faculty/Classroom: 66% of faculty are male; 34%, female. 89% teach undergraduates, 3% do research, and 20% do both. No introductory courses are taught by graduate students. The average class size in an introductory lecture is 23; in a laboratory, 23; and in a regular course, 23.

Requirements: The ACT is required. In addition, a high school diploma or GED is required for admission, along with an interview. High school courses must include 4 years of English and 2 each of foreign language, social science, lab science, and math (algebra and geometry). AP and CLEP credits are accepted. Important factors in the admissions decision are ability to finance college education, advanced placement or honor courses, and recommendations by school officials.

Procedure: Freshmen are admitted to all sessions. Application deadlines are open. Application fee is $20.

Transfer: Applicants must have a minimum GPA of 2.0. Those with fewer than 30 hours of college credit must submit a high school transcript along with college records. 30 of 120 credits required for the bachelor's degree must be completed at UDC.

Visiting: There are guides for informal visits and visitors may sit in on classes. To schedule a visit, contact the Office of Student Recruitment at (202) 282-3350.

Financial Aid: In a recent year, 25% of all full-time freshmen and 35% of continuing full-time students received some form of financial aid. 35% of full-time freshmen and 33% of continuing full-time students received need-based aid. Need-based scholarships or need-based grants averaged $3000 ($19,000 maximum); need-based self-help aid (loans and jobs) averaged $8512 ($8500 maximum); non-need-based athletic scholarships averaged $9000 ($16,370 maximum); and other non-need-based awards and non-need-based scholarships averaged $1000 ($15,000 maximum). UDC is a member of CSS. The CSS/Profile or FFS is required. Check with the school for current application deadlines.

International Students: They must score satisfactorily on the written TOEFL and also take the university's own English, math, and reading tests.

Computers: All students may access the system 24 hours a day. There are no time limits and no fees.

Admissions Contact: LaVerne Hill-Flanagan, Director of Recruitment and Admissions. E-mail: *lflanagan@udc.edu* Web: *universityofdc.org*

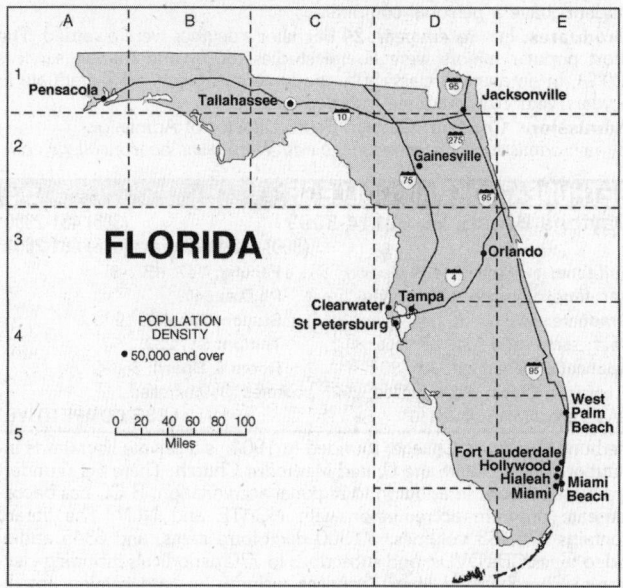

A B C D E

1 Pensacola
Tallahassee
Jacksonville

2 Gainesville

FLORIDA

3 Orlando

POPULATION
DENSITY
Tampa
Clearwater
St Petersburg

4 ● 50,000 and over

West
Palm
Beach

0 20 40 60 80 100
Miles

Fort Lauderdale
Hollywood
Hialeah   Miami
Miami   Beach

5

BARRY UNIVERSITY   E-5
Miami Shores, FL 33161
(305) 899-3100
(800) 695-2279; Fax: (305) 899-2971

Full-time: 1010 men, 2270 women	**Faculty:** 167; IIA, -$
Part-time: 1135 men, 1600 women	**Ph.D.s:** 80%
Graduate: 855 men, 1935 women	**Student/Faculty:** 15 to 1
Year: semesters, summer session	**Tuition:** $17,550
Application Deadline: open	**Room & Board:** $6650
Freshman Class: n/av	
SAT or ACT: required	**LESS COMPETITIVE**

Barry University is an independent Roman Catholic institution of liberal arts and professional studies. Figures in the above capsule and in this profile are approximate. There are 6 undergraduate and 10 graduate schools. In addition to regional accreditation, Barry has baccalaureate program accreditation with CAHEA and NLN. The library contains 290,590 volumes, 512,192 microform items, and 3593 audio/video tapes/CDs/DVDs, and subscribes to 1851 periodicals including electronic. Computerized library services include the card catalog, interlibrary loans, and database searching. Special learning facilities include a learning resource center, radio station, human performance lab, biotechnology lab, photography studios, TV studio, theater, biomechanics lab, and multimedia business classrooms. The 122-acre campus is in a suburban area 14 miles from Fort Lauderdale and 7 miles north of downtown Miami. Including any residence halls, there are 26 buildings.

Student Life: 67% of undergraduates are from Florida. Others are from 46 states, 70 foreign countries, and Canada. 75% are from public schools. 39% are white; 30% Hispanic; 17% African American. 24% are Catholic; 8% Protestant. The average age of freshmen is 19; all undergraduates, 25. 28% do not continue beyond their first year; 48% remain to graduate.

Housing: 715 students can be accommodated in college housing, which includes single-sex and coed dormitories and off-campus apartments. In addition, there are special-interest houses. On-campus housing is guaranteed for the freshman year only, is available on a first-come, first-served basis, and is available on a lottery system for upperclassmen. Priority is given to out-of-town students. 71% of students commute. All students may keep cars.

Activities: 13% of men belong to 3 national fraternities; 4% of women belong to 2 national sororities. There are 82 groups on campus, including cheerleading, chorale, computers, dance, drama, ethnic, honors, international, literary magazine, musical theater, newspaper, photography, political, professional, radio and TV, religious, social, social service, and student government. Popular campus events include Halloween Dance, Festival of Nations, and World AIDS Day.

Sports: There are 5 intercollegiate sports for men and 7 for women. Facilities include baseball, softball, and soccer fields, a health and sports center with an indoor gym, outdoor basketball courts, and racquetball and tennis courts, an outdoor swimming pool, a strength and conditioning center, an athletic training room, a human performance lab, and a biomechanics lab.

Disabled Students: 85% of the campus is accessible. Wheelchair ramps, elevators, special parking, specially equipped rest rooms, special class scheduling, lowered drinking fountains, and lowered telephones are available.

Services: Counseling and information services are available, as is tutoring in most subjects. There is remedial math, reading, and writing.

Campus Safety and Security: Measures include 24-hour foot and vehicle patrol, self-defense education, security escort services, and shuttle buses. There are informal discussions, pamphlets/posters/films, emergency telephones, and lighted pathways/sidewalks.

Programs of Study: Barry confers B.A., B.S., B.F.A., B.L.S., B.P.A., B.P.S., B.S.L.S., B.S.N., B.S.T., and B.S.W. degrees. Master's and doctoral degrees are also awarded. Bachelor's degrees are awarded in BIOLOGICAL SCIENCE (biology/biological science and marine biology), BUSINESS (accounting, international business management, management information systems, management science, marketing/retailing/merchandising, and sports management), COMMUNICATIONS AND THE ARTS (advertising, art, broadcasting, communications, dramatic arts, English, French, music performance, photography, public relations, Spanish, and theater management), COMPUTER AND PHYSICAL SCIENCE (chemistry, computer science, and mathematics), EDUCATION (early childhood and physical), ENGINEERING AND ENVIRONMENTAL DESIGN (preengineering), HEALTH PROFESSIONS (cytotechnology, medical technology, nuclear medical technology, nursing, occupational therapy, predentistry, premedicine, prepharmacy, and ultrasound technology), SOCIAL SCIENCE (criminology, economics, history, international studies, liberal arts/general studies, philosophy, political science/government, prelaw, psychology, sociology, and theological studies). Biology, chemistry, and elementary and early childhood education are the strongest academically. Nursing, elementary and early childhood education, and biology are the largest.

Required: To graduate, students must complete 120 credit hours, including at least 48 in upper-division courses, 40 to 60 in the major, and 45 distributed in these curricular divisions: theology and philosophy, written and oral communication, physical or natural science and math, social and behavior sciences, and humanities and the arts. A minimum GPA of 2.0 must be maintained.

Special: Barry offers junior- or senior-year internships, a Washington semester for prelaw/political science students, on-campus work-study programs in all departments, dual majors, a liberal studies degree, an accelerated degree program in nursing, nondegree study, and pass/fail options. Students may study in 5 European countries. Barry is a member of the College Consortium for International Studies; students can participate in more than 50 programs offered by members. There are 15 national honor societies and a freshman honors program.

Faculty/Classroom: 44% of faculty are male; 56%, female. 69% teach undergraduates. No introductory courses are taught by graduate students. The average class size in an introductory lecture is 17; in a laboratory, 14; and in a regular course, 17.

Requirements: The SAT or ACT is required. In addition, graduation from an accredited secondary school or satisfactory scores on the GED are required for admission. A GPA of 2.0 is required. AP and CLEP credits are accepted.

Procedure: Freshmen are admitted to all sessions. Entrance exams should be taken as early as possible. There are early admissions and rolling admissions plans. Application deadlines are open. Applications are accepted on-line. The fall 2005 application fee was $30.

Transfer: 563 transfer students enrolled in a recent year. Applicants must have earned at least 12 acceptable credit hours with a minimum GPA of 2.0. 30 of 120 credits required for the bachelor's degree must be completed at Barry.

Visiting: There are guides for informal visits and visitors may sit in on classes. To schedule a visit, contact Undergraduate Admissions at (305) 899-3113 or (800) 695-2279.

Financial Aid: In a recent year, 85% of all full-time freshmen and 87% of continuing full-time students received some form of financial aid. 67% of full-time freshmen and 68% of continuing full-time students received need-based aid. The average freshman award was $16,883. 19% of undergraduates worked part time. Average annual earnings from campus work are $2431. The average financial indebtedness of a recent graduate was $17,469. Barry is a member of CSS. The FAFSA is required. Check with the school for current application deadlines.

International Students: In a recent year, there were 321 international students enrolled. The school actively recruits these students. They must score satisfactorily on the written TOEFL.

Computers: All students may access the system 24 hours a day. There are no time limits and no fees. It is strongly recommended that all students have a personal computer. It is required that students in anesthesiology program (graduate degree) have personal computers. IBM ThinkPad or Dell is recommended.

Admissions Contact: Tracy Fontaine, Director of Admissions.
E-mail: *admissions@mail.barry.edu* Web: *www.barry.edu*

BEACON COLLEGE

Leesburg, FL 34748   **(352) 787-7249; Fax: (352) 787-0721**

Full-time: 59 men, 42 women	**Faculty:** n/av
Part-time: none	**Ph.D.s:** n/av
Graduate: none	**Student/Faculty:** 9 to 1
Year: semesters, summer session	**Tuition:** $22,700
Application Deadline: open	**Room & Board:** $6860
Freshman Class: 84 applied, 54 accepted, 34 enrolled	
SAT or ACT: not required	**LESS COMPETITIVE**

Beacon College, founded in 1989, is a private institution that offers undergraduate degrees in liberal studies and human services exclusively for students with learning disabilities. Some information in this profile is approximate. The library contains 20,075 volumes and 554 audio/video tapes/CDs/DVDs, and subscribes to 182 periodicals including electronic. Computerized library services include the card catalog, interlibrary loans, database searching, and Internet access. Special learning facilities include a learning resource center and art gallery. The 2-acre campus is in a small town in the downtown historic district. Including any residence halls, there are 11 buildings.

Student Life: 84% of undergraduates are from out of state, mostly the South. Students are from 25 states and 1 foreign country. 48% are from public schools. 81% are white; 14% African American. The average age of freshmen is 20. 23% do not continue beyond their first year; 76% remain to graduate.

Housing: 130 students can be accommodated in college housing, which includes coed on-campus apartments and off-campus apartments. On-campus housing is guaranteed for all 4 years. All students live on campus; of those, 97% remain on campus on weekends. Alcohol is not permitted. All students may keep cars.

Activities: 38% of women belong to 1 local sorority. There are no fraternities. There are 15 groups on campus, including art, choir, computers, drama, literary magazine, musical theater, newspaper, social, social service, student government, and yearbook.

Disabled Students: 90% of the campus is accessible. Wheelchair ramps, special parking, specially equipped rest rooms, special class scheduling, and special housing are available.

Services: Counseling and information services are available, as is tutoring in every subject. There is remedial math, reading, and writing. There is an Academic Mentoring Program.

Campus Safety and Security: Measures include lighted pathways/sidewalks and school van transportation.

Programs of Study: Beacon College confers the B.A. degree. Associate degrees are also awarded. Bachelor's degrees are awarded in SOCIAL SCIENCE (human services and liberal arts/general studies).

Required: To graduate, students must have 120 credit hours, including 33 credit hours of general education and at least 63 credit hours in their major, and a 2.0 GPA. Students in the liberal studies program must write a thesis and take a comprehensive exam.

Special: Internships, B.A.-B.S. degrees, dual majors, and study abroad are possible.

Faculty/Classroom: All teach undergraduates, 15% both teach and do research. The average class size in an introductory lecture is 8; in a laboratory, 10; and in a regular course, 8.

Admissions: 64% of the 2005-2006 applicants were accepted.

Requirements: Required testing and documentation include a clear diagnosis of learning disability or AD/HD; Wechsler scales (Wais-III are preferred) with full scale, cluster, and subtest scores; and Woodcock Johnson Test of Achievement with age- or grade-equivalency scores in reading, writing, and math. CLEP credit is accepted. Important factors in the admissions decision are evidence of special talent, extracurricular activities record, and geographic diversity.

Procedure: Freshmen are admitted fall and spring. Entrance exams should be taken within 3 years prior to application. There is a rolling admissions plan. Application deadlines are open. Application fee is $50. Applicants receive notification within 2 weeks of completing their file.

Transfer: 15 transfer students enrolled in 2004-2005. Transfer students must meet the same requirements as all incoming students. 60 of 120 credits required for the bachelor's degree must be completed at Beacon College.

Visiting: There are regularly scheduled orientations for prospective students. There are guides for informal visits. To schedule a visit, contact Director of Admissions Carolyn Scott.

Financial Aid: In a recent year, 43% of all full-time freshmen received some form of financial aid, including need-based aid. The average freshman award was $6200. Need-based scholarships or need-based grants averaged $6200 (maximum). The FAFSA and the college's own financial statement are required. Check with the school for current deadlines.

International Students: There were 1 international student enrolled in a recent year. They must take the TOEFL and the college's own entrance exam and WAIS subtests with the GLE in reading, writing, and math.

Computers: All students may access the system during school hours. There are no time limits and no fees. It is strongly recommended that all students have a personal computer.

Graduates: In a recent year, 24 bachelor's degrees were awarded. The most popular majors were liberal studies (80%) and human services (20%). In an average class, 50% graduate in 4 years, 40% graduate in 5 years, and 10% graduate in 6 years.

Admissions Contact: Carolyn Scott, Director of Admissions.
E-mail: *admissions@beaconcollege.edu* Web: *www.beaconcollege.edu*

BETHUNE-COOKMAN COLLEGE   D-2

Daytona Beach, FL 32114-3099   **(386) 481-2600**
(800) 448-0228; Fax: (386) 481-2601

Full-time: 1146 men, 1649 women	**Faculty:** 147; IIB, --$
Part-time: 124 men, 171 women	**Ph.D.s:** 54%
Graduate: none	**Student/Faculty:** 19 to 1
Year: semesters, summer session	**Tuition:** $11,230
Application Deadline: July 30	**Room & Board:** $6692
Freshman Class: 3974 applied, 2925 accepted, 949 enrolled	
SAT Verbal/Math: 410/410*	**LESS COMPETITIVE**

Bethune-Cookman College, founded in 1904, is a private liberal arts institution affiliated with the United Methodist Church. There are 6 undergraduate schools. In addition to regional accreditation, B-CC has baccalaureate program accreditation with NCATE and NLN. The library contains 175,483 volumes, 60,300 microform items, and 6345 audio/video tapes/CDs/DVDs, and subscribes to 770 periodicals including electronic. Computerized library services include the card catalog, interlibrary loans, and database searching. Special learning facilities include a learning resource center, art gallery, radio station, TV station, and observatory. The 70-acre campus is in an urban area 65 miles east of Orlando. Including any residence halls, there are 37 buildings.

Student Life: 65% of undergraduates are from Florida. Others are from 41 states, 32 foreign countries, and Canada. 90% are from public schools. 92% are African American. Most are Protestant. The average age of freshmen is 18; all undergraduates, 21. 24% do not continue beyond their first year; 71% remain to graduate.

Housing: 1772 students can be accommodated in college housing, which includes single-sex dorms. On-campus housing is guaranteed for the freshman year only and is available on a first-come, first-served basis. Priority is given to out-of-town students. 58% of students live on campus; of those, 85% remain on campus on weekends. Alcohol is not permitted. Upperclassmen may keep cars.

Activities: 3% of men belong to 5 national fraternities; 5% of women belong to 4 national sororities. There are 35 groups on campus, including band, cheerleading, choir, chorale, computers, dance, drama, drill team, honors, international, literary magazine, marching band, newspaper, political, professional, radio and TV, religious, social, student government, and yearbook. Popular campus events include Religious Outreach, Career Day, and Founders Day.

Sports: There are 7 intercollegiate sports for men and 8 for women, and 6 intramural sports for men and 7 for women. Facilities include a gym, a weight room, and practice fields.

Disabled Students: 30% of the campus is accessible. Wheelchair ramps, elevators, special parking, specially equipped rest rooms, lowered drinking fountains, and lowered telephones are available.

Services: Counseling and information services are available, as is tutoring in most subjects. There is remedial math, reading, and writing.

Campus Safety and Security: Measures include 24-hour foot and vehicle patrol, security escort services, informal discussions, and pamphlets/posters/films. There are lighted pathways/sidewalks, surveillance cameras, and auto-lock doors.

Programs of Study: B-CC confers B.A. and B.S. degrees. Bachelor's degrees are awarded in BIOLOGICAL SCIENCE (biology/biological science), BUSINESS (accounting, business administration and management, hotel/motel and restaurant management, and international business management), COMMUNICATIONS AND THE ARTS (communications, dramatic arts, English, modern language, and music), COMPUTER AND PHYSICAL SCIENCE (chemistry, computer science, information sciences and systems, mathematics, and physics), EDUCATION (business, education, education of the exceptional child, elementary, English, music, physical, science, and social science), ENGINEERING AND ENVIRONMENTAL DESIGN (computer engineering), HEALTH PROFESSIONS (clinical science and nursing), SOCIAL SCIENCE (criminal justice, gerontology, history, international studies, liberal arts/general studies, political science/government, psychology, religion, and sociology). Business administration, elementary education, and nursing are the strongest academically. Business administration, elementary education, and criminal justice are the largest.

Required: To graduate, students must have a total of 124 credit hours with a minimum GPA of 2.0. All students must complete a total of 49 hours in general education requirements, pass all parts of the College-

Level Academic Skills Test (CLAST), and pass at a specified level a senior exit exam that may include a standardized exam and/or senior area comprehensive exam. They must also complete a senior seminar and senior research paper, and must have 1 year residency, especially the last semester of study at B-CC.

Special: Students may take courses at other institutions with the approval of the area adviser or registrar. B-CC offers cooperative courses in all divisions, internships related to the student's major, work-study programs, an accelerated degree program in business adminstration, nondegree-study, and 3-2 engineering degrees with the Universities of Florida and Central Florida, Tuskegee and Florida Atlantic Universities, and Florida Agriculture and Mechanical University-Florida State University. Study abroad is available in Spain, France, and Germany. There are 8 national honor societies, including Phi Beta Kappa, and a freshman honors program.

Faculty/Classroom: 54% of faculty are male; 46%, female. 93% teach undergraduates and 7% both teach and do research. The average class size in an introductory lecture is 20; in a laboratory, 20; and in a regular course, 18.

Admissions: 74% of the 2005-2006 applicants were accepted. The SAT scores for the 2005-2006 freshman class were: Verbal--87% below 500, 11% between 500 and 599, and 1% between 600 and 700; Math--89% below 500, 9% between 500 and 599, and 1% between 600 and 700. The ACT scores were 96% below 21, and 4% between 21 and 23. 10% of the current freshmen were in the top fifth of their class; 33% were in the top two fifths.

Requirements: The SAT or ACT is required. In addition, graduation from an accredited secondary school or satisfactory scores on the GED are required for admission. High school courses must include 24 credits with 4 of English, 3 each of math and science, 3 of social science and history, and 6 electives; 2 years of a modern language and 1 year of computer literacy are strongly recommended. Students must submit an essay and a letter of recommendation. A GPA of 2.25 is required. AP and CLEP credits are accepted. Important factors in the admissions decision are recommendations by school officials, leadership record, and geographic diversity.

Procedure: Freshmen are admitted to all sessions. Entrance exams should be taken during the fall prior to application. There are early admissions, deferred admissions, and rolling admissions plans. Applications should be filed by July 30 for fall entry, November 30 for spring entry, and April 30 for summer entry, along with a $25 fee. Notification is sent on a rolling basis.

Transfer: 115 transfer students enrolled in 2004-2005. Applicants must submit transcripts from previous institutions attended and a statement of good standing and eligibility to return. A minimum GPA of 2.25 is required. Students having fewer than 12 credit hours must meet the requirements for entering freshmen. 30 of 124 credits required for the bachelor's degree must be completed at B-CC.

Visiting: There are guides for informal visits and visitors may sit in on classes. To schedule a visit, contact the Admissions Office at *ferrier@cookman.edu.*

Financial Aid: In 2005-2006, 97% of all full-time freshmen and 96% of continuing full-time students received some form of financial aid. 82% of full-time freshmen and 76% of continuing full-time students received need-based aid. The average freshman award was $15,200. Need-based scholarships or need-based grants averaged $4800 ($10,000 maximum); need-based self-help aid (loans and jobs) averaged $2855 ($4500 maximum); non-need-based athletic scholarships averaged $13,550 ($17,900 maximum); and other non-need-based awards and non-need-based scholarships averaged $3330 ($17,900 maximum). 71% of undergraduates work part time. Average annual earnings from campus work are $2000. The average financial indebtedness of the 2005 graduate was $26,700. The FAFSA is required. The priority date for freshman financial aid applications for fall entry is April 1.

International Students: There are 109 international students enrolled. The school actively recruits these students. Satisfactory score are required on the written TOEFL and the SAT or the ACT.

Computers: Wireless access is available. Computing labs are available in all academic buildings, Library/Learning Resources Center, and all residential rooms have access to Internet and e-mail. All students may access the system. There are no time limits. The fee is $90.

Graduates: From July 1, 2004 to June 30, 2005, 322 bachelor's degrees were awarded. The most popular majors were business administration (14%), criminal justice (13%), and psychology (11%). In an average class, 5% graduate in 3 years or less, 19% graduate in 4 years or less, 31% graduate in 5 years or less, and 38% graduate in 6 years or less. 125 companies recruited on campus in 2004-2005. Of the 2004 graduating class, 28% were enrolled in graduate school within 6 months of graduation and 75% were employed.

Admissions Contact: Les Ferrier, Director of Admissions. A video is available. E-mail: *ferrierl@cookman.edu*
Web: *www.bethune.cookman.edu*

CARLOS ALBIZU UNIVERSITY   E-5

Miami, FL 33172-2209
(305) 593-1223 ext 160
(800) 672-3246; Fax: (305) 593-1854

Full-time: 38 men, 164 women	**Faculty:** 4
Part-time: 49 men, 202 women	**Ph.D.s:** n/av
Graduate: 135 men, 488 women	**Student/Faculty:** 37 to 1
Year: trimesters, summer session	**Tuition:** $11,109
Application Deadline: open	**Room & Board:** n/app
Freshman Class: 176 applied, 129 accepted, 125 enrolled	
SAT or ACT: not required	**COMPETITIVE**

Carlos Albizu University is a private, specialized institution of higher learning offering degrees at the undergraduate, graduate, and doctoral levels. CAU has campuses in San Juan, Puerto Rico, and Miami, Florida, founded in 1966 and 1980 respectively. There are 3 undergraduate and 3 graduate schools. Some of the figures in the capsule and this profile are approximate. The library contains 23,000 volumes and 1000 audio/video tapes/CDs/DVDs, and subscribes to 350 periodicals including electronic. Computerized library services include the card catalog, interlibrary loans, database searching, and Internet access. Special learning facilities include a learning resource center and an ESOL lab. The 18-acre campus is in an urban area in Miami. There are 2 buildings.

Student Life: 98% of undergraduates are from Florida. Students are from 22 states, 42 foreign countries, and Canada. 72% are Hispanic; 11% African American. The average age of freshmen is 28; all undergraduates, 35. 1% do not continue beyond their first year; 37% remain to graduate.

Housing: There are no residence halls. All students commute. Alcohol is not permitted. All students may keep cars.

Activities: There are no fraternities or sororities. There are 4 groups on campus, including ethnic, gay, honors, newsletter, and student government. Popular campus events include the Excellent Student Award Banquet, the Student Council Initiation Event, and the Student Support Services Cultural Event.

Disabled Students: All of the campus is accessible. Wheelchair ramps, special parking, specially equipped rest rooms, and lowered drinking fountains are available.

Services: Counseling and information services are available, as is tutoring in most subjects. There is a mentoring program and student support services center.

Campus Safety and Security: Measures include 24-hour foot and vehicle patrol, security escort services, emergency telephones, and lighted pathways/sidewalks. There is an annual report on crime statistics.

Programs of Study: CAU confers B.A., B.S., and B.B.A. degrees. Master's and doctoral degrees are also awarded. Bachelor's degrees are awarded in BUSINESS (business administration and management), EDUCATION (elementary), SOCIAL SCIENCE (psychology). Psychology is the largest.

Required: To graduate, students must earn 120 to 124 credits, with 30 to 48 in the major. Foundation courses include English composition, oral communication, math, behaviorial life, physical sciences, humanities, cross-cultural studies, literature, liberal arts, and computing, for a total of 48 credits.

Special: CAU offers cross-registration with other area colleges, internships or practicums in psychology and elementary education, federal work-study, an accelerated degree program in business administration, and dual majors in psychology and elementary education. There is 1 national honor society.

Faculty/Classroom: 43% of faculty are male; 57%, female. All both teach and do research. Graduate students teach 15% of introductory courses. The average class size in an introductory lecture is 12; in a laboratory, 10; and in a regular course, 15.

Admissions: 73% of the 2005-2006 applicants were accepted.

Requirements: A GPA of 2.0 is required. AP and CLEP credits are accepted. Important factors in the admissions decision are advanced placement or honor courses and ability to finance college education.

Procedure: Freshmen are admitted fall, spring, and summer. There is a rolling admissions plan. Application deadlines are open. Application fee is $25.

Transfer: 31 transfer students enrolled in a recent year. Transfer applicants must have an overall GPA of 2.0 and must submit official transcripts from all colleges/universities previously attended. 30 of 120 to 124 credits required for the bachelor's degree must be completed at CAU.

Visiting: There are regularly scheduled orientations for prospective students, consisting of 2 open houses per session. There are guides for informal visits and visitors may sit in on classes. To schedule a visit, contact Dr. Arturo Tigera at (305) 593-1223 ext 149.

Financial Aid: In 2005-2006, 72% of all full-time freshmen and 29% of continuing full-time students received some form of financial aid. 70% of full-time freshmen and 67% of continuing full-time students received need-based aid. The average freshman award was $10,000. The FAFSA and the college's own financial statement are required. Check with the school for current application deadlines.

Computers: All students may access the system from 10 A.M. to 9 P.M. Monday through Friday, and from 9 A.M. to 3 P.M. Saturdays. There are no time limits and no fees. It is strongly recommended that all students have a personal computer.

Graduates: In a recent year, 37 bachelor's degrees were awarded. Of a recent graduating class, 53% were enrolled in graduate school within 6 months of graduation.

Admissions Contact: Priscilliana Berrios, Admissions Officer. E-mail: pberrios@albizu.edu Web: www.albizu.edu

CLEARWATER CHRISTIAN COLLEGE D-4

Clearwater, FL 33759
(727) 726-1153, ext. 228
(800) 348-4463; Fax: (727) 726-8597

Full-time: 275 men, 355 women	**Faculty:** 34
Part-time: 10 men, 10 women	**Ph.D.s:** 56%
Graduate: none	**Student/Faculty:** 18 to 1
Year: semesters, summer session	**Tuition:** $9130
Application Deadline: see profile	**Room & Board:** $4060
Freshman Class: n/av	
SAT or ACT: recommended	**LESS COMPETITIVE**

Clearwater Christian College, founded in 1966, is a private, fundamentalist, nonsectarian institution offering programs in Bible, liberal arts, business, and teacher preparation. Figures in the above capsule and in this profile are approximate. The library contains 103,000 volumes, 198,000 microform items, and 2100 audio/video tapes/CDs/DVDs, and subscribes to 1050 periodicals including electronic. Computerized library services include the card catalog, interlibrary loans, and database searching. Special learning facilities include a learning resource center. The 130-acre campus is in a small town 10 miles west of Tampa. Including any residence halls, there are 7 buildings.

Student Life: 47% of undergraduates are from Florida. Others are from 37 states, 14 foreign countries, and Canada. 27% are from public schools. 89% are white. Most are Protestant. The average age of freshmen is 18; all undergraduates, 20. 39% do not continue beyond their first year; 41% remain to graduate.

Housing: 600 students can be accommodated in college housing, which includes single-sex dormitories. On-campus housing is guaranteed for all 4 years. 81% of students live on campus; of those, all remain on campus on weekends. Alcohol is not permitted. All students may keep cars.

Activities: There are no fraternities or sororities. There are 8 groups on campus, including band, cheerleading, choir, chorale, drama, honors, newspaper, orchestra, pep band, political, professional, religious, student government, and yearbook.

Sports: There are 3 intercollegiate sports for men and 3 for women, and 3 intramural sports for men and 3 for women. Facilities include a gym and a playing field.

Disabled Students: All of the campus is accessible. Wheelchair ramps, elevators, special parking, specially equipped rest rooms, lowered drinking fountains, and lowered telephones are available.

Services: There is a reader service for the blind. as needed.

Campus Safety and Security: Measures include 24-hour foot and vehicle patrol, self-defense education, informal discussions, and pamphlets/posters/films. There are emergency telephones and lighted pathways/sidewalks.

Programs of Study: CCC confers B.A. and B.S. degrees. Associate degrees are also awarded. Bachelor's degrees are awarded in BIOLOGICAL SCIENCE (biology/biological science), BUSINESS (accounting, and business administration and management), COMMUNICATIONS AND THE ARTS (communications, English, and music), COMPUTER AND PHYSICAL SCIENCE (mathematics), EDUCATION (elementary, music, physical, secondary, social studies, and special), HEALTH PROFESSIONS (premedicine), SOCIAL SCIENCE (biblical studies, history, humanities, ministries, pastoral studies, prelaw, psychology, religious education, and religious music). Education and business are the largest.

Required: General education requirements include 25 hours of human adjustment, 19 each of social science and humanities, 12 of arts and communication, and 10 of science and math. Computer science courses are required. A total of 128 credit hours is required, including more than 60 in the major, with a minimum GPA of 2.0. Students must have no grade lower than a C- in any major requirement and maintain satisfactory Christian service involvement throughout the college career.

Special: On occasion, credit from an approved correspondence school may be accepted, or registration at another school for a course to complete degree requirements at CCC may be permitted. Internships are offered in teacher education, business, and psychology. Work-study programs and nondegree study are possible. There is 1 national honor society.

Faculty/Classroom: 68% of faculty are male; 32%, female. All teach undergraduates. The average class size in an introductory lecture is 50; in a laboratory, 20; and in a regular course, 25.

Admissions: In a recent year, there was 1 National Merit finalist and 2 semifinalists. 20 freshmen graduated first in their class.

Requirements: The SAT or ACT is recommended with a satisfactory score on the SAT or on the ACT. Applicants must be high school graduates or have a GED certificate. An essay is required, and an interview is recommended. A GPA of 2.0 is required. AP and CLEP credits are accepted.

Procedure: Freshmen are admitted to all sessions. Entrance exams should be taken in the fall of the senior year. There are deferred admissions and rolling admissions plans. Notification is sent on a rolling basis. The application fee is $35.

Transfer: 59 transfer students enrolled in a recent year. Transfer applicants must submit transcripts from all postsecondary schools attended. Grades of C or better transfer. Applicants must have a minimum cumulative postsecondary GPA of 2.0. 32 of 128 credits required for the bachelor's degree must be completed at CCC.

Visiting: There are regularly scheduled orientations for prospective students. There are guides for informal visits and visitors may sit in on classes and stay overnight. To schedule a visit, contact the Admissions Office.

Financial Aid: The CSS/Profile, FAFSA, or FFS are required, the FFS is preferred. Check with the school for current application deadlines.

International Students: They must score satisfactorily on the written TOEFL and also take the SAT or the ACT. Applicants must also submit a Foreign Student Data Form.

Computers: All students may access the system. There are no time limits. The fee is $30 annually. It is strongly recommended that all students have a personal computer.

Admissions Contact: Benjamin J. Puckett, Dean of Enrollment Services. A video is available. E-mail: benpuckett@clearwater.edu Web: clearwater.edu

DEVRY UNIVERSITY/MIRAMAR

Miramar, FL 33027-4150
(954) 499-9700
(866) 793-3879; Fax: (954) 499-9723

Full-time: 240 men, 85 women	**Faculty:** n/av
Part-time: 310 men, 150 women	**Ph.D.s:** n/av
Graduate: none	**Student/Faculty:** n/av
Year: semesters, summer session	**Tuition:** $12,000
Application Deadline: open	**Room & Board:** n/app
Freshman Class: n/av	
SAT or ACT: n/av	**LESS COMPETITIVE**

Devry University/Miramar, 1 of 67 DeVry University locations in the United States and Canada, opened in 2002. It offers programs in business administration, computer engineering technology, computer information systems, electronics engineering technology, network and communications management, and technical management. Figures in the above capsule and in this profile are approximate. The library contains 8100 volumes and 550 audio/video tapes/CDs/DVDs, and subscribes to 125 periodicals including electronic. The 16-acre campus is .

Student Life: 39% are African American; 38% Hispanic; 11% white.

Housing: There are no residence halls. All students commute.

Activities: There are no fraternities or sororities.

Programs of Study: DeVry confers B.A. degrees. Associate and master's degrees are also awarded. Bachelor's degrees are awarded in BUSINESS (business administration and management), COMMUNICATIONS AND THE ARTS (telecommunications), COMPUTER AND PHYSICAL SCIENCE (information sciences and systems), ENGINEERING AND ENVIRONMENTAL DESIGN (computer engineering, electrical/electronics engineering technology, and technological management).

Required: To graduate, students must achieve a GPA of at least 2.0, complete 48 to 154 credit hours, and satisfactorily complete all curriculum requirements. Course requirements vary according to program. All first-semester students take courses in business organization, computer applications, algebra, psychology, and student success strategies.

Special: Accelerated degree programs, co-op programs, and distance learning are available.

Requirements: Admissions requirements include graduation from a secondary school; the GED is accepted. Applicants must pass the DeVry entrance exam or present satisfactory SAT or ACT scores. An interview is required.

Procedure: Freshmen are admitted fall, spring, and summer. There are early admissions and deferred admissions plans. Application deadlines are open. Check with the school for application fee. Applications are accepted on-line.

Transfer: 25 of 48 credits required for the bachelor's degree must be completed at DeVry University/Miramar.

Financial Aid: In a recent year, 69% of all full-time students received some form of financial aid. 65% of full-time freshmen and 64% of continuing full-time students received need-based aid. The average freshman award was $6506. Need-based scholarships or need-based grants averaged $4035; need-based self-help aid (loans and jobs) averaged $3416; and other non-need-based awards and non-need-based scholarships averaged $6562. The FAFSA is required. The deadline for filing freshman financial aid applications is rolling.

International Students: International students must take the TOEFL and also take the college's own entrance exam.

Graduates: The most popular major was engineering/engineering technologies.

Admissions Contact: Martin Najarro, Director of Admissions.
E-mail: *openhouse@mir.devry.edu* Web: *www.devry.edu/miramar*

DEVRY UNIVERSITY/ORLANDO D-3
Orlando, FL 32839-2426   (407) 370-3131
                                          (866) 353-3879; Fax: (407) 370-3198

Full-time: 600 men, 250 women	**Faculty:** n/av
Part-time: 375 men, 170 women	**Ph.D.s:** n/av
Graduate: none	**Student/Faculty:** n/av
Year: semesters, summer session	**Tuition:** $12,000
Application Deadline: open	**Room & Board:** n/app
Freshman Class: n/av	
SAT or ACT: n/av	**LESS COMPETITIVE**

DeVry University/Orlando, founded in 2000, is a private institution offering hands-on programs in electronics, business administration, computer information systems, telecommunications management, information technology, and computer engineering technology. The school is 1 of 67 DeVry University locations throughout the United States and Canada. Figures in the above capsule and in this profile are approximate. The library contains 14,000 volumes and 1000 audio/video tapes/CDs/DVDs, and subscribes to 65 periodicals including electronic. Computerized library services include the card catalog, interlibrary loans, and database searching. Special learning facilities include a learning resource center and electronics and other labs.

Student Life: 30% are white; 26% African American; 16% Hispanic. The average age of all undergraduates is 25.

Housing: There are no residence halls. All students commute. Alcohol is not permitted. All students may keep cars.

Activities: There are no fraternities or sororities. There are 11 groups on campus, including professional, social, and yearbook. Popular campus events include Model Car Competition, Fun Flicks, and Welcome Picnic.

Sports: There is no sports program at DeVry.

Disabled Students: 98% of the campus is accessible. Special parking, specially equipped rest rooms, lowered drinking fountains, and lowered telephones are available.

Services: Counseling and information services are available, as is tutoring in every subject.

Campus Safety and Security: Measures include security escort services, informal discussions, pamphlets/posters/films, and emergency telephones. There are lighted pathways/sidewalks and off-duty police as security.

Programs of Study: DeVry confers the B.S. degree. Associate and master's degrees are also awarded. Bachelor's degrees are awarded in BUSINESS (business administration and management), COMMUNICATIONS AND THE ARTS (telecommunications), COMPUTER AND PHYSICAL SCIENCE (information sciences and systems), ENGINEERING AND ENVIRONMENTAL DESIGN (computer engineering, electrical/electronics engineering technology, and technological management). Electronics, computer information systems, and telecommunications are the largest.

Required: To graduate, students must achieve a GPA of at least 2.0 and satisfactorily complete all curriculum requirements. Course requirements vary according to program. All first-semester students take courses in business organization, computer applications, algebra, psychology, and student success strategies.

Special: Accelerated degrees, co-op programs, nondegree study, distance learning, and evening and weekend classes are possible.

Faculty/Classroom: All teach undergraduates.

Requirements: Admissions requirements include graduation from a secondary school; the GED is also accepted. Applicants must pass the DeVry entrance exam or present satisfactory ACT or SAT scores. An interview is required. CLEP credit is accepted.

Procedure: Freshmen are admitted fall, winter, and summer. There are early admissions and deferred admissions plans. Application deadlines are open. Check with the school for application fee. Applications are accepted on-line.

Transfer: Applicants must present passing grades in all completed college course work, demonstrate language skills proficiency in at least 24 completed semester hours, and present evidence of math proficiency by appropriate college-level credits. A minimum GPA of 2.0 is required. 25 of 48 credits required for the bachelor's degree must be completed at DeVry.

Visiting: There are regularly scheduled orientations for prospective students. There are guides for informal visits and visitors may sit in on classes. To schedule a visit, contact the New Student Coordinator.

Financial Aid: In a recent year, 68% of all full-time freshmen and 79% of continuing full-time students received some form of financial aid. 67%

of full-time freshmen and 77% of continuing full-time students received need-based aid. The average freshman award was $6351. Need-based scholarships or need-based grants averaged $3859; need-based self-help aid (loans and jobs) averaged $3673; and other non-need-based awards and non-need-based scholarships averaged $10,000. The FAFSA is required. The deadline for filing freshman financial aid applications for fall entry is rolling.

International Students: International students must take the TOEFL and also take the college's own entrance exam.

Graduates: In a recent year, 11 bachelor's degrees were awarded. The most popular majors were business (91%) and electronics engineering technology (9%).

Admissions Contact: Director of Admissions.
E-mail: *krochford@orl.devry.edu* Web: *www.orl.devry.edu*

ECKERD COLLEGE D-4
St. Petersburg, FL 33711   (727) 864-8331
                                          (800) 456-9009; Fax: (727) 866-2304

Full-time: 746 men, 1006 women	**Faculty:** IIB, av$
Part-time: 10 men, 16 women	**Ph.D.s:** n/av
Graduate: none	**Student/Faculty:** 16 to 1
Year: 4-1-4, summer session	**Tuition:** $27,624
Application Deadline: April 1	**Room & Board:** $7868
Freshman Class: 2740 applied, 1962 accepted, 505 enrolled	
SAT or ACT: required	**VERY COMPETITIVE**

Eckerd College, founded in 1958, is a private liberal arts institution affiliated with the Presbyterian Church (U.S.A.). Interdisciplinary programs are an important part of the school's curriculum. This is reflected in the organization of the faculty into collegia, rather than into traditional departments. The college also fosters and encourages strong faculty-student mentoring, service learning, volunteerism, other types of hands-on, practical learning, and environmental and global perspectives. Some figures in this profile are approximate. In addition to regional accreditation, Eckerd has baccalaureate program accreditation with AALE. The library contains 113,850 volumes, 14,606 microform items, and 1941 audio/video tapes/CDs/DVDs, and subscribes to 3009 periodicals including electronic. Computerized library services include the card catalog, interlibrary loans, and database searching. Special learning facilities include an art gallery, radio station, TV station, and a sea mammal necropsy lab. The 267-acre campus is in a suburban area on 1 1/4 miles of waterfront, 5 miles south of St. Petersburg. Including any residence halls, there are 67 buildings.

Student Life: 69% of undergraduates are from out of state, mostly the Northeast. Students are from 50 states, 49 foreign countries, and Canada. 75% are from public schools. 77% are white. 52% are claim no religious affiliation; 24% Protestant; 18% Catholic; 7% Muslim, Hindu, Buddhist, and Greek Orthodox. The average age of freshmen is 18; all undergraduates, 20. 16% do not continue beyond their first year; 64% remain to graduate.

Housing: 1209 students can be accommodated in college housing, which includes single-sex and coed dorms and on-campus apartments. In addition, there are language houses and substance-free houses. On-campus housing is guaranteed for the freshman year only, is available on a first-come, first-served basis, and is available on a lottery system for upperclassmen. 76% of students live on campus; of those, 95% remain on campus on weekends. All students may keep cars.

Activities: There are no fraternities or sororities. There are 74 groups on campus, including cheerleading, chess, choir, chorale, chorus, computers, drama, ethnic, film, gay, honors, international, literary magazine, musical theater, newspaper, photography, political, professional, radio and TV, religious, social, social service, student government, water search and rescue and yearbook. Popular campus events include the Festival of Cultures, Kon-Tiki, and the Festival of Hope.

Sports: There are 6 intercollegiate sports for men and 7 for women, and 11 intramural sports for men and 10 for women. Facilities include a gym, a baseball and softball complex, soccer fields, tennis courts, a weight room, a renovated and modernized fitness room, a swimming pool, and waterfront facilities.

Disabled Students: 90% of the campus is accessible. Wheelchair ramps, elevators, special parking, specially equipped rest rooms, special class scheduling, lowered drinking fountains, and lowered telephones, are available readers are available for the visually impaired as are magnifiers in the library.

Services: Counseling and information services are available, as is tutoring in some subjects, including math, sciences, and foreign languages.

Campus Safety and Security: Measures include 24-hour foot and vehicle patrol, security escort services, informal discussions, and pamphlets/posters/films. There are emergency telephones, lighted pathways/sidewalks, and a security gate at the entrance to the campus.

Programs of Study: Eckerd confers B.A. and B.S. degrees. Bachelor's degrees are awarded in AGRICULTURE (environmental studies), BIOLOGICAL SCIENCE (biology/biological science and marine science), BUSINESS (business administration and management, international business management, and management science), COMMUNICATIONS AND THE ARTS (communications, comparative literature, creative writing, dramatic arts, English, French, German, music, Russian, Spanish, and visual and performing arts), COMPUTER AND PHYSICAL SCIENCE (chemistry, computer science, mathematics, and physics), HEALTH PROFESSIONS (predentistry and premedicine), SOCIAL SCIENCE (American studies, anthropology, economics, history, human development, humanities, international relations, philosophy, political science/government, prelaw, psychology, religion, sociology, and women's studies). Marine science, management, and environmental studies are the largest.

Required: To graduate, students must complete a total of 36 courses or 126 semester hours with a minimum GPA of 2.0. Required courses include 1 each in the arts, humanities, natural and social sciences, and environmental and global perspectives. Students must also demonstrate competencies in writing, speaking, foreign language, computation, and technology and must take a comprehensive exam or submit a thesis or project in the senior year.

Special: Eckerd offers internships, study abroad, work-study programs, dual majors in all subjects, interdisciplinary majors in international relations and environmental studies, student-designed majors, nondegree study, and pass/fail options. Students may earn B.A.-B.S. degrees in biology, chemistry, and marine science. A 3-2 engineering degree is offered with Auburn, Washington, and Columbia Universities and the University of Miami. The Program for Experienced Learners (students 25 and older) offers independent study, weekend courses, and credit for experiential learning. There are 8 national honor societies, including Phi Beta Kappa, a freshman honors program, and 30 departmental honors programs.

Faculty/Classroom: All both teach and do research. The average class size in an introductory lecture is 20; in a laboratory, 15; and in a regular course, 20.

Admissions: 72% of the 2005-2006 applicants were accepted. 37% of the current freshmen were in the top fifth of their class; 73% were in the top two fifths. 4 freshmen graduated first in their class.

Requirements: The SAT or ACT is required. In addition, graduation from an accredited secondary school or satisfactory scores on the GED are required. High school courses must include 4 years of English, 3 each of math and science, 2 each of a foreign language and social studies, and 1 of history. SAT Subject Tests in writing, literature, and math are recommended. An essay is required and an interview is recommended. A GPA of 2.0 is required. AP and CLEP credits are accepted. Important factors in the admissions decision are advanced placement or honor courses, leadership record, and personality/intangible qualities.

Procedure: Freshmen are admitted fall, winter, and spring. Entrance exams should be taken in October, November, or December. There are early admissions and deferred admissions plans. There is a rolling admissions plan. Applications should be filed by April 1 for fall entry, December 1 for winter entry, and December 1 for spring entry, along with a $35 fee. Notification is sent on a rolling basis. A waiting list is an active part of the admissions procedure.

Transfer: 62 transfer students enrolled in 2005-2006. Applicants must have a minimum GPA of 2.5. The SAT or ACT is required. An interview is recommended. A faculty recommendation is required. 63 of 126 credits required for the bachelor's degree must be completed at Eckerd.

Visiting: There are regularly scheduled orientations for prospective students, consisting of an interview and a tour. There are guides for informal visits and visitors may sit in on classes and stay overnight. To schedule a visit, contact Donna Grosso at *admissions@eckerd.edu.*

Financial Aid: In 2005-2006, 90% of all full-time freshmen and 92% of continuing full-time students received some form of financial aid. 59% of full-time freshmen and 54% of continuing full-time students received need-based aid. The average freshman award was $20,160. Need-based scholarships or need-based grants averaged $14,208; need-based self-help aid (loans and jobs) averaged $3528; non-need-based athletic scholarships averaged $15,571; and other non-need-based awards and non-need-based scholarships averaged $9193. 75% of undergraduates work part time. Average annual earnings from campus work are $1500. The average financial indebtedness of a recent year's graduate was $17,500. The FAFSA is required. Check with the school for current deadlines.

International Students: There were 144 international students enrolled in a recent year. The school actively recruits these students. A satisfactory score on the TOEFL is required.

Computers: All students may access the system at any time. There are no time limits and no fees. It is strongly recommended that all students have a personal computer.

Graduates: In a recent year, 345 bachelor's degrees were awarded. The most popular majors were marine science (13%), management (11%), and international business (11%). In an average class, 1% graduate in 3 years or less, 64% graduate in 4 years or less, 65% graduate in 5 years or less, and 67% graduate in 6 years or less. Of a recent graduating class, 28% were enrolled in graduate school within 6 months of graduation and 64% were employed.

Admissions Contact: Laura Martin, Dean of Admissions and Financial Aid. E-mail: *martinle@eckerd.edu* Web: *http://www.eckerd.edu*

EDWARD WATERS COLLEGE   D-1
Jacksonville, FL 32209

(904) 470-8202
(888) 898-3191; Fax: (904) 470-8048

Full-time: 665 men, 600 women	**Faculty:** 44
Part-time: 20 men, 20 women	**Ph.D.s:** 18%
Graduate: none	**Student/Faculty:** 29 to 1
Year: semesters, summer session	**Tuition:** $8355
Application Deadline: see profile	**Room & Board:** $6035
Freshman Class: n/av	
SAT or ACT: recommended	**LESS COMPETITIVE**

Edward Waters College, founded in 1866, is the oldest independent institution of higher learning in Florida. Figures in the above capsule and profile are approximate. Affiliated with the African Methodist Episcopal Church, the college offers programs in the arts and sciences, business, and education. The library contains 65,798 volumes and 2900 audio/video tapes/CDs/DVDs, and subscribes to 1350 periodicals including electronic. Computerized library services include the card catalog, interlibrary loans, database searching, and Internet access. Special learning facilities include a learning resource center, art gallery, and a museum of African art. The 50-acre campus is in an urban area in Jacksonville. Including any residence halls, there are 25 buildings.

Student Life: 90% of undergraduates are from Florida. Others are from 12 states, 4 foreign countries, and Canada. 90% are from public schools. 95% are African American. The average age of freshmen is 18; all undergraduates, 20. 40% do not continue beyond their first year; 60% remain to graduate.

Housing: 584 students can be accommodated in college housing, which includes single-sex dormitories. In addition, there are honors houses. 53% of students live on campus; of those, 45% remain on campus on weekends. Alcohol is not permitted. All students may keep cars.

Activities: 20% of men belong to 4 national fraternities; 35% of women belong to 4 national sororities. There are 20 groups on campus, including band, cheerleading, choir, chorus, dance, drama, drill team, honors, international, jazz band, marching band, newspaper, pep band, photography, political, professional, religious, social service, student government, and yearbook. Popular campus events include Fall and Spring Convocations, Religious Emphasis Week, and African American History Celebration.

Sports: There are 6 intercollegiate sports for men and 5 for women, and 3 intramural sports for men and 3 for women. Facilities are off campus.

Disabled Students: 75% of the campus is accessible. Wheelchair ramps, elevators, special parking, specially equipped rest rooms, and lowered drinking fountains are available.

Services: Counseling and information services are available, as is tutoring in every subject. There is remedial math, reading, and writing. There is a student support services program for students who are academically disadvantaged. Academic career counseling employment services are available.

Campus Safety and Security: Measures include 24-hour foot and vehicle patrol, security escort services, informal discussions, and emergency telephones. There are lighted pathways/sidewalks.

Programs of Study: EWC confers B.A., B.S., and B.B.A. degrees. Bachelor's degrees are awarded in BIOLOGICAL SCIENCE (biology/biological science), BUSINESS (accounting and business administration and management), COMMUNICATIONS AND THE ARTS (communications and English), COMPUTER AND PHYSICAL SCIENCE (computer science and mathematics), EDUCATION (early childhood, elementary, and physical), SOCIAL SCIENCE (criminal justice, history, philosophy, political science/government, psychology, religion, and sociology). Education is the strongest academically. Business administration is the largest.

Required: To graduate, all students must complete at least 120 credit hours, including 30 in the major, with a 2.0 GPA overall and in the major. Weekly chapel service attendance is required.

Special: EWC offers co-op programs, internships in communications, political science, education, and criminal justice, dual and student-designed majors, and work-study programs. A dual law degree with Florida Coastal School of Law and a 3-2 engineering degree with Florida A&M University are offered. There is a freshman honors program.

Faculty/Classroom: 50% of faculty are male; 50%, female. All teach undergraduates.

Requirements: The SAT or ACT is required for some programs. SAT or ACT scores are necessary for unconditional admission. Applicants must be graduates of an accredited secondary school or have a GED certificate, and have taken the California Achievement Test. EWC requires applicants to be in the upper 20% of their class. A GPA of 2.0 is required. AP and CLEP credits are accepted. Important factors in the admissions decision are advanced placement or honor courses, ability to finance college education, and recommendations by school officials.

Procedure: Freshmen are admitted fall and spring. There is a rolling admissions plan.The college accepts all applicants. Notification is sent on a rolling basis. Applications are accepted on-line. The fall 2005 application fee was $25.

Transfer: 30 of 120 credits required for the bachelor's degree must be completed at EWC.

Visiting: There are guides for informal visits. To schedule a visit, contact the Admissions Office.

Financial Aid: In a recent year, 80% of all full-time freshmen and 86% of continuing full-time students received some form of financial aid. 82% of full-time freshmen and 91% of continuing full-time students received need-based aid. The average freshman award was $9550. Need-based scholarships or need-based grants averaged $2400 ($5830 maximum); need-based self-help aid (loans and jobs) averaged $2950 ($9125 maximum); non-need-based athletic scholarships averaged $2095 ($7187 maximum); and other non-need-based awards and non-need-based scholarships averaged $2105 ($4250 maximum). 23% of undergraduates worked part time. Average annual earnings from campus work are $1790. The average financial indebtedness of a recent graduate was $9500. EWC is a member of CSS. The FAFSA is required. Check with the school for current application deadlines.

International Students: In a recent year, there were 39 international students enrolled. The school actively recruits these students. They must take an English profiency and are encouraged to take the TOEFL.

Computers: All students may access the system. There are no time limits and no fees.

Graduates: In a recent year, 126 bachelor's degrees were awarded. The most popular majors were organizational management (69%), business administration (11%), and criminal justice (5%). In an average class, 20% graduate in 4 years or less, 23% graduate in 5 years or less, and 25% graduate in 6 years or less. 250 companies recruited on campus in a recent year.

Admissions Contact: Tony Baldwin, Director of Enrollment. A video is available. E-mail: *tabaldwin@ewc.edu* Web: *www.ewc.edu*

EMBRY-RIDDLE AERONAUTICAL UNIVERSITY   D-2

Daytona Beach, FL 32114   **(386) 226-6112**
                               (800) 862-2416; Fax: (386) 226-7070

Full-time: 3406 men, 687 women	**Faculty:** 248; IIA, av$
Part-time: 229 men, 60 women	**Ph.D.s:** 64%
Graduate: 296 men, 98 women	**Student/Faculty:** 17 to 1
Year: semesters, summer session	**Tuition:** $23,550
Application Deadline: July 1	**Room & Board:** $6730
Freshman Class: 3545 applied, 2982 accepted, 977 enrolled	
SAT Verbal/Math: 540/570*	**ACT:** 23 **COMPETITIVE**

Embry-Riddle Aeronautical University, founded in 1926, is a private institution offering undergraduate programs in aviation, engineering, and business on 2 campuses: one in Daytona Beach and the other, founded in 1978, in Prescott, Arizona. There are 4 undergraduate schools and 1 graduate school. In addition to regional accreditation, ERAU has baccalaureate program accreditation with ABET and ACBSP. The library contains 103,153 volumes, 255,817 microform items, and 5150 audio/video tapes/CDs/DVDs, and subscribes to 835 periodicals including electronic. Computerized library services include the card catalog, interlibrary loans, and database searching. Special learning facilities include a learning resource center, radio station, an airway science simulation lab, and a College of Aviation Building. The 185-acre campus is in an urban area 48 miles northeast of Orlando. Including any residence halls, there are 49 buildings.

Student Life: 68% of undergraduates are from out of state, mostly the South. Students are from 50 states, 85 foreign countries, and Canada. 67% are white. The average age of freshmen is 18; all undergraduates, 21. 24% do not continue beyond their first year; 56% remain to graduate.

Housing: 1917 students can be accommodated in university housing, which includes coed dorms, on-campus apartments, off-campus apartments, and married-student housing. On-campus housing is guaranteed for the freshman year only, is available on a first-come, first-served basis, and is available on a lottery system for upperclassmen. 61% of students commute. All students may keep cars.

Activities: 10% of men belong to 15 national fraternities; 14% of women belong to 5 national sororities. There are 164 groups on campus, including cheerleading, chess, choir, computers, dance, debate, drama, drill team, ethnic, film, gay, honors, international, literary magazine, musical theater, newspaper, pep band, photography, political, professional, radio and TV, religious, social, social service, and student government. Popular campus events include Spring Concert and Hypnotist.

Sports: There are 8 intercollegiate sports for men and 7 for women, and 8 intramural sports for men and 8 for women. Facilities include a field house with a full-size basketball court and 2 practice courts, a fitness center, a weight room, softball and soccer fields, a swimming pool, a Nautilus/weight room, racquetball and tennis courts, and a fitness trail.

Disabled Students: 95% of the campus is accessible. Wheelchair ramps, elevators, special parking, specially equipped rest rooms, lowered drinking fountains, lowered telephones, and ADA-compliant signage and reception counters are available.

Services: Counseling and information services are available, as is tutoring in most subjects. There is remedial math, reading, and writing.

Campus Safety and Security: Measures include 24-hour foot and vehicle patrol, self-defense education, security escort services, and shuttle buses. There are informal discussions, pamphlets/posters/films, emergency telephones, lighted pathways/sidewalks, and and "Call A Ride And Live" (CARAL).

Programs of Study: ERAU confers the B.S. degree. Associate and master's degrees are also awarded. Bachelor's degrees are awarded in BUSINESS (business administration and management and transportation management), COMMUNICATIONS AND THE ARTS (communications), COMPUTER AND PHYSICAL SCIENCE (atmospheric sciences and meteorology, computer science, and software engineering), ENGINEERING AND ENVIRONMENTAL DESIGN (aeronautical engineering, aeronautical science, aeronautical technology, aerospace studies, air traffic control, aviation maintenance management, civil engineering, computer engineering, computer graphics, electrical/electronics engineering, engineering physics, and engineering technology), SOCIAL SCIENCE (safety science). Aerospace engineering is the strongest academically. Aeronautical science (flight) is the largest.

Required: To graduate, students must complete a total of 120 to 136 credit hours, including 60 in the major, with a minimum GPA of 2.0. All students must complete 36 credits of general education requirements, including courses in communication skills, technical report writing, humanities/social sciences, math, physical science, economics, and computer science.

Special: ERAU offers co-op programs and internships in all majors, study abroad in 21countries, work-study programs, credit for life experience, and nondegree study. There are 6 national honor societies, and a freshman honors program.

Faculty/Classroom: 77% of faculty are male; 23%, female. All teach undergraduates, 8% do research, and 8% do both. No introductory courses are taught by graduate students. The average class size in an introductory lecture is 29; in a laboratory, 10; and in a regular course, 27.

Admissions: 84% of the 2005-2006 applicants were accepted. The SAT scores for the 2005-2006 freshman class were: Verbal--31% below 500, 44% between 500 and 599, 22% between 600 and 700, and 4% above 700; Math--18% below 500, 41% between 500 and 599, 34% between 600 and 700, and 7% above 700. The ACT scores were 24% below 21, 27% between 21 and 23, 24% between 24 and 26, 14% between 27 and 28, and 11% above 28. 40% of the current freshmen were in the top fifth of their class; 68% were in the top two fifths. 48 freshmen graduated first in their class.

Requirements: The SAT or ACT is required. In addition, students should complete a competitive academic program in high school, including 16 Carnegie units with at least 3 years of math. Admissions decisions are based on the strength of the academic record, rank in class, standardized test scores, recommendations, and the written statement. AP and CLEP credits are accepted. Important factors in the admissions decision are advanced placement or honor courses, recommendations by school officials, and evidence of special talent.

Procedure: Freshmen are admitted to all sessions. Entrance exams should be taken during spring of the junior year or fall of the senior year. Early decision applications should be filed by December 1; regular applications, by July 1 for fall entry, November 1 for spring entry, and April 1 for summer entry. Notification of early decision is sent December; regular decision, on a rolling basis. Applications are accepted on-line.

Transfer: 260 transfer students enrolled in 2004-2005. A GPA of 2.5 is preferred. 30 of 120 to 136 credits required for the bachelor's degree must be completed at ERAU.

Visiting: There are regularly scheduled orientations for prospective students. There are guides for informal visits and visitors may sit in on classes and stay overnight. To schedule a visit, contact the Admissions Office at (386) 226-6100 or *dbadmit@erau.edu.*

Financial Aid: In 2005-2006, 95% of all full-time freshmen and 78% of continuing full-time students received some form of financial aid. 59% of full-time freshmen and 80% of continuing full-time students received need-based aid. The average freshman award was $21,885. Need-based scholarships or need-based grants averaged $3515 ($11,200 maximum); need-based self-help aid (loans and jobs) averaged $3340 ($3500 maximum); non-need-based athletic scholarships averaged $12,006 ($22,820 maximum); and other non-need-based awards and non-need-based scholarships averaged $21,006 ($39,689 maximum). 35% of undergraduates work part time. Average annual earnings from campus work are $1635. The average financial indebtedness of the 2005 graduate was $52,276. The FAFSA is required. The deadline for filing freshman financial aid applications for fall entry is April 15.

International Students: There are 302 international students enrolled. The school actively recruits these students. They must take the written TOEFL and also take the SAT or the ACT.

Computers: Wireless access is available. All students may access the system at any time. There are no time limits and no fees. It is recommended that students in the computer science program have personal computers.

Graduates: From July 1, 2004 to June 30, 2005, 844 bachelor's degrees were awarded. The most popular majors were aerospace engineering (31%), aeronautical science (30%), and air traffic management (7%). In an average class, 31% graduate in 4 years or less, 54% graduate in 5 years or less, and 58% graduate in 6 years or less. 175 companies recruited on campus in 2004-2005. Of the 2004 graduating class, 20% were enrolled in graduate school within 6 months of graduation and 87% were employed.

Admissions Contact: Director of Admissions. A video is available. E-mail: dbadmit@db.erau.edu Web: www.embryriddle.edu

FLAGLER COLLEGE   D-2

St. Augustine, FL 32084   (904) 829-6481
                                          (800) 304-4208; Fax: (904) 826-0094

Full-time: 797 men, 1297 women	Faculty: 79
Part-time: 28 men, 35 women	Ph.D.s: 62%
Graduate: none	Student/Faculty: 27 to 1
Year: semesters, summer session	Tuition: $8600
Application Deadline: March 1	Room & Board: $5190
Freshman Class: 2248 applied, 560 accepted, 458 enrolled	
SAT Verbal/Math: 570/560*	ACT: 24 VERY COMPETITIVE+

Flagler College, founded in 1968, is an independent liberal arts college that emphasizes undergraduate education in select liberal and preprofessional studies. The library contains 85,654 volumes, 69,158 microform items, and 3516 audio/video tapes/CDs/DVDs, and subscribes to 464 periodicals including electronic. Computerized library services include the card catalog, interlibrary loans, database searching, Internet access, and laptop Internet portals. Special learning facilities include a learning resource center, art gallery, and radio station. The 35-acre campus is in a small town 35 miles south of Jacksonville and 45 miles north of Daytona Beach. Including any residence halls, there are 16 buildings.

Student Life: 67% of undergraduates are from Florida. Others are from 45 states, 34 foreign countries, and Canada. 78% are from public schools. 90% are white. The average age of freshmen is 18; all undergraduates, 21. 27% do not continue beyond their first year; 54% remain to graduate.

Housing: 820 students can be accommodated in college housing, which includes single-sex dorms. On-campus housing is guaranteed for the freshman year only and is available on a first-come, first-served basis. 62% of students commute. Alcohol is not permitted. All students may keep cars.

Activities: There are no fraternities or sororities. There are 37 groups on campus, including art, cheerleading, choir, film, honors, international, literary magazine, newspaper, photography, political, professional, radio and TV, religious, social, social service, and student government. Popular campus events include Spring and Fall Formal Dance, Family Weekend, and tailgating.

Sports: There are 6 intercollegiate sports for men and 6 for women, and 35 intramural sports for men and 35 for women. Facilities include a 17-acre complex for baseball and soccer, 8 tennis courts, a swimming pool, a multipurpose gym, and an outdoor volleyball court.

Disabled Students: 80% of the campus is accessible. Wheelchair ramps, elevators, special parking, specially equipped rest rooms, lowered drinking fountains, lowered telephones, and special housing are available.

Services: Counseling and information services are available. Tutoring is available only by referral and based upon private contract between tutor and student. There is a reader service for the blind, and remedial math, reading, and writing.

Campus Safety and Security: Measures include 24-hour foot and vehicle patrol, self-defense education, informal discussions, and pamphlets/posters/films. There are emergency telephones, lighted pathways/sidewalks, and 2 full-time uniformed police officers.

Programs of Study: Flagler confers B.A., and B.F.A. degrees. Bachelor's degrees are awarded in BUSINESS (accounting, business administration and management, and sports management), COMMUNICATIONS AND THE ARTS (communications, dramatic arts, English, fine arts, graphic design, and Spanish), EDUCATION (art, education of the deaf and hearing impaired, education of the exceptional child, elementary, and secondary), SOCIAL SCIENCE (history, Latin American studies, liberal arts/general studies, philosophy, political science/government, psychology, religion, and sociology). Business, liberal studies, and arts are the strongest academically. Business, communications, and education are the largest.

Required: To graduate, students must complete a minimum of 120 semester hours, including 30 to 90 hours in the major, with a minimum GPA of 2.0. All students must take 6 hours in English composition, 6 hours in math, and 3 hours in speech communication. In addition, students must take 15 hours of courses required by the general education

program in humanities, social sciences, and math/natural sciences. Students must demonstrate basic computer skills and complete a career planning program.

Special: The school offers internships, work-study, and dual majors. Students may participate in study-abroad programs in almost any country. Students majoring in deaf education can work directly with students at the Florida State School for the Deaf and Blind. There are 7 national honor societies, and 5 departmental honors programs.

Faculty/Classroom: 51% of faculty are male; 49%, female. All teach undergraduates. The average class size in an introductory lecture is 30; in a laboratory, 12; and in a regular course, 21.

Admissions: 25% of the 2005-2006 applicants were accepted. The SAT scores for the 2005-2006 freshman class were: Verbal--6% below 500, 58% between 500 and 599, 31% between 600 and 700, and 5% above 700; Math--13% below 500, 61% between 500 and 599, 22% between 600 and 700, and 4% above 700. The ACT scores were 8% below 21, 39% between 21 and 23, 35% between 24 and 26, 13% between 27 and 28, and 5% above 28. 39% of the current freshmen were in the top fifth of their class; 76% were in the top two fifths. 6 freshmen graduated first in their class.

Requirements: The SAT or ACT is required. In addition, graduation from an accredited secondary school, or a satisfactory score on the GED, is required for admission. Students must have a total of 19 academic credits. High school courses must include 4 credits of English, 3 credits each of math and science, and 2 credits of a foreign language. An essay is required, and an interview is recommended. Flagler requires applicants to be in the upper 50% of their class. A GPA of 2.85 is required. AP and CLEP credits are accepted. Important factors in the admissions decision are advanced placement or honor courses, leadership record, and extracurricular activities record.

Procedure: Freshmen are admitted fall and spring. Entrance exams should be taken during the fall of the senior year at the latest. There are early decision and deferred admissions plans. Early decision applications should be filed by January 15; regular applications, by March 1 for fall entry and October 15 for winter entry, along with a $30 fee. Notification of early decision is sent February 1; regular decision, March 15. 347 early decision candidates were accepted for the 2005-2006 class. ; 44 were admitted. Applications are accepted on-line.

Transfer: 95 transfer students enrolled in 2004-2005. Transfer students must have a minimum of 24 semester hours with a satisfactory GPA. Transfers must also present satisfactory scores from the SAT or ACT. 45 of 120 credits required for the bachelor's degree must be completed at Flagler.

Visiting: There are guides for informal visits and visitors may sit in on classes and stay overnight. To schedule a visit, contact the Office of Admissions at admiss@flagler.edu.

Financial Aid: In 2005-2006, 85% of all full-time freshmen and 86% of continuing full-time students received some form of financial aid. 31% of full-time freshmen and 35% of continuing full-time students received need-based aid. The average freshman award was $8381. Need-based scholarships or need-based grants averaged $3168 ($8600 maximum); need-based self-help aid (loans and jobs) averaged $2838 ($6525 maximum); non-need-based athletic scholarships averaged $3602 ($13,790 maximum); and other non-need-based awards and non-need-based scholarships averaged $6906 ($14,145 maximum). 60% of undergraduates work part time. Average annual earnings from campus work are $487. The average financial indebtedness of the 2005 graduate was $14,791. The FAFSA and the college's own financial statement are required. The deadline for filing freshman financial aid applications for fall entry is April 1.

International Students: There are 57 international students enrolled. A satisfactory score is required on the written TOEFL.

Computers: Wireless access is available. All dorm rooms are wired to the Internet and Intranet. There are 150 PCs and 70 Macs in the library for student use. All are Internet accessible. Students can plug in their own laptops in the library for Internet access. All students may access the system during library hours. There are no time limits and no fees.

Graduates: From July 1, 2004 to June 30, 2005, 438 bachelor's degrees were awarded. The most popular majors were business administration (26%), communication (22%), and education (14%). In an average class, 42% graduate in 4 years or less, 53% graduate in 5 years or less, and 54% graduate in 6 years or less. 72 companies recruited on campus in 2004-2005. Of the 2004 graduating class, 20% were enrolled in graduate school within 6 months of graduation and 65% were employed.

Admissions Contact: Marc G. Williar, Director of Admissions. A video is available. E-mail: admiss@flagler.edu Web: www.flagler.edu

FLORIDA AGRICULTURAL AND MECHANICAL UNIVERSITY   C-1

Tallahassee, FL 32307-3200

(850) 599-3796
Fax: (850) 599-3069

Full-time: 4055 men, 5520 women
Part-time: 542 men, 689 women
Graduate: 503 men, 874 women
Year: semesters, summer session
Application Deadline: May 15
Freshman Class: 4507 applied, 3220 accepted, 1459 enrolled
SAT or ACT: required

Faculty: n/av
Ph.D.s: n/av
Student/Faculty: n/av
Tuition: $3297 ($15,286)
Room & Board: $5047

COMPETITIVE

Florida Agricultural and Mechanical University, founded in 1887 and a public institution within the state university system of Florida, offers undergraduate programs in agriculture, allied health science, architecture, the arts and sciences, business and industry, education, engineering, journalism, pharmacy and pharmaceutical sciences, upper-level nursing, and technology. There are 14 undergraduate schools and 1 graduate school. In addition to regional accreditation, Florida A&M has baccalaureate program accreditation with AACSB, ABET, ACEJMC, ACPE, APTA, CSWE, NAAB, NCATE, and NLN. The 6 libraries contain 781,408 volumes, 171,926 microform items, and 75,622 audio/video tapes/CDs/DVDs, and subscribe to 10,137 periodicals including electronic. Computerized library services include the card catalog, interlibrary loans, database searching, and Internet access. Special learning facilities include a learning resource center, art gallery, radio station, TV station, and black archives, and an observatory. The 422-acre campus is in an urban area 169 miles east of Jacksonville. Including any residence halls, there are 155 buildings.
Student Life: 75% of undergraduates are from Florida. Students are from 46 states, 49 foreign countries, and Canada. 95% are from public schools. 93% are African American. The average age of freshmen is 19; all undergraduates, 22. 20% do not continue beyond their first year.
Housing: 3356 students can be accommodated in college housing, which includes single-sex dorms, on-campus apartments, and married-student housing. On-campus housing is guaranteed for the freshman year only and is available on a first-come, first-served basis. Priority is given to out-of-town students. 51% of students commute. Alcohol is not permitted. Upperclassmen may keep cars.
Activities: There are 5 national fraternities and 4 national sororities. There are 147 groups on campus, including cheerleading, choir, chorus, dance, drama, drill team, ethnic, honors, international, jazz band, marching band, newspaper, orchestra, pep band, political, professional, radio and TV, religious, social, social service, student government, symphony, and yearbook. Popular campus events include FAMU Essen-Theater, FAMU Orchesis Dance Theater, and Ebony Fashion Fair.
Sports: There are 9 intercollegiate sports for men and 8 for women and 14 intramural sports for women. Facilities include a 3300-seat gym, a 1600-seat auditorium, a 25,559-seat football stadium, swimming pools, baseball diamonds, softball and track fields, tennis courts, a bowling alley, a pool hall, a student activities center, and a fitness center.
Disabled Students: 90% of the campus is accessible. Wheelchair ramps, elevators, special parking, and specially equipped rest rooms are available.
Services: Counseling and information services are available, as is tutoring in some subjects, including math, English, and reading. There is remedial math, reading, and writing.
Campus Safety and Security: Measures include 24-hour foot and vehicle patrol, self-defense education, security escort services, and informal discussions. There are pamphlets/posters/films and lighted pathways/sidewalks.
Programs of Study: Florida A&M confers B.A., B.S., B.Arch., B.C.J., B.S.Arch. and Constr.E.T., B.S.Arch.E.T., B.S.Studies., B.S.C.E., B.S.C.E.T., B.S.Ch.E., B.S.Constr.E.T., B.S.E.E., B.S.Elect.E.T., B.S.H.C.M., B.S.I.E., B.S.J., B.S.M.E., B.S.M.R.A., B.S.N., B.S.Pharm., B.S.P.T., B.S.R.T., B.S.T., and B.S.W. degrees. Associate, master's, and doctoral degrees are also awarded. Bachelor's degrees are awarded in AGRICULTURE (animal science and horticulture), BIOLOGICAL SCIENCE (biology/biological science), BUSINESS (accounting, banking and finance, business administration and management, and business economics), COMMUNICATIONS AND THE ARTS (dramatic arts, English, fine arts, journalism, and music), COMPUTER AND PHYSICAL SCIENCE (actuarial science, chemistry, computer science, mathematics, and physics), EDUCATION (art, business, early childhood, elementary, industrial arts, music, and science), ENGINEERING AND ENVIRONMENTAL DESIGN (chemical engineering, civil engineering, electrical/electronics engineering, engineering technology, industrial engineering, and mechanical engineering), HEALTH PROFESSIONS (nursing, occupational therapy, pharmacy, physical therapy, predentistry, and premedicine), SOCIAL SCIENCE (criminal justice, economics, history, political science/government, psychology, public administration, social science, social work, and sociology). Business, engineering, and pharmacy are the strongest academically. Business, pharmacy, and arts and sciences are the largest.

Required: General education requirements include 36 credit hours in English, humanities, social science, natural science, American history, foreign language, and math at the college algebra level or above. In order to graduate, students must complete at least 120 credit hours, including 30 in a major field, with a minimum GPA of 2.0.
Special: Cooperative programs and cross-registration are offered in conjunction with Florida State University. Internships are available either on or off campus. Florida A&M also offers a Washington semester for architecture majors, a B.A.-B.S. degree, credit for life experience, and pass/fail options. Nondegree study is possible. There are 10 national honor societies and a freshman honors program.
Admissions: 71% of the 2005-2006 applicants were accepted.
Requirements: A satisfactory score on the SAT or ACT is required. Applicants must be graduates of accredited secondary schools or have earned a GED. The university requires 19 academic credits, including 4 each in English and academic electives, 3 each in math, science, and social studies, and 2 in foreign language. A GPA of 2.0 is required. AP and CLEP credits are accepted. Important factors in the admissions decision are recommendations by school officials, extracurricular activities record, and evidence of special talent.
Procedure: Freshmen are admitted to all sessions. Entrance exams should be taken by the fall of the senior year. There is a deferred admissions and a rolling admissions plan. Applications should be filed by May 15 for fall entry, November 15 for spring entry, and April 1 for summer entry. The fall 2005 application fee was $20. Notification is sent on a rolling basis.
Transfer: Applicants must present a minimum GPA of 2.0 in at least 60 semester hours or 90 quarter hours earned. 30 of 120 credits required for the bachelor's degree must be completed at Florida A&M.
Visiting: There are regularly scheduled orientations for prospective students. There are guides for informal visits and visitors may sit in on classes. To schedule a visit, contact Ms. Sheryl Cooper at (850) 599-3869.
Financial Aid: 1% of undergraduates work part time. Average annual earnings from campus work are $1800. The average financial indebtedness of a recent graduate was $23,000. The university prefers the FAFSA but will accept the CSS Profile. The priority date for freshman financial aid applications for fall entry is March 1. The deadline for filing freshman financial aid applications for fall entry is June 30.
International Students: In a recent year, there are 113 international students enrolled. Satisfactory score are required on the written TOEFL and the SAT or the ACT.
Computers: All students may access the system. There are no time limits and no fees.
Graduates: From July 1, 2004 to June 30, 2005, 1328 bachelor's degrees were awarded. The most popular majors were business administration (18%), psychology (7%), and elementary education (7%). 600 companies recruited on campus in 2004-2005.
Admissions Contact: Barbara Cox, Director.
E-mail: *barbara.cox@famu.edu* Web: *www.famu.edu*

FLORIDA ATLANTIC UNIVERSITY   E-5

Boca Raton, FL 33431-0991

(561) 297-3040
(800) 299-4FAU; Fax: (561) 297-2758

Full-time: 4967 men, 6843 women
Part-time: 3564 men, 6131 women
Graduate: 1532 men, 2667 women
Year: semesters, summer session
Application Deadline: June 1
Freshman Class: 10,363 applied, 5505 accepted, 2478 enrolled
SAT Verbal/Math: 528/530*

Faculty: 1065; I, --$
Ph.D.s: 86%
Student/Faculty: 11 to 1
Tuition: $3259 ($16,391)
Room & Board: $7962
ACT: 22

COMPETITIVE

Florida Atlantic University, founded in 1961, is a publicly funded liberal arts institution in the state university system of Florida. There are 8 undergraduate and 8 graduate schools. In addition to regional accreditation, FAU has baccalaureate program accreditation with AACSB, ABET, ACS, ASLHA, CSAB, CSWE, NAAB, NAACLS, NASM, NASPAA, NCATE, and NLN. The library contains 2,066,155 volumes, 2,074,770 microform items, and 22,414 audio/video tapes/CDs/DVDs, and subscribes to 12,549 periodicals including electronic. Computerized library services include the card catalog, interlibrary loans, database searching, Internet access, and laptop Internet portals. Special learning facilities include a learning resource center, art gallery, radio station, TV station, engineering research labs, a marine sciences research center, a K-8 developmental research school, a nonnative fish research lab, and an environmental sciences center. The 860-acre campus is in a suburban area 17 miles north of Ft. Lauderdale, 45 miles north of Miami, and 22 miles south of Palm Beach. Including any residence halls, there are 88 buildings.
Student Life: 94% of undergraduates are from Florida. Students are from 49 states, 141 foreign countries, and Canada. 71% are from public schools. 58% are white; 17% African American; 16% Hispanic. The average age of freshmen is 18; all undergraduates, 25. 31% do not continue beyond their first year; 37% remain to graduate.

Housing: 2500 students can be accommodated in college housing, which includes single-sex and coed dorms, on-campus apartments, and married-student housing. In addition, there are honors houses, wellness and quiet floors, and apartments for students age 21 and older. On-campus housing is guaranteed for the freshman year only and is available on a first-come, first-served basis. 92% of students commute. All students may keep cars.

Activities: 1% of men belong to 12 national fraternities; 1% of women belong to 9 national sororities. There are 185 groups on campus, including art, band, cheerleading, chess, choir, chorale, chorus, computers, dance, drama, ethnic, film, gay, honors, international, jazz band, literary magazine, marching band, musical theater, newspaper, opera, orchestra, pep band, political, professional, radio and TV, religious, social, social service, and student government. Popular campus events include Luau, African American Festival, and Festival of Nations.

Sports: There are 8 intercollegiate sports for men and 9 for women, and 10 intramural sports for men and 10 for women. Facilities include an athletic center, a gym, a weight room, baseball and softball stadiums, a lighted soccer field, a 25-meter swimming pool with 1- and 10-meter diving boards, lighted outdoor jai alai, a dance area, and 8 tennis, 5 racquetball, 4 badminton, 3 volleyball, and 2 basketball courts.

Disabled Students: All of the campus is accessible. Wheelchair ramps, elevators, special parking, specially equipped rest rooms, lowered drinking fountains, and lowered telephones are available.

Services: Counseling and information services are available, as is tutoring in most subjects. There is a reader service for the blind. Remedial work must be taken at the community college level.

Campus Safety and Security: Measures include 24-hour foot and vehicle patrol, self-defense education, security escort services, and shuttle buses. There are informal discussions, pamphlets/posters/films, emergency telephones, and lighted pathways/sidewalks.

Programs of Study: FAU confers B.A., B.S., B.A.E., B.Arch., B.B.A., B.F.A., B.H.S., B.Mus., B.P.M., B.S.C.E., B.S.C.V., B.S.E., B.S.E.E., B.S.H.S., B.S.M.E., B.S.M.T., B.S.N., B.S.O.E., B.S.W., and B.U.R.P. degrees. Associate, master's, and doctoral degrees are also awarded. Bachelor's degrees are awarded in BIOLOGICAL SCIENCE (biology/biological science and marine biology), BUSINESS (accounting, banking and finance, business administration and management, hospitality management services, human resources, international business management, marketing/retailing/merchandising, real estate, and small business management), COMMUNICATIONS AND THE ARTS (art, communications, dramatic arts, English, fine arts, French, German, graphic design, Italian, journalism, linguistics, multimedia, music, Spanish, and visual and performing arts), COMPUTER AND PHYSICAL SCIENCE (chemistry, computer science, geology, information sciences and systems, mathematics, and physics), EDUCATION (elementary, English, foreign languages, physical, and special), ENGINEERING AND ENVIRONMENTAL DESIGN (architecture, civil engineering, computer engineering, electrical/electronics engineering, mechanical engineering, ocean engineering, and urban planning technology), HEALTH PROFESSIONS (health care administration, health science, medical laboratory technology, and nursing), SOCIAL SCIENCE (anthropology, criminal justice, economics, geography, history, interdisciplinary studies, Judaic studies, liberal arts/general studies, philosophy, political science/government, psychobiology, psychology, public administration, social psychology, social science, social work, and sociology). Engineering, education, and business are the strongest academically. Elementary education, biological science, and management are the largest.

Required: All students must take the College Level Academic Skills Test (CLAST) required by the state. To graduate, students must complete a total of 120 credit hours, with a minimum GPA of 2.0. All students must take the required courses in the core curriculum, including 9 credits each of humanities and social sciences and 6 each of math, communication, and natural sciences, and must demonstrate proficiency in a foreign language.

Special: FAU offers cooperative programs and internships in most majors. Work-study programs, dual and student-designed majors, a general studies degree, credit for military experience, nondegree study, and pass/fail options are available. The school offers a Washington semester, study abroad through all state university system of Florida programs, and an exchange program in ocean engineering with the Polytechnic University of Madrid, Spain; there is also a study abroad center in Salamanca, Spain. Cross-registration is available with all Florida state universities, in science and engineering with Palm Beach and Broward Community Colleges, and in military science with the University of Miami. Students may earn a second baccalaureate degree with 30 additional hours in a number of subjects. There are 15 national honor societies, a freshman honors program, and 9 departmental honors programs.

Faculty/Classroom: 61% of faculty are male; 39%, female. All both teach and do research. Graduate students teach 5% of introductory courses. The average class size in an introductory lecture is 50; in a laboratory, 15; and in a regular course, 25.

Admissions: 53% of the 2005-2006 applicants were accepted. The SAT scores for the 2005-2006 freshman class were: Verbal--36% below 500, 48% between 500 and 599, 14% between 600 and 700, and 2%

above 700; Math--34% below 500, 49% between 500 and 599, 16% between 600 and 700, and 3% above 700. The ACT scores were 40% below 21, 35% between 21 and 23, 16% between 24 and 26, 6% between 27 and 28, and 3% above 28. There was 1 National Merit finalist.

Requirements: A minimum composite score on the SAT or ACT is required. In addition, graduation from an accredited secondary school or satisfactory scores on the GED are required. Students must have 19 academic credits, including 4 units of English, 3 each of math (algebra I and higher), science (including 2 with substantial lab work), and social studies, and 2 of a foreign language, plus 4 of electives in computer science, fine arts, or humanities. A portfolio or an audition may be requested by individual departments. An essay and an interview are required. A GPA of 2.0 is required. AP and CLEP credits are accepted. Important factors in the admissions decision are advanced placement or honor courses, evidence of special talent, and recommendations by school officials.

Procedure: Freshmen are admitted to all sessions. Entrance exams should be taken by June. There are early decision, early admissions, and deferred admissions plans. There is a rolling admissions plan. Applications should be filed by June 1 for fall entry, October 15 for spring entry, and March 15 for summer entry. The fall 2005 application fee was $20. Notification is sent on a rolling basis. 33 early decision candidates were accepted for the 2005-2006 class. Applications are accepted on-line.

Transfer: Students must have a minimum GPA of 2.0, submit official transcripts from the previous schools attended, and be in good standing at those institutions. Applicants from a community or junior college in Florida with an associate degree are automatically admitted. Students with fewer than 60 transferable hours must meet the same criteria as entering freshmen. 30 of 120 credits required for the bachelor's degree must be completed at FAU.

Visiting: There are regularly scheduled orientations for prospective students, consisting of a group tour. There are guides for informal visits. To schedule a visit, contact the Admissions Office.

Financial Aid: FAU is a member of CSS. The FAFSA is required. The deadline for filing freshman financial aid applications for fall entry is March 1.

International Students: There are 484 international students enrolled. The school actively recruits these students. They must take the TOEFL, achieving a satisfactory score, and also take the SAT or the ACT.

Computers: All students may access the system. Labs are open from 8 A.M. to 11 P.M. weekdays and various hours on weekends. There are no time limits and no fees.

Graduates: From July 1, 2004 to June 30, 2005, 4022 bachelor's degrees were awarded. The most popular majors were elementary education (9%), management (7%), and marketing (7%). In an average class, 15% graduate in 4 years or less, 32% graduate in 5 years or less, and 37% graduate in 6 years or less. 200 companies recruited on campus in 2004-2005.

Admissions Contact: Barbar Pletcher, Acting Director of Admissions. A video is available. E-mail: *admisweb@fau.edu* Web: *www.fau.edu*

FLORIDA GULF COAST UNIVERSITY   H-6
Fort Myers, FL 33965-6565   (239) 590-7891
                                        (888) 889-1095; Fax: (239) 590-7894

Full-time: 1752 men, 2849 women	**Faculty:** 253; IIA, --$
Part-time: 533 men, 984 women	**Ph.D.s:** 78%
Graduate: 344 men, 767 women	**Student/Faculty:** 18 to 1
Year: semesters, summer session	**Tuition:** $3373 ($15,361)
Application Deadline: June 1	**Room & Board:** $7460
Freshman Class: 3449 applied, 2617 accepted, 1343 enrolled	
SAT Verbal/Math: 510/520*	**ACT:** 21 **COMPETITIVE**

Florida Gulf Coast University, founded in 1991, is part of the State University System of Florida. There are 5 undergraduate schools. In addition to regional accreditation, FGCU has baccalaureate program accreditation with APTA, CAPTE, CSWE, and NLN. The library contains 176,898 volumes, 556,214 microform items, and 2940 audio/video tapes/CDs/DVDs, and subscribes to 2638 periodicals including electronic. Computerized library services include the card catalog, interlibrary loans, database searching, Internet access, and laptop Internet portals. Special learning facilities include a learning resource center, art gallery, radio station, TV station, chickee huts, computer labs, and a family resource center. The 760-acre campus is in a rural area in southwest Florida in southern Lee County. Including any residence halls, there are 69 buildings.

Student Life: 90% of undergraduates are from Florida. Others are from 47 states, 73 foreign countries, and Canada. 80% are white. The average age of freshmen is 19; all undergraduates, 24. 28% do not continue beyond their first year; 37% remain to graduate.

Housing: 1948 students can be accommodated in college housing, which includes coed on-campus apartments. On-campus housing is available on a first-come, first-served basis. 70% of students commute. Alcohol is not permitted. All students may keep cars.

Activities: 1% of men belong to 3 national fraternities; 1% of women belong to 3 national sororities. There are 106 groups on campus, including cheerleading, chess, choir, dance, debate, drama, ethnic, honors, international, newspaper, professional, religious, social, social service, student government, and yearbook. Popular campus events include Jazz on the Green, Eagle Expo, and University lecture series featuring Mikhail Gorbachev.

Sports: There are 6 intercollegiate sports for men and 7 for women, and 9 intramural sports for men and 9 for women. Facilities include a fitness center, a lakefront, a 4500-seat teaching gym, 2 playing fields, and 12 tennis courts.

Disabled Students: All of the campus is accessible. Wheelchair ramps, elevators, special parking, specially equipped rest rooms, special class scheduling, lowered drinking fountains, lowered telephones, and special housing are available.

Services: Counseling and information services are available, as is tutoring in most subjects.

Campus Safety and Security: Measures include 24-hour foot and vehicle patrol, self-defense education, security escort services, and shuttle buses. There are informal discussions, pamphlets/posters/films, emergency telephones, and lighted pathways/sidewalks.

Programs of Study: FGCU confers B.A., and B.S. degrees. Associate and master's degrees are also awarded. Bachelor's degrees are awarded in BIOLOGICAL SCIENCE (biotechnology), BUSINESS (accounting, banking and finance, business administration and management, management information systems, management science, and marketing and distribution), COMPUTER AND PHYSICAL SCIENCE (computer science and information sciences and systems), EDUCATION (athletic training, early childhood, elementary, secondary, and special), ENGINEERING AND ENVIRONMENTAL DESIGN (engineering), HEALTH PROFESSIONS (community health work, health, health science, nursing, occupational therapy, and physical therapy), SOCIAL SCIENCE (anthropology, criminal justice, criminology, human services, liberal arts/general studies, paralegal studies, political science/government, public affairs, social work, and sociology). Management and criminal justice are the largest.

Required: To graduate, students must have a 2.0 minimum GPA and 120 credit hours that include courses in phys ed, computer science, general education, service learning, and university colloquium.

Special: The university offers cross-registration with the University of Central Florida, study abroad in China, a Washington semester, and work-study programs. There is 1 national honor society (Phi Beta Kappa), a freshman honors program, and 1 departmental honors program.

Faculty/Classroom: 53% of faculty are male; 47%, female. All both teach and do research. No introductory courses are taught by graduate students. The average class size in an introductory lecture is 26; in a laboratory, 23; and in a regular course, 24.

Admissions: 76% of the 2005-2006 applicants were accepted. The SAT scores for the 2005-2006 freshman class were: Verbal--40% below 500, 48% between 500 and 599, 11% between 600 and 700, and 1% above 700; Math--36% below 500, 49% between 500 and 599, 14% between 600 and 700, and 1% above 700. The ACT scores were 44% below 21, 34% between 21 and 23, 16% between 24 and 26, 4% between 27 and 28, and 2% above 28. 39% of the current freshmen were in the top fifth of their class; 71% were in the top two fifths. 3 freshmen graduated first in their class.

Requirements: The SAT or ACT is recommended. A GPA of 2.0 is required. AP and CLEP credits are accepted. Important factors in the admissions decision are recommendations by school officials, leadership record, and evidence of special talent.

Procedure: Freshmen are admitted fall, spring, and summer. Entrance exams should be taken in the junior year. There is a deferred admissions plan. Applications should be filed by June 1 for fall entry, October 15 for spring entry, and March 1 for summer entry, along with a $30 fee. Applications are accepted on-line.

Transfer: 730 transfer students enrolled in 2004-2005. Lower-level transfers must meet the same requirements as regular admissions. Upper-level transfers must have a 2.0 GPA and 60 hours of transferable credit and be in good standing at their last institution. 30 of 120 credits required for the bachelor's degree must be completed at FGCU.

Visiting: There are regularly scheduled orientations for prospective students. There are guides for informal visits and visitors may sit in on classes. To schedule a visit, contact the Admissions Office at (888) 889-1095 or (239) 590-7878 or admissions@fgcu.edu.

Financial Aid: In 2005-2006, 82% of all full-time freshmen and 72% of continuing full-time students received some form of financial aid. 27% of full-time freshmen and 33% of continuing full-time students received need-based aid. The average freshman award was $6014. Need-based scholarships or need-based grants averaged $3048 ($7650 maximum); need-based self-help aid (loans and jobs) averaged $2328 ($6393 maximum); non-need-based athletic scholarships averaged $3841 ($10,359 maximum); and other non-need-based awards and non-need-based scholarships averaged $4571 ($15,561 maximum). 80% of undergraduates work part time. Average annual earnings from campus work are

$2015. The average financial indebtedness of the 2005 graduate was $13,245. FGCU is a member of CSS. The FAFSA is required. The deadline for filing freshman financial aid applications for fall entry is March 15.

International Students: There are 58 international students enrolled. The school actively recruits these students. They must achieve a satisfactory score on the TOEFL and also take the SAT or the ACT.

Computers: More than 300 computers are available in labs throughout the campus, and T1 connections are available in dorms. Wireless connections throughout the campus are available. All students may access the system any time. There are no time limits and no fees.

Graduates: From July 1, 2004 to June 30, 2005, 832 bachelor's degrees were awarded. The most popular majors were liberal arts/liberal studies (34%), elementary education (12%), and nursing (10%). In an average class, 1% graduate in 3 years or less, 12% graduate in 4 years or less, 26% graduate in 5 years or less, and 37% graduate in 6 years or less. Of the 2004 graduating class, 17% were enrolled in graduate school within 6 months of graduation and 77% were employed.

Admissions Contact: Marc Maviolette, Director of Admissions. E-mail: oar@fgcu.edu Web: http://www.fgcu.edu

FLORIDA HOSPITAL COLLEGE OF HEALTH SCIENCES

D-3

Orlando, FL 32803

(407) 303-9798
(800) 500-7747; Fax: (407) 303-9408

Full-time: 5 men, 31 women	Faculty: 49
Part-time: 193 men, 792 women	Ph.Ds: 5%
Graduate: none	Student/Faculty: 22 to 1
Year: semesters, summer session	Tuition: $5770
Application Deadline: July 18	Room & Board: $5382
Freshman Class: n/av	
SAT or ACT: required	SPECIAL

Florida Hospital College of Health Sciences, founded in 1992 and affiliated with the Seventh-day Adventist Church, is a private institution offering associate and baccalaureate degrees in nursing and allied health. Students can also take a variety of general education and prerequisite courses and then transfer to an institution offering degrees that FHCHS does not offer. In addition to regional accreditation, Florida Hospital College of Health Sciences has baccalaureate program accreditation with NLN and JRCERT. The library contains 15,298 volumes and 1835 audio/video tapes/CDs/DVDs, and subscribes to 12,850 periodicals including electronic. Computerized library services include the card catalog, interlibrary loans, database searching, and Internet access. Special learning facilities include a learning resource center and student success center. The 9-acre campus is in an urban area Orlando. Including any residence halls, there are 6 buildings.

Student Life: 74% are white; 10% African American. The average age of freshmen is 37.

Housing: 130 students can be accommodated in college housing, which includes single-sex off-campus apartments. Housing is available on a first-come, first-served basis. Priority is given to out-of-town students. 90% of students commute. Alcohol is not permitted. No one may keep cars.

Activities: There are no fraternities or sororities. There are some groups and organizations on campus, including drama, newspaper, religious, and student government.

Sports: There are 3 intramural sports for men and 3 for women.

Disabled Students: All of the campus is accessible. Wheelchair ramps, elevators, special parking, specially equipped rest rooms, special class scheduling, lowered drinking fountains, lowered telephones, and special housing are available.

Services: Counseling and information services are available, as is tutoring in most subjects. There is remedial math and writing.

Campus Safety and Security: Measures include 24-hour foot and vehicle patrol, security escort services, shuttle buses, and informal discussions. There are pamphlets/posters/films and lighted pathways/sidewalks.

Programs of Study: Florida Hospital College of Health Sciences confers the B.S. degree. Associate degrees are also awarded. Bachelor's degrees are awarded in HEALTH PROFESSIONS (health science, nursing, and radiological science). Nursing and radiologic science are the strongest academically and the largest.

Required: Professional program graduation requirements vary. Check individual program requirements.

Faculty/Classroom: 26% of faculty are male; 74%, female. All teach undergraduates. The average class size in an introductory lecture is 27; in a laboratory, 24; and in a regular course, 27.

Requirements: The SAT or ACT is required. A GPA of 2.5 is required. AP and CLEP credits are accepted. Important factors in the admissions decision are advanced placement or honor courses, recommendations by school officials, and personality/intangible qualities.

Procedure: Freshmen are admitted to all sessions. There is an early decision and a rolling admissions plan. Applications should be filed by July

18 for fall entry, November 28 for winter entry, and March 28 for summer entry. The fall 2005 application fee was $20. a $20 fee. Notification is sent on a rolling basis. A waiting list is an active part of the admissions procedure.

Transfer: Applicants must submit the required data for general college admissions. Transfer credits must be submitted on an official transcript from a regionally accredited institution. The number of credits that must be completed for graduation at Florida Hospital College of Health Science varies by program.

Visiting: There are regularly scheduled orientations for prospective students, including fall and spring open houses. There are guides for informal visits and visitors may sit in on classes. To schedule a visit, contact Katie Shaw at (407) 303-1878 or *katie.shaw@fhchs.edu*.

Financial Aid: In a recent year, 77% of all full-time freshmen and 70% of continuing full-time students received some form of financial aid. 40% of full-time freshmen and 39% of continuing full-time students received need-based aid. The average freshman award was $2650. Need-based scholarships or need-based grants averaged $1739 ($2650 maximum); need-based self-help aid (loans and jobs) averaged $1313 ($1313 maximum); and other non-need-based awards and non-need-based scholarships averaged $451 ($2226 maximum). The FAFSA and the college's own financial statement are required. Check with the school for current deadlines.

International Students: Satisfactory scores are required on the TOEFL and the SAT or the ACT.

Computers: Wireless access is available. All students may access the system during regular hours of operation. There are no time limits and no fees. It is strongly recommended that all students have a PC. Upon acceptance, students should check with the professional program for recommended make and model.

Graduates: From July 1, 2004 to June 30, 2005, 145 bachelor's degrees were awarded. The most popular majors were radiologic science (60%), nursing (39%), and health sciences (1%).

Admissions Contact: Janet Cslderon, Director of Admissions. A video is available. E-mail: *janet.calderon@fhchs.edu* Web: *www.fhchs.edu*

FLORIDA INSTITUTE OF TECHNOLOGY   E-3

Melbourne, FL 32901-6975   (321) 674-8030
                              (800) 888-4348; Fax: (321) 723-9468

Full-time: 1554 men, 710 women	**Faculty:** 166
Part-time: 69 men, 25 women	**Ph.D.s:** 90%
Graduate: 1458 men, 929 women	**Student/Faculty:** 14 to 1
Year: semesters, summer session	**Tuition:** $22,920
Application Deadline: open	**Room & Board:** $6800
Freshman Class: 2463 applied, 2051 accepted, 604 enrolled	
SAT Verbal/Math: 570/610*	**ACT:** 25 **VERY COMPETITIVE**

Florida Institute of Technology, founded in 1958, offers undergraduate degrees in engineering and science, liberal arts, management, psychology, and aeronautics. There are 5 undergraduate and 6 graduate schools. In addition to regional accreditation, Florida Tech has baccalaureate program accreditation with ABET, ACS, APA, CAA, and CSAB. The library contains 419,274 volumes, 315,905 microform items, and 8548 audio/video tapes/CDs/DVDs, and subscribes to 17,148 periodicals including electronic. Computerized library services include the card catalog, interlibrary loans, database searching, Internet access, and laptop Internet portals. Special learning facilities include a learning resource center, radio station, and TV station. The 130-acre campus is in a small town 70 miles east of Orlando. Including any residence halls, there are 75 buildings.

Student Life: 54% of undergraduates are from out of state, mostly the Middle Atlantic. Students are from 47 states, 79 foreign countries, and Canada. 77% are from public schools. 59% are white; 15% foreign nationals. The average age of freshmen is 18; all undergraduates, 20. 21% do not continue beyond their first year; 54% remain to graduate.

Housing: 1420 students can be accommodated in college housing, which includes single-sex and coed dorms and on-campus apartments. On-campus housing is guaranteed for the freshman year only and is available on a first-come, first-served basis. 57% of students live on campus; of those, 78% remain on campus on weekends. All students may keep cars.

Activities: 15% of men belong to 6 national fraternities; 15% of women belong to 3 national sororities. There are 104 groups on campus, including band, cheerleading, chess, chorus, computers, dance, drama, drill team, environmental, ethnic, gay, honors, international, jazz band, literary magazine, newspaper, pep band, political, professional, radio and TV, religious, science fiction, social, social service, and student government. Popular campus events include basketball games, Poor Man's Mardi Gras, and International Affair.

Sports: There are 7 intercollegiate sports for men and 8 for women, and 13 intramural sports for men and 13 for women. Facilities include a sports and recreation center, with 2 basketball courts, a racquetball court, and a 5000-square-foot weight and fitness area with cardiovascular machines, free weights, and specialized weight equipment.

Disabled Students: 90% of the campus is accessible. Wheelchair ramps, elevators, special parking, specially equipped rest rooms, special class scheduling, lowered drinking fountains, and lowered telephones are available.

Services: Counseling and information services are available, as is tutoring in every subject. There is a reader service for the blind, and remedial math, reading, and writing.

Campus Safety and Security: Measures include 24-hour foot and vehicle patrol, self-defense education, security escort services, and informal discussions. There are pamphlets/posters/films, emergency telephones, lighted pathways/sidewalks, and formal "Personal Safety and Security" sessions given to all University Experience classes by security staff.

Programs of Study: Florida Tech confers B.A., and B.S. degrees. Master's and doctoral degrees are also awarded. Bachelor's degrees are awarded in BIOLOGICAL SCIENCE (biochemistry, biology/biological science, ecology, marine biology, and molecular biology), BUSINESS (accounting, business administration and management, and management information systems), COMMUNICATIONS AND THE ARTS (communications), COMPUTER AND PHYSICAL SCIENCE (applied mathematics, astrophysics, atmospheric sciences and meteorology, chemistry, computer science, information sciences and systems, oceanography, physics, and planetary and space science), EDUCATION (computer, mathematics, and science), ENGINEERING AND ENVIRONMENTAL DESIGN (aeronautical engineering, aeronautical science, aviation administration/management, aviation computer technology, chemical engineering, civil engineering, computer engineering, electrical/electronics engineering, environmental science, mechanical engineering, military science, and ocean engineering), HEALTH PROFESSIONS (premedicine), SOCIAL SCIENCE (forensic studies, humanities, interdisciplinary studies, and psychology). Engineering, science, and aeronautics are the strongest academically. Aerospace engineering, aviation, and mechanical engineering are the largest.

Required: To graduate, students must have a minimum 2.0 GPA and 120 to 135 credit hours. The required number of hours in the major varies. All students must take 9 hours in communication and humanities and 3 in English composition. The core curriculum also requires 6 credit hours each in physical or life sciences and math, and 3 hours in computer science and social sciences.

Special: Florida Tech offers co-op programs in all majors. Students may choose to pursue more than 1 degree by completing degree requirements for each major. Internships are available in the senior year for many majors, including psychology, engineering, and aeronautics. Study abroad and work-study programs are available. There are 9 national honor societies.

Faculty/Classroom: 82% of faculty are male; 18%, female. 54% teach undergraduates. Graduate students teach 5% of introductory courses. The average class size in an introductory lecture is 23; in a laboratory, 20; and in a regular course, 20.

Admissions: 83% of the 2005-2006 applicants were accepted. The SAT scores for the 2005-2006 freshman class were: Verbal--18% below 500, 42% between 500 and 599, 32% between 600 and 700, and 8% above 700; Math--8% below 500, 36% between 500 and 599, 43% between 600 and 700, and 13% above 700. The ACT scores were 12% below 21, 23% between 21 and 23, 26% between 24 and 26, 12% between 27 and 28, and 27% above 28. 56% of the current freshmen were in the top fifth of their class; 83% were in the top two fifths. There were 5 National Merit finalists. 12 freshmen graduated first in their class.

Requirements: The SAT or ACT is required. In addition, applicants must be graduates of an accredited secondary school or have a GED certificate. At least 18 academic credits or Carnegie units are required, including 4 years each of English, math, and science. An experiential essay is required and an interview is recommended. A GPA of 2.8 is required. AP and CLEP credits are accepted. Important factors in the admissions decision are advanced placement or honor courses, recommendations by school officials, and extracurricular activities record.

Procedure: Freshmen are admitted fall and spring. Entrance exams should be taken during the junior year or the beginning of the senior year of high school. There are rolling admissions and a deferred admissions plan. Application deadlines are open. The fall 2005 application fee was $40. Applications are accepted on-line.

Transfer: 114 transfer students enrolled in 2004-2005. Applicants must have a minimum 2.5 GPA. If transfer students have fewer than 30 semester hours, high school transcripts and SAT or ACT scores are required. A personal statement is recommended. 30 of 120 credits required for the bachelor's degree must be completed at Florida Tech.

Visiting: There are regularly scheduled orientations for prospective students, including tours and interviews with admissions staff, faculty, or department heads upon request. There are guides for informal visits and visitors may sit in on classes. To schedule a visit, contact the Admissions Office at *admission@fit.edu*.

Financial Aid: In 2005-2006, 99% of all full-time freshmen and 88% of continuing full-time students received some form of financial aid. 72% of full-time freshmen and 59% of continuing full-time students received

need-based aid. The average freshman award was $16,434. Need-based scholarships or need-based grants averaged $14,504 ($36,200 maximum); need-based self-help aid (loans and jobs) averaged $4854 ($12,125 maximum); non-need-based athletic scholarships averaged $11,728 ($19,205 maximum); and other non-need-based awards and non-need-based scholarships averaged $10,130 ($29,050 maximum). 26% of undergraduates work part time. Average annual earnings from campus work are $1468. The average financial indebtedness of the 2005 graduate was $24,234. The FAFSA is required. The priority date for freshman financial aid applications for fall entry is March 15.

International Students: There are 327 international students enrolled. The school actively recruits these students. They must score 550 on the written TOEFL or 213 on the electronic version and also take a math entrance qualifying exam. If students score below 550 on the TOEFL, they take language courses on campus.

Computers: All students may access the system 24 hours per day. There are no time limits and no fees.

Graduates: From July 1, 2004 to June 30, 2005, 461 bachelor's degrees were awarded. The most popular majors were computer engineering (10%), electrical engineering (9%), and computer science (8%). In an average class, 35% graduate in 4 years or less, 52% graduate in 5 years or less, and 54% graduate in 6 years or less. 98 companies recruited on campus in 2004-2005. Of the 2004 graduating class, 29% were enrolled in graduate school within 6 months of graduation and 63% were employed.

Admissions Contact: Judi Marino, Director, Undergraduate Admissions. A video is available. E-mail: *jmarino@fit.edu* Web: *http://www.fit.edu*

FLORIDA INTERNATIONAL UNIVERSITY — E-5

Miami, FL 33199	(305) 348-2363; Fax: (305) 348-3648
Full-time: 8033 men, 10,664 women	Faculty: 757; I, --$
Part-time: 5400 men, 6587 women	Ph.D.s: 97%
Graduate: 2520 men, 3700 women	Student/Faculty: 25 to 1
Year: semesters, summer session	Tuition: $3314 ($15,713)
Application Deadline: open	Room & Board: $5901
Freshman Class: 10,223 applied, 4833 accepted, 2506 enrolled	
SAT Verbal/Math: 560/557*	ACT: 23 VERY COMPETITIVE

Florida International University, founded in 1965, is part of the State University System of Florida. Undergraduate degrees are offered through the Colleges of Arts and Sciences, Business Administration, Education, Engineering, Health, Science, and Urban and Public Affairs; and the Schools of Accounting, Computer Science, Architecture, Hospitality Management, Music, and Journalism and Mass Communication. The North and University Park campuses are in Miami, and there are 2 educational centers in Fort Lauderdale. There are 15 undergraduate and 16 graduate schools. In addition to regional accreditation, FIU has baccalaureate program accreditation with AACSB, ABET, ACCE, ACEJMC, ADA, APTA, ASLA, CSAB, CSWE, NAAB, NASAD, NASM, NCATE, and NLN. The 2 libraries contain 1,939,102 volumes, 3,450,360 microform items, and 46,553 audio/video tapes/CDs/DVDs, and subscribe to 35,149 periodicals including electronic. Computerized library services include the card catalog, interlibrary loans, database searching, and laptop Internet portals. Special learning facilities include a learning resource center, radio station, and an art museum. The 573-acre campus is in an urban area 10 miles west of downtown Miami. Including any residence halls, there are 24 buildings.

Student Life: 93% of undergraduates are from Florida. Students are from 50 states, 148 foreign countries, and Canada. 61% are from public schools. 56% are Hispanic; 18% white; 13% African American. The average age of freshmen is 21; all undergraduates, 24. 14% do not continue beyond their first year; 52% remain to graduate.

Housing: 2200 students can be accommodated in college housing, which includes coed dorms, on-campus apartments, and married-student housing. On-campus housing is available on a first-come, first-served basis. 95% of students commute. All students may keep cars.

Activities: 9% of men belong to 10 national fraternities; 10% of women belong to 1 local and 9 national sororities. There are 150 groups on campus, including band, cheerleading, chorus, drama, ethnic, gay, honors, international, marching band, newspaper, political, professional, radio and TV, religious, social, social service, and student government.

Sports: There are 6 intercollegiate sports for men and 9 for women, and 14 intramural sports for men and 10 for women. Facilities include a 5000-seat arena with basketball and racquetball courts, an aquatic center, baseball and soccer fields, a fitness center with Nautilus machines, and a racquet sports center with lighted tennis and racquetball courts.

Disabled Students: 96% of the campus is accessible. Wheelchair ramps, elevators, special parking, specially equipped rest rooms, special class scheduling, lowered drinking fountains, and lowered telephones, are available. There is also accessible computer equipment for visually impaired students, including talking and large-print computers.

Services: Counseling and information services are available, as is tutoring in most subjects. There is a reader service for the blind, and remedial math, reading, and writing. Note taking, adapted testing, and special registration may be arranged for disabled students.

Campus Safety and Security: Measures include 24-hour foot and vehicle patrol, security escort services, informal discussions, and pamphlets/posters/films. There are emergency telephones and lighted pathways/sidewalks.

Programs of Study: FIU confers B.A., B.S., B.Ac., B.B.A., B.F.A., B.H.S.A., B.I.D., B.M., B.P.A., and B.S.N. degrees. Associate, master's, and doctoral degrees are also awarded. Bachelor's degrees are awarded in BIOLOGICAL SCIENCE (biology/biological science and marine biology), BUSINESS (accounting, banking and finance, business administration and management, hospitality management services, international business management, management information systems, management science, marketing/retailing/merchandising, personnel management, real estate, tourism, and transportation management), COMMUNICATIONS AND THE ARTS (art, art history and appreciation, communications, dance, dramatic arts, English, French, German, music, Portuguese, and Spanish), COMPUTER AND PHYSICAL SCIENCE (applied mathematics, chemistry, computer science, geology, information sciences and systems, mathematics, physics, and statistics), EDUCATION (art, education of the emotionally handicapped, education of the mentally handicapped, elementary, English, foreign languages, health, home economics, mathematics, music, physical, science, social studies, special, specific learning disabilities, and vocational), ENGINEERING AND ENVIRONMENTAL DESIGN (architectural technology, biomedical engineering, chemical engineering, civil engineering, computer engineering, construction management, electrical/electronics engineering, environmental science, industrial engineering, interior design, and mechanical engineering), HEALTH PROFESSIONS (health care administration, health science, nursing, occupational therapy, and rehabilitation therapy), SOCIAL SCIENCE (Asian/Oriental studies, criminal justice, dietetics, economics, geography, history, humanities, international relations, Italian studies, liberal arts/general studies, parks and recreation management, philosophy, political science/government, psychology, public administration, religion, social work, sociology, urban studies, and women's studies). Accounting, engineering, and biology are the strongest academically. Accounting, hospitality management, and elementary education are the largest.

Required: To graduate, students must complete between 120 and 152 hours with a 2.0 GPA. There are also general education and writing requirements. Students admitted with fewer than 48 hours must complete the core curriculum.

Special: FIU offers co-op and work-study programs, and study abroad in 6 countries. Accelerated degree programs, nondegree study, dual majors, and B.A.-B.S. degrees in chemistry, enviromental studies, and geology may also be arranged. There are 34 national honor societies, including Phi Beta Kappa, a freshman honors program, and 20 departmental honors programs.

Faculty/Classroom: 60% of faculty are male; 40%, female. All both teach and do research. Graduate students teach 32% of introductory courses. The average class size in an introductory lecture is 41; in a laboratory, 15; and in a regular course, 23.

Admissions: 47% of the 2005-2006 applicants were accepted. The SAT scores for the 2005-2006 freshman class were: Verbal--17% below 500, 55% between 500 and 599, 25% between 600 and 700, and 3% above 700; Math--16% below 500, 56% between 500 and 599, 25% between 600 and 700, and 3% above 700. The ACT scores were 1% below 21, 24% between 21 and 23, 50% between 24 and 26, 14% between 27 and 28, and 11% above 28. There was 1 National Merit finalist and 2 semifinalists. 9 freshmen graduated first in their class.

Requirements: The SAT or ACT is required. In addition, applicants must be graduates of an accredited secondary school or have a GED certificate. The required academic courses include 4 units in English, 3 each in math, natural science, and social studies, 2 in a foreign language, and 4 in academic electives. The university's placement tests must be taken the semester before attending. An interview may be required. A GPA of 2.0 is required. AP and CLEP credits are accepted. Important factors in the admissions decision are advanced placement or honor courses, evidence of special talent, and recommendations by school officials.

Procedure: Freshmen are admitted fall, spring, and summer. Entrance exams should be taken during the spring of the junior year. There are early admissions deferred admissions, and rolling admissions plans. Application deadlines are open. Application fee is $30. Applications are accepted on-line.

Transfer: 2563 transfer students enrolled in 2004-2005. Applicants with fewer than 60 semester credits must meet regular freshman admissions requirements. All students must pass the CLAST or take the pre-CLAST testing program during the first term of enrollment, fulfill core curriculum or general education requirements, and have a 2.0 GPA. 30 of 120 to 152 credits required for the bachelor's degree must be completed at FIU.

Visiting: There are regularly scheduled orientations for prospective students, including placement tests, advising, a tour, and student activities.

There are guides for informal visits and visitors may sit in on classes. To schedule a visit, contact the Office of Admissions.

Financial Aid: FIU is a member of CSS. The FAFSA is required. The deadline for filing freshman financial aid applications for fall entry is March 1.

International Students: There are 1549 international students enrolled. The school actively recruits these students. A satisfactory score is required on the written TOEFL. Students must also take the SAT or the ACT.

Computers: All students may access the system 8 A.M. to 4 A.M. There are no time limits and no fees.

Graduates: From July 1, 2004 to June 30, 2005, 4862 bachelor's degrees were awarded. The most popular majors were business (34%), health professions (9%), and psychology (6%). In an average class, 1% graduate in 3 years or less, 19% graduate in 4 years or less, 39% graduate in 5 years or less, and 50% graduate in 6 years or less.

Admissions Contact: Carmen Brown, Admissions Director.
E-mail: *brownc@fiu.edu* Web: *www.fiu.edu*

FLORIDA MEMORIAL COLLEGE   E-5

Miami, FL 33054

(305) 626-3750
(800) 822-1362; Fax: (305) 626-3769

Full-time: n/av	**Faculty:** 80
Part-time: n/av	**Ph.D.s:** 40%
Graduate: n/av	**Student/Faculty:** 18 to 1
Year: summer session	**Tuition:** $6010
Application Deadline: open	**Room & Board:** n/app
Freshman Class: n/av	
SAT or ACT: required	LESS COMPETITIVE

Florida Memorial College, founded in 1879, is a private liberal arts institution affiliated with the American Baptist Church. Figures given in above capsule and this profile are approximate. There are 6 undergraduate schools. Figures in the above capsule and the profile are approximate. The library contains 88,000 volumes, and subscribes to 400 periodicals including electronic. Special learning facilities include an aviation center. The 77-acre campus is in an urban area in northwestern Miami. There are 12 buildings.

Programs of Study: Florida Memorial confers B.A., and B.S. degrees. Bachelor's degrees are awarded in BIOLOGICAL SCIENCE (biology/biological science), BUSINESS (accounting, business administration and management, and transportation management), COMMUNICATIONS AND THE ARTS (English, fine arts, and music), COMPUTER AND PHYSICAL SCIENCE (chemistry, computer science, and mathematics), EDUCATION (elementary, physical, and secondary), ENGINEERING AND ENVIRONMENTAL DESIGN (air traffic control, aviation administration/management, and aviation computer technology), SOCIAL SCIENCE (criminal justice, philosophy, political science/government, psychology, public administration, religion, and sociology).

Required: To graduate, all students must complete at least 124 credit hours, including 62 hours of general education requirements, with a minimum overall GPA of 2.0. Students must successfully complete all 4 subtests of the Florida College-Level Academic Skills Test by junior year.

Special: Private sector and college internships, work-study, and a 3-2 engineering program with the University of Miami are available. Pass/fail credit and nondegree options are possible. There is a freshman honors program.

Requirements: The SAT or ACT is required. Applicants must be graduates of an accredited secondary school or have a GED certificate. 1 faculty and 2 personal recommendations, an autobiography, and a health certificate are required. Up to 20% of a freshman class may be admitted for 1 semester on a conditional basis to demonstrate their abilities. A GPA of 2.0 is required.

Procedure: Freshmen are admitted fall and spring. Application deadlines are open.

Transfer: Transcripts must be submitted for all previous college work, as well as high school transcripts for students with fewer than 3 credits. The SAT or ACT is recommended. 30 of 124 credits required for the bachelor's degree must be completed at Florida Memorial.

Financial Aid: The CSS/Profile or FFS is required. Check with the school for current application deadlines.

International Students: They must take the TOEFL.

Computers: All students may access the system. There are no time limits and no fees.

Admissions Contact: Peggy Kelly, Director of Admissions.
Web: *http://www.fmc.edu*

FLORIDA SOUTHERN COLLEGE   D-4

Lakeland, FL 33801-5698

(863) 680-4131
(800) 274-4131; Fax: (863) 680-4120

Full-time: 682 men, 1077 women	**Faculty:** 107; IIB, -$
Part-time: 30 men, 27 women	**Ph.D.s:** 87%
Graduate: 25 men, 80 women	**Student/Faculty:** 16 to 1
Year: semesters, summer session	**Tuition:** $19,165
Application Deadline: August 1	**Room & Board:** $6800
Freshman Class: 1829 applied, 1343 accepted, 464 enrolled	
SAT Verbal/Math: 528/539*	**ACT:** 23 COMPETITIVE

Florida Southern College, founded in 1885, is a private institution affiliated with the United Methodist Church offering undergraduate programs through the divisions of humanities, social sciences, and natural sciences. In addition to regional accreditation, Florida Southern has baccalaureate program accreditation with CAAHEP and CCNE. The library contains 192,684 volumes, 458,541 microform items, and 12,798 audio/video tapes/CDs/DVDs, and subscribes to 641 periodicals including electronic. Computerized library services include the card catalog, interlibrary loans, database searching, and Internet access. Special learning facilities include a learning resource center, art gallery, and planetarium. The 100-acre campus is in a suburban area 30 miles east of Tampa. Including any residence halls, there are 40 buildings.

Student Life: 72% of undergraduates are from Florida. Others are from 44 states, 34 foreign countries, and Canada. 80% are from public schools. 83% are white. 30% are claim no religious affiliation; 24% Protestant; 17% Catholic. The average age of freshmen is 18; all undergraduates, 20. 33% do not continue beyond their first year; 53% remain to graduate.

Housing: 1313 students can be accommodated in college housing, which includes single-sex dorms, married-student housing, fraternity houses, and sorority houses. On-campus housing is guaranteed for all 4 years. 66% of students live on campus; of those, 60% remain on campus on weekends. Alcohol is not permitted. All students may keep cars.

Activities: 5% of men belong to 5 national fraternities; 10% of women belong to 6 national sororities. There are 60 groups on campus, including art, band, cheerleading, chess, choir, chorale, chorus, dance, drama, ethnic, film, forensics, honors, international, jazz band, literary magazine, musical theater, newspaper, opera, orchestra, pep band, photography, political, professional, radio and TV, religious, social, social service, student government, symphony, volunteer, and yearbook. Popular campus events include theater productions, a jazz festival, and the Festival of Fine Art series.

Sports: There are 7 intercollegiate sports for men and 8 for women, and 6 intramural sports for men and 6 for women. Facilities include a 2500-seat air-conditioned field house for basketball and volleyball; fields for soccer, softball, and intramurals; 9 lighted tennis courts and a sand volleyball court; aerobics, weight, and fitness facilities; an intramural gym; a heated competitive-size pool; and a boathouse for waterskiing equipment. Facilities for baseball games and golf matches are off campus.

Disabled Students: 60% of the campus is accessible. Wheelchair ramps, elevators, special parking, specially equipped rest rooms, special class scheduling, lowered drinking fountains, lowered telephones, and special housing are available.

Services: Counseling and information services are available, as is tutoring in some subjects, including math, English, and most general education courses.

Campus Safety and Security: Measures include 24-hour foot and vehicle patrol, security escort services, informal discussions, and pamphlets/posters/films. There are emergency telephones and lighted pathways/sidewalks.

Programs of Study: Florida Southern confers B.A., B.S., B.F.A., B.M.E., B.S.M., and B.S.N. degrees. Master's degrees are also awarded. Bachelor's degrees are awarded in AGRICULTURE (horticulture), BIOLOGICAL SCIENCE (biology/biological science), BUSINESS (accounting, banking and finance, business administration and management, business economics, hotel/motel and restaurant management, international business management, marketing/retailing/merchandising, and personnel management), COMMUNICATIONS AND THE ARTS (advertising, communications, dramatic arts, English, journalism, music, public relations, and Spanish), COMPUTER AND PHYSICAL SCIENCE (chemistry, information sciences and systems, and mathematics), EDUCATION (art, athletic training, early childhood, elementary, foreign languages, middle school, music, science, secondary, and special), ENGINEERING AND ENVIRONMENTAL DESIGN (environmental science), SOCIAL SCIENCE (criminal justice, economics, history, humanities, political science/government, psychology, religion, social science, and sociology). Biology, music, and business/economics are the strongest academically. Business, education, and biology are the largest.

Required: To graduate, all students must have completed a minimum of 124 semester hours of credit, with no more than 42 hours in the major for most programs and a minimum 2.0 GPA. Core requirements include 9 hours of humanities, 8 of natural science, 6 each of English, social sciences, and math, 3 each of history and fine arts, 2 of phys ed, and attendance at faith and life convocation.

Special: Florida Southern offers study abroad in 8 countries, a Washington semester with American University, and a 3-2 engineering degree with Washington University in St. Louis. Students may choose the United Nations semester in cooperation with Drew University in New Jersey, or the May Option Program, which combines study and travel in England for course credit. Internships with corporations in Tampa, Lakeland, and Orlando are offered through most academic departments and are required by many. Credit for military experience, work-study, dual majors, and pass/fail options are available. There are 22 national honor societies, a freshman honors program, and 5 departmental honors programs.

Faculty/Classroom: 63% of faculty are male; 37%, female. All teach undergraduates. No introductory courses are taught by graduate students. The average class size in an introductory lecture is 20; in a laboratory, 15; and in a regular course, 15.

Admissions: 73% of the 2005-2006 applicants were accepted. The SAT scores for the 2005-2006 freshman class were: Verbal--37% below 500, 43% between 500 and 599, 17% between 600 and 700, and 3% above 700; Math--33% below 500, 43% between 500 and 599, 20% between 600 and 700, and 4% above 700. The ACT scores were 29% below 21, 28% between 21 and 23, 22% between 24 and 26, 11% between 27 and 28, and 10% above 28. 46% of the current freshmen were in the top fifth of their class; 75% were in the top two fifths. 5 freshmen graduated first in their class.

Requirements: A satisfactory score is required on the SAT or ACT. Applicants must be graduates of an accredited secondary school or have a GED certificate. An essay is required, and an interview is recommended. AP and CLEP credits are accepted.

Procedure: Freshmen are admitted to all sessions. Entrance exams should be taken starting in the junior year of high school. There are early decision and deferred admissions plans. There is a rolling admissions plan. Applications should be filed by August 1 for fall entry and December 1 for spring entry, along with a $30 fee. Notification is sent on a rolling basis. 43 early decision candidates were accepted for the 2005-2006 class. Applications are accepted on-line.

Transfer: 98 transfer students enrolled in 2004-2005. Transfer students must have a minimum 2.5 GPA and must submit SAT or ACT scores. An associate degree and an interview are recommended. 31 of a minimum of 124 credits required for the bachelor's degree must be completed at Florida Southern.

Visiting: There are regularly scheduled orientations for prospective students, including campuswide open houses. There are guides for informal visits and visitors may sit in on classes and stay overnight. To schedule a visit, contact the Admissions Office.

Financial Aid: In 2005-2006, 96% of all full-time freshmen and 91% of continuing full-time students received some form of financial aid. 65% of full-time freshmen and 68% of continuing full-time students received need-based aid. The average freshman award was $18,403. 78% of undergraduates work part time. Average annual earnings from campus work are $1200. The average financial indebtedness of the 2005 graduate was $16,072. The FAFSA, the college's own financial statement; and the parents' and student's tax returns are required. The deadline for filing freshman financial aid applications for fall entry is March 1.

International Students: There are 75 international students enrolled. The school actively recruits these students. A satisfactory score on the TOEFL is required.

Computers: Wireless access is available in select areas of campus. There are computers for student use in the library and labs. All students may access the system during lab hours. There are no time limits and no fees. It is strongly recommended that all students have a personal computer.

Graduates: From July 1, 2004 to June 30, 2005, 522 bachelor's degrees were awarded. The most popular majors were business (18%), education (10%), and biology (8%). In an average class, 5% graduate in 3 years or less, 40% graduate in 4 years or less, 53% graduate in 5 years or less, and 53% graduate in 6 years or less. 90 companies recruited on campus in 2004-2005. Of the 2004 graduating class, 15% were enrolled in graduate school within 6 months of graduation and 80% were employed.

Admissions Contact: Bill Langston, Director of Admissions. A video is available. E-mail: *fscadm@flsouthern.edu*
Web: *http://www.flsouthern.edu*

FLORIDA STATE UNIVERSITY C-1

Tallahassee, FL 32306-   (850) 644-6200; Fax: (850) 644-0197

Full-time: 11,205 men, 14,760 women	**Faculty:** 1403; I, -$
Part-time: 1675 men, 2000 women	**Ph.D.s:** 92%
Graduate: 3205 men, 4060 women	**Student/Faculty:** 19 to 1
Year: semesters, summer session	**Tuition:** $2865 ($13,900)
Application Deadline: see profile	**Room & Board:** $6170
Freshman Class: n/av	
SAT or ACT: required	**HIGHLY COMPETITIVE**

Florida State University, a public institution founded in 1851, is a residential university designated as a Doctoral Research (Extensive) University by the Carnegie Foundation for the Advancement of Teaching. There are 15 undergraduate and 16 graduate schools. Figures in the above capsule and this profile are approxmite. In addition to regional accreditation, FSU has baccalaureate program accreditation with AACSB, ABET, ADA, AHEA, ASLA, CSWE, FIDER, NASM, NCATE, NLN, and NRPA. The 6 libraries contain 2,620,296 volumes, 9,029,029 microform items, and 73,519 audio/video tapes/CDs/DVDs, and subscribe to 21,598 periodicals including electronic. Computerized library services include the card catalog, interlibrary loans, database searching, and Internet access. Special learning facilities include a learning resource center, art gallery, planetarium, radio station, TV station, nuclear accelerator, x-ray emission lab, marine lab, supercomputers, and the National High Magnetic Field Laboratory. The 448-acre campus is in a suburban area 163 miles west of Jacksonville. Including any residence halls, there are 215 buildings.

Student Life: 82% of undergraduates are from Florida. Others are from 49 states, 118 foreign countries, and Canada. 82% are from public schools. 71% are white; 12% African American. The average age of freshmen is 19; all undergraduates, 21. 16% do not continue beyond their first year.

Housing: 6000 students can be accommodated in college housing, which includes single-sex and coed dormitories, on-campus apartments, married-student housing, fraternity houses, and sorority houses. In addition, there are honors houses, special-interest houses, living and learning centers, music residence, scholarship houses, and academic discipline houses. On-campus housing is available on a first-come, first-served basis. All students may keep cars.

Activities: 15% of men belong to 28 national fraternities; 13% of women belong to 21 national sororities. There are 266 groups on campus, including art, band, cheerleading, chess, choir, chorale, chorus, computers, dance, debate, drama, drill team, ethnic, forensics, gay, honors, international, jazz band, literary magazine, marching band, musical theater, newspaper, opera, orchestra, pep band, political, professional, radio and TV, religious, social, social service, student government, symphony, and yearbook. Popular campus events include Twelve Days of Dance, Parents Weekend, and Seven Days of Opening Nights.

Sports: There are 9 intercollegiate sports for men and 10 for women, and 27 intramural sports for men and 27 for women. Facilities include an 80,000-seat stadium, an aquatic center with a heated outdoor swimming pool, a golf course, a track, courts for basketball, tennis, racquetball, and handball, a student recreation center with an indoor Olympic-size swimming pool, 2 Jacuzzis, a steam room, a sauna, 10 racquetball courts, a squash court, a multipurpose gym, a 3-lane jogging track, aerobic rooms, aerobic exercise machines, and free and fixed weights, and a lakefront recreation area for outdoor water sports.

Disabled Students: 99% of the campus is accessible. Wheelchair ramps, elevators, special parking, specially equipped rest rooms, special class scheduling, lowered drinking fountains, and lowered telephones are available.

Services: Counseling and information services are available, as is tutoring in most subjects. There is a reader service for the blind, and remedial math, reading, and writing.

Campus Safety and Security: Measures include 24-hour foot and vehicle patrol, self-defense education, security escort services, and shuttle buses. There are informal discussions, pamphlets/posters/films, emergency telephones, lighted pathways/sidewalks, a full time police force, a bicycle identification program, a valuables identification program, and a victim advocate program.

Programs of Study: FSU confers B.A., B.S., B.S.N., B.F.A., B.M., and B.M.Ed. degrees. Associate, master's, and doctoral degrees are also awarded. Bachelor's degrees are awarded in AGRICULTURE (environmental studies and plant science), BIOLOGICAL SCIENCE (biochemistry, biology/biological science, cell biology, ecology, evolutionary biology, genetics, marine biology, molecular biology, nutrition, physiology, and zoology), BUSINESS (accounting, banking and finance, business administration and management, entrepreneurial studies, fashion merchandising, hotel/motel and restaurant management, insurance and risk management, international business management, management information systems, management science, marketing/retailing/merchandising, personnel management, recreation and leisure services, recreational facilities management, small business management, and sports management), COMMUNICATIONS AND THE ARTS (advertising, American literature, apparel design, art history and appreciation, broadcasting, classics, communications, creative writing, dance, dramatic arts, English, fiber/textiles/weaving, film arts, French, German, Greek, Italian, jazz, Latin, linguistics, music, music history and appreciation, music performance, music theory and composition, musical theater, piano/organ, public relations, Russian, Spanish, speech/debate/rhetoric, strings, studio art, theater design, voice, and winds), COMPUTER AND PHYSICAL SCIENCE (actuarial science, applied mathematics, atmospheric sciences and meteorology, chemical technology, chemistry, computer science, geology, information sciences and systems, mathematics, physics, and statistics), EDUCATION (art, athletic training, early childhood, education of the emotionally handicapped, education of the mentally handicapped, education of the visually handicapped, elementary, English, foreign languages, health, home economics, mathematics, music, physical, reading, science, social science, and specific learning disabilities), ENGINEERING AND ENVIRONMENTAL DESIGN (bioengineering, biomedical engineering, chemical engineering, civil engineering, computer engineering, electrical/electronics engineering, environmental engineering, environmental science, graphic arts technology, industrial engineering, interior design, materials engineering, and mechanical engineering), HEALTH PROFESSIONS (community health work, music therapy, nursing, predentistry, premedicine, preoptometry, prepharmacy, preveterinary science, rehabilitation therapy, speech pathology/audiology, and sports medicine), SOCIAL SCIENCE (American studies, anthropology, Asian/Oriental studies, Caribbean studies, child care/child and family studies, classical/ancient civilization, clothing and textiles management/production/services, criminology, dietetics, Eastern European studies, economics, family/consumer studies, fashion design and technology, food science, geography, history, home economics, humanities, international relations, Latin American studies, philosophy, political science/government, prelaw, psychology, religion, Russian and Slavic studies, social science, social work, sociology, and women's studies). Biology, meteorology, and physics are the strongest academically. Biology, psychology, and business are the largest.

Required: Students must take the Florida CollegeLevel Academic Skills Test (CLAST) for admission to upper-division status. The required core curriculum includes 6 semester hours in English composition, 6 to 12 history/social science, 5 to 11 humanities/fine arts, and 7 in natural sciences. All academic areas require at least 120 semester hours for graduation.

Special: Cross-registration with Florida Agricultural and Mechanical University and Tallahassee Community College is possible, as is study at FSU centers in London or Florence and in programs in Costa Rica, France, Russia, Spain, Switzerland, and Vietnam, among other countries. FSU offers cooperative programs in engineering, computer science, business, and communication, work-study programs, general studies and combined B.A.-B.S. degrees, dual majors, and accelerated degree programs. Internships are required in criminology, human science, education, nursing, and social work. There are preprofessional programs in health and law. There are 47 national honor societies, including Phi Beta Kappa, a freshman honors program, and 60 departmental honors programs.

Faculty/Classroom: 62% of faculty are male; 38%, female. Graduate students teach 51% of introductory courses. The average class size in an introductory lecture is 41; in a laboratory, 18; and in a regular course, 35.

Requirements: The SAT or ACT is required. In addition, it is recommended that in-state students have at least an A-/B+ weighted average and a satisfactory. SAT score, or 25 on the ACT. Out-of-state students must meet higher standards. Applicants should have at least the following high school units: 4 in English, 3 in math, natural science, and social science, and 2 in a foreign language. Other factors include the number of honors, AP, and IB classes, strength of academic curriculum, class rank, and others. AP and CLEP credits are accepted. Important factors in the admissions decision are advanced placement or honor courses, evidence of special talent, and recommendations by school officials.

Procedure: Freshmen are admitted fall, spring, and summer. Entrance exams should be taken beginning in the second semester of the junior year. There early admissions and rolling admissions plans. Applications should be filed by March 1 for fall entry, November 1 for spring entry, and March 1 for summer entry, along with a $30 fee. Notification is sent on a rolling basis. Applications are accepted on-line.

Transfer: 1875 transfer students enrolled in a recent year. Transfer applicants should present at least a 2.5 cumulative college GPA unless transferring from a Florida public community college with an associate in arts degree, in which case the minimum college GPA needed varies according to major. Applicants with less than 60 semester hours of transferable credit must also meet freshman admission requirements. All transfers must have completed 2 years of the same foreign language in high school or have 8 semester hours at the college level. Students must pass the Florida CLAST Examination. 30 of 120 credits required for the bachelor's degree must be completed at FSU.

Visiting: There are regularly scheduled orientations for prospective students, including campus tours several times daily on weekdays. Walking and riding tours are available and tours are coordinated around an 11:00 admissions information session. There are guides for informal visits and visitors may sit in on classes. To schedule a visit, contact Visitor Services at (850) 644-3246.

Financial Aid: In a recent year, 41% of all full-time students received some form of financial aid. 31% of all full-time students received need-based aid. The average freshman award was $4147. Need-based scholarships or need-based grants averaged $3608; need-based self-help aid (loans and jobs) averaged $2839; non-need-based athletic scholarships averaged $5514; and other non-need-based awards and non-need-based scholarships averaged $2601. 2% of undergraduates worked part time. Average annual earnings from campus work are $1778. The average financial indebtedness of a recent graduate was $17,112. The FAFSA and the college's own financial statement are required. Check with the school for current application deadlines.

International Students: In a recent year, there were 341 international students enrolled. They must score satisfactorily on the written TOEFL or on the electronic version and also take the SAT or the ACT.

Computers: All students may access the system, although use of some machines is restricted to particular majors or graduate students. There are no time limits and no fees. It is strongly recommended that all students have a personal computer. It is recommended that students in engineering programs have personal computers. A PC with a 1.8 GHZ Pentium 4, 128 MB of RAM 606B hard drive, or a MAC 700 HMz 64 is recommended.

Graduates: In a recent year, 6335 bachelor's degrees were awarded. The most popular majors were finance (5%), psychology (5%), and criminology (5%). In an average class, 4% graduate in 3 years or less, 42% graduate in 4 years or less, 58% graduate in 5 years or less, and 63% graduate in 6 years or less.

Admissions Contact: Admissions.
E-mail: *admissions@admin.fsu.edu* Web: *http://admissions.fsu.edu*

INTERNATIONAL COLLEGE
D-5

Naples, FL 34119-7932
(239) 513-1122
(800) 466-8017; Fax: (239) 513-9054

Full-time: 329 men, 764 women	**Faculty:** 51
Part-time: 126 men, 258 women	**Ph.D.s:** 64%
Graduate: 64 men, 121 women	**Student/Faculty:** 19 to 1
Year: trimesters, summer session	**Tuition:** $9500
Application Deadline: open	**Room & Board:** n/app
Freshman Class: n/av	
SAT or ACT: not required	**NONCOMPETITIVE**

International College founded in 1990, is a private institution offering undergraduate and graduate degree programs in business and public administration, accounting, criminal justice, health administration and allied health, computer technology, and paralegal studies. There are 4 undergraduate and 3 graduate schools. The library contains 30,000 volumes and 550 audio/video tapes/CDs/DVDs, and subscribes to 300 periodicals including electronic. Computerized library services include the card catalog, interlibrary loans, database searching, and Internet access. Special learning facilities include an art gallery. The 10-acre campus is in a suburban area 100 miles west of Fort Lauderdale. There is one building.

Student Life: 70% are white; 14% Hispanic; 13% African American. The average age of freshmen is 31; all undergraduates, 33.

Housing: There are no residence halls. 99% of students commute.

Activities: There are no fraternities or sororities. There are some groups and organizations on campus, including literary magazine and student government.

Disabled Students: All of the campus is accessible. Elevators, specially equipped rest rooms, and lowered drinking fountains are available.

Services: There is remedial math and writing.

Campus Safety and Security: Measures include security escort services and lighted pathways/sidewalks.

Programs of Study: International College confers the B.S. degree. Associate and master's degrees are also awarded. Bachelor's degrees are awarded in BUSINESS (accounting and business administration and management), COMPUTER AND PHYSICAL SCIENCE (information sciences and systems), ENGINEERING AND ENVIRONMENTAL DESIGN (computer technology), HEALTH PROFESSIONS (health and health care administration), SOCIAL SCIENCE (criminal justice, interdisciplinary studies, and paralegal studies). Management is the largest.

Required: To graduate, students must complete a minimum of 120 semester hours, with at least 60 in the major and with a minimum GPA of 2.0. At least 48 hours must be upper-division courses. A comprehensive exam is required.

Special: Dual majors, internships, work study, an accelerated degree in management, on-line classes, and credit for life experience are possible.

Faculty/Classroom: 68% of faculty are male; 31%, female. All teach undergraduates. No introductory courses are taught by graduate students. The average class size in an introductory lecture is 14; in a laboratory, 14; and in a regular course, 14.

Requirements: An essay and interview are required. AP and CLEP credits are accepted.

Procedure: Freshmen are admitted fall, winter, and summer. Entrance exams can be taken any time. Application deadlines are open. The fall 2005 application fee was $20. Notification is sent ona rolling basis. Applications are accepted on-line.

Transfer: 645 transfer students enrolled in a recent year. Applicants must submit previous transcripts. Only credits completed with a C or better will transfer. 32 of 120 credits required for the bachelor's degree must be completed at International College.

Visiting: There are regularly scheduled orientations for prospective students, Orientations for undergraduates are held 3 days prior to start of the term.

Financial Aid: In a recent year, 94% of all full-time freshmen and 93% of continuing full-time students received some form of financial aid. 84% of all full-time students received need-based aid. The average freshman award in a recent year was $7888. Need-based scholarships or need-based grants averaged $1400 ($4050 maximum); need-based self-help aid (loans and jobs) averaged $3500 ($6625 maximum); and other non-need-based awards and non-need-based scholarships averaged $2988. 1% of undergraduates work part time. Average annual earnings from campus work are $4000. The average financial indebtedness of the 2005 graduate was $17,000. The FAFSA is required. Check with the school for current deadlines.

International Students: The school actively recruits these students. A satisfactory score are required on the written TOEFL and the CPAT.

Computers: All students may access the system. There are no time limits and no fees.

Graduates: In a recent year, 379 bachelor's degrees were awarded. The most popular majors were management/business (40%), criminal justice (16%), and legal studies (15%). 12 companies recruited on campus in a recent year. Of the recent year's graduating class, 5% were enrolled in graduate school within 6 months of graduation and 94% were employed.

Admissions Contact: Rita Lampus, VP of Student Enrollment.
E-mail: *rlampus@internationalcollege.edu*
Web: *www.internationalcollege.edu*

JACKSONVILLE UNIVERSITY D-1
Jacksonville, FL 32211

(904) 256-7000
(800) 225-2027; Fax: (904) 256-7012

Full-time: 990 men, 915 women	**Faculty:** 125; IIA, -$
Part-time: 120 men, 200 women	**Ph.D.s:** 75%
Graduate: 195 men, 235 women	**Student/Faculty:** 15 to 1
Year: semesters, summer session	**Tuition:** $17,955
Application Deadline: open	**Room & Board:** $6110
Freshman Class: n/av	
SAT or ACT: required	**COMPETITIVE**

Jacksonville University, founded in 1934, is a private institution offering undergraduate and graduate degree programs in the arts and sciences, fine arts and business. There are 3 undergraduate and 4 graduate schools. Figures in the above capsule and this profile are approximate. In addition to regional accreditation, JU has baccalaureate program accreditation with CCNE, NASAD, NASM, and NLN. The library contains 328,900 volumes, 352,608 microform items, and 33,366 audio/video tapes/CDs/DVDs, and subscribes to 326 periodicals including electronic. Computerized library services include the card catalog, interlibrary loans, database searching, and Internet access. Special learning facilities include a learning resource center, art gallery, planetarium, radio station, TV station, a chemistry research lab, and a marine science center. The 260-acre campus is in a suburban area 10 minutes from downtown Jacksonville, near the St. Johns River. Including any residence halls, there are 48 buildings.

Student Life: 66% of undergraduates are from Florida. Others are from 46 states, 61 foreign countries, and Canada. 72% are white; 16% African American. 23% are Protestant; 20% Catholic. The average age of freshmen is 19; all undergraduates, 22. 31% do not continue beyond their first year; 44% remain to graduate.

Housing: 1061 students can be accommodated in college housing, which includes single-sex dormitories and on-campus apartments. On-campus housing is guaranteed for all 4 years. 59% of students live on campus. All students may keep cars.

Activities: 18% of men belong to 6 national fraternities; 15% of women belong to 4 national sororities. There are many groups and organizations on campus, including art, band, cheerleading, choir, chorale, chorus, dance, debate, drama, drill team, ethnic, film, honors, international, jazz band, literary magazine, musical theater, newspaper, orchestra, pep band, photography, political, professional, radio and TV, religious, social, social service, student government, symphony, and yearbook.

Sports: There are 7 intercollegiate sports for men and 10 for women. Facilities include a 1500-seat stadium, a gym, a swimming pool, a boathouse, baseball and softball diamonds, soccer and football fields, and an archery range. There are also tennis, basketball, handball/racquetball,

volleyball, and shuffleboard courts, an all-purpose playing field, a 440-yard track, a 540-seat auditorium, a 220-seat recital hall, and a dance pavilion.

Disabled Students: Wheelchair ramps, elevators, special parking, specially equipped rest rooms, special class scheduling and, lowered drinking fountains are available. Accommodation is made for all students regardless of disability.

Services: Counseling and information services are available, as is tutoring in most subjects. There is a reader service for the blind, and remedial math, reading, and writing. There also is a writer service for note taking in class.

Campus Safety and Security: Measures include 24-hour foot and vehicle patrol, self-defense education, security escort services, and informal discussions. There are pamphlets/posters/films, emergency telephones, and lighted pathways/sidewalks.

Programs of Study: JU confers B.A., B.S., B.F.A., B.G.S., B.Mus., B.Mus.Ed., and B.S.N. degrees. Master's degrees are also awarded. Bachelor's degrees are awarded in BIOLOGICAL SCIENCE (biology/biological science and marine science), BUSINESS (accounting, banking and finance, business administration and management, international business management, and marketing/retailing/merchandising), COMMUNICATIONS AND THE ARTS (art history and appreciation, communications, dance, dramatic arts, English, French, music, music performance, music theory and composition, Spanish, and studio art), COMPUTER AND PHYSICAL SCIENCE (chemistry, computer science, information sciences and systems, mathematics, and physics), EDUCATION (art, dance, education of the exceptional child, elementary, music, and physical), ENGINEERING AND ENVIRONMENTAL DESIGN (aviation administration/management, computer graphics, electrical/electronics engineering, engineering physics, environmental science, and mechanical engineering), HEALTH PROFESSIONS (nursing), SOCIAL SCIENCE (economics, geography, history, humanities, international studies, philosophy, political science/government, psychology, and sociology). Business administration, nursing, and biology are the largest.

Required: All students must complete a core curriculum, including 9 hours of English and literature, 4 hours of lab science, 3 hours each of technology, social science, math, philosophy, information systems, humanities, history, foreign language, fine arts, and economics, and 1 hour of phys ed. A total of 128 hours, with a minimum GPA of 2.0, is needed to graduate.

Special: Internships and work-study are available, as are student-designed majors, and a dual major in music and business. There is a co-op program in art, and a 3-2 engineering degree is available with 7 other universities and technological instititutes. There is a Washington semester and study abroad in 12 countries. Credit is granted for military experience. There are 12 national honor societies, including Phi Beta Kappa and, a freshman honors program.

Faculty/Classroom: 57% of faculty are male; 43%, female. No introductory courses are taught by graduate students. The average class size in an introductory lecture is 17; in a laboratory, 16; and in a regular course, 14.

Requirements: The SAT or ACT is required. In addition, applicants must be graduates of an accredited secondary school and provide an offical copy of their secondary school transcript, or have a GED. At least 18 academic credits are required, including 4 in English, 3 each in math, natural science, and social sciences, and 2 of the same foreign language. Art students must submit a portfolio. Music, theater, and dance students must audition. A GPA of 2.0 is required. AP and CLEP credits are accepted. Important factors in the admissions decision are advanced placement or honor courses, extracurricular activities record, and leadership record.

Procedure: Freshmen are admitted to all sessions. Entrance exams should be taken in the spring of the junior year or the fall or spring of the senior year. There are early admissions, deferred admissions, and rolling admissions plans. Application deadlines are open. Applications are accepted on-line. The fall 2005 application fee was $30

Transfer: 216 transfer students enrolled in a recent year. Transfer students must submit official transcripts from all colleges attended. Art students must submit a portfolio; music and dance students must audition. Transfer applicants must have completed at least one semester at an accredited college or university, be in good standing at the last institution attended, and have a minimum GPA of 2.0. 32 of 128 credits required for the bachelor's degree must be completed at JU.

Visiting: There are regularly scheduled orientations for prospective students, consisting of an interview, a campus tour, advisement, area presentations, registration, a parents program, and mock classes. There are guides for informal visits and visitors may sit in on classes and stay overnight. To schedule a visit, contact the Admissions office.

Financial Aid: In a recent year, 98% of all full-time freshmen received some form of financial aid. 80% of full-time freshmen received need-based aid. JU is a member of CSS. The FAFSA, the college's own financial statement and a federal tax return and W-2 are required. Check with the school for current application deadlines.

International Students: In a recent year, there were 64 international students enrolled. The school actively recruits these students. They must score satisfactorily on the written TOEFL or on the electronic version and also take the SAT or the ACT.

Computers: All students may access the system during lab hours, 7 days a week. There is also dial-in-access. There are no time limits and no fees. It is strongly recommended that all students have a personal computer.

Graduates: IN a recent year, 399 bachelor's degrees were awarded. The most popular majors were business (29%), nursing (14%), and communications (7%). In an average class, 31% graduate in 4 years or less, 41% graduate in 5 years or less, and 44% graduate in 6 years or less. 50 companies recruited on campus in a recent year. Of a recent graduating class, 23% were enrolled in graduate school within 6 months of graduation and 51% were employed.

Admissions Contact: John P. Grundig, Director of Admissions. E-mail: admissions@ju.edu Web: www.ju.edu

JOHNSON AND WALES UNIVERSITY/NORTH MIAMI CAMPUS

North Miami, FL 33181	**(866) 598-3567; Fax: (305) 892-7020**
Full-time: 1076 men, 1241 women	Faculty: 59
Part-time: 66 men, 69 women	Ph.D.s: n/av
Graduate: none	Student/Faculty: 39 to 1
Year: quarters	Tuition: $20,826
Application Deadline: open	Room & Board: $9300
Freshman Class: 5601 accepted	
SATor ACT: required for some programs	**LESS COMPETITIVE**

Johnson & Wales University/North Miami Campus, founded in 1992, offers degree programs in its College of Culinary Ars, College of Business, and Hospitality College. There are 3 undergraduate schools. The library contains 11,642 volumes and 1987 audio/video tapes/CDs/DVDs, and subscribes to 225 periodicals including electronic. Computerized library services include interlibrary loans, database searching, Internet access, and laptop Internet portals. Special learning facilities include a learning resource center and a University-owned/operated hotel. The campus is in an urban area in the heart of North Miami, between Miami and Fort Lauderdale. Including any residence halls, there are 13 buildings.

Student Life: 52% of undergraduates are from Florida. Students are from 50 states, 47 foreign countries, and Canada. 30% are African American; 29% white; 20% Hispanic. The average age of freshmen is 19; all undergraduates, 20.

Housing: 1184 students can be accommodated in college housing, which includes coed dorms and on-campus apartments. Housing is available to freshmen on a first-deposited, first-contract-received basis. On-campus housing is available on a lottery system for upperclassmen. All students may keep cars.

Activities: There are 5 national fraternities and 3 national sororities. There are some groups and organizations on campus, including campus activities board, campus activities board, cheerleading, dance, ethnic, gay, honors, international, newspaper, professional, religious, and social.

Sports: There are 4 intercollegiate sports for men and 4 for women, and 5 intramural sports for men and 5 for women. Facilities include a fitness center located in Biscayne Commons residence hall. The center is equipped with cardio machines, free weights, universal machines, treadmills, and so on and is open 7 days a week.

Disabled Students: Wheelchair ramps, elevators, special parking, specially equipped rest rooms, special class scheduling, lowered drinking fountains, lowered telephones, and special housing are available.

Services: Counseling and information services are available, as is tutoring in every subject.

Campus Safety and Security: Measures include 24-hour foot and vehicle patrol, security escort services, shuttle buses, and informal discussions. There are pamphlets/posters/films and emergency telephones.

Programs of Study: J&W confers the B.S. degree. Associate degrees are also awarded. Bachelor's degrees are awarded in BUSINESS (accounting, business administration and management, entrepreneurial studies, hospitality management services, hotel/motel and restaurant management, marketing management, marketing/retailing/merchandising, recreation and leisure services, sports management, and tourism), ENGINEERING AND ENVIRONMENTAL DESIGN (electrical/electronics engineering and food services technology), SOCIAL SCIENCE (clothing and textiles management/production/services, criminal justice, food production/management/services, paralegal studies, and parks and recreation management).

Required: To graduate, students must complete 180 quarter credit hours, including at least 36 in the major, with a minimum GPA of 2.0. Required classes include English, math, history, economics, science, psychology, sociology, and professional development.

Special: The university offers co-op programs, accelerated degree programs, dual majors, study abroad, and worldwide work-study opportunities in business, hospitality, technology, and culinary arts. Most majors require 11-week internships,.

Admissions: 31% of the current freshmen were in the top fifth of their class; 46% were in the top two fifths.

Requirements: The SAT or ACT is required for some programs. In addition, although SAT and ACT scores are required only for students applying for honors admissions, students who have taken these tests are encouraged to submit their scores. A GPA of 2.0 is required. AP and CLEP credits are accepted. Important factors in the admissions decision are advanced placement or honor courses, extracurricular activities record, and recommendations by school officials.

Procedure: Freshmen are admitted to all sessions. There is a deferred admissions and a rolling admissions plan. Application deadlines are open.

Transfer: 116 transfer students enrolled in 2004-2005. Applications are required to submit official high school and college transcripts and must have earned a minimum college GPA of 2.0.

Visiting: There are regularly scheduled orientations for prospective students, including an introduction to the academic and social aspects of the campus experience through interative sessions. There are guides for informal visits and visitors may sit in on classes and stay overnight. To schedule a visit, contact Admissions.

Financial Aid: In 2005-2006, 83% of all full-time freshmen and 80% of continuing full-time students received some form of financial aid. 77% of full-time freshmen and 73% of continuing full-time students received need-based aid. The average freshman award was $16,742. Need-based scholarships or need-based grants averaged $6734; need-based self-help aid (loans and jobs) averaged $8098; and other non-need-based awards and non-need-based scholarships averaged $4670. The average financial indebtedness of the 2005 graduate was $18,634. J&W is a member of CSS. The FAFSA is required.

International Students: The school actively recruits these students. A satisfactory score is required on the written TOEFL.

Computers: There are general-purpose labs and labs equipped with specialized software applications. The computer labs offer free Internet access, e-mail access, and black-and-white printing. All students may access the system.

Graduates: From July 1, 2004 to June 30, 2005, 190 bachelor's degrees were awarded. The most popular majors were marketing (30%), financial management (22%), and organizational leadership (18%).

Admissions Contact: Jeff Greenip, Director of Admissions. A video is available. E-mail: admissions.fla@jwu.edu Web: wwww.jwu.edu

LYNN UNIVERSITY   E-5

Boca Raton, FL 33431	**(561) 237-7900**
	(800) 888-LYNN; Fax: (561) 237-7100
Full-time: 850 men, 805 women	Faculty: 57
Part-time: 90 men, 165 women	Ph.D.s: 80%
Graduate: 1780men, 175 women	Student/Faculty: 29 to 1
Year: semesters, summer session	Tuition: $22,770
Application Deadline: open	Room & Board: $8010
Freshman Class: n/av	
SAT or ACT: required	**COMPETITIVE**

Lynn University, founded in 1962, is a private, nonsectarian liberal arts college offering graduate and undergraduate programs in the arts and sciences, business, education, hospitality, and preprofessional studies. There are 6 undergraduate and 2 graduate schools. Figures in the above capsule and this profile are approximate. In addition to regional accreditation, LU has baccalaureate program accreditation with ABFSE. The library contains 95,000 volumes, 2000 microform items, and 3500 audio/video tapes/CDs/DVDs, and subscribes to 400 periodicals including electronic. Computerized library services include the card catalog, interlibrary loans, and database searching. Special learning facilities include a learning resource center, art gallery, radio station, and an academic resource center. The 123-acre campus is in a suburban area midway between Fort Lauderdale and Palm Beach. Including any residence halls, there are 17 buildings.

Student Life: 50% of undergraduates are from out of state, mostly the Northeast. Students are from 46 states, 77 foreign countries, and Canada. 34% are from public schools. 27% are white; 17% foreign nationals. The average age of freshmen is 19; all undergraduates, 20. 40% do not continue beyond their first year; 60% remain to graduate.

Housing: 680 students can be accommodated in college housing, which includes single-sex and coed dormitories. On-campus housing is guaranteed for all 4 years. 65% of students live on campus; of those, 74% remain on campus on weekends. All students may keep cars.

Activities: 1% of men belong to 1 national fraternity, 1% of women belong to 1 national sorority. There are 25 groups on campus, including cheerleading, choir, community service, debate, drama, drill team, ethnic, film, honors, international, literary magazine, newspaper, photography, political, professional, radio and TV, religious, social, social service, student government, and yearbook. Popular campus events include Holiday Formal, International Day, and Spring Fling.

Sports: There are 5 intercollegiate sports for men and 7 for women, and 10 intramural sports for men and 6 for women. Facilities include softball, baseball and soccer fields, tennis courts, indoor and outdoor basketball courts, 2 outdoor pools, and a weight facility.

Disabled Students: 90% of the campus is accessible. Wheelchair ramps, elevators, special parking, specially equipped rest rooms, special class scheduling, and lowered drinking fountains are available.

Services: Counseling and information services are available, as is tutoring in most subjects, including There are services for learning disabled students. There is remedial math, reading, and writing.

Campus Safety and Security: Measures include 24-hour foot and vehicle patrol, self-defense education, security escort services, and informal discussions. There are pamphlets/posters/films and lighted pathways/sidewalks.

Programs of Study: LU confers B.A. and B.S. degrees. Associate, master's, and doctoral degrees are also awarded. Bachelor's degrees are awarded in BUSINESS (accounting, business administration and management, fashion merchandising, hotel/motel and restaurant management, marketing/retailing/merchandising, recreational facilities management, sports management, and tourism), COMMUNICATIONS AND THE ARTS (communications, design, fine arts, and graphic design), EDUCATION (early childhood, education, elementary, and secondary), ENGINEERING AND ENVIRONMENTAL DESIGN (aviation administration/management), HEALTH PROFESSIONS (health care administration), SOCIAL SCIENCE (history, human services, humanities, political science/government, prelaw, psychology, and sociology). Accounting, international management, and education are the strongest academically. Business administration and hotel restaurant management are the largest.

Required: Students are required to complete 120 to 128 credits, with 45 to 50 in the major, and must maintain a minimum GPA of 2.0. In addition, all students must complete a core curriculum of 39 semester hours. To graduate, students must complete courses in public forum, academic adventure, and first year experience.

Special: Opportunities are provided for internships, which are required in many majors. There is study abroad in Ireland, Japan, and France. Credit by exam, credit for life experience, and pass/fail options are available. There is a freshman honors program.

Faculty/Classroom: 56% of faculty are male; 44%, female. All teach undergraduates. No introductory courses are taught by graduate students. The average class size in an introductory lecture is 26; in a laboratory, 20; and in a regular course, 22.

Requirements: The SAT or ACT is required. In addition, graduation from an accredited secondary school is required; a GED will be accepted. Applicants must have a minimum high school GPA of 2.0. An essay and an interview are recommended. A GPA of 2.5 is required. AP and CLEP credits are accepted. Important factors in the admissions decision are recommendations by school officials, personality/intangible qualities, and extracurricular activities record.

Procedure: Freshmen are admitted fall and spring. Entrance exams should be taken during the junior or senior year. There are early admissions, deferred admissions, and rolling admissions plans. Application deadlines are open. Application fee is $35. Applications are accepted on-line.

Transfer: 178 transfer students enrolled in a recent year. Transfer students must submit an official transcript from each previous college attended, plus a recommendation from the dean of students. The student must have maintained a minimum GPA of 2.0. An interview is recommended. Most complete an essay and a personal statement. 30 of 120 credits required for the bachelor's degree must be completed at LU.

Visiting: There are guides for informal visits and visitors may sit in on classes. To schedule a visit, contact the Office of Admissions.

Financial Aid: In a recent year, 75% of all full-time freshmen and 50% of continuing full-time students received some form of financial aid. 53% of full-time freshmen and 34% of continuing full-time students received need-based aid. The average freshman award was $16,662. Need-based scholarships or need-based grants averaged $9713 ($20,550 maximum); need-based self-help aid (loans and jobs) averaged $17,505 ($42,625 maximum); non-need-based athletic scholarships averaged $15,940 ($30,000 maximum); and other non-need-based awards and non-need-based scholarships averaged $7677 ($30,000 maximum). 77% of undergraduates work part time. Average annual earnings from campus work were $683. The average financial indebtedness of a recent graduate was $12,572. LU is a member of CSS. The FAFSA or FFS is required. Check with the school for current application deadlines.

International Students: In a recent year, there were 265 international students enrolled. The school actively recruits these students. They must score satisfactorily on the written TOEFL or on the electronic version.

Computers: All students may access the system. There are no time limits and no fees.

Graduates: In a recent year, 355 bachelor's degrees were awarded. The most popular majors were business administration/general manageme (11%), hospitality (8%), and international business (6%). In an average class, 6% graduate in 3 years or less, 30% graduate in 4 years or less, 35% graduate in 5 years or less, and 35% graduate in 6 years or less. 98 companies recruited on campus in a recent year.

Admissions Contact: Alejandra Carvajal, Associate Director of Admission. A video is available. E-mail: *admission@lynn.edu* Web: *www.lynn.edu*

NEW COLLEGE OF FLORIDA
D-4

Sarasota, FL 34243-2197 (941) 359-4269; Fax: (941) 359-4435

Full-time: 266 men, 426 women	Faculty: 63; IIB, av$
Part-time: none	Ph.D.s: 99%
Graduate: none	Student/Faculty: 11 to 1
Year: 4-1-4	Tuition: $3679 ($19,475)
Application Deadline: May 1	Room & Board: $6330
Freshman Class: 708 applied, 454 accepted, 251 enrolled	
SAT Verbal/Math: 680/630*	ACT: 28

HIGHLY COMPETITIVE+

New College of Florida, established in 1960, is the honors college of the State University System of Florida. The library contains 259,886 volumes, 525,736 microform items, and 4635 audio/video tapes/CDs/DVDs. Computerized library services include the card catalog, interlibrary loans, database searching, and Internet access. Special learning facilities include an art gallery and a media and educational technology center, writing resource center, math reading room, marine biology research center, and a living ecosystem teaching and research aquarium. The 144-acre campus is in a suburban area 50 miles south of Tampa, on Sarasota Bay. Including any residence halls, there are 46 buildings.

Student Life: 80% of undergraduates are from Florida. Others are from 38 states, 27 foreign countries, and Canada. 84% are from public schools. 83% are white. The average age of freshmen is 18; all undergraduates, 20. 16% do not continue beyond their first year; 65% remain to graduate.

Housing: 460 students can be accommodated in college housing, which includes single-sex and coed dorms, on-campus apartments, a wellness dorm, apartment-style dorms, and food co-op housing. On-campus housing is guaranteed for the freshman year only. 70% of students live on campus; of those, 70% remain on campus on weekends. All students may keep cars.

Activities: There are no fraternities or sororities. There are 43 groups on campus, including chess, choir, dance, debate, drama, ethnic, film, gay, international, literary magazine, newspaper, photography, political, radio and TV, religious, social, social service, and student government. Popular campus events include Halloween and graduation parties, a diversity discussion service, and a kickball tournament.

Sports: There is no sports program at New College. There is 1 intercollegiate sport for men and 1 for women. Facilities include a soccer field, a softball diamond, a fitness path, outdoor tennis and basketball courts, a volleyball pit, playground equipment, a swimming pool, and a fitness center with Nautilus equipment and indoor facilities for racquetball, aerobics, dance, and yoga.

Disabled Students: 80% of the campus is accessible. Wheelchair ramps, elevators, special parking, specially equipped rest rooms, special class scheduling, lowered drinking fountains, lowered telephones, and special housing are available.

Services: Counseling and information services are available, as is tutoring in most subjects. There is a reader service for the blind. A writing resouce center provides assistance in developing writing skills and strategies.

Campus Safety and Security: Measures include 24-hour foot and vehicle patrol, self-defense education, security escort services, and informal discussions. There are pamphlets/posters/films, emergency telephones, lighted pathways/sidewalks, and 24-hour dispatch/information services, and fire/smoke alarm systems in all dorms.

Programs of Study: New College confers the B.A. degree. Bachelor's degrees are awarded in BIOLOGICAL SCIENCE (biology/biological science), COMMUNICATIONS AND THE ARTS (art history and appreciation, classics, dramatic arts, English, fine arts, Germanic languages and literature, languages, literature, music, and Russian languages and literature), COMPUTER AND PHYSICAL SCIENCE (chemistry, mathematics, natural sciences, and physics), ENGINEERING AND ENVIRONMENTAL DESIGN (environmental science), SOCIAL SCIENCE (anthropology, economics, French studies, history, humanities, international studies, medieval studies, philosophy, political science/government, psychology, public administration, religion, social science, sociology, Spanish studies, urban studies, and women's studies). Psychology, humanities, and chemistry are the largest.

Required: An academic credit system is not used. To qualify for graduation, students must complete 7 semester contracts, which are designed by the student in consultation with faculty; 3 independent study projects completed during January each year, between the fall and spring semesters; a senior thesis, which involves original research or creative work and includes working closely with a faculty committee of the student's choice; and an oral baccalaureate exam, which is primarily a defense of the senior thesis. To fulfill the liberal arts curriculum requirements, students must complete 8 LAC-designated courses, including 1 each in humanities, natural sciences, and social sciences. Exemptions from the LAC requirements are possible through AP exam scores of 4 and 5, IB higher level exam scores of 5 to 7, and transferable college course work at the general education level. Students also must use on-line training to sign up for a college e-mail account and complete the College Level Academic Skills Test or be exempted by appropriate college course work or SAT or ACT scores.

Special: Domestic and international internships, study abroad in 39 countries, accelerated degree programs, student-designed, interdisciplinary and dual majors, and independent study are available. There is a freshman honors program. All departments have honors programs.

Faculty/Classroom: 53% of faculty are male; 47%, female. All teach undergraduates, 95% do research, and 95% do both. The average class size in a regular course is 17.

Admissions: 64% of the 2005-2006 applicants were accepted. The SAT scores for the 2005-2006 freshman class were: Verbal--1% below 500, 5% between 500 and 599, 57% between 600 and 700, and 37% above 700; Math--1% below 500, 28% between 500 and 599, 53% between 600 and 700, and 18% above 700. The ACT scores were 8% between 21 and 23, 26% between 24 and 26, 27% between 27 and 28, and 39% above 28. 11% of the current freshmen were in the top fifth of their class; 95% were in the top two fifths. There were 20 National Merit finalists and 2 semifinalists. 3 freshmen graduated first in their class.

Requirements: The SAT or ACT is required. In addition, graduation from an accredited secondary school (preferred) or the GED is required. High school students should pursue at least 5 academic courses each year, at the most rigorous level available, with a minimum distribution of 4 years of English; 3 years each of math, sciences, and social sciences; 2 consecutive years of the same foreign language; and 3 other academic courses. Application essays must be submitted. A formal interview is recommended for all applicants. A GPA of 3.0 is required. Important factors in the admissions decision are advanced placement or honor courses, evidence of special talent, and recommendations by school officials.

Procedure: Freshmen are admitted fall and spring. Entrance exams should be taken by fall of the senior year. There are deferred admissions and rolling admissions plans. Applications should be filed by May 1 for fall entry and December 31 for spring entry, along with a $30 fee. Notification of regular decision is sent May 1. 23 applicants were on the 2005 waiting list; 15 were admitted. Applications are accepted on-line.

Transfer: In a recent year, 50 transfer students enrolled in 2004-2005. Transfers must be in good academic and financial standing with their previous college(s). Transfers with less than 60 semester hours must submit SAT or ACT scores.

Visiting: There are regularly scheduled orientations for prospective students, including a campus tour, admissions information session, and/or class visits, which must be scheduled individually by the student through Admissions. Visitors may sit in on classes and stay overnight. To schedule a visit, contact the Office of Admissions at *admissions@ncf.edu*.

Financial Aid: In 2005-2006, 88% of all full-time freshmen and 84% of continuing full-time students received some form of financial aid. 34% of full-time freshmen and 39% of continuing full-time students received need-based aid. The average freshman award was $10,983. Need-based scholarships or need-based grants averaged $556 ($6615 maximum); need-based self-help aid (loans and jobs) averaged $2921 ($6125 maximum); and other non-need-based awards and non-need-based scholarships averaged $3600 ($18,800 maximum). 4% of undergraduates work part time. Average annual earnings from campus work are $2049. The average financial indebtedness of the 2005 graduate was $15,045. The FAFSA is required. The deadline for filing freshman financial aid applications for fall entry is March 1.

International Students: There are 38 international students enrolled. The school actively recruits these students. A satisfactory score is required on the written TOEFL. Applicants must also take the SAT or the ACT.

Computers: All students may use the network either on-campus or through a proxy off-campus. Wireless is available in many locations on campus. There are PCs available in the library and in a computer lab. An Apple computer lab is also available to students. All students may access the system 24 hours a day. There are no time limits and no fees.

Graduates: From July 1, 2004 to June 30, 2005, 125 bachelor's degrees were awarded. The most popular majors were political science (7%), psychology (5%), and humanities (5%). In an average class, 59% graduate in 4 years or less, 65% graduate in 5 years or less, and 65% graduate in 6 years or less. 60 companies recruited on campus in 2004-2005. Of the 2004 graduating class, 20% were enrolled in graduate school within 6 months of graduation.

Admissions Contact: Kathy Killion, Dean of Admissions and Financial Aid. E-mail: *admissions@ncf.edu* Web: *www.ncf.edu*

NORTHWOOD UNIVERSITY

West Palm Beach, FL 33409-2911
(561) 478-5500
(800) 458-8325; Fax: (561) 640-3328

E-5

Full-time: 400 men, 260 women	**Faculty:** 14
Part-time: 25 men, 10 women	**Ph.D.s:** 36%
Graduate: none	**Student/Faculty:** 47 to 1
Year: quarters, summer session	**Tuition:** $14,510
Application Deadline: see profile	**Room & Board:** $7050
Freshman Class: n/av	
SAT or ACT: required	**COMPETITIVE**

Northwood University, founded in 1959, is a private institution offering undergraduate degrees in business administration and management. Campuses are located in Florida, Michigan, and Texas. The Florida campus opened in 1982. Figures in the above capsule and this profile are approximate. The library contains 23,000 volumes and 450 audio/video tapes/CDs/DVDs, and subscribes to 130 periodicals including electronic. Computerized library services include the card catalog, database searching, and Internet access. Special learning facilities include a learning resource center, art gallery, and the Ethics Center for Business. The 84-acre campus is in a suburban area 70 miles north of Miami. Including any residence halls, there are 10 buildings.

Student Life: 62% of undergraduates are from out of state, mostly the South. Students are from 35 states, 47 foreign countries, and Canada. 70% are from public schools. 57% are white; 23% foreign nationals. The average age of freshmen is 18; all undergraduates, 21. 40% do not continue beyond their first year; 41% remain to graduate.

Housing: 432 students can be accommodated in college housing, which includes single-sex on-campus apartments. On-campus housing is guaranteed for the freshman year only. 56% of students commute. All students may keep cars.

Activities: There are no fraternities or sororities. There are 15 groups on campus, including art, computers, debate, drama, ethnic, honors, international, newspaper, photography, political, professional, social, social service, student government, and yearbook. Popular campus events include Automotive Industry Show, Diversity Month, and carnival.

Sports: There are 4 intercollegiate sports for men and 5 for women, and 6 intramural sports for men and 6 for women. Facilities include baseball, softball, and soccer fields, a student center, and a recreation center with an outdoor swimming pool and basketball, tennis, and handball/racquetball courts.

Disabled Students: 80% of the campus is accessible. Wheelchair ramps, elevators, special parking, specially equipped rest rooms, special class scheduling, lowered drinking fountains, and lowered telephones are available.

Services: Counseling and information services are available, as is tutoring in every subject, including accounting, math, English, and computers. There is remedial math and writing.

Campus Safety and Security: Measures include 24-hour foot and vehicle patrol, informal discussions, pamphlets/posters/films, and emergency telephones. There are lighted pathways/sidewalks.

Programs of Study: Northwood confers the B.B.A. degree. Associate degrees are also awarded. Bachelor's degrees are awarded in BUSINESS (accounting, banking and finance, business administration and management, hotel/motel and restaurant management, international business management, management information systems, marketing management, sports management, and transportation and travel marketing), COMMUNICATIONS AND THE ARTS (advertising). Accounting and management information systems are the strongest academically. Business management and automotive marketing are the largest.

Required: To graduate, all students must complete a minimum of 180 credit hours, with 36 credit hours in the major. A minimum GPA of 2.0 must be maintained, and 6 credits of computer science management and 2 credits of executive fitness must be completed. Internships for 1 to 6 credits are required in some majors.

Special: Northwood offers cooperative programs and cross-registration with Georgian College in Canada, internships with various automotive and fashion marketing corporations, study abroad in 20 countries, and various work-study programs. Externships are available for all programs and required in 4. Also available are an accelerated degree program in all majors, dual majors, credit for military experience, and nondegree study. There is a freshman honors program.

Faculty/Classroom: 65% of faculty are male; 35%, female. All teach undergraduates. The average class size in an introductory lecture is 27; in a laboratory, 13; and in a regular course, 18.

Requirements: The SAT or ACT is required. In addition, applicants must be graduates of an accredited secondary school or have a GED certificate. An interview is recommended. A GPA of 2.0 is required. AP and CLEP credits are accepted. Important factors in the admissions decision are advanced placement or honor courses, evidence of special talent, and leadership record.

Procedure: Freshmen are admitted to all sessions. Entrance exams should be taken in the fall of the senior year. There are early admissions, deferred admissions, and rolling admissions plans. Applications should be filed by August 1 for fall entry, November 1 for winter entry, February 15 for spring entry, and June 1 for summer entry, along with a $25 fee. Notification is sent on a rolling basis. Applications are accepted on-line.

Transfer: 139 transfer students enrolled in a recent year. Applicants must have a minimum 2.0 GPA, with at least 15 credit hours earned and official transcripts of all completed college-level work. Good academic and social standing are required. An interview is recommended. 45 of 180 credits required for the bachelor's degree must be completed at Northwood.

Visiting: There are regularly scheduled orientations for prospective students, including a fall and spring open house, campus tours, and meetings with students and financial aid and academic staff. There are guides for informal visits and visitors may sit in on classes and stay overnight. To schedule a visit, contact the Admissions Office.

Financial Aid: In a recent year, 91% of all full-time freshmen and 86% of continuing full-time students received some form of financial aid. 55% of full-time freshmen and 50% of continuing full-time students received need-based aid. The average freshman award was $13,030. Need-based scholarships or need-based grants averaged $9183 ($15,434 maximum); need-based self-help aid (loans and jobs) averaged $4318 ($4725 maximum); non-need-based athletic scholarships averaged $4044 ($12,500 maximum); and other non-need-based awards and non-need-based scholarships averaged $1799 ($24,491 maximum). 9% of undergraduates worked part time. Average annual earnings from campus work were $1050. The average financial indebtedness of a recent graduate was $13,495. The FAFSA is required. Check with the school for current application deadlines.

International Students: In a recent year, there were 149 international students enrolled. The school actively recruits these students. They must score satisfactorily on the written TOEFL or on the electronic version.

Computers: All students may access the system. There are no time limits and no fees.

Graduates: In a recent year, 140 bachelor's degrees were awarded. The most popular majors were marketing/management (26%), automotive marketing (23%), and international business (19%). In an average class, 22% graduate in 4 years or less, and 41% graduate in 6 years or less.

Admissions Contact: Jack Letvinchuk, Admissions Director. A video is available. E-mail: *fladmit@northwood.edu* Web: *www.northwood.edu*

NOVA SOUTHEASTERN UNIVERSITY   E-5
Fort Lauderdale, FL 33314

(954) 262-8000
(800) 338-4723, ext. 8000

Full-time: 867 men, 2484 women	Faculty: 70
Part-time: 527 men, 1447 women	Ph.Ds: 89%
Graduate: 6354 men, 13,721 women	Student/Faculty: 48 to 1
Year: trimesters, summer session	Tuition: $17,800
Application Deadline: open	Room & Board: $6520
Freshman Class: n/av	
SAT Verbal/Math: 510/520*	ACT: 21 COMPETITIVE

Nova Southeastern University, founded in 1964, is an independent institution offering degree programs in liberal arts, sciences, business, health sciences, education, and preprofessional studies. The university also offers graduate and first-professional programs. There are 3 undergraduate and 8 graduate schools. In addition to regional accreditation, NSU has baccalaureate program accreditation with NLN. The 3 libraries contain 690,000 volumes, 1,347,411 microform items, and 19,878 audio/video tapes/CDs/DVDs, and subscribe to 11,455 periodicals including electronic. Computerized library services include the card catalog, interlibrary loans, database searching, and Internet access. Special learning facilities include a learning resource center and radio station. The 300-acre campus is in a suburban area 10 miles west of downtown Fort Lauderdale. Including any residence halls, there are 39 buildings.

Student Life: 78% of undergraduates are from Florida. Others are from 21 states, 20 foreign countries, and Canada. 32% are white; 28% Hispanic; 25% African American. The average age of all undergraduates is 30. 33% do not continue beyond their first year.

Housing: 584 students can be accommodated in college housing, which includes coed dorms, on-campus apartments, and married-student housing. On-campus housing is guaranteed for the freshman year only and is available on a first-come, first-served basis. 89% of students commute. Alcohol is not permitted. All students may keep cars.

Activities: There are 3 national fraternities and 2 national sororities. There are 34 groups on campus, including cheerleading, chorus, drama, environmental, ethnic, honors, international, literary magazine, newspaper, political, professional, radio and TV, religious, social, and student government. Popular campus events include Hollywood Squares, Life 101, and Student Life Achievement Awards.

Sports: There are 5 intercollegiate sports for men and 8 for women, and 11 intramural sports for men and 11 for women. Facilities include baseball and soccer fields and a recreational complex with a swimming pool and basketball and tennis courts.

Disabled Students: Wheelchair ramps, elevators, special parking, specially equipped rest rooms, lowered drinking fountains, special housing, and wheelchair lifts in some buildings are available.

Services: Counseling and information services are available, as is tutoring in most subjects. There is remedial math, reading, and writing. Availability of remedial tutoring is contingent on registration in specific courses.

Campus Safety and Security: Measures include 24-hour foot and vehicle patrol, security escort services, shuttle buses, and informal discussions. There are pamphlets/posters/films, emergency telephones, and lighted pathways/sidewalks.

Programs of Study: NSU confers B.A., B.S., B.H. Sc., and B.S.N. degrees. Associate, master's, and doctoral degrees are also awarded. Bachelor's degrees are awarded in AGRICULTURE (environmental studies), BIOLOGICAL SCIENCE (biology/biological science and marine biology), BUSINESS (accounting, banking and finance, business administration and management, and sports management), COMMUNICATIONS AND THE ARTS (dramatic arts and English), COMPUTER AND PHYSICAL SCIENCE (computer science and information sciences and systems), EDUCATION (athletic training, early childhood, education of the exceptional child, elementary, and sports and wellness studies), HEALTH PROFESSIONS (health science, nursing, and physician's assistant), SOCIAL SCIENCE (criminal justice, history, humanities, paralegal studies, prelaw, and psychology). Business and education are the largest.

Required: To graduate, all students must complete at least 120 credit hours. A minimum 2.25 GPA is needed for courses in the major, and a 2.0 for all other courses.

Special: NSU offers internships, study abroad, work-study, accelerated degree programs, and nondegree study. Combined bachelor-professional degree programs and a dual admission program are also available. There are 4 national honor societies, a freshman honors program, and 3 departmental honors programs.

Faculty/Classroom: 57% of faculty are male; 43%, female. No introductory courses are taught by graduate students. The average class size in a regular course is 18.

Admissions: The SAT scores for the 2005-2006 freshman class were: Verbal--42% below 500, 47% between 500 and 599, 9% between 600 and 700, and 1% above 700; Math--41% below 500, 40% between 500 and 599, 17% between 600 and 700, and 2% above 700.

Requirements: The SAT or ACT is required. In addition, applicants must be graduates of an accredited secondary school or have a GED certificate. An interview is recommended. AP and CLEP credits are accepted. Important factors in the admissions decision are advanced placement or honor courses, leadership record, and recommendations by alumni.

Procedure: Freshmen are admitted to all sessions. Entrance exams should be taken by June 15 for the fall semester. There are early admissions and deferred admissions plans. There is a rolling admissions plan. Application deadlines are open. The fall 2005 application fee was $50. Applications are accepted on-line.

Transfer: Applicants must have a minimum 2.5 GPA from a regionally accredited institution. An interview is recommended. At least 50% of credits in the major or specialty must be earned at NSU. 30 of 120 credits required for the bachelor's degree must be completed at NSU.

Visiting: There are regularly scheduled orientations for prospective students. There are guides for informal visits and visitors may sit in on classes. To schedule a visit, contact the Admissions Office at *ncsinfo@nova.edu.*

Financial Aid: In 2005-2006, 78% of all full-time freshmen and 76% of continuing full-time students received some form of financial aid. 77% of full-time freshmen and 73% of continuing full-time students received need-based aid. The average freshman award was $15,923. Need-based scholarships or need-based grants averaged $9297; need-based self-help aid (loans and jobs) averaged $7290; non-need-based athletic scholarships averaged $8384; and other non-need-based awards and non-need-based scholarships averaged $3638. The average financial indebtedness of the 2005 graduate was $26,658. The FAFSA and the college's own financial statement are required. The priority date for freshman financial aid applications for fall entry is April 15.

International Students: There are 149 international students enrolled. The school actively recruits these students. They must score satisfactorily on the TOEFL and also take the MELAB. The SAT with a satisfactory verbal score may replace the TOEFL.

Computers: Wireless access is available. Students must have their own ISP. All students may access the system. There are no time limits and no fees. It is strongly recommended that all students have a personal computer. Students in the law I.D. program are required to provide a personal computer.

Graduates: From July 1, 2004 to June 30, 2005, 1173 bachelor's degrees were awarded. The most popular majors were business (38%), health professions (13%), and education (12%).

Admissions Contact: Maria Dillard, Undergraduate Admissions. E-mail: *ncsinfo@nova.edu* Web: *undergrad.nova.edu/admissions*

PALM BEACH ATLANTIC UNIVERSITY — E-5

West Palm Beach, FL 33416-4708
(561) 803-2100
(888) GO TO PBA; Fax: (561) 803-2115

Full-time: 824 men, 1460 women	**Faculty:** 138
Part-time: 88 men, 114 women	**Ph.Ds:** 74%
Graduate: 218 men, 467 women	**Student/Faculty:** 17 to 1
Year: semesters, summer session	**Tuition:** $17,350
Application Deadline: open	**Room & Board:** $6247
Freshman Class: 2224 applied, 974 accepted, 450 enrolled	
SAT Verbal/Math: 580/575*	**ACT:** 23 **VERY COMPETITIVE**

Palm Beach Atlantic University, founded in 1968, is a comprehensive Christian university. There are 9 undergraduate and 5 graduate schools. In addition to regional accreditation, PBA has baccalaureate program accreditation with ACPE, IACBE, and NASM. The library contains 181,849 volumes, 26,762 microform items, and 5213 audio/video tapes/CDs/DVDs, and subscribes to 40,417 periodicals including electronic. Computerized library services include the card catalog, interlibrary loans, database searching, and Internet access. Special learning facilities include a children's literature collection. The 25-acre campus is in an urban area 60 miles north of Miami. Including any residence halls, there are 18 buildings.

Student Life: 72% of undergraduates are from Florida. Others are from 45 states, 18 foreign countries, and Canada. 68% are white; 15% African American. 82% are Protestant; 9% Catholic; 8% claim no religious affiliation. The average age of freshmen is 22; all undergraduates, 24. 23% do not continue beyond their first year; 43% remain to graduate.

Housing: 1114 students can be accommodated in college housing, which includes single-sex dorms and on-campus apartments. 55% of students commute. Alcohol is not permitted. All students may keep cars.

Activities: There are no fraternities or sororities. There are 38 groups on campus, including art, cheerleading, chess, choir, chorale, chorus, computers, concert band, dance, drama, ethnic, film, honors, international, jazz band, literary magazine, music ensembles, musical theater, newspaper, orchestra, pep band, photography, political, professional, radio and TV, religious, social, social service, student government, symphony, and yearbook. Popular campus events include American Free Enterprise Day and Christival.

Sports: There are 6 intercollegiate sports for men and 6 for women, and 25 intramural sports for men and 25 for women. Facilities include a 60,000-square-foot sports and recreation center, a 1750-seat main arena, and an auxiliary gym for basketball, volleyball, and badminton. Racquetball courts, a weight room, a fitness room, a dance room, and an indoor jogging track are also available.

Disabled Students: 90% of the campus is accessible. Wheelchair ramps, elevators, special parking, and specially equipped rest rooms are available.

Services: Counseling and information services are available, as is tutoring in most subjects. There is remedial math, reading, and writing.

Campus Safety and Security: Measures include 24-hour foot and vehicle patrol, self-defense education, security escort services, and informal discussions. There are pamphlets/posters/films, emergency telephones, and lighted pathways/sidewalks.

Programs of Study: PBA confers B.A., B.S., B.G.S., B.Mus., and B.S.N. degrees. Associate, master's, and doctoral degrees are also awarded. Bachelor's degrees are awarded in BIOLOGICAL SCIENCE (biology/biological science), BUSINESS (banking and finance, business administration and management, entrepreneurial studies, international business management, management science, marketing management, and sports management), COMMUNICATIONS AND THE ARTS (art, broadcasting, communications, dance, dramatic arts, English, film arts, graphic design, journalism, music, music performance, music theory and composition, musical theater, piano/organ, speech/debate/rhetoric, and voice), COMPUTER AND PHYSICAL SCIENCE (computer science, and mathematics), EDUCATION (art, athletic training, drama, elementary, English, mathematics, music, physical, science, secondary, social science, and specific learning disabilities), HEALTH PROFESSIONS (exercise science, and nursing), SOCIAL SCIENCE (biblical studies, Christian studies, crosscultural studies, history, liberal arts/general studies, ministries, philosophy, political science/government, prelaw, psychology, and religious music). Business, psychology, and education are the strongest academically as well as the largest.

Required: Students must complete core requirements and 120 credit hours, with a minimum of 30 credit hours in the major and 42 upper-level hours. A minimum 2.0 GPA is required.

Special: PBA offers work-study, internships, a student-designed interdisciplinary major, dual majors, accelerated degree programs in organizational management and ministry, and a Washington semester and study abroad through the Coalition of Christian Colleges and Universities. A 2-2 engineering degree with the University of Florida, ESL, and teacher certification are also offered. There is a freshman honors program.

Faculty/Classroom: 58% of faculty are male; 42%, female. 88% teach undergraduates. No introductory courses are taught by graduate students. The average class size in an introductory lecture is 30; in a laboratory, 24; and in a regular course, 20.

Admissions: 44% of the 2005-2006 applicants were accepted. The SAT scores for the 2005-2006 freshman class were: Verbal--29% below 500, 46% between 500 and 599, 22% between 600 and 700, and 3% above 700; Math--29% below 500, 47% between 500 and 599, 22% between 600 and 700, and 2% above 700. The ACT scores were 26% below 21, 35% between 21 and 23, 24% between 24 and 26, 10% between 27 and 28, and 5% above 28. 39% of the current freshmen were in the top fifth of their class; 65% were in the top two fifths.

Requirements: A satisfactory score on the SAT or ACT is required for some programs. In addition, applicants must be graduates of an accredited secondary school or have a GED certificate, and have completed 18 academic credits—4 in English, 3 in math, science, social studies, and history, and 2 in a foreign language. An essay and an interview are required. A portfolio is recommended for art students. A GPA of 2.0 is required. AP and CLEP credits are accepted. Important factors in the admissions decision are advanced placement or honor courses, leadership record, and personality/intangible qualities.

Procedure: Freshmen are admitted to all sessions. Entrance exams should be taken in the junior year of high school. There are early admissions and deferred admissions plans. Application deadlines are open. The fall 2005 application fee was $25. Notification is send on a rolling basis beginning December 8. Applications are accepted on-line.

Transfer: 217 transfer students enrolled in 2004-2005. Transfer students must have a minimum 2.0 GPA, a minimum of 12 credit hours, and 2 letters of recommendation. An interview is encouraged. 32 of 120 credits required for the bachelor's degree must be completed at PBA.

Visiting: There are regularly scheduled orientations for prospective students, including a general open house and a school-specific open house. There are guides for informal visits and visitors may sit in on classes and stay overnight. To schedule a visit, contact the Admissions Office.

Financial Aid: In 2005-2006, 95% of all full-time students received some form of financial aid. 78% of full-time freshmen and 29% of continuing full-time students received need-based aid. The average freshman award was $3445. Need-based scholarships or need-based grants averaged $3375 ($8050 maximum); need-based self-help aid (loans and jobs) averaged $2745 ($5500 maximum); non-need-based athletic scholarships averaged $7938 ($18,500 maximum); and other non-need-based awards and non-need-based scholarships averaged $2444 ($13,500 maximum). 13% of undergraduates work part time. Average annual earnings from campus work are $2000. The average financial indebtedness of the 2005 graduate was $24,393. The FAFSA, the state aid form, and the college's own financial statement are required. The deadline for filing freshman financial aid applications for fall entry is April 1.

International Students: There are 78 international students enrolled. The school actively recruits these students. They must score satisfactorily on the written TOEFL.

Computers: Internet access is available through computer labs. All students may access the system. There are no time limits and no fees. It is strongly recommended that all students have a personal computer.

Graduates: From July 1, 2004 to June 30, 2005, 744 bachelor's degrees were awarded. The most popular majors were business/management (42%), communication (12%), and education (9%). In an average class, 2% graduate in 3 years or less, 42% graduate in 5 years or less, and 43% graduate in 6 years or less. 188 companies recruited on campus in 2004-2005.

Admissions Contact: Buck James, Vice President of Enrollment Services. E-mail: admit@pba.edu Web: www.pba.edu

RINGLING SCHOOL OF ART AND DESIGN — D-4

Sarasota, FL 34234-5896
(941) 351-5100
(800) 255-7695; Fax: (941) 359-7517

Full-time: 532 men, 518 women	**Faculty:** 60
Part-time: 22 men, 16 women	**Ph.Ds:** 61%
Graduate: none	**Student/Faculty:** 18 to 1
Year: semesters	**Tuition:** $21,400
Application Deadline: open	**Room & Board:** $9613
Freshman Class: 1059 applied, 782 accepted, 364 enrolled	
SAT Verbal/Math: 540/510*	**ACT:** 23 **SPECIAL**

Ringling School of Art and Design, founded in 1931, is a private art college. In addition to regional accreditation, Ringling School has baccalaureate program accreditation with FIDER and NASAD. The library contains 48,925 volumes and 5565 audio/video tapes/CDs/DVDs, and subscribes to 340 periodicals including electronic. Computerized library services include interlibrary loans, database searching, and Internet access. Special learning facilities include a learning resource center, art gallery, and, a total of 125,000 slides. The 35-acre campus is in an urban area 50 miles south of Tampa. Including any residence halls, there are 69 buildings.

Student Life: 50% of undergraduates are from out of state, mostly the South. Others are from 44 states, 28 foreign countries, and Canada. 77% are white; 11% Hispanic. The average age of freshmen is 19; all undergraduates, 21. 14% do not continue beyond their first year; 70% remain to graduate.

Housing: 523 students can be accommodated in college housing, which includes single-sex and coed dorms, on-campus apartments, and married-student housing. On-campus housing is available on a first-come, first-served basis and is available on a lottery system for upperclassmen. Priority is given to out-of-town students. 52% of students commute. Alcohol is not permitted. All students may keep cars.

Activities: 1% of men belong to 2 national fraternities; 1% of women belong to 1 national sororitiy. There are 22 groups on campus, including art, computers, dance, drama, ethnic, film, gay, international, professional, religious, social, social service, and student government. Popular campus events include All School Welcome Back Beach Party, Valentines Dance, and Latin Ball.

Sports: There are 4 intramural sports for men and 4 for women. Facilities include a recreation room with pool tables.

Disabled Students: 80% of the campus is accessible. Wheelchair ramps, elevators, special parking, specially equipped rest rooms, special class scheduling, lowered telephones, and interpreters for the hearing-impaired are available.

Services: Counseling and information services are available, as is tutoring in some subjects, including English, art history, and history. There is remedial writing.

Campus Safety and Security: Measures include 24-hour foot and vehicle patrol, security escort services, informal discussions, and emergency telephones. There are lighted pathways/sidewalks.

Programs of Study: Ringling School confers the B.F.A. degree. Bachelor's degrees are awarded in COMMUNICATIONS AND THE ARTS (fine arts, graphic design, illustration, and photography), ENGINEERING AND ENVIRONMENTAL DESIGN (computer graphics and interior design). Illustration and computer animation are the strongest academically and have the largest enrollments.

Required: To graduate, all students must complete 123 semester hours, including the CORE studio program, 75 hours of studio art, 30 hours of liberal arts, and 12 hours of art history, with 75 hours in the major. A minimum 2.0 GPA and courses in drawing, 2- and 3-dimensional design, art history, and written communication are required.

Special: The college offers cross-registration with the Association of Independent Colleges of Art and Design (AICAD) and study abroad in France, England, and Ireland. Also available are credit by portfolio, and a nondegree continuing education program.

Faculty/Classroom: 63% of faculty are male; 37%, female. All teach undergraduates. The average class size in liberal arts classes is 25 and in studio courses 17.

Admissions: 74% of the 2005-2006 applicants were accepted. The SAT scores for the 2005-2006 freshman class were: Verbal--32% below 500, 38% between 500 and 599, 26% between 600 and 700, and 4% above 700; Math--44% below 500, 35% between 500 and 599, 20% between 600 and 700, and 1% above 700.

Requirements: Applicants must have received either a standard high school diploma from an accredited secondary school or a GED. Admission is based on the academic record, letters of recommendation, and a portfolio. An essay is required and an interview is recommended. A GPA of 2.0 is required. AP and CLEP credits are accepted. Important factors in the admissions decision are evidence of special talent, advanced placement or honor courses, and recommendations by school officials.

Procedure: Freshmen are admitted in the fall. Applications deadline are open. There is a $35 application fee. Notification is sent on a rolling basis. A waiting list is an active part of the admissions procedure.Applications are accepted on-line.

Transfer: 142 transfer students enrolled in 2004-2005. Transfer students must meet the same criteria as freshmen and must also submit college transcripts. 45 of 123 credits required for the bachelor's degree must be completed at Ringling School.

Visiting: There are guides for informal visits and visitors may sit in on classes. To schedule a visit, contact the Admissions Office.

Financial Aid: In 2005-2006, 76% of all full-time freshmen and 72% of continuing full-time students received some form of financial aid. 66% of full-time freshmen and 61% of continuing full-time students received need-based aid. The average freshman award was $17,183. Need-based scholarships or need-based grants averaged $2450 ($6000 maximum); need-based self-help aid (loans and jobs) averaged $2650 ($10,500 maximum); other non-need-based awards and non-need-based scholarships averaged $28,000; and outside scholarships averaged $2897 ($20,320 maximum). 24% of undergraduates work part time. Average annual earnings from campus work are $1540. The average financial indebtedness of the 2005 graduate was $26,700. The FAFSA and the college's own financial statement are required. The priority date for freshman financial aid applications for fall entry is March 1.

International Students: There are 54 international students enrolled. The school actively recruits these students. They must take the TOEFL and submit a portfolio.

Computers: Ringling provides students with high speed Internet connection and an internal network that is accessible from every dorm room, lab, library, and office. This includes the campus's wireless network that is accessible internally and externally on the entire campus. There are over 600 Windows and Macintosh workstations available in labs. All students may access the system. There are no time limits and no fees.

Graduates: From July 1, 2004 to June 30, 2005, 196 bachelor's degrees were awarded. The most popular majors were illustration (41%), computer animation (18%), and graphic and interactive communication (16%). In an average class, 67% graduate in 4 years or less, 69% graduate in 5 years or less, and 70% graduate in 6 years or less. 49 companies recruited on campus in 2004-2005. Of the 2004 graduating class, 7% were enrolled in graduate school within 6 months of graduation and 85% were employed.

Admissions Contact: James H. Dean, Dean of Admissions.
E-mail: *admissions@ringling.edu* Web: *ringling.edu*

ROLLINS COLLEGE   D-3

Winter Park, FL 32789   (407) 646-2161; Fax: (407) 646-1502

Full-time: 689 men, 1030 women	**Faculty:** 157; IIA, av$
Part-time: none	**Ph.D.s:** 91%
Graduate: 351 men, 423 women	**Student/Faculty:** 11 to 1
Year: semesters	**Tuition:** $29,224
Application Deadline: February 15	**Room & Board:** $9142
Freshman Class: 2958 applied, 1578 accepted, 464 enrolled	
SAT Verbal/Math: 590/590*	**ACT:** 25 **VERY COMPETITIVE**

Rollins College, founded in 1885, is a private, liberal arts institution. In addition to regional accreditation, Rollins has baccalaureate program accreditation with ACS and NASM. The library contains 300,783 volumes, 43,589 microform items, and 5083 audio/video tapes/CDs/DVDs, and subscribes to 15,290 periodicals including electronic. Computerized library services include the card catalog, interlibrary loans, database searching, Internet access, and laptop Internet portals. Special learning facilities include a learning resource center, art gallery, radio station, TV station, art museum, theaters, writing center, and student resource center. The 70-acre campus is in a suburban area 5 miles north of Orlando. Including any residence halls, there are 70 buildings.

Student Life: 54% of undergraduates are from Florida. Others are from 42 states, 23 foreign countries, and Canada. 56% are from public schools. 79% are white. The average age of freshmen is 18; all undergraduates, 20. 16% do not continue beyond their first year; 63% remain to graduate.

Housing: 1274 students can be accommodated in college housing, which includes coed dorms, on-campus apartments, fraternity houses, and sorority houses. In addition, there are honors houses and special-interest houses. On-campus housing is guaranteed for all 4 years. 65% of students live on campus; of those, 90% remain on campus on weekends. Upperclassmen may keep cars.

Activities: 35% of men belong to 1 local fraternity and 4 national fraternities; 37% of women belong to 1 local sorority and 4 national sororities. There are 73 groups on campus, including art, cheerleading, chess, chorale, computers, dance, debate, drama, drill team, drum and bugle corps, ethnic, film, gay, honors, international, literary magazine, musical theater, newspaper, pep band, photography, political, professional, radio and TV, religious, social, social service, student government, and yearbook. Popular campus events include WPRK 91.5 Marathon, Civic Engagement Week, and Sexual Assault Awareness Week.

Sports: There are 10 intercollegiate sports for men and 12 for women, and 18 intramural sports for men and 18 for women. Facilities include a 2500-seat auditorium, a 600-seat stadium, tennis courts, baseball and soccer fields, a field house with a gym that seats 2500, a weight room, a boat house, and a swimming pool.

Disabled Students: 60% of the campus is accessible. Wheelchair ramps, elevators, special parking, specially equipped rest rooms, special class scheduling, lowered drinking fountains, lowered telephones, and special housing are available.

Services: Counseling and information services are available, as is tutoring in every subject. There is a reader service for the blind, and remedial math, reading, and writing.

Campus Safety and Security: Measures include 24-hour foot and vehicle patrol, self-defense education, security escort services, and informal discussions. There are pamphlets/posters/films, emergency telephones, lighted pathways/sidewalks, and 24-hour locked residential units.

Programs of Study: Rollins confers the A.B. degree. Master's degrees are also awarded. Bachelor's degrees are awarded in BIOLOGICAL SCIENCE (biochemistry and biology/biological science), BUSINESS (international business management), COMMUNICATIONS AND THE ARTS (art history and appreciation, dramatic arts, English, French, music performance, Spanish, and studio art), COMPUTER AND PHYSICAL SCIENCE (chemistry, computer science, mathematics, and physics), EDUCATION (elementary), ENGINEERING AND ENVIRONMENTAL DESIGN (environmental science), SOCIAL SCIENCE (anthropology, classical/ancient civilization, economics, European studies, history, international relations, Latin American studies, philosophy, political science/

government, psychology, religion, and sociology). International business, psychology, and economics are the largest.

Required: All students must complete at least 6 skills, including at least 4 cognitive, and at least 2 affective courses, a values requirement, and 3 phys ed courses. A minimum of 140 semester hours, with 48-64 in the course major, and a minimum GPA of 2.0 are required to graduate.

Special: Rollins offers cross-registration with the evening studies division, co-op programs with American University in Washington, D.C., and Duke University School of Forestry and Environmental Studies. Departmental and professional internships, study abroad in 9 countries, and a Washington semester are also options. Also available are an accelerated (3-2) MBA program, a B.A.-B.S. degree in preengineering with Washington University (St. Louis), Auburn, and Columbia Universities, an interdepartmental biochemistry/molecular biology major, dual majors in any combination, and student-designed majors. Nondegree study and pass/fail options are possible. There are 5 national honor societies, a freshman honors program, and 28 departmental honors programs.

Faculty/Classroom: 61% of faculty are male; 39%, female. No introductory courses are taught by graduate students. The average class size in an introductory lecture is 17; in a laboratory, 17; and in a regular course, 17.

Admissions: 53% of the 2005-2006 applicants were accepted. The SAT scores for the 2005-2006 freshman class were: Verbal--7% below 500, 48% between 500 and 599, 38% between 600 and 700, and 7% above 700; Math--9% below 500, 42% between 500 and 599, 41% between 600 and 700, and 8% above 700. The ACT scores were 12% below 21, 30% between 21 and 23, 27% between 24 and 26, 15% between 27 and 28, and 16% above 28. 58% of the current freshmen were in the top fifth of their class; 87% were in the top two fifths. 5 freshmen graduated first in their class.

Requirements: The SAT or ACT is required. The ACT Optional Writing test is also recommended. In addition, applicants must be graduates of an accredited secondary school or have a GED certificate, and have completed 4 years of English, 3 of math, and 2 each of foreign language, science, and social studies. An essay is required. SAT Subject tests in writing, math, and foreign language and an interview are recommended. AP and CLEP credits are accepted. Important factors in the admissions decision are advanced placement or honor courses, evidence of special talent, and extracurricular activities record.

Procedure: Freshmen are admitted fall and spring. Entrance exams should be taken by the first semester of the senior year. There are early decision, early admissions, and deferred admissions plans. Early decision applications should be filed by January 15; regular applications, by February 15 for fall entry and December 1 for spring entry. Notification of early decision is sent February 1; regular decision, April 1. 188 early decision candidates were accepted for the 2005-2006 class. 175 applicants were on the 2005 waiting list; 40 were admitted. Applications are accepted on-line.

Transfer: 59 transfer students enrolled in 2004-2005. Transfer students must satisfy all regular admission requirements and submit official transcripts of college and high school work and SAT or ACT scores. A recommended 3.0 GPA and a year's worth of credit hours earned are required. An interview is recommended. 64 of 140 credits required for the bachelor's degree must be completed at Rollins.

Visiting: There are regularly scheduled orientations for prospective students, including 2 all-campus previews in the fall. There are guides for informal visits and visitors may sit in on classes and stay overnight. To schedule a visit, contact the Office of Admissions at *admissions@rollins.edu.*

Financial Aid: In 2005-2006, 74% of all full-time freshmen and 72% of continuing full-time students received some form of financial aid. 39% of full-time freshmen and 37% of continuing full-time students received need-based aid. The average freshman award was $22,469. Need-based scholarships or need-based grants averaged $17,946 ($34,878 maximum); need-based self-help aid (loans and jobs) averaged $5220 ($6825 maximum); non-need-based athletic scholarships averaged $15,616 ($38,366 maximum); and other non-need-based awards and non-need-based scholarships averaged $8850 ($41,866 maximum). 18% of undergraduates work part time. Average annual earnings from campus work are $1063. The average financial indebtedness of the 2005 graduate was $14,000. Rollins is a member of CSS. The FAFSA and the college's own financial statement are required. The deadline for filing freshman financial aid applications for fall entry is March 1.

International Students: There are 66 international students enrolled. The school actively recruits these students. They must take the TOEFL and also take the SAT or ACT.

Computers: Wireless access is available. There are 8 computer labs on campus with 15 computers per lab. 30% of classrooms allow wire connectivity between student laptops and Internet, and 98% of classrooms allow wireless connectivity between laptops and Internet. Network access is available in dorm rooms and lounges. Rollins permits and provides student Web pages. Students can remotely access the Web and get their e-mail through the college's connection. Students can register for classess and perform additional administrative functions online. All students may

access the system. There are no time limits. The fee is $275. It is strongly recommended that all students have a personal computer.

Graduates: From July 1, 2004 to June 30, 2005, 394 bachelor's degrees were awarded. The most popular majors were psychology (14%), international business (10%), and economics (9%). In an average class, 63% graduate in 6 years or less. Of the 2004 graduating class, 25% were enrolled in graduate school within 6 months of graduation and 62% were employed.

Admissions Contact: David G. Erdmann, Dean of Admission and Student Financial Planning. A video is available.
E-mail: *admission@rollins.edu*
Web: *http://www.rollins/admission/index.shtml*

SAINT LEO UNIVERSITY   D-3
Saint Leo, FL 33574-6665   (352) 588-8283
                                    (800) 334-5532; Fax: (352) 588-8257

Full-time: 600 men, 735 women	**Faculty:** 66
Part-time: 21 men, 28 women	**Ph.D.s:** 77%
Graduate: 347 men, 532 women	**Student/Faculty:** 20 to 1
Year: semesters, summer session	**Tuition:** $14,680
Application Deadline: open	**Room & Board:** $7460
Freshman Class: 3248 applied, 1409 accepted, 454 enrolled	
SAT Verbal/Math: 510/500*	**ACT:** 21 **COMPETITIVE+**

Saint Leo University, a private institution, was founded in 1889 by the Benedictine Order of the Catholic Church. The university offers undergraduate programs in business administration, the humanities, natural sciences, social sciences, education, and preprofessional studies. There are 3 undergraduate and 6 graduate schools. In addition to regional accreditation, Saint Leo has baccalaureate program accreditation with CSWE and IACBE. The library contains 141,521 volumes, 28,290 microform items, and 6437 audio/video tapes/CDs/DVDs, and subscribes to 700 periodicals including electronic. Computerized library services include the card catalog, interlibrary loans, database searching, and Internet access. Special learning facilities include a learning resource center and TV station. The 186-acre campus is in a rural area 40 miles north of Tampa. Including any residence halls, there are 25 buildings.

Student Life: 67% of undergraduates are from Florida. Others are from 38 states, 43 foreign countries, and Canada. 74% are from public schools. 65% are white. 49% are Catholic; 32% Protestant; 13% claim no religious affiliation. The average age of freshmen is 18; all undergraduates, 21. 29% do not continue beyond their first year; 39% remain to graduate.

Housing: 1184 students can be accommodated in college housing, which includes single-sex and coed dorms, on-campus apartments, and sorority houses. On-campus housing is available on a first-come, first-served basis and is available on a lottery system for upperclassmen. 75% of students live on campus; of those, 80% remain on campus on weekends. All students may keep cars.

Activities: 26% of men belong to 4 local and 8 national fraternities; 14% of women belong to 1 local and 3 national sororities. There are 50 groups on campus, including band, cheerleading, chorus, dance, drama, ethnic, honors, international, literary magazine, newspaper, political, professional, radio and TV, religious, social, social service, student government, and yearbook. Popular campus events include Spring Fling, Winter Formal, and Community Service Days (fall and spring).

Sports: There are 7 intercollegiate sports for men and 7 for women, and 15 intramural sports for men and 15 for women. Facilities include a 2000-seat indoor gym, a fitness center, an outdoor swimming pool, a golf course, soccer, softball, baseball, practice fields, basketball, volleyball, lighted tennis, and racquetball courts, and sailing and canoeing.

Disabled Students: 95% of the campus is accessible. Wheelchair ramps, elevators, special parking, specially equipped rest rooms, and lowered drinking fountains are available. Accommodations for persons with disabilities are available on a case-by-case basis with proper documentation.

Services: Counseling and information services are available, as is tutoring in most subjects. There is remedial math and writing.

Campus Safety and Security: Measures include 24-hour foot and vehicle patrol, security escort services, informal discussions, and pamphlets/posters/films. There are emergency telephones and lighted pathways/sidewalks.

Programs of Study: Saint Leo confers B.A., B.S., and B.S.W. degrees. Associate and master's degrees are also awarded. Bachelor's degrees are awarded in BIOLOGICAL SCIENCE (biology/biological science), BUSINESS (accounting, business administration and management, hospitality management services, human resources, management science, and sports management), COMMUNICATIONS AND THE ARTS (communications and English), COMPUTER AND PHYSICAL SCIENCE (information sciences and systems and mathematics), EDUCATION (elementary and middle school), ENGINEERING AND ENVIRONMENTAL DESIGN (environmental science), HEALTH PROFESSIONS (health care administration and medical technology), SOCIAL SCIENCE (criminal justice, history, human services, international studies, political science/

government, psychology, religion, social work, and sociology). Biology, English, and environmental science are the strongest academically. Business administration, criminal justice, and biology are the largest.

Required: To graduate, all students must complete a minimum of 120 academic credits, with 30 to 60 hours in the major, all the requirements of their division and major, and 53 to 56 hours in the general education program. The honors program may be substituted for general education requirements. A minimum 2.0 GPA and capstone course are required, as is a 30-hour residency requirement.

Special: Saint Leo offers internships in most majors, study abroad in 10 countries, work-study programs on campus, dual majors, and credit for military experience. There is a prelaw program, preprofessional programs in medicine, dentistry, and veterinary science, learning enhancement for academic progress, and Air Force and Army ROTC programs. Saint Leo also offers articulation agreements with Nova Southeastern University (osteopathy, dental, pharmacy, nursing), Lake Erie College (osteopathy), Jacksonville University (nursing), and the University of St. Augustine for health sciences (occupational and physical therapy). There are 10 national honor societies and a freshman honors program.

Faculty/Classroom: 63% of faculty are male; 37%, female. All teach undergraduates. No introductory courses are taught by graduate students. The average class size in an introductory lecture is 25; in a laboratory, 10; and in a regular course, 20.

Admissions: 43% of the 2005-2006 applicants were accepted. The SAT scores for the 2005-2006 freshman class were: Verbal--43% below 500, 47% between 500 and 599, and 10% between 600 and 700; Math--45% below 500, 46% between 500 and 599, and 9% between 600 and 700. The ACT scores were 47% below 21, 26% between 21 and 23, 18% between 24 and 26, 8% between 27 and 28, and 1% above 28. 25% of the current freshmen were in the top fifth of their class; 54% were in the top two fifths.

Requirements: The SAT or ACT is required. In addition, applicants must be graduates of an accredited secondary school or have a GED certificate, and have completed 4 credits in English, 3 each in math and social studies, and 2 each in science, foreign language, and electives. A GPA of 2.3 is required. AP and CLEP credits are accepted. Important factors in the admissions decision are advanced placement or honor courses, personality/intangible qualities, and recommendations by school officials.

Procedure: Freshmen are admitted fall and spring. Entrance exams should be taken by the fall of the senior year. There is a deferred admissions plan and a rolling admissions plan. Application deadlines are open. Notification is sent on a rolling basis. The fall 2005 application fee was $35. Applications are accepted on-line.

Transfer: 111 transfer students enrolled in 2004-2005. Applicants must submit an official transcript from each previously attended college, a recommendation from the dean of students of the last institution attended, and a writing sample. A minimum 2.5 GPA is required. If transferring fewer than 24 academic credits, a high school transcript or GED and standardized test scores are required. 30 of 120 credits required for the bachelor's degree must be completed at Saint Leo.

Visiting: There are regularly scheduled orientations for prospective students, consisting of overnight campus visitation programs. There are guides for informal visits and visitors may sit in on classes and stay overnight. To schedule a visit, contact the Office of Admission at *admission@saintleo.edu.*

Financial Aid: In 2005-2006, 99% of all full-time freshmen and 94% of continuing full-time students received some form of financial aid. 96% of full-time freshmen and 89% of continuing full-time students received need-based aid. The average freshman award was $17,017. Need-based scholarships or need-based grants averaged $6775 ($23,190 maximum); need-based self-help aid (loans and jobs) averaged $4775 ($9125 maximum); non-need-based athletic scholarships averaged $7442 ($19,690 maximum); and other non-need-based awards and non-need-based scholarships averaged $4956 ($26,655 maximum). 34% of undergraduates work part time. Average annual earnings from campus work are $2500. The average financial indebtedness of the 2005 graduate was $15,714. Saint Leo is a member of CSS. The FAFSA is required. The priority date for freshman financial aid applications for fall entry is March 1.

International Students: There are 112 international students enrolled. The school actively recruits these students. They must take the TOEFL and also supply a satisfactory SAT Verbal scores, or an IELTS minimum score of 6.

Computers: Wireless access is available. All students who live on campus receive an IBM Thinkpad laptop for their use. The Thinkpad connects to network ports in the residence hall rooms or the wireless network that serves much of the university campus. Support for the program is provided by the Office of Information Technology. This support includes trouble shooting, repairs, and educational services. All students may access the system. There are no time limits and no fees.

Graduates: From July 1, 2004 to June 30, 2005, 180 bachelor's degrees were awarded. The most popular majors were business administration (21%), elementary education (13%), and psychology (9%). In an average class, 28% graduate in 4 years or less, 36% graduate in 5 years or less, and 39% graduate in 6 years or less. 39 companies recruited on campus in 2004-2005. Of a recent graduating class, 57% were enrolled in graduate school within 6 months of graduation and 91% were employed.

Admissions Contact: Gary Bracken, Vice President for Enrollment. E-mail: *admission@saintleo.edu* Web: *www.saintleo.edu*

SAINT THOMAS UNIVERSITY	E-5
Miami, FL 33054	**(305) 628-6546**
	(800) 367-9010; Fax: (305) 628-6591

Full-time: 468 men, 701 women	**Faculty:** n/av
Part-time: none	**Ph.D.s:** n/av
Graduate: 582 men, 767 women	**Student/Faculty:** n/av
Year: semesters, summer session	**Tuition:** $17,850
Application Deadline: open	**Room & Board:** $5640
Freshman Class: 1540 applied, 650 accepted, 343 enrolled	
SAT Verbal/Math: 440/450*	**ACT:** 17 COMPETITIVE

Saint Thomas University, founded in 1961, is a private, liberal arts university affiliated with the Roman Catholic Church and sponsored by the Archdiocese of Miami. There are 2 undergraduate and 2 graduate schools. The 2 libraries contain 200,000 volumes, and subscribe to 1000 periodicals including electronic. Computerized library services include the card catalog, interlibrary loans, database searching, and Internet access. Special learning facilities include a learning resource center and TV station. The 140-acre campus is in a suburban area 10 miles from Miami and Fort Lauderdale. Including any residence halls, there are 15 buildings.

Student Life: 85% of undergraduates are from Florida. Others are from 25 states, 49 foreign countries, and Canada. 70% are from public schools. 39% are Hispanic; 23% African American; 21% white; 18% foreign nationals. 55% are Catholic; 12% claim no religious affiliation. The average age of freshmen is 19; all undergraduates, 25. 30% do not continue beyond their first year; 42% remain to graduate.

Housing: 350 students can be accommodated in college housing, which includes coed dorms. On-campus housing is guaranteed for all 4 years. 80% of students commute. All students may keep cars.

Activities: There are no fraternities or sororities. There are 30 groups on campus, including art, choir, chorus, computers, debate, drama, ethnic, honors, international, literary magazine, newspaper, photography, political, professional, radio and TV, religious, social, social service, student government, and yearbook. Popular campus events include Senior Capping Ceremony, Freshman Investiture Ceremony, and Land and Water Olympics.

Sports: There are 5 intercollegiate sports for men and 4 for women, and 5 intramural sports for men and 5 for women. Facilities include basketball, soccer, and softball fields, tennis courts, a weight room, and a swimming pool.

Disabled Students: 90% of the campus is accessible. Wheelchair ramps, elevators, special parking, specially equipped rest rooms, special class scheduling, lowered drinking fountains, lowered telephones, and special housing are available.

Services: Counseling and information services are available, as is tutoring in most subjects. There is remedial math, reading, and writing. Computer-assisted instruction is available.

Campus Safety and Security: Measures include 24-hour foot and vehicle patrol, self-defense education, security escort services, and informal discussions. There are pamphlets/posters/films, emergency telephones, and lighted pathways/sidewalks.

Programs of Study: STU confers B.A. and B.B.A. degrees. Master's degrees are also awarded. Bachelor's degrees are awarded in BIOLOGICAL SCIENCE (biology/biological science), BUSINESS (accounting, banking and finance, business administration and management, hospitality management services, international business management, marketing/retailing/merchandising, sports management, and tourism), COMMUNICATIONS AND THE ARTS (communications and English), COMPUTER AND PHYSICAL SCIENCE (computer programming and computer science), EDUCATION (elementary, secondary, and social studies), HEALTH PROFESSIONS (predentistry and premedicine), SOCIAL SCIENCE (criminal justice, history, human services, international relations, liberal arts/general studies, political science/government, prelaw, psychology, and religion). Sports administration and accounting are the strongest academically. Business management, psychology, and communications are the largest.

Required: All students must complete at least 120 semester credits with 30 to 60 in the major, and specific courses, including 12 credits in English, 9 each in math/physical science, philosophy, and religion, and 6 each in history, social science, and humanities. Students must maintain a 2.0 overall GPA and a 2.25 GPA in the major subject.

Special: Communication arts, hospitality management, and sports administration internships, study abroad in Italy and Spain, and a general studies degree are available. The university grants credit for life, military, and work experience via the Life Experience Portfolio. There is a freshman honors program.

Admissions: 42% of the 2005-2006 applicants were accepted.

Requirements: The SAT or ACT is required. In addition, applicants should have completed 18 high school units, including 4 units in English, 3 each in math and social science, and 2 in science. STU requires applicants to be in the upper 50% of their class. A GPA of 2.25 is required. AP and CLEP credits are accepted. Important factors in the admissions decision are recommendations by school officials, advanced placement or honor courses, and evidence of special talent.

Procedure: Freshmen are admitted to all sessions. Entrance exams should be taken in December of the senior year of high school. There is a deferred admissions plan. Application deadlines are open. Application fee is $40.

Transfer: Maximum credit hours accepted are 60 from a junior college and 90 from a 4-year institution. No grade of D is acceptable in courses beyond sophomore level or in the major. Students with fewer than 30 credits must submit a high school transcript and SAT or ACT scores. 30 of 120 credits required for the bachelor's degree must be completed at STU.

Visiting: There are regularly scheduled orientations for prospective students. There are guides for informal visits and visitors may sit in on classes and stay overnight. To schedule a visit, contact the Admissions Office.

Financial Aid: Need-based scholarships or need-based grants averaged $1000 ($2000 maximum); need-based self-help aid (loans and jobs) averaged $5000 ($9000 maximum); and non-need-based athletic scholarships averaged $7500 ($17,850 maximum). 15% of undergraduates work part time. Average annual earnings from campus work are $3000. The CSS/Profile or FAFSA, and the college's own financial statement are required. The priority date for freshman financial aid applications for fall entry is April 1.

International Students: 221 international students were enrolled in a recent year. The school actively recruits these students. They must take the TOEFL and also take the SAT or ACT.

Computers: All students may access the system any time it is available. There are no time limits and no fees.

Admissions Contact: Andre Lightbourn, Associate Director of Admissions. A video is available. E-mail: *alightbo@stu.edu*
Web: *www.stu.edu*

SOUTHEASTERN UNIVERSITY D-3
Lakeland, FL 33801

(863) 667-5018
(800) 500-8760; Fax: (863) 667-5200

Full-time: 941 men, 1233 women	Faculty: 54
Part-time: 58 men, 65 women	Ph.D.s: 48%
Graduate: 31 men, 8 women	Student/Faculty: 40 to 1
Year: semesters, summer session	Tuition: $11,500
Application Deadline: see profile	Room & Board: $5680
Freshman Class: 984 applied, 785 accepted, 521 enrolled	
SAT or ACT: required	LESS COMPETITIVE

Southeastern University, formerly Southeastern College, founded in 1935 is a Christian liberal arts institution offering 25 degree programs that equip students to serve in both professional careers and ministry-related fields. The 2 libraries contain 94,000 volumes, 1700 microform items, and 3000 audio/video tapes/CDs/DVDs, and subscribe to 450 periodicals including electronic. Computerized library services include the card catalog, interlibrary loans, and database searching. Special learning facilities include a learning resource center, radio station, TV station, and Pentecostal Research Library. The 56-acre campus is in a small town 30 miles east of Tampa and 45 miles west of Orlando. Including any residence halls, there are 32 buildings.

Student Life: 58% of undergraduates are from Florida. Students are from 40 states, 8 foreign countries, and Canada. 79% are white; 10% Hispanic. Most are Protestant. The average age of freshmen is 18; all undergraduates, 21. 19% do not continue beyond their first year; 35% remain to graduate.

Housing: 910 students can be accommodated in college housing, which includes single-sex dorms and on-campus apartments. On-campus housing is guaranteed for all 4 years. 60% of students live on campus. Alcohol is not permitted. All students may keep cars.

Activities: There are no fraternities or sororities. There are 20 groups on campus, including band, cheerleading, choir, chorale, chorus, computers, drama, ethnic, honors, international, jazz band, newspaper, radio and TV, religious, social service, student government, and yearbook. Popular campus events include Fall Festival, Christmas Social, and Junior-Senior Banquet.

Sports: There are 4 intercollegiate sports for men and 4 for women, and 8 intramural sports for men and 6 for women. Facilities include a gym, baseball and soccer fields, tennis, racquetball, and beach volleyball courts, a weight room, and intramural fields.

Disabled Students: 90% of the campus is accessible. Wheelchair ramps, elevators, special parking, specially equipped rest rooms, special class scheduling, and lowered drinking fountains are available.

Services: Counseling and information services are available, as is tutoring in some subjects, including math, reading, and English. There is remedial math, reading, and writing.

Campus Safety and Security: Measures include 24-hour foot and vehicle patrol, informal discussions, pamphlets/posters/films, lighted pathways/sidewalks, and a main entrance security booth attendant.

Programs of Study: Southeastern confers B.A., B.S., B.M., and B.S.W. degrees. Bachelor's degrees are awarded in BIOLOGICAL SCIENCE (biology/biological science), BUSINESS (accounting, banking and finance, business administration and management, management information systems, marketing/retailing/merchandising, and sports management), COMMUNICATIONS AND THE ARTS (broadcasting, communications, dramatic arts, English, journalism, music, and public relations), COMPUTER AND PHYSICAL SCIENCE (mathematics), EDUCATION (education of the exceptional child, elementary, middle school, music, and secondary), SOCIAL SCIENCE (biblical studies, criminal justice, history, interdisciplinary studies, ministries, pastoral studies, psychology, public administration, religion, religious music, social work, and youth ministry). Religion, education, and business are the strongest academically. Religion is the largest.

Required: Every degree student must complete 125 to 130 hours, including 36 hours of general education and at least 20 hours of religion. Distribution requirements include 6 to 12 hours each in arts and communications, human adjustment, science and math, social sciences, and humanities and fine arts. A minimum GPA of 2.0 must be maintained.

Special: Internships are available in communications, education, ministry, psychology, pastoral studies, Christian education, and business. There are accelerated degree programs in Church leadership and in business and professional leadership, study abroad in 7 countries, and a Washington semester. There are 2 national honor societies and 2 departmental honors programs.

Faculty/Classroom: 69% of faculty are male; 31%, female. 96% teach undergraduates. The average class size in an introductory lecture is 60; in a laboratory, 20; and in a regular course, 32.

Admissions: 80% of the 2005-2006 applicants were accepted.

Requirements: The SAT or ACT is required; the GED is accepted. A GPA of 1.5 is required. AP and CLEP credits are accepted.

Procedure: Freshmen are admitted to all sessions. Entrance exams should be taken prior to enrollment. There are early admissions and rolling admissions plans. Applicantions are accepted on-line.

Transfer: Admission requirements for transfer applicants are the same as for first-time students. 30 of 125 to 130 credits required for the bachelor's degree must be completed at Southeastern.

Visiting: There are regularly scheduled orientations for prospective students, including College Days (fall and spring), which consist of a 24 hour overview of campus life with class visits, faculty reception, admission/financial aid workshops, a student panel discussion, and a worship service. There are guides for informal visits and visitors may sit in on classes and stay overnight. To schedule a visit, contact the Admission Office.

Financial Aid: In 2005-2006, 56% of all full-time freshmen and 68% of continuing full-time students received some form of financial aid. 53% of full-time freshmen and 63% of continuing full-time students received need-based aid. The average freshman award was $6902. Need-based scholarships or need-based grants averaged $5380; and need-based self-help aid (loans and jobs) averaged $2409. The FAFSA and the college's own financial statement are required. Check with the school for current deadlines.

International Students: The school actively recruits these students. A satisfactory score is required on the written TOEFL. Students must also take the SAT or the ACT.

Computers: All students may access the system during designated lab hours or from their residence hall. There are no time limits and no fees.

Admissions Contact: Omar Rashed, Director of Admission.
E-mail: *admission@seuniversity.edu* Web: *http://www.seuniversity.edu*

STATE UNIVERSITY SYSTEM OF FLORIDA

The State University System of Florida, established in 1906, is a public system in Florida. It is governed by a board of regents, whose chief administrator is the chancellor. The primary goal of the system is teaching, research, and public service. The main priorities are to improve the quality of undergraduate education, to solve critical state problems, to forge public-private partnerships, and to increase the efficiency of the system. 4-year campuses are located in Gainesville,, Tallahassee,, Tampa,, Boca Raton,, Pensacola,, Orlando,, Jacksonville,, Miami, and, and Fort Myers. Profiles of the 4-year campuses are included in this section.

STETSON UNIVERSITY   D-2
Deland, FL 32723

	(386) 822-7100
	(800) 688-0101; Fax: (386) 822-7112
Full-time: 898 men, 1262 women	**Faculty:** 181; IIA, +$
Part-time: 39 men, 35 women	**Ph.D.s:** 90%
Graduate: 168 men, 247 women	**Student/Faculty:** 12 to 1
Year: semesters, summer session	**Tuition:** $25,450
Application Deadline: March 1	**Room & Board:** $7275
Freshman Class: 2782 applied, 1918 accepted, 550 enrolled	
SAT Verbal/Math: 573/572*	**ACT:** 24 **VERY COMPETITIVE**

Stetson University, founded in 1883, is an independent institution offering undergraduate programs in liberal arts and sciences, music, and business administration and graduate programs. There are 3 undergraduate and 2 graduate schools. In addition to regional accreditation, Stetson has baccalaureate program accreditation with AACSB, NASM, and NCATE. The 3 libraries contain 392,218 volumes, 406,372 microform items, and 18,364 audio/video tapes/CDs/DVDs, and subscribe to 17,000 periodicals including electronic. Computerized library services include the card catalog, interlibrary loans, database searching, and Internet access. Special learning facilities include an art gallery and a museum of minerals. The 170-acre campus is in a small town 35 miles north of Orlando and 25 miles west of Daytona Beach. Including any residence halls, there are 64 buildings.

Student Life: 76% of undergraduates are from Florida. Others are from 41 states, 40 foreign countries, and Canada. 71% are from public schools. 77% are white. 53% claim no religious affiliation; 24% Protestant. The average age of freshmen is 18; all undergraduates, 20. 23% do not continue beyond their first year; 63% remain to graduate.

Housing: 1868 students can be accommodated in college housing, which includes single-sex and coed dorms, on-campus apartments, fraternity houses, and sorority houses. In addition, there are honors houses, language houses, and special-interest houses. On-campus housing is guaranteed for all 4 years. 63% of students live on campus; of those, 60% remain on campus on weekends. All students may keep cars.

Activities: 23% of men belong to 8 national fraternities; 22% of women belong to 6 national sororities. There are 102 groups on campus, including band, cheerleading, chess, choir, chorale, chorus, computers, dance, drama, ethnic, gay, honors, international, jazz band, literary magazine, musical theater, newspaper, opera, orchestra, political, professional, radio and TV, religious, social, social service, student government, and symphony. Popular campus events include Caribbean Week, Asian Week, and Black History Month.

Sports: There are 7 intercollegiate sports for men and 8 for women, and 12 intramural sports for men and 12 for women. Facilities include 4 racquetball, 6 volleyball, and 8 tennis courts, basketball courts, weight and training rooms, baseball and soccer fields, 2 softball fields, a multipurpose field, a training and exercise science facility, a swimming pool, and a 5000-seat auditorium.

Disabled Students: 80% of the campus is accessible. Wheelchair ramps, elevators, special parking, specially equipped rest rooms, special class scheduling, lowered drinking fountains, and lowered telephones are available.

Services: Counseling and information services are available, as is tutoring in most subjects. There is a reader service for the blind.

Campus Safety and Security: Measures include 24-hour foot and vehicle patrol, self-defense education, security escort services, and informal discussions. There are pamphlets/posters/films, emergency telephones, and lighted pathways/sidewalks.

Programs of Study: Stetson confers B.A., B.S., B.B.A., B.M., and B.M.E. degrees. Master's degrees are also awarded. Bachelor's degrees are awarded in BIOLOGICAL SCIENCE (biochemistry, biology/biological science, marine biology, and molecular biology), BUSINESS (accounting, banking and finance, business administration and management, business economics, electronic business, international business management, management science, marketing/retailing/merchandising, and sports management), COMMUNICATIONS AND THE ARTS (art, communications, dramatic arts, English, French, German, guitar, music, music performance, music theory and composition, piano/organ, Spanish, voice, and winds), COMPUTER AND PHYSICAL SCIENCE (chemistry, computer science, digital arts/technology, mathematics, and physics), EDUCATION (elementary, music, secondary, and social science), ENGINEERING AND ENVIRONMENTAL DESIGN (environmental science), HEALTH PROFESSIONS (health science, medical technology, and rehabilitation therapy), SOCIAL SCIENCE (American studies, economics, geography, history, humanities, international studies, Latin American studies, philosophy, political science/government, prelaw, psychology, religion, Russian and Slavic studies, social science, and sociology). Business, psychology, and education are the largest.

Required: To graduate, all students must complete 120 total credit hours, including 30 to 40 in the major, with a minimum GPA of 2.0. At least 40 hours must be at the 300-400 level, 26 of which must be taken at Stetson. A freshman English sequence and courses in religious studies or philosophy, humanities, natural sciences, and social sciences are required. A senior research project must be completed in most majors.

Special: Stetson offers co-op programs in preengineering, prelaw, premedicine, forestry, environmental studies, and medical technology, internships in most disciplines, study abroad in France, Germany, Spain, Russia, Mexico, Hong Kong, Austria, Australia, New Zealand, and the United Kingdom, and a Washington semester at American University. B.A.-B.S. degrees, dual majors, student-designed majors through the honors programs, 3-2 engineering degrees with the Universities of Florida and Miami, a 3-3 law degree with Stetson College of Law, and pass/fail options are also offered. There is also the Leadership Development Program, the Roland George Investments Program, in which students manage an actual investment portfolio of approximately $2.9 million, and the Family Business Center. There are 6 national honor societies, including Phi Beta Kappa, and a freshman honors program.

Faculty/Classroom: 58% of faculty are male; 42%, female. 97% teach undergraduates. No introductory courses are taught by graduate students. The average class size in an introductory lecture is 22; in a laboratory, 18; and in a regular course, 18.

Admissions: 69% of the 2005-2006 applicants were accepted. The SAT scores for the 2005-2006 freshman class were: Verbal--14% below 500, 49% between 500 and 599, 33% between 600 and 700, and 4% above 700; Math--13% below 500, 52% between 500 and 599, 31% between 600 and 700, and 5% above 700. The ACT scores were 17% below 21, 27% between 21 and 23, 30% between 24 and 26, 17% between 27 and 28, and 9% above 28.

Requirements: The SAT or ACT is required. In addition, applicants must be graduates of an accredited secondary school or have a GED, and have completed 4 years of English, 3 of math and science, and 2 each of foreign language, social sciences, and electives. Auditions are required for music students. A GPA of 2.0 is required. AP and CLEP credits are accepted. Important factors in the admissions decision are advanced placement or honor courses, leadership record, and evidence of special talent.

Procedure: Freshmen are admitted fall, spring, and summer. Entrance exams should be taken in the spring of the junior year or the fall of the senior year. There is a rolling admissions plan. There are early decision and deferred admissions plans. Early decision applications should be filed by November 1; regular applications, by March 1 for fall entry, along with a $40 fee. Notification of early decision is sent November 25; regular decision, on a rolling basis. 38 early decision candidates were accepted for the 2005-2006 class. Applications are accepted on-line.

Transfer: 95 transfer students enrolled in 2004-2005. Transfer students must have completed a semester of academic work in good standing at an accredited college with a minimum 2.0 GPA. A 2.8 GPA and an interview are recommended. 45 of 120 credits required for the bachelor's degree must be completed at Stetson.

Visiting: There are regularly scheduled orientations for prospective students, consisting of a campus tour and orientation, interviews, class visits, and presentations. There are guides for informal visits and visitors may sit in on classes and stay overnight. To schedule a visit, contact the Admissions Office.

Financial Aid: In 2005-2006, 97% of all full-time students received some form of financial aid. 64% of full-time freshmen and 50% of continuing full-time students received need-based aid. The average freshman award was $23,861. Need-based scholarships or need-based grants averaged $18,800 ($23,996 maximum); need-based self-help aid (loans and jobs) averaged $4903 ($9025 maximum); non-need-based athletic scholarships averaged $15,324 ($38,442 maximum); and other non-need-based awards and non-need-based scholarships averaged $14,675 ($25,840 maximum). 40% of undergraduates work part time. Average annual earnings from campus work are $2259. The average financial indebtedness of the 2005 graduate was $21,500. Stetson is a member of CSS. The FAFSA is required. The priority date for freshman financial aid applications for fall entry is March 15.

International Students: There are 77 international students enrolled. The school actively recruits these students. They must achieve a satisfactory score on the TOEFL and also take the SAT or the ACT.

Computers: Wireless access is available at many locations around the campus. All students may access the system. There are no time limits and no fees.

Graduates: From July 1, 2004 to June 30, 2005, 454 bachelor's degrees were awarded. The most popular majors were business (36%), education (6%), and biology (5%). In an average class, 52% graduate in 4 years or less, 62% graduate in 5 years or less, and 63% graduate in 6 years or less. 80 companies recruited on campus in 2004-2005.

Admissions Contact: Deborah Thompson, Vice President for Enrollment Management. E-mail: *admissions@stetson.edu* Web: *www.stetson.edu/admissions*

UNIVERSITY OF CENTRAL FLORIDA D-3

Orlando, FL 32816-0111 (407) 823-3000; Fax: (407) 823-3419

Full-time: 12,798 men, 15,786 women | **Faculty:** 1192; I, --$
Part-time: 4215 men, 4997 women | **Ph.D.s:** 79%
Graduate: 2925 men, 4232 women | **Student/Faculty:** 24 to 1
Year: semesters, summer session | **Tuition:** $3339 ($16,471)
Application Deadline: May 1 | **Room & Board:** $7400
Freshman Class: 20,265 applied, 12,542 accepted, 6359 enrolled
SAT Verbal/Math: 582/595* | **ACT:** 25 **VERY COMPETITIVE**

University of Central Florida, founded in 1963 and part of the State University System of Florida, offers programs in liberal and fine arts, business, engineering, health science, professional training, and teacher preparation, and graduate and research programs in optics, biotechnology, simulation, computer science, and other areas. There are 8 undergraduate and 8 graduate schools. In addition to regional accreditation, UCF has baccalaureate program accreditation with AACSB, ABET, CSAB, CSWE, NASM, NCATE, and NLN. The library contains 1,623,277 volumes, 2,921,975 microform items, and 40,216 audio/video tapes/CDs/DVDs, and subscribes to 16,530 periodicals including electronic. Computerized library services include the card catalog, interlibrary loans, database searching, and Internet access. Special learning facilities include a learning resource center, art gallery, radio station, an observatory, an arboretum, a center for research and education in optics and lasers, an institute for simulation and training, the Florida Solar Energy Center, and the Biomolecular Science Center. The 1415-acre campus is in an urban area 13 miles northeast of downtown Orlando. Including any residence halls, there are 136 buildings.

Student Life: 95% of undergraduates are from Florida. Others are from 49 states, 125 foreign countries, and Canada. 68% are white; 13% Hispanic. The average age of freshmen is 18; all undergraduates, 23. 17% do not continue beyond their first year; 57% remain to graduate.

Housing: 8751 students can be accommodated in college housing, which includes single-sex and coed dorms, on-campus apartments, off-campus apartments, fraternity houses, and sorority houses. In addition, there are honors houses and special-interest houses. On-campus housing is available on a first-come, first-served basis. 77% of students commute. All students may keep cars.

Activities: 11% of men belong to 24 national fraternities; 9% of women belong to 20 national sororities. There are 382 groups on campus, including art, band, cheerleading, chess, choir, chorus, computers, dance, debate, drama, drill team, ethnic, film, forensics, gay, honors, international, jazz band, literary magazine, marching band, musical theater, newspaper, orchestra, pep band, photography, political, pre-profession Medical Society, professional, radio and TV, religious, social, social service, sport clubs, student government, Volunteer UCF, and yearbook. Popular campus events include Student Showcase Week, Wellness Fair, and ethnic awareness festivals.

Sports: There are 7 intercollegiate sports for men and 10 for women, and 49 intramural sports for men and 49 for women. Facilities include 9 multipurpose playing fields, 7 tennis courts, an outdoor adventure challenge course, 8 sand volleyball courts, 3 basketball courts, a disc golf course, and 2 swimming pools, and an 82,000-square-foot arena with basketball/volleyball courts, exercise rooms, 3-lane track, weight room, cardio rooms, and climbing tower.

Disabled Students: 95% of the campus is accessible. Wheelchair ramps, elevators, special parking, specially equipped rest rooms, special class scheduling, lowered drinking fountains, and lowered telephones are available.

Services: Counseling and information services are available, as is tutoring in most subjects, including math, English, reading, physics, statistics, Spanish, biology, chemistry, and economics. There is a reader service for the blind, and remedial math, reading, and writing. Review programs for the College-Level Academic Skills Test (CLAST) and the General Knowledge Exam are also available.

Campus Safety and Security: Measures include 24-hour foot and vehicle patrol, self-defense education, security escort services, and shuttle buses. There are informal discussions, pamphlets/posters/films, emergency telephones and lighted pathways/sidewalks. There is also a college-sponsored transportation system that buses students to and from apartment complexes within a 2- or 3-mile radius of the school.

Programs of Study: UCF confers B.A., B.S., B.A.B.A., B.A.S., B.F.A., B.M., B.M.E., B.S.A.E., B.S.B.A., B.S.C.E., B.S.Cp.E., B.S.E.E., B.S.E.E.T., B.S.Env.E., B.S.E.T., B.S.I.E., B.S.M.E., B.S.N., and B.S.W. degrees. Associate, master's, and doctoral degrees are also awarded. Bachelor's degrees are awarded in BIOLOGICAL SCIENCE (biology/biological science and microbiology), BUSINESS (accounting, banking and finance, business administration and management, hospitality management services, management information systems, management science, and marketing/retailing/merchandising), COMMUNICATIONS AND THE ARTS (advertising, art, broadcasting, communications, dramatic arts, English, film arts, fine arts, French, journalism, languages, music, public relations, and Spanish), COMPUTER AND PHYSICAL SCIENCE (chemistry, computer science, digital arts/technology, mathematics, physics, and statistics), EDUCATION (art, business, early childhood, education of the exceptional child, elementary, English, foreign languages, mathematics, music, physical, science, social science, special, and vocational), ENGINEERING AND ENVIRONMENTAL DESIGN (aeronautical engineering, aerospace studies, civil engineering, computer engineering, electrical/electronics engineering, electrical/electronics engineering technology, engineering technology, environmental engineering, industrial engineering technology, and mechanical engineering), HEALTH PROFESSIONS (health care administration, health science, medical laboratory technology, nursing, radiological science, respiratory therapy, and speech pathology/audiology), SOCIAL SCIENCE (anthropology, criminal justice, economics, forensic studies, history, humanities, law, liberal arts/general studies, philosophy, political science/government, psychology, public administration, social science, social work, and sociology). Engineering, business administration, and computer science are the strongest academically. Business, education, and psychology are the largest.

Required: To graduate, students must complete at least 120 semester hours, with 36 hours in general education program courses, including 9 each in communication foundations and cultural and historical foundations, and 6 each in math foundations, science foundations, and social foundations. Students must maintain a minimum GPA of 2.0. There is a 30 hour residency requirement and the last semester is required in residence.

Special: Internships are available in most majors through UCF's extensive partnerships with area businesses and industries such as NASA, Disney, Universal Studios, and AT&T. Students may participate in study abroad and co-op and work-study programs, earn B.A.-B.S. degrees or a liberal studies degree, or pursue dual majors. Nondegree study and pass/fail options are available. There is a 3-4 medical degree program with the University of South Florida. There are 42 national honor societies, a freshman honors program, and all departments have honors programs.

Faculty/Classroom: 62% of faculty are male; 38%, female. All teach undergraduates, 95% do research, and 95% do both. No introductory courses are taught by graduate students. The average class size in an introductory lecture is 55; in a laboratory, 30; and in a regular course, 38.

Admissions: 62% of the 2005-2006 applicants were accepted. The SAT scores for the 2005-2006 freshman class were: Verbal--15% below 500, 53% between 500 and 599, 28% between 600 and 700, and 4% above 700; Math--10% below 500, 50% between 500 and 599, 35% between 600 and 700, and 5% above 700. The ACT scores were 9% below 21, 23% between 21 and 23, 39% between 24 and 26, 18% between 27 and 28, and 11% above 28. There were 25 National Merit finalists and 7 semifinalists. 21 freshmen graduated first in their class.

Requirements: The SAT or ACT is required. GPA and standardized test scores are rated on a sliding scale. A high school diploma or GED is required. Applicants should have completed 4 units of English, 3 each of math, science (2 with labs), and social studies, and 2 of a foreign language, plus 4 of academic electives. A GPA of 2.0 is required. AP and CLEP credits are accepted. Important factors in the admissions decision are advanced placement or honor courses, evidence of special talent, and leadership record.

Procedure: Freshmen are admitted to all sessions. Entrance exams should be taken during the junior year or the first semester of the senior year. There is a rolling admissions plan. Applications should be filed by May 1 for fall entry, November 1 for spring entry, and March 1 for summer entry, along with a $30 fee. Notification is sent on a rolling basis. 400 applicants were on the 2005 waiting list. Applications are accepted on-line.

Transfer: 5854 transfer students enrolled in 2004-2005. A minimum GPA of 2.0 is required in all college work. Either the SAT or the ACT is required of applicants with fewer than 60 credit hours. Other transfer requirements vary widely depending on credits already earned. 30 of 120 credits required for the bachelor's degree must be completed at UCF.

Visiting: There are regularly scheduled orientations for prospective students, including tours offered twice a day, Monday through Friday, followed by a group information session or personal interview. There are guides for informal visits and visitors may sit in on classes. To schedule a visit, contact the Undergraduate Admissions office.

Financial Aid: In 2005-2006, 96% of all full-time freshmen and 78% of continuing full-time students received some form of financial aid. 29% of full-time freshmen and 17% of continuing full-time students received need-based aid. The average freshman award was $4170. Need-based scholarships or need-based grants averaged $3236 ($9250 maximum); need-based self-help aid (loans and jobs) averaged $2387 ($7820 maximum); non-need-based athletic scholarships averaged $4457 ($10,836 maximum); and other non-need-based awards and non-need-based scholarships averaged $2873 ($22,913 maximum). 49% of undergraduates work part time. Average annual earnings from campus work are $5938. The average financial indebtedness of the 2005 graduate was $12,780. The FAFSA is required. The deadline for filing freshman financial aid applications for fall entry is March 1.

International Students: There are 450 international students enrolled. They must score satisfactorily on the written TOEFL or on the electronic version. Students with fewer than 60 semester hours of college credit must take either the SAT or the ACT.

Computers: Wireless access is available. All UCF students have complete access to the university's wired and wireless network infrastructure and services. The wired network is complemented by wireless network coverage in all of the interior spaces of all buildings, plus considerable outdoor wireless coverage. Students have access to the UCF network from 2,926 personal computers located in public and departmental computer labs. In addition, all UCF residence halls have wireless network service. All students may access the system at all times. There are no time limits and no fees. It is strongly recommended that all students have a personal computer. It is recommended that students in Digital Media have personal computers.

Graduates: From July 1, 2004 to June 30, 2005, 7330 bachelor's degrees were awarded. The most popular majors were business (27%), psychology (10%), and education (9%). In an average class, 2% graduate in 3 years or less, 30% graduate in 4 years or less, 52% graduate in 5 years or less, and 57% graduate in 6 years or less. 801 companies recruited on campus in 2004-2005. Of a recent graduating class, 21% were enrolled in graduate school within 6 months of graduation and 71% were employed.

Admissions Contact: Dr. Gordon Chavis Jr., Assistant Vice President.
E-mail: *admission@mail.ucf.edu*
Web: *http://www.admissions.sdes.ucf.edu*

UNIVERSITY OF FLORIDA — D-2

Gainesville, FL 32611-4000 (352) 392-1365

Full-time and Part-time 49,693 men and women	Faculty: 1686; I, -$
	Ph.D.s: 94%
Graduate: n/av	Student/Faculty: 19 to 1
Year: semesters, summer session	Tuition: $3094 ($17,222)
Application Deadline: January 13	Room & Board: $6260
Freshman Class: 21,511 applied, 12,100 accepted, 7241 enrolled	
SAT or ACT: required	HIGHLY COMPETITIVE

The University of Florida, founded in 1853, is a public liberal arts institution that is part of the state university system of Florida. There are 14 undergraduate and 17 graduate schools. Enrollment figures in the above capsule are approximate. In addition to regional accreditation, UF has baccalaureate program accreditation with AACSB, ABET, ACCE, ACEJ-MC, ACPE, ADA, AHEA, APTA, ASLA, FIDER, NAAB, NASAD, NASM, NCATE, NLN, and SAF. The 15 libraries contain 5,024,637 volumes, 6,701,512 microform items, and 36,078 audio/video tapes/CDs/DVDs, and subscribe to 28,103 periodicals including electronic. Computerized library services include the card catalog, interlibrary loans, and database searching. Special learning facilities include a learning resource center, art gallery, natural history museum, radio station, TV station, a performing arts center, and a teaching hospital. The 2000-acre campus is in a suburban area 75 miles from Jacksonville. Including any residence halls, there are 850 buildings.

Student Life: 95% of undergraduates are from Florida. Others are from 49 states, 114 foreign countries, and Canada. 76% are white; 13% Hispanic. The average age of freshmen is 18; all undergraduates, 21. 7% do not continue beyond their first year; 64% remain to graduate.

Housing: 7351 students can be accommodated in college housing, which includes single-sex and coed dormitories, on-campus apartments, off-campus apartments, married-student housing, fraternity houses, and sorority houses. In addition, there are honors houses special-interest houses quiet floors, Co-ops, special housing for disabled students, wellness floors, and first-year floors. On-campus housing is available on a first-come, first-served basis and is available on a lottery system for upperclassmen. 79% of students commute. All students may keep cars.

Activities: 15% of men belong to 29 national fraternities; 15% of women belong to 18 national sororities. There are 500 groups on campus, including art, band, cheerleading, chess, choir, chorale, chorus, computers, dance, drama, drill team, ethnic, film, gay, honors, international, jazz band, literary magazine, marching band, musical theater, newspaper, orchestra, pep band, photography, political, professional, radio and TV, religious, social, social service, student government, symphony, and yearbook. Popular campus events include Madrigal dinners, student-sponsored cultural programs, and Gator Growl, a student-produced variety show.

Sports: There are 8 intercollegiate sports for men and 10 for women. Facilities include tennis, volleyball, and basketball courts, a 12,000-seat athletic center, a 60,000-square-foot fitness park, an Olympic-size swimming pool, a running track, weight rooms, intramural fields, an 83,000-seat stadium, and lakefront facilities.

Disabled Students: 95% of the campus is accessible. Wheelchair ramps, elevators, special parking, specially equipped rest rooms, special class scheduling, lowered drinking fountains, and lowered telephones are available. There is computer access for blind and visually impaired students.

Services: Counseling and information services are available, as is tutoring in every subject. There is a reader service for the blind. There is a counseling center.

Campus Safety and Security: Measures include 24-hour foot and vehicle patrol, self-defense education, security escort services, and shuttle buses. There are informal discussions, pamphlets/posters/films, emergency telephones, lighted pathways/sidewalks, and an apartment safety program in cooperation with local law enforcement.

Programs of Study: UF confers B.A., B.S., B.A.E., B.F.A., B.H.S., B.M.E., B.Mus., B.S.A., B.S.B.A., B.S.F., B.S.N., and B.S.P. degrees. Master's and doctoral degrees are also awarded. Bachelor's degrees are awarded in AGRICULTURE (agricultural business management, agronomy, animal science, dairy science, forestry and related sciences, horticulture, natural resource management, plant science, and soil science), BIOLOGICAL SCIENCE (botany, entomology, microbiology, wildlife biology, and zoology), BUSINESS (accounting, banking and finance, business administration and management, human resources, insurance, management science, marketing/retailing/merchandising, and recreation and leisure services), COMMUNICATIONS AND THE ARTS (advertising, art, art history and appreciation, dance, East Asian languages and literature, English, French, German, graphic design, journalism, linguistics, music, performing arts, photography, Portuguese, public relations, Russian, Spanish, speech/debate/rhetoric, telecommunications, theater design, and visual and performing arts), COMPUTER AND PHYSICAL SCIENCE (astronomy, chemistry, computer science, earth science, geology, information sciences and systems, mathematics, physics, and statistics), EDUCATION (agricultural, art, elementary, health, and music), ENGINEERING AND ENVIRONMENTAL DESIGN (aeronautical engineering, agricultural engineering, architecture, chemical engineering, civil engineering, computer engineering, construction engineering, electrical/electronics engineering, emergency/disaster science, engineering and applied science, environmental engineering, industrial engineering technology, interior design, landscape architecture/design, materials engineering, mechanical engineering, nuclear engineering, and nuclear engineering technology), HEALTH PROFESSIONS (allied health, exercise science, health science, nursing, occupational therapy, physical therapy, prepharmacy, rehabilitation therapy, and speech pathology/audiology), SOCIAL SCIENCE (American studies, anthropology, Asian/Oriental studies, classical/ancient civilization, criminology, economics, food science, geography, history, home economics, interdisciplinary studies, Judaic studies, philosophy, physical fitness/movement, political science/government, psychology, religion, and sociology). Engineering, pharmacy, and tax law are the strongest academically. Business, finance, and psychology are the largest.

Required: Requirements for graduation vary depending on the major elected, but all students are required to complete a minimum of 120 credits and maintain a minimum 2.0 GPA.

Special: UF offers many internships, dual and student-designed majors, and study abroad in 32 countries. Cross-registration is possible through the Undergraduate Inter-institutional Registration program. Work-study programs, accelerated degree programs, co-op programs, and B.A.-B.S. degrees are available. There are 53 national honor societies, including Phi Beta Kappa, and a freshman honors program.

Faculty/Classroom: 77% of faculty are male; 23%, female. Graduate students teach 10% of introductory courses.

Admissions: 56% of the 2005-2006 applicants were accepted. There were 205 National Merit finalists.

Requirements: The SAT or ACT is required. The SAT is preferred. A satisfactory score on the SAT or on the ACT are required. Candidates should have graduated from an accredited secondary school or have a GED, and have completed 4 years of English, 3 years each of math, science, and social studies, 2 years of a foreign language, and 4 units of academic electives. AP and CLEP credits are accepted. Important factors in the admissions decision are advanced placement or honor courses, parents or siblings attending the school, and recommendations by school officials.

Procedure: Freshmen are admitted to all sessions. Entrance exams should be taken in the junior year. There is a early decision plan. Early decision applications should be filed by October 1; regular applications, by January 13 for fall entry, September 15 for spring entry, and January 12 for summer entry. Notification of early decision is sent December; regular decision, rolling. Applications are accepted on-line. The fall 2005 application fee was $30.

Transfer: 2031 transfer students enrolled in a recent year. Admission requirements for transfer students vary by college. The lower division is highly competitive; applicants are encouraged to apply at the upper-division level. Students should try to complete their associate degrees or 60 semester hours before applying. 30 of 120 credits required for the bachelor's degree must be completed at UF.

Visiting: There are regularly scheduled orientations for prospective students, consisting of general information sessions at 10 A.M. and 2 P.M. Monday through Friday (excluding holidays) and a student-guided walking tour of the central campus. There are guides for informal visits and visitors may sit in on classes and stay overnight. To schedule a visit, contact the Admissions Office.

Financial Aid: In a recent year, 34% of all full-time students received some form of financial aid. 18% of full-time freshmen and 22% of continuing full-time students received need-based aid. The average freshman award was $7873. Need-based scholarships or need-based grants averaged $4036; need-based self-help aid (loans and jobs) averaged $2341; and non-need-based athletic scholarships averaged $8357. 17% of undergraduates worked part time. Average annual earnings from campus work were $1800. The average financial indebtedness of a recent graduate was $14,449. The FAFSA is required. Check with the school for current application deadlines.

International Students: They must score satisfactorily on the written TOEFL or on the electronic version. Freshmen and lower-division transfers must take the SAT or ACT.

Computers: All students may access the system. There is a limit on the IBM systems but no limit on the DEC cluster. There are no fees. All students are required to have personal computers.

Graduates: In a recent year, 7975 bachelor's degrees were awarded. The most popular majors were business/marketing (21%), engineering (11%), and social sciences/history (11%). In an average class, 77% graduate in 6 years or less.

Admissions Contact: Bill Kolb, Director of Admissions.
Web: www.reg.ufl.edu/regadmi.htm

UNIVERSITY OF MIAMI
E-5

Coral Gables, FL 33124

Full-time: 4250 men, 5516 women	(305) 284-4323; Fax: (305) 284-2507
Part-time: 277 men, 494 women	Faculty: 707; I, -$
Graduate: 2603 men, 2534 women	Ph.Ds: 97%
Year: semesters, summer session	Student/Faculty: 14 to 1
Application Deadline: February 1	Tuition: $29,491
	Room & Board: $8906
Freshman Class: 18,812 applied, 8679 accepted, 2277 enrolled	
SAT Verbal/Math: n/av	ACT: n/av MOST COMPETITIVE

The University of Miami, founded in 1925, is a private university that offers degrees in more than 130 majors and areas of study. There are 8 undergraduate and 11 graduate schools. In addition to regional accreditation, UM has baccalaureate program accreditation with AACSB, ABET, ACEJMC, APTA, NAAB, NASM, NCATE, and NLN. The 8 libraries contain 2,463,580 volumes, 3,875,907 microform items, and 116,988 audio/video tapes/CDs/DVDs, and subscribe to 43,939 periodicals including electronic. Computerized library services include the card catalog, interlibrary loans, database searching, Internet access, and laptop Internet portals. Special learning facilities include a learning resource center, art gallery, radio station, TV station, a state-of-the-art research vessel, a sound stage and film studios, a film theater, a performing arts theater, a concert hall, a wellness center, an arboretum, and a palmetum. The 260-acre campus is in a suburban area 6 miles south of Miami. Including any residence halls, there are 113 buildings.

Student Life: 51% of undergraduates are from Florida. Others are from 49 states, 107 foreign countries, and Canada. 69% are from public schools. 56% are white; 27% Hispanic; 10% African American. 47% are Catholic; 29% Protestant; 15% Jewish; 9% Hindu 2%, Muslim 1%. The average age of freshmen is 18; all undergraduates, 21. 11% do not continue beyond their first year; 71% remain to graduate.

Housing: 4234 students can be accommodated in college housing, which includes single-sex and coed dorms, on-campus apartments, and fraternity houses. In addition, there are language houses and special-interest houses. All freshmen living on campus live in residential colleges with live-in resident faculty. On-campus housing is guaranteed for all 4 years. 59% of students commute. All students may keep cars.

Activities: 12% of men belong to 13 national fraternities; 14% of women belong to 13 national sororities. There are 200 groups on campus, including art, band, cheerleading, chess, choir, chorale, chorus, dance, debate, drama, drill team, ethnic, film, gay, honors, international, jazz band, literary magazine, marching band, musical theater, newspaper, opera, orchestra, pep band, political, professional, radio and TV, religious, social, social service, student government, symphony, and yearbook. Popular campus events include International Week, Cinematic Arts Commission (CAC) Film Festival, and Gusman Concert Hall – Festivale Miami.

Sports: There are 8 intercollegiate sports for men and 10 for women, and 21 intramural sports for men and 21 for women. Facilities include a baseball stadium seating 5000, a soccer stadium, a sports complex, a tennis center, a track and field facility, an athletic center, lighted tennis courts, 4 sports fields, and an Olympic-size swimming pool. A 149,000-square foot indoor/outdoor recreational facility includes a multipurpose room, a courtyard, 4 basketball/volleyball courts, an aerobics room, an atrium/fitness room, a floor hockey/indoor soccer gym, a swimming pool, an elevated jogging track, 6 racquetball and 2 squash courts, a spa, and 2 saunas, and a Bank United Center seating 7000.

Disabled Students: 95% of the campus is accessible. Wheelchair ramps, elevators, special parking, specially equipped rest rooms, special class scheduling, lowered drinking fountains, lowered telephones, special housing, and lowered elevator controls are available.

Services: Counseling and information services are available, as is tutoring in every subject. There is a reader service for the blind, and remedial math, reading, and writing.

Campus Safety and Security: Measures include 24-hour foot and vehicle patrol, self-defense education, security escort services, and shuttle buses. There are informal discussions, pamphlets/posters/films, emergency telephones, and lighted pathways/sidewalks. There has been a comprehensive crime prevention program since 1981, including security card access to all residential colleges, office crimewatch, and an adopt a cop program in the residence halls.

Programs of Study: UM confers B.A., B.S., B.Arch., B.B.A., B.C.S., B.F.A., B.F.A.V.C., B.G.S., B.H.S., B.L.A., B. M., B.S.A.E., B.S.B.E., B.S.C., B.S.C.E., B.S.Cp.E., B.S.Ed., B.S.E.E., B.S.I.E., B.S.I.T., B.S.M.E., B.S.M.S., B.S.N., and B.S.S.A. degrees. Master's and doctoral degrees are also awarded. Bachelor's degrees are awarded in BIOLOGICAL SCIENCE (biochemistry, biology/biological science, marine science, and microbiology), BUSINESS (accounting, banking and finance, business administration and management, entrepreneurial studies, human resources, international business management, management information systems, marketing management, and sports management), COMMUNICATIONS AND THE ARTS (advertising, art, art history and appreciation, audio technology, broadcasting, ceramic art and design, communications, creative writing, dramatic arts, English, fine arts, French, German, graphic design, guitar, Italian, jazz, journalism, music, music performance, music theory and composition, musical theater, painting, percussion, photography, piano/organ, printmaking, public relations, sculpture, Spanish, studio art, telecommunications, theater design, theater management, video, and voice), COMPUTER AND PHYSICAL SCIENCE (applied mathematics, chemistry, computer science, geology, mathematics, physics, and systems analysis), EDUCATION (athletic training, elementary, music, secondary, and special), ENGINEERING AND ENVIRONMENTAL DESIGN (aeronautical engineering, architectural engineering, architecture, biomedical engineering, civil engineering, computer engineering, electrical/electronics engineering, engineering, environmental engineering, environmental science, industrial engineering, manufacturing engineering, and mechanical engineering), HEALTH PROFESSIONS (health science, music therapy, nursing, predentistry, premedicine, prepharmacy, and preveterinary science), SOCIAL SCIENCE (African American studies, American studies, anthropology, criminology, economics, geography, history, international studies, Judaic studies, Latin American studies, philosophy, political science/government, prelaw, psychobiology, psychology, religion, sociology, and women's studies). Marine science, international finance and marketing, and music are the strongest academically. Biology, psychology, and business management and organization are the largest.

Required: Requirements for each degree vary, but all students must complete at least 120 credit hours. All students must fulfill general education requirements in English composition, math, writing across the curriculum, natural sciences, social sciences, and arts and humanities. Students must complete 24 to 36 hours in the major and maintain a minimum GPA of 2.0.

Special: UM offers co-op programs in engineering and internships in communications, business, engineering, architecture, and science. There is on- and off-campus work-study, and study abroad in 28 countries. Also available are 3-2 engineering degrees with Jacksonville University and Eckerd College. There are 45 national honor societies, including Phi Beta Kappa, a freshman honors program, and 100 departmental honors programs.

Faculty/Classroom: 63% of faculty are male; 37%, female. 76% teach undergraduates. Graduate students teach 21% of introductory courses. The average class size in an introductory lecture is 32; in a laboratory, 15; and in a regular course, 20.

Admissions: 46% of the 2005-2006 applicants were accepted. 82% of the current freshmen were in the top fifth of their class; 97% were in the top two fifths.

Requirements: The SAT or ACT is required. In addition, it is recommended that applicants have completed 4 years of English, 3 each of math, science, and social sciences, and 2 of foreign language. Also considered in the admissions decision are a recommendation from a high school counselor and an essay. The GED is accepted. AP and CLEP credits are accepted.

Procedure: Freshmen are admitted fall, spring, and summer. Entrance exams should be taken in the fall of the senior year or earlier. There are early decision, early admissions, and deferred admissions plans. Early decision applications should be filed by November 1; regular applications, by February 1 for fall entry and November 1 for spring entry, along with a $65 fee. Notification of early decision is sent December 20; regular decision, April 15. 356 early decision candidates were accepted for the 2005-2006 class. A waiting list is an active part of the admissions procedure. Applications are accepted on-line.

Transfer: 651 transfer students enrolled in 2004-2005. Transfer applicants must have a GPA of at least 2.8; higher admission standards are in effect for most programs. College transcripts and a statement of good standing from previous institutions attended are required. Courses with grades of C or higher may transfer for credit. 45 of 120 credits required for the bachelor's degree must be completed at UM.

Visiting: There are regularly scheduled orientations for prospective students, consisting of several open house programs that enable students to tour the campus and meet with representatives from admission, financial aid, and various university departments. Daily information sessions are offered on campus. There are guides for informal visits and visitors may sit in on classes. To schedule a visit, contact the Admission Office or the specific school or college.

Financial Aid: In 2005-2006, 86% of all full-time freshmen and 87% of continuing full-time students received some form of financial aid. 52% of full-time freshmen and 51% of continuing full-time students received need-based aid. The average freshman award was $23,188. Need-based scholarships or need-based grants averaged $17,512 ($40,830 maximum); need-based self-help aid (loans and jobs) averaged $4833 ($9200 maximum); non-need-based athletic scholarships averaged $23,653 ($39,868 maximum); other non-need-based awards and non-need-based scholarships averaged $14,846 ($58,968 maximum); and need-based parent loans, need-based tuition remission, and need-based athletic scholarships averaged $10,048 ($33,308 maximum). 24% of undergraduates work part time. Average annual earnings from campus work are $2000. The average financial indebtedness of the 2005 graduate was $19,140. UM is a member of CSS. The FAFSA and the state aid form are required. The deadline for filing freshman financial aid applications for fall entry is February 1.

International Students: There are 737 international students enrolled. The school actively recruits these students. They must take the TOEFL if English is not their native language scoring satisfactorily on the written TOEFL or on the electronic version. Students from Amreican schools or IB curriculums must also take the SAT or ACT.

Computers: Wireless access is available. All students may access the system 24 hours a day. There are no time limits and no fees.

Graduates: From July 1, 2004 to June 30, 2005, 2392 bachelor's degrees were awarded. The most popular majors were biology (8%), finance (7%), and psychology (5%). Of the 2004 graduating class, 32% were enrolled in graduate school within 6 months of graduation and 78% were employed. More than 350 companies recruited on campus in 2004-2005.

Admissions Contact: Edward M. Gillis, Assistant Vice President for EM/ Executive Director of Admission. A video is available.
E-mail: *admission@miami.edu* Web: *www.miami.edu/admission*

UNIVERSITY OF NORTH FLORIDA   D-1

Jacksonville, FL 32224	(904) 620-2624; Fax: (904) 620-2414
Full-time: 4014 men, 5510 women	Faculty: 379; II A, -$
Part-time: 1709 men, 2502 women	Ph.D.s: 95%
Graduate: 578 men, 1040 women	Student/Faculty: 25 to 1
Year: semesters, summer session	Tuition: $3268 ($14,911)
Application Deadline: July 2	Room & Board: $6640
Freshman Class: 7047 applied, 4498 accepted, 1804 enrolled	
SAT Verbal/Math: 583/577*	ACT: 22 VERY COMPETITIVE

The University of North Florida, founded in 1965, is a public university that is part of the state university system. There are 5 undergraduate and 5 graduate schools. In addition to regional accreditation, UNF has baccalaureate program accreditation with AACSB, ABET, ACCE, CAAHEP, CAPTE, NASM, NCATE, and NLN. The library contains 746,604 volumes, 1.3 million microform items, and 67,208 audio/video tapes/CDs/DVDs, and subscribes to 3466 periodicals including electronic. Computerized library services include the card catalog, interlibrary loans, and database searching. Special learning facilities include a learning resource center, art gallery, radio station, TV station, a theater, auditorium, and nature preserve. The 1300-acre campus is in an urban area 12 miles southeast of downtown Jacksonville. Including any residence halls, there are 67 buildings.

Student Life: 84% of undergraduates are from Florida. Others are from 48 states, 111 foreign countries, and Canada. 76% are white; 10% African American. Most are claim no religious affiliation. The average age of freshmen is 19; all undergraduates, 24. 25% do not continue beyond their first year; 48% remain to graduate.

Housing: 2445 students can be accommodated in college housing, which includes coed dorms, on-campus apartments, and married-student housing. In addition, there are honors houses. On-campus housing is available on a first-come, first-served basis. 84% of students commute. All students may keep cars.

Activities: 6% of men belong to 8 national fraternities; 6% of women belong to 7 national sororities. There are 172 groups on campus, including art, band, cheerleading, choir, chorale, chorus, computers, dance, drama, ethnic, film, gay, honors, international, jazz band, literary magazine, newspaper, orchestra, pep band, photography, political, professional, radio and TV, religious, social, social service, and student government. Popular campus events include Clubfest, Spring Bash, and Earth Music Fest.

Sports: There are 8 intercollegiate sports for men and 9 for women, and 12 intramural sports for men and 12 for women. Facilities include a baseball stadium, softball, soccer, and multipurpose fields, an aquatic center, a fitness center, jogging trails, racquetball, basketball, volleyball, and tennis courts, a 6,000-seat multipurpose arena, and lakes for canoeing and fishing.

Disabled Students: Wheelchair ramps, elevators, special parking, specially equipped rest rooms, special class scheduling, lowered drinking fountains, and lowered telephones are available. The Disabled Services Office provides specialized assistance and equipment, including priority registration, interpreters for the hearing impaired, and proctored testing are available.

Services: Counseling and information services are available, as is tutoring in some subjects including reading, writing, math, business, accounting, physics, biology, chemistry, Spanish, French, and English as a second language.

Campus Safety and Security: Measures include 24-hour foot and vehicle patrol, self-defense education, security escort services, and informal discussions. There are pamphlets/posters/films, emergency telephones, lighted pathways/sidewalks, and university police presentations at new student orientation.

Programs of Study: UNF confers B.A., B.S., B.A.E., B.B.A., B.F.A., B.M., B.S.E.E., B.S.H., and B.S.N. degrees. Associate, master's, and doctoral degrees are also awarded. Bachelor's degrees are awarded in BIOLOGICAL SCIENCE (biology/biological science), BUSINESS (accounting, banking and finance, business administration and management, business economics, marketing management, and transportation management), COMMUNICATIONS AND THE ARTS (art, communications, English, fine arts, jazz, music, music performance, and Spanish), COMPUTER AND PHYSICAL SCIENCE (chemistry, computer science, information sciences and systems, mathematics, physics, and statistics), EDUCATION (art, athletic training, elementary, mathematics, middle school, music, physical, science, secondary, and special), ENGINEERING AND ENVIRONMENTAL DESIGN (civil engineering, construction management, electrical/electronics engineering, and mechanical engineering), HEALTH PROFESSIONS (health science, nursing, and predentistry), SOCIAL SCIENCE (anthropology, criminal justice, economics, history, philosophy, political science/government, prelaw, psychology, and sociology). Nursing, fine arts, and elementary education are the strongest academically. Elementary education, psychology, and business management are the largest.

Required: Students are required to take general education distribution requirements, including 9 hours of composition and humanities, and 6 each of natural science, math, and social science. There is a core curriculum in Western civilization and cultural diversity. A minimum 2.0 GPA and 120 credit hours, with a minimum of 60 hours in the major, are needed for graduation. All students must take the state-required college-level academic skills test unless exempt.

Special: There are cooperative programs and internships in most majors, and work-study programs with several Jacksonville businesses. Study abroad, a Washington semester, accelerated degree program in nursing, B.A.-B.S. degrees in math, statistics, and psychology, dual majors, and student-designed majors are also available. Credit is given for military experience. There are 5 national honor societies, a freshman honors program, and 10 departmental honors programs.

Faculty/Classroom: 59% of faculty are male; 41%, female. 91% teach undergraduates, 79% do research, and 70% do both. Graduate students teach 1% of introductory courses. The average class size in an introductory lecture is 38; in a laboratory, 17; in a regular course, 34.

Admissions: 64% of the 2005-2006 applicants were accepted. The SAT scores for the 2005-2006 freshman class were: Verbal--7% below 500, 52% between 500 and 599, 38% between 600 and 700, and 3% above 700; Math--7% below 500, 54% between 500 and 599, 37% between 600 and 700, and 2% above 700. The ACT scores were 28% below 21, 50% between 21 and 23, 16% between 24 and 26, 4% between 27 and 28, and 2% above 28. 45% of the current freshmen were in the top fifth of their class; 77% were in the top two fifths. 11 freshmen graduated first in their class.

Requirements: The SAT or ACT is required with a satisfactory score on the SAT or on the ACT. In addition, applicants must be graduates of an accredited secondary school or have a GED. A total of 15 academic credits plus 4 additional academic electives or 19 Carnegie units is required. Secondary school course work must include 4 years of English, 3 each of math, science, and social studies, and 2 of foreign language. A GPA of 2.5 is required. AP and CLEP credits are accepted. Important factors in the admissions decision are advanced placement or honor courses, recommendations by school officials, and evidence of special talent.

Procedure: Freshmen are admitted to all sessions. Entrance exams should be taken during the spring of the junior year or the fall of the senior year. There are early admissions, deferred admissions and rolling admissions plans. Applications should be filed by July 2 for fall entry, November 2 for spring entry, and April 8 for summer entry. Notification is sent on a rolling basis. Applications are accepted on-line. The fall 2005 application fee was $30.

Transfer: 6550 transfer students enrolled in 2004-2005. Transfer applicants with fewer than 60 credit hours must take either the SAT or the ACT and achieve a minimum composite score of 970 on the SAT or 20 on the ACT, and must meet all high school unit requirements. The minimum college GPA for transfers is 2.0. Some programs require 2.5. 30 of

120 credits required for the bachelor's degree must be completed at UNF.

Visiting: There are regularly scheduled orientations for prospective students, consisting of open houses which include tours of the campus and housing, a general information session, financial aid sessions, academic advising, and personal interviews by request. There are guides for informal visits and visitors may sit in on classes. To schedule a visit, contact the Admissions Office at (904) 620-2625.

Financial Aid: In 2005-2006, 84% of all full-time freshmen and 70% of continuing full-time students received some form of financial aid. 28% of full-time freshmen and 32% of continuing full-time students received need-based aid. The average freshman award was $2620. Need-based scholarships or need-based grants averaged $2060 ($4050 maximum); need-based self-help aid (loans and jobs) averaged $2521 ($4000 maximum); non-need-based athletic scholarships averaged $4977 ($13,814 maximum); and other non-need-based awards and non-need-based scholarships averaged $2816 ($25,000 maximum). 5% of undergraduates work part time. Average annual earnings from campus work are $6476. The average financial indebtedness of the 2005 graduate was $16,708. The FAFSA is required. The deadline for filing freshman financial aid applications for fall entry is April 1.

International Students: There are 145 international students enrolled. The school actively recruits these students. They must score satisfactorily on the written TOEFL.

Computers: All students may access the system The general purpose labs are open more than 100 hours per week. There are no time limits and no fees. It is recommended that students in building construction management have personal computers. A Pentium 200 Notebook with 128 MB RAM and a 6 GB hard drive is recommended.

Graduates: From July 1, 2004 to June 30, 2005, 2262 bachelor's degrees were awarded. The most popular majors were communications (10%), business (9%), and psychology (7%). In an average class, 2% graduate in 3 years or less, 20% graduate in 4 years or less, 46% graduate in 5 years or less, and 54% graduate in 6 years or less. 281 companies recruited on campus in 2004-2005.

Admissions Contact: John Yancey, Director of Admissions. A video is available. E-mail: *osprey@unf.edu* Web: *www.unf.edu*

UNIVERSITY OF SOUTH FLORIDA D-1

Tampa, FL 33620   (813) 974-3350; Fax: (813) 974-9689

Full-time: 9804 men, 14,141 women	Faculty: 1724; I, --$
Part-time: 3936 men, 5821 women	Ph.D.s: 93%
Graduate: 3288 men, 5669 women	Student/Faculty: 14 to 1
Year: semesters, summer session	Tuition: $3384 ($16,150)
Application Deadline: May 1	Room & Board: $6900
Freshman Class: 18,307 applied, 10,664 accepted, 4311 enrolled	
SAT Verbal/Math: 560/570*	ACT: 24 VERY COMPETITIVE

The University of South Florida, founded in 1956, is a comprehensive public institution, part of the Florida Division of Colleges and Universities, offering programs in liberal and fine arts, business, engineering, health science, and education. USF also maintains campuses at Lakeland, Sarasota, and St. Petersburg. There are 6 undergraduate and 9 graduate schools. In addition to regional accreditation, USF has baccalaureate program accreditation with AACSB, ABET, ACEJMC, ASLA, CSAB, CSWE, NAAB, NASAD, NASM, NCATE, and NLN. The 5 libraries contain 2.1 million volumes, 4.4 million microform items, and 148,986 audio/video tapes/CDs/DVDs, and subscribe to 20,440 periodicals including electronic. Computerized library services include the card catalog, interlibrary loans, database searching, and Internet access. Special learning facilities include a learning resource center, art gallery, radio station, TV station, mock broadcasting studio, anthropology museum, and botanical gardens. The 1941-acre campus is in an urban area 10 miles northeast of downtown Tampa. Including any residence halls, there are 434 buildings.

Student Life: 96% of undergraduates are from Florida. Others are from 49 states, 132 foreign countries, and Canada. 91% are from public schools. 67% are white; 11% African American; 10% Hispanic. The average age of freshmen is 19; all undergraduates, 22. 18% do not continue beyond their first year; 47% remain to graduate.

Housing: 4229 students can be accommodated in college housing, which includes single-sex and coed dorms, on-campus apartments, married-student housing, fraternity houses, and sorority houses. In addition, there are honors houses, special-interest houses, and graduate students only, medical students, and an internation hall. On-campus housing is available on a first-come, first-served basis. 89% of students commute. All students may keep cars.

Activities: 7% of men belong to 19 national fraternities; 6% of women belong to 11 national sororities. There are 200 groups on campus, including art, band, cheerleading, chess, choir, chorale, chorus, computers, dance, drama, drill team, ethnic, film, gay, honors, international, jazz band, literary magazine, marching band, musical theater, newspaper, opera, orchestra, pep band, photography, political, professional, radio and TV, religious, social, social service, student government, and sym-

phony. Popular campus events include Minority events, International events, and University Lecture Series.

Sports: There are 9 intercollegiate sports for men and 9 for women, and 20 intramural sports for men and 19 for women. Facilities include a 10,000-seat multipurpose arena, 4 pools, tennis and indoor racquetball courts, a track, a jogging course, an indoor recreation center with weight training and aerobics rooms, a soccer stadium, a softball complex, a baseball stadium, and an 18-hole golf course.

Disabled Students: All of the campus is accessible. Wheelchair ramps, elevators, special parking, specially equipped rest rooms, special class scheduling, lowered drinking fountains, and lowered telephones are available.

Services: Counseling and information services are available, as is tutoring in most subjects. There is a reader service for the blind.

Campus Safety and Security: Measures include 24-hour foot and vehicle patrol, self-defense education, security escort services, and shuttle buses. There are informal discussions, pamphlets/posters/films, emergency telephones, lighted pathways/sidewalks, and university police.

Programs of Study: USF confers B.A., B.S., B.F.A., B.I.S., B.M., B.S.W. degrees. Associate, master's, and doctoral degrees are also awarded. Bachelor's degrees are awarded in BIOLOGICAL SCIENCE (biology/biological science and microbiology), BUSINESS (accounting, banking and finance, business administration and management, business economics, management information systems, management science, and marketing/retailing/merchandising), COMMUNICATIONS AND THE ARTS (classics, communications, dance, dramatic arts, English literature, French, German, Italian, music, Russian, Spanish, and speech/debate/rhetoric), COMPUTER AND PHYSICAL SCIENCE (chemistry, geology, mathematics, physical sciences, and physics), EDUCATION (art, business, education, education of the emotionally handicapped, education of the mentally handicapped, elementary, English, foreign languages, mathematics, music, physical, science, social studies, special, and specific learning disabilities), ENGINEERING AND ENVIRONMENTAL DESIGN (chemical engineering, civil engineering, computer engineering, electrical/electronics engineering, engineering, environmental science, industrial engineering, and mechanical engineering), HEALTH PROFESSIONS (medical technology and nursing), SOCIAL SCIENCE (African American studies, American studies, anthropology, criminology, economics, geography, gerontology, history, humanities, international relations, liberal arts/general studies, philosophy, political science/government, psychology, religion, social science, social work, and sociology). Education, business and arts and sciences, are the strongest academically. Business and education are the largest.

Required: To graduate, all students are required to complete at least 120 credit hours, including 36 distributed among English, math, science, social science, historical perspectives, fine arts, and humanities, and 9 of exit requirements in major works/major issues and literature/writing. The number of hours required for each major varies. Students must maintain a minimum GPA of 2.0.

Special: USF offers co-op programs in business and engineering, study abroad, cross-registration, work-study programs, accelerated degree programs in public health and medicine, internships, cross-registration, a Washington semester, dual and student-designed majors, a liberal arts degree, nondegree study, and pass/fail options for some courses. There are 21 national honor societies, a freshman honors program, and 18 departmental honors programs.

Faculty/Classroom: 57% of faculty are male; 43%, female. 48% teach undergraduates and 16% do research. The average class size in an introductory lecture is 30; in a laboratory, 21; and in a regular course, 30.

Admissions: 58% of the 2005-2006 applicants were accepted. The SAT scores for the 2005-2006 freshman class were: Verbal--17% below 500, 55% between 500 and 599, 25% between 600 and 700, and 3% above 700; Math--13% below 500, 55% between 500 and 599, 29% between 600 and 700, and 4% above 700. The ACT scores were 52% below 24, 42% between 24 and 29, and 5% 30 and above. 50% of the current freshmen were in the top fifth of their class; 73% were in the top two fifths. There were 11 National Merit finalists.

Requirements: The SAT or ACT is required. In addition, candidates for admission should have completed 4 units each of English and academic electives, 3 each of math, science, and social studies, and 2 of a foreign language. The GED is accepted. Applicants who do not meet minimum requirements but have important attributes, special talents, or unique circumstances are considered for admission by an academic faculty committee. A GPA of 2.0 is required. AP and CLEP credits are accepted. Important factors in the admissions decision are advanced placement or honor courses, evidence of special talent, and recommendations by school officials.

Procedure: Freshmen are admitted fall, spring, and summer. Entrance exams should be taken at the end of the junior year or the beginning of the senior year. There are early admissions and rolling admissions plans. Applications should be filed by May 1 for fall entry, October 1 for spring entry, and March 1 for summer entry, along with a $30 fee. Notification is sent on a rolling basis. Applications are accepted on-line.

Transfer: 4009 transfer students enrolled in 2004-2005. Applicants must have a cumulative college GPA of 2.0 and be in good standing at their last institution. 30 of 120 to 132 credits required for the bachelor's degree must be completed at USF.

Visiting: There are regularly scheduled orientations for prospective students, including a 2-day program. There are guides for informal visits and visitors may sit in on classes. To schedule a visit, contact the Admissions Office/New Student Orientation at (813) 974-3060.

Financial Aid: The average freshman award was $7824. 23% of undergraduates work part time. The average financial indebtedness of the 2005 graduate was $17,434. The FAFSA is required. The deadline for filing freshman financial aid applications for fall entry is March 1.

International Students: In a recent year, there were 788 international students enrolled. The school actively recruits these students. They must score satisfactorily on the written TOEFL or on the electronic version and also take the SAT or the ACT.

Computers: Wireless access is available. All students may access the system. There are no time limits and no fees.

Graduates: From July 1, 2004 to June 30, 2005, 5179 bachelor's degrees were awarded. The most popular majors were business (25%), social science (12%), and education (10%). In an average class, 1% graduate in 3 years or less, 21% graduate in 4 years or less, 39% graduate in 5 years or less, and 47% graduate in 6 years or less. 700 companies recruited on campus in 2004-2005. Of a recent graduating class, 22% were enrolled in graduate school within 6 months of graduation and 71% were employed.

Admissions Contact: Dewey Holleman, Director of Admissions. A video is available. E-mail: *dhollema@admin.usf.edu* Web: *http://usfweb.usf.edu/enroll/admiss/admiss.htm*

UNIVERSITY OF TAMPA   D-4

Tampa, FL 33606-1490

                                                        (813) 253-6211
                                        (888) 646-2738; Fax: (813) 258-7398

Full-time: 1606 men, 2563 women	**Faculty:** 233; IIB, av$
Part-time: 159 men, 308 women	**Ph.D.s:** 90%
Graduate: 265 men, 301 women	**Student/Faculty:** 18 to 1
Year: semesters, summer session	**Tuition:** $18,848
Application Deadline: open	**Room & Board:** $6936
Freshman Class: 6365 applied, 3207 accepted, 1010 enrolled	
SAT Verbal/Math: 539/542*	**ACT:** 23	**COMPETITIVE**

The University of Tampa, founded in 1931, is a comprehensive, independent institution that offers degree programs in more than 65 undergraduate and preprofessional areas of study, and graduate and evening programs. There are 2 undergraduate and 2 graduate schools. In addition to regional accreditation, UT has baccalaureate program accreditation with AACSB, NASM, and NLN. The library contains 253,640 volumes, 25,337 microform items, and 7909 audio/video tapes/CDs/DVDs, and subscribes to 23,120 periodicals including electronic. Computerized library services include the card catalog, interlibrary loans, database searching, and Internet access. Special learning facilities include a learning resource center, art gallery, radio station, TV station, a fully equipped research vessel for marine science studies, a music facility, writing and language labs, an academic center for excellence, a graphic design studio, a marine science lab, and art studios. The 100-acre campus is in an urban area in Tampa. Including any residence halls, there are 45 buildings.

Student Life: 54% of undergraduates are from out of state, mostly the Northeast. Others are from 50 states, 101 foreign countries, and Canada. 75% are from public schools. 64% are white; 13% foreign nationals. The average age of freshmen is 18; all undergraduates, 21. 23% do not continue beyond their first year; 56% remain to graduate.

Housing: 2505 students can be accommodated in college housing, which includes single-sex and coed dorms on-campus apartments, a special honors floor, a non-traditional floor, a leadership floor, and a substance-free floor. 58% of students live on campus; of those, 85% remain on campus on weekends. All students may keep cars.

Activities: 19% of men belong to 8 national fraternities; 19% of women belong to 9 national sororities. There are 120 groups on campus, including academic leadership, art, band, cheerleading, chess, chorale, chorus, computers, dance, debate, drama, ethnic, gay, honors, international, jazz band, literary magazine, musical theater, newspaper, orchestra, pep band, political, professional, radio and TV, religious, social, social service, special interest, student government, symphony, and yearbook. Popular campus events include Into the Streets (volunteer program) and Global Village Day.

Sports: There are 6 intercollegiate sports for men and 8 for women, and 7 intramural sports for men and 7 for women. Facilities include a sports center, a stadium, baseball, softball, practice, and intramural fields, a boathouse, an Olympic-size pool, 6 lighted tennis courts, volleyball and basketball courts, activity and fitness centers, a dance studio, the student union, and recreation rooms in each residence hall.

Disabled Students: All of the campus is accessible. Wheelchair ramps, elevators, special parking, specially equipped rest rooms, lowered drinking fountains, lowered telephones, and special housing are available.

Services: Counseling and information services are available, as is tutoring in every subject. There is remedial math, reading, and writing.

Campus Safety and Security: Measures include 24-hour foot and vehicle patrol, self-defense education, security escort services, and shuttle buses. There are informal discussions, pamphlets/posters/films, emergency telephones, lighted pathways/sidewalks, and a full-service, on-campus security office.

Programs of Study: UT confers B.A., B.S., B.F.A., B.L.S., B.M., and B.S.N. degrees. Associate and master's degrees are also awarded. Bachelor's degrees are awarded in BIOLOGICAL SCIENCE (biochemistry, biology/biological science, and marine science), BUSINESS (accounting, banking and finance, business administration and management, business economics, international business management, and marketing/retailing/merchandising), COMMUNICATIONS AND THE ARTS (art, communications, creative writing, English, fine arts, graphic design, music, performing arts, and Spanish), COMPUTER AND PHYSICAL SCIENCE (chemistry, information sciences and systems, and mathematics), EDUCATION (elementary and secondary), ENGINEERING AND ENVIRONMENTAL DESIGN (computer graphics and environmental science), HEALTH PROFESSIONS (exercise science and nursing), SOCIAL SCIENCE (criminology, economics, history, international studies, liberal arts/general studies, political science/government, psychology, social science, sociology, and urban studies). Biology and chemistry are the strongest academically. Communication, management, and marketing are the largest.

Required: To graduate, students must maintain a minimum GPA of 2.0 in at least 124 credit hours, including the 2-year Learning Community, 11 hours each in humanities/fine arts and social science, 6 in natural science, global issues, non-Western studies, an art/aesthetics as well as courses in writing-intensive course work. The requirements for individual majors vary.

Special: Students may participate in internships, work-study programs on campus, study abroad in 7 countries, a Washington semester, and an Oxford semester program. UT also offers summer marine science courses at the Gulf Coast Research Laboratory, nondegree study, pass/fail options, dual majors, accelerated degree programs, and credit for life, military, and work experience. There are 22 national honor societies, a freshman honors program, and 16 departmental honors programs.

Faculty/Classroom: 51% of faculty are male; 49%, female. All teach undergraduates. No introductory courses are taught by graduate students. The average class size in an introductory lecture is 22; in a laboratory, 4; and in a regular course, 21.

Admissions: 50% of the 2005-2006 applicants were accepted. The SAT scores for the 2005-2006 freshman class were: Verbal--26% below 500, 54% between 500 and 599, 18% between 600 and 700, and 2% above 700; Math--23% below 500, 57% between 500 and 599, 19% between 600 and 700, and 1% above 700. The ACT scores were 26% below 21, 35% between 21 and 23, 26% between 24 and 26, 8% between 27 and 28, and 5% above 28. 40% of the current freshmen were in the top fifth of their class; 85% were in the top two fifths.

Requirements: The SAT or ACT is required. In addition, candidates for admission should have completed 4 credits in English, 3 each in math, science, and social studies, and 5 in college-preparatory electives. The GED is accepted. A portfolio or an audition is required for specific art and music programs. A GPA of 2.5 is required. AP and CLEP credits are accepted. Important factors in the admissions decision are personality/intangible qualities, evidence of special talent, and recommendations by school officials.

Procedure: Freshmen are admitted fall, spring, and summer. Entrance exams should be taken by the end of the junior year or early in the senior year. There are deferred admissions and rolling admissions plans. Application deadlines are open. Notification of regular decision is sent September 15. Application fee is $35. Applications are accepted on-line.

Transfer: 409 transfer students enrolled in 2004-2005. Applicants should have earned 17 college credits with a minimum GPA of 2.0. 31 of 124 credits required for the bachelor's degree must be completed at UT.

Visiting: There are regularly scheduled orientations for prospective students, including a campus tour and an interview with an admissions counselor, faculty, and others as requested. There are guides for informal visits and visitors may sit in on classes and stay overnight. To schedule a visit, contact the Admissions Office at *admissions@ut.edu*.

Financial Aid: In 2005-2006, 87% of all full-time freshmen and 88% of continuing full-time students received some form of financial aid. 80% of full-time freshmen and 81% of continuing full-time students received need-based aid. The average freshman award was $15,472. Need-based scholarships or need-based grants averaged $6198; need-based self-help aid (loans and jobs) averaged $3731 ($9125 maximum); and other non-need-based awards and non-need-based scholarships averaged $2000 ($2000 maximum). 25% of undergraduates work part time. Average annual earnings from campus work are $2000. The average financial indebtedness of the 2005 graduate was $23,051. The FAFSA is required.

International Students: There are 315 international students enrolled. The school actively recruits these students. A satisfactory score is required on the written TOEFL.

Computers: Wireless access is available. Campus buildings are connected to a high-speed fiber-optic backbone with more than 4500 connections throughout the campus. All residence hall rooms provide network access for each student. Dial-in lines provide remote access. All students may access the system. There are no time limits and no fees. It is strongly recommended that all students have a personal computer.

Graduates: From July 1, 2004 to June 30, 2005, 784 bachelor's degrees were awarded. The most popular majors were communication (11%), management (9%), and marketing (8%). In an average class, 45% graduate in 4 years or less, 54% graduate in 5 years or less, and 56% graduate in 6 years or less. 240 companies recruited on campus in 2004-2005. Of the 2004 graduating class, 8% were enrolled in graduate school within 6 months of graduation and 89% were employed.

Admissions Contact: Barbara P. Strickler, Vice President, Enrollment. E-mail: *admissions@ut.edu* Web: *www.ut.edu*

UNIVERSITY OF WEST FLORIDA A-1

Pensacola, FL 32514-5750

(850) 474-2230
(800) 263-1074; Fax: (850) 474-3360

Full-time: 2276 men, 3364 women	**Faculty:** IIA, --$
Part-time: 862 men, 1279 women	**Ph.D.s:** n/av
Graduate: 407 men, 831 women	**Student/Faculty:** n/av
Year: semesters, summer session	**Tuition:** $2559 ($12,564)
Application Deadline: June 30	**Room & Board:** $6000
Freshman Class: 3366 applied, 2302 accepted, 924 enrolled	
SAT Verbal/Math: 550/545*	**ACT:** 23 COMPETITIVE

The University of West Florida, founded in 1967, is a public, liberal arts institution that is part of the State University system of Florida. Some figures in the above capsule and this profile are approximate. There are 3 undergraduate and 3 graduate schools. In addition to regional accreditation, UWF has baccalaureate program accreditation with AACSB, ABET, CSWE, NCATE, and NLN. The library contains 416,380 volumes, 1,635,474 microform items, and 7311 audio/video tapes/CDs/DVDs, and subscribes to 5032 periodicals including electronic. Computerized library services include the card catalog, interlibrary loans, and database searching. Special learning facilities include a learning resource center, art gallery, radio station, TV station, and an archeology museum. The 1600-acre campus is in a suburban area 10 miles north of downtown Pensacola. Including any residence halls, there are 71 buildings.

Student Life: 87% of undergraduates are from Florida. Others are from 49 states, 82 foreign countries, and Canada. 78% are white; 10% African American. The average age of freshmen is 19; all undergraduates, 25.

Housing: 1250 students can be accommodated in college housing, which includes coed dormitories and on-campus apartments. In addition, there are honors houses. On-campus housing is available on a first-come, first-served basis. 85% of students commute. All students may keep cars.

Activities: There are 6 national fraternities and 5 national sororities. There are 85 groups on campus, including art, band, cheerleading, choir, chorale, chorus, debate, drama, ethnic, film, forensics, gay, honors, international, jazz band, literary magazine, newspaper, orchestra, political, professional, radio and TV, religious, social, social service, student government, and symphony.

Sports: There are 6 intercollegiate sports for men and 7 for women, and 16 intramural sports for men and 16 for women. Facilities include facilities for baseball, track, tennis, racquetball, handball, softball, soccer, swimming, diving, weight lifting, and aerobics.

Disabled Students: All of the campus is accessible. Wheelchair ramps, elevators, special parking, specially equipped rest rooms, special class scheduling, lowered drinking fountains, and special housing are available.

Services: Counseling and information services are available, as is tutoring in most subjects. There is remedial math, reading, and writing. Remedial courses are offered on campus by the local community college.

Campus Safety and Security: Measures include 24-hour foot and vehicle patrol, security escort services, informal discussions, and pamphlets/posters/films. There are emergency telephones, lighted pathways/sidewalks, and a trolley system.

Programs of Study: UWF confers B.A., B.S., B.F.A., B.S.B.A., B.S.C.E., B.S.E.E., and B.S.N degrees. Associate, master's, and doctoral degrees are also awarded. Bachelor's degrees are awarded in BIOLOGICAL SCIENCE (biology/biological science and marine biology), BUSINESS (accounting, banking and finance, business administration and management, business economics, and marketing/retailing/merchandising), COMMUNICATIONS AND THE ARTS (communications, English, music, and studio art), COMPUTER AND PHYSICAL SCIENCE (chemistry, computer science, mathematics, physics, and statistics), EDUCATION (art, early childhood, elementary, health, middle school, music, and secondary), ENGINEERING AND ENVIRONMEN-

TAL DESIGN (computer engineering and electrical/electronics engineering), HEALTH PROFESSIONS (medical laboratory technology, nursing, predentistry, and premedicine), SOCIAL SCIENCE (criminal justice, history, philosophy, political science/government, prelaw, psychology, religion, social science, and social work). Accounting, communication arts, and management are the strongest academically. Communication arts, psychology, and business are the largest.

Required: To graduate, students must maintain a 2.0 GPA and complete 120 semester hours with a minimum of 24 hours in the major and 24 hours in upper-division courses.

Special: Internships are arranged on an individual basis through a student's major department. The college offers pass/fail options and credit for military experience. A 3-2 engineering degree is also offered. There are 5 national honor societies and a freshman honors program.

Admissions: 68% of the 2005-2006 applicants were accepted. The SAT scores for the 2005-2006 freshman class were: Verbal--23% below 500, 48% between 500 and 599, 25% between 600 and 700, and 4% above 700; Math--28% below 500, 45% between 500 and 599, 23% between 600 and 700, and 4% above 700. The ACT scores were 20% below 21, 30% between 21 and 23, 30% between 24 and 26, 15% between 27 and 28, and 5% above 28.

Requirements: The SAT or ACT is required. In addition, students must have completed 4 years of English, 3 each of math (algebra 1 and higher) science, and social studies, and 2 of a foreign language. A GPA of 2.0 is required. AP and CLEP credits are accepted. Important factors in the admissions decision are advanced placement or honor courses, evidence of special talent, and geographic diversity.

Procedure: Freshmen are admitted to all sessions. Entrance exams should be taken by the fall of the senior year. There are early admissions, and deferred admissions and rolling admissions plans. Applications should be filed by June 30 for fall entry, December 1 for spring entry, and April 1 for summer entry, along with a $30 fee. Notification is sent 2 to 4 weeks after the file is complete. Applications are accepted online.

Transfer: 1119 transfer students enrolled in 2004-2005. Applicants must have a 2.0 GPA and a 2.0 at their last institution. Transfer students with fewer than 60 semester hours of transferable credit must meet freshman admission requirements. 30 of 120 credits required for the bachelor's degree must be completed at UWF.

Visiting: There are regularly scheduled orientations for prospective students, including 5 open house programs per year. There are guides for informal visits and visitors may sit in on classes. To schedule a visit, contact the Admissions Office.

Financial Aid: In 2005-2006, 65% of continuing full-time students received some form of financial aid. Need-based scholarships or need-based grants averaged $3470 ($4050 maximum); need-based self-help aid (loans and jobs) averaged $2600 ($3240 maximum); non-need-based athletic scholarships averaged $4111 ($6000 maximum); and other non-need-based awards and non-need-based scholarships averaged $2390 ($5000 maximum). The CSS/Profile and the University of West Florida Request for Financial Aid Consideration form, and SAR are required. Check with the school for current application deadlines.

International Students: They must score satisfactorily on the written TOEFL or on the electronic version or take the MELAB, and also take the SAT or the ACT.

Computers: All students may access the system. There are no time limits and no fees.

Admissions Contact: Dr. Richard Barth, Director of Admissions. E-mail: *admissions@uwf.edu* Web: *www.uwf.edu*

WARNER SOUTHERN COLLEGE D-4

Lake Wales, FL 33859

(863) 638-7212
(800) 309-9563; Fax: (863) 638-7290

Full-time: 340 men, 450 women	**Faculty:** 52
Part-time: 65 men, 365 women	**Ph.D.s:** 54%
Graduate: 40 men, 20 women	**Student/Faculty:** 15 to 1
Year: semesters, summer session	**Tuition:** $12,000
Application Deadline: open	**Room & Board:** $6000
Freshman Class: n/av	
SAT or ACT: required	LESS COMPETITIVE

Warner Southern College is a Christian college in the liberal arts tradition committed to the search for truth in the context of Christian faith and academic excellence. There are 2 undergraduate schools and 1 graduate school. Figures in the above capsule and in this profile are approximate. The library contains 74,000 volumes, 7500 microform items, and 15,000 audio/video tapes/CDs/DVDs, and subscribes to 200 periodicals including electronic. Computerized library services include the card catalog, interlibrary loans, database searching, and Internet access. Special learning facilities include a learning resource center. The 380-acre campus is in a rural area 5 miles south of Lake Wales. Including any residence halls, there are 20 buildings.

Student Life: 88% of undergraduates are from Florida. Others are from 26 states, 18 foreign countries, and Canada. 68% are white; 17% African American. 61% are Protestant; 29% claim no religious affiliation; 7% Catholic. The average age of freshmen is 19; all undergraduates, 22. 62% do not continue beyond their first year; 50% remain to graduate.

Housing: 235 students can be accommodated in college housing, which includes single-sex dorms and off-campus apartments. On-campus housing is guaranteed for all 4 years. 58% of students commute. Alcohol is not permitted. All students may keep cars.

Activities: There are no fraternities or sororities. There are 14 groups on campus, including band, cheerleading, choir, chorale, chorus, computers, honors, newspaper, pep band, photography, religious, social, social service, and student government. Popular campus events include Christmas banquet, Barn Party, and Spring banquet.

Sports: There are 7 intercollegiate sports for men and 8 for women, and 4 intramural sports for men and 3 for women. Facilities include the Turner Athletic Center.

Disabled Students: 90% of the campus is accessible. Wheelchair ramps, special parking, specially equipped rest rooms, lowered drinking fountains, and lowered telephones are available.

Services: Counseling and information services are available, as is tutoring in most subjects. There is remedial math, reading, and writing.

Campus Safety and Security: Measures include 24-hour foot and vehicle patrol, security escort services, shuttle buses, and informal discussions. There are pamphlets/posters/films, emergency telephones, lighted pathways/sidewalks, and special training in CPR/First Aid and emergency response.

Programs of Study: Warner Southern College confers the B.A. degree. Associate and master's degrees are also awarded. Bachelor's degrees are awarded in BIOLOGICAL SCIENCE (biology/biological science), BUSINESS (accounting, banking and finance, business administration and management, business law, institutional management, marketing management, and sports management), COMMUNICATIONS AND THE ARTS (communications and English), COMPUTER AND PHYSICAL SCIENCE (information sciences and systems), EDUCATION (business, education of the exceptional child, elementary, English, music, physical, science, and social science), HEALTH PROFESSIONS (exercise science), SOCIAL SCIENCE (biblical studies, history, pastoral studies, psychology, religious music, and social work). Biblical studies, social work, and teacher education are the strongest academically. Organizational management, church ministry, and teacher education are the largest.

Required: To graduate, students must complete 128 credit hours with a GPA of 2.0 to 2.5, depending on the major. 30 to 80 hours are required in the major. 48 hours of upper-division courses are required, as is a computer application course in the major.

Special: Internships are required in many majors, including teacher education, social work, sports management, and church ministry. An accelerated degree program is available in organizational management. HEART (Hunger Education and Resoure Training) is a missionary training program designed to equip students to serve in missions, community development work, or crosscultural assignments in developing countries. There are 5 national honor societies and 1 departmental honors program.

Faculty/Classroom: 72% of faculty are male; 28%, female. All teach undergraduates, 20% do research, and 20% do both. No introductory courses are taught by graduate students. The average class size in an introductory lecture is 28; in a laboratory, 20; and in a regular course, 18.

Admissions: 70% of the 2005-2006 applicants were accepted. The SAT scores for the 2005-2006 freshman class were: Verbal--69% below 500, 27% between 500 and 599, 21% between 600 and 700, and 2% above 700; Math--69% below 500, 27% between 500 and 599, 2% between 600 and 700, and 2% above 700. The ACT scores were 66% below 21, 16% between 21 and 23, 13% between 24 and 26, 2% between 27 and 28, and 3% above 28. 19% of the current freshmen were in the top fifth of their class; 54% were in the top two fifths. There was 1 National Merit finalist and 1 semifinalist. 2 freshmen graduated first in their class.

Requirements: The SAT or ACT is required. Warner Southern College requires applicants to be in the upper 50% of their class. A GPA of 2.25 is required. AP and CLEP credits are accepted.

Procedure: Freshmen are admitted fall and spring. Entrance exams should be taken in the junior or senior year. There are early admissions and deferred admissions plans. Application deadlines are open. Check with the school for application fee. Applications are accepted on-line.

Transfer: 39 transfer students enrolled in a recent year. Applicants may transfer 24 or more hours from a regionally accredited school and must present a GPA of 2.0 or higher. 36 of 128 credits required for the bachelor's degree must be completed at Warner Southern College.

Visiting: There are regularly scheduled orientations for prospective students, consisiting of Warner Weekend held in the spring. There are guides for informal visits and visitors may sit in on classes and stay overnight. To schedule a visit, contact at admissions@warner.edu.

Financial Aid: In a recent year, 93% of all full-time freshmen and 98% of continuing full-time students received some form of financial aid. 91% of full-time freshmen and 52% of continuing full-time students received need-based aid. Need-based scholarships or need-based grants averaged $12,401; need-based self-help aid (loans and jobs) averaged $14,000; non-need-based athletic scholarships averaged $3736; and other non-need-based awards and non-need-based scholarships averaged $7802. 47% of undergraduates work part time. Average annual earnings from campus work are $1528. The FAFSA and the state aid form are required. Check with the school for current deadlines.

International Students: The school actively recruits international students. They must take the TOEFL.

Computers: All students may access the system 7:30 A.M. to 10:45 P.M., Monday to Friday, and some weekend hours. There are no time limits and no fees. It is strongly recommended that all students have a personal computer.

Graduates: In a recent year, 2005, 368 bachelor's degrees were awarded. The most popular majors were organizational management (63%), elementary education (6%), and business administration (3%). In an average class, 25% graduate in 4 years or less, 32% graduate in 5 years or less, and 35% graduate in 6 years or less.

Admissions Contact: Jason Roe, Director of Admissions. E-mail: admissions@warner.edu Web: www.warner.edu

WEBBER INTERNATIONAL UNIVERSITY   D-3
Babson Park, FL 33827   (863) 638-2930
                                     (800) 741-1844; Fax: (863) 638-1317

Full-time: 325 men, 181 women	**Faculty:** 19
Part-time: 28 men, 23 women	**Ph.D.s:** 87%
Graduate: 31 men, 37 women	**Student/Faculty:** 27 to 1
Year: semesters, summer session	**Tuition:** $13,100
Application Deadline: August 1	**Room & Board:** $4480
Freshman Class: n/av	
SAT or ACT: required	**LESS COMPETITIVE**

Webber International University, is a privately endowed, nonprofit institution founded in 1927, offering undergraduate and graduate degrees in business. In addition to regional accreditation, Webber has baccalaureate program accreditation with IACBE. The library contains 28,000 volumes, 105 microform items, and 5000 audio/video tapes/CDs/DVDs, and subscribes to more than 5000 periodicals including electronic. Computerized library services include the card catalog, interlibrary loans, database searching, and Internet access. Special learning facilities include a learning resource center and an Audubon Society museum. The 110-acre campus is in a small town 50 miles east of Tampa and 50 miles south of Orlando. Including any residence halls, there are 10 buildings.

Student Life: 81% of undergraduates are from Florida. Others are from 14 states, 35 foreign countries, and Canada. 76% are from public schools. 55% are white; 23% African American; 15% foreign nationals. The average age of freshmen is 19; all undergraduates, 21. 44% do not continue beyond their first year; 43% remain to graduate.

Housing: 240 students can be accommodated in college housing, which includes single-sex dorms. On-campus housing is guaranteed for the freshman year only and is available on a first-come, first-served basis. 55% of students commute. All students may keep cars.

Activities: There are no fraternities or sororities. There are 19 groups on campus, including debate, honors, international, newspaper, political, professional, religious, social, social service, and student government. Popular campus events include Webber Weekend, Christmas Party, and International Day.

Sports: There are 9 intercollegiate sports for men and 9 for women, and 4 intramural sports for men and 4 for women. Facilities include 2 gyms, a weight room, 4 tennis courts, a fitness center, a football practice field, a swimming pool, softball, baseball, and soccer fields, beach volleyball courts, football practice field, and a lake for water sports.

Disabled Students: 72% of the campus is accessible. Wheelchair ramps, special parking, specially equipped rest rooms, special class scheduling, lowered drinking fountains, and lowered telephones are available.

Services: Counseling and information services are available, as is tutoring in most subjects. There is remedial math, reading, and writing.

Campus Safety and Security: Measures include security escort services, informal discussions, pamphlets/posters/films, lighted pathways/sidewalks, and a security patrol nights and all weekend.

Programs of Study: Webber confers B.A. and B.S. degrees. Associate and master's degrees are also awarded. Bachelor's degrees are awarded in BUSINESS (accounting, banking and finance, business administration and management, hotel/motel and restaurant management, marketing/retailing/merchandising, and sports management), SOCIAL SCIENCE (prelaw). Business administration is the strongest academically and has the largest enrollment.

Required: To graduate, all students must complete 120 credit hours, including courses in their major, a 40-credit general curriculum, and a 30-credit business core. A GPA of 2.0 or better must be maintained. Students must pass the college's required English courses and meet its writing requirements. All students must take at least 3 computer courses.

Special: Cross-registration with other schools may be arranged. Internships are required for hospitality management and sport management majors. Study abroad is available in 9 countries. There is 1 national honor society and 1 departmental honors program.

Faculty/Classroom: 67% of faculty are male; 33%, female. All teach undergraduates and 15% both teach and do research. The average class size in an introductory lecture is 25; in a laboratory, 10; and in a regular course, 21.

Requirements: The SAT or ACT is required. Applicants should be graduates of accredited secondary schools and have completed 3 years each of English, math, and science and 2 years of social studies. An essay is also required. The GED is accepted. A GPA of 2.0 is required. AP and CLEP credits are accepted. Important factors in the admissions decision are personality/intangible qualities, recommendations by school officials, and leadership record.

Procedure: Freshmen are admitted to all sessions. Entrance exams should be taken during the senior year. There are early decision, early admissions, and deferred admissions plans. There is a rolling admissions plan. Applications should be filed by August 1 for fall entry, December 1 for spring entry, and April 1 for summer entry, along with a $35 fee. Notification is sent on a rolling basis. Applications are accepted on-line.

Transfer: Applicants must have a minimum GPA of 2.0 with 15 credit hours, leave their previous institution in good academic standing, and submit a letter of recommendation and a student essay. Students with fewer than 15 credits must meet freshman requirements. 30 of 120 credits required for the bachelor's degree must be completed at Webber.

Visiting: There are guides for informal visits and visitors may sit in on classes and stay overnight. To schedule a visit, contact the Director of Admissions.

Financial Aid: In a recent year, 97% of all full-time freshmen and 96% of continuing full-time students received some form of financial aid. 61% of full-time freshmen and 60% of continuing full-time students received need-based aid. The average freshman award was $10,742. Need-based scholarships or need-based grants averaged $8377 ($16,000 maximum); need-based self-help aid (loans and jobs) averaged $2480 ($7625 maximum); non-need-based athletic scholarships averaged $4659 ($8000 maximum); and other non-need-based awards and non-need-based scholarships averaged $2041 ($5000 maximum). 46% of undergraduates work part time. Average annual earnings from campus work are $1000. The average financial indebtedness of the 2005 graduate was $11,813. Webber is a member of CSS. The FAFSA is required. Check with the school for curent deadlines.

International Students: The school actively recruits these students. They must score satisfactorily on the TOEFL and also take the SAT or the ACT, scoring satisfactorily.

Computers: Wireless access is available. There are 3 computer labs, 1 of which is open 24 hours. Internet access is available in residence halls. All students may access the system. There are no time limits and no fees. It is strongly recommended that all students have a personal computer.

Graduates: Of the 2004 graduating class, 22% were enrolled in graduate school within 6 months of graduation and 99% were employed.

Admissions Contact: Kathy Wilson, Registrar. A video is available. E-mail: *wilson@webber.edu* Web: *www.webber.edu*

GEORGIA

POPULATION DENSITY
• 50,000 and over

0 20 40 60 80 100
Miles

AGNES SCOTT COLLEGE
B-2

Decatur, GA 30030

(404) 471-6285
(800) 868-8602; Fax: (404) 471-6414

Full-time: 2 men, 877 women	**Faculty:** 81; IIB, av$
Part-time: 8 men, 116 women	**Ph.D.s:** 100%
Graduate: 3 men, 10 women	**Student/Faculty:** 11 to 1
Year: semesters	**Tuition:** $23,570
Application Deadline: March 1	**Room & Board:** $8500
Freshman Class: 1526 applied, 815 accepted, 229 enrolled	
SAT Verbal/Math: 630/600*	**ACT:** 26 **HIGHLY COMPETITIVE**

Agnes Scott College, founded in 1889, is an independent liberal arts college for women and is affiliated with the Presbyterian Church (U.S.A.). The library contains 221,991 volumes, 33,125 microform items, and 18,867 audio/video tapes/CDs/DVDs, and subscribes to 15,049 periodicals including electronic. Computerized library services include the card catalog, interlibrary loans, database searching, and Internet access. Special learning facilities include a learning resource center, art gallery, planetarium, an educational technology center, multimedia classrooms, and centers for writing and speaking. The 100-acre campus is in an urban area 6 miles from downtown Atlanta. Including any residence halls, there are 25 buildings.

Student Life: 51% of undergraduates are from Georgia. Others are from 41 states, 30 foreign countries, and Canada. 71% are from public schools. 54% are white; 19% African American. 37% are Islamic and various others; 31% Protestant; 18% Catholic; 7% claim no religious affiliation. The average age of freshmen is 18; all undergraduates, 20. 16% do not continue beyond their first year; 66% remain to graduate.

Housing: 760 students can be accommodated in college housing, which includes dorms and on-campus apartments. In addition, there are special-interest houses, language wings within residence halls for French and German and CHOICE housing choosing healthy options. In a Community Environment.On-campus housing is guaranteed for all 4 years. 91% of students live on campus; of those, 65% remain on campus on weekends. All students may keep cars.

Activities: There are no sororities. There are 79 groups on campus, including art, cheerleading, choir, chorale, dance, drama, ethnic, gay, honors, international, literary magazine, musical theater, newspaper, orchestra, pep band, political, professional, religious, social, social service,

student government, and yearbook. Popular campus events include Black Cat, holiday parties, and Senior Investiture.

Sports: Facilities include a gym with a regulation basketball court, an 8-lane indoor pool, a soccer field, a tennis facility, a weight room, a track, an aerobics room, and dance studios.

Disabled Students: 90% of the campus is accessible. Wheelchair ramps, elevators, special parking, specially equipped rest rooms, special class scheduling, lowered drinking fountains, lowered telephones, special housing, and lifts are available.

Services: Counseling and information services are available, as is tutoring in some subjects, including classical languages, English, math, physics, biology, psychology, chemistry, and economics. There is a reader service for the blind and centers for writing and speaking.

Campus Safety and Security: Measures include 24-hour foot and vehicle patrol, self-defense education, security escort services, and informal discussions. There are pamphlets/posters/films, emergency telephones, lighted pathways/sidewalks, and reimbursement for emergency taxi service.

Programs of Study: Agnes Scott confers the B.A. degree. Master's degrees are also awarded. Bachelor's degrees are awarded in BIOLOGICAL SCIENCE (biochemistry and biology/biological science), COMMUNICATIONS AND THE ARTS (classical languages, classics, creative writing, dramatic arts, English, fine arts, French, German, music, and Spanish), COMPUTER AND PHYSICAL SCIENCE (astrophysics, chemistry, mathematics, and physics), SOCIAL SCIENCE (anthropology, classical/ancient civilization, economics, history, international relations, philosophy, political science/government, psychology, religion, sociology, and women's studies). Biology, psychology, and history are the largest.

Required: Requirements for graduation include first-year seminar and courses in English composition and reading, foreign language, and phys ed, as well as courses in literature and fine arts, religious or philosophical thought, historical studies or classical civilization, natural science, math, social science, and social and cultural analysis. Students must complete 128 credit hours, including 32 to 52 in the major, with a 2.0 GPA.

Special: There is cross-registration through ARCHE (a 19-member consortium), and more than 300 credit and noncredit internships are available. There is a 3-2 engineering program with the Georgia Institute of Technology, and the college offers dual, student-designed, and interdisciplinary majors. Pass/fail options are also available. Opportunities for study abroad include exchange programs, a Global Awareness program, and Global Connections. Also offered are a Washington semester, an Atlanta semester, the PLEN Public Policy Semester, the Mills College Exchange, a 3-4 architecture degree with Washington University, a 3-2 nursing program with Emory University, and work-study programs. Teacher certification and Language Across the Curriculum programs are offered. B.A. degree requirements may be completed in 3 years. There are 13 national honor societies, including Phi Beta Kappa.

Faculty/Classroom: 40% of faculty are male; 60%, female. All both teach and do research. No introductory courses are taught by graduate students. The average class size in an introductory lecture is 20; in a laboratory, 13; and in a regular course, 15.

Admissions: 53% of the 2005-2006 applicants were accepted. The SAT scores for the 2005-2006 freshman class were: Verbal--4% below 500, 30% between 500 and 599, 43% between 600 and 700, and 22% above 700; Math--7% below 500, 44% between 500 and 599, 43% between 600 and 700, and 7% above 700. The ACT scores were 7% below 21, 16% between 21 and 23, 32% between 24 and 26, 19% between 27 and 28, and 26% above 28. 60% of the current freshmen were in the top fifth of their class; 87% were in the top two fifths. There was 1 National Merit semifinalist. 6 freshmen graduated first in their class.

Requirements: The SAT or ACT is required. In addition, applicants (except early admission) must graduate from an accredited secondary school or have a GED. A total of 16 academic credits is recommended, including 4 years of English, 3 of math, and 2 each of a foreign language, science, and social studies. An essay is required, and an interview is recommended. An audition is required for those seeking a music scholarship. AP credits are accepted. Important factors in the admissions decision are advanced placement or honor courses, recommendations by school officials, and leadership record.

Procedure: Freshmen are admitted fall and spring. Entrance exams should be taken late in the junior year or by January of the senior year. There are early decision, early admissions, and deferred admissions plans. Early decision applications should be filed by November 15; regular applications, by March 1 for fall entry and November 1 for spring entry, along with a $35 fee. Notification of early decision is sent December 15; regular decision, March 1. 13 early decision candidates were accepted for the 2005-2006 class. 13 applicants were on the 2005 waiting list; 2 were admitted. Applications are accepted on-line.

Transfer: 16 transfer students enrolled in 2004-2005. A minimum college GPA of 3.0 is recommended, as is an interview and a letter of recommendation from a professor. 64 of 128 credits required for the bachelor's degree must be completed at Agnes Scott.

Visiting: There are regularly scheduled orientations for prospective students, including classes, tours, interviews, residence hall experiences, and informational sessions. There are guides for informal visits and visitors may sit in on classes and stay overnight. To schedule a visit, contact the Office of Admission at *admission@agnesscott.edu*.

Financial Aid: In 2005-2006, 66% of all full-time freshmen and 62% of continuing full-time students received some form of financial aid. 66% of full-time freshmen and 62% of continuing full-time students received need-based aid. The average freshman award was $23,295. The average financial indebtedness of the 2005 graduate was $22,018. Agnes Scott is a member of CSS. The FAFSA, the college's own financial statement, and the previous year's tax return are required. The priority date for freshman financial aid applications for fall entry is February 15. The deadline for filing freshman financial aid applications for fall entry is May 1.

International Students: There are 66 international students enrolled. The school actively recruits these students. They must score satisfactorily on the TOEFL and also take the SAT or the ACT.

Computers: All students may access the system. There are no time limits and no fees.

Graduates: From July 1, 2004 to June 30, 2005, 184 bachelor's degrees were awarded. The most popular majors were psychology (16%), international relations (10%), and economics/business (9%). In an average class, 1% graduate in 3 years or less, 60% graduate in 4 years or less, 63% graduate in 5 years or less, and 66% graduate in 6 years or less. 27 companies recruited on campus in 2004-2005. Of the 2004 graduating class, 27% were enrolled in graduate school within 6 months of graduation and 72% were employed.

Admissions Contact: Stephanie Balmer, Associate VP for Enrollment/ Dean of Admission. A video is available.
E-mail: *admission@agnesscott.edu* Web: *http://www.agnesscott.edu*

ALBANY STATE UNIVERSITY — B-4
Albany, GA 31705-2796

(229) 430-7862
(800) 822-RAMS; Fax: (229) 430-3936

Full-time: 855 men, 1610 women	**Faculty:** 128
Part-time: 150 men, 410 women	**Ph.D.s:** 52%
Graduate: 115 men, 330 women	**Student/Faculty:** 19 to 1
Year: semesters, summer session	**Tuition:** $2400 ($8030)
Application Deadline: see profile	**Room & Board:** $3370
Freshman Class: 2663 applied, 1310 accepted, 417 enrolled	
SAT or ACT: required	**COMPETITIVE+**

Albany State University, founded in 1903, is a state-supported institution within the University System of Georgia, offering programs in liberal arts, business, health fields, and teacher education. There are 4 undergraduate schools and 1 graduate school. Figures in the above capsule and this profile are approximate. In addition to regional accreditation, Albany State has baccalaureate program accreditation with ACBSP, NCATE, and NLN. The library contains 351,467 volumes, 743,621 microform items, and 3431 audio/video tapes/CDs/DVDs, and subscribes to 169,097 periodicals including electronic. Computerized library services include the card catalog, interlibrary loans, and database searching. Special learning facilities include a radio station. The 144-acre campus is in an urban area 175 miles south of Atlanta. Including any residence halls, there are 28 buildings.

Student Life: 98% of undergraduates are from Georgia. 91% are African American. The average age of all undergraduates is 24.

Housing: College housiong includes single-sex dorms. On-campus housing is available on a first-come, first-served basis and is available on a lottery system for upperclassmen. Alcohol is not permitted. All students may keep cars.

Activities: There are 3 national fraternities and 3 national sororities. There are many groups and organizations on campus, including art, band, cheerleading, choir, chorale, computers, dance, debate, drama, drill team, honors, jazz band, marching band, musical theater, pep band, political, professional, religious, social, social service, student government, and yearbook. Popular campus events include Honors Day and Founders Day.

Sports: There are 5 intercollegiate sports for men and 6 for women, and 2 intramural sports for men and 1 for women. Facilities include tennis courts, baseball and softball fields, an Olympic-size pool, a recreation room, and an all-weather track.

Disabled Students: 90% of the campus is accessible. Wheelchair ramps, elevators, special parking, specially equipped rest rooms, lowered drinking fountains, and lowered telephones are available.

Services: There is remedial math, reading, and writing.

Campus Safety and Security: Measures include 24-hour foot and vehicle patrol, security escort services, pamphlets/posters/films, and emergency telephones. There are lighted pathways/sidewalks.

Programs of Study: Associate and master's degrees are also awarded. Bachelor's degrees are awarded in BIOLOGICAL SCIENCE (biology/ biological science), BUSINESS (accounting, marketing/retailing/ merchandising, and office supervision and management), COMMUNICATIONS AND THE ARTS (art, dramatic arts, English, fine arts, French, music, Spanish, and speech/debate/rhetoric), COMPUTER AND PHYSICAL SCIENCE (chemistry, computer science, information sciences and systems, and mathematics), EDUCATION (early childhood, health, middle school, music, physical, science, and special), HEALTH PROFESSIONS (allied health and nursing), SOCIAL SCIENCE (criminal justice, forensic studies, history, political science/government, psychology, social work, and sociology).

Required: To graduate, all students must complete 120 semester hours, including 30 in the major. The core curriculum includes 12 hours of social science, 10 to 11 of science/math/technology, 9 of essential composition and math skills, 6 of humanities/fine arts, 5 of leadership and global awareness, and 3 of phys ed. Most majors require a minimum GPA of 2.25. Students must take a Regents exam to assess English language skills competency, pass a comprehensive exam in their major, and/or score satisfactorily on the aptitude section of the GRE.

Special: The university offers co-op programs in all majors, 2+2 programs with Darton College, dual majors in social sciences, and 3-2 engineering degrees with the Georgia Institute of Technology. Several work-study programs and a gerontology training program are available. Albany State participates in the Georgian Intern Programs. All language majors are eligible to study abroad. There are 5 national honor societies, a freshman honors program, and 4 departmental honors programs.

Faculty/Classroom: 56% of faculty are male; 44%, female.

Requirements: The SAT or ACT is required. The student must have a satisfactory score on the SAT, or English score of 17 and a math score of 16 on the ACT. Applicants must be graduates of an accredited secondary school and have completed 4 years each of English and math, 3 each of science and social sciences, and 2 of a foreign language. A GED is accepted; however, GED students must take and pass SAT: Subject tests in areas where college-preparatory courses are deficient. A GPA of 2.0 is required. AP and CLEP credits are accepted.

Procedure: Freshmen are admitted to all sessions. Entrance exams should be taken by December of the senior year. There is an early admissions plan. Check with the school for current application deadlines. The fall 2005 application fee was $20.

Transfer: Students must provide official transcripts of all previous college work. Students with fewer than 30 transferable semester hours must meet freshman requirements. 30 of 120 credits required for the bachelor's degree must be completed at Albany State.

Visiting: There are regularly scheduled orientations for prospective students, consisting of summer and fall orientations and planned campus visitations. There are guides for informal visits and visitors may sit in on classes. To schedule a visit, contact the Office of Student Affairs at (229) 430-4742.

Financial Aid: The FAFSA is required. Check with the school for current application deadlines.

International Students: They must score satisfactorily on the written TOEFL and also take the SAT or the ACT.

Computers: All students may access the system. There are no time limits and no fees.

Admissions Contact: Fred Suttles, Assistant Director of Recruitment. A video is available. E-mail: *fsuttles@asurams.edu* Web: *www.asurams.edu*

AMERICAN COLLEGE
(See American InterContinental University)

AMERICAN INTERCONTINENTAL UNIVERSITY — B-2
Atlanta, GA 30326

(404) 965-5721
(800) 999-4248; Fax: (404) 965-5701

Full-time: 285 men, 715 women	**Faculty:** 37
Part-time: none	**Ph.D.s:** 99%
Graduate: none	**Student/Faculty:** 15 to 1
Year: quarters, summer session	**Tuition:** $12,100
Application Deadline: open	**Room & Board:** n/av
Freshman Class: n/av	
SAT or ACT: n/av	**NONCOMPETITIVE**

American InterContinental University, is a private institution founded in 1977. AIU offers undergraduate programs in interior design, visual communication, fashion design, fashion marketing, business, video production, and information technology. Figures in above capsule and in this profile are approximate. In addition to regional accreditation, AIU has baccalaureate program accreditation with FIDER. The library contains 23,000 volumes, 17 microform items, and 600 audio/video tapes/CDs/ DVDs, and subscribes to 300 periodicals including electronic. Computerized library services include the card catalog, interlibrary loans, and database searching. Special learning facilities include a learning resource center and art gallery. The 1-acre campus is in an urban area in north Atlanta. Including any residence halls, there is 1 building.

Student Life: 62% of undergraduates are from out of state, mostly the South. Students are from 40 states, 54 foreign countries, and Canada. 45% are white; 25% African American; 25% foreign nationals. The average age of freshmen is 19; all undergraduates, 24.

Housing: 200 students can be accommodated in college housing, which includes single-sex off-campus apartments. On-campus housing is available on a first-come, first-served basis. Alcohol is not permitted. All students may keep cars.

Activities: There are no fraternities or sororities. There are 6 groups on campus, including newspaper, professional, social, and student government. Popular campus events include International Day, Career Days, and Fashion Association Bazaar.

Sports: There is no sports program at AIU.

Disabled Students: Wheelchair ramps, elevators, special parking, specially equipped rest rooms, special class scheduling, and lowered telephones are available.

Services: There is remedial math, reading, and writing.

Campus Safety and Security: Measures include 24-hour foot and vehicle patrol, security escort services, informal discussions, and pamphlets/posters/films. There are emergency telephones and lighted pathways/sidewalks.

Programs of Study: AIU confers B.B.A. and B.F.A. degrees. Associate degrees are also awarded. Bachelor's degrees are awarded in BUSINESS (business administration and management and fashion merchandising), COMMUNICATIONS AND THE ARTS (video), COMPUTER AND PHYSICAL SCIENCE (information sciences and systems), ENGINEERING AND ENVIRONMENTAL DESIGN (commercial art and interior design), SOCIAL SCIENCE (fashion design and technology). Interior design and visual communication are the strongest academically and are the largest.

Required: In addition to specific requirements for individual programs of study, all students must complete 25 credit hours each in humanities and social sciences and 5 credit hours in math. Students may substitute 10 hours of a foreign language for 10 hours of social science. 190 quarter credit hours are required to graduate, with 140 in the major and a minimum GPA of 2.0.

Special: Students may earn up to 20 credit hours in internships. Study abroad in London and Dubai is offered. All majors offer accelerated degree opportunities. A dual major in fashion marketing and design is available. There is a freshman honors program.

Faculty/Classroom: 39% of faculty are male; 61%, female. All teach undergraduates. The average class size in an introductory lecture is 25; in a laboratory, 16; and in a regular course, 18.

Requirements: Applicants should be graduates of a secondary school and should submit 2 personal references. The GED is accepted. A GPA of 2.0 is required. AP and CLEP credits are accepted. Important factors in the admissions decision are personality/intangible qualities, leadership record, and evidence of special talent.

Procedure: Freshmen are admitted to all sessions. There is an early admissions plan. Application deadlines are open.

Transfer: Transfer students must have a minimum 2.0. GPA. 2 personal references must be submitted. 60 of 190 credits required for the bachelor's degree must be completed at AIU.

Visiting: There are regularly scheduled orientations for prospective students. There are guides for informal visits and visitors may sit in on classes. To schedule a visit, contact Suzanne McBride in Admissions.

Financial Aid: AIU is a member of CSS. The CSS/Profile or FAFSA and the college's own financial statement are required. Check with the school for current applicatiom deadlines.

International Students: The school actively recruits these students. They must score satisfacorily on the written TOEFL and also take the college's own test.

Computers: All students may access the system. There are no time limits and no fees.

Admissions Contact: Marita Carey, Director of Admissions.
E-mail: *mcarey@aiuniv.edu*

ARMSTRONG ATLANTIC STATE UNIVERSITY   E-4
Savannah, GA 31419-1997

	(912) 927-5277
	(800) 633-2349; Fax: (912) 921-5462
Full-time: 1243 men, 2434 women	**Faculty:** 224
Part-time: 637 men, 1601 women	**Ph.D.s:** 59%
Graduate: 187 men, 608 women	**Student/Faculty:** 16 to 1
Year: semesters, summer session	**Tuition:** $2894 ($10,210)
Application Deadline: July 1	**Room & Board:** $4500
Freshman Class: 799 accepted, 799 enrolled	
SAT Verbal/Math: 500/490*	**ACT:** 19 **COMPETITIVE**

Armstrong Atlantic State University, founded in 1935, is a public institution within the University System of Georgia, offering programs in the arts and sciences, education, computing, and the health professions. There are 4 undergraduate and 4 graduate schools. In addition to regional accreditation, AASU has baccalaureate program accreditation with ABET, ACS, ADA, CAHEA, CAPTE, JRCERT, NAACLS, NASM, NCATE, and NLN. The library contains 232,791 volumes, 698,512 microform items, and 11,215 audio/video tapes/CDs/DVDs, and subscribes to 1145 periodicals including electronic. Computerized library services include the card catalog, interlibrary loans, database searching, and Internet access. Special learning facilities include a learning resource center and art gallery. The 268-acre campus is in an urban area. Including any residence halls, there are 30 buildings.

Student Life: 89% of undergraduates are from Georgia. Others are from 46 states, 68 foreign countries, and Canada. 66% are white; 21% African American. The average age of freshmen is 20; all undergraduates, 26. 35% do not continue beyond their first year; 19% remain to graduate.

Housing: 600 students can be accommodated in college housing, which includes single-sex on-campus apartments. On-campus housing is available on a first-come, first-served basis. 90% of students commute. Alcohol is not permitted. All students may keep cars.

Activities: There is 1 local fraternity and 3 national fraternities and 1 local sorority and 4 national sororities. There are 65 groups on campus, including band, cheerleading, choir, chorus, computers, dance, debate, drama, ethnic, gay, honors, international, jazz band, literary magazine, musical theater, newspaper, orchestra, pep band, political, professional, religious, social, social service, and student government. Popular campus events include AASU Celebrates and International Culture Day.

Sports: There are 4 intercollegiate sports for men and 4 for women. Facilities include an indoor pool, a gym, a weight room, an indoor running track, tennis courts, and playing fields.

Disabled Students: 80% of the campus is accessible. Wheelchair ramps, elevators, special parking, specially equipped rest rooms, special class scheduling, lowered drinking fountains, and special housing are available.

Services: Counseling and information services are available, as is tutoring in most subjects. There is a reader service for the blind, and remedial math, reading, and writing.

Campus Safety and Security: Measures include 24-hour foot and vehicle patrol, self-defense education, security escort services, and pamphlets/posters/films. There are emergency telephones and lighted pathways/sidewalks.

Programs of Study: AASU confers B.A., B.S., B.F.A., B.G.S., B.Health Science, B.I.T., B.Mus.Ed., B.S.D.H., B.S.Ed., B.S.M.T., B.S.N. degrees. Associate and master's degrees are also awarded. Bachelor's degrees are awarded in BIOLOGICAL SCIENCE (biology/biological science), COMMUNICATIONS AND THE ARTS (art, dramatic arts, English, music, Spanish, and visual and performing arts), COMPUTER AND PHYSICAL SCIENCE (applied physics, chemistry, computer science, information sciences and systems, and mathematics), EDUCATION (art, business, elementary, middle school, music, physical, secondary, social science, and special), HEALTH PROFESSIONS (dental hygiene, health science, medical technology, nursing, physical therapy, radiological science, respiratory therapy, and speech pathology/audiology), SOCIAL SCIENCE (criminal justice, economics, history, liberal arts/general studies, political science/government, and psychology). Nursing and education are the largest.

Required: The core curriculum consists of 60 hours in humanities, math, natural sciences, and social sciences, and 3 in phys ed. A minimum GPA of 2.0 overall and a grade of C or better in each major course is required. Each student must complete 123 hours, with 29 hours in the major, and must take a comprehensive exam.

Special: AASU offers co-op programs in engineering, study abroad in 26 countries, many dual-degree programs, including a 3-2 degree in forestry and environmental science with Duke University, and 3-2 engineering programs with several colleges, including Georgia Tech. A general studies degree, cross-registration with Savannah State University and Georgia Southern University, on-campus work-study, and credit for military experience are also offered. There are 8 national honor societies, a freshman honors program, and 10 departmental honors programs.

Faculty/Classroom: 47% of faculty are male; 53%, female. 90% both teach and do research. No introductory courses are taught by graduate students. The average class size in an introductory lecture is 23; in a laboratory, 14; and in a regular course, 16.

Admissions: The SAT scores for the 2005-2006 freshman class were: Verbal--47% below 500, 41% between 500 and 599, 11% between 600 and 700, and 1% above 700; Math--54% below 500, 38% between 500 and 599, 8% between 600 and 700, and 1% above 700. The ACT scores were 64% below 21, 23% between 21 and 23, 10% between 24 and 26, 2% between 27 and 28, and 1% above 28.

Requirements: The SAT is required. Applicants should graduate from an accredited secondary school. A GED may be accepted. College preparatory work should include 4 units of English, 3 each of math, science, and social studies, and 2 of foreign language. Art students must submit a portfolio. A GPA of 2.0 is required. AP and CLEP credits are accepted.

Procedure: Freshmen are admitted to all sessions. Applications should be filed by July 1 for fall entry, November 1 for spring entry, and May 1 for summer entry, along with a $20 fee. Notification is sent on a rolling basis. Applications are accepted on-line.

Transfer: 549 transfer students enrolled in 2004-2005. Transfer applicants must submit all transcripts and must be in good standing at the last college attended. 30 of 123 credits required for the bachelor's degree must be completed at AASU.

Visiting: There are regularly scheduled orientations for prospective students, including a tour of the campus and departments. There are guides for informal visits. To schedule a visit, contact Melanie Mirande at (912) 921-5424.

Financial Aid: In a recent year, 80% of all full-time freshmen and 85% of continuing full-time students received some form of financial aid. 60% of full-time freshmen and 69% of continuing full-time students received need-based aid. The average freshman award was $4000. Need-based scholarships or need-based grants averaged $4000; need-based self-help aid (loans and jobs) averaged $2000; non-need-based athletic scholarships averaged $4000; and other non-need-based awards and non-need-based scholarships averaged $3500. Average annual earnings from campus work were $4500. The average financial indebtedness of recent 2005 graduate was $8000. The FAFSA and the college's own financial statement are required. The priority date for freshman financial aid applications for fall entry is March 15. The deadline for filing freshman financial aid applications for fall entry is May 1.

International Students: There are 96 international students enrolled. The school actively recruits these students. They must take the TOEFL and also take the SAT or the ACT.

Computers: All students may access the system. There are no time limits and no fees.

Graduates: From July 1, 2004 to June 30, 2005, 657 bachelor's degrees were awarded. The most popular majors were health professions (31%), education (18%), and general studies (14%). 71 companies recruited on campus in a recent year.

Admissions Contact: Jill H. Bell-Marriott, Associate Director of Admissions. Web: www.armstrong.edu

ART INSTITUTE OF ATLANTA   B-2
Atlanta, GA 30328

(770) 394-8300
(800) 275-4242; Fax: (770) 394-0008

Full-time: 1245 men, 1100 women	Faculty: 91
Part-time: 180 men, 185 women	Ph.D.s: 51%
Graduate: none	Student/Faculty: 26 to 1
Year: quarters, summer session	Tuition: $16,570
Application Deadline: open	Room & Board: $6650
Freshman Class: n/av	
SAT or ACT: not required	**SPECIAL**

The Art Institute of Atlanta, founded in 1949, seeks to educate creative professionals. Figures in the above capsule and this profile are approximate. It offers bachelor's degree programs in advertising, media arts and animation, digital media production, game art and design, graphic design, interior design, multimedia and web design, photographic imaging, and culinary arts management and associate degree programs in culinary arts, graphic design, multimedia and web design, photographic imaging, and video production. In addition to regional accreditation, the Art Institute has baccalaureate program accreditation with ACF and FIDER. The library contains 38,780 volumes and 6100 audio/video tapes/CDs/DVDs, and subscribes to 135 periodicals including electronic. Computerized library services include the card catalog, interlibrary loans, database searching, and Internet access. Special learning facilities include a learning resource center, art gallery, and an academic support center. The 7-acre campus is in a suburban area in the Metro-Atlanta community of Dunwoody, approximately 5 miles north of the city limits. Including any residence halls, there are 2 buildings.

Student Life: 73% of undergraduates are from Georgia. Others are from 44 states, 38 foreign countries, and Canada. 49% are white; 34% African American. The average age of freshmen is 20; all undergraduates, 23.

Housing: College-sponsored housing includes coed off-campus apartments. All students commute. All students may keep cars.

Activities: There are no fraternities or sororities. There are 16 groups on campus, including art, dance, gay, international, photography, professional, social service, and student government. Popular campus events include gallery openings, Quarterly Welcome Week, and Quarterly Portfolio Show.

Sports: There is no sports program at the Art Institute. Facilities include basketball courts and fields for touch football, a swimming pool, and a weight room in student housing.

Disabled Students: All of the campus is accessible. Wheelchair ramps, elevators, special parking, specially equipped rest rooms, lowered drinking fountains, lowered telephones, and special housing are available.

Services: Counseling and information services are available, as is tutoring in most subjects. There is remedial math, reading, and writing. Tutoring is available in computer classes.

Campus Safety and Security: Measures include 24-hour foot and vehicle patrol, self-defense education, shuttle buses, and informal discussions. There are pamphlets/posters/films and lighted pathways/sidewalks.

Programs of Study: The Art Institute confers B.A., B.S., and B.F.A. degrees. Associate degrees are also awarded. Bachelor's degrees are awarded in COMMUNICATIONS AND THE ARTS (advertising, animation, graphic design, multimedia, photography, and video), ENGINEERING AND ENVIRONMENTAL DESIGN (computer graphics and interior design), SOCIAL SCIENCE (culinary arts). Graphic design, culinary arts, and video production are the largest.

Required: The Art Institute requires 192 credit hours for the B.F.A., with a minimum GPA of 2.0. Students in design-based majors complete a portfolio of work prior to graduation. The core curriculum includes foundation art, English, art history, humanities, math, and science courses. Foundation art classes are not required for culinary arts students.

Special: Internships in all programs, independent study, work-study programs, and study abroad are possible.

Faculty/Classroom: 53% of faculty are male; 47%, female. All teach undergraduates. The average class size in a regular course is 16.

Requirements: Students must submit SAT, ACT, ASSET, or COMPASS test scores. (COMPASS testing is offered free at the college to any applicant needing it.) Preference is given to applicants with GPAs of 3.0 or above; a minimum GPA of 2.5 for bachelor's degree applicants is highly recommended. An official transcript showing high school GPA is required; the GED is accepted. An essay and an interview are required. AP and CLEP credits are accepted.

Procedure: Freshmen are admitted to all sessions. Entrance exams should be taken prior to the application closing date. There are early admissions, deferred admissions, and rolling admissions plans. Application deadlines are open. Application fee is $50. Applications are accepted on-line.

Transfer: In addition to fulfilling general admission requirements, transfer students must also submit all previous college transcripts. 96 of 192 credits required for the bachelor's degree must be completed at the Art Institute.

Visiting: There are regularly scheduled orientations for prospective students, including individual tours and interviews. There are guides for informal visits and visitors may sit in on classes. To schedule a visit, contact the Office of Admissions.

Financial Aid: 1% of undergraduates work part time. The FAFSA and the state aid form are required. The deadline for filing freshman financial aid applications for fall entry is rolling.

International Students: In a recent year, there were 84 international students enrolled. The school actively recruits these students. They must score satisfactorily on the written TOEFL or on the electronic version. ASSET, COMPASS, or SAT or ACT scores can be submitted instead.

Computers: All students may access the system. There are no time limits and no fees.

Graduates: In a recent year, 127 bachelor's degrees were awarded. The most popular majors were graphic design (22%), culinary arts (17%), and video production interior design (8%). 174 companies recruited on campus in 2004-2005. Of the 2004 graduating class, 90% were employed within 6 months of graduation.

Admissions Contact: Donna Scott, Director of Admissions. A video is available. E-mail: aiaadm@aii.edu Web: www.aia.artinstitutes.edu

ATLANTA COLLEGE OF ART   B-2
Atlanta, GA 30309

(404) 733-5100
(800) 832-2104; Fax: (404) 733-5107

Full-time: 225 men, 200 women	Faculty: 23
Part-time: 10 men, 10 women	Ph.D.s: 87%
Graduate: none	Student/Faculty: 18 to 1
Year: semesters, summer session	Tuition: $13,020
Application Deadline: open	Room & Board: $5610
Freshman Class: n/av	
SAT or ACT: required	**SPECIAL**

The Atlanta College of Art, founded in 1928, is a private professional art college offering programs in the fine arts, design, and electronic arts. Figures given in above capsule and in this profile are approximate. In addition to regional accreditation, ACA has baccalaureate program accreditation with NASAD. The library contains 29,000 volumes and 100 audio/video tapes/CDs/DVDs, and subscribes to 200 periodicals including electronic. Computerized library services include interlibrary loans and database searching. Special learning facilities include a learning resource center, art gallery, printmaking studio, photography darkrooms, computer labs, and experimental sound lab. There is also a sculpture building with a foundry, forge, and woodworking shop. The 6-acre campus is in an urban area in Atlanta. Including any residence halls, there are 3 buildings.

Student Life: 52% of undergraduates are from out of state, mostly the South. Students are from 21 states and 6 foreign countries. 80% are from public schools. 62% are white; 18% African American. 62% are Muslim and Russian Orthodox; 26% Protestant; 9% Catholic. The average age of freshmen is 18; all undergraduates, 21. 30% do not continue beyond their first year; 55% remain to graduate.

Housing: 120 students can be accommodated in college housing, which includes coed on-campus apartments. On-campus housing is guaranteed for the freshman year only and is available on a first-come, first-served basis. Priority is given to out-of-town students. 70% of students commute. Alcohol is not permitted. All students may keep cars.

Activities: There are no fraternities or sororities. There are 15 groups on campus, including art, ethnic, film, gay, international, photography, social, social service, student government, and yearbook. Popular campus events include Welcome Week, student gallery openings, and Thanksgiving Feast.

Sports: There is no sports program at ACA.

Disabled Students: 95% of the campus is accessible. Wheelchair ramps, elevators, special parking, specially equipped rest rooms, lowered drinking fountains, and lowered telephones are available.

Services: Counseling and information services are available, as is tutoring in some subjects, including liberal arts subjects. A writing lab is available.

Campus Safety and Security: Measures include 24-hour foot and vehicle patrol, self-defense education, security escort services, and informal discussions. There are pamphlets/posters/films, emergency telephones, and lighted pathways/sidewalks.

Programs of Study: ACA confers the B.F.A. degree. Bachelor's degrees are awarded in COMMUNICATIONS AND THE ARTS (advertising, design, drawing, fine arts, graphic design, illustration, painting, photography, printmaking, sculpture, and video), ENGINEERING AND ENVIRONMENTAL DESIGN (computer graphics and interior design). Communication design and electronic arts are the largest.

Required: To graduate, the student must complete 42 credits in liberal arts and 78 in studio art for a total of 120 credit hours. Of the 78 studio credits, 33 to 36 must be in the major. The student must also complete 12 credits each in world cultures and art history, 6 in composition, and 3 each in math, science, social science, and humanities. A GPA of 2.0 in the major and overall and a senior exit review are required.

Special: Students may design their own majors, combining 2 or 3 areas of the arts. Special academic programs include cross-registration with the colleges of the University Center of Georgia and other art schools, highly supervised internships, and a dual degree program with Oglethorpe University.

Faculty/Classroom: 65% of faculty are male; 35%, female. All both teach and do research. The average class size in an introductory lecture is 25 and in a regular course, 12.

Requirements: The SAT or ACT is required. In addition, applicants must have graduated from an accredited secondary school and must submit an essay and portfolio; Either 2 letters of recommendation or 1 letter and an on-campus interview are required. The GED is accepted. ACA requires applicants to be in the upper 50% of their class. A GPA of 2.0 is required. AP credits are accepted. Important factors in the admissions decision are evidence of special talent, personality/intangible qualities, and recommendations by alumni.

Procedure: Freshmen are admitted fall and spring. Entrance exams should be taken during the senior year. There are early admissions, deferred admissions, and rolling admissions plans. Application deadlines are open. Application fee is $30. Applications are accepted on-line.

Transfer: Applicants must have a GPA of at least 2.0 and must submit a portfolio and transcripts from previously attended colleges from which credit was earned. Either 2 letters of recommendation or 1 letter and an on-campus interview are required. 39 of 120 credits required for the bachelor's degree must be completed at ACA.

Visiting: There are regularly scheduled orientations for prospective students, including open houses, general information sessions, workshops, and special events for prospective students. There are guides for informal visits and visitors may sit in on classes. To schedule a visit, contact the Admissions Office.

Financial Aid: ACA is a member of CSS. The FAFSA and the college's own financial statement are required. Check with the school for current application deadlines.

International Students: The school actively recruits these students. They must score satisfactorily on the written TOEFL.

Computers: All students may access the system during scheduled hours. There are no time limits and no fees.

Admissions Contact: Carol Lee Conchar, Director of Enrollment Management. E-mail: *acainfo@woodruff-arts.org* Web: *www.aca.edu*

AUGUSTA STATE UNIVERSITY   D-2

Augusta, GA 30904-2200   (706) 737-1632; Fax: (706) 667-4355

Full-time: 1427 men, 2259 women	**Faculty:** 215; IIA, --$
Part-time: 527 men, 1269 women	**Ph.D.s:** 67%
Graduate: 244 men, 607 women	**Student/Faculty:** 17 to 1
Year: semesters, summer session	**Tuition:** $2920 ($10,236)
Application Deadline: July 21	**Room & Board:** n/app
Freshman Class: 2076 applied, 1305 accepted, 988 enrolled	
SAT Verbal/Math: 492/487*	**COMPETITIVE**

Augusta State University, founded in 1925, is a liberal arts commuter institution within the University System of Georgia. There are 3 undergraduate and 3 graduate schools. In addition to regional accreditation, Augusta State University has baccalaureate program accreditation with AACSB, NASM, NCATE, and NLN. The library contains 542,183 volumes, 1,261,469 microform items, and 4276 audio/video tapes/CDs/DVDs, and subscribes to 4430 periodicals including electronic. Computerized library services include the card catalog, interlibrary loans, database searching, Internet access, and laptop Internet portals. Special learning facilities include a learning resource center, art gallery, and radio station. The 316-acre campus is in an urban area 140 miles east of Atlanta on the Georgia-South Carolina border. Including any residence halls, there are 35 buildings.

Student Life: 89% of undergraduates are from Georgia. Others are from 47 states, 60 foreign countries, and Canada. 95% are from public schools. 66% are white; 24% African American. The average age of freshmen is 19; all undergraduates, 24. 35% do not continue beyond their first year; 21% remain to graduate.

Housing: 508 students can be accommodated in college housing, which is off-campus apartments. All students commute to the campus. Alcohol is not permitted. All students may keep cars.

Activities: 1% of men belong to 3 national fraternities; 1% of women belong to 3 national sororities. There are 64 groups on campus, including art, band, cheerleading, choir, chorus, drama, ethnic, gay, honors, international, jazz band, literary magazine, newspaper, orchestra, pep band, photography, political, professional, religious, social, social service, and student government. Popular campus events include Lyceum, Midnight Madness, and SOS.

Sports: There are 5 intercollegiate sports for men and 6 for women, and 2 intramural sports for men and 2 for women. Facilities include a 2000-seat gym, baseball, soccer, and softball fields, a tennis center, and an 18-hole golf course.

Disabled Students: 90% of the campus is accessible. Wheelchair ramps, elevators, special parking, specially equipped rest rooms, special class scheduling, lowered drinking fountains, and lowered telephones are available.

Services: Counseling and information services are available, as is tutoring in most subjects. There is a reader service for the blind, and remedial math, reading, and writing.

Campus Safety and Security: Measures include 24-hour foot and vehicle patrol, security escort services, informal discussions, and pamphlets/posters/films. There are lighted pathways/sidewalks.

Programs of Study: Augusta State University confers B.A., B.S., B.B.A., B.F.A., B.M., B.S.Ed., and B.S.W. degrees. Associate and master's degrees are also awarded. Bachelor's degrees are awarded in BIOLOGICAL SCIENCE (biology/biological science), BUSINESS (accounting, banking and finance, business administration and management, and marketing/retailing/merchandising), COMMUNICATIONS AND THE ARTS (art, communications, English, French, music, Spanish, and studio art), COMPUTER AND PHYSICAL SCIENCE (chemistry, computer science, mathematics, and physics), EDUCATION (early childhood, education of the mentally handicapped, elementary, health, middle school, music, and special), SOCIAL SCIENCE (criminal justice, history, political science/government, psychology, and sociology). Biology, elementary education, and computer science are the largest.

Required: Students must complete 125 hours, with a minimum GPA of 2.0. All students are required to take 6 courses in phys ed; pass the Regents test in reading and composition; and demonstrate, through course completion or exam, a knowledge of U.S. and Georgia history and their constitutions.

Special: A Washington semester and study abroad may be arranged. The school offers co-op programs with area companies, internships, work-study programs, dual majors, nondegree study, and cross-registration with Paine College. There are 5 national honor societies, a freshman honors program, and 7 departmental honors programs.

Faculty/Classroom: 49% of faculty are male; 51%, female. All teach undergraduates. No introductory courses are taught by graduate students. The average class size in an introductory lecture is 30; in a laboratory, 19; and in a regular course, 27.

Admissions: 63% of the 2005-2006 applicants were accepted. The SAT scores for the 2005-2006 freshman class were: Verbal--56% below 500, 32% between 500 and 599, 11% between 600 and 700, and 1% above 700; Math--55% below 500, 34% between 500 and 599, 10% between 600 and 700, and 1% above 700. The ACT scores were 74% below 21, 18% between 21 and 23, 6% between 24 and 26, 1% between 27 and 28, and 1% above 28.

Requirements: The SAT or ACT is required, with satisfactory scores. Applicants must be graduates of an accredited secondary school. The GED is accepted. Secondary school courses must include 4 units each of English and math, 3 each of science and social science, and 2 of a foreign language. A GPA of 2.0 is required. AP and CLEP credits are accepted.

Procedure: Freshmen are admitted fall, spring, and summer. There is a deferred admissions plan and a rolling admissions plan. Applications should be filed by July 21 for fall entry and December 6 for spring entry, along with a $20 fee. Notification is sent on a rolling basis. Applications are accepted on-line.

Transfer: 418 transfer students enrolled in 2004-2005. Applicants must have completed 30 semester or 45 quarter hours. If fewer than 15 semester hours have been completed, students are considered as entering freshmen and are required to submit appropriate paperwork. 30 of 125 credits required for the bachelor's degree must be completed at Augusta State University.

Visiting: There are regularly scheduled orientations for prospective students. There are guides for informal visits and visitors may sit in on classes. To schedule a visit, contact the Admissions Office.

Financial Aid: In 2005-2006, 88% of all full-time freshmen and 87% of continuing full-time students received some form of financial aid. 53% of full-time freshmen and 65% of continuing full-time students received need-based aid. The average freshman award was $7350, with $2225 ($4650 maximum) from need-based scholarships or grants, $2313 ($4625 maximum) from need-based self-help aid (loans and jobs), $1100 ($3392 maximum) from, non-need-based athletic scholarships,and $1712 ($2750 maximum) from other non-need-based awards and non-need-based scholarships. 94% of undergraduates work part time. Average annual earnings from campus work are $3000. The average financial indebtedness of the 2005 graduate was $14,986. The FAFSA is required. The deadline for filing freshman financial aid applications for fall entry is June 1.

International Students: There are 170 international students enrolled. They must take the written TOEFL and also take the SAT or the ACT.

Computers: Wireless access is available. All students may access the system. There are no time limits and no fees.

Graduates: From July 1, 2004 to June 30, 2005, 529 bachelor's degrees were awarded. The most popular majors were psychology (9%), management (9%), and sociology (8%). In an average class, 1% graduate in 3 years or less, 5% graduate in 4 years or less, 14% graduate in 5 years or less, and 21% graduate in 6 years or less. 100 companies recruited on campus in 2004-2005.

Admissions Contact: Katherine Sweeney, Registrar and Director of Admissions. E-mail: *admissions@aug.edu* Web: *www.aug.edu/admissions*

BERRY COLLEGE
A-2

Mount Berry, GA 30149-0159

(706) 236-2215
(800) BERRYGA; Fax: (706) 290-2178

Full-time: 663 men, 1166 women	Faculty: 130; IIA, --$
Part-time: 15 men, 20 women	Ph.D.s: 88%
Graduate: 31 men, 76 women	Student/Faculty: 14 to 1
Year: semesters, summer session	Tuition: $17,570
Application Deadline: February 1	Room & Board: $6772
Freshman Class: n/av	
SAT or ACT: required	VERY COMPETITIVE

Berry College, founded in 1902, is a private nonsectarian college offering programs in fine and liberal arts and preprofessional programs in education and business. There are 4 undergraduate and 2 graduate schools. In addition to regional accreditation, Berry has baccalaureate program accreditation with NASM and NCATE. The library contains 200,263 volumes, 527,790 microform items, and 3140 audio/video tapes/CDs/DVDs, and subscribes to 1792 periodicals including electronic. Computerized library services include the card catalog, interlibrary loans, database searching, Internet access, and laptop Internet portals. Special learning facilities include a learning resource center, art gallery, TV station, and equine center, forestry center, and beef- and dairy-cattle operations. The 28,000-acre campus is in a suburban area 65 miles northwest of Atlanta. Including any residence halls, there are 38 buildings.

Student Life: 85% of undergraduates are from Georgia. Others are from 33 states, 26 foreign countries, and Canada. 90% are white. 75% are Protestant; 15% Catholic. The average age of freshmen is 18; all undergraduates, 20. 22% do not continue beyond their first year; 62% remain to graduate.

Housing: 1395 students can be accommodated in college housing, which includes single-sex and coed dorms and on-campus apartments. In addition, there are special-interest houses and housing for women in math and science (primarily first-year students). On-campus housing is guaranteed for the freshman year only, is available on a first-come, first-served basis, and is available on a lottery system for upperclassmen. 75% of students live on campus; of those, 60% remain on campus on weekends. Alcohol is not permitted. All students may keep cars.

Activities: There are no fraternities or sororities. There are 73 groups on campus, including cheerleading, chess, choir, chorus, computers, dance, drama, ethnic, forensics, honors, international, jazz band, literary magazine, musical theater, newspaper, orchestra, pep band, political, professional, radio and TV, religious, social, social service, student government, and yearbook. Popular campus events include Mountain Day, Conson Wilson Lecture Series, and BCTC Theater Season.

Sports: There are 8 intercollegiate sports for men and 8 for women, and 16 intramural sports for men and 15 for women. Facilities include running and biking trails, 10 tennis courts, intramural fields, 2 gyms, a weight-training room, an indoor swimming pool, 3 sand volleyball courts, and an equestrian center.

Disabled Students: 75% of the campus is accessible. Wheelchair ramps, elevators, special parking, specially equipped rest rooms, lowered drinking fountains, and special housing are available.

Services: Counseling and information services are available, as is tutoring in most subjects. There is a reader service for the blind and remedial writing.

Campus Safety and Security: Measures include 24-hour foot and vehicle patrol, self-defense education, informal discussions, and pamphlets/posters/films. There are emergency telephones, lighted pathways/sidewalks, shuttle buses (class shuttles) a gated campus, mobile security patrols, identification of valuables, limited access to campus, and on-campus sworn police officers.

Programs of Study: Berry confers B.A., B.S., and B.Mu. degrees. Master's degrees are also awarded. Bachelor's degrees are awarded in AGRICULTURE (animal science), BIOLOGICAL SCIENCE (biology/biological science), BUSINESS (accounting, banking and finance, business administration and management, and marketing management), COMMUNICATIONS AND THE ARTS (art, communications, dramatic arts, English, French, German, music, music performance, Spanish, and studio art), COMPUTER AND PHYSICAL SCIENCE (chemistry, computer science, mathematics, and physics), EDUCATION (art, early childhood, mathematics, middle school, music, and physical), ENGINEERING AND ENVIRONMENTAL DESIGN (environmental science), SOCIAL SCIENCE (economics, history, interdisciplinary studies, international studies, philosophy, political science/government, psychology, religion, social science, and sociology). Business, education, and communication are the largest.

Required: General education requirements include 5 courses in the humanities and fine arts, 3 each in behavioral science, math and natural sciences, communication, and health and phys ed, and 2 in electives. A 2.0 GPA and a total of 124 credits, including at least 30 hours in the major, are required for graduation. All students are also required to attend at least 3 approved cultural events per semester and pass a comprehensive exam or other senior assessment in the major.

Special: The college offers internships, a Washington semester, study abroad in 17 countries, work-study programs, student-designed majors, co-op programs, cross-registration with Shorter College, dual majors, credit by exam, and nondegree study. There are 3-2 engineering degrees and dual degree programs in several fields with the Georgia Institute of Technology and Mercer University. There is also a dual degree program in nursing with Emory University. There are 15 national honor societies, a freshman honors program, and 5 departmental honors programs.

Faculty/Classroom: 66% of faculty are male; 34%, female. 99% both teach and do research. No introductory courses are taught by graduate students. The average class size in an introductory lecture is 20 and in a laboratory, 17.

Admissions: The SAT scores for the 2005-2006 freshman class were: Verbal--14% below 500, 43% between 500 and 599, 39% between 600 and 700, and 4% above 700; Math--14% below 500, 50% between 500 and 599, 32% between 600 and 700, and 4% above 700. The ACT scores were 7% below 21, 26% between 21 and 23, 29% between 24 and 26, 20% between 27 and 28, and 18% above 28. 49% of the current freshmen were in the top fifth of their class; 80% were in the top two fifths.

Requirements: The SAT or ACT is required. The ACT Optional Writing test is also required. In addition, applicants should be graduates of an accredited high school or have a GED. 20 academic credits are required, including 4 units each of English and math (to include algebra I, algebra II, and either geometry or trigonometry), 3 each of science and social studies, and 2 of a foreign language. AP credits are accepted. Important factors in the admissions decision are advanced placement or honor courses, leadership record, and recommendations by school officials.

Procedure: Freshmen are admitted to all sessions. Entrance exams should be taken by the fall of the senior year. There is a rolling admissions plan. Applications should be filed by February 1 for fall entry, along with a $50 fee. Notification is sent on a rolling basis. Applications are accepted on-line.

Transfer: 66 transfer students enrolled in 2004-2005. Applicants must submit official transcripts from all colleges previously attended, have a minimum GPA of 2.5, and be in good standing at the last school attended. 62 of 124 credits required for the bachelor's degree must be completed at Berry.

Visiting: There are regularly scheduled orientations for prospective students, including weekdays and Saturday mornings. Students should schedule their campus visit in advance. Several "Discover Berry" days are held during fall and spring. There are guides for informal visits and visitors may sit in on classes and stay overnight. To schedule a visit, contact the Admissions Office.

Financial Aid: In 2005-2006, 99% of all full-time freshmen and 97% of continuing full-time students received some form of financial aid. 57% of full-time freshmen and 5% of continuing full-time students received need-based aid. The average freshman award was $14,592. Need-based scholarships or need-based grants averaged $11,545; need-based self-help aid (loans and jobs) averaged $3563; non-need-based athletic scholarships averaged $7847; and other non-need-based awards and non-need-based scholarships averaged $15,303. 69% of undergraduates work part time. Average annual earnings from campus work are $2592. The average financial indebtedness of the 2005 graduate was $12,592. The FAFSA is required. The priority date for freshman financial aid applications for fall entry is April 1.

International Students: There are 33 international students enrolled. The school actively recruits these students. A satisfactory score is required on the written TOEFL. Applicants must also take the SAT or the ACT if the student is from an English-speaking country.

Computers: Wireless access is available. In the library approximately 600 simultaneous users can be accommodated at the college. All students may access the system. There are no time limits and no fees.

Graduates: From July 1, 2004 to June 30, 2005, 379 bachelor's degrees were awarded. The most popular majors were psychology (13%), business administration and management (12%), and communication, journalism, and related programs (10%). In an average class, 2% graduate in 3 years or less, 51% graduate in 4 years or less, 62% graduate in 5 years or less, and 62% graduate in 6 years or less. 137 companies recruited on campus in 2004-2005. Of the 2004 graduating class, 25% were enrolled in graduate school within 6 months of graduation and 99% were employed.

Admissions Contact: Garreth Johnson, Director of Admissions. A video is available. E-mail: *admissions@berry.edu* Web: *www.berry.edu*

BRENAU UNIVERSITY WOMEN'S COLLEGE B-2

Gainesville, GA 30501

(770) 534-6100
(800) 252-5119; Fax: (770) 538-4306

Full-time: 670 women	**Faculty:** 72
Part-time: 41 women	**Ph.D.s:** 86%
Graduate: 32 women	**Student/Faculty:** 9 to 1
Year: semesters, summer session	**Tuition:** $15,600
Application Deadline: open	**Room & Board:** $8350
Freshman Class: n/av	
SAT or ACT: required	**VERY COMPETITIVE**

Brenau University Women's College, founded in 1878, is a private undergraduate and graduate liberal arts institution for women. Coed programs are offered as part of the university, in an evening and weekend format. There are 4 undergraduate schools. In addition to regional accreditation, Brenau has baccalaureate program accreditation with FIDER, NCATE, and NLN. The library contains 103,740 volumes, 350,328 microform items, and 16,023 audio/video tapes/CDs/DVDs, and subscribes to 2000 periodicals including electronic. Computerized library services include the card catalog, interlibrary loans, database searching, Internet access, and laptop Internet portals. Special learning facilities include a learning resource center, art gallery, natural history museum, radio station, and TV station. The 57-acre campus is in a suburban area 50 miles northeast of Atlanta. Including any residence halls, there are 50 buildings.

Student Life: 90% of undergraduates are from Georgia. Others are from 20 states, 13 foreign countries, and Canada. 71% are white; 18% African American. The average age of freshmen is 18; all undergraduates, 22. 27% do not continue beyond their first year.

Housing: 400 students can be accommodated in college housing, which includes single-sex dorms, on-campus apartments, and sorority houses. In addition, there are special-interest houses. On-campus housing is guaranteed for all 4 years. 50% of students live on campus. Alcohol is not permitted. All students may keep cars.

Activities: 50% of women belong to 9 national sororities. There are no fraternities. There are 55 groups on campus, including art, choir, chorale, chorus, crew, dance, debate, drama, ethnic, honors, international, literary magazine, musical theater, newspaper, opera, photography, political, professional, radio and TV, religious, social, social service, student government, symphony, and yearbook. Popular campus events include Remember All the Traditions Week, May Day, and Spade Hunt.

Sports: Facilities include a tennis center, a recreation field, a gym, and a natatorium.

Disabled Students: 90% of the campus is accessible. Wheelchair ramps, elevators, special parking, specially equipped rest rooms, special class scheduling, lowered drinking fountains, and lowered telephones are available.

Services: There is remedial math, reading, and writing and there are professional degreed tutors for diagnosed learning-disabled students.

Campus Safety and Security: Measures include 24-hour foot and vehicle patrol, self-defense education, security escort services, and informal discussions. There are pamphlets/posters/films and lighted pathways/sidewalks.

Programs of Study: Brenau confers B.A., B.S., B.B.A., B.F.A., B.Mus., and B.S.N. degrees. Master's degrees are also awarded. Bachelor's degrees are awarded in AGRICULTURE (environmental studies), BIOLOGICAL SCIENCE (biology/biological science), BUSINESS (accounting, business administration and management, fashion merchandising, and marketing/retailing/merchandising), COMMUNICATIONS AND THE ARTS (arts administration/management, communications, dance, dramatic arts, English, fine arts, music performance, musical theater, and studio art), EDUCATION (art, dance, early childhood, middle school, music, and special), ENGINEERING AND ENVIRONMENTAL DESIGN (commercial art, graphic and printing production, and interior design), HEALTH PROFESSIONS (nursing and occupational therapy), SOCIAL SCIENCE (history, international studies, liberal arts/general studies, political science/government, and psychology). Nursing, occupational therapy, and performing arts are the largest.

Required: To graduate, all students must complete at least 120 semester hours of work including 48 to 69 hours in the major. Requirements for each degree vary, but students must maintain a 2.0 GPA overall and a 2.5 GPA in course work required by the major. Most majors either require or encourage internships. In addition to specific requirements, students must take phys ed courses and demonstrate computer as well as oral and written communication proficiency. Courses in women's health and leisure studies are also required.

Special: Cross-registration is possible with the Atlanta Regional Consortium for Higher Education. Students may study abroad in 10 foreign countries. Brenau offers B.A.-B.S. degrees, work-study programs, internships, a general studies degree, and student-designed majors. Students may receive credit for life, military, and work experience. There are 8 national honor societies, a freshman honors program, and 4 departmental honors programs.

Faculty/Classroom: 31% of faculty are male; 69%, female. All teach undergraduates. No introductory courses are taught by graduate students.

Requirements: The SAT or ACT is required. In addition, candidates for admission should have completed 4 units of English, 3 of math, 2 of science, and 7 to 9 of electives. A GPA of 2.0 is required. AP and CLEP credits are accepted. Important factors in the admissions decision are advanced placement or honor courses, extracurricular activities record, and evidence of special talent.

Procedure: Freshmen are admitted fall and spring. Entrance exams should be taken in the fall of the senior year or the spring of the junior year. There is a rolling admissions plan. Application deadlines are open. The fall 2005 application fee was $35. Applications are accepted on-line.

Transfer: 109 transfer students enrolled in 2004-2005. A minimum GPA of 2.0 on transfer credits is required, and transfer students must submit high school transcripts and SAT scores if fewer than 30 hours were earned. The last 45 semester hours, including at least 30 in the major, must be taken at Brenau. Students must maintain a minimum GPA of 2.0 and 2.5 in the major. 45 of 120 credits required for the bachelor's degree must be completed at Brenau.

Visiting: There are regularly scheduled orientations for prospective students, consisting of a campus tour, information sessions, and an interview. There are guides for informal visits and visitors may sit in on classes and stay overnight. To schedule a visit, contact the Admissions Office.

Financial Aid: In 2005-2006, 71% of all full-time freshmen and 73% of continuing full-time students received some form of financial aid, including need-based aid. The average freshman award was $12,587. Need-based scholarships or need-based grants averaged $14,175; need-based self-help aid (loans and jobs) averaged $3138; non-need-based athletic scholarships averaged $7969; and other non-need-based awards and non-need-based scholarships averaged $9460. 12% of undergraduates work part time. The FAFSA is required. The priority date for freshman financial aid applications for fall entry is May 1. The deadline for filing freshman financial aid applications for fall entry is July 15.

International Students: There are 14 international students enrolled. The school actively recruits these students. A satisfactory score on the TOEFL or completion of Level 109 at an ELS Language Center is required. The SAT or ACT only if the TOEFL is not taken.

Computers: All students may access the system 24 hours per day. There are no time limits. The fee is $150 per year.

Graduates: From July 1, 2004 to June 30, 2005, 135 bachelor's degrees were awarded. The most popular majors were health professions

(30%), visual and performing arts (21%), and teacher education (13%). 20 companies recruited on campus in 2004-2005.

Admissions Contact: Christina White, Coordinator of Women's College Admissions. A video is available. E-mail: *cwhite@brenau.edu or wcadmissions@brenau.edu* Web: *www.brenau.edu*

BREWTON-PARKER COLLEGE   C-4
Mt. Vernon, GA 30445-0197   (912) 583-3264
(800) 342-1087; Fax: (912) 583-4498

Full-time: 350 men, 585 women	**Faculty:** 60; IIB, --$
Part-time: 50 men, 140 women	**Ph.D.s:** 54%
Graduate: none	**Student/Faculty:** 15 to 1
Year: semesters, summer session	**Tuition:** $9910
Application Deadline: open	**Room & Board:** $4310
Freshman Class: n/av	
SAT : required for some programs	**ACT:** recommended
	LESS COMPETITIVE

Brewton-Parker College, founded in 1904, is a private institution offering instruction in the liberal arts and sciences. It is affiliated with the Georgia Baptist Convention. Check with the school for current application deadlines. The library contains 80,871 volumes, 2985 microform items, and 5575 audio/video tapes/CDs/DVDs, and subscribes to 350 periodicals including electronic. Computerized library services include the card catalog, interlibrary loans, database searching, and Internet access. Special learning facilities include a learning resource center, art gallery, and a living history museum. The 270-acre campus is in a rural area 90 miles west of Savannah. Including any residence halls, there are 46 buildings.

Student Life: 95% of undergraduates are from Georgia. Others are from 13 states, 11 foreign countries, and Canada. 85% are from public schools. 77% are white; 19% African American. 74% are Protestant; 14% claim no religious affiliation. The average age of freshmen is 19; all undergraduates, 23. 38% do not continue beyond their first year; 17% remain to graduate.

Housing: 450 students can be accommodated in college housing, which includes single-sex dorms. On-campus housing is guaranteed for all 4 years. 68% of students commute. Alcohol is not permitted. All students may keep cars.

Activities: 5% of men belong to 2 local fraternities; 7% of women belong to 3 local sororities. There are 26 groups on campus, including band, cheerleading, choir, chorus, dance, drama, ethnic, honors, international, jazz band, musical theater, newspaper, pep band, professional, religious, social, social service, student government, and yearbook. Popular campus events include Road Rally, Fun Flicks, and the Fine Arts Series.

Sports: There are 3 intercollegiate sports for men and 4 for women, and 6 intramural sports for men and 6 for women. Facilities include softball, baseball, and soccer fields, tennis courts, a swimming pool, a gym, a track, an intramural field, an outdoor volleyball court, a physical fitness building, a game room, and a campus lake.

Disabled Students: 80% of the campus is accessible. Wheelchair ramps, special parking, specially equipped rest rooms, lowered telephones, and special housing are available.

Services: Counseling and information services are available, as is tutoring in most subjects. There is remedial math, reading, and writing. Tutoring in Spanish is available.

Campus Safety and Security: Measures include self-defense education, informal discussions, emergency telephones, and lighted pathways/ sidewalks.

Programs of Study: BPC confers B.A., B.S., B.Min., and B.Mu. degrees. Associate degrees are also awarded. Bachelor's degrees are awarded in BIOLOGICAL SCIENCE (biology/biological science), BUSINESS (accounting and business administration and management), COMMUNICATIONS AND THE ARTS (English, music, music performance, and speech/debate/rhetoric), COMPUTER AND PHYSICAL SCIENCE (mathematics), EDUCATION (early childhood, education, health, mathematics, middle school, music, physical, science, secondary, and social studies), SOCIAL SCIENCE (Christian studies, history, liberal arts/general studies, political science/government, psychology, religion, social science, sociology, and theological studies). Education degree programs are the largest.

Required: The required core curriculum consists of humanities, math and natural science, social science, phys ed, and computer science. Students must maintain a minimum 2.0 GPA with half of the major taken at BPC.

Special: The college offers internships, a general studies degree, B.A.-B.S. degrees, and nondegree study.

Faculty/Classroom: All teach undergraduates. The average class size in an introductory lecture is 28; in a laboratory, 15; and in a regular course, 14.

Requirements: The SAT is required for some programs and the ACT is recommended. A GED is accepted. Students should prepare with 4 years of English, 3 of social studies, and 2 each of foreign language, math, and science. A GPA of 2.0 is required. AP credits are accepted.

Important factors in the admissions decision are personality/intangible qualities, leadership record, and advanced placement or honor courses.

Procedure: Freshmen are admitted to all sessions. Entrance exams should be taken during the senior year of high school. There are early decision and early admissions plans. Application deadlines are open. Application fee is $25. 201 early decision candidates were accepted in a recent year. Applications are accepted on-line.

Transfer: 39 transfer students enrolled in a recent year. Applicants must submit transcripts from previously attended institutions, along with high school transcripts, if they have completed fewer than 30 semester hours. 60 credits required for the bachelor's degree must be completed at BPC.

Visiting: There are regularly scheduled orientations for prospective students, consisting of a campus tour and academic and financial aid sessions. There are guides for informal visits and visitors may sit in on classes and stay overnight. To schedule a visit, contact the Office of Admissions.

Financial Aid: In a recent year, the average freshman award was $8900. Need-based scholarships or need-based grants averaged $2600 ($4850 maximum); need-based self-help aid (loans and jobs) averaged $1124 ($8325 maximum); non-need-based athletic scholarships averaged $1860 ($10,000 maximum); and other non-need-based awards and non-need-based scholarships averaged $1650 ($6000 maximum). 18% of undergraduates worked part time. Average annual earnings from campus work were $750. The average financial indebtedness of a recent graduate was $5000. BPC is a member of CSS. The FAFSA and the college's own financial statement are required. Check with the school for current application deadlines.

International Students: In a recent year, there were 30 international students enrolled. They must take the SAT - Verbal with a satisfactory score.

Computers: All students may access the system. There are no time limits and no fees.

Graduates: In a recent year, 208 bachelor's degrees were awarded. The most popular majors were education (36%), business administration (23%), and psycology (9%). In an average class, 9% graduate in 4 years or less, 5% graduate in 5 years or less, and 2% graduate in 6 years or less. 23 companies recruited on campus in a recent year. Of a recent graduating class, 23% were enrolled in graduate school within 6 months of graduation and 51% were employed.

Admissions Contact: Brad Kissell, Dean of Enrollment Management. E-mail: *admissions@bpc.edu* Web: *bpc.edu*

CLARK ATLANTA UNIVERSITY   B-2
Atlanta, GA 30314   (404) 880-8918
(800) 668-3228; Fax: (404) 880-6174

Full-time: 970 men, 2551 women	**Faculty:** 242
Part-time: 47 men, 103 women	**Ph.D.s:** 78%
Graduate: 257 men, 515 women	**Student/Faculty:** 15 to 1
Year: semesters, summer session	**Tuition:** $14,522
Application Deadline: June 1	**Room & Board:** $6438
Freshman Class: n/av	
SAT or ACT: required	**LESS COMPETITIVE**

Clark Atlanta University was formed in 1988 from the consolidation of Clark College (1869) and Atlanta University (1865). A private, predominantly black college affiliated with the United Methodist Church, CAU offers programs in arts and sciences, business administration, education, and social work. There are 5 undergraduate and 4 graduate schools. In addition to regional accreditation, CAU has baccalaureate program accreditation with AACSB, CAHEA, CSWE, and NCATE. The library contains 742,257 volumes, 836,593 microform items, and 10,555 audio/ video tapes/CDs/DVDs, and subscribes to 1410 periodicals including electronic. Computerized library services include interlibrary loans and database searching. Special learning facilities include a learning resource center, art gallery, radio station, TV station, and a distance learning instructional technology education center. The 113-acre campus is in an urban area 3 miles southwest of Atlanta. Including any residence halls, there are 30 buildings.

Student Life: 73% of undergraduates are from out of state, mostly the South. Students are from 33 states and 14 foreign countries. Most are Protestant. The average age of freshmen is 18; all undergraduates, 20. 22% do not continue beyond their first year; 50% remain to graduate.

Housing: 1682 students can be accommodated in college housing, which includes single-sex and coed dorms, on-campus apartments, and off-campus apartments. On-campus housing is available on a first-come, first-served basis and is available on a lottery system for upperclassmen. 63% of students live on campus. Alcohol is not permitted. All students may keep cars.

Activities: 20% of men belong to 4 national fraternities; 30% of women belong to 4 national sororities. There are 77 groups on campus, including art, band, cheerleading, choir, chorale, chorus, computers, dance, drama, drill team, ethnic, film, honors, international, jazz band, marching band, musical theater, newspaper, orchestra, pep band, photography, political, professional, radio and TV, religious, social, social service, student government, and symphony. Popular campus events include Commencement and Alumni Weekend, Founders Week, and convocations.

Sports: There are 7 intercollegiate sports for men and 7 for women, and 6 intramural sports for men and 6 for women. Facilities include a gym, a stadium, and a student center.

Disabled Students: 70% of the campus is accessible. Wheelchair ramps, elevators, special parking, and specially equipped rest rooms are available.

Services: Counseling and information services are available, as is tutoring in every subject. There is remedial math, reading, and writing.

Campus Safety and Security: Measures include 24-hour foot and vehicle patrol, security escort services, shuttle buses, and informal discussions. There are pamphlets/posters/films, emergency telephones, and lighted pathways/sidewalks.

Programs of Study: CAU confers B.A., B.S., and B.S.W. degrees. Master's and doctoral degrees are also awarded. Bachelor's degrees are awarded in BIOLOGICAL SCIENCE (biology/biological science), BUSINESS (accounting and business administration and management), COMMUNICATIONS AND THE ARTS (art, communications, English, languages, music, and speech/debate/rhetoric), COMPUTER AND PHYSICAL SCIENCE (chemistry, computer science, mathematics, and physics), EDUCATION (business, early childhood, middle school, and physical), ENGINEERING AND ENVIRONMENTAL DESIGN (engineering), HEALTH PROFESSIONS (allied health), SOCIAL SCIENCE (economics, history, philosophy, political science/government, psychology, religion, social work, and sociology). Business administration, physical and biological sciences, and communications are the strongest academically. Biology, business, and communications are the largest.

Required: To graduate, students must complete a minimum of 122 hours of course work, including a prescribed major sequence, with a minimum 2.0 GPA. Beyond the general education core requirements, at least 60% of courses must represent work at or above the 300 level.

Special: Clark Atlanta offers co-op programs, public and private internships, study abroad in 12 countries, accelerated degree programs in biology, chemistry, physics, computer science, math, religion, and accounting, and a Washington semester. There is cross-registration with Atlanta University Center, Georgia Institute of Technology, Georgia State University, and Paine College. B.A.-B.S. degrees may be obtained in business and management, education, and social and natural sciences. Dual majors in allied health and engineering and a 3-2 engineering degree with 7 universities are also available. There are 10 national honor societies and a freshman honors program.

Faculty/Classroom: 64% of faculty are male; 36%, female. 83% teach undergraduates. The average class size in an introductory lecture is 34; in a laboratory, 12; and in a regular course, 17.

Requirements: The SAT or ACT is required. In addition, applicants must be high school graduates or hold the GED. A letter of recommendation is required. A GPA of 2.5 is required. AP and CLEP credits are accepted. Important factors in the admissions decision are advanced placement or honor courses and recommendations by school officials.

Procedure: Freshmen are admitted fall and spring. Entrance exams should be taken by January. There are early admissions, deferred admissions, and rolling admissions plans. Applications should be filed by June 1 for fall entry and October 1 for spring entry, along with a $35 fee. Notification of early decision is sent January 1; regular decision, on a rolling basis. Applications are accepted on-line.

Transfer: 295 transfer students enrolled in a recent year. Applicants must have a 2.3 GPA, be in good standing at the institution previously attended, and have completed at least 12 semester hours. 30 of 122 credits required for the bachelor's degree must be completed at CAU.

Visiting: There are regularly scheduled orientations for prospective students. There are guides for informal visits and visitors may sit in on classes. To schedule a visit, contact Robin Reid, Admission Counselor at (404) 880-8782 or rreid@cau.edu.

Financial Aid: In 2005-2006, 94% of all full-time freshmen and 95% of continuing full-time students received some form of financial aid. 79% of full-time freshmen and 78% of continuing full-time students received need-based aid. The average freshman award was $15,900. Need-based scholarships or need-based grants averaged $3492 ($4000 maximum); need-based self-help aid (loans and jobs) averaged $2988 ($4000 maximum); non-need-based athletic scholarships averaged $11,353 ($18,391 maximum); and other non-need-based awards and non-need-based scholarships averaged $11,307 ($23,062 maximum). 6% of undergraduates work part time. Average annual earnings from campus work are $3705. The average financial indebtedness of the 2005 graduate was $17,798. The FAFSA is required. The priority date for freshman financial aid applications for fall entry is April 1. The deadline for filing freshman financial aid applications for fall entry is July 15.

International Students: There were 38 international students enrolled in a recent year. The school actively recruits these students. A satisfactory score is required on the written TOEFL.

Computers: Those students with assigned user identification codes may access the system any time. There are no time limits and no fees. It is strongly recommended that all students have a PC.

Graduates: In a recent year, 443 bachelor's degrees were awarded. The most popular majors were business administration (22%), mass media arts (18%), and social work (11%). In an average class, 10% graduate in 3 years or less, 36% graduate in 4 years or less, 81% graduate in 5 years or less, and 92% graduate in 6 years or less. 300 companies recruited on campus in a recent year.

Admissions Contact: Julius Dodds, Director of Admissions.
E-mail: jdodds@cau.edu Web: www.cau.edu

CLAYTON COLLEGE AND STATE UNIVERSITY   B-2

Morrow, GA 30260-0285	(770) 961-5100; Fax: (770) 961-3752
Full-time: 820 men, 1610 women	Faculty: 169
Part-time: 915 men, 1875 women	Ph.D.s: 51%
Graduate: none	Student/Faculty: 14 to 1
Year: semesters, summer session	Tuition: $2445 ($9080)
Application Deadline: see profile	Room & Board: n/app
Freshman Class: n/av	
SAT : required	ACT: required

LESS COMPETITIVE

Clayton College and State University, founded in 1969 as a public junior college, has been a 4-year undergraduate college in the University System of Georgia since 1985. The first baccalaureate degrees were awarded in 1989. There are 5 undergraduate schools. Check with the school for current application deadlines. In addition to regional accreditation, Clayton State has baccalaureate program accreditation with ADA, NCATE, and NLN. The library contains 97,835 volumes, 254,014 microform items, and 5113 audio/video tapes/CDs/DVDs, and subscribes to 750 periodicals including electronic. Computerized library services include the card catalog, interlibrary loans, and database searching. Special learning facilities include a learning resource center and a concert facility. The 160-acre campus is in a suburban area 17 miles south of downtown Atlanta near Hartsfield International Airport. There are 12 buildings.

Student Life: 92% of undergraduates are from Georgia. Others are from 28 states, 42 foreign countries, and Canada. The average age of all undergraduates is 28. 37% do not continue beyond their first year.

Housing: There are no residence halls. All of students commute. Alcohol is not permitted. All students may keep cars.

Activities: There are no fraternities or sororities. There are 20 groups on campus, including art, band, cheerleading, choir, chorale, chorus, computers, drama, ethnic, gay, honors, international, jazz band, musical theater, newspaper, professional, religious, social, social service, and student government. Popular campus events include Southern Crescent Festival and Spring Fling.

Sports: There are 4 intercollegiate sports for men and 4 for women. Facilities include a gym, jogging trails, a circuit training facility, a weight room, soccer fields, and tennis, badminton, volleyball, and basketball courts.

Disabled Students: All of the campus is accessible. Wheelchair ramps, elevators, special parking, specially equipped rest rooms, special class scheduling, lowered drinking fountains, and lowered telephones are available.

Services: Counseling and information services are available, as is tutoring in most subjects. There is remedial math, reading, and writing.

Campus Safety and Security: Measures include 24-hour foot and vehicle patrol, self-defense education, security escort services, and pamphlets/posters/films. There are emergency telephones and lighted pathways/sidewalks.

Programs of Study: Clayton State confers B.A., B.S., B.A.S., B.B.A., B.M., and B.S.N. degrees. Associate degrees are also awarded. Bachelor's degrees are awarded in BUSINESS (accounting, business administration and management, and marketing and distribution), COMMUNICATIONS AND THE ARTS (music, music performance, and music theory and composition), COMPUTER AND PHYSICAL SCIENCE (information sciences and systems), EDUCATION (middle school), ENGINEERING AND ENVIRONMENTAL DESIGN (technological management), HEALTH PROFESSIONS (allied health, dental hygiene, health care administration, and nursing), SOCIAL SCIENCE (history and interdisciplinary studies). Nursing, middle school education, and music performance are the strongest academically. Management is the largest.

Required: Students in the baccalaureate program must complete 120 to 126 semester hours, including a 60-hour core curriculum in English and humanities, math or sciences, and social sciences. A 2.0 minimum GPA is required for graduation.

Special: Co-op programs and internships can be arranged in all majors except middle school education. The B.A.S. career program enables associate degree holders to complete the baccalaureate degree. Cross-registration is offered through the University Center Consortium. Dual majors, B.A.-B.S. degrees, study abroad, student-designed majors, and work-study programs are offered. Distance learning opportunities are possible. There are 2 national honor societies and, a freshman honors program.

Faculty/Classroom: 51% of faculty are male; 49%, female. All teach undergraduates.

Requirements: The SAT or ACT is required. Applicants should be graduates of accredited secondary schools. High school preparation should include 4 courses each in English and math, 3 each in science, history, and social studies, and 2 in a foreign language. Students may also be admitted on the strength of their high school academic records. AP and CLEP credits are accepted.

Procedure: Freshmen are admitted to all sessions. Entrance exams should be taken before registration. There are early admissions, deferred admissions, and rolling admissions plans. Applications should be filed by July 1 for fall entry, December 1 for spring entry, and April 1 for summer entry, along with a $40 fee. Notification is sent on a rolling basis. Applications are accepted on-line.

Transfer: 578 transfer students enrolled in a recent year. Applicants with fewer than 30 semester hours or 45 quarter credits must meet the same criteria as entering freshmen. 30 of 120 credits required for the bachelor's degree must be completed at Clayton State.

Visiting: There are regularly scheduled orientations for prospective students, including tours of the campus and the opportunity to meet faculty and staff and learn about the athletic programs, the notebook computers, and campus life. There are guides for informal visits and visitors may sit in on classes. To schedule a visit, contact the Office of Admissions at (770) 961-3500.

Financial Aid: In a recent year, 32% of all full-time freshmen and 48% of continuing full-time students received some form of financial aid. Clayton State is a member of CSS. The FAFSA and the college's own financial statement are required. Check with the school for current application deadlines.

International Students: In a recent year, there were 328 international students enrolled. The school actively recruits these students. They must score satisfactorily on the written TOEFL or on the electronic version and also take the Georgia State Test for English Proficiency (G-STEP) and the SAT or ACT.

Computers: All students may access the system. All students are required to have personal computers.

Graduates: In a recent year, 399 bachelor's degrees were awarded. The most popular majors were business/marketing (36%), nursing/health (29%), and computer information science (17%). 99 companies recruited on campus in a recent year.

Admissions Contact: Jeff Hammer, Director of Admissions.
E-mail: ccsu-info@mail.clayton.edu Web: www.clayton.edu

COLUMBUS STATE UNIVERSITY   A-3

Columbus, GA 31907-5645 (706) 568-2035
(866) 264-2035; Fax: (706) 568-2462

Full-time: 1643 men, 2771 women	Faculty: 201; IIA, --$
Part-time: 874 men, 1336 women	Ph.D.s: 77%
Graduate: 359 men, 492 women	Student/Faculty: 22 to 1
Year: semesters, summer session	Tuition: $2944 ($10,260)
Application Deadline: May 1	Room & Board: $5720
Freshman Class: 3005 applied, 1921 accepted, 1184 enrolled	
SAT Verbal/Math: 503/493*	ACT: 20 COMPETITIVE

Columbus State University, established in 1958, is a public liberal arts institution within the University System of Georgia. There are 4 undergraduate schools and 1 graduate school. In addition to regional accreditation, Columbus State has baccalaureate program accreditation with APTA, CACREP, NASAD, NASM, NCATE, and NLN. The 2 libraries contain 265,103 volumes, 795,279 microform items, and 9589 audio/video tapes/CDs/DVDs, and subscribe to 1450 periodicals including electronic. Computerized library services include the card catalog, interlibrary loans, database searching, and Internet access. Special learning facilities include a learning resource center, art gallery, and archives. The 132-acre campus is in a suburban area 100 miles south of Atlanta. Including any residence halls, there are 26 buildings.

Student Life: 86% of undergraduates are from Georgia. Others are from 35 states, 39 foreign countries, and Canada. 59% are white; 31% African American. The average age of freshmen is 20; all undergraduates, 25. 28% do not continue beyond their first year; 29% remain to graduate.

Housing: 1200 students can be accommodated in college housing, which includes single-sex on-campus apartments and off-campus apartments. In addition, there are special-interest houses. On-campus housing is guaranteed for all 4 years. 83% of students commute. Alcohol is not permitted. All students may keep cars.

Activities: 1% of men belong to 1 local fraternity and 6 national fraternities; 1% of women belong to 2 local and 5 national sororities. There are 50 groups on campus, including art, band, cheerleading, choir, chorale, chorus, computers, dance, drama, drill team, ethnic, film, honors, international, jazz band, literary magazine, musical theater, orchestra, pep band, photography, political, professional, religious, social, social service, student government, symphony, and yearbook. Popular campus events include Black History Month, Halloween, and Greek Week.

Sports: There are 5 intercollegiate sports for men and 5 for women, and 16 intramural sports for men and 16 for women. Facilities include a physical fitness room, tennis courts, baseball, soccer, softball, and intramural multipurpose fields, a walking trail, and volleyball and basketball courts.

Disabled Students: All of the campus is accessible. Wheelchair ramps, elevators, special parking, specially equipped rest rooms, special class scheduling, lowered drinking fountains, lowered telephones, and specially equipped electronic doors are available.

Services: Counseling and information services are available, as is tutoring in most subjects. There is a reader service for the blind, and remedial math, reading, and writing. Scribe and braille services are also available.

Campus Safety and Security: Measures include 24-hour foot and vehicle patrol, self-defense education, security escort services, and shuttle buses. There are informal discussions, pamphlets/posters/films, emergency telephones, lighted pathways/sidewalks, and shuttles for evening students.

Programs of Study: Columbus State confers B.A., B.S. B.B.A., B.F.A., B.M., B.S.Ed. and B.S.N. degrees. Associate and master's degrees are also awarded. Bachelor's degrees are awarded in BIOLOGICAL SCIENCE (biology/biological science), BUSINESS (accounting, banking and finance, business administration and management, management information systems, and marketing/retailing/merchandising), COMMUNICATIONS AND THE ARTS (art, communications, dramatic arts, English, music, music performance, and visual and performing arts), COMPUTER AND PHYSICAL SCIENCE (chemistry, computer science, geology, and mathematics), EDUCATION (art, drama, early childhood, foreign languages, health, middle school, music, secondary, and special), HEALTH PROFESSIONS (exercise science, health science, and nursing), SOCIAL SCIENCE (criminal justice, history, political science/government, psychology, and sociology). Business, biology, and music are the strongest academically. Business, education, and nursing are the largest.

Required: To graduate, all students must maintain a 2.0 GPA and complete a minimum of 123 semester hours, 63 of them in a core curriculum and 60 in the major. 3 semester hours of phys ed are required. All students must pass the Georgia Regents Test for competency in reading and writing, complete English 1101 and 1102 with a C or better, and satisfy the Georgia History and Constitution and U.S. History and Constitution requirement by taking specified courses at a University System of Georgia institution or, for transfers from outside the system, by passing an exemption test. Some majors require a comprehensive exam.

Special: Cooperative programs in computer programming, engineering, nursing, and business, internships, a Washington semester, work-study, and study abroad in 11 countries are possible. A 3-2 engineering degree with the Georgia Institute of Technology and a B.A.-B.S. degree in biology, chemistry, math, or psychology are also available. There are 13 national honor societies and a freshman honors program.

Faculty/Classroom: 51% of faculty are male; 49%, female. 99% teach undergraduates and 90% both teach and do research. Graduate students teach 1% of introductory courses. The average class size in an introductory lecture is 24; in a laboratory, 17; and in a regular course, 20.

Admissions: 64% of the 2005-2006 applicants were accepted. The SAT scores for the 2005-2006 freshman class were: Verbal--46% below 500, 41% between 500 and 599, 11% between 600 and 700, and 2% above 700; Math--52% below 500, 36% between 500 and 599, 10% between 600 and 700, and 2% above 700.

Requirements: A satisfactory score is required on the SAT or ACT; the SAT is preferred. Applicants must be graduates of accredited secondary schools. 16 academic credits are required, including 4 each in English and math, 3 each in science and social studies, and 2 in a foreign language. AP and CLEP credits are accepted.

Procedure: Freshmen are admitted to all sessions. Entrance exams should be taken in the fall of the senior year. There is an early admissions plan. There is a rolling admissions plan. Applications should be filed by May 1 for fall entry, November 1 for spring entry, and March 1 for summer entry, along with a $25 fee. Notification is sent on a rolling basis. Applications are accepted on-line.

Transfer: 512 transfer students enrolled in fall 2005. Transfer students with fewer than 30 hours of credit must meet the same requirements as entering freshmen. Transfer students must have a 2.0 GPA and be eligible to return to the institution last attended. 36 of 123 credits required for the bachelor's degree must be completed at Columbus State.

Visiting: There are regularly scheduled orientations for prospective students. During the fall and spring semesters, there are college visitation programs. Prospective students may arrange a tour on any weekday. There are guides for informal visits and visitors may sit in on classes. To schedule a visit, contact the Admissions Office at www.admission@colstate.edu.

Financial Aid: In 2005-2006, 87% of all full-time freshmen and 72% of continuing full-time students received some form of financial aid. 36% of full-time freshmen and 37% of continuing full-time students received need-based aid. The average freshman award was $4015. Need-based scholarships or need-based grants averaged $3324; need-based self-help aid (loans and jobs) averaged $3872; and non-need-based athletic scholarships averaged $2172. The average financial indebtedness of the 2005 graduate was $20,125. The FAFSA is required. The priority date for freshman financial aid applications for fall entry is May 1.

International Students: There are 86 international students enrolled. The school actively recruits these students. They must achieve a satisfactory score on the TOEFL as well as on the SAT or ACT.

Computers: Wireless access is available. All students may access the system. There are no time limits. The fee is $76.

Graduates: From July 1, 2004 to June 30, 2005, 654 bachelor's degrees were awarded. The most popular majors were business/ marketing (22%), education (15%), and computer and information sciences (11%). In an average class, 27% graduate in 6 years or less. 150 companies recruited on campus in 2004-2005.

Admissions Contact: Susan Lovell, Director of Admissions. A video is available. E-mail: *lovell_susan@colstate.edu* Web: *www.colstate.edu*

COVENANT COLLEGE   D-4
Lookout Mountain, GA 30750   (706) 820-2398
(888) 451-2683; Fax: (706) 820-0893

Full-time: 337 men, 528 women	Faculty: 58; IIB, -$
Part-time: 20 men, 17 women	Ph.D.s: 82%
Graduate: none	Student/Faculty: 15 to 1
Year: semesters, summer session	Tuition: $20,580
Application Deadline: May 1	Room & Board: $5880
Freshman Class: 667 applied, 438 accepted, 262 enrolled	
SAT or ACT: required	VERY COMPETITIVE+

Covenant College, founded in 1955, is a private liberal arts college affiliated with the Presbyterian Church in America (P.C.A.). The library contains 100,000 volumes, 5000 microform items, and 4500 audio/video tapes/CDs/DVDs, and subscribes to 400 periodicals including electronic. Computerized library services include interlibrary loans, database searching, and Internet access. Special learning facilities include a radio station. The 300-acre campus is in a suburban area 12 miles southwest of Chattanooga, Tennessee. Including any residence halls, there are 10 buildings.

Student Life: 75% of undergraduates are from out of state, mostly the South. Students are from 47 states, 29 foreign countries, and Canada. 93% are white. Most are Protestant. The average age of freshmen is 18; all undergraduates, 20. 22% do not continue beyond their first year; 67% remain to graduate.

Housing: 774 students can be accommodated in college housing, which includes single-sex dorms and on-campus apartments. On-campus housing is guaranteed for all 4 years. 86% of students live on campus; of those, 85% remain on campus on weekends. Alcohol is not permitted. All students may keep cars.

Activities: There are no fraternities or sororities. There are 48 groups on campus, including cheerleading, choir, chorale, dance, drama, honors, international, literary magazine, newspaper, photography, professional, religious, social, social service, student government, symphony, and yearbook. Popular campus events include Madrigal Dinner, Spring Banquet, and Kilter Night.

Sports: There are 3 intercollegiate sports for men and 4 for women, and 6 intramural sports for men and 4 for women. Facilities include a gym, a weight room, a swimming pool, tennis courts, 3 soccer fields, running trails, an aerobics room, and a wellness room equipped with a variety of fitness machines.

Disabled Students: All of the campus is accessible. Wheelchair ramps, elevators, special parking, specially equipped rest rooms, lowered drinking fountains, lowered telephones, and special doors for wheelchair access are available.

Services: Counseling and information services are available, as is tutoring in some subjects, including math and writing.

Campus Safety and Security: Measures include lighted pathways/sidewalks and a watchman who maintains campus security at night.

Programs of Study: Covenant confers B.A., B.S., and B.Mus. degrees. Associate and master's degrees are also awarded. Bachelor's degrees are awarded in BIOLOGICAL SCIENCE (biology/biological science), BUSINESS (business administration and management), COMMUNICATIONS AND THE ARTS (applied music, art, English, and music), COMPUTER AND PHYSICAL SCIENCE (chemistry, information sciences and systems, mathematics, natural sciences, and physics), EDUCATION (elementary and middle school), SOCIAL SCIENCE (biblical studies, history, interdisciplinary studies, missions, philosophy, psychology, religion, and sociology). Business, history, and education are the largest.

Required: All students must complete 55 to 63 hours of core and distribution requirements, including course work in Bible studies, interdisciplinary studies, English composition, cross-cultural experience, speech, language, phys ed, computers, lab science, social science, and history. A minimum total of 126 credits and a GPA of 2.0 are required for graduation. All students must also complete an oral interview and a senior integration project, in which they explore a problem in their major field in light of Christian philosophy.

Special: Cross-registration is possible with the Council for Christian Colleges and Universities (CCCU) as are internships in business, psychology, and biology. Students may study abroad in 9 countries or spend a semester in Washington. There is a 3-2 engineering program with Georgia Tech and other universities and technical institutes, and a 13-month degree-completion program for students with 2 years of previous college experience. Juniors and seniors may take classes on a pass/fail basis. There are 2 national honor societies, a freshman honors program, and 2 departmental honors programs.

Faculty/Classroom: 87% of faculty are male; 13%, female. All teach undergraduates. The average class size in an introductory lecture is 19; in a laboratory, 16; and in a regular course, 18.

Admissions: 65% of the 2005-2006 applicants were accepted. 9 freshmen graduated first in their class in a recent year.

Requirements: A minimum composite score on the SAT or ACT is required. Applicants must graduate from an accredited high school or have a GED. Applicants should have 16 total units, including 4 years of high school English, 3 years of math, and 2 years each of foreign language, history, science, and social studies. An essay and an interview are required. A GPA of 2.5 is required. AP and CLEP credits are accepted. Important factors in the admissions decision are advanced placement or honor courses, extracurricular activities record, and leadership record.

Procedure: Freshmen are admitted fall and spring. Entrance exams should be taken either by January of the senior year. There is a rolling admissions plan. Applications should be filed by May 1 for fall entry and November 1 for spring entry, along with a $25 fee. Notification is sent on a rolling basis.

Transfer: 58 transfer students enrolled in 2004-2005. Transfer applicants must take either the SAT I, with a minimum composite score, or the ACT, with a minimum composite of 21. Courses with a grade of C or better that apply toward the selected Covenant program will receive transfer credit. 30 of 126 credits required for the bachelor's degree must be completed at Covenant.

Visiting: There are regularly scheduled orientations for prospective students, consisting of a campus preview weekend during which high school students stay in dorms and attend classes, seminars, and other college activities. There are guides for informal visits and visitors may sit in on classes and stay overnight. To schedule a visit, contact Beth Nedelisky, Admissions Assistant Director at (706) 419-1656.

Financial Aid: In a recent year, 87% of all full-time freshmen and 92% of continuing full-time students received some form of financial aid. 71% of full-time freshmen and 66% of continuing full-time students received need-based aid. The average freshman award was $11,678. 38% of undergraduates work part time. Average annual earnings from campus work are $1854. The FAFSA and the college's own financial statement are required. The priority date for freshman financial aid applications for fall entry is March 1. The deadline for filing freshman financial aid applications for fall entry is March 31.

International Students: There are 7 international students enrolled. The school actively recruits these students. A satisfactory score on the TOEFL is required. Applicants are encouraged to take the SAT or ACT if it is available in their country.

Computers: All students may access the system 8 A.M. to 12 A.M. Monday through Thursday and Saturday and 8 A.M. to 6 P.M. on Friday. There are no time limits. The fee is $60 per semester.

Graduates: In a recent year, 165 bachelor's degrees were awarded. The most popular majors were English (11%), psychology (9%), and biology, history, and Bible studies (8%). In an average class, 1% graduate in 3 years or less, 49% graduate in 4 years or less, 58% graduate in 5 years or less, and 60% graduate in 6 years or less. 25 companies recruited on campus in a recent year.

Admissions Contact: Bryan Pierce, Director, Student Recruitment. E-mail: *admissions@covenant.edu* Web: *covenant.edu*

DEVRY UNIVERSITY/ALPHARETTA   B-2
Alpharetta, GA 30004-2232   (770) 664-9520
(800) 221-4771; Fax: (770) 664-8824

Full-time: 535 men, 290 women	Faculty: n/av
Part-time: 315 men, 155 women	Ph.D.s: n/av
Graduate: none	Student/Faculty: n/av
Year: semesters, summer session	Tuition: $10,675
Application Deadline: open	Room & Board: n/app
Freshman Class: n/av	
SAT or ACT: not required	LESS COMPETITIVE

DeVry University/Alpharetta, founded in 1997, is a private institution offering hands-on programs in electronics, business administration, computer information systems, telecommunications management, technical management, information technology, and computer engineering technology. The school is 1 of 67 DeVry University locations throughout the United States and Canada. Figures in the above capsule and this profile are approximate. In addition to regional accreditation, DeVry has baccalaureate program accreditation with ABET. The library contains 3517 volumes and 221 audio/video tapes/CDs/DVDs, and subscribes to 75 periodicals including electronic. Computerized library services include the card catalog, interlibrary loans, and database searching. Special learning facilities include a learning resource center and electronics and other labs. The 9-acre campus is in a suburban area. There is one building.

Student Life: 32% are African American; 28% white. The average age of all undergraduates is 27.

Housing: There are no residence halls. All students commute. Alcohol is not permitted. All students may keep cars.

Activities: There are no fraternities or sororities. There are 12 groups on campus, including international, newspaper, professional, programming, social, and Toastmasters. Popular campus events include Fall Festival, Spring Fling, and Thanksgiving Dinner.

Sports: There are 4 intramural sports for men and 4 for women.

Disabled Students: 98% of the campus is accessible. Wheelchair ramps, elevators, special parking, specially equipped rest rooms, lowered drinking fountains, and lowered telephones are available.

Services: Counseling and information services are available, as is tutoring in every subject.

Campus Safety and Security: Measures include security escort services, informal discussions, pamphlets/posters/films, and emergency telephones.There is CCTV and video recording.

Programs of Study: DeVry confers the B.S. degree. Associate and master's degrees are also awarded. Bachelor's degrees are awarded in BIOLOGICAL SCIENCE (bioinformatics), BUSINESS (business administration and management), COMMUNICATIONS AND THE ARTS (telecommunications), COMPUTER AND PHYSICAL SCIENCE (information sciences and systems), ENGINEERING AND ENVIRONMENTAL DESIGN (computer engineering, electrical/electronics engineering technology, and technological management). Telecommunications, computer information systems, and business administration are the largest.

Required: To graduate, students must achieve a cumulative GPA of at least 2.0 and satisfactorily complete all curriculum requirements. Course requirements vary according to program. All first-semester students take courses in business organization, computer applications, algebra, psychology, and student success strategies.

Special: Accelerated degrees, co-op programs, nondegree study, distance learning, and evening classes are possible. There are 5 national honor societies.

Faculty/Classroom: All teach undergraduates.

Requirements: Admissions requirements include graduation from a secondary school; the GED is also accepted. Applicants must pass the DeVry entrance exam or present satisfactory ACTor SAT scores. An interview is required. CLEP credit is accepted.

Procedure: Freshmen are admitted fall, spring, and summer. There are early admissions, deferred admissions, and rolling admissions plans. Application deadlines are open. Application fee is $50. Applications are accepted on-line.

Transfer: Applicants must present passing grades in all completed college course work, demonstrate language skills proficiency with at least 24 completed semester hours, and present evidence of math proficiency by appropriate college-level credits. A minimum GPA of 2.0 is required. 25 of 48 credits required for the bachelor's degree must be completed at DeVry.

Visiting: There are regularly scheduled orientations for prospective students. There are guides for informal visits and visitors may sit in on classes. To schedule a visit, contact the New Student Coordinator.

Financial Aid: In a recent year, 51% of all full-time freshmen and 71% of continuing full-time students received some form of financial aid. 49% of full-time freshmen and 68% of continuing full-time students received need-based aid. The average freshman award was $7008. Need-based scholarships or need-based grants averaged $3741; need-based self-help aid (loans and jobs) averaged $3549; and other non-need-based awards and non-need-based scholarships averaged $6349. The FAFSA and are required. The deadline for filing freshman financial aid applications for fall entry is rolling.

International Students: They must score satisfactorily on the written TOEFL or on the electronic version and also take the college's own entrance exam.

Computers: All students may access the system. Students may access the system during lab hours. There are no fees. It is strongly recommended that all students have a personal computer.

Graduates: In a recent year, 283 bachelor's degrees were awarded. The most popular majors were computer information systems (66%), business (27%), and electronics engineering technology (7%). 65 companies recruited on campus in a recent year.

Admissions Contact: Gerry Purcell, Director of Admissions. E-mail: *admissions@devry.edu* Web: *www.atl.devry.edu/alpharetta/*

DEVRY UNIVERSITY/DECATUR   **B-2**
Decatur, GA 30030-2198   (404) 292-2645
                                        (800) 221-4771; Fax: (404) 292-7011

Full-time: 1035 men, 770 women	**Faculty:** n/av
Part-time: 415 men, 350 women	**Ph.D.s:** n/av
Graduate: none	**Student/Faculty:** n/av
Year: semesters, summer session	**Tuition:** $10,680
Application Deadline: open	**Room & Board:** n/app
Freshman Class: n/av	
SAT or ACT: n/av	**LESS COMPETITIVE**

DeVry University/Decatur, a private institution, was established in 1969; there are 66 other DeVry University locations in the United States and Canada. The school offers technology-based undergraduate programs in business administration, electronics, computer information systems, telecommunications management, technical management, information technology, and computer engineering technology. Figures in the above capsule and profile are approximate. In addition to regional accreditation, DeVry has baccalaureate program accreditation with ABET. The library contains 22,094 volumes and 1380 audio/video tapes/CDs/DVDs. Computerized library services include the card catalog, interlibrary loans, and database searching. Special learning facilities include a learning resource center and electronics and other labs. The 18-acre campus is in a suburban area 6 miles from downtown Atlanta. There is one building.

Student Life: The average age of all undergraduates is 27.

Housing: There are no residence halls. All students commute. Alcohol is not permitted. All students may keep cars.

Activities: There are no fraternities or sororities. There are 12 groups on campus, including electronics, ethnic, environmental, film, fitness, ham radio, honors, international, newspaper, professional, and social and Toast masters (speech). Popular campus events include Fall Festival, Spring Fling, and Thanksgiving Dinner.

Sports: There is 1 intercollegiate sport for men, and 4 intramural sports for men and 4 for women.

Disabled Students: 98% of the campus is accessible. Wheelchair ramps, elevators, special parking, specially equipped rest rooms, lowered drinking fountains, and lowered telephones are available.

Services: Counseling and information services are available, as is tutoring in every subject.

Campus Safety and Security: Measures include security escort services, informal discussions, pamphlets/posters/films, and emergency telephones. There are lighted pathways/sidewalks. The campus is patrolled by county police 7:30 A.M. to 8 P.M. Monday through Friday and by DeVry security 6:30 A.M. to 11:30 P.M. Monday through Friday and 8 A.M. to 5 P.M. Saturday.

Programs of Study: DeVry confers the B.S. degree. Associate and master's degrees are also awarded. Bachelor's degrees are awarded in BIOLOGICAL SCIENCE (bioinformatics), BUSINESS (business administration and management), COMMUNICATIONS AND THE ARTS (telecommunications), COMPUTER AND PHYSICAL SCIENCE (information sciences and systems), ENGINEERING AND ENVIRONMENTAL DESIGN (biomedical engineering, computer engineering, electrical/electronics engineering technology, and technological management). Computer information systems and telecommunications are the largest.

Required: To graduate, students must achieve a cumulative GPA of at least 2.0 and satisfactorily complete all curriculum requirements. Course requirements vary according to program. All first-semester students take courses in business organization, computer applications, algebra, psychology, and student success strategies.

Special: Evening and weekend classes, co-op programs, an accelerated degree program, distance learning, and nondegree study are possible. There are 4 national honor societies and 3 departmental honors programs.

Faculty/Classroom: All teach undergraduates.

Requirements: Admissions requirements include graduation from a secondary school; the GED is also accepted. Applicants must pass the DeVry entrance exam or present satisfactory ACT or SAT scores. An interview is required. CLEP credit is accepted.

Procedure: Freshmen are admitted fall, spring, and summer. There are early admissions, deferred admissions, and rolling admissions plans. Application deadlines are open. Application fee is $50. Applications are accepted on-line.

Transfer: Applicants must present passing grades in all completed college course work, demonstrate language skills proficiency with at least 24 completed semester hours, and evidence math proficiency by appropriate college-level credits. A minimum GPA of 2.0 is required. 25 of 48 credits required for the bachelor's degree must be completed at DeVry.

Visiting: There are regularly scheduled orientations for prospective students. There are guides for informal visits and visitors may sit in on classes. To schedule a visit, contact the New Student Coordinator.

Financial Aid: In a recent year, 76% of all full-time freshmen and 85% of continuing full-time students received some form of financial aid. 74% of full-time freshmen and 83% of continuing full-time students received

need-based aid. The average freshman award was $8075. Need-based scholarships or need-based grants averaged $4535; need-based self-help aid (loans and jobs) averaged $3915; and other non-need-based awards and non-need-based scholarships averaged $7861. The FAFSA is required. Check with the school for current application deadlines.

International Students: They must score satisfactorily on the written or electronic version of the TOEFL and also take the college's own entrance exam.

Computers: Students in the computer information systems program may access the system during published lab hours. There are no fees.

Graduates: In a recent year 454 bachelor's degrees were awarded. The most popular majors were computer information systems (63%), business (31%), and electronics engineering technology (8%). 49 companies recruited on campus in a recent year.

Admissions Contact: Tonya Gibson, Director of Admissions.
E-mail: dsilva@admin.atl.devry.edu Web: www.atl.devry.edu

EMORY UNIVERSITY   B-2

Atlanta, GA 30322   (404) 727-6036; (800) 727-6036

Full-time: 2396 men, 3229 women	**Faculty:** 906; I, +$
Part-time: 11 men, 29 women	**Ph.D.s:** 100%
Graduate: 2247 men, 3026 women	**Student/Faculty:** 6 to 1
Year: semesters, summer session	**Tuition:** $30,794
Application Deadline: January 15	**Room & Board:** $9752
Freshman Class: 12,011 applied, 4395 accepted, 1259 enrolled	
SAT Verbal/Math: 670/690*	**ACT:** 29* **MOST COMPETITIVE**

Emory University, founded in 1836, is a private institution affiliated with the United Methodist Church. There are 4 undergraduate and 7 graduate schools. The 8 libraries contain 3,039,000 volumes, 272,000 microform items, and 53,575 audio/video tapes/CDs/DVDs, and subscribe to 54,000 periodicals including electronic. Computerized library services include the card catalog, interlibrary loans, database searching, Internet access, and laptop Internet portals. Special learning facilities include a learning resource center, art gallery, planetarium, radio station, TV station, the Michael C. Carlos Museum, and the Carter Center. The 634-acre campus is in a suburban area 5 miles northeast of downtown Atlanta. Including any residence halls, there are 150 buildings.

Student Life: 80% of undergraduates are from out of state, mostly the South. Students are from 50 states, 47 foreign countries, and Canada. 65% are from public schools. 60% are white; 16% Asian American. 13% are claim no religious affiliation; 11% Jewish; 7% Catholic. The average age of freshmen is 18; all undergraduates, 20. 6% do not continue beyond their first year; 89% remain to graduate.

Housing: 4014 students can be accommodated in college housing, which includes single-sex and coed dorms, on-campus apartments, married-student housing, fraternity houses, and sorority houses. In addition, there are honors houses, language houses, special-interest houses, and theme housing. On-campus housing is guaranteed for all 4 years. 70% of students live on campus; of those, 95% remain on campus on weekends. Upperclassmen may keep cars.

Activities: 31% of men belong to 12 national fraternities; 33% of women belong to 13 national sororities. There are more than 220 groups on campus, including art, bagpipe band, band, cheerleading, chess, choir, chorale, chorus, computers, dance, debate, drama, ethnic, film, gay, honors, international, jazz band, literary magazine, musical theater, newspaper, orchestra, pep band, photography, political, professional, radio and TV, religious, social, social service, student government, symphony, and yearbook. Popular campus events include Heritage Ball, Dooley's Week, and Festival of Nine Lessons.

Sports: There are 8 intercollegiate sports for men and 8 for women, and 20 intramural sports for men and 20 for women. Facilities include a recreation center, which contains a 3000-seat gym with 4 basketball courts, 5 volleyball courts, an Olympic-size swimming pool, indoor track, 2 Nautilus weight rooms, a sheer rock wall, and tennis, racquetball, and squash courts. In addition, there is a soccer field and a 400-meter track, with seating for 2000 spectators.

Disabled Students: 90% of the campus is accessible. Wheelchair ramps, elevators, special parking, specially equipped rest rooms, special class scheduling, lowered drinking fountains, lowered telephones, and special housing are available.

Services: Counseling and information services are available, as is tutoring in most subjects. There is a reader service for the blind.

Campus Safety and Security: Measures include 24-hour foot and vehicle patrol, self-defense education, security escort services, and shuttle buses. There are informal discussions, pamphlets/posters/films, emergency telephones, and lighted pathways/sidewalks, and The campus patrol is a fully accredited police department.

Programs of Study: Emory confers B.A., B.S., B.B.A., and B.S.N. degrees. Associate, master's, and doctoral degrees are also awarded. Bachelor's degrees are awarded in AGRICULTURE (environmental studies), BIOLOGICAL SCIENCE (biology/biological science and neurosciences), BUSINESS (accounting, banking and finance, business administration and management, business economics, and marketing/retailing/

merchandising), COMMUNICATIONS AND THE ARTS (art, art history and appreciation, Chinese, classics, comparative literature, creative writing, dance, dramatic arts, English, film arts, fine arts, French, Greek, Italian, Japanese, journalism, Latin, linguistics, music, Russian languages and literature, and Spanish), COMPUTER AND PHYSICAL SCIENCE (chemistry, computer science, mathematics, and physics), EDUCATION (educational statistics and research), HEALTH PROFESSIONS (nursing), SOCIAL SCIENCE (African American studies, African studies, American studies, anthropology, Asian/American studies, Asian/Oriental studies, Caribbean studies, classical/ancient civilization, economics, French studies, German area studies, history, interdisciplinary studies, international studies, Italian studies, Judaic studies, Latin American studies, medieval studies, Middle Eastern studies, philosophy, political science/government, psychology, religion, Russian and Slavic studies, sociology, and women's studies). Business administration, psychology, and economics are the largest.

Required: To graduate, students must complete 132 semester hours, including courses during the first 2 years in English, science, math, history, the social sciences, health, and phys ed. Students must have a GPA of 1.9 for the first 3 years and 2.0 in the senior year. The number of hours required for the major varies by department. A thesis is required for students in honors or dual B.A./M.A. or B.S./M.S. programs.

Special: Special academic programs include cross-registration with Atlanta area colleges and universities, departmental internships, work-study programs, dual majors, 3-2 and 4-2 engineering degrees with Georgia Tech, and pass/fail options. A Washington semester and B.A.-B.S. degrees are available, and students may study abroad in many countries. There are accelerated degree programs offered in biology, chemistry, math, physics, English, history, philosophy, political science, sociology, and computer science. There are 30 national honor societies, including Phi Beta Kappa.

Faculty/Classroom: 59% of faculty are male; 41%, female. 58% teach undergraduates, 65% do research, and 100% do both. Graduate students teach less than 10% of introductory courses. The average class size in an introductory lecture is 27; in a laboratory, 27; and in a regular course, 20.

Admissions: 37% of the 2005-2006 applicants were accepted. The SAT scores for the 2005-2006 freshman class were: Verbal--10% between 500 and 599, 55% between 600 and 700, and 35% above 700; Math--8% between 500 and 599, 47% between 600 and 700, and 45% above 700. The ACT scores were 4% between 21 and 23, 15% between 24 and 26, 20% between 27 and 28, and 61% above 28. 90% of the current freshmen were in the top fifth of their class; 100% were in the top two fifths. There were 72 National Merit finalists. 8 freshmen graduated first in their class.

Requirements: The SAT or ACT is required. In addition, students must submit a hight school transcript. We invite applicants to submit SAT results, but they are not required unless a student is homeschooled. We look for leadership and/or commitment in extracurricular activities, the required recommendation for the high school couselor, up to two additional letters of recommendations, and the contact an applicant has had with the Office of Admission during the application process. The student must have acquired 16 academic credits in secondary school, including 4 years of English, 3 years of math, and 2 years each of history, science, and foreign language. AP credits are accepted. Important factors in the admissions decision are advanced placement or honor courses, recommendations by school officials, and extracurricular activities record.

Procedure: Freshmen are admitted in the fall. Entrance exams should be taken prior to applying. There are early decision, early admissions, and deferred admissions plans. Early decision applications should be filed by November 1, early decision 11 by January 1; regular applications, by January 15 for fall entry, along with a $50 fee. Notification of early decision is sent December 15, early decision 11 by February 1; regular decision, April 1. 498 early decision candidates were accepted for the 2005-2006 class. 800 applicants were on the 2005 waiting list; 25 were admitted. Applications are accepted on-line.

Transfer: 92 transfer students enrolled in 2004-2005. Applicants must have taken the SAT or ACT and completed at least 1 year of college, with a GPA of 3.0. 64 of 132 credits required for the bachelor's degree must be completed at Emory.

Visiting: There are regularly scheduled orientations for prospective students, including a student-led campus tour and an informational focus session led by a member of our Admission staff. Prospective students may also arrange to sit in on classes, as well as meet with faculty or athletic coaches. There are guides for informal visits and visitors may sit in on classes. To schedule a visit, contact the Office of Undergraduate Admission.

Financial Aid: In 2005-2006, 60% of all full-time freshmen and 59% of continuing full-time students received some form of financial aid. 38% of full-time freshmen and 37% of continuing full-time students received need-based aid. The average freshman award was $25,568. Need-based scholarships or need-based grants averaged $21,616 ($34,326 maximum); need-based self-help aid (loans and jobs) averaged $4147 ($6625 maximum); and other non-need-based awards and non-need-based scholarships averaged $16,047 ($41,546 maximum). Average annual earnings from campus work are $2080. The average financial indebtedness of the 2005 graduate was $22,175. Emory is a member of CSS. The CSS/Profile or FAFSA is required. The deadline for filing freshman financial aid applications for fall entry is February 15.

International Students: There are 266 international students enrolled. The school actively recruits these students. They must take the TOEFL and also take the SAT or the ACT.

Computers: Wireless access is available. All students may access the system 24 hours a day. There are no time limits and no fees.

Graduates: From July 1, 2004 to June 30, 2005, 1476 bachelor's degrees were awarded. The most popular majors were business (12%), economics (9%), and political science (9%). In an average class, 2% graduate in 3 years or less, 84% graduate in 4 years or less, 88% graduate in 5 years or less, and 89% graduate in 6 years or less. 250 companies recruited on campus in 2004-2005. Of the 2004 graduating class, 65% were enrolled in graduate school within 6 months of graduation.

Admissions Contact: Daniel C. Walls, Dean of Admission. A video is available. E-mail: *admiss@emory.edu*
Web: *www.emory.edu/admissions*

FORT VALLEY STATE UNIVERSITY B-3

Fort Valley, GA 31030-3298
(478) 822-7594
(877) 462-3878; Fax: (478) 822-7595

Full-time: 900 men, 1085 women	**Faculty:** 133
Part-time: 115 men, 205 women	**Ph.D.s:** 60%
Graduate: 65 men, 195 women	**Student/Faculty:** 15 to 1
Year: semesters, summer session	**Tuition:** $2795 ($9425)
Application Deadline: see profile	**Room & Board:** $4180
Freshman Class: 2484 applied, 1194 accepted, 511 enrolled	
SAT or ACT: required	**COMPETITIVE**

Fort Valley State University, founded in 1895, is a public land-grant member of the University System of Georgia. The university offers undergraduate programs in the arts and sciences, business, education, agriculture, engineering, and other vocational and technical fields. Graduate programs are offered in early childhood, middle grades education, mental health and rehabilitation counseling, and guidance and counseling. Some information in this capsule and profile is approximate. There are 3 undergraduate schools and 1 graduate school. In addition to regional accreditation, FVSU has baccalaureate program accreditation with NCATE. The library contains 250,000 volumes and 172,000 microform items, and subscribes to 1168 periodicals including electronic. Computerized library services include the card catalog, interlibrary loans, and database searching. Special learning facilities include a learning resource center, radio station, TV station, experimental agricultural plots, animal research centers, and greenhouse complex. The 1375-acre campus is in a rural area 30 miles southwest of Macon. Including any residence halls, there are 35 buildings.

Student Life: 92% of undergraduates are from Georgia. Others are from 29 states and 5 foreign countries. 92% are African American. 50% of freshmen remain to graduate.

Housing: 982 students can be accommodated in college housing, which includes single-sex dorms and on-campus apartments. On-campus housing is guaranteed for the freshman year only and is available on a first-come, first-served basis. 65% of students live on campus. Alcohol is not permitted. All students may keep cars.

Activities: There are 4 national fraternities and 5 national sororities. There are 73 groups on campus, including cheerleading, choir, chorus, dance, drama, honors, international, jazz band, marching band, newspaper, opera, orchestra, political, radio and TV, religious, social service, student government, and yearbook. Popular campus events include Black History month.

Sports: There are 8 intercollegiate sports for men, and 3 intramural sports for men and 3 for women. Facilities include a stadium, a gym, a baseball field, lighted tennis courts, an indoor swimming pool, indoor and outdoor tracks, and shuffleboard courts.

Disabled Students: Wheelchair ramps, elevators, special parking, and specially equipped rest rooms are available.

Services: Counseling and information services are available, as is tutoring in most subjects. There is remedial math, reading, and writing.

Campus Safety and Security: Measures include 24-hour foot and vehicle patrol, informal discussions, and pamphlets/posters/films.

Programs of Study: FVSU confers B.A., B.S., B.B.A., and B.S.W. degrees. Associate and master's degrees are also awarded. Bachelor's degrees are awarded in AGRICULTURE (agricultural economics, animal science, horticulture, and plant science), BIOLOGICAL SCIENCE (biology/biological science, nutrition, and zoology), BUSINESS (accounting, business administration and management, marketing/retailing/merchandising, and office supervision and management), COMMUNICATIONS AND THE ARTS (communications and English), COMPUTER AND PHYSICAL SCIENCE (chemistry, computer science, information sciences and systems, and mathematics), EDUCATION (agricultural, early childhood, home economics, mathematics, middle school, physical, and secondary), ENGINEERING AND ENVIRONMENTAL DESIGN

(agricultural engineering technology, commercial art, and electrical/electronics engineering technology), HEALTH PROFESSIONS (veterinary science), SOCIAL SCIENCE (child psychology/development, criminal justice, economics, political science/government, psychology, social work, and sociology).

Required: Students must complete a minimum of 120 credit hours, plus 5 additional hours to satisfy requirements for freshmen orientation and for military science or phys ed. General education requirements include courses in humanities, social science, and math/science, and courses in the major. The bachelor's degree requires a minimum GPA of 2.0 and no grade below C in the major.

Special: Students may participate in cooperative work-study programs with local industries, cross-register for courses at Robins Residence Center, and study abroad. FVSU also offers a 3-2 dual degree program in chemistry/geosciences with University of Oklahoma, in engineering or other technical fields with Georgia Institute of Technology, and a 3-2 engineering degree with University of Nevada, Las Vegas. There are 5 national honor societies and a freshman honors program.

Faculty/Classroom: 60% of faculty are male; 40%, female. The average class size in a regular course is 25.

Requirements: The SAT or ACT is required. In addition, applicants must be graduates of an accredited secondary school or have earned a GED. The university requires at least 17 academic units of study, including 4 in English, 3 in social science, 3 each in math and science, and 2 of foreign language. A GPA of 2.67 is required. AP and CLEP credits are accepted.

Procedure: Freshmen are admitted to all sessions. There are early admissions and rolling admissions plans. Notification is sent on a rolling basis. Applications are accepted on-line. The application fee is $20.

Transfer: In addition to meeting standard admission requirements, transfers must submit transcripts from all colleges previously attended. Transfer credit is accepted based on a 2.0 minimum GPA, and only courses with a C or better will be accepted. 45 of 125 credits required for the bachelor's degree must be completed at FVSU.

Visiting: There are regularly scheduled orientations for prospective students, including an overview, an introduction of administration and faculty, and a tour. There are guides for informal visits and visitors may sit in on classes. To schedule a visit, contact the Office of Enrollment Management.

Financial Aid: In a recent year, need-based scholarships or need-based grants averaged $2700 ($3040 maximum); need-based self-help aid (loans and jobs) averaged $2362 ($2438 maximum); and non-need-based athletic scholarships averaged $944 ($1000 maximum). The FAFSA is required. Check with the school for current application deadlines.

International Students: They must take the TOEFL and college's own test, and also take the SAT or the ACT.

Computers: There are no time limits and no fees. It is strongly recommended that all students have a personal computer.

Admissions Contact: John D. Jones, Assistant VP/Assessment and Accountability. E-mail: *jonesj@fvsu.edu* Web: *www.fvsu.edu*

GEORGIA COLLEGE AND STATE UNIVERSITY C-3

Milledgeville, GA 31061
(478) 445-5004
(800) 342-0471; Fax: (478) 445-1914

Full-time: 1721 men, 2525 women	**Faculty:** 268; IIA, --$
Part-time: 229 men, 326 women	**Ph.D.s:** 75%
Graduate: 290 men, 571 women	**Student/Faculty:** 16 to 1
Year: semesters, summer session	**Tuition:** $4142 ($14,354)
Application Deadline: April 1	**Room & Board:** $6878
Freshman Class: 3236 applied, 1954 accepted, 1033 enrolled	
SAT Verbal/Math: 550/550*	**ACT:** 22 **COMPETITIVE**

Georgia College and State University, founded in 1889, is the public liberal arts university of Georgia. There are 4 undergraduate schools and 1 graduate school. In addition to regional accreditation, GC&SU has baccalaureate program accreditation with AACSB, NASM, NCATE, and NLN. The library contains 188,977 volumes, 646,107 microform items, and 4880 audio/video tapes/CDs/DVDs, and subscribes to 15,171 periodicals including electronic. Computerized library services include the card catalog, interlibrary loans, database searching, and Internet access. Special learning facilities include a learning resource center, art gallery, radio station, TV station, and museum. The 590-acre campus is in a small town 30 miles from Macon. Including any residence halls, there are 61 buildings.

Student Life: 95% of undergraduates are from Georgia. Others are from 38 states, 38 foreign countries, and Canada. 87% are white. The average age of freshmen is 18; all undergraduates, 21. 17% of the fall 2004 freshman class did not continue beyond their first year; 83% returned.

Housing: 2090 students can be accommodated in college housing, which includes single-sex and coed dorms and off-campus apartments. In addition, there are honors houses, special-interest houses, and a freshman experience house. On-campus housing is available on a first-come, first-served basis. 56% of students commute. All students may keep cars.

Activities: 9% of men belong to 5 national fraternities; 13% of women belong to 5 national sororities. There are 126 groups on campus, including band, Big Brother/Sister, cheerleading, choir, chorale, chorus, dance, debate, drama, ethnic, honors, international, jazz band, literary magazine, musical theater, photography, political, professional, radio and TV, religious, residence hall council, social, social service, student government, and yearbook. Popular campus events include Week of Welcome, Progressive Dinner, and International Week.

Sports: There are 5 intercollegiate sports for men and 5 for women, and 26 intramural sports for men and 26 for women. Facilities include a basketball arena, a gym, a track, racquetball courts, a weight room, aerobics facilities, an indoor rock-climbing wall, a 70-acre phys ed complex, a soccer field, a ball park, a golf course, tennis courts, an indoor and an outdoor pool, a rope/challenge course, and nearby lakes for canoeing, sailing, and skiing.

Disabled Students: 82% of the campus is accessible. Wheelchair ramps, elevators, special parking, specially equipped rest rooms, lowered drinking fountains, lowered telephones, and special housing are available.

Services: Counseling and information services are available, as is tutoring in most subjects. There is a reader service for the blind, and remedial math, reading, and writing.

Campus Safety and Security: Measures include 24-hour foot and vehicle patrol, self-defense education, security escort services, and shuttle buses. There are informal discussions, pamphlets/posters/films, emergency telephones, and lighted pathways/sidewalks.

Programs of Study: GC&SU confers B.A., B.S., B.B.A., B.G.S., B.M., B.M.E., B.M.T., and B.S.N. degrees. Master's degrees are also awarded. Bachelor's degrees are awarded in BIOLOGICAL SCIENCE (biology/biological science), BUSINESS (accounting, business administration and management, international business management, management science, and marketing and distribution), COMMUNICATIONS AND THE ARTS (art, communications, dramatic arts, English, French, music, Spanish, and speech/debate/rhetoric), COMPUTER AND PHYSICAL SCIENCE (chemistry, computer science, information sciences and systems, and mathematics), EDUCATION (early childhood, health, middle school, music, physical, recreation, and special), ENGINEERING AND ENVIRONMENTAL DESIGN (environmental science), HEALTH PROFESSIONS (music therapy and nursing), SOCIAL SCIENCE (criminal justice, economics, history, liberal arts/general studies, political science/government, psychology, and sociology). Chemistry, nursing, and education are the strongest academically. Education and nursing are the largest.

Required: To graduate, students must complete at least 120 semester hours, including 60 in the major and 39 in upper-level courses, with a minimum GPA of 2.0. Core curriculum requirements of 60 semester hours include 12 hours of social science, 11 of math/science, 9 of essential skills, 6 of humanities/fine arts, 4 of global and arts awareness, and 18 of courses related to the major. All B.A. candidates and some B.S. candidates must take foreign language. All students must pass an exam on the history and Constitution of both the U.S. and Georgia, the reading and writing sections of the Regents exam, and a senior exit exam in the major. They must also earn a C or better in English 101.

Special: GC&SU has study-abroad agreements with institutions worldwide, Washington semester, co-op programs, internships, work-study programs, dual majors, independent study, and student-designed majors. There is a 3-2 engineering degree program with the Georgia Institute of Technology. There are 15 national honor societies and a freshman honors program.

Faculty/Classroom: 52% of faculty are male; 48%, female. All teach undergraduates. Graduate students teach 5% of introductory courses. The average class size in an introductory lecture is 23; in a laboratory, 13; and in a regular course, 18.

Admissions: 60% of the 2005-2006 applicants were accepted. The SAT scores for the 2005-2006 freshman class were: Verbal--12% below 500, 60% between 500 and 599, 25% between 600 and 700, and 3% above 700; Math--14% below 500, 60% between 500 and 599, 24% between 600 and 700, and 2% above 700. The ACT scores were 26% below 21, 39% between 21 and 23, 26% between 24 and 26, 6% between 27 and 28, and 4% above 28. 25% of the current freshmen were in the top fifth of their class; 75% were in the top two fifths.

Requirements: The SAT or ACT is required. Applicants must be graduates of an accredited or recognized secondary school and must complete the Georgia college-preparatory curriculum requirements, including 4 units each of English and math, 3 each of social science and science, and 2 of a foreign language. A GPA of 2.0 is required. AP and CLEP credits are accepted. Important factors in the admissions decision are advanced placement or honor courses, evidence of special talent, and leadership record.

Procedure: Freshmen are admitted to all sessions. Entrance exams should be taken by January of the senior year. There are early admissions and deferred admissions plans. There is a rolling admissions plan. Early decision applications should be filed by November 1; regular applications, by April 1 for fall entry, December 1 for spring entry, and May 1 for summer entry, along with a $25 fee. Notification of early decision

is sent December 15; regular decision, on a rolling basis. 139 applicants were on the 2005 waiting list; 16 were admitted. Applications are accepted on-line.

Transfer: 371 transfer students enrolled in 2004-2005. To transfer applicants must have at least a 2.3 GPA, submit official transcripts from all colleges attended, and be eligible to return to their previous institution. Those who have completed fewer than 30 semester hours must meet all freshman admissions requirements. 40 of 120 credits required for the bachelor's degree must be completed at GC&SU.

Visiting: There are regularly scheduled orientations for prospective students, including receptions, tours, school meetings, information sessions, and academic and cocurricular advising and registration. There are guides for informal visits and visitors may sit in on classes. To schedule a visit, contact the Office of Admissions.

Financial Aid: In 2004-2005, 35% of all full-time freshmen received some form of financial aid. 86% of full-time freshmen and 72% of continuing full-time students received need-based aid. Need-based scholarships or need-based grants averaged $2668; need-based self-help aid (loans and jobs) averaged $1206; non-need-based athletic scholarships averaged $2128; and other non-need-based awards and non-need-based scholarships averaged $921. 4% of undergraduates work part time. Average annual earnings from campus work are $2600. The average financial indebtedness of the 2004 graduate was $15,286. The FAFSA is required. The priority date for freshman financial aid applications for fall entry is March.

International Students: There are 95 international students enrolled. The school actively recruits these students. They must score satisfactorily on the TOEFL or take the IELTS or Cambridge Exam, or complete the highest level of an ESL course. To comply with NCAA regulations, international students who will compete in intercolliate athletics must submit official SAT or ACT scores.

Computers: Wireless access is available. Each dorm room 4 jacks for network access. Each student has a wireless account and may access the network on the Milledgeville campus. A centralized student lab is located in the Info Tech Center on the ground floor of the library. During the academic term, the lab is available from Sunday until Friday with some Saturday hours. Various department specialty labs and free-standing public access machines are also available. There are approximately 450 public and student-access machines. All students may access the system. Lab hours vary. There are no time limits. The fee is $38 per semester. It is strongly recommended that all students have a personal computer.

Graduates: From July 1, 2004 to June 30, 2005, 773 bachelor's degrees were awarded. The most popular majors were management (12%), nursing (9%), and psychology (9%). In an average class, 35% graduate in 6 years or less. 46 companies recruited on campus in 2004-2005.

Admissions Contact: Mike Augustine, Director of Admissions. E-mail: *info@gcsu.edu* Web: *www.gcsu.edu*

GEORGIA INSTITUTE OF TECHNOLOGY
B-2

Atlanta, GA 30332 (404) 894-4154; Fax: (404) 894-9511

Full-time: 7886 men, 3106 women	**Faculty:** 831; I, +$
Part-time: 614 men, 235 women	**Ph.D.s:** 96%
Graduate: 3908 men, 1386 women	**Student/Faculty:** 13 to 1
Year: semesters, summer session	**Tuition:** $4648 ($18,990)
Application Deadline: January 15	**Room & Board:** $6802
Freshman Class: 9172 applied, 6191 accepted, 2436 enrolled	
SAT Verbal/Math: 641/687*	**ACT:** 28

HIGHLY COMPETITIVE+

Georgia Institute of Technology, founded in 1885, is a public technological institution offering programs in architecture, management, policy, international affairs, engineering, computing, and science. There are 6 undergraduate and 6 graduate schools. In addition to regional accreditation, Georgia Tech has baccalaureate program accreditation with AACSB, ABET, ACCE, ACS, NAAB, and NASAD. The 2 libraries contain 2,410,964 volumes, 4,495,012 microform items, and 114,338 audio/video tapes/CDs/DVDs, and subscribe to 21,248 periodicals including electronic. Computerized library services include the card catalog, interlibrary loans, database searching, Internet access, and laptop Internet portals. Special learning facilities include a learning resource center, art gallery, and radio station. The 450-acre campus is in an urban area. Including any residence halls, there are 183 buildings.

Student Life: 70% of undergraduates are from Georgia. Others are from 50 states, 84 foreign countries, and Canada. 68% are white; 15% Asian American. The average age of freshmen is 18; all undergraduates, 21. 8% do not continue beyond their first year; 76% remain to graduate.

Housing: 7992 students can be accommodated in college housing, which includes single-sex and coed dorms, on-campus apartments, married-student housing, fraternity houses, and sorority houses. In addition, there are language and special-interest, and freshman experience houses. On-campus housing is guaranteed for the freshman year only, is available on a first-come, first-served basis, and is available on a lottery system for upperclassmen. 64% of students live on campus; of those,

70% remain on campus on weekends. Alcohol is not permitted. All students except first-semester freshmen may keep cars.

Activities: 21% of men and about 1% of women belong to 34 national fraternities; 24% of women belong to 1 local and 13 national sororities. There are more than 350 groups on campus, including art, athletic, band, cheerleading, chess, choir, chorale, chorus, computers, cultural, dance, debate, departmental, drama, drill team, ethnic, gay, honors, international, jazz band, literary magazine, marching band, musical theater, newspaper, orchestra, outdoor, pep band, photography, political, professional, radio and TV, religious, social, social service, student government, symphony, and yearbook. Popular campus events include Greek Week and the Ramblin' Wreck Parade.

Sports: There are 9 intercollegiate sports for men and 8 for women, and 20 intramural sports for men and 20 for women. Facilities include softball fields, a 4000-seat baseball stadium, a 55,000-seat football stadium, a 9100-seat basketball arena, a golf practice facility, an Olympic aquatic center for swimming and diving, outdoor tennis courts, an outdoor turf field featuring flag football fields, 2 outdoor sand volleyball courts, and a recreation center with 6 multipurpose indoor courts, strength training and cardio-fitness, 4 racquetball/wallyball/squash courts, a running track, a climbing wall, and 3 studios for aerobic fitness programs.

Disabled Students: 75% of the campus is accessible. Wheelchair ramps, elevators, special parking, specially equipped rest rooms, special class scheduling, lowered drinking fountains, lowered telephones, visual alarms in housing, assistive listening devices, adapted furniture in computer labs, adaptable living space, and a paid TDD telephone booth are available.

Services: Counseling and information services are available, as is tutoring in most subjects. There is a reader service for the blind. The Learning Assistance Program/ Freshmen Experience provides tutors for calculus, chemistry, particle dynamics, and other advanced core classes; the GT Cable Network provides students with call-in tutoring and 1-to-1 tutoring.

Campus Safety and Security: Measures include 24-hour foot and vehicle patrol, self-defense education, security escort services, and shuttle buses. There are informal discussions, pamphlets/posters/films, emergency telephones, lighted pathways/sidewalks, foot and bike patrols, limited access to dorms, a mobile security patrol, and video cameras.

Programs of Study: Georgia Tech confers B.S. and many specialized bachelor's degrees in science, engineering, computing, architecture, liberal arts, and management. Master's and doctoral degrees are also awarded. Bachelor's degrees are awarded in BIOLOGICAL SCIENCE (biology/biological science), BUSINESS (business administration and management and management science), COMMUNICATIONS AND THE ARTS (industrial design), COMPUTER AND PHYSICAL SCIENCE (applied mathematics, applied physics, chemistry, computer science, earth science, mathematics, physics, and polymer science), ENGINEERING AND ENVIRONMENTAL DESIGN (aeronautical engineering, architecture, biomedical engineering, chemical engineering, civil engineering, computer engineering, construction management, electrical/electronics engineering, industrial engineering, materials engineering, materials science, mechanical engineering, nuclear engineering, technology and public affairs, and textile engineering), SOCIAL SCIENCE (applied psychology, economics, history, international relations, public affairs, and textiles and clothing). Engineering, computer science, and sciences are the strongest academically. Mechanical engineering, management, and industrial engineering are the largest.

Required: All students must fulfill the core curriculum requirements, including 12 hours of science, math, and technology; 12 hours of social sciences, 9 hours of essential skills courses (English composition, calculus), 6 hours of humanitites, and 4 hours of electives. Other course requirements include a U.S. and Georgia history and government course, and a wellness course. Students must maintain a 2.0 GPA in more than 120 hours, and must pass a reading and English composition exam.

Special: Extensive co-op programs, cross-registration with other Atlanta-area colleges, and internships are available. Study abroad in 29 countries is possible. An engineering transfer program is offered within the university system, and a liberal arts–engineering dual degree program serves area colleges and institutions nationwide. Students have access to multidisciplinary and certificate programs outside their major field of study. The Georgia Tech Regional Engineering Program (GTREP) offers undergraduate and graduate degrees in collaboration with Armstrong Atlantic State, Georgia Southern, and Savannah State Universities. There are 13 national honor societies.

Faculty/Classroom: 82% of faculty are male; 18%, female. All teach undergraduates.

Admissions: 67% of the 2005-2006 applicants were accepted. The SAT scores for the 2005-2006 freshman class were: Verbal--2% below 500, 22% between 500 and 599, 59% between 600 and 700, and 17% above 700; Math--1% below 500, 6% between 500 and 599, 56% between 600 and 700, and 37% above 700. The ACT scores were 1% below 21, 6% between 21 and 23, 29% between 24 and 26, 23% between 27 and 28, and 41% above 28. There were 100 National Merit finalists.

Requirements: The SAT or ACT is required. In addition, candidates for admission must have completed 4 units each of English and math, 3 units of social studies, 3 units of science, including 2 units of lab sciences, and 2 units of foreign language. AP credits are accepted.

Procedure: Freshmen are admitted in the fall. Entrance exams should be taken by the end of the junior year. There is an early admissions plan. Applications should be filed by January 15 for fall entry and January 15 for summer entry. The fall 2005 application fee was $50. Notification is sent on a rolling basis. 208 applicants were on the 2005 waiting list; 102 were admitted. Applications are accepted on-line.

Transfer: 759 transfer students enrolled in 2004-2005. Transfer applicants must have completed a minimum of 30 semester hours or 45 quarter hours of course work. All of the specifically required courses on the course requirements chart for the prospective major must be completed. Grades and academic standing must be satisfactory for the last term of enrollment at the prior college. Competitive GPAs are determined according to the projected major. 36 of at least 120 credits required for the bachelor's degree must be completed at Georgia Tech.

Visiting: There are regularly scheduled orientations for prospective students, including the Connect with Tech program, offered 8 times between September and April by invitation only for prospective freshmen and their parents (includes an overnight stay in a freshman hall, a class visit, and a tour). Other programs include The Future Program, Girls Night Out, and Preview Georgia Tech. For more information, go to http://www.visits.gatech.edu/. There are guides for informal. To schedule a visit, contact the Office of Undergraduate Admissions at (404) 894-2691 or *admissions@gatech.edu*.

Financial Aid: In 2005-2006, 84% of all full-time freshmen and 71% of continuing full-time students received some form of financial aid. 40% of full-time freshmen and 41% of continuing full-time students received need-based aid. The average freshman award was $9459. Need-based scholarships or need-based grants averaged $5195 ($10,000 maximum); need-based self-help aid (loans and jobs) averaged $3289 ($6625 maximum); non-need-based athletic scholarships averaged $13,695 ($27,550 maximum); and other non-need-based awards and non-need-based scholarships averaged $5064 ($23,633 maximum). 2% of undergraduates work part time. Average annual earnings from campus work are $2400. The average financial indebtedness of the 2005 graduate was $12,643. The FAFSA and the college's own financial statement are required. The deadline for filing freshman financial aid applications for fall entry is March 1.

International Students: There are 551 international students enrolled. They must score on the written or electronic version of the TOEFL or take the College Board APIEL (Advanced Placement International English Language) exam, and must also take the SAT.

Computers: All students have access to the networkand wireless system, which can be accessed in locations such as labs, classrooms, the library, the student center, and dorms. There are no time limits and no fees. All students are required to have personal computers. Minimum general requirements include at least 512 MB RAM and hard drive. 40-GB specific PC requirements include an Intel Pentium IV, AMD athlon, or higher processor. Specific Mac requirements include a Power Mac G4 or higher.

Graduates: From July 1, 2004 to June 30, 2005, 2512 bachelor's degrees were awarded. The most popular majors were management (14%), computer science (12%), and industrial engineering (11%). In an average class, 29% graduate in 4 years or less, 67% graduate in 5 years or less, and 76% graduate in 6 years or less. 593 companies recruited on campus in 2004-2005.

Admissions Contact: Ingrid Hayes, Director of Undergraduate Admissions. E-mail: *admission@gatech.edu*
Web: *www.admissions.gatech.edu*

GEORGIA SOUTHERN UNIVERSITY   D-3

Statesboro, GA 30460   (912) 681-5391; Fax: (912) 486-7240

Full-time: 6652 men, 6467 women	**Faculty:** 628; IIA, --$
Part-time: 750 men, 781 women	**Ph.D.s:** 76%
Graduate: 598 men, 1398 women	**Student/Faculty:** 21 to 1
Year: semesters, summer session	**Tuition:** $3462 ($10,778)
Application Deadline: July 1	**Room & Board:** $6300
Freshman Class: 8302 applied, 4585 accepted, 2811 enrolled	
SAT Verbal/Math: 546/552*	**ACT:** 22 **COMPETITIVE**

Georgia Southern University, founded in 1906, is a member of the University System of Georgia and offers undergraduate degree programs in education, business, liberal arts and social sciences, information technology, science and technology, and health and human sciences. We also offer graduate degrees in a variety of disciplines. There are 6 undergraduate schools and 1 graduate school. In addition to regional accreditation, Georgia Southern has baccalaureate program accreditation with AACSB, ABET, ACCE, ACS, ADA, CAAHEP, CADE, CCNE, CSAB, FIDER, NAIT, NASAD, NASM, NASPAA, NASPE, NCATE, and NRPA. The library contains 577,172 volumes, 888,272 microform items, and 29,059 audio/video tapes/CDs/DVDs, and subscribes to 2687 periodicals including electronic. Computerized library services include the card catalog, interlibrary loans, database searching, Internet access, and laptop Internet portals. Special learning facilities include a learning resource center, art gallery, natural history museum, planetarium, radio station, wildlife center, botanical gardens, performing arts center, and continuing education center. The 675-acre campus is in a small town 50 miles northwest of Savannah. Including any residence halls, there are 148 buildings.

Student Life: 95% of undergraduates are from Georgia. Others are from 41 states, 78 foreign countries, and Canada. 73% are white; 22% African American. The average age of freshmen is 18; all undergraduates, 21. 22% do not continue beyond their first year; 41% remain to graduate.

Housing: 3920 students can be accommodated in college housing, which includes single-sex and coed dorms, on-campus apartments, fraternity houses, and sorority houses. In addition, there are honors houses, special-interest houses, and theme hall. On-campus housing is available on a first-come, first-served basis and is available on a lottery system for upperclassmen. 74% of students commute. Alcohol is restricted. All students may keep cars.

Activities: 12% of men belong to 18 national fraternities; 12% of women belong to 7 national sororities. There are 150 groups on campus, including art, band, cheerleading, choir, chorale, chorus, computers, dance, debate, drama, drill team, ethnic, gay, honors, international, jazz band, literary magazine, marching band, multicultural, musical theater, newspaper, opera, orchestra, pep band, photography, political, professional, radio, religious, social, social service, student government, and symphony. Popular campus events include Eagle Expo Career Fairs, Welcome Week Activities, and Black History Month.

Sports: There are 6 intercollegiate sports for men and 9 for women, and 12 intramural sports for men and 12 for women. Facilities include football, soccer, and softball fields, basketball, handball, racquetball, tennis, and volleyball courts, a weight training area, golf ranges, an exercise trail, football and baseball stadiums, a field house, swimming pools, a challenge course, an activity center, circuit training and cardiovascular equipment, an indoor walking track, and other facilities.

Disabled Students: 92% of the campus is accessible. Wheelchair ramps, elevators, special parking, specially equipped rest rooms, special class scheduling, lowered drinking fountains, lowered telephones, and special housing are available.

Services: Counseling and information services are available, as is tutoring in most subjects. There is a reader service for the blind, and remedial math, reading, and writing.

Campus Safety and Security: Measures include 24-hour foot and vehicle patrol, self-defense education, security escort services, and shuttle buses. There are informal discussions, pamphlets/posters/films, emergency telephones, lighted pathways/sidewalks, bike police, and environmental safety services.

Programs of Study: Georgia Southern confers B.A., B.S., B.B.A., B.F.A., B.G.S., B.M., B.S.B.I.O., B.S.C.E.T., B.S.C.H.E.M., B.S.Cons., B.S.Ed., B.S.E.E.T., B.S.H.S., B.S.J.S., B.S.K., B.S.Manu., B.S.M.A.T., B.S.M.E.T., B.S.M.T., B.S.N., B.S.Phy., and B.S.P.M.G.T. degrees. Master's and doctoral degrees are also awarded. Bachelor's degrees are awarded in BIOLOGICAL SCIENCE (biology/biological science and nutrition), BUSINESS (accounting, banking and finance, fashion merchandising, hotel/motel and restaurant management, human resources, international economics, logistics, management science, marketing and distribution, marketing/retailing/merchandising, recreation and leisure services, recreational facilities management, sports management, and tourism), COMMUNICATIONS AND THE ARTS (art, broadcasting, communications, dramatic arts, English, French, German, journalism, linguistics, music, music theory and composition, performing arts, public relations, and Spanish), COMPUTER AND PHYSICAL SCIENCE (chemistry, computer science, geology, information sciences and systems, mathematics, and physics), EDUCATION (art, business, early childhood, English, foreign languages, health, home economics, mathematics, middle school, music, science, social science, special, and technical), ENGINEERING AND ENVIRONMENTAL DESIGN (civil engineering technology, construction management, electrical/electronics engineering technology, engineering technology, industrial administration/management, interior design, mechanical engineering technology, and printing technology), HEALTH PROFESSIONS (community health work, exercise science, health, medical technology, nursing, recreation therapy, speech pathology/audiology, and sports medicine), SOCIAL SCIENCE (anthropology, child care/child and family studies, criminal justice, economics, family/consumer studies, food production/management/services, food science, geography, history, international studies, philosophy, political science/government, psychology, rural economics, social work, and sociology). Business, education, and nursing are the largest.

Required: All students must complete a total of 125 semester credit hours, including at least 30 in the major, with a minimum GPA of 2.0. Specific courses must be completed in English, math, history, humanities, science and technology, and social sciences, and a healthful living class, 2 physical activity courses, and an orientation course are also required

Special: GSU offers opportunities for study abroad, internships, work-study programs, B.A.-B.S. degrees, cooperative programs, a general studies degree, cross-registration with Georgia Tech and East Georgia College, a 3-2 engineering degree with Georgia Institute of Technology, pass/fail options, credit for military service, and nondegree study. There are 16 national honor societies, and a freshman honors program.

Faculty/Classroom: 53% of faculty are male; 47%, female. 95% teach undergraduates, 77% do research, and 72% do both. No introductory courses are taught by graduate students.

Admissions: 55% of the 2005-2006 applicants were accepted. The SAT scores for the 2005-2006 freshman class were: Verbal--19% below 500, 60% between 500 and 599, 19% between 600 and 700, and 2% above 700; Math--17% below 500, 58% between 500 and 599, 23% between 600 and 700, and 2% above 700. The ACT scores were 30% below 21, 42% between 21 and 23, 18% between 24 and 26, 4% between 27 and 28, and 3% above 28.

Requirements: A satisfactory score on the SAT or ACT is required. The ACT Optional Writing test is also required. In addition, a high school diploma or the equivalent are required. A minimum of 18 credits in college preparatory courses should include 4 each in English and math, 3 each in social studies and science, 2 in a foreign language, and 2 additional courses. A GPA of 2.0 is required. AP and CLEP credits are accepted.

Procedure: Freshmen are admitted to all sessions. Entrance exams should be taken during the junior year. There is a rolling admissions and a deferred admissions plan. Applications should be filed by July 1 for fall entry, December 1 for spring entry, and May 1 for summer entry, along with a $20 fee. Notification is sent on a rolling basis. Applications are accepted on-line.

Transfer: 752 transfer students enrolled in a recent year. Applicants must have completed at least 30 semester credit hours of college courses with a minimum GPA of 2.0. Those with fewer than 30 hours must meet freshman requirements. Students transferring with an associate degree must have a minimum GPA of 2.0 in a school with a parallel curriculum. 38 of 125 credits required for the bachelor's degree must be completed at Georgia Southern.

Visiting: There are regularly scheduled orientations for prospective students. There are guides for informal visits and visitors may stay overnight. To schedule a visit, contact the Office of Admissions at admissions@georgiasouthern.edu.

Financial Aid: In 2005-2006, 93% of all full-time freshmen and 84% of continuing full-time students received some form of financial aid. 46% of full-time freshmen and 43% of continuing full-time students received need-based aid. The average freshman award was $6148. Need-based scholarships or need-based grants averaged $4871; need-based self-help aid (loans and jobs) averaged $2431; non-need-based athletic scholarships averaged $4677; and other non-need-based awards and non-need-based scholarships averaged $1348. The average financial indebtedness of the 2005 graduate was $17,913. Georgia Southern is a member of CSS. The FAFSA is required. The priority date for freshman financial aid applications for fall entry is March 31. The deadline for filing freshman financial aid applications for fall entry is May 1.

International Students: There are 113 international students enrolled. The school actively recruits these students. They must score satisfactorily on the written or electronic version of the TOEFL. International students whose native language is not English, but whose secondary instruction was exclusively in English, must submit satisfactory SAT or ACT scores.

Computers: Wireless access is available. All students can access the Internet in campus computing labs or their residence hall rooms. We have approximately 1600 lab computers available for student use on campus. All students may access the system 24 hours a day. There are no time limits and no fees.

Graduates: From July 1, 2004 to June 30, 2005, 2172 bachelor's degrees were awarded. The most popular majors were business/marketing (29%), education (11%), and health professions and related sciences (7%). In an average class, 1% graduate in 3 years or less, 12% graduate in 4 years or less, 34% graduate in 5 years or less, and 41% graduate in 6 years or less. 94 companies recruited on campus in 2004-2005.

Admissions Contact: Admissioins Officer. A video is available.
E-mail: admissions@georgiasouthern.edu
Web: http://admissions.georgiasouthern.edu/

GEORGIA SOUTHWESTERN STATE UNIVERSITY   B-4
Americus, GA 31709

(912) 928-1273
(800) 338-0082; Fax: (912) 931-2983

Full-time: 550 men, 900 women	**Faculty:** 128; IIA, --$
Part-time: 170 men, 335 women	**Ph.D.s:** 72%
Graduate: 110 men, 490 women	**Student/Faculty:** 11 to 1
Year: semesters, summer session	**Tuition:** $2240 ($8030)
Application Deadline: see profile	**Room & Board:** $3795
Freshman Class: n/av	
SAT or ACT: required	**COMPETITIVE**

Georgia Southwestern State University, founded in 1906, is a liberal arts, professional and teachers college that is part of the public University System of Georgia. There are 5 undergraduate and 4 graduate schools. Figures in the above capsule and profile are approximate. In addition to regional accreditation, GSW has baccalaureate program accreditation with NCATE and NLN. The library contains 190,000 volumes, 618,842 microform items, and 1849 audio/video tapes/CDs/DVDs, and subscribes to 825 periodicals including electronic. Computerized library services include the card catalog, interlibrary loans, and database searching. Special learning facilities include a learning resource center, art gallery, and TV station. The 225-acre campus is in a small town 38 miles north of Albany. Including any residence halls, there are 37 buildings.

Student Life: 95% of undergraduates are from Georgia. Others are from 18 states, 33 foreign countries, and Canada. 70% are from public schools. 72% are white; 25% African American. The average age of freshmen is 20; all undergraduates, 22. 27% do not continue beyond their first year; 25% remain to graduate.

Housing: 597 students can be accommodated in college housing, which includes single-sex dorms. In addition, there are special-interest houses and independent fraternity and sorority houses. On-campus housing is guaranteed for all 4 years. 62% of students commute. All students may keep cars.

Activities: 13% of men belong to 7 national fraternities; 15% of women belong to 8 national sororities. There are 55 groups on campus, including art, band, cheerleading, choir, chorale, chorus, computers, dance, drama, ethnic, forensics, Habitat for Humanity, honors, international, jazz band, literary magazine, musical theater, newspaper, nursing, orchestra, photography, political, radio and TV, religious, social, social service, and student government. Popular campus events include Convocation Series.

Sports: There are 3 intercollegiate sports for men and 4 for women, and 9 intramural sports for men and 9 for women. Facilities include 2 gyms, tennis courts, an indoor/outdoor pool, a lake for canoeing, and playing fields for baseball, softball, football, and soccer. The larger gym seats 3000; the smaller seats 500.

Disabled Students: 85% of the campus is accessible. Wheelchair ramps, elevators, special parking, specially equipped rest rooms, special class scheduling, lowered drinking fountains, and accessible dorms are available.

Services: Counseling and information services are available, as is tutoring in most subjects. There is a reader service for the blind, and remedial math, reading, and writing.

Campus Safety and Security: Measures include 24-hour foot and vehicle patrol, self-defense education, security escort services, and informal discussions. There are pamphlets/posters/films, emergency telephones, and lighted pathways/sidewalks.

Programs of Study: GSW confers B.A., B.S., B.A.S., B.B.A., B.F.A., B.S. Ed., and B.S.N. degrees. Associate and master's degrees are also awarded. Bachelor's degrees are awarded in BIOLOGICAL SCIENCE (biology/biological science), BUSINESS (accounting, business administration and management, and marketing/retailing/merchandising), COMMUNICATIONS AND THE ARTS (English, fine arts, and music), COMPUTER AND PHYSICAL SCIENCE (chemistry, computer programming, computer science, geology, and mathematics), EDUCATION (art, business, early childhood, elementary, English, foreign languages, mathematics, middle school, music, recreation, science, secondary, social science, and special), ENGINEERING AND ENVIRONMENTAL DESIGN (computer technology), HEALTH PROFESSIONS (nursing), SOCIAL SCIENCE (history, political science/government, psychology, and sociology). Geology, preprofessional health and nursing, and education are the strongest academically. Business, education, and nursing are the largest.

Required: To graduate, students must complete 120 credit hours, including 18 in the major, with a minimum GPA of 2.0. The core curriculum consists of 12 hours each in English and the humanities, science, math, and social science. The student must also complete 4 courses in health and phys ed, including swimming, and pass tests in reading, writing, and geography.

Special: The college offers a 3-2 engineering degree with the Georgia Institute of Technology, cooperative programs with the South Georgia Technical School, a 2-2 degree program in nursing, internships through the Governor's Intern Program, study abroad, and credit for military phys ed and training. There are 15 national honor societies, a freshman honors program, and 1 departmental honors program.

Faculty/Classroom: 56% of faculty are male; 44%, female. All teach undergraduates and 25% do research. No introductory courses are taught by graduate students. The average class size in an introductory lecture is 22; in a laboratory, 19; and in a regular course, 18.

Requirements: The SAT or ACT is required, but the SAT is preferred. Those with low scores may gain acceptance through the Developmental Studies Program. Students must be graduates of an accredited secondary school or have a GED certificate. The college requires 16 academic credits and 21 Carnegie units, based on 4 years of English, 3 of science and 4 of math, 2 each of history and a foreign language, and 1 of social studies. An art portfolio and a music audition are recommended for appropriate majors. A GPA of 2.0 is required. AP and CLEP credits are accepted. Important factors in the admissions decision are advanced placement or honor courses, evidence of special talent, and geographic diversity.

Procedure: Freshmen are admitted to all sessions. There is a rolling admissions plan. Entrance exams should be taken before the end of the senior year. Check with the school for application deadlines. Applications are accepted on-line. The fall 2005 application fee was $20.

Transfer: Applicants should be in good standing at their former institutions. Those with fewer than 30 hours of transfer credit must meet freshman requirements. 30 of 120 credits required for the bachelor's degree must be completed at GSW.

Visiting: There are regularly scheduled orientations for prospective students. There are guides for informal visits and visitors may sit in on classes and stay overnight. To schedule a visit, contact the Admissions Office.

Financial Aid: The FAFSA is required. Check with the school for current application deadlines.

International Students: The school actively recruits these students. They must score satisfactorily on the written TOEFL or on the electronic version.

Computers: All students may access the system 8 A.M. to 12 midnight Monday through Friday and selected hours on weekends. There are no time limits and no fees.

Admissions Contact: Gary Fallis, Director of Admissions. A video is available. E-mail: *gswapps@canes.gsw.edu* Web: *www.gsw.edu*

GEORGIA STATE UNIVERSITY   B-2

Atlanta, GA 30302-3999	(404) 651-2365; Fax: (404) 651-4811
Full-time: 5451 men, 8301 women	**Faculty:** 695; I, --$
Part-time: 2016 men, 3192 women	**Ph.D.s:** 85%
Graduate: 2880 men, 4105 women	**Student/Faculty:** 20 to 1
Year: semesters, summer session	**Tuition:** $4464 ($15,378)
Application Deadline: March 1	**Room & Board:** $6980
Freshman Class: n/av	
SAT or ACT: required	**VERY COMPETITIVE**

Georgia State University, founded in 1913 and a part of the University System of Georgia, is a public residential university offering programs in liberal arts and sciences, business administration, education, law, health sciences, and public policy. There are 5 undergraduate and 6 graduate schools. In addition to regional accreditation, Georgia State has baccalaureate program accreditation with AACSB, ABA, ACS, APA, ADA, APTA, CACREP, CADE, CAHEA, CAPTE, CSWE, NASAD, NASM, NCATE, and NLN. The 2 libraries contain 1,420,068 volumes, 1,695,822 microform items, and 22,551 audio/video tapes/CDs/DVDs, and subscribe to 7788 periodicals including electronic. Computerized library services include interlibrary loans, database searching, Internet access, and laptop Internet portals. Special learning facilities include a learning resource center, art gallery, radio station, TV station, digital arts lab, observatory, instructional technology center, and distance learning classrooms. The 33-acre campus is in an urban area in downtown Atlanta. Including any residence halls, there are 46 buildings.

Student Life: 92% of undergraduates are from Georgia. Others are from 48 states, 139 foreign countries, and Canada. 37% are white; 31% African American; 10% Asian American. The average age of freshmen is 20; all undergraduates, 24. 24% do not continue beyond their first year; 44% remain to graduate.

Housing: 2435 students can be accommodated in college housing, which includes coed on-campus apartments. In addition, there are honors houses and special-interest houses. On-campus housing is available on a first-come, first-served basis. 90% of students commute. All students may keep cars.

Activities: 3% of men belong to 10 national fraternities; 4% of women belong to 11 national sororities. There are 203 groups on campus, including art, band, cheerleading, chess, chorale, chorus, computers, dance, debate, drama, ethnic, film, gay, honors, international, jazz band, literary magazine, musical theater, newspaper, opera, orchestra, outdoor, pep band, photography, political, professional, radio and TV, religious, social, social service, and student government. Popular campus events include International Student Festival, Honors Day, and Greek Week.

Sports: There are 7 intercollegiate sports for men and 8 for women, and 30 intramural sports for men and 30 for women. Facilities include a phys ed complex with 3 gyms, a pool, a diving well, a weight room, indoor and outdoor tennis courts, a climbing wall, a jogging track, exercise rooms, a dance studio, and racquetball courts; the Indian Creek recreation area with a pool, 3 tennis courts, picnic facilities, regular and sand volleyball, basketball courts, and a rope challenge course; and the Panthersville Road athletic fields.

Disabled Students: All of the campus is accessible. Wheelchair ramps, elevators, special parking, specially equipped rest rooms, special class scheduling, lowered drinking fountains, and lowered telephones are available.

Services: Counseling and information services are available, as is tutoring in most subjects. There is a reader service for the blind, and remedial

math, reading, and writing. Programs are available in effective studying, reading comprehension, speed reading, test and note taking, test anxiety, fear of public speaking, and organization and planning.

Campus Safety and Security: Measures include 24-hour foot and vehicle patrol, self-defense education, security escort services, and shuttle buses. There are informal discussions, pamphlets/posters/films, emergency telephones, lighted pathways/sidewalks, 24-hour security at university housing, and a bicycle patrol.

Programs of Study: Georgia State confers B.A., B.S., B.B.A., B.F.A., B.I.S., B.M., B.S.Ed., and B.S.W. degrees. Master's and doctoral degrees are also awarded. Bachelor's degrees are awarded in BIOLOGICAL SCIENCE (biology/biological science and nutrition), BUSINESS (accounting, banking and finance, business administration and management, business economics, hospitality management services, insurance and risk management, management information systems, marketing/retailing/merchandising, office supervision and management, and real estate), COMMUNICATIONS AND THE ARTS (art, art history and appreciation, classics, English, film arts, fine arts, French, German, journalism, music, music business management, Spanish, speech/debate/rhetoric, and studio art), COMPUTER AND PHYSICAL SCIENCE (actuarial science, chemistry, computer science, geology, mathematics, physics, and statistics), EDUCATION (art, early childhood, and physical), HEALTH PROFESSIONS (exercise science, nursing, and respiratory therapy), SOCIAL SCIENCE (African American studies, anthropology, criminal justice, economics, geography, history, interdisciplinary studies, philosophy, political science/government, psychology, religious education, social work, sociology, urban studies, and women's studies). Biological sciences, psychology, and management are the largest.

Required: Students must complete distribution requirements, including courses in English composition, humanities, natural science and math, social science, U.S. history, and political science. A minimum of 120 hours must be completed for graduation with a minimum GPA of 2.0.

Special: There is cross-registration with the Atlanta Regional Consortium for Higher Education (ARCHE). Internships with numerous employers and government agencies can be arranged. Study abroad is available in various countries. Work-study, an accelerated degree program in nursing, and dual majors are available. The Summer Scholar program allows high school seniors to take college-level course work. There is a freshman honors program.

Faculty/Classroom: 56% of faculty are male; 44%, female.

Requirements: The SAT or ACT is required. The ACT Optional Writing Test is also required. Applicants must graduate from a regionally accredited high school. A total of 16 academic credits is required. Students should prepare with 4 years each of English and math, 3 years each of science and social science, and 2 years of the same foreign language. Students must have a minimum 2.8 high school grade point average calculated on the required 16 courses listed above. A GPA of 2.8 is required. AP and CLEP credits are accepted. Important factors in the admissions decision are evidence of special talent, advanced placement or honor courses, and extracurricular activities record.

Procedure: Freshmen are admitted fall, spring, and summer. Entrance exams should be taken during the first semester of the senior year. There is a rolling admissions plan. Applications should be filed by March 1 for fall entry, October 1 for spring entry, and March 1 for summer entry, along with a $50 fee. Notification is sent on a rolling basis beginning October 1. Applications are accepted on-line.

Transfer: 1962 transfer students enrolled in 2004-2005. Transfer applicants must submit official transcripts of all college-level work, have a minimum GPA of 2.5, have earned 30 semester hours, and be in good academic standing. Those with fewer than 30 semester hours earned must meet freshman requirements. 39 of 120 credits required for the bachelor's degree must be completed at Georgia State.

Visiting: There are guides for informal visits and visitors may sit in on classes. To schedule a visit, contact Susan Goodroe, Welcome Center at (404) 651-3900 or sgoodroe@gsu.edu.

Financial Aid: In 2005-2006, 95% of all full-time freshmen and 69% of continuing full-time students received some form of financial aid. 59% of full-time freshmen and 54% of continuing full-time students received need-based aid. The average freshman award was $8641. Need-based scholarships or need-based grants averaged $3227; need-based self-help aid (loans and jobs) averaged $2867; and non-need-based athletic scholarships averaged $2222. 5% of undergraduates work part time. The average financial indebtedness of the 2005 graduate was $11,753. The FAFSA is required. The priority date for freshman financial aid applications for fall entry is April 1. The deadline for filing freshman financial aid applications for fall entry is November 1.

International Students: There are 1059 international students enrolled. The school actively recruits these students. They must take the TOEFL and also take the college's own test. If the TOEFL is not taken, students may take the GSTEP with a passing score of 6, or the SAT with satisfactory verbal score, or the ACT with an English subtest score of 17. Nonnative English speakers must demonstrate sufficient English language proficiency.

Computers: Wireless access is available. The Georgia State University Wireless Communication Infrastructure (CatChat) is designed and imple-

mented as an adjunct to the existing wired data network. Georgia State's open access computer labs are available to all Georgia State faculty, staff, and students. Users are required to enter a password to gain access to workstations and the campus network. There are open-access PC labs in 6 buildings. Additionally, Georgia State maintains 15 classrooms with PC workstations. These rooms have between 27 and 54 PCs installed for student use during class. All students may access the system 24 hours per day. There are no time limits and no fees. It is strongly recommended that all students have a personal computer. Students in Computer Information Systems (CIS) must have personal computers.

Graduates: From July 1, 2004 to June 30, 2005, 3337 bachelor's degrees were awarded. The most popular majors were management (7%), marketing (6%), and journalism (6%). In an average class, 1% graduate in 3 years or less, 13% graduate in 4 years or less, 19% graduate in 5 years or less, and 39% graduate in 6 years or less.

Admissions Contact: Gretchen Young, Associate Director.
E-mail: *admissions@gsu.edu* Web: *www.gsu.edu*

KENNESAW STATE UNIVERSITY   B-2

Kennesaw, GA 30144-5591   (770) 423-6300; Fax: (770) 423-6541

Full-time: 4503 men, 6908 women	**Faculty:** 442; IIA, --$
Part-time: 1957 men, 3371 women	**Ph.D.s:** 74%
Graduate: 681 men, 1136 women	**Student/Faculty:** 26 to 1
Year: semesters, summer session	**Tuition:** $3044 ($10,360)
Application Deadline: see profile	**Room & Board:** $9108
Freshman Class: 6658 applied, 4119 accepted, 2348 enrolled	
SAT Verbal/Math: 535/532*	**ACT:** required **COMPETITIVE**

Kennesaw State University, founded in 1963, is a 4-year public college in the University System of Georgia. There are 6 undergraduate and 4 graduate schools. In addition to regional accreditation, Kennesaw State has baccalaureate program accreditation with AACSB, NASM, NCATE, and NLN. The library contains 550,000 volumes, 1,723,000 microform items, and 9500 audio/video tapes/CDs/DVDs, and subscribes to 4202 periodicals including electronic. Computerized library services include the card catalog, interlibrary loans, and database searching. Special learning facilities include a learning resource center and art gallery. The 185-acre campus is in a suburban area 25 miles north of Atlanta. Including all residence halls, there are 25 buildings.

Student Life: 96% of undergraduates are from Georgia. Students are from 31 states, 129 foreign countries, and Canada. 80% are white; 11% African American. The average age of freshmen is 21; all undergraduates, 25. 30% do not continue beyond their first year.

Housing: 1058 students can be accommodated in college housing, which includes coed on-campus apartments. On-campus housing is available on a first-come, first-served basis. 94% of students commute. Alcohol is not permitted. All students may keep cars.

Activities: 1% of men belong to 3 national fraternities; 7% of women belong to 6 national sororities. There are 112 groups on campus, including art, band, cheerleading, choir, chorale, chorus, computers, drama, ethnic, gay, honors, international, jazz band, literary magazine, newspaper, opera, pep band, political, professional, religious, social, social service, student government, symphony, and yearbook. Popular campus events include KSU Day, Black History Month, and KSU Turkey Trout.

Sports: There are 4 intercollegiate sports for men and 4 for women, and 16 intramural sports for men and 16 for women. Facilities include a gym, a pool, tennis and racquetball courts, and baseball, softball, and soccer fields.

Disabled Students: All of the campus is accessible. Wheelchair ramps, elevators, special parking, specially equipped rest rooms, special class scheduling, lowered drinking fountains, lowered telephones, marked crosswalks with curb cuts, adapted computer equipment with voice synthesizer, a voice-activated computer, screen-enlarging programs, a swimming pool lift, microfilm and microfiche facilities for wheelchair-bound and blind students, a brailler, and enlarged-print machines are available.

Services: Counseling and information services are available, as is tutoring in some subjects, including math, foreign languages, and English. There is a reader service for the blind, and remedial math, reading, and writing.

Campus Safety and Security: Measures include 24-hour foot and vehicle patrol, self-defense education, security escort services, and informal discussions. There are pamphlets/posters/films, emergency telephones, and lighted pathways/sidewalks.

Programs of Study: Kennesaw State confers B.A., B.S., B.B.A., B.F.A., and B.M. degrees. Master's degrees are also awarded. Bachelor's degrees are awarded in BIOLOGICAL SCIENCE (biochemistry, biology/biological science, and biotechnology), BUSINESS (accounting, banking and finance, business economics, management science, marketing/retailing/merchandising, purchasing/inventory management, and sports management), COMMUNICATIONS AND THE ARTS (art, communications, dramatic arts, English, French, music, music performance, and Spanish), COMPUTER AND PHYSICAL SCIENCE (chemistry, computer science, information sciences and systems, and mathematics), EDUCATION (art, early childhood, elementary, English, foreign languages, health, mathematics, middle school, music, physical, science, and social studies), HEALTH PROFESSIONS (nursing), SOCIAL SCIENCE (criminal justice, geography, history, human services, international studies, political science/government, psychology, and sociology). Business, psychology, and education are the strongest academically. Business and education are the largest.

Required: Requirements vary by degree program. Generally, all students must complete 123 semester hours, including 45 to 47 in core curriculum courses and 39 in upper-level courses, with a minimum GPA of 2.0 and grades of C or better in the major and in required English courses. Students must also successfully complete the University System of Georgia Regents' Testing Program and demonstrate (by course or exam) competency in the history and constitutions of the United States and Georgia. 3 hours of Fitness for Living is also required.

Special: Students may register for courses with any of the colleges in the University System of Georgia, study abroad in 2 countries, and participate in work-study programs and internships, some with pass/fail options. Dual majors and nondegree programs also are offered. There are 23 national honor societies, a freshman honors program, and 7 departmental honors programs.

Faculty/Classroom: 50% of faculty are male; 50%, female. 10% both teach and do research. No introductory courses are taught by graduate students. The average class size in an introductory lecture is 38; in a laboratory, 32; and in a regular course, 32.

Admissions: 62% of the 2005-2006 applicants were accepted. The SAT scores for the 2005-2006 freshman class were: Verbal--27% below 500, 57% between 500 and 599, 15% between 600 and 700, and 1% above 700; Math--28% below 500, 58% between 500 and 599, 13% between 600 and 700, and 1% above 700.

Requirements: The SAT or ACT is required. In addition, applicants should be graduates of accredited secondary schools. Secondary preparation should include 4 units of English, 4 of math, 3 of social science, 3 of science, and 2 of a foreign language. A GPA of 2.5 is required. AP and CLEP credits are accepted. Important factors in the admissions decision are advanced placement or honor courses, ability to finance college education, and recommendations by alumni.

Procedure: Freshmen are admitted fall, spring, and summer. There is a rolling admissions plan. Entrance exams should be taken before June 1. Notification is sent on a rolling basis. Applications are accepted online. The fall 2005 application fee was $40. Check with the school for current application deadlines.

Transfer: 1308 transfer students enrolled in 2004-2005. Applicants should have completed 30 semester hours with a GPA of 2.0 or above; those with a lower GPA may be admitted on probation. Grades of D or better (C or better in English) may be transferred by those with a 2.0 cumulative GPA. Students with fewer than 30 hours of credit must meet freshman requirements. 30 of 123 credits required for the bachelor's degree must be completed at Kennesaw State.

Visiting: There are regularly scheduled orientations for prospective students, including Insight Sessions every Tuesday at 4 P.M. and special visits for adult students. There are guides for informal visits. To schedule a visit, contact the Admissions Office.

Financial Aid: The FAFSA is required. Check with the school for current application deadlines.

International Students: In a recent year, there were 1472 international students enrolled. The school actively recruits these students. They must score satisfactory on the electronic TOEFL or take ESL level 109. They must also take the SAT or the ACT.

Computers: All students may access the system 24 hours a day. There are no time limits and no fees.

Admissions Contact: Joe F. Head, Dean of Enrollment Services. A video is available. E-mail: ksuadmit@kennesaw.edu
Web: www.kennesaw.edu

LAGRANGE COLLEGE   A-3
LaGrange, GA 30240

(706) 880-8253
(800) 593-2885; Fax: (706) 880-8010

Full-time: 355 men, 543 women	**Faculty:** 65; IIB, -$
Part-time: 25 men, 63 women	**Ph.D.s:** 82%
Graduate: 16 men, 44 women	**Student/Faculty:** 14 to 1
Year: 4-1-4, summer session	**Tuition:** $16,200
Application Deadline: open	**Room & Board:** $6674
Freshman Class: 1267 applied, 625 accepted, 204 enrolled	
SAT Verbal/Math: 515/500*	**ACT:** 21 COMPETITIVE+

LaGrange College, founded in 1831, is a private liberal arts institution affiliated with the United Methodist Church. Major undergraduate programs include business, art, education, biology, and psychology. In addition to regional accreditation, LaGrange has baccalaureate program accreditation with ACBSP and NLN. The library contains 213,531 volumes, 171,948 microform items, and 4173 audio/video tapes/CDs/DVDs, and subscribes to 378 periodicals including electronic. Computerized library services include the card catalog, interlibrary loans, database searching, and Internet access. Special learning facilities include a learn-

ing resource center, art gallery, 2 music technology labs, and a performing arts theater. The 85-acre campus is in a small town 70 miles southwest of Atlanta. Including any residence halls, there are 22 buildings.

Student Life: 89% of undergraduates are from Georgia. Others are from 15 states and 17 foreign countries. 74% are white; 21% African American. 49% are Protestant; 33% claim no religious affiliation. The average age of freshmen is 18; all undergraduates, 21. 23% do not continue beyond their first year; 49% remain to graduate.

Housing: 656 students can be accommodated in college housing, which includes single-sex and coed dorms and on-campus apartments. On-campus housing is guaranteed for all 4 years. 55% of students commute. Alcohol is not permitted. All students may keep cars.

Activities: 37% of men belong to 3 national fraternities; 28% of women belong to 4 national sororities. There are 48 groups on campus, including art, cheerleading, choir, drama, ethnic, film, honors, international, jazz band, literary magazine, opera, photography, political, professional, religious, social, social service, and student government. Popular campus events include Family Weekend, Greek Week, and Celebrate the Servant Week.

Sports: There are 7 intercollegiate sports for men and 7 for women, and 7 intramural sports for men and 7 for women. Facilities include a fitness center, West Point Lake, an auditorium, indoor and outdoor pools, 3 gyms, 10 lighted tennis courts, and lighted softball, baseball, and soccer fields.

Disabled Students: 75% of the campus is accessible. Wheelchair ramps, elevators, special parking, specially equipped rest rooms, special class scheduling, and lowered drinking fountains are available.

Services: Counseling and information services are available, as is tutoring in most subjects.

Campus Safety and Security: Measures include 24-hour foot and vehicle patrol, pamphlets/posters/films, lighted pathways/sidewalks, and safety awareness seminars during freshman orientation.

Programs of Study: LaGrange confers B.A., B.S., B.B.A., and B.S.N. degrees. Associate and master's degrees are also awarded. Bachelor's degrees are awarded in BIOLOGICAL SCIENCE (biochemistry and biology/biological science), BUSINESS (accounting and business administration and management), COMMUNICATIONS AND THE ARTS (art, dramatic arts, English, fine arts, music, music performance, music technology, and Spanish), COMPUTER AND PHYSICAL SCIENCE (chemistry, computer science, and mathematics), EDUCATION (early childhood and middle school), HEALTH PROFESSIONS (nursing, predentistry, and premedicine), SOCIAL SCIENCE (history, human services, political science/government, prelaw, psychology, religion, religious music, and social work). Business administration, human services, and nursing are the largest.

Required: To graduate, all students must complete 108 semester hours, including 60 in the major. The core curriculum includes Freshman Cornerstone, rhetoric and composition, math, world languages and cultures, natural science, lab science, quantitative reasoning, humanities, fine arts, religion, and the American experience. All students must have a minimum GPA of 2.0.

Special: Internships are offered in business, social work, and political science, including positions in a Congressional office in Washington. Students may study abroad in Ireland, Great Britain, Japan, and France. There is an accelerated degree program in organizational leadership. A 3-2 engineering degree is offered with Georgia Institute of Technology and Auburn University. There are 12 national honor societies, a freshman honors program, and 8 departmental honors programs.

Faculty/Classroom: 54% of faculty are male; 46%, female. All teach undergraduates and 30% both teach and do research. No introductory courses are taught by graduate students. The average class size in an introductory lecture is 13; in a laboratory, 17; and in a regular course, 11.

Admissions: 49% of the 2005-2006 applicants were accepted. The SAT scores for the 2005-2006 freshman class were: Verbal--44% below 500, 42% between 500 and 599, 14% between 600 and 700, and 1% above 700; Math--44% below 500, 43% between 500 and 599, 11% between 600 and 700, and 2% above 700. The ACT scores were 50% below 21, 20% between 21 and 23, 20% between 24 and 26, and 11% between 27 and 28. 35% of the current freshmen were in the top fifth of their class; 69% were in the top two fifths.

Requirements: The SAT or ACT is required. In addition, applicants should be graduates of accredited secondary schools or have a GED certificate. They should have completed a minimum of 4 units of English, 3 of social studies, and 2 each of math and science. A GPA of 2.7 is required. AP credits are accepted. Important factors in the admissions decision are advanced placement or honor courses, leadership record, and personality/intangible qualities.

Procedure: Freshmen are admitted to all sessions. There is a deferred admissions plan and a rolling admissions plan. Application deadlines are open. Application fee is $20.

Transfer: 60 transfer students enrolled in 2004-2005. Transfer students must have a minimum 2.0 GPA and be in good standing with the previous college. 65 of 108 credits required for the bachelor's degree must be completed at LaGrange.

Visiting: There are regularly scheduled orientations for prospective students, including admissions workshops, a student panel, and a guided tour of the campus. There are guides for informal visits and visitors may sit in on classes and stay overnight. To schedule a visit, contact the Admission Office at (706) 880-8005 or *lgcadmis@lagrange.edu.*

Financial Aid: In 2005-2006, 74% of all full-time freshmen and 73% of continuing full-time students received some form of financial aid, including need-based aid. The average freshman award was $17,259. Need-based scholarships or need-based grants averaged $5673 ($13,050 maximum); need-based self-help aid (loans and jobs) averaged $3235 ($7170 maximum); and other non-need-based awards and non-need-based scholarships averaged $8703 ($22,875 maximum). 46% of undergraduates work part time. Average annual earnings from campus work are $1545. The average financial indebtedness of the 2005 graduate was $17,076. LaGrange is a member of CSS. The FAFSA and the college's own financial statement are required. The deadline for filing freshman financial aid applications for fall entry is May 1.

International Students: There are 30 international students enrolled. The school actively recruits these students. They must take the TOEFL.

Computers: Wireless access is available. All students may access the system 24 hours a day. There are no time limits and no fees.

Graduates: From July 1, 2004 to June 30, 2005, 199 bachelor's degrees were awarded. The most popular majors were business (41%), visual and performing arts (11%), and psychology (7%). In an average class, 40% graduate in 4 years or less, 43% graduate in 5 years or less, and 45% graduate in 6 years or less. 10 companies recruited on campus in 2004-2005.

Admissions Contact: Wells Shepard, Director of Admission. E-mail: *ageeter@lagrange.edu* Web: *www.lagrange.edu*

MERCER UNIVERSITY
Macon, GA 31207-0001

C-3

(478) 301-2650
(800) 840-8577; Fax: (478) 301-2828

Full-time: 1320 men, 2515 women	**Faculty:** 282; IIA, av$
Part-time: 210 men, 550 women	**Ph.Ds:** 92%
Graduate: 995 men, 1635 women	**Student/Faculty:** 14 to 1
Year: semesters, summer session	**Tuition:** $20,800
Application Deadline: see profile	**Room & Board:** $6725
Freshman Class: n/av	
SAT or ACT: required	**VERY COMPETITIVE+**

Mercer University, founded in 1833, is a private institution affiliated with the Georgia Baptist Convention. The university offers degree programs in liberal arts, business and economics, education, engineering, and professional studies. Mercer also offers a Great Books program as an alternative to the traditional core curriculum. Figures in the above capsule and in this profile are approximate. There are 5 undergraduate and 7 graduate schools. In addition to regional accreditation, Mercer has baccalaureate program accreditation with ABET, CSAB, and NASM. The 2 libraries contain 418,865 volumes, 3,055,812 microform items, and 57,166 audio/video tapes/CDs/DVDs. Computerized library services include the card catalog, interlibrary loans, and database searching. Special learning facilities include a learning resource center. The 130-acre campus is in a suburban area 85 miles south of Atlanta. Including any residence halls, there are 58 buildings.

Student Life: 77% of undergraduates are from Georgia. Others are from 35 states, 48 foreign countries, and Canada. 73% are white; 19% African American. 62% are Protestant; 19% claim no religious affiliation; 9% Catholic. The average age of freshmen is 18; all undergraduates, 20. 24% do not continue beyond their first year.

Housing: 1208 students can be accommodated in college housing, which includes single-sex and coed dorms, on-campus apartments, married-student housing, fraternity houses, and sorority houses. On-campus housing is guaranteed for the freshman year only, is available on a first-come, first-served basis, and is available on a lottery system for upperclassmen. Priority is given to out-of-town students. 60% of students live on campus; of those, 70% remain on campus on weekends. Alcohol is not permitted. All students may keep cars.

Activities: 15% of men belong to 9 national fraternities; 20% of women belong to 1 local and 7 national sororities. There are 65 groups on campus, including bagpipe band, band, cheerleading, chess, choir, chorale, chorus, computers, dance, debate, drama, ethnic, honors, international, jazz band, literary magazine, musical theater, newspaper, opera, pep band, political, professional, religious, social, social service, student government, and yearbook. Popular campus events include Pilgrimage to Penfield, Spring Concert, and Family Weekend.

Sports: There are 7 intercollegiate sports for men and 7 for women, and 10 intramural sports for men and 10 for women. Facilities include 2 gyms, 3 playing fields, a student center, a swimming pool, a 30-station fitness trail, a lighted intramural complex, and tennis, volleyball, and racquetball courts.

Disabled Students: 85% of the campus is accessible. Wheelchair ramps, elevators, special parking, specially equipped rest rooms, special

class scheduling, lowered drinking fountains, lowered telephones, and assistance with registration are available.

Services: Counseling and information services are available, as is tutoring in most subjects. There is a reader service for the blind, and remedial math, reading, and writing.

Campus Safety and Security: Measures include 24-hour foot and vehicle patrol, self-defense education, security escort services, and shuttle buses. There are informal discussions, pamphlets/posters/films, emergency telephones, lighted pathways/sidewalks, and external CCTV cameras monitored by the police department.

Programs of Study: Mercer confers B.A., B.S., B.B.A., B.M., B.M.D., B.M.E., B.S.E., B.S.M., and B.S.N. degrees. Master's and doctoral degrees are also awarded. Bachelor's degrees are awarded in BIOLOGICAL SCIENCE (biology/biological science), BUSINESS (accounting, banking and finance, business administration and management, and marketing/retailing/merchandising), COMMUNICATIONS AND THE ARTS (English, French, German, Greek, Latin, music, and Spanish), COMPUTER AND PHYSICAL SCIENCE (chemistry, computer science, mathematics, natural sciences, and physics), EDUCATION (early childhood, elementary, music, secondary, and special), ENGINEERING AND ENVIRONMENTAL DESIGN (biomedical engineering, electrical/electronics engineering, environmental engineering, industrial engineering, and mechanical engineering), HEALTH PROFESSIONS (predentistry, premedicine, and prepharmacy), SOCIAL SCIENCE (economics, history, philosophy, political science/government, prelaw, psychology, religion, social science, and sociology). Engineering, chemistry, and English are the strongest academically. Business, English, and engineering are the largest.

Required: To graduate, all students must complete at least 120 to 128 semester hours with a minimum GPA of 2.0.

Special: Mercer offers co-op programs in all majors, cross-registration with Wesleyan and Macon State Colleges, B.A.-B.S. degrees in various science and math fields, internships, student-designed majors, work-study programs, and satisfactory-unsatisfactory options for elective courses. Students may study abroad in Spain, France, Great Britain, Australia, Hong Kong, and Morocco. There are 2 national honor societies, a freshman honors program, and 20 departmental honors programs.

Faculty/Classroom: 61% of faculty are male; 39%, female. All teach undergraduates. No introductory courses are taught by graduate students. The average class size in an introductory lecture is 21; in a laboratory, 15; and in a regular course, 17.

Requirements: The SAT or ACT is required. In addition, applicants must be graduates of an accredited secondary school and have completed 16 academic units. Students should submit their transcript and class rank, a recommendation from a guidance counselor, and a list of extracurricular activities, including employment. A GPA of 3.0 is required. AP and CLEP credits are accepted. Important factors in the admissions decision are advanced placement or honor courses, extracurricular activities record, and evidence of special talent.

Procedure: Freshmen are admitted to all sessions. Entrance exams should be taken in the spring of the junior year or fall of the senior year. There are early admissions, deferred admissions, and rolling admissions plans. Check with the school for application deadlines. The fall 2005 application fee was $50.

Transfer: A minimum GPA of 2.0 is required for all transfer students. Applicants with fewer than 9 semester hours must meet freshman entrance requirements. Those with fewer than 20 semester hours must submit a high school transcript and SAT or ACT scores, and those with more than 20 semester hours must submit transcripts from all colleges attended and be in good academic standing at their present school, or present evidence of satisfactory work in a previously attended college. 30 of 120 credits required for the bachelor's degree must be completed at Mercer.

Visiting: There are regularly scheduled orientations for prospective students, including 26 regional orientation programs in the spring, 3 preorientation sessions during the summer, and a 4-day orientation prior to the beginning of classes. There are guides for informal visits and visitors may sit in on classes and stay overnight. To schedule a visit, contact the Office of Admissions.

Financial Aid: The FAFSA and the college's own financial statement are required. Check with the school for current application deadlines.

International Students: The school actively recruits these students. They must score satisfactorily on the written TOEFL or take Mercer's ELI exit examination. They must also take the SAT or the ACT.

Computers: All students may access the system 24 hours per day if they have dial-in access. There are no time limits and no fees. It is strongly recommended that all students have a personal computer.

Admissions Contact: Allen S. London, Vice President for University Admissions. A video is available. E-mail: *admissions@mercer.edu* Web: *www.mercer.edu* .

MOREHOUSE COLLEGE   B-2

Atlanta, GA 30314   (404) 215-2632
                                    (800) 851-1254; Fax: (404) 524-5635

Full-time: 2856 men	Faculty: 176; IIB, -$
Part-time: 172 men	Ph.D.s: 84%
Graduate: none	Student/Faculty: 16 to 1
Year: semesters, summer session	Tuition: $16,016
Application Deadline: February 15	Room & Board: $9066
Freshman Class: 2520 applied, 1679 accepted, 661 enrolled	
SAT Verbal/Math: 565/523*	ACT: 21 COMPETITIVE

Morehouse College, founded in 1867, is a private men's liberal arts college offering undergraduate programs in the arts and humanities, natural sciences and math, and social sciences and business. In addition to regional accreditation, Morehouse has baccalaureate program accreditation with AACSB. The library contains 550,000 volumes, 15,000 microform items, and 8000 audio/video tapes/CDs/DVDs, and subscribes to 110 periodicals including electronic. Computerized library services include the card catalog, interlibrary loans, and database searching. Special learning facilities include a learning resource center and an academic support center. The 61-acre campus is in an urban area 3 miles southwest of downtown Atlanta. Including any residence halls, there are 36 buildings.

Student Life: 70% of undergraduates are from out of state, mostly the South. Others are from 45 states and 14 foreign countries. 80% are from public schools. 96% are African American. The average age of freshmen is 18; all undergraduates, 20. 15% do not continue beyond their first year; 55% remain to graduate.

Housing: 1676 students can be accommodated in college housing, which includes single-sex dorms and on-campus apartments. On-campus housing is guaranteed for the freshman year only, is available on a first-come, first-served basis, and is available on a lottery system for upperclassmen. 55% of students live on campus; of those, All remain on campus on weekends. Alcohol is not permitted. Upperclassmen may keep cars.

Activities: 3% of men belong to 6 national fraternities. There are no sororities. There are 60 groups on campus, including band, cheerleading, chess, choir, chorus, computers, dance, debate, drama, ethnic, gay, glee club, honors, international, jazz band, literary magazine, marching band, musical theater, newspaper, political, professional, religious, social, social service, speech, student government, and yearbook. Popular campus events include Founders Day, Religious Emphasis Week, and Parents Weekend.

Sports: Facilities include a comprehensive health and phys ed center, a 9000-seat football stadium, a track, and a 5700-seat basketball arena.

Disabled Students: 85% of the campus is accessible. Wheelchair ramps, elevators, special parking, specially equipped rest rooms, lowered drinking fountains, and lowered telephones are available.

Services: Counseling and information services are available, as is tutoring in most subjects. There is remedial math, reading, and writing.

Campus Safety and Security: Measures include 24-hour foot and vehicle patrol, security escort services, shuttle buses, and informal discussions. There are pamphlets/posters/films and lighted pathways/sidewalks.

Programs of Study: Morehouse confers B.A. and B.S. degrees. Bachelor's degrees are awarded in BIOLOGICAL SCIENCE (biology/biological science), BUSINESS (accounting, banking and finance, business administration and management, and marketing/retailing/merchandising), COMMUNICATIONS AND THE ARTS (art, English, French, German, music, and Spanish), COMPUTER AND PHYSICAL SCIENCE (chemistry, computer science, mathematics, and physics), EDUCATION (physical), SOCIAL SCIENCE (African American studies, economics, history, international relations, philosophy, political science/government, psychology, religion, sociology, and urban studies). Engineering, business administration, and English are the strongest academically. Business administration, psychology, and computer science are the largest.

Required: Students must complete a minimum of 120 semester hours, including 53 hours in general studies, plus 8 noncredit hours in Freshman Orientation and College Assembly. A 2.0 GPA is required, with no grade below C in the major.

Special: Morehouse is a member of the Atlanta University Center; students may register for courses at 4 of the 5 member institutions. They may complete a major at Spelman College, one of the 5 member institutions. Atlanta Regional Consortium for Higher Education (ARCHE) enables students to take courses at Atlanta regional colleges. In addition, students may study abroad in Europe or Africa. A dual-degree program is offered in architecture with the University of Michigan and in engineering with Columbia, Dartmouth, Georgia Tech, Rensselaer, and other schools; students in these programs are offered summer internships. Work study is also available. There are 6 national honor societies, including Phi Beta Kappa, a freshman honors program, and 10 departmental honors programs.

Faculty/Classroom: 68% of faculty are male; 32%, female. All teach undergraduates and 20% do research. The average class size in an introductory lecture is 25; in a laboratory, 30; and in a regular course, 20.

Admissions: 67% of the 2005-2006 applicants were accepted. The SAT scores for the 2005-2006 freshman class were: Verbal--38% below 500, 40% between 500 and 599, 21% between 600 and 700, and 1% above 700; Math--36% below 500, 41% between 500 and 599, 22% between 600 and 700, and 1% above 700. The ACT scores were 41% below 21, 28% between 21 and 23, 19% between 24 and 26, 9% between 27 and 28, and 3% above 28. 35% of the current freshmen were in the top fifth of their class; 65% were in the top two fifths. 3 freshmen graduated first in their class.

Requirements: The SAT or ACT is required. In addition, applicants should be graduates of accredited secondary schools or have the GED. Secondary preparation should include 4 units in English, 3 in math, 2 each in natural and social sciences, and 5 in other disciplines. Applicants must write an essay and are urged to seek an interview. A GPA of 2.8 is required. AP and CLEP credits are accepted. Important factors in the admissions decision are advanced placement or honor courses, leadership record, and recommendations by school officials.

Procedure: Freshmen are admitted fall and spring. Entrance exams should be taken by the fall of the senior year. There are early decision, early admissions, and deferred admissions plans. Early decision applications should be filed by October 15; regular applications, by February 15 for fall entry and October 15 for spring entry, along with a $45 fee. Notification of early decision is sent before the Winter Holiday break; regular decision, usually within 30 to 45 days of application . A waiting list is an active part of the admissions procedure. Applications are accepted online.

Transfer: 92 transfer students enrolled in 2004-2005. Transfer applicants must have at least a 2.5 GPA and a minimum of 26 semester hours of credit. 64 of 120 credits required for the bachelor's degree must be completed at Morehouse.

Visiting: There are regularly scheduled orientations for prospective students. There are guides for informal visits and visitors may sit in on classes. To schedule a visit, contact the Admissions Office at (800) 851-1254, ext. 2632.

Financial Aid: In 2005-2006, 55% of all full-time freshmen and 49% of continuing full-time students received some form of financial aid. 52% of full-time freshmen and 42% of continuing full-time students received need-based aid. The average freshman award was $5289. Need-based scholarships or need-based grants averaged $3819 ($7125 maximum); need-based self-help aid (loans and jobs) averaged $3088 ($6028 maximum); non-need-based athletic scholarships averaged $5670 ($9864 maximum); and other non-need-based awards and non-need-based scholarships averaged $6439 ($8903 maximum). 24% of undergraduates work part time. Average annual earnings from campus work are $1500. The average financial indebtedness of the 2005 graduate was $17,125. Morehouse is a member of CSS. The FAFSA and the college's own financial statement are required. The deadline for filing freshman financial aid applications for fall entry is April 1.

International Students: In a recent year, there were 100 international students enrolled. The school actively recruits these students. A satisfactory score is required on the written TOEFL.

Computers: Wireless access is available. There are 420 PCs in academic buildings. All students may access the system.

Graduates: From July 1, 2004 to June 30, 2005, 434 bachelor's degrees were awarded. The most popular majors were business administration (35%), biology (10%), and political science (8%). In an average class, 33% graduate in 4 years or less, 40% graduate in 5 years or less, and 50% graduate in 6 years or less. 60 companies recruited on campus in 2004-2005. Of the 2004 graduating class, 31% were enrolled in graduate school within 6 months of graduation and 58% were employed.

Admissions Contact: Terrance Dixon, Associate Dean, Admissions and Recruitment. E-mail: tdixon@morehouse.edu
Web: www.morehouse.edu

NORTH GEORGIA COLLEGE AND STATE   B-1
UNIVERSITY

Dahlonega, GA 30597   (706) 864-1754
                                    (800) 498-9581; Fax: (706) 864-1478

Full-time: 1270 men, 1885 women	Faculty: n/av
Part-time: 240 men, 570 women	Ph.D.s: 64%
Graduate: 140 men, 440 women	Student/Faculty: n/av
Year: semesters, summer session	Tuition: $2820 ($9450)
Application Deadline: see profile	Room & Board: $4180
Freshman Class: n/av	
SAT: required	ACT: not required COMPETITIVE

North Georgia College and State University, founded in 1873 as a military college, is today a liberal arts college that is part of the public University System of Georgia. One of 4 colleges in the United States classified as military colleges by the Department of the Army, the school requires all male resident students to join its Corps of Cadets; other students are given an option to join. There are 4 undergraduate schools and 1 graduate school. Figures in the above capsule and profile are approximate. In addition to regional accreditation, NGCSU has baccalaureate program accreditation with ACBSP, APTA, NCATE, and NLN. The 2 libraries contain 142,807 volumes, 774,482 microform items, and 3118 audio/video tapes/CDs/DVDs, and subscribe to 2546 periodicals including electronic. Computerized library services include the card catalog, interlibrary loans, database searching, and Internet access. Special learning facilities include an art gallery, planetarium, a math lab, a language lab, and a writing center. The 665-acre campus is in a small town 60 miles north of Atlanta. Including any residence halls, there are 25 buildings.

Student Life: 95% of undergraduates are from Georgia. Others are from 33 states, 8 foreign countries, and Canada. 90% are from public schools. 93% are white. The average age of freshmen is 19; all undergraduates, 22.

Housing: 1200 students can be accommodated in college housing, which includes single-sex dorms and on-campus apartments. On-campus housing is available on a first-come, first-served basis. 69% of students commute. Alcohol is not permitted. All students may keep cars.

Activities: 13% of men belong to 2 local and 4 national fraternities; 10% of women belong to 4 national sororities. There are 52 groups on campus, including band, cheerleading, choir, chorale, chorus, drama, drill team, ethnic, honors, jazz band, literary magazine, marching band, newspaper, pep band, political, professional, religious, student government, symphony, and yearbook. Popular campus events include Spring Jam, frisbee golf, and Military reviews.

Sports: There are 5 intercollegiate sports for men and 6 for women, and 7 intramural sports for men and 7 for women. Facilities include a swimming pool, a track, a fully equipped exercise room, a rappeling tower, a confidence course, a picnic area, a 2000-seat gym, and a 250-seat arena.

Disabled Students: 50% of the campus is accessible. Wheelchair ramps, elevators, special parking, specially equipped rest rooms, and lowered drinking fountains are available.

Services: Counseling and information services are available, as is tutoring in most subjects. There is a reader service for the blind, and remedial math, reading, and writing.

Campus Safety and Security: Measures include 24-hour foot and vehicle patrol, security escort services, informal discussions, and emergency telephones. There are lighted pathways/sidewalks.

Programs of Study: NGCSU confers A.B., B.S., B.B.A., and B.S.N. degrees. Associate and master's degrees are also awarded. Bachelor's degrees are awarded in BIOLOGICAL SCIENCE (biology/biological science), BUSINESS (accounting, banking and finance, business administration and management, business economics, marketing/retailing/merchandising, and recreation and leisure services), COMMUNICATIONS AND THE ARTS (art, arts administration/management, English, French, music, and Spanish), COMPUTER AND PHYSICAL SCIENCE (chemistry, computer science, mathematics, and physics), EDUCATION (art, early childhood, elementary, foreign languages, mathematics, middle school, music, physical, science, secondary, social science, and special), ENGINEERING AND ENVIRONMENTAL DESIGN (preengineering), HEALTH PROFESSIONS (nursing, predentistry, premedicine, prepharmacy, and preveterinary science), SOCIAL SCIENCE (criminal justice, history, political science/government, prelaw, psychology, social science, and sociology). Education and premedicine are the strongest academically. Business and teacher education are the largest.

Required: To graduate, students must complete 120 semester credit hours with a minimum GPA of 2.0. English, math, lab sciences, and social sciences are required.

Special: Special academic programs include a co-op program in business, internships, a 3-2 engineering degree with Georgia Institute of Technology, study abroad in Europe, South America, and Canada, dual majors, and credit for life, military, or work experience. There are 9 national honor societies, including Phi Beta Kappa, a freshman honors program, and 8 departmental honors programs.

Faculty/Classroom: 50% of faculty are male; 50%, female. All teach undergraduates. No introductory courses are taught by graduate students. The average class size in an introductory lecture is 30; in a laboratory, 30; and in a regular course, 30.

Requirements: The SAT is required. In addition, students must have graduated from a secondary school with 4 years of English, 3 each of math, science, and social science, and 2 of a foreign language. The GED is accepted if granted at least 5 years later than expected high school graduation date. SAT: Subject tests are required of home-schooled students. A GPA of 2.0 is required. AP and CLEP credits are accepted. Important factors in the admissions decision are leadership record, advanced placement or honor courses, and evidence of special talent.

Procedure: Freshmen are admitted fall, spring, and summer. Entrance exams should be taken in the junior year. There are deferred admissions and rolling admissions plans. Check with the school for application deadlines. The application fee is $25. Notification is sent on a rolling basis. Applications are accepted on-line.

Transfer: 270 transfer students enrolled in 2004-2005. Transfer students must have maintained a C average and a clear conduct record, and be in good academic standing. Those who have not completed 90

quarter hours of transferable credit must have completed the approved precollege curriculum and must submit high school transcripts and the SAT or ACT results. 45 of 120 credits required for the bachelor's degree must be completed at NGCSU.

Visiting: There are regularly scheduled orientations for prospective students, including an admissions video, college overview, tour, and a meeting with an admissions counselor. There are guides for informal visits and visitors may stay overnight. To schedule a visit, contact the Admissions Office.

Financial Aid: The FAFSA and the college's own financial statement are required. Check with the school for current application deadlines.

International Students: They must score satisfactorily on the written TOEFL or on the electronic version and also take the SAT or the ACT.

Computers: All students may access the system 8 A.M. to 10 P.M. There are no time limits and no fees.

Graduates: In a recent year, 691 bachelor's degrees were awarded. The most popular majors were nursing (16%), early childhood education (10%), and marketing (7%). 71 companies recruited on campus in a recent year. Of a recent graduating class, 6% were enrolled in graduate school within 6 months of graduation and 48% were employed.

Admissions Contact: Robert LaVerriere, Director of Undergraduate Admissions and Recruiting. A video is available.
E-mail: *rlaverriere@ngcsu.edu* Web: *www.ngcsu.edu*

OGLETHORPE UNIVERSITY
B-2
Atlanta, GA 30319-2797
(404) 364-8307
(800) 428-8491; Fax: (404) 364-8500

Full-time: 279 men, 505 women	Faculty: 57; IIB, av$
Part-time: 50 men, 111 women	Ph.D.s: 96%
Graduate: 20 men, 64 women	Student/Faculty: 14 to 1
Year: semesters, summer session	Tuition: $22,300
Application Deadline: open	Room & Board: $8000
Freshman Class: 1236 applied, 794 accepted, 233 enrolled	
SAT Verbal/Math: 560/540*	ACT: 25 VERY COMPETITIVE

Oglethorpe University, founded in 1835, is an independent institution offering programs in the liberal arts, sciences, business, and preprofessional studies. There are 2 undergraduate and 2 graduate schools. In addition to regional accreditation, Oglethorpe has baccalaureate program accreditation with NCATE. The library contains 125,432 volumes, 4189 microform items, and 6786 audio/video tapes/CDs/DVDs, and subscribes to 775 periodicals including electronic. Computerized library services include the card catalog, interlibrary loans, and database searching. Special learning facilities include a learning resource center, art gallery, and radio station. The 118-acre campus is in a suburban area 10 miles northeast of downtown Atlanta. Including any residence halls, there are 25 buildings.

Student Life: 62% of undergraduates are from Georgia. Students are from 36 states and 21 foreign countries. 74% are from public schools. 65% are white; 20% African American. 50% claim no religious affiliation; 44% Protestant; 12% Catholic. The average age of freshmen is 18; all undergraduates, 20. 19% do not continue beyond their first year; 63% remain to graduate.

Housing: 575 students can be accommodated in college housing, which includes single-sex and coed dorms, fraternity houses, and sorority houses. On-campus housing is guaranteed for the freshman year only and is available on a first-come, first-served basis. Priority is given to out-of-town students. 56% of students live on campus; of those, 60% remain on campus on weekends. All students may keep cars.

Activities: 33% of men belong to 4 national fraternities; 25% of women belong to 3 national sororities. There are 51 groups on campus, including art, cheerleading, choir, chorale, chorus, computers, dance, drama, ethnic, gay, honors, international, literary magazine, newspaper, pep band, photography, political, professional, radio and TV, religious, social, social service, student government, and yearbook. Popular campus events include Oglethorpe Day, Liberal Arts Symposium, and "Stomp the Lawn."

Sports: There are 7 intercollegiate sports for men and 7 for women, and 6 intramural sports for men and 6 for women. Facilities include a field house and recreation center, housing basketball and volleyball courts, a running track, handball courts, and a weight room. Outdoor facilities include 6 tennis courts, an all-weather track, an outdoor swimming pool, a sand volleyball court, and soccer, baseball, and intramural fields.

Disabled Students: 80% of the campus is accessible. Wheelchair ramps, elevators, special parking, specially equipped rest rooms, special class scheduling, lowered drinking fountains, and special housing are available.

Services: Counseling and information services are available, as is tutoring in most subjects, including including all core courses, English, writing, accounting, and math.

Campus Safety and Security: Measures include 24-hour foot and vehicle patrol, self-defense education, security escort services, and informal

discussions. There are pamphlets/posters/films and lighted pathways/sidewalks.

Programs of Study: Oglethorpe confers B.A., B.S., B.A.L.S., and B.B.A. degrees. Master's degrees are also awarded. Bachelor's degrees are awarded in BIOLOGICAL SCIENCE (biology/biological science), BUSINESS (accounting and business administration and management), COMMUNICATIONS AND THE ARTS (art, art history and appreciation, communications, English, French, and Spanish), COMPUTER AND PHYSICAL SCIENCE (chemistry, mathematics, and physics), SOCIAL SCIENCE (American studies, behavioral science, biopsychology, economics, history, international studies, philosophy, political science/government, psychology, social work, and sociology). Accounting, biology, and English are the strongest academically. Business administration, biology, and communications and rhetoric are the largest.

Required: To graduate, all students must complete at least 128 credit hours, fulfilling a major as well as completing the core curriculum, and achieve a minimum GPA of 2.0. The core curriculum is a unique 4-year sequence of related interdisciplinary courses, 1 per semester. All freshmen must complete the first-year experience program.

Special: Oglethorpe offers co-op programs in all majors, cross-registration through the Atlanta Regional Consortium for Higher Education, international exchange agreements with several universities in Europe, Asia, and South America, and other study-abroad options. Internships are available in all areas of study, earning up to 15 credit hours for upperclassmen with a minimum 2.8 GPA, and a Washington semester offers internships with Georgia senators and others. There is a dual-degree program with the Atlanta College of Art and a 3-2 engineering program with Georgia Institute of Technology, the Universities of Florida and Southern California, and Auburn University. Accelerated degrees, dual majors, student-designed majors, federal work-study programs, and nondegree study are offered. There are 7 national honor societies. All departments have honors programs.

Faculty/Classroom: 68% of faculty are male; 32%, female. All teach undergraduates. No introductory courses are taught by graduate students. The average class size in an introductory lecture is 20; in a laboratory, 20; and in a regular course, 15.

Admissions: 64% of the 2005-2006 applicants were accepted. The SAT scores for the 2005-2006 freshman class were: Verbal--23% below 500, 41% between 500 and 599, 26% between 600 and 700, and 10% above 700; Math--30% below 500, 40% between 500 and 599, 27% between 600 and 700, and 3% above 700. The ACT scores were 17% below 21, 28% between 21 and 23, 22% between 24 and 26, 18% between 27 and 28, and 15% above 28. 57% of the current freshmen were in the top fifth of their class; 77% were in the top two fifths.

Requirements: The SAT or ACT is required. The ACT Optional Writing test is also recommended. In addition, students should graduate from an accredited high school or have a GED certificate. They should have completed 4 courses in English, 3 each in science and social studies, and a math sequence of algebra I and II and geometry. A counselor's or teacher's recommendation is required, and an essay is required for a scholarship. An interview is recommended. AP and CLEP credits are accepted. Important factors in the admissions decision are recommendations by school officials, extracurricular activities record, and advanced placement or honor courses.

Procedure: Freshmen are admitted to all sessions. Entrance exams should be taken late in the junior year or early in the senior year. There are early action, early admissions, and deferred admissions plans. There is a rolling admisions plan. Early action applications should be filed by December 5; regular application deadlines for fall entry are open. Application fee is $35. Notification is sent on a rolling basis. Applications are accepted on-line.

Transfer: 104 transfer students enrolled in 2004-2005. Applicants who have completed less than a full year of college work must take the SAT or ACT. All transfers must be in good academic standing with a minimum GPA of 2.5. An interview is recommended. 64 of 128 credits required for the bachelor's degree must be completed at Oglethorpe.

Visiting: There are regularly scheduled orientations for prospective students, including placement tests, class registration, an activities fair, and group activities. There are guides for informal visits and visitors may sit in on classes and stay overnight. To schedule a visit, contact the Admissions Office.

Financial Aid: In 2005-2006, 96% of all full-time freshmen and 85% of continuing full-time students received some form of financial aid. 69% of full-time freshmen and 58% of continuing full-time students received need-based aid. The average financial indebtedness of the 2005 graduate was $16,250. Oglethorpe is a member of CSS. The FAFSA is required.

International Students: There are 49 international students enrolled. The school actively recruits these students. They mustachieve a satisfactory score on the TOEFL or demonstrate proficiency in English by other means. They must also take the SAT or the ACT.

Computers: Wireless access is available. Each resident student has a network portal in his or her room and there are several computer labs available on campus, including a 24-hour computer lab. All students are provided an Email address accessible from the network or from the Internet, and all may access the wireless network. There are no time limits and no fees. It is strongly recommended that all students have a personal computer.

Graduates: From July 1, 2004 to June 30, 2005, 175 bachelor's degrees were awarded. In an average class, 2% graduate in 3 years or less, 53% graduate in 4 years or less, 62% graduate in 5 years or less, and 65% graduate in 6 years or less. Of the 2004 graduating class, 35% were enrolled in graduate school within 6 months of graduation and 65% were employed.

Admissions Contact: Kelly Gosnell, Director of Admission. E-mail: *admission@oglethorpe.edu* Web: *www.oglethorpe.edu*

PAINE COLLEGE   D-2
Augusta, GA 30901-3182

(706) 821-8320
(800) 476-7703; Fax: (706) 821-8691

Full-time: 226 men, 534 women	**Faculty:** 74
Part-time: 22 men, 46 women	**Ph.Ds:** 51%
Graduate: none	**Student/Faculty:** 10 to 1
Year: semesters, summer session	**Tuition:** $9690
Application Deadline: August 1	**Room & Board:** $4728
Freshman Class: n/av	
SAT Verbal/Math: 410/400*	**ACT:** 16 **LESS COMPETITIVE**

Paine College, founded in 1882, is a largely African-American private institution affiliated with the Christian Methodist Episcopal Church and the United Methodist Church. It offers programs in liberal arts, business, and teacher preparation. In addition to regional accreditation, Paine has baccalaureate program accreditation with ACBSP. The library contains 72,990 volumes, 114 microform items, and 997 audio/video tapes/CDs/DVDs, and subscribes to 7951 periodicals including electronic. Computerized library services include the card catalog, interlibrary loans, database searching, and Internet access. Special learning facilities include a learning resource center, art gallery, tutorial and enrichment center and mathematics support center. The 55-acre campus is in an urban area 150 miles east of Atlanta and 72 miles west of Columbia, South Carolina. Including any residence halls, there are 25 buildings.

Student Life: 84% of undergraduates are from Georgia. Others are from 27 states and 3 foreign countries. 98% are African American. 64% are claim no religious affiliation; 29% Protestant. The average age of freshmen is 19; all undergraduates, 22. 34% do not continue beyond their first year; 30% remain to graduate.

Housing: 506 students can be accommodated in college housing, which includes single-sex dorms. On-campus housing is available on a first-come, first-served basis. 58% of students live on campus; of those, 2% remain on campus on weekends. Alcohol is not permitted. All students may keep cars.

Activities: 10% of men belong to 4 national fraternities; 10% of women belong to 4 national sororities. There are 43 groups on campus, including band, cheerleading, choir, chorus, dance, drama, honors, international, literary magazine, marching band, NAACP, newspaper, pep band, professional, religious, social, social service, student government, and yearbook. Popular campus events include Founders Day, Religious Emphasis Week, and black history activities.

Sports: There are 5 intercollegiate sports for men and 5 for women, and 7 intramural sports for men and 7 for women. Facilities include a gym, a tennis court, a track, a baseball field, and outside basketball and volleyball courts.

Disabled Students: 60% of the campus is accessible. Wheelchair ramps, elevators, special parking, specially equipped rest rooms, and lowered drinking fountains are available.

Services: Counseling and information services are available, as is tutoring in most subjects. There is remedial math, reading, and writing.

Campus Safety and Security: Measures include 24-hour foot and vehicle patrol, security escort services, informal discussions, and pamphlets/posters/films. There are emergency telephones, lighted pathways/sidewalks, and security cameras.

Programs of Study: Paine confers B.A. and B.S. degrees. Bachelor's degrees are awarded in BIOLOGICAL SCIENCE (biology/biological science), BUSINESS (business administration and management), COMMUNICATIONS AND THE ARTS (communications, English, and music), COMPUTER AND PHYSICAL SCIENCE (chemistry and mathematics), EDUCATION (early childhood, middle school, and secondary), SOCIAL SCIENCE (history, philosophy, psychology, and sociology). Education, natural sciences, and math are the strongest academically. Biology, business, and sociology are the largest.

Required: Common curriculum requirements include 18 hours in world citizenship/society, 14 in science/technology, 9 to 11 in fundamentals, 9 in spiritual and social values, and 6 in the aesthetic heritage. From 42 to 84 hours are required in the major. A minimum GPA of 2.5 in the major is needed. To graduate, at least 124 credits must be completed. A thesis in most programs and comprehensive exams in some programs may also be required, as well as a national standardized test.

Special: Paine has cross-registration with Augusta State University (any department) and Clark Atlanta University (mass communications courses), internships for business administration and sociology majors, and study abroad in France, Africa, and South America. A 3-2 engineering degree is offered with Tuskegee University. There are transfer programs with the Medical University of South Carolina at Charleston School of Nursing and Medical College of Georgia. There are 2 national honor societies and a freshman honors program.

Faculty/Classroom: 68% of faculty are male; 32%, female. All teach undergraduates. The average class size in an introductory lecture is 18; in a laboratory, 12; and in a regular course, 9.

Admissions: The SAT scores for the 2005-2006 freshman class were: Verbal--87% below 500, 9% between 500 and 599, 3% between 600 and 700, and 1% above 700; Math--85% below 500, 13% between 500 and 599, and 2% between 600 and 700. The ACT scores were 94% below 21, 4% between 21 and 23, and 1% between 27 and 28.

Requirements: The SAT is required. In addition, applicants should be graduates of an accredited secondary school or have a GED. A total of 16 academic credits is required, including 4 units of English, 3 each of math, social studies, and science. A GPA of 2.0 is required. AP and CLEP credits are accepted. Important factors in the admissions decision are recommendations by school officials, advanced placement or honor courses, and evidence of special talent.

Procedure: Freshmen are admitted to all sessions. Entrance exams should be taken during summer testing sessions; they are also offered during each orientation period. There are early admissions, deferred admissions, and rolling admissions plans. Applications should be filed by August 1 for fall entry, December 1 for spring entry, and June 1 for summer entry, along with a $20 fee. Notification is sent on a rolling basis. Applications are accepted on-line.

Transfer: 24 transfer students enrolled in 2004-2005. Applicants must meet freshman criteria except for the SAT requirement if they have attained sophomore or higher status. 30 of 124 credits required for the bachelor's degree must be completed at Paine.

Visiting: There are regularly scheduled orientations for prospective students, including meetings with administrators, tours of the city and campus, and placement testing. There are guides for informal visits and visitors may sit in on classes and stay overnight. To schedule a visit, contact Joe Tinsley, Director of Admissions.

Financial Aid: In a recent year, 90% of all full-time students received some form of financial aid. 90% of all full-time students received need-based aid. 60% of undergraduates work part time. Average annual earnings from campus work were $2000. The FAFSA is required. The deadline for filing freshman financial aid applications for fall entry is April 15.

International Students: There are 3 international students enrolled. They must score satisfactorily on the written TOEFL and also take the SAT or the ACT.

Computers: All students may access the system. There are no time limits. The fee is included in the comprehensive fee.

Graduates: From July 1, 2004 to June 30, 2005, 98 bachelor's degrees were awarded. The most popular majors were general sociology (26%), counseling psychology (12%), and biology (11%). In an average class, 13% graduate in 4 years or less, 24% graduate in 5 years or less, and 30% graduate in 6 years or less. 15 companies recruited on campus in a recent year.

Admissions Contact: Joseph Tinsley, Director of Admissions.
E-mail: *tinsleyj@mail.paine.edu* Web: *www.paine.edu*

PIEDMONT COLLEGE   C-1
Demorest, GA 30535

	(706) 778-3000, ext. 1188
	(800) 277-7020; Fax: (706) 776-6635
Full-time: 311 men, 534 women	Faculty: 85
Part-time: 30 men, 64 women	Ph.D.s: 83%
Graduate: 194 men, 805 women	Student/Faculty: 10 to 1
Year: semesters, summer session	Tuition: $15,500
Application Deadline: open	Room & Board: $5000
Freshman Class: 485 applied, 322 accepted, 157 enrolled	
SAT or ACT: required	COMPETITIVE

Piedmont College, founded in 1897, is a private, liberal arts institution affiliated with the Congregational Christian Churches of America and the United Church of Christ. There are 4 undergraduate schools and 1 graduate school. In addition to regional accreditation, Piedmont has baccalaureate program accreditation with NLN. The library contains 124,777 volumes, 48,633 microform items, and 2523 audio/video tapes/CDs/DVDs, and subscribes to 8578 periodicals including electronic. Computerized library services include the card catalog, interlibrary loans, and database searching. Special learning facilities include a learning resource center, art gallery, radio station, TV station, the Georgia Youth Science and Technology Center, and an observatory. The 300-acre campus is in a small town 75 miles northeast of Atlanta. Including any residence halls, there are 30 buildings.

Student Life: 95% of undergraduates are from Georgia. Others are from 8 states and 10 foreign countries. 93% are from public schools.

89% are white. 55% are Protestant; 41% claim no religious affiliation. The average age of freshmen is 18; all undergraduates, 25. 30% do not continue beyond their first year; 32% remain to graduate.

Housing: 450 students can be accommodated in college housing, which includes single-sex and coed dorms and on-campus apartments. On-campus housing is guaranteed for all 4 years and is available on a first-come, first-served basis. 61% of students commute. Alcohol is not permitted. All students may keep cars.

Activities: There are no fraternities or sororities. There are 32 groups on campus, including art, cheerleading, choir, chorale, chorus, debate, drama, film, honors, jazz band, musical theater, newspaper, orchestra, professional, radio and TV, religious, social, social service, student government, and yearbook. Popular campus events include Halloween Dance, Spring Formal Dance, and cultural activities.

Sports: There are 5 intercollegiate sports for men and 6 for women, and 5 intramural sports for men and 5 for women. Facilities include a gym, 8 tennis courts, beach volleyball courts, and regulation baseball, softball, and soccer fields.

Disabled Students: 85% of the campus is accessible. Wheelchair ramps, elevators, special parking, specially equipped rest rooms, and special class scheduling are available.

Services: Counseling and information services are available, as is tutoring in some subjects, including most general education courses, such as math, English, biology, Spanish, chemistry, and history.

Campus Safety and Security: Measures include 24-hour foot and vehicle patrol, self-defense education, security escort services, and informal discussions. There are pamphlets/posters/films, emergency telephones, lighted pathways/sidewalks, and campus patrol by the local police department.

Programs of Study: Piedmont confers B.A., B.S., and B.S.N. degrees. Master's degrees are also awarded. Bachelor's degrees are awarded in AGRICULTURE (environmental studies), BIOLOGICAL SCIENCE (biology/biological science), BUSINESS (business administration and management and sports management), COMMUNICATIONS AND THE ARTS (art, communications, dramatic arts, English, music, and Spanish), COMPUTER AND PHYSICAL SCIENCE (chemistry, computer mathematics, mathematics, and science), EDUCATION (early childhood, middle school, and special), ENGINEERING AND ENVIRONMENTAL DESIGN (environmental science), HEALTH PROFESSIONS (nursing), SOCIAL SCIENCE (criminal justice, history, interdisciplinary studies, philosophy, political science/government, psychology, religion, social science, and sociology). Sociology, music, and English are the strongest academically. Education, business administration, and social sciences are the largest.

Required: To graduate, a minimum of 120 credit hours is required, with a minimum GPA of 2.0, or higher in some majors. Students must complete 24 to 56 credit hours in their major, 23 to 26 in humanities, 14 to 18 in math and natural science, 9 in social science, 3 in fine arts, and 3 in computer science.

Special: Piedmont offers internships in business, psychology, education, art management, criminal justice, sociology, and political science, study abroad in 3 countries, and student-designed majors. There are 4 national honor societies, a freshman honors program, and 1 departmental honors program.

Faculty/Classroom: 49% of faculty are male; 51%, female. 80% teach undergraduates. No introductory courses are taught by graduate students. The average class size in an introductory lecture is 18; in a laboratory, 12; and in a regular course, 14.

Admissions: 66% of the 2005-2006 applicants were accepted.

Requirements: The SAT or ACT is required. In addition, applicants must be graduates of an accredited secondary school or have a GED certificate. Students must have completed a minimum of 21 academic units. Piedmont Scholars are required to submit an essay. A portfolio is required for art scholarship applicants and an audition for music scholarship applicants. An interview is recommended for all students. A GPA of 2.0 is required. AP and CLEP credits are accepted. Important factors in the admissions decision are leadership record, advanced placement or honor courses, and extracurricular activities record.

Procedure: Freshmen are admitted to all sessions. There are deferred admissions and rolling admissions plans. Application deadlines are open.

Transfer: 91 transfer students enrolled in 2004-2005. Applicants must have a GPA of 2.0 at each institution attended. An interview is recommended. 30 of 120 credits required for the bachelor's degree must be completed at Piedmont.

Visiting: There are regularly scheduled orientations for prospective students, consisting of student activities, academic assistance and counseling, resident orientation, and a financial aid presentation. There are guides for informal visits and visitors may sit in on classes and stay overnight. To schedule a visit, contact Jim Clement.

Financial Aid: In 2005-2006, 97% of all full-time freshmen and 96% of continuing full-time students received some form of financial aid. 72% of full-time freshmen and 73% of continuing full-time students received need-based aid. The average freshman award was $10,170. Need-based scholarships or need-based grants averaged $3180 ($11,400 maximum);

need-based self-help aid (loans and jobs) averaged $3058 ($10,668 maximum); and other non-need-based awards and non-need-based scholarships averaged $3926 ($13,600 maximum). 91% of undergraduates work part time. Average annual earnings from campus work are $1576. The average financial indebtedness of the 2005 graduate was $15,537. The FAFSA and the state aid form are required. The priority date for freshman financial aid applications for fall entry is May 1. The deadline for filing freshman financial aid applications for fall entry is July 1.

International Students: There are 17 international students enrolled. Satisfactory scores are required on the written TOEFL and the SAT or the ACT.

Computers: Wireless access is available. All students may access the system more than 90 hours per week. There are no time limits and no fees.

Graduates: From July 1, 2004 to June 30, 2005, 257 bachelor's degrees were awarded. The most popular majors were early childhood education (25%), business administrastion (23%), and social sciences (21%). In an average class, 6% graduate in 3 years or less, 43% graduate in 4 years or less, and 49% graduate in 5 years or less.

Admissions Contact: Cynthia L Peterson, Director of Undergraduate Admissions. A video is available. E-mail: *cpeterson@piedmont.edu* Web: *www.piedmont.edu*

REINHARDT COLLEGE   B-2

Waleska, GA 30183   **(770) 720-5526**
                               1-87REINHARDT; Fax: (770) 720-5899

Full-time: 380 men, 565 women	**Faculty:** 51
Part-time: 60 men, 85 women	**Ph.D.s:** 39%
Graduate: none	**Student/Faculty:** 18 to 1
Year: semesters, summer session	**Tuition:** $11,260
Application Deadline: open	**Room & Board:** $9610
Freshman Class: n/av	
SAT or ACT: required	**COMPETITIVE**

Reinhardt College, founded in 1883, is a private institution affiliated with the Methodist Church and offering undergraduate degrees. There are 4 undergraduate schools. Figures in the above capsule and in this profile are approximate. The library contains 48,000 volumes, 1983 microform items, and 3598 audio/video tapes/CDs/DVDs, and subscribes to 315 periodicals including electronic. Computerized library services include the card catalog, interlibrary loans, database searching, and Internet access. Special learning facilities include an art gallery, natural history museum, radio station, and TV station. The 600-acre campus is in a small town 40 miles north of Atlanta. Including any residence halls, there are 31 buildings.

Student Life: 98% of undergraduates are from Georgia. Others are from 4 states, 6 foreign countries, and Canada. 90% are from public schools. 82% are white. 70% are Protestant; 23% claim no religious affiliation; 6% Catholic. The average age of freshmen is 18; all undergraduates, 23. 36% do not continue beyond their first year; 50% remain to graduate.

Housing: 404 students can be accommodated in college housing, which includes single-sex dorms. On-campus housing is guaranteed for all 4 years. 64% of students commute. Alcohol is not permitted. All students may keep cars.

Activities: There are no fraternities or sororities. There are 14 groups on campus, including cheerleading, honors, newspaper, professional, radio and TV, religious, social, social service, student government, and yearbook. Popular campus events include Spring Day, Spring Formal, and Diversity Days.

Sports: There are 5 intercollegiate sports for men and 4 for women, and 4 intramural sports for men and 4 for women. Facilities include parks, jogging trails, outdoor volleyball, tennis, and basketball courts, soccer and softball fields, a pool, a weight room, a bowling alley, and racquetball courts.

Disabled Students: 90% of the campus is accessible. Wheelchair ramps, elevators, special parking, specially equipped rest rooms, special class scheduling, and lowered drinking fountains are available.

Services: Counseling and information services are available, as is tutoring in every subject.

Campus Safety and Security: Measures include 24-hour foot and vehicle patrol, self-defense education, and lighted pathways/sidewalks.

Programs of Study: Reinhardt confers B.A., B.S., B.F.A., and B.S.B.A. degrees. Associate degrees are also awarded. Bachelor's degrees are awarded in BIOLOGICAL SCIENCE (biology/biological science), BUSINESS (business administration and management), COMMUNICATIONS AND THE ARTS (communications), SOCIAL SCIENCE (liberal arts/general studies). Business and liberal studies are the largest.

Required: To graduate, students must have a core curriculum in the humanities, math and science, social science, lanquage, phys ed, and wellness. A total of 120 semester hours is required, including 65 in the major. A 2.0 GPA must be maintained.

Special: Internships, study abroad, and work-study programs are available. There is an accelerated degree program in organizational leadership. There is 1 national honor society and a freshman honors program.

Faculty/Classroom: 45% of faculty are male; 55%, female. All teach undergraduates. The average class size in an introductory lecture is 17; in a laboratory, 17; and in a regular course, 17.

Requirements: The SAT or ACT is required. The GED is accepted and a placement test may be required. A GPA of 2.0 is required. AP and CLEP credits are accepted. Important factors in the admissions decision are recommendations by alumni, recommendations by school officials, and parents or siblings attending the school.

Procedure: Freshmen are admitted to all sessions. Entrance exams should be taken before acceptance. There are early admissions and rolling admissions plans. Application deadlines are open. Application fee is $25. Applications are accepted on-line.

Transfer: 60 transfer students enrolled in a recent year. A GPA of 2.0 or better may be considered for transfer applicants. 40 of 120 credits required for the bachelor's degree must be completed at Reinhardt.

Visiting: There are regularly scheduled orientations for prospective students. There are guides for informal visits and visitors may sit in on classes.

Financial Aid: In a recent year, 96% of all full-time freshmen and 90% of continuing full-time students received some form of financial aid. 30% of full-time freshmen and 40% of continuing full-time students received need-based aid. The average freshman award was $8200. 20% of undergraduates worked part time. Average annual earnings from campus work were $4883. The average financial indebtedness of a recent graduate was $28,000. Reinhardt is a member of CSS. The FAFSA and are required. Check with the school for current application deadlines.

International Students: In a recent year, there were 42 International students enrolled. They must score satisfactorily on the written TOEFL.

Computers: All students may access the system. There are no time limits and no fees. It is strongly recommended that all students have a personal computer.

Admissions Contact: Julie Cook, Director of Admissions.
E-mail: *admissions@reinhardt.edu* Web: *www.reinhardt.edu*

SAVANNAH COLLEGE OF ART AND DESIGN   E-4

Savannah, GA 31401-3146   **(912) 525-5100**
                               (800) 869-7223; Fax: (912) 525-5995

Full-time: 2642 men, 2886 women	**Faculty:** 366
Part-time: 310 men, 298 women	**Ph.D.s:** 80%
Graduate: 588 men, 632 women	**Student/Faculty:** 15 to 1
Year: quarters, summer session	**Tuition:** $22,100
Application Deadline: open	**Room & Board:** $8700
Freshman Class: 4782 applied, 3251 accepted, 1404 enrolled	
SAT Verbal/Math: 550/536*	**ACT:** 24 **SPECIAL**

Savannah College of Art and Design, founded in 1978, is a private fine arts university emphasizing career preparation in the visual and performing arts, design, building arts, and the history of art and architecture. There are 7 undergraduate schools. In addition to regional accreditation, SCAD has baccalaureate program accreditation with NAAB. The library contains 128,574 volumes, 6134 microform items, and 3473 audio/video tapes/CDs/DVDs, and subscribes to 948 periodicals including electronic. Computerized library services include the card catalog, interlibrary loans, database searching, and Internet access. Special learning facilities include a learning resource center, art gallery, radio station, TV station, international student center, writing center, Internet labs, and the Earle W. Newton Center for British-American Studies. The campus is in an urban area on the southeast coast of Georgia, midway between Charleston, South Carolina, and Jacksonville, Florida. Including any residence halls, there are 50 buildings.

Student Life: 84% of undergraduates are from out of state, mostly the South. Students are from 50 states, 80 foreign countries, and Canada. 43% are white. The average age of freshmen is 18; all undergraduates, 21. 18% do not continue beyond their first year; 63% remain to graduate.

Housing: 2591 students can be accommodated in college housing, which includes single-sex and coed dorms and on-campus apartments. In addition, there are theme houses and living-learning communities. On-campus housing is available on a first-come, first-served basis. 70% of students commute. Alcohol is not permitted. All students may keep cars.

Activities: There are no fraternities or sororities. There are 45 groups on campus, including art, cheerleading, chess, chorale, computers, dance, drama, ethnic, film, international, literary magazine, musical theater, newspaper, orchestra, photography, professional, radio and TV, religious, social service, and student government. Popular campus events include Sidewalk Arts Festival, Beaux Arts Ball, and International Student Festival.

Sports: There are 9 intercollegiate sports for men and 10 for women, and 6 intramural sports for men and 6 for women. Facilities include Club SCAD and Turner fitness center.

Disabled Students: 85% of the campus is accessible. Wheelchair ramps, elevators, special parking, specially equipped rest rooms, special class scheduling, lowered drinking fountains, and lowered telephones are available. Facilities vary by building, but individual situations are accommodated.

Services: Counseling and information services are available, as is tutoring in every subject. There is a sign language interpreter for hearing-impaired students and a coordinator of disability services.

Campus Safety and Security: Measures include 24-hour foot and vehicle patrol, self-defense education, security escort services, and shuttle buses. There are informal discussions, pamphlets/posters/films, emergency telephones, lighted pathways/sidewalks, and video surveillance cameras.

Programs of Study: SCAD confers the B.F.A. degree. Master's degrees are also awarded. Bachelor's degrees are awarded in COMMUNICATIONS AND THE ARTS (advertising, animation, art, art history and appreciation, audio technology, broadcasting, design, fiber/textiles/weaving, film arts, graphic design, historic preservation, illustration, industrial design, media arts, metal/jewelry, painting, photography, and visual effects), ENGINEERING AND ENVIRONMENTAL DESIGN (architectural history, architecture, computer graphics, furniture design, and interior design), SOCIAL SCIENCE (fashion design and technology). Graphic design, photography, and architecture are the largest.

Required: To graduate, students need 30 to 45 credit hours of foundation studies (drawing/design), 65 to 70 of liberal arts, 60 to 70 in the major discipline, and 10 to 20 of electives, for a total of 180 quarter hours. All students must earn at least 5 quarter hours in computer courses. Students must maintain a 2.0 GPA overall and a 3.0 in the major.

Special: The college offers study abroad in France and Italy, on-campus work-study programs, dual majors in all disciplines, sessions for credit in New York and other domestic locations, and internships with artists, designers, museums, agencies, and architectural firms in the United States and abroad. There are 2 national honor societies.

Faculty/Classroom: 58% of faculty are male; 42%, female. All teach undergraduates. No introductory courses are taught by graduate students. The average class size in an introductory lecture is 20 and in a regular course, 11.

Admissions: 68% of the 2005-2006 applicants were accepted. The SAT scores for the 2005-2006 freshman class were: Verbal--28% below 500, 42% between 500 and 599, 24% between 600 and 700, and 6% above 700; Math--32% below 500, 43% between 500 and 599, 21% between 600 and 700, and 3% above 700. The ACT scores were 24% below 21, 26% between 21 and 23, 24% between 24 and 26, 9% between 27 and 28, and 18% above 28.

Requirements: The SAT or ACT is required. In addition, students must submit a completed application and high school transcript indicating successful completion. Preference is given to students with a 3.0 GPA or above and to students whose SAT or ACT scores are above the national average (B.F.A. Architecture candidates with lower math scores, may be admitted to architecture on a conditional basis). 3 recommendations, an interview, and a portfolio are encouraged. SCAD requires applicants to be in the upper 50% of their class. AP and CLEP credits are accepted. Important factors in the admissions decision are evidence of special talent, recommendations by school officials, and leadership record.

Procedure: Freshmen are admitted to all sessions. Entrance exams should be taken by January of the senior year. Application deadlines are open. The application fee is $50. There is a rolling admissions plan. Applications are accepted on-line.

Transfer: 578 transfer students enrolled in a recent year. Transfer students must submit a completed application and college transcripts. (High school transcripts may be required if the number of college credits is insufficient for evaluating performance.) An official report of SAT or ACT scores (architecture majors only) and 3 recommendations are required. A portfolio and an interview are encouraged but not required. 45 of 180 credits required for the bachelor's degree must be completed at SCAD.

Visiting: There are regularly scheduled orientations for prospective students, including check-in, tours, visits with faculty from areas of interest, portfolio reviews, financial aid counseling, admissions counseling, workshops, and a social event. There are guides for informal visits and visitors may sit in on classes. To schedule a visit, contact the Admission Office at *admission@scad.edu.*

Financial Aid: In 2005-2006, 54% of all full-time freshmen and 50% of continuing full-time students received some form of financial aid. 45% of all full-time students received need-based aid. The average freshman award was $10,379. Need-based scholarships or need-based grants averaged $3220; need-based self-help aid (loans and jobs) averaged $2600; non-need-based athletic scholarships averaged $15,000; and other non-need-based awards and non-need-based scholarships averaged $5100. 88% of undergraduates work part time. Average annual earnings from campus work are $1500. The average financial indebtedness of the 2005 graduate was $20,000. SCAD is a member of CSS. The FAFSA, the state aid form, and the college's own financial statement are required. A customized packet of materials is sent to each applicant interested in financial aid. The priority date for freshman financial aid appli-

cations for fall entry is April 1. The deadline for filing freshman financial aid applications for fall entry is September 1.

International Students: There are 358 international students enrolled. The school actively recruits these students. They must score satisfactorily the TOEFL.

Computers: All students may access the system. Students may access the system based on the hours of operation of specific buildings in which computer labs are housed. There are no fees.

Graduates: From July 1, 2004 to June 30, 2005, 1071 bachelor's degrees were awarded. The most popular majors were computer art (12%), graphic design (12%), and photography (9%). In an average class, 14% graduate in 3 years or less, 47% graduate in 4 years or less, 60% graduate in 5 years or less, and 63% graduate in 6 years or less. 45 companies recruited on campus in 2004-2005. Of a recent graduating class, 10% were enrolled in graduate school within 6 months of graduation.

Admissions Contact: Pamela Rhame, Vice President for Admission. A video is available. E-mail: *admission@scad.edu* Web: *www.scad.edu*

SAVANNAH STATE UNIVERSITY   E-4
Savannah, GA 31404
(912) 356-2181
(800) 788-0478; Fax: (912) 356-2256

Full-time: 1022 men, 1352 women	**Faculty:** n/av
Part-time: 274 men, 327 women	**Ph.Ds:** 54%
Graduate: 32 men, 84 women	**Student/Faculty:** n/av
Year: semesters, summer session	**Tuition:** $3056 ($10,372)
Application Deadline: July 1	**Room & Board:** $4716
Freshman Class: 2689 applied, 2084 accepted, 1067 enrolled	
SAT Verbal/Math: 440/430*	**ACT:** 17 **LESS COMPETITIVE**

Savannah State University, founded in 1890, is a liberal arts institution that is part of the University System of Georgia. Undergraduate and graduate degrees are offered through the colleges of business, liberal arts and social sciences, and sciences and technology. Preprofessional programs are available. There are 3 undergraduate and 3 graduate schools. In addition to regional accreditation, Savannah State has baccalaureate program accreditation with ABET, CSWE, and NCATE. The library contains 200,000 volumes, 557,690 microform items, and 4173 audio/video tapes/CDs/DVDs, and subscribes to 832 periodicals including electronic. Computerized library services include the card catalog, interlibrary loans, database searching, and Internet access. Special learning facilities include a learning resource center, radio station, arts center, and marine science lab. The 165-acre campus is in a suburban area 265 miles southeast of Atlanta. Including any residence halls, there are 42 buildings.

Student Life: 84% of undergraduates are from Georgia. Others are from 34 states and 7 foreign countries. 70% are from public schools. 95% are African American. The average age of freshmen is 20; all undergraduates, 23. 33% do not continue beyond their first year; 28% remain to graduate.

Housing: 1260 students can be accommodated in college housing, which includes single-sex dorms, on-campus apartments, and married-student housing. On-campus housing is available on a first-come, first-served basis. 55% of students commute. Alcohol is not permitted. All students may keep cars.

Activities: 15% of men and 3% of women belong to 6 national fraternities; 20% of women belong to 4 national sororities. There are 17 groups on campus, including art, band, cheerleading, choir, chorale, computers, dance, debate, drama, drill team, ethnic, international, jazz band, literary magazine, marching band, newspaper, opera, political, professional, radio and TV, religious, and student government. Popular campus events include drama presentations, a Fine Arts Festival, and Christmas and spring concerts.

Sports: There are 5 intercollegiate sports for men and 4 for women, and 1 intramural sport for men. Facilities include a student center, a gym complex, a swimming pool, a stadium, a field house, tennis court, track, and field.

Disabled Students: 80% of the campus is accessible. Wheelchair ramps, elevators, special parking, specially equipped rest rooms, and lowered drinking fountains are available.

Services: Counseling and information services are available, as is tutoring in every subject. There is remedial math, reading, and writing.

Campus Safety and Security: Measures include 24-hour foot and vehicle patrol, informal discussions, pamphlets/posters/films, and lighted pathways/sidewalks. The campus police department is staffed with public safety officers, building attendants, security guards, safety inspectors, and telephone operators.

Programs of Study: Savannah State confers B.A., B.S., B.B.A., and B.S.W. degrees. Master's degrees are also awarded. Bachelor's degrees are awarded in BIOLOGICAL SCIENCE (biology/biological science and marine biology), BUSINESS (accounting, management information systems, marketing/retailing/merchandising, and recreational facilities management), COMMUNICATIONS AND THE ARTS (broadcasting, communications, English, and music), COMPUTER AND PHYSICAL SCIENCE (chemistry, computer science, mathematics, and physics), ENGINEERING AND ENVIRONMENTAL DESIGN (chemical engineering, civil engineering, electrical/electronics engineering technology, engineering technology, environmental science, mechanical engineering, and petroleum/natural gas engineering), HEALTH PROFESSIONS (predentistry), SOCIAL SCIENCE (criminal justice, history, political science/government, social work, and sociology). Marine science, social work, and computer information systems are the strongest academically. Biology, mass communications, and management are the largest.

Required: To graduate, all students must complete 120 credit hours and fulfill the core curriculum requirements of 30 hours in courses appropriate to the major and 20 hours each of humanities, math and science, and social science. Students must maintain a minimum 2.0 GPA. Students must pass the University System of Georgia Language Skills Exam, 6 hours of phys ed courses, and 3 to 5 hours of a freshman orientation course. Exit competency exams and other requirements may be required.

Special: The college offers co-op programs, cross-registration with Armstrong Atlantic State University, study abroad, a dual degree program with Georgia Institute of Technology, the Georgia Legislative Internship Program, and a variety of other internship programs across the curriculum, on- and off-campus work-study programs, correspondence study, credit for military experience, and nondegree study. There are 7 national honor societies and a freshman honors program.

Faculty/Classroom: 54% of faculty are male; 46%, female. All teach undergraduates. The average class size in an introductory lecture is 28; in a laboratory, 13; and in a regular course, 22.

Admissions: 78% of the 2005-2006 applicants were accepted. The SAT scores for the 2005-2006 freshman class were: Verbal--82% below 500, 16% between 500 and 599, and 2% between 600 and 700; Math--82% below 500, 16% between 500 and 599, and 2% between 600 and 700.

Requirements: The SAT or ACT is required. In addition, applicants must be graduates of an accredited secondary school. Students should have completed 4 units each of English, and math, 3 each of science and social studies, and 2 of 1 foreign language. A GPA of 2.0 is required. AP and CLEP credits are accepted.

Procedure: Freshmen are admitted to all sessions. Entrance exams should be taken early in the senior year. There are early admissions and deferred admissions plans. Applications should be filed by July 1 for fall entry and December 1 for spring entry, along with a $20 fee. Notification is sent rolling.

Transfer: Applicants with at least 45 quarter hours or 30 semester hours of core curriculum credit do not need to submit high school transcripts, but must have a 2.0 average. All transfers must submit college transcripts, standardized test scores, and proof of good standing at the previous institution. 30 of 120 credits required for the bachelor's degree must be completed at Savannah State.

Visiting: There are guides for informal visits and visitors may sit in on classes. To schedule a visit, contact the Office of Admissions.

Financial Aid: In 2005-2006, 90% of all full-time freshmen and 87% of continuing full-time students received some form of financial aid. 80% of full-time freshmen and 90% of continuing full-time students received need-based aid. The average freshman award was $3200. Need-based scholarships or need-based grants averaged $3000 ($4050 maximum); need-based self-help aid (loans and jobs) averaged $2625; non-need-based athletic scholarships averaged $1415 ($7328 maximum); and other non-need-based awards and non-need-based scholarships averaged $1000 ($4000 maximum). The CSS/Profile or FAFSA, the college's own financial statement, and the Scholarship Application Form are required. Check with the school for current application deadlines.

International Students: They must score satisfactorily on the written TOEFL and also take the SAT or the ACT or the Collegiate Placement Exams.

Computers: Wireless access is available. All students may access the system 8 A.M. to 10 P.M. There are no time limits and no fees.

Graduates: The most popular majors were information systems (11%), sociology (7%), and marketing (7%). In an average class, 29% graduate in 6 years or less.

Admissions Contact: Gwendolyn Moore, Associate Director of Admissions. A video is available. E-mail: *mooreg@savstate.edu*
Web: *http://www.savstate.edu*

SHORTER COLLEGE   A-2
Rome, GA 30165-4298

(706) 233-7319
(800) 868-6980; Fax: (706) 233-7224

Full-time: 458 men, 471 women	Faculty: 65; IIB, --$
Part-time: 17 men, 21 women	Ph.D.s: 78%
Graduate: none	Student/Faculty: 14 to 1
Year: semesters, summer session	Tuition: $13,500
Application Deadline: open	Room & Board: $6200
Freshman Class: 1032 applied, 770 accepted, 292 enrolled	
SAT Verbal/Math: 515/510*	ACT: 21 COMPETITIVE

Shorter College, founded in 1873, is a private institution affiliated with the Georgia Baptist Convention and offering undergraduate degree programs in communications, education, business, fine arts, humanities, social sciences, religion, and natural sciences. There are 6 undergraduate schools. In addition to regional accreditation, Shorter has baccalaureate program accreditation with NASM. The library contains 135,806 volumes, 7592 microform items, and 5227 audio/video tapes/CDs/DVDs, and subscribes to 582 periodicals including electronic. Computerized library services include the card catalog, interlibrary loans, database searching, and Internet access. Special learning facilities include a learning resource center, art gallery, natural history museum, radio station, and a college museum and archives. The 150-acre campus is in a small town 70 miles northwest of Atlanta. Including any residence halls, there are 18 buildings.

Student Life: 87% of undergraduates are from Georgia. Others are from 21 states, 27 foreign countries, and Canada. 96% are from public schools. 84% are white. 81% are Protestant; 11% claim no religious affiliation; 6% Catholic. The average age of freshmen is 19; all undergraduates, 21. 27% do not continue beyond their first year; 48% remain to graduate.

Housing: 591 students can be accommodated in college housing, which includes single-sex dorms, on-campus apartments, and married-student housing. On-campus housing is guaranteed for the freshman year only and is available on a first-come, first-served basis. 62% of students live on campus; of those, 56% remain on campus on weekends. Alcohol is not permitted. All students may keep cars.

Activities: 16% of men and about 29% of women belong to 2 national fraternities; 28% of women belong to 1 local and 1 national sorority. There are 44 groups on campus, including art, band, cheerleading, choir, chorale, chorus, dance, drama, ethnic, honors, international, literary magazine, musical theater, newspaper, opera, professional, radio and TV, religious, social service, and student government. Popular campus events include Football games, Christmas Dinners and ShorterFest.

Sports: There are 7 intercollegiate sports for men and 6 for women, and 12 intramural sports for men and 12 for women. Facilities include a 54,000-square foot activities complex that houses a basketball arena, dance and aerobics studios, racquetball courts, a weight room, and an indoor jogging track. In addition, there are tennis courts and a swimming pool.

Disabled Students: 50% of the campus is accessible. Wheelchair ramps, elevators, special parking, specially equipped rest rooms, and lowered drinking fountains are available.

Services: Counseling and information services are available, as is tutoring in most subjects. There is a reader service for the blind, and remedial math, reading, and writing. Computerized study skills assessment and training is offered.

Campus Safety and Security: Measures include 24-hour foot and vehicle patrol, self-defense education, security escort services, and informal discussions. There are pamphlets/posters/films, and lighted pathways/sidewalks. Campus access is controlled via a gatehouse from 6 P.M. to 6 A.M., all weekends and during vacations.

Programs of Study: Shorter confers B.A., B.S., B.B.A., B.C.M., B.F.A., B.M., B.M.Ed., and B.S.E. degrees. Bachelor's degrees are awarded in BIOLOGICAL SCIENCE (biology/biological science), BUSINESS (accounting, business administration and management, and recreational facilities management), COMMUNICATIONS AND THE ARTS (art, communications, dramatic arts, English, French, music, musical theater, piano/organ, public relations, Spanish, and voice), COMPUTER AND PHYSICAL SCIENCE (chemistry, mathematics, and natural sciences), EDUCATION (early childhood, mathematics, middle school, and music), HEALTH PROFESSIONS (medical laboratory technology), SOCIAL SCIENCE (Christian studies, economics, history, parks and recreation management, psychology, religion, religious music, social science, and sociology). Music and natural sciences are the strongest academically. Business, early childhood education, and music are the largest.

Required: To graduate, students must maintain at least a 2.0 overall GPA, or 2.5 for education degrees, in 126 to 138 credits, with grades of C or better in the 27 to 96 credits required for a major. The core curriculum requires 33 hours in English, speech, literature, religion, social science, science, math, phys ed, and the arts. Those seeking B.A. and B.S. degrees will have additional core requirements. In addition, students must complete 42 hours in upper-level courses and pass an English writing exam.

Special: Shorter offers internships in most programs, cross-registration with Berry College, and study abroad in England, China, Austria, and Hong Kong. Dual and student-designed majors and pass/fail options are available. There are 5 national honor societies, a freshman honors program, and all departments have all departments honors programs.

Faculty/Classroom: 63% of faculty are male; 37%, female. All teach undergraduates and 30% both teach and do research. The average class size in an introductory lecture is 22; in a laboratory, 20; and in a regular course, 18.

Admissions: 75% of the 2005-2006 applicants were accepted. The SAT scores for the 2005-2006 freshman class were: Verbal--43% below 500, 39% between 500 and 599, 16% between 600 and 700, and 2% above 700; Math--43% below 500, 41% between 500 and 599, 15% be-

tween 600 and 700, and 1% above 700. The ACT scores were 46% below 21, 28% between 21 and 23, 19% between 24 and 26, and 7% between 27 and 28. 40% of the current freshmen were in the top fifth of their class; 67% were in the top two fifths. 2 freshmen graduated first in their class.

Requirements: The SAT or ACT is required. In addition, applicants should be graduates of accredited secondary schools or have a GED certificate. Secondary preparation should include 4 units in English, 3 each in history or social sciences, math, and natural sciences, and 2 in foreign language. Prospective music majors must audition and take a theory placement test; prospective theater majors must audition. A GPA of 2.25 is required. AP and CLEP credits are accepted. Important factors in the admissions decision are advanced placement or honor courses, evidence of special talent, and extracurricular activities record.

Procedure: Freshmen are admitted to all sessions. There is a rolling admission plan. Entrance exams should be taken by the fall of the senior year. Application deadlines are open. Application fee is $25.

Transfer: Applicants must submit transcripts, a character reference, and catalogs from any out-of-state colleges attended. A minimum 2.0 GPA based on transferable credit is required. 30 of 126 to 138 credits required for the bachelor's degree must be completed at Shorter.

Visiting: There are regularly scheduled orientations for prospective students, consisting of entertainment, financial aid workshops, a student-administration panel discussion, faculty consultations, admissions consultations, and campus/residence hall tours. There are guides for informal visits and visitors may sit in on classes and stay overnight. To schedule a visit, contact the Admissions Office.

Financial Aid: In 2005-2006, 99% of all full-time freshmen and 97% of continuing full-time students received some form of financial aid. 77% of full-time freshmen and 68% of continuing full-time students received need-based aid. The average freshman award was $15,718. Need-based scholarships or need-based grants averaged $10,306 ($20,700 maximum); need-based self-help aid (loans and jobs) averaged $6372 ($20,625 maximum); non-need-based athletic scholarships averaged $5687 ($19,400 maximum); and other non-need-based awards and non-need-based scholarships averaged $3822 ($9942 maximum). 60% of undergraduates work part time. Average annual earnings from campus work are $1290. The average financial indebtedness of the 2005 graduate was $16,718. The FAFSA and the college's own financial statement are required. The deadline for filing freshman financial aid applications for fall entry is April 1.

International Students: There are 43 international students enrolled. The school actively recruits these students. They must score satisfactorily on the written TOEFL or on the electronic version or take the MELAB.

Computers: Wireless access is available. All of the campus has wirelss access. Students are encouraged to use password protected web interface for checking on course assignments and grades. All students may access the system. There are no time limits and no fees.

Graduates: From July 1, 2004 to June 30, 2005, 179 bachelor's degrees were awarded. The most popular majors were business (38%), education (25%), and biology (24%). In an average class, 1% graduate in 3 years or less, 35% graduate in 4 years or less, 46% graduate in 5 years or less, and 48% graduate in 6 years or less.

Admissions Contact: Dr. John Head, Vice President for Enrollment Management. E-mail: admissions@shorter.edu Web: www.shorter.edu

SOUTH UNIVERSITY (Formerly South College)   E-4

Savannah, GA 31406 (912) 201-8018; Fax: (912) 201-8070

Full-time: n/av	Faculty: n/av
Part-time: n/av	Ph.D.s: n/av
Graduate: n/av	Student/Faculty: 20 to 1
Year: quarters, summer session	Tuition: see profile
Application Deadline: open	Room & Board: n/app
Freshman Class: n/av	
SAT or ACT: recommended	LESS COMPETITIVE

South University, formerly South College, a private academic institution founded in 1899, offers undergraduate and graduate programs in business administration and heath-related fields. Figures in the above capsule and this profile are approximate. There are 4 undergraduate and 4 graduate schools. In addition to regional accreditation, South University has baccalaureate program accreditation with APTA and CAHEA. Computerized library services include interlibrary loans, database searching, Internet access, and laptop Internet portals. Special learning facilities include medical labs, computer labs, a physical therapist assistant lab, a pharmacy lab, and a PA lab. The campus is in an urban area in Savannah. Including any residence halls, there are 2 buildings.

Student Life: 98% of undergraduates are from Georgia. Others are from 2 states and 5 foreign countries. 57% are white; 38% African American. The average age of all undergraduates is 30.

Housing: Single-sex and coed off-campus apartments are available. All of students commute. Alcohol is not permitted. All students may keep cars.

Activities: There are no fraternities or sororities. There are more than 15 groups and organizations on campus, including computers, honors, pharmacy, physical therapy assistant, physician assistant, professional, social, social service, and student government. Popular campus events include Business Week, Health Professions Month, and Paralegal Week.

Sports: There is no sports program at South University.

Disabled Students: All of the campus is accessible. Wheelchair ramps, elevators, special parking, specially equipped rest rooms, and lowered telephones are available.

Services: Counseling and information services are available, as is tutoring in most subjects. There is remedial math and writing.

Campus Safety and Security: Measures include 24-hour foot and vehicle patrol, lighted pathways/sidewalks, informal discussions regarding safety and security, and a safety patrol during evening class hours.

Programs of Study: South University confers B.B.A., and B.S. degrees. Associate, master's, and doctoral degrees are also awarded. Bachelor's degrees are awarded in BUSINESS (business administration and management), COMMUNICATIONS AND THE ARTS (graphic design), HEALTH PROFESSIONS (health care administration, health science, industrial hygiene, nursing, and physician's assistant), SOCIAL SCIENCE (criminal justice and law). Paralegal studies, medical assisting, and business administration are the largest.

Special: Internships are available in paralegal studies, medical assisting, physical therapist assistant, business administration, physician assistant, information technology, pharmacy, physicians assistant, healthcare management, and anestheiologist assistant. Work-study programs are offered with various employers and South College, and there are dual majors. There are 5 national honor societies.

Requirements: The SAT or ACT is recommended. The ACT Optional Writing test is also recommended. In addition, students should score satisfactorily on the SAT or on the ACT; they may also take a test administered by the college. Students must have earned a high school diploma or GED. An interview is required. CLEP credit is accepted.

Procedure: Freshmen are admitted to all sessions. Entrance exams should be taken prior to application. There is a rolling admissions plan. Application deadlines are open. The fall 2005 application fee was $25. Check with the school for current deadlines and fee.

Transfer: 73 of 183 credits required for the bachelor's degree must be completed at South University.

Visiting: There are regularly scheduled orientations for prospective students. There are guides for informal visits and visitors may sit in on classes. To schedule a visit, contact the Admissions Department at www.southuniversity.edu.

Financial Aid: The FAFSA is required. Check with the school for current deadlines.

International Students: The school actively recruits these students. A satisfactory score is required on the TOEFL. Students must also take the SAT or the ACT the college's own entrance exam, or the Computerized Placement Test (CPT).

Computers: Wireless access is available. The university has wireless Internet access and a fully equipped computer lab. All students may access the system. There are no time limits and no fees. It is recommended that students in physician's assistant and pharmacy have personal computers.

Admissions Contact: Matthew Mills, Director of Admissions.
E-mail: mmills@southuniversity.edu Web: www.southuniversity.edu

SOUTHERN POLYTECHNIC STATE UNIVERSITY   B-2

Marietta, GA 30060 (678) 915-7778
(800) 635-3204; Fax: (678) 915-7292

Full-time: 1838 men, 354 women	Faculty: 117; II A, av$
Part-time: 907 men, 200 women	Ph.D.s: 63%
Graduate: 308 men, 170 women	Student/Faculty: 15 to 1
Year: semesters, summer session	Tuition: $2760 ($9695)
Application Deadline: August 1	Room & Board: $4870
Freshman Class: 1056 applied, 701 accepted, 448 enrolled	
SAT Verbal/Math: 540/570*	ACT: 21 VERY COMPETITIVE

Southern Polytechnic State University, founded in 1948, is a public institution that is part of the university system of Georgia. The university offers degree programs in computer science, management, engineering, technology, and architecture. There are 3 undergraduate schools. In addition to regional accreditation, Southern Polytechnic has baccalaureate program accreditation with ABET, ACCE, and NAAB. The library contains 119,780 volumes, 57,144 microform items, and 82 audio/video tapes/CDs/DVDs, and subscribes to 1256 periodicals including electronic. Computerized library services include the card catalog, interlibrary loans, database searching, Internet access, and laptop Internet portals. Special learning facilities include a learning resource center and radio station. The 120-acre campus is in a suburban area 15 miles northwest of Atlanta. Including any residence halls, there are 23 buildings.

Student Life: 99% of undergraduates are from Georgia. Others are from 22 states, 93 foreign countries, and Canada. The average age of freshmen is 18; all undergraduates, 24. 32% do not continue beyond their first year.

Housing: 476 students can be accommodated in college housing, which includes single-sex and coed dorms and on-campus apartments. On-campus housing is available on a first-come, first-served basis. 88% of students commute. All students may keep cars.

Activities: 5% of men belong to 1 local and 6 national fraternities; 2% of women belong to 3 national sororities. There are 43 groups on campus, including computers, ethnic, honors, international, political, professional, radio and TV, religious, social, social service, student government, and yearbook. Popular campus events include Fall Party, Spring Fling, and NSBE Awards Dinner.

Sports: There are 3 intercollegiate sports for men and 1 for women, and 23 intramural sports for men and 23 for women. Facilities include a 1000-seat gym, a baseball field, softball fields, 9 tennis courts, a 500-seat auditorium, outdoor areas for basketball and volleyball, a multipurpose soccer field, an outdoor running track, and an indoor recreational facility with a swimming pool, racquetball courts, exercise and weight training rooms, and basketball courts that are suitable for badminton and volleyball.

Disabled Students: 80% of the campus is accessible. Wheelchair ramps, elevators, special parking, specially equipped rest rooms, special class scheduling, lowered drinking fountains, and lowered telephones are available.

Services: Counseling and information services are available, as is tutoring in some subjects, including English, math, and physics. There is a reader service for the blind.

Campus Safety and Security: Measures include 24-hour foot and vehicle patrol, security escort services, informal discussions, and pamphlets/posters/films. There are emergency telephones and lighted pathways/sidewalks.

Programs of Study: Southern Polytechnic confers B.A., B.S., B.Arch., and B.A.S. degrees. Associate and master's degrees are also awarded. Bachelor's degrees are awarded in BIOLOGICAL SCIENCE (biology/biological science), BUSINESS (business administration and management), COMMUNICATIONS AND THE ARTS (technical and business writing), COMPUTER AND PHYSICAL SCIENCE (computer science, information sciences and systems, mathematics, physics, and software engineering), ENGINEERING AND ENVIRONMENTAL DESIGN (architecture, civil engineering technology, computer engineering, construction engineering, electrical/electronics engineering technology, engineering and applied science, industrial engineering technology, manufacturing engineering, mechanical engineering technology, and survey and mapping technology), SOCIAL SCIENCE (international studies). Electrical engineering technology, mechanical engineering technology, and computer science are the strongest academically and have the largest enrollments.

Required: All students must complete a core curriculum of 42 semester hours of English composition, college algebra, humanites and fine arts, math and natural sciences, and social sciences. To graduate students must maintain a minimum 2.0 GPA in 120 to 128 semester hours.

Special: Southern Polytechnic offers cross-registration with the University Center in Georgia, cooperative programs in all majors, dual majors in all disciplines, internships, and study abroad in Germany and Mexico. Credit is given for life experience and by exam. There is 1 national honor society and a freshman honors program.

Faculty/Classroom: 79% of faculty are male; 21%, female. 98% teach undergraduates and 2% do research. No introductory courses are taught by graduate students.

Admissions: 66% of the 2005-2006 applicants were accepted. The SAT scores for the 2005-2006 freshman class were: Verbal--22% below 500, 51% between 500 and 599, 25% between 600 and 700, and 2% above 700; Math--8% below 500, 55% between 500 and 599, 34% between 600 and 700, and 3% above 700. The ACT scores were 35% below 21, 38% between 21 and 23, 22% between 24 and 26, 3% between 27 and 28, and 2% above 28.

Requirements: The SAT or ACT is required. In addition, applicants must be graduates of an accredited secondary school. Students should have completed 18 academic credits, including 4 years of English and math, 3 of science and social studies, and 2 of a foreign language and history. A GPA of 2.5 is required. AP and CLEP credits are accepted.

Procedure: Freshmen are admitted to all sessions. Entrance exams should be taken at the end of the junior year. There is an early admissions plan and a rolling admissions plan. Applications should be filed by August 1 for fall entry, December 1 for spring entry, and May 1 for summer entry, along with a $20 fee. Notification is sent on a rolling basis. Applications are accepted on-line.

Transfer: 429 transfer students enrolled in 2004-2005. Applicants must have a minimum GPA of 2.0. and must submit college transcripts. SAT or ACT scores may be required for some students. 30 of 120 credits required for the bachelor's degree must be completed at Southern Polytechnic.

Visiting: There are regularly scheduled orientations for prospective students. There are guides for informal visits and visitors may sit in on classes. To schedule a visit, contact Jim Cooper at (770) 528-4188 or jcooper@spsu.edu.

Financial Aid: In 2005-2006, 83% of all full-time freshmen and 37% of continuing full-time students received some form of financial aid. At least 24% of full-time freshman and at least 26% of full-time continuing students received need-based aid. The average freshman award was $2284. Need-based scholarships or need-based grants averaged $2364; need-based self-help aid (loans and jobs) averaged $2525; non-need-based athletic scholarships averaged $2752; and other non-need-based awards and non-need-based scholarships averaged $1530. The average financial indebtedness of the 2005 graduate was $12,706. Southern Polytechnic is a member of CSS. The FAFSA is required. The priority date for freshman financial aid applications for fall entry is April 1.

International Students: There are 273 international students enrolled in a recent year. They must score satisfactorily on the written TOEFL.

Computers: All students may access the system. There are no time limits and no fees. It is recommended that students in architecture have personal computers.

Graduates: In a recent year, 386 bachelor's degrees were awarded. The most popular majors were engineering technologies (45%), computer and information sciences (20%), and business/marketing (17%). In an average class, 7% graduate in 4 years or less, 18% graduate in 5 years or less, and 27% graduate in 6 years or less. 135 companies recruited on campus in a recent year.

Admissions Contact: Virginia A. Head, Director of Admissions. E-mail: *admissions@spsu.edu* Web: *spsu.edu*

SPELMAN COLLEGE
Atlanta, GA 30314

B-2

(404) 681-3643
(800) 982-2411; Fax: (404) 215-7788

Full-time: 18 men, 2203 women	**Faculty:** n/av
Part-time: 97 women	**Ph.D.s:** n/av
Graduate: none	**Student/Faculty:** 14 to 1
Year: semesters	**Tuition:** $16,195
Application Deadline: February 1	**Room & Board:** $8455
Freshman Class: 4534 applied, 1771 accepted, 531 enrolled	
SAT Math & Verbal (Composite): 1101* **ACT:** 23	**VERY COMPETITIVE**

Spelman College, founded in 1881, is a private, nonsectarian, liberal arts college for black women. Some figures in the above capsule and in this profile are approximate. In addition to regional accreditation, Spelman has baccalaureate program accreditation with NASM and NCATE. The library contains 500,000 volumes and 385,538 microform items, and subscribes to 1439 periodicals including electronic. Special learning facilities include a learning resource center, art gallery, and a language lab, a media center, and music and art studios. The 32-acre campus is in an urban area 3 miles southwest of downtown Atlanta. Including any residence halls, there are 24 buildings.

Student Life: 71% of undergraduates are from out of state, mostly the South. Students are from 46 states, 21 foreign countries, and Canada. 86% are from public schools. 96% are African American. The average age of freshmen is 18; all undergraduates, 20. 10% do not continue beyond their first year; 72% remain to graduate.

Housing: 1169 students can be accommodated in college housing, which includes dormitories. In addition, there are honors houses. On-campus housing is guaranteed for the freshman year only, is available on a first-come, first-served basis, and is available on a lottery system for upperclassmen. Priority is given to out-of-town students. 60% of students live on campus; of those, 67% remain on campus on weekends. Alcohol is not permitted. Upperclassmen may keep cars.

Activities: 88% of women belong to 4 local and 4 national sororities. There are no fraternities. There are 60 groups on campus, including art, band, cheerleading, choir, chorus, dance, drama, gay, honors, international, jazz band, literary magazine, musical theater, newspaper, political, religious, social, student government, and yearbook. Popular campus events include Founders Day and Martin Luther King Jr.'s Birthday.

Sports: Facilities include a gym, tennis courts, a swimming pool, a weight room, dance studios, and bowling lanes.

Disabled Students: 25% of the campus is accessible. Wheelchair ramps, elevators, special parking, and specially equipped rest rooms are available.

Services: Counseling and information services are available, as is tutoring in every subject.

Campus Safety and Security: Measures include 24-hour foot and vehicle patrol, self-defense education, security escort services, and shuttle buses. There are informal discussions, pamphlets/posters/films, emergency telephones, and lighted pathways/sidewalks.

Programs of Study: Spelman confers B.A. and B.S. degrees. Bachelor's degrees are awarded in BIOLOGICAL SCIENCE (biochemistry and biology/biological science), COMMUNICATIONS AND THE ARTS (art, dramatic arts, English, fine arts, French, music, and Spanish), COMPUTER AND PHYSICAL SCIENCE (chemistry, computer science, mathematics, natural sciences, and physics), EDUCATION (art), ENGINEERING AND ENVIRONMENTAL DESIGN (engineering), SOCIAL SCIENCE (anthropology, child psychology/development, economics, history, philosophy, political science/government, psychology, religion, sociology, and women's studies). Biology and engineering are the strongest academically. Psychology, biology, and English are the largest.

Required: To graduate, students must complete 120 semester hours, including at least 30 or more in the major and maintain a GPA of 2.0. Core requirements include 8 credits of African studies, up to 8 of foreign language, 4 of international or women's studies, up to 4 each of English composition, computer literacy, and math, and 2 to 3 of phys ed, plus freshman orientation and sophomore assembly. Students also must complete 4 credits each of divisional requirements in social science, humanities, natural science, and fine arts. A reading course may be required, based on the placement test scores.

Special: Students may cross-register with Atlanta University Center member institutions. Spelman offers internships, study abroad in several countries, student-designed majors, work-study programs at the school, B.A.-B.S. degrees, and dual majors, as well as a 3-2 engineering degree with Georgia Tech, Rochester Institute of Technology, University of Alabama at Huntsville, Auburn and Boston Universities, and North Carolina Agricultural and Technical State University. The college grants credit for life experience and permits nondegree study. There are 9 national honor societies, including Phi Beta Kappa, and a freshman honors program.

Faculty/Classroom: 36% of faculty are male; 64%, female.

Admissions: 39% of the 2005-2006 applicants were accepted. The SAT scores for the 2005-2006 freshman class were: Verbal--23% below 500, 57% between 500 and 599, 17% between 600 and 700, and 3% above 700; Math--28% below 500, 55% between 500 and 599, 16% between 600 and 700, and 1% above 700. 71% of the current freshmen were in the top fifth of their class; 91% were in the top two fifths.

Requirements: The SAT or ACT is required. In addition, applicants should be high school graduates or have a GED certificate. Students should have earned at least 12 academic credits, including 4 in English, 2 each in foreign language, math (algebra and geometry), social studies, and science (including a lab science). Students with additional years in math, science, and language and with AP and honors courses are considered more competitive. An essay is required. An audition or portfolio is recommended for art majors. A GPA of 2.0 is required. AP and CLEP credits are accepted. Important factors in the admissions decision are advanced placement or honor courses, leadership record, and recommendations by school officials.

Procedure: Freshmen are admitted in the fall. Entrance exams should be taken by December of the senior year. There are early decision, early admissions, and deferred admissions plans. Early decision applications should be filed by November 15; regular applications, by February 1 for fall entry, along with a $35 fee. Notification of early decision is sent December 31; regular decision, April 1. 297 early decision candidates were accepted for the 2005-2006 class. A waiting list is an active part of the admissions procedure.

Transfer: 47 transfer students enrolled in 2004-2005. A 3.0 GPA is recommended, with a minimum 2.0 required. Applicants must submit high school and college transcripts, as well as 2 recommendations from instructors at the last school attended. Students with fewer than 30 semester hours of credit must also submit SAT or ACT scores. 30 of 120 credits required for the bachelor's degree must be completed at Spelman.

Visiting: There are regularly scheduled orientations for prospective students, including a general information session and a campus tour. There are also high school senior days and junior days. There are guides for informal visits. To schedule a visit, contact the Admissions Office at (404) 681-3643, ext. 2188.

Financial Aid: In 2005-2006, 82% of all full-time freshmen received some form of financial aid. 82% of full-time freshmen received need-based aid. Need-based scholarships or need-based grants averaged $2500; need-based self-help aid (loans and jobs) averaged $8500; and other non-need-based awards and non-need-based scholarships averaged $17,000. 20% of undergraduates work part time. Spelman is a member of CSS. The FAFSA and the college's own financial statement are required. Check with the schol for current application deadlines.

International Students: The school actively recruits these students. They must score satisfactorily on the written TOEFL and also take the SAT or the ACT.

Computers: All students may access the system 24 hours a day. There are no time limits. It is strongly recommended that all students have a personal computer.

Admissions Contact: Theodora Riley, Interim Director of Admissions and Orientation Services. E-mail: *admiss@spelman.edu* Web: *www.spelman.edu*

STATE UNIVERSITY OF WEST GEORGIA
(See University of West Georgia)

THOMAS UNIVERSITY   B-5
Thomasville, GA 31792-7499

(229) 226-1621
(800) 538-9784; Fax: (229) 226-1653

Full-time: 165 men, 345 women	Faculty: 38
Part-time: 45 men, 135 women	Ph.D.s: 65%
Graduate: 35 men, 60 women	Student/Faculty: 13 to 1
Year: semesters, summer session	Tuition: $9110
Application Deadline: open	Room & Board: $2410
Freshman Class: n/av	
SAT or ACT: recommended	NONCOMPETITIVE

Thomas University, founded in 1950, is a private institution offering 20 undergraduate degrees and master's programs in business administration and rehabilitation counseling. Figures in the above capsule and this profile are approximate. In addition to regional accreditation, Thomas University has baccalaureate program accreditation with NLN. The library contains 54,209 volumes and 823 audio/video tapes/CDs/DVDs, and subscribes to 413 periodicals including electronic. Computerized library services include the card catalog, interlibrary loans, and database searching. Special learning facilities include a learning resource center. The 25-acre campus is in a rural area 28 miles north of Tallahassee. Including any residence halls, there are 20 buildings.

Student Life: 90% of undergraduates are from Georgia. Others are from 9 states, 11 foreign countries, and Canada. 99% are from public schools. 64% are white; 24% African American. The average age of freshmen is 24; all undergraduates, 27.

Housing: 64 students can be accommodated in college housing, which includes single-sex and coed dorms and off-campus apartments. 89% of students commute. Alcohol is not permitted. All students may keep cars.

Activities: There are no fraternities or sororities. There are 23 groups on campus, including chorus, jazz band, literary magazine, newspaper, religious, social, and student government.

Sports: There are 5 intercollegiate sports for men and 5 for women, and 3 intramural sports for men and 3 for women. The university contracts with the city of Thomasville and other groups to use existing public athletic facilities. On-campus facilities include a soccer field, a tennis court, a beach volleyball court, and an outdoor basketball court.

Disabled Students: 90% of the campus is accessible. Wheelchair ramps, special parking, specially equipped rest rooms, and lowered telephones are available.

Services: Counseling and information services are available, as is tutoring in most subjects. There is a reader service for the blind, and remedial math, reading, and writing.

Campus Safety and Security: Measures include informal discussions, pamphlets/posters/films, lighted pathways/sidewalks, an evening vehicle patrol, and sheriff's deputies on campus.

Programs of Study: Thomas University confers B.A. and B.S. degrees. Associate and master's degrees are also awarded. Bachelor's degrees are awarded in BIOLOGICAL SCIENCE (biology/biological science), BUSINESS (business administration and management), COMMUNICATIONS AND THE ARTS (English), EDUCATION (early childhood, middle school, and secondary), HEALTH PROFESSIONS (nursing and rehabilitation therapy), SOCIAL SCIENCE (criminal justice, humanities, liberal arts/general studies, psychology, social science, and social work). Early childhood education and criminal justice are the largest.

Required: To graduate, students must complete 120 semester hours, including 30 to 60 in the major, with a minimum GPA of 2.0 (2.5 for education majors). Core requirements include 48 to 49 semester hours in English composition, history, biology, math, political science, music or art, and computer science. All students must pass a post test.

Special: There are 6 national honor societies, including Phi Beta Kappa, and 6 departmental honors programs.

Faculty/Classroom: All teach undergraduates. No introductory courses are taught by graduate students. The average class size in an introductory lecture is 16; in a laboratory, 14; and in a regular course, 12.

Requirements: The SAT or ACT is recommended. Students should be graduates of an accredited high school or its equivalent. AP and CLEP credits are accepted.

Procedure: Freshmen are admitted to all sessions. There is a rolling admissions plan. Entrance exams should be taken prior to enrollment. Application deadlines are open. Application fee is $25. Applications are accepted on-line.

Transfer: Applicants should have a minimum college GPA of 2.0 and be in good standing at their current or previous institution. 30 of 120 credits required for the bachelor's degree must be completed at Thomas University.

Visiting: There are regularly scheduled orientations for prospective students. There are guides for informal visits. To schedule a visit, contact Lourena Maxwell.

Financial Aid: In a recent year, 95% of all full-time freshmen and 96% of continuing full-time students received some form of financial aid. 50% of full-time freshmen and 48% of continuing full-time students received need-based aid. The average freshman award was $5500. 2% of undergraduates worked part time. Average annual earnings from campus work were $1593. The average financial indebtedness of a recent graduate was $3328. Thomas University is a member of CSS. The FAFSA and the college's own financial statement are required. The priority date for freshman financial aid applications for fall entry is open.

International Students: In a recent year, there were 44 international students enrolled. The school actively recruits these students. They must score satisfactorily on the written TOEFL or on the electronic version and also take the college's own entrance exam or the MAPS (Multiple Assessment Program/Services).

Computers: All students may access the system 8 A.M. to 9 P.M. Students may access the system 1 hour. There are no fees. It is strongly recommended that all students have a personal computer.

Graduates: In a recent year, 117 bachelor's degrees were awarded. In an average class, 18% graduate in 4 years or less, and 35% graduate in 5 years or less. 19 companies recruited on campus in a recent year.

Admissions Contact: Darla M. Glass, Director of Student Affairs.
Web: *www.thomasu.edu*

TOCCOA FALLS COLLEGE
C-1

Toccoa Falls, GA 30598

(706) 886-6831, ext. 5380
Fax: (706) 282-6012

Full-time: 354 men, 477 women	**Faculty:** 44; IIB, --$
Part-time: 21 men, 18 women	**Ph.D.s:** 55%
Graduate: none	**Student/Faculty:** 19 to 1
Year: 4-1-4, summer session	**Tuition:** $12,525
Application Deadline: August 1	**Room & Board:** $4600
Freshman Class: 662 applied, 433 accepted, 380 enrolled	
SAT Verbal/Math: 524/499*	**ACT:** 22	**COMPETITIVE**

Toccoa Falls College is a private, interdenominational Christian college founded in 1907 that offers programs in Biblical studies, counseling, Christian education, communications, missions, teacher education, theology, music, business administration, and general studies. In addition to regional accreditation, TFC has baccalaureate program accreditation with ABHE, and IACBE. The library contains 148,944 volumes, 6401 microform items, and 4280 audio/video tapes/CDs/DVDs, and subscribes to 20,310 periodicals including electronic. Computerized library services include the card catalog, interlibrary loans, database searching, and Internet access. Special learning facilities include a learning resource center and radio station. The 1100-acre campus is in a small town 90 miles northeast of Atlanta. Including any residence halls, there are 45 buildings.

Student Life: 50% of undergraduates are from out of state, mostly the South. Others are from 45 states, 10 foreign countries, and Canada. 61% are from public schools. 86% are white. Most are Protestant. The average age of freshmen is 18; all undergraduates, 22. 29% do not continue beyond their first year; 38% remain to graduate.

Housing: 677 students can be accommodated in college housing, which includes single-sex dorms, on-campus apartments, off-campus apartments, and married-student housing. On-campus housing is guaranteed for all 4 years. 64% of students live on campus; of those, 50% remain on campus on weekends. Alcohol is not permitted. All students may keep cars.

Activities: There are no fraternities or sororities. There are 17 groups on campus, including band, choir, chorus, drama, ethnic, international, jazz band, newspaper, orchestra, outdoor, photography, radio and TV, religious, social, social service, student government, and yearbook. Popular campus events include Spiritual Emphasis Week, Lecture Series, and World Outreach Conference.

Sports: There are 5 intercollegiate sports for men and 5 for women, and 5 intramural sports for men and 5 for women. Facilities include a gymnatorium with racquetball courts and a weight room, tennis courts, and soccer and baseball fields.

Disabled Students: 70% of the campus is accessible. Wheelchair ramps, elevators, special parking, specially equipped rest rooms, special class scheduling, and special housing are available.

Services: Counseling and information services are available, as is tutoring in most subjects.

Campus Safety and Security: Measures include 24-hour foot and vehicle patrol, security escort services, informal discussions, and pamphlets/posters/films. There are lighted pathways/sidewalks and the campus is closed at night, with a guard at the entrance.

Programs of Study: TFC confers B.A., B.S., and B.M. degrees. Associate degrees are also awarded. Bachelor's degrees are awarded in BIOLOGICAL SCIENCE (biology/biological science), BUSINESS (business administration and management, and international business management), COMMUNICATIONS AND THE ARTS (communications, English, media arts, music, and music performance), EDUCATION (Christian, early childhood, middle school, music, and secondary), SOCIAL SCIENCE (biblical studies, counseling/psychology, crosscultural studies, pastoral studies, philosophy, prelaw, religious music, and youth ministry). Counseling psychology, cross-cultural studies, and teacher education are the strongest academically, and have the largest enrollments.

Required: Students must successfully complete at least 126 semester hours, with an average of 42 hours in the major, maintaining a C- or better, to earn a bachelor's degree. All students must also complete a core curriculum of 69 hours, which includes 30 hours of Bible and doctrine. A GPA of at least 2.0 must be maintained. Additional requirements for graduation include 4 semesters of student ministry and a senior oral comprehensive exam or a thesis.

Special: The college offers dual majors, and B.A.-B.S. degrees are available. An on-campus work-study program and internships for many majors are also provided. There are 2 national honor societies.

Faculty/Classroom: 73% of faculty are male; 27%, female. All teach undergraduates. The average class size in an introductory lecture is 52; in a laboratory, 12; and in a regular course, 26.

Admissions: 65% of the 2005-2006 applicants were accepted. The SAT scores for the 2005-2006 freshman class were: Verbal--42% below 500, 33% between 500 and 599, 21% between 600 and 700, and 4% above 700; Math--47% below 500, 35% between 500 and 599, 17% between 600 and 700, and 1% above 700. The ACT scores were 43% below 21, 18% between 21 and 23, 18% between 24 and 26, 11% between 27 and 28, and 10% above 28. 33% of the current freshmen were in the top fifth of their class; 58% were in the top two fifths. 6 freshmen graduated first in their class.

Requirements: The SAT or ACT is required, as is high school graduation or a GED certificate. A personal reference from the student's pastor and an essay submitted with the student's application are also required. Admission is based on an index found by multiplying high school GPA by the best total standardized test score. A GPA of 2.0 is required. AP and CLEP credits are accepted. Important factors in the admissions decision are personality/intangible qualities, extracurricular activities record, and leadership record.

Procedure: Freshmen are admitted to all sessions. Entrance exams should be taken early in the senior year. There is a deferred admissions plan. Applications should be filed by August 1 for fall entry, January 1 for spring entry, and May 15 for summer entry, along with a $20 fee. Notification is sent on a rolling basis. Applications are accepted on-line.

Transfer: 61 transfer students enrolled in 2004-2005. Transfer students must have successfully completed 12 semester hours of college credit courses and have maintained a minimum GPA of 2.0. Students must also provide 3 references and write an essay. A minimum of 50% of major course hours out of a total of at least 126 hours required for the bachelor's degree must be completed at TFC.

Visiting: There are regularly scheduled orientations for prospective students, including visits to the admissions counselor, school directors, and the financial aid office arranged 2 weeks in advance. There are guides for informal visits and visitors may sit in on classes and stay overnight. To schedule a visit, contact the Office of Admissions at *admissions@tfc.edu*.

Financial Aid: In 2005-2006, 99% of all full-time freshmen and 98% of continuing full-time students received some form of financial aid. 66% of full-time freshmen and 67% of continuing full-time students received need-based aid. The average freshman award was $12,728. Need-based scholarships or need-based grants averaged $2871; need-based self-help aid (loans and jobs) averaged $3340; and other non-need-based awards and non-need-based scholarships averaged $9399. 31% of undergraduates work part time. Average annual earnings from campus work are $1855. The average financial indebtedness of the 2005 graduate was $17,341. The FAFSA, the state aid form, and the college's own financial statement are required. The priority date for freshman financial aid applications for fall entry is May 1. The deadline for filing freshman financial aid applications for fall entry is July 15.

International Students: There are 14 international students enrolled. They must score satisfactorily on the TOEFL. Entrance scholarship students must also take the SAT or the ACT.

Computers: Wireless access is available. TFC provides network and Internet service to all students through in-room network connections, academic labs, library, and dial-in connections. A wireless network is available in the library and a section of the student center. 60 PCs for student use are available in the computer lab and in the library. All students may access the system. There are no time limits and no fees. It is strongly recommended that all students have a personal computer.

Graduates: From July 1, 2004 to June 30, 2005, 148 bachelor's degrees were awarded. The most popular majors were counseling psychology (16%), cross cultural studies (11%), and youth ministries (10%). In an average class, 2% graduate in 3 years or less, 32% graduate in 4 years or less, 43% graduate in 5 years or less, and 46% graduate in 6 years or less. 60 companies recruited on campus in 2004-2005.

Admissions Contact: Christy Meadows, Director of Admissions.
E-mail: *admission@tfc.edu* Web: *www.tfc.edu*

UNIVERSITY OF GEORGIA C-2

Athens, GA 30602

Full-time: 9769 men, 12,846 women	(706) 542-8776; Fax: (706) 542-1466
Part-time: 1068 men, 1189 women	**Faculty:** I, -$
Graduate: 2859 men, 3933 women	**Ph.D.s:** 94%
Year: semesters, summer session	**Student/Faculty:** 18 to 1
Application Deadline: January 15	**Tuition:** $4628 ($16,848)
Freshman Class: 12,326 applied, 7979 accepted, 4654 enrolled	**Room & Board:** $6376
SAT Verbal/Math: 620/620*	**ACT: 27 HIGHLY COMPETITIVE**

The University of Georgia, chartered in 1785 and part of the University System of Georgia, offers degree programs in agricultural and environmental sciences, arts and sciences, business, education, environment and design, family and consumer sciences, forest resources, journalism, mass communication, law, pharmacy, public health, public and international affairs, social work, veterinary medicine, and biomedical and health sciences. There are 11 undergraduate schools and 1 graduate school. In addition to regional accreditation, UGA has baccalaureate program accreditation with AACSB, AAFCS, ABET, ACEJMC, ACPE, ACS, ADA, APA, ASHA, ASLA, CAAHEP, CACREP, CSWE, FIDER, NASAD, NASD, NASPAA, NASPC, NASM, NAST, NCATE, NRPA, and SAF. The 3 libraries contain 4,028,611 volumes, 6,487,755 microform items, and 253,388 audio/video tapes/CDs/DVDs, and subscribe to 67,268 periodicals including electronic. Computerized library services include the card catalog, interlibrary loans, database searching, Internet access, and laptop Internet portals. Special learning facilities include a learning resource center, art gallery, natural history museum, radio station, bioscience learning center, rare book and manuscript library, performing arts center, broadcast newsroom, State Botanical Garden of Georgia, Peabody Awards Archives, Institute for Newspaper Management Studies, and Georgia Museum of Art. The 614-acre campus is in a small town 60 miles northeast of Atlanta. Including any residence halls, there are 372 buildings.

Student Life: 85% of undergraduates are from Georgia. Others are from 49 states, 100 foreign countries, and Canada. 83% are white. 43% are Protestant; 42% claim no religious affiliation; 10% Catholic. The average age of freshmen is 19; all undergraduates, 21. 8% do not continue beyond their first year; 74% remain to graduate.

Housing: 7857 students can be accommodated in college housing, which includes single-sex and coed dorms, on-campus apartments, married-student housing and learning communities within residence halls. On-campus housing is guaranteed for the freshman year only and is available on a first-come, first-served basis. 97% of students live on campus. Alcohol is not permitted. All students may keep cars.

Activities: 19% of men belong to 32 national fraternities; 24% of women belong to 22 national sororities. There are 450 groups on campus, including art, band, cheerleading, chess, choir, chorale, chorus, computers, dance, debate, drama, drill team, ethnic, film, forensics, gay, honors, international, jazz band, literary magazine, marching band, musical theater, newspaper, orchestra, pep band, photography, political, professional, radio and TV, religious, social, social service, student government, symphony, and yearbook. Popular campus events include UGA Health Fair and dance, music, and art series.

Sports: There are 8 intercollegiate sports for men and 11 for women, and 28 intramural sports for men and 27 for women. Facilities include a 92,746-seat stadium, a 12,000-seat basketball arena, a 4500-seat tennis stadium, 4 indoor tennis courts, a 3200-seat baseball field complete football-training facilities, and a sports complex with a lake, a beach, playing fields, and trails. There is also the Ramsey Student Center with 5 gyms, 3 swimming pools, a strength/conditioning room, 10 racquetball courts, an indoor track, and a climbing wall. The Women's Athletic Complex hosts women's soccer and softball programs with 3000-spectator capacity.

Disabled Students: 90% of the campus is accessible. Wheelchair ramps, elevators, special parking, specially equipped rest rooms, special class scheduling, lowered drinking fountains, lowered telephones, wheelchair vans, auxiliary aides, residence hall accommodations, and an adaptive technology lab are available.

Services: Counseling and information services are available, as is tutoring in every subject. There is a reader service for the blind, and remedial math, reading, and writing. Alternate format textbooks and class materials, note takers, modifications for tests and assignments, and counseling and advisement from learning disability specialists are available. There are also sign language interpreters, text type machines, FM/assistive listening devices, and a pilot closed-captioning program.

Campus Safety and Security: Measures include 24-hour foot and vehicle patrol, self-defense education, security escort services, and shuttle buses. There are informal discussions, pamphlets/posters/films, emergency telephones, and lighted pathways/sidewalks.

Programs of Study: UGA confers A.B., B.S., A.B.J., B.B.A., B.F.A., B.L.A., B.Mus., B.S.A., B.S.A.E., B.S.A.B., B.S.B.E., B.S.Chem., B.S.Ed., B.S.E.H., B.S.E.S., B.S.F.R., B.S.C.S., B.S.H.P., and B.S.W. degrees. Associate, master's, and doctoral degrees are also awarded. Bachelor's degrees are awarded in AGRICULTURE (agricultural business management, agricultural communications, agricultural economics, animal science, dairy science, environmental studies, fishing and fisheries, forestry and related sciences, horticulture, natural resource management, plant science, poultry science, and wildlife management), BIOLOGICAL SCIENCE (avian sciences, biochemistry, biology/biological science, biotechnology, cell biology, ecology, entomology, genetics, microbiology, nutrition, and zoology), BUSINESS (accounting, banking and finance, business administration and management, fashion merchandising, insurance and risk management, international business management, management information systems, management science, marketing/retailing/merchandising, real estate, and recreation and leisure services), COMMUNICATIONS AND THE ARTS (advertising, art, art history and appreciation, broadcasting, ceramic art and design, comparative literature, dance, design, digital communications, dramatic arts, drawing, English, fiber/textiles/weaving, film arts, French, German, Germanic languages and literature, Greek, illustration, Italian, journalism, Latin, linguistics, metal/jewelry, music, music performance, music theory and composition, photography, printmaking, public relations, romance languages and literature, Russian, sculpture, Spanish, speech/debate/rhetoric, studio art, and telecommunications), COMPUTER AND PHYSICAL SCIENCE (astronomy, chemistry, computer science, geology, mathematics, physics, and statistics), EDUCATION (agricultural, art, business, early childhood, English, foreign languages, home economics, marketing and distribution, mathematics, middle school, music, physical, science, social science, special, sports studies, and vocational), ENGINEERING AND ENVIRONMENTAL DESIGN (agricultural engineering, bioengineering, environmental science, interior design, landscape architecture/design, preengineering, and technology and public affairs), HEALTH PROFESSIONS (environmental health science, exercise science, music therapy, premedicine, preveterinary science, and speech pathology/audiology), SOCIAL SCIENCE (African American studies, anthropology, child care/child and family studies, classical/ancient civilization, cognitive science, consumer services, criminal justice, dietetics, economics, family/consumer resource management, family/consumer studies, food science, geography, history, interdisciplinary studies, international relations, Japanese studies, philosophy, political science/government, psychology, religion, social work, sociology, water resources, and women's studies). Business, journalism, and genetics are the strongest academically. Biology, psychology , and art are the largest.

Required: Students must have a 2.0 GPA to graduate and must complete a minimum of 120 semester hours, with at least 18 in the major and 42 in general education. Required specific disciplines are grammar, composition, literature, math, biological sciences, history, American government, and environmental literacy. Specific courses include basic phys ed and English 1101 and 1102. UGA also requires all students to pass the Regents Exit Exam, as well as exams on the federal and state constitutions.

Special: UGA offers cross-registration with University Center institutions in urban Atlanta. With the Governor's Intern Program, students may serve a full-time 10-week internship in a state government agency; many other internships are available within the departments, as well as work-study programs within the university and with many area businesses. Students may study abroad in 36 countries. A Washington semester, an accelerated degree program in business, a general studies degree, student-designed majors, dual degrees and double majors, and nondegree study are also available. There are 33 national honor societies, including Phi Beta Kappa, and a freshman honors program.

Faculty/Classroom: 64% of faculty are male; 36%, female.

Admissions: 65% of the 2005-2006 applicants were accepted. The SAT scores for the 2005-2006 freshman class were: Verbal--5% below 500, 33% between 500 and 599, 47% between 600 and 700, and 16% above 700; Math--4% below 500, 31% between 500 and 599, 50% between 600 and 700, and 15% above 700. The ACT scores were 4% below 21, 11% between 21 and 23, 33% between 24 and 26, 23% between 27 and 28, and 30% above 28.

Requirements: The SAT or ACT is required. UGA admits freshmen primarily on the basis of high school curriculum, grades earned, and college admissions test scores. The University may consider qualitative information to determine a student's potential for success. Applicants should be high school graduates or present a GED certificate. Students should have taken 4 years of English, 3 each of math, science, and social studies, and 2 of a foreign language. Students should have a satisfactory SAT verbal score and math score, or subscores of 17 on both the English and math sections of the ACT. An audition is required for music majors. AP and CLEP credits are accepted.

Procedure: Freshmen are admitted fall, spring, and summer. Entrance exams should be taken by January of the senior year. There is an early decision plan. Early decision applications should be filed by October 15; regular applications, by January 15 for fall entry, October 1 for spring entry, and January 15 for summer entry, along with a $50 fee. Notification of early decision is sent December 15; regular decision, April 1. 4557 early decision candidates were accepted for the 2005-2006 class. 355 applicants were on the 2005 waiting list; 13 were admitted. Applications are accepted on-line.

Transfer: 843 transfer students enrolled in 2004-2005. Transfer requirements are subject to change for each semester as the university reviews space availibility for that term. Junior and senior transfer spplicants must have a minimum GPA of 2.5 and sophomore transfer applicants must have a minimum GPA of 3.2, although there is no minimum GPA that guarantees admission. Students with fewer than 30 transferable hours are not eligible for transfer admission. Approximately 45 of 120 credits required for the bachelor's degree must be completed at UGA.

Visiting: There are regularly scheduled orientations for prospective students, including walking and driving tours of the campus and meetings with faculty, staff and students. There are guides for informal visits and visitors may sit in on classes and stay overnight. To schedule a visit, contact the Visitor Center at (706) 542-0842.

Financial Aid: In 2005-2006, 94% of all full-time freshmen and 77% of continuing full-time students received some form of financial aid. 24% of full-time freshmen and 22% of continuing full-time students received need-based aid. The average freshman award was $6628. Need-based scholarships or need-based grants averaged $5768; need-based self-help aid (loans and jobs) averaged $2754; and non-need-based athletic scholarships averaged $8265. 2% of undergraduates work part time. Average annual earnings from campus work are $2632. The average financial indebtedness of the 2005 graduate was $13,209. UGA is a member of CSS. The FAFSA is required. The priority date for freshman financial aid applications for fall entry is March 1.

International Students: They must take the TOEFL and also take the SAT .New international students must take the SAT.

Computers: Computers and Internet access are available to students in the Student Learning Center and many departmental classrooms and labs. Wireless Internet access is available on most of the campus and part of the downtown area. All students may access the system at designated times for the various locations. There are no time limits and no fees.

Graduates: From July 1, 2004 to June 30, 2005, 6160 bachelor's degrees were awarded. The most popular majors were psychology (5%), biology (5%), and political science (5%). In an average class, 2% graduate in 3 years or less, 43% graduate in 4 years or less, 69% graduate in 5 years or less, and 74% graduate in 6 years or less. 1409 companies recruited on campus in 2004-2005. Of the 2004 graduating class, 18% were enrolled in graduate school within 6 months of graduation and 61% were employed.

Admissions Contact: Nancy G. McDuff, Director of Admissions.
E-mail: *adm-info@uga.edu* Web: *http://www.admissions.uga.edu*

UNIVERSITY OF WEST GEORGIA   A-2
(Formerly State University of West Georgia)

Carrollton, GA 30118	**(678) 839-4000; Fax: (678) 839-4747**
Full-time: 2800 men, 4121 women	Faculty: 338; IIA, --$
Part-time: 551 men, 874 women	Ph.D.s: 78%
Graduate: 427 men, 1381 women	Student/Faculty: 20 to 1
Year: semesters, summer session	Tuition: $3270 ($10,586)
Application Deadline: July 1	Room & Board: $5568
Freshman Class: 5175 applied, 2859 accepted, 1983 enrolled	
SAT Verbal/Math: 520/511*	ACT: 20 COMPETITIVE

University of West Georgia, formerly State University of West Georgia, founded in 1906 as part of the University System of Georgia, is a public institution offering degree programs in liberal arts, business, and teacher preparation. There are 3 undergraduate schools and 1 graduate school. In addition to regional accreditation, West Georgia has baccalaureate program accreditation with AACSB, ACS, NASAD, NASM, NASPAA, NAST, NCATE, and NLN. The library contains 521,039 volumes, 1,143,479 microform items, and 10,380 audio/video tapes/CDs/DVDs, and subscribes to 65,517 periodicals including electronic. Computerized library services include the card catalog, interlibrary loans, and database searching. Special learning facilities include a learning resource center, art gallery, radio station, TV station, observatory, state archaeologist office, performing arts center, the Advanced Academy of Georgia, and the Waring Archaeology Laboratory. The 394-acre campus is in a suburban area 50 miles southwest of Atlanta. Including any residence halls, there are 67 buildings.

Student Life: 97% of undergraduates are from Georgia. Students are from 38 states, 73 foreign countries, and Canada. 95% are from public schools. 71% are white; 23% African American. The average age of freshmen is 18; all undergraduates, 21. 30% do not continue beyond their first year; 30% remain to graduate.

Housing: 2500 students can be accommodated in college housing, which includes single-sex and coed dorms and fraternity houses. In addition, there are special-interest houses, a sorority - only residence hall, and housing for Advanced Academy of Georgia students. On-campus housing is guaranteed for the freshman year only, is available on a first-come, first-served basis, and is available on a lottery system for upperclassmen. Priority is given to out-of-town students. 70% of students commute. All students may keep cars.

Activities: 10% of men belong to 12 national fraternities; 10% of women belong to 8 national sororities. There are 71 groups on campus, including band, cheerleading, choir, chorus, dance, debate, drama, drill team, ethnic, gay, honors, international, jazz band, literary magazine, marching band, musical theater, newspaper, opera, pep band, political, professional, radio and TV, religious, social, social service, student government, and yearbook. Popular campus events include Fine Arts Festival, Spring Fling, and International Student Night.

Sports: There are 5 intercollegiate sports for men and 6 for women, and 11 intramural sports for men and 11 for women. Facilities include a weight room, a baseball stadium, an Olympic-size metric track, a football field house, and various intramural and practice fields.

Disabled Students: 85% of the campus is accessible. Wheelchair ramps, elevators, special parking, specially equipped rest rooms, special class scheduling, lowered drinking fountains, and lowered telephones are available.

Services: Counseling and information services are available, as is tutoring in some subjects, including most core subjects. There is a reader service for the blind, and remedial math, reading, and writing. There is also braille equipment and a speech recognition computer.

Campus Safety and Security: Measures include 24-hour foot and vehicle patrol, security escort services, shuttle buses, and informal discussions. There are pamphlets/posters/films, emergency telephones, and lighted pathways/sidewalks.

Programs of Study: West Georgia confers B.A., B.S., B.B.A., B.F.A., B.M., B.S. Chem., B.S.Ed., B.S.E.S., B.S.N., and B.S.Rec. degrees. Master's and doctoral degrees are also awarded. Bachelor's degrees are awarded in AGRICULTURE (environmental studies), BIOLOGICAL SCIENCE (biology/biological science), BUSINESS (accounting, banking and finance, international economics, management information systems, management science, marketing/retailing/merchandising, and real estate), COMMUNICATIONS AND THE ARTS (art, communications, English, fine arts, French, German, music, and Spanish), COMPUTER AND PHYSICAL SCIENCE (chemistry, computer science, earth science, geology, mathematics, and physics), EDUCATION (art, business, early childhood, middle school, music, physical, and special), ENGINEERING AND ENVIRONMENTAL DESIGN (environmental science), HEALTH PROFESSIONS (nursing and speech pathology/audiology), SOCIAL SCIENCE (anthropology, criminology, economics, geography, history, international studies, parks and recreation management, philosophy, political science/government, psychology, and sociology). Economics, music theory, and composition and chemistry/secondary education are the strongest academically. Early childhood education, biology, and nursing are the largest.

Required: To graduate, students must have earned 120 semester credit hours with a minimum GPA of 2.0. Distribution requirements include 39 hours in courses numbered 3000 and above.

Special: The university has cooperative and work-study programs with state, regional, national, and international corporations and offers short-term internships and supervised work experience, usually for credit. Cross-registration with the University of Georgia and Dalton College is available. The student may undertake an accelerated-degree program in any major, a dual major in physics/chemistry or geology/engineering, a 3-2 engineering degree program with Mercer University, Georgia Tech, University of Georgia, or Auburn University, nondegree study for teacher certification, and study abroad in 6 countries. There are 30 national honor societies, including Phi Beta Kappa, a freshman honors program, and 17 departmental honors programs.

Faculty/Classroom: 48% of faculty are male; 52%, female. 90% teach undergraduates, 63% do research, and 63% do both. No introductory courses are taught by graduate students. The average class size in an introductory lecture is 35; in a laboratory, 21; and in a regular course, 23.

Admissions: 55% of the 2005-2006 applicants were accepted. The SAT scores for the 2005-2006 freshman class were: Verbal--44% below 500, 41% between 500 and 599, 14% between 600 and 700, and 1% above 700; Math--47% below 500, 41% between 500 and 599, 10% between 600 and 700, and 2% above 700. The ACT scores were 59% below 21, 26% between 21 and 23, 11% between 24 and 26, 3% between 27 and 28, and 1% above 28.

Requirements: The SAT or ACT is required. Applicants must have completed 16 college preparatory high school units, including 4 each in English and math, 3 each in science and social science, and 2 in foreign language. A GPA of 2.5 is required. AP and CLEP credits are accepted.

Procedure: Freshmen are admitted fall, spring, and summer. There is a rolling admissions plan. Entrance exams should be taken by December of the senior year. Applications should be filed by July 1 for fall entry, December 5 for spring entry, and May 15 for summer entry. Notification is sent on a rolling basis. Applications are accepted on-line. The fall 2005 application fee was $20.

Transfer: 571 transfer students enrolled in 2004-2005. Applicants must have a minimum GPA of 2.0 in all work attempted. 30 of 120 credits required for the bachelor's degree must be completed at West Georgia.

Visiting: There are regularly scheduled orientations for prospective students. There are guides for informal visits and visitors may sit in on classes. To schedule a visit, contact the Director of Admissions.

Financial Aid: In a recent year, 93% of all full-time freshmen and 82% of continuing full-time students received some form of financial aid. 52%

of full-time freshmen and 29% of continuing full-time students received need-based aid. The average freshman award was $3173. Average annual earnings from campus work are $3300. The average financial indebtedness of a recent graduate was $17,000. West Georgia is a member of CSS. The FAFSA is required. The priority date for freshman financial aid applications for fall entry is open.

International Students: There are 100 international students enrolled. The school actively recruits these students. They must score satisfactorily on the written TOEFL or on the electronic version and also take the SAT or the ACT with a satisfactory minimum score on the SAT or on the ACT.

Computers: Wireless access is available. Students have unrestricted access to the internet in over 30 labs, housing approximately 1000 PCs. Wireless access is available in the library and the common areas of the majority of academic buildings. All students may access the system. There are no time limits and no fees. It is strongly recommended that all students have a personal computer.

Graduates: From July 1, 2004 to June 30, 2005, 1137 bachelor's degrees were awarded. The most popular majors were early childhood education (14%), management (8%), and psychology (6%). In an average class, 9% graduate in 4 years or less, 25% graduate in 5 years or less, and 31% graduate in 6 years or less. 88 companies recruited on campus in 2004-2005.

Admissions Contact: Dr. Bobby Johnson, Director of Admissions. E-mail: *rjohnson@westga.edu* Web: *www.westga.edu*

UNIVERSITY SYSTEM OF GEORGIA

The University System of Georgia, established in 1932, is a public system in Georgia. It is governed by a 15-member board of regents, whose chief administrator is the chancellor. The primary goal of the system is teaching, research, and public service. The main priorities are to provide broad access to undergraduate education at a high level of excellence, to provide sound programs of graduate education and research addressing state and national problems and advancing the frontiers of knowledge, and to work cooperatively with all levels and sectors of education to improve the social, cultural, and economic welfare of the state's citizens. The total enrollment of all 34 campuses is usually about 250,000; there were 8000 faculty members. Altogether there are 950 baccalaureate, 582 master's, and 174 doctoral programs offered in University System of Georgia. There is a 4-year campus located in Albany,. Profiles of the 4-year campuses are included in this section.

VALDOSTA STATE UNIVERSITY
Valdosta, GA 31698   C-5

	(229) 333-5791
	(800) 618-1878; Fax: (229) 333-5482
Full-time: 3122 men, 4435 women	Faculty: 402; IIA, --$
Part-time: 639 men, 897 women	Ph.D.s: 76%
Graduate: 337 men, 1073 women	Student/Faculty: 19 to 1
Year: semesters, summer session	Tuition: $3278 ($10,594)
Application Deadline: July 1	Room & Board: $5524
Freshman Class: 5782 applied, 3643 accepted, 1757 enrolled	
SAT Verbal/Math: 511/504*	ACT: 21 COMPETITIVE

Valdosta State University, founded in 1906 and a unit of the University System of Georgia, is a public liberal arts institution offering degrees in arts and sciences, education, business administration, nursing, fine arts, social work, and library science. There are 5 undergraduate schools and 1 graduate school. In addition to regional accreditation, VSU has baccalaureate program accreditation with AACSB, CAAHEP, CCNE, NASAD, NASM, NAST, and NCATE. The library contains 482,617 volumes, 1,100,808 microform items, and 25,120 audio/video tapes/CDs/DVDs, and subscribes to 2788 periodicals including electronic. Computerized library services include the card catalog, interlibrary loans, database searching, and Internet access. Special learning facilities include a learning resource center, art gallery, planetarium, radio station, TV station, and herbarium. The 178-acre campus is in a suburban area in southern Georgia, 3 1/2 hours from Atlanta and from Orlando, Florida. Including any residence halls, there are 85 buildings.

Student Life: 94% of undergraduates are from Georgia. Others are from 43 states, 60 foreign countries, and Canada. 74% are white; 21% African American. The average age of freshmen is 19; all undergraduates, 22.

Housing: 1780 students can be accommodated in college housing, which includes single-sex and coed dorms, on-campus apartments, and married-student housing. On-campus housing is available on a first-come, first-served basis. 80% of students commute. All students may keep cars.

Activities: 10% of men belong to 12 national fraternities; 8% of women belong to 10 national sororities. There are 140 groups on campus, including art, band, cheerleading, choir, chorale, chorus, computers, dance, debate, drama, ethnic, gay, honors, international, jazz band, literary magazine, marching band, musical theater, newspaper, outdoor, pep

band, photography, political, professional, radio and TV, religious, social, social service, student government, and symphony. Popular campus events include Family Day, Beach Trip, and The Happening.

Sports: There are 6 intercollegiate sports for men and 5 for women, and 14 intramural sports for men and 14 for women. Facilities include a phys ed complex with a 5500-seat basketball arena, a health fitness center, a weight-training room, and a human performance lab; and a gym with a weight room, training room, dance studio, auxiliary gym, outdoor pool, climbing wall, racquetball courts, and an indoor track.

Disabled Students: All of the campus is accessible. Wheelchair ramps, elevators, special parking, specially equipped rest rooms, special class scheduling, lowered drinking fountains, lowered telephones, and special housing are available.

Services: Counseling and information services are available, as is tutoring in some subjects, including math, reading, and English at no charge. There is a reader service for the blind.

Campus Safety and Security: Measures include 24-hour foot and vehicle patrol, self-defense education, security escort services, and shuttle buses. There are informal discussions, pamphlets/posters/films, emergency telephones, lighted pathways/sidewalks, a bicycle patrol, security cameras, and electronic key card access.

Programs of Study: VSU confers B.A., B.S., B.A.S., B.B.A., B.F.A., B.G.S., B.M., B.S.Ed., B.S.E.P., and B.S.N. degrees. Associate, master's, and doctoral degrees are also awarded. Bachelor's degrees are awarded in BIOLOGICAL SCIENCE (biology/biological science), BUSINESS (accounting, banking and finance, business administration and management, business economics, and marketing/retailing/merchandising), COMMUNICATIONS AND THE ARTS (American Sign Language, art, dramatic arts, English, French, media arts, music, music performance, Spanish, and speech/debate/rhetoric), COMPUTER AND PHYSICAL SCIENCE (applied mathematics, astronomy, chemistry, computer science, information sciences and systems, mathematics, and physics), EDUCATION (art, business, early childhood, health, middle school, music, physical, secondary, special, and trade and industrial), ENGINEERING AND ENVIRONMENTAL DESIGN (environmental science and interior design), HEALTH PROFESSIONS (exercise science, nursing, speech pathology/audiology, and sports medicine), SOCIAL SCIENCE (anthropology, criminal justice, history, liberal arts/general studies, paralegal studies, philosophy, political science/government, psychology, and sociology). Early childhood education, biology, and nursing are the largest.

Required: To graduate, all students must complete a minimum of 120 semester hours, including 60 in the core curriculum and 20 in a major, with a GPA of 2.0. Reasonable proficiency in written and spoken English is also required.

Special: VSU offers more than 30 dual degrees with the Georgia Institute of Technology and has a co-op program with the Medical College of Georgia. Internships are available, as are work-study programs, study abroad, dual majors, a 3-2 engineering degree, a general studies degree, and credit for life experience. There are 15 national honor societies, including Phi Beta Kappa, and a freshman honors program.

Faculty/Classroom: 52% of faculty are male; 48%, female. 92% teach undergraduates. No introductory courses are taught by graduate students. The average class size in an introductory lecture is 27; in a laboratory, 18; and in a regular course, 24.

Admissions: 63% of the 2005-2006 applicants were accepted. The SAT scores for the 2005-2006 freshman class were: Verbal--43% below 500, 45% between 500 and 599, 10% between 600 and 700, and 1% above 700; Math--45% below 500, 43% between 500 and 599, and 11% between 600 and 700. The ACT scores were 11% between 21 and 23, 78% between 24 and 26, and 12% between 27 and 28. 34% of the current freshmen were in the top fifth of their class.

Requirements: A satisfactory score on the SAT or ACT is required. Applicants must be graduates of accredited high schools and have completed the college preparatory curriculum, including 4 years each of English and math, 3 each of science and social science, and 2 each of a foreign language and academic or arts electives. A GPA of 2.0 is required. AP and CLEP credits are accepted.

Procedure: Freshmen are admitted to all sessions. Entrance exams should be taken so that the results may be received by VSU at least 20 days prior to registration. There are early admissions and deferred admissions plans. There is a rolling admissions plan. Applications should be filed by July 1 for fall entry, December 1 for spring entry, and May 1 for summer entry, along with a $20 fee. Notification is sent on a rolling basis. Applications are accepted on-line.

Transfer: Applicants with fewer than 30 hours of transferable credit must meet the same qualifications as entering freshmen. Applicants with 30 or more hours must submit transcripts from all previously attended colleges and have earned a minimum GPA of 2.0 in all work attempted. 30 of 120 credits required for the bachelor's degree must be completed at VSU.

Visiting: There are regularly scheduled orientations for prospective students, consisting of a Saturday open house 3 times a year, including an academic and activities carousel, a campus tour, and lunch. There are guides for informal visits and visitors may sit in on classes. To schedule a visit, contact the Admissions Office at *http://www.valdosta.edu/admission/contact.html*.

Financial Aid: In 2005-2006, 95% of all full-time freshmen and 71% of continuing full-time students received some form of financial aid. 46% of full-time freshmen and 53% of continuing full-time students received need-based aid. The average freshman award was $11,397. Need-based scholarships or need-based grants averaged $3720 ($5250 maximum); need-based self-help aid (loans and jobs) averaged $1196 ($5625 maximum); non-need-based athletic scholarships averaged $2946 ($9574 maximum); and other non-need-based awards and non-need-based scholarships averaged $6381 ($15,092 maximum). 5% of undergraduates work part time. Average annual earnings from campus work are $2000. The average financial indebtedness of the 2005 graduate was $16,220. VSU is a member of CSS. The FAFSA and the college's own financial statement are required. The deadline for filing freshman financial aid applications for fall entry is June 1.

International Students: There are 249 international students enrolled. A satisfactory score on the TOEFL is required. The SAT may be substituted for the TOEFL if the SAT score is high enough.

Computers: 46 computer labs and classrooms, open during business days and evenings, house 1600 PCs. Wireless connections are available in most academic buildings and residence halls. All students may access the system. There are no time limits and no fees.

Graduates: From July 1, 2004 to June 30, 2005, 1391 bachelor's degrees were awarded. The most popular majors were early childhood education (11%), business management (6%), marketing (6%), and nursing (6%). 211 companies recruited on campus in 2004-2005.

Admissions Contact: Walter H. Peacock, Director of Admissions. A video is available. E-mail: *admissions@valdosta.edu* Web: *www.valdosta.edu*

WESLEYAN COLLEGE   C-3

Macon, GA 31210

(912) 757-5206
(800) 447-6610; Fax: (912) 757-4030

Full-time: 1 man, 399 women	Faculty: 47; IIB, --$
Part-time: 2 men, 149 women	Ph.D.s: 94%
Graduate: 23 men, 66 women	Student/Faculty: 14 to 1
Year: semesters, summer session	Tuition: $12,110
Application Deadline: February 1	Room & Board: $7450
Freshman Class: 214 applied, 202 accepted, 113 enrolled	
SAT Verbal/Math: 540/500*	ACT: 22 COMPETITIVE

Wesleyan College, founded in 1836, is a private, liberal arts college for women, affiliated with the United Methodist Church. It is the world's first college chartered to grant degrees to women. In addition to regional accreditation, Wesleyan has baccalaureate program accreditation with NASM. The library contains 143,071 volumes, 33,438 microform items, and 4267 audio/video tapes/CDs/DVDs, and subscribes to 615 periodicals including electronic. Computerized library services include the card catalog, interlibrary loans, database searching, and Internet access. Special learning facilities include a learning resource center, art gallery, a computerized teaching classroom, language and math labs, collaborative research science labs, and an arboretum. The 200-acre campus is in a suburban area 90 miles south of Atlanta. Including any residence halls, there are 18 buildings.

Student Life: 75% of undergraduates are from Georgia. Others are from 22 states and 24 foreign countries. 90% are from public schools. 48% are white; 30% African American; 14% foreign nationals. 53% are Protestant; 34% claim no religious affiliation; 8% Catholic. The average age of freshmen is 19; all undergraduates, 30. 30% do not continue beyond their first year; 47% remain to graduate.

Housing: 600 students can be accommodated in college housing, which includes single-sex dorms and on-campus apartments. On-campus housing is guaranteed for all 4 years. 85% of students live on campus; of those, 60% remain on campus on weekends. Alcohol is not permitted. All students may keep cars.

Activities: There are no fraternities. There are 47 groups on campus, including art, choir, chorus, computers, dance, debate, drama, ethnic, forensics, gay, honors, international, literary magazine, musical theater, newspaper, photography, political, professional, religious, social, social service, student government, and yearbook. Popular campus events include Casino Night, Benefit Ball, and STUNT.

Sports: Facilities include an equestrian arena, softball and soccer fields, an indoor pool, a gym, a dance studio, a weight room, a lake, a fitness trail, and a fitness center.

Disabled Students: 65% of the campus is accessible. Wheelchair ramps, elevators, special parking, specially equipped rest rooms, special class scheduling, lowered drinking fountains, and lowered telephones are available.

Services: Counseling and information services are available, as is tutoring in some subjects. Free tutors are available upon request, and academic counseling is available. In addition, a writing lab, study skills workshops, and sessions with first-year classes conducted by the director of the academic center are available.

Campus Safety and Security: Measures include 24-hour foot and vehicle patrol, self-defense education, security escort services, and informal discussions. There are pamphlets/posters/films, emergency telephones and lighted pathways/sidewalks. Dorm entrances are locked 24 hours a day, 7 days a week.

Programs of Study: Wesleyan confers A.B. and B.S.B.A. degrees. Master's degrees are also awarded. Bachelor's degrees are awarded in BIOLOGICAL SCIENCE (biology/biological science), BUSINESS (business administration and management and international business management), COMMUNICATIONS AND THE ARTS (advertising, art history and appreciation, communications, English, French, music, Spanish, and studio art), COMPUTER AND PHYSICAL SCIENCE (chemistry, information sciences and systems, mathematics, physical sciences, and physics), EDUCATION (early childhood and middle school), ENGINEERING AND ENVIRONMENTAL DESIGN (environmental science), SOCIAL SCIENCE (American studies, economics, history, humanities, interdisciplinary studies, international relations, philosophy, political science/government, psychology, religion, and social science). Chemistry, biology, and philosophy are the strongest academically. Business, psychology, advertising and marketing are the largest.

Required: To graduate, students must complete 120 credit hours with a minimum GPA of 2.0. Requirements include proficiency in writing, math, and modern foreign language, 10 courses distributed with 2 but no more than 3 from fine arts, humanities, science and math, and social sciences. A first-year seminar, a speech-intensive course, cross-cultural and workplace experience, and integrative experience in the major are also required. All classes are seminar based.

Special: Wesleyan offers cross-registration with Mercer University and a 3-2 engineering degree with Georgia Institute of Technology and Auburn and Mercer Universities. More than 150 internships are available, as are interdisciplinary, student-designed, and dual majors, study abroad in 10 countries, a Washington semester, work-study programs, credit for life experience, nondegree study, and pass/fail options. There are 10 national honor societies, and a freshman honors program.

Faculty/Classroom: 50% of faculty are male; 50%, female. All teach undergraduates and 75% both teach and do research. No introductory courses are taught by graduate students. The average class size in an introductory lecture is 13; in a laboratory, 12; and in a regular course, 11.

Admissions: 94% of the 2005-2006 applicants were accepted. The SAT scores for the 2005-2006 freshman class were: Verbal--24% below 500, 44% between 500 and 599, 26% between 600 and 700, and 6% above 700; Math--48% below 500, 38% between 500 and 599, 12% between 600 and 700, and 2% above 700. The ACT scores were 36% below 21, 27% between 21 and 23, 25% between 24 and 26, 7% between 27 and 28, and 5% above 28. 49% of the current freshmen were in the top fifth of their class; 72% were in the top two fifths. 3 freshmen graduated first in their class.

Requirements: The SAT or ACT is required. In addition, each applicant for admission is reviewed on the following: performance in and quality of a college preparatory curriculum, standardized test score, counselor and teacher recommendation, writing ability, and cocurricular involvement. A minimum of 15 Carnegie units is required, including 4 units of English, 3 each of math, natural sciences, and social sciences, and 2 of foreign language. Admitted students must graduate from an accredited secondary school or have a GED certificate. The admission staff does not require but welcomes the opportunity to interview prospective students. Students who wish to be considered for a performance arts scholarship must submit a portfolio or audition. AP and CLEP credits are accepted. Important factors in the admissions decision are advanced placement or honor courses, evidence of special talent, and leadership record.

Procedure: Freshmen are admitted fall and spring. Entrance exams should be taken by the fall of the senior year. There are early decision, early admissions, deferred admissions, and rolling admissions plans. Early decision applications should be filed by November 15; regular applications, by February 1 for fall entry and December 1 for spring entry, along with a $30 fee. Notification of early decision is sent December 15; regular decision, on a rolling basis. 40 early decision candidates were accepted for the 2005-2006 class. Applications are accepted on-line.

Transfer: 11 transfer students enrolled in a recent year. Applicants with fewer than 24 transferable semester hours must submit a final high school transcript and record of standardized test scores in addition to their college transcripts. An interview is encouraged. 30 of 120 credits required for the bachelor's degree must be completed at Wesleyan.

Visiting: There are regularly scheduled orientations for prospective students, including a campus tour, parent/student panels, class visits, admission and financial aid sessions, and meals in the dining hall. There are guides for informal visits and visitors may sit in on classes and stay overnight. To schedule a visit, contact Sheri Baucom, Admissions.

Financial Aid: In 2005-2006, 99% of all full-time freshmen and 96% of continuing full-time students received some form of financial aid. 71% of full-time freshmen and 58% of continuing full-time students received need-based aid. The average freshman award was $13,842. Need-based

scholarships or need-based grants averaged $10,116; need-based self-help aid (loans and jobs) averaged $3064; and other non-need-based awards and non-need-based scholarships averaged $12,230. 40% of undergraduates work part time. Average annual earnings from campus work are $1000. The average financial indebtedness of the 2005 graduate was $21,872. The FAFSA and the college's own financial statement are required. The priority date for freshman financial aid applications for fall entry is March 1. The deadline for filing freshman financial aid applications for fall entry is May 1.

International Students: There are 79 international students enrolled. The school actively recruits these students. They must score satisfactorily on the written TOEFL or on the electronic version and also take the SAT or the ACT.

Computers: Wireless access is available. The college provides computer labs and electronic classrooms in most disciplines. Internet access is provided to all residential students. Students use the network to gain access to e-mail accounts, the Internet, Intranet, and printers. They also can view unofficial transcripts, register for classes, and pay their college bills online. All students may access the system. There are no time limits. The fee is $300. All full-time traditional students are required to have personal computers. They are given a minimum specification for the hardware and software needed for their academic experience.

Graduates: From July 1, 2004 to June 30, 2005, 94 bachelor's degrees were awarded. The most popular majors were psychology (18%), business administration (13%), and advertising and marketing communication (9%). In an average class, 41% graduate in 4 years or less, 44% graduate in 5 years or less, and 45% graduate in 6 years or less. Of the 2004 graduating class, 22% were enrolled in graduate school within 6 months of graduation and 36% were employed.

Admissions Contact: Patricia M. Gibbs, Vice President of Enrollment Services and Student Affairs. E-mail: *admissions@wesleyancollege.edu* Web: *www.wesleyancollege.edu*

HAWAII

INSET 1

POPULATION DENSITY

● 10,000 and over

0 20 40 60 80 100
Miles

BRIGHAM YOUNG UNIVERSITY/HAWAII   C-2

Laie, HI 96762   (808) 293-3731; Fax: (808) 293-3741

Full-time: 954 men, 1287 women   **Faculty:** n/av
Part-time: 105 men, 146 women   **Ph.D.s:** n/av
Graduate: none   **Student/Faculty:** n/av
Year: semesters, summer session   **Tuition:** $2760 ($4140)
Application Deadline: February 15   **Room & Board:** $4980
Freshman Class: 2128 applied, 243 accepted, 220 enrolled
SAT Verbal/Math: 585/595*   **ACT:** 23

                                        HIGHLY COMPETITIVE+

Bringham Young University/Hawai'I is a private, comprehensive undergraduate institution that educates 2,400 students each year from 70 countries in Asia, the Pacific, the U.S., and other parts of the world. Tuition is $2760 for (Church of Jesus Christ of Latter Day Saints) LDS students, $4140 for non-LDS Students. (see above capsule.) There are 4 undergraduate schools. In addition to regional accreditation, BYU - Hawai'i has baccalaureate program accreditation with NCATE and CSWE. The library contains 3179 volumes, 450,000 microform items, and 9538 audio/video tapes/CDs/DVDs, and subscribes to 2100 periodicals including electronic. Computerized library services include the card catalog, interlibrary loans, database searching, Internet access, and laptop Internet portals. Special learning facilities include a learning resource center, art gallery, and natural history museum. The nearby Polynesian Cultural Center houses an art collection and an artifact collection and provides valuable research opportunities for students in related programs. The 200-acre campus is in a small town 38 miles from Honolulu. Including any residence halls, there are 42 buildings.

Student Life: Students are from 43 states, 74 foreign countries, and Canada. 41% are foreign nationals; 38% white. The average age of freshmen is 20; all undergraduates, 23. 25% do not continue beyond their first year; 40% remain to graduate.

Housing: 1374 students can be accommodated in college housing, which includes single-sex dorms, on-campus apartments, and married-student housing. On-campus housing is guaranteed for the freshman year only and is available on a first-come, first-served basis. 62% of students live on campus. Alcohol is not permitted. All students may keep cars.

Activities: There are no fraternities or sororities. There are 41 groups on campus, including art, band, cheerleading, chess, choir, chorale, computers, dance, drama, ethnic, film, honors, international, jazz band, literary magazine, musical theater, newspaper, pep band, political, professional, religious, social, social service, and student government. Popular campus events include International Food Fest, International Cultural Night, and Talent Show.

Sports: There are 4 intercollegiate sports for men and 4 for women, and 10 intramural sports for men and 10 for women. Facilities include 3 softball fields, 2 soccer fields, a rugby field, 10 tennis and 4 racquetball courts, a swimming pool, a weight room, a bowling alley, a dance studio, pool tables, and 2 basketball gyms.

Disabled Students: 95% of the campus is accessible. Wheelchair ramps, elevators, special parking, specially equipped rest rooms, lowered drinking fountains, and lowered telephones are available.

Services: Counseling and information services are available, as is tutoring in most subjects. There is remedial math, reading, and writing.

Campus Safety and Security: Measures include 24-hour foot and vehicle patrol, security escort services, informal discussions, and pamphlets/posters/films. There are emergency telephones and lighted pathways/sidewalks.

Programs of Study: BYU - Hawai'i confers B.A., B.S., B.F.A., and B.S.W. degrees. Associate degrees are also awarded. Bachelor's degrees are awarded in BIOLOGICAL SCIENCE (biology/biological science), BUSINESS (accounting, hospitality management services, international business management, and tourism), COMMUNICATIONS AND THE ARTS (art, English, fine arts, and music), COMPUTER AND PHYSICAL SCIENCE (computer science, information sciences and systems, and mathematics), EDUCATION (art, business, elementary, English, mathematics, science, social science, special, and teaching English as a second/foreign language (TESOL/TEFOL)), HEALTH PROFESSIONS (predentistry and premedicine), SOCIAL SCIENCE (Hawaiian studies, history, interdisciplinary studies, international studies, Pacific area studies, physical fitness/movement, political science/government, psychology, and social work). Biological science, information systems, and education are the strongest academically. International business management, information systems, and psychology are the largest.

Required: Students must complete the 31- to 43-credit general education curriculum, as well as meet English proficiency, religious education, and exercise science requirements. A total of 120 credit hours, including 40 in the major, must be earned with a minimum GPA of 2.0 for graduation. A thesis is required in certain areas.

Special: BYU-Hawaii offers work-study programs with the Polynesian Cultural Center, internships, cooperative programs in most majors, non-degree study, student-designed majors in interdisciplinary studies, and pass/fail options. There are 5 national honor societies and a freshman honors program.

Admissions: 11% of the 2005-2006 applicants were accepted. The SAT scores for the 2005-2006 freshman class were: Verbal--21% below 500, 29% between 500 and 599, 43% between 600 and 700, and 7% above 700; Math--7% below 500, 43% between 500 and 599, 43% between 600 and 700, and 7% above 700. The ACT scores were 32% below 21, 19% between 21 and 23, 27% between 24 and 26, 9% between 27 and 28, and 13% above 28.

Requirements: The ACT is required and the SAT is recommended. In addition, the applicant should be a high school graduate. Home-schooled and other non-traditional students should call for more information. AP and CLEP credits are accepted. Important factors in the admissions decision are geographic diversity, recommendations by alumni, and personality/intangible qualities.

Procedure: Freshmen are admitted to all sessions. Entrance exams should be taken prior to the application deadline. There is a deferred admissions and rolling admissions plans. Applications should be filed by February 15 for fall entry, October 1 for winter entry, February 15 for spring entry, and February 15 for summer entry. The fall 2005 application fee was $35. Notification is sent April 1. Applications are accepted on-line.

Transfer: Applicants must have 30 hours of college credit, with a minimum GPA of 2.5. 30 of 120 credits required for the bachelor's degree must be completed at BYU - Hawai'i.

Visiting: There are guides for informal visits. To schedule a visit, contact the University Advancement Office at (808) 293-3456 or magaleil@byuh.edu.

Financial Aid: The FAFSA is required. Check with the school for current deadlines.

International Students: There are 1149 international students enrolled. The school actively recruits these students. A satisfactory score is required on the written TOEFL or the MELAB.

Computers: All students may access the system all day. There are no time limits and no fees.

Graduates: From July 1, 2004 to June 30, 2005, 555 bachelor's degrees were awarded. The most popular majors were international business management (13%), information system (10%), and psychology (8%). In an average class, 40% graduate in 6 years or less. 60 companies recruited on campus in 2004-2005.

Admissions Contact: Jeffrey N. Bunker, Dean of Admissions and Records. A video is available. E-mail: adm@byuh.edu
Web: http://www.byuh.edu

CHAMINADE UNIVERSITY OF HONOLULU C-2

Honolulu, HI 96816
(808) 735-4735
(800) 735-3733; Fax: (808) 739-4647

Full-time: 333 men, 725 women	**Faculty:** 82; IIB, -$
Part-time: 10 men, 38 women	**Ph.Ds:** 59%
Graduate: 193 men, 511 women	**Student/Faculty:** 13 to 1
Year: semesters, summer session	**Tuition:** $14,450
Application Deadline: open	**Room & Board:** $8870
Freshman Class: 907 applied, 870 accepted, 268 enrolled	
SAT Verbal/Math: 480/470*	**ACT:** 22 **LESS COMPETITIVE**

Chaminade University of Honolulu, founded in 1955, is a private institution affiliated with the Roman Catholic Church. The school is divided into three major programs: the day undergraduate is on the main campus, the evening undergraduate program is off campus, and the evening graduate program is on campus. There are 5 undergraduate and 5 graduate schools. The library contains 68,256 volumes, 134,000 microform items, and 231 audio/video tapes/CDs/DVDs, and subscribes to 273 periodicals including electronic. Computerized library services include interlibrary loans, database searching, and Internet access. Special learning facilities include a learning resource center, an observatory, and a theater. The 62-acre campus is in an urban area 4 miles east of downtown Honolulu. Including any residence halls, there are 14 buildings.

Student Life: 52% of undergraduates are from out of state, mostly the West. Students are from 42 states, 10 foreign countries, and Canada. 63% are Asian American; 24% white. 41% are Catholic; 33% Protestant; 25% claim no religious affiliation. The average age of freshmen is 19; all undergraduates, 22. 31% do not continue beyond their first year; 38% remain to graduate.

Housing: 395 students can be accommodated in college housing, which includes single-sex and coed dorms, on-campus apartments, and off-campus apartments. On-campus housing is available on a first-come, first-served basis. 65% of students commute. All students may keep cars.

Activities: There are no fraternities or sororities. There are 38 groups on campus, including cheerleading, chorale, computers, drama, ethnic, forensics, honors, international, literary magazine, musical theater, newspaper, orchestra, political, professional, religious, social, social service, student government, and yearbook. Popular campus events include Spring Serendipity, International Extravaganza, and Club Fest.

Sports: There are 4 intercollegiate sports for men and 4 for women. Facilities include volleyball, tennis, and basketball courts, fitness and weight-training facilities, and a student center.

Disabled Students: 75% of the campus is accessible. Wheelchair ramps, special parking, specially equipped rest rooms, special class scheduling, lowered drinking fountains, lowered telephones, and special housing are available.

Services: Counseling and information services are available, as is tutoring in most subjects. There is remedial math, reading, and writing.

Campus Safety and Security: Measures include 24-hour foot and vehicle patrol, self-defense education, security escort services, and informal discussions. There are pamphlets/posters/films, emergency telephones, and lighted pathways/sidewalks.

Programs of Study: Chaminade confers B.A., B.S., and B.F.A. degrees. Associate and master's degrees are also awarded. Bachelor's degrees are awarded in AGRICULTURE (environmental studies), BIOLOGICAL SCIENCE (biology/biological science), BUSINESS (accounting, management science, and marketing/retailing/merchandising), COMMUNICATIONS AND THE ARTS (communications and English), COMPUTER AND PHYSICAL SCIENCE (computer science and information sciences and systems), EDUCATION (early childhood, elementary, and secondary), ENGINEERING AND ENVIRONMENTAL DESIGN (interior design), SOCIAL SCIENCE (behavioral science, criminal justice, forensic studies, history, humanities, international relations, psychology, religion, and social studies). Forensic science, biology, and education are the strongest academically and have the largest enrollments.

Required: To graduate, students must complete 120 credit hours, including 61 in general education courses and at least 24 in the major at the upper-division level. A 2.0 GPA is required in all majors except criminal justice (2.5), communications (2.5), and education (2.75).

Special: Internships are available with local companies through the Career Development Office. Students may design majors toward a B.A. in humanities. There is a sister university exchange program with the University of Dayton and St. Mary's University. There are 7 national honor societies.

Faculty/Classroom: 61% of faculty are male; 39%, female. All teach undergraduates. No introductory courses are taught by graduate students. The average class size in an introductory lecture is 18; in a laboratory, 18; and in a regular course, 18.

Admissions: 96% of the 2005-2006 applicants were accepted. The SAT scores for the 2005-2006 freshman class were: Verbal--58% below 500, 32% between 500 and 599, 9% between 600 and 700, and 1% above 700; Math--58% below 500, 32% between 500 and 599, 9% between 600 and 700, and 1% above 700. 3 freshmen graduated first in their class in a recent year.

Requirements: A satisfactory score on the SAT or ACT is recommended. In addition, students must have earned 16 credits, based on 4 years of English and college preparatory electives, 3 each of math and social studies and 2 of science. The GED is accepted. An essay is required, and an interview is recommended. A GPA of 2.0 is required. AP and CLEP credits are accepted. Important factors in the admissions decision are leadership record, personality/intangible qualities, and extracurricular activities record.

Procedure: Freshmen are admitted fall and spring. Entrance exams should be taken during the first semester of the senior year. There is a rolling admissions plan. Application deadlines are open. Application fee is $50. Notification is sent on a rolling basis. Applications are accepted on-line.

Transfer: 115 transfer students enrolled in a recent year.. Applicants must have a minimum GPA of 2.0. 30 of 120 credits required for the bachelor's degree must be completed at Chaminade.

Visiting: There are guides for informal visits and visitors may sit in on classes. To schedule a visit, contact the Admissions Office.

Financial Aid: In 2005-2006, 96% of all full-time freshmen and 98% of continuing full-time students received some form of financial aid. 82% of full-time freshmen and 70% of continuing full-time students received need-based aid. The average freshman award was $18,401. Need-based scholarships or need-based grants averaged $2935 ($15,197 maximum); need-based self-help aid (loans and jobs) averaged $3526 ($8788 maximum); non-need-based athletic scholarships averaged $5470 ($16,776 maximum); and other non-need-based awards and non-need-based scholarships averaged $9655 ($21,633 maximum). 5% of undergraduates work part time. Average annual earnings from campus work are $1500. The average financial indebtedness of the 2005 graduate was $22,263. Chaminade is a member of CSS. The FAFSA is required. The priority date for freshman financial aid applications for fall entry is March 1.

International Students: There are 20 international students enrolled. They must take the SAT or the ACT.

Computers: All students may access the system. There are no time limits and no fees.

Graduates: From July 1, 2004 to June 30, 2005, 276 bachelor's degrees were awarded. The most popular majors were criminal justice (27%), education (16%), and psychology (11%). In an average class, 4% graduate in 3 years or less, 24% graduate in 4 years or less, 37% graduate in 5 years or less, and 39% graduate in 6 years or less. 40 companies recruited on campus in 2004-2005.

Admissions Contact: Joy Bouey, Dean of Enrollment. A video is available. E-mail: admissions@chaminade.edu
Web: www.chaminade.edu

HAWAII PACIFIC UNIVERSITY C-2

Honolulu, HI 96813
(808) 544-0238
(866) 225-5478; Fax: (808) 544-1136

Full-time: 1329 men, 2431 women	**Faculty:** 227
Part-time: 430 men, 921 women	**Ph.D.s:** 71%
Graduate: 530 men, 561 women	**Student/Faculty:** 17 to 1
Year: semesters, summer session	**Tuition:** $11,630
Application Deadline: open	**Room & Board:** $9450
Freshman Class: 3099 applied, 2544 accepted, 657 enrolled	
SAT Verbal/Math: 508/510*	**ACT:** 22 **COMPETITIVE**

Hawaii Pacific University, founded in 1965, is a private institution offering undergraduate and graduate programs in liberal arts, business, natural sciences, nursing, international studies, and communication There are 7 undergraduate and 6 graduate schools. In addition to regional accreditation, HPU has baccalaureate program accreditation with CSWE and NLN. The 2 libraries contain 10,000 volumes, 390,000 microform items, and 4600 audio/video tapes/CDs/DVDs, and subscribe to 67,000 periodicals including electronic. Computerized library services include the card catalog, interlibrary loans, database searching, Internet access, and laptop Internet portals. Special learning facilities include a learning resource center, art gallery, and and a research vessel (boat). The 135-acre campus is in an urban area downtown Honolulu and suburban Kaneohe on the island of Oahu. Including any residence halls, there are 16 buildings.

Student Life: 52% of undergraduates are from out of state, mostly the West. Others are from 50 states, 99 foreign countries, and Canada. 73% are from public schools. 38% are Asian American; 31% white; 21% foreign nationals. The average age of freshmen is 19; all undergraduates, 25. 34% do not continue beyond their first year; 35% remain to graduate.

Housing: 210 students can be accommodated in college housing, which includes single-sex and coed dorms and a homestay program. The housing office assists students in finding apartments and other living arrangements in Honolulu. On-campus housing is available on a first-come, first-served basis. Priority is given to out-of-town students. 97% of students commute. Alcohol is not permitted. All students may keep cars.

Activities: There are no fraternities or sororities. There are 93 groups on campus, including art, band, cheerleading, chorale, computers, dance, debate, drama, ethnic, film, gay, honors, international, literary magazine, musical theater, newspaper, orchestra, pep band, political, professional, religious, social, social service, and student government. Popular campus events include Intercultural Day, Honors Banquet, and Club Carnival.

Sports: There are 45 intercollegiate sports for men and 45 for women, and 8 intramural sports for men and 8 for women. Facilities include soccer and softball fields, tennis courts and two regulation basketball courts.

Disabled Students: 75% of the campus is accessible. Wheelchair ramps, elevators, special parking, specially equipped rest rooms, special class scheduling, lowered drinking fountains, and lowered telephones are available.

Services: Counseling and information services are available, as is tutoring in most subjects. There is remedial math, reading, and writing.

Campus Safety and Security: Measures include 24-hour foot and vehicle patrol, security escort services, shuttle buses, and informal discussions. There are pamphlets/posters/films, emergency telephones, and lighted pathways/sidewalks.

Programs of Study: HPU confers B.A., B.S., B.S.B.A., B.S.Comp.Sci., B.S.N., and B.S.W. degrees. Associate and master's degrees are also awarded. Bachelor's degrees are awarded in BIOLOGICAL SCIENCE (biology/biological science and marine science), BUSINESS (accounting, banking and finance, business administration and management, business economics, entrepreneurial studies, human resources, international business management, management science, marketing management, personnel management, small business management, and tourism), COMMUNICATIONS AND THE ARTS (advertising, communications, English, journalism, literature, and public relations), COMPUTER AND PHYSICAL SCIENCE (applied mathematics, computer programming, computer science, oceanography, and science), EDUCATION (teaching English as a second/foreign language (TESOL/TEFOL)), ENGINEERING AND ENVIRONMENTAL DESIGN (environmental science and military science), HEALTH PROFESSIONS (nursing and premedicine), SOCIAL SCIENCE (anthropology, classical/ancient civilization, criminal justice, economics, history, human services, humanities, international relations, international studies, Pacific area studies, political science/government, psychology, public administration, social science, social work, and sociology). Marine biology, nursing, and computer science are the strongest academically. Nursing, computer science, and management are the largest.

Required: Seniors who have completed a minimum of 100 semester hours of credit towards their undergraduate degree program, and have a cumulative GPA of at least 3.0, may enroll concurrently in certain graduate degree programs. Students enrolled in this program may earn a maximum of 12 semester hours of dual graduate and undergraduate credit while pursuing both degrees. (MA-TESL allows only 6 AL concurrent credits)

Special: Upperclassmen may participate in internships and work-study programs with numerous companies and study abroad in 4 countries. HPU also offers accelerated degree and co-op programs in all majors, B.A.-B.S. degrees in most majors, student-designed majors, dual majors in all business subjects, a 3-2 engineering degree with Washington University in St. Louis and the University of Southern California, credit for military experience, nondegree study, and pass/fail options. There are 17 national honor societies, a freshman honors program, and 7 departmental honors programs.

Faculty/Classroom: 55% of faculty are male; 45%, female. 95% teach undergraduates, 42% do research, and 42% do both. No introductory courses are taught by graduate students. The average class size in an introductory lecture is 23; in a laboratory, 11; and in a regular course, 19.

Admissions: 82% of the 2005-2006 applicants were accepted. The SAT scores for the 2005-2006 freshman class were: Verbal--46% below 500, 39% between 500 and 599, 13% between 600 and 700, and 2% above 700; Math--45% below 500, 37% between 500 and 599, 17% between 600 and 700, and 1% above 700. The ACT scores were 34% below 21, 24% between 21 and 23, 31% between 24 and 26, 5% between 27 and 28, and 6% above 28. 40% of the current freshmen were in the top fifth of their class; 69% were in the top two fifths. 6 freshmen graduated first in their class.

Requirements: The SAT or ACT is required. In addition, the university prefers completion of 20 credits based on 4 years of English, 2 each of math and social studies, and 2 each of history and science. An essay and an interview are recommended. Certain programs, for example, marine science and nursing, have more specific admission requirements. A GPA of 2.5 is required. AP and CLEP credits are accepted. Important factors in the admissions decision are recommendations by school officials, extracurricular activities record, and evidence of special talent.

Procedure: Freshmen are admitted to all sessions. Entrance exams should be taken during the spring or summer of the junior year or the fall of the senior year. There are deferred admissions and rolling admis-

sions plans. Application deadlines are open. Application fee is $50. Applications are accepted on-line.

Transfer: 613 transfer students enrolled in 2004-2005. Applicants must have a GPA of 2.0 in a minimum of 24 credit hours. The SAT or ACT and an interview are recommended. 30 of 124 credits required for the bachelor's degree must be completed at HPU.

Visiting: There are regularly scheduled orientations for prospective students. There are guides for informal visits and visitors may sit in on classes and stay overnight. To schedule a visit, contact the Admissions Office at *admissions@hpu.edu*.

Financial Aid: In 2005-2006, 80% of all full-time freshmen and 66% of continuing full-time students received some form of financial aid. 42% of full-time freshmen and 36% of continuing full-time students received need-based aid. The average freshman award was $10,239. Need-based scholarships or need-based grants averaged $4066 ($6050 maximum); need-based self-help aid (loans and jobs) averaged $3678 ($17,550 maximum); non-need-based athletic scholarships averaged $8577 ($17,430 maximum); and other non-need-based awards and non-need-based scholarships averaged $6115 ($11,550 maximum). 14% of undergraduates work part time. Average annual earnings from campus work are $2443. The average financial indebtedness of the 2005 graduate was $19,750. The FAFSA is required. The priority date for freshman financial aid applications for fall entry is March 1.

International Students: There are 1414 international students enrolled. The school actively recruits these students. Satisfactory scores are required on the written TOEFL and the college's own test.

Computers: Wireless access is available. Students may access the network from the library, computer labs, residence halls and various wireless zones on campus. All students may access the system 7 days a week during day and evening hours. There are no time limits and no fees. It is strongly recommended that all students have a personal computer.

Graduates: From July 1, 2004 to June 30, 2005, 1012 bachelor's degrees were awarded. The most popular majors were nursing (12%), justice administration (6%), and management (6%). In an average class, 5% graduate in 3 years or less, 25% graduate in 4 years or less, 36% graduate in 5 years or less, and 40% graduate in 6 years or less. 133 companies recruited on campus in 2004-2005. Of the 2004 graduating class, 40% were enrolled in graduate school within 6 months of graduation and 69% were employed.

Admissions Contact: Director of Admissions. A video is available.
E-mail: *admissions@hpu.edu* Web: *http://www.hpu.edu*

UNIVERSITY OF HAWAII SYSTEM

The University of Hawaii System, established in 1907, is a public system in Hawaii. It is governed by a board of regents, whose chief administrator is the president and the chancellor. The primary goal of the system is to provide all qualified people in Hawaii an equal opportunity for quality college and university education, to create knowledge and gain insights through research and scholarship, to preserve and contribute to the artistic and cultural heritage of the community, and to provide other public service through the dissemination of current and new ideas and techniques. The main priorities are serving the state of Hawaii, achieving program quality, establishing Pacific/Asian focus, and adapting to scientific change. The total enrollment of all 10 campuses is usually about 51,000 with 3100 faculty members. Altogether there are 115 baccalaureate, 86 master's, and 49 doctoral programs offered in University of Hawaii System. There are 4-year campuses located in Hilo and Manoa. Profiles of the 4-year campuses are included in this section.

UNIVERSITY OF HAWAII AT HILO   F-4
Hilo, HI 96720-4091

(808) 974-7414
(800) 897-4456; Fax: (808) 933-0861

Full-time: 875 men, 1330 women	**Faculty:** 162; IIB, av$
Part-time: 235 men, 400 women	**Ph.D.s:** 80%
Graduate: 30 men, 75 women	**Student/Faculty:** 14 to 1
Year: semesters, summer session	**Tuition:** $1660 ($7275)
Application Deadline: see profile	**Room & Board:** $4840
Freshman Class: n/av	
SAT or ACT: required	**COMPETITIVE**

The University of Hawaii at Hilo, founded in 1970, is part of the public University of Hawaii and offers degree programs through its Colleges of Agriculture, Arts and Sciences, and Hawaiian language. It has a branch campus at Kealakekua, West Hawaii. Major programs include marine science, volcanology, and astronomy. There are 3 undergraduate and 2 graduate schools. Figures in the above capsule and profile are approximate. In addition to regional accreditation, UH Hilo has baccalaureate program accreditation with NLN. The library contains 240,000 volumes and 11,000 microform items, and subscribes to 1200 periodicals including electronic. Computerized library services include the card catalog, interlibrary loans, and database searching. Special learning facilities include a learning resource center, art gallery, space science center and marine education center. The 115-acre campus is in a small town 200 miles southeast of Honolulu. Including any residence halls, there are 54 buildings.

Student Life: 69% of undergraduates are from Hawaii. Others are from 46 states, 32 foreign countries, and Canada. 76% are from public schools. 31% are white; 27% Asian American; 18% Native American/Eskimo. The average age of all undergraduates is 27. 29% do not continue beyond their first year; 31% remain to graduate.

Housing: 800 students can be accommodated in college housing, which includes coed dorms, on-campus apartments, off-campus apartments, and married-student housing. In addition, there are honors house, special-interest houses, and an educational recreational enrichment hall. On-campus housing is available on a first-come, first-served basis. Priority is given to out-of-town students. 79% of students commute. Alcohol is not permitted. All students may keep cars.

Activities: There are no fraternities or sororities. There are 40 groups on campus, including art, band, cheerleading, chess, choir, chorale, chorus, computers, dance, drama, ethnic, gay, honors, international, jazz band, literary magazine, musical theater, newspaper, pep band, political, professional, religious, social, social service, and student government. Popular campus events include International Night, May Day, and dances.

Sports: There are 5 intercollegiate sports for men and 4 for women, and 10 intramural sports for men and 10 for women. Facilities include a student activities center with billiards and a game room, an athletic complex with basketball courts and a weight room, 8 tennis courts, and baseball, softball, and soccer fields.

Disabled Students: 95% of the campus is accessible. Wheelchair ramps, elevators, special parking, specially equipped rest rooms, special class scheduling, lowered drinking fountains, lowered telephones, specially designed dormitory rooms, cassette recorders, talking calculators, a TDY terminal, a magnifier projector, a large-print typewriter, and taped textbooks are available.

Services: Counseling and information services are available, as is tutoring in most subjects. There is remedial math, reading, and writing.

Campus Safety and Security: Measures include 24-hour foot and vehicle patrol, self-defense education, informal discussions, and emergency telephones. There are lighted pathways/sidewalks.

Programs of Study: UH Hilo confers B.A., B.S., B.B.A., and B.S.N. degrees. Master's degrees are also awarded. Bachelor's degrees are awarded in AGRICULTURE (agriculture), BIOLOGICAL SCIENCE (biology/biological science and marine science), BUSINESS (business administration and management), COMMUNICATIONS AND THE ARTS (art, communications, English, linguistics, and music), COMPUTER AND PHYSICAL SCIENCE (astronomy, chemistry, computer science, geology, mathematics, natural sciences, and physics), HEALTH PROFESSIONS (nursing), SOCIAL SCIENCE (anthropology, criminal justice, economics, geography, Hawaiian studies, history, Japanese studies, liberal arts/general studies, philosophy, political science/government, psychology, and sociology). Business, computer science, and biology are the strongest academically. Business, psychology, and marine science are the largest.

Required: To graduate, students must earn a minimum of 120 semester hours, including at least 30 in the college from which a degree is sought, with a 2.0 GPA overall and in the major. Students also must complete general education requirements, including 10 semester hours of natural sciences with 1 hour of lab, 9 each of humanities and social sciences, 6 of world cultures, and 3 each of English composition and quantitative reasoning. 3 writing-intensive courses and 1 Hawaiian/Asian/Pacific course are also required.

Special: UH Hilo offers cross-registration with Hawaii Community College, a political science legislative internship and other internships in business and psychology, and many work-study programs. Students may study abroad through a variety of programs and other internships in business and psychology. The school permits a student-designed liberal studies major, dual degrees, a 3-2 engineering degree with the University of Hawaii at Manoa, nondegree study, pass/fail options, and credit for military experience. There is a freshman honors program.

Faculty/Classroom: 60% of faculty are male; 40%, female. All both teach and do research. The average class size in an introductory lecture is 25; in a laboratory, 25; and in a regular course, 17.

Requirements: The SAT or ACT is required. In addition, applicants should be high school graduates or present a GED certificate. Students should have earned 22 academic credits, including 4 units of English, 3 of math, 3 of life and physical sciences, and 7 of electives. Applications are accepted on-line. UH Hilo requires applicants to be in the upper 50% of their class. A GPA of 2.5 is required. AP and CLEP credits are accepted. Important factors in the admissions decision are advanced placement or honor courses, recommendations by school officials, and evidence of special talent.

Procedure: Freshmen are admitted fall and spring. Entrance exams should be taken by November of the senior year. There are early admissions and rolling admissions plans. Check with the school for current application deadlines. The application fee is $25. Notification is sent on a rolling basis. Applications are accepted on-line.

Transfer: Applicants must have a GPA of 2.0; those with fewer than 24 college credits must submit their high school transcript and SAT or ACT results. 30 of 120 credits required for the bachelor's degree must be completed at UH Hilo.

Visiting: There are regularly scheduled orientations for prospective students, including a campus tour and a meeting with an admissions counselor. There are guides for informal visits and visitors may sit in on classes. To schedule a visit, contact the Admissions Office at (808) 933-3714.

Financial Aid: In a recent year, 55% of all full-time freshmen and 41% of continuing full-time students received some form of financial aid. 55% of full-time freshmen received need-based aid. The average freshman award was $3853. 70% of undergraduates worked part time. Average annual earnings from campus work were $2600. The average financial indebtedness of a recent graduate was $10,698. UH Hilo is a member of CSS. The FAFSA and the college's own financial statement are required. Check with the school for current application deadlines.

International Students: The school actively recruits these students. They must score satisfactorily on the written TOEFL or on the electronic version and also take the college's own test. The SAT or ACT is not required, but is recommended.

Computers: All students may access the system at posted times in person and any time by modem. There are no time limits and no fees.

Admissions Contact: Admissions Office. A video is available.
E-mail: *uhhadm@hawaii.edu* Web: *www.uhh.hawaii.edu*

UNIVERSITY OF HAWAII AT MANOA   C-2
Honolulu, HI 96822   (808) 956-8975
                              (800) 823-9771; Fax: (808) 956-4148

Full-time: 5255 men, 6602 women	**Faculty:** I, -$
Part-time: 1130 men, 1364 women	**Ph.D.s:** 82%
Graduate: 2617 men, 3676 women	**Student/Faculty:** n/av
Year: semesters, summer session	**Tuition:** $3696 ($10,176)
Application Deadline: May 1	**Room & Board:** $6717
Freshman Class: 6896 applied, 4679 accepted, 2022 enrolled	
SAT Verbal/Math: 530/570*	**ACT:** 23 **VERY COMPETITIVE**

The University of Hawaii at Manoa, founded in 1907, is the major research institution in the University of Hawaii system. The undergraduate programs offered include liberal arts and sciences, business, education, engineering, nursing, tropical agriculture, architecture, travel industry management, physical science, technology, Hawaiian, Asian-Pacific Studies, social work, and medicine. There are 13 undergraduate and 12 graduate schools. In addition to regional accreditation, UHM has baccalaureate program accreditation with AACSB, ABA, ABET, ACS, ADA, APA, ASHLA, CAAHEP, CACREP, CSWE, LCME, NAAB, NAACLS, NASM, NLN, and others. The 2 libraries contain 3.3 million volumes, 4.3 million microform items, and 60,000 audio/video tapes/CDs/DVDs, and subscribe to 30,000 periodicals including electronic. Computerized library services include the card catalog, interlibrary loans, database searching, and Internet access. Special learning facilities include a learning resource center, art gallery, radio station, and TV station. The 320-acre campus is in an urban area in Honolulu. Including any residence halls, there are 247 buildings.

Student Life: 80% of undergraduates are from Hawaii. Others are from 49 states, 65 foreign countries, and Canada. 70% are from public schools. 64% are Asian American; 26% white. The average age of freshmen is 18; all undergraduates, 22. 25% do not continue beyond their first year; 65% remain to graduate.

Housing: 3074 students can be accommodated in college housing, which includes single-sex and coed dorms, on-campus apartments, and married-student housing. In addition, there are special-interest houses, substance free/wellness, first-year experience, technology, and 24-hour quiet halls. On-campus housing is guaranteed for the freshman year only and is available on a lottery system for upperclassmen. Priority is given to out-of-town students. 80% of students commute. All students may keep cars.

Activities: 1% of men belong to 1 local and 2 national fraternities; 1% of women belong to 1 local and 1 national sorority. There are more than 150 groups on campus, including art, band, cheerleading, chess, choir, chorale, chorus, dance, drama, drill team, ethnic, film, gay, honors, international, literary magazine, marching band, musical theater, newspaper, opera, pep band, photography, political, professional, radio and TV, religious, social, social service, student government, and symphony. Popular campus events include noontime concerts, All Niter Programs (Manoa Midnight Madness), and Hawaiian Culture Series.

Sports: There are 7 intercollegiate sports for men and 12 for women, and 20 intramural sports for men and 20 for women. Facilities include a 10,300-seat arena, a 4312-seat baseball stadium, swimming facilities, 2 weight rooms, a turf field and rubberized track, 2 grass fields, 2 gyms, a softball field, and 12 tennis courts.

Disabled Students: 40% of the campus is accessible. Wheelchair ramps, elevators, special parking, specially equipped rest rooms, special class scheduling, lowered drinking fountains and lowered telephones. Disability access information is available on request, and auxiliary aids and program adjustments can be arranged on an individual basis are available.

Services: Counseling and information services are available, as is tutoring in some subjects on a limited basis. There is a reader service for the blind.

Campus Safety and Security: Measures include 24-hour foot and vehicle patrol, security escort services, shuttle buses, and informal discussions. There are pamphlets/posters/films, emergency telephones, lighted pathways/sidewalks, crime alerts via campuswide e-mail, and a campus security web site.

Programs of Study: UHM confers B.A., B.S., B.B.A., B.Ed., B.F.A., B.Mus., and B.S.W. degrees. Master's and doctoral degrees are also awarded. Bachelor's degrees are awarded in AGRICULTURE (animal science, environmental studies, natural resource management, plant protection (pest management), plant science, and soil science), BIOLOGICAL SCIENCE (biology/biological science, botany, marine biology, microbiology, and zoology), BUSINESS (accounting, banking and finance, business administration and management, human resources, international business management, management information systems, management science, marketing/retailing/merchandising, recreation and leisure services, and tourism), COMMUNICATIONS AND THE ARTS (apparel design, art, Chinese, classics, communications, dance, dramatic arts, English, English as a second/foreign language, French, German, Hawaiian, Japanese, journalism, Korean, linguistics, music, musical theater, Russian, Spanish, and speech/debate/rhetoric), COMPUTER AND PHYSICAL SCIENCE (atmospheric sciences and meteorology, chemistry, computer science, geology, geophysics and seismology, information sciences and systems, mathematics, and physics), EDUCATION (elementary, physical, and secondary), ENGINEERING AND ENVIRONMENTAL DESIGN (bioengineering, civil engineering, electrical/electronics engineering, environmental science, and mechanical engineering), HEALTH PROFESSIONS (dental hygiene, exercise science, medical laboratory technology, medical technology, nursing, and speech pathology/audiology), SOCIAL SCIENCE (American studies, anthropology, Asian/Oriental studies, economics, ethnic studies, family/consumer resource management, food science, geography, gerontology, Hawaiian studies, history, interdisciplinary studies, Near Eastern studies, Pacific area studies, peace studies, philosophy, political science/government, psychology, religion, social work, sociology, and women's studies). Psychology, biology, and art are the largest.

Required: In most disciplines, a minimum GPA of 2.0 and a total of 124 credit hours are required for graduation. The total number of hours required in the major varies according to discipline. All students must fulfill general education core requirements.

Special: Internships are available with a variety of employers, including the state legislature, and through 55 different offices as well as academic departments via career services. Co-op and work-study programs and internships are also offered. Dual majors, nondegree study, and pass/fail options are available. The liberal studies program offers student-designed majors. Students may study abroad in any one of 20 countries for a summer, a semester, or a year. There are 7 national honor societies, including Phi Beta Kappa, a freshman honors program, and 4 departmental honors programs.

Faculty/Classroom: 61% of faculty are male; 29%, female. The average class size in an introductory lecture is 40; in a laboratory, 16; and in a regular course, 22.

Admissions: 68% of the 2005-2006 applicants were accepted. The SAT scores for the 2005-2006 freshman class were: Verbal--31% below 500, 49% between 500 and 599, 18% between 600 and 700, and 2% above 700; Math--14% below 500, 51% between 500 and 599, 31% between 600 and 700, and 4% above 700. The ACT scores were 19% below 21, 36% between 21 and 23, 31% between 24 and 26, 8% between 27 and 28, and 7% above 28. 50% of the current freshmen were in the top fifth of their class; 81% were in the top two fifths. 29 freshmen graduated first in their class.

Requirements: The SAT or ACT is required. Applicants must be graduates of an accredited secondary school. The GED is accepted. UHM requires 22 Carnegie units or 17 academic credits, including 4 units of English and 3 units each of math, science, and social studies, as well as 4 additional units of college preparatory courses and 5 electives. UHM requires applicants to be in the upper 40% of their class. A GPA of 2.8 is required. AP and CLEP credits are accepted. Important factors in the admissions decision are advanced placement or honor courses, recommendations by school officials, and leadership record.

Procedure: Freshmen are admitted fall and spring. Entrance exams should be taken by December of the senior year for fall admission. There is a rolling admissions plan. Applications should be filed by May 1 for fall entry and October 1 for spring entry, along with a $50 fee. Notification is sent on a rolling basis. Applications are accepted on-line.

Transfer: 2304 transfer students enrolled in 2004-2005. Applicants must have a total of 24 semester credits with a minimum GPA of 2.5. 30 of 124 credits required for the bachelor's degree must be completed at UHM.

Visiting: There are regularly scheduled orientations for prospective students, including campus tours and information sessions on areas of study, financial aid, and student employment. There are guides for informal visits. To schedule a visit, contact School and College Services at (808) 956-6524 or toll free (877) 447-3233.

Financial Aid: In 2005-2006, 44% of all full-time freshmen and 43% of continuing full-time students received some form of financial aid. 27% of full-time freshmen and 32% of continuing full-time students received need-based aid. The average freshman award was $8556. Need-based scholarships or need-based grants averaged $3544 ($10,254 maximum); need-based self-help aid (loans and jobs) averaged $3585 ($8325 maximum); non-need-based athletic scholarships averaged $12,309 ($18,240 maximum); and other non-need-based awards and non-need-based scholarships averaged $6404 ($20,000 maximum). 29% of undergraduates work part time. Average annual earnings from campus work are $4200. The average financial indebtedness of the 2005 graduate was $9280. The FAFSA and the college's own financial statement are required. The deadline for filing freshman financial aid applications for fall entry is March 1.

International Students: There are 599 international students enrolled. The school actively recruits these students. They must score satisfactorily on the written TOEFL or on the electronic version and also take the SAT or the ACT.

Computers: Wireless access is available. All students may access the system. There are no time limits and no fees. It is strongly recommended that all students have a personal computer.

Graduates: From July 1, 2004 to June 30, 2005, 2647 bachelor's degrees were awarded. The most popular majors were psychology (23%), marketing (11%), and liberal studies (7%). In an average class, 1% graduate in 3 years or less, 12% graduate in 4 years or less, 41% graduate in 5 years or less, and 56% graduate in 6 years or less. 52 companies recruited on campus in 2004-2005.

Admissions Contact: Jan Heu, Interim Director of Admissions and Records. E-mail: *ar-info@hawaii.edu* Web: *www.hawaii.edu/admrec*

IDAHO

POPULATION
DENSITY

● 10,000 and over

0   20   40   60   80   100
Miles

ALBERTSON COLLEGE OF IDAHO   A-5
Caldwell, ID 83605-4432

(208) 459-5305
(800) 224-3246; Fax: (208) 459-5757

Full-time: 317 men, 444 women	Faculty: 66; IIB, --$
Part-time: 11 men, 16 women	Ph.D.s: 86%
Graduate: 4 men, 14 women	Student/Faculty: 12 to 1
Year: 4-1-4	Tuition: $15,765
Application Deadline: June 1	Room & Board: $5330
Freshman Class: 924 applied, 777 accepted, 244 enrolled	
SAT Verbal/Math: 590/580*	ACT: 25 VERY COMPETITIVE

Albertson College of Idaho, founded in 1891, is a private institution offering degree programs in liberal arts education and the sciences. The college runs on a 12-6-12 calendar, with a 6-week intercession. In addition to regional accreditation, ACI has baccalaureate program accreditation with NASDTEC. The library contains 183,308 volumes, 17,000 microform items, and 1717 audio/video tapes/CDs/DVDs, and subscribes to 703 periodicals including electronic. Computerized library services include the card catalog, interlibrary loans, database searching, Internet access, and laptop Internet portals. Special learning facilities include a learning resource center, art gallery, natural history museum, planetarium, and rock and mineral collection. The 43-acre campus is in a small town 25 miles west of Boise. Including any residence halls, there are 21 buildings.

Student Life: 71% of undergraduates are from Idaho. Others are from 29 states, 10 foreign countries, and Canada. 95% are from public schools. 73% are white. Most claim no religious affiliation. The average age of freshmen is 18; all undergraduates, 20. 23% do not continue beyond their first year.

Housing: 410 students can be accommodated in college housing, which includes single-sex and coed dorms, on-campus apartments, and off-campus apartments. In addition there is an honors residence hall and special lifestyle floors (substance free and so on) On-campus housing is guaranteed for the freshman year only, is available on a first-come, first-served basis, and is available on a lottery system for upperclassmen. 52% of students live on campus; of those, 80% remain on campus on weekends. All students may keep cars.

Activities: 12% of men belong to 3 national fraternities; 13% of women belong to 1 local and 3 national sororities. There are 37 groups on campus, including art, band, cheerleading, choir, chorale, chorus, comput-

ers, dance, debate, drama, ethnic, film, gay, honors, international, jazz band, jazz choir, literary magazine, musical theater, newspaper, opera, orchestra, pep band, photography, political, professional, radio and TV, religious, social, social service, student government, and yearbook. Popular campus events include Spring Fling, Student-Alumni Career Forum, and Winterfest.

Sports: There are 8 intercollegiate sports for men and 10 for women, and 12 intramural sports for men and 12 for women. Facilities include an activities center with a 3000-seat gym, a weight room, and a swimming pool, as well as a 6500-seat baseball stadium, softball and soccer fields, an outdoor walking/running path and a climbing wall.

Disabled Students: 75% of the campus is accessible. Wheelchair ramps, elevators, special parking, specially equipped rest rooms, lowered drinking fountains, and special housing are available.

Services: Counseling and information services are available, as is tutoring in most subjects. There is a reader service for the blind, and remedial math, reading, and writing.

Campus Safety and Security: Measures include 24-hour foot and vehicle patrol, self-defense education, security escort services, and informal discussions. There are pamphlets/posters/films, emergency telephones, and lighted pathways/sidewalks.

Programs of Study: ACI confers B.A. and B.S. degrees. Bachelor's degrees are awarded in AGRICULTURE (environmental studies), BIOLOGICAL SCIENCE (biology/biological science), BUSINESS (business administration and management, international business management, international economics, and sports management), COMMUNICATIONS AND THE ARTS (art, creative writing, dramatic arts, English, music, and Spanish), COMPUTER AND PHYSICAL SCIENCE (chemistry and mathematics), EDUCATION (physical), HEALTH PROFESSIONS (exercise science), SOCIAL SCIENCE (anthropology, economics, history, philosophy, political science/government, psychology, and religion). Biology, business, and social sciences/history are the largest.

Required: To graduate, the student must earn 124 credits, including 40 or more in upper-division courses, with a minimum GPA of 2.0. There is a 48-unit liberal arts core curriculum, including 3-credit diversity requirements. Required disciplines include writing, math, Western civilization, cultural diversity, natural sciences, literature, social sciences, philosophy, religion, fine arts, and phys ed. The total number of hours in the major varies, but is usually more than 30. Every major requires a capstone experience, senior seminar, or independent project. A comprehensive exam is required of history and biology majors only. A thesis is required to graduate with honors in a department and as a Gipson Honors Scholar.

Special: ACI offers a 3-2 engineering degree with 4 universities, as well as cross-registration with Northwest Nazarene University. Co-op programs are available in nursing, preengineering, and computer science. Internships with major corporations, work-study programs on campus, a Washington semester, study abroad, pass/fail options, phys ed credit for military experience, an accelerated degree in business, and nondegree study are also available. The Gipson Scholar Program allows freshmen with superior records (minimum GPA of 3.5) to design their own majors. There are 3 national honor societies, a freshman honors program, and honors programs in all departments.

Faculty/Classroom: 58% of faculty are male; 42%, female. All teach undergraduates and all both teach and do research. The average class size in an introductory lecture is 21; in a laboratory, 12; and in a regular course, 16.

Admissions: 84% of the 2005-2006 applicants were accepted. The SAT scores for the 2005-2006 freshman class were: Verbal--16% below 500, 36% between 500 and 599, 35% between 600 and 700, and 14% above 700; Math--16% below 500, 40% between 500 and 599, 33% between 600 and 700, and 11% above 700. The ACT scores were 8% below 21, 21% between 21 and 23, 32% between 24 and 26, 15% between 27 and 28, and 24% above 28. 60% of the current freshmen were in the top fifth of their class; 84% were in the top two fifths.

Requirements: The SAT or ACT is required. In addition, applicants must be high school graduates or present a GED certificate. ACI recommends that students have 4 years of English, 3 each of math, history, and social studies, and 2 of science. An essay and a teacher or guidance counselor recommendation are required. AP credits are accepted. Important factors in the admissions decision are extracurricular activities record, leadership record, and recommendations by school officials.

Procedure: Freshmen are admitted to all sessions. Entrance exams should be taken by the fall of the senior year. There are early admissions and deferred admissions plans. There is a rolling admissions plan. Early decision applications should be filed by November 15; regular applications, by June 1 for fall entry, along with a $50 fee. Notification of early decision is sent December 15; regular decision, on a rolling basis.

Transfer: 52 transfer students enrolled in 2004-2005. Applicants must supply official transcripts and clearance reports from colleges attended, as well as an essay and 1 teacher recommendation. They must also have at least 28 semester hours of college credit. 30 of 124 credits required for the bachelor's degree must be completed at ACI.

Visiting: There are regularly scheduled orientations for prospective students, including an overnight stay with student hosts, class visitations, personal appointments with financial aid counselors, professors, and coaches, social events, and a campus tour. Individual tours can also be arranged. There are guides for informal visits and visitors may sit in on classes and stay overnight. To schedule a visit, contact the Admission Office at *www.albertson.edu*.

Financial Aid: In 2005-2006, 93% of all full-time freshmen and 92% of continuing full-time students received some form of financial aid. 89% of full-time freshmen and 83% of continuing full-time students received need-based aid. Need-based scholarships or need-based grants averaged $3737; need-based self-help aid (loans and jobs) averaged $3650; non-need-based athletic scholarships averaged $3415; and other non-need-based awards and non-need-based scholarships averaged $4080. 40% of undergraduates work part time. Average annual earnings from campus work are $775. The average financial indebtedness of the 2005 graduate was $25,343. The FAFSA and the college's own financial statement are required. The priority date for freshman financial aid applications for fall entry is February 15.

International Students: There are 12 international students enrolled. They must score satisfactorily on the TOEFL or take the MELAB and also take the SAT or the ACT.

Computers: Wireless access is available. All students may access the system at designated times in computer labs; 24 hours in residence halls. There are no time limits and no fees. It is strongly recommended that all students have a personal computer.

Graduates: From July 1, 2004 to June 30, 2005, 174 bachelor's degrees were awarded. The most popular majors were business (21%), history (13%), and social sciences (1%). In an average class, 47% graduate in 4 years or less, 56% graduate in 5 years or less, and 56% graduate in 6 years.

Admissions Contact: Charlene Brown, Director of Admissions. A video is available. E-mail: *admissions@albertson.edu* Web: *www.albertson.edu*

BOISE STATE UNIVERSITY
Boise, ID 83725

B-5

(208) 426-1177
(800) 824-7017; Fax: (208) 426-3765

Full-time: 5032 men, 5713 women	Faculty: 513; IIA, --$
Part-time: 2765 men, 3415 women	Ph.D.s: 78%
Graduate: 705 men, 956 women	Student/Faculty: 22 to 1
Year: semesters, summer session	Tuition: $3872 ($11,280)
Application Deadline: July 12	Room & Board: $5566
Freshman Class: 3556 applied, 3199 accepted, 1782 enrolled	
SAT Verbal/Math: 520/525*	ACT: 22 LESS COMPETITIVE

Boise State University, founded in 1932, is part of the Idaho State System of Higher Education, and offers degree programs in the arts and sciences, business, education, health science, public affairs, technology, and vocational technical education. There are 7 undergraduate schools and 1 graduate school. In addition to regional accreditation, Boise State has baccalaureate program accreditation with AACSB, ABET, CAHEA, CSWE, NASM, NCATE, and NLN. The library contains 615,000 volumes, 1.4 million microform items, and 58,000 audio/video tapes/CDs/DVDs, and subscribes to 4797 periodicals including electronic. Computerized library services include the card catalog, interlibrary loans, and database searching. Special learning facilities include a learning resource center, art gallery, radio station, and technology center. The 170-acre campus is in an urban area in Boise. Including any residence halls, there are 60 buildings.

Student Life: 89% of undergraduates are from Idaho. Students are from 50 states, 48 foreign countries, and Canada. 82% are white. The average age of freshmen is 21; all undergraduates, 26. 39% do not continue beyond their first year; 61% remain to graduate.

Housing: 1200 students can be accommodated in college housing, which includes single-sex and coed dorms, on-campus apartments, and married-student housing. In addition, there are honors houses. On-campus housing is available on a first-come, first-served basis. 93% of students commute. All students may keep cars.

Activities: 1% of men belong to 4 national fraternities; 1% of women belong to 3 national sororities. There are 170 groups on campus, including art, band, cheerleading, chess, choir, chorale, dance, drama, drill team, ethnic, gay, honors, international, jazz band, literary magazine, marching band, newspaper, orchestra, pep band, political, professional, radio and TV, religious, social, social service, and student government. Popular campus events include Spring Fling, Leadership Quest, and Martin Luther King, Jr. Celebration.

Sports: There are 7 intercollegiate sports for men and 7 for women. Facilities include a 30,000-seat stadium, a 12,000-seat indoor arena, a swimming pool, racquetball courts, indoor and outdoor tennis courts, indoor and outdoor tracks, and a weight room.

Disabled Students: 97% of the campus is accessible. Wheelchair ramps, elevators, special parking, specially equipped rest rooms, special class scheduling, lowered drinking fountains, lowered telephones, and electric doors are available.

Services: Counseling and information services are available, as is tutoring in most subjects. There is a reader service for the blind, and remedial math, reading, and writing.

Campus Safety and Security: Measures include 24-hour foot and vehicle patrol, shuttle buses, informal discussions, and pamphlets/posters/films. There are emergency telephones and lighted pathways/sidewalks.

Programs of Study: Boise State confers B.A., B.A.S., B.B.A., B.F.A., B.S., B.S.C.E., B.S.C.M., B.S.E.E., B.S.M.E., and B.Mus. degrees. Associate, master's, and doctoral degrees are also awarded. Bachelor's degrees are awarded in BIOLOGICAL SCIENCE (biology/biological science), BUSINESS (accounting, banking and finance, business administration and management, and marketing/retailing/merchandising), COMMUNICATIONS AND THE ARTS (art, communications, dramatic arts, English, fine arts, and music), COMPUTER AND PHYSICAL SCIENCE (chemistry, geology, geophysics and seismology, information sciences and systems, mathematics, physics, and radiological technology), EDUCATION (art, education, elementary, English, music, physical, and secondary), ENGINEERING AND ENVIRONMENTAL DESIGN (construction management), HEALTH PROFESSIONS (environmental health science, health science, medical laboratory technology, nursing, predentistry, premedicine, and respiratory therapy), SOCIAL SCIENCE (anthropology, criminal justice, economics, history, interdisciplinary studies, philosophy, political science/government, psychology, social science, social work, and sociology). Electrical engineering and computer science are the strongest academically. Business management and elementary education are the largest.

Required: To graduate, students must complete 128 credits with a minimum GPA of 2.0. Core requirements include 6 semester hours in English composition and 12 each in arts and humanities, social sciences, math, and natural sciences. A minimum grade of C is required in all major courses and courses used to meet the core requirements.

Special: Boise State offers internships, work-study programs, dual majors, a general studies degree, nondegree study, pass/fail options, and study abroad in England, France, Germany, and Italy. There is a chapter of Phi Beta Kappa and a freshman honors program.

Faculty/Classroom: 58% of faculty are male; 42%, female. 94% teach undergraduates, and 52% do research as well as teach. Graduate students teach 4% of introductory courses. The average class size in an introductory lecture is 28 and in a laboratory, 21.

Admissions: 90% of the 2005-2006 applicants were accepted. The SAT scores for the 2005-2006 freshman class were: Verbal--38% below 500, 45% between 500 and 599, 16% between 600 and 700, and 1% above 700; Math--36% below 500, 43% between 500 and 599, 19% between 600 and 700, and 2% above 700. The ACT scores were 51% below 21, 22% between 21 and 23, 12% between 24 and 26, 8% between 27 and 28, and 7% above 28. 23% of the current freshmen were in the top fifth of their class; 50% were in the top two fifths. There were 5 National Merit finalists.

Requirements: The SAT or ACT is required. In addition, students must graduate from an accredited high school and have an appropriate GPA and ACT or SAT test score (as rated by the school's admission index). Students must have completed 4 years of English, 3 each of math (algebra I and higher) and natural science, 2 1/2 of social science, 1 of humanities or foreign language, and 1 1/2 in other college-preparatory classes. Students who have not completed all the above classes but meet the other admission requirements will be considered for provisional admission status. AP and CLEP credits are accepted.

Procedure: Freshmen are admitted to all sessions. Applications should be filed by July 12 for fall entry and November 30 for spring entry. Check with school for the current application fee. Notification is sent rolling on a rolling basis. Applications are accepted on-line.

Transfer: A minimum GPA of 2.0 is required for students with at least 14 college credits. Those students with fewer credits must submit SAT or ACT scores and a high school transcript. 30 of 128 credits required for the bachelor's degree must be completed at Boise State.

Visiting: There are guides for informal visits and visitors may sit in on classes. To schedule a visit, contact the New Student Information Center at (208) 385-1820 or (800) 824-7017.

Financial Aid: In a recent year, 58% of all full-time students received some form of financial aid. 38% of full-time freshmen and 39% of continuing full-time students received need-based aid. The average freshman award was $5801. Need-based scholarships or need-based grants averaged $2891; need-based self-help aid (loans and jobs) averaged $2426; and non-need-based athletic scholarships averaged $8254. Boise State is a member of CSS. The CSS/Profile or FAFSA is required. Check with the school for current deadlines.

International Students: There are 159 international students enrolled. The school actively recruits these students. They must score satisfactorily on the written TOEFL or on the electronic version.

Computers: All students may access the system. Students may access the system 2 hours at a time in the labs if overcrowded.

Graduates: From July 1, 2004 to June 30, 2005, 1613 bachelor's degrees were awarded. The most popular majors were nursing (5%), accounting (5%), and criminal justice (5%). 55 companies recruited on campus in 2004-2005. Of the 2004 graduating class, 4% were enrolled in graduate school within 6 months of graduation and 84% were employed.

Admissions Contact: Barbara Fortin, Director of Admissions. A video is available. E-mail: *bsuinfo@boisestate.edu* Web: *www.boisestate.edu*

IDAHO STATE UNIVERSITY   D-6

Pocatello, ID 83209-0009	(208) 282-5822; Fax: (208) 282-4231
Full-time: 3654 men, 4318 women	Faculty: 585; IIA, --$
Part-time: 1513 men, 2414 women	Ph.D.s: 67%
Graduate: 955 men, 1123 women	Student/Faculty: 14 to 1
Year: semesters, summer session	Tuition: $4000 ($11,700)
Application Deadline: August 1	Room & Board: $5030
Freshman Class: 3566 applied, 2731 accepted, 2490 enrolled	
SAT Verbal/Math: 510/540*	ACT: 21 COMPETITIVE

Idaho State University, founded in 1901, is a public institution offering programs in the liberal arts and sciences, business, education, engineering, and health professions. There are 7 undergraduate schools and 1 graduate school. In addition to regional accreditation, ISU has baccalaureate program accreditation with AACSB, ABET, ACPE, APTA, CSWE, NASDTEC, NASM, and NCATE. The library contains 1,279,757 volumes, 1,963,434 microform items, and 4266 audio/video tapes/CDs/DVDs, and subscribes to 4350 periodicals including electronic. Computerized library services include the card catalog, interlibrary loans, database searching, Internet access, and laptop Internet portals. Special learning facilities include a learning resource center, art gallery, natural history museum, planetarium, radio station, and TV station. The 1000-acre campus is in a small town 150 miles north of Salt Lake City. Including any residence halls, there are 61 buildings.

Student Life: 92% of undergraduates are from Idaho. Others are from 46 states, 71 foreign countries, and Canada. 96% are from public schools. 83% are white. 42% are claim no religious affiliation; 36% Latter Day Saints (Mormon); 6% Catholic. The average age of freshmen is 22; all undergraduates, 26. 43% do not continue beyond their first year; 27% remain to graduate.

Housing: 964 students can be accommodated in college housing, which includes single-sex and coed dorms, on-campus apartments, and married-student housing. In addition, there are honors houses and special-interest houses. On-campus housing is available on a first-come, first-served basis. 94% of students commute. Alcohol is not permitted. All students may keep cars.

Activities: 1% of men belong to 2 local fraternities; 1% of women belong to 2 local sororities. There are 128 groups on campus, including band, choir, chorus, computers, dance, debate, drama, ethnic, gay, honors, international, jazz band, marching band, musical theater, newspaper, outdoor, pep band, photography, political, professional, radio and TV, religious, social, student government, symphony, and yearbook. Popular campus events include movies, concerts, and art displays.

Sports: There are 7 intercollegiate sports for men and 9 for women, and 15 intramural sports for men and 15 for women. Facilities include playing fields, a field house, a gym, a recreation center, tennis courts, an athletic arena, a fitness/wellness center, and facilities for bowling and billiards.

Disabled Students: All of the campus is accessible. Wheelchair ramps, elevators, special parking, specially equipped rest rooms, lowered drinking fountains, lowered telephones, special housing, electric doors, and handrails are available.

Services: Counseling and information services are available, as is tutoring in every subject. There is a reader service for the blind, and remedial math, reading, and writing.

Campus Safety and Security: Measures include 24-hour foot and vehicle patrol, self-defense education, security escort services, and shuttle buses. There are informal discussions, pamphlets/posters/films, emergency telephones, lighted pathways/sidewalks, and an e-mail bulletin alert service on campus.

Programs of Study: ISU confers B.A., B.S., B.A.T., B.B.A., B.F.A., B.M., B.M.E., and B.U.S. degrees. Associate, master's, and doctoral degrees are also awarded. Bachelor's degrees are awarded in BIOLOGICAL SCIENCE (biochemistry, biology/biological science, botany, ecology, microbiology, and zoology), BUSINESS (accounting, banking and finance, business administration and management, business systems analysis, human resources, management science, and marketing/retailing/merchandising), COMMUNICATIONS AND THE ARTS (art, communications, dramatic arts, English, French, German, music, music performance, Spanish, and speech/debate/rhetoric), COMPUTER AND PHYSICAL SCIENCE (chemistry, computer science, geology, mathematics, and physics), EDUCATION (early childhood, elementary, health, music, physical, school psychology, secondary, and special), ENGINEERING AND ENVIRONMENTAL DESIGN (civil engineering, electrical/electronics engineering, engineering, engineering management, me-

chanical engineering, and nuclear engineering), HEALTH PROFESSIONS (dental hygiene, health care administration, health science, medical laboratory science, nursing, radiological science, speech pathology/audiology, and speech therapy), SOCIAL SCIENCE (American studies, anthropology, dietetics, economics, family/consumer studies, history, international studies, liberal arts/general studies, philosophy, political science/government, psychology, social work, and sociology). Nursing, elementary education, and secondary education are the strongest academically. Biology is the largest.

Required: Students must satisfy general education requirements in the areas of written and spoken English, math, biological and physical sciences, fine arts, literature, philosophy, U.S. and non-U.S. history, government/economics, foreign language, psychology, anthropology, and sociology. To graduate, students must complete 128 credit hours, including 24 to 50 in the major, with a minimum GPA of 2.0.

Special: ISU participates in the Idaho Dental Education Program and several other medical co-op programs. Students may cross-register through the Western Education Exchange. ISU also offers a work-study program, study abroad in 50 countries, dual and student-designed majors, internships, credit by challenge exam or for life/military/work experience, nondegree study, and a general studies degree. As many as 16 credits of correspondence study may be applied toward the bachelor's degree. There are 3 national honor societies, a freshman honors program, and 6 departmental honors programs.

Faculty/Classroom: 59% of faculty are male; 41%, female.

Admissions: 77% of the 2005-2006 applicants were accepted. The SAT scores for the 2005-2006 freshman class were: Verbal--45% below 500, 37% between 500 and 599, 14% between 600 and 700, and 4% above 700; Math--30% below 500, 44% between 500 and 599, 22% between 600 and 700, and 4% above 700. The ACT scores were 50% below 21, 24% between 21 and 23, 16% between 24 and 26, 5% between 27 and 28, and 4% above 28.

Requirements: The SAT or ACT is required, the ACT is preferred. Applicants must be graduates of an accredited secondary school or have a GED. They should prepare with 4 units of English, 3 each of math and science, 2.5 of social studies, 1.5 of health and humanities, and 1 of foreign language. A GPA of 2.0 is required. AP and CLEP credits are accepted. Important factors in the admissions decision are extracurricular activities record, ability to finance college education, and parents or siblings attending the school.

Procedure: Freshmen are admitted to all sessions. Entrance exams should be taken early in the senior year. There is a deferred admissions and a rolling admissions plan. Applications should be filed by August 1 for fall entry and December 1 for spring entry. Notification is sent on a rolling basis. Applications are accepted on-line. The fall 2005 application fee was $40.

Transfer: 1088 transfer students enrolled in 2004-2005. Applicants must submit a final, official transcript from each college attended. At least 14 credit hours with a minimum GPA of 2.0 is required; students with fewer credit hours are subject to freshman admission requirements. Applicants with fewer than 25 credits must submit high school transcripts. 32 of 128 credits required for the bachelor's degree must be completed at ISU.

Visiting: There are regularly scheduled orientations for prospective students, including a meeting with an administration specialist and a campus tour. After the tour, students meet with a faculty member from their desired program of study. There are guides for informal visits and visitors may sit in on classes and stay overnight. To schedule a visit, contact Enrollment Planning at (208) 282-3277.

Financial Aid: In 2005-2006, 73% of all full-time students received some form of financial aid. 55% of full-time freshmen and 72% of continuing full-time students received need-based aid. Need-based scholarships or need-based grants averaged $2503 ($12,350 maximum); need-based self-help aid (loans and jobs) averaged $2284 ($9225 maximum); non-need-based athletic scholarships averaged $5167 ($17,130 maximum); and other non-need-based awards and non-need-based scholarships averaged $4883 ($16,875 maximum). 12% of undergraduates work part time. The average financial indebtedness of the 2005 graduate was $19,299. The FAFSA is required. The priority date for freshman financial aid applications for fall entry is February 20.

International Students: There are 212 international students enrolled. The school actively recruits these students. They must score satisfactorily on the written TOEFL or on the electronic version or take the IELTS. U.S. high school graduates with an A or B in English are exempted as are students who complete ELS level 112. Students from countries where English is the official language can be exempted depending on academic performance.

Computers: Wireless access is available. Students may check out laptops that are connected to campus wireless network; thay have access to PCs and Macs from the computer labs. All students may access the system. There are no time limits. The fee is $20 per semester.

Graduates: From July 1, 2004 to June 30, 2005, 1040 bachelor's degrees were awarded. The most popular majors were education (18%), business administration (18%), and history (18%). In an average class,

8% graduate in 4 years or less, 20% graduate in 5 years or less, and 26% graduate in 6 years or less. 210 companies recruited on campus in 2004-2005. Of the 2004 graduating class, 24% were enrolled in graduate school within 6 months of graduation and 55% were employed.

Admissions Contact: Nathan Peterson, Associate Director, Recruitment. A video is available. E-mail: *petenath@isu.edu*
Web: *www.isu.edu/departments/enroll/*

LEWIS-CLARK STATE COLLEGE   A-3

Lewiston, ID 83501-2698   **(208) 792-2210**
                                (800) 933-LCSC; Fax: (208) 792-2876

Full-time: 955 men, 1310 women	**Faculty:** 134; IIB, --$
Part-time: 415 men, 805 women	**Ph.D.s:** 71%
Graduate: none	**Student/Faculty:** 17 to 1
Year: semesters, summer session	**Tuition:** $3130 ($9130)
Application Deadline: open	**Room & Board:** $3860
Freshman Class: n/av	
SAT or ACT: required	**COMPETITIVE**

Lewis-Clark State College, founded in 1893 and today part of the Idaho Higher Education System, offers programs in the arts and sciences, business, education, nursing, and preprofessional and technical training. It is named for the famed explorers, who once camped near what is now the campus. There are 8 undergraduate schools. Figures in the above capsule and this profile are approximate. In addition to regional accreditation, Lewis-Clark has baccalaureate program accreditation with AACSB, NASDTEC, NCATE, and NLN. The library contains 253,000 volumes, 53,000 microform items, and 7000 audio/video tapes/CDs/DVDs, and subscribes to 4000 periodicals including electronic. Computerized library services include the card catalog, interlibrary loans, and database searching. Special learning facilities include a learning resource center, art gallery, planetarium, radio station, TV station, and an educational technology center. The 44-acre campus is in an urban area 100 miles southeast of Spokane. Including any residence halls, there are 29 buildings.

Student Life: 86% of undergraduates are from Idaho. Others are from 20 states, 30 foreign countries, and Canada. 82% are white. The average age of freshmen is 21; all undergraduates, 25. 46% do not continue beyond their first year; 28% remain to graduate.

Housing: 300 students can be accommodated in college housing, which includes single-sex and coed dorms, off-campus apartments, and married-student housing. In addition, there are honors houses and language houses. On-campus housing is available on a first-come, first-served basis. 91% of students commute. Alcohol is not permitted. All students may keep cars.

Activities: There are no fraternities or sororities. There are 46 groups on campus, including art, chess, choir, chorale, chorus, computers, dance, debate, departmental, drama, ethnic, honors, international, jazz band, literary magazine, musical theater, newspaper, orchestra, political, professional, radio and TV, religious, social, and student government. Popular campus events include Artists Series and Dogwood Festival.

Sports: There are 5 intercollegiate sports for men and 5 for women, and 8 intramural sports for men and 7 for women. Facilities include a gym, indoor tennis courts, and a baseball field.

Disabled Students: 99% of the campus is accessible. Wheelchair ramps, elevators, special parking, specially equipped rest rooms, and special class scheduling are available.

Services: Counseling and information services are available, as is tutoring in every subject. There is a reader service for the blind, and remedial math, reading, and writing.

Campus Safety and Security: Measures include 24-hour foot and vehicle patrol, self-defense education, security escort services, and shuttle buses. There are lighted pathways/sidewalks.

Programs of Study: Lewis-Clark confers B.A., B.S., B. Applied Sc., B. Applied Tech., B.S.N., and B.S.W. degrees. Associate degrees are also awarded. Bachelor's degrees are awarded in BIOLOGICAL SCIENCE (biology/biological science), BUSINESS (business administration and management), COMMUNICATIONS AND THE ARTS (communications and English), COMPUTER AND PHYSICAL SCIENCE (chemistry, computer science, geoscience, mathematics, and natural sciences), EDUCATION (elementary and secondary), HEALTH PROFESSIONS (nursing), SOCIAL SCIENCE (criminal justice, history, liberal arts/general studies, physical fitness/movement, psychology, social science, and social work). Education, business, and nursing are the strongest academically and are the largest.

Required: Students must earn 128 credit hours, including 38 to 40 in the core curriculum and 48 in their major, with a minimum GPA of 2.0 to graduate.

Special: Lewis-Clark offers cooperative programs and cross-registration with 3 Idaho universities, on-campus internships, work-study programs, student-designed majors, nondegree study, and pass/fail options. The college grants credit for military experience. There are also between-semester and weekend academic programs, and flexible scheduling in a variety of programs. A 3-2 engineering degree is available at Boise or

Idaho State Universities. There is 1 national honor society and a freshman honors program.

Faculty/Classroom: 58% of faculty are male; 42%, female. All teach undergraduates. The average class size in an introductory lecture is 33 and in a laboratory, 25.

Requirements: The SAT or ACT is required if the applicant is under age 21 at the time of college entrance. Lewis-Clark has a liberal admissions policy, but students must be high school graduates or present a GED certificate. They must have fulfilled requirements in English, math, social and natural sciences, fine arts, and speech, with a minimum GPA of 2.0. AP and CLEP credits are accepted.

Procedure: Freshmen are admitted to all sessions. Entrance exams should be taken before registration. There are early admissions, deferred admissions and rolling admissions plans. Application deadlines are open. Application fee is $35. Applications are accepted on-line.

Transfer: 389 transfer students enrolled in a recent year. Applicants who do not have a minimum GPA of 2.0 must submit standardized test scores. 32 of 128 credits required for the bachelor's degree must be completed at Lewis-Clark.

Visiting: There are regularly scheduled orientations for prospective students, including STAR (Student Advising and Registration), and Warrior Discovery Day. There are guides for informal visits and visitors may sit in on classes and stay overnight. To schedule a visit, contact the Office of Recruitment and Retention at (208) 792-2378.

Financial Aid: In a recent year, 68% of all full-time freshmen and 62% of continuing full-time students received some form of financial aid. 52% of full-time freshmen and 50% of continuing full-time students received need-based aid. The average freshman award was $4033. Need-based scholarships or need-based grants averaged $2781 ($4500 maximum); need-based self-help aid (loans and jobs) averaged $2652 ($6625 maximum); non-need-based athletic scholarships averaged $4485 ($8562 maximum); and other non-need-based awards and non-need-based scholarships averaged $2873. 10% of undergraduates worked part time. Average annual earnings from campus work were $1360. Lewis-Clark is a member of CSS. The FAFSA is required. Check with the school for current application deadlines.

International Students: In a recent year there were 94 international students enrolled. The school actively recruits these students. They must score satisfactorily on the written TOEFL or on the electronic version.

Computers: All students may access the system 7 days a week. There are no time limits and no fees.

Graduates: In a recent year, 299 bachelor's degrees were awarded. The most popular majors were business (25%), justice studies (15%), and nursing (14%). Of a recent graduating class, 8% were enrolled in graduate school within 6 months of graduation.

Admissions Contact: Steven J. Bussolini, Director of Admission and Market Development. E-mail: *admissions@lcsc.edu* Web: *www.lcsc.edu*

NORTHWEST NAZARENE UNIVERSITY   A-5

Nampa, ID 83686   **(208) 467-8496; (877) NNU-4-YOU**

Full-time: 1167 men and women	**Faculty:** 109; IIA, --$
Part-time: none	**Ph.D.s:** 69%
Graduate: 460 men and women	**Student/Faculty:** 11 to 1
Year: semesters, summer session	**Tuition:** $17,730
Application Deadline: August 8	**Room & Board:** $4860
Freshman Class: 1199 applied, 597 accepted, 267 enrolled	
SAT: not required	**ACT:** 23 **VERY COMPETITIVE**

Northwest Nazarene University, founded in 1913, is a private liberal arts college affiliated with the Church of the Nazarene. It offers programs in fine arts, language and literature, math and natural science, philosophy and religion, professional studies, and social science. There are 6 undergraduate and 4 graduate schools. In addition to regional accreditation, NNU has baccalaureate program accreditation with CACREP, CCNE, CSWE, NASM, NCATE, and NWCCU. The library contains 120,000 volumes, 19,500 microform items, and 3500 audio/video tapes/CDs/DVDs, and subscribes to 830 periodicals including electronic. Computerized library services include the card catalog, interlibrary loans, database searching, Internet access, and laptop Internet portals. Special learning facilities include a learning resource center, art gallery, and educational media center. The 85-acre campus is in a small town 20 miles west of Boise. Including any residence halls, there are 26 buildings.

Student Life: 56% of undergraduates are from out of state, mostly the Northwest. Students are from 21 states and 4 foreign countries. 77% are white. 81% are Protestant; 9% claim no religious affiliation. The average age of freshmen is 19; all undergraduates, 21. 28% do not continue beyond their first year; 40% remain to graduate.

Housing: 862 students can be accommodated in college housing, which includes single-sex dorms, on-campus apartments, off-campus apartments, and married-student housing. On-campus housing is guaranteed for all 4 years. 70% of students live on campus; of those, 80% remain on campus on weekends. Alcohol is not permitted. All students may keep cars.

Activities: There are no fraternities or sororities. There are 35 groups on campus, including art, band, choir, chorale, chorus, computers, debate, drama, film, forensics, honors, international, jazz band, literary magazine, musical theater, newspaper, orchestra, pep band, photography, political, professional, radio and TV, religious, social, social service, student government, symphony, and yearbook. Popular campus events include Welcome Week, Malibu Days, and Mother-Daughter Weekend.

Sports: There are 5 intercollegiate sports for men and 6 for women, and 6 intramural sports for men and 6 for women. Facilities include a lighted baseball field, 2 soccer fields, outdoor basketball, tennis, and sand volleyball courts, a track-and-field facility, a field house, a park, and a softball field.

Disabled Students: 95% of the campus is accessible. Wheelchair ramps, elevators, special parking, specially equipped rest rooms, special class scheduling, lowered drinking fountains, lowered telephones, special housing, and alternate testing and evaluation methods are available.

Services: Counseling and information services are available, as is tutoring in every subject. There is remedial math, reading, and writing.

Campus Safety and Security: Measures include 24-hour foot and vehicle patrol, security escort services, informal discussions, and pamphlets/posters/films. There are emergency telephones, lighted pathways/sidewalks, and a professional security company, student lock-up-unlock and walk-around-campus teams, and a city police substation.

Programs of Study: NNU confers B.A., B.S., and B.S.N. degrees. Associate and master's degrees are also awarded. Bachelor's degrees are awarded in BIOLOGICAL SCIENCE (biochemistry and biology/biological science), BUSINESS (accounting, business administration and management, international business management, marketing and distribution, and recreation and leisure services), COMMUNICATIONS AND THE ARTS (art, ceramic art and design, communications, English, graphic design, music, painting, sculpture, and Spanish), COMPUTER AND PHYSICAL SCIENCE (chemistry, computer science, mathematics, natural sciences, and physics), EDUCATION (art, elementary, English, foreign languages, mathematics, music, physical, science, and social science), ENGINEERING AND ENVIRONMENTAL DESIGN (engineering physics), HEALTH PROFESSIONS (nursing and premedicine), SOCIAL SCIENCE (economics, history, international studies, liberal arts/general studies, ministries, philosophy, political science/government, psychology, religion, and social work). Biology (nursing), education, and business are the strongest academically are the largest.

Required: All students must complete 124 semester credits, of which 43 must be upper division. Students must show competency in communication and language skills, have a 2.0 GPA, demonstrate math proficiency, complete a major field of study, and take a comprehensive exam. In addition, each student must complete general education requirements, which are divided into three categories: English, speech, wellness, math proficiency, and freshman seminar; Bible history and literature, theology, philosophy, and history; and art history/music literature, literature, science, and social science electives. The core curriculum requires 25 credits in explorations, 16 in contextual disciplines; and 13 in abilities. The number of hours required varies per major, as do senior internships and projects.

Special: There is cross-registration with other Nazarene schools and study abroad in 11 countries. The university also offers internships, which are required in many majors, a work-study program, a general studies degree, dual and student-designed majors, and credit for military experience. An accelerated degree in business is offered, as are B.A.-B.S. degrees. There is a 3-2 engineering program with the University of Idaho, Seattle Pacific University, and Walla Walla College. There are 4 national honor societies, and a freshman honors program.

Faculty/Classroom: 65% of faculty are male; 35%, female. 97% teach undergraduates, and 12% do research. No introductory courses are taught by graduate students. The average class size in an introductory lecture is 21; in a laboratory, 10; and in a regular course, 18.

Admissions: 50% of the 2005-2006 applicants were accepted. The ACT scores for the 2005-2006 freshman class were: 35% below 21, 30% between 21 and 23, 18% between 24 and 26, 10% between 27 and 28, and 8% above 28. 13 freshmen graduated first in their class.

Requirements: The ACT is required. In addition, applicants should be graduates of an accredited secondary school; the GED may also be accepted. Applicants should prepare with 4 years of English, 3 each of math, science, and history or social science, and 2 of foreign language. A GPA of 2.5 is required. AP and CLEP credits are accepted.

Procedure: Freshmen are admitted fall, spring, and summer. Entrance exams should be taken early in the senior year. Early action applications should be filed by December 15; regular applications, by August 8 for fall entry and December 15 for winter entry, along with a $25 fee. Notification is sent on a rolling basis. Applications are accepted on-line.

Transfer: 92 transfer students enrolled in 2004-2005. Students who have earned the equivalent of 12 semester credits may be admitted as transfer students. Official transcripts from all colleges previously attended must be submitted. 32 of 124 credits required for the bachelor's degree must be completed at NNU.

Visiting: There are regularly scheduled orientations for prospective students, including the opportunity to stay in a dorm and have class visits.

There are guides for informal visits. To schedule a visit, contact the Campus Visit Coordinator at *admissions@nnu.edu*.

Financial Aid: In 2005-2006, 95% of all full-time freshmen and 96% of continuing full-time students received some form of financial aid. 79% of full-time freshmen and 64% of continuing full-time students received need-based aid. The average freshman award was $13,238. 66% of undergraduates work part time. Average annual earnings from campus work are $883. The average financial indebtedness of the 2005 graduate was $24,405. The FAFSA is required. The priority date for freshman financial aid applications for fall entry is February 15. The deadline for filing freshman financial aid applications for fall entry is August 25.

International Students: They must score satisfactorily on the written TOEFL or on the electronic version and also take the ACT, scoring 18.

Computers: Wireless access is available. Students can have a computer in dorm rooms; there are 4 computer labs on campus, and some PCs in the library. All students may access the system. There are no time limits and no fees. It is strongly recommended that all students have a personal computer.

Graduates: From July 1, 2004 to June 30, 2005, 241 bachelor's degrees were awarded. The most popular majors were business administration (17%), elementary education (9%), and social work (8%). In an average class, 51% graduate in 6 years or less. 100 companies recruited on campus in 2004-2005.

Admissions Contact: Office of Enrollment Services.
Web: *www.nnu.edu*

UNIVERSITY OF IDAHO A-2

Moscow, ID 83844-2282
(208) 885-6326
(888) 884-3246; Fax: (208) 885-9119

Full-time: 4630 men, 3772 women	Faculty: 507; I, --$
Part-time: 614 men, 534 women	Ph.D.s: 77%
Graduate: 1563 men, 1391 women	Student/Faculty: 17 to 1
Year: semesters, summer session	Tuition: $3968 ($12,738)
Application Deadline: August 1	Room & Board: $5342
Freshman Class: 4091 applied, 3407 accepted, 1657 enrolled	
SAT Verbal/Math: 550/550*	ACT: 23 NONCOMPETITIVE

The University of Idaho, founded in 1889 as a land-grant institution, offers programs in art and architecture, agriculture, business and economics, education, engineering, letters and science, and natural resources, forestry, wildlife, and range sciences. There are 9 undergraduate schools and 1 graduate school. In addition to regional accreditation, UI has baccalaureate program accreditation with AACSB, ABET, ADA, ASLA, CSAB, FIDER, NAAB, NASAD, NASM, NCATE, NRPA, and SAF. The 2 libraries contain 1,666,884 volumes, 107,891 microform items, and 35,206 audio/video tapes/CDs/DVDs, and subscribe to 9183 periodicals including electronic. Computerized library services include the card catalog, interlibrary loans, and database searching. Special learning facilities include a learning resource center, art gallery, radio station, TV station, an electron microscopy center, a lab animal facility, research institutes for water resources and for materials and advanced processing, university farms, and experimental forests. The 800-acre campus is in a small town 90 miles southeast of Spokane, Washington. Including any residence halls, there are 147 buildings.

Student Life: 75% of undergraduates are from Idaho. Others are from 49 states, 82 foreign countries, and Canada. 98% are from public schools. 92% are white. The average age of freshmen is 18; all undergraduates, 22. 18% do not continue beyond their first year; 48% remain to graduate.

Housing: 2850 students can be accommodated in college housing, which includes single-sex and coed dorms, on-campus apartments, off-campus apartments, married-student housing, fraternity houses, and sorority houses. In addition, there are honors houses, special-interest houses, cooperative residence, and alcohol, smoke-free, and quiet communities. On-campus housing is guaranteed for all 4 years. 65% of students commute. Alcohol is not permitted. All students may keep cars.

Activities: 16% of men belong to 19 national fraternities; 13% of women belong to 9 national sororities. There are 132 groups on campus, including art, band, cheerleading, chess, choir, chorale, chorus, computers, dance, drama, drill team, ethnic, film, gay, honors, ice hockey, international, jazz band, literary magazine, marching band, mountaineering club, musical theater, newspaper, opera, orchestra, pep band, photography, political, professional, radio and TV, religious ski club, social, social service, student government, symphony, and yearbook. Popular campus events include Lionel Hampton Jazz Festival, the Borah Symposium, and Palousefest.

Sports: There are 6 intercollegiate sports for men and 7 for women, and 28 intramural sports for men and 27 for women. Facilities include an activity center, a 17,000-seat domed stadium for basketball and football games, indoor and outdoor tracks, a 2-pool swim center, 3 gyms, a 500-seat auditorium, an 18-hole championship golf course, tennis, racquetball, and handball courts, and a student recreation center with a 55-foot climbing wall.·

Disabled Students: 87% of the campus is accessible. Wheelchair ramps, elevators, special parking, specially equipped rest rooms, special class scheduling, lowered drinking fountains, lowered telephones, 2 motorized wheelchairs, plus readers, note takers, and sign language interpreters are available.

Services: Counseling and information services are available, as is tutoring in most subjects. There is a reader service for the blind and remedial math and writing. There is career and professional planning and a Center for Academic Advising.

Campus Safety and Security: Measures include 24-hour foot and vehicle patrol, self-defense education, informal discussions, and pamphlets/posters/films. There are emergency telephones and lighted pathways/sidewalks.

Programs of Study: UI confers B.A., B.S., B.F.A., B.G.S., B.L.Arch., B.Mus., B.N.S., B.S.Ag.Econ., B.S.Ag.Ed., B.S.Ag.Sc.Tech., B.S.A.S.M., B.S.An.Sc., B.S.Arch., B.S.Art Ed., B.S.B.A.E., B.S.Bus., B.S.C.E., B.S.Ch.E., B.S.Comp.E., B.S.C.S., B.S.Dan., B.S.Erly.Chdhd.Dev.Ed., B.S.Ed., B.S.E.E., B.S.Ent., B.S.Env.S., B.S.F.C.S., B.S.Fish.Res., B.S.F.S., B.S.For.Prod., B.S.For.Res., B.S.I.S., B.S.M.B.B., B.S.M.E., B.S.Met.E., B.S.Mfg.E., B.S.M.S.E., B.S.Microbiol., B.S.Ecol.Cons.Biol., B.S.O.Ad., B.S.P.E., B.S.Pl.Sc., B.S.R.L.M., B.S.Rangeland Ecol.-Mgt., B.S.Rec., B.S.Res.Rc., B.S.Soil Sc., B.S.Tech., B.S.Vet.Sc., and B.S.Wildl.Res. degrees. Master's and doctoral degrees are also awarded. Bachelor's degrees are awarded in AGRICULTURE (agricultural business management, agricultural economics, agricultural mechanics, agriculture, animal science, fishing and fisheries, forestry production and processing, horticulture, range/farm management, soil science, and wildlife management), BIOLOGICAL SCIENCE (biology/biological science, botany, entomology, microbiology, molecular biology, and zoology), BUSINESS (accounting, banking and finance, management information systems, marketing/retailing/merchandising, office supervision and management, personnel management, and sports management), COMMUNICATIONS AND THE ARTS (applied music, art, communications, dance, design, dramatic arts, English, fine arts, French, German, journalism, Latin, music, music history and appreciation, music performance, music theory and composition, photography, Spanish, studio art, and telecommunications), COMPUTER AND PHYSICAL SCIENCE (applied mathematics, chemistry, computer science, geology, information sciences and systems, mathematics, and physics), EDUCATION (agricultural, art, business, early childhood, elementary, foreign languages, home economics, industrial arts, marketing and distribution, music, physical, recreation, science, secondary, special, and vocational), ENGINEERING AND ENVIRONMENTAL DESIGN (agricultural engineering, architectural engineering, bioengineering, cartography, chemical engineering, civil engineering, computer engineering, electrical/electronics engineering, geological engineering, interior design, landscape architecture/design, mechanical engineering, metallurgical engineering, and mining and mineral engineering), HEALTH PROFESSIONS (medical laboratory technology and veterinary science), SOCIAL SCIENCE (American studies, anthropology, classical/ancient civilization, criminal justice, dietetics, economics, food science, geography, history, interdisciplinary studies, international relations, Latin American studies, parks and recreation management, philosophy, political science/government, psychology, rural economics, sociology, and textiles and clothing). Electrical engineering, natural resources, and business are the strongest academically. Elementary education and electrical and computer science are the largest.

Required: To graduate, students must complete at least 128 credit hours, including 36 in upper-division courses and 40 in the major, with a minimum GPA of 2.0. The core curriculum requires a total of 30 credits in communications, math, natural and applied sciences, humanities, and social sciences.

Special: UI offers cooperative programs and cross-registration with Washington State University and Idaho State University, internships, extensive study-abroad programs, work-study programs, B.A.-B.S. degrees, dual and student-designed majors, a general studies degree, credit for life and work experience, nondegree study, and pass/fail options. There are 24 national honor societies, including Phi Beta Kappa, a freshman honors program, and a university honors program.

Faculty/Classroom: 64% of faculty are male; 36%, female. 90% teach undergraduates and 95% do research. Graduate students teach 20% of introductory courses. The average class size in an introductory lecture is 39; in a laboratory, 14; and in a regular course, 16.

Admissions: 83% of the 2005-2006 applicants were accepted. The SAT scores for the 2005-2006 freshman class were: Verbal--26% below 500, 42% between 500 and 599, 26% between 600 and 700, and 6% above 700; Math--25% below 500, 43% between 500 and 599, 26% between 600 and 700, and 6% above 700. The ACT scores were 32% below 21, 26% between 21 and 23, 23% between 24 and 26, 9% between 27 and 28, and 11% above 28. 38% of the current freshmen were in the top fifth of their class; 67% were in the top two fifths. There were 8 National Merit finalists. 55 freshmen graduated first in their class.

Requirements: The SAT or ACT is required. In addition, applicants must be graduates of an accredited secondary school. GED certificates are accepted for special admissions only. Students must have completed at least 8 credits in English, 6 each in math and natural science, 5 in social science, 3 in electives, and 2 in humanities/foreign language. A GPA of 2.5 is required. AP and CLEP credits are accepted.

Procedure: Freshmen are admitted to all sessions. Entrance exams should be taken during the junior or senior year. There are deferred admissions and rolling admissions plans. Applications should be filed by August 1 for fall entry, December 15 for spring entry, and May 1 for summer entry, along with a $40 fee. The college accepts all in-state residents. Notification is sent on a rolling basis. Applications are accepted on-line.

Transfer: 751 transfer students enrolled in 2004-2005. Applicants must have completed at least 14 credit hours with a minimum GPA of 2.0, or 2.8 for engineering transfers from outside the state of Idaho. 32 of 128 credits required for the bachelor's degree must be completed at UI.

Visiting: There are regularly scheduled orientations for prospective students, including a visit with faculty and financial aid personnel, a tour of campus, and an overnight stay in the dorms or Greek houses. There are guides for informal visits and visitors may sit in on classes and stay overnight. To schedule a visit, contact the Office of New Student Services at (208) 885-6163.

Financial Aid: In 2005-2006, 57% of all full-time freshmen and 58% of continuing full-time students received some form of financial aid. 43% of full-time freshmen and 42% of continuing full-time students received need-based aid. The average freshman award was $8151. Need-based scholarships or need-based grants averaged $3263; need-based self-help aid (loans and jobs) averaged $3564; non-need-based athletic scholarships averaged $12,442; and other non-need-based awards and non-need-based scholarships averaged $3286. All of undergraduates work part time. The average financial indebtedness of the 2005 graduate was $20,002. UI is a member of CSS. The FAFSA is required. The deadline for filing freshman financial aid applications for fall entry is February 15.

International Students: There are 182 international students enrolled. The school actively recruits these students. They must score satisfactorily on the written TOEFL or on the electronic version and also take the SAT or the ACT.

Computers: All students may access the system 23 hours a day in more than 20 labs. There are no time limits and no fees. It is recommended that students in business, architecture, and law have personal computers.

Graduates: From July 1, 2004 to June 30, 2005, 1924 bachelor's degrees were awarded. The most popular majors were business/marketing (13%), education (12%), and engineering (9%). In an average class, 20% graduate in 4 years or less, 47% graduate in 5 years or less, and 55% graduate in 6 years or less.

Admissions Contact: Daniel D. Davenport, Director, Admissions and Student Financial Aid. A video is available.
E-mail: *admappl@uidaho.edu*
Web: *www.students.uidaho.edu.admissions*

ILLINOIS

Rockford ●
Waukegan
Elgin
Aurora
INSET
Rock Island
Galesburg
Peoria
Springfield   Decatur
E. St. Louis

POPULATION
DENSITY
● 50,000 and over

0 20 40 60 80 100
Miles

INSET

Arlington Heights
Evanston
Oak Park
Oak Lawn Cicero
Berwyn Chicago
Joliet

AUGUSTANA COLLEGE
C-2

Rock Island, IL 61201-2296
(309) 794-7341
(800) 798-8100, ext. 7341; Fax: (309) 794-7422

Full-time: 987 men, 1376 women	**Faculty:** 145; IIB, av$
Part-time: 11 men, 12 women	**Ph.D.s:** 96%
Graduate: none	**Student/Faculty:** 16 to 1
Year: quarters, summer session	**Tuition:** $23,457
Application Deadline: open	**Room & Board:** $6405
Freshman Class: 2921 applied, 2462 accepted, 679 enrolled	
ACT: 26*	**VERY COMPETITIVE+**

Augustana College, founded in 1860, is a private liberal arts institution affiliated with the Evangelical Lutheran Church in America. In addition to regional accreditation, Augustana has baccalaureate program accreditation with NASM and NCATE. The 3 libraries contain 185,026 volumes, 107,037 microform items, and 1741 audio/video tapes/CDs/DVDs, and subscribe to 1200 periodicals including electronic. Computerized library services include the card catalog, interlibrary loans, database searching, Internet access, and laptop Internet portals. Special learning facilities include a learning resource center, art gallery, natural history museum, planetarium, radio station, and a preschool, a center for communicative disorders, a geology museum, a planetarium/observatory, a U.S. Geological Survey map repository, a Swedish immigration research center, 3 outdoor environmental labs, and an educational technology building. The 115-acre campus is in a suburban area 165 miles west of Chicago. Including any residence halls, there are 46 buildings.

Student Life: 88% of undergraduates are from Illinois. Students are from 28 states, 24 foreign countries, and Canada. 91% are white. 39% are Protestant; 35% Catholic. The average age of freshmen is 18; all undergraduates, 20. 14% do not continue beyond their first year; 75% remain to graduate.

Housing: 1605 students can be accommodated in college housing, which includes single-sex and coed dorms, on-campus apartments, and off-campus apartments. In addition, there are special-interest houses. On-campus housing is guaranteed for all 4 years. 68% of students live on campus; of those, 75% remain on campus on weekends. Alcohol is not permitted. All students may keep cars.

Activities: 19% of men belong to 7 local fraternities; 26% of women belong to 6 local sororities. There are 110 groups on campus, including

alcohol responsibility, band, cheerleading, choir, chorale, chorus, computers, dance, debate, drama, environment, ethnic, gay, honors, international, jazz band, literary magazine, musical theater, newspaper, opera, orchestra, pep band, political, professional, radio and TV, religious, social, social service, student government, symphony, volunteer and yearbook. Popular campus events include Messiah performances, Greek Olympics, and Humanities Festival.

Sports: There are 9 intercollegiate sports for men and 8 for women, and 19 intramural sports for men and 18 for women. Facilities include a recreational center with an indoor 200-meter track, courts for basketball, volleyball, racquetball, and tennis, a weight room, and physical conditioning equipment. A phys ed center has courts for basketball, volleyball, racquetball, and badminton, weight and physical conditioning rooms, wrestling facilities, and a swimming pool. There is a lighted field and an all-weather track for football, soccer, and track and field, including stadium seating for 3500. Facilities also include a baseball field, 10 outdoor tennis courts, and a dance studio.

Disabled Students: 75% of the campus is accessible. Wheelchair ramps, elevators, special parking, specially equipped rest rooms, lowered drinking fountains, lowered telephones, special housing, and automatic door openers are available.

Services: Counseling and information services are available, as is tutoring in every subject. There is a reader service for the blind.

Campus Safety and Security: Measures include 24-hour foot and vehicle patrol, self-defense education, security escort services, and informal discussions. There are pamphlets/posters/films, lighted pathways/sidewalks, and vans.

Programs of Study: Augustana confers the B.A. degree. Bachelor's degrees are awarded in BIOLOGICAL SCIENCE (biology/biological science), BUSINESS (accounting and business administration and management), COMMUNICATIONS AND THE ARTS (art, art history and appreciation, classics, dramatic arts, English, French, German, music, music performance, Scandinavian languages, Spanish, speech/debate/rhetoric, and studio art), COMPUTER AND PHYSICAL SCIENCE (chemistry, computer science, earth science, geology, mathematics, and physics), EDUCATION (art, elementary, music, physical, and secondary), ENGINEERING AND ENVIRONMENTAL DESIGN (engineering physics, landscape architecture/design, and preengineering), HEALTH PROFESSIONS (occupational therapy, premedicine, and speech pathology/audiology), SOCIAL SCIENCE (Asian/Oriental studies, economics, geography, history, philosophy, political science/government, psychology, public administration, religion, and sociology). Premedicine, business/accounting, and biology are the largest.

Required: A total of 123 credits with a minimum GPA of 2.0 is required to graduate. Courses in foreign language, religion, writing, phys ed, fine arts, humanities, literature, and the sciences must be completed.

Special: Cooperative degree programs are offered in engineering, environmental management, forestry, landscape architecture, and occupational therapy with Duke, Iowa State, Northwestern, Purdue, and Washington (St. Louis) Universities and the University of Illinois (Urbana-Champaign). Domestic and international internships are offered. Study abroad is possible in 17 countries, including China, Peru, Sweden, Germany, and France, as is fall term study in East Asia, Europe, and Latin America. Interdisciplinary majors are offered in earth science, teaching, Asian studies, and public administration. A B.A.-B.S. degree in occupational therapy is offered, as well as 3-2 engineering programs with the University of Illinois and Purdue, Washington (St. Louis), and Iowa State Universities. Work-study programs, double majors, phys ed credits, and pass/fail options are available. There are 13 national honor societies, including Phi Beta Kappa, a freshman honors program, and 12 departmental honors programs.

Faculty/Classroom: 60% of faculty are male; 40%, female. All teach undergraduates and 60% both teach and do research. The average class size in an introductory lecture is 23; in a laboratory, 17; and in a regular course, 22.

Admissions: 84% of the 2005-2006 applicants were accepted. The ACT scores for the 2005-2006 freshman class were: 4% below 21, 11% between 21 and 23, 30% between 24 and 26, 22% between 27 and 28, and 33% above 28. 55% of the current freshmen were in the top fifth of their class; 85% were in the top two fifths.

Requirements: The SAT or ACT is required. In addition, applicants should be graduates of an accredited secondary school with 16 academic credits, including 4 in English, 3 in math, 2 each in science and social studies, 1 in foreign language, and other science and math courses for appropriate majors. An audition for music majors and an interview are recommended. The GED is accepted. AP credits are accepted. Important factors in the admissions decision are advanced placement or honor courses, evidence of special talent, and recommendations by school officials.

Procedure: Freshmen are admitted fall, winter, and spring. Entrance exams should be taken by fall of the senior year. There are deferred admissions and early admissions plans. Application deadlines are open. The fall 2005 application fee was $25. Notification is sent on a rolling basis. 153 applicants were on the 2005 waiting list; 20 were admitted. Applications are accepted on-line.

Transfer: 63 transfer students enrolled in 2004-2005. A minimum GPA of 2.0 is required. SAT or ACT scores and an interview are recommended. 60 of 123 credits required for the bachelor's degree must be completed at Augustana.

Visiting: There are regularly scheduled orientations for prospective students, including information sessions with speakers, exhibits, campus tours, meetings with faculty, counselors, and students, and social activities. There are guides for informal visits and visitors may sit in on classes and stay overnight. To schedule a visit, contact Kent Brands, Vice President of Enrollment.

Financial Aid: In 2005-2006, 96% of all full-time students received some form of financial aid. 66% of full-time freshmen and 67% of continuing full-time students received need-based aid. The average freshman award was $17,871. Need-based scholarships or need-based grants averaged $12,816; need-based self-help aid (loans and jobs) averaged $3801; and other non-need-based awards and non-need-based scholarships averaged $4241. 80% of undergraduates work part time. Average annual earnings from campus work are $900. The average financial indebtedness of the 2005 graduate was $18,098. Augustana is a member of CSS. The FAFSA and the college's own financial statement are required. The deadline for filing freshman financial aid applications for fall entry is April 5.

International Students: There are 22 international students enrolled. The school actively recruits these students. A staisfactory score is required on the written TOEFL.

Computers: Wireless access is available. An extensive campus network provides intranet services, including e-mail accounts, and Internet access. Residence hall rooms have jacks for each resident. Wireless access is provided in selected buildings, including the library. An educational technology building provides computer classrooms and labs, including specialized equipment for multimedia applications. Computers for student access to the network are widespread on campus. All students may access the system. There are no time limits and no fees. It is strongly recommended that all students have a personal computer.

Graduates: From July 1, 2004 to June 30, 2005, 493 bachelor's degrees were awarded. The most popular majors were business/marketing (20%), biological/life science (15%), and social science (11%). In an average class, 71% graduate in 4 years, 77% graduate in 5 years, and 76% graduate in 6 years. 238 companies recruited on campus in 2004-2005. Of the 2004 graduating class, 34% were enrolled in graduate school within 6 months of graduation and 65% were employed.

Admissions Contact: Kent Brands, Vice President of Enrollment. E-mail: *admissions@augustana.edu* Web: *www.augustana.edu*

AURORA UNIVERSITY   E-2
Aurora, IL 60506-4892

(630) 844-5533
(800) 742-5281; Fax: (630) 844-5535

Full-time: 540 men, 910 women	Faculty: 63; IIA, --$
Part-time: 65 men, 155 women	Ph.D.s: 85%
Graduate: 520 men, 1290 women	Student/Faculty: 23 to 1
Year: quarters, summer session	Tuition: $14,255
Application Deadline: open	Room & Board: $6390
Freshman Class: n/av	
SAT or ACT recommended	COMPETITIVE

Aurora University, founded in 1893, is a private institution that offers graduate and undergraduate degrees in arts and sciences, education, business and information science, communication, nursing and health, recreation, social work, and a professional/staff program. There are 4 undergraduate and 4 graduate schools. Figures in the above capsule and this profile are approximate. In addition to regional accreditation, AU has baccalaureate program accreditation with CSWE, NLN, and NRPA. The library contains 114,144 volumes, 221,286 microform items, and 6791 audio/video tapes/CDs/DVDs, and subscribes to 627 periodicals including electronic. Computerized library services include the card catalog, interlibrary loans, and database searching. Special learning facilities include a learning resource center, art gallery, TV station, a Native-American museum, a lake-front campus, and a natural study area in Wisconsin. The 27-acre campus is in a suburban area 40 miles west of Chicago. Including any residence halls, there are 19 buildings.

Student Life: 96% of undergraduates are from Illinois. Others are from 17 states. 89% are from public schools. 70% are white; 17% African American; 10% Hispanic. 65% claim no religious affiliation; 17% Catholic; 17% Protestant. The average age of freshmen is 18; all undergraduates, 26. 24% do not continue beyond their first year; 50% remain to graduate.

Housing: 415 students can be accommodated in college housing, which includes single-sex and coed dorms. On-campus housing is available on a first-come, first-served basis. 69% of students commute. Alcohol is not permitted. All students may keep cars.

Activities: 2% of men belong to 1 local and 3 national fraternities; 3% of women belong to 2 local and 2 national sororities. There are 40 groups on campus, including cheerleading, choir, chorus, computers, dance, drama, ethnic, film, gay, honors, international, literary magazine, musical theater, newspaper, photography, political, professional, radio and TV, religious, social service, student government, and yearbook. Popular campus events include Spring Fling and annual Native-American Pow Wow.

Sports: There are 6 intercollegiate sports for men and 5 for women, and 7 intramural sports for men and 6 for women. Facilities include a fitness center, a weight room, a 2000-seat gym, football and soccer fields, a racquetball court, and a climbing wall.

Disabled Students: 95% of the campus is accessible. Wheelchair ramps, elevators, special parking, specially equipped rest rooms, and special class scheduling are available.

Services: Counseling and information services are available, as is tutoring in most subjects. There is remedial math, reading, and writing. There are professional and peer tutors, workshops in word processing, and computer-based tutorials.

Campus Safety and Security: Measures include 24-hour foot and vehicle patrol, self-defense education, security escort services, and informal discussions. There are pamphlets/posters/films, emergency telephones, and lighted pathways/sidewalks.

Programs of Study: AU confers B.A., B.S., B.S.N., B.S.P.S., and B.S.W. degrees. Master's and doctoral degrees are also awarded. Bachelor's degrees are awarded in BIOLOGICAL SCIENCE (biology/biological science), BUSINESS (accounting, business administration and management, business economics, management information systems, management science, and marketing/retailing/merchandising), COMMUNICATIONS AND THE ARTS (communications, English, and literature), COMPUTER AND PHYSICAL SCIENCE (computer science and mathematics), EDUCATION (elementary and physical), ENGINEERING AND ENVIRONMENTAL DESIGN (environmental science and industrial administration/management), HEALTH PROFESSIONS (nursing), SOCIAL SCIENCE (criminal justice, history, humanities, parks and recreation management, philosophy, political science/government, psychology, religion, social work, and sociology). Business, education, and protective services are the largest.

Required: To graduate, students must complete 120 semester hours with a minimum GPA of 2.0. Distribution requirements include 12 semester hours each in humanities, social/behavioral science, and natural science/math, 6 in freshman English, and 3 additional in communication. A minimum of 27 hours is required in the major; most require 36 or more.

Special: AU offers cross-registration with North Central College and Benedictine University, field-related job experience, work-study programs, study abroad in England, Germany, and Mexico, internships, student designed and dual majors, nondegree study, and a B.A.-B.S. degree. Pass/fail options, and credit for life, military, or work experience are also available. There are 3 national honor societies.

Faculty/Classroom: 40% of faculty are male; 60%, female. All teach undergraduates. No introductory courses are taught by graduate students. The average class size in an introductory lecture is 24; in a laboratory, 18; and in a regular course, 16.

Requirements: The SAT or ACT is recommended. In addition, applicants must be graduates of an accredited secondary school or have earned the GED. A GPA of 2.0 is required. AP and CLEP credits are accepted. Important factors in the admissions decision are leadership record, advanced placement or honor courses, and extracurricular activities record.

Procedure: Freshmen are admitted fall, winter, and spring. Entrance exams should be taken by late in the junior year or early in the senior year. There are early decision, early admissions, deferred admissions and rolling admissions plans. Application deadlines are open. Applications are accepted on-line. The fall 2005 application fee was $25.

Transfer: 320 transfer students enrolled in a recent year. Applicants are required to have a minimum GPA of 2.0 and must have completed at least 15 semester hours. 30 of 120 credits required for the bachelor's degree must be completed at AU.

Visiting: There are regularly scheduled orientations for prospective students. There are guides for informal visits and visitors may sit in on classes and stay overnight. To schedule a visit, contact the Admissions Office.

Financial Aid: In a recent year, 97% of all full-time freshmen and 73% of continuing full-time students received some form of financial aid. 79% of full-time freshmen and 62% of continuing full-time students received need-based aid. The average freshman award was $13,855. Need-based scholarships or need-based grants averaged $5886 ($7000 maximum); need-based self-help aid (loans and jobs) averaged $3275 ($6124 maximum); and other non-need-based awards and non-need-based scholarships averaged $7258 ($9000 maximum). 11% of undergraduates worked part time. Average annual earnings from campus work were $849. The average financial indebtedness of a recent graduate was $6925. The FAFSA is required. Check with the school for current application deadlines.

International Students: They must score satisfactorily on the written TOEFL.

Computers: All students may access the system until midnight. There are no time limits and no fees. It is strongly recommended that all students have a personal computer.

Graduates: In a recent year, 357 bachelor's degrees were awarded. The most popular majors were business (21%), education (17%), and criminal justice (16%). In an average class, 39% graduate in 4 years or less, 52% graduate in 5 years or less, and 54% graduate in 6 years or less. 41 companies recruited on campus in a recent year. Of a recent graduating class, 15% were enrolled in graduate school within 6 months of graduation and 90% were employed.

Admissions Contact: Linda Gebhard, Enrollment Information Manager. A video is available. E-mail: *admission@aurora.edu* Web: *http://www.aurora.edu*

BENEDICTINE UNIVERSITY   E-2

Lisle, IL 60532	(630) 829-6300; Fax: (630) 829-6301
Full-time: 653 men, 865 women	Faculty: 77; IIA, -$
Part-time: 279 men, 523 women	Ph.Ds: 89%
Graduate: 375 men, 705 women	Student/Faculty: 20 to 1
Year: semesters, summer session	Tuition: $19,210
Application Deadline: open	Room & Board: $6500
Freshman Class: 975 applied, 801 accepted, 311 enrolled	
ACT: 23	COMPETITIVE

Benedictine University, founded in 1887, is a private, Roman Catholic liberal arts and sciences institution. There are 4 undergraduate and 4 graduate schools. In addition to regional accreditation, Benedictine has baccalaureate program accreditation with ADA and NLN. The library contains 166,537 volumes, 355,089 microform items, and 9404 audio/video tapes/CDs/DVDs, and subscribes to 16,186 periodicals including electronic. Computerized library services include the card catalog, interlibrary loans, database searching, Internet access, and laptop Internet portals. Special learning facilities include a learning resource center, art gallery, natural history museum, and TV station. The 108-acre campus is in a suburban area 25 miles west of Chicago. Including any residence halls, there are 11 buildings.

Student Life: 95% of undergraduates are from Illinois. Others are from 31 states, 9 foreign countries, and Canada. 42% are white; 14% Asian American; 10% African American. The average age of freshmen is 18; all undergraduates, 25. 24% do not continue beyond their first year; 52% remain to graduate.

Housing: On-campus housing is available on a first-come, first-served basis. All students may keep cars.

Activities: There are no fraternities or sororities. There are 38 groups on campus, including art, band, cheerleading, choir, chorus, computers, dance, debate, ethnic, honors, international, jazz band, literary magazine, musical theater, newspaper, pep band, political, professional, radio and TV, religious, social, social service, and student government. Popular campus events include Family Weekend, Homecoming, and Senior Week.

Sports: There are 8 intercollegiate sports for men and 8 for women, and 16 intramural sports for men and 16 for women. Facilities include a recreation center housing a main arena, a pool, a weight room, and a dance room; racquetball and tennis courts; a sports complex that includes a football/soccer/track stradium, a baseball stadium and a softball stadium.

Disabled Students: All of the campus is accessible. Wheelchair ramps, elevators, special parking, specially equipped rest rooms, and lowered drinking fountains are available.

Services: Counseling and information services are available, as is tutoring in most subjects. There is a reader service for the blind, and remedial math, reading, and writing.

Campus Safety and Security: Measures include 24-hour foot and vehicle patrol, self-defense education, security escort services, and informal discussions. There are pamphlets/posters/films, emergency telephones, and lighted pathways/sidewalks.

Programs of Study: Benedictine confers B.A., B.S., B.B.A., and B.S.N. degrees. Associate, master's, and doctoral degrees are also awarded. Bachelor's degrees are awarded in BIOLOGICAL SCIENCE (biochemistry, biology/biological science, molecular biology, and nutrition), BUSINESS (accounting, banking and finance, business administration and management, business economics, international business management, management information systems, marketing management, marketing/retailing/merchandising, and organizational behavior), COMMUNICATIONS AND THE ARTS (arts administration/management, communications, literature, music, publishing, Spanish, and studio art), COMPUTER AND PHYSICAL SCIENCE (chemistry, computer science, mathematics, and physics), EDUCATION (elementary and special), ENGINEERING AND ENVIRONMENTAL DESIGN (engineering and applied science and environmental science), HEALTH PROFESSIONS (clinical science, health care administration, health science, nuclear medical technology, nursing, and radiation therapy), SOCIAL SCIENCE

(economics, history, international studies, philosophy, political science/government, psychology, social science, and sociology). Biology, health science, and psychology are the largest.

Required: To graduate students must complete 120 semester hours, including 36 in their major, and maintain a minimum GPA of 2.0. They must complete 12 hours in the arts and humanities, 9 each in social sciences, natural sciences, and cultural heritage, 6 in rhetoric, and 3 each in speech, math, and freshman seminar. A thesis, capstone course or project, or comprehensive exam is required in specific departments.

Special: There is cross-registration with North Central College, Aurora University, and the Illinois Institute of Technology. Benedictine offers study abroad in 9 countries, and exchange programs can be arranged through other colleges. There are 3-2 preengineering degrees with Marquette University and the Universities of Illinois, Detroit, and Notre Dame, and an engineering degree with the Illinois Institute of Technology. Preprofessional programs including prepodiatry, pre-physical therapy, and prenursing are offered. Work-study programs with a number of surrounding firms, internships, an accelerated degree programs in management, credit for work and life experience, and dual majors are also offered. There are 11 national honor societies and a freshman honors program.

Faculty/Classroom: 66% of faculty are male; 34%, female. All both teach and do research. No introductory courses are taught by graduate students. The average class size in an introductory lecture is 19; in a laboratory, 16; and in a regular course, 18.

Admissions: 82% of the 2005-2006 applicants were accepted. The ACT scores for the 2005-2006 freshman class were: 37% below 21, 24% between 21 and 23, 23% between 24 and 26, 6% between 27 and 28, and 10% above 28. 39% of the current freshmen were in the top fifth of their class; 64% were in the top two fifths. 3 freshmen graduated first in their class.

Requirements: The ACT is required. In addition, to be admitted, students must complete 4 years of English, 3 each of social studies, math, and lab science, and 2 of foreign language. The GED is accepted. Benedictine requires applicants to be in the upper 50% of their class. AP and CLEP credits are accepted.

Procedure: Freshmen are admitted fall and spring. There is a rolling admissions plans. Application deadlines are open. Application fee is $40. Applications are accepted on-line.

Transfer: 300 transfer students enrolled in 2004-2005. Applicants must have a C average. A minimum GPA of 2.0 is necessary, and an interview is required in some cases. Students who have completed fewer than 20 semester hours must submit ACT or SAT scores. 30 of 120 credits required for the bachelor's degree must be completed at Benedictine.

Visiting: There are regularly scheduled orientations for prospective students, including a regularly scheduled Visit Day and open houses each semester. There are guides for informal visits and visitors may sit in on classes and stay overnight. To schedule a visit, contact the Enrollment Center at (630) 829-6300.

Financial Aid: In a recent year, 98% of all full-time freshmen and 95% of continuing full-time students received some form of financial aid. The FAFSA and the college's own financial statement are required.

International Students: There are 18 international students enrolled. The school actively recruits these students. They must score satisfactorily on the written TOEFL or on the electronic version.

Computers: Wireless access is available. Students can access the Internet from their rooms in the residence halls, in the library, the student center, and the 3 classroom buildings. Two of the classroom buildings have wireless access. There are approximately 200 PCs available for student use. All students may access the system. Students may use the PC labs 24 hours a day. There are no time limits. The fee is $150 per term.

Graduates: From July 1, 2004 to June 30, 2005, 443 bachelor's degrees were awarded. The most popular majors were management (14%), psychology (9%), and health science (7%). In an average class, 32% graduate in 4 years or less, 48% graduate in 5 years or less, and 52% graduate in 6 years or less.

Admissions Contact: Kari A. Cranmer, Director of Admissions. A video is available. E-mail: *admissions@ben.edu* Web: *www.ben.edu*

BLACKBURN COLLEGE   C-4

Carlinville, IL 62626	(217) 854-3231
	(800) 233-3550; Fax: (217) 854-3713
Full-time: 250 men, 310 women	Faculty: 32
Part-time: 5 men, 10 women	Ph.D.s: 72%
Graduate: none	Student/Faculty: 17 to 1
Year: semesters, summer session	Tuition: $9475
Application Deadline: open	Room & Board: $4275
Freshman Class: n/av	
SAT or ACT: required	COMPETITIVE

Blackburn College, founded in 1837, is a private liberal arts institution affiliated with the Presbyterian Church (U.S.A.). The college is noted for its work program, which allows resident students to reduce their education costs and develop useful skills by managing and administering all essential campus services. Figures in the above capsule and profile are approximate. The library contains 80,000 volumes, and subscribes to 400 periodicals including electronic. Computerized library services include interlibrary loans and database searching. Special learning facilities include a learning resource center and art gallery. The 80-acre campus is in a rural area 60 miles north of St. Louis. Including any residence halls, there are 13 buildings.

Student Life: 85% of undergraduates are from Illinois. Others are from 12 states and 9 foreign countries. 85% are from public schools. 81% are white; 11% African American. 50% are Protestant; 45% Catholic. The average age of freshmen is 18; all undergraduates, 20. 30% do not continue beyond their first year.

Housing: 480 students can be accommodated in college housing, which includes single-sex and coed dorms and a quiet residence hall. On-campus housing is guaranteed for all 4 years. 76% of students live on campus; of those, 60% remain on campus on weekends. All students may keep cars.

Activities: There are no fraternities or sororities. There are 15 groups on campus, including band, cheerleading, choir, chorale, chorus, drama, ethnic, international, jazz band, literary magazine, newspaper, religious, social, student government, and yearbook.

Sports: There are 6 intercollegiate sports for men and 6 for women, and 9 intramural sports for men and 9 for women. Facilities include a gym, a swimming pool, racquetball and tennis courts, weight and wrestling rooms, an outdoor track, and lighted playing fields.

Disabled Students: 65% of the campus is accessible. Wheelchair ramps, elevators, special parking, specially equipped rest rooms, special class scheduling, lowered drinking fountains, and lowered telephones are available.

Services: Counseling and information services are available, as is tutoring in most subjects.

Campus Safety and Security: Measures include self-defense education, security escort services, lighted pathways/sidewalks, and student-run security through the work program.

Programs of Study: Blackburn confers the B.A. degree. Bachelor's degrees are awarded in BIOLOGICAL SCIENCE (biology/biological science), BUSINESS (accounting, business administration and management, international business management, and international economics), COMMUNICATIONS AND THE ARTS (American literature, art, English literature, music business management, music performance, and Spanish), COMPUTER AND PHYSICAL SCIENCE (chemistry, computer science, and mathematics), EDUCATION (art, elementary, English, music, physical, secondary, and social science), HEALTH PROFESSIONS (medical laboratory technology), SOCIAL SCIENCE (history, political science/government, psychology, and public administration). Life sciences and physical sciences are the strongest academically. Biology, education, and business are the largest.

Required: To graduate, students must complete 122 semester hours with a minimum 2.0 GPA. Requirements include interdisciplinary courses, intercultural courses in foreign languages or English, and foundation courses in writing, literature, math, philosophy or religion, analysis, fine arts, and phys ed. Work program participation is required of resident students. All students must complete their last year in residence.

Special: Blackburn offers supervised off-campus internships related to student majors, co-op programs, work-study programs, and a semester in Mexico, Great Britain, or Washington, D.C. A 3-2 engineering degree with Washington University in St. Louis is offered. Students may design their own majors. There is 1 national honor society.

Faculty/Classroom: 65% of faculty are male; 35%, female. All teach undergraduates. The average class size in an introductory lecture is 25; in a laboratory, 20; and in a regular course, 18.

Requirements: The SAT or ACT is required. In addition, applicants should be graduates of an accredited secondary school or have a GED certificate. Blackburn recommends completion of 4 years of English, 2 to 4 of math, and 2 each of lab sciences, social sciences, and foreign language. A personal essay is required. Blackburn requires applicants to be in the upper 60% of their class. A GPA of 2.0 is required. AP and CLEP credits are accepted. Important factors in the admissions decision are leadership record, personality/intangible qualities, and recommendations by school officials.

Procedure: Freshmen are admitted fall and spring. There is a rolling admissions plan. Entrance exams should be taken in the junior year or early in the senior year. Application deadlines are open. Applications are accepted on-line.

Transfer: Applicants must submit official transcripts of college-level work and be in good standing at the previous institution attended. Students from accredited colleges may receive credit for grades of C or better; those with associate degrees may transfer some D grades. Credit for work at unaccredited institutions may be accepted provisionally. 30 of 122 credits required for the bachelor's degree must be completed at Blackburn.

Visiting: There are regularly scheduled orientations for prospective students, including a campus tour and meetings with an admissions representative, the financial aid director, and a department head. There are

guides for informal visits and visitors may sit in on classes and stay overnight. To schedule a visit, contact the Admissions Office.

Financial Aid: Blackburn is a member of CSS. The FAFSA is required. Check with the school for current application deadlines.

International Students: The school actively recruits these students. They must score satisfactorily on the written TOEFL or on the electronic version.

Computers: All students may access the system every day during lab hours. There are no time limits and no fees.

Admissions Contact: John C. Malin, Director of Admissions. E-mail: *jmali@mail.blackburn.edu* Web: *www.blackburn.edu*

BRADLEY UNIVERSITY — D-3
Peoria, IL 61625

(309) 677-1000
(800) 447-6460; Fax: (309) 677-2797

Full-time: 2263 men, 2792 women	**Faculty:** 326; II A, av$
Part-time: 128 men, 186 women	**Ph.D.s:** 85%
Graduate: 388 men, 397 women	**Student/Faculty:** 16 to 1
Year: semesters, summer session	**Tuition:** $18,830
Application Deadline: open	**Room & Board:** $6450
Freshman Class: 4218 applied, 3820 accepted, 1136 enrolled	
SAT Verbal/Math: 560/570*	**ACT:** 25 **VERY COMPETITIVE**

Bradley University, founded in 1897, is an independent, privately endowed institution. Bradley offers a full range of baccalaureate and graduate-level programs, as well as personal attention, from a faculty dedicated to student learning. There are 5 undergraduate schools and 1 graduate school. In addition to regional accreditation, Bradley has baccalaureate program accreditation with AACSB, ABET, ACCE, ADA, NASAD, NASM, NCATE, and NLN. The library contains 541,995 volumes, 816,601 microform items, and 9907 audio/video tapes/CDs/DVDs, and subscribes to 25,011 periodicals including electronic. Computerized library services include the card catalog, interlibrary loans, and database searching. Special learning facilities include a learning resource center, art gallery, radio station, and TV station. The 75-acre campus is in an urban area 160 miles southwest of Chicago. Including any residence halls, there are 41 buildings.

Student Life: 89% of undergraduates are from Illinois. Others are from 42 states, 55 foreign countries, and Canada. 82% are white. 42% are Protestant; 34% Catholic; 14% claim no religious affiliation; 6% are Jewish. The average age of freshmen is 18; all undergraduates, 20. 11% do not continue beyond their first year; 72% remain to graduate.

Housing: 2200 students can be accommodated in college housing, which includes single-sex and coed dorms, on-campus apartments, fraternity houses, and sorority houses. On-campus housing is guaranteed for all 4 years. 97% of students live on campus; of those, 99% remain on campus on weekends. Upperclassmen may keep cars.

Activities: 28% of men belong to 16 national fraternities; 25% of women belong to 12 national sororities. There are 223 groups on campus, including art, band, cheerleading, chess, choir, chorale, chorus, computers, dance, drama, drill team, ethnic, forensics, gay, honors, international, jazz band, literary magazine, musical theater, newspaper, orchestra, pep band, photography, political, professional, radio and TV, religious; social, social service, student government, symphony, and yearbook. Popular campus events include Founders Day, Greek Week, and Garret Week.

Sports: There are 6 intercollegiate sports for men and 7 for women, and 24 intramural sports for men and 24 for women. Facilities include tennis courts, a civic center, playing fields, a field house, outdoor lighted basketball courts, and a 6500-seat gym.

Disabled Students: 80% of the campus is accessible. Wheelchair ramps, elevators, special parking, specially equipped rest rooms, and lowered drinking fountains are available.

Services: Counseling and information services are available, as is tutoring in most subjects, including introductory subjects and selected higher-level classes. There is remedial math and writing.

Campus Safety and Security: Measures include 24-hour foot and vehicle patrol, security escort services, informal discussions, and pamphlets/posters/films. There are emergency telephones, lighted pathways/sidewalks, engravers for marking personal property, and a medical escort service.

Programs of Study: Bradley confers B.A., B.S., B.F.A., B.M., B.S.C., B.S.C.E., B.S.E.E., B.S.I.E., B.S.M.E., B.S.M.F.E., B.S.M.F.E.T., and B.S.N. degrees. Master's degrees are also awarded. Bachelor's degrees are awarded in BIOLOGICAL SCIENCE (biochemistry, biology/biological science, and molecular biology), BUSINESS (accounting, banking and finance, business administration and management, entrepreneurial studies, insurance and risk management, international business management, management information systems, and marketing/retailing/merchandising), COMMUNICATIONS AND THE ARTS (art history and appreciation, communications, dramatic arts, English, French, German, graphic design, multimedia, music, music business management, music performance, music theory and composition, photography, printmaking, sculpture, Spanish, studio art, and visual and performing arts), COMPUTER AND PHYSICAL SCIENCE (actuarial science, chemistry, computer science, geoscience, information sciences and systems, mathematics, and physics), EDUCATION (art, drama, early childhood, elementary, home economics, music, secondary, and special), ENGINEERING AND ENVIRONMENTAL DESIGN (civil engineering, construction engineering, electrical/electronics engineering, engineering physics, environmental science, industrial engineering, manufacturing engineering, manufacturing technology, and mechanical engineering), HEALTH PROFESSIONS (health science, medical technology, and nursing), SOCIAL SCIENCE (criminal justice, dietetics, economics, family/consumer studies, history, international studies, philosophy, political science/government, psychology, religion, social work, and sociology). Business, engineering, and natural sciences are the strongest academically. Communication, elementary education, and psychology are the largest.

Required: To graduate, the student must complete the school's basic skills and general education curriculum. Overall, the university requires 124 total credit hours, with 32 hours in the student's major and a minimum GPA of 2.0.

Special: Special academic programs include, co-op programs, internships, a Washington semester, work-study programs, study abroad in 30 countries, B.A.-B.S. degrees in most majors, dual majors, and leadership fellowships. There are 31 national honor societies and a freshman honors program.

Faculty/Classroom: 65% of faculty are male; 35%, female. All both teach and do research. No introductory courses are taught by graduate students. The average class size in a laboratory is 14 and in a regular course, 20.

Admissions: 91% of the 2005-2006 applicants were accepted. The SAT scores for the 2005-2006 freshman class were: Verbal--25% below 500, 41% between 500 and 599, 30% between 600 and 700, and 4% above 700; Math--13% below 500, 43% between 500 and 599, 38% between 600 and 700, and 6% above 700. The ACT scores were 10% below 21, 23% between 21 and 23, 33% between 24 and 26, 16% between 27 and 28, and 17% above 28. 50% of the current freshmen were in the top fifth of their class; 83% were in the top two fifths. 36 freshmen graduated first in their class.

Requirements: The SAT or ACT is required. A GPA of 2.0 is required. AP and CLEP credits are accepted. Important factors in the admissions decision are advanced placement or honor courses, extracurricular activities record, and evidence of special talent.

Procedure: Freshmen are admitted to all sessions. Entrance exams should be taken in the spring of the junior year or the fall of the senior year. There is a rolling admissions plan. Application deadlines are open. Application fee is $35. A waiting list is an active part of the admissions procedure.60 applicatns were on the waiting list; 9 were admitted.

Transfer: 320 transfer students enrolled in 2004-2005. Transfer students must have a minimum GPA of 2.0. Those with fewer than 15 hours of college credit must submit their ACT or SAT scores and a high school transcript. 30 of 124 credits required for the bachelor's degree must be completed at Bradley.

Visiting: There are regularly scheduled orientations for prospective students, including class visits, campus tours, admissions information, financial assistance seminars, lunch, and student and parent meetings. There are guides for informal visits and visitors may sit in on classes and stay overnight. To schedule a visit, contact the Office of Undergraduate Admissions.

Financial Aid: In 2005-2006, 97% of all full-time freshmen and 86% of continuing full-time students received some form of financial aid. 64% of full-time freshmen and 56% of continuing full-time students received need-based aid. The average freshman award was $17,712. Need-based scholarships or need-based grants averaged $11,162 ($18,700 maximum); need-based self-help aid (loans and jobs) averaged $4431 ($5425 maximum); non-need-based athletic scholarships averaged $13,101 ($25,280 maximum); and other non-need-based awards and non-need-based scholarships averaged $9626 ($10,500 maximum). 22% of undergraduates work part time. Average annual earnings from campus work are $950. The average financial indebtedness of the 2005 graduate was $14,760. Bradley is a member of CSS. The FAFSA is required. The deadline for filing freshman financial aid applications for fall entry is March 1.

International Students: In a recent year, there were 96 international students enrolled. The school actively recruits these students. They must score 500 on the written TOEFL or 173 on the electronic version.

Computers: Wireless access is available. Students have access to hishspeed wired networking form residence halls, the library, and other public spaces such as meeting rooms. There are approximately 900 computers available for student use in public and academic labs. All students may access the system 24 hours a day. There are no time limits and no fees.

Graduates: From July 1, 2004 to June 30, 2005, 1329 bachelor's degrees were awarded. The most popular majors were elementary education (5%), communications(advertising) (5%), and psychology (4%). In an average class, 62% graduate in 4 years or less, 71% graduate in 5

years or less, and 72% graduate in 6 years or less. 251 companies recruited on campus in 2004-2005. Of the 2004 graduating class, 16% were enrolled in graduate school within 6 months of graduation and 74% were employed.

Admissions Contact: Angela (Nickie) Roberson, Associate Provost for Enrollment Management. A video is available.
E-mail: *admissions@bradley.edu* Web: *www.bradley.edu/admissions/*

CHICAGO STATE UNIVERSITY E-2
Chicago, IL 60628

(773) 995-2513
(800) 278-3011; Fax: (773) 995-3820

Full-time: 910 men, 2300 women	**Faculty:** IIA, --$
Part-time: 415 men, 1295 women	**Ph.D.s:** 62%
Graduate: 675 men, 1470 women	**Student/Faculty:** n/av
Year: semesters, summer session	**Tuition:** $4390 ($10,800)
Application Deadline: See profile	**Room & Board:** $6525
Freshman Class: n/av	
ACT: required	**COMPETITIVE+**

Chicago State University, founded in 1867, is a public commuter and residential institution controlled by the State of Illinois. It offers day and evening undergraduate programs through the Colleges of Arts and Sciences, Health Sciences, Business Administration, Education, and Non-Traditional Programs. There are 5 undergraduate and 2 graduate schools. Figures in the above capsule and profile are approximate. In addition to regional accreditation, Chicago State has baccalaureate program accreditation with ADA, CAHEA, NCATE, and NLN. The library contains 26,000 volumes and 388,028 microform items, and subscribes to 1734 periodicals including electronic. Computerized library services include the card catalog, interlibrary loans, and database searching. Special learning facilities include a learning resource center, art gallery, radio station, and a TV studio. The 161-acre campus is in an urban area 12 miles south of downtown Chicago. Including any residence halls, there are 11 buildings.

Student Life: 98% of undergraduates are from Illinois. Others are from 24 states, 21 foreign countries, and Canada. 80% are African American; 10% white. The average age of freshmen is 21; all undergraduates, 29.

Housing: 360 students can be accommodated in college housing, which includes coed dorms. On-campus housing is available on a first-come, first-served basis. Alcohol is not permitted. All students may keep cars.

Activities: 12% of men and about 15% of women belong to 4 national fraternities and 4 national sororities. There are 17 groups on campus, including cheerleading, choir, dance, drama, drill team, honors, international, jazz band, literary magazine, musical theater, newspaper, photography, political, professional, radio and TV, religious, social, student government, and yearbook. Popular campus events include Welcome Week activities, Black Writers Conference, and Hispanic Heritage Month.

Sports: There are 6 intercollegiate sports for men and 6 for women, and 4 intramural sports for men and 2 for women. Facilities include tennis courts, indoor/outdoor tracks, an Olympic-size swimming pool, weight rooms, basketball courts, a fitness center, dance studio, and a baseball field.

Disabled Students: All of the campus is accessible. Wheelchair ramps, elevators, special parking, specially equipped rest rooms, lowered drinking fountains, and lowered telephones are available.

Services: Counseling and information services are available, as is tutoring in some subjects, including math, science, and accounting . There is remedial math, reading, and writing.

Campus Safety and Security: Measures include 24-hour foot and vehicle patrol, security escort services, informal discussions, and pamphlets/posters/films. There are emergency telephones and lighted pathways/sidewalks.

Programs of Study: Chicago State confers B.A., B.S., B.M.E., and B.S.Ed. degrees. Master's degrees are also awarded. Bachelor's degrees are awarded in BIOLOGICAL SCIENCE (biochemistry and biology/biological science), BUSINESS (accounting, banking and finance, business administration and management, management science, marketing/retailing/merchandising, and recreation and leisure services), COMMUNICATIONS AND THE ARTS (art, broadcasting, English, music, Spanish, and speech/debate/rhetoric), COMPUTER AND PHYSICAL SCIENCE (chemistry, computer science, information sciences and systems, mathematics, and physics), EDUCATION (art, bilingual/bicultural, business, early childhood, elementary, industrial arts, music, physical, secondary, and vocational), HEALTH PROFESSIONS (health, health care administration, health science, nursing, predentistry, and premedicine), SOCIAL SCIENCE (African American studies, criminal justice, economics, geography, history, political science/government, prelaw, psychology, and sociology). Business administration and computer science are the strongest academically. Elementary education is the largest.

Required: All students must complete 120 credit hours, including 40 hours in the major, maintain a 2.0 GPA, and fulfill a foreign language requirement. They must complete a 39-hour core curriculum as well as examinations in English, math, reading, and the U.S. Constitution.

Special: Chicago State offers a combined B.A.-B.S. degree, a board of governors degree program, a University Without Walls Program, and an individualized curriculum program. Study abroad in Liberia and life experience credits are also provided. There is a freshman honors program.

Faculty/Classroom: 99% teach undergraduates. The average class size in an introductory lecture is 60; in a laboratory, 26; and in a regular course, 35.

Requirements: The ACT is required, but scores need not be submitted if the applicant is over 23 years of age. Graduation from an accredited secondary school is required; a GED will be accepted. Minimum credits submitted should include 4 units of English, 3 of math, 3 of science, and 3 of social sciences. A GPA of 2.0 is required. AP and CLEP credits are accepted.

Procedure: Freshmen are admitted to all sessions. There is a rolling admission plan. Applications should be filed by July 15 for fall entry, November 1 for spring entry, and May 1 for summer entry, along with a $25 fee. Notification is sent on a rolling basis.

Transfer: 630 transfer students enrolled in a recent year. Transfer students must have a minimum GPA of 2.0, and those with fewer than 24 hours must also meet freshman admission requirements. 30 of 120 credits required for the bachelor's degree must be completed at Chicago State.

Visiting: There are regularly scheduled orientations for prospective students, including a tour of campus, admissions overview, and financial aid information. To schedule a visit, contact the Office of Admissions.

Financial Aid: In a recent year, 68% of all full-time freshmen and 77% of continuing full-time students received some form of financial aid. 67% of full-time freshmen and 75% of continuing full-time students received need-based aid. The average freshman award was $3589. Need-based scholarships or need-based grants averaged $3174 ($5450 maximum); need-based self-help aid (loans and jobs) averaged $1949 ($8002 maximum); and non-need-based athletic scholarships averaged $5431 ($8005 maximum). Average annual earnings from campus work were $2700. The average financial indebtedness of a recent graduate was $23,000. The FAFSA is required. Check with school for current application deadlines.

International Students: In a recent year there were 50 international students enrolled. They must score satisfactorily on the written TOEFL or on the electronic version and also take the college's own test. They must also take the SAT or the ACT.

Computers: All students may access the system 8:30 A.M. to 10 P.M. Monday through Friday, 8:30 A.M. to 5 P.M. Saturday, and 1 p.m to 8 P.M. Sunday. There are no time limits. The fee $5. It is strongly recommended that all students have a personal computer.

Graduates: In a recent year, 1110 bachelor's degrees were awarded. The most popular majors were elementary education (6%), nursing (5%), and criminal justice (5%).

Admissions Contact: Addie Epps, Director of Admissions.
E-mail: *ug-admissions@csu.edu* Web: *www.csu.edu*

COLUMBIA COLLEGE CHICAGO — E-2

Chicago, IL 60605

(312) 663-1600, ext. 7133
(800) 838-1226; Fax: (312) 344-8024

Full-time: 3780 men, 4020 women	Faculty: 286; IIA, av$
Part-time: 720 men, 760 women	Ph.Ds: 35%
Graduate: 170 men, 485 women	Student/Faculty: 27 to 1
Year: semesters, summer session	Tuition: $15,285
Application Deadline: see profile	Room & Board: $9840
Freshman Class: n/av	
SAT or ACT: not required	LESS COMPETITIVE

Columbia College Chicago, founded in 1890, is a private liberal arts institution with special emphasis on educating students for creative occupations in the visual, performing, and media and commununication arts. There are 3 undergraduate schools and 1 graduate school. Figures in the above capsule and profile are approximate. The library contains 2054 volumes, 128,615 microform items, and 13,772 audio/video tapes/CDs/DVDs, and subscribes to 1204 periodicals including electronic. Computerized library services include the card catalog, interlibrary loans, and database searching. Special learning facilities include a learning resource center, art gallery, radio station, TV station, and contemporary photography museum. The campus is in an urban area in Chicago. Including any residence halls, there are 15 buildings.

Student Life: 75% of undergraduates are from Illinois. Others are from 49 states, 51 foreign countries, and Canada. 80% are from public schools. 63% are white; 16% African American; 11% Hispanic. The average age of freshmen is 19; all undergraduates, 22.

Housing: 500 students can be accommodated in college housing, which includes coed dormitories. On-campus housing is available on a first-come, first-served basis. Priority is given to out-of-town students. 95% of students commute. Alcohol is not permitted. All students may keep cars.

Activities: There are no fraternities or sororities. There are 27 groups on campus, including art, chorus, computers, dance, drama, ethnic, film, gay, international, jazz band, literary magazine, musical theater, photography, political, professional, radio and TV, religious, social service, student government, and yearbook. Popular campus events include African Heritage, Dr. Martin Luther King Jr.'s Birthday, and Women in the Arts.

Disabled Students: 95% of the campus is accessible. Wheelchair ramps, elevators, specially equipped rest rooms, special class scheduling, and lowered telephones are available.

Services: Counseling and information services are available, as is tutoring in some subjects. There is a reader service for the blind, and remedial math, reading, and writing.

Campus Safety and Security: Measures include self-defense education, security escort services, informal discussions, and pamphlets/posters/films. There are emergency telephones and lighted pathways/sidewalks.

Programs of Study: Columbia confers B.A. and B.F.A. degrees. Master's degrees are also awarded. Bachelor's degrees are awarded in BUSINESS (marketing management), COMMUNICATIONS AND THE ARTS (advertising, art, audio technology, creative writing, dance, dramatic arts, film arts, journalism, multimedia, music, music business management, photography, and radio/television technology), EDUCATION (early childhood), ENGINEERING AND ENVIRONMENTAL DESIGN (computer graphics), SOCIAL SCIENCE (crosscultural studies and interpreter for the deaf). Art, film/video, and management are the largest.

Required: To graduate, all students must complete 124 semester hours of study with a minimum 2.0 GPA. General studies distribution consists of 9 hours each of literature/humanities and science/math, 6 each of English, history, and social science, and 3 each of computer applications, oral communications, senior seminar, and electives; 1 intensive writing course also is required.

Special: Columbia offers study abroad in 2 countries, independent study, internships, work-study programs, student-designed majors, and a general studies degree.

Faculty/Classroom: 56% of faculty are male; 44%, female. All teach undergraduates. No introductory courses are taught by graduate students. The average class size in a regular course is 16.

Requirements: Applicants should be graduates of accredited secondary schools. The GED is also accepted. An interview is recommended. AP and CLEP credits are accepted.

Procedure: Freshmen are admitted to all sessions. There are deferred admissions and rolling admissions plans. Applications should be filed by August 15 for fall entry, along with a $35 fee. The college accepts all applicants. Notification is sent on a rolling basis. Applications are accepted on-line.

Transfer: 1325 transfer students enrolled in a recent year. Up to 88 credit hours are accepted with a grade of C or better; up to 62 credit hours from 2-year colleges with a grade of C or better are accepted. 36 of 124 credits required for the bachelor's degree must be completed at Columbia.

Visiting: There are regularly scheduled orientations for prospective students. There are guides for informal visits and visitors may sit in on classes. To schedule a visit, contact the Undergraduate Admissions Office.

Financial Aid: The FAFSA is required. Check with the school for current application deadlines.

International Students: In a recent year there were 250 international students enrolled. The school actively recruits these students. They must score satisfactorily on the written TOEFL.

Graduates: In a recent year, 1370 bachelor's degrees were awarded. The most popular majors were film/video (12%), marketing (9%), and art and design (9%).

Admissions Contact: Murphy Monroe, Director of Admissions.
E-mail: *admissions@popmail.colum.edu*

CONCORDIA UNIVERSITY, RIVER FOREST — E-1

River Forest, IL 60305

(708) 209-3101
(866) GO-2-CURF; Fax: (708) 209-3473

Full-time: 351 men, 610 women	Faculty: 74; IIB, --$
Part-time: 21 men, 50 women	Ph.Ds: 65%
Graduate: 428 men, 1323 women	Student/Faculty: 13 to 1
Year: semesters, summer session	Tuition: $20,000
Application Deadline: open	Room & Board: $6300
Freshman Class: 680 applied, 628 accepted, 210 enrolled	
ACT: required	COMPETITIVE

Concordia University, founded in 1864, is a private liberal arts institution affiliated with the Lutheran Church, Missouri Synod. There are 3 undergraduate schools and 1 graduate school. In addition to regional accreditation, Concordia University has baccalaureate program accreditation with NCATE and NLN. The library contains 140,000 volumes, 480,000 microform items, and 2250 audio/video tapes/CDs/DVDs, and subscribes to 235 periodicals including electronic. Computerized library services include the card catalog, interlibrary loans, database searching, Internet access, and laptop Internet portals. Special learning facilities include a learning resource center, art gallery, natural history museum, radio station, TV station, and early childhood resource center, human performance lab, language lab, computer center, and weather station. The 40-acre campus is in a suburban area 10 miles west of downtown Chicago. Including any residence halls, there are 24 buildings.

Student Life: 65% of undergraduates are from Illinois. Others are from 21 states, 1 foreign country, and Canada. 66% are from public schools. 51% are white; 10% African American. 59% are includes undeclared; 31% Protestant; 13% Catholic. The average age of freshmen is 18; all undergraduates, 22. 27% do not continue beyond their first year; 53% remain to graduate.

Housing: 775 students can be accommodated in college housing, which includes single-sex and coed dorms and married-student housing. On-campus housing is guaranteed for all 4 years. 65% of students live on campus; of those, 75% remain on campus on weekends. Alcohol is not permitted. All students may keep cars.

Activities: There are no fraternities or sororities. There are 43 groups on campus, including band, cheerleading, choir, chorale, chorus, dance, drama, ethnic, honors, jazz band, literary magazine, musical theater, newspaper, pep band, professional, religious, social, social service, student government, symphony, and yearbook. Popular campus events include Orientation Week, Campus Awareness Day, and Family Weekend.

Sports: There are 7 intercollegiate sports for men and 7 for women, and 12 intramural sports for men and 12 for women. Facilities include 2 gyms, an indoor swimming pool, weight training room, human performance lab, football and soccer fields, tennis courts, baseball and softball fields, track, first aid training room, table tennis, billiards, and table games.

Disabled Students: 74% of the campus is accessible. Wheelchair ramps, elevators, special parking, specially equipped rest rooms, special class scheduling, lowered drinking fountains, and lowered telephones are available.

Services: Counseling and information services are available, as is tutoring in every subject. There is remedial math, reading, and writing.

Campus Safety and Security: Measures include 24-hour foot and vehicle patrol, self-defense education, security escort services, and shuttle buses. There are informal discussions, pamphlets/posters/films, emergency telephones, and lighted pathways/sidewalks.

Programs of Study: Concordia University confers B.A., B.Mus., and B.Mus.Ed. degrees. Master's and doctoral degrees are also awarded. Bachelor's degrees are awarded in BIOLOGICAL SCIENCE (biology/ biological science), BUSINESS (accounting, and business administration and management), COMMUNICATIONS AND THE ARTS (art, communications, English, and music), COMPUTER AND PHYSICAL SCIENCE (chemistry, computer programming, computer science, mathematics, natural sciences, and physical sciences), EDUCATION (computer, early childhood, elementary, middle school, music, physical, science, and secondary), HEALTH PROFESSIONS (premedicine), SOCIAL SCIENCE (geography, history, physical fitness/movement, political science/ government, prelaw, psychology, religion, social science, social work, sociology, and theological studies). Elementary education, exercise science, and theology are the strongest academically. Elementary education, business, and psychology are the largest.

Required: All students are required to take 2 years of liberal arts, including humanities, English, science, religion, and social science, and 5 quarter hours of phys ed. A 2.0 to 2.25 GPA and a total of 128 to 150 quarter hours are required. The number of hours required for the major varies by program.

Special: Cross-registration is possible with Dominican University and the Chicago Consortium of Colleges. Concordia also offers internships for liberal arts majors in the Chicago area, which provides numerous opportunities, study abroad in England, and pass/fail options. Work-study is possible, as is an accelerated degree program in organizational management. There are 3 national honor societies, including Phi Beta Kappa, and a freshman honors program.

Faculty/Classroom: 50% of faculty are male; 50%, female. 82% teach undergraduates and 100% both teach and do research. No introductory courses are taught by graduate students. The average class size in an introductory lecture is 20; in a laboratory, 18; and in a regular course, 25.

Admissions: 92% of the 2005-2006 applicants were accepted. The ACT scores for the 2005-2006 freshman class were: 36% below 21, 23% between 21 and 23, 20% between 24 and 26, 9% between 27 and 28, and 12% above 28. 30% of the current freshmen were in the top fifth of their class; 41% were in the top two fifths.

Requirements: The ACT is required. In addition, applicants should have 15 units of credit, with 11 units in college preparatory courses, including English, math, lab science, and social studies. A letter of recommendation is required, as is a minimum GPA of 2.0 in the college preparatory subjects and a ranking in the top half of their graduating class. Concordia University requires applicants to be in the upper 50% of their class. A GPA of 2.0 is required. AP and CLEP credits are accepted. Important factors in the admissions decision are advanced placement or honor courses, recommendations by school officials, and leadership record.

Procedure: Freshmen are admitted to all sessions. Entrance exams should be taken in the spring of the junior year or fall of the senior year. There is a rolling admissions plan. Application deadlines are open. Notification is sent on a rolling basis. Applications are accepted on-line.

Transfer: 90 transfer students enrolled in 2004-2005. A cumulative GPA of 2.0 or higher at all previous colleges plus a letter of recommendation are required. 48 of 128 to 150 credits required for the bachelor's degree must be completed at Concordia University.

Visiting: There are regularly scheduled orientations for prospective students, consisting of daily planned activities during orientation in the first week of the fall semester. There are guides for informal visits and visitors may sit in on classes and stay overnight. To schedule a visit, contact the Office of Admission at crtadmis.edu.

Financial Aid: In a recent year, 93% of all full-time freshmen and 87% of continuing full-time students received some form of financial aid. 85% of full-time freshmen and 67% of continuing full-time students received need-based aid. The average freshman award was $12,000. The average financial indebtedness of the 2005 graduate was $12,000. The FAFSA, the college's own financial statement, and the student and parent 1040 U.S. tax forms are required.

International Students: There are 5 international students enrolled. A satisfactory score is required on the written TOEFL. Applicants must also take the MELAB or successfully complete Level 109 at an ELS language center.

Computers: Wireless access is available. All students may access the system 24 hours per day. There are no time limits and no fees.

Graduates: From July 1, 2004 to June 30, 2005, 216 bachelor's degrees were awarded. The most popular majors were education (34%), business (8%), and sociology/social work (4%). In an average class, 36% graduate in 4 years, 41% graduate in 5 years, and 41% graduate in 6 years. Of the 2004 graduating class, 23% were enrolled in graduate school within 6 months of graduation and 98% were employed.

Admissions Contact: James P. Malley, Director of Admission.
E-mail: *crfmalleyjp@curf.edu* Web: *www.curf.edu*

DEPAUL UNIVERSITY   E-2

Chicago, IL 60604   (312) 362-8300
                          (800) 4-DEPAUL; Fax: (312) 362-5749

Full-time: 4913 men, 6468 women	**Faculty:** 615; I, -$
Part-time: 1389 men, 1970 women	**Ph.D.s:** 80%
Graduate: 3602 men, 3627 women	**Student/Faculty:** 18 to 1
Year: quarters, summer session	**Tuition:** $20,970
Application Deadline: February 1	**Room & Board:** $8865
Freshman Class: 9779 applied, 6963 accepted, 2400 enrolled	
SAT Verbal/Math: 570/560*	**ACT:** 24 **VERY COMPETITIVE**

DePaul University, founded by the Vincentian Order in 1898, is a private Catholic institution with 2 main campuses: the Lincoln Park Campus houses undergraduate programs in liberal arts and sciences, education, theater, and music, and the Loop Campus, offers programs in commerce, law, and computer science, telecommunications, and information systems (CTI). DePaul also has 6 suburban campuses. There are 8 undergraduate and 9 graduate schools. In addition to regional accreditation, DePaul has baccalaureate program accreditation with AACSB, NASM, NCATE, and NLN. The 7 libraries contain 886,843 volumes, 290,188 microform items, and 26,818 audio/video tapes/CDs/DVDs, and subscribe to 25,786 periodicals including electronic. Computerized library services include the card catalog, interlibrary loans, database searching, Internet access, and laptop Internet portals. Special learning facilities include a learning resource center, art gallery, radio station, performing arts center, recording studio, and a marketing research center. The 36-acre campus is in an urban area in Chicago. Including any residence halls, there are 39 buildings.

Student Life: 85% of undergraduates are from Illinois. Students are from 50 states, 74 foreign countries, and Canada. 74% are from public schools. 60% are white; 13% Hispanic; 10% African American. 33% are Catholic; 12% claim no religious affiliation. The average age of freshmen is 18; all undergraduates, 21. 15% do not continue beyond their first year; 64% remain to graduate.

Housing: 3000 students can be accommodated in college housing, which includes coed dorms and on-campus apartments. In addition, there are honors houses, limited off-campus apartments, and the University Center of Chicago (UCC), which features private studios and apartments as well as traditional residence-style units. On-campus housing is available on a first-come, first-served basis and is available on a lottery system for upperclassmen. Priority is given to out-of-town students. 75% of students commute. All students may keep cars.

Activities: 2% of men and less than 1% of women belong to 10 national fraternities; 3% of women belong to 11 national sororities. There are 170 groups on campus, including band, cheerleading, choir, chorale, chorus, computers, dance, drama, drill team, ethnic, gay, honors, international, jazz band, marching band, musical theater, newspaper, opera, orchestra, pep band, political, professional, radio and TV, religious, social, social service, student government, and symphony. Popular campus events include Hispanic Awareness Month, Women's History Month, and Annual Spring Concert (FEST).

Sports: There are 6 intercollegiate sports for men and 7 for women, and 10 intramural sports for men and 10 for women. Facilities include a 120,000-square-foot fitness and recreation center with a 4-court gym, a 6-lane, 25-yard pool, a 4-lane, 200-meter track, group fitness studios, a spin studio, and a conditioning area. An athletic field is used for intramural sports.

Disabled Students: 95% of the campus is accessible. Wheelchair ramps, elevators, special parking, specially equipped rest rooms, lowered drinking fountains, lowered telephones, and a disabled student services department are available.

Services: Counseling and information services are available, as is tutoring in most subjects. There is a reader service for the blind, and remedial math, reading, and writing. A writing center, a productive learning strategies program, and a student development center are also available.

Campus Safety and Security: Measures include 24-hour foot and vehicle patrol, self-defense education, security escort services, and shuttle buses. There are informal discussions, pamphlets/posters/films, emergency telephones, lighted pathways/sidewalks, and a crime prevention office.

Programs of Study: DePaul confers B.A., B.S., B.F.A, B.M., and B.S.C. degrees. Master's and doctoral degrees are also awarded. Bachelor's degrees are awarded in BIOLOGICAL SCIENCE (biology/biological science), BUSINESS (accounting, banking and finance, business administration and management, business economics, and marketing/retailing/merchandising), COMMUNICATIONS AND THE ARTS (applied music, art, communications, comparative literature, dramatic arts, English, fine arts, French, German, Italian, jazz, music, music business management, Spanish, and theater design), COMPUTER AND PHYSICAL SCIENCE (chemistry, computer science, information sciences and systems, mathematics, and physics), EDUCATION (early childhood, elementary, foreign languages, music, physical, and secondary), ENGINEERING AND ENVIRONMENTAL DESIGN (environmental science), HEALTH PROFESSIONS (medical laboratory technology), SOCIAL SCIENCE (American studies, economics, geography, history, international studies, Judaic studies, Latin American studies, philosophy, political science/government, psychology, religion, social science, social studies, sociology, urban studies, and women's studies). Commerce, liberal arts and science, and computer science are the largest.

Required: All students must complete general education requirements, including 4 courses in behavioral and social sciences, 3 each in natural sciences and math, 2 each in English composition, world civilization, and philosophy and religion, and 1 each in art, music, and literature. A total of 192 quarter hour credits, including a minimum of 52 in the student's major, and a minimum GPA of 2.0 are required to graduate.

Special: A co-op program in Jewish studies is offered with Spertus College of Judaica. Numerous internships in communications, commerce, computer science, and social sciences are possible. Study abroad is offered in 11 countries and in a West European Seminar in Comparative Business Practices. Accelerated degree programs, dual majors, a certificate program in acting and costume construction, pass/fail options, and concentrations within the theater major, including acting, costume design, general theater studies, lighting design, playwriting, production theater management, and theater technology, are available. The School for New Learning provides evening and weekend degree programs for adult learners, with credit given for life and work experience. There are 21 national honor societies, a freshman honors program, and 29 departmental honors programs.

Faculty/Classroom: 56% of faculty are male; 44%, female. 84% teach undergraduates. Graduate students teach less than 3% of introductory courses. The average class size in an introductory lecture is 18; in a laboratory, 18; and in a regular course, 16.

Admissions: 71% of the 2005-2006 applicants were accepted. The SAT scores for the 2005-2006 freshman class were: Verbal--17% below 500, 48% between 500 and 599, 30% between 600 and 700, and 5% above 700; Math--23% below 500, 47% between 500 and 599, 26% between 600 and 700, and 4% above 700. The ACT scores were 25% below 21, 22% between 21 and 23, 28% between 24 and 26, 14% between 27 and 28, and 11% above 28. 24% of the current freshmen were in the top fifth of their class; 45% were in the top two fifths. 19 freshmen graduated first in their class.

Requirements: The SAT or ACT is required. In addition, applicants should have completed 16 Carnegie units or submit the GED. A portfolio is required for theater majors and an audition for acting and music majors. DePaul requires applicants to be in the upper 50% of their class. A GPA of 2.5 is required. AP and CLEP credits are accepted. Important factors in the admissions decision are advanced placement or honor courses, leadership record, and personality/intangible qualities.

Procedure: Freshmen are admitted to all sessions. Entrance exams should be taken by the spring of the junior year. There are early admissions and deferred admissions plans. There is a rolling admissions plan. Applications should be filed by February 1 for fall entry, December 1 for winter entry, and February 1 for spring entry. Application fee is $40 ($25

for on-line applications). Notification of early decision is sent January 1; regular decision, May 1. Applications are accepted on-line.

Transfer: 1229 transfer students enrolled in 2004-2005. A 2.0 GPA is required for most programs; a 2.5 in commerce. Applicants with fewer than 30 semester hours or 44 quarter hours should submit high school transcripts and SAT or ACT scores. An audition is required for music and theater majors. 64 of 192 credits required for the bachelor's degree must be completed at DePaul.

Visiting: There are regularly scheduled orientations for prospective students, including a 2-day program offered throughout the summer that provides academic advising, assessment testing, and registration, in addition to information on social activities and residence life. There are guides for informal visits and visitors may sit in on classes and stay overnight. To schedule a visit, contact the Admissions Office.

Financial Aid: In 2005-2006, 60% of all full-time freshmen and 62% of continuing full-time students received some form of financial aid. 47% of full-time freshmen and 49% of continuing full-time students received need-based aid. The average freshman award was $16,928. Need-based scholarships or need-based grants averaged $11,558 ($27,639 maximum); need-based self-help aid (loans and jobs) averaged $12,136 ($38,625 maximum); non-need-based athletic scholarships averaged $16,882 ($40,018 maximum); and other non-need-based awards and non-need-based scholarships averaged $8300 ($21,500 maximum). The average financial indebtedness of the 2005 graduate was $21,061. The FAFSA is required. The deadline for filing freshman financial aid applications for fall entry is May 1.

International Students: There are 730 international students enrolled. They must score achieve a satisfactory score on the TOEFL and also take the SAT or the ACT.

Computers: Wireless access is available. Students have access to the network via campus computer labs, stations, and libraries as well as in dorm rooms. All students may access the system 24 hours a day. There are no time limits and no fees. It is strongly recommended that all students have a personal computer.

Graduates: From July 1, 2004 to June 30, 2005, 2683 bachelor's degrees were awarded. The most popular majors were finance (12%), marketing (8%), and clinical lab science (7%). In an average class, 40% graduate in 4 years or less, 66% graduate in 5 years or less, and 71% graduate in 6 years or less. 144 companies recruited on campus in 2004-2005. Of the 2004 graduating class, 19% were enrolled in graduate school within 6 months of graduation and 89% were employed.

Admissions Contact: Carlene Klaas, Director of Undergraduate Admissions. E-mail: *admitdpu@depaul.edu* Web: *www.depaul.edu*

DEVRY UNIVERSITY/ADDISON (DUPAGE COUNTY)   E-2
Addison, IL 60101-6106

(630) 953-2000
(800) 346-5420; Fax: (630) 953-1236

Full-time: 1655 men, 715 women	**Faculty:** n/av
Part-time: 1540 men, 925 women	**Ph.D.s:** n/av
Graduate: none	**Student/Faculty:** n/av
Year: semesters, summer session	**Tuition:** $10,800
Application Deadline: open	**Room & Board:** n/app
Freshman Class: n/av	
SAT or ACT: n/av	**LESS COMPETITIVE**

DeVry University/Addison (DuPage County), a private institution, opened in 1982; there are 66 other DeVry University locations in the United States and Canada. Figures in the above capsule and profile are approximate. The school offers hands-on technology-based programs in electronics, business administration, telecommunications management, computer information systems, technical management, information technology, and computer engineering technology. In addition to regional accreditation, DeVry has baccalaureate program accreditation with ABET. The library contains 16,606 volumes and 676 audio/video tapes/CDs/DVDs, and subscribes to 109 periodicals including electronic. Computerized library services include the card catalog, interlibrary loans, and database searching. Special learning facilities include a learning resource center and electronics and other labs. The 15-acre campus is in a suburban area 20 miles west of Chicago. There is one building.

Student Life: 52% are white; 13% African American. The average age of all undergraduates is 26.

Housing: There are no residence halls. Housing referrals can be obtained though the Student Housing Office. There are private apartments, student-plan housing, and private rooms. All students commute. Alcohol is not permitted. All students may keep cars.

Activities: There are no fraternities or sororities. There are 11 groups on campus, including computers, ethnic, honors, international, literary magazine, newspaper, professional, religious, and social service. Popular campus events include Summer Fest, Casino Night, and Santa Day.

Sports: There are 5 intramural sports for men and 5 for women. Facilities include a weight room, a gym, an indoor and outdoor track, baseball diamonds, and an outdoor pool, all available not far from DeVry.

Disabled Students: 90% of the campus is accessible. Wheelchair ramps, elevators, special parking, specially equipped rest rooms, and lowered drinking fountains are available.

Services: Counseling and information services are available, as is tutoring in every subject.

Campus Safety and Security: Measures include lighted pathways/sidewalks. During business hours, the campus is patrolled by student assistants. An alarm system is in operation during other hours.

Programs of Study: DeVry confers the B.S. degree. Associate degrees are also awarded. Bachelor's degrees are awarded in BUSINESS (business administration and management), COMMUNICATIONS AND THE ARTS (telecommunications), COMPUTER AND PHYSICAL SCIENCE (information sciences and systems), ENGINEERING AND ENVIRONMENTAL DESIGN (computer engineering, electrical/electronics engineering technology, and technological management). Computer information systems, telecommunications, and electronics engineering technology are the largest.

Required: To graduate, students must achieve a cumulative GPA of at least 2.0 and satisfactorily complete all curriculum requirements. Course requirements vary according to program. All first-semester students take courses in business organization, computer applications, algebra, psychology, and student success strategies.

Special: Nondegree study, co-op programs, an accelerated degree program, evening and weekend classes, and distance learning are available. There are 3 national honor societies and 3 departmental honors programs.

Faculty/Classroom: All teach undergraduates.

Requirements: Admissions requirements include graduation from a secondary school; the GED is also accepted. Applicants must pass the DeVry entrance exam or present satisfactory ACT or SAT scores. An interview is required. CLEP credit is accepted.

Procedure: Freshmen are admitted fall, spring, and summer. There are early admissions, deferred admissions and rolling admissions plans. Application deadlines are open. Application fee is $50. Applications are accepted on-line.

Transfer: Applicants must present passing grades in all completed college course work, demonstrate language skills proficiency with at least 24 completed semester hours, and evidence math proficiency by appropriate college-level credits. A minimum GPA of 2.0 is required. 25 of 48 credits required for the bachelor's degree must be completed at DeVry.

Visiting: There are regularly scheduled orientations for prospective students. There are guides for informal visits and visitors may sit in on classes. To schedule a visit, contact Billy Bungert, New Student Coordinator at (708) 953-0610.

Financial Aid: In a recent year, 24% of all full-time freshmen and 49% of continuing full-time students received some form of financial aid. 24% of full-time freshmen and 48% of continuing full-time students received need-based aid. The average freshman award was $6723. Need-based scholarships or need-based grants averaged $5099; need-based self-help aid (loans and jobs) averaged $3495; and other non-need-based awards and non-need-based scholarships averaged $6930. DeVry is a member of CSS. The FAFSA is required. Check with the school for current application deadlines.

International Students: They must score satisfactorily on the written TOEFL or on the electronic version or also take the MELAB, the Comprehensive English Language Test, or the college's own test and also take the SAT or the ACT or the college's own entrance exam.

Computers: Students in the computer information systems program may access the system during published lab hours. There are no time limits and no fees.

Graduates: In a recent year, 719 bachelor's degrees were awarded. The most popular majors were computer information systems (71%), business (17%), and electronics engineering technology (12%). 55 companies recruited on campus in 2004-2005.

Admissions Contact: Ted Kulawiak, Director of Admissions. E-mail: *mbutler@dpg.devry.edu* Web: *www.dpg.devry.edu*

DEVRY UNIVERSITY/CHICAGO — E-2

Chicago, IL 60618-5994

(773) 929-6550
(800) 383-3879; Fax: (773) 697-2710

Full-time: 1200 men, 620 women	Faculty: n/av
Part-time: 660 men, 425 women	Ph.D.s: n/av
Graduate: none	Student/Faculty: n/av
Year: semesters, summer session	Tuition: $10,800
Application Deadline: open	Room & Board: n/app
Freshman Class: n/av	
SAT or ACT: n/av	LESS COMPETITIVE

DeVry University/Chicago, founded in 1931, is a private institution offering hands-on programs in electronics, computer engineering technology, information technology, business administration, telecommunications, technical management, and computer information systems. Figures in the above capsule and profile are approximate. The school is a part of DeVry University, Inc., an organization administering the 67 DeVry University locations throughout the United States and Canada. In addition to regional accreditation, DeVry has baccalaureate program accreditation with ABET. The library contains 19,524 volumes and 1136 audio/video tapes/CDs/DVDs, and subscribes to 26 periodicals including electronic. Computerized library services include the card catalog, interlibrary loans, and database searching. Special learning facilities include a learning resource center and electronics and other labs. The 14-acre campus is in an urban area in northwest Chicago. There is one building.

Student Life: 34% are African American; 31% Hispanic; 22% white; 11% Asian American. The average age of all undergraduates is 26.

Housing: There are no residence halls. Housing referrals may be obtained through the Student Housing Office. There are private apartments, student-plan housing, and private rooms. All of students commute. Alcohol is not permitted. All students may keep cars.

Activities: There are no fraternities or sororities. There are 16 groups on campus, including computers, ethnic, honors, international, newspaper, professional, and religious. Popular campus events include Megaflicks and Freaky Photos, Taste of Chicago, and Welcome Week.

Sports: There is no sports program at DeVry.

Disabled Students: 70% of the campus is accessible. Elevators, special parking, specially equipped rest rooms, lowered drinking fountains, and lowered telephones are available.

Services: Counseling and information services are available, as is tutoring in every subject.

Campus Safety and Security: Measures include 24-hour foot and vehicle patrol and lighted pathways/sidewalks. Security guards are on duty Monday through Friday 7 A.M. to midnight. There is 24-hour security on weekends and holidays.

Programs of Study: DeVry confers the B.S. degree. Associate degrees are also awarded. Bachelor's degrees are awarded in BUSINESS (business administration and management), COMMUNICATIONS AND THE ARTS (telecommunications), COMPUTER AND PHYSICAL SCIENCE (information sciences and systems), ENGINEERING AND ENVIRONMENTAL DESIGN (computer engineering, electrical/electronics engineering technology, and technological management). Computer information systems and electronics engineering technology are the largest.

Required: To graduate, students must achieve a cumulative GPA of at least 2.0 and satisfactorily complete all curriculum requirements. Course requirements vary according to program. All first-semester students take courses in business organization, computer applications, algebra, psychology, and student success strategies.

Special: Accelerated degrees, co-op programs, evening and weekend classes, and nondegree study are possible. There are 3 national honor societies and 3 departmental honors programs.

Faculty/Classroom: All teach undergraduates.

Requirements: Admission requirements include graduation from a secondary school; the GED is also accepted. Applicants must pass the DeVry entrance exam or present satisfactory ACT or SAT I scores. An interview is required. CLEP credit is accepted.

Procedure: Freshmen are admitted fall, spring, and summer. There are early admissions, deferred admissions and rolling admissions plans. Application deadlines are open. Application fee is $50. Applications are accepted on-line.

Transfer: Applicants must present passing grades in all completed college course work, demonstrate language skills proficiency with at least 24 completed semester hours, and evidence math proficiency by appropriate college-level credits. A minimum GPA of 2.0 is required. 25 of 48 credits required for the bachelor's degree must be completed at DeVry.

Visiting: There are regularly scheduled orientations for prospective students. There are guides for informal visits and visitors may sit in on classes. To schedule a visit, contact the Enrollment Services Coordinator at (773) 929-8500.

Financial Aid: In a recent year, 35% of all full-time freshmen and 64% of continuing full-time students received some form of financial aid. 34% of full-time freshmen and 63% of continuing full-time students received need-based aid. The average freshman award was $9238. Need-based scholarships or need-based grants averaged $6630; need-based self-help aid (loans and jobs) averaged $3792; and other non-need-based awards and non-need-based scholarships averaged $7112. The FAFSA is required. The deadline for filing freshman financial aid applications for fall entry is rolling.

International Students: They must score satisfactorily on the written TOEFL on the electronic version and also take the college's own entrance exam.

Computers: Computer information systems students may access the system during lab hours. There are no fees.

Graduates: In a recent year, 577 bachelor's degrees were awarded. The most popular majors were computer information systems (56%), business administration (26%), and electronics technology (18%). 115 companies recruited on campus in 2004-2005.

Admissions Contact: Christine Hierl, Director of Admissions. E-mail: *admissions2@devry.edu* Web: *www.chi.devry.edu*

DEVRY UNIVERSITY/TINLEY PARK
E-2
Tinley Park, IL 60477-6243
(708) 342-3100
(877) 305-8184; Fax: (708) 342-3505

Full-time: 700 men, 250 women	**Faculty:** n/av
Part-time: 320 men, 175 women	**Ph.D.s:** n/av
Graduate: none	**Student/Faculty:** n/av
Year: semesters, summer session	**Tuition:** $12,000
Application Deadline: open	**Room & Board:** n/app
Freshman Class: n/av	
SAT or ACT: n/av	**LESS COMPETITIVE**

DeVry University/Tinley Park, founded in 2000, is 1 of 67 DeVry University locations throughout the United States and Canada. The private institution offers career-oriented degree programs with hands-on training in various fields of business and technology. Figures in the above capsule and in this profile are approximate. The library contains 11,000 volumes and 600 audio/video tapes/CDs/DVDs, and subscribes to 70 periodicals including electronic. Computerized library services include the card catalog, interlibrary loans, and database searching. Special learning facilities include a learning resource center and electronics and other labs. .

Student Life: 53% are white; 30% African American. The average age of all undergraduates is 26.

Housing: There are no residence halls. All of students commute. All students may keep cars.

Activities: There are no fraternities or sororities. There are 6 groups on campus, including computers, professional, and social. Popular campus events include Anniversary Celebration.

Sports: There is no sports program at DeVry.

Disabled Students: All of the campus is accessible. Wheelchair ramps, elevators, special parking, specially equipped rest rooms, special class scheduling, lowered drinking fountains, and lowered telephones are available.

Services: Counseling and information services are available, as is tutoring in every subject.

Campus Safety and Security: Measures include security escort services, informal discussions, emergency telephones, and lighted pathways/sidewalks. There are 24-hour emergency telephone/alarm devices, and 16-hour patrols by trained security personnel.

Programs of Study: DeVry confers the B.S. degree. Associate and master's degrees are also awarded. Bachelor's degrees are awarded in BUSINESS (business administration and management), COMMUNICATIONS AND THE ARTS (telecommunications), COMPUTER AND PHYSICAL SCIENCE (information sciences and systems), ENGINEERING AND ENVIRONMENTAL DESIGN (computer engineering, electrical/electronics engineering technology, and technological management). Telecommunications management and computer information systems are the largest.

Required: To graduate, students must achieve a GPA of at least 2.0 and complete all curriculum requirements. Course requirements may vary according to program. All first-semester students take courses in business organization, computer applications, algebra, psychology, and student success strategies.

Special: Accelerated degree programs are offered in business administration and telecommunications management. Co-op programs, nondegree study, distance learning, and evening and weekend classes are possible.

Faculty/Classroom: All teach undergraduates.

Requirements: Admissions requirements include graduation from a secondary school; the GED is also accepted. Applicants must pass the DeVry entrance exam or present satisfactory ACT or SAT scores. An interview is required. CLEP credit is accepted.

Procedure: Freshmen are admitted to all sessions. There are early admissions and deferred admissions plans. Application deadlines are open. Check with the school for application fee. Applications are accepted online.

Transfer: Applicants must submit official transcripts from all previous colleges attended indicating passing grades in all completed course work, demonstrate language skills proficiency in at least 24 completed semester hours, and present evidence of math proficiency by appropriate college-level credits. A minimum GPA of 2.0 is required. 25 of 48 credits required for the bachelor's degree must be completed at DeVry.

Visiting: There are regularly scheduled orientations for prospective students. There are guides for informal visits and visitors may sit in on classes. To schedule a visit, contact New Student Coordinator.

Financial Aid: In a recent year, 49% of all full-time freshmen and 72% of continuing full-time students received some form of financial aid. 49% of full-time freshmen and 72% of continuing full-time students received need-based aid. The average freshman award was $7533. Need-based scholarships or need-based grants averaged $5844; need-based self-help aid (loans and jobs) averaged $3747; and other non-need-based awards and non-need-based scholarships averaged $8740. The FAFSA is required.

International Students: International students must take the TOEFL and also take the college's own entrance exam.

Graduates: In a recent year, 180 bachelor's degrees were awarded. The most popular majors were computer information systems (89%), electronics engineering technology (9%), and business (3%).

Admissions Contact: Angela Howard, Director of Admissions. E-mail: *imccauley@tp.devry.edu* Web: *www.tp.devry.edu*

DOMINICAN UNIVERSITY
E-2
River Forest, IL 60305
(708) 524-6800
(800) 828-8475; Fax: (708) 524-6864

Full-time: 354 men, 742 women	**Faculty:** 89; IIA, -$
Part-time: 54 men, 137 women	**Ph.D.s:** 88%
Graduate: 476 men, 1437 women	**Student/Faculty:** 12 to 1
Year: semesters, summer session	**Tuition:** $20,050
Application Deadline: open	**Room & Board:** $6320
Freshman Class: 993 applied, 808 accepted, 269 enrolled	
ACT: 23	**COMPETITIVE**

Dominican University, founded in 1901, is an independent liberal arts institution affiliated with the Roman Catholic Church and sponsored by the Sinsinawa Dominicans. There are 2 undergraduate and 4 graduate schools. In addition to regional accreditation, Dominican University has baccalaureate program accreditation with ACBSP and ADA. The library contains 300,000 volumes, 46,000 microform items, and 4170 audio/video tapes/CDs/DVDs, and subscribes to 5800 periodicals including electronic. Computerized library services include the card catalog, interlibrary loans, and database searching. Special learning facilities include a learning resource center, art gallery, language lab, and writing center. The 30-acre campus is in a suburban area 10 miles west of Chicago. Including any residence halls, there are 8 buildings.

Student Life: 91% of undergraduates are from Illinois. Others are from 23 states and 16 foreign countries. 60% are from public schools. 60% are white; 19% Hispanic. 66% are Catholic; 16% claim no religious affiliation; 13% Protestant. The average age of freshmen is 18; all undergraduates, 22. 17% do not continue beyond their first year; 65% remain to graduate.

Housing: 490 students can be accommodated in college housing, which includes single-sex and coed dorms and suites reserved for service learning groups. On-campus housing is guaranteed for all 4 years. 65% of students commute. All students may keep cars.

Activities: There are no fraternities or sororities. There are 30 groups on campus, including art, cheerleading, choir, computers, dance, drama, ethnic, honors, international, literary magazine, musical theater, newspaper, photography, political, professional, religious, social, social service, and student government. Popular campus events include Founders Day, Spring Fling, and Candle and Rose Ceremony.

Sports: There are 5 intercollegiate sports for men and 6 for women, and 5 intramural sports for men and 5 for women. Facilities include a gym, an indoor running track, an indoor swimming pool, a weight room, a training room, a fitness center, a dance room, racquetball courts, and soccer fields.

Disabled Students: All of the campus is accessible. Wheelchair ramps, elevators, special parking, specially equipped rest rooms, special class scheduling, lowered drinking fountains, and special housing are available.

Services: Counseling and information services are available, as is tutoring in most subjects. There is remedial math and writing.

Campus Safety and Security: Measures include 24-hour foot and vehicle patrol, security escort services, shuttle buses, and informal discussions. There are pamphlets/posters/films, emergency telephones, lighted pathways/sidewalks, and door alarms.

Programs of Study: Dominican University confers B.A. and B.S. degrees. Master's degrees are also awarded. Bachelor's degrees are awarded in BIOLOGICAL SCIENCE (biochemistry, biology/biological science, and nutrition), BUSINESS (accounting, business administration and management, fashion merchandising, and international business management), COMMUNICATIONS AND THE ARTS (art, communications, dramatic arts, English, fine arts, French, graphic design, Italian, journalism, music, performing arts, photography, and Spanish), COMPUTER AND PHYSICAL SCIENCE (chemistry, computer science, information sciences and systems, and mathematics), ENGINEERING AND ENVIRONMENTAL DESIGN (engineering and environmental science), SOCIAL SCIENCE (American studies, criminology, dietetics, fashion design and technology, food production/management/services, food science, history, international relations, philosophy, political science/government, psychology, religion, social science, and sociology). English, psychology, and sciences are the strongest academically. Business administration, psychology, sociology, and English are the largest.

Required: To graduate, students must complete 124 credit hours with a minimum GPA of 2.0. A total of 30 to 56 hours is required in the major. All students must demonstrate proficiency, through a placement exam or the completion of specified courses in English composition, math, computer competency, and library skills. In addition, students must take 1 interdisciplinary seminar at each academic level and 1 course each in natural sciences, history, fine arts and literature, social sciences, theology, and philosophy. 1 course must meet the multicultural requirement.

Special: Co-op programs in nursing with Rush University, cross-registration with Concordia University, internships, study abroad in 7 countries and a Washington semester are offered. Student-designed majors and interdisciplinary majors, including computer information systems, math and computer science, environmental science, and environmental management, credit for prior learning, and pass/fail options are possible. There is an accelerated degree program in organizational leadership, and a joint B.A.-B.S. in engineering with the Illinios Institute of Technology, and a dual admission program with Midwestern University. There are 11 national honor societies and a freshman honors program.

Faculty/Classroom: 39% of faculty are male; 61%, female. 80% teach undergraduates and 100% both teach and do research. No introductory courses are taught by graduate students. The average class size in an introductory lecture is 23; in a laboratory, 12; and in a regular course, 20.

Admissions: 81% of the 2005-2006 applicants were accepted. The ACT scores for the 2005-2006 freshman class were: 34% below 21, 29% between 21 and 23, 23% between 24 and 26, 8% between 27 and 28, and 5% above 28. 42% of the current freshmen were in the top fifth of their class; 74% were in the top two fifths. 5 freshmen graduated first in their class.

Requirements: The SAT or ACT is required. The ACT Optional Writing test is also required for some programs. In addition, graduation from an accredited secondary school or satisfactory scores on the GED are required for admission. The school requires 14 academic credits or 16 Carnegie units. High school courses should include English, math, foreign language, social science, and lab science. An essay is required and an interview is recommended. Dominican University requires applicants to be in the upper 50% of their class. A GPA of 2.75 is required. AP and CLEP credits are accepted. Important factors in the admissions decision are advanced placement or honor courses, recommendations by school officials, and leadership record.

Procedure: Freshmen are admitted to all sessions. Entrance exams should be taken in the junior year. There is a deferred admissions plan. Application deadlines are open. Application fee is $25. Applications are accepted on-line.

Transfer: 161 transfer students enrolled in a recent year. Applicants must have a minimum of 12 credit hours with a GPA of 2.5. An interview is recommended. The high school record will be evaluated if GPA is below 2.5 at the previous college. 34 of 124 credits required for the bachelor's degree must be completed at Dominican University.

Visiting: There are regularly scheduled orientations for prospective students, including visiting day and open house programs, which consist of faculty and student presentations, tours, and an academic and co-curricular fair. Special events are also held in the summer. There are guides for informal visits and visitors may sit in on classes and stay overnight. To schedule a visit, contact the Undergraduate Admissions Office at domadmis@dom.edu.

Financial Aid: In 2005-2006, 95% of all full-time freshmen and 85% of continuing full-time students received some form of financial aid. 87% of full-time freshmen and 81% of continuing full-time students received need-based aid. The average freshman award was $18,408. Need-based scholarships or need-based grants averaged $10,324 ($15,381 maximum); need-based self-help aid (loans and jobs) averaged $4317 ($6825 maximum); and other non-need-based awards and non-need-based scholarships averaged $4143 ($10,000 maximum). 28% of undergraduates work part time. Average annual earnings from campus work are $1862. The average financial indebtedness of the 2005 graduate was $14,300. Dominican University is a member of CSS. The FAFSA and tax returns are required. The priority date for freshman financial aid applications for fall entry is April 15. The deadline for filing freshman financial aid applications for fall entry is September 1.

International Students: There are 23 international students enrolled. They must score satisfactorily on the written TOEFL or on the electronic version or take the MELAB, the Comprehensive English Language Test, or the college's own test. The TOEFL is preferred.

Computers: Wireless access is available. All residence rooms have Internet access as do commuter lounges. There are numerous PCs on campus and a MAC lab. The library has wireless access and there are ports for laptops in the Cybercafe. All students may access the system 24/7. There are no time limits and no fees. It is strongly recommended that all students have a personal computer.

Graduates: In a recent year, 279 bachelor's degrees were awarded. The most popular majors were business (15%), psychology (9%), and sociology (5%). In an average class, 55% graduate in 4 years or less, 62% graduate in 5 years or less, and 63% graduate in 6 years or less. Of a recent graduating class, 12% were enrolled in graduate school within 6 months of graduation and 95% were employed.

Admissions Contact: Glenn Hamilton, Director of Freshman Admission. E-mail: domadmis@dom.edu Web: www.dom.edu

EASTERN ILLINOIS UNIVERSITY   E-4
Charleston, IL 61920-3099   (217) 581-2223
                                   (800) 252-5711; Fax: (217) 581-7060

Full-time: 4029 men, 5264 women	**Faculty:** IIA, -$
Part-time: 358 men, 724 women	**Ph.D.s:** 70%
Graduate: 647 men, 1107 women	**Student/Faculty:** n/av
Year: semesters, summer session	**Tuition:** $6373 ($15,631)
Application Deadline: open	**Room & Board:** $6196
Freshman Class: 7682 applied, 5975 accepted, 1719 enrolled	
ACT: 22	**COMPETITIVE**

Eastern Illinois University, founded in 1895, is a state-assisted school offering undergraduate and graduate degrees in arts and sciences and professional studies. There are 4 undergraduate schools and 1 graduate school. In addition to regional accreditation, EIU has baccalaureate program accreditation with AACSB, ACEJMC, ADA, NASAD, NASM, NCATE, and NRPA. The library contains 1,060,899 volumes, 1,382,016 microform items, and 28,375 audio/video tapes/CDs/DVDs, and subscribes to 5292 periodicals including electronic. Computerized library services include the card catalog, interlibrary loans, database searching, Internet access, and laptop Internet portals. Special learning facilities include a learning resource center, art gallery, radio station, and TV station. The 320-acre campus is in a small town 50 miles south of Champaign-Urbana. Including any residence halls, there are 90 buildings.

Student Life: 98% of undergraduates are from Illinois. Others are from 29 states, 42 foreign countries, and Canada. 85% are white. The average age of freshmen is 18; all undergraduates, 22. 19% do not continue beyond their first year; 62% remain to graduate.

Housing: 5533 students can be accommodated in college housing, which includes single-sex and coed dorms, on-campus apartments, married-student housing, fraternity houses, and sorority houses. In addition, there are honors houses. On-campus housing is guaranteed for all 4 years. 57% of students commute. All students may keep cars.

Activities: 14% of men belong to 12 national fraternities; 14% of women belong to 12 national sororities. There are 155 groups on campus, including art, band, cheerleading, choir, chorale, chorus, computers, dance, debate, drama, drill team, ethnic, forensics, gay, honors, international, jazz band, literary magazine, marching band, musical theater, newspaper, orchestra, pep band, political, professional, radio and TV, religious, social, social service, student government, symphony, and yearbook. Popular campus events include Family Weekend, Greek Week, and an arts festival.

Sports: There are 11 intercollegiate sports for men and 11 for women, and 16 intramural sports for men and 16 for women. Facilities include a swimming pool, a gym, a student recreation center, a track, tennis courts, racquetball courts, and a jogging trail.

Disabled Students: 75% of the campus is accessible. Wheelchair ramps, elevators, special parking, specially equipped rest rooms, special class scheduling, lowered drinking fountains, and lowered telephones are available.

Services: Counseling and information services are available, as is tutoring in most subjects. There is a reader service for the blind, and remedial math, reading, and writing. An academic assistance center advises freshmen and students with undeclared majors. Term paper clinics, study skills seminars, and stress management workshops are also available.

Campus Safety and Security: Measures include 24-hour foot and vehicle patrol, self-defense education, security escort services, and shuttle buses. There are informal discussions, pamphlets/posters/films, emergency telephones, and lighted pathways/sidewalks.

Programs of Study: EIU confers B.A., B.S., B.M., B.S.Bus., and B.S.Ed. degrees. Master's degrees are also awarded. Bachelor's degrees are awarded in BIOLOGICAL SCIENCE (biology/biological science), BUSINESS (accounting, banking and finance, business administration and management, and marketing/retailing/merchandising), COMMUNICATIONS AND THE ARTS (art, communications, dramatic arts, English, journalism, languages, and music), COMPUTER AND PHYSICAL SCIENCE (chemistry, computer science, geology, mathematics, and physics), EDUCATION (early childhood, elementary, middle school, physical, secondary, social science, and special), ENGINEERING AND ENVIRONMENTAL DESIGN (industrial engineering technology), HEALTH PROFESSIONS (medical laboratory science and speech pathology/audiology), SOCIAL SCIENCE (African American studies, economics, geography, history, philosophy, political science/government, psychology, and sociology). Education is the strongest academically. Elementary education, phys ed, and family and consumer sciences are the largest.

Required: A total of 120 credit hours, with a minimum of 40 hours in upper-division courses, must be completed for graduation. The minimum GPA required for graduation is 2.0 (2.5 in education). A core curriculum of 40 to 46 hours includes courses in language, quantitative reasoning and problem solving, scientific awareness, foreign languages, cultural experience, foundations of civilizations, human behavior, social interaction and well-being, U.S. Constitution, and a senior seminar.

Special: EIU offers a co-op program in clinical laboratory science and an engineering co-op program with the University of Illinois at Champaign-Urbana. Internships, study abroad in 12 countries, dual majors, nondegree study, B.A.-B.S. degrees in athletic training and industrial technology, and pass/fail options are available. Credit for life experience may be granted through the Board of Trustees program and the Career Occupations program. There are 39 national honor societies, a freshman honors program, and 22 departmental honors programs.

Faculty/Classroom: 53% of faculty are male; 47%, female. The average class size in a regular course is 22.

Admissions: 78% of the 2005-2006 applicants were accepted. The ACT scores for the 2005-2006 freshman class were: 39% below 21, 33% between 21 and 23, 19% between 24 and 26, 5% between 27 and 28, and 4% above 28. 18% of the current freshmen were in the top fifth of their class; 46% were in the top two fifths.

Requirements: The SAT or ACT is required with a minimum composite scores based on students' rank in the class. The ACT Optional Writing test is also recommended. SAT Subject Tests are also accepted. Applicants must be graduates of an accredited secondary school. The GED is accepted. 13 academic credits are required and should include 4 years of English and 3 years each of math, science, and social studies, including 1 year of U.S. history. EIU requires applicants to be in the upper 75% of their class. A GPA of 2.25 is required. AP and CLEP credits are accepted.

Procedure: Freshmen are admitted fall, spring, and summer. Entrance exams should be taken by spring of the junior year. There is an early admissions plan. There is a rolling admissions plan. Application deadlines are open. Application fee is $30. Applications are accepted on-line.

Transfer: 1009 transfer students enrolled in 2004-2005. Transfer students must have earned 30 credit hours with a minimum GPA of 2.0. An associate degree is recommended. 42 of 120 credits required for the bachelor's degree must be completed at EIU.

Visiting: There are regularly scheduled orientations for prospective students, including open houses, scheduled several times in the spring and fall, which provide an opportunity to meet with representatives of colleges and academic departments and student services personnel and go on student-led campus tours. There are guides for informal visits and visitors may sit in on classes and stay overnight. To schedule a visit, contact the Office of Orientation at (217) 581-6435 or night@www.eiu.edu.

Financial Aid: In 2005-2006, 49% of all full-time freshmen and 46% of continuing full-time students received some form of financial aid. 22% of all full-time students received need-based aid. The average freshman award was $9412. Need-based scholarships or need-based grants averaged $2750; need-based self-help aid (loans and jobs) averaged $2211; non-need-based athletic scholarships averaged $5198; and other non-need-based awards and non-need-based scholarships averaged $5976. 20% of undergraduates work part time. The average financial indebtedness of the 2005 graduate was $15,538. The FAFSA, parent and student income tax forms, and an institutional verification form are required. The priority date for freshman financial aid applications for fall entry is March 1.

International Students: There are 44 international students enrolled. The school actively recruits these students. They must achieve a satisfactory score on the TOEFL or achieve a proficiency level of 9 from a U.S. ESL center. They must also take the SAT or the ACT.

Computers: Wireless access is available. 100 wireless points were added in fall 2005. 200 more are to be installed, bringing the total to 300. There are 11 computer labs on campus. All students may access the system. There are no time limits and no fees.

Graduates: From July 1, 2004 to June 30, 2005, 1970 bachelor's degrees were awarded. The most popular majors were elementary education (12%), general studies (8%), and family and consumer sciences (6%). In an average class, 34% graduate in 4 years or less, 57% graduate in 5 years or less, and 62% graduate in 6 years or less. 523 companies recruited on campus in 2004-2005.

Admissions Contact: Brenda Major, Director of Admissions. A video is available. E-mail: *admissions@eiu.edu* Web: *http://www.eiu.edu*

EAST-WEST UNIVERSITY   E-2
Chicago, IL 60605   (312) 939-0111
                                        (877) 398-9376; Fax: (312) 939-0083

Full-time: 370 men, 620 women	**Faculty:** 11
Part-time: 10 men, 20 women	**Ph.D.s:** 8%
Graduate: none	**Student/Faculty:** 89 to 1
Year: quarters, summer session	**Tuition:** $10,375
Application Deadline: open	**Room & Board:** n/app
Freshman Class: n/av	
ACT: required	**LESS COMPETITIVE**

East-West University, founded in 1978, is a private commuter institution offering undergraduate programs in the arts and sciences, business, computer science, and engineering. Figures given in the above capsule and in this profile are approximate. The library contains 21,500 volumes and 8500 microform items, and subscribes to 95 periodicals including elec-

tronic. The campus is in an urban area in Chicago. There is one building.

Student Life: 85% are from in state. Students are from 1 state and 9 foreign countries. 97% are from public schools. 75% are African American; 13% Hispanic. The average age of freshmen is 19; all undergraduates, 20.

Housing: There are no residence halls. Alcohol is not permitted.

Activities: There are no fraternities or sororities. There are 3 groups on campus, including drama, international, and student government. Popular campus events include International Day, Mother's Day Banquet, and Black History Celebration.

Sports: There is no sports program at East-West.

Disabled Students: 50% of the campus is accessible. Elevators and specially equipped rest rooms are available.

Services: Counseling and information services are available, as is tutoring in most subjects. There is remedial math, reading, and writing.

Programs of Study: East-West confers B.A. and B.S. degrees. Associate degrees are also awarded. Bachelor's degrees are awarded in BUSINESS (business administration and management), COMMUNICATIONS AND THE ARTS (communications, and English), COMPUTER AND PHYSICAL SCIENCE (computer science), ENGINEERING AND ENVIRONMENTAL DESIGN (electrical/electronics engineering technology), SOCIAL SCIENCE (behavioral science). Business administration is the largest.

Required: General education requirements vary according to the degree program. To graduate, students must complete at least 180 quarter hours, including 60 in a major field, with a minimum GPA of 2.0.

Special: East-West offers co-op programs in all majors.

Faculty/Classroom: All teach undergraduates. The average class size in an introductory lecture is 15; in a laboratory, 15; and in a regular course, 15.

Requirements: The ACT is required. In addition, applicants must be graduates of accredited secondary schools or have earned a GED. Placement exams are required in math and English. A GPA of 2.5 is required. AP and CLEP credits are accepted.

Procedure: Freshmen are admitted to all sessions. There is a rolling admissions plan. Application deadlines are open.

Transfer: East-West accepts only courses with grades of C or better. 48 of 180 credits required for the bachelor's degree must be completed at East-West.

Visiting: There are regularly scheduled orientations for prospective students. There are guides for informal visits and visitors may sit in on classes.

Financial Aid: In a recent year, 90% of all full-time students received some form of financial aid. 90% of all full-time students received need-based aid. The average freshman award was $9021. Need-based scholarships or need-based grants averaged $2970; and need-based self-help aid (loans and jobs) averaged $2625. The CSS/Profile is required. Check with the school for current application deadlines.

International Students: The school actively recruits these students. They must take the college's own test. Applicants are encouraged but not required to submit TOEFL scores.

Computers: There are no time limits.

Admissions Contact: William Link, Director of Admissions.
E-mail: *williaml@eastwest.edu* Web: *eastwest.edu*

ELMHURST COLLEGE   E-2
Elmhurst, IL 60126-3296   (630) 617-3400
                                        (800) 697-1871; Fax: (630) 617-5501

Full-time: 700 men, 1370 women	**Faculty:** 110; IIB, +$
Part-time: 125 men, 210 women	**Ph.D.s:** 85%
Graduate: 110 men, 90 women	**Student/Faculty:** 19 to 1
Year: 4-1-4, summer session	**Tuition:** $18,650
Application Deadline: see profile	**Room & Board:** $6035
Freshman Class: n/av	
SAT or ACT: required	**COMPETITIVE**

Elmhurst College, founded in 1871, is a private liberal arts college affiliated with the United Church of Christ. Figures in the above capsule and profile are approximate. In addition to regional accreditation, Elmhurst has baccalaureate program accreditation with NCATE and NLN. The library contains 222,441 volumes, 50,605 microform items, and 7532 audio/video tapes/CDs/DVDs, and subscribes to 2010 periodicals including electronic. Computerized library services include the card catalog, interlibrary loans, and database searching. Special learning facilities include a learning resource center, art gallery, radio station, a 16-track, 34-channel board recording studio, an electron microscopy lab, and an accelerator lab. The 38-acre campus is in a suburban area 15 miles west of Chicago. Including any residence halls, there are 23 buildings.

Student Life: 92% of undergraduates are from Illinois. Others are from 26 states, 21 foreign countries, and Canada. 82% are from public schools. 76% are white. 41% are Catholic; 26% claim no religious affiliation; 22% Protestant; 10% Muslim, Hindu, and Buddhist. The average

age of freshmen is 18; all undergraduates, 24. 17% do not continue beyond their first year; 70% remain to graduate.

Housing: 805 students can be accommodated in college housing, which includes coed dorms, on-campus apartments, and off-campus apartments. In addition, there are honors houses. On-campus housing is guaranteed for all 4 years. 62% of students commute. All students may keep cars.

Activities: 5% of men belong to 3 national fraternities; 11% of women belong to 2 local and 4 national sororities. There are 100 groups on campus, including art, band, cheerleading, chess, choir, chorale, chorus, computers, dance, drama, ethnic, film, gay, honors, international, jazz band, literary magazine, musical theater, newspaper, orchestra, pep band, political, professional, radio and TV, religious, social, social service, student government, symphony, and yearbook. Popular campus events include Midwest Jazz Festival, Spring Fling and Family Day.

Sports: There are 8 intercollegiate sports for men and 8 for women, and 7 intramural sports for men and 7 for women. Facilities include a phys ed center, weight rooms, and courts for tennis, racquetball, and handball.

Disabled Students: 95% of the campus is accessible. Wheelchair ramps, elevators, special parking, specially equipped rest rooms, special class scheduling, lowered drinking fountains and lowered telephones are available.

Services: Counseling and information services are available, as is tutoring in most subjects.

Campus Safety and Security: Measures include 24-hour foot and vehicle patrol, security escort services, informal discussions, and pamphlets/posters/films. There are emergency telephones and lighted pathways/sidewalks.

Programs of Study: Elmhurst confers B.A., B.S., B.L.S., and B.Mus. degrees. Master's degrees are also awarded. Bachelor's degrees are awarded in BIOLOGICAL SCIENCE (biology/biological science), BUSINESS (accounting, banking and finance, business administration and management, international business management, marketing/retailing/merchandising, recreational facilities management, and transportation management), COMMUNICATIONS AND THE ARTS (art, communications, dramatic arts, English, French, German, music, music business management, and Spanish), COMPUTER AND PHYSICAL SCIENCE (chemistry, computer science, information sciences and systems, mathematics, and physics), EDUCATION (art, athletic training, drama, early childhood, elementary, mathematics, music, physical, secondary, and special), ENGINEERING AND ENVIRONMENTAL DESIGN (environmental science), HEALTH PROFESSIONS (nursing and speech pathology/audiology), SOCIAL SCIENCE (American studies, economics, geography, history, liberal arts/general studies, philosophy, political science/government, psychology, religion, sociology, and urban studies). Biology, English, and education are the strongest academically. Business administration, nursing, and education-related programs are the largest.

Required: All students are required to take a minimum of 11 general education courses in the following 11 categories: writing and reasoning; Western culture; fine arts; literature; people, power and politics; the natural world; issues and inquiry in science and technology; human behavior; global society; the search for human values; and the Judeo-Christian heritage and religious faith. Students must maintain a 2.0 GPA and complete 128 semester hours. The total number of hours required for the major varies from 32 to 72.

Special: There are cooperative programs in all majors. The Center for Professioal Excellence provides internships and mentoring experiences. Internships varying from 1 month to 1 term are available in approximately 20 major fields. Students may study abroad in 10 countries. Elmhurst also offers a Washington semester and a 3-2 engineering degree with the Illinois Institute of Technology, Washington University, and the Universities of Illinois and Southern California. There are accelerated degree programs in business administration, managerial communication, information technology, and psychology. Credit for life, military, and work experience, nondegree study and pass/fail options are possible. There are 20 national honor societies, a freshman honors program, and 22 departmental honors programs.

Faculty/Classroom: 54% of faculty are male; 46%, female. All both teach and do research. No introductory courses are taught by graduate students. The average class size in an introductory lecture is 19; in a laboratory, 15; and in a regular course, 16.

Requirements: The SAT or ACT is required, with the ACT preferred. Candidates for admission must have completed 16 academic units of credit including at least 3 in English and 2 each of math, social science, and natural science lab courses. 2 years of a foreign language are recommended. AP and CLEP credits are accepted. Important factors in the admissions decision are advanced placement or honor courses, leadership record, and extracurricular activities record.

Procedure: Freshmen are admitted fall and spring. Entrance exams should be taken by the spring of the senior year. There are early admissions, and deferred admissions and rolling admissions plans. Applications should be filed by April 1 for fall entry and January 15 for spring entry. Notification is sent on a rolling basis. Applications are accepted on-line. The fall 2005 application fee was $25.

Transfer: 265 transfer students enrolled in a recent year. Applicants must have a 2.4 GPA and be in good standing at the most recent college attended. A higher GPA is required for nursing, athletic training, and education. 32 of 128 credits required for the bachelor's degree must be completed at Elmhurst.

Visiting: There are regularly scheduled orientations for prospective students, including an admissions interview, a campus tour, and faculty meetings if desired. There are guides for informal visits and visitors may sit in on classes and stay overnight. To schedule a visit, contact The Office of Admission.

Financial Aid: In a recent year, 88% of all full-time freshmen and 75% of continuing full-time students received some form of financial aid. 74% of full-time freshmen and 65% of continuing full-time students received need-based aid. The average freshman award was $15,525. Need-based scholarships or need-based grants averaged $5800 ($14,000 maximum); need-based self-help aid (loans and jobs) averaged $2100 ($4000 maximum); and other non-need-based awards and non-need-based scholarships averaged $7300 ($12,400 maximum). 63% of undergraduates worked part time. Average annual earnings from campus work were $1160. The average financial indebtedness of a recent graduate was $14,700. Elmhurst is a member of CSS. The FAFSA and the college's own financial statement are required. Check with the school for current application deadlines.

International Students: In a recent year, there were 31 international students enrolled. The school actively recruits these students. They must score satisfactorily on the written TOEFL or on the electronic version or take the MELAB.

Computers: All students may access the system Remote access is available 7 days a week, 24 hours a day. Labs are available 98 hours per week. There are no time limits and no fees.

Graduates: In a recent year, 608 bachelor's degrees were awarded. The most popular majors were business and marketing (33%), education (16%), and health professions (7%). In an average class, 1% graduate in 3 years or less, 57% graduate in 4 years or less, 69% graduate in 5 years or less, and 72% graduate in 6 years or less. Of a recent graduating class, 17% were enrolled in graduate school within 6 months of graduation and 90% were employed.

Admissions Contact: Andrew B. Sison, Director of Admission.
E-mail: *admit@elmhurst.edu* Web: *www.elmhurst.edu*

EUREKA COLLEGE
D-3
Eureka, IL 61530

(309) 467-6350
(888) 4-EUREKA; Fax: (309) 467-6576

Full-time: 540 men and women	**Faculty:** 44; IIB, --$
Part-time: 10 men and women	**Ph.Ds:** 85%
Graduate: none	**Student/Faculty:** 12 to 1
Year: semesters, summer session	**Tuition:** $13,400
Application Deadline: August 1	**Room & Board:** $5880
Freshman Class: 900 applied, 600 accepted, 140 enrolled	
ACT: 23	**COMPETITIVE**

Eureka College, founded in 1855, is a small, private, liberal arts college affiliated with the Christian Church (Disciples of Christ). There is 1 undergraduate school. In addition to regional accreditation, E.C. has baccalaureate program accreditation with NCATE. The library contains 85,000 volumes, 4989 microform items, and 977 audio/video tapes/CDs/DVDs, and subscribes to 343 periodicals including electronic. Computerized library services include interlibrary loans, database searching, and Internet access. Special learning facilities include a learning resource center, art gallery, and the Ronald Reagan Museum. The 112-acre campus is in a small town 20 minutes east of Peoria, 20 minutes west of Bloomington, and 2 hours south of Chicago. Including any residence halls, there are 23 buildings.

Student Life: 90% of undergraduates are from Illinois. Others are from 17 states and 3 foreign countries. 80% are from public schools. 87% are white. 37% claim no religious affiliation; 31% Protestant; 28% Catholic. The average age of freshmen is 18; all undergraduates, 21. 25% do not continue beyond their first year; 65% remain to graduate.

Housing: 550 students can be accommodated in college housing, which includes single-sex and coed dorms, fraternity houses, and sorority houses. On-campus housing is guaranteed for all 4 years. 80% of students live on campus; of those, 70% remain on campus on weekends. All students may keep cars.

Activities: 35% of men belong to 3 national fraternities; 35% of women belong to 1 local and 2 national sororities. There are 41 groups on campus, including art, band, cheerleading, choir, chorale, chorus, computers, dance, drama, ethnic, honors, international, literary magazine, musical theater, newspaper, pep band, photography, political, professional, religious, social, social service, student government, and yearbook. Popular campus events include Pride Day, Tree Lighting Ceremony, and Ivy Ceremony.

Sports: There are 8 intercollegiate sports for men and 8 for women, and 6 intramural sports for men and 6 for women. Facilities include a

gym, a pool, a weight room, tennis courts, football, softball, and baseball fields, and a wellness center.

Disabled Students: 50% of the campus is accessible. Wheelchair ramps, elevators, special parking, and specially equipped rest rooms are available.

Services: Counseling and information services are available, as is tutoring in most subjects. There is remedial reading and writing. There is a writing center and math lab located within the Learning Center.

Campus Safety and Security: Measures include informal discussions, pamphlets/posters/films, and lighted pathways/sidewalks. A city police officer provides campus security in the evenings and on weekends.

Programs of Study: E.C. confers B.A. and B.S. degrees. Bachelor's degrees are awarded in BIOLOGICAL SCIENCE (biology/biological science), BUSINESS (accounting, business administration and management, business economics, and management information systems), COMMUNICATIONS AND THE ARTS (communications, dramatic arts, English, fine arts, and music), COMPUTER AND PHYSICAL SCIENCE (chemistry, computer science, mathematics, and physical sciences), EDUCATION (athletic training, education, elementary, music, physical, science, and secondary), HEALTH PROFESSIONS (medical laboratory technology), SOCIAL SCIENCE (child care/child and family studies, history, liberal arts/general studies, philosophy, physical fitness/movement, political science/government, psychology, religion, social science, and sociology). Chemistry, biology, and business administration are the strongest academically. Business administration, education, and psychology are the largest.

Required: All students must take English composition, biological and physical sciences, general studies, math, phys ed, Western civilization, 3 humanities courses, 3 social science courses, and a global awareness component. A total of at least 124 hours is required for graduation, including 32 hours in the major. A minimum GPA of 2.0 is required.

Special: Cooperative programs include a 3-2 engineering degree with Washington University in St. Louis and Illinois Institute of Technology, a 2-2 B.S.N. with Mennonite College of Nursing or St. Francis College of Nursing, and a 3-1 clinical lab science degree with St. Francis or St. John's School of Clinical Laboratory Science. Students may study abroad in most countries. Professional programs in arts management, art therapy, communications, prelaw, premedicine, preministry, and teacher education are offered. An interdisciplinary major in arts and letters combines visual, performing, and literary arts. Internships, student-designed, and dual majors are offered in various areas. A Washington semester is available. There are 7 national honor societies and a freshman honors program, all departments have honors programs.

Faculty/Classroom: 64% of faculty are male; 36%, female. All teach undergraduates. The average class size in an introductory lecture is 15; in a laboratory, 10; and in a regular course, 15.

Admissions: 67% of the 2005-2006 applicants were accepted. 35% of the current freshmen were in the top fifth of their class; 65% were in the top two fifths.

Requirements: The SAT or ACT is required. The ACT Optional Writing test is also recommended. In addition, applicants should be graduates of accredited secondary schools or have the GED. E.C. requires applicants to be in the upper 50% of their class. A GPA of 2.3 is required. AP and CLEP credits are accepted. Important factors in the admissions decision are recommendations by school officials, extracurricular activities record, and leadership record.

Procedure: Freshmen are admitted to all sessions. Entrance exams should be taken by December of the senior year. There is a deferred admissions and a rolling admissions plan. Applications should be filed by August 1 for fall entry, the first day of classes for winter entry. Notification is sent on a rolling basis. Applications are accepted on-line.

Transfer: 90 transfer students enrolled in 2004-2005. Applicants must have at least a 2.0 GPA in previous college work. Those with fewer than 30 hours of transferable credit must submit high school transcripts and ACT scores. Courses with grades below C are not accepted. 30 of 124 credits required for the bachelor's degree must be completed at E.C.

Visiting: There are regularly scheduled orientations for prospective students, including visits with admissions and financial aid advisers, observing student panels, meetings with faculty and coaches, and campus tours. There are guides for informal visits and visitors may sit in on classes and stay overnight. To schedule a visit, contact the Office of Admissions admissions@eureka.edu.

Financial Aid: In 2005-2006, 98% of all full-time students received some form of financial aid. 30% of all full-time students received need-based aid. The average freshman award was $4000. 49% of undergraduates work part time. Average annual earnings from campus work are $1000. The average financial indebtedness of the 2005 graduate was $8500. E.C. is a member of CSS. The FAFSA is required. The priority date for freshman financial aid applications for fall entry is April 1. The deadline for filing freshman financial aid applications for fall entry is August 1.

International Students: There are 12 international students enrolled. The school actively recruits these students. They must score satisfactorily on the TOEFL.

Computers: Wireless access is available. Internet access includes pillow to port for all residence halls, wireless access, a 24-hour computer lab, and 5 open labs. All students may access the system. There are no time limits and no fees. It is strongly recommended that all students have a personal computer.

Graduates: From July 1, 2004 to June 30, 2005, 131 bachelor's degrees were awarded. The most popular majors were education (24%), business (23%), and psychology (15%). In an average class, 2% graduate in 3 years or less, 58% graduate in 4 years or less, and 5% graduate in 5 years or less. 65 companies recruited on campus in 2004-2005. Of the 2004 graduating class, 20% were enrolled in graduate school within 6 months of graduation and 75% were employed.

Admissions Contact: Dr. Brian Sajko, Dean of Admissions and Financial Aid. A video is available. E-mail: admissions@eureka.edu Web: www.eureka.edu

GREENVILLE COLLEGE — D-4

Greenville, IL 62246-0159
(618) 664-7130
(800) 345-4440; Fax: (618) 664-9841

Full-time: 544 men, 631 women	**Faculty:** 61; IIB, --$
Part-time: 10 men, 30 women	**Ph.D.s:** 61%
Graduate: 45 men, 90 women	**Student/Faculty:** 19 to 1
Year: 4-1-4, summer session	**Tuition:** $17,242
Application Deadline: August 1	**Room & Board:** $5904
Freshman Class: 633 applied, 570 accepted, 251 enrolled	
SAT Verbal/Math: 518/496*	**ACT:** 22 COMPETITIVE

Greenville College, founded in 1892, is a private liberal arts institution affiliated with the Free Methodist Church. It offers bachelor's degree programs in the humanities; mathematics, natural sciences, and information science technologies; social sciences; and the educational arts and sciences, and master's degrees in leadership and ministry, education, and teaching. The library contains 131,425 volumes, 13,909 microform items, and 3546 audio/video tapes/CDs/DVDs, and subscribes to 498 periodicals including electronic. Computerized library services include the card catalog, interlibrary loans, database searching, and Internet access. Special learning facilities include a learning resource center, art gallery, radio station, and the Bock Museum. The 25-acre campus is in a small town 50 miles east of St. Louis. Including any residence halls, there are 47 buildings.

Student Life: 68% of undergraduates are from Illinois. Others are from 38 states, 13 foreign countries, and Canada. 85% are white. 81% are Protestant; 14% claim no religious affiliation. The average age of freshmen is 18; all undergraduates, 24. 27% do not continue beyond their first year; 48% remain to graduate.

Housing: 740 students can be accommodated in college housing, which includes single-sex dorms and on-campus apartments. On-campus housing is guaranteed for all 4 years. 66% of students live on campus; of those, 60% remain on campus on weekends. Alcohol is not permitted. All students may keep cars.

Activities: There are no fraternities or sororities. There are 20 groups on campus, including art, band, cheerleading, choir, chorale, chorus, drama, ethnic, honors, jazz band, musical theater, newspaper, pep band, professional, radio and TV, religious, social, social service, student government, and yearbook. Popular campus events include Agape Music Festival, All College Hike, and Back to School Bash.

Sports: There are 7 intercollegiate sports for men and 7 for women, and 6 intramural sports for men and 6 for women. Facilities include a gym, a sports training annex, a recreational center, 6 tennis courts, a fitness pool, an all-weather track, and softball, baseball, football, soccer, and practice fields.

Disabled Students: 25% of the campus is accessible. Wheelchair ramps, elevators, special parking, specially equipped rest rooms, special class scheduling, and lowered drinking fountains are available.

Services: Counseling and information services are available, as is tutoring in some subjects, including lower-division general education courses. There is remedial math, reading, and writing. There is a program for at-risk freshmen.

Campus Safety and Security: Measures include self-defense education, security escort services, informal discussions, and pamphlets/posters/films. There are emergency telephones, lighted pathways/sidewalks, and alarm systems in some buildings.

Programs of Study: Greenville confers B.A., B.S., and B.Mus.Ed. degrees. Master's degrees are also awarded. Bachelor's degrees are awarded in BIOLOGICAL SCIENCE (biology/biological science and environmental biology), BUSINESS (accounting, business administration and management, management information systems, marketing/retailing/merchandising, and recreation and leisure services), COMMUNICATIONS AND THE ARTS (art, communications, contemporary Christian music, dramatic arts, English, media arts, music, music business management, public relations, Spanish, and speech/debate/rhetoric), COMPUTER AND PHYSICAL SCIENCE (chemistry, computer science, digital arts/technology, mathematics, and physics), EDUCATION (early childhood, elementary, English, mathematics, music, physical, and special),

SOCIAL SCIENCE (criminal justice, history, liberal arts/general studies, ministries, pastoral studies, philosophy, political science/government, psychology, religion, social work, sociology, and youth ministry). Biology, chemistry, physics, and math are the strongest academically. Education, music, and information science and technology are the largest.

Required: A minimum of 126 credits and a 2.0 GPA are required for graduation. All students must successfully complete the core requirements in addition to specific courses in communication, English, history, phys ed, and foreign language (B.A. only). Other degree requirements are fulfilled by in-depth study in biblical studies, cross-cultural experience, physical fitness activities, lab science, math, literature, philosophy, fine arts, psychology, sociology, and a writing-intensive course.

Special: The college provides opportunities for dual majors in such areas as psychology/religion, B.A.-B.S. degrees, student-designed programs, work-study programs, study abroad, credit by exam, internships, a general studies degree, pass/fail options, and nondegree study. A 3-2 engineering degree with the University of Illinois and Washington University, a 2-2 degree with St. John's College of Nursing, and an American Studies program in Washington, D.C. are also available. Cross-registration is offered within the Wesleyan Urban Coalition, the Christian College Consortium, and the Council of Christian Colleges and Universities. There are 7 national honor societies, and a freshman honors program.

Faculty/Classroom: 67% of faculty are male; 33%, female. All teach undergraduates. The average class size in an introductory lecture is 20; in a laboratory, 16; and in a regular course, 19.

Admissions: 90% of the 2005-2006 applicants were accepted. The SAT scores for the 2005-2006 freshman class were: Verbal--54% below 500, 26% between 500 and 599, 18% between 600 and 700, and 2% above 700; Math--54% below 500, 38% between 500 and 599, 3% between 600 and 700, and 5% above 700. The ACT scores were 35% below 21, 21% between 21 and 23, 27% between 24 and 26, 9% between 27 and 28, and 8% above 28.

Requirements: The SAT or ACT. Applicants must have completed a minimum of 16 high school units; recommended are 4 units in English, 2 each in a foreign language and math, and 1 each in a lab science and American history. A GED certificate will be accepted. An essay is also required. Greenville requires applicants to be in the upper 50% of their class. A GPA of 2.0 is required. AP and CLEP credits are accepted. Important factors in the admissions decision are leadership record, advanced placement or honor courses, and personality/intangible qualities.

Procedure: Freshmen are admitted to all sessions. Entrance exams should be taken in the spring of the junior year. There is a rolling admissions plan. Applications should be filed by August 1 for fall entry, December 1 for winter entry, December 1 for spring entry, and April 1 for summer entry, along with a $25 fee. Notification is sent on a rolling basis. Applications are accepted on-line.

Transfer: 83 transfer students enrolled in 2004-2005. A minimum average grade of C or better is required. An associate degree will be accepted for transfer. 40 of 126 credits required for the bachelor's degree must be completed at Greenville.

Visiting: There are regularly scheduled orientations for prospective students, including campus visits during scheduled preview days. There are guides for informal visits and visitors may sit in on classes and stay overnight. To schedule a visit, contact the Admissions Office at (800) 345-4440 or (618) 664-7100 or *admissions@greenville.edu.*

Financial Aid: In 2005-2006, 95% of all full-time freshmen and 94% of continuing full-time students received some form of financial aid. 88% of full-time freshmen and 82% of continuing full-time students received need-based aid. The average freshman award was $18,626. Need-based scholarships or need-based grants averaged $7747; need-based self-help aid (loans and jobs) averaged $5881; and other non-need-based awards and non-need-based scholarships averaged $6185. 40% of undergraduates work part time. Average annual earnings from campus work are $981. The average financial indebtedness of the 2005 graduate was $18,789. Greenville is a member of CSS. The FAFSA is required. The deadline for filing freshman financial aid applications for fall entry is July 1.

International Students: There are 13 international students enrolled. A satisfactory score on the TOEFL is required.

Computers: Wireless access is available. GC has several computer labs on campus, some open for student use 24 hours a day. Students are able to view and print class schedules, unofficial transcripts, and bills; check grades; turn in work; and evaluate courses via Internet-based programs. All students may access the system 24 hours a day. There are no time limits and no fees. It is strongly recommended that all students have a personal computer, specifically a Dell Latitude.

Graduates: From July 1, 2004 to June 30, 2005, 294 bachelor's degrees were awarded. The most popular majors were education (13%), music (6%), and information science and technology (6%). In an average class, 1% graduate in 3 years or less, 40% graduate in 4 years or less, 47% graduate in 5 years or less, and 48% graduate in 6 years or less.

Admissions Contact: Michael Ritter, Director of Admissions.
E-mail: *admissions@greenville.edu* Web: *http://www.greenville.edu*

ILLINOIS COLLEGE C-3
Jacksonville, IL 62650-2299

(217) 245-3030
(866) 464-5265; Fax: (217) 245-3034

Full-time: 475 men, 534 women	**Faculty:** 72; IIB, --$
Part-time: 3 men, 18 women	**Ph.D.s:** 83%
Graduate: none	**Student/Faculty:** 14 to 1
Year: semesters	**Tuition:** $15,500
Application Deadline: open	**Room & Board:** $6400
Freshman Class: 868 applied, 811 accepted, 256 enrolled	
SAT Verbal/Math: 550/580*	**ACT:** 24	**COMPETITIVE+**

Illinois College, founded in 1829, is a private liberal arts institution with historical ties to the Presbyterian Church (U.S.A.) and the United Church of Christ. The library contains 166,968 volumes, 8049 microform items, and 4041 audio/video tapes/CDs/DVDs, and subscribes to 631 periodicals including electronic. Computerized library services include the card catalog, interlibrary loans, database searching, Internet access, and laptop Internet portals. Special learning facilities include an art gallery, a theater, and television studio. The 62-acre campus is in a small town 35 miles west of Springfield. Including any residence halls, there are 33 buildings.

Student Life: 91% of undergraduates are from Illinois. Students are from 21 states, 14 foreign countries, and Canada. 92% are white. 62% are Protestant; 26% Catholic; 11% claim no religious affiliation. The average age of freshmen is 18; all undergraduates, 21. 26% do not continue beyond their first year; 56% remain to graduate.

Housing: 742 students can be accommodated in college housing, which includes single-sex and coed dorms and off-campus apartments. In addition, there are honors houses and language houses. On-campus housing is guaranteed for all 4 years. 67% of students live on campus; of those, 65% remain on campus on weekends. All students may keep cars.

Activities: There are no fraternities or sororities. There are 72 groups on campus, including art, band, cheerleading, chess, choir, chorale, computers, debate, drama, ethnic, forensics, gay, honors, international, literary magazine, newspaper, photography, political, professional, radio and TV, religious, social, social service, student government, and yearbook. Popular campus events include Osage Orange Picnic, Honors Retreat, and McGaw Fine Arts Series.

Sports: There are 9 intercollegiate sports for men and 8 for women, and 5 intramural sports for men and 5 for women. 53% of men and 27% of women participate in intramurals and 48% of men and 19% of women participate in intercollegiate. Facilities include a fitness center with a large swimming pool, whirl pool and sauna, several gyms, and expansive weight and exercise room, and aerobics room, 5 basketball courts, volleyball courts, playing fields for football and baseball, an all-weather track, and 6 tennis court.

Disabled Students: 34% of the campus is accessible. Wheelchair ramps, elevators, special parking, specially equipped rest rooms, special class scheduling, lowered drinking fountains, lowered telephones, and special housing are available.

Services: Counseling and information services are available, as is tutoring in most subjects. There is a reader service for the blind. Note takers, scribes, and test readers are also available.

Campus Safety and Security: Measures include 24-hour foot and vehicle patrol, self-defense education, security escort services, and shuttle buses. There are informal discussions, pamphlets/posters/films, emergency telephones, and lighted pathways/sidewalks.

Programs of Study: IC confers B.A. and B.S. degrees. Bachelor's degrees are awarded in BIOLOGICAL SCIENCE (biology/biological science), BUSINESS (accounting and business administration and management), COMMUNICATIONS AND THE ARTS (communications, dramatic arts, English, fine arts, French, German, music, Spanish, and speech/debate/rhetoric), COMPUTER AND PHYSICAL SCIENCE (chemistry, computer science, information sciences and systems, mathematics, and physics), EDUCATION (elementary, foreign languages, physical, science, and secondary), ENGINEERING AND ENVIRONMENTAL DESIGN (environmental science), HEALTH PROFESSIONS (medical laboratory technology), SOCIAL SCIENCE (economics, history, international relations, philosophy, political science/government, pre-law, psychology, religion, and sociology). Life sciences is the strongest academically. Business , education, and biology are the largest.

Required: To graduate, all students must fulfill general graduation and convocation requirements and complete at least 120 semester hours, including 24 hours of electives outside of the major discipline. Other requirements include 1 unit in public speaking, 1 unit in writing, 1 unit of library research methods, and a first-year seminar. Students must also attend 30 cultural, artistic, or public affairs events. A 2.0 GPA is required.

Special: The college offers study abroad in various countries, on- and off-campus work-study programs, and internships through the departments of communication, computer science and information systems, economics and business administration, English, and political science. Also available are student-designed and dual majors, B.A.-B.S. degrees, a 3-2 engineering degree with the University of Illinois, Washington University, or Southern Illinois University-Edwardsville, and a 3-2 occupational therapy program with Washington University. The Intercultural Exchange Program with Ritsumeikan University in Kyoto, Japan, Model United Nations simulations, and the Urban Studies Program of Associated Colleges of the Midwest in Chicago are offered. There are 12 national honor societies, including Phi Beta Kappa and 11 departmental honors programs.

Faculty/Classroom: 57% of faculty are male; 43%, female. All teach undergraduates. The average class size in an introductory lecture is 40; in a laboratory, 20; and in a regular course, 16.

Admissions: 93% of the 2005-2006 applicants were accepted. The SAT scores for the 2005-2006 freshman class were: Verbal--12% below 500, 47% between 500 and 599, 35% between 600 and 700, and 6% above 700; Math--6% below 500, 41% between 500 and 599, 47% between 600 and 700, and 6% above 700. The ACT scores were 22% below 21, 23% between 21 and 23, 27% between 24 and 26, 16% between 27 and 28, and 11% above 28. 43% of the current freshmen were in the top fifth of their class; 75% were in the top two fifths. 15 freshmen graduated first in their class.

Requirements: The SAT or ACT is required. The ACT Optional Writing test is also required. In addition, applicants must be graduates of an accredited secondary school or have a GED certificate. Students should have completed at least 15 academic credits, including 3 in English and 7 from the following: English, foreign language, history, lab science, math, and social studies. 1 recommendation and 1 essay or 2 letters of recommendation are required. IC requires applicants to be in the upper 50% of their class. A GPA of 2.5 is required. AP and CLEP credits are accepted.

Procedure: Freshmen are admitted to all sessions. Entrance exams should be taken in the spring of the junior year of high school. There is a rolling admissions plan. Application deadlines are open. Application fee is $25. Applications are accepted on-line.

Transfer: 40 transfer students enrolled in 2004-2005. Transfer students must have a minimum 2.0 GPA and submit SAT or ACT scores and transcripts of completed college work. 36 of 120 credits required for the bachelor's degree must be completed at IC.

Visiting: There are regularly scheduled orientations for prospective students, including general information sessions, meeting with faculty, a campus tour, and lunch. There are guides for informal visits and visitors may sit in on classes and stay overnight. To schedule a visit, contact the Admissions Office.

Financial Aid: In 2005-2006, 99% of all full-time freshmen and 97% of continuing full-time students received some form of financial aid. 77% of full-time freshmen and 75% of continuing full-time students received need-based aid. The average freshman award was $14,400. Need-based scholarships or need-based grants averaged $10,757 ($21,663 maximum); need-based self-help aid (loans and jobs) averaged $4724 ($7375 maximum); and other non-need-based awards and non-need-based scholarships averaged $6575 ($15,500 maximum). 84% of undergraduates work part time. Average annual earnings from campus work are $1034. The average financial indebtedness of the 2005 graduate was $11,105. The FAFSA is required. The priority date for freshman financial aid applications for fall entry is March 1. The deadline for filing freshman financial aid applications for fall entry is May 1.

International Students: There are 20 international students enrolled. They must score satisfactorily on the written TOEFL or on the electronic version.

Computers: Wireless access is available. Students use the college network for access to the Internet and campus resources to do research and share information. All students may access the system in labs from 7 A.M. to midnight and any time from dorm rooms. There are no time limits and no fees.

Graduates: From July 1, 2004 to June 30, 2005, 170 bachelor's degrees were awarded. The most popular majors were business (17%), education (14%), and biology (12%). In an average class, 1% graduate in 3 years or less, 46% graduate in 4 years or less, 54% graduate in 5 years or less, and 56% graduate in 6 years or less. 6 companies recruited on campus in 2004-2005. Of the 2004 graduating class, 20% were enrolled in graduate school within 6 months of graduation and 81% were employed.

Admissions Contact: Vice President for Enrollment. Web: *www.ic.edu*

ILLINOIS INSTITUTE OF TECHNOLOGY   E-2

Chicago, IL 60616   (312) 567-3025
                                   (800) 448-2329; Fax: (312) 567-6939

Full-time: 1250 men, 450 women	**Faculty:** 241
Part-time: 220 men, 55 women	**Ph.D.s:** 99%
Graduate: 2785 men, 1445 women	**Student/Faculty:** 7 to 1
Year: semesters, summer session	**Tuition:** $20,340
Application Deadline: open	**Room & Board:** $6130
Freshman Class: n/av	
SAT or ACT: required	**HIGHLY COMPETITIVE+**

Illinois Institute of Technology, founded in 1890, is a private institution offering undergraduate programs in architecture, engineering, applied math, biology, chemistry, physics, computing, political science, business and psychology. There are 5 undergraduate and 7 graduate schools. Figures in the above capsule and profile are approximate. In addition to regional accreditation, IIT has baccalaureate program accreditation with ABET. The 3 libraries contain 594,294 volumes, 184,377 microform items, and 54,274 audio/video tapes/CDs/DVDs, and subscribe to 666 periodicals including electronic. Computerized library services include the card catalog, interlibrary loans, and database searching. Special learning facilities include a learning resource center and radio station. The 120-acre campus is in an urban area 3 miles south of downtown Chicago. Including any residence halls, there are 33 buildings.

Student Life: 53% of undergraduates are from Illinois. Others are from 49 states, 96 foreign countries, and Canada. 80% are from public schools. 43% are white; 33% foreign nationals; 10% Asian American. The average age of freshmen is 19; all undergraduates, 23. 19% do not continue beyond their first year; 62% remain to graduate.

Housing: 1251 students can be accommodated in college housing, which includes single-sex and coed dorms, on-campus apartments, married-student housing, fraternity houses, and sorority houses. On-campus housing is guaranteed for all 4 years. 58% of students live on campus; of those, 80% remain on campus on weekends. All students may keep cars.

Activities: 21% of men belong to 7 national fraternities; 15% of women belong to 2 local and 1 national sorority. There are 80 groups on campus, including art, chess, choir, chorus, computers, dance, drama, ethnic, film, gay, honors, international, jazz band, literary magazine, musical theater, newspaper, photography, professional, radio and TV, religious, social, social service, student government, and yearbook. Popular campus events include International Fest, Greek Week, and Spring Formal.

Sports: There are 5 intercollegiate sports for men and 5 for women, and 6 intramural sports for men and 6 for women. Facilities include tennis, basketball, volleyball, racquetball, and squash courts, soccer and softball fields, a swimming pool, an exercise room, a weight room, a bowling alley, and a game room.

Disabled Students: Wheelchair ramps, elevators, special parking, specially equipped rest rooms, and lowered drinking fountains are available.

Services: Counseling and information services are available, as is tutoring in some subjects, including lower division science, math, engineering, and writing courses. There is a reader service for the blind.

Campus Safety and Security: Measures include 24-hour foot and vehicle patrol, security escort services, shuttle buses, and informal discussions. There are pamphlets/posters/films, emergency telephones, and lighted pathways/sidewalks.

Programs of Study: IIT confers B.S., and B.Arch. degrees. Master's and doctoral degrees are also awarded. Bachelor's degrees are awarded in BIOLOGICAL SCIENCE (biochemistry, biology/biological science, biophysics, and molecular biology), COMMUNICATIONS AND THE ARTS (technical and business writing), COMPUTER AND PHYSICAL SCIENCE (applied mathematics, chemistry, computer science, information sciences and systems, physics, and web technology), ENGINEERING AND ENVIRONMENTAL DESIGN (aeronautical engineering, architectural engineering, architecture, chemical engineering, civil engineering, computer engineering, electrical/electronics engineering, manufacturing technology, mechanical engineering, and metallurgical engineering), SOCIAL SCIENCE (political science/government and psychology). All engineering programs is the strongest academically. Architecture and engineering are the largest.

Required: To graduate, students must have completed a total of 126 to 142 credit hours with a minimum cumulative GPA and a minimum major GPA of 2.0. General education requirements include 21 hours of social studies or humanities, 11 hours of science, 5 hours of math, 1 course each in industrial culture and computer science, and 6 hours of interdisciplinary project work

Special: IIT offers co-op programs in engineering, dual majors, study abroad, and an accelerated degree program in prelaw. There are 3 national honor societies.

Faculty/Classroom: 86% of faculty are male; 14%, female. No introductory courses are taught by graduate students. The average class size in an introductory lecture is 18; in a laboratory, 12; and in a regular course, 18.

Requirements: The SAT or ACT is required, in addition graduation from an accredited secondary school is required for admission. The school requires 16 academic credits, including 4 units each of English and math, 3 of lab science, and 2 of history or social science. A GPA of 3.0 is required. AP credits are accepted. Important factors in the admissions decision are advanced placement or honor courses, leadership record, and recommendations by school officials.

Procedure: Freshmen are admitted fall and spring. There are deferred admissions and rolling admissions plans. Application deadlines are open. Applications are accepted on-line. The fall 2005 application fee was $30.

Transfer: 83 transfer students enrolled in a recent year. A minimum 3.0 GPA is required. 45 of 126 credits required for the bachelor's degree must be completed at IIT.

Visiting: There are regularly scheduled orientations for prospective students, including accompanying current students, visiting classes, and attending department receptions. There are guides for informal visits and visitors may sit in on classes and stay overnight. To schedule a visit, contact Emily Staples at (312) 567-5193.

Financial Aid: In a recent year, 99% of all full-time freshmen and 98% of continuing full-time students received some form of financial aid. 56% of full-time freshmen and 45% of continuing full-time students received need-based aid. The average freshman award was $19,117. Need-based scholarships or need-based grants averaged $2757 ($13,466 maximum); need-based self-help aid (loans and jobs) averaged $2891 ($7625 maximum); non-need-based athletic scholarships averaged $157 ($9000 maximum); and other non-need-based awards and non-need-based scholarships averaged $15,239 ($34,000 maximum). 24% of undergraduates worked part time. Average annual earnings from campus work were $2604. The average financial indebtedness of a recent graduate was $14,370. IIT is a member of CSS. The FAFSA is required. Check with the school for current application deadlines.

International Students: In a recent year, there were 263 international students enrolled. The school actively recruits these students. They must score satisfactorily on the written TOEFL and also take the SAT or the ACT.

Computers: All students may access the system. There are no time limits and no fees. It is strongly recommended that all students have a personal computer.

Graduates: In a recent year, 267 bachelor's degrees were awarded. The most popular majors were computer engineering (16%), computer science (15%), and electrical engineering (12%). In an average class, 4% graduate in 3 years or less, 28% graduate in 4 years or less, 63% graduate in 5 years or less, and 67% graduate in 6 years or less. 63 companies recruited on campus in a recent year. Of a recent graduating class, 43% were enrolled in graduate school within 6 months of graduation and 51% were employed.

Admissions Contact: Brent Benner, Director of Admissions.
E-mail: *admission@iit.edu* Web: *www.iit.edu*

ILLINOIS STATE UNIVERSITY   D-3

Normal, IL 61761

(309) 438-2181
(800) 366-2478; Fax: (309) 438-3932

Full-time: 7021 men, 9614 women	Faculty: 829; I, --$
Part-time: 560 men, 663 women	Ph.D.s: 84%
Graduate: 990 men, 1805 women	Student/Faculty: 20 to 1
Year: semesters, summer session	Tuition: $7091 ($12,971)
Application Deadline: March 1	Room & Board: $5748
Freshman Class: 10,414 applied, 8030 accepted, 3179 enrolled	
SAT: not required	ACT: 24 COMPETITIVE+

Illinois State University, founded in 1857, is a public institution offering instruction through schools of applied science and technology, arts and sciences, business, education, fine arts, and nursing. There are 6 undergraduate schools and 1 graduate school. In addition to regional accreditation, ISU has baccalaureate program accreditation with AACSB, ADA, AHEA, CSWE, NASAD, NASM, NCATE, NLN, and NRPA. The library contains 1,566,327 volumes, 1,882,332 microform items, and 24,716 audio/video tapes/CDs/DVDs, and subscribes to 12,254 periodicals including electronic. Computerized library services include the card catalog, interlibrary loans, and database searching. Special learning facilities include a learning resource center, art gallery, planetarium, radio station, TV station, and a distance-learning classroom. The 850-acre campus is in an urban area 125 miles south of Chicago and 180 miles north of St. Louis. Including any residence halls, there are 153 buildings.

Student Life: 99% of undergraduates are from Illinois. Others are from 48 states, 76 foreign countries, and Canada. 88% are from public schools. 84% are white. The average age of freshmen is 18; all undergraduates, 21. 15% do not continue beyond their first year; 63% remain to graduate.

Housing: 6896 students can be accommodated in college housing, which includes single-sex and coed dorms, on-campus apartments, and married-student housing. In addition, there are honors houses and special-interest houses. On-campus housing is available on a first-come, first-served basis. All students may keep cars.

Activities: 10% of men belong to 21 national fraternities; 9% of women belong to 17 national sororities. There are 250 groups on campus, including art, band, cheerleading, chess, choir, chorale, chorus, computers, dance, debate, drama, drill team, ethnic, film, forensics, gay, honors, international, jazz band, literary magazine, marching band, musical theater, newspaper, opera, orchestra, pep band, photography, political, professional, radio and TV, religious, social, social service, student government, symphony, and yearbook. Popular campus events include Festival ISU, International Fair, and Madrigal Dinners.

Sports: There are 8 intercollegiate sports for men and 11 for women, and 9 intramural sports for men and 9 for women. Facilities include a student recreational building, a basketball arena, a football stadium, a field house, baseball diamonds, tennis courts, Olympic-size pools, an 18-hole golf course, a soccer and softball field, and a bowling and billiards center.

Disabled Students: All of the campus is accessible. Wheelchair ramps, elevators, special parking, specially equipped rest rooms, special class scheduling, lowered drinking fountains, lowered telephones, a telecommunication device, 2 rooms in the library for visually disabled students, and a learning lab with a braille thermoform and a variable speed lexicon are available.

Services: Counseling and information services are available, as is tutoring in every subject. There is a reader service for the blind, and remedial math, reading, and writing. Interpreters for the hearing impaired, note takers, taped lectures, and braillists are available.

Campus Safety and Security: Measures include 24-hour foot and vehicle patrol, self-defense education, security escort services, and shuttle buses. There are informal discussions, pamphlets/posters/films, emergency telephones, and lighted pathways/sidewalks.

Programs of Study: ISU confers B.A., B.S., B.F.A., B.Mu., B.Mu.E., B.M.Ed., B.S.Ed., and B.S.W. degrees. Master's and doctoral degrees are also awarded. Bachelor's degrees are awarded in AGRICULTURE (agriculture), BIOLOGICAL SCIENCE (biochemistry and biology/ biological science), BUSINESS (accounting, banking and finance, business administration and management, insurance, international business management, management science, and marketing/retailing/ merchandising), COMMUNICATIONS AND THE ARTS (art, communications, dramatic arts, English, French, German, journalism, music, music performance, public relations, Spanish, speech/debate/rhetoric, and telecommunications), COMPUTER AND PHYSICAL SCIENCE (chemistry, computer science, digital arts/technology, geology, information sciences and systems, mathematics, and physics), EDUCATION (athletic training, business, early childhood, elementary, health, middle school, music, physical, and special), ENGINEERING AND ENVIRONMENTAL DESIGN (industrial engineering technology), HEALTH PROFESSIONS (environmental health science, exercise science, health care administration, medical laboratory technology, nursing, and speech pathology/ audiology), SOCIAL SCIENCE (anthropology, criminal justice, economics, family/consumer studies, fashion design and technology, geography, history, home economics, interdisciplinary studies, parks and recreation management, philosophy, political science/government, psychology, safety management, social science, social work, and sociology). Elementary education, business administration, and special education are the largest.

Required: Students must complete 45 hours of general education and a total of 120 credit hours with a minimum GPA of 2.0. In addition, they must pass a writing exam and exams on the Constitutions of the U.S. and the State of Illinois, and one on the proper use of the American flag.

Special: There are numerous cooperative programs and internships, dual majors, student-designed majors, and work-study programs both on campus and with nonprofit organizations. There is also a general studies degree, a 3-2 engineering program with the University of Illinois, a BS/ MPA, and study abroad in 11 countries. Pass/fail options are available and credit is given for military experience. ISU is part of the National Student Exchange, enabling qualifying juniors and seniors to study for up to 1 year at one of several hundred colleges around the country. There are 25 national honor societies, including Phi Beta Kappa, a freshman honors program, and 43 departmental honors programs.

Faculty/Classroom: 54% of faculty are male; 46%, female. All teach undergraduates. Graduate students teach 13% of introductory courses. The average class size in an introductory lecture is 37; in a laboratory, 22; and in a regular course, 32.

Admissions: 77% of the 2005-2006 applicants were accepted. The ACT scores for the 2005-2006 freshman class were: 13% below 21, 35% between 21 and 23, 35% between 24 and 26, 11% between 27 and 28, and 6% above 28. 29% of the current freshmen were in the top fifth of their class; 68% were in the top two fifths. There were 3 National Merit finalists. 33 freshmen graduated first in their class.

Requirements: The ACT is required. In addition, applicants must be graduates of an accredited secondary school or have a GED. Admission is based on a combination of factors, including class rank and ACT or SAT score. ISU requires applicants to be in the upper 50% of their class. AP and CLEP credits are accepted.

Procedure: Freshmen are admitted to all sessions. Entrance exams should be taken in the fall of the junior year. There is a rolling admissions plan. Applications should be filed by March 1 for fall entry, along with a $30 fee. Notification is sent on a rolling basis. Applications are accepted on-line.

Transfer: 2472 transfer students enrolled in 2004-2005. Graduates of Illinois community colleges holding associate degrees are admitted pending receipt of transcripts. Other students must meet the requirements for beginning freshmen with a minimum 2.0 GPA. 30 of 120 credits required for the bachelor's degree must be completed at ISU.

Visiting: There are regularly scheduled orientations for prospective students. There are guides for informal visits and visitors may sit in on classes and stay overnight. To schedule a visit, contact the Admissions Office at (309) 438-8486 or *preview@ilstu.edu* or go to *www.ilstu.edu/preview.*

Financial Aid: In 2005-2006, 44% of all full-time students received some form of financial aid. 29% of all full-time students received need-based aid. The average freshman award was $7684. Need-based scholarships or need-based grants averaged $6091; need-based self-help aid (loans and jobs) averaged $4033; non-need-based athletic scholarships averaged $8579; and other non-need-based awards and non-need-based scholarships averaged $3907. Average annual earnings from campus work are $2250. The average financial indebtedness of the 2005 graduate was $14,620. The CSS/Profile, FAFSA, FFS, or SFS is required. The deadline for filing freshman financial aid applications for fall entry is March 1.

International Students: There are 149 international students enrolled. The school actively recruits these students. They must score satisfactorily on the TOEFL.

Computers: Wireless access is available. Ulabs at Illinois State is comprised of seven computer labs containing a total of over 400 seats around campus open to Illinois State University students. These labs are located in Milner Library, Stevenson 250, Manchester Hall, Walker Hall, Watterson Towers, Whitten Hall, and Wright Hall. Supported by Computer Infrastructure Support Services, the labs are equipped with state-of-the-art computers, printers, and copy machines. The mainframe is available to those taking courses involving its use. Students may access the system 24 hours a day. There are no time limits and no fees. All new students are required to have personal computers.

Graduates: From July 1, 2004 to June 30, 2005, 4274 bachelor's degrees were awarded. The most popular majors were elementary education (8%), marketing (5%), and business administration (5%). In an average class, 36% graduate in 4 years or less, 59% graduate in 5 years or less, and 63% graduate in 6 years or less. 261 companies recruited on campus in 2004-2005.

Admissions Contact: Molly Arnold, Interim Director of Admissions. A video is available. E-mail: *admissions@ilstu.edu* Web: *www.ilstu.edu*

ILLINOIS WESLEYAN UNIVERSITY — D-3

Bloomington, IL 61702-2900 (309) 556-3031; (800) 332-2498

Full-time: 917 men, 1223 women	Faculty: 161; IIB, +$
Part-time: 5 men, 1 woman	Ph.D.s: 93%
Graduate: none	Student/Faculty: 13 to 1
Year: n/app	Tuition: $27,624
Application Deadline: March 1	Room & Board: $6426
Freshman Class: 2770 applied, 1580 accepted, 564 enrolled	
SAT Verbal/Math: 630/645*	ACT: 29

HIGHLY COMPETITIVE+

Illinois Wesleyan University, founded in 1850, is a private institution offering 35 major programs in liberal arts, fine arts, and nursing. There are 5 undergraduate schools. In addition to regional accreditation, Illinois Wesleyan has baccalaureate program accreditation with NASM and CCNE. The library contains 317,889 volumes, 23,484 microform items, and 15,866 audio/video tapes/CDs/DVDs, and subscribes to 1046 periodicals including electronic. Computerized library services include the card catalog, interlibrary loans, database searching, Internet access, and laptop Internet portals. Special learning facilities include a learning resource center, art gallery, radio station, TV station, and an observatory, a multicultural center, and a 20-acre tract of virgin timberland. The 80-acre campus is in a suburban area 130 miles from Chicago and 160 miles from St. Louis. Including any residence halls, there are 52 buildings.

Student Life: 84% of undergraduates are from Illinois. Students are from 36 states, 15 foreign countries, and Canada. 86% are from public schools. 82% are white. The average age of freshmen is 18; all undergraduates, 20. 8% do not continue beyond their first year; 82% remain to graduate.

Housing: 1740 students can be accommodated in college housing, which includes coed dorms, fraternity houses, and sorority houses. In addition, there are honors houses, language houses, special-interest houses and internationalism, environmentism, art, and interfaith learning housing areas. On-campus housing is guaranteed for all 4 years. 81% of students live on campus; of those, 80% remain on campus on weekends. All students may keep cars.

Activities: 33% of men belong to 6 national fraternities; 25% of women belong to 1 local and 4 national sororities. There are 160 groups on campus, including art, band, cheerleading, chess, choir, chorale, chorus, computers, dance, drama, ethnic, film, gay, honors, international, jazz band, literary magazine, marching band, musical theater, newspaper, opera, orchestra, pep band, political, professional, radio and TV, religious, social, social service, student government, symphony, and yearbook. Popular campus events include Family Days, comedy clubs, and international festivals from many regions of the world.

Sports: There are 9 intercollegiate sports for men and 9 for women, and 9 intramural sports for men and 9 for women. Facilities include a fitness center with weight/exercise equipment and racquetball courts; a swimming pool with 1- and 3-meter diving boards; an activity center with a 200-meter, 6-lane indoor track and courts for tennis, recreational basketball, and volleyball; a separate gym for intercollegiate and other activities; an outdoor track; and softball, baseball, and soccer fields.

Disabled Students: 90% of the campus is accessible. Wheelchair ramps, elevators, special parking, specially equipped rest rooms, special class scheduling, lowered drinking fountains, lowered telephones, and special housing are available.

Services: Counseling and information services are available, as is tutoring in every subject. There is a reader service for the blind. Assistance in writing and study skills is also available, but not at the remedial level.

Campus Safety and Security: Measures include 24-hour foot and vehicle patrol, self-defense education, security escort services, and informal discussions. There are pamphlets/posters/films, emergency telephones, lighted pathways/sidewalks, and And emergency response team of key executives and staff members has developed policies and procedures for natural disasters and other crises.

Programs of Study: Illinois Wesleyan confers B.A., B.S., B.F.A., B.Mus., B.Mus.Ed., and B.S.N. degrees. Bachelor's degrees are awarded in AGRICULTURE (environmental studies), BIOLOGICAL SCIENCE (biology/biological science), BUSINESS (accounting, business administration and management, insurance and risk management, and international business management), COMMUNICATIONS AND THE ARTS (dramatic arts, English, French, German, music, music theory and composition, musical theater, piano/organ, Spanish, visual and performing arts, and voice), COMPUTER AND PHYSICAL SCIENCE (chemistry, computer science, mathematics, and physics), HEALTH PROFESSIONS (nursing), SOCIAL SCIENCE (American studies, anthropology, economics, Hispanic American studies, history, interdisciplinary studies, international studies, philosophy, political science/government, psychology, religion, sociology, and women's studies). The life sciences, music, and business and economics are the largest.

Required: For B.A., B.S., B.S.N., and B.F.A. degrees, a total of 32 course units (128 semester hours) is required for the bachelor's degree with a 2.0 GPA. General education requirements include 2 course units in natural sciences and 1 each in literature, intellectual traditions, formal reasoning, cultural and historical change, contemporary social institutions, the arts, analysis of values, and Gateway Colloquium, plus demonstrated proficiency in a foreign language. 2 additional writing-intensive courses are required, as in coursework focusing on U.S. and global diversity issues. 2 degree programs (B.M.Ed.and B.M.) require more than 32 course units because of additional requirements in the major. Phys ed is a noncredit graduation requirement.

Special: There are several combined degree programs, including a 3-2 degree in forestry and environmental studies with Duke University and a 2-2 engineering degree with the University of Illinois. Students may study abroad in many locations throughout the world through the Institute for the International Education of Students (IES), Pembroke College, Keio University, University of Oxford, Arcadia University Center for Study Abroad, and many other programs. Illinois Wesleyan also offers its own semester-long programs in London and Madrid. The university also offers on-campus work-study, both credit and noncredit internships in many areas, Washington and United Nations semesters, B.A.-B.S. degress, dual and student-designed majors, pass/fail options, and an honor research program for upperclass students. There are 29 national honor societies, including Phi Beta Kappa. All departments have honors programs.

Faculty/Classroom: 58% of faculty are male; 42%, female. 100% both teach and do research. The average class size in an introductory lecture is 24; in a laboratory, 15; and in a regular course, 18.

Admissions: 57% of the 2005-2006 applicants were accepted. The SAT scores for the 2005-2006 freshman class were: Verbal--1% below 500, 23% between 500 and 599, 53% between 600 and 700, and 23% above 700; Math--2% below 500, 25% between 500 and 599, 49% between 600 and 700, and 24% above 700. The ACT scores were 6% between 21 and 23, 20% between 24 and 26, 24% between 27 and 28, and 50% above 28. 72% of the current freshmen were in the top fifth of their class; 96% were in the top two fifths. There were 6 National Merit finalists and 28 semifinalists. 28 freshmen graduated first in their class.

Requirements: The SAT or ACT is required. In addition, applicants should graduate from an accredited secondary school, though a GED may be accepted. 15 academic credits are required. It is strongly recommended that these units include 4 units of English, 3 each of natural science, math, and a foreign language, and 2 of social science. An audition is required for theater and music majors and a portfolio for art majors. Illinois Wesleyan requires applicants to be in the upper 35% of their class. A GPA of 3.0 is required. AP credits are accepted. Important factors in the admissions decision are advanced placement or honor courses, evidence of special talent, and personality/intangible qualities.

Procedure: Freshmen are admitted fall and spring. Entrance exams should be taken in the spring of the junior year. There are early admissions and deferred admissions plans. Applications should be filed by March 1 for fall entry and November 1 for spring entry. Notification is sent on a rolling basis. 55 applicants were on the 2005 waiting list; 44 were admitted. Applications are accepted on-line.

Transfer: 27 transfer students enrolled in 2004-2005. Applicants must submit all high school and college transcripts. A GPA of at least 2.5 is required. 16 of 32 course units (64 of 128 semester hours), required for the bachelor's degree must be completed at Illinois Wesleyan.

Visiting: There are regularly scheduled orientations for prospective students, including a 1 to 1-1/2 hour guided tour in small groups, and interviews with an admissions couselor and departmental faculty members may be scheduled. Accepted applicants may visit classes or stay overnight. There are guides for informal visits and visitors may sit in on classes and stay overnight. To schedule a visit, contact the Admissions Office at iwuadmit@iwu.edu.

Financial Aid: In 2005-2006, 89% of all full-time freshmen and 90% of continuing full-time students received some form of financial aid. 54% of full-time freshmen and 52% of continuing full-time students received need-based aid. The average freshman award was $17,199. Need-based scholarships or need-based grants averaged $16,150 ($27,474 maximum); need-based self-help aid (loans and jobs) averaged $5286 ($6825 maximum); and other non-need-based awards and non-need-based scholarships averaged $10,216 ($27,474 maximum). 46% of undergraduates work part time. Average annual earnings from campus work are $1853. The average financial indebtedness of the 2005 graduate was $21,846. Illinois Wesleyan is a member of CSS. The CSS/Profile or FAFSA and the college's own financial statement are required. The deadline for filing freshman financial aid applications for fall entry is March 1.

International Students: There are 39 international students enrolled. The school actively recruits these students. Satisfactory scores are required on the written TOEFL and the SAT or the ACT.

Computers: Wireless access is available. Students have access to 420 networked public access computers in various academic buildings. Wireless network access is available in the student center and library. There are 20 laptop computers as well as digital project equipment, such as cameras, camcorders, and scanners available for student checkout in the library. Digital video stations are provided for students working on video projects and e-portfolios in both campus libraries. All residence halls and sorority/fraternity houses are wired to the campus network. IWU does not have a technology fee, and all laser color printing is free for students. All students may access the system. There are no time limits and no fees.

Graduates: From July 1, 2004 to June 30, 2005, 473 bachelor's degrees were awarded. The most popular majors were business administration (20%), psychology (10%), and biology (9%). In an average class, 1% graduate in 3 years or less, 77% graduate in 4 years or less, 81% graduate in 5 years or less, and 82% graduate in 6 years or less. 75 companies recruited on campus in 2004-2005. Of the 2004 graduating class, 32% were enrolled in graduate school within 6 months of graduation and 67% were employed.

Admissions Contact: Tony Bankston, Dean of Admissions. A video is available. E-mail: iwuadmit@titan.iwu.edu Web: www.iwu.edu

JUDSON COLLEGE E-1
Elgin, IL 60123-1498

(847) 628-2500
(800) 879-5376; Fax: (847) 695-0216

Full-time: 394 men, 521 women	Faculty: 54; IIB, -$
Part-time: 106 men, 174 women	Ph.D.s: 65%
Graduate: 27 men, 23 women	Student/Faculty: 17 to 1
Year: semesters	Tuition: $18,530
Application Deadline: open	Room & Board: $6600
Freshman Class: 626 applied, 484 accepted, 221 enrolled	
SAT or ACT: required	COMPETITIVE

Judson College is an evangelical Christian college of the liberal arts, sciences, and professions. In addition to regional accreditation, Judson has baccalaureate program accreditation with NAAB. The library contains 92,000 volumes, 27,000 microform items, and 17,000 audio/video tapes/CDs/DVDs, and subscribes to 470 periodicals including electronic. Computerized library services include the card catalog, interlibrary loans, database searching, and Internet access. Special learning facilities include a learning resource center, art gallery, and radio station. The 90-acre campus is in a suburban area 40 miles west of Chicago. Including any residence halls, there are 16 buildings.

Student Life: 65% of undergraduates are from Illinois. Others are from 21 states, 25 foreign countries, and Canada. 71% are white. 80% are

Protestant; 8% Catholic; 7% claim no religious affiliation. The average age of freshmen is 18; all undergraduates, 20. 22% do not continue beyond their first year; 50% remain to graduate.

Housing: 670 students can be accommodated in college housing, which includes single-sex dorms, on-campus apartments, and married-student housing. On-campus housing is guaranteed for all 4 years. 65% of students live on campus. Alcohol is not permitted. All students may keep cars.

Activities: There are no fraternities or sororities. There are 23 groups on campus, including art, band, cheerleading, choir, chorale, chorus, computers, drama, ethnic, honors, international, literary magazine, newspaper, orchestra, photography, political, radio and TV, religious, social, social service, and student government. Popular campus events include Spiritual Enrichment Week, Fall Orientation, and Christmas by Candlelight.

Sports: There are 3 intercollegiate sports for men and 4 for women, and 9 intramural sports for men and 8 for women. Facilities include a fitness center, a 1500-seat gym, a soccer field, lighted baseball and softball diamonds, lighted tennis courts, racquetball and handball courts, indoor and outdoor running tracks, and a Nautilus and free-weight room.

Disabled Students: 80% of the campus is accessible. Wheelchair ramps, elevators, special parking, specially equipped rest rooms, special class scheduling, lowered drinking fountains, lowered telephones, and special housing are available.

Services: Counseling and information services are available, as is tutoring in some subjects, including core courses. There is remedial math, reading, and writing.

Campus Safety and Security: Measures include 24-hour foot and vehicle patrol, security escort services, emergency telephones, and lighted pathways/sidewalks.

Programs of Study: Judson confers the B.A. degree. Master's degrees are also awarded. Bachelor's degrees are awarded in BIOLOGICAL SCIENCE (biology/biological science), BUSINESS (accounting, business administration and management, international business management, and sports management), COMMUNICATIONS AND THE ARTS (communications, dramatic arts, English, fine arts, media arts, and music), COMPUTER AND PHYSICAL SCIENCE (chemistry, computer science, and mathematics), EDUCATION (early childhood, elementary, English, mathematics, music, physical, science, and secondary), ENGINEERING AND ENVIRONMENTAL DESIGN (preengineering), HEALTH PROFESSIONS (medical laboratory technology, nursing, predentistry, and premedicine), SOCIAL SCIENCE (anthropology, history, political science/government, prelaw, psychology, sociology, and youth ministry). Architecture, visual communications/graphic design, and education are the strongest academically.

Required: Most students must have a GPA of 2.0; education majors must have a 2.5. Students must complete at least 126 credit hours, including 45 to 66 in the major, and take the college's core courses of Bible study, writing, speech, literature, math, science, history, fine arts, human relations, and phys ed, as well as a course in either psychology or sociology.

Special: The college has co-op programs with North Park College, Rush University, and the Mennonite College of Nursing, cross-registration with the Christian College Coalition, and work-study programs with many businesses. Students may serve internships in art and business, take a Washington semester, a film studies semester in Hollywood, an ecology studies semester at Sable Institute in Michigan, or study abroad in numerous external programs recognized by Judson. The college allows dual majors, student-designed majors, and accelerated degrees in business leadership and management, human services, human resource management, and criminal justice management. There is 1 national honor society, a freshman honors program, and 2 departmental honors programs.

Faculty/Classroom: 66% of faculty are male; 34%, female. 80% teach undergraduates and 20% both teach and do research. The average class size in an introductory lecture is 28; in a laboratory, 9; and in a regular course, 14 to 16.

Admissions: 77% of the 2005-2006 applicants were accepted.

Requirements: The SAT or ACT is required. The GED is accepted. Judson requires applicants to be in the upper 50% of their class. A GPA of 2.0 is required. AP and CLEP credits are accepted.

Procedure: Freshmen are admitted to all sessions. Entrance exams should be taken in the spring of the junior year or the fall of the senior year. There is a deferred admissions plan, and a rolling admissions plan. There is a early admissions plan for the architecture program only. Application deadlines are open. Application fee is $35. Applications are accepted on-line.

Transfer: 86 transfer students enrolled in 2004-2005. Students with fewer than 28 hours of college credit must submit high school transcripts showing a GPA of at least 2.0, as well as, satisfactory ACT or SAT results. Transfer students with more than 28 hours must have a GPA of at least 2.0. 30 of 126 credits required for the bachelor's degree must be completed at Judson.

Visiting: There are regularly scheduled orientations for prospective students, including a tour, class visits, individual meetings with professors, coaches, choir and or band director, and other campus administrators if requested. Students may have lunch or dinner in the cafeteria, meet current students, and stay a night in the dorms. There are guides for informal visits and visitors may sit in on classes. To schedule a visit, contact the Enrollment Services Office at (847) 628-2510 or *admission@judsoncollege.edu*.

Financial Aid: In 2005-2006, 90% of all full-time students received some form of financial aid. 90% of all full-time students received need-based aid. The average freshman award was $9486. Need-based scholarships or need-based grants averaged $7212; need-based self-help aid (loans and jobs) averaged $8568; and non-need-based athletic scholarships averaged $8999. The average financial indebtedness of the 2005 graduate was $19,216. The FAFSA is required, as is the Verification worksheet or Professional Judgement Worksheet, if requested. The priority date for freshman financial aid applications for fall entry is rolling but preferred by February 15.

International Students: There are 44 international students enrolled. The school actively recruits these students. They must take the TOEFL.

Computers: Wireless access is available. All students may access the system. There are no time limits and no fees.

Graduates: From July 1, 2004 to June 30, 2005, 339 bachelor's degrees were awarded. In an average class, 46% graduate in 4 years or less, and 48% graduate in 5 years or less.

Admissions Contact: Philip G. Guth, Vice President for Enrollment Management and Technology Services. A video is available. E-mail: *admissions@judsoncollege.edu* Web: *www.judsoncollege.edu*

KENDALL COLLEGE
Chicago, IL 60622

E-1

(312) 752-2160
(877) 588-8860; Fax: (312) 752-2021

Full-time: 242 men, 255 women	**Faculty:** 23
Part-time: 77 men, 206 women	**Ph.D.s:** 18%
Graduate: none	**Student/Faculty:** 22 to 1
Year: quarters, summer session	**Tuition:** $19,800
Application Deadline: open	**Room & Board:** $9000
Freshman Class: n/av	
SAT Verbal/Math: 515/520*	**ACT:** 22 NONCOMPETITIVE

Kendall College, founded in 1934, is a private institution affiliated with the United Methodist Church. It offers programs in liberal arts, business, and professional training, as well as culinary arts. There are 4 undergraduate schools. The library contains 36,500 volumes and 1500 audio/video tapes/CDs/DVDs, and subscribes to 200 periodicals including electronic. Computerized library services include interlibrary loans, database searching, and Internet access. Special learning facilities include a learning resource center and an art gallery. The 1-acre campus is in an urban area in Chicago. Including any residence halls, there are 2 buildings.

Student Life: 92% of undergraduates are from Illinois. Students are from 19 states, 13 foreign countries, and Canada. 70% are from public schools. 69% are white; 10% Hispanic. The average age of freshmen is 24; all undergraduates, 27. 25% do not continue beyond their first year; 26% remain to graduate.

Housing: 180 students can be accommodated in college housing, which includes single-sex and coed off-campus apartments. On-campus housing is available on a first-come, first-served basis. 65% of students commute. Alcohol is not permitted. All students may keep cars.

Activities: There are no fraternities or sororities. There are some groups and organizations on campus, including computers, ethnic, honors, international, newspaper, professional, social service, student government, and yearbook.

Sports: There is no sports program at Kendall.

Disabled Students: All of the campus is accessible. Wheelchair ramps, elevators, special parking, and specially equipped rest rooms are available.

Services: Counseling and information services are available, as is tutoring in most subjects. There is remedial math, reading, and writing.

Campus Safety and Security: Measures include 24-hour foot and vehicle patrol and lighted pathways/sidewalks.

Programs of Study: Kendall confers the B.A. degree. Associate degrees are also awarded. Bachelor's degrees are awarded in BUSINESS (business administration and management, hospitality management services, and hotel/motel and restaurant management), EDUCATION (early childhood), SOCIAL SCIENCE (culinary arts and food production/management/services). Culinary Arts, early childhood education, and hospitality management are the strongest academically. Culinary arts and hospitality management are the largest.

Required: A 2.0 GPA is required to graduate.

Special: All majors require internships. Study abroad in 3 countries and work-study programs are available. Accelerated degree programs, B.A.-B.S. degrees, and student-designed majors are also possible.

Faculty/Classroom: 64% of faculty are male; 36%, female. All teach undergraduates. The average class size in an introductory lecture is 25; in a laboratory, 15; and in a regular course, 13.

Admissions: The ACT scores for the 2005-2006 freshman class were: 37% below 21, 35% between 21 and 23, 22% between 24 and 26, 4% between 27 and 28, and 1% above 28.

Requirements: The SAT or ACT is required. However, there is a placement test for students who do not meet the minimum requirement. Applicants should be graduates of an accredited secondary school or have a GED. High school students should prepare with 4 years of high school math, 2 years each of history, science, and social studies, and 1 year of a foreign language. An interview is recommended. A GPA of 2.0 is required. AP and CLEP credits are accepted. Important factors in the admissions decision are ability to finance college education, recommendations by school officials, and leadership record.

Procedure: Freshmen are admitted to all sessions. Entrance exams should be taken as soon as requested. There are deferred admissions and rolling admissions plans. Application deadlines are open. Application fee is $75. A waiting list is an active part of the admissions procedure. Applications are accepted on-line.

Transfer: 217 transfer students enrolled in 2004-2005. The minimum GPA for transfer applicants is 2.0. An interview is recommended. 26 credits per quarter of 192 total quarter hours required for the bachelor's degree must be completed at Kendall.

Visiting: There are regularly scheduled orientations for prospective students. There are guides for informal visits and visitors may sit in on classes and stay overnight. To schedule a visit, contact the Admissions Office at (312) 752-2020 (866) 6KENDALL or *admissions@kendall.edu*.

Financial Aid: In 2005-2006, 87% of all full-time students received some form of financial aid. The FAFSA and the college's own financial statement are required. Check with the school for deadlines.

International Students: The school actively recruits these students. Satisfactory scores are required on the written TOEFL and the SAT or the ACT.

Computers: Wireless access is available. All students may access the system. There are no time limits and no fees.

Graduates: From July 1, 2004 to June 30, 2005, 45 bachelor's degrees were awarded. The most popular majors were hospitality management (48%), early childhood education (33%), and business and technology (14%). In an average class, 35% graduate in 4 years or less.

Admissions Contact: Thomas P FitzGibbon, Director of Admissions. A video is available. E-mail: *admissions@kendall.edu* Web: *www.kendall.edu*

KNOX COLLEGE
Galesburg, IL 61401

C-2

(309) 341-7123
(800) 678-KNOX; Fax: (309) 341-7070

Full-time: 550 men, 651 women	**Faculty:** 95; IIB, -$
Part-time: 2 men, 2 women	**Ph.D.s:** 94%
Graduate: none	**Student/Faculty:** 13 to 1
Year: trimesters	**Tuition:** $26,100
Application Deadline: February 1	**Room & Board:** $6285
Freshman Class: 1582 applied, 1339 accepted, 325 enrolled	
SAT Verbal/Math: 640/600*	**ACT:** 28 VERY COMPETITIVE+

Knox College, founded in 1837, is an independent liberal arts college. The 3 libraries contain 311,715 volumes, 98,723 microform items, and 7497 audio/video tapes/CDs/DVDs, and subscribe to 12,782 periodicals including electronic. Computerized library services include the card catalog, interlibrary loans, database searching, and Internet access. Special learning facilities include a learning resource center, natural history museum, radio station, and a 760-acre biological field station near the campus. The 82-acre campus is in a small town 180 miles southwest of Chicago. Including any residence halls, there are 42 buildings.

Student Life: 55% of undergraduates are from Illinois. Others are from 46 states, 46 foreign countries, and Canada. 93% are from public schools. 74% are white. The average age of freshmen is 18; all undergraduates, 20. 15% do not continue beyond their first year; 71% remain to graduate.

Housing: 1119 students can be accommodated in college housing, which includes single-sex and coed dorms, on-campus apartments, and fraternity houses. In addition, there are special-interest houses. On-campus housing is guaranteed for all 4 years. 95% of students live on campus; of those, 80% remain on campus on weekends. All students may keep cars.

Activities: 21% of men belong to 4 national fraternities; 11% of women belong to 2 national sororities. There are 99 groups on campus, including art, band, chess, choir, chorus, computers, dance, drama, ethnic, gay, honors, international, jazz band, literary magazine, newspaper, orchestra, photography, political, professional, radio and TV, religious, social, social service, student government, symphony, and yearbook. Popular campus events include International Fair, Black Culture Month, and Flunk Day.

Sports: There are 11 intercollegiate sports for men and 10 for women, and 4 intramural sports for men and 4 for women. Facilities include 6 outdoor playing fields, 2 gyms, a swimming pool, tennis courts, and an outdoor track. The campus stadium seats 5000; the gym, 3000. There are club sports in men's volleyball, lacrosse, and water polo. The field house contains a 200-meter indoor track, tennis and volleyball courts, and multiuse space.

Disabled Students: 60% of the campus is accessible. Wheelchair ramps, elevators, special parking, specially equipped rest rooms, and special class scheduling are available.

Services: Counseling and information services are available, as is tutoring in most subjects. There is a reader service for the blind and remedial writing. The Center for Teaching and Learning provides academic support to students in most subjects, particularly development of writing skills.

Campus Safety and Security: Measures include 24-hour foot and vehicle patrol, security escort services, informal discussions, and pamphlets/posters/films. There are emergency telephones and lighted pathways/sidewalks.

Programs of Study: Knox confers the B.A. degree. Bachelor's degrees are awarded in BIOLOGICAL SCIENCE (biochemistry and biology/biological science), COMMUNICATIONS AND THE ARTS (art history and appreciation, classics, creative writing, dramatic arts, English literature, French, German, modern language, music, Spanish, and studio art), COMPUTER AND PHYSICAL SCIENCE (chemistry, computer science, mathematics, and physics), EDUCATION (elementary and secondary), ENGINEERING AND ENVIRONMENTAL DESIGN (environmental science), SOCIAL SCIENCE (African American studies, American studies, anthropology, economics, history, international relations, philosophy, political science/government, psychology, sociology, and women's studies). Biology, chemistry, and math are the strongest academically. Creative writing, anthropology-sociology, and psychology are the largest.

Required: Students must take a 1-term interdisciplinary preceptorial emphasizing writing and discussion skills. In addition to this, 2 writing intensive courses and 1 course emphasizing oral presentation are required. One course focusing on diversity is also required, as well as documentation of a significant experiential learning project outside the classroom. Breadth requirements include 1 course each in the 4 areas of arts, humanities, math, and natural science, and an additional field of concentration, minor or major, not in the department of the major.

Special: The normal academic load is 3 courses per term, with 3 terms per year. Cooperative programs are offered with Washington University in St. Louis in architecture and engineering; Columbia University in engineering and law; University of Illinois at Urbana-Champaign and Rensselaer Polytechnic Institute in engineering; Rush University in medicine, nursing, and medical technology; Duke University in forestry and environmental management; and University of Chicago in law and social work. Study abroad is available in 20 countries. Other programs include a Washington semester, an urban studies semester, science and library research programs, work-study programs, and numerous internships. Dual majors, student-designed majors, and pass/fail options are available. Early admission to George Washington University Medical School and Rush Medical College is possible. Nondegree study is possible. Knox College participates in the Kemper Scholars Program. There are 7 national honor societies, including Phi Beta Kappa, and 39 departmental honors programs.

Faculty/Classroom: 56% of faculty are male; 44%, female. All both teach and do research. The average class size in an introductory lecture is 32; in a laboratory, 15; and in a regular course, 17.

Admissions: 85% of the 2005-2006 applicants were accepted. The SAT scores for the 2005-2006 freshman class were: Verbal--7% below 500, 22% between 500 and 599, 42% between 600 and 700, and 29% above 700; Math--7% below 500, 39% between 500 and 599, 39% between 600 and 700, and 15% above 700. The ACT scores were 3% below 21, 14% between 21 and 23, 18% between 24 and 26, 21% between 27 and 28, and 44% above 28. 61% of the current freshmen were in the top fifth of their class; 89% were in the top two fifths. There were 8 National Merit finalists and 11 semifinalists. 10 freshmen graduated first in their class.

Requirements: An essay is required of all applicants. Applicants should be graduates of an accredited secondary school with a minimum of 15 academic credits (18-20 are recommended). An interview is strongly recommended. The submission of ACT/SAT scores is optional; scores will be considered if submitted. AP credits are accepted. Important factors in the admissions decision are advanced placement or honor courses, recommendations by school officials, and extracurricular activities record.

Procedure: Freshmen are admitted in the fall. Entrance exams should be taken by December 15. There is a deferred admissions plan. Early decision applications should be filed by December 1; regular applications, by February 1 for fall entry, November 1 for winter entry, and January 15 for spring entry, along with a $40 fee. Notification of early decision is sent December 31; regular decision, March 31. 69 applicants were on the 2005 waiting list; 5 were admitted. Applications are accepted on-line.

Transfer: 38 transfer students enrolled in 2004-2005. A 3.0 GPA is expected. An interview is recommended. 13 of 36 credits required for the bachelor's degree must be completed at Knox.

Visiting: There are regularly scheduled orientations for prospective students, including a summer open house in early August, fall open houses

in October and November, and a winter open house in January. Open House programs include campus tours, class visits, lunch with students and professors, and informational sessions. Interviews are available on request. Students are also welcome to visit at other times of the year that are more convenient to them. There are guides for informal visits and visitors may sit in on classes and stay overnight. To schedule a visit, contact Admission Office at (309) 341-7100.

Financial Aid: In 2005-2006, 98% of all full-time freshmen and 97% of continuing full-time students received some form of financial aid. 68% of all full-time students received need-based aid. The average freshman award was $18,690. Need-based scholarships or need-based grants averaged $16,591 ($32,333 maximum); need-based self-help aid (loans and jobs) averaged $5950 ($7750 maximum); and other non-need-based awards and non-need-based scholarships averaged $10,445 ($25,815 maximum). 64% of undergraduates work part time. Average annual earnings from campus work are $1176. The average financial indebtedness of the 2005 graduate was $18,642. Knox is a member of CSS. The FAFSA, the college's own financial statement, and the student and parent tax returns are required. The priority date for freshman financial aid applications for fall entry is February 15.

International Students: There are 88 international students enrolled. The school actively recruits these students. They must score satisfactorily on the written TOEFL.

Computers: Wireless access is available. The entire campus is in range of the wireless network, and all living units and academic buildings have Internet connections. Several campus labs exist, from which the network may also be accessed. All students may access the system A large student computer lab is open 24 hours. Others are open until midnight. There are no time limits and no fees.

Graduates: From July 1, 2004 to June 30, 2005, 224 bachelor's degrees were awarded. The most popular majors were psychology (13%), political science (9%), and anthropology-sociology (9%). In an average class, 64% graduate in 4 years or less, 70% graduate in 5 years or less, and 75% graduate in 6 years or less. 98 companies recruited on campus in 2004-2005. Of the 2004 graduating class, 29% were enrolled in graduate school within 6 months of graduation and 61% were employed.

Admissions Contact: Paul Steenis, Director of Admission.
E-mail: *admission@knox.edu* Web: *www.knox.edu*

LAKE FOREST COLLEGE E-1
Lake Forest, IL 60045-2399

(847) 735-5000
(800) 828-4751; Fax: (847) 735-6271

Full-time: 586 men, 812 women	**Faculty:** 89; IIB, +$
Part-time: 10 men, 10 women	**Ph.D.s:** 98%
Graduate: 6 men, 11 women	**Student/Faculty:** 16 to 1
Year: semesters, summer session	**Tuition:** $27,334
Application Deadline: February 15	**Room & Board:** $6526
Freshman Class: 2195 applied, 1431 accepted, 358 enrolled	
SAT Verbal/Math: 590/590*	**ACT:** 25 **VERY COMPETITIVE**

Lake Forest College, founded in 1857, is a private liberal arts institution affiliated by heritage with the Presbyterian Church (U.S.A.). The library contains 263,708 volumes, 104,151 microform items, and 5534 audio/video tapes/CDs/DVDs. Computerized library services include the card catalog, interlibrary loans, database searching, Internet access, and laptop Internet portals. Special learning facilities include a learning resource center, art gallery, radio station, and a multimedia language lab, and an electronic music studio with practice rooms. The 107-acre campus is in a suburban area 30 miles north of Chicago. Including any residence halls, there are 30 buildings.

Student Life: 53% of undergraduates are from out of state, mostly the Midwest. Students are from 47 states, 53 foreign countries, and Canada. 67% are from public schools. 76% are white. The average age of freshmen is 18; all undergraduates, 20. 18% do not continue beyond their first year; 70% remain to graduate.

Housing: 1096 students can be accommodated in college housing, which includes single-sex and coed dorms and on-campus apartments. In addition, there are special-interest houses and options for 24-hour quiet hours and substance-free housing. On-campus housing is guaranteed for the freshman year only. 81% of students live on campus; of those, 95% remain on campus on weekends. Upperclassmen may keep cars.

Activities: 8% of men belong to 1 local and 2 national fraternities; 17% of women belong to 5 national sororities. There are 86 groups on campus, including art, band, cheerleading, chess, choir, chorus, computers, dance, debate, drama, ethnic, film, gay, honors, international, jazz band, literary magazine, musical theater, newspaper, orchestra, pep band, photography, political, professional, radio and TV, religious, social, social service, student government, and yearbook. Popular campus events include Festival of Ra, Big Chill Weekend, and poet, writer, artist, and scholar-residence programs.

Sports: There are 8 intercollegiate sports for men and 9 for women, and 10 intramural sports for men and 10 for women. Facilities include a gym, tennis courts, indoor and outdoor basketball courts, and racquetball, handball, squash, and outdoor sand volleyball courts. There are also weight and exercise rooms, a pool, an indoor ice rink, and baseball, football, soccer, and intramural fields.

Disabled Students: 80% of the campus is accessible. Wheelchair ramps, elevators, special parking, specially equipped rest rooms, special class scheduling, lowered drinking fountains, and lowered telephones are available.

Services: Counseling and information services are available, as is tutoring in every subject.

Campus Safety and Security: Measures include 24-hour foot and vehicle patrol, self-defense education, security escort services, and shuttle buses. There are informal discussions, pamphlets/posters/films, emergency telephones, and lighted pathways/sidewalks.

Programs of Study: Lake Forest confers the B.A. degree. Master's degrees are also awarded. Bachelor's degrees are awarded in BIOLOGICAL SCIENCE (biology/biological science), BUSINESS (business economics), COMMUNICATIONS AND THE ARTS (art, communications, English, French, music, and Spanish), COMPUTER AND PHYSICAL SCIENCE (chemistry, computer science, mathematics, and physics), EDUCATION (education), ENGINEERING AND ENVIRONMENTAL DESIGN (environmental science), SOCIAL SCIENCE (American studies, anthropology, area studies, Asian/Oriental studies, economics, history, international relations, Latin American studies, philosophy, political science/government, psychology, and sociology). Business/economics, communications and psychology are the largest.

Required: All students are required to complete 32 courses with a minimum GPA of 2.0. General education requirements include 2 courses in natural science or math, 2 cultural diversity courses, and 1 course each in freshman studies, freshman writing, humanities, social science, and senior studies.

Special: Lake Forest offers cross-registration with Associated Colleges of the Midwest, an extensive internship program, through Chicago Alliance and Outreach Programs, a student-designed Independent Scholar Program, and study abroad in 10 countries. Dual and interdisciplinary majors, including American studies, Asian studies, area studies, art (studio and art history), and environmental studies, are available. There is a Washington semester with American University and a work-study program. A 3-2 engineering degree with Washington University at St. Louis and a 3-2 extended degree program in social service with the University of Chicago School of Social Service Administration are offered. Several minors and a pass/fail option are available. A program in marine biology is offered in the Bahamas. There are 11 national honor societies, including Phi Beta Kappa, and a freshman honors program.

Faculty/Classroom: 58% of faculty are male; 42%, female. All both teach and do research. No introductory courses are taught by graduate students. The average class size in an introductory lecture is 20; in a laboratory, 12; and in a regular course, 18.

Admissions: 65% of the 2005-2006 applicants were accepted. The SAT scores for the 2005-2006 freshman class were: Verbal--10% below 500, 42% between 500 and 599, 36% between 600 and 700, and 12% above 700; Math--10% below 500, 42% between 500 and 599, 35% between 600 and 700, and 13% above 700. The ACT scores were 12% below 21, 21% between 21 and 23, 32% between 24 and 26, 14% between 27 and 28, and 21% above 28. 47% of the current freshmen were in the top fifth of their class; 78% were in the top two fifths. There were 4 National Merit finalists and 25 semifinalists. 11 freshmen graduated first in their class.

Requirements: The SAT or ACT is required. In addition, applicants are advised to complete a minimum of 16 academic credits, including 4 in English, 3 in math, 2 to 4 each in social and natural sciences, and study in 1 or more foreign languages. A GED is accepted. An interview is encouraged. AP credits are accepted. Important factors in the admissions decision are advanced placement or honor courses, evidence of special talent, and extracurricular activities record.

Procedure: Freshmen are admitted fall and spring. Entrance exams should be taken in the junior or senior year. There are early decision, early admissions, and deferred admissions plans. Early decision applications should be filed by December 1; regular applications, by February 15 for fall entry and December 1 for spring entry, along with a $40 fee. Notification of early decision is sent December 21; regular decision, March 21. 25 early decision candidates were accepted for the 2005-2006 class. 46 applicants were on the 2005 waiting list; 22 were admitted. Applications are accepted on-line.

Transfer: 61 transfer students enrolled in 2004-2005. Transfer applicants should have a minimum C average in all college work and should be in good standing with their previous institution. High school and college transcripts and a letter of recommendation from the academic dean or a teacher at the most recent college attended are required. 16 of 32 credits required for the bachelor's degree must be completed at Lake Forest.

Visiting: There are regularly scheduled orientations for prospective students, consisting of class visitation, panel presentations, tours and individual appointments with faculty and/or admission officers. There are guides for informal visits and visitors may sit in on classes and stay overnight. To schedule a visit, contact the Admissions Office.

Financial Aid: In 2005-2006, 90% of all full-time freshmen and 93% of continuing full-time students received some form of financial aid. 82% of full-time freshmen and 78% of continuing full-time students received need-based aid. The average freshman award was $21,385. Need-based scholarships or need-based grants averaged $18,006 ($27,000 maximum); need-based self-help aid (loans and jobs) averaged $5298 ($7500 maximum); and other non-need-based awards and non-need-based scholarships averaged $9544 ($27,000 maximum). All of undergraduates work part time. Average annual earnings from campus work are $1900. The average financial indebtedness of the 2005 graduate was $18,800. Lake Forest is a member of CSS. The FAFSA and the Federal Income Tax Return 1040 are required. The priority date for freshman financial aid applications for fall entry is February 15. The deadline for filing freshman financial aid applications for fall entry is April 1.

International Students: There are 117 international students enrolled. The school actively recruits these students. They must score satisfactorily on the written TOEFL or on the electronic version.

Computers: Wireless access is available. All students may access the system 24 hours a day, 7 days a week. There are no time limits and no fees. It is strongly recommended that all students have a personal computer.

Graduates: From July 1, 2004 to June 30, 2005, 306 bachelor's degrees were awarded. The most popular majors were business/economics (19%), communications (16%), and psychology (7%). In an average class, 2% graduate in 3 years or less, 63% graduate in 4 years or less, and 69% graduate in 5 years or less. 66 companies recruited on campus in 2004-2005. Of the 2004 graduating class, 33% were enrolled in graduate school within 6 months of graduation and 71% were employed.

Admissions Contact: William G. Motzer, Vice President for Admissions and Career Services. E-mail: *admissions@lfc.edu*
Web: *http://www.lfc.edu*

LEWIS UNIVERSITY   E-2

Romeoville, IL 60446   (815) 838-0500, ext. 5250
(800) 897-9000; Fax: (815) 836-5002

Full-time: 1020 men, 1240 women	**Faculty:** 141; IIA, -$
Part-time: 320 men, 650 women	**Ph.D.s:** 57%
Graduate: 470 men, 795 women	**Student/Faculty:** 16 to 1
Year: semesters, summer session	**Tuition:** $16,000
Application Deadline: open	**Room & Board:** $7,050
Freshman Class: n/av	
SAT or ACT: required	**COMPETITIVE+**

Lewis University, founded in 1932, is a private institution affiliated with the Roman Catholic Church and sponsored by the De La Salle Christian Brothers. A comprehensive liberal arts university, Lewis offers classes at its main campus and at more than 20 satellite locations in the Chicago metropolitan area. There are 4 undergraduate and 11 graduate schools. Figures in the above capsule and profile are approximate. In addition to regional accreditation, Lewis has baccalaureate program accreditation with NCATE and NLN. The library contains 180,000 volumes, 13,100 microform items, and 2300 audio/video tapes/CDs/DVDs, and subscribes to 800 periodicals including electronic. Computerized library services include the card catalog, interlibrary loans, database searching, and Internet access. Special learning facilities include a learning resource center, art gallery, radio station, TV station, and aviation building and airport. The 350-acre campus is in a suburban area 30 miles southwest of downtown Chicago. Including any residence halls, there are 21 buildings.

Student Life: 97% of undergraduates are from Illinois. Others are from 24 states, 30 foreign countries, and Canada. 75% are from public schools. 71% are white; 14% African American. Most are Catholic. The average age of freshmen is 19; all undergraduates, 28. 19% do not continue beyond their first year.

Housing: 900 students can be accommodated in college housing, which includes single-sex and coed dorms. On-campus housing is available on a first-come, first-served basis and is available on a lottery system for upperclassmen. Priority is given to out-of-town students. 73% of students commute. All students may keep cars.

Activities: 3% of men belong to 4 local and 5 national fraternities; 2% of women belong to 3 national sororities. There are 27 groups on campus, including band, cheerleading, choir, chorale, chorus, dance, debate, drama, ethnic, forensics, honors, international, jazz band, literary magazine, musical theater, newspaper, orchestra, pep band, photography, political, professional, radio and TV, religious, social, social service, student government, symphony, and yearbook. Popular campus events include Fall and Spring Formals, Greek Stock, and International Student Food Festival.

Sports: There are 9 intercollegiate sports for men and 9 for women, and 10 intramural sports for men and 10 for women. Facilities include a recreation center containing a field house with 4 multipurpose courts, a fitness center, an aerobics studio, an 8-lane pool, and an indoor track; a tennis complex; an outdoor track; and baseball, softball, and soccer fields.

Disabled Students: 95% of the campus is accessible. Wheelchair ramps, elevators, special parking, specially equipped rest rooms, special class scheduling, lowered drinking fountains, and lowered telephones are available.

Services: Counseling and information services are available, as is tutoring in most subjects. There is remedial math, reading, and writing. The University Success Program provides assistance to those students who do not meet the outright scholastic requirements.

Campus Safety and Security: Measures include 24-hour foot and vehicle patrol, security escort services, informal discussions, and pamphlets/posters/films. There are emergency telephones and lighted pathways/sidewalks.

Programs of Study: Lewis confers B.A., B.S., B.E.S., and B.S.N. degrees. Associate and master's degrees are also awarded. Bachelor's degrees are awarded in BIOLOGICAL SCIENCE (biochemistry and biology/biological science), BUSINESS (accounting, banking and finance, business administration and management, human resources, management information systems, marketing/retailing/merchandising, and sports management), COMMUNICATIONS AND THE ARTS (broadcasting, communications, communications technology, dramatic arts, drawing, English, illustration, journalism, multimedia, music, music business management, painting, public relations, radio/television technology, and studio art), COMPUTER AND PHYSICAL SCIENCE (atmospheric sciences and meteorology, chemistry, computer science, mathematics, and physics), EDUCATION (athletic training, elementary, secondary, special, and speech correction), ENGINEERING AND ENVIRONMENTAL DESIGN (aircraft mechanics, airline piloting and navigation, aviation administration/management, computer graphics, environmental science, and pre-engineering), HEALTH PROFESSIONS (community health work, health care administration, nursing, physical therapy, predentistry, premedicine, preoptometry, prepharmacy, and preveterinary science), SOCIAL SCIENCE (Christian studies, criminal justice, economics, history, liberal arts/general studies, philosophy, political science/government, prelaw, psychology, public administration, religion, safety and security technology, social work, and sociology). Aviation, criminal social justice, and nursing education are the strongest academically and have the largest enrollments.

Required: All students must earn 128 credit hours in courses acceptable for graduation, with one third of these courses in the core curriculum. Students must maintain a minimum GPA of 2.0. At least 4 upper-division courses must be taken in the major. Students must complete the Introduction to the College Experience course and pass a writing proficiency exam.

Special: Lewis offers a general education degree, co-op programs with Chicago College of Pharmacy and Logan Chiropractic College, student-designed majors, B.A.-B.S. degrees in nursing, pass/fail options, dual majors, work-study programs, and nondegree study. Internships are required for some majors and optional for all others. There are accelerated-degree programs in business administration, computer network administration, health care leadership, RN-BSN, social and community studies, and nursing. The aviation program permits graduates to qualify for the FAA Airframe and Powerplant certificate. There are 10 national honor societies, a freshman honors program, and 10 departmental honors programs.

Faculty/Classroom: 57% of faculty are male; 43%, female. All teach undergraduates. No introductory courses are taught by graduate students. The average class size in an introductory lecture is 14; in a laboratory, 11; and in a regular course, 13.

Requirements: The SAT or ACT is required. The ACT is preferred, with a minimum composite score of 20. Applicants should be graduates of an accredited secondary school. The GED is accepted. Students should have 18 units consisting of 3 in English and 15 in other college preparatory subjects. A GPA of 2.0 is required. AP and CLEP credits are accepted. Important factors in the admissions decision are advanced placement or honor courses, leadership record, and extracurricular activities record.

Procedure: Freshmen are admitted to all sessions. There is a rolling admission plan. Entrance exams should be taken prior to enrollment. Application deadlines are open. Applications are accepted on-line. The fall 2005 application fee was $35.

Transfer: 487 transfer students enrolled in a recent year. Applicants must have a 2.0 GPA in transferable course work of at least 12 semester hours, submit official transcripts from all colleges attended, and be in good standing at the previous institution. 32 of 128 credits required for the bachelor's degree must be completed at Lewis.

Visiting: There are regularly scheduled orientations for prospective students, consisting of 1- or 2-day sessions (overnight optional) and parent orientation followed by a welcome weekend before the first class day in the fall. There are guides for informal visits and visitors may sit in on classes and stay overnight. To schedule a visit, contact the Admissions Office at *admissions@lewisu.edu*.

Financial Aid: Lewis is a member of CSS. The FAFSA is required. Check with the school for current application deadlines.

International Students: The school actively recruits these students. They must score satisfactorily on the written TOEFL and also take the SAT or the ACT.

Computers: All students may access the system. There are no time limits.

Admissions Contact: Patrick Hughes, Dean of Admission. E-mail: *admissions@lewisu.edu* Web: *www.lewisu.edu*

LOYOLA UNIVERSITY CHICAGO · E-2

Chicago, IL 60611

(312) 915-6500
(800) 262-2373; Fax: (312) 915-7216

Full-time: 2911 men, 5407 women	**Faculty:** 481; I, -$
Part-time: 358 men, 564 women	**Ph.D.s:** 98%
Graduate: 2033 men, 3491 women	**Student/Faculty:** 17 to 1
Year: semesters, summer session	**Tuition:** $23,836
Application Deadline: April 1	**Room & Board:** $9060
Freshman Class: 13,163 applied, 10,722 accepted, 2080 enrolled	
SAT Verbal/Math: 590/585*	**ACT:** 25 VERY COMPETITIVE

Loyola University Chicago, founded in 1870, is a private Roman Catholic (Jesuit) university offering undergraduate curricula in the arts and sciences, business, nursing, social work, and education. There are 5 undergraduate and 9 graduate schools. In addition to regional accreditation, Loyola has baccalaureate program accreditation with AACSB, CSWE, NCATE, and NLN. The 3 libraries contain 1,412,380 volumes, 1,625,782 microform items, and 15,984 audio/video tapes/CDs/DVDs, and subscribe to 19,295 periodicals including electronic. Computerized library services include the card catalog, interlibrary loans, database searching, Internet access, and laptop Internet portals. Special learning facilities include a learning resource center, art gallery, radio station, a nursing resource center, theater, seismograph station, and an electron microscope. The 105-acre campus is in an urban area in Chicago. Including any residence halls, there are 130 buildings.

Student Life: 61% of undergraduates are from Illinois. Students are from 50 states, 82 foreign countries, and Canada. 61% are from public schools. 67% are white; 12% Asian American; 11% Hispanic. 65% are Catholic; 8% Protestant; 7% claim no religious affiliation. The average age of freshmen is 18; all undergraduates, 21. 16% do not continue beyond their first year; 66% remain to graduate.

Housing: 3273 students can be accommodated in college housing, which includes single-sex and coed dorms and on-campus apartments. In addition, there are special-interest houses a 24-hour quiet center, and a living-learning center. On-campus housing is guaranteed for the freshman and sophomore years only. 79% of students live on campus; of those, 70% remain on campus on weekends. All students may keep cars.

Activities: 6% of men belong to 6 national fraternities; 5% of women belong to 1 local sorority and 5 national sororities. There are 136 groups on campus, including cheerleading, choir, chorus, drama, enviromental, ethnic, gay, honors, international, jazz band, literary magazine, newspaper, political, professional, radio and TV, religious, social, social service, and student government. Popular campus events include Hunger Week, Harmony Colors Festival, and President's and Valentine's Balls.

Sports: There are 7 intercollegiate sports for men and 8 for women, and 31 intramural sports for men and 31 for women. Facilities include racquetball courts, a dance studio, swimming pools, saunas, an elevated jogging track, weight rooms, an arena, a gym, and a soccer/softball field.

Disabled Students: 95% of the campus is accessible. Wheelchair ramps, elevators, special parking, specially equipped rest rooms, special class scheduling, lowered drinking fountains, and lowered telephones are available.

Services: Counseling and information services are available, as is tutoring in some subjects, including general education courses. There is a reader service for the blind and remedial writing. A writing center is also available for student use.

Campus Safety and Security: Measures include 24-hour foot and vehicle patrol, self-defense education, security escort services, and shuttle buses. There are informal discussions, pamphlets/posters/films, emergency telephones, and lighted pathways/sidewalks.

Programs of Study: Loyola confers B.A., B.S., B.A.Classics, B.B.A., B.S.Ed., B.S.N, and B.S.W. degrees. Master's and doctoral degrees are also awarded. Bachelor's degrees are awarded in AGRICULTURE (environmental studies), BIOLOGICAL SCIENCE (bioinformatics and biology/biological science), BUSINESS (accounting, banking and finance, business administration and management, business economics, international business management, marketing/retailing/merchandising, operations management, organizational behavior, organizational leadership and management, and sports management), COMMUNICATIONS AND THE ARTS (advertising, communications, dramatic arts, English, film arts, fine arts, French, German, Greek, Italian, journalism, Latin, media arts, music, and Spanish), COMPUTER AND PHYSICAL SCIENCE (chemistry, computer mathematics, computer science, computer security and information assurance, mathematics, physics, and statistics), EDUCATION (bilingual/bicultural, elementary, mathematics, secondary, and special), ENGINEERING AND ENVIRONMENTAL DESIGN (environmental science), HEALTH PROFESSIONS (nursing), SOCIAL SCIENCE (anthropology, applied psychology, classical/ancient civilization, criminal justice, dietetics, economics, forensic studies, history, human services, international studies, philosophy, political science/government, psychology, religion, social work, sociology, and theological studies). Biology, psychology, and nursing are the largest.

Required: To graduate, students must have a total of 128 credit hours with a minimum GPA of 2.0. The number of hours required in the major varies. For the core requirement, all students must take 9 hours each of theology, philosophy, and social sciences and 6 hours each of English composition and humanities.

Special: Sophomores and juniors may study in 19 countries through 31 different programs. Dual majors, a Washington semester, nondegree study, and pass/fail options are available. The school also offers a B.A.-B.S. degree in chemistry and a 2-3 engineering degree with the University of Illinois at Urbana-Champaign and Washington University. There is a chapter of Phi Beta Kappa and a freshman honors program.

Faculty/Classroom: 51% of faculty are male; 49%, female. 93% teach undergraduates and all do research. No introductory courses are taught by graduate students. The average class size in an introductory lecture is 25; in a laboratory, 2; and in a regular course, 15.

Admissions: 81% of the 2005-2006 applicants were accepted. The SAT scores for the 2005-2006 freshman class were: Verbal--11% below 500, 41% between 500 and 599, 40% between 600 and 700, and 8% above 700; Math--14% below 500, 42% between 500 and 599, 36% between 600 and 700, and 8% above 700. The ACT scores were 12% below 21, 25% between 21 and 23, 29% between 24 and 26, 17% between 27 and 28, and 18% above 28. 53% of the current freshmen were in the top fifth of their class; 86% were in the top two fifths. There were 12 National Merit finalists. 31 freshmen graduated first in their class.

Requirements: The SAT or ACT is required. In addition, graduation from an accredited secondary school or satisfactory scores on the GED are required for admission. 15 academic credits are required. Secondary school courses should include 4 credits of English, 2 of math, and 1 each of science and social studies. An interview is recommended, but an essay is not required. AP and CLEP credits are accepted. Important factors in the admissions decision are recommendations by school officials, leadership record, and advanced placement or honor courses.

Procedure: Freshmen are admitted to all sessions. Entrance exams should be taken as early as possible, normally in the spring of the junior year. There is a rolling admissions plan. Applications should be filed by April 1 for fall entry, along with a $25 fee. Notification is sent on a rolling basis. A waiting list is an active part of the admissions procedure. Applications are accepted on-line.

Transfer: 614 transfer students enrolled in 2004-2005. Transfer students must have 20 transferable semester hours of credit, with a minimum GPA of 2.0 for the schools of arts and sciences and education. A minimum GPA of 2.5 is required for the schools of nursing and business administration. If transfers have fewer then 20 hours, students must meet the same requirements as entering freshmen. 45 of 128 credits required for the bachelor's degree must be completed at Loyola.

Visiting: There are regularly scheduled orientations for prospective students, including interviews and tours; students may attend classes if previous arrangements have been made. There are guides for informal visits and visitors may sit in on classes and stay overnight. To schedule a visit, contact the Undergraduate Admissions Office.

Financial Aid: In 2005-2006, 96% of all full-time freshmen and 92% of continuing full-time students received some form of financial aid. 82% of full-time freshmen and 83% of continuing full-time students received need-based aid. The average freshman award was $21,950. Need-based scholarships or need-based grants averaged $11,760 ($37,564 maximum); need-based self-help aid (loans and jobs) averaged $5147 ($10,000 maximum); non-need-based athletic scholarships averaged $17,692 ($34,195 maximum); and other non-need-based awards and non-need-based scholarships averaged $7205. 10% of undergraduates work part time. Average annual earnings from campus work are $1739. The average financial indebtedness of the 2005 graduate was $23,238. The FAFSA is required. The deadline for filing freshman financial aid applications for fall entry is March 1.

International Students: There are 122 international students enrolled. The school actively recruits these students. They must achieve a satisfactory score on the TOEFL and also take the SAT or the ACT.

Computers: Wireless access is available. All students may access the system whenever facilities are available. Connection is available from dorm rooms. There are no time limits and no fees.

Graduates: From July 1, 2004 to June 30, 2005, 1616 bachelor's degrees were awarded. The most popular majors were biology (11%), psychology (8%), and nursing (7%). In an average class, 1% graduate in 3 years or less, 41% graduate in 4 years or less, 65% graduate in 5 years or less, and 66% graduate in 6 years or less. 360 companies recruited on campus in 2004-2005.

Admissions Contact: April Hansen, Director, Undergraduate Admissions. A video is available. E-mail: *admission@luc.edu* Web: *http://www.luc.edu*

MACMURRAY COLLEGE C-3
Jacksonville, IL 62650 (217) 479-7056
(800) 252-7485; Fax: (217) 291-0702

Full-time: 267 men, 375 women	Faculty: 45
Part-time: 15 men, 44 women	Ph.D.s: 62%
Graduate: none	Student/Faculty: 14 to 1
Year: semesters, summer session	Tuition: $15,250
Application Deadline: open	Room & Board: $5505
Freshman Class: 1421 applied, 806 accepted, 186 enrolled	
SAT Verbal/Math: 470/600*	ACT: 21 COMPETITIVE

MacMurray College, founded in 1846, is a private liberal arts institution affiliated with the United Methodist Church. In addition to regional accreditation, MacMurray has baccalaureate program accreditation with CCNE and CSWE. The library contains 1,817,284 volumes, 28,093 microform items, and 1085 audio/video tapes/CDs/DVDs, and subscribes to 130 periodicals including electronic. Computerized library services include the card catalog, interlibrary loans, database searching, Internet access, and laptop Internet portals. Special learning facilities include a learning resource center and art gallery. The 60-acre campus is in a small town 30 miles west of Springfield. Including any residence halls, there are 17 buildings.

Student Life: 88% of undergraduates are from Illinois. Others are from 17 states, 3 foreign countries, and Canada. 90% are from public schools. 79% are white; 11% African American. 78% are Protestant; 18% Catholic. The average age of freshmen is 19; all undergraduates, 22. 40% do not continue beyond their first year; 56% remain to graduate.

Housing: 725 students can be accommodated in college housing, which includes single-sex and coed dorms. On-campus housing is guaranteed for all 4 years. 54% of students live on campus; of those, 70% remain on campus on weekends. All students may keep cars.

Activities: 9% of men belong to 1 local and 2 national fraternities; 15% of women belong to 3 local sororities. There are 31 groups on campus, including art, bagpipe band, band, cheerleading, choir, chorale, chorus, dance, drama, ethnic, gay, international, literary magazine, musical theater, newspaper, orchestra, pep band, photography, professional, religious, social, social service, student government, and yearbook. Popular campus events include spring formal, Sigma Tau Gamma Day, and midnight breakfasts.

Sports: There are 9 intercollegiate sports for men and 8 for women, and 15 intramural sports for men and 15 for women. Facilities include a gym, 3 basketball courts, tennis and outdoor basketball courts, a competition-size swimming pool, a weight room, a wrestling room, dance studios, a game room, and a TV lounge.

Disabled Students: 90% of the campus is accessible. Wheelchair ramps, elevators, special parking, specially equipped rest rooms, special class scheduling, and special housing are available.

Services: Counseling and information services are available, as is tutoring in every subject. There is remedial math, reading, and writing. The college provides services to visually and hearing impaired students through interpreters, readers, and note takers.

Campus Safety and Security: Measures include security escort services, informal discussions, pamphlets/posters/films, and emergency telephones. There are lighted pathways/sidewalks, evening patrols, and evening sign-in at dorms.

Programs of Study: MacMurray confers B.A., B.S., B.S.N., and B.S.W. degrees. Associate degrees are also awarded. Bachelor's degrees are awarded in BIOLOGICAL SCIENCE (biology/biological science), BUSINESS (accounting, business administration and management, management information systems, marketing/retailing/merchandising, and sports management), COMMUNICATIONS AND THE ARTS (art, dramatic arts, English, music, and Spanish), COMPUTER AND PHYSICAL SCIENCE (chemistry, computer science, mathematics, and physics), EDUCATION (education of the deaf and hearing impaired, elementary, music, physical, science, secondary, and special), ENGINEERING AND ENVIRONMENTAL DESIGN (preengineering), HEALTH PROFESSIONS (nursing, predentistry, premedicine, and preveterinary science), SOCIAL SCIENCE (criminal justice, history, interpreter for the deaf, liberal arts/general studies, philosophy, political science/government, prelaw, psychology, religion, social work, and youth ministry). Education of the hearing impaired and nursing are the strongest academically. Business, education, and criminal justice are the largest.

Required: To graduate, students must complete 120 semester hours with a minimum GPA of 2.0. All students must take 3 courses in rhetorical skills, and a 3-course sequence on major ideas in Western civilization, and a course in Diversity and the American Experience, and must satisfy the requirements of the breadth component, a 16-hour distribution of nonmajor courses. They also must pass a proficiency exam in writing, given when students attain junior standing.

Special: The school has co-op programs in modern languages and international studies and cross-registration with 5 colleges through the West Central Illinois Foreign Language Consortium. A 3-2 engineering degree with Washington and Columbia Universities, a Washington semester, internships in all majors, work-study programs, dual majors, and pass/fail options are available. Students may study abroad in England, Germany, Japan, or Russia. There are 4 national honor societies, a freshman honors program, and 5 departmental honors programs.

Faculty/Classroom: 42% of faculty are male; 58%, female. All teach undergraduates. The average class size in an introductory lecture is 41; in a laboratory, 14; and in a regular course, 17.

Admissions: 57% of the 2005-2006 applicants were accepted. The SAT scores for the 2005-2006 freshman class were: Verbal--17% below 500, 75% between 500 and 599, and 8% between 600 and 700; Math--17% below 500, 75% between 500 and 599, and 8% between 600 and 700. The ACT scores were 50% below 21, 28% between 21 and 23, 15% between 24 and 26, 4% between 27 and 28, and 3% above 28. 28% of the current freshmen were in the top fifth of their class; 50% were in the top two fifths. 3 freshmen graduated first in their class.

Requirements: The SAT or ACT is required. In addition, applicants must be graduates of an accredited secondary school. The GED is accepted. Secondary school courses should include 4 years of English, 3 years of math, and 2 years each of science, foreign language, and social studies. MacMurray requires applicants to be in the upper 50% of their class. A GPA of 2.5 is required. AP and CLEP credits are accepted. Important factors in the admissions decision are advanced placement or honor courses, extracurricular activities record, and leadership record.

Procedure: Freshmen are admitted to all sessions. Entrance exams should be taken in the spring of the junior year. There is a rolling admissions and a deferred admissions plan. Application deadlines are open. Notification is sent on a rolling basis. Applications are accepted on-line.

Transfer: 101 transfer students enrolled in 2004-2005. Transfer students must have a minimum GPA of 2.0 in at least 28 transferable semester credits. Nursing applicants must have a GPA of 2.75 and a satisfactory score on the ACT. 30 of 120 credits required for the bachelor's degree must be completed at MacMurray.

Visiting: There are regularly scheduled orientations for prospective students, including a financial aid conference, a tour, and faculty appointments. There are guides for informal visits and visitors may sit in on classes and stay overnight. To schedule a visit, contact the Office of Admissions at (217) 470-7056 or *admissions@mac.edu*.

Financial Aid: In 2005-2006, 99% of all full-time students received some form of financial aid. 92% of full-time freshmen and 80% of continuing full-time students received need-based aid. The average freshman award was $16,385. Need-based scholarships or need-based grants averaged $5512 ($15,000 maximum); need-based self-help aid (loans and jobs) averaged $4607 ($5500 maximum); and other non-need-based awards and non-need-based scholarships averaged $11,279 ($15,300 maximum). 55% of undergraduates work part time. Average annual earnings from campus work is $1134. The average financial indebtedness of the 2005 graduate was $13,926. MacMurray is a member of CSS. The FAFSA is required. The deadline for filing freshman financial aid applications for fall entry is open.

International Students: There are 8 international students enrolled. They must score satisfactorily on the written or electronic version of the TOEFL.

Computers: Wireless access is available. There are 2 computer labs, each having approximately 30 computers, each with Internet access. Every room in the residence halls has Internet access. The library has laptops that students may check out. All students may access the system at designated hours throughout the week (8 A.M. to 11 P.M. Monday through Friday). There are no time limits and no fees.

Graduates: From July 1, 2004 to June 30, 2005, 115 bachelor's degrees were awarded. The most popular majors were social work (12%), nursing (10%), and psychology (10%). In an average class, 36% graduate in 4 years or less, 45% graduate in 5 years or less, and 52% graduate in 6 years or less. 75 companies recruited on campus in 2004-2005. Of the 2004 graduating class, 15% were enrolled in graduate school within 6 months of graduation and 90% were employed.

Admissions Contact: Rhonda Cors, Vice President for Enrollment. A video is available. E-mail: *admiss@mac.edu* Web: *www.mac.edu*

MCKENDREE COLLEGE   C-5

Lebanon, IL 62254   **(618) 537-6835**
                                    (800) BEARCAT; Fax: (618) 537-6496

Full-time: 763 men, 854 women	**Faculty:** 74; IIB, -$
Part-time: 234 men, 406 women	**Ph.D.s:** 81%
Graduate: 75 men, 253 women	**Student/Faculty:** 22 to 1
Year: semesters, summer session	**Tuition:** $17,800
Application Deadline: open	**Room & Board:** $7000
Freshman Class: 1465 applied, 968 accepted, 274 enrolled	
ACT: 25	**VERY COMPETITIVE**

McKendree College, founded in 1828, is the oldest college in Illinois. It is a private liberal arts institution affiliated with the United Methodist Church. In addition to regional accreditation, McKendree has baccalaureate program accreditation with CAAHEP, IACBE, NCATE, and NLN. The library contains 140,000 volumes, 40,000 microform items, and 30,000 audio/video tapes/CDs/DVDs, and subscribes to 9000 periodicals

including electronic. Computerized library services include the card catalog, interlibrary loans, database searching, Internet access, and laptop Internet portals. Special learning facilities include a learning resource center, a greenhouse, and archives. The 115-acre campus is in a suburban area 23 miles east of St. Louis. Including any residence halls, there are 34 buildings.

Student Life: 83% of undergraduates are from Illinois. Others are from 23 states, 20 foreign countries, and Canada. 92% are from public schools. 81% are white; 10% African American. 41% are Protestant; 30% claim no religious affiliation; 25% Catholic. The average age of freshmen is 18; all undergraduates, 21. 20% do not continue beyond their first year; 62% remain to graduate.

Housing: 692 students can be accommodated in college housing, which includes coed dorms, on-campus apartments, and off-campus apartments. On-campus housing is guaranteed for all 4 years. 54% of students live on campus; of those, 75% remain on campus on weekends. Alcohol is not permitted. All students may keep cars.

Activities: 6% of men belong to 2 local and 3 national fraternities; 10% of women belong to 3 local sororities. There are 67 groups on campus, including art, band, cheerleading, choir, chorale, chorus, computers, dance, debate, drama, ethnic, film, forensics, gay, honors, international, jazz band, literary magazine, marching band, musical theater, newspaper, pep band, photography, political, professional, religious, social, social service, student government, and yearbook. Popular campus events include Model United Nations, Family Festival, and Midnight Breakfast.

Sports: There are 10 intercollegiate sports for men and 10 for women, and 13 intramural sports for men and 13 for women. Facilities include a 1600-seat gym, an intramural gym, a fitness center, tennis courts, a student center with table tennis and billiards, an all-weather track, a 3000-seat football stadium, and playing fields for baseball, softball, and intramurals.

Disabled Students: 80% of the campus is accessible. Wheelchair ramps, elevators, special parking, specially equipped rest rooms, special class scheduling, and lowered drinking fountains are available.

Services: Counseling and information services are available, as is tutoring in every subject. There is remedial reading and writing.

Campus Safety and Security: Measures include 24-hour foot and vehicle patrol, security escort services, shuttle buses, and informal discussions. There are pamphlets/posters/films, emergency telephones, and lighted pathways/sidewalks.

Programs of Study: McKendree confers B.A., B.S., B.B.A., B.F.A., B.S.Ed., and B.S.N. degrees. Master's degrees are also awarded. Bachelor's degrees are awarded in BIOLOGICAL SCIENCE (biology/biological science), BUSINESS (accounting, banking and finance, business administration and management, and marketing/retailing/merchandising), COMMUNICATIONS AND THE ARTS (art, English, music, music history and appreciation, public relations, and speech/debate/rhetoric), COMPUTER AND PHYSICAL SCIENCE (chemistry, computer science, information sciences and systems, and mathematics), EDUCATION (art, athletic training, business, elementary, music, and physical), HEALTH PROFESSIONS (medical laboratory technology and nursing), SOCIAL SCIENCE (criminal justice, economics, gerontology, history, international relations, philosophy, political science/government, psychology, religion, religious music, social science, social work, and sociology). Business, math, and computer science are the strongest academically. Business, education, and nursing are the largest.

Required: To graduate, students must complete 128 semester hours, with a minimum GPA of 2.0. The 51-credit-hour core curriculum includes 9 credits of social science, 7 of science, 6 of freshman English, 3 each of speech, math, ethics, philosophy or religion, history, cross-cultural studies, literature, fine or performing arts, and computer competency, and 1 to 2 of phys ed. In addition, 2 writing-intensive courses and a writing proficiency exam must be taken. A thesis is required for biology majors seeking a B.S. degree.

Special: McKendree offers internships, work-study programs, study abroad in England, Ireland, and France, a Washington semester, dual and student-designed majors, and nondegree study, as well as a 3-2 program in occupational therapy with Washington University in St. Louis. There are 10 national honor societies, a freshman honors program, and 1 departmental honors program.

Faculty/Classroom: 52% of faculty are male; 48%, female. All both teach and do research. No introductory courses are taught by graduate students. The average class size in an introductory lecture is 20; in a laboratory, 15; and in a regular course, 12.

Admissions: 66% of the 2005-2006 applicants were accepted. The ACT scores for the 2005-2006 freshman class were: 21% below 21, 27% between 21 and 23, 27% between 24 and 26, 13% between 27 and 28, and 10% above 28. 49% of the current freshmen were in the top fifth of their class; 82% were in the top two fifths. There was 1 National Merit finalist. 12 freshmen graduated first in their class.

Requirements: The SAT or ACT is required. In addition, students must be high school graduates or submit the GED certificate. Completion of at least 15 units of high school work is recommended. A recommendation from the secondary school counselor is required. McKendree requires applicants to be in the upper 50% of their class. A GPA of 2.5 is required. AP and CLEP credits are accepted. Important factors in the admissions decision are advanced placement or honor courses, leadership record, and evidence of special talent.

Procedure: Freshmen are admitted to all sessions. Entrance exams should be taken in the junior year. There is a rolling admissions plan. Application deadlines are open. Application fee is $40. Applications are accepted on-line.

Transfer: 210 transfer students enrolled in a recent year. Applicants must have a minimum 2.25 GPA from all colleges previously attended. 64 of 128 credits required for the bachelor's degree must be completed at McKendree.

Visiting: There are regularly scheduled orientations for prospective students, consisting of Preview Days, where faculty members and personnel from several departments answer questions. Student-led tours of the campus and various other events are also available. There are guides for informal visits and visitors may sit in on classes and stay overnight. To schedule a visit, contact Jan Mallich at (800) 232-7228, ext. 6831 or *inquiry@mckendree.edu.*

Financial Aid: In 2005-2006, 99% of all full-time freshmen and 89% of continuing full-time students received some form of financial aid. 78% of full-time freshmen and 77% of continuing full-time students received need-based aid. The average freshman award was $13,940. Need-based scholarships or need-based grants averaged $14,846 ($17,500 maximum); need-based self-help aid (loans and jobs) averaged $3091 ($6125 maximum); and non-need-based athletic scholarships averaged $4940 ($24,800 maximum). 23% of undergraduates work part time. Average annual earnings from campus work are $913. The average financial indebtedness of the 2005 graduate was $16,322. The FAFSA is required. The priority date for freshman financial aid applications for fall entry is May 15.

International Students: There are 46 international students enrolled. The school actively recruits these students. They must score satisfactorily on the TOEFL and also take the SAT or the ACT, scoring 20 on the ACT.

Computers: Wireless access is available. Students have access to more than 220 networked lab computers located throughtout the campus. Students can use these computers to access McKendree's web-based systems, including the Intranet, WebAdvisor, Webmail, and Blackboard. All students may access the system. There are no time limits and no fees.

Graduates: From July 1, 2004 to June 30, 2005, 513 bachelor's degrees were awarded. The most popular majors were education (10%), management (10%), and heath professions (10%). In an average class, 1% graduate in 3 years or less, 37% graduate in 4 years or less, 57% graduate in 5 years or less, and 60% graduate in 6 years or less. 150 companies recruited on campus in 2004-2005. Of the 2004 graduating class, 22% were enrolled in graduate school within 6 months of graduation and 96% were employed.

Admissions Contact: Mark Campbell, Enrollment Management. A video is available. E-mail: *mecampbell@mckendree.edu* Web: *www.mckendree.edu*

MILLIKIN UNIVERSITY   D-3
Decatur, IL 62522-2084   (217) 424-6210
                              (800) 373-7733; Fax: (217) 425-4669

Full-time: 1100 men, 1415 women	**Faculty:** 154; IIB, -$
Part-time: 35 men, 60 women	**Ph.D.s:** 88%
Graduate: 25 men, 10 women	**Student/Faculty:** 16 to 1
Year: semesters, summer session	**Tuition:** $19,260
Application Deadline: open	**Room & Board:** $6330
Freshman Class: n/av	
SAT or ACT: required	**COMPETITIVE**

Millikin University, founded in 1901, is a private university affiliated with the Presbyterian Church (U.S.A.) offering undergraduate programs in arts and sciences, nursing, fine arts, and business. Figures in the above capsule and profile are approximate. There are 4 undergraduate schools. In addition to regional accreditation, Millikin has baccalaureate program accreditation with NASM and NLN. The library contains 212,145 volumes, 21,432 microform items, and 2305 audio/video tapes/CDs/DVDs, and subscribes to 580 periodicals including electronic. Computerized library services include the card catalog, interlibrary loans, and database searching. Special learning facilities include a learning resource center, art gallery, radio station, television lab, computer imaging center, audio/video recording studio, and museum of decorative arts. The 70-acre campus is in a suburban area 180 miles southwest of Chicago, 130 miles northeast of St. Louis, Missouri. Including any residence halls, there are 28 buildings.

Student Life: 85% of undergraduates are from Illinois. Others are from 33 states and 13 foreign countries. 85% are from public schools. 84% are white. 53% are Protestant; 24% Catholic; 18% claim no religious affiliation. The average age of freshmen is 18; all undergraduates, 21. 21% do not continue beyond their first year.

Housing: 1425 students can be accommodated in college housing, which includes single-sex and coed dorms, on-campus apartments, off-campus apartments, fraternity houses, and sorority houses. In addition, there are special-interest houses, Greek houses provided by their own organizations, and smoke-free, academic, and freshman floors in residence halls. On-campus housing is available on a first-come, first-served basis and is available on a lottery system for upperclassmen. 75% of students live on campus; of those, 80% remain on campus on weekends. Upperclassmen may keep cars.

Activities: 16% of men belong to 9 national fraternities; 10% of women belong to 3 national sororities. There are 91 groups on campus, including art, band, cheerleading, chess, choir, chorale, chorus, computers, dance, drama, ethnic, film, gay, honors, international, jazz band, literary magazine, musical theater, newspaper, opera, orchestra, pep band, photography, political, professional, radio and TV, religious, social, social service, student government, symphony, and yearbook. Popular campus events include Springfest, Fall Family Weekend, and Millipalooza.

Sports: There are 10 intercollegiate sports for men and 9 for women, and 12 intramural sports for men and 12 for women. Facilities include a phys ed center with a 6-lane, 25-yard pool, a fitness/wellness center, a sand volleyball court, a playing field for football and track, and an indoor sports center.

Disabled Students: 65% of the campus is accessible. Wheelchair ramps, elevators, special parking, specially equipped rest rooms, special class scheduling, lowered drinking fountains, and lowered telephones are available.

Services: Counseling and information services are available, as is tutoring in most subjects. A writing center and a basic review course in English fundamentals are available.

Campus Safety and Security: Measures include 24-hour foot and vehicle patrol, self-defense education, security escort services, and informal discussions. There are pamphlets/posters/films, emergency telephones, and lighted pathways/sidewalks.

Programs of Study: Millikin confers B.A., B.S., B.F.A., B.M., and B.S.N. degrees. Master's degrees are also awarded. Bachelor's degrees are awarded in BIOLOGICAL SCIENCE (biology/biological science), BUSINESS (accounting, banking and finance, business administration and management, international business management, management information systems, and marketing/retailing/merchandising), COMMUNICATIONS AND THE ARTS (art, arts administration/management, communications, creative writing, dramatic arts, English, French, German, modern language, music, music performance, musical theater, and Spanish), COMPUTER AND PHYSICAL SCIENCE (chemistry, computer science, mathematics, and physics), EDUCATION (art, elementary, foreign languages, middle school, music, physical, science, and secondary), ENGINEERING AND ENVIRONMENTAL DESIGN (commercial art and industrial administration/management), HEALTH PROFESSIONS (art therapy and nursing), SOCIAL SCIENCE (American studies, economics, experimental psychology, history, human services, international studies, philosophy, political science/government, psychology, religion, social science, and sociology). Business, music, and theater are the strongest academically. Accounting, biology, and education are the largest.

Required: Requirements for graduation include courses in critical reading, writing, and research, humanities, fine arts, natural sciences/math, and global and U.S. studies. An off-campus learning experience and a university capstone course are also required. The minimum GPA is 2.0. Students must complete 124 to 136 credit hours, with 33 to 88 in the major.

Special: Millikin offers internships, a Washington semester through American University, study abroad at 22 foreign sites, student-designed majors, a 3-2 engineering degree with Washington University, B.A.-B.S. degrees, credit by exam, and pass/fail options. There are preprofessional programs in engineering, law, optometry, dentistry, medicine, veterinary science, occupational therapy, medical technology, physical therapy, and pharmacy. Students are also offered a United Nations semester at Drew University, affiliate research with the U.S. Department of Energy, affiliate agreements in occupational therapy and medical technology, and an Urban Life Studies Center semester in Chicago. There are 9 national honor societies, a freshman honors program, and 5 departmental honors programs.

Faculty/Classroom: 67% of faculty are male; 33%, female. All both teach and do research. The average class size in an introductory lecture is 25; in a laboratory, 15; and in a regular course, 21.

Requirements: The SAT or ACT is required. In addition, applicants should be graduates of an accredited secondary school or have a GED. They should prepare with 4 units of high school English, 3 each of history, math, and science, and 2 of foreign language. An audition is required for music-theater, music, or theater majors. A portfolio is required for art majors. Millikin requires applicants to be in the upper 50% of their class. AP and CLEP credits are accepted. Important factors in the admissions decision are recommendations by school officials, personality/intangible qualities, and evidence of special talent.

Procedure: Freshmen are admitted to all sessions. Entrance exams should be taken in April. There are deferred admissions and rolling admissions plans. Application deadlines are open. Applications are accepted on-line.

Transfer: 130 transfer students enrolled in a recent year. Applicants must provide official transcripts from previous institutions, must be in good standing at the previous institution, and must have earned at least a C average in all college study previously attempted. Submission of official high school transcripts and testing is requested. 33 of 124 credits required for the bachelor's degree must be completed at Millikin.

Visiting: There are regularly scheduled orientations for prospective students, consisting of meetings with faculty and coaches, honors, curriculum, housing, and financial aid presentations, and campus tours. There is also an opportunity for students to audition or have portfolios reviewed. There are guides for informal visits and visitors may sit in on classes and stay overnight. To schedule a visit, contact the Admission Office.

Financial Aid: In a recent year, 83% of all full-time freshmen and 61% of continuing full-time students received some form of financial aid. 77% of full-time freshmen and 55% of continuing full-time students received need-based aid. The average freshman award was $17,086. Need-based scholarships or need-based grants averaged $11,990; need-based self-help aid (loans and jobs) averaged $1175; and other non-need-based awards and non-need-based scholarships averaged $6546. The average financial indebtedness of a recent year graduate was $17,100. Millikin is a member of CSS. The FAFSA and the college's own financial statement are required. Check with the school for current application deadlines.

International Students: In a recent year, there were 9 international students enrolled. The school actively recruits these students. They must score satisfactorily on the written TOEFL.

Computers: All students may access the system. There are no time limits and no fees.

Graduates: In a recent year, 536 bachelor's degrees were awarded. The most popular majors were communications (24%), visual and performing arts (18%), and engineering (15%). In an average class, 60% graduate in 4 years or less, and 61% graduate in 6 years or less. Of a recent graduating class, 14% were enrolled in graduate school within 6 months of graduation and 98% were employed.

Admissions Contact: Patrick Hues, Dean of Admission.
E-mail: *admis@mail.millikin.edu* Web: *www.millikin.edu*

MONMOUTH COLLEGE C-2
Monmouth, IL 61462

(309) 457-2131
(800) 747-2687; Fax: (309) 457-2141

Full-time: 565 men, 595 women	**Faculty:** 69; IIB, av$
Part-time: 2 men, 5 women	**Ph.D.s:** 83%
Graduate: none	**Student/Faculty:** 17 to 1
Year: semesters	**Tuition:** $18,650
Application Deadline: open	**Room & Board:** $5050
Freshman Class: n/av	
SAT or ACT: required	**COMPETITIVE**

Monmouth College, founded in 1853, is a private liberal arts institution affiliated with the Presbyterian Church (U.S.A.). Figures in the above capsule and profile are approximate. The library contains 181,875 volumes, 237,502 microform items, and 7818 audio/video tapes/CDs/DVDs, and subscribes to 547 periodicals including electronic. Computerized library services include the card catalog, interlibrary loans, and database searching. Special learning facilities include a learning resource center, art gallery, radio station, TV station, a biology field station on the Mississippi River, and a prairie plot of native flora. The 70-acre campus is in a small town 45 miles south of Rock Island and Moline. Including any residence halls, there are 26 buildings.

Student Life: 89% of undergraduates are from Illinois. Others are from 20 states, 18 foreign countries, and Canada. 88% are from public schools. 87% are white. 35% are Protestant; 22% Catholic; 20% claim no religious affiliation. The average age of freshmen is 18; all undergraduates, 20. 19% do not continue beyond their first year; 62% remain to graduate.

Housing: 1196 students can be accommodated in college housing, which includes single-sex and coed dormitories and fraternity houses. In addition, there are honors houses and special-interest houses. On-campus housing is guaranteed for all 4 years. 96% of students live on campus; of those, 75% remain on campus on weekends. All students may keep cars.

Activities: 22% of men belong to 3 national fraternities; 24% of women belong to 3 national sororities. There are 60 groups on campus, including art, bagpipe band, band, cheerleading, chess, choir, chorale, chorus, computers, dance, debate, drama, ethnic, gay, honors, international, jazz band, literary magazine, musical theater, photography, political, professional, radio and TV, religious, social, social service, and student government. Popular campus events include Greek Week, Women's Week, and Family Weekend.

Sports: There are 10 intercollegiate sports for men and 10 for women, and 14 intramural sports for men and 14 for women. Facilities include a track, 2 gyms, weight rooms, a fitness/wellness center, football, base-

ball, soccer, and softball fields, a climbing wall, a pool and sauna, a putting green, all-purpose indoor courts, and an outdoor tennis stadium.

Disabled Students: 20% of the campus is accessible. Wheelchair ramps, elevators, special parking, specially equipped rest rooms, special class scheduling, lowered drinking fountains, and special housing are available.

Services: Counseling and information services are available, as is tutoring in most subjects. There is remedial math, reading, and writing.

Campus Safety and Security: Measures include self-defense education, security escort services, informal discussions, and pamphlets/posters/films. There are emergency telephones, lighted pathways/sidewalks, and 12-hour foot and vehicle patrols.

Programs of Study: MC confers the B.A. degree. Bachelor's degrees are awarded in BIOLOGICAL SCIENCE (biochemistry and biology/biological science), BUSINESS (accounting, business administration and management, business economics, international business management, and management information systems), COMMUNICATIONS AND THE ARTS (art, classics, communications, dramatic arts, English, French, Greek, Latin, music, and Spanish), COMPUTER AND PHYSICAL SCIENCE (chemistry, computer programming, computer science, mathematics, and physics), EDUCATION (elementary, physical, and secondary), ENGINEERING AND ENVIRONMENTAL DESIGN (environmental science), SOCIAL SCIENCE (anthropology, biopsychology, history, international studies, philosophy, political science/government, psychology, religion, and sociology). Education, sciences, and business are the strongest academically. Business and education are the largest.

Required: To graduate, all students must complete 124 credit hours with a minimum GPA of 2.0. A major program must be completed with a minimum of C in all courses. Students must also fulfill 38 hours of the general education program and pass Introduction to Liberal Arts and a senior seminar.

Special: Monmouth offers 3-2 nursing programs with Rush Hospital, a 3-2 engineering degree with Washington University, Case Western Reserve, and the University of Southern California, and B.A.-B.S. degrees in nursing and engineering. Students have the opportunity to study in more than 15 countries in Europe, Asia, and Africa. Internships, a Washington semester, and dual and student-designed synoptic majors are available. There are 12 national honor societies, a freshman honors program, and 8 departmental honors programs.

Faculty/Classroom: 54% of faculty are male; 46%, female. All teach undergraduates. The average class size in an introductory lecture is 22; in a laboratory, 15; and in a regular course, 20.

Requirements: The SAT or ACT is required. Applicants must be graduates of accredited high schools and have completed 4 years of English, 3 each of math and social studies, 2 each of science, including 1 of lab, and a foreign language, and 1 of history. A GED is also accepted. MC requires applicants to be in the upper 50% of their class. A GPA of 2.5 is required. AP credits are accepted. Important factors in the admissions decision are advanced placement or honor courses, evidence of special talent, and recommendations by school officials.

Procedure: Freshmen are admitted fall and spring. There is a rolling admissions plan. Entrance exams should be taken by the spring of the junior year. Application deadlines are open. Applications are accepted on-line.

Transfer: 54 transfer students enrolled in a recent year. Students must have a minimum GPA of 2.5. A satisfactory score on the SAT or 19 on the ACT is recommended. 62 of 124 credits required for the bachelor's degree must be completed at MC.

Visiting: There are regularly scheduled orientations for prospective students, including tours, admissions and financial aid discussions, faculty appointments, lunch and entertainment, and a talk with the president. There are guides for informal visits and visitors may sit in on classes and stay overnight. To schedule a visit, contact the Admission Office.

Financial Aid: In a recent year, 98% of all full-time freshmen and 94% of continuing full-time students received some form of financial aid. 83% of all full-time students received need-based aid. The average freshman award was $15,772. Need-based scholarships or need-based grants averaged $12,808; and need-based self-help aid (loans and jobs) averaged $4278. 36% of undergraduates worked part time. Average annual earnings from campus work were $900. The average financial indebtedness of a recent graduate was $18,286. The FAFSA is required. Check with the school for current application deadlines.

International Students: In a recent year there were 20 international students enrolled. The school actively recruits these students. They must score satisfactorily on the written TOEFL.

Computers: All students may access the system 24 hours a day. There are no time limits and no fees.

Graduates: In a recent year, 224 bachelor's degrees were awarded. The most popular majors were business (29%), education (25%), and communication/theater arts (16%). In an average class, 55% graduate in 4 years or less, 60% graduate in 5 years or less, and 62% graduate in 6 years or less. 59 companies recruited on campus in a recent year. Of a recent graduating class, 28% were enrolled in graduate school within 6 months of graduation and 99% were employed.

Admissions Contact: John Klockentager, Vice President of Admission. A video is available. E-mail: *admit@monm.edu*
Web: *www.monm.edu*

NAES COLLEGE OF EASTERN ILLINIOS UNIVERSITY E-2
(Formerly NAES College)

Chicago, IL 60659   (773) 761-5000; Fax: (773) 761-3808

Full-time: 70 men and women	**Faculty:** 3
Part-time: 20 men and women	**Ph.D.s:** 20%
Graduate: none	**Student/Faculty:** 22 to 1
Year: semesters, summer session	**Tuition:** 5150
Application Deadline: open	**Room & Board:** n/app
Freshman Class: n/av	
SAT or ACT: not required	**SPECIAL**

NAES College of Eastern Illinois University, formerly NAES College, founded in 1974, is an independent commuter institution offering a program in community studies for Native Americans employed in Indian programs and agencies. The multicampus college has evening classes. Figures in above capsule and in this profile are approximate. There are 4 undergraduate schools. The library contains 13,000 volumes, 5 microform items, and 500 audio/video tapes/CDs/DVDs, and subscribes to 55 periodicals including electronic. Computerized library services include the card catalog. The 1-acre campus is in an urban area in Chicago. There is one building.

Student Life: All are from public schools. 96% are Native American/Eskimo. The average age of freshmen is 34; all undergraduates, 37. 85% of freshmen remain to graduate.

Housing: There are no residence halls. All students commute. Alcohol is not permitted. All students may keep cars.

Activities: There are no fraternities or sororities.

Sports: There is no sports program at NAES.

Disabled Students: All of the campus is accessible. Special class scheduling is available.

Services: Counseling and information services are available, as is tutoring in most subjects.

Campus Safety and Security: Measures include pamphlets/posters/films, emergency telephones, and lighted pathways/sidewalks.

Programs of Study: NAES confers the B.A. degree. Bachelor's degrees are awarded in SOCIAL SCIENCE (community services).

Required: To graduate, students must maintain a 2.0 GPA and complete 120 credit hours, including a core curriculum of 6 6-credit courses, with 57 hours in the major. Students are required to complete courses in art, math, science, English literature, tribal language, composition, and speech, and demonstrate computer competence. A field project in the American Indian community is also required.

Special: Cross-registration with Northeastern Illinois University is available and students may receive credit for prior learning.

Faculty/Classroom: 61% of faculty are male; 39%, female. The average class size in an introductory lecture is 10 and in a regular course, 10.

Requirements: The SAT or ACT is not required. Applicants must be graduates of an accredited secondary school or have a GED certificate and be employed or a volunteer at an Indian organization or agency that serves Indian people in the community where the campus is located or in which the student lives. Applicants must be at least 24 years old or have an associate of art or science degree, or have completed at least 60 semester hours of transferable credit. CLEP credit is accepted. Important factors in the admissions decision are parents or siblings attending the school, advanced placement or honor courses, and personality/intangible qualities.

Procedure: Freshmen are admitted to all sessions. There are early admissions and rolling admissions plans. Application deadlines are open.

Transfer: Transfer students must satisfy the same requirements as other applicants. 54 of 120 credits required for the bachelor's degree must be completed at NAES.

Visiting: There are regularly scheduled orientations for prospective students. Visitors may sit in on classes. To schedule a visit, contact the campus administrator.

Financial Aid: NAES is a member of CSS. The CSS/Profile, FAFSA, FFS, or SFS is required. Check with the school for current deadlines.

Computers: All students may access the system 9 A.M. to 8 P.M. There are no time limits and no fees.

Admissions Contact: Campus Administrator. Web: *www.naes.edu*

NATIONAL-LOUIS UNIVERSITY E-1

Chicago, IL 60603   (312) 621-9650; (888) NLU TODAY

Full-time: 433 men, 1137 women	**Faculty:** 100
Part-time: 83 men, 431 women	**Ph.D.s:** n/av
Graduate: 1098 men, 3637 women	**Student/Faculty:** 16 to 1
Year: quarters, summer session	**Tuition:** $16,915
Application Deadline: open	**Room & Board:** n/app
Freshman Class: n/av	
SAT or ACT: required	**LESS COMPETITIVE**

National-Louis University, founded in 1886, is an independent institution offering programs in education, liberal arts, health science, business, and human services for the traditional and the adult student. 4 Chicago-area campuses, in Evanston, Wheaton, Wheeling, and the Chicago Loop, accommodate commuters, and academic centers in Elgin, Illinois, Virginia, Missouri, Georgia, Florida, Wisconsin, and Germany offer selected programs for working adults. There are 3 undergraduate and 3 graduate schools. In addition to regional accreditation, NLU has baccalaureate program accreditation with CAHEA and NCATE. The library contains 137,620 volumes, 1 million microform items, and 7130 audio/video tapes/CDs/DVDs, and subscribes to 2872 periodicals including electronic. Computerized library services include the card catalog, interlibrary loans, database searching, and Internet access. Special learning facilities include a learning resource center and a pre-K through 8 elementary demonstration school. The 12-acre campus is in a suburban area 12 miles north of Chicago. Including any residence halls, there are 3 buildings.

Student Life: 99% of undergraduates are from Illinois. Others are from 30 states and 4 foreign countries. 39% are white; 15% African American. The average age of freshmen is 25; all undergraduates, 33. 39% do not continue beyond their first year.

Housing: 160 students can be accommodated in college housing, which includes coed dorms. On-campus housing is available on a first-come, first-served basis. Priority is given to out-of-town students. 99% of students commute. Alcohol is not permitted. Upperclassmen may keep cars.

Activities: There are no fraternities or sororities. There are 30 groups on campus, including chorus, drama, ethnic, honors, musical theater, newspaper, professional, religious, and student government. Popular campus events include cultural clubs celebrating various holidays (e.g., Chinese New Year).

Sports: There is no sports program at NLU. Facilities include a 300-seat gym, a 700-seat auditorium, and a swimming pool.

Disabled Students: 90% of the campus is accessible. Wheelchair ramps, elevators, and special parking are available.

Services: Counseling and information services are available, as is tutoring in most subjects. There is remedial math, reading, and writing. A center for academic development provides services to academically at-risk students.

Campus Safety and Security: Measures include security escort services, informal discussions, pamphlets/posters/films, and emergency telephones. There are lighted pathways/sidewalks and security guards when campus buildings are open.

Programs of Study: NLU confers B.A. and B.S. degrees. Master's and doctoral degrees are also awarded. Bachelor's degrees are awarded in BIOLOGICAL SCIENCE (biology/biological science), BUSINESS (business administration and management and management science), COMMUNICATIONS AND THE ARTS (English and fine arts), COMPUTER AND PHYSICAL SCIENCE (information sciences and systems, mathematics, and science), EDUCATION (early childhood and elementary), HEALTH PROFESSIONS (health care administration and medical laboratory technology), SOCIAL SCIENCE (anthropology, crosscultural studies, human development, human services, psychology, and social science). Education and business are the strongest academically. Management and education are the largest.

Required: Students must take courses in humanities, natural sciences, and behavioral sciences, for a minimum of 50 hours in general education requirements. Other course requirements vary by program. All students must pass an English competency writing exam. A minimum 2.0 GPA and 180 quarter hours, including 45 in the major, are required to graduate. There is a 45 quarter-hour residency requirement.

Special: NLU offers credit by exam and for experiential learning, internships in teaching and human services, and limited nondegree and pass/fail options. There are special completion programs for adults in management, applied behavioral science, and health care leadership. In addition, NLU offers several programs in the field as well as customized programs for working adults. There is 1 national honor society, including Phi Beta Kappa.

Faculty/Classroom: 33% of faculty are male; 67%, female. No introductory courses are taught by graduate students. The average class size in an introductory lecture is 16 and in a regular course, 16.

Requirements: The SAT or ACT is required for first-time freshman under 21 years of age. Applicants should graduate from an accredited secondary school with 15 academic credits, including 4 in English, 3 in social studies, and 2 each in math and science. The GED is accepted. 2 letters of recommendation, with 1 from the high school counselor are required; an interview is strongly encouraged. NLU requires applicants to be in the upper 50% of their class. AP and CLEP credits are accepted. Important factors in the admissions decision are recommendations by school officials, leadership record, and evidence of special talent.

Procedure: Freshmen are admitted fall, winter, and spring. Entrance exams should be taken the winter before application. There is a deferred admissions plan and a rolling admissions plan. Application deadlines are open. Application fee is $95.

Transfer: 1046 transfer students enrolled in a recent year. A minimum GPA of 2.0 is required. Applicants must be in good standing at the college previously attended. Official transcripts from previously attended colleges and letters of recommendation are required. Personal interviews are strongly encouraged. 45 of 180 quarter hours required for the bachelor's degree must be completed at NLU.

Visiting: There are regularly scheduled orientations for prospective students, including campus tours, meeting with students and key administrators, attending typical campus entertainment, and visiting classes. There are guides for informal visits and visitors may sit in on classes. To schedule a visit, contact the Undergraduate Enrollment Office.

Financial Aid: In 2005-2006, 68% of all full-time freshmen and 57% of continuing full-time students received some form of financial aid. 60% of full-time freshmen and 53% of continuing full-time students received need-based aid. Need-based scholarships or need-based grants averaged $6940 ($12,171 maximum); need-based self-help aid (loans and jobs) averaged $3000 ($6625 maximum); and non-need-based athletic scholarships averaged $9915 ($25,173 maximum). 5% of undergraduates work part time. Average annual earnings from campus work are $3000. The average financial indebtedness of the 2005 graduate was $9875. NLU is a member of CSS. The FAFSA is required. Students must complete financial aid applications prior to their last term of the current academic year.

International Students: They must take the college's own test.

Computers: All students may access the system. There are no time limits and no fees.

Graduates: From July 1, 2004 to June 30, 2005, 879 bachelor's degrees were awarded. The most popular majors were management (44%), applied behavorial sciences (27%), and education (10%). In an average class, 3% graduate in 3 years or less, 23% graduate in 4 years or less, 32% graduate in 5 years or less, and 44% graduate in 6 years or less.

Admissions Contact: Patricia Petillo, Admissions Director.
E-mail: *nluinfo@nl.edu* Web: *www.nl.edu*

NORTH CENTRAL COLLEGE   E-2
Naperville, IL 60566   **(630) 637-5800**
                          (800) 411-1861; Fax: (630) 637-5819

Full-time: 784 men, 1126 women	**Faculty:** 111; IIA, -$
Part-time: 110 men, 113 women	**Ph.D.s:** 86%
Graduate: 161 men, 178 women	**Student/Faculty:** 17 to 1
Year: quarters, summer session	**Tuition:** $21,993
Application Deadline: open	**Room & Board:** $6993
Freshman Class: 1936 applied, 1348 accepted, 425 enrolled	
SAT Verbal/Math: 570/590*	**ACT:** 24 **VERY COMPETITIVE**

North Central College, founded in 1861, is a private comprehensive liberal arts institution affiliated with the United Methodist Church. In addition to regional accreditation, North Central has baccalaureate program accreditation with ACS. The library contains 150,777 volumes, 212,624 microform items, and 3961 audio/video tapes/CDs/DVDs, and subscribes to 603 periodicals including electronic. Computerized library services include the card catalog, interlibrary loans, database searching, and Internet access. Special learning facilities include a learning resource center, art gallery, radio station, an advising center, a foreign language lab, and a writing center. The 54-acre campus is in a suburban area 30 miles west of Chicago. Including any residence halls, there are 24 buildings.

Student Life: 92% of undergraduates are from Illinois. Others are from 30 states and 24 foreign countries. 80% are white. 35% claim no religious affiliation; 35% Protestant; 26% Catholic. The average age of freshmen is 18; all undergraduates, 21. 21% do not continue beyond their first year; 63% remain to graduate.

Housing: 1009 students can be accommodated in college housing, which includes single-sex and coed dorms and on-campus apartments. On-campus housing is available on a lottery system for upperclassmen. 52% of students commute. All students may keep cars.

Activities: There are no fraternities or sororities. There are 50 groups on campus, including art, band, cheerleading, choir, chorale, chorus, dance, drama, ethnic, forensics, gay, honors, international, jazz band, literary magazine, musical theater, newspaper, pep band, photography, political, professional, radio and TV, religious, social, social service, student government, and yearbook. Popular campus events include Family Weekend, Winter Carnival, and Arts and Letters Festival.

Sports: There are 10 intercollegiate sports for men and 9 for women, and 12 intramural sports for men and 12 for women. Facilities include indoor and outdoor tracks, a weight room, football and baseball stadiums, soccer fields, a swimming pool, tennis courts, an athletic training facility, and a human performance lab.

Disabled Students: 60% of the campus is accessible. Wheelchair ramps, elevators, special parking, specially equipped rest rooms, special class scheduling, lowered drinking fountains, lowered telephones, and special housing are available.

Services: Counseling and information services are available, as is tutoring in most subjects. There is a reader service for the blind, remedial math and limited technology for students with disabilities.

Campus Safety and Security: Measures include 24-hour foot and vehicle patrol, self-defense education, security escort services, and informal discussions. There are pamphlets/posters/films, emergency telephones, and lighted pathways/sidewalks.

Programs of Study: North Central confers B.A. and B.S. degrees. Master's degrees are also awarded. Bachelor's degrees are awarded in BIOLOGICAL SCIENCE (biochemistry and biology/biological science), BUSINESS (accounting, banking and finance, business administration and management, international business management, and marketing/retailing/merchandising), COMMUNICATIONS AND THE ARTS (broadcasting, communications, English, fine arts, French, German, Japanese, music, Spanish, and speech/debate/rhetoric), COMPUTER AND PHYSICAL SCIENCE (actuarial science, applied mathematics, chemistry, computer science, mathematics, and physics), EDUCATION (elementary and secondary), ENGINEERING AND ENVIRONMENTAL DESIGN (preengineering), HEALTH PROFESSIONS (predentistry, premedicine, and preveterinary science), SOCIAL SCIENCE (anthropology, classical/ancient civilization, economics, history, philosophy, political science/government, prelaw, psychology, religion, social science, and sociology). Business and education are the largest.

Required: All students must complete a general education core, including 9 hours in humanities and fine arts, 9 hours in social sciences, 6.5 hours in life and physical sciences, 3 to 6 hours in composition, and 3 hours each in speech communication and math. In addition, all students take an intercultural seminar, a leadership, ethics, and values seminar, and a course in religion and ethics. A GPA of 2.0 and a total of 120 credit hours are required for graduation, with 24 to 51 credits taken in the major.

Special: North Central offers co-op programs in medical technology, nursing, radiation therapy, and nuclear medicine technology, cross-registration with Benedictine University, Elmhurst College, and Aurora University, a Washington semester, and study abroad. Internships in most subject areas, work-study programs, a 3-2 engineering degree with Washington and Marquette Universities and the Universities of Minnesota and Illinois at Urbana-Champaign, experiential credit, and nondegree study are available. Dual majors, accelerated degree programs, and student-designed majors are also offered. There are 2 national honor societies and a freshman honors program.

Faculty/Classroom: 55% of faculty are male; 45%, female. All teach undergraduates. No introductory courses are taught by graduate students. The average class size in an introductory lecture is 24; in a laboratory, 19; and in a regular course, 21.

Admissions: 70% of the 2005-2006 applicants were accepted. The SAT scores for the 2005-2006 freshman class were: Verbal--16% below 500, 44% between 500 and 599, 35% between 600 and 700, and 5% above 700; Math--13% below 500, 42% between 500 and 599, 36% between 600 and 700, and 9% above 700. The ACT scores were 15% below 21, 29% between 21 and 23, 25% between 24 and 26, 13% between 27 and 28, and 17% above 28. 40% of the current freshmen were in the top fifth of their class; 71% were in the top two fifths. 6 freshmen graduated first in their class.

Requirements: A satisfactory score is required on the SAT or ACT. Minimum requirements also include a GPA of at least 2.5 and involvement in school and/or community. An admission essay and/or admission interview may be recommended. The GED is accepted. The recommended secondary school courses are 4 years of English and 3 years each of math, science, social science, and foreign language. North Central requires applicants to be in the upper 50% of their class. AP and CLEP credits are accepted.

Procedure: Freshmen are admitted to all sessions. Entrance exams should be taken in the spring of the junior year or the fall of the senior year. There is a deferred admissions plan. There is a rolling admissions plan. Application deadlines are open. Application fee is $25. Applications are accepted on-line.

Transfer: 350 transfer students enrolled in 2004-2005. Applicants need to have maintained a 2.25 transferable GPA or better and earned 27 transferable semester hours. If they have not earned 27 transferable hours, their high school transcripts and ACT/SAT scores are also considered. 30 of 120 credits required for the bachelor's degree must be completed at North Central.

Visiting: There are regularly scheduled orientations for prospective students, including presentations on academic programs, student life, admission guidelines, and financial aid. Prospective students may also take a campus tour and talk with a professor. Orientation sessions for all incoming freshmen are offered during the summer. There are guides for informal visits and visitors may sit in on classes and stay overnight. To schedule a visit, contact the Office of Admissions.

Financial Aid: In 2005-2006, 94% of all full-time freshmen and 89% of continuing full-time students received some form of financial aid. 68% of full-time freshmen and 65% of continuing full-time students received need-based aid. The average freshman award was $17,447. 33% of undergraduates work part time. Average annual earnings from campus work are $1300. The average financial indebtedness of the 2005 graduate was $14,608. The FAFSA and the college's own financial statement are required. The deadline for filing freshman financial aid applications for fall entry is September 1.

International Students: There are 33 international students enrolled. The school actively recruits these students. A satisfactory score is required on the TOEFL.

Computers: Wireless access is available. Every room in every building is cabled for Internet service as are residence halls. The library, Boiler-House, and the student center are completely wireless as is the main spine of campus and the areas outside of residence halls. There are labs in 4 buildings. There are 325 PCs on campus available to students. All students may access the system 7 A.M. to midnight in the computer center or at any time from residence hall rooms and labs. There are no time limits and no fees.

Graduates: From July 1, 2004 to June 30, 2005, 503 bachelor's degrees were awarded. The most popular majors were business (27%), education (15%), and social sciences (10%). In an average class, 1% graduate in 3 years or less, 55% graduate in 4 years or less, 63% graduate in 5 years or less, and 63% graduate in 6 years or less.

Admissions Contact: Marty Sauer, Dean of Admission and Financial Aid. A video is available. E-mail: admissions@noctrl.edu Web: www.northcentralcollege.edu

NORTH PARK UNIVERSITY   E-2

Chicago, IL 60625-4987   (312) 583-2700; (800) 888-6728

Full-time: 500 men, 760 women	Faculty: 81
Part-time: 110 men, 220 women	Ph.Ds: 41%
Graduate: 270 men, 485 women	Student/Faculty: 15 to 1
Year: semesters, summer session	Tuition: $17,800
Application Deadline: open	Room & Board: $6250
Freshman Class: n/av	
SAT or ACT: recommended	COMPETITIVE

North Park University, founded in 1891, is a private liberal arts college affiliated with the Evangelical Covenant Church offering undergraduate programs in the arts and sciences, business, music, and education. There are 5 undergraduate and 3 graduate schools. Figures in the above capsule and profile are approximate. In addition to regional accreditation, North Park has baccalaureate program accreditation with NLN. The 2 libraries contain 220,000 volumes, 93,000 microform items, and 6500 audio/video tapes/CDs/DVDs, and subscribe to 950 periodicals including electronic. Computerized library services include the card catalog, interlibrary loans, and database searching. Special learning facilities include a learning resource center, art gallery, and an herbarium. The 30-acre campus is in an urban area 10 miles north of downtown Chicago. Including any residence halls, there are 25 buildings.

Student Life: 68% of undergraduates are from Illinois. Others are from 38 states, 38 foreign countries, and Canada. 55% are white. 57% are Protestant; 16% claim no religious affiliation; 13% Catholic. The average age of freshmen is 18; all undergraduates, 21. 30% do not continue beyond their first year; 65% remain to graduate.

Housing: 943 students can be accommodated in college housing, which includes single-sex dorms, on-campus apartments, off-campus apartments, and married-student housing. In addition, there are honors houses, language houses, special-interest houses, and an international living center. On-campus housing is guaranteed for all 4 years. 60% of students live on campus; of those, 90% remain on campus on weekends. Alcohol is not permitted. All students may keep cars.

Activities: There are no fraternities or sororities. There are 40 groups on campus, including art, band, cheerleading, choir, chorale, chorus, computers, drama, ethnic, honors, international, jazz band, literary magazine, musical theater, newspaper, opera, orchestra, pep band, photography, political, professional, religious, social, social service, student government, symphony, and yearbook. Popular campus events include dances, concerts, and film festivals.

Sports: There are 8 intercollegiate sports for men and 8 for women, and 5 intramural sports for men and 5 for women. Facilities include football, baseball, track, and soccer fields, tennis courts, a weight room, a gym, a fitness center, and a swimming pool.

Disabled Students: 90% of the campus is accessible. Wheelchair ramps, elevators, specially equipped rest rooms, lowered drinking fountains, and lowered telephones are available.

Services: Counseling and information services are available, as is tutoring in every subject. There is a reader service for the blind, and remedial

math, reading, and writing. An extended orientation program is available.

Campus Safety and Security: Measures include 24-hour foot and vehicle patrol, self-defense education, security escort services, and informal discussions. There are pamphlets/posters/films, emergency telephones, and lighted pathways/sidewalks.

Programs of Study: North Park confers B.A., B.S., B.Mus., and B.S.Med.Tech. degrees. Master's and doctoral degrees are also awarded. Bachelor's degrees are awarded in BIOLOGICAL SCIENCE (biology/biological science), BUSINESS (accounting, banking and finance, business administration and management, international business management, and marketing/retailing/merchandising), COMMUNICATIONS AND THE ARTS (communications, English, music, and Spanish), COMPUTER AND PHYSICAL SCIENCE (chemistry, mathematics, and physics), EDUCATION (early childhood, elementary, and secondary), HEALTH PROFESSIONS (medical laboratory technology, nursing, occupational therapy, physical therapy, predentistry, and premedicine), SOCIAL SCIENCE (anthropology, economics, history, international relations, philosophy, political science/government, prelaw, psychology, religion, and sociology). Music, sciences, and premedicine are the strongest academically. Nursing, education, and psychology are the largest.

Required: Students must successfully complete 120 semester hours with a minimum 2.0 GPA. The required number of hours in the major varies. Students must meet a general requirement of 17 core courses.

Special: Cross-registration with Christian College Coalition schools is possible. Opportunities are provided for a co-op program in occupational therapy, internships, work-study, a Washington semester, 3-2 engineering degrees, accelerated degree programs in organization management and nursing, credit by examination, dual majors, student-designed majors, B.A.-B.S. degrees, pass/fail options, and study abroad. There are 6 national honor societies, a freshman honors program, and 25 departmental honors programs.

Faculty/Classroom: 50% of faculty are male; 50%, female. All teach undergraduates. The average class size in an introductory lecture is 35; in a laboratory, 20; and in a regular course, 25.

Requirements: The SAT or ACT is recommended. Graduation from an accredited secondary school is required; a GED will be accepted. Students should have completed course work in a foreign language, 4 years of English, and 3 years each of math, science, and social studies. Recommendations from teachers should also be submitted. An essay and an audition are required. An interview is recommended. A GPA of 2.0 is required. AP and CLEP credits are accepted. Important factors in the admissions decision are evidence of special talent, personality/intangible qualities, and parents or siblings attending the school.

Procedure: Freshmen are admitted to all sessions. There are rolling admissions plans. Entrance exams should be taken during spring of the junior year or fall of the senior year. Application deadlines are open. The fall 2005 application fee was $20.

Transfer: To be eligible for transfer admission, students must submit a reference from a faculty member, counselor, or administrator, and official transcripts from the previous college, and must have maintained a minimum GPA of 2.0. An interview is also recommended. 30 of 120 credits required for the bachelor's degree must be completed at North Park.

Visiting: There are regularly scheduled orientations for prospective students. There are guides for informal visits and visitors may sit in on classes and stay overnight. To schedule a visit, contact Campus Visitation Coordinator at (312) 244-5500.

Financial Aid: The CSS/Profile or FFS, the college's own financial statement, and student and parent federal income tax returns are required. Check with the school for application deadlines.

International Students: The school actively recruits these students. They must score satisfactorily on the written TOEFL.

Computers: All students may access the system at any time. There are no time limits and no fees.

Admissions Contact: John Baworowski, Vice President for Admissions. Web: http://www.northpark.edu/afao

NORTHEASTERN ILLINOIS UNIVERSITY   E-2

Chicago, IL 60625   (773) 442-4044; Fax: (773) 442-4020

Full-time: 1985 men, 3222 women	Faculty: n/av
Part-time: 1570 men, 2641 women	Ph.Ds: n/av
Graduate: 944 men, 1865 women	Student/Faculty: 14 to 1
Year: semesters, summer session	Tuition: $3000 ($7800)
Application Deadline: July 1	Room & Board: n/app
Freshman Class: 3071 applied, 2298 accepted, 1058 enrolled	
ACT: 21	COMPETITIVE

Northeastern Illinois University, founded in 1867, is a public liberal arts institution offering degree programs in arts and sciences, business management, and education. Some figures in the above capsule and this profile are approximate. There are 4 undergraduate schools and 1 graduate school. In addition to regional accreditation, Northeastern has baccalaureate program accreditation with NCATE. The library contains

459,191 volumes, 749,370 microform items, and 1001 audio/video tapes/CDs/DVDs, and subscribes to 73,503 periodicals including electronic. Computerized library services include interlibrary loans and database searching. Special learning facilities include a learning resource center, art gallery, and radio station. The 63-acre campus is in an urban area in northwest Chicago. There are 10 buildings.

Student Life: 99% of undergraduates are from Illinois. Students are from 22 states and 9 foreign countries. 55% are from public schools. 44% are white; 27% Hispanic; 14% Asian American; 13% African American. The average age of freshmen is 20; all undergraduates, 28. 45% do not continue beyond their first year; 36% remain to graduate.

Housing: There are no residence halls. All of students commute. Alcohol is not permitted. All students may keep cars.

Activities: There are 1 local sorority. There are no fraternities. There are 50 groups on campus, including art, band, cheerleading, chess, choir, chorus, computers, dance, drama, ethnic, film, gay, honors, international, jazz band, literary magazine, musical theater, newspaper, opera, orchestra, photography, political, professional, radio and TV, religious, social, social service, and student government. Popular campus events include International Day, fairs, and the Visiting Lecture Series.

Sports: There are 10 intramural sports for men and 10 for women. Facilities include basketball, tennis, and racquetball courts, indoor and outdoor tracks, a pool, a weight room, and baseball and softball fields.

Disabled Students: 94% of the campus is accessible. Wheelchair ramps, elevators, special parking, specially equipped rest rooms, special class scheduling, lowered drinking fountains, lowered telephones, and a Handicap Education Liaison Program (HELP) that allows priority registration are available.

Services: Counseling and information services are available, as is tutoring in most subjects. There is a reader service for the blind, and remedial math, reading, and writing.

Campus Safety and Security: Measures include 24-hour foot and vehicle patrol, security escort services, pamphlets/posters/films, and emergency telephones. There are lighted pathways/sidewalks.

Programs of Study: Northeastern confers B.A. and B.S. degrees. Master's degrees are also awarded. Bachelor's degrees are awarded in AGRICULTURE (environmental studies), BIOLOGICAL SCIENCE (biology/biological science), BUSINESS (accounting, business administration and management, and marketing/retailing/merchandising), COMMUNICATIONS AND THE ARTS (English, fine arts, French, music, Spanish, and speech/debate/rhetoric), COMPUTER AND PHYSICAL SCIENCE (chemistry, computer science, earth science, mathematics, and physics), EDUCATION (bilingual/bicultural, early childhood, elementary, physical, secondary, and special), SOCIAL SCIENCE (anthropology, criminal justice, economics, geography, history, philosophy, political science/government, psychology, social work, and sociology). Education, business, and computer science are the strongest academically. Business and education are the largest.

Required: All students are required to take at least 120 semester hours, including 39 hours of foundational general education, 30 to 60 hours in the major, and 12 hours each in social and natural sciences, 9 in humanities, and 6 in fine arts. A 2.0 overall GPA is required for graduation. An overall GPA and college major GPA of 2.5 are required within the College of Business Management and the College of Education.

Special: Alternative degree and nondegree programs are available, as is cross-registration with Governors State University. Some departments offer internships. A dual major in elementary and early childhood or special education is offered. There are pass/fail options. Honors classes are available. There are 12 national honor societies, a freshman honors program, and 18 departmental honors programs.

Faculty/Classroom: 63% of faculty are male; 37%, female. 90% teach undergraduates. No introductory courses are taught by graduate students. The average class size in an introductory lecture is 80; in a laboratory, 20; and in a regular course, 30.

Admissions: 75% of the 2005-2006 applicants were accepted. The ACT scores for the 2005-2006 freshman class were: 40% below 21, 49% between 21 and 23, 9% between 24 and 26, 9% between 27 and 28, and 1% above 28. 16% of the current freshmen were in the top fourth of their class; 55% were in the top half.

Requirements: The ACT is required, for freshmen under 21 years of age. Applicants must have graduated from a regionally accredited high school or passed the GED. High school preparation should total at least 12 credits, including 4 years in English, 3 each in math, sciences, and social studies, and 2 in foreign language, music, art, fine arts, or vocational education (only 1 vocational course is accepted). Northeastern requires applicants to be in the upper 50% of their class. AP and CLEP credits are accepted. Important factors in the admissions decision are evidence of special talent, advanced placement or honor courses, and recommendations by school officials.

Procedure: Freshmen are admitted to all sessions. Entrance exams should be taken . There are deferred admissions and rolling admissions plans. Applications should be filed by July 1 for fall entry, November 1 for spring entry, and April 1 for summer entry, along with a $25 fee. The college accepts all applicants. Notification is sent on a rolling basis. Applications are accepted on-line.

Transfer: 1200 transfer students enrolled in 2004-2005. Applicants are considered if they have completed at least 30 semester hours of study with a C average. Those with fewer than 30 hours of credit must meet freshman admissions requirements. 30 of 120 credits required for the bachelor's degree must be completed at Northeastern.

Visiting: There are guides for informal visits and visitors may sit in on classes. To schedule a visit, contact the Admissions Counseling and Recruitment Office at (773) 442-4050.

Financial Aid: In 2005-2006, 62% of all full-time freshmen and 64% of continuing full-time students received some form of financial aid. The average freshman award was $6890. Need-based scholarships or need-based grants averaged $2231; need-based self-help aid (loans and jobs) averaged $955; and other non-need-based awards and non-need-based scholarships averaged $204. The FAFSA and the college's own financial statement are required. The deadline for filing freshman financial aid applications for fall entry is April 1.

International Students: They must score satisfactorily on the written TOEFL or on the electronic version.

Computers: Those students enrolled in specific courses or doing research may access the system posted times, which vary from 12 to 15 hours daily. There are no time limits and no fees.

Admissions Contact: Marcia Boyd, Associate Director of Enrollment Services. E-mail: m-boyd@neiu.edu Web: www.neiu.edu

NORTHERN ILLINOIS UNIVERSITY	D-2
DeKalb, IL 60115	(815) 753-0446
	(800) 892-3050; Fax: (815) 753-1783

Full-time: 7950 men, 8659 women	Faculty: 901; I, --$
Part-time: 868 men, 990 women	Ph.D.s: 83%
Graduate: 2747 men, 3994 women	Student/Faculty: 18 to 1
Year: semesters, summer session	Tuition: $7228 ($12,290)
Application Deadline: August 1	Room & Board: $5950
Freshman Class: 15,007 applied, 9917 accepted, 3165 enrolled	
ACT: 22	COMPETITIVE

Northern Illinois University, founded in 1895, is a publicly funded institution offering undergraduate and graduate programs in a comprehensive range of disciplines. There are 6 undergraduate and 2 graduate schools. In addition to regional accreditation, NIU has baccalaureate program accreditation with AACSB, ABET, ACEJMC, APTA, ASLA, CAHEA, NASAD, NASM, NCATE, and NLN. The 3 libraries contain 2,068,449 volumes, 4,048,896 microform items, and 54,688 audio/video tapes/CDs/DVDs, and subscribe to 18,456 periodicals including electronic. Computerized library services include the card catalog, interlibrary loans, and database searching. Special learning facilities include an art gallery, radio station, TV station, and anthropology museum. The 755-acre campus is in a small town 65 miles west of Chicago. Including any residence halls, there are 55 buildings.

Student Life: 95% of undergraduates are from Illinois. Others are from 50 states, 95 foreign countries, and Canada. 84% are from public schools. 74% are white; 13% African American. 47% are Catholic; 31% Protestant; 14% claim no religious affiliation. The average age of freshmen is 18; all undergraduates, 22. 22% do not continue beyond their first year; 78% remain to graduate.

Housing: 6000 students can be accommodated in college housing, which includes single-sex and coed dorms, on-campus apartments, and married-student housing. In addition, there are honors houses, language houses, and special-interest houses in law, computer science, music, political science, and health professions. On-campus housing is guaranteed for the freshman year only and is available on a first-come, first-served basis. 67% of students live on campus; of those, 60% remain on campus on weekends. All students may keep cars.

Activities: 15% of men belong to 22 national fraternities; 11% of women belong to 15 national sororities. There are 200 groups on campus, including art, band, cheerleading, chess, choir, chorale, chorus, computers, dance, drama, drill team, ethnic, film, gay, honors, international, jazz band, literary magazine, marching band, musical theater, newspaper, orchestra, pep band, photography, political, professional, radio and TV, religious, social, social service, student government, and symphony. Popular campus events include Unity in Diversity Week, Greek Week, and Springfest.

Sports: There are 8 intercollegiate sports for men and 8 for women, and 15 intramural sports for men and 15 for women. Facilities include a sports stadium, a recreation center and field house with facilities for basketball, volleyball, badminton, table tennis, tennis, racquetball/handball, and weight training, and 2 swimming pools.

Disabled Students: 85% of the campus is accessible. Wheelchair ramps, elevators, special parking, specially equipped rest rooms, special class scheduling, lowered drinking fountains, lowered telephones, special housing, and transportation are available.

Services: Formal tutoring is provided for eligible students.

Campus Safety and Security: Measures include 24-hour foot and vehicle patrol, self-defense education, security escort services, and shuttle buses. There are informal discussions, pamphlets/posters/films, emergency telephones, lighted pathways/sidewalks, and a bicycle patrol.

Programs of Study: NIU confers B.A., B.S., B.F.A., B.G.S., B.M., and B.S.Ed. degrees. Master's and doctoral degrees are also awarded. Bachelor's degrees are awarded in BIOLOGICAL SCIENCE (biology/ biological science and nutrition), BUSINESS (accounting, banking and finance, business administration and management, and marketing/ retailing/merchandising), COMMUNICATIONS AND THE ARTS (art, art history and appreciation, communications, dramatic arts, English, French, German, journalism, music, Russian, Spanish, and studio art), COMPUTER AND PHYSICAL SCIENCE (atmospheric sciences and meteorology, chemistry, computer science, geology, geoscience, information sciences and systems, mathematics, and physics), EDUCATION (art, early childhood, elementary, health, music, physical, and special), ENGINEERING AND ENVIRONMENTAL DESIGN (electrical/electronics engineering, industrial engineering, mechanical engineering, and technological management), HEALTH PROFESSIONS (clinical science, community health work, health science, nursing, and speech pathology/ audiology), SOCIAL SCIENCE (anthropology, child care/child and family studies, dietetics, early childhood studies, economics, geography, history, liberal arts/general studies, philosophy, physical fitness/movement, political science/government, psychology, sociology, and textiles and clothing). Business, engineering, and sciences are the strongest academically. Business, education, and communications are the largest.

Required: To graduate, students must have a minimum of 124 credit hours and a minimum GPA of 2.0. All students must take English 103 and 104 and Communication Studies 100. In addition, they must take Math 101 or obtain at least a C in Math 155, 201, 206, 210, 211, or 229. The school also requires that students complete 29 hours in distributive studies areas, consisting of 9 to 12 hours in the humanities and arts, 7 to 11 hours in science and math, 6 to 9 hours in social science, and 3 to 6 hours in interdisciplinary studies.

Special: NIU offers internships in several areas. Students may study abroad in 30 countries. A physics/engineering degree is offered in cooperation with the University of Illinois. Either a B.A. or a B.S. may be obtained in the social science programs. Work-study programs, a general studies degree, co-op programs, pass/fail options, and student-designed majors are available. There are 5 national honor societies, a freshman honors program, and 18 departmental honors programs.

Faculty/Classroom: 57% of faculty are male; 43%, female. Graduate students teach 20% of introductory courses. The average class size in an introductory lecture is 37; in a laboratory, 17; and in a regular course, 30.

Admissions: 66% of the 2005-2006 applicants were accepted. The ACT scores for the 2005-2006 freshman class were: 35% below 21, 32% between 21 and 23, 23% between 24 and 26, 7% between 27 and 28, and 4% above 28. 24% of the current freshmen were in the top fifth of their class; 56% were in the top two fifths.

Requirements: The ACT is required. Students must have a minimum score of 19 on the ACT and be in the top half of their class, or have an ACT score of 23 and be in the upper two thirds of their class. Graduation from an accredited secondary school or satisfactory scores on the GED are required for admission. Secondary school courses must include 4 years of English and 2 to 3 years each of math, science, and social studies. In addition, students must have completed 1 to 2 years of art, film, foreign language, music, or theater. AP and CLEP credits are accepted.

Procedure: Freshmen are admitted to all sessions. Entrance exams should be taken during the junior year. Applications should be filed by August 1 for fall entry, December 15 for spring entry, and May 15 for summer entry. Notification is sent on a rolling basis. 496 applicants were on the 2005 waiting list. Applications are accepted on-line.

Transfer: 2229 transfer students enrolled in 2004-2005. Transfer students with 24 or more credit hours must have a minimum GPA of 2.0. The core competency requirement in English, math, and speech must be satisfied by all transfer students. 30 of 124 credits required for the bachelor's degree must be completed at NIU.

Visiting: There are regularly scheduled orientations for prospective students, including open house programs, bus tours, faculty meetings, residence hall tours, and department receptions. There are guides for informal visits and visitors may sit in on classes and stay overnight. To schedule a visit, contact the Office of Orientation and Student Assistance at (815) 753-1535.

Financial Aid: 57% of full-time freshmen and 51% of continuing full-time students received need-based aid. Need-based scholarships or need-based grants averaged $6149 ($11,870 maximum); need-based self-help aid (loans and jobs) averaged $2676 ($7485 maximum); non-need-based athletic scholarships averaged $11,591 ($23,148 maximum); and other non-need-based awards and non-need-based scholarships averaged $3126 ($15,213 maximum). 30% of undergraduates work part time. Average annual earnings from campus work are $2925. The average financial indebtedness of the 2005 graduate was $17,168. The FAFSA and the college's own financial statement are required. The priority date for freshman financial aid applications for fall entry is March 1.

International Students: There are 128 international students enrolled. They must score satisfactorily on the written TOEFL.

Computers: All students may access the system. Computer labs are open more than 150 hours per week. There are no time limits and no fees.

Graduates: From July 1, 2004 to June 30, 2005, 3626 bachelor's degrees were awarded. The most popular majors were teacher education (11%), communication studies (7%), and accountancy (5%). In an average class, 23% graduate in 4 years or less, 48% graduate in 5 years or less, and 51% graduate in 6 years or less. 800 companies recruited on campus in 2004-2005. Of the 2004 graduating class, 19% were enrolled in graduate school within 6 months of graduation and 89% were employed.

Admissions Contact: Robert Burk, Director of Admissions.
E-mail: *admissions-info@niu.edu* Web: *http://www.niu.edu/*

NORTHWESTERN UNIVERSITY

E-1

Evanston, IL 60208   **(847) 491-7271**

Full-time: 3700 men, 4110 women	Faculty: 900; I, ++$
Part-time: 90 men, 120 women	Ph.D.s: 100%
Graduate: 4000 men, 2890 women	Student/Faculty: 9 to 1
Year: quarters, summer session	Tuition: $28,625
Application Deadline: see profile	Room & Board: $8970
Freshman Class: n/av	
SAT or ACT required	**MOST COMPETITIVE**

Northwestern University, founded in 1851, is an independent, nonprofit liberal arts institution offering undergraduate study in the arts and sciences, education and social policy, journalism, music, communication, and engineering and applied science. There are 6 undergraduate and 7 graduate schools. Figures in the above capsule and profile are approximate. In addition to regional accreditation, Northwestern has baccalaureate program accreditation with AACSB, ABET, ACEJMC, APTA, and NASM. The 3 libraries contain 4,315,314 volumes, 4,225,339 microform items, and 75,358 audio/video tapes/CDs/DVDs, and subscribe to 39,310 periodicals including electronic. Computerized library services include the card catalog, interlibrary loans, database searching, and Internet access. Special learning facilities include an art gallery, radio station, TV station, and an observatory. The 231-acre campus is in a suburban area 12 miles north of Chicago on the shores of Lake Michigan. Including any residence halls, there are 180 buildings.

Student Life: 75% of undergraduates are from out of state, mostly the Midwest. Students are from 50 states, 51 foreign countries, and Canada. 73% are from public schools. 60% are white; 17% Asian American. 33% are Protestant; 25% claim no religious affiliation; 23% Catholic; 16% Jewish. The average age of freshmen is 19; all undergraduates, 20. 3% do not continue beyond their first year; 93% remain to graduate.

Housing: 4250 students can be accommodated in college housing, which includes single-sex and coed dorms, fraternity houses, and sorority houses. In addition, there are special-interest houses. On-campus housing is guaranteed for the freshman year only. 65% of students live on campus; of those, 95% remain on campus on weekends. Upperclassmen may keep cars.

Activities: 30% of men belong to 22 national fraternities; 39% of women belong to 19 national sororities. There are 415 groups on campus, including art, band, cheerleading, chess, choir, chorale, chorus, dance, debate, drama, ethnic, film, gay, honors, international, jazz band, literary magazine, marching band, musical theater, newspaper, opera, orchestra, pep band, photography, political, professional, radio and TV, religious, social, social service, student government, symphony, and yearbook. Popular campus events include Waa-Mu Variety Show, Armadillo Day, and Dance Marathon.

Sports: There are 9 intercollegiate sports for men and 12 for women, and 21 intramural sports for men and 19 for women. Facilities include a stadium, an arena, a gym, lakefront playing fields for soccer, field hockey, and Frisbee, a boat house, and recreation and sports centers housing basketball, volleyball, tennis, racquetball, swimming, badminton, weight training, jogging, squash, fitness facilities, and a golf center.

Disabled Students: All of the campus is accessible. Wheelchair ramps, elevators, special parking, specially equipped rest rooms, special class scheduling, lowered drinking fountains, lowered telephones, and special housing are available.

Services: There is a reader service for the blind and one-on-one compensation, remediation, ADHD coaching, note taking, and real-time captioning.

Campus Safety and Security: Measures include 24-hour foot and vehicle patrol, self-defense education, security escort services, and shuttle buses. There are informal discussions, pamphlets/posters/films, emergency telephones, lighted pathways/sidewalks, and a security keycard system in residence halls.

Programs of Study: Northwestern confers B.A., B.S., B.A.C.M.N., B.A.Mus., B.M.E., B.Mus., B.Ph., B.P.H.C., B.S.A.M., B.S.B.M., B.S.C.H., B.S.C.I., B.S.C.M.N., B.S.C.O., B.S.C.S., B.S.Ed., B.S.E.E., B.S.E.N., B.S.E.S., B.S.G.E., B.S.G.S., B.S.I.E., B.S.J., B.S.M.,

B.S.M.D., B.S.M.E., B.S.M.F., B.S.M.T., B.S.S.E., and B.S.S.P. degrees. Master's and doctoral degrees are also awarded. Bachelor's degrees are awarded in BIOLOGICAL SCIENCE (biology/biological science, ecology, molecular biology, and neurosciences), BUSINESS (organizational behavior), COMMUNICATIONS AND THE ARTS (art, art history and appreciation, classics, communications, communications technology, comparative literature, dance, dramatic arts, English, fine arts, French, German, Italian, jazz, journalism, linguistics, music, music performance, music technology, music theory and composition, percussion, performing arts, piano/organ, radio/television technology, Slavic languages, Spanish, strings, voice, and winds), COMPUTER AND PHYSICAL SCIENCE (applied mathematics, astronomy, chemistry, computer science, geology, information sciences and systems, mathematics, physics, and statistics), EDUCATION (education, mathematics, music, and secondary), ENGINEERING AND ENVIRONMENTAL DESIGN (biomedical engineering, chemical engineering, civil engineering, computer engineering, electrical/electronics engineering, engineering, environmental engineering, environmental science, industrial engineering, manufacturing engineering, materials engineering, materials science, and mechanical engineering), HEALTH PROFESSIONS (premedicine and speech pathology/audiology), SOCIAL SCIENCE (African American studies, American studies, anthropology, cognitive science, economics, ethics, politics, and social policy, European studies, gender studies, geography, history, human development, international studies, philosophy, political science/government, psychology, religion, science and society, sociology, and urban studies). Journalism, communications, and physical and life sciences are the strongest academically. Economics, political science, and engineering are the largest.

Required: Requirements for graduation vary by school and degree program. Students must maintain a minimum 2.0 GPA and complete a total of 45 to 48 quarter units (courses).

Special: The university offers cooperative engineering programs throughout the country, many off-campus field studies and research opportunities, internships in the arts, journalism, and teaching, study abroad in 46 countries around the world, a Washington semester, and numerous work-study programs both on and off campus. There is an accelerated degree program in medical education, and B.A.-B.S. degrees in liberal arts and engineering, liberal arts and music, and music and engineering. An integrated science program, an interdisciplinary study in mathematical methods in social sciences and numerous other interdisciplinary majors, a variety of dual and student-designed majors, pass/fail options, and a teaching media program are also available. There are 23 national honor societies, including Phi Beta Kappa, a freshman honors program, and 40 departmental honors programs.

Faculty/Classroom: 71% of faculty are male; 29%, female. All both teach and do research. Graduate students teach 3% of introductory courses. The average class size in an introductory lecture is 35; in a laboratory, 14; and in a regular course, 22.

Requirements: The SAT or ACT is required. In addition, applicants must be graduates of an accredited secondary school or have a GED certificate, and have completed a minimum of 16 units, including 4 units of English, 3 of math, 2 or 3 each of a foreign language and history, and 2 of lab sciences. SAT: Subject tests are required for the accelerated honors program in medical education and the integrated science program. Auditions are required for applicants to the School of Music. AP credits are accepted. Important factors in the admissions decision are advanced placement or honor courses, recommendations by school officials, and extracurricular activities record.

Procedure: Freshmen are admitted to all sessions. Entrance exams should be taken by December of the senior year. There are early decision and deferred admissions plans. Early decision applications should be filed by November 1; regular applications, by January 1 for fall entry, November 1 for winter entry, February 1 for spring entry, and May 1 for summer entry, along with a $65 fee. Notification of early decision is sent December 15; regular decision, April 15. Applications are accepted online.

Transfer: 129 transfer students enrolled in a recent year. Transfer students need a minimum 3.0 GPA, SAT or ACT scores, high school record, 1 essay, and the dean's reference form. Applicants are required to have a minimum of 1 year of completed college work to apply to Northwestern. 23 of 45 credits required for the bachelor's degree must be completed at Northwestern.

Visiting: There are regularly scheduled orientations for prospective students, including daily information sessions Monday through Friday. There are guides for informal visits and visitors may sit in on classes and stay overnight. To schedule a visit, contact the Admission Office.

Financial Aid: In a recent year, 55% of all full-time freshmen and 60% of continuing full-time students received some form of financial aid. 45% of full-time freshmen and 50% of continuing full-time students received need-based aid. The average freshman award was $23,587. 32% of undergraduates worked part time. Average annual earnings from campus work were $1842. The average financial indebtedness of a recent graduate was $15,136. Northwestern is a member of CSS. The CSS/Profile or FAFSA and tax returns under certain conditions are required. Check with the school for current application deadlines.

International Students: In a recent year, there were 415 international students enrolled. The school actively recruits these students. They must score satisfactorily on the written TOEFL or on the electronic version and also take the SAT or the ACT.

Computers: All students may access the system 24 hours per day. There are no time limits and no fees. It is recommended that students in engineering have personal computers.

Graduates: In a recent year, 2022 bachelor's degrees were awarded. The most popular majors were engineering (15%), economics (11%), and journalism (7%). In an average class, 84% graduate in 4 years or less, 92% graduate in 5 years or less, and 93% graduate in 6 years or less. 350 companies recruited on campus in a recent year.

Admissions Contact: Carol Lunkenheimer, Dean of Undergraduate Admission. A video is available.
E-mail: *ug-admission@northwestern.edu*
Web: *www.ugadm.northwestern.edu*

OLIVET NAZARENE UNIVERSITY   E-2
Bourbonnais, IL 60914 (815) 939-5203
(800) 648-1463; Fax: (815) 935-4998

Full-time: 995 men, 1407 women	**Faculty:** 80; IIA, --$
Part-time: none	**Ph.D.s:** 74%
Graduate: 539 men, 1544 women	**Student/Faculty:** 30 to 1
Year: semesters, summer session	**Tuition:** $16,490
Application Deadline: May 15	**Room & Board:** $6100
Freshman Class: 2747 applied, 1758 accepted, 703 enrolled	
SAT Verbal/Math: 550/540*	**ACT:** 23 **COMPETITIVE**

Olivet Nazarene University, established in 1907, is a private comprehensive institution affiliated with the Church of the Nazarene. Its undergraduate and graduate programs emphasize the liberal arts, business, communication, health science, art and fine arts, engineering, music, Bible and relgious studies, and teacher preparation in an atmosphere of Christian culture. There are 5 undergraduate schools and 1 graduate school. In addition to regional accreditation, Olivet has baccalaureate program accreditation with ABET, ADA, CAAHEP, CCNE, CSWE, IACBE, NASM, NCATE and NLN. The library contains 529,092 volumes, 312,729 microform items, and 7703 audio/video tapes/CDs/DVDs, and subscribes to 12,100 periodicals including electronic. Computerized library services include the card catalog, interlibrary loans, database searching, Internet access, and laptop Internet portals. Special learning facilities include a learning resource center, art gallery, natural history museum, planetarium, radio station, TV station, smart board classrooms, a greenhouse, a solar telescope, and observation rooms. The 225-acre campus is in a suburban area 60 miles south of Chicago. Including any residence halls, there are 53 buildings.

Student Life: 55% of undergraduates are from out of state, mostly the Midwest. Students are from 40 states, 18 foreign countries, and Canada. 88% are white. 76% are Protestant; 13% Catholic. The average age of freshmen is 18; all undergraduates, 20. 25% do not continue beyond their first year; 51% remain to graduate.

Housing: 1550 students can be accommodated in college housing, which includes single-sex dorms, on-campus apartments, and married-student housing. In addition, there are honors houses. On-campus housing is guaranteed for all 4 years. 93% of students live on campus; of those, 80% remain on campus on weekends. Alcohol is not permitted. All students may keep cars.

Activities: There are no fraternities or sororities. There are 79 groups on campus, including art, Athletic Booster Club, band, cheerleading, choir, chorale, chorus, computers, drama, ethnic, FCA, film, honors, international, jazz band, literary magazine, marching band, newspaper, orchestra, pep band, photography, political, professional, radio and TV, religious, social, social service, student government, and yearbook. Popular campus events include Revival Services, TWIRP weekends, and the annual Christmas Banquet.

Sports: There are 9 intercollegiate sports for men and 8 for women, and 14 intramural sports for men and 14 for women. Facilities include a 3000-seat gym with basketball, volleyball, and racquetball courts, a pool, a weight-lifting room, and an indoor track; a 2500-seat stadium with a track; and an athletic park with softball, baseball, and soccer fields, a jogging track, track and field facilities, an ice rink, and tennis courts.

Disabled Students: 90% of the campus is accessible. Wheelchair ramps, elevators, special parking, specially equipped rest rooms, lowered drinking fountains, and lowered telephones are available.

Services: There is remedial math and writing. In addition to many counseling and information services, tutoring is available in economics, psychology, sociology, chemistry, and Old and New Testament studies.

Campus Safety and Security: Measures include 24-hour foot and vehicle patrol, security escort services, informal discussions, and pamphlets/posters/films. There are emergency telephones, lighted pathways/sidewalks, and an on-campus security service.

Programs of Study: Olivet confers B.A., B.S., B.A.T., and B.S.T. degrees. Associate and master's degrees are also awarded. Bachelor's degrees are awarded in BIOLOGICAL SCIENCE (biology/biological science and zoology), BUSINESS (accounting, business administration and management, and fashion merchandising), COMMUNICATIONS AND THE ARTS (art, English, music, romance languages and literature, and speech/debate/rhetoric), COMPUTER AND PHYSICAL SCIENCE (chemistry, computer science, geology, mathematics, physical sciences, and science technology), EDUCATION (Christian, early childhood, elementary, and physical), ENGINEERING AND ENVIRONMENTAL DESIGN (engineering, environmental design, and environmental science), HEALTH PROFESSIONS (clinical science and nursing), SOCIAL SCIENCE (dietetics, economics, family/consumer studies, history, liberal arts/general studies, philosophy, political science/government, psychology, public affairs, religion, social science, social work, and sociology). Engineering and physical science are the strongest academically. Business administration and education are the largest.

Required: To graduate, students must complete 128 semester hours of credit, with fulfillment of a major and a minimum of 40 hours of credit in upper-division courses, (50 to 64 in the major) and maintain a minimum GPA of 2.0. The required general education studies, 50 to 61 hours, include 12 credit hours of Christianity, 9 to 10 of communication, 7 to 11 of natural science and math, 9 of social sciences, 6 to 8 of international culture, 6 of literature and the arts, and 4 to 5 of personal health. Participation in the Senior Outcomes testing program in general education is required.

Special: Special academic programs include a work-study program, which can be arranged with other institutions, and a general studies degree. A 4-year engineering program (ABET) is available. There are 6 national honor societies and 5 departmental honors programs.

Faculty/Classroom: 57% of faculty are male; 43%, female.

Admissions: 64% of the 2005-2006 applicants were accepted. The SAT scores for the 2005-2006 freshman class were: Verbal--29% below 500, 39% between 500 and 599, 29% between 600 and 700, and 3% above 700; Math--30% below 500, 45% between 500 and 599, 19% between 600 and 700, and 6% above 700. The ACT scores were 29% below 21, 25% between 21 and 23, 26% between 24 and 26, 10% between 27 and 28, and 10% above 28.

Requirements: The ACT is required. With a minimum score. Olivet requires graduation from an accredited secondary school. Olivet does not have any specific high school course requirements, but there are some suggestions for high school courses. College preparatory courses, completed with a C or above, are recommended. In general, you should have 3 years of English, and 2 years each of math, foreign language and natural or social science. To enroll in the nursing program, you need 1 year of biology and 1 year of chemistry. In choosing high school courses, you should also take into consideration the career/major you intend to pursue. The GED is accepted. 2 certificates of recommendation must be submitted along with an application. Olivet requires applicants to be in the upper 50% of their class. A GPA of 2.0 is required. AP and CLEP credits are accepted.

Procedure: Freshmen are admitted fall, spring, and summer. Entrance exams should be taken during the spring of the junior year or during the senior year. There is a rolling admissions plan. Applications should be filed by May 15 for fall entry and December 1 for spring entry. Notification is sent on a rolling basis. Applications are accepted on-line.

Transfer: 272 transfer students enrolled in 2004-2005. Transcripts of all college work must be submitted. 30 of 128 credits required for the bachelor's degree must be completed at Olivet.

Visiting: There are regularly scheduled orientations for prospective students, including class visits, financial aid, information tour, lunch, professor meetings, and an optional overnight stay. There are guides for informal visits and visitors may sit in on classes and stay overnight. To schedule a visit, contact Jean Milton, the Campus Visit Coordinator in the Admissions Office at jmilton@olivet.edu.

Financial Aid: In 2005-2006, 99% of all full-time freshmen and 97% of continuing full-time students received some form of financial aid. 77% of full-time freshmen and 69% of continuing full-time students received need-based aid. The average freshman award was $19,670. Need-based scholarships or need-based grants averaged $4979 ($8971 maximum); need-based self-help aid (loans and jobs) averaged $1944 ($5125 maximum); non-need-based athletic scholarships averaged $479 ($16,590 maximum); and other non-need-based awards and non-need-based scholarships averaged $4446 ($21,640 maximum). 29% of undergraduates work part time. Average annual earnings from campus work are $1099. The average financial indebtedness of the 2005 graduate was $16,325. The FAFSA and the college's own financial statement are required. The deadline for filing freshman financial aid applications for fall entry is March 1.

International Students: There are 31 international students enrolled. A satisfactory score is required on the written TOEFL. Students must also take the ACT, scoring 17.

Computers: Wireless access is available. Data network connections exist in all of the residence hall rooms and university owned apartments. Students must use PCs equipped with Ethernet cards to access the Internet from these locations. Olivet Nazarene University provides SBC Global high-speed Internet access and campus connectivity to your residential computer, lab computer, faculty office or employee workstation, and virtually any place else on campus. All students may access the system. There are no time limits and no fees. It is strongly recommended that all students have a PC. An Intel Pentium IV 2.8 GHz, AMD Athlon XP 2800+, or Macintosh G5 is recommended.

Graduates: From July 1, 2004 to June 30, 2005, 455 bachelor's degrees were awarded. The most popular majors were elementary education (8%), nursing (7%), and business/marketing (6%). In an average class, 52% graduate in 6 years or less. Of the 2004 graduating class, 24% were enrolled in graduate school within 6 months of graduation and 64% were employed.

Admissions Contact: Brian Parker, Director of Admissions.
E-mail: *admissions@olivet.edu* Web: *http://www.olivet.edu*

PRINCIPIA COLLEGE   C-4

Elsah, IL 62028   (618) 374-5181
                                   (800) 277-4648; Fax: (618) 374-4000

Full-time: 254 men, 282 women	**Faculty:** 55; IIB, -$
Part-time: none	**Ph.D.s:** 68%
Graduate: none	**Student/Faculty:** 10 to 1
Year: quarters	**Tuition:** $20,415
Application Deadline: March 1	**Room & Board:** $7350
Freshman Class: 242 applied, 216 accepted, 139 enrolled	
SAT or ACT: required	**VERY COMPETITIVE+**

Principia College, founded in 1910, is a private liberal arts and sciences college for Christian Scientists. It is the only college in the world strictly for Christian Scientists. In addition to regional accreditation, Prin has baccalaureate program accreditation with NCATE. The library contains 217,257 volumes, 115,665 microform items, and 4847 audio/video tapes/CDs/DVDs, and subscribes to 12,813 periodicals including electronic. Computerized library services include the card catalog, interlibrary loans, database searching, and Internet access. Special learning facilities include a learning resource center, art gallery, planetarium, radio station, and TV station. The 2600-acre campus is in a rural area 30 miles northeast of St. Louis. Including any residence halls, there are 33 buildings.

Student Life: 90% of undergraduates are from out of state, mostly the Midwest. Others are from 34 states, 27 foreign countries, and Canada. 61% are from public schools. 81% are white; 15% foreign nationals. The average age of freshmen is 18; all undergraduates, 20. 12% do not continue beyond their first year; 75% remain to graduate.

Housing: 625 students can be accommodated in college housing, which includes single-sex dormitories, on-campus apartments, and married-student housing. In addition, there are language houses and special-interest houses. On-campus housing is guaranteed for all 4 years. 99% of students live on campus; of those, All remain on campus on weekends. Alcohol is not permitted. All students may keep cars.

Activities: There are no fraternities or sororities. There are 34 groups on campus, including art, cheerleading, choir, chorus, computers, dance, drama, ethnic, honors, international, jazz band, literary magazine, musical theater, newspaper, orchestra, photography, political, radio and TV, religious, social, social service, student government, and yearbook. Popular campus events include athletic events, dances, and drama and dance performances.

Sports: There are 8 intercollegiate sports for men and 7 for women, and 3 intramural sports for men and 3 for women. Facilities include 2 gyms, a pool, indoor and outdoor tennis courts, a racquetball court, basketball/volleyball courts, a dance studio, a weight room, baseball, football, soccer, and practice fields, and a 6-lane track.

Disabled Students: 80% of the campus is accessible. Wheelchair ramps, elevators, special parking, specially equipped rest rooms, and lowered drinking fountains are available.

Services: There is remedial reading and writing. Assistance in study skills is available.

Campus Safety and Security: Measures include 24-hour foot and vehicle patrol, informal discussions, emergency telephones, and lighted pathways/sidewalks.

Programs of Study: Prin confers B.A. and B.S. degrees. Bachelor's degrees are awarded in BIOLOGICAL SCIENCE (biology/biological science), BUSINESS (business administration and management and sports management), COMMUNICATIONS AND THE ARTS (communications, dramatic arts, English, fine arts, French, languages, music, Spanish, and studio art), COMPUTER AND PHYSICAL SCIENCE (chemistry, computer science, mathematics, and physics), EDUCATION (elementary), ENGINEERING AND ENVIRONMENTAL DESIGN (environmental science), SOCIAL SCIENCE (economics, German area studies, history, international relations, philosophy, political science/government, religion, and sociology). Education, studio art, and biology are the strongest academically. Business administration, studio art, and education are the largest.

Required: All students must complete a minimum of 180 quarter hours, with 45 to 93 quarter hours in the major (10 to 15 courses) and at least a 2.0 overall GPA. Courses in foreign language, literature, arts, religion and philosophy, history, social science, math, and natural sciences are required. In addition, students must be certified as proficient in written English, pass a moral reasoning seminar, earn 4 credits in individual and team phys ed activities, and pass a survival swim test.

Special: Students may design their own majors, study abroad or in San Francisco, or pursue a B.A.-B.S. degree. Internships, student-planned with a professor, independent study, work-study, and an interdisciplinary major, global studies, are available. A 3-2 engineering program with Washington University in St. Louis, Southern Illinois University at Carbondale, the University of Southern California, or another university with approval is also possible. A San Francisco field program in business administration is offered. There is 1 national honor society, a freshman honors program, and 3 departmental honors program.

Faculty/Classroom: 60% of faculty are male; 40%, female. All teach undergraduates and 60% do research. The average class size in an introductory lecture is 13; in a laboratory, 12; and in a regular course, 10.

Admissions: 89% of the 2005-2006 applicants were accepted. 48% of the current freshmen were in the top fifth of their class; 68% were in the top two fifths. There was 1 National Merit finalist and 3 semifinalists. 2 freshmen graduated first in their class.

Requirements: The SAT or ACT is required; the SAT is preferred. An essay is required. SAT: Subject tests in foreign language and math are recommended. High school preparation should include 4 years of English, 3 of math (including algebra II), 2 to 3 of a foreign language, 2 of natural sciences, history or social sciences, and electives. A GPA of 2.3 is required. AP and CLEP credits are accepted. Important factors in the admissions decision are advanced placement or honor courses, recommendations by school officials, and recommendations by alumni.

Procedure: Freshmen are admitted fall and winter. Entrance exams should be taken in the spring of the junior year and again in the fall of the senior year. There is a deferred admissions and a rolling admissions plan. Early decision applications should be filed by November 15; regular applications, by March 1 for fall entry, November 1 for winter entry, and March 1 for spring entry. The application deadline for students applying for an academic merit scholarship is January 15. Notification of early decision is sent December 1; regular decision March 15. Applications are accepted on-line.

Transfer: 17 transfer students enrolled in 2004-2005. Applicants must be in good standing at their previous college or university. 45 of 180 quarter hours required for the bachelor's degree must be completed at Prin.

Visiting: There are regularly scheduled orientations for prospective students, including a visit to classes, meeting professors, living in a dorm, and meeting students (3-day weekend). There are guides for informal visits and visitors may sit in on classes and stay overnight. To schedule a visit, contact Alison Reid at (618) 374-5175 (800) 277-4648 ext.2804 or *alison.reid@principia.edu.*

Financial Aid: In 2005-2006, 86% of all full-time students received some form of financial aid. 62% of full-time freshmen and 58% of continuing full-time students received need-based aid. The average freshman award was $19,801. Need-based scholarships or need-based grants averaged $13,552 ($27,265 maximum); need-based self-help aid (loans and jobs) averaged $5169 ($7500 maximum); and other non-need-based awards and non-need-based scholarships averaged $10,254 ($20,140 maximum). 52% of undergraduates work part time. Average annual earnings from campus work are $1368. The average financial indebtedness of the 2005 graduate was $12,740. Prin is a member of CSS. The CSS/Profile and the college's own financial statement are required. The priority date for freshman financial aid applications for fall entry is March 1. The deadline for filing freshman financial aid applications for fall entry is June 1.

International Students: There are 61 international students enrolled. The school actively recruits these students. Satisfactory scores are required on the written TOEFL and the SAT or the ACT.

Computers: All students may access the system 24 hours a day.

Graduates: In a recent year, 121 bachelor's degrees were awarded. The most popular majors in a recent year were business administration (17%), studio art (13%), and mass communication (7%). In an average class, 74% graduate in 4 years, 72% graduate in 5 years, and 78% graduate in 6 years. 20 companies recruited on campus in 2004-2005. Of the 2004 graduating class, 7% were enrolled in graduate school within 6 months of graduation and 92% were employed.

Admissions Contact: Martha Green Quirk, Dean of Admissions. A video is available. E-mail: *martha.quirk@principia.edu*
Web: *www.prin.edu/college/admissions*

QUINCY UNIVERSITY   B-3

Quincy, IL 62301-2699   (217) 228-5210
(800) 688-4295; Fax: (217) 228-5479

Full-time: 407 men, 520 women	**Faculty:** 54; IIB, --$
Part-time: 57 men, 91 women	**Ph.D.s:** 83%
Graduate: 79 men, 205 women	**Student/Faculty:** 17 to 1
Year: semesters, summer session	**Tuition:** $18,330
Application Deadline: open	**Room & Board:** $6590
Freshman Class: 986 applied, 926 accepted, 202 enrolled	
SAT or ACT: 23	**COMPETITIVE**

Quincy University, established in 1860, is a private liberal arts institution conducted by the Franciscan Friars of the Roman Catholic Church. There are 3 undergraduate and 2 graduate schools. In addition to regional accreditation, Quincy has baccalaureate program accreditation with NLN. The library contains 202,142 volumes, 188,589 microform items, and 6065 audio/video tapes/CDs/DVDs, and subscribes to 455 periodicals including electronic. Computerized library services include the card catalog, interlibrary loans, database searching, and Internet access. Special learning facilities include a learning resource center, art gallery, radio station, and TV station. The 75-acre campus is in a small town 120 miles north of St. Louis. Including any residence halls, there are 41 buildings.

Student Life: 71% of undergraduates are from Illinois. Others are from 26 states, 6 foreign countries, and Canada. 48% are from public schools. 78% are white. 52% are Catholic; 21% claim no religious affiliation; 20% Protestant. The average age of freshmen is 18; all undergraduates, 23. 31% do not continue beyond their first year; 55% remain to graduate.

Housing: 831 students can be accommodated in college housing, which includes single-sex and coed dorms, on-campus apartments, married-student housing, fraternity houses, and sorority houses. In addition, there are special-interest houses. On-campus housing is guaranteed for all 4 years. 70% of students live on campus; of those, 80% remain on campus on weekends. All students may keep cars.

Activities: 4% of men belong to 1 national fraternity; 11% of women belong to 2 national sororities. There are 43 groups on campus, including band, cheerleading, choir, chorale, chorus, computers, dance, drama, honors, international, jazz band, literary magazine, musical theater, newspaper, opera, orchestra, pep band, political, professional, radio and TV, religious, social, social service, student government, and symphony. Popular campus events include Fall Fest, Hawk Pride Weekend, and Septemberfest.

Sports: There are 9 intercollegiate sports for men and 8 for women, and 11 intramural sports for men and 11 for women. Facilities include a health and fitness center, 2 gyms, a football/baseball stadium, a soccer stadium, a weight room, a college athletic field, and outdoor basketball/volleyball courts.

Disabled Students: 95% of the campus is accessible. Wheelchair ramps, elevators, special parking, specially equipped rest rooms, special class scheduling, lowered drinking fountains, and lowered telephones are available.

Services: Counseling and information services are available, as is tutoring in every subject. There is a reader service for the blind and remedial math and writing. Skill development and motivation workshops and courses are available.

Campus Safety and Security: Measures include 24-hour foot and vehicle patrol, self-defense education, security escort services, and shuttle buses. There are informal discussions, pamphlets/posters/films, emergency telephones, and lighted pathways/sidewalks.

Programs of Study: Quincy confers B.A., B.S., B.F.A., and B.S.N. degrees. Associate and master's degrees are also awarded. Bachelor's degrees are awarded in BIOLOGICAL SCIENCE (biology/biological science), BUSINESS (accounting, banking and finance, business administration and management, marketing/retailing/merchandising, and sports management), COMMUNICATIONS AND THE ARTS (art, communications, English, music, and music business management), COMPUTER AND PHYSICAL SCIENCE (chemistry, computer science, information sciences and systems, and mathematics), EDUCATION (elementary, music, physical, science, secondary, and special), ENGINEERING AND ENVIRONMENTAL DESIGN (aviation administration/management), HEALTH PROFESSIONS (medical laboratory technology and nursing), SOCIAL SCIENCE (criminal justice, history, human services, humanities, interpreter for the deaf, political science/government, psychology, religious education, and social work). Business, education, and science are the strongest academically. Elementary education, nursing, and management are the largest.

Required: Each student is required to complete a minimum of 124 credit hours, with at least 27 in the major and average of 36 in upper-level courses. In addition, students must complete required courses in rhetoric, science or math, social sciences, humanities, fine arts, theology, and phys ed; complete a senior comprehensive seminar; and maintain a minimum GPA of 2.0.

Special: Dual majors, study abroad in 27 countries, credit by exam, and upper-class and early exploratory internships are available. Pass/fail options, credit for life experience, student-designed majors, and a 3-2 degree with Washington University in St. Louis are also offered. There are 6 national honor societies, a freshman honors program, and 5 departmental honors programs.

Faculty/Classroom: 57% of faculty are male; 43%, female. All teach undergraduates. No introductory courses are taught by graduate students. The average class size in an introductory lecture is 40; in a laboratory, 20; and in a regular course, 20.

Admissions: 94% of the 2005-2006 applicants were accepted. The ACT scores for the 2005-2006 freshman class were: 36% below 21, 35% between 21 and 23, 20% between 24 and 26, 6% between 27 and 28, and 3% above 28. 23% of the current freshmen were in the top fifth of their class; 51% were in the top two fifths. 2 freshmen graduated first in their class.

Requirements: The SAT or ACT is required. The GED is accepted. College preparatory courses totaling 16 credits should include 4 years of English, 3 each of math and science, and 2 each of a foreign language, history, and social studies. Art students must submit a portfolio, and music students are required to audition. AP and CLEP credits are accepted. Important factors in the admissions decision are leadership record, evidence of special talent, and recommendations by school officials.

Procedure: Freshmen are admitted fall and spring. Entrance exams should be taken in October of the senior year. There is a deferred admissions and a rolling admissions plan. Application deadlines are open. Application fee is $25. Applications are accepted on-line.

Transfer: 100 transfer students enrolled in a recent year. Applicants must have a minimum GPA of 2.0. Grades of C or better transfer for credit. 30 of 124 credits required for the bachelor's degree must be completed at Quincy.

Visiting: There are regularly scheduled orientations for prospective students, including weekend advising and registration programs throughout the summer. There are guides for informal visits and visitors may sit in on classes and stay overnight. To schedule a visit, contact the Admissions Office at (800) 688-4295.

Financial Aid: In 2005-2006, 99% of all full-time freshmen and 95% of continuing full-time students received some form of financial aid. 82% of full-time freshmen and 89% of continuing full-time students received need-based aid. The average freshman award was $17,635. 43% of undergraduates work part time. Average annual earnings from campus work are $1050. The average financial indebtedness of the 2005 graduate was $17,000. Quincy is a member of CSS. The FAFSA and are required. The priority date for freshman financial aid applications for fall entry is February 15.

International Students: There are 12 international students enrolled. The school actively recruits these students. They must score satisfactorily on the written TOEFL and also take the SAT or the ACT.

Computers: Wireless access is available. Students have unlimited access to the univeristy's network which includes 9 computer labs, a learning center, 190 PCs and network connections in all residence halls. All students may access the system. There are no time limits and no fees. It is strongly recommended that all students have a personal computer.

Graduates: From July 1, 2004 to June 30, 2005, 228 bachelor's degrees were awarded. The most popular majors were elementary education (14%), nursing (13%), and marketing (7%). In an average class, 37% graduate in 4 years or less, 52% graduate in 5 years or less, and 55% graduate in 6 years or less. 38 companies recruited on campus in 2004-2005. Of the 2004 graduating class, 20% were enrolled in graduate school within 6 months of graduation and 75% were employed.

Admissions Contact: Mark Clynes, VP for Enrollment Management. E-mail: clynes@quincy.edu Web: www.quincy.edu

ROCKFORD COLLEGE	D-1
Rockford, IL 61108	**(815) 226-4140**
	(800) 892-2984; Fax: (815) 226-4169

Full-time: 290 men, 415 women	**Faculty:** 80
Part-time: 85 men, 120 women	**Ph.D.s:** 45%
Graduate: 215 men, 305 women	**Student/Faculty:** 9 to 1
Year: semesters, summer session	**Tuition:** $20,220
Application Deadline: open	**Room & Board:** $8110
Freshman Class: n/av	
ACT: required	**SAT:** not required
	VERY COMPETITIVE

Rockford College, founded in 1847, is a private institution offering undergraduate and graduate instruction in liberal arts and professional programs. Figures in the above capsule and in this profile are approximate. In addition to regional accreditation, Rockford College has baccalaureate program accreditation with NLN. The library contains 167,983 volumes, 7590 microform items, and 9855 audio/video tapes/CDs/DVDs, and subscribes to 815 periodicals including electronic. Computerized library services include the card catalog, interlibrary loans, and database searching. Special learning facilities include a learning resource center and art gallery. The 130-acre campus is in a suburban area 90 miles west of Chicago. Including any residence halls, there are 26 buildings.

Student Life: 88% of undergraduates are from Illinois. Others are from 9 states and 2 foreign countries. 75% are from public schools. 83% are white. The average age of freshmen is 18; all undergraduates, 23. 36% do not continue beyond their first year.

Housing: 560 students can be accommodated in college housing, which includes single-sex and coed dorms. In addition, there are special-interest houses. On-campus housing is guaranteed for all 4 years. 64% of students commute. All students may keep cars.

Activities: There are no fraternities or sororities. There are 28 groups on campus, including art, cheerleading, chorus, computers, dance, drama, ethnic, gay, honors, international, literary magazine, musical theater, newspaper, political, professional, religious, social, social service, and student government. Popular campus events include Snowball Dance, Kids and Sibs Weekend, and Family Weekend.

Sports: There are 6 intercollegiate sports for men and 5 for women, and 12 intramural sports for men and 12 for women. Facilities include a swimming pool, athletic fields, tennis courts, and a fitness center with free weights and Nautilus weight rooms.

Disabled Students: 85% of the campus is accessible. Wheelchair ramps, elevators, special parking, specially equipped rest rooms, special class scheduling, lowered drinking fountains, and lowered telephones are available.

Services: Counseling and information services are available, as is tutoring in most subjects. There is a reader service for the blind, and remedial math, reading, and writing. Diagnostic testing is available.

Campus Safety and Security: Measures include 24-hour foot and vehicle patrol, security escort services, informal discussions, and pamphlets/posters/films. There are emergency telephones and lighted pathways/sidewalks.

Programs of Study: Rockford College confers B.A., B.S., B.F.A., and B.S.N. degrees. Master's degrees are also awarded. Bachelor's degrees are awarded in BIOLOGICAL SCIENCE (biology/biological science), BUSINESS (accounting and business administration and management), COMMUNICATIONS AND THE ARTS (art, art history and appreciation, classical languages, dramatic arts, English, fine arts, French, German, music, and Spanish), COMPUTER AND PHYSICAL SCIENCE (chemistry, computer science, mathematics, and science), EDUCATION (athletic training, early childhood, elementary, and physical), ENGINEERING AND ENVIRONMENTAL DESIGN (military science and preengineering), HEALTH PROFESSIONS (nursing, predentistry, premedicine, prepharmacy, and preveterinary science), SOCIAL SCIENCE (anthropology, criminal justice, economics, history, human services, humanities, philosophy, political science/government, prelaw, psychology, religion, social science, social work, sociology, and urban studies). Business, education, and psychology are the largest.

Required: To graduate, students must have a total of at least 124 credit hours and a minimum GPA of 2.0 (nursing 2.5). The required hours for each major varies between 28 and 44. Students are required to take 12 hours of social sciences, 8 to 12 of science, math, and computer science, 8 of language and literature, 6 to 9 of freshman English, 6 of art, and 2 hours each of phys ed. Requirements for some degree programs may vary. All students must complete a senior seminar or project and must demonstrate proficiency in writing or public speaking, either by exam or by enrollment in a course that meets the requirement.

Special: The school offers junior and senior year internships, study abroad in 9 countries, a Washington semester at American University, and work-study programs. Dual majors, student-designed majors, non-degree study, and a 3-2 engineering degree with Washington University in St. Louis, the Universities of Southern California and Illinois, and Illinois Institute of Technology also are available. There are 5 national honor societies, including Phi Beta Kappa and a freshman honors program.

Faculty/Classroom: 57% of faculty are male; 43%, female. All teach undergraduates. No introductory courses are taught by graduate students. The average class size in an introductory lecture is 25; in a laboratory, 12; and in a regular course, 18.

Requirements: The ACT is required. Applicants must graduate from an accredited secondary school or demonstrate satisfactory scores on the GED. 16 academic credits are required, including 4 years of English, 2 of math, and 1 each of a foreign language, history, and laboratory science. An essay and an interview are recommended. For performing arts students, an audition is recommended. Rockford College requires applicants to be in the upper 50% of their class. A GPA of 2.65 is required. AP and CLEP credits are accepted. Important factors in the admissions decision are advanced placement or honor courses, recommendations by school officials, and leadership record.

Procedure: Freshmen are admitted to all sessions. Entrance exams should be taken by the fall of the senior year. There are deferred admissions and rolling admissions plans. Application deadlines are open. Application fee is $35.

Transfer: Applicants must have a minimum GPA of 2.2. Nursing transfer students' minimum GPA is 2.5. 30 of 124 credits required for the bachelor's degree must be completed at Rockford College.

Visiting: There are regularly scheduled orientations for prospective students, consisting of a tour, a meeting with faculty members and other students, class visits, and social/athletic programs. A week-long orientation program is required for all freshmen the week before fall classes begin. There are guides for informal visits and visitors may sit in on classes and stay overnight. To schedule a visit, contact the Admissions Office.

Financial Aid: In a recent year, 98% of all full-time students received some form of financial aid. 28% of undergraduates worked part time. Average annual earnings from campus work were $1500. The FAFSA is required. Check with school for current application deadlines.

International Students: The school actively recruits these students. They must score satisfactorily on the written TOEFL. Students can be conditionally admitted, then tested for English proficiency at the school's English Language Study Center.

Computers: All students may access the system. There are no time limits and no fees. It is strongly recommended that all students have a personal computer.

Admissions Contact: Anna Krug, Assistant Vice President for Public Affairs and Strategic Market. A video is available.
E-mail: *akrug@rockford.edu* Web: *www.rockford.edu*

ROOSEVELT UNIVERSITY E-2

Chicago, IL 60605

(847) 619-8620
(877) APPLYRU; Fax: (847) 619-8636

Full-time: 680 men, 1180 women	**Faculty:** 190; IIA, +$
Part-time: 745 men, 1695 women	**Ph.D.s:** 85%
Graduate: 1035 men, 2205 women	**Student/Faculty:** 10 to 1
Year: semesters, summer session	**Tuition:** $15,445
Application Deadline: open	**Room & Board:** $7160
Freshman Class: n/av	
SAT or ACT: required	**VERY COMPETITIVE**

Roosevelt University, founded in 1945, an independent, comprehensive university. Figures in the above capsule and in this profile are approximate. There are 5 undergraduate and 5 graduate schools. In addition to regional accreditation, Roosevelt has baccalaureate program accreditation with AACSB, NASM, and NCATE. The 2 libraries contain 405,022 volumes, 130,233 microform items, and 10,000 audio/video tapes/CDs/DVDs, and subscribe to 1601 periodicals including electronic. Computerized library services include the card catalog, interlibrary loans, and database searching. Special learning facilities include a learning resource center and radio station. The campus is in an urban area downtown Chicago. Including any residence halls, there are 2 buildings.

Student Life: 90% of undergraduates are from Illinois. Others are from 24 states, 70 foreign countries, and Canada. 44% are white; 27% African American; 12% Hispanic; 10% foreign nationals. The average age of freshmen is 21; all undergraduates, 27.

Housing: 300 students can be accommodated in college housing, which includes coed dorms. On-campus housing is available on a first-come, first-served basis. 94% of students commute.

Activities: 1% of men belong to 1 local fraternity; 1% of women belong to 1 local sorority. There are 45 groups on campus, including band, choir, chorale, chorus, computers, cultural, drama, ethnic, honors, international, jazz band, literary magazine, model United Nations, musical theater, newspaper, opera, orchestra, political, professional, radio and TV, religious, social service, student government, and symphony.

Sports: There is 1 intramural sport for men and 1 for women. Facilities include a fitness center and a recreational gym for basketball, volleyball, soccer, and intramural activities.

Disabled Students: All of the campus is accessible. Wheelchair ramps, elevators, specially equipped rest rooms, special class scheduling, and lowered telephones are available. For special needs, contact the Disabled Student Services Office.

Services: Counseling and information services are available, as is tutoring in most subjects. There is remedial math, reading, and writing, arranged counseling, and testing. Emphasis is placed on individual program planning.

Campus Safety and Security: Measures include shuttle buses and lighted pathways/sidewalks.

Programs of Study: Roosevelt confers B.A., B.S., B.A.Comp.Sci., B.A.Ed., B.F.A.Mus.Theater, B.G.S., B.M., B.S.B.A., B.S. in Hospitality Mgt., and B.S.Telecomm. degrees. Master's and doctoral degrees are also awarded. Bachelor's degrees are awarded in BIOLOGICAL SCIENCE (biology/biological science), BUSINESS (accounting, banking and finance, business administration and management, hotel/motel and restaurant management, insurance, insurance and risk management, management science, marketing/retailing/merchandising, and personnel management), COMMUNICATIONS AND THE ARTS (advertising, art history and appreciation, broadcasting, communications, dramatic arts, English, French, guitar, jazz, journalism, languages, literature, media arts, music, music history and appreciation, music performance, music theory and composition, musical theater, percussion, performing arts, piano/organ, public relations, Spanish, strings, telecommunications, theater design, theater management, voice, and winds), COMPUTER AND PHYS-

ICAL SCIENCE (actuarial science, chemistry, computer science, information sciences and systems, mathematics, and statistics), EDUCATION (early childhood, elementary, music, and secondary), ENGINEERING AND ENVIRONMENTAL DESIGN (electrical/electronics engineering technology and environmental science), HEALTH PROFESSIONS (allied health, medical technology, nuclear medical technology, predentistry, premedicine, prepharmacy, and preveterinary science), SOCIAL SCIENCE (African American studies, American studies, economics, history, international studies, liberal arts/general studies, philosophy, political science/government, prelaw, psychology, public administration, social science, sociology, urban studies, and women's studies). Journalism, accounting, and psychology are the strongest academically.

Required: For graduation, students must complete 120 credit hours, including 54 in the major, with a minimum GPA of 2.0, or 2.5 in the College of Education. The core curriculum consists of courses in the social sciences, natural sciences, and humanities, including English 101 and 102. The last 54 hours must be from a 4-year school.

Special: Roosevelt offers internships in approximately 20 subject areas, on-campus work-study, study abroad in 4 countries, dual and student-designed majors, pass/fail options, and noncredit courses. Adults older than 25 years of age may earn a Bachelor of General Studies through an accelerated degree program. Credit for life, military, and work experience is available in some majors through continuing education. The Roosevelt Scholars Program is offered. There are 4 national honor societies, a freshman honors program, and 20 departmental honors programs.

Faculty/Classroom: All teach undergraduates. No introductory courses are taught by graduate students.

Requirements: The SAT or ACT is required. In addition, students must have completed 15 academic units, including 4 of English, 3 of math, 2 each of science, social studies, and foreign language, and 1 each of history and electives. An interview is recommended for all applicants, and an audition is required for music and theater candidates. Roosevelt requires applicants to be in the upper 50% of their class. A GPA of 2.3 is required. AP and CLEP credits are accepted. Important factors in the admissions decision are advanced placement or honor courses, evidence of special talent, and extracurricular activities record.

Procedure: Freshmen are admitted to all sessions. There are early decision, early admissions, deferred admissions and rolling admissions plans. Application deadlines are open. Applications are accepted on-line. The fall 2005 application fee was $25.

Transfer: Applicants must have earned a minimum GPA of 2.0 in all accredited college course work. Offical transcripts must be received from each college where course work was attempted. 30 of 120 credits required for the bachelor's degree must be completed at Roosevelt.

Visiting: There are regularly scheduled orientations for prospective students, including open houses and Transfer Days. There are guides for informal visits and visitors may sit in on classes. To schedule a visit, contact the Undergraduate Admissions Office.

Financial Aid: In a recent year, 85% of all full-time freshmen and 65% of continuing full-time students received some form of financial aid. 75% of full-time freshmen and 65% of continuing full-time students received need-based aid. The average freshman award was $10,500. Need-based scholarships or need-based grants averaged $7725; need-based self-help aid (loans and jobs) averaged $7170; and other non-need-based awards and non-need-based scholarships averaged $5220. The FAFSA and the college's own financial statement are required. Check with the school for current application deadlines.

International Students: The school actively recruits these students. They must score satisfactorily on the written TOEFL and also take the college's own test.

Computers: All students may access the system. Students may access the system 1 hour when demand is great. There are no fees.

Admissions Contact: Gwen Kanelos, Assistant Vice President for Enrollment Services. E-mail: *applyru@roosevelt.edu*
Web: *www.roosevelt.edu*

SAINT XAVIER UNIVERSITY E-2

Chicago, IL 60655

(773) 298-3050
(800) 462-9288; Fax: (773) 298-3076

Full-time: 705 men, 1630 women	**Faculty:** 160; IIA, av$
Part-time: 170 men, 565 women	**Ph.D.s:** 86%
Graduate: 510 men, 1995 women	**Student/Faculty:** 15 to 1
Year: semesters, summer session	**Tuition:** $16,690
Application Deadline: see profile	**Room & Board:** $6470
Freshman Class: n/av	
ACT: required	**COMPETITIVE**

Saint Xavier University is a private institution founded by the Sisters of Mercy in 1846 and affiliated with the Roman Catholic Church. There are 4 undergraduate and 4 graduate schools. Figures in the above capsule and this profile are approximate. In addition to regional accreditation, SXU has baccalaureate program accreditation with NASM and NLN. The library contains 172,104 volumes, 10,519 microform items, and

2282 audio/video tapes/CDs/DVDs, and subscribes to 798 periodicals including electronic. Computerized library services include the card catalog, interlibrary loans, database searching, and Internet access. Special learning facilities include a learning resource center, art gallery, and radio station. The 70-acre campus is in an urban area 15 miles southwest of Chicago's loop. Including any residence halls, there are 16 buildings.

Student Life: 96% of undergraduates are from Illinois. Others are from 21 states and 4 foreign countries. 50% are from public schools. 63% are white; 18% African American; 11% Hispanic. 80% are Catholic; 16% Protestant. The average age of freshmen is 18; all undergraduates, 23. 24% do not continue beyond their first year.

Housing: 630 students can be accommodated in college housing, which includes single-sex and coed dorms. On-campus housing is guaranteed for all 4 years. 81% of students commute. Alcohol is not permitted. All students may keep cars.

Activities: There are no fraternities or sororities. There are 37 groups on campus, including art, band, cheerleading, choir, chorus, computers, drama, ethnic, honors, international, jazz band, literary magazine, marching band, musical theater, newspaper, pep band, political, professional, radio and TV, religious, social service, student government, and yearbook. Popular campus events include Xavierfest, Boat Bash, and Octoberfest.

Sports: There are 4 intercollegiate sports for men and 5 for women, and 4 intramural sports for men and 4 for women. Facilities include baseball and softball diamonds, an outdoor sports facility, and a football field. The convocation and athletic center seats 2200 in the main arena with 4 additional competition courts. It also has racquetball courts, an indoor running track, training rooms, and a health and fitness center.

Disabled Students: 98% of the campus is accessible. Wheelchair ramps, elevators, special parking, specially equipped rest rooms, special class scheduling, lowered drinking fountains, and lowered telephones are available.

Services: Counseling and information services are available, as is tutoring in every subject. There are reading and language clinics and a center for learning disabilities.

Campus Safety and Security: Measures include 24-hour foot and vehicle patrol, self-defense education, security escort services, and shuttle buses. There are emergency telephones and lighted pathways/sidewalks.

Programs of Study: SXU confers B.A., B.S., and B.M. degrees. Master's degrees are also awarded. Bachelor's degrees are awarded in BIOLOGICAL SCIENCE (biology/biological science), BUSINESS (accounting, banking and finance, business administration and management, international business management, and marketing/retailing/merchandising), COMMUNICATIONS AND THE ARTS (communications, English, French, music, and Spanish), COMPUTER AND PHYSICAL SCIENCE (chemistry, computer science, and mathematics), EDUCATION (art, early childhood, elementary, foreign languages, middle school, music, science, and secondary), HEALTH PROFESSIONS (nursing, predentistry, premedicine, prepharmacy, and speech pathology/audiology), SOCIAL SCIENCE (criminal justice, history, philosophy, political science/government, prelaw, psychology, religion, social science, and sociology). Business, nursing, and education are the strongest programs academically and have the largest enrollments.

Required: To graduate, the student must complete 120 credit hours, including the school's 57-semester-hour core curriculum, and earn a GPA of 2.0. The credit hours required in the student's major vary by subject.

Special: The university offers internships and study abroad in England, Ireland, and Italy. There is a freshman honors program.

Faculty/Classroom: 44% of faculty are male; 56%, female. All teach undergraduates. The average class size in an introductory lecture is 20; in a laboratory, 15; and in a regular course, 16.

Admissions: 38% of the current freshmen were in the top fifth of their class; 70% were in the top two fifths.

Requirements: The ACT is required. In addition, students must be graduates of an accredited secondary school and have earned 16 specific academic credits, including 4 years each of English and the natural and social sciences, 3 each of math and academic electives, and 2 years of a foreign language. The GED is accepted. AP and CLEP credits are accepted.

Procedure: Freshmen are admitted fall and spring. Entrance exams should be taken during the spring of the junior year. There are deferred admissions and rolling admissions plans. Applications should be filed by August 15 for fall entry and January 15 for spring entry. Notification is sent on a rolling basis. Applications are accepted on-line. The fall 2005 application fee was $25.

Transfer: 471 transfer students enrolled in a recent year. Applicants must have completed 12 semester hours with a GPA of 2.25. An interview is recommended. 30 of 120 credits required for the bachelor's degree must be completed at SXU.

Visiting: There are regularly scheduled orientations for prospective students. There are guides for informal visits and visitors may sit in on classes and stay overnight. To schedule a visit, contact the Director of Admissions.

Financial Aid: In a recent year, 88% of all full-time freshmen and 82% of continuing full-time students received some form of financial aid. 64%

of full-time freshmen and 65% of continuing full-time students received need-based aid. The average freshman award was $15,197. Need-based scholarships or need-based grants averaged $10,123; need-based self-help aid (loans and jobs) averaged $5271; and non-need-based athletic scholarships averaged $4297. 12% of undergraduates worked part time. The average financial indebtedness of a recent graduate was $19,374. The FAFSA is required. Check with the school for current application deadlines.

International Students: The school actively recruits these students. They must score satisfactorily on the written TOEFL.

Computers: All students may access the system. There are no time limits and no fees.

Graduates: In a recent year, 617 bachelor's degrees were awarded. The most popular majors were education (20%), business (20%), and nursing (17%). In an average class, 30% graduate in 3 years or less, 74% graduate in 4 years or less, 49% graduate in 5 years or less, and 56% graduate in 6 years or less. Of a recent graduating class, 23% were enrolled in graduate school within 6 months of graduation and 98% were employed.

Admissions Contact: Beth Gierach, Director of Enrollment Services. E-mail: *admissions@sxu.edu* Web: *www.sxu.edu.admission*

SCHOOL OF THE ART INSTITUTE OF CHICAGO   E-2

Chicago, IL 60603
(312) 899-5219
(800) 232-7242; Fax: (312) 899-1840

Full-time: 665 men, 1221 women	**Faculty:** n/av
Part-time: 33 men, 89 women	**Ph.Ds:** 87%
Graduate: 190 men, 390 women	**Student/Faculty:** n/av
Year: semesters, summer session	**Tuition:** $29,200
Application Deadline: September 1	**Room & Board:** $8600
Freshman Class: n/av	
SAT or ACT: required	**SPECIAL**

The School of the Art Institute of Chicago, founded in 1866, offers a comprehensive college education centered in the visual and related arts. In addition to regional accreditation, SAIC has baccalaureate program accreditation with NASAD. The library contains 7100 volumes, 157 microform items, and 4000 audio/video tapes/CDs/DVDs, and subscribes to 350 periodicals including electronic. Computerized library services include the card catalog, interlibrary loans, and database searching. Special learning facilities include a learning resource center, art gallery, TV station, the Gene Siskel Film Center, the Video Data Bank, the Fashion Resource Center, student galleries, the Poetry center, Free Radio SAIC, Roger Brown Study Collection, the Joan Flasch Artists Book Collection, and the Collection of the Art Institute of Chicago. The campus is in an urban area in downtown Chicago. Including any residence halls, there are 5 buildings.

Student Life: 77% of undergraduates are from out of state, mostly the Midwest. Students are from 47 states, 28 foreign countries, and Canada. 59% are white; 16% foreign nationals; 10% Asian American. The average age of freshmen is 19; all undergraduates, 22. 23% do not continue beyond their first year.

Housing: 706 students can be accommodated in college housing, which includes coed dorms. On-campus housing is available on a first-come, first-served basis and is available on a lottery system for upperclassmen. 64% of students commute. Alcohol is not permitted. All students may keep cars.

Activities: There are no fraternities or sororities. There are 28 groups on campus, including art, dance, ethnic, film, gay, international, literary magazine, newspaper, performance, political, professional, radio and TV, religious, social, social service, and student government. Popular campus events include film center screenings, visiting artist lectures, and holiday and spring art sales.

Sports: There is no sports program at SAIC.

Disabled Students: 98% of the campus is accessible. Wheelchair ramps, elevators, special parking, specially equipped rest rooms, special class scheduling, lowered drinking fountains, and lowered telephones are available. Assistance in other areas is available on an individual basis.

Services: Counseling and information services are available, as is tutoring in every subject. There is remedial reading and writing. Tutoring for students with learning disabilities is provided through the learning center.

Campus Safety and Security: Measures include 24-hour foot and vehicle patrol, self-defense education, security escort services, and informal discussions. There are pamphlets/posters/films, emergency telephones, and lighted pathways/sidewalks.

Programs of Study: SAIC confers B.A., B.F.A., and B.I.A. degrees. Master's degrees are also awarded. Bachelor's degrees are awarded in COMMUNICATIONS AND THE ARTS (art history and appreciation, audio technology, ceramic art and design, creative writing, design, drawing, fiber/textiles/weaving, film arts, painting, photography, printmaking, sculpture, video, and visual and performing arts), COMPUTER AND PHYSICAL SCIENCE (digital arts/technology), EDUCATION (art), ENGINEERING AND ENVIRONMENTAL DESIGN (drafting and design technology and interior design), SOCIAL SCIENCE (fashion design and technology).

Required: All students are required to take 72 credit hours of studio courses, 30 hours of liberal arts, 18 hours of art history, and 12 hours of electives. A total of 132 credit hours must be completed to graduate. All students are required to take English literature and composition, natural science, social science, and humanities courses as well as course work in the first-year experience.

Special: The school offers internships, student-designed majors, a credit/no-credit grading system, visual arts co-op programs, cross-registration with Roosevelt University, and many cooperative work-study opportunities. Dual and student-designed majors, 6 undergraduate degrees, and study abroad in 20 countries with active exchange programs are possible.

Faculty/Classroom: 55% of faculty are male; 45%, female.

Requirements: The SAT or ACT is required. In addition, a satisfactory score is required on the verbal section of the SAT or an English score of 20 required on the ACT. Applicants must be graduates of an accredited secondary school. The GED is accepted. All students must submit a portfolio and an essay. An interview is recommended. AP and CLEP credits are accepted. Important factors in the admissions decision are evidence of special talent, recommendations by school officials, and personality/intangible qualities.

Procedure: Freshmen are admitted fall and spring. There are early admissions, deferred admissions and rolling admissions plans. Early admissions applications should be filed by January 2; regular applications, by September 1 for fall entry and February 1 for spring entry, along with a $65 fee. Notification of early decision is sent on a rolling basis; regular decision, on a rolling basis.

Transfer: Transfer students must take the SAT or ACT. A satisfactory score is required on the verbal section of the SAT and a minimum English score of 20 is required on the ACT. Students must submit a portfolio. 36 of 132 credits required for the bachelor's degree must be completed at SAIC.

Visiting: There are regularly scheduled orientations for prospective students, including tours and meetings with faculty counselors Monday through Friday. There are guides for informal visits. To schedule a visit, contact the Office of Admissions.

Financial Aid: In 2005-2006, 70% of all full-time freshmen and 74% of continuing full-time students received some form of financial aid. The average freshman award was $17,189. The average financial indebtedness of the 2005 graduate was $28,959. The FAFSA is required. The priority date for freshman financial aid applications for fall entry is March 15.

International Students: The school actively recruits these students. They must score 527 on the written TOEFL.

Computers: Wireless access is available. All students may access the system. There are no time limits and no fees. SAIC requires that all incoming students have PCs. An Apple G4 is recommended.

Graduates: From July 1, 2004 to June 30, 2005, 379 bachelor's degrees were awarded.

Admissions Contact: Pat Lally, Associate Director of Admissions. E-mail: *admiss@artic.edu* Web: *http://www.artic.edu/saic*

SHIMER COLLEGE   C-1
Waukegan, IL 60085   (847) 623-8400
                                    (800) 215-7173; Fax: (847) 249-8798

Full-time: 52 men, 41 women	**Faculty:** 15
Part-time: 11 men; 3 women	**Ph.Ds:** 94%
Graduate: none	**Student/Faculty:** 6 to 1
Year: semesters, summer session	**Tuition:** $19,525
Application Deadline: July 31	**Room & Board:** $7000
Freshman Class: 23 applied, 22 accepted, 19 enrolled	
SAT or ACT: recommended	**LESS COMPETITIVE**

Shimer College, the Great Books College of the Midwest, is a private liberal arts institution founded in 1853 that offers a curriculum based on original sources and a Socratic teaching method in discussion classes of 12 or fewer students. The library contains 20,000 volumes. Computerized library services include the card catalog, interlibrary loans, database searching, and Internet access. Special learning facilities include a radio station. The 3-acre campus is in an urban area one hour north of Chicago. Including any residence halls, there are 10 buildings.

Student Life: 75% of undergraduates are from Illinois. Others are from 14 states and 4 foreign countries. 75% are from public schools. 88% are white. The average age of freshmen is 19; all undergraduates, 24.

Housing: 65 students can be accommodated in college housing, which includes coed dorms and on-campus apartments. In addition, there is a suvstance-free (no smoking, no alcohol) house. On-campus housing is guaranteed for the freshman year only and is available on a first-come, first-served basis. Priority is given to out-of-town students. 50% of students live on campus; of those, 95% remain on campus on weekends. All students may keep cars.

Activities: There are no fraternities or sororities. There are some groups and organizations on campus, including art, chess, computers, drama, literary magazine, newspaper, photography, and student government. Popular campus events include community lunch; poetry readings; and talent show.

Sports: There is no sports program at Shimer. Facilities include a gym and arrangements with local YMCA for additional recreational facilities.

Disabled Students: 20% of the campus is accessible. Wheelchair ramps are available.

Services: Counseling and information services are available, as is tutoring in every subject.

Campus Safety and Security: Measures include security escort services and informal discussions.

Programs of Study: Shimer confers B.A. and B.S. degrees. Bachelor's degrees are awarded in COMPUTER AND PHYSICAL SCIENCE (natural sciences), SOCIAL SCIENCE (humanities, liberal arts/general studies, and social science). Humanities and social science are the strongest academically. Humanities is the largest.

Required: To graduate, students must earn 125 credit hours with a GPA of 2.0, complete 2 comprehensive exams, and submit a thesis. The school requires 60 credit hours in the major for the B.S. degree, 40 for the B.A.; 65 in the core curriculum for the B.S., 85 for the B.A.

Special: Shimer offers internships in all areas of study and study abroad at Oxford in England. There is an accelerated degree program, a B.A.-B.S. degree, dual majors in all areas, student-designed majors, and a general studies degree. Nondegree study and pass/fail options are possible.

Faculty/Classroom: 64% of faculty are male; 26%, female. All teach undergraduates. The average class size in a regular course is 7.

Admissions: 96% of the 2005-2006 applicants were accepted.

Requirements: The SAT or ACT is recommended. Essays, letters of recommendation, and an interview are required. Important factors in the admissions decision are evidence of special talent, personality/intangible qualities, and recommendations by school officials.

Procedure: Freshmen are admitted fall and spring. There are early admissions, deferred admissions and rolling admissions plans. Applications should be filed by July 31 for fall entry and January 15 for spring entry, along with a $25 fee. Notification is sent on a rolling basis. Applications are accepted on-line.

Transfer: 11 transfer students enrolled in 2004-2005. The requirements are the same as for all other applicants plus all post-secondary transcripts. A minimum of 65 to 125 semester hours required for the bachelor's degree must be completed at Shimer.

Visiting: There are regularly scheduled orientations for prospective students, consisting of class visits, lunch, and an admissions interview. There are guides for informal visits and visitors may sit in on classes and stay overnight. To schedule a visit, contact Ann Penway.

Financial Aid: In 2005-2006, 90% of all full-time students received some form of financial aid. Need-based scholarships or need-based grants averaged $4000; and need-based self-help aid (loans and jobs) averaged $2625. Average annual earnings from campus work are $1800. The average financial indebtedness of the 2005 graduate was $25,000. Shimer is a member of CSS. The FAFSA is required. The priority date for freshman financial aid applications for fall entry is April 15. The deadline for filing freshman financial aid applications for fall entry is July 30.

International Students: There are 5 international students enrolled. The school actively recruits these students. They must score satisfactorily on the written TOEFL.

Computers: Wireless access is available. Students must register as authorized users with the Director of Information Technology to use the wireless network on campus on their own laptops. 4 desktops are available in the PC lab 24 hours a day. Portable memory devices are available to registered users. All students may access the system 24 hours a day. There are no time limits and no fees.

Graduates: From July 1, 2004 to June 30, 2005, 16 bachelor's degrees were awarded. The most popular majors were humanities (55%), social sciences (35%), and natural sciences (10%). In an average class, 7% graduate in 3 years or less, 50% graduate in 4 years or less, 53% graduate in 5 years or less, and 58% graduate in 6 years or less. Of the 2004 graduating class, 20% were enrolled in graduate school within 6 months of graduation and 70% were employed.

Admissions Contact: Anne Penway, Director of Admissions. E-mail: *info@shimer.edu* Web: *www.shimer.edu*

SOUTHERN ILLINOIS UNIVERSITY SYSTEM

The Southern Illinois University System, established in 1965, is 1 of 2 public senior university systems in Illinois. It has two campuses: Southern Illinois University Carbondale, with a School of Medicine in Springfield and Southern Illinois University Edwardsville, with a School of Dental Medicine in Alton and a center in East St. Louis. The university offers degree programs from the associate through the doctorate, and professional degrees in law, medicine, dentistry, and pharmacy. The SIU Board of Trustees is the legal entity with overall responsibility for the organization and governance of the university and its constituent institutions. The chief executive officer is the president. Dedicated to the traditional academic pursuits of instruction, scholarship, and public service, the university assigns priority to achieving excellence in undergraduate and graduate education, encourages and supports scholarly research and creative achievement, and strives to achieve and maintain cultural diversity. The recent total enrollment of both campuses was 34,581; there were 1,685 full-time instructional faculty members. Altogether, there are 4 associate, 124 baccalaureate, 109 master's, and 36 doctoral and professional degree programs offered through the Southern Illinois University System. For more information, visit Southern Illinois University on the web at www.siu.edu.

SOUTHERN ILLINOIS UNIVERSITY CARBONDALE   D-5

Carbondale, IL 62901   (618) 453-2908; Fax: (618) 453-3250

Full-time: 8557 men, 6405 women	**Faculty:** 901; I, --$
Part-time: 998 men, 737 women	**Ph.D.s:** 79%
Graduate: 2290 men, 2454 women	**Student/Faculty:** 17 to 1
Year: semesters, summer session	**Tuition:** $6831 ($14,796)
Application Deadline: open	**Room & Board:** $5560
Freshman Class: 9285 applied, 7173 accepted, 2470 enrolled	
ACT: 23	**COMPETITIVE**

Southern Illinois University Carbondale, founded in 1869, is a public institution that is part of the Southern Illinois University system. The multicampus university offers undergraduate programs in the Colleges of Applied Sciences and Arts, Agricultural Sciences, Business and Administration, College of Education and Human Services, Engineering, Liberal Arts, Mass Communication and Media Arts, and Science. There is also a graduate school, and schools of law and medicine. There are 8 undergraduate and 3 graduate schools. In addition to regional accreditation, SIUC has baccalaureate program accreditation with AACSB, ABET, ABFSE, ACEJMC, ADA, APTA, CAHEA, CSWE, FIDER, NASAD, NASM, NCATE, NRPA, and SAF. The 2 libraries contain 2,670,736 volumes, 4,515,319 microform items, and 14,229 audio/video tapes/CDs/DVDs, and subscribe to 34,404 periodicals including electronic. Computerized library services include the card catalog, interlibrary loans, database searching, Internet access, and laptop Internet portals. Special learning facilities include a learning resource center, natural history museum, radio station, student-run newspaper, farms and timberlands, greenhouses, livestock facilities, archeological center, aviation program, crime study center, wildlife lab, international programs and services, broadcasting division that operates public television and radio stations, a dental lab, and a child development lab. The 1133-acre campus is in a rural area 96 miles southeast of St. Louis. Including any residence halls, there are 256 buildings.

Student Life: 86% of undergraduates are from Illinois. Others are from 49 states, 104 foreign countries, and Canada. 71% are white; 16% African American. The average age of freshmen is 19; all undergraduates, 24. 30% do not continue beyond their first year; 70% remain to graduate.

Housing: 5464 students can be accommodated in college housing, which includes single-sex and coed dorms, on-campus apartments, married-student housing, fraternity houses, and sorority houses. In addition, there are honors houses, special-interest houses, family housing, over-21 residence halls, and residence halls that stay open during breaks. On-campus housing is guaranteed for the freshman year only and is available on a first-come, first-served basis. 72% of students commute. All students may keep cars.

Activities: 5% of men belong to 1 local and 18 national fraternities; 5% of women belong to 11 national sororities. There are 392 groups on campus, including art, band, cheerleading, chess, choir, chorale, chorus, computers, dance, debate, drama, drill team, drum and bugle corps, ethnic, film, forensics, gay, honors, international, jazz band, literary magazine, marching band, musical theater, opera, orchestra, pep band, photography, political, professional, radio and TV, religious, social, social service, student government, symphony, and yearbook. Popular campus events include Cardboard Boat Regatta, International Festival, and Hispanic Month.

Sports: There are 9 intercollegiate sports for men and 9 for women, and 25 intramural sports for men and 25 for women. Facilities include a 17,324-seat stadium, a 10,014-seat arena, a skate park, a women's softball field, a baseball field, 700-seat gym, a lake and beach with boat docks, tennis courts, and a cross-country course. The 214,000-square-foot student recreation center houses an Olympic-size pool, indoor tracks, racquetball, squash, tennis courts, aerobics equipment, a weight room, Nautilus room and numerous exercise stations. The center also offers volleyball, basketball, badminton, handball, indoor soccer, climbing wall, dance studio, boxing practice room, and martial arts practice room.

Disabled Students: 99% of the campus is accessible. Wheelchair ramps, elevators, special parking, specially equipped rest rooms, special class scheduling, lowered drinking fountains, lowered telephones, special housing, classroom accommodations, and disability support services are available.

Services: Counseling and information services are available, as is tutoring in most subjects. There is a reader service for the blind. There is new student orientation, a mentoring program, a writing skills lab, premajor advisement, student development programs, and career counseling. Students often are required to pay for tutorial assistance.

Campus Safety and Security: Measures include 24-hour foot and vehicle patrol, self-defense education, security escort services, and shuttle buses. There are informal discussions, pamphlets/posters/films, emergency telephones, and lighted pathways/sidewalks. Campus security is operated by law enforcement officers, supplemented with a student patrol program.

Programs of Study: SIUC confers B.A., B.S., B.F.A., and B.Mus. degrees. Associate, master's, and doctoral degrees are also awarded. Bachelor's degrees are awarded in AGRICULTURE (agricultural economics, agriculture, animal science, forestry and related sciences, and plant science), BIOLOGICAL SCIENCE (avian sciences, biology/biological science, botany, microbiology, physiology, and zoology), BUSINESS (accounting, banking and finance, business administration and management, business economics, business systems analysis, fashion merchandising, funeral home services, management science, marketing/retailing/merchandising, and recreation and leisure services), COMMUNICATIONS AND THE ARTS (art, broadcasting, classics, design, dramatic arts, English, English literature, film arts, fine arts, French, German, journalism, linguistics, music, photography, radio/television technology, Russian, Spanish, and speech/debate/rhetoric), COMPUTER AND PHYSICAL SCIENCE (chemistry, computer science, geology, information sciences and systems, mathematics, physics, and radiological technology), EDUCATION (business, early childhood, elementary, health, physical, special, and vocational), ENGINEERING AND ENVIRONMENTAL DESIGN (architecture, automotive technology, aviation administration/management, aviation computer technology, civil engineering, computer engineering, electrical/electronics engineering, electrical/electronics engineering technology, engineering management, engineering technology, industrial engineering technology, interior design, mechanical engineering, mining and mineral engineering, and technological management), HEALTH PROFESSIONS (dental hygiene, dental laboratory technology, health care administration, physician's assistant, rehabilitation therapy, respiratory therapy, and speech pathology/audiology), SOCIAL SCIENCE (anthropology, clothing and textiles management/production/services, criminal justice, dietetics, economics, family/consumer resource management, fire protection, food science, geography, German area studies, history, international relations, law, liberal arts/general studies, paralegal studies, parks and recreation management, philosophy, political science/government, psychology, social science, social studies, social work, and sociology). Workforce education, French, and fire science management are the strongest academically. Psychology, radio and television, and workforce education are the largest.

Required: To graduate, all students must meet the university and program requirements, maintain a minimum 2.0 GPA, and complete a minimum of 120 semester hours. The total number of hours in the major varies, and students must complete a university core curriculum.

Special: The university offers internships through the Washington center and study abroad in 40 countries, including Europe, Africa, Australia, British Isles, Latin America, Ireland, and Spain. Also available are a Washington semester, student-designed majors, work-study programs, accelerated degree programs, dual majors, and B.A.-B.S. degrees in numerous programs. The College of Applied Sciences and Arts offers technically oriented programs, co-op programs, and work-study. Nondegree study is available through the Community Listeners Permit and Elderhostel. A combined total of 40 hours may be earned through proficiency exams and credit for work experience. There are 27 national honor societies and a freshman honors program.

Faculty/Classroom: 64% of faculty are male; 36%, female. Graduate students teach 30% of introductory courses. The average class size in an introductory lecture is 215; in a laboratory, 23; and in a regular course, 23.

Admissions: 77% of the 2005-2006 applicants were accepted. The ACT scores for the 2005-2006 freshman class were: 21% below 21, 38% between 21 and 23, 25% between 24 and 26, 9% between 27 and 28, and 7% above 28. 23% of the current freshmen were in the top fifth of their class; 49% were in the top two fifths. 5 freshmen graduated first in their class.

Requirements: The ACT is required. In addition, applicants must be graduates of an accredited secondary high school or have a GED certificate, with 4 years of English, 3 years each of math, lab science, and social science, and 2 years of electives, which may include art, music, foreign language, or vocational education. For general admission, high school transcripts or GED test scores, ACT or SAT scores and immunization records are required . Some programs require additional materials and/or screening. AP and CLEP credits are accepted.

Procedure: Freshmen are admitted fall, spring, and summer. Entrance exams should be taken during spring of the junior year. There is a deferred admissions and rolling admissions plan. Application deadlines are open. Application fee is $30. Applications are accepted on-line.

Transfer: 2833 transfer students enrolled in 2004-2005. All transfer students must have a minimum 2.0 GPA. Students are required to meet freshman admission requirements if they are under 21 years old and have fewer than 26 credit hours of acceptable transfer work. Some academic programs have higher admission requirements. 30 of 120 credits required for the bachelor's degree must be completed at SIUC.

Visiting: There are regularly scheduled orientations for prospective students, including admission counseling, academic program exhibits, student organization exhibits, workshops on financial aid and housing, and tours of the campus, academic departments, and residence halls. There are guides for informal visits and visitors may sit in on classes. To schedule a visit, contact New Student Admission Services at (618) 453-7141.

Financial Aid: In 2005-2006, 80% of all full-time freshmen and 83% of continuing full-time students received some form of financial aid. 77% of full-time freshmen and 78% of continuing full-time students received need-based aid. The average freshman award was $7801 with $3332 from need-based scholarships or need-based grants $2535 from need-based self-help aid (loans and jobs) $107 from non-need-based athletic scholarships and $1827 from other non-need-based awards and non-need-based scholarships. Average annual earnings from campus work are $2091. The average financial indebtedness of the 2005 graduate was $14,708. The FAFSA is required. The deadline for filing freshman financial aid applications for fall entry is April 1.

International Students: There are 291 international students enrolled. The school actively recruits these students. They must score satisfactorily on the written TOEFL or on the electronic version and also take the SAT or ACT and their own country's standardized college entrance exam.

Computers: Wireless access is available. There are more than 1000 PCs in student labs on campus; all residence halls have Internet access. Half of the buildings have wireless access. All students may access the system all the time, all year. There are no time limits and no fees. It is strongly recommended that all students have a personal computer.

Graduates: From July 1, 2004 to June 30, 2005, 4373 bachelor's degrees were awarded. The most popular majors were workforce education and development (16%), industrial technology (4%), and health care management (4%). In an average class, 21% graduate in 4 years or less, 38% graduate in 5 years or less, and 43% graduate in 6 years or less. 259 companies recruited on campus in 2004-2005. Of the 2004 graduating class, 10% were enrolled in graduate school within 6 months of graduation.

Admissions Contact: Anne DeLuca, Assistant Vice Chancellor Affairs and Enrollment Management and. A video is available.
E-mail: *adeluca@siu.edu* Web: *www.siuc.edu*

SOUTHERN ILLINOIS UNIVERSITY EDWARDSVILLE   C-4

Edwardsville, IL 62026-1600   (618) 650-3705
                          (800) 447-SIUE; Fax: (618) 650-5013

Full-time: 4127 men, 5105 women	**Faculty:** 508; IIA, -$
Part-time: 801 men, 312 women	**Ph.D.s:** 83%
Graduate: 948 men, 1567 women	**Student/Faculty:** 18 to 1
Year: semesters, summer session	**Tuition:** $5203 ($11,728)
Application Deadline: May 1	**Room & Board:** $5819
Freshman Class: 5379 applied, 4149 accepted, 1748 enrolled	
ACT: required	**COMPETITIVE**

Southern Illinois University Edwardsville, founded in 1957, is part of the Southern Illinois University system and offers undergraduate programs in business, education, engineering, arts and sciences, and nursing. Graduate programs also are offered in 34 subject areas, including professional programs in pharmacy and dental medicine. There are 5 undergraduate schools and 1 graduate school. In addition to regional accreditation, SIUE has baccalaureate program accreditation with AACSB, ABET, ACCE, ACEJMC, ADA, ASLA, CCNE, CSWE, NASM, NCATE, and NLN. The library contains 839,239 volumes, 1,658,339 microform items, and 31,099 audio/video tapes/CDs/DVDs, and subscribes to 24,601 periodicals including electronic. Computerized library services include the card catalog, interlibrary loans, database searching, and Internet access. Special learning facilities include a learning resource center, art gallery, radio station, TV station, recording studio, engineering labs, anthropology museum, greenhouse, arboretum, and nursing psychomotor skills lab. The 2660-acre campus is in a suburban area 18 miles northeast of downtown St. Louis, Missouri. Including any residence halls, there are 25 buildings.

Student Life: 88% of all students are from Illinois. Others are from 43 states, 48 foreign countries, and Canada. 84% are white. The average age of all undergraduates is 22. 24% do not continue beyond their first year; 45% remain to graduate.

Housing: 3000 students can be accommodated in college housing, which includes coed dorms, on-campus apartments, married-student housing, and fraternity houses. In addition there are honors wings and special-interest wings. On-campus housing is available on a first-come,

first-served basis. Priority is given to out-of-town students. 73% of students commute. All students may keep cars.

Activities: 7% of men belong to 9 national fraternities; 5% of women belong to 7 national sororities. There are 170 groups on campus, including art, band, cheerleading, choir, chorale, chorus, dance, drama, ethnic, gay, honors, international, jazz band, literary magazine, musical theater, newspaper, opera, orchestra, pep band, photography, political, professional, radio and TV, religious, social, social service, student government, and symphony. Popular campus events include Welcome Week, Arts and Issues Series, and International Week.

Sports: There are 8 intercollegiate sports for men and 8 for women, and 17 intramural sports for men and 17 for women. Facilities include the Vadalabene Center and Student Fitness Center, which offer racquetball, basketball, aquatics, volleyball, indoor track, exercise, and weight training; the University Center, which features restaurants, a recreation center, billiards, and a bowling alley; an outdoor swimming pool; a lake for canoeing and sailing; an outdoor track and field and soccer stadium; baseball, softball, and soccer fields; extensive walking and biking trails; and a Frisbee course.

Disabled Students: All of the campus is accessible. Wheelchair ramps, elevators, special parking, specially equipped rest rooms, special class scheduling, lowered drinking fountains, lowered telephones, a Visualtek large-screen TV, Kurzweil readers, test-taking facilities, accessible weight-training equipment, and a swimming pool are available.

Services: Counseling and information services are available, as is tutoring in most subjects. There is a reader service for the blind, and remedial math, reading, and writing.

Campus Safety and Security: Measures include 24-hour foot and vehicle patrol, self-defense education, security escort services, and shuttle buses. There are informal discussions, pamphlets/posters/films, emergency telephones, lighted pathways/sidewalks, and and emergency blue lights located throughout campus.

Programs of Study: SIUE confers B.A., B.S., B.F.A., B.L.S., B.M., and B.S.A. degrees. Master's degrees are also awarded. Bachelor's degrees are awarded in BIOLOGICAL SCIENCE (biology/biological science), BUSINESS (accounting, business administration and management, business economics, and management information systems), COMMUNICATIONS AND THE ARTS (art, communications, dance, design, dramatic arts, English, languages, music, and speech/debate/rhetoric), COMPUTER AND PHYSICAL SCIENCE (chemistry, computer science, mathematics, and physics), EDUCATION (early childhood, elementary, health, science, and special), ENGINEERING AND ENVIRONMENTAL DESIGN (civil engineering, computer engineering, construction engineering, electrical/electronics engineering, industrial engineering, manufacturing engineering, and mechanical engineering), HEALTH PROFESSIONS (exercise science, nursing, and speech pathology/audiology), SOCIAL SCIENCE (anthropology, criminal justice, economics, geography, history, liberal arts/general studies, philosophy, political science/government, psychology, social work, and sociology). Business administration, biological sciences, and nursing are the largest.

Required: To graduate, students must complete a total of 124 semester hours with a minimum GPA of 2.0. Students must fulfill general education requirements, including 9 hours of math/science, and complete a senior project.

Special: SIUE offers cross-registration with the University of Missouri at St. Louis, co-op programs, internships, which are required by several majors, including mass communications and sociology, work-study programs, dual majors, B.A.-B.S. degrees, student-designed majors (available to specific honors students only), study abroad in 5 countries (England, France, Germany, the Netherlands, and Mexico) by formal exchange agreements and in a wide variety of others, a liberal studies degree, and a 5-year (3+2) program in dental medicine. There are 20 national honor societies, a freshman honors program, and 15 departmental honors programs.

Faculty/Classroom: 56% of full-time faculty are male; 44%, female. 88% teach undergraduates. Graduate students teach 5% of introductory courses. The average class size in a regular course is 31.

Admissions: 77% of the 2005-2006 applicants were accepted. The ACT scores for the 2005-2006 freshman class were: 29% below 21, 34% between 21 and 23, 23% between 24 and 26, 7% between 27 and 28, and 6% above 28. 35% of the current freshmen were in the top fifth of their class; 66% were in the top two fifths.

Requirements: The ACT is required. In addition, applicants must be graduates of an accredited secondary school or have a GED certificate. They must have completed 15 academic credits, based on 4 years of English, 3 each of math and lab science, 2 years of any combination of art, foreign language, music, and vocational education, at least 2 years of government and/or history, plus 1 more year of social studies. A GPA of 2.5 is required. AP and CLEP credits are accepted.

Procedure: Freshmen are admitted to all sessions. Entrance exams should be taken before high school graduation. There is a rolling admissions plan. Applications should be filed by May 1 for fall entry, December 15 for spring entry, and May 3 for summer entry, along with a $30 fee. Notification is sent on a rolling basis. Applications are accepted on-line.

Transfer: 1325 transfer students enrolled in 2004-2005. Applicants must have a minimum 2.0 GPA in at least 30 semester hours earned. 30 of 124 credits required for the bachelor's degree must be completed at SIUE.

Visiting: There are regularly scheduled orientations for prospective students, including visits before the semester starts. There are guides for informal visits and visitors may sit in on classes. To schedule a visit, contact the Office of Admissions.

Financial Aid: In a recent year, 49% of all full-time students received some form of financial aid. 38% of all full-time students received need-based aid. The average freshman award was $5304. Need-based scholarships or need-based grants averaged $4211 ($9215 maximum); need-based self-help aid (loans and jobs) averaged $3421 ($5220 maximum); non-need-based athletic scholarships averaged $1986 ($8875 maximum); and other non-need-based awards and non-need-based scholarships averaged $1100 ($2911 maximum). 26% of undergraduates work part time. Average annual earnings from campus work are $1574. The average financial indebtedness of a recent year's graduate was $12,222. The FAFSA is required. The deadline for filing freshman financial aid applications for fall entry is March 1.

International Students: There are 119 international students enrolled. The school actively recruits these students. A satisfactory score on the TOEFL is required.

Computers: Wireless access is available. All students may access the system daily at designated hours with some labs open 24 hours. There are no time limits and no fees.

Graduates: From July 1, 2004 to June 30, 2005, 1883 bachelor's degrees were awarded. The most popular majors were business administration (15%), psychology (7%), and elementary education (6%). In an average class, 19% graduate in 4 years or less, 37% graduate in 5 years or less, and 45% graduate in 6 years or less. 546 companies recruited on campus in 2004-2005. Of the 2004 graduating class, 30% were employed within 6 months of graduation.

Admissions Contact: Admission Counseling. A video is available. E-mail: *admissions@siue.edu* Web: *siue.edu*

TRINITY CHRISTIAN COLLEGE   E-2
Palos Heights, IL 60463

(708) 597-3000
(800) 748-0085; Fax: (708) 385-5665

Full-time: 381 men, 668 women	**Faculty:** 76
Part-time: 55 men, 176 women	**Ph.D.s:** 64%
Graduate: none	**Student/Faculty:** 14 to 1
Year: semesters, summer session	**Tuition:** $17,045
Application Deadline: August 15	**Room & Board:** $6600
Freshman Class: 559 applied, 535 accepted, 229 enrolled	
ACT: 22	**COMPETITIVE**

Trinity Christian College, founded in 1959, is a private college offering programs in arts and sciences, business, health science, liberal arts, music, religion, and teacher preparation. In addition to regional accreditation, Trinity has baccalaureate program accreditation with AACSB, CCNE, CSWE, and NLN. The library contains 79,375 volumes, 41,379 microform items, and 894 audio/video tapes/CDs/DVDs, and subscribes to 435 periodicals including electronic. Computerized library services include the card catalog, interlibrary loans, database searching, Internet access, and laptop Internet portals. Special learning facilities include a learning resource center, art gallery, and a Dutch heritage collection. The 53-acre campus is in a suburban area 20 miles southwest of the Chicago Loop. Including any residence halls, there are 23 buildings.

Student Life: 57% of undergraduates are from Illinois. Others are from 33 states, 6 foreign countries, and Canada. 36% are from public schools. 84% are white. 92% are Protestant; 8% Catholic. The average age of freshmen is 18; all undergraduates, 24. 20% do not continue beyond their first year; 54% remain to graduate.

Housing: 726 students can be accommodated in college housing, which includes coed dorms and off-campus apartments. On-campus housing is guaranteed for all 4 years. 66% of students live on campus; of those, 45% remain on campus on weekends. Alcohol is not permitted. All students may keep cars.

Activities: There are no fraternities or sororities. There are 18 groups on campus, including art, band, cheerleading, choir, chorale, chorus, dance, drama, ethnic, honors, jazz band, literary magazine, newspaper, pep band, photography, political, professional, religious, social, social service, student government, and yearbook. Popular campus events include the Opus fine arts festival and the Trollstock Concert.

Sports: There are 6 intercollegiate sports for men and 6 for women, and 7 intramural sports for men and 7 for women. Facilities include a gym, a track, a stadium, a baseball diamond, and softball and soccer fields.

Disabled Students: 95% of the campus is accessible. Wheelchair ramps, elevators, special parking, specially equipped rest rooms, and lowered drinking fountains are available.

Services: Counseling and information services are available, as is tutoring in every subject.

Campus Safety and Security: Measures include 24-hour foot and vehicle patrol, self-defense education, security escort services, and informal discussions. There are emergency telephones and lighted pathways/sidewalks.

Programs of Study: Trinity confers B.A. B.S., B.S.N., and B.S.W. degrees. Bachelor's degrees are awarded in BIOLOGICAL SCIENCE (biology/biological science), BUSINESS (accounting and business administration and management), COMMUNICATIONS AND THE ARTS (applied music, art, communications, English, music, music performance, Spanish, and studio art), COMPUTER AND PHYSICAL SCIENCE (chemistry, computer science, information sciences and systems, and mathematics), EDUCATION (art, education, elementary, music, and special), HEALTH PROFESSIONS (nursing, predentistry, premedicine, and preoptometry), SOCIAL SCIENCE (biblical studies, history, philosophy, prelaw, psychology, social work, sociology, and theological studies). Business, education, and nursing are the strongest academically and have the largest enrollments.

Required: All students must take 9 credits in English, 6 each in philosophy, history, and theology, as well as distribution requirements in cross-cultural studies, natural sciences, social sciences, fine arts, math, and phys ed. Students must complete 125 credit hours and maintain a minimum GPA of 2.0 to graduate.

Special: Students may have various part-time or full-time internships in their major field. There is a study-abroad program Spain. Pass/fail options exist. Dual majors are offered. There is 1 national honor society and a freshman honors program.

Faculty/Classroom: 60% of faculty are male; 40%, female. All both teach and do research. The average class size in an introductory lecture is 24; in a laboratory, 17; and in a regular course, 15.

Admissions: 96% of the 2005-2006 applicants were accepted. The ACT scores for the 2005-2006 freshman class were: 34% below 21, 29% between 21 and 23, 20% between 24 and 26, 7% between 27 and 28, and 10% above 28. 28% of the current freshmen were in the top fifth of their class; 52% were in the top two fifths. 3 freshmen graduated first in their class.

Requirements: The ACT is recommended. In addition, applicants should graduate from an accredited high school or have a GED. They should prepare with 3 or 4 years of high school English, 3 years of math, science, and social studies, or 2 years each of a combination of two subject areas chosen among foreign language, math, science, or social studies. An interview is required. Trinity requires applicants to be in the upper 60% of their class. A GPA of 2.0 is required. AP and CLEP credits are accepted. Important factors in the admissions decision are advanced placement or honor courses, leadership record, and recommendations by school officials.

Procedure: Freshmen are admitted fall and spring. Entrance exams should be taken during the last semester of the junior year. There is a rolling admissions plan. Applications should be filed by August 15 for fall entry and January 15 for spring entry. Notification is sent on a rolling basis. The fall application fee was $20.

Transfer: 93 transfer students enrolled in 2004-2005. Applicants must have 24 hours of acceptable credits and a minimum 2.3 GPA. Associate degrees are recognized for transfer. 30 of 125 credits required for the bachelor's degree must be completed at Trinity.

Visiting: There are regularly scheduled orientations for prospective students, including a tour, an interview, a seminar, and class visits. There are guides for informal visits and visitors may sit in on classes and stay overnight. To schedule a visit, contact the Admissions Office at (866) 874-6463.

Financial Aid: In 2005-2006, 98% of all full-time freshmen and 92% of continuing full-time students received some form of financial aid. 78% of full-time freshmen and 71% of continuing full-time students received need-based aid. The average freshman award was $7452. Need-based scholarships or need-based grants averaged $6194 ($16,070 maximum); need-based self-help aid (loans and jobs) averaged $3496 ($7126 maximum); and non-need-based athletic scholarships averaged $5120 ($10,000 maximum). 50% of undergraduates work part time. Average annual earnings from campus work are $1300. The average financial indebtedness of the 2005 graduate was $14,000. The FAFSA is required. The deadline for filing freshman financial aid applications for fall entry is February 15.

International Students: There are 10 international students enrolled. They must score satisfactorily on the written TOEFL or on the electronic version. The SAT is accepted, but we recommend the ACT.

Computers: All students may access the system. There are no time limits and no fees. It is strongly recommended that all students have a personal computer.

Graduates: From July 1, 2004 to June 30, 2005, 279 bachelor's degrees were awarded. The most popular majors were elemetary education (25%), business (14%), and nursing (7%). In an average class, 47% graduate in 4 years or less, 53% graduate in 5 years or less, and 54% graduate in 6 years or less. 10 companies recruited on campus in 2004-2005. Of the 2004 graduating class, 13% were enrolled in graduate school within 6 months of graduation and 96% were employed.

Admissions Contact: Pete Hamstra, Vice President for Admissions and Advancement. E-mail: *admissions@trnty.edu* Web: *www.trnty.edu*

TRINITY COLLEGE OF NURSING AND HEALTH SCIENCES   C-2

Rock Island, IL 61201-5317	(309) 779-7812; Fax: (309) 779-7748
Full-time: 190 men and women	**Faculty:** 14
Part-time: none	**Ph.D.s:** 20%
Graduate: none	**Student/Faculty:** n/av
Year: semesters, summer session	**Tuition:** $4620
Application Deadline: open	**Room & Board:** n/app
Freshman Class: n/av	
SAT or ACT: required	SPECIAL

Trinity College of Nursing and Health Sciences, founded in 1994, is a private institution offering degrees in nursing , radiography, and emergency medical services. Figures in the above capsule and this profile are approximate. The library contains 4200 volumes, and subscribes to 64 periodicals including electronic. Computerized library services include the card catalog, interlibrary loans, database searching, and Internet access. Special learning facilities include learning lab for all programs. The 2-acre campus is in an urban area part of the Illinois/Iowa Quad-Cities on the Mississippi River. There is one building.

Student Life: 82% of undergraduates are from Illinois. Others are from 3 states. 95% are white. The average age of freshmen is 25. 14% do not continue beyond their first year; 86% remain to graduate.

Housing: There are no residence halls. . College-sponsored housing is coed. All of students commute. Alcohol is not permitted. All students may keep cars.

Activities: There are no fraternities or sororities. There are 5 groups on campus, including honors, social, and student government and student Nurses Association. Popular campus events include Visiting Artists cultural presentations.

Sports: There is no sports program at Trinity College.

Disabled Students: 95% of the campus is accessible. Wheelchair ramps, elevators, special parking, specially equipped rest rooms, and special class scheduling are available.

Services: Counseling and information services are available, as is tutoring in every subject. There is remedial math, reading, and writing.

Campus Safety and Security: Measures include informal discussions, pamphlets/posters/films, emergency telephones, and lighted pathways/sidewalks. There is a safety and security overview during orientation, and a foot and vehicle patrol.

Programs of Study: Trinity College confers the B.S.N. degree. Associate degrees are also awarded. Bachelor's degrees are awarded in HEALTH PROFESSIONS (nursing).

Required: Students must complete a mininum of 127 semester hours, including general education courses, and maintain a 2.0 GPA.

Special: There is 1 national honor society and 1 departmental honors program.

Faculty/Classroom: All of faculty are female. All teach undergraduates. The average class size in an introductory lecture is 40 and in a laboratory, 25.

Requirements: The SAT or ACT is required. They should be high school graduates or have the GED. Official transcripts from all high school and postsecondary institutions are required, as is fluency in the English language. Applicants should have the physical ability to provide safe and effective client care and should have CPR certification for health care professionals. A GPA of 2.5 is required. AP and CLEP credits are accepted.

Procedure: Freshmen are admitted in the fall. There is a rolling admissions plan. Entrance exams should be taken in the senior year. Application deadlines are open. Application fee is $50. A waiting list is an active part of the admissions procedure.

Transfer: Applicants should have official transcripts, fluency in the English language, confirmed physical/mental ability to provide safe and effective client care, and CPR certification. They should also complete the nursing transition course with a grade of C or higher. 19 of 127 credits required for the bachelor's degree must be completed at Trinity College.

Visiting: There are regularly scheduled orientations for prospective students, consisting of a 2-day orientation 2 weeks prior to the start of the fall term. There are guides for informal visits and visitors may sit in on classes and stay overnight. To schedule a visit, contact Barb Kimpe, Admissions Representative.

Financial Aid: In a recent year, 75% of all full-time freshmen and 80% of continuing full-time students received some form of financial aid. 70% of full-time freshmen and 80% of continuing full-time students received need-based aid. The average freshman award was $6375. Need-based scholarships or need-based grants averaged $6000 ($8968 maximum); need-based self-help aid (loans and jobs) averaged $4063 ($10,500 maximum); and other non-need-based awards and non-need-based scholarships averaged $500 ($500 maximum). 55% of undergraduates worked part time. The average financial indebtedness of a recent gradu-

ate was $19,125. The FAFSA is required. Check with the school for current application deadlines.

International Students: They must score satisfactorily on the written TOEFL.

Computers: All students may access the system. There are no time limits and no fees.

Admissions Contact: Barb Kimpe, Admissions Representative. E-mail: *kimpeb@trinityqc.com* Web: *www.trinityqc.edu*

TRINITY INTERNATIONAL UNIVERSITY   E-1

Deerfield, IL 60015	(847) 317-7000
	(800) 822-3225; Fax: (847) 317-7081
Full-time: 452 men, 630 women	**Faculty:** 41; IIA, --$
Part-time: 55 men, 117 women	**Ph.D.s:** 84%
Graduate: 1077 men, 496 women	**Student/Faculty:** 26 to 1
Year: semesters, summer session	**Tuition:** $19,366
Application Deadline: open	**Room & Board:** $6320
Freshman Class: 459 applied, 377 accepted, 159 enrolled	
SAT Verbal/Math: 519/545*	**ACT:** 23 COMPETITIVE

Trinity International University, established in 1897 by the Evangelical Free Church, is a Christian, liberal arts institution offering undergraduate, graduate, and doctoral programs. There are 8 undergraduate and 3 graduate schools. In addition to regional accreditation, Trinity has baccalaureate program accreditation with ATS, and CAAHEP. The library contains 155,000 volumes, 141,000 microform items, and 4300 audio/video tapes/CDs/DVDs, and subscribes to 1332 periodicals including electronic. Computerized library services include the card catalog, interlibrary loans, database searching, and Internet access. Special learning facilities include a learning resource center. The 111-acre campus is in a suburban area 25 miles north of Chicago. Including any residence halls, there are 34 buildings.

Student Life: 52% of undergraduates are from Illinois. Students are from 33 states, 38 foreign countries, and Canada. 66% are from public schools. 65% are white. Most are Protestant. The average age of freshmen is 18; all undergraduates, 21. 22% do not continue beyond their first year; 52% remain to graduate.

Housing: 700 students can be accommodated in college housing, which includes single-sex dorms, on-campus apartments, and married-student housing. On-campus housing is guaranteed for all 4 years. 58% of students live on campus; of those, 75% remain on campus on weekends. Alcohol is not permitted. Upperclassmen may keep cars.

Activities: There are no fraternities or sororities. There are 36 groups on campus, including art, band, cheerleading, choir, chorale, computers, debate, drama, ethnic, gospel choir, handbell choir, honors, international, jazz band, literary magazine, newspaper, orchestra, pep band, political, religious, social service, student government, symphony, and yearbook. Popular campus events include Santa Lucia Festival, Fine Arts Series, and Day of Prayer.

Sports: There are 4 intercollegiate sports for men and 4 for women, and 6 intramural sports for men and 6 for women. Facilities include a student center, a sports complex, and football and soccer fields. Students have access to a nearby indoor tennis and racquetball club.

Disabled Students: 75% of the campus is accessible. Wheelchair ramps, elevators, special parking, specially equipped rest rooms, and special class scheduling are available.

Services: Counseling and information services are available, as is tutoring in every subject. There is a reader service for the blind, and remedial math, reading, and writing.

Campus Safety and Security: Measures include 24-hour foot and vehicle patrol, self-defense education, security escort services, and informal discussions. There are emergency telephones and lighted pathways/sidewalks.

Programs of Study: Trinity confers the B.A. degree. Master's and doctoral degrees are also awarded. Bachelor's degrees are awarded in BIOLOGICAL SCIENCE (biology/biological science), BUSINESS (accounting, business administration and management, human resources, international business management, marketing/retailing/merchandising, and sports management), COMMUNICATIONS AND THE ARTS (communications, English, and music), COMPUTER AND PHYSICAL SCIENCE (chemistry and mathematics), EDUCATION (athletic training, elementary, physical, and secondary), HEALTH PROFESSIONS (physical therapy, premedicine, and sports medicine), SOCIAL SCIENCE (biblical studies, Christian studies, history, humanities, liberal arts/general studies, philosophy, psychology, social science, and youth ministry). Music, education, and biblical studies are the strongest academically. Business, Christian ministries, and education are the largest.

Required: To graduate, all students must complete 126 semester hours, including 58 general education hours and a variable 36 to 54 hours in the major. A GPA of 2.0 is required. Chapel attendance, Christian service, Bible study, and science are also required.

Special: Students can cross-register with the Christian College Consortium and at Trinity Evangelical Divinity School. Trinity offers 3 levels of internships, study abroad in 7 countries, and an opportunity through the

American Studies Program to spend a semester in Washington. Dual majors, a general studies degree, and nondegree study are offered. There are 2 national honor societies, a freshman honors program, and 15 departmental honors programs.

Faculty/Classroom: 79% of faculty are male; 21%, female. 45% teach undergraduates. No introductory courses are taught by graduate students. The average class size in an introductory lecture is 40; in a laboratory, 20; and in a regular course, 15.

Admissions: 82% of the 2005-2006 applicants were accepted. The SAT scores for the 2005-2006 freshman class were: Verbal--44% below 500, 38% between 500 and 599, 13% between 600 and 700, and 5% above 700; Math--23% below 500, 56% between 500 and 599, 15% between 600 and 700, and 6% above 700. The ACT scores were 26% below 21, 34% between 21 and 23, 20% between 24 and 26, 7% between 27 and 28, and 13% above 28. 30% of the current freshmen were in the top fifth of their class; 60% were in the top two fifths. 4 freshmen graduated first in their class.

Requirements: A satisfactory score on the SAT or ACT is required, the ACT is preferred. In addition, applicants should be graduates of an accredited high school and have completed 15 academic credits in art, a foreign language, math, music, science, social studies, and English. A GED is accepted. Recommendations from a pastor must be submitted. A GPA of 2.5 is required. AP and CLEP credits are accepted. Important factors in the admissions decision are personality/intangible qualities, leadership record, and advanced placement or honor courses.

Procedure: Freshmen are admitted fall and spring. Entrance exams should be taken during spring of the junior year or fall of the senior year. Application deadlines are open. There is a rolling admissions plan. Application fee is $25. Applications are accepted on-line.

Transfer: 72 transfer students enrolled in 2004-2005. Applicants must submit college transcripts and have a cumulative college GPA of 2.0 or higher. 30 of 126 credits required for the bachelor's degree must be completed at Trinity.

Visiting: There are regularly scheduled orientations for prospective students, including class visits, meetings with professors and admission counselors, and a dorm visit. There are guides for informal visits and visitors may sit in on classes and stay overnight. To schedule a visit, contact the Campus Visit Coordinator at *visits@tiu.edu.*

Financial Aid: In 2005-2006, 76% of all full-time freshmen and 64% of continuing full-time students received some form of financial aid. 46% of full-time freshmen and 43% of continuing full-time students received need-based aid. The average freshman award was $14,902. Need-based scholarships or need-based grants averaged $5897 ($12,000 maximum); need-based self-help aid (loans and jobs) averaged $4302 ($5625 maximum); and non-need-based athletic scholarships averaged $8334 ($22,980 maximum). 53% of undergraduates work part time. Average annual earnings from campus work are $875. The average financial indebtedness of the 2005 graduate was $17,129. Trinity is a member of CSS. The FAFSA is required. The deadline for filing freshman financial aid applications for fall entry is April 15.

International Students: There were 19 international students enrolled in a recent year. They must score satisfactorily on the written TOEFL or on the electronic version and also take the SAT or the ACT.

Computers: Wireless access is available. Students may access the network and the Internet in their dorm rooms, via a number of computer kiosks, by using one of the 75 computers in the 3 computer labs, and in 3 buildings equipped with wireless access. All students may access the system. There are no time limits and no fees. It is strongly recommended that all students have a personal computer.

Graduates: From July 1, 2004 to June 30, 2005, 210 bachelor's degrees were awarded. The most popular majors were elementary education (10%), youth ministry (9%), and psychology (6%). 20 companies recruited on campus in 2004-2005. Of the 2004 graduating class, 21% were enrolled in graduate school within 6 months of graduation and 55% were employed.

Admissions Contact: Matthew Yoder, Director of Undergraduate Admissions. E-mail: *tcdadm@tiu.edu* Web: *www.tiu.edu*

UNIVERSITY OF CHICAGO   E-2

Chicago, IL 60637	(773) 702-8662; Fax: (773) 702-4199
Full-time: 2258 men, 2324 women	Faculty: 827; I, ++$
Part-time: 37 men, 19 women	Ph.Ds: 98%
Graduate: 5071 men, 3334 women	Student/Faculty: 6 to 1
Year: quarters, summer session	Tuition: $32,265
Application Deadline: January 1	Room & Board: $10,104
Freshman Class: 9011 applied, 3628 accepted, 1205 enrolled	
SAT or ACT: required	MOST COMPETITIVE

The University of Chicago, founded in 1891, is a private liberal arts institution offering undergraduate and graduate programs with emphases on the biological and physical sciences, the humanities, and the social sciences. In addition to regional accreditation, Chicago has baccalaureate program accreditation with NCATE. The 7 libraries contain 7 million volumes, and subscribe to 47,000 periodicals including electronic. Comput-

erized library services include the card catalog, interlibrary loans, database searching, Internet access, and laptop Internet portals. Special learning facilities include a learning resource center, art gallery, radio station, film studies center, language labs, museum of Near Eastern antiquities, and Renaissance Society (contemporary art). The 204-acre campus is in an urban area in Chicago. Including any residence halls, there are 243 buildings.

Student Life: 85% of undergraduates are from out of state, mostly the Northeast. Students are from 48 states, 53 foreign countries, and Canada. 70% are from public schools. 52% are white; 14% Asian American. The average age of freshmen is 18; all undergraduates, 20. 5% do not continue beyond their first year; 90% remain to graduate.

Housing: College housing includes single-sex and coed dormitories on-campus apartments and on international house. On-campus housing is guaranteed for all 4 years. 93% of students live on campus; of those, 95% remain on campus on weekends. Upperclassmen may keep cars.

Activities: There are 11 national fraternities and 4 national sororities. There are 350 groups on campus, including art, bagpipe band, band, cheerleading, chess, choir, chorale, chorus, college bowl, computers, dance, debate, drama, ethnic, film, gay, honors, international, jazz band, literary magazine, model UN, musical theater, newspaper, orchestra, pep band, photography, political, professional, radio and TV, religious, social, social service, student government, and symphony. Popular campus events include Summer Breeze Festival, Kuviasungnerk Winter Festival, and Festival of the Arts.

Sports: There are 10 intercollegiate sports for men and 9 for women, and 18 intramural sports for men and 18 for women. Facilities include a field house, a 1500-seat stadium, a 1500-seat arena, and a student activities center housing a movie theater, TV and pool rooms, and a pub.

Disabled Students: Wheelchair ramps, elevators, special parking, specially equipped rest rooms, special class scheduling, lowered drinking fountains, and lowered telephones are available.

Services: Counseling and information services are available, as is tutoring in some subjects, including math, physics, chemistry, writing, and biology. There is a reader service for the blind.

Campus Safety and Security: Measures include 24-hour foot and vehicle patrol, security escort services, shuttle buses, and informal discussions. There are pamphlets/posters/films, emergency telephones, and lighted pathways/sidewalks.

Programs of Study: Chicago confers B.A. and B.S. degrees. Master's and doctoral degrees are also awarded. Bachelor's degrees are awarded in BIOLOGICAL SCIENCE (biochemistry and biology/biological science), COMMUNICATIONS AND THE ARTS (art history and appreciation, classics, comparative literature, East Asian languages and literature, English, film arts, fine arts, German, Japanese, Korean, linguistics, media arts, music, romance languages and literature, Russian, Slavic languages, and visual and performing arts), COMPUTER AND PHYSICAL SCIENCE (applied mathematics, astronomy, astrophysics, chemistry, computer science, geoscience, mathematics, physics, and statistics), ENGINEERING AND ENVIRONMENTAL DESIGN (environmental science), SOCIAL SCIENCE (African American studies, anthropology, Asian/Oriental studies, Christian studies, classical/ancient civilization, economics, gender studies, geography, history, humanities, international studies, Judaic studies, Latin American studies, law, medieval studies, Near Eastern studies, philosophy, political science/government, psychology, public affairs, religion, social science, sociology, and South Asian studies). Social sciences, biological and biomedical sciences, and foreign language and literature are the largest.

Required: To graduate, students must complete 42 quarter courses, including 9 to 13 courses in the major, with an overall GPA of 1.75 and 2.0 in the major. The core curriculum includes sequences in humanities, social sciences, biological and physical sciences, civilization, and foreign languages. Also required are 2 quarters of math, 1 of art or music, and 1 year of noncredit phys ed.

Special: Special academic programs include cross-registration through the Committee on Institutional Cooperation, a summer internship in Washington, and study abroad in 19 countries. B.A.-B.S. and general studies degrees are offered, as are student-designed majors. Nondegree study and pass/fail options are possible. There are 2 national honor societies, including Phi Beta Kappa.

Faculty/Classroom: 70% of faculty are male; 30%, female. All both teach and do research. The average class size in a regular course is 25.

Admissions: 40% of the 2005-2006 applicants were accepted. The SAT scores for the 2005-2006 freshman class were: Verbal--4% between 500 and 599, 28% between 600 and 700, and 68% above 700; Math--5% between 500 and 599, 31% between 600 and 700, and 64% above 700. The ACT scores were 4% between 21 and 23, 9% between 24 and 26, 13% between 27 and 28, and 74% above 28. 95% of the current freshmen were in the top fifth of their class. There were 203 National Merit finalists.

Requirements: The SAT or ACT is required. In addition, other admissions criteria include a recommended secondary school curriculum of 4 years of English, 3 to 4 years each of history, social studies, math, and science, and 3 years of a foreign language. The GED is accepted. An essay must be submitted, and an interview is recommended. AP credits are accepted. Important factors in the admissions decision are advanced placement or honor courses, personality/intangible qualities, and extracurricular activities record.

Procedure: Freshmen are admitted in the fall. Entrance exams should be taken during the junior or senior year. There are early admissions and deferred admissions plans. Early decision applications should be filed by November 1; regular applications, by January 1 for fall entry, along with a $60 fee. Notification of early decision is sent December 15; regular decision, April 1. 1545 applicants were on the 2005 waiting list; 42 were admitted. Applications are accepted on-line.

Transfer: 73 transfer students enrolled in 2004-2005. Proven ability and interest in liberal arts education is considered. Essay, broad course work, and solid performance at home institution is considered critical. A recommendation is required from a secondary school, instructors, and dean of previous institution. A 2 year residency is a requirement. 18 of 42 quarter courses required for the bachelor's degree must be completed at Chicago.

Visiting: There are regularly scheduled orientations for prospective students, including meeting with an admissions counselor and students, sitting in on classes, visiting faculty, and staying in a residence hall. There are guides for informal visits and visitors may sit in on classes and stay overnight. To schedule a visit, contact College Admissions at (773) 702-8650.

Financial Aid: Chicago is a member of CSS. The CSS/Profile or FAFSA and the college's own financial statement are required. Check with the school for current application deadlines.

International Students: There are 429 international students enrolled. The school actively recruits these students. They must score satisfactorily on the written TOEFL or on the electronic version and also take the SAT or the ACT.

Computers: Wireless access is available. All students may access the system any time. There are no time limits and no fees.

Graduates: From July 1, 2004 to June 30, 2005, 1072 bachelor's degrees were awarded. The most popular majors were social sciences (39%), biological science (11%), and psychology (6%). In an average class, 85% graduate in 4 years or less, and 90% graduate in 6 years or less.

Admissions Contact: Theodore O'Neill, Dean, College Admissions. E-mail: *toneill@uchicgo.edu* Web: *www.uchicago.edu*

UNIVERSITY OF ILLINOIS SYSTEM

The University of Illinois System, established in 1867, is a public system in Illinois. It is governed by a board of trustees, whose chief administrator is the president. The primary goal of the system is to provide undergraduate and graduate education, conduct research, and provide public service. The total enrollment of both campuses is usually about 60,000 with 5600 faculty members. Altogether there are some 174 baccalaureate, 164 master's, and 106 doctoral programs offered in University of Illinois System. There are 4-year campuses located in Chicago and Urbana-Champaign. Profiles of the 4-year campuses are included in this section.

UNIVERSITY OF ILLINOIS AT CHICAGO   E-2

Chicago, IL 60680	**(312) 996-4350; Fax: (312) 413-7628**
Full-time: 6344 men, 7389 women	**Faculty:** I, av$
Part-time: 704 men, 713 women	**Ph.D.s:** n/av
Graduate: 4025 men, 5637 women	**Student/Faculty:** n/av
Year: semesters, summer session	**Tuition:** $8302 ($20,692)
Application Deadline: January 15	**Room & Board:** $7954
Freshman Class: 12,692 applied, 7418 accepted, 2776 enrolled	
ACT: 23	**VERY COMPETITIVE**

The University of Illinois at Chicago, founded in 1946, is a public institution with undergraduate and graduate programs in the liberal arts, art and fine arts, business, engineering, architecture, health sciences, music, teacher preparation, social work, and professional training in dentistry, medicine, and pharmacy. There are 8 undergraduate schools and 1 graduate school. In addition to regional accreditation, UIC has baccalaureate program accreditation with AACSB, ABET, ACPE, ADA, APTA, CSAB, CSWE, NAAB, NASAD, CCNE, CAAHEP, AHIMA, and CAADE. The 3 libraries contain 2,284,649 volumes and 3,903,703 microform items, and subscribe to 39,350 periodicals including electronic. Computerized library services include the card catalog, interlibrary loans, database searching, Internet access, and laptop Internet portals. Special learning facilities include a learning resource center, art gallery, radio station, and Jane Addams Hull House, which is a restored settlement house, and the James Woodworth Prairie Reserve. The 240-acre campus is in an urban area just west of downtown Chicago. Including any residence halls, there are 113 buildings.

Student Life: 97% of undergraduates are from Illinois. Others are from 42 states, 52 foreign countries, and Canada. 79% are from public schools. 43% are white; 24% Asian American; 17% Hispanic. The aver-

age age of freshmen is 18; all undergraduates, 21. 23% do not continue beyond their first year; 49% remain to graduate.

Housing: 3100 students can be accommodated in college housing, which includes coed dormitories and on-campus apartments. In addition, there are honors houses. On-campus housing is available on a first-come, first-served basis. 88% of students commute. All students may keep cars.

Activities: 1% of men belong to 5 local and 6 national fraternities; 1% of women belong to 10 national sororities. There are 220 groups on campus, including art, band, cheerleading, chess, choir, chorus, computers, dance, drama, ethnic, gay, honors, international, jazz band, literary magazine, musical theater, newspaper, political, professional, religious, social, social service, and student government. Popular campus events include Activities and Services Fair, VIC Fashion Show, and Women's Heritage Month.

Sports: There are 8 intercollegiate sports for men and 8 for women, and 15 intramural sports for men and 14 for women. Facilities include a 12,000-seat sports pavilion, 2 sports and fitness centers, a recreation centers, a 1000-seat gym, 3 pools, racquetball and tennis courts, a baseball, softball, and soccer fields, a bowling alley, indoor and outdoor tracks, and weight rooms.

Disabled Students: 80% of the campus is accessible. Wheelchair ramps, elevators, special parking, specially equipped rest rooms, special class scheduling, lowered drinking fountains, and lowered telephones are available.

Services: Counseling and information services are available, as is tutoring in most subjects. There is a reader service for the blind, and remedial math, reading, and writing. a writing center, and academic skills classes.

Campus Safety and Security: Measures include 24-hour foot and vehicle patrol, self-defense education, security escort services, and shuttle buses. There are informal discussions, pamphlets/posters/films, emergency telephones, lighted pathways/sidewalks, and emergency call buttons across campus.

Programs of Study: UIC confers B.A., B.S., B.Arch., B.F.A., B.S.C. and E., B.S.C.E., B.S.Ch.E., B.S.E.E., B.S.E.M., B.S.E.M.A.N., B.S.M.E., B.S.N., and B.S.W. degrees. Master's and doctoral degrees are also awarded. Bachelor's degrees are awarded in BIOLOGICAL SCIENCE (biochemistry, biology/biological science, and nutrition), BUSINESS (accounting, banking and finance, entrepreneurial studies, management science, and marketing/retailing/merchandising), COMMUNICATIONS AND THE ARTS (art history and appreciation, classics, design, dramatic arts, French, graphic design, industrial design, Italian, literature, music, photography, Polish, Russian, Spanish, speech/debate/rhetoric, and studio art), COMPUTER AND PHYSICAL SCIENCE (chemistry, computer science, geology, information sciences and systems, mathematics, physics, and statistics), EDUCATION (art, education, elementary, English, foreign languages, mathematics, physical, science, and secondary), ENGINEERING AND ENVIRONMENTAL DESIGN (architecture, bioengineering, chemical engineering, civil engineering, computer engineering, electrical/electronics engineering, engineering management, engineering physics, industrial engineering technology, and mechanical engineering), HEALTH PROFESSIONS (medical laboratory science, and nursing), SOCIAL SCIENCE (African American studies, anthropology, classical/ancient civilization, criminal justice, economics, German area studies, history, Latin American studies, philosophy, political science/government, psychology, social work, and sociology). Math, nursing, and philosophy are the strongest academically. Accounting, engineering, and psychology are the largest.

Required: Students must demonstrate proficiency in written English through either course work or testing, and complete 24 hours of general education, including 6 hours each of humanities, social sciences, and natural sciences. The remaining 6 hours may be spread across the 3 categories. A minimum overall GPA of 2.0 on a 4.0 scale is required. Total number of hours to graduate varies by major but is always at least 120.

Special: Special academic programs include a wide variety of co-op and program internships, work-study with some 70 on- and off-campus employers, and study abroad opportunities at accredited foreign universities, as well as special programs in France, Italy, Canada, Austria, Spain, and Mexico. There is cross-registration with the City Colleges of Chicago. Interdisciplinary majors are offered in architectural studies, communications and theater, math and computer science, bioengineering, and information and decision sciences. Students may pursue a 3-2 engineering degree with Chicago State, Eastern Illinois, Illinois State, Northeastern Illinois, and Western Illinois Universities. Up to 4 semester hours of credit may be granted for military experience. Dual and student-designed majors, nondegree study, and pass/fail options are available. There are 21 national honor societies, including Phi Beta Kappa, a freshman honors program.

Admissions: 58% of the 2005-2006 applicants were accepted. The ACT scores for the 2005-2006 freshman class were: 27% below 21, 27% between 21 and 23, 26% between 24 and 26, 10% between 27 and 28, and 10% above 28. 47% of the current freshmen were in the top fifth of their class; 82% were in the top two fifths.

Requirements: The SAT or ACT is required. In addition, applicants should be graduates of an accredited secondary school; the GED is accepted. The recommended secondary school curriculum varies according to the college program chosen, but 16 high school credits are required as follows: English: 4: Mathematics: 3; Science: 3: Foreign Language: 2: and Social Studies: 3: Electives: 1. AP and CLEP credits are accepted. Important factors in the admissions decision are recommendations by school officials, evidence of special talent, and advanced placement or honor courses.

Procedure: Freshmen are admitted in the fall. Entrance exams should be taken in the spring of the junior year or the fall of the senior year. Applications should be filed by January 15 for fall entry and October 1 for spring entry, along with a $40 fee. Notification is sent on a rolling basis. A waiting list is an active part of the admissions procedure.Applications are accepted on-line.

Transfer: 1307 transfer students enrolled in 2004-2005. Transferable hours and minimum GPA vary according to program. 30 of 120 credits required for the bachelor's degree must be completed at UIC.

Visiting: There are regularly scheduled orientations for prospective students, consisting of a general meeting, a college meeting, and campus tours. There are guides for informal visits and visitors may sit in on classes. To schedule a visit, contact the Office of Undergraduate Admissions at uicadmit@uic.edu.

Financial Aid: In 2005-2006, 57% of all full-time freshmen and 67% of continuing full-time students received some form of financial aid. 44% of full-time freshmen received need-based aid. The average freshman award was $10,169. Need-based scholarships or need-based grants averaged $8860; need-based self-help aid (loans and jobs) averaged $3518; and non-need-based athletic scholarships averaged $11,117. The average financial indebtedness of the 2005 graduate was $16,800. UIC is a member of CSS. The FAFSA is required.

International Students: There are 210 international students enrolled. They must score 520 on the written TOEFL or 190 on the electronic version and also take the SAT, ACTor for freshmen. Minimum required scores depend on the specific college.

Computers: Wireless access is available. The Academic Computing and Communications Center (ACCC) supports the educational and research needs of the UIC community by providing a variety of computing and communications resources. Student have ready access to both Unix systems and personal PCs. Through 1100 workstations, ACCC provides internet connections for students living in residence halls, in the libraries, and student centers. A wireless network in public areas on campus is also available. All students may access the system 24 hours daily. There are no time limits and no fees. It is strongly recommended that all students have a personal computer.

Graduates: From July 1, 2004 to June 30, 2005, 3149 bachelor's degrees were awarded. The most popular majors were business/marketing (20%), builogical/life sciences (11%), and engineering (10%). In an average class, 20% graduate in 4 years or less, 22% graduate in 5 years or less, and 50% graduate in 6 years or less. 175 companies recruited on campus in 2004-2005.

Admissions Contact: Thomas E. Glenn, Executive Director of Admissions and Records. E-mail: uicadmit@uic.edu
Web: http://www.uic.edu/depts/oar

UNIVERSITY OF ILLINOIS AT URBANA-CHAMPAIGN   E-3

Urbana, IL 61801   (217) 333-0302; Fax: (217) 244-0903

Full-time: 15,948 men, 13,957 women	Faculty: 2149; I, +$
Part-time: 292 men, 256 women	Ph.D.s: 88%
Graduate: 5441 men, 4776 women	Student/Faculty: 14 to 1
Year: semesters, summer session	Tuition: $8624 ($22,710)
Application Deadline: January 2	Room & Board: $7176
Freshman Class: n/av	
SAT Verbal/Math: 620/680*	ACT: 28

HIGHLY COMPETITIVE+

The University of Illinois at Urbana-Champaign, founded in 1867, is the oldest and largest campus in the University of Illinois system, offering some 150 undergraduate and more than 100 graduate degree programs. There are 16 undergraduate schools. In addition to regional accreditation, Illinois has baccalaureate program accreditation with AACSB, AALE, ABA, ABET, ACBSP, ACEJMC, ADA, AHEA, APA, ASLA, ASLHA, AVMA, CSAB, CSWE, NAAB, NASAD, NASD, NASM, NAST, NCACS, NCATE, NISAB, NRPA, and SAF. The 41 libraries contain 10,015,321 volumes, 9,201,301 microform items, and 169,894 audio/video tapes/CDs/DVDs, and subscribe to 89,444 periodicals including electronic. Computerized library services include the card catalog, interlibrary loans, database searching, Internet access, and laptop Internet portals. Special learning facilities include a learning resource center, art gallery, natural history museum, radio station, TV station, language learning lab, performing arts center, graphic technologies lab, world history and cultural museum, rehabilitation-education center, center for American music, Japan House and gardens, and rare books and special collections libraries. The 3909-acre campus is in a small town 130 miles south of Chicago. Including any residence halls, there are 345 buildings.

Student Life: 89% of undergraduates are from Illinois. Others are from 50 states, 121 foreign countries, and Canada. 63% are white; 12% foreign nationals; 11% Asian American. The average age of freshmen is 19; all undergraduates, 21. 7% do not continue beyond their first year; 80% remain to graduate.

Housing: 10,970 students can be accommodated in college housing, which includes single-sex and coed dorms, on-campus apartments, and married-student housing. In addition, there are language houses and special-interest houses. On-campus housing is guaranteed for all 4 years. 82% of students commute. All students may keep cars.

Activities: 20% of men belong to 3 local and 56 national fraternities; 22% of women belong to 3 local and 32 national sororities. There are 1000 groups on campus, including art, band, cheerleading, choir, chorale, chorus, computers, dance, debate, drama, drill team, ethnic, film, forensics, gay, honors, international, jazz band, literary magazine, marching band, musical theater, newspaper, opera, orchestra, pep band, photography, political, professional, radio and TV, religious, social, social service, student government, symphony, and yearbook. Popular campus events include Quad Day to introduce campus organizations, Dad's Weekend, and Mom's Weekend.

Sports: There are 10 intercollegiate sports for men and 12 for women, and 22 intramural sports for men and 22 for women. Facilities include major varsity sports facilities, one of the world's largest intramural sports and recreation buildings, numerous student union facilities, and 42 acres of outdoor playing fields.

Disabled Students: All of the campus is accessible. Wheelchair ramps, elevators, special parking, specially equipped rest rooms, special class scheduling, lowered drinking fountains, lowered telephones, special housing, adjustable tables and labs, textbook and supply services and fitness equipment for all students with disabilities, including wheelchair sports such as basketball, and track, and sport camps are available.

Services: Counseling and information services are available, as is tutoring in every subject. There is a reader service for the blind, and remedial math, reading, and writing. Transportation and rehabilitation services are offered, as well as interpreters, note taking, taped lectures, priority registration, and modified test times.

Campus Safety and Security: Measures include 24-hour foot and vehicle patrol, self-defense education, security escort services, and shuttle buses. There are informal discussions, pamphlets/posters/films, emergency telephones, lighted pathways/sidewalks, a safe rides program, safety presentations, and evaluations by campus police.

Programs of Study: Illinois confers A.B., B.S., B.A.U.P., B.F.A., B.Land.Arch., B.Mus., B.S.Ed., B.S.J., B.S.W., and B.V.M. degrees. Master's and doctoral degrees are also awarded. Bachelor's degrees are awarded in AGRICULTURE (agricultural business management, agricultural communications, agricultural economics, agricultural mechanics, agronomy, animal science, forestry and related sciences, horticulture, natural resource management, range/farm management, and wildlife management), BIOLOGICAL SCIENCE (biology/biological science, biophysics, biotechnology, botany, cell biology, entomology, microbiology, molecular biology, nutrition, physiology, plant physiology, and wildlife biology), BUSINESS (accounting, banking and finance, entrepreneurial studies, hospitality management services, human resources, insurance, labor studies, logistics, management information systems, management science, marketing and distribution, marketing management, marketing/retailing/merchandising, operations research, organizational behavior, personnel management, purchasing/inventory management, real estate, and recreation and leisure services), COMMUNICATIONS AND THE ARTS (advertising, art history and appreciation, broadcasting, classics, communications, comparative literature, crafts, dance, dramatic arts, East Asian languages and literature, English, English literature, film arts, fine arts, French, Germanic languages and literature, graphic design, Hebrew, industrial design, Italian, journalism, linguistics, media arts, music, music history and appreciation, music performance, music theory and composition, painting, photography, Portuguese, Russian languages and literature, sculpture, Spanish, speech/debate/rhetoric, and voice), COMPUTER AND PHYSICAL SCIENCE (actuarial science, astronomy, chemistry, computer management, computer mathematics, computer programming, geology, mathematics, physics, and statistics), EDUCATION (agricultural, art, athletic training, computer, early childhood, education, education of the multiply handicapped, elementary, English, foreign languages, mathematics, music, physical, science, secondary, and vocational), ENGINEERING AND ENVIRONMENTAL DESIGN (aeronautical engineering, agricultural engineering, airline piloting and navigation, architectural engineering, architecture, aviation administration/management, bioengineering, ceramic engineering, chemical engineering, city/community/regional planning, civil engineering, computational sciences, computer engineering, computer technology, electrical/electronics engineering, engineering, engineering mechanics, engineering physics, geological engineering, industrial administration/management, industrial engineering, landscape architecture/design, materials engineering, materials science, mechanical engineering, metallurgical engineering, nuclear engineering, and plastics engineering), HEALTH PROFESSIONS (biomedical science, community health work, exercise science, health care administration, preveterinary science, public health, and rehabilitation therapy), SOCIAL SCIENCE (anthropology, child psychology/development, dietetics, East Asian studies, economics, family/consumer studies, food production/management/services, food science, geography, history, human development, humanities, international studies, Latin American studies, liberal arts/general studies, parks and recreation management, philosophy, political science/government, prelaw, psychology, religion, Russian and Slavic studies, sociology, textiles and clothing, and women's studies). Accounting, engineering, and music are the strongest academically. Psychology, accountancy, and electrical and computer engineering are the largest.

Required: All students must demonstrate satisfactory proficiency in the use of the English and 6 hours each in approved composition classes, western/nonwestern cultural studies, arts and humanities, social sciences/behavior, natural sciences/technology, and quantitative reasoning. Successful completion of either the third or fourth year (depending on college) of a language other than the student's primary language is required. Students must maintain a minimum GPA of 2.0 while completing 120 to 132 credit hours (depending on the major) in order to graduate.

Special: Illinois offers cooperative engineering programs with many midwestern liberal arts colleges; summer, semester, and full-year programs abroad and numerous exchange opportunities. Unusual opportunities include a leisure studies semester in Scotland and a summer parliamentary internship in London. Dual degrees are offered, as well as student-designed majors and a 3-2 engineering program with numerous universities. Work-study and pass/fail options are possible. There are 89 national honor societies, including Phi Beta Kappa, a freshman honors program, and honors programs in all departments.

Faculty/Classroom: 67% of faculty are male; 33%, female. 95% teach undergraduates, 100% do research, and 95% do both. Graduate students teach 50% of introductory courses. The average class size in an introductory lecture is 19; in a laboratory, 22; and in a regular course, 29.

Admissions: The SAT scores for the 2005-2006 freshman class were: Verbal--11% below 500, 33% between 500 and 599, 42% between 600 and 700, and 14% above 700; Math--3% below 500, 17% between 500 and 599, 41% between 600 and 700, and 39% above 700. The ACT scores were 5% below 21, 11% between 21 and 23, 27% between 24 and 26, 23% between 27 and 28, and 33% above 28. 76% of the current freshmen were in the top fifth of their class; 96% were in the top two fifths.

Requirements: The SAT or ACT is recommended. The ACT Optional Writing test is also required. In addition, applicants should be graduates of accredited secondary schools or have the GED. Advanced placement tests are encouraged and accepted. High school preparation must include 4 years of English, 3 or more of math, 2 each of lab science and social studies, 2 years of the same foreign language, and 2 years of flexible academic units. A personal and professional essay is required. Visual arts applicants must submit a portfolio; performing arts applicants are required to audition. AP credits are accepted. Important factors in the admissions decision are advanced placement or honor courses, evidence of special talent, and geographic diversity.

Procedure: Freshmen are admitted in the fall. There are early admissions and deferred admissions plans. Applications should be filed by January 2 for fall entry, along with a $40 fee. Notification of regular decision is December through March. 503 applicants were on the 2005 waiting list. Applications are accepted on-line.

Transfer: 1094 transfer students enrolled in 2004-2005. Transfer application requirements differ by degree program. Generally, students transferring should have junior standing of 60 hours. Admission is also subject to the number of places available. 30 of 136 credits required for the bachelor's degree must be completed at Illinois.

Visiting: There are regularly scheduled orientations for prospective students, consisting of presentations, videotape, and tours given by the admissions staff at 10 A.M. and 1 P.M. daily on weekdays and 10 A.M. on Saturdays. There are guides for informal visits and visitors may sit in on classes. To schedule a visit, contact the Campus Visitors Center at (217) 333-0824 or *visits@oar.vivc.edu.*

Financial Aid: In 2005-2006, 65% of all full-time freshmen and 60% of continuing full-time students received some form of financial aid. 38% of all full-time students received need-based aid. The average freshman award was $4649. Need-based scholarships or need-based grants averaged $3609 ($7313 maximum); need-based self-help aid (loans and jobs) averaged $1781 ($3500 maximum); non-need-based athletic scholarships averaged $8032 ($24,290 maximum); and other non-need-based awards and non-need-based scholarships averaged $1972 ($14,086 maximum). 35% of undergraduates work part time. Average annual earnings from campus work are $1772. The average financial indebtedness of the 2005 graduate was $15,536. The FAFSA is required. The deadline for filing freshman financial aid applications for fall entry is March 15.

International Students: There are 1445 international students enrolled. The school actively recruits these students. They must take the written TOEFL and also take the SAT or ACT, if the student has attended a U.S. institution for 2 or more years.

Computers: Wireless access is available. All students may use the college network in residence halls, classrooms, computer labs, or public spaces on campus. There are 1,336 general access computers in on-campus computer labs, residence hall labs, and libraries. There are also E-mail kiosks scattered over the campus, as well as wireless access in the library, the Student Union, and many other buildings across campus. There are approximately another 1000 computers accessible in various departmental laboratories. All students may access the system 24 hours a day. Students may access the system 20 hours per week on dial-in access only. There are no fees. It is strongly recommended that all students have a personal computer.

Graduates: From July 1, 2004 to June 30, 2005, 6763 bachelor's degrees were awarded. The most popular majors were finance (7%), psychology (6%), and accounting (5%). In an average class, 2% graduate in 3 years or less, 58% graduate in 4 years or less, 78% graduate in 5 years or less, and 81% graduate in 6 years or less. 4611 companies recruited on campus in 2004-2005. Of the 2004 graduating class, 31% were enrolled in graduate school within 6 months of graduation and 86% were employed.

Admissions Contact: Stacey Kostell, Director, Undergraduate Admissions. A video is available.
E-mail: *undergraduate@admissions.uiuc.edu* Web: *www.apply.uiuc.edu*

UNIVERSITY OF SAINT FRANCIS   E-2
Joliet, IL 60435   (815) 740-3400
                                     (800) 735-7500; Fax: (815) 740-5032

Full-time: 360 men, 778 women	**Faculty:** 70
Part-time: 38 men, 100 women	**Ph.D.s:** 59%
Graduate: 180 men, 606 women	**Student/Faculty:** 16 to 1
Year: semesters, summer session	**Tuition:** $18,530
Application Deadline: August 1	**Room & Board:** $6900
Freshman Class: n/av	
ACT: required	**COMPETITIVE**

The University of Saint Francis, founded as a college in 1920, is a private liberal arts and professional institution affiliated with the Roman Catholic Church. There are 5 undergraduate and 4 graduate schools. In addition to regional accreditation, USF has baccalaureate program accreditation with CSWE, NLN, and NRPA. The library contains 107,457 volumes, 1761 microform items, and 6366 audio/video tapes/CDs/DVDs, and subscribes to 342 periodicals including electronic. Computerized library services include the card catalog, interlibrary loans, database searching, Internet access, and laptop Internet portals. Special learning facilities include a learning resource center, art gallery, radio station, TV station, greenhouse, and wireless education classroom. The 22-acre campus is in a suburban area 35 miles southwest of Chicago. Including any residence halls, there are 7 buildings.

Student Life: 98% of undergraduates are from Illinois. Others are from 9 states. 86% are from public schools. 75% are white. 55% are Catholic; 27% Protestant. The average age of freshmen is 18; all undergraduates, 23. 20% do not continue beyond their first year; 56% remain to graduate.

Housing: 331 students can be accommodated in college housing, which includes coed dorms. On-campus housing is guaranteed for the freshman year only, is available on a first-come, first-served basis, and is available on a lottery system for upperclassmen. Priority is given to out-of-town students. 74% of students live on campus; of those, 50% remain on campus on weekends. All students may keep cars.

Activities: There are no fraternities or sororities. There are 37 groups on campus, including art, business, cheerleading, chess, choir, chorale, chorus, dance, drama, education, environmental, ethnic, honors, literary magazine, musical theater, newspaper, nursing, orchestra, political, professional, radio and TV, religious, social, social service, and student government. Popular campus events include Ballet Folklorico Mexico, African Dance, and Exchanging Cultures night.

Sports: There are 6 intercollegiate sports for men and 8 for women, and 6 intramural sports for men and 6 for women. A 10,000-seat football stadium and a 5,000-seat minor league baseball stadium are among the many off-campus facilities, as well as a six-field, lighted softball complex, three golf courses, two soccer fields and an indoor/outdoor tennis complex. On campus, a recreation center houses a 1,200-seat gymnasium, a state of the art fitness center features facilities for swimming, weight training and aerobic training, and an indoor and outdoor walking track.

Disabled Students: 90% of the campus is accessible. Wheelchair ramps, elevators, special parking, specially equipped rest rooms, special class scheduling, lowered drinking fountains, and lowered telephones are available.

Services: Counseling and information services are available, as is tutoring in most subjects. There is remedial math. The writing center provides help with papers. Numerous computerized tutorial programs for courses are also available.

Campus Safety and Security: Measures include 24-hour foot and vehicle patrol, self-defense education, security escort services, and shuttle

buses. There are informal discussions, pamphlets/posters/films, emergency telephones, lighted pathways/sidewalks, and sexual assault counseling, and routine fire inspection.

Programs of Study: USF confers B.A., B.S., B.B.A., and B.S.N and B.S.W. degrees. Master's degrees are also awarded. Bachelor's degrees are awarded in BIOLOGICAL SCIENCE (biology/biological science), BUSINESS (accounting, banking and finance, business administration and management, marketing/retailing/merchandising, and recreational facilities management), COMMUNICATIONS AND THE ARTS (communications, English, journalism, music, and visual and performing arts), COMPUTER AND PHYSICAL SCIENCE (computer programming, computer science, information sciences and systems, mathematics, and web technology), EDUCATION (elementary, secondary, and special), ENGINEERING AND ENVIRONMENTAL DESIGN (computer technology and environmental science), HEALTH PROFESSIONS (allied health, health, medical technology, nuclear medical technology, nursing, predentistry, premedicine, preveterinary science, radiation therapy, and radiograph medical technology), SOCIAL SCIENCE (history, liberal arts/general studies, political science/government, psychology, social work, and theological studies). Biology and education are the strongest academically. Business, nursing, and education are the largest.

Required: To graduate, students are required to complete 128 credit hours with a minimum of 40 hours in the major while maintaining a GPA of 2.0. The required liberal education core includes courses in the following areas: literacy, literary inquiry and aesthetic awareness, numerical understanding and scientific inquiry, historical understanding, social awareness, ethical understanding, philosophical inquiry, and religious foundations. A thesis or other senior capstone experience is also required.

Special: Internships, on- and off-campus, paid and unpaid, are available in most majors. Dual and interdisciplinary majors, a pass/fail option, a Washington semester, study abroad , and credit for life, military, and work experience are available. There are 12 national honor societies and a freshman honors program.

Faculty/Classroom: 46% of faculty are male; 54%, female. 78% teach undergraduates. No introductory courses are taught by graduate students. The average class size in an introductory lecture is 18; in a laboratory, 14; and in a regular course, 17.

Admissions: The ACT scores for the 2005-2006 freshman class were: 39% below 21, 31% between 21 and 23, 19% between 24 and 26, 9% between 27 and 28, and 2% above 28. 38% of the current freshmen were in the top fifth of their class; 70% were in the top two fifths.

Requirements: The ACT is required. Admission requirements also include 4 years of English, 3 of either art, music, foreign language, or computer science, and 2 each of math, including geometry, science (1 lab), and social studies. USF requires applicants to be in the upper 50% of their class. A GPA of 2.0 is required. AP and CLEP credits are accepted. Important factors in the admissions decision are personality/intangible qualities, advanced placement or honor courses, and leadership record.

Procedure: Freshmen are admitted fall and spring. Entrance exams should be taken in the spring of the junior year or the fall of the senior year. There is a deferred admissions plan. Applications should be filed by August 1 for fall entry, along with a $30 fee. Notification is sent on a rolling basis. Applications are accepted on-line.

Transfer: 179 transfer students enrolled in 2004-2005. Transfer students must have a GPA of 2.0 and must submit transcripts from colleges previously attended; applicants with fewer than 30 semester hours must also submit high school transcripts. Applicants must have taken English at the college level, math at the intermediate algebra level, and present a high school diploma or GED. 32 of 128 credits required for the bachelor's degree must be completed at USF.

Visiting: There are regularly scheduled orientations for prospective students, including orientation, meeting faculty, a tour, and student presentations. There are guides for informal visits and visitors may sit in on classes and stay overnight. To schedule a visit, contact the Admissions Office at *information@stfrancis.edu.*

Financial Aid: In 2005-2006, 99% of all full-time freshmen and 91% of continuing full-time students received some form of financial aid. 76% of full-time freshmen and 71% of continuing full-time students received need-based aid. The average freshman award was $16,007. Need-based scholarships or need-based grants averaged $7030; need-based self-help aid (loans and jobs) averaged $3752; non-need-based athletic scholarships averaged $8704; and other non-need-based awards and non-need-based scholarships averaged $6098. 67% of undergraduates work part time. Average annual earnings from campus work are $1279. The average financial indebtedness of the 2005 graduate was $14,650. The FAFSA and the college's own financial statement are required. The priority date for freshman financial aid applications for fall entry is May 1.

International Students: There are 8 international students enrolled. They must take on the TOEFL and also take the SAT or the ACT.

Computers: Wireless access is available. The University of St. Francis has over 300 PC workstations located in classrooms, general student labs, science labs, and specialized teaching classrooms that provide students full access to network services, programs, and the Internet. The

University library provides both wired and wireless access to the Internet and the institutional intranet. There are 34 wired research stations for use and the entire building provides wireless access to the Internet and web library services. In addition, the University residence halls have study rooms with 16 wired stations providing access to the campus intranet and print services. Wireless access to the Internet is provided in the main student lounge in the Marian Hall dormitory, as well as two other lounges located in the main academic building on campus. All students may access the system 24 hours a day. There are no time limits and no fees.

Graduates: From July 1, 2004 to June 30, 2005, 288 bachelor's degrees were awarded. The most popular majors were education (25%), business (19%), and nursing (17%). In an average class, 36% graduate in 4 years or less, 53% graduate in 5 years or less, and 55% graduate in 6 years or less. Of the 2004 graduating class, 15% were enrolled in graduate school within 6 months of graduation and 78% were employed.

Admissions Contact: Meghan Connolly, Director of Undergraduate Admissions. A video is available. E-mail: *informations@stfrancis.edu* Web: *www.stfrancis.edu*

VANDERCOOK COLLEGE OF MUSIC E-2

Chicago, IL 60616-3731 (312) 225-6288
(800) 448-2655; Fax: (312) 225-5211

Full-time: 50 men, 35 women	**Faculty:** 11
Part-time: 1 man, 3 women	**Ph.Ds:** 70%
Graduate: 32 men, 38 women	**Student/Faculty:** 7 to 1
Year: semesters	**Tuition:** $13,820
Application Deadline: see profile	**Room & Board:** $5610
Freshman Class: n/av	
SAT or ACT: required	**SPECIAL**

VanderCook College of Music, founded in 1909, is devoted solely to the preparation of music educators. There is 1 undergraduate school. Figures in the above capsule and in this profile are approximate. In addition to regional accreditation, VCM has baccalaureate program accreditation with NASM. The 2 libraries contain 20,000 volumes, 2000 microform items, and 5000 audio/video tapes/CDs/DVDs, and subscribe to 80 periodicals including electronic. Computerized library services include the card catalog, interlibrary loans, and database searching. Special learning facilities include a learning resource center. The 1-acre campus is in an urban area 3 miles from the center of Chicago. Including any residence halls, there is 1 building.

Student Life: 60% of undergraduates are from Illinois. Others are from 11 states, 1 foreign countries, and Canada. 80% are from public schools. 63% are white; 32% African American. The average age of freshmen is 19; all undergraduates, 21. 8% do not continue beyond their first year; 80% remain to graduate.

Housing: 100 students can be accommodated in college housing, which includes single-sex and coed dorms, on-campus apartments, married-student housing, and fraternity houses. On-campus housing is guaranteed for all 4 years. 60% of students live on campus; of those, 90% remain on campus on weekends. Alcohol is not permitted. All students may keep cars.

Activities: 50% of men belong to 2 local and 1 national fraternity, 20% of women belong to 2 local and 1 national sorority. There are 9 groups on campus, including band, choir, chorale, chorus, jazz band, musical theater, orchestra, pep band, religious, and student government.

Sports: There is no sports program at VCM. Facilities include a swimming pool, a gym, and tennis courts.

Disabled Students: Special parking and special class scheduling are available.

Campus Safety and Security: Measures include 24-hour foot and vehicle patrol, self-defense education, security escort services, and shuttle buses. There are informal discussions, emergency telephones, and lighted pathways/sidewalks.

Programs of Study: VCM confers the B.M.Ed degree. Master's degrees are also awarded. Bachelor's degrees are awarded in EDUCATION (music).

Required: To graduate, students must complete a total of 134 semester hours distributed in the 5 major categories of general education, professional education, applied music performance, fundamentals and theory, and music education. They must also pass performance proficiency exams on 17 instruments and a vocal proficiency exam.

Faculty/Classroom: 44% of faculty are male; 56%, female. All teach undergraduates. No introductory courses are taught by graduate students. The average class size in an introductory lecture is 15; in a laboratory, 15; and in a regular course, 15.

Requirements: The SAT or ACT is required. Graduation from an accredited secondary school or a satisfactory score on the GED is required for admission. Secondary school courses must include 3 units each of English and science, 2 each of math, social studies, music, and a foreign language, and 1 each of history and art. An audition and an interview are required. VCM requires applicants to be in the upper 75% of their class. A GPA of 2.0 is required. AP and CLEP credits are accepted. Important factors in the admissions decision are evidence of special talent, recommendations by alumni, and extracurricular activities record.

Procedure: Freshmen are admitted fall and spring. Entrance exams should be taken during the junior year. There are early decision, early admissions, deferred admissions, and rolling admissions plans. Early decision applications should be filed by May 1; regular applications, by June 1 for fall entry and October 1 for spring entry, along with a $35 fee. The college accepts all applicants. Notification is sent on a rolling basis. 8 early decision candidates were accepted for the 2005-2006 class.

Transfer: Transfer students must have a minimum GPA of 2.5. An audition and an interview are required. Courses taken at other institutions in performance, theory, and history must be validated.

Visiting: There are regularly scheduled orientations for prospective students, including the opportunity to observe a class, meet students and faculty, and tour the campus. There are guides for informal visits and visitors may sit in on classes and stay overnight. To schedule a visit, contact James Malley, Director of Admission.

Financial Aid: 30% of undergraduates work part time. The FAFSA is required. Check with the school for current application deadlines.

International Students: They must score satisfactorily on the written TOEFL.

Computers: All students may access the system. There are no time limits and no fees.

Admissions Contact: James P. Malley, Jr., Director of Admissions. E-mail: *jmalley@vandercook.edu*

WESTERN ILLINOIS UNIVERSITY C-3
Macomb, IL 61455-1390

(309) 298-3157
(877) PICK WIU; Fax: (309) 298-3111

Full-time: 5327 men, 4990 women	**Faculty:** 641; IIA, -$
Part-time: 464 men, 503 women	**Ph.D.s:** 70%
Graduate: 816 men, 1304 women	**Student/Faculty:** 16 to 1
Year: semesters, summer session	**Tuition:** $6899 ($9383)
Application Deadline: May 15	**Room & Board:** $6143
Freshman Class: 7286 applied, 5224 accepted, 1823 enrolled	
ACT: 22	**COMPETITIVE**

Western Illinois University, founded in 1899, is a public institution with 5 colleges, a school of graduate studies, and and a school of music. There are 6 undergraduate schools and 1 graduate school. In addition to regional accreditation, WIU has baccalaureate program accreditation with AACSB, ADA, ASLA, CAHEA, CSWE, NASM, NCATE, and NRPA. The 5 libraries contain 998,041 volumes, 1,342,620 microform items, and 3445 audio/video tapes/CDs/DVDs, and subscribe to 3200 periodicals including electronic. Computerized library services include the card catalog, interlibrary loans, database searching, Internet access, and laptop Internet portals. Special learning facilities include an art gallery, natural history museum, radio station, TV station, and international studies center. The 1050-acre campus is in a rural area 76 miles from Peoria and 151 miles from St. Louis. Including any residence halls, there are 52 buildings.

Student Life: 93% of undergraduates are from Illinois. Students are from 33 states, 50 foreign countries, and Canada. 89% are from public schools. 81% are white. The average age of freshmen is 18; all undergraduates, 22. 20% do not continue beyond their first year; 55% remain to graduate.

Housing: 5045 students can be accommodated in college housing, which includes single-sex and coed dorms, on-campus apartments, and married-student housing. In addition, there are honors houses, special-interest houses, and academic majors, honors, and wellness floors in residence halls. On-campus housing is guaranteed for all 4 years. 52% of students commute. Alcohol is not permitted. All students may keep cars.

Activities: 8% of men belong to 18 national fraternities; 8% of women belong to 10 national sororities. There are 254 groups on campus, including art, band, cheerleading, chess, choir, chorale, chorus, computers, dance, drama, drill team, ethnic, gay, honors, international, jazz band, literary magazine, marching band, musical theater, newspaper, opera, orchestra, pep band, photography, political, professional, radio and TV, religious, social, social service, student government, and symphony. Popular campus events include Family Weekend, Summer Music Theater, and International Bazaar.

Sports: There are 10 intercollegiate sports for men and 10 for women, and 25 intramural sports for men and 25 for women. Facilities include an 18-hole golf course, tennis courts, a basketball court, a swimming pool, a recreation center, and softball, soccer, and football fields.

Disabled Students: 95% of the campus is accessible. Wheelchair ramps, elevators, special parking, specially equipped rest rooms, special class scheduling, lowered drinking fountains, and lowered telephones are available.

Services: Counseling and information services are available, as is tutoring in some subjects, including business, art, English, math, computer science, science, social sciences, and humanities. There is a reader service for the blind and remedial math and writing.

Campus Safety and Security: Measures include 24-hour foot and vehicle patrol, self-defense education, security escort services, and shuttle buses. There are informal discussions, pamphlets/posters/films, emergency telephones, lighted pathways/sidewalks, and and a beacon system.

Programs of Study: WIU confers B.A., B.S., B.B., B.F.A., B.S.Ed., and B.S.W. degrees. Master's degrees are also awarded. Bachelor's degrees are awarded in AGRICULTURE (agriculture), BIOLOGICAL SCIENCE (biology/biological science), BUSINESS (accounting, banking and finance, business administration and management, management information systems, marketing/retailing/merchandising, and personnel management), COMMUNICATIONS AND THE ARTS (art, communications, dramatic arts, English, French, journalism, media arts, music, and Spanish), COMPUTER AND PHYSICAL SCIENCE (chemistry, computer science, geology, mathematics, and physics), EDUCATION (bilingual/bicultural, elementary, industrial arts, physical, special, and technical), ENGINEERING AND ENVIRONMENTAL DESIGN (industrial engineering technology and manufacturing technology), HEALTH PROFESSIONS (health science, medical technology, and speech pathology/audiology), SOCIAL SCIENCE (economics, family/consumer studies, geography, history, law enforcement and corrections, parks and recreation management, philosophy, political science/government, psychology, social work, and sociology). Accounting, chemistry, and human resource management are the strongest academically. Law enforcement and justice administration and elementary education are the largest.

Required: To graduate, all students must complete at least 120 credit hours with 32 hours in the major, and have a minimum 2.0 GPA. Students must take 44 hours in the fields of basic skills, well-being, natural science and math, historical and social foundations, and humanities.

Special: WIU offers internships in business, law enforcement, and physical training, study abroad in 9 countries, and dual programs in engineering, dentistry, medicine, and medical technology. Student-designed majors and independent study are available through the Experimental Studies, Board of Trustees, and Interdisciplinary Studies programs. The Board of Trustees degree program offers credit for work experience. Also available are a field campus and a life science station on the Mississippi River, a 3-2 engineering program with the University of Illinois, and various preprofessional programs. There are 30 national honor societies, a freshman honors program, and 34 departmental honors programs.

Faculty/Classroom: 55% of faculty are male; 45%, female. 99% teach undergraduates and 90% do research. Graduate students teach 3% of introductory courses. The average class size in an introductory lecture is 34; in a laboratory, 25; and in a regular course, 25.

Admissions: 72% of the 2005-2006 applicants were accepted. The ACT scores for the 2005-2006 freshman class were: 46% below 21, 32% between 21 and 23, 16% between 24 and 26, 4% between 27 and 28, and 2% above 28. 16% of the current freshmen were in the top fifth of their class; 41% were in the top two fifths. 12 freshmen graduated first in their class.

Requirements: The SAT or ACT is required. Students must have 4 years of English, 3 years each of math, science, and social studies, and 2 electives in art, film, foreign language, music, speech, theater, journalism, religion, philosophy, or vocational education. Academic Services is a program for selected students who do not meet regular admission requirements. WIU requires applicants to be in the upper 40% of their class. A GPA of 2.2 is required. AP and CLEP credits are accepted.

Procedure: Freshmen are admitted to all sessions. Entrance exams should be taken by April of the senior year. There is a deferred admissions and a rolling admissions plan. Applications should be filed by May 15 for fall entry, along with a $30 fee. Notification is sent on a rolling basis. Applications are accepted on-line.

Transfer: 1403 transfer students enrolled in 2004-2005. Students transferring fewer than 24 semester credits or 36 quarter credits must meet freshman admissions standards, have a combined C average for all hours attempted, and be in good standing at their previous college. 30 of 120 credits required for the bachelor's degree must be completed at WIU.

Visiting: There are regularly scheduled orientations for prospective students. There are guides for informal visits and visitors may sit in on classes and stay overnight. To schedule a visit, contact the Admissions Office at (309) 298-3140.

Financial Aid: In 2005-2006, 76% of all full-time students received some form of financial aid. 52% of full-time freshmen and 51% of continuing full-time students received need-based aid. The average freshman award was $6800. With $2090 from need-based scholarships or need-based grants; $1490 from need-based self-help aid (loans and jobs); $320 from non-need-based athletic scholarships; $1230 from other non-need-based awards and non-need-based scholarships; and $1670 from non-need based loans and jobs. 19% of undergraduates work part time. Average annual earnings from campus work is $1280. The average financial indebtedness of the 2005 graduate was $14,750. The FAFSA is required. The priority date for freshman financial aid applications for fall entry is February 15. The deadline for filing freshman financial aid applications for fall entry is open.

International Students: There are 251 international students enrolled. The school actively recruits these students. They must score satisfactory on the written TOEFL or successfully complete WIU's ESL program.

Computers: Wireless access is available. Computer access is available in all residence hall rooms, residence hall lounges, the library, and computer labs in academic buildings. The wireless system is currently available in the library, 1 residence hall, and 7 academic buildings. All students may access the system any time. There are no time limits and no fees.

Graduates: From July 1, 2004 to June 30, 2005, 2376 bachelor's degrees were awarded. The most popular majors were law enforcement and justice administration (13%), Board of Trustees degree (13%), and elementary education (8%). In an average class, 32% graduate in 4 years or less, 52% graduate in 5 years or less, and 55% graduate in 6 years or less. 105 companies recruited on campus in a recent year. Of a recent graduating class, 14% were enrolled in graduate school within 6 months of graduation and 78% were employed.

Admissions Contact: Admissions Office. A video is available. E-mail: *wiuadm@wiu.edu* Web: *www.wiu.edu*

WHEATON COLLEGE E-2

Wheaton, IL 60187-5593

(630) 752-5005
(800) 222-2419; Fax: (630) 752-5285

Full-time: 1139 men, 1198 women	**Faculty:** 191; IIB, +$
Part-time: 25 men, 30 women	**Ph.D.s:** 70%
Graduate: 178 men, 244 women	**Student/Faculty:** 12 to 1
Year: semesters, summer session	**Tuition:** $21,100
Application Deadline: January 15	**Room & Board:** $6660
Freshman Class: 2163 applied, 1097 accepted, 578 enrolled	
SAT or ACT: required	**HIGHLY COMPETITIVE**

Wheaton College, founded in 1860, is a private, nondenominational institution committed to providing students with a Christian education. Basically a liberal arts school, it offers undergraduate programs in business, the arts and fine arts, music, teacher preparation, and religious and Bible studies. In addition to regional accreditation, Wheaton has baccalaureate program accreditation with NASM and NCATE. The 2 libraries contain 342,746 volumes, 674,827 microform items, and 32,761 audio/video tapes/CDs/DVDs, and subscribe to 3264 periodicals including electronic. Computerized library services include the card catalog, interlibrary loans, and database searching. Special learning facilities include a radio station and a communications resource center with TV and audio studios, a special collection of British authors books and papers, an evangelical museum with document archives, and the Center for Applied Christian Ethics. The 80-acre campus is in a suburban area 25 miles west of Chicago. Including any residence halls, there are 35 buildings.

Student Life: 72% of undergraduates are from out of state, mostly the Midwest. Students are from 50 states, 13 foreign countries, and Canada. 67% are from public schools. 73% are white. 94% are Protestant; 6% affiliation unknown. The average age of freshmen is 18; all undergraduates, 20. 5% do not continue beyond their first year; 86% remain to graduate.

Housing: 2091 students can be accommodated in college housing, which includes single-sex dorms, on-campus apartments, off-campus apartments, and married-student housing. In addition, the college owns and rents houses to groups of students. On-campus housing is guaranteed for the freshman year only and is available on a lottery system for upperclassmen. 90% of students live on campus; of those, 95% remain on campus on weekends. Alcohol is not permitted. Upperclassmen may keep cars.

Activities: There are no fraternities or sororities. There are 71 groups on campus, including band, cheerleading, chess, choir, chorale, chorus, debate, drama, drill team, ethnic, forensics, international, jazz band, literary magazine, newspaper, orchestra, pep band, radio and TV, religious, social, social service, student government, symphony, and yearbook. Popular campus events include Air Jam and an artist concert series.

Sports: There are intercollegiate and intramural sports programs.

Disabled Students: Wheelchair ramps, elevators, special parking, specially equipped rest rooms, special class scheduling, lowered drinking fountains, and lowered telephones are available. Housing for disabled students is provided as needed.

Services: There is a reader service for the blind and a writing center. Other services are provided as needed.

Campus Safety and Security: Measures include 24-hour foot and vehicle patrol, self-defense education, security escort services, and informal discussions. There are pamphlets/posters/films, emergency telephones, and lighted pathways/sidewalks.

Programs of Study: Wheaton confers B.A., B.S., B.M., and B.M.E. degrees. Master's and doctoral degrees are also awarded. Bachelor's degrees are awarded in BIOLOGICAL SCIENCE (biology/biological science), BUSINESS (business economics), COMMUNICATIONS AND THE ARTS (art, communications, English, French, German, music, and Spanish), COMPUTER AND PHYSICAL SCIENCE (chemistry, computer science, geology, mathematics, physical sciences, and physics), EDUCATION (elementary, music, science, and secondary), ENGINEERING AND ENVIRONMENTAL DESIGN (environmental science), SOCIAL SCIENCE (anthropology, archeology, biblical studies, economics, history, interdisciplinary studies, philosophy, physical fitness/movement, political science/government, psychology, religion, social science, and sociology).

Required: To graduate, students must complete 124 semester hours, 36 in upper-division courses, with a varying number of hours in a major, and maintain at least a 2.0 GPA. General education requirements include competency in a foreign language, math, speech, writing, and Bible studies; distribution requirements include fine arts, history, literature, sciences, physical sciences, English, humanities, philosophy, social science, and sport/fitness.

Special: Special academic programs include internships, study abroad in 8 countries, an urban semester in Chicago and a Washington semester. Dual majors are available in all areas, as are student-designed majors. A 3-2 engineering degree is offered with the Illinois Institute of Technology, University of Illinois, Case Western Reserve University School of Engineering, and Washington University School of Engineering and Applied Science; transfer to other engineering schools is also possible. A 3-2 nursing degree is offered with Emory University, Goshen Nursing School, University of Rochester, and Rush University. Pass/fail options are available. There are 10 national honor societies and 11 departmental honors programs.

Faculty/Classroom: 67% of faculty are male; 33%, female. No introductory courses are taught by graduate students.

Admissions: 51% of the 2005-2006 applicants were accepted. There were 59 National Merit finalists. 64 freshmen graduated first in their class.

Requirements: The SAT or ACT is required. The ACT Optional Writing test is also required. In addition, a high school diploma is required and the GED is accepted. Wheaton requires a general college preparatory program of 18 units, including 4 of English, 3 to 4 of math, science, and social studies, and 2 to 3 of a foreign language. AP and CLEP credits are accepted. Personality/intangible qualities is an important factor in the admission decision.

Procedure: Freshmen are admitted in the fall. Entrance exams should be taken November of the senior year. There is a deferred admissions plan. Applications should be filed by January 15 for fall entry, along with a $50 fee. Notification is sent April 1. 349 applicants were on the 2005 waiting list; 39 were admitted.

Transfer: 75 transfer students enrolled in 2004-2005. Applicants must have completed 15 semester hours with a 3.0 average and present a high school transcript, college transcript, and an essay or personal statement. An interview is required. 48 of 124 credits required for the bachelor's degree must be completed at Wheaton.

Visiting: There are regularly scheduled orientations for prospective students, consisting of presentations by faculty, administrators, students, and financial aid and admissions staff, as well as social activities. There are guides for informal visits and visitors may sit in on classes and stay overnight. To schedule a visit, contact the Admissions Office at (630) 752-5600.

Financial Aid: In 2005-2006, 49% of all full-time students received some form of financial aid. At least 40% of full-time freshmen and at least 41% of continuing full-time students received need-based aid. The average freshman award was $19,128. Need-based scholarships or need-based grants averaged $13,546; need-based self-help aid (loans and jobs) averaged $4748; and other institutional non-need-based awards and non-need-based scholarships averaged $3251. The average financial indebtedness of the 2005 graduate was $17,936. The FAFSA and the college's own financial statement are required. The priority date for freshman financial aid applications for fall entry is February 15.

International Students: The school actively recruits these students. They must score satisfactorily on the TOEFL and also take the TSE and TWE.

Computers: All students may access the system 24 hours a day. Students may access the system 2 hours at one sitting if there is a waiting list; otherwise, there is no limit. There are no fees.

Graduates: From July 1, 2004 to June 30, 2005, 584 bachelor's degrees were awarded. The most popular majors were social science (15%), education (9%), and theology and religion vocations (9%). In an average class, 75% graduate in 4 years or less, 82% graduate in 5 years or less, and 86% graduate in 6 years or less.

Admissions Contact: Director of Admissions. E-mail: *admissions@wheaton.edu* Web: *http://www.wheaton.edu*

INDIANA

POPULATION DENSITY
● 50,000 and over

0 20 40 60 80 100
Miles

ANDERSON UNIVERSITY · C-3

Anderson, IN 46012

(765) 641-4080
(800) 428-6414; Fax: (765) 641-3851

Full-time: 921 men, 1228 women	**Faculty:** 126; IIB, --$
Part-time: 66 men, 122 women	**Ph.D.s:** 64%
Graduate: 302 men, 172 women	**Student/Faculty:** 17 to 1
Year: semesters, summer session	**Tuition:** $18,900
Application Deadline: open	**Room & Board:** $6150
Freshman Class: n/av	
SAT or ACT: required	**LESS COMPETITIVE**

Anderson University, founded in 1917, is a private liberal arts institution affiliated with the Church of God. The university offers programs in theoretical and applied science, social and professional studies, and arts, culture, and religion. There are 3 undergraduate and 3 graduate schools. In addition to regional accreditation, Anderson has baccalaureate program accreditation with ACBSP, CSWE, NASM, NCATE, and NLN. The library contains 243,543 volumes, 193,660 microform items, and 402 audio/video tapes/CDs/DVDs, and subscribes to 754 periodicals including electronic. Computerized library services include the card catalog, interlibrary loans, and database searching. Special learning facilities include a learning resource center, art gallery, radio station, and the Museum of the Bible and the Ancient Near East. The 100-acre campus is in a suburban area 40 miles northeast of Indianapolis. Including any residence halls, there are 26 buildings.

Student Life: 60% of undergraduates are from Indiana. Others are from 42 states, 22 foreign countries, and Canada. 97% are from public schools. 91% are white. 83% are Protestant; 13% claim no religious affiliation. The average age of freshmen is 18; all undergraduates, 21. 24% do not continue beyond their first year; 56% remain to graduate.

Housing: 1343 students can be accommodated in college housing, which includes single-sex dorms, on-campus apartments, off-campus apartments, and married-student housing. On-campus housing is guaranteed for all 4 years. 63% of students live on campus; of those, 50% remain on campus on weekends. Alcohol is not permitted. All students may keep cars.

Activities: There are no fraternities or sororities. There are 41 groups on campus, including art, band, cheerleading, choir, chorale, debate, drama, ethnic, film, honors, international, jazz band, literary magazine, musical theater, newspaper, opera, orchestra, photography, political, professional, radio and TV, religious, social, social service, student government, and symphony. Popular campus events include Christmas Carols, Celebration Weekend, and Black Awareness.

Sports: There are 8 intercollegiate sports for men and 8 for women, and 8 intramural sports for men and 8 for women. Facilities include 2 gyms, football, baseball/softball, and soccer fields, an 8-lane all-weather track, tennis courts, a bowling alley, and a game room. The campus stadium seats 4200 and the indoor gym seats 2400.

Disabled Students: 97% of the campus is accessible. Wheelchair ramps, elevators, special parking, specially equipped rest rooms, special class scheduling, lowered drinking fountains, and lowered telephones are available.

Services: Counseling and information services are available, as is tutoring in most subjects. There is a reader service for the blind, and remedial math, reading, and writing.

Campus Safety and Security: Measures include 24-hour foot and vehicle patrol, self-defense education, security escort services, and informal discussions. There are pamphlets/posters/films, emergency telephones, and lighted pathways/sidewalks. Indiana State police academy graduates are security officers.

Programs of Study: Anderson confers B.A., B.Mus, and B.S.N. degrees. Associate, master's, and doctoral degrees are also awarded. Bachelor's degrees are awarded in BIOLOGICAL SCIENCE (biology/biological science), BUSINESS (accounting, banking and finance, business administration and management, management science, marketing/retailing/merchandising, and sports management), COMMUNICATIONS AND THE ARTS (communications, dramatic arts, English, fine arts, French, German, graphic design, music business management, music performance, and Spanish), COMPUTER AND PHYSICAL SCIENCE (chemistry, computer science, mathematics, and physics), EDUCATION (art, Christian, elementary, foreign languages, health, music, physical, science, and social studies), HEALTH PROFESSIONS (medical laboratory technology and nursing), SOCIAL SCIENCE (criminal justice, economics, family/consumer studies, history, philosophy, political science/government, psychology, religion, social work, and sociology). Physical sciences is the strongest academically. Business, education, and music are the largest.

Required: Requirements for graduation include the general education core, consisting of 55 hours, a minimum 2.0 GPA overall and in the major, 124 total credit hours, and a minimum of 36 hours in the major. All students must complete a liberal arts seminar. The last 24 credit hours must be taken in residence.

Special: Anderson offers co-op programs with Purdue University, internships through the Center for Public Service, study abroad in 25 countries through the International Studies Program, and a Washington semester. Also available are credit for military experience and pass/fail options. Courses in electronic engineering may be taken through the Purdue Anderson campus. Pre-professional programs are offered in medicial, podiatry, dentistry, law, engineering, seminary, and several allied health fields. There are 12 national honor societies, a freshman honors program, and 10 departmental honors programs.

Faculty/Classroom: 55% of faculty are male; 45%, female. 92% teach undergraduates. No introductory courses are taught by graduate students. The average class size in an introductory lecture is 34; in a laboratory, 17; and in a regular course, 20.

Admissions: 24 freshmen graduated first in their class.

Requirements: The SAT or ACT is required. In addition, applicants must be graduates of an accredited secondary school or have a GED certificate, and submit a photograph, references, and a health form. A GPA of 2.0 is required. AP and CLEP credits are accepted. Important factors in the admissions decision are leadership record, parents or siblings attending the school, and personality/intangible qualities.

Procedure: Freshmen are admitted fall and spring. Entrance exams should be taken in the fall of the junior year. There is a rolling admissions plan. Application deadlines are open. The fall 2005 application fee was $20. Applications are accepted on-line.

Transfer: Applicants must have a minimum 2.0 GPA, satisfactory SAT or ACT scores, and transcripts for all previously attended colleges. 24 of 124 credits required for the bachelor's degree must be completed at Anderson.

Visiting: There are regularly scheduled orientations for prospective students, including a campus tour, an academic overview, a financial aid and athletics overview, and appointments with professors and departmental chairs. There are guides for informal visits and visitors may sit in on classes and stay overnight. To schedule a visit, contact the Admissions Office.

Financial Aid: Anderson is a member of CSS. The FAFSA is required. Check with the school for current deadlines.

International Students: Satisfactory scores are required on the written TOEFL and the SAT.

Computers: All students may access the system. There are no time limits and no fees.

Graduates: Of the 2004 graduating class, 20% were enrolled in graduate school within 6 months of graduation.

Admissions Contact: Admissions Counselor.
E-mail: *info@anderson.edu* Web: *www.anderson.edu*

BALL STATE UNIVERSITY   B-3
Muncie, IN 47306   (765) 285-8300
(800) 482-4BSU; Fax: (765) 285-1632

Full-time: 14,780 men and women	Faculty: 806; I, --$
Part-time: 1123 men and women	Ph.D.s: 76%
Graduate: 1825 men and women	Student/Faculty: 18 to 1
Year: semesters, summer session	Tuition: $6568 ($16,328)
Application Deadline: March 1	Room & Board: $6570
Freshman Class: 7944 accepted, 3347 enrolled	
SAT Verbal/Math: 525/526*	ACT: 22 COMPETITIVE

Ball State University, founded in 1918, is a public university offering undergraduate and graduate programs through 7 academic colleges in applied sciences and technology; architecture and planning; business; communication, information, and media; fine arts; sciences and humanities; and teacher education. The Honors College and the University College are interdisciplinary colleges. There are 7 undergraduate schools and 1 graduate school. Some of the figures in this capsule and in this profile are approximate. In addition, to regional accreditation, Ball State has baccalaureate program accreditation with AACSB, ACEJMC, ADA, AHEA, CAHEA, CSAB, CSWE, NAAB, NASAD, NASM, NCATE, and NLN. The 3 libraries contain 1.1 million volumes, 1 million microform items, and 500,000 audio/video tapes/CDs/DVDs, and subscribe to 3000 periodicals including electronic. Computerized library services include interlibrary loans and database searching. Special learning facilities include a learning resource center, art gallery, planetarium, radio station, TV station, and research centers in solar energy, human performance, and international programs. The 955-acre campus is in a suburban area 56 miles northwest of Indianapolis. Including any residence halls, there are 57 buildings.

Student Life: 91% of undergraduates are from Indiana. Students are from 49 states, 86 foreign countries, and Canada. 90% are white. The average age of freshmen is 18; all undergraduates, 21. 23% do not continue beyond their first year.

Housing: 6400 students can be accommodated in college housing, which includes single-sex and coed dorms, on-campus apartments, married-student housing, and fraternity houses. In addition, there are honors houses, special-interest houses, and wellness halls. On-campus housing is guaranteed for the freshman year only. 60% of students commute. Alcohol is not permitted. All students may keep cars.

Activities: 10% of men belong to 19 national fraternities; 10% of women belong to 1 local and 15 national sororities. There are 300 groups on campus, including art, band, cheerleading, chess, choir, chorale, chorus, computers, dance, debate, drama, drill team, ethnic, film, forensics, gay, honors, international, jazz band, literary magazine, marching band, musical theater, newspaper, orchestra, pep band, photography, political, professional, radio and TV, religious, social, social service, student government, symphony, and yearbook. Popular campus events include Watermelon Bust, Unity Week, and Family Weekend.

Sports: There are 9 intercollegiate sports for men and 10 for women, and 43 intramural sports for men and 41 for women. Facilities include an 11,500-seat basketball and volleyball arena, 2 gyms, a field sports building, tennis courts, and an aquatic center. The campus stadium seats 16,320.

Disabled Students: All of the campus is accessible. Wheelchair ramps, elevators, special parking, specially equipped rest rooms, special class scheduling, lowered drinking fountains and lowered telephones are available. A special resource guide, an accessibility map (including tactile), and text telephones (TDD) in all key offices are also available.

Services: Counseling and information services are available, as is tutoring in most subjects. There is a reader service for the blind.

Campus Safety and Security: Measures include 24-hour foot and vehicle patrol, self-defense education, security escort services, and shuttle buses. There are informal discussions, pamphlets/posters/films, emergency telephones, and lighted pathways/sidewalks.

Programs of Study: Ball State confers B.A., B.S., B.Arch., B.F.A., B.G.S., B.Land.Arch., B.Mus., B.S.W., and B.Urban Planning and Development degrees. Associate, master's, and doctoral degrees are also awarded. Bachelor's degrees are awarded in AGRICULTURE (fishing and fisheries and natural resource management), BIOLOGICAL SCIENCE (biology/biological science, botany, cell biology, genetics, microbiology, molecular biology, wildlife biology, and zoology), BUSINESS (accounting, banking and finance, business administration and management, business economics, insurance, management science, marketing/retailing/merchandising, personnel management, real estate, and sports management), COMMUNICATIONS AND THE ARTS (art, broadcasting, classical languages, classics, communications, dance, dra-

matic arts, English, film arts, fine arts, French, German, graphic design, guitar, journalism, music, music performance, photography, piano/organ, Spanish, speech/debate/rhetoric, telecommunications, and voice), COMPUTER AND PHYSICAL SCIENCE (actuarial science, chemistry, computer science, geology, mathematics, and physics), EDUCATION (art, business, early childhood, education of the deaf and hearing impaired, educational media, elementary, foreign languages, health, home economics, industrial arts, journalism, middle school, music, science, secondary, social studies, special, and technical), ENGINEERING AND ENVIRONMENTAL DESIGN (architecture, environmental design, graphic arts technology, landscape architecture/design, and urban planning technology), HEALTH PROFESSIONS (health science, medical laboratory technology, nursing, predentistry, premedicine, prepharmacy, and speech pathology/audiology), SOCIAL SCIENCE (anthropology, criminal justice, dietetics, economics, food production/management/services, geography, history, home economics, Latin American studies, liberal arts/general studies, paralegal studies, parks and recreation management, philosophy, physical fitness/movement, political science/government, prelaw, psychology, religion, social work, and sociology). Architecture, business, and education are the strongest academically. Elementary education and business are the largest.

Required: All students must take at least 126 credits and maintain a 2.0 GPA for graduation. Required courses are in English composition, math, speech, history, physical sciences, social or behavioral sciences, humanities or fine arts, global studies, and 3 hours of phys ed. In addition, all juniors must pass a writing competency exam.

Special: Nearly all undergraduate disciplines offer internships. Study abroad is possible at the university's London center and in 20 other programs; students may also spend a semester in Washington, D.C., and co-op and work-study programs are available. Most disciplines offer dual majors. There is a 3-2 program in engineering, an award-winning program in entrepreneurship, a general studies degree, nondegree study, and pass/fail options. There are 40 national honor societies and a freshman honors program.

Faculty/Classroom: 63% of faculty are male; 37%, female. 94% teach undergraduates, 75% do research, and 73% do both. No introductory courses are taught by graduate students. The average class size in an introductory lecture is 50; in a laboratory, 18; and in a regular course, 30.

Requirements: The SAT or ACT is required. The ACT Optional Writing test is also required. Admission is based on strength of the applicant's curriculum, grades in English, math, lab sciences, social sciences, and foreign language, curricula patterns and grade trends, and the SAT or ACT scores. AP and CLEP credits are accepted. Important factors in the admissions decision are advanced placement or honor courses, recommendations by school officials, and personality/intangible qualities.

Procedure: Freshmen are admitted fall, spring, and summer. Entrance exams should be taken during the spring of the junior year or early in the senior year. There are deferred admissions and rolling admissions plans. Applications should be filed by March 1 for fall entry, December 1 for spring entry, and April 1 for summer entry, along with a $25 fee. Notification is sent on a rolling basis.

Transfer: 800 transfer students enrolled in 2004-2005. Transfer applicants should have earned a 2.0 GPA on a 4.0 scale (as computed by Ball State) to be considered for admission. An official high school transcript or GED score report and official transcripts from each postsecondary institution are required. 63 of 126 credits required for the bachelor's degree must be completed at Ball State.

Visiting: There are regularly scheduled orientations for prospective students, including a 10 A.M. presentation, on 11 A.M. tour, and lunch. There are guides for informal visits and visitors may sit in on classes and stay overnight. To schedule a visit, contact the Admissions Visitors Desk at (765) 285-5683 or (866) 770-3163.

Financial Aid: In 2005-2006, 90% of all full-time freshmen and 83% of continuing full-time students received some form of financial aid. 55% of full-time freshmen and 53% of continuing full-time students received need-based aid. The average freshman award was $5496. Need-based scholarships or need-based grants averaged $1931 ($11,388 maximum); need-based self-help aid (loans and jobs) averaged $1278 ($7525 maximum); non-need-based athletic scholarships averaged $200 ($23,298 maximum); and other non-need-based awards and non-need-based scholarships averaged $2087 ($21,371 maximum). Ball State is a member of CSS. The FAFSA is required. Check with the shool for current application deadlines.

International Students: The school actively recruits these students. They must score satisfactory on the written TOEFL.

Computers: All students may access the system at any time except Friday from 5 P.M. to 8 A.M. Saturday. There are no time limits and no fees.

Admissions Contact: Lawrence Waters, Dean of Admissions and Enrollment Services. E-mail: *askus@.bsu.edu* Web: *www.bsu.edu/admissions*

BETHEL COLLEGE

Mishawaka, IN 46545

C-1

(574) 257-3339
(800) 422-4101; Fax: (574) 257-3335

Full-time: 515 men, 780 women	**Faculty:** 59; IIB, --$
Part-time: 125 men, 330 women	**Ph.D.s:** 74%
Graduate: 60 men, 50 women	**Student/Faculty:** 22 to 1
Year: semesters, summer session	**Tuition:** $15,000
Application Deadline: open	**Room & Board:** $4685
Freshman Class: n/av	
SAT or ACT: required	**COMPETITIVE**

Bethel College, founded in 1947, is a private institution affiliated with the Missionary Church, offering a liberal arts education with a Christian perspective. Figures in the above capsule and this profile are approximate. In addition to regional accreditation, Bethel has baccalaureate program accreditation with NCATE and NLN. The library contains 104,076 volumes, 4374 microform items, and 3970 audio/video tapes/CDs/DVDs, and subscribes to 450 periodicals including electronic. Computerized library services include the card catalog, interlibrary loans, database searching, and Internet access. Special learning facilities include a learning resource center, art gallery, and radio station. The 70-acre campus is in a suburban area 90 miles east of Chicago. Including any residence halls, there are 50 buildings.

Student Life: 67% of undergraduates are from Indiana. Others are from 32 states, 13 foreign countries, and Canada. 78% are from public schools. 83% are white; 10% African American. 84% are Protestant; 8% Catholic; 7% claim no religious affiliation. The average age of freshmen is 19; all undergraduates, 26. 13% do not continue beyond their first year; 60% remain to graduate.

Housing: 810 students can be accommodated in college housing, which includes single-sex dorms, on-campus apartments, and married-student housing. In addition, there is a cultural awareness house and a missions house. On-campus housing is guaranteed for all 4 years. 54% of students commute. Alcohol is not permitted. Upperclassmen may keep cars.

Activities: There are no fraternities or sororities. There are 18 groups on campus, including art, band, cheerleading, choir, chorale, chorus, computers, drama, Fellowship of Christian Athletes, Hawaii Fellowship, honors, international, jazz band, literary magazine, musical theater, newspaper, orchestra, pep band, professional, radio and TV, religious, social, social service, student government, and yearbook. Popular campus events include Christmas Banquet, Junior-Senior Banquet, and Spiritual Emphasis Week.

Sports: There are 9 intercollegiate sports for men and 9 for women, and 15 intramural sports for men and 15 for women. Facilities include a gym, a weight room, exercise, baseball and training facilities, baseball, softball, and soccer fields, tennis courts, and a practice track.

Disabled Students: 78% of the campus is accessible. Wheelchair ramps, elevators, special parking, specially equipped rest rooms, lowered drinking fountains, and special housing are available.

Services: Counseling and information services are available, as is tutoring in every subject. There is remedial math, reading, and writing.

Campus Safety and Security: Measures include 24-hour foot and vehicle patrol, security escort services, informal discussions, and pamphlets/posters/films. There are emergency telephones and lighted pathways/sidewalks.

Programs of Study: Bethel confers B.A., B.S., and B.S.N. degrees. Associate and master's degrees are also awarded. Bachelor's degrees are awarded in BIOLOGICAL SCIENCE (biology/biological science and environmental biology), BUSINESS (accounting, business administration and management, and sports management), COMMUNICATIONS AND THE ARTS (art, communications, dramatic arts, English, graphic design, music, music performance, photography, and video), COMPUTER AND PHYSICAL SCIENCE (applied physics, chemistry, computer science, digital arts/technology, mathematics, physics, and web technology), EDUCATION (business, elementary, English, mathematics, music, physical, science, secondary, and social studies), ENGINEERING AND ENVIRONMENTAL DESIGN (aeronautical engineering, chemical engineering, civil engineering, electrical/electronics engineering, interior design, and mechanical engineering), HEALTH PROFESSIONS (exercise science, nursing, predentistry, and premedicine), SOCIAL SCIENCE (biblical studies, criminal justice, history, human services, international studies, interpreter for the deaf, liberal arts/general studies, ministries, missions, philosophy, prelaw, psychology, religion, religious music, social science, sociology, and youth ministry).

Required: To graduate, students must complete 124 credits, including 24 to 52 in the major, with a minimum 2.0 GPA. Also required are 4 semesters of phys ed, 10 credits in Bible and religion, courses in communication skills, social science and history, fine arts and humanities, and natural sciences and math, and a course called Lifelong Physical Awareness. Computer proficiency is also required.

Special: A cooperative program is offered with the University of Notre Dame, and students may cross-register for courses at various local colleges including Northern Indiana Consortium for Education (NICE). Also available are a B.A.-B.S. degree in engineering, a 3-2 engineering degree with the University of Notre Dame and Tri-State University (Angola), a liberal arts degree, and an accelerated degree in organizational management (for students age 25 and over). Bethel also offers nondegree courses, a pass/fail option, student teaching, some business and computer internships, study in Ecuador, China, Russia, New Zealand, Australia, and Jamaica, double majors, and work-study programs. There is a freshman honors program.

Faculty/Classroom: 52% of faculty are male; 48%, female. All teach undergraduates and 10% both teach and do research. No introductory courses are taught by graduate students. The average class size in an introductory lecture is 50; in a laboratory, 15; and in a regular course, 16.

Admissions: 30% of the current freshmen were in the top fifth of their class; 59% were in the top two fifths. There was 1 National Merit semifinalist. 4 freshmen graduated first in their class.

Requirements: The SAT or ACT is required. In addition, applicants should be graduates of accredited secondary schools or have the GED. Required secondary school credits include 8 units in English, 6 each in math, lab science, and social science, and 4 in a foreign language. Chemistry is required for nursing majors. An interview is recommended. An audition is required of music program applicants. A GPA of 2.0 is required. AP and CLEP credits are accepted.

Procedure: Freshmen are admitted to all sessions. Entrance exams should be taken as early as possible in the junior or senior year. There are early admissions, deferred admissions and rolling admissions plans. Application deadlines are open. Application fee is $25. Applications are accepted on-line.

Transfer: 145 transfer students enrolled in a recent year. Grades of C or better are eligible for transfer; students without a minimum GPA of 2.0 may be admitted on probation. Other admission requirements are the same as for entering freshmen. 30 of 124 credits required for the bachelor's degree must be completed at Bethel.

Visiting: There are regularly scheduled orientations for prospective students, including an interview, chapel visit, tour, lunch, and a class or professor visit as requested. There are guides for informal visits and visitors may sit in on classes and stay overnight. To schedule a visit, contact the Office of Admissions at (800) 422-4101.

Financial Aid: Bethel is a member of CSS. The FAFSA, the college's own financial statement and the SAR are required. Check with the school for current application deadlines.

International Students: In a recent year there were 34 international students enrolled. They must score satisfactorily on the written TOEFL or on the electronic version.

Computers: All students may access the system Monday through Friday 8 A.M. to midnight and Saturday 8 A.M. to 7 P.M. in the computer labs. There are no time limits and no fees. It is strongly recommended that all students have a personal computer.

Graduates: In a recent year, 307 bachelor's degrees were awarded. The most popular majors were business areas (31%), nursing (17%), and education (16%). In an average class, 2% graduate in 3 years or less, 49% graduate in 4 years or less, 55% graduate in 5 years or less, and 66% graduate in 6 years or less. 68 companies recruited on campus in a recent year. Of a recent graduating class, 12% were enrolled in graduate school within 6 months of graduation and 70% were employed.

Admissions Contact: Randy Beachy, Assistant Vice President of Enrollment and Marketing. E-mail: *beachyr@bethelcollege.edu* Web: *www.bethelcollege.edu*

BUTLER UNIVERSITY

Indianapolis, IN 46208

C-3

(317) 940-8100
(888) 940-8100; Fax: (317) 940-8150

Full-time: 1414 men, 2387 women	**Faculty:** 253; IIA, -$
Part-time: 42 men, 36 women	**Ph.D.s:** 85%
Graduate: 239 men, 266 women	**Student/Faculty:** 15 to 1
Year: semesters, summer session	**Tuition:** $23,774
Application Deadline: open	**Room & Board:** $8170
Freshman Class: n/av	
SAT Verbal/Math: 592/599*	**ACT:** 27 **VERY COMPETITIVE+**

Butler University, founded in 1855, is an independent, private institution offering programs in liberal arts and sciences, business administration, fine arts, pharmacy, health sciences, and education. There are 5 undergraduate and 5 graduate schools. In addition to regional accreditation, Butler has baccalaureate program accreditation with AACSB, ACPE, NASM, and NCATE. The 2 libraries contain 309,511 volumes, 180,107 microform items, and 14,407 audio/video tapes/CDs/DVDs, and subscribe to 2126 periodicals including electronic. Computerized library services include the card catalog, interlibrary loans, and database searching. Special learning facilities include a learning resource center, planetarium, TV station, and an observatory. The 290-acre campus is in a suburban area 5 miles from downtown Indianapolis. Including any residence halls, there are 19 buildings.

Student Life: 57% of undergraduates are from Indiana. Others are from 46 states, 63 foreign countries, and Canada. 86% are from public schools. 90% are white. 52% are Protestant; 31% Catholic; 11% claim no religious affiliation. The average age of freshmen is 18; all undergraduates, 20. 13% do not continue beyond their first year; 72% remain to graduate.

Housing: 1500 students can be accommodated in college housing, which includes single-sex and coed dorms, on-campus apartments, fraternity houses, and sorority houses. In addition, there are special-interest houses and special-interest units are available in the residence halls. On-campus housing is guaranteed for all 4 years. 56% of students live on campus; of those, 50% remain on campus on weekends. Alcohol is not permitted. All students may keep cars.

Activities: 24% of men belong to 8 national fraternities; 29% of women belong to 8 national sororities. There are 97 groups on campus, including band, cheerleading, choir, chorale, chorus, dance, debate, drama, drill team, ethnic, gay, honors, international, jazz band, literary magazine, marching band, newspaper, opera, orchestra, pep band, photography, political, professional, radio and TV, religious, social, social service, student government, and symphony. Popular campus events include Geneva Stunts, Spring Sing, and Spring Sports Spectacular.

Sports: There are 10 intercollegiate sports for men and 9 for women, and 23 intramural sports for men and 23 for women. Facilities include a 10,000-seat field house, a 20,000-seat football stadium, tennis courts, indoor and outdoor tracks, a weight-training room, an aerobics/exercise room, intramural fields, and baseball, softball, and soccer fields.

Disabled Students: 90% of the campus is accessible. Wheelchair ramps, elevators, special parking, specially equipped rest rooms, special class scheduling, and lowered drinking fountains are available.

Services: Counseling and information services are available, as is tutoring in every subject. There is a reader service for the blind. A writer's studio offers assistance in all areas of the writing process.

Campus Safety and Security: Measures include 24-hour foot and vehicle patrol, self-defense education, security escort services, and informal discussions. There are pamphlets/posters/films, emergency telephones, and lighted pathways/sidewalks.

Programs of Study: Butler confers B.A., B.S., B.F.A., B.M., B.S.H.S., and B.S.P. degrees. Master's and doctoral degrees are also awarded. Bachelor's degrees are awarded in BIOLOGICAL SCIENCE (biology/ biological science), BUSINESS (accounting, banking and finance, international business management, and marketing/retailing/merchandising), COMMUNICATIONS AND THE ARTS (arts administration/ management, communications, dance, dramatic arts, English, French, German, Greek, journalism, Latin, music, music business management, music performance, music theory and composition, performing arts, Spanish, speech/debate/rhetoric, and telecommunications), COMPUTER AND PHYSICAL SCIENCE (actuarial science, chemistry, computer science, mathematics, and physics), EDUCATION (elementary, music, and secondary), HEALTH PROFESSIONS (pharmacy, physician's assistant, and speech pathology/audiology), SOCIAL SCIENCE (anthropology, criminal justice, economics, history, international studies, philosophy, political science/government, psychology, religion, science and society, sociology, and urban studies). Pharmacy, chemistry, and biology are the strongest academically. Business, education, and pharmacy are the largest.

Required: The core curriculum includes specific courses in English, speech, computer literacy, phys ed, and interdisciplinary studies, as well as distribution requirements in humanities, fine arts, social science, natural science, and quantitative reasoning. To graduate, students must complete 126 to 166 semester hours with a minimum GPA of 2.0.

Special: Butler offers cross-registration with the 4 other members of the Consortium for Urban Education, co-op programs in business administration, and internships in pharmacy, arts administration, and business programs. A 3-2 degree program in engineering with Purdue University, extensive study-abroad programs, and work-study programs are available. There are dual majors including French, German, and Spanish combined with business studies, student-designed majors, a general studies degree, pass/fail options, and nondegree study. There are 5 national honor societies and a freshman honors program.

Faculty/Classroom: 58% of faculty are male; 42%, female. 91% teach undergraduates and 75% both teach and do research. No introductory courses are taught by graduate students. The average class size in an introductory lecture is 24; in a laboratory, 18; and in a regular course, 19.

Admissions: The SAT scores for the 2005-2006 freshman class were: Verbal--7% below 500, 48% between 500 and 599, 37% between 600 and 700, and 8% above 700; Math--9% below 500, 37% between 500 and 599, 44% between 600 and 700, and 10% above 700. The ACT scores were 3% below 21, 14% between 21 and 23, 29% between 24 and 26, 22% between 27 and 28, and 32% above 28. 68% of the current freshmen were in the top fifth of their class; 87% were in the top two fifths. There were 12 National Merit finalists and 26 semifinalists. 49 freshmen graduated first in their class.

Requirements: The SAT or ACT is required. In addition, applicants should be graduates of an accredited secondary school, but Butler will consider talented or gifted students without a diploma. Students should have earned at least 17 academic units, based on 4 years of English, 3 each of math and lab science, 2 each of a foreign language and history/ social science, and the rest of electives. An audition is required for dance, music, and theater majors, and an interview is required for radio/ TV majors. Butler requires applicants to be in the upper 50% of their class. A GPA of 2.0 is required. AP and CLEP credits are accepted. Important factors in the admissions decision are advanced placement or honor courses, evidence of special talent, and leadership record.

Procedure: Freshmen are admitted to all sessions. Entrance exams should be taken during the junior year. There are deferred admissions and rolling admissions plans. Application deadlines are open. Application fee is $35. Applications are accepted on-line.

Transfer: 95 transfer students enrolled in 2004-2005. Applicants who have completed more than 12 hours of college work must present transcripts from all previous colleges attended, indicating good standing and a minimum GPA of 2.0, and an official high school transcript showing a posted date of graduation. Those students with fewer than 12 hours must also submit SAT or ACT scores. Students wishing to transfer into pharmacy or physician assistant programs should contact the Office of Admission for requirements and deadlines. 45 of 126 to 166 credits required for the bachelor's degree must be completed at Butler.

Visiting: There are regularly scheduled orientations for prospective students, including a campus tour, faculty visit, and financial aid interview. There are guides for informal visits and visitors may sit in on classes and stay overnight. To schedule a visit, contact the Office of Admission.

Financial Aid: In 2005-2006, 90% of all full-time freshmen and 86% of continuing full-time students received some form of financial aid. 43% of full-time freshmen and 45% of continuing full-time students received need-based aid. 40% of undergraduates work part time. Average annual earnings from campus work are $1200. Butler is a member of CSS. The FAFSA and the college's own financial statement are required. The deadline for filing freshman financial aid applications for fall entry is March 1.

International Students: There are 82 international students enrolled. The school actively recruits these students. They must score satisfactorily on the written TOEFL or on the electronic version or complete level 5 at the American Language Academy on Butler's campus.

Computers: All students may access the system 24 hours a day. There are no time limits and no fees. It is strongly recommended that all students have a personal computer.

Graduates: From July 1, 2004 to June 30, 2005, 814 bachelor's degrees were awarded. The most popular majors were marketing (16%), pharmacy (16%), and communications (13%). In an average class, 63% graduate in 4 years or less, 69% graduate in 5 years or less, and 72% graduate in 6 years or less. 300 companies recruited on campus in 2004-2005. Of the 2004 graduating class, 19% were enrolled in graduate school within 6 months of graduation and 74% were employed.

Admissions Contact: Scott McIntyre, Director of Admission. A video is available. E-mail: *admission@butler.edu* Web: *www.butler.edu*

CALUMET COLLEGE OF ST. JOSEPH   B-1

Whiting, IN 46394   (219) 473-4739
                            (877) 700-9100; Fax: (219) 473-4259

Full-time: 145 men, 305 women	**Faculty:** 23; IIB, --$
Part-time: 340 men, 380 women	**Ph.Ds:** 50%
Graduate: 90 men, 30 women	**Student/Faculty:** 19 to 1
Year: semesters, summer session	**Tuition:** $9500
Application Deadline: open	**Room & Board:** n/app
Freshman Class: n/av	
SAT or ACT: not required	**LESS COMPETITIVE**

Calumet College of St. Joseph, founded in 1951, is a private, Catholic institution offering commuting students a liberal arts education in a Christian environment. Figures in the above capsule are approximate. The library contains 93,055 volumes, 3035 microform items, and 6412 audio/video tapes/CDs/DVDs, and subscribes to 354 periodicals including electronic. Computerized library services include interlibrary loans and database searching. Special learning facilities include a learning resource center and art gallery. The 256-acre campus is in an urban area 15 miles southeast of Chicago in northwest Indiana. There is one building.

Student Life: 70% of undergraduates are from Indiana. Others are from 2 states. 65% are from public schools. 46% are white; 33% African American; 19% Hispanic. Most are Catholic. The average age of freshmen is 21; all undergraduates, 35. 42% do not continue beyond their first year; 58% remain to graduate.

Housing: There are no residence halls. All students commute. Alcohol is not permitted. All students may keep cars.

Activities: There are no fraternities or sororities. There are 15 groups on campus, including cheerleading, drama, ethnic, literary magazine, musical theater, newspaper, photography, professional, religious, social, social service, and student government. Popular campus events include Thanksgiving Ethnicfest and Student Appreciation Week.

Sports: There are 3 intercollegiate sports for men and 4 for women, and 1 intramural sport for men.

Disabled Students: All of the campus is accessible. Wheelchair ramps, elevators, special parking, and specially equipped rest rooms are available.

Services: Counseling and information services are available, as is tutoring in most subjects. There is remedial math, reading, and writing.

Campus Safety and Security: Measures include emergency telephones and lighted pathways/sidewalks.

Programs of Study: CCSJ confers B.A., B.S., B.S.Ed., and B.S.M.T. degrees. Associate and master's degrees are also awarded. Bachelor's degrees are awarded in BUSINESS (accounting, business administration and management, and institutional management), COMMUNICATIONS AND THE ARTS (English and media arts), COMPUTER AND PHYSICAL SCIENCE (information sciences and systems), EDUCATION (elementary and secondary), HEALTH PROFESSIONS (health care administration), SOCIAL SCIENCE (criminal justice, human services, law enforcement and corrections, liberal arts/general studies, paralegal studies, psychology, religion, theological studies, and urban studies). Management, accounting, and criminal justice are the strongest academically. Management, human services, and education are the largest.

Required: All students must complete 42 semester hours of general education courses, including English composition, economics, speech, theology, philosophy, communication and fine arts, science and math, and social and behavioral science. A total of 124 semester hours with a minimum GPA of 2.0 is required to graduate.

Special: The college offers a cooperative 3-1 baccalaureate degree in medical technology with the schools of St. Margaret-Mercy Hospital in Indiana, where students complete their study and a clinical internship. Accelerated degree programs in organizational management, health-care mangement, and law enforcement management are possible. The LEAP program offers credit for life experience. Study abroad, internships, work-study programs, a general studies degree, pass/fail options, and nondegree study are possible.

Faculty/Classroom: 75% of faculty are male; 25%, female. All teach undergraduates. The average class size in an introductory lecture is 25; in a laboratory, 20; and in a regular course, 20.

Requirements: Applicants should have completed 4 years of high school English, 3 to 4 of math, 2 to 3 of science, and 2 of social studies. The GED is accepted. An essay and an interview are recommended. The Vocabulary and Reading Assessment Test is required. A GPA of 2.0 is required. AP and CLEP credits are accepted. Important factors in the admissions decision are extracurricular activities record, leadership record, and evidence of special talent.

Procedure: Freshmen are admitted to all sessions. There are deferred admissions and rolling admissions plans. Application deadlines are open. Applications are accepted on-line.

Transfer: 382 transfer students enrolled in a recent year. A 2.0 GPA is required. An interview is recommended. The Vocabulary and Reading Assessment Test is required. 30 of 124 credits required for the bachelor's degree must be completed at CCSJ.

Visiting: There are regularly scheduled orientations for prospective students. There are guides for informal visits and visitors may sit in on classes. To schedule a visit, contact Chuck Walz, Director of Admissions at (219) 473-4379.

Financial Aid: CCSJ is a member of CSS. The FAFSA and the college's own financial statement are required. Check with the school for application deadlines.

International Students: They must score satisfactorily on the TOEFL.

Computers: All students may access the system Monday through Friday from 8 A.M. to 10 P.M., except during class lab times. There are no time limits and no fees. It is strongly recommended that all students have a personal computer.

Admissions Contact: Chuck Walz, Director of Admissions.
Web: *www.ccsj.edu*

DEPAUW UNIVERSITY B-3
Greencastle, IN 46135

	(765) 658-4006
	(800) 447-2495; Fax: (765) 658-4007
Full-time: 1060 men, 1270 women	**Faculty:** 209; IIB, +$
Part-time: 15 men, 30 women	**Ph.D.s:** 93%
Graduate: none	**Student/Faculty:** 11 to 1
Year: 4-1-4	**Tuition:** $25,000
Application Deadline: see profile	**Room & Board:** $7100
Freshman Class: n/av	
SAT or ACT: required	**HIGHLY COMPETITIVE**

DePauw University, founded in 1837, is a private institution affiliated with the United Methodist Church offering programs in the fields of liberal arts and music. There are 2 undergraduate schools. Figures in the above capsule are approximate. In addition to regional accreditation, DePauw has baccalaureate program accreditation with ACS, CAAHEP, NASM, and NCATE. The 3 libraries contain 283,735 volumes, 371,852 microform items, and 15,659 audio/video tapes/CDs/DVDs, and subscribe to 4017 periodicals including electronic. Computerized library services include the card catalog, interlibrary loans, database searching, and Internet access. Special learning facilities include a learning resource center, art gallery, natural history museum, radio station, TV station, an observatory, an arboretum, a digital video studio, and a digital media lab. The 175-acre campus is in a small town 45 miles west of Indianapolis. Including any residence halls, there are 81 buildings.

Student Life: 50% of undergraduates are from out of state, mostly the Midwest. Students are from 41 states and 19 foreign countries. 88% are from public schools. 85% are white. 45% are Protestant; 22% Catholic; 6% claim no religious affiliation. The average age of freshmen is 19; all undergraduates, 20. 7% do not continue beyond their first year; 77% remain to graduate.

Housing: 1275 students can be accommodated in college housing, which includes coed dorms, on-campus apartments, off-campus apartments, fraternity houses, and sorority houses. In addition, there are special-interest houses. On-campus housing is guaranteed for all 4 years. 98% of students live on campus. All students may keep cars.

Activities: 76% of men belong to 12 national fraternities; 70% of women belong to 10 national sororities. There are 80 groups on campus, including art, band, cheerleading, chess, choir, chorale, chorus, computers, dance, debate, drama, ethnic, film, forensics, gay, honors, international, jazz band, literary magazine, musical theater, newspaper, opera, orchestra, pep band, political, professional, radio and TV, religious, social, social service, student government, symphony, and yearbook. Popular campus events include Little 5 track meet, Monon Bell football game, and Old Gold Day.

Sports: There are 17 intercollegiate sports for men and 16 for women, and 14 intramural sports for men and 12 for women. Facilities include a recreation center, a 4000-seat stadium, baseball, soccer, and field hockey fields, 3 basketball courts, indoor/outdoor tennis courts and tracks, a pool, a fitness center, volleyball and badminton courts, and a 3200-seat indoor gym.

Disabled Students: 85% of the campus is accessible. Wheelchair ramps, elevators, special parking, specially equipped rest rooms, special class scheduling, lowered drinking fountains, and lowered telephones are available.

Services: Counseling and information services are available, as is tutoring in most subjects. There is a reader service for the blind.

Campus Safety and Security: Measures include 24-hour foot and vehicle patrol, self-defense education, security escort services, and shuttle buses. There are informal discussions, pamphlets/posters/films, emergency telephones, and lighted pathways/sidewalks.

Programs of Study: DePauw confers B.A., B.M.A., B.M.E., and B.Mu. degrees. Bachelor's degrees are awarded in BIOLOGICAL SCIENCE (biochemistry and biology/biological science), COMMUNICATIONS AND THE ARTS (art history and appreciation, classical languages, communications, English, English literature, French, German, Greek, Latin, music, music business management, music performance, music theory and composition, romance languages and literature, Spanish, and studio art), COMPUTER AND PHYSICAL SCIENCE (chemistry, computer science, earth science, geology, mathematics, and physics), EDUCATION (elementary and music), ENGINEERING AND ENVIRONMENTAL DESIGN (environmental science and preengineering), SOCIAL SCIENCE (African American studies, anthropology, classical/ancient civilization, East Asian studies, economics, geography, history, interdisciplinary studies, peace studies, philosophy, physical fitness/movement, political science/government, psychology, religion, Russian and Slavic studies, sociology, and women's studies). English, economics, and communications are the largest.

Required: Students must demonstrate competence in oral communications, quantitative reasoning, and writing. Successful completion of 124 semester hours, including 32 to 40 in the major, is required for graduation. In addition, students must fulfill distribution requirements in natural sciences and math, social and behavioral sciences, literature and the arts, historical and philosophical understanding, foreign language, and self-expression. A comprehensive exam, thesis, or seminar is required for each major.

Special: DePauw offers dual majors in any 2 disciplines, student-designed majors, internships for honors programs and winter-term projects, unlimited study-abroad options through cooperative arrangements with other universities, a Washington semester, pass/fail options, and credit by departmental examination. Also available are 3-2 engineering degrees with Case Western Reserve, Columbia, and Washington Universities and a 3-2 nursing program with Rush University Hospital in Chicago. The Media Fellows, Management Fellows, and Science Research Fellows programs offer majors in any discipline, plus a semester-long internship. There are 13 national honor societies, including Phi Beta Kappa, a freshman honors program, and 12 departmental honors programs.

Faculty/Classroom: 58% of faculty are male; 42%, female. All teach undergraduates and 82% both teach and do research. The average class size in an introductory lecture is 20; in a laboratory, 14; and in a regular course, 18.

Requirements: The SAT or ACT is required. In addition, graduation from an accredited secondary school or a GED is required for admission. Course distribution must include 4 in English, 3 to 4 each in math, social studies, and science (2 or more with lab), and 2 to 4 in a foreign language. An essay is required, and an interview is strongly recommended. Applicants for the School of Music must audition. AP credits are accepted. Important factors in the admissions decision are advanced placement or honor courses, recommendations by school officials, and personality/intangible qualities.

Procedure: Freshmen are admitted fall and spring. Entrance exams should be taken as early as possible. There are early decision, early admissions, and deferred admissions plans. Applications are accepted online. Check with the school for application deadlines.

Transfer: 13 transfer students enrolled in a recent year. Applicants must submit either the SAT or ACT scores. High school and college transcripts are required, and a minimum GPA on previous college work of 3.0 is preferred. 60 of 124 credits required for the bachelor's degree must be completed at DePauw.

Visiting: There are regularly scheduled orientations for prospective students, consisting of daylong student/parent programs that include campus tours, faculty viewpoints, conversations with students, admissions information, financial aid and career planning sessions, and a meal in a residence hall. There are guides for informal visits and visitors may sit in on classes and stay overnight. To schedule a visit, contact Anna Logan, Admission Program and Visit Coordinator.

Financial Aid: In a recent year, 94% of all full-time freshmen and 96% of continuing full-time students received some form of financial aid. 56% of full-time freshmen and 51% of continuing full-time students received need-based aid. The average freshman award was $23,343. Need-based scholarships or need-based grants averaged $9151 ($25,675 maximum); need-based self-help aid (loans and jobs) averaged $4414 ($5825 maximum); and other non-need-based awards and non-need-based scholarships averaged $9778 ($2400 maximum). 39% of undergraduates worked part time. Average annual earnings from campus work were $630. The average financial indebtedness of a recent graduate was $15,635. DePauw is a member of CSS. The CSS/Profile or FAFSA and the college's own financial statement are required. Check with the school for application deadlines.

International Students: In a recent year, there were 47 international students enrolled. The school actively recruits these students. They must score satisfactorily on the TOEFL and also take the SAT or the ACT.

Computers: All students may access the system 24 hours a day.

Graduates: In a recent year, 537 bachelor's degrees were awarded. The most popular majors were communications (16%), creative writing (11%), and economics (10%). In an average class, 73% graduate in 4 years or less, 78% graduate in 5 years or less, and 79% graduate in 6 years or less. 50 companies recruited on campus in a recent year. Of a recent graduating class, 21% were enrolled in graduate school within 6 months of graduation and 79% were employed.

Admissions Contact: Madeleine R. Eagon, Vice President for Admission and Financial Aid. A video is available.
E-mail: *admissions@depauw.edu* Web: *http://www.depauw.edu*

EARLHAM COLLEGE
D-3

Richmond, IN 47374

(765) 983-1600
(800) 327-5426; Fax: (765) 983-1560

Full-time: 495 men, 683 women	**Faculty:** 93; IIB, av$
Part-time: 1 man, 6 women	**Ph.D.s:** 97%
Graduate: 29 men, 28 women	**Student/Faculty:** 13 to 1
Year: semesters and May term	**Tuition:** $27,684
Application Deadline: February 15	**Room & Board:** $5920
Freshman Class: 1554 applied, 1090 accepted, 324 enrolled	
SAT Verbal/Math: 640/600*	**ACT:** 26 **HIGHLY COMPETITIVE**

Earlham College, established in 1847 by the Society of Friends, is a private liberal arts college that emphasizes Quaker values. It offers undergraduate programs in humanities, fine arts, social sciences and natural sciences. The 2 libraries contain 404,760 volumes, 246,307 microform items, and 52,997 audio/video tapes/CDs/DVDs, and subscribe to 2213 periodicals including electronic. Computerized library services include the card catalog, interlibrary loans, database searching, Internet access, and laptop Internet portals. Special learning facilities include a learning resource center, art gallery, natural history museum, planetarium, radio station, observatory, herbarium, and greenhouse. The 800-acre campus is in a small town 70 miles east of Indianapolis and 40 miles west of Dayton, Ohio. Including any residence halls, there are 57 buildings.

Student Life: 75% of undergraduates are from out of state, mostly the Midwest. Students are from 49 states, 51 foreign countries, and Canada. 68% are from public schools. 75% are white. 38% claim no religious affiliation; 21% Protestant; 12% other non-Protestant (Buddhist, Islamic, etc.); 6% Catholic. The average age of freshmen is 18; all undergraduates, 20. 10% do not continue beyond their first year; 70% remain to graduate.

Housing: 978 students can be accommodated in college housing, which includes single-sex and coed dorms. In addition, there are language houses, special-interest houses, a service learning house, a Jewish culture center, an African American culture center, and a International Culture Center. On-campus housing is guaranteed for all 4 years. 88% of students live on campus; of those, 84% remain on campus on weekends. Alcohol is not permitted. All students may keep cars.

Activities: There are no fraternities or sororities. There are 64 groups on campus, including art, cheerleading, choir, chorale, chorus, computers, dance, drama, ethnic, film, gay, honors, international, jazz band, literary magazine, musical theater, newspaper, orchestra, photography, political, radio and TV, religious, social, social service, student government, symphony, and yearbook. Popular campus events include Reggae Festival, Japanese Spring Festival, and Women's Spring Festival.

Sports: There are 8 intercollegiate sports for men and 8 for women, and 7 intramural sports for men and 7 for women. Facilities include a fitness center with cardiovascular equipment and weights, group fitness and dance rooms, a field house with 4 indoor courts for tennis, volleyball, and basketball, 2 racquetball courts, an indoor climbing wall, an indoor running track, a 25-meter pool, a performance gym, and a massage therapist. Outdoor facilities include a natural grass football field, 10 all-weather tennis courts, basketball courts, a trail for cross-country running and skiing, and baseball, softball, soccer, lacrosse, and field hockey fields.

Disabled Students: 90% of the campus is accessible. Wheelchair ramps, elevators, special parking, specially equipped rest rooms, lowered drinking fountains, lowered telephones, and special housing are available.

Services: Counseling and information services are available, as is tutoring in some subjects, including humanities sciences, languages, some math and other subjects on request. There is a reader service for the blind.

Campus Safety and Security: Measures include 24-hour foot and vehicle patrol, self-defense education, security escort services, and shuttle buses. There are informal discussions, pamphlets/posters/films, emergency telephones, and lighted pathways/sidewalks.

Programs of Study: Earlham confers the B.A. degree. Master's degrees are also awarded. Bachelor's degrees are awarded in BIOLOGICAL SCIENCE (biochemistry and biology/biological science), BUSINESS (business administration and management), COMMUNICATIONS AND THE ARTS (art, dramatic arts, English, French, German, journalism, languages, music, and Spanish), COMPUTER AND PHYSICAL SCIENCE (astronomy, chemistry, computer science, geoscience, mathematics, and physics), ENGINEERING AND ENVIRONMENTAL DESIGN (environmental science), SOCIAL SCIENCE (African American studies, anthropology, classical/ancient civilization, economics, history, human development, international studies, Japanese studies, Latin American studies, peace studies, philosophy, political science/government, psychobiology, psychology, religion, sociology, and women's studies). Natural sciences and psychology are the strongest academically. Biology, psychology, and economics are the largest.

Required: To graduate, all students must complete the general education curriculum (scientific inquiry, analytical reasoning, the arts, domestic diversity, international diversity, and wellness). Students must also maintain a minimum GPA of 2.0 and complete a total of 122 semester hours, including 32 semester hours in the major and at least 36-upper level semester hours and 40 outside the major division. A senior capstone experience is required.

Special: Opportunities are provided for dual majors, cross-registration with Indiana University East, internships, work-study programs, accelerated degree programs, nondegree study, and student-designed majors. Study off-campus is available through 24 foreign and domestic programs. Pre-professional and professional options are offered in law and medicine. There is a 3-2 engineering degree with Case Western Reserve University, Columbia University, University of Rochester, and Rensselaer Polytechnic Institute. There are 2 national honor societies, including Phi Beta Kappa.

Faculty/Classroom: 56% of faculty are male; 44%, female. All teach undergraduates, 75% do research, and 75% do both. No introductory courses are taught by graduate students. The average class size in an introductory lecture is 30; in a laboratory, 15; and in a regular course, 19.

Admissions: 70% of the 2005-2006 applicants were accepted. The SAT scores for the 2005-2006 freshman class were: Verbal--9% below 500, 24% between 500 and 599, 40% between 600 and 700, and 27% above 700; Math--17% below 500, 31% between 500 and 599, 43% between 600 and 700, and 9% above 700. 53% of the current freshmen were in the top fifth of their class; 79% were in the top two fifths. There were 6 National Merit finalists. 8 freshmen graduated first in their class.

Requirements: The ACT is required and the SAT is recommended. The ACT Optional Writing test is also required. In addition, in most cases, graduation from an accredited secondary school is required; a GED will be accepted. Home-schooled students are not required to take the GED or have a high school diploma. Students must have completed at least 15 academic credits, including 4 years of English, 3 of math, and 2 each of science, history or social studies, and a foreign language. Students are required to submit an essay and letters of recommendation from a teacher and guidance counselor. An interview is recommended. AP credits are accepted. Important factors in the admissions decision are advanced placement or honor courses, evidence of special talent, and extracurricular activities record.

Procedure: Freshmen are admitted fall, winter, and spring. Entrance exams should be taken during the spring of the junior year or early fall of the senior year. There are early decision, early admissions, and deferred admissions plans. Early decision applications should be filed by December 1; regular applications, by February 15 for fall entry, November 15 for winter entry, and November 15 for spring entry. Notification of early decision is sent December 15; regular decision, March 15. 40 early decision candidates were accepted for the 2005-2006 class. 72 applicants were on the 2005 waiting list; 12 were admitted. Applications are accepted on-line. The fall 2005 application fee was $30.

Transfer: 14 transfer students enrolled in 2004-2005. Applicants must take the SAT or ACT and have a minimum GPA of 2.3 in college course work. An interview is recommended. High school and college transcripts, an essay, and a statement of good standing from the prior institution are required. 60 of 120 credits required for the bachelor's degree must be completed at Earlham.

Visiting: There are regularly scheduled orientations for prospective students, including class visitation, an admissions interview, a tour, and special appointments with faculty. There are guides for informal visits and visitors may sit in on classes and stay overnight. To schedule a visit, contact the Admissions Office at 800-EARLHAM.

Financial Aid: In 2004-2005, 83% of all full-time freshmen and 85% of continuing full-time students received some form of financial aid. 62% of full-time freshmen and 63% of continuing full-time students received need-based aid. The average freshman award was $19,989. Need-based scholarships or need-based grants averaged $12,422 ($26,500 maximum); need-based self-help aid (loans and jobs) averaged $3905 ($7730 maximum); and other non-need-based awards and non-need-based scholarships averaged $6150 ($10,000 maximum). 50% of undergraduates work part time. Average annual earnings from campus work are $1120. The average financial indebtedness of the 2005 graduate was $18,900. Earlham is a member of CSS. The FAFSA and the college's own financial statement are required. The deadline for filing freshman financial aid applications for fall entry is March 1.

International Students: There are 128 international students enrolled. The school actively recruits these students. They must score satisfactorily on the written TOEFL and also take the SAT.

Computers: Wireless access is available. 8 public computing labs provide 133 Dell PCs and 31 Macs for student use. One of the labs with 25 PCs and 6 Macs is open 24 hours a day. There also are 12 other discipline-specific labs throughout the campus providing an additional 72 PCs. Undergraduates with their own units can connect to the campus network from network ports in their residence hall rooms or via the wireless network from one of 40 access points around campus. Students can check out laptops from the library for use within the building for up to 3 hours, or from the instructional technology and media center for use around campus for up to 3 days. All students may access the system 24 hours per day. There are no time limits and no fees.

Graduates: From July 1, 2004 to June 30, 2005, 226 bachelor's degrees were awarded. The most popular majors were social sciences and history (18%), biology (15%), and interdisciplinary studies (11%). In an average class, 59% graduate in 4 years or less, 67% graduate in 5 years or less, and 70% graduate in 6 years or less. 86 companies recruited on campus in 2004-2005. Of the 2004 graduating class, 42% were enrolled in graduate school within 6 months of graduation and 60% were employed.

Admissions Contact: Jeff Rickey, Dean of Admissions and Financial Aid. A video is available. E-mail: *admission@earlham.edu* Web: *http://www.earlham.edu*

FRANKLIN COLLEGE   C-4
Franklin, IN 46131-2623

(317) 738-8062
(800) 852-0232; Fax: (317) 738-8274

Full-time: 487 men, 459 women	Faculty: 60; IIB, --$
Part-time: 34 men, 23 women	Ph.D.s: 92%
Graduate: none	Student/Faculty: 16 to 1
Year: 4-1-4, summer session	Tuition: $19,365
Application Deadline: open	Room & Board: $5730
Freshman Class: 1009 applied, 790 accepted, 273 enrolled	
SAT Verbal/Math: 510/520*	ACT: 21 COMPETITIVE

Franklin College, founded in 1834, is a private liberal arts college affiliated with the American Baptist Churches, U.S.A. In addition to regional accreditation, Franklin College has baccalaureate program accreditation with CAAHEP and NCATE. The library contains 124,661 volumes, 295,251 microform items, and 7432 audio/video tapes/CDs/DVDs, and subscribes to 806 periodicals including electronic. Computerized library services include the card catalog, interlibrary loans, and database searching. Special learning facilities include a learning resource center, radio

station, and TV station. The 74-acre campus is in a small town 20 miles south of Indianapolis. Including any residence halls, there are 20 buildings.

Student Life: 94% of undergraduates are from Indiana. Others are from 16 states and 7 foreign countries. 83% are white. 51% are Protestant; 32% claim no religious affiliation; 16% are Catholic. The average age of freshmen is 19; all undergraduates, 23. 24% do not continue beyond their first year; 58% remain to graduate.

Housing: 814 students can be accommodated in college housing, which includes single-sex and coed dorms and fraternity houses. In addition, there is a substance-and-alcohol-free residence hall living area. On-campus housing is available on a first-come, first-served basis and is available on a lottery system for upperclassmen. 74% of students live on campus. All students may keep cars.

Activities: 49% of men belong to 5 national fraternities; 42% of women belong to 4 national sororities. There are 60 groups on campus, including art, cheerleading, choir, chorus, drama, ethnic, film, honors, international, literary magazine, musical theater, newspaper, photography, political, professional, radio and TV, religious, social, social service, student government, and yearbook. Popular campus events include Grizzly Grand Prix, Annual Kite Carnival, and Greek Week.

Sports: There are 8 intercollegiate sports for men and 8 for women, and 6 intramural sports for men and 6 for women. Facilities include athletic and soccer fields, tennis courts, a phys ed center, and a fitness center.

Disabled Students: All of the campus is accessible. Wheelchair ramps, elevators, special parking, specially equipped rest rooms, special class scheduling, lowered drinking fountains, and special housing are available.

Services: Counseling and information services are available, as is tutoring in most subjects. There is a reader service for the blind, and remedial math, reading, and writing.

Campus Safety and Security: Measures include 24-hour foot and vehicle patrol, security escort services, pamphlets/posters/films, and emergency telephones. There are lighted pathways/sidewalks.

Programs of Study: Franklin College confers the B.A. degree. Bachelor's degrees are awarded in BIOLOGICAL SCIENCE (biology/biological science), BUSINESS (accounting, business administration and management, and recreation and leisure services), COMMUNICATIONS AND THE ARTS (dramatic arts, English, French, journalism, music, and Spanish), COMPUTER AND PHYSICAL SCIENCE (chemistry, computer science, information sciences and systems, and mathematics), EDUCATION (elementary, English, health, journalism, mathematics, physical, science, secondary, and social studies), SOCIAL SCIENCE (American studies, Canadian studies, economics, history, philosophy, political science/government, psychology, religion, and sociology). Journalism, education, and business are the strongest academically and have the largest enrollments.

Required: Requirements for graduation include 96 hours outside the major, including general education, a minimum of 24 hours in the major, and 128 total credit hours. Each student must maintain a minimum GPA of 2.0 and must pass the Senior Competency Test, which is administered by the department in which the student completes a major. All students must complete a leadership winter term course.

Special: Cooperative programs in nursing, political science, Canadian studies, forestry, and engineering are available, as are January and summer internships. Study abroad in 16 countries and cross-registration with 7 Indiana universities and colleges and the Indianapolis Museum of Art are permitted. A 3-2 engineering degree with Washington University at St. Louis is possible. There are 10 national honor societies.

Faculty/Classroom: 59% of faculty are male; 41%, female. All teach undergraduates. The average class size in an introductory lecture is 18; in a laboratory, 15; and in a regular course, 16.

Admissions: 78% of the 2005-2006 applicants were accepted. The SAT scores for the 2005-2006 freshman class were: Verbal--43% below 500, 42% between 500 and 599, 13% between 600 and 700, and 2% above 700; Math--37% below 500, 45% between 500 and 599, 17% between 600 and 700, and 1% above 700. The ACT scores were 35% below 21, 30% between 21 and 23, 19% between 24 and 26, 11% between 27 and 28, and 5% above 28. 41% of the current freshmen were in the top fifth of their class; 72% were in the top two fifths. 5 freshmen graduated first in their class in a recent year.

Requirements: The SAT or ACT is required. The ACT Optional Writing test is also required. In addition, candidates for admission should have completed 4 years of English, 3 to 4 of math, 2 to 3 of science, 2 each of art and music, social studies, and a foreign language, and typing and basic computing skill courses. The GED is accepted, and an essay is required. AP and CLEP credits are accepted. Important factors in the admissions decision are leadership record, recommendations by school officials, and advanced placement or honor courses.

Procedure: Freshmen are admitted to all sessions. Entrance exams should be taken in spring of the junior year or fall of the senior year. Application deadlines are open. Application fee is $30. Applications are accepted on-line.

Transfer: 59 transfer students enrolled in a recent year. Transfer students must have at least a 2.0 cumulative GPA and submit official transcripts from previously attended colleges. 30 of 128 credits required for the bachelor's degree must be completed at Franklin College.

Visiting: There are regularly scheduled orientations for prospective students, including academic presentations, admissions and financial presentations, a student life presentation, campus tours, lunch, and opportunities to talk to professors . There are guides for informal visits and visitors may sit in on classes and stay overnight. To schedule a visit, contact the Admissions Office at *admissions@franklincollege.edu.*

Financial Aid: In 2005-2006, 98% of all full-time freshmen and all continuing full-time students received some form of financial aid. 60% of full-time freshmen and 58% of continuing full-time students received need-based aid. The average freshman award was $12,753. Need-based scholarships or need-based grants averaged $3944 ($15,064 maximum); and need-based self-help aid (loans and jobs) averaged $3663 ($8125 maximum). 64% of undergraduates work part time. Average annual earnings from campus work are $840. The average financial indebtedness of the 2005 graduate was $21,263. The FAFSA and the college's own financial statement are required. The deadline for filing freshman financial aid applications for fall entry is March 1.

International Students: There were 7 international students enrolled in a recent year. They must score satisfactorily on the written TOEFL, and completion of level 109 in an English language service (ELS) center is also necessary.

Computers: Wireless access is available. All resident students have network access in dorm rooms. There are approximately 85 desktops in public areas for student use, 25 desktops for lab use only, 20 laptops for student checkout, and 90 laptops for lab use only. All have access to the college's network and the Internet. All students may access the system 8 A.M. to midnight (24 hours in one lab). 20 laptops may be checked out 24 hours. There are no time limits and no fees.

Graduates: From July 1, 2004 to June 30, 2005, 204 bachelor's degrees were awarded. The most popular majors were journalism (21%), elementary education (14%), and sociology (13%). In an average class, 1% graduate in 3 years or less, 50% graduate in 4 years or less, 54% graduate in 5 years or less, and 56% graduate in 6 years or less. 40 companies recruited on campus in 2004-2005.

Admissions Contact: Alan Hill, Vice President for Enrollment and Student Affairs. E-mail: *admissions@franklincollege.edu*
Web: *http://www.franklincollege.edu/admissions_index.htm*

GOSHEN COLLEGE   C-1

Goshen, IN 46526

(574) 535-7535
(800) 348-7422; Fax: (574) 535-7609

Full-time: 320 men, 470 women	**Faculty:** 72
Part-time: 40 men, 100 women	**Ph.D.s:** 59%
Graduate: none	**Student/Faculty:** 11 to 1
Year: semesters, summer session	**Tuition:** $16,850
Application Deadline: see profile	**Room & Board:** $6000
Freshman Class: n/av	
SAT or ACT: required	**VERY COMPETITIVE**

Goshen College, founded in 1894, is a private liberal arts institution affiliated with the Mennonite Church. Figures in the above capsule are approximate. In addition to regional accreditation, Goshen has baccalaureate program accreditation with CSWE, NCATE, and NLN. The library contains 120,000 volumes, 140,000 microform items, and 1500 audio/video tapes/CDs/DVDs, and subscribes to 900 periodicals including electronic. Computerized library services include the card catalog, interlibrary loans, and database searching. Special learning facilities include a learning resource center, art gallery, and radio station. The 135-acre campus is in a small town 120 miles east of Chicago. Including any residence halls, there are 25 buildings.

Student Life: 52% of undergraduates are from Indiana. Others are from 29 states, 30 foreign countries, and Canada. 83% are white. Most are Protestant. The average age of freshmen is 18; all undergraduates, 21. 19% do not continue beyond their first year; 66% remain to graduate.

Housing: 696 students can be accommodated in college housing, which includes single-sex and coed dorms, off-campus apartments, married-student housing and small-group special-interest houses. On-campus housing is guaranteed for all 4 years. 69% of students live on campus; of those, 85% remain on campus on weekends. Alcohol is not permitted. All students may keep cars.

Activities: There are no fraternities or sororities. There are 26 groups on campus, including chess, choir, chorale, chorus, drama, ethnic, honors, international, jazz band, literary magazine, musical theater, newspaper, opera, orchestra, photography, professional, radio and TV, religious, social, social service, student government, and yearbook. Popular campus events include February Fest, Fall Fest, and Celebrate Service Day.

Sports: There are 7 intercollegiate sports for men and 7 for women, and 8 intramural sports for men and 8 for women. Facilities include a fit-

ness center with an indoor track and swimming pool, 3 basketball courts, a soccer field, tennis courts, a sand volleyball court, a 400-meter, all-weather track, and baseball and softball diamonds.

Disabled Students: All of the campus is accessible. Wheelchair ramps, elevators, special parking, specially equipped rest rooms, special class scheduling, lowered drinking fountains, and lowered telephones are available.

Services: Counseling and information services are available, as is tutoring in every subject. There is a reader service for the blind, and remedial math, reading, and writing.

Campus Safety and Security: Measures include 24-hour foot and vehicle patrol, self-defense education, security escort services, and informal discussions. There are pamphlets/posters/films and lighted pathways/sidewalks.

Programs of Study: Goshen confers B.A., B.S., and B.S.N. degrees. Bachelor's degrees are awarded in BIOLOGICAL SCIENCE (biology/biological science and molecular biology), BUSINESS (accounting, business administration and management, institutional management, and management information systems), COMMUNICATIONS AND THE ARTS (American Sign Language, communications, dramatic arts, English, music, and Spanish), COMPUTER AND PHYSICAL SCIENCE (chemistry, computer programming, information sciences and systems, mathematics, and physics), EDUCATION (art, business, elementary, foreign languages, middle school, music, physical, science, and secondary), ENGINEERING AND ENVIRONMENTAL DESIGN (environmental science and preengineering), HEALTH PROFESSIONS (nursing, predentistry, premedicine, prepharmacy, and preveterinary science), SOCIAL SCIENCE (biblical studies, history, peace studies, psychology, religion, social work, and sociology). Nursing, elementary education, and biology are the largest.

Required: All students must complete the general education program, including courses in literature and communication, fine arts, Bible, religion, philosophy, natural science, math, social science, and history, and 12 hours of international education in the Study Service Term and 1 hour of phys ed. A total of 120 credit hours with a minimum GPA of 2.0 is required to graduate.

Special: A semester abroad internship in the required Study Service Term is possible in China, Indonesia, Germany, Ivory Coast, Cuba, and the Dominican Republic. Cross-registration is offered with member colleges of the Northern Indiana Consortium for Education. A Washington semester, dual majors, student-designed majors, and a 3-2 engineering degree with the University of Illinois, Washington University in St. Louis, and Case Western Reserve University are available. Credit for life experience, pass/fail options, and nondegree study are possible. There is 1 national honor society, a freshman honors program, and 1 departmental honors program.

Faculty/Classroom: 56% of faculty are male; 44%, female. All both teach and do research. The average class size in an introductory lecture is 28; in a laboratory, 14; and in a regular course, 22.

Requirements: The SAT or ACT is required. In addition, applicants should be graduates of an accredited secondary school or have a GED equivalent, with 4 years of high school English, 2 to 4 years of math, and 2 years each of foreign language, science, history, and social studies. An interview is recommended. AP and CLEP credits are accepted. Important factors in the admissions decision are advanced placement or honor courses, recommendations by school officials, and recommendations by alumni.

Procedure: Freshmen are admitted to all sessions. Entrance exams should be taken by fall of the senior year. There is a deferred admissions plan and a rolling admissions plan. Check with the school for application deadlines. Notification is sent on a rolling basis. Applications are accepted on-line. The fall 2005 application fee was $25.

Transfer: 65 transfer students enrolled in a recent year. A GPA of 2.0 or higher is required on previous college work. 30 of 120 credits required for the bachelor's degree must be completed at Goshen.

Visiting: There are regularly scheduled orientations for prospective students, consisting of a campus tour, a parents session, talks with professors, a financial aid session, visitation, an overnight stay in the dorms, a student panel, and a campus interview. There are guides for informal visits and visitors may sit in on classes and stay overnight. To schedule a visit, contact the Admissions Office.

Financial Aid: In a recent year, 99% of all full-time students received some form of financial aid. 75% of full-time freshmen and 71% of continuing full-time students received need-based aid. The average freshman award was $16,036. Need-based scholarships or need-based grants averaged $11,781 ($23,700 maximum); need-based self-help aid (loans and jobs) averaged $4527 ($16,425 maximum); non-need-based athletic scholarships averaged $2400 ($3000 maximum); and other non-need-based awards and non-need-based scholarships averaged $10,167 ($21,000 maximum). 72% of undergraduates worked part time. Average annual earnings from campus work were $1470. The average financial indebtedness of a recent graduate was $15,689. Goshen is a member of CSS. The FAFSA and the college's own financial statement are required. Check with the school for application deadlines.

International Students: In a recent year, there were 77 international students enrolled. The school actively recruits these students. They must score satisfactorily on the TOEFL and also take the SAT or the ACT.

Computers: All students may access the system. There are no time limits and no fees.

Graduates: In a recent year, 229 bachelor's degrees were awarded. The most popular majors were organizational management (10%), elementary education (8%), and nursing (5%). In an average class, 46% graduate in 4 years or less, 65% graduate in 5 years or less, and 66% graduate in 6 years or less. 28 companies recruited on campus in a recent year. Of a recent graduating class, 30% were enrolled in graduate school within 6 months of graduation and 70% were employed.

Admissions Contact: Karen Lee Raftus, Director of Admission. A video is available. E-mail: *admission@goshen.edu* Web: *www.goshen.edu*

GRACE COLLEGE
C-2

Winona Lake, IN 46590

(574) 372-5100, ext. 6004
(800) 54-GRACE; Fax: (574) 372-5120

Full-time: 300 men, 464 women	**Faculty:** 45
Part-time: 43 men, 61 women	**Ph.D.s:** 63%
Graduate: 10 men, 27 women	**Student/Faculty:** 21 to 1
Year: semesters, summer session	**Tuition:** $16,020
Application Deadline: August 1	**Room & Board:** $6150
Freshman Class: 700 applied, 529 accepted, 217 enrolled	
SAT Verbal/Math: 532/579*	**ACT:** 23 **COMPETITIVE**

Grace College, founded in 1948, is a Christian liberal arts institution affiliated with the Fellowship of Grace Brethren Churches. In addition to regional accreditation, Grace has baccalaureate program accreditation with CSWE, NASM, and NCATE. The library contains 150,843 volumes, 26,000 microform items, and 3714 audio/video tapes/CDs/DVDs, and subscribes to 19,360 periodicals including electronic. Computerized library services include the card catalog, interlibrary loans, database searching, Internet access, and laptop Internet portals. Special learning facilities include a learning resource center and art gallery. The 150-acre campus is in a small town 40 miles west of Fort Wayne. Including any residence halls, there are 15 buildings.

Student Life: 58% of undergraduates are from Indiana. Others are from 27 states, 5 foreign countries, and Canada. 74% are from public schools. 91% are white. Most are Protestant. The average age of freshmen is 18; all undergraduates, 23. 17% do not continue beyond their first year; 58% remain to graduate.

Housing: 684 students can be accommodated in college housing, which includes single-sex dorms and on-campus apartments. On-campus housing is available on a first-come, first-served basis and is available on a lottery system for upperclassmen. Priority is given to out-of-town students. 75% of students live on campus; of those, 80% remain on campus on weekends. Alcohol is not permitted. All students may keep cars.

Activities: There are no fraternities or sororities. There are 14 groups on campus, including band, cheerleading, choir, chorale, drama, honors, international, musical theater, newspaper, orchestra, pep band, religious, social, student government, and yearbook. Popular campus events include Fall Fest, Heart of the Holidays, and VIP Days.

Sports: There are 8 intercollegiate sports for men and 8 for women, and 3 intramural sports for men and 3 for women. Facilities include a gym, soccer fields, tennis courts, softball and baseball diamonds, and a recreation center with basketball courts, indoor track, and weight and exercise rooms.

Disabled Students: 80% of the campus is accessible. Wheelchair ramps, elevators, special parking, and specially equipped rest rooms are available.

Services: Counseling and information services are available, as is tutoring in most subjects. There is remedial math, reading, and writing.

Campus Safety and Security: Measures include 24-hour foot and vehicle patrol, security escort services, and lighted pathways/sidewalks.

Programs of Study: Grace confers B.A., B.S., B.M., and B.S.W. degrees. Associate and master's degrees are also awarded. Bachelor's degrees are awarded in BIOLOGICAL SCIENCE (biology/biological science), BUSINESS (accounting, business administration and management, and management information systems), COMMUNICATIONS AND THE ARTS (art, communications, English, French, German, graphic design, journalism, music, and Spanish), COMPUTER AND PHYSICAL SCIENCE (mathematics and science), EDUCATION (art, business, elementary, English, foreign languages, journalism, mathematics, music, physical, science, and special), HEALTH PROFESSIONS (predentistry and premedicine), SOCIAL SCIENCE (biblical studies, counseling/psychology, criminal justice, prelaw, psychology, religion, social work, sociology, and youth ministry). Biology, psychology, and business are the strongest academically. Psychology, elementary education, and biblical studies are the largest.

Required: To graduate, students must complete 124 hours, including 36 to 54 in the major, and have a minimum GPA of 2.0. The required core curriculm of 56 hours consists of languages/literature, humanities, religion/philosophy, education, social sciences, and natural sciences.

Special: Students may study abroad in 5 countries. A B.A.-B.S. degree is available in all majors except languages, English, and biblical studies. Dual majors are offered in psychology, sociology, communication, business, accounting, youth ministries, and management information technology. There is 1 national honor society and a freshman honors program.

Faculty/Classroom: 72% of faculty are male; 23%, female. All teach undergraduates and 10% both teach and do research. No introductory courses are taught by graduate students. The average class size in an introductory lecture is 48; in a laboratory, 14; and in a regular course, 17.

Admissions: 76% of the 2005-2006 applicants were accepted. The SAT scores for the 2005-2006 freshman class were: Verbal--32% below 500, 44% between 500 and 599, 19% between 600 and 700, and 5% above 700; Math--36% below 500, 40% between 500 and 599, 21% between 600 and 700, and 3% above 700. The ACT scores were 25% below 21, 29% between 21 and 23, 28% between 24 and 26, 8% between 27 and 28, and 10% above 28. 38% of the current freshmen were in the top fifth of their class; 58% were in the top two fifths. 13 freshmen graduated first in their class.

Requirements: A satisfactory score is recommended on the SAT or ACT is recommended. In addition, applicants must have completed 15 Carnegie units, including 4 of English, 3 each of math and science, 2 each of a foreign language and social studies, and 1 of history. A GED is accepted. Grace requires applicants to be in the upper 50% of their class. A GPA of 2.3 is required. AP and CLEP credits are accepted. Important factors in the admissions decision are advanced placement or honor courses, leadership record, and personality/intangible qualities.

Procedure: Freshmen are admitted to all sessions. Entrance exams should be taken in October, December, or February. There is a deferred admissions plan and a rolling admissions plan. Applications should be filed by August 1 for fall entry and December 1 for spring entry, along with a $25 fee. Notification is sent on a rolling basis. Applications are accepted on-line.

Transfer: 61 transfer students enrolled in a recent year. Transfer applicants should have a minimum 2.0 GPA in addition to fulfilling freshman entrance requirements. 60 of 124 credits required for the bachelor's degree must be completed at Grace.

Visiting: There are regularly scheduled orientations for prospective students, including tours, class visits, and meetings with professors. There are guides for informal visits and visitors may sit in on classes and stay overnight. To schedule a visit, contact the Visitors Center at (574) 372-5100, ext. 6003.

Financial Aid: In 2005-2006, 82% of all full-time freshmen and 93% of continuing full-time students received some form of financial aid. 76% of full-time freshmen and 94% of continuing full-time students received need-based aid. The average freshman award was $13,472. Need-based scholarships or need-based grants averaged $8219 ($12,900 maximum); need-based self-help aid (loans and jobs) averaged $4724 ($7925 maximum); non-need-based athletic scholarships averaged $3243 ($6000 maximum); and other non-need-based awards and non-need-based scholarships averaged $3081 ($5420 maximum). 47% of undergraduates work part time. Average annual earnings from campus work are $1300. The average financial indebtedness of a recent graduate was $19,709. The FAFSA is required. The priority date for freshman financial aid applications for fall entry is March 10.

International Students: There were 15 international students enrolled in a recent year. They must take the written TOEFL and also take the SAT or the ACT, scoring stisfactorily.

Computers: All students may access the system when the classrooms and labs are open. There are no time limits and no fees. It is strongly recommended that all students have a personal computer.

Graduates: From July 1, 2004 to June 30, 2005, 238 bachelor's degrees were awarded. The most popular majors were elementary education (14%), psychology (8%), and business administration (7%). In an average class, 46% graduate in 4 years or less, 56% graduate in 5 years or less, and 58% graduate in 6 years or less.

Admissions Contact: Ken Moyer, Dean of Enrollment Management. E-mail: *moyerkp@grace.edu* Web: *http://www.grace.edu*

HANOVER COLLEGE
D-5

Hanover, IN 47243

(812) 866-7022
(800) 213-2178; Fax: (812) 866-7098

Full-time: 438 men, 566 women	**Faculty:** 95; IIB, av$
Part-time: 1 man, 3 women	**Ph.D.s:** 95%
Graduate: none	**Student/Faculty:** 11 to 1
Year: 4-1-4	**Tuition:** $21,650
Application Deadline: March 1	**Room & Board:** $6500
Freshman Class: n/av	
SAT Verbal/Math: 590/600*	**ACT:** 26 **HIGHLY COMPETITIVE**

Hanover College, founded in 1827 and the oldest private college in Indiana, is a liberal arts school affiliated with the United Presbyterian

Church. In addition to regional accreditation, Hanover has baccalaureate program accreditation with NCATE. The library contains 222,782 volumes, 44,951 microform items, and 10,015 audio/video tapes/CDs/DVDs, and subscribes to 1667 periodicals including electronic. Computerized library services include the card catalog, interlibrary loans, database searching, Internet access, and laptop Internet portals. Special learning facilities include a learning resource center, art gallery, planetarium, radio station, TV station, and a geology museum. The 650-acre campus is in a rural area 45 miles north of Louisville, Kentucky. Including any residence halls, there are 35 buildings.

Student Life: 64% of undergraduates are from Indiana. Others are from 28 states and 17 foreign countries. 84% are from public schools. 88% are white. 50% are claim no religious affiliation; 35% Protestant; 14% Catholic. The average age of freshmen is 18; all undergraduates, 19. 23% do not continue beyond their first year; 70% remain to graduate.

Housing: 1050 students can be accommodated in college housing, which includes single-sex and coed dorms, on-campus apartments, fraternity houses, and sorority houses. In addition, there are honors houses, special-interest houses, and a multicultural center. On-campus housing is guaranteed for all 4 years. 94% of students live on campus. Alcohol is not permitted. Upperclassmen may keep cars.

Activities: 42% of men belong to 5 national fraternities; 59% of women belong to 4 national sororities. There are 46 groups on campus, including band, cheerleading, choir, chorus, computers, dance, debate, drama, ethnic, film, gay, honors, international, jazz band, literary magazine, musical theater, newspaper, orchestra, pep band, photography, political, professional, radio and TV, religious, social, social service, student government, and yearbook. Popular campus events include a community artist series, a foreign film series, and Spring Fling.

Sports: There are 8 intercollegiate sports for men and 8 for women, and 10 intramural sports for men and 10 for women. Facilities include a health and recreation center consisting of a 2000-seat performance gym, a multisports forum, a suspended running track, racquetball and squash courts, a weight room, a training room, and a physiology lab. There also is an outdoor athletic complex consisting of a 5000-seat stadium and performance and practice fields.

Disabled Students: 75% of the campus is accessible. Wheelchair ramps, elevators, special parking, special class scheduling, lowered drinking fountains, and lowered telephones are available.

Services: Counseling and information services are available, as is tutoring in most subjects. There is remedial writing.

Campus Safety and Security: Measures include 24-hour foot and vehicle patrol, self-defense education, security escort services, and shuttle buses. There are informal discussions, pamphlets/posters/films, emergency telephones, and lighted pathways/sidewalks.

Programs of Study: Hanover confers the B.A. degree. Bachelor's degrees are awarded in BIOLOGICAL SCIENCE (biology/biological science), BUSINESS (business administration and management), COMMUNICATIONS AND THE ARTS (art, art history and appreciation, classics, communications, dramatic arts, English, French, German, music, and Spanish), COMPUTER AND PHYSICAL SCIENCE (chemistry, computer science, geology, mathematics, and physics), HEALTH PROFESSIONS (exercise science), SOCIAL SCIENCE (anthropology, economics, history, international studies, Latin American studies, medieval studies, philosophy, political science/government, psychology, sociology, and theological studies). Arts and sciences and interdisciplinary studies are the strongest academically. Psychology and sociology are the largest.

Required: Students must complete 37 units of credit, including 8 to 12 in the major, maintain a GPA of 2.0, pass a comprehensive exam, participate in a culminating experience in the major, as well as complete a senior capstone.

Special: Internships, study abroad, a Washington semester, an experiential program at the Philadelphia Center, and student-designed majors in international studies and Latin American studies, along with self-designed majors including 2 or more disciplines, are offered. The Center for Business Preparation provides preparation for a career in business, built on a liberal arts foundation. There are 8 national honor societies.

Faculty/Classroom: 64% of faculty are male; 36%, female. All teach undergraduates. The average class size in an introductory lecture is 15; in a laboratory, 16; and in a regular course, 12.

Admissions: 70% of the 2005-2006 applicants were accepted. The SAT scores for the 2005-2006 freshman class were: Verbal--9% below 500, 42% between 500 and 599, 34% between 600 and 700, and 15% above 700; Math--7% below 500, 42% between 500 and 599, 43% between 600 and 700, and 8% above 700. The ACT scores were 2% below 21, 25% between 21 and 23, 25% between 24 and 26, 14% between 27 and 28, and 34% above 28. 69% of the current freshmen were in the top fifth of their class; 91% were in the top two fifths. 11 freshmen graduated first in their class.

Requirements: The SAT or ACT is required. Admission is competitive, based on the applicant pool. The college requires 16 academic credits, including 4 years of English and 2 each of a foreign language, math, science, and either history or social studies. The GED is accepted. The col-

lege also requires a foreign language achievement test for those who wish to meet their world language requirement in the language they studied in high school, as well as an essay; an interview is recommended. AP credits are accepted. Important factors in the admissions decision are recommendations by school officials, advanced placement or honor courses, and extracurricular activities record.

Procedure: Freshmen are admitted fall and winter. Entrance exams should be taken late in the spring of the junior year. There is a deferred admissions plan. There is a rolling admissions plan. Applications should be filed before March 1 for fall entry, along with a $30 fee. Notification is sent on a rolling basis by March 1. 54 applicants were on the 2005 waiting list; 38 were admitted. Applications are accepted on-line.

Transfer: 29 transfer students enrolled in a recent year. Transfer students must submit transcripts from all colleges attended and must have performed successfully. SAT or ACT scores and high school record may also be taken into consideration. 17 of 37 units credit required for the bachelor's degree must be completed at Hanover.

Visiting: There are regularly scheduled orientations for prospective students. There are guides for informal visits and visitors may sit in on classes and stay overnight. To schedule a visit, contact the Office of Admissions.

Financial Aid: In 2005-2006, 80% of all full-time freshmen and 85% of continuing full-time students received some form of financial aid. 80% of full-time freshmen and 72% of continuing full-time students received need-based aid. The average freshman award was $16,453. Need-based scholarships or need-based grants averaged $14,421; need-based self-help aid (loans and jobs) averaged $3478; and other non-need-based awards and non-need-based scholarships averaged $14,452. 26% of undergraduates work part time. Average annual earnings from campus work are $1418. The average financial indebtedness of the 2005 graduate was $16,514. The FAFSA is required. The deadline for filing freshman financial aid applications for fall entry is March 1.

International Students: There are 52 international students enrolled. The school actively recruits these students. They must achieve a satisfactory score on the TOEFL and also take the SAT or the ACT.

Computers: Wireless access is available. All students may access the system in computer labs, 8 A.M. to 11 P.M. Monday through Thursday and Sunday, and 8 A.M. to 5 P.M. Friday and Saturday. The library has a 24-hour lab. There are no time limits and no fees.

Graduates: From July 1, 2004 to June 30, 2005, 196 bachelor's degrees were awarded. The most popular majors were business administration (11%), psychology (11%), and biology (9%). In an average class, 68% graduate in 4 years or less, 69% graduate in 5 years or less, and 70% graduate in 6 years or less. 49 companies recruited on campus in 2004-2005. Of the 2004 graduating class, 29% were enrolled in graduate school within 6 months of graduation and 61% were employed.

Admissions Contact: William Preble, Dean of Admission and Financial Assistance. A video is available. E-mail: *admission@hanover.edu* Web: *www.hanover.edu*

HUNTINGTON UNIVERSITY (Formerly Huntington College)   D-2

Huntington, IN 46750

(260) 358-4000
(800) 642-6493; Fax: (260) 358-3699

Full-time: 376 men, 454 women	**Faculty:** 59; IIB, --$
Part-time: 45 men, 74 women	**Ph.D.s:** 76%
Graduate: 46 men, 24 women	**Student/Faculty:** 14 to 1
Year: 4-1-4, summer session	**Tuition:** $18,490
Application Deadline: August 15	**Room & Board:** $6340
Freshman Class: 783 applied, 714 accepted, 268 enrolled	
SAT or ACT: required	**COMPETITIVE**

Huntington University, formerly Huntington College, founded in 1897, is a private Christian liberal arts university offering graduate and undergraduate programs in more than 70 academic concentrations. It is affiliated with the church of the United Brethren in Christ. In addition to regional accreditation, Huntington has baccalaureate program accreditation with NASM and NCATE. The library contains 171,721 volumes, 2250 microform items, and 4269 audio/video tapes/CDs/DVDs, and subscribes to 300 periodicals including electronic. Computerized library services include the card catalog, interlibrary loans, database searching, and Internet access. Special learning facilities include a learning resource center, art gallery, radio station, TV station, a writing center, and an arboretum. The 170-acre campus is in a small town 20 miles southwest of Fort Wayne. Including any residence halls, there are 25 buildings.

Student Life: 65% of undergraduates are from Indiana. Students are from 28 states, 16 foreign countries, and Canada. 85% are from public schools. 96% are white. Most are Protestant. The average age of freshmen is 18; all undergraduates, 20. 22% do not continue beyond their first year; 78% remain to graduate.

Housing: 680 students can be accommodated in college housing, which includes single-sex dorms, on-campus apartments, and married-student housing. On-campus housing is guaranteed for all 4 years. 75% of students live on campus. Alcohol is not permitted. All students may keep cars.

Activities: 77% of women belong to 1 local sorority. There are no fraternities. There are 30 groups on campus, including art, band, cheerleading, choir, chorale, chorus, computers, drama, ethnic, film, honors, international, jazz band, literary magazine, musical theater, newspaper, opera, orchestra, pep band, photography, professional, radio and TV, religious, social, social service, student government, symphony, and yearbook. Popular campus events include Chapel series, Forester Lecture Series, and Missions Emphasis Week.

Sports: There are 7 intercollegiate sports for men and 7 for women, and 5 intramural sports for men and 4 for women. Facilities include a field house with an indoor running track, 3 basketball courts, indoor and outdoor tennis courts, a swimming pool, softball and baseball diamonds, an outdoor track, soccer and intramural fields, rollerblading, and a gym.

Disabled Students: 90% of the campus is accessible. Wheelchair ramps, elevators, special parking, specially equipped rest rooms, lowered drinking fountains, and special housing are available.

Services: Counseling and information services are available, as is tutoring in some subjects, including English, math, and others. There is a reader service for the blind and remedial math and writing.

Campus Safety and Security: Measures include self-defense education, security escort services, informal discussions, and emergency telephones. There are lighted pathways/sidewalks and security on duty from 6 P.M. to 6 A.M.

Programs of Study: Huntington confers B.A., B.S., B.Mus., and B.S.Sc. degrees. Associate and master's degrees are also awarded. Bachelor's degrees are awarded in BIOLOGICAL SCIENCE (biology/biological science), BUSINESS (business administration and management, entrepreneurial studies, nonprofit/public organization management, and organizational behavior), COMMUNICATIONS AND THE ARTS (art, communications, dramatic arts, English, music business management, music performance, music theory and composition, public relations, and theater design), COMPUTER AND PHYSICAL SCIENCE (chemistry, computer science, information sciences and systems, and mathematics), EDUCATION (art, education, elementary, English, mathematics, music, physical, science, and social studies), ENGINEERING AND ENVIRONMENTAL DESIGN (environmental science), HEALTH PROFESSIONS (exercise science, medical laboratory technology, nursing, and premedicine), SOCIAL SCIENCE (biblical studies, history, ministries, parks and recreation management, philosophy, prelaw, psychology, religious music, social work, sociology, and youth ministry). Education, youth ministries, and business are the strongest academically. Business and elementary education are the largest.

Required: Students must complete a minimum of 128 credit hours including 24 in the major, and maintain a GPA of 2.0 overall and in the major. Students must pass an English competency exam, complete a program in general education, and take 36 hours in upper-division courses numbered 300 or above, 3 hours of computers, 2 hours of phys ed, and 3 January term courses in at least 2 departments. Courses in Bible are required.

Special: Companies in the area offer internships in business, social work, education, design, music, and recreation, and a work-study program is available. Students may study abroad in England, Costa Rica, Jamaica, Israel, Spain, and Africa. A Washington semester, a Hollywood semester, dual majors, correspondence courses with other schools, an accelerated degree program in organizational management, and pass/fail options are available. There are 7 national honor societies, including Phi Beta Kappa and a freshman honors program.

Faculty/Classroom: 70% of faculty are male; 30%, female. All teach undergraduates, 30% do research, and 30% do both. No introductory courses are taught by graduate students. The average class size in an introductory lecture is 30; in a laboratory, 15; and in a regular course, 25.

Admissions: 91% of the 2005-2006 applicants were accepted. The SAT scores for the 2005-2006 freshman class were: Verbal--33% below 500, 42% between 500 and 599, 18% between 600 and 700, and 7% above 700; Math--33% below 500, 41% between 500 and 599, 19% between 600 and 700, and 7% above 700. The ACT scores were 31% below 21, 29% between 21 and 23, 18% between 24 and 26, 11% between 27 and 28, and 11% above 28. 39% of the current freshmen were in the top fifth of their class; 68% were in the top two fifths. There were 2 National Merit finalists. 38 freshmen graduated first in their class.

Requirements: The SAT or ACT is required. In addition, secondary school courses should include 4 years of English, 3 of college-preparatory math, and 3 of social studies, including 1 each of American and world history. Huntington requires applicants to be in the upper 50% of their class. A GPA of 2.3 is required. AP and CLEP credits are accepted. Important factors in the admissions decision are recommendations by school officials, recommendations by alumni, and personality/intangible qualities.

Procedure: Freshmen are admitted to all sessions. Entrance exams should be taken before or during the fall semester of the senior year. There are deferred admissions and rolling admissions plans. Applications should be filed by August 15 for fall entry, along with a $20 fee. Notification is sent on a rolling basis. Applications are accepted on-line.

Transfer: 47 transfer students enrolled in 2004-2005. Transfer applicants should be in good standing at the college previously attended and have maintained a GPA of 2.0. Courses with a grade of C or better transfer. All transcripts and an essay are required. 30 of 128 credits required for the bachelor's degree must be completed at Huntington.

Visiting: There are regularly scheduled orientations for prospective students, available on 3 days notice. There are guides for informal visits and visitors may sit in on classes and stay overnight. To schedule a visit, contact Carlene Peters at (260) 359-4020.

Financial Aid: In 2005-2006, 78% of all full-time freshmen and 73% of continuing full-time students received some form of financial aid. 74% of full-time freshmen and 67% of continuing full-time students received need-based aid. Need-based scholarships or need-based grants averaged $11,883 ($22,000 maximum); need-based self-help aid (loans and jobs) averaged $4097 ($16,600 maximum); and non-need-based athletic scholarships averaged $6252 ($24,830 maximum). 63% of undergraduates work part time. Average annual earnings from campus work are $1003. The average financial indebtedness of the 2005 graduate was $18,290. The FAFSA and the college's own financial statement are required. The priority date for freshman financial aid applications for fall entry is March 1. The deadline for filing is open.

International Students: There are 31 international students enrolled. They must score satisfactory on the written TOEFL or on the electronic version.

Computers: Wireless access is available. The University provides 3 student general purpose computer labs that include a total of 68 PC. There are university provided PC in each residence hall and in commuter lounges totaling 38 computers. 12 laptop PC are available for checkout from the library and student union. Students can access the university's network and the Internet from these computing facilities and from their own computers if equipped with wireless technology. The university provides network storage and e-mail accounts to all registered students. Other departmental labs and departmental notebook computers are available to students in support of specific academic programs. All students may access the system The mainframe computer system may be used from 9 A.M. to 11 P.M. Monday through Thursday, 9 A.M. to 5 P.M. Friday, and 9 A.M. to 2 P.M. Saturday. There are no time limits and no fees. It is strongly recommended that all students have a personal computer.

Graduates: From July 1, 2004 to June 30, 2005, 182 bachelor's degrees were awarded. The most popular majors were business/marketing (21%), education (20%), and philosophy, religion, theology (13%). In an average class, 3% graduate in 3 years or less, 50% graduate in 4 years or less, 61% graduate in 5 years or less, and 69% graduate in 6 years or less. 30 companies recruited on campus in 2004-2005. Of the 2004 graduating class, 10% were enrolled in graduate school within 6 months of graduation and 74% were employed.

Admissions Contact: Jeff Berggren, Vice President for Enrollment Management & Marketing. A video is available.
E-mail: *admissions@huntington.edu* Web: *www.huntington.edu*

INDIANA INSTITUTE OF TECHNOLOGY
D-2

Fort Wayne, IN 46803-1297

(260) 422-5561, ext. 2206
(800) 937-2448; Fax: (260) 422-7696

Full-time: 736 men, 842 women	**Faculty:** 35
Part-time: 499 men, 751 women	**Ph.D.s:** 40%
Graduate: 203 men, 169 women	**Student/Faculty:** 45 to 1
Year: semesters, summer session	**Tuition:** $16,680
Application Deadline: open	**Room & Board:** $6750
Freshman Class: 2225 applied, 1145 accepted, 229 enrolled	
SAT Verbal/Math: 460/500*	**ACT:** 18 COMPETITIVE

Indiana Institute of Technology, established in 1930, is a private institution offering degrees primarily in business, engineering, and computer science. There are 3 undergraduate and 2 graduate schools. In addition to regional accreditation, Indiana Tech has baccalaureate program accreditation with ABET and IACBE. The library contains 33,000 volumes, 1000 microform items, and 150 audio/video tapes/CDs/DVDs, and subscribes to 160 periodicals including electronic. Computerized library services include the card catalog, interlibrary loans, and database searching. Special learning facilities include a learning resource center, an amphitheater, a movie theatre with auditorium-style seating, and engineering and computer networking labs. The 37-acre campus is in an urban area 150 miles east of Chicago. Including any residence halls, there are 11 buildings.

Student Life: 87% of undergraduates are from Indiana. Others are from 31 states and 3 foreign countries. 68% are white; 19% African American. The average age of freshmen is 20; all undergraduates, 34. 42% do not continue beyond their first year; 31% remain to graduate.

Housing: 272 students can be accommodated in college housing, which includes coed dorms and fraternity houses. On-campus housing is guaranteed for the freshman year only and is available on a first-come, first-served basis. Priority is given to out-of-town students. 60% of students commute. Alcohol is not permitted. All students may keep cars.

Activities: 15% of men belong to 4 national fraternities; 5% of women belong to 1 local sorority. There are 20 groups on campus, including cheerleading, chess, choir, computers, dance, ethnic, honors, international, newspaper, pep band, professional, religious, social, social service, and student government. Popular campus events include Cosmic Bowling and intramurals.

Sports: There are 3 intercollegiate sports for men and 3 for women, and 6 intramural sports for men and 6 for women. Facilities include basketball, badminton, and volleyball courts, a weight room, and an indoor field house for soccer, softball, and baseball.

Disabled Students: 90% of the campus is accessible. Wheelchair ramps, elevators, special parking, specially equipped rest rooms, lowered drinking fountains, lowered telephones, and special housing are available.

Services: Counseling and information services are available, as is tutoring in most subjects. There is remedial math, reading, and writing.

Campus Safety and Security: Measures include 24-hour foot and vehicle patrol, security escort services, lighted pathways/sidewalks, and card access and camera surveillance.

Programs of Study: Indiana Tech confers B.A., B.S. degrees. Associate and master's degrees are also awarded. Bachelor's degrees are awarded in BUSINESS (accounting, business administration and management, and sports management), COMMUNICATIONS AND THE ARTS (communications), COMPUTER AND PHYSICAL SCIENCE (computer science, information sciences and systems, and web services), ENGINEERING AND ENVIRONMENTAL DESIGN (biomedical engineering, computer engineering, electrical/electronics engineering, industrial engineering, and mechanical engineering), HEALTH PROFESSIONS (recreation therapy), SOCIAL SCIENCE (criminal justice, human services, parks and recreation management, and psychology). Engineering and computer science are the strongest academically. Business administration is the largest.

Required: To graduate, students must complete a minimum of 120 credit hours, including at least 35 in the major, with a 2.0 minimum GPA. General education requirements include at least 18 hours in social science/humanities and 9 in English.

Special: The school offers internships, work-study programs, and accelerated degree programs in business administration and accounting. Credit for life experience is offered through the College of Professional Studies. Dual majors and nondegree studies are available. There is 1 national honor society.

Faculty/Classroom: 61% of faculty are male; 37%, female. 98% teach undergraduates. No introductory courses are taught by graduate students. The average class size in an introductory lecture is 30; in a laboratory, 22; and in a regular course, 21.

Admissions: 51% of the 2005-2006 applicants were accepted. The SAT scores for the 2005-2006 freshman class were: Verbal--63% below 500, 30% between 500 and 599, 6% between 600 and 700, and 1% above 700; Math--47% below 500, 34% between 500 and 599, 18% between 600 and 700, and 1% above 700. The ACT scores were 65% below 21, 21% between 21 and 23, 3% between 24 and 26, and 8% between 27 and 28. 13% of the current freshmen were in the top fifth of their class; 34% were in the top two fifths.

Requirements: The SAT or ACT is required. In addition, applicants must be graduates of an accredited secondary school. The GED is accepted. At least 13 academic credits are required, including 4 to 6 units of social studies, 4 units of English, 3 to 6 units of math, and 2 units of a lab science. An interview is recommended. Indiana Tech requires applicants to be in the upper 50% of their class. A GPA of 2.0 is required. AP and CLEP credits are accepted. Important factors in the admissions decision are leadership record, parents or siblings attending the school, and recommendations by alumni.

Procedure: Freshmen are admitted to all sessions. Entrance exams should be taken by January of the senior year. There are early admissions, deferred admissions, and rolling admissions plans. Application deadlines are open. Application fee is $50. Applications are accepted on-line.

Transfer: 57 transfer students enrolled in 2004-2005. Applicants must be in good standing and have a minimum GPA of 2.0. The SAT is recommended. 30 of 120 credits required for the bachelor's degree must be completed at Indiana Tech.

Visiting: There are regularly scheduled orientations for prospective students, including a campus tour, classroom visits, and meetings with financial aid personnel, coaches, and current students. There are guides for informal visits and visitors may sit in on classes. To schedule a visit, contact Allison Carnahan at (800) 937-2448, ext. 2206.

Financial Aid: In 2005-2006, 93% of all full-time freshmen and 95% of continuing full-time students received some form of financial aid. 93% of full-time freshmen and 92% of continuing full-time students received need-based aid. The average freshman award was $18,523. Need-based scholarships or need-based grants averaged $6210 ($7000 maximum); need-based self-help aid (loans and jobs) averaged $4812 ($8000 maxi-

mum); non-need-based athletic scholarships averaged $4870 ($10,000 maximum); and other non-need-based awards and non-need-based scholarships averaged $2631 ($7000 maximum). 38% of undergraduates work part time. Average annual earnings from campus work are $1600. The average financial indebtedness of the 2005 graduate was $15,800. The FAFSA and the college's own financial statement are required. The deadline for filing freshman financial aid applications for fall entry is March 10.

International Students: In a recent year, there were 8 international students enrolled. The school actively recruits these students. They must score satisfactorily on the written TOEFL and also take the SAT or the ACT.

Computers: All students may access the system 7 days a week, 24 hours a day. There are no time limits and no fees. All students are required to have personal computers.

Graduates: From July 1, 2004 to June 30, 2005, 388 bachelor's degrees were awarded. The most popular majors were business (93%), engineering (4%), and computer studies (3%). In an average class, 8% graduate in 3 years or less, 24% graduate in 4 years or less, 31% graduate in 5 years or less, and 33% graduate in 6 years or less. 5 companies recruited on campus in 2004-2005. Of the 2004 graduating class, 6% were enrolled in graduate school within 6 months of graduation.

Admissions Contact: Allison Carnahan, Vice President of Enrollment Management. A video is available.
E-mail: *agcarnahan@indianatech.edu* Web: *http://www.indtech.edu*

INDIANA STATE UNIVERSITY   B-4
Terre Haute, IN 47809

(812) 237-2121
(800) 742-0891; Fax: (812) 237-8023

Full-time: 3747 men, 3881 women	Faculty: 431; I, --$
Part-time: 441 men, 601 women	Ph.Ds: 77%
Graduate: 887 men, 1122 women	Student/Faculty: 18 to 1
Year: semesters, summer session	Tuition: $5864 ($12,860)
Application Deadline: August 1	Room & Board: $5740
Freshman Class: 5351 applied, 4279 accepted, 1642 enrolled	
SAT Verbal/Math: 477/473*	ACT: 20	COMPETITIVE

Indiana State University, founded in 1865, is a publicly supported institution offering undergraduate and graduate study in liberal arts and sciences, business, health, phys ed and recreation, education, nursing, and technology. There are 6 undergraduate schools and 1 graduate school. In addition to regional accreditation, ISU has baccalaureate program accreditation with AACSB, ADA, AHEA, CAHEA, CSWE, FIDER, NASAD, NASM, NCATE, NLN,NLNAC, and NRPA . The library contains 1,354,000 volumes, 997,000 microform items, and 38,000 audio/video tapes/CDs/DVDs, and subscribes to 2800 periodicals including electronic. Computerized library services include the card catalog, interlibrary loans, database searching, and Internet access. Special learning facilities include a learning resource center, art gallery, planetarium, radio station, and an African American cultural center. The 235-acre campus is in an urban area 75 miles west of Indianapolis. Including any residence halls, there are 55 buildings.

Student Life: 89% of undergraduates are from Indiana. Others are from 49 states, 61 foreign countries, and Canada. 80% are white; 11% African American. The average age of freshmen is 19; all undergraduates, 23. 33% do not continue beyond their first year; 44% remain to graduate.

Housing: 3471 students can be accommodated in college housing, which includes single-sex and coed dorms, married-student housing, fraternity houses, and sorority houses. In addition, there are honors houses special-interest houses, and special freshman dorms. On-campus housing is guaranteed for all 4 years. 66% of students commute. Alcohol is not permitted. All students may keep cars.

Activities: 12% of men belong to 19 national fraternities; 11% of women belong to 13 national sororities. There are 180 groups on campus, including art, band, cheerleading, choir, chorale, chorus, computers, drama, drill team, ethnic, film, gay, honors, international, jazz band, marching band, musical theater, newspaper, opera, orchestra, pep band, political, professional, radio and TV, religious, social, social service, student government, and symphony. Popular campus events include a contemporary music festival, Theaterfest, and Black History Month.

Sports: There are 7 intercollegiate sports for men and 9 for women, and 29 intramural sports for men and 29 for women. Facilities include a 20,000-seat football stadium, a 10,000-seat basketball arena, 2 softball diamonds, a baseball field, a soccer field, 2 indoor and outdoor tracks, 2 pools, indoor and outdoor basketball and tennis courts, racquetball, sand volleyball, and volleyball courts, a physical fitness center with weight training facilities, a climbing wall, and 3 fitness and wellness facilities located in 2 residence halls and the student union.

Disabled Students: 98% of the campus is accessible. Wheelchair ramps, elevators, special parking, specially equipped rest rooms, special class scheduling, lowered drinking fountains, lowered telephones, special housing, and special dining hall facilities are available.

Services: Counseling and information services are available, as is tutoring in most subjects. There is a reader service for the blind. A learning skills center, an academic advisement center, a counseling center, student support services, a math lab, and a writing lab are available.

Campus Safety and Security: Measures include 24-hour foot and vehicle patrol, self-defense education, security escort services, and informal discussions. There are pamphlets/posters/films, emergency telephones, lighted pathways/sidewalks, and bicycle and car registration.

Programs of Study: ISU confers B.A., B.S., B.F.A., B.M., B.M.E., and B.S.W. degrees. Associate, master's, and doctoral degrees are also awarded. Bachelor's degrees are awarded in BIOLOGICAL SCIENCE (biology/biological science), BUSINESS (accounting, banking and finance, business administration and management, insurance, management information systems, marketing and distribution, marketing/retailing/merchandising, office supervision and management, recreation and leisure services, and sports management), COMMUNICATIONS AND THE ARTS (art history and appreciation, broadcasting, communications, dramatic arts, English, film arts, fine arts, French, German, journalism, music, Spanish, and studio art), COMPUTER AND PHYSICAL SCIENCE (chemistry, computer science, geology, mathematics, and physics), EDUCATION (art, business, early childhood, educational media, elementary, foreign languages, health, home economics, industrial arts, middle school, music, physical, science, secondary, social studies, and special), ENGINEERING AND ENVIRONMENTAL DESIGN (aeronautical technology, airline piloting and navigation, computer technology, construction technology, electrical/electronics engineering technology, industrial engineering technology, interior design, manufacturing technology, and mechanical engineering technology), HEALTH PROFESSIONS (environmental health science, medical laboratory technology, nursing, and speech pathology/audiology), SOCIAL SCIENCE (African American studies, anthropology, child care/child and family studies, criminology, dietetics, economics, food science, geography, history, home economics, interdisciplinary studies, liberal arts/general studies, parks and recreation management, philosophy, political science/government, psychology, safety management, social work, sociology, and textiles and clothing). Safety management, criminology, and business are the strongest academically. Criminology, communication, and elementary education are the largest.

Required: All students must complete the general education program, as well as a minimum of 50 hours of upper-division course work. Specific courses required include phys ed, English, speech, math, foreign language, and computer science. A minimum GPA of 2.0 (2.5 for education majors) and a total of 124 credit hours are required for graduation. The number of hours required in the major varies.

Special: The school has cross-registration with the Rose-Hulman Institute of Technology, Saint Mary-of-the-Woods College, and Ivy Tech State College. Internships are available in athletic training, criminology, environmental health, political science, safety management, and sports studies. There is a co-op program, and summer and winter work-study is available. The school offers a general studies degree, study abroad in 40 countries, credit for life experience, and nondegree study. There is a freshman honors program and all departments have honors programs.

Faculty/Classroom: 59% of faculty are male; 41%, female. 86% teach undergraduates, 45% do research, and 38% do both. Graduate students teach 8% of introductory courses.

Admissions: 80% of the 2005-2006 applicants were accepted. The SAT scores for the 2005-2006 freshman class were: Verbal--60% below 500, 32% between 500 and 599, 7% between 600 and 700, and 1% above 700; Math--62% below 500, 30% between 500 and 599, 7% between 600 and 700, and 1% above 700. The ACT scores were 61% below 21, 16% between 21 and 23, 17% between 24 and 26, 4% between 27 and 28, and 2% above 28. 21% of the current freshmen were in the top fifth of their class; 48% were in the top two fifths. 10 freshmen graduated first in their class.

Requirements: The SAT or ACT is required. In addition, the applicant must be a graduate of an accredited secondary school. The GED is accepted. An essay is not required. Applicants are reviewed based on a combination of class rank, grade point average, strength of curriculum, academic progress, and standardized test scores. Those students who rank in the top 50% of their class are routinely admitted, whereas those in the bottom 50% of their class are reviewed on an individual basis. Routine admission does not guarantee admission to specific majors. A GPA of 2.5 is required. AP and CLEP credits are accepted. Important factors in the admissions decision are advanced placement or honor courses, leadership record, and extracurricular activities record.

Procedure: Freshmen are admitted fall, spring, and summer. Entrance exams should be taken before January 1. There are deferred admissions and rolling admissions plans. Applications should be filed by August 1 for fall entry, December 1 for spring entry, and May 1 for summer entry. Notification of early decision is sent rolling ; regular decision, on a rolling basis. Applications are accepted on-line. The fall 2005 application fee was $25.

Transfer: 675 transfer students enrolled in 2004-2005. Transfer students must have a minimum GPA of 2.0. 30 of 124 credits required for the bachelor's degree must be completed at ISU.

Visiting: There are regularly scheduled orientations for prospective students, consisting of Sycamore Preview Days, which include campus tours, opportunities to meet with academic advisers in the majors students are considering, and formal sessions with representatives from financial aid and the career center. There are guides for informal visits and visitors may sit in on classes and stay overnight. To schedule a visit, contact the Admissions Office.

Financial Aid: In a recent year, 59% of all full-time freshmen and 52% of continuing full-time students received some form of financial aid. 37% of full-time freshmen and 36% of continuing full-time students received need-based aid. The average freshman award was $5793. Need-based scholarships or need-based grants averaged $4277; need-based self-help aid (loans and jobs) averaged $2901; non-need-based athletic scholarships averaged $8455; other non-need-based awards and non-need-based scholarships averaged $3326; and other awards averaged $2602. The average financial indebtedness of a recent graduate was $16,242. The FAFSA is required. The deadline for filing freshman financial aid applications for fall entry is March 1.

International Students: There are 134 international students enrolled. The school actively recruits these students. They must score satisfactorily on the written or electronic version of the TOEFL.

Computers: Wireless access is available. All students may access the system.

Graduates: From July 1, 2004 to June 30, 2005, 1459 bachelor's degrees were awarded. The most popular majors were criminology (9%), elementary education (7%), and psychology (4%). In an average class, 3% graduate in 3 years or less, 22% graduate in 4 years or less, 39% graduate in 5 years or less, and 42% graduate in 6 years or less. 203 companies recruited on campus in 2004-2005. Of the 2004 graduating class, 18% were enrolled in graduate school within 6 months of graduation and 77% were employed.

Admissions Contact: Richard Toomey, Director.
E-mail: *admissions@indstate.edu*
Web: *http://web.indstate.edu/admissions/*

INDIANA UNIVERSITY SYSTEM

Indiana University, established in 1820, is a public university governed by a board of trustees. The chief administrator is the president. The primary missions of the university are instruction, research, and service. Total enrollment of all 8 campuses generally exceeds 98,000, with over 6,900 faculty members. There are 356 baccalaureate, 232 master's, and 104 doctoral programs offered within the university. Four-year campuses are located in Bloomington, Indianapolis, Kokomo, South Bend, Gary, New Albany, and Richmond. Indiana University manages the Indianapolis campus while Purdue University manages the Fort Wayne campus. Profiles of some of these campuses are included in this section.

INDIANA UNIVERSITY BLOOMINGTON   C-4
Bloomington, IN 47405-1106   (812) 855-0661
                                                   Fax: (812) 855-5102

Full-time: 13,452 men, 14,522 women	**Faculty:** I, av$
Part-time: 787 men, 801 women	**Ph.D.s:** 86%
Graduate: 4073 men, 4323 women	**Student/Faculty:** n/av
Year: semesters, summer session	**Tuition:** $7112 ($19,508)
Application Deadline: February 1	**Room & Board:** $6244
Freshman Class: n/av	
SAT Verbal/Math: 550/560*	**ACT:** 24 **VERY COMPETITIVE**

Indiana University Bloomington, founded in 1820, is a comprehensive institution that is part of the Indiana University system. The university offers undergraduate programs in arts and sciences, allied health sciences, business, dentistry, education, health, physical education, recreation, journalism, music, nursing, optometry, public and environmental affairs, social work ,and informatics. In addition to regional accreditation, IU has baccalaureate program accreditation with AACSB, ACBSP, ACEJMC, ADA, APTA, ASLA, CAHEA, CSWE, FIDER, NASAD, NASM, NCATE, and NLN. The 22 libraries contain 6,647,355 volumes, 4,902,515 microform items, and 252,970 audio/video tapes/CDs/DVDs, and subscribe to 59,439 periodicals including electronic. Computerized library services include the card catalog, interlibrary loans, and database searching. Special learning facilities include a learning resource center, art gallery, natural history museum, radio station, TV station, observatory, arboretum, museum of world cultures, garden and nature center, musical arts center, and more than 70 research centers. The 1931-acre campus is in a small town 50 miles southwest of Indianapolis. Including any residence halls, there are 490 buildings.

Student Life: 67% of undergraduates are from Indiana. Others are from 50 states, 150 foreign countries, and Canada. 84% are white. The average age of freshmen is 19; all undergraduates, 21. 13% do not continue beyond their first year.

Housing: 12,167 students can be accommodated in college housing, which includes single-sex and coed dorms, off-campus apartments, and married-student housing. In addition, there are honors houses, language houses, special-interest houses, living-learning , international, women's, wellness centers, freshmen interest group, and thematic communities. On-campus housing is guaranteed for all 4 years. 58% of students commute. Alcohol is not permitted. All students may keep cars.

Activities: 16% of men belong to fraternities; 18% of women belong to sororities. There are 400 groups on campus, including art, band, cheerleading, chess, choir, chorale, chorus, computers, dance, debate, drama, drill team, ethnic, film, gay, honors, international, jazz band, literary magazine, marching band, musical theater, newspaper, opera, orchestra, pep band, photography, political, professional, radio and TV, religious, social, social service, student government, and symphony. Popular campus events include Little 500 and Founder's Day.

Sports: There are 10 intercollegiate sports for men and 12 for women, and 27 intramural sports for men and 27 for women. Facilities include a 52,000-seat football stadium, an 18,000-seat soccer/bicycle stadium, an 18,000-seat indoor gym, a 2,300-seat auditorium, an assembly hall, indoor/outdoor swimming pools, a tennis pavilion, an indoor practice facility, a golf driving range, and a student recreation and aquatics center.

Disabled Students: 95% of the campus is accessible. Wheelchair ramps, elevators, special parking, specially equipped rest rooms, special class scheduling, lowered drinking fountains, lowered telephones, and scheduled transportation are available.

Services: Counseling and information services are available, as is tutoring in most subjects. There is a reader service for the blind, and remedial math, reading, and writing. Skills workshops are also offered.

Campus Safety and Security: Measures include 24-hour foot and vehicle patrol, self-defense education, security escort services, and shuttle buses. There are informal discussions, pamphlets/posters/films, emergency telephones, lighted pathways/sidewalks, and safety awareness education.

Programs of Study: IU confers B.A., B.S., B.F.A., B.G.S., B.M., B.S.E., B.S.N., B.S.P.A., B.S.P.H., and B.S.W. degrees. Associate, master's, and doctoral degrees are also awarded. Bachelor's degrees are awarded in AGRICULTURE (environmental studies), BIOLOGICAL SCIENCE (biochemistry, biology/biological science, ecology, microbiology, and nutrition), BUSINESS (accounting, apparel and accessories marketing, banking and finance, business administration and management, business economics, entrepreneurial studies, international business management, labor studies, management information systems, management science, marketing/retailing/merchandising, operations research, real estate, recreation and leisure services, sports management, and tourism), COMMUNICATIONS AND THE ARTS (art history and appreciation, audio technology, ballet, ceramic art and design, classics, communications, comparative literature, creative writing, dramatic arts, Dutch, East Asian languages and literature, English, fine arts, folklore and mythology, French, German, graphic design, Greek, guitar, Italian, jazz, journalism, Latin, linguistics, media arts, metal/jewelry, music, music performance, music theory and composition, opera, painting, photography, piano/organ, Portuguese, printmaking, Spanish, speech/debate/rhetoric, studio art, telecommunications, visual and performing arts, and voice), COMPUTER AND PHYSICAL SCIENCE (astronomy, astrophysics, atmospheric sciences and meteorology, chemistry, computer science, digital arts/technology, geology, hydrology, information sciences and systems, mathematics, physics, and statistics), EDUCATION (athletic training, early childhood, educational media, elementary, health, music, physical, science, social studies, and special), ENGINEERING AND ENVIRONMENTAL DESIGN (aerospace studies, environmental science, geological engineering, interior design, and occupational safety and health), HEALTH PROFESSIONS (exercise science, health care administration, nursing, public health, and speech pathology/audiology), SOCIAL SCIENCE (African American studies, anthropology, classical/ancient civilization, cognitive science, criminal justice, dietetics, East Asian studies, economics, ethics, politics, and social policy, family/consumer studies, gender studies, geography, history, human development, international studies, Judaic studies, law, liberal arts/general studies, Near Eastern studies, parks and recreation management, philosophy, physical fitness/movement, political science/government, psychology, public administration, public affairs, religion, Russian and Slavic studies, social work, sociology, textiles and clothing, and urban studies).

Required: The general requirements for graduation include courses in English and writing, math, foreign language, arts and humanities, social and behavioral sciences, natural sciences, and culture studies. Students must complete 122 credit hours, with approximately 36 hours in the major. Many degrees have intensive writing requirements, and the minimum GPA requirement varies by department. Liberal arts requirements are common throughout all degree programs.

Special: IU offers cooperative programs with universities in many countries, including the People's Republic of China, a variety of internships, and study abroad in more than 25 countries. A Washington semester, work-study programs, B.A.-B.S. degrees in the sciences and liberal arts, dual majors, and the general studies degree through the School of Continuing Studies are available. Student-designed majors through the Individualized Major Program, credit for military experience, nondegree study through the School of Continuing Studies, and pass/fail options

are also available. There are 18 national honor societies, and a freshman honors program.

Faculty/Classroom: 65% of faculty are male; 35%, female.

Admissions: The SAT scores for the 2005-2006 freshman class were: Verbal--27% below 500, 44% between 500 and 599, 25% between 600 and 700, and 4% above 700; Math--23% below 500, 43% between 500 and 599, 29% between 600 and 700, and 5% above 700. The ACT scores were 18% below 21, 24% between 21 and 23, 29% between 24 and 26, 14% between 27 and 28, and 15% above 28. 47% of the current freshmen were in the top fifth of their class; 83% were in the top two fifths. There were 26 National Merit finalists. 121 freshmen graduated first in their class.

Requirements: The SAT or ACT is required. In addition, applicants must be graduates of an accredited secondary high school or have a GED certificate. SAT Subject tests are recommended for credit and placement. Auditions for music majors are required. An interview is recommended for information purposes. AP and CLEP credits are accepted. Important factors in the admissions decision are advanced placement or honor courses, parents or siblings attending the school, and recommendations by school officials.

Procedure: Freshmen are admitted to all sessions. Entrance exams should be taken in the late junior year or early senior year. There is a deferred admissions plan. Applications should be filed by February 1 for fall entry, November 1 for spring entry, and February 1 for summer entry. The fall 2005 application fee was $50. Notification is sent on a rolling basis. Applications are accepted on-line.

Transfer: 838 transfer students enrolled in 2004-2005. Admission for transfers is selective. Most successful applicants have a 2.5 or higher GPA and no grades below C in recent work. Applicants with less than 1 year of transfer work (fewer than 26 credit hours) must also meet freshman admission standards. 30 of 122 credits required for the bachelor's degree must be completed at IU.

Visiting: There are regularly scheduled orientations for prospective students, including admissions counseling and answers to students' questions about the school. There are guides for informal visits and visitors may sit in on classes and stay overnight. To schedule a visit, contact the scheduling director at (812) 855-3512.

Financial Aid: In 2005-2006, 42% of all full-time freshmen and 37% of continuing full-time students received some form of financial aid. 27% of full-time freshmen and 21% of continuing full-time students received need-based aid. The average freshman award was $10,512. Need-based scholarships or need-based grants averaged $4964; need-based self-help aid (loans and jobs) averaged $1788; non-need-based athletic scholarships averaged $15,450; and other non-need-based awards and non-need-based scholarships averaged $3721. The average financial indebtedness of the 2005 graduate was $18,423. The FAFSA is required. The deadline for filing freshman financial aid applications for fall entry is March 1.

International Students: There are were 1143 international students enrolled in a recent year. The school actively recruits these students.

Computers: Wireless access is available. All students may access the system 24 hours a day. There are no time limits. There is a $372 technology fee. It is strongly recommended that all students have a personal computer.

Graduates: From July 1, 2004 to June 30, 2005, 6069 bachelor's degrees were awarded. The most popular majors were business/marketing (20%), education (16%), and communications/journalism (10%).

Admissions Contact: Mary Ellen Anderson, Director of Admissions. E-mail: *iuadmit@indiana.edu* Web: *http://www.indiana.edu/~iuadmit*

INDIANA UNIVERSITY EAST   D-3
Richmond, IN 47374-1289

(765) 973-8208
(800) 959-4485; Fax: (765) 973-8288

Full-time: 406 men, 886 women	Faculty: 87; IIB, -$
Part-time: 369 men, 731 women	Ph.D.s: n/av
Graduate: 12 men, 55 women	Student/Faculty: 15 to 1
Year: semesters, summer session	Tuition: $4806 ($11,484)
Application Deadline: open	Room & Board: n/app
Freshman Class: n/av	
SAT Verbal/Math: 470/450*	ACT: 19 LESS COMPETITIVE

Indiana University East, established in 1971, is a public institution serving a commuter student body. The university offers undergraduate degree programs in humanities, natural science and math, behavioral and social sciences, education, business and technology, nursing, public and environmental affairs, social work, and continuing studies. In addition to regional accreditation, IU East has baccalaureate program accreditation with NCATE and NLN. The library contains 69,204 volumes, 53,013 microform items, and 2219 audio/video tapes/CDs/DVDs, and subscribes to 76 periodicals including electronic. Computerized library services include the card catalog, interlibrary loans, and database searching. Special learning facilities include an art gallery. The 194-acre campus is in a small town 40 miles west of Dayton, Ohio, and 70 miles east of Indianapolis. There are 10 buildings.

Student Life: 87% of undergraduates are from Indiana. Others are from 10 states, 8 foreign countries, and Canada. 92% are white. The average age of freshmen is 22; all undergraduates, 26. 46% do not continue beyond their first year.

Housing: There are no residence halls. All students commute. Alcohol is not permitted.

Activities: There is 1 national fraternity and 1 national sorority. There are 20 groups on campus, including art, cheerleading, drama, ethnic, newspaper, photography, political, professional, radio and TV, religious, social, social service, and student government. Popular campus events include fall and spring festivals and a Wednesday lunch program.

Sports: There are 4 intramural sports for men and 4 for women. Facilities include a softball field, tennis and sand volleyball courts, and a field house.

Disabled Students: 98% of the campus is accessible. Wheelchair ramps, elevators, special parking, lowered drinking fountains, lowered telephones, special testing accommodations, and note taking are available.

Services: Counseling and information services are available, as is tutoring in some subjects, including several freshman-level courses. There is a reader service for the blind, and remedial math, reading, and writing.

Campus Safety and Security: Measures include security escort services, informal discussions, pamphlets/posters/films, and emergency telephones. There are lighted pathways/sidewalks and a 14-hour foot and vehicle patrol.

Programs of Study: IU East confers B.A., B.S., B.G.S., and B.S.W. degrees. Associate degrees are also awarded. Bachelor's degrees are awarded in BIOLOGICAL SCIENCE (biology/biological science), BUSINESS (business administration and management), COMMUNICATIONS AND THE ARTS (communications, English, and fine arts), COMPUTER AND PHYSICAL SCIENCE (information sciences and systems, mathematics, and natural sciences), EDUCATION (elementary and secondary), HEALTH PROFESSIONS (nursing), SOCIAL SCIENCE (behavioral science, criminal justice, humanities, liberal arts/general studies, and social work). Nursing, business, and education are the largest.

Required: To graduate, students must satisfactorily complete courses in English composition, humanities, biological or physical science, and social science, as well as demonstrate computer literacy, and complete a minimum of 120 semester hours with a GPA of at least 2.0.

Special: IU East offers a cooperative program in criminal justice with Indiana University-Purdue University and an organizational leadership program through Purdue's Statewide Technology program. IU East also offers cross-registration with Earlham College, dual majors, independent study, an internship in social work, pass/fail options, study abroad through Indiana University Bloomington, and credit for life experience. Nondegree study is possible. There is 1 national honor society.

Faculty/Classroom: 40% of faculty are male; 60%, female.

Admissions: The SAT scores for the 2005-2006 freshman class were: Verbal--67% below 500, 26% between 500 and 599, and 7% between 600 and 700; Math--68% below 500, 26% between 500 and 599, 5% between 600 and 700, and 1% above 700. The ACT scores were 78% below 21, 13% between 21 and 23, 4% between 24 and 26, and 4% between 27 and 28. 18% of the current freshmen were in the top fifth of their class; 43% were in the top two fifths.

Requirements: The SAT or ACT is recommended. In addition, a minimum GPA of 2.0 is required for applicants who have graduated from high school in the preceding 3 years. Applicants must be graduates of accredited secondary schools or have earned a GED. They must have completed 15 academic credits, including 4 in English, 2 each in math, social studies, and foreign language, and 1 in science, as well as an additional 4 units of academic study. 4 credits in a foreign language are strongly recommended. AP and CLEP credits are accepted.

Procedure: Freshmen are admitted to all sessions. Entrance exams should be taken during the junior or senior year. There are early admissions and deferred admissions, and rolling admissions plans. Application deadlines are open. The fall 2005 application fee was $25.

Transfer: 177 transfer students enrolled in 2004-2005. Applicants must have a GPA of 2.0 (2.5 for out-of-state transfer applicants) and submit college transcripts. Grades of C or better transfer for credit. 30 of 120 credits required for the bachelor's degree must be completed at IU East.

Visiting: There are regularly scheduled orientations for prospective students, including tours, counseling, registration, and financial aid sessions. There are guides for informal visits and visitors may sit in on classes. To schedule a visit, contact the Admissions Office.

Financial Aid: In a recent year, 61% of all full-time freshmen and 67% of continuing full-time students received some form of financial aid. 46% of full-time freshmen and 53% of continuing full-time students received need-based aid. The average freshman award was $4156. Need-based scholarships or need-based grants averaged $4408; need-based self-help aid (loans and jobs) averaged $2635; and other non-need-based awards and non-need-based scholarships averaged $1185. The average financial indebtedness of the 2005 graduate was $17,547. The FAFSA and the college's own financial statement are required. The deadline for filing freshman financial aid applications for fall entry is March 1.

International Students: There are 2 international students enrolled. A satisfactory score is required on the TOEFL. Applicants must also take the SAT or the ACT.

Computers: All students may access the system during the operating hours of the university. There are no time limits. The fee is $234.

Graduates: From July 1, 2004 to June 30, 2005, 158 bachelor's degrees were awarded. The most popular majors were education (21%), health professions (18%), and philosophy and religious studies (15%).

Admissions Contact: James Bland, Acting Director of Student Recruitment. E-mail: *admit@indiana.edu*
Web: *http://www.iue.indiana.edu/admissions/*

INDIANA UNIVERSITY KOKOMO   C-2

Kokomo, IN 46904-9003

(765) 455-9216
(888) 875-4485; Fax: (765) 455-9537

Full-time: 428 men, 995 women	**Faculty:** IIB, -$
Part-time: 375 men, 939 women	**Ph.D.s:** n/av
Graduate: 74 men, 84 women	**Student/Faculty:** n/av
Year: semesters, summer session	**Tuition:** $4835 ($11,513)
Application Deadline: August 3	**Room & Board:** n/app
Freshman Class: n/av	
SAT Verbal/Math: 490/490*	**ACT:** 19 LESS COMPETITIVE

Indiana University Kokomo, founded in 1945 and part of the Indiana University System, offers a wide range of programs that emphasize liberal arts, business, education, and nursing. In addition to regional accreditation, IUK has baccalaureate program accreditation with ABET, NCATE, and NLN. The library contains 133,433 volumes, 466,693 microform items, and 1445 audio/video tapes/CDs/DVDs, and subscribes to 1448 periodicals including electronic. Computerized library services include interlibrary loans, database searching, and Internet access. Special learning facilities include a learning resource center, art gallery, and and an observatory. The 51-acre campus is in a small town 45 miles north of Indianapolis. There are 17 buildings.

Student Life: 99% of undergraduates are from Indiana. Others are from 14 states, 9 foreign countries, and Canada. 91% are white. The average age of freshmen is 21; all undergraduates, 26. 44% do not continue beyond their first year.

Housing: There are no residence halls. 100% of students commute. Alcohol is not permitted.

Activities: There are no fraternities or sororities. There are 20 groups on campus, including chorale, computers, drama, ethnic, honors, political, religious, social service, and student government. Popular campus events include International Festival.

Sports: There is no sports program at IUK.

Disabled Students: All of the campus is accessible. Wheelchair ramps, elevators, special parking, specially equipped rest rooms, special class scheduling, lowered drinking fountains, and lowered telephones are available.

Services: There is remedial math, reading, and writing. Students who do not meet regular admissions standards can be admitted under the Guided Study Program, which includes courses in basic skills as needed, counseling and tutoring, and a seminar on studying.

Campus Safety and Security: Measures include security escort services, emergency telephones, lighted pathways/sidewalks, and Campus police are on duty from 7 A.M. to 10 P.M.

Programs of Study: IUK confers B.A., B.S., B.G.S., B.S.Bus., B.S.Ed., and B.S.N. degrees. Associate and master's degrees are also awarded. Bachelor's degrees are awarded in BIOLOGICAL SCIENCE (biology/biological science), BUSINESS (accounting, business administration and management, business economics, electronic business, labor studies, and marketing management), COMMUNICATIONS AND THE ARTS (communications, and English), COMPUTER AND PHYSICAL SCIENCE (chemistry, information sciences and systems, mathematics, and physical sciences), EDUCATION (elementary), HEALTH PROFESSIONS (cytotechnology, health care administration, medical laboratory technology, nuclear medical technology, nursing, occupational therapy, radiation therapy, radiograph medical technology, radiological science, and respiratory therapy), SOCIAL SCIENCE (behavioral science, criminal justice, gerontology, humanities, liberal arts/general studies, psychology, public affairs, social science, and sociology). Education, business, and nursing are the largest.

Required: All students must maintain a minimum GPA of 2.0 while taking 120 credit hours. All students must complete course work in English, computer, and math.

Special: Student-designed majors, a general studies degree, internships, study abroad, joint programs with other Indiana University campuses and with Purdue University, pass/fail options, nondegree study, and credit for military experience and by exam are available. There is 1 national honor society, a freshman honors program.

Faculty/Classroom: 42% of faculty are male; 58%, female. All teach undergraduates. No introductory courses are taught by graduate students.

Admissions: The SAT scores for the 2005-2006 freshman class were: Verbal--56% below 500, 34% between 500 and 599, 9% between 600 and 700, and 1% above 700; Math--52% below 500, 40% between 500 and 599, and 7% between 600 and 700. The ACT scores were 69% below 21, 19% between 21 and 23, 10% between 24 and 26, and 2% between 27 and 28. 15% of the current freshmen were in the top fifth of their class; 39% were in the top two fifths.

Requirements: The SAT or ACT is required. In addition, admissions requirements include 14 academic credits, including 4 units of English, 3 units of math, 2 units of social sciences, and 1 unit of science. In addition, 2 units each of a foreign language and history are recommended. The GED is accepted. In-state students should be in the top half of the graduating class; out-of-state students should be in the top one third. AP and CLEP credits are accepted. Important factors in the admissions decision are recommendations by school officials and advanced placement or honor courses.

Procedure: Freshmen are admitted to all sessions. Entrance exams should be taken prior to registration. There is a deferred admissions plan. Applications should be filed by August 3 for fall entry, December 1 for spring entry, and April 15 for summer entry. Notification is sent on a rolling basis.

Transfer: 211 transfer students enrolled in 2004-2005. Transfer applicants must have at least 7 credits with a minimum GPA of 2.0 and clear records of conduct from previously attended colleges. Transcripts are required. Transfers are considered on a case-by-case basis. Contact the Admissions Office for more information. 30 of 120 credits required for the bachelor's degree must be completed at IUK.

Visiting: There are regularly scheduled orientations for prospective students. There are guides for informal visits and visitors may sit in on classes. To schedule a visit, contact the Admissions Office.

Financial Aid: In 2005-2006, 40% of all full-time freshmen and 41% of continuing full-time students received some form of financial aid. 29% of full-time freshmen and 30% of continuing full-time students received need-based aid. The average freshman award was $5619. Need-based scholarships or need-based grants averaged $4476; need-based self-help aid (loans and jobs) averaged $2319; and other non-need-based awards and non-need-based scholarships averaged $1783. The average financial indebtedness of the 2005 graduate was $11,681. The FAFSA, the college's own financial statement and the are required. The deadline for filing freshman financial aid applications for fall entry is March 1.

International Students: There are 4 international students enrolled. They must score satisfactorily on the written TOEFL and also take the SAT or the ACT.

Computers: may access the system. There are no time limits. The fee is $280 technology fee.

Graduates: From July 1, 2004 to June 30, 2005, 558 bachelor's degrees were awarded. The most popular majors were education (19%), liberal arts/general studies (18%), and health professions (18%).

Admissions Contact: Jackie Kennedy-Fletcher, Director of Admissions. E-mail: *iuadmis@iuk.edu*
Web: *http://www.iuk.edu/student-services/admissions*

INDIANA UNIVERSITY NORTHWEST   B-1
Gary, IN 46408-1197

(219) 980-6991
(888) 968-7486; Fax: (219) 981-4219

Full-time: 790 men, 1679 women	**Faculty:** IIA, -$
Part-time: 515 men, 1403 women	**Ph.D.s:** n/av
Graduate: 167 men, 433 women	**Student/Faculty:** n/av
Year: semesters, summer session	**Tuition:** $4902 ($11,580)
Application Deadline: August 1	**Room & Board:** n/app
Freshman Class: n/av	
SAT Verbal/Math: 450/450*	**ACT:** 18 **LESS COMPETITIVE**

Indiana University Northwest, established in 1948, is one of 8 campuses of the Indiana University system. A public commuter school, it offers liberal arts and professional programs. In addition to regional accreditation, IUN has baccalaureate program accreditation with AACSB, ADA, NCATE, and NLN. The library contains 252,137 volumes, 340,849 microform items, and 331 audio/video tapes/CDs/DVDs, and subscribes to 1527 periodicals including electronic. Computerized library services include interlibrary loans. Special learning facilities include a learning resource center and art gallery. The 38-acre campus is in an urban area 30 miles southeast of Chicago. There are 22 buildings.

Student Life: 99% of undergraduates are from Indiana. Others are from 14 states, 34 foreign countries, and Canada. 62% are white; 22% African American; 12% Hispanic. The average age of freshmen is 22; all undergraduates, 25. 42% do not continue beyond their first year.

Housing: There are no residence halls. All students commute. Alcohol is not permitted. All students may keep cars.

Activities: There are 3 national fraternities and 3 national sororities. There are 70 groups on campus, including chess, chorale, drama, ethnic, honors, literary magazine, musical theater, newspaper, political, professional, social, student government, and yearbook. Popular campus events include Student/Faculty Dinner Dance and Health Fair.

Sports: There are 3 intercollegiate sports for men and 3 for women, and 8 intramural sports for men and 5 for women.

Disabled Students: 90% of the campus is accessible. Wheelchair ramps, elevators, special parking, specially equipped rest rooms, special class scheduling, lowered drinking fountains, and lowered telephones are available.

Services: Counseling and information services are available, as is tutoring in some subjects, including biology, anatomy and physiology, Spanish I, chemistry, sociology, and math. There is a reader service for the blind, and remedial math, reading, and writing.

Campus Safety and Security: Measures include 24-hour foot and vehicle patrol, security escort services, emergency telephones, and lighted pathways/sidewalks.

Programs of Study: IUN confers B.A., B.S., and B.G.S. degrees. Associate and master's degrees are also awarded. Bachelor's degrees are awarded in BIOLOGICAL SCIENCE (biology/biological science), BUSINESS (accounting, business administration and management, and labor studies), COMMUNICATIONS AND THE ARTS (communications, dramatic arts, English, fine arts, French, and Spanish), COMPUTER AND PHYSICAL SCIENCE (actuarial science, chemistry, geology, information sciences and systems, and mathematics), EDUCATION (elementary and secondary), ENGINEERING AND ENVIRONMENTAL DESIGN (engineering technology), HEALTH PROFESSIONS (health care administration, nursing, and radiological science), SOCIAL SCIENCE (African American studies, criminal justice, economics, history, liberal arts/general studies, philosophy, political science/government, psychology, public administration, and sociology). Business and nursing are the strongest academically.

Required: Each division sets its own degree requirements. All students must maintain a minimum GPA of 2.0 and complete at least 120 credit hours to graduate. Students must take courses in computer literacy, English, foreign language, humanities, math, science, and social science.

Special: IUN offers cross-registration with Purdue University, work-study, dual majors, independent study, internships, study abroad in 25 countries, credit for life, military, and work experience, nondegree study, accelerated degree programs, student-designed majors, and pass/fail options. There are 2 national honor societies.

Faculty/Classroom: 47% of faculty are male; 53%, female.

Admissions: The SAT scores for the 2005-2006 freshman class were: Verbal--70% below 500, 25% between 500 and 599, and 5% between 600 and 700; Math--68% below 500, 26% between 500 and 599, and 6% between 600 and 700. The ACT scores were 65% below 21, 23% between 21 and 23, 8% between 24 and 26, and 4% between 27 and 28. 16% of the current freshmen were in the top fifth of their class; 38% were in the top two fifths.

Requirements: The SAT or ACT is required for all incoming freshmen and for all students who graduated in the last 3 years. A satisfactory score is required on the SAT. Applicants must be graduates of an accredited secondary school, with 16 academic units, including 4 each in English and academic electives, 3 in math, 2 each in social studies and foreign language (recommended) and 1 in science. The GED is accepted. The university recommends an interview. AP and CLEP credits are accepted. Important factors in the admissions decision are advanced placement or honor courses, leadership record, and recommendations by school officials.

Procedure: Freshmen are admitted fall, spring, and summer. Entrance exams should be taken as early as possible. There are deferred admissions and rolling admissions plans. Applications should be filed by August 1 for fall entry, December 1 for spring entry, and May 1 for summer entry. The fall 2005 application fee was $35. Notification is sent on a rolling basis.

Transfer: 350 transfer students enrolled in 2004-2005. Residents of Indiana must have a 2.0 GPA. Out-of-state transfers must have a C+ average or higher. The SAT or ACT is recommended. Grades of C or better transfer for credit. High school and college transcripts are required. 30 of 120 credits required for the bachelor's degree must be completed at IUN.

Visiting: There are regularly scheduled orientations for prospective students. There are guides for informal visits and visitors may sit in on classes. To schedule a visit, contact the Admissions Office.

Financial Aid: In a recent year, 35% of all full-time freshmen and 43% of continuing full-time students received some form of financial aid. 25% of full-time freshmen and 31% of continuing full-time students received need-based aid. The average freshman award was $6515. Need-based scholarships or need-based grants averaged $4569; need-based self-help aid (loans and jobs) averaged $2842; and other non-need-based awards and non-need-based scholarships averaged $2155. The average financial indebtedness of the 2005 graduate was $14,444. The FAFSA and the college's own financial statement are required. The priority date for freshman financial aid applications for fall entry is March 1.

International Students: There are 6 international students enrolled. A satisfactory score is required on the SAT or the ACT.

Computers: All students may access the system any time. There are no time limits. The fee is $320.

Graduates: From July 1, 2004 to June 30, 2005, 367 bachelor's degrees were awarded. The most popular majors were business/marketing (16%), education (15%), and health professions (15%).
Admissions Contact: Linda Templeton, Director of Admissions.
E-mail: *admit@iun.edu* Web: *www.iun.edu/~admit*

INDIANA UNIVERSITY SOUTH BEND   C-1
South Bend, IN 46634-7111

(574) 237-4839
(877) GO-2-IUSB; Fax: (574) 237-4834

Full-time: 1382 men, 2254 women	**Faculty:** IIA, --$
Part-time: 1021 men, 1667 women	**Ph.D.s:** n/av
Graduate: 383 men, 752 women	**Student/Faculty:** n/av
Year: semesters, summer session	**Tuition:** $4989 ($12,408)
Application Deadline: open	**Room & Board:** n/app
Freshman Class: n/av	
SAT Verbal/Math: 480/480*	**ACT:** 20 **LESS COMPETITIVE**

Indiana University South Bend, a commuter institution of the state-supported university system, was founded in 1941 and offers undergraduate programs in arts and sciences, business and economics, dental health, education, music, nursing, and public and environmental affairs. In addition to regional accreditation, IUSB has baccalaureate program accreditation with ADA, NCATE, and NLN. The library contains 303,203 volumes, 451,621 microform items, and 7524 audio/video tapes/CDs/DVDs, and subscribes to 1713 periodicals including electronic. Computerized library services include the card catalog, interlibrary loans, and database searching. Special learning facilities include a learning resource center, art gallery, science labs, studios for fine and performing arts, instructional media services, and academic resource center. The 80-acre campus is in a suburban area 90 miles east of Chicago. There are 57 buildings.
Student Life: 96% of undergraduates are from Indiana. Others are from 31 states, 71 foreign countries, and Canada. 84% are white. The average age of freshmen is 20; all undergraduates, 25. 35% do not continue beyond their first year.
Housing: There are no residence halls. There are on-campus and off-campus apartments. In addition, there is special housing for international students. All students commute. Alcohol is not permitted. No one may keep cars.
Activities: There are no fraternities. There are 52 groups on campus, including art, cheerleading, chorus, drama, ethnic, film, gay, honors, international, jazz band, literary magazine, musical theater, newspaper, opera, orchestra, pep band, political, professional, religious, social, social service, student government, and symphony. Popular campus events include Job Fair, club days, and new student welcome day.
Sports: There is 1 intercollegiate sport for men and 1 for women, and 7 intramural sports for men and 7 for women. Facilities include a running club for men and women.
Disabled Students: 95% of the campus is accessible. Wheelchair ramps, elevators, special parking, specially equipped rest rooms, special class scheduling, lowered drinking fountains, and lowered telephones are available.
Services: Counseling and information services are available, as is tutoring in every subject. There is remedial math, reading, and writing. Taped texts, note takers, and interpreters or transcription services are available.
Campus Safety and Security: Measures include 24-hour foot and vehicle patrol, security escort services, informal discussions, and pamphlets/posters/films. There are emergency telephones and lighted pathways/sidewalks.
Programs of Study: IUSB confers B.S., B.A., B.M., B.M.E., and B.S.Ed. degrees. Associate and master's degrees are also awarded. Bachelor's degrees are awarded in AGRICULTURE (environmental studies), BIOLOGICAL SCIENCE (biology/biological science), BUSINESS (accounting, banking and finance, business administration and management, human resources, labor studies, marketing/retailing/merchandising, and organizational behavior), COMMUNICATIONS AND THE ARTS (advertising, communications, dramatic arts, English, fine arts, French, German, journalism, music, music theory and composition, performing arts, piano/organ, public relations, Spanish, speech/debate/rhetoric, and voice), COMPUTER AND PHYSICAL SCIENCE (actuarial science, applied mathematics, chemistry, computer science, digital arts/technology, information sciences and systems, mathematics, and physics), EDUCATION (early childhood, elementary, English, mathematics, music, science, secondary, social studies, and special), ENGINEERING AND ENVIRONMENTAL DESIGN (industrial administration/management and preengineering), HEALTH PROFESSIONS (allied health, health care administration, nursing, predentistry, premedicine, preoptometry, prepharmacy, and preveterinary science), SOCIAL SCIENCE (applied psychology, counseling/psychology, criminal justice, economics, history, human services, liberal arts/general studies, philosophy, political science/government, prelaw, psychology, public administration, public affairs, social work, sociology, and women's studies). Accounting, management, and marketing are the strongest academically. Business, education, and liberal arts and sciences are the largest.

Required: All students must complete divisional requirements and general education and concentration courses, including English composition, fine arts, computer literacy, humanities, math, physical or biological science, and social science. A total of 120 to 123 semester hours, with a minimum GPA of 2.0, is required to graduate.
Special: Cross-registration with the Northern Indiana Consortium for Education (NICE), internships, study abroad, accelerated degree programs, and dual majors are possible. There is a freshman honors program.
Faculty/Classroom: 51% of faculty are male; 49%, female. No introductory courses are taught by graduate students.
Admissions: The SAT scores for the 2005-2006 freshman class were: Verbal--57% below 500, 34% between 500 and 599, 8% between 600 and 700, and 1% above 700; Math--57% below 500, 34% between 500 and 599, and 8% between 600 and 700. The ACT scores were 60% below 21, 20% between 21 and 23, 17% between 24 and 26, and 3% between 27 and 28. 17% of the current freshmen were in the top fifth of their class; 46% were in the top two fifths.
Requirements: The SAT or ACT is required. In addition, applicants should have completed 13 units including 4 units in English, 3 in math, 2 in social sciences, and 1 in science, or have the GED equivalent with a minimum composite of 52. An interview is recommended. CLEP credit is accepted. Important factors in the admissions decision are advanced placement or honor courses, extracurricular activities record, and leadership record.
Procedure: Freshmen are admitted to all sessions. Entrance exams should be taken 1 year to 6 months before entering the university. There is a deferred admissions plan. Applications should be filed by July 1st for fall entry. The fall 2005 application fee was $40. Notification is sent on a rolling basis.
Transfer: 529 transfer students enrolled in 2004-2005. A 2.0 GPA is required. College transcripts must be submitted. 30 of 120 to 123 credits required for the bachelor's degree must be completed at IUSB.
Visiting: There are regularly scheduled orientations for prospective students, including a visit to the admissions office, a campus tour, professor meetings, and information on financial aid. There are guides for informal visits and visitors may sit in on classes. To schedule a visit, contact the Admissions Office at (219) 237-4839.
Financial Aid: In a recent year, 45% of full-time freshmen and 34% of continuing full-time students received some form of financial aid. 31% of full-time freshmen and 34% of full-time continuing students received need-based aid. The average freshman award was $4895. Need-based scholarships or need-based grants averaged $3448; need-based self-help aid (loans and jobs) averaged $2539; non-need-based athletic scholarships averaged $4300; and other non-need-based awards and non-need-based scholarships averaged $1298. The average financial indebtedness of a recent graduate was $16,334. The FAFSA and the college's own financial statement are required. The deadline for filing freshman financial aid applications for fall entry is March 1.
International Students: There are 82 international students enrolled. The school actively recruits these students. They must score satisfactorily on the written TOEFL.
Computers: All students may access the system 7 days a week. There are no time limits. The fee is $300.
Graduates: From July 1, 2004 to June 30, 2005, 580 bachelor's degrees were awarded. The most popular majors were education (22%), business/marketing (16%), and liberal arts/general studies (13%).
Admissions Contact: Jeff Johnston, Director of Admissions.
E-mail: *admissio@iusb.edu* Web: *www.iusb.edu/~admissio/*

INDIANA UNIVERSITY SOUTHEAST   C-5
New Albany, IN 47150

(812) 941-2212
(800) 852-8835; Fax: (812) 941-2595

Full-time: 1179 men, 2041 women	**Faculty:** 189; IIA, -$
Part-time: 755 men, 1325 women	**Ph.D.s:** n/av
Graduate: 307 men, 557 women	**Student/Faculty:** 17 to 1
Year: semesters, summer session	**Tuition:** $4880 ($11,558)
Application Deadline: July 15	**Room & Board:** n/app
Freshman Class: n/av	
SAT Verbal/Math: 480/470*	**ACT:** 20 **LESS COMPETITIVE**

Indiana University Southeast, established in 1941, is a state-supported institution, part of the Indiana University system, and offers undergraduate and graduate programs in humanities, social sciences, natural sciences, business and economics, education, general studies, and nursing. In addition to regional accreditation, IUS has baccalaureate program accreditation with AACSB, NCATE, and NLN. The library contains 223,181 volumes, 356,077 microform items, and 9497 audio/video tapes/CDs/DVDs, and subscribes to 951 periodicals including electronic. Computerized library services include the card catalog, interlibrary loans, and database searching. Special learning facilities include an art gallery. The 177-acre campus is in a suburban area 7 miles northwest of Louisville, Kentucky, and 114 miles south of Indianapolis. There are 20 buildings.

Student Life: 77% of undergraduates are from Indiana. Others are from 9 states, 26 foreign countries, and Canada. 90% are white. The average age of freshmen is 20; all undergraduates, 25. 35% do not continue beyond their first year.

Housing: There are no residence halls. All students commute. Alcohol is not permitted.

Activities: There are 2 national fraternities and 4 national sororities. There are 50 groups on campus, including academic, art, band, cheerleading, choir, chorus, computers, drama, ethnic, film, gay, honors, literary magazine, newspaper, orchestra, political, religious, social, special interest, student government, and yearbook.

Sports: There are 4 intercollegiate sports for men and 4 for women, and 5 intramural sports for men and 5 for women. Facilities include a 1600-seat activities building with a basketball court, facilities for jogging, badminton, volleyball, weightlifting, and gymnastics, 6 tennis courts, baseball and softball fields, and playing fields.

Disabled Students: All of the campus is accessible. Wheelchair ramps, elevators, special parking, specially equipped rest rooms, lowered drinking fountains, lowered telephones, and special accommodations as needed are available.

Services: Counseling and information services are available, as is tutoring in every subject. There is a reader service for the blind, and remedial math, reading, and writing. The coordinator for services to students with disabilities provides information and coordination of needed services.

Campus Safety and Security: Measures include 24-hour foot and vehicle patrol, self-defense education, pamphlets/posters/films, emergency telephones, and lighted pathways/sidewalks. There is a police department on campus.

Programs of Study: IUS confers B.A., B.S., and B.G.S. degrees. Associate and master's degrees are also awarded. Bachelor's degrees are awarded in BIOLOGICAL SCIENCE (biology/biological science), BUSINESS (accounting, banking and finance, business administration and management, business economics, management science, marketing/retailing/merchandising, and organizational behavior), COMMUNICATIONS AND THE ARTS (communications, English, fine arts, French, German, journalism, music, and Spanish), COMPUTER AND PHYSICAL SCIENCE (chemistry, computer science, and mathematics), EDUCATION (elementary, English, mathematics, secondary, social studies, and special), HEALTH PROFESSIONS (clinical science, medical technology, and nursing), SOCIAL SCIENCE (criminal justice, economics, geography, history, liberal arts/general studies, philosophy, political science/government, psychology, and sociology). Education, business, and continuing studies are the largest.

Required: Students must complete 120 credit hours, with 30 in upper-level courses and at least 25 in the major, and must maintain a minimum cumulative GPA of 2.0. In addition, all students must complete a core curriculum that includes courses in English composition, math, computer literacy, arts and humanities, and social and natural sciences.

Special: Cross-registration with Metroversity is possible, and opportunities are provided for study abroad in 17 locations, internships, work-study programs, dual majors, a general studies degree, credit by exam, nondegree study, accelerated degree programs, and pass/fail options.

Faculty/Classroom: 54% of faculty are male; 46%, female.

Admissions: The SAT scores for the 2005-2006 freshman class were: Verbal--59% below 500, 31% between 500 and 599, and 10% between 600 and 700; Math--60% below 500, 34% between 500 and 599, and 6% between 600 and 700. The ACT scores were 58% below 21, 28% between 21 and 23, 10% between 24 and 26, and 4% between 27 and 28. 20% of the current freshmen were in the top fifth of their class; 51% were in the top two fifths.

Requirements: The SAT or ACT is required. These requirements are waived if the applicant has been out of high school for 3 or more years. Graduation from an accredited secondary school is required; the GED is accepted. Applicants must have completed 14 academic units, including 4 in English, 3 in math, 2 in social studies, 1 in lab science, and 4 academic electives. 2 units in foreign language are recommended. AP and CLEP credits are accepted.

Procedure: Freshmen are admitted to all sessions. Entrance exams should be taken during high school. There are deferred admissions, and rolling admissions plans. Applications should be filed by July 15 for fall entry, December 1 for spring entry, and April 15 for summer entry. Notification is sent on a rolling basis.

Transfer: 347 transfer students enrolled in a recent year. A GPA of 2.0 is required for Indiana residents, 2.5 for out-of-state applicants. If the student has fewer than 26 transferable semester hours, the high school record should reflect compliance with freshman admission requirements. 30 of 120 credits required for the bachelor's degree must be completed at IUS.

Visiting: There are regularly scheduled orientations for prospective students, including an opportunity for students to apply for admission, financial aid, and scholarships, a faculty perspective, a student perspective, and a campus tour. There are guides for informal visits and visitors may sit in on classes. To schedule a visit, contact the Office of Admissions.

Financial Aid: In a recent year, 41% of all full-time freshmen and 43% of continuing full-time students received some form of financial aid. 29% of full-time freshmen and 31% of continuing full-time students received need-based aid. The average freshman award was $5023. Need-based scholarships or need-based grants averaged $4202; need-based self-help aid (loans and jobs) averaged $2257; non-need-based athletic scholarships averaged $827; and other non-need-based awards and non-need-based scholarships averaged $1744. The average financial indebtedness of the 2005 graduate was $12,973. The FAFSA and the college's own financial statement are required. The deadline for filing freshman financial aid applications for fall entry is March 1.

International Students: There are 10 international students enrolled. A satisfactory score is required on the written TOEFL. Applicants must also take special tests as directed.

Computers: All students may access the system. There are no time limits. The fee is $300.

Graduates: From July 1, 2004 to June 30, 2005, 618 bachelor's degrees were awarded. The most popular majors were business/marketing (24%), education (23%), and liberal arts (16%).

Admissions Contact: David B. Campbell, Director of Admissions. E-mail: *admissions@ius.edu* Web: *www.ius.edu/Admissions*

INDIANA UNIVERSITY-PURDUE UNIVERSITY FORT WAYNE
D-2

Fort Wayne, IN 46805-1499

(260) 481-6812
(800) 324-4739; Fax: (260) 481-6880

Full-time: 3027 men, 3786 women	Faculty: 352; IIA, -$
Part-time: 1740 men, 2475 women	Ph.D.s: 90%
Graduate: 293 men, 474 women	Student/Faculty: 19 to 1
Year: semesters, summer session	Tuition: $5067 ($11,686)
Application Deadline: August 1	Room & Board: n/av
Freshman Class: 2786 applied, 2681 accepted, 1895 enrolled	
SAT Verbal/Math: 485/497*	ACT: 21 LESS COMPETITIVE

In 1964, Indiana University at Fort Wayne, founded in 1917, joined Purdue University at Fort Wayne, founded in 1944. The combined school, a state-controlled institution, offers programs in liberal arts, science, business, education, health sciences, engineering, technology, and public affairs. There are 9 undergraduate and 6 graduate schools. In addition to regional accreditation, IPFW has baccalaureate program accreditation with AACSB, ABET, CSAB, NASM, NCATE, and NLN. The library contains 474,802 volumes, 542,026 microform items, and 6525 audio/video tapes/CDs/DVDs, and subscribes to 22,782 periodicals including electronic. Computerized library services include the card catalog, interlibrary loans, database searching, and Internet access. Special learning facilities include a learning resource center, art gallery, and TV station. The 622-acre campus is in a suburban area 113 miles north of Indianapolis. Including any residence halls, there are 18 buildings.

Student Life: 96% of undergraduates are from Indiana. Others are from 44 states, 74 foreign countries, and Canada. 80% are from public schools. 88% are white. The average age of freshmen is 23. 37% do not continue beyond their first year; 19% remain to graduate.

Housing: 568 students can be accommodated in college housing, which includes coed on-campus apartments. On-campus housing is available on a first-come, first-served basis. 95% of students commute. Alcohol is not permitted. All students may keep cars.

Activities: 1% of men belong to 2 local fraternities. There are no sororities. There are 99 groups on campus, including art, ASID, band, cheerleading, chess, choir, chorus, dance, debate, drama, ethnic, forensics, gay, honors, international, jazz band, literary magazine, musical theater, newspaper, orchestra, pep band, political, professional, radio and TV, religious, social, social service, Society of Women Engineers, and student government. Popular campus events include Mastodon Stomp and Mastodon Roast.

Sports: There are 7 intercollegiate sports for men and 9 for women, and 13 intramural sports for men and 13 for women. Facilities include a physical fitness center with a gym, 3 basketball courts, an indoor track, a weight room, 4 racquetball courts, 1 Wallyball court, a fencing and dance room, baseball and soccer fields, and an indoor soccer facility.

Disabled Students: All of the campus is accessible. Wheelchair ramps, elevators, special parking, specially equipped rest rooms, lowered drinking fountains, lowered telephones, and special housing are available.

Services: Counseling and information services are available, as is tutoring in most subjects. There is a reader service for the blind, and remedial math, reading, and writing.

Campus Safety and Security: Measures include 24-hour foot and vehicle patrol, self-defense education, security escort services, and pamphlets/posters/films. There are emergency telephones and lighted pathways/sidewalks.

Programs of Study: IPFW confers B.A., B.S., B.C.L.S., B.F.A., B.G.S., B.M.T.P., B.Mus., B.Mus.Ed., B.S.B., B.S.C., B.S.C.E., B.S.Ed., B.S.E.E., B.S.G., B.S.L.S., B.S.M.E., and B.S.P.A. degrees. Associate and master's degrees are also awarded. Bachelor's degrees are awarded in BIOLOGICAL SCIENCE (biology/biological science), BUSINESS (accounting, banking and finance, business economics, hospitality management services, labor studies, management science, and marketing/retailing/merchandising), COMMUNICATIONS AND THE ARTS (broadcasting, communications, dramatic arts, English, fine arts, French, German, Spanish, speech/debate/rhetoric, and telecommunications), COMPUTER AND PHYSICAL SCIENCE (chemistry, computer programming, computer science, earth science, geology, information sciences and systems, mathematics, and physics), EDUCATION (art, early childhood, elementary, foreign languages, music, science, and secondary), ENGINEERING AND ENVIRONMENTAL DESIGN (computer engineering, electrical/electronics engineering, engineering, engineering technology, industrial engineering technology, mechanical engineering, and mechanical engineering technology), HEALTH PROFESSIONS (health care administration, medical technology, music therapy, nursing, predentistry, premedicine, and speech pathology/audiology), SOCIAL SCIENCE (anthropology, criminal justice, economics, history, human services, liberal arts/general studies, philosophy, political science/government, prelaw, psychology, public administration, social science, sociology, and women's studies). Engineering and biology are the strongest academically. Business and education are the largest.

Required: All bachelor's degree students must complete 120 credits, including 36 general education hours, with a GPA of 2.0, and take English composition, speech communication, and math to graduate.

Special: There are continuing education, co-op, and work-study programs, as well as study abroad in 5 countries. An accelerated general studies degree, cross-registration with other Fort Wayne colleges, B.A.-B.S. degrees, dual majors, a Washington semester for public affairs students, internships, and credit for military experience are available. Non-degree study and pass/fail options are possible. There are 9 national honor societies and a freshman honors program.

Faculty/Classroom: 55% of faculty are male; 45%, female. All teach undergraduates and 92% do research. Graduate students teach 3% of introductory courses. The average class size in an introductory lecture is 22; in a laboratory, 15; and in a regular course, 22.

Admissions: 96% of the 2005-2006 applicants were accepted. The SAT scores for the 2005-2006 freshman class were: Verbal--58% below 500, 31% between 500 and 599, 9% between 600 and 700, and 2% above 700; Math--51% below 500, 36% between 500 and 599, 11% between 600 and 700, and 2% above 700. The ACT scores were 48% below 21, 26% between 21 and 23, 18% between 24 and 26, 5% between 27 and 28, and 3% above 28. 22% of the current freshmen were in the top fifth of their class; 51% were in the top two fifths. 7 freshmen graduated first in their class.

Requirements: A satisfactory score is required on the SAT or ACT. Applicants should have 20 academic credits, including 4 years of English, 3 years of math, and a 3-year combination of science, social studies, and foreign language. The GED is accepted. AP and CLEP credits are accepted. Important factors in the admissions decision are recommendations by school officials, evidence of special talent, and advanced placement or honor courses.

Procedure: Freshmen are admitted fall, spring, and summer. Entrance exams should be taken in the senior year of high school. There is a rolling admissions plan. Applications should be filed by August 1 for fall entry, December 15 for spring entry, and May 1 for summer entry, along with a $30 fee. Notification is sent on a rolling basis. Applications are accepted on-line.

Transfer: 708 transfer students enrolled in 2004-2005. Transfer applicants must have a minimum GPA of 2.0. Grades of C or better transfer for credit. 32 of 120 credits required for the bachelor's degree must be completed at IPFW.

Visiting: There are regularly scheduled orientations for prospective students. There are guides for informal visits and visitors may sit in on classes. To schedule a visit, contact the Admissions Office.

Financial Aid: In 2005-2006, 57% of all full-time freshmen and 58% of continuing full-time students received some form of financial aid. 39% of full-time freshmen and 48% of continuing full-time students received need-based aid. The average freshman award was $5176. Need-based scholarships or need-based grants averaged $3786 ($10,193 maximum); need-based self-help aid (loans and jobs) averaged $2380 ($10,841 maximum); non-need-based athletic scholarships averaged $5052 ($23,015 maximum); and other non-need-based awards and non-need-based scholarships averaged $2134 ($4957 maximum). 1% of undergraduates work part time. Average annual earnings from campus work are $2000. The average financial indebtedness of the 2005 graduate was $16,395. IPFW is a member of CSS. The FAFSA is required. The priority date for freshman financial aid applications for fall entry is March 10.

International Students: There are 139 international students enrolled. The school actively recruits these students. A satisfactory score on the TOEFL is required. Students must also have a satisfactory SAT score, pass level 109 of an ESL program, or receive a B at 0 level of G.C.E. The ACT may be substituted for the SAT.

Computers: Wireless access is available. There are 6 open-use computer labs, as well as departmental computer labs. All students may access the system. There are no time limits and no fees.

Graduates: From July 1, 2004 to June 30, 2005, 907 bachelor's degrees were awarded. The most popular majors were education (15%), general studies (11%), and nursing (8%). In an average class, 3% graduate in 4 years or less, 10% graduate in 5 years or less, and 19% graduate in 6 years or less. 110 companies recruited on campus in 2004-2005.

Admissions Contact: Carol Isaacs, Director of Admissions.
E-mail: *ipfwadms@ipfw.edu* Web: *www.ipfw.edu*

INDIANA UNIVERSITY-PURDUE UNIVERSITY INDIANAPOLIS   C-3

Indianapolis, IN 46202-5143   (317) 274-4591
                                                  Fax: (317) 278-1862

Full-time: 5566 men, 8170 women	**Faculty:** 2132; IIA, av$
Part-time: 3244 men, 4458 women	**Ph.D.s:** 89%
Graduate: 3760 men, 4735 women	**Student/Faculty:** 6 to 1
Year: semesters, summer session	**Tuition:** $6219 ($16,547)
Application Deadline: open	**Room & Board:** $4740
Freshman Class: n/av	
SAT Verbal/Math: 490/500*	**ACT:** 20 **COMPETITIVE**

Indian University-Purdue University Indianapolis is a large, comprehensive urban research university created in 1969 as a partnership by and between Indiana and Purdue Universities, with IU as the managing partner. IUPUI has approximately 201 authorized IU degree programs in both the health division and the general academic division and operates satellite sites in Carmel and Glendale as well as an education center in Columbus. There are 16 undergraduate and 17 graduate schools. In addition to regional accreditation, IUPUI has baccalaureate program accreditation with AACSB, ABET, ACCE, ACEJMC, ADA, APTA, CAHEA, CSWE, NASAD, NASM, NCATE, and NLN. The 4 libraries contain 1,592,144 volumes, 2,461,513 microform items, and 1591 audio/video tapes/CDs/DVDs, and subscribe to 10,159 periodicals including electronic. Computerized library services include the card catalog and database searching. Special learning facilities include an art gallery, an 85-acre medical center, and an electronic classroom. The 513-acre campus is in an urban area near downtown Indianapolis. Including any residence halls, there are 100 buildings.

Student Life: 97% of undergraduates are from Indiana. Others are from 41 states, 116 foreign countries, and Canada. 81% are white; 11% African American. The average age of freshmen is 20; all undergraduates, 22. 35% do not continue beyond their first year.

Housing: 350 students can be accommodated in college housing, which includes coed dorms, on-campus apartments, off-campus apartments, and married-student housing. In addition, there are special-interest houses. On-campus housing is available on a first-come, first-served basis. 99% of students commute. Alcohol is not permitted. All students may keep cars.

Activities: 1% of men belong to 3 national fraternities; 1% of women belong to 2 national sororities. There are 200 groups on campus, including cheerleading, chorale, chorus, dance, debate, drama, ethnic, gay, honors, international, jazz band, literary magazine, newspaper, opera, pep band, political, professional, radio and TV, religious, social, social service, student government, and yearbook. Popular campus events include Career Day and Activities Fair.

Sports: There are 6 intercollegiate sports for men and 8 for women. Facilities include a 12,000-seat track and field stadium, a 3-pool natatorium, softball fields, a tennis center, and the National Institute for Fitness and Sport.

Disabled Students: All of the campus is accessible. Wheelchair ramps, elevators, special parking, specially equipped rest rooms, special class scheduling, lowered drinking fountains, lowered telephones, classroom aids, and sign language interpreters are available.

Services: Counseling and information services are available, as is tutoring in most subjects. There is a reader service for the blind, and remedial math, reading, and writing.

Campus Safety and Security: Measures include 24-hour foot and vehicle patrol, self-defense education, security escort services, and shuttle buses. There are informal discussions, pamphlets/posters/films, emergency telephones, and lighted pathways/sidewalks.

Programs of Study: IUPUI confers B.A., B.S., B.A.E., B.F.A., B.G.S., B.S.E., B.S.E.E., B.S.M.E., and B.S.W. degrees. Associate, master's, and doctoral degrees are also awarded. Bachelor's degrees are awarded in BIOLOGICAL SCIENCE (biology/biological science), BUSINESS (accounting, banking and finance, business administration and management, business economics, human resources, labor studies, marketing and distribution, marketing/retailing/merchandising, office supervision and management, and tourism), COMMUNICATIONS AND THE ARTS (American Sign Language, art history and appreciation, ceramic art and design, communications, English, fine arts, French, German, journalism, media arts, painting, photography, printmaking, sculpture, and Spanish), COMPUTER AND PHYSICAL SCIENCE (chemistry, computer science, geology, information sciences and systems, mathematics, and physics), EDUCATION (art, drama, elementary, English, foreign languages, health, mathematics, physical, science, secondary, and social studies),

ENGINEERING AND ENVIRONMENTAL DESIGN (biomedical engineering, computer engineering, computer graphics, computer technology, construction technology, electrical/electronics engineering, electrical/electronics engineering technology, engineering, furniture design, manufacturing technology, mechanical engineering, and mechanical engineering technology), HEALTH PROFESSIONS (clinical science, cytotechnology, dental hygiene, health care administration, medical laboratory technology, nuclear medical technology, nursing, physical therapy, predentistry, premedicine, preoptometry, preosteopathy, prepharmacy, preveterinary science, public health, radiation therapy, and respiratory therapy), SOCIAL SCIENCE (anthropology, criminal justice, economics, geography, history, international studies, liberal arts/general studies, philosophy, political science/government, prelaw, psychology, public affairs, religion, social work, and sociology). Engineering and technology, nursing, and education are the largest.

Required: All students must complete courses in computer, humanities, math, science, and social science toward the 122 to 126 credits required for the bachelor's degree.

Special: There is a metropolitan studies program for career work in the city and cross-registration with the Consortium for Urban Education. IUPUI also offers study abroad, combined B.A.-B.S. degree programs, internships, work-study programs, dual and student-designed majors, nondegree study, nontraditional programs for adult learners, and interdisciplinary majors such as business economics and public policy, health occupations education, and interdisciplinary engineering. There is a freshman honors program.

Faculty/Classroom: 64% of faculty are male; 36%, female.

Admissions: The SAT scores for the 2005-2006 freshman class were: Verbal--52% below 500, 36% between 500 and 599, 11% between 600 and 700, and 1% above 700; Math--49% below 500, 38% between 500 and 599, 12% between 600 and 700, and 1% above 700. The ACT scores were 54% below 21, 25% between 21 and 23, 12% between 24 and 26, 7% between 27 and 28, and 2% above 28. 24% of the current freshmen were in the top fifth of their class; 57% were in the top two fifths.

Requirements: The SAT or ACT is required for recent high school graduates. The SAT is preferred. Applicants should be graduates of an accredited high school, rank in the upper half of their class, and have completed 14 Carnegie units, including 4 in English, 3 in math, 2 in social studies, and 1 in lab science. 2 units of a foreign language are recommended. The GED is accepted. The university accepts applications on computer disk. AP and CLEP credits are accepted.

Procedure: Freshmen are admitted to all sessions. Entrance exams should be taken by the end of junior year or fall of senior year. There is a deferred admissions and rolling admissions plans. Application deadlines are open. The fall 2005 application fee was $50.

Transfer: 1823 transfer students enrolled in 2004-2005. Transfers who are Indiana residents must present a minimum GPA of 2.0 in all previous college work; out-of-state residents need a minimum 2.5. All applicants must be in good standing at their former schools. 30 of 122 to 126 credits required for the bachelor's degree must be completed at IUPUI.

Visiting: There are regularly scheduled orientations for prospective students, consisting of a campus tour and talks with students. There are guides for informal visits and visitors may sit in on classes. To schedule a visit, contact Enrollment Center.

Financial Aid: In a recent year, 51% of all full-time freshmen and 52% of continuing full-time students received some form of financial aid. 32% of full-time freshmen and 35% of continuing full-time students received need-based aid. The average freshman award was $6074. Need-based scholarships or need-based grants averaged $4984; need-based self-help aid (loans and jobs) averaged $2486; non-need-based athletic scholarships averaged $2822; and other non-need-based awards and non-need-based scholarships averaged $2088. The average financial indebtedness of the 2005 graduate was $19,660. The FAFSA is required. The deadline for filing freshman financial aid applications for fall entry is March 1.

International Students: There are 285 international students enrolled. They must score satisfactorily on written TOEFL and also take the SAT or the ACT.

Computers: All students may access the system up to 24 hours a day in some clusters. There are no time limits. The fee is $354.

Graduates: From July 1, 2004 to June 30, 2005, 2759 bachelor's degrees were awarded. The most popular majors were business (17%), health profession (14%), and liberal arts (14%).

Admissions Contact: Mike Donahue, Director of Admissions.
E-mail: *apply@iupui.edu* Web: *www.enroll.iupui.edu/*

INDIANA WESLEYAN UNIVERSITY	C-2
Marion, IN 46953-4974	**(765) 677-2138**
	(800) 332-6901; Fax: (765) 677-2333

Full-time: 1004 men, 1613 women	**Faculty:** 127
Part-time: 85 men, 128 women	**Ph.D.s:** 56%
Graduate: none	**Student/Faculty:** 21 to 1
Year: semesters, summer session	**Tuition:** $16,184
Application Deadline: August 1	**Room & Board:** $5890
Freshman Class: 2105 applied, 1721 accepted, 736 enrolled	
SAT Verbal/Math: 544/541*	**ACT:** 24 **COMPETITIVE+**

Indiana Wesleyan University, founded in 1920, is a private institution affiliated with the Methodist Church. The university offers undergraduate programs in the arts and sciences, business, education, fine arts, nursing, professional training, and religious studies. There are 2 undergraduate schools and 1 graduate school. In addition to regional accreditation, IWU has baccalaureate program accreditation with CAHEA, CCNE, CSWE, NCATE, and NLN. The library contains 133,396 volumes, 200,530 microform items, and 10,657 audio/video tapes/CDs/DVDs, and subscribes to 919 periodicals including electronic. Computerized library services include the card catalog, interlibrary loans, database searching, Internet access, and laptop Internet portals. Special learning facilities include a learning resource center, art gallery, radio station, and TV station. The 325-acre campus is in an urban area 60 miles north of Indianapolis. Including any residence halls, there are 114 buildings.

Student Life: 54% of undergraduates are from Indiana. Others are from 44 states, 21 foreign countries, and Canada. 76% are from public schools. 98% are white. Most are Protestant. The average age of freshmen is 18; all undergraduates, 20. 22% do not continue beyond their first year; 68% remain to graduate.

Housing: 2202 students can be accommodated in college housing, which includes single-sex dorms and on-campus apartments. On-campus housing is guaranteed for all 4 years. 77% of students live on campus; of those, 50% remain on campus on weekends. Alcohol is not permitted. All students may keep cars.

Activities: There are no fraternities or sororities. There are 35 groups on campus, including art, cheerleading, choir, chorale, chorus, drama, film, honors, international, jazz band, literary magazine, musical theater, newspaper, orchestra, pep band, photography, political, professional, radio and TV, religious, social service, student government, symphony, and yearbook. Popular campus events include Campus Visit Days and "Friday Night Live" comedy event.

Sports: There are 7 intercollegiate sports for men and 7 for women, and 21 intramural sports for men and 21 for women. Facilities include a gym, racquetball courts, a weight room, and a 65-acre outdoor athletic complex with a track.

Disabled Students: All of the campus is accessible. Wheelchair ramps, elevators, special parking, specially equipped rest rooms, special class scheduling, lowered drinking fountains, lowered telephones, special housing, amplified telephones, and TTY are available.

Services: Counseling and information services are available, as is tutoring in most subjects. There is a reader service for the blind and remedial reading and writing. External testing, a note taker service, and advocacy are available.

Campus Safety and Security: Measures include 24-hour foot and vehicle patrol, self-defense education, security escort services, and informal discussions. There are pamphlets/posters/films, emergency telephones, and lighted pathways/sidewalks.

Programs of Study: IWU confers B.A. and B.S. degrees. Associate, master's, and doctoral degrees are also awarded. Bachelor's degrees are awarded in BIOLOGICAL SCIENCE (biology/biological science), BUSINESS (accounting, banking and finance, business administration and management, management science, marketing/retailing/merchandising, and recreational facilities management), COMMUNICATIONS AND THE ARTS (art, ceramic art and design, communications, creative writing, English, illustration, music, music theory and composition, painting, photography, printmaking, Spanish, and studio art), COMPUTER AND PHYSICAL SCIENCE (chemistry, computer science, information sciences and systems, mathematics, and science), EDUCATION (art, athletic training, elementary, English, mathematics, music, nursing, physical, science, secondary, social studies, and special), ENGINEERING AND ENVIRONMENTAL DESIGN (computer graphics), HEALTH PROFESSIONS (health, medical laboratory technology, and premedicine), SOCIAL SCIENCE (addiction studies, biblical studies, criminal justice, economics, history, liberal arts/general studies, ministries, political science/government, prelaw, psychology, religion, religious music, social studies, social work, and sociology). Education, religion, and nursing are the strongest academically.

Required: Students must attend chapel services 3 times a week. A 52-credit general education core includes 12 credit hours of humanities, 10 of math and science, 9 each of English and history or social studies, 6 of biblical literature, and 3 each of intercultural experience and phys ed. Foreign language courses are required for the B.A., computer literacy courses for the B.S. To graduate, students must complete at least 124 semester hours, including 40 to 60 in a major field of study, with a minimum GPA of 2.0 overall and 2.25 in the major. A thesis is required for the honors college.

Special: Students may study abroad in 20 countries. IWU also offers business, pastoral, nursing, and social work internships, cross-registration with CCCU, a Washington semester, work-study programs with the Economic Growth Council, pass/fail options, and nondegree study. Accelerated degree programs are available in accounting, business administration, business information, management, and nursing. Students may earn a B.A.-B.S. degree in management, business, and education. Dual majors and student-designed majors are available. Adult learners may earn credit for life experience toward bachelor's degrees in business. There are 6 national honor societies, a freshman honors program, and 12 departmental honors programs.

Faculty/Classroom: 64% of faculty are male; 36%, female. All both teach and do research. The average class size in an introductory lecture is 30; in a laboratory, 15; and in a regular course, 21.

Admissions: 82% of the 2005-2006 applicants were accepted. The SAT scores for the 2005-2006 freshman class were: Verbal--30% below 500, 42% between 500 and 599, 24% between 600 and 700, and 4% above 700; Math--28% below 500, 45% between 500 and 599, 24% between 600 and 700, and 3% above 700. The ACT scores were 12% below 21, 26% between 21 and 23, 28% between 24 and 26, 23% between 27 and 28, and 11% above 28. 25% of the current freshmen were in the top fifth of their class; 50% were in the top two fifths. 43 freshmen graduated first in their class.

Requirements: The SAT or ACT is required. In addition, applicants should be graduates of accredited secondary schools or have earned a GED. The university requires 10 units of college preparatory study that includes courses in English, science, social science, math, and foreign language. Recommendations are also required. A GPA of 2.0 is required. AP and CLEP credits are accepted.

Procedure: Freshmen are admitted to all sessions. Entrance exams should be taken in the junior year or early in the senior year. There is a deferred admissions plan and a roling admissions plan. Applications should be filed by August 1 for fall entry. The fall 2005 application fee was $25. Notification is sent on a rolling basis. Applications are accepted on-line.

Transfer: 131 transfer students enrolled in 2004-2005. In addition to standard admissions requirements, transfers must submit transcripts of all previous college work and be in good standing at their former school. 60 of 124 credits required for the bachelor's degree must be completed at IWU.

Visiting: There are regularly scheduled orientations for prospective students, including appointments with admissions counselors and professors, campus tours, classroom visits, and meals. There are guides for informal visits and visitors may sit in on classes and stay overnight. To schedule a visit, contact the Admissions Office at *admissions@indwes.edu.*

Financial Aid: In 2005-2006, 95% of all full-time freshmen and 87% of continuing full-time students received some form of financial aid. 73% of full-time freshmen and 63% of continuing full-time students received need-based aid. The average freshman award was $16,102. Need-based scholarships or need-based grants averaged $4524; need-based self-help aid (loans and jobs) averaged $3116; non-need-based athletic scholarships averaged $4423; and other non-need-based awards and non-need-based scholarships averaged $8168. The FAFSA and the college's own financial statement are required. The deadline for filing freshman financial aid applications for fall entry is March 1.

International Students: There are 21 international students enrolled. The school actively recruits these students. They must take the TOEFL and also take the SAT or the ACT.

Computers: Wireless access is available. Students can access the university network from dedicated ports for each student in residence halls, through wireless access points in campus buildings, and in various labs on campus. There are more than 400 computers accessible in discipline-specific and general access labs. All computers on the network can access IWU network resources (portal) and also the Internet. All students may access the system any time.

Graduates: From July 1, 2004 to June 30, 2005, 453 bachelor's degrees were awarded. The most popular majors were religion and philosophy (16%), nursing (14%), and business (11%). In an average class, 56% graduate in 4 years or less, 61% graduate in 5 years or less, and 70% graduate in 6 years or less. 218 companies recruited on campus in 2004-2005.

Admissions Contact: Jerry Shephard, Vice President for Enrollment Management. A video is available. E-mail: *admissions@indwes.edu* Web: *www.indwes.edu*

MANCHESTER COLLEGE   C-2
North Manchester, IN 46962-0365   (260) 982-5055
                              (800) 852-3648; Fax: (260) 982-5239

Full-time: 500 men, 600 women	**Faculty:** 68; IIB, -$
Part-time: 5 men, 15 women	**Ph.D.s:** 93%
Graduate: 10 men 10 women	**Student/Faculty:** 16 to 1
Year: 4-1-4, summer session	**Tuition:** $17,120
Application Deadline: open	**Room & Board:** $6350
Freshman Class: n/av	
SAT or ACT: required	**COMPETITIVE**

Manchester College, established in 1889, is a private liberal arts college affiliated with the Church of the Brethren offering undergraduate and graduate major programs in accounting, business and economics, premedicine, education, psychology, the social sciences, and the humanities. Figures in the above capsule are approximate. In addition to regional accreditation, Manchester has baccalaureate program accreditation with CSWE and NCATE. The library contains 174,078 volumes, 23,014 microform items, and 5258 audio/video tapes/CDs/DVDs, and subscribes to 973 periodicals including electronic. Computerized library services include the card catalog, interlibrary loans, database searching, and Internet access. Special learning facilities include a learning resource center, planetarium, radio station, and a 100-acre nature preserve. The 124-acre campus is in a small town 35 miles west of Fort Wayne in northeastern Indiana. Including any residence halls, there are 44 buildings.

Student Life: 83% of undergraduates are from Indiana. Others are from 29 states, 33 foreign countries, and Canada. 99% are from public schools. 87% are white. 61% are Protestant; 20% claim no religious affiliation; 12% Catholic; 7%, includes Muslim and unknown. The average age of freshmen is 18; all undergraduates, 20. 25% do not continue beyond their first year; 55% remain to graduate.

Housing: 979 students can be accommodated in college housing, which includes single-sex and coed dormitories, on-campus apartments, off-campus apartments, and married-student housing. In addition, there are special-interest houses. Theme units for students interested in science, health, and international issues are located within the residence hall system. On-campus housing is guaranteed for all 4 years. 77% of students live on campus; of those, 50% remain on campus on weekends. Alcohol is not permitted. All students may keep cars.

Activities: There are no fraternities or sororities. There are 55 groups on campus, including band, cheerleading, choir, chorale, chorus, computers, dance, drama, ethnic, gay, honors, international, jazz band, literary magazine, musical theater, newspaper, orchestra, pep band, photography, political, professional, radio and TV, religious, social, social service, student government, symphony, and yearbook. Popular campus events include Parents Weekend, Sibling Weekend, and International Fair.

Sports: There are 9 intercollegiate sports for men and 8 for women, and 13 intramural sports for men and 12 for women. Facilities include a phys ed and recreation center with an 1800-seat gym, racquetball courts, and a fitness center; tennis courts; a cross-country and an all-weather track; and athletic fields for baseball, softball, soccer, and football.

Disabled Students: 20% of the campus is accessible. Wheelchair ramps, elevators, special parking, specially equipped rest rooms, special class scheduling, lowered drinking fountains, and lowered telephones are available.

Services: Counseling and information services are available, as is tutoring in every subject. There is a reader service for the blind. There is also a learning center with an academic assistance program, and a seminar to enhance study and learning skills and time and project management.

Campus Safety and Security: Measures include 24-hour foot and vehicle patrol, security escort services, informal discussions, and pamphlets/posters/films. There are emergency telephones and lighted pathways/sidewalks.

Programs of Study: Manchester confers B.A. and B.S. degrees. Associate and master's degrees are also awarded. Bachelor's degrees are awarded in BIOLOGICAL SCIENCE (biochemistry and biology/biological science), BUSINESS (accounting, banking and finance, and business administration and management), COMMUNICATIONS AND THE ARTS (art, communications, English, French, German, music, and Spanish), COMPUTER AND PHYSICAL SCIENCE (chemistry, computer science, mathematics, and physics), EDUCATION (art, elementary, health, middle school, and secondary), ENGINEERING AND ENVIRONMENTAL DESIGN (engineering), HEALTH PROFESSIONS (medical laboratory technology), SOCIAL SCIENCE (economics, history, interdisciplinary studies, peace studies, philosophy, political science/government, prelaw, psychology, religion, social work, and sociology). Education, accounting, and biology-chemistry are the strongest academically. Education, accounting, and communication studies are the largest.

Required: Students must complete a general studies curriculum, including requirements in humanities, social sciences, and natural sciences, as well as specific courses in English composition, public communication, Western civilization, and physical fitness. In order to graduate, students must complete a minimum of 128 semester hours, including 26 to 52 hours in a major field, with a GPA of at least 2.0 (2.5 for the education major). A comprehensive exam in the major is also required. A thesis for honors students is optional.

Special: The college offers cooperative programs in nursing and engineering science. The Brethren Colleges Abroad program allows study abroad in 12 countries, including Ecuador, China, England, France, Germany, Japan, Mexico, and Spain. Manchester also offers B.A.-B.S. degrees, internships, work-study programs, dual majors, student-designed majors, a 3-2 engineering program, pass/fail options, and non-degree study. Other special academic features include independent study, required study in non-Western culture, and interdisciplinary programs in both peace studies and environmental studies. A January interterm permits internships, travel abroad, and concentrated classes on campus. There are 6 national honor societies, a freshman honors program, and 5 departmental honors programs.

Faculty/Classroom: 63% of faculty are male; 37%, female. All teach undergraduates. No introductory courses are taught by graduate students. The average class size in an introductory lecture is 30; in a laboratory, 15; and in a regular course, 20.

Requirements: The SAT or ACT is required. Each application is reviewed on an individual basis. The GED is accepted. For high school students, the college recommends completion of 28 academic credits, based on 4 years each of English, math, and science, and 2 years each of foreign language, history, and social studies. Manchester requires applicants to be in the upper 50% of their class. A GPA of 2.3 is required. AP and CLEP credits are accepted. Important factors in the admissions decision are advanced placement or honor courses, leadership record, and recommendations by school officials.

Procedure: Freshmen are admitted to all sessions. Entrance exams should be taken by November of the senior year. There are early admissions deferred admissions, and rolling admissions plans. Application deadlines are open. Application fee is $20.

Transfer: 31 transfer students enrolled in a recent year. Transfer students must present a minimum GPA of 2.0 in all previous college work. 96 of 128 credits required for the bachelor's degree must be completed at Manchester.

Visiting: There are regularly scheduled orientations for prospective students, including meetings about financial aid, with faculty and admissions, and campus tours. Visitors may also eat meals on campus, sit in on classes, and meet with current students. There are guides for informal visits and visitors may sit in on classes and stay overnight. To schedule a visit, contact Jill Biehl, Campus Visit Coordinator.

Financial Aid: The FAFSA is required. The deadline for filing freshman financial aid applications for fall entry is rolling.

International Students: The school actively recruits these students. They must score satisfactorily on the TOEFL.

Computers: All students may access the system any time. There are no time limits and no fees.

Admissions Contact: Jolane Rohr, Director of Admissions.
E-mail: *admitinfo@manchester.edu* Web: *www.manchester.edu*

MARIAN COLLEGE	C-3
Indianapolis, IN 46222	**(317) 955-6300**
	(800) 772-7264; Fax: (317) 955-6401
Full-time: 315 men, 773 women	**Faculty:** 83
Part-time: 125 men, 453 women	**Ph.D.s:** 58%
Graduate: 4 men, 8 women	**Student/Faculty:** 13 to 1
Year: semesters, summer session	**Tuition:** $19,760
Application Deadline: August 1	**Room & Board:** $6400
Freshman Class: 835 applied, 558 accepted, 191 enrolled	
SAT Verbal/Math: 520/520*	**ACT:** 21 COMPETITIVE

Marian College, a private institution, was founded in 1851 by the Sisters of St. Francis and is today affiliated with the Roman Catholic Church. The college offers undergraduate programs in the arts and sciences, business, education, fine arts, and the health professions. In addition to regional accreditation, Marian has baccalaureate program accreditation with AHEA, CAHEA, CCNE, IACBE, NCATE, and NLN. The library contains 149,000 volumes, 39 microform items, and 4900 audio/video tapes/CDs/DVDs, and subscribes to 606 periodicals including electronic. Computerized library services include the card catalog, interlibrary loans, database searching, and Internet access. Special learning facilities include a learning resource center, art gallery, and the 35-acre Wetlands Ecology Laboratory. The 114-acre campus is in a suburban area 6 miles from downtown Indianapolis. Including any residence halls, there are 22 buildings.

Student Life: 90% of undergraduates are from Indiana. Others are from 19 states, 17 foreign countries, and Canada. 69% are from public schools. 65% are white; 17% African American. 50% are Catholic; 45% Protestant. The average age of freshmen is 19; all undergraduates, 25. 30% do not continue beyond their first year; 47% remain to graduate.

Housing: 532 students can be accommodated in college housing, which includes single-sex and coed dorms, on-campus apartments, off-

campus apartments, and married-student housing. On-campus housing is guaranteed for all 4 years. 55% of students commute. Alcohol is not permitted. All students may keep cars.

Activities: There are no fraternities or sororities. There are 33 groups on campus, including art, band, cheerleading, choir, chorale, chorus, computers, drama, drill team, ethnic, honors, international, jazz band, literary magazine, musical theater, newspaper, pep band, photography, political, professional, religious, social, social service, student government, and yearbook. Popular campus events include Global Speaker Series, Field Day, and Knightly Music Awards.

Sports: There are 8 intercollegiate sports for men and 9 for women, and 10 intramural sports for men and 10 for women. Facilities include varsity and intramural gyms, racquetball courts, a fitness center, a weight-training room, and a phys ed assessment lab.

Disabled Students: 90% of the campus is accessible. Wheelchair ramps, elevators, special parking, specially equipped rest rooms, and special class scheduling are available.

Services: Counseling and information services are available, as is tutoring in most subjects. There is a reader service for the blind, and remedial math, reading, and writing. Study skills training and peer tutoring are available.

Campus Safety and Security: Measures include 24-hour foot and vehicle patrol, security escort services, shuttle buses, and informal discussions. There are pamphlets/posters/films and lighted pathways/sidewalks.

Programs of Study: Marian confers B.A., B.S., and B.S.N. degrees. Associate and master's degrees are also awarded. Bachelor's degrees are awarded in BIOLOGICAL SCIENCE (biology/biological science), BUSINESS (accounting, banking and finance, business administration and management, and sports management), COMMUNICATIONS AND THE ARTS (art history and appreciation, communications, English, French, graphic design, music, Spanish, and studio art), COMPUTER AND PHYSICAL SCIENCE (chemistry and mathematics), EDUCATION (elementary, physical, and special), ENGINEERING AND ENVIRONMENTAL DESIGN (environmental science), HEALTH PROFESSIONS (nursing), SOCIAL SCIENCE (economics, history, pastoral studies, philosophy, political science/government, psychology, religious education, sociology, and theological studies). Accounting, nursing, and biology are the strongest academically. Nursing, business administration, and education are the largest.

Required: To graduate, students must complete 128 semester hours, including 30 to 40 in the major, with a minimum GPA of 2.0 overall and in the major. General education requirements include 14 semester hours in cultural awareness, 10 to 12 in scientific and quantitative reasoning, 9 to 17 in written and oral communication and foreign language, and 9 each in moral reasoning and individual and social awareness.

Special: Co-op programs in accounting, finance, business administration, chemistry, management information systems, and sociology, and cross-registration through the Consortium for Urban Education are offered. A dual degree program in math and computer science , a 3-2 engineering degree, and accelerated degrees in nursing and business administration are also offered. Internships, study abroad, work-study, independent study, dual and student-designed majors, and pass/fail options are available. There are 12 national honor societies, a freshman honors program, and 7 departmental honors programs.

Faculty/Classroom: 49% of faculty are male; 51%, female. All teach undergraduates. No introductory courses are taught by graduate students. The average class size in an introductory lecture is 20; in a laboratory, 15; and in a regular course, 14.

Admissions: 67% of the 2005-2006 applicants were accepted. The SAT scores for the 2005-2006 freshman class were: Verbal--39% below 500, 47% between 500 and 599, 13% between 600 and 700, and 1% above 700; Math--33% below 500, 48% between 500 and 599, 17% between 600 and 700, and 2% above 700. The ACT scores were 48% below 21, 26% between 21 and 23, 20% between 24 and 26, 3% between 27 and 28, and 3% above 28. 4 freshmen graduated first in their class.

Requirements: The SAT or ACT is required. The ACT Optional Writing test is also required. In addition, applicants must be graduates of an accredited secondary school or have a GED. Marian requires 20 academic units, including 4 units in English, 2 each in a foreign language and math, of which algebra and geometry are recommended, and 2 each in a lab science and social studies. A GPA of 2.3 is required. AP and CLEP credits are accepted. Important factors in the admissions decision are recommendations by school officials, recommendations by alumni, and leadership record.

Procedure: Freshmen are admitted to all sessions. Entrance exams should be taken at the end of the junior year or the beginning of the senior year. There is a rolling admissions plan. Applications should be filed by August 1 for fall entry, December 15 for spring entry, and April 15 for summer entry, along with a $20 fee. Notification is sent on a rolling basis. Applications are accepted on-line.

Transfer: 255 transfer students enrolled in 2004-2005. In addition to meeting standard admissions requirements, applicants must submit transcripts of all college work and be in good standing at their former school. Students transferring must have a 2.0 GPA. 30 of 128 credits required for the bachelor's degree must be completed at Marian.

Visiting: There are regularly scheduled orientations for prospective students, including a campus tour, visits with faculty and coaches, and financial aid information. There are guides for informal visits and visitors may sit in on classes and stay overnight. To schedule a visit, contact the Office of Admissions at *admissions@marian.edu.*

Financial Aid: In 2005-2006, 97% of all full-time freshmen and 90% of continuing full-time students received some form of financial aid. 83% of full-time freshmen and 80% of continuing full-time students received need-based aid. The average freshman award was $18,534. Need-based scholarships or need-based grants averaged $6924 ($21,814 maximum); need-based self-help aid (loans and jobs) averaged $3457 ($10,125 maximum); non-need-based athletic scholarships averaged $6350 ($18,400 maximum); and other non-need-based awards and non-need-based scholarships averaged $7673 ($18,400 maximum). 56% of undergraduates work part time. Average annual earnings from campus work are $1500. The average financial indebtedness of the 2005 graduate was $12,661. The FAFSA and the college's own financial statement are required. The deadline for filing freshman financial aid applications for fall entry is March 1.

International Students: There are 19 international students enrolled. The school actively recruits these students. A satisfactory score is required on the written TOEFL.

Computers: Wireless access is available. All students may access the system 24 hours a day 7 days a week. There are no time limits and no fees. It is strongly recommended that all students have a personal computer.

Graduates: The most popular majors were business/marketing (34%), nursing (17%), and education (9%). In an average class, 1% graduate in 3 years or less, 33% graduate in 4 years or less, 47% graduate in 5 years or less, and 48% graduate in 6 years or less. 150 companies recruited on campus in 2004-2005. Of the 2004 graduating class, 5% were enrolled in graduate school within 6 months of graduation and 87% were employed.

Admissions Contact: Luann Brames, Director of Enrollment.
E-mail: *admissions@marian.edu* Web: *www.marian.edu*

MARTIN UNIVERSITY — C-3

Indianapolis, IN 46218 — (317) 543-3237; Fax: (317) 543-4790

Full-time: 45 men, 180 women	Faculty: 36
Part-time: 105 men, 260 women	Ph.D.s: 36%
Graduate: 30 men, 50 women	Student/Faculty: 6 to 1
Year: semesters, summer session	Tuition: $10,300
Application Deadline: open	Room & Board: n/app
Freshman Class: n/av	
ACT or SAT: not required	SPECIAL

Martin University, established in 1977, is a private liberal arts institution offering undergraduate programs primarily to low-income minority-group adults. Figures in the above capsule are approximate. It also offers graduate degrees in community psychology and urban ministry studies. Computerized library services include interlibrary loans and database searching. Special learning facilities include a learning resource center and English and math labs. The 8-acre campus is in an urban area in Indianapolis. There are 4 buildings.

Student Life: 90% are from public schools. 90% are African American. The average age of freshmen is 33; all undergraduates, 38.

Housing: There are no residence halls. All students commute. Alcohol is not permitted. No one may keep cars.

Activities: There are no fraternities or sororities. There are some groups and organizations on campus, including choir, civil rights, computers, drama, newspaper, opera, and social service. Popular campus events include internal and external conferences, St. Martin de Porres Feast Day, and Fine Arts Festival.

Sports: There is no sports program at Martin U.

Disabled Students: 90% of the campus is accessible. Wheelchair ramps, elevators, special parking, specially equipped rest rooms, lowered drinking fountains, and lowered telephones are available.

Services: Counseling and information services are available, as is tutoring in most subjects. There is remedial math, reading, and writing and addiction services.

Campus Safety and Security: Measures include 24-hour foot and vehicle patrol, security escort services, pamphlets/posters/films, and lighted pathways/sidewalks.

Programs of Study: Martin U confers B.A. and B.S. degrees. Master's degrees are also awarded. Bachelor's degrees are awarded in BIOLOGICAL SCIENCE (biology/biological science), BUSINESS (accounting, business administration and management, insurance, and marketing/retailing/merchandising), COMMUNICATIONS AND THE ARTS (communications, fine arts, music, and Spanish), COMPUTER AND PHYSICAL SCIENCE (chemistry and mathematics), EDUCATION (early childhood, education, and vocational), ENGINEERING AND ENVIRONMENTAL DESIGN (computer technology and environmental science), SOCIAL SCIENCE (African American studies, community services, counseling/psychology, criminal justice, history, humanities, politi-

cal science/government, psychology, religion, and sociology). Humanities and psychology are the strongest academically. Business is the largest.

Required: Students must successfully complete 134 credits, including 36 in the humanities, 12 in English, and 6 each in social science and math, with at least 36 in the major and a minimum GPA of 2.0. Other required courses include computer science and critical thinking, and a foreign language for the B.A. Students must complete a final project in their major.

Special: Cross-registration is permitted with 7 schools in the Consortium of Urban Education in the area. Opportunities are provided for internships, student-designed majors, and credit based on assessment of prior learning.

Faculty/Classroom: 55% of faculty are male; 45%, female. All teach undergraduates and 10% do research. No introductory courses are taught by graduate students. The average class size in an introductory lecture is 13 and in a laboratory, 8.

Requirements: Graduation from an accredited secondary school is required; a GED will be accepted. No specific number of academic credits is required. An essay, an interview, and diagnostic testing are required. CLEP credit is accepted.

Procedure: Freshmen are admitted to all sessions. There is a rolling admissions plan. Entrance exams should be taken at the time of admission. Application deadlines are open. Application fee is $25.

Transfer: 49 transfer students enrolled in a recent year. Transfers are accepted from accredited regional schools. 34 of 134 credits required for the bachelor's degree must be completed at Martin U.

Visiting: There are regularly scheduled orientations for prospective students, consisting of 4 3-hour sessions. There are guides for informal visits and visitors may sit in on classes. To schedule a visit, contact the Recruitment Office at (317) 543-3865.

Financial Aid: In a recent year, 89% of all full-time freshmen and 94% of continuing full-time students received some form of financial aid. 88% of full-time freshmen and 90% of continuing full-time students received need-based aid. The average freshman award was $9121. Average annual earnings from campus work were $2769. The average financial indebtedness of a recent graduate was $29,782. The FAFSA is required. Check with the school for application deadlines.

International Students: They must score satisfactorily on the TOEFL.

Computers: All students may access the system. There are no time limits and no fees. It is strongly recommended that all students have a personal computer.

Graduates: In a recent year, 55 bachelor's degrees were awarded. The most popular majors were business administration (27%), social sciences (20%), and religious studies (14%).

Admissions Contact: Brenda Shaheed, Director of Admissions.
E-mail: *bshaheed@martin.edu* Web: *www.martin.edu*

OAKLAND CITY UNIVERSITY — A-5

Oakland City, IN 47660 — (812) 749-1217
(800) 737-5125; Fax: (812) 749-1233

Full-time: 1900 men and women	Faculty: n/av
Part-time: none	Ph.D.s: 71%
Graduate: none	Student/Faculty: n/av
Year: semesters, summer session	Tuition: $14,220
Application Deadline: open	Room & Board: $5400
Freshman Class: n/av	
SAT or ACT: required	NONCOMPETITIVE

Oakland City University, founded in 1885, is a private liberal arts institution affiliated with the General Association of General Baptists. There are 6 undergraduate and 2 graduate schools. In addition to regional accreditation, OCU has baccalaureate program accreditation with NCATE. The library contains 83,404 volumes, 100,318 microform items, and 2576 audio/video tapes/CDs/DVDs, and subscribes to 8000 periodicals including electronic. Computerized library services include the card catalog, interlibrary loans, database searching, and Internet access. Special learning facilities include a learning resource center and archives and a curriculum lab. The 20-acre campus is in a small town 30 miles north of Evansville, Illinois. Including any residence halls, there are 15 buildings.

Student Life: 88% of undergraduates are from Indiana. Students are from 18 states and 15 foreign countries. 90% are from public schools. 96% are white. 76% are Protestant; 30% claim no religious affiliation; 13% Catholic. The average age of freshmen is 19; all undergraduates, 24. 30% do not continue beyond their first year; 70% remain to graduate.

Housing: 246 students can be accommodated in college housing, which includes single-sex dorms and on-campus apartments. In addition, there are honors houses and special-interest houses. On-campus housing is available on a first-come, first-served basis. 57% of students commute. Alcohol is not permitted. All students may keep cars.

Activities: There are no fraternities or sororities. There are 19 groups on campus, including art, cheerleading, choir, chorus, computers, drama, honors, international, musical theater, newspaper, pep band, photography, professional, religious, social, social service, student government, and yearbook. Popular campus events include Fall Festival Week, Spring Fling, and Fine Arts Festival.

Sports: There are 6 intercollegiate sports for men and 7 for women, and 14 intramural sports for men and 14 for women. Facilities include a gym, a health and phys ed center with a 1600-seat gym, a soccer field, a baseball field, and a tennis complex.

Disabled Students: 99% of the campus is accessible. Wheelchair ramps, elevators, special parking, specially equipped rest rooms, lowered drinking fountains, and special housing are available.

Services: Counseling and information services are available, as is tutoring in every subject. There is a reader service for the blind, and remedial math, reading, and writing.

Campus Safety and Security: Measures include self-defense education, security escort services, informal discussions, and pamphlets/posters/films. There are emergency telephones, lighted pathways/sidewalks, and security in the evenings.

Programs of Study: OCU confers B.A. and B.S. degrees. Associate and master's degrees are also awarded. Bachelor's degrees are awarded in BIOLOGICAL SCIENCE (biology/biological science), BUSINESS (accounting and business administration and management), COMMUNICATIONS AND THE ARTS (English, fine arts, and music), COMPUTER AND PHYSICAL SCIENCE (mathematics), EDUCATION (art, business, elementary, middle school, music, science, and secondary), HEALTH PROFESSIONS (premedicine), SOCIAL SCIENCE (prelaw and religion). Education is the strongest academically and is the largest.

Required: Liberal arts students must take a general studies core, including 1 computer science course and 2 hours of phys ed. A minimum GPA of 2.0 (2.5 in the major) and 120 total semester hours are needed.

Special: OCU offers campus work-study programs, an accelerated business degree program, business and networking internships, a B.A.-B.S. degree, dual majors, credit for significant work or service experience, nondegree study, pass/fail options, and a general studies degree. There are 3 national honor societies.

Faculty/Classroom: 58% of faculty are male; 42%, female. All both teach and do research. The average class size in an introductory lecture is 25; in a laboratory, 16; and in a regular course, 25.

Requirements: The SAT or ACT is required. Preparatory programs usually include 4 units of English, 2 each of social science and science, 2 to 4 of a foreign language, and 3 to 4 of math. An interview is recommended. The GED is accepted. AP and CLEP credits are accepted. Important factors in the admissions decision are personality/intangible qualities, evidence of special talent, and extracurricular activities record.

Procedure: Freshmen are admitted to all sessions. Entrance exams should be taken in the fall of the senior year. There is a deferred admissions plan. Application deadlines are open. Application fee is $35.

Transfer: Transfer applicants need a minimum GPA of 2.0 and a satisfactory score on the SAT or 18 on the ACT. An interview is recommended. 35 of 120 credits required for the bachelor's degree must be completed at OCU.

Visiting: There are regularly scheduled orientations for prospective students. There are guides for informal visits and visitors may sit in on classes and stay overnight. To schedule a visit, contact the Admissions Office at bharris@oak.edu.

Financial Aid: In a recent year, 92% of all full-time freshmen and 87% of continuing full-time students received some form of financial aid. 62% of full-time freshmen received need-based aid. The average freshman award was $13,500. 32% of undergraduates work part time. Average annual earnings from campus work are $2200. The average financial indebtedness of the recent graduate was $11,600. OCU is a member of CSS. The FAFSA and the college's own financial statement are required. The priority date for freshman financial aid applications for fall entry is March 1. The deadline for filing freshman financial aid applications for fall entry is open.

International Students: There were 25 international students enrolled in a recent year. The school actively recruits these students. They must take the TOEFL also take the SAT or the ACT.

Computers: Wireless access is available. All students may access the system.

Graduates: The most popular majors in a recent year were education (70%), seminary (15%), and business (10%). In an average class, 1% graduate in 3 years or less, 15% graduate in 4 years or less, 72% graduate in 5 years or less, and 5% graduate in 6 years or less. 12 companies recruited on campus in a recent year. Of a recent graduating class, 3% were enrolled in graduate school within 6 months of graduation and 71% were employed.

Admissions Contact: Brian Baker, Director of Admissions.
E-mail: bbaker@oak.edu Web: www.oak.edu

PURDUE UNIVERSITY SYSTEM

Purdue University was founded in 1869 as a land-grant institution in West Lafayette, Indiana. Since opening its doors to 39 students in 1874,

Purdue has grown to a statewide system whose priorities are learning, discovery, and engagement. The total enrollment of all 5 campuses is approximately 68,700 students with more than 38,600 at the main campus in West Lafayette. Purdue offers nearly 6100 courses in more than 200 specializations. Graduate students can work toward a master's or doctoral degree in approximately 60 different departmental programs. Among the 25 largest colleges and universities in the nation, Purdue maintains a tradition of providing students with an excellent, affordable education.

PURDUE UNIVERSITY/CALUMET

B-1

Hammond, IN 46323

(219) 989-2213
(800) HI PURDUE; Fax: (219) 989-2775

Full-time: 2203 men, 2826 women	**Faculty:** IIA, --$
Part-time: 1956 men, 1374 women	**Ph.D.s:** 90%
Graduate: 339 men, 604 women	**Student/Faculty:** n/av
Year: semesters, summer session	**Tuition:** $5127ª ($11,019)
Application Deadline: see profile	**Room & Board:** $5764
Freshman Class: n/av	
SAT or ACT: required	**LESS COMPETITIVE**

Purdue University/Calumet, established in 1946, is a public commuter institution offering undergraduate degrees in general studies, liberal arts, and professional studies. There are 7 undergraduate schools and 1 graduate school. In addition to regional accreditation, Purdue Cal has baccalaureate program accreditation with ABET, NCATE, and NLN. The library contains 269,648 volumes, 764,621 microform items, and 998 audio/video tapes/CDs/DVDs, and subscribes to 228 periodicals including electronic. Computerized library services include the card catalog, interlibrary loans, database searching, and Internet access. Special learning facilities include a learning resource center, art gallery, a computer education building, and an educational media lab. The 167-acre campus is in an urban area 25 miles southeast of Chicago. Including any residence halls, there are 21 buildings.

Student Life: 91% of undergraduates are from Indiana. Others are from 30 states and 27 foreign countries. 72% are from public schools. 68% are white; 15% African American; 14% Hispanic. The average age of freshmen is 19; all undergraduates, 25. 64% do not continue beyond their first year; 24% remain to graduate.

Housing: 376 students can be accommodated in college housing. College-sponsored housing is coed. On-campus housing is available on a first-come, first-served basis. 97% of students commute. Alcohol is not permitted. All students may keep cars.

Activities: There are 2 national fraternities and 2 local and 2 national sororities. There are 40 groups on campus, including art, cheerleading, chorus, computers, dance, drama, ethnic, film, gay, honors, international, literary magazine, musical theater, newspaper, political, professional, religious, social, social service, special interest, student government, and Student Organization Executive Board. Popular campus events include Orientation, Latin Culture Month, and Black History Month.

Sports: There are 2 intercollegiate sports for men and 2 for women, and 22 intramural sports for men and 22 for women. Facilities include a 1500-seat gym, racquetball courts, an outdoor volleyball court, a running track, a weight room, and a total fitness center.

Disabled Students: All of the campus is accessible. Wheelchair ramps, elevators, special parking, specially equipped rest rooms, special class scheduling, lowered drinking fountains, and lowered telephones are available. There are electric door openers on all but one student building.

Services: Counseling and information services are available, as is tutoring in most subjects. There is a reader service for the blind, and remedial math, reading, and writing.

Campus Safety and Security: Measures include 24-hour foot and vehicle patrol, self-defense education, security escort services, and informal discussions. There are pamphlets/posters/films, emergency telephones, lighted pathways/sidewalks, and student patrols.

Programs of Study: Purdue Cal confers B.A., B.S., B.A.B., B.S.A., B.S.Chm., B.S.E., and B.S.I.M. degrees. Associate and master's degrees are also awarded. Bachelor's degrees are awarded in BIOLOGICAL SCIENCE (biology/biological science, biotechnology, and microbiology), BUSINESS (accounting, banking and finance, business economics, hotel/motel and restaurant management, and marketing/retailing/merchandising), COMMUNICATIONS AND THE ARTS (broadcasting, communications, English, English literature, French, German, public relations, and Spanish), COMPUTER AND PHYSICAL SCIENCE (chemistry, computer programming, computer science, information sciences and systems, mathematics, and physics), EDUCATION (early childhood, elementary, foreign languages, science, and secondary), ENGINEERING AND ENVIRONMENTAL DESIGN (computer engineering, computer graphics, computer technology, construction technology, electrical/electronics engineering, electrical/electronics engineering technology, engineering, engineering technology, industrial engineering technology, mechanical engineering, and mechanical engineering technology), HEALTH PROFESSIONS (medical laboratory technology, nursing, optometry, and physical therapy), SOCIAL SCIENCE (criminal justice, history, philosophy, political science/government, psychology, and sociology). Education, nursing, and foreign language are the strongest academically. Management, behavioral sciences, and manufacturing engineering are the largest.

Required: Graduation requirements vary depending on the program. The total number of credit hours required for a degree varies from 126 to 136, with 24 to 73 in the major. All students must take English composition and 36 hours of general education courses and maintain a C average.

Special: Some cooperative programs, internships, and work-study programs are available to students. Purdue Cal offers cross-registration in philosophy, study in Spain, and credit for military experience, as well as non-degree study and pass/fail options. There are 7 national honor societies and a freshman honors program. All departments have honors programs.

Faculty/Classroom: 51% of faculty are male; 49%, female. The average class size in an introductory lecture is 26; in a laboratory, 16; and in a regular course, 21.

Requirements: The SAT or ACT is required. The ACT Optional Writing test is also required. In addition, the SAT Subject Test in math is required. Applicants must be graduates of an accredited secondary school. The GED is accepted. 33 Carnegie units are required for admission. Required courses vary, depending on the curriculum, and include 3 or 4 years of English, 2 or 3 years of math, 2 years of foreign language, and 1 year of history or social studies. Purdue Cal requires applicants to be in the upper 66% of their class. A GPA of 2.0 is required. AP and CLEP credits are accepted. Important factors in the admissions decision are recommendations by school officials, advanced placement or honor courses, and personality/intangible qualities.

Procedure: Freshmen are admitted to all sessions. Entrance exams should be taken any time during junior and senior years in high school. There are early admissions, deferred admissions and rolling admissions plans. Notification is sent on rolling basis. Applications are accepted online. There are August 15 and January 1 application deadlines for remedial programs. Acceptance letters are mailed upon admission.

Transfer: Applicants must have a minimum GPA of 2.0 for transfer credit. 32 of 126 to 136 credits required for the bachelor's degree must be completed at Purdue Cal.

Visiting: There are regularly scheduled orientations for prospective students. There are guides for informal visits and visitors may sit in on classes at the instructor's discretion. To schedule a visit, contact the Office of Admissions and Recruitment at (219) 989-2289 or *adms@calumet.purdue.edu*.

Financial Aid: In 2005-2006, 61% of all full-time freshmen and 62% of continuing full-time students received some form of financial aid. 52% of full-time freshmen and 57% of continuing full-time students received need-based aid. The average freshman award was $3409. Need-based scholarships or need-based grants averaged $2246 ($5065 maximum); need-based self-help aid (loans and jobs) averaged $2099 ($5173 maximum); non-need-based athletic scholarships averaged $1929 ($3000 maximum); and other non-need-based awards and non-need-based scholarships averaged $2248 ($9661 maximum). 6% of undergraduates work part time. Average annual earnings from campus work are $3723. The average financial indebtedness of the 2005 graduate was $14,820. Purdue Cal is a member of CSS. The priority date for freshman financial aid applications for fall entry is March 10.

International Students: There are 112 international students enrolled. The school actively recruits these students. They must take the TOEFL or the MELAB. International students can take the SAT in place of the TOEFL.

Computers: Wireless access is available. All students may access the system. There are no time limits and no fees.

Graduates: From July 1, 2004 to June 30, 2005, 773 bachelor's degrees were awarded. The most popular majors were management (19%), behavioral sciences (16%), and computer information systems and information technology (8%). In an average class, 3% graduate in 4 years or less, 11% graduate in 5 years, and 8% graduate in 6 years. Of the 2004 graduating class, 52% were enrolled in graduate school within 6 months of graduation and 14% were employed.

Admissions Contact: Paul McGuinness, Admissions Director. E-mail: *adms.@calumet.purdue.edu* Web: *www.calumet.purdue.edu*

PURDUE UNIVERSITY/WEST LAFAYETTE   B-3

West Lafayette, IN 47907   (765) 494-1776; Fax: (765) 494-0544

Full-time: 17,383 men, 11,813 women	**Faculty:** 1911; I, av$
Part-time: 867 men, 812 women	**Ph.D.s:** 99%
Graduate: 4564 men, 3273 women	**Student/Faculty:** 15 to 1
Year: semesters, summer session	**Tuition:** $6458 ($19,824)
Application Deadline: open	**Room & Board:** $7000
Freshman Class: 24,052 applied, 20,430 accepted, 7191 enrolled	
SAT Verbal/Math: 557/593*	**ACT:** 25 **VERY COMPETITIVE**

Purdue University, founded in 1869, is a publicly supported institution offering degree programs with an emphasis on engineering, business, communications, arts, and social sciences. There are 12 undergraduate schools and 1 graduate school. In addition to regional accreditation, Purdue has baccalaureate program accreditation with AACSB, ABET, ACCE, ACPE, ADA, ASLA, NCATE, NLN, and SAF. The 15 libraries contain 2,459,943 volumes, 3,183,942 microform items, and 3756 audio/video tapes/CDs/DVDs, and subscribe to 20,829 periodicals including electronic. Computerized library services include the card catalog, interlibrary loans, database searching, and Internet access. Special learning facilities include a learning resource center, art gallery, and radio station. The 2307-acre campus is in a suburban area 65 miles northwest of Indianapolis. Including any residence halls, there are 377 buildings.

Student Life: 67% of undergraduates are from Indiana. Others are from 50 states, 126 foreign countries, and Canada. 76% are white; 13% foreign nationals. 79% claim no religious affiliation; 10% Protestant; 7% Catholic. The average age of freshmen is 18; all undergraduates, 21. 16% do not continue beyond their first year; 68% remain to graduate.

Housing: 11,523 students can be accommodated in college housing, which includes single-sex and coed dorms, on-campus apartments, married-student housing, fraternity houses, and sorority houses. There are also 3 floors in a women's hall for women in engineering or women in science, and other floors for living and learning communities. On-campus housing is available on a first-come, first-served basis. 64% of students commute. Alcohol is not permitted. Upperclassmen may keep cars.

Activities: 17% of men belong to 1 local and 49 national fraternities; 17% of women belong to 3 local and 26 national sororities. There are 730 groups on campus, including band, cheerleading, chess, choir, chorale, chorus, computers, dance, debate, drama, ethnic, gay, honors, international, jazz band, literary magazine, marching band, newspaper, orchestra, pep band, photography, political, professional, radio and TV, religious, social, social service, student government, symphony, and yearbook. Popular campus events include Grand Prix Race, Old Masters, and Gala week.

Sports: There are 10 intercollegiate sports for men and 10 for women, and 27 intramural sports for men and 26 for women. Facilities include a 14,000-seat arena, a 62,000-seat stadium, an intercollegiate athletic facility, a recreational gym, a field house, an athletic center, intramural playing fields, 2 golf courses, and baseball, softball, track, and women's soccer fields.

Disabled Students: 90% of the campus is accessible. Wheelchair ramps, elevators, special parking, specially equipped rest rooms, special class scheduling, lowered drinking fountains, lowered telephones, and a lab with assistive technology and special computers are available.

Services: Counseling and information services are available, as is tutoring in every subject. There is a reader service for the blind, and remedial math, reading, and writing.

Campus Safety and Security: Measures include 24-hour foot and vehicle patrol, self-defense education, security escort services, and shuttle buses. There are informal discussions, pamphlets/posters/films, emergency telephones, lighted pathways/sidewalks, and public transportation routes throughout campus.

Programs of Study: Purdue confers B.A., B.S., B.P.E, B.S.A.A.E., B.S.A.B.E., B.S.C.E., B.S.C.E.M., B.S.Ch., B.S.Ch.E., B.S.C.M.P.E., B.S.E., B.S.E.E., B.S.E.H., B.S.I.E., B.S.I.E.D., B.S.I.M., B.S.L.A., B.S.L.S.E., B.S.M.E., B.S.M.S.E., and B.S.N.E. degrees. Associate, master's, and doctoral degrees are also awarded. Bachelor's degrees are awarded in AGRICULTURE (agricultural business management, agricultural economics, agricultural mechanics, agriculture, agronomy, animal science, conservation and regulation, fishing and fisheries, forestry and related sciences, horticulture, natural resource management, plant protection (pest management), plant science, soil science, wildlife management, and wood science), BIOLOGICAL SCIENCE (biochemistry, biology/biological science, cell biology, ecology, entomology, nutrition, and plant genetics), BUSINESS (accounting, hospitality management services, hotel/motel and restaurant management, management science, marketing management, office supervision and management, operations research, organizational behavior, recreation and leisure services, and retailing), COMMUNICATIONS AND THE ARTS (apparel design, art history and appreciation, classics, communications, comparative literature, crafts, creative writing, design, dramatic arts, English, film arts, fine arts, French, German, graphic design, industrial design, Japanese, journalism, languages, Latin, linguistics, media arts, photography, public relations, Russian, Spanish, telecommunications, and theater design), COMPUTER AND PHYSICAL SCIENCE (actuarial science, applied mathematics, applied physics, atmospheric sciences and meteorology, chemistry, computer science, earth science, geology, information sciences and systems, mathematics, natural sciences, physics, science, and statistics), EDUCATION (agricultural, art, athletic training, early childhood, educational media, elementary, English, foreign languages, health, industrial arts, mathematics, physical, science, secondary, social studies, and special), ENGINEERING AND ENVIRONMENTAL DESIGN (aeronautical engineering, aeronautical technology, agricultural engineering, architectural engineering, aviation administration/management, aviation computer technology, biomedical engineering, chemical engineering, civil engineering, computer engineering, computer graphics, computer technology, construction engineering, construction technology, electrical/electronics engineering, electrical/electronics engineering technology, engineering, geological engineering, graphic arts technology, industrial administration/management, industrial engineering, industrial engineering technology, interior design, landscape architecture/design, materials engineering, mechanical engineering, mechanical engineering technology, nuclear engineering, occupational safety and health, ocean engineering, preengineering, surveying engineering, systems engineering, and transportation engineering), HEALTH PROFESSIONS (community health work, environmental health science, exercise science, health science, medical technology, nursing, pharmacy, predentistry, premedicine, prepharmacy, preveterinary science, radiological science, speech pathology/audiology, and veterinary science), SOCIAL SCIENCE (African American studies, American studies, anthropology, Asian/American studies, child care/child and family studies, consumer services, dietetics, economics, family and community services, food production/management/services, food science, history, interdisciplinary studies, Italian studies, Judaic studies, law, liberal arts/general studies, medieval studies, philosophy, political science/government, prelaw, psychology, religion, sociology, urban studies, and women's studies). Mechanical and civil engineering, management, psychology, and elementary education are the strongest academically and the largest.

Required: To graduate, students must complete approximately 128 hours and earn a minimum GPA of 2.0. In most majors, students must take courses in English, math, science, computer science, and social sciences.

Special: Cooperative programs are available in engineering, technology, agriculture, science, and consumer and family sciences. Cross-registration with Purdue's regional campuses, numerous internships, study abroad in 46 countries, dual majors, student-designed majors, nondegree study, and pass/fail options are also offered. There are 14 national honor societies, including Phi Beta Kappa, a freshman honors program, and 10 departmental honors programs.

Faculty/Classroom: 71% of faculty are male; 29%, female. The average class size in an introductory lecture is 50; in a laboratory, 22; and in a regular course, 30.

Admissions: 85% of the 2005-2006 applicants were accepted. The SAT scores for the 2005-2006 freshman class were: Verbal--27% below 500, 47% between 500 and 599, 22% between 600 and 700, and 4% above 700; Math--17% below 500, 40% between 500 and 599, 33% between 600 and 700, and 10% above 700. The ACT scores were 12% below 21, 22% between 21 and 23, 29% between 24 and 26, 17% between 27 and 28, and 20% above 28. 50% of the current freshmen were in the top fifth of their class; 82% were in the top two fifths. There were 86 National Merit finalists. 240 freshmen graduated first in their class.

Requirements: The SAT or ACT is required. In addition, Purdue recommends that most students have 15 semester credits, including 4 years of English, 3 to 4 of math, 2 to 4 of lab science, and 4 semesters of a foreign language. The GED is accepted. AP and CLEP credits are accepted. Important factors in the admissions decision are advanced placement or honor courses, recommendations by school officials, and parents or siblings attending the school.

Procedure: Freshmen are admitted to all sessions. Entrance exams should be taken at the end of the junior year. Application deadlines are open. There is a rolling admissions plan. Application fee is $30. Applications are accepted on-line.

Transfer: 1726 transfer students enrolled in 2004-2005. Transfer students must file a regular application at least 30 days before the start of the semester and submit SAT/ACT results and high school and college transcripts. Students must be in good academic standing and meet the same subject-matter requirements as a beginning student. A minimum 2.2 GPA is required; many programs require a higher average, and some have subject requirements. 32 of 128 credits required for the bachelor's degree must be completed at Purdue.

Visiting: There are regularly scheduled orientations for prospective students, including fall and spring preview days, which consist of admission, financial aid, housing, and school sessions, a campus tour, and dorm visits. The Summer Visit Program consists of a counselor's orientation and campus and residence hall visits. There are guides for informal visits and visitors may sit in on classes. To schedule a visit, contact the Office of Admissions at *admissions@purdue.edu.*

Financial Aid: In 2005-2006, at least 44% of all full-time freshmen and 40% of continuing full-time students received some form of financial aid. At least 36% of all full-time students received need-based aid. The average freshman award was $9990. Need-based scholarships or need-based grants averaged $8946; need-based self-help aid (loans and jobs) averaged $3208; institutional non-need-based athletic scholarships averaged $17,039; and other institutional non-need-based awards and non-need-based scholarships averaged $12,724. 12% of undergraduates work part time. Average annual earnings from campus work are $859. The average financial indebtedness of the 2005 graduate was $17,510. The FAFSA is required. The deadline for filing freshman financial aid applications for fall entry is March 1.

International Students: There are 1746 international students enrolled. The school actively recruits these students. They must take the TOEFL.

Computers: Wireless access is available. All students may access the system 24 hours daily. There are no time limits and no fees.

Graduates: From July 1, 2004 to June 30, 2005, 6197 bachelor's degrees were awarded. The most popular majors were management (7%), mechanical engineering (4%), and psychology (4%). In an average class, 4% graduate in 3 years or less, 36% graduate in 4 years or less, 62% graduate in 5 years or less, and 68% graduate in 6 years or less. 545 companies recruited on campus in 2004-2005.

Admissions Contact: Dr. Douglas L. Christiansen, Director, Admissions. E-mail: *admissions@purdue.edu* Web: *www.purdue.edu/*

ROSE-HULMAN INSTITUTE OF TECHNOLOGY   B-4

Terre Haute, IN 47803

(812) 877-1511
(800) 248-7448; Fax: (812) 877-8941

Full-time: 1439 men, 326 women	**Faculty:** 148; IIB, +$
Part-time: 3 men	**Ph.Ds:** 100%
Graduate: 99 men, 12 women	**Student/Faculty:** 12 to 1
Year: quarters, summer session	**Tuition:** $27,138
Application Deadline: March 1	**Room & Board:** $7419
Freshman Class: n/av	
SAT Verbal/Math: 630/680*	**ACT:** 29

HIGHLY COMPETITIVE+

Rose-Hulman Institute of Technology, founded in 1874, is a private college emphasizing engineering, science, and math. In addition to regional accreditation, Rose-Hulman has baccalaureate program accreditation with ABET. The library contains 79,060 volumes, 532 microform items, and 711 audio/video tapes/CDs/DVDs, and subscribes to 33,335 periodicals including electronic. Computerized library services include the card catalog, interlibrary loans, database searching, and Internet access. Special learning facilities include a learning resource center, art gallery, planetarium, and radio station. The 200-acre campus is in a suburban area on the east side of Terre Haute. Including any residence halls, there are 35 buildings.

Student Life: 56% of undergraduates are from out of state, mostly the Midwest. Students are from 50 states and 18 foreign countries. 82% are from public schools. 91% are white. The average age of freshmen is 18; all undergraduates, 20. 8% do not continue beyond their first year; 81% remain to graduate.

Housing: 1099 students can be accommodated in college housing, which includes single-sex and coed dorms, on-campus apartments, fraternity houses, and sophomore residence halls. On-campus housing is guaranteed for the freshman year only, is available on a first-come, first-served basis, and is available on a lottery system for upperclassmen. 60% of students live on campus; of those, 60% remain on campus on weekends. All students may keep cars.

Activities: 37% of men belong to 8 national fraternities; 43% of women belong to 2 national sororities. There are 60 groups on campus, including band, cheerleading, chess, chorale, chorus, computers, dance, debate, drama, drill team, ethnic, gay, honors, international, jazz band, literary magazine, musical theater, newspaper, pep band, photography, political, professional, radio and TV, religious, social, social service, and student government. Popular campus events include art shows, concerts, and plays.

Sports: There are 12 intercollegiate sports for men and 11 for women, and 14 intramural sports for men and 14 for women. Facilities include a field house, a recreational center, a swimming pool, tennis courts, and intramural fields.

Disabled Students: 95% of the campus is accessible. Wheelchair ramps, elevators, special parking, specially equipped rest rooms, special class scheduling, and lowered drinking fountains are available.

Services: Counseling and information services are available, as is tutoring in most subjects.

Campus Safety and Security: Measures include 24-hour foot and vehicle patrol, security escort services, informal discussions, and pamphlets/posters/films. There are emergency telephones, lighted pathways/sidewalks, medical transports, and free traffic assistance.

Programs of Study: Rose-Hulman confers the B.S. degree. Master's degrees are also awarded. Bachelor's degrees are awarded in BIOLOGI-

CAL SCIENCE (biology/biological science), COMPUTER AND PHYSICAL SCIENCE (chemistry, computer science, mathematics, physics, and software engineering), ENGINEERING AND ENVIRONMENTAL DESIGN (biomedical engineering, chemical engineering, civil engineering, computer engineering, electrical/electronics engineering, engineering physics, mechanical engineering, and optical engineering), SOCIAL SCIENCE (economics). Engineering, science, and mathematics are the strongest academically. Mechanical engineering, chemical engineering, and electrical engineering are the largest.

Required: All students must complete at least 192 to 195 quarter hours with a minimum GPA of 2.0 and 36 hours in the humanities and social sciences. Freshmen are required to take math, biology, chemistry, or physics. The total number of hours required in the major varies.

Special: The Institute offers co-op programs, independent study, cross-registration with Indiana State University and Saint Mary-of-the-Woods College, summer industrial internships, study abroad in 8 countries, and dual majors. Pass/fail options also are available. There are 10 national honor societies and 6 departmental honors programs.

Faculty/Classroom: 82% of faculty are male; 18%, female. All teach undergraduates and 20% do research. No introductory courses are taught by graduate students. The average class size in an introductory lecture is 19; in a laboratory, 20; and in a regular course, 20.

Admissions: 69% of the 2005-2006 applicants were accepted. The SAT scores for the 2005-2006 freshman class were: Verbal--2% below 500, 33% between 500 and 599, 52% between 600 and 700, and 13% above 700; Math--10% between 500 and 599, 55% between 600 and 700, and 35% above 700. The ACT scores were 1% below 21, 5% between 21 and 23, 18% between 24 and 26, 20% between 27 and 28, and 56% above 28. 87% of the current freshmen were in the top fifth of their class; 99% were in the top two fifths. There were 17 National Merit finalists. 34 freshmen graduated first in their class.

Requirements: The SAT or ACT is required. In addition, candidates should have at least 16 units of credit, including 4 in English, 2 in social sciences, and 1 each in math, chemistry, physics, and electives. An essay and interview are recommended. Rose-Hulman requires applicants to be in the upper 25% of their class. AP credits are accepted. Important factors in the admissions decision are advanced placement or honor courses, recommendations by school officials, and extracurricular activities record.

Procedure: Freshmen are admitted in the fall. Entrance exams should be taken in the fall of the senior year or spring of the junior year. Applications should be filed by March 1 for fall entry, along with a $40 fee. There is a rolling admissions plan. Notification is sent on a rolling basis. Applications are accepted on-line.

Transfer: 21 transfer students enrolled in 2004-2005. Applicants need 1 year each of calculus, physics, and chemistry and a minimum GPA of 3.0. An interview is recommended. 60 of 192 to 195 quarter hours required for the bachelor's degree must be completed at Rose-Hulman.

Visiting: There are regularly scheduled orientations for prospective students, including interviews, campus tours, and academic meetings. There are guides for informal visits and visitors may sit in on classes and stay overnight. To schedule a visit, contact the Admissions Office at (812) 877-8213 or admis.ofc@rose-hulman.edu.

Financial Aid: In 2005-2006, 98% of all full-time students received some form of financial aid. 71% of full-time freshmen and 65% of continuing full-time students received need-based aid. The average freshman award was $20,504. Need-based scholarships or need-based grants averaged $15,271 ($40,187 maximum); need-based self-help aid (loans and jobs) averaged $10,582 ($33,887 maximum); and other non-need-based awards and non-need-based scholarships averaged $9127 ($34,688 maximum). 65% of undergraduates work part time. Average annual earnings from campus work are $1569. The average financial indebtedness of the 2005 graduate was $33,105. Rose-Hulman is a member of CSS. The FAFSA is required. The priority date for freshman financial aid applications for fall entry is March 1.

International Students: There are 25 international students enrolled. The school actively recruits these students. They must take the TOEFL and also take the SAT or the ACT.

Computers: Wireless access is available. Three is ubiquitous access with more than 8000 wired ports, including all classrooms, 2 ports per pillow in residence halls, and wireless 802.11 a/b/g throughout the academic complex. Free public printers are located throughout campus. All students may access the system. There are no time limits and no fees. All students must purchase a school-selected laptop as a condition of registration. A Dell Precision Workstation M70 is recommended.

Graduates: From July 1, 2004 to June 30, 2005, 368 bachelor's degrees were awarded. The most popular majors were mechanical engineering (31%), chemical engineering (15%), and electrical engineering (14%). In an average class, 1% graduate in 3 years or less, 74% graduate in 4 years or less, 81% graduate in 5 years or less, and 82% graduate in 6 years or less. 218 companies recruited on campus in 2004-2005. Of the 2004 graduating class, 19% were enrolled in graduate school within 6 months of graduation and 98% were employed.

Admissions Contact: James Goecker, Dean of Admissions and Financial Aid. E-mail: admis.ofc@rose-hulman.edu
Web: www.rose-hulman.edu

SAINT JOSEPH'S COLLEGE — B-2
Rensselaer, IN 47978

(219) 866-6170
(800) 447-8781; Fax: (219) 866-6122

Full-time: 366 men, 520 women	**Faculty:** 56; IIB, --$
Part-time: 15 men, 102 women	**Ph.D.s:** 79%
Graduate: none	**Student/Faculty:** 16 to 1
Year: semesters, summer session	**Tuition:** $20,120
Application Deadline: open	**Room & Board:** $6480
Freshman Class: 1363 applied, 1061 accepted, 233 enrolled	
SAT Verbal/Math: 499/498*	**ACT:** 22 **COMPETITIVE**

St. Joseph's College, founded in 1889, is a private Catholic institution providing a liberal arts core curriculum with an interdisciplinary approach and practical, career-oriented experiences. In addition to regional accreditation, SJC has baccalaureate program accreditation with NCATE. The library contains 156,044 volumes, 69,864 microform items, and 22,906 audio/video tapes/CDs/DVDs, and subscribes to 399 periodicals including electronic. Computerized library services include the card catalog, interlibrary loans, database searching, Internet access, and laptop Internet portals. Special learning facilities include a learning resource center, radio station, and TV station. The 180-acre campus is in a small town 80 miles south of Chicago and 90 miles north of Indianapolis. Including any residence halls, there are 26 buildings.

Student Life: 71% of undergraduates are from Indiana. Others are from 19 states, 4 foreign countries, and Canada. 87% are white. 46% are Catholic; 38% Protestant; 11% claim no religious affiliation. The average age of freshmen is 19; all undergraduates, 22. 29% do not continue beyond their first year; 54% remain to graduate.

Housing: 806 students can be accommodated in college housing, which includes single-sex and coed dorms, on-campus apartments housing for nontraditional or adult students, and special interest floors. On-campus housing is guaranteed for all 4 years. 68% of students live on campus; of those, 70% remain on campus on weekends. All students may keep cars.

Activities: There are no fraternities or sororities. There are 41 groups on campus, including art, band, cheerleading, chess, choir, chorale, chorus, computers, dance, debate, drama, ethnic, film, forensics, honors, jazz band, literary magazine, marching band, musical theater, newspaper, orchestra, pep band, photography, political, professional, radio and TV, religious, social, social service, and student government. Popular campus events include the Little 500 Go-Kart Race and Little Siblings Weekend.

Sports: There are 9 intercollegiate sports for men and 9 for women, and 6 intramural sports for men and 6 for women. Facilities include a field house, a 2500-seat gym, a recreation center, a baseball complex, a lighted soccer field, a football facility, and a lake with a sand beach.

Disabled Students: 74% of the campus is accessible. Wheelchair ramps, elevators, special parking, specially equipped rest rooms, special class scheduling, lowered drinking fountains, and lowered telephones are available.

Services: Counseling and information services are available, as is tutoring in every subject. There is a reader service for the blind, and remedial math, reading, and writing.

Campus Safety and Security: Measures include 24-hour foot and vehicle patrol, security escort services, informal discussions, and pamphlets/posters/films. There are lighted pathways/sidewalks.

Programs of Study: SJC confers B.A., B.S., and B.S.N. degrees. Associate and master's degrees are also awarded. Bachelor's degrees are awarded in BIOLOGICAL SCIENCE (biology/biological science), BUSINESS (accounting, business administration and management, and management information systems), COMMUNICATIONS AND THE ARTS (art, creative writing, dramatic arts, English, journalism, music, and music business management), COMPUTER AND PHYSICAL SCIENCE (chemistry, computer science, and mathematics), EDUCATION (art, elementary, middle school, music, physical, and secondary), HEALTH PROFESSIONS (medical technology, nursing, predentistry, and premedicine), SOCIAL SCIENCE (criminal justice, economics, history, international studies, ministries, philosophy, political science/government, prelaw, psychology, religion, social work, and sociology). Accounting, biology-chemistry, and education are the strongest academically. Business administration, education, and nursing, are the largest.

Required: Students must complete 45 hours in the general education program and 36 hours in the major. A total of 120 credit hours with a minimum GPA of 2.0 is required to graduate.

Special: Cross-registration with Saint Elizabeth's School of Nursing is offered. Internships in all fields, a Washington semester, accelerated degree programs, and study abroad throughout Europe and Latin America are available. Dual majors are offered in biology/chemistry, management/information systems, and math/computer science. Credit for life, military, and work experience, nondegree study, student-designed majors, and pass/fail options are offered. The core program consists of lectures and discussions over a 4-year period. There are 4 national honor societies and a freshman honors program.

Faculty/Classroom: 58% of faculty are male; 42%, female. All teach undergraduates. The average class size in an introductory lecture is 16; in a laboratory, 18; and in a regular course, 14.

Admissions: 78% of the 2005-2006 applicants were accepted. The SAT scores for the 2005-2006 freshman class were: Verbal--49% below 500, 37% between 500 and 599, 13% between 600 and 700, and 1% above 700; Math--48% below 500, 43% between 500 and 599, and 9% between 600 and 700. The ACT scores were 35% below 21, 36% between 21 and 23, 13% between 24 and 26, 14% between 27 and 28, and 2% above 28. 30% of the current freshmen were in the top fifth of their class; 61% were in the top two fifths. 3 freshmen graduated first in their class.

Requirements: The SAT or ACT is required, with satisfactory scores. Applicants should be graduates of an accredited secondary school or have earned the GED. They should have completed 15 academic credits, 10 of which must be from the following academic fields: English, foreign language, social studies, math, and natural sciences. An interview is recommended. AP and CLEP credits are accepted. Important factors in the admissions decision are advanced placement or honor courses, recommendations by school officials, and recommendations by alumni.

Procedure: Freshmen are admitted fall and winter. Entrance exams should be taken by January of the senior year. There is a deferred admissions plan and a rolling admissions plan. Notification is sent beginning December 15. Application deadlines are open. Application fee is $25. Applications are accepted on-line.

Transfer: 34 transfer students enrolled in 2004-2005. Applicants must have a GPA of 2.0 and satisfactory SAT or ACT scores. Grades of C or better transfer for credit. 30 of 120 credits required for the bachelor's degree must be completed at SJC.

Visiting: There are regularly scheduled orientations for prospective students, consisting of Discover Days, Special Interest Days, early registration, and freshman orientation. There are guides for informal visits and visitors may sit in on classes and stay overnight. To schedule a visit, contact the Admissions Office at *admissions@saintjoe.edu*.

Financial Aid: In 2005-2006, 97% of all full time students received some form of financial aid. 84% of full-time freshmen and 80% of continuing full-time students received need-based aid. The average freshman award was $17,314, with $5367 ($28,350 maximum) from need-based scholarships or grants, $1212 ($28,350 maximum) from need-based self-help aid (loans and jobs), $2251 ($26,440 maximum) from non-need-based athletic scholarships, $6233 ($28,350 maximum) from other non-need based awards and non-need based scholarships, and $2251 from non-need self-help awards. 33% of undergraduates work part time. Average annual earnings from campus work are $1500. The average financial indebtedness of the 2005 graduate was $23,417. SJC is a member of CSS. The FAFSA and combined admission and financial aid applications are required. The deadline for filing freshman financial aid applications for fall entry is March 1.

International Students: There are 9 international students enrolled. They must take TOEFL.

Computers: Wireless access is available. 69 computers are available for student use in 4 labs. All buildings on campus are connected to the campus network with Internet access. Each dorm room has Internet access and the majority have wireless capability. 2 main academic facilities are equipped for a wireless network. All students may access labs from 8 A.M. to midnight Monday through Thursday, Friday 8 A.M., to 4 P.M., and Sunday 1 P.M. to 10 P.M.; Saturday access is in the library only, or by special request. Dorm room access is 24 hours/day. There are no time limits and no fees.

Graduates: From July 1, 2004 to June 30, 2005, 167 bachelor's degrees were awarded. The most popular majors were business (20%), education (16%), and criminal justice (7%). In an average class, 49% graduate in 4 years or less, 54% graduate in 5 years or less, and 55% graduate in 6 years or less. 31 companies recruited on campus in 2004-2005. Of the 2004 graduating class, 14% were enrolled in graduate school within 6 months of graduation and 98% were employed.

Admissions Contact: Karen Raftus, Director of Admissions.
E-mail: *admissions@saintjoe.edu* Web: *www.saintjoe.edu*

SAINT MARY-OF-THE-WOODS COLLEGE   B-4

St. Mary-of-the-Woods, IN 47876   (812) 535-5106
                                        (800) 926-SMWC; Fax: (812) 535-4900

Full-time: 1 man, 509 women	**Faculty:** IIB, --$
Part-time: 21 men, 1095 women	**Ph.D.s:** 70%
Graduate: 17 men, 114 women	**Student/Faculty:** n/av
Year: varies by program, summer session	**Tuition:** $18,660
	Room & Board: $6820
Application Deadline: July 15	
Freshman Class: n/av	
SAT Verbal/Math: 516/499*	**ACT:** 21 **COMPETITIVE**

Saint Mary-of-the-Woods, founded in 1840, is a private, liberal arts women's college affiliated with the Roman Catholic Church. In addition to regional accreditation, The Woods has baccalaureate program accreditation with NASM and NCATE. The library contains 142,000 volumes and 1676 microform items, and subscribes to 460 periodicals including electronic. Computerized library services include the card catalog, interlibrary loans, database searching, and Internet access. Special learning facilities include a learning resource center and art gallery. The 200-acre campus is in a rural area 5 miles northwest of Terre Haute. Including any residence halls, there are 10 buildings.

Student Life: 80% of undergraduates are from Indiana. Others are from 50 states, 5 foreign countries, and Canada. 80% are from public schools. 92% are white. The average age of freshmen is 18; all undergraduates, 32. 27% do not continue beyond their first year; 61% remain to graduate.

Housing: 500 students can be accommodated in college housing, which includes single-sex dorms. Housing for student mothers with young children is available. On-campus housing is guaranteed for all 4 years. 80% of students live on campus; of those, 75% remain on campus on weekends. Alcohol is not permitted. All students may keep cars.

Activities: There are no fraternities. There are 30 groups on campus, including band, chorale, chorus, computers, dance, drama, ethnic, honors, international, jazz band, literary magazine, musical theater, orchestra, professional, religious, social, social service, and student government. Popular campus events include Ring Day and Pops Concert.

Sports: Facilities include stables, an athletic field, a gym, tennis and volleyball courts, a pool, a weight room, a fitness course, and soccer fields.

Disabled Students: All of the campus is accessible. Wheelchair ramps, elevators, special parking, specially equipped rest rooms, and special class scheduling are available.

Services: Counseling and information services are available, as is tutoring in every subject. There is remedial math and writing.

Campus Safety and Security: Measures include 24-hour foot and vehicle patrol, self-defense education, informal discussions, and pamphlets/posters/films. There are emergency telephones and lighted pathways/sidewalks.

Programs of Study: The Woods confers B.A. and B.S. degrees. Associate and master's degrees are also awarded. Bachelor's degrees are awarded in AGRICULTURE (equine science), BIOLOGICAL SCIENCE (biology/biological science), BUSINESS (accounting, business administration and management, electronic business, human resources, and marketing/retailing/merchandising), COMMUNICATIONS AND THE ARTS (English, fine arts, French, graphic design, journalism, languages, music, photography, and Spanish), COMPUTER AND PHYSICAL SCIENCE (computer science, information sciences and systems, and mathematics), EDUCATION (art, early childhood, elementary, foreign languages, middle school, music, science, secondary, and special), HEALTH PROFESSIONS (medical technology, music therapy, predentistry, premedicine, and preveterinary science), SOCIAL SCIENCE (gerontology, history, human services, humanities, international studies, liberal arts/general studies, paralegal studies, political science/government, prelaw, psychology, religious education, social science, social work, and theological studies). Education, biology/preprofessional, and equine studies are the strongest academically. Education and business are the largest.

Required: All students must complete a 54 to 56 credit-hour general studies curriculum, which includes a freshman course in lifelong learning; courses in writing, speech, phys ed, computer science, and math; selected courses in religion, fine arts, philosophy, science, and social sciences; and 3 capstone interdisciplinary integrative courses. Completion of 125 credit hours with a minimum GPA of 2.0 is necessary for graduation. A minimum of 42 hours is required in the major.

Special: The college offers cross-registration with Indiana State University and Rose-Hulman Institute of Technology, student-designed majors, study abroad in Spain, Taiwan, and the U.K., a B.A.-B.S. degree, dual majors, internships, pass/fail options, on-campus work-study, an accelerated degree, and nondegree study. The Woods' External Degree program, offering more than 20 majors, provides educational opportunities to students who study mostly at home.

Faculty/Classroom: 10% of faculty are male; 90%, female. 95% teach undergraduates, 3% do research, and 3% do both. No introductory

courses are taught by graduate students. The average class size in an introductory lecture is 15; in a laboratory, 15; and in a regular course, 12.

Admissions: 56% of the 2005-2006 applicants were accepted. 40% of the current freshmen were in the top fifth of their class; 55% were in the top two fifths.

Requirements: The SAT or ACT is required. In addition, candidates should be graduates of an accredited secondary school. The GED is accepted. Documents needed for acceptance include an application for admission, letter of recommendation, and a high school transcript. Students should have completed 4 years of English, 3 years each of social sciences, lab science, and math (algebra 1, algebra 2, and geometry), and 2 years of a foreign language. The Woods requires applicants to be in the upper 50% of their class. A GPA of 2.5 is required.

Procedure: Freshmen are admitted fall and winter. Entrance exams should be taken in the fall semester of the senior year. There is a rolling admissions plan. Applications should be filed by July 15 for fall entry and December 1 for spring entry. Notification is sent on a rolling basis. The fall 2005 application fee was $30.

Transfer: 9 transfer students enrolled in 2004-2005. Transfer students should be in good academic standing at their most recent institution with a minimum GPA of 2.0. 30 of 125 credits required for the bachelor's degree must be completed at The Woods.

Visiting: There are regularly scheduled orientations for prospective students, including a campus tour, class visit, and meetings with faculty, financial aid, and admissions staff. There are guides for informal visits and visitors may sit in on classes and stay overnight. To schedule a visit, contact the Office of Admissions at *admissions@smwc.edu*.

Financial Aid: In 2005-2006, 92% of all full-time freshmen and 75% of continuing full-time students received some form of financial aid. 66% of full-time freshmen and 60% of continuing full-time students received need-based aid. The average freshman award was $10,000. 70% of undergraduates work part time. The average financial indebtedness of the 2005 graduate was $16,000. The FAFSA is required.

International Students: There were 5 international students enrolled in a recent year. The school actively recruits these students. They must take the TOEFL. The SAT or ACT is recommended if English is the Student's first language.

Computers: Wireless access is available. Several labs across campus contain more than 90 machines. All students may access the system during posted lab hours, or access can be made by PCs at any time. There are no time limits and no fees.

Graduates: In a recent year, 145 bachelor's degrees were awarded. The most popular majors were elementary education (12%), psychology (10%), and business administration (8%). In an average class, 53% graduate in 4 years or less, 60% graduate in 5 years or less, and 61% graduate in 6 years or less.

Admissions Contact: Theresa Denton, Director of Admission. A video is available. E-mail: *smwcadms@smwc.edu* Web: *www.smwc.edu*

SAINT MARY'S COLLEGE   C-1

Notre Dame, IN 46556

	(574) 284-4587
	(800) 551-7621; Fax: (574) 284-4716
Full-time: 1366 women	Faculty: 125; IIB, av$
Part-time: 1 man, 30 women	Ph.D.s: 77%
Graduate: none	Student/Faculty: 11 to 1
Year: semesters, summer session	Tuition: $24,358
Application Deadline: March 1	Room & Board: $8180
Freshman Class: 997 applied, 807 accepted, 377 enrolled	
SAT Verbal/Math: 570/570*	ACT: 25 VERY COMPETITIVE

Saint Mary's College, established in 1844, was founded and sponsored by the Congregation of the Sisters of the Holy Cross. It is a Catholic comprehensive college for women in the liberal arts tradition. In addition to regional accreditation, Saint Mary's has baccalaureate program accreditation with CSWE, NASAD, NASM, NCATE, and NLN. The library contains 228,012 volumes, 14,920 microform items, and 2641 audio/video tapes/CDs/DVDs, and subscribes to 634 periodicals including electronic. Computerized library services include the card catalog, interlibrary loans, database searching, Internet access, and laptop Internet portals. Special learning facilities include an art gallery and TV station. The 275-acre campus is in a suburban area 90 miles east of Chicago, in Notre Dame, Indiana. Including any residence halls, there are 18 buildings.

Student Life: 70% of undergraduates are from out of state, mostly the Midwest. Students are from 45 states and 9 foreign countries. 54% are from public schools. 91% are white. 82% are Catholic; 14% Protestant. The average age of freshmen is 18; all undergraduates, 20. 13% do not continue beyond their first year; 74% remain to graduate.

Housing: 1575 students can be accommodated in college housing, which includes single-sex dorms and on-campus apartments. In addition, there is an independent living residence floor for seniors and a multicultural living floor. On-campus housing is guaranteed for all 4 years and is available on a first-come, first-served basis. 84% of students live on

campus; of those, 80% remain on campus on weekends. All students may keep cars.

Activities: There are no fraternities. There are 101 groups on campus, including art, band, cheerleading, choir, chorale, chorus, dance, drama, drill team, ethnic, gay, honors, international, jazz band, literary magazine, marching band, musical theater, newspaper, orchestra, pep band, political, professional, radio and TV, religious, social, social service, and student government. Popular campus events include Fall Festival, winter carnival, and spring celebration.

Sports: Facilities include an athletic facility, outdoor tennis and volleyball courts, a soccer field, a softball field, and a swimming pool.

Disabled Students: 99% of the campus is accessible. Wheelchair ramps, elevators, special parking, specially equipped rest rooms, and lowered drinking fountains are available.

Services: Counseling and information services are available, as is tutoring in most subjects. A writing center is also available.

Campus Safety and Security: Measures include 24-hour foot and vehicle patrol, self-defense education, security escort services, and shuttle buses. There are informal discussions, pamphlets/posters/films, emergency telephones, lighted pathways/sidewalks, key cards for residence hall entry, and underground tunnels connecting buildings.

Programs of Study: Saint Mary's confers B.A., B.S., B.B.A., B.F.A., and B.Mus. degrees. Bachelor's degrees are awarded in BIOLOGICAL SCIENCE (biology/biological science), BUSINESS (accounting, business administration and management, and management information systems), COMMUNICATIONS AND THE ARTS (art, communications, dramatic arts, English, fine arts, French, music, and Spanish), COMPUTER AND PHYSICAL SCIENCE (chemistry and mathematics), EDUCATION (elementary), HEALTH PROFESSIONS (nursing), SOCIAL SCIENCE (economics, history, humanities, philosophy, political science/government, psychology, religion, social work, and sociology). Art, business, and English are the strongest academically. Business, education, and communications are the largest.

Required: Students must successfully complete 128 credits, with at least 24 in the major, and must maintain a minimum GPA of 2.0. Students must also complete distribution requirements in fine arts, history, language, literature, math, philosophy, science, religion, and other selected disciplines. Advanced proficiency in composition within the student's major must also be demonstrated, and a comprehensive exam in the major area is required by the end of the senior year.

Special: Cross-registration is permitted with the University of Notre Dame and a consortium of 6 northern Indiana colleges. Opportunities are provided for internships, a Washington semester, an accelerated degree program in nursing, dual and student-designed majors, a 3-2 engineering degree with the University of Notre Dame, nondegree study, pass/fail options, and study abroad in 20 countries. There are 9 national honor societies.

Faculty/Classroom: 36% of faculty are male; 64%, female. All teach undergraduates. The average class size in an introductory lecture is 17; in a laboratory, 13; and in a regular course, 14.

Admissions: 81% of the 2005-2006 applicants were accepted. The SAT scores for the 2005-2006 freshman class were: Verbal--15% below 500, 47% between 500 and 599, 32% between 600 and 700, and 6% above 700; Math--15% below 500, 52% between 500 and 599, 32% between 600 and 700, and 2% above 700. The ACT scores were 7% below 21, 28% between 21 and 23, 34% between 24 and 26, 19% between 27 and 28, and 12% above 28. 41% of the current freshmen were in the top fifth of their class; 62% were in the top two fifths. 18 freshmen graduated first in their class.

Requirements: The SAT or ACT is required. In addition, SAT: Subject tests are required in writing, math, and foreign language. The ACT writing test is required if the SAT's are not taken. Graduation from an accredited secondary school is required; a GED will be accepted. Applicants must have completed 16 academic credits, including 4 in English, 3 in math, 2 in a foreign language, 2 in history or social studies, 1 in science, and the remainder from college preparatory electives in the above areas. An essay is required. AP and CLEP credits are accepted. Important factors in the admissions decision are advanced placement or honor courses, evidence of special talent, and recommendations by school officials.

Procedure: Freshmen are admitted fall and spring. Entrance exams should be taken between March of the junior year and December of the senior year. There are early decision, deferred admissions and rolling admissions plans. Early decision applications should be filed by November 15; regular applications, by March 1 for fall entry and November 15 for spring entry, along with a $30 fee. Notification of early decision is sent December 15; regular decision, on a rolling basis. 87 early decision candidates were accepted for the 2005-2006 class. Applications are accepted on-line.

Transfer: 40 transfer students enrolled in 2004-2005. Students must submit a transcript from high school and each previous college attended, along with an essay, a recommendation from a college adviser, and SAT or ACT test scores if the student has fewer than 30 semester hours of transferable credit. All transfer applicants must have maintained a minimum GPA of 3.0. An interview is recommended. 60 of 128 credits required for the bachelor's degree must be completed at Saint Mary's.

Visiting: There are regularly scheduled orientations for prospective students, including campus tours and visits with admissions and financial aid counselors and faculty and athletic staff. There are guides for informal visits and visitors may sit in on classes and stay overnight. To schedule a visit, contact the Campus Visit Coordinator.

Financial Aid: In 2005-2006, 89% of all full-time freshmen and 60% of continuing full-time students received some form of financial aid. 80% of full-time freshmen and 77% of continuing full-time students received need-based aid. Need-based scholarships or need-based grants averaged $9557; need-based self-help aid (loans and jobs) averaged $4236; and other non-need-based awards and non-need-based scholarships averaged $8055. 45% of undergraduates work part time. Average annual earnings from campus work are $1800. The average financial indebtedness of the 2005 graduate was $24,617. The CSS/Profile or FAFSA is required. The deadline for filing freshman financial aid applications for fall entry is March 1.

International Students: There are 11 international students enrolled. The school actively recruits these students. They must take the TOEFL and also take the SAT or the ACT.

Computers: Wireless access is available. All students may access the system 24 hours a day, 7 days a week. There are no time limits and no fees. It is strongly recommended that all students have a personal computer.

Graduates: From July 1, 2004 to June 30, 2005, 376 bachelor's degrees were awarded. The most popular majors were elementary education (15%), communications (11%), and business administration (10%). In an average class, 69% graduate in 4 years or less, and 74% graduate in 5 years or less. 36 companies recruited on campus in 2004-2005. Of the 2004 graduating class, 44% were enrolled in graduate school within 6 months of graduation and 79% were employed.

Admissions Contact: Mona Bowe, Director of Admission. A video is available. E-mail: *admission@saintmarys.edu*
Web: *www.saintmarys.edu*

TAYLOR UNIVERSITY — D-3
Upland, IN 46989-1001

(765) 998-5134
(800) 882-3456; Fax: (765) 998-4925

Full-time: 805 men, 991 women	**Faculty:** 128; IIB, --$
Part-time: 32 men, 25 women	**Ph.D.s:** 73%
Graduate: 7 men, 7 women	**Student/Faculty:** 14 to 1
Year: 4-1-4, summer session	**Tuition:** $20,746
Application Deadline: January 15	**Room & Board:** $5630
Freshman Class: 1402 applied, 1237 accepted, 461 enrolled	
SAT Verbal/Math: 590/610*	**ACT:** 26 **VERY COMPETITIVE+**

Taylor University, founded in 1846, is a private Christian interdenominational liberal arts institution. In addition to regional accreditation, Taylor has baccalaureate program accreditation with CSWE, NASM, and NCATE. The library contains 186,441 volumes, 10,915 microform items, and 8398 audio/video tapes/CDs/DVDs, and subscribes to 13,000 periodicals including electronic. Computerized library services include the card catalog, interlibrary loans, database searching, and Internet access. Special learning facilities include a learning resource center, art gallery, radio station, TV station, a 65-acre arboretum, C. S. Lewis Collection, and an observatory. The 250-acre campus is in a rural area 70 miles north of Indianapolis. Including any residence halls, there are 32 buildings.

Student Life: 67% of undergraduates are from out of state, mostly the Midwest. Students are from 46 states, 22 foreign countries, and Canada. 79% are from public schools. 93% are white. Most are Protestant. The average age of freshmen is 19; all undergraduates, 20. 12% do not continue beyond their first year; 80% remain to graduate.

Housing: 1520 students can be accommodated in college housing, which includes single-sex dorm, off-campus apartments, and married-student housing. On-campus housing is guaranteed for all 4 years. 97% of students live on campus; of those, 90% remain on campus on weekends. Alcohol is not permitted. All students may keep cars.

Activities: There are no fraternities or sororities. There are 100 groups on campus, including art, band, choir, chorale, chorus, computers, drama, ethnic, film, honors, international, jazz band, literary magazine, musical theater, newspaper, opera, orchestra, pep band, photography, political, professional, radio and TV, religious, social, social service, student government, and symphony. Popular campus events include Taylathon, Youth Conference, and Spiritual Renewal and Emphasis Weeks.

Sports: There are 8 intercollegiate sports for men and 7 for women, and 14 intramural sports for men and 14 for women. Facilities include a gym, a field house, a wellness center, tennis and racquetball courts, an indoor and outdoor track, and a lake for swimming and ice skating.

Disabled Students: 65% of the campus is accessible. Wheelchair ramps, elevators, special parking, specially equipped rest rooms, special class scheduling, lowered drinking fountains, and lowered telephones are available.

Services: Counseling and information services are available, as is tutoring in most subjects. There is a reader service for the blind, and remedial math, reading, and writing.

Campus Safety and Security: Measures include 24-hour foot and vehicle patrol, self-defense education, security escort services, and informal discussions. There are pamphlets/posters/films and lighted pathways/sidewalks.

Programs of Study: Taylor confers B.A., B.S., and B.Mus. degrees. Associate and master's degrees are also awarded. Bachelor's degrees are awarded in BIOLOGICAL SCIENCE (biology/biological science and environmental biology), BUSINESS (accounting, banking and finance, international business management, management information systems, management science, marketing and distribution, recreation and leisure services, and sports management), COMMUNICATIONS AND THE ARTS (art, communications, dramatic arts, English, French, journalism, music, Spanish, and visual and performing arts), COMPUTER AND PHYSICAL SCIENCE (chemistry, computer science, environmental geology, mathematics, natural sciences, and physics), EDUCATION (art, Christian, early childhood, elementary, English, foreign languages, mathematics, music, physical, science, and social studies), ENGINEERING AND ENVIRONMENTAL DESIGN (computer engineering, computer graphics, engineering physics, environmental engineering, and environmental science), HEALTH PROFESSIONS (exercise science and health science, and premedicine), SOCIAL SCIENCE (biblical studies, economics, geography, history, international studies, philosophy, political science/government, psychology, social work, and sociology). Computer science, environmental science, and engineering physics are the strongest academically. Business, education, and premedicine are the largest.

Required: Students must complete at least 128 total hours, of which at least 42 must be upper division. To graduate, students must have a minimum cumulative GPA of 2.0, a 2.3 GPA in all majors and minors and must demonstrate proficiencies in writing, math, and reading. Students must also complete a senior paper, exam, or project in their major(s). Students must complete general education requirements that include courses in Bible, religion, philosophy, phys. ed., speech, expository writing, fine arts, computer science, literature, science, history, math, social science, and a course designated as cross-cultural. The bachelor of arts degree requires the equivalent of 2 years of 1 foreign language. Most bachelor of science degrees must be combined with curriculum requirements in systems or education.

Special: Opportunities are provided for internships, cooperative programs, a Washington semester, study abroad in 12 countries, work-study programs, dual majors, student-designed majors, B.A.-B.S. degrees, and a 3-2 engineering degree. There is cross-registration with the other members of the Council for Christian Colleges and Universities and the Christian College Consortium. There are 7 national honor societies, including Phi Beta Kappa, a freshman honors program, and 19 departmental honors programs.

Faculty/Classroom: 74% of faculty are male; 26%, female. All teach undergraduates. The average class size in an introductory lecture is 35; in a laboratory, 12; and in a regular course, 20.

Admissions: 88% of the 2005-2006 applicants were accepted. The SAT scores for the 2005-2006 freshman class were: Verbal--10% below 500, 41% between 500 and 599, 35% between 600 and 700, and 14% above 700; Math--11% below 500, 34% between 500 and 599, 39% between 600 and 700, and 16% above 700. The ACT scores were 9% below 21, 16% between 21 and 23, 26% between 24 and 26, 23% between 27 and 28, and 25% above 28. 60% of the current freshmen were in the top fifth of their class; 85% were in the top two fifths. There were 4 National Merit finalists. 21 freshmen graduated first in their class.

Requirements: The SAT or ACT is required. In addition, graduation from an accredited secondary school is required; a GED will be accepted. It is recommended that applicants complete 4 years of English, 3 to 4 each of math and lab science, 2 each of social studies and a foreign language, and course work in computing, typing/keyboarding, and the arts. An interview is recommended for all students, and an audition is required for music majors. Taylor requires applicants to be in the upper 40% of their class. A GPA of 2.8 is required. AP and CLEP credits are accepted. Important factors in the admissions decision are recommendations by school officials, extracurricular activities record, and leadership record.

Procedure: Freshmen are admitted fall and spring. Entrance exams should be taken during the spring of the junior year or fall of the senior year. There are early admissions and deferred admissions plans. Early admissions applications should be filed by November 1; regular applications, by January 15 for fall entry, along with a $25 fee. Notification is sent February 5. 91 applicants were on the 2005 waiting list; 31 were admitted. Applications are accepted on-line.

Transfer: 46 transfer students enrolled in 2004-2005. Applicants must have maintained a minimum GPA of 2.5 and have completed at least 12 credit hours at the previous college. An interview is recommended. 48 of 128 credits required for the bachelor's degree must be completed at Taylor.

Visiting: There are regularly scheduled orientations for prospective students, including a campus tour, lunch, class meetings, faculty meetings, a financial aid session, and an admissions interview. There are guides for informal visits and visitors may sit in on classes and stay overnight. To schedule a visit, contact Kathy Thornburg, the Campus Visit Coordinator at *admissions_uataylor.edu*.

Financial Aid: In 2005-2006, 89% of all full-time freshmen and 87% of continuing full-time students received some form of financial aid. 58% of full-time freshmen and 56% of continuing full-time students received need-based aid. The average freshman award was $13,164, with $3343 (15,390 maximum) from need-based scholarships or grants $2718 ($6025 maximum) from need-based self-help aid (loans and jobs) $596 ($20,520 maximum) from non-need-based athletic scholarships, $4566 ($28,776 maximum) from other non-need-based awards and non-need-based scholarships and $1941(28,776 maximum) from other non-based student loan. 28% of undergraduates work part time. Average annual earnings from campus work are $1135. The average financial indebtedness of the 2005 graduate was $17,910. Taylor is a member of CSS. The FAFSA is required. The deadline for filing freshman financial aid applications for fall entry is March 10.

International Students: There are 30 international students enrolled. The school actively recruits these students. They must take the TOEFL and also take the SAT or ACT. The school will accept the TOEFL in lieu of the SAT or the ACT.

Computers: All students may access the system. There are no time limits and no fees. It is strongly recommended that all students have a personal computer.

Graduates: From July 1, 2004 to June 30, 2005, 429 bachelor's degrees were awarded. The most popular majors were business (10%), psychology (7%), and education (6%). In an average class, 2% graduate in 3 years or less, 72% graduate in 4 years or less, 76% graduate in 5 years or less, and 77% graduate in 6 years or less. 86 companies recruited on campus in 2004-2005. Of the 2004 graduating class, 16% were enrolled in graduate school within 6 months of graduation and 77% were employed.

Admissions Contact: Stephen Mortland, Director of Admissions. E-mail: *admissions_u@tayloru.edu* Web: *www.tayloru.edu*

TRI-STATE UNIVERSITY-MAIN CAMPUS   D-1

Angola, IN 46703

(260) 665-4365
(800) 347-4878; Fax: (260) 665-4578

Full-time: 701 men, 299 women	**Faculty:** IIB, --$
Part-time: 65 men, 103 women	**Ph.D.s:** 71%
Graduate: 2 men, 2 women	**Student/Faculty:** n/av
Year: semesters, summer session	**Tuition:** $20,200
Application Deadline: June 1	**Room & Board:** $6000
Freshman Class: n/av	
SAT Verbal/Math: n/av	**ACT:** n/av **COMPETITIVE**

Tri-State University, founded in 1884, is a private, independent university with 45 schools: Allen School of Engineering and Technology, Ketner School of Business, School of Education, School of Arts and Sciences, and the School of Professional Studies. There are 5 undergraduate schools and 1 graduate school. In addition to regional accreditation, Tri-State has baccalaureate program accreditation with ABET. The library contains 141,543 volumes, 15,439 microform items, and 6087 audio/video tapes/CDs/DVDs, and subscribes to 162 periodicals including electronic. Computerized library services include the card catalog, interlibrary loans, database searching, Internet access, and laptop Internet portals. Special learning facilities include a learning resource center, radio station, and an 18-hole golf course. The 400-acre campus is in a small town 30 miles north of Ft. Wayne. Including any residence halls, there are 25 buildings.

Student Life: 60% of undergraduates are from Indiana. Others are from 23 states and 13 foreign countries. 80% are from public schools. 87% are white. The average age of freshmen is 19; all undergraduates, 22. 25% do not continue beyond their first year; 51% remain to graduate.

Housing: 649 students can be accommodated in college housing, which includes coed dormitories and on-campus apartments. In addition, there are honors houses. On-campus housing is guaranteed for all 4 years. 53% of students commute. Alcohol is not permitted. All students may keep cars.

Activities: 25% of men belong to 8 national fraternities; 15% of women belong to 6 local sororities. There are 35 groups on campus, including cheerleading, choir, computers, drama, ethnic, honors, international, newspaper, pep band, professional, radio and TV, religious, social service, student government, and yearbook.

Sports: There are 9 intercollegiate sports for men and 8 for women, and 6 intramural sports for men and 5 for women. Facilities include a gym with indoor and outdoor tracks, basketball and racquetball courts, an 18-hole golf course, tennis court, and a football stadium.

Disabled Students: 98% of the campus is accessible. Wheelchair ramps, elevators, special parking, specially equipped rest rooms, special class scheduling, lowered drinking fountains, lowered telephones, and special housing are available.

Services: Counseling and information services are available, as is tutoring in some subjects, including math, business, engineering, accounting, and English. There is remedial math.

Campus Safety and Security: Measures include pamphlets/posters/films, emergency telephones, and lighted pathways/sidewalks.

Programs of Study: Tri-State confers B.A. and B.S. degrees. Associate and master's degrees are also awarded. Bachelor's degrees are awarded in BIOLOGICAL SCIENCE (biology/biological science), BUSINESS (accounting, banking and finance, business administration and management, management information systems, management science, marketing/retailing/merchandising, recreation and leisure services, recreational facilities management, and sports management), COMMUNICATIONS AND THE ARTS (communications), COMPUTER AND PHYSICAL SCIENCE (chemistry, computer science, information sciences and systems, mathematics, and physical sciences), EDUCATION (elementary, English, mathematics, physical, science, secondary, and social science), ENGINEERING AND ENVIRONMENTAL DESIGN (chemical engineering, civil engineering, computer engineering, drafting and design technology, electrical/electronics engineering, engineering management, environmental science, industrial administration/management, and mechanical engineering), HEALTH PROFESSIONS (premedicine), SOCIAL SCIENCE (criminal justice, forensic studies, psychology, and social science). Engineering, math/computer science, and science are the strongest academically. Engineering, arts sciences, and business are the largest.

Required: Candidates for graduation must complete 120 to 132 semester hours, satisfying general education, program, and major requirements and maintaining a minimum overall GPA of 2.0. Required courses vary by degree sought. All students must complete a general education curriculum including science, math, American studies, social science, global studies, English composition, humanistics, computer literacy, and oral communication course work. Some majors have senior design projects. The number of hours in the major varies from 40 to 60.

Special: Cooperative education programs are available in engineering, business, and computer science. Opportunities exist for internships and work-study programs with the university and many companies. There are 12 national honor societies and a freshman honors program.

Faculty/Classroom: 75% of faculty are male; 25%, female. All teach undergraduates and 10% both teach and do research. No introductory courses are taught by graduate students. The average class size in an introductory lecture is 30; in a laboratory, 16; and in a regular course, 18.

Admissions: 36% of the current freshmen were in the top fifth of their class; 64% were in the top two fifths. 5 freshmen graduated first in their class.

Requirements: The SAT or ACT is required. In addition, candidates for admission should be graduates of accredited secondary schools. The GED is accepted. Most students should have 4 years of English and 3 years each of science, social studies, and math. Tri-State requires applicants to be in the upper 50% of their class. A GPA of 2.0 is required. AP and CLEP credits are accepted. Important factors in the admissions decision are advanced placement or honor courses, recommendations by school officials, and leadership record.

Procedure: Freshmen are admitted to all sessions. Entrance exams should be taken in the junior or senior year. There are deferred admissions and rolling admissions plans. Early decision applications should be filed by March 1; regular applications, by June 1 for fall entry. Notification is sent on a rolling basis. Applications are accepted on-line.

Transfer: 45 transfer students enrolled in 2004-2005. In addition to meeting the university's requirements for freshmen, applicants must have satisfactory records from previous institutions. 30 of 120 to 132 credits required for the bachelor's degree must be completed at Tri-State.

Visiting: There are regularly scheduled orientations for prospective students, including meetings with faculty, administrators, financial aid personnel, and a coach (if the student is an athlete), and a campus tour. There are guides for informal visits and visitors may sit in on classes and stay overnight. To schedule a visit, contact the Admissions Office at (260) 665-4132.

Financial Aid: 48% of undergraduates work part time. Average annual earnings from campus work are $500. The FAFSA is required.

International Students: There are 13 international students enrolled. The school actively recruits these students. They must score satisfactorily on the written TOEFL and also take the MELAB, or the Comprehensive English Language Test, or the college's own test Applicants not transferring credits in math or English must be tested in those subjects.

Computers: Wireless access is available. There are more than 150 Pcs across campus in labs and the library as well as wireless access in several locations. All residence halls have a computer connection for each student. The library catalog is on-line and also has many full-text resources. All students may access the system. There are no time limits and no fees.

Graduates: From July 1, 2004 to June 30, 2005, 212 bachelor's degrees were awarded. The most popular majors were engineering (38%), education (17%), and business (16%). In an average class, 35% graduate in 4 years or less, 45% graduate in 5 years or less, and 51% graduate in 6 years or less. 25 companies recruited on campus in 2004-2005. Of the 2004 graduating class, 20% were enrolled in graduate school within 6 months of graduation and 85% were employed.

Admissions Contact: Scott Goplin, Dean of Admission.
E-mail: *admit@tristate.edu* Web: *www.tristate.edu*

UNIVERSITY OF EVANSVILLE — A-5
Evansville, IN 47722

(812) 488-2468
(800) 423-8633; Fax: (812) 474-4076

Full-time: 926 men, 1507 women	Faculty: 177; IIA, -$
Part-time: 59 men, 60 women	Ph.D.s: 87%
Graduate: 24 men, 45 women	Student/Faculty: 14 to 1
Year: semesters, summer session	Tuition: $21,660
Application Deadline: February 1	Room & Board: $6660
Freshman Class: 2583 applied, 2339 accepted, 670 enrolled	
SAT Verbal/Math: 580/570*	ACT: 25 VERY COMPETITIVE

The University of Evansville, founded in 1854, is a private institution affiliated with the United Methodist Church. The university offers undergraduate degree programs in arts and sciences, business administration, education, and health sciences, and engineering and computer sciences. There are 4 undergraduate and 3 graduate schools. In addition to regional accreditation, UE has baccalaureate program accreditation with ABET, APTA, CAAHEP, NASM, NCATE, and NLN. The library contains 286,163 volumes, 468,108 microform items, and 11,395 audio/video tapes/CDs/DVDs, and subscribes to 970 periodicals including electronic. Computerized library services include interlibrary loans, database searching, Internet access, and laptop Internet portals. Special learning facilities include a learning resource center, art gallery, and radio station. The 75-acre campus is in an urban area 120 miles west of Louisville. Including any residence halls, there are 40 buildings.

Student Life: 60% of undergraduates are from Indiana. Others are from 41 states, 42 foreign countries, and Canada. 71% are white. 65% of students that declared a religion are Protestant; 41% claim no religious affiliation; 32% Catholic. The average age of freshmen is 18; all undergraduates, 20. 19% do not continue beyond their first year; 60% remain to graduate.

Housing: 1862 students can be accommodated in college housing, which includes single-sex and coed dorms, on-campus apartments, off-campus apartments, and fraternity houses. In addition, there are honors houses, special-interest houses, and a international house. On-campus housing is available on a first-come, first-served basis and is available on a lottery system for upperclassmen. Priority is given to out-of-town students. 71% of students live on campus; of those, 85% remain on campus on weekends. Alcohol is not permitted. All students may keep cars.

Activities: 22% of men belong to 6 national fraternities; 23% of women belong to 4 national sororities. There are 146 groups on campus, including art, band, cheerleading, choir, chorale, chorus, computers, dance, drama, drill team, ethnic, film, gay, honors, international, jazz band, literary magazine, musical theater, newspaper, opera, orchestra, pep band, photography, political, professional, radio and TV, religious, social, social service, student government, and yearbook. Popular campus events include Greek Week, Bike Race, and International Bazaar.

Sports: There are 6 intercollegiate sports for men and 8 for women, and 27 intramural sports for men and 27 for women. Facilities include a 12,000-seat basketball arena, 2500-seat soccer stadium, 600-seat softball stadium, 1200-seat baseball stadium, and a volleyball arena. The university fitness center includes a 25-meter pool, conditioning room, aerobics room, free weight room, and indoor track, outdoor tennis courts, a 1/2 mile security lighted jogging trail, and basketball, racquetball, and volleyball courts.

Disabled Students: 87% of the campus is accessible. Wheelchair ramps, elevators, special parking, and specially equipped rest rooms are available.

Services: Counseling and information services are available, as is tutoring in some subjects, including especially sciences and math; others by request. There is remedial writing.

Campus Safety and Security: Measures include 24-hour foot and vehicle patrol, self-defense education, security escort services, and informal discussions. There are pamphlets/posters/films, emergency telephones, and lighted pathways/sidewalks.

Programs of Study: UE confers B.A., B.S., B.F.A., B.L.S., and B.M. degrees. Associate and master's degrees are also awarded. Bachelor's degrees are awarded in BIOLOGICAL SCIENCE (biochemistry and biology/biological science), BUSINESS (accounting, banking and finance, business administration and management, international business management, marketing/retailing/merchandising, and sports management), COMMUNICATIONS AND THE ARTS (art, art history and appreciation, communications, creative writing, dramatic arts, French, German, graphic design, literature, music, music business management, music performance, Spanish, studio art, theater design, and theater management), COMPUTER AND PHYSICAL SCIENCE (applied mathematics, chemistry, computer science, mathematics, and physics), EDUCATION (art, athletic training, drama, elementary, English, foreign languages, mathematics, music, physical, science, social studies, and special), ENGINEERING AND ENVIRONMENTAL DESIGN (civil engineering, computer engineering, electrical/electronics engineering, engineering management,

environmental science, and mechanical engineering), HEALTH PROFESSIONS (exercise science, health care administration, music therapy, nursing, physical therapy, predentistry, premedicine, preoptometry, prepharmacy, preveterinary science, and sports medicine), SOCIAL SCIENCE (archeology, biblical studies, classical/ancient civilization, cognitive science, economics, history, interdisciplinary studies, international studies, liberal arts/general studies, philosophy, political science/government, prelaw, psychobiology, psychology, sociology, and theological studies). Theater, physical therapy, and engineering are the strongest academically. Elementary education, physical therapy, and theater are the largest.

Required: To graduate, students must complete at least 120 semester hours with a minimum 2.0 cumulative and in their major, generally with 36 to 40 hours in the major. All students must take a core of 6 hours each of world cultures and foreign language, 7 hours of natural sciences, 15 hours divided among the humanities, fine arts, and social sciences, 1 hour of health and wellness, and 3 hours each of math and senior seminar. 2 years of foreign language are required for the B.A. A demonstration of writing proficiency, a capstone course in the major, and a demonstration of foreign language proficiency are required for graduation.

Special: Students may study abroad at the University of Evansville British campus, Harlaxton College, and more than 100 other sites. There is also Italian archeological excavation program, a British Parliament internship, a U.S. Pentagon internship, an accelerated Bachelor of Liberal Studies degree combined bachelors/graduate degrees, cooperative education, distance learning, dual enrollment of high school students, ESL, and teacher certification, as well as exchange student, external degree, honors, and independent study programs, internships, and student-designed majors. There are 19 national honor societies, and a freshman honors program.

Faculty/Classroom: 67% of faculty are male; 33%, female. All teach undergraduates. No introductory courses are taught by graduate students.

Admissions: 91% of the 2005-2006 applicants were accepted. The SAT scores for the 2005-2006 freshman class were: Verbal--17% below 500, 40% between 500 and 599, 34% between 600 and 700, and 8% above 700; Math--20% below 500, 38% between 500 and 599, 35% between 600 and 700, and 7% above 700. The ACT scores were 14% below 21, 24% between 21 and 23, 25% between 24 and 26, 14% between 27 and 28, and 23% above 28. 56% of the current freshmen were in the top fifth of their class; 82% were in the top two fifths. There were 7 National Merit finalists and 9 semifinalists. 88 freshmen graduated first in their class.

Requirements: The SAT or ACT is required. The ACT Optional Writing test is also required. Applicants must be graduates of accredited secondary schools; applicants who have been home-schooled are also considered. The university requires completion of 4 years of college-preparatory English, 3 years of math (algebra I and II, geometry) 2 years of science (biology with a lab), and 1 year of history. Two years of a foreign language; trigonometry, pre-calculus, or calculus; and physics are recommended. An interview is recommended, but not required. A GPA of 3.0 is required. AP and CLEP credits are accepted. Important factors in the admissions decision are advanced placement or honor courses, leadership record, and recommendations by school officials.

Procedure: Freshmen are admitted fall and spring. Entrance exams should be taken by the junior year of high school. There is a deferred admissions plan, and a rolling admissions plan. Early decision applications should be filed by December 1; regular applications, by February 1 for fall entry, along with a $35 fee. Notification of early decision is sent December 15; regular decision, February 15. Applications are accepted online.

Transfer: 70 transfer students enrolled in 2004-2005. Applicants must have a minimum GPA of 2.0 in all previous college work. High transcripts are reviewed for strength of curriculum and acdemic performance. Comments from the Dean of Students Recommendation Form included with the application for admission are also considered. 63 of 120 credits required for the bachelor's degree must be completed at UE.

Visiting: There are regularly scheduled orientations for prospective students, campus tour, faculty academic sessions, financial aid and admission appointments, and study abroad and honors program sessions. There are guides for informal visits and visitors may sit in on classes and stay overnight. To schedule a visit, contact the Office of Admissions at (800) 423-8633, ext. 2468 or *admission@evansville.edu*.

Financial Aid: In 2005-2006, 99% of all full-time freshmen and 95% of continuing full-time students received some form of financial aid. 71% of full-time freshmen and 69% of continuing full-time students received need-based aid. The average freshman award was $17,147. Need-based scholarships or need-based grants averaged $6730 ($25,710 maximum); need-based self-help aid (loans and jobs) averaged $3900 ($7925 maximum); and non-need-based athletic scholarships averaged $17,700 ($28,900 maximum). 19% of undergraduates work part time. Average annual earnings from campus work are $1300. The average financial indebtedness of the 2005 graduate was $17,400. UE is a member of CSS.

The FAFSA is required. The deadline for filing freshman financial aid applications for fall entry is March 1.

International Students: There are 118 international students enrolled. The school actively recruits these students. They must score satisfactorily on the TOEFL and also take a writing placement test upon arrival at the university before registration for classes. The SAT or ACT is required if participating in NCAA Division I athletics.

Computers: Students access e-mail, daily university news, grades, and online class discussions using their personal account on the university intranet. They also preregister for classes online. There are 7 public computer labs, several departmental computer clusters, and a small computer lab in each of the residence halls. All classrooms are wired for computer and projection systems for instructional use. All students may access the system at any time. There are no time limits and no fees. It is strongly recommended that all students have a personal computer, especially students in engineering and computer science programs.

Graduates: From July 1, 2004 to June 30, 2005, 396 bachelor's degrees were awarded. The most popular majors were health professions and related sciences (14%), visual and performing arts (12%), and business/marketing (11%). In an average class, 45% graduate in 4 years or less, 59% graduate in 5 years or less, and 60% graduate in 6 years or less. 129 companies recruited on campus in 2004-2005. Of the 2004 graduating class, 18% were enrolled in graduate school within 6 months of graduation and 99% were employed.

Admissions Contact: Dr. Tom Bear, Vice President for Enrollment. A video is available. E-mail: *admission@evansville.edu* Web: *http://www.evansville.edu*

UNIVERSITY OF INDIANAPOLIS — C-3

Indianapolis, IN 46227-3697 (317) 788-3517
(800) 232-8634; Fax: (317) 788-3300

Full-time: 863 men, 1526 women	**Faculty:** 135; IIA, --$
Part-time: 217 men, 755 women	**Ph.Ds:** 74%
Graduate: 310 men, 791 women	**Student/Faculty:** 18 to 1
Year: semesters, summer session	**Tuition:** $18,080
Application Deadline: open	**Room & Board:** $7010
Freshman Class: 3519 applied, 2685 accepted, 727 enrolled	
SAT Verbal/Math: 510/510*	**ACT:** 22 **COMPETITIVE**

The University of Indianapolis, established in 1902, is a private liberal arts school affiliated with the United Methodist Church. It provides undergraduate and graduate studies with an emphasis on education, business, nursing, and arts and sciences. There are 7 undergraduate and 7 graduate schools. In addition to regional accreditation, U of I has baccalaureate program accreditation with ACBSP, APA, APTA, CSWE, NASAD, NASM, NCATE, and NLN. The library contains 182,000 volumes, 20,600 microform items, and 4056 audio/video tapes/CDs/DVDs, and subscribes to 972 periodicals including electronic. Computerized library services include the card catalog, interlibrary loans, database searching, Internet access, and laptop Internet portals. Special learning facilities include a learning resource center, art gallery, planetarium, radio station, and an archeology lab. The 65-acre campus is in a suburban area on the south side of Indianapolis. Including any residence halls, there are 30 buildings.

Student Life: 83% of undergraduates are from Indiana. Others are from 35 states, 38 foreign countries, and Canada. 80% are white; 11% African American. 55% are Protestant; 24% Catholic; 20% claim no religious affiliation. The average age of freshmen is 18; all undergraduates, 20. 26% do not continue beyond their first year; 53% remain to graduate.

Housing: 1214 students can be accommodated in college housing, which includes single-sex and coed dorms, on-campus apartments, off-campus apartments, and married-student housing. In addition, there are honors houses. On-campus housing is guaranteed for all 4 years. 51% of students live on campus. Alcohol is not permitted. All students may keep cars.

Activities: There are no fraternities or sororities. There are 45 groups on campus, including academic, art, cheerleading, chess, choir, chorale, chorus, computers, dance, debate, drama, ethnic, forensics, gay, honors, international, jazz band, literary magazine, musical theater, newspaper, orchestra, pep band, photography, political, professional, radio and TV, religious, social, social service, and student government. Popular campus events include winter and spring formals, Ceremony of the. Flags, and Midnight Breakfast.

Sports: There are 11 intercollegiate sports for men and 10 for women, and 7 intramural sports for men and 6 for women. Facilities include a health and fitness center with a 3500-seat gym, an Olympic-size swimming pool, racquetball courts, a weight room, and a dance studio.

Disabled Students: 90% of the campus is accessible. Wheelchair ramps, elevators, special parking, specially equipped rest rooms, special class scheduling, lowered drinking fountains, and lowered telephones are available.

Services: Counseling and information services are available, as is tutoring in every subject. There is remedial math and writing. There is a special learning disabled program.

Campus Safety and Security: Measures include 24-hour foot and vehicle patrol, self-defense education, security escort services, and emergency telephones. There are lighted pathways/sidewalks.

Programs of Study: U of I confers B.A., B.S., B.F.A., B.M., B.S.N., and B.S.W. degrees. Associate, master's, and doctoral degrees are also awarded. Bachelor's degrees are awarded in BIOLOGICAL SCIENCE (biology/biological science), BUSINESS (accounting, banking and finance, business administration and management, business communications, business economics, entrepreneurial studies, international business management, management information systems, marketing/retailing/merchandising, and sports management), COMMUNICATIONS AND THE ARTS (art, broadcasting, communications, dramatic arts, English, French, German, journalism, music, music performance, musical theater, public relations, Spanish, speech/debate/rhetoric, and studio art), COMPUTER AND PHYSICAL SCIENCE (chemistry, computer science, earth science, mathematics, and physics), EDUCATION (art, athletic training, business, drama, elementary, English, foreign languages, mathematics, middle school, music, physical, science, secondary, and social studies), ENGINEERING AND ENVIRONMENTAL DESIGN (commercial art, electrical/electronics engineering, environmental science, and mechanical engineering), HEALTH PROFESSIONS (art therapy, exercise science, medical laboratory technology, nursing, and respiratory therapy), SOCIAL SCIENCE (anthropology, archeology, corrections, economics, history, international relations, law enforcement and corrections, philosophy, political science/government, psychology, religion, social science, social work, sociology, and youth ministry). Education, nursing, and science (biology/chemistry) are the strongest academically. Business is the largest.

Required: All undergraduate students must complete at least 124 hours, including 24 hours or more in the major with a GPA of 2.0 or better. Requirements include a core curriculum in which 8 learning goals must be met. Students must also take a health and phys ed course and 1 spring term, and attend lecture/performance events. Specific courses include math, social inquiry, history, and cross-cultural understanding and global awareness.

Special: Cross-registration is offered in conjunction with 6 area colleges. Cooperative programs, internships, various work-study programs, study abroad, dual and student-designed majors, accelerated programs in liberal studies and organizational leadership, pass/fail options, and a 3-2 engineering degree with Indiana University-Purdue University at Indianapolis are available. A fleximester, which is a 3-week spring term, and 27-week summer sessions, are also offered. There are 14 national honor societies and a freshman honors program.

Faculty/Classroom: 45% of faculty are male; 55%, female. 93% teach undergraduates. No introductory courses are taught by graduate students. The average class size in an introductory lecture is 19; in a laboratory, 18; and in a regular course, 19.

Admissions: 76% of the 2005-2006 applicants were accepted. The SAT scores for the 2005-2006 freshman class were: Verbal--44% below 500, 39% between 500 and 599, 15% between 600 and 700, and 2% above 700; Math--40% below 500, 43% between 500 and 599, 16% between 600 and 700, and 1% above 700. The ACT scores were 42% below 21, 26% between 21 and 23, 15% between 24 and 26, 14% between 27 and 28, and 3% above 28. 42% of the current freshmen were in the top fifth of their class; 74% were in the top two fifths. 13 freshmen graduated first in their class.

Requirements: The SAT or ACT is required. In addition, each applicant should have at least 24 academic credits, including at least 12 units total from English and literature (not including speech), history, foreign language, math lab science, and social studies. The GED is accepted. An interview is recommended. U of I requires applicants to be in the upper 50% of their class. A GPA of 2.25 is required. AP and CLEP credits are accepted. Important factors in the admissions decision are recommendations by school officials, extracurricular activities record, and recommendations by alumni.

Procedure: Freshmen are admitted to all sessions. There is a deferred admissions plan and a rolling admissions plan. Application deadlines are open. Application fee is $20. 15 applicants were on the 2005 waiting list; 15 were admitted. Applications are accepted on-line.

Transfer: 120 transfer students enrolled in 2004-2005. No ACT or SAT is needed if applicants have a GPA of C and 20 semester hours of credit. 30 of 124 credits required for the bachelor's degree must be completed at U of I.

Visiting: There are regularly scheduled orientations for prospective students, including campus visits and tours. There are guides for informal visits and visitors may sit in on classes and stay overnight. To schedule a visit, contact the Admissions Office at (800) 232-8634, ext. 3526 or *Winslow@uindy.edu*.

Financial Aid: In 2005-2006, 82% of all full-time freshmen and 87% of continuing full-time students received some form of financial aid. 71% of full-time freshmen and 78% of continuing full-time students received need-based aid. The average freshman award was $15,940. Need-based

scholarships or need-based grants averaged $7850; need-based self-help aid (loans and jobs) averaged $3052; and non-need-based athletic scholarships averaged $9532. 50% of undergraduates work part time. Average annual earnings from campus work are $1400. The average financial indebtedness of the 2005 graduate was $24,650. U of I is a member of CSS. The FAFSA, the college's own financial statement, and parent and student tax returns are required. The deadline for filing freshman financial aid applications for fall entry is March 10.

International Students: There are 152 international students enrolled. The school actively recruits these students. They must take the TOEFL or the MELAB, IELTS or Cambridge Exam.

Computers: Wireless access is available. There are approximately 200 PCs located in 4 buildings for student use. Wireless service is available in academic buildings for anyone with a valid e-mail account. All students may access the system 7 days per week. There are no time limits and no fees.

Graduates: From July 1, 2004 to June 30, 2005, 454 bachelor's degrees were awarded. The most popular majors were business (25%), education (16%), and biology (13%). In an average class, 2% graduate in 3 years or less, 40% graduate in 4 years or less, 51% graduate in 5 years or less, and 53% graduate in 6 years or less. 180 companies recruited on campus in 2004-2005. Of the 2004 graduating class, 25% were enrolled in graduate school within 6 months of graduation and 81% were employed.

Admissions Contact: Ron Wilks, Director of Admissions. E-mail: *rwilks@uindy.edu* Web: *www.uindy.edu*

UNIVERSITY OF NOTRE DAME   C-1

Notre Dame, IN 46556   (574) 631-7505

Full-time: 4383 men, 3877 women	**Faculty:** I,
Part-time: 10 men, 5 women	**Ph.D.s:** n/av
Graduate: 1968 men, 1174 women	**Student/Faculty:** 11 to 1
Year: semesters, summer session	**Tuition:** $31,542
Application Deadline: December 31	**Room & Board:** $8010
Freshman Class: 11,317 applied, 3582 accepted, 1995 enrolled	
SAT Verbal/Math: 667/693*	**ACT:** 31 **MOST COMPETITIVE**

The University of Notre Dame, founded in 1842, is a private institution affiliated with the Roman Catholic Church offering undergraduate programs in architecture, arts and letters, business administration, engineering, and science. Some information in this profile is approximate. There are 5 undergraduate and 6 graduate schools. In addition to regional accreditation, Notre Dame has baccalaureate program accreditation with AACSB, ABET, and NAAB. The 8 libraries contain 2.7 million volumes, 2.1 million microform items, and 25,513 audio/video tapes/CDs/DVDs, and subscribe to 17,239 periodicals including electronic. Computerized library services include the card catalog, interlibrary loans, and database searching. Special learning facilities include a learning resource center, art gallery, radio station, and art museum. The 1250-acre campus is in a suburban area 90 miles east of Chicago. Including any residence halls, there are 175 buildings.

Student Life: 91% of undergraduates are from out of state, mostly the Midwest. Students are from 50 states, 100 foreign countries, and Canada. 48% are from public schools. 76% are white. 84% are Catholic; 9% Eastern religions (Eastern Islam, Eastern Orthodox); 7% Protestant. The average age of freshmen is 18; all undergraduates, 20. 3% do not continue beyond their first year; 95% remain to graduate.

Housing: 6255 students can be accommodated in college housing, which includes single-sex dorms. On-campus housing is guaranteed for the freshman year only and is available on a lottery system for upperclassmen. 81% of students live on campus; of those, 90% remain on campus on weekends. Upperclassmen may keep cars.

Activities: There are no fraternities or sororities. There are 264 groups on campus, including art, bagpipe band, band, cheerleading, chess, choir, chorale, chorus, computers, dance, debate, drama, ethnic, film, forensics, honors, international, jazz band, literary magazine, marching band, musical theater, newspaper, orchestra, pep band, photography, political, professional, radio, religious, social, social service, student government, symphony, and yearbook. Popular campus events include a spring festival, home football weekends, and the Collegiate Jazz Festival.

Sports: There are 13 intercollegiate sports for men and 13 for women, and 22 intramural sports for men and 22 for women. Facilities include an athletic and convocation center with an 11,500-seat basketball arena and a hockey arena, a tennis pavilion, a golf course, an indoor sports center, a recreational sports center, and an aquatic center. The campus football stadium seats 80,225. There are general-purpose playing fields, stadiums for track, lacrosse, and baseball, and soccer and softball fields.

Disabled Students: 85% of the campus is accessible. Wheelchair ramps, elevators, special parking, specially equipped rest rooms, special class scheduling, lowered drinking fountains, and lowered telephones are available.

Services: Counseling and information services are available, as is tutoring in most subjects. There is a reader service for the blind.

Campus Safety and Security: Measures include 24-hour foot and vehicle patrol, self-defense education, security escort services, and shuttle buses. There are informal discussions, pamphlets/posters/films, emergency telephones, and lighted pathways/sidewalks.

Programs of Study: Notre Dame confers B.A., B.S., B.Arch., B.B.A., AND B.F.A. degrees. Master's and doctoral degrees are also awarded. Bachelor's degrees are awarded in BIOLOGICAL SCIENCE (biochemistry and biology/biological science), BUSINESS (accounting, banking and finance, management information systems, management science, and marketing/retailing/merchandising), COMMUNICATIONS AND THE ARTS (art history and appreciation, Chinese, English, film arts, French, German, Greek, Italian, Japanese, Latin, music, romance languages and literature, Russian, Spanish, and studio art), COMPUTER AND PHYSICAL SCIENCE (applied physics, chemistry, computer science, mathematics, and physics), EDUCATION (science), ENGINEERING AND ENVIRONMENTAL DESIGN (aeronautical engineering, architecture, chemical engineering, civil engineering, computer engineering, electrical/electronics engineering, environmental engineering, environmental science, and mechanical engineering), HEALTH PROFESSIONS (predentistry and premedicine), SOCIAL SCIENCE (American studies, anthropology, classical/ancient civilization, economics, history, liberal arts/general studies, medieval studies, philosophy, political science/government, psychology, sociology, and theological studies). Engineering, theology, and business are the strongest academically. Political science, finance, and English are the largest.

Required: All students must complete courses in English, philosophy, science, history, theology, math, social science, and phys ed. A total of 125 semester hours with a minimum GPA of 2.0 is required to graduate.

Special: Cross-registration is offered with Saint Mary's College. Study abroad is possible in 20 countries. A 5-year arts and letters/engineering B.A.-B.S. degree is offered. There is a program of liberal studies, centered on the discussion of great books. Internships, an accelerated degree program, a Washington semester, dual majors, 3-2 engineering degrees, and pass/fail options are available. There are 9 national honor societies, including Phi Beta Kappa, and 2 departmental honors programs.

Admissions: 32% of the 2005-2006 applicants were accepted. The SAT scores for the 2005-2006 freshman class were: Verbal--12% between 500 and 599, 41% between 600 and 700, and 47% above 700; Math--6% between 500 and 599, 37% between 600 and 700, and 57% above 700. 97% of the current freshmen were in the top fifth of their class; All were in the top two fifths.

Requirements: The SAT or ACT is required. In addition, applicants should be graduates of an accredited secondary school with 16 Carnegie credits completed, including 4 years of English, 3 of math, and 2 each of science, foreign language, and history. The SAT: subject test in a foreign language is recommended. An essay is required. An audition or a portfolio is recommended for some majors. AP credits are accepted.

Procedure: Freshmen are admitted in the fall. Entrance exams should be taken by fall of the senior year. There is a deferred admissions plan. Early decision applications should be filed by November 1; regular applications, by December 31 for fall entry. Notification of early decision is sent December 15; regular decision, April 1. 787 applicants were on the 2005 waiting list; 98 were admitted. Applications are accepted on-line. The fall 2005 application fee was $50.

Transfer: 115 transfer students enrolled in 2004-2005. Applicants should have completed at least 27 semester hours of transferable credit and maintained a 3.0 GPA in all courses. Admission depends on openings in each undergraduate college. 60 of 125 credits required for the bachelor's degree must be completed at Notre Dame.

Visiting: There are regularly scheduled orientations for prospective students, including small group sessions for students, larger sessions for parents, and tours for all. Visitors may sit in on classes and stay overnight. To schedule a visit, contact the Admissions telephone receptionists.

Financial Aid: Notre Dame is a member of CSS. The CSS/Profile or FAFSA and federal income tax return are required. Check with the school for current application deadlines.

International Students: In a recent year, there were 302 international students enrolled. The school actively recruits these students. They must score satisfactory on the written TOEFL.

Computers: All students may access the system 24 hours a day. There are no time limits and no fees. It is strongly recommended that all students have a personal computer.

Graduates: In a recent year, 2094 bachelor's degrees were awarded. The most popular majors were finance (10%), government (9%), and accountancy (9%). In an average class, 88% graduate in 4 years or less, 94% graduate in 5 years or less, and 95% graduate in 6 years or less. 340 companies recruited on campus in a recent year. Of a recent graduating class, 66% were employed within 6 months of graduation.

Admissions Contact: Daniel J. Saracino, Assistant Provost for Enrollment. E-mail: *admissio.1@nd.edu* Web: *http://admissions.nd.edu*

UNIVERSITY OF SAINT FRANCIS
D-2
Fort Wayne, IN 46808

(260) 434-3178
(800) 729-4732; Fax: (260) 434-7590

Full-time: 415 men, 815 women	**Faculty:** 94
Part-time: 60 men, 325 women	**Ph.D.s:** 46%
Graduate: 60 men, 170 women	**Student/Faculty:** 13 to 1
Year: semesters, summer session	**Tuition:** $15,520
Application Deadline: open	**Room & Board:** $5500
Freshman Class: n/av	
SAT or ACT: required	COMPETITIVE

University of Saint Francis is a private Roman Catholic liberal arts college founded in 1890 by the sisters of Saint Francis. Figures in the above capsule are approximate. In addition to regional accreditation, USF has baccalaureate program accreditation with CAHEA, CSWE, NCATE, and NLN. The 2 libraries contain 85,544 volumes, 618,843 microform items, and 1487 audio/video tapes/CDs/DVDs, and subscribe to 520 periodicals including electronic. Computerized library services include the card catalog, interlibrary loans, database searching, and Internet access. Special learning facilities include a learning resource center, art gallery, and planetarium. The 75-acre campus is in an urban area on the west side of Fort Wayne. Including any residence halls, there are 21 buildings.

Student Life: 91% of undergraduates are from Indiana. Others are from 8 states and 3 foreign countries. 90% are white. 40% are Protestant; 30% claim no religious affiliation; 28% Catholic. The average age of freshmen is 24; all undergraduates, 25. 33% do not continue beyond their first year; 54% remain to graduate.

Housing: 240 students can be accommodated in college housing, which includes coed dormitories. On-campus housing is guaranteed for the freshman year only and is available on a first-come, first-served basis. 84% of students commute. Alcohol is not permitted. All students may keep cars.

Activities: There are no fraternities or sororities. There are 25 groups on campus, including art, cheerleading, choir, dance, drama, ethnic, film, honors, musical theater, newspaper, pep band, professional, radio and TV, religious, social, social service, and student government. Popular campus events include Little Regatta and Spring Fling.

Sports: There are 8 intercollegiate sports for men and 8 for women, and 4 intramural sports for men and 4 for women. Facilities include a gym with 2 basketball courts or 3 volleyball courts, a weight room, a baseball diamond, a beach volleyball pit, a football stadium, and soccer, baseball, and softball fields.

Disabled Students: 85% of the campus is accessible. Wheelchair ramps, elevators, special parking, specially equipped rest rooms, and lowered drinking fountains are available.

Services: Counseling and information services are available, as is tutoring in most subjects. There is remedial math, reading, and writing, help for the learning disabled, individual counseling, and peer tutoring.

Campus Safety and Security: Measures include 24-hour foot and vehicle patrol, security escort services, pamphlets/posters/films, and emergency telephones. There are lighted pathways/sidewalks.

Programs of Study: USF confers B.A., B.S., B.B.A., B.L.S., B.S.Ed., B.S.N., and B.S.W. degrees. Associate and master's degrees are also awarded. Bachelor's degrees are awarded in BIOLOGICAL SCIENCE (biology/biological science), BUSINESS (accounting and business administration and management), COMMUNICATIONS AND THE ARTS (communications, English, and fine arts), COMPUTER AND PHYSICAL SCIENCE (chemistry and science), EDUCATION (art, business, elementary, English, health, science, secondary, social studies, and special), ENGINEERING AND ENVIRONMENTAL DESIGN (environmental science), HEALTH PROFESSIONS (medical laboratory technology, nursing, predentistry, and premedicine), SOCIAL SCIENCE (history, liberal arts/general studies, ministries, psychology, religion, and social work). Nursing, education, and history are the strongest academically. Business, art, and nursing are the largest.

Required: All students must complete courses in humanities, social and behavioral science, religious studies, life and physical sciences, oral and written communication, phys ed, computer science, and math. 128 semester hours with a minimum GPA of 2.0 and at least 30 hours in the major are required to graduate. A comprehensive exam is required in biology and business administration and a thesis is required in history.

Special: Internships in art, business, and communication are available, as well as nondegree study. Students also can receive credit for life experience. Cross-registration with the Fort Wayne Higher Education Consortium is available, as well as dual and student-designed majors. There is 1 national honor society, a freshman honors program, and 1 departmental honors program.

Faculty/Classroom: 39% of faculty are male; 61%, female. 94% teach undergraduates. No introductory courses are taught by graduate students. The average class size in an introductory lecture is 30; in a laboratory, 11; and in a regular course, 20.

Requirements: The SAT or ACT is required. USF requires applicants to be in the upper 50% of their class. A GPA of 2.0 is required. AP and

CLEP credits are accepted. Important factors in the admissions decision are recommendations by school officials, advanced placement or honor courses, and extracurricular activities record.

Procedure: Freshmen are admitted to all sessions. Entrance exams should be taken in the spring of the junior year or fall of the senior year. There are deferred admissions and rolling admissions plans. Application deadlines are open. Application fee is $20.

Transfer: 286 transfer students enrolled in a recent year. Applicants need a minimum cumulative GPA of 2.0 and must submit all college transcripts. 32 of 128 credits required for the bachelor's degree must be completed at USF.

Visiting: There are regularly scheduled orientations for prospective students, including meetings with faculty and staff and student tours. There are guides for informal visits and visitors may sit in on classes and stay overnight. To schedule a visit, contact the Admissions Office at (260) 434-3279.

Financial Aid: In a recent year, 87% of all full-time freshmen and 94% of continuing full-time students received some form of financial aid. 87% of full-time freshmen and 94% of continuing full-time students received need-based aid. The average freshman award was $13,228. Need-based scholarships or need-based grants averaged $2163 ($5000 maximum); need-based self-help aid (loans and jobs) averaged $3460 ($2625 maximum); non-need-based athletic scholarships averaged $4401 ($20,938 maximum); and other non-need-based awards and non-need-based scholarships averaged $2613 ($7000 maximum). 9% of undergraduates worked part time. Average annual earnings from campus work were $877. USF is a member of CSS. The FAFSA and are required. Check with the school for application deadlines.

International Students: In a recent year, there were 3 international students enrolled. They must score satisfactorily on the TOEFL.

Computers: All students may access the system 7 days a week.

Graduates: In a recent year, 192 bachelor's degrees were awarded. The most popular majors were business (15%), education (13%), and nursing (12%). In an average class, 3% graduate in 3 years or less, 33% graduate in 4 years or less, 39% graduate in 5 years or less, and 40% graduate in 6 years or less. Of a recent graduating class, 4% were enrolled in graduate school within 6 months of graduation and 95% were employed.

Admissions Contact: Matthew P. Nettleton, Director of Admissions. A video is available. E-mail: *mnettleton@sf.edu* Web: *www.sf.edu*

UNIVERSITY OF SOUTHERN INDIANA
A-5
Evansville, IN 47712

(812) 464-1765
(800) 467-1965; Fax: (812) 465-7154

Full-time: 3080 men, 4397 women	**Faculty:** IIA, --$
Part-time: 637 men, 1138 women	**Ph.D.s:** n/av
Graduate: 181 men, 571 women	**Student/Faculty:** n/av
Year: semesters, summer session	**Tuition:** $6222 ($12,230)
Application Deadline: see profile	**Room & Board:** $6368
Freshman Class: 4807 applied, 4356 accepted, 2148 enrolled	
SAT Verbal/Math: 476/483*	**ACT:** 20 LESS COMPETITIVE

The University of Southern Indiana, founded in 1965, is a public institution offering undergraduate programs in business, education and human service, liberal arts, nursing and health professions, and science and engineering. There are 5 undergraduate schools and 1 graduate school. In addition to regional accreditation, USI has baccalaureate program accreditation with AACSB, ABET, ADA, CSWE, and NCATE. The library contains 326,660 volumes, 580,298 microform items, and 5659 audio/video tapes/CDs/DVDs, and subscribes to 13,537 periodicals including electronic. Computerized library services include the card catalog, interlibrary loans, database searching, and Internet access. Special learning facilities include a learning resource center, radio station, and TV station. The 300-acre campus is in a suburban area 150 miles south of Indianapolis. Including any residence halls, there are 76 buildings.

Student Life: 91% of undergraduates are from Indiana. Others are from 32 states, 29 foreign countries, and Canada. 93% are white. The average age of freshmen is 19; all undergraduates, 22. 34% do not continue beyond their first year; 33% remain to graduate.

Housing: 3227 students can be accommodated in college housing, which includes single-sex and coed dorms, on-campus apartments, off-campus apartments, married-student housing, fraternity houses, and sorority houses. In addition, there are honors houses and special-interest houses. On-campus housing is available on a first-come, first-served basis. Priority is given to out-of-town students. 70% of students commute. Alcohol is not permitted. All students may keep cars.

Activities: 4% of men belong to 6 national fraternities; 4% of women belong to 4 national sororities. There are 108 groups on campus, including art, cheerleading, chess, choir, chorus, computers, dance, drama, ethnic, film, gay, honors, international, jazz band, literary magazine, musical theater, newspaper, pep band, photography, political, professional, radio and TV, religious, social, social service, student government, and yearbook. Popular campus events include Eagle Gran Prix Bike Race, Spring Fling, and Oksoberfest.

Sports: There are 7 intercollegiate sports for men and 8 for women, and 11 intramural sports for men and 11 for women. Facilities include a physical activities center with a swimming pool, a weight room, 6 tennis courts, and a 3000-seat multipurpose area and a recreation and fitness center with weights, cardiovascular equipment, and exercise programs.

Disabled Students: 93% of the campus is accessible. Wheelchair ramps, elevators, special parking, specially equipped rest rooms, special class scheduling, lowered drinking fountains, lowered telephones, and student assistance through the counseling center are available.

Services: Counseling and information services are available, as is tutoring in most subjects. There is a reader service for the blind, and remedial math, reading, and writing.

Campus Safety and Security: Measures include 24-hour foot and vehicle patrol, self-defense education, security escort services, and shuttle buses. There are pamphlets/posters/films, emergency telephones, and lighted pathways/sidewalks.

Programs of Study: USI confers B.A., B.S., B.G.S., B.S.E., B.S.N., and B.S.W. degrees. Associate and master's degrees are also awarded. Bachelor's degrees are awarded in BIOLOGICAL SCIENCE (biology/ biological science and biophysics), BUSINESS (accounting, banking and finance, business administration and management, business economics, electronic business, and marketing/retailing/merchandising), COMMUNI- CATIONS AND THE ARTS (broadcasting, communications, dramatic arts, English, German, journalism, Spanish, and speech/debate/rhetoric), COMPUTER AND PHYSICAL SCIENCE (chemistry, and mathematics), EDUCATION (art, business, elementary, middle school, science, secondary, and special), ENGINEERING AND ENVIRONMENTAL DESIGN (engineering), HEALTH PROFESSIONS (nursing, occupational therapy, predentistry, and premedicine), SOCIAL SCIENCE (economics, history, philosophy, political science/government, prelaw, psychology, social work, and sociology). Math and German are the strongest academically. Business administration, education, and nursing are the largest.

Required: The university core curriculum's goals focus on four areas: The Mind (enhancement of cognitive abilities), The Self (enhancement of individual development), The World (enhancement of cultural and natural awareness), and The Synthesis (the integration and application of knowledge). These are then subdivided into 13 objectives concerned with critical thinking, oral and written communication, math, information processing, ethics, the arts, health and lifestyle, history, individual development and social behavior, science, Western culture, global communities, and interdisciplinary studies. A total of 50 credit hours is distributed among the objectives with a total of 124 credit hours needed to graduate. A minimum cumulative 2.0 GPA is required.

Special: Students may participate in cooperative programs, internships in business and communications, and work-study programs. Study abroad, dual majors, pass/fail options, and B.A.-B.S. degrees are possible. There are 12 national honor societies and a freshman honors program.

Faculty/Classroom: All teach undergraduates. No introductory courses are taught by graduate students. The average class size in an introductory lecture is 100; in a laboratory, 25; and in a regular course, 30.

Admissions: 91% of the 2005-2006 applicants were accepted. The SAT scores for the 2005-2006 freshman class were: Verbal--61% below 500, 31% between 500 and 599, 7% between 600 and 700, and 1% above 700; Math--56% below 500, 34% between 500 and 599, 9% between 600 and 700, and 1% above 700. The ACT scores were 55% below 21, 25% between 21 and 23, 14% between 24 and 26, 3% between 27 and 28, and 3% above 28. 18% of the current freshmen were in the top fifth of their class; 41% were in the top two fifths. 33 freshmen graduated first in their class.

Requirements: The SAT or ACT is required. In addition, applicants must be graduates of an accredited secondary school. The GED is accepted. An interview is recommended if the student is below admissions standards. A GPA of 2.0 is required. AP and CLEP credits are accepted. Important factors in the admissions decision are advanced placement or honor courses, evidence of special talent, and leadership record.

Procedure: Freshmen are admitted fall, spring, and summer. Entrance exams should be taken in the spring term of the junior year. Check with the school for current application deadlines. The application fee is $25. Notification is sent on a rolling basis. Applications are accepted on-line.

Transfer: 658 transfer students enrolled in 2004-2005. Grades of C and above will transfer for credit. 30 of 124 credits required for the bachelor's degree must be completed at USI.

Visiting: There are regularly scheduled orientations for prospective students, including meetings with counselors and faculty and campus tours. There are guides for informal visits and visitors may sit in on classes and stay overnight. To schedule a visit, contact the Office of Admission at enroll@usi.edu.

Financial Aid: In 2005-2006, 78% of all full-time freshmen and 69% of continuing full-time students received some form of financial aid. 62% of full-time freshmen and 54% of continuing full-time students received need-based aid. The average freshman award was $6672. Need-based scholarships or need-based grants averaged $4240 ($15,028 maximum);

need-based self-help aid (loans and jobs) averaged $4658 ($14,625 maximum); non-need-based athletic scholarships averaged $3939 ($15,359 maximum); and other non-need-based awards and non-need-based scholarships averaged $2418 ($21,625 maximum). 10% of undergraduates work part time. Average annual earnings from campus work are $3296. The average financial indebtedness of the 2005 graduate was $15,724. The FAFSA and the college's own financial statement are required. The deadline for filing freshman financial aid applications for fall entry is March 1.

International Students: There are 43 international students enrolled. They must score satisfactorily on the TOEFL and also take the SAT or ACT.

Computers: All students may access the system. There are no time limits and no fees.

Graduates: From July 1, 2004 to June 30, 2005, 1151 bachelor's degrees were awarded. The most popular majors were elementary education (11%), business administration (5%), and psychology (5%). In an average class, 14% graduate in 4 years or less, 28% graduate in 5 years or less, and 33% graduate in 6 years or less. 244 companies recruited on campus in 2004-2005. Of the 2004 graduating class, 16% were enrolled in graduate school within 6 months of graduation and 88% were employed.

Admissions Contact: Eric Otto, Director of Admission.
E-mail: *eotto@usi.edu* Web: *www.usi.edu*

VALPARAISO UNIVERSITY
B-1
Valparaiso, IN 46383

(219) 464-5011
(888) GO-VALPO; Fax: (219) 464-6898

Full-time: 1374 men, 1451 women	**Faculty:** 216; IIA, av$
Part-time: 42 men, 99 women	**Ph.D.s:** 88%
Graduate: 428 men, 472 women	**Student/Faculty:** 13 to 1
Year: semesters, summer session	**Tuition:** $22,750
Application Deadline: August 15	**Room & Board:** $6220
Freshman Class: n/a	
SAT or ACT: required	**VERY COMPETITIVE+**

Valparaiso University, founded in 1859, is an independent institution affiliated with the Lutheran Church and offering degree programs in arts and sciences, business administration, engineering, nursing, and law. There are 5 undergraduate and 3 graduate schools. In addition to regional accreditation, Valpo has baccalaureate program accreditation with AACSB, ABA, ABET, ACS, CCNE, CSWE, NASM, and NCATE. The 2 libraries contain 635,508 volumes, 1,562,938 microform items, and 5212 audio/video tapes/CDs/DVDs, and subscribe to 25,463 periodicals including electronic. Computerized library services include the card catalog, interlibrary loans, database searching, Internet access, and laptop Internet portals. Special learning facilities include a learning resource center, art gallery, planetarium, radio station, TV station, observatory, weather station, and center for visual and performing arts. The 310-acre campus is in a small town 55 miles southeast of Chicago. Including any residence halls, there are 47 buildings.

Student Life: 65% of undergraduates are from out of state, mostly the Midwest. Students are from 48 states, 45 foreign countries, and Canada. 80% are from public schools. 89% are white. 66% are Protestant; 21% Catholic; 9% other; 6% claim no religious affiliation. The average age of freshmen is 19; all undergraduates, 21. 14% do not continue beyond their first year; 73% remain to graduate.

Housing: 2007 students can be accommodated in college housing, which includes single-sex and coed dorms, on-campus apartments, off-campus apartments, fraternity houses, and sorority houses. In addition, there are language houses and special-interest houses. On-campus housing is guaranteed for all 4 years. 67% of students live on campus. Alcohol is not permitted. Upperclassmen may keep cars.

Activities: 25% of men belong to 9 national fraternities; 18% of women belong to 6 national sororities. There are 74 groups on campus, including art, band, cheerleading, chess, choir, chorale, chorus, computers, dance, debate, drama, ethnic, film, gay, honors, international, jazz band, literary magazine, musical theater, newspaper, orchestra, pep band, photography, political, professional, radio and TV, religious, social, social service, student government, symphony, and yearbook. Popular campus events include Christmas Concert, Martin Luther King Day Celebration, and Jazz Festival.

Sports: There are 8 intercollegiate sports for men and 8 for women, and 20 intramural sports for men and 20 for women. Facilities include a 5000-seat arena, swimming pool, 7 additional playing floors, a track, 4 racquetball/handball courts, a cardio room, weight rooms, a training room, a football stadium, tennis courts, a soccer stadium, a baseball field, and indoor batting facilities.

Disabled Students: 60% of the campus is accessible. Wheelchair ramps, elevators, special parking, specially equipped rest rooms, and lowered drinking fountains are available.

Services: Counseling and information services are available, as is tutoring in most subjects. There is a reader service for the blind. A writing center provides assistance.

Campus Safety and Security: Measures include 24-hour foot and vehicle patrol, security escort services, shuttle buses, and informal discussions. There are pamphlets/posters/films, emergency telephones, and lighted pathways/sidewalks.

Programs of Study: Valpo confers B.A., B.S., B.Mus., B.Mus.Ed., B.S.Acc., B.S.Bus.Adm., B.S.C.E., B.S.Comp.Eng., B.S.Ed., B.S.E.E., B.S.F.A., B.S.M.E., B.S.N., B.S.P.E., and B.S.W. degrees. Associate, master's, and doctoral degrees are also awarded. Bachelor's degrees are awarded in BIOLOGICAL SCIENCE (biochemistry and biology/biological science), BUSINESS (accounting, banking and finance, business administration and management, international business management, international economics, marketing/retailing/merchandising, and sports management), COMMUNICATIONS AND THE ARTS (art, classics, communications, creative writing, dramatic arts, English, French, German, journalism, music, music performance, music theory and composition, public relations, radio/television technology, Spanish, and technical and business writing), COMPUTER AND PHYSICAL SCIENCE (actuarial science, atmospheric sciences and meteorology, chemistry, computer science, geology, information sciences and systems, mathematics, and physics), EDUCATION (elementary, middle school, music, physical, and secondary), ENGINEERING AND ENVIRONMENTAL DESIGN (civil engineering, computer engineering, electrical/electronics engineering, environmental science, and mechanical engineering), HEALTH PROFESSIONS (exercise science and nursing), SOCIAL SCIENCE (American studies, Asian/Oriental studies, criminology, economics, geography, history, international public service, ministries, philosophy, political science/government, psychology, religion, religious music, social work, sociology, and theological studies). Meteorology, engineering, and business are the strongest academically. Business, engineering, and education are the largest.

Required: General education requirements include the 10-credit Valpo core plus 3 courses in math/natural and behavioral sciences, 2 each of theology, literature/fine arts, and social analysis, and 1 each of philosophy/history, global perspectives, U.S. diversity, and phys ed; requirements may vary by degree program. To graduate, students must complete at least 124 credit hours, including a minimum of 25 in the major, with a GPA of at least 2.0.

Special: There is cross-registration with Indiana University Northwest at the undergraduate level in the geological and geographical sciences. Off-campus study programs in the United States include 2 Washington semester programs, a United Nations semester, and a Chicago urban semester. Students may also study abroad in 9 countries including Greece, England, Spain, China, Japan, Namibia, France, Germany, and Mexico. Co-op programs, internships, the B.A.-B.S. degree, work-study programs, dual and student-designed majors, an accelerated degree program in numerous majors, pass/fail options, and non-degree study are also available. Other special academic features include Christ College, which is an autonomous honors college. There are 8 national honor societies, including Phi Beta Kappa, a freshman honors program, and 25 departmental honors programs.

Faculty/Classroom: 60% of faculty are male; 40%, female. 88% teach undergraduates. No introductory courses are taught by graduate students. The average class size in an introductory lecture is 26; in a laboratory, 18; and in a regular course, 20.

Admissions: 54% of the current freshmen were in the top fifth of their class; 77% were in the top two fifths. There were 7 National Merit finalists. 28 freshmen graduated first in their class.

Requirements: The SAT or ACT is required. The ACT Optional Writing test is also required. In addition, applicants must be graduates of accredited secondary schools or have earned a GED. Valpo requires completion of 4 years of English, 3 to 4 years of math, 2 to 3 years of lab science, 2 years each of history and foreign language, and 3 years of additional academic courses. An application essay is required and an interview are recommended for all applicants, an audition is required for music majors. AP and CLEP credits are accepted. Important factors in the admissions decision are advanced placement or honor courses, extracurricular activities record, and evidence of special talent.

Procedure: Freshmen are admitted fall, spring, and summer. Entrance exams should be taken prior to the senior year. There is a deferred admissions plans. There is a rolling admissions plan. Applications should be filed by August 15 for fall entry. The fall 2005 application fee was $30. Notification is sent on a rolling basis. Applications are accepted on-line.

Transfer: 126 transfer students enrolled in 2004-2005. Applicants must submit official transcripts from all colleges attended. To be considered for admission, a minimum 2.0 cumulative grade point average in college coursework is required for most programs. However, some programs require a minimum 3.0 grade point average for transfer students. If the applicant has completed fewer than 24 credit hours, entrance exam scores and a high school transcript are required. A completed transfer evaluation form from the Dean of Students of the current institution must also be submitted. An interview is recommended. 30 of 124 credits required for the bachelor's degree must be completed at Valpo.

Visiting: There are regularly scheduled orientations for prospective students, including a campus tour conducted by a current student, an interview with a counselor, and the option to meet with professors, attend a class, and meet with coaches. There are guides for informal visits and visitors may sit in on classes and stay overnight. To schedule a visit, contact Office of Admission at *undergrad.admissions@valpo.edu.*

Financial Aid: In 2005-2006, 96% of all full-time freshmen and 93% of continuing full-time students received some form of financial aid. 71% of full-time freshmen and 68% of continuing full-time students received need-based aid. The average freshman award was $18,070. Need-based scholarships or need-based grants averaged $13,799 ($21,000 maximum); need-based self-help aid (loans and jobs) averaged $4860 ($8625 maximum); non-need-based athletic scholarships averaged $19,110 ($31,945 maximum); and other non-need-based awards and non-need-based scholarships averaged $7145 ($22,000 maximum). 40% of undergraduates work part time. Average annual earnings from campus work are $1000. The average financial indebtedness of the 2005 graduate was $23,853. The FAFSA is required. The deadline for filing freshman financial aid applications for fall entry is March 1.

International Students: There are 61 international students enrolled. The school actively recruits these students.Students must score satisfactorily on the TOEFL or take IELTS, GCE or GCSE English Exam, IB Higher Level English Exam, or complete the interlink program, an intensive English language program on Valpo's campus.

Computers: Wireless access is available. A campuswide network is in place with wired and partial wireless access, and provides students access to the Internet, e-mail, library resources, the campus Web space and intranet, personal Web pages, personal and shared file spaces, the course management system, registration, degree audit, grade retreival, and a variety of software. The University offers free enrichment courses in specific applications, Web resources, e-mail, and basic computer skills. There are 820 computers available for student use in 63 computer labs and classrooms. All housing units are wired for high-speed Internet access. All computer labs have access to the wireless network. All students may access the system 7 days a week. There are no time limits and no fees. It is recommended that students in engineering have personal computers. Pentium IV (2.4 GHz), 512 MB memory, 40 GB hard drive is recommended.

Graduates: From July 1, 2004 to June 30, 2005, 654 bachelor's degrees were awarded. The most popular majors were nursing (9%), elementary education (6%), and psychology and English (5%). In an average class, 1% graduate in 3 years or less, 61% graduate in 4 years or less, 72% graduate in 5 years or less, and 73% graduate in 6 years or less. 167 companies recruited on campus in 2004-2005. Of the 2004 graduating class, 25% were enrolled in graduate school within 6 months of graduation and 70% were employed.

Admissions Contact: Office of Admissions.
E-mail: *undergrad.admissions@valpo.edu* Web: *www.valpo.edu*

WABASH COLLEGE — B-3

Crawfordsville, IN 47933-0352   (765) 361-6253
(800) 345-5385; Fax: (765) 361-6437

Full-time: 871 men	Faculty: 87; IIB, +$
Part-time: 6 men	Ph.D.s: 96%
Graduate: none	Student/Faculty: 10 to 1
Year: semesters	Tuition: $23,388
Application Deadline: February 1	Room & Board: $6728
Freshman Class: 1392 applied, 676 accepted, 250 enrolled	
SAT Verbal/Math: 592/604*	ACT: 26 HIGHLY COMPETITIVE

Wabash College, founded in 1832, is a private liberal arts men's college with a strong emphasis on preprofessional programs. In addition to regional accreditation, Wabash has baccalaureate program accreditation with NCATE. The library contains 431,942 volumes, 11,359 microform items, and 15,909 audio/video tapes/CDs/DVDs, and subscribes to 4776 periodicals including electronic. Computerized library services include the card catalog, interlibrary loans, database searching, and Internet access. Special learning facilities include a learning resource center, art gallery, radio station, and an archival center, and research centers for the study of theology and religion and inquiry in the liberal arts. The 60-acre campus is in a small town 45 miles northwest of Indianapolis. Including any residence halls, there are 55 buildings.

Student Life: 71% of undergraduates are from Indiana. Others are from 30 states and 22 foreign countries. 94% are from public schools. 81% are white. The average age of freshmen is 18; all undergraduates, 20. 11% do not continue beyond their first year; 70% remain to graduate.

Housing: 840 students can be accommodated in college housing, which includes single-sex dormitories, on-campus apartments, off-campus apartments, and fraternity houses. In addition, there are language houses. On-campus housing is guaranteed for all 4 years. 91% of students live on campus; of those, 65% remain on campus on weekends. All students may keep cars.

Activities: 65% of men belong to 10 national fraternities. There are 50 groups on campus, including art, band, cheerleading, chess, choir, chorus, computers, debate, drama, drum corps, ethnic, film, foreign language, forensics, gay, honors, international, jazz band, literary magazine, musical theater, newspaper, orchestra, pep band, photography, political, professional, radio, religious, social, social service, student government, symphony, and yearbook. Popular campus events include Pan-Hel Weekend, Monon Bell, and Chapel Sing.

Sports: Facilities include a 4200-seat stadium, indoor and outdoor tennis courts, football, baseball, and soccer fields, a swimming pool, an indoor track, an all-weather track, wrestling and weight rooms, racquetball and handball courts, a ropes challenge course, an 1800-seat basketball arena, a wellness center, and an aerobics studio.

Disabled Students: 60% of the campus is accessible. Wheelchair ramps, elevators, special parking, specially equipped rest rooms, lowered drinking fountains and lowered telephones. A counseling service is also provided.

Services: Counseling and information services are available, as is tutoring in most subjects. There is a reader service for the blind, and remedial math, reading, and writing. There is a quantitative skills center as well as a writing center where, under professional supervision, students help each other.

Campus Safety and Security: Measures include 24-hour foot and vehicle patrol, security escort services, pamphlets/posters/films, and emergency telephones. There are lighted pathways/sidewalks.

Programs of Study: Wabash confers the A.B. degree. Bachelor's degrees are awarded in BIOLOGICAL SCIENCE (biology/biological science), COMMUNICATIONS AND THE ARTS (art, classics, dramatic arts, English, French, German, Greek, Latin, music, Spanish, and speech/debate/rhetoric), COMPUTER AND PHYSICAL SCIENCE (chemistry, mathematics, and physics), SOCIAL SCIENCE (economics, history, philosophy, political science/government, psychology, and religion). Preprofessional studies, economics, and religion are the strongest academically. English, history, and biology are the largest.

Required: All students must complete at least 3 courses each in literature/fine arts, behavioral science, and natural science/math, 2 in history, philosophy, or religion, and 1 in quantitative skills. To graduate, students must maintain a minimum 2.0 GPA for 136 credit hours (34 courses), which include a freshman tutorial and 2 semesters of cultures and traditions. The student must pass a written comprehensive exam in the major as well as a senior oral exam and must demonstrate proficiency in English and proficiency in a foreign language at a level equivalent to 2 college courses.

Special: Wabash offers internships with off-campus organizations, study abroad in an unlimited number of countries, a Washington semester with American University, dual majors, a B.A.-B.S. degree in engineering, and both a 3-2 engineering program and a 3-3 law program with Columbia University and Washington University in St. Louis. A tuition-free Ninth Semester Teacher Education Program is also available. There are 9 national honor societies, including Phi Beta Kappa and 7 departmental honors programs.

Faculty/Classroom: 81% of faculty are male; 19%, female. All teach undergraduates. The average class size in an introductory lecture is 21; in a laboratory, 15; and in a regular course, 13.

Admissions: 49% of the 2005-2006 applicants were accepted. The SAT scores for the 2005-2006 freshman class were: Verbal--11% below 500, 40% between 500 and 599, 41% between 600 and 700, and 8% above 700; Math--10% below 500, 33% between 500 and 599, 45% between 600 and 700, and 12% above 700. 60% of the current freshmen were in the top fifth of their class; 87% were in the top two fifths. There were 6 National Merit semifinalists. 12 freshmen graduated first in their class.

Requirements: The SAT or ACT is required. Wabash recommends applicants have 4 high school courses in English, 3 to 4 in math, and 2 each in foreign language, lab science, and social studies. An essay is required, and an interview is recommended. AP and CLEP credits are accepted. Important factors in the admissions decision are advanced placement or honor courses, leadership record, and extracurricular activities record.

Procedure: Freshmen are admitted fall and spring. Entrance exams should be taken by the spring of the junior year or fall of the senior year. There are early decision, early action, early admissions, deferred admissions, and rolling admissions plans. Early decision applications should be filed by November 15; early action by December 15; regular applications, by February 1 for fall entry and December 1 for spring entry, along with a $30 fee. Notification of early decision is sent December 15; early action january 31; regular decision February 28. 40 early decision candidates were accepted for the 2005-2006 class. 58 applicants were on the 2005 waiting list; 1 was admitted. Applications are accepted on-line.

Transfer: 2 transfer students enrolled in 2004-2005. Applicants must submit official transcripts of all college courses attended. Wabash strongly considers the overall high school and college background of applicants. Courses must be liberal arts in nature with a minimum GPA of 2.0 to transfer. Recommendations from the college adviser and dean of students at the previous college attended and a personal written statement are required, with an interview strongly recommended. 17 of 34 course credits required for the bachelor's degree must be completed at Wabash.

Visiting: There are regularly scheduled orientations for prospective students, consisting of a tour, lunch, opportunity to meet faculty, coaches, and alumni, and panel discussions on academics, extracurricular activities, and financial aid. There are guides for informal visits and visitors may sit in on classes and stay overnight. To schedule a visit, contact Mary Skelton of the Admissions Office at (765) 361-6276.

Financial Aid: In 2005-2006, 72% of all full-time freshmen and 76% of continuing full-time students received some form of financial aid. 71% of full-time freshmen and 70% of continuing full-time students received need-based aid. The average freshman award was $22,859. Need-based scholarships or need-based grants averaged $17,396; and need-based self-help aid (loans and jobs) averaged $4046. 65% of undergraduates work part time. Average annual earnings from campus work are $1500. The average financial indebtedness of the 2005 graduate was $17,328. Wabash is a member of CSS. The CSS/Profile or FAFSA and federal tax form with W-2 statements are required. The priority date for freshman financial aid applications for fall entry is February 15. The deadline for filing freshman financial aid applications for fall entry is March 1.

International Students: There are 34 international students enrolled. The school actively recruits these students. They must score satisfactorily on the written TOEFL or on the electronic version, or take the MELAB, and also take the SAT or the ACT.

Computers: Wireless access is available. Every classroom building has publicly accessible computers, with more than 300 such computers on campus. There are 6 public computer labs, some open 24 hours a day. A wireless network is available in most buildings. Students have unlimited access to the Internet from their rooms. All students may access the system 24 hours per day or at designated times for specific computers. There are no time limits and no fees.

Graduates: From July 1, 2004 to June 30, 2005, 163 bachelor's degrees were awarded. The most popular majors were English (17%), history (14%), and psychology (11%). In an average class, 69% graduate in 4 years or less, 72% graduate in 5 years or less, and 75% graduate in 6 years or less. 40 companies recruited on campus in 2004-2005. Of the 2004 graduating class, 37% were enrolled in graduate school within 6 months of graduation and 60% were employed.

Admissions Contact: Steve Klein, Director of Admissions. A video is available. E-mail: *admissions@wabash.edu* Web: *www.wabash.edu*

IOWA

POPULATION
DENSITY
• 25,000 and over

0   20   40   60   80   100

Miles

ALLEN COLLEGE
D-2

Waterloo, IA 50703

(319) 226-2002; Fax: (319) 226-2051

Full-time: 19 men, 299 women	**Faculty:** IIA, --$
Part-time: 4 men, 52 women	**Ph.D.s:** 17%
Graduate: 1 man, 29 women	**Student/Faculty:** 14 to 1
Year: semesters, summer session	**Tuition:** $12,548
Application Deadline: March 1	**Room & Board:** $5519

Freshman Class: 265 applied, 37 accepted, 18 enrolled

ACT: 22

SPECIAL

Allen College, founded in 1989, is a private institution offering a baccalaureate program in nursing and is part of the Iowa Health System. In addition to regional accreditation, Allen College has baccalaureate program accreditation with NLN. The library contains 1853 volumes and 225 audio/video tapes/CDs/DVDs, and subscribes to 104 periodicals including electronic. Computerized library services include the card catalog, interlibrary loans, database searching, and Internet access. The 20-acre campus is in a suburban area in Waterloo. Including any residence halls, there are 3 buildings.

Student Life: 97% of undergraduates are from Iowa. Others are from 3 states. 98% are white. The average age of freshmen is 18; all undergraduates, 24. 24% do not continue beyond their first year; 75% remain to graduate.

Housing: 24 students can be accommodated in college housing, which includes coed on-campus apartments. Living facilities are available at cooperative colleges. On-campus housing is available on a first-come, first-served basis. 90% of students commute. Alcohol is not permitted. All students may keep cars.

Activities: There are no fraternities or sororities. There are 6 groups on campus, including newspaper and student government. Popular campus events include Fall Fling and Winter Party.

Sports: There is no sports program at Allen College.

Disabled Students: All of the campus is accessible. Wheelchair ramps, elevators, special parking, specially equipped rest rooms, and lowered drinking fountains are available.

Services: Counseling and information services are available, as is tutoring in some subjects, including science courses and lower division major courses.

Campus Safety and Security: Measures include informal discussions, pamphlets/posters/films, and lighted pathways/sidewalks.

Programs of Study: Allen College confers the B.S.N. degree. Associate and master's degrees are also awarded. Bachelor's degrees are awarded in HEALTH PROFESSIONS (nursing).

Required: To graduate, all students must complete general education courses in humanities, social science, natural science, and electives, and maintain a 2.0 GPA; 124 credits are required, with 73 in the major.

Special: Cross-registration is available with the University of Northern Iowa and Wartburg College. Co-op programs in nursing and radiography are also available.

Faculty/Classroom: 4% of faculty are male; 96%, female. 89% teach undergraduates. The average class size in an introductory lecture is 60; in a laboratory, 8; and in a regular course, 30.

Admissions: 14% of the 2005-2006 applicants were accepted. The ACT scores for the 2005-2006 freshman class were: 44% below 21, 44% between 21 and 23, 6% between 24 and 26, and 6% between 27 and 28. 50% of the current freshmen were in the top fifth of their class; 78% were in the top two fifths.

Requirements: A satisfactorily score is required on the ACT. An essay, a letter of recommendation, and class rank in the upper 50th percentile are required. Core high school courses including 4 years of English, 3 each of math and social studies, and 1 each of chemistry, biology, and 1 other science are required. Students must earn grades of C or better. A GPA of 3.0 is required. AP and CLEP credits are accepted.

Procedure: Freshmen are admitted fall, spring, and summer. Entrance exams should be taken early in the senior year of high school. There is an early admissions plan. Applications should be filed by March 1 for fall entry, September 1 for spring entry, and February 1 for summer entry, along with a $50 fee. Notification is sent March 15 and September 15. A waiting list is an active part of the admissions procedure. Applications are accepted on-line.

Transfer: 81 transfer students enrolled in 2004-2005. Students must have a college GPA of 3.0 and submit an essay and a letter of recommendation. 30 of 124 credits required for the bachelor's degree must be completed at Allen College.

Visiting: There are regularly scheduled orientations for prospective students, including an opportunity to speak to the Director of Admissions, the Director of Financial Aid, and department chairs, and to tour campus. There are guides for informal visits and visitors may sit in on classes. To schedule a visit, contact Allen College Admissions at (319) 226-2000 or *AllenCollegeAdmissions@ihs.org*.

Financial Aid: In 2005-2006, 83% of all full-time freshmen and 81% of continuing full-time students received some form of financial aid. 67% of full-time freshmen and 71% of continuing full-time students received need-based aid. The average freshman award was $7347. Need-based scholarships or need-based grants averaged $1976 ($12,966 maximum); need-based self-help aid (loans and jobs) averaged $1123 ($5626 maximum); and other non-need-based awards and non-need-based scholarships averaged $4248 ($20,596 maximum). 4% of undergraduates work part time. Average annual earnings from campus work are $2000. The average financial indebtedness of the 2005 graduate was $22,948. The FAFSA and the college's own financial statement are required. The priority date for freshman financial aid applications for fall entry is May 1.

International Students: International students must score satisfactorily on the TOEFL and on the SAT or the ACT.

Computers: All students may access the system 24 hours a day. There are no time limits. The fee is $110 per semester. It is strongly recommended that all students have a personal computer.

Graduates: From July 1, 2004 to June 30, 2005, 45 bachelor's degrees were awarded. In an average class, 65% graduate in 4 years or less, 75% graduate in 5 years or less, and 75% graduate in 6 years or less. 40 companies recruited on campus in 2004-2005. Of the 2004 graduating class, all were employed within 6 months of graduation.

Admissions Contact: Holly Risetter, Admissions Counselor.
E-mail: *AllenCollegeAdmissions@ihs.org*
Web: *http://www.allencollege.edu*

ASHFORD UNIVERSITY F-3
(Formerly The Franciscan University)
Clinton, IA 52733-2967
(563) 243-6102
(800) 242-4153; Fax: (563) 242-2003

Full-time: 159 men, 176 women	**Faculty:** 42
Part-time: 18 men, 23 women	**Ph.D.s:** n/av
Graduate: 8 men, 32 women	**Student/Faculty:** 8 to 1
Year: semesters, summer session	**Tuition:** $14,770
Application Deadline: August 15	**Room & Board:** $5600
Freshman Class: n/av	**ACT:** required **COMPETITIVE**

Ashford University, formerly The Franciscan University, is a private liberal arts college founded in 1918. The library contains 80,759 volumes, 73,405 microform items, and 2458 audio/video tapes/CDs/DVDs, and subscribes to 645 periodicals including electronic. Computerized library services include the card catalog, interlibrary loans, database searching, Internet access, and laptop Internet portals. Special learning facilities include a learning resource center, art gallery, and a living lab adjacent to the campus. The 25-acre campus is in a small town 135 miles west of Chicago, Illinois. Including any residence halls, there are 6 buildings.

Student Life: 53% of undergraduates are from Iowa. Students are from 10 states, 8 foreign countries, and Canada. 86% are white.

Housing: 242 students can be accommodated in college housing, which includes single-sex and coed dorms. On-campus housing is guaranteed for all 4 years. 68% of students commute. Alcohol is not permitted. All students may keep cars.

Activities: There are no fraternities or sororities. There are 20 groups on campus, including band, choir, computers, drama, ethnic, gay, honors, international, musical theater, newspaper, professional, religious, social, SISEA (Iowa State Education Association) social service, and student government. Popular campus events include Family Weekend, Matriculation Ceremony, and Earth Day.

Sports: There are 6 intercollegiate sports for men and 6 for women, and 6 intramural sports for men and 6 for women. Facilities include an arena with 2 regulation-size basketball courts, a fitness center, a 4-lane perimeter track, 2 locker rooms plus 2 rooms and 1 training room. The gym is located on campus. There is a soccer field.

Disabled Students: 95% of the campus is accessible. Wheelchair ramps, elevators, special parking, specially equipped rest rooms, lowered drinking fountains, and special doors for the disabled are available.

Services: Counseling and information services are available, as is tutoring in most subjects. There is a reader service for the blind, and remedial math, reading, and writing. There is also voice-activated computer software, proctoring exams, and prep courses for the GRE and MCAT.

Campus Safety and Security: Measures include self-defense education, security escort services, informal discussions, and pamphlets/posters/films. There are emergency telephones, lighted pathways/sidewalks, and 24-hour security through the Clinton Police Department. On-campus security is available Sunday to Wednesday 4 P.M.-12 A.M. and Thursday to Saturday 6 P.M.-2 A.M.

Programs of Study: AU confers B.A., B.S., B.A.S., and B.G.S degrees. Associate and master's degrees are also awarded. Bachelor's degrees are awarded in BIOLOGICAL SCIENCE (biology/biological science), BUSINESS (accounting, business administration and management, management information systems, marketing management, and sports management), COMMUNICATIONS AND THE ARTS (English and visual and performing arts), COMPUTER AND PHYSICAL SCIENCE (computer mathematics and computer science), EDUCATION (business, elementary, and science), ENGINEERING AND ENVIRONMENTAL DESIGN (computer graphics), HEALTH PROFESSIONS (clinical science, cytotechnology, and nuclear medical technology), SOCIAL SCIENCE (criminal justice, interdisciplinary studies, psychology, religion, and social science). Accounting, business administration, and elementary education are the strongest academically. Liberal arts, elementary education, and business administration are the largest.

Required: Students must complete 122 semester hours, including 34 semester hours of general education requirements, plus 12 hours of competencies (computer/writing/math), and 30 hours in a major, with a minimum 2.0 GPA; a higher GPA is required for some programs. A final exam, report, or project is required in every course.

Special: Special academic programs include a dual major in accounting and business. There are 2 national honor societies, a freshman honors program, and 1 departmental honors program.

Faculty/Classroom: All teach undergraduates. No introductory courses are taught by graduate students.

Requirements: The ACT is required; the SAT is accepted. In addition, applicants must be graduates of an accredited secondary school or have earned a GED and must meet 2 of the following requirements: a GPA of 2.0 in college preparatory or regular high school courses, rank in the upper half of the graduating class, and a minimum ACT composite score of 18 or a satisfactory SAT composite score. AU requires applicants to be in the upper 50% of their class. A GPA of 2.0 is required. AP and CLEP credits are accepted.

Procedure: Freshmen are admitted to all sessions. Entrance exams should be taken before enrolling. There are deferred admissions and rolling admissions plans. Applications should be filed by August 15 for fall entry, January 10 for spring entry, and June 1 for summer entry, along with a $20 fee. Notification is sent on a rolling basis. Applications are accepted on-line.

Transfer: Applicants may have 64 semester hours of 100-level or higher courses from a 2-year school, and up to 90 semester hours maximum. 30 of 122 credits required for the bachelor's degree must be completed at AU.

Visiting: There are regularly scheduled orientations for prospective students, including 2-day orientation sessions held prior to the first week of classes for students and parents. There are guides for informal visits and visitors may sit in on classes and stay overnight. To schedule a visit, contact the Admissions Office at (563) 242-4023.

Financial Aid: AU is a member of CSS. The FAFSA and parents' and student's income tax form are required. The deadline for filing freshman financial aid applications for fall entry is June 1.

International Students: The school actively recruits these students. A satisfactory score is required on the written TOEFL.

Computers: Wireless access is available. All students may access the system. There are no time limits and no fees. All students are required to have PCs.

Graduates: From July 1, 2004 to June 30, 2005, 91 bachelor's degrees were awarded.

Admissions Contact: Waunita M. Sullivan, Director of Enrollment. A video is available. E-mail: *admissions@ashford.edu*
Web: *http://www.ashford.edu*

BRIAR CLIFF UNIVERSITY B-2
Sioux City, IA 51104-0100
(712) 279-5200
(800) 662-3303; Fax: (712) 279-1632

Full-time: 398 men, 572 women	**Faculty:** 53; IIB, --$
Part-time: 37 men, 89 women	**Ph.D.s:** 72%
Graduate: 6 men, 23 women	**Student/Faculty:** 18 to 1
Year: trimesters, summer session	**Tuition:** $17,985
Application Deadline: open	**Room & Board:** $5565
Freshman Class: 1275 applied, 971 accepted, 251 enrolled	
SAT Verbal/Math: 498/435*	**ACT:** 22 **LESS COMPETITIVE**

Briar Cliff University, founded in 1930, is a private Roman Catholic-Franciscan liberal arts institution. In addition to regional accreditation, Briar Cliff has baccalaureate program accreditation with AACSB, CSWE, and NLN. The library contains 84,540 volumes, 21,652 microform items, and 10,769 audio/video tapes/CDs/DVDs, and subscribes to 10,573 periodicals including electronic. Computerized library services include the card catalog, interlibrary loans, database searching, and Internet access. Special learning facilities include a learning resource center, art gallery, radio station, TV station, an integrated multimedia center, a nursing simulation lab, and a human anatomy/cadaver lab. The 70-acre campus is in a suburban area minutes from downtown Sioux City. Including any residence halls, there are 13 buildings.

Student Life: 66% of undergraduates are from Iowa. Others are from 23 states, 2 foreign countries, and Canada. 91% are white. 51% are Catholic; 32% claim no religious affiliation; 17% Protestant. The average age of freshmen is 18; all undergraduates, 24. 29% do not continue beyond their first year; 52% remain to graduate.

Housing: 583 students can be accommodated in college housing, which includes coed dormitories. In addition, there are special-interest houses. On-campus housing is guaranteed for the freshman year only. 53% of students live on campus. All students may keep cars.

Activities: There are no fraternities or sororities. There are 36 groups on campus, including art, cheerleading, choir, chorale, chorus, computers, dance, drama, ethnic, film, honors, literary magazine, musical theater, newspaper, pep band, photography, professional, radio and TV, religious, social, social service, student government, and yearbook. Popular campus events include Cliffstock, Family Weekend, and Little Brother Little Sister Weekend.

Sports: There are 8 intercollegiate sports for men and 8 for women, and 15 intramural sports for men and 15 for women. Facilities include baseball, softball, and soccer fields, and a recreation center with 2 racquetball courts, a running track, tennis courts, 2 basketball/volleyball courts, and weight-lifting facilities.

Disabled Students: 90% of the campus is accessible. Wheelchair ramps, elevators, special parking, specially equipped rest rooms, lowered drinking fountains, and lowered telephones are available.

Services: Counseling and information services are available, as is tutoring in most subjects. There is remedial math, reading, and writing.

Campus Safety and Security: Measures include 24-hour foot and vehicle patrol, security escort services, informal discussions, and pamphlets/posters/films. There are emergency telephones and lighted pathways/sidewalks.

Programs of Study: Briar Cliff confers B.A., B.S., B.S.N., and B.S.W. degrees. Associate and master's degrees are also awarded. Bachelor's degrees are awarded in BIOLOGICAL SCIENCE (biology/biological science), BUSINESS (accounting, business administration and management, and human resources), COMMUNICATIONS AND THE ARTS (art, communications, dramatic arts, English, graphic design, journalism, media arts, music, and Spanish), COMPUTER AND PHYSICAL SCIENCE (chemistry, computer science, information sciences and systems, mathematics, and radiological technology), EDUCATION (elementary, health, and secondary), ENGINEERING AND ENVIRONMENTAL DESIGN (environmental science), HEALTH PROFESSIONS (medical technology, nursing, and sports medicine), SOCIAL SCIENCE (criminal justice, history, political science/government, psychology, social work, sociology, and theological studies). Biology, business administration, and education are the strongest academically. Education, nursing, and business administration are the largest.

Required: To graduate, students must complete a minimum of 124 semester hours, maintain a GPA of 2.0 with no more than 1 D or D+ in the major, complete the three components of Briar Cliff's general educational program. and complete a major field of concentration.

Special: Internships in Chicago, study abroad, dual majors, work-study programs, accelerated degree programs in business administration, human resource management, and professional studies, student-designed interdisciplinary majors, and pass/fail options are available. Students may earn a 3-2 engineering degree with Iowa State University. There is a freshman honors program.

Faculty/Classroom: 45% of faculty are male; 55%, female. All teach undergraduates. The average class size in an introductory lecture is 20; in a laboratory, 15; and in a regular course, 20.

Admissions: 76% of the 2005-2006 applicants were accepted. The SAT scores for the 2005-2006 freshman class were: Verbal--57% below 500, 29% between 500 and 599, and 14% between 600 and 700; Math--63% below 500, and 38% between 500 and 599. The ACT scores were 45% below 21, 27% between 21 and 23, 16% between 24 and 26, 8% between 27 and 28, and 4% above 28. 30% of the current freshmen were in the top fifth of their class; 54% were in the top two fifths.

Requirements: The SAT or ACT is required, the ACT is preferred, and a satisfactory score qualifies for automatic acceptance review. Applicants need not be graduates of an accredited secondary school. The GED is accepted. Admission to freshman standing requires 4 years each of English and math, 3 of science, 2 of history, and 1 of social studies. 2 years of foreign language is recommended. A GPA of 2.0 is required. AP and CLEP credits are accepted. Important factors in the admissions decision are leadership record, extracurricular activities record, and advanced placement or honor courses.

Procedure: Freshmen are admitted to all sessions. Entrance exams should be taken by October for scholarship consideration, and by April for admission there is a rolling admissions plan. Application deadlines are open. Application fee is $20. Applications are accepted on-line.

Transfer: 129 transfer students enrolled in 2004-2005. Applicants must have a minimum GPA of 2.0 with at least 10 credit hours earned and satisfactory dismissal from the previous institution. Grades of D or better transfer for credit. 30 of 124 credits required for the bachelor's degree must be completed at Briar Cliff.

Visiting: There are regularly scheduled orientations for prospective students, including a presidential welcome, a meeting with faculty and student panels, a luncheon, campus tours, a slide show, and financial aid information. There are guides for informal visits and visitors may sit in on classes and stay overnight. To schedule a visit, contact the Admissions Office at (800) 662-3303, ext. 5200.

Financial Aid: In 2005-2006, all of full-time freshmen and 97% of continuing full-time students received some form of financial aid. All of full-time freshmen and 97% of continuing full-time students received need-based aid. The average freshman award was $24,500. Need-based scholarships or need-based grants averaged $2377 ($8000 maximum); need-based self-help aid (loans and jobs) averaged $4533 ($8125 maximum); non-need-based athletic scholarships averaged $3463 ($17,490 maximum); and other non-need-based awards and non-need-based scholarships averaged $6324 ($17,490 maximum). 25% of undergraduates work part time. Average annual earnings from campus work are $675. The average financial indebtedness of the 2005 graduate was $22,964. The FAFSA is required. The priority date for freshman financial aid applications for fall entry is March 1.

International Students: There are 2 international students enrolled. They must score satisfactorily on the written TOEFL.

Computers: Wireless access is available. Briar Cliff University's campus-wide network of PCs offers students access to the Internet, Office 2003 (including Access, Excel, Front Page, Outlook, PowerPoint, Publisher, and Word), and Web Advisor access to Datatel's student information system. Briar Cliff University currently has 114 PC's located in labs throughout the campus, including a lab on each residence hall floor, in the library, the student center, and three classroom/labs in the main academic building. Wireless network access is available in the student center, the science wing of the main academic building, and the main athletic facility. All students may access the system 24 hours each day. There are no time limits and no fees.

Graduates: From July 1, 2004 to June 30, 2005, 181 bachelor's degrees were awarded. The most popular majors were business administration (16%), education (14%), and nursing (11%). In an average class, 40% graduate in 4 years or less, 51% graduate in 5 years or less, and 52% graduate in 6 years or less. Of the 2004 graduating class, 16% were enrolled in graduate school within 6 months of graduation and 81% were employed.

Admissions Contact: Sharisue Wilcoxon, Vice President/Enrollment Management. E-mail: *Sharisue.Wilcoxon@briarcliff.edu* Web: *www.briarcliff.edu*

BUENA VISTA UNIVERSITY
B-2

Storm Lake, IA 50588
(712) 749-2235
(800) 383-9600; Fax: (712) 749-2037

Full-time: 574 men, 624 women	Faculty: 82
Part-time: 8 men, 8 women	Ph.D.s: 82%
Graduate: 16 men, 53 women	Student/Faculty: 15 to 1
Year: 4-1-4, summer session	Tuition: $21,688
Application Deadline: open	Room & Board: $6054
Freshman Class: n/av	
ACT: 22	COMPETITIVE

Buena Vista University, founded in 1891, is a private institution affiliated with the Presbyterian Church (U.S.A.). The university offers undergraduate degree programs in business, education, communication and arts, science, social science, philosophy, and religion, and an accredited master's program in education. Programs emphasize career education with a liberal arts foundation. There are 5 undergraduate schools and 1 graduate school. In addition to regional accreditation, Buena Vista has baccalaureate program accreditation with CSWE. The library contains 132,000 volumes, 41,348 microform items, and 3920 audio/video tapes/CDs/DVDs, and subscribes to 675 periodicals including electronic. Computerized library services include the card catalog, interlibrary loans, database searching, and Internet access. Special learning facilities include a learning resource center, art gallery, radio station, TV station, and student newspaper desktop production lab. The 60-acre campus is in a small town 65 miles east of Sioux City. Including any residence halls, there are 16 buildings.

Student Life: 78% of undergraduates are from Iowa. Students are from 16 states and 1 foreign country. 92% are from public schools. 92% are white. 55% are Protestant; 27% Catholic; 12% claim no religious affiliation. The average age of freshmen is 18; all undergraduates, 20. 24% do not continue beyond their first year; 62% remain to graduate.

Housing: 1142 students can be accommodated in college housing, which includes single-sex and coed dorms and on-campus apartments. In addition, there are honors houses and special-interest houses. On-campus housing is guaranteed for all 4 years. 88% of students live on campus; of those, 60% remain on campus on weekends. All students may keep cars.

Activities: There are no fraternities or sororities. There are 50 groups on campus, including art, band, cheerleading, choir, chorale, chorus, computers, debate, drama, drill team, environmental, ethnic, gay, gender, honors, international, jazz band, literary magazine, musical theater, newspaper, orchestra, pep band, photography, political, professional, radio and TV, religious, social, social service, student government, and yearbook. Popular campus events include Winter Olympics, Academic and Cultural Events Series, and Buenafication Day.

Sports: There are 10 intercollegiate sports for men and 9 for women, and 10 intramural sports for men and 10 for women. Facilities include a 380-seat auditorium, a 1000-seat auditorium, a 4000-seat stadium, a field house with a 4000-seat gym, basketball, volleyball, racquetball, and tennis courts, football, softball, and baseball fields, a track, facilities for weight training and other recreational activities, an Olympic-size indoor pool, and a game room.

Disabled Students: 90% of the campus is accessible. Wheelchair ramps, elevators, special parking, specially equipped rest rooms, special class scheduling, lowered drinking fountains, lowered telephones, and automatic/remote-controlled doors are available.

Services: Counseling and information services are available, as is tutoring in most subjects. There is a reader service for the blind, and remedial math, reading, and writing.

Campus Safety and Security: Measures include 24-hour foot and vehicle patrol, self-defense education, security escort services, and shuttle buses. There are informal discussions, pamphlets/posters/films, emergency telephones, lighted pathways/sidewalks, and and an enhanced 911 system on campus.

Programs of Study: Buena Vista confers B.A. and B.S. degrees. Master's degrees are also awarded. Bachelor's degrees are awarded in BIOLOGICAL SCIENCE (biology/biological science), BUSINESS (accounting, banking and finance, business administration and management, business economics, international business management, marketing/retailing/merchandising, and sports management), COMMUNICATIONS AND THE ARTS (art, arts administration/management, communications, English, graphic design, music, Spanish, and speech/debate/rhetoric), COMPUTER AND PHYSICAL SCIENCE (chemistry, computer science, mathematics, physics, and science), EDUCATION (art, business, elementary, middle school, music, science, secondary, and special), SOCIAL SCIENCE (criminal justice, economics, history, philosophy, physical fitness/movement, political science/government, psychology, public administration, religion, social science, and social work). Biology, mass communication, and business are the strongest academically. Education, biology, and management are the largest.

Required: All students must complete 6 semester hours each of natural sciences, humanities, social sciences, communication, and writing, and 3 semester hours of fine arts. In addition, students must successfully complete English 100 and 200, demonstrate proficiency by exam in math and writing, and participate in the Academic and Cultural Events Series, through which they attend lectures and performances by national and world leaders. The bachelor's degree requires a minimum of 128 semester hours, including 30 to 62 hours in the major, with a GPA of at least 2.0, or 2.5 for education majors.

Special: Special academic offerings include a work-study program with Marriott Corporation, and a 3-2 engineering degree program with Washington University in St. Louis. Students may study abroad in Japan, Taiwan, Australia, and Europe. Buena Vista offers dual and student-designed majors, credit for life experience, and pass/fail options in courses outside the major field. Nondegree study is possible. Internships are required in many majors and encouraged in most. The J. Leslie Rollins Fellowship allows 1 or 2 students each year to design an internship anywhere in the world. There is 1 national honor society and a freshman honors program.

Faculty/Classroom: 56% of faculty are male; 44%, female. All teach undergraduates. The average class size in an introductory lecture is 30; in a laboratory, 25; and in a regular course, 18.

Admissions: The ACT scores for the 2005-2006 freshman class were: 35% below 21, 29% between 21 and 23, 23% between 24 and 26, 5% between 27 and 28, and 8% above 28. 28% of the current freshmen were in the top fifth of their class; 60% were in the top two fifths. There were 20 National Merit semifinalists. 22 freshmen graduated first in their class.

Requirements: The ACT is recommended. SAT scores may be submitted instead. Minimum score should be 21 on the ACT. Applicants must be graduates of an accredited secondary school or have earned a GED. The college requires 13 academic credits, including 4 of English and 3 each of math, social studies, and science. Campus visits and an interview are recommended. A GPA of 2.75 is required. AP and CLEP credits are accepted. Important factors in the admissions decision are advanced placement or honor courses, leadership record, and recommendations by school officials.

Procedure: Freshmen are admitted fall, winter, and spring. Entrance exams should be taken during the spring of the junior year or October of the senior year. There are deferred admissions and rolling admissions plans. Application deadlines are open. Applications are accepted on-line.

Transfer: 42 transfer students enrolled in 2004-2005. A high school diploma and a minimum GPA of 2.5 from the applicant's college are required. 30 of 128 credits required for the bachelor's degree must be completed at Buena Vista.

Visiting: There are regularly scheduled orientations for prospective students, including a campus tour and meetings with an admissions counselor, faculty representatives, coaches, and activity representatives in the student's areas of interest. There are guides for informal visits and visitors may sit in on classes and stay overnight. To schedule a visit, contact the Director of Admissions.

Financial Aid: The average freshman award was $20,022. 60% of undergraduates work part time. Average annual earnings from campus work are $787. The average financial indebtedness of the 2005 graduate was $26,759. The FAFSA and the college's own financial statement are required. The deadline for filing freshman financial aid applications for fall entry is June 1.

International Students: There are 4 international students enrolled. The school actively recruits these students. They must score satisfactory on the written TOEFL.

Computers: Wireless access is available. All students may access the system. There are no time limits and no fees.

Graduates: In a recent year, 253 bachelor's degrees were awarded. In an average class, 1% graduate in 3 years or less, 51% graduate in 4 years or less, 60% graduate in 5 years or less, and 62% graduate in 6 years or less. 40 companies recruited on campus in a recent year. Of a recent graduating class, 14% were enrolled in graduate school within 6 months of graduation and 98% were employed.

Admissions Contact: Chris Coons, Director of Admissions. A video is available. E-mail: *admissions@bvu.edu* Web: *www.bvu.edu*

CENTRAL COLLEGE   D-3

Pella, IA 50219

(641) 628-5285
(877) 462-3687; Fax: (641) 628-5316

Full-time: 702 men, 899 women	Faculty: 95; IIB, --$
Part-time: 19 men, 15 women	Ph.D.s: 88%
Graduate: none	Student/Faculty: 17 to 1
Year: semesters, summer session	Tuition: $19,928
Application Deadline: March 1	Room & Board: $6846
Freshman Class: n/av	
ACT: 24	VERY COMPETITIVE

Central College, founded in 1853, is a private institution affiliated with the Reformed Church in America. The college offers undergraduate degree programs in applied arts, behavioral sciences, cross-cultural studies, fine arts, humanities, and natural sciences. In addition to regional accreditation, Central has baccalaureate program accreditation with NASM and NCATE. The 3 libraries contain 229,223 volumes, 51,952 microform items, and 8500 audio/video tapes/CDs/DVDs, and subscribe to 925 periodicals including electronic. Computerized library services include the card catalog, interlibrary loans, database searching, Internet access, and laptop Internet portals. Special learning facilities include a learning resource center, art gallery, radio station, and a fiber-optic classroom. The 133-acre campus is in a suburban area 45 miles southeast of Des Moines. Including any residence halls, there are 45 buildings.

Student Life: 79% of undergraduates are from Iowa. Others are from 39 states and 17 foreign countries. 98% are from public schools. 88% are white. 67% are Protestant; 14% Catholic; 11% claim no religious affiliation. The average age of freshmen is 18; all undergraduates, 20. 20% do not continue beyond their first year.

Housing: 1415 students can be accommodated in college housing, which includes single-sex and coed dorms, on-campus apartments, married-student housing, fraternity houses, and sorority houses. In addition, there are honors houses, language houses, and special-interest houses. On-campus housing is guaranteed for all 4 years. 87% of students live on campus; of those, 70% remain on campus on weekends. Alcohol is not permitted. All students may keep cars.

Activities: 12% of men belong to 4 local fraternities; 5% of women belong to 3 local sororities. There are 71 groups on campus, including art, band, cheerleading, choir, chorus, drama, drill team, ethnic, gay, honors, international, jazz band, literary magazine, marching band, musical theater, newspaper, opera, orchestra, pep band, photography, political, professional, radio and TV, religious, social, social service, student government, and symphony. Popular campus events include Career Day, Interdisciplinary Research Symposium, and Academic Seminar.

Sports: There are 10 intercollegiate sports for men and 9 for women, and 12 intramural sports for men and 12 for women. Facilities include an athletic complex with a 4000-seat stadium and 2500-seat gym, a 700-seat auditorium, a golf driving range, several practice and competition fields, tennis courts, a field house with an indoor track, a cross-country course, and a 7000-square-foot fitness center.

Disabled Students: 90% of the campus is accessible. Wheelchair ramps, elevators, special parking, specially equipped rest rooms, special class scheduling, lowered drinking fountains, and lowered telephones are available.

Services: Counseling and information services are available, as is tutoring in every subject. There is a reader service for the blind.

Campus Safety and Security: Measures include 24-hour foot and vehicle patrol, self-defense education, security escort services, and informal discussions. There are pamphlets/posters/films, emergency telephones, and lighted pathways/sidewalks.

Programs of Study: Central confers the B.A. degree. Bachelor's degrees are awarded in BIOLOGICAL SCIENCE (biology/biological science), BUSINESS (accounting, business administration and management, and international business management), COMMUNICATIONS AND THE ARTS (communications, dramatic arts, English, fine arts, French, German, languages, linguistics, music, and Spanish), COMPUTER AND PHYSICAL SCIENCE (chemistry, computer science, mathematics, and physics), EDUCATION (elementary, music, and secondary), ENGINEERING AND ENVIRONMENTAL DESIGN (environmental science), HEALTH PROFESSIONS (exercise science), SOCIAL SCIENCE (anthropology, economics, history, international studies, philosophy, political science/government, psychology, religion, and sociology). Business management, elementary education, and exercise science are the largest.

Required: General education requirements include 44 semester hours, including 11 in cultural awareness, 6 each in central foundations and core focus, and 3 each in art, historical perspectives, mathematical reasoning, religion, scientific inquiry, social and behavioral inquiry, and textual interpretation. Each department also establishes a communication skill requirement, and foreign language proficiency must be demonstrated. To graduate, students must complete a minimum of 120 semester hours with a GPA of at least 2.0.

Special: Nearly half the students participate in study-abroad programs in London, Paris, Vienna, Mexico, Spain, Wales, England, China, and the Netherlands. Central also offers a Washington semester, a Chicago program, numerous internship opportunities, and work-study. A 3-4 program in architecture and a 3-2 degree program in engineering are offered with Washington University in St. Louis. A general studies degree, student-designed majors, and pass/no-credit options are possible. There is 1 national honor society and a freshman honors program.

Faculty/Classroom: 64% of faculty are male; 36%, female. All both teach and do research. The average class size in an introductory lecture is 19; in a laboratory, 15; and in a regular course, 20.

Admissions: The ACT scores for the 2005-2006 freshman class were: 21% below 21, 30% between 21 and 23, 26% between 24 and 26, 11% between 27 and 28, and 12% above 28. 49% of the current freshmen were in the top fifth of their class; 71% were in the top two fifths. 18 freshmen graduated first in their class.

Requirements: The SAT or ACT is required. In addition, applicants must be graduates of an accredited secondary school or have earned a GED. Central requires 16 academic credits and recommends that they include 4 years of English, 3 each of lab science, social studies, and math, including 2 in algebra and 1 in geometry, and 2 of foreign language. An interview is required and an essay is recommended. Central requires applicants to be in the upper 50% of their class. A GPA of 2.7 is required. AP and CLEP credits are accepted. Important factors in the admissions decision are leadership record, recommendations by school officials, and evidence of special talent.

Procedure: Freshmen are admitted to all sessions. Entrance exams should be taken in the spring of the junior year. There is a deferred admissions plan and a rolling admissions plan. Applications should be filed by March 1 for fall entry, November 1 for spring entry, and May 1 for summer entry, along with a $25 fee. Notification is sent on a rolling basis. Applications are accepted on-line.

Transfer: Each tranfer student is considered individually. Interviews are encouraged. 30 of 120 credits required for the bachelor's degree must be completed at Central.

Visiting: There are regularly scheduled orientations for prospective students, including a campus tour, a registration session with academic advisers, and presentations by the academic dean, student life dean, financial aid director, and admissions staff. There are guides for informal visits and visitors may sit in on classes and stay overnight. To schedule a visit, contact the Admissions Office at *admission@central.edu*.

Financial Aid: In 2005-2006, all full-time students received some form of financial aid. 83% of full-time freshmen and 81% of continuing full-time students received need-based aid. The average freshman award was $16,233, with $10,533 ($25,100 maximum) from need-based scholarships or grants, $2,779 ($6,125 maximum) from need-based self-help aid (loans and jobs), $2,155 ($22,675 maximum) from other non-need-based awards and non-need-based scholarships and $766 ($5520 maximum) from grants, scholarships, and no-need work and loans. 82% of undergraduates work part time. Average annual earnings from campus work are $713. The average financial indebtedness of the 2005 graduate was $19,851. Central is a member of CSS. The FAFSA is required. The deadline for filing freshman financial aid applications for fall entry is April 1.

International Students: There are 29 international students enrolled. The school actively recruits these students. They must take the TOEFL.

Computers: Wireless access is available. Central provides 392 computers for student use in labs and classrooms plus another 194 in the library and for special academic use. More than 90% of Central students bring their own computers to campus and Central provides a dedicated high-speed Internet connection for each student in residence halls. The science center has wireless network access and the school has a 12 Mpbs connection to the Internet including 8 Mbps dedicated to residential use. All students may access the system. There are no time limits. The fee is $250 per year.

Graduates: From July 1, 2004 to June 30, 2005, 368 bachelor's degrees were awarded. The most popular majors were business management (13%), elementary education (12%), and exercise science (11%). In an average class, 66% graduate in 4 years or less. 80 companies recruited on campus in 2004-2005. Of the 2004 graduating class, 18% were enrolled in graduate school within 6 months of graduation and 90% were employed.

Admissions Contact: Carol Williams, Dean of Admission.
E-mail: *admissions@central.edu* Web: *www.central.edu*

CLARKE COLLEGE E-2
Dubuque, IA 52001

(563) 588-6316
(800) 383-2345; Fax: (563) 588-6789

Full-time: 248 men, 609 women	Faculty: 83
Part-time: 48 men, 116 women	Ph.D.s: 54%
Graduate: 48 men, 177 women	Student/Faculty: 10 to 1
Year: semesters, summer session	Tuition: $18,945
Application Deadline: open	Room & Board: $6445
Freshman Class: 478 accepted, 158 enrolled	
SAT Verbal/Math: 559/548*	ACT: 23 COMPETITIVE

Clarke College, established in 1843, is a private Catholic institution. A strong liberal arts core is integrated into all majors and preprofessional programs. In addition to regional accreditation, Clarke has baccalaureate program accreditation with APTA, CSWE, NASM, NCATE, and NLN. The library contains 128,598 volumes, 11,792 microform items, and 1530 audio/video tapes/CDs/DVDs, and subscribes to 14,046 periodicals including electronic. Computerized library services include the card catalog, interlibrary loans, database searching, and Internet access. Special learning facilities include a learning resource center, art gallery, planetarium, an art slide library, electronic music studio, and several computer-integrated specialized departmental labs. The 55-acre campus is in an urban area 150 miles west of Chicago. Including any residence halls, there are 13 buildings.

Student Life: 65% of undergraduates are from Iowa. Others are from 30 states and 9 foreign countries. 80% are from public schools. 92% are white. 51% are Catholic; 30% claim no religious affiliation; 12% Protestant. The average age of freshmen is 18; all undergraduates, 26. 22% do not continue beyond their first year; 58% remain to graduate.

Housing: 585 students can be accommodated in college housing, which includes single-sex and coed dorms, on-campus apartments, a residence hall reserved for upperclassmen, and an apartment building reserved for juniors and seniors. On-campus housing is guaranteed for all 4 years. 60% of students live on campus; of those, 33% remain on campus on weekends. All students may keep cars.

Activities: There are no fraternities or sororities. There are 50 groups on campus, including art, cheerleading, choir, chorus, computers, drama, ethnic, honors, international, jazz band, literary magazine, newspaper, pep band, photography, political, professional, religious, social, social service, student government, and yearbook. Popular campus events include Family Weekend, New Year's Dance, and Midnight Pancake Breakfast.

Sports: There are 8 intercollegiate sports for men and 8 for women, and 15 intramural sports for men and 13 for women. Facilities include a 1000-seat gym, a 700-seat arena, an indoor track, a swimming pool, a soccer field, basketball, volleyball, tennis, and racquetball courts, a fitness trail, weight and aerobics rooms, and an indoor batting cage/pitching mound area. There are baseball/softball fields and 2 alpine ski courses nearby, plus a municipal golf course adjacent to the campus.

Disabled Students: 90% of the campus is accessible. Wheelchair ramps, elevators, special parking, specially equipped rest rooms, special class scheduling, lowered drinking fountains, and lowered telephones are available.

Services: Counseling and information services are available, as is tutoring in most subjects. There is remedial math, reading, and writing.

Campus Safety and Security: Measures include 24-hour foot and vehicle patrol, informal discussions, pamphlets/posters/films, and emergency telephones. There are lighted pathways/sidewalks.

Programs of Study: Clarke confers B.A., B.S., and B.F.A. degrees. Associate, master's, and doctoral degrees are also awarded. Bachelor's degrees are awarded in BIOLOGICAL SCIENCE (biochemistry, bioinformatics, and biology/biological science), BUSINESS (accounting, business administration and management, and marketing management), COMMUNICATIONS AND THE ARTS (advertising, art, art history and appreciation, communications, dramatic arts, English, music, Spanish, and studio art), COMPUTER AND PHYSICAL SCIENCE (chemistry, computer science, information sciences and systems, and mathematics), EDUCATION (art, elementary, music, secondary, and special), HEALTH PROFESSIONS (nursing and physical therapy), SOCIAL SCIENCE (history, liberal arts/general studies, philosophy, physical fitness/movement, political science/government, psychology, religion, social work, and sociology). Biology, education, and computer science are the strongest academically. Business administration, education,and psychology are the largest.

Required: To graduate, all students must complete 124 semester hours, with 30 to 70 in the major, and maintain a GPA of 2.0 (2.5 for education majors or 3.25 for physical therapy majors). Students must complete Cornerstone I and II, a Capstone course, and 6 hours each in religious studies, philosophy, fine arts, humanities, math and natural sciences, and social sciences

Special: There are co-op programs in most majors, cross-registration with Loras College and the University of Dubuque, and study abroad. Clarke also offers internships in chemistry, biology, and communications; an accelerated degree program in many majors for nontraditional, evening students; a B.A.-B.S. degree in biology, chemistry, psychology, business, and computer science; and a B.F.A.-B.A. program in art. There are also on- and off-campus work-study programs, dual majors, student-designed majors, and a freshman-entry 6-year physical therapy program. There are 4 national honor societies, a freshman honors program, and 3 departmental honors programs.

Faculty/Classroom: 39% of faculty are male; 61%, female. 100% both teach and do research. No introductory courses are taught by graduate students. The average class size in an introductory lecture is 24; in a laboratory, 11; and in a regular course, 14.

Admissions: The SAT scores for the 2005-2006 freshman class were: Verbal--40% below 500, 30% between 500 and 599, 10% between 600 and 700, and 20% above 700; Math--50% below 500, 10% between 500 and 599, 20% between 600 and 700, and 20% above 700. 34% of the current freshmen were in the top fifth of their class; 75% were in the top two fifths. 16 freshmen graduated first in their class.

Requirements: The SAT or ACT is required. In addition, the high school transcript should include 4 years of English, 3 each of math, history/social science, and science (4 for human biology and physical therapy majors), 2 of the same foreign language, and 5 of electives. Clarke requires applicants to be in the upper 50% of their class. A GPA of 2.0 is required. AP and CLEP credits are accepted. Advanced placement or honor courses are an important factor in the admission decision.

Procedure: Freshmen are admitted to all sessions. Entrance exams should be taken in the spring of the junior year or the fall of the senior year. There is a deferred admissions plan. Application deadlines are open. Applications are accepted on-line.

Transfer: 66 transfer students enrolled in 2004-2005. Applicants must submit a transcript and a recommendation from the dean of students for each college attended. Students with fewer than 24 completed semester hours must also submit a high school transcript and SAT or ACT scores. 30 of 124 credits required for the bachelor's degree must be completed at Clarke.

Visiting: There are guides for informal visits and visitors may sit in on classes and stay overnight. To schedule a visit, contact the Admissions Office at *admissions@clarke.edu.*

Financial Aid: In 2005-2006, 100% of all full-time freshmen and 98% of continuing full-time students received some form of financial aid. 93% of full-time freshmen and 86% of continuing full-time students received need-based aid. The average freshman award was $18,968. Need-based scholarships or need-based grants averaged $16,125; need-based self-help aid (loans and jobs) averaged $3366; non-need-based athletic scholarships averaged $2776; and other non-need-based awards and non-need-based scholarships averaged $12,252. 75% of undergraduates work part time. Average annual earnings from campus work are $904. The average financial indebtedness of the 2005 graduate was $18,000. The FAFSA is required.

International Students: There are 11 international students enrolled. The school actively recruits these students. They must take the written TOEFL.

Computers: Wireless network is available in the library, atrium, and in some classrooms. All students may access the system at any time. There are no time limits. The fee is $150 per year.

Graduates: From July 1, 2004 to June 30, 2005, 191 bachelor's degrees were awarded. The most popular majors were business administration (17%), education (9%), and psychology (9%). In an average class, 45% graduate in 4 years or less, 56% graduate in 5 years or less, and 58% graduate in 6 years or less. 50 companies recruited on campus in 2004-2005. Of the 2004 graduating class, 23% were enrolled in graduate school within 6 months of graduation and 69% were employed.

Admissions Contact: Sharon Lyons, Director of Admissions.
E-mail: *Sharon.lyons@clarke.edu* Web: *http://www.clarke.edu*

COE COLLEGE
Cedar Rapids, IA 52402 E-3

(319) 399-8500
(877) CALL-COE; Fax: (319) 399-8816

Full-time: 510 men, 670 women	Faculty: 74; IIB, av$
Part-time: 55 men, 60 women	Ph.D.s: 95%
Graduate: 5 men, 25 women	Student/Faculty: 16 to 1
Year: semesters, summer session	Tuition: $21,650
Application Deadline: see profile	Room & Board: $5790
Freshman Class: n/a	
SAT or ACT: required	VERY COMPETITIVE

Coe College, founded in 1851, is a private liberal arts institution affiliated with the Presbyterian Church (U.S.A.). Figures in the above capsule are approximate. In addition to regional accreditation, Coe has baccalaureate program accreditation with CAAHEP, NASM, and NLN. The 2 libraries contain 216,699 volumes, 5828 microform items, and 9044 audio/video tapes/CDs/DVDs, and subscribe to 1380 periodicals including electronic. Computerized library services include the card catalog, interlibrary loans, database searching, and Internet access. Special learning facilities include a learning resource center, art gallery, radio station, and an ornithological wing. The 53-acre campus is in an urban area 225

miles west of Chicago. Including any residence halls, there are 22 buildings.

Student Life: 68% of undergraduates are from Iowa. Others are from 34 states and 16 foreign countries. 90% are from public schools. 92% are white. The average age of freshmen is 18; all undergraduates, 22. 19% do not continue beyond their first year; 70% remain to graduate.

Housing: 1036 students can be accommodated in college housing, which includes single-sex and coed dormitories and on-campus apartments. In addition, there are special-interest houses and a substance-free facility. On-campus housing is guaranteed for all 4 years. 85% of students live on campus; of those, 75% remain on campus on weekends. All students may keep cars.

Activities: 26% of men belong to 5 national fraternities; 19% of women belong to 3 national sororities. There are 60 groups on campus, including art, band, cheerleading, choir, chorale, chorus, computers, dance, drama, ethnic, gay, honors, international, jazz band, literary magazine, newspaper, orchestra, pep band, political, professional, religious, social, social service, student government, and yearbook. Popular campus events include Coe Olympics, International Student Banquet and Cultural Show, and Flunk Day.

Sports: There are 11 intercollegiate sports for men and 10 for women, and 24 intramural sports for men and 24 for women. Facilities include a racquet center with 4 indoor and 6 outdoor tennis courts, 4 racquetball courts, 2 squash courts, and a 200-meter indoor track; and a field house with an indoor natatorium, an indoor track, a wrestling room, a fitness center, a rock climbing wall, courts for basketball and volleyball, and batting cages for baseball and softball. There also is a 400-meter outdoor track, softball diamond, and 1100-seat football/soccer stadium.

Disabled Students: 40% of the campus is accessible. Wheelchair ramps, elevators, special parking, specially equipped rest rooms, and special class scheduling are available.

Services: Counseling and information services are available, as is tutoring in most subjects. There is a reader service for the blind. A writing center and an educational support program are available.

Campus Safety and Security: Measures include 24-hour foot and vehicle patrol, security escort services, informal discussions, and pamphlets/posters/films. There are emergency telephones and lighted pathways/sidewalks.

Programs of Study: Coe confers B.A., B.Mus., and B.S.N. degrees. Master's degrees are also awarded. Bachelor's degrees are awarded in BIOLOGICAL SCIENCE (biochemistry, biology/biological science, and molecular biology), BUSINESS (accounting and business administration and management), COMMUNICATIONS AND THE ARTS (art, dramatic arts, English, French, German, literature, music, public relations, and Spanish), COMPUTER AND PHYSICAL SCIENCE (chemistry, computer science, mathematics, physics, and science), EDUCATION (athletic training, elementary, music, physical, and secondary), ENGINEERING AND ENVIRONMENTAL DESIGN (environmental science and preengineering), HEALTH PROFESSIONS (medical laboratory technology, nursing, physical therapy, predentistry, and premedicine), SOCIAL SCIENCE (African American studies, American studies, Asian/Oriental studies, classical/ancient civilization, economics, history, human services, interdisciplinary studies, philosophy, political science/government, prelaw, psychology, religion, sociology, and women's studies). Chemistry, physics, and psychology are the strongest academically. Business administration, psychology, and biology are the largest.

Required: All students must take 4 writing-emphasis courses, a first-year seminar, and a distribution of courses in fine arts, natural science, social science, and Western and foreign culture. A minimum of 32 course credits, including 9 to 12 in the major, and a 2.0 GPA are required for graduation. Students in an honors program must submit a thesis, and psychology and physics majors must pass a comprehensive examination. All students are required to do an internship, practicum, independent research project, or off-campus study program.

Special: Coe offers cross-registration with nearby Mount Mercy College and the University of Iowa; a cooperative program in architecture; Washington and New York semesters; and study abroad in 17 countries. Non-degree study, and dual and student-designed majors also are possible. Practicum experience is required. Core course instructors serve as students' mentors. There are 8 national honor societies, including Phi Beta Kappa, a freshman honors program, and all departments have honors programs.

Faculty/Classroom: 58% of faculty are male; 42%, female. All teach undergraduates and 95% both teach and do research. No introductory courses are taught by graduate students. The average class size in an introductory lecture is 13; in a laboratory, 14; and in a regular course, 16.

Requirements: The SAT or ACT is required. In addition, Coe recommends that applicants have 4 years in English, 3 each in math, history, science, and social studies, and 2 in foreign language. All students must submit an essay. In addition, fine arts students need a portfolio or audition. The GED is accepted. Coe requires applicants to be in the upper 60% of their class. A GPA of 2.75 is required. AP and CLEP credits are accepted. Important factors in the admissions decision are advanced placement or honor courses, recommendations by school officials, and extracurricular activities record.

Procedure: Freshmen are admitted fall and spring. Entrance exams should be taken in the spring of the junior year or the fall of the senior year. There is a deferred admissions plan. Check with the school for application deadlines. Applications are accepted on-line.

Transfer: 49 transfer students enrolled in a reent year. Applicants must be high school graduates, have a minimum GPA of 2.5, and submit either the SAT or ACT scores. An associate degree and an interview also are recommended. 8 of 32 credits required for the bachelor's degree must be completed at Coe.

Visiting: There are regularly scheduled orientations for prospective students, consisting of tours, a luncheon, and informational sessions on admission, financial aid, and student life. There are guides for informal visits and visitors may sit in on classes and stay overnight. To schedule a visit, contact Sharon Fair, Campus Visit Coordinator.

Financial Aid: In a recent year, 98% of all full-time freshmen and 95% of continuing full-time students received some form of financial aid. 80% of full-time freshmen and 79% of continuing full-time students received need-based aid. The average freshman award was $19,879. Need-based scholarships or need-based grants averaged $14,657 ($21,280 maximum); need-based self-help aid (loans and jobs) averaged $5492 ($8225 maximum); and other non-need-based awards and non-need-based scholarships averaged $9396 ($13,000 maximum). 43% of undergraduates worked part time. Average annual earnings from campus work were $1400. The average financial indebtedness of a recent graduate was $22,157. The FAFSA is required. Check with the school for application deadlines.

International Students: In a recent year, there were 66 international students enrolled. The school actively recruits these students. They must score satisfactorily on the TOEFL and also take the SAT or the ACT.

Computers: All students may access the system 24 hours a day. There are no time limits and no fees.

Graduates: In a recent year, 307 bachelor's degrees were awarded. The most popular majors were economics and business administration (16%), psychology (7%), and biology (5%). In an average class, 63% graduate in 4 years or less, and 69% graduate in 5 years or less. 81 companies recruited on campus in a recent year. Of a recent graduating class, 28% were enrolled in graduate school within 6 months of graduation and 70% were employed.

Admissions Contact: John Sullivan, Executive Director of Admission and Financial Aid. E-mail: *jsulliva@coe.edu* Web: *www.coe.edu*

CORNELL COLLEGE · E-3
Mount Vernon, IA 52314-1098
(319) 895-4215
(800) 747-1112; Fax: (319) 895-4451

Full-time: 524 men, 642 women	Faculty: 94; IIB, -$
Part-time: 4 men, 9 women	Ph.D.s: 91%
Graduate: none	Student/Faculty: 12 to 1
Year: n/app	Tuition: $23,680
Application Deadline: February 1	Room & Board: $6430
Freshman Class: 1653 applied, 1096 accepted, 319 enrolled	
SAT Verbal/Math: 630/620*	ACT: 26 VERY COMPETITIVE+

Cornell College, founded in 1853, is private institution affiliated with the United Methodist Church. Its emphases are on the liberal arts and on student service and leadership. Cornell has a 1-course-at-a-time calendar in which the year is divided into nine 3 1/2 week terms. In addition to regional accreditation, Cornell has baccalaureate program accreditation with NASM. The library contains 177,554 volumes, 75,514 microform items, and 7358 audio/video tapes/CDs/DVDs, and subscribes to 779 periodicals including electronic. Computerized library services include the card catalog, interlibrary loans, database searching, Internet access, and laptop Internet portals. Special learning facilities include a learning resource center, art gallery, natural history museum, and radio station. The 129-acre campus is in a small town 15 miles east of Cedar Rapids. Including any residence halls, there are 44 buildings.

Student Life: 70% of undergraduates are from out of state, mostly the Midwest. Students are from 45 states, 16 foreign countries, and Canada. 89% are from public schools. 85% are white. 48% are claim no religious affiliation; 35% Protestant; 15% Catholic. The average age of freshmen is 18; all undergraduates, 20. 19% do not continue beyond their first year; 66% remain to graduate.

Housing: 1088 students can be accommodated in college housing, which includes single-sex and coed dormitories and on-campus apartments. In addition, there are special-interest houses and living and learning communities. On-campus housing is guaranteed for all 4 years. 90% of students live on campus; of those, 70% remain on campus on weekends. All students may keep cars.

Activities: 30% of men belong to 8 local fraternities; 32% of women belong to 7 local sororities. There are 76 groups on campus, including art, band, cheerleading, chess, choir, chorale, chorus, computers, dance, debate, drama, environmental, ethnic, gay, honors, international, jazz band, leadership development, literary magazine, musical theater, newspaper, opera, orchestra, pep band, performing arts, photography, political, professional, radio and TV, religious, social, social service, student government, and yearbook. Popular campus events include Knock Your Block Off.

Sports: There are 10 intercollegiate sports for men and 9 for women, and 40 intramural sports for men and 40 for women. Facilities include a multisport center, including a 2100-seat basketball and volleyball arena, sports fitness and training facilities, 6-lane track, 4 multipurpose courts for tennis, basketball, and volleyball, batting cages, golf hitting nets; a 2500-seat football and track stadium; and baseball, soccer, softball, and football practice fields and 6 outdoor tennis courts.

Disabled Students: 43% of the campus is accessible. Wheelchair ramps, elevators, special parking, specially equipped rest rooms, special class scheduling, lowered drinking fountains, and lowered telephones are available.

Services: Counseling and information services are available, as is tutoring in every subject. There is a reader service for the blind.

Campus Safety and Security: Measures include 24-hour foot and vehicle patrol, self-defense education, security escort services, and informal discussions. There are pamphlets/posters/films, emergency telephones and lighted pathways/sidewalks. A foot and vehicle patrol runs 24 hours on weekends and 4 P.M. to 7 A.M. during weekdays.

Programs of Study: Cornell confers B.A., B.Mus., B.Ph., and B.S.S. degrees. Bachelor's degrees are awarded in BIOLOGICAL SCIENCE (biology/biological science), BUSINESS (international business management), COMMUNICATIONS AND THE ARTS (dramatic arts, English, fine arts, French, German, languages, music, Russian, and Spanish), COMPUTER AND PHYSICAL SCIENCE (chemistry, computer science, geology, mathematics, and physics), EDUCATION (art, elementary, foreign languages, music, science, and secondary), ENGINEERING AND ENVIRONMENTAL DESIGN (environmental science), SOCIAL SCIENCE (anthropology, classical/ancient civilization, economics, history, international relations, Latin American studies, medieval studies, philosophy, political science/government, psychology, religion, sociology, and women's studies). Art, geology, and philosophy are the strongest academically. Psychology, education, and economics are the largest.

Required: To graduate, all students must complete 32 course credits (128 semester hours), with 7 to 15 in a faculty-approved major, and maintain at least a 2.0 GPA; at least one writing course is required. B.A. candidates must complete 4 courses in humanities, 2 each in science (1 with a lab) and social science, 1 each in fine arts and math, and 1 to 4 in a foreign language. B.S.S. candidates need not meet all of the above requirements.

Special: Special academic programs include study abroad in 25 countries, internships including a Washington semester, double majors, student-designed majors, and interdisciplinary majors in biochemistry and molecular biology, environmental studies, international relations, and women's studies. A cooperative degree program in nursing and allied health services with Rush University, a 3-2 engineering program and a 3-4 architecture program with Washington University, and a 3-2 forestry or environmental management program with Duke University are also available. Nondegree study is possible. There are 9 national honor societies, including Phi Beta Kappa.

Faculty/Classroom: 52% of faculty are male; 48%, female. All teach undergraduates, 75% do research, and 75% do both. The average class size in an introductory lecture is 20; in a laboratory, 16; and in a regular course, 17.

Admissions: 66% of the 2005-2006 applicants were accepted. The SAT scores for the 2005-2006 freshman class were: Verbal--5% below 500, 29% between 500 and 599, 49% between 600 and 700, and 17% above 700; Math--6% below 500, 34% between 500 and 599, 45% between 600 and 700, and 15% above 700. The ACT scores were 2% below 21, 23% between 21 and 23, 28% between 24 and 26, 17% between 27 and 28, and 30% above 28. 45% of the current freshmen were in the top fifth of their class; 80% were in the top two fifths. There were 3 National Merit finalists. 40 freshmen graduated first in their class.

Requirements: The SAT or ACT is required. In addition, applicants should be graduates of an accredited secondary school, with a recommended 4 years each of English and history/social studies, 3 each of math and science, 2 to 4 of a foreign language, and 1 each of art and music. The GED is accepted. An essay is required, and an interview is advised. Cornell requires applicants to be in the upper 50% of their class. A GPA of 2.8 is required. AP and CLEP credits are accepted. Important factors in the admissions decision are leadership record, evidence of special talent, and advanced placement or honor courses.

Procedure: Freshmen are admitted to all sessions. There are early decision, early admissions, deferred admissions and rolling admissions plans. Early decision applications should be filed by December 1; regular applications, by February 1 for fall entry. Notification of early decision is sent December 20; regular decision, on a rolling basis. 65 applicants were on the 2005 waiting list; 11 were admitted. Applications are accepted on-line. The fall 2005 application was $40.

Transfer: 59 transfer students enrolled in 2004-2005. Applicants must provide all items required of traditional students; in addition, they must submit official college transcripts from all other institutions they have attended. 8 of 32 courses required for the bachelor's degree must be completed at Cornell.

Visiting: There are regularly scheduled orientations for prospective students, including campus tours and meetings with an informational panel, a student panel, financial aid staff, and faculty and coaches as requested. There are guides for informal visits and visitors may sit in on classes and stay overnight. To schedule a visit, contact Judy Penn, Visit Coordinator at (319) 895-4161.

Financial Aid: In 2005-2006, 97% of all full-time freshmen and 96% of continuing full-time students received some form of financial aid. 71% of full-time freshmen and 70% of continuing full-time students received need-based aid. The average freshman award was $18,300. Need-based scholarships or need-based grants averaged $16,745 ($20,000 maximum); need-based self-help aid (loans and jobs) averaged $3855 ($6125 maximum); and other non-need-based awards and non-need-based scholarships averaged $10,115 ($20,000 maximum). 65% of undergraduates work part time. Average annual earnings from campus work are $1200. The average financial indebtedness of the 2005 graduate was $17,970. Cornell is a member of CSS. The FAFSA and the college's own financial statement are required. The deadline for filing freshman financial aid applications for fall entry is March 1.

International Students: There are 33 international students enrolled. The school actively recruits these students. They must score satisfactorily on the written TOEFL and also take the college's own test.

Computers: Wireless access is available. There is Internet access in all residence halls, many labs, some classrooms, and the library. All students may access the system. There are no time limits and no fees.

Graduates: From July 1, 2004 to June 30, 2005, 221 bachelor's degrees were awarded. The most popular majors were psychology (13%), economics and business (13%), and history (10%). In an average class, 3% graduate in 3 years or less, 63% graduate in 4 years or less, 65% graduate in 5 years or less, and 66% graduate in 6 years or less. 10 companies recruited on campus in 2004-2005. Of the 2004 graduating class, 31% were enrolled in graduate school within 6 months of graduation and 63% were employed.

Admissions Contact: Jonathan Stroud, Vice President of Enrollment. A video is available. E-mail: *admissions@cornellcollege.edu* Web: *http://www.cornellcollege.edu/*

DORDT COLLEGE
B-1

Sioux Center, IA 51250

(712) 722-6080
(800) 34-DORDT; Fax: (712) 722-1967

Full-time: 565 men, 675 women	Faculty: 75; IIB, av$
Part-time: 30 men, 30 women	Ph.D.s: 85%
Graduate: 20 men, 55 women	Student/Faculty: 16 to 1
Year: semesters	Tuition: $15,825
Application Deadline: n/av	Room & Board: $4500
Freshman Class: n/av	
SAT or ACT: required	VERY COMPETITIVE

Dordt College, founded in 1955, is a private institution affiliated with the Christian Reformed Church. Figures in the above capsule are approximate. The curriculum, which is designed to reflect the principles of the Christian faith, leads to degrees in liberal arts, agriculture, art, music, business, engineering, and teaching preparation. In addition to regional accreditation, Dordt has baccalaureate program accreditation with ABET and CSWE. The library contains 185,000 volumes, 14,819 microform items, and 5000 audio/video tapes/CDs/DVDs, and subscribes to 700 periodicals including electronic. Computerized library services include the card catalog and interlibrary loans. Special learning facilities include a learning resource center, planetarium, radio station, and 2 observatories, as well as a 160-acre agriculture stewardship center just north of the campus. The 110-acre campus is in a rural area 42 miles north of Sioux City. Including any residence halls, there are 22 buildings.

Student Life: 58% of undergraduates are from out of state, mostly the Midwest. Students are from 32 states, 12 foreign countries, and Canada. 40% are from public schools. 98% are white. Most are Protestant. The average age of freshmen is 18; all undergraduates, 21. 17% do not continue beyond their first year; 68% remain to graduate.

Housing: 1250 students can be accommodated in college housing, which includes single-sex and coed dormitories, on-campus apartments, and off-campus apartments. On-campus housing is guaranteed for all 4 years. 90% of students live on campus; of those, 80% remain on campus on weekends. Alcohol is not permitted. All students may keep cars.

Activities: There are no fraternities or sororities. There are 25 groups on campus, including band, choir, chorale, computers, dance, drama, drill team, forensics, international, jazz band, literary magazine, newspaper, opera, orchestra, pep band, professional, radio and TV, religious, social, social service, student government, symphony, and yearbook. Popular campus events include Parents Day in October.

Sports: There are 7 intercollegiate sports for men and 7 for women, and 10 intramural sports for men and 10 for women. Facilities include a 2500-seat gym with 2 courts; an 85,000-square-foot recreation center, which includes a 200-meter indoor track, 3 courts adaptable for basketball, volleyball, and tennis, 3 racquetball courts, weight lifting and exercise equipment rooms, and a golf simulation room; an outdoor track;

tennis courts; soccer, softball, and baseball fields; and an indoor pool and ice arena adjacent to the campus.

Disabled Students: All of the campus is accessible. Wheelchair ramps, elevators, special parking, specially equipped rest rooms, special class scheduling, lowered drinking fountains, lowered telephones, and special housing are available.

Services: Counseling and information services are available, as is tutoring in most subjects. There is a reader service for the blind, and remedial math, reading, and writing.

Campus Safety and Security: Measures include 24-hour foot and vehicle patrol and lighted pathways/sidewalks.

Programs of Study: Dordt confers B.A., B.S., B.S.N., and B.S.W. degrees. Associate and master's degrees are also awarded. Bachelor's degrees are awarded in BIOLOGICAL SCIENCE (biology/biological science), BUSINESS (accounting and business administration and management), COMMUNICATIONS AND THE ARTS (broadcasting, communications, dramatic arts, Dutch, English, fine arts, German, graphic design, journalism, languages, music, Spanish, and speech/debate/rhetoric), COMPUTER AND PHYSICAL SCIENCE (chemistry, computer programming, computer science, information sciences and systems, mathematics, and physics), EDUCATION (art, business, elementary, foreign languages, music, and secondary), ENGINEERING AND ENVIRONMENTAL DESIGN (chemical engineering, electrical/electronics engineering, engineering, environmental science, and mechanical engineering), HEALTH PROFESSIONS (health science, medical laboratory technology, nursing, predentistry, and premedicine), SOCIAL SCIENCE (criminal justice, history, philosophy, political science/government, prelaw, psychology, religion, social science, social work, sociology, and youth ministry). Engineering, business administration, and social work are the strongest academically. Education is the largest.

Required: All students must complete a college introductory course and a distribution of 14 other courses in the various academic disciplines, including General Education 300. Proficiency requirements must be met in English, math, and phys ed. To graduate, students must complete a minimum of 126 credits with a 2.0 GPA.

Special: Students may study abroad in 10 countries. Dordt also offers a Washington semester, a Chicago Metro semester, a joint nursing degree program with St. Luke's School of Nursing, a B.S.N. with Briar Cliff University, B.A.-B.S. degrees in engineering and agriculture, and numerous internships in all majors. Dual majors, student-designed majors, and pass/fail options are available. There is a freshman honors program.

Faculty/Classroom: 85% of faculty are male; 15%, female. All teach undergraduates. The average class size in an introductory lecture is 30; in a laboratory, 20; and in a regular course, 25.

Requirements: The SAT or ACT is required. In addition, applicants must be graduates of accredited secondary schools or have earned a GED. The college requires 18 academic credits, including 4 in English and 2 each in foreign language, math, science, and social studies. A GPA of 2.25 is required. AP and CLEP credits are accepted. Important factors in the admissions decision are advanced placement or honor courses, evidence of special talent, and leadership record.

Procedure: Freshmen are admitted fall and spring. There is a rolling admissions plan Entrance exams should be taken by October of the senior year and no later than April. Notification is sent on a rolling basis. Applications are accepted on-line. The fall 2005 application fee was $25.

Transfer: 47 transfer students enrolled in a recent year. Transfer students must have a GPA of 2.0. 62 of 126 credits required for the bachelor's degree must be completed at Dordt.

Visiting: There are regularly scheduled orientations for prospective students, including tours, class visits, personal visits with professors and coaches, and a financial aid session. There are guides for informal visits and visitors may sit in on classes and stay overnight. To schedule a visit, contact the Admissions Office.

Financial Aid: In a recent year, 98% of all full-time students received some form of financial aid. 95% of all full-time students received need-based aid. The average freshman award was $13,500. Need-based scholarships or need-based grants averaged $6500; need-based self-help aid (loans and jobs) averaged $6000; non-need-based athletic scholarships averaged $2000; and other non-need-based awards and non-need-based scholarships averaged $3000. 80% of undergraduates worked part time. Average annual earnings from campus work were $1300. The average financial indebtedness of a recent graduate was $15,100. The FAFSA and the college's own financial statement are required. Check with the school for application deadlines.

International Students: In a recent year, there were 139 international students enrolled. The school actively recruits these students. They must score satisfactorily on the TOEFL and also take the SAT or the ACT.

Computers: All students may access the system. There are no time limits and no fees.

Graduates: In a recent year, 282 bachelor's degrees were awarded. The most popular majors were education (26%), business (18%), and engineering (8%). In an average class, 68% graduate in 4 years or less. 50 companies recruited on campus in a recent year. Of a recent graduating class, 8% were enrolled in graduate school within 6 months of graduation and 97% were employed.

Admissions Contact: Quentin Van Essen, Executive Director of Admissions. E-mail: *admissions@dordt.edu* Web: *www.dordt.edu*

DRAKE UNIVERSITY   C-3
Des Moines, IA 50311   **(515) 271-3181**
                                        (800) 44-DRAKE; Fax: (515) 271-2831

Full-time: 1255 men, 1658 women	**Faculty:** 203; IIA, av$
Part-time: 102 men, 126 women	**Ph.D.s:** 96%
Graduate: 770 men, 1366 women	**Student/Faculty:** 14 to 1
Year: semesters, summer session	**Tuition:** $21,462
Application Deadline: March 1	**Room & Board:** $6170
Freshman Class: 3668 applied, 3006 accepted, 809 enrolled	
SAT Verbal/Math: 600/590*	**ACT:** 26 **VERY COMPETITIVE+**

Drake University, founded in 1881, is a private institution offering undergraduate and graduate programs in arts and sciences, business and public administration, pharmacy and health sciences, journalism and mass communication, education, fine arts, and law. There are 5 undergraduate schools and 1 graduate school. In addition to regional accreditation, Drake has baccalaureate program accreditation with AACSB, ACEJMC, ACPE, NASAD, and NASM. The library contains 501,567 volumes, 1,901,935 microform items, and 2766 audio/video tapes/CDs/DVDs, and subscribes to 15,000 periodicals including electronic. Computerized library services include the card catalog, interlibrary loans, database searching, and Internet access. Special learning facilities include a learning resource center, art gallery, radio station, TV station, an observatory, and the Henry G. Harmon Fine Arts Center. The 120-acre campus is in a suburban area in Des Moines. Including any residence halls, there are 49 buildings.

Student Life: 70% of undergraduates are from out of state, mostly the Midwest. Students are from 40 states, 53 foreign countries, and Canada. 89% are from public schools. 81% are white. The average age of freshmen is 18; all undergraduates, 21. 15% do not continue beyond their first year; 85% remain to graduate.

Housing: 1714 students can be accommodated in college housing, which includes coed dorms, on-campus apartments, and fraternity houses. On-campus housing is available on a first-come, first-served basis and is available on a lottery system for upperclassmen. 90% of students live on campus; of those, 80% remain on campus on weekends. All students may keep cars.

Activities: 28% of men belong to 8 national fraternities; 23% of women belong to 4 national sororities. There are 160 groups on campus, including art, band, cheerleading, chess, choir, chorale, chorus, computers, dance, drama, drill team, ethnic, gay, honors, international, jazz band, literary magazine, marching band, musical theater, newspaper, opera, orchestra, pep band, photography, political, professional, radio and TV, religious, social, social service, student government, and symphony. Popular campus events include Drake Relays, Supreme Court Days, and Parents Weekend.

Sports: There are 8 intercollegiate sports for men and 10 for women, and 24 intramural sports for men and 24 for women. Facilities include a football stadium, an indoor swimming pool, an aerobics room, 2 weight rooms, basketball, volleyball, and badminton courts, 2 indoor tracks and 1 outdoor track, 4 racquetball courts, and 6 indoor and 6 outdoor tennis courts. A recreation and sports facility seats 7000.

Disabled Students: 80% of the campus is accessible. Wheelchair ramps, elevators, special parking, specially equipped rest rooms, special class scheduling, lowered drinking fountains, lowered telephones, an IBM-compatible computer and scanner that includes a voice and screen enlargement program, closed-caption television, and TDD at multiple locations are available.

Services: There is a reader service for the blind. The Student Disability Service works with Recordings for the Blind dyslexic students.

Campus Safety and Security: Measures include 24-hour foot and vehicle patrol, self-defense education, security escort services, and shuttle buses. There are informal discussions, pamphlets/posters/films, emergency telephones, and lighted pathways/sidewalks.

Programs of Study: Drake confers B.A., B.S., B.A.Journ. and Mass Comm., B.F.A., B.Mus., B.Mus.Ed., B.S.B.A., and B.S.Ed. degrees. Master's and doctoral degrees are also awarded. Bachelor's degrees are awarded in BIOLOGICAL SCIENCE (biology/biological science and neurosciences), BUSINESS (accounting, banking and finance, business administration and management, international business management, management science, and marketing management), COMMUNICATIONS AND THE ARTS (advertising, art history and appreciation, broadcasting, communications, dramatic arts, English, graphic design, journalism, music, music business management, music performance, printmaking, public relations, speech/debate/rhetoric, and studio art), COMPUTER AND PHYSICAL SCIENCE (actuarial science, chemistry, computer science, information sciences and systems, mathematics, and physics), EDUCATION (elementary, mathematics, music, and secondary), ENGINEERING AND ENVIRONMENTAL DESIGN (environmental science), HEALTH PROFESSIONS (pharmacy), SOCIAL SCIENCE (economics, ethics, politics, and social policy, history, international rela-

tions, philosophy, political science/government, psychology, religion, and sociology). Actuarial science, pharmacy, and physics/astronomy are the strongest academically. Pharmacy, accounting, and music peformance are the largest.

Required: Undergraduates must take a first-year seminar and general education courses, satisfy 11 areas of inquiry requirements that include writing, critical thinking, artistic experience, historical consciousness, information and technical literacy, multicultural experience, scientific and quantitative literacy, values and ethics, and the engaged citizen. A capstone demonstration is required. For graduation, 124 credit hours are required with 27 to 36 hours in the major. The minimum GPA is 2.0.

Special: Study abroad is available in 67 countries and at sea. The university offers cross-registration with Des Moines area colleges, including Grand View, internships, a Washington semester, cooperative programs in computer science, and work-study programs. Dual majors, B.A.-B.S. degrees, a 3-2 engineering degree with Washington University, student-designed majors, credit for military experience, and nondegree study are possible. Students may take a maximum of 12 hours of course work on a credit/no credit basis. There are 25 national honor societies, including Phi Beta Kappa, a freshman honors program, and 19 departmental honors programs.

Faculty/Classroom: 57% of faculty are male; 43%, female. 79% teach undergraduates and 90% do research. No introductory courses are taught by graduate students. The average class size in an introductory lecture is 29; in a laboratory, 14; and in a regular course, 27.

Admissions: 82% of the 2005-2006 applicants were accepted. The SAT scores for the 2005-2006 freshman class were: Verbal--14% below 500, 34% between 500 and 599, 43% between 600 and 700, and 10% above 700; Math--18% below 500, 32% between 500 and 599, 37% between 600 and 700, and 14% above 700. The ACT scores were 4% below 21, 18% between 21 and 23, 21% between 24 and 26, 31% between 27 and 28, and 25% above 28. 63% of the current freshmen were in the top fifth of their class; 86% were in the top two fifths. There were 7 National Merit finalists. 40 freshmen graduated first in their class.

Requirements: The SAT or ACT is required. In addition, applicants must be graduates of an accredited secondary school. The GED is accepted. Students must have completed 4 years of English, 2 years of math, and 10 other units to be selected from English, foreign languages, social studies, math, lab sciences, and others. A portfolio is required for art majors and for those seeking scholarship consideration. An audition is necessary for admission to the music program. Tapes are accepted. Drake requires applicants to be in the upper 60% of their class. A GPA of 2.5 is required. AP and CLEP credits are accepted. Important factors in the admissions decision are advanced placement or honor courses, extracurricular activities record, and leadership record.

Procedure: Freshmen are admitted to all sessions. Entrance exams should be taken during the spring of the junior year or early fall of the senior year. There is a deferred admissions plan and a rolling admissions plan. Applications should be filed by March 1 for fall entry and December 1 for spring entry, along with a $25 fee. Notification is sent on a October 1. Applications are accepted on-line.

Transfer: 125 transfer students enrolled in 2004-2005. Applicants must have a minimum GPA of 2.0 and have completed 24 credit hours for evaluation. Grades of C or better transfer for credit. There is no assurance that all courses transferred will apply toward the major requirement. The final 30 hours must be completed in residence. Transfer students are admitted in the fall, spring, and summer. 30 of 124 credits required for the bachelor's degree must be completed at Drake.

Visiting: There are regularly scheduled orientations for prospective students, including an opportunity for students and parents to confer with professors, meet with current students, and attend information sessions on academic programs, financial aid, housing, and the Drake campus. Also included are a walking tour and lunch. There are guides for informal visits and visitors may sit in on classes and stay overnight. To schedule a visit, contact the Visit Coordinator in the Office of Admission at *admission@drake.edu*.

Financial Aid: In 2005-2006, 98% of all full-time freshmen and 97% of continuing full-time students received some form of financial aid. 66% of full-time freshmen and 63% of continuing full-time students received need-based aid. The average freshman award was $17,839. Need-based scholarships or need-based grants averaged $11,768 ($21,077 maximum); need-based self-help aid (loans and jobs) averaged $6238 ($7625 maximum); non-need-based athletic scholarships averaged $18,167 ($26,870 maximum); and other non-need-based awards and non-need-based scholarships averaged $9638 ($26,470 maximum). 29% of undergraduates work part time. Average annual earnings from campus work are $1556. The average financial indebtedness of the 2005 graduate was $18,029. Drake is a member of CSS. The FAFSA is required. The deadline for filing freshman financial aid applications for fall entry is March 1.

International Students: There are 143 international students enrolled. The school actively recruits these students. They must score satisfactorily on the TOEFL.

Computers: Wireless access is available. All students may access the system. There are no time limits. The fee is $250. It is strongly recommended that all students have a personal computer.

Graduates: From July 1, 2004 to June 30, 2005, 647 bachelor's degrees were awarded. The most popular majors were journalism and mass communications (17%), marketing and management (14%), and biology (7%). In an average class, 62% graduate in 4 years or less, 69% graduate in 5 years or less, and 66% graduate in 6 years. 40 companies recruited on campus in 2004-2005. Of the 2004 graduating class, 22% were enrolled in graduate school within 6 months of graduation and 68% were employed.

Admissions Contact: Laura Linn, Director of Admission. E-mail: *admission@drake.edu* Web: *www.choose.drake.edu*

GRACELAND UNIVERSITY   C-4
Lamoni, IA 50140

(641) 784-5118
(866) 472-2352; Fax: (641) 784-5480

Full-time: 575 men, 775 women	Faculty: 94; IIB, -$
Part-time: 135 men, 560 women	Ph.D.s: 47%
Graduate: 70 men, 260 women	Student/Faculty: 14 to 1
Year: 4-1-4, summer session	Tuition: $14,900
Application Deadline: see profile	Room & Board: $4800
Freshman Class: n/av	
SAT or ACT: required	**COMPETITIVE**

Graceland University, established in 1895, is a private liberal arts college sponsored by the Community of Christ. Graceland also maintains a campus in Independence, MO. There are 4 undergraduate and 4 graduate schools. Figures in the above capsule are approximate. In addition to regional accreditation, Graceland has baccalaureate program accreditation with CCNE, NCATE, and NLN. The library contains 199,447 volumes, 914 microform items, and 3658 audio/video tapes/CDs/DVDs, and subscribes to 624 periodicals including electronic. Computerized library services include the card catalog, interlibrary loans, database searching, and Internet access. Special learning facilities include a learning resource center, art gallery, and a center for the study of the Korean War. The 167-acre campus is in a small town 80 miles south of Des Moines. Including any residence halls, there are 28 buildings.

Student Life: 60% of undergraduates are from out of state, mostly the Midwest. Students are from 49 states, 35 foreign countries, and Canada. 64% are white. 16% are Protestant; 6% Catholic. The average age of freshmen is 18; all undergraduates, 20. 30% do not continue beyond their first year; 47% remain to graduate.

Housing: 715 students can be accommodated in college housing, which includes single-sex dormitories and married-student housing. On-campus housing is guaranteed for all 4 years. 64% of students live on campus; of those, 68% remain on campus on weekends. Alcohol is not permitted. All students may keep cars.

Activities: There are no fraternities or sororities. There are 54 groups on campus, including art, band, cheerleading, chess, choir, chorale, chorus, computers, dance, drama, drill team, entreprenuial, environmental, ethnic, gay, honors, international, jazz band, musical theater, newspaper, orchestra, pep band, political, professional, radio and TV, religious, social, social service, student government, symphony, and yearbook. Popular campus events include Renaissance Week, Multi-Cultural Week, and New Year's in November.

Sports: There are 9 intercollegiate sports for men and 8 for women, and 17 intramural sports for men and 17 for women. Facilities include a sports complex with an all-weather track and lighted soccer and football fields; a phys ed center with an indoor junior Olympic-size pool, a 5-court gym, an indoor track, a weight room, and courts for racquetball, basketball, volleyball, and tennis; an intramural sports complex; 8 lighted tennis courts; an 18-hole disc golf course; and 2 small lakes.

Disabled Students: 86% of the campus is accessible. Wheelchair ramps, elevators, special parking, specially equipped rest rooms, special class scheduling, lowered drinking fountains, lowered telephones, and automatic doors are available.

Services: Counseling and information services are available, as is tutoring in most subjects. There is a reader service for the blind, and remedial math, reading, and writing.

Campus Safety and Security: Measures include 24-hour foot and vehicle patrol, security escort services, informal discussions, and pamphlets/posters/films. There are emergency telephones, lighted pathways/sidewalks, and night security personnel.

Programs of Study: Graceland confers B.A., B.S., and B.S.N. degrees. Master's degrees are also awarded. Bachelor's degrees are awarded in BIOLOGICAL SCIENCE (biology/biological science), BUSINESS (accounting, business administration and management, international business management, recreation and leisure services, and recreational facilities management), COMMUNICATIONS AND THE ARTS (communications, dramatic arts, English, German, graphic design, literature, modern language, music, Spanish, speech/debate/rhetoric, and studio art), COMPUTER AND PHYSICAL SCIENCE (chemistry, computer science, information sciences and systems, mathematics, and science),

EDUCATION (athletic training, elementary, music, and physical), ENGINEERING AND ENVIRONMENTAL DESIGN (commercial art), HEALTH PROFESSIONS (health, medical laboratory technology, nursing, predentistry, premedicine, and preveterinary science), SOCIAL SCIENCE (addiction studies, criminal justice, economics, history, human services, international studies, liberal arts/general studies, philosophy, psychology, religion, social science, and sociology). Business administration, education, and nursing are the largest.

Required: To graduate, students must complete 128 credit hours, including 39 in upper-division courses and an average of 40 in the major, and maintain a minimum GPA of 2.0 overall and in the major. General education requirements include studies in humanities, social sciences, natural sciences, behavioral sciences, ethics, math, computer science, leadership, thinking skills, human diversity, and the arts.

Special: Internships are required in business, education, recreation, communications, and publication design. Graceland offers study abroad, cross-registration, B.A.-B.S. degrees, work-study, dual and student-designed majors, and a general studies degree. Credit for life, military, or work experience is possible. A pass/fail option is available for 2 courses each semester. The university also offers nondegree study, home study in addiction studies and nursing, a program for students with learning disabilities, an accelerated degree program in nursing, and a 3-2 engineering degree with the University of Iowa and the University of Missouri-Rolla. There are 3 national honor societies, a freshman honors program, and 6 departmental honors programs.

Faculty/Classroom: 47% of faculty are male; 53%, female. 93% teach undergraduates and 10% do research. The average class size in an introductory lecture is 24; in a laboratory, 24; and in a regular course, 11.

Requirements: The SAT or ACT is required. In addition, Graceland requires applicants to meet 2 of these 3 criteria: rank in the upper 50% of their class, a GPA of 2.5, and a satisfactory score on the SAT or 21 on the ACT. Applicants must be graduates of an accredited secondary school. The GED is accepted. An interview is recommended. Graceland requires applicants to be in the upper 50% of their class. A GPA of 2.5 is required. AP and CLEP credits are accepted. Important factors in the admissions decision are advanced placement or honor courses, evidence of special talent, and leadership record.

Procedure: Freshmen are admitted to all sessions. There is a rolling admissions plan. Entrance exams should be taken in the junior or senior year. Check with the school for application deadlines. Notification is sent on a rolling basis. Applications are accepted on-line.

Transfer: 121 transfer students enrolled in a recent year. Applicants must submit official transcripts from all colleges attended and from high school. The required GPA varies by the number of hours of college study completed. Transfer students are admitted every term. 32 of 128 credits required for the bachelor's degree must be completed at Graceland.

Visiting: There are regularly scheduled orientations for prospective students, including a campus tour and opportunities to meet students, faculty, and campus personnel. There are guides for informal visits and visitors may sit in on classes and stay overnight. To schedule a visit, contact Helen Caples at (641) 784-5127.

Financial Aid: The FAFSA is required. Check with the school for application deadlines.

International Students: In a recent year, there were 147 international students enrolled. The school actively recruits these students. They must score satisfactorily on the TOEFL.

Computers: All students may access the system any time. There are no time limits and no fees. It is strongly recommended that all students have a personal computer.

Admissions Contact: James R. Simpson, Vice Provost for Enrollment. E-mail: *admissions@graceland.edu* Web: *www.graceland.edu*

GRAND VIEW COLLEGE   C-3
Des Moines, IA 50316-1599

(515) 263-2810
(800) 444-6083; Fax: (515) 263-2974

Full-time: 441 men, 931 women	Faculty: 86
Part-time: 109 men, 280 women	Ph.D.s: 37%
Graduate: none	Student/Faculty: 16 to 1
Year: semesters, summer session	Tuition: $16,060
Application Deadline: open	Room & Board: $5422
Freshman Class: 438 applied, 421 accepted, 217 enrolled	
ACT: 20	**COMPETITIVE**

Grand View College, founded in 1896, is a private liberal arts college affiliated with the Evangelical Lutheran Church in America, that focuses on connecting liberal arts with career preparation. In addition to regional accreditation, Grand View has baccalaureate program accreditation with NLN. The library contains 105,146 volumes, 11,170 microform items, and 4482 audio/video tapes/CDs/DVDs, and subscribes to 394,000 periodicals including electronic. Computerized library services include interlibrary loans, database searching, and Internet access. Special learning facilities include a learning resource center, radio station, and TV station. The 25-acre campus is in an urban area in a residential area of Des Moines. Including any residence halls, there are 22 buildings.

Student Life: 90% of undergraduates are from Iowa. Others are from 30 states, 7 foreign countries, and Canada. 88% are white. 46% are Protestant; 24% Catholic. The average age of freshmen is 18; all undergraduates, 26. 26% do not continue beyond their first year.

Housing: 451 students can be accommodated in college housing, which includes coed dormitories and on-campus apartments. In addition, there are special-interest houses. On-campus housing is guaranteed for the freshman year only and is available on a first-come, first-served basis. 66% of students commute. All students may keep cars.

Activities: There are no fraternities or sororities. There are 19 groups on campus, including art, band, cheerleading, choir, chorale, chorus, dance departmental, drama, ethnic, honors, international, newspaper, professional, radio and TV, religious, social service, and student government. Popular campus events include Stundenterfest.

Sports: There are 6 intercollegiate sports for men and 8 for women, and 8 intramural sports for men. Facilities include a 1200-seat phys ed building with facilities for varsity athletics and recreation programs, tennis courts, and an athletic field.

Disabled Students: 90% of the campus is accessible. Wheelchair ramps, elevators, special parking, specially equipped rest rooms, special class scheduling, lowered drinking fountains, lowered telephones, and support services for the disabled are available.

Services: Counseling and information services are available, as is tutoring in every subject. Support services for the blind and hearing-impaired also are available.

Campus Safety and Security: Measures include 24-hour foot and vehicle patrol, security escort services, shuttle buses, and informal discussions. There are pamphlets/posters/films, emergency telephones, and lighted pathways/sidewalks.

Programs of Study: Grand View confers B.A. and B.S.N. degrees. Associate degrees are also awarded. Bachelor's degrees are awarded in BIOLOGICAL SCIENCE (biology/biological science), BUSINESS (accounting and business administration and management), COMMUNICATIONS AND THE ARTS (broadcasting, communications, English, graphic design, journalism, music, and visual and performing arts), COMPUTER AND PHYSICAL SCIENCE (applied mathematics, computer science, and information sciences and systems), EDUCATION (art, elementary, music, and secondary), HEALTH PROFESSIONS (nursing), SOCIAL SCIENCE (criminal justice, human services, political science/government, and psychology). Art, nursing, and education are the strongest academically. Business, nursing, and education are the largest.

Required: Students must complete core requirements, including courses in English, public speaking, liberal arts, integrating seminar, other culture encounter, religion or philosophy, history or other humanities, laboratory science, and social science. Students must complete at least 124 hours of work, including 60 hours in courses other than the major and 24 hours in the major. Students must maintain an overall GPA of 2.0 and a 2.2 GPA in the major. Students must also demonstrate computer proficiency.

Special: Co-op programs, cross-registration with Drake University and Des Moines Area Community College, student-designed majors, study abroad, and internships for most majors are available. Dual majors, a B.A.-B.S. degree, a Washington semester, work-study programs, and an accelerated degree program in business administration are offered. Non-degree study, a liberal arts degree, a certificate in art therapy, and pass/fail options are possible. There are 4 national honor societies and a freshman honors program.

Faculty/Classroom: 42% of faculty are male; 58%, female. All teach undergraduates and 40% both teach and do research. The average class size in an introductory lecture is 25; in a laboratory, 15; and in a regular course, 25.

Admissions: 96% of the 2005-2006 applicants were accepted. The ACT scores for the 2005-2006 freshman class were: 60% below 21, 25% between 21 and 23, 11% between 24 and 26, 3% between 27 and 28, and 1% above 28. 24% of the current freshmen were in the top fifth of their class; 80% were in the top two fifths. 6 freshmen graduated first in their class.

Requirements: The ACT is required and the SAT is recommended. Students must be graduates of an accredited secondary school. The GED is also accepted. Grand View recommends that students should have completed 4 courses in English, 3 courses each in math, science, and social science, and 2 courses in a foreign language. A GPA of 2.0 is required. AP and CLEP credits are accepted.

Procedure: Freshmen are admitted fall, spring, and summer. Entrance exams should be taken during the second semester of the junior year. There are deferred admissions and rolling admissions plans. Application deadlines are open. Applications are accepted on-line. The fall 2005 application fee was $35.

Transfer: 229 transfer students enrolled in 2004-2005. Applicants must submit transcripts from each college attended. 30 of 124 credits required for the bachelor's degree must be completed at Grand View.

Visiting: There are regularly scheduled orientations for prospective students, including placement tests, a financial aid session, lunch, advisor

meetings, and a registration session. There are guides for informal visits and visitors may sit in on classes and stay overnight. To schedule a visit, contact the Admissions Office.

Financial Aid: In a recent year, 99% of all full-time freshmen and 98% of continuing full-time students received some form of financial aid. 90% of full-time freshmen and 80% of continuing full-time students received need-based aid. The average freshman award was $20,600. 95% of undergraduates work part time. Average annual earnings from campus work are $1500. The average financial indebtedness of the 2005 graduate was $18,463. The FAFSA is required. The deadline for filing freshman financial aid applications for fall entry is April 15.

International Students: They must score satisfactorily on the written TOEFL or on the electronic version and also take the SAT or the ACT.

Computers: All students may access the system. There are no time limits and no fees.

Graduates: From July 1, 2004 to June 30, 2005, 362 bachelor's degrees were awarded. In a recent year the most popular majors were business administration (18%), education (18%), and nursing (16%). In an average class, 25% graduate in 4 years or less, 35% graduate in 5 years or less, and 37% graduate in 6 years or less. 66 companies recruited on campus in a recent year. Of the 2004 graduating class, 5% were enrolled in graduate school within 6 months of graduation and 99% were employed.

Admissions Contact: Diane Schafer Johnson, Director of Admissions. E-mail: djohnson@gvc.edu Web: gvc.edu

GRINNELL COLLEGE

D-3

Grinnell, IA 50112

(641) 269-3600
(800) 247-0113; Fax: (641) 269-4937

Full-time: 701 men, 845 women	Faculty: 156; IIB, +$
Part-time: 13 men, 18 women	Ph.D.s: 96%
Graduate: none	Student/Faculty: 10 to 1
Year: semesters	Tuition: $27,504
Application Deadline: January 20	Room & Board: $7310
Freshman Class: 3121 applied, 1398 accepted, 387 enrolled	
SAT or ACT: required	HIGHLY COMPETITIVE+

Grinnell College, founded in 1846, is a private institution that offers undergraduate degree programs in the arts and sciences. Some figures in the above capsule and in this profile are approximate. The 3 libraries contain 500,000 volumes, 375,000 microform items, and 30,000 audio/video tapes/CDs/DVDs, and subscribe to 3000 periodicals including electronic. Computerized library services include the card catalog, interlibrary loans, database searching, and Internet access. Special learning facilities include a learning resource center, art gallery, an observatory, physics museum, and print and drawing gallery. The 127-acre campus is in a small town 55 miles east of Des Moines. Including any residence halls, there are 63 buildings.

Student Life: 87% of undergraduates are from out of state, mostly the Midwest. Students are from 50 states, 52 foreign countries, and Canada. 82% are from public schools. 69% are white; 10% foreign nationals. 40% are claim no religious affiliation; 30% Protestant; 10% Catholic; 8% Jewish. The average age of freshmen is 18; all undergraduates, 20. 8% do not continue beyond their first year; 85% remain to graduate.

Housing: 1265 students can be accommodated in college housing, which includes single-sex and coed dorms. In addition, there are language houses and special-interest houses. On-campus housing is guaranteed for all 4 years. 86% of students live on campus; of those, 96% remain on campus on weekends. All students may keep cars.

Activities: There are no fraternities or sororities. There are 168 groups on campus, including art, chess, choir, chorale, chorus, computers, dance, debate, drama, ethnic, film, forensics, gay, honors, international, jazz band, literary magazine, musical theater, newspaper, orchestra, photography, political, radio and TV, religious, social, social service, student government, and yearbook. Popular campus events include Winter Waltz, Spring Waltz, and Disco.

Sports: There are 10 intercollegiate sports for men and 10 for women, and 11 intramural sports for men and 11 for women. Facilities include a phys ed complex, a gym, 5 sports fields, a track, and 3 intramural fields.

Disabled Students: 80% of the campus is accessible. Wheelchair ramps, elevators, special parking, specially equipped rest rooms, special class scheduling, lowered drinking fountains, and lowered telephones are available.

Services: Counseling and information services are available, as is tutoring in every subject. There is a reader service for the blind. There are reading, writing, math, and science labs.

Campus Safety and Security: Measures include 24-hour foot and vehicle patrol, self-defense education, security escort services, and informal discussions. There are pamphlets/posters/films, emergency telephones, lighted pathways/sidewalks, fire drills, and a committee on personal safety education. Security information and reports are released to the entire campus when incidents occur.

Programs of Study: Grinnell confers the B.A. degree. Bachelor's degrees are awarded in BIOLOGICAL SCIENCE (biochemistry and biology/biological science), COMMUNICATIONS AND THE ARTS (art, Chinese, classics, dramatic arts, English, French, German, music, Russian, and Spanish), COMPUTER AND PHYSICAL SCIENCE (chemistry, computer science, mathematics, physics, and science), SOCIAL SCIENCE (anthropology, economics, history, philosophy, political science/government, psychology, religion, and sociology). English, history, and biology are the largest.

Required: All students are required to take a tutorial in the first semester focusing on writing. All students must also complete a major field, which includes between 32 and 48 credits in most departments. Of the total 124 credits needed for the bachelor's degree, no more than 48 may be earned in any one department or 92 in any one division, and a minimum 2.0 GPA must be maintained.

Special: Students may participate in 63 study-abroad programs in 32 countries or in off-campus study at selected locations in the United States. Grinnell offers cooperative programs in architecture with Washington University in St. Louis and a 3-2 engineering program with California Institute of Technology, Columbia University, and Rensselaer Polytechnic Institute. There is also an extensive internship program, a Washington semester, a general studies degree in science, student-designed majors, and S/D/F grading options in selected courses. Grinnell's special "plus-2" option permits students to add 2 credits to a regular course through independent study. Students may pursue one of 10 interdisciplinary concentrations in addition to their major. Accelerated degree programs of 6 to 7 semesters may be approved on an individual basis. There are 2 national honor societies, including Phi Beta Kappa. All departments have honors programs.

Faculty/Classroom: 53% of faculty are male; 47%, female. All both teach and do research. The average class size in an introductory lecture is 20; in a laboratory, 13; and in a regular course, 16.

Admissions: 45% of the 2005-2006 applicants were accepted. The ACT scores were 7% between 18 and 23, 28% between 24 and 29, and 66% between 30 and 36. 73% of the current freshmen were in the top tenth of their class; 93% were in the top quarter; 99% were in the top half. 32 freshmen graduated first in their class.

Requirements: The SAT or ACT is required. In addition, applicants must be graduates of accredited secondary schools. The college recommends 20 Carnegie units, 4 each in English and math, and 3-4 each in lab science, social studies or history, and a foreign language. An essay is required and an interview is recommended. AP credits are accepted. Important factors in the admissions decision are advanced placement or honor courses, extracurricular activities record, and leadership record.

Procedure: Freshmen are admitted in the fall. Entrance exams should be taken during the second semester of the junior year or early in the fall semester of the senior year. There are early decision, early admissions, and deferred admissions plans. Early decision applications should be filed by November 20; regular applications, by January 20 for fall entry, along with a $30 fee. Notification of early decision is sent December 20; regular decision, April 1. 93 early decision candidates were accepted for the 2005-2006 class. 598 applicants were on the 2005 waiting list; 30 were admitted. Applications are accepted on-line.

Transfer: 19 transfer students enrolled in 2005-2006. Students must submit all college transcripts and have a 3.0 GPA. 62 of 124 credits required for the bachelor's degree must be completed at Grinnell.

Visiting: There are regularly scheduled orientations for prospective students, including a campus tour, an interview with a member of the admissions staff, an opportunity to attend classes, presentations/discussions with students and faculty from a number of academic departments, overnight accommodations, and complimentary meals. There are guides for informal visits and visitors may sit in on classes and stay overnight. To schedule a visit, contact the Admissions Office.

Financial Aid: In 2005-2006, 95% of all full-time freshmen and 86% of continuing full-time students received some form of financial aid. 61% of full-time freshmen and 53% of continuing full-time students received need-based aid. Need-based scholarships or need-based grants averaged $18,952; need-based self-help aid (loans and jobs) averaged $5074; and other non-need-based awards and non-need-based scholarships averaged $10,888. The FAFSA and the college's own financial statement are required. Check with the school for current deadlines.

International Students: There are 154 international students enrolled. The school actively recruits these students. A satisfactory score is required on the written TOEFL. Students must also take the SAT or the ACT.

Computers: All students may access the system 24 hours a day. There are no time limits and no fees.

Graduates: In a recent year, 317 bachelor's degrees were awarded. The most popular majors were biology (11%), English (9%), and sociology (8%). In an average class, 83% graduate in 4 years or less, 84% graduate in 5 years or less, and 85% graduate in 6 years or less. 113 companies recruited on campus in a recent year. Of the recent year's graduating class, 30% were enrolled in graduate school within 6 months of graduation and 50% were employed.

Admissions Contact: James Sumner, Dean for Admission and Financial Aid. A video is available. E-mail: *askgrin@grinnell.edu* Web: *http://www.grinnell.edu*

IOWA BOARD OF REGENTS

The Iowa Board of Regents, established in 1905, is a public system in Iowa. It is governed by Iowa State Board of Regents, whose chief administrator is Executive Director. The primary goal of the system is teaching, research, and public service. The main priorities are Teaching Research Service. The total enrollment is usually about 70,000, with 5,000 faculty members. Altogether there are some 300 baccalaureate, 300 master's, and 200 doctoral programs offered in Iowa Board of Regents. Profiles of the 4-year campuses are included in this section.

IOWA STATE UNIVERSITY
C-3

Ames, IA 50011-2011

(515) 294-5836
(800) 262-3810; Fax: (515) 294-2592

Full-time: 11,236 men, 8768 women	**Faculty:** 1040; I, -$
Part-time: 747 men, 603 women	**Ph.D.s:** 88%
Graduate: 2817 men, 2209 women	**Student/Faculty:** 19 to 1
Year: semesters, summer session	**Tuition:** $5634 ($15,724)
Application Deadline: August 1	**Room & Board:** $6197
Freshman Class: 9101 applied, 8216 accepted, 3769 enrolled	
ACT: 24	**VERY COMPETITIVE**

Iowa State University, established in 1858, is a public land-grant institution offering undergraduate and graduate programs in agriculture, business, design, engineering, human sciences, liberal arts and sciences, and veterinary medicine. There are 7 undergraduate schools and 1 graduate school. In addition to regional accreditation, Iowa State has baccalaureate program accreditation with AACSB, ABET, ACEJMC, ACS, ADA, AHEA, APA, ASLA, CSAB, FIDER, NAAB, NASM, and SAF. The library contains 2,416,670 volumes, 3,445,603 microform items, and 64,524 audio/video tapes/CDs/DVDs, and subscribes to 29,850 periodicals including electronic. Computerized library services include the card catalog, interlibrary loans, and database searching. Special learning facilities include a learning resource center, art gallery, natural history museum, planetarium, radio station, and TV station. The 1788-acre campus is in an urban area 30 miles north of Des Moines. Including any residence halls, there are 284 buildings.

Student Life: 77% of undergraduates are from Iowa. Others are from 50 states, 115 foreign countries, and Canada. 94% are from public schools. 84% are white. The average age of freshmen is 18; all undergraduates, 21. 14% do not continue beyond their first year; 68% remain to graduate.

Housing: 10,000 students can be accommodated in college housing, which includes single-sex and coed dorms, on-campus apartments, married-student housing, fraternity houses, and sorority houses. In addition, there are honors houses and special-interest houses. On-campus housing is guaranteed for all 4 years. 52% of students live on campus. All students may keep cars.

Activities: 13% of men belong to 1 local and 29 national fraternities; 12% of women belong to 1 local and 17 national sororities. There are 687 groups on campus, including art, band, cheerleading, chess, choir, chorale, chorus, computers, dance, debate, drama, drum and bugle corps, ethnic, film, forensics, gay, honors, international, jazz band, literary magazine, marching band, musical theater, newspaper, opera, orchestra, pep band, photography, political, professional, radio and TV, recreation, religious, social, social service, student government, and symphony. Popular campus events include VEISHEA, spring festival, and Honors Week.

Sports: There are 7 intercollegiate sports for men and 12 for women, and 43 intramural sports for men and 43 for women. Facilities include a coliseum, a stadium/field, a baseball and softball complex, a track complex, a tennis complex, multipurpose gyms, swimming pools, an ice center, a phys ed building, recreation centers, multipurpose intramural-recreation fields, and a soccer competitive site.

Disabled Students: 95% of the campus is accessible. Wheelchair ramps, elevators, special parking, specially equipped rest rooms, special class scheduling, lowered drinking fountains, lowered telephones, voice-recognition and output computer systems, accessible public transportation, and adaptive recreational equipment are available.

Services: Counseling and information services are available, as is tutoring in most subjects. There is a reader service for the blind and remedial math and writing. A Kurzweil reader, an Arkanstone reader, enlargement services, talking and braille text from the Iowa Commission for the Blind, a braille printer, loaner computers, steno-captioning service, a TTY telecommunications device, FM listeners, and sign interpreters are also available.

Campus Safety and Security: Measures include 24-hour foot and vehicle patrol, self-defense education, security escort services, and shuttle buses. There are informal discussions, pamphlets/posters/films, emergency telephones, lighted pathways/sidewalks, and a Help Van for motorists.

Programs of Study: Iowa State confers B.A, B.S., B.Arch., B.B.A., B.F.A., B.L.A., B.L.S., and B.Mus. degrees. Master's and doctoral degrees are also awarded. Bachelor's degrees are awarded in AGRICULTURE (agricultural business management, agriculture, agronomy, animal science, dairy science, forestry and related sciences, horticulture, international agriculture, plant protection (pest management), and plant science), BIOLOGICAL SCIENCE (biochemistry, biology/biological science, biophysics, entomology, genetics, microbiology, nutrition, and plant pathology), BUSINESS (accounting, banking and finance, business administration and management, fashion merchandising, hotel/motel and restaurant management, international business management, management science, marketing/retailing/merchandising, and transportation management), COMMUNICATIONS AND THE ARTS (advertising, communications, design, English, fine arts, French, German, graphic design, journalism, linguistics, music, Russian, Spanish, and speech/debate/rhetoric), COMPUTER AND PHYSICAL SCIENCE (atmospheric sciences and meteorology, chemistry, computer science, earth science, geology, mathematics, physics, and statistics), EDUCATION (agricultural, early childhood, elementary, health, industrial arts, music, physical, and secondary), ENGINEERING AND ENVIRONMENTAL DESIGN (aeronautical engineering, agricultural engineering, architecture, chemical engineering, city/community/regional planning, civil engineering, computer engineering, construction engineering, electrical/electronics engineering, engineering, engineering technology, environmental science, industrial engineering technology, interior design, landscape architecture/design, materials engineering, and mechanical engineering), SOCIAL SCIENCE (anthropology, child care/child and family studies, child psychology/development, dietetics, economics, family/consumer resource management, family/consumer studies, fashion design and technology, food science, history, international relations, liberal arts/general studies, philosophy, political science/government, psychology, religion, sociology, and textiles and clothing). Engineering, agriculture, and statistics, are the strongest academically. Engineering, business, and agriculture are the largest.

Required: A minimum of 120 1/2 to 169 1/2 credit hours, depending on the major, and a GPA of 2.0 are required for graduation. All students must take freshman English, library instruction, 3 credits in U.S. diversity, and 3 credits in internationalization.

Special: Iowa State offers cooperative programs in engineering, forestry, agronomy, chemistry, computer science, economics, agricultural systems technology, business administration, industrial technology, and performing arts, and cross-registration with the Universities of Iowa and Northern Iowa. Internships, study abroad in 38 countries, dual majors, the B.A.-B.S. degree, student-designed majors, and accelerated degree programs are available. Interdisciplinary studies include agricultural biochemistry, agricultural systems technology, animal ecology, public service and administration in agriculture, and engineering operations. There are work-study programs, a Washington semester, nondegree study, and pass/no pass options. There are 16 national honor societies, including Phi Beta Kappa, and a freshman honors program.

Faculty/Classroom: 66% of faculty are male; 34%, female. 85% teach undergraduates, and 95% do research. Graduate students teach 15% of introductory courses. The average class size in a laboratory is 18 and in a regular course, 31.

Admissions: 90% of the 2005-2006 applicants were accepted. The SAT scores for the 2005-2006 freshman class were: Verbal--19% below 500, 35% between 500 and 599, 33% between 600 and 700, and 13% above 700; Math--12% below 500, 28% between 500 and 599, 40% between 600 and 700, and 21% above 700. The ACT scores were 15% below 21, 25% between 21 and 23, 26% between 24 and 26, 16% between 27 and 28, and 17% above 28. 46% of the current freshmen were in the top fifth of their class; 90% were in the top two fifths. There were 59 National Merit finalists.

Requirements: The SAT or ACT is required. In addition, applicants must graduate from an accredited secondary school. The GED is accepted. For admission to freshman standing, students must have completed 4 years of English, 3 each of math and science, and 2 to 3 of social studies. For the College of Liberal Arts and Sciences, 2 years of a single foreign language are also required. Iowa State requires applicants to be in the upper 50% of their class. AP and CLEP credits are accepted.

Procedure: Freshmen are admitted to all sessions. Entrance exams should be taken during the spring of the junior year or the fall of the senior year. There is a deferred admissions plan. Applications should be filed by August 1 for fall entry and December 1 for spring entry, along with a $30 fee. Notification is sent on a rolling basis. Applications are accepted on-line.

Transfer: 1429 transfer students enrolled in 2004-2005. Applicants must have a minimum GPA of 2.0 and at least 24 semester credits of acceptable transfer course work. They must also submit standardized test scores and provide a statement of good standing from prior institutions. 32 of 120 1/2 to 169 1/2 credits required for the bachelor's degree must be completed at Iowa State.

Visiting: There are regularly scheduled orientations for prospective students, including presentations on academics, admissions, residence hall living, fraternity and sorority life, and financial aid. There is also a group session with an adviser and a tour of the campus. There are guides for informal visits and visitors may sit in on classes and stay overnight. To schedule a visit, contact Phil Caffrey, Admissions Office at (515) 294-0821.

Financial Aid: In 2005-2006, 63% of all full-time freshmen and 85% of continuing full-time students received some form of financial aid. Need-based scholarships or need-based grants averaged $3399; need-based self-help aid (loans and jobs) averaged $3408; and non-need-based athletic scholarships averaged $13,672. 27% of undergraduates work part time. Average annual earnings from campus work are $3580. The average financial indebtedness of the 2005 graduate was $25,851. The FAFSA is required. The deadline for filing freshman financial aid applications for fall entry is March 1.

International Students: There are 741 international students enrolled. The school actively recruits these students. They must score satisfactorily on the TOEFL and take the college's own test.

Computers: Wireless access is available. All students may access the system all the time. There are no time limits and no fees.

Graduates: From July 1, 2004 to June 30, 2005, 4679 bachelor's degrees were awarded. The most popular majors were business (20%), engineering (19%), and agriculture (12%). In an average class, 1% graduate in 3 years or less, 31% graduate in 4 years or less, 63% graduate in 5 years or less, and 68% graduate in 6 years or less. 250 companies recruited on campus in 2004-2005. Of the 2004 graduating class, 20% were enrolled in graduate school within 6 months of graduation and 75% were employed.

Admissions Contact: Phil Caffrey, Associate Director, Admissions. E-mail: *admissions@iastate.edu* Web: *www.iastate.edu*

IOWA WESLEYAN COLLEGE E-4
Mount Pleasant, IA 52641

(319) 385-6231
(800) 582-2383; Fax: (319) 385-6240

Full-time: 279 men, 335 women	**Faculty:** 43
Part-time: 53 men, 182 women	**Ph.Ds:** n/av
Graduate: none	**Student/Faculty:** 14 to 1
Year: semesters, summer session	**Tuition:** $16,950
Application Deadline: open	**Room & Board:** $5190
Freshman Class: 727 applied, 426 accepted, 135 enrolled	
ACT: 19	COMPETITIVE

Iowa Wesleyan College, founded in 1842, is a private institution affiliated with the United Methodist Church. The college offers undergraduate degree programs in business, education, fine arts, human studies, language and literature, nursing, and science. There are 7 undergraduate schools. In addition to regional accreditation, IWC has baccalaureate program accreditation with NLN. The library contains 110,000 volumes, 26,757 microform items, and 3492 audio/video tapes/CDs/DVDs, and subscribes to 400 periodicals including electronic. Computerized library services include the card catalog, interlibrary loans, database searching, and Internet access. Special learning facilities include a learning resource center, art gallery, and radio station. The 60-acre campus is in a small town 45 miles south of Iowa City. Including any residence halls, there are 16 buildings.

Student Life: 54% of undergraduates are from Iowa. Others are from 22 states, 16 foreign countries, and Canada. 65% are white; 19% African American. 46% claim no religious affiliation; 9% Catholic; 8% Protestant. The average age of freshmen is 19; all undergraduates, 28. 47% do not continue beyond their first year; 38% remain to graduate.

Housing: 493 students can be accommodated in college housing, which includes single-sex dormitories. On-campus housing is guaranteed for all 4 years. 60% of students live on campus. All students may keep cars.

Activities: 8% of men belong to 1 national fraternity; 12% of women belong to 1 national sorority. There are 40 groups on campus, including art, band, cheerleading, choir, chorus, dance, drama, ethnic, film, honors, international, jazz band, literary magazine, newspaper, orchestra, pep band, photography, professional, radio and TV, religious, social, social service, student government, symphony, and yearbook. Popular campus events include Forum, Winterfest, and Spring Thing.

Sports: There are 6 intercollegiate sports for men and 6 for women, and 11 intramural sports for men and 11 for women. Facilities include a 32-acre complex with baseball, softball, and football fields and an all-weather quarter-mile track. There is also a gym, a swimming pool, and a basketball court.

Disabled Students: 77% of the campus is accessible. Wheelchair ramps, elevators, special parking, and special class scheduling are available.

Services: Counseling and information services are available, as is tutoring in every subject. There is remedial math, reading, and writing.

Campus Safety and Security: Measures include 24-hour foot and vehicle patrol, self-defense education, security escort services, and informal discussions. There are pamphlets/posters/films, emergency telephones, and lighted pathways/sidewalks.

Programs of Study: IWC confers B.A., B.S., B.G.S., B.M.E., and B.S.N. degrees. Bachelor's degrees are awarded in BIOLOGICAL SCIENCE (biology/biological science and life science), BUSINESS (accounting, business administration and management, and sports management), COMMUNICATIONS AND THE ARTS (communications, English, fine arts, and music), COMPUTER AND PHYSICAL SCIENCE (chemistry, computer science, and mathematics), EDUCATION (art, early childhood, elementary, music, physical, science, and secondary), ENGINEERING AND ENVIRONMENTAL DESIGN (preengineering), HEALTH PROFESSIONS (environmental health science, nursing, predentistry, premedicine, preoptometry, and preveterinary science), SOCIAL SCIENCE (criminal justice, history, prelaw, psychology, religion, and sociology). English, communications, and art are the strongest academically. Business, elementary education, and nursing are the largest.

Required: General education requirements of 35 to 40 hours include 6 of English, 4 of science, and 3 each of computer science, math, communication, civic issues, fine arts, religion, English literature, and global issues. Students must complete English 102 with a minimum of C-, satisfy a safety and survival requirement, complete 6 semester hours of service learning, and 6 to 14 semester hours of a field experience in the major. A minimum of 124 semester hours is required for the bachelor's degree, 28 or more must be in the major.

Special: The college maintains a cooperative program with Southeastern Community College. There are also internships in every major, a study-abroad program in Japan, China, and Mexico, a selective studies option, a general studies degree, credit in nursing through challenge exam, and satisfactory/unsatisfactory grade options. Work-study programs on campus and a Washington semester are also available. Cross-registration is available with Southeastern, Muscatine, and Indian Hills Community Colleges. There are 5 national honor societies and 2 departmental honors programs.

Faculty/Classroom: 51% of faculty are male; 49%, female. All teach undergraduates. The average class size in an introductory lecture is 22; in a laboratory, 24; and in a regular course, 14.

Admissions: 59% of the 2005-2006 applicants were accepted. The ACT scores for the 2005-2006 freshman class were: 80% below 21, 11% between 21 and 23, and 9% between 24 and 26. 14% of the current freshmen were in the top fifth of their class; 35% were in the top two fifths.

Requirements: The SAT or ACT is required. The ACT Optional Writing test is also recommended. In addition, applicants must be graduates of accredited secondary schools or have earned a GED. IWC requires applicants to be in the upper 50% of their class. A GPA of 2.0 is required. AP and CLEP credits are accepted. Important factors in the admissions decision are geographic diversity, extracurricular activities record, and evidence of special talent.

Procedure: Freshmen are admitted fall, winter, and spring. Entrance exams should be taken in April of the junior year or in June, October, or December of the senior year. There are early admissions, deferred admissions, and rolling admissions plans. Application deadlines are open. Applications are accepted on-line.

Transfer: 131 transfer students enrolled in 2004-2005. A minimum cumulative college GPA of 2.0 is required. 30 of 124 credits required for the bachelor's degree must be completed at IWC.

Visiting: There are regularly scheduled orientations for prospective students, including meetings with admissions, financial aid, and academic staff, as well as social activities. There are guides for informal visits and visitors may sit in on classes and stay overnight. To schedule a visit, contact the Admissions Office at (800) 582-2383, ext. 6388.

Financial Aid: In 2005-2006, 98% of all full-time freshmen and 97% of continuing full-time students received some form of financial aid. 90% of all full-time students received need-based aid. The average freshman award was $13,218. Need-based scholarships or need-based grants averaged $6180 ($14,350 maximum); need-based self-help aid (loans and jobs) averaged $3583 ($7418 maximum); non-need-based athletic scholarships averaged $4435 ($9000 maximum); and other non-need-based awards and non-need-based scholarships averaged $4682 ($19,990 maximum). 56% of undergraduates work part time. Average annual earnings from campus work are $1000. The average financial indebtedness of the 2005 graduate was $21,766. IWC is a member of CSS. The FAFSA and the college's own financial statement are required. The priority date for freshman financial aid applications for fall entry is January 1. The deadline for filing freshman financial aid applications for fall entry is open.

International Students: The school actively recruits these students. They must score satisfactorily on the written or electronic TOEFL.

Computers: All students may access the system 8 A.M. to 10 P.M. There are no time limits and no fees.

Admissions Contact: Cary A. Owens, Associate VP and Dean of Enrollment Management. E-mail: *admit@iwc.edu* Web: *www.iwc.edu*

LORAS COLLEGE
E-2

Dubuque, IA 52004-0178

(563) 588-7236
(800) 245-6727; Fax: (563) 588-7119

Full-time: 762 men, 750 women	**Faculty:** 111; IIB, --$
Part-time: 31 men, 51 women	**Ph.D.s:** 98%
Graduate: 32 men, 57 women	**Student/Faculty:** 14 to 1
Year: semesters, summer session	**Tuition:** $21,098
Application Deadline: open	**Room & Board:** $6095
Freshman Class: 1402 applied, 1152 accepted, 366 enrolled	
SAT Verbal/Math: 517/556*	**ACT:** 22 **COMPETITIVE**

Loras College, founded in 1839, is a private Roman Catholic liberal arts institution offering degree programs in humanities, social and behavioral studies, natural sciences, philosophy and religious studies, and professional studies. In addition to regional accreditation, Loras has baccalaureate program accreditation with ACS and NCATE. The library contains 347,351 volumes, 10,256 microform items, and 1356 audio/video tapes/CDs/DVDs, and subscribes to 11,032 periodicals including electronic. Computerized library services include the card catalog, interlibrary loans, database searching, Internet access, and laptop Internet portals. Special learning facilities include a learning resource center, art gallery, planetarium, radio station, TV station, and a Center for Dubuque History. The 60-acre campus is in a small town 180 miles west of Chicago and 250 miles south of Minneapolis. Including any residence halls, there are 18 buildings.

Student Life: 54% of undergraduates are from Iowa. Others are from 26 states and 7 foreign countries. 58% are from public schools. 92% are white. 59% are Catholic; 31% claim no religious affiliation; 8% Methodist and Lutheran. The average age of freshmen is 18; all undergraduates, 21. 22% do not continue beyond their first year; 66% remain to graduate.

Housing: 1030 students can be accommodated in college housing, which includes single-sex and coed dormitories, on-campus apartments, and off-campus apartments. In addition, there are honors houses. On-campus housing is guaranteed for all 4 years and is available on a lottery system for upperclassmen. 60% of students live on campus; of those, 65% remain on campus on weekends. All students may keep cars.

Activities: 33% of women belong to 1 national sorority. There are no fraternities. There are 59 groups on campus, including band, cheerleading, choir, chorus, computers, dance, debate, drama, ethnic, film, forensics, gay, honors, international, jazz band, literary magazine, musical theater, newspaper, photography, political, professional, programming board, radio and TV, religious, social, social service, student government, and yearbook. Popular campus events include Family Weekend, Tri-College Free Day, and Awareness Week.

Sports: There are 11 intercollegiate sports for men and 10 for women, and 73 intramural sports for men and 73 for women. Facilities include a sports center with 3 gym floors, a swimming pool, 4 racquetball courts, and an 8-lane Olympic indoor/outdoor track. There are also 5 outdoor tennis courts, a field house for basketball games, a football field, a soccer field, and a softball field. The campus stadium seats 3500.

Disabled Students: 65% of the campus is accessible. Wheelchair ramps, elevators, special parking, specially equipped rest rooms, special class scheduling, lowered drinking fountains, lowered telephones and special housing. An LD program is designed for helping physically disabled students.

Services: Counseling and information services are available, as is tutoring in every subject. There is a reader service for the blind and remedial math and writing.

Campus Safety and Security: Measures include 24-hour foot and vehicle patrol, security escort services, informal discussions, and pamphlets/posters/films. There are lighted pathways/sidewalks.

Programs of Study: Loras confers B.A., B.S., and B.M. degrees. Associate and master's degrees are also awarded. Bachelor's degrees are awarded in BIOLOGICAL SCIENCE (biochemistry and biology/biological science), BUSINESS (accounting, banking and finance, business administration and management, international business management, management information systems, marketing/retailing/merchandising, personnel management, and sports management), COMMUNICATIONS AND THE ARTS (broadcasting, creative writing, English literature, journalism, media arts, music, public relations, Spanish, speech/debate/rhetoric, studio art, and visual and performing arts), COMPUTER AND PHYSICAL SCIENCE (chemistry, computer science, mathematics, and science), EDUCATION (art, athletic training, early childhood, elementary, foreign languages, music, physical, science, secondary, and special), ENGINEERING AND ENVIRONMENTAL DESIGN (electrical/electronics engineering), HEALTH PROFESSIONS (exercise science), SOCIAL SCIENCE (classical/ancient civilization, criminal justice, economics, history, international studies, philosophy, political science/government, psychology, religion, social work, and sociology). Accounting and business, education, social sciences and history are the largest.

Required: To earn any degree students must complete a total of 120 hours with a minimum GPA of 2.0, and 36 to 37 hours of general education. There are additional requirements for a bachelor of music degree. All students must complete and present 2 1-credit student portfolios for review. A thesis and/or comprehensive exam is required for some majors.

Special: The college offers cross-registration with Clarke College and the University of Dubuque and study abroad in 10 countries. Also available are various internships, on-campus work-study programs, a 3-2 engineering degree, a Washington semester, pass/fail options, combined liberal arts-preprofessional programs, dual and student-designed majors, and adult degree programs offering a B.A.-B.S. degree. There are 6 national honor societies and a freshman honors program.

Faculty/Classroom: 65% of faculty are male; 35%, female. All teach undergraduates. No introductory courses are taught by graduate students. The average class size in an introductory lecture is 20; in a laboratory, 13; and in a regular course, 15.

Admissions: 82% of the 2005-2006 applicants were accepted. The SAT scores for the 2005-2006 freshman class were: Verbal--39% below 500, 44% between 500 and 599, and 17% between 600 and 700; Math--22% below 500, 39% between 500 and 599, and 39% between 600 and 700. The ACT scores were 34% below 21, 34% between 21 and 23, 19% between 24 and 26, 9% between 27 and 28, and 6% above 28. 27% of the current freshmen were in the top fifth of their class; 53% were in the top two fifths. 41 freshmen graduated first in their class.

Requirements: The SAT or ACT is required. In addition, applicants must be graduates of an accredited secondary school or have a GED certificate, and have completed 4 units of English and 3 each of math, science, social studies, and history. An essay and an interview are recommended. Loras requires applicants to be in the upper 50% of their class. A GPA of 2.5 is required. AP and CLEP credits are accepted. Important factors in the admissions decision are evidence of special talent, advanced placement or honor courses, and leadership record.

Procedure: Freshmen are admitted fall and spring. Entrance exams should be taken in April or June before the senior year or October of the senior year. There is a rolling admissions plan. Application deadlines are open. Application fee is $25. Applications are accepted on-line.

Transfer: 250 transfer students enrolled in 2005-2006. Transfer students must have a minimum 2.0 GPA and submit transcripts of previous college work. Other requirements apply. 30 of the last 40 hours of 120 credits required for the bachelor's degree must be completed at Loras.

Visiting: There are regularly scheduled orientations for prospective students, consisting of 5 fall visitation days for all students and 7 programs for specific geographic locations. There are guides for informal visits and visitors may sit in on classes and stay overnight. To schedule a visit, contact the Office of Admissions.

Financial Aid: In 2005-2006, all of full-time freshmen and 98% of continuing full-time students received some form of financial aid. 55% of full-time freshmen and 48% of continuing full-time students received need-based aid. The average freshman award was $9116. Need-based scholarships or need-based grants averaged $3356 ($12,500 maximum); need-based self-help aid (loans and jobs) averaged $3599 ($7125 maximum); and other non-need-based awards and non-need-based scholarships averaged $6195 ($15,000 maximum). 35% of undergraduates work part time. Average annual earnings from campus work are $940. The average financial indebtedness of the 2005 graduate was $17,190. The FAFSA is required. The deadline for filing freshman financial aid applications for fall entry is April 15.

International Students: There are 47 international students enrolled. The school actively recruits these students. They must score satisfactorily on the written or electronic version of the TOEFL.

Computers: Wireless access is available. PCs are available throughout the campus to connect to the wireless system. All students may access the system. All computer equipment is available for student use on all school days. There are no time limits and no fees. All students are required to have personal computers.

Graduates: From July 1, 2004 to June 30, 2005, 319 bachelor's degrees were awarded. The most popular majors were business (32%), education (30%), and social science and history (9%). In an average class, 55% graduate in 4 years or less, 65% graduate in 5 years or less, and 66% graduate in 6 years or less. 85 companies recruited on campus in 2004-2005. Of the 2004 graduating class, 20% were enrolled in graduate school within 6 months of graduation and 75% were employed.

Admissions Contact: Mary K. Weck, Director of Admissions. A video is available. E-mail: adms@loras.edu Web: www.loras.edu

LUTHER COLLEGE
E-1
Decorah, IA 52101
(563) 387-1287
(800) 458-8437; Fax: (563) 387-2159

Full-time: 1026 men, 1450 women	**Faculty:** 179; IIB, -$
Part-time: 34 men, 35 women	**Ph.Ds:** 79%
Graduate: none	**Student/Faculty:** 14 to 1
Year: 4-1-4, summer session	**Tuition:** $24,570
Application Deadline: open	**Room & Board:** $4230
Freshman Class: 2121 applied, 1593 accepted, 631 enrolled	
SAT Verbal/Math: 610/630*	**ACT:** 26 **VERY COMPETITIVE+**

Luther College, affiliated with the Evangelical Lutheran Church in America, is a private liberal arts institution founded in 1861. In addition to regional accreditation, Luther has baccalaureate program accreditation with CSWE, NASM, NCATE, and NLN. The library contains 339,085 volumes, 25,004 microform items, and 24,000 audio/video tapes/CDs/DVDs, and subscribes to 1612 periodicals including electronic. Computerized library services include the card catalog, interlibrary loans, database searching, and Internet access. Special learning facilities include a learning resource center, art gallery, natural history museum, planetarium, and radio station. The 200-acre campus is in a small town 70 miles south of Rochester, Minnesota. Including any residence halls, there are 35 buildings.

Student Life: 64% of undergraduates are from out of state, mostly the Midwest. Students are from 36 states and 25 foreign countries. 90% are from public schools. 89% are white. 72% are Protestant; 15% Catholic; 11% claim no religious affiliation. The average age of freshmen is 18; all undergraduates, 20. 15% do not continue beyond their first year; 77% remain to graduate.

Housing: 2148 students can be accommodated in college housing, which includes coed dorms, on-campus apartments, off-campus apartments, and married-student housing. In addition, there are language houses, dialogue floors, and wellness floors. On-campus housing is guaranteed for all 4 years. 84% of students live on campus; of those, 90% remain on campus on weekends. All students may keep cars.

Activities: 7% of men belong to 4 local fraternities; 9% of women belong to 4 local sororities. There are 139 groups on campus, including art, band, cheerleading, choir, chorale, chorus, computers, dance, drama, drill team, ethnic, forensics, gay, honors, international, jazz band, literary magazine, musical theater, newspaper, opera, orchestra, pep band, photography, political, professional, radio and TV, religious, social, social service, student government, symphony, and yearbook. Popular campus events include Christmas at Luther, the Ethnic Arts Fair, and Parents Weekend.

Sports: There are 10 intercollegiate sports for men and 9 for women, and 45 intramural sports for men and 45 for women. Facilities include 5 hardwood basketball courts, an indoor swimming pool, 4 batting cages, a fitness center, a climbing wall, 3 soccer fields, a golf driving range, a dance studio, a 4000-seat stadium and 3500-seat gym, 6 indoor tennis courts, 3 racquetball courts, an indoor 6-lane 200-meter track, an outdoor 8-lane polyurethane 400-meter track, and 9 outdoor tennis courts.

Disabled Students: 95% of the campus is accessible. Wheelchair ramps, elevators, special parking, specially equipped rest rooms, lowered drinking fountains, lowered telephones, and special housing are available.

Services: Counseling and information services are available, as is tutoring in every subject. There is a reader service for the blind and remedial reading and writing. Reading machines, tape recorders, note taking, and a learning center are available.

Campus Safety and Security: Measures include 24-hour foot and vehicle patrol, self-defense education, security escort services, and informal discussions. There are pamphlets/posters/films, emergency telephones, and lighted pathways/sidewalks.

Programs of Study: Luther confers the B.A. degree. Bachelor's degrees are awarded in BIOLOGICAL SCIENCE (biology/biological science), BUSINESS (accounting, management information systems, and management science), COMMUNICATIONS AND THE ARTS (art, classical languages, communications, dance, dramatic arts, English, French, German, music, Spanish, and speech/debate/rhetoric), COMPUTER AND PHYSICAL SCIENCE (chemistry, computer science, mathematics, physics, and statistics), EDUCATION (athletic training, elementary, and physical), HEALTH PROFESSIONS (health and nursing), SOCIAL SCIENCE (African American studies, anthropology, biblical languages, economics, history, philosophy, political science/government, psychology, religion, Scandinavian studies, social work, and sociology). Biology, music, and English are the strongest academically. Biology, management, and elementary education are the largest.

Required: Students must complete 11 hours of interdisciplinary English and history, 9 hours of religion/philosophy, 6 to 9 of foreign language, 7 of natural science, 7 of social science, 3 each of fine arts, global studies, and quantitative/symbolic reasoning, and 2 of phys ed. The B.A. requires 128 semester hours with a GPA of at least 2.0 in the major. A senior project and writing course are required. Foreign language proficiency must be demonstrated.

Special: Internships in all disciplines, work-study programs, a Washington semester, study-abroad plans in numerous countries, pass/fail options, student-designed and dual majors, and 3-2 engineering degrees with Washington University in St. Louis and the University of Minnesota are available. There are 10 national honor societies, including Phi Beta Kappa, and a freshman honors program.

Faculty/Classroom: 57% of faculty are male; 43%, female. All teach undergraduates. The average class size in an introductory lecture is 30; in a laboratory, 13; and in a regular course, 21.

Admissions: 75% of the 2005-2006 applicants were accepted. The SAT scores for the 2005-2006 freshman class were: Verbal--12% below 500, 26% between 500 and 599, 45% between 600 and 700, and 17% above 700; Math--7% below 500, 30% between 500 and 599, 47% between 600 and 700, and 16% above 700. The ACT scores were 11% below 21, 21% between 21 and 23, 25% between 24 and 26, 18% between 27 and 28, and 24% above 28. 55% of the current freshmen were in the top fifth of their class; 78% were in the top two fifths. There were 10 National Merit finalists and 10 semifinalists. 40 freshmen graduated first in their class.

Requirements: The SAT or ACT is required. In addition, high school applicants should have 4 years of English, 3 each of math and social studies, and 2 of science. An essay is required, and an interiew is recommended. The GED is accepted. Luther requires applicants to be in the upper 50% of their class. A GPA of 2.5 is required. AP and CLEP credits are accepted. Important factors in the admissions decision are advanced placement or honor courses, evidence of special talent, and extracurricular activities record.

Procedure: Freshmen are admitted to all sessions. Entrance exams should be taken by the fall of the senior year. There are early admissions and deferred admissions plans. Application deadlines are open. Application fee is $25. Applications are accepted on-line.

Transfer: 84 transfer students enrolled in 2004-2005. Applicants must meet the same high school standards and the SAT or ACT requirements as entering freshmen, with a minimum GPA of 2.5 in parallel college course work. 32 of 128 credits required for the bachelor's degree must be completed at Luther.

Visiting: There are regularly scheduled orientations for prospective students. There are guides for informal visits and visitors may sit in on classes and stay overnight. To schedule a visit, contact the Admissions Office at *visit@luther.edu.*

Financial Aid: In 2005-2006, 99% of all full-time students received some form of financial aid. 73% of full-time freshmen and 71% of continuing full-time students received need-based aid. The average freshman award was $16,824. Need-based scholarships or need-based grants averaged $18,463 ($31,150 maximum); need-based self-help aid (loans and jobs) averaged $5603 ($7375 maximum); and other non-need-based awards and non-need-based scholarships averaged $8563 ($14,500 maximum). 79% of undergraduates work part time. Average annual earnings from campus work were $1684. The average financial indebtedness of the 2005 graduate was $18,504. Luther is a member of CSS. The FAFSA, the college's own financial statement, and the a family tax return are required. The priority date for freshman financial aid applications for fall entry is March 1.

International Students: There are 64 international students enrolled. The school actively recruits these students. They must take the written TOEFL or the IELTS.

Computers: Wireless access is available in certain campus locations. All students may access the system anytime. There are no time limits and no fees.

Graduates: From July 1, 2004 to June 30, 2005, 570 bachelor's degrees were awarded. The most popular majors were biology (10%), management (9%), and psychology (8%). In an average class, 65% graduate in 4 years or less, 74% graduate in 5 years or less, and 75% graduate in 6 years or less. 192 companies recruited on campus in 2004-2005. Of the 2004 graduating class, 21% were enrolled in graduate school within 6 months of graduation and 62% were employed.

Admissions Contact: Jon Lund, Vice President for Enrollment Management. A video is available. E-mail: *admissions@luther.edu* Web: *www.luther.edu*

MAHARISHI UNIVERSITY OF MANAGEMENT   E-4
Fairfield, IA 52557
(641) 472-1110
(800) 369-6480; Fax: (641) 472-1179

Full-time: 125 men, 120 women	**Faculty:** 53
Part-time: 10 men, 5 women	**Ph.Ds:** 70%
Graduate: 383 men, 160 women	**Student/Faculty:** 5 to 1
Year: semesters	**Tuition:** $24,150
Application Deadline: open	**Room & Board:** $5300
Freshman Class: n/av	
SAT or ACT: required	**VERY COMPETITIVE**

Maharishi University of Management, established in 1971, is a private institution offering undergraduate and graduate programs in a broad range of disciplines. The University provides Consciousness-Based education and incorporates the group practice of the Maharishi Transcendental Meditation technique into a traditional academic program. There are 5 undergraduate and 5 graduate schools. Figures in the above capsule are approximate. The 2 libraries contain 148,000 volumes, 59,900 microform items, and 24,114 audio/video tapes/CDs/DVDs, and subscribe to 14,000 periodicals including electronic. Computerized library services include the card catalog, interlibrary loans, database searching, and Internet access. Special learning facilities include a learning resource center, art gallery, radio station, psychophysiology, electronic engineering, visual technology, and physics labs, and a scanning electron microscope. The 272-acre campus is in a small town 114 miles southeast of Des Moines. Including any residence halls, there are 50 buildings.

Student Life: 60% of undergraduates are from out of state, mostly the Middle Atlantic. Students are from 21 states, 29 foreign countries, and Canada. 61% are white; 30% foreign nationals. The average age of freshmen is 20; all undergraduates, 23. 29% do not continue beyond their first year; 37% remain to graduate.

Housing: Housing includes single-sex dormitories, on-campus apartments, and married-student housing. In addition, there are special-interest houses and privately owned, on-campus family housing for studnets with families. On-campus housing is guaranteed for all 4 years. 73% of students live on campus; of those, 93% remain on campus on weekends. Alcohol is not permitted. All students may keep cars.

Activities: There are no fraternities or sororities. There are 15 groups on campus, including art, chess, chorale, dance, drama, ecology, entrepreneurial, ethnic, international, musical theater, newspaper, permaculture, photography, political, professional, radio and TV, religious, social, social service, student government, and yearbook. Popular campus events include sports festivals, seasonal celebrations, and International Cultural Exchange Festival.

Sports: There are 2 intercollegiate sports for men and 1 for women, and 5 intramural sports for men and 5 for women. Facilities include outdoor and indoor tennis, basketball, and volleyball courts, a gym, a weight-training room, a field house, a swimming pool, a table tennis room, baseball batting and golf driving cages, a golf putting range, an indoor 4-lane jogging track, a dance studio, and a rock-climbing wall.

Disabled Students: All of the campus is accessible. Wheelchair ramps, special parking, specially equipped rest rooms, and lowered telephones are available.

Services: Counseling and information services are available, as is tutoring in every subject. There is remedial math, reading, and writing.

Campus Safety and Security: Measures include 24-hour foot and vehicle patrol, security escort services, informal discussions, and emergency telephones. There are lighted pathways/sidewalks.

Programs of Study: Maharishi University of Management confers B.A., B.S., and B.F.A. degrees. Master's and doctoral degrees are also awarded. Bachelor's degrees are awarded in AGRICULTURE (environmental studies), BUSINESS (management science), COMMUNICATIONS AND THE ARTS (dramatic arts, fine arts, and literature), COMPUTER AND PHYSICAL SCIENCE (computer science, mathematics, and web services), EDUCATION (education). Math, computer science, and management science are the strongest academically. Fine arts and management are the largest.

Required: Students must complete 166 credit units with a minimum of 60 credits in the major and must also complete the core curriculum of 18 units as well as 20 units in a distribution of academic fields. All students must maintain a minimum GPA of 2.0. Additional requirements include health and fitness courses, the Science of Creative Intelligence course with its applied aspect, the Transcendental Meditation program, and courses in math and writing. The 42-week school year and block scheduling system allow students to take 1 course at a time.

Special: Opportunities are provided for internships, B.A.-B.S. degrees in environmental sciences and computer science, study abroad, and nondegree study. Systematic programs are offered in the Science of Creative Intelligence, by which students apply knowledge to practical professional values. There are several 1-month blocks a year during which students may study, for example, art in Italy, literature in Switzerland, or business in Japan. There is a freshman honors program.

Faculty/Classroom: 67% of faculty are male; 33%, female. All teach undergraduates, 20% do research, and 20% do both. No introductory courses are taught by graduate students. The average class size in an introductory lecture is 35 and in a regular course, 10.

Requirements: The SAT or ACT is required. In addition, applicants must graduate from an accredited secondary school or have a GED. An essay and 2 personal recommendations are required. An interview is recommended. A GPA of 2.5 is required. AP and CLEP credits are accepted. Important factors in the admissions decision are personality/intangible qualities, recommendations by school officials, and leadership record.

Procedure: Freshmen are admitted fall and spring. There is a rolling admissions plans. Entrance exams should be taken in the fall of the senior year or spring of the junior year. Application deadlines are open. Application fee is $25. Applications are accepted on-line.

Transfer: 24 transfer students enrolled in a recent year. Students must have a 2.5 GPA, acceptable recommendations, and meet all standards set by the university. 66 of 166 credits required for the bachelor's degree must be completed at Maharishi University of Management.

Visiting: There are regularly scheduled orientations for prospective students, including campus tours, visits to classes, interviews, student panels, and informal dinners. There are guides for informal visits and visitors may sit in on classes and stay overnight. To schedule a visit, contact Julie Beaufort, Director of guest services.

Financial Aid: In a reent year, 95% of all full-time freshmen and 98% of continuing full-time students received some form of financial aid. 87% of full-time freshmen and 90% of continuing full-time students received need-based aid. The average freshman award was $26,577. Need-based scholarships or need-based grants averaged $18,657 ($21,000 maximum); need-based self-help aid (loans and jobs) averaged $6297 ($20,000 maximum); and other non-need-based awards and non-need-based scholarships averaged $1623 ($5000 maximum). 75% of undergraduates worked part time. Average annual earnings from campus work were $1600. The average financial indebtedness of a recent graduate was $18,996. The FAFSA is required. Check with the school for application deadlines.

International Students: In a recent year, there were 75 international students enrolled. The school actively recruits these students. They must score satisfactorily on the TOEFL and also take the college's own test.

Computers: All students may access the system daytime and evenings. There are no time limits and no fees. All students are required to have personal computers.

Graduates: In a recent year, 48 bachelor's degrees were awarded. The most popular majors were management (31%), fine arts (25%), and computer science (8%). In an average class, 28% graduate in 4 years or less, and 47% graduate in 6 years or less. Of a recent graduating class, 22% were enrolled in graduate school within 6 months of graduation and 75% were employed.

Admissions Contact: Richard Neate, Director of Admissions. A video is available. E-mail: *admissions@mum.edu* Web: *www.mum.edu*

MERCY COLLEGE OF HEALTH SCIENCES	C-8
Des Moines, IA 50309-1239	(515) 643-6715
	(800) 637-2994; Fax: (515) 643-6698

Full-time: 37 men, 378 women	**Faculty:** 36
Part-time: 22 men, 219 women	**Ph.D.s:** 22%
Graduate: none	**Student/Faculty:** 12 to 1
Year: semesters, summer session	**Tuition:** $11,700
Application Deadline: n/av	**Room & Board:** n/app
Freshman Class: 582 applied, 549 accepted, 278 enrolled	
ACT: required	SPECIAL

Mercy College of Health Sciences was founded in 1995 and is a private school affiliated with the Religious Sisters of Mercy (RSM), a religious order of Roman Catholic women. There are 4 undergraduate schools. The 2 libraries contain 9505 volumes and 1313 audio/video tapes/CDs/DVDs, and subscribe to 96 periodicals including electronic. Computerized library services include the card catalog, interlibrary loans, database searching, and Internet access. Special learning facilities include a learning resource center and clinical labs. The 4-acre campus is in an urban area in Des Moines. There are 3 buildings.

Student Life: 95% of undergraduates are from Iowa. Others are from 3 states. 91% are white. The average age of freshmen is 28; all undergraduates, 28.

Housing: There are no residence halls. All students commute. Alcohol is not permitted. All students may keep cars.

Activities: There are no fraternities or sororities. There are 5 groups on campus, including professional and student government. Popular campus events include Mercy Day and Student Appreciation Day.

Sports: There is no sports program at Mercy College of Health Sciences.

Disabled Students: All of the campus is accessible. Wheelchair ramps, elevators, special parking, specially equipped rest rooms, and lowered drinking fountains are available.

Services: Counseling and information services are available, as is tutoring in most subjects.

Campus Safety and Security: Measures include 24-hour foot and vehicle patrol, security escort services, shuttle buses, and informal discussions. There are pamphlets/posters/films and lighted pathways/sidewalks.

Programs of Study: Mercy College of Health Sciences confers B.S.H.C.M., and B.S.N. degrees. Associate degrees are also awarded. Bachelor's degrees are awarded in HEALTH PROFESSIONS (health care administration and nursing). Radiologic technology and diagnostic sonography are the strongest academically. Nursing is the largest.

Required: There is a community service requirement, and a caring course is also required. Students must complete a communication portfolio and credit hours must be completed to graduate.

Special: Internships offering clinical expierience are available. There are 2 national honor societies.

Faculty/Classroom: 11% of faculty are male; 89%, female.

Admissions: 74% of the 2005-2006 applicants were accepted.

Requirements: The ACT is required. A GPA of 2.5 is required. AP and CLEP credits are accepted.

Procedure: Freshmen are admitted fall, spring, and summer. There is a rolling admissions plan. Notification is sent on a rolling basis. The application fee is $25.

Transfer: 329 transfer students enrolled in 2004-2005. Requirements vary by program.

Visiting: There are guides for informal visits. To schedule a visit, contact Sandi Nagel or Sara Pratt at (515) 643-3180.

Financial Aid: In 2005-2006, 93% of all full-time freshmen and 88% of continuing full-time students received some form of financial aid. 78% of full-time freshmen and 79% of continuing full-time students received need-based aid. Need-based scholarships or need-based grants averaged $5760 ($17,550 maximum); need-based self-help aid (loans and jobs) averaged $1432 ($2625 maximum); and other non-need-based awards and non-need-based scholarships averaged $7525 ($21,000 maximum). 1% of undergraduates work part time. Average annual earnings from campus work are $910. The average financial indebtedness of the 2005 graduate was $16,976. The FAFSA is required. The priority date for freshman financial aid applications for fall entry is April 15. The deadline for filing freshman financial aid applications for fall entry is July 1.

Computers: There are no time limits and no fees.

Graduates: From July 1, 2004 to June 30, 2005, 41 bachelor's degrees were awarded. The most popular majors were nursing (49%), surgical technology (11%), and radiologic technology (11%).

Admissions Contact: Admissions Officer.
E-mail: *admissions@mchs.edu* Web: *www.mchs.edu*

MORNINGSIDE COLLEGE	B-2
Sioux City, IA 51106	(712) 274-5111
	(800) 831-0806; Fax: (712) 274-5101

Full-time: 493 men, 573 women	**Faculty:** 63; IIB, --$
Part-time: 31 men, 52 women	**Ph.D.s:** 84%
Graduate: 51 men, 240 women	**Student/Faculty:** 17 to 1
Year: semesters, summer session	**Tuition:** $18,080
Application Deadline: open	**Room & Board:** $5624
Freshman Class: 1467 applied, 1073 accepted, 349 enrolled	
ACT: 22	COMPETITIVE

Morningside College, founded in 1894, is a private college affiliated with the United Methodist Church. Its curriculum includes the liberal arts and preprofessional and professional programs of study. In addition to regional accreditation, Morningside has baccalaureate program accreditation with NASM, NCATE, and NLN. The library contains 114,861 volumes, 287,113 microform items, and 5513 audio/video tapes/CDs/DVDs, and subscribes to 543 periodicals including electronic. Computerized library services include the card catalog, interlibrary loans, database searching, and Internet access. Special learning facilities include a learning resource center, art gallery, radio station, TV station, and an observatory, and a theater. The 41-acre campus is in a suburban area 100 miles north of Omaha on Interstate 29, at the convergence of the states of South Dakota, Iowa, and Nebraska. Including any residence halls, there are 19 buildings.

Student Life: 70% of undergraduates are from Iowa. Others are from 23 states and 8 foreign countries. 92% are from public schools. 90% are white. 49% are Protestant; 30% claim no religious affiliation; 21% Catholic. The average age of freshmen is 18; all undergraduates, 21. 36% do not continue beyond their first year; 59% remain to graduate.

Housing: 720 students can be accommodated in college housing, which includes coed dorms, on-campus apartments, and freshman halls. On-campus housing is guaranteed for all 4 years. 70% of students live on campus; of those, 60% remain on campus on weekends. All students may keep cars.

Activities: 12% of men belong to 2 national fraternities; 3% of women belong to 1 national sorority. There are 36 groups on campus, including art, band, cheerleading, choir, chorale, chorus, computers, dance, drama, ethnic, honors, international, jazz band, literary magazine, newspaper, orchestra, pep band, photography, political, professional, radio and TV, religious, social, student government, and yearbook. Popular campus events include Friday is Writing Day, Academic and Cultural Arts Series, and Christmas at Morningside.

Sports: There are 8 intercollegiate sports for men and 9 for women, and 12 intramural sports for men and 12 for women. Facilities include an 8000-seat stadium, a football field, a campus recreation center with basketball, volleyball, badminton, tennis, and racquetball/handball courts, an elevated track, a weight room, and a 6-lane, 25-meter swimming pool.

Disabled Students: 80% of the campus is accessible. Wheelchair ramps, elevators, special parking, specially equipped rest rooms, special class scheduling, and lowered telephones are available.

Services: Counseling and information services are available, as is tutoring in most subjects. There is a reader service for the blind, and remedial math, reading, and writing.

Campus Safety and Security: Measures include self-defense education, security escort services, informal discussions, and pamphlets/posters/films. There are emergency telephones, and lighted pathways/sidewalks. The college is in compliance with the Crime Awareness and Campus Security Act of 1990.

Programs of Study: Morningside confers B.A., B.S., B.Mus., B.Mus.Ed., and B.S.N. degrees. Master's degrees are also awarded. Bachelor's degrees are awarded in BIOLOGICAL SCIENCE (biology/biological science), BUSINESS (accounting and business administration and management), COMMUNICATIONS AND THE ARTS (art, communications, dramatic arts, English, graphic design, music, photography, and Spanish), COMPUTER AND PHYSICAL SCIENCE (chemistry, computer science, mathematics, and physics), EDUCATION (art, business, elementary, English, mathematics, music, science, social studies, and special), HEALTH PROFESSIONS (nursing), SOCIAL SCIENCE (history, philosophy, political science/government, psychology, and religion). Business administration, education, and biology are the largest.

Required: The total number of credit hours required for graduation is 124, with 44 hours of core curriculum in liberal arts and 30 hours minimum in the major. Students must have a minimum GPA of 2.0 to graduate.

Special: There is a co-op program in medical technology. Internships are available in all departments. Study abroad in 3 countries, a Washington semester, work-study programs, both on campus and with 20 nonprofit agencies, a dual major in philosophy/religious studies, and student-designed majors are available. There are 15 national honor societies, and a freshman honors program.

Faculty/Classroom: 59% of faculty are male; 41%, female. All teach undergraduates and 20% do research. No introductory courses are taught by graduate students. The average class size in an introductory lecture is 24; in a laboratory, 10; and in a regular course, 12.

Admissions: 73% of the 2005-2006 applicants were accepted. The SAT scores for the 2005-2006 freshman class were: Verbal--47% below 500, 26% between 500 and 599, and 26% between 600 and 700; Math--42% below 500, 26% between 500 and 599, 26% between 600 and 700, and 5% above 700. The ACT scores were 38% below 21, 28% between 21 and 23, 21% between 24 and 26, 7% between 27 and 28, and 6% above 28. 34% of the current freshmen were in the top fifth of their class; 65% were in the top two fifths. 11 freshmen graduated first in their class.

Requirements: The ACT is required. In addition, applicants must also be graduates of an accredited secondary school. The GED is accepted. A portfolio is required for all studio art majors and an audition for performing music majors. Applicants graduating from high school 5 years or more prior to entering college are exempted from submitting the ACT scores. Those entering from a homeschooled environment must submit a completed Home School Credit Evaluation form, which may be obtained in the Office of Admissions. Morningside requires applicants to be in the upper 50% of their class. A GPA of 2.5 is required. AP and CLEP credits are accepted. Important factors in the admissions decision are recommendations by school officials, evidence of special talent, and advanced placement or honor courses.

Procedure: Freshmen are admitted to all sessions. Entrance exams should be taken in the junior year. There is a rolling admissions plan. Application deadlines are open. Application fee is $25. Applications are accepted on-line.

Transfer: 64 transfer students enrolled in a recent year. Transfer applicants must take the ACT and have an interview. They must have 24 semester hours with a 2.0 or above cumulative average. They must present official transcripts of previous collegiate records. 30 of 124 credits required for the bachelor's degree must be completed at Morningside.

Visiting: There are regularly scheduled orientations for prospective students, consisting of a campus tour, appointments with faculty and financial aid, and an interview with an admissions counselor. There are guides for informal visits and visitors may sit in on classes and stay overnight. To schedule a visit, contact the Office of Admissions at (800) 831-0806, ext. 5111.

Financial Aid: In a recent year, 100% of all full-time freshmen and 99% of continuing full-time students received some form of financial aid.

79% of all full-time students received need-based aid. The average freshman award was $18,916. Need-based scholarships or need-based grants averaged $6305 ($14,050 maximum); need-based self-help aid (loans and jobs) averaged $5515 ($8343 maximum); non-need-based athletic scholarships averaged $2702 ($6700 maximum); and other non-need-based awards and non-need-based scholarships averaged $9428 ($23,735 maximum). Average annual earnings from campus work are $1501. The average financial indebtedness of the 2005 graduate was $18,648. The FAFSA is required. The priority date for freshman financial aid applications for fall entry is March 1.

International Students: There are 22 international students enrolled. A satisfactory score is required on the written TOEFL.

Computers: All students may access the system. There are no time limits and no fees. It is strongly recommended that all students have a personal computer.

Graduates: In a recent year, 164 bachelor's degrees were awarded. The most popular majors were education (27%), business (18%), and nursing (6%). In an average class, 1% graduate in 3 years or less, 38% graduate in 4 years or less, 49% graduate in 5 years or less, and 52% graduate in 6 years or less. 19 companies recruited on campus in 2004-2005. Of the 2004 graduating class, 12% were enrolled in graduate school within 6 months of graduation and 81% were employed.

Admissions Contact: Joel Weyand, Director of Admissions.
E-mail: mscadm@morningside.edu Web: www.morningside.edu

MOUNT MERCY COLLEGE E-3
Cedar Rapids, IA 52402

(319) 368-6460
(800) 248-4504; Fax: (319) 363-5270

Full-time: 252 men, 767 women	**Faculty:** 73; IIB, --$
Part-time: 151 men, 320 women	**Ph.D.s:** 59%
Graduate: none	**Student/Faculty:** 14 to 1
Year: 4-1-4, summer session	**Tuition:** $18,030
Application Deadline: August 15	**Room & Board:** $5640
Freshman Class: 478 applied, 376 accepted, 181 enrolled	
ACT: 22	COMPETITIVE

Mount Mercy College, founded in 1928, is a Catholic college providing student focused education in the spirit of the Sisters of Mercy. In addition to regional accreditation, Mount Mercy has baccalaureate program accreditation with CSWE and NLN. The library contains 127,471 volumes, 46,339 microform items, and 4811 audio/video tapes/CDs/DVDs, and subscribes to 711 periodicals including electronic. Computerized library services include the card catalog, interlibrary loans, database searching, Internet access, and laptop Internet portals. Special learning facilities include a learning resource center, art gallery, and video media room. The 40-acre campus is in an urban area in Cedar Rapids in eastern Iowa. Including any residence halls, there are 19 buildings.

Student Life: 94% of undergraduates are from Iowa. Others are from 20 states and 6 foreign countries. 88% are white. The average age of freshmen is 18; all undergraduates, 25. 24% do not continue beyond their first year; 61% remain to graduate.

Housing: 510 students can be accommodated in college housing, which includes single-sex and coed dormitories and on-campus apartments. On-campus housing is guaranteed for all 4 years. 74% of students commute. All students may keep cars.

Activities: There are no fraternities or sororities. There are 34 groups on campus, including academic art, cheerleading, choir, chorale, chorus, drama, drill team, film, honors, international, literary magazine, musical theater, newspaper, political, professional, religious, social, social service, and student government. Popular campus events include Hillfest, Spring Fling, Halloween on the Hill, and Friends and Family Weekend.

Sports: There are 6 intercollegiate sports for men and 7 for women, and 10 intramural sports for men and 10 for women. Facilities include a 2,000-seat recreation center, an indoor hitting facility, a weight room, an aerobics area, a cardio room, 2 racquetball courts, and a fitness center.

Disabled Students: 95% of the campus is accessible. Wheelchair ramps, elevators, special parking, specially equipped rest rooms, and lowered drinking fountains are available.

Services: Counseling and information services are available, as is tutoring in most subjects, including all communication skills. There is a reader service for the blind, and remedial math, reading, and writing.

Campus Safety and Security: Measures include 24-hour foot and vehicle patrol, self-defense education, security escort services, and informal discussions. There are pamphlets/posters/films, emergency telephones, lighted pathways/sidewalks, evening and weekend foot patrol, cameras at residence hall entrances, and a patrolled parking area.

Programs of Study: Mount Mercy confers B.A., B.S., B.A.A., B.A.S., B.B.A., and B.S.N. degrees. Bachelor's degrees are awarded in BIOLOGICAL SCIENCE (biology/biological science), BUSINESS (accounting, business administration and management, and marketing/retailing/merchandising), COMMUNICATIONS AND THE ARTS (art, communications, dramatic arts, English, music, speech/debate/rhetoric, and visual and performing arts), COMPUTER AND PHYSICAL SCIENCE (computer science, information sciences and systems, and mathematics), EDUCATION (elementary, music, and secondary), HEALTH PROFESSIONS (health care administration, medical laboratory technology, and nursing), SOCIAL SCIENCE (criminal justice, history, international studies, philosophy, political science/government, psychology, religion, social work, sociology, and urban studies). Business, education, and nursing are the largest.

Required: To graduate, students must complete 123 semester hours, with at least 30 hours in the major, and maintain at least a 2.0 GPA. General education requirements include a total of 12 courses in philosophy, religious studies, English, speech, arts, social and natural sciences, history, and multicultural studies.

Special: Mount Mercy offers internships in many majors, study abroad in the Czech Republic, work-study programs on campus, cross-registration with Coe College for courses not offered, accelerated programs in business, accounting, marketing, and health services administration, an accelerated degree completion program for RNs, and student-designed, interdisciplinary majors. Credit for prior experiential learning may be granted, and pass/fail options are available. There are 3 national honor societies, a freshman honors program, and all departments have honors programs.

Faculty/Classroom: 41% of faculty are male; 59%, female. All teach undergraduates. The average class size in an introductory lecture is 25; in a laboratory, 14; and in a regular course, 25.

Admissions: 79% of the 2005-2006 applicants were accepted. The ACT scores for the 2005-2006 freshman class were: 41% below 21, 33% between 21 and 23, 20% between 24 and 26, 4% between 27 and 28, and 2% above 28. 34% of the current freshmen were in the top fifth of their class; 53% were in the top two fifths. 4 freshmen graduated first in their class.

Requirements: The SAT or ACT is required. Other admissions requirements include graduation from an accredited secondary school, with 16 Carnegie units, including 4 of English, 3 of social studies, and 2 each of math, history, and foreign language. A recommendation from a high school teacher or counselor and an essay or personal statement are also required. Mount Mercy requires applicants to be in the upper 50% of their class. A GPA of 2.5 is required. AP and CLEP credits are accepted. Extracurricular activities record is an important factor in the admission decision.

Procedure: Freshmen are admitted to all sessions. Entrance exams should be taken in the junior year or the fall of the senior year. There is a deferred admissions and a rolling addmissions plan. Applications should be filed by August 15 for fall entry, December 30 for winter entry, and February for spring entry, along with a $20 fee. Notification is sent on a rolling basis within 3 days. Applications are accepted on-line.

Transfer: 203 transfer students enrolled in 2004-2005. Applicants must have at least a 2.0 GPA. Associate degree holders must submit transcripts from all previous colleges attended; students with fewer credits earned must also submit a high school transcript. An interview is recommended. 30 of 123 credits required for the bachelor's degree must be completed at Mount Mercy.

Visiting: There are regularly scheduled orientations for prospective students, consisting of a presidential welcome, campus tour, student panel, faculty academic fair, presentations on college selection and admission requirements, and student evaluation. There are guides for informal visits and visitors may sit in on classes and stay overnight. To schedule a visit, contact the Admissions Office.

Financial Aid: In 2005-2006, all of full-time freshmen and 96% of continuing full-time students received some form of financial aid. 83% of full-time freshmen and 84% of continuing full-time students received need-based aid. The average freshman award was $15,203. Need-based scholarships or need-based grants averaged $11,614; need-based self-help aid (loans and jobs) averaged $4738; and other non-need-based awards and non-need-based scholarships averaged $13,461. 29% of undergraduates work part time. Average annual earnings from campus work are $1500. The average financial indebtedness of the 2005 graduate was $22,530. The FAFSA is required. The deadline for filing freshman financial aid applications for fall entry is March 1.

International Students: There are 10 international students enrolled. They must take the TOEFL and also take the SAT or the ACT, for athletic eligibility.

Computers: Wireless access is available. Students have access to 135 lab computers that are open for public use. 60 PCs are located in the computer center, 10 in the library, and 40 in the business department building; 25 PCs are distributed in 3 separate residence hall labs. Every public building is equipped with free Wi-Fi Internet access. Most residence rooms are equipped with Ethernet ports, and every room is provided with free high-speed Internet access that is protected by a firewall and virus protection. All students may access the system 24 hours a day. There are no time limits and no fees.

Graduates: From July 1, 2004 to June 30, 2005, 389 bachelor's degrees were awarded. The most popular majors were business administrative management (22%), nursing (12%), and elementary education (12%). In an average class, 1% graduate in 3 years or less, and 61%

graduate in 6 years or less. 32 companies recruited on campus in 2004-2005. Of the 2004 graduating class, 5% were enrolled in graduate school within 6 months of graduation and 94% were employed.

Admissions Contact: James E. Krystofiak, Dean of Admission.
E-mail: *admission@.mtmercy.edu* Web: *www.mtmercy.edu*

NORTHWESTERN COLLEGE OF IOWA   B-2

Orange City, IA 51041   (712) 707-7130
(800) 747-4757; Fax: (712) 707-7164

Full-time: 465 men, 761 women	**Faculty:** 77; IIB, --$
Part-time: 19 men, 28 women	**Ph.Ds:** 81%
Graduate: none	**Student/Faculty:** 16 to 1
Year: semesters, summer session	**Tuition:** $17,260
Application Deadline: open	**Room & Board:** $4914
Freshman Class: 1269 applied, 1101 accepted, 374 enrolled	
ACT: 24	**COMPETITIVE+**

Northwestern College, founded in 1882, is a private college affiliated with the Reformed Church in America and offers liberal arts and teacher education programs. In addition to regional accreditation, Northwestern has baccalaureate program accreditation with CSWE and NCATE. The library contains 107,878 volumes, 153,000 microform items, and 6564 audio/video tapes/CDs/DVDs, and subscribes to 18,978 periodicals including electronic. Computerized library services include the card catalog, interlibrary loans, database searching, Internet access, and laptop Internet portals. Special learning facilities include a learning resource center, art gallery, and TV station. The 100-acre campus is in a small town 40 miles northeast of Sioux City, and 75 miles southeast of Sioux Falls, South Dakota. Including any residence halls, there are 30 buildings.

Student Life: 56% of undergraduates are from Iowa. Others are from 30 states and 16 foreign countries. 79% are from public schools. 98% are white. Most are Protestant. The average age of freshmen is 18; all undergraduates, 20. 22% do not continue beyond their first year; 63% remain to graduate.

Housing: 1156 students can be accommodated in college housing, which includes single-sex dormitories and on-campus apartments. In addition, there are language houses and special-interest houses. On-campus housing is guaranteed for all 4 years. 89% of students live on campus; of those, 60% remain on campus on weekends. Alcohol is not permitted. All students may keep cars.

Activities: There are no fraternities or sororities. There are 46 groups on campus, including art, band, cheerleading, chess, choir, chorus, dance, drama, drill team, film, honors, international, jazz band, literary magazine, musical theater, newspaper, orchestra, pep band, photography, political, professional, radio and TV, religious, SIFE (students in free enterprise), social, social service, student government, symphony, and yearbook. Popular campus events include Winter Carnival, Spring Fest, and a Model Arab League.

Sports: There are 9 intercollegiate sports for men and 8 for women, and 11 intramural sports for men and 11 for women. Facilities include an athletic field, a 3000-seat stadium, a 2200-seat arena, a 176-meter indoor track, 4 handball/racquetball courts, 4 basketball/volleyball courts, archery, gymnastics rooms, and an outdoor 8-lane track.

Disabled Students: 90% of the campus is accessible. Wheelchair ramps, elevators, special parking, specially equipped rest rooms, and lowered drinking fountains are available.

Services: Counseling and information services are available, as is tutoring in most subjects. There is remedial math, reading, and writing.

Campus Safety and Security: Measures include informal discussions, pamphlets/posters/films, and lighted pathways/sidewalks.

Programs of Study: Northwestern confers the B.A. degree. Bachelor's degrees are awarded in AGRICULTURE (agricultural business management), BIOLOGICAL SCIENCE (biology/biological science), BUSINESS (accounting, business administration and management, and business economics), COMMUNICATIONS AND THE ARTS (communications, dramatic arts, literature, music, and Spanish), COMPUTER AND PHYSICAL SCIENCE (actuarial science, chemistry, computer science, information sciences and systems, and mathematics), EDUCATION (art, athletic training, business, Christian, early childhood, elementary, foreign languages, middle school, music, physical, science, secondary, and special), HEALTH PROFESSIONS (medical laboratory technology, predentistry, and premedicine), SOCIAL SCIENCE (economics, history, philosophy, physical fitness/movement, political science/government, prelaw, psychology, religion, religious music, social work, sociology, and youth ministry). Biology, education, and religion are the strongest academically. Business and education are the largest.

Required: All students are required to take 46 to 60 credits in the core curriculum, including courses in Bible, language, history, math, literature, writing, philosophy, social and natural sciences, fine arts, speech and phys ed. Students must maintain a 2.0 GPA for 124 total credits, with 36-42 in the major, and pass both writing and math competency levels.

Special: Northwestern offers co-op programs in engineering, cross-registration with Dordt College, numerous internships, a Washington semester, student-designed majors, and study abroad in 15 countries, including Spain, France, and the Netherlands. There is a 3-2 engineering degree with Washington University at St. Louis. There are 2 national honor societies, a freshman honors program, and 30 departmental honors programs.

Faculty/Classroom: 69% of faculty are male; 31%, female. All teach undergraduates, 69% do research, and 69% do both. The average class size in an introductory lecture is 22; in a laboratory, 16; and in a regular course, 21.

Admissions: 87% of the 2005-2006 applicants were accepted. The ACT scores for the 2005-2006 freshman class were: 18% below 21, 25% between 21 and 23, 27% between 24 and 26, 13% between 27 and 28, and 17% above 28. 49% of the current freshmen were in the top fifth of their class; 74% were in the top two fifths. 28 freshmen graduated first in their class.

Requirements: The SAT or ACT is required. In addition, applicants with a satisfactory ACT, in the top half of their high school class, and with a 2.4 GPA are generally accepted. Applicants should be graduates of an accredited secondary school. The suggested distribution of high school courses is 4 years of English, 3 years each of math, foreign language, and social studies, and 2 of natural science. An interview is recommended. The GED is accepted. Northwestern requires applicants to be in the upper 75% of their class. A GPA of 2.0 is required. AP and CLEP credits are accepted. Important factors in the admissions decision are personality/intangible qualities, leadership record, and evidence of special talent.

Procedure: Freshmen are admitted to all sessions. Entrance exams should be taken in the spring of the junior year. There is a rolling admissions plan. Application deadlines are open. Application fee is $25. Applications are accepted on-line.

Transfer: 49 transfer students enrolled in a recent year. Transfer applicants must submit a transcript and letter of recommendation. A minimum college GPA of 2.0 is required. 30 of 124 credits required for the bachelor's degree must be completed at Northwestern.

Visiting: There are regularly scheduled orientations for prospective students. There are guides for informal visits and visitors may sit in on classes and stay overnight. To schedule a visit, contact Julie Wynia at the Admissions Office at (712) 707-7142 or (800) 747-4757.

Financial Aid: In 2005-2006, all of full-time freshmen and 98% of continuing full-time students received some form of financial aid. 93% of all students received need-based aid. The average freshman award was $14,246. 28% of undergraduates work part time. Average annual earnings from campus work are $1062. The average financial indebtedness of the 2005 graduate was $21,404. The FAFSA is required. The priority date for freshman financial aid applications for fall entry is April 1. The deadline for filing freshman financial aid applications for fall entry is June 30.

International Students: There are 28 international students enrolled. The school actively recruits these students. They must score satisfactorily on the written TOEFL or on the electronic version.

Computers: Wireless access is available. The college maintains 450 of its own PCs in various academic buildings and campus housing. Many of these PCs are accessible to students 24/7 and are used to access the network and Internet. All students may access the system 24 hours a day in residence halls; 7 A.M. to 12 P.M. in academic buildings. There are no time limits and no fees.

Graduates: From July 1, 2004 to June 30, 2005, 284 bachelor's degrees were awarded. The most popular majors were business administration (19%), elementary education (17%), and biology (7%). In an average class, 1% graduate in 3 years or less, 54% graduate in 4 years or less, 63% graduate in 5 years or less, and 63% graduate in 6 years or less. 52 companies recruited on campus in 2004-2005. Of the 2004 graduating class, 20% were enrolled in graduate school within 6 months of graduation and 75% were employed.

Admissions Contact: Mark Bloemendaal, Director of Admissions. A video is available. E-mail: *markb@nwciowa.edu* Web: *admissions@nwciowa.edu*

SAINT AMBROSE UNIVERSITY — E-3
Davenport, IA 52803

	(563) 333-6311
	(800) 383-2627; Fax: (563) 333-6297
Full-time: 916 men, 1285 women	Faculty: 157; IIB, -$
Part-time: 166 men, 332 women	Ph.D.s: 71%
Graduate: 360 men, 565 women	Student/Faculty: 14 to 1
Year: 4-1-4, summer session	Tuition: $18,530
Application Deadline: open	Room & Board: $6965
Freshman Class: 1634 applied, 1373 accepted, 474 enrolled	
ACT: 22	COMPETITIVE

St. Ambrose University, a private institution founded in 1882 in affiliation with the Roman Catholic Church, offers degree programs through the colleges of arts and sciences, business, education and health sci-

ences, and professional studies. There also is a college-level seminary. There are 4 undergraduate and 15 graduate schools. In addition to regional accreditation, St. Ambrose has baccalaureate program accreditation with ABET, ACBSP, ACOTE, AOTA, APTE/APTA, CCNE, and CSWE. The library contains 147,083 volumes, 6836 microform items, and 3869 audio/video tapes/CDs/DVDs, and subscribes to 41,736 periodicals including electronic. Computerized library services include the card catalog, interlibrary loans, database searching, Internet access, and laptop Internet portals. Special learning facilities include a learning resource center, art gallery, radio station, TV station, and an observatory. The 48-acre campus is in an urban area 180 miles west of Chicago. Including any residence halls, there are 29 buildings.

Student Life: 56% of undergraduates are from Iowa. Students are from 22 states, 18 foreign countries, and Canada. 67% are from public schools. 91% are white. 65% are Catholic; 35% Protestant. The average age of freshmen is 18; all undergraduates, 24. 20% do not continue beyond their first year; 80% remain to graduate.

Housing: 1422 students can be accommodated in college housing, which includes single-sex and coed dorms, on-campus apartments, off-campus apartments, and townhouse residences for upper-division students. On-campus housing is guaranteed for all 4 years. 50% of students live on campus; of those, 70% remain on campus on weekends. All students may keep cars.

Activities: There are no fraternities or sororities. There are 24 groups on campus, including art, band, cheerleading, choir, chorale, chorus, computers, dance, debate, drama, ethnic, gay, honors, international, jazz band, literary magazine, musical theater, newspaper, opera, orchestra, pep band, photography, political, professional, radio and TV, religious, social, social service, student government, and symphony. Popular campus events include Multicultural Weeks, Parents Weekend, and Brother/Sister Weekend.

Sports: There are 9 intercollegiate sports for men and 9 for women, and 10 intramural sports for men and 10 for women. Facilities include tennis, handball/racquetball, and volleyball courts, a swimming pool, a golf room, an archery range, a gym, a weight-lifting room, and a running track.

Disabled Students: 96% of the campus is accessible. Wheelchair ramps, elevators, special parking, specially equipped rest rooms, special class scheduling, lowered drinking fountains, and special housing are available.

Services: Counseling and information services are available, as is tutoring in most subjects. There is a reader service for the blind, and remedial math, reading, and writing.

Campus Safety and Security: Measures include 24-hour foot and vehicle patrol, self-defense education, security escort services, and informal discussions. There are pamphlets/posters/films, emergency telephones, and lighted pathways/sidewalks.

Programs of Study: St. Ambrose confers B.A., B.S., B.A.M.T., B.B.A., B.B.A.A., B.E.D., B.E.S., B.M.E., B.S.I.E., B.S.N., B.S.O.T., and B.S.S. degrees. Master's and doctoral degrees are also awarded. Bachelor's degrees are awarded in BIOLOGICAL SCIENCE (biology/biological science), BUSINESS (accounting, business administration and management, business economics, international business management, management science, marketing/retailing/merchandising, and sports management), COMMUNICATIONS AND THE ARTS (communications, English, fine arts, French, German, graphic design, music, Spanish, and speech/debate/rhetoric), COMPUTER AND PHYSICAL SCIENCE (chemistry, computer science, mathematics, and physics), EDUCATION (art, early childhood, elementary, music, physical, and secondary), ENGINEERING AND ENVIRONMENTAL DESIGN (engineering physics and industrial engineering), HEALTH PROFESSIONS (health science), SOCIAL SCIENCE (criminal justice, criminology, economics, history, philosophy, political science/government, psychology, public administration, sociology, and theological studies). Biology, chemistry, and engineering physics are the strongest academically. Business, psychology, and elementary education are the largest.

Required: To graduate, all students must complete at least 120 credit hours, including 45 outside the major and 30 in upper-level courses. A minimum GPA of 2.0 is required. Students must also complete developmental courses and demonstrate proficiency in English composition, math, public speaking, and library skills, among other requirements.

Special: The university offers co-op and work-study programs, study abroad in England, Ireland, Ecuador, Italy, Spain, Austria, and Germany, internships, a 3-2 engineering degree with the University of Iowa and Iowa State University, accelerated degree programs, combined B.A.-B.S. degrees, dual majors and student-designed majors. Credit for life, military, and work experience, nondegree study, and pass/fail options also are available. There are 10 national honor societies and 5 departmental honors programs.

Faculty/Classroom: 56% of faculty are male; 44%, female. All both teach and do research. No introductory courses are taught by graduate students. The average class size in an introductory lecture is 21; in a laboratory, 19; and in a regular course, 17.

Admissions: 84% of the 2005-2006 applicants were accepted. The ACT scores for the 2005-2006 freshman class were: 41% below 21, 25%

between 21 and 23, 18% between 24 and 26, 7% between 27 and 28, and 9% above 28. 28% of the current freshmen were in the top fifth of their class; 50% were in the top two fifths. 29 freshmen graduated first in their class.

Requirements: The ACT is required. The ACT Optional Writing test is also required. In addition, the SAT, with a satisfactory score, may be substituted. Applicants must be graduates of an accredited secondary school; the GED is accepted. An interview is recommended. St. Ambrose requires applicants to be in the upper 50% of their class. A GPA of 2.5 is required. AP and CLEP credits are accepted. Important factors in the admissions decision are recommendations by school officials, leadership record, and parents or siblings attending the school.

Procedure: Freshmen are admitted to all sessions. Entrance exams should be taken in the spring of the junior year. There are early decision, deferred admissions and rolling admissions plans. Application deadlines are open. Application fee is $25. 602 early decision candidates were accepted for the 2005-2006 class. Applications are accepted on-line. Undergraduates do not have to pay an application fee if they apply on-line.

Transfer: 298 transfer students enrolled in 2004-2005. Applicants must have a college GPA of 2.0. 30 of 120 credits required for the bachelor's degree must be completed at St. Ambrose.

Visiting: There are regularly scheduled orientations for prospective students, including breakfast, welcome, testing, panel given by current students, student and parent meeting with faculty mentor, evening meeting and activity; on the next day, there is advising and registration. Parents follow their own agenda (with panels and tours). There are guides for informal visits and visitors may sit in on classes and stay overnight. To schedule a visit, contact the Admissions Office at (563) 333-6300 or admit@sau.edu.

Financial Aid: In 2005-2006, 99% of all full-time freshmen and 97% of continuing full-time students received some form of financial aid. 86% of full-time freshmen and 79% of continuing full-time students received need-based aid. The average freshman award was $17,875. Need-based scholarships or need-based grants averaged $9150 ($18,530 maximum); need-based self-help aid (loans and jobs) averaged $3702 ($10,500 maximum); non-need-based athletic scholarships averaged $3042 ($5000 maximum); and other non-need-based awards and non-need-based scholarships averaged $6815 ($9500 maximum). 95% of undergraduates work part time. Average annual earnings from campus work are $1547. The average financial indebtedness of the 2005 graduate was $24,728. St. Ambrose is a member of CSS. The FAFSA is required. The deadline for filing freshman financial aid applications for fall entry is March 15.

International Students: There are 30 international students enrolled. The school actively recruits these students. A satisfactory score is required on the written TOEFL.

Computers: Wireless access is available. The student union has wireless access for anyone that is in the building. All of the rooms in our residence halls are wired for access to the Internet. There are computer labs that have 200 PCs which can be used by the students. The library is also set up to work with student laptops. All students may access the system 24 hours a day. There are no time limits and no fees.

Graduates: From July 1, 2004 to June 30, 2005, 571 bachelor's degrees were awarded. The most popular majors were business (30%), psychology (11%), and elementary education (8%). In an average class, 1% graduate in 3 years or less, 53% graduate in 4 years or less, 63% graduate in 5 years or less, and 64% graduate in 6 years or less. 48 companies recruited on campus in 2004-2005. Of the 2004 graduating class, 22% were enrolled in graduate school within 6 months of graduation and 85% were employed.

Admissions Contact: Meg Higgins, Director of Admissions. A video is available. E-mail: higginsmegf@sau.edu
Web: http://www.sau.edu/sau.html

SIMPSON COLLEGE   C-3
Indianola, IA 50125

(515) 961-1624
(800) 362-2454; Fax: (515) 961-1870

Full-time: 623 men, 862 women	Faculty: 87; IIB, -$
Part-time: 210 men, 340 women	Ph.D.s: 90%
Graduate: none	Student/Faculty: 17 to 1
Year: 4-1-4, summer session	Tuition: $20,911
Application Deadline: open	Room & Board: $5922
Freshman Class: 1216 applied, 1055 accepted, 336 enrolled	
ACT: 24	VERY COMPETITIVE

Simpson College, founded in 1860, is a private liberal arts institution affiliated with the United Methodist Church. In addition to regional accreditation, Simpson has baccalaureate program accreditation with NASM. The 2 libraries contain 159,938 volumes, 12,497 microform items, and 5552 audio/video tapes/CDs/DVDs, and subscribe to 16,264 periodicals including electronic. Computerized library services include the card catalog, interlibrary loans, database searching, Internet access, and laptop Internet portals. Special learning facilities include a learning resource center, art gallery, radio station, science reference library, and an extensive collection from the Antebellum era. The 63-acre campus is in a suburban area 12 miles south of Des Moines. Including any residence halls, there are 35 buildings.

Student Life: 92% of undergraduates are from Iowa. Students are from 20 states and 12 foreign countries. 97% are from public schools. 94% are white. 55% are Protestant; 26% claim no religious affiliation; 19% Catholic. The average age of freshmen is 18; all undergraduates, 23. 16% do not continue beyond their first year; 61% remain to graduate.

Housing: 1205 students can be accommodated in college housing, which includes single-sex and coed dorms, on-campus apartments, fraternity houses, and sorority houses, and tjheme houses. In addition, there are honors houses, language houses, and special-interest houses. On-campus housing is guaranteed for all 4 years and is available on a lottery system for upperclassmen. 85% of students live on campus; of those, 85% remain on campus on weekends. All students may keep cars.

Activities: 18% of men belong to 1 local and 3 national fraternities; 25% of women belong to 4 national sororities. There are 80 groups on campus, including art, band, cheerleading, choir, chorale, chorus, computers, drama, drill team, ethnic, gay, honors, international, jazz band, literary magazine, musical theater, newspaper, opera, pep band, political, professional, radio and TV, religious, social, social service, student government, and yearbook. Popular campus events include Campus Day, Greek Week, and Minority Emphasis Week.

Sports: There are 9 intercollegiate sports for men and 9 for women, and 50 intramural sports for men and 50 for women. Facilities include a gym and an athletic center with a field house containing 2 racquetball courts, a wrestling practice room, a weight room, indoor batting facilities, a training room, a pool and sauna, 3 indoor tennis courts, and 2 running tracks. Outdoor facilities include a football stadium, an 8-lane track, 6 tennis courts, 2 basketball courts, a sand volleyball court, and football, soccer, baseball, and softball fields.

Disabled Students: 85% of the campus is accessible. Wheelchair ramps, elevators, special parking, specially equipped rest rooms, special class scheduling, lowered drinking fountains, and special housing are available.

Services: Counseling and information services are available, as is tutoring in every subject. There is a reader service for the blind.

Campus Safety and Security: Measures include self-defense education, security escort services, informal discussions, and pamphlets/posters/films. There are emergency telephones, lighted pathways/sidewalks, and and a campus patrol during day and evening hours.

Programs of Study: Simpson confers B.A. and B.Mus. degrees. Bachelor's degrees are awarded in BIOLOGICAL SCIENCE (biochemistry, and biology/biological science), BUSINESS (accounting international business management, marketing/retailing/merchandising, and sports management), COMMUNICATIONS AND THE ARTS (art, communications, dramatic arts, English, French, German, journalism, music, music performance, Spanish, and speech/debate/rhetoric), COMPUTER AND PHYSICAL SCIENCE (chemistry, computer science, information sciences and systems, mathematics, and physics), EDUCATION (athletic training, business, drama, elementary, music, and physical), ENGINEERING AND ENVIRONMENTAL DESIGN (environmental science), SOCIAL SCIENCE (criminal justice, economics, forensic studies, history, international relations, philosophy, political science/government, psychology, religion, and sociology). Natural sciences, management, and visual and performing arts are the strongest academically. Management, education, and biology are the largest.

Required: Graduation requirements include at least 128 credit hours for a B.A. and 132 credit hours for a B.Mus., with a GPA of 2.0. Students must satisfactorily complete the Cornerstone Studies in Liberal Arts, including a senior colloquium; fulfill 84 hours in the major division and 30 to 42 hours in the major department; take a May term course each year; and demonstrate competency in writing, math, and foreign language.

Special: Simpson offers a 3-2 engineering degree with Washington University at St. Louis, cross-registration at American and Drew Universities, internships in all majors, a Washington semester, study abroad in 15 to 20 countries, and work-study programs. Also available are dual majors, student-designed majors, nondegree study, credit for life, military, and work experience, and a pass/fail option for 1 course per year. There are preprofessional programs in nursing, optometry, physical therapy, dentistry, medicine, pharmacy, and veterinary medicine. There are 13 national honor societies, a freshman honors program, and 8 departmental honors programs.

Faculty/Classroom: 62% of faculty are male; 38%, female. All teach undergraduates. The average class size in an introductory lecture is 26; in a laboratory, 22; and in a regular course, 22.

Admissions: 87% of the 2005-2006 applicants were accepted. The ACT scores for the 2005-2006 freshman class were: 12% below 21, 28% between 21 and 23, 33% between 24 and 26, 13% between 27 and 28, and 14% above 28. 50% of the current freshmen were in the top fifth of their class; 79% were in the top two fifths. 30 freshmen graduated first in their class.

Requirements: The SAT or ACT is required. In addition, applicants must be graduates of an accredited secondary school. The GED is accepted. Test scores, counselor recommendations, GPA, college prep course grades, and class rank are all considered in a selective admissions process. The college strongly recommends that applicants complete 4 years of English and 3 each of math, lab science, social science, and a foreign language. The college requires an audition for music and theater scholarships. A portfolio is required for art scholarships. AP and CLEP credits are accepted. Important factors in the admissions decision are advanced placement or honor courses, recommendations by school officials, and leadership record.

Procedure: Freshmen are admitted to all sessions. Entrance exams should be taken in the junior or senior year. There are deferred and rolling admissions plans. Application deadlines are open. Applications are accepted on-line. Notication is sent by on a arollimg basis.

Transfer: 70 transfer students enrolled in 2004-2005. In addition to freshman requirements, transfer applicants are considered on the basis of college work taken and grades received. Applicants must take either the SAT or ACT. The recommended GPA is 2.5, and grades of 2.0 and above transfer for credit. The school admits transfer students every term. 32 of 128 credits required for the bachelor's degree must be completed at Simpson.

Visiting: There are regularly scheduled orientations for prospective students, including a full-day orientation program scheduled 3 times during the summer, when students meet with an academic adviser, register for classes, and participate in activity information sessions. Parents are encouraged to attend. There are guides for informal visits, and visitors may sit in on classes and stay overnight. To schedule a visit, contact the Office of Admissions at (800) 362-2454, ext. 1660 or *dyerb@simpson.edu*.

Financial Aid: In 2005-2006, All full-time freshmen and 99% of continuing full-time students received some form of financial aid. 86% of full-time freshmen and 84% of continuing full-time students received need-based aid. The average freshman award was $20,552. Need-based scholarships or need-based grants averaged $15,212 ($27,200 maximum); need-based self-help aid (loans and jobs) averaged $6481 ($22,379 maximum); and other non-need-based awards and non-need-based scholarships averaged $9272 ($27,943 maximum). 59% of undergraduates work part time. Average annual earnings from campus work are $1004. The average financial indebtedness of the 2005 graduate was $21,199. The FAFSA is required. The deadline for filing freshman financial aid applications for fall entry is July 1.

International Students: There are 25 international students enrolled. The school actively recruits these students. A satisfactory score is required on the written TOEFL. Students must also take the SAT or the ACT.

Computers: Wireless access is available. The campus is equipped with 286 computers in 35 computer labs offering high-speed Internet access from 8 A.M. to midnight. Internet access is available in residence halls 24 hours a day. Wireless access is available in 4 areas on campus. All students may access the system 24 hours a day. There are no time limits and no fees.

Graduates: From July 1, 2004 to June 30, 2005, 342 bachelor's degrees were awarded. The most popular majors were management (12%), accounting (11%), and elementary education (7%). In an average class, 61% graduate in 4 years or less, 69% graduate in 5 years or less, and 70% graduate in 6 years or less. 116 companies recruited on campus in 2004-2005. Of the 2004 graduating class, 16% were enrolled in graduate school within 6 months of graduation and 78% were employed.

Admissions Contact: Deborah Tierney, Vice President for Enrollment. A video is available. E-mail: *admiss@simpson.edu*
Web: *http://www.simpson.edu*

THE FRANCISCAN UNIVERSITY
(See Ashford University)

UNIVERSITY OF DUBUQUE
E-2

Dubuque, IA 52001

(563) 589-3214
(800) 722-5583; Fax: (563) 589-3690

Full-time: 708 men, 416 women	Faculty: 70
Part-time: 25 men, 30 women	Ph.D.s: 80%
Graduate: 165 men, 97 women	Student/Faculty: 16 to 1
Year: semesters, summer session	Tuition: $17,440
Application Deadline: May 1	Room & Board: $5950
Freshman Class: 885 applied, 681 accepted, 308 enrolled	
SAT Verbal/Math: 500/500*	ACT: 23　　　　COMPETITIVE

The University of Dubuque, established in 1852, is a private, liberal arts institution affiliated with the Presbyterian Church (U.S.A.). Strengths in the undergraduate curriculum include environmental science, business, aviation, education, and computer graphics/interactive media. There are 3 undergraduate and 2 graduate schools. The library contains 164,859 volumes, 20,739 microform items, and 2180 audio/video tapes/CDs/DVDs, and subscribes to 801 periodicals including electronic. Computerized library services include the card catalog, interlibrary loans, database

searching, and Internet access. Special learning facilities include a learning resource center, art gallery, and planetarium. The 56-acre campus is in a suburban area 180 miles northwest of Chicago. Including any residence halls, there are 24 buildings.

Student Life: 60% of undergraduates are from out of state, mostly the Midwest. Students are from 35 states and 21 foreign countries. 90% are from public schools. 79% are white; 12% African American. 50% are Catholic; 40% Protestant; 35% claim no religious affiliation. The average age of freshmen is 18; all undergraduates, 22. 12% do not continue beyond their first year; 59% remain to graduate.

Housing: 600 students can be accommodated in college housing, which includes coed dormitories, on-campus apartments, and married-student housing. In addition, there are special-interest houses. On-campus housing is guaranteed for all 4 years. 50% of students live on campus; of those, 75% remain on campus on weekends. Alcohol is not permitted. All students may keep cars.

Activities: 11% of men belong to 5 local fraternities; 10% of women belong to 3 local sororities. There are 50 groups on campus, including art, cheerleading, choir, chorale, chorus, computers, dance, drama, ecology, ethnic, honors, international, musical theater, newspaper, pep band, political, professional, religious, social, social service, and student government. Popular campus events include Founder's Day Ball, Annual Gala, and Family Weekend.

Sports: There are 10 intercollegiate sports for men and 9 for women, and 13 intramural sports for men and 13 for women. Facilities include a sports center with basketball and volleyball courts, 2 racquetball courts, a wrestling room, and an athletic training room; a football field and track; baseball and softball fields; and a practice football/intramural field; and a cardiovascular workout center.

Disabled Students: 50% of the campus is accessible. Wheelchair ramps, elevators, special parking, specially equipped rest rooms, special class scheduling, and lowered drinking fountains are available.

Services: Counseling and information services are available, as is tutoring in some subjects, including English, math, economics, accounting, and computer literacy. There is remedial math, reading, and writing.

Campus Safety and Security: Measures include 24-hour foot and vehicle patrol, self-defense education, security escort services, and shuttle buses. There are informal discussions, pamphlets/posters/films, emergency telephones, lighted pathways/sidewalks, and security-locked residence halls.

Programs of Study: UD confers B.A., B.S., and B.B.A. degrees. Associate, master's, and doctoral degrees are also awarded. Bachelor's degrees are awarded in BIOLOGICAL SCIENCE (biology/biological science), BUSINESS (accounting and business administration and management), COMMUNICATIONS AND THE ARTS (English and speech/debate/rhetoric), COMPUTER AND PHYSICAL SCIENCE (computer science), EDUCATION (education and physical), ENGINEERING AND ENVIRONMENTAL DESIGN (aviation administration/management, computer graphics, and environmental science), HEALTH PROFESSIONS (nursing), SOCIAL SCIENCE (philosophy, psychology, religion, and sociology). Nursing, computer graphics, and business are the strongest academically. Business, aviation management/flight operations, and computer graphics are the largest.

Required: As part of our mission, the University aims to prepare students for successful, professional careers and fulfilling lives by providing them with an education that encourages their growth as whole persons. A total of 120 credits must be earned, with a minimum GPA of 2.0 (2.5 for education majors) for graduation. At UD, we combine professional preparation and the liberal arts to create programs that serve our students.

Special: UD offers cross-registration with Loras and Clarke Colleges, internships, study abroad through the Maastricht Center for Transatlantic Studies, work-study programs, accelerated degree programs, B.A.-B.S. degrees, dual and student-designed majors, credit for life, military, and work experience, nondegree study, and pass/fail options. B.A.-M.A. programs are offered in conjunction with the university's theological seminary. Adult degree programs and an environmental field trip to Colorado and New Mexico are available. There are 8 national honor societies and 2 departmental honors programs.

Faculty/Classroom: 55% of faculty are male; 45%, female. All teach undergraduates. No introductory courses are taught by graduate students. The average class size in an introductory lecture is 25; in a laboratory, 16; and in a regular course, 17.

Admissions: 77% of the 2005-2006 applicants were accepted. The SAT scores for the 2005-2006 freshman class were: Verbal--26% below 500, 64% between 500 and 599, 9% between 600 and 700, and 1% above 700; Math--17% below 500, 68% between 500 and 599, and 15% between 600 and 700. 23% of the current freshmen were in the top fifth of their class; 50% were in the top two fifths. 10 freshmen graduated first in their class.

Requirements: The SAT or ACT is required. In addition, applicants must graduate from an accredited secondary school with a minimum of 4 years in English and 3 each in math, social sciences, and natural sciences. Other academic areas, such as foreign languages, business courses, computer programming, and the fine and performing arts, are also considered. The GED is accepted. Essays and recommendations are required. Auditions are required for music scholarship candidates. UD requires applicants to be in the upper 50% of their class. A GPA of 2.5 is required. AP and CLEP credits are accepted. Important factors in the admissions decision are leadership record, recommendations by school officials, and extracurricular activities record.

Procedure: Freshmen are admitted fall and spring. Entrance exams should be taken before the senior year. There are deferred admissions and rolling admissions plans. Applications should be filed by May 1 for fall entry. Notification is sent on a rolling basis. Applications are accepted on-line. The fall 2005 application fee was $25.

Transfer: 136 transfer students enrolled in 2004-2005. A minimum GPA of 2.0 is required. The applicant must be in good standing at all previously attended institutions. 30 of 120 credits required for the bachelor's degree must be completed at UD.

Visiting: There are regularly scheduled orientations for prospective students, including a campus tour and visits with coaches, faculty, admissions, and financial aid advisers. There are guides for informal visits and visitors may sit in on classes and stay overnight. To schedule a visit, contact Jesse James, Admission Director.

Financial Aid: In 2005-2006 all full-time students received some sort of financial aid and 33% of all full-time students received need-based aid. The average freshman award was $17,723. Need-based scholarships or need-based grants averaged $9189; need-based self-help aid (loans and jobs) averaged $9951; and other non-need-based awards and non-need-based scholarships averaged $9302. 65% of undergraduates work part time. Average annual earnings from campus work are $1500. The average financial indebtedness of the 2005 graduate was $17,620. The FAFSA is required. The priority date for freshman financial aid applications for fall entry is February 1. The deadline for filing freshman financial aid applications for fall entry is April 1.

International Students: In a recent year, there were 70 international students enrolled. The school actively recruits these students. They must score satisfactorily on the written TOEFL or on the electronic version and also take the college's own test.

Computers: All resident halls are wired with fiber-optic. There are many PC labs across campus. All students may access the system 24 hours a day, 7 days a week. There are no time limits and no fees.

Graduates: From July 1, 2004 to June 30, 2005, 180 bachelor's degrees were awarded. The most popular majors were computer information systems (26%), business administration (15%), and aviation (15%). In an average class, 2% graduate in 3 years or less, 50% graduate in 4 years or less, 55% graduate in 5 years or less, and 60% graduate in 6 years or less. 50 companies recruited on campus in 2004-2005. Of the 2004 graduating class, 15% were enrolled in graduate school within 6 months of graduation and 85% were employed.

Admissions Contact: Jesse L. James, Admission Director.
E-mail: jjames@dbq.edu Web: www.dbq.edu

UNIVERSITY OF IOWA   E-3
Iowa City, IA 52242-1396

(319) 335-3847
(800) 553-IOWA; Fax: (319) 335-1535

Full-time: 8485 men, 9709 women	Faculty: 1598; I, av$
Part-time: 964 men, 1142 women	Ph.D.s: 97%
Graduate: 3892 men, 4234 women	Student/Faculty: 11 to 1
Year: semesters, summer session	Tuition: $5612 ($16,998)
Application Deadline: April 1	Room & Board: $6560
Freshman Class: 13,241 applied, 11,122 accepted, 3849 enrolled	
SAT Verbal/Math: 590/600*	ACT: 25 VERY COMPETITIVE

The University of Iowa, founded in 1847, is a comprehensive, public institution. Its undergraduate and graduate programs emphasize the liberal and fine arts, business, engineering, health science, and the professions. There are 6 undergraduate and 5 graduate schools. In addition to regional accreditation, Iowa has baccalaureate program accreditation with AACSB, ABET, ACEJMC, ACPE, ADA, AHEA, APTA, CAHEA, CSWE, NASM, NCATE, and NLN. The 13 libraries contain 4,555,217 volumes, 7,131,140 microform items, and 34,133 audio/video tapes/CDs/DVDs, and subscribe to 50,214 periodicals including electronic. Computerized library services include the card catalog, interlibrary loans, database searching, and Internet access. Special learning facilities include an art gallery, natural history museum, radio station, and UI hospitals and clinics, the Iowa Center for the Arts, and a driving simulator. The 1900-acre campus is in a small town 110 miles east of Des Moines and 220 miles west of Chicago. Including any residence halls, there are 125 buildings.
Student Life: 69% of undergraduates are from Iowa. Others are from 49 states, 59 foreign countries, and Canada. 91% are from public schools. 86% are white. The average age of freshmen is 18; all undergraduates, 21. 16% do not continue beyond their first year; 66% remain to graduate.
Housing: 5600 students can be accommodated in college housing, which includes coed dorms, on-campus apartments, and married-student housing. In addition, there are honors houses, language houses,

special-interest houses, a quiet house, upperclas floors, floors for women in science and engineering, and for men is engineering, health science, business, performing arts, honors and writing. On-campus housing is available on a first-come, first-served basis. 73% of students commute. Alcohol is not permitted. All students may keep cars.
Activities: 7% of men belong to 16 national fraternities; 12% of women belong to 13 national sororities. There are 400 groups on campus, including art, bagpipe band, band, cheerleading, chess, choir, chorale, chorus, computers, dance, debate, drama, drill team, ethnic, film, forensics, gay, honors, international, jazz band, literary magazine, marching band, musical theater, newspaper, opera, orchestra, pep band, photography, political, professional, radio and TV, religious, social, social service, student government, and symphony. Popular campus events include Riverfest, Greek Week, and Weeks of Welcome.
Sports: There are 10 intercollegiate sports for men and 12 for women, and 29 intramural sports for men and 29 for women. Facilities include a 70,397-seat stadium, a 15,500-seat arena, softball and baseball stadiums, an 18-hole golf course, a pool, basketball, racquetball and handball courts, outdoor and indoor tennis courts and running tracks, weight and fitness rooms, a 1000-seat field hockey stadium, a field campus for hiking, cross-country skiing, canoeing, and a soccer field.
Disabled Students: 98% of the campus is accessible. Wheelchair ramps, elevators, special parking, specially equipped rest rooms, special class scheduling, lowered drinking fountains, lowered telephones, special housing, and a transportation service are available.
Services: Counseling and information services are available, as is tutoring in most subjects. There is a reader service for the blind, and remedial math, reading, and writing.
Campus Safety and Security: Measures include 24-hour foot and vehicle patrol, self-defense education, security escort services, and shuttle buses. There are informal discussions, pamphlets/posters/films, emergency telephones, and lighted pathways/sidewalks.
Programs of Study: Iowa confers B.A., B.S., B.A.S., B.B.A., B.F.A., B.L.S., B.M., B.S.E., B.S.M., and B.S.N. degrees. Master's and doctoral degrees are also awarded. Bachelor's degrees are awarded in BIOLOGICAL SCIENCE (biochemistry, biology/biological science, and microbiology), BUSINESS (accounting, banking and finance, business administration and management, business economics, management science, marketing/retailing/merchandising, and recreation and leisure services), COMMUNICATIONS AND THE ARTS (art, art history and appreciation, broadcasting, classics, communications, comparative literature, dance, dramatic arts, English, film arts, fine arts, French, German, Greek, Italian, journalism, Latin, linguistics, music, Portuguese, Russian, Spanish, and speech/debate/rhetoric), COMPUTER AND PHYSICAL SCIENCE (actuarial science, astronomy, chemistry, computer science, geology, information sciences and systems, mathematics, physics, and statistics), EDUCATION (art, elementary, foreign languages, health, middle school, music, science, and secondary), ENGINEERING AND ENVIRONMENTAL DESIGN (biomedical engineering, chemical engineering, civil engineering, computer engineering, electrical/electronics engineering, engineering, environmental science, industrial administration/management, industrial engineering, and mechanical engineering), HEALTH PROFESSIONS (medical laboratory technology, nuclear medical technology, nursing, pharmacy, predentistry, premedicine, and speech pathology/audiology), SOCIAL SCIENCE (African American studies, American studies, anthropology, Asian/Oriental studies, classical/ancient civilization, economics, geography, history, liberal arts/general studies, parks and recreation management, philosophy, political science/government, prelaw, psychology, religion, Russian and Slavic studies, social science, social work, and sociology). Business, engineering, and psychology are the largest.
Required: To graduate, students must complete at least 120 semester hours, with a GPA of 2.0. The general education program includes rhetoric, historical perspectives, foreign language, quantitative and formal reasoning, humanities, and natural and social sciences. In addition, students choose 2 of the following to satisfy a distributed general education area: cultural diversity, fine arts, foreign civilization and culture, phys ed, social science, humanities, or historical perspectives.
Special: The University of Iowa offers cooperative education programs and internships in more than 70 academic departments, combined degree programs in liberal arts and engineering; liberal arts and business; liberal arts and nursing; and study abroad in more than 40 countries. Dual and student-designed majors, B.A.- B.S. degrees, certificate programs including Native American studies, global studies, international business, and women's studies, credit for military experience, and pass/nonpass options are also available. There are 21 national honor societies, including Phi Beta Kappa, a freshman honors program, and 55 departmental honors programs.
Faculty/Classroom: 73% of faculty are male; 27%, female.
Admissions: 84% of the 2005-2006 applicants were accepted. The SAT scores for the 2005-2006 freshman class were: Verbal--16% below 500, 36% between 500 and 599, 36% between 600 and 700, and 12% above 700; Math--12% below 500, 34% between 500 and 599, 39% between 600 and 700, and 15% above 700. The ACT scores were 11% below 21, 25% between 21 and 23, 33% between 24 and 26, 16% be-

tween 27 and 28, and 13% above 28. 43% of the current freshmen were in the top fifth of their class; 79% were in the top two fifths. There were 27 National Merit finalists. 174 freshmen graduated first in their class.

Requirements: The SAT or ACT is required. In addition, Iowa residents must rank in the upper 50% of their high school class (nonresidents in the upper 30%) or must meet an acceptable combination of class rank and test scores. All applicants must have completed 4 years of high school English, 3 years each of social studies, science, and math (including 2 years of algebra and 1 of geometry), and 2 years of a single foreign language. Music students must audition. AP and CLEP credits are accepted.

Procedure: Freshmen are admitted to all sessions. Entrance exams should be taken in the junior year. There is a deferred admissions plan and a rolling admissions plan. Applications should be filed by April 1 for fall entry, November 15 for spring entry, and April 1 for summer entry. Notification is sent on a rolling basis. 149 applicants were on the 2005 waiting list; 142 were admitted. Applications are accepted on-line.

Transfer: 1338 transfer students enrolled in 2004-2005. For the College of Liberal Arts, a GPA of at least 2.25 is required for applicants with 24 or more semester hours of credit. Those with fewer credits are considered on the same criteria as freshmen. Other colleges have different requirements. 30 of 120 credits required for the bachelor's degree must be completed at Iowa.

Visiting: There are regularly scheduled orientations for prospective students, including information sessions, campus tours, and visits to departments, residence halls, and classrooms. There are guides for informal visits and visitors may sit in on classes. To schedule a visit, contact the Admission Visitors Center at (319) 335-1566 or *admission@uiowa.edu*.

Financial Aid: In 2005-2006, 80% of all full-time freshmen and 90% of continuing full-time students received some form of financial aid. 36% of full-time freshmen and 42% of continuing full-time students received need-based aid. The average freshman award was $5150. Need-based scholarships or need-based grants averaged $2400 ($10,000 maximum); need-based self-help aid (loans and jobs) averaged $2100 ($8500 maximum); non-need-based athletic scholarships averaged $9000 ($10,500 maximum); and other non-need-based awards and non-need-based scholarships averaged $2700 ($12,500 maximum). 65% of undergraduates work part time. Average annual earnings from campus work are $2200. The average financial indebtedness of the 2005 graduate was $16,500. The FAFSA and the college's own financial statement are required. The priority date for freshman financial aid applications for fall entry is January 1.

International Students: There are 340 international students enrolled. The school actively recruits these students. They must score satisfactorily on the TOEFL. International students must submit TOEFL for admission purposes and may be asked to take a proficiency exam after arriving on campus.

Computers: Wireless access is available. All residence halls have Internet access. Many campus buildings and classrooms have wireless access. There are 52 computer labs on campus with more than 1700 PCs. All students may access the system 24 hours a day, 7 days a week. There are no time limits. The fee varies by college.

Graduates: From July 1, 2004 to June 30, 2005, 4041 bachelor's degrees were awarded. The most popular majors were communication studies (7%), English (6%), and psychology (6%). In an average class, 1% graduate in 3 years or less, 38% graduate in 4 years or less, 62% graduate in 5 years or less, and 66% graduate in 6 years or less. 272 companies recruited on campus in 2004-2005.

Admissions Contact: Michael Barron, Assistant Provost for Enrollment Services and Director of Admissions.
E-mail: *admission@uiowa.edu* Web: *http://www.uiowa.edu*

UNIVERSITY OF NORTHERN IOWA   D-2
Cedar Falls, IA 50614-0018   **(319) 273-2281**
                              (800) 772-2037; Fax: (319) 273-2885

Full-time: 4174 men, 5608 women	Faculty: 596; IIA, av$
Part-time: 520 men, 650 women	Ph.D.s: 73%
Graduate: 525 men, 1036 women	Student/Faculty: 16 to 1
Year: semesters, summer session	Tuition: $5602 ($13,214)
Application Deadline: August 15	Room & Board: $5531
Freshman Class: 4360 applied, 3422 accepted, 1737 enrolled	
SAT Verbal/Math: 549/568*	ACT: 23 COMPETITIVE

The University of Northern Iowa, established in 1876, is a public institution offering degree programs in business administration, education, humanities and fine arts, natural science, and social and behavioral sciences. There are 5 undergraduate schools and 1 graduate school. In addition to regional accreditation, UNI has baccalaureate program accreditation with AACSB, ACS, ADA, ASLA, CSWE, NASAD, NASM, and NRPA. The library contains 950,130 volumes, 1,113,402 microform items, and 19,946 audio/video tapes/CDs/DVDs, and subscribes to 3910 periodicals including electronic. Computerized library services include the card catalog, interlibrary loans, database searching, Internet access, and laptop Internet portals. Special learning facilities include a learning

resource center, art gallery, natural history museum, planetarium, radio station, and observatory. The university also sponsors a laboratory school, the Native Roadside Vegetation Center, the Iowa Center for Immigrant Leadership and Integration, a waste reduction center, a performing arts center, and several research institutes. The 910-acre campus is in a small town about 100 miles north of Des Moines. Including any residence halls, there are 64 buildings.

Student Life: 91% of undergraduates are from Iowa. Others are from 48 states, 73 foreign countries, and Canada. 87% are white. The average age of freshmen is 18; all undergraduates, 21. 19% do not continue beyond their first year; 65% remain to graduate.

Housing: 4939 students can be accommodated in university housing, which includes single-sex and coed dormitories, on-campus apartments, and married-student housing. In addition, there are honors houses and special-interest houses. On-campus housing is guaranteed for all 4 years. 64% of students commute. All students may keep cars.

Activities: 3% of men belong to 6 national fraternities; 3% of women belong to 4 national sororities. There are 170 groups on campus, including art, band, cheerleading, choir, chorale, chorus, computers, dance, debate, drama, drill team, ethnic, film, forensics, gay, honors, international, jazz band, literary magazine, marching band, musical theater, newspaper, nontraditional students, opera, orchestra, pep band, political, professional, radio and TV, religious, social, social service, student government, symphony, and yearbook. Popular campus events include Celebrate the Seasons, Welcome Week, and Diversity Week.

Sports: There are 9 intercollegiate sports for men and 9 for women, and 25 intramural sports for men and 24 for women. Facilities include a domed stadium, a field house, a basketball facility, and a wellness and recreation center with an 8-lane swimming pool, 6 handball/racquetball courts, a climbing wall, weight rooms, and basketball courts.

Disabled Students: 95% of the campus is accessible. Wheelchair ramps, elevators, special parking, specially equipped rest rooms, special class scheduling, lowered drinking fountains, lowered telephones, and special housing are available.

Services: Counseling and information services are available, as is tutoring in some subjects, including liberal arts core courses, accounting, art, biology, business, chemistry, communications, education, mathematics. music, physics, political science, Spanish, science, psychology, textile, apparel and interior designs, and TESOL. There is a reader service for the blind, and remedial math, reading, and writing.

Campus Safety and Security: Measures include 24-hour foot and vehicle patrol, self-defense education, security escort services, and shuttle buses. There are informal discussions, pamphlets/posters/films, emergency telephones, and lighted pathways/sidewalks.

Programs of Study: UNI confers B.A., B.S., B.F.A., B.L.S., and B.Mus. degrees. Master's and doctoral degrees are also awarded. Bachelor's degrees are awarded in BIOLOGICAL SCIENCE (bioinformatics, biology/biological science, biotechnology, microbiology, and nutrition), BUSINESS (accounting, banking and finance, management information systems, management science, marketing/retailing/merchandising, real estate, and recreation and leisure services), COMMUNICATIONS AND THE ARTS (art history and appreciation, broadcasting, communications, dramatic arts, English, fine arts, French, German, graphic design, music, music performance, music theory and composition, public relations, Spanish, speech/debate/rhetoric, studio art, and theater design), COMPUTER AND PHYSICAL SCIENCE (chemistry, computer management, computer science, earth science, geology, information sciences and systems, mathematics, physics, and science), EDUCATION (art, athletic training, business, early childhood, elementary, foreign languages, health, middle school, music, physical, science, special, teaching English as a second/foreign language (TESOL/TEFOL), and technical), ENGINEERING AND ENVIRONMENTAL DESIGN (computer technology, construction management, electromechanical technology, energy management technology, industrial engineering technology, and manufacturing technology), HEALTH PROFESSIONS (speech pathology/audiology), SOCIAL SCIENCE (American studies, anthropology, Asian/Oriental studies, clothing and textiles management/production/services, criminology, dietetics, economics, European studies, family and community services, geography, history, humanities, Latin American studies, liberal arts/general studies, philosophy, political science/government, psychology, public administration, religion, Russian and Slavic studies, social science, social work, and sociology). Accounting, management, and education are the strongest academically. Accounting and elementary education are the largest.

Required: Degree requirements include completion of 120 to 130 credits, with 30 to 60 in the major. Liberal arts majors must maintain a minimum GPA of 2.0 (2.5 for business, communication, and education majors). General education requirements include 11 hours of civilizations and cultures, 9 each of natural science/technology, social science, and communication, 6 of arts/literature/philosophy/religion, and 3 of personal wellness. Students must meet requirements in foreign language and complete a capstone course in environment, technology, and society. Education students must complete a 32-credit professional sequence.

Special: Internships and co-op programs are offered through all colleges of the university. Students may study abroad in 19 countries and may participate in a Washington semester. Interdisciplinary majors include safety education, chemistry/marketing, design/human environment, and natural history interpretation. Cross-registration, work-study programs, a general studies degree, dual and student-designed majors, nondegree study, and pass/fail options are also available. There are 25 national honor societies and a freshman honors program.

Faculty/Classroom: 56% of faculty are male; 44%, female. 97% both teach and do research. Graduate students teach 1% of introductory courses. The average class size in an introductory lecture is 49; in a laboratory, 18; and in a regular course, 26.

Admissions: 78% of the 2005-2006 applicants were accepted. The SAT scores for the 2005-2006 freshman class were: Verbal--35% below 500, 40% between 500 and 599, 17% between 600 and 700, and 8% above 700; Math--29% below 500, 37% between 500 and 599, 26% between 600 and 700, and 8% above 700. The ACT scores were 28% below 21, 31% between 21 and 23, 26% between 24 and 26, 9% between 27 and 28, and 6% above 28. 37% of the current freshmen were in the top fifth of their class; 70% were in the top two fifths. 66 freshmen graduated first in their class.

Requirements: The ACT is required. In addition, applicants must graduate from an approved secondary school. The GED, with a minimum standard score average of 570, and no single score below 500, is accepted. High school requirements include 4 years of English, 3 years each of math, social studies, and science, and 2 years or more of electives, which may include foreign language and fine arts. UNI requires applicants to be in the upper 50% of their class. AP and CLEP credits are accepted. Important factors in the admissions decision are advanced placement or honor courses, evidence of special talent, and leadership record.

Procedure: Freshmen are admitted to all sessions. Entrance exams should be taken by October of the senior year. Applications should be filed by August 15 for fall entry, December 31 for spring entry, and May 15 for summer entry, along with a $30 fee. Notification is sent on a rolling basis. Applications are accepted on-line.

Transfer: 1421 transfer students enrolled in 2004-2005. Applicants must have a minimum GPA of 2.0 to 2.5, depending on the number of credits they wish to transfer. Other applicants may be admitted on academic probation. 32 of 120 credits required for the bachelor's degree must be completed at UNI.

Visiting: There are regularly scheduled orientations for prospective students, including a student panel, lunch, a campus tour, and presentations by admissions, financial aid, housing, and academic departments. There are guides for informal visits and visitors may sit in on classes and stay overnight. To schedule a visit, contact the Admissions Office.

Financial Aid: In 2005-2006, 84% of all full-time freshmen and 64% of continuing full-time students received some form of financial aid. 53% of full-time freshmen and 67% of continuing full-time students received need-based aid. The average freshman award was $14,686. Need-based scholarships or need-based grants averaged $2598 ($7650 maximum); need-based self-help aid (loans and jobs) averaged $2924 ($6625 maximum); non-need-based athletic scholarships averaged $6721 ($18,833 maximum); and other non-need-based awards and non-need-based scholarships averaged $1687 ($7612 maximum). 32% of undergraduates work part time. Average annual earnings from campus work are $2109. The average financial indebtedness of the 2005 graduate was $20,239. The FAFSA is required. The deadline for filing freshman financial aid applications for fall entry is open.

International Students: There are 232 international students enrolled. The school actively recruits these students. They must take the written TOEFL or take the MELAB, the Comprehensive English Language Test, or the college's own test.

Computers: The network is available to students through more than 800 PCs located in 7 public access labs and through dial-up ports. Nearly all buildings have wireless access. All students may have accounts on the VMS system and Internet priviliges. All students may access the system 24 hours a day. There are no time limits and no fees.

Graduates: From July 1, 2004 to June 30, 2005, 2669 bachelor's degrees were awarded. The most popular majors were elementary education (14%), accounting (5%), and psychology (5%). In an average class, 1% graduate in 3 years or less, 32% graduate in 4 years or less, 62% graduate in 5 years or less, and 65% graduate in 6 years or less. 150 companies recruited on campus in 2004-2005.

Admissions Contact: Ronald Carillo, Executive Director of Enrollment Services. E-mail: *admissions@uni.edu* Web: *www.uni.edu*

UPPER IOWA UNIVERSITY
E-2
Fayette, IA 52142-1857

(563) 425-5281
(800) 553-4150; Fax: (563) 425-5323

Full-time: 405 men, 270 women	**Faculty:** 36; IIB, --$
Part-time: 10 men, 15 women	**Ph.D.s:** 75%
Graduate: none	**Student/Faculty:** 19 to 1
Year: n/app	**Tuition:** $15,100
Application Deadline: open	**Room & Board:** $5030
Freshman Class: n/av	
SAT or ACT: required	**COMPETITIVE**

Upper Iowa University, founded in 1857, is a private institution with a liberal arts focus. Figures in the above capsule are approximate. The library contains 132,175 volumes, 8895 microform items, and 2040 audio/video tapes/CDs/DVDs, and subscribes to 287 periodicals including electronic. Computerized library services include interlibrary loans and database searching. Special learning facilities include a learning resource center and art gallery. The 100-acre campus is in a rural area 65 miles north of Cedar Rapids. Including any residence halls, there are 14 buildings.

Student Life: 60% of undergraduates are from Iowa. Others are from 14 states, 5 foreign countries, and Canada. 90% are from public schools. 75% are white; 13% African American. The average age of freshmen is 19; all undergraduates, 22. 32% do not continue beyond their first year; 68% remain to graduate.

Housing: 515 students can be accommodated in college housing, which includes single-sex dormitories and on-campus apartments. On-campus housing is guaranteed for all 4 years. 70% of students live on campus; of those, 50% remain on campus on weekends. All students may keep cars.

Activities: 19% of men belong to 5 local and 1 national fraternity; 40% of women belong to 5 local sororities. There are 31 groups on campus, including art, cheerleading, computers, drama, enviromental, international, newspaper, outdoor pursuits, political, religious, social, social service, student government, and yearbook. Popular campus events include Winterfest, Greek Week, and Springfest.

Sports: There are 9 intercollegiate sports for men and 8 for women, and 4 intramural sports for men and 4 for women. Facilities include a recreation center, a golf course, an indoor swimming pool, a rock climbing wall, a weight room, and nearby cross-country skiing areas.

Disabled Students: 70% of the campus is accessible. Wheelchair ramps, elevators, special parking, specially equipped rest rooms, special class scheduling, lowered drinking fountains, and lowered telephones are available. The school will make accommodations when necessary.

Services: Counseling and information services are available, as is tutoring in most subjects. There is remedial math, reading, and writing.

Campus Safety and Security: Measures include security escort services, informal discussions, pamphlets/posters/films, and emergency telephones. There are lighted pathways/sidewalks and a security officer living in each residence hall.

Programs of Study: Upper Iowa confers B.A. and B.S. degrees. Associate and master's degrees are also awarded. Bachelor's degrees are awarded in AGRICULTURE (conservation and regulation), BIOLOGICAL SCIENCE (biology/biological science), BUSINESS (accounting, banking and finance, business administration and management, management information systems, management science, marketing/retailing/merchandising, and recreation and leisure services), COMMUNICATIONS AND THE ARTS (art, arts administration/management, communications, English, fine arts, and graphic design), COMPUTER AND PHYSICAL SCIENCE (chemistry, mathematics, and science), EDUCATION (athletic training, elementary, and physical), HEALTH PROFESSIONS (health and health care administration), SOCIAL SCIENCE (American studies, criminology, human services, physical fitness/movement, psychology, social science, and sociology). Business, education, and preprofessional science are the strongest academically. Conservation management, education, and management information systems are the largest.

Required: All students must complete at least 120 semester hours with a GPA of 2.0 overall and 2.5 in the major. Distribution requirements include 9 hours each in English and speech, 6 each in arts and humanities, natural sciences, and social science, and 3 each in math, computer skills, and cultures.

Special: Internships, a work-study program, study abroad, a 3-year B.A. degree in any major except education, and student-designed majors are available. There are 3 national honor societies and a freshman honors program.

Faculty/Classroom: 55% of faculty are male; 45%, female. All teach undergraduates, 20% do research, and 20% do both. The average class size in an introductory lecture is 30; in a laboratory, 10; and in a regular course, 15.

Requirements: The SAT or ACT is required. In addition, recommendations from counselors and extracurricular activities in school, church, and community are considered in the admissions process. A GPA of 2.0 is required. AP and CLEP credits are accepted.

Procedure: Freshmen are admitted to all sessions. There is a rolling admission plans. Entrance exams should be taken in the spring of junior year. Application deadlines are open. Application fee is $15.

Transfer: 128 transfer students enrolled in a recent year. The prime consideration for transfer students is continued good standing in an accredited institution. Credit is generally given for all lecture and lab courses. 30 of 120 credits required for the bachelor's degree must be completed at Upper Iowa.

Visiting: There are regularly scheduled orientations for prospective students, including campus tours, meals, and visits with faculty and admissions counselors. There are guides for informal visits and visitors may sit in on classes and stay overnight. To schedule a visit, contact Admissions Administrative Assistant/Office Manager.

Financial Aid: The FAFSA and the college's own financial statement are required. Check with the school for application deadlines.

International Students: The school actively recruits these students. They must score satisfactorily on the TOEFL.

Computers: All students may access the system. There are no time limits and no fees.

Admissions Contact: Linda Hoopes, Director of Admissions. E-mail: *admissions@uiu.edu* Web: *www.uiu.edu*

WARTBURG COLLEGE   D-2

Waverly, IA 50677-0903

(319) 352-8264
(800) 772-2085; Fax: (319) 352-8579

Full-time: 823 men, 909 women	Faculty: 106; IIB, -$
Part-time: 30 men, 49 women	Ph.D.s: 94%
Graduate: none	Student/Faculty: 15 to 1
Year: , summer session	Tuition: $21,130
Application Deadline: September 1	Room & Board: $6185
Freshman Class: 1405 applied, 1370 accepted, 491 enrolled	
SAT Verbal/Math: 560/600*	ACT: 23 NONCOMPETITIVE

Wartburg College, established in 1852, is a private liberal arts institution affiliated with the Evangelical Lutheran Church in America. In addition to regional accreditation, Wartburg has baccalaureate program accreditation with CSWE, NASM, and NCATE. The library contains 147,044 volumes, 7774 microform items, and 4245 audio/video tapes/CDs/DVDs, and subscribes to 829 periodicals including electronic. Computerized library services include the card catalog, interlibrary loans, database searching, Internet access, and laptop Internet portals. Special learning facilities include a learning resource center, radio station, TV station, business center, classroom technology center, fine arts center, journalism lab, symbolic computation lab, music computer lab, Center for Community Engagement, 6 acres of native grasses and prairie plants, and more than 100 acres of native timber used for field trips and research. The 118-acre campus is in a small town 15 miles north of Waterloo/Cedar Falls. Including any residence halls, there are 37 buildings.

Student Life: 74% of undergraduates are from Iowa. Students are from 24 states and 37 foreign countries. 85% are white. 68% are Protestant; 26% Catholic. The average age of freshmen is 18; all undergraduates, 20. 19% do not continue beyond their first year; 67% remain to graduate.

Housing: 1443 students can be accommodated in college housing, which includes single-sex and coed dorms and on-campus apartments. In addition, there are language houses and special-interest houses. On-campus housing is guaranteed for all 4 years. 79% of students live on campus; of those, 60% remain on campus on weekends. All students may keep cars.

Activities: There are no fraternities or sororities. There are 93 groups on campus, including art, band, cheerleading, choir, chorale, chorus, computers, dance, debate, drama, ethnic, forensics, gay, honors, international, jazz band, literary magazine, musical theater, newspaper, opera, orchestra, pep band, photography, political, professional, radio and TV, religious, social, social service, student government, and symphony. Popular campus events include art series, convocations, and family weekend.

Sports: There are 10 intercollegiate sports for men and 9 for women, and 8 intramural sports for men and 8 for women. Facilities include a phys ed center that includes a field house, handball/racquetball/squash courts, basketball and tennis/badminton/volleyball courts, an indoor track, a weight room, a cardiovascular room, and an aerobics and wrestling room; a 5000-seat stadium with a football field and all-weather track; a 2000-seat gym; a lighted baseball park; football, soccer, and softball fields; and outdoor tennis courts.

Disabled Students: 85% of the campus is accessible. Wheelchair ramps, elevators, special parking, specially equipped rest rooms, special class scheduling, lowered drinking fountains, lowered telephones, and special housing are available.

Services: Counseling and information services are available, as is tutoring in most subjects. There is remedial math. There is a comprehensive academic support center, a supplemental instruction program, and assistance with speech writing and delivery. A writing and reading center is also available.

Campus Safety and Security: Measures include 24-hour foot and vehicle patrol, self-defense education, security escort services, and informal discussions. There are pamphlets/posters/films, emergency telephones, lighted pathways/sidewalks, night vehicle patrol, part of 24-hour patrol, and student escort service.

Programs of Study: Wartburg confers B.A., B.A.A., B.A.S., B.M., and B.M.E. degrees. Bachelor's degrees are awarded in BIOLOGICAL SCIENCE (biochemistry and biology/biological science), BUSINESS (accounting, banking and finance, business administration and management, international business management, marketing/retailing/merchandising, and recreation and leisure services), COMMUNICATIONS AND THE ARTS (applied music, art, arts administration/management, broadcasting, communications, creative writing, dramatic arts, English, French, German, graphic design, journalism, music, music performance, music theory and composition, public relations, and Spanish), COMPUTER AND PHYSICAL SCIENCE (chemistry, computer science, information sciences and systems, mathematics, and physics), EDUCATION (art, elementary, English, foreign languages, journalism, mathematics, music, physical, science, secondary, and social studies), ENGINEERING AND ENVIRONMENTAL DESIGN (engineering and applied science), HEALTH PROFESSIONS (medical laboratory technology, music therapy, and occupational therapy), SOCIAL SCIENCE (economics, French studies, German area studies, history, international relations, philosophy, political science/government, psychology, religion, religious music, social work, and sociology). Math, biology, and psychology are the strongest academically. Business, communication arts, and biology are the largest.

Required: Degree requirements include a minimum cumulative and major GPA of 2.0 and completion of 36 course credits (128 semester hours), including 4 May term course credits. All students must complete the Wartburg Plan of Essential Education, an integrative and interdisciplinary program of study, based on course work in thinking strategies, reasoning skills, faith and reflection, health and wellness, and literacy in writing, diversity, and a foreign lanaguage. Students must also demonstrate proficiency in information systems and in oral communication and must complete a Capstone course. Inquiry Studies 101/201 are required of all students.

Special: Special academic programs at Wartburg include those in leadership education and global and multicultural studies. Internships are available in all majors and there are internship programs in Denver, Washington, D.C., and abroad. Study abroad in 21 countries, on and off campus work-study, dual majors in any combination, and individualized majors are possible. 3-1 degrees are possible in medical technology and a 3-1 degree in occupational therapy. A deferred admit program with the University of Iowa College of Dentistry is offered, as is an array of experiential learning opportunities. There are 11 national honor societies and a freshman honors program.

Faculty/Classroom: 58% of faculty are male; 42%, female. All teach undergraduates and 42% do research. The average class size in an introductory lecture is 29; in a laboratory, 19; and in a regular course, 19.

Admissions: 98% of the 2005-2006 applicants were accepted. The SAT scores for the 2005-2006 freshman class were: Verbal--20% below 500, 44% between 500 and 599, 24% between 600 and 700, and 12% above 700; Math--20% below 500, 28% between 500 and 599, 36% between 600 and 700, and 16% above 700. The ACT scores were 23% below 21, 28% between 21 and 23, 24% between 24 and 26, 13% between 27 and 28, and 12% above 28. 52% of the current freshmen were in the top fifth of their class; 80% were in the top two fifths. There were 2 National Merit finalists. 40 freshmen graduated first in their class.

Requirements: The SAT or ACT is required. The ACT Optional Writing test is also recommended. Candidates for admission must be graduates of an accredited secondary school, having completed 4 years of English, 3 each of math, and science, 2 each of social studies and foreign language, and 1 of introduction to computers. The GED is accepted, with an average of 50 or above expected. Wartburg requires applicants to be in the upper 50% of their class. A GPA of 2.2 is required. AP and CLEP credits are accepted. Important factors in the admissions decision are advanced placement or honor courses, recommendations by school officials, and leadership record.

Procedure: Freshmen are admitted fall and winter. Entrance exams should be taken before the senior year. Early decision applications should be filed by December 1; regular applications, by September 1 for fall entry, January 1 for winter entry, May 1 for spring entry, and June 1 for summer entry. There is a rolling admissions plan. Notification of early decision and regular decision is on a rolling basis. Applications are accepted on-line. The fall 2005 application fee was $20.

Transfer: 42 transfer students enrolled in 2004-2005. Applicants must have earned an associate degree or have maintained a minimum GPA of 2.0 in previous college work for 1 year. The ACT or the SAT must be taken; the minimum acceptable ACT score is 19. Students must submit official transcripts from all colleges attended. 7 of 36 credits required for the bachelor's degree must be completed at Wartburg.

Visiting: There are regularly scheduled orientations for prospective students, including an introduction to academic and student life conducted by administrators, faculty, and students, and advising and registration.

There are guides for informal visits and visitors may sit in on classes and stay overnight. To schedule a visit, contact the Admissions Office.

Financial Aid: In 2005-2006, 99% of all full-time freshmen and 100% of continuing full-time students received some form of financial aid. 73% of full-time freshmen and 69% of continuing full-time students received need-based aid. The average freshman award was $17,927. Need-based scholarships or need-based grants averaged $5581 ($21,700 maximum); need-based self-help aid (loans and jobs) averaged $3094 ($6625 maximum); and other non-need-based awards and non-need-based scholarships averaged $9252 ($28,625 maximum). 68% of undergraduates work part time. Average annual earnings from campus work are $1138. The average financial indebtedness of the 2005 graduate was $13,506. The FAFSA is required.

International Students: There are 92 international students enrolled. The school actively recruits these students. They must score satisfactory on the written TOEFL. SAT or ACT scores are not required, but are useful in admissions.

Computers: Wireless access is available. Students access the Internet and the college network either by connecting (Ethernet cable or wireless card) with their own computer by using a college-owned computer in one of the classrooms or one of the 200 college-owned PCs in 10 computer labs on campus. Network jacks exist in every residence hall room, classroom, and gathering area. All students may access the system. There are no time limits. The fee is $125 per tem.

Graduates: From July 1, 2004 to June 30, 2005, 368 bachelor's degrees were awarded. The most popular majors were business adminstration (20%), communication arts (14%), and biology (11%). In an average class, 1% graduate in 3 years or less, 56% graduate in 4 years or less, 63% graduate in 5 years or less, and 68% graduate in 6 years or less. 105 companies recruited on campus in 2004-2005. Of the 2004 graduating class, 19% were enrolled in graduate school within 6 months of graduation and 73% were employed.

Admissions Contact: Doug Bowman, Dean of Admissions and Financial Aid. A video is available. E-mail: *admissions@wartburg.edu* Web: *www.wartburg.edu*

WILLIAM PENN UNIVERSITY   D-3

Oskaloosa, IA 52577

(641) 673-1012
(800) 779-7366; Fax: (641) 673-1396

Full-time: 750 men, 630 women	Faculty: 43
Part-time: 65 men, 110 women	Ph.D.s: 40%
Graduate: none	Student/Faculty: 32 to 1
Year: semesters, summer session	Tuition: $13,375
Application Deadline: open	Room & Board: $4310
Freshman Class: n/av	
SAT or ACT:: required	**LESS COMPETITIVE**

William Penn University, founded in 1873, is a private liberal arts institution affiliated with the Society of Friends (Quakers). There are 2 undergraduate schools. Figures in the above capsule are approximate. In addition to regional accreditation, William Penn has baccalaureate program accreditation with NCATE. The library contains 66,500 volumes, 2879 microform items, and 423 audio/video tapes/CDs/DVDs, and subscribes to 345 periodicals including electronic. Computerized library services include the card catalog, interlibrary loans, and database searching. Special learning facilities include a learning resource center, art gallery, radio station, and Mideast collection. The 40-acre campus is in a rural area 58 miles southeast of Des Moines. Including any residence halls, there are 13 buildings.

Student Life: 73% of undergraduates are from Iowa. Others are from 41 states, 10 foreign countries, and Canada. 90% are from public schools. 83% are white; 10% African American. 44% are Protestant; 39% claim no religious affiliation; 13% Catholic. The average age of freshmen is 19; all undergraduates, 25. 35% do not continue beyond their first year; 40% remain to graduate.

Housing: 500 students can be accommodated in college housing, which includes single-sex and coed dormitories. On-campus housing is guaranteed for all 4 years. 60% of students commute. Alcohol is not permitted. All students may keep cars.

Activities: 5% of men belong to 2 local fraternities; 5% of women belong to 3 local sororities. There are 30 groups on campus, including band, cheerleading, choir, chorale, chorus, computers, drama, ethnic, honors, international, jazz band, literary magazine, musical theater,

newspaper, pep band, photography, professional, radio, religious, social, social service, student government, and yearbook. Popular campus events include Multicultural Day and Campus Beautification Day.

Sports: There are 8 intercollegiate sports for men and 6 for women, and 6 intramural sports for men and 6 for women. Facilities include include a gym with 2 regulation-size basketball courts and wrestling and weight training rooms, baseball and softball fields, 3 tennis courts, and football and soccer practice fields.

Disabled Students: 70% of the campus is accessible. Wheelchair ramps, elevators, special parking, specially equipped rest rooms, and special class scheduling are available.

Services: Counseling and information services are available, as is tutoring in most subjects. There is remedial math, reading, and writing.

Campus Safety and Security: Measures include 24-hour foot and vehicle patrol, informal discussions, emergency telephones, and lighted pathways/sidewalks.

Programs of Study: William Penn confers the B.A. degree. Associate degrees are also awarded. Bachelor's degrees are awarded in BIOLOGICAL SCIENCE (biology/biological science and biotechnology), BUSINESS (accounting, business administration and management, recreation and leisure services, and sports management), COMMUNICATIONS AND THE ARTS (communications, English, fine arts, journalism, and public relations), COMPUTER AND PHYSICAL SCIENCE (computer science), EDUCATION (elementary, health, physical, science, secondary, and special), ENGINEERING AND ENVIRONMENTAL DESIGN (environmental science, industrial administration/management, and industrial engineering technology), SOCIAL SCIENCE (criminology, history, human services, political science/government, psychology, and sociology). Elementary and secondary education, industrial technology, and business are the strongest academically. Education and business are the largest.

Required: To graduate, students must complete 124 hours, with 30 to 75 hours in the major. A GPA of 2.0 overall and in major and minor courses is required. Leadership core requirements total 47 hours in English/communications, math, natural science, social science, religion, fine arts, and philosophy.

Special: William Penn offers internships, work-study programs with local businesses, dual majors, nondegree study, pass/fail options, and 3-2 engineering degree programs with Iowa State and Washington Universities. Preprofessional studies, driver and safety education, and endorsements in numerous secondary education subjects are also offered. There are 2 national honor societies, including Phi Beta Kappa.

Faculty/Classroom: 57% of faculty are male; 43%, female. All teach undergraduates. The average class size in an introductory lecture is 25.

Requirements: The SAT or ACT is required. In addition, applicants must be graduates of an accredited secondary and should have completed 15 high school units. The GED is accepted. Applications are accepted on-line via the school's web site. A GPA of 2.0 is required. AP and CLEP credits are accepted. Important factors in the admissions decision are evidence of special talent, extracurricular activities record, and leadership record.

Procedure: Freshmen are admitted to all sessions. Entrance exams should be taken late in the junior year or early in the senior year. There are early admissions, deferred admissions, and rolling admissions plans. Application deadlines are open. Application fee is $20. Applications are accepted on-line.

Transfer: Applicants must be in good standing at their previous institution and submit official transcripts from previously attended schools. 30 of 124 credits required for the bachelor's degree must be completed at William Penn.

Visiting: There are regularly scheduled orientations for prospective students, including a 1-day visit comprised of meetings with faculty, student services, financial aid, personnel, and people who share students' interests. There are guides for informal visits and visitors may sit in on classes and stay overnight. To schedule a visit, contact the Director of Admissions.

Financial Aid: The FAFSA is required. Check with the school for application deadlines.

International Students: The school actively recruits these students. They must score satisfactorily on the TOEFL.

Computers: All students may access the system. There are no time limits and no fees.

Admissions Contact: John Ottosson, Director of Admissions.
E-mail: *admissions@wmpenn.edu* Web: *www.wmpenn.edu*

KANSAS

POPULATION
DENSITY
• 25,000 and over

0 20 40 60 80 100
Miles

BAKER UNIVERSITY
E-2

Baldwin City, KS 66006

(785) 594-8386
(800) 873-4282; Fax: (785) 594-8372

Full-time: 408 men, 452 women	**Faculty:** 73; IIB, --$
Part-time: 27 men, 29 women	**Ph.D.s:** 71%
Graduate: none	**Student/Faculty:** 12 to 1
Year: 4-1-4, summer session	**Tuition:** $16,560
Application Deadline: open	**Room & Board:** $5630
Freshman Class: 1051 applied, 666 accepted, 239 enrolled	
ACT: 23	**COMPETITIVE**

Baker University, founded in 1858, is a private liberal arts institution affiliated with the United Methodist Church. There are 4 undergraduate schools and 1 graduate school. In addition to regional accreditation, Baker has baccalaureate program accreditation with ACBSP, NASM, NCATE, and NLN. The library contains 96,000 volumes, 11,370 microform items, and 5229 audio/video tapes/CDs/DVDs, and subscribes to 376 periodicals including electronic. Computerized library services include the card catalog, interlibrary loans, database searching, and Internet access. Special learning facilities include a learning resource center, art gallery, natural history museum, radio station, TV station, greenhouse, and wetlands. The 26-acre campus is in a rural area 35 miles southwest of Kansas City and 15 miles south of Lawrence in a small community. Including any residence halls, there are 26 buildings.

Student Life: 74% of undergraduates are from Kansas. Others are from 18 states and 5 foreign countries. 95% are from public schools. 84% are white. 63% are Protestant; 18% Catholic; 15% claim no religious affiliation. The average age of freshmen is 18; all undergraduates, 20. 25% do not continue beyond their first year; 55% remain to graduate.

Housing: 524 students can be accommodated in college housing, which includes single-sex and coed dorms, on-campus apartments, fraternity houses, and sorority houses. On-campus housing is guaranteed for all 4 years. 84% of students live on campus; of those, 75% remain on campus on weekends. Alcohol is not permitted. All students may keep cars.

Activities: 39% of men belong to 1 local and 3 national fraternities; 45% of women belong to 4 national sororities. There are 70 groups on campus, including art, band, cheerleading, chess, choir, chorale, chorus, computers, dance, debate, drama, drill team, ethnic, forensics, honors, international, jazz band, literary magazine, musical theater, newspaper, opera, orchestra, pep band, photography, political, professional, radio and TV, religious, social, social service, student government, and yearbook. Popular campus events include Maple Leaf, Festival Day, and Founders Day.

Sports: There are 9 intercollegiate sports for men and 9 for women, and 5 intramural sports for men and 5 for women. Facilities include a 3500-seat football/track stadium, a 2500-seat gym, a 500-seat baseball stadium, practice and varsity fields for football, track, soccer, softball and baseball, 2 basketball courts, 4 racquetball courts, 4 tennis courts, a jogging track, a wellness facility, and a weight room.

Disabled Students: 45% of the campus is accessible. Wheelchair ramps, elevators, special parking, specially equipped rest rooms, special class scheduling, lowered drinking fountains, lowered telephones, and special housing are available.

Services: Counseling and information services are available, as is tutoring in most subjects. There is a reader service for the blind, and remedial math, reading, and writing.

Campus Safety and Security: Measures include 24-hour foot and vehicle patrol, security escort services, informal discussions, and lighted pathways/sidewalks. There is a patrol from 5 P.M. to 6 A.M.

Programs of Study: Baker confers B.A., B.S., and B.M.E. degrees. Master's degrees are also awarded. Bachelor's degrees are awarded in BIOLOGICAL SCIENCE (biology/biological science, molecular biology, and wildlife biology), BUSINESS (accounting, business administration and management, business economics, and international business management), COMMUNICATIONS AND THE ARTS (art history and appreciation, communications, dramatic arts, English, fine arts, French, German, music, Spanish, and studio art), COMPUTER AND PHYSICAL SCIENCE (chemistry, computer science, information sciences and systems, mathematics, and physics), EDUCATION (art, business, elementary, music, and physical), SOCIAL SCIENCE (economics, history, international studies, philosophy, political science/government, psychology, religion, and sociology). Computer information systems, physics, and mathematics are the strongest academically. Business, biology, and mass communication are the largest.

Required: To graduate, all students must complete 132 credit hours, including 24 to 30 hours in the major, a cornerstone liberal arts core, 42 hours in 6 basic areas of study, and a minimal level of proficiency in written and oral communication and math. A minimum GPA of 2.0 is required.

Special: Internships are encouraged for students in most majors. Baker also offers study abroad, work-study, B.A.-B.S. degrees, accelerated degrees, and dual and student-designed majors. A 3-2 engineering degree may be earned in conjunction with Washington University in St. Louis or the University of Kansas. Interdisciplinary majors are offered in molecular bioscience and international studies. There are 15 national honor societies, a freshman honors program, and 9 departmental honors programs.

Faculty/Classroom: 59% of faculty are male; 41%, female. All teach undergraduates and 33% both teach and do research. The average class size in an introductory lecture is 19; in a laboratory, 15; and in a regular course, 14.

Admissions: 63% of the 2005-2006 applicants were accepted. The SAT scores for the 2005-2006 freshman class were: Verbal--44% below 500, 35% between 500 and 599, 18% between 600 and 700, and 3% above 700; Math--53% below 500, 24% between 500 and 599, 21% between 600 and 700, and 3% above 700. The ACT scores were 25% below 21, 28% between 21 and 23, 28% between 24 and 26, 8% between 27 and 28, and 11% above 28. 43% of the current freshmen were in the top fifth of their class; 69% were in the top two fifths.

Requirements: The SAT or ACT is required. In addition, candidates for admission must graduate from an accredited secondary school or earn a GED. High school course work in English, a foreign language, social studies, math, and natural science is recommended. Applications of students not meeting these requirements will be reviewed, and students may be admitted on a probationary basis. Students are required to submit ACT or SAT scores. AP and CLEP credits are accepted.

Procedure: Freshmen are admitted fall and spring. Entrance exams should be taken in the fall of the senior year. There is a rolling admissions plan. Application deadlines are open. Applications are accepted on-line.

Transfer: 75 transfer students enrolled in 2004-2005. Transfer applicants must supply a recommendation form, available from the Baker Admissions Office. The ACT or the SAT score, official high school transcript, and official transcripts of all college courses are required. The minimum GPA is 2.3. 31 of 132 credits required for the bachelor's degree must be completed at Baker.

Visiting: There are regularly scheduled orientations for prospective students, including Preview Days scheduled for both freshman and transfers in spring and fall. Individual visits are scheduled daily. There are guides for informal visits and visitors may sit in on classes and stay overnight. To schedule a visit, contact the Admissions Office at *admissions@bakeru.edu*.

Financial Aid: In 2005-2006, 98% of all full-time freshmen and 95% of continuing full-time students received some form of financial aid. 77% of full-time freshmen and 79% of continuing full-time students received need-based aid. The average freshman award was $24,022. Need-based scholarships or need-based grants averaged $7981; need-based self-help aid (loans and jobs) averaged $15,598; non-need-based athletic scholarships averaged $1812; and other non-need-based awards and non-need-based scholarships averaged $6901. 38% of undergraduates work part time. Average annual earnings from campus work are $1000. The average financial indebtedness of the 2005 graduate was $19,602. The FAFSA and the college's own financial statement are required. The priority date for freshman financial aid applications for fall entry is March 1. The deadline for filing freshman financial aid applications for fall entry is rolling.

International Students: There are 4 international students enrolled. The school actively recruits these students. They must score satisfactorily on the TOEFL.

Computers: Wireless access is available. PCs are available in library labs and common areas as well as in on-campus housing and in some classroom buildings; wireless access is available in the library and in on-campus housing. All students may access the system. There are no time limits. The fee is $150.

Graduates: From July 1, 2004 to June 30, 2005, 152 bachelor's degrees were awarded. The most popular majors were business (18%), biology (9%), and mass communication/elementary education (9%). In an average class, 2% graduate in 3 years or less, 42% graduate in 4 years or less, 55% graduate in 5 years or less, and 57% graduate in 6 years or less. Of the 2004 graduating class, 28% were enrolled in graduate school within 6 months of graduation and 68% were employed.

Admissions Contact: Charly Edmonds, Director of Admissions. A video is available. E-mail: *admissions@bakeru.edu*
Web: *www.bakeru.edu*

BENEDICTINE COLLEGE
Atchison, KS 66002

		E-1
	(913) 367-5340, ext. 2476	
	(800) 467-5340; Fax: (913) 367-6102	
Full-time: 588 men, 580 women	**Faculty:** 54	
Part-time: 86 men, 139 women	**Ph.D.s:** 79%	
Graduate: 33 men, 19 women	**Student/Faculty:** 22 to 1	
Year: semesters, summer session	**Tuition:** $15,760	
Application Deadline: open	**Room & Board:** $6208	
Freshman Class: n/av		
ACT: required		**COMPETITIVE**

Benedictine College, established in 1971, is a liberal arts, Catholic, Benedictine institution. In addition to regional accreditation, Benedictine has baccalaureate program accreditation with NASM and NCATE. The library contains 366,936 volumes, 36,440 microform items, and 839 audio/video tapes/CDs/DVDs, and subscribes to 350 periodicals including electronic. Computerized library services include the card catalog, interlibrary loans, and database searching. Special learning facilities include a learning resource center. The 225-acre campus is in a small town 45 miles north of Kansas City. Including any residence halls, there are 18 buildings.

Student Life: 53% of undergraduates are from Kansas. Others are from 38 states and 18 foreign countries. 55% are from public schools. 81% are white. 68% are Catholic; 14% Protestant; 10% claim no religious affiliation. The average age of freshmen is 18; all undergraduates, 23. 25% do not continue beyond their first year; 51% remain to graduate.

Housing: 725 students can be accommodated in college housing, which includes single-sex dorms. On-campus housing is guaranteed for all 4 years. 82% of students live on campus. All students may keep cars.

Activities: There are no fraternities or sororities. There are 25 groups on campus, including band, cheerleading, choir, chorale, computers, drama, drill team, ethnic, honors, international, jazz band, literary magazine, musical theater, newspaper, orchestra, pep band, photography, political, professional, religious, social, social service, student government, symphony, and yearbook. Popular campus events include Discovery Week, Parents Weekend, and All School Mass.

Sports: There are 7 intercollegiate sports for men and 8 for women, and 7 intramural sports for men and 7 for women. Facilities include a

gym, weight rooms, a football and track stadium, baseball, softball, and track fields, and an isometrics training room.

Disabled Students: 80% of the campus is accessible. Wheelchair ramps, elevators, special parking, specially equipped rest rooms, special class scheduling, and lowered drinking fountains are available.

Services: Counseling and information services are available, as is tutoring in most subjects. There is remedial math, reading, and writing.

Campus Safety and Security: Measures include 24-hour foot and vehicle patrol, informal discussions, pamphlets/posters/films, and lighted pathways/sidewalks.

Programs of Study: Benedictine confers B.A., B.S., and B.Mus.Ed. degrees. Associate and master's degrees are also awarded. Bachelor's degrees are awarded in BIOLOGICAL SCIENCE (biochemistry and biology/biological science), BUSINESS (accounting and business administration and management), COMMUNICATIONS AND THE ARTS (art, dramatic arts, English, French, journalism, music, Spanish, and theater management), COMPUTER AND PHYSICAL SCIENCE (astronomy, chemistry, computer science, mathematics, natural sciences, and physics), EDUCATION (athletic training, elementary, music, physical, secondary, and special), SOCIAL SCIENCE (economics, history, liberal arts/general studies, philosophy, political science/government, psychology, religion, social science, sociology, and youth ministry). Physical science, biology, and history are the strongest academically. Biology, education, and sociology are the largest.

Required: To graduate, students must complete 128 semester hours, pass a comprehensive exam in their major, and earn a minimum GPA of 2.0 overall and in the major. Curriculum requirements include 9 hours each in philosophy and religious studies, 8 hours each in English, natural science, and foreign language, 6 each in Western civilization and social science, 4 in math, 3 in fine arts, and 2 each in speech communication and phys ed. A dean's colloquium and a comprehensive exam are also required.

Special: Benedictine offers cross-registration with the 14 other members of the Kansas City Regional Council for Higher Education and study abroad in several countries. The school also offers a 3-2 occupational therapy program with Washington University in St. Louis and a 3-2 engineering degree. Internships, work-study programs, dual majors, an interdisciplinary music marketing major, student-designed majors, pass/fail options, and nondegree study are also available. There are 4 national honor societies and 4 departmental honors programs.

Faculty/Classroom: 66% of faculty are male; 34%, female. 96% teach undergraduates. No introductory courses are taught by graduate students. The average class size in an introductory lecture is 25; in a laboratory, 20; and in a regular course, 20.

Admissions: 27% of recent freshmen were in the top fifth of their class; 65% were in the top two fifths.

Requirements: The ACT is required. In addition, applicants should graduate in the upper 50% of their class at an accredited secondary school. Students should have 16 academic units, including 4 in English, 3 to 4 in math, 2 to 4 in foreign language and science, 2 in social science, and 1 in history. An interview is recommended. Counselor recommendations are required. A GPA of 2.0 is required. AP and CLEP credits are accepted. Important factors in the admissions decision are advanced placement or honor courses, recommendations by school officials, and recommendations by alumni.

Procedure: Freshmen are admitted to all sessions. Entrance exams should be taken before the July following graduation from high school. There is a deferred admissions plan and a rolling admissions plan. Application deadlines are open. Notification is sent on a rolling basis. Application fee is $25. Applications are accepted on-line.

Transfer: 99 transfer students enrolled in a recent year. Applicants must submit transcripts from all colleges attended, a statement of courses in progress, and, if transferring with fewer than 60 hours, a high school transcript and ACT score. A minimum GPA of 2.0 is required. 30 of 128 credits required for the bachelor's degree must be completed at Benedictine.

Visiting: There are regularly scheduled orientations for prospective students, consisting of an advanced placement exam, preregistration, meetings with the dean and student affairs, business office, and financial aid representatives, and campus tours. The orientations are scheduled for April, June, and July. There are guides for informal visits and visitors may sit in on classes and stay overnight. To schedule a visit, contact the Admissions Office at *bcadmiss@benedictine.edu*.

Financial Aid: In a recent year, 98% of all full-time freshmen and 95% of continuing full-time students received some form of financial aid. 74% of full-time freshmen and 75% of continuing full-time students received need-based aid. The average freshman award was $14,395. Need-based scholarships or need-based grants averaged $6480 ($13,500 maximum); need-based self-help aid (loans and jobs) averaged $5425 ($7625 maximum); non-need-based athletic scholarships averaged $6885 ($13,500 maximum); and other non-need-based awards and non-need-based scholarships averaged $2500 ($4000 maximum). 41% of undergraduates work part time. Average annual earnings from campus work are $900. The average financial indebtedness of a recent graduate was

$20,822. Benedictine is a member of CSS. The FAFSA and the college's own financial statement are required. The deadline for filing freshman financial aid applications for fall entry is April 1.

International Students: There are 38 international students enrolled. The school actively recruits these students. They must take the TOEFL or the MELAB and also take the SAT or the ACT, scoring 18 on the ACT.

Computers: All students may access the system 24 hours a day in residence halls, and 7:45 A.M. to 11 P.M. weekdays, with shorter hours on weekends. There are no time limits and no fees.

Graduates: From July 1, 2004 to June 30, 2005, 166 bachelor's degrees were awarded. The most popular majors were business/marketing (23%), religious studies/philosophy (23%), and education (19%). In an average class, 36% graduate in 4 years or less, 45% graduate in 5 years or less, and 46% graduate in 6 years or less. 26 companies recruited on campus in 2004-2005. Of the 2004 graduating class, 15% were enrolled in graduate school within 6 months of graduation and 75% were employed.

Admissions Contact: Kelly Vowels, Dean of Enrollment Management. E-mail: *kvowels@raven.benedictine.edu* Web: *www.benedictine.edu*

BETHANY COLLEGE
D-2

Lindsborg, KS 67456

(785) 227-3311
(800) 826-2281; Fax: (785) 227-2004

Full-time: 298 men, 254 women	**Faculty:** 44; IIB, --$
Part-time: 23 men, 13 women	**Ph.D.s:** 63%
Graduate: none	**Student/Faculty:** 13 to 1
Year: 4-1-4, summer session	**Tuition:** $15,460
Application Deadline: May 1	**Room & Board:** $5200
Freshman Class: n/av	
ACT: required	**LESS COMPETITIVE**

Bethany College, founded in 1881, is a private small liberal arts institution affiliated with the Evangelical Lutheran Church in America. In addition to regional accreditation, Bethany has baccalaureate program accreditation with CSWE, NASM, and NCATE. The library contains 110,000 volumes, 59,000 microform items, and 3800 audio/video tapes/CDs/DVDs, and subscribes to 200 periodicals including electronic. Computerized library services include interlibrary loans and database searching. Special learning facilities include a learning resource center and art gallery. The 80-acre campus is in a small town 65 miles north of Wichita and 20 miles south of Salina. Including any residence halls, there are 17 buildings.

Student Life: 59% of undergraduates are from Kansas. Students are from 27 states, 15 foreign countries, and Canada. 98% are from public schools. 81% are white. 61% are Protestant; 25% claim no religious affiliation; 14% Catholic. The average age of freshmen is 18; all undergraduates, 20. 22% do not continue beyond their first year; 45% remain to graduate.

Housing: 605 students can be accommodated in college housing, which includes single-sex and coed dorms. In addition, there are special-interest houses. On-campus housing is available on a first-come, first-served basis. 72% of students live on campus; of those, 80% remain on campus on weekends. Alcohol is not permitted. All students may keep cars.

Activities: 15% of men belong to 3 local fraternities; 18% of women belong to 3 local sororities. There are 62 groups on campus, including art, band, cheerleading, chess, choir, chorale, chorus, dance, drama, drill team, ethnic, gay, honors, international, jazz band, musical theater, newspaper, orchestra, pep band, photography, professional, religious, social, social service, student government, symphony, and yearbook. Popular campus events include the Messiah Festival of Art and Music Holy Week Festival.

Sports: There are 8 intercollegiate sports for men and 7 for women, and 15 intramural sports for men and 15 for women. Facilities include a 1500-seat gym, a 4000-seat stadium, tennis courts, track and field facilities, handball/racquetball courts, a weight training area, 2 softball diamonds and 1 baseball diamond, a soccer field, and a 2-court practice gym.

Disabled Students: 98% of the campus is accessible. Wheelchair ramps, elevators, special parking, specially equipped rest rooms, special class scheduling, and lowered drinking fountains are available.

Services: Counseling and information services are available, as is tutoring in every subject.

Campus Safety and Security: Measures include self-defense education, security escort services, informal discussions, and pamphlets/posters/films. There are emergency telephones, lighted pathways/sidewalks, and a campus patrol at night; residence halls are locked from midnight to 9 A.M.

Programs of Study: Bethany confers the B.A. degree. Bachelor's degrees are awarded in BIOLOGICAL SCIENCE (biology/biological science), BUSINESS (business administration and management and business economics), COMMUNICATIONS AND THE ARTS (art, communications, English, fine arts, and music), COMPUTER AND

PHYSICAL SCIENCE (chemistry and mathematics), EDUCATION (art, athletic training, business, Christian, elementary, English, mathematics, middle school, music, physical, science, and secondary), HEALTH PROFESSIONS (predentistry and premedicine), SOCIAL SCIENCE (criminal justice, economics, history, ministries, parks and recreation management, prelaw, psychology, social science, and social work). Chemistry, English, and education are the strongest academically. Business and education are the largest.

Required: All students must complete 28 to 39 semester hours of general education requirements and the courses Thinking and Writing and Christianity in the Global Context. A total of 34 semester hours must be in 300-level courses. A total of 128 credit hours with a minimum GPA of 2.0 is required for graduation.

Special: Bethany offers co-op programs and cross-registration through the Associated Colleges of Central Kansas and a 3-2 engineering degree with Wichita State University. Internships, a Chicago semester, a Washington semester, work-study programs, accelerated degree programs in economics/business and preengineering, dual majors, including history-political science and religion-philosophy, student-designed majors, and limited pass/fail options are also available. There are 6 national honor societies and a freshman honors program.

Faculty/Classroom: 61% of faculty are male; 39%, female. All teach undergraduates. The average class size in an introductory lecture is 30; in a laboratory, 8; and in a regular course, 22.

Admissions: 26% of the current freshmen were in the top fifth of their class; 58% were in the top two fifths. 8 freshmen graduated first in their class.

Requirements: The ACT is required. In addition, applicants should be graduates of an accredited secondary school, with 4 years of English, 3 of social studies, 2 each of math and science, and 1 each of foreign language and phys ed. The GED is accepted. An interview is recommended, along with a portfolio or an audition for some majors. Bethany requires applicants to be in the upper 50% of their class. A GPA of 2.5 is required. AP and CLEP credits are accepted. Important factors in the admissions decision are advanced placement or honor courses, leadership record, and evidence of special talent.

Procedure: Freshmen are admitted to all sessions. There is a rolling admissions plan. Applications should be filed by May 1 for fall entry, December 15 for winter entry, and January 15 for spring entry, along with a $20 fee. Notification is sent on a rolling basis. Applications are accepted on-line.

Transfer: 68 transfer students enrolled in 2004-2005. A GPA of 2.3 in 24 credit hours is required. 32 of 128 credits required for the bachelor's degree must be completed at Bethany.

Visiting: There are regularly scheduled orientations for prospective students, including campus tours, a faculty visit, class enrollment, and a financial aid visit. There are guides for informal visits and visitors may sit in on classes and stay overnight. To schedule a visit, contact the Office of Admissions.

Financial Aid: In 2005-2006, of all full-time freshmen and 98% of continuing full-time students received some form of financial aid. 79% of full-time freshmen and 83% of continuing full-time students received need-based aid. The average freshman award was $16,682. Need-based scholarships or need-based grants averaged $4499 ($10,000 maximum); need-based self-help aid (loans and jobs) averaged $5534 ($8125 maximum); non-need-based athletic scholarships averaged $4610 ($10,000 maximum); and other non-need-based awards and non-need-based scholarships averaged $6914 ($15,250 maximum). 88% of undergraduates work part time. Average annual earnings from campus work are $1500. The average financial indebtedness of the 2005 graduate was $16,925. The priority date for freshman financial aid applications for fall entry is March 15. The deadline for filing freshman financial aid applications for fall entry is August 1.

International Students: There are 20 international students enrolled. The school actively recruits these students. They must take the TOEFL, achieving a satisfactory score, and also take the SAT or the ACT.

Computers: All students may access the system from 6 A.M. to midnight. There are no time limits and no fees.

Graduates: From July 1, 2004 to June 30, 2005, 129 bachelor's degrees were awarded. The most popular majors were economics and business (31%), education (24%), and biology (13%). In an average class, 1% graduate in 3 years or less, 39% graduate in 4 years or less, 45% graduate in 5 years or less, and 47% graduate in 6 years or less. 3 companies recruited on campus in 2004-2005. Of the 2004 graduating class, 24% were enrolled in graduate school within 6 months of graduation and 47% were employed.

Admissions Contact: Thandabantu Maceo, Dean of Enrollment Management. A video is available. E-mail: *admissions@bethanylb.edu* Web: *www.bethanylb.edu*

BETHEL COLLEGE
D-3

North Newton, KS 67117
(316) 284-5230
(800) 522-1887, ext. 230; Fax: (316) 284-5870

Full-time: 241 men, 235 women	**Faculty:** 47; IIB, --$
Part-time: 11 men, 27 women	**Ph.D.s:** 57%
Graduate: none	**Student/Faculty:** 10 to 1
Year: 4-1-4, summer session	**Tuition:** $15,550
Application Deadline: open	**Room & Board:** $6100
Freshman Class: n/av	**COMPETITIVE**

Bethel College, established in 1887, is a private liberal arts institution affiliated with the Mennonite Church U.S.A. In addition to regional accreditation, Bethel has baccalaureate program accreditation with CCNE, CSWE, and NCATE. The 2 libraries contain 140,408 volumes, 14,001 microform items, and 6204 audio/video tapes/CDs/DVDs, and subscribe to 19,422 periodicals including electronic. Computerized library services include the card catalog, interlibrary loans, database searching, Internet access, and laptop Internet portals. Special learning facilities include a learning resource center, art gallery, natural history museum, radio station, and an observatory. The 60-acre campus is in a suburban area 25 miles north of Wichita. Including any residence halls, there are 21 buildings.

Student Life: 71% of undergraduates are from Kansas. Others are from 23 states, 15 foreign countries, and Canada. 94% are from public schools. 82% are white. 34% are Protestant; 19% claim no religious affiliation; 10% Catholic. The average age of freshmen is 18; all undergraduates, 22. 34% do not continue beyond their first year; 53% remain to graduate.

Housing: 473 students can be accommodated in college housing, which includes single-sex and coed dorms, off-campus apartments, and married-student housing. On-campus housing is guaranteed for all 4 years. 67% of students live on campus; of those, 80% remain on campus on weekends. Alcohol is not permitted. All students may keep cars.

Activities: There are no fraternities or sororities. There are 22 groups on campus, including art, chess, choir, chorale, chorus, computers, dance, debate, drama, ethnic, forensics, gay, international, jazz band, literary magazine, musical theater, newspaper, opera, orchestra, pep band, political, professional, radio and TV, religious, social, social service, student government, symphony, and yearbook. Popular campus events include Fall Festival, Christmas Gala, and Spring Fling.

Sports: There are 6 intercollegiate sports for men and 6 for women, and 7 intramural sports for men and 7 for women. Facilities include 2 indoor gyms, 2 weight rooms, a cardio-exercise room, 8 tennis courts, 2 soccer practice fields, an all-weather track, outdoor stadium complex for football, soccer and track with an 8 lane track and artificial field turf, and 1 football practice field, an outdoor basketball court, an outdoor sand volleyball court, and a nature trail.

Disabled Students: 75% of the campus is accessible. Wheelchair ramps, elevators, special parking, specially equipped rest rooms, special class scheduling, lowered drinking fountains, and special housing are available.

Services: Counseling and information services are available, as is tutoring in most subjects. There is a reader service for the blind, and remedial math, reading, and writing.

Campus Safety and Security: Measures include informal discussions, emergency telephones, and lighted pathways/sidewalks.

Programs of Study: Bethel confers B.A., B.S., B.S.N., and B.S.S.W. degrees. Bachelor's degrees are awarded in BIOLOGICAL SCIENCE (biology/biological science), BUSINESS (business administration and management), COMMUNICATIONS AND THE ARTS (art, communications, English, German, music, and Spanish), COMPUTER AND PHYSICAL SCIENCE (chemistry, computer science, mathematics, natural sciences, and physics), EDUCATION (athletic training, elementary, and health), HEALTH PROFESSIONS (nursing), SOCIAL SCIENCE (history, psychology, religion, and social work). English, biology, and psychology are the strongest academically. Nursing, elementary education, and psychology are the largest.

Required: To graduate, students must earn a total of 124 credits, including 24 to 50 in the major, 12 to 50 of those in upper-level courses, with a GPA of 2.0. Students must also meet general education requirements that include demonstrating competency in writing, math, speech, computers, and foreign language. Additional distribution requirements include convocation, religious studies, natural sciences, math or philosophy, cross-cultural learning, social sciences, humanities, fine arts, and physical education.

Special: Students may cross-register with Associated Colleges of Central Kansas (ACCK) institutions and Hesston College. Internships are required in many majors. Work-study programs, study abroad in 17 countries, dual majors, and a Washington semester are available. The college offers a 3-2 engineering degree with University of Kansas, Kansas State University, and Wichita State University.

Faculty/Classroom: 52% of faculty are male; 48%, female. All teach undergraduates, 50% do research, and 50% do both. The average class size in an introductory lecture is 24; in a laboratory, 16; and in a regular course, 18.

Admissions: 39% of the current freshmen were in the top fifth of their class; 66% were in the top two fifths. 7 freshmen graduated first in their class.

Requirements: A satisfactorily score is required on the SAT or ACT, along with a minimum GPA of 2.5 for automatic admission. The GED is accepted. Auditions are required of candidates applying for some scholarships, and interviews are recommended for all applicants. Specific departmental requirements may vary. CLEP, AP, and International Baccalaureate credit may be awarded. A GPA of 2.0 is required. Important factors in the admissions decision are evidence of special talent, recommendations by alumni, and parents or siblings attending the school.

Procedure: Freshmen are admitted to all sessions. Entrance exams should be taken by the fall of the senior year. There is a rolling admissions plan. Application deadlines are open. Notification is sent on a rolling basis. Application fee is $20. Applications are accepted on-line.

Transfer: 113 transfer students enrolled in 2004-2005. A high school transcript (or GED), or official college transcript (minimum 2.0 GPA), ACT or SAT scores (waived if the student has more than 24 hours accepted in transfer to Bethel College), and a transfer recommendation are required. Automatic admission requires a cumulative GPA of 2.0 and a satisfactorily ACT or SAT score. 30 of 124 credits required for the bachelor's degree must be completed at Bethel.

Visiting: There are regularly scheduled orientations for prospective students, including a campus tour, classroom observations, visits with faculty, an interview with an admissions counselor, lunch, and overnight residence hall lodging. There are guides for informal visits and visitors may sit in on classes and stay overnight. To schedule a visit, contact the Admissions Office.

Financial Aid: In 2005-2006, 99% of all full-time freshmen and 90% of continuing full-time students received some form of financial aid. 92% of full-time freshmen and 67% of continuing full-time students received need-based aid. The average freshman award was $17,570. Need-based scholarships or need-based grants averaged $4425; need-based self-help aid (loans and jobs) averaged $5294; and non-need-based athletic scholarships averaged $3253. 82% of undergraduates work part time. Average annual earnings from campus work are $787. The average financial indebtedness of the 2005 graduate was $15,765. The FAFSA is required. The priority date for freshman financial aid applications for fall entry is August 15.

International Students: There are 25 international students enrolled. They must score satisfactorily on the TOEFL.

Computers: Wireless access is available. Students have 2 network jacks in their dorm rooms that are high speed connection to the Internet. File storage is available on the network along with an e-mail account. The wireless network covers most of the campus and all of the areas where students congregate to work and play. There are 2 computer labs with a total of 28 PCs. The library also has public use PCs. All students may access the system 18 hours a day. There are no time limits and no fees.

Graduates: From July 1, 2004 to June 30, 2005, 113 bachelor's degrees were awarded. The most popular majors were nursing (24%), business administration (8%), and social work (7%). In an average class, 43% graduate in 4 years, 8% graduate in 5 years, and 2% graduate in 6 years.

Admissions Contact: Allan Bartel, Director of Admissions & Enrollment. A video is available. E-mail: *admissions@bethelks.edu* Web: *http://www.bethelks.edu*

EMPORIA STATE UNIVERSITY
E-2

Emporia, KS 66801-5087
(620) 341-5465
(877) GO-TO-ESU; Fax: (620) 341-5599

Full-time: 1468 men, 2329 women	**Faculty:** 252; IIA, --$
Part-time: 204 men, 350 women	**Ph.D.s:** 81%
Graduate: 566 men, 1371 women	**Student/Faculty:** 15 to 1
Year: semesters, summer session	**Tuition:** $3306 ($10,658)
Application Deadline: open	**Room & Board:** $4787
Freshman Class: 1188 applied, 931 accepted, 739 enrolled	
ACT: 22	**COMPETITIVE**

Emporia State University, founded in 1863, is a state-supported institution that offers degree programs in liberal arts, business, teacher education, and vocational fields, as well as various graduate programs. There are 4 undergraduate schools and 1 graduate school. In addition to regional accreditation, ESU has baccalaureate program accreditation with AACSB, ACS, CAAHEP, NASAD, NASM, NCATE, and NLN. The library contains 569,802 volumes, 1,173,546 microform items, and 8180 audio/video tapes/CDs/DVDs, and subscribes to 1233 periodicals including electronic. Computerized library services include the card catalog, interlibrary loans, database searching, and Internet access. Special learning facilities include a learning resource center, art gallery, natural history museum, planetarium, and theaters, geology museum, and Great Plains study center. The 207-acre campus is in a small town 110 miles from

Kansas City in the Bluestem Region of the Flint Hills. Including any residence halls, there are 20 buildings.

Student Life: 95% of undergraduates are from Kansas. Others are from 43 states, 36 foreign countries, and Canada. 82% are white. The average age of freshmen is 19; all undergraduates, 22. 33% do not continue beyond their first year; 67% remain to graduate.

Housing: 1131 students can be accommodated in college housing, which includes single-sex and coed dorms, on-campus apartments, fraternity houses, and sorority houses. In addition, there are honors houses and special-interest houses. On-campus housing is guaranteed for the freshman year only and is available on a first-come, first-served basis. Priority is given to out-of-town students. 80% of students commute. All students may keep cars.

Activities: 13% of men belong to 6 national fraternities; 9% of women belong to 4 national sororities. There are 131 groups on campus, including art, band, cheerleading, choir, chorale, chorus, computers, debate, drama, drill team, ethnic, film, gay, honors, international, jazz band, literary magazine, marching band, musical theater, newspaper, opera, orchestra, pep band, political, professional, religious, social, social service, student government, symphony, and yearbook. Popular campus events include Family Day.

Sports: There are 7 intercollegiate sports for men and 8 for women, and 12 intramural sports for men and 12 for women. Facilities include a 7000-seat stadium, a recreation center, an Olympic-size pool, 5 gyms, 6 handball courts, exercise, physical therapy, and dance rooms, a sports complex with 3 softball fields and 1 baseball diamond, an all-weather 8-lane track, and 3 additional softball fields separate from the sports complex.

Disabled Students: All of the campus is accessible. Wheelchair ramps, elevators, special parking, specially equipped rest rooms, special class scheduling, lowered drinking fountains, lowered telephones, and special housing are available.

Services: There is a reader service for the blind, and remedial math, reading, and writing.

Campus Safety and Security: Measures include 24-hour foot and vehicle patrol, security escort services, informal discussions, and pamphlets/posters/films. There are emergency telephones, lighted pathways/sidewalks, motorist-assist programs, safety and self-awareness programs for students and parents, 24-hour residence hall monitoring, and smoke detectors in residence halls.

Programs of Study: ESU confers B.A., B.S., B.F.A., B.I.S., B Mus., B.Mus.Ed., B.S.Bus., B.S.Ed., and B.S.N. degrees. Master's and doctoral degrees are also awarded. Bachelor's degrees are awarded in BIOLOGICAL SCIENCE (biology/biological science), BUSINESS (accounting, business administration and management, marketing/retailing/merchandising, and recreation and leisure services), COMMUNICATIONS AND THE ARTS (art, communications, dramatic arts, English, modern language, and music), COMPUTER AND PHYSICAL SCIENCE (chemistry, computer science, earth science, information sciences and systems, mathematics, physical sciences, and physics), EDUCATION (art, athletic training, business, elementary, foreign languages, health, music, physical, and secondary), HEALTH PROFESSIONS (health care administration, nursing, and rehabilitation therapy), SOCIAL SCIENCE (economics, history, liberal arts/general studies, political science/government, psychology, social science, and sociology). Elementary education is the largest.

Required: To graduate, all students must complete at least 124 credit hours, including 40 in upper-division courses, with a minimum GPA of 2.0. Students must also pass competency exams in reading, math, and writing and complete the general education program for their field of study, which includes courses in math, physical and applied science, humanities, history, speech, cultural diversity, and fitness and phys ed.

Special: ESU offers internships in many majors, study abroad in 34 countries, work-study programs, on-campus and on-line general studies degrees, B.A.-B.S. degrees, dual and student-designed majors, 3-2 engineering degrees with Kansas State University, Wichita State University, and the University of Kansas, credit for military experience, nondegree study, independent study, evening and Saturday classes, and pass/no credit options. There is also a law librarian graduate degree program with the University of Kansas. There are 17 national honor societies and a freshman honors program.

Faculty/Classroom: 60% of faculty are male; 40%, female. All teach undergraduates. Graduate students teach 9% of introductory courses. The average class size in an introductory lecture is 22; in a laboratory, 16; and in a regular course, 20.

Admissions: 78% of the 2005-2006 applicants were accepted. The ACT scores for the 2005-2006 freshman class were: 38% below 21, 28% between 21 and 23, 21% between 24 and 26, 9% between 27 and 28, and 4% above 28.

Requirements: The ACT is required. In addition, applicants must meet 1 of these 3 criteria: a satisfactory ACT score, class rank in the top third, or a 2.0 GPA in the Kansas core curriculum in-state; 2.5 for out-of-state applicants. Students should have completed 4 units of English, 3 each of natural science, math, and social science, and 1 of computer technol-

ogy. Applicants may also be admitted through an exceptions window and are encouraged to apply. A GPA of 2.0 is required. AP and CLEP credits are accepted.

Procedure: Freshmen are admitted to all sessions. Entrance exams should be taken in October or December of the senior year. There is a deferred admissions and a rolling admissions plan. The fall 2005 application fee was $30. Application deadlines are open. A waiting list is an active part of the admissions procedure for the exceptions window only. Applications are accepted on-line.

Transfer: 481 transfer students enrolled in 2004-2005. Applicants must submit official transcripts of all previous college work. The minimum GPA depends on the number of semester hours earned. Physical activity requirements must be met. 30 of 124 credits required for the bachelor's degree must be completed at ESU.

Visiting: There are regularly scheduled orientations for prospective students, including campus and residence hall tours, meetings with admissions and financial aid personnel, and appointments with academic and extracurricular personnel, if desired. There are guides for informal visits and visitors may sit in on classes and stay overnight. To schedule a visit, contact Laura Eddy, Director of Admissions at go2esu@emporia.edu.

Financial Aid: In 2004-2005, 93% of all full-time freshmen and 84% of continuing full-time students received some form of financial aid. 59% of all full-time students received need-based aid. The average freshman award was $4480. Need-based scholarships or need-based grants averaged $1474; need-based self-help aid (loans and jobs) averaged $2118; and non-need-based athletic scholarships averaged $1812. 17% of undergraduates work part time. Average annual earnings from campus work are $2655. The average financial indebtedness of the 2005 graduate was $16,197. The FAFSA and the state aid form are required. The priority date for freshman financial aid applications for fall entry is March 15.

International Students: There are 120 international students enrolled. The school actively recruits these students. They must score satisfactorily on the TOEFL, MELAB, or the college's own test and also take the ACT.

Computers: All students may access the system 24 hours per day. There are no time limits. The fee is $100.

Graduates: From July 1, 2004 to June 30, 2005, 741 bachelor's degrees were awarded. The most popular majors were education (29%), business administration (19%), and sociology (12%). In an average class, 19% graduate in 4 years or less, 38% graduate in 5 years or less, and 44% graduate in 6 years or less. 185 companies recruited on campus in 2004-2005. Of the 2004 graduating class, 18% were enrolled in graduate school within 6 months of graduation and 58% were employed.

Admissions Contact: Laura Eddy, Director of Admissions.
E-mail: go2esu@emporia.edu Web: www.emporia.edu

FORT HAYS STATE UNIVERSITY

C-2

Hays, KS 67601-4099

(785) 628-5666
(800) 628-FHSU; Fax: (785) 628-4014

Full-time: 1946 men, 2278 women	**Faculty:** IIA, --$
Part-time: 1540 men, 1991 women	**Ph.D.s:** 77%
Graduate: 503 men, 866 women	**Student/Faculty:** n/av
Year: semesters, summer session	**Tuition:** $2442 ($7660)
Application Deadline: open	**Room & Board:** $5196
Freshman Class: 1407 accepted, 882 enrolled	
ACT: 22	**COMPETITIVE**

Fort Hays State University, established in 1902, is a public liberal arts institution offering programs in arts and sciences, business and leadership, education, health and life sciences, and preprofessional study. There are 4 undergraduate schools and 1 graduate school. In addition to regional accreditation, FHSU has baccalaureate program accreditation with AACSB, NASM, NCATE, and NLN. The library contains 300,000 volumes, 500,000 microform items, and 1480 audio/video tapes/CDs/DVDs, and subscribes to 3100 periodicals including electronic. Computerized library services include the card catalog, interlibrary loans, and database searching. Special learning facilities include an art gallery, radio station, TV station, and an English lab. The 200-acre campus is in a small town 180 miles northwest of Wichita. Including any residence halls, there are 44 buildings.

Student Life: 93% of undergraduates are from Kansas. Others are from 36 states, 32 foreign countries, and Canada. 95% are from public schools. 87% are white. The average age of freshmen is 18; all undergraduates, 23. 61% do not continue beyond their first year; 40% remain to graduate.

Housing: 1000 students can be accommodated in college housing, which includes single-sex and coed dorms, on-campus apartments, married-student housing, fraternity houses, sorority houses, apartments for students with families, and apartments for nontraditional-age students. 82% of students commute. All students may keep cars.

Activities: 1% of men belong to 3 national fraternities; 1% of women belong to 3 national sororities. There are 85 groups on campus, including art, band, cheerleading, choir, chorale, chorus, computers, dance, debate, drama, drill team, ethnic, film, gay, honors, international, jazz band, literary magazine, marching band, musical theater, newspaper, opera, orchestra, pep band, photography, political, professional, radio and TV, religious, social, social service, student government, symphony, and yearbook. Popular campus events include Octoberfest and Parents Day.

Sports: There are 8 intercollegiate sports for men and 7 for women, and 40 intramural sports for men and 40 for women. Facilities include a 6300-seat stadium, tennis courts, and a coliseum containing a 6800-seat basketball arena, a track, and wrestling and training rooms.

Disabled Students: 95% of the campus is accessible. Wheelchair ramps, elevators, special parking, specially equipped rest rooms, special class scheduling, lowered drinking fountains, lowered telephones, an Arkenstone reader, TDD, and voice dictation programs are available.

Services: Counseling and information services are available, as is tutoring in most subjects. There is remedial math and reading.

Campus Safety and Security: Measures include 24-hour foot and vehicle patrol, security escort services, informal discussions, and emergency telephones. There are lighted pathways/sidewalks.

Programs of Study: FHSU confers B.A., B.S., B.B.A., B.F.A., B.G.S., B.M., and B.S.W. degrees. Associate and master's degrees are also awarded. Bachelor's degrees are awarded in AGRICULTURE (agricultural business management and agriculture), BIOLOGICAL SCIENCE (biology/biological science), BUSINESS (accounting, banking and finance, business administration and management, management information systems, marketing/retailing/merchandising, and office supervision and management), COMMUNICATIONS AND THE ARTS (art, communications, English, fine arts, French, German, modern language, music, music performance, music theory and composition, Spanish, and telecommunications), COMPUTER AND PHYSICAL SCIENCE (chemistry, computer science, geology, information sciences and systems, mathematics, physical sciences, physics, radiological technology, and science), EDUCATION (art, elementary, music, physical, and technical), HEALTH PROFESSIONS (nursing, and speech pathology/audiology), SOCIAL SCIENCE (criminal justice, economics, history, liberal arts/general studies, philosophy, political science/government, psychology, social work, and sociology). Speech pathology is the strongest academically. Interdisciplinary studies, teacher education, and business administration are the largest.

Required: To graduate, students must earn an overall minimum GPA of 2.0 or higher in some departments for 124 credit hours, including 40 hours in upper-level study, and 30 hours minimum in the major. The 55-hour liberal arts general education curriculum includes courses addressing personal wellness, analysis and communication, international studies, humanities, math, and natural, social, and behavioral sciences.

Special: Students may, with approval, earn their degrees through a cooperative program with FHSU and another accredited institution, or a correspondence or extension school. Cross-registration with several community colleges, internships, study abroad, work-study programs, a 3-2 engineering degree with Kansas State University, B.A.-B.S. degrees, a general studies degree, and pass/fail options are available. There are 21 national honor societies, and a freshman honors program.

Faculty/Classroom: 59% of faculty are male; 41%, female. All teach undergraduates. The average class size in an introductory lecture is 17; in a laboratory, 17; and in a regular course, 18.

Admissions: The ACT scores for the 2005-2006 freshman class were: 47% below 21, 24% between 21 and 23, 18% between 24 and 26, 6% between 27 and 28, and 5% above 28.

Requirements: The ACT is recommended. In addition, candidates for admission who are residents of Kansas must graduate from an accredited secondary school or earn a GED. A GPA of 2.0 is required. Nonresidents must have earned better than a 2.0 GPA as well. AP and CLEP credits are accepted.

Procedure: Freshmen are admitted fall, spring, and summer. Entrance exams should be taken in the senior year. Application deadlines are open. Application fee is $30. Applications are accepted on-line.

Transfer: 567 transfer students enrolled in a recent year. Applicants must have a minimum college GPA of 2.0 and submit official college transcripts from all institutions previously attended. 30 of 124 credits required for the bachelor's degree must be completed at FHSU.

Visiting: There are regularly scheduled orientations for prospective students. There are guides for informal visits and visitors may sit in on classes and stay overnight. To schedule a visit, contact the office of Admissions, Campus Tour Coordinator.

Financial Aid: 66% of undergraduates work part time. The FFS and the college's own financial statement are required.

International Students: 117 international students enrolled in a recent year. The school actively recruits these students. They must take the TOEFL.

Computers: All students may access the system The modem pool may be used 24 hours a day, the labs until 11 P.M. There are no time limits and no fees.

Graduates: In a recent year, 936 bachelor's degrees were awarded. The most popular majors were elementary education (12%), nursing

(9%), and management (5%). 160 companies recruited on campus. Of a recent graduating class, 16% were enrolled in graduate school within 6 months of graduation and 90% were employed.

Admissions Contact: Roger Schieferecke, Director of Admissions. A video is available. E-mail: *tigers@fhsu.edu* Web: *www.fhsu.edu*

FRIENDS UNIVERSITY D-3
Wichita, KS 67213

(316) 295-5100
(800) 577-2233; Fax: (316) 295-5101

Full-time: 400 men, 525 women	**Faculty:** IIA, --$
Part-time: 100 men and women	**Ph.D.s:** n/av
Graduate: 275 men, 290 women	**Student/Faculty:** n/av
Year: semesters, summer session	**Tuition:** $12,500
Application Deadline: open	**Room & Board:** $3750
Freshman Class: n/av	
SAT or ACT: required	**LESS COMPETITIVE**

Friends University, established in 1898, is an interdenominational institution offering undergraduate and graduate degrees through the Colleges of Arts and Sciences, Business and Information Technology, and Adult and Professional Studies. There are 3 undergraduate and 3 graduate schools. Figures in the above capsule and profile are approximate. In addition to regional accreditation, Friends has baccalaureate program accreditation with NASM and NCATE. The library contains 75,540 volumes, 319,861 microform items, and 13,135 audio/video tapes/CDs/DVDs, and subscribes to 321 periodicals including electronic. Computerized library services include the card catalog, interlibrary loans, and database searching. Special learning facilities include a learning resource center, art gallery, and observatory. The 54-acre campus is in an urban area 200 miles southwest of Kansas City. Including any residence halls, there are 15 buildings.

Student Life: 71% are white. 86% are Protestant; 10% Catholic. The average age of freshmen is 19; all undergraduates, 21.

Housing: 326 students can be accommodated in college housing, which includes single-sex dormitories, on-campus apartments, and off-campus apartments. On-campus housing is available on a first-come, first-served basis. Alcohol is not permitted. All students may keep cars.

Activities: There is 1 local fraternity and 1 national sorority. There are many groups and organizations on campus, including art, band, cheerleading, choir, chorale, chorus, computers, dance, drama, ethnic, honors, international, jazz band, musical theater, orchestra, pep band, photography, political, professional, religious, social, social service, student government, symphony, yearbook, and yell-leading. Popular campus events include Christian Emphasis Week, Cherry Carnival, and Symphony of Spring.

Sports: There are 9 intercollegiate sports for men and 8 for women, and 6 intramural sports for men and 6 for women. Facilities include a 2600-seat stadium and athletic field for football and soccer, a phys ed center with basketball and racquetball courts, an intramural gym, and tennis courts.

Disabled Students: 95% of the campus is accessible. Wheelchair ramps, elevators, special parking, specially equipped rest rooms, special class scheduling, lowered drinking fountains, and lowered telephones are available.

Services: Counseling and information services are available, as is tutoring in most subjects.

Campus Safety and Security: Measures include 24-hour foot and vehicle patrol, pamphlets/posters/films, and lighted pathways/sidewalks.

Programs of Study: Friends confers B.A., B.S., B.B.A., B.F.A., and B.Mus. degrees. Associate and master's degrees are also awarded. Bachelor's degrees are awarded in BIOLOGICAL SCIENCE (biology/biological science and zoology), BUSINESS (accounting, business administration and management, international business management, and management information systems), COMMUNICATIONS AND THE ARTS (art, ballet, English, fine arts, music, musical theater, and Spanish), COMPUTER AND PHYSICAL SCIENCE (chemistry, computer science, information sciences and systems, mathematics, and radiological technology), EDUCATION (art, business, elementary, English, foreign languages, health, music, science, secondary, and social science), ENGINEERING AND ENVIRONMENTAL DESIGN (environmental science), HEALTH PROFESSIONS (premedicine), SOCIAL SCIENCE (history, human services, political science/government, psychology, and religion). Science is the strongest academically. Business and education are the largest.

Required: To graduate, students must complete 124 credit hours, including 33 to 54 in general education (varies by degree sought) and 24 to 45 in the major, with a minimum GPA of 2.0. Distribution requirements include course work in humanities, fine arts, religion and philosophy, behavioral science, and natural science.

Special: Students may cross-register with Newman University, and they can pursue internships in their majors. A study-abroad program is available in Cancun, Mexico, and several Asian countries. Friends offers accelerated degree programs in business management, organizational management and leadership, computer information systems, criminal justice, and electronic commerce management, as well as dual majors in accounting/business administration, and math/computer science. There is a 3-2 engineering degree program with Wichita State University. Friends also offers a general studies degree, credit for life, military, and work experience, nondegree study, and pass/fail options are possible. For working adults, the College of Adult and Professional Studies offers undergraduate degrees and certificate programs. There is 1 national honor society, a freshman honors program, and 1 departmental honors program.

Faculty/Classroom: 92% teach undergraduates. No introductory courses are taught by graduate students. The average class size in an introductory lecture is 35; in a laboratory, 18; and in a regular course, 25.

Requirements: The SAT or ACT is required. In addition, candidates for admission must graduate from an accredited secondary school or earn a GED, having completed 4 courses in English, 2 each in history and math, and 1 each in science and social studies. The composite ACT score or converted SAT score is multiplied by the high school GPA. A result of 45 is the minimum for full admission; students scoring lower may be admitted provisionally. Interviews are recommended; portfolios and auditions are advised in appropriate instances. A GPA of 2.0 is required. CLEP credit is accepted.

Procedure: Freshmen are admitted fall and spring. Entrance exams should be taken in the spring of the junior year or fall of the senior year. There are early admissions plans and rolling admissions. Application deadlines are open. The fall 2005 application fee was $15.

Transfer: Applicants with fewer than 15 semester hours must submit ACT or SAT scores and high school and college transcripts. 30 of 124 credits required for the bachelor's degree must be completed at Friends.

Visiting: There are regularly scheduled orientations for prospective students, including half-day classroom visits, individual instructor visits, discussion with current students, a tour, lunch, and a financial aid session. There are guides for informal visits and visitors may sit in on classes and stay overnight. To schedule a visit, contact the Admissions Office.

Financial Aid: The FAFSA is required. Check with the school for current application deadlines.

International Students: The school actively recruits these students. They must score satisfactorily on the written TOEFL or on the electronic version unless they are either native speakers of English or non-native speakers who attended an English-speaking high school.

Computers: All students may access the system. There are no time limits and no fees. It is strongly recommended that all students have a personal computer.

Admissions Contact: Tony Myers, Director of Admissions.
E-mail: *tmyers@friends.edu* Web: *www.friends.edu*

KANSAS STATE UNIVERSITY   E-2

Manhattan, KS 66506   (785) 532-6250; Fax: (785) 532-6393

Full-time: 8497 men, 8022 women	Faculty: 1199; I, --$
Part-time: 1077 men, 1242 women	Ph.D.s: 81%
Graduate: 1776 men, 2568 women	Student/Faculty: 14 to 1
Year: semesters, summer session	Tuition: $5124 ($14,454)
Application Deadline: open	Room & Board: $5392
Freshman Class: 8207 applied, 4806 accepted, 3309 enrolled	
ACT: required	VERY COMPETITIVE

Kansas State University, established in 1863, is a land-grant institution offering degree programs in agriculture, arts and sciences, business, engineering, human ecology, architecture, education, veterinary medicine, and technology. There are 9 undergraduate schools and 1 graduate school. In addition to regional accreditation, K-State has baccalaureate program accreditation with AACSB, ABET, ACCE, AHEA, CSWE, FIDER, NAAB, NASM, NCATE, and NRPA. The 5 libraries contain 2,520,114 volumes, 2,687,566 microform items, and 29,137 audio/video tapes/CDs/DVDs, and subscribe to 12,247 periodicals including electronic. Computerized library services include the card catalog, interlibrary loans, and database searching. Special learning facilities include a learning resource center, art gallery, planetarium, radio station, TV station, nuclear reactor, laser center, cancer research center, and telecommunications satellite teaching. The 668-acre campus is in a suburban area 125 miles west of Kansas City. Including any residence halls, there are 96 buildings.

Student Life: 87% of undergraduates are from Kansas. Others are from 50 states, 66 foreign countries, and Canada. 85% are white. The average age of freshmen is 18; all undergraduates, 21. 20% do not continue beyond their first year; 59% remain to graduate.

Housing: 4300 students can be accommodated in college housing, which includes single-sex and coed dorms, on-campus apartments, off-campus apartments, married-student housing, fraternity houses, and sorority houses. In addition, there are honors houses and special-interest houses. On-campus housing is available on a first-come, first-served basis. 25% of students live on campus. Alcohol is not permitted. All students may keep cars.

Activities: 17% of men belong to 28 national fraternities; 18% of women belong to 16 national sororities. There are 402 groups on campus, including band, cheerleading, chess, choir, chorale, chorus, computers, dance, drama, drill team, ethnic, film, gay, honors, international, jazz band, literary magazine, marching band, musical theater, newspaper, orchestra, pep band, photography, political, professional, radio and TV, religious, social, social service, student government, symphony, and yearbook. Popular campus events include Family Weekend, K-State Open House, and Winterfest.

Sports: There are 6 intercollegiate sports for men and 8 for women, and 49 intramural sports for men and 49 for women. Facilities include indoor and outdoor tracks, baseball fields, tennis courts, basketball courts, swimming pools, a football stadium, and an indoor practice field. A multipurpose recreation facility is open 16 hours a day.

Disabled Students: 90% of the campus is accessible. Wheelchair ramps, elevators, special parking, specially equipped rest rooms, special class scheduling, lowered drinking fountains, lowered telephones, and a campus shuttle service are available.

Services: Counseling and information services are available, as is tutoring in every subject. There is a reader service for the blind, and remedial math, reading, and writing.

Campus Safety and Security: Measures include 24-hour foot and vehicle patrol, self-defense education, security escort services, and shuttle buses. There are informal discussions, pamphlets/posters/films, emergency telephones, lighted pathways/sidewalks, and televised monitors in parking lots, CPR classes, and vehicle assistance devices.

Programs of Study: K-State confers B.A., B.S., B.Arch., B.F.A., B.Int.Arch., B.L.A., B.M., and B.M.E. degrees. Associate, master's, and doctoral degrees are also awarded. Bachelor's degrees are awarded in AGRICULTURE (agricultural business management, agricultural economics, agronomy, animal science, fish and game management, and horticulture), BIOLOGICAL SCIENCE (biochemistry, biology/biological science, entomology, life science, microbiology, nutrition, plant pathology, and wildlife biology), BUSINESS (accounting, apparel and accessories marketing, banking and finance, business administration and management, hotel/motel and restaurant management, management information systems, and marketing/retailing/merchandising), COMMUNICATIONS AND THE ARTS (apparel design, applied music, art, communications, dramatic arts, English, journalism, modern language, and music), COMPUTER AND PHYSICAL SCIENCE (chemistry, computer science, geology, information sciences and systems, mathematics, physical sciences, physics, and statistics), EDUCATION (agricultural, art, athletic training, elementary, music, and secondary), ENGINEERING AND ENVIRONMENTAL DESIGN (aeronautical technology, agricultural engineering, agricultural engineering technology, airline piloting and navigation, architectural engineering, architecture, chemical engineering, civil engineering, computer engineering, construction management, electrical/electronics engineering, electrical/electronics engineering technology, engineering management, engineering technology, industrial engineering, interior design, landscape architecture/design, manufacturing engineering, and mechanical engineering), HEALTH PROFESSIONS (medical technology), SOCIAL SCIENCE (anthropology, child psychology/development, dietetics, economics, family and community services, family/consumer studies, food science, geography, history, human development, humanities, parks and recreation management, philosophy, physical fitness/movement, political science/government, psychology, social science, social work, sociology, and textiles and clothing). Architecture, engineering, and accounting are the strongest academically. Journalism, elementary education, and mechanical engineering are the largest.

Required: To graduate, students must complete 120 to 167 credits with a minimum GPA of 2.0. All students must take expository writing and public speaking. General education requirements vary by major but include at least 18 hours of approved courses.

Special: K-State offers co-op programs, internships, and dual degrees and majors through most of its colleges. Cross-registration is available with Kansas State at Salina and Kansas Wesleyan University, as is study abroad in more than 100 countries. A 3-2 engineering degree program, nondegree study, and pass/fail options are also available. There are 78 national honor societies, including Phi Beta Kappa, a freshman honors program, and 7 departmental honors programs.

Faculty/Classroom: 66% of faculty are male; 34%, female. The average class size in a regular course is 29.

Admissions: 59% of the 2005-2006 applicants were accepted. The ACT scores for the 2005-2006 freshman class were: 23% below 21, 26% between 21 and 23, 26% between 24 and 26, 11% between 27 and 28, and 13% above 28.

Requirements: The ACT is required. In addition, applicants must meet 1 of these 3 criteria: an ACT score of 21 or above, class rank in the top third, or a 2.0 GPA in the Kansas core curriculum. It is recommended that students complete 4 units of English, 3 each of natural science, math, and social studies, and 1 of computer technology. The GED is accepted. AP and CLEP credits are accepted.

Procedure: Freshmen are admitted to all sessions. Entrance exams should be taken in the junior and senior years. There is a rolling admissions plan. Application deadlines are open. Notifications are sent on a rolling basis. The fall 2005 application fee was $30. Applications are accepted on-line.

Transfer: 1725 transfer students enrolled in 2004-2005. Applicants must have a minimum of 24 credit hours and a college GPA of 2.0 or otherwise meet freshman requirements. Students must submit official transcripts from previous colleges attended. 30 of 120 to 167 credits required for the bachelor's degree must be completed at K-State.

Visiting: There are regularly scheduled orientations for prospective students, including campus tours and visits with academic advisers and admissions representatives. There are guides for informal visits and visitors may sit in on classes and stay overnight. To schedule a visit, contact New Student Services at (785) 532-6318.

Financial Aid: In 2005-2006, 70% of all full-time students received some form of financial aid. 55% of all full-time students received need-based aid. Need-based scholarships or need-based grants averaged $3034; and need-based self-help aid (loans and jobs) averaged $2900. The average financial indebtedness of the 2005 graduate was $18,907. K-State is a member of CSS. The FAFSA is required. The deadline for filing freshman financial aid applications for fall entry is March 15.

International Students: Satisfactory scores are required on the written TOEFL and on the SAT or the ACT. Applicants must also take the college's own entrance exam or an English proficiency test given at the university.

Computers: Wireless access is available. All students may access the system 24 hours a day. There are no time limits. The fee is $11 per credit hour.

Graduates: From July 1, 2004 to June 30, 2005, 3612 bachelor's degrees were awarded. The most popular majors were business (17%), engineering (12%), and education (11%). In an average class, 24% graduate in 4 years or less, 49% graduate in 5 years or less, and 59% graduate in 6 years or less.

Admissions Contact: Larry Moeder, Director of Admissions. A video is available. E-mail: *kstate@k-state.edu* Web: *www.k-state.edu*

KANSAS WESLEYAN UNIVERSITY — D-2

Salina, KS 67401-6196
(785) 827-5541, ext. 1285
(800) 874-1154, ext. 1285; Fax: (785) 827-0927

Full-time: 279 men, 385 women	Faculty: IIB, --$
Part-time: 33 men, 94 women	Ph.D.s: n/av
Graduate: 38 men, 25 women	Student/Faculty: n/av
Year: semesters, summer session	Tuition: $15,800
Application Deadline: open	Room & Board: $5600
Freshman Class: 1078 applied, 678 accepted, 351 enrolled	
ACT: 22	VERY COMPETITIVE

Kansas Wesleyan, founded in 1886, is affiliated with the United Methodist Church. The college offers undergraduate programs in the arts and sciences, business, and education. In addition to regional accreditation, Kansas Wesleyan has baccalaureate program accreditation with NCATE and NLN. The library contains 82,000 volumes, 33,505 microform items, and 984 audio/video tapes/CDs/DVDs, and subscribes to 421 periodicals including electronic. Computerized library services include the card catalog, interlibrary loans, database searching, and Internet access. Special learning facilities include a learning resource center, art gallery, planetarium, and TV station. The 25-acre campus is in an urban area 85 miles north of Wichita. Including any residence halls, there are 12 buildings.

Student Life: 75% of undergraduates are from Kansas. Others are from 14 states, 3 foreign countries, and Canada. 92% are from public schools. 85% are white. 48% are Protestant; 39% claim no religious affiliation; 13% Catholic. The average age of freshmen is 21; all undergraduates, 25. 33% do not continue beyond their first year.

Housing: 450 students can be accommodated in college housing, which includes single-sex dorms, on-campus apartments, and married-student housing. On-campus housing is guaranteed for all 4 years. 83% of students commute. Alcohol is not permitted. All students may keep cars.

Activities: 10% of men belong to 1 local and 1 national fraternity; 5% of women belong to 1 local sorority. There are 38 groups on campus, including art, band, cheerleading, choir, chorale, chorus, computers, dance, drama, ethnic, film, honors, international, literary magazine, musical theater, newspaper, pep band, photography, professional, radio and TV, religious, social, social service, student government, and yearbook. Popular campus events include Lilac Fete, Sweetheart Dance, and Family Weekend.

Sports: There are 7 intercollegiate sports for men and 7 for women, and 8 intramural sports for men and 6 for women. Facilities include a gym, a sand volleyball court, football practice and game fields, a multipurpose courtyard, a track, and a weight room.

Disabled Students: 90% of the campus is accessible. Wheelchair ramps, elevators, special parking, specially equipped rest rooms, special class scheduling, lowered drinking fountains, and lowered telephones are available.

Services: Counseling and information services are available, as is tutoring in most subjects. There is remedial reading and writing.

Campus Safety and Security: Measures include self-defense education, security escort services, informal discussions, and pamphlets/posters/films. There are lighted pathways/sidewalks, random security checks and private service security guards.

Programs of Study: Kansas Wesleyan confers B.A., B.S., and B.S.N. degrees. Associate and master's degrees are also awarded. Bachelor's degrees are awarded in BIOLOGICAL SCIENCE (biology/biological science), BUSINESS (accounting and business economics), COMMUNICATIONS AND THE ARTS (communications, dramatic arts, English, music, Spanish, speech/debate/rhetoric, and studio art), COMPUTER AND PHYSICAL SCIENCE (chemistry, computer science, mathematics, and physics), EDUCATION (art, music, physical, secondary, and special), HEALTH PROFESSIONS (nursing), SOCIAL SCIENCE (addiction studies, criminal justice, history, prelaw, psychology, religion, religious education, and sociology). Premedicine, nursing, and preengineering are the strongest academically. Education, nursing, and business are the largest.

Required: Students must demonstrate proficiency in English and math and must fulfill distribution requirements in 15 liberal arts components, including environmental awareness, biblical heritage, and lifetime recreation. Courses in phys ed and computers are required. To graduate, students must complete at least 126 credit hours, including 30 to 40 in a major field of study, with a minimum GPA of 2.0.

Special: Cross-registration is available with other members of the Associated Colleges of Central Kansas and the Salina College Consortium. Cooperative degree programs are offered in agriculture, cytotechnology, engineering, environmental studies, and medical technology. Kansas Wesleyan also offers January interterm study trips throughout the United States and abroad, Washington, D.C., and UN semesters, internships, dual majors, student designed majors, credit for life experience, and nondegree study. A 3-2 engineering degree is offered with Columbia University and Washington University at St. Louis. There are 4 national honor societies.

Faculty/Classroom: 65% both teach and do research. The average class size in an introductory lecture is 23; in a laboratory, 7; and in a regular course, 13.

Admissions: 63% of the 2005-2006 applicants were accepted. 10 freshmen graduated first in their class.

Requirements: The SAT or ACT is required. Applicants must be graduates of accredited secondary schools or have earned a GED. An interview is recommended. A GPA of 2.5 is required. AP and CLEP credits are accepted.

Procedure: Freshmen are admitted to all sessions. Entrance exams should be taken as early as possible. There are deferred admissions and rolling admissions plans. Application deadlines are open. Notification is sent on a rolling basis.

Transfer: Transfers must submit transcripts from all colleges previously attended. Those students transferring fewer than 15 credit hours must submit ACT scores and a high school transcript. A minimum GPA of 2.0 is recommended. 63 of 126 credits required for the bachelor's degree must be completed at Kansas Wesleyan.

Visiting: There are regularly scheduled orientations for prospective students. There are guides for informal visits and visitors may sit in on classes and stay overnight. To schedule a visit, contact the Admissions Office.

Financial Aid: The FAFSA and tax forms are required.

International Students: The school actively recruits these students. A satisfactory score is required on the written TOEFL .

Computers: All students may access the system at any time. There are no time limits and no fees.

Admissions Contact: Admissions Office.
E-mail: *admissions@kwu.edu*

MCPHERSON COLLEGE — D-2

McPherson, KS 67460
(620) 241-0731
(800) 365-7402; Fax: (620) 241-8443

Full-time: 270 men, 152 women	Faculty: 35
Part-time: 20 men, 24 women	Ph.D.s: 56%
Graduate: none	Student/Faculty: 12 to 1
Year: 4-1-4, summer session	Tuition: $15,160
Application Deadline: open	Room & Board: $5850
Freshman Class: 495 applied, 421 accepted, 108 enrolled	
SAT Verbal/Math: 485/495*	ACT: 21 COMPETITIVE

McPherson College, founded in 1887 and affiliated with the Church of the Brethren, is a private, nonprofit institution offering undergraduate programs in the arts and sciences, business, and education. The library contains 89,946 volumes, 60,561 microform items, and 4465 audio/video tapes/CDs/DVDs, and subscribes to 4056 periodicals including electronic. Computerized library services include the card catalog, interlibrary loans, and database searching. Special learning facilities include a learning resource center, art gallery, natural history museum, and automobile restoration center. The 23-acre campus is in a small town 60 miles north of Wichita. Including any residence halls, there are 15 buildings.

Student Life: 50% of undergraduates are from out of state, mostly the Midwest. Students are from 30 states and 6 foreign countries. 99% are from public schools. 85% are white; 11% African American. Most are Catholic. The average age of freshmen is 18; all undergraduates, 21.

Housing: 392 students can be accommodated in college housing, which includes single-sex and coed dorms. On-campus housing is guaranteed for all 4 years. 72% of students live on campus; of those, 65% remain on campus on weekends. Alcohol is not permitted. All students may keep cars.

Activities: There are no fraternities or sororities. There are 26 groups on campus, including art, band, cheerleading, choir, chorus, computers, drama, ethnic, honors, international, musical theater, newspaper, orchestra, pep band, professional, religious, social service, student government, and yearbook. Popular campus events include Family Weekend.

Sports: There are 5 intercollegiate sports for men and 6 for women, and 4 intramural sports for men and 4 for women. Facilities include a sports center with 2 full-size courts, a racquetball court, and a fitness center with an open weight-training room.

Disabled Students: 95% of the campus is accessible. Wheelchair ramps, elevators, special parking, specially equipped rest rooms, special class scheduling, lowered drinking fountains, and special housing are available.

Services: Counseling and information services are available, as is tutoring in most subjects. There is remedial reading and writing.

Campus Safety and Security: Measures include informal discussions, pamphlets/posters/films, emergency telephones, and lighted pathways/sidewalks.

Programs of Study: McPherson confers B.A. and B.S. degrees. Bachelor's degrees are awarded in AGRICULTURE (agricultural economics, agronomy, and animal science), BIOLOGICAL SCIENCE (biology/biological science), BUSINESS (accounting and business administration and management), COMMUNICATIONS AND THE ARTS (art, English, music, Spanish, and speech/debate/rhetoric), COMPUTER AND PHYSICAL SCIENCE (chemistry, computer science, mathematics, and physics), EDUCATION (elementary, physical, secondary, and special), ENGINEERING AND ENVIRONMENTAL DESIGN (industrial engineering technology), SOCIAL SCIENCE (history, philosophy, psychology, religion, and sociology). Natural/physical science, education, and business are the strongest academically. Business and education are the largest.

Required: To graduate, students must complete 124 credits, including 32 in the major, with a GPA of 2.0. All students must fulfill general education requirements in the following areas: written and oral communication, aesthetics, history, society, natural sciences, technology and culture, and religion/beliefs/values. Students must also participate in an integrative seminar and a service experience, and must complete a global/intercultural experience, which may include intercultural studies courses or modern language courses.

Special: Cross-registration with other colleges is available through the Associated Colleges of Central Kansas. McPherson also offers internships, study abroad in 10 countries, credit by exam, a general studies degree, student-designed majors, and pass/fail options. There are preprofessional programs in health, engineering, law, forestry, veterinary medicine, nursing and medicine, optometry, and dentistry. There are 3 national honor societies, including Phi Beta Kappa, and 3 departmental honors programs.

Faculty/Classroom: 71% of faculty are male; 29%, female. All teach undergraduates. The average class size in an introductory lecture is 30; in a laboratory, 12; and in a regular course, 12.

Admissions: 85% of the 2005-2006 applicants were accepted. The SAT scores for the 2005-2006 freshman class were: Verbal--58% below 500, 25% between 500 and 599, and 17% between 600 and 700; Math--63% below 500, 21% between 500 and 599, 12% between 600 and 700, and 4% above 700. The ACT scores were 37% below 21, 31% between 21 and 23, 20% between 24 and 26, 6% between 27 and 28, and 8% above 28. 2 freshmen graduated first in their class.

Requirements: The SAT or ACT is required. In addition, the GED is accepted. A GPA of 2.0 is required. AP and CLEP credits are accepted. Important factors in the admissions decision are recommendations by school officials, evidence of special talent, and parents or siblings attending the school.

Procedure: Freshmen are admitted fall, winter, and spring. Entrance exams should be taken in the junior year. There is a deferred admissions plan. Application deadlines are open. Application fee is $25. Notification is sent on a rolling basis. Applications are accepted on-line.

Transfer: 60 transfer students enrolled in 2004-2005. Applicants must have satisfactorily completed 12 credit hours of college course work covering 3 academic areas with a 2.0 GPA. 32 of 124 credits required for the bachelor's degree must be completed at McPherson.

Visiting: There are regularly scheduled orientations for prospective students, consisting of campus tours, meetings with admissions personnel, and class attendance. There are guides for informal visits and visitors may stay overnight. To schedule a visit, contact the Admissions Office.

Financial Aid: In 2005-2006, 98% of all full-time freshmen and 95% of continuing full-time students received some form of financial aid. 87%

of full-time freshmen and 84% of continuing full-time students received need-based aid. The average freshman award was $16,265. Need-based scholarships or need-based grants averaged $5246; need-based self-help aid (loans and jobs) averaged $5034; and other non-need-based awards and non-need-based scholarships averaged $7833. The average financial indebtedness of the 2005 graduate was $18,010. The FAFSA is required. The priority date for freshman financial aid applications for fall entry is April 1.

International Students: There are 6 international students enrolled. They must score satisfactorily on the written TOEFL and also take the ACT, scoring 18.

Computers: All students may access the system. There are no time limits and no fees.

Graduates: From July 1, 2004 to June 30, 2005, 63 bachelor's degrees were awarded. The most popular majors were business/marketing (24%), arts (11%), and education (9%).

Admissions Contact: Carol Williams, Director of Admissions and Financial Aid. E-mail: *admiss@mcpherson.edu*
Web: *www.mcpherson.edu*

MIDAMERICA NAZARENE UNIVERSITY   F-2
Olathe, KS 66062-1899   (913) 791-3380
(800) 800-8887; Fax: (913) 791-3487

Full-time: 573 men, 625 women	**Faculty:** 75
Part-time: 84 men, 108 women	**Ph.D.s:** 47%
Graduate: 116 men, 273 women	**Student/Faculty:** 16 to 1
Year: semesters, summer session	**Tuition:** $14,754
Application Deadline: August 1	**Room & Board:** $5830
Freshman Class: n/av	
SAT: required	**ACT:** required

LESS COMPETITIVE

MidAmerica Nazarene University was founded in 1966 as a private liberal arts institution affiliated with the Church of the Nazarene. In addition to regional accreditation, MNU has baccalaureate program accreditation with ACBSP, NASM, and NLN. The library contains 120,520 volumes, 354,309 microform items, and 4640 audio/video tapes/CDs/DVDs, and subscribes to 225 periodicals including electronic. Computerized library services include the card catalog, interlibrary loans, database searching, Internet access, and laptop Internet portals. Special learning facilities include a learning resource center and radio station. The 105-acre campus is in a suburban area 19 miles southwest of downtown Kansas City, Missouri. Including any residence halls, there are 21 buildings.

Student Life: 66% of undergraduates are from Kansas. Others are from 38 states and 10 foreign countries. 88% are from public schools. 71% are white. 76% are Protestant; 15% claim no religious affiliation; 8% Catholic. The average age of freshmen is 18; all undergraduates, 24. 33% do not continue beyond their first year; 45% remain to graduate.

Housing: 752 students can be accommodated in college housing, which includes single-sex dormitories, on-campus apartments, and off-campus apartments. On-campus housing is guaranteed for all 4 years. 59% of students live on campus; of those, 75% remain on campus on weekends. Alcohol is not permitted. All students may keep cars.

Activities: There are no fraternities or sororities. There are 43 groups on campus, including agriculture, cheerleading, choir, chorus, computers, drama, ethnic, honors, international, jazz band, newspaper, orchestra, pep band, political, professional, psychology, radio and TV, religious, student government, writers, and yearbook. Popular campus events include Mr. MNU and Welcome Week.

Sports: There are 6 intercollegiate sports for men and 6 for women, and 6 intramural sports for men and 6 for women. Facilities include a weight room, a football stadium, a gym, a track, tennis and sand volleyball courts, and softball, baseball, and soccer fields.

Disabled Students: 90% of the campus is accessible. Wheelchair ramps, elevators, special parking, specially equipped rest rooms, special class scheduling, and lowered drinking fountains are available.

Services: Counseling and information services are available, as is tutoring in most subjects. There is a reader service for the blind, and remedial math, reading, and writing. There are also test-taking accommodations, interpreters for the hearing impaired, and note takers for the blind, hearing impaired, and learning disabled.

Campus Safety and Security: Measures include 24-hour foot and vehicle patrol, self-defense education, security escort services, and informal discussions. There are pamphlets/posters/films, emergency telephones, and lighted pathways/sidewalks.

Programs of Study: MNU confers B.A., B.M.Ed., and B.S.N. degrees. Associate and master's degrees are also awarded. Bachelor's degrees are awarded in AGRICULTURE (international agriculture), BIOLOGICAL SCIENCE (biology/biological science), BUSINESS (accounting, business administration and management, international business management, marketing/retailing/merchandising, and sports management), COMMUNICATIONS AND THE ARTS (communications, dramatic arts, English, graphic design, modern language, music, music performance, and Spanish), COMPUTER AND PHYSICAL SCIENCE (chemistry, computer science, mathematics, and physics), EDUCATION (athletic training, business, Christian, elementary, English, health, mathematics, music, physical, science, social studies, and speech correction), HEALTH PROFESSIONS (nursing), SOCIAL SCIENCE (criminal justice, history, ministries, missions, psychology, sociology, urban studies, and youth ministry). Management and human relations, elementary education, and business administration are the largest.

Required: All students must meet core curriculum requirements in humanities-communications, natural sciences-math, social sciences, religion-philosophy, and phys ed. Students must maintain a minimum GPA of 2.0 and complete 126 semester hours to graduate.

Special: MNU offers nondegree study, cross-registration with the Christian College Coalition, study abroad in 4 countries, internships, and a Washington semester. There are accelerated degree programs in management and human relations and in nursing. There is 1 national honor society and 4 departmental honors programs.

Faculty/Classroom: 62% of faculty are male; 38%, female. All teach undergraduates. No introductory courses are taught by graduate students. The average class size in an introductory lecture is 15; in a laboratory, 33; and in a regular course, 17.

Requirements: The SAT or ACT is required. Candidates for admission should be graduates of an accredited secondary school. The GED is accepted. Students should have completed 15 units of study, including 4 units of English and 3 each of natural science, social studies, and math. An essay is optional. AP and CLEP credits are accepted.

Procedure: Freshmen are admitted to all sessions. Entrance exams should be taken during the senior year. There is a rolling admissions plan. Applications should be filed by August 1 for fall entry and December 15 for winter entry, along with a $25 fee. Notification is sent on a rolling basis.

Transfer: 119 transfer students enrolled in 2004-2005. Transfer applicants should have earned 24 or more hours at an accredited institution and not be on academic or disciplinary probation. ACT or SAT scores are required. 30 of 126 credits required for the bachelor's degree must be completed at MNU.

Visiting: There are regularly scheduled orientations for prospective students, including an academic fair, advising, class visitation, informational meetings, social activities, and experiencing residential life. There are guides for informal visits and visitors may sit in on classes and stay overnight. To schedule a visit, contact the Office of Admissions.

Financial Aid: In 2005-2006, 99% of all full-time freshmen and 95% of continuing full-time students received some form of financial aid. 75% of full-time freshmen and 73% of continuing full-time students received need-based aid. The average freshman award was $12,555. Need-based scholarships or need-based grants averaged $6727 ($16,594 maximum); need-based self-help aid (loans and jobs) averaged $4271 ($7911 maximum); non-need-based athletic scholarships averaged $4438 ($12,377 maximum); and other non-need-based awards and non-need-based scholarships averaged $4018 ($10,987 maximum). Average annual earnings from campus work are $1201. The average financial indebtedness of the 2005 graduate was $15,111. The FAFSA and the college's own financial statement are required. The deadline for filing freshman financial aid applications for fall entry is March 1.

International Students: There are 25 international students enrolled. They must score satisfactorily on the written TOEFL and also take the ACT and/or the SAT if from a world area where English is the official first language. There are placement tests for incoming freshmen.

Computers: Wireless access is available. There are student PCs in dorm rooms, lab PCs in library and dorms; and additional labs available for specific majors. There is wireless network in all academic buildings, including the library. All students may access the system 7:30 A.M. to 11 P.M. Monday to Thursday and to 5 P.M. Friday; 10 A.M. for the library. Dorm rooms and dorm labs are available 24/7. There are no time limits. The fee is $200. It is recommended that students in OIS and MET have personal computers.

Graduates: From July 1, 2004 to June 30, 2005, 345 bachelor's degrees were awarded. In a recent year, the most popular majors were human resources management (38%), elementary education (8%), and business administration (7%). In an average class, 49% graduate in 6 years or less. 100 companies recruited on campus in a recent year.

Admissions Contact: Tammy Laird, Applicant Secretary. A video is available. E-mail: admissions@mnu.edu
Web: www.mnu.edu/admissions

NEWMAN UNIVERSITY D-3

Wichita, KS 67213
(316) 942-4291, ext. 144
(877) NEWMANU; Fax: (316) 942-4483

Full-time: 434 men, 689 women	**Faculty:** 76
Part-time: 241 men, 368 women	**Ph.D.s:** 55%
Graduate: 102 men, 269 women	**Student/Faculty:** 15 to 1
Year: semesters, summer session	**Tuition:** $15,822
Application Deadline: open	**Room & Board:** $5284
Freshman Class: 148 applied, 141 accepted, 137 enrolled	
SAT Verbal/Math: 600/500*	**ACT:** 23 COMPETITIVE

Newman University established in 1933, is a private, liberal arts institution affiliated with the Roman Catholic Church. There are 5 undergraduate schools and 1 graduate school. In addition to regional accreditation, NU has baccalaureate program accreditation with ACOTE, CAAHEP, CANEAP, CCNE, CoARC, CSWE, JRCERT, and NLN. The library contains 108,000 volumes, 134,000 microform items, and 2142 audio/video tapes/CDs/DVDs, and subscribes to 466 periodicals including electronic. Computerized library services include the card catalog, interlibrary loans, database searching, and Internet access. Special learning facilities include a learning resource center, art gallery, planetarium, and allied health and nursing labs. The 61-acre campus is in an urban area in Wichita west of downtown. Including any residence halls, there are 13 buildings.

Student Life: 87% of undergraduates are from Kansas. Others are from 25 states, 37 foreign countries, and Canada. 56% are from public schools. 75% are white. 59% are Protestant; 41% Catholic. The average age of freshmen is 18; all undergraduates, 25. 41% do not continue beyond their first year; 45% remain to graduate.

Housing: 259 students can be accommodated in college housing, which includes single-sex and coed dormitories, on-campus apartments, and married-student housing. On-campus housing is guaranteed for all 4 years. 89% of students commute. Alcohol is not permitted. All students may keep cars.

Activities: There are no fraternities or sororities. There are 39 groups on campus, including cheerleading, choir, chorale, computers, dance, drama, ethnic, forensics, honors, international, newspaper, political, professional, religious, social, social service, and student government. Popular campus events include Family Weekend, Take-off Week, and Midnight Madness.

Sports: There are 9 intercollegiate sports for men and 9 for women, and 3 intramural sports for men and 3 for women. Facilities include a baseball stadium, a softball stadium, a field for soccer and lacrosse, and a gym with 1 main basektball court, 2 side-by-side courts, 6 locker rooms, a weight room, an a erobics room, a training room, and athletic offices.

Disabled Students: All of the campus is accessible. Wheelchair ramps, elevators, special parking, specially equipped rest rooms, special class scheduling, lowered drinking fountains, and lowered telephones are available.

Services: Counseling and information services are available, as is tutoring in most subjects. There is remedial math and writing.

Campus Safety and Security: Measures include 24-hour foot and vehicle patrol, security escort services, informal discussions, and pamphlets/posters/films. There are emergency telephones and lighted pathways/sidewalks.

Programs of Study: NU confers B.A., B.S., B.B.A., and B.S.N. degrees. Associate and master's degrees are also awarded. Bachelor's degrees are awarded in BIOLOGICAL SCIENCE (biochemistry and biology/biological science), BUSINESS (accounting, banking and finance, business administration and management, management information systems, management science, and marketing and distribution), COMMUNICATIONS AND THE ARTS (art, communications, English, and music), COMPUTER AND PHYSICAL SCIENCE (chemistry, information sciences and systems, and mathematics), EDUCATION (elementary and secondary), ENGINEERING AND ENVIRONMENTAL DESIGN (preengineering), HEALTH PROFESSIONS (nursing, occupational therapy, physical therapy, predentistry, premedicine, preoptometry, prepharmacy, preveterinary science, and ultrasound technology), SOCIAL SCIENCE (counseling/psychology, criminal justice, history, liberal arts/general studies, pastoral studies, prelaw, psychology, sociology, and theological studies). Nursing, biology, and chemistry are the strongest academically. Nursing, business, and education are the largest.

Required: Degree requirements include completion of 124 credit hours, 30 of which must be upper division. The number of credits required in the major varies. A minimum GPA of 2.0 is required for graduation, and students must fulfill the college's liberal arts requirement, including courses in philosophy and theology.

Special: NU offers co-op programs in most majors through Friends University, internships, study abroad in Great Britain, the Netherlands, Ireland, and Italy, nondegree study, and dual majors. Course requirements for majors in counseling, business management, education, nursing, and liberal studies can be satisfied through evening and weekend classes. There are 3 national honor societies.

Faculty/Classroom: 48% of faculty are male; 52%, female. 85% teach undergraduates. No introductory courses are taught by graduate students. The average class size in a regular course is 11.

Admissions: 95% of the 2005-2006 applicants were accepted. The SAT scores for the 2005-2006 freshman class were: Verbal--45% below 500, 31% between 500 and 599, 17% between 600 and 700, and 7% above 700; Math--45% below 500, 41% between 500 and 599, 7% between 600 and 700, and 7% above 700. The ACT scores were 26% below 21, 33% between 21 and 23, 25% between 24 and 26, 7% between 27 and 28, and 9% above 28. 40% of the current freshmen were in the top fifth of their class; 68% were in the top two fifths.

Requirements: The SAT or ACT is required, of entering freshmen who have not been out of high school longer than 3 years, with a minimum composite score of 18 on the ACT. Candidates for admission must graduate from an accredited secondary school with 23 high school academic credits, including 4 credits of English and 3 each of math, science, and social studies. 2 credits of a foreign language are recommended. A GPA of 2.0 is required. AP and CLEP credits are accepted.

Procedure: Freshmen are admitted fall, spring, and summer. Entrance exams should be taken during the spring of the junior year or fall of the senior year. There are early admissions, deferred admissions, and rolling admissions plans. Application deadlines are open. Application fee is $20. Applications are accepted on-line.

Transfer: 303 transfer students enrolled in 2004-2005. A minimum GPA of 2.0 is required. 30 of 124 credits required for the bachelor's degree must be completed at NU.

Visiting: There are regularly scheduled orientations for prospective students, including meetings with faculty, athletic coaches, co-curricular sponsors, financial aid counselors, admissions counselors, and a campus tour. There are guides for informal visits and visitors may sit in on classes and stay overnight. To schedule a visit, contact the Admissions Office at (316) 942-4291, ext.2129.

Financial Aid: In 2005-2006, of all full-time freshmen and 96% of continuing full-time students received some form of financial aid. 58% of full-time freshmen and 75% of continuing full-time students received need-based aid. The average freshman award was $13,800. Need-based scholarships or need-based grants averaged $4360 ($11,450 maximum); need-based self-help aid (loans and jobs) averaged $2206 ($3610 maximum); non-need-based athletic scholarships averaged $2856 ($4300 maximum); and other non-need-based awards and non-need-based scholarships averaged $9684 ($24,966 maximum). 13% of undergraduates work part time. Average annual earnings from campus work are $600. The average financial indebtedness of the 2005 graduate was $18,939. The FAFSA and the college's own financial statement are required. The priority date for freshman financial aid applications for fall entry is March 1.

International Students: There are 150 to 170 international students enrolled. The school actively recruits these students. They must score satisfactorily on the written TOEFL or on the electronic version.

Computers: Wireless access is available. The student union is a wireless hot spot. 3 computer classroom labs are available, and an open computer lab is accessible in Student Support Services. All students may access the system. There are no time limits and no fees.

Graduates: From July 1, 2004 to June 30, 2005, 311 bachelor's degrees were awarded. The most popular majors were elementary education (23%), nursing (19%), and business management (10%). In an average class, 35% graduate in 4 years or less, and 45% graduate in 6 years or less. 20 companies recruited on campus in 2004-2005.

Admissions Contact: Jann Reusser, Admissions Secretary/Receptionist. E-mail: *admissions@newmanu.edu* Web: *www.newmanu.edu*

OTTAWA UNIVERSITY
Ottawa, KS 66067-3399

E-2

Full-time: 260 men, 190 women	**Faculty:** 21; IIB, --$
Part-time: 10 men, 15 women	**Ph.D.s:** 54%
Graduate: none	**Student/Faculty:** 20 to 1
Year: semesters, summer session	**Tuition:** $12,000
Application Deadline: open	**Room & Board:** n/app
Freshman Class: n/av	**ACT:** required
	LESS COMPETITIVE

(785) 242-5200, ext. 5555
(800) 755-5200,; Fax: (785) 229-1008

Ottawa University, founded in 1865 and affiliated with the American Baptist Churches, is a private institution offering programs through the divisions of arts and humanities, natural sciences, and social and behavioral sciences. Figures in the above capsule and in this profile are approximate. The library contains 90,000 volumes, and subscribes to 400 periodicals including electronic. Computerized library services include interlibrary loans and database searching. Special learning facilities include a learning resource center, art gallery, and radio station. The 64-acre campus is in a small town 45 miles southwest of Kansas City. Including any residence halls, there are 15 buildings.

Student Life: 55% of undergraduates are from Kansas. Others are from 18 states, 5 foreign countries, and Canada. 99% are from public schools.

77% are white; 11% African American. 64% are Protestant; 20% claim no religious affiliation; 13% Catholic. The average age of freshmen is 19; all undergraduates, 22. 25% do not continue beyond their first year; 30% remain to graduate.

Housing: 428 students can be accommodated in college housing, which includes single-sex dormitories, on-campus apartments, and married-student housing. On-campus housing is guaranteed for all 4 years. 58% of students live on campus; of those, 65% remain on campus on weekends. Alcohol is not permitted. All students may keep cars.

Activities: There are no fraternities or sororities. There are 35 groups on campus, including cheerleading, choir, chorale, chorus, computers, dance, debate, drama, ethnic, forensics, honors, international, jazz band, musical theater, newspaper, orchestra, pep band, photography, professional, radio and TV, religious, social, social service, student government, and yearbook. Popular campus events include Family Day, Charter Day, and Christmas Feast.

Sports: There are 7 intercollegiate sports for men and 7 for women, and 12 intramural sports for men and 12 for women. Facilities include a field, a sports complex, an athletic center, and a gym with a wellness center.

Disabled Students: 50% of the campus is accessible. Wheelchair ramps, elevators, special parking, specially equipped rest rooms, and special class scheduling are available.

Services: Counseling and information services are available, as is tutoring in most subjects. There is remedial math, reading, and writing.

Campus Safety and Security: Measures include self-defense education, security escort services, pamphlets/posters/films, and lighted pathways/sidewalks and a night security guard. In addition, students are issued individual residence hall security and room keys.

Programs of Study: OU confers the B.A. degree. Bachelor's degrees are awarded in BIOLOGICAL SCIENCE (biology/biological science), BUSINESS (accounting, business administration and management, and management information systems), COMMUNICATIONS AND THE ARTS (art, communications, dramatic arts, English, and music), COMPUTER AND PHYSICAL SCIENCE (chemistry, information sciences and systems, and mathematics), EDUCATION (elementary and physical), SOCIAL SCIENCE (history, human services, political science/government, psychology, religion, and sociology). English, business, and math are the strongest academically. Business, teacher education, and human services are the largest.

Required: To graduate, students must complete 9 courses in 8 academic areas with a minimum GPA of 2.0. The university requires students to complete 124 semester hours, with 24 to 40 in the major. Three interdisciplinary general education seminars must be completed. In addition, students must attend 10 University Program events each semester for 6 semesters.

Special: Internships are available, especially in business, human services, and teacher education. Student-designed majors are an option. 3/2 engineering degrees with Kansas state and the University of Kansas, 3 +1 degree in medical technology, and preprofessional programs in premedicine, predentistry, prelaw, and preministry are available. Work-study programs are also offered. There are 2 national honor societies.

Faculty/Classroom: 60% of faculty are male; 40%, female. All teach undergraduates. The average class size in a laboratory is 12.

Requirements: The ACT is required. The GED is accepted. There are no specific high school courses required, but a sound college preparatory curriculum is highly recommended. OU requires applicants to be in the upper 50% of their class. A GPA of 2.5 is required. AP and CLEP credits are accepted. Important factors in the admissions decision are parents or siblings attending the school, recommendations by alumni, and recommendations by school officials.

Procedure: Freshmen are admitted to all sessions. There is a rolling admissions plan. Entrance exams should be taken as early as possible. Application deadlines are open. The fall 2005 application fee was $15.

Transfer: Transfer applicants must submit transcripts from all colleges attended and must have a 2.0 GPA and 12 hours of college credit, or else they must meet freshman requirements. 30 of 124 credits required for the bachelor's degree must be completed at OU.

Visiting: There are regularly scheduled orientations for prospective students, including Discovery Day in the early spring, which gives prospective students a chance to meet faculty, students, and staff and to learn more about Ottawa University, the admissions process, and financial aid. There are guides for informal visits and visitors may sit in on classes and stay overnight. To schedule a visit, contact D'Nette Orr or Marikay Galutia of the Admissions Office at (913) 242-5200, ext. 5541, or (800) 755-5200.

Financial Aid: In a recent year, 99% of all full-time freshmen and 95% of continuing full-time students received some form of financial aid. 88% of full-time freshmen and 90% of continuing full-time students received need-based aid. The average freshman award was $12,800. 80% of undergraduates worked part time. Average annual earnings from campus work were $1500. The average financial indebtedness of a recent graduate was $12,000. The FAFSA and the college's own financial statement are required. Check with the school for current application deadlines.

International Students: The school actively recruits these students. They must score satisfactorily on the written TOEFL or take the MELAB.
Computers: All students may access the system. There are no time limits and no fees.
Graduates: In a recent year, 56 bachelor's degrees were awarded. The most popular majors were business administration (30%), elementary education (16%), and biology (12%). In an average class, 13% graduate in 4 years or less, 28% graduate in 5 years or less, and 30% graduate in 6 years or less. 53 companies recruited on campus in a recent year.
Admissions Contact: Tim Albers, Director of Admissions. A video is available. E-mail: admiss@ottawa.edu Web: www.ottawa.edu

PITTSBURG STATE UNIVERSITY F-3
Pittsburg, KS 66762

(620) 235-4251
(800) 854-PITT; Fax: (620) 235-6003

Full-time: 2653 men, 2480 women	Faculty: 291; IIA, --$
Part-time: 204 men, 206 women	Ph.D.s: 78%
Graduate: 381 men, 704 women	Student/Faculty: 18 to 1
Year: semesters, summer session	Tuition: $3562 ($10,444)
Application Deadline: open	Room & Board: $4550
Freshman Class: 1935 applied, 1738 accepted, 991 enrolled	
ACT: 22	COMPETITIVE

Pittsburg State University, founded in 1903, is a state-supported institution offering programs in arts and sciences, business, education, and technology. There are 4 undergraduate schools and 1 graduate school. In addition to regional accreditation, Pitt State has baccalaureate program accreditation with AACSB, ABET, CACREP, CCNE, CSWE, NASM, and NCATE. The 2 libraries contain 796,123 volumes, 848,212 microform items, and 1850 audio/video tapes/CDs/DVDs, and subscribe to 24,427 periodicals including electronic. Computerized library services include the card catalog, interlibrary loans, database searching, Internet access, and laptop Internet portals. Special learning facilities include a learning resource center, art gallery, planetarium, radio station, TV station, a dedicated channel on local cable television, Nature Reach, and Veterans Memorial Amphitheater. The 233-acre campus is in a small town 120 miles south of Kansas City. Including any residence halls, there are 34 buildings.
Student Life: 71% of undergraduates are from Kansas. Others are from 41 states and 37 foreign countries. 87% are white. The average age of freshmen is 19; all undergraduates, 22. 23% do not continue beyond their first year.
Housing: 1015 students can be accommodated in college housing, which includes coed dorms and married-student housing. On-campus housing is available on a first-come, first-served basis. 84% of students commute. Alcohol is not permitted. All students may keep cars.
Activities: 3% of men belong to 7 national fraternities; 3% of women belong to 3 national sororities. There are 140 groups on campus, including art, band, cheerleading, chess, choir, chorale, chorus, computers, dance, debate, drama, drill team, ethnic, film forensics, gay, honors, international, jazz band, literary magazine, marching band, newspaper, opera, orchestra, pep band, photography, political, professional, radio and TV, religious, social, social service, student government, symphony, and yearbook. Popular campus events include Greek Week, Multicultural Month, and Apple Day.
Sports: There are 6 intercollegiate sports for men and 5 for women, and 7 intramural sports for men and 7 for women. Facilities include a football stadium, indoor and outdoor tracks, a basketball arena, softball diamonds, a baseball field, a weight room, a dance studio, an Olympic-size pool, volleyball, racquetball, and badminton courts, indoor and outdoor tennis courts, and sand volleyball courts.
Disabled Students: 70% of the campus is accessible. Wheelchair ramps, elevators, special parking, specially equipped rest rooms, special class scheduling, lowered drinking fountains, and lowered telephones are available.
Services: Counseling and information services are available, as is tutoring in some subjects, including accounting, biology, chemistry, elementary education, English, modern language, math, music, computers, physics, psychology, reading/study, and writing. There are also counseling services, a learning center, and a writing center.
Campus Safety and Security: Measures include 24-hour foot and vehicle patrol, security escort services, informal discussions, and pamphlets/posters/films. There are emergency telephones, lighted pathways/sidewalks, crime prevention programs, and an engraving program for valuables.
Programs of Study: Pitt State confers B.A., B.S., B.A.S. Tech., B.B.A., B.F.A., B.Gen.Studies, B.M.Ed., B.Music, B.S.Ed., B.S.E.T., B.S.Med. Tech., B.S.N., and B.S.T. degrees. Associate and master's degrees are also awarded. Bachelor's degrees are awarded in AGRICULTURE (wood science), BIOLOGICAL SCIENCE (biology/biological science), BUSINESS (accounting, banking and finance, business administration and management, international business management, marketing management, and recreation and leisure services), COMMUNICATIONS AND THE ARTS (art, communications, English, French, music, and

Spanish), COMPUTER AND PHYSICAL SCIENCE (chemistry, computer science, information sciences and systems, mathematics, and physics), EDUCATION (art, elementary, English, foreign languages, mathematics, music, physical, psychology, science, social studies, technical, and vocational), ENGINEERING AND ENVIRONMENTAL DESIGN (automotive technology, commercial art, construction management, electrical/electronics engineering technology, engineering technology, graphic arts technology, mechanical engineering technology, and technological management), HEALTH PROFESSIONS (medical technology and nursing), SOCIAL SCIENCE (criminal justice, economics, family/consumer studies, geography, history, international studies, liberal arts/general studies, political science/government, psychology, social science, social work, and sociology). Education, business, and technology are the largest.
Required: To graduate, students must complete more than 124 semester hours, including 36 to 60 hours in the major, with a minimum GPA of 2.0. General education requirements total 45 to 54 hours (up to 54 for education majors) and include courses in English, speech, math, computer science, humanities, social and behavioral sciences, natural and physical sciences, producing and consuming, nutrition, and health/well-being.
Special: Co-op and work-study programs by arrangement, internships in psychology and social work and by arrangement elsewhere, a general studies degree, B.A.-B.S. degrees, dual majors, a 3-2 engineering degree with the University of Kansas and Kansas State University, credit by exam, nondegree study, student-designed majors, and pass/fail options are available. Pitt State has student exchange programs with 70 countries. There are 11 national honor societies, a freshman honors program, and 26 departmental honors programs.
Faculty/Classroom: 57% of faculty are male; 43%, female. The average class size in an introductory lecture is 34; in a laboratory, 14; and in a regular course, 20.
Admissions: 90% of the 2005-2006 applicants were accepted. The ACT scores for the 2005-2006 freshman class were: 40% below 21, 29% between 21 and 23, 20% between 24 and 26, 6% between 27 and 28, and 5% above 28. 36 freshmen graduated first in their class.
Requirements: The ACT is required. In addition, applicants must meet 1 of these 3 criteria: an ACT score of 21 or above, class rank in the top third, or a 2.0 GPA in the Kansas core curriculum (2.5 GPA for out-of-state students). Candidates may also be accepted through an exceptions window. The GED is accepted. A GPA of 2.0 is required. AP and CLEP credits are accepted. Important factors in the admissions decision are advanced placement or honor courses, geographic diversity, and ability to finance college education.
Procedure: Freshmen are admitted to all sessions. Entrance exams should be taken before or during the first semester of the freshman year of college. There is a rolling admissions plan. Application deadlines are open. The fall 2005 application fee was $30. Applications are accepted on-line.
Transfer: 539 transfer students enrolled in 2004-2005. Applicants must have 24 credit hours and a college GPA of 2.0 or else meet freshman admissions requirements. 30 of more than 124 credits required for the bachelor's degree must be completed at Pitt State.
Visiting: There are regularly scheduled orientations for prospective students. There are guides for informal visits and visitors may sit in on classes. To schedule a visit, contact the Admissions Office.
Financial Aid: In 2005-2006, 83% of all full-time freshmen and 84% of continuing full-time students received some form of financial aid. 52% of full-time freshmen and 54% of continuing full-time students received need-based aid. The average freshman award was $6487. Need-based scholarships or need-based grants averaged $3770; need-based self-help aid (loans and jobs) averaged $2611; non-need-based athletic scholarships averaged $3400; and other non-need-based awards and non-need-based scholarships averaged $1642. 27% of undergraduates work part time. The average financial indebtedness of the 2005 graduate was $10,761. The FAFSA is required. The priority date for freshman financial aid applications for fall entry is March 1.
International Students: There are 249 international students enrolled. The school actively recruits these students. A satisfactory score on the TOEFL is required. The SAT, ACT, or IELTS may be substituted for the TOEFL.
Computers: Wireless access and computer labs are available campuswide. All students may access the system. There are no time limits and no fees.
Graduates: From July 1, 2004 to June 30, 2005, 1081 bachelor's degrees were awarded. The most popular majors were education (18%), business/marketing (13%), and science technologies (12%).
Admissions Contact: Director of Admission and Enrollment Services. A video is available. E-mail: psuadmit@pittstate.edu Web: www.pittstate.edu

SOUTHWESTERN COLLEGE — D-3
Winfield, KS 67156-2499

(620) 229-6210
(800) 846-1543; Fax: (620) 229-6344

Full-time: 271 men, 298 women	**Faculty:** 46; IIB, --$
Part-time: 364 men, 330 women	**Ph.D.s:** 50%
Graduate: 57 men, 96 women	**Student/Faculty:** 12 to 1
Year: semesters, summer session	**Tuition:** $16,218
Application Deadline: August 1	**Room & Board:** $5258
Freshman Class: 285 applied, 268 accepted, 136 enrolled	
SAT Verbal/Math: 480/490*	**ACT:** 22 **COMPETITIVE**

Southwestern College, established in 1885, is a private institution affiliated with the Kansas West Conference of the United Methodist Church. In addition to regional accreditation, Southwestern has baccalaureate program accreditation with CSWE, NASM, NCATE, and NLN. The 3 libraries contain 60,967 volumes, 5712 microform items, and 4571 audio/video tapes/CDs/DVDs, and subscribe to 11,379 periodicals including electronic. Computerized library services include the card catalog, interlibrary loans, database searching, and Internet access. Special learning facilities include a learning resource center, art gallery, radio station, TV station, and biological field station. The 82-acre campus is in a small town 45 miles southeast of Wichita. Including any residence halls, there are 20 buildings.

Student Life: 70% of undergraduates are from Kansas. Others are from 36 states and 10 foreign countries. 65% are white. 68% are claim no religious affiliation; 17% Protestant. The average age of freshmen is 19; all undergraduates, 29. 31% do not continue beyond their first year; 51% remain to graduate.

Housing: 551 students can be accommodated in college housing, which includes single-sex and coed dorms, on-campus apartments, and married-student housing. In addition, there are honors houses. On-campus housing is guaranteed for the freshman year only and is available on a first-come, first-served basis. 70% of students commute. Alcohol is not permitted. All students may keep cars.

Activities: 4% of men and about 1% of women belong to 1 local and 1 national fraternity; 6% of women belong to 1 local and 1 national sorority. There are 28 groups on campus, including band, cheerleading, choir, chorus, dance, debate, drama, drill team, ethnic, film, forensics, honors, international, jazz band, literary magazine, musical theater, newspaper, orchestra, pep band, photography, political, professional, radio and TV, religious, social, social service, student government, and symphony. Popular campus events include Movie Nights, Spring Formal, and Kickback Day.

Sports: There are 7 intercollegiate sports for men and 8 for women, and 2 intramural sports for men and 2 for women. Facilities include a 2400-seat stadium, tennis and basketball courts, playing floors, exercise rooms, a gym, an indoor swimming pool, a running track, a soccer field, a weight room, and a Frisbee golf course.

Disabled Students: 80% of the campus is accessible. Wheelchair ramps, elevators, special parking, specially equipped rest rooms, special class scheduling, lowered drinking fountains, and lowered telephones are available.

Services: Counseling and information services are available, as is tutoring in every subject. There is remedial math, reading, and writing. A reader service is available for dyslexic students.

Campus Safety and Security: Measures include 24-hour foot and vehicle patrol, self-defense education, security escort services, and informal discussions. There are emergency telephones and lighted pathways/sidewalks.

Programs of Study: Southwestern confers B.A., B.S., B.B.A., B.G.S., B.L.S., B.Mus., B.Ph., and B.S.N. degrees. Master's degrees are also awarded. Bachelor's degrees are awarded in BIOLOGICAL SCIENCE (biochemistry, biology/biological science, and marine biology), BUSINESS (accounting, business administration and management, business communications, entrepreneurial studies, human resources, management information systems, management science, marketing management, nonprofit/public organization management, operations management, purchasing/inventory management, and sports management), COMMUNICATIONS AND THE ARTS (communications, dramatic arts, English, and music), COMPUTER AND PHYSICAL SCIENCE (chemistry, computer programming, computer science, digital arts/technology, mathematics, and physics), EDUCATION (athletic training, business, drama, early childhood, elementary, English, mathematics, music, physical, and science), ENGINEERING AND ENVIRONMENTAL DESIGN (computer technology and manufacturing technology), HEALTH PROFESSIONS (nursing), SOCIAL SCIENCE (criminal justice, history, liberal arts/general studies, pastoral studies, philosophy and religion, and psychology). Biology, education, and nursing are the strongest academically and have the largest enrollments.

Required: To graduate, students must earn 124 credits, fulfill all requirements of the major, and maintain a GPA of 2.0. Students must complete the integrative studies requirements.

Special: Southwestern offers internships in industry and social and civic agencies and a Washington semester through the Institute for Experiential Learning. Exchange programs are available through the University of Kansas. A music and theater dual major is available and other combinations or degrees are possible with approval from the Academic Affairs Committee. There is a 3-2 engineering degree program with Washington University in St. Louis. Work-study programs, an accelerated degree program in 9 majors, credit for life, military, and work experience, nondegree study, and pass/fail options are also available. There are 4 national honor societies, including Phi Beta Kappa, a freshman honors program, and 3 departmental honors programs.

Faculty/Classroom: 57% of faculty are male; 43%, female. All teach undergraduates. No introductory courses are taught by graduate students. The average class size in an introductory lecture is 39; in a laboratory, 10; and in a regular course, 13.

Admissions: 94% of the 2005-2006 applicants were accepted. The SAT scores for the 2005-2006 freshman class were: Verbal--58% below 500, 37% between 500 and 599, and 5% above 700; Math--58% below 500, 26% between 500 and 599, 11% between 600 and 700, and 5% above 700. The ACT scores were 37% below 21, 20% between 21 and 23, 26% between 24 and 26, 10% between 27 and 28, and 7% above 28. 32% of the current freshmen were in the top fifth of their class; 33% were in the top two fifths.

Requirements: The ACT is required and the SAT is recommended. In addition, all candidates for admission must graduate from an accredited secondary school with a specified college-bound curriculum. The GED is accepted and an essay is required. Interviews are recommended. A GPA of 2.5 is required. AP and CLEP credits are accepted.

Procedure: Freshmen are admitted fall, spring, and summer. There is a deferred admissions plan and a rolling admissions plan.. Applications should be filed by August 1 for fall entry and January 1 for spring entry, along with a $20 fee. Notification is sent on a rolling basis. Applications are accepted on-line.

Transfer: Applicants must have a college GPA of 2.0 and must submit an essay. 30 of 124 credits required for the bachelor's degree must be completed at Southwestern.

Visiting: There are regularly scheduled orientations for prospective students, including 4 Explore More events. There are guides for informal visits and visitors may sit in on classes and stay overnight. To schedule a visit, contact the Admissions Office at (620) 229-6236 or jcombs@sckans.edu.

Financial Aid: In 2005-2006, 99% of all full-time freshmen and 91% of continuing full-time students received some form of financial aid. 68% of all full-time students received need-based aid. The average freshman award was $13,937. Need-based scholarships or need-based grants averaged $2927 ($6300 maximum); need-based self-help aid (loans and jobs) averaged $4067 ($6625 maximum); non-need-based athletic scholarships averaged $2760 ($3000 maximum); other non-need-based awards and non-need-based scholarships averaged $6168 ($17,000 maximum); and outside private scholarships averaged $1466 ($7000 maximum). Average annual earnings from campus work are $700. The average financial indebtedness of the 2005 graduate was $15,206. The FAFSA and the college's own financial statement are required.

International Students: There are 36 international students enrolled. The school actively recruits these students. They must score satisfactorily on the TOEFL.

Computers: Wireless access is available. All students are provided laptops during their college career. All common areas of dorms, classrooms, and public access areas are wireless. Wired connections are in each dorm room - 1 port per pillow. Certain labs are available (computer science, publications) that have more powerful desktop computers installed for higher resource, media-rich applications. All students may access the system 24 hours a day, 7 days a week. There are no time limits and no fees.

Graduates: From July 1, 2004 to June 30, 2005, 347 bachelor's degrees were awarded. The most popular majors were business (57%), computer (15%), and nursing (8%). In an average class, 2% graduate in 3 years or less, 36% graduate in 4 years or less, 45% graduate in 5 years or less, and 52% graduate in 6 years or less. 15 companies recruited on campus in 2004-2005. Of the 2004 graduating class, 16% were enrolled in graduate school within 6 months of graduation and 90% were employed.

Admissions Contact: Todd Moore, Director of Admission. A video is available. E-mail: tmoore@sckans.edu Web: www.sckans.edu

STERLING COLLEGE

Sterling, KS 67579

D-3

(316) 278-4275
(800) 346-1017; Fax: (316) 278-4416

Full-time: 231 men, 202 women	**Faculty:** 40
Part-time: 32 men, 51 women	**Ph.D.s:** 50%
Graduate: none	**Student/Faculty:** 11 to 1
Year: 4-1-4	**Tuition:** $13,906
Application Deadline: open	**Room & Board:** $6086
Freshman Class: 541 applied, 305 accepted, 127 enrolled	
SAT Verbal/Math: 470/470*	**ACT:** 21*

COMPETITIVE

Sterling College, established in 1887, is a private liberal arts institution affiliated with the Presbyterian Church (U.S.A.), offering undergraduate curricula in 17 majors plus teacher preparation. The library contains 61,430 volumes, 2120 microfilm items, and 2125 audio/video tapes/CDs/DVDs, and subscribes to 846 periodicals including electronic. Computerized library services include the card catalog, interlibrary loans, database searching, and Internet access. Special learning facilities include a learning resource center, art gallery, radio station, TV station, a museum, and a theater. The 43-acre campus is in a rural area 70 miles northwest of Wichita. Including any residence halls, there are 19 buildings.

Student Life: 59% of undergraduates are from Kansas. Students are from 30 states, 5 foreign countries, and Canada. 85% are from public schools. 83% are white; 45% Hispanic. 74% are Protestant; 29% claim no religious affiliation; 6% Catholic. The average age of freshmen is 18; all undergraduates, 20. 35% do not continue beyond their first year; 45% remain to graduate.

Housing: 509 students can be accommodated in college housing, which includes single-sex dorms. On-campus housing is guaranteed for all 4 years. 80% of students live on campus; of those, 70% remain on campus on weekends. Alcohol is not permitted. All students may keep cars.

Activities: There are no fraternities or sororities. There are 23 groups on campus, including art, band, cheerleading, choir, chorus, debate, drama, ethnic, forensics, honors, international, jazz band, literary magazine, musical theater, newspaper, pep band, photography, political, professional, religious, social, social service, student government, and yearbook. Popular campus events include Habitat for Humanity Week, community picnic, and Missions and International Peacemaker Convocations/Events.

Sports: There are 6 intercollegiate sports for men and 6 for women, and 6 intramural sports for men and 6 for women. Facilities include a weight-training facility, exercise deck, swimming pool, track, football field and stadium, baseball diamond, soccer field, practice fields, basketball, handball, and tennis courts, sand volleyball, outdoor basketball, and horseshoe pits.

Disabled Students: 88% of the campus is accessible. Wheelchair ramps, elevators, special parking, specially equipped rest rooms, and special class scheduling are available.

Services: Counseling and information services are available, as is tutoring in every subject. There is remedial math, reading, and writing. Special accommodations are provided on an as-needed basis.

Campus Safety and Security: Measures include informal discussions, pamphlets/posters/films, lighted pathways/sidewalks, and evening and nighttime foot and vehicle patrol.

Programs of Study: Sterling confers B.A. and B.S. degrees. Bachelor's degrees are awarded in BIOLOGICAL SCIENCE (biology/biological science), BUSINESS (business administration and management), COMMUNICATIONS AND THE ARTS (art, communications, dramatic arts, English, and music), COMPUTER AND PHYSICAL SCIENCE (chemistry, computer science, and mathematics), EDUCATION (athletic training, elementary, and music), HEALTH PROFESSIONS (exercise science), SOCIAL SCIENCE (behavioral science, history, religious education, and theological studies). Biology, behavioral science, and education are the strongest academically. Biology, business administration, and exercise science are the largest.

Required: To graduate, students must complete 52 to 57 credits in a general education curriculum including writing, math, science, social science, philosophy, computers, fine arts, and religion. They must have an overall GPA of 2.0, with 2.5 in the major. A total of 124 credits must be earned, with 39 to 59 in the major. Chapel/convocation requirements must also be met.

Special: Sterling offers cross-registration with the Associated Colleges of Central Kansas and the Council of Christian Colleges and Universities. Internships are available in most majors, as is study abroad in 7 countries. A Washington semester and work-study programs are offered. Student-designed majors and a dual degree program in biology and medical technology with Wichita State University are possible. There are 3 national honor societies and a freshman honors program.

Faculty/Classroom: 63% of faculty are male; 37%, female. 98% teach undergraduates and 2% do research. The average class size in an introductory lecture is 30; in a laboratory, 20; and in a regular course, 15.

Admissions: 56% of the 2005-2006 applicants were accepted. The SAT scores for the 2005-2006 freshman class were: Verbal--62% below 500, 29% between 500 and 599, and 10% between 600 and 700; Math--67% below 500, 29% between 500 and 599, and 5% between 600 and 700. The ACT scores were 40% below 21, 28% between 21 and 23, 18% between 24 and 26, 6% between 27 and 28, and 8% above 28. 7 freshmen graduated first in their class.

Requirements: The SAT or ACT is required. In addition, applicants must graduate from an accredited secondary school or have a GED. An interview is recommended. A GPA of 2.2 is required. AP and CLEP credits are accepted. Important factors in the admissions decision are personality/intangible qualities, extracurricular activities record, and leadership record.

Procedure: Freshmen are admitted fall and spring. Entrance exams should be taken in the spring of the junior year. There is a early admissions plan. Application deadlines are open. Application fee is $25. Applications are accepted on-line.

Transfer: 67 transfer students enrolled in 2004-2005. Transfer students must have a minimum composite ACT score of 18 or a combined SAT I score of 860 if they have fewer than 12 hours of college credit; and a 2.2 GPA. 24 of 124 credits required for the bachelor's degree must be completed at Sterling.

Visiting: There are regularly scheduled orientations for prospective students, including visits with admissions, financial aid, current students, and faculty and campus and housing tours. There are guides for informal visits and visitors may sit in on classes and stay overnight. To schedule a visit, contact the Admissions Office at (620) 278-4314.

Financial Aid: In 2005-2006, 100% of all full-time freshmen and 98% of continuing full-time students received some form of financial aid. 86% of full-time freshmen and 82% of continuing full-time students received need-based aid. The average freshman award was $12,944. Need-based scholarships or need-based grants averaged $6296; need-based self-help aid (loans and jobs) averaged $2305; and non-need-based athletic scholarships averaged $15,528. 58% of undergraduates work part time. Average annual earnings from campus work are $1200. The average financial indebtedness of the 2005 graduate was $15,099. The FAFSA is required. The deadline for filing freshman financial aid applications for fall entry is April 1.

International Students: There are 6 international students enrolled. They must score satisfactorily on the written TOEFL or on the electronic version and also take the ACT or SAT.

Computers: Wireless access is available. Students can use the network throughout the campus classrooms, library, and residence halls. 2 residence halls and 3 classrooms have access to the wireless system. All students may access the system 16 hours per day in the library and academic buildings and 24 hours per day in residence halls. There are no time limits. The fee is $100.

Graduates: From July 1, 2004 to June 30, 2005, 80 bachelor's degrees were awarded. The most popular majors were elementary education (23%), business administration (10%), and biology (9%). In an average class, 39% graduate in 4 years or less, 44% graduate in 5 years or less, and 5% graduate in 6 years or less.

Admissions Contact: Dennis Dutton, VP for Enrollment Services. A video is available. E-mail: admissions@sterling.edu Web: www.sterling.edu

TABOR COLLEGE

Hillsboro, KS 67063

D-2

(620) 947-3121, ext. 1723
(800) TABOR-99; Fax: (620) 947-6276

Full-time: 266 men, 214 women	**Faculty:** 32; IIB, --$
Part-time: 35 men, 81 women	**Ph.D.s:** 70%
Graduate: 4 men, 4 women	**Student/Faculty:** 13 to 1
Year: 4-1-4	**Tuition:** $15,944
Application Deadline: see profile	**Room & Board:** $5670
Freshman Class: n/av	
ACT: required	

NONCOMPETITIVE

Tabor College, established in 1908, is a private liberal arts facility affiliated with the Mennonite Brethren Church. There are 2 undergraduate schools. Some figures in this capsule and profile are approximate. In addition to regional accreditation, Tabor has baccalaureate program accreditation with CSWE and NASM. The library contains 80,099 volumes, 435 microform items, and 1640 audio/video tapes/CDs/DVDs, and subscribes to 265 periodicals including electronic. Computerized library services include the card catalog, interlibrary loans, database searching, and Internet access. Special learning facilities include a learning resource center and a writing center. The 26-acre campus is in a rural area 50 miles north of Wichita. Including any residence halls, there are 28 buildings.

Student Life: 68% of undergraduates are from Kansas. Students are from 23 states, 5 foreign countries, and Canada. 90% are from public schools. 89% are white. 89% are Protestant; 6% unspecified. The average age of freshmen is 18; all undergraduates, 20. 10% do not continue beyond their first year; 87% remain to graduate.

Housing: 210 students can be accommodated in college housing, which includes single-sex dorms and off-campus apartments. On-campus housing is guaranteed for all 4 years. 78% of students live on campus; of those, 85% remain on campus on weekends. Alcohol is not permitted. All students may keep cars.

Activities: There are no fraternities or sororities. There are 18 groups on campus, including art, band, cheerleading, choir, chorale, chorus, computers, drama, drill team, ethnic, honors, international, jazz band, musical theater, newspaper, pep band, photography, political, religious, social service, student government, and yearbook. Popular campus events include Service Emphasis Week and Mission Emphasis Week.

Sports: There are 8 intercollegiate sports for men and 8 for women, and 10 intramural sports for men and 10 for women. Facilities include 4 lighted tennis courts, 2 racquetball courts, lighted football and baseball fields, several practice fields, a soccer field, a curbed metric all-weather track, a gym with 2 playing floors, a practice/intramural gym, an indoor soccer court, and aerobic exercise, athletic training, and weight rooms.

Disabled Students: 75% of the campus is accessible. Wheelchair ramps, elevators, special parking, specially equipped rest rooms, special class scheduling, lowered drinking fountains, and lowered telephones are available.

Services: Counseling and information services are available, as is tutoring in most subjects. Tutoring is available for most learning disabled students and for those on academic probation.

Campus Safety and Security: Measures include lighted pathways/sidewalks.

Programs of Study: Tabor confers B.A. and B.S. degrees. Associate degrees are also awarded. Bachelor's degrees are awarded in BIOLOGICAL SCIENCE (biology/biological science), BUSINESS (accounting, business administration and management, marketing/retailing/merchandising, and office supervision and management), COMMUNICATIONS AND THE ARTS (applied art, communications, English, graphic design, and music), COMPUTER AND PHYSICAL SCIENCE (chemistry, computer science, mathematics, and natural sciences), EDUCATION (athletic training, business, elementary, health, middle school, music, physical, science, secondary, and special), SOCIAL SCIENCE (biblical studies, history, humanities, international studies, ministries, philosophy, psychology, religion, social science, and sociology). The sciences are the strongest academically. Business and education are the largest.

Required: All students must complete 47 to 59 hours of general education courses including biblical and religious studies, history of diverse cultures, creative expression, natural and mathematical systems, values, social sciences, language, communication, computer literacy, physical fitness, and a college success seminar. A total of 124 credits, 16 of which must be in the major, with a minimum GPA of 2.0, is required in order to graduate.

Special: Cross-registration is offered with the Association of Colleges of Central Kansas. Study abroad in 5 countries is possible. Dual majors, student-designed majors, internships, a Washington semester for juniors or seniors, and pass/fail options are available, as is a 3-2 engineering degree with Wichita State University. An accelerated degree program in management organizational development and preprofessional curricula in allied health, law, and medicine are also offered. There is a freshman honors program.

Faculty/Classroom: 65% of faculty are male; 35%, female. All teach undergraduates. No introductory courses are taught by graduate students. The average class size in an introductory lecture is 32; in a laboratory, 12; and in a regular course, 20.

Requirements: The ACT is required. In addition, an essay is required and an interview is recommended. A GPA of 2.0 is required. AP and CLEP credits are accepted.

Procedure: Freshmen are admitted to all sessions. There is a rolling admissions plan. Entrance exams should be taken in October of the senior year. Notification is sent on a rolling basis. Applications are accepted online. Check with the school for current application deadlines.

Transfer: 47 transfer students enrolled in 2004-2005. A minimum 2.0 GPA is required and an interview is recommended. 33 of 124 credits required for the bachelor's degree must be completed at Tabor.

Visiting: There are regularly scheduled orientations for prospective students, including a tour, admissions interview, and faculty, class, and financial aid visits. If requested, an audition or tryout will be scheduled. There are guides for informal visits and visitors may sit in on classes and stay overnight. To schedule a visit, contact Admissions Counselors.

Financial Aid: In a recent year, All full-time students received some form of financial aid. 82% of full-time freshmen and 77% of continuing full-time students received need-based aid. The average freshman award was $5022. Need-based scholarships or need-based grants averaged $4488; and non-need-based athletic scholarships averaged $1672. 43% of undergraduates worked part time. Average annual earnings from campus work were $1000. The average financial indebtedness of a recent graduate was $17,914. The FAFSA, a federal income tax form, and W-2 forms are required. Check with the school for current application deadlines.

International Students: They must score satisfactory on the written TOEFL and also take the SAT or the ACT.

Computers: All students may access the system. There are no time limits and no fees.

Graduates: In a recent year, 101 bachelor's degrees were awarded. The most popular majors were business marketing (22%), philosophy, religion, theology (21%), and education (14%).

Admissions Contact: Rusty Allen, Director of Admissions.
E-mail: *admissions@.tabor.edu* Web: *www.tabor.edu*

UNIVERSITY OF KANSAS   E-2
Lawrence, KS 66045

(785) 864-3911
(888) 686-7323; Fax: (785) 864-5017

Full-time: 9133 men, 9554 women	**Faculty:** 1161; I, -$
Part-time: 1347 men, 1309 women	**Ph.D.s:** 95%
Graduate: 3325 men, 4237 women	**Student/Faculty:** 16 to 1
Year: semesters, summer session	**Tuition:** $5413 ($13,866)
Application Deadline: April 1	**Room & Board:** $5502
Freshman Class: 10,442 applied, 7228 accepted, 4269 enrolled	
ACT: 24	**VERY COMPETITIVE**

The University of Kansas, founded in 1866, is a public, comprehensive institution. Its undergraduate and graduate programs emphasize the liberal arts, business, fine arts, music, teacher preparation, journalism, engineering, architecture, social welfare, law, and health science, including pharmacy. Its medical center campus is located in Kansas City. There are 11 undergraduate and 3 graduate schools. In addition to regional accreditation, KU has baccalaureate program accreditation with AACN, AACSB, ABET, ACEJMC, ACPE, AOTA, APTA, CAAHEP, CSWE, NAAB, NAACLS, NASAD, NASM, and NCATE. The 12 libraries contain 4,039,645 volumes, 4,108,857 microform items, and 50,126 audio/video tapes/CDs/DVDs, and subscribe to 41,830 periodicals including electronic. Computerized library services include the card catalog, interlibrary loans, database searching, Internet access, and laptop Internet portals. Special learning facilities include a learning resource center, art gallery, natural history museum, radio station, TV station, observatory, film studio, space technology center, state-of-the-art performing arts center, art, natural history, classics, entomology, and invertebrate paleontology museums, organ recital hall, Robert J.Dole Institute of Politics and Hall Center for the Humanities. The 1100-acre campus is in a suburban area 40 miles west of Kansas City. Including any residence halls, there are 218 buildings.

Student Life: 73% of undergraduates are from Kansas. Others are from 49 states, 113 foreign countries, and Canada. 82% are white. The average age of freshmen is 18; all undergraduates, 21. 17% do not continue beyond their first year; 57% remain to graduate.

Housing: 5135 students can be accommodated in college housing, which includes single-sex and coed dorms, on-campus apartments, and married-student housing. In addition, there are honors houses, special interest floors, and 1 residence hall with a fine arts emphasis. On-campus housing is available on a first-come, first-served basis. 78% of students commute. Alcohol is not permitted. All students may keep cars.

Activities: 14% of men belong to 24 national fraternities; 17% of women belong to 17 national sororities. There are 400 groups on campus, including art, band, cheerleading, chess, choir, chorale, chorus, computers, dance, debate, drama, environmental, ethnic, film, gay, honors, international, jazz band, literary magazine, marching band, musical theater, newspaper, opera, orchestra, pep band, photography, political, professional, radio and TV, religious, social, social service, student government, symphony, and yearbook. Popular campus events include Holiday Vespers, music and theater presentations, and Rock Chalk Revue.

Sports: There are 7 intercollegiate sports for men and 11 for women, and 20 intramural sports for men and 20 for women. Facilities include a field house with an indoor track and basketball and volleyball courts; a 52,000-seat football stadium with an outdoor track; a sports pavilion with an indoor football field; a health and phys ed center housing 2 indoor pools, handball and racquetball courts, and gyms; baseball, lacrosse, ultimate, cricket, football, soccer, and rugby fields; tennis courts; a bowling alley; and a student recreation center containing an indoor climbing wall, a gym, a suspended jogging track, 2 racquetball courts, a free weight/cardiovascular gym area, and aerobic and martial arts rooms.

Disabled Students: 95% of the campus is accessible. Wheelchair ramps, elevators, special parking, specially equipped rest rooms, special class scheduling, lowered drinking fountains, and lowered telephones are available.

Services: Counseling and information services are available, as is tutoring in most subjects, including how-to sessions on study and organizational skills and a workshop. There is a reader service for the blind and remedial math. A writing center is available to students.

Campus Safety and Security: Measures include 24-hour foot and vehicle patrol, security escort services, shuttle buses, and informal discussions. There are pamphlets/posters/films, emergency telephones, and lighted pathways/sidewalks.

Programs of Study: KU confers B.A., B.S., B.A.E., B.Arch., B.F.A., B.G.S., B.M., B.M.E., B.S.E., B.S.N., and B.S.W. degrees. Master's and doctoral degrees are also awarded. Bachelor's degrees are awarded in AGRICULTURE (environmental studies), BIOLOGICAL SCIENCE (biochemistry, biology/biological science, microbiology, and molecular biology), BUSINESS (accounting, banking and finance, and business administration and management), COMMUNICATIONS AND THE ARTS (art, art history and appreciation, ceramic art and design, classical languages, dance, design, dramatic arts, East Asian languages and literature, english, French, German, Germanic languages and literature, industrial design, journalism, linguistics, metal/jewelry, music history and appreciation, music performance, music theory and composition, painting, printmaking, sculpture, Slavic languages, Spanish, speech/debate/rhetoric, theater design, and voice), COMPUTER AND PHYSICAL SCIENCE (astronomy, atmospheric sciences and meteorology, chemistry, computer science, geology, information sciences and systems, mathematics, and physics), EDUCATION (art, athletic training, elementary, middle school, music, and physical), ENGINEERING AND ENVIRON-MENTAL DESIGN (aeronautical engineering, architectural engineering, architecture, chemical engineering, civil engineering, computer engineering, electrical/electronics engineering, engineering physics, interior design, mechanical engineering, petroleum/natural gas engineering, and textile engineering), HEALTH PROFESSIONS (clinical science, community health work, cytotechnology, health, music therapy, nursing, occupational therapy, pharmacy, respiratory therapy, speech pathology/audiology, and sports medicine), SOCIAL SCIENCE (African American studies, African studies, American studies, anthropology, archeology, behavioral science, economics, European studies, geography, history, humanities, international studies, Latin American studies, philosophy, political science/government, psychology, public administration, religion, Russian and Slavic studies, social work, sociology, and women's studies). Business, pharmacy, and engineering are the strongest academically. Engineering, biological sciences, and psychology are the largest.

Required: To graduate with a B.A., B.S., or B.G.S. degree, all students must complete at least 124 credit hours, including 27 to 50 in the major, and maintain a GPA of at least 2.0. These, as well as curricula and distribution requirements, vary according to the school and the major. English composition and literature must be taken.

Special: Special academic programs include internships, study abroad in more than 50 countries, a Washington semester, and work-study programs with the university. A cooperative program in engineering is offered, as are B.A.-B.S. degrees in many combinations, interdisciplinary majors, and dual majors in any approved combination. General studies degrees are available in many areas, and student-designed majors are possible. Nondegree study and pass/fail options are offered. There are 12 national honor societies, including Phi Beta Kappa, and a freshman honors program.

Faculty/Classroom: 66% of faculty are male; 34%, female. 98% teach undergraduates, and all do research. Graduate students teach 18% of introductory courses. The average class size in a laboratory is 20 and in a regular course, 24.

Admissions: 69% of the 2005-2006 applicants were accepted. The ACT scores for the 2005-2006 freshman class were: 15% below 21, 27% between 21 and 23, 28% between 24 and 26, 13% between 27 and 28, and 17% above 28. 56% of the current freshmen were in the top fifth of their class; 87% were in the top two fifths. There were 57 National Merit finalists.

Requirements: The SAT or ACT is required. In addition, Kansas resident applicants must have a minimum 2.0 GPA in the qualified admissions college preparatory curriculum; or have an ACT composite score of 21 or a comparable SAT score; or rank in the top third of their high school class. College preparatory curriculum includes 4 units of English, 3 of college preparatory math, 3 of natural science (1 must be chemistry or physics), 3 of social sciences, and 1 of computer technology. 2 units of foreign language and 1 of fine or performing arts are recommended. Nonresidents have the same curriculum requirements but they must have a minimum GPA of 2.5; or an ACT composite score of 24 or a comparable SAT score with 2.0 GPA; or be on the top third of their high school class. AP and CLEP credits are accepted. Important factors in the admissions decision are advanced placement or honor courses, evidence of special talent, and recommendations by school officials.

Procedure: Freshmen are admitted to all sessions. Entrance exams should be taken by the end of the junior year. There is a deferred admissions plan. Applications should be filed by April 1 for fall entry, December 1 for spring entry, and February 1 for summer entry. The fall 2005 application fee was $30. Notification is sent on a rolling basis. 126 applicants were on the 2005 waiting list; 93 were admitted. Applications are accepted on-line.

Transfer: 1499 transfer students enrolled in 2004-2005. For entrance to the College of Liberal Arts and Sciences, transfer students must have at least 24 credit hours with a minimum GPA of 2.0 in state or 2.5 out of state. The criteria vary widely within the other KU schools, some of which may also consider the ACT score and course work. 30 of 124 credits required for the bachelor's degree must be completed at KU.

Visiting: There are regularly scheduled orientations for prospective students, consisting of a summer orientation program that includes a 1-day campus visit. There are guides for informal visits and visitors may sit in on classes and stay overnight. To schedule a visit, contact the KU Visitor Center at (785) 864-5135 or *visitku@ku.edu*.

Financial Aid: In 2005-2006, 47% of all full-time freshmen and 46% of continuing full-time students received some form of financial aid. 36% of all full-time students received need-based aid. The average freshman award was $5933. Need-based scholarships or need-based grants averaged $3752; need-based self-help aid (loans and jobs) averaged $2720; non-need-based athletic scholarships averaged $12,057; and other non-need-based awards and non-need-based scholarships averaged $2538. 18% of undergraduates work part time. Average annual earnings from campus work are $4160. The average financial indebtedness of the 2005 graduate was $17,243. The FAFSA is required. The deadline for filing freshman financial aid applications for fall entry is March 1.

International Students: There are 646 international students enrolled. The school actively recruits these students. Students must take the university's own test upon arrival. A high TOEFL score may be accepted in place of this test.

Computers: Wireless access is available. All students may access the system 24 hours a day, 7 days a week. There are no time limits and no fees.

Graduates: From July 1, 2004 to June 30, 2005, 3864 bachelor's degrees were awarded. The most popular majors were business (11%), psychology (8%), and journalism (7%). In an average class, 1% graduate in 3 years or less, 26% graduate in 4 years or less, 51% graduate in 5 years or less, and 57% graduate in 6 years or less. 500 companies recruited on campus in 2004-2005. Of a recent graduating class, 19% were enrolled in graduate school within 6 months of graduation and 46% were employed.

Admissions Contact: Lisa Pinamonti Kress, Director of Admissions and Scholarships. A video is available. E-mail: *adm@ku.edu* Web: *www.admissions.ku.edu*

UNIVERSITY OF SAINT MARY   F-2
Leavenworth, KS 66048
(913) 758-6165
(800) 752-7043; Fax: (913) 758-6140

Full-time: 210 men, 185 women	**Faculty:** 46
Part-time: 60 men, 135 women	**Ph.D.s:** 61%
Graduate: 20 men, 290 women	**Student/Faculty:** 8 to 1
Year: semesters, summer session	**Tuition:** $13,600
Application Deadline: open	**Room & Board:** $5300
Freshman Class: n/av	
SAT: required	**ACT:** required **COMPETITIVE**

The University of Saint Mary, founded in 1923, is a private liberal arts institution affiliated with the Roman Catholic Church and sponsored by the Sisters of Charity of Leavenworth. There is 1 graduate school. Figures in the above capsule and profile are approximate. In addition to regional accreditation, USM has baccalaureate program accreditation with NCATE and IACBE. The library contains 120,000 volumes and 1675 microform items, and subscribes to 301 periodicals including electronic. Computerized library services include the card catalog, interlibrary loans, database searching, and Internet access. Special learning facilities include a learning resource center, art gallery, and several special library collections. The 240-acre campus is in a small town 25 miles northwest of Kansas City, Missouri. Including any residence halls, there are 10 buildings.

Student Life: 75% of undergraduates are from Kansas. Students are from 31 states, 7 foreign countries, and Canada. 73% are white. The average age of freshmen is 18; all undergraduates, 26. 64% do not continue beyond their first year; 43% remain to graduate.

Housing: 333 students can be accommodated in college housing, which includes single-sex and coed dorms. On-campus housing is guaranteed for all 4 years. 62% of students commute. All students may keep cars.

Activities: There are no fraternities or sororities. There are 25 groups on campus, including art, cheerleading, choir, chorale, chorus, computers, dance, drama, honors, literary magazine, musical theater, newspaper, opera, political, professional, religious, social, social service, and student government. Popular campus events include Fall Convocation, Founders Day, and Family Weekend.

Sports: There are 4 intercollegiate sports for men and 4 for women, and 10 intramural sports for men and 10 for women. Facilities include a 500-seat sports center, soccer and softball fields, a multipurpose field, 3 tennis courts, a sandlot volleyball court, 2 racquetball courts, a weight and exercise room, a swimming pool, a dance and aerobics space, a walking trail, and an indoor jogging track.

Disabled Students: 90% of the campus is accessible. Wheelchair ramps, elevators, special parking, and specially equipped rest rooms are available.

Services: Counseling and information services are available, as is tutoring in most subjects.

Campus Safety and Security: Measures include self-defense education, informal discussions, pamphlets/posters/films, and lighted pathways/sidewalks. There are 14-hour foot and vehicle patrols, and controlled access to residence halls.

Programs of Study: USM confers B.A. and B.S. degrees. Associate and master's degrees are also awarded. Bachelor's degrees are awarded in BIOLOGICAL SCIENCE (biology/biological science), BUSINESS (accounting, business administration and management, business systems analysis, and sports management), COMMUNICATIONS AND THE ARTS (art, dramatic arts, and English), COMPUTER AND PHYSICAL SCIENCE (chemistry, information sciences and systems, and mathematics), EDUCATION (elementary), HEALTH PROFESSIONS (medical technology), SOCIAL SCIENCE (applied psychology, child psychology/development, history, interdisciplinary studies, international studies, liberal arts/general studies, pastoral studies, political science/government, psychology, sociology, and theological studies). Elementry education, business administration, and information sciences are the strongest academically.

Required: To graduate, students must complete all general education requirements and earn at least 128 credits, including 30 to 42 in the major, with a minimum GPA of 2.0. The core curriculum includes freshman humanities, colloquium in human communities, introduction to fine arts, and a senior integration project. Distribution requirements include 3 courses each in English, math, and natural science, and social and behavioral sciences, 2 courses each in theology, philosophy, history,and foreign language, plus an additional literature course, a fine arts course, a learning communities course, and an elective in arts. Completion of a writing portfolio is also required. Students must also fulfill cultural literacy and lifetime physical wellness requirements.

Special: The university offers study abroad at various locations in Europe, Latin America, or Austrailia. CLEP and credit for life experience, internships in most major programs, evening and weekend study programs, pass/fail option, and dual majors are also available. There are 2 national honor societies.

Faculty/Classroom: 45% of faculty are male; 55%, female. All teach undergraduates. The average class size in an introductory lecture is 25 and in a laboratory, 12.

Requirements: The SAT or ACT is required. In addition, applicants should be graduates of an accredited secondary school. The GED is accepted. A GPA of 2.5 is required. AP and CLEP credits are accepted. Important factors in the admissions decision are parents or siblings attending the school, recommendations by alumni, and recommendations by school officials.

Procedure: Freshmen are admitted fall and spring. Entrance exams should be taken in the spring of the junior year and fall of the senior year. There are early decision,early admissions and rolling admissions plans. Application deadlines are open. Application fee is $25.

Transfer: 54 transfer students enrolled in a recent year. A college GPA of 2.0 is required. 30 of 128 credits required for the bachelor's degree must be completed at USM.

Visiting: There are regularly scheduled orientations for prospective students, including interviews with faculty and financial aid representatives, and touring the campus. There are guides for informal visits and visitors may sit in on classes. To schedule a visit, contact the Admissions Office at (913) 682-5151 ext. 6118.

Financial Aid: In a recent year, 95% of all full-time freshmen received some form of financial aid. 85% of full-time freshmen and 65% of continuing full-time students received need-based aid. The average freshman award was $11,100. 27% of undergraduates worked part time. Average annual earnings from campus work were $627. The average financial indebtedness of a recent graduate was $15,000. USM is a member of CSS. The FAFSA is required. Check with the school for current application deadlines.

International Students: In a recent year, there were 11 international students enrolled. The school actively recruits these students. They must score satisfactorily on the written TOEFL or on the electronic version.

Computers: All students may access the system. There are no time limits and no fees. It is strongly recommended that all students have a personal computer. Incoming freshmen are issued laptops.

Admissions Contact: Judy Weidower, Director of Admissions. A video is available. E-mail: admiss@stmary.edu Web: www.stmary.edu

WASHBURN UNIVERSITY — E-2
Topeka, KS 66621

(785) 670-1030
(800) 332-0291; Fax: (785) 670-1048

Full-time: 1650 men, 2501 women	**Faculty:** 231; IIA, -$
Part-time: 791 men, 1482 women	**Ph.D.s:** 86%
Graduate: 375 men, 462 women	**Student/Faculty:** 18 to 1
Year: semesters, summer session	**Tuition:** $4982 ($11,192)
Application Deadline: August 1	**Room & Board:** $4752
Freshman Class: n/av	
ACT: required	**NONCOMPETITIVE**

Washburn University is a publicly funded, independently governed, state-coordinated university. Established in 1865, the school offers more than 190 programs leading to certification, associate, bachelor's, master's, and juris doctor degrees through the College of Arts and Sciences and the Schools of Law, Business, Nursing, and Applied Studies. There are 4 undergraduate and 5 graduate schools. In addition to regional accreditation, Washburn has baccalaureate program accreditation with ACS, APTA, CAAHEP, CAHEA, CSWE, NASAD, NASM, and NCATE. The 2 libraries contain 338,794 volumes, 578,828 microform items, and 18,018 audio/video tapes/CDs/DVDs, and subscribe to 9659 periodicals including electronic. Computerized library services include the card catalog, interlibrary loans, database searching, and Internet access. Special learning facilities include a learning resource center, art gallery, planetarium, and TV station. The 160-acre campus is in an urban area 60 miles west of Kansas City. Including any residence halls, there are 29 buildings.

Student Life: 94% of undergraduates are from Kansas. Students are from 40 states, 180 foreign countries, and Canada. 87% are from public schools. The average age of freshmen is 22; all undergraduates, 25. 30% do not continue beyond their first year; 65% remain to graduate.

Housing: 674 students can be accommodated in college housing, which includes coed dorms, on-campus apartments, fraternity houses, and sorority houses. In addition, there are special-interest houses. On-campus housing is available on a first-come, first-served basis. Priority is given to out-of-town students. 90% of students commute. Alcohol is not permitted. All students may keep cars.

Activities: 12% of men belong to 1 local fraternity and 3 national fraternities; 8% of women belong to 5 national sororities. There are 90 groups on campus, including art, band, campus activities board, cheerleading, chess, choir, chorus, computers, dance, debate, drama, drill team, drum and bugle corps, ethnic, forensics, gay, honors, international, jazz band, literary magazine, marching band, musical theater, newspaper, orchestra, peer educators, pep band, political, professional, radio and TV, religious, social, social service, student government, symphony, and yearbook. Popular campus events include Greek Week, Student Activities Fair, and the Annual Music Festival.

Sports: There are 6 intercollegiate sports for men and 6 for women, and 7 intramural sports for men and 7 for women. Facilities include a recreation and wellness center with rock-climbing wall, indoor track, gym, and cardiovascular and resistance training area, a 2700-seat field house for indoor sports, a 7200-seat stadium for intercollegiate football, and a health center with a 6-lane swimming pool.

Disabled Students: 95% of the campus is accessible. Wheelchair ramps, elevators, special parking, specially equipped rest rooms, special class scheduling, lowered drinking fountains, lowered telephones, special housing, note takers, readers, library assistance, recorders, reading machines, videotaped classes, oral tests, a learning center, tutors, and extended time for tests are available.

Services: Counseling and information services are available, as is tutoring in most subjects. There is a reader service for the blind and remedial math and writing.

Campus Safety and Security: Measures include 24-hour foot and vehicle patrol, self-defense education, security escort services, and informal discussions. There are pamphlets/posters/films, emergency telephones, lighted pathways/sidewalks, a whistle campaign, operation ID, a textbook ID program, a bicycle patrol, and fire safety programs for residential living facilities.

Programs of Study: Washburn confers B.A., B.S., B.A.S., B.B.A., B.Ed., B.F.A., B.H.S., B.I.S., B.M., B.P.A., B.S.C.J., B.S.N., and B.S.W. degrees. Associate, master's, and doctoral degrees are also awarded. Bachelor's degrees are awarded in BIOLOGICAL SCIENCE (biology/biological science), BUSINESS (accounting, banking and finance, business administration and management, business economics, and marketing/retailing/merchandising), COMMUNICATIONS AND THE ARTS (art, art history and appreciation, communications, dramatic arts, English, French, German, media arts, music, music performance, Spanish, speech/debate/rhetoric, and theater design), COMPUTER AND PHYSICAL SCIENCE (chemistry, computer programming, computer science, information sciences and systems, mathematics, physics, and science), EDUCATION (art, business, early childhood, education, elementary, music, physical, and secondary), ENGINEERING AND ENVIRONMENTAL DESIGN (technological management), HEALTH PROFESSIONS (medical laboratory technology and nursing), SOCIAL SCIENCE (anthropology, corrections, economics, history, human services, law enforcement and corrections, liberal arts/general studies, philosophy, political science/government, psychology, public administration, religion, social work, and sociology). Natural sciences, art, and music are the strongest academically. Business administration, criminal justice, and nursing are the largest.

Required: Students must complete courses in the arts and humanities, English composition, natural sciences, math, social sciences, and phys ed. A minimum GPA of 2.0 is required over 124 credit hours, including 30 to 40 in the major, for graduation.

Special: Washburn offers a co-op program in computer information science, engineering, social/behavioral sciences, education, and health profession, internships in numerous departments, and study abroad in 15 countries. Dual and student-designed majors, B.A.-B.S. degrees, an integrated studies degree, credit by exam, nondegree study, and pass/fail options are also available. A 3-2 engineering degree is possible in conjunction with the University of Kansas and Kansas State University. There are 9 national honor societies, a freshman honors program, and 22 departmental honors programs.

Faculty/Classroom: 53% of faculty are male; 47%, female. 91% teach undergraduates. No introductory courses are taught by graduate students. The average class size in an introductory lecture is 27; in a laboratory, 16; and in a regular course, 18.

Admissions: 34% of the current freshmen were in the top fifth of their class; 72% were in the top two fifths. 24 freshmen graduated first in their class.

Requirements: The ACT is required. In addition, applicants should be graduates of an accredited secondary school or have the GED. AP and CLEP credits are accepted.

Procedure: Freshmen are admitted to all sessions. Entrance exams should be taken during the junior year. There is a rolling admissions plan. Applications should be filed by August 1 for fall entry, January 3 for spring entry, and May 5 for summer entry. The fall 2005 application fee was $20. Notification is sent on a rolling basis. Applications are accepted on-line.

Transfer: 633 transfer students enrolled in 2004-2005. Applicants must meet the same requirements as incoming freshmen. 30 of 124 credits required for the bachelor's degree must be completed at Washburn.

Visiting: There are regularly scheduled orientations for prospective students, consisting of a campus visit program Monday through Friday at 9:30 A.M. or 1:30 P.M. that includes a tour, visits with faculty, financial aid information, and the opportunity to have all questions answered. There are guides for informal visits and visitors may sit in on classes and stay overnight. To schedule a visit, contact the Admissions Office.

Financial Aid: In 2004-2005, 59% of all full-time freshmen and 62% of continuing full-time students received some form of financial aid. 32% of full-time freshmen and 36% of continuing full-time students received need-based aid. The average freshman award was $5174. Need-based scholarships or need-based grants averaged $3179; need-based self-help aid (loans and jobs) averaged $2719; and other non-need-based awards and non-need-based scholarships averaged $2078. 8% of undergraduates work part time. Average annual earnings from campus work are $3700. The average financial indebtedness of the 2004 graduate was $13,125. Washburn is a member of CSS. The FAFSA and the admission/scholarship application are required. The priority date for freshman financial aid applications for fall entry is February 15. The deadline for filing freshman financial aid applications for fall entry is July 1.

International Students: There are 99 international students enrolled. The school actively recruits these students. A satisfactory score on the TOEFL is required.

Computers: Wireless access is available. All students may access the system 7 A.M. until midnight on campus; by dial-up, 24 hours a day. There are no time limits and no fees.

Graduates: From July 1, 2004 to June 30, 2005, 739 bachelor's degrees were awarded. The most popular majors were business (23%), nursing (12%), and criminal justice (12%). In an average class, 42% graduate in 4 years or less, 51% graduate in 5 years or less, and 60% graduate in 6 years or less. 90 companies recruited on campus in 2004-2005. Of the 2004 graduating class, 15% were enrolled in graduate school within 6 months of graduation and 98% were employed.

Admissions Contact: Kirk Haskins, Director of Admissions. E-mail: admissions@washburn.edu Web: www.washburn.edu

WICHITA STATE UNIVERSITY
D-3

Wichita, KS 67260

(316) 978-3085
(800) 362-2594; Fax: (316) 978-3174

Full-time: 3265 men, 4115 women	**Faculty:** 460; I, --$
Part-time: 1830 men, 2500 women	**Ph.D.s:** 78%
Graduate: 1470 men, 1740 women	**Student/Faculty:** 16 to 1
Year: semesters, summer session	**Tuition:** $3500 ($11,000)
Application Deadline: open	**Room & Board:** $5000
Freshman Class: n/av	
SAT or ACT: required	**COMPETITIVE**

Wichita State University, established in 1895, is a public institution offering programs in the liberal arts and sciences, business, engineering, education, and health professions. There are 6 undergraduate schools and 1 graduate school. Figures in the above capsule and profile are approximate. In addition to regional accreditation, WSU has baccalaureate program accreditation with AACSB, ABET, ADA, APTA, CAHEA, CSWE, NASM, NCATE, and NLN. The library contains 1,649,694 volumes, 1,135,688 microform items, and 31,442 audio/video tapes/CDs/DVDs, and subscribes to 17,545 periodicals including electronic. Computerized library services include the card catalog, interlibrary loans, database searching, and Internet access. Special learning facilities include a learning resource center, art gallery, natural history museum, radio station, TV station, electronic classroom, telecourses, the National Institute for Aviation Research, museum of art, and public observatory. The 330-acre campus is in an urban area in the metropolitan Wichita area. Including any residence halls, there are 61 buildings.

Student Life: 92% of undergraduates are from Kansas. Others are from 46 states, 81 foreign countries, and Canada. 69% are white. The average age of freshmen is 21; all undergraduates, 25. 29% do not continue beyond their first year; 37% remain to graduate.

Housing: 1236 students can be accommodated in college housing, which includes coed dormitories, on-campus apartments, married-student housing, fraternity houses, and sorority houses. In addition, there are honors houses. On-campus housing is available on a first-come, first-served basis. 90% of students commute. All students may keep cars.

Activities: 8% of men belong to 10 national fraternities; 5% of women belong to 8 national sororities. There are 99 groups on campus, including art, band, cheerleading, chess, choir, chorus, computers, dance, debate, drama, ethnic, film, gay, honors, international, jazz band, literary magazine, musical theater, newspaper, opera, orchestra, pep band, photography, political, professional, radio and TV, religious, social, social service, student government, and symphony. Popular campus events include Hippodrome, International Week, and Shocktoberfest.

Sports: There are 7 intercollegiate sports for men and 8 for women, and 24 intramural sports for men and 24 for women. Facilities include a 10,656-seat arena, 2 stadiums, an 18-hole golf course, a baseball field, a tennis complex, and a recreation and sports center.

Disabled Students: 98% of the campus is accessible. Wheelchair ramps, elevators, special parking, specially equipped rest rooms, special class scheduling, lowered drinking fountains, lowered telephones, and wheelchairs, and braille typewriters are available. Interpreters for the hearing impaired, note taking, and typing services are also offered.

Services: Counseling and information services are available, as is tutoring in most subjects. There is a reader service for the blind, and remedial math, reading, and writing. Group and individual psychological services are available for students and their families.

Campus Safety and Security: Measures include 24-hour foot and vehicle patrol, self-defense education, security escort services, and shuttle buses. There are informal discussions, pamphlets/posters/films, emergency telephones, lighted pathways/sidewalks, and a bicycle patrol.

Programs of Study: WSU confers B.A., B.S., B.A.E., B.B.A., B.F.A., B.G.S., B.H.S., B.M., B.M.E., B.S.A.E., B.S.E., B.S.E.E., B.S.I.E., B.S.M.E., and B.S.N. degrees. Associate, master's, and doctoral degrees are also awarded. Bachelor's degrees are awarded in BIOLOGICAL SCIENCE (biology/biological science), BUSINESS (accounting, banking and finance, business administration and management, entrepreneurial studies, human resources, international business management, management science, marketing/retailing/merchandising, and sports management), COMMUNICATIONS AND THE ARTS (art, art history and appreciation, communications, English, French, graphic design, Latin, music, Spanish, studio art, and visual and performing arts), COMPUTER AND PHYSICAL SCIENCE (chemistry, computer science, geology, mathematics, and physics), EDUCATION (art, elementary, music, physical, secondary, and special), ENGINEERING AND ENVIRONMENTAL DESIGN (aeronautical engineering, computer engineering, electrical/electronics engineering, industrial engineering, manufacturing engineering, and mechanical engineering), HEALTH PROFESSIONS (health care administration, medical laboratory technology, nursing, physician's assistant, and speech pathology/audiology), SOCIAL SCIENCE (anthropology, criminal justice, economics, ethnic studies, gerontology, history, liberal arts/general studies, philosophy, political science/government, psychology, social work, sociology, and women's studies). Physician's assistant, music theater, and speech pathology are the strongest academically. Management, nursing, and elementry education are the largest.

Required: To graduate, students need at least 124 credit hours, with a GPA of 2.0 to 2.5, depending on the major. Specific distribution requirements, as well as department requirements, must also be met. The core curriculum consists of 14 courses (42 hours) in general education.

Special: WSU offers co-op programs, internships, study abroad, work-study programs, and a Washington semester. Dual and student-designed majors, a general studies degree, credit by exam, nondegree study, and pass/fail options are also available. There are 14 national honor societies and a freshman honors program.

Faculty/Classroom: 63% of faculty are male; 37%, female. 85% both teach and do research. The average class size in an introductory lecture is 20; in a laboratory, 14; and in a regular course, 24.

Requirements: The SAT or ACT is required, rank in the top one third of their high school graduating class, and have a 2.0 GPA (nonresidents, 2.5). Requirements include 4 years of English, 3 each of math, natural and social sciences, and 1 of computer technology. AP and CLEP credits are accepted.

Procedure: Freshmen are admitted to all sessions. There are early admissions, deferred admissions and rolling admissions plans. Application deadlines are open. Applications are accepted on-line. The fall 2005 application fee was $30.

Transfer: 1304 transfer students enrolled in a recent year. Applicants must have a minimum GPA of 2.0 to 2.5, depending on the WSU college they wish to enter. 30 of 124 credits required for the bachelor's degree must be completed at WSU.

Visiting: There are regularly scheduled orientations for prospective students, Students may schedule their visit online through the school's web site. There are guides for informal visits and visitors may sit in on classes and stay overnight. To schedule a visit, contact the Admissions Office.

Financial Aid: The FAFSA is required. Check with the school for current application deadlines.

International Students: In a recent year, there were 556 international students enrolled. The school actively recruits these students. .

Computers: All students may access the system 24 hours a day. There are no fees.

Graduates: In a recent year, 1760 bachelor's degrees were awarded. The most popular majors were elementary education (7%), nursing (5%), and business administration (4%). In an average class, 11% graduate in 4 years or less, 28% graduate in 5 years or less, and 37% graduate in 6 years or less. 58 companies recruited on campus in a recent year. Of a recent graduating class, 21% were enrolled in graduate school within 6 months of graduation and 96% were employed.

Admissions Contact: Gina Crabtree, Director of Admissions. A video is available. E-mail: *admissions@wichita.edu*
Web: *http://www.wichita.edu*

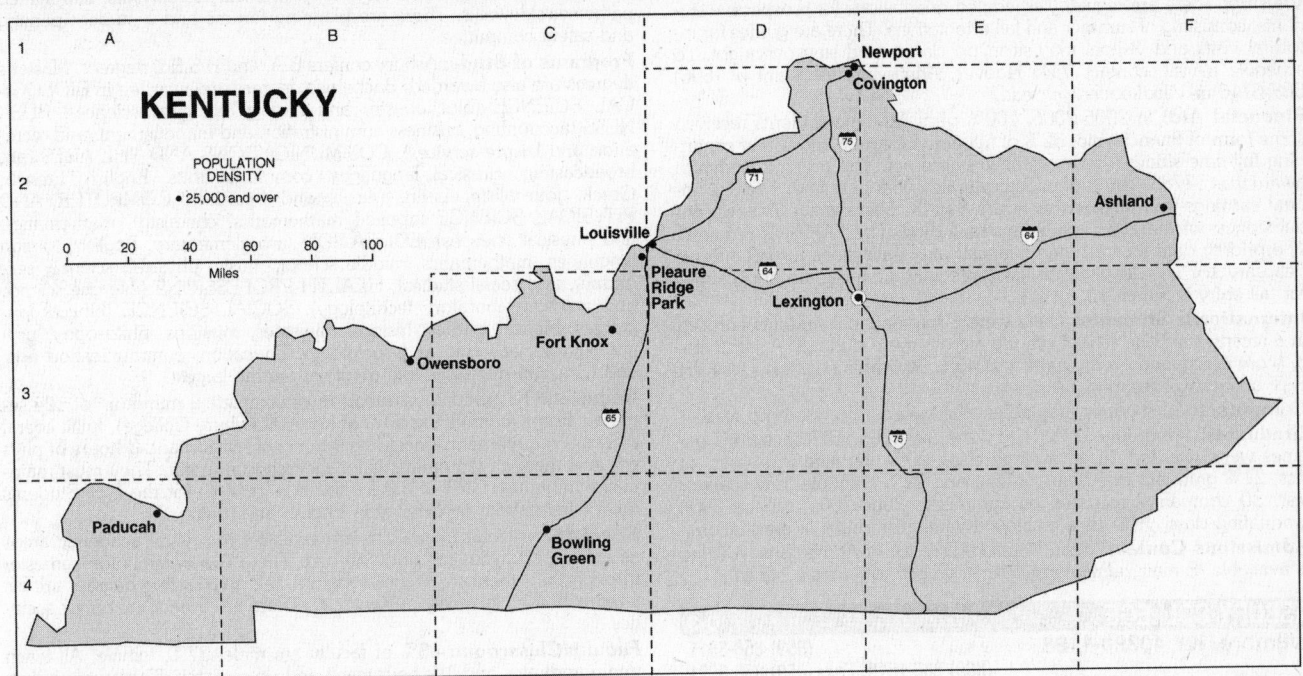

KENTUCKY

POPULATION
DENSITY
● 25,000 and over

0 20 40 60 80 100
Miles

ALICE LLOYD COLLEGE   E-4
Pippa Passes, KY 41844

(606) 368-6036, ext. 6134
(888) 280-4252; Fax: (606) 368-6215

Full-time: 281 men, 308 women

Part-time: 11 men, 12 women

Graduate: none

Year: semesters

Application Deadline: open

Freshman Class: n/av

ACT: 20

Faculty: 27

Ph.D.s: 65%

Student/Faculty: 22 to 1

Tuition: $1190 ($7550)

Room & Board: $3710

COMPETITIVE

Alice Lloyd College, founded in 1923, is a private liberal arts facility emphasizing Christian values and serving the Appalachian community. Within a 108-county area, which includes most of eastern Kentucky and parts of Ohio, Tennessee, West Virginia, and Virginia, annual fees are approximately $1,190, plus room and board; outside of this 108-county area, tuition and fees are approximately $7,500, plus room and board. Students within this service area receive the Appalachian Leaders College Scholarship, which covers the full cost of tuition. In addition to regional accreditation, ALC has baccalaureate program accreditation with NCATE. The library contains 62,000 volumes, 1500 microform items, and 300 audio/video tapes/CDs/DVDs, and subscribes to 300 periodicals including electronic. Computerized library services include the card catalog, interlibrary loans, database searching, and Internet access. Special learning facilities include a learning resource center, art gallery, radio station, TV station and a performing arts center. The 225-acre campus is in a rural area in the eastern part of the state. Including any residence halls, there are 38 buildings.

Student Life: 85% of undergraduates are from Kentucky. Others are from 7 states and 2 foreign countries. 90% are from public schools. 97% are white. The average age of freshmen is 18; all undergraduates, 20. 37% do not continue beyond their first year.

Housing: 451 students can be accommodated in college housing, which includes single-sex dorms. On-campus housing is guaranteed for all 4 years. Also available is a Caney Cottage scolarship program, which provides housing for students to continue their education after the undergraduate level .78% of students live on campus; of those, 35% remain on campus on weekends. Alcohol is not permitted. All students may keep cars.

Activities: There are no fraternities or sororities. There are 16 groups on campus, including art, cheerleading, choir, chorus, computers, drama, honors, newspaper, pep band, photography, professional, radio and TV, religious, social, student government, and yearbook. Popular campus events include Religious Emphasis Week, Alcohol Awareness Week, and Appalachia Day.

Sports: There are 5 intercollegiate sports for men and 5 for women, and 11 intramural sports for men and 11 for women. Facilities include an indoor pool, weight rooms, a 1500-seat gym, recreation areas, 2 tennis courts, a baseball/athletic field, and 2 racquetball courts.

Disabled Students: 95% of the campus is accessible. Wheelchair ramps, elevators, special parking, specially equipped rest rooms, and special class scheduling are available.

Services: Counseling and information services are available, as is tutoring in every subject. There is remedial math, reading, and writing.

Campus Safety and Security: Measures include 24-hour foot and vehicle patrol, self-defense education, security escort services, and informal discussions. There are pamphlets/posters/films, emergency telephones, and lighted pathways/sidewalks.

Programs of Study: ALC confers B.A. and B.S. degrees. Bachelor's degrees are awarded in BIOLOGICAL SCIENCE (biology/biological science), BUSINESS (business administration and management), COMMUNICATIONS AND THE ARTS (English), EDUCATION (elementary, middle school, physical, secondary, and social studies), ENGINEERING AND ENVIRONMENTAL DESIGN (preengineering), HEALTH PROFESSIONS (prepharmacy), SOCIAL SCIENCE (history). Biology, education, and business administration are the strongest academically. Biology is the largest.

Required: To graduate, students must complete a work-study requirement extending through each semester and a 49-semester-hour general education requirement, including phys ed, health, composition, philosophy, and speech. 128 credit hours are required. Students must maintain a 2.0 GPA (2.5 for education majors) to graduate. The number of hours required in the major varies.

Special: Special arrangements include a 2-2 engineering degree with the Universities of Kentucky, Louisville, and West Virginia. Credit by exam is possible. There is 1 national honor society, Phi Beta Kappa.

Faculty/Classroom: 74% of faculty are male; 26%, female. All teach undergraduates and 10% do research. The average class size in an introductory lecture is 25; in a laboratory, 12; and in a regular course, 17.

Admissions: The ACT scores for the 2005-2006 freshman class were: 48% below 21, 35% between 21 and 23, 13% between 24 and 26, 3% between 27 and 28, and 1% above 28. 50% of the current freshmen were in the top fifth of their class; 82% were in the top two fifths. 6 freshmen graduated first in their class.

Requirements: The SAT or ACT is required. In addition, applicants must be graduates of an accredited secondary school or have a GED, having successfully completed 12 academic credits, including 4 in English, 3 each in math and science, and 2 in social studies. A GPA of 2.25 is required. AP and CLEP credits are accepted. Important factors in the admissions decision are leadership record, recommendations by alumni, and recommendations by school officials.

Procedure: Freshmen are admitted fall and spring. Entrance exams should be taken in the fall of the senior year. There is a rolling admissions plan. Application deadlines are open. 31 applicants were on the 2005 waiting list; 22 were admitted. Applications are accepted on-line.

Transfer: 35 transfer students enrolled in 2004-2005. Applicants must have a minimum 2.0 GPA, 2.5 for some majors, be in good standing at their previous school, and have a minimum ACT score of 17. 30 of 128 credits required for the bachelor's degree must be completed at ALC.

Visiting: There are regularly scheduled orientations for prospective students, consisting of summer and fall orientations. There are guides for informal visits and visitors may sit in on classes and stay overnight. To schedule a visit, contact Vikki Hoover, Admissions Assistant at (606) 368-6146 or *Vikkihoover@alc.edu*.

Financial Aid: In 2005-2006, 100% of all full-time students received some form of financial aid. 52% of full-time freshmen and 4% of continuing full-time students received need-based aid. The average freshman award was $7783. 100% of undergraduates work part time. Average annual earnings from campus work are $1648. The average financial indebtedness of the 2005 graduate was $1060. The FAFSA is required. The priority date for freshman financial aid applications for fall entry is February 15. The deadline for filing freshman financial aid applications for fall entry is March 15.

International Students: There were 3 international students enrolled in a recent year. The school actively recruits these students. A satisfactory score is required on the written TOEFL. Aplicants must also take the SAT or the ACT, scoring 17.

Computers: All students may access the system. There are no fees.

Graduates: From July 1, 2004 to June 30, 2005, 107 bachelor's degrees were awarded. In an average class, 20% graduate in 4 years or less, 21% graduate in 5 years or less, and 22% graduate in 6 years or less. 30 companies recruited on campus in 2004-2005. Of the 2004 graduating class, 96% were employed within 6 months of graduation.

Admissions Contact: Sean Damron, Director of Admissions. A video is available. E-mail: *admissions@alicelloyd.edu* Web: *www.alc.edu*

ASBURY COLLEGE   D-3
Wilmore, KY 40390-1198

	(859) 858-3511
	(800) 888-1818; Fax: (859) 858-3921
Full-time: 464 men, 660 women	Faculty: 88; IIB, --$
Part-time: 44 men, 61 women	Ph.D.s: 75%
Graduate: 22 men, 42 women	Student/Faculty: 13 to 1
Year: semesters, summer session	Tuition: $18,956
Application Deadline: open	Room & Board: $4806
Freshman Class: 797 applied, 589 accepted, 277 enrolled	
SAT Verbal/Math: 593/560*	ACT: 24 VERY COMPETITIVE

Asbury College, founded in 1890, is an independent nondenominational liberal arts institution. In addition to regional accreditation, Asbury has baccalaureate program accreditation with CSWE, NASM, and NCATE. The library contains 145,913 volumes, 22,845 microform items, and 9197 audio/video tapes/CDs/DVDs, and subscribes to 517 periodicals including electronic. Computerized library services include the card catalog, interlibrary loans, database searching, and Internet access. Special learning facilities include a learning resource center, art gallery, radio station, TV station, and media and fine arts centers. The 65-acre campus is in a small town 20 miles south of Lexington. Including any residence halls, there are 30 buildings.

Student Life: 66% of undergraduates are from out of state, mostly the South. Students are from 47 states, 11 foreign countries, and Canada. 67% are from public schools. 95% are white. 93% are Protestant; 6% claim no religious affiliation. The average age of freshmen is 18; all undergraduates, 20. 20% do not continue beyond their first year; 69% remain to graduate.

Housing: 1255 students can be accommodated in college housing, which includes single-sex dorms, on-campus apartments, off-campus apartments, and married-student housing. In addition, there are language houses and leadership development/community service houses. On-campus housing is guaranteed for all 4 years. 84% of students live on campus; of those, 75% remain on campus on weekends. Alcohol is not permitted. Upperclassmen may keep cars.

Activities: There are no fraternities or sororities. There are 42 groups on campus, including art, band, choir, chorale, chorus, computers, debate, drama, ethnic, film, forensics, honors, international, jazz band, literary magazine, missionary, musical theater, newspaper, opera, orchestra, political, radio and TV, religious, social service, student government, and yearbook. Popular campus events include Parents Weekend, Artists Series, and Jym Jamboree.

Sports: There are 6 intercollegiate sports for men and 7 for women, and 10 intramural sports for men and 10 for women. Facilities include a 1,500-seat gym, athletic fields, tennis courts, an indoor swimming pool, and indoor/outdoor basketball courts.

Disabled Students: 80% of the campus is accessible. Wheelchair ramps, elevators, special parking, specially equipped rest rooms, special class scheduling, lowered drinking fountains, and lowered telephones are available.

Services: Counseling and information services are available, as is tutoring in most subjects. There is remedial writing. For students on academic probation, there are mentors who provide help in such areas as time

management and test-taking skills. There is some help available for the visually impaired, such as tapes and agencies that offer aid.

Campus Safety and Security: Measures include 24-hour foot and vehicle patrol, security escort services, pamphlets/posters/films, and lighted pathways/sidewalks. There are planning forums and a student parking and safety committee.

Programs of Study: Asbury confers B.A. and B.S.Ed. degrees. Master's degrees are also awarded. Bachelor's degrees are awarded in BIOLOGICAL SCIENCE (biochemistry and biology/biological science), BUSINESS (accounting, business administration and management, and recreation and leisure services), COMMUNICATIONS AND THE ARTS (art, broadcasting, classical languages, communications, English, French, Greek, journalism, Latin, music, and Spanish), COMPUTER AND PHYSICAL SCIENCE (applied mathematics, chemistry, mathematics, and physical sciences), EDUCATION (art, elementary, English, foreign languages, mathematics, middle school, music, physical, science, secondary, and social studies), HEALTH PROFESSIONS (exercise science and medical laboratory technology), SOCIAL SCIENCE (biblical languages, biblical studies, history, ministries, missions, philosophy, psychology, social work, and sociology). Education, communication arts, and Christian ministries and theology are the largest.

Required: To graduate, students must complete a minimum of 124 semester hours (completing 50% of hours at Asbury College), fulfill liberal arts core requirements (including 9 hours of religion and 3 hours of phys ed) and meet all requirements for their chosen major. They must maintain a minimum GPA of 2.0 for the B.A. or 2.75 for the B.S. Students must demonstrate proficiency in English and math.

Special: For-credit internships are available in several academic areas as are opportunities for study abroad. There is a Washington semester through the American Studies Program. 3-2 engineering degrees are offered with the University of Kentucky. There are 6 national honor societies.

Faculty/Classroom: 63% of faculty are male; 37%, female. All teach undergraduates and 1% both teach and do research. The average class size in an introductory lecture is 22; in a laboratory, 15; and in a regular course, 12.

Admissions: 74% of the 2005-2006 applicants were accepted. The SAT scores for the 2005-2006 freshman class were: Verbal--17% below 500, 32% between 500 and 599, 35% between 600 and 700, and 16% above 700; Math--22% below 500, 37% between 500 and 599, 33% between 600 and 700, and 8% above 700. The ACT scores were 21% below 21, 27% between 21 and 23, 19% between 24 and 26, 13% between 27 and 28, and 19% above 28. 61% of the current freshmen were in the top fifth of their class; 77% were in the top two fifths. There were 7 National Merit finalists. 20 freshmen graduated first in their class.

Requirements: The SAT or ACT is required for all new students and for transfer students with fewer than 30 college credit hours. In addition, an official high school transcript or the GED is required. Applicants should have completed 15 high school academic credits, including 4 units of English, 3 of math, and 2 each of lab science, social studies, and a foreign language. A GPA of 2.5 is required. AP and CLEP credits are accepted.

Procedure: Freshmen are admitted to all sessions. Entrance exams should be taken in the junior year or in the first semester of the senior year. There are early admissions and deferred admissions plans. There is a rolling admission plan. Application deadlines are open. Application fee is $30. Notification is sent on a rolling basis. A waiting list is an active part of the admissions procedure. Applications are accepted on-line.

Transfer: 65 transfer students enrolled in 2004-2005. Applicants with 12 quarter hours or 8 semester hours of college work or more are considered transfers. They must have an overall minimum GPA of 2.5 and be in good standing at each previous institution attended. Transfers with fewer than 30 semester hours of college work must submit a high school transcript. 49 of 124 hours required for the bachelor's degree must be completed at Asbury if they are transferred from a 4-year college (64 hours if from a 2-year or unaccredited institution).

Visiting: There are regularly scheduled orientations for prospective students, including visits, scheduled individually or during planned visitation weekends, in which students stay overnight in dorms, visit classes, attend departmental open houses and financial aid sessions, and participate in chapel and campus events. There are guides for informal visits and visitors may sit in on classes and stay overnight. To schedule a visit, contact the Admissions Office at (859) 858-3511, ext. 2374.

Financial Aid: In 2004-2005, 72% of all full-time freshmen and 71% of continuing full-time students received some form of financial aid. 72% of full-time freshmen and 70% of continuing full-time students received need-based aid. The average freshman award was $13,644. Need-based scholarships or need-based grants averaged $7937; need-based self-help aid (loans and jobs) averaged $4195; and other non-need-based awards and non-need-based scholarships averaged $10,856. 58% of undergraduates work part time. Average annual earnings from campus work are $1210. The average financial indebtedness of the 2004 graduate was $18,972. The FAFSA and the college's own financial statement are required. The priority date for freshman financial aid applications for fall entry is March 1. The deadline for filing freshman financial aid applications for fall entry is May 1.

International Students: There are 16 international students enrolled. They must achieve a satisfactory score on the TOEFL and also take the SAT or the ACT.

Computers: Wireless access is available. High-speed Internet connections are available in all dorms, and e-mail accounts are provided for all students. There are 189 computers for use in classrooms, computer labs, the student center, and the library. All students may access the system. There are no time limits and no fees. It is strongly recommended that all students have a personal computer.

Graduates: From July 1, 2004 to June 30, 2005, 294 bachelor's degrees were awarded. The most popular majors were media communication (35%), applied communication (24%), and psychology (20%). In an average class, 1% graduate in 3 years or less, 61% graduate in 4 years or less, 69% graduate in 5 years or less, and 69% graduate in 6 years or less.

Admissions Contact: Ronald Anderson, Director of Admissions and Director of Financial Aid. A video is available.
E-mail: *admissions@asbury.edu* Web: *www.asbury.edu*

BELLARMINE UNIVERSITY   D-2

Louisville, KY 40205

(502) 452-8131
(800) 274-4723; Fax: (502) 452-8002

Full-time: 602 men, 1135 women	Faculty: 106; IIA, -$
Part-time: 100 men, 167 women	Ph.D.s: 80%
Graduate: 177 men, 367 women	Student/Faculty: 16 to 1
Year: semesters, summer session	Tuition: $21,500
Application Deadline: February 1	Room & Board: $6150
Freshman Class: 2024 applied, 1427 accepted, 431 enrolled	
SAT Verbal/Math: 551/552*	ACT: 24	COMPETITIVE+

Bellarmine University, founded in 1950, is a private liberal arts institution affiliated with the Roman Catholic Church. There are 4 undergraduate and 3 graduate schools. In addition to regional accreditation, Bellarmine has baccalaureate program accreditation with AACSB, NCATE, and NLN. The library contains 117,421 volumes, 693,875 microform items, and 4835 audio/video tapes/CDs/DVDs, and subscribes to 547 periodicals including electronic. Computerized library services include the card catalog, interlibrary loans, and database searching. Special learning facilities include a learning resource center, art gallery, and the Thomas Merton Center, a collection of works by and about Thomas Merton. The 135-acre campus is in a suburban area in Louisville. Including any residence halls, there are 28 buildings.

Student Life: 78% of undergraduates are from Kentucky. Students are from 32 states, 15 foreign countries, and Canada. 56% are from public schools. 79% are white. 42% are Catholic; 37% Muslim, Hindu, other; 20% Protestant; 17% claim no religious affiliation. The average age of freshmen is 18; all undergraduates, 22. 16% do not continue beyond their first year; 64% remain to graduate.

Housing: 725 students can be accommodated in college housing, which includes single-sex and coed dorms and off-campus apartments. On-campus housing is guaranteed for all 4 years. 64% of students commute. Alcohol is not permitted. All students may keep cars.

Activities: 2% of men and about 3% of women belong to 3 national fraternities; 2% of women belong to 1 national sorority. There are 61 groups on campus, including art, band, cheerleading, chess, choir, chorale, chorus, computers, dance, debate, drama, ethnic, gay, honors, international, jazz band, literary magazine, mock trial team, musical theater, newspaper, opera, pep band, photography, political, professional, radio and TV, religious, social, social service, student government, wind ensemble, and yearbook. Popular campus events include Hillside Concerts, Midnight Breakfast, and Family Weekend.

Sports: There are 9 intercollegiate sports for men and 10 for women, and 8 intramural sports for men and 8 for women. Facilities include a basketball arena, weight rooms, indoor and outdoor tennis courts, a par 3 golf course, exercise and aerobics rooms in residence halls, a track, and softball, baseball, field hockey and soccer fields.

Disabled Students: 85% of the campus is accessible. Wheelchair ramps, elevators, special parking, specially equipped rest rooms, special class scheduling, lowered drinking fountains, lowered telephones, and special housing are available.

Services: Counseling and information services are available, as is tutoring in every subject. The Academic Resource Center provides one-on-one or group tutoring for all 100- and 200-level courses. Disability Services provides notetakers, distraction-reduced testing environments, extended time, books on tape, and scribe services.

Campus Safety and Security: Measures include 24-hour foot and vehicle patrol, self-defense education, security escort services, and shuttle buses. There are informal discussions, pamphlets/posters/films, emergency telephones, lighted pathways/sidewalks, 24-hour locked residence halls, security alert bulletins, CPR-certified security, and security cameras in residence halls and in the parking lot.

Programs of Study: Bellarmine confers B.A., B.S., and B.H.S. degrees. Master's degrees are also awarded. Bachelor's degrees are awarded in BIOLOGICAL SCIENCE (biology/biological science), BUSINESS (accounting, business administration and management, and international business management), COMMUNICATIONS AND THE ARTS (art, arts administration/management, communications, English, and music), COMPUTER AND PHYSICAL SCIENCE (actuarial science, chemistry, computer science, information science and systems, and mathematics), EDUCATION (elementary, middle school, secondary, and special), ENGINEERING AND ENVIRONMENTAL DESIGN (computer engineering and preengineering), HEALTH PROFESSIONS (cytotechnology, medical technology, nursing, physical therapy, predentistry, premedicine, prepharmacy, preveterinary science, and respiratory therapy), SOCIAL SCIENCE (criminal justice, economics, history, international studies, liberal arts/general studies, philosophy, political science/government, prelaw, psychology, sociology, and theological studies). Premedicine, accounting, and business are the strongest academically. Accounting, business, and nursing are the largest.

Required: To graduate, students must complete a minimum of 126 credit hours with a minimum GPA of 2.0. Between 24 and 51 hours are required in the major. All students must fulfill 49 credit hours of core requirements, including English, philosophy, theology, math, social sciences, natural sciences, fine arts, Western civilization, American experience, transcultural experience, and freshman and senior seminars. Students in the honors program must complete a senior honors thesis.

Special: Cross-registration may be arranged through Kentuckiana Metroversity, a consortium of colleges in Kentucky and southern Indiana. Bellarmine also offers study abroad in more than 43 countries, internships in most majors, a Washington semester, a liberal studies degree, dual majors, accelerated degree programs, credit for life experience, pass/fail options during the junior and senior years, and a marine biology program in the Bahamas. There is also an honors program and the Brown Leadership Program. There are 5 national honor societies and a freshman honors program.

Faculty/Classroom: 53% of faculty are male; 47%, female. 94% teach undergraduates, 70% do research, and 70% do both. No introductory courses are taught by graduate students. The average class size in an introductory lecture is 25; in a laboratory, 18; and in a regular course, 19.

Admissions: 71% of the 2005-2006 applicants were accepted. The SAT scores for the 2005-2006 freshman class were: Verbal--26% below 500, 49% between 500 and 599, 19% between 600 and 700, and 6% above 700; Math--20% below 500, 48% between 500 and 599, 27% between 600 and 700, and 3% above 700. The ACT scores were 20% below 21, 32% between 21 and 23, 28% between 24 and 26, 12% between 27 and 28, and 10% above 28. 43% of the current freshmen were in the top fifth of their class; 71% were in the top two fifths. There was 1 National Merit finalist.

Requirements: The SAT or ACT is required. In addition, applicants should have a minimum high school GPA of 2.0. The GED is accepted. High school courses should include 4 years of English, 3 years of math, and 2 years each of science and social studies. An essay is required. A GPA of 2.0 is required. AP and CLEP credits are accepted. Important factors in the admissions decision are advanced placement or honor courses, extracurricular activities record, and recommendations by school officials.

Procedure: Freshmen are admitted to all sessions. Entrance exams should be taken by December of the senior year. There is a deferred admissions plan. Applications should be filed by February 1 for fall entry, along with a $25 fee. Notification is sent on a rolling basis. Applications are accepted on-line.

Transfer: 80 transfer students enrolled in a recent year. Applicants should have a minimum college GPA of 2.0 and submit high school transcripts from all postsecondary schools attended. 36 of 126 credits required for the bachelor's degree must be completed at Bellarmine.

Visiting: There are regularly scheduled orientations for prospective students, including an admissions and financial aid session, a campus tour, interviews with faculty, and participation in a student panel. There are guides for informal visits and visitors may sit in on classes and stay overnight. To schedule a visit, contact the Office of Admission.

Financial Aid: In 2005-2006, 100% of all full-time freshmen and 97% of continuing full-time students received some form of financial aid. 43% of full-time freshmen and 46% of continuing full-time students received need-based aid. The average freshman award was $18,463. Need-based scholarships or need-based grants averaged $4550 ($11,500 maximum); need-based self-help aid (loans and jobs) averaged $3898 ($8625 maximum); non-need-based athletic scholarships averaged $2186 ($11,340 maximum); and other non-need-based awards and non-need-based scholarships averaged $16,659 ($30,931 maximum). 90% of undergraduates work part time. Average annual earnings from campus work are $1571. The average financial indebtedness of the 2005 graduate was $12,263. The FAFSA is required. The priority date for freshman financial aid applications for fall entry is March 1. The deadline for filing freshman financial aid applications for fall entry is May 1.

International Students: There are 37 international students enrolled. The school actively recruits these students. A satisfactory score is required on the written TOEFL.

Computers: All students may access the system. There are no time limits. The fee is $250 per full-time semester.

Graduates: From July 1, 2004 to June 30, 2005, 413 bachelor's degrees were awarded. The most popular majors were nursing (21%), general business (10%), and liberal studies (8%). In an average class, 1% graduate in 3 years or less, 46% graduate in 4 years or less, 59% graduate in 5 years or less, and 62% graduate in 6 years or less. 35 companies recruited on campus in a recent year. Of the recent year's graduating class, 15% were enrolled in graduate school within 6 months of graduation and 90% were employed.

Admissions Contact: Timothy Sturgeon, Dean of Admission. E-mail: *admissions@bellarmine.edu* Web: *http://www.bellarmine.edu*

BEREA COLLEGE
Berea, KY 40404

D-3

(859) 985-3500
(800) 326-5948; Fax: (859) 985-3512

Full-time: 617 men, 912 women	Faculty: 130; IIB, av$
Part-time: 39 men, 27 women	Ph.D.s: 91%
Graduate: none	Student/Faculty: 12 to 1
Year: 4-1-4, summer session	Tuition: $516 (fee)
Application Deadline: open	Room & Board: $4980
Freshman Class: 1908 applied, 511 accepted, 378 enrolled	
SAT Verbal/Math: 565/550*	ACT: 23* VERY COMPETITIVE+

Berea College, founded in 1855, is a private liberal arts institution. Berea combines college, federal, and state grants, as well as outside scholarships earned by students, to provide every admitted student with a 4-year, full-tuition scholarship. Therefore, no student pays tuition at Berea College. The college provides a laptop for every student; students are expected to pay $300 to offset the cost of networking and other related expenses, and the laptop becomes the property of the student at graduation. As part of these scholarship agreements, each student is expected to perform some of the labor required in maintaining the institution while carrying a normal academic load. For participation in the student labor program, each student is credited with a labor grant that is incorporated into the full-tuition scholarship. Room, board, and fees are assessed on a sliding scale according to how much each family can afford. Enrollment figures include both degree- and nondegree-seeking students. In addition to regional accreditation, Berea has baccalaureate program accreditation with ADA, NCATE, and NLN. The library contains 331,406 print volumes with 42,501 e-books, 133,230 microform items, and 10,491 audio/video tapes/CDs/DVDs, and subscribes to 1508 periodicals including electronic. Computerized library services include the card catalog, interlibrary loans, database searching, and Internet access. Special learning facilities include a learning resource center, art gallery, planetarium, and a geology museum. The 140-acre campus is in a small town 40 miles south of Lexington. Including any residence halls, there are 58 buildings.

Student Life: 64% of undergraduates are from out of state, mostly the South. Students are from 41 states and 67 foreign countries. 69% are white; 19% African American. The average age of freshmen is 18; all undergraduates, 20. 18% do not continue beyond their first year; 62% remain to graduate.

Housing: 1416 students can be accommodated in college housing, which includes single-sex dorms, on-campus apartments, and married-student housing. In addition, there are special-interest houses and a single-parent house. On-campus housing is guaranteed for all 4 years. 84% of students live on campus. Alcohol is not permitted.

Activities: There are no fraternities or sororities. There are 70 groups on campus, including art, band, cheerleading, chess, choir, chorus, dance, debate, drama, ethnic, gay, honors, international, jazz band, literary magazine, newspaper, orchestra, pep band, photography, political, professional, religious, social, social service, student government, and yearbook. Popular campus events include Mountain Day and Labor Day.

Sports: There are 9 intercollegiate sports for men and 8 for women, and 78 intramural sports for men and 78 for women. Facilities include 2 gyms, an indoor swimming pool, 5 racquetball courts, 15 tennis courts, playing fields, a dance studio, a 3-lane indoor walking track, an 8-lane all-weather track, and weight training and cardiovascular exercise rooms.

Disabled Students: 50% of the campus is accessible. Wheelchair ramps, elevators, special parking, specially equipped rest rooms, special class scheduling, lowered drinking fountains, lowered telephones, electronic doors, and a lift chair for the indoor pool are available.

Services: Counseling and information services are available, as is tutoring in some subjects. There is a reader service for the blind, and remedial math, reading, and writing. The Learning Center offers individual consultation in writing, reading, listening, speaking, learning strategies and styles, and study skills. Berea's tutorial labs assist with study skills, project development, homework assignments, clarification of concepts, skills development, and software application.

Campus Safety and Security: Measures include 24-hour foot and vehicle patrol, self-defense education, security escort services, and informal discussions. There are pamphlets/posters/films, emergency telephones, lighted pathways/sidewalks, and Berea has ongoing programs on campus safety, theft prevention, assault and rape prevention, fire prevention, defensive driving, and occupational safety, including work with hazardous materials.

Programs of Study: Berea confers B.A. and B.S. degrees. Bachelor's degrees are awarded in AGRICULTURE (agriculture), BIOLOGICAL SCIENCE (biology/biological science), BUSINESS (business administration and management), COMMUNICATIONS AND THE ARTS (art, classical languages, dramatic arts, English, French, German, industrial design, music, Spanish, and speech/debate/rhetoric), COMPUTER AND PHYSICAL SCIENCE (chemistry, mathematics, and physics), EDUCATION (art, early childhood, elementary, foreign languages, home economics, middle school, music, physical, and secondary), ENGINEERING AND ENVIRONMENTAL DESIGN (industrial engineering technology), HEALTH PROFESSIONS (nursing and speech pathology/audiology), SOCIAL SCIENCE (child care/child and family studies, dietetics, economics, history, philosophy, political science/government, psychology, religion, sociology, and women's studies). Business administration and child and family studies are the largest.

Required: Students must complete a 15-course general education program, including courses in wellness, cultural studies, arts, Western traditions, recent world issues, contemporary Christianity, quantitative reasoning, and natural and social sciences, and courses emphasizing reading and written communication. 3 short-term (January) courses are required. All students will be automatically enrolled in a one-quarter-credit convocation course during each of their regular terms of enrollment, with the exception of the final term of enrollment, for a maximum of 8 such terms. To graduate, students must complete 33 courses, including 8 to 12 in the major, with a minimum GPA of 2.0 overall and in the major. Nursing majors must complete 35 courses.

Special: Students may study abroad in many countries. Internships, work-study programs, dual degrees, independent and team-initiated studies, and dual and student-designed majors are available. A 3-2 engineering degree is offered with Washington University and the University of Kentucky. All students participate in an on-campus work program 10 to 15 hours per week. There are 17 national honor societies.

Faculty/Classroom: 59% of faculty are male; 41%, female. All teach undergraduates. The average class size in a laboratory is 20 and in a regular course, 20.

Admissions: 27% of the 2005-2006 applicants were accepted. The SAT scores for the 2005-2006 freshman class were: Verbal--18% below 500, 40% between 500 and 599, 33% between 600 and 700, and 9% above 700; Math--20% below 500, 48% between 500 and 599, 27% between 600 and 700, and 5% above 700. The ACT scores were 22% below 21, 35% between 21 and 23, 29% between 24 and 26, 9% between 27 and 28, and 5% above 28. 55% of the current freshmen were in the top fifth of their class; 83% were in the top two fifths. 11 freshmen graduated first in their class.

Requirements: The SAT or ACT is required. In addition, applicants should be graduates of an accredited secondary school. The GED is accepted. Homeschooled students are also encouraged to apply. Financial need is a requirement for admission. Berea recommends that applicants present as part of their high school record 4 units in English, 3 in math, and 2 each in science and social studies. Work in a foreign language is highly desirable. AP and CLEP credits are accepted. Important factors in the admissions decision are ability to finance college education, geographic diversity, and advanced placement or honor courses.

Procedure: Freshmen are admitted fall and spring. Entrance exams should be taken late in the junior year or early in the senior year. There is a rolling admissions plan. Application deadlines are open. Applications are accepted on-line.

Transfer: 84 transfer students enrolled in 2004-2005. Applicants must be in good standing at the last college attended and have a minimum GPA of 2.4. 8 of 33 credits required for the bachelor's degree must be completed at Berea.

Visiting: There are regularly scheduled orientations for prospective students, consisting of welcome, admissions, and student and residence life sessions, departmental visits, a campus tour, a musical performance, and lunch. There are guides for informal visits and visitors may sit in on classes and stay overnight. To schedule a visit, contact Sarah Boggs, Campus Visit Coordinator at (800) 326-5948 or (859) 985-3500 or *sarah_boggs@berea.edu*.

Financial Aid: In 2005-2006, of all full-time students received some form of financial aid and need-based aid. The average freshman award was $27,511. Need-based scholarships or need-based grants averaged $26,190; and need-based self-help aid (loans and jobs) averaged $1321. All of undergraduates work part time. Average annual earnings from campus work are $2248. The average financial indebtedness of the 2005 graduate was $7299. The FAFSA is required. The deadline for filing freshman financial aid applications for fall entry is April 1.

International Students: There are 109 international students enrolled. They must score satisfactorily on the TOEFL.

Computers: Wireless access is available. There is campus-wide network with computer access in residence halls, classrooms, the library, and other campus locations. Students integrate the use of computer technology with their learning, work, and social experiences. All students receive a labtop computer. At the end of the third year, students turn in their labtops for new models and keep them after graduation. All students may access the system 24 hours a day, 7 days a week. There are no time limits. The fee is $150 per semester.

Graduates: From July 1, 2004 to June 30, 2005, 314 bachelor's degrees were awarded. The most popular majors were business administration (11%), industrial/manufacturing (9%), and child and family studies (8%). In an average class, 35% graduate in 4 years or less, 60% graduate in 5 years or less, and 62% graduate in 6 years or less. 80 companies recruited on campus in 2004-2005.

Admissions Contact: Jamie Ealy, Director of Admissions.
E-mail: *jamie_ealy@berea.edu* Web: *www.berea.edu*

BRESCIA UNIVERSITY
B-3

Owensboro, KY 42301 — (270) 686-4241; Fax: (270) 686-4314

Full-time: 200 men, 340 women	Faculty: 43; IIB, --$
Part-time: 105 men, 165 women	Ph.D.s: 70%
Graduate: 15 men, 25 women	Student/Faculty: 12 to 1
Year: semesters, summer session	Tuition: $9850
Application Deadline: open	Room & Board: $4390
Freshman Class: n/av	
SAT or ACT: required	COMPETITIVE

Brescia University, founded in 1925 as a women's junior college, became a 4-year, coeducational liberal arts institution in 1950. It is a private school affiliated with the Roman Catholic Church. The university offers certificates, associate, baccalaureate, and master's degrees through semester and weekend classes. Figures in the above capsule and profile are approximate. The library contains 183,406 volumes, 364,553 microform items, and 6580 audio/video tapes/CDs/DVDs, and subscribes to 5334 periodicals including electronic. Computerized library services include the card catalog, interlibrary loans, and database searching. Special learning facilities include a learning resource center and art gallery. The 6-acre campus is in an urban area 32 miles southeast of Evansville, Indiana, and 125 miles from both Louisville and Nashville. Including any residence halls, there are 14 buildings.

Student Life: 78% of undergraduates are from Kentucky. Others are from 18 states, 18 foreign countries, and Canada. 89% are white. 39% are Catholic; 32% Protestant; 27% claim no religious affiliation. The average age of freshmen is 20; all undergraduates, 30. 33% do not continue beyond their first year.

Housing: 224 students can be accommodated in college housing, which includes single-sex and coed dormitories and on-campus apartments. On-campus housing is available on a first-come, first-served basis. 73% of students commute. Alcohol is not permitted. All students may keep cars.

Activities: There are no fraternities or sororities. There are 23 groups on campus, including choir, chorus, computers, creative writing, drama, honors, international, literary magazine, newspaper, philosophy, professional, religious, social, social service, student government, and yearbook. Popular campus events include Family Weekend, Opening Year Mass, and Inaugural Ball.

Sports: There are 4 intercollegiate sports for men and 5 for women, and 11 intramural sports for men and 11 for women. Facilities include 2 tennis courts, a gym, a weight room, a game room, a cardiovascular workout room, a racquetball court, a batting cage, and a baseball field.

Disabled Students: 95% of the campus is accessible. Wheelchair ramps, elevators, special parking, specially equipped rest rooms, lowered drinking fountains, and lowered telephones are available.

Services: Counseling and information services are available, as is tutoring in most subjects. There is remedial math, reading, and writing.

Campus Safety and Security: Measures include security escort services, informal discussions, emergency telephones, lighted pathways/sidewalks, and night security.

Programs of Study: Brescia confers B.A., B.S., and B.S.W. degrees. Associate and master's degrees are also awarded. Bachelor's degrees are awarded in BIOLOGICAL SCIENCE (biology/biological science), BUSINESS (accounting, banking and finance, business administration and management, business economics, and human resources), COMMUNICATIONS AND THE ARTS (art, English, and graphic design), COMPUTER AND PHYSICAL SCIENCE (chemistry, computer science, mathematics, and physical sciences), EDUCATION (art, elementary, and special), HEALTH PROFESSIONS (art therapy, medical technology, and speech pathology/audiology), SOCIAL SCIENCE (history, human development, liberal arts/general studies, pastoral studies, psychology, religion, social studies, and social work). Education, business, and English are the strongest academically. Business, social work, and education are the largest.

Required: All students must earn 128 credit hours, including 42 upper-division hours, and 30 or more hours in the major, while maintaining an overall GPA of 2.0 and 2.5 in the major. Distribution requirements include 18 hours in aesthetics, language, and literature, 12 in social science, 9 each in fine arts, science, and math, 6 in religious studies, and 3 in philosophy. Students must also demonstrate computer competency.

Special: Brescia offers a combined engineering degree with the University of Kentucky and the University of Louisville. Work-study programs, student-designed majors, nondegree study, dual majors, study abroad in Mexico, an internship in professional writing, pass/fail options and cross-registration with Kentucky Wesleyan are available. The Weekend College offers four 9-week modules of study. There are 2 national honor societies and a freshman honors program.

Faculty/Classroom: 47% of faculty are male; 53%, female. All teach undergraduates. No introductory courses are taught by graduate students. The average class size in an introductory lecture is 14; in a laboratory, 10; and in a regular course, 12.

Requirements: The SAT or ACT is required. In addition, essays and recommendations are helpful. High school units should include 4 of English, 3 of math, and 2 each in social studies, science, foreign language, fine arts, and computer science. Brescia requires applicants to be in the upper 50% of their class. A GPA of 2.5 is required. AP and CLEP credits are accepted. Important factors in the admissions decision are advanced placement or honor courses and recommendations by school officials.

Procedure: Freshmen are admitted to all sessions. There is a rolling admissions plan. Entrance exams should be taken at the end of the junior year. Application deadlines are open. Applications are accepted on-line. The fall 2005 application fee was $25.

Transfer: Transfer students must have a minimum GPA of 2.0. 42 of 128 credits required for the bachelor's degree must be completed at Brescia.

Visiting: There are regularly scheduled orientations for prospective students, including spring and fall open houses for freshmen and a spring transfer open house. There are guides for informal visits and visitors may sit in on classes and stay overnight. To schedule a visit, contact the Admissions Director.

Financial Aid: Brescia is a member of CSS. The FAFSA is required. Check with the school for current application deadlines.

International Students: The school actively recruits these students. They must score satisfactorily on the written TOEFL or on the electronic version and also take the SAT or the ACT.

Computers: All students may access the system. There are no time limits. The fee is $10 per semester.

Admissions Contact: Sister Mary Austin Blank, Director of Admissions. A video is available. E-mail: *admissions@brescia.edu* Web: *www.brescia.edu*

CAMPBELLSVILLE UNIVERSITY
D-3

Campbellsville, KY 42718-2799 — (270) 789-5220
(800) 264-6014; Fax: (270) 789-5071

Full-time: 606 men, 663 women	Faculty: 85; IIB, --$
Part-time: 195 men, 367 women	Ph.D.s: 66%
Graduate: 165 men, 253 women	Student/Faculty: 15 to 1
Year: semesters, summer session	Tuition: $15,460
Application Deadline: see profile	Room & Board: $5868
Freshman Class: 1351 applied, 922 accepted, 354 enrolled	
ACT: 21	COMPETITIVE

Campbellsville University, founded in 1906, is a private, comprehensive institution affiliated with the Kentucky Baptist Convention. There are 6 undergraduate and 7 graduate schools. In addition to regional accreditation, Campbellsville has baccalaureate program accreditation with NASM. The 2 libraries contain 108,000 volumes, 24,000 microform items, and 8000 audio/video tapes/CDs/DVDs, and subscribe to 360 periodicals including electronic. Computerized library services include the card catalog, interlibrary loans, and database searching. Special learning facilities include a learning resource center, art gallery, radio station, TV station, a teacher resource center, the Kentuckiana Collection, Clay Hill Memorial Forest, and The American Civil War Institute. The 80-acre campus is in a small town 85 miles southwest of Lexington and 85 miles southeast of Louisville. Including any residence halls, there are 48 buildings.

Student Life: 87% of undergraduates are from Kentucky. Others are from 29 states, 28 foreign countries, and Canada. 95% are from public schools. 86% are white. 60% are Protestant; 12% claim no religious affiliation; 7% Catholic. The average age of freshmen is 19; all undergraduates, 35. 35% do not continue beyond their first year; 40% remain to graduate.

Housing: 802 students can be accommodated in college housing, which includes single-sex dorms and on-campus apartments. In addition, there are honors houses and special-interest houses. On-campus housing is guaranteed for all 4 years. 64% of students commute. Alcohol is not permitted. All students may keep cars.

Activities: There are no fraternities or sororities. There are 45 groups on campus, including art, band, cheerleading, choir, chorale, chorus, computers, dance, drama, ethnic, honors, international, jazz band, literary magazine, marching band, musical theater, newspaper, opera, orchestra, pep band, photography, political, professional, radio and TV, religious, social, social service, student government, symphony, and yearbook. Popular campus events include Valentine Banquet, a Christmas celebration, and Heritage Day.

Sports: There are 8 intercollegiate sports for men and 7 for women, and 10 intramural sports for men and 10 for women. Facilities include a swimming pool, a 1700-seat gym, a football stadium, a baseball field, an intramural activities center with skating facilities and large game rooms, softball and soccer fields, and an indoor practice field.

Disabled Students: 85% of the campus is accessible. Wheelchair ramps, elevators, special parking, specially equipped rest rooms, special class scheduling, lowered drinking fountains, lowered telephones, and widened doorways are available.

Services: Counseling and information services are available, as is tutoring in most subjects. There is remedial math, reading, and writing. There is also an AIDS education program and a study skills program.

Campus Safety and Security: Measures include 24-hour foot and vehicle patrol, self-defense education, security escort services, and informal discussions. There are pamphlets/posters/films, emergency telephones, and lighted pathways/sidewalks.

Programs of Study: Campbellsville confers B.A., B.S., B.M., B.S.B.A., B.S.Med.Tech, and B.S.W. degrees. Associate and master's degrees are also awarded. Bachelor's degrees are awarded in BIOLOGICAL SCIENCE (biology/biological science), BUSINESS (accounting, business administration and management, and office supervision and management), COMMUNICATIONS AND THE ARTS (art, communications, English, and music), COMPUTER AND PHYSICAL SCIENCE (chemistry, information sciences and systems, and mathematics), EDUCATION (athletic training, elementary, middle school, physical, and recreation), HEALTH PROFESSIONS (medical laboratory technology and sports medicine), SOCIAL SCIENCE (Christian studies, economics, history, political science/government, psychology, religious education, religious music, social work, and sociology). Biology, chemistry, and music are the strongest academically. Elementary education, business administration, and music are the largest.

Required: All candidates must be of good moral character. All students must complete a minimum of 128 semester hours, including 30 in the major, 21 in the minor, and 51 in general education courses. The minimum GPA is 2.5 for education majors, 2.1 for all others. All students must fulfill an English composition requirement.

Special: Legislative and public administration internships, a Washington semester, and federal work-study programs are available. The university also offers a semester in London program, a 3-2 engineering degree with the University of Kentucky, dual majors, credit by exam, credit for life, military, and work experience, nondegree study, and pass/fail options. There is a freshman honors program.

Faculty/Classroom: 52% of faculty are male; 48%, female. All teach undergraduates. No introductory courses are taught by graduate students. The average class size in an introductory lecture is 25; in a laboratory, 13; and in a regular course, 18.

Admissions: 68% of the 2005-2006 applicants were accepted. The ACT scores for the 2005-2006 freshman class were: 47% below 21, 30% between 21 and 23, 17% between 24 and 26, 3% between 27 and 28, and 3% above 28. 45% of the current freshmen were in the top fifth of their class; 75% were in the top two fifths.

Requirements: The ACT is required and the SAT is recommended. In addition, the SAT may be substituted for the ACT. Applicants must be graduates of an accredited secondary school with a GPA of 2.0. The GED is accepted. An interview is recommended. A GPA of 2.0 is required. AP and CLEP credits are accepted. Important factors in the admissions decision are evidence of special talent, leadership record, and advanced placement or honor courses.

Procedure: Freshmen are admitted to all sessions. Entrance exams should be taken no later than February of the senior year. There are deferred and rolling admissions plans. The fall 2005 application fee was $20. Notification is sent on a rolling basis. Applications are accepted online. Check with the school for current application deadlines.

Transfer: Of the 128 credits needed to graduate, all students must complete one third of the credits required for the major and the minor at the university; the last year must be completed in residence. 32 of 128 credits required for the bachelor's degree must be completed at Campbellsville.

Visiting: There are regularly scheduled orientations for prospective students, consisting of visitation days held in October, February, and April. There are guides for informal visits and visitors may sit in on classes and stay overnight. To schedule a visit, contact the Admissions Office.

Financial Aid: 47% of undergraduates work part time. Average annual earnings from campus work are $1700. The FAFSA is required. The priority date for freshman financial aid applications for fall entry is March 15. The deadline for filing freshman financial aid applications for fall entry is April 1.

International Students: In a recent year, 91 international students were enrolled. The school actively recruits these students. Satisfactory scores are required on the written TOEFL and the SAT or the ACT.

Computers: All students may access the system 24 hours a day or during lab hours. Students may access the system 45 hours monthly on dial-in access only. The fee is $200.

Graduates: From July 1, 2004 to June 30, 2005, 219 bachelor's degrees were awarded. In an average class, 42% graduate in 6 years or less.

Admissions Contact: David Walters, Vice President for Admissions. A video is available. E-mail: *admissions@campbellsville.edu* Web: *www.campbellsville.edu*

CENTRE COLLEGE
D-3

Danville, KY 40422

(859) 238-5350
(800) 423-6236; Fax: (859) 238-5373

Full-time: 510 men, 550 women	Faculty: IIB, av$
Part-time: 5 women	Ph.D.s: 97%
Graduate: none	Student/Faculty: n/av
Year: 4-1-4	Tuition: $23,110
Application Deadline: February 1	Room & Board: $7700
Freshman Class: 1259 applied, 1063 accepted, 272 enrolled	
SAT or ACT: required	VERY COMPETITIVE

Centre College, founded in 1819 by the Presbyterian Church (U.S.A.), is a private liberal arts and sciences institution. Enrollment figures in the above capsule are approximate. The library contains 217,751 volumes, 52,512 microform items, and 3500 audio/video tapes/CDs/DVDs, and subscribes to 2076 periodicals including electronic. Computerized library services include the card catalog, interlibrary loans, database searching, Internet access, and laptop Internet portals. Special learning facilities include an art gallery, natural history museum, and a performing arts center. The 115-acre campus is in a small town 35 miles southwest of Lexington and 80 miles southeast of Louisville. Including any residence halls, there are 60 buildings.

Student Life: 65% of undergraduates are from Kentucky. Students are from 38 states, 7 foreign countries, and Canada. 69% are from public schools. 95% are white. 61% are Protestant; 19% claim no religious affiliation; 18% Catholic. The average age of freshmen is 18; all undergraduates, 20. 10% do not continue beyond their first year; 80% remain to graduate.

Housing: 970 students can be accommodated in college housing, which includes single-sex and coed dorms, on-campus apartments, fraternity houses, and sorority houses. There is an International students house. On-campus housing is guaranteed for all 4 years. 95% of students live on campus; of those, 90% remain on campus on weekends. All students may keep cars.

Activities: 58% of men belong to 5 national fraternities; 65% of women belong to 4 national sororities. There are 105 groups on campus, including art, band, cheerleading, choir, chorus, computers, dance, debate, drama, ethnic, film, forensics, gay, honors, international, jazz band, literary magazine, musical theater, newspaper, orchestra, pep band, photography, political, professional, radio and TV, religious, social, social service, student government, and yearbook. Popular campus events include Carnival, Honors Convocation, and Honor Walk.

Sports: There are 9 intercollegiate sports for men and 10 for women, and 15 intramural sports for men and 15 for women. Facilities include a complex with a 1500-seat gym, 3 basketball courts, 2 volleyball courts, a training room, a game room, a sauna, a weight room, fitness center, and racquetball/handball courts. There is also a 2500-seat stadium, tennis courts, and playing fields for football, track, baseball, softball, soccer, field hockey, and other sports. The natatorium has a 25-yard, 6-lane swimming pool. Golf teams compete at the local country club.

Disabled Students: 65% of the campus is accessible. Wheelchair ramps, elevators, special parking, specially equipped rest rooms, special class scheduling, lowered drinking fountains, and electronic doors are available.

Services: Counseling and information services are available, as is tutoring in most subjects. There is a reader service for the blind.

Campus Safety and Security: Measures include 24-hour foot and vehicle patrol, self-defense education, security escort services, and informal discussions. There are pamphlets/posters/films, emergency telephones, lighted pathways/sidewalks, and a working relationship with outside agencies.

Programs of Study: Centre confers B.A. and B.S. degrees. Bachelor's degrees are awarded in BIOLOGICAL SCIENCE (biochemistry, biology/biological science, and molecular biology), COMMUNICATIONS AND THE ARTS (dramatic arts, English, fine arts, French, German, music, and Spanish), COMPUTER AND PHYSICAL SCIENCE (chemistry, computer science, mathematics, physical chemistry, and physics), EDUCATION (elementary), SOCIAL SCIENCE (anthropology, classical/ancient civilization, economics, history, international relations, philosophy, political science/government, psychobiology, psychology, religion, and sociology). English, economics, and history are the strongest academically and have the largest enrollments.

Required: All students must earn an overall GPA of 2.0 and complete a minimum of 111 credit hours. Students also must demonstrate competency in writing, foreign language, and math plus 1 course beyond basic skills in math, foreign language, or computer science. A freshman humanities program and a freshman seminar must be completed. Core curriculum requirements include 2 courses each in the humanities or art from the aesthetic context; the scientific/technological context; the social context; and the fundamental questions context. 2 phys ed courses must be completed by the end of sophomore year.

Special: Centre offers internships, study abroad in 9 countries, a Washington semester through American University, work-study, and a 3-2 engineering degree with Vanderbilt University, Washington University in St. Louis, Columbia University, and the University of Kentucky. Student-designed majors, interdisciplinary majors including chemical physics, secondary education certification, and prelaw, prebusiness, and premedicine programs are available. Pass/fail options also are available. There are 8 national honor societies, including Phi Beta Kappa.

Faculty/Classroom: 58% of faculty are male; 42%, female. All both teach and do research. The average class size in an introductory lecture is 20; in a laboratory, 14; and in a regular course, 17.

Admissions: 63% of the 2005-2006 applicants were accepted. There was 1 National Merit finalist and 13 semifinalists in a recent year. 22 freshmen graduated first in their class, ina recent year.

Requirements: The SAT or ACT is required. The ACT Optional Writing test is also recommended. No minimum test scores are required. Students should have completed a minimum of 15 academic credits, including 4 years each in English and math, 3 years each in science and social studies, 2 years in foreign language, and 1 year in an art- or music-related course. An essay is required, and an interview is strongly recommended. AP credits are accepted. Important factors in the admissions decision are advanced placement or honor courses, extracurricular activities record, and leadership record.

Procedure: Freshmen are admitted in the fall. Entrance exams should be taken by February of the senior year. There are early admissions and deferred admissions plans. Applications should be filed by February 1 for fall entry. Notification of early decision is sent March 15. The fall 2005 application fee was $40. A waiting list is an active part of the admissions procedure. Applications are accepted on-line.

Transfer: 14 transfer students enrolled in a recent year. Applicants for transfer must have all previous college transcripts on file and a recommendation from the dean of the most recent college attended. If the student has completed fewer than 2 years of college work, high school records must also be submitted. 45 of 111 credits required for the bachelor's degree must be completed at Centre.

Visiting: There are regularly scheduled orientations for prospective students, including a campus tour, an interview, class visits, faculty appointments, and an overnight stay, if requested. There are guides for informal visits and visitors may sit in on classes and stay overnight. To schedule a visit, contact the Office of Admission at admission@centre.edu.

Financial Aid: In a recent year, 90% of all full-time students received some form of financial aid. 70% of full-time freshmen and 66% of continuing full-time students received need-based aid. The average freshman award was $17,922. 49% of undergraduates work part time. Average annual earnings from campus work are $1312. The average financial indebtedness of thea recent graduate was $14,300. Centre is a member of CSS. The FAFSA and the college's own financial statement are required. The priority date for freshman financial aid applications for fall entry is February 15. The deadline for filing freshman financial aid applications for fall entry is March 1.

International Students: There were 16 international students enrolled in a recent year. They must take the TOEFL submit SAT or ACT scores.

Computers: Wireless access is available. All students may access the system. There are no time limits and no fees.

Admissions Contact: J. Carey Thompson, Dean of Admission and Student Financial Planning. A video is available.
E-mail: admission@centre.edu Web: www.centre.edu

CUMBERLAND COLLEGE
(See University of the Cumberlands)

EASTERN KENTUCKY UNIVERSITY   E-3
Richmond, KY 40475

	(859) 622-2106
	(800) 465-9191; Fax: (859) 622-3024
Full-time: 3890 men, 5800 women	Faculty: 574; IIA, -$
Part-time: 1400 men, 2290 women	Ph.Ds: 70%
Graduate: none	Student/Faculty: 17 to 1
Year: semesters, summer session	Tuition: $3200 ($8800)
Application Deadline: see profile	Room & Board: $4525
Freshman Class: n/av	ACT: required COMPETITIVE

Eastern Kentucky University, established in 1906, is a public, state-supported institution offering degree programs in the arts and sciences, business, environmental studies, health fields, education, and public service occupations. There are 5 undergraduate schools and 1 graduate school. Figures in the above capsule and profile are approximate. In ad-

dition to regional accreditation, EKU has baccalaureate program accreditation with AACSB, ADA, AHEA, CSWE, FIDER, NASM, NCATE, NLN, and NRPA. The 3 libraries contain 837,945 volumes, 1,410,522 microform items, and 4221 audio/video tapes/CDs/DVDs, and subscribe to 3565 periodicals including electronic. Computerized library services include the card catalog, interlibrary loans, database searching, and Internet access. Special learning facilities include a learning resource center, art gallery, natural history museum, planetarium, radio station, TV station, and a law enforcement complex that includes a training tank for underwater rescue and recovery. The 628-acre campus is in a small town 20 miles south of Lexington. Including any residence halls, there are 98 buildings.

Student Life: 90% of undergraduates are from Kentucky. Others are from 45 states, 49 foreign countries, and Canada. 90% are from public schools. 91% are white. The average age of freshmen is 18; all undergraduates, 21. 35% do not continue beyond their first year.

Housing: 5646 students can be accommodated in college housing, which includes single-sex and coed dormitories, on-campus apartments, and married-student housing. In addition, there are honors houses, special-interest houses, and special accomodations for senior home economics students. On-campus housing is guaranteed for all 4 years. 67% of students commute. Alcohol is not permitted. All students may keep cars.

Activities: 4% of men belong to 12 national fraternities; 4% of women belong to 10 national sororities. There are 151 groups on campus, including art, band, cheerleading, choir, chorale, chorus, computers, dance, debate, drama, drill team, ethnic, film, gay, honors, international, jazz band, marching band, musical theater, newspaper, orchestra, pep band, photography, political, professional, radio and TV, religious, social service, student government, symphony, and yearbook. Popular campus events include Hanging of the Greens at Christmas, International Month, and fraternity/sorority competitions.

Sports: There are 8 intercollegiate sports for men and 8 for women, and 12 intramural sports for men and 12 for women. Facilities include 5 gyms, 1 outdoor and 2 indoor swimming pools, 19 outdoor hard-court and 4 indoor tennis courts, handball and racquetball courts, training rooms, a dance studio, a martial arts room, a wellness center, a 7000-seat basketball arena, a 20,000-seat stadium, an 8-lane outdoor track, a field hockey area, an 18-hole golf course, fields for baseball, softball, soccer, weight facilities, and a conditioning center.

Disabled Students: 85% of the campus is accessible. Wheelchair ramps, elevators, special parking, specially equipped rest rooms, special class scheduling, lowered drinking fountains, and lowered telephones are available.

Services: Counseling and information services are available, as is tutoring in some subjects, including math, English, and reading. There is a reader service for the blind, and remedial math, reading, and writing. Tutoring is available in other fields upon request.

Campus Safety and Security: Measures include 24-hour foot and vehicle patrol, self-defense education, security escort services, and shuttle buses. There are informal discussions, pamphlets/posters/films, emergency telephones, lighted pathways/sidewalks, and 16 crime-prevention programs.

Programs of Study: EKU confers B.A., B.S., B.B.A., B.F.A., B.I.S., B.M., B.M.Ed., B.S.N., and B.S.W. degrees. Associate and master's degrees are also awarded. Bachelor's degrees are awarded in AGRICULTURE (agriculture, horticulture, and wildlife management), BIOLOGICAL SCIENCE (biology/biological science and microbiology), BUSINESS (accounting, banking and finance, business administration and management, and marketing/retailing/merchandising), COMMUNICATIONS AND THE ARTS (art, broadcasting, dramatic arts, English, French, journalism, music, performing arts, public relations, Spanish, and speech/debate/rhetoric), COMPUTER AND PHYSICAL SCIENCE (chemistry, computer programming, computer science, geology, mathematics, and statistics), EDUCATION (art, business, education of the deaf and hearing impaired, elementary, foreign languages, health, home economics, industrial arts, middle school, music, physical, secondary, special, and technical), ENGINEERING AND ENVIRONMENTAL DESIGN (airline piloting and navigation, construction technology, environmental science, interior design, and manufacturing technology), HEALTH PROFESSIONS (environmental health science, health care administration, nursing, and occupational therapy), SOCIAL SCIENCE (anthropology, child care/child and family studies, corrections, dietetics, economics, fire protection, forensic studies, geography, history, paralegal studies, philosophy, political science/government, psychology, social work, and sociology). Occupational therapy, psychology, and nursing are the strongest academically. Education, nursing, and law enforcement are the largest.

Required: All students must complete 51 credit hours of general education requirements, including courses in phys ed, health, English, natural science, social science, math, and the humanities. Students must complete a total of 128 credit hours, including 45 to 60 credits in the major, with a minimum GPA of 2.0.

Special: EKU offers cooperative programs with all academic colleges, internships, and study abroad in various European countries. Students may opt for credit by exam, nondegree study, pass/fail options, student-designed and dual majors, and a general studies degree. There are 30 national honor societies, including Phi Beta Kappa, a freshman honors program, and 1 departmental honors program.

Faculty/Classroom: 55% of faculty are male; 45%, female. 98% teach undergraduates and 25% both teach and do research. The average class size in an introductory lecture is 30; in a laboratory, 15; and in a regular course, 25.

Requirements: The ACT is required. A GPA of 2.0 is required. AP and CLEP credits are accepted. Important factors in the admissions decision are evidence of special talent, extracurricular activities record, and leadership record.

Procedure: Freshmen are admitted to all sessions. There is a rolling admissions plan. Entrance exams should be taken prior to enrollment. Check with the school for current application deadlines. The application fee is $25. Notification is sent on a rolling basis. Applications are accepted on-line.

Transfer: Applicants must have a 2.0 cumulative GPA from all accredited institutions previously attended and must not have been dismissed. 30 of 128 credits required for the bachelor's degree must be completed at EKU.

Visiting: There are regularly scheduled orientations for prospective students, consisting of a 1-day program during the summer prior to fall enrollment. There are guides for informal visits and visitors may sit in on classes and stay overnight. To schedule a visit, contact the Admissions Office.

Financial Aid: EKU is a member of CSS. The CSS/Profile and the college's own financial statement are required. Figures in the above capsule and profile are approximate.

International Students: The school actively recruits these students. They must score satisfactorily on the written TOEFL and also take the ACT or the SAT for those applicants from states where the SAT is dominant.

Computers: All students may access the system. There are no time limits and no fees.

Admissions Contact: Stephen A. Byrn, Director of Admissions. E-mail: admissions@eku.edu Web: http://www.admissions.eku.edu

GEORGETOWN COLLEGE

D-2

Georgetown, KY 40324-1696

(502) 863-8009
(800) 788-9985; Fax: (502) 868-7733

Full-time: 586 men, 723 women	**Faculty:** 109; IIB, --$
Part-time: 15 men, 8 women	**Ph.D.s:** 86%
Graduate: 95 men, 392 women	**Student/Faculty:** 12 to 1
Year: semesters, summer session	**Tuition:** $19,170
Application Deadline: open	**Room & Board:** $5780
Freshman Class: 1063 applied, 1009 accepted, 416 enrolled	
ACT: 25*	**COMPETITIVE+**

Georgetown College, founded in 1829, is a private liberal arts college affiliated with the Kentucky Baptist Convention. The library contains 163,950 volumes, 189,541 microform items, and 6169 audio/video tapes/CDs/DVDs, and subscribes to 32,509 periodicals including electronic. Computerized library services include the card catalog, interlibrary loans, database searching, Internet access, and laptop Internet portals. Special learning facilities include a learning resource center, art gallery, and planetarium. The 104-acre campus is in a suburban area 12 miles north of Lexington. Including any residence halls, there are 40 buildings.

Student Life: 84% of undergraduates are from Kentucky. Others are from 23 states and 8 foreign countries. 90% are from public schools. 94% are white. 78% are Protestant; 12% Catholic; 6% claim no religious affiliation. The average age of freshmen is 18; all undergraduates, 20. 15% do not continue beyond their first year; 57% remain to graduate.

Housing: 1255 students can be accommodated in college housing, which includes single-sex dormitories, on-campus apartments, married-student housing, fraternity houses, and sorority houses. On-campus housing is guaranteed for all 4 years. 93% of students live on campus; of those, 78% remain on campus on weekends. Alcohol is not permitted. All students may keep cars.

Activities: 25% of men belong to 1 local and 4 national fraternities; 35% of women belong to 4 national sororities. There are 101 groups on campus, including academic, art, band, cheerleading, choir, chorale, chorus, computers, dance, drama, ethnic, forensics, honors, international, jazz band, literary magazine, musical theater, newspaper, pep band, photography, political, professional, radio and TV, religious, social, social service, and student government. Popular campus events include Festival of Song, Parents Day, and Hanging of the Green (Christmas).

Sports: There are 8 intercollegiate sports for men and 8 for women, and 11 intramural sports for men and 11 for women. Facilities include a 3000-seat stadium, 8 tennis courts, soccer, baseball, football, softball, and intramural fields, a 1550-seat gym, racquetball courts, a training room, and a fitness center housing a Nautilus area, a weight lifting area, basketball courts, a recreation room, and dressing rooms.

Disabled Students: 70% of the campus is accessible. Wheelchair ramps, elevators, special parking, specially equipped rest rooms, and special class scheduling are available.

Services: Counseling and information services are available, as is tutoring in every subject.

Campus Safety and Security: Measures include 24-hour foot and vehicle patrol, self-defense education, security escort services, and shuttle buses. There are informal discussions, pamphlets/posters/films, emergency telephones, and lighted pathways/sidewalks.

Programs of Study: Georgetown confers B.A., B.S., B.M., and B.M.E. degrees. Master's degrees are also awarded. Bachelor's degrees are awarded in BIOLOGICAL SCIENCE (biology/biological science), BUSINESS (accounting, banking and finance, business economics, international business management, management information systems, and marketing/retailing/merchandising), COMMUNICATIONS AND THE ARTS (art, communications, dramatic arts, English, French, German, music, performing arts, and Spanish), COMPUTER AND PHYSICAL SCIENCE (chemistry, computer science, mathematics, and physics), EDUCATION (athletic training, elementary, foreign languages, and music), ENGINEERING AND ENVIRONMENTAL DESIGN (environmental science), HEALTH PROFESSIONS (exercise science), SOCIAL SCIENCE (American studies, European studies, history, liberal arts/general studies, philosophy, political science/government, psychology, religion, religious music, and sociology). Biology and English are the strongest academically. Business and communication are the largest.

Required: All students are required to complete 56 semester hours of general education courses, including 16 in fine arts and humanities, 9 in foreign language and culture (or otherwise demonstrate proficiency), 8 in communication, 6 each in religion, natural sciences, and social sciences, 3 in math, and 2 in phys ed. A minimum of 120 semester hours, including 33 to 60 in the major, with a minimum GPA of 2.0, is required to graduate, as is successful completion of a comprehensive exam in the major.

Special: Georgetown offers cross-registration with the University of Kentucky Air Force ROTC for aerospace studies. A 3-2 engineering degree is available with the University of Kentucky and Washington University in St. Louis. Internships, co-op programs in math and computer science, study abroad in 28 countries, work-study programs, dual and student-designed majors, and pass/fail options are available. Interdisciplinary majors include business administration/communication arts and business administration/ethics. A dual degree is offered in liberal studies. Nondegree study is possible. There are 20 national honor societies and a freshman honors program.

Faculty/Classroom: 57% of faculty are male; 43%, female. All teach undergraduates. No introductory courses are taught by graduate students. The average class size in an introductory lecture is 20 and in a regular course, 18.

Admissions: 95% of the 2005-2006 applicants were accepted. The ACT scores for the 2005-2006 freshman class were: 22% below 21, 31% between 21 and 23, 26% between 24 and 26, 11% between 27 and 28, and 10% above 28. 49% of the current freshmen were in the top fifth of their class; 78% were in the top two fifths. 23 freshmen graduated first in their class.

Requirements: The SAT or ACT is required. In addition, applicants should have completed 4 high school credits in English, 3 each in math and science, 2 in a foreign language, and 1 each in social studies and history, with additional credits in electives strongly encouraged. A student essay is required; Kentucky high school applicants may substitute a writing portfolio entry. A GPA of 2.0 is required. AP and CLEP credits are accepted. Important factors in the admissions decision are advanced placement or honor courses, evidence of special talent, and leadership record.

Procedure: Freshmen are admitted to all sessions. Entrance exams should be taken from December of the junior year through October of the senior year. Early decision applications should be filed by December 1, along with a $30 fee. Notification is sent on a rolling basis. Applications are accepted on-line.

Transfer: 31 transfer students enrolled in 2004-2005. Applicants must be in good standing at the school most recently attended and must submit official college and high school transcripts. 30 of 120 credits required for the bachelor's degree must be completed at Georgetown.

Visiting: There are regularly scheduled orientations for prospective students, consisting of campus tours and information on admissions, financial assistance, student life, and academic programs. There are guides for informal visits and visitors may sit in on classes and stay overnight. To schedule a visit, contact Johnnie Johnson, Director of Admissions at admissions@georgetowncollege.edu.

Financial Aid: In 2005-2006, 98% of all full-time freshmen and 97% of continuing full-time students received some form of financial aid. 64% of full-time freshmen and 66% of continuing full-time students received need-based aid. The average freshman award was $18,350. Need-based scholarships or need-based grants averaged $14,359 ($25,750 maximum); need-based self-help aid (loans and jobs) averaged $3652 ($7825 maximum); non-need-based athletic scholarships averaged

$5704 ($24,950 maximum); and other non-need-based awards and non-need-based scholarships averaged $9139 ($25,750 maximum). 47% of undergraduates work part time. Average annual earnings from campus work are $1200. The average financial indebtedness of the 2005 graduate was $15,081. The FAFSA is required. The priority date for freshman financial aid applications for fall entry is February 1. The deadline for filing freshman financial aid applications for fall entry is March 1.

International Students: There are 16 international students enrolled. The school actively recruits these students. They must score satisfactorily on the written or electronic version of the TOEFL.

Computers: All students may access the system. There are no time limits and no fees.

Graduates: From July 1, 2004 to June 30, 2005, 250 bachelor's degrees were awarded. The most popular majors were business (16%), communication arts (10%), and psychology (10%). In an average class, 46% graduate in 4 years or less, 59% graduate in 5 years or less, and 61% graduate in 6 years or less. 60 companies recruited on campus in 2004-2005. Of the 2004 graduating class, 45% were enrolled in graduate school within 6 months of graduation and 88% were employed.

Admissions Contact: Johnnie Johnson, Director of Admissions.
E-mail: *admissions@georgetowncollege.edu*
Web: *http://www.georgetowncollege.edu*

KENTUCKY CHRISTIAN COLLEGE   F-2
Grayson, KY 41143

	(606) 474-6613
	(800) KCC-3181; Fax: (606) 474-3155

Full-time: 270 men, 290 women	**Faculty:** 27; IIB, --$
Part-time: 10 men, 15 women	**Ph.D.s:** 92%
Graduate: 15 men, 1 woman	**Student/Faculty:** 21 to 1
Year: semesters, summer session	**Tuition:** $8550
Application Deadline: open	**Room & Board:** $4130
Freshman Class: n/av	
SAT or ACT: required	**COMPETITIVE**

Kentucky Christian College, established in 1919, is a private Christian college affiliated with the Church of Christ, offering undergraduate programs in Christian ministry, psychology, social work, business administration, teacher education, music, history, and intercultural studies. Figures in the above capsule and profile are approximate. In addition to regional accreditation, KCC has baccalaureate program accreditation with CSWE. The library contains 101,859 volumes, 738 microform items, and 3547 audio/video tapes/CDs/DVDs, and subscribes to 439 periodicals including electronic. Computerized library services include interlibrary loans and database searching. Special learning facilities include a learning resource center and radio station. The 121-acre campus is in a small town 20 miles from Ashland and 90 miles east of Lexington. Including any residence halls, there are 16 buildings.

Student Life: 69% of undergraduates are from out of state, mostly the Midwest. Others are from 24 states, 8 foreign countries, and Canada. 94% are white. Most are Protestant. The average age of freshmen is 18; all undergraduates, 20. 34% do not continue beyond their first year.

Housing: 556 students can be accommodated in college housing, which includes single-sex dormitories, on-campus apartments, and married-student housing. On-campus housing is guaranteed for all 4 years. 91% of students live on campus. Alcohol is not permitted. All students may keep cars.

Activities: There are no fraternities or sororities. There are 14 groups on campus, including cheerleading, choir, chorale, drama, jazz band, musical theater, newspaper, pep band, professional, radio and TV, religious, social service, student government, and yearbook. Popular campus events include Feast of Christmas, Days of Future Knights, and Summer in the Son.

Sports: There are 4 intercollegiate sports for men and 4 for women, and 16 intramural sports for men and 16 for women. Facilities include a gym, soccer and recreational fields, a baseball diamond, a student life recreational center, and racquetball and tennis courts.

Disabled Students: 95% of the campus is accessible. Wheelchair ramps, elevators, special parking, specially equipped rest rooms, lowered drinking fountains, and lowered telephones are available.

Services: Counseling and information services are available, as is tutoring in some subjects, including RAs on campus serve as dorm tutors in various subjects. There is a reader service for the blind, and remedial math, reading, and writing.

Campus Safety and Security: Measures include security escort services, informal discussions, emergency telephones, and lighted pathways/sidewalks. There are and a full-time security guard.

Programs of Study: KCC confers B.A. and B.S. degrees. Associate and master's degrees are also awarded. Bachelor's degrees are awarded in BUSINESS (business administration and management), COMMUNICATIONS AND THE ARTS (literature, music, and music performance), COMPUTER AND PHYSICAL SCIENCE (mathematics, and science), EDUCATION (elementary, middle school, and music), SOCIAL SCIENCE (biblical studies, counseling/psychology, history, ministries, philos-

ophy, psychology, religious music, social work, and youth ministry). Teacher education and ministry are the largest.

Required: To graduate, students must complete 132 semester hours with at least 30 hours in the major and a minimum GPA of 2.0. Required courses include freshman orientation, phys ed, English, history, Introduction to Christian Doctrine, and Survey of Biblical Literature. Candidates for the B.A. degree must fulfill a 14-hour language requirement. All students are Bible majors, and most complete the requirements of a second major or a minor. Students must also participate in a Christian service program.

Special: Internships, work-study programs, B.A.-B.S. degrees, and dual majors are offered. Internships are required in business, education, ministry, and social work. Nondegree study is available. There is a chapter of Phi Beta Kappa.

Faculty/Classroom: 81% of faculty are male; 19%, female. All teach undergraduates and 25% both teach and do research. The average class size in an introductory lecture is 30; in a laboratory, 15; and in a regular course, 17.

Admissions: 3 freshmen graduated first in their class.

Requirements: The SAT or ACT is required. Applicants with lower test scores who have a high school GPA of 2.5 or higher will be considered. Applicants must graduate from an accredited secondary school or have a GED. Essays are required. Applications are accepted on-line at the school's web site. A GPA of 2.0 is required. AP and CLEP credits are accepted.

Procedure: Freshmen are admitted to all sessions. There are early decision and deferred admissions plans. Application deadlines are open. Applications are accepted on-line.

Transfer: 37 transfer students enrolled in 2004-2005. Applicants must have a cumulative GPA of 2.0. They must submit transcripts from all previous institutions and must be in good standing at the last college attended. 32 of 132 credits required for the bachelor's degree must be completed at KCC.

Visiting: There are regularly scheduled orientations for prospective students, consisting of an interview, a campus tour, lunch, and attending classes. Also, a semester-long orientation class is offered for all first-time freshmen. There are guides for informal visits and visitors may sit in on classes and stay overnight. To schedule a visit, contact Leslie Arnold, Assistant to the Director of Admissions.

Financial Aid: In 2005-2006, 76% of all full-time freshmen and 71% of continuing full-time students received some form of financial aid. 41% of full-time freshmen and 49% of continuing full-time students received need-based aid. The average freshman award was $6621. 54% of undergraduates work part time. Average annual earnings from campus work are $1586. The average financial indebtedness of the 2005 graduate was $19,497. The FAFSA and the college's own financial statement are required. The deadline for filing freshman financial aid applications for fall entry is April 1.

International Students: There are 13 international students enrolled. They must score 500 on the written TOEFL and also take the SAT or the ACT.

Computers: All students may access the system. There are no time limits. The fee is $100.

Graduates: From July 1, 2004 to June 30, 2005, 76 bachelor's degrees were awarded. The most popular majors were Christian ministry (29%), teacher education (24%), and business administration (17%). In an average class, 45% graduate in 4 years or less, and 50% graduate in 6 years or less.

Admissions Contact: Sandra Deakins, Director of Admissions.
E-mail: *knights@email.kcc.edu* Web: *www.kcc.edu*

KENTUCKY STATE UNIVERSITY   D-2
Frankfort, KY 40601

	(502) 597-6322
	(800) 325-1716; Fax: (502) 597-5814

Full-time: 704 men, 916 women	**Faculty:** 152
Part-time: 268 men, 363 women	**Ph.D.s:** n/av
Graduate: 65 men, 70 women	**Student/Faculty:** 11 to 1
Year: semesters, summer session	**Tuition:** $4468 ($10,910)
Application Deadline: open	**Room & Board:** $5621
Freshman Class: 1430 accepted, 460 enrolled	
SAT Verbal/Math: 418/426*	**ACT:** 17 **LESS COMPETITIVE**

Kentucky State University, founded in 1886, is a public liberal arts institution that emphasizes student involvement in seminars and course planning. There are 4 undergraduate schools and 1 graduate school. In addition to regional accreditation, KSU has baccalaureate program accreditation with AACSB, ADA, AHEA, CSWE, NASM, NCATE, and NLN. The library contains 438,355 volumes, 323,864 microform items, and 3453 audio/video tapes/CDs/DVDs, and subscribes to 1160 periodicals including electronic. Computerized library services include the card catalog, interlibrary loans, database searching, and Internet access. Special learning facilities include a learning resource center, art gallery, and a 167-acre agricultural research farm. The 308-acre campus is in a small town 25 miles west of Lexington. Including any residence halls, there are 34 buildings.

Student Life: 62% of undergraduates are from Kentucky. Others are from 34 states, 29 foreign countries, and Canada. 99% are from public schools. 60% are African American; 34% white. The average age of freshmen is 21; all undergraduates, 25. 44% do not continue beyond their first year; 35% remain to graduate.

Housing: 849 students can be accommodated in college housing, which includes single-sex dorms and on-campus apartments. In addition, there are special-interest houses. On-campus housing is guaranteed for the freshman year only and is available on a first-come, first-served basis. 67% of students commute. Alcohol is not permitted. All students may keep cars.

Activities: 3% of men belong to 6 national fraternities; 4% of women belong to 5 national sororities. There are 70 groups on campus, including art, band, cheerleading, choir, chorale, computers, dance, drama, drill team, honors, international, jazz band, literary magazine, marching band, musical theater, newspaper, opera, orchestra, political, professional, religious, social, social service, student government, and symphony. Popular campus events include plays, concerts, and talent shows.

Sports: There are 7 intercollegiate sports for men and 6 for women. Facilities include a 6500-seat football stadium, an indoor swimming pool, tennis courts, a bowling alley, training and weight rooms, a field house, and baseball, track, and field complexes.

Disabled Students: Wheelchair ramps, elevators, special parking, specially equipped rest rooms, lowered drinking fountains, lowered telephones, and electric doors are available.

Services: Counseling and information services are available, as is tutoring in every subject. There is a reader service for the blind, and remedial math, reading, and writing.

Campus Safety and Security: Measures include 24-hour foot and vehicle patrol, self-defense education, and lighted pathways/sidewalks.

Programs of Study: KSU confers B.A. and B.S. degrees. Associate and master's degrees are also awarded. Bachelor's degrees are awarded in BIOLOGICAL SCIENCE (biology/biological science), BUSINESS (apparel and accessories marketing and business administration and management), COMMUNICATIONS AND THE ARTS (art, English, fine arts, music performance, and studio art), COMPUTER AND PHYSICAL SCIENCE (applied mathematics, chemistry, computer science, and mathematics), EDUCATION (art, early childhood, elementary, mathematics, music, physical, secondary, and social studies), HEALTH PROFESSIONS (nursing), SOCIAL SCIENCE (criminal justice, history, liberal arts/general studies, political science/government, psychology, public administration, social work, and sociology).

Required: A total of 128 credits is required to graduate, with 64 in the major and a minimum 2.0 GPA. An assessment may include, but is not limited to, a portfolio, written exam, presentation, recital, and/or capstone course.

Special: There is 1 national honor society, a freshman honors program, and 10 departmental honors programs.

Faculty/Classroom: 95% teach undergraduates.

Requirements: A satisfactory score on the SAT or ACT is required. In addition applicants are required to have 4 years in English, 3 in math, 2 each in science and history, and 9 additional precollege curriculum classes. The GED is accepted. A GPA of 2.0 is required. AP and CLEP credits are accepted.

Procedure: Freshmen are admitted to all sessions. Entrance exams should be taken from October to April. There are early admissions and deferred admissions plans. There is a rolling admissions plan. Application deadlines are open. The fall 2005 application fee was $22. Notification is sent on a rolling basis. Applications are accepted on-line.

Transfer: 109 transfer students enrolled in 2004-2005. Transfer applicants must have a 2.0 minimum GPA at previous colleges. Only C grades or higher transfer. If fewer than 30 semester credits are transferable, applicants must meet freshman criteria. 45 of 128 credits required for the bachelor's degree must be completed at KSU.

Visiting: There are regularly scheduled orientations for prospective students, including tours and meetings with faculty and financial aid officers. There are guides for informal visits and visitors may sit in on classes. To schedule a visit, contact Admissions at *admission@kysu.edu*.

Financial Aid: In a recent year, 80% of all full-time freshmen and 85% of continuing full-time students received some form of financial aid. 65% of full-time freshmen and 60% of continuing full-time students received need-based aid. The average freshman award was $6500. Need-based scholarships or need-based grants averaged $500 ($800 maximum); need-based self-help aid (loans and jobs) averaged $3040 ($5500 maximum); non-need-based athletic scholarships averaged $7426 ($14,500 maximum); and other non-need-based awards and non-need-based scholarships averaged $1950 ($14,500 maximum). 55% of undergraduates work part time. Average annual earnings from campus work are $1000. The average financial indebtedness of a recent year's graduate was $12,000. KSU is a member of CSS. The FAFSA and the college's own financial statement are required. The priority date for freshman financial aid applications for fall entry is April 15.

International Students: They must take the TOEFL, achieving a satisfactory score, and also take the SAT or the ACT.

Computers: All students may access the system 13 hours a day. There are no time limits and no fees. All students are required to have personal computers.

Graduates: From July 1, 2004 to June 30, 2005, 330 bachelor's degrees were awarded. The most popular majors were business (15%), computer science (7%), and criminal justice (7%).

Admissions Contact: James Burrell, Director of Admissions. A video is available. E-mail: *james.burrell@kysu.edu* Web: *www.kysu.edu*.

KENTUCKY WESLEYAN COLLEGE
Owensboro, KY 42302-1039   B-3

(270) 852-3122
(800) 999-0592; Fax: (270) 852-3133

Full-time: 368 men, 349 women	**Faculty:** 36; IIB, --$
Part-time: 18 men, 20 women	**Ph.D.s:** 75%
Graduate: none	**Student/Faculty:** 20 to 1
Year: semesters, summer session	**Tuition:** $12,990
Application Deadline: open	**Room & Board:** $5600
Freshman Class: 1074 applied, 828 accepted, 209 enrolled	
SAT Verbal/Math: 490/520*	**ACT:** 21 COMPETITIVE

Kentucky Wesleyan College, founded in 1858, is a private liberal arts institution affiliated with the United Methodist Church. KWC offers undergraduate programs in natural sciences, humanities and fine arts, and social sciences. Additionally, academic programs are offered in criminal justice, human resources administration, mass communication, and computer science. In addition to regional accreditation, KWC has baccalaureate program accreditation with NLN. The library contains 108,356 volumes, 148,285 microform items, and 3672 audio/video tapes/CDs/DVDs, and subscribes to 322 periodicals including electronic. Computerized library services include the card catalog, interlibrary loans, database searching, and Internet access. Special learning facilities include a learning resource center, art gallery, and radio station. The 55-acre campus is in an urban area 95 miles southwest of Louisville and 120 miles north of Nashville. Including any residence halls, there are 15 buildings.

Student Life: 80% of undergraduates are from Kentucky. Others are from 26 states, 6 foreign countries, and Canada. 93% are from public schools. 79% are white; 10% African American. 56% are Protestant; 22% claim no religious affiliation; 18% Catholic. The average age of freshmen is 18; all undergraduates, 20. 29% do not continue beyond their first year; 47% remain to graduate.

Housing: 425 students can be accommodated in college housing, which includes single-sex and coed dorms, on-campus apartments, fraternity houses, and sorority houses. On-campus housing is guaranteed for all 4 years. 54% of students commute. Alcohol is not permitted. All students may keep cars.

Activities: 15% of men belong to 3 national fraternities; 20% of women belong to 2 national sororities. There are 42 groups on campus, including art, band, cheerleading, choir, chorale, chorus, computers, dance, drama, ethnic, jazz band, literary magazine, marching band, musical theater, newspaper, pep band, political, professional, radio and TV, religious, social, social service, student government, and yearbook. Popular campus events include Family Weekend, theater productions, and Madrigal Dinner.

Sports: There are 5 intercollegiate sports for men and 6 for women, and 7 intramural sports for men and 7 for women. Facilities include a health and recreation center, which houses an 800-seat gym, a fully equipped weight-training center, racquetball courts, batting and pitching facilities for softball and baseball, and a multipurpose auxiliary gym. Outdoor facilities include a baseball park, a softball park, a soccer field, a football field, and additional practice fields for football and soccer. Varsity basketball games are played in the 5,000-seat Owensboro Sports Center.

Disabled Students: 70% of the campus is accessible. Wheelchair ramps, elevators, special parking, specially equipped rest rooms, special class scheduling, and lowered drinking fountains are available.

Services: Counseling and information services are available, as is tutoring in most subjects. There is a reader service for the blind, and remedial math, reading, and writing.

Campus Safety and Security: Measures include 24-hour foot and vehicle patrol, security escort services, informal discussions, and pamphlets/posters/films. There are lighted pathways/sidewalks.

Programs of Study: KWC confers B.A., B.S., B.M., B.M.E., and B.M.P. degrees. Bachelor's degrees are awarded in BIOLOGICAL SCIENCE (biology/biological science and zoology), BUSINESS (accounting, business administration and management, business economics, human resources, and sports management), COMMUNICATIONS AND THE ARTS (art, communications, dramatic arts, English, fine arts, music, music business management, and Spanish), COMPUTER AND PHYSICAL SCIENCE (chemistry, computer science, and physics), EDUCATION (art, elementary, middle school, music, physical, and secondary), ENGINEERING AND ENVIRONMENTAL DESIGN (preengineering), HEALTH PROFESSIONS (predentistry and premedicine), SOCIAL SCI-

ENCE (criminal justice, early childhood studies, history, political science/government, prelaw, psychology, public administration, and sociology). Natural sciences, education, and business are the strongest academically. Business administration, biology, and general education are the largest.

Required: All students are required to complete the following general education program of skills and content requirements: 9 hours each in humanities and communication skills, 7 in natural science, 6 hours each in aesthetics and social sciences, and 3 hours each in math, religion, multicultural studies and phys ed. Students must demonstrate proficiency in math, computing, and oral and written communication. To graduate, students must complete a total of 128 credit hours, including 36 in the major, with a 2.0 GPA.

Special: Internships, dual majors, and student-designed majors are available in many programs and are established on an individual basis. A 3-2 degree in engineering is offered with Auburn University and the University of Kentucky. A Washington semester and study abroad in 5 countries are also available. There are 8 national honor societies and 7 departmental honors programs.

Faculty/Classroom: 70% of faculty are male; 30%, female. All teach undergraduates and 30% do research. The average class size in an introductory lecture is 22; in a laboratory, 16; and in a regular course, 12.

Admissions: 77% of the 2005-2006 applicants were accepted. The SAT scores for the 2005-2006 freshman class were: Verbal--50% below 500, 36% between 500 and 599, and 14% between 600 and 700; Math--36% below 500, 39% between 500 and 599, 22% between 600 and 700, and 3% above 700. The ACT scores were 44% below 21, 26% between 21 and 23, 18% between 24 and 26, 7% between 27 and 28, and 5% above 28.

Requirements: The SAT or ACT is required. In addition, applicants should have completed 13 high school units in college preparatory English, math, science, social studies, and a foreign language, or the GED equivalent. Applicants are considered individually. A GPA of 2.25 is required. AP and CLEP credits are accepted. Important factors in the admissions decision are advanced placement or honor courses, evidence of special talent, and leadership record.

Procedure: Freshmen are admitted to all sessions. Entrance exams should be taken during the spring of the junior year or the fall of the senior year. There is a deferred admissions plan. There is a rolling admissions plan. Application deadlines are open. Notification is sent on a rolling basis. Applications are accepted on-line.

Transfer: 76 transfer students enrolled in 2004-2005. Transfer applicants should have a minimum GPA of 2.0 in all course work and be in good standing at the previously attended institution. 32 of 128 credits required for the bachelor's degree must be completed at KWC.

Visiting: There are regularly scheduled orientations for prospective students, including a campus tour, meetings with faculty and students, and dining on campus. There are guides for informal visits and visitors may sit in on classes and stay overnight. To schedule a visit, contact the Admissions Office.

Financial Aid: In 2005-2006, 92% of all full-time freshmen and 86% of continuing full-time students received some form of financial aid. 69% of full-time freshmen and 60% of continuing full-time students received need-based aid. The average freshman award was $15,455. 47% of undergraduates work part time. The FAFSA and the college's own financial statement are required. The priority date for freshman financial aid applications for fall entry is March 15. The deadline for filing freshman financial aid applications for fall entry is August 1.

International Students: There are 8 international students enrolled. A satisfactory score is required on the TOEFL. SAT or ACT scores are required of international students who do not have a TOEFL score or who want to play NCAA sports.

Computers: All students may access the system. There are no time limits and no fees.

Graduates: From July 1, 2004 to June 30, 2005, 108 bachelor's degrees were awarded. The most popular majors were communication arts (15%), business administration (14%), and criminal justice (8%). In an average class, 44% graduate in 5 years or less, and 44% graduate in 6 years or less. 17 companies recruited on campus in 2004-2005. Of the 2004 graduating class, 21% were enrolled in graduate school within 6 months of graduation and 84% were employed.

Admissions Contact: Claude Bacon, Dean of Admissions and Financial Aid. A video is available. E-mail: *cbacon@kwc.edu* Web: *www.kwc.edu*

LINDSEY WILSON COLLEGE — D-3

Columbia, KY 42728
(270) 384-8504
(800) 264-0138; Fax: (270) 384-8591

Full-time: 480 men, 765 women	**Faculty:** 44; IIB, --$
Part-time: 35 men, 110 women	**Ph.D.s:** 57%
Graduate: 10 men, 30 women	**Student/Faculty:** 27 to 1
Year: semesters, summer session	**Tuition:** $11,600
Application Deadline: open	**Room & Board:** $4825
Freshman Class: n/av	
SAT or ACT: recommended	**LESS COMPETITIVE**

Lindsey Wilson College, founded in 1903, is a private liberal arts college affiliated with the United Methodist Church, offering undergraduate programs in arts and sciences, business administration, education, human services, and pre-health. Figures in the above capsule and in this profile are approximate. In addition to regional accreditation, Lindsey has baccalaureate program accreditation with NCATE. The library contains 85,000 volumes, 68,000 microform items, and 3650 audio/video tapes/CDs/DVDs, and subscribes to 35 periodicals including electronic. Computerized library services include the card catalog, interlibrary loans, database searching, and Internet access. Special learning facilities include a learning resource center and art gallery. The 40-acre campus is in a small town 100 miles southeast of Louisville. Including any residence halls, there are 35 buildings.

Student Life: 89% of undergraduates are from Kentucky. Others are from 15 states, 23 foreign countries, and Canada. 90% are from public schools. 89% are white. 78% are Protestant; 16% claim no religious affiliation; 6% Catholic. The average age of freshmen is 19; all undergraduates, 24. 46% do not continue beyond their first year.

Housing: 650 students can be accommodated in college housing, which includes single-sex dormitories, on-campus apartments, and married-student housing. In addition, there are honors houses. On-campus housing is guaranteed for all 4 years. 51% of students commute. Alcohol is not permitted. All students may keep cars.

Activities: There are no fraternities or sororities. There are 30 groups on campus, including art, cheerleading, choir, chorale, chorus, computers, dance, drama, film, honors, international, literary magazine, musical theater, newspaper, pep band, photography, political, professional, religious, social, social service, student government, and yearbook. Popular campus events include Hanging of the Greens, Parent Day, Tradition Day, and Founders Day.

Sports: There are 8 intercollegiate sports for men and 8 for women, and 15 intramural sports for men and 15 for women. Facilities include a sports center with a 1000-seat gym and a weight-training room, a sand volleyball court, and the student union building.

Disabled Students: 80% of the campus is accessible. Wheelchair ramps, elevators, special parking, specially equipped rest rooms, special class scheduling, and lowered drinking fountains are available.

Services: Counseling and information services are available, as is tutoring in every subject. There is remedial math, reading, and writing.

Campus Safety and Security: Measures include security escort services, informal discussions, pamphlets/posters/films, lighted pathways/sidewalks and 12-hour foot and vehicle patrol.

Programs of Study: Lindsey confers the B.A. degree. Associate and master's degrees are also awarded. Bachelor's degrees are awarded in BIOLOGICAL SCIENCE (biology/biological science), BUSINESS (accounting and business administration and management), COMMUNICATIONS AND THE ARTS (art, communications, and English), EDUCATION (elementary and secondary), SOCIAL SCIENCE (American studies, criminal justice, history, human services, liberal arts/general studies, and social science). Business, elementary education, and human services are the strongest academically and are the largest.

Required: All students must complete general education core requirements, including courses in communication of ideas, math, natural science, religion, humanities, fine arts, social behavioral science, and phys ed, as well as a 1-hour personal development career seminar. A total of 128 semester hours, with a minimum GPA of 2.0, is required to graduate.

Special: Human services majors are offered a social services practicum in their field of study. Internships, work-study programs, a general studies degree, and pass/fail options in some courses are available. Study abroad is possible through Lindsey in London and the Northern Ireland Exchange. There is a freshman honors program.

Faculty/Classroom: 47% of faculty are male; 53%, female. All teach undergraduates. No introductory courses are taught by graduate students. The average class size in an introductory lecture is 26; in a laboratory, 20; and in a regular course, 26.

Requirements: The SAT or ACT is recommended. Applicants should have completed 20 academic high school credits or the GED equivalent. A GPA of 2.8 is required. AP and CLEP credits are accepted. Important factors in the admissions decision are geographic diversity, recommendations by alumni, and recommendations by school officials.

Procedure: Freshmen are admitted fall and spring. Entrance exams should be taken during the junior year. There are early decision and rolling admissions plans. Application deadlines are open.

Transfer: Transfer applicants are required to submit an official transcript from schools previously attended. An interview is recommended. 30 of 128 credits required for the bachelor's degree must be completed at Lindsey.

Visiting: There are regularly scheduled orientations for prospective students. There are guides for informal visits and visitors may sit in on classes and stay overnight. To schedule a visit, contact the Admissions Office.

Financial Aid: Lindsey is a member of CSS. The CSS/Profile and the college's own financial statement are required. Check with the school for current application deadlines.

International Students: The school actively recruits these students. They must score satisfactorily on the written TOEFL or take the MELAB.

Computers: Mainly those enrolled in computing courses may access the system. There are no time limits and no fees.

Admissions Contact: Claude Bacon. E-mail: *bacon@lindsey.edu* Web: *www.lindsey.edu*

MIDWAY COLLEGE D-3

Midway, KY 40347-1120

(859) 846-5346
(800) 755-0031; Fax: (859) 846-5822

Full-time: 87 men, 789 women	**Faculty:** 50; III, --$
Part-time: 87 men, 316 women	**Ph.D.s:** 22%
Graduate: none	**Student/Faculty:** 18 to 1
Year: semesters, summer session	**Tuition:** $13,950
Application Deadline: open	**Room & Board:** $6200
Freshman Class: 423 applied, 319 accepted, 159 enrolled	
SAT Verbal/Math: 576/529*	**ACT:** 20 COMPETITIVE

Midway College, founded in 1847, is a private institution affiliated with the Disciples of Christ. The day college is for women only and the evening program is an accelerated coed program. The library contains 52,000 volumes, 57,000 microform items, and 8900 audio/video tapes/CDs/DVDs, and subscribes to 450 periodicals including electronic. Computerized library services include the card catalog, interlibrary loans, and database searching. Special learning facilities include a learning resource center. The 105-acre campus is in a rural area in Woodford County. 15 minutes from Lexington. Including any residence halls, there are 10 buildings.

Student Life: 88% of undergraduates are from Kentucky. Others are from 31 states, 5 foreign countries, and Canada. 87% are white. The average age of freshmen is 23; all undergraduates, 27.

Housing: 225 students can be accommodated in college housing, which includes single-sex dorms. On-campus housing is guaranteed for the freshman year only and is available on a first-come, first-served basis. 87% of students commute. Alcohol is not permitted. All students may keep cars.

Activities: There are no fraternities or sororities. There are 15 groups on campus, including art, chorale, honors, newspaper, professional, religious, social, social service, student government, and yearbook.

Sports: There are 4 intercollegiate sports for women. Facilities include a full service gym, a weight room, tennis courts, soccer and softball fields, and an equine arena.

Disabled Students: 65% of the campus is accessible. Wheelchair ramps, elevators, special parking, specially equipped rest rooms, special class scheduling, lowered drinking fountains, and lowered telephones are available.

Services: Counseling and information services are available, as is tutoring in most subjects. There are writing and math labs.

Campus Safety and Security: Measures include 24-hour foot and vehicle patrol, emergency telephones, and lighted pathways/sidewalks.

Programs of Study: Midway College confers B.A. and B.S. degrees. Associate degrees are also awarded. Bachelor's degrees are awarded in AGRICULTURE (equine science), BIOLOGICAL SCIENCE (biology/biological science), BUSINESS (business administration and management, human resources, and sports management), COMMUNICATIONS AND THE ARTS (English), COMPUTER AND PHYSICAL SCIENCE (chemistry and mathematics), EDUCATION (education), ENGINEERING AND ENVIRONMENTAL DESIGN (environmental science), HEALTH PROFESSIONS (nursing), SOCIAL SCIENCE (liberal arts/general studies and psychology). Biology, nursing, and equine science education are the strongest academically. Nursing, equine science, and business education are the largest.

Required: All students must complete 130 credits, including 82 to 91 major and elective credits and 38 to 48 general education credits. Core requirements include courses in math, computing, science, communication, and composition. A 2.0 GPA must be maintained.

Special: A cooperative program in teacher education and an accelerated degree program in management and education are offered. There are 2 national honor societies, including Phi Beta Kappa, and a freshman honors program.

Faculty/Classroom: 37% of faculty are male; 63%, female. All teach undergraduates and do research. The average class size in an introductory lecture is 16; in a laboratory, 9; and in a regular course, 13.

Admissions: 75% of the 2005-2006 applicants were accepted. The SAT scores for the 2005-2006 freshman class were: Verbal--31% below 500, 31% between 500 and 599, 13% between 600 and 700, and 25% above 700; Math--49% below 500, 13% between 500 and 599, 25% between 600 and 700, and 13% above 700. The ACT scores were 62% below 21, 21% between 21 and 23, 10% between 24 and 26, 3% between 27 and 28, and 4% above 28. 35% of the current freshmen were in the top quarter of their class; 61% were in the top half. 2 freshmen graduated first in their class.

Requirements: The SAT or ACT is required. In addition, a score of 50 or better on the GED is required for acceptance. A GPA of 2.2 is required. AP and CLEP credits are accepted. Important factors in the admissions decision are leadership record, extracurricular activities record, and recommendations by school officials.

Procedure: Freshmen are admitted fall, spring, and summer. SAT or ACT scores must be received by the school by August 1. Application deadlines are open.

Transfer: 249 transfer students enrolled in 2004-2005. Applicants must have a minimum college GPA of 2.0. 39 of 130 credits required for the bachelor's degree must be completed at Midway College.

Visiting: There are regularly scheduled orientations for prospective students, including campus tours, faculty and student conferences, and the president's address. There are guides for informal visits and visitors may sit in on classes. To schedule a visit, contact Stacy Sharp at *ssharpn@midway.edu*.

Financial Aid: In 2005-2006, 81% of all full-time freshmen and 80% of continuing full-time students received some form of financial aid. 81% of full-time freshmen and 69% of continuing full-time students received need-based aid. The average freshman award was $12,678. Need-based scholarships or need-based grants averaged $6530; need-based self-help aid (loans and jobs) averaged $2860; non-need-based athletic scholarships averaged $1250; and other non-need-based awards and non-need-based scholarships averaged $2594. 9% of undergraduates work part time. Average annual earnings from campus work are $1372. The average financial indebtedness of the 2005 graduate was $15,407. Midway College is a member of CSS. The FAFSA is required. The deadline for filing freshman financial aid applications for fall entry is April 15.

International Students: There are 9 international students enrolled. They must take the TOEFL and also take the SAT or the ACT.

Computers: All students may access the system. There are no time limits and no fees.

Graduates: From July 1, 2004 to June 30, 2005, 218 bachelor's degrees were awarded. The most popular majors were business/organizational management (38%), teacher education (34%), and nursing (12%). In an average class, 20% graduate in 4 years or less. 8 companies recruited on campus in 2004-2005.

Admissions Contact: Stacy Sharp, Director of Women's College Admissions. A video is available. E-mail: *ssharp@midway.edu* Web: *www.midway.edu*

MOREHEAD STATE UNIVERSITY E-2

Morehead, KY 40351

(606) 783-2000
(800) 354-2090; Fax: (606) 783-5038

Full-time: 2514 men, 3450 women	**Faculty:** 378; IIA, --$
Part-time: 367 men, 1213 women	**Ph.D.s:** 68%
Graduate: 467 men, 1051 women	**Student/Faculty:** 16 to 1
Year: semesters, summer session	**Tuition:** $4320 ($11,480)
Application Deadline: open	**Room & Board:** $4830
Freshman Class: 5092 applied, 3528 accepted, 1300 enrolled	
ACT: 20	COMPETITIVE

Morehead State University, founded in 1922, is a public institution offering degree programs in applied science and technology, humanities, educational and behavioral sciences, and business. There are 4 undergraduate schools and 1 graduate school. In addition to regional accreditation, MSU has baccalaureate program accreditation with AACSB, ACBSP, CSWE, NASM, NCATE, and NLN. The library contains 522,673 volumes, 819,736 microform items, and 22,194 audio/video tapes/CDs/DVDs, and subscribes to 3046 periodicals including electronic. Computerized library services include the card catalog, interlibrary loans, database searching, Internet access, and laptop Internet portals. Special learning facilities include a learning resource center, art gallery, planetarium, radio station, TV station, a 320-acre farm complex, the space science center, and robotics lab. The 1016-acre campus is in a small town 60 miles east of Lexington. Including any residence halls, there are 140 buildings.

Student Life: 86% of undergraduates are from Kentucky. Others are from 37 states, 22 foreign countries, and Canada. 95% are from public schools. 95% are white. The average age of freshmen is 19; all undergraduates, 24. 39% do not continue beyond their first year.

Housing: 3250 students can be accommodated in college housing, which includes single-sex and coed dorms, on-campus apartments, married-student housing, and fraternity houses. In addition, there are honors houses, a cross-cultural house, and housing for farm students. On-campus housing is guaranteed for all 4 years. 70% of students commute. Alcohol is not permitted. All students may keep cars.

Activities: 20% of men belong to 12 national fraternities; 20% of women belong to 9 national sororities. There are 95 groups on campus, including art, band, cheerleading, choir, chorale, chorus, computers, dance, drama, drill team, drum and bugle corps, ethnic, honors, international, jazz band, marching band, musical theater, newspaper, orchestra, pep band, photography, political, professional, radio and TV, religious, social, social service, student government, symphony, and yearbook. Popular campus events include Greek Week, Black History Month, and Appalachian Celebration.

Sports: There are 9 intercollegiate sports for men and 9 for women, and 24 intramural sports for men and 24 for women. Facilities include an athletic complex, a 6500-seat gym, a 10,000-seat stadium, a pool, bowling lanes, and a wellness/fitness center.

Disabled Students: 85% of the campus is accessible. Wheelchair ramps, elevators, special parking, specially equipped rest rooms, special class scheduling, lowered drinking fountains, lowered telephones, and special housing are available.

Services: Counseling and information services are available, as is tutoring in most subjects. There is a reader service for the blind, and remedial math, reading, and writing.

Campus Safety and Security: Measures include 24-hour foot and vehicle patrol, security escort services, shuttle buses, and informal discussions. There are emergency telephones and lighted pathways/sidewalks.

Programs of Study: MSU confers A.B., B.S., B.B.A., B.M., B.M.Ed., B.S.N., B.S.W., and B.U.S. degrees. Associate and master's degrees are also awarded. Bachelor's degrees are awarded in AGRICULTURE (agriculture), BIOLOGICAL SCIENCE (biology/biological science and ecology), BUSINESS (accounting, banking and finance, business economics, management information systems, management science, marketing management, and real estate), COMMUNICATIONS AND THE ARTS (communications, dramatic arts, English, music, and speech/debate/rhetoric), COMPUTER AND PHYSICAL SCIENCE (chemistry, computer science, earth science, geology, mathematics, and physics), EDUCATION (agricultural, business, elementary, health, home economics, industrial arts, middle school, physical, and special), ENGINEERING AND ENVIRONMENTAL DESIGN (industrial engineering technology), HEALTH PROFESSIONS (medical technology and nursing), SOCIAL SCIENCE (geography, history, liberal arts/general studies, paralegal studies, philosophy, political science/government, psychology, social science, social work, and sociology). Elementary education is the largest.

Required: All students must complete 42 semester hours (45 for teacher certification) of general education courses, including 15 hours in communications and humanities, 12 in natural and mathematical sciences, 12 in social and behavioral sciences, and 3 in health or phys ed. A total of 128 semester hours, with a minimum GPA of 2.0, is required to graduate.

Special: Cross-registration is offered with the University of Kentucky. Students may earn specialist certification in education. Study abroad in 3 countries, a Washington semester, a 3-2 engineering degree, dual and student-designed majors, a general studies degree, credit for life experience, pass/fail options, and nondegree study are available. There are 12 national honor societies and a freshman honors program.

Faculty/Classroom: 55% of faculty are male; 45%, female. All teach undergraduates. No introductory courses are taught by graduate students. The average class size in a regular course is 19.

Admissions: 69% of the 2005-2006 applicants were accepted. The ACT scores for the 2005-2006 freshman class were: 55% below 21, 26% between 21 and 23, 13% between 24 and 26, 4% between 27 and 28, and 2% above 28. 33% of the current freshmen were in the top fifth of their class; 58% were in the top two fifths.

Requirements: The SAT or ACT is required. In addition, applicants should have completed the Kentucky Pre-College Curriculum requirement. An interview is recommended. A GPA of 2.0 is required. AP and CLEP credits are accepted.

Procedure: Freshmen are admitted fall, spring, and summer. Entrance exams should be taken in the spring of the junior year. Application deadlines are open. Applications are accepted on-line.

Transfer: 379 transfer students enrolled in 2004-2005. Applicants should have a minimum GPA of 2.0 with at least 12 credit hours earned and be in good standing at their previous institution. They must have completed a precollege curriculum or meet any deficiencies. 32 of 128 credits required for the bachelor's degree must be completed at MSU.

Visiting: There are regularly scheduled orientations for prospective students, consisting of registration for classes, advisement, and an overview of MSU. There are guides for informal visits and visitors may sit in on classes. To schedule a visit, contact Enrollment Services at *admissions@moreheadstate.edu.*

Financial Aid: In 2005-2006, 98% of all full-time freshmen received some form of financial aid. 60% of full-time freshmen received need-based aid. The average freshman award was $7778. Need-based scholarships or need-based grants averaged $2174 ($4050 maximum); need-based self-help aid (loans and jobs) averaged $1985 ($2625 maximum); non-need-based athletic scholarships averaged $3645 ($9688 maximum); and other non-need-based awards and non-need-based scholarships averaged $2095 ($6000 maximum). 16% of undergraduates work part time. Average annual earnings from campus work are $1496. The average financial indebtedness of the 2005 graduate was $16,431. The FAFSA and the college's own financial statement are required. The deadline for filing freshman financial aid applications for fall entry is April 1.

International Students: There are 44 international students enrolled. They must score satisfactorily on the TOEFL and also take the SAT or ACT, with the ACT preferred.

Computers: Wireless access is available. Students can access the Internet a variety of ways including high-speed Internet access in residence halls; approximately 1000 desktop PCs distributed across campus in academic classrooms and labs; and mobile access via an extensive wireless computing network located in all classroom buildings, the library, and many outside common areas. In fall of 2005 the University implemented a portable computing imitative for students providing access to wireless enabled tablet computers with approximately 500 Gateway Tablet PCs placed in student hands during the first semester. All students may access the system days and evenings. There are no time limits and no fees. It is strongly recommended that all students have a Gateway personal computer.

Graduates: From July 1, 2004 to June 30, 2005, 1038 bachelor's degrees were awarded. The most popular majors were management and marketing (18%), elementary education (17%), and general studies (10%). In an average class, 40% graduate in 6 years or less. 70 companies recruited on campus in 2004-2005.

Admissions Contact: Joel Pace, Director, Admissions.
E-mail: *admissions@moreheadstate.edu* Web: *www.moreheadstate.edu*

MURRAY STATE UNIVERSITY

B-4

Murray, KY 42071

(270) 809-3741
(800) 272-4678; Fax: (270) 809-3780

Full-time: 3114 men, 4041 women	**Faculty:** 386; IIA, --$
Part-time: 441 men, 871 women	**Ph.D.s:** 78%
Graduate: 531 men, 1158 women	**Student/Faculty:** 19 to 1
Year: semesters, summer session	**Tuition:** $4428 ($6100)
Application Deadline: August 1	**Room & Board:** $4472
Freshman Class: 3057 applied, 2509 accepted, 1337 enrolled	
ACT: 23	**VERY COMPETITIVE**

Murray State University, founded in 1922, is a public institution offering degree programs in business and public affairs, education, health sciences and human services, humanities and fine arts, engineering, technology and science, and agriculture. There are 6 undergraduate and 6 graduate schools. In addition to regional accreditation, MSU has baccalaureate program accreditation with AACSB, ABET, ACEJMC, ACS, ADA, ASLA, AVMA, CSWE, NASAD, NASM, NCATE, and NLN. The 2 libraries contain 400,000 volumes, 200,800 microform items, and 10,500 audio/video tapes/CDs/DVDs, and subscribe to 2500 periodicals including electronic. Computerized library services include the card catalog, interlibrary loans, database searching, and Internet access. Special learning facilities include a learning resource center, art gallery, natural history museum, radio station, TV station, biological station, interactive telecommunications network, and web-based courses. The 253-acre campus is in a small town 130 miles northwest of Nashville. Including any residence halls, there are 96 buildings.

Student Life: 72% of undergraduates are from Kentucky. Others are from 45 states, 52 foreign countries, and Canada. 80% are from public schools. 88% are white. The average age of freshmen is 19; all undergraduates, 23. 20% do not continue beyond their first year; 56% remain to graduate.

Housing: 3000 students can be accommodated in college housing, which includes single-sex and coed dorms, on-campus apartments, married-student housing, residential colleges, and sorority houses. On-campus housing is available on a first-come, first-served basis. 62% of students commute. Alcohol is not permitted. All students may keep cars.

Activities: 16% of men belong to 3 local and 14 national fraternities; 12% of women belong to 1 local and 8 national sororities. There are 210 groups on campus, including art, band, cheerleading, chess, choir, chorale, chorus, computers, dance, debate, drama, drill team, ethnic, film, forensics, honors, international, jazz band, literary magazine, marching band, musical theater, newspaper, orchestra, pep band, photography, political, professional, radio and TV, religious, social, social service, student government, symphony, and yearbook. Popular campus events include Racer Regatta, Mr. MSU, and Miss MSU.

Sports: There are 10 intercollegiate sports for men and 11 for women, and 8 intramural sports for men and 8 for women. Facilities include a 73,00-square-foot recreation and wellness center, a 16,500-seat stadium, 2 gyms seating 6000, gymnastics and weight rooms, an indoor jogging track, racquetball courts, a swimming pool, outdoor tennis, basketball, and volleyball courts, a golf course, a physical fitness trail, and the 8500-seat Regional Special Events Center. A physical fitness center includes 2 pools, 3 gyms, racquetball courts, jogging and walking tracks, cardio and weight areas, an Interent lounge, aerobic studios, and a fitness assessment center.

Disabled Students: 96% of the campus is accessible. Wheelchair ramps, elevators, special parking, specially equipped rest rooms, special class scheduling, lowered drinking fountains, lowered telephones, and special housing are available.

Services: Counseling and information services are available, as is tutoring in most subjects. There is a reader service for the blind, and remedial math, reading, and writing.

Campus Safety and Security: Measures include 24-hour foot and vehicle patrol, self-defense education, security escort services, and informal discussions. There are pamphlets/posters/films, emergency telephones, and lighted pathways/sidewalks.

Programs of Study: MSU confers B.A., B.S., B.A.B., B.F.A., B.I.S., B.M., B.M.E., B.S.A., B.S.B., B.S.N., B.S.V.T.E., and B.S.W. degrees. Associate and master's degrees are also awarded. Bachelor's degrees are awarded in AGRICULTURE (agricultural mechanics, agriculture, animal science, fishing and fisheries, and horticulture), BIOLOGICAL SCIENCE (biochemistry, biology/biological science, and wildlife biology), BUSINESS (accounting, banking and finance, business administration and management, business economics, marketing/retailing/merchandising, personnel management, and recreation and leisure services), COMMUNICATIONS AND THE ARTS (advertising, broadcasting, communications, dramatic arts, English, fine arts, French, German, journalism, languages, music, public relations, Spanish, speech/debate/rhetoric, and telecommunications), COMPUTER AND PHYSICAL SCIENCE (chemistry, computer programming, computer science, earth science, geology, information sciences and systems, mathematics, and physics), EDUCATION (agricultural, art, business, early childhood, elementary, foreign languages, health, home economics, industrial arts, middle school, music, secondary, and special), ENGINEERING AND ENVIRONMENTAL DESIGN (civil engineering technology, computer technology, construction technology, electrical/electronics engineering technology, engineering technology, occupational safety and health, and technological management), HEALTH PROFESSIONS (exercise science, nursing, predentistry, premedicine, speech pathology/audiology, and veterinary science), SOCIAL SCIENCE (criminal justice, crosscultural studies, dietetics, economics, geography, history, international studies, liberal arts/general studies, parks and recreation management, philosophy, political science/government, prelaw, psychology, social work, and sociology). Premedicine, engineering, and physics are the strongest academically. Business, communication, and education technologies are the largest.

Required: All students must complete University Studies requirements, including courses in communications and basic skills, lab sciences and math, humanities and fine arts, social sciences and foreign language for the B.A. degree. A total of 120 semester hours, including at least 30 in the major, with a minimum GPA of 2.0 are required to graduate.

Special: MSU offers cooperative programs in all majors, cross-registration through the National Student Exchange, internships, study abroad in 25 countries, work-study, dual majors, B.A.-B.S. degrees, and 3-2 engineering degrees with the University of Louisville and the University of Kentucky. Credit for life experience and a degree in independent studies are also offered. Nondegree study is possible. There are 25 national honor societies, including Phi Beta Kappa, a freshman honors program, and 20 departmental honors programs.

Faculty/Classroom: 59% of faculty are male; 41%, female. All teach undergraduates. The average class size in an introductory lecture is 21 and in a laboratory, 20.

Admissions: 82% of the 2005-2006 applicants were accepted. The ACT scores for the 2005-2006 freshman class were: 20% below 21, 30% between 21 and 23, 30% between 24 and 26, 12% between 27 and 28, and 8% above 28. 56% of the current freshmen were in the top fifth of their class; 89% were in the top two fifths. 55 freshmen graduated first in their class.

Requirements: A satisfactory score is required on the ACT. Applicants must rank in the top half of their class or have a 3.0 GPA. Applicants should have completed 22 high school academic credits, including 4 units in English, 3 in math, 2 each in science and social studies, and 9 in electives; in addition, MSU strongly recommends a fourth year of math, 2 of foreign language, 2 in foreign language, 1 in art appreciation, 1/2 in health, 1/2 in phys ed and 5 in electives. A portfolio or audition is required for art and music majors. An interview is recommended. AP and CLEP credits are accepted. Important factors in the admissions decision are advanced placement or honor courses and leadership record.

Procedure: Freshmen are admitted to all sessions. Entrance exams should be taken before January of the enrollment year. There are early admissions and rolling admissions plans. Applications should be filed by August 1 for fall entry, December 1 for spring entry, and May 1 for summer entry, along with a $30 fee. Notification is sent on a rolling basis. Applications are accepted on-line.

Transfer: 662 transfer students enrolled in 2004-2005. Applicants must have a minimum GPA of 2.0 in at least 12 hours of degree credit. 36 of 120 credits required for the bachelor's degree must be completed at MSU.

Visiting: There are regularly scheduled orientations for prospective students, in the fall and spring. There are guides for informal visits and visitors may sit in on classes and stay overnight. To schedule a visit, contact the School Relations Office at (270) 809-2896 or *paul.radke@murraystate.edu.*

Financial Aid: In 2005-2006, 81% of all full-time freshmen and 77% of continuing full-time students received some form of financial aid. 45% of all full-time students received need-based aid. The average freshman award was $4591. Need-based scholarships or need-based grants averaged $3077 ($3552 maximum); need-based self-help aid (loans and jobs) averaged $3526 ($3612 maximum); non-need-based athletic scholarships averaged $7310 ($14,252 maximum); and other non-need-based awards and non-need-based scholarships averaged $3077 ($9804 maximum). 18% of undergraduates work part time. Average annual earnings from campus work are $3000. The average financial indebtedness of the 2005 graduate was $14,488. The FAFSA and the college's own financial statement are required. The deadline for filing freshman financial aid applications for fall entry is April 1.

International Students: There are 122 international students enrolled. The school actively recruits these students. A satisfactory score is required on the written TOEFL. Applicants must also complete level 5 in MSU's English Language Institute and take the ACT.

Computers: Wireless access is available. PCs are available throughout the campus, including residential colleges, libraries, classrooms and labs. All students may access the system. There are no time limits and no fees. It is strongly recommended that all students have a personal computer.

Graduates: From July 1, 2004 to June 30, 2005, 1372 bachelor's degrees were awarded. The most popular majors were education (18%), business (15%), and journalism (12%). In an average class, 35% graduate in 4 years or less, 52% graduate in 5 years or less, and 57% graduate in 6 years or less. 715 companies recruited on campus in a recent year.

Admissions Contact: Mary E. Smith, Director of Admissions Services. E-mail: *mary.smith@murraystate.edu* Web: *http://www.murraystate.edu*

NORTHERN KENTUCKY UNIVERSITY   D-1
Highland Heights, KY 41099   (859) 572-5220
                        (800) 637-9948; Fax: (859) 572-6665

Full-time: 7675 men and women	**Faculty:** IIA, --$
Part-time: 3165 men and women	**Ph.D.s:** 82%
Graduate: 875 men and women	**Student/Faculty:** n/av
Year: semesters, summer session	**Tuition:** $2470 ($6710)
Application Deadline: see profile	**Room & Board:** $4000
Freshman Class: n/av	
SAT or ACT: required	**NONCOMPETITIVE**

Northern Kentucky University, founded in 1968, is a publicly controlled institution offering programs in arts and sciences, business, and professional studies. There are 4 undergraduate and 4 graduate schools. Figures in the above capsule and profile are approximate. In addition to regional accreditation, NKU has baccalaureate program accreditation with CAHEA, CSWE, NASM, and NLN. The 3 libraries contain 267,257 volumes, 135,257 microform items, and 2133 audio/video tapes/CDs/DVDs, and subscribe to 4423 periodicals including electronic. Computerized library services include the card catalog, interlibrary loans, and database searching. Special learning facilities include a learning resource center, art gallery, radio station, TV station, and a biology and geology museum. The 300-acre campus is in a suburban area 7 miles southeast of Cincinnati, Ohio. Including any residence halls, there are 42 buildings.

Student Life: 77% of undergraduates are from Kentucky. Others are from 35 states, 40 foreign countries, and Canada. 80% are white. The average age of freshmen is 20; all undergraduates, 26. 35% do not continue beyond their first year.

Housing: 1140 students can be accommodated in college housing, which includes single-sex and coed dormitories and on-campus apartments. On-campus housing is available on a first-come, first-served basis. Priority is given to out-of-town students. 91% of students commute. Alcohol is not permitted. All students may keep cars.

Activities: 4% of men belong to 6 national fraternities; 4% of women belong to 7 national sororities. There are 80 groups on campus, including art, cheerleading, chorale, chorus, computers, dance, drama, drill team, ethnic, film, gay, honors, international, jazz band, literary magazine, musical theater, newspaper, pep band, photography, political, professional, radio and TV, religious, social, social service, and student government. Popular campus events include Northern Noel, Musicfest, and Kentucky Awareness Week.

Sports: There are 6 intercollegiate sports for men and 5 for women, and 15 intramural sports for men and 13 for women. Facilities include a 2000-seat gym, baseball and soccer fields, tennis and racquetball courts, a track, a weight room, and a swimming pool.

Disabled Students: All of the campus is accessible. Elevators, special parking, specially equipped rest rooms, special class scheduling, lowered drinking fountains, and lowered telephones are available.

Services: Counseling and information services are available, as is tutoring in most subjects. There is a reader service for the blind, and remedial math, reading, and writing. There are also developmental education courses.

Campus Safety and Security: Measures include 24-hour foot and vehicle patrol, security escort services, informal discussions, and pamphlets/posters/films. There are emergency telephones and lighted pathways/sidewalks.

Programs of Study: NKU confers B.A., B.S., B.Mus., B.Mus.Ed., B.S.N., and B.S.W. degrees. Associate and master's degrees are also awarded. Bachelor's degrees are awarded in BIOLOGICAL SCIENCE (biology/biological science), BUSINESS (accounting, labor studies, management science, marketing/retailing/merchandising, and organizational behavior), COMMUNICATIONS AND THE ARTS (art, dramatic arts, English, French, graphic design, journalism, music, performing arts, radio/television technology, Spanish, and speech/debate/rhetoric), COMPUTER AND PHYSICAL SCIENCE (chemistry, computer science, geology, information sciences and systems, mathematics, and physics), EDUCATION (art, business, elementary, industrial arts, middle school, physical, science, and secondary), ENGINEERING AND ENVIRONMENTAL DESIGN (construction technology, industrial engineering technology, manufacturing engineering, manufacturing technology, and pre-engineering), HEALTH PROFESSIONS (mental health/human services, nursing, predentistry, premedicine, prepharmacy, and preveterinary science), SOCIAL SCIENCE (anthropology, economics, geography, history, international studies, philosophy, physical fitness/movement, political science/government, prelaw, psychology, public administration, social science, social work, and sociology). Education, nursing, and biology are the largest.

Required: All students must complete 54 semester hours of general studies, including English composition and speech, the arts, computer literacy, history, humanities, math, philosophy, sciences, and social sciences, along with major and minor requirements. A total of 128 semester hours, with a minimum GPA of 2.0, is required to graduate.

Special: A 3-2 engineering degree is offered with the University of Kentucky. Cross-registration is possible through the Greater Cincinnati Area Consortium of colleges and universities. Study abroad in 6 countries, a Washington semester, internships for communication majors, on-campus work-study programs, an accelerated degree program, an interdisciplinary honors program, B.A.-B.S. degrees, dual majors, and pass/fail options are offered. There are co-op programs in most majors. Student-designed majors and credit for work experience are available. Nondegree study is possible. There are 8 national honor societies and a freshman honors program.

Faculty/Classroom: 52% of faculty are male; 48%, female. All teach undergraduates. No introductory courses are taught by graduate students. The average class size in a regular course is 26.

Requirements: The SAT or ACT is required. Students who score satisfactorily and who meet all precollege curriculum requirements, including 4 units of English, 3 of math (algebra I, geometry, algebra II), 2 of U.S. history, world civilization (for Kentucky residents only), and 2 of science (biology and chemistry or physics), are granted regular admission. Others may be admitted with a stipulation or restriction on their admission. A high school diploma is required; the GED is accepted. AP and CLEP credits are accepted.

Procedure: Freshmen are admitted to all sessions. Entrance exams should be taken prior to enrollment. There are early decision, early admissions, deferred admissions and rolling admissions plans. Check with the school for current application deadlines. The application fee is $25. The college accepts all applicants. Notification is sent on a rolling basis. Applications are accepted on-line.

Transfer: Students must be eligible to return to their previous institution. College transcripts from previous institutions are required. 30 of 128 credits required for the bachelor's degree must be completed at NKU.

Visiting: There are regularly scheduled orientations for prospective students, consisting of a 1-day program with sessions on student services and financial aid, activities, a campus tour, and academic information, advising, and registration. There are guides for informal visits and visitors may sit in on classes and stay overnight. To schedule a visit, contact the Office of Admissions.

Financial Aid: The FAFSA and the college's own financial statement are required. Check with the school for current application deadlines.

International Students: The school actively recruits these students. They must score satisfactorily on the written TOEFL and also take the MELAB.

Computers: All students may access the system 7 days a week. There are no time limits. The fee $15 per semester.

Admissions Contact: Melissa Gorbrandt, Admissions Director of Admissions. E-mail: *gorbrandt@nku.edu* Web: *www.nku.edu*

PIKEVILLE COLLEGE   F-3
Pikeville, KY 41501   (606) 218-5251
                              (866) 232-7700; Fax: (606) 218-5255

Full-time: 377 men, 401 women	**Faculty:** 54; IIB, --$
Part-time: 27 men, 39 women	**Ph.Ds:** 52%
Graduate: 162 men, 123 women	**Student/Faculty:** 14 to 1
Year: semesters, summer session	**Tuition:** $11,500
Application Deadline: August 16	**Room & Board:** $5000
Freshman Class: 520 applied, 520 accepted, 208 enrolled	
ACT: 19	**NONCOMPETITIVE**

Pikeville College, founded in 1889 by the Prebyterian Church, is a private institution that offers a broad liberal arts and sciences education. The 2 libraries contain 72,673 volumes, 39,128 microform items, and 1811 audio/video tapes/CDs/DVDs, and subscribe to 219 periodicals including electronic. Computerized library services include the card catalog, interlibrary loans, database searching, and Internet access. Special learning facilities include a learning resource center and art gallery. The 27-acre campus is in a small town 20 miles from the Virginia border in the eastern Kentucky hills. Including any residence halls, there are 16 buildings.

Student Life: 81% of undergraduates are from Kentucky. Others are from 32 states, 7 foreign countries, and Canada. 99% are from public schools. 91% are white. Most are Protestant. The average age of freshmen is 18; all undergraduates, 22. 43% do not continue beyond their first year; 37% remain to graduate.

Housing: 525 students can be accommodated in college housing, which includes single-sex and coed dorms, on-campus apartments, and married-student housing. On-campus housing is guaranteed for all 4 years. 66% of students commute. Alcohol is not permitted. All students may keep cars.

Activities: There are no fraternities or sororities. There are 40 groups on campus, including art, band, cheerleading, choir, chorus, computers, dance, debate, drama, honors, jazz band, newspaper, pep band, political, professional, religious, social service, student government, and yearbook. Popular campus events include Founders Day.

Sports: There are 8 intercollegiate sports for men and 8 for women, and 10 intramural sports for men and 10 for women. Facilities include a gym, basketball, volleyball, and tennis courts, softball and baseball fields, and a football stadium.

Disabled Students: 95% of the campus is accessible. Wheelchair ramps, elevators, special parking, specially equipped rest rooms, lowered drinking fountains, and an elevator from the main parking lot to the upper campus are available.

Services: Counseling and information services are available, as is tutoring in most subjects, including math, English, biology, all physical sciences, computers, accounting, and Spanish. There is remedial math, reading, and writing.

Campus Safety and Security: Measures include 24-hour foot and vehicle patrol, lighted pathways/sidewalks, and night security guards.

Programs of Study: PC confers B.A., B.S., and B.B.A. degrees. Associate degrees are also awarded. Bachelor's degrees are awarded in BIOLOGICAL SCIENCE (biology/biological science), BUSINESS (business administration and management), COMMUNICATIONS AND THE ARTS (art, communications, and English), COMPUTER AND PHYSICAL SCIENCE (chemistry, computer science, and mathematics), EDUCATION (elementary, middle school, and secondary), SOCIAL SCIENCE (criminal justice, history, human services, political science/government, psychology, religion, social science, and sociology). Math, English, and religion are the strongest academically. Business, biology, and education are the largest.

Required: All students must complete core courses in humanities, English, social sciences, natural sciences, and math, as well as 2 courses each in religion, phys ed, and history and 1 course in computer science. Additional requirements include 6 hours in a foreign language for the B.A. degree and 2 lab science courses for the B.S. degree. An overall GPA of 2.0 is required. To graduate, students must complete 128 semester hours, with 30 to 60 hours in the major.

Special: Students may earn up to 6 credits at other institutions while enrolled at the college. Internships, B.A.-B.S. degrees, credit for life, military, and work experience, and pass/fail options are offered. Nondegree study is possible. There are 7 national honor societies and 7 departmental honors programs.

Faculty/Classroom: 43% of faculty are male; 57%, female. All teach undergraduates and 10% both teach and do research. No introductory courses are taught by graduate students. The average class size in an introductory lecture is 25; in a laboratory, 13; and in a regular course, 18.

Admissions: All of the 2005-2006 applicants were accepted. The ACT scores for the 2005-2006 freshman class were: 62% below 21, 23% between 21 and 23, 10% between 24 and 26, 3% between 27 and 28, and 2% above 28.

Requirements: The ACT is required. In addition, applicants must graduate from an accredited secondary school or have a GED. An interview is recommended. AP and CLEP credits are accepted.

Procedure: Freshmen are admitted to all sessions. Entrance exams should be taken in October of the year preceding entry. There are early admissions, rolling admissions and deferred admissions plans. Applications should be filed by August 16 for fall entry, January 10 for spring entry, and June for summer entry. The college accepts all applicants. Notification is sent on a rolling basis. Applications are accepted on-line.

Transfer: 106 transfer students enrolled in 2004-2005. All college transcripts and a review of students on suspension and probation are required. 30 of 128 credits required for the bachelor's degree must be completed at PC.

Visiting: There are regularly scheduled orientations for prospective students, consisting of a campus tour and lunch. There are guides for informal visits and visitors may sit in on classes and stay overnight. To schedule a visit, contact Paula Thompson at (606) 218-5257 or pthompso@pc.edu.

Financial Aid: In 2005-2006, 97% of all full-time students received some form of financial aid. 97% of full-time freshmen and 96% of continuing full-time students received need-based aid. The average freshman award was $11,903. Need-based scholarships or need-based grants averaged $10,040; and need-based self-help aid (loans and jobs) averaged $3227. 98% of undergraduates work part time. Average annual earnings from campus work are $1633. The average financial indebtedness of the 2005 graduate was $15,208. The FAFSA and the college's own financial statement are required. The deadline for filing freshman financial aid applications for fall entry is March 15.

International Students: There are 13 international students enrolled. They must score satisfactorily on the TOEFL and also take the ACT for placement purposes only.

Computers: Wireless access is available. Pikeville College maintains several public access facilities located throughout the campus including 136 PCs. The facilities are available for open access computing and for classroom instruction. All students may access the system 8 A.M. to 11 P.M. There are no time limits and no fees.

Graduates: From July 1, 2004 to June 30, 2005, 140 bachelor's degrees were awarded. The most popular majors were psychology /human services (20%), business (19%), and education (16%). In an average class, 22% graduate in 4 years or less, 35% graduate in 5 years or less, and 37% graduate in 6 years or less. 112 companies recruited on campus in 2004-2005. Of the 2004 graduating class, 33% were enrolled in graduate school within 6 months of graduation and 83% were employed.

Admissions Contact: Paula Thompson, Assistant Director of Admissions. E-mail: wewantyou@pc.edu Web: http://www.pc.edu

SPALDING UNIVERSITY D-2

Louisville, KY 40203-2188
(502) 585-7111
(800) 896-8941, ext. 2111; Fax: (502) 585-7128

Full-time: 645 men and women	**Faculty:** 58
Part-time: 258 men and women	**Ph.Ds:** 65%
Graduate: 747 men and women	**Student/Faculty:** 11 to 1
Year: term, summer session	**Tuition:** $15,000
Application Deadline: open	**Room & Board:** $3882
Freshman Class: n/av	
SAT or ACT: required	**COMPETITIVE**

Spalding University, established in 1814, is a private institution affiliated with the Roman Catholic Church and offers undergraduate degrees in the social sciences, humanities, health and natural sciences, business, communication studies, and education. There are 4 undergraduate and 4 graduate schools. In addition to regional accreditation, Spalding has baccalaureate program accreditation with CSWE, NCATE, and NLN. The library contains 220,232 volumes, 16,246 microform items, and 8669 audio/video tapes/CDs/DVDs, and subscribes to 601 periodicals including electronic. Computerized library services include the card catalog, interlibrary loans, database searching, and Internet access. Special learning facilities include a learning resource center, art gallery, video production facilities, and a digital media center. The 5-acre campus is in an urban area in downtown Louisville. Including any residence halls, there are 8 buildings.

Student Life: 82% of undergraduates are from Kentucky. Others are from 18 states, 25 foreign countries, and Canada. 85% are from public schools. 75% are white; 15% African American. 40% claim no religious affiliation; 31% Protestant; 29% Catholic. The average age of freshmen is 21; all undergraduates, 28. 37% do not continue beyond their first year; 51% remain to graduate.

Housing: 276 students can be accommodated in college housing, which includes coed dormitories. On-campus housing is guaranteed for all 4 years. 89% of students commute. Alcohol is not permitted. All students may keep cars.

Activities: There are no fraternities or sororities. There are 15 groups on campus, including art, drama, ethnic, gay, honors, international, political, professional, recreational, religious, social, social service, student government, and yearbook. Popular campus events include Annual

Running of the Rodents, Moonlight in the Mansion, and Community Service Fair.

Sports: There are 3 intercollegiate sports for men and 4 for women, and 4 intramural sports for men and 4 for women. Facilities include a gym and an exercise room.

Disabled Students: 80% of the campus is accessible. Wheelchair ramps, elevators, special parking, specially equipped rest rooms, special class scheduling, lowered drinking fountains, note takers, extended test taking time, oral testing, and special classroom accommodations are available.

Services: Counseling and information services are available, as is tutoring in every subject.

Campus Safety and Security: Measures include 24-hour foot and vehicle patrol, self-defense education, security escort services, and informal discussions. There are pamphlets/posters/films, emergency telephones, lighted pathways/sidewalks, and direct access to campus security from campus phones.

Programs of Study: Spalding confers B.A., B.S., B.S.B.A., B.S.Ed., B.S.N., and B.S.S.W. degrees. Associate, master's, and doctoral degrees are also awarded. Bachelor's degrees are awarded in BUSINESS (accounting and business administration and management), COMMUNICATIONS AND THE ARTS (communications), COMPUTER AND PHYSICAL SCIENCE (natural sciences), EDUCATION (education, elementary, and middle school), HEALTH PROFESSIONS (nursing and occupational therapy), SOCIAL SCIENCE (humanities, pastoral studies, psychology, social science, and social work). Nursing, education, psychology, and business administration are the strongest academically and have the largest enrollments.

Required: To graduate, students must earn 125 credits, with a maximum of 40 credits in the major for the B.A. degree and 50 credits for the B.S. degree, and a minimum overall GPA of 2.0. All students must complete a university studies requirement of 15 credits in humanities, 12 credits in social sciences, 12 credits in commnication, 9 credits in natural sciences and math, 6 credits in religious studies, and a 1-credit general introduction to the college.

Special: Cross-registration is offered with the Kentuckiana Metroversity Consortium. Internships, study abroad, B.A.-B.S. degrees, dual majors, work-study programs, and accelerated degree programs in business, psychology, and nursing are available. Credit is given for military experience and pass/fail options are available. The SAIL program enables students to earn a bachelor's degree by attending classes only on weekends and evenings. There are 8 national honor societies and 6 departmental honors programs.

Faculty/Classroom: 39% of faculty are male; 61%, female. 83% teach undergraduates. The average class size in an introductory lecture is 20; in a laboratory, 10; and in a regular course, 20.

Requirements: The SAT or ACT is required. In addition, applicants must be graduates of an accredited secondary school and should have completed 4 years of high school English and 2 years each of a foreign language, math, science, and social studies. A GED may be substituted for the high school degree. A GPA of 2.5 is required. AP and CLEP credits are accepted. Important factors in the admissions decision are advanced placement or honor courses, recommendations by school officials, and evidence of special talent.

Procedure: Freshmen are admitted to all sessions. Entrance exams should be taken by August 1. There is a rolling admissions plan. Application deadlines are open. Application fee is $20. Applications are accepted on-line.

Transfer: 117 transfer students enrolled in a recent year. It is preferred that applicants have a 2.5 GPA. 32 of 125 credits required for the bachelor's degree must be completed at Spalding.

Visiting: There are regularly scheduled orientations for prospective students. There are guides for informal visits and visitors may sit in on classes and stay overnight. To schedule a visit, contact the Office of University Admission.

Financial Aid: In a recent year, 74% of all full-time freshmen and 94% of continuing full-time students received some form of financial aid. 67% of full-time freshmen and 83% of continuing full-time students received need-based aid. The average freshman award was $14,513. 13% of undergraduates worked part time. Average annual earnings from campus work were $1046. The average financial indebtedness of a recent graduate was $15,106. The FAFSA is required. Check with the school for current application deadlines.

International Students: In a recent year there were 69 international students enrolled. The school actively recruits these students. A satisfactory score is required on the written TOEFL and also take the SAT or the ACT.

Computers: All students may access the system. There are no time limits and no fees. It is strongly recommended that all students have a personal computer.

Graduates: In a recent year, 178 bachelor's degrees were awarded. The most popular majors were nursing (23%), business (18%), and education (12%). In an average class, 34% graduate in 4 years or less, 45% graduate in 5 years or less, and 47% graduate in 6 years or less. 10 companies recruited on campus in a recent year.

Admissions Contact: Vicki Prince, Director of Admissions.
E-mail: *admissions@spalding.edu* Web: *www.spalding.edu*

THOMAS MORE COLLEGE — D-1
Crestview Hills, KY 41017-3495
(859) 344-3332
(800) 825-4557; Fax: (859) 344-3638

Full-time: 572 men, 555 women	Faculty: 71
Part-time: 85 men, 130 women	Ph.D.s: 72%
Graduate: 51 men, 40 women	Student/Faculty: 16 to 1
Year: semesters, summer session	Tuition: $18,320
Application Deadline: August 15	Room & Board: $6150
Freshman Class: 1007 applied, 637 accepted, 227 enrolled	
SAT Verbal/Math: 537/538*	ACT: 22	COMPETITIVE

Thomas More College, founded in 1921 as Villa Madonna College, is a private Catholic institution offering undergraduate programs in liberal arts and sciences, and an M.B.A in business administration. In addition to regional accreditation, Thomas More has baccalaureate program accreditation with NLN. The library contains 121,795 volumes, 14,116 microform items, and 2266 audio/video tapes/CDs/DVDs, and subscribes to 505 periodicals including electronic. Computerized library services include the card catalog, interlibrary loans, database searching, and Internet access. Special learning facilities include a learning resource center, art gallery, and observatory and biology field station on the Ohio River. The 100-acre campus is in a suburban area 8 miles south of Cincinnati. Including any residence halls, there are 9 buildings.

Student Life: 62% of undergraduates are from Kentucky. Others are from 12 states and 5 foreign countries. 71% are from public schools. 91% are white; 11% Asian American. 49% are Catholic; 49% unknown; 38% Protestant. The average age of freshmen is 18; all undergraduates, 26. 37% do not continue beyond their first year; 55% remain to graduate.

Housing: 400 students can be accommodated in college housing, which includes single-sex and coed dorms. On-campus housing is available on a first-come, first-served basis. Priority is given to out-of-town students. 70% of students commute. All students may keep cars.

Activities: There are no fraternities or sororities. There are 29 groups on campus, including art, cheerleading, chorus, computers, debate, drama, ethnic, honors, international, literary magazine, newspaper, political, professional, religious, social, social service, and student government. Popular campus events include fall and spring formals, Spring Pig Roast, and International Awareness Week.

Sports: There are 6 intercollegiate sports for men and 6 for women, and 6 intramural sports for men and 6 for women. Facilities include an athletic/convocation center with a 1,500-seat indoor gym and a 2,100-seat arena, plus baseball, football, softball, and soccer fields, 16 tennis courts (8 indoor), 4 racquetball courts, an indoor pool, a track, and weight and exercise rooms.

Disabled Students: 99% of the campus is accessible. Wheelchair ramps, elevators, special parking, and specially equipped rest rooms are available.

Services: Counseling and information services are available, as is tutoring in every subject. There is a reader service for the blind, and remedial math, reading, and writing. Signing for the hearing impaired is available.

Campus Safety and Security: Measures include 24-hour foot and vehicle patrol, self-defense education, security escort services, and informal discussions. There are pamphlets/posters/films and lighted pathways/sidewalks.

Programs of Study: Thomas More confers B.A., B.S., B.B.A., B.E.S., and B.S.N. degrees. Associate and master's degrees are also awarded. Bachelor's degrees are awarded in BIOLOGICAL SCIENCE (biology/biological science), BUSINESS (accounting and business administration and management), COMMUNICATIONS AND THE ARTS (art, communications, dramatic arts, English, fine arts, and speech/debate/rhetoric), COMPUTER AND PHYSICAL SCIENCE (chemistry, computer science, mathematics, and physics), EDUCATION (elementary, middle school, and secondary), HEALTH PROFESSIONS (medical laboratory technology and nursing), SOCIAL SCIENCE (criminal justice, economics, forensic studies, history, humanities, international studies, liberal arts/general studies, philosophy, political science/government, psychology, sociology, and theological studies). Business, biology, and education are the largest.

Required: All students must complete 56 to 61 hours of core requirements, including 6 credits each in English, theology, social sciences, global history, fine arts, philosophy, and natural sciences, and 3 each in foreign language, speech, and math. A total of 128 credit hours, including 36 to 76 in the major, with a minimum GPA of 2.0 is required to graduate.

Special: There are co-op programs in all majors except nursing and education, and 3-2 engineering degrees with the Universities of Cincinnati, Dayton, Detroit, Kentucky, and Notre Dame. Cross-registration is possible through the Greater Cincinnati Consortium. The college offers dual majors in international studies with a second major of the student's choice. There are also internships, study abroad in 15 countries, B.A.-

B.S. degrees, student-designed majors, work-study programs, credit for life experience, and pass/fail options. The Bachelor of Elected Studies degree provides adult learners with an individualized program. Nondegree study is possible. There are 6 national honor societies, a freshman honors program, and all departments have honors programs.

Faculty/Classroom: 56% of faculty are male; 44%, female. All teach undergraduates. No introductory courses are taught by graduate students. The average class size in an introductory lecture is 20; in a laboratory, 10; and in a regular course, 13.

Admissions: 63% of the 2005-2006 applicants were accepted. The SAT scores for the 2005-2006 freshman class were: Verbal--34% below 500, 36% between 500 and 599, 25% between 600 and 700, and 5% above 700; Math--36% below 500, 39% between 500 and 599, 22% between 600 and 700, and 3% above 700. The ACT scores were 37% below 21, 34% between 21 and 23, 16% between 24 and 26, 6% between 27 and 28, and 7% above 28. 28% of the current freshmen were in the top fifth of their class; 57% were in the top two fifths. 2 freshmen graduated first in their class.

Requirements: The SAT or ACT is required. In addition, applicants should have completed 16 high school academic credits, including 4 years of English and 2 each of math, science, social studies, and foreign language. Thomas More requires applicants to be in the upper 50% of their class. A GPA of 2.0 is required. AP and CLEP credits are accepted. Important factors in the admissions decision are advanced placement or honor courses, leadership record, and personality/intangible qualities.

Procedure: Freshmen are admitted to all sessions. Entrance exams should be taken in the spring of the junior year or in the fall of the senior year. There are early admissions and deferred admissions plans. Applications should be filed by August 15 for fall entry and January 5 for spring entry, along with a $25 fee. Notification is sent on a rolling basis. Applications are accepted on-line.

Transfer: 28 transfer students enrolled in 2004-2005. Applicants should be in good academic standing and have a minimum GPA of 2.0 in 24 semester hours earned. 38 of 128 credits required for the bachelor's degree must be completed at Thomas More.

Visiting: There are regularly scheduled orientations for prospective students, including a campus tour and meetings with an admissions counselor, a professor in one's major field (if decided), and financial aid staff. There are guides for informal visits and visitors may sit in on classes and stay overnight. To schedule a visit, contact the Admissions Office at *admissions@thomasmore.edu*.

Financial Aid: In 2005-2006, 100% of all full-time students received some form of financial aid. 92% of full-time freshmen and 93% of continuing full-time students received need-based aid. The average freshman award was $16,235. Need-based scholarships or need-based grants averaged $1990; need-based self-help aid (loans and jobs) averaged $2900; and other non-need-based awards and non-need-based scholarships averaged $4600. 101% of undergraduates work part time. The average financial indebtedness of the 2005 graduate was $17,125. The FAFSA, the college's own financial statement and the are required. The deadline for filing freshman financial aid applications for fall entry is March 15.

International Students: There are 7 international students enrolled. The school actively recruits these students. They must score 515 on the written TOEFL or 187 on the electronic version.

Computers: Wireless access is available. All students may access the system any time. There are no time limits. The fee is $150 per semester.

Graduates: From July 1, 2004 to June 30, 2005, 228 bachelor's degrees were awarded. The most popular majors were business (47%), social sciences and history (16%), and communications (5%). In an average class, 36% graduate in 4 years or less, 52% graduate in 5 years or less, and 56% graduate in 6 years or less. 84 companies recruited on campus in 2004-2005. Of the 2004 graduating class, 22% were enrolled in graduate school within 6 months of graduation and 78% were employed.

Admissions Contact: Angela Griffin Jones, Vice President for Enrollment Management. A video is available.
E-mail: *jim.harter@thomasmore.edu* Web: *www.thomasmore.edu*

TRANSYLVANIA UNIVERSITY — D-3
Lexington, KY 40508-1797
(859) 233-8242
(800) 872-6798; Fax: (859) 233-8797

Full-time: 452 men, 683 women	Faculty: 82; IIB, av$
Part-time: 12 men, 4 women	Ph.D.s: 97%
Graduate: none	Student/Faculty: 14 to 1
Year: 4-1-4, summer session	Tuition: $19,650
Application Deadline: February 1	Room & Board: $6590
Freshman Class: 1276 applied, 1065 accepted, 344 enrolled	
SAT Verbal/Math: 599/589*	ACT: 26	VERY COMPETITIVE+

Transylvania University, founded in 1780, is an independent liberal arts institution affiliated with the Christian Church (Disciples of Christ). In addition to regional accreditation, Transy has baccalaureate program accreditation with NCATE. The library contains 120,000 volumes, 57 microform items, and 2431 audio/video tapes/CDs/DVDs, and subscribes to 12,000 periodicals including electronic. Computerized library services include the card catalog, interlibrary loans, database searching, Internet access, and laptop Internet portals. Special learning facilities include a learning resource center, art gallery, natural history museum, and radio station. The 48-acre campus is in an urban area 80 miles east of Louisville and 80 miles south of Cincinnati, Ohio. Including any residence halls, there are 24 buildings.

Student Life: Students are from 35 states and 1 foreign countries. 85% are from public schools. 87% are white. 59% are Protestant; 21% claim no religious affiliation; 18% Catholic. The average age of freshmen is 18; all undergraduates, 20. 11% do not continue beyond their first year; 70% remain to graduate.

Housing: 900 students can be accommodated in college housing, which includes single-sex and coed dormitories and on-campus apartments. In addition, there are language houses. On-campus housing is guaranteed for all 4 years. 76% of students live on campus; of those, 80% remain on campus on weekends. All students may keep cars.

Activities: 50% of men belong to 4 national fraternities; 50% of women belong to 4 national sororities. There are 46 groups on campus, including art, band, cheerleading, choir, chorale, chorus, computers, dance, debate, drama, ethnic, forensics, gay, honors, international, jazz band, literary magazine, musical theater, newspaper, opera, orchestra, pep band, political, professional, radio and TV, religious, social, social service, student government, and yearbook. Popular campus events include the Presentation Ball, Madrigal Dinner, and the Kenan Lecture Series.

Sports: There are 7 intercollegiate sports for men and 9 for women, and 10 intramural sports for men and 10 for women. Facilities include a 1300-seat performance gym, 2 recreation gyms, a dance/aerobics room, an indoor jogging track, a swimming pool, basketball and racquetball/handball courts, 6 tennis courts, 3 athletic fields (baseball, men's soccer/field hockey, and women's soccer/softball), and weight and fitness rooms.

Disabled Students: 90% of the campus is accessible. Wheelchair ramps, elevators, special parking, specially equipped rest rooms, special class scheduling, and lowered drinking fountains are available. Arrangements are made according to individual needs.

Services: Counseling and information services are available, as is tutoring in every subject. A computing center provides individual help.

Campus Safety and Security: Measures include 24-hour foot and vehicle patrol, self-defense education, security escort services, and shuttle buses. There are informal discussions, pamphlets/posters/films, emergency telephones, lighted pathways/sidewalks, and a security presentation during freshman orientation.

Programs of Study: Transy confers the B.A. degree. Bachelor's degrees are awarded in BIOLOGICAL SCIENCE (biology/biological science), BUSINESS (accounting and business administration and management), COMMUNICATIONS AND THE ARTS (dramatic arts, English, French, music, Spanish, and studio art), COMPUTER AND PHYSICAL SCIENCE (chemistry, computer science, mathematics, and physics), EDUCATION (elementary and middle school), HEALTH PROFESSIONS (exercise science), SOCIAL SCIENCE (anthropology, economics, history, philosophy, political science/government, psychology, religion, and sociology). Business, biology, and psychology are the largest.

Required: All students must complete general education requirements in foundations of the liberal arts, academic career skills, humanities, lifetime fitness, fine arts, natural sciences, math, Western and non-Western cultural traditions, social sciences, and foreign language. 4 upper-level liberal arts classes are also required. Most majors have a capstone course requirement. A total of 36 course units, including 10 to 14 in the major, with a minimum GPA of 2.0, is required to graduate.

Special: 3-2 engineering degrees with the University of Kentucky, Vanderbilt University, and Washington University in St. Louis are offered. Cross-registration with May Term Consortium schools, internships, study abroad in 17 countries, work-study programs, a Washington semester, dual majors, and student-designed majors are available. There are 9 national honor societies.

Faculty/Classroom: 63% of faculty are male; 37%, female. All teach undergraduates. The average class size in an introductory lecture is 21; in a laboratory, 14; and in a regular course, 18.

Admissions: 83% of the 2005-2006 applicants were accepted. The SAT scores for the 2005-2006 freshman class were: Verbal--15% below 500, 35% between 500 and 599, 35% between 600 and 700, and 15% above 700; Math--17% below 500, 33% between 500 and 599, 39% between 600 and 700, and 11% above 700. The ACT scores were 6% below 21, 15% between 21 and 23, 27% between 24 and 26, 23% between 27 and 28, and 29% above 28. 76% of the current freshmen were in the top fifth of their class; 94% were in the top two fifths. There were 5 National Merit finalists. 24 freshmen graduated first in their class.

Requirements: The SAT or ACT is required. 1 essay and 2 recommendations are required. An interview is strongly recommended. Transy requires applicants to be in the upper 50% of their class. A GPA of 3.0 is required. AP credits are accepted. Important factors in the admissions decision are advanced placement or honor courses, recommendations by school officials, and extracurricular activities record.

Procedure: Freshmen are admitted fall and winter. Entrance exams should be taken during the junior year and no later than December of the senior year for scholarship consideration or February for general admission. There are early admissions and deferred admissions plans. Early decision applications should be filed by December 1; regular applications, by February 1 for fall entry and December 5 for winter entry, along with a $30 fee. Notification of early decision is sent January 15; regular decision, March 15. A waiting list is an active part of the admissions procedure. Applications are accepted on-line.

Transfer: 12 transfer students enrolled in 2005-2006. Applicants must have a minimum college GPA of 2.75 and should submit official copies of all college transcripts, 2 recommendations, and 1 essay. A high school transcript of GED is required 18 of 36 courses required for the bachelor's degree must be completed at Transy.

Visiting: There are regularly scheduled orientations for prospective students, consisting of campus open houses in fall and winter for high school juniors and seniors, including a welcome program, an academic information fair, campus tours, a luncheon, a financial aid session, and a faculty session. There are guides for informal visits and visitors may sit in on classes and stay overnight. To schedule a visit, contact Tammie Williams.

Financial Aid: In 2005-2006, 99% of all full-time freshmen and 98% of continuing full-time students received some form of financial aid. 64% of full-time freshmen and 60% of continuing full-time students received need-based aid. The average freshman award was $15,086. Need-based scholarships or need-based grants averaged $12,719 ($28,740 maximum); need-based self-help aid (loans and jobs) averaged $4124 ($6425 maximum); and other non-need-based awards and non-need-based scholarships averaged $11,890 ($28,740 maximum). 29% of undergraduates work part time. Average annual earnings from campus work are $1265. The average financial indebtedness of the 2005 graduate was $15,673. Transy is a member of CSS. The FAFSA is required. The deadline for filing freshman financial aid applications for fall entry is March 1.

International Students: There is 1 international students enrolled. They must score satisfactorily on the written TOEFL or on the electronic version and take the TWE. They must also take the SAT or the ACT.

Computers: Wireless access is available. There are 262 PCs in student labs; all residential rooms have access, and there are 30 wireless access points. All students may access the system 24 hours a day. There are no time limits and no fees. It is strongly recommended that all students have a personal computer.

Graduates: From July 1, 2004 to June 30, 2005, 232 bachelor's degrees were awarded. The most popular majors were business administration (17%), biology (13%), and psychology (8%). In an average class, 1% graduate in 3 years or less, 65% graduate in 4 years or less, 70% graduate in 5 years or less, and 70% graduate in 6 years or less. 13 companies recruited on campus in 2004-2005. Of the 2004 graduating class, 40% were enrolled in graduate school within 6 months of graduation and 41% were employed.

Admissions Contact: Deana Ison, Interim Director of Admissions. A video is available. E-mail: *admissions@transy.edu* Web: *www.transy.edu*

UNION COLLEGE   E-4
Barbourville, KY 40906-9989

(606) 546-1657
(800) 489-8646; Fax: (606) 546-1667

Full-time: 321 men, 232 women	**Faculty:** 42
Part-time: 21 men, 37 women	**Ph.D.s:** 74%
Graduate: 213 men, 400 women	**Student/Faculty:** 13 to 1
Year: semesters, summer session	**Tuition:** $14,520
Application Deadline: open	**Room & Board:** $4400
Freshman Class: 521 accepted, 261 enrolled	
SAT or ACT: required	**COMPETITIVE**

Union College, founded in 1879, is a private liberal arts institution affiliated with the United Methodist Church. The library contains 110,197 volumes, 447,333 microform items, and 5196 audio/video tapes/CDs/DVDs, and subscribes to 14,453 periodicals including electronic. Computerized library services include the card catalog, interlibrary loans, database searching, Internet access, and laptop Internet portals. Special learning facilities include a learning resource center and TV station. The 100-acre campus is in a small town 95 miles south of Lexington and 85 miles north of Knoxville, Tennessee. Including any residence halls, there are 20 buildings.

Student Life: 77% of undergraduates are from Kentucky. Students are from 21 states, 14 foreign countries, and Canada. 93% are from public schools. 83% are white. 65% are Protestant; 11% Catholic; 7% claim no religious affiliation. The average age of freshmen is 19; all undergraduates, 22. 44% do not continue beyond their first year; 33% remain to graduate.

Housing: 328 students can be accommodated in college housing, which includes single-sex and coed dorms, on-campus apartments, and married-student housing. On-campus housing is guaranteed for all 4 years. 50% of students live on campus; of those, 60% remain on campus on weekends. Alcohol is not permitted. All students may keep cars.

Activities: There are no fraternities or sororities. There are 20 groups on campus, including band, cheerleading, chess, choir, chorale, chorus, computers, drama, ethnic, honors, international, literary magazine, newspaper, orchestra, pep band, professional, religious, social, social service, student government, and yearbook. Popular campus events include Springfest, Student Holiday Dinner, and CIRCLES ceremony.

Sports: There are 9 intercollegiate sports for men and 9 for women. There are 5 intramural sports for men, 3 for women, and 2 coed. Facilities include a 3000-seat campus stadium, an 1800-seat gym, an indoor pool with bleachers for 300, 6 tennis courts, a weight-training center, an athletic training center, a 500-seat baseball stadium with 3 batting cages and a practice infield, a soccer field with stands for 250, a softball frield with stand for 150, and practice fields for football and soccer.

Disabled Students: 80% of the campus is accessible. Wheelchair ramps, elevators, special parking, specially equipped rest rooms, special class scheduling, lowered drinking fountains, and lowered telephones are available.

Services: Counseling and information services are available, as is tutoring in most subjects. There is a tutoring lab with computer support. There is remedial reading and writing.

Campus Safety and Security: Measures include 24-hour foot and vehicle patrol, self-defense education, security escort services, and informal discussions. There are pamphlets/posters/films, emergency telephones, and lighted pathways/sidewalks.

Programs of Study: Union confers B.A., and B.S. degrees. Associate and master's degrees are also awarded. Bachelor's degrees are awarded in BIOLOGICAL SCIENCE (biology/biological science), BUSINESS (accounting, business administration and management, recreational facilities management, and sports management), COMMUNICATIONS AND THE ARTS (dramatic arts and English), COMPUTER AND PHYSICAL SCIENCE (chemistry and mathematics), EDUCATION (education, elementary, middle school, physical, secondary, and special), ENGINEERING AND ENVIRONMENTAL DESIGN (computer technology), HEALTH PROFESSIONS (health), SOCIAL SCIENCE (criminal justice, history, ministries, political science/government, psychology, religion, and sociology). Education, sciences, and social sciences are the strongest academically. Education, business, and social sciences are the largest.

Required: All students are required to complete 43 credits in a liberal education core, including 21 hours in humanities, 7 to 8 of general science, 6 of social science, and 3 each of wellness, math, and cultural studies.

Special: A 3-2 enginering degree is offered with the University of Kentucky and Auburn University. Work-study programs, study abroad in 7 countries, an accelerated business degree completion program, and internships in business, sociology, psychology, recreational management, and mass communications are available.

Faculty/Classroom: 64% of faculty are male; 36%, female. 85% teach undergraduates. No introductory courses are taught by graduate students. The average class size in an introductory lecture is 17; in a laboratory, 14; and in a regular course, 11.

Requirements: The SAT or ACT is required (standardized text scores are not required for students 25 years or older). All first-year students should have completed a precollege high school curriculum that includes 4 units of English, 3 of math, 2 each of lab science and social science, and the study of a foreign language. An official, sealed high school transcript or an official GED score report is also required. Union requires applicants to be in the upper 50% of their class. A GPA of 2.0 is required. AP and CLEP credits are accepted. Important factors in the admissions decision are evidence of special talent, geographic diversity, and advanced placement or honor courses.

Procedure: Freshmen are admitted to all sessions. Entrance exams should be taken by January of the senior year. There is a deferred admissions and a rolling admissions plan. Application deadlines are open. Application fee is $10. Notificaion is sent on a rolling basis. Applications are accepted on-line.

Transfer: 61 transfer students enrolled in 2004-2005. Applicants should have a minimum GPA of 2.0. 32 of 128 credits required for the bachelor's degree must be completed at Union.

Visiting: There are regularly scheduled orientations for prospective students, consisting of advising and registration, parent sessions, and breakout sessions. There are guides for informal visits and visitors may sit in on classes and stay overnight. To schedule a visit, contact Admissions.

Financial Aid: In 2005-2006, 84% of all full-time freshmen and 91% of continuing full-time students received some form of financial aid. 84% of full-time freshmen and 89% of continuing full-time students received need-based aid. The average freshman award was $14,254. Need-based scholarships or need-based grants averaged $5050; need-based self-help aid (loans and jobs) averaged $4125; non-need-based athletic scholarships averaged $18,920; and other non-need-based awards and non-need-based scholarships averaged $18,920. 44% of undergraduates work part time. Average annual earnings from campus work are $750. The average financial indebtedness of the 2005 graduate was $11,681.

Union is a member of CSS. The CSS/Profile or FAFSA is required. The deadline for filing freshman financial aid applications for fall entry is March 15.

International Students: There are 22 international students enrolled. The school actively recruits these students. Satisfactory scores are required on the written TOEFL. Students must also complete an ELS program at level 109 submit a satisfactory score on the SAT or the ACT.

Computers: Wireless access is available. All residence halls are wired; the library, the student center, and other key buildings have wireless. There are 2 labs for student use on campus. The library has 15 laptops for student use. All students may access the system. There are no time limits and no fees.

Graduates: From July 1, 2004 to June 30, 2005, 132 bachelor's degrees were awarded. The most popular majors were education (30%), business (28%), and psychology (12%). In an average class, 23% graduate in 4 years or less, 30% graduate in 5 years or less, and 33% graduate in 6 years or less. 6 companies recruited on campus in 2004-2005.

Admissions Contact: Jamirae Hammons, Associate Dean of Admissions. A video is available. E-mail: *enrollme@unionky.edu* Web: *www.unionky.edu*

UNIVERSITY OF KENTUCKY   D-3

Lexington, KY 40506-0032   (606) 257-2000; Fax: (606) 257-3823

Full-time: 7145 men, 7720 women	**Faculty:** 1239; I, -$
Part-time: 975 men, 1025 women	**Ph.D.s:** 98%
Graduate: 2875 men, 3355 women	**Student/Faculty:** 12 to 1
Year: semesters, summer session	**Tuition:** $3750 ($10,300)
Application Deadline: see profile	**Room & Board:** $4050
Freshman Class: n/av	
SAT or ACT: required	COMPETITIVE

The University of Kentucky, founded in 1865, is a public land-grant institution offering undergraduate and graduate programs in a variety of areas. Figures in the above capsule and in this profile are approximate. There are 13 undergraduate schools and 1 graduate school. In addition to regional accreditation, UK has baccalaureate program accreditation with AACSB, ABET, ACEJMC, ACPE, ADA, AHEA, APTA, ASLA, CAHEA, CSWE, FIDER, NAAB, NASAD, NASM, NCATE, NLN, NRPA, and SAF. The 13 libraries contain 2,792,293 volumes, 5,872,795 microform items, and 73,600 audio/video tapes/CDs/DVDs, and subscribe to 26,539 periodicals including electronic. Computerized library services include the card catalog and database searching. Special learning facilities include a learning resource center, art gallery, natural history museum, radio station, and TV station. The 764-acre campus is in a suburban area 75 miles south of Cincinnati. Including any residence halls, there are 335 buildings.

Student Life: 83% of undergraduates are from Kentucky. Others are from 49 states, 114 foreign countries, and Canada. 85% are from public schools. 87% are white. The average age of freshmen is 18; all undergraduates, 22. 20% do not continue beyond their first year; 50% remain to graduate.

Housing: 6166 students can be accommodated in college housing, which includes single-sex and coed dormitories, on-campus apartments, married-student housing, fraternity houses, and sorority houses. In addition, there are honors houses, language houses, and special-interest houses. On-campus housing is available on a first-come, first-served basis. 69% of students commute. Alcohol is not permitted. All students may keep cars.

Activities: 15% of men belong to 22 national fraternities; 17% of women belong to 16 national sororities. There are 272 groups on campus, including band, cheerleading, chess, choir, chorale, chorus, computers, dance, debate, drama, drill team, ethnic, gay, honors, international, jazz band, literary magazine, marching band, musical theater, newspaper, orchestra, pep band, photography, political, professional, radio and TV, religious, social, social service, student government, symphony, and yearbook. Popular campus events include Little Kentucky Derby, Cultural Diversity Week, and Spotlight Jazz Series.

Sports: There are 11 intercollegiate sports for men and 12 for women, and 22 intramural sports for men and 22 for women. Facilities include a 58,000-seat football stadium, a 24,500-seat arena for basketball and other activities, an aquatic center and swimming pool, baseball fields, a training center, indoor tennis courts, and a field house.

Disabled Students: 90% of the campus is accessible. Wheelchair ramps, elevators, special parking, specially equipped rest rooms, special class scheduling, lowered drinking fountains, and lowered telephones are available.

Services: There is a reader service for the blind and remedial math.

Campus Safety and Security: Measures include 24-hour foot and vehicle patrol, self-defense education, security escort services, and shuttle buses. There are informal discussions, pamphlets/posters/films, emergency telephones, and lighted pathways/sidewalks.

Programs of Study: UK confers B.A., B.S., B.Arch., B.B.A., B.F.A., B.H.S., and B.M. degrees. Master's and doctoral degrees are also awarded. Bachelor's degrees are awarded in AGRICULTURE (agricultural economics, agriculture, animal science, and forestry and related sciences), BIOLOGICAL SCIENCE (biology/biological science, botany, and zoology), BUSINESS (accounting, banking and finance, business economics, hotel/motel and restaurant management, and marketing/retailing/merchandising), COMMUNICATIONS AND THE ARTS (advertising, art history and appreciation, arts administration/management, communications, dramatic arts, English, French, German, Italian, journalism, linguistics, music, music performance, Russian, Spanish, and telecommunications), COMPUTER AND PHYSICAL SCIENCE (chemistry, computer science, geology, mathematics, and physics), EDUCATION (agricultural, art, business, early childhood, elementary, foreign languages, health, mathematics, middle school, music, physical, science, secondary, social studies, and special), ENGINEERING AND ENVIRONMENTAL DESIGN (chemical engineering, civil engineering, electrical/electronics engineering, landscape architecture/design, materials engineering, mechanical engineering, and mining and mineral engineering), HEALTH PROFESSIONS (nursing, physical therapy, and physician's assistant), SOCIAL SCIENCE (anthropology, economics, food science, geography, history, Latin American studies, philosophy, political science/government, psychology, social work, sociology, and textiles and clothing). Pharmacy, architecture, and allied health are the strongest academically. Finance, accounting, and marketing are the largest.

Required: All students must maintain a minimum 2.0 GPA and complete at least 120 credit hours. Students must demonstrate competency in math, foreign language, writing, and oral communications. Required studies include courses in basic skills, inference, and communicative skills, along with disciplinary and cross-disciplinary studies.

Special: Co-op programs are offered in engineering, business, computer science, math, and agriculture. The Academic Common Market allows students in 14 southern states to study outside the university. Internships in a variety of fields, study abroad in 36 countries, work-study programs with the university and local businesses, and credit for life experience are also available. An accelerated degree program, B.A.-B.S. degrees, dual and double majors, a general studies degree, student-designed majors, a 3-2 engineering degree with several smaller schools in Kentucky, non-degree study, and pass/fail options are also offered. There are 12 national honor societies, including Phi Beta Kappa, and a freshman honors program.

Faculty/Classroom: 70% of faculty are male; 30%, female. 66% teach undergraduates.

Requirements: The SAT or ACT is required. Minimum scores vary with the GPA. Applicants must complete 20 Carnegie units, including 4 years of English, 3 of math, and 2 each of science and social studies. A fourth year of math, 2 years of foreign language, and 1 year of fine arts also are recommended. A portfolio is required for art studio courses, and an audition is required for music performance. A GPA of 2.0 is required. AP and CLEP credits are accepted.

Procedure: Freshmen are admitted to all sessions. There is a rolling admissions plan. Entrance exams should be taken before Christmas of the senior year. Check with the school for current application deadlines. Notification of early decision is sent rolling; regular decision, on a rolling basis.

Transfer: Transfer students need a minimum GPA of 2.0. If they have fewer than 24 credit hours, they must meet freshmen admission standards. With 24 credits or more, the SAT or ACT is not required. 30 of 120 credits required for the bachelor's degree must be completed at UK.

Visiting: There are regularly scheduled orientations for prospective students, including a campus tour and information on admissions, housing, financial aid, and campus activities. There are guides for informal visits and visitors may sit in on classes. To schedule a visit, contact the UK Visitor Center at (606) 257-3595.

Financial Aid: UK is a member of CSS. The FAFSA is required. Check with the school for current application deadlines.

International Students: The school actively recruits these students. They must score satisfactorily on the written TOEFL.

Computers: All students may access the system 24 hours daily in the computing center and various hours in labs. There are no time limits and no fees.

Admissions Contact: Randy Mills, Associate Director for Recruitment. E-mail: *admissio@uky.edu* Web: *www.uky.edu*

UNIVERSITY OF LOUISVILLE   D-2
Louisville, KY 40292   (502) 852-6531
(800) 334-8635; Fax: (502) 852-4476

Full-time: 5208 men, 6017 women	Faculty: 802; I, --$
Part-time: 1365 men, 1303 women	Ph.D.s: 68%
Graduate: 1777 men, 2219 women	Student/Faculty: 14 to 1
Year: semesters, summer session	Tuition: $5532 ($15,092)
Application Deadline: August 21	Room & Board: $4868
Freshman Class: 5712 applied, 4515 accepted, 2009 enrolled	
ACT: 23	VERY COMPETITIVE

The University of Louisville, founded in 1798, is a public institution offering a wide range of undergraduate and academic graduate programs.

There are 7 undergraduate and 7 graduate schools. In addition to regional accreditation, U of L has baccalaureate program accreditation with AACSB, ABET, ACEJMC, ASLA, CAHEA, NAAB, NASM, NCATE, and NLN. The 7 libraries contain 2,026,840 volumes, 2,190,246 microform items, and 38,628 audio/video tapes/CDs/DVDs, and subscribe to 24,720 periodicals including electronic. Computerized library services include the card catalog, interlibrary loans, and database searching. Special learning facilities include a learning resource center, art gallery, planetarium, and radio station. The campus is in an urban area.

Student Life: 86% of undergraduates are from Kentucky. Others are from 50 states, 80 foreign countries, and Canada. 90% are from public schools. 62% are white; 10% African American. The average age of freshmen is 18; all undergraduates, 24. 24% do not continue beyond their first year; 37% remain to graduate.

Housing: 2400 students can be accommodated in college housing, which includes coed dorms, on-campus apartments, off-campus apartments, married-student housing, fraternity houses, and sorority houses. In addition, there are honors houses, special-interest houses, and suites. On-campus housing is available on a first-come, first-served basis. Priority is given to out-of-town students. 91% of students commute. All students may keep cars.

Activities: 3% of men belong to 14 national fraternities; 3% of women belong to 1 local and 9 national sororities. There are 49 groups on campus, including art, band, cheerleading, chess, choir, chorale, chorus, computers, ethnic, gay, honors, international, jazz band, literary magazine, marching band, newspaper, opera, orchestra, pep band, photography, political, professional, radio, religious, social, social service, student government, and symphony.

Sports: There are 9 intercollegiate sports for men and 12 for women, and 34 intramural sports for men and 34 for women. Facilities include a 19,400-seat gym and a football stadium.

Disabled Students: 90% of the campus is accessible. Wheelchair ramps, elevators, special parking, specially equipped rest rooms, special class scheduling, lowered drinking fountains, lowered telephones, and special housing are available.

Services: Counseling and information services are available, as is tutoring in every subject.

Campus Safety and Security: Measures include 24-hour foot and vehicle patrol, security escort services, shuttle buses, and informal discussions. There are pamphlets/posters/films, emergency telephones, and lighted pathways/sidewalks.

Programs of Study: U of L confers B.A., B.S., and B.F.A. degrees. Associate, master's, and doctoral degrees are also awarded. Bachelor's degrees are awarded in AGRICULTURE (equine science), BIOLOGICAL SCIENCE (biology/biological science), BUSINESS (accounting, banking and finance, business administration and management, business economics, management science, marketing/retailing/merchandising, and sports management), COMMUNICATIONS AND THE ARTS (art, art history and appreciation, communications, dramatic arts, English, French, linguistics, music, and Spanish), COMPUTER AND PHYSICAL SCIENCE (chemistry, computer science, information sciences and systems, mathematics, and physics), EDUCATION (art, business, early childhood, elementary, foreign languages, middle school, music, physical, science, secondary, and teaching English as a second/foreign language (TESOL/TEFOL)), ENGINEERING AND ENVIRONMENTAL DESIGN (chemical engineering, civil engineering, computer engineering, electrical/electronics engineering, engineering, engineering management, industrial engineering, and mechanical engineering), HEALTH PROFESSIONS (health, medical laboratory technology, medical science, and nursing), SOCIAL SCIENCE (African studies, anthropology, criminal justice, geography, history, humanities, liberal arts/general studies, paralegal studies, philosophy, political science/government, psychology, sociology, and women's studies). Engineering, health professional, and business management are the strongest academically. The arts and sciences, business, and education are the largest.

Required: Distribution requirements include at least 6 hours each in social sciences, natural sciences, the history of world civilizations, and humanities. Freshmen are required to take college writing or advanced composition, and 2 phys ed courses. A total of 123 semester hours, including 46 to 60 hours in the major, with a minimum GPA of 2.5 (2.0 in education, 2.75 in engineering) is required in order to graduate.

Special: Cross-registration with other schools, study abroad in 5 countries, work-study programs, and B.A.-B.S. degrees are offered. A general studies degree, nondegree study, and pass/fail options are available. Co-op programs in engineering and business and internships are also possible. There is a freshman honors program.

Faculty/Classroom: 59% of faculty are male; 41%, female. The average class size in an introductory lecture is 31 and in a regular course, 29.

Admissions: 79% of the 2005-2006 applicants were accepted. The ACT scores for the 2005-2006 freshman class were: 25% below 21, 30% between 21 and 23, 23% between 24 and 26, 11% between 27 and 28, and 11% above 28. There were 4 National Merit finalists and 5 semifinalists.

Requirements: The SAT or ACT is required. In addition, applicants must be graduates from accredited high school or have received a GED and completed pre-college curriculum with a GPA of 2.5 and at least one of the following: Earn a composite ACT score of 20 or a satisfactory SAT score; have completed U of L enhanced pre-college curriculum (PCC) with a minimum GPA of 2.5, or rank in the top 15% of the high school graduating class. A GPA of 2.5 is required. AP and CLEP credits are accepted.

Procedure: Freshmen are admitted fall, spring, and summer. Entrance exams should be taken in spring or summer of junior year. There are early admissions and deferred admissions plans. There is a rolling admissions plan. Applications should be filed by August 21 for fall entry, along with a $30 fee. Notification is sent on a rolling basis. Applications are accepted on-line.

Transfer: 949 transfer students enrolled in 2004-2005. Transfer students must have a minimum GPA of 2.0. 30 of 123 credits required for the bachelor's degree must be completed at U of L.

Visiting: There are regularly scheduled orientations for prospective students. There are guides for informal visits and visitors may sit in on classes. To schedule a visit, contact Admissions at (502) 852-5516 or (800) 334-8635.

Financial Aid: In 2005-2006, 56% of all full-time freshmen and 50% of continuing full-time students received some form of financial aid. At least 30% of full-time freshmen and at least 37% of continuing full-time students received need-based aid. The average freshman award was $8229. Need-based scholarships or need-based grants averaged $5876 ($19,342 maximum); need-based self-help aid (loans and jobs) averaged $3082 ($22,641 maximum); non-need-based athletic scholarships averaged $12,264 ($22,329 maximum); and other institutional non-need-based awards and non-need-based scholarships averaged $5541 ($23,590 maximum). The average financial indebtedness of the 2005 graduate was $15,128. The FAFSA is required. The priority date for freshman financial aid applications for fall entry is March 15.

International Students: There are 221 international students enrolled. They must score satisfactorily on the written TOEFL and also take the ACT.

Computers: Wireless access is available. All students may access the system. There are no time limits and no fees.

Graduates: From July 1, 2004 to June 30, 2005, 2148 bachelor's degrees were awarded. The most popular majors were business/marketing (22%), social sciences (10%), and engineering (9%). In an average class, 13% graduate in 4 years or less, 30% graduate in 5 years or less, and 37% graduate in 6 years or less.

Admissions Contact: Jenny Sawyer, Director of Admissions.
E-mail: *admitme@gwise.louisville.edu* Web: *http://www.louisville.edu*

UNIVERSITY OF THE CUMBERLANDS   E-4
(Formerly Cumberland College)

Williamsburg, KY 40769

(606) 539-4241
(800) 343-1609; Fax: (606) 539-4303

Full-time: 684 men, 726 women	Faculty: 92
Part-time: 98 men, 122 women	Ph.D.s: 72%
Graduate: 49 men, 161 women	Student/Faculty: 15 to 1
Year: semesters, summer session	Tuition: $12,658
Application Deadline: open	Room & Board: $5526

Freshman Class: 984 applied, 818 accepted, 431 enrolled
SAT Verbal/Math: 510/520*   ACT: 22*   COMPETITIVE

University of the Cumberlands, formerly Cumberland College, founded in 1888, is a private liberal arts institution affiliated with the Kentucky Baptist Convention. The library contains 188,281 volumes, 805,102 microform items, and 3759 audio/video tapes/CDs/DVDs, and subscribes to 1360 periodicals including electronic. Computerized library services include the card catalog, interlibrary loans, database searching, Internet access, and laptop Internet portals. Special learning facilities include a learning resource center, art gallery, natural history museum, radio station, TV station, and a distance learning lab. The 50-acre campus is in a small town 100 miles south of Lexington and 65 miles north of Knoxville. Including any residence halls, there are 30 buildings.

Student Life: 57% of undergraduates are from Kentucky. Students are from 37 states, 21 foreign countries, and Canada. 95% are from public schools. 90% are white. 15% claim no religious affiliation; 8% Protestant. The average age of freshmen is 18; all undergraduates, 21. 40% do not continue beyond their first year; 40% remain to graduate.

Housing: 1100 students can be accommodated in college housing, which includes single-sex dorms. On-campus housing is guaranteed for all 4 years. 68% of students live on campus; of those, 60% remain on campus on weekends. Alcohol is not permitted. All students may keep cars.

Activities: There are no fraternities or sororities. There are 45 groups on campus, including art, band, cheerleading, choir, chorale, chorus, dance, debate, drama, drill team, forensics, honors, jazz band, literary magazine, marching band, musical theater, newspaper, pep band, political, professional, radio and TV, religious, social, social service, and student government. Popular campus events include Madrigal Dinner, Hanging of the Greens, and Valentine's Dance.

Sports: There are 12 intercollegiate sports for men and 12 for women, and 6 intramural sports for men and 6 for women. Facilities include a gym for intramurals and recreation, an athletic complex with facilities for men's and women's basketball and volleyball, a weight room, and a swimming pool, a game room, tennis court, baseball, football,soccer, softball fields, a practice soccer and football fields, and a wrestling gym.

Disabled Students: 75% of the campus is accessible. Wheelchair ramps, elevators, special parking, specially equipped rest rooms, special class scheduling, and lowered drinking fountains are available.

Services: Counseling and information services are available, as is tutoring in every subject.

Campus Safety and Security: Measures include 24-hour foot and vehicle patrol, self-defense education, security escort services, and informal discussions. There are pamphlets/posters/films and lighted pathways/sidewalks.

Programs of Study: University of the Cumberlands confers B.A., B.S., B.G.S., and B.M. degrees. Master's degrees are also awarded. Bachelor's degrees are awarded in BIOLOGICAL SCIENCE (biology/biological science), BUSINESS (accounting, business administration and management, and office supervision and management), COMMUNICATIONS AND THE ARTS (art, communications, dramatic arts, English, and music), COMPUTER AND PHYSICAL SCIENCE (chemistry, information sciences and systems, mathematics, and physics), EDUCATION (art, business, elementary, English, health, mathematics, middle school, music, physical, science, social studies, and special), HEALTH PROFESSIONS (health, medical laboratory technology, and public health), SOCIAL SCIENCE (history, political science/government, psychology, religion, religious music, and social work). Biology, business, and chemistry are the strongest academically. Biology, business, and education are the largest.

Required: All students must complete 128 semester hours, including 49 hours of liberal arts courses and an average of 36 hours in a major, while maintaining an overall GPA of 2.0 (2.5 for those seeking teacher certification). General education requirements include courses from the areas of physical fitness, art, music, theater, speech, religion, English composition, literature, history, math, natural and social sciences, community service, and fine arts or philosophy. A comprehensive exam may be required. Programs presented for graduation must include 2 majors, 1 major and 1 minor, 1 major with 15 hours of restricted electives, or 3 minors.

Special: Internships, study abroad in England and China, a Washington semester, and work-study programs with the university, local businesses, and other educational institutions are available. The university offers B.A.-B.S. degrees in all majors except music, dual majors in all major fields, a general studies degree, and nondegree study. There are 11 national honor societies, a freshman honors program, and 10 departmental honors programs.

Faculty/Classroom: 62% of faculty are male; 38%, female. All teach undergraduates. No introductory courses are taught by graduate students. The average class size in an introductory lecture is 30; in a laboratory, 15; and in a regular course, 21.

Admissions: 83% of the 2005-2006 applicants were accepted. The SAT scores for the 2005-2006 freshman class were: Verbal--47% below 500, 40% between 500 and 599, 13% between 600 and 700, and 1% above 700; Math--44% below 500, 39% between 500 and 599, 16% between 600 and 700, and 1% above 700. The ACT scores were 43% below 21, 29% between 21 and 23, 16% between 24 and 26, 8% between 27 and 28, and 4% above 28. 34% of the current freshmen were in the top fifth of their class; 66% were in the top two fifths. 8 freshmen graduated first in their class.

Requirements: The SAT or ACT is required, with satisfactory scores. Consideration is given to those with lower ACT scores, provided the high school GPA is 2.5 or above in college prep classes. Although each application is considered individually, students must have fulfilled general high school requirements of 4 years of English, 3 each of math and science, and 2 of social studies. A completed Teacher Recommendation Form from a current teacher, a completed High School Information Form signed by the guidance counselor, and a high school transcript are required. The university also recommends an interview. The GED is accepted. A GPA of 2.0 is required. AP and CLEP credits are accepted. Important factors in the admissions decision are leadership record, recommendations by school officials, and advanced placement or honor courses.

Procedure: Freshmen are admitted to all sessions. Entrance exams should be taken prior to admission consideration. There is a rolling admissions plan. Application deadlines are open. Notification is sent within a few days of the decision. Application fee is $30. Applications are accepted on-line.

Transfer: 68 transfer students enrolled in 2004-2005. Applicants must have verification from their previous school that they are eligible to return. Students with fewer than 30 semester or 45 quarter hours must meet freshman admissions requirements. 30 of 128 credits required for the bachelor's degree must be completed at University of the Cumberlands.

Visiting: There are regularly scheduled orientations for prospective students, consisting of a tour, a departmental conference, an advising session, adjustment information, and general information. There are guides for informal visits and visitors may sit in on classes and stay overnight. To schedule a visit, contact the Admissions Office at *admiss@ucumberlands.edu.*

Financial Aid: In 2005-2006, 97% of all full-time freshmen and 94% of continuing full-time students received some form of financial aid. 74% of full-time freshmen and 71% of continuing full-time students received need-based aid. The average freshman award was $15,235. Need-based scholarships or need-based grants averaged $6511 ($13,258 maximum); need-based self-help aid (loans and jobs) averaged $4173 ($8625 maximum); non-need-based athletic scholarships averaged $3768 ($18,184 maximum); and other non-need-based awards and non-need-based scholarships averaged $4319 ($18,184 maximum). 80% of undergraduates work part time. Average annual earnings from campus work are $1770. The average financial indebtedness of the 2005 graduate was $16,083. The FAFSA is required. The priority date for freshman financial aid applications for fall entry is March 1.

International Students: There are 26 international students enrolled. They must take the TOEFL, the SAT or ACT and the English Placement Examination.

Computers: Wireless access is available. Labs are located in several buildings on campus including the dorms; students may use their own computers in dorm rooms, library, campus grill, and cafeteria. Wireless access is available in the dining hall and grill. All students may access the system 24 hours a day, 7 days a week. There are no time limits. The fee is $260 per year.

Graduates: From July 1, 2004 to June 30, 2005, 257 bachelor's degrees were awarded. The most popular majors were elementary education (20%), biology (11%), and business (10%). In an average class, 1% graduate in 3 years or less, 21% graduate in 4 years or less, 36% graduate in 5 years or less, and 40% graduate in 6 years or less. 10 companies recruited on campus in 2004-2005. Of the 2004 graduating class, 20% were enrolled in graduate school within 6 months of graduation and 75% were employed.

Admissions Contact: Erica Harris, Director of Admissions. A video is available. E-mail: *admiss@ucumberlands.edu*
Web: *www.ucumberlands.edu*

WESTERN KENTUCKY UNIVERSITY — C-4

Bowling Green, KY 42101-3576

(270) 745-2551
(800) 495-8463; Fax: (270) 745-6133

Full-time: 5682 men, 7371 women	Faculty: 621; IIA, --$
Part-time: 1027 men, 1898 women	Ph.D.s: 74%
Graduate: 796 men, 1871 women	Student/Faculty: 21 to 1
Year: semesters, summer session	Tuition: $5316 ($12,732)
Application Deadline: August 1	Room & Board: $4876
Freshman Class: 6781 applied, 6220 accepted, 3150 enrolled	
SAT Verbal/Math: 500/500*	ACT: 20	COMPETITIVE

Western Kentucky University, founded in 1906, is a public institution that provides students with rigorous academic programs in the liberal arts and sciences and traditional and emerging professional programs, with emphasis at the baccalaureate level, complemented by relevant associate and graduate-level programs. There are 6 undergraduate schools and 1 graduate school. In addition to regional accreditation, Western has baccalaureate program accreditation with AACSB, ABET, ACEJMC, ACS, ADA, AHIMA, AMA, ASHLA, CCNE, CSAB, CSWE, NAIT, NASAD, NASM, NCATE, NLN, and NRPA. The 3 libraries contain 656,517 volumes, 2,020,100 microform items, and 19,805 audio/video tapes/CDs/DVDs, and subscribe to 13,912 periodicals including electronic. Computerized library services include the card catalog, interlibrary loans, database searching, Internet access, and laptop Internet portals. Special learning facilities include a learning resource center, art gallery, planetarium, radio station, TV station, and Kentucky Museum. The 200-acre campus is in a suburban area 65 miles north of Nashville, Tennessee, and 110 miles south of Louisville. Including any residence halls, there are 66 buildings.

Student Life: 83% of undergraduates are from Kentucky. Others are from 46 states, 55 foreign countries, and Canada. 85% are white. The average age of freshmen is 19; all undergraduates, 23. 27% do not continue beyond their first year; 41% remain to graduate.

Housing: 4662 students can be accommodated in college housing, which includes single-sex and coed dorms. In addition, there are honors houses and special-interest houses. On-campus housing is available on a first-come, first-served basis. 68% of students commute. Alcohol is not permitted. All students may keep cars.

Activities: 9% of men belong to 16 national fraternities; 7% of women belong to 12 national sororities. There are 251 groups on campus, including art, band, cheerleading, chess, choir, chorale, chorus, computers, dance, debate, drama, drill team, ethnic, film, forensics, gay, honors, international, jazz band, literary magazine, marching band, musical theater, newspaper, opera, orchestra, pep band, photography, political,

professional, radio and TV, religious, social, social service, student government, symphony, and yearbook. Popular campus events include Step Show, Concerts, and Cultural Enhancement Series.

Sports: There are 11 intercollegiate sports for men and 10 for women, and 17 intramural sports for men and 16 for women. Facilities include a 17,500-seat football stadium, a basketball arena, baseball fields, softball fields, a soccer complex, and tennis courts. The Preston Center adds a weight room, a fitness room, a gym, a dance studio, racquetball courts, a swimming pool, a pro shop, the Outdoor Recreation & Adventure Center, and a health and fitness lab.

Disabled Students: 75% of the campus is accessible. Wheelchair ramps, elevators, special parking, specially equipped rest rooms, special class scheduling, and lowered telephones are available. Services are available for students with special needs through the Equal Opportunity/504 ADA Compliance Office.

Services: Counseling and information services are available, as is tutoring in some subjects, with both departmental and freelance tutoring offered. The Student Support Services program offers tutoring in general education courses. There is a reader service for the blind, and remedial math, reading, and writing.

Campus Safety and Security: Measures include 24-hour foot and vehicle patrol, security escort services, shuttle buses, and informal discussions. There are pamphlets/posters/films, emergency telephones, and lighted pathways/sidewalks.

Programs of Study: Western confers A.B., B.S., B.F.A., B.G.S., B.M., and B.S.N. degrees. Associate and master's degrees are also awarded. Bachelor's degrees are awarded in AGRICULTURE (agriculture), BIOLOGICAL SCIENCE (biochemistry, biology/biological science, and genetics), BUSINESS (accounting, banking and finance, business economics, hospitality management services, management engineering, management information systems, management science, marketing and distribution, and recreation and leisure services), COMMUNICATIONS AND THE ARTS (advertising, broadcasting, communications, design, dramatic arts, English, French, German, journalism, language arts, music, performing arts, public relations, Spanish, and visual and performing arts), COMPUTER AND PHYSICAL SCIENCE (chemistry, computer science, geology, mathematics, and physics), EDUCATION (art, business, early childhood, education of the exceptional child, elementary, home economics, marketing and distribution, middle school, physical, technical, and vocational), ENGINEERING AND ENVIRONMENTAL DESIGN (civil engineering, construction management, electrical/electronics engineering, electromechanical technology, industrial engineering technology, mechanical engineering, and technology and public affairs), HEALTH PROFESSIONS (dental hygiene, environmental health science, health care administration, medical technology, nursing, public health, and speech pathology/audiology), SOCIAL SCIENCE (anthropology, economics, geography, history, liberal arts/general studies, philosophy, political science/government, psychology, religion, social studies, social work, sociology, and textiles and clothing). Elementary education, psychology, and nursing have the largest enrollments.

Required: To graduate, all students must complete at least 128 semester hours, with a varying number of hours in the major, and maintain a minimum GPA of 2.0. Curricula must include 44 semester hours of general education requirements and 42 semester hours in upper-division courses, including 6 semester hours of English composition and 3 semester hours each of Western civilization, foreign language, speech, and literature.

Special: Internships in many areas, study abroad in 34 countries, work-study programs, and cooperative programs with the Universities of Louisville and Kentucky and Eastern Kentucky University are offered. Accelerated degree programs are available in some majors. Dual majors include math and physical science, and physics and engineering. A general studies degree, student-designed majors, a Washington semester, and a 3-2 engineering degree are offered. Credit for life, military, or work experience may be granted, and nondegree study is possible. There are 36 national honor societies and a freshman honors program.

Faculty/Classroom: 56% of faculty are male; 44%, female.

Admissions: 92% of the 2005-2006 applicants were accepted. The SAT scores for the 2005-2006 freshman class were: Verbal--48% below 500, 35% between 500 and 599, and 17% between 600 and 700; Math--45% below 500, 41% between 500 and 599, 11% between 600 and 700, and 3% above 700. The ACT scores were 52% below 21, 24% between 21 and 23, 14% between 24 and 26, 6% between 27 and 28, and 4% above 28. 30% of the current freshmen were in the top fifth of their class; 55% were in the top two fifths. 76 freshmen graduated first in their class.

Requirements: The SAT or ACT is required. In addition, other admissions requirements include graduation from an accredited secondary school and a minimum college preparatory curriculum that includes 4 years of English, 3 years each of math, social studies, and science, 2 years of a foregin language, and one-half year each of health, phys ed, and visual or performing arts. The GED is accepted. A GPA of 2.5 is required. AP and CLEP credits are accepted.

Procedure: Freshmen are admitted to all sessions. Entrance exams should be taken by fall of the senior year. There are early admissions and deferred admissions plans. There is a rolling admissions plan. Applications should be filed by August 1 for fall entry, January 1 for spring entry, and May 1 for summer entry, along with a $35 fee. Notification is sent on a rolling basis. Applications are accepted on-line.

Transfer: 865 transfer students enrolled in 2004-2005. Transfer students must have a minimum GPA 2.0 for the last semester or term of full-time work, a cumulative GPA of 2.0, and be in good standing at the institution from which they are transferring. Students with fewer than 24 hours earned are required to have completed the precollege curriculum. 32 of 128 credits required for the bachelor's degree must be completed at Western.

Visiting: There are regularly scheduled orientations for prospective students, including campus tours, informational sessions, presentations, departmental visits, residence hall visits, and a video. There are guides for informal visits and visitors may sit in on classes and stay overnight. To schedule a visit, contact the Office of Admissions at *tours@wku.edu*.

Financial Aid: In 2005-2006, 57% of all full-time freshmen and 54% of continuing full-time students received some form of financial aid. 35% of all full-time students received need-based aid. The average freshman award was $6769. Need-based scholarships or need-based grants averaged $3650; need-based self-help aid (loans and jobs) averaged $2492; non-need-based athletic scholarships averaged $7387; and other non-need-based awards and non-need-based scholarships averaged $2296. 8% of undergraduates work part time. Average annual earnings from campus work are $2098. The average financial indebtedness of the 2005 graduate was $12,250. Western is a member of CSS. The FAFSA is required. The deadline for filing freshman financial aid applications for fall entry is April 1.

International Students: There are 201 international students enrolled. They must take the TOEFL, achieving a satisfactory score, or take the MELAB. They must also take the SAT or the ACT.

Computers: Wireless access is available. WKU provides open computer labs for all students at locations across the university. In addition to 6 labs on the main campus, there is one at each extended campus location and another at the South Campus (Community College). Labs are equipped with hardware, software, scanners, and free laser printing. One location, in the Mass Media and Technology Hall, is open 24 hours a day, 7 days a week while classes are in session. All students may access the system. See *http://atech.wku.edu/page.php?PageName=Student+Technology+Lab+Hours* for a full listing of hours. There are no time limits and no fees.

Graduates: From July 1, 2004 to June 30, 2005, 2166 bachelor's degrees were awarded. The most popular majors were education (19%), business (16%), and communications/journalism (11%). In an average class, 27% graduate in 4 years, 14% graduate in 5 years, and 4% graduate in 6 years. 202 companies recruited on campus in 2004-2005.

Admissions Contact: Dr. Dean R. Kahler, Admissions and Academic Services Director. A video is available. E-mail: *admission@wku.edu* Web: *www.wku.edu*

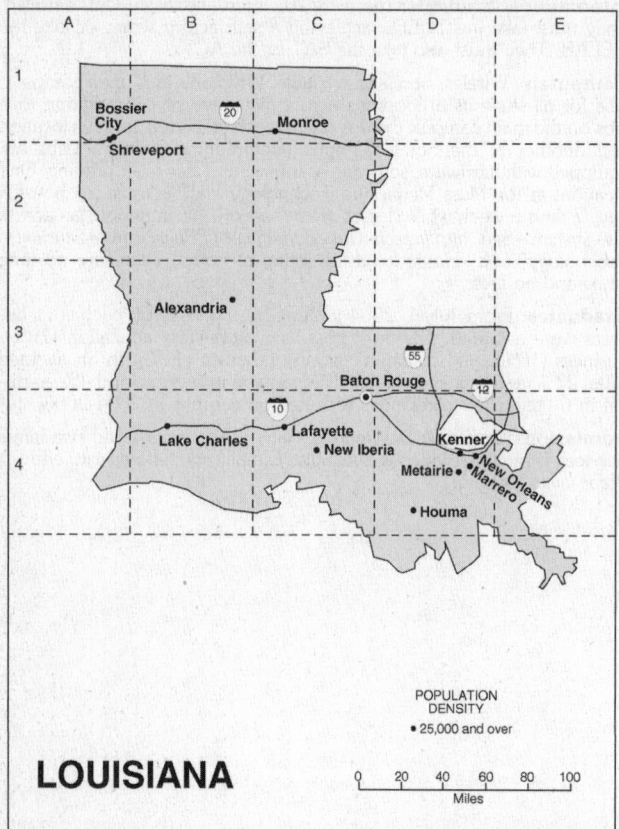

LOUISIANA

POPULATION
DENSITY

● 25,000 and over

0   20   40   60   80   100
Miles

CENTENARY COLLEGE OF LOUISIANA   A-1
Shreveport, LA 71104   (318) 869-5131
                              (800) 234-4440; Fax: (318) 869-5005

Full-time: 334 men, 548 women	Faculty: 72; IIB, -$
Part-time: 9 men, 13 women	Ph.D.s: 94%
Graduate: 49 men, 91 women	Student/Faculty: 12 to 1
Year: semesters, summer session	Tuition: $18,390
Application Deadline: August 1	Room & Board: $6370
Freshman Class: 1006 applied, 856 accepted, 233 enrolled	
SAT Verbal/Math: 580/570*	ACT: 25 VERY COMPETITIVE

Centenary College of Louisiana, founded in 1825, is a private institution affiliated with the United Methodist Church, offering degrees in the liberal arts, music, business, sciences, and education. In addition to regional accreditation, Centenary has baccalaureate program accreditation with NASM. The 2 libraries contain 180,000 volumes, 310,671 microform items, and 425 audio/video tapes/CDs/DVDs, and subscribe to 942 periodicals including electronic. Computerized library services include the card catalog, interlibrary loans, and database searching. Special learning facilities include a radio station, a theater, and an art museum. The 65-acre campus is in an urban area in the northwest corner of Louisiana, 180 miles east of Dallas, Texas. Including any residence halls, there are 23 buildings.

Student Life: 62% of undergraduates are from Louisiana. Others are from 31 states, 13 foreign countries, and Canada. 83% are white. 60% are Protestant; 20% Catholic; 14% claim no religious affiliation; 6% Hindu, Unitarian, Mormon, Muslim, and Buddhist. The average age of freshmen is 18; all undergraduates, 20. 26% do not continue beyond their first year; 55% remain to graduate.

Housing: 616 students can be accommodated in college housing, which includes single-sex and coed dorms and on-campus apartments. On-campus housing is guaranteed for all 4 years and is available on a first-come, first-served basis. 67% of students live on campus; of those, 80% remain on campus on weekends. Alcohol is not permitted. All students may keep cars.

Activities: 23% of men belong to 4 national fraternities; 26% of women belong to 2 national sororities. There are 61 groups on campus, including band, cheerleading, choir, chorale, chorus, dance, drama, environmental, film, forensics, gay, honors, jazz band, literary magazine, musical theater, newspaper, opera, orchestra, pep band, photography, political,

professional, radio and TV, religious, social, social service, student government, symphony, and yearbook. Popular campus events include Spring Fling, President's Convocation, and Freak Week.

Sports: There are 7 intercollegiate sports for men and 9 for women, and 16 intramural sports for men and 16 for women. Facilities include a 3000-seat gym, 2 weight rooms, basketball, racquetball, volleyball, and tennis courts, baseball, soccer, and softball fields, a fitness center with aerobic exercise and strengthening equipment, and a natatorium.

Disabled Students: 90% of the campus is accessible. Wheelchair ramps, elevators, special parking, specially equipped rest rooms, special class scheduling, lowered drinking fountains, lowered telephones, and lowered security phones are available.

Services: Counseling and information services are available, as is tutoring in most subjects.

Campus Safety and Security: Measures include 24-hour foot and vehicle patrol, security escort services, informal discussions, and pamphlets/posters/films. There are emergency telephones and lighted pathways/sidewalks.

Programs of Study: Centenary confers B.A., B.S., and B.M. degrees. Master's degrees are also awarded. Bachelor's degrees are awarded in BIOLOGICAL SCIENCE (biochemistry, biology/biological science, biophysics, and neurosciences), BUSINESS (accounting, banking and finance, business administration and management, and business economics), COMMUNICATIONS AND THE ARTS (art, communications, dance, dramatic arts, English, French, German, Latin, music, music performance, and Spanish), COMPUTER AND PHYSICAL SCIENCE (chemistry, geology, mathematics, and physics), EDUCATION (elementary, foreign languages, music, physical, and social studies), ENGINEERING AND ENVIRONMENTAL DESIGN (environmental science), HEALTH PROFESSIONS (exercise science), SOCIAL SCIENCE (economics, history, interdisciplinary studies, liberal arts/general studies, philosophy, political science/government, psychology, religion, religious music, and sociology). Physical sciences, life sciences, and political science are the strongest academically. Business, biology, and psychology are the largest.

Required: To graduate, all students must complete 124 semester hours, with a maximum of 45 in a non-interdisciplinary major and a minimum of 30 at the upper-division level, including a writing and speaking class in the major at the junior level, and maintain a minimum GPA of 2.0. There are 48 to 52 hours of distribution requirements. Core curriculum requirements include courses in the humanities, social sciences, hard sciences, and math. In addition, freshmen must take a liberal arts orientation course. All students must complete a community service project, participate in cultural perspective events, study or live in a different culture, or study abroad, and fulfill career explorations.

Special: Centenary offers study abroad in 7 countries, cross-registration with Associated Colleges of the South, internships in all majors, a Washington semester, and a work-study program within the college. A 3-1 communications disorders degree with Louisiana State University Medical Center is possible, as is a 3-2 engineering degree with Washington University in St. Louis, University of Southern California, Columbia University, Texas A&M University, Louisiana Tech, and Case Western Reserve Universities. A 3-2 applied science preprofessional degree combines with health administration or medical school. Preveterinary studies, general studies and interdisciplinary degrees, and student-designed majors are available. There are 7 national honor societies and 15 departmental honors programs.

Faculty/Classroom: 60% of faculty are male; 40%, female. 93% teach undergraduates. No introductory courses are taught by graduate students. The average class size in an introductory lecture is 25; in a laboratory, 24; and in a regular course, 20.

Admissions: 85% of the 2005-2006 applicants were accepted. The SAT scores for the 2005-2006 freshman class were: Verbal--22% below 500, 30% between 500 and 599, 37% between 600 and 700, and 11% above 700; Math--22% below 500, 39% between 500 and 599, 37% between 600 and 700, and 2% above 700. The ACT scores were 13% below 21, 23% between 21 and 23, 31% between 24 and 26, 14% between 27 and 28, and 1% above 28. 61% of the current freshmen were in the top fifth of their class; 85% were in the top two fifths. 20 freshmen graduated first in their class.

Requirements: The SAT or ACT is required. In addition, applicants should be high school graduates. Secondary school preparation should include 15 academic credits, including 4 of English, 3 each of math and science, 2 each of a foreign language and history, 1 of social studies, and electives. Music students must audition; art students are advised to present a portfolio. A GPA of 2.0 is required. AP credits are accepted. Important factors in the admissions decision are advanced placement or honor courses, extracurricular activities record, and personality/intangible qualities.

Procedure: Freshmen are admitted fall, spring, and summer. Entrance exams should be taken by the fall of the senior year. There are early decision, rolling admissions, and early admissions plans. Early decision applications should be filed by December 1; regular applications, by August 1 for fall entry, December 1 for spring entry, and June 1 for summer entry. Notification of early decision is sent January 1; regular decision, on a rolling basis. 33 early decision candidates were accepted for the 2005-2006 class. Applications are accepted on-line.

Transfer: 48 transfer students enrolled in 2004-2005. Transfer applicants must have a minimum GPA of 2.0 and demonstrate good performance in a liberal arts curriculum. 45 of 124 credits required for the bachelor's degree must be completed at Centenary.

Visiting: There are regularly scheduled orientations for prospective students, consisting of information sessions with a counselor, a tour of the campus, a visit to a class or with faculty, and lunch. There are guides for informal visits and visitors may sit in on classes and stay overnight. To schedule a visit, contact the Admissions Office at or *tcrowley@centenary.edu.*

Financial Aid: The FAFSA and the college's own financial statement are required. The priority date for freshman financial aid applications for fall entry is February 15.

International Students: There are 21 international students enrolled. The school actively recruits these students. They must score satisfactorily on the TOEFL.

Computers: Wireless access is available. All students may access the system. There are no time limits. The fee is $60. It is strongly recommended that all students have a personal computer.

Graduates: From July 1, 2004 to June 30, 2005, 184 bachelor's degrees were awarded. The most popular majors were business (15%), biology (8%), and psychology (6%). In an average class, 1% graduate in 3 years or less, 42% graduate in 4 years or less, 54% graduate in 5 years or less, and 55% graduate in 6 years or less.

Admissions Contact: Tim Crowley, Director of Admissions.
E-mail: *tcrowley@centenary.edu* Web: *www.centenary.edu*

DILLARD UNIVERSITY   ○   θ   D-4
New Orleans, LA 70122-3097   **(504) 816-4670**
                               (800) 216-6637; Fax: (504) 816-4895

Full-time: 2200 men and women	**Faculty:** 143
Part-time: 115 men and women	**Ph.D.s:** 52%
Graduate: none	**Student/Faculty:** 15 to 1
Year: semesters, summer session	**Tuition:** $11,000
Application Deadline: see profile	**Room & Board:** $6500
Freshman Class: n/av	
SAT or ACT: recommended	**VERY COMPETITIVE**

Dillard University, established in 1930, is an independent, nonsectarian, liberal arts institution, affiliated with the United Church of Christ and the United Methodist Church. It offers undergraduate programs in business, education, humanities, natural sciences, nursing, and social sciences. There are 6 undergraduate schools. Figures in the above capsule and profile are approximate. In addition to regional accreditation, Dillard has baccalaureate program accreditation with NLN. The library contains 104,615 volumes, 21,638 microform items, and 426 audio/video tapes/CDs/DVDs, and subscribes to 295 periodicals including electronic. Computerized library services include the card catalog, interlibrary loans, and database searching. Special learning facilities include a learning resource center, art gallery, and radio station. The 55-acre campus is in an urban area in New Orleans. Including any residence halls, there are 21 buildings.

Student Life: 54% of undergraduates are from out of state, mostly the South. Students are from 31 states, 13 foreign countries, and Canada. 98% are African American. 28% do not continue beyond their first year.

Housing: 1058 students can be accommodated in college housing, which includes single-sex dormitories, on-campus apartments, and off-campus apartments. On-campus housing is guaranteed for the freshman year only, is available on a first-come, first-served basis, and is available on a lottery system for upperclassmen. Priority is given to out-of-town students. Alcohol is not permitted. All students may keep cars.

Activities: 4% of men belong to 4 national fraternities; 11% of women belong to 4 national sororities. There are 64 groups on campus, including art, cheerleading, chess, choir, chorus, dance, drama, ethnic, honors, professional, religious, social service, student government, and yearbook. Popular campus events include Coronation, Avenue of the Oaks Gala, and Founder's Day.

Sports: There are 3 intercollegiate sports for men and 3 for women. Facilities include a gym, a swimming pool, a Nautilus room, tennis courts, dance facility, and game room.

Disabled Students: 70% of the campus is accessible. Wheelchair ramps, special parking, specially equipped rest rooms, and special class scheduling are available.

Services: Counseling and information services are available, as is tutoring in every subject. There is remedial math, reading, and writing.

Campus Safety and Security: Measures include 24-hour foot and vehicle patrol, shuttle buses, informal discussions, and pamphlets/posters/films. There are lighted pathways/sidewalks.

Programs of Study: Dillard confers B.A., B.S., and B.S.N. degrees. Bachelor's degrees are awarded in BIOLOGICAL SCIENCE (biology/biological science), BUSINESS (accounting and business administration and management), COMMUNICATIONS AND THE ARTS (art, communications, English, French, languages, music, music business management, music performance, and Spanish), COMPUTER AND PHYSICAL SCIENCE (chemistry, computer science, mathematics, and physics), EDUCATION (elementary, secondary, and special), HEALTH PROFESSIONS (nursing and public health), SOCIAL SCIENCE (African studies, economics, history, Japanese studies, political science/government, psychology, sociology, and urban studies). Biological sciences is the largest.

Required: Students must successfully complete 125 semester hours and maintain a minimum overall GPA of 2.0 and a GPA of 2.0 or better in all courses in the major. In addition, all students must complete 35 semester hours in the core curriculum, which includes courses in English composition, world literature, English literature, math, natural sciences, world history, political science, economics, university assembly, phys ed, and academic orientation. Additionally, each student must engage in a minimum of 120 clock hours of volunteer service in the community.

Special: Opportunities are provided for internships, work-study programs, credit by exam, nondegree study, and pass/fail options. All social science majors are encouraged to pursue a double major. There is a 4-year co-op degree in music therapy with Loyola University, a clinical public health curriculum with Howard University, a 5-year joint degree in urban studies with Columbia University, and preengineering dual degree programs with the Georgia Institute of Technology and Auburn and Columbia Universities. There are 3 national honor societies.

Faculty/Classroom: 45% of faculty are male; 55%, female. All teach undergraduates. The average class size in an introductory lecture is 30.

Requirements: The SAT or ACT is recommended. In addition, graduation from an accredited secondary school is required; a GED will be accepted. Applicants must submit an academic record of 20 units, distributed as follows: 4 units in English, 3 each in math and natural sciences, 2 in social studies, and 8 in other academic electives. Recommendations from a high school teacher and the principal or a student counselor are required. A GPA of 2.2 is required. AP credits are accepted. Important factors in the admissions decision are recommendations by school officials, leadership record, and personality/intangible qualities.

Procedure: Freshmen are admitted in the spring. Entrance exams should be taken between April of the junior year and December of the senior year. There are early admissions, deferred admissions, and rolling admissions plans. Check with the school for current application deadlines. The application fee is $20. Notification is sent on a rolling basis. Applications are accepted on-line.

Transfer: 53 transfer students enrolled in a recent year. Applicants for transfer must submit a secondary school record or equivalent, transcripts from previous colleges showing an average grade of C, and personal recommendations. No more than 60 semester hours may be submitted for transfer credit. 65 of 125 credits required for the bachelor's degree must be completed at Dillard.

Visiting: There are regularly scheduled orientations for prospective students, scheduled on individual basis. There are guides for informal visits and visitors may sit in on classes and stay overnight. To schedule a visit, contact the Campus Visit Coordinator.

Financial Aid: In a recent year, 98% of all full-time students received some form of financial aid. 85% of full-time freshmen and 97% of continuing full-time students received need-based aid. The average freshman award was $14,003. Need-based scholarships or need-based grants averaged $3081 ($4050 maximum); need-based self-help aid (loans and jobs) averaged $2458 ($15,000 maximum); and non-need-based athletic scholarships averaged $18,585 ($20,025 maximum). 1% of undergraduates worked part-time. Average annual earnings from campus work were $2000. The average financial indebtedness of a recent graduate was $18,000. Dillard is a member of CSS. The FAFSA and the college's own financial statement are required. Check with the school for current application deadlines.

International Students: In a recent year, there were 42 international students enrolled. They must score satisfactorily on the written TOEFL or on the electronic version and also take the SAT or the ACT, scoring 18.

Computers: There are no time limits. The fee is $150. It is strongly recommended that all students have a personal computer.

Graduates: In a recent year, 278 bachelor's degrees were awarded. The most popular majors were public health (16%), biology (13%), and mass communications (9%). Of a recent graduating class, 45% were enrolled in graduate school within 6 months of graduation and 45% were employed.

Admissions Contact: Linda G. Nash, Director of Admissions.
Web: *www.dillard.edu*

GRAMBLING STATE UNIVERSITY
B-1

Grambling, LA 71245

(318) 274-6423
(888) 863-3655; Fax: (318) 274-3292

Full-time and Part-time: 4700 men and women	**Faculty:** 227
	Ph.D.s: 64%
Graduate: n/av none	**Student/Faculty:** n/av
Year: semesters, summer session	**Tuition:** $3200 ($8600)
Application Deadline: open	**Room & Board:** $3500
Freshman Class: n/av	
SAT or ACT: required	**NONCOMPETITIVE**

Founded in 1901, Grambling State University, a constituent member of the University of Louisiana System, is a historically and predominantly black comprehensive university, offering degrees ranging from associate to doctorate. There are 6 undergraduate schools and 1 graduate school. Figures in the above capsule and profile are approximate. In addition to regional accreditation, GSU has baccalaureate program accreditation with AACSB, ABET, ACEJMC, ACS, CSAB, CSWE, NASAD, NASM, NASPAA, NCATE, NLN, and NRPA. The library contains 306,990 volumes, 121,954 microform items, and 6282 audio/video tapes/CDs/DVDs, and subscribes to 109,517 periodicals including electronic. Computerized library services include the card catalog, interlibrary loans, database searching, and Internet access. Special learning facilities include a learning resource center, radio station, TV station, and student technology labs. The 383-acre campus is in a small town 60 miles from Shreveport. Including any residence halls, there are 85 buildings.

Student Life: 65% of undergraduates are from Louisiana. Others are from 41 states, 14 foreign countries, and Canada. 95% are African American. 80% are Protestant; 15% Catholic. The average age of freshmen is 18; all undergraduates, 20.

Housing: 2611 students can be accommodated in college housing, which includes single-sex dormitories. In addition, there are honors houses and private room floors. On-campus housing is guaranteed for all 4 years. 55% of students commute. Alcohol is not permitted. All students may keep cars.

Activities: 2% of men belong to 4 national fraternities; 7% of women belong to 4 national sororities. There are 81 groups on campus, including art, band, cheerleading, choir, computers, dance, drama, honors, international, jazz band, marching band, newspaper, orchestra, political, professional, radio and TV, religious, social, social service, student government, symphony, and yearbook. Popular campus events include Founders Day, Black History Month, and Springfest.

Sports: There are 8 intercollegiate sports for men and 9 for women, and 6 intramural sports for men and 3 for women. Facilities include a gym, tennis courts, a 20,000-seat football stadium, an intramural center, a baseball field, a softball field, and an 1,850-seat basketball gym.

Disabled Students: 80% of the campus is accessible. Wheelchair ramps, elevators, special parking, specially equipped rest rooms, special class scheduling, lowered drinking fountains, and lowered telephones are available.

Services: Counseling and information services are available, as is tutoring in some subjects, including biology, English, chemistry, history, math, and physics. There is remedial math, reading, and writing.

Campus Safety and Security: Measures include 24-hour foot and vehicle patrol, security escort services, pamphlets/posters/films, and emergency telephones. There are lighted pathways/sidewalks.

Programs of Study: GSU confers B.A., B.S., B.A.S.W., B.P.A., and B.S.N. degrees. Associate, master's, and doctoral degrees are also awarded. Bachelor's degrees are awarded in BIOLOGICAL SCIENCE (biology/biological science), BUSINESS (accounting, business administration and management, business economics, hotel/motel and restaurant management, marketing/retailing/merchandising, and recreation and leisure services), COMMUNICATIONS AND THE ARTS (art, communications, dramatic arts, English, French, music, and Spanish), COMPUTER AND PHYSICAL SCIENCE (chemistry, computer science, information sciences and systems, mathematics, and physics), EDUCATION (art, business, drama, early childhood, elementary, English, foreign languages, home economics, industrial arts, mathematics, music, physical, science, and special), ENGINEERING AND ENVIRONMENTAL DESIGN (engineering technology), HEALTH PROFESSIONS (nursing, premedicine, and speech pathology/audiology), SOCIAL SCIENCE (criminal justice, food production/management/services, history, political science/government, prelaw, psychology, public administration, social work, and sociology). Nursing, education, and computer science are the strongest academically. Business management is the largest.

Required: To graduate, students must complete a minimum of 125 semester hours, with a minimum GPA of 2.0. Students also must earn a passing grade in each part of the general education integration seminar and pass the senior comprehensive competency exam. An exam is also required in the sophomore year. General education requirements include courses in English, math, computer literacy, natural sciences, arts, humanities, and social studies for a total of 42 semester hours.

Special: B.A.-B.S. degrees in some subjects, work-study programs, nondegree study, and cross-registration with Louisiana Tech University

are offered. The university sponsors Project Rescue for disadvantaged students. Internships, study abroad, accelerated degree programs, dual majors, and student-designed majors are also possible. There are 15 national honor societies, and a freshman honors program.

Faculty/Classroom: 83% teach undergraduates and 3% do research. The average class size in an introductory lecture is 26; in a laboratory, 20; and in a regular course, 30.

Requirements: The SAT or ACT is required. In addition, applicants must be graduates of an accredited high school. The GED is accepted. AP and CLEP credits are accepted. Important factors in the admissions decision are ability to finance college education, parents or siblings attending the school, and personality/intangible qualities.

Procedure: Freshmen are admitted fall, spring, and summer. There are early admissions and rolling admissions plans. Application deadlines are open. Application fee is $20. Applications are accepted on-line.

Transfer: Applicants must submit official transcripts from all previously attended colleges and be in good standing at the school most recently attended. 30 of 128 credits required for the bachelor's degree must be completed at GSU.

Visiting: There are regularly scheduled orientations for prospective students. There are guides for informal visits and visitors may sit in on classes and stay overnight. To schedule a visit, contact Nora D. Bingaman Taylor.

Financial Aid: The FAFSA, the college's own financial statement, and the Singlefile Form are required. Check with the school for current application deadlines.

International Students: There are 21 international students enrolled. The school actively recruits these students. They must score satisfactorily on the written TOEFL and also take the SAT or the ACT.

Computers: All students may access the system. There are no time limits and no fees.

Admissions Contact: Nora D. Bingaman Taylor, Director of Admissions. E-mail: *bingnamann@gram.edu* Web: *www.gram.edu*

LOUISIANA COLLEGE
B-3

Pineville, LA 71359

(318) 487-7259
(800) 487-1906; Fax: (318) 487-7550

Full-time: 440 men, 540 women	**Faculty:** 68; IIB, --$
Part-time: 25 men, 50 women	**Ph.D.s:** 60%
Graduate: none	**Student/Faculty:** 14 to 1
Year: semesters, summer session	**Tuition:** $9750
Application Deadline: open	**Room & Board:** $3700
Freshman Class: n/av	
SAT or ACT: required	**COMPETITIVE**

Louisiana College, founded in 1906, is a private liberal arts college affiliated with the Southern Baptist Churches of Louisiana. Some figures in the above in the capsule are approximate. In addition to regional accreditation, LC has baccalaureate program accreditation with AACSB, CSWE, NASM, and NLN. The library contains 135,443 volumes, 112,275 microform items, and 2500 audio/video tapes/CDs/DVDs, and subscribes to 10,235 periodicals including electronic. Computerized library services include the card catalog, interlibrary loans, database searching, and Internet access. Special learning facilities include a learning resource center, art gallery, radio station, and a performing arts center. The 81-acre campus is in a small town 1 mile northeast of Alexandria. Including any residence halls, there are 16 buildings.

Student Life: 92% of undergraduates are from Louisiana. Others are from 17 states and 5 foreign countries. 88% are white. 66% are Protestant; 18% claim no religious affiliation; 13% Catholic. The average age of freshmen is 18; all undergraduates, 22. 36% do not continue beyond their first year; 43% remain to graduate.

Housing: 726 students can be accommodated in college housing, which includes single-sex dorms, on-campus apartments, and married-student housing. On-campus housing is guaranteed for all 4 years. 54% of students live on campus. Alcohol is not permitted. All students may keep cars.

Activities: 5% of men belong to 4 local fraternities; 15% of women belong to 4 local sororities. There are 57 groups on campus, including art, band, breaking all Barriers (diversity), cheerleading, choir, chorale, chorus, debate, drama, honors, international, jazz band, literary magazine, musical theater, newspaper, opera, pep band, political, professional, religious, social, social service, student government, symphony, Union Board (campus programming) and yearbook. Popular campus events include Gala Christmas, Sanders Lecture Series, and Miss LC Pageant.

Sports: There are 5 intercollegiate sports for men and 5 for women, and 11 intramural sports for men and 11 for women. Facilities include a field house for basketball, a baseball field, a fitness/wellness center, a jogging trail, tennis courts, an intramural/soccer/football field, an outdoor beach volleyball court, softball field, and a practice football field.

Disabled Students: 95% of the campus is accessible. Wheelchair ramps, elevators, special parking, specially equipped rest rooms, and lowered telephones are available.

Services: Counseling and information services are available, as is tutoring in most subjects. There is a reader service for the blind and remedial math and writing. PASS (Program to Assist Student Success) offers services for students with documented learning disabilities.

Campus Safety and Security: Measures include 24-hour foot and vehicle patrol, self-defense education, security escort services, and informal discussions. There are pamphlets/posters/films and lighted pathways/sidewalks.

Programs of Study: LC confers B.A., B.S., B.G.S., B.M., B.S.N., and B.S.W. degrees. Bachelor's degrees are awarded in BIOLOGICAL SCIENCE (biology/biological science), BUSINESS (business administration and management), COMMUNICATIONS AND THE ARTS (communications, dramatic arts, English, French, graphic design, journalism, languages, multimedia, music, speech/debate/rhetoric, and studio art), COMPUTER AND PHYSICAL SCIENCE (chemistry and mathematics), EDUCATION (art, athletic training, business, elementary, English, health, mathematics, music, science, secondary, social studies, and special), HEALTH PROFESSIONS (exercise science, medical laboratory technology, music therapy, nursing, predentistry, premedicine, preoptometry, and preveterinary science), SOCIAL SCIENCE (criminal justice, economics, history, philosophy, prelaw, psychology, public administration, religion, religious education, religious music, social work, and sociology). Education, biology, and business are the largest.

Required: To graduate, students must complete 127 total credit hours, 42 of which must be junior-senior level, including a central core of 56 hours in all degree programs, and maintain a minimum GPA of 2.0, 2.25 in the major. They must also complete Cultural/Intellectual and Spiritual Enrichment requirements and earn at least 25% of credit applied toward degree through instruction offered by LC. They must complete the last 30 hours of course work at LC, and take 3 hours each of phys ed and computer applications.

Special: Study abroad in London and Hong Kong, interdisciplinary studies, work-study programs, nondegree study, internships, dual majors, and pass/fail options are offered. There are 13 national honor societies and a freshman honors program.

Faculty/Classroom: 54% of faculty are male; 46%, female. All teach undergraduates. The average class size in an introductory lecture is 30; in a laboratory, 20; and in a regular course, 18.

Admissions: Un a recent year there was 1 National Merit finalist and 2 semifinalists; 20 freshmen graduated first in their class.

Requirements: The SAT or ACT is required. In addition, candidates for admission must have completed 17 units, which must include 4 of English, 3 of math (algebra I, II, and geometry), 3 of social studies, and 3 of science (2 with lab). Graduates of accredited high schools must meet one of the following requirements for unconditional admission: (1) Score satisfactorily on the ACT or the SAT and possess a GPA of 2.0 on a 4.0 scale; or (2) possess an academic GPA of 2.0 on a 4.0 scale and rank in the upper 50% of their graduating class with an acceptable ACT or SAT score. LC requires applicants to be in the upper 50% of their class. A GPA of 2.0 is required. AP and CLEP credits are accepted. Important factors in the admissions decision are extracurricular activities record, leadership record, and advanced placement or honor courses.

Procedure: Freshmen are admitted fall, spring, and summer. Entrance exams should be taken during the junior or senior year. There is a rolling admission plan. Application deadlines are open. The fall 2005 application fee was $25. Applications are accepted on-line.

Transfer: 99 transfer students enrolled in a recent year. Applicants must have an overall minimum GPA of 2.0 and finish all remedial course work prior to transfer. 30 of 127 credits required for the bachelor's degree must be completed at LC.

Visiting: There are regularly scheduled orientations for prospective students, consisting of spring and fall campus preview days and a 2-day orientation and pre-registration in June. There are guides for informal visits and visitors may sit in on classes and stay overnight. To schedule a visit, contact the Office of Admissions at admissions@lacollege.edu.

Financial Aid: In a recent year, 98% of all full-time freshmen and 95% of continuing full-time students received some form of financial aid. 46% of full-time freshmen and 34% of continuing full-time students received need-based aid. The average freshman award was $6356. Need-based scholarships or need-based grants averaged $2161; need-based self-help aid (loans and jobs) averaged $3869; other non-need-based awards and non-need-based scholarships averaged $2152; and other awards averaged $4162. 19% of undergraduates work part time. The average financial indebtedness of a recent graduate was $18,000. The FAFSA or FFS and the college's own financial statement are required. Check with the school for current deadlines.

International Students: There were 12 international students enrolled in a recent year. They must score satisfactorily on the TOEFL. The TOEFL is waived for students taking the SAT who earn a certain score on the verbal section.

Computers: All students may access the system. There are no time limits and no fees.

Graduates: In a recent year, 158 bachelor's degrees were awarded. The most popular majors were nursing (9%), biology (9%), and social

work (8%). In an average class, 24% graduate in 4 years or less, 41% graduate in 5 years or less, and 45% graduate in 6 years or less. 65 companies recruited on campus in a recent year.

Admissions Contact: Director of Admissions.
E-mail: admissions@lacollege.edu Web: www.lacollege.edu

LOUISIANA STATE UNIVERSITY SYSTEM

The Louisiana State University System, established in 1860, is a public system in Louisiana. It is governed by a board of supervisors, whose chief administrator is the president. The primary goal of the system is to foster excellence in teaching, research, and public service. The main priorities are undergraduate education, graduate education, and economic development. The total enrollment is usually about 60,000, with 3500 faculty members. Altogether there are 228 baccalaureate, 220 master's, and 86 doctoral programs offered in Louisiana State University System. 4-year campuses are located in Baton Rouge,, Shreveport, and, and New Orleans. Profiles of the 4-year campuses are included in this section.

LOUISIANA STATE UNIVERSITY AND AGRICULTURAL AND MECHANICAL COLLEGE C-4

Baton Rouge, LA 70803 (225) 578-1175; Fax: (225) 578-4433

Full-time: 11,426 men, 12,340 women	**Faculty:** 1158; I, --$
Part-time: 891 men, 1048 women	**Ph.Ds:** 82%
Graduate: 2648 men, 2911 women	**Student/Faculty:** 21 to 1
Year: semesters, summer session	**Tuition:** $4419 ($12,719)
Application Deadline: April 15	**Room & Board:** $6330
Freshman Class: 10,825 applied, 7927 accepted, 4970 enrolled	
SAT Verbal/Math: 589/608*	**ACT:** 25 **VERY COMPETITIVE**

Louisiana State University and Agricultural and Mechanical College, a public institution founded in 1860, and part of the Louisiana State University System, offers programs in agriculture, arts and sciences, basic sciences, business administration, art and design, education, engineering, music and dramatic arts, and mass communication. There are 10 undergraduate and 4 graduate schools. In addition to regional accreditation, LSU has baccalaureate program accreditation with AACSB, ABET, ACCE, ACEJMC, ADA, ASLA, CSWE, FIDER, NAAB, NASAD, NASM, NCATE, and SAF. The 2 libraries contain 3,213,314 volumes, 6,606,164 microform items, and 24,803 audio/video tapes/CDs/DVDs, and subscribe to 28,387 periodicals including electronic. Computerized library services include the card catalog, interlibrary loans, database searching, and Internet access. Special learning facilities include a learning resource center, art gallery, natural history museum, radio station, TV station, 3 herbaria, and museums of natural science, natural history, geoscience, rural life, and art. The 2000-acre campus is in an urban area in Baton Rouge, Louisiana. Including any residence halls, there are 250 buildings.

Student Life: 85% of undergraduates are from Louisiana. Others are from 50 states, 120 foreign countries, and Canada. 77% are white. 39% are Catholic; 29% Protestant; 28% claim no religious affiliation. The average age of freshmen is 18; all undergraduates, 21. 17% do not continue beyond their first year; 58% remain to graduate.

Housing: 7504 students can be accommodated in college housing, which includes single-sex and coed dorms, on-campus apartments, married-student housing, fraternity houses, and sorority houses. In addition, there are honors houses and special-interest houses. 79% of students commute. All students may keep cars.

Activities: 10% of men belong to 20 national fraternities; 17% of women belong to 15 national sororities. There are 335 groups on campus, including art, band, cheerleading, choir, chorus, computers, dance, debate, drama, ethnic, gay, honors, international, jazz band, literary magazine, marching band, musical theater, newspaper, opera, orchestra, pep band, political, professional, radio and TV, religious, social, social service, student government, symphony, and yearbook. Popular campus events include Fall Fest, Martin Luther King Day Celebration, and LSU Union Ice Cream/Watermelon Giveaways.

Sports: There are 8 intercollegiate sports for men and 10 for women, and 18 intramural sports for men and 17 for women. Facilities include a 91,600-seat football stadium, a 14,237-seat domed sports center, a 7700-seat baseball stadium, a 400-meter track with seating for 5600, a natatorium with an 8-lane Olympic pool and diving well, an indoor track, and courts for handball, badminton, vollyball, and tennis. The recreational sports facility provides a multifaceted program that includes aquatics, sports clubs, informal recreation, instructional sports, intramural sports, outdoor recreation, special-events activities, and sports medicine. There is also an indoor practice facility for football, a soccer field that seats 1200, and a softball stadium that seats 1500.

Disabled Students: 70% of the campus is accessible. Wheelchair ramps, elevators, special parking, specially equipped rest rooms, special class scheduling, lowered drinking fountains, lowered telephones, telecommunication devices for the deaf, and power doors are available.

Services: Counseling and information services are available, as is tutoring in some subjects, including English, math, foreign languages, and sciences. There is remedial reading and writing. There are designated sections of math and Latin for students with learning disabilities.

Campus Safety and Security: Measures include 24-hour foot and vehicle patrol, self-defense education, security escort services, and shuttle buses. There are informal discussions, pamphlets/posters/films, emergency telephones, lighted pathways/sidewalks, and specialized crime prevention programs.

Programs of Study: LSU confers B.A., B.S., B.A. in M.C., B.Arch., B.F.A., B.G.S., B.Int.Design, B.Land.Arch., B.M., B.M.Ed., B.S.B.E., B.S.C.E., B.S.Ch.E., B.S.Cons.M., B.S.E.E., B.S.Env.Engineering, B.S.F., B.S.I.E., B.S. in Geol., B.S.M.E., and B.S. PETE degrees. Master's and doctoral degrees are also awarded. Bachelor's degrees are awarded in AGRICULTURE (agricultural business management, animal science, dairy science, fish and game management, forestry and related sciences, plant science, and poultry science), BIOLOGICAL SCIENCE (biochemistry, biology/biological science, microbiology, and nutrition), BUSINESS (accounting, banking and finance, business administration and management, business economics, international economics, and marketing/retailing/merchandising), COMMUNICATIONS AND THE ARTS (communications, dramatic arts, English, fine arts, French, German, Latin, music, Spanish, and speech/debate/rhetoric), COMPUTER AND PHYSICAL SCIENCE (chemistry, computer science, geology, information sciences and systems, mathematics, and physics), EDUCATION (elementary, music, secondary, and vocational), ENGINEERING AND ENVIRONMENTAL DESIGN (architecture, bioengineering, chemical engineering, civil engineering, computer engineering, construction management, electrical/electronics engineering, environmental engineering, environmental science, industrial engineering, interior design, landscape architecture/design, mechanical engineering, and petroleum/natural gas engineering), HEALTH PROFESSIONS (speech pathology/audiology), SOCIAL SCIENCE (anthropology, clothing and textiles management/production/services, early childhood studies, economics, family/consumer studies, food science, gender studies, geography, history, international studies, liberal arts/general studies, philosophy, physical fitness/movement, political science/government, psychology, sociology, textiles and clothing, and women's studies). Biological sciences, mass communication, and chemistry are the strongest academically. Biological sciences, mass communication, and general studies are the largest.

Required: To graduate, all students must have a minimum overall 2.0 GPA in 120 to 163 credit hours. They must complete a general education component of 38 to 39 semester hours in approved courses in 6 major areas, including 9 hours in humanities, 8 to 9 in natural sciences, 6 each in English composition, analytical reasoning, and social sciences, and 3 in the arts. Students must earn at least 25% of required hours for degree at LSU and meet college residency requirements.

Special: Co-op programs in numerous majors, cross-registration with Southern University and Baton Rouge Community College, study abroad, and work-study programs are offered. B.A.-B.S. degrees, dual majors, a general studies degree, nondegree study, an evening school, a program of study for adult learners, and pass/fail options are available. There are 32 national honor societies, including Phi Beta Kappa, a freshman honors program, and 17 departmental honors programs.

Faculty/Classroom: 65% of faculty are male; 35%, female. 85% teach undergraduates, 74% do research, and 70% do both. Graduate students teach 22% of introductory courses. The average class size in an introductory lecture is 50; in a laboratory, 20; and in a regular course, 41.

Admissions: 73% of the 2005-2006 applicants were accepted. The SAT scores for the 2005-2006 freshman class were: Verbal--11% below 500, 42% between 500 and 599, 40% between 600 and 700, and 7% above 700; Math--6% below 500, 36% between 500 and 599, 49% between 600 and 700, and 9% above 700. The ACT scores were 5% below 21, 28% between 21 and 23, 34% between 24 and 26, 17% between 27 and 28, and 16% above 28. 41% of the current freshmen were in the top fifth of their class; 70% were in the top two fifths. There were 41 National Merit finalists and 14 semifinalists. 150 freshmen graduated first in their class.

Requirements: The SAT or ACT is required. The ACT Optional Writing test is also required. In addition, applicants must be graduates of an accredited secondary school. GED certificates may be accepted in unusual circumstances. Students must have completed 4 credits in English, 3 each in specific math, science, and social studies courses, 2 credits in a foreign language, 1/2 credit in computer skills, and 2 1/2 additional credits from the above categories or certain courses in the visual and performing arts (18 total units). A GPA of 3.0 is required. AP and CLEP credits are accepted. Important factors in the admissions decision are advanced placement or honor courses, extracurricular activities record, recommendations by school officials, and geographic diversity.

Procedure: Freshmen are admitted to all sessions. Entrance exams should be taken in spring of the junior year or fall of the senior year. There is an early admissions plan. There is a rolling admissions plan. Applications should be filed by April 15 for fall and summer entry and December 1 for spring entry, along with a $40 fee. Notification is sent on a rolling basis. Applications are accepted on-line.

Transfer: 924 transfer students enrolled in 2004-2005. Transfer students must submit an official transcript from each previously attended school. Requirements are 30 or more semester hours with a minimum 2.5 GPA, and a college level English and math course. 30 of 120 to 163 credits required for the bachelor's degree must be completed at LSU.

Visiting: There are regularly scheduled orientations for prospective students, including an information session and a tour of campus. Department appointments can be arranged. There are guides for informal visits and visitors may sit in on classes and stay overnight. To schedule a visit, contact the Office of Recruitment and Tours at (225) 578-6652 or *pmhowar@lsu.edu.*

Financial Aid: In 2005-2006, 94% of all full-time freshmen and 86% of continuing full-time students received some form of financial aid. 24% of full-time freshmen and 30% of continuing full-time students received need-based aid. The average freshman award was $6179. Need-based scholarships or need-based grants averaged $2947; need-based self-help aid (loans and jobs) averaged $2428; non-need-based athletic scholarships averaged $10,840; and other non-need-based awards and non-need-based scholarships averaged $3941. 23% of undergraduates work part time. Average annual earnings from campus work are $2083. The average financial indebtedness of the 2005 graduate was $19,258. The FAFSA is required. The deadline for filing freshman financial aid applications for fall entry is February 1.

International Students: There are 467 international students enrolled. The school actively recruits these students. They must take the TOEFL and also take the SAT or ACT scoring satisfactorily.

Computers: Wireless access is available. There are 450 PCs in 8 general access PC labs, several restricted-use PC labs (Business, Engineering, Art and Design, Mass Comm, Residence Halls), internet ports in dorm rooms, 600 Wireless Access Points (plus 140 more stages for deployment) covering all major areas of campus (union, library, quad, dorms, classroom buildings, PC labs). All students may access the system. There are no time limits and no fees.

Graduates: From July 1, 2004 to June 30, 2005, 4449 bachelor's degrees were awarded. The most popular majors were general studies (9%), biological sciences (7%), and psychology (5%). In an average class, 25% graduate in 4 years or less, 50% graduate in 5 years or less, and 58% graduate in 6 years or less. 952 companies recruited on campus in 2004-2005.

Admissions Contact: Cleve Brooks, Admissions Director. A video is available. E-mail: *admissions@lsu.edu* Web: *www.lsu.edu*

LOUISIANA STATE UNIVERSITY IN SHREVEPORT   A-1
Shreveport, LA 71115

(318) 797-5061
(800) 229-5957; Fax: (318) 797-5286

Full-time: 1000 men, 1565 women	**Faculty:** 127; IIA, --$
Part-time: 410 men, 670 women	**Ph.D.s:** 73%
Graduate: 220 men, 510 women	**Student/Faculty:** 20 to 1
Year: semesters, summer session	**Tuition:** $2900 ($7220)
Application Deadline: see profile	**Room & Board:** n/av
Freshman Class: n/av	
SAT: not required	**ACT:** required

NONCOMPETITIVE

Louisiana State University in Shreveport, established in 1965, is a state-supported, primarily commuter institution offering undergraduate and graduate programs through the colleges of liberal arts, business, education, and sciences. There are 4 undergraduate and 4 graduate schools. Figures in the above capsule and profile are approximate. In addition to regional accreditation, LSUS has baccalaureate program accreditation with AACSB, CSAB, and NCATE. The library contains 279,821 volumes, 364,744 microform items, and 1914 audio/video tapes/CDs/DVDs, and subscribes to 2000 periodicals including electronic. Computerized library services include the card catalog, interlibrary loans, database searching, and Internet access. Special learning facilities include an art gallery, natural history museum, radio station, pioneer heritage center, and museum of life sciences. The 200-acre campus is in an urban area 7 miles south of downtown Shreveport. Including any residence halls, there are 18 buildings.

Student Life: 95% of undergraduates are from Louisiana. Others are from 28 states, 6 foreign countries, and Canada. 95% are from public schools. 65% are white; 21% African American. The average age of freshmen is 19; all undergraduates, 25. 47% do not continue beyond their first year; 23% remain to graduate.

Housing: 480 students can be accommodated in college housing, which includes single-sex and coed on-campus apartments and married-student housing. On-campus housing is available on a first-come, first-served basis. 94% of students commute. All students may keep cars.

Activities: 5% of men belong to 1 national fraternity 3% of women belong to 3 national sororities. There are 40 groups on campus, including cheerleading, computers, dance, debate, drama, ethnic, film, forensics, honors, international, literary magazine, photography, political, professional, religious, social, social service, student activities board, student government, and yearbook. Popular campus events include Fall Fest, Spring Fling, and Welcome Back Bash.

Sports: There are 2 intercollegiate sports for men and 1 for women. Facilities include tennis and racquetball courts, sand or volleyball courts, a swimming pool, gym, weight room, dance studio, football fields, softball diamonds, and a soccer field.

Disabled Students: All of the campus is accessible. Wheelchair ramps, elevators, special parking, specially equipped rest rooms, special class scheduling, lowered drinking fountains, lowered telephones, special housing, and lowered computer terminals are available.

Services: Counseling and information services are available, as is tutoring in some subjects, including math and English. There is remedial math and writing.

Campus Safety and Security: Measures include 24-hour foot and vehicle patrol, self-defense education, security escort services, and informal discussions. There are emergency telephones, lighted pathways/sidewalks, and commissioned University police officers.

Programs of Study: LSUS confers B.A., B.S., B.C.J., B.G.S. degrees. Master's degrees are also awarded. Bachelor's degrees are awarded in BIOLOGICAL SCIENCE (biochemistry and biology/biological science), BUSINESS (accounting, banking and finance, business administration and management, business economics, management science, and marketing/retailing/merchandising), COMMUNICATIONS AND THE ARTS (communications, English, fine arts, French, journalism, Spanish, and speech/debate/rhetoric), COMPUTER AND PHYSICAL SCIENCE (chemistry, computer science, mathematics, and physics), EDUCATION (art, elementary, and secondary), ENGINEERING AND ENVIRONMENTAL DESIGN (environmental science), SOCIAL SCIENCE (economics, geography, history, liberal arts/general studies, political science/government, psychology, and sociology). Biochemical science and math are the strongest academically. Elementary education, psychology, and biology are the largest.

Required: All students must take a computer course. A minimum of 128 semester hours, with a minimum GPA of 2.0, is required for the bachelor's degree.

Special: Opportunities are provided for cross-registration with Southern University/Shreveport, internships, a Washington semester, a general studies degree, a 3-2 engineering degree with Louisiana Tech University, credit for military service schools, nondegree study, and pass/fail options. There are 5 national honor societies.

Faculty/Classroom: 63% of faculty are male; 37%, female. 80% teach undergraduates, 70% do research, and 70% do both. No introductory courses are taught by graduate students. The average class size in an introductory lecture is 30; in a laboratory, 18; and in a regular course, 19.

Requirements: The ACT is required, with a minimum composite score of 18. Graduation from an accredited secondary school is required. The GED will be accepted. Conditional admission is granted to those who do not meet minimum requirements. A GPA of 2.3 is required. AP and CLEP credits are accepted.

Procedure: Freshmen are admitted to all sessions. Entrance exams should be taken at least 2 months before start of the current semester. There is a rolling admissions plam. Application fee is $10. Check with the school for application deadlines. Notification is sent on a rolling basis.

Transfer: Transfers must be in good academic standing, with a GPA of 2.0, or they may enter on probation. They must be eligible to continue at the last institution attended. 30 of 128 credits required for the bachelor's degree must be completed at LSUS.

Visiting: There are regularly scheduled orientations for prospective students, including a preview program during the spring semester for high school juniors and seniors, students may stay overnight for this scheduled visit. There are guides for informal visits. To schedule a visit, contact O.L. Kelly, Lisa Branch, Alison White, or Andranell Watley at (318) 797-5061.

Financial Aid: In a recent year, 90% of all full-time freshmen and 80% of continuing full-time students received some form of financial aid. 65% of full-time freshmen and 60% of continuing full-time students received need-based aid. Need-based scholarships or need-based grants averaged $2100 ($4050 maximum); non-need-based athletic scholarships averaged $2000 ($5000 maximum); and other non-need-based awards and non-need-based scholarships averaged $1000 ($3000 maximum). 90% of undergraduates worked part time. Average annual earnings from campus work were $3200. The FAFSA is required. Check with the school for application deadlines. The priority date for freshman financial aid applications for fall entry is June 1. The deadline for filing freshman financial aid applications for fall entry is June 1.

International Students: In a recent year, there were 10 international students enrolled. They must score satisfactorily on the written TOEFL and also take the SAT or the ACT, scoring 18.

Computers: All students may access the system. There are no time limits.

Admissions Contact: Kelli Stevens, Admission Counselor.
E-mail: *kstevens@pilot.lsus.edu* Web: *www.lsus.edu*

LOUISIANA TECH UNIVERSITY
B-3
Ruston, LA 71272
(318) 257-3036
(800) LATECH-1; Fax: (318) 257-2499

Full-time: 4220 men, 3730 women	**Faculty:** 397; IIA, -$
Part-time: 800 men, 1000 women	**Ph.D.s:** 80%
Graduate: 820 men, 1410 women	**Student/Faculty:** 20 to 1
Year: quarters, summer session	**Tuition:** $3560 ($7350)
Application Deadline: see profile	**Room & Board:** $3810
Freshman Class: n/av	
ACT: required	**COMPETITIVE**

Louisiana Tech University, founded in 1894, is a public institution offering programs in arts and sciences, business, agriculture, engineering, health science, education, fine and liberal arts, and human ecology. There are 5 undergraduate and 5 graduate schools. Some figures in the above capsule and profile are approximate. In addition to regional accreditation, Tech has baccalaureate program accreditation with AACSB, ABET, ADA, AHEA, ASLA, CAHEA, FIDER, NAAB, NASAD, NASM, NCATE, NLN, and SAF. The library contains 1,131,558 volumes, 2,140,172 microform items, and 511 audio/video tapes/CDs/DVDs, and subscribes to 2932 periodicals including electronic. Computerized library services include the card catalog, interlibrary loans, and database searching. Special learning facilities include a learning resource center, art gallery, natural history museum, planetarium, and radio station. The 235-acre campus is in a small town 30 miles west of Monroe and 90 miles east of Shreveport. Including any residence halls, there are 146 buildings.

Student Life: 85% of undergraduates are from Louisiana. Others are from 48 states, 70 foreign countries, and Canada. 70% are white; 16% African American. 51% are Protestant; 12% Catholic. The average age of freshmen is 19; all undergraduates, 20. 22% do not continue beyond their first year; 49% remain to graduate.

Housing: 3067 students can be accommodated in college housing, which includes single-sex and coed dorms and married-student housing. In addition, there are honors houses. On-campus housing is guaranteed for all 4 years. 74% of students commute. Alcohol is not permitted. All students may keep cars.

Activities: 7% of men belong to 9 national fraternities; 11% of women belong to 5 national sororities. There are 121 groups on campus, including art, band, cheerleading, choir, chorale, chorus, computers, dance, debate, drama, drill team, drum and bugle corps, ethnic, film, honors, international, jazz band, marching band, musical theater, newspaper, opera, orchestra, pep band, photography, political, professional, radio and TV, religious, social, social service, student government, symphony, and yearbook. Popular campus events include International Student Festival, Spring Fling, and Little Theater concerts.

Sports: There are 5 intercollegiate sports for men and 5 for women, and 10 intramural sports for men and 10 for women. Facilities include a football stadium, a coliseum, an intramural complex, a natatorium, a 9-hole golf course, and 10 lighted tennis courts.

Disabled Students: 95% of the campus is accessible. Wheelchair ramps, elevators, special parking, specially equipped rest rooms, lowered drinking fountains, and lowered telephones are available.

Services: Counseling and information services are available, as is tutoring in some subjects. There is a reader service for the blind, and remedial math, reading, and writing.

Campus Safety and Security: Measures include 24-hour foot and vehicle patrol, self-defense education, security escort services, and informal discussions. There are emergency telephones and lighted pathways/sidewalks.

Programs of Study: Tech confers B.A., B.S., B. Arch., B.F.A., and B.G.S. degrees. Associate, master's, and doctoral degrees are also awarded. Bachelor's degrees are awarded in AGRICULTURE (agricultural business management, animal science, forestry and related sciences, and wildlife management), BIOLOGICAL SCIENCE (biology/biological science), BUSINESS (accounting, banking and finance, business administration and management, business economics, business systems analysis, management science, marketing/retailing/merchandising, and personnel management), COMMUNICATIONS AND THE ARTS (English, fine arts, French, journalism, music, music performance, Spanish, and speech/debate/rhetoric), COMPUTER AND PHYSICAL SCIENCE (chemistry, computer science, geology, mathematics, and physics), EDUCATION (art, early childhood, elementary, foreign languages, music, physical, secondary, and special), ENGINEERING AND ENVIRONMENTAL DESIGN (airline piloting and navigation, architecture, aviation administration/management, biomedical engineering, chemical engineering, civil engineering, construction engineering, electrical/electronics engineering technology, environmental science, industrial engineering, and mechanical engineering), HEALTH PROFESSIONS (medical laboratory technology, medical records administration/services, and speech pathology/audiology), SOCIAL SCIENCE (dietetics, geography, history, liberal arts/general studies, political science/government, psychology, and sociology). Business and engineering are the strongest academically and the largest.

Required: All students must complete 45 quarter hours of general education courses, including 12 hours in humanities, 9 each in natural and social sciences, 6 each in English and math, and 3 in arts or computer literacy. A total of 120 to 142 quarter hours, with a minimum GPA of 2.0, is required to graduate.

Special: Co-op programs are available in engineering and applied and natural sciences, and cross-registration with Grambling State University is offered. Internships in agriculture, engineering, dietetics, and human ecology are offered. Study abroad, work-study programs, dual majors, a general studies degree, nondegree study, and pass/fail options are available. There is a chapter of Phi Beta Kappa and a freshman honors program.

Faculty/Classroom: 65% of faculty are male; 35%, female. 95% teach undergraduates and 75% both teach and do research. Graduate students teach 2% of introductory courses. The average class size in an introductory lecture is 40; in a laboratory, 20; and in a regular course, 26.

Admissions: There were 5 National Merit finalists in a recent year.

Requirements: The ACT is required. In addition, applicants must be graduates of an accredited secondary school or have a GED. Tech requires applicants to be in the upper 35% of their class. A GPA of 2.3 is required. AP credits are accepted.

Procedure: Freshmen are admitted to all sessions. There is a rollling admissions plan. Check with the school for current application deadlines. The fall 2005 application fee was $20. Notification is sent on a rolling basis.

Transfer: 526 transfer students enrolled in a recent year. Transfer applicants should have a 2.0 GPA and be eligible to enroll in the school from which they are transferring. 30 of 120 credits required for the bachelor's degree must be completed at Tech.

Visiting: There are regularly scheduled orientations for prospective students. There are guides for informal visits and visitors may stay overnight. To schedule a visit, contact the Admissions Office.

Financial Aid: 27% of undergraduates work part time. The FAFSA is required. Check with the school for current deadlines.

International Students: There are 139 international students enrolled. The school actively recruits these students. They must score satisfactorily on the written TOEFL. And have a minimum GPA of 2.5.

Computers: All students may access the system 24 hours a day, 7 days a week. There are no time limits.

Graduates: In a recent year, 1401 bachelor's degrees were awarded. The most popular majors were business (22%), engineering (17%), and education (11%). In an average class, 29% graduate in 4 years or less, 49% graduate in 5 years or less, and 55% graduate in 6 years or less. 632 companies recruited on campus in a recent year.

Admissions Contact: Jan Albritton, Admissions Office. A video is available. E-mail: *bulldog@latech.edu* Web: *http://www.latech.edu*

LOYOLA UNIVERSITY NEW ORLEANS — D-4

New Orleans, LA 70118-6195
(504) 865-3240
(800) 4-LOYOLA; Fax: (504) 865-3383

Full-time: 1260 men, 2030 women	Faculty: 238; IIA, +$
Part-time: 120 men, 250 women	Ph.D.s: 88%
Graduate: 240 men, 590 women	Student/Faculty: 14 to 1
Year: semesters, summer session	Tuition: $23,050
Application Deadline: see profile	Room & Board: $8000
Freshman Class: n/av	
SAT or ACT: required	VERY COMPETITIVE+

Loyola University New Orleans, founded in 1912, is a private institution operated by the Society of Jesus and affiliated with the Roman Catholic Church. There are 4 undergraduate schools and 1 graduate school. Some figures in the above capsule are approximate. In addition to regional accreditation, Loyola has baccalaureate program accreditation with AACSB, ACS, NASM, and NLN.. The 2 libraries contain 447,380 volumes, 671,775 microform items, and 14,872 audio/video tapes/CDs/DVDs, and subscribe to 1339 periodicals including electronic. Computerized library services include the card catalog, interlibrary loans, database searching, and Internet access. Special learning facilities include a learning resource center, art gallery, TV station, and theater, humanities lab with Perseus Project and TLG TV and radio production studios, multimedia classrooms, graphics lab, visual arts lab, ad club/communications lab, computer business lab, audio recording studio, and multimedia training center for nonprofit communication. The 20-acre campus is in an urban area 5 miles from downtown New Orleans. Including any residence halls, there are 24 buildings.

Student Life: 55% of undergraduates are from out of state, mostly the South. Students are from 50 states, 55 foreign countries, and Canada. 40% are from public schools. 66% are white; 11% Hispanic. Most are Catholic. The average age of freshmen is 18; all undergraduates, 20. 20% do not continue beyond their first year; 59% remain to graduate.

Housing: 1381 students can be accommodated in college housing, which includes single-sex and coed dorms and on-campus apartments. In addition, there are special-interest houses. On-campus housing is available on a first-come, first-served basis. Priority is given to out-of-town students. 60% of students commute. Upperclassmen may keep cars.

Activities: 17% of men belong to 2 local and 6 national fraternities; 18% of women belong to 6 national sororities. There are 140 groups on campus, including art, band, cheerleading, choir, chorale, chorus, computers, dance, drama, ethnic, film, gay, honors, international, jazz band, literary magazine, musical theater, newspaper, opera, orchestra, photography, political, professional, radio and TV, religious, social, social service, student government, symphony, and yearbook. Popular campus events include Loyolapalooza Spring Music Festival, Swamp Stomp, and Wolves on the Prowl Community Service Day.

Sports: There are 5 intercollegiate sports for men and 6 for women, and 20 intramural sports for men and 20 for women. Facilities include a sports complex with an arena, 6 multipurpose courts for basketball, tennis, volleyball, badminton, and floor hockey, 3 racquetball courts, an Olympic-style natatorium, a jogging track, and a weight-lifting and conditioning area.

Disabled Students: 99% of the campus is accessible. Wheelchair ramps, elevators, special parking, specially equipped rest rooms, lowered drinking fountains, lowered telephones, special housing, and special class relocation to provide accessibility are available.

Services: Counseling and information services are available, as is tutoring in most subjects. There is remedial math and writing. Peer tutoring is available in all introductory common curriculum courses. A reader service for the blind is provided for all exams and for course work if books on tape are not sufficient.

Campus Safety and Security: Measures include 24-hour foot and vehicle patrol, self-defense education, security escort services, and shuttle buses. There are informal discussions, pamphlets/posters/films, emergency telephones, lighted pathways/sidewalks, and CCTV coverage, card access control, intrusion alarm monitoring, first aid medical assistance, motor vehicle assistance, bicycle registration, finger printing services, and crime prevention services.

Programs of Study: Loyola confers B.A., B.S., B.Acc., B.A.S., B.B.A., B.C.J., B.F.A., B.L.S., B.Mus., B.Mus.Ed., B.Mus. Therapy, and B.S.N. degrees. Master's degrees are also awarded. Bachelor's degrees are awarded in BIOLOGICAL SCIENCE (biology/biological science), BUSINESS (accounting, banking and finance, business administration and management, international business management, management science, marketing/retailing/merchandising, and organizational behavior), COMMUNICATIONS AND THE ARTS (communications, communications technology, creative writing, dramatic arts, English, fine arts, French, German, graphic design, jazz, music business management, music performance, music theory and composition, piano/organ, Russian, Spanish, studio art, and visual and performing arts), COMPUTER AND PHYSICAL SCIENCE (chemistry, computer science, information sciences and systems, mathematics, and physics), EDUCATION (elementary and music), HEALTH PROFESSIONS (music therapy and nursing), SOCIAL SCIENCE (anthropology, classical/ancient civilization, criminal justice, economics, forensic studies, history, philosophy, political science/government, psychology, religion, religious education, social science, and sociology). Biology, chemistry, and English are the strongest academically. Communications, psychology, and biology are the largest.

Required: All students must complete a core curriculum that includes courses in English composition and literature, math, philosophy, science, world civilization, and religious studies; the number of credit hours varies by college. At least 120 credit hours, with at least 30 in the major, and a minimum GPA of 2.0 are required to graduate.

Special: Cross-registration is available with Xavier University, Notre Dame Seminary, the University of New Orleans, Tulane University, and Southern University of New Orleans. Internships with the New Orleans business community are also available. Study abroad in 7 countries, dual and student-designed majors, nondegree studies, and a general studies degree are offered. A Washington semester through American University and a 3-2 engineering degree with Tulane University are also offered. There are 24 national honor societies, a freshman honors program, and 9 departmental honors programs.

Faculty/Classroom: 58% of faculty are male; 42%, female. 89% teach undergraduates and 90% do research. No introductory courses are taught by graduate students. The average class size in an introductory lecture is 26; in a laboratory, 38; and in a regular course, 18.

Requirements: The SAT or ACT is required. In addition, candidates for admission must be graduates of an accredited secondary school or have a GED. They should have completed 4 units in high school English and 3 each in math, science, and social sciences, along with 4 academic electives; 2 units in a foreign language are recommended. A portfolio is required for fine arts students; an audition for music majors. An interview is recommended for scholarship consideration. AP and CLEP credits are accepted. Important factors in the admissions decision are advanced placement or honor courses, recommendations by school officials, and evidence of special talent.

Procedure: Freshmen are admitted to all sessions. Entrance exams should be taken during the junior or senior year. There is an early admissions and rolling admissions plan. Check with the school for current application deadlines. The fall 2005 application fee was $20. Notification is sent on a rolling basis. Applications are accepted on-line.

Transfer: 140 transfer students enrolled in a recent year. Applicants must have a minimum 2.25 GPA on all attempted college-level work; 12 credit hours are needed for consideration. 30 of 120 credits required for the bachelor's degree must be completed at Loyola.

Visiting: There are regularly scheduled orientations for prospective students, including class and department visits, a student panel, a tour, a financial aid session, a campus support panel, meetings with faculty members, and an overnight stay. There are guides for informal visits and visitors may sit in on classes and stay overnight. To schedule a visit, contact the Admissions Office.

Financial Aid: In a recent year, 59% of all full-time freshmen and 55% of continuing full-time students received some form of financial aid. 59% of full-time freshmen and 54% of continuing full-time students received need-based aid. The average freshman award was $18,470. Need-based scholarships or need-based grants averaged $13,693; need-based self-help aid (loans and jobs) averaged $2952; and other non-need-based awards and non-need-based scholarships averaged $10,197. The average financial indebtedness of a recent graduate was $18,125. The FAFSA is required. Check with the school for current deadlines.

International Students: There were 141 international students enrolled in a recent year. The school actively recruits these students. They must score satisfactorily on the TOEFL and also take the college's own test and the SAT or the ACT.

Computers: All students may access the system at any time. There are no time limits. The fee is $125. It is strongly recommended that all students have a personal computer.

Graduates: In a recent year, 815 bachelor's degrees were awarded. The most popular majors were communications (14%), psychology (9%), and biology (5%). In an average class, 49% graduate in 4 years or less, 57% graduate in 5 years or less, and 59% graduate in 6 years or less. 298 companies recruited on campus in a recent year. Of a recent graduating class, 28% were enrolled in graduate school within 6 months of graduation and 51% were employed.

Admissions Contact: Deborah C. Stieffel, Dean of Admissions and Enrollment Management. A video is available.
E-mail: *admit@loyno.edu* Web: *www.loyno.edu*

MCNEESE STATE UNIVERSITY   B-4
Lake Charles, LA 70609-2495

(337) 475-5148
(800) 622-3352; Fax: (337) 475-5189

Full-time: 2390 men, 3310 women	**Faculty:** 262; IIA, --$
Part-time: 430 men, 725 women	**Ph.Ds:** 64%
Graduate: 285 men, 655 women	**Student/Faculty:** 22 to 1
Year: semesters, summer session	**Tuition:** $2520 ($8900)
Application Deadline: open	**Room & Board:** $2750
Freshman Class: n/av	
ACT: required	**LESS COMPETITIVE**

McNeese State University, founded in 1939, and part of the University of Louisiana System, is a public institution offering programs in business, agriculture, engineering, education, firn arts, science, liberal arts, and nursing. There are 6 undergraduate schools and 1 graduate school. Figures in the above capsule and profile are approximate. In addition to regional accreditation, MSU has baccalaureate program accreditation with AACSB, AAFCS, ABET, ACS, ADA, CAHEA, CSAB, NAACLS, NASM, NCATE, and NLN. The library contains 546,183 volumes, 1,437,496 microform items, and 1382 audio/video tapes/CDs/DVDs, and subscribes to 1808 periodicals including electronic. Computerized library services include the card catalog, interlibrary loans, and database searching. Special learning facilities include a learning resource center, art gallery, planetarium, a farm, a vertebrate museum, and a communicty health care clinic. The 580-acre campus is in a suburban area 120 miles west of Baton Rouge and 60 miles east of Beaumont, Texas. Including any residence halls, there are 95 buildings.

Student Life: 92% of undergraduates are from Louisiana. Others are from 33 states, 51 foreign countries, and Canada. 78% are white; 17% African American. The average age of freshmen is 22; all undergraduates, 24. 34% do not continue beyond their first year.

Housing: 850 students can be accommodated in college housing, which includes single-sex and coed dormitories, on-campus apartments, and married-student housing. In addition, there are honors houses and a 12-month hall for out-of-state and internatiional students who can not go home. On-campus housing is guaranteed for all 4 years. 90% of students commute. Alcohol is not permitted. All students may keep cars.

Activities: 5% of men belong to 7 national fraternities; 5% of women belong to 6 national sororities. There are 93 groups on campus, including art, band, cheerleading, choir, chorale, chorus, computers, dance, debate, drama, drill team, ethnic, honors, international, jazz band, marching band, musical theater, newspaper, orchestra, pep band, political, professional, religious, social, social service, student government, symphony, and yearbook. Popular campus events include Spring Fling.

Sports: There are 7 intercollegiate sports for men and 9 for women, and 15 intramural sports for men and 15 for women. Facilities include a football stadium, softball and intramural fields, an indoor/outdoor track, a 50-meter pool, a coliseum, a baseball complex, outdoor tennis courts, an 8,000-square-foot weight room, racquetball courts, and 3 regulation basketball courts.

Disabled Students: 94% of the campus is accessible. Wheelchair ramps, elevators, special parking, specially equipped rest rooms, lowered drinking fountains, academic planning and registration assistance, and classroom and testing accommodations are available.

Services: Counseling and information services are available, as is tutoring in some subjects, including English, math, chemistry, physics, and biology. There is remedial math, reading, and writing and a study skills course.

Campus Safety and Security: Measures include 24-hour foot and vehicle patrol, security escort services, informal discussions, and pamphlets/posters/films. There are lighted pathways/sidewalks, security guards posted at the residence halls from 11 P.M. until 7 A.M., and a crime stoppers program.

Programs of Study: MSU confers B.A., B.S., B.Mus., B.Mus.Ed., and B.S.N. degrees. Associate and master's degrees are also awarded. Bachelor's degrees are awarded in AGRICULTURE (agricultural business management, agriculture, animal science, and wildlife management), BIOLOGICAL SCIENCE (biology/biological science), BUSINESS (accounting, banking and finance, business administration and management, and marketing/retailing/merchandising), COMMUNICATIONS AND THE ARTS (broadcasting, communications, dramatic arts, English, fine arts, languages, music, speech/debate/rhetoric, and visual and performing arts), COMPUTER AND PHYSICAL SCIENCE (chemistry, computer science, geology, information sciences and systems, mathematics, physics, and radiological technology), EDUCATION (business, early childhood, elementary, foreign languages, guidance, health, home economics, science, and special), ENGINEERING AND ENVIRONMENTAL DESIGN (chemical engineering, civil engineering, electrical/electronics engineering, environmental science, and mechanical engineering), HEALTH PROFESSIONS (medical laboratory technology and nursing), SOCIAL SCIENCE (criminal justice, economics, family/consumer studies, history, liberal arts/general studies, psychology, and sociology). Education, nursing, and engineering are the largest.

Required: The general requirements for graduation include 9 hours each in the humanities and natural sciences, 6 each in English, math, and social sciences, 3 in arts and computer literacy, and 1 in orientation, for a total of 43 core hours. A total of 120 credit hours with a minimum GPA equivalent of C is needed.

Special: MSU offers co-op programs in engineering, internships in medical technology, radiologic technology, and education, dual majors, a general studies degree, nondegree study, and credit for military experience. There are 13 national honor societies and a freshman honors program.

Faculty/Classroom: 58% of faculty are male; 42%, female. 94% teach undergraduates and 11% both teach and do research. The average class size in an introductory lecture is 38; in a laboratory, 25; and in a regular course, 27.

Requirements: The ACT is required. In addition, applicants must have a high school GPA of at least 3.0 or an Act score of at least 20. AP and CLEP credits are accepted.

Procedure: Freshmen are admitted to all sessions. Entrance exams should be taken prior to enrolling. There are early admissions and rolling admissions plans. Application deadlines are open. Application fee is $20. Applications are accepted on-line.

Transfer: Transferees must be eligible for readmission to the last collegiate institution attended. 30 of 120 credits required for the bachelor's degree must be completed at MSU.

Visiting: There are regularly scheduled orientations for prospective students. There are guides for informal visits and visitors may sit in on classes and stay overnight. To schedule a visit, contact John Martin, Enrollment Information Center at (377) 475-5504.

Financial Aid: The FAFSA or FFS and the college's own financial statement are required. Check with the school for application deadlines.

International Students: The school actively recruits these students. They must score satisfactorily on the written TOEFL or on the electronic version and also take the SAT or the ACT.

Computers: All students may access the system during lab operating hours. There are no time limits and no fees.

Admissions Contact: Tammie Pettis, Director of Admissions.
E-mail: *tpettis@mail.mcneese.edu* Web: *mcneese.edu*

NICHOLLS STATE UNIVERSITY D-4
Thibodaux, LA 70310

(504) 448-4507
(877) 642-4655; Fax: (504) 448-4929

Full-time: 2065 men, 3245 women	Faculty: 285
Part-time: 395 men, 830 women	Ph.D.s: 53%
Graduate: 190 men, 555 women	Student/Faculty: 19 to 1
Year: semesters, summer session	Tuition: $3000 ($8500)
Application Deadline: open	Room & Board: $3500
Freshman Class: n/av	
SAT : not required	ACT: recommended

NONCOMPETITIVE

Nicholls State University, established in 1948, and part of the University of Louisiana System, is a public liberal arts institution offering instruction in health sciences, fine arts, business, teacher preparation, and agricultural and technical disciplines. There are 6 undergraduate and 4 graduate schools. Figures in the above capsule and profile are approximate. In addition to regional accreditation, Nicholls has baccalaureate program accreditation with AACSB, AAFCS, ACEJMC, ADA, AHEA, CAAHEP, CSAB, IAME, NASM, NCATE, and NLN. The library contains 436,079 volumes, 340,970 microform items, and 3797 audio/video tapes/CDs/DVDs, and subscribes to 1281 periodicals including electronic. Computerized library services include the card catalog, interlibrary loans, database searching, and Internet access. Special learning facilities include a learning resource center, art gallery, radio station, TV station, a culinary institute, a rural development institute, and centers for the study of dyslexia, women and government, and economic education. The 210-acre campus is in a small town 50 miles southwest of New Orleans and 60 miles southeast of Baton Rouge. Including any residence halls, there are 47 buildings.

Student Life: 96% of undergraduates are from Louisiana. Others are from 30 states, 29 foreign countries, and Canada. 76% are white; 17% African American. 62% claim no religious affiliation; 27% Catholic; 9% Protestant. The average age of freshmen is 19; all undergraduates, 23. 43% do not continue beyond their first year.

Housing: 1056 students can be accommodated in college housing, which includes single-sex and coed dormitories and married-student housing. On-campus housing is guaranteed for the freshman year only and is available on a first-come, first-served basis. 85% of students commute. Alcohol is not permitted. All students may keep cars.

Activities: 5% of men belong to 8 national fraternities; 4% of women belong to 7 national sororities. There are 92 groups on campus, including art, band, cheerleading, chess, choir, chorale, chorus, computers, dance, debate, drama, drill team, ethnic, gay, honors, international, jazz band, literary magazine, marching band, musical theater, newspaper, pep band, photography, political, professional, radio and TV, religious, social, social service, student government, symphony, and yearbook. Popular campus events include Midterm Exam Week Breakfast, Family Day, and Crawfish Boil.

Sports: There are 7 intercollegiate sports for men and 8 for women, and 6 intramural sports for men and 4 for women. Facilities include a stadium, 2 gyms, tennis and raquetball courts, a soccer field, a swimming pool, baseball and softball fields, and a weight room.

Disabled Students: Wheelchair ramps, elevators, special parking, specially equipped rest rooms, special class scheduling, lowered drinking fountains, and lowered telephones are available.

Services: Counseling and information services are available, as is tutoring in most subjects. There is a reader service for the blind and remedial math and writing.

Campus Safety and Security: Measures include 24-hour foot and vehicle patrol, self-defense education, security escort services, and informal discussions. There are pamphlets/posters/films, emergency telephones, and lighted pathways/sidewalks.

Programs of Study: Nicholls confers B.A., B.S., B.G.S., B.M.E., and B.S.N. degrees. Associate and master's degrees are also awarded. Bachelor's degrees are awarded in AGRICULTURE (agricultural business management), BIOLOGICAL SCIENCE (biology/biological science), BUSINESS (accounting, banking and finance, business administration and management, marketing/retailing/merchandising, and personnel management), COMMUNICATIONS AND THE ARTS (art, communications, English, French, journalism, and music), COMPUTER AND PHYSICAL SCIENCE (chemistry, computer science, information sciences and systems, and mathematics), EDUCATION (business, elementary, music, secondary, and special), ENGINEERING AND ENVIRONMENTAL DESIGN (manufacturing technology and petroleum/natural gas engineering), HEALTH PROFESSIONS (health science, nursing, and speech pathology/audiology), SOCIAL SCIENCE (dietetics, family/consumer studies, food production/management/services, history, political science/government, psychology, and sociology). Language and literature, art, and economics and finance are the strongest academically. Teacher education, general studies, and nursing are the largest.

Required: All students must complete general education requirements, including 9 hours each in English, natural sciences, and humanities, 6 hours each in social sciences and math, 3 hours each in the arts, and student development, 2 semesters of health and phys ed, and a computer literacy course. At least 125 total credit hours, plus a minimum of 24 hours in the major, with a minimum GPA of 2.0, are required to graduate.

Special: Internships are offered in business areas, government, home economics, computer science, and psychology. A Washington semester congressional internship, dual majors in education, and student-designed majors in general studies are available. Nondegree study and credit for military experience are possible. There is a 7-on/7-off degree program for offshore oil field workers. There are 12 national honor societies, a freshman honors program, and 1 departmental honors program.

Faculty/Classroom: 55% of faculty are male; 45%, female. 98% teach undergraduates, 12% do research, and 12% do both. Graduate students teach 1% of introductory courses. The average class size in an introductory lecture is 38; in a laboratory, 17; and in a regular course, 29.

Requirements: The ACT is recommended. Applicants must be graduates of an accredited secondary school or have the GED. Institutional placement tests are given for English, math, and reading. Nicholls requires applicants to be in the upper 50% of their class. A GPA of 2.25 is required. AP and CLEP credits are accepted.

Procedure: Freshmen are admitted to all sessions. Entrance exams should be taken as early as possible. There are early admissions and rolling admissions plans. Application deadlines are open. Applications are accepted on-line. The fall 2005 application fee was $20.

Transfer: 348 transfer students enrolled in a recent year. Transfer applicants must be eligible to return to the institution from which they are transferring. 31 of 125 credits required for the bachelor's degree must be completed at Nicholls.

Visiting: There are regularly scheduled orientations for prospective students. There are guides for informal visits and visitors may sit in on classes and stay overnight. To schedule a visit, contact Admissions Information.

Financial Aid: In a recent year, 83% of all full-time freshmen and 73% of continuing full-time students received some form of financial aid. 52% of full-time freshmen and 46% of continuing full-time students received need-based aid. The average freshman award was $4223. 9% of undergraduates worked part time. Average annual earnings from campus work were $1234. The FAFSA or FFS and are required. Check with the school for application deadlines.

International Students: The school actively recruits these students. They must score satisfactorily on the written TOEFL or on the electronic version.

Computers: All students may access the system 24 hours a day. There are no time limits and no fees.

Graduates: In a recent year, 752 bachelor's degrees were awarded. The most popular majors were education (25%), general studies (9%), and nursing (6%). In an average class, 22% graduate in 6 years or less. 134 companies recruited on campus in a recent year.

Admissions Contact: Becky L. Durocher, Director of Admissions. E-mail: *esai-bl@nicholls.edu* Web: *www.nicholls.edu*

NORTHWESTERN STATE UNIVERSITY OF LOUISIANA B-2
Natchitoches, LA 71497

(318) 357-4503
(800) 327-1903; Fax: (318) 357-5567

Full-time: 2397 men, 4063 women	Faculty: 269; IIA, --$
Part-time: 513 men, 1815 women	Ph.D.s: 56%
Graduate: 224 men, 835 women	Student/Faculty: 24 to 1
Year: semesters, summer session	Tuition: $3394 ($9471)
Application Deadline: July 6	Room & Board: $3750
Freshman Class: 2910 applied, 1988 accepted, 1318 enrolled	
SAT Verbal/Math: 500/500*	ACT: 20

COMPETITIVE

Northwestern State University of Louisiana, founded in 1884, offers undergraduate programs in business, education, liberal arts, nursing, and science and technology. There are 7 undergraduate schools and 1 graduate school. In addition to regional accreditation, NSU has baccalaureate program accreditation with AACSB, AAFCS, ABET, ACEJMC, ACS, CAHEA, CCNE, CSWE, JRCERT, NASAD, NASM, NASPE, NAST, NCATE, and NLN. The library contains 320,554 volumes. Computerized library services include the card catalog, interlibrary loans, database searching, and Internet access. Special learning facilities include an art gallery, natural history museum, radio station, TV station, and the Cammie G. Henry Research Center. The 916-acre campus is in a small town in central Louisiana, 60 miles south of Shreveport. Including any residence halls, there are 35 buildings.

Student Life: 92% of undergraduates are from Louisiana. Others are from 43 states, 24 foreign countries, and Canada. 61% are white; 30% African American. The average age of freshmen is 20; all undergraduates, 24. 40% do not continue beyond their first year; 31% remain to graduate.

Housing: 1506 students can be accommodated in college housing, which includes coed dorms, on-campus apartments, married-student housing, fraternity houses, and sorority houses. In addition, there are honors houses. CAPA has its own wing in a dorm for music practice. On-campus housing is available on a first-come, first-served basis. 80% of students commute. Alcohol is not permitted. All students may keep cars.

Activities: 9% of men belong to 10 national fraternities; 5% of women belong to 8 national sororities. There are 78 groups on campus, including art, band, cheerleading, choir, chorale, chorus, computers, dance, drama, drill team, ethnic, gay, honors, international, jazz band, literary magazine, marching band, musical theater, newspaper, opera, orchestra, pep band, photography, political, professional, radio and TV, religious, social, social service, student government, symphony, and yearbook. Popular campus events include Spring Fling Weeks, Greek Week, and Welcome Week.

Sports: There are 5 intercollegiate sports for men and 7 for women and 35 intramural sports for both men and women. Facilities include a 16,000-seat football stadium, a 5000-seat indoor gym, sports training and basketball centers, a track, and a coliseum. The largest auditorium/arena seats 1500. NSU also has a wellness, recreation, and activity center that contains 2 gyms with 4 basketball courts, a 3000-square-foot-free weights area, a 2800-square-foot strength machine weight area, a 2800-square-foot cardio-equipment area, a group exercise studio, a spin cycle class studio, a fitness assessment lab, 2 game rooms, 3 racquetball courts, men's and women's locker areas, steam rooms, a massage room, an equipment service center, a student café, meeting rooms, and an indoor track.

Disabled Students: 97% of the campus is accessible. Wheelchair ramps, elevators, special parking, specially equipped rest rooms, special class scheduling, lowered drinking fountains, lowered telephones, and special housing are available.

Services: Counseling and information services are available, as is tutoring in most subjects. There is remedial math, reading, and writing.

Campus Safety and Security: Measures include 24-hour foot and vehicle patrol, security escort services, shuttle buses, and informal discussions. There are pamphlets/posters/films, emergency telephones, and lighted pathways/sidewalks.

Programs of Study: NSU confers B.A., B.S., B.F.A., B.G.S., B.M., B.M.Ed., B.S.N., and B.S.W. degrees. Associate and master's degrees are also awarded. Bachelor's degrees are awarded in BIOLOGICAL SCIENCE (biology/biological science), BUSINESS (accounting, business administration and management, and hospitality management services), COMMUNICATIONS AND THE ARTS (dramatic arts, English, fine arts, journalism, and music), COMPUTER AND PHYSICAL SCIENCE (chemistry, information sciences and systems, mathematics, and physics), EDUCATION (early childhood, elementary, health, music, and secondary), ENGINEERING AND ENVIRONMENTAL DESIGN (electrical/electronics engineering technology and industrial engineering technology), HEALTH PROFESSIONS (nursing and radiological science), SOCIAL SCIENCE (addiction studies, criminal justice, family/consumer studies, history, liberal arts/general studies, political science/government, psychology, social work, and sociology). Nursing, CAPA, and educational technology are the strongest academically. Nursing, business administration, and liberal arts/general studies are the largest.

Required: To graduate, all students must complete their senior year in residence, plus an approved 44-hour core curriculum, the university education requirement, and a minimum of 120 semester hours, with at least 30 semester hours in the major field. Distribution requirements include 9 credits each of communications, social sciences, and natural sciences, 6 each of fine arts and math, and 4 of personal fitness, as well as a 1-hour orientation course. A minimum 2.0 GPA is needed for all hours taken at NSU.

Special: NSU offers cooperative programs with local businesses, internships, study abroad on 5 continents, and work-study programs. A general studies degree, credit for experience, nondegree study, dual majors, and pass/fail options are available. There is a freshman honors program.

Faculty/Classroom: 46% of faculty are male; 54%, female. 87% teach undergraduates. Graduate students teach 3% of introductory courses. The average class size in an introductory lecture is 33; in a laboratory, 21; and in a regular course, 26.

Admissions: 68% of the 2005-2006 applicants were accepted. The SAT scores for the 2005-2006 freshman class were: Verbal--45% below 500, 36% between 500 and 599, 17% between 600 and 700, and 1% above 700; Math--44% below 500, 43% between 500 and 599, 11% between 600 and 700, and 2% above 700. The ACT scores were 58% below 21, 24% between 21 and 23, 12% between 24 and 26, 3% between 27 and 28, and 2% above 28. 29% of the current freshmen were in the top fifth of their class; 53% were in the top two fifths. 23 freshmen graduated first in their class.

Requirements: The SAT or ACT is required. In addition, applicants must complete 4 units of English, 3 units each of math and science, 2 units each of foreign language and social studies, 1 unit each of history and fine arts, and 1/2 unit of computer literacy. Students must have a satisfactory score on the SAT or ACT, be in the top half of their graduating class, and have a 2.0 high school GPA, and they must need no more than 1 development course. Different admission standards apply for students who are out of state, homeschooled, over 21, and other groups.

Certain GED students can be admitted. Developmental needs can be met by taking the COMPASS. Exceptions are available for some students. The Louisiana Scholars' College has more stringent admission criteria. AP and CLEP credits are accepted.

Procedure: Freshmen are admitted fall, spring, and summer. Entrance exams should be taken before the semester begins. There is a deferred admissions plan. There is a rolling admissions plan. Applications should be filed by July 6 for fall entry, November 2 for spring entry, and April 5 for summer entry, along with a $20 fee. Notification is sent on a rolling basis. A waiting list is an active part of the admissions procedure. Applications are accepted on-line.

Transfer: 460 transfer students enrolled in 2004-2005. Transfer students must be eligible for readmission to their former university or college in order to enter NSU, and they must submit college transcripts and a statement of good standing. Students also must have a need for no more than 1 developmental course and must have a 2.0 nondevelopmental college GPA. Students with less than 12 hours of nondevelopmental classes must also meet the freshman admission standards. 30 of 120 credits required for the bachelor's degree must be completed at NSU.

Visiting: There are regularly scheduled orientations for prospective students, consisting of a campus tour, with special focus on financial aid, housing and board, academic requirements, selecting a major, registration, campus organizations, and adapting to the college. There are guides for informal visits and visitors may sit in on classes. To schedule a visit, contact the Director of University Recruiting.

Financial Aid: In 2005-2006, 81% of all full-time freshmen and 73% of continuing full-time students received some form of financial aid. 43% of full-time freshmen and 46% of continuing full-time students received need-based aid. Need-based scholarships or need-based grants averaged $7865; need-based self-help aid (loans and jobs) averaged $2551; non-need-based athletic scholarships averaged $6592; and other non-need-based awards and non-need-based scholarships averaged $4682. The average financial indebtedness of the 2005 graduate was $18,832. NSU is a member of CSS. The FAFSA and the college's own financial statement are required. The priority date for freshman financial aid applications for fall entry is May 1.

International Students: There are 38 international students enrolled. They must achieve a satisfactory score on the TOEFL and also take the SAT or the ACT.

Computers: Wireless access is available. Computer labs are avilable throughout the main campus as well as on other campuses. Students can access free dial-up service on their computers. All students may access the system at all times. There are no time limits and no fees.

Graduates: From July 1, 2004 to June 30, 2005, 1061 bachelor's degrees were awarded. The most popular majors were nursing (13%), general studies (13%), and business administration (11%). In an average class, 14% graduate in 4 years or less, 26% graduate in 5 years or less, and 31% graduate in 6 years or less.

Admissions Contact: Jana Lucky, Director of University Recruiting.
E-mail: *admissions@nsula.edu*
Web: *http://www.nsula.edu/enrollmentservices/recruiting*

OUR LADY OF HOLY CROSS COLLEGE D-4

New Orleans, LA 70131-7399
(504) 394-7744
(800) 259-7744; Fax: (504) 391-2421

Full-time: 603 men and women	**Faculty:** n/av
Part-time: 709 men and women	**Ph.Ds:** n/av
Graduate: 101 men and women	**Student/Faculty:** n/av
Year: semesters, summer session	**Tuition:** $8090
Application Deadline: July 20	**Room & Board:** n/app
Freshman Class: n/av	
ACT: required	**LESS COMPETITIVE**

Our Lady of Holy Cross College, founded in 1916, is a private commuter college affiliated with the Roman Catholic Church. In addition to regional accreditation, OLHCC has baccalaureate program accreditation with CACREP, IACBE, JRCERT, and NLN. The library contains 56,700 volumes, 136,015 microform items, and 13,598 audio/video tapes/CDs/DVDs, and subscribes to 601 periodicals including electronic. Computerized library services include the card catalog, interlibrary loans, and database searching. The 15-acre campus is in an urban area in New Orleans. There are 2 buildings.

Student Life: 99% of undergraduates are from Louisiana. Others are from 4 states. 39% are from public schools. 74% are white; 15% African American. 74% are Catholic; 14% Protestant; 8% claim no religious affiliation. The average age of freshmen is 18; all undergraduates, 25. 10% do not continue beyond their first year; 70% remain to graduate.

Housing: There are no residence halls. Off-campus apartments are available. All students commute. Alcohol is not permitted. All students may keep cars.

Activities: There are no fraternities or sororities. There are 11 groups on campus, including choir, chorus, computers, drama, ethnic, honors, international, literary magazine, professional, social, social service, and student government. Popular campus events include Fall Fest, Crawfish Boil, and Christmas dances.

Sports: There are 5 intramural sports for men and 4 for women.

Disabled Students: All of the campus is accessible. Wheelchair ramps, elevators, special parking, specially equipped rest rooms, lowered drinking fountains, and lowered telephones are available.

Services: There is remedial math, reading, and writing.

Campus Safety and Security: Measures include self-defense education, security escort services, pamphlets/posters/films, and emergency telephones. There are lighted pathways/sidewalks. There is a foot patrol inside and outside of the building from 7:30 A.M. to 10 P.M.

Programs of Study: OLHCC confers B.A. and B.S. degrees. Associate and master's degrees are also awarded. Bachelor's degrees are awarded in BIOLOGICAL SCIENCE (biology/biological science), BUSINESS (accounting, business administration and management, and marketing and distribution), COMMUNICATIONS AND THE ARTS (English), EDUCATION (elementary and secondary), HEALTH PROFESSIONS (health science and nursing), SOCIAL SCIENCE (behavioral science, history, liberal arts/general studies, social psychology, and social science). Nursing is the strongest academically. Nursing, business, and education are the largest.

Required: A total of 128 credit hours, with 33 to 36 hours in the major, and a minimum GPA of 2.0 are required to graduate. All students must take courses in theology, philosophy, literature, English composition, math, natural sciences, library orientation, social sciences, speech, fine arts, and computer science.

Special: Co-op programs in business, internships with the Navy Civilian Personnel Office, study abroad in France, and credit for life, military, and work experience are offered.

Faculty/Classroom: 20% of faculty are male; 80%, female. 98% teach undergraduates and 2% do research. The average class size in an introductory lecture is 25; in a laboratory, 24; and in a regular course, 20.

Requirements: The ACT is required. The GED is accepted. A GPA of 2.0 is required. AP and CLEP credits are accepted. Important factors in the admissions decision are leadership record, recommendations by school officials, and recommendations by alumni.

Procedure: Freshmen are admitted to all sessions. Entrance exams should be taken a week before registration. Applications should be filed by July 20 for fall entry, December 20 for spring entry, and May 1 for summer entry. The fall 2005 application fee was $15.

Transfer: Transfer applicants must have an overall 2.0 GPA for unconditional admission. 30 of 128 credits required for the bachelor's degree must be completed at OLHCC.

Visiting: There are regularly scheduled orientations for prospective students. There are guides for informal visits and visitors may sit in on classes. To schedule a visit, contact the Office of Enrollment Services at *admissions@olhcc.edu*.

Financial Aid: 3% of undergraduates work part time. Average annual earnings from campus work are $1000. The FAFSA and the college's own financial statement are required. The deadline for filing freshman financial aid applications for fall entry is April 15.

International Students: A satisfactory score is required on the written TOEFL.

Computers: All students may access the system. There are no time limits and no fees.

Admissions Contact: Kristine H. Kopecky, V.P. for Student Affairs. A video is available. E-mail: *kkopecky@olhcc.edu* Web: *www.olhcc.edu*

SOUTHEASTERN LOUISIANA UNIVERSITY　D-3

Hammond, LA 70402　　　　　　　　　　　　　　**(985) 549-2066**
　　　　　　　　　　　　(800) 222-7358; Fax: (985) 549-5632

Full-time: 4597 men, 7047 women	Faculty: 464; IIA, --$
Part-time: 1840 men, 879 women	Ph.D.s: 61%
Graduate: 1123 men, 582 women	Student/Faculty: 25 to 1
Year: semesters, summer session	Tuition: $3341 ($8669)
Application Deadline: July 15	Room & Board: $5180
Freshman Class: 3286 applied, 3111 accepted, 2578 enrolled	
ACT: 21	LESS COMPETITIVE

Southeastern Louisiana University, founded in 1925, is a public university offering courses in liberal arts, fine arts, and professional studies. There are 6 undergraduate schools and 1 graduate school. In addition to regional accreditation, Southeastern has baccalaureate program accreditation with AACSB, ABET, CSWE, NASM, NCATE, NLN, ACS, AAFCS, CAAHEP, and NAIT. The library contains 386,715 volumes, 795,999 microform items, and 51,541 audio/video tapes/CDs/DVDs, and subscribes to 2901 periodicals including electronic. Computerized library services include the card catalog, interlibrary loans, database searching, Internet access, and laptop Internet portals. Special learning facilities include a learning resource center, art gallery, radio station, and TV station. The 365-acre campus is in a small town 60 miles northwest of New Orleans and 50 miles east of Baton Rouge. Including any residence halls, there are 100 buildings.

Student Life: 97% of undergraduates are from Louisiana. Others are from 43 states, 66 foreign countries, and Canada. 77% are white; 17% African American. The average age of freshmen is 20; all undergraduates, 23. 38% do not continue beyond their first year; 26% remain to graduate.

Housing: 2100 students can be accommodated in college housing, which includes coed dormitories, on-campus apartments, fraternity houses, and sorority houses. In addition, there are honors houses. On-campus housing is available on a first-come, first-served basis. Priority is given to out-of-town students. 85% of students commute. All students may keep cars.

Activities: 3% of men belong to 9 national fraternities; 5% of women belong to 9 national sororities. There are 95 groups on campus, including art, band, cheerleading, chess, choir, chorale, chorus, computers, dance, debate, drama, drum and bugle corps, ethnic, film, gay, honors, international, jazz band, literary magazine, marching band, musical theater, newspaper, opera, orchestra, pep band, photography, political, professional, radio and TV, religious, social, social service, student government, symphony, and yearbook. Popular campus events include Fanfare (cultural events month).

Sports: There are 8 intercollegiate sports for men and 8 for women, and 34 intramural sports for men and 34 for women. Facilities include weight, fitness, and aerobics rooms, an outdoor elevated track, basketball, volleyball, badminton, tennis, and racquetball courts, multipurpose fields, a pool, gym, a football stadium, and baseball and soccer fields.

Disabled Students: 90% of the campus is accessible. Wheelchair ramps, elevators, special parking, specially equipped rest rooms, special class scheduling, lowered drinking fountains, lowered telephones, and services for the mobility and learning impaired, and those with physical disability are available.

Services: Counseling and information services are available, as is tutoring in some subjects, including math, English, biology, physics, chemistry, and social sciences. There is remedial math, reading, and writing.

Campus Safety and Security: Measures include 24-hour foot and vehicle patrol, self-defense education, security escort services, and informal discussions. There are pamphlets/posters/films, emergency telephones, lighted pathways/sidewalks, and community policing, bicycle patrols, and video cameras.

Programs of Study: Southeastern confers B.A., B.S., B.G.S., B.M., and B.M.E. degrees. Associate and master's degrees are also awarded. Bachelor's degrees are awarded in AGRICULTURE (horticulture), BIOLOGICAL SCIENCE (biology/biological science), BUSINESS (accounting, banking and finance, business administration and management, and marketing/retailing/merchandising), COMMUNICATIONS AND THE ARTS (art, arts administration/management, communications, English, French, music, and Spanish), COMPUTER AND PHYSICAL SCIENCE (chemistry, computer science, mathematics, and physics), EDUCATION (art, athletic training, early childhood, elementary, English, foreign languages, health, mathematics, middle school, music, physical, science, social studies, and special), ENGINEERING AND ENVIRONMENTAL DESIGN (industrial engineering technology and occupational safety and health), HEALTH PROFESSIONS (health, nursing, and speech pathology/audiology), SOCIAL SCIENCE (criminal justice, family/consumer studies, history, liberal arts/general studies, political science/government, psychology, social work, and sociology). Teacher education, nursing, and biological sciences are the largest.

Required: To graduate, students must complete 125 credits in a core curriculum in English composition, literature, math, computer literacy, social, behavioral, and natural sciences, arts, history, and humanities and maintain a 2.0 GPA (2.5 in some majors).

Special: Southeastern offers a general studies degree, co-op programs, study abroad in Costa Rica, France, Brazil, Canada, Honduras, England, Italy, and Austria, internships, nondegree study, and pass/fail options. Cross-registration is possible with Louisiana State and McNeese State Universities, and the University of Southwestern Louisiana. There are 18 national honor societies, a freshman honors program, and 24 departmental honors programs.

Faculty/Classroom: 45% of faculty are male; 55%, female. 90% teach undergraduates. Graduate students teach 1% of introductory courses. The average class size in an introductory lecture is 39; in a laboratory, 16; and in a regular course, 25.

Admissions: 95% of the 2005-2006 applicants were accepted. The ACT scores for the 2005-2006 freshman class were: 49% below 21, 32% between 21 and 23, 14% between 24 and 26, 3% between 27 and 28, and 2% above 28. 20% of the current freshmen were in the top fifth of their class; 47% were in the top two fifths.

Requirements: The ACT is required. In addition, applicants should have completed the Regents High School core curriculum, have no more than 1 developmental course requirement, rank in the upper 50% of their class or have a GPA of 2.0. AP and CLEP credits are accepted.

Procedure: Freshmen are admitted fall, spring, and summer. Entrance exams should be taken prior to registering for classes. There is a deferred admissions plan. Applications should be filed by July 15 for fall entry, December 1 for spring entry, and May 1 for summer entry, along with a $20 fee. Notification is sent on a rolling basis. Applications are accepted on-line.

Transfer: 742 transfer students enrolled in 2004-2005. Applicants with less than 12 hours must meet freshman entrance requirements. Those with more must have a GPA of 2.0. All must be eligible to attend the last institution. 30 of 125 credits required for the bachelor's degree must be completed at Southeastern.

Visiting: There are regularly scheduled orientations for prospective students, including a 2-day program of credit exams, academic advising, class registration, social programs, and session presentations. There are guides for informal visits and visitors may sit in on classes and stay overnight. To schedule a visit, contact the Office of Admission and Financial Aid at *admission@selu.edu.*

Financial Aid: In 2005-2006, 84% of all full-time freshmen and 75% of continuing full-time students received some form of financial aid. 41% of full-time freshmen and 47% of continuing full-time students received need-based aid. The average freshman award was $4974. Need-based scholarships or need-based grants averaged $2955 ($4050 maximum); need-based self-help aid (loans and jobs) averaged $2480 ($3500 maximum); non-need-based athletic scholarships averaged $2558 ($3790 maximum); and other non-need-based awards and non-need-based scholarships averaged $3179 ($12,000 maximum). 14% of undergraduates work part time. Average annual earnings from campus work are $1348. The average financial indebtedness of the 2005 graduate was $10,908. The FAFSA is required. The priority date for freshman financial aid applications for fall entry is May 1.

International Students: There are 121 international students enrolled. They must take the TOEFL and the ACT.

Computers: Southeastern has a total of 1,453 computers available for student use. Of these, 94 are in open labs, 11 in service labs, 496 in restricted labs, 116 in PC classrooms, 736 in departmental labs, and 113 in the library. All PCs have access to the Internet. Wireless Internet access is available in over 50 indoor and outdoor locations throughout campus. All students may access the system. There are no time limits and no fees.

Graduates: From July 1, 2004 to June 30, 2005, 1601 bachelor's degrees were awarded. The most popular majors were management (11%), general studies (9%), and general business (9%). In an average class, 6% graduate in 4 years or less, 19% graduate in 5 years or less, and 25% graduate in 6 years or less. 180 companies recruited on campus in 2004-2005.

Admissions Contact: Richard Beaugh, Director of Admissions. A video is available. E-mail: *admissions@selu.edu*
Web: *http://www.selu.edu/ProspectiveStudents.html*

SOUTHERN UNIVERSITY SYSTEM

The Southern University System, the nation's only historically black university system, was established in 1975. It is governed by the Southern University Board of Supervisors and the Louisiana Board of Regents, whose chief administrator is the president. The primary goal of the system is teaching. The main priorities are teaching, public service, and research. The total enrollment of all 3 campuses is usually about 16,000 with 2,400 faculty and staff members. Altogether there are 152 degree programs ranging from certificates to doctorates. There is a 4-year campus located in Baton Rouge and New Orleans. Profiles of the 4-year campuses are included in this section.

SOUTHERN UNIVERSITY AND A&M COLLEGE   C-4
Baton Rouge, LA 70813   **(504) 771-2430**
                                     (800) 256-1531; Fax: (504) 772-2500

Full-time: 3051 men, 4678 women	**Faculty:** 352; IIA, --$
Part-time: 286 men, 561 women	**Ph.D.s:** 68%
Graduate: 368 men, 997 women	**Student/Faculty:** 22 to 1
Year: semesters, summer session	**Tuition:** $3592 ($9384)
Application Deadline: July 1	**Room & Board:** $4646
Freshman Class: 4703 applied, 2479 accepted, 1485 enrolled	
SAT Verbal/Math: 433/427*	**ACT:** 18 **LESS COMPETITIVE**

Southern University and A&M College, founded in 1880, is a publicly supported, nonsectarian, land-grant institution offering degree programs in agriculture, family and consumer science, arts and humanities, architecture, business, education, engineering, nursing, public policy and urban affairs, sciences, and university college. There are 11 undergraduate schools and 1 graduate school. In addition to regional accreditation, Southern has baccalaureate program accreditation with AACSB, AAFCS, ABET, ACEJMC, ACS, ADA, CSAB, CSWE, NAAB, NASM, NASPAA, NCATE, and NLN. The 2 libraries contain 514,498 volumes, 730,781 microform items, and 42,438 audio/video tapes/CDs/DVDs, and subscribe to 2032 periodicals including electronic. Computerized library services include interlibrary loans and database searching. Special learning facilities include a learning resource center, art gallery, Black Heritage Collection, and museum of art. The 884-acre campus is in an

urban area of Baton Rouge. Including any residence halls, there are 180 buildings.

Student Life: 83% of undergraduates are from Louisiana. Students are from 42 states, 45 foreign countries, and Canada. 96% are African American. The average age of freshmen is 18; all undergraduates, 22. 28% do not continue beyond their first year; 29% remain to graduate.

Housing: 2945 students can be accommodated in college housing, which includes single-sex dorms. 66% of students commute. Alcohol is not permitted. Upperclassmen may keep cars.

Activities: 2% of men belong to 5 national fraternities; 1% of women belong to 4 national sororities. There are 55 groups on campus, including art, band, cheerleading, chess, choir, chorale, computers, drama, ethnic, honors, international, jazz band, marching band, newspaper, political, professional, religious, social, student government, and yearbook. Popular campus events include Founder's Day and Bayou Classic football game at the New Orleans Super Dome.

Sports: There are 8 intercollegiate sports for men and 10 for women, and 7 intramural sports for men and 7 for women. Facilities include a center around the main activity complex, which accommodates theater, convocations, and athletic contests.

Disabled Students: All of the campus is accessible. Wheelchair ramps, elevators, special parking, specially equipped rest rooms, special class scheduling, and special housing are available.

Services: Counseling and information services are available, as is tutoring in every subject. There is a reader service for the blind, and remedial math, reading, and writing.

Campus Safety and Security: Measures include 24-hour foot and vehicle patrol, informal discussions, pamphlets/posters/films, and emergency telephones. There are lighted pathways/sidewalks.

Programs of Study: Southern confers B.A., B.S., B.A.R., B.M.E., B.S.C.E., B.S.E.E., B.S.M.E., and B.S.N. degrees. Associate, master's, and doctoral degrees are also awarded. Bachelor's degrees are awarded in AGRICULTURE (agricultural economics, agriculture, and forestry and related sciences), BIOLOGICAL SCIENCE (biology/biological science), BUSINESS (accounting, banking and finance, business administration and management, business economics, electronic business, and marketing/retailing/merchandising), COMMUNICATIONS AND THE ARTS (communications, dramatic arts, English, fine arts, French, music, and Spanish), COMPUTER AND PHYSICAL SCIENCE (chemistry, computer science, mathematics, and physics), EDUCATION (early childhood, elementary, middle school, music, secondary, and special), ENGINEERING AND ENVIRONMENTAL DESIGN (architecture, civil engineering, electrical/electronics engineering, engineering technology, and mechanical engineering), HEALTH PROFESSIONS (nursing, recreation therapy, rehabilitation therapy, speech pathology/audiology, and speech therapy), SOCIAL SCIENCE (criminal justice, family/consumer studies, history, political science/government, psychology, social work, and sociology). Nursing, engineering and chemistry are the strongest academically. Nursing, business management, and biology are the largest.

Required: All students must pass a general competency exam measuring proficiency in communication, computation, logical thinking, and general knowledge. Courses in English composition and literature, math, natural sciences, arts, humanities, social sciences, health, and phys ed are required, as well as 60 hours of community service and 3 hours of African-American studies. All students also must take the GRE at the end of the junior year. To graduate, they must complete 124 semester hours (at least 31 in the major) with a minimum GPA of 2.0 overall and in the major.

Special: Cross-registration, nondegree study, credit for military experience, accelerated degrees, co-op education, study abroad, internships, work-study, and an exchange program and dual majors in chemistry/chemical engineering with Louisiana State University are available. There are 9 national honor societies, a freshman honors program, and 1 departmental honors program.

Faculty/Classroom: 52% of faculty are male; 48%, female. 87% teach undergraduates. No introductory courses are taught by graduate students. The average class size in a regular course is 30.

Admissions: 53% of the 2005-2006 applicants were accepted. The SAT scores for the 2005-2006 freshman class were: Verbal--80% below 500, 15% between 500 and 599, and 2% between 600 and 700; Math--80% below 500, 15% between 500 and 599, and 2% between 600 and 700. The ACT scores were 85% below 21, 11% between 21 and 23, 3% between 24 and 26, 1% between 27 and 28, and 1% above 28. 39% of the current freshmen were in the top fifth of their class; 60% were in the top two fifths. 1 freshman graduated first in their class.

Requirements: The SAT or ACT is required. In addition, southern requires the following core courses: English (4), math (3), science (3), foreign languages (2), social studies (2) history (1), fine arts (1) and computer literacy (.5). Also required are: a high school GPA of 2.0, a satisfactory ACT score or a satisfactory SAT score or be in the top 50% of graduating class, and require no more than 1 remedial class. A GPA of 2.0 is required. AP and CLEP credits are accepted.

Procedure: Freshmen are admitted to all sessions. Entrance exams should be taken in 11th grade. There is an early admissions and a rolling admissions plan. Applications should be filed by July 1 for fall entry, December 1 for spring entry, and April 1 for summer entry. Notification is sent on a rolling basis. Applications are accepted on-line. The fall 2005 application fee was $20.

Transfer: 273 transfer students enrolled in 2004-2005. Students having less than 24 hours must meet regular admission requirements. If applicants have 24 or more hours they must have a 2.0 GPA based on 4.0 scale. All transcripts must be received within 30 days. 31 of 124 credits required for the bachelor's degree must be completed at Southern.

Visiting: There are regularly scheduled orientations for prospective students, consisting of summer and fall orientation programs. There are guides for informal visits. To schedule a visit, contact the Office of Admissions.

Financial Aid: In 2005-2006, 90% of all full-time students received some form of financial aid. 90% of all full-time students received need-based aid. The average freshman award was $6868. Need-based scholarships or need-based grants averaged $400 ($5200 maximum); need-based self-help aid (loans and jobs) averaged $2625 ($2625 maximum); non-need-based athletic scholarships averaged $3740 ($3740 maximum); and other non-need-based awards and non-need-based scholarships averaged $2625 ($2625 maximum). 12% of undergraduates work part time. Average annual earnings from campus work are $1850. The average financial indebtedness of the 2005 graduate was $23,000. The FAFSA is required. The deadline for filing freshman financial aid applications for fall entry is May 31.

International Students: There are 57 international students enrolled. The school actively recruits these students. They must score satisfactorily on the written TOEFL or on the electronic version and also take the SAT or the ACT.

Computers: Wireless access is available. Wireless access is available in the library. All students may access the system. There are no time limits and no fees.

Graduates: From July 1, 2004 to June 30, 2005, 923 bachelor's degrees were awarded. The most popular majors were computer science (7%), business management (6%), and criminal justice (6%). In an average class, 7% graduate in 4 years or less, 19% graduate in 5 years or less, and 29% graduate in 6 years or less. 198 companies recruited on campus in 2004-2005. Of the 2004 graduating class, 15% were enrolled in graduate school within 6 months of graduation and 33% were employed.

Admissions Contact: Tracie Abraham, Director of Admissions. E-mail: *tracie_abraham@cxs.subr.edu* Web: *www.subr.edu*

SOUTHERN UNIVERSITY AT NEW ORLEANS   D-4
New Orleans, LA 70126 (504) 286-5314

Full-time: 450 men and women	**Faculty:** n/av
Part-time: none	**Ph.D.s:** n/av
Graduate: 70 men and women	**Student/Faculty:** n/av
Year: semesters, summer session	**Tuition:** $1000 ($1900)
Application Deadline: see profile	**Room & Board:** n/app
Freshman Class: n/av	
ACT: required	**NONCOMPETITIVE**

Southern University at New Orleans, established in 1956, is a public commuter institution offering programs in liberal arts and sciences, business, education, and the technologies. Figures given in the above capsule are approximate. In addition to regional accreditation, SUNO has baccalaureate program accreditation with CSWE. The library contains 300,000 volumes. The 22-acre campus is in a suburban area. There are 10 buildings.

Programs of Study: Bachelor's degrees are awarded in BIOLOGICAL SCIENCE (biology/biological science), BUSINESS (accounting, business administration and management, secretarial studies/office management, and transportation management), COMMUNICATIONS AND THE ARTS (English, fine arts, journalism, Spanish, and speech/debate/rhetoric), COMPUTER AND PHYSICAL SCIENCE (chemistry, computer science, mathematics, and physics), EDUCATION (art, business, education of the deaf and hearing impaired, elementary, English, foreign languages, mathematics, music, physical, recreation, science, secondary, and social studies), ENGINEERING AND ENVIRONMENTAL DESIGN (technological management), HEALTH PROFESSIONS (health care administration), SOCIAL SCIENCE (addiction studies, criminal justice, economics, history, political science/government, psychology, social work, and sociology).

Requirements: The ACT is required.

Procedure: There is a rolling admissions plan. Check with the school for current application deadlines and fee. Notification is sent on a rolling basis.

Financial Aid: The SAR is required. Check with the school for current deadlines.

International Students: They must score satisfactorily on the TOEFL.

Computers: All students may access the system. There are no time limits and no fees.

Admissions Contact: Director of Admissions and Registrar. Web: *www.suno.edu*

TULANE UNIVERSITY   D-4
New Orleans, LA 70118 (504) 865-5731
(800) 873-9283; Fax: (504) 862-8715

Full-time: 3030 men, 3123 women	**Faculty:** I, -$
Part-time: 738 men, 1087 women	**Ph.D.s:** 90%
Graduate: 1463 men, 1635 women	**Student/Faculty:** n/av
Year: semesters, summer session	**Tuition:** $32,946
Application Deadline: January 15	**Room & Board:** $8152
Freshman Class: 17,572 applied, 7867 accepted, 1602 enrolled	
SAT or ACT: required	**MOST COMPETITIVE**

Tulane University, founded in 1834, is a private institution offering degree programs in liberal arts and sciences, business, architecture, and engineering, and social work. Enrollment figures in the above capsule and in this profile are approximate. There are 6 undergraduate and 8 graduate schools. In addition to regional accreditation, Tulane has baccalaureate program accreditation with AACSB, ABET, ACS, CSAB, CSWE, and NAAB. The 9 libraries contain 2,368,701 volumes, 2,652,736 microform items, and 96,642 audio/video tapes/CDs/DVDs, and subscribe to 16,588 periodicals including electronic. Computerized library services include the card catalog, interlibrary loans, and database searching. Special learning facilities include a learning resource center, art gallery, natural history museum, radio station, TV station, an observatory, Middle American Reseach Institute, Amisted Research Center, Tulane Jazz Archives, Latin American Library, and Tullane Center for Research on Women. The 110-acre campus is in an urban area in uptown New Orleans. Including any residence halls, there are 70 buildings.

Student Life: 70% of undergraduates are from out of state, mostly the Northeast. Students are from 50 states, 100 foreign countries, and Canada. 50% are from public schools. 79% are white; 10% African American. The average age of freshmen is 18; all undergraduates, 22. 12% do not continue beyond their first year; 88% remain to graduate.

Housing: College housing includes single-sex and coed dormitories, on-campus apartments, and married-student housing. In addition, there are honors houses and special interest floors. On-campus housing is guaranteed for the freshman year only and is available on a lottery system for upperclassmen. 65% of students live on campus; of those, 95% remain on campus on weekends. Upperclassmen may keep cars.

Activities: 35% of men belong to 14 national fraternities; 40% of women belong to 9 national sororities. There are 250 groups on campus, including art, band, cheerleading, chess, choir, chorale, chorus, computers, dance, drama, drill team, ethnic, film, gay, honors, international, jazz band, literary magazine, marching band, musical theater, newspaper, opera, orchestra, pep band, photography, political, professional, radio and TV, religious, social, social service, student government, and symphony. Popular campus events include Newcomb College Spring Arts Week, International Festival, and Student Activites Expo.

Sports: There are 8 intercollegiate sports for men and 8 for women, and 30 intramural sports for men and 30 for women. Facilities include a baseball diamond, a track complex, a tennis facility, and a recreation center with indoor and outdoor pools, an indoor track, squash and racquetball courts, a gymnastics area, a weight room, and exercise rooms and equipment.

Disabled Students: 60% of the campus is accessible. Wheelchair ramps, elevators, special parking, specially equipped rest rooms, lowered drinking fountains, lowered telephones, and special housing are available.

Services: Counseling and information services are available, as is tutoring in some subjects, including high-demand math and science classes and some languages.

Campus Safety and Security: Measures include 24-hour foot and vehicle patrol, self-defense education, security escort services, and shuttle buses. There are informal discussions, pamphlets/posters/films, emergency telephones, lighted pathways/sidewalks, trained student patrols, and programs about living safely off campus. Victim resources include academic assistance, legal counseling, emergency housing, and security review of home and personal security habits. In addition, there are bike patrols, limited dorm access, smoke detectors in dorms, and surveillance cameras.

Programs of Study: Tulane confers B.A., B.S., B. Arch., B.B.S., B.F.A., B.G.S., B.S.C., B.S.E., and B.S.M. degrees. Associate, master's, and doctoral degrees are also awarded. Bachelor's degrees are awarded in BIOLOGICAL SCIENCE (biochemistry, cell biology, ecology, and evolutionary biology), BUSINESS (accounting, business administration and management, management science, and marketing management), COMMUNICATIONS AND THE ARTS (art history and appreciation, classics, communications, dance, English, French, German, Italian, linguistics, media arts, music, Portuguese, Russian, Spanish, and studio art), COMPUTER AND PHYSICAL SCIENCE (chemistry, computer science, earth science, geology, information sciences and systems, mathematics, and physics), ENGINEERING AND ENVIRONMENTAL DESIGN (architecture, biomedical engineering, chemical engineering, civil engineering, computer engineering, electrical/electronics engineering, engineering, environmental engineering, environmental science, and mechanical engineering), HEALTH PROFESSIONS (exercise science), SOCIAL SCIENCE (African studies, American studies, anthropology, Asian/Oriental studies, cognitive science, economics, history, Judaic studies, Latin American studies, medieval studies, philosophy, political science/government, psychology, religion, Russian and Slavic studies, sociology, and women's studies). Environmental sciences, political economy, and preprofessional programs are the strongest academically. Business, social sciences, and engineering are the largest.

Required: All students in the liberal arts and sciences must meet proficiency requirements in English, foreign language, and math. They must take a distribution component including courses in humanities and fine arts, social sciences, and sciences and math. A total of 120 credits, including at least 24 in the major, with a minimum cumulative GPA of 2.0, is required to graduate.

Special: Students may pursue cross-registration with Loyola and Xavier Universities, numerous internships, study abroad in 23 countries, work-study programs, a Washington semester, and B.A.-B.S. degrees in liberal arts, engineering, and architecture. Tulane also offers accelerated joint degrees with its schools of medicine, law, business, and public health; student-designed, dual, and interdisciplinary majors, including art and biology, Greek and Latin, mathematical economics, political economy, and cognitive studies; a 3-2 engineering degree with Xavier University of Louisiana, joint graduate/professional programs, and 4+1 programs. There are 32 national honor societies, including Phi Beta Kappa, and a freshman honors program.

Faculty/Classroom: 64% of faculty are male; 36%, female. All both teach and do research. The average class size in an introductory lecture is 30; in a laboratory, 20; and in a regular course, 25.

Admissions: 45% of the 2005-2006 applicants were accepted. The SAT scores for the 2005-2006 freshman class were: Verbal--4% below 500, 8% between 500 and 599, 52% between 600 and 700, and 36% above 700; Math--2% below 500, 18% between 500 and 599, 47% between 600 and 700, and 33% above 700. 81% of the current freshmen were in the top fifth of their class; 98% were in the top two fifths.

Requirements: The SAT or ACT is required. The ACT Optional Writing test is also required. In addition, applicants must be graduates of an accredited secondary school or have a GED certificate. It is recommended that students have completed 4 years each of high school English and math, and 3 each of foreign language, social studies, and the sciences. SAT: Subject tests in writing, math, and foreign language are recommended for placement purposes and are required for home-schooled applicants. An essay is required. A portfolio is recommended for architecture applicants only. AP credits are accepted. Important factors in the admissions decision are advanced placement or honor courses, recommendations by school officials, and extracurricular activities record.

Procedure: Freshmen are admitted fall and spring. Entrance exams should be taken during the spring of the junior year or the fall of the senior year. There are early decision, early admissions, deferred admissions, and rolling admissions plans. Early decision applications should be filed by November 1; regular applications, by January 15 for fall entry and November 1 for spring entry, along with a $55 fee. Notification of early decision is sent December 15; regular decision, by April 1. 92 early decision candidates were accepted for the 2005-2006 class. 2337 applicants were on the 2005 waiting list; 6 were admitted. Applications are accepted on-line.

Transfer: 212 transfer students enrolled in 2004-2005. Applicants must submit SAT or ACT scores, high school transcripts, proof of good standing at previously attended institutions, and transcripts (with course descriptions) from all colleges or universities attended. A minimum 3.0 GPA is recommended. 60 of 120 credits required for the bachelor's degree must be completed at Tulane.

Visiting: There are regularly scheduled orientations for prospective students, including 3 on-campus Saturday programs in the fall, daily information sessions, and tours Monday through Friday and Saturday mornings during the academic year. Also, selected classes are open to visitors. In the spring semester, more structured programs are available daily. There are guides for informal visits and visitors may sit in on classes and stay overnight. To schedule a visit, contact the Office of Undergraduate Admission at *undergrad.admission@tulane.edu.*

Financial Aid: In 2005-2006, 82% of all full-time freshmen received some form of financial aid. 32% of full-time freshmen and 30% of continuing full-time students received need-based aid. The average freshman award was $23,547. 45% of undergraduates work part time. Average annual earnings from campus work are $2500. The average financial indebtedness of the 2005 graduate was $21,679. Tulane is a member of CSS. The CSS/Profile or FAFSA, is required . In addition, the Noncustodial Parents Statement and the Business/Farm Supplement (as applicable) are required. The deadline for filing freshman financial aid applications for fall entry is December 15.

International Students: There are 188 international students enrolled. The school actively recruits these students. Satisfactory scores are required on the written TOEFL and the SAT or the ACT.

Computers: Wireless access is available. All students may access the system 24 hours a day. There are no time limits and no fees. It is strongly recommended that all students have a personal computer.

Graduates: In a recent year, 1504 bachelor's degrees were awarded. The most popular majors were business (21%), social sciences (17%), and engineering (9%). 134 companies recruited on campus in 2004-2005.

Admissions Contact: Richard Whiteside, VP for Enrollment Management. A video is available. E-mail: *undergrad.admission@tulane.edu* Web: *www.tulane.edu*

UNIVERSITY OF LOUISIANA AT LAFAYETTE C-4

Lafayette, LA 70504   (337) 482-6473; Fax: (337) 482-6195

Full-time: 5290 men, 6740 women	Faculty: 666; I, --$
Part-time: 920 men, 1640 women	Ph.D.s: 79%
Graduate: 700 men, 930 women	Student/Faculty: 18 to 1
Year: semesters, summer session	Tuition: $2700 ($8960)
Application Deadline: open	Room & Board: $3130
Freshman Class: n/av	
SAT or ACT: required	COMPETITIVE

The University of Louisiana at Lafayette founded in 1898, is a public institution offering degree programs in liberal arts, fine arts, business, agriculture, technical disciplines, health science, engineering, and teacher preparation. There are 9 undergraduate schools and 1 graduate school. Figures in the above capsule are approximate. In addition to regional accreditation, UL Lafayette has baccalaureate program accreditation with AACSB, ABET, ACEJMC, ADA, AHEA, ASLA, CAHEA, CSAB, FIDER, NAAB, NASM, NCATE, and NLN. The library contains 873,173 volumes, 1,768,368 microform items, and 255,992 audio/video tapes/CDs/DVDs, and subscribes to 4965 periodicals including electronic. Computerized library services include the card catalog, interlibrary loans, and database searching. Special learning facilities include a learning resource center, art gallery, radio station, and numerous research centers for environmental, business, science, computer, and business studies. The 1375-acre campus is in an urban area 129 miles west of New Orleans. Including any residence halls, there are 239 buildings.

Student Life: 95% of undergraduates are from Louisiana. Others are from 48 states, 102 foreign countries, and Canada. 74% are white; 17% African American. 50% are Catholic; 31% claim no religious affiliation; 12% Protestant. The average age of freshmen is 19; all undergraduates, 24. 28% do not continue beyond their first year; 30% remain to graduate.

Housing: 1860 students can be accommodated in college housing, which includes single-sex dorms, on-campus apartments, and married-student housing. In addition, there are residence halls for athletes and Pan-Hellenic groups. On-campus housing is guaranteed for all 4 years. 89% of students commute. All students may keep cars.

Activities: 3% of men and about 3% of women belong to 14 national fraternities; 5% of women belong to 8 national sororities. There are 200 groups on campus, including band, cheerleading, choir, chorus, computers, dance, debate, drama, drum and bugle corps, ethnic, forensics, gay, honors, international, jazz band, marching band, musical theater, newspaper, opera, orchestra, photography, political, professional, radio and TV, religious, social, social service, student government, and yearbook. Popular campus events include Rajun Roar, Black Expo Week, and Entertainment Week.

Sports: There are 8 intercollegiate sports for men and 7 for women, and 16 intramural sports for men and 16 for women. Facilities include a 31,000-seat stadium, a 12,000-seat basketball arena, a gym, a track, a softball park, tennis courts, various playing fields, and a health and phys ed complex.

Disabled Students: 90% of the campus is accessible. Wheelchair ramps, elevators, special parking, specially equipped rest rooms, special class scheduling, TDDs, an adaptive computer lab with voice synthesizer, visual-tech, and brailler are available.

Services: Counseling and information services are available, as is tutoring in most subjects. There is remedial math, reading, and writing. An entering freshman can only be in 1 remedial course.

Campus Safety and Security: Measures include 24-hour foot and vehicle patrol, security escort services, shuttle buses, and informal discussions. There are pamphlets/posters/films, emergency telephones, and lighted pathways/sidewalks.

Programs of Study: UL Lafayette confers B.A., B.S., B.A.M., B.F.A., B.G.S., B.M.E., B.M.P., B.M.P.P., B.S.A., B.S.A.E., B.S.B.A., B.S.C.E., B.S.C.I.E., B.S.E.E., B.S.I.T., B.S.M.E., B.S.N., and B.S.P.E. degrees. Master's and doctoral degrees are also awarded. Bachelor's degrees are awarded in BUSINESS (accounting, banking and finance, business administration and management, fashion merchandising, hotel/motel and restaurant management, management science, marketing/retailing/merchandising, and personnel management), COMMUNICATIONS AND THE ARTS (advertising, broadcasting, communications, dance, dramatic arts, English, fine arts, French, music, public relations, Spanish, and telecommunications), COMPUTER AND PHYSICAL SCIENCE (chemistry, computer science, geology, mathematics, physics, and statistics), EDUCATION (agricultural, art, elementary, English, foreign languages, health, home economics, industrial arts, mathematics, music, science, secondary, social studies, and special), ENGINEERING AND ENVIRONMENTAL DESIGN (chemical engineering, civil engineering, computer engineering, electrical/electronics engineering, industrial engineering, interior design, land use management and reclamation, mechanical engineering, and petroleum/natural gas engineering), HEALTH PROFESSIONS (nursing, and speech pathology/audiology), SOCIAL SCIENCE (anthropology, criminal justice, dietetics, economics, history, philosophy, political science/government, psychology, and sociology). Computer science, engineering, and math/statistics/physical sciences are the strongest academically. Nursing, elementary education, and business administration are the largest.

Required: Students are required to complete 42 semester hours of general education courses in the arts, literature, history, math, sciences, behavioral sciences, and composition. Phys ed is required in all but engineering and nursing programs. A minimum of 124 semester hours, with at least 33 in the major, is required for graduation. A minimum GPA of 2.0 is needed; some majors require higher GPAs.

Special: Various internships are available, including a Washington semester. Students may study in France, Canada, Belgium, Japan, and Mexico. UL Lafayette also offers an accelerated degree program in nursing, B.A.-B.S. degrees, and dual majors. There are 6 national honor societies and a freshman honors program.

Faculty/Classroom: 59% of faculty are male; 41%, female.

Requirements: The SAT or ACT is required. In addition, admissions criteria are based on a sliding scale of standardized test scores and GPA. Students should be graduates of accredited secondary schools or have the GED. UL Lafayette requires that students have at least 4 units in English, 3 each in math, science, and social studies, and 4 1/2 in electives, recommended to include 2 in foreign language, 1 each in fine arts and speech, and 1/2 in computer studies. A GPA of 2.0 is required. AP and CLEP credits are accepted.

Procedure: Freshmen are admitted to all sessions. There are early admissions, rolling admissions, and deferred admissions plans. Application deadlines are open. The fall 2005 application fee was $20.

Transfer: 740 transfer students enrolled in a recent year. A cumulative GPA of 2.0 is required. 30 of 124 credits required for the bachelor's degree must be completed at UL Lafayette.

Visiting: There are regularly scheduled orientations for prospective students, including campus tours. There are guides for informal visits. To schedule a visit, contact the Secretary of High School Relations at (337) 482-6553 or *enroll@louisiana.edu.*

Financial Aid: 30% of undergraduates work part time. Average annual earnings from campus work are $1250. UL Lafayette is a member of CSS. The FAFSA is required. Check with the school for current deadlines.

International Students: There were 259 international students enrolled in a recent year. The school actively recruits these students. They must score satisfactorily on the TOEFL and also take the SAT or the ACT. Students must take SAT: Subject tests in math and English.

Computers: All students may access the system anytime. There are no time limits and no fees.

Graduates: In a recent year, 2025 bachelor's degrees were awarded. The most popular majors were business (20%), general studies (14%), and education (14%). In an average class, 7% graduate in 4 years or less, 21% graduate in 5 years or less, and 29% graduate in 6 years or less. 114 companies recruited on campus in a recent year.

Admissions Contact: Leroy Broussard, Director of Admissions. A video is available. E-mail: *admissions@louisiana.edu* Web: *www.louisiana.edu*

UNIVERSITY OF LOUISIANA AT MONROE   C-1
Monroe, LA 71209

(318) 342-5430
(800) 372-5127; Fax: (318) 342-1915

Full-time: 2494 men, 4398 women	Faculty: 467; IIA, --$
Part-time: 482 men, 1072 women	Ph.D.s: 50%
Graduate: 259 men, 640 women	Student/Faculty: 15 to 1
Year: semesters, summer session	Tuition: $3353 ($9305)
Application Deadline: open	Room & Board: $3750
Freshman Class: n/av	
ACT: required	COMPETITIVE

The University of Louisiana at Monroe, founded in 1931, is a public institution offering programs in business, education, liberal arts, pharmacy and health sciences, and pure and applied science. There are 5 undergraduate schools and 1 graduate school. In addition to regional accreditation, ULM has baccalaureate program accreditation with AACSB, ABET, ACCE, ACEJMC, ACPE, ADA, AOTA, ASLHA, CACREP, CCNE, CSWE, JRCERT, NASM, NASPE, and NCATE. The library contains 647,785 volumes, 821,181 microform items, and 152 audio/video tapes/CDs/DVDs, and subscribes to 12,000 periodicals including electronic. Computerized library services include the card catalog, interlibrary loans, database searching, Internet access, and laptop Internet portals. Special learning facilities include a learning resource center, art gallery, natural history museum, planetarium, radio station, herbarium,

---

state poison control center, and state tumor registry. The 238-acre campus is in an urban area 90 miles east of Shreveport on I-20. Including any residence halls, there are 75 buildings.

Student Life: 91% of undergraduates are from Louisiana. Others are from 44 states, 50 foreign countries, and Canada. 66% are white; 28% African American. The average age of freshmen is 21; all undergraduates, 24.

Housing: 1751 students can be accommodated in college housing, which includes single-sex and coed dorms and on-campus apartments. On-campus housing is available on a first-come, first-served basis. 82% of students commute. Alcohol is not permitted. All students may keep cars.

Activities: 4% of men belong to 1 local fraternity and 6 national fraternities; 4% of women belong to 7 national sororities. There are 118 groups on campus, including art, band, cheerleading, choir, chorale, chorus, computers, dance, debate, drama, drill team, drum corps, ethnic, film, honors, international, jazz band, literary magazine, marching band, musical theater, newspaper, opera, orchestra, pep band, political, professional, radio and TV, religious, social, social service, student government, symphony, and yearbook. Popular campus events include Week of Welcome, Lyceum Series, and Casino Night.

Sports: There are 7 intercollegiate sports for men and 9 for women, and 44 intramural sports for men and 31 for women. Facilities include 2 stadiums, a natatorium, a coliseum, tennis courts, a softball complex, an activity center, a baseball complex, and a bayou.

Disabled Students: 98% of the campus is accessible. Wheelchair ramps, elevators, special parking, specially equipped rest rooms, special class scheduling, lowered drinking fountains, and specially equipped dorm rooms are available.

Services: Counseling and information services are available, as is tutoring in most subjects. There is remedial math, reading, and writing.

Campus Safety and Security: Measures include 24-hour foot and vehicle patrol, security escort services, emergency telephones, and lighted pathways/sidewalks.

Programs of Study: ULM confers B.A., B.S., B.B.A., B.F.A., B.G.S., B.M., and B.M.E. degrees. Associate, master's, and doctoral degrees are also awarded. Bachelor's degrees are awarded in AGRICULTURE (agricultural business management), BIOLOGICAL SCIENCE (biology/biological science and toxicology), BUSINESS (accounting, banking and finance, business administration and management, entrepreneurial studies, insurance, management science, and marketing/retailing/merchandising), COMMUNICATIONS AND THE ARTS (art, communications, English, French, music, Spanish, and speech/debate/rhetoric), COMPUTER AND PHYSICAL SCIENCE (atmospheric sciences and meteorology, chemistry, computer science, geology, geoscience, information sciences and systems, mathematics, and radiological technology), EDUCATION (art, early childhood, elementary, English, foreign languages, mathematics, music, physical, reading, science, and social studies), ENGINEERING AND ENVIRONMENTAL DESIGN (aeronautical science and aviation administration/management), HEALTH PROFESSIONS (clinical science, dental hygiene, health, nursing, occupational therapy, and pharmacy), SOCIAL SCIENCE (child care/child and family studies, criminal justice, economics, family/consumer studies, history, law, liberal arts/general studies, political science/government, prelaw, psychology, social work, and sociology). Pharmacy, occupational therapy, and dental hygiene are the strongest academically. Pharmacy, nursing, and general studies are the largest.

Required: Students are required to take the freshman-year seminar, 9 hours each of natural/physical sciences and humanities, 6 each of English, social sciences, and math, and 3 of the arts. An overall minimum GPA of 2.0 is required for graduation along with a total number of credits that varies by degree.

Special: Internships in accounting, information sciences, pharmacy, nursing, clinical laboratory science, radiological technology, dental hygiene, occupational therapy, and communication disorders are available. There are 22 national honor societies, a freshman honors program, and 2 departmental honors programs.

Faculty/Classroom: 58% of faculty are male; 42%, female. The average class size in a laboratory is 24.

Admissions: The SAT scores for the 2005-2006 freshman class were: Verbal--61% below 500, 32% between 500 and 599, 6% between 600 and 700, and 1% above 700; Math--63% below 500, 24% between 500 and 599, 11% between 600 and 700, and 2% above 700. The ACT scores were 56% below 21, 26% between 21 and 23, 12% between 24 and 26, 4% between 27 and 28, and 3% above 28.

Requirements: The ACT is required. In addition, applicants must be graduates of an accredited high school or have a GED. ULM requires applicants to be in the upper 50% of their class. A GPA of 2.0 is required. CLEP credit is accepted.

Procedure: Freshmen are admitted to all sessions. Entrance exams should be taken by April 1. There is a rolling admissions plan. Application deadlines are open. The fall 2005 application fee was $20. Notification is sent on a rolling basis. Applications are accepted on-line.

Transfer: 729 transfer students enrolled in 2004-2005. Applicants must have a minimum overall GPA of 2.0 from a regionally accredited institution and at least 12 semester hours of college-level credit above the remedial level, including a math and an English course. Students who have completed fewer than 12 semster hours of college credit must meet ULM freshman admission requirements. 30 credits required for the bachelor's degree must be completed at ULM.

Visiting: There are regularly scheduled orientations for prospective students, consisting of the mandatory PREP program, which includes campus tours, meetings with deans/advisers, class registration, and placement exams. There are guides for informal visits and visitors may sit in on classes. To schedule a visit, contact Recruitment and Admissions at *recruitment@ulm.edu*.

Financial Aid: The FAFSA is required.

International Students: There are 83 international students enrolled. The school actively recruits these students. A satisfactory score on the TOEFL is required. Only athletes are required to submit ACT/SAT scores due to NCAA requirements.

Computers: The University offers 7 full-time open labs and 12 labs that are open when classes are not in session. There are also 9 computer labs throughout the dorms as well as wireless access in several of the buildings on campus. All students may access the system 24 hours a day. There are no time limits. The fee is $60.

Graduates: From July 1, 2004 to June 30, 2005, 1361 bachelor's degrees were awarded. The most popular majors were general studies (8%), pharmacy (6%), and nursing (6%).

Admissions Contact: Frances Self, Assisantant Director of Admissions. E-mail: *self@ulm.edu* Web: *www.ulm.edu*

UNIVERSITY OF NEW ORLEANS   D-4
New Orleans, LA 70148

(504) 280-6595
(800) 256-5866; Fax: (504) 280-5522

Full-time: 4270 men, 5330 women	Faculty: 557; I, --$
Part-time: 1570 men, 2180 women	Ph.D.s: 87%
Graduate: 1640 men, 2390 women	Student/Faculty: 17 to 1
Year: semesters, summer session	Tuition: $3240 ($10,280)
Application Deadline: see profile	Room & Board: $4130
Freshman Class: n/av	
SAT or ACT: required	COMPETITIVE

University of New Orleans, founded in 1958, is a public liberal arts institution. There are 7 undergraduate schools and 1 graduate school. Figures in the above capsule are approximate. In addition to regional accreditation, UNO has baccalaureate program accreditation with AACSB, ABET, ABFSE, ACS, CACREP, NASM, NAST, and NCATE. The library contains 896,000 volumes, 2,385,500 microform items, and 125,600 audio/video tapes/CDs/DVDs, and subscribes to 4950 periodicals including electronic. Computerized library services include interlibrary loans and database searching. Special learning facilities include a learning resource center, art gallery, and radio station. The 395-acre campus is in an urban area in a residential area of New Orleans. Including any residence halls, there are 30 buildings.

Student Life: 72% of undergraduates are from Louisiana. Others are from 49 states, 95 foreign countries, and Canada. 62% are from public schools. 56% are white; 23% African American. 65% claim no religious affiliation; 22% Catholic; 10% Protestant. The average age of freshmen is 19; all undergraduates, 24. 33% do not continue beyond their first year.

Housing: 1425 students can be accommodated in college housing, which includes coed dorms and married-student housing. On-campus housing is available on a first-come, first-served basis. 91% of students commute. All students may keep cars.

Activities: 1% of men belong to 7 national fraternities; 1% of women belong to 7 national sororities. There are 125 groups on campus, including art, band, cheerleading, chess, choir, chorale, chorus, computers, dance, drama, ethnic, film, gay, honors, international, jazz band, literary magazine, newspaper, opera, orchestra, pep band, photography, political, professional, radio and TV, religious, social, social service, student government, and yearbook. Popular campus events include Fall Fest, April Fest, and Ambassadors Fishing Rodeo.

Sports: There are 5 intercollegiate sports for men and 5 for women, and 7 intramural sports for men and 7 for women. Facilities include the UNO Lakefront Arena, Privateer Park, 12 tennis courts, a swimming pool, and a health and phys ed center. A recreation and fitness center has free weights, cardiovascular equipment, an indoor track, exercise classes, 2 dry saunas, racquetball courts, basketball courts, a lap pool (indoor), an outdoor pool, and equipment accessible to the disabled.

Disabled Students: 96% of the campus is accessible. Wheelchair ramps, elevators, special parking, specially equipped rest rooms, special class scheduling, lowered drinking fountains, and lowered telephones are available.

Services: Counseling and information services are available, as is tutoring in most subjects. There is a reader service for the blind, and remedial math, reading, and writing.

Campus Safety and Security: Measures include 24-hour foot and vehicle patrol, security escort services, informal discussions, and pamphlets/posters/films. There are emergency telephones, lighted pathways/sidewalks, and monitored parking.

Programs of Study: UNO confers B.A., B.S., and B.G.S. degrees. Master's and doctoral degrees are also awarded. Bachelor's degrees are awarded in BIOLOGICAL SCIENCE (biology/biological science), BUSINESS (accounting, banking and finance, business administration and management, business economics, hotel/motel and restaurant management, marketing/retailing/merchandising, and tourism), COMMUNICATIONS AND THE ARTS (art, communications, dramatic arts, English, fine arts, French, music, and Spanish), COMPUTER AND PHYSICAL SCIENCE (chemistry, computer science, geology, geophysics and seismology, mathematics, and physics), EDUCATION (business, elementary, English, foreign languages, mathematics, music, physical, science, and secondary), ENGINEERING AND ENVIRONMENTAL DESIGN (civil engineering, electrical/electronics engineering, marine engineering, mechanical engineering, and naval architecture and marine engineering), HEALTH PROFESSIONS (medical technology, premedicine, and preveterinary science), SOCIAL SCIENCE (anthropology, economics, geography, history, philosophy, political science/government, psychology, sociology, and urban studies). Business administration, drama, and communications are the largest.

Required: Requirements for graduation include 12 hours in social science and the humanities, 11 hours in science, and 6 hours each in English composition and literature, and in math. To graduate, students must complete 128 hours with a minimum GPA of 2.0.

Special: Students may participate in co-op programs with LSU Medical Center and may cross-register with Southern University in New Orleans, Elaine P. Nunez Community College, and Delgado Community College. Internships are required in most professional programs and work-study programs are available with various federal agencies and private companies. Students may study abroad in 7 countries or participate in a Washington semester. UNO also offers dual and student-designed majors, B.A.-B.S. degrees, preprofessional programs in nursing and physical therapy, and nondegree study. Pass/fail options and limited credit for life, military, and work experience are available. There are 5 national honor societies, a freshman honors program, and 28 departmental honors programs.

Faculty/Classroom: 61% of faculty are male; 39%, female. 96% teach undergraduates and 87% do research. Graduate students teach 16% of introductory courses. The average class size in an introductory lecture is 35; in a laboratory, 23; and in a regular course, 24.

Requirements: The SAT or ACT is required. In addition, applicants must be high school graduates with a college preparatory program of 4 units in English, 3 each in math and science, 2 each in foreign language, history, and academic social studies, and 1/2 in computer science. A GPA of 2.0 is required. AP and CLEP credits are accepted. Important factors in the admissions decision are advanced placement or honor courses, recommendations by school officials, and evidence of special talent.

Procedure: Freshmen are admitted to all sessions. Entrance exams should be taken at least 6 months prior to enrollment. There is an early admissions and rolling admissions plan. Check with school for current application deadlines. The fall 2005 application fee was $20. Notification is sent on a rolling basis.

Transfer: A minimum college GPA of 2.0 is required. Applicants with fewer than 24 semester hours of credit must take the SAT I or the ACT. 30 of 128 credits required for the bachelor's degree must be completed at UNO.

Visiting: There are guides for informal visits and visitors may sit in on classes and stay overnight. To schedule a visit, contact the Office of Admissions.

Financial Aid: In a recent year, 75% of all full-time freshmen and 61% of continuing full-time students received some form of financial aid. 37% of full-time freshmen and 36% of continuing full-time students received need-based aid. The average freshman award was $5166. 2% of undergraduates work part time. Average annual earnings from campus work are $2009. UNO is a member of CSS. The FAFSA is required. Check with the school for current deadlines.

International Students: There were 316 international students enrolled in a recent year. The school actively recruits these students. They must score satisfactorily on the TOEFL and also take the college's own test and the SAT or the ACT.

Computers: All students may access the system for class assignments and course research. There are no time limits and no fees.

Graduates: In a recent year, 1579 bachelor's degrees were awarded. The most popular majors were business (16%), general studies (13%), and elementary education (6%). In an average class, 4% graduate in 4 years or less, 16% graduate in 5 years or less, and 22% graduate in 6 years or less. 200 companies recruited on campus in a recent year.

Admissions Contact: Office of Admissions.
E-mail: *admissions@uno.edu* Web: *http://www.uno.edu*

XAVIER UNIVERSITY OF LOUISIANA

New Orleans, LA 70125   D-4

	(504) 520-7388; Fax: (504) 520-7941
Full-time: 730 men, 2270 women	**Faculty:** n/av
Part-time: 50 men, 110 women	**Ph.D.s:** 90%
Graduate: 40 men, 220 women	**Student/Faculty:** n/av
Year: semesters, summer session	**Tuition:** $11,400
Application Deadline: see profile	**Room & Board:** $6200
Freshman Class: n/av	
SAT or ACT: required	**COMPETITIVE**

Xavier University of Louisiana, founded in 1925, is a private, historically black liberal arts university affiliated with the Roman Catholic Church. Some figures in the above capsule are approximate. In addition to regional accreditation, Xavier has baccalaureate program accreditation with ACPE, NASM, and NCATE. The library contains 230,548 volumes, 776,442 microform items, and 5893 audio/video tapes/CDs/DVDs, and subscribes to 1825 periodicals including electronic. Computerized library services include the card catalog, interlibrary loans, and database searching. Special learning facilities include a learning resource center, TV station, and electronic classrooms. The 29-acre campus is in an urban area 2 miles from downtown New Orleans. Including any residence halls, there are 38 buildings.

Student Life: 51% of undergraduates are from Louisiana. 80% are from public schools. 83% are African American. 31% are Baptist; 27% Catholic; 15% claim no religious affiliation. The average age of freshmen is 18; all undergraduates, 20. 27% do not continue beyond their first year.

Housing: 1071 students can be accommodated in college housing, which includes single-sex and coed dorms and on-campus apartments. In addition, there are honors houses. On-campus housing is available on a first-come, first-served basis. Priority is given to out-of-town students. 73% of students commute. Alcohol is not permitted. All students may keep cars.

Activities: 2% of men belong to 4 national fraternities; 6% of women belong to 4 national sororities. There are 80 groups on campus, including art, band, cheerleading, chess, choir, chorus, computers, dance, drill team, ethnic, honors, international, jazz band, literary magazine, newspaper, opera, pep band, political, professional, religious, social, social service, student government, symphony, TV station, and yearbook. Popular campus events include Wellness Week, Octoberfest, and Culturefest.

Sports: There are 3 intercollegiate sports for men and 3 for women, and 22 intramural sports for men and 22 for women. Facilities include a gym, a swimming pool, tennis courts, and a recreation room.

Disabled Students: 99% of the campus is accessible. Wheelchair ramps, elevators, special parking, specially equipped rest rooms, special class scheduling, lowered drinking fountains, and lowered telephones are available.

Services: Counseling and information services are available, as is tutoring in every subject. There is a reader service for the blind, and remedial math, reading, and writing.

Campus Safety and Security: Measures include 24-hour foot and vehicle patrol, security escort services, shuttle buses, and informal discussions. There are pamphlets/posters/films, emergency telephones, and lighted pathways/sidewalks.

Programs of Study: Xavier confers B.A., B.S., and B.M. degrees. Master's and doctoral degrees are also awarded. Bachelor's degrees are awarded in BIOLOGICAL SCIENCE (biochemistry, biology/biological science, microbiology, and toxicology), BUSINESS (accounting, banking and finance, business administration and management, business economics, marketing/retailing/merchandising, and personnel management), COMMUNICATIONS AND THE ARTS (communications, English, fine arts, French, music, and Spanish), COMPUTER AND PHYSICAL SCIENCE (chemistry, computer science, mathematics, physics, and statistics), EDUCATION (art, early childhood, elementary, English, mathematics, music, physical, science, secondary, and social studies), HEALTH PROFESSIONS (predentistry, premedicine, and speech pathology/audiology), SOCIAL SCIENCE (history, philosophy, political science/government, prelaw, psychology, sociology, and theological studies). Science, education, and English are the strongest academically. Pharmacy, biology, and business are the largest.

Required: Requirements for graduation include 9 semester hours in English, 6 each in history, social science, language, theology, philosophy, and natural sciences, 3 each in speech, math, and the arts, and 1 in health and phys ed. Students must complete 128 to 132 total credit hours, including 24 to 54 total hours in the major. Students must maintain a minimum GPA of 2.0, take Introduction to African American History/Culture, pass a comprehensive exam, and by the beginning of the junior year declare a minor in an academic discipline other than the major.

Special: The university offers cooperative programs in any major and 3-2 engineering degrees with Tulane, Louisiana State, Morgan State, and Southern Universities as well as the Universities of Wisconsin, Maryland, New Orleans, and Detroit, and Georgia Institute of Technology. In addition, students may cross-register at colleges of the New Orleans Consortium. Internships are available in legal, political, and pharmaceutical areas. Students may earn an accelerated degree in biology, chemistry, psychology, or political science, pursue dual majors in engineering and biostatistics, opt for nondegree study, and earn a B.A.-B.S. degree in almost any combination. Students may study abroad in 6 countries or participate in an exchange program with Notre Dame University. There are 7 national honor societies, a freshman honors program, and 7 departmental honors programs.

Faculty/Classroom: 57% of faculty are male; 43%, female. No introductory courses are taught by graduate students. The average class size in an introductory lecture is 25; in a laboratory, 21; and in a regular course, 21.

Requirements: The SAT or ACT is required. In addition candidates for admission must have completed 4 units of English, 2 of math, 1 each of science and social studies, and 8 of academic electives. The GED is accepted. A GPA of 2.0 is required. AP and CLEP credits are accepted. Important factors in the admissions decision are advanced placement or honor courses, recommendations by school officials, and evidence of special talent.

Procedure: Freshmen are admitted fall, spring, and summer. Entrance exams should be taken in the spring of the junior year or the fall of the senior year. There is an early decision plan. Check with school for current application deadlines. The fall 2005 application fee was $25. Applications are accepted on-line.

Transfer: 159 transfer students enrolled in a recent year. Applicants must submit college transcripts; high school transcripts are required of applicants with fewer than 30 transferable credits. 30 of 128 credits required for the bachelor's degree must be completed at Xavier.

Visiting: There are guides for informal visits and visitors may sit in on classes and stay overnight. To schedule a visit, contact the Admissions Office at (504) 520-7578.

Financial Aid: In a recent year, 83% of all full-time freshmen and 80% of continuing full-time students received some form of financial aid. 8% of full-time freshmen and 54% of continuing full-time students received need-based aid. The average freshman award was $4438. Need-based self-help aid (loans and jobs) averaged $1406; non-need-based athletic scholarships averaged $6983; and other non-need-based awards and non-need-based scholarships averaged $2988. The average financial indebtedness of a recent graduate was $15,292. Xavier is a member of CSS. The FAFSA is required. Check with the school for current deadlines.

International Students: They must score satisfactorily on the TOEFL and also take the SAT or the ACT.

Computers: All students may access the system. There are no time limits and no fees.

Graduates: In a recent year, 458 bachelor's degrees were awarded. The most popular majors were biology (40%), psychology (14%), and physical sciences (11%). In an average class, 38% graduate in 4 years or less, 48% graduate in 5 years or less, and 50% graduate in 6 years or less.

Admissions Contact: Winston D. Brown, Dean of Admissions. E-mail: *apply@xula.edu* Web: *www.xula.edu*

MAINE

BATES COLLEGE
B-5

Lewiston, ME 04240   (207) 786-6000; Fax: (207) 786-6025

Full-time: 829 men, 855 women	**Faculty:** 180; IIB, +$
Part-time: none	**Ph.D.s:** 99%
Graduate: none	**Student/Faculty:** 9 to 1
Year: 4-1-4	**Tuition:** see profile
Application Deadline: January 1	**Room & Board:** n/app
Freshman Class: 4356 applied, 1272 accepted, 490 enrolled	
SAT Verbal/Math: 675/680*	**MOST COMPETITIVE**

Bates College, founded in 1855, is a private liberal arts institution offering undergraduate and graduate programs in humanities, social sciences, and natural sciences. There is a single comprehensive fee of $42100, which includes tuition, room and board, and fees. The library contains 591,630 volumes, 300,775 microform items, and 34,267 audio/video tapes/CDs/DVDs, and subscribes to 25,703 periodicals including electronic. Computerized library services include the card catalog, interlibrary loans, database searching, and Internet access. Special learning facilities include a learning resource center, art gallery, planetarium, radio station, TV station, a 654-acre mountain conservation area, observatory, language resource center, and the Edmund S. Muskie archives. The 109-acre campus is in a small town 35 miles north of Portland. Including any residence halls, there are 78 buildings.

Student Life: 89% of undergraduates are from out of state, mostly the Northeast. Students are from 47 states, 67 foreign countries, and Canada. 54% are from public schools. 82% are white. The average age of freshmen is 18; all undergraduates, 20. 6% do not continue beyond their first year; 89% remain to graduate.

Housing: 1593 students can be accommodated in college housing, which includes single-sex and coed dorms. In addition, there are special-interest houses. On-campus housing is guaranteed for all 4 years. 93% of students live on campus; of those, 95% remain on campus on weekends. All students may keep cars.

Activities: There are no fraternities or sororities. There are 101 groups on campus, including art, chess, choir, chorale, chorus, computers, dance, debate, drama, ethnic, film, gay, honors, international, jazz band, literary magazine, musical theater, newspaper, orchestra, outdoor, pep band, photography, political, professional, radio and TV, religious, social, social service, student government, and yearbook. Popular campus events include Winter Carnival, international dinners, and ocean clambakes.

Sports: There are 15 intercollegiate sports for men and 16 for women, and 8 intramural sports for men and 8 for women. Facilities include a pool, a field house, indoor and outdoor tracks, indoor and outdoor tennis courts, 3 basketball courts, 3 volleyball courts, dance and fencing space, squash and racquetball courts, training rooms, a rock-climbing

wall, a boathouse, a winter sports arena, a weight room, and football, soccer, baseball, softball, and lacrosse fields.

Disabled Students: 60% of the campus is accessible. Wheelchair ramps, elevators, special parking, specially equipped rest rooms, special class scheduling, and lowered telephones are available.

Services: Counseling and information services are available, as is tutoring in every subject. There is a reader service for the blind and remedial math and writing.

Campus Safety and Security: Measures include 24-hour foot and vehicle patrol, self-defense education, security escort services, and shuttle buses. There are informal discussions, pamphlets/posters/films, emergency telephones, lighted pathways/sidewalks, and electronic access control in residence halls and all major buildings on campus, and an automated 911 telephone system.

Programs of Study: Bates confers B.A. and B.S. degrees. Bachelor's degrees are awarded in AGRICULTURE (environmental studies), BIOLOGICAL SCIENCE (biochemistry, biology/biological science, and neurosciences), COMMUNICATIONS AND THE ARTS (art, Chinese, dramatic arts, English, French, German, Japanese, music, Russian, Spanish, and speech/debate/rhetoric), COMPUTER AND PHYSICAL SCIENCE (chemistry, geology, mathematics, and physics), ENGINEERING AND ENVIRONMENTAL DESIGN (engineering), SOCIAL SCIENCE (African American studies, American studies, anthropology, classical/ancient civilization, East Asian studies, economics, gender studies, history, interdisciplinary studies, medieval studies, philosophy, political science/government, psychology, religion, sociology, and women's studies). Psychology, economics, and political science are the largest.

Required: Requirements for graduation include 5 courses in humanities, 3 each in natural science and social science, and 1 each in quantitative techniques and phys ed. The total number of hours in the major varies by department, but students should take at least 32 courses, plus 2 short terms, and maintain a minimum GPA of 2.0. A senior thesis is required.

Special: Co-op programs in engineering, internships, research apprenticeships, work-study programs, study abroad, and a Washington semester are possible. Dual, student-designed, and interdisciplinary majors, and a 3-2 engineering degree with Columbia University, Dartmouth College, Case Western Reserve University, Rensselaer Polytechnic Institute, and Washington University in St. Louis are available. Students in any major may graduate in 3 years, and a B.A.-B.S. is possible in all majors. Students may also participate in the Williams-Mystic Seaport program in marine biology and maritime history, and exchanges with Spelman College, Morehouse College, Washington and Lee University, and McGill University are possible. There are 2 national honor societies, including Phi Beta Kappa. All departments have honors programs.

Faculty/Classroom: 54% of faculty are male; 46%, female. All both teach and do research. The average class size in an introductory lecture is 35; in a laboratory, 16; and in a regular course, 21.

Admissions: 29% of the 2005-2006 applicants were accepted. The SAT scores for the 2005-2006 freshman class were: Verbal--7% between 500 and 599, 55% between 600 and 700, and 37% above 700; Math--6% between 500 and 599, 65% between 600 and 700, and 29% above 700. 85% of the current freshmen were in the top fifth of their class; 99% were in the top two fifths.

Requirements: Candidates for admission should have completed at least 4 years of English, 3 each of math, social science, and a foreign language, and 2 of lab science. Essays are required, and an interview on or off campus is strongly recommended. The submission of test scores is optional. AP credits are accepted. Important factors in the admissions decision are advanced placement or honor courses, evidence of special talent, and leadership record.

Procedure: Freshmen are admitted fall and winter. There are early decision, early admissions, and deferred admissions plans. Early decision applications should be filed by November 15; regular applications, by January 1 for fall entry and November 1 for winter entry, along with a $60 fee. Notification of early decision is sent December 20; regular decision, by March 31. 203 early decision candidates were accepted for the 2005-2006 class. A waiting list is an active part of the admissions procedure. Applications are accepted on-line.

Transfer: 20 transfer students enrolled in 2005-2006. More weight is given to the student's college record than to high school credentials. Applicants must submit official college and final high school transcripts, a statement of good standing, 3 letters of recommendation, and an essay. An interview is strongly recommended. 16 of 32 courses required for the bachelor's degree must be completed at Bates.

Visiting: There are guides for informal visits and visitors may sit in on classes and stay overnight. To schedule a visit, contact the Admissions Office.

Financial Aid: In 2005-2006, 37% of all full-time freshmen and 39% of continuing full-time students received some form of financial aid, including need-based aid. The average freshman award was $27,686.

50% of undergraduates work part time. Average annual earnings from campus work are $1600. The average financial indebtedness of the 2005 graduate was $13,636. Bates is a member of CSS. The CSS/Profile or FAFSA and parent and student tax returns and W-2 forms are required. The deadline for filing freshman financial aid applications for fall entry is February 1.

International Students: There are 93 international students enrolled. The school actively recruits these students. They must take an English proficiency exam; the TOEFL is preferred.

Computers: Wireless access is available. There are 100 MB network connections in residence halls for each student, network access in every classroom, and wireless in some, plus 400 open ports on campus. More than 400 college-owned computers are available for student use. All students may access the system. There are no time limits and no fees.

Graduates: From July 1, 2004 to June 30, 2005, 517 bachelor's degrees were awarded. The most popular majors were psychology (13%), economics (13%), and political science (11%). In an average class, 84% graduate in 4 years or less, 88% graduate in 5 years or less, and 89% graduate in 6 years or less. Of the 2004 graduating class, 16% were enrolled in graduate school within 6 months of graduation and 79% were employed.

Admissions Contact: Wylie L. Mitchell, Dean of Admissions. E-mail: *admissions@bates.edu* Web: *www.bates.edu*

BOWDOIN COLLEGE
B-5

Brunswick, ME 04011 (207) 725-3100; Fax: (207) 725-3101

Full-time: 823 men, 838 women	Faculty: 152; IIB, ++$
Part-time: 1 man, 4 women	Ph.D.s: 99%
Graduate: none	Student/Faculty: 11 to 1
Year: semesters	Tuition: $32,990
Application Deadline: January 1	Room & Board: $8670
Freshman Class: 5026 applied, 1232 accepted, 478 enrolled	
SAT Verbal/Math: 700/700*	MOST COMPETITIVE

Bowdoin College, established in 1794, is a private liberal arts institution. In addition to regional accreditation, Bowdoin has baccalaureate program accreditation with ASC. The 8 libraries contain 996,694 volumes, 112,453 microform items, and 23,162 audio/video tapes/CDs/DVDs, and subscribe to 4498 periodicals including electronic. Computerized library services include the card catalog, interlibrary loans, database searching, Internet access, and laptop Internet portals. Special learning facilities include a learning resource center, art gallery, radio station, TV station, a museum of art, arctic museum, language media center, women's resource center, electronic classroom, coastal studies center, African American center, craft center ceramics studio and photography darkroom, scientific station, located in the Bay of Fundy, educational research and development program, theaters, music hall, community service resource center, environmental studies center, and visual arts center. The 200-acre campus is in a small town 25 miles northeast of Portland. Including any residence halls, there are 121 buildings.

Student Life: 88% of undergraduates are from out of state, mostly the Northeast. Students are from 48 states, 24 foreign countries, and Canada. 55% are from public schools. 69% are white; 12% Asian American. 33% are claim no religious affiliation; 29% Protestant; 23% Catholic; 8% Jewish; 7% other religion (unspecified), Buddhist, Hindu, and Muslim. The average age of freshmen is 18; all undergraduates, 20. 2% do not continue beyond their first year; 91% remain to graduate.

Housing: 1639 students can be accommodated in college housing, which includes single-sex and coed dormitories, on-campus apartments, and off-campus apartments. In addition, there are special-interest houses. All first-year student participate in the new College House System; their residence hall is associated with lot 6 campus house. All uperclass students are eligible to participate. On-campus housing is available on a lottery system for upperclassmen. 94% of students live on campus; of those, 99% remain on campus on weekends. All students may keep cars.

Activities: There are no fraternities or sororities. There are 110 groups on campus, including art, band, cheerleading, choir, chorale, chorus, computers, dance, debate, drama, environmental awareness groups, ethnic, film, gay, honors, improvisational comedy, international, jazz band, literary magazine, musical theater, newspaper, orchestra, organic garden club, outing club, peer counseling and advising, photography, political, professional, radio and TV, religious, science clubs, social, social service, student government, symphony, volunteer programs and yearbook. Popular campus events include Sara and James Bowdoin Day, and Asian Week.

Sports: There are 13 intercollegiate sports for men and 15 for women, and 12 intramural sports for men and 11 for women. Facilities include an ice arena, a field house, a swimming pool, 2 gyms, indoor and outdoor track facilities, tennis and squash courts, a climbing wall, a boathouse, outdoor leadership center, and cross-country ski trails. There are also weight and aerobics rooms and 60 acres of playing fields for football, baseball, softball, lacrosse, field hockey, and soccer. The fitness center includes Cybex ergonometric equipment, free weights, and various fitness machines.

Disabled Students: 60% of the campus is accessible. Wheelchair ramps, elevators, special parking, specially equipped rest rooms, lowered drinking fountains, lowered telephones and special housing.

Services: Counseling and information services are available, as is tutoring in most subjects. There is a reader service for the blind. A counselor is available to assist students with accommodations as needed. Tutoring is available through the Quantitative Skills Program and the Writing Skills Project.

Campus Safety and Security: Measures include 24-hour foot and vehicle patrol, self-defense education, security escort services, and shuttle buses. There are informal discussions, pamphlets/posters/films, emergency telephones, lighted pathways/sidewalks, and emergency warning whistles. Residences are locked 24 hours a day, and a staffed communications center is available around the clock.

Programs of Study: Bowdoin confers the A.B. degree. Bachelor's degrees are awarded in BIOLOGICAL SCIENCE (biochemistry, biology/biological science, and neurosciences), COMMUNICATIONS AND THE ARTS (art history and appreciation, classics, dramatic arts, English, French, German, music, romance languages and literature, Russian, Spanish, and visual and performing arts), COMPUTER AND PHYSICAL SCIENCE (chemical physics, chemistry, computer science, geochemistry, geology, geophysics and seismology, mathematics, and physics), ENGINEERING AND ENVIRONMENTAL DESIGN (environmental science), SOCIAL SCIENCE (African studies, anthropology, archeology, Asian/Oriental studies, classical/ancient civilization, economics, history, interdisciplinary studies, Latin American studies, philosophy, political science/government, psychology, religion, sociology, and women's studies). Biology, economics, government and legal studies are the strongest academically. Government and legal studies, economics, and history are the largest.

Required: Degree requirements include 32 courses, with at least 2 semesters in natural science and math, social and behavioral sciences, humanities and fine arts, and non-Eurocentric studies, and completion of major requirements.

Special: Students may take advantage of about 100 approved programs all over the world, including Intercollegiate Center for Classical Studies in Rome, Intercollegiate Sri Lanka Education (ISLE), South India Term Abroad (SITA), The Swedish Program, Semester in Environmental Science at the Marine Biological Laboratory, Woods Hole, and the Twelve College Exchange (including Williams College-Mystic Seaport and National Theater Institute). Dual majors in any combination, internships, interdisciplinary majors, student-designed majors, B.A.-B.S. degrees, and pass/fail options are available. The college offers a 3-2 engineering degree with the California Institute of Technology and Columbia University and 3-3 legal studies with Columbia University Law School. There is 1 national honor society, including Phi Beta Kappa, and 34 departmental honors programs.

Faculty/Classroom: 54% of faculty are male; 46%, female. All both teach and do research. The average class size in an introductory lecture is 25; in a laboratory, 12; and in a regular course, 16.

Admissions: 25% of the 2005-2006 applicants were accepted. The SAT scores for the 2005-2006 freshman class were: Verbal--1% below 500, 5% between 500 and 599, 52% between 600 and 700, and 42% above 700; Math--9% between 500 and 599, 44% between 600 and 700, and 47% above 700. There were 27 National Merit finalists.

Requirements: There are no specific academic requirements, but typical applicants for admission will have 4 years each of English, social studies, foreign language, and math, 3 1/2 years of science, and 1 course each in art, music, and history. A high school record, 2 teacher recommendations, and an essay are required. AP credits are accepted.

Procedure: Freshmen are admitted in the fall. Entrance exams should be taken by the late summer before the freshman year. There are early decision and deferred admissions plans. Early decision applications should be filed by November 15; regular applications, by January 1 for fall entry, along with a $60 fee. Notification of early decision is sent December 15; regular decision, April 15. 183 early decision candidates were accepted for the 2005-2006 class. A waiting list is an active part of the admissions procedure. Applications are accepted on-line.

Transfer: 3 transfer students enrolled in 2004-2005. College grades of B or better are required to transfer. Applicants should submit high school and college transcripts, a dean's or adviser's statement from the most recent college attended, and 2 recommendations from recent professors. 16 of 32 credits required for the bachelor's degree must be completed at Bowdoin.

Visiting: There are regularly scheduled orientations for prospective students, in which students should be prepared to talk informally about their academic record, interests, talents, and goals. There are guides for informal visits and visitors may sit in on classes and stay overnight. To schedule a visit, contact the Admissions Office.

Financial Aid: In 2005-2006, 45% of all full-time freshmen and 46% of continuing full-time students received some form of financial aid. 41% of full-time freshmen and 42% of continuing full-time students received need-based aid. The average freshman award was $30,768. Need-based scholarships or need-based grants averaged $28,346 ($44,900 maximum); need-based self-help aid (loans and jobs) averaged $3585 ($5300 maximum); and other non-need-based awards and non-need-based scholarships averaged $1000 ($2000 maximum). 51% of undergraduates work part time. Average annual earnings from campus work are $1577. The average financial indebtedness of the 2005 graduate was $15,300. Bowdoin is a member of CSS. The CSS/Profile or FAFSA and the college's own financial statement are required. The deadline for filing freshman financial aid applications for fall entry is February 15.

International Students: There are 47 international students enrolled. The school actively recruits these students. They must score satisfactorily on the written TOEFL or on the electronic version. SAT scores must be submitted at matriculation for counseling and placement.

Computers: Wireless access is available. Computer equipment and network and Internet access are available to all students in computer labs (150 stations), all residence halls, the library (250 stations), the student center and classrooms (500 stations). Students have access to the wireless network, available in all libraries, some classrooms, computer labs and some residence halls. Students may check out labtops and wireless cards from the library. All students may access the system 24 hours a day. There are no time limits and no fees. It is strongly recommended that all students have a personal computer.

Graduates: From July 1, 2004 to June 30, 2005, 408 bachelor's degrees were awarded. The most popular majors were government and legal studies (19%), economics (13%), and history (10%). In an average class, 84% graduate in 4 years or less, 90% graduate in 5 years or less, and 91% graduate in 6 years or less. 350 companies recruited on campus in 2004-2005. Of the 2004 graduating class, 11% were enrolled in graduate school within 6 months of graduation and 71% were employed.

Admissions Contact: Richard E. Steele, Dean of Admissions/Student Aid. A video is available. E-mail: *admissions@bowdoin.edu* Web: *www.bowdoin.edu/admissions/*

COLBY COLLEGE
B-4

Waterville, ME 04901-8841

(207) 872-3168
(800) 723-3032; Fax: (207) 859-4828

Full-time: 870 men, 1001 women	**Faculty:** 161; IIB, ++$
Part-time: none	**Ph.D.s:** 96%
Graduate: none	**Student/Faculty:** 12 to 1
Year: 4-1-4	**Tuition:** $41,770
Application Deadline: January 1	**Room & Board:** see profile
Freshman Class: 3874 applied, 1454 accepted, 511 enrolled	
SAT Verbal/Math: 680/680*	**ACT:** 29 **MOST COMPETITIVE**

Colby College, founded in 1813, is a private liberal arts college. Students are charged a comprehensive fee of $41,770 annually, which includes tuition, room and board, and required fees. In addition to regional accreditation, Colby has baccalaureate program accreditation with ACS. The 3 libraries contain 1,009,896 volumes, 419,330 microform items, and 20,037 audio/video tapes/CDs/DVDs, and subscribe to 7976 periodicals including electronic. Computerized library services include the card catalog, interlibrary loans, database searching, Internet access, and laptop Internet portals. Special learning facilities include a learning resource center, art gallery, radio station, observatory, astronomy classroom, arboretum, state wildlife management area, and electronic-research classroom. The 714-acre campus is in a small town 75 miles north of Portland. Including any residence halls, there are 59 buildings.

Student Life: 89% of undergraduates are from out of state, mostly the Northeast. Students are from 44 states, 66 foreign countries, and Canada. 55% are from public schools. 83% are white. The average age of freshmen is 19; all undergraduates, 20. 7% do not continue beyond their first year; 88% remain to graduate.

Housing: 1702 students can be accommodated in college housing, which includes coed dorms and on-campus apartments. In addition, there are special-interest houses, substance-free halls, quiet residence halls, and apartments for seniors. On-campus housing is guaranteed for all 4 years. 94% of students live on campus. All students may keep cars.

Activities: There are no fraternities or sororities. There are 106 groups on campus, including art, band, cheerleading, choir, chorale, chorus, computers, dance, debate, drama, environmental, ethnic, film, gay, honors, human rights, international, jazz band, literary magazine, musical theater, newspaper, orchestra, outdoor, photography, political, professional, radio and TV, religious, social, social service, student government, symphony, women's, woodsmen's team, and yearbook. Popular campus events include Winter Carnival, Foss Arts Festival, and International Extravaganza.

Sports: There are 16 intercollegiate sports for men and 17 for women, and 8 intramural sports for men and 8 for women. Facilities include an athletic center with fitness, weight-training, and exercise areas; a gym with badminton, volleyball, and basketball courts; a hockey and skating rink; a field house for track and field, climbing wall, soccer, baseball, softball, tennis, lacrosse, and golf; a swimming pool and saunas; and squash and handball courts. There are also outdoor playing fields, tennis courts, an all-weather track, cross-country skiing, and running trails.

Disabled Students: 90% of the campus is accessible. Wheelchair ramps, elevators, special parking, specially equipped rest rooms, special class scheduling, lowered drinking fountains, and lowered telephones are available.

Services: Counseling and information services are available, as is tutoring in every subject. There is a reader service for the blind. There is also a writing center and a support program for learning-disabled students.

Campus Safety and Security: Measures include 24-hour foot and vehicle patrol, self-defense education, security escort services, and shuttle buses. There are informal discussions, pamphlets/posters/films, emergency telephones, lighted pathways/sidewalks, a women's safety program, a property identification program, party monitors (security officers), a student emergency response team, courtesy rides, and keycard dorm access.

Programs of Study: Colby confers the B.A. degree. Bachelor's degrees are awarded in BIOLOGICAL SCIENCE (biology/biological science), COMMUNICATIONS AND THE ARTS (art, classics, creative writing, English, German, Germanic languages and literature, music, performing arts, and Spanish), COMPUTER AND PHYSICAL SCIENCE (applied mathematics, chemistry, computer science, geology, mathematics, physics, and science technology), ENGINEERING AND ENVIRONMENTAL DESIGN (environmental science), SOCIAL SCIENCE (American studies, anthropology, classical/ancient civilization, East Asian studies, economics, French studies, history, international studies, Latin American studies, philosophy, political science/government, psychology, religion, sociology, and women's studies). Biology, economics, and chemistry are the strongest academically. Economics, biology, and English are the largest.

Required: To graduate, all students must take English composition and fulfill a foreign language requirement. They must also take 2 courses in the natural sciences and 1 course each in the arts, historical studies, literature, quantitative reasoning, the social sciences, and human or cultural diversity and meet Colby's wellness requirement by attending 8 lectures. Students must complete a total of 128 credit hours, including 3 January term courses, and maintain a GPA of 2.0.

Special: Colby offers study abroad in numerous countries. Colby also offers Washington semester programs through American University and the Washington Center, on-campus work-study, exchange programs with various colleges and universities, a 3-2 engineering degree with Dartmouth College, and maritime and oceanographic studies programs. Dual and student-designed majors are possible. There are 9 national honor societies, including Phi Beta Kappa, and 22 departmental honors programs.

Faculty/Classroom: 56% of faculty are male; 44%, female. All both teach and do research. The average class size in a regular course is 17.

Admissions: 38% of the 2005-2006 applicants were accepted. The SAT scores for the 2005-2006 freshman class were: Verbal--1% below 500, 9% between 500 and 599, 48% between 600 and 700, and 42% above 700; Math--1% below 500, 8% between 500 and 599, 55% between 600 and 700, and 36% above 700. The ACT scores were 3% between 21 and 23, 17% between 24 and 26, 23% between 27 and 28, and 57% above 28. 88% of the current freshmen were in the top fifth of their class; 97% were in the top two fifths. 9 freshmen graduated first in their class.

Requirements: The SAT or ACT is required. In addition, candidates should be high school graduates with a recommended academic program of 4 years of English, 3 each of foreign language and math, and 2 each of science (including lab work), social studies/history, and other college-preparatory courses. AP credits are accepted. Important factors in the admissions decision are leadership record, advanced placement or honor courses, and extracurricular activities record.

Procedure: Freshmen are admitted fall and spring. Entrance exams should be taken by January of the senior year. There are early decision, early admissions, and deferred admissions plans. Applications should be filed by January 1 for fall entry. The fall 2005 applicatioin fee was $55.Notification is sent April 1. 220 early decision candidates were accepted for the 2005-2006 class. 320 applicants were on the 2005 waiting list; 1 was admitted. Applications are accepted on-line.

Transfer: 11 transfer students enrolled in 2004-2005. Applicants must have a minimum GPA of 3.0 and, as a rule, have earned enough credit hours to qualify for at least sophomore standing. They must be in good academic and social standing and should submit references from a faculty member and a dean of their current school. If the SAT or ACT has been taken, the results must be submitted as well. 64 of 128 credits required for the bachelor's degree must be completed at Colby.

Visiting: There are regularly scheduled orientations for prospective students, including panel discussions, tours, class visits, complimentary meals, interviews, and information sessions. There are guides for informal visits and visitors may sit in on classes and stay overnight. To schedule a visit, contact the Overnight Host Hotline.

Financial Aid: In 2005-2006, 42% of all full-time freshmen and 38% of continuing full-time students received some form of financial aid, including need-based aid. The average freshman award was $27,177. Need-based scholarships or need-based grants averaged $27,190; and need-based self-help aid (loans and jobs) averaged $3531. 67% of undergraduates work part time. Average annual earnings from campus work are $1020. The average financial indebtedness of the 2005 graduate was $18,479. Colby is a member of CSS. The CSS/Profile or FAFSA and the college's own financial statement are required. The deadline for filing freshman financial aid applications for fall entry is February 1.

International Students: There are 193 international students enrolled. The school actively recruits these students. A satisfactory score on the TOEFL is required.

Computers: Wireless access is available in all dorm rooms and in many public locations. More than 300 public PCs with Internet access and a loaner PC program are also available. All students may access the system 24 hours a day. There are no time limits and no fees. It is strongly recommended that all students have a personal computer; see http://www.colby.edu/info.tech/fall2005/advice2005.html for the model of personal computer that is currently recommended.

Graduates: From July 1, 2004 to June 30, 2005, 484 bachelor's degrees were awarded. The most popular majors were biology (13%), English (11%), and government (10%). In an average class, 84% graduate in 4 years or less, 87% graduate in 5 years or less, and 88% graduate in 6 years or less. 91 companies recruited on campus in 2004-2005. Of the 2004 graduating class, 22% were enrolled in graduate school within 6 months of graduation and 76% were employed.

Admissions Contact: Parker J. Beverage, Dean of Admissions and Financial Aid. E-mail: admissions@colby.edu Web: www.colby.edu

COLLEGE OF THE ATLANTIC   D-5
Bar Harbor, ME 04609

(207) 288-5015
(800) 528-0025; Fax: (207) 288-4126

Full-time: 106 men, 187 women	**Faculty:** 19
Part-time: 3 men, 9 women	**Ph.D.s:** 100%
Graduate: 1 man, 5 women	**Student/Faculty:** 15 to 1
Year: trimesters	**Tuition:** $26,613
Application Deadline: February 15	**Room & Board:** $7089
Freshman Class: 284 applied, 188 accepted, 82 enrolled	
SAT Verbal/Math: 627/579*	**ACT:** 26 HIGHLY COMPETITIVE

College of the Atlantic, founded in 1969, is a private liberal arts college dedicated to the study of human ecology. The library contains 38,500 volumes, 274 microform items, and 1950 audio/video tapes/CDs/DVDs, and subscribes to 400 periodicals including electronic. Computerized library services include the card catalog, interlibrary loans, database searching, and Internet access. Special learning facilities include a learning resource center, art gallery, natural history museum, and writing center, taxidermy lab, photography lab, marine mammal research center, 2 greenhouses, 80-acre organic farm, and 2 offshore research stations. The 34-acre campus is in a small town 45 miles southeast of Bangor, along the Atlantic Ocean shoreline. Including any residence halls, there are 15 buildings.

Student Life: 23% of undergraduates are from Maine. Others are from 36 states, 35 foreign countries, and Canada. 74% are from public schools. The average age of freshmen is 19; all undergraduates, 21. 4% do not continue beyond their first year; 62% remain to graduate.

Housing: 100 students can be accommodated in college housing, which includes coed dorms and a substance-free house. On-campus housing is guaranteed for the freshman year only, is available on a first-come, first-served basis, and is available on a lottery system for upperclassmen. Priority is given to out-of-town students. 60% of students commute. Alcohol is not permitted. All students may keep cars.

Activities: There are no fraternities or sororities. There are 20 groups on campus, including art, chess, chorus, computers, dance, debate, drama, environmental, film, gay, international, jazz band, literary magazine, musical theater, newspaper, orchestra, photography, political, social, social service, and student government. Popular campus events include the annual Bar Island swim, contra dances, and Winter Carnival.

Sports: There are 4 intramural sports for men and 4 for women. All students are members of the local YMCA and may use its pool, Nautilus equipment, and volleyball and basketball facilities, as well as nearby tennis courts. Acadia National Park offers seasonal outdoor activities. The college has camping and outdoor equipment and canoes, sea kayaks, and sailboats for student use and offers a sailing class, sea kayaking class, and wilderness first responder class.

Disabled Students: 80% of the campus is accessible. Wheelchair ramps, elevators, special parking, specially equipped rest rooms, lowered drinking fountains, lowered telephones, and specially equipped residence hall rooms are available.

Services: Counseling and information services are available, as is tutoring in some subjects, including writing, math, language, photography, and computer use. There is remedial math and writing.

Campus Safety and Security: Measures include 24-hour foot and vehicle patrol, security escort services, shuttle buses, and informal discussions. There are pamphlets/posters/films, emergency telephones, and lighted pathways/sidewalks.

Programs of Study: COA confers the B.A. degree. Master's degrees are also awarded. Bachelor's degrees are awarded in SOCIAL SCIENCE (human ecology).

Required: Students design their own program. They must complete a total of 36 COA credits, including 2 interdisciplinary core courses and 2 courses each in environmental science, human studies, and arts and design. Also required are group study, a 3-credit internship, a human ecology essay, participation in a 3-credit senior project, and community service.

Special: Teacher certification is offered in elementary, and secondary, science, English, and social studies education. Students may cross-register with the University of Maine and other local nautical schools. Eco League exchanges are available with Alaska Pacific University and Green Mountain, Northland, Antioch, and Prescott Colleges. Study abroad is available in Uruguay, Mexico, the Czech Republic, and Guatemala. Students arrange internships with a broad range of employers. Pass/fail grading options are available.

Faculty/Classroom: 55% of faculty are male; 45%, female. All teach undergraduates and 75% do research. The average class size in an introductory lecture is 17; in a laboratory, 12; and in a regular course, 12.

Admissions: 66% of the 2005-2006 applicants were accepted. The SAT scores for the 2005-2006 freshman class were: Verbal--4% below 500, 27% between 500 and 599, 54% between 600 and 700, and 15% above 700; Math--10% below 500, 50% between 500 and 599, 27% between 600 and 700, and 12% above 700. The ACT scores were 9% below 21, 18% between 21 and 23, 32% between 24 and 26, 23% between 27 and 28, and 18% above 28. 67% of the current freshmen were in the top fifth of their class; 92% were in the top two fifths. There were 2 National Merit finalists and 7 semifinalists.

Requirements: Candidates for admission must be high school graduates who have completed 4 years of English, 3 to 4 of math, 2 to 3 of science, 2 of a foreign language, and 1 of history. AP and CLEP credits are accepted. Important factors in the admissions decision are personality/intangible qualities, extracurricular activities record, and advanced placement or honor courses.

Procedure: Freshmen are admitted fall, winter, and spring. Entrance exams should be taken in the junior or senior year. There are early decision and deferred admissions plans. Early decision applications should be filed by December 1; regular applications, by February 15 for fall entry, November 15 for winter entry, and February 15 for spring entry, along with a $45 fee. Notification of early decision is sent December 15; regular decision, April 1. 37 early decision candidates were accepted for the 2005-2006 class. 3 applicants were on the 2005 waiting list; 1 was admitted. Applications are accepted on-line.

Transfer: 18 transfer students enrolled in 2004-2005. 18 of 36 credits required for the bachelor's degree must be completed at COA.

Visiting: There are regularly scheduled orientations for prospective students, including an annual fall tour for high school seniors on Columbus Day. Contact the Office of Admission for further information. There are guides for informal visits and visitors may sit in on classes and stay overnight. To schedule a visit, contact Donna McFarland at dlm@coa.edu.

Financial Aid: In 2005-2006, 91% of all full-time freshmen and 88% of continuing full-time students received some form of financial aid. 79% of full-time freshmen and 83% of continuing full-time students received need-based aid. The average freshman award was $23,500. Need-based scholarships or need-based grants averaged $24,260 ($38,650 maximum); need-based self-help aid (loans and jobs) averaged $4275 ($4725 maximum); and other non-need-based awards and non-need-based scholarships averaged $4745 ($7500 maximum). 75% of undergraduates work part time. Average annual earnings from campus work are $1600. The average financial indebtedness of the 2005 graduate was $16,082. COA is a member of CSS. The FAFSA and the college's own financial statement are required. The deadline for filing freshman financial aid applications for fall entry is February 15.

International Students: There are 59 international students enrolled. The school actively recruits these students. They must score satisfactorily on the written TOEFL or on the electronic version and also take or submit SAT scores or the IB English exam score.

Computers: Wireless access is available. All students may access the system 24 hours a day. There are no time limits and no fees. It is strongly recommended that all students have a personal computer.

Graduates: From July 1, 2004 to June 30, 2005, 59 bachelor's degrees were awarded. In an average class, 3% graduate in 3 years or less, 32% graduate in 4 years or less, 62% graduate in 5 years or less, and 63% graduate in 6 years or less. Of the 2004 graduating class, 12% were enrolled in graduate school within 6 months of graduation and 90% were employed.

Admissions Contact: Sarah G. Baker, Director of Admission. E-mail: inquiry@coa.edu Web: www.coa.edu

HUSSON COLLEGE
Bangor, ME 04401-2999

C-4

(207) 941-7100
(800) 448-7766; Fax: (207) 941-7935

Full-time: 619 men, 966 women	Faculty: 50
Part-time: 114 men, 178 women	Ph.D.s: 100%
Graduate: 95 men, 173 women	Student/Faculty: 32 to 1
Year: semesters, summer session	Tuition: $11,380
Application Deadline: open	Room & Board: $6030
Freshman Class: 1128 applied, 1073 accepted, 590 enrolled	
SAT Verbal/Math: 459/469*	ACT: 20 LESS COMPETITIVE

Husson College, founded in 1898, is a private institution offering business, health careers, teaching, and other professional training. There are 4 undergraduate and 2 graduate schools. In addition to regional accreditation, Husson has baccalaureate program accreditation with ACOTE, CAPTE, CCNE and IACBE. The library contains 37,916 volumes, 14,059 microform items, and 129 audio/video tapes/CDs/DVDs, and subscribes to 490 periodicals including electronic. Computerized library services include the card catalog, interlibrary loans, database searching, and Internet access. Special learning facilities include a learning resource center, art gallery, and radio station. The 200-acre campus is in an urban area in the city of Bangor. Including any residence halls, there are 8 buildings.

Student Life: 87% of undergraduates are from Maine. Students are from 18 states, 11 foreign countries, and Canada. 90% are from public schools. 92% are white. The average age of freshmen is 20; all undergraduates, 22. 32% do not continue beyond their first year.

Housing: 840 students can be accommodated in college housing, which includes coed dorms. In addition, there are honors houses. On-campus housing is guaranteed for all 4 years. 54% of students commute. All students may keep cars.

Activities: 1% of men belong to 1 national fraternity; 1% of women belong to 3 local sororities. There are 29 groups on campus, including cheerleading, choir, computers, drama, ethnic, international, literary magazine, newspaper, pep band, professional, radio and TV, religious, social, social service, and student government. Popular campus events include Spring Fling, Winter Carnival, and Greek Alumni Weekend.

Sports: There are 5 intercollegiate sports for men and 6 for women, and 8 intramural sports for men and 8 for women. Facilities include a gym, an Olympic-size swimming pool, weight training and mat rooms, a health and fitness center, basketball and tennis courts, a baseball complex, and a soccer field.

Disabled Students: 80% of the campus is accessible. Wheelchair ramps, elevators, special parking, specially equipped rest rooms, lowered drinking fountains, and lowered telephones are available.

Services: Counseling and information services are available, as is tutoring in most subjects. There is remedial math and writing.

Campus Safety and Security: Measures include 24-hour foot and vehicle patrol, security escort services, informal discussions, and pamphlets/posters/films. There are lighted pathways/sidewalks.

Programs of Study: Husson confers the B.S. degree. Associate, master's, and doctoral degrees are also awarded. Bachelor's degrees are awarded in BIOLOGICAL SCIENCE (biology/biological science), BUSINESS (accounting, banking and finance, business administration and management, business systems analysis, hospitality management services, marketing/retailing/merchandising, and sports management), COMPUTER AND PHYSICAL SCIENCE (computer programming), EDUCATION (physical), HEALTH PROFESSIONS (nursing), SOCIAL SCIENCE (criminal justice, paralegal studies, and psychology). Accounting, nursing, and physical therapy are the strongest academically. Business administration is the largest.

Required: Requirements for graduation vary by program, but a total of 120 credit hours with a minimum GPA of 2.0 is necessary. A course in computer information systems is required in the first year for most programs.

Special: Experiential learning is part of the core curriculum in all majors. Internships are incorporated in accounting, computer information systems, sports management, hospitality management, nursing, physical therapy, occupational therapy, international business, and family business. Co-op programs, externships, and clinicals are included in the curriculum in all other majors. Students can go a fifth year and obtain a master's in business in accounting, business administration, or CIS, and in phys ed with a concentration in sports management. An accelerated degree program, dual majors, and student-designed majors are also available.

Faculty/Classroom: 48% of faculty are male; 52%, female. All teach undergraduates. No introductory courses are taught by graduate students. The average class size in an introductory lecture is 20; in a laboratory, 16; and in a regular course, 19.

Admissions: 95% of the 2005-2006 applicants were accepted. The SAT scores for the 2005-2006 freshman class were: Verbal--74% below 500, 23% between 500 and 599, and 3% between 600 and 700; Math--66% below 500, 29% between 500 and 599, and 5% between 600 and

700. The ACT scores were 88% below 21, 8% between 21 and 23, and 4% between 24 and 26. 19% of the current freshmen were in the top fifth of their class; 48% were in the top two fifths. In a recent year, 4 freshmen graduated first in their class.

Requirements: The SAT is required. In addition, applicants must be graduates of an accredited secondary school or have earned a GED. A recommendation from a high school counselor is required. Husson requires applicants to be in the upper 50% of their class. A GPA of 2.0 is required. AP and CLEP credits are accepted. Important factors in the admissions decision are advanced placement or honor courses, recommendations by school officials, and leadership record.

Procedure: Freshmen are admitted to all sessions. Entrance exams should be taken prior to enrollment. There is a deferred admissions and a rolling admissionds plan. Application deadlines are open. Application fee is $25. Notification is sent on a rolling basis. A waiting list is an active part of the admissions procedure. Applications are accepted on-line.

Transfer: 114 transfer students enrolled in 2004-2005. Applicants must have a 2.0 GPA. Courses with a C grade or better transfer. 30 of 120 credits required for the bachelor's degree must be completed at Husson.

Visiting: There are regularly scheduled orientations for prospective students, including an interview and campus tour. There are guides for informal visits and visitors may sit in on classes and stay overnight. To schedule a visit, contact the Admissions Office at admit@husson.edu.

Financial Aid: 80% of undergraduates work part time. Husson is a member of CSS. The FAFSA is required. The deadline for filing freshman financial aid applications for fall entry is open.

International Students: There are 25 international students enrolled. The school actively recruits these students. Satisfactory scores are required on the written TOEFL and the SAT or ACT. Students who score unsatisfactory on the TOEFL may be accepted conditionally and must enroll in a full-time intensive English program.

Computers: Wireless access is available. Students have access in their dorm rooms, various labs, which have 100 PCs available for student use, and the library. All students may access the system 24 hours a day. There are no time limits and no fees.

Graduates: From July 1, 2004 to June 30, 2005, 317 bachelor's degrees were awarded. In a recent year, the most popular majors were business administration (35%), nursing (10%), and accounting (10%). In an average class, 62% graduate in 4 years or less, 43% graduate in 5 years or less, and 45% graduate in 6 years or less. 50 companies recruited on campus in 2004-2005. Of the 2004 graduating class, 2% were enrolled in graduate school within 6 months of graduation and 95% were employed.

Admissions Contact: Jane Goodwin, Director of Admissions. A video is available. E-mail: admit@husson.edu Web: http://www.husson.edu

MAINE COLLEGE OF ART
Portland, ME 04101

B-6

(207) 775-5157, ext. 254
(800) 639-4808; Fax: (207) 772-5069

Full-time: 130 men, 220 women	Faculty: 30
Part-time: 20 men, 30 women	Ph.D.s: 93%
Graduate: 20 men, 20 women	Student/Faculty: 11 to 1
Year: semesters	Tuition: $21,140
Application Deadline: open	Room & Board: $7680
Freshman Class: n/av	
SAT or ACT: required	SPECIAL

Maine College of Art, established in 1882, is a private, independent visual art college. Some figures in the above capsule are approximate. In addition to regional accreditation, MECA has baccalaureate program accreditation with NASAD. The library contains 18,500 volumes and 150 audio/video tapes/CDs/DVDs, and subscribes to 100 periodicals including electronic. Computerized library services include the card catalog, interlibrary loans, and database searching. Special learning facilities include an art gallery. The campus is in an urban area 100 miles north of Boston in downtown Portland. Including any residence halls, there are 6 buildings.

Student Life: 65% of undergraduates are from out of state, mostly the Northeast. Students are from 29 states and 6 foreign countries. 94% are white. The average age of freshmen is 20; all undergraduates, 22. 30% do not continue beyond their first year.

Housing: 100 students can be accommodated in college housing, which includes coed dorms and on-campus apartments. On-campus housing is available on a first-come, first-served basis. 75% of students commute. Alcohol is not permitted. All students may keep cars.

Activities: There are no fraternities or sororities. There are 5 groups on campus, including art, computers, dance, drama, gay, international, newspaper, photography, social, and student government. Popular campus events include annual art sale, art auction, and Earth Day celebration.

Sports: There is no sports program at MECA.

Disabled Students: 65% of the campus is accessible. Wheelchair ramps, elevators, specially equipped rest rooms, and lowered drinking fountains are available.

Services: Counseling and information services are available, as is tutoring in every subject. There is remedial math, reading, and writing. Academic support for writing papers, study skills, and time management is available, as is help for students with learning disabilities.

Campus Safety and Security: Measures include self-defense education, informal discussions, pamphlets/posters/films, and emergency telephones. There is also safety training by local police.

Programs of Study: MECA confers the B.F.A. degree. Master's degrees are also awarded. Bachelor's degrees are awarded in COMMUNICATIONS AND THE ARTS (graphic design, media arts, metal/jewelry, painting, photography, printmaking, and sculpture), ENGINEERING AND ENVIRONMENTAL DESIGN (ceramic science). Painting, photography, and ceramics are the largest.

Required: All students must take 2 years of studio foundation courses and 2 years in the studio major, as well as 5 semesters of art history, 3 of humanities or social science, 2 each of English composition, natural science, and Western civilization, and 1 of critical issues. 129 total credit hours are necessary, with 36 in the major. Students must maintain a minimum GPA of 2.0. A senior thesis is required.

Special: Cross-registration with Bowdoin College, the Greater Portland Alliance of Colleges and Universities, and AICAD Mobility is available, as are internships utilizing professional artists and design and photography studios. An internship coordinator supervises the formal program for elective credit. There are also Art in Service internships. The continuing studies program provides for nondegree study. Minors in art history, drawing, and illustration are also offered, as are dual and student-designed majors.

Faculty/Classroom: 50% of faculty are male; 50%, female. All teach undergraduates. No introductory courses are taught by graduate students. The average class size in an introductory lecture is 36; in a laboratory, 18; and in a regular course, 20.

Requirements: The SAT or ACT is required. In addition, it is recommended that candidates for admission complete 4 years of English, 3 years each of art and math, and 2 years each of foreign language, science, and social studies. AP credits are accepted. Important factors in the admissions decision are personality/intangible qualities, advanced placement or honor courses, and evidence of special talent.

Procedure: Freshmen are admitted fall and spring. Entrance exams should be taken in the fall of the senior year. There is a deferred admissions and rolling admissions plan. Application deadlines are open. The fall 2005 application fee was $40.

Transfer: 46 transfer students enrolled in a recent year. Transfers must submit an official copy of their college transcripts. 65 of 129 credits required for the bachelor's degree must be completed at MECA.

Visiting: There are regularly scheduled orientations for prospective students, including a tour, a portfolio review, and a faculty-student panel, and opportunities to observe classes and meet with an admissions counselor or other staff. There are guides for informal visits and visitors may sit in on classes. To schedule a visit, contact Kate Quin-Easter in the Admissions Office at (800) 639-4808 or (207) 775-5157, ext. 226 or kquin-easter@meca.edu.

Financial Aid: 21% of undergraduates work part time. Average annual earnings from campus work are $1341. MECA is a member of CSS. The FAFSA is required. Check with the school for current deadlines.

International Students: There were 12 international students enrolled in a recent year. The school actively recruits these students. They must score satisfactorily on the TOEFL and also take the SAT or the ACT.

Computers: All students may access the system. Time is scheduled around classroom use. There are no time limits and no fees.

Graduates: In a recent year, 60 bachelor's degrees were awarded. The most popular majors were graphic design (21%), painting (18%), and sculpture (17%). In an average class, 33% graduate in 4 years or less, 38% graduate in 5 years or less, and 48% graduate in 6 years or less.

Admissions Contact: Joshua Bergey, Dean of Admissions. A video is available. E-mail: admissions@meca.edu Web: www.meca.edu

MAINE MARITIME ACADEMY		C-5
Castine, ME 04420		**(207) 326-2215**
	(800) 227-8465; Fax: (207) 326-2515	
Full-time: 675 men, 121 women	**Faculty:** 66	
Part-time: 7 men, 2 women	**Ph.Ds:** 37%	
Graduate: 10 men, 2 women	**Student/Faculty:** 12 to 1	
Year: semesters	**Tuition:** $7620 ($13,550)	
Application Deadline: July 1	**Room & Board:** $6720	
Freshman Class: n/av		
SAT Verbal/Math: 520/540*	**ACT:** 21	**COMPETITIVE**

Maine Maritime Academy, founded in 1941, is a public institution offering degree programs in ocean and marine-oriented studies with emphasis on engineering, transportation, business management, and ocean sciences, as well as preparing graduates for the merchant marine and uniformed services of the United States. The academic calendar consists of 2 semesters plus a 2- to 3-month annual training cruise. There are 4 undergraduate schools and 1 graduate school. In addition to regional accreditation, MMA has baccalaureate program accreditation with ABET. The library contains 88,490 volumes, 5000 microform items, and 808 audio/video tapes/CDs/DVDs, and subscribes to 1311 periodicals including electronic. Computerized library services include the card catalog, interlibrary loans, database searching, Internet access, and laptop Internet portals. Special learning facilities include a natural history museum, planetarium, more than 60 vessels, and bridge, radar, power plant, and cargo system simulators. The 50-acre campus is in a small town 38 miles south of Bangor on the east coast of Penobscot Bay. Including any residence halls, there are 14 buildings.

Student Life: 65% of undergraduates are from Maine. Others are from 35 states, 7 foreign countries, and Canada. 90% are from public schools. 97% are white. The average age of freshmen is 19; all undergraduates, 24. 12% do not continue beyond their first year; 75% remain to graduate.

Housing: 600 students can be accommodated in college housing, which includes coed dorms and on-campus apartments. On-campus housing is guaranteed for all 4 years. 85% of students live on campus; of those, 40% remain on campus on weekends. Alcohol is not permitted. All students may keep cars.

Activities: 6% of men and about 25% of women belong to 1 national fraternity. There are no sororities. There are 30 groups on campus, including amateur radio, bagpipe band, band, billiards, chess, drama, drill team, ethnic, international, marching band, newspaper, outing, pep band, photography, professional, rifle/pistol, scuba, social, social service, and student government. Popular campus events include Daisy Day, Klondike Derby, and Family Weekend.

Sports: There are 6 intercollegiate sports for men and 6 for women, and 10 intramural sports for men and 10 for women. Facilities include 2 weight rooms, an Olympic pool, a field house, a gym, racquetball and squash courts, an aerobics room, and a multisports athletic field.

Disabled Students: All of the campus is accessible. Wheelchair ramps, elevators, special parking, and specially equipped rest rooms are available.

Services: Counseling and information services are available, as is tutoring in most subjects. There is remedial math, reading, and writing.

Campus Safety and Security: Measures include 24-hour foot and vehicle patrol, informal discussions, pamphlets/posters/films, and lighted pathways/sidewalks. There are and medical counseling services.

Programs of Study: MMA confers the B.S. degree. Associate and master's degrees are also awarded. Bachelor's degrees are awarded in BUSINESS (international business management), COMPUTER AND PHYSICAL SCIENCE (oceanography), ENGINEERING AND ENVIRONMENTAL DESIGN (engineering, engineering technology, marine engineering, maritime science, and transportation technology). Marine systems engineering is the strongest academically. Marine engineering technology is the largest.

Required: A minimum GPA of 2.0 in an average of 140 total credit hours is required for graduation. A comprehensive exam is required for USCG license candidates.

Special: The annual training cruise gives students practical experience aboard the academy's 500-foot ship or on assigned merchant ships. Co-op programs and internships are offered, as is study abroad through special agreements with other maritime colleges worldwide. Dual and student-designed majors are possible.

Faculty/Classroom: 76% of faculty are male; 24%, female. All teach undergraduates. No introductory courses are taught by graduate students. The average class size in an introductory lecture is 30; in a laboratory, 15; and in a regular course, 25.

Requirements: The SAT or ACT is required. In addition, candidates for admission must have completed 4 years of English, 3 years of math, and 2 years of lab science. Courses must include algebra I, algebra II or trigonometry, geometry, and either chemistry or physics with a lab. A GPA of 2.0 is required. AP and CLEP credits are accepted. Important factors in the admissions decision are advanced placement or honor courses, evidence of special talent, and leadership record.

Procedure: Freshmen are admitted fall and spring. Entrance exams should be taken as early as possible in the senior year. There are early decision, early admissions, and deferred admissions plans. There is a rolling admissions plan. Early decision applications should be filed by December 20; regular applications, by July 1 for fall entry and November 1 for spring entry. The fall 2005 application fee was $15. Notification is sent on a rolling basis. 25 early decision candidates were accepted for a recent class. Applications are accepted on-line.

Transfer: 16 transfer students enrolled in a recent year. Applicants must have a minimum 2.0 GPA in previous college work and meet the same prerequisites as entering freshmen.

Visiting: There are regularly scheduled orientations for prospective students, consisting of 3 open houses per year; campus visits are available weekdays throughout the year. There are guides for informal visits and visitors may sit in on classes and stay overnight. To schedule a visit, contact the Admissions Office at (207) 326-2206 or admissions@mma.edu.

Financial Aid: The FAFSA, student and parent tax returns, and a verification worksheet are required. The deadline for filing freshman financial aid applications for fall entry is March 1.

International Students: A satisfactory score on the TOEFL is required.

Computers: All students may access the system. There are no time limits. The fee is $100. All students are required to have personal computers.

Graduates: In a recent year, 130 bachelor's degrees were awarded. The most popular majors were marine engineering (42%), marine transportation (20%), and power engineering (12%). In an average class, 75% graduate in 4 years, 4% graduate in 5 years, and 1% graduate in 6 years.

Admissions Contact: Jeff Wright, Director of Admissions. A video is available. E-mail: *admissions@mma.edu*
Web: *www.mainemaritime.edu*

SAINT JOSEPH'S COLLEGE OF MAINE
A-6

Standish, ME 04084-5263

(207) 893-7746
(800) 338-7057; Fax: (207) 893-7862

Full-time: 337 men, 588 women	**Faculty:** 63
Part-time: 9 men, 21 women	**Ph.D.s:** 98%
Graduate: none	**Student/Faculty:** 15 to 1
Year: semesters, summer session	**Tuition:** $20,605
Application Deadline: open	**Room & Board:** $8580
Freshman Class: n/av	
SAT Verbal/Math: 518/521*	**ACT:** 21 **COMPETITIVE**

Saint Joseph's College of Maine, , founded in 1912, is a private, Roman Catholic institution offering liberal arts and preprofessional programs. In addition to regional accreditation, Saint Joseph's College of Maine has baccalaureate program accreditation with CCNE. The library contains 98,626 volumes, 29,010 microform items, and 1000 audio/video tapes/CDs/DVDs, and subscribes to 11,461 periodicals including electronic. Computerized library services include interlibrary loans, database searching, and Internet access. Special learning facilities include a learning resource center, radio station, and telescope observatory. The 350-acre campus is in a rural area 18 miles west of Portland. Including any residence halls, there are 20 buildings.

Student Life: 60% of undergraduates are from Maine. Others are from 15 states, 3 foreign countries, and Canada. 82% are white. The average age of freshmen is 18; all undergraduates, 20. 18% do not continue beyond their first year; 59% remain to graduate.

Housing: 829 students can be accommodated in college housing, which includes single-sex and coed dormitories and substance-free housing. On-campus housing is guaranteed for all 4 years. 83% of students live on campus; of those, 65% remain on campus on weekends. All students may keep cars.

Activities: There are no fraternities or sororities. There are 28 groups on campus, including campus activities board, campus minisry council, cheerleading, choir, chorale, computers, dance, drama, ethnic, habitat for humanity, high adventure club, honors, international, literary magazine, musical theater, newspaper, pep band, photography, political, professional, radio and TV, religious, social, social service, student government, superkids, and yearbook. Popular campus events include Family Weekend, Christmas Benefit Concert, and Spring Fling.

Sports: There are 5 intercollegiate sports for men and 6 for women, and 12 intramural sports for men and 12 for women. Facilities include a multipurpose facility housing a gym, a workout room with free weights, Nautilus and other weight-training equipment, a cardiovascular workout room, dance aerobics rooms, a climbing wall, a 25-meter pool, saunas, and an elevated jogging track. There are also soccer and field hockey fields, a private beach on a lake, lighted athletic fields for baseball and softball, cross-country running and ski trails, and a low ropes course.

Disabled Students: 75% of the campus is accessible. Wheelchair ramps, elevators, special parking, specially equipped rest rooms, special class scheduling, and lowered drinking fountains are available.

Services: Counseling and information services are available, as is tutoring in every subject. There is a reader service for the blind.

Campus Safety and Security: Measures include 24-hour foot and vehicle patrol, self-defense education, security escort services, and informal discussions. There are pamphlets/posters/films, emergency telephones, lighted pathways/sidewalks, and and round-the-clock security officers.

Programs of Study: Saint Joseph's College of Maine confers B.A., B.S., B.S.B.A., and B.S.N. degrees. Associate degrees are also awarded. Bachelor's degrees are awarded in BIOLOGICAL SCIENCE (biology/biological science), BUSINESS (business administration and management), COMMUNICATIONS AND THE ARTS (communications, and English), COMPUTER AND PHYSICAL SCIENCE (chemistry and mathematics), EDUCATION (elementary and physical), ENGINEERING AND ENVIRONMENTAL DESIGN (environmental science), HEALTH PROFESSIONS (nursing and prepharmacy), SOCIAL SCIENCE (criminal justice, history, philosophy, psychology, sociology, and theological studies). Business, nursing, and biology are the strongest academically. Elementary education, business, and nursing are the largest.

Required: To graduate, students must complete 128 credit hours with a minimum GPA of 2.0, including 8 hours of English, history, theology, and a foreign language, 4 each of science and math, and 8 of electives.

Special: Saint Joseph's offers internships, cross-registration with 4 southern Maine colleges, study abroad in 5 countries, a semester at sea, dual majors, work-study programs, and non-degree study. There are 2 national honor societies, a freshman honors program, and 6 departmental honors programs.

Faculty/Classroom: 48% of faculty are male; 52%, female. All teach undergraduates, 39% do research, and 38% do both. The average class size in an introductory lecture is 25; in a laboratory, 12; and in a regular course, 18.

Admissions: The SAT scores for the 2005-2006 freshman class were: Verbal--50% below 500, 38% between 500 and 599, and 12% between 600 and 700; Math--53% below 500, 36% between 500 and 599, and 11% between 600 and 700. 2 freshmen graduated first in their class.

Requirements: The SAT or ACT is required. In addition, candidates for admission must be high school graduates who have completed a college preparatory curriculum with a recommended 4 units in English, 3 to 4 in math, 2 in foreign language, and 1 to 3 each in history, science, and social studies. A GPA of 2.0 is required. AP and CLEP credits are accepted. Important factors in the admissions decision are advanced placement or honor courses, recommendations by school officials, and extracurricular activities record.

Procedure: Freshmen are admitted fall and spring. Entrance exams should be taken by January of the senior year. There are early admissions, and deferred admissions, and rolling admissions plans. Application deadlines are open. 45 applicants were on the 2005 waiting list; 25 were admitted. Applications are accepted on-line. The fall 2005 application fee was $40.

Transfer: 40 transfer students enrolled in a recent year. Transfer students should have a minimum GPA of 2.0. 32 of 128 credits required for the bachelor's degree must be completed at Saint Joseph's College of Maine.

Visiting: There are regularly scheduled orientations for prospective students, including Application and Acceptance Day programs, visits on 5 fall Saturdays, and summer visits. There are guides for informal visits and visitors may sit in on classes and stay overnight. To schedule a visit, contact the Office of Admission.

Financial Aid: In 2005-2006, 99% of all full-time students received some form of financial aid. 80% of full-time freshmen and 81% of continuing full-time students received need-based aid. The average freshman award was $17,086. Need-based scholarships or need-based grants averaged $12,302 ($25,700 maximum); need-based self-help aid (loans and jobs) averaged $5772 ($6625 maximum); and other non-need-based awards and non-need-based scholarships averaged $13,398 ($20,390 maximum). 35% of undergraduates work part time. Average annual earnings from campus work are $896. The average financial indebtedness of the 2005 graduate was $16,020. St. Joseph's College of Maine is a member of CSS. The FAFSA and the college's own financial statement are required. The priority date for freshman financial aid applications for fall entry is March 1.

International Students: There are 3 international students enrolled. They must score satisfactorily on the written TOEFL or on the electronic version and also take the SAT, or ACT. For non-English speaking we require the TOEFL exam. Students may also include the SAT or ACT. For English speaking international students, the SAT or ACT is required.

Computers: Wireless access is available. All students may access the system 24 hours a day in all labs and until 10 P.M. in the library. There are no time limits and no fees. It is strongly recommended that all students have a personal computer.

Graduates: From July 1, 2004 to June 30, 2005, 213 bachelor's degrees were awarded. The most popular majors were education (20%), business (20%), and nursing (12%). In an average class, 54% graduate in 4 years or less, 60% graduate in 5 years or less, and 61% graduate in 6 years or less. 43 companies recruited on campus in 2004-2005. Of the 2004 graduating class, 15% were enrolled in graduate school within 6 months of graduation and 89% were employed.

Admissions Contact: Vincent Kloskowski, Dean of Admissions.
E-mail: *admission@sjcme.edu* Web: *http://www.sjcme.edu*

THOMAS COLLEGE
B-4

Waterville, ME 04901

(207) 877-0101
(800) 339-7001; Fax: (207) 877-0114

Full-time: 321 men, 277 women	**Faculty:** 23; IIB, --$
Part-time: 36 men, 98 women	**Ph.D.s:** 48%
Graduate: 64 men, 80 women	**Student/Faculty:** 26 to 1
Year: semesters, summer session	**Tuition:** $16,690
Application Deadline: open	**Room & Board:** $7080
Freshman Class: 651 applied, 487 accepted, 235 enrolled	
SAT Verbal/Math: 464/468*	**LESS COMPETITIVE**

Thomas College, founded in 1894, is a private institution offering undergraduate programs in liberal arts and business. The library contains

21,938 volumes and 770 audio/video tapes/CDs/DVDs, and subscribes to 18,430 periodicals including electronic. Computerized library services include the card catalog, interlibrary loans, database searching, Internet access, and laptop Internet portals. Special learning facilities include a learning resource center and art gallery. The 70-acre campus is in a rural area 75 miles north of Portland. Including any residence halls, there are 11 buildings.

Student Life: 84% of undergraduates are from Maine. Others are from 10 states. 85% are from public schools. 96% are white. The average age of freshmen is 19; all undergraduates, 25. 39% do not continue beyond their first year; 56% remain to graduate.

Housing: 375 students can be accommodated in college housing, which includes coed dorms and off-campus apartments. On-campus housing is guaranteed for the freshman year only, is available on a first-come, first-served basis, and is available on a lottery system for upperclassmen. 65% of students live on campus; of those, 60% remain on campus on weekends. All students may keep cars.

Activities: 3% of men belong to 1 national fraternity; 5% of women belong to 1 national and 2 local sororities. There are 30 groups on campus, including art, chorale, computers, drama, honors, international, newspaper, professional, religious, social, social service, student government, and yearbook. Popular campus events include Winter Carnival, Spring Fling, and Welcome Week.

Sports: There are 6 intercollegiate sports for men and 6 for women, and 6 intramural sports for men and 6 for women. Facilities include a gym, a basketball court, a weight, fitness, and aerobics room, soccer, baseball, field hockey, and softball fields, a training area, an intramural field, and cross-country skiing and snowshoe trails. Facilities for swimming, indoor tennis, racquetball, and hockey are available locally.

Disabled Students: 80% of the campus is accessible. Wheelchair ramps, special parking, specially equipped rest rooms, special class scheduling, and special housing are available.

Services: Counseling and information services are available, as is tutoring in most subjects. There is remedial math, reading, and writing.

Campus Safety and Security: Measures include 24-hour foot and vehicle patrol, informal discussions, pamphlets/posters/films, and lighted pathways/sidewalks.

Programs of Study: Thomas confers the B.A. and B.S. degrees. Associate and master's degrees are also awarded. Bachelor's degrees are awarded in BUSINESS (accounting, business administration and management, business economics, management information systems, management science, marketing management, and sports management), COMMUNICATIONS AND THE ARTS (communications), COMPUTER AND PHYSICAL SCIENCE (information sciences and systems), EDUCATION (business and elementary), SOCIAL SCIENCE (criminal justice, international studies, and psychology). Accounting and management information systems are the strongest academically. Accounting, management, and computer information systems are the largest.

Required: To graduate, students must achieve a minimum GPA of 2.0, fulfill all course requirements, and complete a minimum of 120 total credit hours of study, including 30 hours in the major.

Special: Students may cross-register with Colby College and Kennebec Valley Community College. There are co-op programs and internships available in most majors. The college also offers study in Canada through the New England - Quebec Exchange and in France and Australia. 5-year degrees are offered in most majors where a B.S. is available. There are 2 national honor societies.

Faculty/Classroom: 65% of faculty are male; 35%, female. All teach undergraduates. The average class size in an introductory lecture is 22 and in a regular course, 14.

Admissions: 75% of the 2005-2006 applicants were accepted. The SAT scores for the 2005-2006 freshman class were: Verbal--67% below 500, 27% between 500 and 599, 5% between 600 and 700, and 1% above 700; Math--64% below 500, 28% between 500 and 599, 7% between 600 and 700, and 1% above 700. The ACT scores were 100% below 21. 13% of the current freshmen were in the top fifth of their class; 30% were in the top two fifths.

Requirements: The SAT is required. In addition, candidates for admission must be high school graduates with an academic program that includes 4 years of English, 3 of each math, sciences, 2 each of social studies, foreign language, and 2 other. A letter of recommendation from a secondary school counselor is required. An interview is highly recommended. A GPA of 2.0 is required. AP and CLEP credits are accepted. Important factors in the admissions decision are advanced placement or honor courses, recommendations by school officials, and personality/intangible qualities.

Procedure: Freshmen are admitted to all sessions. Entrance exams should be taken by the fall of the senior year. There is a deferred admissions plan and a rolling admissions plan. Application deadlines are open. Application fee is $35. Applications are accepted on-line.

Transfer: 35 transfer students enrolled in 2004-2005. Applicants should have a minimum college GPA of 2.0. The school recommends the SAT as well as an interview. Official transcripts from all previously attended postsecondary institutions are required. 60 of 120 credits required for the bachelor's degree must be completed at Thomas.

Visiting: There are regularly scheduled orientations for prospective students, including 3 to 4 open houses and 1 new student orientation/preregistration. There are guides for informal visits and visitors may sit in on classes. To schedule a visit, contact the Admissions Office.

Financial Aid: In 2005-2006, 94% of all full-time freshmen and 90% of continuing full-time students received some form of financial aid. 89% of full-time freshmen and 87% of continuing full-time students received need-based aid. The average freshman award was $18,168. All undergraduates work part time. Average annual earnings from campus work are $2200. The average financial indebtedness of the 2005 graduate was $19,000. The FAFSA is required. The deadline for filing freshman financial aid applications for fall entry is open.

International Students: The school actively recruits these students. They must take the TOEFL and take the SAT.

Computers: Wireless access is available. Campuswide network ports and wireless access points along with more than 130 workstations in various computer labs and clusters provide students 24/7 access. All students may access the system 24 hours a day. There are no time limits and no fees. It is strongly recommended that all students have a personal computer. A Dell Latitude D610 is recommended.

Graduates: From July 1, 2004 to June 30, 2005, 118 bachelor's degrees were awarded. The most popular majors were management (23%), computer information systems (13%), and sports management (13%). In an average class, 43% graduate in 4 years, and 10% graduate in 5 years. 60 companies recruited on campus in 2004-2005. Of the 2004 graduating class, 11% were enrolled in graduate school within 6 months of graduation and 91% were employed.

Admissions Contact: Wendy Martin, Director of Admissions. E-mail: *admiss@thomas.edu* Web: *www.thomas.edu*

UNITY COLLEGE — C-4

Unity, ME 04988-0532 (207) 948-3131; Fax: (207) 948-6277

Full-time: 321 men, 196 women	**Faculty:** 32
Part-time: 5 men, 5 women	**Ph.D.s:** 63%
Graduate: none	**Student/Faculty:** 16 to 1
Year: semesters, summer session	**Tuition:** $17,690
Application Deadline: open	**Room & Board:** $6630
Freshman Class: 410 applied, 373 accepted, 154 enrolled	
SAT Verbal/Math: 510/500*	**COMPETITIVE**

Unity College, founded in 1965, is a private, independent institution offering undergraduate programs in environmental science, natural resource management, and wilderness-based outdoor recreation. In addition to regional accreditation, Unity has baccalaureate program accreditation with SAF. The library contains 46,000 volumes and 750 audio/video tapes/CDs/DVDs, and subscribes to 651 periodicals including electronic. Computerized library services include the card catalog, interlibrary loans, and database searching. Special learning facilities include a learning resource center and art gallery. The 205-acre campus is in a rural area 18 miles east of Waterville. Including any residence halls, there are 18 buildings.

Student Life: 67% of undergraduates are from out of state, mostly the Northeast. Students are from 30 states and 1 foreign country. 97% are from public schools. 98% are white. 57% are Catholic; 30% Protestant. The average age of freshmen is 18; all undergraduates, 20. 35% do not continue beyond their first year; 47% remain to graduate.

Housing: 335 students can be accommodated in college housing, which includes single-sex and coed dorms and on-campus apartments. On-campus housing is guaranteed for all 4 years. 90% of students live on campus; of those, 68% remain on campus on weekends. All students may keep cars.

Activities: There are no fraternities or sororities. There are 36 groups on campus, including art, drama, environmental, literary magazine, newspaper, outdoor, photography, student government, and yearbook. Popular campus events include Regional Woodsman's Meet in October.

Sports: There are 3 intercollegiate sports for men and 2 for women, and 10 intramural sports for men and 8 for women. Facilities include a gym, a weight-training room, playing fields, a nature trail, and game rooms.

Disabled Students: 80% of the campus is accessible. Wheelchair ramps, special parking, and special class scheduling are available.

Services: Counseling and information services are available, as is tutoring in every subject. There is remedial math, reading, and writing. A full-time learning disability specialist is on staff.

Campus Safety and Security: Measures include 24-hour foot and vehicle patrol, informal discussions, and emergency telephones.

Programs of Study: Unity confers B.A. and B.S. degrees. Associate degrees are also awarded. Bachelor's degrees are awarded in AGRICULTURE (conservation and regulation and fishing and fisheries), BIOLOGICAL SCIENCE (ecology, environmental biology, and wildlife biology), EDUCATION (environmental), ENGINEERING AND ENVIRONMENTAL DESIGN (environmental science), HEALTH PROFESSIONS (environmental health science), SOCIAL SCIENCE (human ecology, interdisciplinary studies, and parks and recreation management). Aquaculture, fisheries, and ecology are the strongest academically. Conservation law enforcement, wilderness-based recreation, and wildlife are the largest.

Required: General education requirements include 38 credits in English composition, oral communication, math, computer science, life science, physical science, and electives, as well as 9 credits in a specialization outside the major field. Students must complete at least 120 credit hours with a minimum GPA of 2.0. An internship, thesis, or seminar is required in all bachelor's degree programs.

Special: The college offers co-op programs, credit-bearing internships, study abroad, a Washington semester, work-study programs, accelerated degree programs, dual and student-designed majors, and credit for life experience. A mentor program, in which a faculty member assists a student with research, is available to those students who earn a minimum GPA of 3.33 in their first 30 credit hours. There is 1 national honor society and a freshman honors program.

Faculty/Classroom: 68% of faculty are male; 32%, female. All teach undergraduates.

Admissions: 91% of the 2005-2006 applicants were accepted. The SAT scores for the 2005-2006 freshman class were: Verbal--48% below 500, 32% between 500 and 599, 17% between 600 and 700, and 1% above 700; Math--50% below 500, 43% between 500 and 599, and 7% between 600 and 700. 20% of the current freshmen were in the top fifth of their class; 55% were in the top two fifths.

Requirements: The SAT or ACT scores, though not required, should be submitted, if available, for placement purposes. Applicants must be graduates of an accredited secondary school with a minimum GPA of 2.0. The GED is accepted. An essay is required, and an interview is recommended. AP and CLEP credits are accepted. Important factors in the admissions decision are advanced placement or honor courses, recommendations by alumni, and leadership record.

Procedure: Freshmen are admitted fall and spring. Entrance exams should be taken in the junior or senior year. There is a deferred admissions plan. There is a rolling admissions plan. Application deadlines are open. Application fee is $25. Notification is sent on a rolling basis. A waiting list is an active part of the admissions procedure.

Transfer: 42 transfer students enrolled in 2004-2005. Applicants must present a minimum college GPA of 2.0 and are encouraged to submit SAT scores. 30 of 120 credits required for the bachelor's degree must be completed at Unity.

Visiting: There are regularly scheduled orientations for prospective students. There are guides for informal visits and visitors may sit in on classes and stay overnight. To schedule a visit, contact the Admissions Office.

Financial Aid: The CSS/Profile or FAFSA and the college's own financial statement are required. Check with the school for current application deadlines.

International Students: The school actively recruits these students. A satisfactory score on the TOEFL is required.

Computers: All students may access the system. There are no time limits and no fees.

Graduates: From July 1, 2004 to June 30, 2005, 93 bachelor's degrees were awarded. The most popular majors were conservation law (25%), wildlife (16%), and forestry (9%). In an average class, 10% graduate in 3 years or less, 35% graduate in 4 years or less, 39% graduate in 5 years or less, and 47% graduate in 6 years or less. 76 companies recruited on campus in 2004-2005. Of the 2004 graduating class, 13% were enrolled in graduate school within 6 months of graduation and 90% were employed.

Admissions Contact: Holly A. Hein, Dean of Enrollment and Retention Services/Registrar. E-mail: *hein@unity.edu* Web: *www.unity.edu*

UNIVERSITY OF MAINE SYSTEM

The University of Maine System, established in 1968, is a private system in Maine. It is governed by a board of trustees, whose chief administrator is chancellor. The primary goal of the system is teaching, research, and public service. The main priorities are to strengthen human services through programs in education, health, and social services; to provide international exchange and foreign language programs; and to conduct science and technology education and basic and applied research. The total enrollment is usually about 32,000 with 1500 faculty members. Altogether there are some 200 baccalaureate, 75 master's, and 25 doctoral programs offered in University of Maine System. Profiles of the 4-year campuses are included in this section.

UNIVERSITY OF MAINE
C-4
Orono, ME 04473-9966

(207) 581-1561
(877) 486-2364; Fax: (207) 581-1213

Full-time: 3875 men, 3742 women	**Faculty:** I, --$
Part-time: 574 men, 988 women	**Ph.D.s:** 85%
Graduate: 764 men, 1492 women	**Student/Faculty:** n/av
Year: semesters, summer session	**Tuition:** $6910 ($17,050)
Application Deadline: open	**Room & Board:** $6732
Freshman Class: 5702 applied, 4508 accepted, 1800 enrolled	
SAT Verbal/Math: 540/540*	**ACT:** 23 **COMPETITIVE**

The University of Maine, established in 1865, is a publicly funded, land-grant institution in the University of Maine system. The university offers degree programs in the arts and sciences, business, public policy, health fields, engineering, education, forestry, and agriculture. There are 5 undergraduate schools and 1 graduate school. In addition to regional accreditation, U-Maine has baccalaureate program accreditation with AACSB, ABET, ACS, ADA, AHEA, APA, ASLHA, CCNE, CSAB, CSWE, NASM, NASPAA, NCATE, NLN, and SAF. The library contains 1,034,248 volumes, 1,6 million microform items, and 26,647 audio/video tapes/CDs/DVDs, and subscribes to 3889 periodicals including electronic. Computerized library services include the card catalog, interlibrary loans, database searching, Internet access, and laptop Internet portals. Special learning facilities include an art gallery, natural history museum, planetarium, radio station, concert hall and other music facilities, 2 theaters, a digital media lab, an anthropology museum, and a laboratory for surface science and technology. The 3300-acre campus is in a small town 8 miles north of Bangor. Including any residence halls, there are 204 buildings.

Student Life: 85% of undergraduates are from Maine. Others are from 47 states, 76 foreign countries, and Canada. 93% are white. The average age of freshmen is 19; all undergraduates, 22. 21% do not continue beyond their first year; 56% remain to graduate.

Housing: 3500 students can be accommodated in college housing, which includes coed dorms, on-campus apartments, off-campus apartments, and married-student housing. In addition, there are honors houses, language houses, special-interest houses, Substance-free housing, quiet sections, and graduate, family, and academic wings. On-campus housing is guaranteed for the freshman year only and is available on a first-come, first-served basis. 57% of students commute. All students may keep cars.

Activities: There are 1 local and 12 national fraternities and 6 national sororities. There are 226 groups on campus, including art, band, cheerleading, chess, choir, chorale, chorus, computers, dance, debate, drama, drill team, ethnic, film, gay, honors, international, jazz band, literary magazine, marching band, musical theater, newspaper, opera, orchestra, pep band, photography, political, professional, radio and TV, religious, social, social service, student government, symphony, and yearbook. Popular campus events include Maine Day, Family and Friends Weekend, and International Week.

Sports: There are 9 intercollegiate sports for men and 10 for women, and 35 intramural sports for men and 35 for women. Facilities include a sports arena for hockey and basketball, a field house, an indoor climbing center, a fitness center, a swimming pool, a weight room, an indoor track, a dance studio, basketball, volleyball, badminton, squash, tennis, and racquetball courts, and baseball, softball, soccer, field hockey, and football fields.

Disabled Students: 90% of the campus is accessible. Wheelchair ramps, elevators, special parking, specially equipped rest rooms, special class scheduling, lowered drinking fountains, lowered telephones, and a transport van are available.

Services: Counseling and information services are available, as is tutoring in some subjects, including 100- and 200-level courses. There is a reader service for the blind. Developmental courses are offered in remedial math, reading, and writing.

Campus Safety and Security: Measures include 24-hour foot and vehicle patrol, self-defense education, security escort services, and informal discussions. There are pamphlets/posters/films, emergency telephones, and lighted pathways/sidewalks.

Programs of Study: U-Maine confers B.A., B.S., B.F.A., B.M.E., and B.U.S. degrees. Master's and doctoral degrees are also awarded. Bachelor's degrees are awarded in AGRICULTURE (agriculture, animal science, fishing and fisheries, forest engineering, forestry and related sciences, horticulture, natural resource management, wildlife management, and wood science), BIOLOGICAL SCIENCE (biochemistry, biology/biological science, biotechnology, botany, cell biology, marine biology, marine science, microbiology, molecular biology, nutrition, and zoology), BUSINESS (business administration and management and business economics), COMMUNICATIONS AND THE ARTS (art, communications, dramatic arts, English, French, German, journalism, Latin, media arts, modern language, music, music performance, romance languages and literature, Spanish, speech/debate/rhetoric, and studio art), COMPUTER AND PHYSICAL SCIENCE (chemistry, computer science, earth science, information sciences and systems, mathematics, and physics),

EDUCATION (art, elementary, health, music, physical, recreation, and secondary), ENGINEERING AND ENVIRONMENTAL DESIGN (bioengineering, chemical engineering, civil engineering, computer engineering, construction technology, electrical/electronics engineering, electrical/electronics engineering technology, engineering physics, environmental science, mechanical engineering, mechanical engineering technology, paper and pulp science, and surveying engineering), HEALTH PROFESSIONS (clinical science, medical laboratory technology, nursing, and speech pathology/audiology), SOCIAL SCIENCE (anthropology, child care/child and family studies, economics, food science, history, interdisciplinary studies, international studies, parks and recreation management, philosophy, political science/government, psychology, public administration, social work, sociology, and women's studies). Education, engineering, and biology are the largest.

Required: To graduate, students must complete a minimum of 120 credit hours, including a minimum of 48 in the major, with a minimum GPA of 2.0. 40 credits in approved courses must be taken. General education requirements include 18 credits in human values and social context, 6 credits in math/statistics/computer science, 2 courses in science, and at least 1 course in ethics. English composition is required. Students must demonstrate writing competency, and complete a capstone.

Special: A Professional Preparation Team program is offered by the College of Education. Cross-registration through the National Student Exchange and at other University of Maine campuses, internships at the upper level, a Washington semester, work-study programs both on- and off-campus, dual majors, a general studies degree, and pass/fail options are available. Students may study abroad in more than 40 countries. Cooperative programs are available in most majors, and accelerated degrees may be arranged. There are 43 national honor societies, including Phi Beta Kappa, and a freshman honors program.

Faculty/Classroom: 60% of faculty are male; 40%, female. Graduate students teach 6% of introductory courses. The average class size in an introductory lecture is 24; in a laboratory, 16; and in a regular course, 21.

Admissions: 79% of the 2005-2006 applicants were accepted. The SAT scores for the 2005-2006 freshman class were: Verbal--28% below 500, 48% between 500 and 599, 21% between 600 and 700, and 3% above 700; Math--27% below 500, 46% between 500 and 599, 22% between 600 and 700, and 5% above 700. The ACT scores were 30% below 21, 28% between 21 and 23, 25% between 24 and 26, 11% between 27 and 28, and 6% above 28. 43% of the current freshmen were in the top fifth of their class; 74% were in the top two fifths. There were 3 National Merit finalists. 33 freshmen graduated first in their class.

Requirements: The SAT or ACT is required.The GED is accepted. The number of academic or Carnegie credits required varies according to the program. The required secondary school courses also vary with each program but should include 4 credits of English, 3 of math, 2 of lab science, 2 social studies, 2 in a foreign language, and 3 of electives. Guidance counselor recommendation is required for high school students. An essay is required. An audition is required for music majors. AP and CLEP credits are accepted. Important factors in the admissions decision are advanced placement or honor courses, recommendations by school officials, and evidence of special talent.

Procedure: Freshmen are admitted fall and spring. Entrance exams should be taken by January of the senior year. There are early admissions, rolling sdmissions, and deferred admissions plans. Application deadlines are open. The application fee is $40. 68 applicants were on the 2005 waiting list. Applications are accepted on-line.

Transfer: 453 transfer students enrolled in 2004-2005. Applicants must submit transcripts of all college and high school records. A minimum GPA of 2.0 is required. 30 of 120 credits (or more, for some programs) required for the bachelor's degree must be completed at U-Maine.

Visiting: There are regularly scheduled orientations for prospective students, includes an opening welcome, campus tours, registration, department tours, student panel, admissions, financial aid, student life sessions, performing arts presentation, and music auditions. There are guides for informal visits and visitors may sit in on classes. To schedule a visit, contact the Visitors' Center at (207) 581-3740 or *um-admit@maine.edu.*

Financial Aid: In 2005-2006, 82% of all full-time freshmen and 83% of continuing full-time students received some form of financial aid. 63% of all full-time students received need-based aid. The average freshman award was $9667. Need-based scholarships or need-based grants averaged $5880; need-based self-help aid (loans and jobs) averaged $4219; non-need-based athletic scholarships averaged $14,845; and other non-need-based awards and non-need-based scholarships averaged $4126. 60% of undergraduates work part time. Average annual earnings from campus work are $2000. The average financial indebtedness of the 2005 graduate was $20,930. The FAFSA is required. The deadline for filing freshman financial aid applications for fall entry is March 1.

International Students: There are 138 international students enrolled. The school actively recruits these students. They must score satisfactorily on the TOEFL and also take the SAT or ACT. The SAT is preferred.

Computers: Wireless access is available. All dorms have wired connectivity. All academic buildings and some administrative buildings have wireless access. Public and private PC clusters are set up throughout campus with the largest clusters in the library and the student union. There are approximately 500 PCs and Macs available in the clusters. All students may access the system 24 hours a day. There are no time limits and no fees. All students are required to have Apple i Book computers.

Graduates: From July 1, 2004 to June 30, 2005, 1601 bachelor's degrees were awarded. The most popular majors were eduacation (13%), engineering (12%), and business (11%). In an average class, 30% graduate in 4 years or less, 51% graduate in 5 years or less, and 56% graduate in 6 years or less. 178 companies recruited on campus in 2004-2005. Of the 2004 graduating class, 24% were enrolled in graduate school within 6 months of graduation and 88% were employed.

Admissions Contact: Sharon M. Oliver, Director of Admissions. E-mail: *um-admit@maine.edu* Web: *www.umaine.edu*

UNIVERSITY OF MAINE AT AUGUSTA B-5

Augusta, ME 04430
(207) 621-3390
(877) UMA-1234; Fax: (207) 621-3333

Full-time: 469 men, 1075 women	**Faculty:** 95; IIB, -$
Part-time: 940 men, 3010 women	**Ph.D.s:** 38%
Graduate: none	**Student/Faculty:** 16 to 1
Year: semesters, summer session	**Tuition:** $5025 ($11,115)
Application Deadline: June 15	**Room & Board:** n/app
Freshman Class: 2090 applied, 2090 accepted, 1342 enrolled	
SAT or ACT: not required	**NONCOMPETITIVE**

The University of Maine at Augusta, founded in 1965, offers both associate and baccalaureate degrees and is part of the University of Maine System. There are 3 undergraduate schools. In addition to regional accreditation, UMA has baccalaureate program accreditation with ADA, NEASC, and NLN. The 2 libraries contain 78,985 volumes, 6502 microform items, and 3568 audio/video tapes/CDs/DVDs, and subscribe to 560 periodicals including electronic. Computerized library services include the card catalog, interlibrary loans, database searching, Internet access, and laptop Internet portals. Special learning facilities include a learning resource center, art gallery, and an interactive television system. The 159-acre campus is in a small town 50 miles north of Portland. There are 15 buildings.

Student Life: 98% of undergraduates are from Maine. Others are from 34 states and 7 foreign countries. 99% are from public schools. 96% are white. The average age of freshmen is 27; all undergraduates, 33. 40% do not continue beyond their first year; 30% remain to graduate.

Housing: There are no residence halls. All of students commute. Alcohol is not permitted. All students may keep cars.

Activities: There are no fraternities or sororities. There are 17 groups on campus, including art, gay, honors, international, jazz band, newspaper, pep band, professional, religious, social, social service, and student government. Popular campus events include Mile of Art, Jazz Week, and Plunkett Poetry Festival.

Sports: There is 1 intercollegiate sport for men and 2 for women, and 4 intramural sports for men and 4 for women. Facilities include the UMA Community Outdoor Leisure Center, which is also open to the public. Facilities provide for seasonal activities and feature a running and cross-country skiing trail, tennis courts, a soccer field, and a softball field. Indoor facilities include a small gym, a racquetball court, and a small fitness center.

Disabled Students: 90% of the campus is accessible. Wheelchair ramps, elevators, special parking, specially equipped rest rooms, special class scheduling, lowered drinking fountains, and lowered telephones are available.

Services: Counseling and information services are available, as is tutoring in some subjects, including developmental and introductory level courses. There is a reader service for the blind, and remedial math, reading, and writing. There are workshops on a variety of student success skills, such as effective learning and reducing test anxiety.

Campus Safety and Security: Measures include security escort services, pamphlets/posters/films, emergency telephones, and lighted pathways/sidewalks.

Programs of Study: UMA confers B.A., B.S., and B.Mus., B.A.S. degrees. Associate degrees are also awarded. Bachelor's degrees are awarded in BIOLOGICAL SCIENCE (biology/biological science), BUSINESS (accounting and business administration and management), COMMUNICATIONS AND THE ARTS (art, English, and jazz), COMPUTER AND PHYSICAL SCIENCE (applied science and information sciences and systems), EDUCATION (library science), ENGINEERING AND ENVIRONMENTAL DESIGN (architecture), HEALTH PROFESSIONS (dental hygiene and mental health/human services), SOCIAL SCIENCE (interdisciplinary studies, law enforcement and corrections, liberal arts/general studies, public administration, and social science). Mental health and human services are the largest.

Required: All students must complete at least 120 hours, including 30 to 40 in the major, with a minimum GPA of 2.0. All degree programs require courses in English and communications, humanities, math and computer sciences, social sciences, fine arts, and college writing. Specific course requirements differ by degree program.

Special: Work-study and internship programs with local employers, study abroad, a general studies degree, nondegree study, and pass/fail options are available. Cross-registration is offered with University of Maine System campuses. There is 1 national honor society.

Faculty/Classroom: 49% of faculty are male; 51%, female. All teach undergraduates. The average class size in an introductory lecture is 22; in a laboratory, 18; and in a regular course, 19.

Admissions: 100% of the 2005-2006 applicants were accepted. 12% of the current freshmen were in the top fifth of their class; 63% were in the top two fifths.

Requirements: Students are encouraged to submit SAT scores for placement only. Applicants should have a high school diploma or the GED. Recommended secondary preparation varies according to the degree program. Applicants for the B.M. program must audition. UMA requires applicants to be in the upper 25% of their class. A GPA of 2.0 is required. AP and CLEP credits are accepted.

Procedure: Freshmen are admitted fall and spring. There are early admissions deferred admissions and rolling admissions plans. Applications should be filed by June 15 for fall entry and October 15 for spring entry, along with a $40 fee. Notification is sent on a rolling basis. A waiting list is an active part of the admissions procedure. Applications are accepted on-line.

Transfer: 506 transfer students enrolled in a recent year. High school/college transcripts and a statement of good standing from prior institutions are required. Standardized test scores are required for some students, and an interview is recommended. 30 of 120 credits required for the bachelor's degree must be completed at UMA.

Visiting: There are regularly scheduled orientations for prospective students, during the month before the beginning of a semester. There are guides for informal visits and visitors may sit in on classes. To schedule a visit, contact the Admissions Office at (207 621-3465).

Financial Aid: In 2005-2006, 82% of all full-time freshmen and 89% of continuing full-time students received some form of financial aid. 73% of full-time freshmen and 74% of continuing full-time students received need-based aid. The average freshman award was $5749. Need-based scholarships or need-based grants averaged $4129 ($6500 maximum); need-based self-help aid (loans and jobs) averaged $2780 ($6625 maximum); and other non-need-based awards and non-need-based scholarships averaged $3181 ($4000 maximum). 5% of undergraduates work part time. Average annual earnings from campus work are $1358. The average financial indebtedness of the 2005 graduate was $11,811. The FAFSA is required. The priority date for freshman financial aid applications for fall entry is March 1.

International Students: There are 4 international students enrolled. They must score satisfactorily on the written TOEFL or on the electronic version.

Computers: Wireless access is available. Wireless Internet access is available anywhere on campus and in all PC classrooms and student labs. All students may access the system 24 hours a day at home, 8 A.M. to 9 P.M. in a shared lab, and 24 hours wireless. There are no time limits and no fees.

Graduates: From July 1, 2004 to June 30, 2005, 222 bachelor's degrees were awarded. The most popular majors were mental health/human services (41%), business administration (19%), and social sciences (11%). 10 companies recruited on campus in 2004-2005.

Admissions Contact: Sheri Fraser, Director of Admissions. A video is available. E-mail: *fraser@maine.edu* Web: *www.uma.maine.edu*

UNIVERSITY OF MAINE AT FARMINGTON
Farmington, ME 04938-1990

B-4

(207) 778-7050
Fax: (207) 778-8182

Full-time: 728 men, 1395 women	Faculty: 118; IIB, --$
Part-time: 100 men, 229 women	Ph.D.s: 91%
Graduate: none	Student/Faculty: 18 to 1
Year: semesters, summer session	Tuition: $5531 ($12,761)
Application Deadline: open	Room & Board: $5984
Freshman Class: 1602 applied, 1190 accepted, 575 enrolled	
SAT Verbal/Math: 528/511*	COMPETITIVE

The University of Maine at Farmington, founded in 1863 and part of the University of Maine System, is a public liberal arts institution offering programs in arts and sciences, teacher education, and human services. There are 2 undergraduate schools. In addition to regional accreditation, UMF has baccalaureate program accreditation with NCATE. The library contains 100,464 volumes, 89,977 microform items, and 7857 audio/video tapes/CDs/DVDs, and subscribes to 1768 periodicals including electronic. Computerized library services include the card catalog, interlibrary loans, database searching, and Internet access. Special learning facilities include a learning resource center, art gallery, radio station, an instructional media center, an archeology research center, a 20-workstation electronic classroom, an observatory, on-site nursery school and day care teaching labs, and a multimedia graphic lab. The 50-acre campus is in a small town 38 miles northwest of Augusta, 80 miles north of Portland. Including any residence halls, there are 35 buildings.

Student Life: 83% of undergraduates are from Maine. Others are from 32 states, 8 foreign countries, and Canada. 88% are from public schools. 95% are white. The average age of all undergraduates is 23. 21% do not continue beyond their first year; 54% remain to graduate.

Housing: 1100 students can be accommodated in college housing, which includes single-sex and coed dorms and on-campus apartments. There is also an international guest house, a wellness floor, and scholar areas. On-campus housing is guaranteed for all 4 years. 60% of students commute. All students may keep cars.

Activities: There are no fraternities or sororities. There are 53 groups on campus, including chamber choir, cheerleading, choir, chorus, club sports, commuter, computers, dance, drama, enviromental, film, gay, history, honors, international, languages, literary magazine, musical theater, newspaper, orchestra, pep band, photography, political, professional, radio and TV, religious, social, social service, and student government. Popular campus events include Parents and Alumni weekends, Winter Carnival Weekend, and Student Symposium Day.

Sports: There are 5 intercollegiate sports for men and 6 for women, and 12 intramural sports for men and 12 for women. Facilities include a 500-seat gym, baseball, softball, and soccer fields, a field house with an indoor jogging track, 4 multipurpose courts, a swimming pool, and a weight-training center. A ski area, mountain climbing, canoeing, fishing, white water rafting, and mountain biking opportunities are nearby.

Disabled Students: 55% of the campus is accessible. Wheelchair ramps, elevators, special parking, specially equipped rest rooms, special class scheduling, lowered drinking fountains, lowered telephones, an accessible van, a swimming pool, and TDD are available.

Services: Counseling and information services are available, as is tutoring in every subject. There is a reader service for the blind, and remedial math, reading, and writing.

Campus Safety and Security: Measures include 24-hour foot and vehicle patrol, self-defense education, security escort services, and informal discussions. There are pamphlets/posters/films, emergency telephones, lighted pathways/sidewalks, and safety whistles.

Programs of Study: UMF confers B.A., B.S., B.F.A., and B.G.S. degrees. Bachelor's degrees are awarded in BIOLOGICAL SCIENCE (biology/biological science), BUSINESS (business economics), COMMUNICATIONS AND THE ARTS (art, creative writing, English, language arts, music, and visual and performing arts), COMPUTER AND PHYSICAL SCIENCE (computer science, geochemistry, geology, and mathematics), EDUCATION (early childhood, elementary, health, secondary, and special), ENGINEERING AND ENVIRONMENTAL DESIGN (environmental science), HEALTH PROFESSIONS (community health work and rehabilitation therapy), SOCIAL SCIENCE (geography, history, interdisciplinary studies, international studies, liberal arts/general studies, philosophy, political science/government, psychology, sociology, and women's studies). Education, environmental science, and creative writing are the strongest academically. Elementary education, psychology, and interdisciplinary studies are the largest.

Required: All students must maintain a minimum GPA of 2.0 while earning 120 semester hours, including 30 in their major. Core requirements include 9 hours each in social and behavioral sciences and the humanities, 8 in natural science, 4 in English composition, 3 each in math, health, and phys ed, and a foreign language.

Special: Study abroad in 4 countries, as well as numerous opportunities through the National Student Exchange program, work-study with UMF, and student-designed majors are available. Study abroad is possible through other universities as well. Internships are required in rehabilitation and health and are available in all disciplines. Student teaching is required of all education majors. Also possible is interdisciplinary field study in many disciplines, a ski industry certificate, nondegree study, and pass/fail options. There are 2 national honor societies, a freshman honors program, and 10 departmental honors programs.

Faculty/Classroom: 49% of faculty are male; 51%, female. All teach undergraduates. The average class size in an introductory lecture is 45; in a laboratory, 20; and in a regular course, 19.

Admissions: 74% of the 2005-2006 applicants were accepted. The SAT scores for the 2005-2006 freshman class were: Verbal--42% below 500, 37% between 500 and 599, 18% between 600 and 700, and 2% above 700; Math--47% below 500, 37% between 500 and 599, 13% between 600 and 700, and 1% above 700. 3 freshmen graduated first in their class in a recent year.

Requirements: Applicants are required to have 16 to 19 college preparatory courses including 4 in English, 3 to 5 in math, 3 electives, 2 to 3 in lab science, and 2 each in social science and foreign language. An essay and a counselor recommendation are required, and an interview is recommended. The GED is accepted for older, highly motivated students. AP and CLEP credits are accepted. Important factors in the admissions decision are advanced placement or honor courses, recommendations by school officials, and leadership record.

Procedure: Freshmen are admitted fall and spring. There are early admissions and deferred admissions plans. There is a rolling admissions plan. Application deadlines are open. The fall 2005 application fee was $40. Notification of early admissions is sent December 15, regular decision, on a rolling basis. Applications are accepted on-line.

Transfer: 116 transfer students enrolled in 2004-2005. Applicants must have a minimum GPA of 2.0 (2.5 for some majors). 30 of 120 credits required for the bachelor's degree must be completed at UMF.

Visiting: There are regularly scheduled orientations for prospective students, including sessions on financial aid, majors, student life, the admissions process, and special opportunities such as study abroad, and tours of the campus. There are guides for informal visits and visitors may sit in on classes. To schedule a visit, contact the Admissions Office at *umfadmit@maine.edu*.

Financial Aid: In 2005-2006, 91% of all full-time freshmen and 67% of continuing full-time students received some form of financial aid. 70% of full-time freshmen and 67% of continuing full-time students received need-based aid. The average freshman award was $8497. Need-based scholarships or need-based grants averaged $4496; need-based self-help aid (loans and jobs) averaged $3282; and other non-need-based awards and non-need-based scholarships averaged $2885. 45% of undergraduates work part time. Average annual earnings from campus work are $1631. The average financial indebtedness of the 2005 graduate was $17,482. UMF is a member of CSS. The FAFSA is required. The deadline for filing freshman financial aid applications for fall entry is March 1.

International Students: There were 9 international students enrolled in a recent year. The school actively recruits these students. They must take the TOEFL. The SAT is optional but recommended for placement.

Computers: Wireless access is available. All residence halls have Ethernet hookups for each resident, free Internet, and e-mail. 128 stations in the computer center are available 24/7. All students may access the system. About 50 stations are available 24 hours a day; 125 other stations are available 80 hours per week. There are no time limits. The fee is $65 per semester.

Graduates: From July 1, 2004 to June 30, 2005, 381 bachelor's degrees were awarded. The most popular majors were education (40%), interdisciplinary (19%), and English (10%). In an average class, 33% graduate in 4 years or less, 52% graduate in 5 years or less, and 58% graduate in 6 years or less. 35 companies recruited on campus in 2004-2005. Of a recent graduating class, 18% were enrolled in graduate school within 6 months of graduation and 92% were employed.

Admissions Contact: William Geller, Director of Admissions.
E-mail: *umfadmit@maine.edu* Web: *www.umf.maine.edu*

UNIVERSITY OF MAINE AT FORT KENT   D-1
Fort Kent, ME 04743

	(207) 834-7600
	(888) TRY-UMFK; Fax: (207) 834-7609
Full-time: 310 men, 452 women	Faculty: 38; IIB, --$
Part-time: 96 men, 335 women	Ph.D.s: 70%
Graduate: none	Student/Faculty: 20 to 1
Year: semesters, summer session	Tuition: $4844 ($10,934)
Application Deadline: open	Room & Board: $5988 ($17,822)
Freshman Class: 770 applied, 603 accepted, 364 enrolled	
SAT Verbal/Math: 444/445*	ACT: 20 LESS COMPETITIVE

The University of Maine at Fort Kent, founded in 1878, is a publicly funded liberal arts institution within the University of Maine system. There are 7 undergraduate and 2 graduate schools. In addition to regional accreditation, UMFK has baccalaureate program accreditation with NLN and SAF. The library contains 67,137 volumes and 1300 audio/video tapes/CDs/DVDs, and subscribes to 333 periodicals including electronic. Computerized library services include the card catalog, interlibrary loans, database searching, and Internet access. Special learning facilities include a learning resource center, radio station, a greenhouse, and biological park. The 52-acre campus is in a small town 200 miles north of Bangor. Including any residence halls, there are 16 buildings.

Student Life: 69% of undergraduates are from Maine. Students are from 15 states, 2 foreign countries, and Canada. 96% are from public schools. 71% are white; 26% foreign nationals. The average age of freshmen is 20; all undergraduates, 26. 30% do not continue beyond their first year; 40% remain to graduate.

Housing: 300 students can be accommodated in college housing, which includes coed dorms. On-campus housing is guaranteed for all 4 years. 80% of students commute. Alcohol is not permitted. All students may keep cars.

Activities: 2% of men belong to 1 national fraternity; fewer than 1% of women belong to 1 national sorority. There are 25 groups on campus, including cheerleading, chorale, chorus, computers, dance, drama, environmental, international, literature, literary magazine, musical theater, newspaper, outing, professional, radio and TV, religious, and student government. Popular campus events include French Heritage Festival, Spring Meltdown, and Winter Carnival.

Sports: There are 4 intercollegiate sports for men and 5 for women, and 10 intramural sports for men and 10 for women. Facilities include an 11,500-square-foot gym, racquetball courts, soccer field, weight room, cardiovascular room, intramural fields, and game rooms in the residence halls.

Disabled Students: 80% of the campus is accessible. Wheelchair ramps, elevators, special parking, specially equipped rest rooms, special

class scheduling, lowered drinking fountains, lowered telephones, and special housing are available.

Services: Counseling and information services are available, as is tutoring in every subject. There is a reader service for the blind, and remedial math, reading, and writing.

Campus Safety and Security: Measures include informal discussions, pamphlets/posters/films, lighted pathways/sidewalks, and night watchmen 11 P.M. to 7 A.M.

Programs of Study: UMFK confers B.A., B.S., B.S.E.S, B.S.N., and B.U.S. degrees. Associate degrees are also awarded. Bachelor's degrees are awarded in BIOLOGICAL SCIENCE (biology/biological science), BUSINESS (business administration and management), COMMUNICATIONS AND THE ARTS (English and French), COMPUTER AND PHYSICAL SCIENCE (computer science), EDUCATION (elementary), ENGINEERING AND ENVIRONMENTAL DESIGN (environmental science), HEALTH PROFESSIONS (nursing), SOCIAL SCIENCE (behavioral science, liberal arts/general studies, safety management, and social science). Environmental studies, nursing, and biology are the strongest academically. Education, nursing, and behavioral science are the largest.

Required: A minimum GPA of 2.0 and a total of 120 credit hours (2.5 GPA and 127 credit hours for nursing, 128 credit hours for business management) are required for graduation. Curricula and distribution requirements vary by major.

Special: Internships are required for business majors, nursing (clinicals), social sciences, public safety administration, and education (student teaching). A general studies degree, a B.A.-B.S. degree in bilingual-bicultural studies, credit for life experience, nondegree study, and an accelerated nursing program are available. Students may cross-register with the College Universitaire St. Louis Maillet in New Brunswick. Study abroad may be arranged in Canada, France, and Mexico through the University of Maine at Farmington. Interactive TV courses broadcast from other universities are available on campus. There is 1 national honor society.

Faculty/Classroom: 53% of faculty are male; 47%, female. All teach undergraduates. The average class size in an introductory lecture is 20; in a laboratory, 15; and in a regular course, 25.

Admissions: 78% of the 2005-2006 applicants were accepted. The SAT scores for the 2005-2006 freshman class were: Verbal--70% below 500, 24% between 500 and 599, and 6% between 600 and 700; Math--71% below 500, 21% between 500 and 599, and 6% between 600 and 700. The ACT scores were 100% below 21. 20% of the current freshmen were in the top fifth of their class; 54% were in the top two fifths.

Requirements: The SAT is required for some programs. The ACT Optional Writing test is also required. In addition, applicants should be graduates of an accredited secondary school. The GED is accepted. Required secondary school courses include 4 years of English and 2 each of social studies, math, and lab science. A foreign language is suggested. An essay and an interview are recommended. A GPA of 2.0 is required. AP and CLEP credits are accepted. Important factors in the admissions decision are recommendations by school officials, advanced placement or honor courses, and evidence of special talent.

Procedure: Freshmen are admitted fall and spring. Entrance exams should be taken before March of the senior year. There are early decision, early admissions, deferred admissions and rolling admissions plans. Application deadlines are open. Application fee is $40. Applications are accepted on-line.

Transfer: 269 transfer students enrolled in 2004-2005. Applicants must submit transcripts from each college and secondary school attended. The SAT and an interview are recommended. 30 of 120 credits required for the bachelor's degree must be completed at UMFK.

Visiting: There are regularly scheduled orientations for prospective students, including placement testing, meetings with advisers, campus tours, and get-acquainted activities. There are guides for informal visits and visitors may sit in on classes and stay overnight. To schedule a visit, contact the Admissions Office.

Financial Aid: 47% of full-time freshmen and 30% of continuing full-time students received need-based aid. Need-based scholarships or need-based grants averaged $3218; need-based self-help aid (loans and jobs) averaged $2881; and other non-need-based awards and non-need-based scholarships averaged $3141. 54% of undergraduates work part time. Average annual earnings from campus work are $1500. The average financial indebtedness of the 2005 graduate was $12,204. The FAFSA and income tax forms are required. The deadline for filing freshman financial aid applications for fall entry is March 1.

International Students: There are 312 international students enrolled. The school actively recruits these students. They must score satisfactorily on the written TOEFL. SAT scores may be submitted in place of the TOEFL.

Computers: Wireless access is available. All students may access the system from 8 A.M. to 11 P.M. in the library and computer centers, and 24 hours a day in the dorms. There are no time limits. The fee is $5.

Graduates: From July 1, 2004 to June 30, 2005, 254 bachelor's degrees were awarded. The most popular majors were education (75%), nursing (9%), and business (5%). In an average class, 25% graduate in

4 years or less, 18% graduate in 5 years or less, and 3% graduate in 6 years or less. 2 companies recruited on campus in 2004-2005. Of the 2004 graduating class, 5% were enrolled in graduate school within 6 months of graduation and 90% were employed.

Admissions Contact: Douglas Barley, Director of Admissions. A video is available. E-mail: *umfkadm@maine.edu* Web: *www.umfk.maine.edu*

UNIVERSITY OF MAINE AT MACHIAS   E-4

Machias, ME 04654   (207) 255-1318
                           (888) 468-6866; Fax: (207) 255-1363

Full-time: 159 men, 303 women	**Faculty:** 31; IIB, --$
Part-time: 145 men, 542 women	**Ph.D.s:** 71%
Graduate: none	**Student/Faculty:** 15 to 1
Year: semesters, summer session	**Tuition:** $4845 ($12,195)
Application Deadline: open	**Room & Board:** $5678
Freshman Class: 374 applied, 312 accepted, 120 enrolled	
SAT Verbal/Math: 500/480*	**ACT:** 22 **COMPETITIVE**

The University of Maine at Machias, founded in 1909, is a publicly funded liberal arts institution in the University of Maine system. In addition to regional accreditation, UMM has baccalaureate program accreditation with NRPA. The library contains 82,000 volumes, 5000 microform items, and 3000 audio/video tapes/CDs/DVDs, and subscribes to 320 periodicals including electronic. Computerized library services include the card catalog, interlibrary loans, database searching, and Internet access. Special learning facilities include a learning resource center, art gallery, radio station, and aquariums for marine and aquaculture studies. The 42-acre campus is in a rural area 85 miles east of Bangor. Including any residence halls, there are 8 buildings.

Student Life: 82% of undergraduates are from Maine. Students are from 26 states, 16 foreign countries, and Canada. 98% are from public schools. 90% are white. The average age of freshmen is 20; all undergraduates, 29. 28% do not continue beyond their first year; 45% remain to graduate.

Housing: 353 students can be accommodated in college housing, which includes single-sex and coed dorms. On-campus housing is guaranteed for all 4 years. 76% of students commute. All students may keep cars.

Activities: 7% of men belong to 2 local and 2 national fraternities; 3% of women belong to 1 local and 3 national sororities. There are 34 groups on campus, including art, cheerleading, chorale, chorus, computers, dance, drama, gay, honors, international, literary magazine, musical theater, pep band, photography, professional, radio and TV, religious, social service, and student government. Popular campus events include Winter Carnival, Spring Weekend, and Family Weekend.

Sports: There are 3 intercollegiate sports for men and 4 for women, and 10 intramural sports for men and 10 for women. Facilities include 2 gyms, weight/exercise rooms, handball/raquetball courts, a pool, and a 64-acre recreational center with a lodge and cabins on the lake.

Disabled Students: 85% of the campus is accessible. Wheelchair ramps, elevators, special parking, specially equipped rest rooms, lowered drinking fountains, and automatic doors are available.

Services: Counseling and information services are available, as is tutoring in every subject. There is remedial math, reading, and writing. The Student Resource Coordinator provides one-on-one services, including learning strategies, study skills, and assistance with papers and learning styles.

Campus Safety and Security: Measures include self-defense education, security escort services, informal discussions, and pamphlets/posters/films. There are lighted pathways/sidewalks, a keyless entry system for residence halls, and a security patrol from 5 P.M. to 5 A.M. daily.

Programs of Study: UMM confers B.A., B.S., and B.C.S. degrees. Bachelor's degrees are awarded in BIOLOGICAL SCIENCE (biology/biological science and marine biology), BUSINESS (accounting, business administration and management, marketing/retailing/merchandising, and recreation and leisure services), COMMUNICATIONS AND THE ARTS (English and fine arts), EDUCATION (business and elementary), ENGINEERING AND ENVIRONMENTAL DESIGN (environmental science), SOCIAL SCIENCE (behavioral science, history, human services, and liberal arts/general studies). Elementary education, marine biology, and environmental studies are the strongest academically. Elementary education, business administration, and behavioral science are the largest.

Required: To graduate, students must complete a minimum of 120 credit hours with a GPA of 2.0. The core curriculum consists of 40-43 hours in the areas of communication skills, science and math, humans in social context, fine arts, historical and cultural perspectives, and lifetime fitness.

Special: Co-op programs in all majors except education, cross-registration, internships, work-study programs, a B.A.-B.S. degree, study abroad in England and Wales, and a student designed concentration in environmental science are available. UMM also offers a Bachelor of College Studies program, credit for prior learning, nondegree study, and a pass/fail option in certain courses. There is a freshman honors program.

Faculty/Classroom: 54% of faculty are male; 46%, female. All teach undergraduates. The average class size in an introductory lecture is 21; in a laboratory, 16; and in a regular course, 17.

Admissions: 83% of the 2005-2006 applicants were accepted. The SAT scores for the 2005-2006 freshman class were: Verbal--49% below 500, 36% between 500 and 599, 13% between 600 and 700, and 2% above 700; Math--59% below 500, 30% between 500 and 599, 9% between 600 and 700, and 1% above 700. The ACT scores were 43% below 21, 14% between 21 and 23, 29% between 24 and 26, 7% between 27 and 28, and 7% above 28. 23% of the current freshmen were in the top fifth of their class; 53% were in the top two fifths.

Requirements: The SAT or ACT is required. In addition, all candidates must be graduates of an accredited secondary school, although the GED is accepted. UMM recommends that students place in the top half of their graduating class and that composite SAT scores be satisfactory. UMM also recommends completion of 4 units of English, 3 of math, 2 each of lab science, social science/history, and fine arts or foreign language, and 3 of electives. An essay is required and an interview is strongly recommended. UMM requires applicants to be in the upper 50% of their class. A GPA of 2.0 is required. AP and CLEP credits are accepted. Important factors in the admissions decision are extracurricular activities record, leadership record, and recommendations by school officials.

Procedure: Freshmen are admitted fall, spring, and summer. There are early admissions, deferred admissions, and rolling admissions plans. Application deadlines are open. Application fee is $40. Notification is sent on a rolling basis. Applications are accepted on-line.

Transfer: 36 transfer students enrolled in 2004-2005. A minimum college GPA of 2.0 and evidence of good standing are required of transfer applicants. 30 of 120 credits required for the bachelor's degree must be completed at UMM.

Visiting: There are regularly scheduled orientations for prospective students, consisting of traditional orientations prior to the fall and spring semesters, which include programming to guide students in all aspects of starting college—academic, student services and activities, and administrative. UMM also offers two summer student orientations, which include aspects of the fall orientations plus a parent orientation. There are guides for informal visits and visitors may sit in on classes. To schedule a visit, contact the Admissions Office.

Financial Aid: In 2005-2006, 88% of all full-time freshmen and 80% of continuing full-time students received some form of financial aid. 78% of full-time freshmen and 82% of continuing full-time students received need-based aid. The average freshman award was $8488. Need-based scholarships or need-based grants averaged $5884; need-based self-help aid (loans and jobs) averaged $3439; and other non-need-based awards and non-need-based scholarships averaged $6420. The FAFSA is required. The deadline for filing freshman financial aid applications for fall entry is March 1.

International Students: There were 50 international students enrolled in a recent year. The school actively recruits these students. A satisfactory score is required on the written TOEFL. Students must also take the SAT or the ACT.

Computers: All students may access the system 24 hours a day, 7 days a week in dorms and the 24-hour room. Other computer labs are open during library hours. There is no set time limit, but students must yield a machine for academic priorities. There are no fees.

Graduates: In a recent year, 100 bachelor's degrees were awarded. The most popular majors were behavioral science (15%), business administration (13%), and recreation management (13%). In an average class, 19% graduate in 4 years or less, 42% graduate in 5 years or less, and 46% graduate in 6 years or less. 10 companies recruited on campus in a recent year.

Admissions Contact: Sarah Guancial, Admissions Counselor. A video is available. E-mail: *ummadmissions@maine.edu* Web: *www.umm.maine.edu*

UNIVERSITY OF MAINE AT PRESQUE ISLE   D-2

Presque Isle, ME 04769-2888   (207) 768-9453
                                        Fax: (207) 768-9777

Full-time: 408 men, 704 women	**Faculty:** 54; IIB, --$
Part-time: 119 men, 317 women	**Ph.D.s:** 56%
Graduate: none	**Student/Faculty:** 21 to 1
Year: semesters, summer session	**Tuition:** $4820 ($11,210)
Application Deadline: open	**Room & Board:** $5246
Freshman Class: 483 applied, 417 accepted, 212 enrolled	
SAT or ACT: not required	**LESS COMPETITIVE**

The University of Maine at Presque Isle, founded in 1903, is a public institution within the University of Maine system offering liberal arts, teacher education, and professional programs leading to post-secondary certificates, associate and bachelor's degrees. There are 2 undergraduate schools. In addition to regional accreditation, UM-Presque Isle has baccalaureate program accreditation with CAAHEP, CSWE, and NAACLS. The library contains 75,000 volumes, 750,000 microform items, and 1400 audio/video tapes/CDs/DVDs, and subscribes to 2000 periodicals including electronic. Computerized library services include the card catalog, interlibrary loans, database searching, and Internet access. Special learning facilities include a learning resource center, art gallery, natural history museum, radio station, and a theater. The 150-acre campus is in a rural area 150 miles north of Bangor. Including any residence halls, there are 11 buildings.

Student Life: 73% of undergraduates are from Maine. Others are from 14 states, 5 foreign countries, and Canada. 67% are white. The average age of freshmen is 20; all undergraduates, 26. 45% do not continue beyond their first year; 28% remain to graduate.

Housing: 359 students can be accommodated in college housing, which includes coed dorms, off-campus apartments, and married-student housing. On-campus housing is guaranteed for all 4 years. 78% of students commute. All students may keep cars.

Activities: 2% of men belong to 1 national fraternity; 1% of women belong to 1 national sorority. There are 25 groups on campus, including A Capella Group, Activities Board, band, chess, chorale, debate, Diversity Club, drama, ethnic, gay, honors, international, newspaper, Non-traditional Students Club, professional, radio and TV, religious, social, social service, and student government. Popular campus events include Spring Ball, Winter Blast, and Spring Fest.

Sports: There are 6 intercollegiate sports for men and 6 for women, and 15 intramural sports for men and 15 for women. Facilities include a facility that houses a swimming pool, gymnasium, track, fitness room, and climbing wall. Another multifunctional structure houses a gym, a weight room, phys ed labs, a sports medicine facility, Athletic Hall of Fame, and an auditorium. A large playing field contains baseball, soccer, and tennis courts. There are also hiking trails, a bike path, and a ropes course. The campus also hosts a club ice hockey team.

Disabled Students: All of the campus is accessible. Wheelchair ramps, elevators, special parking, specially equipped rest rooms, special class scheduling, lowered drinking fountains, and lowered telephones are available.

Services: Counseling and information services are available, as is tutoring in most subjects. There is remedial math, reading, and writing.

Campus Safety and Security: Measures include security escort services, informal discussions, pamphlets/posters/films, and lighted pathways/sidewalks.

Programs of Study: UM-Presque Isle confers B.A., B.S., B.A.A.E., B.F.A., B.L.S., and B.S.W. degrees. Associate degrees are also awarded. Bachelor's degrees are awarded in BIOLOGICAL SCIENCE (biology/biological science), BUSINESS (accounting, business administration and management, and recreation and leisure services), COMMUNICATIONS AND THE ARTS (art and English), EDUCATION (elementary, health, physical, and secondary), ENGINEERING AND ENVIRONMENTAL DESIGN (environmental science), SOCIAL SCIENCE (behavioral science, criminal justice, international studies, liberal arts/general studies, and social work). Education, social work, and criminal justice are the largest.

Required: Core requirements for the B.A. degrees include 18 credits in humanities, 12 in social science, 11 in math/science, and 4 in phys ed/health. The student must complete a minimum number of credits, which varies according to major, with a cumulative GPA of 2.0 in 120 to 128 credit hours. Requirements for the B.S. and other degrees vary considerably with each major.

Special: The university participates in transfer programs in agriculture, nutrition science, animal and veterinary science. There is a nursing program with the University of Maine at Fort Kent. There are study-abroad programs in France, Ireland, Canada (other countries are available), and internships in many majors. UM-Presque Isle offers work-study programs, dual and student-designed majors, a B.A.-B.S. degree, and non-degree study. Students can apply for credit by exam and credit for life, military, and work experience. A credit/no credit option is available. There is 1 national honor society, a freshman honors program, and 5 departmental honors program.

Faculty/Classroom: 56% of faculty are male; 44%, female. All teach undergraduates. The average class size in an introductory lecture is 20; in a laboratory, 12; and in a regular course, 15.

Admissions: 86% of the 2005-2006 applicants were accepted. The SAT scores for the 2005-2006 freshman class were: Verbal--65% below 500, 27% between 500 and 599, and 8% between 600 and 700; Math--69% below 500, 29% between 500 and 599, 1% between 600 and 700, and 1% above 700. 16% of the current freshmen were in the top fifth of their class; 38% were in the top two fifths.

Requirements: Applicants should have completed 16 academic credits at an accredited secondary school, including 4 in English, 3 each in math and social studies, and 2 each in science with a lab, foreign language, and electives. A GED certificate may be substituted. The university recommends an essay and an interview for all candidates. Art majors must submit a portfolio. AP and CLEP credits are accepted. Important factors in the admissions decision are advanced placement or honor courses, recommendations by school officials, and extracurricular activities record.

Procedure: Freshmen are admitted fall, spring, and summer. Entrance exams should be taken by January 1. There are early decision, deferred

admissions and rolling admissions plans. Application deadlines are open. The fall 2005 application fee was $40. Applications are accepted on-line.

Transfer: 203 transfer students enrolled in 2004-2005. Applicants must have a 2.0 GPA from a regionally accredited two or four year college. Applicants must submit official transcripts from all colleges attended, along with an official ranscript from the high school from which they graduated. 30 of 120 to 128 credits required for the bachelor's degree must be completed at UM-Presque Isle.

Visiting: There are regularly scheduled orientations for prospective students, including advisement, a campus tour, and meetings with faculty and coaches. There are guides for informal visits and visitors may sit in on classes and stay overnight. To schedule a visit, contact Beverly A. McAvaddy at (207) 768-9532 or mcavaddy@umpi.maine.edu.

Financial Aid: In 2005-2006, 74% of all full-time freshmen and 79% of continuing full-time students received some form of financial aid. 89% of all full-time students received need-based aid. The average freshman award was $6790. Need-based scholarships or need-based grants averaged $5287; need-based self-help aid (loans and jobs) averaged $3095; and other awards averaged $4389. The average financial indebtedness of the 2005 graduate was $5193. The FAFSA is required. The deadline for filing freshman financial aid applications for fall entry is April 1.

International Students: There are 368 international students enrolled. The school actively recruits these students. A satisfactory score is required on the written TOEFL.

Computers: Wireless access is available. Wireless can be accessed everywhere inside except for the dorms. The University owns 500 PC's which can all access the internet. All students may access the system. There are no time limits. The fee is nominal.

Graduates: From July 1, 2004 to June 30, 2005, 300 bachelor's degrees were awarded. The most popular majors were liberal arts/general studies (45%), education (18%), and business management and administrative (8%). In an average class, 7% graduate in 4 years or less, 21% graduate in 5 years or less, and 28% graduate in 6 years or less. 35 companies recruited on campus in 2004-2005. Of the 2004 graduating class, 7% were enrolled in graduate school within 6 months of graduation.

Admissions Contact: Erin V. Benson, Director of Enrollment Management and University Relations. A video is available.
E-mail: adventure@umpi.maine.edu Web: www.umpi.maine.edu

UNIVERSITY OF NEW ENGLAND   A-6
Biddeford, ME 04005   (207) 283-0171
                                          (800) 477-4863; Fax: (207) 286-3678

Full-time: 356 men, 1163 women	**Faculty:** 113; IIA, --$
Part-time: 53 men, 164 women	**Ph.D.s:** 85%
Graduate: 493 men, 1083 women	**Student/Faculty:** 13 to 1
Year: semesters, summer session	**Tuition:** $22,275
Application Deadline: November 15	**Room & Board:** $8730
Freshman Class: 2398 applied, 2182 accepted, 610 enrolled	
SAT Verbal/Math: 520/520*	**COMPETITIVE**

University of New England, founded in 1831, offers undergraduate degrees in the health sciences, natural sciences, social sciences, liberal arts, education and business administration; graduate degrees in professional and occupational programs; teacher education, doctor of osteopathic medicine, continuing education, and summer sessions. There are 2 undergraduate and 8 graduate schools. In addition to regional accreditation, UNE has baccalaureate program accreditation with ADA, AOA, APTA, CAAHEP, CSWE, and NLN. The 2 libraries contain 143,278 volumes, 6371 microform items, and 10,532 audio/video tapes/CDs/DVDs, and subscribe to 25,063 periodicals including electronic. Computerized library services include the card catalog, interlibrary loans, database searching, Internet access, and laptop Internet portals. Special learning facilities include a learning resource center and art gallery. The 623-acre campus is in a rural area. Including any residence halls, there are 47 buildings.

Student Life: 59% of undergraduates are from out of state, mostly the Northeast. Students are from 33 states, 4 foreign countries, and Canada. 96% are white. The average age of freshmen is 22; all undergraduates, 22. 25% do not continue beyond their first year; 57% remain to graduate.

Housing: 1071 students can be accommodated in college housing, which includes single-sex and coed dorms. On-campus housing is guaranteed for the freshman year only. 65% of students live on campus. Upperclassmen may keep cars.

Activities: There are no fraternities or sororities. There are 44 groups on campus, including environmental, gay, honors, international, literary magazine, newspaper, professional, religious, sailing, social, social service, student government, and yearbook. Popular campus events include welcome week, family and friends weekend, and full leadership retreat.

Sports: There are 5 intercollegiate sports for men and 8 for women, and 17 intramural sports for men and 17 for women. Facilities include a 1500-seat gym, a fitness center, a pool, racquetball courts, soccer and softball fields, outdoor volleyball facilities, and multipurpose recreational field.

Disabled Students: 85% of the campus is accessible. Wheelchair ramps, elevators, special parking, specially equipped rest rooms, special class scheduling, lowered drinking fountains, lowered telephones, and stair climbers are available.

Services: Counseling and information services are available, as is tutoring in most subjects. There is a reader service for the blind, and remedial math, reading, and writing.

Campus Safety and Security: Measures include 24-hour foot and vehicle patrol, self-defense education, security escort services, and informal discussions. There are pamphlets/posters/films, emergency telephones, and lighted pathways/sidewalks. A safe-ride program provides drivers for students.

Programs of Study: UNE confers B.A., B.S., and B.S.N. degrees. Associate, master's, and doctoral degrees are also awarded. Bachelor's degrees are awarded in AGRICULTURE (environmental studies), BIOLOGICAL SCIENCE (biochemistry, biology/biological science, marine biology, and marine science), BUSINESS (business administration and management and sports management), COMMUNICATIONS AND THE ARTS (communications and English), COMPUTER AND PHYSICAL SCIENCE (chemistry and mathematics), EDUCATION (art, athletic training, education, and elementary), ENGINEERING AND ENVIRONMENTAL DESIGN (environmental science), HEALTH PROFESSIONS (biomedical science, dental hygiene, health care administration, health science, nursing, and preventive/wellness health care), SOCIAL SCIENCE (American studies, history, liberal arts/general studies, political science/government, psychobiology, psychology, and sociology). Medical biology, marine biology, and athletic training are the largest.

Required: A total of at least 120 credits with a minimum GPA of 2.0 is required for graduation. Some programs require more than 120 credits. Students must take 43 credits in a liberal arts core curriculum of humanities, sciences, and social sciences. Most majors require 1-semester internships. Courses in English composition, human traditions,environmental studies, lab science, creative arts, and math are required.

Special: UNE offers cross-registration with the Greater Portland Alliance of Colleges and Universities, internships in all majors, work-study programs, study abroad, dual majors in all departments, a 3-4 medical program, and a 3-2 pre-physician assistant program. There are 2 national honor societies.

Faculty/Classroom: 50% of faculty are male; 50%, female. 81% teach undergraduates. No introductory courses are taught by graduate students. The average class size in an introductory lecture is 25; in a laboratory, 18; and in a regular course, 22.

Admissions: 91% of the 2005-2006 applicants were accepted. The SAT scores for the 2005-2006 freshman class were: Verbal--36% below 500, 50% between 500 and 599, 13% between 600 and 700, and 2% above 700; Math--35% below 500, 45% between 500 and 599, 19% between 600 and 700, and 1% above 700. 40% of the current freshmen were in the top fifth of their class; 76% were in the top two fifths.

Requirements: The SAT is required. In addition, applicants should be high school graduates with 4 years of English, 3 years each of math and science, and 2 years each of history and social studies. The GED is accepted. A personal interview is recommended. AP and CLEP credits are accepted. Important factors in the admissions decision are advanced placement or honor courses, recommendations by school officials, and leadership record.

Procedure: Freshmen are admitted fall and spring. Entrance exams should be taken in the spring of the junior year or the fall of the senior year. There is a deferred admissions plan. There is a rolling admissions plan. Early decision applications should be filed by November 15, along with a $40 fee. Notification of early decision is sent December 15; regular decision, on a rolling basis. Applications are accepted on-line.

Transfer: 142 transfer students enrolled in 2004-2005. Transfer applicants should present a GPA of at least 2.5 in college work. An interview is recommended. 30 of at least 120 credits required for the bachelor's degree must be completed at UNE.

Visiting: There are regularly scheduled orientations for prospective students, including a tour and information session, and an interview if the student has formally applied. There are guides for informal visits and visitors may sit in on classes. To schedule a visit, contact the Admissions Office at admission@une.edu.

Financial Aid: In 2005-2006, 83% of all full-time students received some form of financial aid. 72% of full-time freshmen and 76% of continuing full-time students received need-based aid. The average freshman award was $18,574. Need-based scholarships or need-based grants averaged $11,382, and need-based self-help aid (loans and jobs) averaged $4554. The average financial indebtedness of the 2005 graduate was $37,507. The FAFSA is required. The deadline for filing freshman financial aid applications for fall entry is May 1.

International Students: There are 5 international students enrolled. They must score satisfactorily on the TOEFL.

Computers: Wireless access is available. All students may access the system. There are no time limits and no fees.

Graduates: From July 1, 2004 to June 30, 2005, 210 bachelor's degrees were awarded. The most popular majors were health science

(24%), medical biology (10%), and marine biology (10%). In an average class, 49% graduate in 4 years or less.

Admissions Contact: Robert Pecchia, Associate Dean of Admissions. E-mail: *admissions@une.edu* Web: *www.une.edu*

UNIVERSITY OF SOUTHERN MAINE   B-6

Gorham, ME 04038-1088   (207) 780-5670
(800) 800-4876; Fax: (207) 780-5640

Full-time: 2006 men, 2782 women	Faculty: 402; IIA, av$
Part-time: 1504 men, 2330 women	Ph.D.s: 74%
Graduate: 740 men, 1612 women	Student/Faculty: 12 to 1
Year: semesters, summer session	Tuition: $5858 ($14,678)
Application Deadline: February 15	Room & Board: $6756
Freshman Class: 3305 applied, 2848 accepted, 1009 enrolled	
SAT Verbal/Math: 510/501*	ACT: 20 COMPETITIVE

The University of Southern Maine, founded in 1878, is a publicly funded, multicampus, comprehensive, residential, liberal arts institution serving the University of Maine system. There are 5 undergraduate and 8 graduate schools. In addition to regional accreditation, USM has baccalaureate program accreditation with AACSB, ABET, CSAB, CSWE, NASM, NCATE, NLN, and NRPA. The 3 libraries contain 570,000 volumes, 1,046,878 microform items, and 2705 audio/video tapes/CDs/DVDs, and subscribe to 3200 periodicals including electronic. Computerized library services include the card catalog, interlibrary loans, and database searching. Special learning facilities include a learning resource center, art gallery, planetarium, radio station, TV station, and cartography collections. The 144-acre campus is in an urban area 110 miles north of Boston and 10 miles west of the urban Portland campus. Including any residence halls, there are 66 buildings.

Student Life: 90% of undergraduates are from Maine. Others are from 35 states, 27 foreign countries, and Canada. 97% are white. The average age of freshmen is 19; all undergraduates, 25.

Housing: 1500 students can be accommodated in university housing, which includes coed dorm, on-campus apartments, and married-student housing. In addition, there are honors houses and special-interest houses. On-campus housing is guaranteed for all 4 years. 78% of students commute. All students may keep cars.

Activities: 4% of men belong to 1 local fraternity and 3 national fraternities; 4% of women belong to 2 local and 2 national sororities. There are 100 groups on campus, including art, band, cheerleading, chess, choir, chorale, chorus, computers, dance, drama, ethnic, film, gay, honors, international, jazz band, literary magazine, musical theater, newspaper, opera, orchestra, photography, political, professional, radio and TV, religious, social, social service, and student government. Popular campus events include Winter Weekend, Spring Fling, and comedy nights.

Sports: There are 12 intercollegiate sports for men and 13 for women, and 14 intramural sports for men and 14 for women. Facilities include gyms, tennis courts, athletic fields, racquetball and squash courts, cross-country ski trails, two weight-training and fitness facilities, an ice arena, a field house, and an indoor track.

Disabled Students: All of the campus is accessible. Wheelchair ramps, elevators, special parking, specially equipped rest rooms, special class scheduling, lowered drinking fountains, and lowered telephones are available.

Services: Counseling and information services are available, as is tutoring in most subjects. There is a reader service for the blind, and remedial math, reading, and writing.

Campus Safety and Security: Measures include 24-hour foot and vehicle patrol, self-defense education, security escort services, and shuttle buses. There are informal discussions, pamphlets/posters/films, emergency telephones, lighted pathways/sidewalks, and preventive programs within residence halls.

Programs of Study: USM confers B.A., B.S., B.F.A., and B.M. degrees. Associate, master's, and doctoral degrees are also awarded. Bachelor's degrees are awarded in BIOLOGICAL SCIENCE (biology/biological science), BUSINESS (accounting and business administration and management), COMMUNICATIONS AND THE ARTS (communications, dramatic arts, English, fine arts, French, music, and music performance), COMPUTER AND PHYSICAL SCIENCE (chemistry, computer science, geology, geoscience, mathematics, and physics), EDUCATION (music and technical), ENGINEERING AND ENVIRONMENTAL DESIGN (electrical/electronics engineering, environmental science, and industrial engineering technology), HEALTH PROFESSIONS (environmental health science, health science, nursing, recreation therapy, and sports medicine), SOCIAL SCIENCE (anthropology, economics, geography, history, philosophy, political science/government, psychology, social work, sociology, and women's studies). Electrical engineering, computer science, and nursing are the strongest academically. Business administration, nursing, and psychology are the largest.

Required: A total of 120 hours, of which 36 to 94 are in the major, and a minimum GPA of 2.0 are required for graduation. All students must fulfill the distribution requirements of the 3-part core curriculum: basic competence, methods of inquiry/ways of knowing, and interdisciplinary studies.

Special: Cross-registration within the University of Maine system and 4 Greater Portland colleges, a Washington semester, and study abroad in more than 12 countries are offered. Internships, co-op and work-study programs, a B.A.-B.S. degree, dual and student-designed majors, a 2-2 engineering program with the University of Maine, credit for life experience, nondegree study, and pass/fail options are also available. There is a January intersession. There are 2 national honor societies, a freshman honors program, and 1 departmental honors program.

Faculty/Classroom: 57% of faculty are male; 43%, female. 80% teach undergraduates, 100% do research, and 80% do both. No introductory courses are taught by graduate students. The average class size in an introductory lecture is 50; in a laboratory, 20; and in a regular course, 22.

Admissions: 86% of the 2005-2006 applicants were accepted. The SAT scores for the 2005-2006 freshman class were: Verbal--46% below 500, 38% between 500 and 599, 14% between 600 and 700, and 1% above 700; Math--48% below 500, 40% between 500 and 599, 12% between 600 and 700, and 1% above 700. The ACT scores were 54% below 21, 25% between 21 and 23, 15% between 24 and 26, and 5% between 27 and 28. 23% of the current freshmen were in the top fifth of their class; 57% were in the top two fifths. 5 freshmen graduated first in their class.

Requirements: The SAT or ACT is required. In addition, in addition, applicants must be graduates of an accredited secondary school. The GED is accepted. Either 41 academic credits or 20 1/2 Carnegie units are required. Secondary school courses should include 4 years of English, 3 of math, 2 each of a foreign language and lab science, and 1 each of history and social studies. An essay is required, as are auditions for music applicants and interviews for applicants to the School of Applied Science. Guidance counselor recommendations are required for those students applying during their senior year. USM requires applicants to be in the upper 50% of their class. A GPA of 2.0 is required. AP and CLEP credits are accepted. Important factors in the admissions decision are advanced placement or honor courses, recommendations by school officials, and extracurricular activities record.

Procedure: Freshmen are admitted fall and spring. Entrance exams should be taken between May of the junior year and January of the senior year. There is a deferred admissions plan. Applications should be filed by February 15 for fall entry and December 1 for spring entry. Notification is sent on a rolling basis. Applications are accepted on-line.

Transfer: 784 transfer students enrolled in 2004-2005. Applicants must have a minimum GPA of 2.0 or 2.75 for those from nonregionally accredited institutions. Students who have been out of high school for less than 3 years must submit SAT scores. 30 of 120 credits required for the bachelor's degree must be completed at USM.

Visiting: There are regularly scheduled orientations for prospective students, including regularly scheduled campus tours and group information sessions, as well as special events such as fall open houses. Interviews are also available on request. There are guides for informal visits and visitors may sit in on classes. To schedule a visit, contact the Office of Admission.

Financial Aid: The FAFSA is required. The deadline for filing freshman financial aid applications for fall entry is February 15.

International Students: International students must take the TOEFL.

Computers: Wireless access is available. There are approximately 250 PCs available. All students may access the system 16 hours per day. There are no time limits and no fees.

Graduates: From July 1, 2004 to June 30, 2005, 1000 bachelor's degrees were awarded. The most popular majors were nursing (14%), business (9%), and psychology (6%).

Admissions Contact: Dee Gardner, Director of Admission. E-mail: *usmadm@maine.maine.edu* Web: *http://www.usm.maine.edu*

MARYLAND

POPULATION
DENSITY
● 25,000 and over

0 10 20 30 40 50
Miles

BALTIMORE HEBREW UNIVERSITY　　　D-2

Baltimore, MD 21215-3996

(410) 578-6903
(888) 248-7420; Fax: (410) 578-6940

Full-time: 10 men, 20 women	**Faculty:** 8
Part-time: 10 men, 50 women	**Ph.D.s:** 90%
Graduate: 20 men, 60 women	**Student/Faculty:** 3 to 1
Year: semesters, summer session	**Tuition:** $8900
Application Deadline: see profile	**Room & Board:** n/app
Freshman Class: n/av	
SAT or ACT: not required	**SPECIAL**

Baltimore Hebrew University, founded in 1919, is a private nonsectarian institution of Jewish higher education and a major center of advanced Jewish study in the United States. There is 1 graduate school. Some figures in the above capsule are approximate. The library contains 100,000 volumes, 7500 microform items, and 1100 audio/video tapes/CDs/DVDs, and subscribes to 225 periodicals including electronic. Computerized library services include the card catalog, interlibrary loans, database searching, and Internet access. Special learning facilities include a language lab. The 2-acre campus is in an urban area in residential northwest Baltimore. There is 1 building.

Student Life: 96% of undergraduates are from Maryland. Others are from 8 states, 4 foreign countries, and Canada. 98% are white. Most are Jewish. The average age of all undergraduates is 44.

Housing: There are no residence halls. All of students commute. Alcohol is not permitted. All students may keep cars.

Activities: There are no fraternities or sororities. Popular campus events include film series, singles brunches, and concerts.

Sports: There is no sports program at BHU.

Disabled Students: Wheelchair ramps and special parking are available.

Services: Counseling and information services are available, as is tutoring in some subjects, including Hebrew, Yiddish, and Russian.

Campus Safety and Security: Measures include security escort services, pamphlets/posters/films, lighted pathways/sidewalks, a lighted parking lot, and guards during open building hours.

Programs of Study: BHU confers the B.A. degree. Master's and doctoral degrees are also awarded. Bachelor's degrees are awarded in SOCIAL SCIENCE (Judaic studies).

Required: To graduate, students must earn a minimum GPA of 2.0 in a total of 120 credits, including 60 of Jewish studies in literature, philosophy, and history, and 60 of general studies in social and behavioral sciences, arts and humanities, literature, physical or biological science, math, and English composition.

Special: BHU offers study abroad in Israel, cross-registration with Johns Hopkins and Towson Universities and Goucher College, and co-op programs with Johns Hopkins University, University of Maryland/Baltimore County, and University of Maryland School of Social Work.

Faculty/Classroom: 50% of faculty are male; 50%, female. 85% teach undergraduates and 90% do research. No introductory courses are taught by graduate students. The average class size in an introductory lecture is 10 and in a regular course, 10.

Requirements: A candidate's high school record is reviewed by the dean, who also conducts a personal interview. A GPA of 3.0 is required. AP and CLEP credits are accepted. Important factors in the admissions decision are recommendations by school officials, personality/intangible qualities, and evidence of special talent.

Procedure: Freshmen are admitted fall and spring.There is a rolling admissions plan. Check with the school for current application deadlines. The fall 2005 application fee was $50. Notification is sent on a rolling basis.

Transfer: Applicants must meet freshman requirements. 30 of 120 credits required for the bachelor's degree must be completed at BHU.

Visiting: There are regularly scheduled orientations for prospective students. There are guides for informal visits and visitors may sit in on classes. To schedule a visit, contact Director of Admissions.

Financial Aid: In a recent year 80% of full-time freshmen received need-based aid. The FAFSA and the college's own financial statement are required.

International Students: They must score satisfactorily on the TOEFL and also take the college's own test.

Computers: All students may access the system. There are no time limits and no fees.

Admissions Contact: Director of Admissions. E-mail: *bhu@bhu.edu* Web: *www.bhu.edu*

BOWIE STATE UNIVERSITY　　　D-3

Bowie, MD 20715　　　(301) 860-3421; Fax: (301)860-3438

Full-time: 1190 men, 1940 women	**Faculty:** 158; IIA, av$
Part-time: 290 men, 580 women	**Ph.D.s:** n/av
Graduate: 380 men, 1090 women	**Student/Faculty:** 20 to 1
Year: semesters, summer session	**Tuition:** $4860 ($12,470)
Application Deadline: see profile	**Room & Board:** $6020
Freshman Class: n/av	
SAT or ACT: required	**COMPETITIVE+**

Bowie State University, founded in 1865, is a historically black, publicly supported comprehensive liberal arts institution within the University System of Maryland. There are 3 undergraduate schools and 1 graduate school. Some figures in the above capsule are approximate. In addition to regional accreditation, BSU has baccalaureate program accreditation with ACBSP, CSAB, CSWE, NCATE, and NLN. The library contains 242,907 volumes, 424,056 microform items, and 6104 audio/video tapes/CDs/DVDs, and subscribes to 748 periodicals including electronic. Computerized library services include the card catalog, interlibrary loans, database searching, and Internet access. Special learning facilities include a learning resource center, art gallery, radio station, TV station, media center, and satellite operations and control center. The 312-acre campus is in a suburban area 18 miles north of Washington, D.C. Including any residence halls, there are 26 buildings.

Student Life: 89% of undergraduates are from Maryland. Others are from 31 states, 39 foreign countries, and Canada. 95% are from public schools. 90% are African American. The average age of all undergraduates is 24. 30% do not continue beyond their first year; 70% remain to graduate.

Housing: 890 students can be accommodated in college housing, which includes single-sex and coed dorms and off-campus apartments. In addition, there are honors houses. On-campus housing is available on a first-come, first-served basis. Priority is given to out-of-town students. 78% of students commute. Alcohol is not permitted. All students may keep cars.

Activities: 2% of men belong to 6 national fraternities; 2% of women belong to 4 national sororities. There are 52 groups on campus, including art, band, cheerleading, choir, chorale, commuter, computers, dance, drama, drill team, honors, international, jazz band, literary magazine, marching band, musical theater, NAACP, pep band, political, professional, radio and TV, religious, social, social service, student government, urban league and yearbook. Popular campus events include Black History Month Convocation, Parents/Founders Day, and Honors Convocation.

Sports: There are 4 intercollegiate sports for men and 6 for women. Facilities include an athletic complex with a basketball arena, an Olympic-size pool, 8 handball/racquetball courts, a wrestling room, weight training rooms, a dance studio, a gymnastics room, a 4500-seat football/soccer stadium, a baseball diamond, 6 outdoor tennis courts, 4 outdoor basketball courts, and a track-and-field facility with a walking/jogging lane.

Disabled Students: All of the campus is accessible. Wheelchair ramps, elevators, special parking, specially equipped rest rooms, lowered drinking fountains, lowered telephones, and wide doors are available.

Services: Counseling and information services are available, as is tutoring in most subjects. There is a reader service for the blind, and remedial math, reading, and writing.

Campus Safety and Security: Measures include 24-hour foot and vehicle patrol, self-defense education, security escort services, and shuttle buses. There are informal discussions, pamphlets/posters/films, emergency telephones, and lighted pathways/sidewalks.

Programs of Study: BSU confers B.A., B.S. degrees. Master's and doctoral degrees are also awarded. Bachelor's degrees are awarded in BIOLOGICAL SCIENCE (biology/biological science), BUSINESS (business administration and management), COMMUNICATIONS AND THE ARTS (broadcasting, English, and fine arts), COMPUTER AND PHYSICAL SCIENCE (computer science and mathematics), EDUCATION (early childhood, elementary, English, and science), ENGINEERING AND ENVIRONMENTAL DESIGN (computer technology), HEALTH PROFESSIONS (nursing), SOCIAL SCIENCE (criminal justice, history, interdisciplinary studies, political science/government, psychology, social work, and sociology). Business administration, computer science, and elementary education are the largest.

Required: A total of 120 credit hours with a minimum GPA of 2.0 is required for graduation. The number of hours that must be taken in a student's major varies. General education requirements include 12 credits in social science, 9 in arts and humanities, 7 to 8 in sciences, 6 in English compositions, and 3 each in math, computer literacy, health and wellness, and freshman seminar.

Special: BSU offers cooperative programs, internships in communications and practice teaching, work-study programs, B.A.-B.S. degrees, dual majors, credit for life experience, and a 3-2 engineering degree. Dual-degree programs in engineering and dentistry are available at the University of Maryland. Cross-registration is offered with other members of the University System of Maryland. There are 16 national honor societies and a freshman honors program.

Faculty/Classroom: 57% of faculty are male; 43%, female. 23% do research and 23% both teach and do research. No introductory courses are taught by graduate students. The average class size in an introductory lecture is 30; in a laboratory, 20; and in a regular class, 25.

Requirements: The SAT or ACT is required. Applicants should be graduates of an accredited secondary school. The GED is accepted. Students should have completed 15 academic units, including 4 of English, 3 each of math, sciences, and social science/history, and 2 of a foreign language or advanced technology. A GPA of 2.0 is required. AP and CLEP credits are accepted. Important factors in the admissions decision are advanced placement or honor courses, extracurricular activities record, and leadership record.

Procedure: Freshmen are admitted fall and spring. Entrance exams should be taken before the end of January. There is a deferred admissions and a rolling admissions plan. Applications are accepted on-line.

Check with the school for current application deadlines. The fall 2005 application fee was $40.

Transfer: 394 transfer students enrolled in a receny year. Applicants must have a minimum GPA of 2.0. The SAT is required if fewer than 24 credit hours are being transferred. 30 of 120 credits required for the bachelor's degree must be completed at BSU.

Visiting: There are regularly scheduled orientations for prospective students. There are guides for informal visits. To schedule a visit, contact Vonetta Rector at (301) 860-3428 or ugradadmissions@bowiestate.edu.

Financial Aid: In a recent year, 58% of all full-time freshmen received some form of financial aid. 52% of full-time freshmen and 50% of continuing full-time students received need-based aid. The average freshman award was $5846. Need-based scholarships or need-based grants averaged $1200 ($4890 maximum); need-based self-help aid (loans and jobs) averaged $5125 ($6530 maximum); non-need-based athletic scholarships averaged $3289 ($5000 maximum); and other non-need-based awards and non-need-based scholarships averaged $2000 ($2999 maximum). 3% of undergraduates work part time. Average annual earnings from campus work are $2500. The FAFSA and the college's own financial statement are required. Check with the school for current deadlines.

International Students: There were 41 international students enrolled in a recent year. The school actively recruits these students. They must score satisfactorily on the written TOEFL and also take the SAT, ACT, or the college's own entrance exam.

Computers: All students may access the system 24 hours a day. There are no time limits. The fee is $120.

Graduates: In a recent year, 540 bachelor's degrees were awarded. The most popular major was psychology (10%). In an average class, 2% graduate in 3 years or less, 12% graduate in 4 years or less, 30% graduate in 5 years or less, and 38% graduate in 6 years or less. Of a recent graduating class, 46% were enrolled in graduate school within 6 months of graduation and 68% were employed.

Admissions Contact: Shingiral Chanaiwa, Director of Admissions. E-mail: schanaiwa@bowiestate.edu Web: www.bowiestate.edu

CAPITOL COLLEGE
Laurel, MD 20708

D-3

(301) 953-3200
(800) 950-1992; Fax: (301) 953-1442

Full-time: 110 men, 40 women	**Faculty:** n/av
Part-time: 130 men, 30 women	**Ph.D.s:** n/av
Graduate: 340 men, 130 women	**Student/Faculty:** n/av
Year: semesters, summer session	**Tuition:** $17,400
Application Deadline: open	**Room & Board:** $3850
Freshman Class: n/av	
SAT: required	**COMPETITIVE**

Capitol College was founded in 1927 as the Capitol Radio Engineering Institute, a correspondence school. Today it is a private college offering undergraduate programs in engineering and computer technology, as well as graduate programs in management and electronic commerce. Some figures in the above capsule are approximate. In addition to regional accreditation, Capitol has baccalaureate program accreditation with ABET. The library contains 10,000 volumes, and subscribes to 100 periodicals including electronic. Computerized library services include the card catalog, interlibrary loans, and database searching. Special learning facilities include a learning resource center and state-of-the-art labs. The 52-acre campus is in a rural area 19 miles north of Washington, D.C. Including any residence halls, there are 9 buildings.

Student Life: 72% of undergraduates are from Maryland. Others are from 16 states and 21 foreign countries. 43% are white; 39% African American. The average age of freshmen is 23; all undergraduates, 28. 41% do not continue beyond their first year.

Housing: 100 students can be accommodated in college housing, which includes coed on-campus apartments. On-campus housing is available on a first-come, first-served basis. Priority is given to out-of-town students. 87% of students commute. All students may keep cars.

Activities: There are no fraternities or sororities. There are 17 groups on campus, including chess, computers, literary magazine, newspaper, professional, and student government. Popular campus events include Octoberfest and Spring Bash.

Sports: Facilities include an off-campus gym, a basketball court, a student center, and an athletic field.

Disabled Students: All of the campus is accessible. Wheelchair ramps, elevators, special parking, specially equipped rest rooms, and lowered drinking fountains are available.

Services: Counseling and information services are available, as is tutoring in most subjects, including math, electronics, English, and developmental English.

Campus Safety and Security: Measures include lighted pathways/sidewalks.

Programs of Study: Capitol confers the B.S. degree. Associate and master's degrees are also awarded. Bachelor's degrees are awarded in

COMMUNICATIONS AND THE ARTS (telecommunications), COMPUTER AND PHYSICAL SCIENCE (optics), ENGINEERING AND ENVIRONMENTAL DESIGN (computer engineering, electrical/electronics engineering, and engineering technology). Electrical/electronics engineering is the strongest academically and has the largest enrollment.

Required: A minimum GPA of 2.0 and 130 to 137 credit hours are required for graduation. Additional curriculum requirements vary with the major.

Special: Internships and work-study programs are offered through the school's cooperative education program. There are 2 national honor societies.

Faculty/Classroom: All teach undergraduates. No introductory courses are taught by graduate students. The average class size in an introductory lecture is 20 and in a regular course, 22.

Requirements: The SAT is required. Applicants should be graduates of an accredited secondary school. The GED is accepted. 20 academic credits or 20 Carnegie units are required. Secondary school courses must include 4 units of English, 3 of math, and 2 each of science and social studies. An essay and an interview are recommended. Capitol requires applicants to be in the upper 50% of their class. A GPA of 2.8 is required. AP and CLEP credits are accepted. Important factors in the admissions decision are advanced placement or honor courses, recommendations by school officials, and extracurricular activities record.

Procedure: Freshmen are admitted to all sessions. Entrance exams should be taken by March 1. Application deadlines are open. The fall 2005 application fee was $25. Applications are accepted on-line.

Transfer: Transfer students must have earned 15 college credits and a minimum GPA of 2.0. 40 of 130 credits required for the bachelor's degree must be completed at Capitol.

Visiting: There are regularly scheduled orientations for prospective students. There are guides for informal visits and visitors may sit in on classes and stay overnight. To schedule a visit, contact the Admissions Office.

Financial Aid: Capitol is a member of CSS. The CSS/Profile is required.

International Students: The school actively recruits these students. They must score satisfactorily on the TOEFL.

Computers: All students may access the system. There are no time limits and no fees.

Admissions Contact: Darnell Edwards, Director of Admissions.
E-mail: *admissions@capitol-college.edu* Web: *www.capitol-college.edu*

COLLEGE OF NOTRE DAME OF MARYLAND   D-2
Baltimore, MD 21210

(410) 532-5330
(800) 435-0300; Fax: (410) 532-6287

Full-time: 1 man, 630 women	Faculty: 74; IIB, av$
Part-time: 90 men, 880 women	Ph.D.s: 65%
Graduate: 270 men, 1190 women	Student/Faculty: 8 to 1
Year: 4-1-4, summer session	Tuition: $20,300
Application Deadline: open	Room & Board: $7400
Freshman Class: n/av	
SAT or ACT: required	COMPETITIVE

The College of Notre Dame of Maryland, founded in 1873, is a private liberal arts institution primarily for women and affiliated with the Catholic Church. Some figures in the above capsule are approximate. In addition to regional accreditation, Notre Dame has baccalaureate program accreditation with NLN. The library contains 290,000 volumes, 378,138 microform items, and 24,000 audio/video tapes/CDs/DVDs, and subscribes to 2000 periodicals including electronic. Computerized library services include the card catalog and database searching. Special learning facilities include a learning resource center, art gallery, planetarium, radio station, TV station, graphic arts studio, roof-top greenhouse, and cultural center. The 58-acre campus is in a suburban area 10 miles north of Baltimore. Including any residence halls, there are 11 buildings.

Student Life: 70% of undergraduates are from Maryland. Others are from 21 states.

Housing: 450 students can be accommodated in college housing, which includes single-sex dorms. On-campus housing is guaranteed for all 4 years. 65% of students live on campus; of those, 60% remain on campus on weekends. Alcohol is not permitted. All students may keep cars.

Activities: There are no fraternities or sororities. There are 24 groups on campus, including art, choir, dance, drama, ethnic, honors, international, literary magazine, newspaper, political, professional, radio and TV, religious, social, social service, student government, and yearbook. Popular campus events include Honors Convocation, Antostal Day, and Multicultural Awareness Week.

Sports: Facilities include a sports/activities complex that houses racquetball courts, a dance studio, a fitness center, an indoor walking track, a game room, an activities resource center, and a basketball court.

Disabled Students: 98% of the campus is accessible. Wheelchair ramps, elevators, special parking, specially equipped rest rooms, and lowered drinking fountains are available.

Services: Counseling and information services are available, as is tutoring in most subjects.

Campus Safety and Security: Measures include 24-hour foot and vehicle patrol, self-defense education, security escort services, and informal discussions. There are pamphlets/posters/films and lighted pathways/sidewalks.

Programs of Study: Notre Dame confers B.A. and B.S. degrees. Master's degrees are also awarded. Bachelor's degrees are awarded in BIOLOGICAL SCIENCE (biology/biological science), BUSINESS (accounting, banking and finance, business administration and management, international business management, and marketing/retailing/merchandising), COMMUNICATIONS AND THE ARTS (art history and appreciation, classics, communications, English, graphic design, modern language, music, photography, and studio art), COMPUTER AND PHYSICAL SCIENCE (chemistry, computer science, information sciences and systems, mathematics, and physics), EDUCATION (art, early childhood, elementary, foreign languages, music, science, secondary, and special), ENGINEERING AND ENVIRONMENTAL DESIGN (preengineering), HEALTH PROFESSIONS (nursing, predentistry, premedicine, and prepharmacy), SOCIAL SCIENCE (economics, history, interdisciplinary studies, international relations, liberal arts/general studies, political science/government, prelaw, psychology, and religion). Business, education, and communication arts are the strongest academically.

Required: To graduate, students must complete a total of 128 credit hours with a minimum GPA of 2.0 (2.5 in many majors). All students must fulfill the distribution requirements in the general education core, the major, and electives, and must demonstrate proficiency in writing, public speaking, computer literacy, and library research. In most majors, a minimum of 42 hours is required. All students must take a speech course and 2 courses in phys ed, and some majors require senior practicums.

Special: The college offers cross-registration with Johns Hopkins, Towson State, and Morgan State Universities; Coppin State, Goucher, and Loyola Colleges; and the Maryland Institute College of Art. Study abroad, internships, dual bachelor's degrees in nursing and engineering, 3-2 engineering degrees with Johns Hopkins University and the University of Maryland, and pass/fail options are available. Notre Dame's Weekend College offers bachelor's degree programs for employed adults. There are 8 national honor societies, a freshman honors program, and 4 departmental honors programs.

Faculty/Classroom: 30% of faculty are male; 70%, female. All teach undergraduates. The average class size in an introductory lecture is 30; in a laboratory, 20; and in a regular course, 20.

Requirements: The SAT or ACT is required for scholarship purposes. In addition, applicants should be graduates of an accredited secondary school. 18 academic credits are required, including 4 units of English, 3 each of math and a foreign language, and 2 each of history and science, plus 4 electives. An essay is required and an interview is recommended. A GPA of 2.5 is required. AP credits are accepted. Important factors in the admissions decision are recommendations by school officials, advanced placement or honor courses, and leadership record.

Procedure: Freshmen are admitted fall and spring. Entrance exams should be taken no later than January of the senior year. There are early decision, early admissions, rolling admissions and deferred admissions plans. Application deadlines are open. Applications are accepted on-line.

Transfer: Notre Dame requires a minimum GPA of 2.5 for transfer students but recommends a GPA of 3.0. Students must also submit a letter of recommendation and an essay. 60 of 128 credits required for the bachelor's degree must be completed at Notre Dame.

Visiting: There are regularly scheduled orientations for prospective students, consisting of programs in June and January, each of which includes a stay in the dormitory, registration, and advisement. There are guides for informal visits and visitors may sit in on classes. To schedule a visit, contact the Office of Admissions.

Financial Aid: In a recent year, 85% of all full-time freshmen and 89% of continuing full-time students received some form of financial aid. 80% of full-time freshmen and 75% of continuing full-time students received need-based aid. The average freshman award was $20,796. Need-based scholarships or need-based grants averaged $15,600 ($22,750 maximum); need-based self-help aid (loans and jobs) averaged $4011 ($6125 maximum); and other non-need-based awards and non-need-based scholarships averaged $9202 ($18,700 maximum). Notre Dame is a member of CSS. The CSS/Profile or FAFSA is required.

International Students: The school actively recruits these students. They must the college's own entrance exam for placement purposes.

Computers: All students may access the system 7 days a week. There are no time limits and no fees.

Admissions Contact: Sharon Bogdan, Director of Admissions.
E-mail: *admiss@ndm.edu* Web: *www.ndm.edu*

COLUMBIA UNION COLLEGE   D-3
Takoma Park, MD 20912

(301) 891-4080
(800) 835-4212; Fax: (301) 891-4230

Full-time: 269 men, 461 women	Faculty: 53; IIB, --$
Part-time: 101 men, 187 women	Ph.Ds: 51%
Graduate: 12 men, 17 women	Student/Faculty: 14 to 1
Year: semesters, summer session	Tuition: $17,586
Application Deadline: August 1	Room & Board: $5950
Freshman Class: 1351 applied, 752 accepted, 172 enrolled	
SAT or ACT required	**LESS COMPETITIVE**

Columbia Union College, founded in 1904, is a private liberal arts institution affiliated with the Seventh-day Adventist Church. In addition to regional accreditation, CUC has baccalaureate program accreditation with CAHEA and NLN. The library contains 141,152 volumes and 7500 audio/video tapes/CDs/DVDs, and subscribes to 9000 periodicals including electronic. Computerized library services include the card catalog, interlibrary loans, database searching, and Internet access. Special learning facilities include a learning resource center and radio station. The 19-acre campus is in a suburban area 7 miles north of Washington, D.C. Including any residence halls, there are 17 buildings.

Student Life: 56% of undergraduates are from Maryland. Students are from 40 states, 22 foreign countries, and Canada. 53% are from public schools. 57% are African American; 17% white. The average age of freshmen is 18; all undergraduates, 27. 38% do not continue beyond their first year; 62% remain to graduate.

Housing: 440 students can be accommodated in college housing, which includes single-sex dorms and married-student housing. On-campus housing is guaranteed for all 4 years. 52% of students commute. Alcohol is not permitted. All students may keep cars.

Activities: There are no fraternities or sororities. There are 11 groups on campus, including band, choir, chorale, ethnic, honors, newspaper, orchestra, radio and TV, religious, student government, and yearbook. Popular campus events include Intercultural Communication Week, Parents Weekend, and Taste of Takoma.

Sports: There are 6 intercollegiate sports for men and 5 for women, and 5 intramural sports for men and 4 for women. Facilities include a swimming pool, a gym, racquetball and tennis courts, a sports field, a student lounge, and a weight room.

Disabled Students: 1% of the campus is accessible. Elevators and specially equipped rest rooms are available.

Services: Counseling and information services are available, as is tutoring in some subjects, including all English, math, accounting, and chemistry courses. There is a reader service for the blind and remedial math and writing.

Campus Safety and Security: Measures include 24-hour foot and vehicle patrol, security escort services, informal discussions, and pamphlets/posters/films. There are lighted pathways/sidewalks.

Programs of Study: CUC confers B.A., B.S., and B.M. degrees. Associate and master's degrees are also awarded. Bachelor's degrees are awarded in BIOLOGICAL SCIENCE (biochemistry), BUSINESS (accounting, business administration and management, management science, and personnel management), COMMUNICATIONS AND THE ARTS (communications, English, journalism, and music), COMPUTER AND PHYSICAL SCIENCE (chemistry, computer science, information sciences and systems, and mathematics), EDUCATION (elementary, English, and mathematics), HEALTH PROFESSIONS (health care administration, nursing, predentistry, premedicine, and respiratory therapy), SOCIAL SCIENCE (history, liberal arts/general studies, prelaw, psychology, and religion). Communications, business, and psychology are the largest.

Required: To graduate, students must earn 120 to 128 credit hours, including 36 upper division, with a minimum GPA of 2.0 overall and 2.5 in the major. Students must take 12 hours of religion, 9 of social sciences, 8 of physical sciences, natural sciences, and math, 6 of humanities and practical and applied arts, and 3 of phys ed and health. Courses in English, communication, and computer science are also required.

Special: CUC offers co-op programs in business, communication, computer science, English, biochemistry, and math, internships in counseling psychology, history and political science, and through a Washington D.C. experience, work-study programs, a general studies degree, student-designed majors, credit for life experience, nondegree study, a Washington semester, and pass/fail options. Dual majors are available in engineering/chemistry and math, and a 3-2 engineering degree is offered with the University of Maryland. Students may study abroad in France, Spain, Austria and several other countries. There is an adult evening program for degree completion as well as an external (correspondence) degree. Accelerated degrees are available for adult learners only. There are 6 national honor societies.

Faculty/Classroom: 57% of faculty are male; 43%, female. All teach undergraduates and 10% both teach and do research. No introductory courses are taught by graduate students. The average class size in an introductory lecture is 30; in a laboratory, 16; and in a regular course, 12.

Admissions: 56% of the 2005-2006 applicants were accepted. The SAT scores for the 2005-2006 freshman class were: Verbal--77% below 500, 17% between 500 and 599, 6% between 600 and 700, and 1% above 700; Math--79% below 500, 19% between 500 and 599, and 2% between 600 and 700.

Requirements: A satisfactory score on the SAT or ACT is required. In addition, applicants must be graduates of an accredited secondary school. The GED is accepted. 21 Carnegie units are required, including 4 years of high school English and 2 years each of history, math, and lab science. An essay is recommended. A GPA of 2.5 is required. AP and CLEP credits are accepted. Important factors in the admissions decision are advanced placement or honor courses, leadership record, and recommendations by school officials.

Procedure: Freshmen are admitted to all sessions. Entrance exams should be taken in the fall semester of the senior year. There is a rolling admissions plan. There are early admissions and deferred admissions plans. Applications should be filed by August 1 for fall entry and December 1 for spring entry, along with a $25 fee. Notification is sent on a rolling basis. Applications are accepted on-line.

Transfer: 83 transfer students enrolled in 2004-2005. Transfer students must have at least 12 hours of college credit and a minimum GPA of 2.0. 30 of 120 to 128 credits required for the bachelor's degree must be completed at CUC.

Visiting: There are regularly scheduled orientations for prospective students. There are guides for informal visits and visitors may sit in on classes and stay overnight. To schedule a visit, contact the Office of Enrollment Services at enroll@cuc.edu.

Financial Aid: In 2005-2006, 98% of all full-time freshmen and 92% of continuing full-time students received some form of financial aid. The FAFSA is required. The deadline for filing freshman financial aid applications for fall entry is July 1.

International Students: There are 34 international students enrolled. They must score satisfactorily on the written TOEFL or on the electronic version a and also take the SAT or the ACT.

Computers: All students may access the system. It is strongly recommended that all students have a personal computer.

Graduates: From July 1, 2004 to June 30, 2005, 255 bachelor's degrees were awarded. The most popular majors were psychology (22%), business/marketing (14%), and nursing (8%). In an average class, 33% graduate in 6 years or less.

Admissions Contact: Emile John, Director of Admissions.
E-mail: enroll@cuc.edu Web: www.cuc.edu

COPPIN STATE COLLEGE   D-2
Baltimore, MD 21216

(410) 951-3600
(800) 635-3674; Fax: (410) 523-7351

Full-time: 635 men, 1790 women	Faculty: 110; IIB, av$
Part-time: 170 men, 690 women	Ph.Ds: 64%
Graduate: 160 men, 670 women	Student/Faculty: 22 to 1
Year: semesters, summer session	Tuition: $42340($10,100)
Application Deadline: see profile	Room & Board: $5960
Freshman Class: n/av	
SAT or ACT: required	**LESS COMPETITIVE**

Coppin State College, founded in 1900 and part of the University System of Maryland, offers undergraduate programs in liberal arts, teacher education, and nursing. There are 3 undergraduate schools and 1 graduate school. Figures in the above capsule and profile are approximate. In addition to regional accreditation, Coppin has baccalaureate program accreditation with NCATE and NLN. The library contains 200,000 volumes and 233,000 microform items, and subscribes to 715 periodicals including electronic. Computerized library services include the card catalog, interlibrary loans, and Internet access. Special learning facilities include a learning resource center, art gallery, radio station, TV station, and an on-campus video production company. The 45-acre campus is in an urban area in Baltimore. Including any residence halls, there are 9 buildings.

Student Life: 90% of undergraduates are from Maryland. Others are from 10 states and 5 foreign countries. 90% are from public schools. 80% are African American; 10% white. The average age of freshmen is 19; all undergraduates, 23.

Housing: 690 students can be accommodated in college housing, which includes coed dormitories. The housing office maintains lists of community housing available. On-campus housing is guaranteed for all 4 years. 93% of students commute. Alcohol is not permitted. All students may keep cars.

Activities: 20% of men and about 30% of women belong to 5 national fraternities; 27% of women belong to 4 national sororities. There are 40 groups on campus, including art, cheerleading, choir, chorus, computers, dance, drama, ethnic, film, honors, international, musical theater, newspaper, political, professional, radio and TV, religious, social, social service, student government, and yearbook. Popular campus events include the Lyceum Series, the Honors Program, and Black History Month.

Sports: There are 7 intercollegiate sports for men and 7 for women, and 5 intramural sports for men and 5 for women. Facilities include a 2500-seat gym, an indoor swimming pool, handball and racquetball courts, a soccer field, a dance studio, a weight room, a track, and a baseball field.

Disabled Students: 95% of the campus is accessible. Wheelchair ramps, elevators, special parking, specially equipped rest rooms, lowered drinking fountains, lowered telephones, and individual attention for students requiring specialized materials, equipment, or instructional style accommodation are available.

Services: Counseling and information services are available, as is tutoring in every subject. There is remedial math, reading, and writing.

Campus Safety and Security: Measures include 24-hour foot and vehicle patrol, security escort services, shuttle buses, and pamphlets/posters/films. There are emergency telephones and lighted pathways/sidewalks.

Programs of Study: Coppin confers B.A., B.S., and B.S.N. degrees. Master's degrees are also awarded. Bachelor's degrees are awarded in BIOLOGICAL SCIENCE (biology/biological science), BUSINESS (business administration and management, marketing management, and sports management), COMMUNICATIONS AND THE ARTS (English), COMPUTER AND PHYSICAL SCIENCE (chemistry, computer science, and mathematics), EDUCATION (elementary and special), ENGINEERING AND ENVIRONMENTAL DESIGN (preengineering), HEALTH PROFESSIONS (nursing, predentistry, and prepharmacy), SOCIAL SCIENCE (criminal justice, history, liberal arts/general studies, psychology, social science, and social work). Management science, education, and nursing are the strongest academically. Management science, education, and criminal justice are the largest.

Required: To graduate, all students must have a minimum 2.0 GPA and a minimum of 120 credit hours, with 36 to 40 hours in the major. Students must complete about 50 hours of liberal arts courses in English, math, speech, history, health, phys ed, natural and social sciences, and philosophy. All seniors must take a standardized exit exam relevant to their major.

Special: The college offers co-op programs with Dundalk Community College and Morgan University, internships in criminal justice, management science, and sociology, dual majors in engineering, pharmacy, physical therapy, and dentistry, study abroad and B.A.-B.S. degrees in all majors. Work-study is also available. There are 3 national honor societies, including Phi Beta Kappa, and a freshman honors program.

Faculty/Classroom: 54% of faculty are male; 46%, female. The average class size in a regular course is 25.

Requirements: The SAT or ACT is required. In addition, applicants must be graduates of an accredited secondary school with a minimum GPA of 2.0, or have a GED certificate. Students must have completed 4 courses in English, 2 courses each in history, math, science, and social studies, and 1 course in foreign language. Up to 15% of a freshman class may be admitted conditionally without these requirements, and those students who graduated high school more than 5 years ago will be reviewed individually. A GPA of 2.5 is required. CLEP credit is accepted. Important factors in the admissions decision are advanced placement or honor courses, extracurricular activities record, and evidence of special talent.

Procedure: Freshmen are admitted to all sessions. There are early decision, early admissions and rolling admissions plans. Check with the school for application deadlines. Notification is sent on a rolling basis. Applications are accepted on-line.

Transfer: Transfer students must have a minimum 2.0 GPA and be in good academic standing at the former institution. Applicants with fewer than 25 credits must meet freshman requirements. 30 of 120 credits required for the bachelor's degree must be completed at Coppin.

Visiting: There are regularly scheduled orientations for prospective students, consisting of open houses. There are guides for informal visits and visitors may sit in on classes. To schedule a visit, contact Admissions.

Financial Aid: Coppin is a member of CSS. The FAFSA and the college's own financial statement are required. Check with the school for application deadlines.

International Students: They must score satisfactorily on the written TOEFL or on the electronic version.

Computers: All students may access the system. There are no time limits and no fees.

Admissions Contact: Michelle Gross, Director of Admissions. E-mail: *admissions@coppin.edu* Web: *http://www.coppin.edu/*

FROSTBURG STATE UNIVERSITY B-1

Frostburg, MD 21532   (301) 687-4201; Fax: (301) 687-7074

Full-time: 2080 men, 1973 women	**Faculty:** 233; IIA, -$
Part-time: 137 men, 131 women	**Ph.D.s:** 85%
Graduate: 251 men, 469 women	**Student/Faculty:** 17 to 1
Year: semesters, summer session	**Tuition:** $6230 ($14,480)
Application Deadline: open	**Room & Board:** $6442
Freshman Class: n/av	
SAT: required	**COMPETITIVE**

Frostburg State University, founded in 1898, is a part of the University System of Maryland. The university offers programs through the colleges of liberal arts and sciences, business, and education. There are 3 undergraduate and 10 graduate schools. In addition to regional accreditation, FSU has baccalaureate program accreditation with AACSB, CSWE, NCATE, and NRPA. The library contains 356,200 volumes, 300,203 microform items, and 71,985 audio/video tapes/CDs/DVDs, and subscribes to 3390 periodicals including electronic. Computerized library services include the card catalog, interlibrary loans, and database searching. Special learning facilities include a learning resource center, art gallery, planetarium, radio station, TV station, environmental lab, and distance education labs. The 260-acre campus is in a small town about 150 miles west of Baltimore and northwest of Washington D.C. Including any residence halls, there are 32 buildings.

Student Life: 89% of undergraduates are from Maryland. Students are from 27 states, 20 foreign countries, and Canada. 80% are white; 13% African American. The average age of freshmen is 18; all undergraduates, 21. 29% do not continue beyond their first year; 47% remain to graduate.

Housing: 1700 students can be accommodated in college housing, which includes single-sex and coed dorms. In addition, there are honors houses, special-interest houses, and international houses. On-campus housing is guaranteed for all 4 years. 65% of students commute. All students may keep cars.

Activities: 10% of men belong to 5 national fraternities; 10% of women belong to 5 national sororities. There are 150 groups on campus, including art, band, cheerleading, choir, chorale, chorus, computers, dance, drama, drill team, ethnic, gay, honors, international, jazz band, literary magazine, marching band, musical theater, newspaper, orchestra, pep band, photography, political, professional, radio and TV, religious, social, social service, student government, symphony, and yearbook. Popular campus events include cultural events series, and Welcome Week.

Sports: There are 9 intercollegiate sports for men and 10 for women, and 5 intramural sports for men and 4 for women. Facilities include a game room, a 3600-seat main arena, a practice gym, 5 athletic fields, 2 intramural fields, an indoor swimming pool, a dance studio, a wellness room, 6 lighted tennis courts, weight rooms, a dance lab, a football stadium, an 8-lane 400-meter track, training rooms, team rooms, and baseball, racquetball, squash, and archery rooms.

Disabled Students: All of the campus is accessible. Wheelchair ramps, elevators, special parking, specially equipped rest rooms, special class scheduling, lowered drinking fountains, lowered telephones, and special housing are available.

Services: Counseling and information services are available, as is tutoring in every subject. There is a reader service for the blind, and remedial math, reading, and writing.

Campus Safety and Security: Measures include 24-hour foot and vehicle patrol, self-defense education, security escort services, and shuttle buses. There are informal discussions, pamphlets/posters/films, emergency telephones, lighted pathways/sidewalks, and bicycle patrol.

Programs of Study: FSU confers B.A., B.S., B.F.A., B.T.P., and B.U.R. degrees. Master's degrees are also awarded. Bachelor's degrees are awarded in AGRICULTURE (fish and game management and wildlife management), BIOLOGICAL SCIENCE (biology/biological science), BUSINESS (accounting, business administration and management, and recreation and leisure services), COMMUNICATIONS AND THE ARTS (communications, design, dramatic arts, English, languages, and music), COMPUTER AND PHYSICAL SCIENCE (chemistry, computer science, mathematics, physics, and science), EDUCATION (early childhood, elementary, middle school, and physical), ENGINEERING AND ENVIRONMENTAL DESIGN (environmental science), SOCIAL SCIENCE (criminal justice, economics, geography, history, international studies, law enforcement and corrections, liberal arts/general studies, philosophy, political science/government, psychology, social science, social work, and sociology). Business, education, and the natural sciences are the strongest academically. Education, business, and computer science are the largest.

Required: A minimum GPA of 2.0 and 120 credit hours are required to graduate. All students must complete 7 to 14 credits in natural science, 6 to 9 credits in humanities and social sciences, and 3 to 6 credits in creative and performing arts. Courses in computer science, speech and composition, personalized health fitness, and math are also required.

Special: FSU offers co-op programs in applied physics, electrical engineering, and mechanical engineering with the University of Maryland, internships through individual departments, study abroad in Ireland, England, Germany, Denmark, and Ecuador through the International Student Exchange Program, work-study and accelerated degree programs, B.A.-B.S. degrees in all majors, and a dual major in engineering. The 3-2 engineering degree is coordinated with the University of Maryland at College Park. Cross-registration, nondegree study, and pass/fail options are also available. Distance learning and an advanced degree program are available. There are 18 national honor societies, a freshman honors program, and 15 departmental honors programs.

Faculty/Classroom: 57% of faculty are male; 43%, female. All teach undergraduates. No introductory courses are taught by graduate students. The average class size in an introductory lecture is 25; in a laboratory, 15; and in a regular course, 20.

Admissions: 76% of the 2005-2006 applicants were accepted. The SAT scores for the 2005-2006 freshman class were: Verbal--52% below 500, 37% between 500 and 599, 10% between 600 and 700, and 1% above 700; Math--46% below 500, 42% between 500 and 599, 11% between 600 and 700, and 1% above 700. The ACT scores were 64% below 21, 16% between 21 and 23, 13% between 24 and 26, 5% between 27 and 28, and 2% above 28. 25% of the current freshmen were in the top fifth of their class; 56% were in the top two fifths.

Requirements: The SAT is required. In addition, applicants must be graduates of an accredited secondary school or have the GED. Secondary preparation should include 4 units of English, 3 each of math and social studies, and 2 of a foreign language and science. An interview is recommended. A GPA of 2.0 is required. AP and CLEP credits are accepted. Important factors in the admissions decision are recommendations by school officials, extracurricular activities record, and advanced placement or honor courses.

Procedure: Freshmen are admitted to all sessions. Entrance exams should be taken in the junior or senior year. There are early decision, early admissions, and rolling admissions plans. Application deadlines are open. Application fee is $30. Applications are accepted on-line.

Transfer: 323 transfer students enrolled in 2004-2005. Transfer students with 12 to 23 credits must have a minimum GPA of 2.5 and provide an official high school transcript and SAT scores. Students with 24 or more credits must have a minimum GPA of 2.0. 30 of 120 credits required for the bachelor's degree must be completed at FSU.

Visiting: There are regularly scheduled orientations for prospective students, including tours Monday through Friday at 11 A.M. and 12 noon. There are guides for informal visits and visitors may sit in on classes. To schedule a visit, contact the Office of Admissions.

Financial Aid: In 2005-2006, 72% of all full-time freshmen and 65% of continuing full-time students received some form of financial aid. 49% of full-time freshmen and 47% of continuing full-time students received need-based aid. The average freshman award was $8699. Need-based scholarships or need-based grants averaged $4441 ($9400 maximum); need-based self-help aid (loans and jobs) averaged $2379 ($2625 maximum); and other non-need-based awards and non-need-based scholarships averaged $5884 ($20,259 maximum). 13% of undergraduates work part time. Average annual earnings from campus work are $484. The average financial indebtedness of the 2005 graduate was $15,678. The FAFSA and the college's own financial statement are required. The deadline for filing freshman financial aid applications for fall entry is March 1.

International Students: There are 38 international students enrolled. The school actively recruits these students. Satisfactory scores are required on the written TOEFL and the SAT or the ACT.

Computers: Wireless access is available. All students may access the system 8 A.M. to midnight. There are no time limits and no fees. It is strongly recommended that all students have a PC.

Graduates: From July 1, 2004 to June 30, 2005, 834 bachelor's degrees were awarded. The most popular majors were business administration (12%), education (11%), and psychology (7%). In an average class, 21% graduate in 4 years or less, 43% graduate in 5 years or less, and 47% graduate in 6 years or less. 61 companies recruited on campus in 2004-2005.

Admissions Contact: Trisha Gregory, Director of Admissions. E-mail: *fsuadmissions@frostburg.edu* Web: *www.frostburg.edu*

GOUCHER COLLEGE

D-2

Baltimore, MD 21204

(410) 337-6100
(800) 468-2437; Fax: (410) 337-6354

Full-time: 439 men, 867 women	**Faculty:** 113; IIB, +$
Part-time: 11 men, 29 women	**Ph.D.s:** 90%
Graduate: 201 men, 686 women	**Student/Faculty:** 12 to 1
Year: semesters	**Tuition:** $27,525
Application Deadline: February 1	**Room & Board:** $8700
Freshman Class: 2976 applied, 1991 accepted, 340 enrolled	
SAT Verbal/Math: 616/592*	**VERY COMPETITIVE**

Goucher College, founded in 1885, is an independent institution offering programs based on the interdisciplinary traditions of the liberal arts with an international perspective. The college offers 31 majors, many minors,

and emphasizes international and intercultural awareness throughout the curriculum. In addition to regional accreditation, Goucher has baccalaureate program accreditation with NCATE. The library contains 301,795 volumes, 25,019 microform items, and 4544 audio/video tapes/CDs/DVDs, and subscribes to 18,200 periodicals including electronic. Computerized library services include the card catalog, interlibrary loans, database searching, and Internet access. Special learning facilities include a learning resource center, art gallery, radio station, TV station, TV studio, theater, technology/learning center, international technology and media center, and centers for writing, math, and politics. The 287-acre campus is in a suburban area 8 miles north of Baltimore. Including any residence halls, there are 19 buildings.

Student Life: 69% of undergraduates are from out of state, mostly the Middle Atlantic. Students are from 44 states and 9 foreign countries. 64% are from public schools. 67% are white. The average age of freshmen is 18; all undergraduates, 20. 16% do not continue beyond their first year; 66% remain to graduate.

Housing: 1100 students can be accommodated in college housing, which includes single-sex and coed dorms and on-campus apartments. In addition, there are language houses, special-interest houses, and quiet, medical needs, and substance-free housing. On-campus housing is guaranteed for all 4 years. 80% of students live on campus; of those, 77% remain on campus on weekends. All students may keep cars.

Activities: There are no fraternities or sororities. There are 58 groups on campus, including art, chorale, chorus, computers, dance, drama, environmental, ethnic, film, gay, honors, international, jazz band, literary magazine, martial arts, newspaper, orchestra, political, professional, radio and TV, religious, social, social service, student government, symphony, and yearbook. Popular campus events include Get into Goucher Day, Spring Gala, and Blind Date Ball.

Sports: There are 8 intercollegiate sports for men and 10 for women, and 11 intramural sports for men and 11 for women. Facilities include 2 gyms, an indoor swimming pool, a weight room, a dance studio, a training room, racquetball, squash, and tennis courts, and indoor and outdoor equestrian facilities.

Disabled Students: All of the campus is accessible. Wheelchair ramps, elevators, special parking, specially equipped rest rooms, special class scheduling, special housing, and an auditorium loop for the hearing impaired are available.

Services: Counseling and information services are available, as is tutoring in most subjects. There is a reader service for the blind. Many academic support options are available through the college's Academic Center for Excellence (ACE).

Campus Safety and Security: Measures include 24-hour foot and vehicle patrol, self-defense education, security escort services, and shuttle buses. There are informal discussions, pamphlets/posters/films, emergency telephones, lighted pathways/sidewalks, a whistle-alert program, a student safety and security committee, and a manned guard/gatehouse during evening hours.

Programs of Study: Goucher confers the B.A. degree. Master's degrees are also awarded. Bachelor's degrees are awarded in BIOLOGICAL SCIENCE (biology/biological science), BUSINESS (management science), COMMUNICATIONS AND THE ARTS (art, communications, dance, dramatic arts, English, French, historic preservation, music, Russian, and Spanish), COMPUTER AND PHYSICAL SCIENCE (chemistry, computer science, mathematics, and physics), EDUCATION (elementary and special), SOCIAL SCIENCE (American studies, anthropology, economics, history, interdisciplinary studies, international relations, peace studies, philosophy, political science/government, psychology, religion, sociology, and women's studies). Biology, chemistry, and history are the strongest academically. English, communication, and psychology are the largest.

Required: To graduate, all students must complete 120 hours, with a minimum GPA of 2.0. The number of hours in the major varies, with a minimum of 30. Requirements include 1 lab-related course in the natural sciences, 1 course each in the humanities, social sciences, math, and the arts, and the first-year colloquium course for freshmen. Students are also required to demonstrate proficiency in computers, writing, and a foreign language. Other requirements include a 4-class distribution requirement in phys ed, a transitions course, and at least 3 semester hours of an off-campus experience.

Special: Goucher offers internships, study abroad in 14 countries, and other off-campus experiences. The college also collaborates with many of the 22 other colleges in the Baltimore Collegetown Network (*www.colltown.org*). Students may cross-register with Johns Hopkins University, Towson University, College of Notre Dame, Peabody Institute, Villa Julie College, Coppin State College, University of Maryland Baltimore, University of Maryland Baltimore County, Loyola College, and Maryland Institute, College of Art. An advanced degree program with the Monterey Institute for International Studies and a 3-2 engineering degree with Johns Hopkins are offered. Dual majors are an option, and student-designed majors and pass/no pass options are also available. There is 1 national honor society, Phi Beta Kappa.

Faculty/Classroom: 36% of faculty are male; 64%, female. All teach undergraduates.

Admissions: 67% of the 2005-2006 applicants were accepted. The SAT scores for the 2005-2006 freshman class were: Verbal--6% below 500, 34% between 500 and 599, 41% between 600 and 700, and 19% above 700; Math--9% below 500, 45% between 500 and 599, 36% between 600 and 700, and 10% above 700. The ACT scores were 14% below 21, 22% between 21 and 23, 31% between 24 and 26, 15% between 27 and 28, and 18% above 28. 51% of the current freshmen were in the top fifth of their class; 74% were in the top two fifths.

Requirements: The SAT or ACT is required. In addition, applicants should be graduates of an accredited high school or have earned the GED. Secondary preparation should include at least 16 academic units, preferably 4 in English, 3 in math (algebra I and II and geometry) and social studies, and 2 each in the same foreign language, lab science, and electives. A personal essay is required, and an interview is recommended. Prospective arts majors are urged to seek an audition or submit a portfolio. AP credits are accepted. Important factors in the admissions decision are extracurricular activities record, recommendations by school officials, and advanced placement or honor courses.

Procedure: Freshmen are admitted fall and spring. Entrance exams should be taken in spring of the junior year or fall of the senior year. There are early admissions and deferred admissions plans. Applications should be filed by February 1 for fall entry and December 1 for spring entry, along with a $40 fee. Notification of early decision is sent January 15; regular decision, April 1. 266 applicants were on the 2005 waiting list; 61 were admitted. Applications are accepted on-line.

Transfer: 39 transfer students enrolled in a recent year. Applicants must present a GPA of at least 2.5 in 30 hours of college work. An interview, a personal essay, and recommendations from college teachers or counselors are also required, as is a graded paper. 60 of 120 credits required for the bachelor's degree must be completed at Goucher.

Visiting: There are regularly scheduled orientations for prospective students, including an academic presentation, a student panel, discussions, a campus tour, an interview, and an opportunity to sit in on classes and to meet with faculty, coaches, and other staff. There are guides for informal visits and visitors may sit in on classes and stay overnight. To schedule a visit, contact the Office of Admissions.

Financial Aid: In 2005-2006, 82% of all full-time freshmen and 75% of continuing full-time students received some form of financial aid. 69% of full-time freshmen and 77% of continuing full-time students received need-based aid. The average freshman award was $19,739. Need-based scholarships or need-based grants averaged $16,497; need-based self-help aid (loans and jobs) averaged $4978; and other non-need-based awards and non-need-based scholarships averaged $13,652. 46% of undergraduates work part time. Average annual earnings from campus work are $1200. The average financial indebtedness of the 2005 graduate was $19,982. Goucher is a member of CSS. The CSS/Profile or FAFSA and the college's own financial statement are required. The deadline for filing freshman financial aid applications for fall entry is February 15.

International Students: There are 12 international students enrolled. The school actively recruits these students. They must achieve a satisfactory score on the TOEFL and also take the SAT or the ACT.

Computers: Goucher has 140 public computer workstations, some of which are located within 24-hour computer labs. There are wireless network Internet capabilities in most locations throughout the campus. All students may access the system. Some facilities are available around the clock. There are no time limits and no fees.

Graduates: From July 1, 2004 to June 30, 2005, 274 bachelor's degrees were awarded. The most popular majors were psychology (15%), English (11%), and communication (9%). In an average class, 1% graduate in 3 years or less, 56% graduate in 4 years or less, 62% graduate in 5 years or less, and 63% graduate in 6 years or less. 60 companies recruited on campus in 2004-2005. Of the 2004 graduating class, 26% were enrolled in graduate school within 6 months of graduation and 90% were employed.

Admissions Contact: Carlton E. Surbeck, Director of Admissions. A video is available. E-mail: admissions@goucher.edu
Web: www.goucher.edu

HOOD COLLEGE
C-2
Frederick, MD 21701-8575

(301) 696-3400
(800) 922-1599; Fax: (301) 696-3819

Full-time: 238 men, 7 women	**Faculty:** 81; IIA, --$
Part-time: 60 men, 116 women	**Ph.D.s:** 96%
Graduate: 258 men, 676 women	**Student/Faculty:** 12 to 1
Year: semesters, summer session	**Tuition:** $22,335
Application Deadline: February 15	**Room & Board:** $7750
Freshman Class: 1852 applied, 938 accepted, 237 enrolled	
SAT Verbal/Math: 559/553*	**ACT:** 22 **VERY COMPETITIVE**

Hood College, founded in 1893, is an independent, comprehensive college that offers an integration of the liberal arts and professional preparation, as well as undergraduate majors in the natural sciences. In addition to regional accreditation, Hood has baccalaureate program accreditation with CSWE. The library contains 207,285 volumes, 738,716 microform items, and 5313 audio/video tapes/CDs/DVDs, and subscribes to 457 periodicals including electronic. Computerized library services include the card catalog, interlibrary loans, database searching, and Internet access. Special learning facilities include a learning resource center, art gallery, radio station, an aquatic center, a child development lab, an observatory, and an information technology center. The 50-acre campus is in a suburban area 45 miles northwest of Washington, D.C. and 45 miles west of Baltimore. Including any residence halls, there are 31 buildings.

Student Life: 81% of undergraduates are from Maryland. Others are from 28 states, 26 foreign countries, and Canada. 85% are from public schools. 74% are white; 12% African American. 30% are Protestant; 15% Catholic. The average age of freshmen is 18; all undergraduates, 23. 13% do not continue beyond their first year; 87% remain to graduate.

Housing: 640 students can be accommodated in college housing, which includes single-sex and coed dorms. In addition, there are language houses in a living/learning floor, and a community service floor. On-campus housing is guaranteed for the freshman year only and is available on a lottery system for upperclassmen. 52% of students live on campus; of those, 60% remain on campus on weekends. All students may keep cars.

Activities: There are no fraternities or sororities. There are 93 groups on campus, including art, band, cheerleading, choir, chorale, chorus, computers, dance, drama, ethnic, environmental gay, honors, international, literary magazine, musical theater, newspaper, orchestra, political, professional, radio, religious, social, social service, student government, and yearbook. Popular campus events include Ring Formal, performance of "The Messiah" with the U.S. Naval Academy, and Spirit Week.

Sports: There are 7 intercollegiate sports for men and 10 for women, and 1 intramural sport for men and 1 for women. Facilities include a gym with regulation basketball and volleyball courts, a weight room, an aerobics room, indoor and outdoor swimming pools, a 1-mile par course, a softball diamond, 6 tennis courts, an outdoor volleyball court, and 3 multiuse fields (field hockey, soccer, and lacrosse).

Disabled Students: 60% of the campus is accessible. Wheelchair ramps, elevators, special parking, specially equipped rest rooms, and special class scheduling are available.

Services: Counseling and information services are available, as is tutoring in some subjects, including readers for the blind and interpreters for the hearing impaired. There is remedial math. There are also services for students with learning disabilities, a writing lab, a language lab, and courses in time management and study skills.

Campus Safety and Security: Measures include 24-hour foot and vehicle patrol, self-defense education, security escort services, and informal discussions. There are pamphlets/posters/films, emergency telephones, lighted pathways/sidewalks, and an electronic access control system with 24-hour monitoring in all residence halls.

Programs of Study: Hood confers B.A. and B.S. degrees. Master's degrees are also awarded. Bachelor's degrees are awarded in BIOLOGICAL SCIENCE (biochemistry and biology/biological science), BUSINESS (business administration and management and management science), COMMUNICATIONS AND THE ARTS (art, communications, English, French, German, music, and Spanish), COMPUTER AND PHYSICAL SCIENCE (chemistry, computer science, and mathematics), EDUCATION (early childhood, elementary, English, foreign languages, mathematics, science, secondary, and special), ENGINEERING AND ENVIRONMENTAL DESIGN (environmental science), SOCIAL SCIENCE (archeology, economics, history, Latin American studies, law, philosophy, political science/government, psychology, religion, social work, and sociology). Biology, math, and computer science are the strongest academically. Biology, psychology, and management are the largest.

Required: To graduate, students must complete a total of 124 credit hours, with a minimum GPA of 2.0, and a 2.0 GPA in the major. 24 to 52 credits are required in a student's major. All students must complete 42 to 48 credits in the core curriculum, which includes English, math, and language courses, courses in methods of inquiry, and interdisciplinary courses in Western civilization, non-Western civilization and society, science, and technology. Phys ed courses are also required. Enrollment in the final 30 credits must be on the Hood Campus as a degree candidate.

Special: The college offers a Washington semester with American University, dual majors, student-designed majors, a B.A.-B.S. degree in engineering/math, credit for life experience, nondegree study, an accelerated degree program, pass/fail options, and cross-registration with area colleges and the Duke University Marine Sciences Education Consortium. Internships of up to 15 credits are available in all majors at more than 100 sites throughout the United States and abroad. Students may study abroad in the Dominican Republic, Japan, Spain, France, and other countries. There is a 4-year honors program featuring 1 interdisciplinary course per semester and special cocurricular activities. There are 14 national honor societies and a freshman honors program.

Faculty/Classroom: 48% of faculty are male; 52%, female. 100% both teach and do research. The average class size in an introductory lecture is 17; in a laboratory, 15; and in a regular course, 17.

Admissions: 51% of the 2005-2006 applicants were accepted. The SAT scores for the 2005-2006 freshman class were: Verbal--19% below 500, 51% between 500 and 599, 27% between 600 and 700, and 3% above 700; Math--21% below 500, 50% between 500 and 599, 26% between 600 and 700, and 3% above 700. The ACT scores were 33% below 21, 33% between 21 and 23, 20% between 24 and 26, 9% between 27 and 28, and 5% above 28. 53% of the current freshmen were in the top fifth of their class; 87% were in the top two fifths. 5 freshmen graduated first in their class.

Requirements: The SAT or ACT is required. In addition, applicants should be graduates of an accredited secondary school. The GED is accepted. Hood recommends the completion of at least 16 academic credits in high school, including courses in English, social sciences, natural sciences, foreign languages, and math. A GPA of 2.5 is required. AP and CLEP credits are accepted. Important factors in the admissions decision are advanced placement or honor courses, leadership record, and extra-curricular activities record.

Procedure: Freshmen are admitted fall and spring. Entrance exams should be taken in spring of the junior year or fall of the senior year. There are early admissions and deferred admissions plans. Applications should be filed by February 15 (priority date) for fall entry and December 31 (priority date) for spring entry. Notification is sent on a rolling basis beginning October 15. Applications are accepted on-line.

Transfer: 140 transfer students enrolled in 2004-2005. Applicants must have at least 12 college credits and a minimum GPA of 2.5. A total of 70 credits may be transferred. 30 of 124 credits required for the bachelor's degree must be completed at Hood.

Visiting: There are regularly scheduled orientations for prospective students, including tours and meetings with faculty, students, and administrators; and admissions interviews. There are guides for informal visits and visitors may sit in on classes and stay overnight. To schedule a visit, contact the Admissions Office at *admissions@hood.edu*.

Financial Aid: In 2005-2006, 99% of all full-time students received some form of financial aid. 76% of full-time freshmen and 78% of continuing full-time students received need-based aid. The average freshman award was $19,565. Need-based scholarships or need-based grants averaged $16,092 ($26,000 maximum); need-based self-help aid (loans and jobs) averaged $4425 ($7237 maximum); and other non-need-based awards and non-need-based scholarships averaged $14,517. 26% of undergraduates work part time. Average annual earnings from campus work are $1700. The average financial indebtedness of the 2005 graduate was $16,295. Hood is a member of CSS. The FAFSA is required. The priority date for freshman financial aid applications for fall entry is February 15.

International Students: There are 41 international students enrolled. The school actively recruits these students. They must take the TOEFL and also take the SAT or ACT. SAT scores may be substituted for the TOEFL.

Computers: Wireless access is available. The Campus Whitaker Center, library, and residence halls are all wireless. There are 2 labs and 5 simple machines for student access in those locations, plus 4 to 5 per residence hall. There are more than 150 computers in labs available for student use. All students may access the system 24 hours per day, 7 days a week. There are no time limits and no fees. It is strongly recommended that all students have a personal computer. A Pentium 4 class machine with WinXP Pro, 256 MB memory is recommended.

Graduates: From July 1, 2004 to June 30, 2005, 189 bachelor's degrees were awarded. The most popular majors were psychology (14%), English (12%), and early childhood education (11%). In an average class, 5% graduate in 3 years or less, 67% graduate in 4 years or less, 69% graduate in 5 years or less, and 70% graduate in 6 years or less. 64 companies recruited on campus in 2004-2005. Of the 2004 graduating class, 42% were enrolled in graduate school within 6 months of graduation and 94% were employed.

Admissions Contact: Glen Thomas, Dean of Admissions. A video is available. E-mail: *admissions@hood.edu* Web: *www.hood.edu*

JOHNS HOPKINS UNIVERSITY   D-2
Baltimore, MD 21218   (410) 516-8341; Fax: (410) 516-6025

Full-time: 2359 men, 1992 women	**Faculty:** 480; I, av$
Part-time: 32 men, 34 women	**Ph.D.s:** 96%
Graduate: 1017 men, 591 women	**Student/Faculty:** 9 to 1
Year: 4-1-4, summer session	**Tuition:** $32,120
Application Deadline: January 1	**Room & Board:** $9924
Freshman Class: 11,274 applied, 3907 accepted, 1133 enrolled	
SAT Verbal/Math: 685/710*	**ACT:** 30 **MOST COMPETITIVE**

The Johns Hopkins University, founded in 1876, is a private multicampus institution offering undergraduate degrees at the Homewood campus through the Zanvyl Krieger School of Arts and Sciences, the Whiting School of Engineering, and the Peabody Institute (music). There are 5 undergraduate and 8 graduate schools. In addition to regional accreditation, Johns Hopkins has baccalaureate program accreditation with ABET. The 4 libraries contain 2,600,000 volumes, 4,100,000 microform items, and 9707 audio/video tapes/CDs/DVDs, and subscribe to 30,120 periodicals including electronic. Computerized library services include the card catalog, interlibrary loans, database searching, Internet access, and laptop Internet portals. Special learning facilities include an art gallery, radio station, and Space Telescope Science Institute. The 140-acre campus is in a suburban area in a residential setting in northern Baltimore. Including any residence halls, there are 36 buildings.

Student Life: 85% of undergraduates are from out of state, mostly the Middle Atlantic. Students are from 50 states, 49 foreign countries, and Canada. 60% are from public schools. 62% are white; 22% Asian American. The average age of freshmen is 18; all undergraduates, 20. 4% do not continue beyond their first year; 90% remain to graduate.

Housing: 2800 students can be accommodated in college housing, which includes single-sex and coed dorms, on-campus apartments, and off-campus apartments. In addition, there are special-interest houses and non-university-sponsored fraternity and sorority houses. On-campus housing is guaranteed for freshman and sophomore years only and is available on a lottery system for upperclassmen. 51% of students live on campus. Upperclassmen may keep cars.

Activities: 21% of men belong to 11 national fraternities; 17% of women belong to 7 national sororities. There are 250 groups on campus, including art, band, cheerleading, chess, choir, chorale, chorus, computers, dance, debate, drama, ethnic, film, forensics, gay, honors, international, jazz band, literary magazine, marching band, musical theater, newspaper, opera, orchestra, pep band, photography, political, professional, radio and TV, religious, social, social service, student government, symphony, volunteer organizations, and yearbook. Popular campus events include Culturefest, Spring Fair, and Milton E. Eisenhower Symposium.

Sports: There are 14 intercollegiate sports for men and 12 for women, and 20 intramural sports for men and 20 for women. Facilities include a recreation center with a swimming pool and diving pool, wrestling and fencing roooms, a varsity weight room, a fitness center, saunas, a climbing wall, an indoor jogging track, and courts for basketball, badminton, squash, volleyball, and handball. There is also a 4000-seat stadium, outdoor playing fields, and tennis courts.

Disabled Students: Wheelchair ramps, elevators, special parking, specially equipped rest rooms, special class scheduling, lowered drinking fountains, and lowered telephones are available JHU works with all individuals to ensure access to all programs.

Services: Counseling and information services are available, as is tutoring in most subjects. There is a reader service for the blind.

Campus Safety and Security: Measures include 24-hour foot and vehicle patrol, self-defense education, security escort services, and shuttle buses. There are informal discussions, pamphlets/posters/films, emergency telephones, and lighted pathways/sidewalks.

Programs of Study: Johns Hopkins confers B.A. and B.S. degrees. Master's and doctoral degrees are also awarded. Bachelor's degrees are awarded in BIOLOGICAL SCIENCE (biology/biological science, biophysics, cell biology, molecular biology, and neurosciences), COMMUNICATIONS AND THE ARTS (art history and appreciation, classics, creative writing, English, French, German, Italian, media arts, romance languages and literature, and Spanish), COMPUTER AND PHYSICAL SCIENCE (applied mathematics, chemistry, computer science, earth science, mathematics, natural sciences, and physics), ENGINEERING AND ENVIRONMENTAL DESIGN (biomedical engineering, chemical engineering, civil engineering, computer engineering, electrical/electronics engineering, engineering, engineering mechanics, environmental engineering, environmental science, industrial engineering, materials engineering, materials science, and mechanical engineering), SOCIAL SCIENCE (African studies, anthropology, cognitive science, East Asian studies, economics, history, history of science, humanities, interdisciplinary studies, international studies, Latin American studies, Near Eastern studies, philosophy, political science/government, psychology, social science, and sociology). Neuroscience, international studies, and biomedical engineering are the largest.

Required: Although there is no required core curriculum, all students must take 40 hours in the major and 30 hours outside their major field. The B.A. requires a total of 120 hours; the B.S. in engineering requires 120 to 128 hours, depending on the major. A GPA of at least 2.0 is required for graduation. All students must take at least 4 courses (2 for engineers) with a writing-intensive component to graduate.

Special: Internships, dual majors in music and arts and sciences and engineering, cross-registration with all Baltimore-area colleges and all Johns Hopkins divisions, a cooperative 5-year civil engineering program, a student-designed semester at the Johns Hopkins School of International Studies in Washington, D.C., and various multidisciplinary programs are offered. Students may enroll at Johns Hopkins in Bologna, Italy, or Nanjing, China, or arrange programs in Europe, South America, the Far East, or Australia. Students may earn combined B.A.-B.S. degrees in physics, computer, science, applied math, and statistics or a combined B.A.-B.M. through the Peabody Institute. Pass/fail options are available in nonmajor courses. There are 4 national honor societies, including Phi Beta Kappa, and 25 departmental honors programs.

Faculty/Classroom: 78% of faculty are male; 22%, female.

Admissions: 35% of the 2005-2006 applicants were accepted. The SAT scores for the 2005-2006 freshman class were: Verbal--2% below 500, 10% between 500 and 599, 48% between 600 and 700, and 40% above 700; Math--1% below 500, 5% between 500 and 599, 40% between 600 and 700, and 54% above 700. The ACT scores were 1% below 21, 3% between 21 and 23, 13% between 24 and 26, 14% between 27 and 28, and 69% above 28. 92% of the current freshmen were in the top fifth of their class; 99% were in the top two fifths. There were 52 National Merit finalists. 75 freshmen graduated first in their class.

Requirements: The SAT or ACT with ACT Optional Writing Test is required. For those submitting SAT scores, Johns Hopkins recommends that applicants also submit three SAT subject tests. In addition, applicants should be graduates of an accredited secondary school or have the GED. The university recommends that secondary preparation include 4 years each of English and math, 2 (prefer 3) of social science or history and lab science, and 3 to 4 of a foreign language (2 for engineering majors). 2 personal essays are required, and an interview is recommended. AP credits are accepted. Important factors in the admissions decision are advanced placement or honor courses, extracurricular activities record, and personality/intangible qualities.

Procedure: Freshmen are admitted in the fall. Entrance exams should be taken by December for regular decision, or November for early decision. There are early decision and deferred admissions plans. Early decision applications should be filed by November 15; regular applications, by January 1 for fall entry, along with a $60 fee. Notification of early decision is sent December 15; regular decision, by April 1. 379 early decision candidates were accepted for the 2005-2006 class. 1025 applicants were on the 2005 waiting list; 4 were admitted. Applications are accepted on-line.

Transfer: 34 transfer students enrolled in 2004-2005. Applicants should have sophomore or junior standing and at least a B average in previous college work. Applications must include a written essay and at least 1 letter of recommendation. High school records are also required. 60 of 120 credits required for the bachelor's degree must be completed at Johns Hopkins.

Visiting: There are regularly scheduled orientations for prospective students, including scheduled open house programs, campus tours and group information sessions offered weekday mornings and afternoons, and individual day visits with a current student. A schedule of events and a virtual tour is available at http://apply.jhu.edu/visit/tour.html. There are guides for informal visits and visitors may sit in on classes and stay overnight. To schedule a visit, contact the Office of Undergraduate Admissions at (410) 516-8171 or *gotojhu@jhu.edu.*

Financial Aid: In 2005-2006, 48% of all full-time freshmen and 49% of continuing full-time students received some form of financial aid. 42% of full-time freshmen and 41% of continuing full-time students received need-based aid. The average freshman award was $29,472. Need-based scholarships or need-based grants averaged $22,713; need-based self-help aid (loans and jobs) averaged $3513; and non-need-based athletic scholarships averaged $21,645. The average financial indebtedness of the 2005 graduate was $14,000. Johns Hopkins is a member of CSS. The CSS/Profile or FAFSA is required. The deadline for filing freshman financial aid applications for fall entry is February 1.

International Students: There are 280 international students enrolled. The school actively recruits these students. They must score satisfactorily on the TOEFL and also take the SAT or the ACT. Three SAT Subject Tests are recommended.

Computers: Wireless access is available. All students may access the system 24 hours a day, 7 days a week. There are no time limits. The fee is $112 per semester.

Graduates: From July 1, 2004 to June 30, 2005, 1412 bachelor's degrees were awarded. The most popular majors were biomedical engineering (10%), international studies (7%), and economics (4%). In an average class, 5% graduate in 3 years or less, 81% graduate in 4 years or less, 89% graduate in 5 years or less, and 90% graduate in 6 years or less. 224 companies recruited on campus in 2004-2005. Of the 2004 graduating class, 41% were enrolled in graduate school within 6 months of graduation and 42% were employed.

Admissions Contact: Dr. John Latting, Director of Undergraduate Admissions. E-mail: *gotojhu@jhu.edu* Web: *http://apply.jhu.edu*

LOYOLA COLLEGE IN MARYLAND — D-2
Baltimore, MD 21210

(410) 617-5012
(800) 221-9107; Fax: (410) 617-2176

Full-time: 1472 men, 2017 women	**Faculty:** 305; IIA, +$
Part-time: 18 men, 26 women	**Ph.D.s:** 84%
Graduate: 959 men, 1575 women	**Student/Faculty:** 11 to 1
Year: semesters, summer session	**Tuition:** $29,683
Application Deadline: January 15	**Room & Board:** $9215
Freshman Class: 7393 applied, 4691 accepted, 899 enrolled	
SAT Verbal/Math: 600/590*	**ACT:** 25 **HIGHLY COMPETITIVE**

Loyola College, founded in 1852, is a private liberal arts college affiliated with the Roman Catholic Church and the Jesuit tradition. It offers degree programs in arts and sciences, business, and management. There are 2 undergraduate and 2 graduate schools. In addition to regional accreditation, Loyola College has baccalaureate program accreditation with AAC-SB, ABET, CSAB, NASDTEC, and NCATE. The library contains 437,571 volumes, 338,337 microform items, and 39,422 audio/video tapes/CDs/DVDs, and subscribes to 14,901 periodicals including electronic. Computerized library services include the card catalog, interlibrary loans, and database searching. Special learning facilities include an art gallery and radio station. The 89-acre campus is in an urban area 3 miles from downtown Baltimore. Including any residence halls, there are 29 buildings.

Student Life: 83% of undergraduates are from out of state, mostly the Middle Atlantic. Students are from 38 states, 15 foreign countries, and Canada. 86% are white. 78% are Catholic; 9% Protestant; 9% Christian Orthodox and other. The average age of freshmen is 18; all undergraduates, 20. 10% do not continue beyond their first year; 83% remain to graduate.

Housing: 2798 students can be accommodated in college housing, which includes coed dormitories and on-campus apartments. In addition, there are honors houses and special-interest houses. On-campus housing is guaranteed for the freshman year only and is available on a first-come, first-served basis. 79% of students live on campus. Alcohol is not permitted. Upperclassmen may keep cars.

Activities: There are no fraternities or sororities. There are 101 groups on campus, including art, band, cheerleading, chess, choir, chorale, chorus, computers, dance, drama, ethnic, honors, international, jazz band, literary magazine, musical theater, newspaper, orchestra, pep band, photography, political, professional, radio, religious, social, social service, student government, symphony, and yearbook.

Sports: There are 7 intercollegiate sports for men and 8 for women, and 15 intramural sports for men. Facilities include a pool, a sauna, a weight room, racquetball, tennis, and squash courts, a 3000-seat arena, a 2000-seat multipurpose outdoor facility, and a fitness center.

Disabled Students: 99% of the campus is accessible. Wheelchair ramps, elevators, special parking, specially equipped rest rooms, special class scheduling, lowered drinking fountains, and lowered telephones are available.

Services: Counseling and information services are available, as is tutoring in most subjects. There is a reader service for the blind and remedial math.

Campus Safety and Security: Measures include 24-hour foot and vehicle patrol, self-defense education, security escort services, and shuttle buses. There are informal discussions, pamphlets/posters/films, emergency telephones, and lighted pathways/sidewalks.

Programs of Study: Loyola College confers B.A., B.S., B.B.A., B.S.E.E., and B.S.E.S. degrees. Master's and doctoral degrees are also awarded. Bachelor's degrees are awarded in BIOLOGICAL SCIENCE (biology/biological science), BUSINESS (accounting and business administration and management), COMMUNICATIONS AND THE ARTS (communications, creative writing, English, fine arts, French, German, Latin, and Spanish), COMPUTER AND PHYSICAL SCIENCE (chemistry, computer science, mathematics, and physics), EDUCATION (elementary), ENGINEERING AND ENVIRONMENTAL DESIGN (electrical/electronics engineering and engineering), HEALTH PROFESSIONS (speech pathology/audiology), SOCIAL SCIENCE (classical/ancient civilization, economics, history, philosophy, political science/government, psychology, sociology, and theological studies). General business, psychology, and communication are the largest.

Required: All students must complete 120 hours, including 36 in the major, with at least a 2.0 GPA. The required core curriculum includes 2 courses each in history, language (at the second-year level), literature, philosophy, social sciences, and theology; 1 course each in composition, ethics, fine arts, math, humanities, and natural sciences; and 1 additional course in math, natural science, or computer science.

Special: Loyola offers cross-registration with Johns Hopkins, Towson, and Morgan State Universities, Goucher College, the College of Notre Dame, Maryland Art Institute, and Peabody Conservatory. Credit-bearing internships are available in most majors and study abroad is possible in 36 countries. Work-study programs and dual majors are also offered. There are 23 national honor societies, including Phi Beta Kappa, a freshman honors program, and 1 departmental honors program.

Faculty/Classroom: 56% of faculty are male; 44%, female. 90% teach undergraduates, 98% do research, and 87% do both. No introductory courses are taught by graduate students. The average class size in an introductory lecture is 25; in a laboratory, 16; and in a regular course, 21.

Admissions: 63% of the 2005-2006 applicants were accepted. The SAT scores for the 2005-2006 freshman class were: Verbal--6% below 500, 38% between 500 and 599, 48% between 600 and 700, and 9% above 700; Math--6% below 500, 31% between 500 and 599, 53% between 600 and 700, and 10% above 700. The ACT scores were 5% below 21, 19% between 21 and 23, 42% between 24 and 26, 19% between 27 and 28, and 16% above 28. 65% of the current freshmen were in the top fifth of their class; 92% were in the top two fifths. 10 freshmen graduated first in their class.

Requirements: The SAT or ACT is required. In addition, applicants should have graduated from an accredited secondary school or have earned the GED. Secondary preparation should include 4 years of English, 3 to 4 each of math, foreign language, natural science, and classical or modern foreign language, and 2 to 3 of history. A personal essay is required; an interview is recommended. AP and CLEP credits are accepted. Important factors in the admissions decision are advanced placement or honor courses, recommendations by school officials, and extracurricular activities record.

Procedure: Freshmen are admitted fall, spring, and summer. Entrance exams should be taken by December of the senior year. There are early admissions and deferred admissions plans. Applications should be filed by January 15 for fall entry and December 15 for spring entry, along with a $50 fee. Notification is sent April 1. 1682 applicants were on the 2005 waiting list; 484 were admitted.

Transfer: 27 transfer students enrolled in 2004-2005. Transfer applicants should have at least a 2.5 GPA in previous college work and should submit SAT scores. Other factors considered include types of college courses taken and the secondary school record. 60 of 120 credits required for the bachelor's degree must be completed at Loyola College.

Visiting: There are regularly scheduled orientations for prospective students, including a general information session, an interview, and a campus tour. There are guides for informal visits and visitors may sit in on classes. To schedule a visit, contact the Admissions Office.

Financial Aid: In 2005-2006, 50% of all full-time freshmen and 42% of continuing full-time students received some form of financial aid. At least 39% of full-time freshmen and at least 31% of continuing full-time students received need-based aid. The average freshman award was $21,375. Need-based scholarships or need-based grants averaged $13,545 ($26,010 maximum); need-based self-help aid (loans and jobs) averaged $7830 ($7950 maximum); non-need-based athletic scholarships averaged $21,705 ($36,985 maximum); and institutional non-need-based awards and non-need-based scholarships averaged $10,076. 15% of undergraduates work part time. Average annual earnings from campus work are $1380. The average financial indebtedness of the 2005 graduate was $15,680. Loyola College is a member of CSS. The CSS/Profile or FAFSA and if applicable, a noncustodial parent's statement and business/farm supplement are required. The deadline for filing freshman financial aid applications for fall entry is February 15.

International Students: In a recent year, there were 30 international students enrolled. The school actively recruits these students. They must score satisfactorily on the written TOEFL and also take the SAT.

Computers: All students may access the system. There are no time limits and no fees.

Graduates: From July 1, 2004 to June 30, 2005, 766 bachelor's degrees were awarded. The most popular majors were health professions and related scienes (34%), communication (13%), and psychology (8%). In an average class, 78% graduate in 4 years or less, 82% graduate in 5 years or less, and 83% graduate in 6 years or less.

Admissions Contact: William Bossemeyer, Dean of Admissions. A video is available. Web: *www.loyola.edu*

MARYLAND INSTITUTE COLLEGE OF ART   D-2

Baltimore, MD 21217	**(410) 225-2222; Fax: (410) 225-2337**
Full-time: 559 men, 919 women	**Faculty:** 106
Part-time: 8 men, 11 women	**Ph.D.s:** 86%
Graduate: 82 men, 138 women	**Student/Faculty:** 14 to 1
Year: semesters, summer session	**Tuition:** $26,920
Application Deadline: February 15	**Room & Board:** $7530
Freshman Class: 2487 applied, 1118 accepted, 396 enrolled	
SAT Verbal/Math: 590/570*	**SPECIAL**

Maryland Institute College of Art, founded in 1826, is a private accredited institution offering undergraduate and graduate degrees in the fine arts. In addition to regional accreditation, MICA has baccalaureate program accreditation with NASAD. The library contains 76,500 volumes and 4700 audio/video tapes/CDs/DVDs, and subscribes to 315 periodicals including electronic. Computerized library services include the card catalog, interlibrary loans, database searching, Internet access, and laptop Internet portals. Special learning facilities include a learning resource center, 12 large art galleries, open to the public year-round, and featuring work by MICA faculty, students, and nationally and internationally known artists, a slide library containing 215,000 slides, and 8 other galleries for undergraduate and graduate exhibitions. The 13-acre campus is in an urban area in the Mt. Royal cultural center of Baltimore. Including any residence halls, there are 25 buildings.

Student Life: 80% of undergraduates are from out of state, mostly the Northeast. Others are from 47 states, 46 foreign countries, and Canada. 76% are from public schools. 68% are white. The average age of freshmen is 18; all undergraduates, 20. 13% do not continue beyond their first year; 72% remain to graduate.

Housing: 629 students can be accommodated in college housing, which includes coed dorms, on-campus apartments, and off-campus apartments. Residence halls include project rooms where students can do artwork 24 hours a day. On-campus housing is guaranteed for the freshman year only, is available on a first-come, first-served basis, and is available on a lottery system for upperclassmen. 88% of students live on campus; of those, 95% remain on campus on weekends. Alcohol is not permitted. All students may keep cars.

Activities: There are no fraternities or sororities. There are 20 groups on campus, including art, choir, computers, dance, drama, ethnic, film, gay, international, literary magazine, outdoor club (camping, skiing, biking), photography, playwriting club, political, professional, religious, social, social service, and student government. Popular campus events include Regular bus trips to galleries and museums in New York and Washington, D.C., dances, and exhibition openings.

Sports: There are 4 intramural sports for men and 4 for women. Facilities include an outdoor volleyball court and a fitness center for weightlifting and aerobics on campus. There is also a recreation center 5 blocks from campus with a basketball court and other fitness equipment.

Disabled Students: 85% of the campus is accessible. Wheelchair ramps, elevators, special parking, specially equipped rest rooms, special class scheduling, lowered drinking fountains, lowered telephones, and lowered fire extinguishers are available.

Services: Counseling and information services are available, as is tutoring in some subjects, including writing and study skills. There is remedial writing.

Campus Safety and Security: Measures include 24-hour foot and vehicle patrol, self-defense education, security escort services, and shuttle buses. There are informal discussions, pamphlets/posters/films, emergency telephones, lighted pathways/sidewalks, building monitors in most buildings, and periodic discussions and seminars on safety.

Programs of Study: MICA confers the B.F.A. degree. Master's degrees are also awarded. Bachelor's degrees are awarded in COMMUNICATIONS AND THE ARTS (animation, ceramic art and design, drawing, fiber/textiles/weaving, fine arts, graphic design, illustration, media arts, painting, photography, printmaking, sculpture, and video), ENGINEERING AND ENVIRONMENTAL DESIGN (environmental design and interior design). Painting, illustration and graphic design are the strongest academically.

Required: All students complete a foundation program in their first year, including courses in painting, drawing, two- and three-dimensional design, liberal arts, and electronic arts. Of a total 126 credits, students must take one third of the courses in liberal arts and two-thirds in studio arts, with 60 credits in the major and a minimum 2.0 GPA. Seniors must complete a focused, professionally oriented body of work.

Special: Exchange programs are offered with Goucher College, Loyola and Notre Dame Colleges, Johns Hopkins University, the Peabody Conservatory of Music, the University of Baltimore, the University of Maryland Baltimore County, Towson University, Morgan State University, and Baltimore Hebrew College. Cross-registration is possible with any member schools in the Alliance of Independent Colleges of Art and the East Coast Art Schools Consortium. A New York studio semester is available as well as a semester of study with any member schools in the Association of Independent Colleges of Art and Design. Study abroad is possible in the junior year in any of 12 countries including MICA's Center for Advanced Art and Culture in Aix-en-Provence, France. Dual and student-designed majors are available, and there are work-study programs. Juniors and seniors who meet prerequisites are eligible for credit-earning internships locally and nationally.

Faculty/Classroom: 51% of faculty are male; 49%, female. 89% teach undergraduates. No introductory courses are taught by graduate students. The average class size in an introductory lecture is 24 and in a regular course, 17.

Admissions: 45% of the 2005-2006 applicants were accepted. The SAT scores for the 2005-2006 freshman class were: Verbal--10% below 500, 43% between 500 and 599, 33% between 600 and 700, and 14% above 700; Math--19% below 500, 45% between 500 and 599, 29% between 600 and 700, and 7% above 700. 42% of the current freshmen were in the top fifth of their class; 81% were in the top two fifths. There were 4 National Merit finalists and 1 semifinalist.

Requirements: The SAT is required. In addition, admission is based on a comprehensive set of criteria with the most emphasis placed on artistic ability as demonstrated in the portfolio, and on academic achievement as demonstrated in test scores, GPA, and level of coursework. Essays, recommendations, interview, and extra curricular activities are also considered. AP credits are accepted. Important factors in the admissions decision are extracurricular activities record, advanced placement or honor courses, and evidence of special talent.

Procedure: Freshmen are admitted fall and spring. Entrance exams should be taken in the spring of the junior year. There are early decision, early admissions, and deferred admissions plans. Early decision applications should be filed by November 15; regular applications, by February 15 for fall entry and December 1 for spring entry, along with a $50 fee. Notification of early decision is sent December 15; regular decision, March 15. 36 early decision candidates were accepted for the 2005-2006 class. 12 applicants were on the 2005 waiting list; 3 were admitted.

Transfer: 62 transfer students enrolled in 2004-2005. Transfer applicants must submit high school and college transcripts, a personal essay, a portfolio of artwork, and letters of recommendation and course descriptions. 63 of 126 credits required for the bachelor's degree must be completed at MICA.

Visiting: There are regularly scheduled orientations for prospective students, including campus visits, presentations about curriculum, student life, courses in art, admission, and financial aid. There are guides for informal visits and visitors may sit in on classes. To schedule a visit, contact the Office of Undergraduate Admission at *admissions@mica.edu*.

Financial Aid: In 2005-2006, 85% of all full-time students received some form of financial aid. 65% of all full-time students received need-based aid. The average freshman award was $12,526. 60% of undergraduates work part time. Average annual earnings from campus work are $1100. The average financial indebtedness of the 2005 graduate was $13,368. MICA is a member of CSS. The FAFSA and the college's own financial statement are required. The deadline for filing freshman financial aid applications for fall entry is March 1.

International Students: There are 74 international students enrolled. The school actively recruits these students. A satisfactory score is required on the written TOEFL. Applicants must also take the Comprehensive English Language Test or the college's own test, or take the SAT.

Computers: Wireless access is available. Over 350 PCs are available in more than 30 classrooms, labs, and public areas. Sixty percent of the campus has wireless access. Students can use the student portal, Web galleries, student blogs, e-mail, and blackboard e-learning. All students may access the system 24 hours a day. There are no time limits and no fees. It is strongly recommended that all students have a personal computer. Laptops are preferred; either a Mac or Dell PC is recommended, depending on the student's major.

Graduates: From July 1, 2004 to June 30, 2005, 284 bachelor's degrees were awarded. The most popular majors were general fine arts (24%), graphic design (14%), and illustration (14%). In an average class, 66% graduate in 4 years or less, 71% graduate in 5 years or less, and 72% graduate in 6 years or less. 30 companies recruited on campus in 2004-2005. Of the 2004 graduating class, 23% were enrolled in graduate school within 6 months of graduation and 89% were employed.

Admissions Contact: Theresa Lynch Bedoya, Vice President and Dean of Admission. E-mail: *admissions@mica.edu*
Web: *www.mica.edu*

MCDANIEL COLLEGE D-1
Westminster, MD 21157-4390
(410) 857-2230
(800) 638-5005; Fax: (410) 857-2757

Full-time: 705 men, 942 women	Faculty: 131; IIB, +$
Part-time: 23 men, 25 women	Ph.D.s: 98%
Graduate: 414 men, 1415 women	Student/Faculty: 13 to 1
Year: 4-1-4	Tuition: $26,010
Application Deadline: February 1	Room & Board: $5600
Freshman Class: 2008 applied, 1782 accepted, 449 enrolled	
SAT Verbal/Math: 550/560*	VERY COMPETITIVE

McDaniel College, founded in 1867 as Western Maryland College, is a private college offering programs in the liberal arts. There is 1 undergraduate and 1 graduate school. In addition to regional accreditation, The Hill has baccalaureate program accreditation with ACS, CSWE, and NCATE. The library contains 197,286 volumes, 1,444,720 microform items, and 162,540 audio/video tapes/CDs/DVDs, and subscribes to 4342 periodicals including electronic. Computerized library services include the card catalog, interlibrary loans, database searching, Internet access, and laptop Internet portals. Special learning facilities include an art gallery, radio station, TV station, physics observatory, and student research science labs. The 160-acre campus is in a suburban area 30 miles northwest of Baltimore. Including any residence halls, there are 62 buildings.

Student Life: 72% of undergraduates are from Maryland. Others are from 30 states and 17 foreign countries. 80% are white. Most claim no religious affiliation. The average age of freshmen is 18; all undergraduates, 20. 19% do not continue beyond their first year; 73% remain to graduate.

Housing: 1314 students can be accommodated in college housing, which includes single-sex and coed dorms and on-campus apartments. In addition, there are honors houses, language houses, special-interest houses, fraternity and sorority floors, academic clusters, and substance-free floors. On-campus housing is guaranteed for all 4 years. 77% of students live on campus; of those, 85% remain on campus on weekends. Upperclassmen may keep cars.

Activities: 16% of men belong to 2 local and 3 national fraternities; 12% of women belong to 2 local and 2 national sororities. There are 128 groups on campus, including art, band, cheerleading, choir, chorale, chorus, computers, drama, ethnic, film, forensics, gay, honors, international, jazz band, musical theater, newspaper, orchestra, pep band, photography, political, professional, radio and TV, religious, social, social service, student government, and ultimate frisbee. Popular campus events include Spring Fling, Senior Week, and Families Weekend.

Sports: There are 11 intercollegiate sports for men and 11 for women, and 13 intramural sports for men and 12 for women. Facilities include a 9-hole golf course, tennis courts, a swimming pool, a football stadium with a track, a squash/racquetball court, a weight training center, basketball and volleyball courts, and soccer, softball, and lacrosse fields.

Disabled Students: 85% of the campus is accessible. Wheelchair ramps, elevators, special parking, specially equipped rest rooms, special class scheduling, lowered drinking fountains, lowered telephones, special housing, and interpreting and TTY services are available.

Services: Counseling and information services are available, as is tutoring in most subjects. There is a reader service for the blind, and remedial math, reading, and writing.

Campus Safety and Security: Measures include 24-hour foot and vehicle patrol, security escort services, informal discussions, and pamphlets/posters/films. There are emergency telephones and lighted pathways/sidewalks.

Programs of Study: The Hill confers the B.A. degree. Master's degrees are also awarded. Bachelor's degrees are awarded in BIOLOGICAL SCIENCE (biology/biological science), BUSINESS (business administration and management), COMMUNICATIONS AND THE ARTS (art history and appreciation, communications, dramatic arts, English, fine arts, French, German, music, and Spanish), COMPUTER AND PHYSICAL SCIENCE (chemistry, computer science, mathematics, and physics), EDUCATION (physical), ENGINEERING AND ENVIRONMENTAL DESIGN (environmental science), SOCIAL SCIENCE (economics, history, philosophy, political science/government, psychology, religion, social work, and sociology). Business administration, psychology, and biology are the largest.

Required: Distribution requirements for all students include cross-cultural studies, literature and fine arts, humanities, natural sciences, quantitative analysis, and social sciences. All students must take English composition, foreign language, and phys ed (4 courses) and pass a math proficiency exam. A total of 128 credit hours is required for graduation, including 38 to 50 in the major. The college uses a 4-course system, with most courses 4 credits. The minimum GPA for graduation is 2.0.

Special: Internships are available in all majors. Study abroad is available around the world including McDaniel's program in Budapest. There is a Washington semester in conjunction with American University and 3-2 engineering programs with Washington University and the University of Maryland. The college offers work-study programs, dual and student-designed majors, credit by exam (in foreign languages), and pass/fail options. McDaniel College has a 5-year deaf education program and offers certification in elementary and secondary education. The college also offers advanced standing for international baccalaureate recipients. There are 20 national honor societies, including Phi Beta Kappa, a freshman honors program, and 24 departmental honors programs.

Faculty/Classroom: 55% of faculty are male; 45%, female. All teach undergraduates. No introductory courses are taught by graduate students. The average class size in an introductory lecture is 18; in a laboratory, 17; and in a regular course, 17.

Admissions: 89% of the 2005-2006 applicants were accepted. The SAT scores for the 2005-2006 freshman class were: Verbal--26% below 500, 46% between 500 and 599, 23% between 600 and 700, and 5% above 700; Math--21% below 500, 45% between 500 and 599, 27% between 600 and 700, and 6% above 700. 52% of the current freshmen were in the top fifth of their class; 87% were in the top two fifths. 24 freshmen graduated first in their class.

Requirements: The SAT is required. Applicants must be graduates of an accredited secondary school or have a GED. 16 academic credits are required, including 4 years of English, 3 each of foreign language, math, and social studies, and 2 of a lab science. SAT Subject tests and an interview are recommended. An essay is required. The Hill requires applicants to be in the upper 50% of their class. A GPA of 2.5 is required. AP and CLEP credits are accepted. Important factors in the admissions decision are advanced placement or honor courses, leadership record, and evidence of special talent.

Procedure: Freshmen are admitted fall and spring. Entrance exams should be taken at the end of the junior year. There is a deferred admissions plan. Applications should be filed by February 1 for fall entry and January 15 for spring entry, along with a $50 fee. Notification is sent April 1. 49 applicants were on the 2005 waiting list; 10 were admitted. Applications are accepted on-line.

Transfer: 69 transfer students enrolled in 2004-2005. A minimum college GPA of 2.5 is required. 30 of 128 credits required for the bachelor's degree must be completed at The Hill.

Visiting: There are regularly scheduled orientations for prospective students, including meeting the president, a panel of faculty, and a panel of students. Tours of the campus for parents are conducted by faculty members; students tour with current students. There are guides for informal visits and visitors may sit in on classes and stay overnight. To schedule a visit, contact the Admissions Office at *admissions@mcdaniel.edu*.

Financial Aid: In 2005-2006, 67% of all full-time freshmen and 63% of continuing full-time students received some form of financial aid. 63% of full-time freshmen and 62% of continuing full-time students received

need-based aid. The average freshman award was $18,574. Need-based scholarships or need-based grants averaged $9330; need-based self-help aid (loans and jobs) averaged $4702; and other non-need-based awards and non-need-based scholarships averaged $7640. 15% of undergraduates work part time. Average annual earnings from campus work are $652. The average financial indebtedness of the 2005 graduate was $21,416. The CSS/Profile, FAFSA, FFS or SFS and the college's own financial statement are required. The priority date for freshman financial aid applications for fall entry is March 1. The deadline for filing freshman financial aid applications for fall entry is March 1.

International Students: There are 22 international students enrolled. The school actively recruits these students. A satisfactory score is required on the TOEFL.

Computers: Wireless access is available. All students may access the system One lab is open 24 hours per day; other labs are open 8:30 A.M. to midnight daily. The network is available 24 hours per day. There are no time limits and no fees.

Graduates: From July 1, 2004 to June 30, 2005, 352 bachelor's degrees were awarded. The most popular majors were sociology (12%), economics and business (11%), and psychology (10%). In an average class, 2% graduate in 3 years or less, 63% graduate in 4 years or less, 72% graduate in 5 years or less, and 74% graduate in 6 years or less. 49 companies recruited on campus in 2004-2005. Of the 2004 graduating class, 45% were enrolled in graduate school within 6 months of graduation and 74% were employed.

Admissions Contact: Martha O'Connell, Dean of Admissions.
E-mail: *admissions@mcdaniel.edu* Web: *www.mcdaniel.edu*

MORGAN STATE UNIVERSITY   D-2
Baltimore, MD 21251   (443) 885-3000
(800) 332-6674; Fax: (443) 319-3684

Full-time: 2075 men, 2945 women	**Faculty:** 243
Part-time: 355 men, 445 women	**Ph.D.s:** 80%
Graduate: 205 men, 300 women	**Student/Faculty:** 21 to 1
Year: semesters, summer session	**Tuition:** $5080 ($12,100)
Application Deadline: see profile	**Room & Board:** $7000
Freshman Class: n/av	
SAT or ACT: required	**COMPETITIVE**

Morgan State University, founded in 1867, is a comprehensive public institution offering undergraduate and graduate programs leading to liberal arts, preprofessional, and professional degrees. Figures given in the above capsule and in this profile are approximate. There are 6 undergraduate and 4 graduate schools. In addition to regional accreditation, Morgan State has baccalaureate program accreditation with AACSB, ABET, ADA, ASLA, CSWE, NAAB, NASAD, NASM, and NCATE. The library contains 389,516 volumes, 738,311 microform items, and 45,855 audio/video tapes/CDs/DVDs, and subscribes to 3011 periodicals including electronic. Computerized library services include the card catalog, interlibrary loans, and database searching. Special learning facilities include a learning resource center, art gallery, radio station, and TV station. The 140-acre campus is in a suburban area in the northeast corner of Baltimore. Including any residence halls, there are 41 buildings.

Student Life: 60% of undergraduates are from Maryland. Others are from 40 states, 20 foreign countries, and Canada. 91% are from public schools. 92% are African American. The average age of freshmen is 18; all undergraduates, 21. 24% do not continue beyond their first year; 45% remain to graduate.

Housing: 1800 students can be accommodated in college housing, which includes single-sex dormitories and on-campus apartments. In addition, there are honors houses. On-campus housing is guaranteed for the freshman year only and is available on a first-come, first-served basis. 70% of students commute. Alcohol is not permitted. All students may keep cars.

Activities: 4% of men belong to 2 local and 4 national fraternities; 3% of women belong to 3 local and 4 national sororities. There are 132 groups on campus, including art, band, cheerleading, chess, choir, chorale, chorus, computers, dance, debate, drama, drill team, drum and bugle corps, ethnic, film, forensics, gay, honors, international, jazz band, literary magazine, marching band, musical theater, newspaper, opera, orchestra, pep band, photography, political, professional, radio and TV, religious, social, social service, student government, symphony, and yearbook. Popular campus events include Kwanzaa and I Love Morgan Day.

Sports: There are 6 intercollegiate sports for men and 6 for women, and 17 intramural sports for men and 16 for women. Facilities include a field house, a gym, a weight room, a swimming pool, tennis and racquetball courts, and various playing fields.

Disabled Students: 90% of the campus is accessible. Wheelchair ramps, elevators, special parking, specially equipped rest rooms, special class scheduling, and lowered drinking fountains are available.

Services: Counseling and information services are available, as is tutoring in every subject. There is a reader service for the blind, and remedial math, reading, and writing. There are also note takers and sign language interpreters for disabled students.

Campus Safety and Security: Measures include 24-hour foot and vehicle patrol, self-defense education, security escort services, and shuttle buses. There are informal discussions, pamphlets/posters/films, emergency telephones, and lighted pathways/sidewalks.

Programs of Study: Morgan State confers B.A., B.S., A.B., and B.S.Ed. degrees. Master's and doctoral degrees are also awarded. Bachelor's degrees are awarded in BIOLOGICAL SCIENCE (biology/biological science), BUSINESS (accounting, business administration and management, hospitality management services, and marketing/retailing/merchandising), COMMUNICATIONS AND THE ARTS (dramatic arts, English, fine arts, music, speech/debate/rhetoric, and telecommunications), COMPUTER AND PHYSICAL SCIENCE (chemistry, computer science, information sciences and systems, mathematics, and physics), EDUCATION (elementary, health, and physical), ENGINEERING AND ENVIRONMENTAL DESIGN (civil engineering, electrical/electronics engineering, engineering physics, and industrial engineering technology), HEALTH PROFESSIONS (medical laboratory technology and mental health/human services), SOCIAL SCIENCE (African American studies, economics, history, home economics, philosophy, political science/government, psychology, religion, social work, and sociology). Engineering, chemistry, and social work are the strongest academically. Business administration, accounting, and electrical engineering are the largest.

Required: To graduate, students must complete at least 120 credit hours, including 74 in the major, with a 2.0 GPA. All students must pass speech and writing proficiency exams prior to their senior year. The 46-credit general education requirement includes courses in English, humanities, logic, history, behavioral science, science, math, African American history, and health and phys ed. Seniors must pass a proficiency exam in their major.

Special: Co-op programs in public and private institutions may be arranged for pharmacy honors, predentistry, premedicine, and special education students. The university also offers internships for juniors and seniors, study abroad in 3 countries, work-study programs, and preprofessional physical therapy and prelaw programs. Dual majors may be pursued, but do not lead to a dual degree. There are 28 national honor societies, including Phi Beta Kappa, and a freshman honors program.

Faculty/Classroom: 67% of faculty are male; 33%, female. All teach undergraduates and 76% do research. No introductory courses are taught by graduate students. The average class size in an introductory lecture is 25; in a laboratory, 26; and in a regular course, 21.

Requirements: The SAT or ACT is required, with a satisfactory score on the SAT. In addition, applicants should be high school graduates, or have earned the GED, and are encouraged to have 4 years of English, 3 of math, 2 each of science, social studies, and history, and 1 of a foreign language. A personal essay is recommended and, when appropriate, an audition. A GPA of 2.5 is required. AP and CLEP credits are accepted. Important factors in the admissions decision are recommendations by school officials, evidence of special talent, and parents or siblings attending the school.

Procedure: Freshmen are admitted fall and spring. Entrance exams should be taken during the fall semester of the junior or senior year. There are early admissions and rolling admissions plans. Check with the school for application deadlines. Notification is sent on a rolling basis. The fall 2005 application fee was $25.

Transfer: 411 transfer students enrolled in a recent year. Applicants with fewer than 24 credits must submit high school transcripts; those with fewer than 12 credits must also submit SAT scores. Applicants are expected to have at least a 2.0 GPA in all college work attempted and be in good standing at the last institution attended. 30 of 120 credits required for the bachelor's degree must be completed at Morgan State.

Visiting: There are regularly scheduled orientations for prospective students, including placement testing and academic advising. There are guides for informal visits and visitors may sit in on classes and stay overnight. To schedule a visit, contact Cheryl Hopson at (443) 885-1922.

Financial Aid: In a recent year, 87% of all full-time freshmen and 85% of continuing full-time students received some form of financial aid. 74% of full-time freshmen and 75% of continuing full-time students received need-based aid. Morgan State is a member of CSS. The FAFSA and the college's own financial statement are required. Check with the school for application deadlines.

International Students: They must score satisfactorily on the written TOEFL or take the ALIGU and also take the SAT or the ACT. Students who have not attended any school during the preceding 3 years are not required to submit standardized test scores.

Computers: All students may access the system. There are no time limits and no fees.

Graduates: In a recent year, 818 bachelor's degrees were awarded. In an average class, 12% graduate in 4 years or less, and 12% graduate in 5 years or less. 79 companies recruited on campus in 2004-2005.

Admissions Contact: Edwin T. Johnson, Director of Admission and Recruitment. A video is available. E-mail: *Admissions@morgan.edu* Web: *www.morgan.edu*

MOUNT SAINT MARY'S UNIVERSITY   D-1
(Formerly Mount Saint Mary's College)

Emmitsburg, MD 21727   (301) 447-5214
(800) 448-4347; Fax: (301) 447-5860

Full-time: 611 men, 874 women	**Faculty:** 95; II A, --$
Part-time: 42 men, 129 women	**Ph.D.s:** 89%
Graduate: 307 men, 213 women	**Student/Faculty:** 16 to 1
Year: semesters, summer session	**Tuition:** $22,900
Application Deadline: March 1	**Room & Board:** $8030

Freshman Class: 2190 applied, 1847 accepted, 439 enrolled
SAT Verbal/Math: 540/540*   **COMPETITIVE**

Mount Saint Mary's University, founded in 1808, is a private liberal arts institution affiliated with the Roman Catholic Church. In addition to regional accreditation, the Mount has baccalaureate program accreditation with NASDTEC. The library contains 209,770 volumes, 24,186 microform items, and 2455 audio/video tapes/CDs/DVDs, and subscribes to 935 periodicals including electronic. Computerized library services include the card catalog, interlibrary loans, database searching, Internet access, and laptop Internet portals. Special learning facilities include a learning resource center, art gallery, radio station, TV station, and archives. The 1400-acre campus is in a rural area 60 miles northwest of Washington, D.C., and 50 miles west of Baltimore. Including any residence halls, there are 25 buildings.

Student Life: 61% of undergraduates are from Maryland. Others are from 27 states and 12 foreign countries. 55% are from public schools. 87% are white. 83% are Catholic; 16% Protestant. The average age of freshmen is 18; all undergraduates, 20. 16% do not continue beyond their first year; 68% remain to graduate.

Housing: 1181 students can be accommodated in college housing, which includes coed dorms and on-campus apartments. In addition, there are special-interest houses, wellness floors, and quiet floors. On-campus housing is guaranteed for all 4 years. 81% of students live on campus; of those, 80% remain on campus on weekends. All students may keep cars.

Activities: There are no fraternities or sororities. There are 70 groups on campus, including art, band, cheerleading, chess, choir, chorale, computers, dance, drama, ethnic, honors, international, literary magazine, musical theater, newspaper, photography, political, professional, radio and TV, religious, social, social service, student government, and yearbook. Popular campus events include Spring Fling, Family Fest, and Christmas Dance.

Sports: There are 9 intercollegiate sports for men and 10 for women, and 20 intramural sports for men and 20 for women. Facilities include multipurpose indoor courts, a track, a pool, aerobics facilities, a sauna, a weight room, a basketball arena, lighted tennis courts, and playing fields.

Disabled Students: 60% of the campus is accessible. Wheelchair ramps, elevators, special parking, specially equipped rest rooms, special class scheduling, lowered drinking fountains, and lowered telephones are available.

Services: Counseling and information services are available, as is tutoring in every subject. There is a reader service for the blind and remedial math. There is a study skills and language lab and a writing center. Closed-caption TV and software for sight-impaired students are also available.

Campus Safety and Security: Measures include 24-hour foot and vehicle patrol, security escort services, informal discussions, and pamphlets/posters/films. There are emergency telephones, lighted pathways/sidewalks, and access control.

Programs of Study: The Mount confers B.A. and B.S. degrees. Master's degrees are also awarded. Bachelor's degrees are awarded in BIOLOGICAL SCIENCE (biochemistry and biology/biological science), BUSINESS (accounting, business administration and management, and sports management), COMMUNICATIONS AND THE ARTS (communications, English, fine arts, French, German, and Spanish), COMPUTER AND PHYSICAL SCIENCE (chemistry, computer science, information sciences and systems, and mathematics), EDUCATION (elementary and secondary), SOCIAL SCIENCE (criminal justice, economics, history, interdisciplinary studies, international studies, philosophy, political science/government, psychology, social studies, sociology, and theological studies). Business and finance, elementary education, and biology are the largest.

Required: Students are required to take a 4-year, 52-credit core curriculum (with an additional foreign language proficiency requirement) in liberal arts, which includes a freshman seminar, a 4-course Western civilization sequence including art and literature, and courses in science and math, American culture, philosophy, theology, non-Western culture, and ethics. Graduation requirements include 120 credits, with most majors requiring 36 credits (30 to 36 in the major) and a minimum GPA of 2.0.

Special: Mount Saint Mary's offers cross-registration with an area community college, study abroad in the U.K., Europe, and South America, and secondary teacher certification in art, math, and social science. Dual

majors, interdisciplinary majors in biopsychology, American culture, and classical studies, a general studies degree, 3 dual degree programs, and nondegree and accelerated study are possible. A number of independently designed internships, work-study programs, and pass/fail options are available. There also is an integrated freshman year program. There are 16 national honor societies, a freshman honors program, and 14 departmental honors programs.

Faculty/Classroom: 59% of faculty are male; 41%, female. 88% teach undergraduates, and 82% both teach and do research. No introductory courses are taught by graduate students. The average class size in an introductory lecture is 24; in a laboratory, 16; and in a regular course, 20.

Admissions: 84% of the 2005-2006 applicants were accepted. The SAT scores for the 2005-2006 freshman class were: Verbal--24% below 500, 49% between 500 and 599, 25% between 600 and 700, and 2% above 700; Math--25% below 500, 47% between 500 and 599, 25% between 600 and 700, and 3% above 700. 40% of the current freshmen were in the top fifth of their class; 72% were in the top two fifths. 4 freshmen graduated first in their class.

Requirements: The SAT is required. In addition, applicants should be graduates of an accredited secondary school or hold the GED. Secondary preparation should include 4 years of English, 3 each of math, history, natural science, and social sciences, and 2 of a foreign language. An interview is recommended. AP and CLEP credits are accepted. Important factors in the admissions decision are recommendations by school officials, advanced placement or honor courses, and extracurricular activities record.

Procedure: Freshmen are admitted fall and spring. Entrance exams should be taken by January of the senior year. There are early action and deferred admissions plans. There is a rolling admissions plan. Early action applications should be filed by December 1; regular applications, by March 1 for fall entry and December 1 for spring entry. The fall 2005 application fee was $35. Notification of early action is made by December 15; regular decision, on a rolling basis. Applications are accepted online.

Transfer: 49 transfer students enrolled in 2004-2005. Transfer applicants should have at least a 2.0 GPA in previous college work, be in good academic and disciplinary standing, and account for all time elapsed since graduation from high school. 30 of 120 credits required for the bachelor's degree must be completed at the Mount.

Visiting: There are regularly scheduled orientations for prospective students, including campus tours and information sessions on academic programs, community life, admissions, and financial aid. There are guides for informal visits and visitors may sit in on classes and stay overnight. To schedule a visit, contact the Admissions Office.

Financial Aid: In 2005-2006, 98% of all full-time freshmen and 95% of continuing full-time students received some form of financial aid. 65% of full-time freshmen and 66% of continuing full-time students received need-based aid. The average freshman award was $16,514. Need-based scholarships or need-based grants averaged $3823 ($18,850 maximum); need-based self-help aid (loans and jobs) averaged $3917 ($5625 maximum); and non-need-based athletic scholarships averaged $7199 ($30,930 maximum). 32% of undergraduates work part time. Average annual earnings from campus work are $1032. The average financial indebtedness of the 2005 graduate was $15,964. The FAFSA and the college's own financial statement are required. The deadline for filing freshman financial aid applications for fall entry is March 15.

International Students: There are 13 international students enrolled. They must achieve a satisfactory score on the TOEFL and also take the SAT or the ACT.

Computers: Wireless access is available. All students may access the system 24 hours per day. There are no time limits and no fees. It is strongly recommended that all students have a personal computer.

Graduates: From July 1, 2004 to June 30, 2005, 329 bachelor's degrees were awarded. The most popular majors were business (31%), elementary education (11%), and sociology (8%). In an average class, 1% graduate in 3 years or less, 64% graduate in 4 years or less, 68% graduate in 5 years or less, and 68% graduate in 6 years or less. 100 companies recruited on campus in 2004-2005. Of the 2004 graduating class, 28% were enrolled in graduate school within 6 months of graduation and 99% were employed.

Admissions Contact: Stephen Neitz, Executive Director of Admissions and Financial Aid. A video is available.
E-mail: *admissions@msmary.edu* Web: *http://www.msmary.edu*

SAINT JOHN'S COLLEGE E-3

Annapolis, MD 21404
(410) 626-2523
(800) 727-9238; Fax: (410) 269-7916

Full-time: 256 men, 223 women	Faculty: 61; IIB, +$
Part-time: none	Ph.D.s: 69%
Graduate: 60 men, 34 women	Student/Faculty: 8 to 1
Year: semesters, summer session	Tuition: $32,575
Application Deadline: open	Room & Board: $7876
Freshman Class: 494 applied, 375 accepted, 149 enrolled	
SAT or ACT: not required	HIGHLY COMPETITIVE+

St. John's College, founded as King William's School in 1696 and chartered as St. John's in 1784, is a private institution that offers a single all-required curriculum sometimes called the Great Books Program. Students and faculty work together in small discussion classes without lecture courses, written finals, or emphasis on grades. The program is a rigorous interdisciplinary curriculum based on the great works of literature, math, philosophy, theology, sciences, political theory, music, history, and economics. There is also a campus in Santa Fe, New Mexico. The 2 libraries contain 120,000 volumes, 412 microform items, and 5000 audio/video tapes/CDs/DVDs, and subscribe to 127 periodicals including electronic. Computerized library services include the card catalog, interlibrary loans, database searching, Internet access, and laptop Internet portals. Special learning facilities include an art gallery and planetarium. The 36-acre campus is in a small town 35 miles east of Washington, D.C., and 32 miles south of Baltimore. Including any residence halls, there are 18 buildings.

Student Life: 87% of undergraduates are from out of state, mostly the South. Students are from 46 states, 3 foreign countries, and Canada. 60% are from public schools. 89% are white. 62% claim no religious affiliation; 20% Protestant; 12% Catholic. The average age of freshmen is 19; all undergraduates, 20. 18% do not continue beyond their first year; 77% remain to graduate.

Housing: 375 students can be accommodated in college housing, which includes single-sex and coed dormitories. In addition, there are special-interest houses. On-campus housing is guaranteed for the freshman year only and is available on a lottery system for upperclassmen. 83% of students live on campus; of those, 95% remain on campus on weekends. Upperclassmen may keep cars.

Activities: There are no fraternities or sororities. There are 49 groups on campus, including art, chess, chorus, christian fellowship, community garden, computers, dance, drama, fencing, film, gay, international, literary magazine, newspaper, orchestra, photography, poetry. political, religious, social, social service, student government, swing club, vegetarian club, waltz and swing parties, woodshop, and yearbook. Popular campus events include Reality Weekend, Senior Prank, and College Navy Croquet Match.

Sports: There are 4 intercollegiate sports for men and 4 for women, and 19 intramural sports for men and 19 for women. Facilities include a gym with a weight room, cardio room, and indoor running track, tennis courts, a boathouse for sailing and crew, and playing fields.

Disabled Students: 70% of the campus is accessible. Wheelchair ramps, elevators, special parking, specially equipped rest rooms, special class scheduling, lowered drinking fountains, lowered telephones, and special housing are available.

Services: Counseling and information services are available, as is tutoring in most subjects. There is remedial math and writing.

Campus Safety and Security: Measures include 24-hour foot and vehicle patrol, self-defense education, security escort services, and informal discussions. There are pamphlets/posters/films, emergency telephones, and lighted pathways/sidewalks.

Programs of Study: St. John's confers the B.A. degree. Master's degrees are also awarded. Bachelor's degrees are awarded in SOCIAL SCIENCE (liberal arts/general studies, Western civilization/culture, and Western European studies).

Required: The common curriculum, equivalent to 132 credits, covers a range of classic to modern works. Students attend small seminars; 9-week preceptorials on specific works or topics; language, music, and math tutorials; and a 3-year natural sciences lab. Active learning occurs through discussion, translations, writing, experiment, mathematical demonstration, and musical analysis. Students take oral exams each semester and submit annual essays. Sophomores also take a math exam and seniors an oral exam that admits them to degree candidacy. Seniors also present a final essay to the faculty and take a 1-hour public oral exam.

Faculty/Classroom: 73% of faculty are male; 27%, female. All teach undergraduates. No introductory courses are taught by graduate students. The average class size in a laboratory is 15 and in a regular course, 15.

Admissions: 76% of the 2005-2006 applicants were accepted. 65% of the current freshmen were in the top fifth of their class; 83% were in the top two fifths. There were 5 National Merit finalists and 6 semifinalists.

Requirements: Applicants need not be high school graduates; some students are admitted before they complete high school. Test scores may be submitted but are not required. Secondary preparation should include 4 years of English, 3 years of math, and 2 years each of foreign language, science, and history. Applicants must submit written essays, which are critical to the admissions decision, and are strongly urged to schedule an interview. Important factors in the admissions decision are recommendations by school officials, advanced placement or honor courses, and personality/intangible qualities.

Procedure: Freshmen are admitted fall and spring. There are early admissions, deferred admissions, and rolling admissions plans. Application deadlines are open. Applications are accepted on-line.

Transfer: 22 transfer students enrolled in 2004-2005. Transfer students may enter only as freshmen and must complete the entire program at St. John's. The admissions criteria are the same as for regular students. Students in good academic standing may transfer to the Santa Fe campus at the beginning of any academic year. 132 of 132 credits required for the bachelor's degree must be completed at St. John's.

Visiting: There are regularly scheduled orientations for prospective students, consisting of an overnight stay on campus, class visits, and a tour. There are guides for informal visits and visitors may sit in on classes and stay overnight. To schedule a visit, contact the Admission Office at (410) 626-2522.

Financial Aid: In 2005-2006, 54% of all full-time freshmen and 63% of continuing full-time students received some form of financial aid. 54% of full-time freshmen and 63% of continuing full-time students received need-based aid. The average freshman award was $23,520. Need-based scholarships or need-based grants averaged $18,135; and need-based self-help aid (loans and jobs) averaged $5385. 75% of undergraduates work part time. Average annual earnings from campus work are $2700. The average financial indebtedness of the 2005 graduate was $18,375. St. John's is a member of CSS. The CSS/Profile or FAFSA and parent and student federal tax returns are required. The deadline for filing freshman financial aid applications for fall entry is February 15.

International Students: There are 3 international students enrolled. The school actively recruits these students. They must take the TOEFL and also take the SAT.

Computers: Wireless access is available. All students may access the system 24 hours a day. There are no time limits and no fees.

Graduates: From July 1, 2004 to June 30, 2005, 93 bachelor's degrees were awarded. The most popular major was liberal arts (100%). In an average class, 67% graduate in 4 years or less, 75% graduate in 5 years or less, and 77% graduate in 6 years or less. 5 companies recruited on campus in 2004-2005. Of the 2004 graduating class, 11% were enrolled in graduate school within 6 months of graduation and 60% were employed.

Admissions Contact: John Christensen, Director of Admissions. E-mail: admissions@sjca.edu Web: http://www.sjca.edu

SAINT MARY'S COLLEGE OF MARYLAND E-4

St. Marys City, MD 20686
(240) 895-5000
(800) 492-7181; Fax: (240) 895-5001

Full-time: 788 men, 1061 women	Faculty: 129; IIB, av$
Part-time: 50 men, 65 women	Ph.D.s: 96%
Graduate: none	Student/Faculty: 14 to 1
Year: semesters, summer session	Tuition: $10,833 ($19,710)
Application Deadline: January 15	Room & Board: $8043
Freshman Class: 2200 applied, 1503 accepted, 488 enrolled	
SAT Verbal/Math: 630/610*	VERY COMPETITIVE+

St. Mary's College of Maryland, founded in 1840, is a small public liberal arts college in the Maryland State College and University System. The library contains 158,318 volumes, 43,783 microform items, and 11,242 audio/video tapes/CDs/DVDs, and subscribes to 14,211 periodicals including electronic. Computerized library services include the card catalog, interlibrary loans, database searching, and Internet access. Special learning facilities include a learning resource center, art gallery, radio station, TV station, historic archeological site, and estuarine research facilities. The 319-acre campus is in a rural area 70 miles south of Washington, D.C. Including any residence halls, there are 47 buildings.

Student Life: 81% of undergraduates are from Maryland. Others are from 36 states, 32 foreign countries, and Canada. 79% are from public schools. 82% are white. 38% are claim no religious affiliation; 34% Protestant; 19% Catholic; 6% Islam, Buddhist, and other. The average age of freshmen is 18; all undergraduates, 20. 11% do not continue beyond their first year; 79% remain to graduate.

Housing: 1488 students can be accommodated in college housing, which includes single-sex and coed dorms and on-campus apartments. In addition, there are language houses and special-interest houses. On-campus housing is guaranteed for all 4 years. 85% of students live on campus; of those, 75% remain on campus on weekends. All students may keep cars.

Activities: There are no fraternities or sororities. There are 78 groups on campus, including academic, art, band, cheerleading, chess, choir, chorale, chorus, computers, dance, drama, ethnic, film, gay, honors, international, jazz band, literary magazine, musical theater, newspaper, orchestra, outdoors, photography, political, professional, radio and TV, religious, social, social service, student government, symphony, and yearbook. Popular campus events include World Carnival and River Concert Series.

Sports: There are 7 intercollegiate sports for men and 8 for women, and 12 intramural sports for men and 12 for women. Facilities include an Olympic-size 50-meter pool, a 25-yard swimming pool, a 1,200-seat basketball and volleyball arena, an expanded health and fitness center, a weight room, a training room, an exercise room, 2 gyms, and locker and team rooms. Physical education, athletics, and recreation facilities also include 5 varsity practice fields, a track, 6 lighted tennis courts, an outdoor stadium, and baseball facilities.

Disabled Students: 92% of the campus is accessible. Wheelchair ramps, elevators, special parking, specially equipped rest rooms, special class scheduling, lowered drinking fountains, lowered telephones, and Living suites that meet ADA standards are available.

Services: Counseling and information services are available, as is tutoring in some subjects, including math, writing, physics, foreign languages, chemistry, economics, and English. There is a reader service for the blind.

Campus Safety and Security: Measures include 24-hour foot and vehicle patrol, self-defense education, security escort services, and informal discussions. There are pamphlets/posters/films, emergency telephones, lighted pathways/sidewalks, student security-assistant foot patrols, and a nighthawk program from 8 P.M. until midnight.

Programs of Study: St. Mary's confers the B.A. degree. Bachelor's degrees are awarded in BIOLOGICAL SCIENCE (biochemistry and biology/biological science), COMMUNICATIONS AND THE ARTS (art, art history and appreciation, dramatic arts, English, languages, and music), COMPUTER AND PHYSICAL SCIENCE (chemistry, computer science, mathematics, natural sciences, and physics), EDUCATION (education), SOCIAL SCIENCE (anthropology, economics, history, human development, philosophy, political science/government, psychology, public affairs, religion, and sociology). Economics, biology, and psychology are strongest academically and have the largest enrollments.

Required: Students must complete general education requirements in writing, math, foreign language, history, the arts, literature, physical, biological, behavioral, and policy sciences, philosophy, and an interdisciplinary seminar. There is a senior project. Students must meet additional requirements in their major fields and complete 128 semester hours with at least a 2.0 GPA.

Special: St. Mary's offers a co-op program in computer science, internships, study abroad, national and international exchange programs, and work-study. Dual and student-designed majors and a 3-2 engineering degree with the University of Maryland, College Park, also are offered. Nondegree study and pass/fail options are possible. There are 8 national honor societies, including Phi Beta Kappa, a freshman honors program, and 6 departmental honors programs.

Faculty/Classroom: 54% of faculty are male; 46%, female. All both teach and do research. The average class size in an introductory lecture is 23; in a laboratory, 14; and in a regular course, 18.

Admissions: 22% of the 2005-2006 applicants were accepted. The SAT scores for the 2005-2006 freshman class were: Verbal--7% below 500, 27% between 500 and 599, 48% between 600 and 700, and 18% above 700; Math--7% below 500, 36% between 500 and 599, 51% between 600 and 700, and 6% above 700. 57% of the current freshmen were in the top fifth of their class; 89% were in the top two fifths.

Requirements: The SAT or ACT is required. In addition, applicants should have graduated from an accredited secondary school or earned the GED. Minimum high school preparation should include 4 units of English, 3 each of math, social studies, and science, and 7 electives. An essay, a resume of cocurricular activities, and 2 letters of recommendation are required. A GPA of 2.0 is required. AP and CLEP credits are accepted. Important factors in the admissions decision are recommendations by school officials, extracurricular activities record, and leadership record.

Procedure: Freshmen are admitted fall and spring. Entrance exams should be taken in May of the junior year or November of the senior year. There are early decision and early admissions plans. Early decision applications should be filed by December 1; regular applications, by January 15 for fall entry and October 15 for spring entry, along with a $40 fee. Notification of early decision is sent January 1; regular decision, April 1. 164 early decision candidates were accepted for the 2005-2006 class. 215 applicants were on the 2005 waiting list; 29 were admitted. Applications are accepted on-line.

Transfer: 69 transfer students enrolled in 2004-2005. Transfer applicants with a minimum of 24 credits should have at least a 2.0 GPA. Those with fewer credits should have at least a 2.5 GPA. 38 of 128 credits required for the bachelor's degree must be completed at St. Mary's.

Visiting: There are regularly scheduled orientations for prospective students, including group presentations, interaction with faculty and students, and campus tours. There are guides for informal visits and visitors may sit in on classes and stay overnight. To schedule a visit, contact the Admissions Office.

Financial Aid: In 2005-2006, 75% of all full-time freshmen and 71% of continuing full-time students received some form of financial aid. 27% of full-time freshmen and 40% of continuing full-time students received need-based aid. The average freshman award was $6200. Need-based scholarships or need-based grants averaged $1500 ($6000 maximum); need-based self-help aid (loans and jobs) averaged $1000 ($2625 maximum); and other non-need-based awards and non-need-based scholarships averaged $2700 ($6625 maximum). 25% of undergraduates work part time. Average annual earnings from campus work are $1000. The average financial indebtedness of the 2005 graduate was $17,125. St. Mary's is a member of CSS. The FAFSA is required. The deadline for filing freshman financial aid applications for fall entry is March 1.

International Students: There are 49 international students enrolled. They must achieve a satisfactory score on the TOEFL.

Computers: Wireless access is available. Throughout the campus, there are approximately 255 PCs in many general-purpose computer labs featuring Microsoft Windows XP and the Mac OS operating systems. These computer labs are available to all students for word processing, spreadsheet, and database work. There are also several smart classrooms and discipline-specific labs on campus. All of the computer labs have access to the library system, e-mail, and the Internet. There is also wireless access in all academic building areas of the campus for those who own wireless-ready laptop computers. All students may access the system during all lab hours. There are no time limits and no fees.

Graduates: From July 1, 2004 to June 30, 2005, 465 bachelor's degrees were awarded. The most popular majors were psychology (14%), economics (12%), and political science (11%). In an average class, 1% graduate in 3 years or less, 72% graduate in 4 years or less, 75% graduate in 5 years or less, and 75% graduate in 6 years or less. 68 companies recruited on campus in 2004-2005. Of the 2004 graduating class, 35% were enrolled in graduate school within 6 months of graduation and 99% were employed.

Admissions Contact: Dr. Wesley P. Jordan, Director of Admissions. A video is available. E-mail: *admissions@smcm.edu*
Web: *http://www.smcm.edu*

SALISBURY UNIVERSITY   F-4

Salisbury, MD 21801   (410) 543-6161; Fax: (410) 546-6016

Full-time: 2546 men, 3252 women	**Faculty:** 323; IIA, -$
Part-time: 286 men, 353 women	**Ph.D.s:** 82%
Graduate: 141 men, 431 women	**Student/Faculty:** 18 to 1
Year: 4-1-4, summer session	**Tuition:** $6376 ($14,054)
Application Deadline: January 15	**Room & Board:** $6752
Freshman Class: 5550 applied, 3011 accepted, 958 enrolled	
SAT Verbal/Math: 560/570*	**ACT:** 24 **VERY COMPETITIVE**

Salisbury University, founded in 1925, is a public comprehensive university providing undergraduate programs in the liberal arts, sciences, pre-professional and professional programs, and select, mostly applied, graduate programs in business, education, nursing, psychology, English, and history. There are 4 undergraduate schools and 1 graduate school. In addition to regional accreditation, SU has baccalaureate program accreditation with AACSB, ACS, CAAHEP, CSWE, NCATE, NAACLS, NEHSPAC, and NLN. The library contains 263,295 volumes, 750,272 microform items, and 1013 audio/video tapes/CDs/DVDs, and subscribes to 1252 periodicals including electronic. Computerized library services include the card catalog, interlibrary loans, database searching, and Internet access. Special learning facilities include a learning resource center, art gallery, radio station, TV station, Research Center for Delmarva History and Culture, Enterprise Development Group, Shorecan Small Business Resources Center, and Scarborough Leadership Center. The 145-acre campus is in a small town 110 miles southeast of Baltimore and 100 miles east of Washington, D.C. Including any residence halls, there are 55 buildings.

Student Life: 82% of undergraduates are from Maryland. Others are from 28 states, 30 foreign countries, and Canada. 83% are white; 10% African American. The average age of freshmen is 19; all undergraduates, 21. 17% do not continue beyond their first year; 83% remain to graduate.

Housing: 1704 students can be accommodated in university housing, which includes single-sex and coed dorms and off-campus apartments. On-campus housing is available on a first-come, first-served basis and is available on a lottery system for upperclassmen. 74% of students commute. Upperclassmen may keep cars.

Activities: 5% of men belong to 4 national fraternities; 6% of women belong to 4 national sororities. There are 104 groups on campus, including art, band, cheerleading, chess, choir, chorale, chorus, computers, dance, drama, ethnic, film, gay, honors, international, jazz band, literary magazine, musical theater, newspaper, orchestra, pep band, political, professional, radio and TV, religious, social, social service, student government, symphony, and yearbook. Popular campus events include October Fest, Spring Fling, and Festival of Culture.

Sports: There are 10 intercollegiate sports for men and 11 for women, and 20 intramural sports for men and 20 for women. Facilities include

a 3000-seat stadium, a 2000-seat gym, a multipurpose gym, a 25-meter, 6-lane swimming pool, indoor climbing walls, a dance studio, racquetball and indoor and outdoor tennis courts, a baseball diamond, varsity and practice fields, an all-weather track, a fitness center, a strength room, lighted intramural fields, and outdoor sand volleyball courts.

Disabled Students: 90% of the campus is accessible. Wheelchair ramps, elevators, special parking, specially equipped rest rooms, special class scheduling, lowered drinking fountains, lowered telephones, and emergency phones are available.

Services: Counseling and information services are available, as is tutoring in some subjects. There is a reader service for the blind, and remedial math, reading, and writing. and extended test-taking time.

Campus Safety and Security: Measures include 24-hour foot and vehicle patrol, self-defense education, security escort services, and shuttle buses. There are informal discussions, pamphlets/posters/films, emergency telephones, and lighted pathways/sidewalks.

Programs of Study: SU confers B.A., B.S., B.A.S.W., and B.F.A. degrees. Master's degrees are also awarded. Bachelor's degrees are awarded in AGRICULTURE (environmental studies), BIOLOGICAL SCIENCE (biology/biological science), BUSINESS (accounting, banking and finance, business administration and management, management information systems, and marketing/retailing/merchandising), COMMUNICATIONS AND THE ARTS (art, communications, English, fine arts, French, music, Spanish, and theater management), COMPUTER AND PHYSICAL SCIENCE (chemistry, computer science, mathematics, and physics), EDUCATION (athletic training, elementary, health, and physical), HEALTH PROFESSIONS (environmental health science, exercise science, medical technology, nursing, and respiratory therapy), SOCIAL SCIENCE (economics, geography, history, interdisciplinary studies, international studies, peace studies, philosophy, political science/government, psychology, social work, and sociology). Chemistry, business, and education are the strongest academically. Business administration, elementary education, and biology are the largest.

Required: Students must complete 45 semester hours of general education requirements, including specific courses in English composition and literature, world civilization, humanities, social studies, math, and phys ed. The core curriculum also includes courses in art and physical or life science. The bachelor's degree requires completion of at least 120 semester hours, including 30 or more in the major field, with a minimum GPA of 2.0. Some majors may have higher requirements. 30 of the last 37 credit hours must be completed at SU, except for special co-op programs.

Special: Cross-registration with schools in the University System of Maryland, and study abroad in numerous countries are offered. SU also offers an Annapolis semester, a Washington semester, internships, work-study programs, accelerated degree programs in dentistry, optometry, podiatric medicine, and pharmacy, dual majors in biology/environmental marine science, social work/sociology, and physical engineering, interdisciplinary and student-designed majors including physics/microelectronics, a 3-2 engineering degree with the University of Maryland at College Park, Old Dominion University, and Widener University, a co-op program in electrical engineering, and pass/fail options. There are 20 national honor societies, a freshman honors program, and 15 departmental honors programs.

Faculty/Classroom: 55% of faculty are male; 45%, female. All teach undergraduates and 16% both teach and do research. Graduate students teach 1% of introductory courses. The average class size in an introductory lecture is 28; in a laboratory, 18; and in a regular course, 27.

Admissions: 54% of the 2005-2006 applicants were accepted. The SAT scores for the 2005-2006 freshman class were: Verbal--13% below 500, 59% between 500 and 599, 26% between 600 and 700, and 2% above 700; Math--9% below 500, 55% between 500 and 599, 34% between 600 and 700, and 2% above 700. The ACT scores were 30% below 21, 18% between 21 and 23, 33% between 24 and 26, 14% between 27 and 28, and 5% above 28. 52% of the current freshmen were in the top fifth of their class; 89% were in the top two fifths. There were 3 National Merit finalists. 9 freshmen graduated first in their class.

Requirements: The SAT is required. The ACT Optional Writing test is also required. In addition, applicants must be graduates of accredited secondary schools or have earned a GED. The university requires 14 academic credits or 20 Carnegie units, including 4 in English, 3 each in math and social studies, 3 in science (2 with labs), and 2 in foreign language. Auditions are required for admission into the music and B.F.A. programs once admission to the university is granted. Essays are recommended, but are not required. A campus visit is recommended for all students. A GPA of 2.0 is required. AP and CLEP credits are accepted. Important factors in the admissions decision are advanced placement or honor courses, leadership record, and extracurricular activities record.

Procedure: Freshmen are admitted to all sessions. Entrance exams should be taken by December of the senior year. Early decision applications should be filed by December 15; regular applications, by January 15 for fall entry and January 1 for spring entry. Notification of early decision is sent January 15; regular decision, March 15. Applications are accepted on-line.

Transfer: 986 transfer students enrolled in 2004-2005. Applicants must present a minimum GPA of 2.0 in at least 24 transferable credit hours earned. Students with fewer than 24 credit hours must be eligible for freshman admission in addition to maintaining at least a 2.0 GPA in college courses. 30 of 120 credits required for the bachelor's degree must be completed at SU.

Visiting: There are regularly scheduled orientations for prospective students, including presentations, tours, meetings with faculty and staff, and Saturday open house programs. There are guides for informal visits and visitors may sit in on classes. To schedule a visit, contact the Admissions Office.

Financial Aid: In 2004-2005, 68% of all full-time freshmen and 83% of continuing full-time students received some form of financial aid. 38% of full-time freshmen and 50% of continuing full-time students received need-based aid. The average freshman award was $9279. Need-based scholarships or need-based grants averaged $4791 ($17,200 maximum); need-based self-help aid (loans and jobs) averaged $9443 ($23,554 maximum); and other non-need-based awards and non-need-based scholarships averaged $2763 ($14,430 maximum). 30% of undergraduates work part time. Average annual earnings from campus work are $2000. The average financial indebtedness of the 2005 graduate was $15,831. The FAFSA is required. The priority date for freshman financial aid applications for fall entry is February 1. The deadline for filing freshman financial aid applications for fall entry is March 1.

International Students: There are 43 international students enrolled. They must take the TOEFL, provide proof of visa, and also take the SAT or ACT.

Computers: Wireless access is available. Wired network connections are available to students in all dorm rooms, at the library, classrooms, computer labs, and elsewhere in the university. The wireless network can accommodate 460 simultaneous users. All students may access the system 24 hours daily via modem or in residence halls. There are no time limits. The fee is $144. It is strongly recommended that all students have a personal computer.

Graduates: From July 1, 2004 to June 30, 2005, 1313 bachelor's degrees were awarded. The most popular majors were business administration (17%), education (12%), and social sciences and history (12%). In an average class, 47% graduate in 4 years or less, 65% graduate in 5 years or less, and 67% graduate in 6 years or less. 250 companies recruited on campus in 2004-2005. Of the 2004 graduating class, 29% were enrolled in graduate school within 6 months of graduation and 92% were employed.

Admissions Contact: Laura T. Thorpe, Director of Admissions.
E-mail: *ltthorpe@salisbury.edu*
Web: *http://www.salisbury.edu/admissions*

SOJOURNER-DOUGLASS COLLEGE D-2

Baltimore, MD 21201	(410) 276-0306; Fax: (410) 675-1810
Full-time: 40 men, 150 women	Faculty: 14
Part-time: 20 men, 40 women	Ph.D.s: 18%
Graduate: none	Student/Faculty: 13 to 1
Year: trimesters	Tuition: $4200
Application Deadline: open	Room & Board: n/app
Freshman Class: n/av	
SAT or ACT: not required	LESS COMPETITIVE

Sojourner-Douglass College, established in 1980, is a private institution offering undergraduate programs in administration, human and social resources, and human growth and development to a predominantly black student body. Figures given in the above capsule and in this profile are approximate. The library contains 20,000 volumes. Special learning facilities include a learning resource center. The campus is in an urban area in Baltimore.

Housing: There are no residence halls. All of students commute. Alcohol is not permitted.

Activities: There are no fraternities or sororities. There are 5 groups on campus, including student government and yearbook.

Sports: There is no sports program at Sojourner-Douglass.

Disabled Students: Wheelchair ramps, elevators, and special parking are available.

Services: Counseling and information services are available, as is tutoring in some subjects, including reading, writing, math, and study skills.

Programs of Study: Sojourner-Douglass confers the B.A. degree. Bachelor's degrees are awarded in BUSINESS (business administration and management and tourism), COMMUNICATIONS AND THE ARTS (broadcasting), EDUCATION (early childhood), HEALTH PROFESSIONS (health care administration), SOCIAL SCIENCE (criminal justice, gerontology, psychology, public administration, and social work).

Required: In order to graduate, students must earn 63 to 66 general education credits, with 15 credits in English literature and composition; 15 credits in political science, history, economics, sociology, geography, psychology, and anthropology; 12 credits in the humanities; 9 credits in natural science and math; and 3 credits each in career planning and personal development, psychology of the black family in America, and psychology of racism. 12 credits must be earned in a project that demonstrates competence in the major. 6 credits must be earned in the sociology of work. There is also a 3-credit education seminar requirement. A total of 132 credits is needed to graduate, with 54 to 69 in the major.

Special: Credit may be granted for life, military and work experience. Faculty supervised independent study is possible for adult students.

Requirements: The SAT or ACT is not required. Applicants must be graduates of an accredited secondary school or have a GED certificate. They must have completed 4 years of English and 2 years each of math, history, and social studies. Autobiographical essays, resumes, and interviews are required.

Procedure: Freshmen are admitted to all sessions. There is a rolling admissions plan. Application deadlines are open.

Transfer: Transfer criteria are the same as for entering freshmen; however, transfers are not accepted to all classes.

Visiting: There are regularly scheduled orientations for prospective students. To schedule a visit, contact the Office of Admissions at (410) 276-0306.

Financial Aid: The CSS/Profile, FAFSA, FFS or SFS and Federal income tax form are required. Check with the school for current application deadlines.

Computers: There are no time limits and no fees.

Admissions Contact: LaVerne B. Cawthorne, Coord, Admissions.

TOWSON UNIVERSITY   D-2

Towson, MD 21252-0001

(410) 704-2113
(888) 4-TOWSON; Fax: (410) 704-3030

Full-time: 4882 men, 7930 women	**Faculty:** 663; IIA, -$
Part-time: 766 men, 917 women	**Ph.D.s:** 52%
Graduate: 877 men, 2639 women	**Student/Faculty:** 19 to 1
Year: semesters, summer session	**Tuition:** 7096 ($16,030)
Application Deadline: May 2	**Room & Board:** $7112
Freshman Class: 11,746 applied, 7497 accepted, 2310 enrolled	
SAT Verbal/Math: 540/550*	**VERY COMPETITIVE**

Towson University, founded in 1866, is part of the University System of Maryland and offers undergraduate and graduate programs in liberal arts and sciences, allied health sciences, education, fine arts, communication, and business and economics. There are 7 undergraduate schools and 1 graduate school. In addition to regional accreditation, Towson has baccalaureate program accreditation with AACSB, CAHEA, NASDTEC, NASM, and NLN. The library contains 364,468 volumes, 830,286 microform items, and 14,174 audio/video tapes/CDs/DVDs, and subscribes to 2164 periodicals including electronic. Computerized library services include the card catalog, interlibrary loans, database searching, and Internet access. Special learning facilities include a learning resource center, art gallery, planetarium, radio station, TV station, curriculum center, herbarium, animal museum, observatory, and greenhouse. The 321-acre campus is in a suburban area 2 miles north of Baltimore.

Student Life: 84% of undergraduates are from Maryland. Others are from Canada. 87% are white; 11% African American. The average age of all undergraduates is 21. 14% do not continue beyond their first year.

Housing: 3310 students can be accommodated in college housing, which includes coed dorms and on-campus apartments. In addition, there are honors houses, and international house, and separate floors that are alcohol-free, smoke-free, substance-free, leadership, quiet, or co-ed. On-campus housing is available on a first-come, first-served basis and is available on a lottery system for upperclassmen. Priority is given to out-of-town students. 77% of students commute. Upperclassmen may keep cars.

Activities: There are many groups and organizations on campus, including art, band, cheerleading, choir, chorale, chorus, computers, dance, debate, drama, drill team, ethnic, forensics, honors, international, jazz band, literary magazine, marching band, musical theater, newspaper, orchestra, pep band, photography, political, radio and TV, religious, social, student government, symphony, and yearbook. Popular campus events include fraternity and sorority dances, Ethics Forum, and Tiger Fest.

Sports: Facilities include an athletic center, a stadium with artificial turf, baseball and softball fields, tennis courts, a pool, a soccer field, and 3 practice fields. Recreation facilities include 3 gyms, a weight room, a pool, lighted playing fields, and an indoor climbing wall.

Disabled Students: 85% of the campus is accessible. Wheelchair ramps, elevators, special parking, specially equipped rest rooms, special class scheduling, lowered drinking fountains, lowered telephones, special housing, automatic doors, assistive listening devices in theaters and concert halls, and interior and exterior signage are available.

Services: Counseling and information services are available, as is tutoring in most subjects. There is a reader service for the blind, and remedial math, reading, and writing. There are also note takers, English language and tutorial services centers, a writing lab, and signers for the hearing impaired.

Campus Safety and Security: Measures include 24-hour foot and vehicle patrol, self-defense education, security escort services, and shuttle buses. There are informal discussions, pamphlets/posters/films, emergency telephones, lighted pathways/sidewalks, and Operation ID, and a police dog on campus.

Programs of Study: Towson confers B.A., B.S., B.F.A., and B.M. degrees. Master's and doctoral degrees are also awarded. Bachelor's degrees are awarded in BIOLOGICAL SCIENCE (biology/biological science and molecular biology), BUSINESS (accounting, business administration and management, and sports management), COMMUNICATIONS AND THE ARTS (art, communications, dance, English, French, German, media arts, music, Spanish, and theater design), COMPUTER AND PHYSICAL SCIENCE (chemistry, computer science, earth science, geology, geoscience, information sciences and systems, mathematics, and physics), EDUCATION (art, athletic training, dance, early childhood, education, education of the deaf and hearing impaired, elementary, music, physical, and special), ENGINEERING AND ENVIRONMENTAL DESIGN (environmental science), HEALTH PROFESSIONS (exercise science, health care administration, health science, medical laboratory technology, nursing, occupational therapy, speech pathology/audiology, and sports medicine), SOCIAL SCIENCE (anthropology, crosscultural studies, economics, family/consumer studies, geography, gerontology, history, interdisciplinary studies, international studies, law, philosophy, political science/government, psychology, religion, social science, sociology, and women's studies). Fine arts, business, and education are the strongest academically. Business disciplines, mass communications, and psychology are the largest.

Required: Students must complete course work in the arts, English, humanities, math, biological or physical science, social science, information technology, and global awareness.

Special: Towson University offers cooperative programs with other institutions in the University System of Maryland and at Loyola College, the College of Notre Dame, or Johns Hopkins University, cross-registration at more than 80 colleges through the National Student Exchange, and study abroad. Students may pursue a dual major in physics and engineering, an interdisciplinary studies degree, which allows them to design their own majors, a 3-2 engineering program with the University of Maryland at College Park, or nondegree study. There are pass/fail options, extensive evening offerings, and opportunities to earn credits between semesters. Internships are available in most majors and work-study programs are offered both on and off campus. There are 20 national honor societies, a freshman honors program, and 12 departmental honors programs.

Faculty/Classroom: 53% of faculty are male; 47%, female. The average class size in an introductory lecture is 25; in a laboratory, 24; and in a regular course, 25.

Admissions: 64% of the 2005-2006 applicants were accepted. The SAT scores for the 2005-2006 freshman class were: Verbal--27% below 500, 53% between 500 and 599, 18% between 600 and 700, and 2% above 700; Math--21% below 500, 53% between 500 and 599, 25% between 600 and 700, and 2% above 700. 41% of the current freshmen were in the top fifth of their class; 78% were in the top two fifths.

Requirements: The SAT or ACT is required, the ACT is recommended and will be accepted in lieu of the SAT. In addition, applicants should have graduated from an accredited secondary school or earned the GED. Secondary preparation should include 4 years of English, 3 each of math, lab science, and social studies, and 2 of foreign language. Prospective music and dance majors must audition. AP and CLEP credits are accepted. Important factors in the admissions decision are advanced placement or honor courses, recommendations by school officials, and leadership record.

Procedure: Freshmen are admitted fall and spring. Entrance exams should be taken in the junior and senior year. There are deferred admissions plan and a rolliing admissions plan. Applications should be filed by May 2 for fall entry (priority date December 1). The fall 2005 application fee was $45. Notification is sent on a rolling basis. Applications are accepted on-line.

Transfer: 1141 transfer students enrolled in a recent year. Transfer applicants should have earned at least 30 academic credits. For those with less than 30 attempted, freshmen requirements must be met. Minimum GPA requirements range from 2.0 to 2.5, depending on the number of credits completed. Transcripts are required and a personal statement and interview aew recommended. 30 of 120 credits required for the bachelor's degree must be completed at Towson.

Visiting: There are regularly scheduled orientations for prospective students, including campus tours, a session for parents, a session on the admissions process for transfers and freshmen, and a roundtable discussion. There are guides for informal visits. To schedule a visit, contact the Admissions Office.

Financial Aid: In a recent year, 45% of all full-time freshmen and 38% of continuing full-time students received some form of financial aid. 55% of all full-time freshmen and 51% of continuing full time students received need-based aid. The average freshman award was $7260. Need-based scholarships or need-based grants averaged $4393; need-based self-help aid (loans and jobs) averaged $3211; non-need-based athletic scholarships averaged $8467; and other non-need-based awards and non-need-based scholarships averaged $4237. 72% of undergraduates work part time. Average annual earnings from campus work are $1185. The average financial indebtedness of a recent graduate was $15,530. The FAFSA is required. The priority date for freshman financial aid applications for fall entry is March 1.

International Students: The school actively recruits these students. The TOEFL is required at pre-admission; a college test is required at post-admission. The SAT or ACT is also required, but the school accepts the TOEFL as a substitute for the verbal SAT. Graduates of the campus English language center are not required to take the TOEFL.

Computers: Wireless access is available. All students may access the system 24 hours daily except 5 P.M. to 9 P.M. Fridays. There are no time limits and no fees.

Graduates: From July 1, 2004 to June 30, 2005, 2984 bachelor's degrees were awarded. The most popular majors were business administration (19%), education (12%), and social sciences/history (11%). 115 companies recruited on campus in a recent year.

Admissions Contact: Louise Shulack, Director of Admissions. A video is available. E-mail: *admissions@towson.edu* Web: *www.towson.edu*

UNITED STATES NAVAL ACADEMY   E-3
Annapolis, MD 21402-5018

(410) 293-1858
(800) 638-9156; Fax: (410) 293-4348

Full-time: 3600 men, 600 women	**Faculty:** 600; IIB, ++$
Part-time: none	**Ph.D.s:** 90%
Graduate: none	**Student/Faculty:** 7 to 1
Year: semesters, summer session	**Tuition:** 0
Application Deadline: open	**Room & Board:** n/app
Freshman Class: 4769 applied, 1450 accepted, 1245 enrolled	
SAT Verbal/Math: 650/670*	**ACT:** 29 **MOST COMPETITIVE**

The United States Naval Academy, founded in 1845, is a national military service college offering undergraduate degree programs and professional training in aviation, surface ships, submarines, and various military, maritime, and technical fields. The U.S. Navy pays tuition, room and board, medical and dental care, and a monthly stipend to all Naval Academy students. Some figures given in the above capsule are approximate. In addition to regional accreditation, Annapolis has baccalaureate program accreditation with ABET and CSAB. The library contains 530,000 volumes, and subscribes to 2000 periodicals including electronic. Computerized library services include the card catalog, interlibrary loans, and database searching. Special learning facilities include a learning resource center, art gallery, planetarium, radio station, TV station, a propulsion lab, a nuclear reactor, an oceanographic research vessel, towing tanks, a flight simulator, and a naval history museum. The 329-acre campus is in a small town 30 miles southeast of Baltimore and 35 miles east of Washington, D.C. Including any residence halls, there are 25 buildings.

Student Life: 97% of undergraduates are from out of state, mostly the Northeast. Students are from 50 states and 21 foreign countries. 80% are white. 50% are Protestant; 49% Catholic. The average age of freshmen is 18; all undergraduates, 20. 11% do not continue beyond their first year; 77% remain to graduate.

Housing: 4200 students can be accommodated in college housing, which includes coed dorms. On-campus housing is guaranteed for all 4 years. 100% of students live on campus; of those, 75% remain on campus on weekends. Alcohol is not permitted. Upperclassmen may keep cars.

Activities: There are no fraternities or sororities. There are 75 groups on campus, including bagpipe band, cheerleading, chess, choir, chorus, computers, debate, drama, drill team, drum and bugle corps, ethnic, honors, international, jazz band, literary magazine, marching band, musical theater, pep band, photography, professional, radio and TV, religious, social, social service, student government, and yearbook. Popular campus events include Commissioning Week, which includes the Plebe Recognition Ceremony, Ring Dance, and graduation.

Sports: There are 20 intercollegiate sports for men and 9 for women, and 23 intramural sports for men and 10 for women. Facilities include a 30,000-seat stadium, a 5000-seat basketball arena, an Olympic pool with a diving well for 10-meter diving boards, a wrestling arena, a 200-meter indoor track, a 400-meter outdoor track, an indoor ice rink, 6 Nautilus and weight rooms, and facilities for gymnastics, boxing, fencing, and other sports.

Disabled Students: All of the campus is accessible. Wheelchair ramps, elevators, special parking, and specially equipped rest rooms are available.

Services: Counseling and information services are available, as is tutoring in most subjects. There is remedial math, reading, and writing.

Campus Safety and Security: Measures include 24-hour foot and vehicle patrol, self-defense education, shuttle buses, and emergency telephones. There are lighted pathways/sidewalks and gate guards.

Programs of Study: Annapolis confers the B.S. degree. Bachelor's degrees are awarded in COMMUNICATIONS AND THE ARTS (English),

COMPUTER AND PHYSICAL SCIENCE (chemistry, computer science, mathematics, oceanography, physics, and science), ENGINEERING AND ENVIRONMENTAL DESIGN (aeronautical engineering, electrical/electronics engineering, engineering, marine engineering, mechanical engineering, naval architecture and marine engineering, ocean engineering, and systems engineering), SOCIAL SCIENCE (economics, history, and political science/government). Chemistry, aeronautical engineering, and systems engineering are the strongest academically. Mechanical engineering, math, and oceanography are the largest.

Required: Students must complete 140 semester hours, including core requirements in engineering, natural sciences, humanities, and social sciences. Phys ed is required during all 4 years. Physical readiness testing must be passed. During required summer training sessions, students train aboard U.S. ships, submarines, and aircraft. Graduates serve at least 5 years on active duty as commissioned officers of the Navy or Marine Corps.

Special: Study in Washington, D.C., is available during 1 semester of the senior year. A voluntary graduate program is available for those who complete requirements early and wish to begin master's work at nearby institutions, such as Georgetown or Johns Hopkins Universities. Trident Scholars may spend their senior year in independent research. There are 10 national honor societies and 5 departmental honors programs.

Faculty/Classroom: 80% of faculty are male; 20%, female. All teach undergraduates. The average class size in an introductory lecture is 23; in a laboratory, 10; and in a regular course, 15.

Admissions: 30% of the 2005-2006 applicants were accepted. The SAT scores for the 2005-2006 freshman class were: Verbal--2% below 500, 25% between 500 and 599, 45% between 600 and 700, and 28% above 700; Math--13% between 500 and 599, and 34% above 700. 82% of the current freshmen were in the top fifth of their class; 94% were in the top two fifths.

Requirements: The SAT or ACT is required. The ACT Optional Writing test is also required. In addition, candidates must be unmarried with no dependents, U.S. citizens of good moral character, and between 17 and 23 years of age. Candidates should have a sound secondary school background, including 4 years each of English and math, 2 years of a foreign language, and 1 year each of U.S. history, world or European history, chemistry, physics, and computer literacy. Candidates must obtain an official nomination from congressional or military sources. An interview is conducted, and medical and physical exams must be passed to qualify for admission. AP credits are accepted. Important factors in the admissions decision are advanced placement or honor courses, recommendations by school officials, and leadership record.

Procedure: Freshmen are admitted in the summer. Entrance exams should be taken after December of the junior year. There is a rolling admissions plan. Application deadlines are open. There is no application fee. Notification is sent by April 15.

Transfer: 81 transfer students enrolled in 2004-2005. All students enter as freshmen. 140 of 140 credits required for the bachelor's degree must be completed at Annapolis.

Visiting: There are regularly scheduled orientations for prospective students, including visitation weekends for candidates likely to be accepted, summer seminars, and Admissions Day. Visitors may sit in on classes.

International Students: International students must take the TOEFL and the SAT or the ACT.

Computers: All students may access the system. There are no time limits and no fees.

Graduates: Of the 2004 graduating class, 100% were employed within 6 months of graduation.

Admissions Contact: Candidate Guidance Office.
Web: *www.usna.edu*

UNIVERSITY OF MARYLAND/BALTIMORE COUNTY   D-2
Baltimore, MD 21250

(410) 455-2291
UMBC-4U2; Fax: (410) 455-1094

Full-time: 4240 men, 3800 women	**Faculty:** 464; I, -$
Part-time: 835 men, 795 women	**Ph.D.s:** 85%
Graduate: 1025 men, 1205 women	**Student/Faculty:** 17 to 1
Year: 4-1-4, summer session	**Tuition:** $8250 ($16,596)
Application Deadline: see profile	**Room & Board:** $8122
Freshman Class: n/av	
SAT or ACT: required	**VERY COMPETITIVE+**

UMBC, founded in 1966, is a public research university offering programs in liberal arts and sciences and engineering. There are 3 undergraduate and 2 graduate schools. Figures in the above capsule and profile are approximate. In addition to regional accreditation, UMBC has baccalaureate program accreditation with ABET, CSWE, and NCATE. The library contains 938,653 volumes, 1,078,767 microform items, and 1,925,000 audio/video tapes/CDs/DVDs, and subscribes to 4302 periodicals including electronic. Computerized library services include the card catalog, interlibrary loans, database searching, and Internet access. Special learning facilities include a learning resource center, art gallery, radio station, centers for imaging research, earth systems technology, and telecommunications research, and institutes for medicine and policy analysis and research. The 530-acre campus is in a suburban area 5 miles southwest of Baltimore and 35 miles north of Washington, D.C. Including any residence halls, there are 50 buildings.

Student Life: 88% of undergraduates are from Maryland. Others are from 48 states, 108 foreign countries, and Canada. 84% are from public schools. 55% are white; 17% Asian American; 14% African American. The average age of freshmen is 18; all undergraduates, 23. 18% do not continue beyond their first year; 53% remain to graduate.

Housing: 3432 students can be accommodated in college housing, which includes single-sex and coed dormitories and on-campus apartments. In addition, there are honors houses, language houses, special-interest houses, wellness and quiet-study floors, and same-sex floors. On-campus housing is guaranteed for the freshman year only and is available on a first-come, first-served basis. 67% of students commute. Alcohol is not permitted. All students may keep cars.

Activities: 3% of men belong to 11 national fraternities; 3% of women belong to 8 national sororities. There are 180 groups on campus, including band, cheerleading, chess, choir, chorus, computers, Council of Majors, dance, debate, drama, ethnic, film, gay, honors, international, Intellectual Sports Council, jazz band, literary magazine, model United Nations, musical theater, newspaper, opera, orchestra, pep band, political, professional, radio and TV, religious, social, social service, student government, symphony, and yearbook. Popular campus events include Quadmania, Welcome Week, and Family Weekend.

Sports: There are 8 intercollegiate sports for men and 10 for women, and 16 intramural sports for men and 16 for women. Facilities include a multipurpose arena, an aquatic center, a fitness center, tennis courts, a 4500-seat stadium, playing and practice fields, an indoor track, an outdoor cross-country course, a golf driving range, a track and field complex, and a soccer stadium.

Disabled Students: 95% of the campus is accessible. Wheelchair ramps, elevators, special parking, specially equipped rest rooms, special class scheduling, lowered drinking fountains, lowered telephones, a Braille writer, tape recorders, talking book machines, TTY, talking calculators, Optacon, and information on the talking computer are available.

Services: Counseling and information services are available, as is tutoring in most subjects. There is a reader service for the blind, and remedial math, reading, and writing. Other services include notetakers, readers, mobility training, American Sign Language interpreters, and scribes for students who have a need based on a manual or learning disability.

Campus Safety and Security: Measures include self-defense education, security escort services, shuttle buses, and pamphlets/posters/films. There are emergency telephones, lighted pathways/sidewalks, a 24-hour police department, and a campus risk management department.

Programs of Study: UMBC confers B.A., B.S., B.F.A., and B.S.E. degrees. Master's and doctoral degrees are also awarded. Bachelor's degrees are awarded in AGRICULTURE (environmental studies), BIOLOGICAL SCIENCE (biochemistry, and biology/biological science), COMMUNICATIONS AND THE ARTS (dance, dramatic arts, English, fine arts, French, German, linguistics, modern language, music, Russian, Spanish, theater design, and visual and performing arts), COMPUTER AND PHYSICAL SCIENCE (chemistry, computer science, information sciences and systems, mathematics, physics, and statistics), ENGINEERING AND ENVIRONMENTAL DESIGN (chemical engineering, computer engineering, environmental science, and mechanical engineering), HEALTH PROFESSIONS (emergency medical technologies, and health science), SOCIAL SCIENCE (African American studies, American studies, anthropology, classical/ancient civilization, economics, geography, history, interdisciplinary studies, philosophy, political science/government, psychology, social work, and sociology). Information systems, computer science, and biological sciences are the largest.

Required: To graduate, students are required to complete at least 120 credits, including 45 at the upper-division level, with a minimum GPA of 2.0. The core curriculum includes courses in arts and humanities, social sciences, math and natural sciences, phys ed, and modern or classical language and culture. Students must pass an English composition course with a C or better.

Special: Dual and student-designed majors, cooperative education programs in all majors, a Washington semester, the Sondheim Public Affairs Scholars Program, cross-registration with University of Maryland schools and Johns Hopkins University, internships, both paid and nonpaid, in public, private, and nonprofit organizations, study abroad in 19 countries, work-study programs, B.A.-B.S. degrees, pass/fail options, and nondegree study are available. UMBC also offers various opportunities in interdisciplinary studies and in such fields as artificial intelligence and optical communications. There are 15 national honor societies, including Phi Beta Kappa, a freshman honors program, and 17 departmental honors programs.

Faculty/Classroom: 66% of faculty are male; 34%, female. All both teach and do research. The average class size in an introductory lecture is 36; in a laboratory, 19; and in a regular course, 27.

Requirements: The SAT or ACT is required. In addition, minimum high school preparation should include 4 years of English, 3 years each

of social science/history and math, including algebra I and II and geometry, 3 years of lab sciences and 2 of a foreign language. An essay is required of all freshman applicants. A GPA of 3.0 is required. AP and CLEP credits are accepted. Important factors in the admissions decision are advanced placement or honor courses, recommendations by school officials, and leadership record.

Procedure: Freshmen are admitted to all sessions. Entrance exams should be taken by fall of the senior year. There is an early decision plan. Check with the school for current application deadlines. The application fee is $50. Applications are accepted on-line.

Transfer: 1133 transfer students enrolled in a recent year. A 2.5 cumulative GPA for all previous college work is recommended. Applicants with fewer than 30 semester hours should submit SAT scores and the high school transcript; they must also meet freshman admission requirements. 30 of 120 credits required for the bachelor's degree must be completed at UMBC.

Visiting: There are regularly scheduled orientations for prospective students, including a group information session with an admissions counselor followed by a student-guided walking tour of campus. Saturday information sessions and 4 campus open houses are also scheduled each fall. Summer preview days are available for incoming freshmen. There are guides for informal visits and visitors may sit in on classes and stay overnight. To schedule a visit, contact the Office of Undergraduate Admissions.

Financial Aid: The FAFSA is required. Check with the school for current application deadlines.

International Students: In a recent year, there were 466 international students enrolled. They must score satisfactorily on the electronic TOEFL.

Computers: All students may access the system. There is a 200 hour per month limit for modem dial-up access. All other access is unlimited. There are no fees. It is strongly recommended that all students have a personal computer.

Graduates: In a recent year, 1729 bachelor's degrees were awarded. The most popular majors were information systems (22%), psychology (10%), and computer science (8%). In an average class, 1% graduate in 3 years or less, 28% graduate in 4 years or less, 48% graduate in 5 years or less, and 53% graduate in 6 years or less. 997 companies recruited on campus in a recent year. Of a recent graduating class, 39% were enrolled in graduate school within 6 months of graduation and 93% were employed.

Admissions Contact: Yvette Mozie-Ross, Director of Admissions.
E-mail: *admissions@umbc.edu* Web: *http://www.umbc.edu*

UNIVERSITY OF MARYLAND/COLLEGE PARK   D-3
College Park, MD 20742   (301) 314-8385
                                   (800) 422-5867; Fax: (301) 314-9693

Full-time: 11,768 men, 11,495 women	**Faculty:** 1508; I, +$
Part-time: 1194 men, 985 women	**Ph.D.s:** n/av
Graduate: 5074 men, 4853 women	**Student/Faculty:** 15 to 1
Year: semesters, summer session	**Tuition:** $7821 ($20,145)
Application Deadline: January 20	**Room & Board:** $8215
Freshman Class: 22,462 applied, 11,034 accepted, 4212 enrolled	
SAT or ACT: required	**HIGHLY COMPETITIVE**

University of Maryland/College Park, founded in 1856, is a land-grant institution, the flagship campus of the state's university system, offering undergraduate and graduate degrees. There are 11 undergraduate and 13 graduate schools. In addition to regional accreditation, Maryland has baccalaureate program accreditation with AACSB, ABET, ACEJMC, ASLA, ASLHA, CADE, NAST, NAAB, NASM, NAST, and NCATE. The 7 libraries contain 3,016,940 volumes, 5,676,082 microform items, and 257,016 audio/video tapes/CDs/DVDs, and subscribe to 33,348 periodicals including electronic. Computerized library services include the card catalog, interlibrary loans, database searching, and Internet access. Special learning facilities include a learning resource center, art gallery, radio station, TV station, and an observatory. The 1250-acre campus is in a suburban area 3 miles northeast of Washington, D.C., and 35 miles south of Baltimore. Including any residence halls, there are 273 buildings.

Student Life: 75% of undergraduates are from Maryland. Others are from 49 states, 139 foreign countries, and Canada. 57% are white; 14% Asian American; 13% African American. The average age of freshmen is 18; all undergraduates, 21. 7% do not continue beyond their first year; 76% remain to graduate.

Housing: 10,630 students can be accommodated in college housing, which includes single-sex and coed dormitories, on-campus apartments, fraternity houses, and sorority houses. In addition, there are honors houses, language houses, and special-interest houses. On-campus housing is available on a lottery system for upperclassmen. 58% of students commute. Alcohol is not permitted. Upperclassmen may keep cars.

Activities: 9% of men belong to 30 national fraternities; 11% of women belong to 24 national sororities. There are 544 groups on campus, including art, band, cheerleading, chess, choir, chorale, chorus, computers, dance, debate, drama, drill team, ethnic, film, forensics, gay, honors, international, jazz band, literary magazine, marching band, musical theater, newspaper, opera, orchestra, pep band, photography, political, professional, radio and TV, religious, social, social service, student government, symphony, and yearbook. Popular campus events include Art Attack, Union All-Niter, and Maryland Day.

Sports: There are 12 intercollegiate sports for men and 15 for women, and 15 intramural sports for men and 15 for women. Facilities include 2 indoor and 2 outdoor swimming pools, intramural fields, tennis, squash, racquetball, volleyball, and basketball courts, a fitness center including weight rooms, aerobic rooms, martial arts rooms, saunas, and an indoor track, a bowling alley, a golf course, and an outdoor artificial turf field. Athletic facilities include a 51,000-seat stadium, a 17,950-seat gym, and indoor and outdoor artificial turf practice fields.

Disabled Students: 95% of the campus is accessible. Wheelchair ramps, elevators, special parking, specially equipped rest rooms, special class scheduling, lowered drinking fountains, lowered telephones, a special shuttle service, and electronic doors are available.

Services: Counseling and information services are available, as is tutoring in most subjects, including all 100- and 200-level courses. There is a reader service for the blind and remedial math.

Campus Safety and Security: Measures include 24-hour foot and vehicle patrol, self-defense education, security escort services, and shuttle buses. There are informal discussions, pamphlets/posters/films, emergency telephones, lighted pathways/sidewalks, and video surveillance.

Programs of Study: Maryland confers B.A., B.S., B.L.A., B.M., and B.M.E. degrees. Master's and doctoral degrees are also awarded. Bachelor's degrees are awarded in AGRICULTURE (agricultural business management, agricultural economics, agriculture, animal science, horticulture, and natural resource management), BIOLOGICAL SCIENCE (biochemistry, biology/biological science, microbiology, and nutrition), BUSINESS (accounting, banking and finance, business administration and management, human resources, international business management, logistics, management information systems, management science, marketing management, operations management, supply chain management, and transportation management), COMMUNICATIONS AND THE ARTS (art history and appreciation, Chinese, classics, communications, dance, dramatic arts, English, English literature, French, Germanic languages and literature, Japanese, journalism, linguistics, music, music performance, music theory and composition, romance languages and literature, Russian, Spanish, and studio art), COMPUTER AND PHYSICAL SCIENCE (astronomy, chemistry, computer science, geology, information sciences and systems, mathematics, physical sciences, and physics), EDUCATION (art, drama, early childhood, education, elementary, English, foreign languages, mathematics, music, physical, science, secondary, social studies, and special), ENGINEERING AND ENVIRONMENTAL DESIGN (aeronautical engineering, architecture, bioresource engineering, chemical engineering, civil engineering, computer engineering, electrical/electronics engineering, engineering, environmental science, fire protection engineering, landscape architecture/design, materials engineering, and mechanical engineering), HEALTH PROFESSIONS (community health work, preveterinary science, speech pathology/audiology, and veterinary science), SOCIAL SCIENCE (African American studies, American studies, anthropology, criminal justice, criminology, dietetics, economics, family/consumer studies, food science, geography, history, Italian studies, Judaic studies, philosophy, physical fitness/movement, political science/government, psychology, Russian and Slavic studies, sociology, and women's studies). Engineering, computer science, and business are the strongest academically. Criminology and criminal justice, government, politics and psychology are the largest.

Required: Most programs require a minimum of 120 credits for graduation; the number of hours required in the major varies. All students must take 43 to 46 credits in a multidisciplinary core curriculum, including 10 in math and science, 9 each in social sciences, and humanities and the arts, 6 in advanced studies, and 3 diversity credits. Freshman and junior composition are also required, and students must maintain a 2.0 GPA.

Special: Each of the 11 undergraduate schools offers special programs, and there is a campuswide co-op education program offering engineering and other majors. In addition, the university offers cross-registration with other colleges in the Consortium of Universities of the Washington Metropolitan Area, several Living-Learning programs for undergraduates, the B.A./B.S. degree in most majors, dual and student-designed majors, nondegree study, and accelerated veterinary medicine program, varied study-abroad opportunities, work-study programs with government and nonprofit organizations, and internship opportunities with federal and state legislators, the local media, and various federal agencies. There are 49 national honor societies, including Phi Beta Kappa, a freshman honors program, and 39 departmental honors programs.

Faculty/Classroom: 64% of faculty are male; 36%, female. 55% teach undergraduates and 45% do research. Graduate students teach 21% of introductory courses. The average class size in an introductory lecture is 41; in a laboratory, 16; and in a regular course, 36.

Admissions: 49% of the 2005-2006 applicants were accepted. The SAT scores for the 2005-2006 freshman class were: Verbal--7% below 500, 22% between 500 and 599, 51% between 600 and 700, and 17%

above 700; Math--5% below 500, 17% between 500 and 599, 49% between 600 and 700, and 29% above 700.

Requirements: The SAT or ACT is required. The university evaluates exam scores along with GPA, curriculum, and other criteria. Applicants should be graduates of accredited secondary schools or have the GED. Secondary preparation should include 4 years of English, 3 of history or social sciences, 2 of algebra and 1 of plane geometry, and 2 of lab sciences. An essay and counselor recommendation are required. Music majors must also audition. AP and CLEP credits are accepted. Important factors in the admissions decision are advanced placement or honor courses, recommendations by school officials, and evidence of special talent.

Procedure: Freshmen are admitted fall, spring, and summer. Entrance exams should be taken at the end of the junior year or the beginning of the senior year. There are early admissions, deferred admissions and rolling admissions plans. Early decision applications should be filed by December 1; regular applications, by January 20 for fall entry and December 1 for spring entry. Notification of early decision is sent February 15; regular decision, on a rolling basis. 3208 applicants were on the 2005 waiting list; 45 were admitted for fall, 1987 for spring 2006. Applications are accepted on-line. The fall 2005 application fee was $55.

Transfer: 2652 transfer students enrolled in fall 2005. Transfer applicants from regionally accredited institutions should have attempted at least 12 credits and have earned at least a 2.5 GPA, although this requirement varies depending on space available. Applicants from Maryland community colleges may be given special consideration. 30 of 120 credits required for the bachelor's degree must be completed at Maryland.

Visiting: There are regularly scheduled orientations for prospective students, consisting of 3 fall and 4 spring open house programs for admitted students, as well as regularly scheduled information sessions followed by a campus tour. There are guides for informal visits and visitors may sit in on classes and stay overnight. To schedule a visit, contact the Office of Undergraduate Admissions at (800) 422-5867.

Financial Aid: 18% of undergraduates work part time. Average annual earnings from campus work are $5200. The average financial indebtedness of the 2005 graduate was $13,243. The FAFSA is required. The priority date for freshman financial aid applications for fall entry is February 15.

International Students: There are 521 international students enrolled. They must score satisfactorily on the written TOEFL or take the APIEL or ELPT and also take the SAT or the ACT.

Computers: Wireless access is available. All students may access the system 24 hours a day, 7 days a week. There are no time limits and no fees.

Graduates: From July 1, 2004 to June 30, 2005, 6263 bachelor's degrees were awarded. The most popular majors were criminology and criminal justice (7%), government and politics (6%), and economics (5%). In an average class, 50% graduate in 4 years or less, 73% graduate in 5 years or less, and 76% graduate in 6 years or less. 331 companies recruited on campus in 2004-2005.

Admissions Contact: Admissions Officer. A video is available. E-mail: um-admit@uga.umd.edu Web: www.maryland.edu

UNIVERSITY OF MARYLAND/EASTERN SHORE   F-4

Princess Anne, MD 21853   (410) 651-6410; Fax: (410) 651-7922

Full-time: 1225 men, 1810 women	Faculty: 90
Part-time: 125 men, 175 women	Ph.D.s: 80%
Graduate: 185 men, 255 women	Student/Faculty: 34 to 1
Year: semesters, summer session	Tuition: $5080 ($10,000)
Application Deadline: see profile	Room & Board: $6130
Freshman Class: n/av	
SAT: required	COMPETITIVE

University of Maryland/Eastern Shore, founded in 1886, is a public university, part of the University of Maryland System, offering undergraduate and graduate programs in the arts and sciences, professional studies, and agricultural sciences. There are 3 undergraduate schools and 1 graduate school. Figures in the above capsule and profile are approximate. The library contains 150,000 volumes. Computerized library services include the card catalog, interlibrary loans, and database searching. Special learning facilities include a learning resource center, art gallery, and radio station. The 700-acre campus is in a rural area 15 miles south of Salisbury. Including any residence halls, there are 40 buildings.

Student Life: 71% of undergraduates are from Maryland. Others are from 32 states, 48 foreign countries, and Canada. 85% are from public schools. 76% are African American; 18% white. 90% are Protestant; 10% claim no religious affiliation. The average age of freshmen is 18; all undergraduates, 24. 25% do not continue beyond their first year; 36% remain to graduate.

Housing: 1530 students can be accommodated in college housing, which includes single-sex dormitories, on-campus apartments, and off-campus apartments. In addition, there are honors houses, and a residential campus. On-campus housing is available on a first-come, first-served basis and is available on a lottery system for upperclassmen. 50% of students live on campus; of those, 30% remain on campus on weekends. All students may keep cars.

Activities: 20% of men belong to 4 national fraternities; 20% of women belong to 4 national sororities. There are 25 groups on campus, including art, band, cheerleading, choir, chorale, chorus, computers, dance, drama, drill team, ethnic, honors, international, jazz band, literary magazine, musical theater, newspaper, pep band, photography, political, professional, radio and TV, religious, social, social service, student government, and yearbook. Popular campus events include Parents Day, Spring Festival, and Ethnic Festival.

Sports: There are 5 intercollegiate sports for men and 5 for women, and 4 intramural sports for men and 4 for women. Facilities include an indoor swimming pool and a 3000-seat stadium.

Disabled Students: 20% of the campus is accessible. Wheelchair ramps, elevators, special parking, specially equipped rest rooms, special class scheduling, lowered drinking fountains, and lowered telephones are available.

Services: Counseling and information services are available, as is tutoring in every subject. There is remedial math, reading, and writing.

Campus Safety and Security: Measures include 24-hour foot and vehicle patrol, security escort services, shuttle buses, and informal discussions. There are pamphlets/posters/films, emergency telephones, lighted pathways/sidewalks, and a student security team.

Programs of Study: UMES confers B.A., B.S., B.G.S., and B.M. degrees. Master's and doctoral degrees are also awarded. Bachelor's degrees are awarded in AGRICULTURE (agriculture and poultry science), BIOLOGICAL SCIENCE (biology/biological science), BUSINESS (accounting, business administration and management, and hotel/motel and restaurant management), COMMUNICATIONS AND THE ARTS (English), COMPUTER AND PHYSICAL SCIENCE (chemistry, computer science, and mathematics), EDUCATION (agricultural, art, business, elementary, health, home economics, industrial arts, mathematics, music, physical, science, secondary, and social science), ENGINEERING AND ENVIRONMENTAL DESIGN (aeronautical science, construction technology, engineering technology, and environmental science), HEALTH PROFESSIONS (physical therapy and rehabilitation therapy), SOCIAL SCIENCE (criminal justice, history, home economics, liberal arts/general studies, and sociology). Physical therapy, engineering, and environmental science are the strongest academically. Business, hotel restaurant management, and biology are the largest.

Required: Students must complete 122 hours, including 36 hours in the major, 15 in communicative and quantitative skills, 9 in humanities, 7 in natural sciences, 6 in social sciences, and 4 in health and phys ed. A minimum 2.0 overall GPA is required.

Special: Students may cross-register at Salisbury State University. A cooperative education program, internships, a winter term, work-study programs, a general studies degree, and dual and student-designed majors are offered. Also available are an accelerated degree program and a 3-2 engineering degree with the University of Maryland/College Park. There are pass/fail options. There is 1 national honor society, a freshman honors program, and 10 departmental honors programs.

Faculty/Classroom: 45% of faculty are male; 55%, female. 85% teach undergraduates and 15% do research. Graduate students teach 1% of introductory courses. The average class size in an introductory lecture is 75; in a laboratory, 18; and in a regular course, 30.

Requirements: The SAT is required. In addition, applicants should be graduates of accredited secondary schools or have the GED. High school preparation should include 4 years of English, 3 each of social science or history and math, including 2 of algebra and 1 of geometry, and 2 of laboratory science. An essay and interview are recommended. UMES recommends that prospective art education majors submit a portfolio. Students may earn credit by examination. A GPA of 2.5 is required. AP and CLEP credits are accepted. Important factors in the admissions decision are advanced placement or honor courses, leadership record, and recommendations by school officials.

Procedure: Freshmen are admitted to all sessions. Entrance exams should be taken April. There are early decision, early admissions, deferred admissions and rolling admissions plans. Check with the school for current application deadlines. The application fee is $25. Notification is sent on a rolling basis.

Transfer: 129 transfer students enrolled in a recent year. Transfer applicants must have attempted at least 9 credits at another institution and have at least a cumulative GPA of 2.0, or have earned an associate degree or completed 56 hours of community college work. 75 of 122 credits required for the bachelor's degree must be completed at UMES.

Visiting: There are regularly scheduled orientations for prospective students, including 2 formal orientation sessions and 9 visitation/open house days. There are guides for informal visits and visitors may sit in on classes. To schedule a visit, contact the Office of Recruitment at (410) 651-6178.

Financial Aid: UMES is a member of CSS. The college's own financial statement is required. Check with the school for current application deadlines.

International Students: They must score satisfactorily on the written TOEFL and also take the SAT.

Computers: There are no fees. It is strongly recommended that all students have a personal computer.

Admissions Contact: Cheryll Collier-Mills, Director of Admissions and Recruitment. E-mail: *ccmills@mail.umes.edu* Web: *www.umes.edu*

UNIVERSITY OF MARYLAND/UNIVERSITY COLLEGE D-3
Adelphi, MD 20783
(301) 985-7000
(800) 285-6832; Fax: (301) 985-7364

Full-time: 1053 men, 1727 women	Faculty: 221
Part-time: 6692 men, 9528 women	Ph.D.s: 81%
Graduate: 3917 men, 4512 women	Student/Faculty: 13 to 1
Year: semesters, summer session	Tuition: $5640 ($10,272)
Application Deadline: open	Room & Board: n/app
Freshman Class: n/av	
SAT or ACT: not required	SPECIAL

University of Maryland/University College was founded in 1947 to serve the needs of the adult continuing education student. It offers evening and weekend courses in the liberal arts and sciences and in business at more than 17 locations throughout the Washington, D.C.-Baltimore area and the state of Maryland. The library contains 2900 volumes, and subscribes to 28 periodicals including electronic. Computerized library services include the card catalog, interlibrary loans, database searching, and Internet access. Special learning facilities include a learning resource center, art gallery, and TV station. The campus is in an urban area.

Student Life: 82% of undergraduates are from Maryland. Students are from 50 states, 65 foreign countries, and Canada. 50% are white; 36% African American. The average age of all undergraduates is 34.

Housing: There are no residence halls. All of students commute. Alcohol is not permitted. All students may keep cars.

Activities: There are no fraternities or sororities.

Sports: There is no sports program at UMUC.

Disabled Students: Wheelchair ramps, elevators, special parking, specially equipped rest rooms, special class scheduling, and lowered drinking fountains are available.

Services: Counseling and information services are available, as is tutoring in some subjects, including math, writing, accounting, and computing. There is a reader service for the blind. Referrals are available for tutoring in other subjects.

Campus Safety and Security: Measures include 24-hour foot and vehicle patrol, security escort services, and emergency telephones.

Programs of Study: UMUC confers B.A. and B.S. degrees. Associate, master's, and doctoral degrees are also awarded. Bachelor's degrees are awarded in BUSINESS (accounting, business administration and management, human resources, management science, and marketing management), COMMUNICATIONS AND THE ARTS (communications and English), COMPUTER AND PHYSICAL SCIENCE (computer science and information sciences and systems), ENGINEERING AND ENVIRONMENTAL DESIGN (computer technology and environmental science), SOCIAL SCIENCE (criminal justice, fire science, history, humanities, liberal arts/general studies, paralegal studies, psychology, and social science).

Required: A general education requirement of 30 semester hours includes courses in communications, humanities, social sciences, and math/science. The B.A. degree requires 12 semester hours of a foreign language. A minimum 2.0 GPA and 120 semester hours of credit are required to graduate.

Special: UMUC offers cooperative programs in interdisciplinary studies. There are a number of work-study programs with local employers. Credit by exam, credit for life/work experience, nondegree study, and pass/fail options are available. Through UMUC's open learning program, a number of independent learning courses are available. There are 4 national honor societies.

Faculty/Classroom: 60% of faculty are male; 40%, female. All teach undergraduates. The average class size in a regular course is 22.

Requirements: Students should be graduates of an accredited secondary school or have a GED equivalent. AP and CLEP credits are accepted.

Procedure: Freshmen are admitted to all sessions. There is a rolling admissions plan. Application deadlines are open. Application fee is $30. Applications are accepted on-line.

Transfer: 9126 transfer students enrolled in 2004-2005. 30 of 120 credits required for the bachelor's degree must be completed at UMUC.

Financial Aid: The FAFSA and SAR (for Pell grants) are required. Check with the school for current deadlines.

International Students: There are 61 international students enrolled. They must achieve a satisfactory score on the TOEFL and also take the college's own test.

Computers: Wireless access is available. All students may access the system. There are no time limits and no fees.

Graduates: From July 1, 2004 to June 30, 2005, 2677 bachelor's degrees were awarded. The most popular majors were business and management (29%), computer and information science (15%), and information systems management (13%).

Admissions Contact: Technical Director, Admission and Information. E-mail: *umucinfo@nova.umuc.edu* Web: *http://www.umuc.edu*

UNIVERSITY SYSTEM OF MARYLAND

The University System of Maryland, established in 1807, is a public system in Maryland. It is governed by a Board of Regents, whose chief administrator is chancellor. The primary goals of the system are research, teaching, and public service. The total enrollment of all 13 campuses is usually about 128,000; there were about 10,000 faculty members. Altogether more than 600 academic programs are offered in University System of Maryland. Profiles of the 4-year campuses are included in this section.

VILLA JULIE COLLEGE   D-2
Stevenson, MD 21153

(410) 486-7001
(877) 468-6852; Fax: (410) 602-6600

Full-time: 689 men, 1615 women	Faculty: 93; IIB, av$
Part-time: 112 men, 391 women	Ph.D.s: 67%
Graduate: 59 men, 90 women	Student/Faculty: 25 to 1
Year: semesters, summer session	Tuition: $15,674
Application Deadline: open	Room & Board: $9548
Freshman Class: 2166 applied, 1509 accepted, 542 enrolled	
SAT Verbal/Math: 500/500*	COMPETITIVE

Villa Julie College, founded in 1947, is an independent, comprehensive college offering a liberal arts education combined with career preparation. In addition to regional accreditation, VJC has baccalaureate program accreditation with ABA, NAACLS, NCATE and NLN. The library contains 74,092 volumes, 167,735 microform items, and 2481 audio/video tapes/CDs/DVDs, and subscribes to 718 periodicals including electronic. Computerized library services include the card catalog, interlibrary loans, database searching, and Internet access. Special learning facilities include a learning resource center, art gallery, a theater, and a video studio. The 60-acre campus is in a suburban area 10 miles northwest of Baltimore. Including any residence halls, there are 24 buildings.

Student Life: 96% of undergraduates are from Maryland. Others are from 17 states and 7 foreign countries. 76% are from public schools. 75% are white; 15% African American. The average age of freshmen is 18; all undergraduates, 24. 21% do not continue beyond their first year.

Housing: 752 students can be accommodated in college housing, which includes coed dorms and on-campus apartments. On-campus housing is available on a first-come, first-served basis. 73% of students commute. Alcohol is not permitted. All students may keep cars.

Activities: 22% of women belong to 1 national sorority. There are no fraternities. There are 30 groups on campus, including academic, art, band, cheerleading, chess, chorus, computers, dance, drama, enviromental, ethnic, film, gay, honors, jazz band, literary magazine, newspaper, orchestra, pep band, photography, political, professional, religious, service learning, social, social service, student government, and wilderness. Popular campus events include Welcome Picnic, SGA Haunted Trail and Bonfire, and NY City Bus Trip.

Sports: There are 8 intercollegiate sports for men and 9 for women, and 6 intramural sports for men and 5 for women. Facilities include tennis courts and an athletic field, a 1000-seat gym, a fitness center, a NATA-certified training room, and an aerobics room.

Disabled Students: 95% of the campus is accessible. Wheelchair ramps, elevators, special parking, specially equipped rest rooms, special class scheduling, lowered drinking fountains, lowered telephones, and special housing are available.

Services: Counseling and information services are available, as is tutoring in most subjects. There is remedial math, reading, and writing. Free individual tutoring as well as study groups led by a tutor, peer tutoring, paraprofessional tutoring, and faculty tutoring is available.

Campus Safety and Security: Measures include self-defense education, security escort services, shuttle buses, and informal discussions. There are pamphlets/posters/films, emergency telephones, and lighted pathways/sidewalks. There are also 15-hour foot and vehicle patrols during VJC's operating hours.

Programs of Study: VJC confers B.A.and B.S. degrees. Master's degrees are also awarded. Bachelor's degrees are awarded in BIOLOGICAL SCIENCE (biology/biological science and biotechnology), BUSINESS (business administration and management and business systems analysis), COMMUNICATIONS AND THE ARTS (design, English, film arts, and visual design), COMPUTER AND PHYSICAL SCIENCE (applied mathematics, chemistry, and information sciences and systems), EDUCATION (elementary), HEALTH PROFESSIONS (nursing), SOCIAL SCIENCE (family/consumer studies, interdisciplinary studies, liberal arts/general studies, paralegal studies, and psychology). Education, nursing, and paralegal are the strongest academically. Paralegal, nursing, and business are the largest.

Required: The core curriculum includes courses in writing, communication, fine arts, social sciences, math, natural science, humanities, and phys ed. Courses in computer information systems are also required. Students must complete a minimum of 120 hours, including 45 hours in upper-level courses, with at least a 2.0 overall GPA. The number of hours required per major varies. Many majors require a capstone course and an internship.

Special: VJC offers co-op programs in several majors as well as cross-registration through the Baltimore Student Exchange Program. Also offered are supervised internships for second-year students in several majors, which require a minimum of 120 hours per semester, and Washington Center internships. There are work-study programs, and study abroad is possible in 4 countries through programs offered at other colleges. There also are accelerated degree programs in nursing, paralegal studies, and business administration. Student-designed majors are possible, as are interdisciplinary majors, including liberal arts and technology, computer accounting, and business information systems. Education courses for state cerification are available, and students may earn credit by exam. There are 6 national honor societies, a freshman honors program, and 6 departmental honors programs.

Faculty/Classroom: 46% of faculty are male; 54%, female. 99% teach undergraduates. No introductory courses are taught by graduate students. The average class size in an introductory lecture is 18; in a laboratory, 14; and in a regular course, 18.

Admissions: 70% of the 2005-2006 applicants were accepted. The SAT scores for the 2005-2006 freshman class were: Verbal--45% below 500, 42% between 500 and 599, 12% between 600 and 700, and 1% above 700; Math--44% below 500, 41% between 500 and 599, 14% between 600 and 700, and 1% above 700. 33% of the current freshmen were in the top fifth of their class; 64% were in the top two fifths. 6 freshmen graduated first in their class.

Requirements: The SAT or ACT is required. In addition, applicants must be graduates of an accredited secondary school. Although a secondary transcript is required, particular secondary preparation is not stipulated for all programs. Some degree programs do require specific high school courses, however. An essay is required and an interview is recommended. AP and CLEP credits are accepted. Important factors in the admissions decision are advanced placement or honor courses, recommendations by school officials, and leadership record.

Procedure: Freshmen are admitted fall, spring, and summer. Entrance exams should be taken between September and November of the senior year. There are deferred admissions and rolling admissions plans. Application deadlines are open. Applications are accepted on-line.The fall 2005 application fee was $25.

Transfer: 258 transfer students enrolled in 2004-2005. Transfer applicants must provide both college and secondary school transcripts and have a minimum 2.5 GPA. Grades earned at other institutions are not include in calculating the GPA required for graduation. Transfer students with a 2.0 cumulative GPA and other accomplishments or experience may be granted conditional admission to the college. 30 of 120 credits required for the bachelor's degree must be completed at VJC.

Visiting: There are regularly scheduled orientations for prospective students, including a general overview, information on how to apply and how to finance a college education, special academic presentations, tours, meetings with faculty and students, and lunch. There are guides for informal visits and visitors may sit in on classes. To schedule a visit, contact the Admissions Office at *admissions@mail.vjc.edu*.

Financial Aid: In 2005-2006, 58% of all full-time freshmen and 76% of continuing full-time students received some form of financial aid. 52% of full-time freshmen and 68% of continuing full-time students received need-based aid. The average freshman award was $9362. Need-based scholarships or need-based grants averaged $7806; and need-based self-help aid (loans and jobs) averaged $2527. 6% of undergraduates work part time. Average annual earnings from campus work are $1319. The average financial indebtedness of the 2005 graduate was $15,679. VJC is a member of CSS. The FAFSA is required. The priority date for freshman financial aid applications for fall entry is February 15. The deadline for filing freshman financial aid applications for fall entry is March 1.

International Students: There are 8 international students enrolled. A satisfactory score is required on the written TOEFL.

Computers: Wireless access is available. All students may access the system at all times. There are no time limits and no fees.

Graduates: From July 1, 2004 to June 30, 2005, 487 bachelor's degrees were awarded. The most popular majors were nursing (19%), computer and information systems (15%), and business administration (11%). In an average class, 44% graduate in 4 years or less, and 65% graduate in 6 years or less. 93 companies recruited on campus in 2004-2005. Of the 2004 graduating class, 7% were enrolled in graduate school within 6 months of graduation and 96% were employed.

Admissions Contact: Mark J. Hergan, Dean of Admissions. A video is available. E-mail: *admissions@vjc.edu* Web: *www.vjc.edu*

WASHINGTON COLLEGE
Chestertown, MD 21620-1197
E-2

(410) 778-7700
(800) 422-1782; Fax: (410) 778-7287

Full-time: 1312 men and women	**Faculty:** 86; IIB, +$
Part-time: 29 men and women	**Ph.D.s:** 92%
Graduate: 33 men, 38 women	**Student/Faculty:** 16 to 1
Year: semesters	**Tuition:** $28,790
Application Deadline: March 1	**Room & Board:** $6200
Freshman Class: 2224 applied, 1312 accepted, 343 enrolled	
SAT Verbal/Math: 578/567*	**ACT:** 23 **VERY COMPETITIVE**

Washington College, founded in 1782, is an independent college offering programs in the liberal arts and sciences, business management, and teacher preparation. The library contains 244,000 volumes, 250,000 microform items, and 6500 audio/video tapes/CDs/DVDs, and subscribes to 900 periodicals including electronic. Computerized library services include the card catalog, interlibrary loans, database searching, and Internet access. Special learning facilities include a learning resource center, the Center for the American Experience, and the Center for Environment and Society. The 112-acre campus is in a small town 75 miles from Baltimore. Including any residence halls, there are 52 buildings.

Student Life: 53% of undergraduates are from Maryland. Students are from 37 states, 36 foreign countries, and Canada. 66% are from public schools. 82% are white. The average age of freshmen is 19; all undergraduates, 21. 16% do not continue beyond their first year; 66% remain to graduate.

Housing: 1130 students can be accommodated in college housing, which includes single-sex and coed dorms and on-campus apartments. In addition, there are special-interest houses. On-campus housing is guaranteed for the freshman year only and is available on a lottery system for upperclassmen. 78% of students live on campus; of those, 65% remain on campus on weekends. All students may keep cars.

Activities: 20% of men belong to 3 national fraternities; 20% of women belong to 3 national sororities. There are 52 groups on campus, including cheerleading, chorale, chorus, dance, debate, drama, ethnic, gay, honors, international, jazz band, literary magazine, newspaper, opera, orchestra, photography, political, professional, religious, social, social service, student government, and yearbook. Popular campus events include fall and spring convocations, George Washington Birthday Ball, and May Day.

Sports: There are 15 intercollegiate sports for men and 15 for women, and 12 intramural sports for men and 11 for women. Facilities include a swim center, a gym, a field house, squash and racquetball courts, a fitness center, playing and practice fields, and a boat house. There are riding facilities nearby.

Disabled Students: 80% of the campus is accessible. Wheelchair ramps, elevators, special parking, specially equipped rest rooms, special class scheduling, lowered drinking fountains, lowered telephones, motorized carts, and curb cuts are available.

Services: Counseling and information services are available, as is tutoring in every subject. There is remedial math and writing, a writing center, a math lab, a study skills tutor, and peer tutors.

Campus Safety and Security: Measures include 24-hour foot and vehicle patrol, security escort services, informal discussions, and pamphlets/posters/films. There are emergency telephones, lighted pathways/sidewalks, and peer education through student groups.

Programs of Study: WC confers B.A. and B.S. degrees. Master's degrees are also awarded. Bachelor's degrees are awarded in BIOLOGICAL SCIENCE (biology/biological science), BUSINESS (business administration and management), COMMUNICATIONS AND THE ARTS (art, dramatic arts, English, fine arts, French, German, music, and Spanish), COMPUTER AND PHYSICAL SCIENCE (chemistry, computer science, mathematics, and physics), ENGINEERING AND ENVIRONMENTAL DESIGN (environmental science), SOCIAL SCIENCE (American studies, anthropology, economics, history, humanities, international studies, philosophy, political science/government, psychology, and sociology). English, psychology, and business management are the strongest academically.

Required: All students are required to take 2 freshman seminars, and 11 courses distributed among the social sciences, natural sciences, humanities, quantitative studies, foreign langauges, and a writing requirement. The senior obligation consists of a comprehensive exam, thesis, or independent project. Students must complete 128 credit hours, including at least 32 in the major, to graduate. A minimum GPA of 2.0 is required.

Special: Internships are available in all majors. There is study abroad in 20 countries and a Washington semester at American University. The college offers a 3-2 engineering degree with the University of Maryland at College Park, as well as a 3-2 nursing program with Johns Hopkins University, credit by exam, pass/fail options, and student-designed majors. There are 7 national honor societies.

Faculty/Classroom: 56% of faculty are male; 44%, female. 97% teach undergraduates. No introductory courses are taught by graduate students. The average class size in an introductory lecture is 24; in a laboratory, 16; and in a regular course, 16.

Admissions: 59% of the 2005-2006 applicants were accepted. The SAT scores for the 2005-2006 freshman class were: Verbal--12% below 500, 48% between 500 and 599, 29% between 600 and 700, and 11% above 700; Math--12% below 500, 54% between 500 and 599, 30% between 600 and 700, and 4% above 700.

Requirements: The SAT or ACT is required. In addition, applicants must be graduates of an accredited secondary school or have a GED. 16 Carnegie units are required. Applicants should take high school courses in English, foreign language, history, math, science, and social studies. An essay is required, and an interview is recommended. A GPA of 2.5 is required. AP and CLEP credits are accepted. Important factors in the admissions decision are advanced placement or honor courses, recommendations by school officials, and leadership record.

Procedure: Freshmen are admitted fall and spring. Entrance exams should be taken in the spring of the junior year or fall of the senior year. There is an early decision plan and a rolling admissions plan. Early decision applications should be filed by November 1; regular applications, by March 1 for fall entry and December 1 for spring entry, along with a $45 fee. Notification is sent on a rolling basis. A waiting list is an active part of the admissions procedure. Applications are accepted on-line.

Transfer: A minimum GPA of 2.5 is required. An associate degree and interview are recommended. 56 of 128 credits required for the bachelor's degree must be completed at WC.

Visiting: There are regularly scheduled orientations for prospective students, consisting of weekday visits. There are guides for informal visits and visitors may sit in on classes and stay overnight. To schedule a visit, contact the Admissions Office.

Financial Aid: In 2005-2006, 85% of all full-time freshmen received some form of financial aid. The average freshman award was $14,484. 50% of undergraduates work part time. Average annual earnings from campus work are $760. The average financial indebtedness of the 2005 graduate was $17,711. WC is a member of CSS. The FAFSA, the college's own financial statement and parent's and student's federal income tax returns are required. Check eith the school for current deadlines.

International Students: The school actively recruits these students. A satisfactory score on the TOEFL is required. They must also take the SAT or the ACT.

Computers: All students may access the system. There are no time limits and no fees. It is strongly recommended that all students have a personal computer.

Graduates: In a recent year, 227 bachelor's degrees were awarded. The most popular majors were psychology (13%), business management (12%), and English (11%). In an average class, 2% graduate in 3 years or less, 63% graduate in 4 years or less, 65% graduate in 5 years or less, and 66% graduate in 6 years or less. 35 companies recruited on campus in a recent year. Of a recent graduating class, 38% were enrolled in graduate school within 6 months of graduation and 84% were employed.

Admissions Contact: Kevin Coveney, Vice President of Admissions. A video is available. E-mail: *adm-off@washcoll.edu* Web: *www.washcoll.edu*

MASSACHUSETTS

POPULATION DENSITY
● 50,000 and over

0 10 20 30 40
Miles

AMERICAN INTERNATIONAL COLLEGE   B-3

Springfield, MA 01109
(413) 205-3201
(800) 242-3142; Fax: (413) 205-3051

Full-time: 508 men, 706 women	**Faculty:** 70
Part-time: 64 men, 120 women	**Ph.D.s:** 70%
Graduate: 115 men, 302 women	**Student/Faculty:** 17 to 1
Year: semesters, summer session	**Tuition:** $19,800
Application Deadline: open	**Room & Board:** $8910
Freshman Class: 1333 applied, 1118 accepted, 331 enrolled	
SAT Verbal/Math: 475/505*	**ACT:** 20 **LESS COMPETITIVE**

American International College, founded in 1885, is an independent institution offering programs in liberal arts, business, health science, and teacher preparation. There are 4 undergraduate and 3 graduate schools. In addition to regional accreditation, AIC has baccalaureate program accreditation with ACOTE, APTA, IACBE, NASDTEC, and NLN. The library contains 118,000 volumes, 450,000 microform items, and 1380 audio/video tapes/CDs/DVDs, and subscribes to 425 periodicals including electronic. Computerized library services include the card catalog, interlibrary loans, database searching, and Internet access. Special learning facilities include a learning resource center, art gallery, radio station, TV station, and an anatomical lab for health sciences. The 58-acre campus is in an urban area 75 miles west of Boston. Including any residence halls, there are 22 buildings.

Student Life: 60% of undergraduates are from Massachusetts. Students are from 30 states, 15 foreign countries, and Canada. 85% are from public schools. 66% are white; 25% African American. 66% are Catholic; 26% Protestant; 6% Jewish. The average age of freshmen is 19; all undergraduates, 23. 56% of freshmen remain to graduate.

Housing: 680 students can be accommodated in college housing, which includes single-sex and coed dorms. On-campus housing is guaranteed for all 4 years. 60% of students live on campus; of those, 65% remain on campus on weekends. Alcohol is not permitted. All students may keep cars.

Activities: There are no fraternities or sororities. There are 40 groups on campus, including cheerleading, chorale, computers, dance, drama, ethnic, honors, international, literary magazine, musical theater, newspaper, political, professional, radio and TV, religious, social, social service, student government, and yearbook. Popular campus events include holiday semi-formals and international festival.

Sports: There are 9 intercollegiate sports for men and 7 for women, and 9 intramural sports for men and 8 for women. Facilities include 2 gyms, a football stadium, tennis courts, playing fields, and a health and fitness center.

Disabled Students: 75% of the campus is accessible. Wheelchair ramps, elevators, special parking, specially equipped rest rooms, special class scheduling, and lowered drinking fountains are available.

Services: Counseling and information services are available, as is tutoring in every subject. There is remedial math and writing.

Campus Safety and Security: Measures include 24-hour foot and vehicle patrol, self-defense education, security escort services, and shuttle buses. There are informal discussions, pamphlets/posters/films, and lighted pathways/sidewalks.

Programs of Study: AIC confers B.A., B.S., B.B.A., B.S.B.A., B.S.N., and B.S.O.T. degrees. Associate, master's, and doctoral degrees are also awarded. Bachelor's degrees are awarded in BIOLOGICAL SCIENCE (biochemistry and biology/biological science), BUSINESS (accounting, business administration and management, business economics, entrepreneurial studies, human resources, international business management, and marketing/retailing/merchandising), COMMUNICATIONS AND THE ARTS (advertising, communications, English, and Spanish), COMPUTER AND PHYSICAL SCIENCE (chemistry, mathematics, and science), EDUCATION (early childhood, elementary, foreign languages, middle school, science, secondary, and special), HEALTH PROFESSIONS (medical laboratory technology, nursing, occupational therapy, physical therapy, predentistry, and premedicine), SOCIAL SCIENCE (criminal justice, economics, history, international relations, liberal arts/general studies, philosophy, political science/government, prelaw, psychology, public administration, and sociology). Psychology, preprofessional, and health sciences are the strongest academically. Criminal justice, physical therapy, and nursing are the largest.

Required: Distribution requirements include 12 credits of social sciences, 9 of English, 8 of lab science, 6 of humanities, and 3 each of math and computer-oriented courses. A total of 120 credit hours is required for graduation, with 30 to 36 hours in the major. A minimum 2.0 GPA is required for graduation. Students must take 4 credits of phys ed.

Special: Cross-registration with the Cooperative Colleges of Greater Springfield is permitted. Internships are available in all programs, for up to 6 credits in every major, and study abroad is offered, as is a Washington semester. AIC also offers dual majors, credit by exam, credit for life/military/work experience, nondegree study, and for lower-division students, pass/fail options. There are 2 national honor societies, a freshman honors program, and 9 departmental honors programs.

Faculty/Classroom: 48% of faculty are male; 52%, female. All teach undergraduates, 15% do research, and 15% do both. No introductory courses are taught by graduate students. The average class size in an introductory lecture is 27; in a laboratory, 16; and in a regular course, 19.

Admissions: 84% of the 2005-2006 applicants were accepted. The SAT scores for the 2005-2006 freshman class were: Verbal--50% below 500, 40% between 500 and 599, and 10% between 600 and 700; Math--50% below 500, 45% between 500 and 599, and 5% between 600 and 700. The ACT scores were 15% below 21, 80% between 21 and 23, and 5% between 24 and 26. 20% of the current freshmen were in the top fifth of their class; 45% were in the top two fifths.

Requirements: The SAT or ACT is required. In addition, students must be graduates of an accredited secondary school or have a GED. They must have completed 16 academic credits of secondary school work with a minimum of 4 years of English, 2 each of history, math, and science, and 1 of social studies. An interview is recommended. AP and CLEP credits are accepted.

Procedure: Freshmen are admitted fall and spring. Entrance exams should be taken by March of the senior year. There is a deferred admissions plan and a rolling admissions plan. Early decision applications should be filed by November 15; regular decision application deadlines are open. Application fee is $25. Applications are accepted on-line.

Transfer: 180 transfer students enrolled in 2004-2005. Transfer applicants must have at least a 2.0 GPA. 30 of 120 credits required for the bachelor's degree must be completed at AIC.

Visiting: There are regularly scheduled orientations for prospective students, including open houses with faculty, a student life panel, departmental faculty presentations, a financial aid presentation, a tour, and brunch. There are guides for informal visits and visitors may sit in on classes and stay overnight. To schedule a visit, contact the Admissions Office at *ccote@acad.aic.edu*.

Financial Aid: In 2005-2006, 98% of all full-time freshmen and 97% of continuing full-time students received some form of financial aid. 95% of full-time freshmen and 79% of continuing full-time students received need-based aid. The average freshman award was $21,668. Need-based scholarships or need-based grants averaged $12,821; need-based self-help aid (loans and jobs) averaged $6087; and other non-need-based awards and non-need-based scholarships averaged $7499. The FAFSA is required. The deadline for filing freshman financial aid applications for fall entry is May 1.

International Students: There were 50 international students enrolled in a recent year. The school actively recruits these students. A satisfactory score is required on the written TOEFL. Students must also take the SAT or the ACT.

Computers: All students may access the system 7 days per week. There are no time limits and no fees.

Graduates: In a recent year, 226 bachelor's degrees were awarded. The most popular majors were business (22%), health professions (22%), and criminal justice (15%). In an average class, 40% graduate in 4 years or less, 45% graduate in 5 years or less, and 50% graduate in 6 years or less. 50 companies recruited on campus in a recent year. Of the recent year's graduating class, 21% were enrolled in graduate school within 6 months of graduation and 81% were employed.

Admissions Contact: Peter Miller, Vice President Admission Services. E-mail: *inquiry@acad.aic.edu* Web: *www.aic.edu*

AMHERST COLLEGE

B-2

Amherst, MA 01002-5000

(413) 542-2328; Fax: (413) 542-2040

Full-time: 836 men, 787 women	Faculty: 190; IIB, ++$
Part-time: none	Ph.D.s: 94%
Graduate: none	Student/Faculty: 9 to 1
Year: semesters	Tuition: $33,005
Application Deadline: January 1	Room & Board: $8585
Freshman Class: 6281 applied, 1176 accepted, 431 enrolled	
SAT or ACT: required	MOST COMPETITIVE

Amherst College, founded in 1821, is a private liberal arts institution. The 5 libraries contain 1,003,887 volumes, 530,038 microform items, and 60,826 audio/video tapes/CDs/DVDs, and subscribe to 5563 periodicals including electronic. Computerized library services include the card catalog, interlibrary loans, database searching, and Internet access. Special learning facilities include a learning resource center, art gallery, natural history museum, planetarium, radio station, an observatory, the Emily Dickinson Museum, and the Amherst Center for Russian Culture. The 1015-acre campus is in a small town 90 miles west of Boston. Including any residence halls, there are 75 buildings.

Student Life: 81% of undergraduates are from out of state, mostly the Middle Atlantic. Students are from 50 states, 31 foreign countries, and Canada. 58% are from public schools. 44% are white; 13% Asian American; 10% African American. The average age of freshmen is 18; all undergraduates, 19. 3% do not continue beyond their first year; 97% remain to graduate.

Housing: 1650 students can be accommodated in college housing, which includes single-sex and coed dorms. In addition, there are language houses, special-interest houses and 1 cooperative house. On-campus housing is guaranteed for all 4 years. 98% of students live on campus; of those, 95% remain on campus on weekends. Upperclassmen may keep cars.

Activities: There are no fraternities or sororities. There are 110 groups on campus, including art, band, chess, choir, chorale, chorus, computers, dance, debate, drama, ethnic, film, gay, honors, international, jazz band, literary magazine, mock trial, musical theater, newspaper, opera, orchestra, pep band, photography, political, professional, radio and TV, religious, social, social service, student government, and symphony. Popular campus events include Newport Jazz, Harlem Renaissance, and Spring Weekend Concert.

Sports: There are 13 intercollegiate sports for men and 14 for women, and 6 intramural sports for men and 6 for women. Facilities include 2 gyms, a pool, a field house, a hockey rink, an outdoor track, a fitness center, 10 international squash courts, an indoor jogging track, 3 indoor and 30 outdoor tennis courts, baseball and softball diamonds, a 9-hole golf course, and playing fields.

Disabled Students: Wheelchair ramps, elevators, special parking, specially equipped rest rooms, special class scheduling, lowered drinking fountains, and lowered telephones are available.

Services: Counseling and information services are available, as is tutoring in every subject. There is a reader service for the blind. A quantitative skills center and a writing center are also available.

Campus Safety and Security: Measures include 24-hour foot and vehicle patrol, self-defense education, security escort services, and shuttle buses. There are informal discussions, pamphlets/posters/films, emergency telephones, lighted pathways/sidewalks, ACEMS (Amherst College Emergency Medical Service), access code pad security to dorms, and "blue light" emergency telephones placed in 19 locations around campus.

Programs of Study: Amherst confers the B.A. degree. Bachelor's degrees are awarded in BIOLOGICAL SCIENCE (biology/biological science and neurosciences), COMMUNICATIONS AND THE ARTS (classics, dance, dramatic arts, English, fine arts, French, German, Greek, Latin, music, Russian, and Spanish), COMPUTER AND PHYSICAL SCIENCE (astronomy, chemistry, computer science, geology, mathematics, and physics), SOCIAL SCIENCE (African American studies, American studies, anthropology, Asian/Oriental studies, economics, European studies, history, interdisciplinary studies, law, philosophy, political science/government, psychology, religion, sociology, and women's studies). English, psychology, and economics are the largest.

Required: To earn the B.A., all students must complete 32 courses, equivalent to 128 credits, 8 to 14 of which are in the major, with at least a C average. Other than a 1-semester freshman seminar in liberal studies, there are no specific course requirements. A thesis or comparable work is required for honors candidates.

Special: Students may cross-register through the Five College Consortium, the other members of which are all within 10 miles of Amherst, or through the Twelve College Exchange Program. A number of interterm and summer internships are available, as is study-abroad in 40 countries. Dual majors, student-designed interdisciplinary majors based on independent study as of junior or senior year, and work-study programs are possible. There are limited pass/fail options. There are 2 national honor societies, including Phi Beta Kappa, and 30 departmental honors programs.

Faculty/Classroom: 57% of faculty are male; 43%, female. All both teach and do research. The average class size in a laboratory is 18 and in a regular course, 15.

Admissions: 19% of the 2005-2006 applicants were accepted. The SAT scores for the 2005-2006 freshman class were: Verbal--4% between 500 and 599, 29% between 600 and 700, and 67% above 700; Math--6% between 500 and 599, 26% between 600 and 700, and 68% above 700. The ACT scores were 4% between 24 and 26, 13% between 27 and 28, and 83% above 28. 92% of the current freshmen were in the top fifth of their class; 100% were in the top two fifths. There were 95 National Merit semifinalists. 38 freshmen graduated first in their class.

Requirements: The SAT or ACT is required. In addition, 2 SAT: Subject tests are required for admission. Amherst strongly recommends that applicants take 4 years of English, math through calculus, 3 or 4 years of a foreign language, 2 years of history and social science, and at least 2 years of natural science, including a lab science. 2 essays are required. Important factors in the admissions decision are advanced placement or honor courses, recommendations by school officials, and evidence of special talent.

Procedure: Freshmen are admitted in the fall. Entrance exams should be taken no later than December of the senior year. There are early decision and deferred admissions plans. Early decision applications should be filed by November 15; regular applications, by January 1 for fall entry, along with a $55 fee. Notification of early decision is sent December 15; regular decision, April 1. 127 early decision candidates were accepted for the 2005-2006 class. 1162 applicants were on the 2005 waiting list. Applications are accepted on-line.

Transfer: 11 transfer students enrolled in 2004-2005. Applicants must have full sophomore standing prior to applying and a minimum 3.0 GPA in previous college work. Transfers are accepted for the sophomore and junior classes only, and Amherst recommends that they submit SAT or ACT scores, plus high school and college transcripts, and seek a personal interview. 64 of 128 credits required for the bachelor's degree must be completed at Amherst.

Visiting: There are regularly scheduled orientations for prospective students, consisting of information sessions led by a dean and student-led tours. There are guides for informal visits and visitors may sit in on classes and stay overnight. To schedule a visit, contact the Admission Office.

Financial Aid: In 2005-2006, 48% of all full-time students received some form of financial aid. 48% of full-time freshmen and 46% of continuing full-time students received need-based aid. The average freshman award was $23,487. Need-based scholarships or need-based grants averaged $29,373 ($40,342 maximum); and need-based self-help aid (loans and jobs) averaged $2842 ($5050 maximum). 60% of undergraduates work part time. Average annual earnings from campus work are $1250. The average financial indebtedness of the 2005 graduate was $12,109. The CSS/Profile or FAFSA is required. The deadline for filing freshman financial aid applications for fall entry is February 15.

International Students: There are 129 international students enrolled. The school actively recruits these students. A satisfactory score is required on the written TOEFL or the MELAB, or the SAT: ELAP if English is not the applicant's first language. Students must also take the SAT or the ACT.

Computers: Wireless access is available. All dorm rooms provide Internet access as well as libraries and academic buildings. All libraries and academic resource centers provide wireless Internet along with a handful of outdoor areas. There are approximately 270 PC terminals available for student use. All students may access the system 24 hours a day.

Graduates: From July 1, 2004 to June 30, 2005, 409 bachelor's degrees were awarded. The most popular majors were English (14%), psychology (10%), and economics (9%). In an average class, 89% graduate in 4 years or less, 95% graduate in 5 years or less, and 97% graduate in 6 years or less. 38 companies recruited on campus in 2004-2005. Of the 2004 graduating class, 29% were enrolled in graduate school within 6 months of graduation and 60% were employed.

Admissions Contact: Katherine L. Fretwell, Director of Admission.
E-mail: *admission@amherst.edu* Web: *http://www.amherst.edu*

ANNA MARIA COLLEGE C-2

Paxton, MA 01612-1198
(508) 849-3360
(800) 344-4586; Fax: (508) 849-3362

Full-time: 205 men, 335 women	**Faculty:** 38; IIB, --$
Part-time: 84 men, 89 women	**Ph.D.s:** 43%
Graduate: 84 men, 166 women	**Student/Faculty:** 14 to 1
Year: semesters, summer session	**Tuition:** $21,880
Application Deadline: open	**Room & Board:** $7935
Freshman Class: 557 applied, 501 accepted, 169 enrolled	
SAT Verbal/Math: 470/460*	**ACT:** 19 **LESS COMPETITIVE**

Anna Maria College, founded in 1946, is a small, comprehensive Catholic college offering career-oriented programs in liberal and fine arts, business, and teacher preparation. In addition to regional accreditation, AMC has baccalaureate program accreditation with CSWE and NLN. The library contains 81,010 volumes, 1702 microform items, and 6095 audio/video tapes/CDs/DVDs, and subscribes to 277 periodicals including electronic. Computerized library services include the card catalog and database searching. Special learning facilities include a learning resource center, art gallery, and , an audiovisual center, and a nature trail. The 180-acre campus is in a rural area 8 miles northwest of Worcester. Including any residence halls, there are 13 buildings.

Student Life: 79% of undergraduates are from Massachusetts. Others are from 11 states, 7 foreign countries, and Canada. 70% are from public schools. 91% are white. The average age of freshmen is 18; all undergraduates, 20. 41% do not continue beyond their first year; 54% remain to graduate.

Housing: 394 students can be accommodated in college housing, which includes coed dorms. In addition there is substance free housing. On-campus housing is guaranteed for the freshman year only, is available on a first-come, first-served basis, and is available on a lottery system for upperclassmen. Priority is given to out-of-town students. 68% of students live on campus. All students may keep cars.

Activities: There are no fraternities or sororities. There are 25 groups on campus, including art, cheerleading, choir, chorus, computers, drama, ethnic, gay, honors, international, jazz band, musical theater, newspaper, political, professional, religious, social, social service, student government, and yearbook. Popular campus events include Harvest Weekend, Winter Semi-Formal, and Spring Weekend.

Sports: There are 5 intercollegiate sports for men and 6 for women, and 2 intramural sports for men and 2 for women. Facilities include an activities center with a basketball court, locker rooms, and weight and fitness equipment; soccer, baseball, and softball fields; an outdoor basketball court; and a fitness trail.

Disabled Students: 93% of the campus is accessible. Wheelchair ramps, elevators, special parking, specially equipped rest rooms, special class scheduling, and special housing are available.

Services: Counseling and information services are available, as is tutoring in every subject, through a tutoring lab. There is a reader service for the blind, and remedial math, reading, and writing.

Campus Safety and Security: Measures include 24-hour foot and vehicle patrol, security escort services, shuttle buses, and informal discussions. There are pamphlets/posters/films, emergency telephones, and lighted pathways/sidewalks.

Programs of Study: AMC confers B.A., B.S., B.B.A., B.F.A., B.M., and B.S.N. degrees. Associate and master's degrees are also awarded. Bachelor's degrees are awarded in BIOLOGICAL SCIENCE (biology/biological science), BUSINESS (business administration and management), COMMUNICATIONS AND THE ARTS (art, English, music, music performance, and studio art), EDUCATION (art, early childhood, elementary, and music), HEALTH PROFESSIONS (art therapy, music therapy, and nursing), SOCIAL SCIENCE (criminal justice, fire science, history, human development, liberal arts/general studies, paralegal studies, political science/government, psychology, social science, and social work). Criminal justice, education, and business are the largest.

Required: The 60-credit core curriculum consists of classes in English, literature, math, computers, natural science, foreign language, fine arts, history, philosophy, social/behavioral sciences, and religious studies. A total of 120 credits is required for graduation, with a minimum of 30 in the major, and a 2.0 GPA.

Special: Cross-registration with the Colleges of the Worcester Consortium, internships in all majors, and a 3-2 engineering degree in conjunction with the Worcester Polytechnic Institute are available. The art and business major results in a B.F.A. degree. There are preprofessional concentrations in law, dentistry, medicine, and veterinary science. The college offers study abroad, a Washington semester, student designed majors, accelerated degree programs, a general studies degree, credit by exam, work-study programs, and 5-year advanced degree programs in business, counseling psychology, and criminal justice. There are 5 national honor societies and 2 departmental honors programs.

Faculty/Classroom: 53% of faculty are male; 47%, female. All teach undergraduates. No introductory courses are taught by graduate students. The average class size in an introductory lecture is 20; in a laboratory, 20; and in a regular course, 13.

Admissions: 90% of the 2005-2006 applicants were accepted. The SAT scores for the 2005-2006 freshman class were: Verbal--71% below 500, 25% between 500 and 599, and 3% between 600 and 700; Math--64% below 500, 32% between 500 and 599, 3% between 600 and 700, and 1% above 700. The ACT scores were 84% below 21, 8% between 21 and 23, and 8% between 27 and 28. 9% of the current freshmen were in the top fifth of their class; 27% were in the top two fifths.

Requirements: The SAT or ACT is required. In addition,16 academic units are recommended, including 4 years of English, 2 years each of foreign language, history, math, and sciences, and 1 year of social studies. A GED is accepted. An interview is recommended. When applicable, an audition and portfolio are required. Students who have been out of high school for 3 or more years, or transfer students with 10 or more college-level courses, do not need to submit standardized test scores. An essay is required. A GPA of 2.0 is required. AP and CLEP credits are accepted. Important factors in the admissions decision are advanced placement or honor courses, evidence of special talent, and leadership record.

Procedure: Freshmen are admitted fall and spring. Entrance exams should be taken in the spring of the junior year and in the fall of the senior year. There are deferred admissions and rolling admissions plans. Application deadlines are open. Application fee is $40. Notification is sent on a rolling basis beginning December 15. Applications are accepted on-line.

Transfer: 24 transfer students enrolled in 2004-2005. Transfers with a minimum GPA of 2.0 are accepted for upper-division work. High school and college transcripts are required. An essay or personal statement and a statement of good standing from prior institutions are also required. 45 of 120 credits required for the bachelor's degree must be completed at AMC.

Visiting: There are regularly scheduled orientations for prospective students, including on-campus interviews, campus tours, day visitation program by appointment, and a fall open house. There are guides for informal visits and visitors may sit in on classes and stay overnight. To schedule a visit, contact the Undergraduate Admission Office at *admission@annamaria.edu*.

Financial Aid: In 2005-2006, 80% of all full-time freshmen and 81% of continuing full-time students received some form of financial aid. At least 78% of all full-time students received need-based aid. The average freshman award was $16,855. Need-based scholarships or need-based grants averaged $11,071; need-based self-help aid (loans and jobs) averaged $3110; and other non-need-based awards and institutional non-need-based scholarships averaged $8226. The average financial indebtedness of the 2005 graduate was $23,513. The FAFSA and the state aid form are required. The priority date for freshman financial aid applications for fall entry is March 1.

International Students: There are 8 international students enrolled. The school actively recruits these students. A satisfactory score is required on the written TOEFL. Students who score below the satisfactory level on the TOEFL may be admitted to the college's ESL program.

Graduates: From July 1, 2004 to June 30, 2005, 140 bachelor's degrees were awarded. The most popular majors were criminal justice (39%), social sevices (13%), and business/marketing (12%). In an average class, 43% graduate in 4 years, 61% graduate in 5 years, and 63% graduate in 6 years.

Admissions Contact: Wylie Culhane, Director of Admission.
E-mail: *admission@annamaria.edu* Web: *www.annamaria.edu*

ART INSTITUTE OF BOSTON AT LESLEY UNIVERSITY

E-2

Boston, MA 02215-2598

(617) 585-6710
(800) 773-0494; Fax: (617) 585-6720

Full-time: 200 men, 260 women	**Faculty:** 24
Part-time: 30 men, 35 women	**Ph.Ds:** 79%
Graduate: none	**Student/Faculty:** 19 to 1
Year: semesters, summer session	**Tuition:** $18,800
Application Deadline: see profile	**Room & Board:** $9400
Freshman Class: n/av	
SAT or ACT : required for some programs	**SPECIAL**

The Art Institute of Boston at Lesley University, founded in 1912, is a private institution offering undergraduate visual art programs leading to baccalaureate degree, 3-year diplomas, and Advanced Professional Certificates, as well as continuing and professional education, intensive workshops, and precollege courses. There is 1 graduate school. Figures in the above capsule and profile are approximate. In addition to regional accreditation, AIB has baccalaureate program accreditation with NASAD. The 2 libraries contain 120,254 volumes, 878,187 microform items, and 55,799 audio/video tapes/CDs/DVDs, and subscribe to 684 periodicals including electronic. Computerized library services include the card catalog, interlibrary loans, database searching, and Internet access. Special learning facilities include a learning resource center, art gallery, computer labs, state-of-the-art animation lab, print-making studio, clay studio, wood-working studio, photo lab, and digital-printing lab. The 2-acre campus is in an urban area in the Kenmore Square area of Boston. Including any residence halls, there are 2 buildings.

Student Life: 57% of undergraduates are from Massachusetts. Others are from 35 states, 23 foreign countries, and Canada. 78% are white; 10% foreign nationals. The average age of freshmen is 19; all undergraduates, 21. 33% do not continue beyond their first year; 72% remain to graduate.

Housing: 142 students can be accommodated in college housing, which includes single-sex and coed dormitories. On-campus housing is available on a first-come, first-served basis. 73% of students commute. Alcohol is not permitted. No one may keep cars.

Activities: There are no fraternities or sororities. There are 6 groups on campus, including art, chorale, chorus, drama, ethnic, gay, international, literary magazine, musical theater, religious, social service, and student government. Popular campus events include student lunches, student and faculty coffee hours, and Edible Art.

Sports: There are 5 intercollegiate sports for women and 3 intramural sports for women. Facilities include an outdoor tennis court, a fitness center with Nautilus circuit, free weights, and cardiovascular equipment on the main campus. In addition, students may also use an Olympic-size swimming pool at a nearby school and local playing field facilities.

Disabled Students: 75% of the campus is accessible. Wheelchair ramps, elevators, specially equipped rest rooms, special class scheduling, and lowered drinking fountains are available.

Services: Counseling and information services are available, as is tutoring in some subjects. There is a reader service for the blind and remedial math and writing.

Campus Safety and Security: Measures include 24-hour foot and vehicle patrol, security escort services, shuttle buses, and informal discussions. There are pamphlets/posters/films, emergency telephones, lighted pathways/sidewalks, alarms, and electronically operated entrances in some buildings.

Programs of Study: AIB confers the B.F.A. degree. Master's degrees are also awarded. Bachelor's degrees are awarded in COMMUNICATIONS AND THE ARTS (design, fine arts, illustration, and photography). Design and photography are the strongest academically. Illustration/animation is the largest.

Required: All students must complete 124 to 128 credits, including 31 credits in the foundation program and 82 or more in the major. Juniors and seniors must maintain minimum GPA of 2.3; freshmen and sophomores, 2.0. Senior juries are required.

Special: There is cross-registration with Lesley University. Internships are required for design majors and encouraged for all other majors. Accelerated degree programs in all majors, study abroad in Italy and Ireland and dual majors in fine art/illustration, design/illustration, illustration/animation, and art education are offered. There is a freshman honors program.

Faculty/Classroom: 58% of faculty are male; 42%, female. All teach undergraduates. The average class size in an introductory lecture is 25; in a laboratory, 12; and in a regular course, 15.

Requirements: The SAT or ACT is required for some programs. In addition, applicants must submit an official high school transcript, an essay, and do a portfolio review. Letters of recommendation and a campus tour are encouraged. A GPA of 2.0 is required. AP and CLEP credits are accepted. Important factors in the admissions decision are evidence of special talent, personality/intangible qualities, and advanced placement or honor courses.

Procedure: Freshmen are admitted fall and spring. Entrance exams should be taken by February 15. There is a deferred admissions plan. Check with the school for current application deadlines. A waiting list is an active part of the admissions procedure. Applications are accepted on-line. The fall 2005 application fee was $40.

Transfer: 52 transfer students enrolled in a recent year. High school and college transcripts, a portfolio review, an essay, and SAT/ACT scores (if graduated since 1995) are required. 45 of 124 credits required for the bachelor's degree must be completed at AIB.

Visiting: There are regularly scheduled orientations for prospective students, meeting with faculty and students. There are guides for informal visits and visitors may sit in on classes. To schedule a visit, contact Office of Admissions.

Financial Aid: In a recent year, 68% of all full-time freshmen and 55% of continuing full-time students received some form of financial aid. 51% of full-time freshmen and 34% of continuing full-time students received need-based aid. The average freshman award was $7753. Need-based scholarships or need-based grants averaged $4283; and need-based self-help aid (loans and jobs) averaged $4523. 18% of undergraduates worked part time. Average annual earnings from campus work were $2000. The average financial indebtedness of a recent graduate was $14,110. The FAFSA and the college's own financial statement are required. Check with the school for current application deadlines.

International Students: In a recent year, there were 63 international students enrolled. The school actively recruits these students. They must score satisfactorily on the written TOEFL or on the electronic version.

Computers: All students may access the system. There are no time limits and no fees.

Graduates: In a recent year, 100 bachelor's degrees were awarded. The most popular majors were illustration (33%), design (24%), and photography (21%). In an average class, 19% graduate in 4 years or less, 34% graduate in 5 years or less, and 36% graduate in 6 years or less. Of a recent graduating class, 8% were enrolled in graduate school within 6 months of graduation and 79% were employed.

Admissions Contact: Bradford White, Director of Admissions.
E-mail: *admissions@aiboston.edu* Web: *www.aiboston.edu*

ASSUMPTION COLLEGE

C-2

Worcester, MA 01609-1296

(508) 767-7285
(888) 882-7786; Fax: (508) 799-4412

Full-time: 839 men, 1256 women	**Faculty:** 133; IIB, -$
Part-time: 4 men, 6 women	**Ph.Ds:** 94%
Graduate: 78 men, 249 women	**Student/Faculty:** 16 to 1
Year: semesters, summer session	**Tuition:** $24,095
Application Deadline: February 15	**Room & Board:** $8780
Freshman Class: 3357 applied, 2538 accepted, 565 enrolled	
SAT Verbal/Math: 540/540*	**ACT:** 21	**COMPETITIVE**

Assumption College, founded in 1904 by Augustinians of the Assumption, offers a Catholic, liberal arts and sciences education to undergraduates, along with programs for graduate and continuing education students. The library contains 219,685 volumes, 20,285 microform items, and 2577 audio/video tapes/CDs/DVDs, and subscribes to 1902 periodicals including electronic. Computerized library services include the card catalog, interlibrary loans, database searching, and Internet access. Special learning facilities include a learning resource center and TV station. The 175-acre campus is in a suburban area 45 miles west of Boston. Including any residence halls, there are 46 buildings.

Student Life: 68% of undergraduates are from Massachusetts. Others are from 24 states, 9 foreign countries, and Canada. 68% are from public schools. 83% are white. The average age of freshmen is 18; all undergraduates, 20. 16% do not continue beyond their first year; 71% remain to graduate.

Housing: 1962 students can be accommodated in college housing, which includes single-sex dorms and on-campus apartments. In addition, there are special-interest houses, freshman dorms, substance-free dorms, and a living/learning center. On-campus housing is guaranteed for all 4 years. 89% of students live on campus; of those, 80% remain on campus on weekends. Upperclassmen may keep cars.

Activities: There are no fraternities or sororities. There are 47 groups on campus, including art, band, cheerleading, choir, chorale, chorus, computers, dance, drama, ethnic, film, honors, international, literary magazine, musical theater, newspaper, pep band, photography, political, professional, radio and TV, religious, social, social service, student government, and yearbook. Popular campus events include Sibling Weekend, Holiday Ball, and Family Weekend.

Sports: There are 11 intercollegiate sports for men and 10 for women, and 16 intramural sports for men and 16 for women. Facilities include a 1200-seat multi-sports stadium, a 3000-seat gym, baseball and softball diamonds, a field hockey area, a soccer field, and tennis courts. A recreation center houses a 6-lane swimming pool, a jogging/walking track, 4 racquetball courts, an aerobics/dance studio, fully equipped Bodymaster and free-weight rooms, a fitness center, and a field house with 3 multipurpose courts for basketball, volleyball, and floor hockey.

Disabled Students: 71% of the campus is accessible. Wheelchair ramps, elevators, special parking, specially equipped rest rooms, special class scheduling, lowered drinking fountains, lowered telephones, and special housing are available.

Services: Counseling and information services are available, as is tutoring in most subjects. There is a reader service for the blind, signing for the deaf, and technology services for the disabled.

Campus Safety and Security: Measures include 24-hour foot and vehicle patrol, self-defense education, security escort services, and shuttle buses. There are informal discussions, pamphlets/posters/films, emergency telephones, and lighted pathways/sidewalks.

Programs of Study: Assumption confers the B.A. degree. Master's degrees are also awarded. Bachelor's degrees are awarded in BIOLOGICAL SCIENCE (biology/biological science), BUSINESS (accounting, business administration and management, international business management, international economics, and marketing management), COMMUNICATIONS AND THE ARTS (classics, English, French, languages, Spanish, and visual and performing arts), COMPUTER AND PHYSICAL SCIENCE (chemistry, computer science, and mathematics), ENGINEERING AND ENVIRONMENTAL DESIGN (environmental science), HEALTH PROFESSIONS (rehabilitation therapy), SOCIAL SCIENCE (economics, French studies, history, international studies, Latin American studies, philosophy, political science/government, psychology, sociology, Spanish studies, and theological studies). Natural sciences, political science, and philosophy are the strongest academically. Business studies, English, and math and natural sciences are the largest.

Required: Students must complete a core curriculum of 3 courses from different disciplines in social science: 2 courses in 1 and 1 course in another of the 3 areas of math, natural science, and foreign languages; 2 courses each of English composition, philosophy, and theology; 1 each of literature, history, and either art, music, or theater arts, and 1 additional course in 2 of the 3 areas of philosophy and theology, literature, and history. A minimum of 120 semester credit hours, with a minimum of 38 semester courses, must be completed; 8 to 14 courses must be in the upper division of the major. A minimum 2.0 GPA is required.

Special: There are co-op programs in gerontology studies and marine studies. Cross-registration with the Worcester Consortium and a 3-2 engineering program with Worcester Polytechnic Institute are offered. The college offers internships, study abroad, a Washington semester, student-designed and dual majors, credit by exam, and credit for military experience. There are 11 national honor societies and a freshman honors program.

Faculty/Classroom: 60% of faculty are male; 40%, female. All teach undergraduates. No introductory courses are taught by graduate students. The average class size in an introductory lecture is 22; in a laboratory, 15; and in a regular course, 21.

Admissions: 76% of the 2005-2006 applicants were accepted. The SAT scores for the 2005-2006 freshman class were: Verbal--27% below 500, 52% between 500 and 599, 19% between 600 and 700, and 2% above 700; Math--27% below 500, 50% between 500 and 599, 22% between 600 and 700, and 1% above 700. The ACT scores were 40% below 21, 38% between 21 and 23, 16% between 24 and 26, 5% between 27 and 28, and 1% above 28. 27% of the current freshmen were in the top fifth of their class; 66% were in the top two fifths. 4 freshmen graduated first in their class.

Requirements: The SAT is required. In addition, all applicants must graduate from an accredited secondary school or have a GED. 18 academic units are required, including 4 years of English, 3 of math, and 2 each of history, science, and foreign language. An essay and an interview are recommended. AP and CLEP credits are accepted. Important factors in the admissions decision are advanced placement or honor courses, recommendations by school officials, and leadership record.

Procedure: Freshmen are admitted fall and spring. Entrance exams should be taken in May of the junior year or November of the senior year. There are early decision, deferred admissions and rolling admissions plans. Early decision applications should be filed by November 15; regular applications, by February 15 for fall entry and December 1 for spring entry, along with a $50 fee. Notification of early decision is sent December 15; regular decision, on a rolling basis. 52 early decision candidates were accepted for the 2005-2006 class. 415 applicants were on the 2005 waiting list; 55 were admitted. Applications are accepted online.

Transfer: 55 transfer students enrolled in 2004-2005. Transfer students must have maintained a minimum 2.5 GPA at their previous college. SAT scores and high school and college transcripts are required. 60 of 120 credits required for the bachelor's degree must be completed at Assumption.

Visiting: There are regularly scheduled orientations for prospective students, consisting of new student orientation, meetings with future classmates, choosing roommates, registration, testing, conferences with academic advisers, and discussions of aspects of college life. There are guides for informal visits and visitors may sit in on classes. To schedule a visit, contact The Office of Admissions at 888-882-7786 or admiss@assumption.edu.

Financial Aid: In 2005-2006, 93% of all full-time freshmen and 92% of continuing full-time students received some form of financial aid. 64% of full-time freshmen and 67% of continuing full-time students received need-based aid. The average freshman award was $14,355. Need-based scholarships or need-based grants averaged $7706 ($25,600 maximum); need-based self-help aid (loans and jobs) averaged $3577 ($5125 maximum); non-need-based athletic scholarships averaged $33,588 ($33,678 maximum); and other non-need-based awards and non-need-based scholarships averaged $9708 ($23,930 maximum). 83% of undergraduates work part time. Average annual earnings from campus work are $800. The average financial indebtedness of the 2005 graduate was $20,356. The FAFSA is required. The deadline for filing freshman financial aid applications for fall entry is February 1.

International Students: There are 5 international students enrolled. The school actively recruits these students. A satisfactory score is required on the TOEFL. In addition, students may be requested to submit SAT or ACT scores.

Computers: Wireless access is available. Students have full ethernet access to the Internet and campus networked information systems in all classrooms, dorm rooms, the computer center, the library, and other areas. There are 1700 computers connected to the network. Roughly 160 of these are public cluster machines spread throughout the campus. All access the web and e-mail as well as a full suite of applications. All students may access the system. There are no time limits and no fees.

Graduates: From July 1, 2004 to June 30, 2005, 457 bachelor's degrees were awarded. The most popular majors were psychology (12%), English (10%), and management (8%). In an average class, 68% graduate in 4 years or less, 70% graduate in 5 years or less, and 71% graduate in 6 years or less. Of the 2004 graduating class, 23% were enrolled in graduate school within 6 months of graduation and 73% were employed.

Admissions Contact: Kathleen Murphy, Dean of Enrollment. A video is available. E-mail: admiss@assumption.edu Web: www.assumption.edu

ATLANTIC UNION COLLEGE · C-2

South Lancaster, MA 01561 (978) 368-2235
(800) 282-2030; Fax: (978) 368-2517

Full-time: 152 men, 237 women	**Faculty:** 40; IIB, --$
Part-time: 11 men, 31 women	**Ph.D.s:** 42%
Graduate: 2 men, 7 women	**Student/Faculty:** 10 to 1
Year: semesters, summer session	**Tuition:** $13,500
Application Deadline: August 1	**Room & Board:** $4100
Freshman Class: 316 applied, 158 accepted, 82 enrolled	
SAT Verbal/Math: 430/400*	**ACT:** 17 LESS COMPETITIVE

Atlantic Union College, established in 1882, is a private liberal arts institution associated with the Seventh-day Adventist Church, offering professional and preprofessional programs. In addition to regional accreditation, AUC has baccalaureate program accreditation with CSWE, NASM, and NLN. The library contains 139,000 volumes, 17,336 microform items, and 4754 audio/video tapes/CDs/DVDs, and subscribes to 469 periodicals including electronic. Computerized library services include the card catalog, interlibrary loans, database searching, and Internet access. Special learning facilities include a learning resource center, art gallery, model elementary and secondary schools, and music conservatory. The 135-acre campus is in a small town 50 miles west of Boston. Including any residence halls, there are 54 buildings.

Student Life: 55% of undergraduates are from out of state, mostly the Northeast. Students are from 14 states, 21 foreign countries, and Canada. 53% are African American; 22% Hispanic; 20% white; 15% foreign nationals. 10% claim no religious affiliation; 6% Catholic. The average age of freshmen is 21; all undergraduates, 23. 27% do not continue beyond their first year.

Housing: 469 students can be accommodated in college housing, which includes single-sex dorms, on-campus apartments, and married-student housing. On-campus housing is guaranteed for all 4 years. 56% of students live on campus; of those, 85% remain on campus on weekends. Alcohol is not permitted. All students may keep cars.

Activities: There are no fraternities or sororities. There are 13 groups on campus, including art, band, choir, chorale, drama, ethnic, honors, newspaper, orchestra, religious, social, student government, and yearbook. Popular campus events include fall picnic, Cultural Heritage Weeks, and Fine Arts Week.

Sports: There are 7 intramural sports for men and 7 for women. Facilities include a gym and field house with a weight room and tennis/volleyball/badminton, racquetball/handball, and basketball courts, a swimming pool, and athletic fields for flag football, soccer, softball, and baseball.

Disabled Students: 73% of the campus is accessible. Wheelchair ramps, elevators, special parking, specially equipped rest rooms, special class scheduling, and lowered drinking fountains are available.

Services: Counseling and information services are available, as is tutoring in most subjects. There is remedial math, reading, and writing. Additional services are provided upon request.

Campus Safety and Security: Measures include self-defense education, security escort services, informal discussions, and lighted pathways/sidewalks.

Programs of Study: AUC confers B.A., B.S., and B.M. degrees. Associate and master's degrees are also awarded. Bachelor's degrees are awarded in BIOLOGICAL SCIENCE (biology/biological science and life science), BUSINESS (accounting and business administration and management), COMMUNICATIONS AND THE ARTS (art, English, and music), COMPUTER AND PHYSICAL SCIENCE (computer science, information sciences and systems, and mathematics), EDUCATION (early childhood, elementary, and music), HEALTH PROFESSIONS (nursing), SOCIAL SCIENCE (culinary arts, history, liberal arts/general studies, ministries, psychology, religion, social work, and theological studies). Nursing, business, and psychology are the strongest academically. Nursing, business, and education are the largest.

Required: Students must complete 12 hours in religion/ethics and 9 hours each in humanities, science, and social science. Foreign language proficiency, a phys ed requirement, 40 hours of community service, and a course in college writing must also be completed. AUC requires 128 to 143 credit hours for the bachelor's degree, with 30 to 60 in the major, and a 2.0 GPA.

Special: There is cross-registration with Mount Wachusett Community College and the Colleges of Worcester Consortium. Students may study abroad in 6 countries. AUC also offers newspaper and biology research internships, cooperative programs in several majors, pass/fail options, and nondegree study. The Summer Advantage in New England program offers precollege credit to high school honor students. There is also an adult degree program, in which most study is done at home and in which student-designed majors are permitted. Dual majors, an accelerated degree in management and professional studies, a 1-3 engineering degree with Walla Walla College, and preprofessional curricula in dentistry, dental hygiene, medicine, respiratory therapy, radiologic technology, and veterinary medicine in conjunction with Loma Linda University are offered. There are 3 national honor societies, a freshman honors program, and 4 departmental honors programs.

Faculty/Classroom: 45% of faculty are male; 55%, female. All teach undergraduates and 10% both teach and do research. No introductory courses are taught by graduate students. The average class size in an introductory lecture is 18; in a laboratory, 30; and in a regular course, 16.

Admissions: 50% of the 2005-2006 applicants were accepted. The SAT scores for the 2005-2006 freshman class were: Verbal--60% below 500, 32% between 500 and 599, and 6% between 600 and 700; Math--72% below 500, 21% between 500 and 599, and 4% between 600 and 700. The ACT scores were 64% below 21, 24% between 21 and 23, 6% between 24 and 26, 3% between 27 and 28, and 3% above 28.

Requirements: The SAT or ACT is required. In addition, applicants should be graduates of an accredited secondary school. The GED is accepted with a minimum score of 250. Required academic credits include 4 years of high school English and 2 years each of a foreign language, math, history, and science. A GPA of 2.2 is required. AP and CLEP credits are accepted. Important factors in the admissions decision are recommendations by school officials, recommendations by alumni, and personality/intangible qualities.

Procedure: Freshmen are admitted fall and spring. Entrance exams should be taken during the senior year of high school. There is a rolling admissions plan. Applications should be filed by August 1 for fall entry and January 2 for spring entry, along with a $25 fee. Notification is sent on a rolling basis. Applications are accepted on-line.

Transfer: 33 transfer students enrolled in 2004-2005. Applicants who have completed at least 24 semester hours are not required to submit SAT or ACT scores. Applicants from junior colleges may receive credit for up to 72 semester hours. Only a grade of C or better transfers for credit. 30 of 128 to 143 credits required for the bachelor's degree must be completed at AUC.

Visiting: There are regularly scheduled orientations for prospective students, including campus tours, class visits, and financial aid and admissions information sessions. There are guides for informal visits and visitors may sit in on classes and stay overnight. To schedule a visit, contact Wayne Dunbar at (978) 368-2259 or wdunbar@atlanticuc.edu.

Financial Aid: In a recent year, 88% of all full-time freshmen and 84% of continuing full-time students received some form of financial aid. 75% of full-time freshmen and 77% of continuing full-time students received need-based aid. The average freshman award was $12,823. Need-based scholarships or need-based grants averaged $7635; need-based self-help aid (loans and jobs) averaged $6050; and other non-need-based awards and non-need-based scholarships averaged $6347. 60% of undergraduates work part time. Average annual earnings from campus work are $2210. The average financial indebtedness of a recent year's graduate was $16,398. AUC is a member of CSS. The FAFSA is required. The deadline for filing freshman financial aid applications for fall entry is May 1.

International Students: There are 66 international students enrolled. The school actively recruits these students. They must achieve a satisfactory score on the TOEFL and the ACT.

Computers: Students may apply for network and/or wireless access separately. Both allow Internet access. Access is also accomplished by using their laptops (wireless labs only) or campus labs (network) located in the science complex (3 main computer labs), the library, and the dorms. Some academic departments also have small labs. All students may access the system. There are no time limits. Wireless access is $25 per semester. It is strongly recommended that all students have a personal computer.

Graduates: From July 1, 2004 to June 30, 2005, 84 bachelor's degrees were awarded. The most popular majors were nursing (14%), religion (9%), and psychology (9%). In an average class, 29% graduate in 3 years or less, 56% graduate in 4 years or less, 81% graduate in 5 years or less, and 91% graduate in 6 years or less. Of the 2004 graduating class, 10% were enrolled in graduate school within 6 months of graduation and 93% were employed.

Admissions Contact: Rosita Lashley, Director of Admissions. A video is available. E-mail: *enroll@atlanticuc.edu* Web: *www.atlanticuc.edu*

BABSON COLLEGE   D-2
Babson Park, MA 02457

(781) 239-5522
(800) 488-3696; Fax: (781) 239-4135

Full-time: 1056 men, 669 women	**Faculty:** IIB, ++$
Part-time: none	**Ph.D.s:** 91%
Graduate: 1055 men, 430 women	**Student/Faculty:** n/av
Year: semesters, summer session	**Tuition:** $30,496
Application Deadline: February 1	**Room & Board:** $10,792
Freshman Class: 3168 applied, 1164 accepted, 420 enrolled	
SAT Verbal/Math: 604/648*	**HIGHLY COMPETITIVE**

Babson College, founded in 1919, is a private business school. All students start their own businesses during their freshman year with money loaned by the college. In addition to regional accreditation, Babson has baccalaureate program accreditation with AACSB. The library contains 132,024 volumes, 346,941 microform items, and 4645 audio/video tapes/CDs/DVDs, and subscribes to 511 periodicals including electronic. Computerized library services include the card catalog, interlibrary loans, database searching, and Internet access. Special learning facilities include a learning resource center, art gallery, radio station, performing arts theater, and centers for entrepreneurial studies, management, language and culture, writing, math, visual arts, executive education, and women's leadership. The 370-acre campus is in a suburban area 14 miles west of Boston. Including any residence halls, there are 53 buildings.

Student Life: 70% of undergraduates are from out of state, mostly the Northeast. Students are from 47 states, 60 foreign countries, and Canada. 55% are from public schools. 44% are white; 18% foreign nationals. The average age of freshmen is 18; all undergraduates, 20. 5% do not continue beyond their first year; 85% remain to graduate.

Housing: 1441 students can be accommodated in college housing, which includes single-sex and coed dorms, on-campus apartments, and married-student housing. In addition, there are special-interest houses. On-campus housing is guaranteed for all 4 years. 81% of students live on campus; of those, 70% remain on campus on weekends. All students may keep cars.

Activities: 10% of men belong to 4 national fraternities; 12% of women belong to 3 national sororities. There are 60 groups on campus, including a cappella, art, band, cheerleading, choir, chorus, dance, drama, ethnic, gay, honors, international, jazz band, literary magazine, musical theater, newspaper, photography, political, professional, radio and TV, religious, social, social service, student government, and yearbook. Popular campus events include Multicultural Week.

Sports: There are 11 intercollegiate sports for men and 11 for women, and 11 intramural sports for men and 11 for women. Facilities include a sports complex with an indoor pool, a 200-meter, 6-lane indoor track, a 1500-square-foot field house, a 600-seat gym with 3 basketball courts, 5 squash and 2 racquetball courts, a fitness center, a dance aerobics studio, locker rooms with saunas, and a sports medicine facility.

Disabled Students: 75% of the campus is accessible. Wheelchair ramps, elevators, special parking, specially equipped rest rooms, special class scheduling, lowered drinking fountains, and special housing are available.

Services: Counseling and information services are available, as is tutoring in most subjects. There are writing/speech skills and math/science skills centers.

Campus Safety and Security: Measures include 24-hour foot and vehicle patrol, self-defense education, security escort services, and shuttle buses. There are informal discussions, pamphlets/posters/films, emergency telephones, lighted pathways/sidewalks, a motorist assist program, a transportation service for the cross-registration program, vans available to students for school activities, and crime prevention programs.

Programs of Study: Babson confers the B.S.M. degree. Master's degrees are also awarded. Bachelor's degrees are awarded in BUSINESS (business administration and management).

Required: Students must complete a curriculum of general management and liberal arts, with 50% in management and 50% in liberal arts. A total of 128 semester hours is required for graduation. A minimum GPA of 2.0 is required. The curriculum focuses on rhetoric, numeracy, ethics/social responsibility, international/multicultural perspectives, and leadership/teamwork/creativity competencies. Students specialize in certain aspects of business.

Special: There is cross-registration with Brandeis University, Wellesley College, and F.W. Olin College of Engineering. Internships and study abroad in 23 countries are available. There is a freshman honors program.

Faculty/Classroom: 69% of faculty are male; 31%, female. No introductory courses are taught by graduate students. The average class size in an introductory lecture is 34; in a laboratory, 20; and in a regular course, 27.

Admissions: 37% of the 2005-2006 applicants were accepted. The SAT scores for the 2005-2006 freshman class were: Verbal--3% below 500, 35% between 500 and 599, 50% between 600 and 700, and 12% above 700; Math--17% between 500 and 599, 58% between 600 and 700, and 24% above 700. 80% of the current freshmen were in the top fifth of their class.

Requirements: The SAT or ACT is required. In addition, applicants must be graduates of an accredited secondary school or have a GED. 16 academic courses are required, including 4 credits of English, 3 of math, 2 of social studies, and 1 of science. A fourth year of math is strongly recommended. Essays are required. An SAT subject test in math is recommended. AP and CLEP credits are accepted. Important factors in the admissions decision are advanced placement or honor courses, evidence of special talent, and leadership record.

Procedure: Freshmen are admitted in the fall. Entrance exams should be taken prior to application (SAT or ACT). There are early decision, early admissions, and deferred admissions plans. Early decision applications should be filed by November 15; regular applications, by February 1 for fall entry. The fall 2005 application fee was $60. Notification of early decision is sent December 15; regular decision, April 1. 138 early decision candidates were accepted for the 2005-2006 class. 320 applicants were on the 2005 waiting list; 35 were admitted. Applications are accepted on-line.

Transfer: 47 transfer students enrolled in 2004-2005. Transfer applicants are expected to demonstrate solid academic performance at their prior institution and must submit 1 essay and 1 recommendation from a college teacher or administrator, in addition to a high school transcript and SAT I scores. They must also submit course descriptions and syllabi for any courses they have taken. 64 of 128 credits required for the bachelor's degree must be completed at Babson.

Visiting: There are regularly scheduled orientations for prospective students, including an open house each year, personal interviews, campus tours, group information sessions, and Fall Preview Days (select Saturdays--"mini Open House"). There are guides for informal visits. To schedule a visit, contact the Admission Office at least 2 weeks in advance.

Financial Aid: In 2005-2006, 45% of all full-time freshmen and 44% of continuing full-time students received some form of financial aid. 41% of all full-time students received need-based aid. The average freshman award was $26,171. Need-based scholarships or need-based grants averaged $21,633; and need-based self-help aid (loans and jobs) averaged $4538. 32% of undergraduates work part time. Average annual earnings from campus work are $1580. The average financial indebtedness of the 2005 graduate was $24,900. The CSS/Profile or FAFSA and tax returns are required. The priority date for freshman financial aid applications for fall entry is December 1. The deadline for filing freshman financial aid applications for fall entry is February 15.

International Students: There were 318 international students enrolled in a recent year. The school actively recruits these students. They must score satisfactorily on the written or electronic version of the TOEFL or take the English Language Proficiency Test and must also take the SAT or the ACT. An SAT Subject test in math is recommended.

Computers: Wireless access is available. All students may access the system. There are no time limits and no fees. It is strongly recommended that all students have a personal computer.

Graduates: From July 1, 2004 to June 30, 2005, 424 bachelor's degrees were awarded. In an average class, 80% graduate in 4 years or less, and 85% graduate in 5 years or less. 301 companies recruited on campus in a recent year. Of the 2004 graduating class, 3% were enrolled in graduate school within 6 months of graduation and 92% were employed.

Admissions Contact: Alan Kines, Dean of Undergraduate Admission. A video is available. E-mail: ugradadmission@babson.edu Web: www.babson.edu

BAY PATH COLLEGE

Longmeadow, MA 01106

(413) 565-1331
(800) 782-7284; Fax: (413) 565-1105

Full-time: 1020 women	Faculty: 36
Part-time: 230 women	Ph.D.s: 54%
Graduate: 20 men 55 women	Student/Faculty: 31 to 1
Year: semesters	Tuition: $20,606
Application Deadline: open	Room & Board: $8756
Freshman Class: 573 applied, 404 accepted, 129 enrolled	
SAT Verbal/Math: 515/495*	COMPETITIVE

Bay Path College, founded in 1897, is a comprehensive, private college offering innovative undergraduate programs for women onnly and graduate programs for men and women. In addition to regional accreditation, Bay Path has baccalaureate program accreditation with ABA and AOTA. The library contains 47,415 volumes, 4326 microform items, and 3632 audio/video tapes/CDs/DVDs, and subscribes to 156 periodicals including electronic. Computerized library services include the card catalog, interlibrary loans, database searching, and Internet access. Special learning facilities include a learning resource center, radio station, and TV station. The 48-acre campus is in a suburban area 3 miles south of Springfield. Including any residence halls, there are 17 buildings.

Student Life: 59% of undergraduates are from Massachusetts. Others are from 15 states and 6 foreign countries. 93% are from public schools. 79% are white; 11% African American. The average age of freshmen is 18; all undergraduates, 35.

Housing: 376 students can be accommodated in college housing, which includes single-sex dorms. On-campus housing is guaranteed for all 4 years. 66% of students live on campus; of those, 60% remain on campus on weekends. Alcohol is not permitted. All students may keep cars.

Activities: There are no fraternities. There are 39 groups on campus, including cheerleading, choir, chorale, computers, dance, drama, ethnic, forensics, Habitat for Humanity, gay, honors, international, literary magazine, musical theater, newspaper, political, professional, radio and TV, religious, social, social service, student government, Winter Guard and yearbook. Popular campus events include father/daughter and mother/daughter banquets, Karaoke Unplugged, and Dinner with the President.

Sports: Facilities include a fitness center that houses a weight-training room, a dance studio, and an aerobics room and a nearby 12-acre playing field with soccer and softball fields, a walking/jogging track, and a field house.

Disabled Students: 50% of the campus is accessible. Wheelchair ramps, elevators, special parking, and specially equipped rest rooms are available.

Services: Counseling and information services are available, as is tutoring in every subject.

Campus Safety and Security: Measures include 24-hour foot and vehicle patrol, self-defense education, security escort services, and informal discussions. There are pamphlets/posters/films, emergency telephones, lighted pathways/sidewalks, and fire, vehicle, and driving safety education programs.

Programs of Study: Bay Path confers B.A. and B.S. degrees. Associate and master's degrees are also awarded. Bachelor's degrees are awarded in BIOLOGICAL SCIENCE (biology/biological science), BUSINESS (business administration and management, international business management, and marketing/retailing/merchandising), COMMUNICATIONS AND THE ARTS (communications), EDUCATION (early childhood and elementary), ENGINEERING AND ENVIRONMENTAL DESIGN (interior design), HEALTH PROFESSIONS (occupational therapy), SOCIAL SCIENCE (child psychology/development, criminal justice, forensic studies, law, liberal arts/general studies, and psychology).

Required: To graduate, students must complete at least 120 credits with a minimum GPA of 2.0. The 46-hour core curriculum includes course work in communication, science, social science, math, and fine and performing arts.

Special: Co-op programs in busines, internships, a Washington semester, and dual majors are available. Cross-registration is possible with other member schools of the Cooperating Colleges of Greater Springfield Consortium. Bay Path's capital of the world program allows students to visit a different world center during each spring break.

Faculty/Classroom: 40% of faculty are male; 60%, female. All teach undergraduates. No introductory courses are taught by graduate students.

Admissions: 71% of the 2005-2006 applicants were accepted. The SAT scores for the 2005-2006 freshman class were: Verbal--39% below 500, 47% between 500 and 599, and 14% between 600 and 700; Math--56% below 500, 38% between 500 and 599, and 6% between 600 and 700.

Requirements: The SAT or ACT is required. In addition, applicants should have completed at least 4 academic courses each year, including 4 years of English, 3 of math, at least 2 each of social studies and lab sciences, and 2 of a foreign language. An essay is required, as are letters of recommendation from a guidance counselor and a teacher. An interview is strongly recommended. A GPA of 2.0 is required. AP and CLEP credits are accepted.

Procedure: Freshmen are admitted fall and spring. Entrance exams should be taken in the spring of the junior year or by December of the senior year. There is a rolling admissions plan. There is a deferred admissions plan. Application deadlines are open. Application fee is $25. Notification is sent September 15. Applications are accepted on-line.

Transfer: 35 transfer students enrolled in 2004-2005. Applicants must be in good standing at their previous school and are encouraged to arrange for an interview at Bay Path. Students who have earned fewer than 12 credits must submit SAT or ACT scores. 30 of 120 credits required for the bachelor's degree must be completed at Bay Path.

Visiting: There are regularly scheduled orientations for prospective students. There are guides for informal visits and visitors may sit in on classes and stay overnight. To schedule a visit, contact Lisa Casassa, Director of Admissions.

Financial Aid: In 2005-2006, 78% of all full-time freshmen and 69% of continuing full-time students received some form of financial aid. The average freshman award was $12,570. Need-based scholarships or need-based grants averaged $7247 ($16,550 maximum); need-based self-help aid (loans and jobs) averaged $5322 ($8625 maximum); and other non-need-based awards and non-need-based scholarships averaged $11,498 ($13,550 maximum). 39% of undergraduates work part time. Average annual earnings from campus work are $400. The average financial indebtedness of the 2005 graduate was $21,312. Bay Path is a member of CSS. The FAFSA, the college's own financial statement and parent and student income tax forms are required. The priority date for freshman financial aid applications for fall entry is May 1.

International Students: There are 12 international students enrolled. The school actively recruits these students. They must achieve a satisfactory score on the TOEFL and also take the SAT or the ACT.

Computers: Wireless access is available. All students may access the system. There are no time limits and no fees.

Graduates: From July 1, 2004 to June 30, 2005, 206 bachelor's degrees were awarded. The most popular majors were business (35%), liberal studies (19%), and psychology (14%). In an average class, 44% graduate in 5 years or less. 5 companies recruited on campus in 2004-2005. Of the 2004 graduating class, 54% were employed within 6 months of graduation.

Admissions Contact: Lisa Casassa, Director of Admissions.
E-mail: *admiss@baypath.edu* Web: *www.baypath.edu*

BECKER COLLEGE
C-2
Worcester, MA 01615-0071

(508) 791-9241, ext. 245
(877) 523-2537; Fax: (508) 890-1500

Full-time: 185 men, 625 women	**Faculty:** 40
Part-time: 120 men, 550 women	**Ph.D.s:** 33%
Graduate: none	**Student/Faculty:** 19 to 1
Year: semesters, summer session	**Tuition:** $16,500
Application Deadline: open	**Room & Board:** $7800
Freshman Class: n/av	
SAT Verbal/Math: required	**ACT;** recommended

LESS COMPETITIVE

Becker College, founded in 1887, is an independent undergraduate liberal arts and sciences institution offering baccalaureate degrees in various programs. Figures in the above capsule and profile are approximate. In addition to regional accreditation, Becker College has baccalaureate program accreditation with NLN. The 2 libraries contain 75,000 volumes, and subscribe to 253 periodicals including electronic. Computerized library services include the card catalog, interlibrary loans, database searching, and Internet access. Special learning facilities include a learning resource center, a day care center, a veterinary clinic, and a preschool facility. The Worcester campus is in an urban area 40 miles west of Boston. The Leicester campus is in a small town 45 miles west of Boston. Including any residence halls, there are 27 buildings.

Student Life: 68% of undergraduates are from Massachusetts. Others are from 18 states and 6 foreign countries. 52% are white. The average age of all undergraduates is 22. 36% do not continue beyond their first year; 30% remain to graduate.

Housing: 200 students can be accommodated in college housing, which includes single-sex and coed dormitories and 21 and over housing. On-campus housing is guaranteed for all 4 years. 60% of students commute. All students may keep cars.

Activities: There are no fraternities or sororities. There are 22 groups on campus, including animal club, art, chorus, dance, drama, ethnic, gay, honors, international, newspaper, outdoors, photography, professional, social, social service, student government, and yearbook. Popular campus events include Family Day, Class Day, and Spree Day.

Sports: There are 6 intercollegiate sports for men and 8 for women, and 5 intramural sports for men and 5 for women. Facilities include a gym, on-campus field hockey and soccer fields, and tennis courts.

Disabled Students: 80% of the campus is accessible. Wheelchair ramps, elevators, special parking, specially equipped rest rooms, lowered drinking fountains, lowered telephones, and special housing are available. All classes are accessible.

Services: Counseling and information services are available, as is tutoring in most subjects. There is remedial math and writing. There is also an academic support center for students.

Campus Safety and Security: Measures include 24-hour foot and vehicle patrol, self-defense education, security escort services, and shuttle buses. There are informal discussions, pamphlets/posters/films, emergency telephones, and lighted pathways/sidewalks.

Programs of Study: Becker College confers B.A. and B.S. degrees. Associate degrees are also awarded. Bachelor's degrees are awarded in BUSINESS (accounting, banking and finance, business administration and management, hospitality management services, human resources, marketing and distribution, and sports management), COMMUNICATIONS AND THE ARTS (communications, design, and graphic design), EDUCATION (early childhood and elementary), ENGINEERING AND ENVIRONMENTAL DESIGN (interior design), HEALTH PROFESSIONS (exercise science, health, and veterinary science), SOCIAL SCIENCE (criminal justice, human development, law, and psychology). Nursing and veterinary science are the strongest academically. Business administration is the largest.

Required: To graduate, baccalaureate students must complete 122 semester hours and maintain a 2.0 minimum GPA. Distribution requirements vary with the program of study.

Special: Cross-registration is offered through the Worcester Consortium of Higher Education. There are co-op programs, internships, study abroad, student-designed majors, work-study programs, and B.A.-B.S. degrees. There is 1 national honor society and a freshman honors program.

Faculty/Classroom: 31% of faculty are male; 69%, female. All teach undergraduates. The average class size in an introductory lecture is 20; in a laboratory, 15; and in a regular course, 25.

Requirements: The SAT is required and the ACT is recommended. In addition, a high school transcript is required. A GPA of 2.0 is required. AP and CLEP credits are accepted.

Procedure: Freshmen are admitted to all sessions. Entrance exams should be taken before submitting the application There is a rolling admissions plan. Application deadlines are open. Applications are accepted on-line. The fall 2005 application fee was $30.

Transfer: 150 transfer students enrolled in a recent year. Requirements for transfer students depend on the program. 62 of 122 credits required for the bachelor's degree must be completed at Becker College.

Visiting: There are regularly scheduled orientations for prospective students, consisting of 2 open houses each year and group tours. There are guides for informal visits and visitors may sit in on classes. To schedule a visit, contact the Admissions Receptionist.

Financial Aid: In a recent year, 82% of all full-time freshmen and 80% of continuing full-time students received some form of financial aid. 78% of full-time freshmen and 76% of continuing full-time students received need-based aid. The average freshman award was $6054. Need-based scholarships or need-based grants averaged $2868 ($4500 maximum); need-based self-help aid (loans and jobs) averaged $5381 ($10,500 maximum); and private loans and private alternative loans averaged $12,381. 40% of undergraduates worked part time. Average annual earnings from campus work were $1000. The average financial indebtedness of a recent graduate was $17,125. The FAFSA is required. Check with the current application deadlines.

International Students: In a recent year, there were 6 international students enrolled. The school actively recruits these students. They must score satisfactorily on the written TOEFL or on the electronic version. The ELPT is also accepted. The SAT or the ACT is also required.

Computers: All students may access the system. There are no time limits and no fees.

Graduates: In a recent year, 101 bachelor's degrees were awarded. The most popular major wasbusiness administration (31%). In an average class, 40% graduate in 3 years or less, 8% graduate in 4 years or less, 3% graduate in 5 years or less, and 1% graduate in 6 years or less. 45 companies recruited on campus in a recent year. Of a recent graduating class, 43% were enrolled in graduate school within 6 months of graduation and 67% were employed.

Admissions Contact: Karen Schedin, Director of Recruitment and Admissions. E-mail: *admissions@beckercollege.edu*
Web: *www.beckercollege.edu*

BENJAMIN FRANKLIN INSTITUTE OF TECHNOLOGY   E-2

Boston, MA 02116 (617) 423-4630; Fax: (617) 482-3706

Full-time: 388 men and women	**Faculty:** n/av
Part-time: none	**Ph.D.s:** 3%
Graduate: none	**Student/Faculty:** n/av
Year: semesters, summer session	**Tuition:** $14,039
Application Deadline: August 15	**Room & Board:** $9000
Freshman Class: n/av	
SAT or ACT: not required	**SPECIAL**

Benjamin Franklin Institute of Technology, founded in 1908, is a private technical college offering degree programs in industrial and engineering technologies. Some information in this capsule and profile is approximate. In addition to regional accreditation, BFIT has baccalaureate program accreditation with ABET. The library contains 10,000 volumes, and subscribes to 70 periodicals including electronic. Computerized library services include the card catalog, interlibrary loans, database searching, and Internet access. Special learning facilities include a learning resource center. The 3-acre campus is in an urban area. Including any residence halls, there are 3 buildings.

Student Life: 95% of undergraduates are from Massachusetts. Students are from 7 states and 7 foreign countries. 35% are African American; 35% white; 14% Hispanic; 12% Asian American. The average age of freshmen is 22; all undergraduates, 22.

Housing: 20 students can be accommodated in college housing, which includes single-sex dorms. On-campus housing is available on a first-come, first-served basis. Priority is given to out-of-town students. All students commute. Alcohol is not permitted. No one may keep cars.

Activities: There are no fraternities or sororities. There are 2 groups on campus, including student government and women's. Popular campus events include Technology Olympics and International Culture Day.

Sports: There are 2 intercollegiate sports for men and 2 intramural sports for men.

Disabled Students: 50% of the campus is accessible. Elevators and specially equipped rest rooms are available.

Services: Counseling and information services are available, as is tutoring in every subject. There is remedial math, reading, and writing.

Programs of Study: BFIT confers the B.S. degree. Associate degrees are also awarded. Bachelor's degrees are awarded in ENGINEERING AND ENVIRONMENTAL DESIGN (automotive technology). Mechanical and electrical engineering technology are the strongest academically. Automotive and computers are the largest.

Required: To graduate, students must earn a minimum cumulative GPA of 2.0. 2 college English courses are required.

Special: If qualified, 2-year BFIT graduates may transfer to Northeastern University. Automotive technology management students have access to Northeastern's facilities and resources.

Faculty/Classroom: 74% of faculty are male; 26%, female. All teach undergraduates. The average class size in an introductory lecture is 30; in a laboratory, 12; and in a regular course, 25.

Requirements: The ACT Optional Writing test is required. In addition, applicants should be high school graduates or have the GED. A GPA of 2.0 is required.

Procedure: Freshmen are admitted fall and spring. There is a rolling admissions plan. Applications should be filed by August 15 for fall entry and January 1 for spring entry, along with a $25 fee. Notification is sent on a rolling basis.

Visiting: Visitors may sit in on classes. To schedule a visit, contact the Office of Admission at (617) 423-4630, ext. 121.

Financial Aid: In a recent year, 94% of all full-time freshmen and 90% of continuing full-time students received some form of financial aid. BFIT is a member of CSS. The FAFSA and federal tax returns are required. The priority date for freshman financial aid applications for fall entry is April 15.

International Students: A satisfactory score is required on the written TOEFL or the college's own test, or satisfactorily complete Franklin's or another recognized ESL program. Students must also take the college's own entrance exam.

Computers: All students may access the system. There are no time limits and no fees. It is strongly recommended that all students have a PC.

Admissions Contact: Norman Kraft, Dean of Enrollment Services. E-mail: *nkraft@bfit.edu* Web: *www.bfit.edu*

BENTLEY COLLEGE   D-2

Waltham, MA 02452-4705 (781) 891-2244
(800) 523-2354; Fax: (781) 891-3414

Full-time: 2349 men, 1609 women	**Faculty:** 270; IIA, ++$
Part-time: 187 men, 149 women	**Ph.D.s:** 82%
Graduate: 698 men, 573 women	**Student/Faculty:** 15 to 1
Year: semesters, summer session	**Tuition:** $28,614
Application Deadline: February 1	**Room & Board:** $10,170
Freshman Class: 5802 applied, 2516 accepted, 937 enrolled	
SAT Verbal/Math: 590/630*	**HIGHLY COMPETITIVE**

Bentley College is a private institution that offers advanced business education along with a strong foundation in the arts and sciences. In addition to regional accreditation, Bentley has baccalaureate program accreditation with AACSB. The library contains 137,031 volumes, 2930 microform items, and 6400 audio/video tapes/CDs/DVDs, and subscribes to 30,660 periodicals including electronic. Computerized library services include the card catalog, interlibrary loans, database searching, Internet access, and laptop Internet portals. Special learning facilities include a learning resource center, art gallery, planetarium, radio station, TV station, the Accounting Center for Electronic Learning and Business Management, the Center for Languages and International Collaboration, the Center for Marketing Technology, the Design and Usability Testing Center, an academic technology center, and a trading room. The 163-acre campus is in a suburban area 10 miles west of Boston. Including any residence halls, there are 43 buildings.

Student Life: 50% of undergraduates are from out of state, mostly the Northeast. Students are from 39 states, 73 foreign countries, and Canada. 79% are from public schools. 69% are white. The average age of freshmen is 18; all undergraduates, 21. 6% do not continue beyond their first year; 81% remain to graduate.

Housing: 3258 students can be accommodated in college housing, which includes coed dormitories, on-campus apartments, and off-campus apartments. In addition, there are special-interest and substance-free houses. On-campus housing is guaranteed for all 4 years. 76% of students live on campus. Upperclassmen may keep cars.

Activities: There are 4 local and 2 national fraternities and 5 national sororities. There are 90 groups on campus, including alcohol awareness, art, band, Bentley Investment Group, cheerleading, choir, chorale, chorus, computers, dance, debate, drama, ethnic, film, forensics, gay, honors, international, jazz band, literary magazine, martial arts, musical theater, newspaper, pep band, photography, poker club, political, professional, radio and TV, religious, social, social service, student government, and yearbook. Popular campus events include Monte Carlo Night,"drive-in movie" film series, and Midnight Madness.

Sports: There are 12 intercollegiate sports for men and 11 for women, and 8 intramural sports for men and 8 for women. Facilities include a basketball court; a competition-size swimming pool with a diving tank; saunas and a steam bath; volleyball courts; baseball batting and golf cages; racquetball/handball courts; an indoor track; a dance studio; a 10,000-square-foot fitness facility.

Disabled Students: 75% of the campus is accessible. Wheelchair ramps, elevators, special parking, specially equipped rest rooms, special class scheduling, lowered drinking fountains, lowered telephones, and special housing are available.

Services: Counseling and information services are available, as is tutoring in most subjects. There is remedial math, reading, and writing. There is a Kurzweil 3000, Dragon Naturally Speaking available and additional assistive programs upon request.

Campus Safety and Security: Measures include 24-hour foot and vehicle patrol, self-defense education, security escort services, and shuttle buses. There are informal discussions, pamphlets/posters/films, emergency telephones, and lighted pathways/sidewalks.

Programs of Study: Bentley confers B.A. and B.S. degrees. Associate and master's degrees are also awarded. Bachelor's degrees are awarded in BUSINESS (accounting, banking and finance, business administration and management, business communications, business economics, management information systems, and marketing management), COMMUNICATIONS AND THE ARTS (communications, design, and English), COMPUTER AND PHYSICAL SCIENCE (information sciences and systems and mathematics), ENGINEERING AND ENVIRONMENTAL DESIGN (computer information systems), SOCIAL SCIENCE (history, international studies, liberal arts/general studies, and philosophy). Corporate finance and accounting, accountancy, and economics finance are the strongest academically. Management, marketing, and finance are the largest.

Required: All undergraduate students complete general education courses in areas such as expository writing, mathematical sciences, natural sciences, humanities, behavioral sciences, information technology, political science, history, philosophy, and economics. Students in B.S. programs take a common core of 10 courses covering major business areas such as accounting, business law, and marketing. All students take elective courses that fulfill a diversity, international, and communicatin intensive requirement. A total of 122 credit hours is required for graduation, with a minimum GPA of 2.0. All students must take a first-year seminar .

Special: There is cross-registration with Regis College and Brandeis University, and internships are available in business and public service. The college offers study abroad in 11 countries, a Washington semester, work-study programs, accelerated degree programs, student-designed majors, credit by exam, and nondegree study. There is also a minor concentration program through which business majors can broaden their exposure to the arts and sciences, and arts and science majors can minor in business or interdisciplinary topics. There is 1 national honor society, a freshman honors program, and 17 departmental honors programs.

Faculty/Classroom: 62% of faculty are male; 38%, female. All teach undergraduates. No introductory courses are taught by graduate students. The average class size in a regular course is 25.

Admissions: 43% of the 2005-2006 applicants' were accepted. The SAT scores for the 2005-2006 freshman class were: Verbal--7% below 500, 48% between 500 and 599, 42% between 600 and 700, and 3% above 700; Math--1% below 500, 21% between 500 and 599, 63% between 600 and 700, and 15% above 700. 71% of the current freshmen were in the top fifth of their class; 96% were in the top two fifths. 11 freshmen graduated first in their class.

Requirements: The SAT or ACT is required. In addition, applicants must be graduates of an accredited high school or have a GED. Recommended high school preparation is 4 units each in English and math, including algebra I and II, geometry, and a senior-year math course; 3 units in lab science; 3 units in a foreign language; 3 units in history / social science; and 2 additional units in English, math, social science or lab science, foreign langauage, or speech. AP and CLEP credits are accepted. Important factors in the admissions decision are advanced placement or honor courses, recommendations by school officials, and leadership record.

Procedure: Freshmen are admitted in fall and spring. Entrance exams should be taken prior to January 1. There are early decision, early admissions, and deferred admissions plans. Early decision applications should be filed by November 15; regular applications, by February 1 for fall entry and November 15 for spring entry, along with a $50 fee. Notification of early decision is sent December 22; regular decision, April 1. 96 early decision candidates were accepted for the 2005-2006 class. 923 applicants were on the 2005 waiting list; 5 were admitted. Applications are accepted on-line.

Transfer: 150 transfer students enrolled in 2004-2005. The SAT or the ACT is required of all applicants who have completed fewer than 30 college credits. All official college transcripts must be submitted. 60 of 122 credits required for the bachelor's degree must be completed at Bentley.

Visiting: There are regularly scheduled orientations for prospective students, including fall, spring, and summer open house programs. Interviews are arranged by appointment; campus tours and group information sessions take place regularly throughout the year. Visits are available during the week and some selected Saturdays. There are guides for informal visits and visitors may sit in on classes. To schedule a visit, contact the Office of Undergraduate Admission.

Financial Aid: In 2005-2006, 76% of all full-time freshmen and 71% of continuing full-time students received some form of financial aid. 55% of full-time freshmen and 70% of continuing full-time students received need-based aid. The average freshman award was $22,288. Need-based scholarships or need-based grants averaged $16,755; need-based self-help aid (loans and jobs) averaged $5374; non-need-based athletic scholarships averaged $32,478; and other non-need-based awards and non-need-based scholarships averaged $11,409. 24% of undergraduates work part time. Average annual earnings from campus work are $1192. The average financial indebtedness of the 2005 graduate was $27,132. Bentley is a member of CSS. The CSS/Profile or FAFSA and federal tax returns, including all schedules for parents and student are required. The deadline for filing freshman financial aid applications for fall entry is February 1.

International Students: There are 340 international students enrolled. The school actively recruits these students. They must score satisfactorily on the written TOEFL or on the electronic version and also take the SAT or the ACT.

Computers: Wireless access is available. Every undergraduate student has a labtop, and all residence halls provide port per seat and wireless access to the network. All classrooms have wireless access, and about half have port per seat. There are several computer labs, including a media lab. All students may access the system 24/7. There are no time limits and no fees. All students are required to have personal computers. In All full-time undergraduate students receive 2 laptop computers, 1 as freshmen and a second replacement unit at the beginning of their junior year (which they keep upon graduation). The IBM ThinkPad T43 and Toshiba Techra Tablet are recommended.

Graduates: From July 1, 2004 to June 30, 2005, 1019 bachelor's degrees were awarded. The most popular majors were finance (20%), marketing (19%), and management (11%). In an average class, 78% graduate in 4 years or less, 81% graduate in 5 years or less, and 82% graduate in 6 years or less. 262 companies recruited on campus in 2004-2005. Of the 2004 graduating class, 16% were enrolled in graduate school within 6 months of graduation and 84% were employed.

Admissions Contact: Kenton W. Rinehart, Director of Undergraduate Admission. E-mail: *ugadmission@bentley.edu*
Web: *www.bentley.edu/undergraduate*

BERKLEE COLLEGE OF MUSIC   E-2

Boston, MA 02215-3693

(617) 266-1400, ext. 2222
(800) BERKLEE; Fax: (617) 747-2047

Full-time: 2981 men, 1056 women	**Faculty:** n/av
Part-time: none	**Ph.D.s:** n/av
Graduate: none	**Student/Faculty:** 20 to 1
Year: semesters, summer session	**Tuition:** $26,089
Application Deadline: February 1	**Room & Board:** $11,690
Freshman Class: 2964 applied, 1703 accepted, 861 enrolled	
SAT or ACT: required	**SPECIAL**

Berklee College of Music, founded in 1945, is a private institution offering programs in music production and engineering, film scoring, music business/management, composition, music synthesis, music education, music therapy, performance, contemporary writing and production, jazz composition, songwriting, and professional music. Some information in this profile is approximate. The library contains 31,274 volumes and 22,974 audio/video tapes/CDs/DVDs, and subscribes to 122 periodicals including electronic. Computerized library services include the card catalog, database searching, and Internet access. Special learning facilities include a learning resource center, 12 recording studios, 5 performance venues, and film scoring, music synthesis, and songwriting labs. The campus is in an urban area in the Fenway Cultural District, Back Bay, Boston. Including any residence halls, there are 16 buildings.

Student Life: 82% of undergraduates are from out of state, mostly the Northeast. Students are from 50 states, 73 foreign countries, and Canada. 73% are white; 25% foreign nationals. The average age of all undergraduates is 22. 20% do not continue beyond their first year; 60% remain to graduate.

Housing: 840 students can be accommodated in college housing, which includes coed dormitories. On-campus housing is available on a first-come, first-served basis and is available on a lottery system for upperclassmen. 88% of students commute. Alcohol is not permitted. No one may keep cars.

Activities: There are no fraternities or sororities. There are 62 groups on campus, including art, band, choir, chorale, chorus, computers, ethnic, gay, international, jazz band, musical theater, newspaper, orchestra, professional, religious, social, social service, and student government. Popular campus events include International Night, daily recitals and concerts, and Singer Showcase.

Sports: There are 4 intramural sports for men and 4 for women. Discount memberships at the YMCA, a student rate at the Massachusetts College of Art fitness room, and membership at the Sheraton Fitness Center and the Tennis and Racquet Club of Boston are available.

Disabled Students: All of the campus is accessible. Wheelchair ramps, elevators, special class scheduling, lowered drinking fountains, and lowered telephones are available.

Services: Counseling and information services are available, as is tutoring in every subject. There is a reader service for the blind. tape recorders, untimed testing, and learning center resources.

Campus Safety and Security: Measures include 24-hour foot and vehicle patrol, security escort services, informal discussions, and pamphlets/posters/films. There are emergency telephones and lighted pathways/sidewalks.

Programs of Study: Berklee confers the B.M. degree. Master's degrees are also awarded. Bachelor's degrees are awarded in COMMUNICATIONS AND THE ARTS (audio technology, jazz, music, music business management, music performance, and music theory and composition), EDUCATION (music), HEALTH PROFESSIONS (music therapy). Performance, professional music, and music production and engineering are the largest.

Required: Students working toward a degree must take general education courses in English composition/literature, history, physical science, and social sciences. Music course programs vary by specialization. A total of 120 credits must be completed with a minimum GPA of 2.0.

Special: Berklee offers cross-registration with the Pro-Arts Consortium, study abroad in the Netherlands, internships in music education and music production and engineering, 5-year dual majors, and a 4-year professional (nondegree) diploma program. Work-study programs, an accelerated degree program, student-designed majors, and credit by exam are available.

Faculty/Classroom: 82% of faculty are male; 18%, female. All teach undergraduates. The average class size in an introductory lecture is 30; in a laboratory, 8; and in a regular course, 14.

Admissions: 57% of the 2005-2006 applicants were accepted.

Requirements: The SAT or ACT is required. The ACT Optional Writing test is also required. In addition, applicants must be graduates of an accredited secondary school that has a college preparatory program or have their GED. An audition and interview are recommended. Applicants must also submit a detailed reference letter regarding their training and experience in music, a letter from a private instructor, school music director, or professional musician. A GPA of 2.0 is required. AP credits are accepted. Important factors in the admissions decision are evidence of special talent, extracurricular activities record, and recommendations by alumni.

Procedure: Freshmen are admitted to all sessions. Entrance exams should be taken in the fall of the senior year of high school. There are early decision and deferred admissions plans. There is a rolling admissions plan for spring and summer semesters. Early decision applications should be filed by November 1; regular applications, by February 1 for fall entry, along with a $100 fee. Notification of early decision is sent January 30; regular decision, on a rolling basis. A waiting list is an active part of the admissions procedure. Applications are accepted on-line.

Transfer: 237 transfer students enrolled in 2005-2006. Applicants must go through the same application procedures as entering freshmen, as well as submit all previous college records. 60 of 120 credits required for the bachelor's degree must be completed at Berklee.

Visiting: There are regularly scheduled orientations for prospective students, consisting of 2 tours scheduled daily during semesters, with the morning tour followed by an information session given by an admissions counselor. There are guides for informal visits. To schedule a visit, contact the Admissions Office.

Financial Aid: Need-based scholarships or need-based grants averaged $15,414; and need-based self-help aid (loans and jobs) averaged $2946. The CSS/Profile or FFS and the college's own financial statement are required. Check with the school for current application deadlines.

International Students: In a recent year, there were 955 international students enrolled. The school actively recruits these students. They must take the college's own test and also take the SAT, or the ACT.

Computers: All students may access the system. There are no time limits and no fees. It is strongly recommended that all students have a personal computer. An Apple Titanium 64 Power Book is recommended.

Graduates: In the recent year, 650 bachelor's degrees were awarded.

Admissions Contact: Damien Bracken, Director of Admissions. A video is available. E-mail: *admissions@berklee.edu*
Web: *www.berklee.edu*

BOSTON ARCHITECTURAL CENTER E-2

Boston, MA 02115	(617) 262-5000; Fax: (617) 585-0121
Full-time: 310 men, 115 women	**Faculty:** n/av
Part-time: 55 men, 15 women	**Ph.D.s:** 80%
Graduate: 110 men, 80 women	**Student/Faculty:** n/av
Year: semesters, summer session	**Tuition:** $6500 ($7500)
Application Deadline: open	**Room & Board:** n/app
Freshman Class: n/av	
SAT or ACT: not required	**SPECIAL**

Boston Architectural Center, founded in 1889 as the Boston Architectural Club, is an independent, commuter institution offering professional programs in architecture and interior design. Students work in architectural and interior design offices during the day and attend classes at night. There are 2 undergraduate and 2 graduate schools. Figures in the above capsule and profile are approximate. In addition to regional accreditation, BAC has baccalaureate program accreditation with NAAB. The library contains 25,000 volumes, and subscribes to 140 periodicals including electronic. Computerized library services include the card catalog and database searching. Special learning facilities include an art gallery. The campus is in an urban area in Boston. There are 2 buildings.

Student Life: 53% of undergraduates are from Massachusetts. Others are from 43 states and 1 foreign country. 88% are white. The average age of freshmen is 26; all undergraduates, 26. 47% do not continue beyond their first year; 25% remain to graduate.

Housing: There are no residence halls. All of students commute. Alcohol is not permitted.

Activities: There are no fraternities or sororities. There are 4 groups on campus, including newspaper, professional, student government, and yearbook.

Sports: There is no sports program at BAC.

Disabled Students: All of the campus is accessible. Wheelchair ramps, elevators, special parking, and specially equipped rest rooms are available.

Services: Counseling and information services are available, as is tutoring in most subjects. The writing center provides one-on-one writing assistence and special services for ESL students.

Campus Safety and Security: Measures include pamphlets/posters/films, lighted pathways/sidewalks, and full time building security during operating hours.

Programs of Study: BAC confers B.Arch. and B.Int.Design. degrees. Master's degrees are also awarded. Bachelor's degrees are awarded in ENGINEERING AND ENVIRONMENTAL DESIGN (architecture and interior design).

Required: To graduate, all students must complete 123 academic credits, 93 of which must be in professional subjects and 30 in general education courses; 21 credits must be earned in liberal arts courses. Students must earn 54 additional credits by working in architectural or interior-design offices or related fields. Academic study is divided into 3 segments, the final segment being the thesis year, which consists of 2 semesters of student-designed study under the guidance of a faculty adviser. A minimum 2.5 GPA is required.

Special: BAC offers study abroad and cross-registration with schools in the Professional Arts Consortium in Boston and with the Art Institute of Boston for studio and professional courses. The participating schools are BAC, Berklee College of Music, Boston Conservation, Emerson College, Massachusetts College of Art and School of the MFA.

Faculty/Classroom: 86% of faculty are male; 14%, female. All teach undergraduates. The average class size in an introductory lecture is 33 and in a laboratory, 8.

Requirements: All applicants who have graduated from high school or have a college degree are admitted on a first-come, first-served basis. Official transcripts from previously attended secondary schools and colleges must be submitted to determine qualification for admission and advanced placement. Applications are accepted on-line at BAC's Web site. AP credits are accepted.

Procedure: Freshmen are admitted fall and spring. There are deferred admissions and rolling admissions plans. Application deadlines are open. The fall 2005 application fee was $50.

Transfer: Applicants for transfer must have a 2.0 GPA to receive transfer credit in most courses; 3.0 in math and physics. 47 of 123 credits required for the bachelor's degree must be completed at BAC.

Visiting: There are regularly scheduled orientations for prospective students, consisting of monthly presentations. There are guides for informal visits and visitors may sit in on classes. To schedule a visit, contact the Admissions Office at (617) 585-0123.

Financial Aid: BAC is a member of CSS. The FAFSA and the college's own financial statement are required.Check with the school for current application deadlines.

International Students: They must score satisfactorily on the written TOEFL.

Computers: All students may access the system. There are no time limits. The fee is $75 lab fee for certain courses.

Admissions Contact: William Dunfey, Director of Admissions.
E-mail: *admissions@the-bac.edu* Web: *www.the-bac.edu*

BOSTON COLLEGE E-2

Chestnut Hill, MA 02467	(617) 552-3100
	(800) 360-2522; Fax: (617) 552-0798
Full-time: 4314 men, 4705 women	**Faculty:** 595; I, +$
Part-time: none	**Ph.D.s:** 98%
Graduate: 1949 men, 2787 women	**Student/Faculty:** 23 to 1
Year: semesters, summer session	**Tuition:** $31,438
Application Deadline: January 2	**Room & Board:** $10,170
Freshman Class: n/av	
SAT or ACT: required	**MOST COMPETITIVE**

Boston College, founded in 1863, is an independent institution affiliated with the Roman Catholic Church and the Jesuit Order. It offers undergraduate programs in the arts and sciences, business, nursing, and education, and graduate and professional programs. There are 4 undergraduate and 7 graduate schools. In addition to regional accreditation, BC has baccalaureate program accreditation with AACSB, CSWE, NCATE, and NLN. The 6 libraries contain 2,076,844 volumes, 3,976,235 microform items, and 171,099 audio/video tapes/CDs/DVDs, and subscribe to 32,936 periodicals including electronic. Computerized library services include the card catalog, interlibrary loans, database searching, and Internet access. Special learning facilities include a learning resource center, art gallery, radio station, and TV station. The 257-acre campus is in a suburban area 6 miles west of Boston. Including any residence halls, there are 113 buildings.

Student Life: 71% of undergraduates are from out of state, mostly the Northeast. Students are from 46 states, 58 foreign countries, and Canada. 61% are from public schools. 73% are white. 71% are Catholic; 24% Protestant; 13% claim no religious affiliation. The average age of freshmen is 18; all undergraduates, 20. 4% do not continue beyond their first year; 89% remain to graduate.

Housing: 7248 students can be accommodated in college housing, which includes single-sex and coed dormitories and on-campus apartments. In addition, there are honors houses, language houses, special-interest houses, community and multicultural housing,quiet residence, single-sex freshman halls, perspectives academic housing, and a substance-free house. On-campus housing is guaranteed for the freshman year only and is available on a lottery system for upperclassmen. 80% of students live on campus; of those, 80% remain on campus on weekends. Upperclassmen may keep cars.

Activities: There are no fraternities or sororities. There are 200 groups on campus, including art, band, cheerleading, chess, choir, chorale, chorus, computers, dance, debate, drama, ethnic, film, honors, international, jazz band, literary magazine, marching band, musical theater, newspaper, orchestra, pep band, photography, political, professional, radio and TV, religious, social, social service, student government, symphony, and yearbook. Popular campus events include Middlemarch Ball, Christmas Chorale, and Senior Week.

Sports: There are 12 intercollegiate sports for men and 15 for women, and 22 intramural sports for men and 19 for women. Facilities include a 44,500 seat stadium, a forum that seats 8500 for basketball and 7600 for ice hockey, a field, a track, and a student recreation complex.

Disabled Students: 95% of the campus is accessible. Wheelchair ramps, elevators, special parking, specially equipped rest rooms, special class scheduling, lowered drinking fountains, lowered telephones, and special housing are available.

Services: Counseling and information services are available, as is tutoring in most subjects. There is a reader service for the blind and an academic development center that serves all students.

Campus Safety and Security: Measures include 24-hour foot and vehicle patrol, self-defense education, security escort services, and shuttle buses. There are informal discussions, pamphlets/posters/films, emergency telephones, lighted pathways/sidewalks, and safety seminars and safety walking tours are offered for incoming students during orientation.

Programs of Study: BC confers B.A. and B.S. degrees. Master's and doctoral degrees are also awarded. Bachelor's degrees are awarded in BIOLOGICAL SCIENCE (biochemistry and biology/biological science), BUSINESS (accounting, banking and finance, business administration and management, business economics, human resources, management science, marketing/retailing/merchandising, and operations research), COMMUNICATIONS AND THE ARTS (art history and appreciation, classics, communications, dramatic arts, English, film arts, French, Italian, linguistics, music, romance languages and literature, and studio art), COMPUTER AND PHYSICAL SCIENCE (chemistry, computer science, geology, geophysics and seismology, information sciences and systems, mathematics, and physics), EDUCATION (early childhood, elementary, secondary, and special), ENGINEERING AND ENVIRONMENTAL DESIGN (environmental science), HEALTH PROFESSIONS (nursing), SOCIAL SCIENCE (classical/ancient civilization, economics, German area studies, Hispanic American studies, history, human development, philosophy, political science/government, psychology, Russian and Slavic studies, sociology, and theological studies). Finance, economics, history, and political science are the strongest academically. Finance, communications, and English are the largest.

Required: Core requirements include 2 courses each in natural science, social science, history, philosophy, and theology, and 1 course each in literature, writing, math, cultural diversity, and the arts. To graduate, students must complete 114 credits (121 in nursing), including at least 30 in the major, with a minimum 1.667 GPA (1.5 in management). Computer science is required for management majors, intermediate-level foreign language proficiency for arts and sciences and management students, and a freshman writing seminar for all students except Honors and AP students.

Special: There are internship programs in arts and sciences. Students may cross-register with Boston University, Brandeis University, Hebrew College, Pine Manor College, Regis College, and Tufts University. BC also offers a Washington semester with American University, work-study programs with nonprofit agencies, study abroad in more than 70 countries, dual and student-designed majors, credit by exam, and pass/fail options. Students may pursue a 3-2 engineering program with Boston University and accelerated programs in business, social work, and education. There are also special programs in social work and philosophy/theology, in language immersion, capstone courses, and in exploring fundamental questions of faith, peace, and justice. There are 12 national honor societies, including Phi Beta Kappa, a freshman honors program, and 4 departmental honors programs.

Faculty/Classroom: 62% of faculty are male; 38%, female. All both teach and do research. Graduate students teach 14% of introductory courses. The average class size in a laboratory is 15 and in a regular course, 30.

Admissions: 95% of the current freshmen were in the top fifth of their class; 99% were in the top two fifths. There were 7 National Merit finalists.

Requirements: The SAT or ACT is required. The ACT Optional Writing test is also required. In addition, students must take the SAT test and two subject tests of their choice. Applicants must be graduates of an accredited high school completing 4 units each of English, foreign language, and math, and 4 units of science. Those students applying to the School of Nursing must complete at least 2 years of a lab science, including 1 unit of chemistry. Applicants to the School of Management are strongly encouraged to take 4 years of college preparatory math. An essay is required.

Procedure: Freshmen are admitted fall and spring. Entrance exams should be taken no later than January of the senior year. There are early admissions and deferred admissions plans. Early decision applications should be filed by November 1; regular applications, by January 2 for fall entry and November 1 for spring entry, along with a $70 fee. Notifi-

cation of early decision is sent December 25; regular decision, April 15. 5000 applicants were on the 2005 waiting list; 225 were admitted. Applications are accepted on-line.

Transfer: 106 transfer students enrolled in 2004-2005. Applicants must have a current GPA of at least 3.0 and must have earned a minimum of 9 semester hours. High school transcripts, letters of recommendation, and SAT or ACT scores are required. 54 of 114 credits required for the bachelor's degree must be completed at BC.

Visiting: There are regularly scheduled orientations for prospective students, consisting of group information sessions and campus tours Monday through Friday. There are guides for informal visits and visitors may sit in on classes. To schedule a visit, contact the Office of Undergraduate Admission.

Financial Aid: In 2004-2005, 71% of all full-time freshmen and 73% of continuing full-time students received some form of financial aid. 42% of full-time freshmen and 40% of continuing full-time students received need-based aid. The average freshman award was $26,489. Need-based scholarships or need-based grants averaged $19,072 ($34,800 maximum); need-based self-help aid (loans and jobs) averaged $4911 ($6925 maximum); non-need-based athletic scholarships averaged $29,130 ($40,800 maximum); and other non-need-based awards and non-need-based scholarships averaged $10,085 ($28,940 maximum). 26% of undergraduates work part time. Average annual earnings from campus work are $1700. The average financial indebtedness of the 2005 graduate was $16,732. BC is a member of CSS. The CSS/Profile or FAFSA and the federal IRS income tax form, W-2s, Divorced/Separated Statement (when applicable) are required. The deadline for filing freshman financial aid applications for fall entry is February 1.

International Students: There are 252 international students enrolled. The school actively recruits these students. They must score satisfactorily on the written TOEFL or on the electronic version and also take the SAT or the ACT. Students must take the SAT and 2 of the SAT subject tests of the student's choice.

Computers: Wireless access is available. All dorm rooms are wired for the college's network and wireless coverage is available in most buildings on campus including classrooms, cafeterias, and administration buildings. All students may access the system at all times. There are no time limits and no fees. It is strongly recommended that all students have a personal computer.

Graduates: From July 1, 2004 to June 30, 2005, 3033 bachelor's degrees were awarded. The most popular majors were finance (10%), communications (9%), and English (9%). In an average class, 87% graduate in 4 years or less, and 89% graduate in 6 years or less. 300 companies recruited on campus in 2004-2005. Of the 2004 graduating class, 26% were enrolled in graduate school within 6 months of graduation and 67% were employed.

Admissions Contact: John L. Mahoney Jr., Dir, Undergraduate Admission. A video is available.
E-mail: *undergraduate.admission@bc.edu* Web: *www.bc.edu*

BOSTON CONSERVATORY
Boston, MA 02215

E-2

(617) 536-6340; Fax: (617) 536-3176

Full-time: 100 men, 240 women	Faculty: 17
Part-time: 10 men, 15 women	Ph.Ds: 1%
Graduate: 130 men and women	Student/Faculty: 15 to 1
Year: semesters, summer session	Tuition: $20,500
Application Deadline: open	Room & Board: $7000
Freshman Class: n/av	
SAT: recommended	ACT: recommended SPECIAL

The Boston Conservatory, founded in 1867, is a private, coeducational college providing degree programs in music, musical theater, and dance. Figures given in the above capsule and in this profile are approximate. In addition to regional accreditation, the conservatory has baccalaureate program accreditation with NASM. The library contains 40,000 volumes, and subscribes to 120 periodicals including electronic. Computerized library services include interlibrary loans and database searching. The campus is in an urban area in Boston's Back Bay. Including any residence halls, there are 7 buildings.

Student Life: 20% of undergraduates are from Massachusetts. Others are from 36 states, 29 foreign countries, and Canada. 90% are white. The average age of freshmen is 18. 23% do not continue beyond their first year; 44% remain to graduate.

Housing: 164 students can be accommodated in college housing, which includes single-sex and coed dormitories. In addition, there are special-interest houses and international housing. On-campus housing is guaranteed for all 4 years. 67% of students commute. Alcohol is not permitted. All students may keep cars.

Activities: There is 1 national fraternity and 2 national sororities. There are 19 groups on campus, including band, choir, chorale, chorus, dance, drama, ethnic, gay, international, musical theater, newspaper, opera, orchestra, political, professional, religious, social service, student government, and yearbook. Popular campus events include Parents Weekend.

Sports: There is no sports program at the conservatory.

Disabled Students: 20% of the campus is accessible. Elevators are available.

Services: Counseling and information services are available, as is tutoring in every subject. A fee is required.

Campus Safety and Security: Measures include 24-hour foot and vehicle patrol, self-defense education, and informal discussions.

Programs of Study: The conservatory confers B.F.A. and B.Mus. degrees. Bachelor's degrees are awarded in COMMUNICATIONS AND THE ARTS (dance, guitar, music, music performance, music theory and composition, musical theater, opera, and piano/organ), EDUCATION (music). Music is the largest.

Required: All students must successfully complete the curriculum with no more than 12 credit hours of D-grade work. In addition, music performance majors must present recitals, music education majors must present a recital from memory, and composition majors must pass an exam on their primary instrument, present a portfolio of original composition, and perform a recital.

Special: There are 3 national honor societies and 1 departmental honors program.

Faculty/Classroom: All teach undergraduates. No introductory courses are taught by graduate students. The average class size in an introductory lecture is 15; in a laboratory, 5; and in a regular course, 15.

Requirements: The SAT or ACT is recommended and scores are reviewed. An audition is required. An academic high school diploma or GED also is required. A GPA of 2.0 is required. AP and CLEP credits are accepted. Important factors in the admissions decision are evidence of special talent, extracurricular activities record, and personality/intangible qualities.

Procedure: Freshmen are admitted in the fall. Entrance exams should be taken as early as possible. There is a deferred admissions and rolling admissions plans. Application deadlines are open.

Transfer: A successful audition and a 2.0 GPA are required. Transfer credits are determined by exam or review by the division head and the dean. The high school transcript is required if fewer than 30 college credits have been earned.

Visiting: Visitors may sit in on classes. To schedule a visit, contact the Admissions Office at (617) 536-6340.

Financial Aid: The conservatory is a member of CSS. The CSS/Profile and the college's own financial statement are required. Check with the school for current application deadlines.

International Students: The school actively recruits these students. They must take the TOEFL, the MELAB, or the college's own test, or the SAT. An audition also is required.

Computers: There are no time limits and no fees.

Admissions Contact: Halley Shefler, Director of Enrollment Management.

BOSTON UNIVERSITY

E-2

Boston, MA 02215 (617) 353-2300; Fax: (617) 353-9695

Full-time: 7097 men, 10,287 women	Faculty: 1360; I, +$
Part-time: 672 men, 638 women	Ph.Ds: 85%
Graduate: 5658 men, 6605 women	Student/Faculty: 13 to 1
Year: semesters, summer session	Tuition: $31,966
Application Deadline: January 1	Room & Board: $10,080
Freshman Class: 31,431 applied, 17,810 accepted, 4212 enrolled	
SAT Verbal/Math: 630/650*	ACT: 28

HIGHLY COMPETITIVE+

Boston University, founded in 1839, is a private institution offering undergraduate and graduate programs in basic studies, liberal arts, communication, hotel and food administration, allied health education management, and fine arts. There are 11 undergraduate and 15 graduate schools. In addition to regional accreditation, BU has baccalaureate program accreditation with ABET and NASM. The 23 libraries contain 2,396,362 volumes, 4,502,635 microform items, and 72,542 audio/video tapes/CDs/DVDs, and subscribe to 34,214 periodicals including electronic. Computerized library services include the card catalog, interlibrary loans, and database searching. Special learning facilities include a learning resource center, art gallery, planetarium, radio station, TV station, an astronomy observatory, 20th century archives, a theater and theater company in residence, a scientific computing and visualization lab, the Geddes language lab, a speech, language, and hearing clinic, a hotel/food administration culinary center, a performance center, a multimedia center, a center for photonics research, a center for remote sensing, and the Metcalf Center for Science and Engineering. The 132-acre campus is in an urban area on the Charles River in Boston's Back Bay. Including any residence halls, there are 349 buildings.

Student Life: 77% of undergraduates are from out of state, mostly the Middle Atlantic. Others are from 50 states, 135 foreign countries, and Canada. 75% are from public schools. 57% are white; 13% Asian American. 34% are Catholic; 23% Protestant; 20% claim no religious affiliation; 13% Jewish; 10% Buddhist, Hindu, Islamic, and Eastern Rite Orthodox. The average age of freshmen is 19; all undergraduates, 21. 9% do not continue beyond their first year; 77% remain to graduate.

Housing: 10,616 students can be accommodated in college housing, which includes single-sex and coed dorms, on-campus apartments, off-campus apartments, and married-student housing. In addition, there are honors houses, language houses, special-interest houses, international floors and houses, and student residences. On-campus housing is guaranteed for all 4 years. 66% of students live on campus; of those, 80% remain on campus on weekends. All students may keep cars.

Activities: 3% of men belong to 1 local and 8 national fraternities; 5% of women belong to 9 national sororities. There are more than 400 groups on campus, including art, band, cheerleading, chess, choir, chorale, chorus, computers, dance, drama, ethnic, film, gay, honors, international, jazz band, literary magazine, marching band, multicultural, musical theater, newspaper, opera, orchestra, pep band, photography, political, professional, radio and TV, religious, social, social service, sports, student government, symphony, and yearbook. Popular campus events include the Fall Welcome (Splash), World Fair and Culture Fest, and Head of the Charles River Regatta.

Sports: There are 12 intercollegiate sports for men and 14 for women, and 23 intramural sports for men and 23 for women. Facilities include 2 gyms, an ice-skating rink, saunas, a pool, a dance studio, a crew tank, a weight room, indoor and outdoor tracks, tennis and volleyball courts, multipurpose playing fields, and a boathouse.

Disabled Students: 90% of the campus is accessible. Wheelchair ramps, elevators, special parking, specially equipped rest rooms, special class scheduling, lowered drinking fountains, lowered telephones, special housing, and on-campus transportation, relocation of classes/events for access, tactile and access maps, visual fire alarms for the deaf, adaptive computers, and readers, notetakers and ASL interpreters are available.

Services: Counseling and information services are available, as is tutoring in most subjects, including liberal arts, science, engineering, and management. There is a reader service for the blind. Comprehensive learning strategy for learning disabled is available.

Campus Safety and Security: Measures include 24-hour foot and vehicle patrol, self-defense education, security escort services, and shuttle buses. There are informal discussions, pamphlets/posters/films, emergency telephones, lighted pathways/sidewalks, and and a mountain bicycle patrol system. There is a uniformed safety/security assistant on duty 24 hours a day in large residence halls and there are 60 academy-trained officers in the university police department.

Programs of Study: BU confers B.A., B.S., B.F.A., B.L.S., B.Mus., and B.S.B.A. degrees. Master's and doctoral degrees are also awarded. Bachelor's degrees are awarded in AGRICULTURE (environmental studies), BIOLOGICAL SCIENCE (biochemistry, biology/biological science, ecology, environmental biology, neurosciences, nutrition, and physiology), BUSINESS (accounting, banking and finance, business administration and management, entrepreneurial studies, hotel/motel and restaurant management, international business management, management information systems, management science, marketing/retailing/merchandising, operations research, and organizational behavior), COMMUNICATIONS AND THE ARTS (apparel design, classics, communications, dramatic arts, East Asian languages and literature, English, film arts, French, German, Germanic languages and literature, graphic design, Greek (classical), Greek (modern), Italian, journalism, Latin, linguistics, music, music history and appreciation, music performance, music theory and composition, painting, performing arts, public relations, sculpture, Spanish, theater design, and theater management), COMPUTER AND PHYSICAL SCIENCE (astronomy, astrophysics, chemistry, computer science, earth science, geophysics and seismology, mathematics, physics, and planetary and space science), EDUCATION (art, athletic training, bilingual/bicultural, drama, early childhood, education, education of the deaf and hearing impaired, elementary, English, foreign languages, mathematics, music, physical, science, social studies, and special), ENGINEERING AND ENVIRONMENTAL DESIGN (aeronautical engineering, biomedical engineering, computer engineering, electrical/electronics engineering, engineering, environmental science, manufacturing engineering, and mechanical engineering), HEALTH PROFESSIONS (exercise science, health, health science, physical therapy, rehabilitation therapy, and speech pathology/audiology), SOCIAL SCIENCE (American studies, anthropology, archeology, Asian/Oriental studies, classical/ancient civilization, East Asian studies, Eastern European studies, economics, French studies, geography, Hispanic American studies, history, interdisciplinary studies, international relations, Italian studies, Japanese studies, Latin American studies, philosophy, physical fitness/movement, political science/government, psychology, religion, sociology, and urban studies). The University Professors Program, accelerated medical and dental programs, and the management honors program are the strongest academically. Communications, business, and marketing are the largest.

Required: Most students are required to complete 128 credit hours to qualify for graduation. Hours in the major, specific disciplines, curricula, distribution requirements, and minimum GPA vary, depending on the school or college of BU attended. In addition, students in the College of Arts and Sciences must complete the College Writing Program: 1 full year of formal instruction in writing, reading, research and speaking.

Special: Cross-registration is permitted with Brandeis University, Tufts University, Boston College, and Hebrew College in Massachusetts. Opportunities are provided for internships, co-op programs in engineering, a Washington semester, on- and off-campus work-study, accelerated degree programs, B.A.-B.S. degrees, dual majors, student-designed majors, credit by exam, nondegree studies, pass/fail options, and study abroad in 18 countries. A 3-2 engineering degree is offered with 16 schools, and 2-2 engineering agreements with 6 schools, plus 107 other 2-2 agreements. The University Professors Program offers a creative cross-disciplinary approach, and the College of Basic Studies offers team teaching. There are 16 national honor societies, a freshman honors program, and 6 departmental honors programs.

Faculty/Classroom: 69% of faculty are male; 31%, female. 56% teach undergraduates. The average class size in an introductory lecture is 58; in a laboratory, 16; and in a regular course, 19.

Admissions: 57% of the 2005-2006 applicants were accepted. The SAT scores for the 2005-2006 freshman class were: Verbal--4% below 500, 27% between 500 and 599, 54% between 600 and 700, and 15% above 700; Math--21% between 500 and 599, 60% between 600 and 700, and 19% above 700. The ACT scores were 1% below 21, 9% between 21 and 23, 27% between 24 and 26, 22% between 27 and 28, and 41% above 28. 81% of the current freshmen were in the top fifth of their class; 97% were in the top two fifths. There were 81 National Merit finalists. 121 freshmen graduated first in their class.

Requirements: The SAT or ACT is required. The ACT Optional Writing test is also required. In addition, applicants are evaluated on an individual basis. Evidence of strong academic performance in a college prep curriculum, including 4 years of English, at least 3 years of math (through pre-calculus), 3 years of lab sciences, and 3 years of social studies/history with at least 2 years of a foreign language, will be the most important aspect of a student's application review. Subject tests in chemistry and math (level 2) are required for the accelerated medical and dental programs. Students planning to take the SAT are required to submit the SAT with the writing section along with two SAT Subject Tests in different subject areas of their choice. Students selected as finalists in the accelerated programs in medicine and dentistry will be invited to interview in Boston. Candidates for the College of Fine Arts must present a portfolio or participate in an audition. AP and CLEP credits are accepted (prior approval required). Advanced placement or honor courses is an important factor in the admission decision.

Procedure: Freshmen are admitted fall and spring. Entrance exams should be taken in the junior year or early in the senior year. There are early decision, early admissions, and deferred admissions plans. Early decision applications should be filed by November 1; regular applications, by January 1 for fall entry, along with a $70 fee. Notification of early decision is sent December 15; regular decision, late March through mid-April. 391 early decision candidates were accepted for the 2005-2006 class. 3551 applicants were on the 2005 waiting list; 9 were admitted. Applications are accepted on-line.

Transfer: 236 transfer students enrolled in 2004-2005. College transcripts, SAT (with writing test) or ACT scores, and a complete high school transcript (or GED) should be submitted. Recommendations and an essay are also recommended. Students must also submit a Transfer Student Status Report from all undergraduate institutions attended. The number of credits that must be completed at BU for graduation varies by school and college.

Visiting: There are regularly scheduled orientations for prospective students, The Admissions Reception Center is open Monday through Friday from 9 AM to 5 PM. We are also open some Saturdays during the academic year from 9 AM to 2 PM. Appointments must be made in advance for class visits or lunch with current students. Campus Tours and "Meet Boston University" information sessions are also offered. There are guides for informal visits and visitors may sit in on classes and stay overnight (available on a limited basis). To schedule a visit, contact the Admissions Reception Center at (617) 353-2318.

Financial Aid: In 2005-2006, 73% of all full-time freshmen and 66% of continuing full-time students received some form of financial aid. 55% of full-time freshmen and 50% of continuing full-time students received need-based aid. The average freshman award was $27,009. Need-based scholarships or need-based grants averaged $19,149 ($36,200 maximum); need-based self-help aid (loans and jobs) averaged $4228 ($7000 maximum); non-need-based athletic scholarships averaged $32,554 ($42,300 maximum); and other non-need-based awards and non-need-based scholarships averaged $15,849 ($30,402 maximum). 72% of undergraduates work part time. Average annual earnings from campus work are $1637. The average financial indebtedness of the 2005 graduate was $21,196. BU is a member of CSS. The CSS/Profile or FAFSA and are required. The priority date for freshman financial aid applications for fall entry is February 15.

International Students: There are 1440 international students enrolled. The school actively recruits these students. A satisfactory score is required on the written TOEFL. Applicants must also take the SAT or the ACT. Students must take SAT: Subject tests in any two areas for most majors; chemistry and math level 2 are required for accelerated medical and dental programs.

Computers: Wireless access is available. A shared cluster of UNIX systems consisting of several IBM RS/600 machines support the approximately 40,000 users. The Boston University campus network provides direct access to the Internet, e-mail, the Web and many other resources. Tens of thousands of ports support communications that are available throughout the campus, including residence halls. Boston University continues to extend its secure wireless network, currently available at several Charles River campus locations. All students may access the system 24 hours a day.

Graduates: From July 1, 2004 to June 30, 2005, 3541 bachelor's degrees were awarded. The most popular majors were business and management (17%), social sciences (17%), and communications (17%). In an average class, 2% graduate in 3 years, 63% graduate in 4 years, 10% graduate in 5 years, and 2% graduate in 6 years. 325 companies recruited on campus in 2004-2005. Of the 2004 graduating class, 29% were enrolled in graduate school within 6 months of graduation and 65% were employed.

Admissions Contact: Kelly Walter, Director, Undergraduate Admissions. E-mail: *admissions@bu.edu, or intadmis@bu.edu*
Web: *www.bu.edu*

BRANDEIS UNIVERSITY   D-2
Waltham, MA 02454

	(781) 736-3500
	(800) 622-0622; Fax: (781) 736-3536

Full-time: 1446 men, 1796 women	**Faculty:** 342; I, av$
Part-time: 7 men, 18 women	**Ph.D.s:** 91%
Graduate: 983 men, 939 women	**Student/Faculty:** 9 to 1
Year: semesters, summer session	**Tuition:** $32,501
Application Deadline: January 15	**Room & Board:** $9050
Freshman Class: 7343 applied, 2794 accepted, 739 enrolled	
SAT Verbal/Math: 680/690*	**MOST COMPETITIVE**

Brandeis University, founded in 1948, is a private liberal arts institution. The 3 libraries contain 1,761,920 volumes, 936,899 microform items, and 34,405 audio/video tapes/CDs/DVDs, and subscribe to 46,274 periodicals including electronic. Computerized library services include the card catalog, interlibrary loans, database searching, and Internet access. Special learning facilities include a learning resource center, art gallery, radio station, TV station, astronomical observatory, cultural center, treasure hall, art museum, and an audiovisual center. The 235-acre campus is in a suburban area 10 miles west of Boston. Including any residence halls, there are 98 buildings.

Student Life: 63% of undergraduates are from out of state, mostly the Northeast. Students are from 39 states, 52 foreign countries, and Canada. 70% are from public schools. 75% are white. The average age of freshmen is 18; all undergraduates, 20. 6% do not continue beyond their first year; 88% remain to graduate.

Housing: 2542 students can be accommodated in college housing, which includes coed dorms, on-campus apartments, and off-campus apartments. In addition, there are special-interest houses. On-campus housing is available on a first-come, first-served basis and is available on a lottery system for upperclassmen. 80% of students live on campus; of those, 90% remain on campus on weekends. Upperclassmen may keep cars.

Activities: There are no fraternities or sororities. There are 246 groups on campus, including art, cheerleading, chess, choir, chorale, chorus, computers, dance, debate, drama, ethnic, film, gay, honors, international, jazz band, literary magazine, musical theater, newspaper, orchestra, pep band, photography, political, professional, radio and TV, religious, social, social service, student government, symphony, and yearbook. Popular campus events include Community Service Day, Intercultural Center Open House, and Midnight Madness.

Sports: There are 10 intercollegiate sports for men and 10 for women, and 12 intramural sports for men and 12 for women. Facilities include a 7000-seat field house, a basketball arena, an indoor swimming pool, 3 indoor tennis courts, 10 squash and racquetball courts, an indoor track, several multipurpose rooms for fencing, aerobics, dance, and wrestling, sauna and steam rooms, Nautilus and free weight rooms, soccer and practice fields, baseball and softball diamonds, a cross-country and fitness trail, and 10 outdoor tennis courts.

Disabled Students: 78% of the campus is accessible. Wheelchair ramps, elevators, special parking, specially equipped rest rooms, special class scheduling, lowered drinking fountains, lowered telephones are available, Libraries, student centers, several other buildings, sports facilities, and the majority of residence halls are fully accessible.

Services: Counseling and information services are available, as is tutoring in most subjects.

Campus Safety and Security: Measures include 24-hour foot and vehicle patrol, self-defense education, security escort services, and shuttle buses. There are informal discussions, pamphlets/posters/films, emergency telephones, and lighted pathways/sidewalks.

Programs of Study: Brandeis confers B.A. and B.S. degrees. Master's and doctoral degrees are also awarded. Bachelor's degrees are awarded in BIOLOGICAL SCIENCE (biochemistry, biology/biological science, biophysics, and neurosciences), COMMUNICATIONS AND THE ARTS (American literature, art history and appreciation, classics, comparative literature, dramatic arts, English, English literature, fine arts, French, German, linguistics, music, performing arts, Russian, and Spanish), COMPUTER AND PHYSICAL SCIENCE (chemistry, computer science, mathematics, physics, and science), SOCIAL SCIENCE (African American studies, African studies, American studies, anthropology, archeology, economics, European studies, history, Islamic studies, Judaic studies, Latin American studies, Middle Eastern studies, Near Eastern studies, philosophy, political science/government, psychology, and sociology). Sciences, history, and English are the strongest academically. Economics, biology, and politics are the largest.

Required: For the bachelor's degree, all students must complete 3 interrelated semester courses from an approved cluster, including selections from at least 2 different schools of the university. They must also complete 1 course from the University Seminar in Humanistic Inquiries and 1 in non-Western or cross-cultural studies, as well as a 1-semester course in each of the university's schools of creative arts, humanities, science, and social science. Writing, quantitative reasoning, and foreign language requirements also must be met. A total of 32 semester courses must be completed to graduate.

Special: Students may pursue interdepartmental programs in 18 different fields. Students may cross-register with Boston, Wellesley, Babson, and Bentley Colleges, and Boston and Tufts Universities. Study abroad is possible in 68 countries. Internships are available in virtually every field, and a work-study program is also provided. Dual and student-designed majors can be arranged. The university also offers credit by exam, nondegree study, and pass/fail options. Opportunities for early acceptance to area medical schools are offered to Brandeis students. There are 4 national honor societies, including Phi Beta Kappa, a freshman honors program, and 51 departmental honors programs.

Faculty/Classroom: 58% of faculty are male; 42%, female. All both teach and do research. Graduate students teach 10% of introductory courses. The average class size in a regular course is 28.

Admissions: 38% of the 2005-2006 applicants were accepted. The SAT scores for the 2005-2006 freshman class were: Verbal--2% below 500, 11% between 500 and 599, 50% between 600 and 700, and 37% above 700; Math--3% below 500, 10% between 500 and 599, 46% between 600 and 700, and 41% above 700. 90% of the current freshmen were in the top fifth of their class; 99% were in the top two fifths. 7 freshmen graduated first in their class.

Requirements: The SAT or ACT is required. In addition, Brandeis requires the SAT Reasoning Test with Writing and 2 SAT Subject tests of different subjects. Sudents may submit the ACT with writing as a substitute for the SAT Reasoning test and SAT Subject tests. Applicants should prepare with 4 years of high school. English, 3 each of foreign language and math, and at least 1 each of science and social studies. An essay is required, and an interview is recommended. AP credits are accepted. Important factors in the admissions decision are advanced placement or honor courses, recommendations by school officials, and extracurricular activities record.

Procedure: Freshmen are admitted fall and spring. Entrance exams should be taken by January of the senior year. There is an early decision plan. Early decision applications should be filed by January 1; regular applications, by January 15 for fall entry and January 15 for spring entry, along with a $55 fee. Notification of early decision is sent December 15; regular decision, April 1. 171 early decision candidates were accepted for the 2005-2006 class. 408 applicants were on the 2005 waiting list; 74 were admitted. Applications are accepted on-line.

Transfer: 52 transfer students enrolled in 2004-2005. Major consideration is given to the quality of college-level work completed, the secondary school record, testing, professors' and deans' evaluations, and the impression made by the candidate. Because there is a 2-year residence requirement, students should apply before entering their junior year. 16 of 32 credits required for the bachelor's degree must be completed at Brandeis.

Visiting: There are regularly scheduled orientations for prospective students, including year-round student-led campus tours and, in the summer, information sessions given by the admissions staff. There are guides for informal visits and visitors may sit in on classes and stay overnight. To schedule a visit, contact the Office of Admissions at *admissions@bradeis.edu.*

Financial Aid: In 2005-2006, 54% of all full-time freshmen and 47% of continuing full-time students received some form of financial aid. 51% of full-time freshmen and 45% of continuing full-time students received need-based aid. The average freshman award was $25,856. Need-based scholarships or need-based grants averaged $19,252; need-based self-help aid (loans and jobs) averaged $4777; and other non-need-based awards and non-need-based scholarships averaged $18,159. 40% of undergraduates work part time. Average annual earnings from campus work are $1588. Brandeis is a member of CSS. The CSS/Profile or FAFSA and copies of student and parent income tax returns for matriculating students. are required. The priority date for freshman financial aid applications for fall entry is January 15. The deadline for filing freshman financial aid applications for fall entry is April 1.

International Students: There are 245 international students enrolled. The school actively recruits these students. They must score satisfactorily on the TOEFL applicants whose native language is English must take the SAT and SAT: Subject tests.

Computers: Wireless access is available. All students may access the system. There are no time limits and no fees.

Graduates: From July 1, 2004 to June 30, 2005, 722 bachelor's degrees were awarded. The most popular majors were economics (18%), biological/life sciences (11%), and psychology (10%). In an average class, 83% graduate in 4 years or less, 87% graduate in 5 years or less, and 88% graduate in 6 years or less. 60 companies recruited on campus in 2004-2005.

Admissions Contact: Gil J. Villanueva, Dean of Admissions. E-mail: *admissions@brandeis.edu* Web: *http://www.brandeis.edu*

BRIDGEWATER STATE COLLEGE   E-3

Bridgewater, MA 02325	**(508) 531-1237; Fax: (508) 531-1746**
Full-time: 2606 men, 3829 women	**Faculty:** 261; IIA, -$
Part-time: 561 men, 855 women	**Ph.D.s:** 51%
Graduate: 436 men, 1362 women	**Student/Faculty:** 25 to 1
Year: semesters, summer session	**Tuition:** $5506 ($11,646)
Application Deadline: February 15	**Room & Board:** $6614
Freshman Class: 5446 applied, 4369 accepted, 1332 enrolled	
SAT Verbal/Math: 510/509*	**ACT:** 21 **COMPETITIVE**

Bridgewater State College, founded in 1840, is a state-supported college offering undergraduate and graduate programs in liberal arts, education, business, aviation science, and preprofessional studies. There are 3 undergraduate schools and 1 graduate school. In addition to regional accreditation, The college has baccalaureate program accreditation with ACS, CAAHEP, CSWE, IACBE, and NCATE. The library contains 290,426 volumes, 3949 microform items, and 10,923 audio/video tapes/CDs/DVDs, and subscribes to 1064 periodicals including electronic. Computerized library services include the card catalog, interlibrary loans, and database searching. Special learning facilities include a learning resource center, art gallery, radio station, an astronomical observatory, a human performance lab and flight simulators, electronic classrooms, a teleconferencing facility with a satellite dish, and a children's developmental clinic. The 235-acre campus is in a suburban area 28 miles south of Boston. Including any residence halls, there are 41 buildings.

Student Life: 97% of undergraduates are from Massachusetts. Others are from 22 states, 13 foreign countries, and Canada. 71% are white. The average age of freshmen is 18; all undergraduates, 21. 25% do not continue beyond their first year; 48% remain to graduate.

Housing: 1745 students can be accommodated in college housing, which includes single-sex and coed dorms and on-campus apartments. In addition, there is break housing for athletes, student teachers, and international students. On-campus housing is guaranteed for all 4 years. 71% of students commute. All students may keep cars.

Activities: 2% of women belong to 2 local and 3 national fraternities and 3 national sororities. There are 74 groups on campus, including band, cheerleading, choir, chorale, computers, dance, drama, ethnic, gay, honors, international, jazz band, literary magazine, marching band, musical ensembles, musical theater, newspaper, pep band, photography, political, professional, religious, social, social service, student government, and yearbook. Popular campus events include Convocation, Multiculture Day, and Christmas and Spring balls.

Sports: There are 10 intercollegiate sports for men and 11 for women, and 6 intramural sports for men and 4 for women. Facilities include 2 gyms, an Olympic-size swimming pool, tennis courts, a football stadium, a 9-lane track, soccer, lacrosse, and field hockey fields, and a baseball and softball complex.

Disabled Students: 95% of the campus is accessible. Wheelchair ramps, elevators, special parking, specially equipped rest rooms, special class scheduling, lowered drinking fountains, lowered telephones, special housing, a handicapped van service, and a college-operated transit system are available.

Services: Counseling and information services are available, as is tutoring in most subjects. There is a reader service for the blind, and remedial math, reading, and writing. There are taped texts, classroom interpreters, scribes and note takers, testing accommodations, and a speech/hearing/language center.

Campus Safety and Security: Measures include 24-hour foot and vehicle patrol, self-defense education, security escort services, and shuttle buses. There are informal discussions, pamphlets/posters/films, emergency telephones, lighted pathways/sidewalks, a college-operated transit system that runs from 7 A.M. to midnight, Monday through Friday, and a safety-escort van that runs from 6 P.M. to 3 A.M.

Programs of Study: The college confers B.A., B.S., and B.S.Ed. degrees. Master's degrees are also awarded. Bachelor's degrees are awarded in BIOLOGICAL SCIENCE (biology/biological science), BUSINESS (accounting and management science), COMMUNICATIONS AND THE ARTS (art, communications, English, music, and Spanish), COMPUTER AND PHYSICAL SCIENCE (chemistry, computer science, earth science, geology, mathematics, and physics), EDUCATION (early childhood, elementary, health, physical, and special), ENGINEERING AND ENVIRONMENTAL DESIGN (aviation administration/management), SOCIAL SCIENCE (anthropology, criminal justice, economics, geography, history, philosophy, political science/government, psychology, social work, and sociology). Management science, aviation science, and education are the strongest academically. Management science, psychology, and education are the largest.

Required: Students are required to complete a minimum of 120 semester hours, with 30 to 36 hours in the major and 52 to 55 hours in general education courses. Students must maintain a minimum GPA of 2.0 and must complete an introduction to information resources course.

Special: Opportunities are provided for cross-registration with other Massachusetts schools, internships in most majors, dual majors in any two subjects, core requirement credit for military service and work experience, nondegree study, and study abroad in England and Canada. A Washington semester offers possible internship experience in political science. There are 11 national honor societies, a freshman honors program, and 14 departmental honors programs.

Faculty/Classroom: 54% of faculty are male; 46%, female. All teach undergraduates. No introductory courses are taught by graduate students. The average class size in an introductory lecture is 32; in a laboratory, 18; and in a regular course, 24.

Admissions: 80% of the 2005-2006 applicants were accepted. The SAT scores for the 2005-2006 freshman class were: Verbal--43% below 500, 45% between 500 and 599, 11% between 600 and 700, and 1% above 700; Math--42% below 500, 45% between 500 and 599, 12% between 600 and 700, and 1% above 700. The ACT scores were 53% below 21, 23% between 21 and 23, and 23% between 24 and 26. 16% of the current freshmen were in the top fifth of their class; 42% were in the top two fifths.

Requirements: The SAT or ACT is required. In addition, graduation from an accredited secondary school is required; a GED will be accepted. Applicants must have successfully completed 16 Carnegie units, including 4 years of English, 3 of math, 3 of science with 2 lab sciences, 2 of a foreign language, 1 each of history and social studies, and 2 in other college preparatory electives. An essay is recommended. A GPA of 2.0 is required. AP and CLEP credits are accepted. Important factors in the admissions decision are advanced placement or honor courses, leadership record, and extracurricular activities record.

Procedure: Freshmen are admitted fall and spring. Entrance exams should be taken no later than January. There is a deferred admissions plan. Applications should be filed by February 15 for fall entry and December 1 for spring entry. The fall 2005 application fee was $25. Notification is sent on a rolling basis. Applications are accepted on-line.

Transfer: 704 transfer students enrolled in 2004-2005. Transfer students must have maintained a minimum GPA of 2.5 12-24 credits or 2.0 more than 24 credits at the previous college, although this alone does not guarantee admission. College transcripts and an essay are required of all transfer students; some students must submit high school transcripts and standardized test scores. 30 of 120 credits required for the bachelor's degree must be completed at the college.

Visiting: There are regularly scheduled orientations for prospective students, including tours Monday through Friday at 11 A.M. and 3 P.M. and information sessions on Fridays at 10 A.M. when college is in session. Visitations are available on a limited basis Saturdays during the fall. Campus tours are available year round. There are guides for informal visits and visitors may sit in on classes. To schedule a visit, contact the Office of Admissions.

Financial Aid: In 2005-2006, 58% of all full-time freshmen and 52% of continuing full-time students received some form of financial aid. At least 53% of full-time freshmen and 48% of continuing full-time students received need-based aid. The average freshman award was $5375. Need-based scholarships or need-based grants averaged $2356; need-based self-help aid (loans and jobs) averaged $3415; and other institutional non-need-based awards and non-need-based scholarships averaged $3069. 22% of undergraduates work part time. Average annual earnings from campus work are $4000. The average financial indebtedness of the 2005 graduate was $15,065. The college is a member of CSS. The FAFSA and the parents' tax returns are required. The priority date for freshman financial aid applications for fall entry is March 1.

International Students: There are 157 international students enrolled. They must score satisfactorily on the written TOEFL and also take the SAT or ACT.

Computers: All students may access the system 7 days a week. There are no time limits and no fees.

Graduates: From July 1, 2004 to June 30, 2005, 1185 bachelor's degrees were awarded. The most popular majors were psychology (15%), business/marketing (14%), and education (12%). In an average class, 1% graduate in 3 years or less, 19% graduate in 4 years or less, 43% graduate in 5 years or less, and 48% graduate in 6 years or less. 83 companies recruited on campus in 2004-2005. Of the 2004 graduating class, 16% were enrolled in graduate school within 6 months of graduation and 92% were employed.

Admissions Contact: Gregg Meyer, Director of Admissions.
E-mail: *admission@bridgew.edu* Web: *www.bridgew.edu*

CAMBRIDGE COLLEGE — D-2
Cambridge, MA 02138
(617) 868-1000
(800) 877-4723; Fax: (617) 868-1124

Full-time: 345 men and women	**Faculty:** n/av
Part-time: 1078 men and women	**Ph.D.s:** n/av
Graduate: 6429 men and women	**Student/Faculty:** n/av
Year: semesters, summer session	**Tuition:** $11,055
Application Deadline: open	**Room & Board:** n/app
Freshman Class: n/av	
SAT or ACT: not required	**SPECIAL**

Cambridge College, founded in 1971, is a private college with 1 undergraduate school and 3 graduate schools. There is an on-line library. Students also have access to Gutman Library at Harvard University. Students have access to museums at Harvard University and in the Boston area. The campus is in an urban area. There are 2 buildings.

Student Life: 56% of undergraduates are from Massachusetts. 36% are white; 32% African American; 11% Hispanic.

Housing: There are no residence halls. All of students commute. Alcohol is not permitted.

Activities: There are no fraternities or sororities.

Disabled Students: All of the campus is accessible. Elevators, specially equipped rest rooms, and special class scheduling are available.

Services: There is remedial math and writing.

Programs of Study: Cambridge College confers B.A. and B.S. degrees. Master's degrees are also awarded. Bachelor's degrees are awarded in BUSINESS (management science), SOCIAL SCIENCE (human services, interdisciplinary studies, and psychology).

Required: Students must complete 120 credit hours with 36 in the major to graduate. They also must complete 9 hours each in arts and humanities, natural and physical sciences, and social sciences, and complete a final capstone.

Faculty/Classroom: 42% of faculty are male; 58%, female. All teach undergraduates. No introductory courses are taught by graduate students.

Requirements: CLEP credit is accepted.

Procedure: Freshmen are admitted to all sessions. Application deadlines are open. The fall 2005 application fee was $30.

Transfer: 30 of 120 credits required for the bachelor's degree must be completed at Cambridge College.

Financial Aid: In 2005-2006, 77% of all full-time freshmen received some form of financial aid. The FAFSA is required.

International Students: The school actively recruits these students. A satisfactory score on the TOEFL is required.

Computers: Wireless access is available. Students are given e-mail accounts. They can use computers and access the Internet at the college's computer labs. All students may access the system.

Admissions Contact: Dr. Ezat Parnia, Executive Vice President. A video is available. Web: *www.cambridgecollege.edu*

CLARK UNIVERSITY — C-2
Worcester, MA 01610-1477
(508) 793-7431
(800) 462-5275; Fax: (508) 793-8821

Full-time: 835 men, 1262 women	**Faculty:** 167; IIA, +$
Part-time: 72 men, 86 women	**Ph.D.s:** 98%
Graduate: 393 men, 470 women	**Student/Faculty:** 13 to 1
Year: semesters, summer session	**Tuition:** $29,565
Application Deadline: January 15	**Room & Board:** $5600
Freshman Class: 4463 applied, 2748 accepted, 560 enrolled	
SAT Verbal/Math: 610/590*	**ACT:** 26 **VERY COMPETITIVE+**

Clark University, founded in 1887, is an independent liberal arts and research institution. There are 2 undergraduate and 3 graduate schools. In addition to regional accreditation, Clark has baccalaureate program accreditation with AACSB and NASDTEC. The 6 libraries contain 605,421 volumes, 60,043 microform items, and 1185 audio/video tapes/CDs/DVDs, and subscribe to 1303 periodicals including electronic. Computerized library services include the card catalog, interlibrary loans, database searching, Internet access, and laptop Internet portals. Special learning facilities include a learning resource center, art gallery, radio station, a TV studio, campus cable network, center for music with 2 studios for electronic music, 2 theaters, and magnetic resonance imaging facility. The 50-acre campus is in an urban area 50 miles west of Boston. Including any residence halls, there are 56 buildings.

Student Life: 64% of undergraduates are from out of state, mostly the Northeast. Others are from 44 states, 58 foreign countries, and Canada. 72% are from public schools. 65% are white. 38% are claim no religious affiliation; 22% Protestant; 18% Catholic; 11% Jewish. The average age of freshmen is 19; all undergraduates, 20. 14% do not continue beyond their first year; 70% remain to graduate.

Housing: 1621 students can be accommodated in college housing, which includes single-sex and coed dorms and on-campus apartments. In addition, there are special-interest houses nonsmoking, quiet, substance awareness, and year-round houses. On-campus housing is guaranteed for the freshman year only and is available on a lottery system for upperclassmen. 77% of students live on campus. All students may keep cars.

Activities: There are no fraternities or sororities. There are approximately 80 groups on campus, including art, band, chess, choir, chorale, chorus, dance, debate, drama, ethnic, film, gay, honors, international, jazz band, literary magazine, musical theater, newspaper, orchestra, pep band, photography, political, professional, radio and TV, religious, social, social service, student government, symphony, and yearbook. Popular campus events include Gryphon & Pleiades Honor Society Variety Show, International Gala, and Speaker's Forum.

Sports: There are 8 intercollegiate sports for men and 9 for women, and 14 intramural sports for men and 14 for women. Facilities include an athletic center with a 2000-seat gym, a pool, a fitness center, tennis courts, outdoor fields, and baseball and softball diamonds.

Disabled Students: 95% of the campus is accessible. Wheelchair ramps, elevators, special parking, specially equipped rest rooms, special class scheduling, lowered drinking fountains, lowered telephones, and special housing are available.

Services: Counseling and information services are available, as is tutoring in some subjects, including math, biology, chemistry, economics, and psychology. For learning-disabled students, the university provides early orientation, alternative test-taking accommodations, and a learning specialist.

Campus Safety and Security: Measures include 24-hour foot and vehicle patrol, self-defense education, security escort services, and shuttle buses. There are informal discussions, pamphlets/posters/films, emergency telephones, and lighted pathways/sidewalks.

Programs of Study: Clark confers the B.A. degree. Master's and doctoral degrees are also awarded. Bachelor's degrees are awarded in BIOLOGICAL SCIENCE (biochemistry and biology/biological science), BUSINESS (business administration and management), COMMUNICATIONS AND THE ARTS (art history and appreciation, communications, comparative literature, dramatic arts, English, film arts, fine arts, French, languages, music, romance languages and literature, Spanish, studio art, and visual and performing arts), COMPUTER AND PHYSICAL SCIENCE (chemistry, computer science, mathematics, and physics), ENGINEERING AND ENVIRONMENTAL DESIGN (environmental science), HEALTH PROFESSIONS (predentistry and premedicine), SOCIAL SCIENCE (classical/ancient civilization, economics, geography, history, international relations, international studies, philosophy, political science/government, prelaw, psychology, and sociology). Psychology, biology, and government and international relations are the strongest academically. English, psychology, and government/international relations are the largest.

Required: Each student is required to complete 2 critical thinking courses in 2 categories of verbal expression and formal analysis, and 6 perspectives courses, representing the categories of aesthetics, comparative, historical, language and culture, science, and values. A student must receive passing grades in a minimum of 32 full courses, with a C- or better in at least 24 of these courses, and maintain a minimum 2.0 GPA to graduate.

Special: For-credit internships are available in all disciplines with private corporations and small businesses, medical centers, and government agencies. There is cross-registration with members of the Worcester Consortium, including Holy Cross and Worcester Polytechnic Institute. Clark also offers study abroad in 11 countries, a Washington semester with American University, work-study programs, accelerated degree programs, dual and student-designed majors, pass/no record options, and a 3-2 engineering degree with Columbia University, Washington University, and Worcester Polytechnic Institute. A gerontology certificate is offered with the Worcester Consortium for Higher Education. There are 8 national honor societies, including Phi Beta Kappa, and 17 departmental honors programs.

Faculty/Classroom: 62% of faculty are male; 38%, female. 100% both teach and do research. No introductory courses are taught by graduate students. The average class size in an introductory lecture is 18; in a laboratory, 15; and in a regular course, 15.

Admissions: 62% of the 2005-2006 applicants were accepted. The SAT scores for the 2005-2006 freshman class were: Verbal--10% below 500, 36% between 500 and 599, 44% between 600 and 700, and 10% above 700; Math--12% below 500, 39% between 500 and 599, 40% between 600 and 700, and 9% above 700. The ACT scores were 9% below 21, 15% between 21 and 23, 35% between 24 and 26, 21% between 27 and 28, and 20% above 28. 59% of the current freshmen were in the top fifth of their class; 91% were in the top two fifths. 7 freshmen graduated first in their class.

Requirements: The SAT or ACT is required. In addition, the SAT: Writing test is also recommended. Applicants must graduate from an accredited secondary school or have a GED. 16 Carnegie units are required, including 4 years of English, 3 each of math and science, and 2

each of foreign language and social studies, including history. An interview is recommended. AP credits are accepted. Important factors in the admissions decision are advanced placement or honor courses, recommendations by alumni, and recommendations by school officials.

Procedure: Freshmen are admitted fall and spring. Entrance exams should be taken by November of the senior year. There are early decision and deferred admissions plans. Early decision applications should be filed by November 15; regular applications, by January 15 for fall entry and November 15 for spring entry, along with a $50 fee. Notification of early decision is sent January 1; regular decision, April 1. 85 early decision candidates were accepted for the 2005-2006 class. 60 applicants were on the 2005 waiting list; 8 were admitted. Applications are accepted on-line.

Transfer: 39 transfer students enrolled in 2004-2005. Applicants should have a minimum GPA of about 2.8. At least one full semester of college course work is required. High school and college transcripts, recent SAT or ACT test scores, a staement of good standing from previous institutions attended, and a transfer statement are required. Grades of C or better in comparable course work transfer for credit. 16 of 32 course units required for the bachelor's degree must be completed at Clark.

Visiting: There are regularly scheduled orientations for prospective students, consisting of open houses during fall and spring semesters, which include tours, information sessions, and talks with faculty, administration, and coaches. There are guides for informal visits and visitors may sit in on classes. To schedule a visit, contact the Admissions Office.

Financial Aid: In 2005-2006, 82% of all full-time freshmen and 79% of continuing full-time students received some form of financial aid. 56% of all full-time students received need-based aid. The average freshman award was $18,305. 70% of undergraduates work part time. Average annual earnings from campus work are $1700. The average financial indebtedness of the 2005 graduate was $18,990. The CSS/Profile or FAFSA is required. The deadline for filing freshman financial aid applications for fall entry is February 1.

International Students: There are 157 international students enrolled. The school actively recruits these students. Satisfactory scores are required on the written TOEFL and the SAT or the ACT.

Computers: Wireless access is available. All students may access the system 7 days per week. There are no time limits and no fees. It is strongly recommended that all students have a personal computer.

Graduates: From July 1, 2004 to June 30, 2005, 439 bachelor's degrees were awarded. The most popular majors were psychology (19%), government and international relations (12%), and biology and biochemistry (12%). In an average class, 1% graduate in 3 years, 63% graduate in 4 years, 69% graduate in 5 years, and 70% graduate in 6 years. 40 companies recruited on campus in 2004-2005. Of the 2004 graduating class, 33% were enrolled in graduate school within 6 months of graduation.

Admissions Contact: Harold M. Wingood, Dean of Admissions. E-mail: *admissions@clarku.edu*

COLLEGE OF OUR LADY OF THE ELMS   B-3
Chicopee, MA 01013

(413) 592-3189
(800) 255-ELMS; Fax: (413) 594-2781

Full-time: 65 men, 360 women	**Faculty:** 38
Part-time: 25 men, 190 women	**Ph.D.s:** 76%
Graduate: 15 men, 80 women	**Student/Faculty:** 11 to 1
Year: semesters	**Tuition:** $15,000
Application Deadline: open	**Room & Board:** $6000
Freshman Class: n/av	
SAT or ACT: required	**COMPETITIVE**

College of Our Lady of the Elms, founded in 1928, is a Roman Catholic institution offering undergraduate degrees in liberal arts and sciences and graduate degrees in liberal arts, education, and theology. Figures in the above capsule and profile are approximate. In addition to regional accreditation, Elms College has baccalaureate program accreditation with CSWE and NLN. The library contains 103,136 volumes, 77,784 microform items, and 2208 audio/video tapes/CDs/DVDs, and subscribes to 695 periodicals including electronic. Computerized library services include the card catalog, interlibrary loans, and database searching. Special learning facilities include a learning resource center, art gallery, radio station, TV station, and rare books collection. The 32-acre campus is in a suburban area 2 miles north of Springfield and 90 miles west of Boston. Including any residence halls, there are 11 buildings.

Student Life: 85% of undergraduates are from Massachusetts. Others are from 9 states and 10 foreign countries. 74% are from public schools. 80% are white. 60% are Catholic; 9% Protestant. The average age of freshmen is 20; all undergraduates, 22. 11% do not continue beyond their first year.

Housing: 315 students can be accommodated in college housing, which includes single-sex and coed dormitories. On-campus housing is guaranteed for all 4 years. 60% of students commute. All students may keep cars.

Activities: There are no fraternities or sororities. There are 41 groups on campus, including art, choir, chorale, chorus, computers, dance, drama, ethnic, honors, international, literary magazine, musical theater, newspaper, photography, professional, radio and TV, religious, social, social service, student government, and yearbook. Popular campus events include Soph Show, Cap and Gown, and Ring Ceremony.

Sports: There are 6 intercollegiate sports for men and 9 for women, and 6 intramural sports for men and 6 for women. Facilities include a fitness and athletic center housing a suspended indoor track, a 25-meter, 6-lane pool, a weight and aerobics room, a multipurpose arena, a basketball court, and a volleyball court.

Disabled Students: 40% of the campus is accessible. Wheelchair ramps, elevators, special parking, specially equipped rest rooms, special class scheduling, lowered drinking fountains, lowered telephones, and automated doors are available.

Services: Counseling and information services are available, as is tutoring in every subject. There is a reader service for the blind, and remedial math, reading, and writing. There also is an academic advising and resource center, a counseling service office, career services, wellness services, student activities, a campus ministry office, and resident advisers.

Campus Safety and Security: Measures include 24-hour foot and vehicle patrol, self-defense education, security escort services, and informal discussions. There are pamphlets/posters/films, emergency telephones and, lighted pathways/sidewalks. A safety and security manual is published each year, and there is a safety and security committee of administrators, students, faculty, and staff.

Programs of Study: Elms College confers B.A. and B.S. degrees. Associate and master's degrees are also awarded. Bachelor's degrees are awarded in BIOLOGICAL SCIENCE (biology/biological science), BUSINESS (accounting, business administration and management, international business management, and marketing/retailing/merchandising), COMMUNICATIONS AND THE ARTS (English, fine arts, and Spanish), COMPUTER AND PHYSICAL SCIENCE (chemistry, computer science, mathematics, and natural sciences), EDUCATION (bilingual/bicultural, early childhood, elementary, foreign languages, middle school, science, secondary, special, and teaching English as a second/foreign language (TESOL/TEFOL), HEALTH PROFESSIONS (health science, medical laboratory technology, nursing, predentistry, premedicine, and speech pathology/audiology), SOCIAL SCIENCE (American studies, international studies, paralegal studies, prelaw, psychology, religion, social work, and sociology). Nursing, education, and biology are the strongest academically. Education, business, and nursing are the largest.

Required: To graduate; all students must complete 120 hours with a 2.0 GPA. 54 hours are required in courses in rhetoric, computer science, history, religion, phys ed, philosophy, sociology, fine arts, humanities, foreign language, math, senior seminar, and service learning experience.

Special: Students may cross-register at any of the Cooperating Colleges of Greater Springfield or Consortium of Sisters of St. Joseph Colleges. Internships are available with local hospitals, businesses, and schools. Study abroad, student-designed interdepartmental majors, accelerated degree programs, work-study, dual majors, nondegree study, and pass/fail options are offered. There are 5 national honor societies, including Phi Beta Kappa, and a freshman honors program.

Faculty/Classroom: 35% of faculty are male; 65%, female. 90% teach undergraduates, 93% do research, and 92% do both. No introductory courses are taught by graduate students. The average class size in an introductory lecture is 13; in a laboratory, 8; and in a regular course, 11.

Requirements: The SAT or ACT is required. The college prefers SAT with a satisfactory score. Applicants should be graduates of accredited high schools or have earned the GED. Secondary preparation should include 4 units of English, 3 each of math and science, and 2 each of foreign language, history, and social studies. A personal essay is required; an interview is recommended. Elms College requires applicants to be in the upper 50% of their class. A GPA of 2.5 is required. AP and CLEP credits are accepted. Important factors in the admissions decision are advanced placement or honor courses, recommendations by school officials, and extracurricular activities record.

Procedure: Freshmen are admitted fall and spring. Entrance exams should be taken no later than November of the senior year. There are early admissions, deferred admissions and rolling admissions plans. Application deadlines are open. Applications are accepted on-line. The fal 2005 application fee wae $30.

Transfer: Applicants must have a minimum 2.0 GPA. 45 of 120 credits required for the bachelor's degree must be completed at Elms College.

Visiting: There are regularly scheduled orientations for prospective students, including tours and interviews scheduled weekdays between 9 A.M. and 4 P.M. as well as 2 open houses in the fall and 1 in the spring. There are guides for informal visits and visitors may sit in on classes and stay overnight. To schedule a visit, contact the Admission Office.

Financial Aid: Elms College is a member of CSS. The FAFSA and the college's own financial statement are required. Check with the school for current application deadlines.

International Students: The school actively recruits these students. The college requires either the TOEFL, with a satisfactory score, or the SAT.

Computers: All students may access the system 8 A.M. to 10 P.M. Monday through Friday, 12 noon to 9 P.M. Saturday and Sunday, and residence hall labs are open 24 hours. There are no time limits and no fees.

Admissions Contact: Joseph P. Wagner, Director of Admission.
E-mail: *admissions@elms.edu* Web: *www.elms.edu*

COLLEGE OF THE HOLY CROSS   C-2
Worcester, MA 01610   (508) 793-2443
                                      (800) 442-2421; Fax: (508) 793-3888

Full-time: 1267 men, 1521 women	**Faculty:** 240; IIB, +$
Part-time: 4 men, 24 women	**Ph.Ds:** 92%
Graduate: none	**Student/Faculty:** 12 to 1
Year: semesters	**Tuition:** $31,444
Application Deadline: January 15	**Room & Board:** $9220
Freshman Class: 4744 applied, 2270 accepted, 723 enrolled	
SAT Verbal/Math: 632/634*	**MOST COMPETITIVE**

College of the Holy Cross, founded in 1843, is a private liberal arts college affiliated with the Jesuit order of the Roman Catholic Church. In addition to regional accreditation, Holy Cross has baccalaureate program accreditation with NAST. The 4 libraries contain 591,658 volumes, 16,081 microform items, and 27,397 audio/video tapes/CDs/DVDs, and subscribe to 1649 periodicals including electronic. Computerized library services include the card catalog, interlibrary loans, database searching, Internet access, and laptop Internet portals. Special learning facilities include an art gallery, radio station, greenhouses, facilities for aquatic research, and a multimedia resource center. The 174-acre campus is in a suburban area 45 miles west of Boston. Including any residence halls, there are 33 buildings.

Student Life: 63% of undergraduates are from out of state, mostly the Northeast. Students are from 45 states, 15 foreign countries, and Canada. 51% are from public schools. 75% are white. 77% are Catholic; 13% Protestant; 7% claim no religious affiliation. The average age of freshmen is 18; all undergraduates, 20. 3% do not continue beyond their first year; 97% remain to graduate.

Housing: 2353 students can be accommodated in college housing, which includes coed dormitories and on-campus apartments. In addition, there are special-interest houses, substance-free housing, and first-year living and learning housing. On-campus housing is guaranteed for all 4 years. 88% of students live on campus; of those, 90% remain on campus on weekends. Upperclassmen may keep cars.

Activities: There are no fraternities or sororities. There are 102 groups on campus, including art, band, cheerleading, choir, chorale, chorus, computers, dance, debate, drama, drill team, ethnic, film, gay, honors, international, jazz band, literary magazine, marching band, musical theater, newspaper, orchestra, pep band, photography, political, professional, radio, religious, social, social service, student government, and yearbook. Popular campus events include Spring Weekend, Family Weekend, and Senior Week.

Sports: There are 13 intercollegiate sports for men and 14 for women, and 6 intramural sports for men and 6 for women. Facilities include an astroturf playing field, baseball, football fields, and soccer stadiums, indoor and outdoor running tracks, a swimming pool, an ice rink, indoor crew tanks, a basketball arena, weight and exercise rooms, a wellness center and tennis, squash, and racquetball courts.

Disabled Students: 85% of the campus is accessible. Wheelchair ramps, elevators, special parking, specially equipped rest rooms, special class scheduling, lowered drinking fountains, lowered telephones, special housing, special diets, tutors, readers, interpreters, note takers, academic accommodations, and library and laboratory assistance are available.

Services: Counseling and information services are available, as is tutoring in some subjects, including calculus, chemistry, physics, economics, classics, Spanish writing, and writing.

Campus Safety and Security: Measures include 24-hour foot and vehicle patrol, self-defense education, security escort services, and shuttle buses. There are informal discussions, pamphlets/posters/films, emergency telephones, lighted pathways/sidewalks, and a card access control system.

Programs of Study: Holy Cross confers the B.A. degree. Bachelor's degrees are awarded in AGRICULTURE (environmental studies), BIOLOGICAL SCIENCE (biology/biological science), COMMUNICATIONS AND THE ARTS (art history and appreciation, classics, dramatic arts, English, French, German, Italian, literature, music, Russian, Spanish, and studio art), COMPUTER AND PHYSICAL SCIENCE (chemistry, computer science, mathematics, and physics), SOCIAL SCIENCE (anthropology, Asian/Oriental studies, economics, German area studies, history, medieval studies, Middle Eastern studies, philosophy, political science/government, psychology, religion, Russian and Slavic studies, and sociology). Economics, political science, and history are the largest.

Required: Distribution requirements include social science, natural and mathematical science, cross-cultural studies, religious and philosophical studies, historical studies and the arts, and literature. In addition, students must demonstrate competence in a classical or modern language or American sign language. A total of 32 courses worth at least 1 unit each is required for graduation, with 10 to 14 courses in the major. The minimum GPA for graduation is 2.0.

Special: Local academic internships are available through the Center for Interdisciplinary and Special Studies in health and education, law and business, journalism, social service, state and local government, scientific research, and cultural affairs. Student-designed majors, dual majors including economics-accounting, a Washington semester, and study abroad are possible. There is a 3-2 engineering program with Columbia University or Dartmouth College, an honors program, and a premedicine and predentistry program. Students may cross-register with other universities in the Colleges of Worcester Consortium. Nondegree study is possible. There are 18 national honor societies, including Phi Beta Kappa, and 4 departmental honors programs.

Faculty/Classroom: 54% of faculty are male; 46%, female. All both teach and do research. The average class size in an introductory lecture is 23; in a laboratory, 16; and in a regular course, 20.

Admissions: 48% of the 2005-2006 applicants were accepted. The SAT scores for the 2005-2006 freshman class were: Verbal--4% below 500, 23% between 500 and 599, 54% between 600 and 700, and 19% above 700; Math--3% below 500, 20% between 500 and 599, 57% between 600 and 700, and 20% above 700. 90% of the current freshmen were in the top fifth of their class; 98% were in the top two fifths. There were 3 National Merit finalists. 15 freshmen graduated first in their class.

Requirements: Applicants should be graduates of an accredited secondary school or hold the GED. Recommended preparatory courses include English, foreign language, history, math, and science. An essay is required. Students have the option to submit standardized test scores if they believe the results represent a fuller picture of their achievements and potential; students who opt not to submit scores will not be at any disadvantage in admissions decisions. An interview is recommended. AP credits are accepted. Important factors in the admissions decision are advanced placement or honor courses, recommendations by school officials, and evidence of special talent.

Procedure: Freshmen are admitted in the fall. Entrance exams should be taken by December of the senior year. There are early decision, early admissions, and deferred admissions plans. Early decision applications should be filed by December 15; regular applications, by January 15 for fall entry. Notification of early decision is sent January 1; regular decision, April 1. The fall 2005 application fee was $50. 205 early decision candidates were accepted for the 2005-2006 class. 274 applicants were on the 2005 waiting list; 29 were admitted. Applications are accepted on-line.

Transfer: 16 transfer students enrolled in 2004-2005. Transfer students must have a minimum GPA of 3.2. The SAT is not required but applicants must provide transcripts and 2 teacher recommendations. Personal interviews are highly recommended. 64 (16 courses) of 128 credits (32 courses) required for the bachelor's degree must be completed at Holy Cross.

Visiting: There are regularly scheduled orientations for prospective students, including fall open houses in October and November consisting of informational panels on academics, admissions, financial aid, and student life, as well as tours of the facilities. There are guides for informal visits and visitors may sit in on classes and stay overnight. To schedule a visit, contact the Admissions Office at *admissions@holycross.edu*.

Financial Aid: In 2005-2006, 63% of all full-time freshmen and 58% of continuing full-time students received some form of financial aid. 46% of full-time freshmen and 41% of continuing full-time students received need-based aid. The average freshman award was $21,188. Need-based scholarships or need-based grants averaged $16,126 ($40,180 maximum); need-based self-help aid (loans and jobs) averaged $5187 ($7025 maximum); non-need-based athletic scholarships averaged $40,664 (maximum); and other non-need-based awards and non-need-based scholarships averaged $20,062 ($30,960 maximum). 35% of undergraduates work part time. Average annual earnings from campus work are $1700. The average financial indebtedness of the 2005 graduate was $19,380. Holy Cross is a member of CSS. The CSS/Profile or FAFSA and student and parent federal tax returns are required. The deadline for filing freshman financial aid applications for fall entry is February 1.

International Students: There are 34 international students enrolled. The school actively recruits these students. They must score satisfactorily on the TOEFL.

Computers: Wireless access is available. Students have full access to the college's computer network system, including broadband Internet access in all residential rooms and common areas as well as 480 college-provided PCs and Macs located throughout the campus. All students may access the system 24 hours per day. There are no time limits and no fees.

Graduates: From July 1, 2004 to June 30, 2005, 646 bachelor's degrees were awarded. The most popular majors were economics (16%), politcal science (13%), and history (11%). In an average class, 88% graduate in 4 years or less, 91% graduate in 5 years or less, and 91% graduate in 6 years or less. 54 companies recruited on campus in 2004-2005. Of the 2004 graduating class, 25% were enrolled in graduate school within 6 months of graduation and 64% were employed.

Admissions Contact: Admissions Office. A video is available.
E-mail: *admissions@holycross.edu* Web: *www.holycross.edu*

CURRY COLLEGE
Milton, MA 02186-9984

E-2

(617) 333-2210
(800) 669-0686; Fax: (617) 333-2114

Full-time: 615 men, 610 women	**Faculty:** 80; IIB, av$
Part-time: 500 men, 590 women	**Ph.D.s:** 53%
Graduate: 65 men, 60 women	**Student/Faculty:** 15 to 1
Year: semesters, summer session	**Tuition:** $18,900
Application Deadline: see profile	**Room & Board:** $7220
Freshman Class: n/av	
SAT or ACT: required	**LESS COMPETITIVE**

Curry College, founded in 1879, is a private liberal arts institution. Figures in above capsule and in this profile are approximate. In addition to regional accreditation, Curry has baccalaureate program accreditation with NLN. The library contains 90,000 volumes, 14,000 microform items, and 190 audio/video tapes/CDs/DVDs, and subscribes to 625 periodicals including electronic. Computerized library services include the card catalog, interlibrary loans, and database searching. Special learning facilities include a learning resource center and radio station. The 131-acre campus is in a suburban area 7 miles southwest of Boston. Including any residence halls, there are 36 buildings.

Student Life: 79% of undergraduates are from Massachusetts. Others are from 31 states, 12 foreign countries, and Canada. 68% are from public schools. 71% are white. The average age of freshmen is 18; all undergraduates, 20. 30% do not continue beyond their first year; 51% remain to graduate.

Housing: 826 students can be accommodated in college housing, which includes single-sex and coed dormitories. In addition, there are honors houses special-interest houses and a 9-month house for international students. On-campus housing is available on a first-come, first-served basis and is available on a lottery system for upperclassmen. 66% of students live on campus; of those, 80% remain on campus on weekends. All students may keep cars.

Activities: There are no fraternities or sororities. There are 20 groups on campus, including cheerleading, chorale, dance, drama, ethnic, film, honors, international, literary magazine, musical theater, newspaper, photography, political, professional, radio and TV, religious, social, social service, student government, and yearbook. Popular campus events include formal dances, a concert series, and Career Day.

Sports: There are 7 intercollegiate sports for men and 6 for women, and 5 intramural sports for men and 5 for women. Facilities include a 500-seat gym, a dance studio, 13 outdoor tennis courts, an outdoor pool, 5 athletic fields, a 1000-seat stadium, a 500-seat auditorium, and a 5000-meter cross-country trail.

Disabled Students: 60% of the campus is accessible. Wheelchair ramps, elevators, special parking, specially equipped rest rooms, and special class scheduling are available.

Services: Counseling and information services are available, as is tutoring in most subjects. There is a reader service for the blind, and remedial math, reading, and writing. General development courses in writing, reading, and math are designed to develop the student's basic skills. LD tutoring, an Essential Skills Center, and the Program for Advancement of Learning are also available.

Campus Safety and Security: Measures include 24-hour foot and vehicle patrol, security escort services, shuttle buses, and informal discussions. There are pamphlets/posters/films, emergency telephones, and lighted pathways/sidewalks. A campus safety office offers security services.

Programs of Study: Curry confers B.A. and B.S.N. degrees. Master's degrees are also awarded. Bachelor's degrees are awarded in BIOLOGICAL SCIENCE (biology/biological science), BUSINESS (business administration and management), COMMUNICATIONS AND THE ARTS (communications, English, and visual and performing arts), COMPUTER AND PHYSICAL SCIENCE (chemistry and physics), EDUCATION (early childhood, elementary, health, and special), ENGINEERING AND ENVIRONMENTAL DESIGN (environmental science), HEALTH PROFESSIONS (nursing), SOCIAL SCIENCE (criminal justice, history, philosophy, psychology, and sociology). Nursing is the strongest academically. Business, communications, and criminal justice are the largest.

Required: Successful completion of the liberal arts core curriculum and a total of 120 semester hours (121 for nursing), with at least 30 in the major, and a minimum 2.0 GPA, are required for graduation. Nursing students must pass a comprehensive exam.

Special: Curry offers internships in all majors, an accelerated degree with approval of the dean, study abroad, work-study programs, dual and student-designed majors, credit by exam and for life, work, and military experience, nondegree study, and pass/fail options. There are 2 national honor societies.

Faculty/Classroom: 43% of faculty are male; 57%, female. All teach undergraduates. No introductory courses are taught by graduate students. The average class size in an introductory lecture is 20; in a laboratory, 12; and in a regular course, 20.

Requirements: The SAT or ACT is required. Applicants must be graduates of an accredited secondary school or have a GED. 16 credits are required, including 4 years of English, 2 each of foreign language, history, science, and social studies, and 3 of math. An essay is required, and an interview recommended. A portfolio where appropriate is also advised. A GPA of 2.0 is required. AP and CLEP credits are accepted. Important factors in the admissions decision are recommendations by school officials, extracurricular activities record, and evidence of special talent.

Procedure: Freshmen are admitted fall and spring. Entrance exams should be taken in the junior year or in November of the senior year. There are early decision, early admissions, deferred admissions and rolling admissions plans. Check with the school for current application deadlines. Notification of early decision is sent rolling ; regular decision, on a rolling basis. The application fee is $40.

Transfer: Transfer applicants must be in good academic standing at their previous college with a minimum GPA of 2.0. An interview is recommended. 30 of 120 credits required for the bachelor's degree must be completed at Curry.

Visiting: There are regularly scheduled orientations for prospective students, consisting of interviews with an admissions counselor and tours with a student. There are guides for informal visits and visitors may sit in on classes and stay overnight. To schedule a visit, contact the Admissions Office.

Financial Aid: Curry is a member of CSS. The FAFSA and the college's own financial statement are required. Check with the school for current applicatin deadlines.

International Students: The school actively recruits these students. They must score satisfactorily on the written TOEFL and also take the SAT or the ACT.

Computers: All students may access the system. There are no time limits and no fees. It is strongly recommended that all students have a personal computer.

Admissions Contact: Michael Poll, Dean of Admissions and Financial Aid. E-mail: *curryadm@curry.edu* Web: *www.curry.edu*

EASTERN NAZARENE COLLEGE E-2

Quincy, MA 02170 (617) 745-3711
(800) 883-6288; Fax: (617) 745-3980

Full-time: 245 men, 355 women	**Faculty:** 52
Part-time: 15 men, 25 women	**Ph.D.s:** 57%
Graduate: 30 men, 140 women	**Student/Faculty:** 13 to 1
Year: 4-1-4, summer session	**Tuition:** $14,500
Application Deadline: see profile	**Room & Board:** $5000
Freshman Class: n/av	
SAT: required	**ACT:** required
	LESS COMPETITIVE

Eastern Nazarene College, founded in 1918, is a private college affiliated with the Church of the Nazarene. It offers a program in the liberal arts. Figures in above capsule and in this profile are approximate. In addition to regional accreditation, ENC has baccalaureate program accreditation with CSWE. The library contains 115,000 volumes, and subscribes to 600 periodicals including electronic. Computerized library services include interlibrary loans and database searching. Special learning facilities include a learning resource center and radio station. The 15-acre campus is in a suburban area 6 miles south of Boston. Including any residence halls, there are 16 buildings.

Student Life: 55% of undergraduates are from out of state, mostly the Northeast. Students are from 27 states, 24 foreign countries, and Canada. 88% are white. 88% are Protestant; 6% Catholic; 6% claim no religious affiliation. The average age of freshmen is 18; all undergraduates, 20. 25% do not continue beyond their first year; 60% remain to graduate.

Housing: 638 students can be accommodated in college housing, which includes single-sex dormitories and married-student housing. On-campus housing is guaranteed for all 4 years. 75% of students live on campus; of those, 75% remain on campus on weekends. Alcohol is not permitted. All students may keep cars.

Activities: There are no fraternities or sororities. There are 34 groups on campus, including band, cheerleading, choir, chorale, chorus, drama, jazz band, literary magazine, musical theater, newspaper, pep band, photography, professional, radio and TV, religious, social service, student government, and yearbook. Popular campus events include Freshmen Breakout, All-School Outing, and Junior/Senior Banquet.

Sports: There are 5 intercollegiate sports for men and 5 for women, and 4 intramural sports for men and 5 for women. Facilities include a phys ed center equipped with a basketball area, batting cage, and playing courts.

Disabled Students: 65% of the campus is accessible. Wheelchair ramps, elevators, special parking, and specially equipped rest rooms are available.

Services: Counseling and information services are available, as is tutoring in most subjects. There is remedial math, reading, and writing.

Campus Safety and Security: Measures include 24-hour foot and vehicle patrol, self-defense education, security escort services, and informal discussions. There are pamphlets/posters/films, emergency telephones, and lighted pathways/sidewalks.

Programs of Study: ENC confers B.A. and B.S. degrees. Associate and master's degrees are also awarded. Bachelor's degrees are awarded in BIOLOGICAL SCIENCE (biology/biological science and marine biology), BUSINESS (accounting and business administration and management), COMMUNICATIONS AND THE ARTS (advertising, broadcasting, communications, dramatic arts, English, French, journalism, literature, music, music performance, Spanish, and speech/debate/rhetoric), COMPUTER AND PHYSICAL SCIENCE (chemistry, computer science, mathematics, physics, and science), EDUCATION (athletic training, education, elementary, music, science, and social science), ENGINEERING AND ENVIRONMENTAL DESIGN (computer engineering, engineering physics, and environmental science), HEALTH PROFESSIONS (sports medicine), SOCIAL SCIENCE (child psychology/development, Christian studies, clinical psychology, history, ministries, physical fitness/movement, psychology, religion, religious music, social studies, social work, and sociology). Chemistry, physics, and history are the strongest academically. Education, business, and psychology are the largest.

Required: All students must complete the core curriculum of writing and rhetoric, biblical history, social science, science or math, symbolic systems and intercultural awareness, philosophy and religion, and phy ed. A total of 130 credits is required for the B.A. or B.S., with 32 to 40 in the major. Minimum GPA for graduation is 2.0.

Special: Internships are available in the metropolitan Boston area. Study abroad in Costa Rica, a Washington semester, a 3-2 engineering degree with Boston University, and a cooperative program with the Massachusetts College of Pharmacy are offered. Work-study programs, dual majors, credit for life/military/work experience, and pass/fail options are available. An off-campus degree-completion program for adults in business administration is offered. There is 1 national honor society.

Faculty/Classroom: 72% of faculty are male; 28%, female. 83% teach undergraduates. No introductory courses are taught by graduate students. The average class size in an introductory lecture is 75; in a laboratory, 20; and in a regular course, 22.

Requirements: The SAT or ACT is required. In addition, applicants must be graduates of an accredited secondary school or have a GED. They must have a minimum of 16 academic credits, including 4 of English, 2 to 4 each of math and foreign language, 1 to 4 of science, and 1 to 2 each of history and social studies. Music students must audition. An essay and interview are recommended. A GPA of 2.3 is required. AP and CLEP credits are accepted. Important factors in the admissions decision are advanced placement or honor courses, recommendations by school officials, and leadership record.

Procedure: Freshmen are admitted to all sessions. Entrance exams should be taken in the spring of the junior year. There are deferred admissions and rolling admissions plans. Check with the school for current application deadlines. Notification is sent on a rolling basis. The fall 2005 application fee was $25.

Transfer: A minimum 2.0 GPA is required. An interview is recommended. 60 of 130 credits required for the bachelor's degree must be completed at ENC.

Visiting: There are regularly scheduled orientations for prospective students. There are guides for informal visits and visitors may sit in on classes and stay overnight. To schedule a visit, contact the Office of Admissions.

Financial Aid: ENC is a member of CSS. The FAFSA and the college's own financial statement are required. Check with the school for current application deadlines.

International Students: They must score satisfactorily on the written TOEFL.

Computers: All students may access the system. There are no time limits. The fee is $5.

Admissions Contact: James Heyward, Director of Admissions. E-mail: *admissio@enc.edu* Web: *www.enc.edu*

EMERSON COLLEGE E-2

Boston, MA 02116-4624 (617) 824-8600; Fax: (617) 824-8609

Full-time: 1349 men, 1743 women	**Faculty:** 143; IIA, +$
Part-time: 113 men, 168 women	**Ph.D.s:** 74%
Graduate: 214 men, 739 women	**Student/Faculty:** 22 to 1
Year: semesters, summer session	**Tuition:** $24,656
Application Deadline: January 5	**Room & Board:** $10,420
Freshman Class: 5008 applied, 2278 accepted, 709 enrolled	
SAT Verbal/Math: 630/605*	**ACT:** 27 **HIGHLY COMPETITIVE**

Emerson College, founded in 1880, is a private, independent college for the study of commmunication and performing arts. There are 2 undergraduate and 2 graduate schools. The library contains 173,513 volumes, 10,341 microform items, and 9760 audio/video tapes/CDs/DVDs, and subscribes to 642 periodicals including electronic. Computerized library services include the card catalog, interlibrary loans, database searching, Internet access, and laptop Internet portals. Special learning facilities include a learning resource center, radio station, TV station, and film production facilities, DVD authoring and digital production labs, speech-language-hearing clinics, a proscenium stage theater, two radio stations, marketing research suite, and a digital newsroom. The campus is in an urban area in the Theater District on Boston Common. Including any residence halls, there are 10 buildings.

Student Life: 63% of undergraduates are from out of state, mostly the Middle Atlantic. Others are from 45 states, 35 foreign countries, and Canada. 72% are from public schools. 77% are white. The average age of freshmen is 18; all undergraduates, 20. 11% do not continue beyond their first year.

Housing: 1207 students can be accommodated in college housing, which includes coed dormitories.In addition, there are living and learning communities such a writer's block and digital culture floor. On-campus housing is available on a first-come, first-served basis and is available on a lottery system for upperclassmen. 52% of students commute. No one may keep cars.

Activities: 3% of men belong to 2 local and 1 national fraternity; 3% of women belong to 2 local and 1 national sorority. There are 60 groups on campus, including computers, dance, debate, digital media, drama, ethnic, film, forensics, gay, honors, international, literary magazine, marketing/pr, musical theater, newspaper, performance troupes, photography, political, professional, radio and TV, religious, social, social service, student government, and yearbook. Popular campus events include Evvy's Award Show, Family Weekend, and Hand-Me-Down Night.

Sports: There are 6 intercollegiate sports for men and 7 for women. Facilities include a 10,000-square-foot fitness center, a lighted athletic field and fieldhouse, and a gym.

Disabled Students: 50% of the campus is accessible. Wheelchair ramps, elevators, specially equipped rest rooms, special class scheduling, and special housing are available.

Services: Counseling and information services are available, as is tutoring in most subjects. There is remedial math, reading, and writing.

Campus Safety and Security: Measures include 24-hour foot and vehicle patrol, self-defense education, security escort services, and shuttle buses. There are informal discussions, pamphlets/posters/films, emergency telephones, and lighted pathways/sidewalks.

Programs of Study: Emerson confers B.A., B.S., B.F.A., and B.S.Sp. degrees. Master's and doctoral degrees are also awarded. Bachelor's degrees are awarded in BUSINESS (marketing management), COMMUNICATIONS AND THE ARTS (advertising, broadcasting, communications, creative writing, dramatic arts, film arts, journalism, media arts, musical theater, performing arts, public relations, publishing, radio/television technology, speech/debate/rhetoric, theater design, and theater management), HEALTH PROFESSIONS (speech pathology/audiology), SOCIAL SCIENCE (interdisciplinary studies). Visual and media arts, writing, and literature and publishing are the strongest academically. Visual and media arts, performing arts, and communication are the largest.

Required: All students must complete 128 credit hours, with 40 to 64 in their major and a minimum GPA of 2.0. The general education curriculum consists of 4 foundations courses (oral and written communication and quantitative reasoning), 7 courses from liberal arts perspectives, and 2 global/U.S. diversity courses.

Special: Student-designed, interdisciplinary, and dual majors are available. Cross-registration is offered with the 6-member Boston ProArts consortium, and Suffolk University. 700 internships are possible in Boston and 250 in Los Angeles. Internships bear credit and are graded. Emerson has nondegree study and pass/fail options, as well as study abroad in the Netherlands and a summer film program in Prague. There is 1 national honor society, and a freshman honors program.

Faculty/Classroom: 57% of faculty are male; 43%, female. All teach undergraduates. Graduate students teach 4% of introductory courses. The average class size in an introductory lecture is 35; in a laboratory, 18; and in a regular course, 24.

Admissions: 45% of the 2005-2006 applicants were accepted. The SAT scores for the 2005-2006 freshman class were: Verbal--1% below 500, 26% between 500 and 599, 56% between 600 and 700, and 17% above 700; Math--4% below 500, 43% between 500 and 599, 45% between 600 and 700, and 8% above 700. The ACT scores were 3% below 21, 12% between 21 and 23, 40% between 24 and 26, 27% between 27 and 28, and 18% above 28. 75% of the current freshmen were in the top fifth of their class; 85% were in the top two fifths. 5 freshmen graduated first in their class.

Requirements: The SAT or ACT is required. The ACT Optional Writing test is also required. In addition, candidates must be graduates of an accredited secondary school or hold a GED certificate. They must have completed 16 Carnegie units, including 4 in English and 3 each in science, social studies, foreign language, and math. An essay is required. Candidates for performing arts programs are required to submit a theatre-related resume and either audition or interview, or submit a portfolio, or essay. AP and CLEP credits are accepted. Important factors in the admissions decision are advanced placement or honor courses, evidence of special talent, and recommendations by school officials.

Procedure: Freshmen are admitted fall and spring. Entrance exams should be taken before January of the senior year. There is a deferred admissions plan. Early action applications should be filed by November 1; regular applications, by January 5 for fall entry and November 1 for spring entry, along with a $60 fee. Notification of early action is sent December 15; regular decision, April 1. 440 applicants were on the 2005 waiting list. Applications are accepted on-line.

Transfer: 182 transfer students enrolled in 2004-2005. Official transcripts from high school (or a GED), all college course work, a letter of recommendation and a dean's report of good standing are required. SAT or ACT scores must be submitted, unless the candidate possesses an associate degree or has been out of school 3 or more years. 32 of 128 credits required for the bachelor's degree must be completed at Emerson.

Visiting: There are regularly scheduled orientations for prospective students, including an information session with an admission representative and a tour lead by a currently enrolled student. There are guides for informal visits and visitors may sit in on classes. To schedule a visit, contact Visits may be scheduled on-line at *http://visit.emerson.edu*.

Financial Aid: In 2005-2006, 77% of all full-time freshmen and 66% of continuing full-time students received some form of financial aid. 47% of full-time freshmen and 41% of continuing full-time students received need-based aid. The average freshman award was $13,843. Need-based scholarships or need-based grants averaged $11,814; need-based self-help aid (loans and jobs) averaged $4158; and other non-need-based awards and non-need-based scholarships averaged $9590. 60% of undergraduates work part time. Average annual earnings from campus work are $1600. The average financial indebtedness of the 2005 graduate was $22,200. The CSS/Profile or FAFSA is required. The deadline for filing freshman financial aid applications for fall entry is March 1.

International Students: There are 80 international students enrolled. The school actively recruits these students. They must score satisfactorily on the written TOEFL or on the electronic version and also take or take the IELTS.They must also take the SAT or the ACT.

Computers: Wireless access is available. There are very few restrictions on network or wireless access with over 3000 ports on campus. All students may access the system 24 hours a day. There are no time limits and no fees. It is strongly recommended that all students have a personal computer.

Graduates: From July 1, 2004 to June 30, 2005, 715 bachelor's degrees were awarded. The most popular majors were media production/film (20%), writing, literature and publishing (17%), and performing arts (15%). In an average class, 66% graduate in 4 years or less, 69% graduate in 5 years or less, and 70% graduate in 6 years or less. 100 companies recruited on campus in 2004-2005. Of the 2004 graduating class, 13% were enrolled in graduate school within 6 months of graduation and 76% were employed.

Admissions Contact: Sara S. Ramirez, Director of Undergraduate Admission. E-mail: *admission@emerson.edu* Web: *www.emerson.edu*

EMMANUEL COLLEGE E-2

Boston, MA 02115 (617) 735-9715; Fax: (617) 735-9801

Full-time: 396 men, 1107 women	**Faculty:** IIB, av$
Part-time: 119 men, 474 women	**Ph.D.s:** 85%
Graduate: 56 men, 144 women	**Student/Faculty:** n/av
Year: semesters, summer session	**Tuition:** $23,000
Application Deadline: March 1	**Room & Board:** $9700
Freshman Class: 3107 applied, 1181 accepted, 438 enrolled	
SAT Verbal/Math: 531/510*	**ACT:** 22* COMPETITIVE+

Emmanuel College, founded in 1919 by the Sisters of Notre Dame de Namar, is a Catholic college offering a liberal arts and sciences curriculum that prepares students with the skills to succeed in tomorrow's world and the social conscience to make a difference in that world. At Emmanuel, students become engaged learners and develop leadership skills through participation in campus life. In addition to regional accreditation, Emmanuel College has baccalaureate program accreditation with ACPE, NLN, and CCNE. The library contains 97,907 volumes, 2104 microform items, and 527 audio/video tapes/CDs/DVDs, and subscribes to 396 periodicals including electronic. Computerized library services include the card catalog, interlibrary loans, database searching, and Internet access. Special learning facilities include a learning resource center and art gallery. The 17-acre campus is in an urban area in Boston. Including any residence halls, there are 10 buildings.

Student Life: 72% of undergraduates are from Massachusetts. Others are from 33 states, 31 foreign countries, and Canada. 72% are from public schools. 65% are white. The average age of freshmen is 18; all undergraduates, 24. 17% do not continue beyond their first year; 53% remain to graduate.

Housing: 1101 students can be accommodated in college housing, which includes single-sex and coed dorms. On-campus housing is guaranteed for all 4 years. 82% of students live on campus; of those, 95% remain on campus on weekends. Alcohol is not permitted. Upperclassmen may keep cars.

Activities: There are no fraternities or sororities. There are 50 groups on campus, including art, cheerleading, chorus, dance, drama, ethnic, gay, honors, international, literary magazine, musical theater, newspaper, orchestra, pep band, political, professional, religious, social, social service, and student government. Popular campus events include Moonlight Breakfast, Clam Bake, and Casino Night.

Sports: There are 6 intercollegiate sports for men and 8 for women, and 2 intramural sports for men and 2 for women. Facilities include a gymnasium housed in the Jean Yawkey Center with one NCAA regulation court or two full-size practice courts that also serves as the largest meeting room on the campus for gatherings of the entire college community, with seating totaling 2500. The center is equipped with cardiovascular machines (including treadmills, elliptical machines and steppers), as well as circuit training machines and free weights. The athletic training room contains training facilities and a hydrotherapy area for athletes, and overlooking the gymnasium, the Booster Room is suitable for small gatherings during athletic events.

Disabled Students: 75% of the campus is accessible. Wheelchair ramps, elevators, special parking, specially equipped rest rooms, special class scheduling, and lowered telephones are available.

Services: Counseling and information services are available, as is tutoring in most subjects. There is a reader service for the blind and remedial math and writing.

Campus Safety and Security: Measures include 24-hour foot and vehicle patrol, self-defense education, security escort services, and shuttle buses. There are informal discussions, pamphlets/posters/films, lighted pathways/sidewalks, 24-hour staffed residence hall desks, and closed circuit surveillance in public areas.

Programs of Study: Emmanuel College confers B.A., B.S., and B.F.A. degrees. Master's degrees are also awarded. Bachelor's degrees are awarded in BIOLOGICAL SCIENCE (biochemistry and biology/biological science), BUSINESS (business administration and management), COMMUNICATIONS AND THE ARTS (communications, English, English literature, Spanish, and studio art), COMPUTER AND PHYSICAL SCIENCE (chemistry and mathematics), EDUCATION (elementary and secondary), ENGINEERING AND ENVIRONMENTAL DESIGN (graphic arts technology), HEALTH PROFESSIONS (art therapy and nursing), SOCIAL SCIENCE (American studies, counseling/psychology, developmental psychology, history, interdisciplinary studies, international studies, liberal arts/general studies, political science/government, psychology, religion, and sociology). Biology is the strongest academically. Business administration, psychology, and English are the largest.

Required: Students must have foundational skills in English, information technology, and math, and must take two consecutive semesters of a foreign language or American sign language. Domains of knowledge includes 3 courses of scientific inquiry and quantitative analysis, 3 of religious thought and moral reasoning, 2 of aesthetic inquiry and social analysis, and 1 of historical conciousness. A total of 128 credit hours, with a minimum of 10 courses in the major, and a minimum GPA of 2.0 are required for graduation. A first-year seminar program and a capstone experience are required.

Special: There is cross-registration with Wheelock College, Simmons College, Massachusetts College of Art, Massachusetts College of Pharmacy, Wentworth Institute of Technology, and Andover-Newton Theological School. The college offers internships, study abroad, a Washington semester, work-study programs on campus and in Boston-area organizations, an accelerated degree program in business administration, a B.A.-B.S. degree in biology, dual and student-designed majors, a general studies degree, prelaw/prehealth preparation, and pass/fail options. There are 6 national honor societies and a freshman honors program, and all departments have honors programs.

Faculty/Classroom: 48% of faculty are male; 52%, female. No introductory courses are taught by graduate students. The average class size in an introductory lecture is 18 and in a laboratory, 11.

Admissions: 38% of the 2005-2006 applicants were accepted. The SAT scores for the 2005-2006 freshman class were: Verbal--26% below 500, 4% between 500 and 599, 23% between 600 and 700, and 5% above 700; Math--35% below 500, 43% between 500 and 599, 20% between 600 and 700, and 2% above 700. The ACT scores were 30% below 21, 28% between 21 and 23, 26% between 24 and 26, 12% between 27 and 28, and 4% above 28. 33% of the current freshmen were in the top fifth of their class; 64% were in the top two fifths.

Requirements: The SAT or ACT is required. In addition, applicants must be graduates of an accredited secondary school or have a GED. 16 academic credits are required, including 4 years of English, 3 years of math, and 2 years each of foreign language, lab science, and social studies. An essay and an interview are required. AP and CLEP credits are accepted. Important factors in the admissions decision are advanced placement or honor courses, recommendations by school officials, and parents or siblings attending the school.

Procedure: Freshmen are admitted fall and spring. Entrance exams should be taken by November of the senior year. There are early decision and deferred admissions plans. Early decision applications should be filed by November 1; regular applications, by March 1 for fall entry,

along with a $40 fee. Notification of early decision is sent December 1. 3 early decision candidates were accepted for the 2005-2006 class. A waiting list is an active part of the admissions procedure. Applications are accepted on-line.

Transfer: 61 transfer students enrolled in 2004-2005. Students must submit essays, college and high school transcripts, and 2 letters of recommendation. They must be financially and academically eligible to return to the previously attended institution. 64 of 128 credits required for the bachelor's degree must be completed at Emmanuel College.

Visiting: There are regularly scheduled orientations for prospective students. There are guides for informal visits and visitors may sit in on classes and stay overnight. To schedule a visit, contact the Admissions Office at *enroll@emmanuel.edu.*

Financial Aid: In 2005-2006, 91% of all full-time freshmen and 84% of continuing full-time students received some form of financial aid. 77% of full-time freshmen and 75% of continuing full-time students received need-based aid. 4% of undergraduates work part time. Average annual earnings from campus work are $750. The FAFSA, the college's own financial statement, and parents' and students' income tax forms are required. The priority date for freshman financial aid applications for fall entry is April 1.

International Students: There are 53 international students enrolled. The school actively recruits these students. They must score 550 on the written TOEFL or 213 on the electronic version, or take ELS level 109 or the equivalent, and must also take the SAT or the ACT.

Computers: Wireless access is available. All students may access the system. There are no time limits and no fees.

Graduates: From July 1, 2004 to June 30, 2005, 326 bachelor's degrees were awarded. The most popular majors were business administration/management (35%), education (8%), and psychology (7%). In an average class, 1% graduate in 3 years or less, 45% graduate in 4 years or less, 52% graduate in 5 years or less, and 53% graduate in 6 years or less. 20 companies recruited on campus in 2004-2005.

Admissions Contact: Sandra Robbins, Dean of Enrollment.
E-mail: *enroll@emmanuel.edu* Web: *www.emmanuel.edu*

ENDICOTT COLLEGE   E-2
Beverly, MA 01915   (978) 921-1000
                              (800) 325-1114; Fax: (978) 232-2520

Full-time: 687 men, 1030 women	**Faculty:** 68; IIB, av$
Part-time: 180 men and women	**Ph.D.s:** 49%
Graduate: 1419 men and women	**Student/Faculty:** 25 to 1
Year: 4-1-4, summer session	**Tuition:** $20,390
Application Deadline: February 15	**Room & Board:** $9766
Freshman Class: 3293 applied, 1526 accepted, 545 enrolled	
SAT Verbal/Math: 535/537*	**COMPETITIVE+**

Endicott College, founded in 1939, is a private institution offering programs in arts and sciences, business and communications, health sciences, sports science and hospitality, education, art and design, criminal justice, and computer science. There are 7 undergraduate schools and 1 graduate school. In addition to regional accreditation, Endicott College has baccalaureate program accreditation with FIDER and NLN. The library contains 116,800 volumes, 23,500 microform items, and 475 audio/video tapes/CDs/DVDs, and subscribes to 34,283 periodicals including electronic. Computerized library services include the card catalog, interlibrary loans, database searching, and Internet access. Special learning facilities include a learning resource center, art gallery, radio station, TV station, and an archives museum. The 210-acre campus is in a suburban area 20 miles north of Boston. Including any residence halls, there are 41 buildings.

Student Life: 53% of undergraduates are from out of state, mostly the Northeast. Students are from 28 states, 35 foreign countries, and Canada. 86% are white. The average age of freshmen is 18; all undergraduates, 20. 17% do not continue beyond their first year; 50% remain to graduate.

Housing: 1498 students can be accommodated in college housing, which includes single-sex and coed dorms, on-campus apartments, off-campus apartments, and international housing. On-campus housing is guaranteed for the freshman year only, is available on a first-come, first-served basis, and is available on a lottery system for upperclassmen. 86% of students live on campus; of those, 65% remain on campus on weekends. All students may keep cars.

Activities: There are no fraternities or sororities. There are 30 groups on campus, including adventure, art, campus activities board, cheerleading, chorus, computers, dance, ethnic, film, fitness, gay, honors, international, jazz band, literary magazine, newspaper, professional, radio and TV, religious, sailing, social, social service, student government, and yearbook. Popular campus events include hypnotist and comedian acts, performing arts events, and Founders Day.

Sports: There are 10 intercollegiate sports for men and 10 for women, and 6 intramural sports for men and 6 for women. Facilities include a 1400-seat gym with a racquetball and basketball courts, weight, fitness, and aerobics rooms, indoor track, and field house. Outdoor facilities include 6 tennis courts, and field hockey, softball, lighted baseball, lacrosse, and soccer fields, and a 2200-seat multipurpose football stadium.

Disabled Students: 90% of the campus is accessible. Wheelchair ramps, elevators, special parking, specially equipped rest rooms, special class scheduling, and lowered drinking fountains are available.

Services: Counseling and information services are available, as is tutoring in every subject. There is a reader service for the blind, and remedial math, reading, and writing. An interpreter service for hearing-impaired students is available.

Campus Safety and Security: Measures include 24-hour foot and vehicle patrol, self-defense education, security escort services, and shuttle buses. There are informal discussions, pamphlets/posters/films, emergency telephones, and lighted pathways/sidewalks.

Programs of Study: Endicott College confers B.A., B.S., and B.F.A. degrees. Associate and master's degrees are also awarded. Bachelor's degrees are awarded in AGRICULTURE (environmental studies), BUSINESS (business administration and management, hotel/motel and restaurant management, and sports management), COMMUNICATIONS AND THE ARTS (communications, English, fine arts, and Spanish), COMPUTER AND PHYSICAL SCIENCE (computer science), EDUCATION (athletic training, education, and physical), ENGINEERING AND ENVIRONMENTAL DESIGN (interior design), HEALTH PROFESSIONS (nursing), SOCIAL SCIENCE (criminal justice, history, human services, international studies, liberal arts/general studies, and psychology). Business is the largest.

Required: To graduate, students must complete 128 credit hours with a minimum GPA of 2.0 (2.5 in education and nursing). Core requirements include 9 credits in science, humanities, social sciences, math, and writing courses, 12 upper-division electives, 3 credits in first-year seminar, senior seminar, thesis, and capstone.

Special: Cross-registration is available with NECCUM and internships are required in every major. Students may study abroad, and there are accelerated degree programs in business administration and psychology. Student-designed majors are available in liberal studies. There are 4 national honor societies, a freshman honors program, and 3 departmental honors programs.

Faculty/Classroom: 48% of faculty are male; 52%, female. All teach undergraduates. No introductory courses are taught by graduate students. The average class size in an introductory lecture is 19; in a laboratory, 19; and in a regular course, 19.

Admissions: 46% of the 2005-2006 applicants were accepted. The SAT scores for the 2005-2006 freshman class were: Verbal--27% below 500, 57% between 500 and 599, 15% between 600 and 700, and 1% above 700; Math--25% below 500, 57% between 500 and 599, 17% between 600 and 700, and 1% above 700. 36% of the current freshmen were in the top quarter of their class; 89% were in the top half.

Requirements: The SAT is required. In addition, essays and 2 science and math recommendations are required for nursing (including chemistry) and athletic training majors. AP and CLEP credits are accepted. Important factors in the admissions decision are leadership record, recommendations by school officials, and extracurricular activities record.

Procedure: Freshmen are admitted fall and spring. Entrance exams should be taken in fall of the senior year. There is a deferred admissions plan, and a rolling admissions plan. Applications should be filed by February 15 for fall entry and December 15 for spring entry, along with a $40 fee. 147 applicants were on the 2005 waiting list. Applications are accepted on-line.

Transfer: 42 transfer students enrolled in 2004-2005. The SAT or ACT is required, as are official high school and college transcripts, and a letter of recommendation. 24 of 128 credits required for the bachelor's degree must be completed at Endicott College.

Visiting: There are regularly scheduled orientations for prospective students, including testing, preregistration, and an introduction to general student life. There are guides for informal visits and visitors may sit in on classes and stay overnight. To schedule a visit, contact the Admission Office at admissio@endicott.edu.

Financial Aid: In 2005-2006, 78% of all full-time freshmen received some form of financial aid. 25% of undergraduates work part time. Average annual earnings from campus work are $1500. Endicott College is a member of CSS. The FAFSA and the college's own financial statement are required. The priority date for freshman financial aid applications for fall entry is March 15.

International Students: There are 84 international students enrolled. The school actively recruits these students. They must score satisfactorily on the written TOEFL.

Computers: Wireless access is available. Cybercafe is available 24 hours a day, 7 days a week. All students may access the system 24 hours a day, 7 days a week. There are no time limits. The fee is $400. Business majors are required to have personal computers. It is recommended that all other students have personal computers.

Graduates: From July 1, 2004 to June 30, 2005, 399 bachelor's degrees were awarded. The most popular majors were business administration (25%), art and design (22%), and communications (12%). In an average class, 56% graduate in 6 years or less. Of the 2004 graduating

class, 12% were enrolled in graduate school within 6 months of graduation and 77% were employed.

Admissions Contact: Thomas J. Redman, VP, Admissions. A video is available. E-mail: admissio@endicott.edu Web: www.endicott.edu

FITCHBURG STATE COLLEGE   C-2
Fitchburg, MA 01420-2697

(978) 665-3144
(800) 705-9692; Fax: (978) 665-4540

Full-time: 1336 men, 1619 women	**Faculty:** 166
Part-time: 291 men, 414 women	**Ph.D.s:** 90%
Graduate: 381 men, 1304 women	**Student/Faculty:** 18 to 1
Year: semesters	**Tuition:** $5002 ($10,266)
Application Deadline: April 1	**Room & Board:** $6274
Freshman Class: 3860 applied, 2787 accepted, 980 enrolled	
SAT Verbal/Math: 510/500*	**ACT:** 20 **COMPETITIVE**

Fitchburg State College, founded in 1894, is a public college offering programs in liberal arts, business, communications, health sciences, and education. In addition to regional accreditation, Fitchburg State has baccalaureate program accreditation with CCNE, IACBE, and NCATE. The library contains 243,711 volumes and 457,283 microform items, and subscribes to 2256 periodicals including electronic. Computerized library services include the card catalog, interlibrary loans, database searching, and Internet access. Special learning facilities include a learning resource center, art gallery, radio station, a campus school, a graphics center, and a TV studio. The 45-acre campus is in a suburban area 45 miles west of Boston. Including any residence halls, there are 33 buildings.

Student Life: 93% of undergraduates are from Massachusetts. Students are from 19 states and 4 foreign countries. 80% are from public schools. 91% are white. The average age of freshmen is 18; all undergraduates, 20. 23% do not continue beyond their first year; 55% remain to graduate.

Housing: 1488 students can be accommodated in college housing, which includes coed dorms and on-campus apartments. In addition, there are special-interest houses. Priority for on-campus housing is given to out-of-town students. 55% of students commute. All students may keep cars.

Activities: 3% of men belong to 4 national fraternities; 3% of women belong to 1 local and 2 national sororities. There are 65 groups on campus, including band, cheerleading, choir, chorus, computers, dance, drama, ethnic, film, gay, honors, international, jazz band, literary magazine, newspaper, photography, political, professional, radio and TV, religious, social, social service, student government, and yearbook. Popular campus events include Falcon Fest and Center Stage Performing Arts Series.

Sports: There are 8 intercollegiate sports for men and 7 for women, and 8 intramural sports for men and 8 for women. Facilities include a 1000-seat gym, an indoor/outdoor track, a weight room, varsity and intramural fields, the student union, volleyball, basketball, racquetball, and tennis courts, a swimming pool, and a dance studio.

Disabled Students: 80% of the campus is accessible. Wheelchair ramps, elevators, special parking, specially equipped rest rooms, special class scheduling, lowered drinking fountains, lowered telephones, special housing, and an adaptive computer lab are available.

Services: Counseling and information services are available, as is tutoring in most subjects. There is a reader service for the blind, and remedial math, reading, and writing.

Campus Safety and Security: Measures include 24-hour foot and vehicle patrol, self-defense education, security escort services, and shuttle buses. There are informal discussions, pamphlets/posters/films, emergency telephones, and lighted pathways/sidewalks.

Programs of Study: Fitchburg State confers B.A., B.S., and B.S.Ed. degrees. Master's degrees are also awarded. Bachelor's degrees are awarded in BIOLOGICAL SCIENCE (biology/biological science), BUSINESS (business administration and management), COMMUNICATIONS AND THE ARTS (communications and English), COMPUTER AND PHYSICAL SCIENCE (computer science, earth science, and mathematics), EDUCATION (early childhood, elementary, industrial arts, middle school, secondary, and special), ENGINEERING AND ENVIRONMENTAL DESIGN (industrial engineering technology), HEALTH PROFESSIONS (exercise science and nursing), SOCIAL SCIENCE (criminal justice, economics, geography, history, human services, liberal arts/general studies, political science/government, psychology, and sociology). Communications and English are the strongest academically. Business administration, communications, and nursing are the largest.

Required: All students must complete a minimum of 120 credit hours with a GPA of at least 2.0 overall and in the major. Distribution requirements include courses from the categories of ideas and events, human behavior, health and fitness, computer literacy, literature/language/arts, and the quantitative/scientific area. Two introductory semesters of writing are also required.

Special: Students may cross-register at any other Massachusetts state college. Internships in a variety of fields, study abroad in 11 countries, accelerated degree programs, B.A.-B.S. degrees, dual majors, and a student-designed interdiaciplinary studies major are offered. There are 6 national honor societies, a freshman honors program, and 7 departmental honors programs.

Faculty/Classroom: 55% of faculty are male; 45%, female. All teach undergraduates. No introductory courses are taught by graduate students. The average class size in an introductory lecture is 25; in a laboratory, 15; and in a regular course, 20.

Admissions: 72% of the 2005-2006 applicants were accepted. The SAT scores for the 2005-2006 freshman class were: Verbal--44% below 500, 42% between 500 and 599, 13% between 600 and 700, and 1% above 700; Math--43% below 500, 44% between 500 and 599, 12% between 600 and 700, and 1% above 700. The ACT scores were 55% below 21, 25% between 21 and 23, 14% between 24 and 26, 3% between 27 and 28, and 3% above 28.

Requirements: The SAT or ACT is required. In addition, applicants should be graduates of accredited high schools or have the GED. Secondary preparation should include 4 years of English, 3 years each of math and liberal arts or phys ed, and 2 years each of a foreign language, social studies including U.S. history, and science. A GPA of 2.0 is required. AP and CLEP credits are accepted. Important factors in the admissions decision are advanced placement or honor courses, leadership record, and extracurricular activities record.

Procedure: Freshmen are admitted fall and spring. Entrance exams should be taken in the junior or senior year. There is a deferred admissions and a rolling admissions plan. Applications should be filed by April 1 for fall entry and December 1 for spring entry, along with a $10 fee. Notification is sent on a rolling basis. Applications are accepted on-line.

Transfer: 286 transfer students enrolled in 2004-2005. Applicants should present a minimum GPA of 2.0 in at least 12 credits of transferable college work. 45 of 120 credits required for the bachelor's degree must be completed at Fitchburg State.

Visiting: There are regularly scheduled orientations for prospective students, including tours of the campus and residence halls, admissions/financial aid information, and academic program advising. There are guides for informal visits and visitors may sit in on classes. To schedule a visit, contact the Admissions Office.

Financial Aid: The FAFSA and the college's own financial statement are required. The deadline for filing freshman financial aid applications for fall entry is March 1.

International Students: There are 21 international students enrolled. The school actively recruits these students. They must score satisfactory on the written TOEFL or on the electronic version and also take the SAT or the ACT.

Computers: Wireless access is available. Open PC and Mac labs are available to students; wireless Internet access is available in the library campus center and all classroom buildings. All students may access the system 24 hours per day. There are no time limits and no fees.

Graduates: From July 1, 2004 to June 30, 2005, 489 bachelor's degrees were awarded. The most popular majors were business administration (18%), communications (17%), and nursing (9%). In an average class, 22% graduate in 4 years or less, 47% graduate in 5 years or less, and 55% graduate in 6 years or less. Of the 2004 graduating class, 10% were enrolled in graduate school within 6 months of graduation and 94% were employed.

Admissions Contact: Director of Admissions. A video is available. E-mail: admissions@fsc.edu Web: www.fsc.edu

FRAMINGHAM STATE COLLEGE   D-2
Framingham, MA 01701-9101

| | (508) 626-4500 |
| | Fax: (508) 626-4017 |

Full-time: 1003 men, 2042 women	**Faculty:** 163
Part-time: 275 men, 452 women	**Ph.D.s:** 84%
Graduate: 468 men, 1634 women	**Student/Faculty:** 19 to 1
Year: semesters, summer session	**Tuition:** $4999 ($11,079)
Application Deadline: February 15	**Room & Board:** $6157
Freshman Class: 3955 applied, 2518 accepted, 675 enrolled	
SAT Verbal/Math: 532/530*	**COMPETITIVE**

Framingham State College, founded in 1839, is a comprehensive public institution offering degree programs based on a liberal arts foundation that includes unique career programs. In addition to regional accreditation, FSC has baccalaureate program accreditation with ADA and NLN. The library contains 204,828 volumes, 670,850 microform items, and 3433 audio/video tapes/CDs/DVDs, and subscribes to 419 periodicals including electronic. Computerized library services include the card catalog, interlibrary loans, database searching, and Internet access. Special learning facilities include a learning resource center, art gallery, planetarium, radio station, a greenhouse, TV studio, early childhood demonstration lab, curriculum library, and McAuliffe Challenger Learning Center. The 73-acre campus is in a suburban area 20 miles west of Boston. Including any residence halls, there are 19 buildings.

Student Life: 96% of undergraduates are from Massachusetts. Students are from 12 states, 29 foreign countries, and Canada. 80% are from public schools. 88% are white. The average age of freshmen is 19; all

undergraduates, 21. 25% do not continue beyond their first year; 42% remain to graduate.

Housing: 1518 students can be accommodated in college housing, which includes single-sex and coed dorms. On-campus housing is available on a first-come, first-served basis. 51% of students commute. Alcohol is not permitted. Upperclassmen may keep cars.

Activities: There are no fraternities or sororities. There are 50 groups on campus, including art, cheerleading, chorale, chorus, computers, dance, drama, ethnic, gay, honors, international, literary magazine, newspaper, political, professional, radio and TV, religious, social, social service, student government, and yearbook. Popular campus events include the Sandbox Festival, Semi-Formal Dance, and Black History Month events.

Sports: There are 6 intercollegiate sports for men and 7 for women, and 10 intramural sports for men and 10 for women. Facilities include an athletic and recreation center, a gym, and a student center. An all-weather turf field for soccer, football, field hockey, and intramural sports are available on lower campus fields.

Disabled Students: 95% of the campus is accessible. Wheelchair ramps, elevators, special parking, specially equipped rest rooms, special class scheduling, lowered drinking fountains, and lowered telephones are available.

Services: Counseling and information services are available, as is tutoring in most subjects. There is a reader service for the blind, and remedial math, reading, and writing. The College Skills Center offers free tutoring in writing, math, and reading. Subject tutoring may be arranged for an hourly fee.

Campus Safety and Security: Measures include 24-hour foot and vehicle patrol, self-defense education, security escort services, and shuttle buses. There are informal discussions, pamphlets/posters/films, emergency telephones, lighted pathways/sidewalks, and security cameras, residence hall security, card access, and resident hall desk attendants.

Programs of Study: FSC confers B.A., B.S., and B.S.Ed degrees. Master's degrees are also awarded. Bachelor's degrees are awarded in BIOLOGICAL SCIENCE (biology/biological science and nutrition), BUSINESS (business administration and management and fashion merchandising), COMMUNICATIONS AND THE ARTS (art history and appreciation, communications, English, Spanish, and studio art), COMPUTER AND PHYSICAL SCIENCE (chemistry, computer science, and mathematics), EDUCATION (business, early childhood, and elementary), HEALTH PROFESSIONS (nursing), SOCIAL SCIENCE (economics, family/consumer studies, fashion design and technology, food science, geography, history, interdisciplinary studies, political science/government, psychology, sociology, and textiles and clothing). Business administration, elementary/early childhood education, and food sciences and nutrition are the largest.

Required: The college's goal-based general education model includes: writing; math; language; literature or philosophy; visual or performing arts; physical science; life science; historical studies; social and behavioral sciences; forces in the United States; study of Constitutions, gender, class, and race; and non-Western studies. Every student must take 12 general education courses and fulfill all required goals. A total of 128 credits (32 courses), including 40 to 68 credits in the major, and a 2.0 GPA is required to graduate.

Special: The college offers a 2-3 pre-engineering program in cooperation with the University of Massachusetts at Amherst, Lowell, and Dartmouth. Cross-registration is possible at any of the state colleges. Study abroad in 11 countries, a Washington semester, and various internships are available. Pass/fail options are limited to 2 courses. There are 6 national honor societies, a freshman honors program, and 6 departmental honors programs.

Faculty/Classroom: 45% of faculty are male; 54%, female. All teach undergraduates. No introductory courses are taught by graduate students. The average class size in an introductory lecture is 16 and in a laboratory, 30.

Admissions: 64% of the 2005-2006 applicants were accepted. The SAT scores for the 2005-2006 freshman class were: Verbal--27% below 500, 57% between 500 and 599, 15% between 600 and 700, and 1% above 700; Math--29% below 500, 55% between 500 and 599, 15% between 600 and 700, and 1% above 700. 25% of the current freshmen were in the top fifth of their class; 58% were in the top two fifths. 2 freshmen graduated first in their class.

Requirements: The SAT is required. In addition, applicants must have a high school diploma or the GED. Secondary preparation must total 16 college-preparatory credits, including 4 years of English, 3 each of math and science (2 with lab), and 2 each of foreign language and social science. The required 2 years of electives may include additional academic subjects or art, music, or computer courses. Prospective studio art majors must submit a portfolio. A GPA of 3.0 is required. AP and CLEP credits are accepted. Important factors in the admissions decision are advanced placement or honor courses, leadership record, and recommendations by school officials.

Procedure: Freshmen are admitted fall and spring. Entrance exams should be taken in the spring of the junior year or fall of the senior year.

There is a deferred admissions and a rolling admissions plan. Applications should be filed by February 15 for fall entry and December 1 for spring entry, along with a $25 fee. Notification is sent on a rolling basis. Applications are accepted on-line.

Transfer: 533 transfer students enrolled in 2004-2005. Applicants with more than 24 college credits must present a college GPA of at least 2.5; those with fewer than 24 credits must also meet freshman admission requirements. Official transcripts must be submitted from all colleges previously attended at the time of application. 32 of 128 credits required for the bachelor's degree must be completed at FSC.

Visiting: There are regularly scheduled orientations for prospective students, including campus tours and information sessions. There are guides for informal visits and visitors may sit in on classes. To schedule a visit, contact the Admissions Office.

Financial Aid: In 2005-2006, 78% of all full-time freshmen and 58% of continuing full-time students received some form of financial aid. 55% of full-time freshmen and 41% of continuing full-time students received need-based aid. The average freshman award was $5637. Need-based scholarships or need-based grants averaged $2122; need-based self-help aid (loans and jobs) averaged $2336; and other non-need-based awards and non-need-based scholarships averaged $1179. 60% of undergraduates work part time. Average annual earnings from campus work are $982. The average financial indebtedness of the 2005 graduate was $12,200. The FAFSA is required. The priority date for freshman financial aid applications for fall entry is March 1.

International Students: There are 46 international students enrolled. They must score satisfactory on the written TOEFL or on the electronic version and also take the SAT or the ACT.

Computers: Wireless access is available. Students have 24 hour wireless access in all of the campus environs. In addition, there are 6 academic computer labs, 5 general labs and PC classrooms, each of the 6 residence halls has a computer lab, and there is a 24 hour lab in the commuter lounge of the College Center. All students may access the system at any time. There are no time limits and no fees. All students are required to have PC. Dell or a compatible PC is required.

Graduates: From July 1, 2004 to June 30, 2005, 658 bachelor's degrees were awarded. The most popular majors were business and management (16%), psychology (11%), and sociology and communications (9%). In an average class, 44% graduate in 6 years or less. Of the 2004 graduating class, 15% were enrolled in graduate school within 6 months of graduation and 85% were employed.

Admissions Contact: Elizabeth Canella, Associate Dean of Admissions. E-mail: *admiss@frc.mass.edu* Web: *http://www.framingham.edu*

GORDON COLLEGE

Wenham, MA 01984   E-2

(978) 867-4217
866 464-6736; Fax: 978 867-4682

Full-time: 558 men, 1029 women	Faculty: 93; IIB, av$
Part-time: 9 men, 21 women	Ph.D.s: 71%
Graduate: 14 men, 41 women	Student/Faculty: 17 to 1
Year: semesters	Tuition: $22,924
Application Deadline: March 1	Room & Board: $6270
Freshman Class: 1098 applied, 921 accepted, 414 enrolled	
SAT Verbal/Math: 607/593*	ACT: 25 COMPETITIVE+

Gordon College, founded in 1889, is a private nondenominational Christian college offering liberal arts and sciences. In addition to regional accreditation, Gordon has baccalaureate program accreditation with CSWE, NASDTEC, and NASM. The library contains 191,404 volumes, 31,666 microform items, and 5225 audio/video tapes/CDs/DVDs, and subscribes to 510 periodicals including electronic. Computerized library services include the card catalog, interlibrary loans, database searching, Internet access, and laptop Internet portals. Special learning facilities include a learning resource center and art gallery. The 440-acre campus is in a small town 25 miles north of Boston. Including any residence halls, there are 30 buildings.

Student Life: 74% of undergraduates are from out of state, mostly the Northeast. Students are from 45 states, 24 foreign countries, and Canada. 91% are white. Most are Protestant. The average age of freshmen is 18; all undergraduates, 20. 12% do not continue beyond their first year; 70% remain to graduate.

Housing: 1468 students can be accommodated in college housing, which includes single-sex dorms, on-campus apartments, and married-student housing. In addition, there are special-interest houses. On-campus housing is guaranteed for all 4 years. 88% of students live on campus; of those, 70% remain on campus on weekends. Alcohol is not permitted. All students may keep cars.

Activities: There are no fraternities or sororities. There are 35 groups on campus, including art, bagpipe band, band, cheerleading, choir, chorale, chorus, dance, debate, drama, ethnic, film, honors, international, jazz band, literary magazine, musical theater, newspaper, off-campus ministries, opera, orchestra, pep band, photography, political, professional, religious, social, social service, student government, student outreach, symphony, and yearbook. Popular campus events include Genesis Week, International Week, and an artist series.

Sports: There are 8 intercollegiate sports for men and 9 for women, and 15 intramural sports for men and 15 for women. Facilities include a gym, weight rooms, tennis courts, athletic fields, a training room, a swimming pool, a climbing wall, racquetball courts, an aerobics room, ski/running trails, an outdoor ropes course, a sauna, and a walking track.

Disabled Students: 90% of the campus is accessible. Wheelchair ramps, elevators, special parking, specially equipped rest rooms, special class scheduling, lowered drinking fountains, lowered telephones, special housing, and electric doors are available.

Services: Counseling and information services are available, as is tutoring in some subjects, including math, writing, and core science. There is a reader service for the blind, and remedial math, reading, and writing. There are writing and academic support centers. Gordon also provides special advising, study skills help, support groups for some liberal arts core courses, walk-in help, and assistance finding volunteer note takers.

Campus Safety and Security: Measures include 24-hour foot and vehicle patrol, self-defense education, security escort services, and informal discussions. There are pamphlets/posters/films, emergency telephones, and lighted pathways/sidewalks.

Programs of Study: Gordon confers B.A., B.S., and B.Mu. degrees. Master's degrees are also awarded. Bachelor's degrees are awarded in BIOLOGICAL SCIENCE (biology/biological science), BUSINESS (accounting, banking and finance, business administration and management, and recreation and leisure services), COMMUNICATIONS AND THE ARTS (art, communications, dramatic arts, English, French, German, languages, music, music performance, and Spanish), COMPUTER AND PHYSICAL SCIENCE (chemistry, computer science, mathematics, and physics), EDUCATION (early childhood, elementary, middle school, music, secondary, and special), SOCIAL SCIENCE (biblical studies, economics, history, international studies, philosophy, physical fitness/movement, political science/government, psychology, social work, sociology, and youth ministry). English, biology, and psychology are the strongest academically. English, business administration, and communications are the largest.

Required: All students must demonstrate competency in writing, speech, and foreign language. The core curriculum consists of 8 credits in biblical studies, 8 in social and behavioral sciences, 8 in natural sciences, math, and computer science, 6 in humanities, and 4 each in fine arts and freshman seminar. A total of 124 credits is required for graduation, with 18 or more in the major and a minimum GPA of 2.0.

Special: Gordon offers cooperative education, internships, and cross-registration with other institutions in the Northeast Consortium of Colleges and Universities in Massachusetts. There is a 3-2 engineering program with the University of Massachusetts at Lowell and a 2-2 program in allied health with the Thomas Jefferson College of Allied Health Science in Philadelphia. B.A.-B.S. degrees, dual majors, student-designed majors, nondegree study, and pass/fail options are all available. Off-campus study opportunities include a Washington semester, the Christian College Consortium Visitor Program, the LaVida Wilderness Expedition, the Nova Scotia Student Exchange Program, and study abroad in Europe, the Middle East, China, the Philippines, and Latin America. There are 2 national honor societies, and 12 departmental honors programs.

Faculty/Classroom: 71% of faculty are male; 29%, female. All teach undergraduates. No introductory courses are taught by graduate students. The average class size in an introductory lecture is 26; in a laboratory, 14; and in a regular course, 21.

Admissions: 84% of the 2005-2006 applicants were accepted. The SAT scores for the 2005-2006 freshman class were: Verbal--8% below 500, 33% between 500 and 599, 48% between 600 and 700, and 11% above 700; Math--10% below 500, 54% between 500 and 599, 49% between 600 and 700, and 7% above 700. 43% of the current freshmen were in the top fifth of their class; 62% were in the top two fifths. There were 17 National Merit finalists and 1 semifinalist.

Requirements: The SAT or ACT is required. In addition, applicants must graduate from an accredited secondary school or have a GED. A minimum of 17 Carnegie units is required, including 4 English courses and 2 courses each in math, science, and social studies. Foreign language is a recommended elective. An essay, a personal reference, and an interview are required. Music majors must audition. AP and CLEP credits are accepted. Important factors in the admissions decision are advanced placement or honor courses, leadership record, and personality/intangible qualities.

Procedure: Freshmen are admitted fall and spring. Entrance exams should be taken in the spring of the junior year and the fall of the senior year. There are early decision, rolling admissions, and deferred admissions plans. Early decision applications should be filed by November 15; regular applications, by March 1 for fall entry, November 1 for spring entry, and December 1 for summer entry, along with a $50 fee. Notification of early decision is sent December 15; regular decision, on a rolling basis. 67 early decision candidates were accepted for the 2005-2006 class. Applications are accepted on-line.

Transfer: 59 transfer students enrolled in 2004-2005. Applicants must have a minimum GPA of 2.5. College transcripts, high school transcripts, and SAT or ACT scores if the applicant has completed less than 1 year of full-time study, an essay, an interview, and personal and academic references are required. 32 of 124 credits required for the bachelor's degree must be completed at Gordon.

Visiting: There are regularly scheduled orientations for prospective students, consisting of 5 open house programs throughout the fall, winter, and spring. There are guides for informal visits and visitors may sit in on classes and stay overnight. To schedule a visit, contact Sasha Moen, Visitation Coordinator at (978) 867-4022 or *sasha.moen@gordon.edu.*

Financial Aid: In 2005-2006, 50% of all full-time freshmen and 52% of continuing full-time students received some form of financial aid. At least 43% of full-time freshmen and 46% of continuing full-time students received need-based aid. The average freshman award was $14,314. Need-based scholarships or need-based grants averaged $10,938; and need-based self-help aid (loans and jobs) averaged $4140. Gordon is a member of CSS. The CSS/Profile or FAFSA is required. The deadline for filing freshman financial aid applications for fall entry is March 1.

International Students: There were 53 international students enrolled in a recent year. The school actively recruits these students. They must score satisfactorily on the TOEFL and also take or take the SAT or ACT.

Computers: Wireless access is available. All students may access the system at any time. There are no time limits and no fees.

Graduates: In a recent year, 404 bachelor's degrees were awarded. The most popular majors were education (13%), English (12%), and social sciences (10%).

Admissions Contact: Nancy Mering, Dean of Admissions. E-mail: *nancy.mering@gordon.edu* Web: *www.gordon.edu*

HAMPSHIRE COLLEGE   B-2

Amherst, MA 01002   (413) 559-5471; Fax: (413) 559-5631

Full-time: 560 men, 775 women	**Faculty:** 115; IIB,
Part-time: none	**Ph.D.s:** 90%
Graduate: none	**Student/Faculty:** 12 to 1
Year: 4-1-4	**Tuition:** $29,420
Application Deadline: see profile	**Room & Board:** $7700
Freshman Class: n/av	
SAT or ACT: not required	**HIGHLY COMPETITIVE**

Hampshire College, founded in 1965, is a private institution offering a liberal arts education with an emphasis on independent research, creative work, and multidisciplinary study. Figures in the above capsule are approximate. The library contains 124,710 volumes, 4534 microform items, and 8727 audio/video tapes/CDs/DVDs, and subscribes to 731 periodicals including electronic. Computerized library services include the card catalog, interlibrary loans, and database searching. Special learning facilities include an art gallery multimedia center, farm center, music and dance studios, optics lab, electronics shop, integrated greenhouse and aquaculture facility, fabrication shop, and performing arts center. The 800-acre campus is in a rural area 20 miles north of Springfield. Including any residence halls, there are 28 buildings.

Student Life: 86% of undergraduates are from out of state, mostly the Northeast. All are from 46 states, 25 foreign countries, and Canada. 76% are white. The average age of freshmen is 18; all undergraduates, 20. 21% do not continue beyond their first year.

Housing: 1100 students can be accommodated in college housing, which includes single-sex and coed dormitories and on-campus apartments. In addition, there are special-interest houses. On-campus housing is guaranteed for all 4 years. 92% of students live on campus. All students may keep cars.

Activities: There are no fraternities or sororities. There are 80 groups on campus, including art, chorus, computers, dance, drama, ethnic, film, gay, international, literary magazine, musical theater, orchestra, photography, political, radio and TV, religious, social, social service, and student government. Popular campus events include Southern Exposure, Spring Jam, and Casino Night.

Sports: There are 3 intercollegiate sports for men and 2 for women, and 18 intramural sports for men and 18 for women. Facilities include 2 multipurpose sports centers housing a glass-enclosed swimming pool, a 12,000-square-foot playing floor, a 30-foot climbing wall, a weight lifting area, 4 indoor tennis courts, and a jogging track. Other facilities include soccer fields, 10 outdoor tennis courts, 2 softball diamonds, and a 2-mile nature trail.

Disabled Students: 90% of the campus is accessible. Wheelchair ramps, elevators, special parking, specially equipped rest rooms, special class scheduling, lowered drinking fountains and lowered telephones are availabel. The college provides a variety of support services to meet individual special needs.

Services: Counseling and information services are available, as is tutoring in most subjects. There is a reader service for the blind, an advising center, a writing and reading program, and a lab quantitative skills program.

Campus Safety and Security: Measures include 24-hour foot and vehicle patrol, security escort services, informal discussions, and pamphlets/posters/films. There are lighted pathways/sidewalks, an EMT oncall program, and dorm doors accessible by students only.

Programs of Study: Hampshire confers the B.A. degree. Bachelor's degrees are awarded in AGRICULTURE (agriculture and animal science), BIOLOGICAL SCIENCE (biology/biological science, botany, ecology, marine biology, nutrition, and physiology), COMMUNICATIONS AND THE ARTS (art history and appreciation, communications, comparative literature, creative writing, dance, dramatic arts, film arts, fine arts, journalism, linguistics, literature, media arts, music, performing arts, photography, and video), COMPUTER AND PHYSICAL SCIENCE (chemistry, computer science, geology, mathematics, physics, and science), EDUCATION (education), ENGINEERING AND ENVIRONMENTAL DESIGN (architecture, environmental design, and environmental science), HEALTH PROFESSIONS (health science and premedicine), SOCIAL SCIENCE (African American studies, African studies, American studies, anthropology, Asian/Oriental studies, cognitive science, crosscultural studies, economics, family/consumer studies, geography, history, humanities, international relations, international studies, Judaic studies, Latin American studies, law, Middle Eastern studies, peace studies, philosophy, political science/government, psychology, religion, sociology, urban studies, and women's studies). Film/photography/video is the strongest academically. Social sciences is the largest.

Required: All students must complete 3 divisions of study. In Division I, Basic Studies, students work in each of Hampshire's 5 schools: Cognitive Science; Humanities, Arts and Cultural studies; Natural Science; Interdisciplinary Arts; and Social Science, and must complete 2 courses or the Division I exam project. In Division II, the Concentration, students explore their field or fields of emphasis through individually designed internships or field studies. In Division III, Advanced Studies, students complete a major independent study project, centered on a specific topic, question, or idea. Students must also include service to the college or the surrounding community and consider some aspect of their work from a non-Western perspective.

Special: Cross-registration is possible with other members of the Five-College Consortium (Amherst College, the University of Massachusetts, Smith College, and Mount Holyoke). Internships, multidisciplinary dual majors, and study abroad (in the ISEP program, Tibetan Center, or a Costa Rica semester) are offered. All majors are student-designed. Students may complete their programs in fewer than 4 years.

Faculty/Classroom: 50% of faculty are male; 50%, female. All teach undergraduates. The average class size in a regular course is 17.

Requirements: Applicants must submit all transcripts from 9th grade on or GED/state equivalency exam results. Students are required to submit a personal statement and an analytic essay or academic paper. An interview is recommended. AP credits are accepted. Important factors in the admissions decision are personality/intangible qualities, evidence of special talent, and extracurricular activities record.

Procedure: Freshmen are admitted fall and spring. There are early decision, early admissions, and deferred admissions plans. Check with the school or application deadlines. Notification of early decision is sent December 15; regular decision, April 1. The fall 2005 application fee was $55. Applications are accepted on-line.

Transfer: 33 transfer students enrolled in a recent year. A proposed program of study, high school and college transcripts, and 1 recommendation must be submitted.

Visiting: There are regularly scheduled orientations for prospective students, including interviews, information sessions, campus tours, Discover Hampshire Days, Campus Visitation Days, and an overnight program. There are guides for informal visits and visitors may sit in on classes and stay overnight. To schedule a visit, contact the Admissions Office.

Financial Aid: In a recent year, 60% of all full-time freshmen and 54% of continuing full-time students received some form of financial aid. 60% of full-time freshmen and 54% of continuing full-time students received need-based aid. The average freshman award was $26,700. Average annual earnings from campus work were $2300. The average financial indebtedness of the 2005 graduate was $16,975. Hampshire is a member of CSS. The CSS/Profile or FAFSA, the college's own financial statement and the non-custodial parent statement are required. Check with the school for application deadlines.

International Students: In a recent year, there were 43 international students enrolled. The school actively recruits these students. They must score satisfactorily on the TOEFL.

Computers: All students may access the system 24 hours per day via their own PCs or at designated hours in the labs, generally 8 A.M. to midnight, but up to 24 hours at semester's end. There are no time limits and no fees.

Graduates: In a recent year, 273 bachelor's degrees were awarded. The most popular majors were art (9%), film/photo (9%), and theater (6%).

Admissions Contact: Karen S. Parker, Director of Admissions. E-mail: *admissions@hampshire.edu* Web: *www.hampshire.edu*

HARVARD UNIVERSITY/HARVARD COLLEGE D-2

Cambridge, MA 02138 (617) 495-1551; Fax: (617) 495-8821

Full-time: 3505 men, 3135 women	**Faculty:** 837; I, ++$
Part-time: 10 men, 10 women	**Ph.D.s:** 99%
Graduate: 5555 men, 4805 women	**Student/Faculty:** 8 to 1
Year: semesters, summer session	**Tuition:** $32,360
Application Deadline: see profile	**Room & Board:** $13,500
Freshman Class: n/av	
SAT or ACT: required	**MOST COMPETITIVE**

Harvard College is the undergraduate college of Harvard University. Harvard College was founded in 1636. Harvard University also has 10 graduate schools. Figures in the above capsule are approximate. In addition to regional accreditation, Harvard has baccalaureate program accreditation with ABET. The 97 libraries contain 13 million volumes, and subscribe to 100,000 periodicals including electronic. Computerized library services include the card catalog, interlibrary loans, and database searching. Special learning facilities include a learning resource center, art gallery, natural history museum, planetarium, and radio station. The 380-acre campus is in an urban area across the Charles River from Boston. Including any residence halls, there are 400 buildings.

Student Life: 81% of undergraduates are from out of state, mostly the Middle Atlantic. Students are from 50 states, 118 foreign countries, and Canada. 67% are from public schools. 43% are white; 17% Asian American. The average age of freshmen is 18; all undergraduates, 20. 96% of freshmen remain to graduate.

Housing: 6325 students can be accommodated in college housing, which includes coed dormitories and on-campus apartments. On-campus housing is guaranteed for all 4 years. 97% of students live on campus. All students may keep cars.

Activities: There are no fraternities or sororities. There are 250 groups on campus, including art, band, cheerleading, chess, choir, chorale, chorus, computers, dance, debate, drama, ethnic, film, gay, honors, international, jazz band, literary magazine, marching band, musical theater, newspaper, opera, orchestra, pep band, photography, political, professional, radio and TV, religious, social, social service, student government, symphony, and yearbook. Popular campus events include Harvard/Yale football, Head of the Charles crew regatta, and Cultural Rhythms Festival.

Sports: There are 21 intercollegiate sports for men and 20 for women, and 16 intramural sports for men and 16 for women. Facilities include several gyms and athletic centers, pools, a track, boat houses, a sailing center, a hockey rink, and various courts and playing fields.

Disabled Students: Wheelchair ramps, elevators, special parking, specially equipped rest rooms, special class scheduling, lowered drinking fountains, lowered telephones, tutors, adaptive equipment in the field of information technology, TDD/TTY, shuttle van service, a student support organization called ABLE, and an adaptive technology lab are available.

Services: Counseling and information services are available, as is tutoring in every subject. There is a reader service for the blind.

Campus Safety and Security: Measures include 24-hour foot and vehicle patrol, self-defense education, security escort services, and shuttle buses. There are informal discussions, pamphlets/posters/films, emergency telephones, and lighted pathways/sidewalks.

Programs of Study: Harvard confers A.B. and S.B. degrees. Master's and doctoral degrees are also awarded. Bachelor's degrees are awarded in BIOLOGICAL SCIENCE (biochemistry, biology/biological science, and biophysics), COMMUNICATIONS AND THE ARTS (art history and appreciation, Chinese, classics, creative writing, English, fine arts, folklore and mythology, French, German, Greek, Hebrew, Italian, Japanese, Latin, linguistics, literature, music, Portuguese, Russian, and Spanish), COMPUTER AND PHYSICAL SCIENCE (applied mathematics, astronomy, chemistry, computer science, geology, geophysics and seismology, mathematics, physical sciences, physics, and statistics), ENGINEERING AND ENVIRONMENTAL DESIGN (engineering, environmental design, environmental science, and preengineering), SOCIAL SCIENCE (African American studies, American studies, anthropology, Asian/Oriental studies, economics, European studies, history, humanities, Middle Eastern studies, philosophy, political science/government, psychology, religion, Russian and Slavic studies, Sanskrit and Indian studies, social science, social studies, sociology, and women's studies). Economics, government, and biology are the largest.

Required: In 8 semesters, students must pass a minimum of 32 1-semester courses. The average course load is 4 courses per semester, but the course rate may be varied for special reasons. A typical balanced program devotes about one fourth of its courses to core curriculum requirements, one half to the concentration (or major field), and the remaining one fourth to electives.

Special: Students may cross-register with MIT and with other schools within the university, and may design their own concentrations or enroll for nondegree study. Internships and study abroad may be arranged. Accelerated degree programs, dual majors, a 3-2 engineering degree, and a combined A.B.-S.B. in engineering are offered. There are pass/fail options. There is a chapter of Phi Beta Kappa.

Faculty/Classroom: 98% teach undergraduates, 97% do research, and 95% do both. No introductory courses are taught by graduate students. The average class size in a regular course is 25.

Requirements: The SAT or ACT is required, as well as 3 SAT: Subject tests. Applicants need not be high school graduates but are expected to be well prepared academically. An essay and an interview are required, in addition to a transcript, a counselor report, and 2 teacher recommendations from academic disciplines. AP credits are accepted. Important factors in the admissions decision are evidence of special talent, personality/intangible qualities, and recommendations by school officials.

Procedure: Freshmen are admitted in the fall. Entrance exams should be taken by January of the senior year. There are early decision, early admissions, and deferred admissions plans. Check with the school for application deadlines. A waiting list is an active part of the admissions procedure. The fall 2005 application fee was $60.

Transfer: Transfer applicants must have completed at least 1 full year of daytime study in a degree-granting program at 1 institution. Students are required to submit the SAT or ACT, 2 letters of recommendation, high school and college transcripts with a dean's report, and several essays. 16 of 32 credits required for the bachelor's degree must be completed at Harvard.

Visiting: There are regularly scheduled orientations for prospective students, consisting of group information sessions and tours. There are guides for informal visits and visitors may sit in on classes and stay overnight. To schedule a visit, contact the Undergraduate Admissions Office.

Financial Aid: In a recent year, 80% of all full-time freshmen and 69% of continuing full-time students received some form of financial aid. 51% of full-time freshmen and 46% of continuing full-time students received need-based aid. The average freshman award was $26,465. Need-based scholarships or need-based grants averaged $24,904; and need-based self-help aid (loans and jobs) averaged $1561. 70% of undergraduates worked part time. Harvard is a member of CSS. The CSS/Profile or FAFSA, the college's own financial statement and the federal tax forms are required. Check with the school for application deadlines.

International Students: The school actively recruits these students. They must take the TOEFL and also take the SAT or the ACT. Students must take SAT: Subject tests in any 3 subjects.

Computers: All students may access the system 24 hours per day. There are no time limits and no fees.

Admissions Contact: Marlyn McGrath Lewis, Director of Admissions. A video is available. E-mail: *college@harvard.edu* Web: *www.college.harvard.edu*

HELLENIC COLLEGE/HOLY CROSS GREEK ORTHODOX SCHOOL OF THEOLOGY D-2

Brookline, MA 02445 (617) 731-3500, ext.1260 Fax: (617) 850-1460

Full-time: 51 men, 33 women	**Faculty:** 13
Part-time: none	**Ph.D.s:** 90%
Graduate: 95 men, 19 women	**Student/Faculty:** 6 to 1
Year: semesters	**Tuition:** $15,715
Application Deadline: May 1	**Room & Board:** $9260
Freshman Class: 37 applied, 34 accepted, 20 enrolled	
SAT or ACT: required	**COMPETITIVE**

Hellenic College, founded in 1937, is a private college affiliated with the Greek Orthodox Church. It offers programs in the classics, elementary education, religious studies, human development, and management and leadership. In addition to regional accreditation, HCHC has baccalaureate program accreditation with NASDTEC. The library contains 75,000 volumes, 863 microform items, and 2849 audio/video tapes/CDs/DVDs, and subscribes to 723 periodicals including electronic. Computerized library services include the card catalog, interlibrary loans, database searching, and Internet access. Special learning facilities include archives, rare books, a Greek cultural center, a language lab, and a museum. The 52-acre campus is in an urban area 4 miles southwest of Boston. Including any residence halls, there are 7 buildings.

Student Life: 95% of undergraduates are from out of state, mostly the Midwest. Students are from 29 states and 8 foreign countries. 98% are from public schools. 97% are white; 20% foreign nationals. Most are Greek or Eastern Orthodox.; 10% Catholic; 10% claim no religious affiliation. The average age of freshmen is 20; all undergraduates, 25. 3% do not continue beyond their first year; 93% remain to graduate.

Housing: 220 students can be accommodated in college housing, which includes coed dorms, on-campus apartments, and married-student housing. On-campus housing is guaranteed for all 4 years. 95% of students live on campus; of those, 95% remain on campus on weekends. Alcohol is not permitted. All students may keep cars.

Activities: There are no fraternities or sororities. There are 9 groups on campus, including choir, ethnic, photography, religious, social, social service, student government, and yearbook. Popular campus events include Feast of the Holy Cross, Matriculation Day, and Campus Christmas Party.

Sports: There are 4 intramural sports for men and 3 for women. Facilities include a gym, tennis, basketball, and racquetball courts, and a soccer field.

Disabled Students: 10% of the campus is accessible. Wheelchair ramps, elevators, special parking, specially equipped rest rooms, and lowered drinking fountains are available.

Services: Counseling and information services are available, as is tutoring in some subjects, including Greek and music writing and composition. There is remedial math, reading, and writing.

Campus Safety and Security: Measures include shuttle buses, informal discussions, pamphlets/posters/films, lighted pathways/sidewalks, and a 16-hour security patrol.

Programs of Study: HCHC confers the B.A. degree. Master's degrees are also awarded. Bachelor's degrees are awarded in BUSINESS (business administration and management), COMMUNICATIONS AND THE ARTS (classics), EDUCATION (elementary), SOCIAL SCIENCE (human development and religion). Religious studies and elementary education are the strongest academically. Religious studies and human development are the largest.

Required: To graduate, students must complete 129 credits, with 39 in the major, and maintain a minimum overall GPA of 2.0. General education requirements include 72 credits, with courses in English language and literature, music, history, science, philosophy, and social science.

Special: The college offers cross-registration with Boston Theological Institute, Newbury College, and Boston College, credit by examination, and study abroad in Greece.

Faculty/Classroom: 50% of faculty are male; 50%, female. All teach undergraduates. No introductory courses are taught by graduate students. The average class size in an introductory lecture is 20; in a laboratory, 20; and in a regular course, 15.

Admissions: 92% of the 2005-2006 applicants were accepted. The SAT scores for the 2005-2006 freshman class were: Verbal--30% below 500, 50% between 500 and 599, and 20% between 600 and 700; Math--40% below 500, 30% between 500 and 599, and 30% between 600 and 700. There were 2 National Merit finalists in a recent year.

Requirements: The SAT or ACT is required. In addition, applicants should graduate from an accredited secondary school or have a GED. 15 academic credits are required, including 4 units of English, 2 each of math, foreign language, and social studies, and 1 of science. An essay is required. A GPA of 2.5 is required. AP and CLEP credits are accepted. Important factors in the admissions decision are recommendations by school officials, advanced placement or honor courses, and recommendations by alumni.

Procedure: Freshmen are admitted fall and spring. There are early decision and deferred admissions plans. There is a rolling admission plan. Early decision applications should be filed by December 1; regular applications, by May 1 for fall entry and December 1 for spring entry. The fall 2005 application fee was $50. Notification of early decision is sent February 1; regular decision, on a rolling basis. 12 early decision candidates were accepted for the 2005-2006 class.

Transfer: 9 transfer students enrolled in 2004-2005. The SAT, an essay, recommendation letters, high school transcripts, an interview, and a health certificate are required. 60 of 129 credits required for the bachelor's degree must be completed at HCHC.

Visiting: There are regularly scheduled orientations for prospective students, including observation of classroom and student life. There are guides for informal visits and visitors may sit in on classes and stay overnight. To schedule a visit, contact Agnes Desses, Office of Admissions at *admissions@hchc.edu.*

Financial Aid: In 2005-2006, 95% of all full-time students received some form of financial aid. 95% of all full-time students received need-based aid. Need-based scholarships or need-based grants averaged $13,000 ($18,000 maximum), and need-based self-help aid (loans and jobs) averaged $3500 ($7500 maximum). 34% of undergraduates work part time. The average financial indebtedness of the 2005 graduate was $31,000. The FAFSA and the college's own financial statement are required. The priority date for freshman financial aid applications for fall entry is April 1. The deadline for filing freshman financial aid applications for fall entry is July 1.

International Students: There are 16 international students enrolled. They must score satisfactorily on the written TOEFL .

Computers: All students may access the system. There are no time limits and no fees.

Graduates: From July 1, 2004 to June 30, 2005, 21 bachelor's degrees were awarded. The most popular majors were religious studies (50%), elementary education (25%), and human development (25%). In an average class, 97% graduate in 4 years or less, and 100% graduate in 5 years or less. Of the 2004 graduating class, 60% were enrolled in graduate school within 6 months of graduation and 30% were employed.

Admissions Contact: Agnes Desses, Assistant Director, Admissions. A video is available. E-mail: *admissions@hchc.edu* Web: *www.hchc.edu*

LASELL COLLEGE — D-2

Newton, MA 02466

(617) 243-2225
(888) LASELL-4; Fax: (617) 243-2380

Full-time: 285 men, 775 women	**Faculty:** 46; IIB, -$
Part-time: 15 men, 20 women	**Ph.D.s:** 38%
Graduate: 20 men and women	**Student/Faculty:** 23 to 1
Year: semesters	**Tuition:** $17,700
Application Deadline: open	**Room & Board:** $8550
Freshman Class: n/av	
SAT Verbal/Math: required	**COMPETITIVE**

Lasell College, founded in 1851, is a private nonsecular institution whose curriculum combines classroom study with practical experience in the sciences, business, education, and health fields. There are 3 undergraduate schools and 1 graduate school. Figures in the above capsule are approximate. In addition to regional accreditation, Lasell has baccalaureate program accreditation with CAAHEP, NAEYC. The library contains 55,335 volumes, 48,197 microform items, and 2560 audio/video tapes/CDs/DVDs, and subscribes to 494 periodicals including electronic. Computerized library services include the card catalog, interlibrary loans, database searching, and Internet access. Special learning facilities include a learning resource center, art gallery, an early childhood curriculum library, Lasell Village (retirement community), a nursery school, and a daycare center. The 50-acre campus is in a suburban area 8 miles west of Boston. Including any residence halls, there are 42 buildings.

Student Life: 56% of undergraduates are from Massachusetts. Others are from 20 states, 8 foreign countries, and Canada. 95% are from public schools. 73% are white. 39% are Catholic; 30% Protestant; 25% claim no religious affiliation. The average age of freshmen is 18; all undergraduates, 21. 32% do not continue beyond their first year; 55% remain to graduate.

Housing: 850 students can be accommodated in college housing, which includes single-sex and coed dormitories and on-campus apartments. In addition, there are special-interest houses. On-campus housing is guaranteed for all 4 years. 80% of students live on campus; of those, 80% remain on campus on weekends. All students may keep cars.

Activities: There are no fraternities or sororities. There are 30 groups on campus, including cheerleading, chorale, chorus, dance, drama, ethnic, gay, honors, international, literary magazine, newspaper, political, professional, social, social service, student government, and yearbook. Popular campus events include River Day, Torchlight Parade, and Awards Night.

Sports: There are 5 intercollegiate sports for men and 7 for women, and 3 intramural sports for men and 3 for women. Facilities include an athletic center with a basketball court, a volleyball court, an indoor track, a dance studio, an exercise room, locker rooms, and 2 athletic fields.

Disabled Students: 50% of the campus is accessible. Wheelchair ramps, elevators, special parking, specially equipped rest rooms, lowered drinking fountains, and lowered telephones are available.

Services: Counseling and information services are available, as is tutoring in most subjects. There is remedial math and writing, and books on tape.

Campus Safety and Security: Measures include 24-hour foot and vehicle patrol, self-defense education, shuttle buses, and informal discussions. There are pamphlets/posters/films, emergency telephones, and lighted pathways/sidewalks.

Programs of Study: Lasell confers B.A. and B.S. degrees. Master's degrees are also awarded. Bachelor's degrees are awarded in BUSINESS (accounting, banking and finance, business administration and management, fashion merchandising, hospitality management services, hotel/motel and restaurant management, international business management, management information systems, marketing/retailing/merchandising, sports management, and tourism), COMPUTER AND PHYSICAL SCIENCE (computer science), EDUCATION (athletic training, early childhood, elementary, and secondary), HEALTH PROFESSIONS (exercise science and health care administration), SOCIAL SCIENCE (child care/child and family studies, criminal justice, fashion design and technology, human services, law, liberal arts/general studies, paralegal studies, physical fitness/movement, psychology, and sociology). Allied health is the strongest academically. Business, education, and criminal justice are the largest.

Required: To graduate, students must complete 124 credit hours with a minimum GPA of 2.0. Requirements include 2 courses in writing and math, one course in literature, art, music, or drama, one in history, philosophy, or language, one in social science, one in science, and a computer literacy course. An internship is also required.

Special: Internships are built into the curriculum, and work-study programs are available on campus. Student-designed majors and student-arranged study-abroad programs are possible. All programs feature connected learning, which is an ongoing practical application of classroom theory. There is a freshman honors program.

Faculty/Classroom: 33% of faculty are male; 67%, female. All teach undergraduates. No introductory courses are taught by graduate stu-

dents. The average class size in an introductory lecture is 20; in a laboratory, 11; and in a regular course, 15.

Requirements: The SAT is required. In addition, applicants should have completed 16 Carnegie units of high school study. The GED is accepted. A letter of recommendation is required and an interview is recommended. A GPA of 2.0 is required. AP and CLEP credits are accepted. Important factors in the admissions decision are advanced placement or honor courses, personality/intangible qualities, and leadership record.

Procedure: Freshmen are admitted fall and spring. Application deadlines are open. There is a rolling admissionsplan. Application fee is Freshmen are admitted fall and spring. Application deadlines are open. There is a rolling admissions plan. Application fee is $40. Applications are accepted on-line.

Transfer: 73 transfer students enrolled in a recent year. Applicants must have a minimum of 2.0 GPA. 45 of 124 credits required for the bachelor's degree must be completed at Lasell.

Visiting: There are regularly scheduled orientations for prospective students, consisting of the president's welcome, faculty presentations, tours, and student panels. There are guides for informal visits and visitors may sit in on classes and stay overnight. To schedule a visit, contact the Office of Admission.

Financial Aid: In a recent year, 89% of all full-time freshmen and 88% of continuing full-time students received some form of financial aid. 82% of full-time freshmen and 86% of continuing full-time students received need-based aid. The average freshman award was $15,800. 32% of undergraduates worked part time. Lasell is a member of CSS. The FAFSA and the college's own financial statement are required. Check with the school for application deadlines.

International Students: In a recent year there were 30 international students enrolled. They must score satisfactorily on the TOEFL.

Computers: All students may access the system 24 hours/day, 7 days/week. There are no time limits and no fees.

Graduates: In a recent year, 67 bachelor's degrees were awarded. The most popular majors were business (26%), education (21%), and fashion (18%). In an average class, 55% graduate in 4 years or less. Of a recent graduating class, 20% were enrolled in graduate school within 6 months of graduation and 90% were employed.

Admissions Contact: James M. Tweed, Director of Admission. E-mail: *info@lasell.edu* Web: *www.lasell.edu*

LESLEY UNIVERSITY	D-2
Cambridge, MA 02138-2790	**(617) 349-8800**
	(800) 999-1959; Fax: (617) 349-8810

Full-time: 232 men, 791 women	Faculty: 53
Part-time: 61 men, 181 women	Ph.Ds: 78%
Graduate: 755 men, 5278 women	Student/Faculty: 19 to 1
Year: semesters, summer session	Tuition: $24,450
Application Deadline: March 1	Room & Board: $10,500
Freshman Class: 1664 applied, 1116 accepted, 361 enrolled	
SAT Verbal/Math: 538/510*	COMPETITIVE

Lesley University, founded in 1909, is a private, primarily women's undergraduate institution, offering degree programs in education, human services, and the arts. Expanded resources, course work, and opportunities are available to students through the larger coeducational Lesley University system, including cross-registration with the Art Institute of Boston There are 3 undergraduate and 2 graduate schools. In addition to regional accreditation, Lesley has baccalaureate program accreditation with AACTE, CACREP, NASAD, and TEAC.. The 2 libraries contain 113,861 volumes, 878,562 microform items, and 46,600 audio/video tapes/CDs/DVDs, and subscribe to 861 periodicals including electronic. Computerized library services include the card catalog, interlibrary loans, database searching, Internet access, and laptop Internet portals. Special learning facilities include a learning resource center, art gallery, center for teaching resources, media production facility, instructional computing, and math achievement center. The 5-acre campus is in an urban area just outside of Harvard Square in Cambridge. Including any residence halls, there are 53 buildings.

Student Life: 52% of undergraduates are from out of state, mostly the Northeast. Students are from 34 states, 10 foreign countries, and Canada. 83% are from public schools. 73% are white. The average age of freshmen is 18; all undergraduates, 21. 21% do not continue beyond their first year; 79% remain to graduate.

Housing: 600 students can be accommodated in college housing, which includes single-sex dorms. In addition, there are special-interest houses, a wellness floor, a substance-free floor, and a mind, body, and spirit house. On-campus housing is guaranteed for all 4 years. No one may keep cars.

Activities: There are no fraternities or sororities. There are 25 groups on campus, including choir, chorus, dance, drama, ethnic, gay, international, literary magazine, musical theater, newspaper, photography, political, professional, religious, Second Start, Student Athlete Advisory Committee, social, social service, student government, and Third Wave

(a women's group). Popular campus events include Family and Friends Weekend, Quad Fest, and World Fest.

Sports: There are 4 intercollegiate sports for men and 5 for women, and 3 intramural sports for men and 3 for women. Facilities include outdoor tennis courts, and a fitness center with Nautilus circuit, free weights, and cardiovascular equipment. Students may also use an Olympic-size swimming pool at a nearby school as well as the indoor and outdoor facilities at a nearby school, including two full size basketball courts, two racquetball courts, a rowing tank, a softball court, an indoor track, and a lighted outdoor soccer field.

Disabled Students: 85% of the campus is accessible. Wheelchair ramps, elevators, special parking, specially equipped rest rooms, special class scheduling, and lowered drinking fountains. The Disability Services Office provides document review and arranges for reasonable accommodations for special needs students.

Services: Counseling and information services are available, as is tutoring in most subjects. There is a reader service for the blind remedial math, study skills, and interpreter services.

Campus Safety and Security: Measures include 24-hour foot and vehicle patrol, self-defense education, security escort services, and shuttle buses. There are informal discussions, pamphlets/posters/films, emergency telephones, lighted pathways/sidewalks, and and watch tours.

Programs of Study: Lesley confers B.S., B.F.A. degrees. Associate, master's, and doctoral degrees are also awarded. Bachelor's degrees are awarded in BUSINESS (management science), COMMUNICATIONS AND THE ARTS (visual and performing arts), COMPUTER AND PHYSICAL SCIENCE (natural sciences), EDUCATION (early childhood, elementary, middle school, and special), SOCIAL SCIENCE (human services, humanities, psychology, and social science). Education, counseling, and photography and art therapy are the largest.

Required: Students must complete 45 hours of general education requirements, including 15 of humanities, 12 of natural science, 9 of social science, 6 of multicultural perspectives, and 3 of first-year seminar; emphasis is given to cross-curriculum components in writing, critical and quantitative reasoning, global perspectives, and leadership and ethics. Art Institute of Boston students must also complete a foundation year. To graduate, students need 128 total credit hours, including 30 to 33 in the liberal arts majors or 41 to 43 in professional majors, with a minimum 2.0 GPA.

Special: Study abroad in Cuba, England, and Sweden, and 6 others by arrangement, a Washington Justice semester, and on-campus work-study programs are offered. All students participate in at least 3 field placement experiences, beginning in their freshman year. There are combined accelerated degree programs in management, counseling, and education majors. Dual majors and student-designed majors are also available. Accelerated and weekend course programs as well as cross-registration with AIB are offered for Adult Baccalaureate College and School of Management degree programs. There is a freshman honors program.

Faculty/Classroom: 45% of faculty are male; 55%, female. All both teach and do research. No introductory courses are taught by graduate students. The average class size in an introductory lecture is 20; in a laboratory, 14; and in a regular course, 14.

Admissions: 67% of the 2005-2006 applicants were accepted. The SAT scores for the 2005-2006 freshman class were: Verbal--30% below 500, 43% between 500 and 599, 26% between 600 and 700, and 1% above 700; Math--42% below 500, 43% between 500 and 599, and 15% between 600 and 700. 50% of the current freshmen were in the top fifth of their class; 78% were in the top two fifths.

Requirements: The SAT or ACT is required. In addition, it is recommended that students complete 20 academic units in high school, including 4 in English, 3 in science, 3 in math, and 2 in U.S. history. SAT or ACT scores, a writing sample, and 2 recommendations are also required as part of the application; a personal interview is recommended. Applicants must have a high school diploma from an accredited secondary school or a GED. AP and CLEP credits are accepted. Important factors in the admissions decision are advanced placement or honor courses, leadership record, and recommendations by school officials.

Procedure: Freshmen are admitted fall and spring. Entrance exams should be taken by March 1. There are early action, deferred admissions, and rolling admissions plans. Early action applications should be filed by December 1; regular applications, by March 1 for fall entry and December 15 for spring entry, along with a $40 fee. Notification of early action is sent January 1; regular decision, on a rolling basis. 18 applicants were on the 2005 waiting list; 6 were admitted. Applications are accepted on-line.

Transfer: 94 transfer students enrolled in 2004-2005. Applicants must have a minimum 2.5 GPA, provide high school and college transcripts, complete an essay or personal statement, and have a statement of good standing from prior institution. An interview is recommended for all Lesley College students and required of all Art Institute of Boston students. 68 of 128 credits required for the bachelor's degree must be completed at Lesley.

Visiting: There are regularly scheduled orientations for prospective students, includes personal interviews with professional staff, student campus tours, information sessions, class visits, and meetings with financial aid. There are guides for informal visits and visitors may sit in on classes and stay overnight. To schedule a visit, contact Lesley College Admissions, AIB Admissions at *lcadmissions@lesley.edu* or *admissions@aiboston.edu*.

Financial Aid: In 2005-2006, 92% of all full-time freshmen and 81% of continuing full-time students received some form of financial aid. 76% of full-time freshmen and 67% of continuing full-time students received need-based aid. The average freshman award was $16,791. Need-based scholarships or need-based grants averaged $12,741; need-based self-help aid (loans and jobs) averaged $4329; and other non-need-based awards and non-need-based scholarships averaged $5938. 27% of undergraduates work part time. Average annual earnings from campus work are $1800. The average financial indebtedness of the 2005 graduate was $13,650. The FAFSA, the college's own financial statement and the parent and student federal tax returns are required. The priority date for freshman financial aid applications for fall entry is March 1.

International Students: There are 33 international students enrolled. The school actively recruits these students. A satisfactory score is required on the written TOEFL.

Computers: Wireless access is available. The university offers students 12 computer labs, each with an average of 15 computers. In addition, Internet access is provided in all classrooms, dorms and lounge areas and wireless access is available in 50% of all classrooms. A campuswide network is in place which gives all students access to course and extracurricular activity information free of charge. All students may access the system 24/7, except for some computer labs. There are no time limits and no fees.

Graduates: From July 1, 2004 to June 30, 2005, 422 bachelor's degrees were awarded. The most popular majors were education/liberal studies (40%), business/marketing (22%), and visual and performing arts (20%). In an average class, 72% graduate in 4 years or less, 91% graduate in 5 years or less, and 98% graduate in 6 years or less. 28 companies recruited on campus in 2004-2005. Of the 2004 graduating class, 38% were enrolled in graduate school within 6 months of graduation and 91% were employed.

Admissions Contact: Deb Kocar, Director of Admissions, Lesley College or Bonnie Roth Director of Admissions, Art Institute of Boston. E-mail:*lcadmission@lesley.edu, admissions@aiboston.edu*
Web: *http://www.lesley.edu/Ichttp://www.aiboston.edu*

MASSACHUSETTS BOARD OF HIGHER EDUCATION

The Massachusetts Board of Higher Education, established in 1980, is a public system in Massachusetts. It is governed by a 16-member board of regents appointed by the governor., whose chief administrator is chancellor. The primary goal of the system is the central governing authority for the state's public higher education system. The total enrollment in fall 2005 of all 29 campuses is usually about 170,000. Profiles of the 4-year campuses are included in this section.

MASSACHUSETTS COLLEGE OF ART   E-2

Boston, MA 02115	(617) 879-7222; Fax: (617) 879-7250
Full-time: 497 men, 862 women	Faculty: 86
Part-time: 69 men, 121 women	Ph.D.s: 71%
Graduate: 41 men, 88 women	Student/Faculty: 16 to 1
Year: semesters, summer session	Tuition: $6850 ($19,200)
Application Deadline: February 15	Room & Board: $9800
Freshman Class: 1210 applied, 735 accepted, 265 enrolled	
SAT Verbal/Math: 570/540*	ACT: 23 SPECIAL

Massachusetts College of Art, founded in 1873, is a public institution offering undergraduate and graduate programs in art, design, and education. In addition to regional accreditation, MassArt has baccalaureate program accreditation with NASAD. The library contains 231,586 volumes and 8700 microform items, and subscribes to 757 periodicals including electronic. Computerized library services include the card catalog, interlibrary loans, database searching, and Internet access. Special learning facilities include an art gallery, a computer arts center, performance spaces, and film viewing rooms. The 5-acre campus is in an urban area in Boston. Including any residence halls, there are 6 buildings.

Student Life: 71% of undergraduates are from Massachusetts. Others are from 27 states, 28 foreign countries, and Canada. 85% are from public schools. 70% are white. The average age of freshmen is 18; all undergraduates, 23. 15% do not continue beyond their first year; 65% remain to graduate.

Housing: 375 students can be accommodated in college housing, which includes coed dorms and on-campus apartments. In addition, there is a visual art college residence hall with ventilated workrooms, a visiting artist suite, and gallery space. On-campus housing is guaranteed for the freshman year only, is available on a first-come, first-served basis, and is available on a lottery system for upperclassmen. Priority is given to out-of-town students. 74% of students commute. Alcohol is not permitted. No one may keep cars.

Activities: There are no fraternities or sororities. There are 30 groups on campus, including art, computers, ethnic, film, gay, international, literary magazine, newspaper, photography, political, professional, radio and TV, social, social service, student government, and yearbook. Popular campus events include Eventworks, First Night Ice Sculpture, and gallery exhibitions and openings.

Sports: There are 7 intercollegiate sports for men and 6 for women, and 8 intramural sports for men and 6 for women. Facilities include a gym, a fitness center, and courts for squash, volleyball, and basketball.

Disabled Students: 95% of the campus is accessible. Wheelchair ramps, elevators, special parking, specially equipped rest rooms, special class scheduling, lowered drinking fountains, and lowered telephones are available.

Services: There is remedial reading and writing.

Campus Safety and Security: Measures include 24-hour foot and vehicle patrol, self-defense education, security escort services, and shuttle buses. There are informal discussions, pamphlets/posters/films, emergency telephones, and lighted pathways/sidewalks.

Programs of Study: MassArt confers the B.F.A. degree. Master's degrees are also awarded. Bachelor's degrees are awarded in COMMUNICATIONS AND THE ARTS (animation, art history and appreciation, ceramic art and design, fiber/textiles/weaving, film arts, fine arts, glass, graphic design, illustration, industrial design, media arts, metal/jewelry, painting, photography, printmaking, sculpture, and studio art), EDUCATION (art), ENGINEERING AND ENVIRONMENTAL DESIGN (architecture), SOCIAL SCIENCE (fashion design and technology). Painting, illustration, and graphic design are the largest.

Required: A total of 120 semester credits is required for graduation; the minimum GPA varies by major. Typically, students take 42 credits in liberal arts, 18 in studio foundations, 36 in the major, and 24 in electives. Beginning in the sophomore year, the student's work is reviewed by panels of faculty and visiting artists.

Special: MassArt offers cross-registration with several consortiums, internships for advanced students, on- and off-campus work-study programs, study-abroad and foreign-exchange programs, an open major for exceptional students, and dual majors in most combinations of concentrations.

Faculty/Classroom: 51% of faculty are male; 49%, female. All teach undergraduates. No introductory courses are taught by graduate students. The average class size in an introductory lecture is 23; in a laboratory, 12; and in a regular course, 14.

Admissions: 61% of the 2005-2006 applicants were accepted. The SAT scores for the 2005-2006 freshman class were: Verbal--17% below 500, 50% between 500 and 599, 29% between 600 and 700, and 4% above 700; Math--32% below 500, 49% between 500 and 599, 18% between 600 and 700, and 1% above 700. The ACT scores were 9% below 21, 45% between 21 and 23, 36% between 24 and 26, and 10% between 27 and 28. 40% of the current freshmen were in the top fifth of their class; 73% were in the top two fifths.

Requirements: The SAT is required. In addition, applicants should be graduates of an accredited secondary school or have earned the GED. College preparatory studies should include as a minimum 4 years of English; 2 each of social studies, math, and science; 2 academic electives, 1 each of math or science and 1 art elective; and a foreign language. A personal essay and portfolio are required, and an interview and letters of reference are recommended. A GPA of 3.0 is required. AP and CLEP credits are accepted. Important factors in the admissions decision are evidence of special talent, recommendations by school officials, and personality/intangible qualities.

Procedure: Freshmen are admitted fall and spring. Entrance exams should be taken in early fall of the senior year. There are early decision, early admissions, and deferred admissions plans. There is a rolling admissions plan. Early decision applications should be filed by December 1; regular applications--by February 15 for fall entry and November 1 for spring entry, along with a $30 fee ($65 for out-of-state applicants). Notification of early decision is sent December 20; regular decision, April 1. 13 early decision candidates were accepted for a recent year. A waiting list is an active part of the admissions procedure. Applications are accepted on-line.

Transfer: 176 transfer students enrolled in 2004-2005. Applicants must submit secondary school and postsecondary school transcripts, a statement of purpose, and a portfolio of at least 15 pieces, preferably in slides. An interview is recommended. 60 of 120 credits required for the bachelor's degree must be completed at MassArt.

Visiting: There are regularly scheduled orientations for prospective students, including an information session and a campus tour. There are guides for informal visits and visitors may sit in on classes. To schedule a visit, contact the Admissions Office.

Financial Aid: In a recent year, 75% of all full-time freshmen and 65% of continuing full-time students received some form of financial aid. 60% of full-time freshmen and 68% of continuing full-time students received need-based aid. The average freshman award was $9741. Need-based scholarships or need-based grants averaged $3603; need-based self-help aid (loans and jobs) averaged $3194; and other non-need-based awards and non-need-based scholarships averaged $3083. 84% of undergraduates work part time. Average annual earnings from campus work are $1000. The average financial indebtedness of a recent year's graduate was $18,337. The CSS/Profile, FAFSA, FFS, or SFS is required. The deadline for filing freshman financial aid applications for fall entry is May 1.

International Students: There are 56 international students enrolled. They are required to take the TOEFL. They may take the SAT or ACT in lieu of the TOEFL.

Computers: Wireless access is available. All students may access the system. There are no time limits.

Graduates: From July 1, 2004 to June 30, 2005, 285 bachelor's degrees were awarded. The most popular majors were painting (11%), graphic design/studio for interrelated media (10%), and photography (10%). In an average class, 1% graduate in 3 years or less, 25% graduate in 4 years or less, 45% graduate in 5 years or less, and 53% graduate in 6 years or less. 8 companies recruited on campus in 2004-2005. Of the 2004 graduating class, 2% were enrolled in graduate school within 6 months of graduation and 91% were employed.

Admissions Contact: Kay Ransdell, Dean of Admissions. A video is available. E-mail: *admissions@massart.edu*
Web: *http://www.massart.edu*

MASSACHUSETTS COLLEGE OF LIBERAL ARTS   A-1
North Adams, MA 01247-4100   **(413) 662-5410**
         (800) 292-6632; Fax: (413) 662-5179

Full-time: 450 men, 640 women	**Faculty:** 84
Part-time: 100 men, 210 women	**Ph.D.s:** 73%
Graduate: 50 men, 80 women	**Student/Faculty:** 13 to 1
Year: semesters, summer session	**Tuition:** $3500 ($11,900)
Application Deadline: open	**Room & Board:** $5225
Freshman Class: n/av	
SAT or ACT: required	**LESS COMPETITIVE**

Massachusetts College of Liberal Arts, founded in 1894, is a liberal arts institution emphasizing business and education courses. Figures in above capsule and in this profile are approximate. In addition to regional accreditation, MCLA has baccalaureate program accreditation with NCATE. The library contains 168,225 volumes, 312,298 microform items, and 6645 audio/video tapes/CDs/DVDs, and subscribes to 583 periodicals including electronic. Computerized library services include the card catalog, interlibrary loans, and database searching. Special learning facilities include a learning resource center, art gallery, radio station, and TV station. The 80-acre campus is in a rural area 45 miles east of Albany. Including any residence halls, there are 19 buildings.

Student Life: 84% of undergraduates are from Massachusetts. Others are from 20 states, 5 foreign countries, and Canada. 80% are from public schools. 91% are white. The average age of freshmen is 19; all undergraduates, 24. 28% do not continue beyond their first year; 35% remain to graduate.

Housing: 1100 students can be accommodated in college housing, which includes single-sex and coed dormitories and on-campus apartments. On-campus housing is guaranteed for all 4 years. Upperclassmen may keep cars.

Activities: 4% of men belong to 2 local and 1 national fraternity; 9% of women belong to 2 local and 3 national sororities. There are 50 groups on campus, including band, cheerleading, choir, chorus, computers, dance, drama, ethnic, gay, honors, international, jazz band, literary magazine, musical theater, newspaper, photography, political, professional, radio and TV, religious, social, social service, student government, and yearbook. Popular campus events include Parents Weekend and Winter Carnival.

Sports: There are 6 intercollegiate sports for men and 6 for women, and 10 intramural sports for men and 10 for women. Facilities include a campus center with a swimming pool, weight rooms, a fitness center, and handball, squash, and racquetball courts; an outdoor complex with tennis courts and soccer, baseball, and softball fields; a 1750-seat gym; and a 5-mile cross-country running trail.

Disabled Students: 80% of the campus is accessible. Wheelchair ramps, elevators, special parking, specially equipped rest rooms, and special class scheduling are available.

Services: Counseling and information services are available, as is tutoring in some subjects, including most general education requirements. There is remedial math, reading, and writing. The Tutoring Exchange Network has qualified peers tutoring small groups.

Campus Safety and Security: Measures include 24-hour foot and vehicle patrol, self-defense education, security escort services, and informal discussions. There are pamphlets/posters/films, emergency telephones, and lighted pathways/sidewalks.

Programs of Study: MCLA confers B.A. and B.S. degrees. Master's degrees are also awarded. Bachelor's degrees are awarded in BIOLOGICAL SCIENCE (biology/biological science), BUSINESS (business administration and management), COMMUNICATIONS AND THE ARTS (English and fine arts), COMPUTER AND PHYSICAL SCIENCE (com-

puter science, mathematics, and physics), EDUCATION (education), SOCIAL SCIENCE (history, interdisciplinary studies, philosophy, psychology, and sociology). English, education, and biology are the strongest academically. Business and education are the largest.

Required: All students must complete at least 120 credits, including 50 in a core curriculum, and maintain a GPA of at least 2.0. Phys ed and computer science courses are required.

Special: MCLA offers cross-registration with Williams College and Berkshire Community College, dual majors, internships in all majors, and study abroad in many countries within the International College Program. Student-designed majors, pass/fail options, nondegree study, and independent study also are available. There are 8 national honor societies, a freshman honors program, and 6 departmental honors programs.

Faculty/Classroom: 69% of faculty are male; 31%, female. All teach undergraduates. No introductory courses are taught by graduate students. The average class size in an introductory lecture is 20; in a laboratory, 9; and in a regular course, 19.

Requirements: The SAT or ACT is required. An eligibility index is used to determine a minimum SAT score. Applicants should have completed 16 Carnegie units, including 4 courses in English, 3 each in science and math, and 2 each in foreign language, history/social science, and electives. The GED is accepted. A GPA of 2.0 is required. AP and CLEP credits are accepted. Important factors in the admissions decision are advanced placement or honor courses, evidence of special talent, and parents or siblings attending the school.

Procedure: Freshmen are admitted fall and spring. Entrance exams should be taken by January of the senior year. There are early decision deferred admissions and rolling admissions plans. Application deadlines are open. Application fee is $25.

Transfer: Applicants who have a minimum of 12 semester hours from an accredited college are eligible. Students are evaluated on the basis of past college records, which must include a GPA of at least 2.5 with fewer than 25 credits or a 2.0 with 25 credits or more. 30 of 120 credits required for the bachelor's degree must be completed at MCLA.

Visiting: There are regularly scheduled orientations for prospective students, including a 2-day, overnight program for students who have been accepted. There are guides for informal visits and visitors may sit in on classes. To schedule a visit, contact the Admissions Office.

Financial Aid: MCLA is a member of CSS. The FAFSA, the college's own financial statement are required. Check with the school for application deadlines.

International Students: The school actively recruits these students. They must score satisfactorily on the TOEFL and also take the SAT.

Computers: All students may access the system. Students may access the system Limits on student access to the system vary with the time of year. The fee is $25 per year.

Admissions Contact: Denise C. Richardello, Dean of Enrollment Management. A video is available. E-mail: *admissions@mcla.mass.edu*
Web: *www.mcla.mass.edu*

MASSACHUSETTS COLLEGE OF PHARMACY AND HEALTH SCIENCES   E-2
Boston, MA 02115   **(617) 732-2850**
         (800) 225-5506; Fax: (617) 732-2118

Full-time: 556 men, 1208 women	**Faculty:** 162
Part-time: 34 men, 88 women	**Ph.D.s:** 83%
Graduate: 323 men, 687 women	**Student/Faculty:** 18 to 1
Year: semesters, summer session	**Tuition:** $21,050
Application Deadline: February 1	**Room & Board:** $10,970
Freshman Class: 1200 applied, 917 accepted, 423 enrolled	
SAT Verbal/Math: 532/575*	**ACT:** 22 **SPECIAL**

The Massachusetts College of Pharmacy and Health Sciences, established in 1823, is a private institution offering undergraduate programs in chemistry, the pharmaceutical sciences, and the health sciences. There are 3 undergraduate schools and 1 graduate school. In addition to regional accreditation, MCPHS has baccalaureate program accreditation with ACPE, ADA, ARC-PA, CCNE, JRCNMT and JRCERT.. The library contains 15,000 volumes and 525 audio/video tapes/CDs/DVDs, and subscribes to 125 periodicals including electronic. Computerized library services include the card catalog, interlibrary loans, database searching, Internet access, laptop Internet portals and access to 1.5 million documents through consortium resources. Special learning facilities include a learning resource center and a pharmacy lab, and a dental hygeine clinic. The 2-acre campus is in an urban area 1 mile from Boston's center. Including any residence halls, there are 3 buildings.

Student Life: 55% of undergraduates are from Massachusetts. Others are from 35 states, 34 foreign countries, and Canada. 50% are white; 33% Asian American. The average age of freshmen is 18; all undergraduates, 21. 12% do not continue beyond their first year; 77% remain to graduate.

Housing: 720 students can be accommodated in college housing, which includes single-sex and coed dormitories and on-campus apartments. On-campus housing is guaranteed for the freshman year only, is available on a first-come, first-served basis, and is available on a lottery system for upperclassmen. 66% of students commute. Alcohol is not permitted. No one may keep cars.

Activities: 5% of men belong to 6 national fraternities; 5% of women belong to 2 national sororities. There are 39 groups on campus, including academic chorale, dance, drama, ethnic, gay, honors, international, newspaper, professional, religious, social service, student government, and yearbook. Popular campus events include International Fair and Mission Hill Walk for Health.

Sports: There are 6 intramural sports for men and 6 for women. MCPHS shares facilities with the Massachusetts College of Art, which include a wellness center with weight training equipment and a gym with court space for basketball, volleyball, and badminton.

Disabled Students: All of the campus is accessible. Wheelchair ramps, elevators, special parking, specially equipped rest rooms, lowered drinking fountains, lowered telephones, and special housing are available. All dorm rooms have elevator access and meet ADA requirements.

Services: Counseling and information services are available, as is tutoring in some subjects. Tutoring free of charge and includes both group and individual peer tutoring.

Campus Safety and Security: Measures include self-defense education, security escort services, shuttle buses, and informal discussions. There are pamphlets/posters/films, lighted pathways/sidewalks, security guards at all entrances, and admission to all buildings by means of a security pass worn by all students, faculty, and staff.

Programs of Study: MCPHS confers the B.S. degree. Associate, master's, and doctoral degrees are also awarded. Bachelor's degrees are awarded in COMPUTER AND PHYSICAL SCIENCE (chemistry and radiological technology), HEALTH PROFESSIONS (dental hygiene, health, nuclear medical technology, nursing, pharmacy, and premedicine), SOCIAL SCIENCE (psychology). Pharmacy, physicians assistant, and dental hygiene are the largest.

Required: Graduation requirements vary by program. Students must complete course work in expository writing, history and politics, psychology, sociology, interpersonal communications in the health professions, evolution of the health professions, biomedical ethics, and humanities. Students must maintain a minimum GPA of 2.0 overall and a professional GPA that varies by program.

Special: MCPHS offers cross-registration with the other colleges of the Fenway Consortium, cooperative programs with Simmons College and Western New England College, an externship program in radiopharmacy in conjunction with Massachusetts General Hospital, internships, and work-study programs. Accelerated degrees and dual majors are available in some programs. There are 2 national honor societies.

Faculty/Classroom: 39% of faculty are male; 61%, female. All both teach and do research. No introductory courses are taught by graduate students. The average class size in a regular course is 14.

Admissions: 76% of the 2005-2006 applicants were accepted. The SAT scores for the 2005-2006 freshman class were: Verbal--32% below 500, 51% between 500 and 599, 16% between 600 and 700, and 1% above 700; Math--13% below 500, 50% between 500 and 599, 32% between 600 and 700, and 5% above 700. The ACT scores were 34% below 21, 38% between 21 and 23, 19% between 24 and 26, 7% between 27 and 28, and 2% above 28. 55% of the current freshmen were in the top fifth of their class; 84% were in the top two fifths.

Requirements: The SAT is required. In addition, applicants must graduate from an accredited secondary school with 16 units, including 4 of English, 3 of math, 2 of lab science, 1 of history, and 6 of other college-preparatory subjects. The college also advises advanced chemistry or physics with lab and an extra unit of math. Interviews are recommended. Letters of reference from a guidance counselor and a science or math teacher and 2 student essays are required. AP and CLEP credits are accepted. Important factors in the admissions decision are evidence of special talent, recommendations by school officials, and advanced placement or honor courses.

Procedure: Freshmen are admitted in the fall. Entrance exams should be taken by December of the senior year. There are early action, early admissions, and deferred admissions plans. Early decision applications should be filed by November 1; regular applications, by February 1 for fall entry. Notification of early decision is sent December 15; regular decision, April 1. 30 early decision candidates were accepted for the 2005-2006 class. Applications are accepted on-line. The fall 2005 application fee was $70.

Transfer: 249 transfer students enrolled in 2005-2006. Applicants must have a minimum GPA of 2.5. Those with 1 year or less of college credit must submit secondary school transcripts.

Visiting: There are regularly scheduled orientations for prospective students, including a campus tour and information sessions. There are guides for informal visits and visitors may sit in on classes. To schedule a visit, contact the Admissions Office.

Financial Aid: 20% of undergraduates work part time. Average annual earnings from campus work are $1200. MCPHS is a member of CSS. The FAFSA is required. The deadline for filing freshman financial aid applications for fall entry is March 15.

International Students: The school actively recruits these students. They must score satisfactorily on the written TOEFL or on the electronic version and also take the college's own test and the SAT or the ACT.

Computers: Wireless access is available. MPCHS provides Internet access in dorms and the library. There are 217 PCs available in Boston; 42, in Manchester; and 100, in Worcester. All students may access the system. There are no time limits and no fees. It is strongly recommended that all students have a personal computer.

Graduates: From July 1, 2004 to June 30, 2005, 99 bachelor's degrees were awarded. The most popular majors were pharmacy (66%), physician assistant (12%), and dental hygiene (9%). In an average class, 31% graduate in 4 years or less, 62% graduate in 5 years or less, and 77% graduate in 6 years or less. 77 companies recruited on campus in 2004-2005.

Admissions Contact: William Dunfey, Executive Director of Admissions. A video is available. E-mail: *admissions@bos.mcphs.edu* Web: *www.mcphs.edu*

MASSACHUSETTS INSTITUTE OF TECHNOLOGY   D-2

Cambridge, MA 02139	(617) 253-4791; Fax: (617) 258-8304
Full-time: 2261 men, 1753 women	Faculty: 982; I, ++$
Part-time: 40 men, 12 women	Ph.D.s: 97%
Graduate: 4355 men, 1785 women	Student/Faculty: 4 to 1
Year: 4-1-4	Tuition: $32,300
Application Deadline: January 1	Room & Board: $9500
Freshman Class: 10,440 applied, 1494 accepted, 996 enrolled	
SAT Verbal/Math: 730/780*	ACT: 33 MOST COMPETITIVE

Massachusetts Institute of Technology, founded in 1861, is a private, independent, institution offering programs in architecture and planning, engineering, humanities, arts, and social sciences, management, science, and health sciences, and technology. There are 5 undergraduate and 6 graduate schools. In addition to regional accreditation, MIT has baccalaureate program accreditation with AACSB, ABET, and CSAB. The 10 libraries contain 2,782,406 volumes, 2,391,503 microform items, and 53,683 audio/video tapes/CDs/DVDs, and subscribe to 22,991 periodicals including electronic. Computerized library services include the card catalog, interlibrary loans, database searching, Internet access, and laptop Internet portals. Special learning facilities include an art gallery, radio station, TV station, and numerous labs and centers. The 168-acre campus is in an urban area 1 mile north of Boston. Including any residence halls, there are 144 buildings.

Student Life: 91% of undergraduates are from out of state, mostly the Middle Atlantic. Students are from 50 states, 84 foreign countries, and Canada. 36% are white; 27% Asian American; 11% Hispanic. The average age of freshmen is 18; all undergraduates, 20. 2% do not continue beyond their first year; 94% remain to graduate.

Housing: Approximately 3000 undergraduates can be recommodated in residence halls. Other housing includes single-sex and coed dormitories, on-campus apartments, married-student housing, fraternity houses, and sorority houses. In addition, there are language houses, special-interest houses, off-campus independent living groups, and non-Greek cooperative houses. On-campus housing is guaranteed for 8 continuous semesters as long as it is the first 8 items of the undergraduate. Students time at MIT. All freshman are required to live on campus during their first year at MIT. 94% of students live on campus. Upperclassmen may keep cars.

Activities: 55% of men belong to 2 local and 24 national fraternities, plus 2 colonies; 26% of women belong to 5 national sororities. There are more than 300 groups on campus, including art, band, cheerleading, chess, choir, chorale, chorus, computers, dance, debate, drama, ethnic, film, gay, honors, international, jazz band, literary magazine, marching band, musical theater, newspaper, orchestra, photography, political, professional, radio and TV, religious, social, social service, student government, symphony, and yearbook. Popular campus events include Rush/Orientation Week, Senior Week, and Spring Weekend.

Sports: There are 23 intercollegiate sports for men and 19 for women, and 22 intramural sports for men and 22 for women. Facilities include an athletic complex with 10 buildings and 26 acres of playing fields.

Disabled Students: Wheelchair ramps, elevators, special parking, specially equipped rest rooms, special class scheduling, lowered drinking fountains, lowered telephones, wheelchair lifts, and automatic doors are available. An adaptive technology lab and special library services are also in place.

Services: Counseling and information services are available, as is tutoring in every subject, including . There is a reader service for the blind. Accommodations for students with documented disabilities are determined on an individual basis.

Campus Safety and Security: Measures include 24-hour foot and vehicle patrol, self-defense education, security escort services, and shuttle buses. There are informal discussions, pamphlets/posters/films, emergency telephones, and lighted pathways/sidewalks.

Programs of Study: MIT confers the B.S. degree. Master's and doctoral degrees are also awarded. Bachelor's degrees are awarded in BIOLOGI-

CAL SCIENCE (biology/biological science), BUSINESS (management science), COMMUNICATIONS AND THE ARTS (creative writing, linguistics, literature, and music), COMPUTER AND PHYSICAL SCIENCE (chemistry, computer science, earth science, mathematics, physics, and science technology), ENGINEERING AND ENVIRONMENTAL DESIGN (aeronautical engineering, architecture, chemical engineering, civil engineering, electrical/electronics engineering, environmental engineering, materials engineering, materials science, mechanical engineering, nuclear engineering, and ocean engineering), SOCIAL SCIENCE (anthropology, archeology, cognitive science, economics, French studies, history, humanities, philosophy, political science/government, Spanish studies, and urban studies). Engineering is the largest.

Required: To graduate, students must fulfill the General Institute Requirements, as well as communication and phys ed requirements, and earn an additional 180 to 198 credit units, while fulfilling departmental program requirements. A GPA of 3.0 on a scale of 5.0 should be maintained. The General Institute Requirements consist of 8 courses in humanities, arts, and social sciences, 6 in science, including chemistry, physics, calculus, and biology, 2 in restricted science and technology electives, and 1 lab, for a total of 17 courses.

Special: MIT offers cross-registration with Harvard, Wellesley, the Massachusetts College of Art, and the School of the Museum of Fine Arts. Internships are offered in a number of programs. Study abroad is offered at Cambridge University in England as part of the Cambridge-MIT Undergraduate Exchange. The Department of Aeronautics and Astronautics also offers study at several European schools, while the Department of Architecture has an exchange program with Delft University of Technology in the Netherlands. The Undergraduate Research Opportunities Program (UROP) offers students research work with faculty. There are 11 national honor societies, including Phi Beta Kappa.

Faculty/Classroom: 82% of faculty are male; 18%, female. All both teach and do research. No introductory courses are taught by graduate students.

Admissions: 14% of the 2005-2006 applicants were accepted. The SAT scores for the 2005-2006 freshman class were: Verbal--1% below 500, 4% between 500 and 599, 27% between 600 and 700, and 68% above 700; Math--7% between 600 and 700, and 92% above 700. The ACT scores were 1% between 21 and 23, 1% between 24 and 26, 4% between 27 and 28, and 94% above 28. 99% of the current freshmen were in the top fifth of their class; all were in the top two fifths. 215 freshmen graduated first in their class.

Requirements: The SAT or ACT is required. In addition, 2 SAT Subject Tests, including math, a science, and an English or history are required. 14 academic units are recommended, including 4 each of English, math, and science, 2 of social studies, and a foreign language. The GED is accepted. Essays, 2 teacher evaluations, an official transcript, and a guidance counselor report are required. An interview is strongly recommended. AP credits are accepted. Important factors in the admissions decision are evidence of special talent, leadership record, and extracurricular activities record.

Procedure: Freshmen are admitted in the fall. Entrance exams should be taken by the January test date. There are early action and deferred admissions plans. Early action applications should be filed by November 1; regular applications, by January 1 for fall entry, along with a $65 fee. Notification of early action is sent mid-December; regular decision, March 25. 401 applicants were on the 2005 waiting list. Applications are accepted on-line.

Transfer: 9 transfer students enrolled in 2004-2005. Transfer applicants must have completed 2 or more terms at an accredited college, university, technical institute, military academy, or community college and be in good standing there. They must have taken 1 year of college-level calculus and calculus-based physics and 1 semester each of biology and chemistry. They must also submit scores for the SAT Subject Tests in math and science. Nonnative English speakers may substitute the TOEFL for the SAT. Competitive applicants have a 3.5 GPA or above. 3 semesters required for the bachelor's degree must be completed at MIT. 17 General Institute Requirement subjects plus 180 to 198 departmental program units are required for the bachelor's degree.

Visiting: There are regularly scheduled orientations for prospective students, including daily tours (Monday through Friday) preceded by an information session with admissions staff. Visitors may sit in on classes and stay overnight. To schedule a visit, contact the Office of Admissions at (617) 258-5515.

Financial Aid: In 2005-2006, 77% of all full-time freshmen and 68% of continuing full-time students received some form of financial aid. 63% of full-time freshmen and 62% of continuing full-time students received need-based aid. The average freshman award was $29,808. Need-based scholarships or need-based grants averaged $27,526 ($45,350 maximum); and need-based self-help aid (loans and jobs) averaged $4155 ($5500 maximum). 55% of undergraduates work part time. Average annual earnings from campus work are $1720. The average financial indebtedness of the 2005 graduate was $15,833. MIT is a member of CSS. The CSS/Profile or FAFSA and parent W-2s, 1040s, and the business tax form are required. The deadline for filing freshman financial aid applications for fall entry is March 1.

International Students: There are 306 international students enrolled. They must take the SAT or ACT. Non-English speakers may substitute the TOEFL for the SAT or ACT. Students must take SAT: Subject tests in a math and a science.

Computers: Wireless access is available. Students may use the wireless network with their own computers; students in dorms can access wireless as well as wired networks. All students have their own computers and/or loaners. In, addition there are more than 1000 public access PCs on campus. All students may access the system at all times. There are no time limits and no fees. It is strongly recommended that all students have a personal computer.

Graduates: From July 1, 2004 to June 30, 2005, 1220 bachelor's degrees were awarded. The most popular majors were computer science and engineering (10%), electrical engineering and computer scie (10%), and management science (9%). In an average class, 3% graduate in 3 years or less, 82% graduate in 4 years or less, 92% graduate in 5 years or less, and 94% graduate in 6 years or less. 481 companies recruited on campus in 2004-2005. Of the 2005 graduating class, 47% were enrolled in graduate school within 6 months of graduation and 40% were employed.

Admissions Contact: Admissions Officers.
Web: *http://web.mit.edu/admissions/*

MASSACHUSETTS MARITIME ACADEMY   E-4
Buzzards Bay, MA 02532-1803

(508) 830-5000
(800) 544-3411; Fax: (508) 830-5077

Full-time: 820 men, 103 women	**Faculty:** n/av
Part-time: 37 men, 9 women	**Ph.D.s:** n/av
Graduate: 37 men, 1 women	**Student/Faculty:** n/av
Year: semesters	**Tuition:** $5107 ($15,912)
Application Deadline: open	**Room & Board:** $6464
Freshman Class: 800 applied, 520 accepted, 326 enrolled	
SAT Verbal/Math: 520/540*	**ACT:** 21 **COMPETITIVE**

Massachusetts Maritime Academy, founded in 1891, is the oldest continuously operating maritime academy in the country. Cooperative educational learning and leadership training opportunities prepare graduates for professional positions within private industry or, if opted, military commissions. In addition to the tuition stated in the above capsule, all freshmen are required to participate in a winter sea term at the cost of $2929. Some figures in this profile are approximate. The library contains 40,171 volumes, 11,674 microform items, and 1113 audio/video tapes/CDs/DVDs, and subscribes to 505 periodicals including electronic. Computerized library services include the card catalog, interlibrary loans, database searching, and Internet access. Special learning facilities include a learning resource center, planetarium, a full bridge-training simulator, oil-spill management simulator, liquid cargo-handling simulator, and computer-aided design lab. The 55-acre campus is in a small town 60 miles south of Boston. Including any residence halls, there are 9 buildings.

Student Life: 70% of undergraduates are from Massachusetts. Students are from 26 states and 11 foreign countries. 73% are from public schools. 90% are white. The average age of freshmen is 18; all undergraduates, 21. 15% do not continue beyond their first year; 70% remain to graduate.

Housing: 800 students can be accommodated in college housing, which includes coed dorms. On-campus housing is guaranteed for all 4 years. 97% of students live on campus; of those, 35% remain on campus on weekends. Alcohol is not permitted. All students may keep cars.

Activities: There are no fraternities or sororities. There are 15 groups on campus, including band, choir, chorus, computers, drill team, jazz band, marching band, newspaper, photography, professional, religious, scuba, social service, student government, and yearbook. Popular campus events include Ring Dance, Emory Rice Day, and Recognition.

Sports: There are 8 intercollegiate sports for men and 6 for women, and 13 intramural sports for men and 5 for women. Facilities include football and baseball fields, a pistol range, outdoor tennis and basketball courts, a sailing center, an Olympic-size swimming pool, 2 weight rooms, 3 multipurpose handball courts, and wrestling courts and fitness rooms. An indoor gym/auditorium seats 2500.

Disabled Students: 90% of the campus is accessible. Wheelchair ramps, elevators, special parking, and specially equipped rest rooms are available.

Services: Counseling and information services are available, as is tutoring in most subjects.

Campus Safety and Security: Measures include 24-hour foot and vehicle patrol and lighted pathways/sidewalks.

Programs of Study: MMA confers the B.S. degree. Master's degrees are also awarded. Bachelor's degrees are awarded in BUSINESS (international business management and transportation management), and ENGINEERING AND ENVIRONMENTAL DESIGN (environmental engineering, industrial engineering, and marine engineering). Marine engineering is the strongest academically and is the largest.

Required: All students must complete 164 credit hours with a minimum of 60 hours in the major and a GPA of 2.0. Requirements include 4 courses in phys ed, 2 each in chemistry and naval science, and 1 each in algebra/trigonometry, introduction to computers, English composition, American literature, Western civilization, economics, analysis, American government, first aid, admiralty law, introduction to marine transportation, introduction to marine engineering, sea term/deck, sea term/engine, and calculus.

Special: MMA offers a junior-year internship in a commercial shipping program. Educational experience includes a minimum of 120 days aboard a training ship, with visits to foreign ports. There are cooperative programs in facilities and environmental engineering and in marine safety and environmental protection. A dual major is available in marine engineering and marine transportaton. A concentration is available in emergency management.

Faculty/Classroom: 96% of faculty are male; 4%, female. All teach undergraduates and 3% do research. The average class size in an introductory lecture is 25; in a laboratory, 12; and in a regular course, 22.

Requirements: The SAT or ACT is required. In addition, applicants must have graduated from an accredited secondary school or hold a GED certificate. They should have completed 16 Carnegie units, including 4 in English, 3 in math, and 2 each in a foreign language, science, and social science. An essay is required, and an interview is strongly recommended. A GPA of 2.0 is required. AP and CLEP credits are accepted. Important factors in the admissions decision are advanced placement or honor courses, leadership record, and extracurricular activities record.

Procedure: Freshmen are admitted in the fall. There are early application, deferred admissions, and rolling admissions plans. Early applications should be filed by November 1; regular applications, by June 15, along with a $50 fee. Notification of early application is sent December 15. Applications are accepted on-line. The application fee is waived for on-line applications.

Transfer: 78 transfer students enrolled in 2004-2005. Students must have a minimum GPA of 2.0. 30 of 164 credits required for the bachelor's degree must be completed at MMA.

Visiting: There are regularly scheduled orientations for prospective students, including a campus tour and an admissions interview. An optional overnight visit can arranged. There are Open House Programs. There are guides for informal visits and visitors may sit in on classes and stay overnight. To schedule a visit, contact Anne Ford at (800) 544-3400.

Financial Aid: MMA is a member of CSS. The CSS/Profile or FAFSA and the college's own financial statement are required. Check with the school for application deadlines. Check with the school for current deadlines.

International Students: A satisfactory score is required on the TOEFL. Students must also take the SAT or the ACT.

Computers: All students may access the system 8 A.M. to 11 P.M. There are no time limits and no fees. All students are required to have PCs.

Graduates: In a recent year, 180 bachelor's degrees were awarded. The most popular majors were marine engineering (45%), marine safety environmental protection (20%), and marine transportation (10%). In an average class, 70% graduate in 4 years or less. 60 companies recruited on campus in a recent year. Of a recent graduating class, 100% were employed within 6 months of graduation.

Admissions Contact: Francis McDonald, Dean of Enrollment Services. A video is available. E-mail: *admissions@maritime.edu* Web: *www.maritime.edu*

MERRIMACK COLLEGE E-2

North Andover, MA 01845 (978) 837-5100; Fax: (978) 837-5133

Full-time: 893 men, 1057 women	**Faculty:** 150
Part-time: 118 men, 86 women	**Ph.D.s:** 77%
Graduate: 3 men, 31 women	**Student/Faculty:** 13 to 1
Year: semesters, summer session	**Tuition:** $24,650
Application Deadline: February 1	**Room & Board:** $9730
Freshman Class: 3413 applied, 2436 accepted, 544 enrolled	
SAT Verbal/Math: 540/540*	**ACT:** 21 COMPETITIVE

Merrimack College, founded in 1947 by the Augustinian clergy of the Roman Catholic Church, is a private institution that offers undergraduate programs in science, engineering, business administration, and liberal arts. In addition to regional accreditation, Merrimack has baccalaureate program accreditation with ABET and CAAHEP. The library contains 117,681 volumes, 11,997 microform items, and 1777 audio/video tapes/CDs/DVDs, and subscribes to 526 periodicals including electronic. Computerized library services include the card catalog, interlibrary loans, and database searching. Special learning facilities include a learning resource center, art gallery, planetarium, TV station, a chemistry center, an urban resource institute, a center for the arts, and a learning center. The 220-acre campus is in a suburban area 25 miles north of Boston. Including any residence halls, there are 34 buildings.

Student Life: 71% of undergraduates are from Massachusetts. Students are from 27 states, 15 foreign countries, and Canada. 60% are from public schools. 80% are white. The average age of freshmen is 18; all

undergraduates, 20. 20% do not continue beyond their first year; 74% remain to graduate.

Housing: 1590 students can be accommodated in college housing, which includes coed dorms and on-campus apartments. In addition, there are special-interest houses, international, wellness, engineering, and theme housing. On-campus housing is guaranteed for all 4 years. 76% of students live on campus; of those, 90% remain on campus on weekends. Upperclassmen may keep cars.

Activities: 3% of men belong to 3 national fraternities; 5% of women belong to 3 national sororities. There are 45 groups on campus, including art, cheerleading, choir, chorale, chorus, computers, dance, drama, ethnic, gay, honors, international, jazz band, literary magazine, musical theater, newspaper, pep band, photography, political, professional, radio and TV, religious, social, social service, student government, and yearbook. Popular campus events include Springfest, Peace and Social Justice Awareness Week, and Global Village.

Sports: There are 8 intercollegiate sports for men and 8 for women, and 6 intramural sports for men and 6 for women. Facilities include an athletic complex, including an ice rink, a basketball court, an aerobics studio, and a well-equipped exercise room, and outdoor facilities including 2 sets of tennis courts, baseball, football, softball, soccer, lacrosse, and field hockey fields, and a turf field.

Disabled Students: All of the campus is accessible. Wheelchair ramps, elevators, special parking, specially equipped rest rooms, special class scheduling, lowered drinking fountains, and lowered telephones are available.

Services: Counseling and information services are available, as is tutoring in every subject. Math, science, and writing resource centers are available to all students.

Campus Safety and Security: Measures include 24-hour foot and vehicle patrol, security escort services, shuttle buses, and informal discussions. There are pamphlets/posters/films, emergency telephones, lighted pathways/sidewalks, and Rape Aggressive Defense is available through police services.

Programs of Study: Merrimack confers B.A. and B.S. degrees. Associate and master's degrees are also awarded. Bachelor's degrees are awarded in BIOLOGICAL SCIENCE (biochemistry and biology/biological science), BUSINESS (accounting, business administration and management, business economics, international business management, and marketing/retailing/merchandising), COMMUNICATIONS AND THE ARTS (communications, English, and modern language), COMPUTER AND PHYSICAL SCIENCE (chemistry, computer science, mathematics, and physics), EDUCATION (elementary and secondary), ENGINEERING AND ENVIRONMENTAL DESIGN (civil engineering, electrical/electronics engineering, and environmental science), HEALTH PROFESSIONS (allied health, predentistry, premedicine, and sports medicine), SOCIAL SCIENCE (economics, history, philosophy, political science/government, prelaw, psychology, religion, and sociology). Science, engineering, and business are the strongest academically. Business, psychology, and liberal arts are the largest.

Required: All students are required to emphasize liberal arts with a variety of courses that must include 3 each in humanities, social science, and math and science, 2 each in theology and philosophy, and 1 each in English composition and freshman seminar. Students also must maintain a minimum GPA of 2.0 while taking a total of 120 credit hours, including 30 in the major.

Special: Merrimack offers cooperative programs in business, engineering, liberal arts, and computer science, cross-registration through the Northeast Consortium, internships in all arts and science programs, study abroad in 15 countries, and a Washington semester at American University. Work-study programs, a 5-year combined B.A.-B.S. degree in many major fields, and dual and self-designed majors are available. General studies, nondegree study, and pass/fail options are possible. There are 7 national honor societies, and 3 departmental honors programs.

Faculty/Classroom: 58% of faculty are male; 42%, female. All teach undergraduates, 60% do research, and 60% do both. No introductory courses are taught by graduate students. The average class size in an introductory lecture is 25; in a laboratory, 15; and in a regular course, 15.

Admissions: 71% of the 2005-2006 applicants were accepted. The SAT scores for the 2005-2006 freshman class were: Verbal--18% below 500, 67% between 500 and 599, 12% between 600 and 700, and 3% above 700; Math--14% below 500, 65% between 500 and 599, 15% between 600 and 700, and 6% above 700. The ACT scores were 38% below 21, 34% between 21 and 23, 22% between 24 and 26, 4% between 27 and 28, and 2% above 28. 36% of the current freshmen were in the top fifth of their class; 75% were in the top two fifths. 4 freshmen graduated first in their class.

Requirements: The SAT or ACT is required. In addition, for business administration, humanities, and social science majors, Merrimack recommends that applicants complete 4 units of English, 3 each of math and science, 2 of social studies, and a foreign language. For other majors, an additional math course and 1 additional course in science are needed. An essay is required, and an interview is recommended. Applicants should have completed 16 Carnegie units. Merrimack requires applicants to be in the upper 50% of their class. A GPA of 2.7 is required. AP and CLEP credits are accepted. Important factors in the admissions decision are advanced placement or honor courses, recommendations by school officials, and leadership record.

Procedure: Freshmen are admitted fall and spring. Entrance exams should be taken during the spring of the junior year and the fall of the senior year. There are early action and deferred admissions plans. Early decision applications should be filed by November 30; regular applications, by February 1 for fall entry and December 15 for spring entry, along with a $50 fee. Notification of early decision is sent December 15; regular decision, April 1. 406 applicants were on the 2005 waiting list; 130 were admitted. Applications are accepted on-line.

Transfer: 123 transfer students enrolled in fall 2005. Applicants must have maintained a minimum 2.5 GPA while accumulating 30 credits. The SAT, an interview, and a letter of recommendation are recommended. 45 of 120 credits required for the bachelor's degree must be completed at Merrimack.

Visiting: There are regularly scheduled orientations for prospective students, including 10 information sessions on Saturdays in the fall and 4 financial aid information sessions throughout the year. There are guides for informal visits and visitors may sit in on classes and stay overnight. To schedule a visit, contact the Office of Admissions.

Financial Aid: In 2005-2006, 81% of all full-time freshmen and 69% of continuing full-time students received some form of financial aid. 74% of full-time freshmen and 61% of continuing full-time students received need-based aid. The average freshman award was $17,500. Need-based scholarships or need-based grants averaged $13,000; need-based self-help aid (loans and jobs) averaged $4625; non-need-based athletic scholarships averaged $20,000; and other non-need-based awards and non-need-based scholarships averaged $10,000. 80% of undergraduates work part time. Average annual earnings from campus work are $2200. The average financial indebtedness of the 2005 graduate was $17,125. Merrimack is a member of CSS. The FAFSA is required. The deadline for filing freshman financial aid applications for fall entry is February 1.

International Students: There are 31 international students enrolled. The school actively recruits these students. A satisfactory score is required on the written TOEFL.

Computers: Wireless access is available. The campus center has computers available for commuter students, and the library has several computer labs available to all students. Both buildings are wireless. All students may access the system. There are no time limits and no fees. It is strongly recommended that all students have a personal computer. Students in the business school which provides a laptop as part of its tuition.

Graduates: From July 1, 2004 to June 30, 2005, 524 bachelor's degrees were awarded. The most popular majors were management (11%), marketing (11%), and psychology (8%). In an average class, 53% graduate in 4 years or less, 70% graduate in 5 years or less, and 71% graduate in 6 years or less. 130 companies recruited on campus in 2004-2005. Of the 2004 graduating class, 11% were enrolled in graduate school within 6 months of graduation and 87% were employed.

Admissions Contact: Mary Lou Retelle, Vice President for Enrollment Management. E-mail: admissions@merrimack.edu
Web: www.merrimack.edu

MONTSERRAT COLLEGE OF ART   E-2

Beverly, MA 01915
(978) 921-4242
(800) 836-0487; Fax: (978) 921-4241

Full-time: 102 men, 177 women	**Faculty:** 24
Part-time: 7 men, 13 women	**Ph.D.s:** 16%
Graduate: none	**Student/Faculty:** 12 to 1
Year: semesters	**Tuition:** $20,629
Application Deadline: open	**Room & Board:** $5300
Freshman Class: n/av	
SAT or ACT: required	**SPECIAL**

Montserrat College of Art, founded in 1970, is a private residential, professional institution offering degrees in painting and drawing, fine arts, printmaking, graphic design, illustration, photography, and sculpture, with a complementary program in art education. In addition to regional accreditation, Montserrat has baccalaureate program accreditation with ACBSP and NASAD. The library contains 11,484 volumes and 677 audio/video tapes/CDs/DVDs, and subscribes to 79 periodicals including electronic. Computerized library services include the card catalog, interlibrary loans, and database searching. Special learning facilities include a learning resource center and art gallery. The 10-acre campus is in a suburban area 26 miles north of Boston. Including any residence halls, there are 17 buildings.

Student Life: 50% of undergraduates are from out of state, mostly the Northeast. Students are from 19 states. 93% are white. The average age of freshmen is 19; all undergraduates, 23. 49% do not continue beyond their first year; 49% remain to graduate.

Housing: 162 students can be accommodated in college housing, which includes single-sex and coed on-campus apartments and quiet housing. All housing is smoke free. On-campus housing is available on

a first-come, first-served basis and is available on a lottery system for upperclassmen. 52% of students commute. Alcohol is not permitted. All students may keep cars.

Activities: There are no fraternities or sororities. There are 6 groups on campus, including art, international, literary magazine, newspaper, radio and TV, social, and student government. Popular campus events include Forum Days, Halloween and holiday parties, and gallery openings.

Sports: There are 2 intramural sports for men and 2 for women. Montserrat uses the facilities of the local YMCA.

Disabled Students: 50% of the campus is accessible. Wheelchair ramps, elevators, special parking, specially equipped rest rooms, and special class scheduling are available.

Services: Counseling and information services are available, as is tutoring in some subjects, including art history. There is remedial writing and a reader service for students with dyslexia.

Campus Safety and Security: Measures include informal discussions, pamphlets/posters/films, emergency telephones, and lighted pathways/sidewalks. In addition, there is a security guard in the main building and resident assistants trained in first aid and CPR who patrol the buildings.

Programs of Study: Montserrat confers the B.F.A. degree. Bachelor's degrees are awarded in COMMUNICATIONS AND THE ARTS (fine arts, graphic design, illustration, painting, photography, printmaking, and sculpture), EDUCATION (art).

Required: To graduate, all students are required to complete 120 credits, including 78 in studio courses and 42 in liberal arts courses, with a 2.0 GPA. Requirements include 12 credits in art history, 9 in humanitites, and 6 each in English composition, and liberal arts. Distribution requirements include 33 credits freshman year, 30 during sophomore and junior year, and 27 in senior year. To enter the senior program, Montserrat students must have a portfolio. During semester-end evaluations, each student displays work from all courses and is evaluated by a faculty panel.

Special: Montserrat is a member of the Northeast Consortium of Colleges and Universities in Massachusetts, which allows students to take classes at any member college for the same cost. Credit study is available through the continuing education department. Montserrat also offers internships, summer study in New York City or Italy, dual and student-designed majors in fine arts and in art education, and a mobility program that allows students to spend a semester at another school within the Association of Independent Colleges of Art and Design.

Faculty/Classroom: 44% of faculty are male; 55%, female. All teach undergraduates. The average class size in a regular course is 15.

Requirements: The SAT or ACT is required. In addition, students must submit an artist's statement, a portfolio, 2 letters of recommendation, and a high school transcript, although no specific program of study is required. A portfolio interview is strongly recommended. A GPA of 2.25 is required. AP and CLEP credits are accepted. Important factors in the admissions decision are evidence of special talent, advanced placement or honor courses, and personality/intangible qualities.

Procedure: Freshmen are admitted fall and spring. There are deferred admissions and rolling admissions plans. Application deadlines are open. Application fee is $40.

Transfer: 19 transfer students enrolled in 2004-2005. Applicants are required to submit a portfolio, transcripts from a previous college, and an artist's statement. They should also be interviewed. 60 of 120 credits required for the bachelor's degree must be completed at Montserrat.

Visiting: There are regularly scheduled orientations for prospective students, including tours of college studios, observation of classes, and portfolio consultations. There are guides for informal visits and visitors may sit in on classes. To schedule a visit, contact the Admissions Coordinator.

Financial Aid: In 2005-2006, 94% of all full-time freshmen and 87% of continuing full-time students received some form of financial aid. 74% of full-time freshmen and 77% of continuing full-time students received need-based aid. The average freshman award was $5082. Need-based scholarships or need-based grants averaged $2168 ($5000 maximum); need-based self-help aid (loans and jobs) averaged $2708 ($4000 maximum); and institutional scholarship and awards averaged $2820 ($5000 maximum). 14% of undergraduates work part time. Average annual earnings from campus work are $847. The FAFSA and the college's own financial statement are required. The priority date for freshman financial aid applications for fall entry is March 1. The deadline for filing freshman financial aid applications for fall entry is June 1.

International Students: The school actively recruits these students. They must score satisfactorily on the written TOEFL or on the electronic version.

Computers: Wireless access is available. The college offers computer labs for work in design, illustration, photography, and video as well as for research, writing, and communication. Computers are available in classroom and studio spaces across campus. "Smart classroom" gives instructors interactive control over visuals from electronic media. Printing is available at several campus locations. Wireless access is available in the senior design and sculpture studios. All students may access the system 8 A.M. to 11 P.M. daily. There are no time limits and no fees.

Graduates: From July 1, 2004 to June 30, 2005, 78 bachelor's degrees were awarded. The most popular majors were painting/graphic design

(22%) and illustration (19%). In an average class, 38% graduate in 4 years or less, and 49% graduate in 6 years or less.

Admissions Contact: Jessica Sarin-Perry, Dean of Admissions & Enrollment Management. E-mail: *admiss@montserrat.edu* Web: *www.montserrat.edu*

MOUNT HOLYOKE COLLEGE   B-3
South Hadley, MA 01075   (413) 538-2023; Fax: (413) 538-2409

Full-time: 2052 women	**Faculty:** 207; IIB, ++$
Part-time: 5 men, 68 women	**Ph.D.s:** 94%
Graduate: 2 women	**Student/Faculty:** 10 to 1
Year: semesters	**Tuition:** $32,598
Application Deadline: January 15	**Room & Board:** $9550
Freshman Class: 2924 applied, 1530 accepted, 505 enrolled	
SAT Verbal/Math: 667/650*	**ACT:** 29

HIGHLY COMPETITIVE+

Mount Holyoke, founded in 1837, is the oldest institution of higher learning for women in the United States. An independent, liberal arts college, it affords students great freedom in selecting course studies. The 3 libraries contain 721,223 volumes, 23,431 microform items, and 7260 audio/video tapes/CDs/DVDs, and subscribe to 3805 periodicals including electronic. Computerized library services include the card catalog, interlibrary loans, database searching, and Internet access. Special learning facilities include a learning resource center, art gallery, radio station, an observatory, child study center, a center for foreign languages, a center for leadership, a botanical garden and greenhouse, and an equestrian center. The 800-acre campus is in a small town 90 miles west of Boston and 160 miles north of New York City. Including any residence halls, there are 62 buildings.

Student Life: 75% of undergraduates are from out of state, mostly the Northeast. Students are from 48 states, 66 foreign countries, and Canada. 57% are from public schools. 52% are white; 15% foreign nationals; 12% Asian American. The average age of freshmen is 18; all undergraduates, 20. 6% do not continue beyond their first year; 94% remain to graduate.

Housing: 2031 students can be accommodated in college housing, which includes single-sex dorm and on-campus apartments. Special accommodations are available by need. On-campus housing is guaranteed for all 4 years. 92% of students live on campus. All students may keep cars.

Activities: There are no fraternities or sororities. There are 145 groups on campus, including art, band, cheerleading, choir, chorale, chorus, computers, dance, debate, drama, ethnic, film, gay, honors, international, jazz band, literary magazine, musical theater, newspaper, orchestra, photography, political, radio and TV, religious, social, social service, student government, and symphony. Popular campus events include Festival of Diversity, Glascock Intercollegiate Poetry Contest, and the Founders Day Ceremony.

Sports: Facilities include a sports and dance complex that houses 2 rehearsal dance studios, a performance dance studio, and classroom; a gym with basketball, volleyball, and badminton courts; an 8-lane, 25-meter pool and separate diving tank; a 3100 square-foot weight room; and a field house with 1/8 mile 4-lane track, indoor pole vault pit, indoor long jump pit, 6 tennis courts, cardiovascular area, 5 international squash courts, and 2 racquetball courts. Outdoor facilities include 12 tennis courts, 1/4 mile 6-lane track, field hockey, soccer, lacrosse, rugby, and softball fields, a rowing tank, a cross-country course, an equestrian center with 2 indoor arenas, and a golf course.

Disabled Students: 95% of the campus is accessible. Wheelchair ramps, elevators, special parking, specially equipped rest rooms, and special class scheduling are available.

Services: Counseling and information services are available, as is tutoring in every subject. The writing center is available to all students at all levels. There is a reader service for the blind. Special testing accommodations, diagnostic testing services, and note-taking services, as well as readers and tutors, are available. There is also an adaptive technology lab.

Campus Safety and Security: Measures include 24-hour foot and vehicle patrol, self-defense education, security escort services, and shuttle buses. There are informal discussions, pamphlets/posters/films, emergency telephones, and lighted pathways/sidewalks.

Programs of Study: Mount Holyoke confers the A.B. degree. Master's degrees are also awarded. Bachelor's degrees are awarded in AGRICULTURE (environmental studies), BIOLOGICAL SCIENCE (biochemistry, biology/biological science, and neurosciences), COMMUNICATIONS AND THE ARTS (art history and appreciation, classics, dance, dramatic arts, English, film arts, French, Greek, Italian, Latin, music, romance languages and literature, Russian, Spanish, and studio art), COMPUTER AND PHYSICAL SCIENCE (astronomy, chemistry, computer science, geology, mathematics, physics, and statistics), EDUCATION (education), ENGINEERING AND ENVIRONMENTAL DESIGN (architecture, and engineering), SOCIAL SCIENCE (African American studies, American studies, anthropology, Asian/Oriental studies, classical/ancient civiliza-

tion, economics, ethics, politics, and social policy, European studies, geography, German area studies, history, international relations, Judaic studies, Latin American studies, medieval studies, philosophy, political science/government, psychobiology, religion, sociology, and women's studies). Sciences, social sciences, and international relations are the strongest academically. English, biology, and psychology are the largest.

Required: Students must maintain a minimum GPA of 2.0 while taking 128 total credits, with 32 to 56 in the major. Students must complete 3 courses in the humanities, 2 courses each in science/math and social studies, a foreign language, a multicultural perspective course, and 6 credits in phys ed. A minor field of study is necessary for those not pursuing a double major, or an interdisciplinary major.

Special: Mount Holyoke offers students cross-registration through the Five-College Consortium. The college also offers dual-degree opportunities, including a 3-2 engineering program and a 3-2 program in public health, both with the University of Massachusetts at Amherst, and 3-2 programs in engineering with Dartmouth College and Caltech. Other opportunities include the 12-College Exchange Program, science and international studies internships, study-abroad programs (semester or full-year), a Washington semester, work-study, student-designed majors, dual majors, a January program, accelerated degrees, nondegree study, and pass/fail options. A B.A.-B.S. degree in nursing at Johns Hopkins and a teacher licensure program are available. There are 2 national honor societies, including Phi Beta Kappa. All departments have honors programs.

Faculty/Classroom: 47% of faculty are male; 53%, female. All both teach and do research. No introductory courses are taught by graduate students. The average class size in an introductory lecture is 15; in a laboratory, 12; and in a regular course, 15.

Admissions: 52% of the 2005-2006 applicants were accepted. The SAT scores for the 2005-2006 freshman class were: Verbal--1% below 500, 10% between 500 and 599, 56% between 600 and 700, and 33% above 700; Math--2% below 500, 15% between 500 and 599, 59% between 600 and 700, and 24% above 700. The ACT scores were 5% between 21 and 23, 14% between 24 and 26, 20% between 27 and 28, and 60% above 28. 75% of the current freshmen were in the top fifth of their class; 95% were in the top two fifths.

Requirements: The school recommends that applicants have 4 years each of English and foreign language, 3 each of math and science, and 2 of social studies. An essay is required and an interview is strongly recommended. AP credits are accepted. Important factors in the admissions decision are recommendations by school officials, leadership record, and advanced placement or honor courses.

Procedure: Freshmen are admitted in the fall. Entrance exams should be taken before the application deadline. There are early decision and deferred admissions plans. Early decision applications should be filed by November 15; regular applications, by January 15 for fall entry, along with a $60 fee. Notification of early decision is sent December 31; regular decision, April 1. 136 early decision candidates were accepted for the 2005-2006 class. 188 applicants were on the 2005 waiting list, none were admitted. Applications are accepted on-line.

Transfer: 25 transfer students enrolled in 2004-2005. A statement of good standing, transcripts of secondary school or college-level work, and an essay are required of transfer applicants. An interview is recommended. SAT scores will be considered if submitted, but are not required. 64 of 128 credits required for the bachelor's degree must be completed at Mount Holyoke.

Visiting: There are regularly scheduled orientations for prospective students, including tours, on campus interviews, overnight stays, and meetings with professors and coaches. There are guides for informal visits and visitors may sit in on classes and stay overnight. To schedule a visit, contact the Admission Office at *admission@mtholyoke.edu*.

Financial Aid: In 2005-2006, 53% of all full-time freshmen and 67% of continuing full-time students received some form of financial aid. 56% of full-time freshmen and 60% of continuing full-time students received need-based aid. The average freshman award was $27,525. Need-based scholarships or need-based grants averaged $24,079; and need-based self-help aid (loans and jobs) averaged $6851. 55% of undergraduates work part time. Average annual earnings from campus work was $1800. The average financial indebtedness of the 2005 graduate was $19,877. Mount Holyoke is a member of CSS. The CSS/Profile, FAFSA, parent and student tax returns, and the noncustodial parent form if applicable are required. The priority date for freshman financial aid applications for fall entry is January 15. The deadline for filing freshman financial aid applications for fall entry is February 1.

International Students: There are 315 international students enrolled. The school actively recruits these students. They must take the TOEFL if English is not their first language.

Computers: Wireless access is available. There are 561 publicly accessible PC workstations available for students on campus; students can access both the regular network and wireless system in the library, student center, dorms and other locations through out campus. All students may access the system. There are no time limits and no fees.

Graduates: From July 1, 2004 to June 30, 2005, 553 bachelor's degrees were awarded. The most popular majors were social sciences

(27%), biological sciences (11%), and psychology (11%). In an average class, 74% graduate in 4 years or less, 78% graduate in 5 years or less, and 80% graduate in 6 years or less. 47 companies recruited on campus in 2004-2005. Of the 2004 graduating class, 21% were enrolled in graduate school within 6 months of graduation and 88% were employed.

Admissions Contact: Diane C. Anci, Dean of Admission.
E-mail: *admission@mtholyoke.edu* Web: *mtholyoke.edu*

MOUNT IDA COLLEGE	D-2
Newton, MA 02459	**(617) 928-4553; Fax: (617) 928-4507**
Full-time: 400 men, 700 women	**Faculty:** 56; IIB, -$
Part-time: 10 men, 20 women	**Ph.D.s:** 61%
Graduate: none	**Student/Faculty:** 19 to 1
Year: semesters, summer session	**Tuition:** $17,000
Application Deadline: open	**Room & Board:** $9000
Freshman Class: n/av	
SAT or ACT: required	**LESS COMPETITIVE**

Mount Ida College, founded in 1899, is an independent baccalaureate college that prepares students for a profession through a curriculum that emphasizes career studies integrated with liberal learning. There are 5 undergraduate schools. Figures in the above capsule and in this profile are approximate. In addition to regional accreditation, Mount Ida has baccalaureate program accreditation with ABFSE, ADA, FIDER, and NASAD. The library contains 62,500 volumes, 70 microform items, and 2000 audio/video tapes/CDs/DVDs, and subscribes to 500 periodicals including electronic. Computerized library services include the card catalog, interlibrary loans, database searching, and Internet access. Special learning facilities include a learning resource center, art gallery, radio station, TV station, communication lab, darkroom, sewing rooms, blueprint-making facility, and dental labs. The 72-acre campus is in a suburban area 8 miles west of downtown Boston. Including any residence halls, there are 18 buildings.

Student Life: 54% of undergraduates are from Massachusetts. Others are from 23 states, 33 foreign countries, and Canada. 80% are from public schools. 63% are white; 16% African American; 10% foreign nationals. The average age of freshmen is 19; all undergraduates, 21.

Housing: 803 students can be accommodated in college housing, which includes single-sex and coed dormitories. In addition, there are honors houses and housing for students over age 21. On-campus housing is guaranteed for all 4 years. 60% of students live on campus. Upperclassmen may keep cars.

Activities: There are no fraternities or sororities. There are 25 groups on campus, including AIGA, art, cheerleading, chess, choir, commuter, dance, drama, equestrian, ethnic, fashion, gay, honors, international, literary magazine, newspaper, photography, professional, radio and TV, religious, social, social service, student government, travel, veterinary, and yearbook. Popular campus events include Welcome Week, Spring Fling, and Senior Week.

Sports: There are 7 intercollegiate sports for men and 6 for women, and 8 intramural sports for men and 10 for women. Facilities include a gym, playing fields, a fitness center, tennis courts, an outdoor swimming pool, athletic fields, and an athletic center.

Disabled Students: 75% of the campus is accessible. Wheelchair ramps, elevators, special parking, specially equipped rest rooms, special class scheduling, lowered drinking fountains, lowered telephones, and special housing are available.

Services: Counseling and information services are available, as is tutoring in most subjects. There is remedial math, reading, and writing. There is a program for learning disabled students, for which a fee is charged. Studies skills courses are also available. The Learning Circle is another innovative campuswide initiative that provides a professional learning specialist to assist students and monitor their academic progress.

Campus Safety and Security: Measures include 24-hour foot and vehicle patrol, self-defense education, security escort services, and shuttle buses. There are informal discussions, pamphlets/posters/films, emergency telephones, and lighted pathways/sidewalks.

Programs of Study: Mount Ida confers B.A., B.S., and B.L.S. degrees. Associate degrees are also awarded. Bachelor's degrees are awarded in AGRICULTURE (equine science), BUSINESS (business administration and management, fashion merchandising, funeral home services, hospitality management services, marketing/retailing/merchandising, retailing, and small business management), COMMUNICATIONS AND THE ARTS (communications, graphic design, journalism, media arts, and radio/television technology), EDUCATION (early childhood), ENGINEERING AND ENVIRONMENTAL DESIGN (interior design), HEALTH PROFESSIONS (veterinary science), SOCIAL SCIENCE (child psychology/development, criminal justice, fashion design and technology, law, and liberal arts/general studies). Veterinary technology, dental hygiene, and funeral service are the strongest academically. Business and veterinary technology are the largest.

Required: Candidates for a bachelor's degree require 128 credits with a 2.0 GPA. The distribution requirement varies for each major. 1 phys ed course is required. The all-college curriculum includes these common

experiences for all students: a college success course, a junior year interdisciplinary seminar, and a senior capstone project.

Special: Internships in the form of work experience are available in each department. Work-study provided by the college, student-designed majors, study abroad in 14 countries, an exchange program with Strasbourg, France, a general studies degree, an interdisciplinary major in legal studies, nondegree study, and an accelerated degree program in funeral service are also available. There are 4 national honor societies, a freshman honors program, and 4 departmental honors programs.

Faculty/Classroom: 46% of faculty are male; 54%, female. All teach undergraduates. The average class size in an introductory lecture is 25; in a laboratory, 16; and in a regular course, 20.

Requirements: The SAT or ACT is required. In addition, applicants are required to have 4 units of English, 2 of social studies, and 3 each of math and science. A portfolio is recommended for certain programs, while an interview is recommended for all applicants. The GED is accepted. A GPA of 2.0 is required. AP and CLEP credits are accepted. Important factors in the admissions decision are advanced placement or honor courses, evidence of special talent, and recommendations by school officials.

Procedure: Freshmen are admitted fall and spring. Entrance exams should be taken as early as possible by the junior year. There are early admissions and deferred admissions plans. There is a rolling admissions plan. Application deadlines are open. The fall 2005 application fee was $35. Applications are accepted on-line.

Transfer: 144 transfer students enrolled in a recent year. Applicants need a minimum grade average of C and must submit college and high school transcripts. 32 of 120 credits required for the bachelor's degree must be completed at Mount Ida.

Visiting: There are regularly scheduled orientations for prospective students, consisting of fall and spring open houses, Saturday sessions, and weekday appointments. There are guides for informal visits and visitors may sit in on classes and stay overnight. To schedule a visit, contact the Admissions Office.

Financial Aid: 70% of undergraduates work part time. Average annual earnings from campus work are $1500. The average financial indebtedness of a recent graduate was $19,268. Mount Ida is a member of CSS. The FAFSA is required. Check with the school for current deadlines.

International Students: There were 93 international students enrolled in a recent year. The school actively recruits these students. They must score satisfactorily on the written TOEFL or on the electronic version and also take the SAT or the ACT.

Computers: All students may access the system. There are no time limits and no fees. It is strongly recommended that all students have a personal computer.

Graduates: In a recent year, 128 bachelor's degrees were awarded. The most popular majors were criminal justice (16%), graphic design (13%), and management (11%).

Admissions Contact: Judith A. Kaufman.
E-mail: *admissions@mountida.edu* Web: *www.mountida.edu*

NEW ENGLAND CONSERVATORY OF MUSIC	E-2
Boston, MA 02115	**(617) 585-1101; Fax: (617) 585-1115**
Full-time: 208 men, 160 women	**Faculty:** IIA
Part-time: 6 men, 9 women	**Ph.D.s:** n/av
Graduate: 167 men, 233 women	**Student/Faculty:** 4 to 1
Year: semesters	**Tuition:** $27,800
Application Deadline: December 1	**Room & Board:** $10,950
Freshman Class: 925 applied, 294 accepted, 85 enrolled	
SAT or ACT: required	**SPECIAL**

The New England Conservatory of Music, founded in 1867, is the oldest private school of its kind in the United States. It combines classroom study of music with an emphasis on performance for talented young musicians. Some figures in the above capsule and this profile are approximate. In addition to regional accreditation, NEC has baccalaureate program accreditation with NASM. The 3 libraries contain 80,000 volumes, 500 microform items, and 50,000 audio/video tapes/CDs/DVDs, and subscribe to 275 periodicals including electronic. Computerized library services include the card catalog and interlibrary loans. Special learning facilities include an electronic music studio. The 8-acre campus is in an urban area 2 miles south of downtown Boston. Including any residence halls, there are 4 buildings.

Student Life: 71% of undergraduates are from out of state, mostly the Northeast. Students are from 47 states, 39 foreign countries, and Canada. 75% are from public schools. 57% are white; 24% foreign nationals. The average age of freshmen is 18; all undergraduates, 21.

Housing: 169 students can be accommodated in college housing, which includes coed dormitories. On-campus housing is guaranteed for the freshman year only. 79% of students commute. Alcohol is not permitted. No one may keep cars.

Activities: There are no fraternities or sororities. There are 8 groups on campus, including band, choir, chorale, chorus, computers, gay, international, jazz band, opera, orchestra, political, religious, student government, and symphony. Popular campus events include visits of guest performers, and 600 NEC concerts per year.

Sports: There is no sports program at NEC.

Disabled Students: All of the campus is accessible. Elevators, special parking, specially equipped rest rooms, and lowered drinking fountains are available.

Services: Counseling and information services are available, as is tutoring in most subjects. There is remedial writing.

Campus Safety and Security: Measures include security escort services, informal discussions, pamphlets/posters/films, and 24-hour security at the residence hall.

Programs of Study: NEC confers the B.Mus. degree. Master's and doctoral degrees are also awarded. Bachelor's degrees are awarded in COMMUNICATIONS AND THE ARTS (applied music, jazz, music, music history and appreciation, music performance, music theory and composition, and visual and performing arts).

Required: Requirements for graduation include a minimum 2.0 GPA, an average of 120 total credits, and a senior recital.

Special: NEC offers cross-registration with Northeastern and Tufts Universities, and Simmons College, as well as a 5 year double major degree program with Tufts University. There is a freshman honors program.

Faculty/Classroom: 64% of faculty are male; 36%, female. All teach undergraduates. The average class size in an introductory lecture is 30 and in a regular course, 15.

Admissions: 32% of the 2005-2006 applicants were accepted.

Requirements: The SAT or ACT is required. In addition, the applicant must be a graduate of an accredited secondary school or have a GED. An essay is required, as is an audition after submitting the formal application. In some cases, taped auditions are accepted; these must be submitted with the admissions application. Applicants are expected to have reached an advanced level of musical accomplishment. A GPA of 2.75 is required. AP and CLEP credits are accepted. Important factors in the admissions decision are evidence of special talent, recommendations by school officials, and parents or siblings attending the school.

Procedure: Freshmen are admitted fall and spring. Entrance exams should be taken by March 1. There is a deferred admissions plan. Applications should be filed by December 1 for fall entry and November 1 for spring entry, along with a $100 fee. Notification is sent by April 1. 337 applicants were on the 2005 waiting list; 21 were admitted. Applications are accepted on-line.

Transfer: 19 transfer students enrolled in 2004-2005. Transfer students must audition and submit all college-level transcripts and a transfer statement. 60 of 120 credits required for the bachelor's degree must be completed at NEC.

Visiting: There are regularly scheduled orientations for prospective students, consisting of tours offered regularly during the week. Visitors may sit in on classes. To schedule a visit, contact the Admissions Office.

Financial Aid: In 2005-2006, 88% of all full-time freshmen and 81% of continuing full-time students received some form of financial aid. 84% of full-time freshmen and 87% of continuing full-time students received need-based aid. The average freshman award was $9640. Need-based scholarships or need-based grants averaged $9640 ($24,500 maximum); and need-based self-help aid (loans and jobs) averaged $2625 ($2625 maximum). In a recent year, 55% of undergraduates worked part time. Average annual earnings from campus work were $1120. The average financial indebtedness of a recent graduate was $36,040. NEC is a member of CSS. The FAFSA and the college's own financial statement are required. Check with the school for current application deadlines.

International Students: In a recent year there were 45 international students enrolled. The school actively recruits these students. They must score satisfactorily on the written TOEFL or on the electronic version and also take the SAT or the ACT.

Computers: All students may access the system. There are no time limits and no fees.

Graduates: In a recent year, 76 bachelor's degrees were awarded. The most popular majors were performance (72%) and composition (4%). In an average class, All graduate in 5 years or less. 50 companies recruited on campus in 2004-2005. Of a recent graduating class, 85% were enrolled in graduate school within 6 months of graduation.

Admissions Contact: Thomas Novak, Dean of Admissions and Financial Aid. E-mail: *admissions@newenglandconservatory.edu* Web: *www.newenglandconservatory.edu*

NEWBURY COLLEGE D-2
Brookline, MA 02445-5796

(617) 730-7007
(800) NEWBURY; Fax: (617) 731-9618

Full-time: 450 men, 500 women	**Faculty:** 54
Part-time: 390 men and women	**Ph.D.s:** 20%
Graduate: none	**Student/Faculty:** 18 to 1
Year: semesters, summer session	**Tuition:** $16,600
Application Deadline: March 1	**Room & Board:** $9000
Freshman Class: 1800 applied, 1460 accepted, 360 enrolled	
ACT: 20	**COMPETITIVE**

Newbury College, founded in 1962, is a private institution offering career-relevant degree programs in business, graphic design, legal studies, computer science, interior design, communication, culinary arts, hotel and restaurant management, and psychology. There are 3 undergraduate schools. In addition to regional accreditation, Newbury has baccalaureate program accreditation with FIDER. The library contains 32,459 volumes, 74,000 microform items, and 1900 audio/video tapes/CDs/DVDs, and subscribes to 127,000 periodicals including electronic. Computerized library services include the card catalog, interlibrary loans, and database searching. Special learning facilities include a learning resource center, art gallery, radio station, and TV station. The 10-acre campus is in a suburban area 3 miles west of Boston. Including any residence halls, there are 10 buildings.

Student Life: 64% of undergraduates are from Massachusetts. Others are from 20 states, 42 foreign countries, and Canada. 60% are from public schools. 52% are white; 24% foreign nationals; 14% African American. The average age of freshmen is 19; all undergraduates, 21. 10% do not continue beyond their first year; 85% remain to graduate.

Housing: 202 students can be accommodated in college housing, which includes single-sex and coed dormitories. In addition, there are special-interest houses. On-campus housing is guaranteed for the freshman year only, is available on a first-come, first-served basis, and is available on a lottery system for upperclassmen. Priority is given to out-of-town students. 50% of students live on campus; of those, 80% remain on campus on weekends. Alcohol is not permitted. Upperclassmen may keep cars.

Activities: There are no fraternities or sororities. There are 20 groups on campus, including debate, drama, ethnic, gay, honors, international, jazz band, literary magazine, professional, radio and TV, religious, social, social service, and student government. Popular campus events include Multicultural Week, Spring Fling, and Fall Fest.

Sports: There are 6 intercollegiate sports for men and 6 for women, and 9 intramural sports for men and 9 for women. Facilities include an off-site gym and a cardiovascular/weight room.

Disabled Students: 80% of the campus is accessible. Wheelchair ramps, elevators, special parking, and specially equipped rest rooms are available.

Services: Counseling and information services are available, as is tutoring in every subject. There is a reader service for the blind, and remedial math, reading, and writing.

Campus Safety and Security: Measures include 24-hour foot and vehicle patrol, security escort services, shuttle buses, and pamphlets/posters/films. There are lighted pathways/sidewalks.

Programs of Study: Newbury confers the B.S. degree. Associate degrees are also awarded. Bachelor's degrees are awarded in BUSINESS (accounting, business administration and management, hotel/motel and restaurant management, and international business management), COMMUNICATIONS AND THE ARTS (communications and graphic design), COMPUTER AND PHYSICAL SCIENCE (computer science), ENGINEERING AND ENVIRONMENTAL DESIGN (interior design), HEALTH PROFESSIONS (health care administration), SOCIAL SCIENCE (criminal justice, food production/management/services, paralegal studies, prelaw, and psychology). Legal studies and hotel and restaurant management are the strongest academically. Business administration, culinary arts, and interior design are the largest.

Required: Candidates for a bachelor's degree must earn 120 credits or 60 credits beyond the associate degree, with a 2.0 GPA. Distribution requirements include courses in math, lab science, literature, and social science, as well as 3 additional credits in arts and sciences.

Special: Internships are part of the bachelor degree program. Dual majors are available. Credits earned for associate degrees in professional areas can be applied toward the college's bachelor degree programs. There is a 3-3 law program with Massachusetts School of Law and study abroad in many countries. A fashion merchandising concentration is possible within the business administration B.S. degree. There is a freshman honors program.

Faculty/Classroom: 51% of faculty are male; 49%, female. All teach undergraduates. The average class size in an introductory lecture is 20; in a laboratory, 10; and in a regular course, 16.

Admissions: 81% of the 2005-2006 applicants were accepted.

Requirements: The SAT or ACT is recommended. Applicants must submit an application, 2 letters of recommendation, high school transcripts, and an essay. A personal interview is strongly recommended. A GPA of 2.0 is required. AP and CLEP credits are accepted. Important factors in the admissions decision are leadership record, recommendations by alumni, and extracurricular activities record.

Procedure: Freshmen are admitted fall and spring. Entrance exams should be taken following acceptance. There are early admissions, deferred admissions and rolling admissions plans. Early decision applications should be filed by December 1; regular applications, by March 1 for fall entry and November 1 for spring entry, along with a $50 fee. Notification of early decision is sent January 1; regular decision, on a rolling basis. Applications are accepted on-line.

Transfer: 35 transfer students enrolled in 2004-2005. Transfer students must submit an application, 2 recommendations, high school and college transcripts, and an essay. 30 of 120 credits required for the bachelor's degree must be completed at Newbury.

Visiting: There are regularly scheduled orientations for prospective students, including fall and spring open houses, daily interviews, and campus tours. There are guides for informal visits and visitors may sit in on classes. To schedule a visit, contact the Office of Admission.

Financial Aid: In a recent year, 80% of all full-time freshmen and 78% of continuing full-time students received some form of financial aid. 75% of all full-time students received need-based aid. 58% of undergraduates work part time. Average annual earnings from campus work were $1250. Newbury is a member of CSS. The FAFSA and the college's own financial statement are required. The priority date for freshman financial aid applications for fall entry is November 1. The deadline for filing freshman financial aid applications for fall entry is March 1.

International Students: There are 230 international students enrolled. The school actively recruits these students. They must score satisfactorily on the written TOEFL or on the electronic version.

Computers: All students may access the system. There are no time limits and no fees.

Graduates: From July 1, 2004 to June 30, 2005, 115 bachelor's degrees were awarded. The most popular majors were business management (34%), hotel and restaurant management (24%), and computer science (10%). 60 companies recruited on campus in 2004-2005. Of the 2004 graduating class, 12% were enrolled in graduate school within 6 months of graduation and 96% were employed.

Admissions Contact: Salvadore Liberto, Vice President.
E-mail: *info@newbury.edu* Web: *www.newbury.edu*

NICHOLS COLLEGE	C-3
Dudley, MA 01571	**(508) 943-2055**
	(800) 470-3379; Fax: (508) 943-9885
Full-time: 600 men, 300 women	**Faculty:** 33
Part-time: 200 men, 300 women	**Ph.D.s:** 61%
Graduate: 200 men, 100 women	**Student/Faculty:** 25 to 1
Year: semesters, summer session	**Tuition:** $20,000
Application Deadline: open	**Room & Board:** $8000
Freshman Class: n/av	
SAT or ACT: required	**LESS COMPETITIVE**

Nichols College, founded in 1931, is a private institution emphasizing business and liberal arts. There are campuses in Dudley, Auburn, and Marlborough. Figures in the above capsule and in this profile are approximate. The library contains 44,000 volumes, 3800 microform items, and 1700 audio/video tapes/CDs/DVDs, and subscribes to 200 periodicals including electronic. Computerized library services include the card catalog, interlibrary loans, database searching, and Internet access. Special learning facilities include a learning resource center, radio station, and the Robert C. Fischer Policy and Cultural Institute. The 200-acre campus is in a rural area 20 miles south of Worcester. Including any residence halls, there are 27 buildings.

Student Life: 70% of undergraduates are from Massachusetts. Others are from 20 states and 3 foreign countries. 91% are white. The average age of freshmen is 18; all undergraduates, 21. 36% do not continue beyond their first year; 45% remain to graduate.

Housing: 737 students can be accommodated in college housing, which includes coed dorms. In addition, there is substance=free housing. On-campus housing is guaranteed for all 4 years and is available on a lottery system for upperclassmen. 80% of students live on campus; of those, 65% remain on campus on weekends. All students may keep cars.

Activities: There are no fraternities or sororities. There are 32 groups on campus, including cheerleading, chess, computers, departmental, drama, ethnic, honors, international, literary magazine, newspaper, political, professional, radio and TV, religious, student government, and yearbook. Popular campus events include Spring Weekend and 100 Days Social.

Sports: There are 8 intercollegiate sports for men and 7 for women, and 5 intramural sports for men and 4 for women. Facilities include a field house with basketball courts, a sauna, aerobics and weight training rooms, and athletic training facilities. There is also an athletic complex with a gym, a suspended jogging track, 2 racquetball courts, a squash

court, an indoor climbing wall, and 2 fitness rooms. Outdoor facilities include 6 tennis courts, a volleyball court, and a basketball court.

Disabled Students: 67% of the campus is accessible. Wheelchair ramps, elevators, special parking, specially equipped rest rooms, special class scheduling, lowered drinking fountains, and special housing are available. The college makes every effort to accommodate students with special needs.

Services: Counseling and information services are available, as is tutoring in most subjects. There is remedial math and writing and ESL assistance by appointment.

Campus Safety and Security: Measures include 24-hour foot and vehicle patrol, self-defense education, security escort services, and informal discussions. There are pamphlets/posters/films and lighted pathways/sidewalks.

Programs of Study: Nichols confers B.A. and B.S.B.A. degrees. Associate and master's degrees are also awarded. Bachelor's degrees are awarded in BUSINESS (accounting, banking and finance, business administration and management, management information systems, marketing/retailing/merchandising, personnel management, and sports management), COMMUNICATIONS AND THE ARTS (English), COMPUTER AND PHYSICAL SCIENCE (mathematics), SOCIAL SCIENCE (economics, history, and psychology). Accounting, management, and marketing are the strongest academically. Sports management and accounting are the largest.

Required: All students must complete a program of study within 10 semesters and maintain a GPA of 2.0 overall and in their major. Business students need 33 hours of business core classes out of the total 122 hours required of all students for graduation. Students must complete 2 writing-intensive upper-level courses, and they must attend 28 events within the Cultural Experience: The Arts, Sciences, and Public Policy program.

Special: Nichols offers cross-registration with the Worecester Consortium of Colleges, internships designed with departmental approval, study abroad at Regents College in London and at the University of Nova Scotia, a Washington semester, a general business degree, a teacher certification program, an accelerated degree program in business administration, and nondegree study. There are 5 national honor societies and 8 departmental honors programs.

Faculty/Classroom: 62% of faculty are male; 38%, female. All teach undergraduates and 45% do research. No introductory courses are taught by graduate students. The average class size in an introductory lecture is 21; in a laboratory, 18; and in a regular course, 23.

Admissions: 87% of recent applicants were accepted. The SAT scores for a recent freshman class were: Verbal--76% below 500, 23% between 500 and 599, and 1% between 600 and 700; Math--70% below 500, 27% between 500 and 599, and 3% between 600 and 700. 5% of freshmen were in the top fifth of their class; 24% were in the top two fifths.

Requirements: The SAT or ACT is required. In addition, applicants must be graduates of accredited secondary schools or have earned a GED. Recommended preparation includes 4 years of high school English, 3 of math, 2 each of science and social studies, and 5 of academic electives. A GPA of 2.0 is required. AP and CLEP credits are accepted. Important factors in the admissions decision are advanced placement or honor courses, recommendations by school officials, and personality/intangible qualities.

Procedure: Freshmen are admitted fall and spring. Entrance exams should be taken by November of the senior year. There is a deferred admissions plan. There is a rolling admissions plan. Application deadlines are open. The fall 2005 application fee was $25. Applications are accepted on-line.

Transfer: 30 transfer students enrolled in a recent year. Applicants need a minimum GPA of 2.0 in courses to be transferred and must submit official transcripts of all previous college study. 30 of 122 credits required for the bachelor's degree must be completed at Nichols.

Visiting: There are regularly scheduled orientations for prospective students, including meetings with faculty members and preregistration; separate orientation programs are tailored for transfers only. There are guides for informal visits and visitors may sit in on classes and stay overnight. To schedule a visit, contact the Admissions Office.

Financial Aid: In a recent year, 91% of all full-time freshmen and 96% of continuing full-time students received some form of financial aid. 80% of full-time freshmen and 77% of continuing full-time students received need-based aid. The average freshman award was $14,718. Need-based scholarships or need-based grants averaged $9561 ($21,476 maximum); need-based self-help aid (loans and jobs) averaged $5555 ($12,000 maximum); and other non-need-based awards and non-need-based scholarships averaged $10,860 ($19,400 maximum). 27% of undergraduates work part time. Average annual earnings from campus work were $828. The average financial indebtedness of a recent graduate was $21,996. The FAFSA is required. Check with the schol for current deadlines.

International Students: There were 6 international students enrolled in a recent year. The school actively recruits these students. They must score satisfactorily on the written TOEFL or on the electronic version or have acceptable scores on the SAT or ACT.

Computers: All students may access the system 24 hours a day. There are no time limits and no fees. All students are required to have personal computers.

Admissions Contact: Director of Admissions and Financial Aid. E-mail: *admissions@nichols.edu* Web: *www.nichols.edu*

NORTHEASTERN UNIVERSITY   E-2
Boston, MA 02115   **(617) 373-2200; Fax: (617) 373-8780**

Full-time: 7209 men, 7521 women	**Faculty:** 853; I, av$
Part-time: none	**Ph.D.s:** 88%
Graduate: 2265 men, 2546 women	**Student/Faculty:** 17 to 1
Year: semesters, summer session	**Tuition:** $25,192
Application Deadline: January 15	**Room & Board:** $10,550
Freshman Class: 25,467 applied, 11,958 accepted, 2831 enrolled	
SAT Verbal/Math: 603/623*	**ACT:** recommended

HIGHLY COMPETITIVE

Northeastern University, founded in 1898, is a private, nonsectarian institution offering programs that include an experiential learning component and that integrate professional work experience with classroom study. The academic program usually requires 5 years to complete. There are 6 undergraduate and 8 graduate schools. In addition to regional accreditation, Northeastern has baccalaureate program accreditation with AACSB, ABET, ACPE, ADA, APTA, CAHEA, CSAB, and NLN. The 4 libraries contain 987,658 volumes, 230,795 microform items, and 17,765 audio/video tapes/CDs/DVDs, and subscribe to 7397 periodicals including electronic. Computerized library services include the card catalog, interlibrary loans, database searching, Internet access, and laptop Internet portals. Special learning facilities include a learning resource center, art gallery, and radio station. The 67-acre campus is in an urban area in the heart of the Back Bay section of Boston. Including any residence halls, there are 69 buildings.

Student Life: 66% of undergraduates are from out of state, mostly the Northeast. Students are from 50 states, 94 foreign countries, and Canada. 74% are white. The average age of freshmen is 18; all undergraduates, 21. 10% do not continue beyond their first year.

Housing: 7305 students can be accommodated in college housing, which includes single-sex and coed dorms, on-campus apartments, and fraternity houses. In addition, there are honors houses and special-interest houses, and quiet, living and learning, international, and wellness halls. On-campus housing is guaranteed for the freshman year only, is available on a first-come, first-served basis, and is available on a lottery system for upperclassmen. Upperclassmen may keep cars.

Activities: 4% of men belong to 4 local and 9 national fraternities; 4% of women belong to 9 national sororities. There are 223 groups on campus, including art, band, cheerleading, chess, chorale, chorus, computers, dance, debate, disabled student, drama, ethnic, gay, honors, international, jazz band, literary magazine, musical theater, newspaper, orchestra, outing, pep band, photography, political, professional, radio and TV, religious, social, social service, student government, and symphony. Popular campus events include SpringFest, International Carnevale, and Nataraj.

Sports: There are 9 intercollegiate sports for men and 11 for women, and 14 intramural sports for men and 14 for women. Facilities include outdoor and indoor tracks, a football stadium, an indoor hockey arena, a swimming pool, indoor and outdoor tennis courts, racquetball, squash, volleyball, and basketball courts, and exercise and weight machines.

Disabled Students: 95% of the campus is accessible. Wheelchair ramps, elevators, special parking, specially equipped rest rooms, special class scheduling, lowered drinking fountains, lowered telephones, and special housing are available.

Services: Counseling and information services are available, as is tutoring in most subjects. The Academic Assistance Center offers tutoring services in reading, language, vocabulary, note taking, test preparation, and related study skills. Individualized computer instruction is available. There is a reader service for the blind, and remedial math, reading, and writing.

Campus Safety and Security: Measures include 24-hour foot and vehicle patrol, self-defense education, security escort services, and pamphlets/posters/films. There are emergency telephones, lighted pathways/sidewalks, and awareness programs on rape prevention, alcohol abuse, personal safety, and crime prevention. A state-of-the-art fire and security alarm center monitors residence halls, academic buildings, and athletic facilities.

Programs of Study: Northeastern confers B.A., and B.S. degrees. Associate, master's, and doctoral degrees are also awarded. Bachelor's degrees are awarded in BIOLOGICAL SCIENCE (biochemistry, biology/biological science, neurosciences, and toxicology), BUSINESS (accounting, business administration and management, human resources, international business management, management information systems, and marketing/retailing/merchandising), COMMUNICATIONS AND THE ARTS (advertising, art, communications, dramatic arts, English, French, journalism, languages, linguistics, music, performing arts, public relations, and Spanish), COMPUTER AND PHYSICAL SCIENCE (ap-

plied physics, chemistry, computer programming, computer science, geology, information sciences and systems, mathematics, and physics), EDUCATION (athletic training, early childhood, and elementary), ENGINEERING AND ENVIRONMENTAL DESIGN (architecture, chemical engineering, civil engineering, computer engineering, computer technology, electrical/electronics engineering, electrical/electronics engineering technology, engineering, engineering technology, industrial engineering, mechanical engineering, and mechanical engineering technology), HEALTH PROFESSIONS (health science, medical laboratory science, nursing, pharmacy, physical therapy, rehabilitation therapy, and speech pathology/audiology), SOCIAL SCIENCE (African American studies, anthropology, criminal justice, economics, history, human services, interdisciplinary studies, international relations, interpreter for the deaf, philosophy, physical fitness/movement, political science/government, psychology, and sociology). Engineering, computer science, and business administration are the strongest academically. Arts and sciences and business administration are the largest.

Required: Although each college has its own requirements, students must generally complete an upper-division writing proficiency requirement in addition to at least 132 semester hours with a minimum GPA of 2.0. Students must also fulfill a diversity requirement.

Special: Northeastern offers paid professional internships with area companies in Boston, around the country, and throughout the world to integrate classroom instruction with professional experience. Cross-registration with the New England Conservatory of Music and Hebrew College, among other universities and colleges, study abroad in dozens of countries, a Washington semester, work-study through the university and in neighboring public and private agencies, and dual majors and student-designed majors in the arts and sciences are also offered. Non-degree adult and continuing education are available, as are programs and scholarships for racial minorities and women, and accelerated degrees in engineering, nursing, the arts and sciences, pharmacy, and business. There are 26 national honor societies, a freshman honors program, and all departments have honors programs.

Faculty/Classroom: 65% of faculty are male; 35%, female. All both teach and do research.

Admissions: 47% of the 2005-2006 applicants were accepted. The SAT scores for the 2005-2006 freshman class were: Verbal--8% below 500, 34% between 500 and 599, 48% between 600 and 700, and 10% above 700; Math--5% below 500, 26% between 500 and 599, 55% between 600 and 700, and 14% above 700. 73% of the current freshmen were in the top fourth of their class; 94% were in the top half.

Requirements: The SAT is required and the ACT is recommended. In addition, northeastern recommends that applicants have 17 academic units, including 4 in English, 3 each in math, science, and social studies, and 2 each in foreign language and history. An essay is required. AP credits are accepted. Important factors in the admissions decision are advanced placement or honor courses, leadership record, and recommendations by school officials.

Procedure: Freshmen are admitted fall and spring. Entrance exams should be taken from May of the junior year through December of the senior year. There are early admissions and deferred admissions plans. Early decision applications should be filed by November 15; regular applications, by January 15 for fall entry. Notification of early decision is sent December 31; regular decision, April 1. 5406 applicants were on the 2005 waiting list. Applications are accepted on-line. The fall 2005 application fee was $75.

Transfer: 584 transfer students enrolled in fall 2005. The most successful transfer students have earned a cumulative GPA of 3.0. Students have also completed the introductory level courses for their intended major. Transfer students with less than 27 semester hours of college-level credit must also submit their high school transcript and SAT or ACT scores. 32 of 128 credits required for the bachelor's degree must be completed at Northeastern.

Visiting: There are regularly scheduled orientations for prospective students. There are guides for informal visits. To schedule a visit, contact the Office of Undergraduate Admissions at (617) 373-2211.

Financial Aid: In 2005-2006, 83% of all full-time freshmen and 72% of continuing full-time students received some form of financial aid. The average freshman award was $17,884. Need-based scholarships or need-based grants averaged $13,352; need-based self-help aid (loans and jobs) averaged $4435; and non-need-based athletic scholarships averaged $20,628. 30% of undergraduates work part time. The CSS/Profile or FAFSA is required. The deadline for filing freshman financial aid applications for fall entry is February 15.

International Students: In a recent year, there were 758 international students enrolled. The school actively recruits these students. They must score satisfactory on the written TOEFL and also take the SAT or ACT. Minimum scores vary by and within the program.

Computers: All students may access the system 24 hours daily. There are no time limits and no fees.

Graduates: From July 1, 2004 to June 30, 2005, 2583 bachelor's degrees were awarded. The most popular majors were business (28%), engineering (11%), and health sciences (8%). In an average class, 61%

graduate in 6 years or less. 81 companies recruited on campus in 2004-2005. Of the 2004 graduating class, 19% were enrolled in graduate school within 6 months of graduation and 84% were employed.

Admissions Contact: Ronne A. Patrick, Director of Admissions. A video is available. E-mail: *admissions@neu.edu* Web: *www.northeastern.edu*

PINE MANOR COLLEGE
E-2

Chestnut Hill, MA 02467

(617) 731-7104
(800) 762-1357; Fax: (617) 731-7102

Full-time: 447 women	**Faculty:** 30; IIB, --$
Part-time: 8 women	**Ph.D.s:** 77%
Graduate: none	**Student/Faculty:** 15 to 1
Year: semesters, summer session	**Tuition:** $15,538
Application Deadline: open	**Room & Board:** $9500
Freshman Class: 387 applied, 364 accepted, 138 enrolled	
SAT or ACT: required	**LESS COMPETITIVE**

Pine Manor College, established in 1911, is a private liberal arts college for women. The library contains 65,632 volumes, 62,386 microform items, and 1944 audio/video tapes/CDs/DVDs, and subscribes to 272 periodicals including electronic. Computerized library services include the card catalog, interlibrary loans, database searching, and Internet access. Special learning facilities include a learning resource center, art gallery, radio station, TV station, and a language lab. The 60-acre campus is in a suburban area 5 miles west of Boston. Including any residence halls, there are 28 buildings.

Student Life: 66% of undergraduates are from Massachusetts. Others are from 28 states, 22 foreign countries, and Canada. 33% are African American; 23% white. The average age of freshmen is 18; all undergraduates, 20. 36% do not continue beyond their first year; 40% remain to graduate.

Housing: 481 students can be accommodated in college housing, which includes single-sex dorms. In addition, there are special-interest houses, nonsmoking dorms, and a wellness floor (no alcohol allowed). On-campus housing is guaranteed for all 4 years. 78% of students live on campus; of those, 80% remain on campus on weekends. All students may keep cars.

Activities: There are no fraternities. There are 25 groups on campus, including chorus, dance, diversity drama, ethnic, gay, honors, interior design (ASID), international, literary magazine, minority (ALANA) musical theater, newspaper, political, professional, psychology, radio and TV, religious, social, social service, student government, student health (SHAB), and yearbook. Popular campus events include Late Night Breakfast during finals, Stressbusters, and Casino Night.

Sports: Facilities include a modern gym, softball and soccer fields, cross-country trails, tennis courts, a dance studio, and a weight room.

Disabled Students: 40% of the campus is accessible. Wheelchair ramps, elevators, special parking, specially equipped rest rooms, and lowered drinking fountains are available.

Services: Counseling and information services are available, as is tutoring in every subject. There is remedial math, reading, and writing. The learning resource center has professional and peer tutoring and workshops.

Campus Safety and Security: Measures include 24-hour foot and vehicle patrol, self-defense education, security escort services, and shuttle buses. There are informal discussions, pamphlets/posters/films, emergency telephones, and lighted pathways/sidewalks.

Programs of Study: PMC confers the B.A. degree. Associate degrees are also awarded. Bachelor's degrees are awarded in BIOLOGICAL SCIENCE (biology/biological science), BUSINESS (business administration and management), COMMUNICATIONS AND THE ARTS (art, communications, and English), SOCIAL SCIENCE (ethics, politics and social policy, history, liberal arts/general studies, and psychology). Psychology, visual arts, and business administration are the largest.

Required: An outcomes-based general education program, with portfolio assessment, is a college requirement. A 4-year leadership program complements the portfolio program. This assists students in exploring inclusive and socially responsible leadership. In addition, students must maintain a minimum GPA of 2.0 and take a total of 132 semester hours.

Special: Pine Manor offers cross-registration with area colleges, internships at more than 1000 sites, and study abroad throughout the world and at sea. A Washington semester, work-study programs, dual majors, student-designed majors, a B.A.-B.S. degree, nondegree study within continuing education, and pass/fail options for 1 course each semester also are available, as is the English Language Institute for students whose native language is not English. There is 1 national honor society and a freshman honors program.

Faculty/Classroom: 26% of faculty are male; 74%, female. All teach undergraduates. The average class size in an introductory lecture is 16; in a laboratory, 16; and in a regular course, 13.

Admissions: 94% of the 2005-2006 applicants were accepted.

Requirements: The SAT or ACT is required. In addition, applicants are required to have taken 4 courses in English and 3 in math. Additional courses in foreign language, social science, natural science, and elective areas are recommended. An essay is also required. An interview is recommended. The GED is accepted. AP and CLEP credits are accepted. Important factors in the admissions decision are advanced placement or honor courses, leadership record, and recommendations by school officials.

Procedure: Freshmen are admitted fall and spring. There are deferred admissions and rolling admissions plans. Application deadlines are open. Notification is sent on a rolling basis. Application fee is $25. Applications are accepted on-line.

Transfer: 24 transfer students enrolled in 2004-2005. Pine Manor requires transfer students to submit 2 letters of recommendation (1 from a professor) and college transcripts and recommends high school transcripts. The SAT or ACT also is recommended. 32 of 132 credits required for the bachelor's degree must be completed at PMC.

Visiting: There are regularly scheduled orientations for prospective students, including a campus tour and interview. There are guides for informal visits and visitors may sit in on classes and stay overnight. To schedule a visit, contact the Admissions Office at *admissions@pmc.edu*.

Financial Aid: In 2005-2006, 95% of all full-time freshmen received some form of financial aid. The average freshman award was $15,961. Need-based scholarships or need-based grants averaged $11,413; and need-based self-help aid (loans and jobs) averaged $5212. Average annual earnings from campus work are $1500. The FAFSA is required. The priority date for freshman financial aid applications for fall entry is May 1.

International Students: There are 39 international students enrolled. The school actively recruits these students. .

Computers: Wireless access is available. Pine Manor College enjoys high-speed computing network. Students have access to e-mail, the Internet, a campus PC network, and PCs located throughout the campus. Labtop connections are also available in some areas. Software for word processing, spreadsheets, databases, statistics, Web page development, graphic design, desktop and electronic publishing, digital media, and specialized course software is available for student use on college PCs in classrooms and labs. Students are provided with an e-mail account, network storage space for files, and 25MB of Web space on our community Web site. All students may access the system. There are no time limits and no fees.

Graduates: From July 1, 2004 to June 30, 2005, 89 bachelor's degrees were awarded. The most popular majors were psychology (25%), business administration (19%), and biology (18%). In an average class, 33% graduate in 4 years or less, 38% graduate in 5 years or less, and 40% graduate in 6 years or less.

Admissions Contact: Robin Engel, Dean of Admissions and Financial Aid. E-mail: *admissions@pmc.edu* Web: *www.pmc.edu*

REGIS COLLEGE
D-2

Weston, MA 02493-1571

(781) 768-7100
(866) 438-7344; Fax: (781) 768-7071

Full-time: 4 men, 617 women	**Faculty:** 48; IIB, --$
Part-time: 21 men, 201 women	**Ph.D.s:** 78%
Graduate: 30 men, 430 women	**Student/Faculty:** 13 to 1
Year: semesters, summer session	**Tuition:** $21,525
Application Deadline: n/av	**Room & Board:** $9825
Freshman Class: 908 applied, 688 accepted, 161 enrolled	
SAT Verbal/Math: 480/460*	**LESS COMPETITIVE**

Regis College, founded in 1927, is a private liberal arts institution for women, affiliated with the Roman Catholic Church. In addition to regional accreditation, Regis has baccalaureate program accreditation with CSWE, NASDTEC, and NLN. The library contains 139,837 volumes and 5867 audio/video tapes/CDs/DVDs, and subscribes to 787 periodicals including electronic. Computerized library services include the card catalog, interlibrary loans, database searching, and Internet access. Special learning facilities include a learning resource center, art gallery, radio station, museum of stamps and postal history, and fine arts center. The 131-acre campus is in a suburban area 12 miles west of Boston. Including any residence halls, there are 15 buildings.

Student Life: 89% of undergraduates are from Massachusetts. Others are from 18 states and 9 foreign countries. 74% are from public schools. 40% are white; 14% African American; 10% Hispanic. The average age of freshmen is 18; all undergraduates, 22. 22% do not continue beyond their first year; 65% remain to graduate.

Housing: 465 students can be accommodated in college housing, which includes single-sex dormitories and quiet housing floors. On-campus housing is guaranteed for all 4 years. 64% of students live on campus; of those, 50% remain on campus on weekends. All students may keep cars.

Activities: There are no fraternities. There are 30 groups on campus, including art, choir, chorale, chorus, commuter association, computers, dance, drama, ethnic, honors, international, literary magazine, musical theater, newspaper, photography, political, professional, radio and TV, religious, social, social service, student government, and yearbook. Popular campus events include Father/Daughter Dance, Mother/Daughter Brunch, and Family Weekend.

Sports: Facilities include a softball diamond, a soccer field, 4 tennis courts, and an athletic facility with a gym, an aerobics and dance studio, squash courts, a pool, and a sauna and Jacuzzi. A fitness center provides a full range of cardiovascular machines as well as free weights and Nautilus equipment.

Disabled Students: 87% of the campus is accessible. Wheelchair ramps, elevators, special parking, specially equipped rest rooms, special class scheduling, lowered drinking fountains, lowered telephones, and special housing are available.

Services: Counseling and information services are available, as is tutoring in every subject. There is a reader service for the blind and remedial math and writing. There are academic support services for learning-disabled students.

Campus Safety and Security: Measures include 24-hour foot and vehicle patrol, self-defense education, security escort services, and shuttle buses. There are informal discussions, pamphlets/posters/films, emergency telephones, and lighted pathways/sidewalks.

Programs of Study: Regis confers B.A., B.S.N., and B.S.W. degrees. Associate and master's degrees are also awarded. Bachelor's degrees are awarded in BIOLOGICAL SCIENCE (biochemistry and biology/biological science), BUSINESS (management science), COMMUNICATIONS AND THE ARTS (communications, dramatic arts, English, graphic design, public relations, and Spanish), COMPUTER AND PHYSICAL SCIENCE (computer science and information sciences and systems), EDUCATION (mathematics and museum studies), HEALTH PROFESSIONS (nursing), SOCIAL SCIENCE (history, international relations, law, liberal arts/general studies, political science/government, psychology, social work, and sociology). Nursing, communication, and biology are the largest.

Required: To graduate, students must complete a total of 36 4-credit courses (144 credits), including 8 to 12 in the major, as well as the General Education Program requirements with a minimum GPA of 2.0.

Special: Cross-registration with Boston, Babson, and Bentley Colleges and through the Sisters of St. Joseph Consortium is offered. Students may study abroad at Regis affiliates in London, Ireland, and in Kyoto, Japan, or through programs of other American colleges. Regis also offers internships, an accelerated degree program, a Washington semester at American University, dual and self-designed majors, work-study, nondegree study, and pass/fail options. Students have the option of pursuing a minor in addition to their major field of study. There are 8 national honor societies, a freshman honors program, and all departments have honors programs.

Faculty/Classroom: 23% of faculty are male; 77%, female. 87% teach undergraduates. No introductory courses are taught by graduate students. The average class size in an introductory lecture is 19; in a laboratory, 17; and in a regular course, 12.

Admissions: 76% of the 2005-2006 applicants were accepted. The SAT scores for the 2005-2006 freshman class were: Verbal--55% below 500, 40% between 500 and 599, 4% between 600 and 700, and 1% above 700; Math--62% below 500, 32% between 500 and 599, and 6% between 600 and 700. 50% of the current freshmen were in the top fifth of their class; 78% were in the top two fifths.

Requirements: The SAT is required. In addition, applicants should have 4 years of English, 3 or 4 of electives, 3 of math, and 2 each of foreign language, social studies, and natural science, including a lab science. An essay and 2 letters of recommendation are required. An interview is strongly encouraged. The GED is accepted. Regis requires applicants to be in the upper 50% of their class. A GPA of 2.5 is required. AP and CLEP credits are accepted. Important factors in the admissions decision are recommendations by school officials, extracurricular activities record, and ability to finance college education.

Procedure: Freshmen are admitted fall and spring. Entrance exams should be taken during the fall before enrollment. There are deferred admissions and rolling admissions plans. Applications should be filed by December 1 for spring entry. Notification is sent on a rolling basis. Applications are accepted on-line. The fall 2005 application fee was $30.

Transfer: 55 transfer students enrolled in 2004-2005. Transfer students need an admission application and fee; an official high school transcript if fewer than 9 college courses have been completed; an official college transcript; 1 letter of recommendation from a professor at the previous college attended; the academic catalog of the previous college; an essay; the SAT scores if fewer than 16 courses have been completed; and health records. 64 of 144 credits required for the bachelor's degree must be completed at Regis.

Visiting: There are regularly scheduled orientations for prospective students, including a welcome tour, lunch, speaker panels, and overnight programs offering class participation. There are guides for informal visits and visitors may sit in on classes and stay overnight. To schedule a visit, contact the Admissions Office.

Financial Aid: In 2005-2006, 87% of all full-time freshmen and 81% of continuing full-time students received some form of financial aid. 82% of full-time freshmen and 72% of continuing full-time students received

need-based aid. The average freshman award was $20,803. Need-based scholarships or need-based grants averaged $11,396 ($25,000 maximum); need-based self-help aid (loans and jobs) averaged $6041 ($15,500 maximum); other non-need-based awards and non-need-based scholarships averaged $8769 ($1400 maximum); and a sibling discount of 25% between both students averaged $3769 ($5381 maximum). 48% of undergraduates work part time. Average annual earnings from campus work are $1234. The average financial indebtedness of the 2005 graduate was $24,094. Regis is a member of CSS. The FAFSA and the college's own financial statement are required. The priority date for freshman financial aid applications for fall entry is February 15.

International Students: There are 9 international students enrolled. The school actively recruits these students. They must score satisfactorily on the written TOEFL or on the electronic version and also take the SAT or the ACT.

Computers: Students can access network resources including e-mail, Blackboard, the Internet and web access to registration and grades either from their dorm room, a computer lab or from off campus through the Internet. All students may access the system. There are no time limits and no fees.

Graduates: From July 1, 2004 to June 30, 2005, 234 bachelor's degrees were awarded. The most popular majors were nursing (35%), management (11%), and biology (9%). In an average class, 63% graduate in 4 years or less, 65% graduate in 5 years or less, and 65% graduate in 6 years or less. 20 companies recruited on campus in 2004-2005.

Admissions Contact: Regis College, Office of Admission.
E-mail: *admission@regiscollege.edu* Web: *www.regiscollege.edu*

SALEM STATE COLLEGE   E-2

Salem, MA 01970   (978) 542-6200; Fax: (978) 542-6893

Full-time: 2043 men, 3425 women	**Faculty:** 296
Part-time: 631 men, 1197 women	**Ph.D.s:** 77%
Graduate: 579 men, 1988 women	**Student/Faculty:** 18 to 1
Year: semesters, summer session	**Tuition:** $5594 ($11,734)
Application Deadline: open	**Room & Board:** $7567
Freshman Class: 4827 applied, 4324 accepted, 1226 enrolled	
SAT or ACT: required	**LESS COMPETITIVE**

Salem State College, founded in 1854, is a public institution offering programs in liberal arts, business, education, and nursing. There are 5 undergraduate schools and 1 graduate school. In addition to regional accreditation, Salem State has baccalaureate program accreditation with CSWE, NASAD, NCATE, and NLN. The library contains 301,876 volumes and 566,592 microform items, and subscribes to 1145 periodicals including electronic. Computerized library services include the card catalog, interlibrary loans, database searching, and Internet access. Special learning facilities include a learning resource center, art gallery, radio station, TV station, and an observatory. The 62-acre campus is in an urban area 18 miles northeast of Boston. Including any residence halls, there are 19 buildings.

Student Life: 90% of undergraduates are from Massachusetts. Others are from 20 states, 40 foreign countries, and Canada. 98% are from public schools. 83% are white. The average age of freshmen is 19; all undergraduates, 24. 25% do not continue beyond their first year; 36% remain to graduate.

Housing: 1470 students can be accommodated in college housing, which includes single-sex and coed dorms and on-campus apartments. On-campus housing is available on a first-come, first-served basis. Priority is given to out-of-town students. 78% of students commute. Alcohol is not permitted. Upperclassmen may keep cars.

Activities: There are no fraternities or sororities. There are 44 groups on campus, including art, band, cheerleading, choir, chorale, chorus, computers, dance, drama, ethnic, gay, honors, international, jazz band, literary magazine, musical theater, newspaper, photography, political, radio and TV, religious, social, social service, and student government. Popular campus events include Welcome Week, Arts Festival, and Senior Week.

Sports: There are 10 intercollegiate sports for men and 10 for women, and 15 intramural sports for men and 15 for women. Facilities include an athletic center with 27 facilities, including a 1600-seat gym, a 2800-seat ice rink, an 8-lane swimming pool, 4 tennis courts, a weight room, a dance studio, and a wellness fitness center.

Disabled Students: 90% of the campus is accessible. Wheelchair ramps, elevators, special parking, specially equipped rest rooms, lowered drinking fountains, and lowered telephones are available.

Services: Counseling and information services are available, as is tutoring in every subject. There is a reader service for the blind, and remedial math, reading, and writing.

Campus Safety and Security: Measures include 24-hour foot and vehicle patrol, self-defense education, security escort services, and shuttle buses. There are informal discussions, pamphlets/posters/films, emergency telephones, and lighted pathways/sidewalks.

Programs of Study: Salem State confers B.A., B.S., B.F.A., B.G.S., B.S.B.A., B.S.Ed., B.S.N., and B.S.W. degrees. Master's degrees are also awarded. Bachelor's degrees are awarded in BIOLOGICAL SCIENCE (biology/biological science), BUSINESS (accounting, banking and finance, business administration and management, and marketing/retailing/merchandising), COMMUNICATIONS AND THE ARTS (advertising, communications, design, dramatic arts, English, fine arts, and photography), COMPUTER AND PHYSICAL SCIENCE (chemistry, computer programming, earth science, geology, and mathematics), EDUCATION (art, business, education, science, and secondary), ENGINEERING AND ENVIRONMENTAL DESIGN (cartography), HEALTH PROFESSIONS (medical laboratory technology and nursing), SOCIAL SCIENCE (criminal justice, economics, geography, history, psychology, social work, and sociology). Sciences is the strongest academically. Business administration is the largest.

Required: All students must demonstrate basic competence in reading, math, and computer literacy, and are required to take a distribution of classes that includes 36 to 38 credits in humanities, sciences, and social sciences. Specific courses required are English composition, speech, phys ed, and the first-year seminar. All core and distribution requirements may be waived if the student passes a departmentally prescribed exemption exam. A minimum GPA of 2.0 and a total of 127 credits, with 36 in the major, are needed to graduate.

Special: Study abroad is available in 3 countries. Cross-registration through a consortium, internships, work-study programs, a Washington semester, student-designed and dual majors, B.A.-B.S. degrees, and a general studies degree are offered. Life experience credit, nondegree study, and pass/fail options also are possible. There are 13 national honor societies, a freshman honors program, and 9 departmental honors programs.

Faculty/Classroom: All teach undergraduates. The average class size in an introductory lecture is 22; in a laboratory, 12; and in a regular course, 17.

Admissions: 90% of the 2005-2006 applicants were accepted. The SAT scores for the 2005-2006 freshman class were: Verbal--52% below 500, 38% between 500 and 599, 9% between 600 and 700, and 1% above 700; Math--56% below 500, 36% between 500 and 599, 7% between 600 and 700, and 1% above 700.

Requirements: The SAT or ACT is required. In addition, Salem State requires that applicants earn 16 credits, including 4 years of English, 3 years each of math and science, and 2 years each of foreign language and history. Courses in music, art, drama, computer science, and psychology are suggested. Art majors must provide a portfolio. A GED is acceptable. Students with a GED, those out of school more than 3 years, and the learning disabled do not need the SAT. A GPA of 2.0 is required. AP and CLEP credits are accepted. Important factors in the admissions decision are advanced placement or honor courses, evidence of special talent, and recommendations by school officials.

Procedure: Freshmen are admitted in the fall. Entrance exams should be taken November and December of the senior year. There is a deferred admissions and a rolling admissions plan. Application deadlines are open. Application fee is $25. Applications are accepted on-line.

Transfer: 809 transfer students enrolled in 2004-2005. Transfer students are required to have a minimum GPA of 2.0 with more than 24 credits; 2.5 with fewer than 24 credits. 30 of 127 credits required for the bachelor's degree must be completed at Salem State.

Visiting: There are regularly scheduled orientations for prospective students. There are guides for informal visits and visitors may sit in on classes. To schedule a visit, contact the Admissions Office at admissions@salemstate.edu.

Financial Aid: 86% of undergraduates work part time. Average annual earnings from campus work are $1600. The FAFSA is required. Check with the school for current deadlines.

International Students: There are 258 international students enrolled. The school actively recruits these students. Satisfactory score are required on the written TOEFL and the SAT or the ACT.

Computers: Wireless access is available. All students may access the system 7 days a week. There are no time limits and no fees. All students are required to have personal computers.

Graduates: From July 1, 2004 to June 30, 2005, 845 bachelor's degrees were awarded. The most popular majors were business marketing (20%), education (12%), and psychology (10%).

Admissions Contact: Nate Bryant, Director of Admissions.
E-mail: admissions@salem.mass.edu Web: www.salemstate.edu

SIMMONS COLLEGE E-2
Boston, MA 02115 (617) 521-2051
(800) 345-8468; Fax: (617) 521-3190

Full-time: 1688 women	Faculty: 130; IIA, +$
Part-time: 27 men, 250 women	Ph.D.s: 65%
Graduate: 420 men, 2420 women	Student/Faculty: 13 to 1
Year: semesters, summer session	Tuition: $24,880
Application Deadline: April 1	Room & Board: $10,760
Freshman Class: 2303 applied, 1469 accepted, 413 enrolled	
SAT Verbal/Math: 561/545*	ACT: 23 VERY COMPETITIVE

Simmons College, founded in 1899, is a private institution primarily for women that offers a comprehensive education combining the arts, sciences, and humanities with preprofessional training. Most graduate programs are co-ed. There are 3 undergraduate and 5 graduate schools. In addition to regional accreditation, Simmons has baccalaureate program accreditation with ADA, APTA, CSWE, and NLN. The library contains 251,494 volumes, 72,894 microform items, and 7054 audio/video tapes/CDs/DVDs, and subscribes to 1595 periodicals including electronic. Computerized library services include the card catalog, interlibrary loans, database searching, Internet access, and laptop Internet portals. Special learning facilities include an art gallery TV studio, modern language lab, physical therapy motion lab, nursing lab, and library science technology center. The 12-acre campus is in an urban area in Boston. Including any residence halls, there are 26 buildings.

Student Life: 60% of undergraduates are from Massachusetts. Others are from 38 states and 26 foreign countries. 78% are from public schools. 79% are white. The average age of freshmen is 18; all undergraduates, 20. 13% do not continue beyond their first year; 75% remain to graduate.

Housing: 1150 students can be accommodated in college housing, which includes single-sex and coed dormitories and off-campus apartments. In addition, there are special-interest houses. On-campus housing is guaranteed for all 4 years. 70% of students live on campus; of those, 75% remain on campus on weekends. No one may keep cars.

Activities: There are no fraternities or sororities. There are 70 groups on campus, including chorale, dance, debate, drama, ethnic, film, gay, honors, international, literary magazine, newspaper, political, professional, religious, social, social service, and student government. Popular campus events include Spring Spree, May Day Breakfast, and Culture Shock.

Sports: There are 8 intercollegiate sports for women and 4 intramural sports for women. Facilities include an 8-lane pool, a spa and sauna, 2 racquetball and 2 squash courts, 2 rowing tanks, 3 fitness rooms, a dance studio, an indoor track, and a gym with 3 badminton courts, 2 volleyball courts, and a basketball court.

Disabled Students: All of the campus is accessible. Wheelchair ramps, elevators, special parking, specially equipped rest rooms, special class scheduling, lowered drinking fountains, and lowered telephones are available.

Services: Counseling and information services are available, as is tutoring in some subjects, including basic freshman courses, languages, biology, chemistry, psychology, and math. There is a reader service for the blind and remedial math and writing. The school also provides study groups, individual tutoring, help with study skills and time management, and assistance for students with learning disabilities and special needs.

Campus Safety and Security: Measures include 24-hour foot and vehicle patrol, self-defense education, security escort services, and shuttle buses. There are informal discussions, pamphlets/posters/films, emergency telephones, lighted pathways/sidewalks, closed-circuit TV, ID card access, and security training in first response and crisis intervention.

Programs of Study: Simmons confers B.A. and B.S. degrees. Master's and doctoral degrees are also awarded. Bachelor's degrees are awarded in BIOLOGICAL SCIENCE (biochemistry, biology/biological science, and nutrition), BUSINESS (banking and finance, management information systems, and marketing/retailing/merchandising), COMMUNICATIONS AND THE ARTS (advertising, art, arts administration/management, communications, English, English as a second/foreign language, French, music, and Spanish), COMPUTER AND PHYSICAL SCIENCE (chemistry, computer science, and mathematics), EDUCATION (early childhood, elementary, secondary, and special), ENGINEERING AND ENVIRONMENTAL DESIGN (environmental science), HEALTH PROFESSIONS (nursing, physical therapy, and premedicine), SOCIAL SCIENCE (African American studies, dietetics, East Asian studies, economics, food science, history, human services, international relations, philosophy, political science/government, prelaw, psychobiology, psychology, sociology, and women's studies). Physical therapy, biology, and communication are the strongest academically. Physical therapy, psychology, and communication are the largest.

Required: To graduate, students must complete 128 semester hours, including 24 to 48 in the major, and maintain a minimum GPA of 2.0. 8 semester hours in a supervised independent learning experience or an internship are also required. 6 modes of inquiry courses are required. They must also fulfill foreign language and math competency requirements. In addition to completing the multidisciplinary core course, students must complete 1 course from each of the following categories: creative and performing arts; language, literature, and culture; quantitative analysis and reasoning; social and historical perspectives; and psychological and ethical development. A thesis is optional.

Special: Cross-registration is available with the New England Conservatory of Music, Hebrew, Emmanuel, and Wheelock Colleges, Massachusetts College of Art, Massachusetts College of Pharmacy and Health Sciences, and Wentworth Institute of Technology. Simmons offers study abroad in Europe through the Institute of European studies. A Washington semester at American University, accelerated degree programs, profit and nonprofit internship programs, a B.A.-B.S. degree, dual majors, interdisciplinary majors, student-designed majors, work-study programs, and pass/fail options are also offered. There is a dual-degree program in chemistry, pharmacy, and physician's assistant with Massachusetts College of Pharmacy and Health Sciences. There is a freshman honors program.

Faculty/Classroom: 30% of faculty are male; 70%, female. All both teach and do research. No introductory courses are taught by graduate students. The average class size in an introductory lecture is 40; in a laboratory, 20; and in a regular course, 19.

Admissions: 64% of the 2005-2006 applicants were accepted. The SAT scores for the 2005-2006 freshman class were: Verbal--18% below 500, 49% between 500 and 599, 29% between 600 and 700, and 4% above 700; Math--23% below 500, 55% between 500 and 599, 21% between 600 and 700, and 1% above 700. 49% of the current freshmen were in the top fifth of their class; 78% were in the top two fifths. There were 7 National Merit semifinalists.

Requirements: The SAT or ACT is required. In addition, Simmons recommends that applicants have 4 years of English, 3 each of math, science, and social studies, and 2 of foreign language. An essay is required, and an interview is strongly recommended. A GPA of 3.0 is required. AP and CLEP credits are accepted. Important factors in the admissions decision are advanced placement or honor courses, recommendations by school officials, and extracurricular activities record.

Procedure: Freshmen are admitted fall and spring. Entrance exams should be taken by February 1 of the senior year. There are early admissions and deferred admissions plans. Early decision applications should be filed by December 1; regular applications, by April 1 for fall entry and December 1 for spring entry, along with a $35 fee. Notification of early decision is sent January 20; regular decision, April 15. 13 applicants were on the 2005 waiting list; 1 was admitted. Applications are accepted on-line.

Transfer: 108 transfer students enrolled in 2004-2005. Applicants should have a GPA of 2.8, at least 9 college-level credit hours, official transcripts from all colleges attended, and a faculty recommendation and dean's report from the previous college attended. 48 of 128 credits required for the bachelor's degree must be completed at Simmons.

Visiting: There are regularly scheduled orientations for prospective students, including a campus tour, class attendance, an interview, and meetings with faculty and students. There are guides for informal visits and visitors may sit in on classes and stay overnight. To schedule a visit, contact the Admissions Office.

Financial Aid: In 2005-2006, 74% of all full-time freshmen and 69% of continuing full-time students received some form of financial aid. 65% of all full-time students received need-based aid. The average freshman award was $17,312. Need-based scholarships or need-based grants averaged $11,751 ($16,500 maximum); and need-based self-help aid (loans and jobs) averaged $4018 ($8625 maximum). 75% of undergraduates work part time. Average annual earnings from campus work are $4800. The average financial indebtedness of the 2005 graduate was $26,300. Simmons is a member of CSS. The FAFSA and federal tax returns or W2 forms are required. The priority date for freshman financial aid applications for fall entry is April 1.

International Students: There are 19 international students enrolled. The school actively recruits these students. They must score satisfactorily on the written TOEFL or on the electronic version and also take the SAT or the ACT.

Computers: Wireless access is available. All students may access the system. There are no time limits and no fees. It is strongly recommended that all students have a personal computer.

Graduates: From July 1, 2004 to June 30, 2005, 428 bachelor's degrees were awarded. The most popular majors were nursing (19%), sociology (18%), and communications (9%). In an average class, 61% graduate in 4 years or less, 65% graduate in 5 years or less, and 66% graduate in 6 years or less. 25 companies recruited on campus in 2004-2005. Of the 2004 graduating class, 75% were employed within 6 months of graduation.

Admissions Contact: Catherine Childs-Capolupo, Director of Undergraduate Admission. E-mail: *ugadm@simmons.edu* Web: *www.simmons.edu*

SIMON'S ROCK COLLEGE OF BARD   A-2

Great Barrington, MA 01230-9702   (413) 528-7313
(800) 235-7186; Fax: (413) 528-7334

Full-time: 162 men, 210 women	**Faculty:** 37
Part-time: 3 men, 14 women	**Ph.D.s:** 89%
Graduate: none	**Student/Faculty:** 10 to 1
Year: semesters	**Tuition:** $33,334
Application Deadline: open	**Room & Board:** $8654
Freshman Class: 236 applied, 190 accepted, 145 enrolled	
SAT Verbal/Math: 645/605*	**ACT:** 23 **VERY COMPETITIVE+**

Simon's Rock College of Bard, founded in 1964, is a private liberal arts school especially designed to permit students who have completed the 10th or 11th grades to enroll for collegiate studies in 8 interdisciplinary majors. The library contains 70,791 volumes, 7550 microform items, and 4382 audio/video tapes/CDs/DVDs, and subscribes to 437 periodicals including electronic. Computerized library services include the card catalog, interlibrary loans, database searching, and Internet access. Special learning facilities include a learning resource center, art gallery, radio station, TV station, language lab, greenhouse, and community garden. The 275-acre campus is in a small town 50 miles west of Springfield. Including any residence halls, there are 47 buildings.

Student Life: 80% of undergraduates are from out of state, mostly the Middle Atlantic. Students are from 44 states and 4 foreign countries. 67% are from public schools. 74% are white. The average age of freshmen is 17; all undergraduates, 18. 22% do not continue beyond their first year.

Housing: 356 students can be accommodated in college housing, which includes single-sex and coed dorms and on-campus apartments. In addition, there are special-interest houses. On-campus housing is guaranteed for all 4 years. 85% of students live on campus; of those, 85% remain on campus on weekends. Alcohol is not permitted. Upperclassmen may keep cars.

Activities: There are no fraternities or sororities. There are 21 groups on campus, including art, chorus, computers, dance, debate, drama, ethnic, film, gay, jazz band, labor coalition, literary magazine, math, multicultural, newspaper, orchestra, photography, political, radio and TV, religious, social, social service, student government, women's center, and yearbook. Popular campus events include Winter Solstice, May Fest, and Prom nite.

Sports: There are 3 intercollegiate sports for men and 3 for women, and 7 intramural sports for men and 7 for women. Facilities include an 8-lane swimming pool, a multicourt gym, 3 racquetball courts, an elevated running track, a fitness and weight-training center, a rock-climbing wall, a soccer field, 4 tennis courts, and hiking trails.

Disabled Students: 80% of the campus is accessible. Wheelchair ramps, elevators, special parking, specially equipped rest rooms, special class scheduling, and lowered drinking fountains are available.

Services: Counseling and information services are available, as is tutoring in most subjects. Study skills instruction is available.

Campus Safety and Security: Measures include self-defense education, security escort services, informal discussions, and pamphlets/posters/films. There are emergency telephones, lighted pathways/sidewalks, and security officers from 4 P.M. to 8 P.M. weekdays and 24 hours a day on weekends.

Programs of Study: Simon's Rock confers the B.A. degree. Associate degrees are also awarded. Bachelor's degrees are awarded in BIOLOGICAL SCIENCE (biology/biological science and ecology), COMMUNICATIONS AND THE ARTS (art, art history and appreciation, creative writing, dance, dramatic arts, drawing, English literature, fine arts, French, German, Germanic languages and literature, literature, modern language, music history and appreciation, music performance, music theory and composition, painting, performing arts, photography, Spanish, studio art, and visual and performing arts), COMPUTER AND PHYSICAL SCIENCE (applied mathematics, chemistry, mathematics, natural sciences, physics, quantitative methods, and science), HEALTH PROFESSIONS (premedicine), SOCIAL SCIENCE (African American studies, American studies, Asian/Oriental studies, crosscultural studies, East Asian studies, Eastern European studies, ethics, politics, and social policy, European studies, French studies, German area studies, interdisciplinary studies, Latin American studies, philosophy, political science/government, psychology, and Russian and Slavic studies). Cross-cultural relations, psychology, and music are the strongest academically. Politics, law, and society; cross-cultural relations; and theater are the largest.

Required: All students must complete a writing and thinking workshop, a 2-semester freshman seminar, a sophomore seminar, and a cultural perspectives seminar. The core curriculum also includes distribution requirements in the arts, math, natural sciences, foreign languages, and phys ed. A total of 120 credits, including at least 32 in the major, plus an interdisciplinary B.A. seminar, an 8-credit senior thesis, and a minimum 2.0 GPA are needed for the B.A. in liberal arts.

Special: A major consists of selecting 2 concentrations from the 36 available; one concentration may be self-designed. Independent study internships in many fields, study abroad, a cooperative program with

Bard College, and a 3-2 engineering degree with Columbia University, Dartmouth College, or Washington University in St. Louis are available.

Faculty/Classroom: 63% of faculty are male; 37%, female. All both teach and do research. The average class size in an introductory lecture is 14; in a laboratory, 10; and in a regular course, 10.

Admissions: 81% of the 2005-2006 applicants were accepted. The SAT scores for the 2005-2006 freshman class were: Verbal--1% below 500, 31% between 500 and 599, 44% between 600 and 700, and 24% above 700; Math--22% below 500, 26% between 500 and 599, 31% between 600 and 700, and 21% above 700. The ACT scores were 53% between 21 and 23, 13% between 24 and 26, 13% between 27 and 28, and 20% above 28.

Requirements: The SAT is required and the ACT is recommended. In addition, the admissions committee looks more toward the required interview, essay, recommendations, and special talent. The school recommends that prospective students finish 2 years each of English, foreign languages, history, math, science, and social studies. A GPA of 2.0 is required. AP credits are accepted. Important factors in the admissions decision are advanced placement or honor courses, recommendations by school officials, and evidence of special talent.

Procedure: Freshmen are admitted fall and spring. Entrance exams should be taken prior to June 10. There are early admissions and deferred admissions plans. There is a rolling admissions plan. Applications deadlines are open for fall entry. Application fee is $50. Notification is sent on a rolling basis. A waiting list is an active part of the admissions procedure.

Transfer: Transfer students must be evaluated by the dean of academic affairs and registrar. 60 of 120 credits required for the bachelor's degree must be completed at Simon's Rock.

Visiting: There are regularly scheduled orientations for prospective students, including attending a class, a campus tour, and an interview. There are guides for informal visits and visitors may sit in on classes. To schedule a visit, contact Barbara Shultis, Receptionist, Office of Admission, at (413) 528-7312 or (800) 235-7186.

Financial Aid: In 2005-2006, 85% of all full-time freshmen and 84% of continuing full-time students received some form of financial aid. 60% of full-time freshmen and 40% of continuing full-time students received need-based aid. The average freshman award was $18,021. Need-based scholarships or need-based grants averaged $14,472 ($18,730 maximum); need-based self-help aid (loans and jobs) averaged $2625; and work contracts averaged $1373. 40% of undergraduates work part time. Average annual earnings from campus work are $1500. The average financial indebtedness of the 2005 graduate was $13,525. Simon's Rock is a member of CSS. The CSS/Profile or FAFSA is required. The deadline for filing freshman financial aid applications for fall entry is June 15.

International Students: There were 4 international students enrolled in a recent year. A satisfactory score on the TOEFL is required.

Computers: All students may access the system. There are no time limits and no fees. It is strongly recommended that all students have a personal computer.

Graduates: In a recent year, 45 bachelor's degrees were awarded. The most popular majors were politics, law, and society (13%), cross-cultural relations (13%), and theater (9%). In an average class, 77% graduate in 4 years or less, 86% graduate in 5 years or less, and 91% graduate in 6 years or less.

Admissions Contact: Mary-King Austin, Dean of Admission. A video is available. E-mail: admit@simons-rock.edu
Web: http://www.simons-rock.edu/

SMITH COLLEGE   B-2

Northampton, MA 01063   (413) 585-2500; Fax: (413) 585-2527

Full-time: 2625 women	Faculty: 274; IIB, ++$
Part-time: 40 women	Ph.D.s: 96%
Graduate: 56 men, 391 women	Student/Faculty: 10 to 1
Year: semesters	Tuition: $30,754
Application Deadline: January 16	Room & Board: $10,720
Freshman Class: n/av	
SAT Verbal/Math: 660/640*	ACT: 28 MOST COMPETITIVE

Smith College, founded in 1871, is the largest independent women's college in the United States and offers a liberal arts education. The 4 libraries contain 1,268,443 volumes, 139,674 microform items, and 64,126 audio/video tapes/CDs/DVDs, and subscribe to 2775 periodicals including electronic. Computerized library services include the card catalog, interlibrary loans, database searching, Internet access, and laptop Internet portals. Special learning facilities include a learning resource center, art gallery, radio station, TV station, astronomy observatories, center for foreign languages and culture, digital design studio, plant and horticultural labs, art studios with casting, printmaking, and darkroom facilities, and specialized libraries for science, music, and art. The 125-acre campus is in a small town 90 miles west of Boston. Including any residence halls, there are 105 buildings.

Student Life: 77% of undergraduates are from out of state, mostly the Middle Atlantic. Students are from 50 states, 53 foreign countries, and

Canada. 66% are from public schools. 71% are white. 21% claim no religious affiliation; 17% Protestant; 14% Catholic; 13% including Bahai, Buddhist, Eastern Orthodox, Hindu, Mormon, and; 10% Jewish. The average age of freshmen is 18; all undergraduates, 21. 8% do not continue beyond their first year; 85% remain to graduate.

Housing: 2453 students can be accommodated in college housing, which includes single-sex dormitories and on-campus apartments. In addition, there are language houses, special-interest houses, nonsmoking houses, 2 cooperative houses, housing for nontraditional-age students, an apartment complex for a limited number of juniors and seniors, a senior house, and a French-speaking house. On-campus housing is guaranteed for all 4 years. 96% of students live on campus. Upperclassmen may keep cars.

Activities: There are no fraternities. There are 102 groups on campus, including art, chess, choir, chorale, chorus, computers, dance, debate, drama, ethnic, film, gay, honors, international, literary magazine, musical theater, newspaper, orchestra, photography, political, professional, radio and TV, religious, social, social service, student government, symphony, and yearbook. Popular campus events include International Student Day, Spring and Winter Weekends, and Rally Day.

Sports: Facilities include indoor and outdoor tracks and tennis courts, riding rings, 2 gyms, a climbing wall, an indoor swimming pool with 1- and 3-meter diving boards, 2 weight-training rooms, a dance studio, 2 athletic training rooms, a human performance lab, squash courts, and field hockey, soccer, lacrosse, and softball fields. There is a performing arts center and a concert hall.

Disabled Students: 75% of the campus is accessible. Wheelchair ramps, elevators, special parking, specially equipped rest rooms, special class scheduling, lowered drinking fountains, lowered telephones, communications-accessible rooms, and accessible van service are available.

Services: Counseling and information services are available, as is tutoring in every subject. There is a reader service for the blind. Numerous services are provided for learning-disabled students, including note taking, oral tests, readers, tutors, books on tape, reading software, voice recognition, tape recorders, extended-timed tests, and writing counselors.

Campus Safety and Security: Measures include 24-hour foot and vehicle patrol, self-defense education, security escort services, and shuttle buses. There are informal discussions, pamphlets/posters/films, emergency telephones, and lighted pathways/sidewalks. First-year students are required to attend panel discussions on campus safety. Specialized personal safety presentations, including self defense and sexual assault information, are provided to various houses and organizations. There are crime prevention programs including bicycle registration.

Programs of Study: Smith confers A.B. and B.S.E.S degrees. Master's and doctoral degrees are also awarded. Bachelor's degrees are awarded in BIOLOGICAL SCIENCE (biochemistry, biology/biological science, and neurosciences), COMMUNICATIONS AND THE ARTS (art history and appreciation, classics, comparative literature, dance, dramatic arts, East Asian languages and literature, English, French, Germanic languages and literature, Greek, Italian, Latin, music, Russian, Spanish, and studio art), COMPUTER AND PHYSICAL SCIENCE (astronomy, chemistry, computer science, geology, mathematics, and physics), EDUCATION (early childhood, education, and elementary), ENGINEERING AND ENVIRONMENTAL DESIGN (architecture and engineering), SOCIAL SCIENCE (African American studies, American studies, anthropology, classical/ancient civilization, economics, French studies, history, Latin American studies, Luso-Brazilian studies, medieval studies, philosophy, political science/government, psychology, religion, Russian and Slavic studies, sociology, and women's studies). Government, psychology, and art are the largest.

Required: All students plan individual programs in consultation with faculty advisers and take 64 credits outside their major and 36 to 64 credits in the major. Students must maintain a minimum 2.0 GPA in all academic work and during the senior year. A total of 128 credits is needed to graduate. A writing-intensive course is required for first-year students. A thesis is required for departmental honors programs. Distribution requirements are necessary for Latin honors eligibility.

Special: Smith offers study abroad in more than 50 countries including the Smith College programs in Italy, France, Germany, and Switzerland, affiliated programs in India, Japan, Russia, China, South Africa, Peru, Brazil, Spain, and many others. Other opportunities include cross-registration with 5 area colleges, a Washington semester, Smithsonian internships, exchanges with historically Black colleges and other liberal arts colleges, and at BioSphere2. A 3-2 engineering degree is offered with Dartmouth College. Support for nontraditional-age students and for international students is provided, and funding for a summer internship is available for every undergraduate. Accelerated degree programs, student-designed majors, dual majors, and non-degree study are offered. There are 3 national honor societies, including Phi Beta Kappa.

Faculty/Classroom: 48% of faculty are male; 52%, female. All both teach and do research. No introductory courses are taught by graduate students. The average class size in an introductory lecture is 24; in a laboratory, 13; and in a regular course, 16.

Admissions: The SAT scores for the 2005-2006 freshman class were: Verbal--2% below 500, 23% between 500 and 599, 45% between 600

and 700, and 30% above 700; Math--5% below 500, 34% between 500 and 599, 44% between 600 and 700, and 17% above 700. The ACT scores were 10% below 21, 12% between 21 and 23, 12% between 24 and 26, 13% between 27 and 28, and 53% above 28. 84% of the current freshmen were in the top fifth of their class; 98% were in the top two fifths. 19 freshmen graduated first in their class.

Requirements: The SAT or ACT is required. In addition, Smith highly recommends that applicants have 4 years of English, 3 years each of math, science, and a foreign language, and 2 years of history. SAT Subject Tests, especially in writing, are strongly recommended, as are personal interviews. The GED is accepted. AP credits are accepted. Important factors in the admissions decision are advanced placement or honor courses, recommendations by school officials, and leadership record.

Procedure: Freshmen are admitted in the fall. Entrance exams should be taken before January of the senior year. There are early decision, early admissions, and deferred admissions plans. Early decision applications should be filed by November 15; regular applications, by January 16 for fall entry, along with a $60 fee. Notification of early decision is sent December 15; regular decision, April 1. 152 early decision candidates were accepted for the 2005-2006 class. 531 applicants were on the 2005 waiting list; 120 were admitted. Applications are accepted on-line.

Transfer: 91 transfer students enrolled in 2004-2005. Criteria for transfer students are similar to those for entering freshmen, with more emphasis on the college record. 64 of 128 credits required for the bachelor's degree must be completed at Smith.

Visiting: There are regularly scheduled orientations for prospective students, including student-guided tours available 4 times a day, Monday through Friday, when school is in full session and on Saturday mornings from September to January. Interviews may also be scheduled during these times. Information sessions are offered twice daily most of the year. There are guides for informal visits and visitors may sit in on classes and stay overnight. To schedule a visit, contact the Office of Admissions receptionist.

Financial Aid: In 2005-2006, 59% of all full-time freshmen and 64% of continuing full-time students received some form of financial aid. 59% of full-time freshmen and 64% of continuing full-time students received need-based aid. The average freshman award was $23,770. Need-based scholarships or need-based grants averaged $25,318 ($42,986 maximum); need-based self-help aid (loans and jobs) averaged $4188 ($9525 maximum); and other non-need-based awards and non-need-based scholarships averaged $3360 ($15,260 maximum). 56% of undergraduates work part time. Average annual earnings from campus work are $2128. The average financial indebtedness of the 2005 graduate was $19,945. Smith is a member of CSS. The CSS/Profile or FAFSA is required. The deadline for filing freshman financial aid applications for fall entry is February 1.

International Students: In a recent year, there were 185 international students enrolled. The school actively recruits these students. They must take the TOEFL and also take the SAT or the ACT if the language of instruction is English.

Computers: Wireless access is available. All students may access the system. There are no time limits and no fees.

Graduates: From July 1, 2004 to June 30, 2005, 734 bachelor's degrees were awarded. The most popular majors were government (16%), psychology (15%), and art (12%). In an average class, 1% graduate in 3 years or less, 82% graduate in 4 years or less, 83% graduate in 5 years or less, and 86% graduate in 6 years or less. 58 companies recruited on campus in 2004-2005. Of the 2004 graduating class, 16% were enrolled in graduate school within 6 months of graduation and 68% were employed.

Admissions Contact: Debra Shaver, Director of Admission.
E-mail: *admission@smith.edu* Web: *smith.edu*

SPRINGFIELD COLLEGE

B-3

Springfield, MA 01109

(413) 748-3136
(800) 343-1257; Fax: (413) 748-3694

Full-time: 2100 men and women	Faculty: 210; IIA, --$
Part-time: 100 men and women	Ph.D.s: 62%
Graduate: 900 men and women	Student/Faculty: 10 to 1
Year: semesters, summer session	Tuition: $18,000
Application Deadline: see profile	Room & Board: $7000
Freshman Class: n/av	
SAT or ACT: required	COMPETITIVE

Springfield College, established in 1885, is a private liberal arts and sciences institution. There are 3 undergraduate schools and 1 graduate school. Figures in the above capsule and in this profile are approximate. In addition to regional accreditation, S.C. has baccalaureate program accreditation with APTA, CAHEA, and NRPA. The library contains 168,300 volumes, 736,100 microform items, and 3200 audio/video tapes/CDs/DVDs, and subscribes to 800 periodicals including electronic. Computerized library services include the card catalog, interlibrary loans, and database searching. Special learning facilities include an art gallery, radio station, an outdoor center. The 160-acre campus is in a suburban area 26 miles north of Hartford, Connecticut. Including any residence halls, there are 38 buildings.

Student Life: Students are from 30 states, 12 foreign countries, and Canada. 83% are from public schools. 93% are white. The average age of freshmen is 18; all undergraduates, 21. 12% do not continue beyond their first year.

Housing: 1980 students can be accommodated in college housing, which includes single-sex and coed dorms, on-campus apartments, off-campus apartments, and married-student housing. In addition, there are special-interest houses and a wellness dorm. On-campus housing is guaranteed for all 4 years. 85% of students live on campus; of those, 70% remain on campus on weekends. Alcohol is not permitted. Upperclassmen may keep cars.

Activities: There are no fraternities or sororities. There are 58 groups on campus, including art, band, cheerleading, choir, chorus, club sports, computers, dance, drama, ethnic, film, gay, honors, international, jazz band, literary magazine, musical theater, newspaper, pep band, professional, radio and TV, religious, social, social service, student government, and yearbook. Popular campus events include Parents Weekend and Stepping Up Day.

Sports: There are 13 intercollegiate sports for men and 11 for women, and 10 intramural sports for men and 10 for women. Facilities include a 2000-seat stadium, a 2000-seat gym, a Superturf football/soccer/lacrosse/field hockey field, 8 tennis courts, baseball and softball fields, and free weight and Nautilus rooms.

Disabled Students: 75% of the campus is accessible. Wheelchair ramps, elevators, special parking, specially equipped rest rooms, special class scheduling, and lowered drinking fountains are available.

Services: Counseling and information services are available, as is tutoring in every subject. There is remedial math and writing.

Campus Safety and Security: Measures include 24-hour foot and vehicle patrol, self-defense education, security escort services, and shuttle buses. There are informal discussions, pamphlets/posters/films, emergency telephones, and lighted pathways/sidewalks.

Programs of Study: S.C. confers B.A. and B.S. degrees. Master's and doctoral degrees are also awarded. Bachelor's degrees are awarded in BIOLOGICAL SCIENCE (biochemistry, biology/biological science, and biotechnology), BUSINESS (business administration and management and sports management), COMMUNICATIONS AND THE ARTS (English and fine arts), COMPUTER AND PHYSICAL SCIENCE (chemistry, information sciences and systems, and mathematics), EDUCATION (early childhood, elementary, health, middle school, physical, science, and secondary), ENGINEERING AND ENVIRONMENTAL DESIGN (computer graphics), HEALTH PROFESSIONS (art therapy, emergency medical technologies, environmental health science, health care administration, predentistry, premedicine, recreation therapy, and rehabilitation therapy), SOCIAL SCIENCE (gerontology, history, human services, parks and recreation management, physical fitness/movement, political science/government, prelaw, psychology, and sociology). Physical therapy and athletic training are the strongest academically. Physical education is the largest.

Required: To graduate, students must complete a total of 130 credits with a 2.0 GPA. Core requirements include 50 semester hours in English, social and natural sciences, health, religion, philosophy, and art, and 4 credits in phys ed.

Special: There is a co-op program and cross-registration with cooperating colleges in the greater Springfield area. Internships are required in most majors, and there is limited study abroad. There are 2 national honor societies.

Faculty/Classroom: 52% of faculty are male; 48%, female. No introductory courses are taught by graduate students. The average class size in an introductory lecture is 125; in a laboratory, 20; and in a regular course, 30.

Requirements: The SAT or ACT is required. In addition, applicants must be graduates of an accredited secondary school and have completed 4 years of English and 3 years each of history, math, and science. The school accepts the GED. An essay is required and an interview is recommended. AP and CLEP credits are accepted. Important factors in the admissions decision are advanced placement or honor courses, leadership record, and extracurricular activities record.

Procedure: Freshmen are admitted fall and spring. Entrance exams should be taken by November of the senior year. There are early decision, early admissions, and deferred admissions plans. Check with the school for current application deadlines. The fall 2005 application fee was $40. Notification of regular decision is sent on a rolling basis. A waiting list is an active part of the admissions procedure. Applications are accepted on-line.

Transfer: Grades of 2.0 transfer for credit. Transfer students are admitted in the fall and spring.

Visiting: There are guides for informal visits and visitors may sit in on classes and stay overnight. To schedule a visit, contact the Admissions Office.

Financial Aid: The CSS/Profile or FAFSA and tax returns for parents and the student are required. Check with the school for current deadlines.

International Students: The school actively recruits these students. They must score satisfactorily on the written TOEFL and also take the SAT or the ACT.

Computers: All students may access the system. There are no time limits and no fees.

Admissions Contact: Mary N. DeAngelo, Director of Admissions. A video is available. E-mail: *admissions@spfldcol.edu* Web: *www.springfieldcollege.edu*

STONEHILL COLLEGE   E-3

Easton, MA 02357	**(508) 565-1373; Fax: (508) 565-1545**
Full-time: 925 men, 1335 women	Faculty: IIB, +$
Part-time: 50 men, 121 women	Ph.D.s: 85%
Graduate: 6 men, 6 women	Student/Faculty: n/av
Year: semesters, summer session	Tuition: $25,540
Application Deadline: January 15	Room & Board: $10,564
Freshman Class: 4847 applied, 2744 accepted, 618 enrolled	
SAT Verbal/Math: 590/600*	ACT: 25*

HIGHLY COMPETITIVE

Stonehill College, founded in 1948 by the Holy Cross Fathers, is a private Roman Catholic college offering undergraduate degrees in liberal arts and sciences, business, and other preprofessional disciplines. The library contains 205,600 volumes, 368,178 microform items, and 6723 audio/video tapes/CDs/DVDs, and subscribes to 2210 periodicals including electronic. Computerized library services include the card catalog, interlibrary loans, database searching, Internet access, and laptop Internet portals. Special learning facilities include a learning resource center, art gallery, radio station, an observatory, an institute for the study of law and society, and several archives and special collections. The 375-acre campus is in a suburban area 20 miles south of Boston. Including any residence halls, there are 26 buildings.

Student Life: 60% of undergraduates are from Massachusetts. Others are from 28 states, 9 foreign countries, and Canada. 67% are from public schools. 90% are white. 67% are Catholic; 15% claim no religious affiliation; 10% Protestant. The average age of freshmen is 18; all undergraduates, 21. 10% do not continue beyond their first year; 85% remain to graduate.

Housing: 1825 students can be accommodated in college housing, which includes single-sex and coed dorms. In addition, there are special-interest house, substance-free wellness housing, and community service housing.. On-campus housing is guaranteed for all 4 years. 89% of students live on campus; of those, 85% remain on campus on weekends. Upperclassmen may keep cars.

Activities: There are no fraternities or sororities. There are 79 groups on campus, including academic, ACES (Active, Concerned, and Educated Students), art, band, cheerleading, chess, choir, chorale, chorus, computers, dance, drama, environmental, ethnic, film, gay, honors, international, literary magazine, musical theater, newspaper, pep band, photography, political, professional, radio and TV, religious, social, social service, student government, and yearbook. Popular campus events include Fall Concert, Spring Weekend, and Halloween Mixer.

Sports: There are 9 intercollegiate sports for men and 11 for women, and 22 intramural sports for men and 22 for women. Facilities include a 2000-seat stadium for football, field hockey, and lacrosse, a 2000-seat field for men's and women's soccer, a gym with basketball and volleyball courts, a 4200-square-foot weight and cardiovascular fitness area, a recreational and intramural sports complex, tennis courts, baseball, softball, and field hockey practice areas, and 3 recreational fields for intramural and club sports.

Disabled Students: 85% of the campus is accessible. Wheelchair ramps, elevators, special parking, specially equipped rest rooms, special class scheduling, lowered drinking fountains, lowered telephones, telecommunication devices for the deaf, and 10 dorm rooms designed specifically for disabled students are available.

Services: Counseling and information services are available, as is tutoring in most subjects. There is an LD specialist and free diagnostic testing. There is a reader service for the blind and remedial writing.

Campus Safety and Security: Measures include 24-hour foot and vehicle patrol, self-defense education, security escort services, and informal discussions. There are pamphlets/posters/films, emergency telephones, lighted pathways/sidewalks, bicycle patrols, and a weekend guest sign-in policy.

Programs of Study: Stonehill confers B.A., B.S., and B.S.B.A. degrees. Master's degrees are also awarded. Bachelor's degrees are awarded in BIOLOGICAL SCIENCE (biochemistry and biology/biological science), BUSINESS (accounting, banking and finance, business administration and management, international business management, and marketing/retailing/merchandising), COMMUNICATIONS AND THE ARTS (communications, English, fine arts, and languages), COMPUTER AND PHYSICAL SCIENCE (chemistry, computer science, and mathematics), EDUCATION (education), ENGINEERING AND ENVIRONMENTAL DESIGN (computer engineering), HEALTH PROFESSIONS (health care administration), SOCIAL SCIENCE (American studies, criminology, economics, gender studies, history, interdisciplinary studies, international studies, philosophy, political science/government, psychology, public administration, religion, and sociology). Biology, computer science, and chemistry are the strongest academically. Business, psychology, and education are the largest.

Required: All students must complete a cornerstone program, which consists of 4 common courses within history/literature and philosophy/religious studies; a learning community consisting of 2 linked courses and a third integrated course; a moral reasoning course, and a senior capstone experience. Distribution requirements include 1 course each in natural science, social science, and statistical reasoning, and 1 year of a foreign language. Students must complete 120 hours, or 40 3- to 4-credit courses, while maintaining a minimum GPA of 2.0.

Special: On-campus work-study, international and domestic internships, a Washington semester through the Washington Center, and a semester in New York City in cooperation with Fordham University are available. Cross-registration with 8 other Massachusetts schools in the SACHEM consortium is also available. A 3-2 computer engineering degree is offered with the University of Notre Dame. Opportunities for study abroad include a Stonehill-Quebec Exchange and a worldwide Foreign Studies Program. Nondegree, directed, and field study are available as is a pass/fail option for upperclassmen. Programs in early childhood, elementary, and secondary education lead to the state's provisional teacher certification. Stonehill is also a member of the Marine Studies Consortium. Preprofessional preparation is available in medicine, dentistry, law, and theology. There are 13 national honor societies, a freshman honors program, and 7 departmental honors programs.

Faculty/Classroom: 62% of faculty are male; 38%, female. All both teach and do research. No introductory courses are taught by graduate students. The average class size in an introductory lecture is 21; in a laboratory, 17; and in a regular course, 20.

Admissions: 57% of the 2005-2006 applicants were accepted. The SAT scores for the 2005-2006 freshman class were: Verbal--5% below 500, 46% between 500 and 599, 45% between 600 and 700, and 4% above 700; Math--5% below 500, 40% between 500 and 599, 50% between 600 and 700, and 5% above 700. The ACT scores were 8% below 21, 18% between 21 and 23, 46% between 24 and 26, 19% between 27 and 28, and 9% above 28. 79% of the current freshmen were in the top fifth of their class; 97% were in the top two fifths. 4 freshmen graduated first in their class.

Requirements: The SAT or ACT is required. The ACT Optional Writing Test is also required. In addition, applicants should be graduates of an accredited high school or have earned the GED. Secondary preparation should include 4 units of English; 3 combined units of history, political science, and social sciences, 2 units of the same foreign language, 2 units of algebra, 1 unit of a lab science, and 1 unit of geometry. To these units elective subjects are to be added. Additional units in math are generally suggested, especially for business and science majors. An essay, school report, and teacher evaluations are also required. AP and CLEP credits are accepted. Important factors in the admissions decision are advanced placement or honor courses, leadership record, and extracurricular activities record.

Procedure: Freshmen are admitted fall and spring. Entrance exams should be taken in October. There are early decision, early admissions, and deferred admissions plans. Early decision applications should be filed by November 1; regular applications, by January 15 for fall entry and November 1 for spring entry, along with a $50 fee. Notification of early decision is sent December 15; regular decision, by April 1. 51 early decision candidates were accepted for the 2005-2006 class. 660 applicants were on the 2005 waiting list; 183 were admitted. Applications are accepted on-line.

Transfer: 41 transfer students enrolled in 2004-2005. Applicants must have a minimum GPA of 2.0, with 3.0 to 4.0 recommended. Official high school and college transcripts, along with catalogs with course descriptions from all colleges attended, are required. SAT or ACT scores are required and an interview is recommended. 60 of 120 credits required for the bachelor's degree must be completed at Stonehill.

Visiting: There are regularly scheduled orientations for prospective students, consisting of group information sessions and guided campus tours available by appointment throughout the year. Visitors may sit in on classes. To schedule a visit, contact the Admissions Office.

Financial Aid: In 2005-2006, 91% of all full-time freshmen and 90% of continuing full-time students received some form of financial aid. 63% of full-time freshmen and 62% of continuing full-time students received need-based aid. The average freshman award was $16,946. Need-based scholarships or need-based grants averaged $7019 ($34,604 maximum); need-based self-help aid (loans and jobs) averaged $6997 ($8625 maximum); non-need-based athletic scholarships averaged $8168 ($36,104 maximum); and other non-need-based awards and non-need-based scholarships averaged $6355 ($25,540 maximum). 36% of undergraduates work part time. Average annual earnings from campus work are $876. The average financial indebtedness of the 2005 graduate was $17,390. Stonehill is a member of CSS. The CSS/Profile and FAFSA are required. The deadline for filing freshman financial aid applications for fall entry is February 1.

International Students: There are 14 international students enrolled. The school actively recruits these students. They must take the TOEFL and also take the SAT or ACT.

Computers: Wireless access is available. The college has 12 computer labs with more than 300 desktop and laptop computers connected to the Internet through the wired and wireless network. Labs also include scanners and printers available for student use, software titles required for coursework, and other tools. Many labs are open 7 days a week, and all labs offer open access for all students. Wireless access is available throughout the campus and in all residence halls. All students may access the system 7 days a week, 24 hours a day. There are no time limits and no fees. It is strongly recommended that all students have a personal computer.

Graduates: From July 1, 2004 to June 30, 2005, 559 bachelor's degrees were awarded. The most popular majors were business (25%), education (8%), and communication (6%). In an average class, 81% graduate in 4 years or less, 83% graduate in 5 years or less, and 85% graduate in 6 years or less. 75 companies recruited on campus in 2004-2005. Of the 2004 graduating class, 16% were enrolled in graduate school within 6 months of graduation and 79% were employed.

Admissions Contact: Brian P. Murphy, Dean of Admissions and Enrollment. E-mail: *admissions@stonehill.edu* Web: *www.stonehill.edu*

SUFFOLK UNIVERSITY — E-2
Boston, MA 02108-2770
(617) 573-8460
(800) 6SUFFOL; Fax: (617) 742-4291

Full-time: 1645 men, 2325 women	**Faculty:** 268; IIA, ++$
Part-time: 164 men, 206 women	**Ph.D.s:** 92%
Graduate: 656 men, 928 women	**Student/Faculty:** 15 to 1
Year: semesters, summer session	**Tuition:** $21,220
Application Deadline: March 1	**Room & Board:** $11,940
Freshman Class: 6234 applied, 5134 accepted, 1136 enrolled	
SAT Verbal/Math: 520/510*	**ACT:** 21	**COMPETITIVE**

Suffolk University, founded in 1906, is a private institution offering undergraduate and graduate degrees in the arts and sciences, business, and law. There are 2 undergraduate and 3 graduate schools. In addition to regional accreditation, Suffolk has baccalaureate program accreditation with AACSB, AALS, ABA, ABET, ACS, APA, FIDER, NASAD and NASPAA. The 3 libraries contain 122,681 volumes, 136,147 microform items, and 945 audio/video tapes/CDs/DVDs, and subscribe to 15,034 periodicals including electronic. Computerized library services include the card catalog, interlibrary loans, database searching, Internet access, and laptop Internet portals. Special learning facilities include a learning resource center, art gallery, radio station, and TV station. The 2-acre campus is in an urban area in the Beacon Hill area of downtown Boston. Including any residence halls, there are 17 buildings.

Student Life: 67% of undergraduates are from Massachusetts. Others are from 39 states, 56 foreign countries, and Canada. 69% are from public schools. 63% are white; 10% foreign nationals. The average age of freshmen is 18; all undergraduates, 21. 25% do not continue beyond their first year; 56% remain to graduate.

Housing: 771 students can be accommodated in college housing, which includes coed dorms. On-campus housing is available on a first-come, first-served basis and is available on a lottery system for upperclassmen. 83% of students commute. Alcohol is not permitted. No one may keep cars.

Activities: 1% of men belong to 1 national fraternity; 1% of women belong to 1 local sorority. There are 75 groups on campus, including art, choir, chorale, chorus, computers, dance, debate, drama, ethnic, evening students, film, forensics, gay, honors, international, jazz band, literary magazine, musical theater, newspaper, orientation, photography, political, professional, radio and TV, recycling, religious, social, social service, student government, transfer students and yearbook. Popular campus events include Hispanic Fiesta, Fallfest Talent Show, and Temple Street Fair.

Sports: There are 7 intercollegiate sports for men and 6 for women, and 2 intramural sports for men and 1 for women. Facilities include a gym for basketball, volleyball, aerobics, intramurals, and indoor baseball/softball practice and a fully equipped fitness center.

Disabled Students: 95% of the campus is accessible. Wheelchair ramps, elevators, specially equipped rest rooms, special class scheduling, lowered drinking fountains, and lowered telephones are available.

Services: Counseling and information services are available, as is tutoring in every subject. There is a reader service for the blind, and remedial math, reading, and writing.

Campus Safety and Security: Measures include 24-hour foot and vehicle patrol, self-defense education, security escort services, and informal discussions. There are pamphlets/posters/films, emergency telephones, and lighted pathways/sidewalks.

Programs of Study: Suffolk confers B.A., B.S., B.F.A., B.S.B.A., B.S.G.S., and B.S.J. degrees. Associate, master's, and doctoral degrees are also awarded. Bachelor's degrees are awarded in BIOLOGICAL SCIENCE (biochemistry, biology/biological science, biotechnology, life science, and marine science), BUSINESS (accounting, banking and finance, entrepreneurial studies, international business management, international economics, management science, and marketing/retailing/merchandising), COMMUNICATIONS AND THE ARTS (advertising, art history and appreciation, broadcasting, communications, creative writing, dramatic arts, English, film arts, fine arts, French, graphic design, journalism, media arts, music history and appreciation, performing arts, public relations, Spanish, and speech/debate/rhetoric), COMPUTER AND PHYSICAL SCIENCE (chemistry, computer programming, computer science, information sciences and systems, mathematics, and physics), EDUCATION (business, elementary, English, mathematics, and science), ENGINEERING AND ENVIRONMENTAL DESIGN (computer engineering, electrical/electronics engineering, environmental engineering, environmental engineering technology, environmental science, and interior design), HEALTH PROFESSIONS (medical laboratory technology, medical science, and radiological science), SOCIAL SCIENCE (African American studies, American studies, criminal justice, economics, European studies, German area studies, history, human development, human services, humanities, international relations, paralegal studies, philosophy, political science/government, psychology, public administration, social science, sociology, and women's studies). Business, sociology, and criminal justice are the strongest academically. Business , sociology, and communications are the largest.

Required: All students must complete 122 semester hours with at least a 2.0 GPA. Distribution requirements vary by degree program.

Special: Numerous cooperative education and work-study programs are available in the Boston area. Cross-registration is offered with Emerson College. Study abroad in 31 countries and a semester internship in Washington, D.C., as well as local and international internships, are possible. B.A. and B.S. degrees in business and public administration, majors in medical biophysics and radiation biology taught in collaboration with Massachusetts General Hospital, dual and student-designed majors, and a lawyer's assistant certificate program are also available. Also, Suffolk has campuses in Spain and Senegal. There are 19 national honor societies, a freshman honors program, and 12 departmental honors programs.

Faculty/Classroom: 57% of faculty are male; 42%, female. 97% teach undergraduates and 90% both teach and do research. The average class size in an introductory lecture is 24; in a laboratory, 14; and in a regular course, 21.

Admissions: 82% of the 2005-2006 applicants were accepted. The SAT scores for the 2005-2006 freshman class were: Verbal--39% below 500, 44% between 500 and 599, 15% between 600 and 700, and 2% above 700; Math--42% below 500, 45% between 500 and 599, and 13% between 600 and 700. The ACT scores were 38% below 21, 36% between 21 and 23, 18% between 24 and 26, 7% between 27 and 28, and 1% above 28. 24% of the current freshmen were in the top fifth of their class; 54% were in the top two fifths.

Requirements: The SAT or ACT is required. The ACT Optional Writing test is also required. In addition, applicants should have a high school diploma or the GED. Recommended secondary preparation includes 4 years of English, 3 of math, 2 each of a foreign language and science, and 1 of American history. Exact requirements differ by degree program. A personal essay is required, and an interview is recommended. A GPA of 2.0 is required. AP and CLEP credits are accepted. Important factors in the admissions decision are advanced placement or honor courses, recommendations by school officials, and leadership record.

Procedure: Freshmen are admitted fall, spring, and summer. Entrance exams should be taken by December of the senior year. There are early action, early admissions, and deferred admissions plans. Early action applications should be filed by November 15; regular applications for priority consideration, by March 1 for fall entry and December 15 for spring entry, along with a $50 fee. Notification of early action is sent by December 15; regular decision, between January 15 and April 15. 223 applicants were on the 2005 waiting list; 177 were admitted. Applications are accepted on-line.

Transfer: 338 transfer students enrolled in 2004-2005. Applicants should have a minimum 2.5 GPA from an accredited college. Those with fewer than 15 college credits must submit a high school transcript. 30 of 122 credits required for the bachelor's degree must be completed at Suffolk.

Visiting: There are regularly scheduled orientations for prospective students, including a general presentation and an overview panel presentation of student life, career and co-op opportunities, learning center services, and athletics, academic department meetings, and campus tours. There are guides for informal visits and visitors may sit in on classes. To schedule a visit, contact the Admissions Office.

Financial Aid: In 2005-2006, 79% of all full-time freshmen and 73% of continuing full-time students received some form of financial aid. 68% of full-time freshmen and 56% of continuing full-time students received need-based aid. The average freshman award was $15,784. Need-based scholarships or need-based grants averaged $6685 ($33,360 maximum); need-based self-help aid (loans and jobs) averaged $5068 ($10,750 maximum); and other non-need-based awards and non-need-based scholarships averaged $5552 ($23,765 maximum). 56% of undergraduates work part time. Average annual earnings from campus work are $1500. The average financial indebtedness of the 2005 graduate was $19,102. The FAFSA, the college's own financial statement and the verification of income are required. The deadline for filing freshman financial aid applications for fall entry is March 1.

International Students: There are 400 international students enrolled. The school actively recruits these students. They must score satisfactorily on the TOEFL and also take the SAT, ACT, or the college's own entrance exam.

Computers: Wireless access is available. The library supports an 802.11 a/b/g network. Students with their own laptops may complete a form available at the circulation desk and register their laptop's wireless network interface card to acquire access to the library's wireless network. All students may access the system. There are no time limits and no fees.

Graduates: From July 1, 2004 to June 30, 2005, 807 bachelor's degrees were awarded. The most popular majors were communications (16%), sociology (10%), and management (9%). In an average class, 2% graduate in 3 years or less, 35% graduate in 4 years or less, 52% graduate in 5 years or less, and 56% graduate in 6 years or less. 43 companies recruited on campus in 2004-2005. Of the 2004 graduating class, 28% were enrolled in graduate school within 6 months of graduation and 85% were employed.

Admissions Contact: John Hamel, Director of Undergraduate Admissions. A video is available. E-mail: *admission@suffolk.edu* Web: *www.suffolk.edu*

TUFFS UNIVERSITY   D-2

Medford, MA 02155   (617) 627-3170; Fax: (617) 627-3860

Full-time: 2374 men, 2594 women	Faculty: 416; I, av$
Part-time: 50 men, 60 women	Ph.D.s: 95%
Graduate: 2019 men, 2811 women	Student/Faculty: 12 to 1
Year: semesters, summer session	Tuition: $32,621
Application Deadline: January 1	Room & Board: $9397
Freshman Class: 15,536 applied, 4398 accepted, 1365 enrolled	
SAT or ACT: n/av	**MOST COMPETITIVE**

Tufts University, founded in 1852, is a private institution offering undergraduate programs in liberal arts and sciences and engineering. There are 2 undergraduate and 8 graduate schools. In addition to regional accreditation, Tufts has baccalaureate program accreditation with ABET, ADA, and CAHEA. The 2 libraries contain 1,134,520 volumes, 1,232,000 microform items, and 38,000 audio/video tapes/CDs/DVDs, and subscribe to 5861 periodicals including electronic. Computerized library services include the card catalog, interlibrary loans, database searching, and Internet access. Special learning facilities include a learning resource center, art gallery, radio station, TV station, and theater in the round. The 140-acre campus is in a suburban area 5 miles northwest of Boston. Including any residence halls, there are 167 buildings.

Student Life: 75% of undergraduates are from out of state, mostly the Middle Atlantic. Students are from 50 states, 65 foreign countries, and Canada. 60% are from public schools. 57% are white; 13% Asian American. The average age of freshmen is 18; all undergraduates, 20. 4% do not continue beyond their first year; 91% remain to graduate.

Housing: 3550 students can be accommodated in college housing, which includes single-sex and coed dorms, on-campus apartments, and fraternity houses. In addition, there are language houses, cooperative houses, and special-interest houses. On-campus housing is available on a lottery system for upperclassmen. 97% of students live on campus. Upperclassmen may keep cars.

Activities: 15% of men belong to 10 national fraternities; 3% of women belong to 3 national sororities. There are 160 groups on campus, including art, band, cheerleading, chess, choir, chorale, chorus, computers, dance, debate, drama, environmental, ethnic, film, forensics, gay, honors, international, jazz band, literary magazine, marching band, musical theater, newspaper, orchestra, outdoors, pep band, photography, political, professional, radio and TV, religious, social, social service, student government, and symphony. Popular campus events include a dramatic arts series, national and international forums, and an international affairs symposium.

Sports: There are 17 intercollegiate sports for men and 16 for women, and 10 intramural sports for men and 6 for women. Facilities include a football stadium, 2 gyms, an 8-lane all-weather track, 9 tennis courts, a field house, an indoor cage, an indoor track, 7 squash courts, a swimming pool, a dance room, a weight room, a sauna, a sailing center, an exercise center, and baseball, softball, and playing fields.

Disabled Students: 90% of the campus is accessible. Wheelchair ramps, elevators, special parking, specially equipped rest rooms, special class scheduling, lowered drinking fountains, lowered telephones, and other special services as needed are available.

Services: Counseling and information services are available, as is tutoring in some subjects as needed through the Academic Resources Center. There is a reader service for the blind. Services are also available through the women's center, and African American, Hispanic, and Asian culture houses.

Campus Safety and Security: Measures include 24-hour foot and vehicle patrol, security escort services, shuttle buses, and informal discussions. There are pamphlets/posters/films, emergency telephones, and lighted pathways/sidewalks.

Programs of Study: Tufts confers B.A., B.S., B.S.C.E., B.S.Ch.E., B.S. Comp. Eng., B.S.E., B.S.E.E., B.S.E.S., B.S. Environmental Eng., B.S.M.E., B.S.B.M.E., and B.S.C.S degrees. Master's and doctoral degrees are also awarded. Bachelor's degrees are awarded in BIOLOGICAL SCIENCE (biochemistry, biology/biological science, and biotechnology), COMMUNICATIONS AND THE ARTS (art history and appreciation, Chinese, classics, dramatic arts, English, French, German, Greek, Japanese, Latin, music, Russian, and Spanish), COMPUTER AND PHYSICAL SCIENCE (applied physics, astrophysics, chemistry, computer science, geology, mathematics, and physics), EDUCATION (early childhood), ENGINEERING AND ENVIRONMENTAL DESIGN (architecture, biomedical engineering, chemical engineering, civil engineering, computer engineering, electrical/electronics engineering, engineering, engineering and applied science, engineering physics, environmental science, and mechanical engineering), SOCIAL SCIENCE (American studies, anthropology, archeology, Asian/Oriental studies, biopsychology, child psychology/development, clinical psychology, economics, experimental psychology, German area studies, history, international relations, Judaic studies, Middle Eastern studies, peace studies, philosophy, political science/government, psychology, religion, Russian and Slavic studies, sociology, and women's studies). International relations, economics, and political science are the largest.

Required: Liberal arts students must complete 34 courses, 10 of them in the area of concentration. Requirements include foundation courses in writing and foreign language or culture and courses in humanities, arts, social sciences, math, and natural sciences. Requirements for engineering students include a total of 38 courses, 12 of them in the area of concentration, and distribution requirements in English, math and science, humanities, and social sciences.

Special: The university offers cross-registration at Swarthmore College, Boston University, Boston College, and Brandeis University, a Washington semester, and study abroad in England, Spain, France, Chile, Japan, Ghana, China, Hong Kong, and Germany. Many internships are available. Double majors in the liberal arts are common; student-designed majors are possible. There is a 5-year B.A./M.A. or B.S./M.S. program in engineering or liberal arts, a B.A.-B.F.A. program with the Museum School of Fine Arts, and a B.A.-B.M. program with the New England Conservatory of Music. Pass/fail options are offered. There are 4 national honor societies, including Phi Beta Kappa.

Faculty/Classroom: 60% of faculty are male; 40%, female. All both teach and do research. No introductory courses are taught by graduate students. The average class size in a regular course is 20.

Admissions: 28% of the 2005-2006 applicants were accepted. The SAT scores for the 2005-2006 freshman class were: Verbal--9% between 500 and 599, 39% between 600 and 700, and 52% above 700; Math--3% between 500 and 599, 33% between 600 and 700, and 64% above 700. The ACT scores were 3% between 21 and 23, 8% between 24 and 26, 14% between 27 and 28, and 75% above 28. 94% of the current freshmen were in the top fifth of their class; 99% were in the top two fifths. There were 46 National Merit finalists.

Requirements: In addition, the university accepts either the SAT Reasoning Test and the results of 2 SAT : Subject tests, or the ACT. Liberal arts applicants should take the 2 SAT : Subject tests of their choice; engineering applicants should take a math level I or II, and either physics or chemistry. In addition, all applicants should be high school graduates or hold the GED. Academic preparation is expected to include 4 years of English, 3 years each of humanities and a foreign language, 2 years each of social and natural sciences, and 1 year of history. AP credits are accepted. Important factors in the admissions decision are advanced placement or honor courses, recommendations by school officials, and extracurricular activities record.

Procedure: Freshmen are admitted in the fall. Entrance exams should be taken by January of the senior year. There are early decision, early admissions, and deferred admissions plans. Round 1 early decision applications should be filed by November 15; round 2 by January 1; regular applications, by January 1 for fall entry, along with a $70 fee. Notification of round 1 early decision is sent December 15; round 2 February 1; regular decision, April 1. 460 early decision candidates were accepted for the 2005-2006 class. A waiting list is an active part of the admissions procedure. Applications are accepted on-line.

Transfer: 39 transfer students enrolled in 2004-2005. Admission is competitive. Primary consideration is given to college and secondary school achievement and record of personal involvement. 17 of 34 courses required for the bachelor's degree must be completed at Tufts.

Visiting: There are regularly scheduled orientations for prospective students, including orientation sessions twice a day, Monday through Friday, April 1 to early December, followed by campus tours. There are additional orientation sessions and tours on selected Saturday mornings during the fall. There are guides for informal visits and visitors may sit in on classes and stay overnight. To schedule a visit, contact the Admissions Office at *admissions.inquiry@ase.tufts.edu*.

Financial Aid: In 2005-2006, 46% of all full-time freshmen and 38% of continuing full-time students received some form of financial aid. 36% of all full-time students received need-based aid. The average freshman award was $25,199. 40% of undergraduates work part time. The average financial indebtedness of the 2005 graduate was $14,400. Tufts is a member of CSS. The CSS/Profile or FAFSA and parent and student federal income tax forms are required. The deadline for filing freshman financial aid applications for fall entry is February 15.

International Students: There are 315 international students enrolled. The school actively recruits these students. They must take the TOEFL if English is not their first language and also take the ACT or the SAT Reasoning Test and 2 SAT subject tests.

Computers: Wireless access is available. All students may access the system 24 hours a day. There are no time limits and no fees.

Graduates: From July 1, 2004 to June 30, 2005, 1240 bachelor's degrees were awarded. The most popular majors were international relations (10%), economics (9%), and political science (7%). In an average class, 91% graduate in 6 years or less. 150 companies recruited on campus in 2004-2005.

Admissions Contact: Lee A. Coffin, Dean of Admissions.
E-mail: *admissions.inquiry@ase.tufts.edu* Web: *www.tufts.edu*

UNIVERSITY OF MASSACHUSETTS AMHERST   B-2

Amherst, MA 01003   (413) 545-0222; Fax: (413) 545-4312

Full-time: 9079 men, 8806 women	**Faculty:** 1148; I, av$
Part-time: 399 men, 528 women	**Ph.D.s:** 93%
Graduate: 2392 men, 2498 women	**Student/Faculty:** 16 to 1
Year: semesters, summer session	**Tuition:** $9456 ($17,079)
Application Deadline: January 15	**Room & Board:** $6517
Freshman Class: 20,205 applied, 16,240 accepted, 4427 enrolled	
SAT Verbal/Math: 560/580*	**COMPETITIVE+**

Established in 1863, University of Massachusetts Amherst is a major public, research, land-grant institution offering nearly 100 academic majors. There are 9 undergraduate and 9 graduate schools. In addition to regional accreditation, UMass has baccalaureate program accreditation with AACSB, ABET, ASLA, FIDER, NASM, NCATE, NLN, and SAF. The 3 libraries contain 3,444,741 volumes, 2,517,808 microform items, and 21,934 audio/video tapes/CDs/DVDs, and subscribe to 15,427 periodicals including electronic. Computerized library services include the card catalog, interlibrary loans, database searching, and Internet access. Special learning facilities include a learning resource center, art gallery, radio station, TV station, and botanical gardens. The 1463-acre campus is in a small town 90 miles west of Boston and 60 miles north of Hartford, Connecticut. Including any residence halls, there are 200 buildings.

Student Life: 81% of undergraduates are from Massachusetts. Others are from 49 states, 37 foreign countries, and Canada. 81% are white. The average age of freshmen is 18; all undergraduates, 20. 16% do not continue beyond their first year; 66% remain to graduate.

Housing: 11,000 students can be accommodated in college housing, which includes single-sex and coed dormitories, on-campus apartments, married-student housing, fraternity houses, and sorority houses. In addition, there are honors houses, language houses, special-interest houses, international students housing, and first-year experience housing. On-campus housing is guaranteed for the freshman year only and is available on a lottery system for upperclassmen. 62% of students live on campus. All students may keep cars.

Activities: 1% of men belong to 20 national fraternities; 1% of women belong to 1 local and 12 national sororities. There are 200 groups on campus, including art, band, cheerleading, chess, choir, chorale, chorus, computers, dance, debate, drama, ethnic, film, gay, honors, international, jazz band, literary magazine, marching band, musical theater, newspaper, opera, orchestra, pep band, photography, political, professional, radio and TV, religious, social, social service, student government, student owned businesses, symphony, and yearbook. Popular campus events include First Week, Family Day, and Oozefest (annual mud volleyball tournament).

Sports: There are 10 intercollegiate sports for men and 11 for women, and 12 intramural sports for men and 14 for women. Facilities include 120 acres of multipurpose fields, a football stadium, a track, and 22 tennis courts. Indoor facilities include 3 pools, 3 handball/squash courts, weight rooms, fitness centers, basketball/volleyball/badminton courts, and a track.

Disabled Students: Wheelchair ramps, elevators, special parking, specially equipped rest rooms, special class scheduling, lowered drinking fountains, and lowered telephones are available. All programs are made accessible through accommodations.

Services: Counseling and information services are available, as is tutoring in most subjects. There is a reader service for the blind and remedial math and reading.

Campus Safety and Security: Measures include 24-hour foot and vehicle patrol, self-defense education, shuttle buses, and informal discussions. There are pamphlets/posters/films, emergency telephones, lighted pathways/sidewalks, and tight restrictions on residence hall access.

Programs of Study: UMass confers B.A., B.S., B.B.A., B.F.A., B.G.S., and B.Mus. degrees. Associate, master's, and doctoral degrees are also awarded. Bachelor's degrees are awarded in AGRICULTURE (animal science, forestry and related sciences, natural resource management, plant science, soil science, and wildlife management), BIOLOGICAL SCIENCE (biochemistry, biology/biological science, microbiology, and nutrition), BUSINESS (accounting, banking and finance, business administration and management, hospitality management services, marketing management, and sports management), COMMUNICATIONS AND THE ARTS (art history and appreciation, Chinese, classics, communications, comparative literature, dance, design, dramatic arts, English, French, German, Japanese, journalism, linguistics, music, Portuguese, Spanish, and studio art), COMPUTER AND PHYSICAL SCIENCE (astronomy, chemistry, computer science, earth science, geology, mathematics, physics, and science), EDUCATION (early childhood, elementary, and secondary), ENGINEERING AND ENVIRONMENTAL DESIGN (chemical engineering, civil engineering, computer engineering, construction technology, electrical/electronics engineering, environmental design, environmental science, industrial engineering, landscape architecture/design, and mechanical engineering), HEALTH PROFESSIONS (exercise science, medical laboratory technology, nursing, predentistry, premedicine, preveterinary science, and speech pathology/audiology), SOCIAL SCIENCE (African American studies, anthropology, economics, ethics, politics and social policy, food science, geography, history, interdisciplinary studies, Italian studies, Judaic studies, law, liberal arts/general studies, Middle Eastern studies, philosophy, political science/government, prelaw, psychology, Russian and Slavic studies, sociology, and women's studies). Engineering, computer science, and management are the strongest academically. Psychology, communication, and biology are the largest.

Required: For graduation, students must complete 120 credit hours and maintain a minimum GPA of 2.0 overall and in the major, with at least 2 courses with a diversity requirement. The general education requirements for all students include courses in English, including composition, humanities, foreign languages, history, arts/fine arts, social and cultural diversity, biological and physical science, math and social science.

Special: Cross-registration is possible with Smith, Mount. Holyoke, Hampshire, and Amherst Colleges. Co-op programs accelerated degrees, internships in every major, study abroad in more than 30 countries, a Washington semester, work-study programs, dual and student-designed majors, and B.A.-B.S. degrees are available. The Bachelor's Degree with Individual Concentration (BDIC) is also available. The Commonwealth College welcomes honor students who meet entrance requirements. There are also teacher certification, distance learning, independent study, and ESL programs. There are 25 national honor societies, including Phi Beta Kappa, a freshman honors program, and all departments have honors programs.

Faculty/Classroom: 66% of faculty are male; 34%, female. All both teach and do research.

Admissions: 80% of the 2005-2006 applicants were accepted. 39% of the current freshmen were in the top fifth of their class; 76% were in the top two fifths.

Requirements: The SAT or ACT is required. In addition, applicants must be graduates of an accredited secondary school, or have the GED. The university recommends that students complete 16 Carnegie units, including 4 years of English, 3 years each of math, and science (including 2 years lab), and 2 years each of electives, foreign language, and social studies. 4 years of math are required for business, computer science, and engineering majors. Students must present a portfolio for admission to the art program and must audition for admission to music and dance. A GPA of 2.0 is required. AP and CLEP credits are accepted. Important factors in the admissions decision are extracurricular activities record, evidence of special talent, and personality/intangible qualities.

Procedure: Freshmen are admitted fall and spring. Entrance exams should be taken before February 1. There are early action, deferred admissions and rolling admissions plans. Early action applications should be filed by November 1; regular applications, by January 15 for fall entry and October 15 for spring entry, along with a $40 fee for in-state $50 for out-of-state, $60 for international. Notification of early decision is sent beginning December 15; regular decision, on a rolling basis. 329 applicants were on the 2005 waiting list; 86 were admitted. Applications are accepted on-line.

Transfer: 1067 transfer students enrolled in 2004-2005. Transfer applicants must submit transcripts from all colleges or universities attended, and an essay. Those with fewer than 30 credits must submit high school transcripts and SAT scores. Priority is given to students with an associate degree. Grades of C- or better transfer for credit. Students must present a 2.5 GPA to transfer. 45 of 120 credits required for the bachelor's degree must be completed at UMass.

Visiting: There are regularly scheduled orientations for prospective students, including twice-daily guided tours and daily information sessions. There are guides for informal visits and visitors may sit in on classes and stay overnight. To schedule a visit, contact the University Tour Service at (413) 545-4237.

Financial Aid: In 2005-2006, 39% of all full-time freshmen and 51% of continuing full-time students received some form of financial aid. At least 37% of full-time freshmen and at least 48% of continuing full-time students received need-based aid. The average freshman award was $9590. Need-based scholarships or need-based grants averaged $6366; need-based self-help aid (loans and jobs) averaged $9645; non-need-based athletic scholarships averaged $9560; and other institutional non-need-based awards and non-need-based scholarships averaged $4829. The average financial indebtedness of the 2005 graduate was $14,672. UMass is a member of CSS. The FAFSA is required. The priority date for freshman financial aid applications for fall entry is March 1.

International Students: They must score satisfactorily on the written TOEFL or on the electronic version.

Computers: Wireless access is available. The University offes centralized computing services through the Office of Information Technologies (OIT). All students are required to have an OITaccount. This account provides students with access to numerous computers available for teaching and public use, a campuswide network accessible from residence halls, public buildings, and off campus, an e-mail account, the campus on-line course management system, and the campus wireless network, which is currently available at many on-campus locations. Registration, grades, and student information are available on-line. There is also a high technology Learning Commons in the W.E.B. DuBois Library, an open learning space with computer terminals, work areas, printers, and support staff. All students may access the system. There are no time limits and no fees. It is strongly recommended that all students have a personal computer.

Graduates: From July 1, 2004 to June 30, 2005, 4262 bachelor's degrees were awarded. The most popular majors were business/marketing (14%), social science (13%), and education (7%). In an average class, 45% graduate in 4 years or less, 62% graduate in 5 years or less, and 66% graduate in 6 years or less. Of the 2004 graduating class, 22% were enrolled in graduate school within 6 months of graduation.

Admissions Contact: Kevin Kelly, Director of Admissions. A video is available. E-mail: *kk@admissions.umass.edu* Web: *www.umas.edu/admissions*

UNIVERSITY OF MASSACHUSETTS BOSTON	E-2
Boston, MA 02125-3393	(617) 287-6100; Fax: (617) 287-6242
Full-time: 2322 men, 3206 women	Faculty: 437; I, -$
Part-time: 1501 men, 1929 women	Ph.D.s: 92%
Graduate: 883 men, 2021 women	Student/Faculty: 13 to 1
Year: semesters, summer session	Tuition: $8024 ($18,756)
Application Deadline: January 1	Room & Board: n/app
Freshman Class: 2903 applied, 1553 accepted, 563 enrolled	
SAT Verbal/Math: 510/510*	COMPETITIVE

The University of Massachusetts Boston, established in 1964, is a public commuter institution offering undergraduate studies in arts and sciences and in preprofessional training. There are 5 undergraduate and 7 graduate schools. In addition to regional accreditation, UMass Boston has baccalaureate program accreditation with AACSB, ACS, APA, CCNE, and NCATE. The library contains 584,015 volumes, 827,171 microform items, and 1902 audio/video tapes/CDs/DVDs, and subscribes to 2779 periodicals including electronic. Computerized library services include the card catalog, interlibrary loans, database searching, Internet access, and laptop Internet portals. Special learning facilities include a learning resource center, art gallery, planetarium, radio station, tropical greenhouse, observatory, adaptive computer lab, languages lab, and applied language and math center. The 177-acre campus is in an urban area 5 miles south of downtown Boston. There are 10 buildings.

Student Life: 92% of undergraduates are from Massachusetts. Others are from 31 states, 8 foreign countries, and Canada. 47% are white; 14% African American. The average age of freshmen is 19; all undergraduates, 25. 29% do not continue beyond their first year; 28% remain to graduate.

Housing: There are no residence halls. All of students commute. Alcohol is not permitted. All students may keep cars.

Activities: There are no fraternities or sororities. There are 75 groups on campus, including art, band, cheerleading, chess, choir, chorale, chorus, computers, dance, drama, ethnic, film, gay, honors, international, jazz band, literary magazine, musical theater, newspaper, orchestra, photography, political, professional, radio and TV, religious, social, social service, and student government. Popular campus events include Convocation Day, seasonal festivals, and lecture series.

Sports: There are 7 intercollegiate sports for men and 7 for women, and 16 intramural sports for men and 16 for women. Facilities include an athletic center with a 3500-seat gym with 4 basketball and 2 volleyball courts, an ice rink that seats 1000, an Olympic-size swimming pool with high-dive area, a multipurpose weight room, and a sports medicine area; an 8-lane, 400-meter track; 8 tennis courts; a softball diamond, 3 multipurpose fields primarily used for soccer and lacrosse, and several other recreational fields; a boat house, dock and fleet of sailboats and rowing dories; and a fitness center with strength-training equipment.

Disabled Students: All of the campus is accessible. Wheelchair ramps, elevators, special parking, specially equipped rest rooms, special class scheduling, lowered drinking fountains, lowered telephones, amplified phones, powered doors, indoor-connected building access, an accessible shuttle bus, an adaptive computer lab, and a center for students with disabilities are available.

Services: Counseling and information services are available, as is tutoring in every subject. There is a reader service for the blind, and remedial math, reading, and writing. There are also reading study skills workshops and a math resource center available.

Campus Safety and Security: Measures include 24-hour foot and vehicle patrol, self-defense education, security escort services, and shuttle buses. There are informal discussions, pamphlets/posters/films, emergency telephones, lighted pathways/sidewalks, and Operation ID, motorist assistance, and crime prevention programs.

Programs of Study: UMass Boston confers B.A. and B.S. degrees. Master's and doctoral degrees are also awarded. Bachelor's degrees are awarded in BIOLOGICAL SCIENCE (biochemistry and biology/biological science), BUSINESS (labor studies and management science), COMMUNICATIONS AND THE ARTS (art, classical languages, classics, dramatic arts, English, French, Italian, music, Russian, and Spanish), COMPUTER AND PHYSICAL SCIENCE (chemistry, computer science, earth science, mathematics, and physics), EDUCATION (physical), ENGINEERING AND ENVIRONMENTAL DESIGN (engineering and engineering physics), HEALTH PROFESSIONS (medical technology and nursing), SOCIAL SCIENCE (African American studies, American studies, anthropology, community services, criminal justice, economics, ethics, politics, and social policy, geography, German area studies, gerontology, Hispanic American studies, history, human services, paralegal studies, philosophy, political science/government, psychology, sociology, and women's studies). Management, nursing, and psychology are the largest.

Required: For graduation, students must complete 120 credit hours (123 hours in the College of Nursing) and maintain a minimum GPA of 2.0. Distribution requirements vary by college. All students must demonstrate writing proficiency.

Special: Students may cross-register with Boston Public Colleges, Massachusetts College of Art, Bunker Hill Community College, Roxbury Community College, and Hebrew College. UMass Boston also offers cooperative programs, internships, study abroad, work-study programs, student-designed majors, B.A.-B.S. degrees, nondegree study, pass/fail options, and dual and interdisciplinary majors, including anthropology/history, biology/medical technology, philosophy/public policy, and psychology/sociology. Also available are 3-1 and 2-2 engineering programs with various area institutions. The College of Public and Community Service provides social-oriented education,. There are 3 national honor societies, and a freshman honors program.

Faculty/Classroom: 52% of faculty are male; 48%, female. 100% both teach and do research. No introductory courses are taught by graduate students. The average class size in an introductory lecture is 21; in a laboratory, 14; and in a regular course, 20.

Admissions: 53% of the 2005-2006 applicants were accepted. The SAT scores for the 2005-2006 freshman class were: Verbal--42% below 500, 41% between 500 and 599, 13% between 600 and 700, and 4% above 700; Math--39% below 500, 46% between 500 and 599, 13% between 600 and 700, and 2% above 700.

Requirements: The SAT or ACT is required. Test scores are not required of students who have been out of high school for 3 or more years. Applicants should be graduates of an accredited secondary school. The GED is accepted. The university requires the completion of 16 Carnegie units, including 4 years of English, 3 of college preparatory math and science, 2 each of a foreign language and social studies, and 2 electives in the above academic areas or in humanities, arts, or computer science. An essay is recommended. A GPA of 3.0 is required. AP and CLEP credits are accepted. Important factors in the admissions decision are advanced placement or honor courses, evidence of special talent, and recommendations by school officials.

Procedure: Freshmen are admitted fall and spring. Entrance exams should be taken by the fall of the senior year. There is a deferred admissions plan. Applications should be filed by January 1 for fall entry and July 1 for spring entry, along with a $40 fee. Notification is sent on a rolling basis. Applications are accepted on-line.

Transfer: 1193 transfer students enrolled in 2004-2005. Applicants with fewer than 24 credits must meet freshman requirements. To transfer, students must have a minimum GPA of 3.0. Grades of C- or better transfer for credit. 30 of 120 credits required for the bachelor's degree must be completed at UMass Boston.

Visiting: There are regularly scheduled orientations for prospective students, including general information sessions about the university and the admissions process and a tour of the campus. There are guides for informal visits and visitors may sit in on classes. To schedule a visit, contact Marketing and Information Services at (617) 287-6000.

Financial Aid: In 2005-2006, 65% of all full-time freshmen and 57% of continuing full-time students received some form of financial aid. 52%

of full-time freshmen and 45% of continuing full-time students received need-based aid. The average freshman award was $5831. The FAFSA is required.

International Students: There are 355 international students enrolled. The school actively recruits these students. They must take the TOEFL and also take the SAT or ACT if the language of instruction is English,

Computers: Wireless access is available. All students may access the system 24 hours a day. There are no time limits and no fees.

Graduates: From July 1, 2004 to June 30, 2005, 1543 bachelor's degrees were awarded. The most popular majors were management (24%), social science (17%), and psychology (13%). In an average class, 1% graduate in 3 years or less, 12% graduate in 4 years or less, 24% graduate in 5 years or less, and 28% graduate in 6 years or less.

Admissions Contact: Liliana Mickle, Director, Undergraduate Admissions. E-mail: *undergrad@umb.edu* Web: *www.umb.edu*

UNIVERSITY OF MASSACHUSETTS DARTMOUTH   E-4

North Dartmouth, MA 02747-2300   **(508) 999-8605**
                                       Fax: (508) 999-8755

Full-time: 3285 men, 3164 women	**Faculty:** 348; IIA, +$
Part-time: 431 men, 639 women	**Ph.D.s:** 89%
Graduate: 454 men, 576 women	**Student/Faculty:** 19 to 1
Year: semesters, summer session	**Tuition:** $8036 ($17,536)
Application Deadline: open	**Room & Board:** $7949
Freshman Class: 6435 applied, 4733 accepted, 1548 enrolled	
SAT Verbal/Math: 530/540*	**ACT:** 21 **COMPETITIVE**

University of Massachusetts Dartmouth, founded in 1895, is a public institution that provides undergraduate and graduate programs in the liberal and creative arts and sciences and in professional training. There are 5 undergraduate schools and 1 graduate school. In addition to regional accreditation, UMass Dartmouth has baccalaureate program accreditation with AACSB, ABET, ACS, CSAB, NAACLS, NASAD, NASDTEC, and NLN. The library contains 455,323 volumes, 810,127 microform items, and 12,980 audio/video tapes/CDs/DVDs, and subscribes to 2925 periodicals including electronic. Computerized library services include the card catalog, interlibrary loans, database searching, and Internet access. Special learning facilities include a learning resource center, art gallery, radio station, observatory, marine research vessels, and a number of cultural and research centers. The 710-acre campus is in a suburban area approximately 60 miles south of Boston, 35 miles east of Providence, Rhode Island, and 3 miles west of Cape Cod. Including any residence halls, there are 27 buildings.

Student Life: 95% of undergraduates are from Massachusetts. Others are from 23 states and 17 foreign countries. 85% are from public schools. 87% are white. The average age of freshmen is 18; all undergraduates, 22. 24% do not continue beyond their first year; 50% remain to graduate.

Housing: 3955 students can be accommodated in college housing, which includes coed dorms and on-campus apartments. In addition, there are honors houses, a quiet house, and apartments for upperclassmen. On-campus housing is guaranteed for the freshman year only, is available on a first-come, first-served basis, and is available on a lottery system for upperclassmen. Priority is given to out-of-town students. 55% of students live on campus; of those, 35% remain on campus on weekends. Alcohol is permitted in designated areas only. All students may keep cars.

Activities: 1% of men belong to 1 local and 2 national fraternities; 1% of women belong to 1 national sorority. There are 90 groups on campus, including art, band, cheerleading, choir, chorale, chorus, computers, drama, ethnic, film, gay, honors, international, jazz band, literary magazine, musical theater, newspaper, orchestra, pep band, political, professional, radio and TV, religious, social, social service, student government, symphony, and yearbook. Popular campus events include Welcome Back Week, Winterfest, and Spring Fling Week.

Sports: There are 11 intercollegiate sports for men and 12 for women, and 10 intramural sports for men and 10 for women. Facilities include a 3000-seat gym, an 1850-seat football stadium, an aquatic sports center, 13 tennis courts, a weight room, a running track, and soccer, softball, and intramural fields.

Disabled Students: 94% of the campus is accessible. Wheelchair ramps, elevators, special parking, specially equipped rest rooms, special class scheduling, lowered drinking fountains, lowered telephones, special housing, mobility assistance, note takers/readers, alternative testing, and an office of disabled student services are available.

Services: Counseling and information services are available, as is tutoring in most subjects, through the writing/reading, science/engineering, math/business, and academic resource centers. There is a reader service for the blind, and remedial math, reading, and writing.

Campus Safety and Security: Measures include 24-hour foot and vehicle patrol, self-defense education, security escort services, and shuttle buses. There are pamphlets/posters/films, emergency telephones, lighted pathways/sidewalks, and a bicycle patrol.

Programs of Study: UMass Dartmouth confers B.A., B.S., and B.F.A. degrees. Master's and doctoral degrees are also awarded. Bachelor's degrees are awarded in BIOLOGICAL SCIENCE (biochemistry, biology/biological science, and marine biology), BUSINESS (accounting, banking and finance, business administration and management, management information systems, and marketing/retailing/merchandising), COMMUNICATIONS AND THE ARTS (art history and appreciation, ceramic art and design, design, English, fiber/textiles/weaving, French, graphic design, illustration, metal/jewelry, music, painting, photography, Portuguese, sculpture, Spanish, and technical and business writing), COMPUTER AND PHYSICAL SCIENCE (chemistry, computer science, mathematics, and physics), EDUCATION (art), ENGINEERING AND ENVIRONMENTAL DESIGN (civil engineering, computer engineering, electrical/electronics engineering, materials science, mechanical engineering, and textile technology), HEALTH PROFESSIONS (medical laboratory science and nursing), SOCIAL SCIENCE (anthropology, criminal justice, economics, history, humanities and social science, interdisciplinary studies, philosophy, political science/government, psychology, and sociology). Engineering, physical/life sciences, and design/fine arts are the strongest academically. Design, psychology, and nursing are the largest.

Required: The core curriculum requires 9 credits each of communication skills, cultural and artistic literacy, and math/science/technology, 6 each of global awareness and information/computer literacy, and 3 of ethics. A freshman English composition course is required. Colleges set some additional distribution course requirements. The B.A. requires foreign language study. To graduate, students must complete 120 to 132 credit hours and maintain a 2.0 GPA.

Special: The university permits cross-registration through the SACHEM Consortium of 9 schools in Massachusetts. Study abroad in 9 countries, an engineering or business co-op program, a Washington semester, internships, numerous work-study programs, dual majors, and student-designed majors are available. Teacher certification in elementary and secondary education is available as is a 3+3 law degree with a local law school. Nondegree study, pass/fail options, B.S.-M.S. degrees in chemistry, nursing, computer science, electrical engineering, computer engineering, and mechanical engineering, a B.A.-M.A. in psychology, and credit for life experience are possible. There are 5 national honor societies and a freshman honors program.

Faculty/Classroom: 63% of faculty are male; 37%, female. All teach undergraduates and 60% do research. Graduate students teach 1% of introductory courses. The average class size in an introductory lecture is 26; in a laboratory, 16; and in a regular course, 26.

Admissions: 74% of the 2005-2006 applicants were accepted. The SAT scores for the 2005-2006 freshman class were: Verbal--34% below 500, 49% between 500 and 599, 16% between 600 and 700, and 1% above 700; Math--27% below 500, 50% between 500 and 599, 22% between 600 and 700, and 1% above 700. The ACT scores were 34% below 21, 40% between 21 and 23, 20% between 24 and 26, 2% between 27 and 28, and 4% above 28. 3 freshmen graduated first in their class.

Requirements: The SAT is required. In addition, applicants should have 4 years of English, 3 each of science and math, 2 of the same foreign language, 1 each of social studies and U.S. history, and 2 of college-preparatory electives. The GED is accepted. An audition is necessary for music majors, and a portfolio is recommended for studio arts and design applicants. All applicants must submit an essay. A GPA of 3.0 is required. AP and CLEP credits are accepted. Important factors in the admissions decision are recommendations by school officials, advanced placement or honor courses, and evidence of special talent.

Procedure: Freshmen are admitted fall and spring. Entrance exams should be taken during the spring of the junior year or early fall of the senior year. There are early decision, deferred admissions, and rolling admissions plans. Application deadlines for early admissions should be filed by November 15; regular application deadlines are open. Application fee is $35 for in-state applicants and $55 for out-of-state applicants. 62 early decision candidates were accepted for the 2005-2006 class. Applications are accepted on-line.

Transfer: 487 transfer students enrolled in 2004-2005. Applicants must submit all official college transcripts and must take the SAT unless they graduated from high school more than 3 years prior to applying. Those with fewer than 30 transferable credits must submit high school records. 45 of 120 to 132 credits required for the bachelor's degree must be completed at UMass Dartmouth.

Visiting: There are regularly scheduled orientations for prospective students, including scheduled campus tours Monday through Friday and most Saturdays. There are guides for informal visits and visitors may sit in on classes. To schedule a visit, contact the Admissions Office, or sign up through the school's web site at *www.umassd.edu/toursignup2.cfm*

Financial Aid: The FAFSA is required. The priority date for freshman financial aid applications for fall entry is March 1.

International Students: There are 30 international students enrolled. Satisfactory scores are required on the written TOEFL and the SAT.

Computers: Wireless access is available. PCs and Macs are located in the library and academic buildings. Wireless access is available, as is Internet hookups in dorms. All students may access the system during the day and evening as well as on weekends. There are no time limits and no fees. It is strongly recommended that all students have a personal computer.

Graduates: From July 1, 2004 to June 30, 2005, 1042 bachelor's degrees were awarded. The most popular majors were psychology (9%), sociology (8%), and marketing (8%). In an average class, 26% graduate in 4 years or less, 46% graduate in 5 years or less, and 50% graduate in 6 years or less. 400 companies recruited on campus in 2004-2005.

Admissions Contact: Steve Briggs, Director of Admissions.
E-mail: *admissions@umassd.edu* Web: *www.umassd.edu/admissions*

UNIVERSITY OF MASSACHUSETTS LOWELL — D-1

Lowell, MA 01854 (978) 934-3931 or (978) 934-3931
(800) 410-4607; Fax: (978) 934-3086

Full-time: 3342 men, 2349 women	**Faculty:** 383; I, +$
Part-time: 1665 men, 9451 women	**Ph.D.s:** 94%
Graduate: 1265 men, 1100 women	**Student/Faculty:** 15 to 1
Year: semesters, summer session	**Tuition:** $8166 ($19,016)
Application Deadline: open	**Room & Board:** $6161
Freshman Class: 6488 applied, 4128 accepted, 1768 enrolled	
SAT(composite): 1094*	**VERY COMPETITIVE**

The University of Massachussetts Lowell, founded in 1895, is a public institution offering undergraduate and graduate programs through the schools of arts and sciences, engineering, health professions, management science, and music, and graduate programs in education. There are 5 undergraduate schools and 1 graduate school. In addition to regional accreditation, UMass Lowell has baccalaureate program accreditation with AACSB, ABET, APTA, CAHEA, CSAB, NASAD, NASM, NCATE, and NLN. The 3 libraries contain 401,941 volumes, 90,376 microform items, and 13,824 audio/video tapes/CDs/DVDs, and subscribe to 12,569 periodicals including electronic. Computerized library services include the card catalog, interlibrary loans, database searching, Internet access, and laptop Internet portals. Special learning facilities include a learning resource center, art gallery, radio station, many experimental and investigative labs, and the Research Foundation, which includes a materials testing division and centers for atmospheric research and tropical disease. The 100-acre campus is in an urban area 30 miles northwest of Boston. Including any residence halls, there are 37 buildings.

Student Life: 89% of undergraduates are from Massachusetts. Others are from 41 states, 68 foreign countries, and Canada. 62% are white. The average age of freshmen is 18; all undergraduates, 23. 26% do not continue beyond their first year; 44% remain to graduate.

Housing: 2536 students can be accommodated in college housing, which includes single-sex and coed dorms, off-campus apartments, and married-student housing. In addition, there are special-interest houses. On-campus housing is available on a first-come, first-served basis. 67% of students commute. All students may keep cars.

Activities: There are no fraternities or sororities. There are 100 groups on campus, including art, band, cheerleading, computers, drama, ethnic, gay, honors, international, marching band, musical theater, newspaper, pep band, photography, political, professional, radio and TV, religious, social, social service, student government, and yearbook.

Sports: There are 15 intercollegiate sports for men and 10 for women, and 34 intramural sports for men and 34 for women. Facilities include a 2000-seat gym, a pool, weight-training facilities, and areas for gymnastics, wrestling, and judo. There are also courts for handball, squash, and tennis, and various playing fields.

Disabled Students: 70% of the campus is accessible. Wheelchair ramps, elevators, special parking, specially equipped rest rooms, special class scheduling, lowered drinking fountains, and lowered telephones are available.

Services: Counseling and information services are available, as is tutoring in most subjects. There is a reader service for the blind and remedial writing.

Campus Safety and Security: Measures include 24-hour foot and vehicle patrol, security escort services, shuttle buses, and informal discussions. There are pamphlets/posters/films, emergency telephones, and lighted pathways/sidewalks.

Programs of Study: UMass Lowell confers B.A., B.S., B.F.A., B.L.A., B.M., B.S.B.A., B.S.E., B.S.E.T., B.S.I.M., and B.S.I.T. degrees. Associate, master's, and doctoral degrees are also awarded. Bachelor's degrees are awarded in BIOLOGICAL SCIENCE (biology/biological science), BUSINESS (business administration and management), COMMUNICATIONS AND THE ARTS (English, fine arts, modern language, and music performance), COMPUTER AND PHYSICAL SCIENCE (applied mathematics, chemistry, computer science, information sciences and systems, mathematics, and physics), ENGINEERING AND ENVIRONMENTAL DESIGN (chemical engineering, civil engineering, electrical/electronics engineering, engineering technology, environmental science, industrial administration/management, industrial engineering technology, mechanical engineering, and plastics engineering), HEALTH PROFESSIONS (clinical science, community health work, exercise science, and nursing), SOCIAL SCIENCE (American studies, criminal jus-

tice, economics, history, liberal arts/general studies, philosophy, political science/government, psychology, and sociology). Engineering and management are the largest.

Required: All students must complete a minimum of 120 credits with a 2.0 GPA. Core requirements include 6 credits of English composition, 3 credits of human values, and an area distribution requirement of 27 to 29 credits outside the major in behavioral and social science, fine arts and the humanities, and math and the sciences.

Special: Cross-registration, co-op, and work-study programs are available, as are opportunities for study abroad. The university offers a combined B.A.-B.S. degree in engineering, dual majors, nondegree study, and pass/fail options. There are 2 national honor societies, a freshman honors program, and honors programs in all departments.

Faculty/Classroom: 68% of faculty are male; 32%, female. 99% teach undergraduates and 1% do research.

Admissions: 64% of the 2005-2006 applicants were accepted. 2 freshmen graduated first in their class.

Requirements: The SAT or ACT is required, the SAT is preferred. In addition, applicants should have a high school diploma or the GED. The university recommends that secondary preparation include 4 courses in English, 3 each in social science/history and math, 2 each in science and a foreign language, and 2 academic electives. Prospective music majors must audition, and an interview is recommended for all students. A GPA of 3.0 is required. AP and CLEP credits are accepted.

Procedure: Freshmen are admitted fall and spring. Entrance exams should be taken by January of the senior year. There is a deferred admissions plan and a rolling admissions plan. Application deadlines are open. Application fee is $20 out-of-state. Applications are accepted online.

Transfer: 680 transfer students enrolled in 2004-2005. Transfer applicants must present at least a 2.0 GPA in previous college work. Those with fewer than 30 credits must meet freshman admission requirements. 30 of 120 credits required for the bachelor's degree must be completed at UMass Lowell.

Visiting: There are regularly scheduled orientations for prospective students. To schedule a visit, contact the Office of Student Services at (978) 934-2105.

Financial Aid: In 2005-2006, approximately 94% of all full-time freshmen received some form of financial aid. 94% of full-time freshmen received need-based aid. The average freshman award was $8192. Need-based scholarships or need-based grants averaged $3720; need-based self-help aid (loans and jobs) averaged $3530; non-need-based athletic scholarships averaged $5376; other non-need-based awards and non-need-based scholarships averaged $3298; and other need-based loans (excluding PLUS loans, unsubsidized loans, and private alternative loans) averaged $2545. 16% of undergraduates work part time. Average annual earnings from campus work are $3084. The FAFSA is required. The priority date for freshman financial aid applications for fall entry is March 1.

International Students: There are 80 international students enrolled. They must score satisfactorily TOEFL and also take the SAT.

Computers: Wireless access is available. All students may access the system. There are no time limits and no fees.

Graduates: From July 1, 2004 to June 30, 2005, 1324 bachelor's degrees were awarded. The most popular majors were business administration (23%), computer science (13%), and engineering (10%).

Admissions Contact: Michael Belcher or Kerrie Mead, Co-directors, Admissions. E-mail: *admissions@uml.edu* Web: *www.uml.edu*

WELLESLEY COLLEGE — D-2

Wellesley, MA 02481 (781) 283-2270; Fax: (781) 283-3678

Full-time and Part-time 2300 students	**Faculty:** IIB, ++$
Graduate: none	**Ph.D.s:** n/av
Year: semesters	**Student/Faculty:** n/av
Application Deadline: January 15	**Tuition:** $31,348
	Room & Board: $9682
Freshman Class: 4466 applied, 1463 accepted, 605 enrolled	
SAT Verbal/Math: 700/685*	**ACT:** 30 **MOST COMPETITIVE**

Wellesley College, established in 1870, is a small, private, diverse liberal arts and sciences college for women. The 5 libraries contain 1.3 million volumes, and subscribe to 2500 periodicals including electronic. Computerized library services include the card catalog, interlibrary loans, and database searching. Special learning facilities include a learning resource center, art gallery, radio station, a science center, a botanic greenhouse, an observatory, a center for developmental studies and services, centers for research on women and child study, and a media and technology center. The 500-acre campus is in a suburban area 12 miles west of Boston. Including any residence halls, there are 64 buildings.

Student Life: 80% of undergraduates are from out of state, mostly the Middle Atlantic. Students are from 50 states, 52 foreign countries, and Canada. 63% are from public schools. 48% are white; 25% Asian American. The average age of freshmen is 18; all undergraduates, 20. 5% do not continue beyond their first year; 87% remain to graduate.

Housing: 2120 students can be accommodated in college housing, which includes single-sex dorms. In addition, there are language houses, language corridors, co-ops, and special-interest houses. On-campus housing is guaranteed for all 4 years. 97% of students live on campus. Upperclassmen may keep cars.

Activities: There are no fraternities. There are 170 groups on campus, including art, choir, chorus, computers, dance, debate, drama, ethnic, film, gay, honors, international, jazz band, literary magazine, musical theater, newspaper, orchestra, photography, political, professional, radio and TV, religious, social, social service, student government, symphony, and yearbook. Popular campus events include Parent and Family Weekend, Spring Weekend, and International Week.

Sports: Facilities include an indoor pool, dance studios, a weight room, an indoor track, a golf course, and courts for racquetball, squash, tennis, and volleyball.

Disabled Students: All of the campus is accessible. Wheelchair ramps, elevators, special parking, specially equipped rest rooms, special class scheduling, lowered drinking fountains, lowered telephones, special housing, and signage in braille are available.

Services: Counseling and information services are available, as is tutoring in every subject. There is a reader service for the blind.

Campus Safety and Security: Measures include 24-hour foot and vehicle patrol, self-defense education, security escort services, and shuttle buses. There are informal discussions, pamphlets/posters/films, emergency telephones, and lighted pathways/sidewalks.

Programs of Study: Wellesley confers the B.A. degree. Bachelor's degrees are awarded in AGRICULTURE (environmental studies), BIOLOGICAL SCIENCE (biochemistry, biology/biological science, and neurosciences), COMMUNICATIONS AND THE ARTS (art history and appreciation, Chinese, comparative literature, dramatic arts, English, film arts, French, German, Greek, Japanese, Latin, music, Russian, Russian languages and literature, Spanish, and studio art), COMPUTER AND PHYSICAL SCIENCE (astronomy, astrophysics, chemistry, computer science, geology, mathematics, and physics), ENGINEERING AND ENVIRONMENTAL DESIGN (architecture), SOCIAL SCIENCE (African American studies, American studies, anthropology, archeology, Asian/Oriental studies, classical/ancient civilization, cognitive science, economics, French studies, German area studies, history, international relations, Italian studies, Japanese studies, Judaic studies, Latin American studies, medieval studies, Middle Eastern studies, peace studies, philosophy, political science/government, psychology, religion, sociology, and women's studies). Psychology, English, and economics are the largest.

Required: All students must complete 32 units, at least 8 of which are in the major field, with a minimum 2.0 GPA. Requirements include 3 courses each in humanities, social science, and natural science and math; 1 multicultural course; 1 semester of expository writing in any department; and 8 credits in phys ed. Students must also possess proficiency in a modern or ancient foreign language. A thesis is required for departmental honors. A quantitative reasoning requirement must be satisfied by all students.

Special: Students may cross-register at MIT, Brandeis University, or Babson College. Exchange programs are available with Spelman College in Georgia and Mills College in California, with members of the Twelve College Exchange Program, with Williams College's maritime studies program, and with Connecticut College's National Theater Institute. Study abroad is possible through Wellesley-administered programs in France and Austria, exchange programs in Argentina, Japan, Korea, and the United Kingdom, and other programs in Italy, Japan, Spain, South Africa, and China. There are summer internship programs in Boston and Washington, D.C. Dual majors, student-designed majors, nondegree study, and pass/fail options are possible. A 3-2 program with MIT awards a B.A.-B.S. degree. There are 2 national honor societies, including Phi Beta Kappa, and 51 departmental honors programs.

Admissions: 33% of the 2005-2006 applicants were accepted. The SAT scores for the 2005-2006 freshman class were: Verbal--7% between 500 and 599, 55% between 600 and 700, and 38% above 700; Math--6% between 500 and 599, 45% between 600 and 700, and 49% above 700. The ACT scores were 69% above 28. 92% of the current freshmen were in the top fifth of their class.

Requirements: The SAT or ACT is required. In addition, SAT Reasoning Test and 2 SAT subject tests, or the ACT with Writing are required. Wellesley College does not require a fixed plan of secondary school course preparation. Entering students normally have completed 4 years of college preparatory studies in secondary school that include training in clear and coherent writing and interpreting literature; history; principles of math (typically 4 years); competence in at least 1 foreign language, ancient or modern (usually 4 years of study); and experience in at least 2 lab sciences. An essay is required, and an interview is recommended. AP credits are accepted. Important factors in the admissions decision are advanced placement or honor courses, extracurricular activities record, and recommendations by school officials.

Procedure: Freshmen are admitted in the fall. Entrance exams should be taken during the spring of the junior year or fall of the senior year (no later than December). There are early decision, early admissions, and deferred admissions plans. Early decision applications should be filed by

November 1; regular applications, by January 15 for fall entry. Notification of early decision is sent December 15; regular decision, April 1. 117 early decision candidates were accepted for the 2005-2006 class. 430 applicants were on the 2005 waiting list; 45 were admitted. The fall 2005 application fee was $50 (waived for online applications). Applications are accepted on-line.

Transfer: 30 transfer students enrolled in 2004-2005. Applicants must provide high school and college transcripts, SAT or ACT scores, a personal statement, and a statement of good standing from institutions previously attended. An interview is required. 16 of 32 credits required for the bachelor's degree must be completed at Wellesley.

Visiting: There are guides for informal visits and visitors may sit in on classes and stay overnight. To schedule a visit, contact the Admissions Office.

Financial Aid: In 2005-2006, 56% of all full-time freshmen and 54% of continuing full-time students received some form of financial aid. 56% of full-time freshmen and 54% of continuing full-time students received need-based aid. The average freshman award was $22,614. Average annual earnings from campus work are $2000. Wellesley is a member of CSS. The CSS/Profile or FAFSA, the college's own financial statement, and the most recent income tax returns of parents and student are required. The deadline for filing freshman financial aid applications for fall entry is January 15.

International Students: The school actively recruits these students. They must score satisfactorily on the TOEFL and also take the SAT or the ACT.

Computers: All students may access the system. There are no time limits and no fees.

Admissions Contact: Dean of Admission. A video is available. E-mail: *admission@wellesley.edu* Web: *www.wellesley.edu*

WENTWORTH INSTITUTE OF TECHNOLOGY   E-2
Boston, MA 02115

(617) 989-4000
(800) 556-0610; Fax: (617) 989-4010

Full-time: 2486 men, 655 women	**Faculty:** 122
Part-time: 463 men, 72 women	**Ph.D.s:** 30%
Graduate: none	**Student/Faculty:** 22 to 1
Year: semesters, summer session	**Tuition:** $18,500
Application Deadline: see profile	**Room & Board:** $9000
Freshman Class: 3040 applied, 1825 accepted, 832 enrolled	
SAT Verbal/Math: 517/556*	**ACT:** 23 **COMPETITIVE**

Wentworth Institute of Technology, founded in 1904, is a private college specializing in architecture, design, engineering, technology, and management. Some of the figures in this capsule and profile are approximate. In addition, to regional accreditation, Wentworth has baccalaureate program accreditation with ABET, ACCE, FIDER, IACBE, and NAAB. The library contains 77,000 volumes, 90 microform items, and 750 audio/video tapes/CDs/DVDs, and subscribes to 500 periodicals including electronic. Computerized library services include the card catalog, interlibrary loans, database searching, and Internet access. Special learning facilities include a learning resource center, radio station, printed-circuit lab, CAD/CAM/CAE labs, design studios, and numerically controlled manufacturing systems. The 35-acre campus is in an urban area in Boston. Including any residence halls, there are 27 buildings.

Student Life: 65% are white. The average age of freshmen is 20; all undergraduates, 22. 31% do not continue beyond their first year; 52% remain to graduate.

Housing: 1665 students can be accommodated in college housing, which includes coed dorms and on-campus apartments. On-campus housing is available on a first-come, first-served basis and is available on a lottery system for upperclassmen. Priority is given to out-of-town students. 60% of students live on campus. Alcohol is not permitted. Upperclassmen may keep cars.

Activities: There are no fraternities or sororities. There are 40 groups on campus, including computers, dance, drama, ethnic, gay, honors, international, literary magazine, musical theater, newspaper, orchestra, professional, radio and TV, religious, social, social service, student government, and yearbook. Popular campus events include Design Lecture Series, Beaux Arts Ball, and Women's History Month.

Sports: There are 9 intercollegiate sports for men and 6 for women, and 5 intramural sports for men and 5 for women. Facilities include gyms, tennis courts, a riflery range, a fitness center, an outdoor basketball court, and softball, soccer, and lacrosse playing fields.

Disabled Students: 30% of the campus is accessible. Wheelchair ramps, elevators, special parking, specially equipped rest rooms, special class scheduling, lowered drinking fountains, and lowered telephones are available.

Services: Counseling and information services are available, as is tutoring in every subject. There is remedial math and writing. Free tutoring is available to all students through the learning center.

Campus Safety and Security: Measures include 24-hour foot and vehicle patrol, self-defense education, security escort services, and shuttle buses. There are pamphlets/posters/films, emergency telephones and lighted pathways/sidewalks. All campus police officers have emergency medical training.

Programs of Study: Wentworth confers B.S. and B.Arch. degrees. Associate degrees are also awarded. Bachelor's degrees are awarded in COMMUNICATIONS AND THE ARTS (industrial design), COMPUTER AND PHYSICAL SCIENCE (computer science, and information sciences and systems), ENGINEERING AND ENVIRONMENTAL DESIGN (architectural technology, architecture, civil engineering technology, computer technology, construction management, construction technology, electrical/electronics engineering technology, electromechanical technology, environmental engineering, industrial administration/management, interior design, mechanical engineering technology, and technological management). Architectural engineering technology, computer science, and electronic engineering technology are the largest.

Required: For a bachelor's degree, students must complete a total of 136 to 176 hours, depending on the major, with a minimum GPA of 2.0 overall and 2.5 in the major. An introductory computer course is required of all students. All full-time bachelor's degree candidates must complete 2 semesters of co-op, beginning after the first 2 years of study. A writing competency assessment is required at the end of the sophomore year.

Special: Wentworth offers extensive cooperative programs; cross-registration with other members of the Colleges of the Fenway Consortium; study abroad, including study in France for third-year architecture students; interdisciplinary majors, including engineering technology and facilities planning and management; a dual major in technical management; and nondegree study. Most students at the bachelor's level attend school in the summer, as most cooperative work occurs during the academic year. There is 1 national honor society.

Faculty/Classroom: 76% of faculty are male; 24%, female. All teach undergraduates. The average class size in an introductory lecture is 25; in a laboratory, 25; and in a regular course, 22.

Admissions: 60% of the 2005-2006 applicants were accepted.

Requirements: The SAT or ACT is required. In addition, applicants must be graduates of an accredited secondary school or have the GED. High school course requirements vary by major. AP and CLEP credits are accepted. Important factors in the admissions decision are advanced placement or honor courses, leadership record, and extracurricular activities record.

Procedure: Freshmen are admitted fall and spring. Entrance exams should be taken in the spring of the junior year or the fall of the senior year. There are a deferred admissions and rolling admissions plans. Notification is sent on a rolling basis. A waiting list is an active part of the admissions procedure for certain majors. Applications are accepted on-line. Check with the school for current application deadlines.

Transfer: 163 transfer students enrolled in 2004-2005. Requirements for transfer students vary by program. All applicants must submit official college and high school transcripts. Portfolios and faculty reviews are recommended of applicants to industrial design, interior design, and architecture programs. Grades of C or better transfer for credit. Transfer students must take 50% of the course work in their degree program at Wentworth to graduate.

Visiting: There are regularly scheduled orientations for prospective students, including daily tours and information programs, Monday to Friday. There are guides for informal visits and visitors may sit in on classes. To schedule a visit, contact the Admissions Office.

Financial Aid: In 2005-2006, 80% of all full-time students received some form of financial aid. 60% of full-time freshmen and 65% of continuing full-time students received need-based aid. Need-based scholarships or need-based grants averaged $4382 ($6750 maximum); need-based self-help aid (loans and jobs) averaged $4225; and other non-need-based awards and non-need-based scholarships averaged $3000. 29% of undergraduates work part time. The FAFSA and are required. Check with the school for current applicant deadlines.

International Students: The school actively recruits these students. They must score satisfactory on the written TOEFL or on the electronic version take the MELAB, the Comprehensive English Language Test, or the college's own test. They must also take the SAT or the ACT, the SAT is recommended.

Computers: All students may access the system. There are no time limits and no fees. It is strongly recommended that all students have a personal computer.

Admissions Contact: Office of Admissions.
E-mail: *admissions@wit.edu* Web: *www.wit.edu*

WESTERN NEW ENGLAND COLLEGE B-3

Springfield, MA 01119 (413) 782-1321
(800) 325-1122 ext. 1321; Fax: (413) 782-1777

Full-time: 1428 men, 935 women	**Faculty:** 133; IIA, +$
Part-time: 346 men, 146 women	**Ph.D.s:** 92%
Graduate: 476 men, 413 women	**Student/Faculty:** 18 to 1
Year: semesters, summer session	**Tuition:** $22,164
Application Deadline: open	**Room & Board:** $8890
Freshman Class: n/av	
SAT Verbal/Math: 520/540*	**COMPETITIVE**

Western New England College, founded in 1919, is a private nonsecretarian institution offering undergraduate programs in business, engineering, and liberal arts. There are 3 undergraduate and 2 graduate schools. In addition to regional accreditation, WNEC has baccalaureate program accreditation with AACSB, ABET, and CSWE. The library contains 123,475 volumes and 364,075 microform items, and subscribes to 176 periodicals including electronic. Computerized library services include the card catalog, interlibrary loans, database searching, and Internet access. Special learning facilities include an art gallery and radio station. The 215-acre campus is in a suburban area 90 miles west of Boston. Including any residence halls, there are 22 buildings.

Student Life: 51% of undergraduates are from out of state, mostly the Northeast. Others are from 29 states and 6 foreign countries. 85% are white. 78% are claim no religious affiliation; 15% Catholic. The average age of freshmen is 18; all undergraduates, 20. 25% do not continue beyond their first year; 60% remain to graduate.

Housing: 1960 students can be accommodated in college housing, which includes coed dorms and on-campus apartments. Students are often grouped by academic interest or theme housing. On-campus housing is guaranteed for all 4 years. 79% of students live on campus. All students may keep cars.

Activities: There are no fraternities or sororities. There are 60 groups on campus, including art, cheerleading, chorus, computers, dance, drama, ethnic, gay, honors, international, jazz band, literary magazine, newspaper, pep band, photography, political, professional, radio and TV, religious, social, social service, student government, and yearbook. Popular campus events include Spring Week, Family and Friends Weekend, and Winter Week.

Sports: There are 10 intercollegiate sports for men and 9 for women, and 9 intramural sports for men and 9 for women. Facilities include a healthful living center equipped for basketball (2000 seats), wrestling, racquetball, squash, aerobics, fitness, and volleyball, as well as a weight room, an 8-lane pool, and a track.

Disabled Students: 90% of the campus is accessible. Wheelchair ramps, elevators, special parking, specially equipped rest rooms, special class scheduling, lowered drinking fountains, and lowered telephones are available.

Services: Counseling and information services are available, as is tutoring in most subjects.

Campus Safety and Security: Measures include 24-hour foot and vehicle patrol, self-defense education, security escort services, and informal discussions. There are pamphlets/posters/films, emergency telephones, lighted pathways/sidewalks, security cameras, medical response, fire response, and a comprehensive public safety awareness program.

Programs of Study: WNEC confers B.A., B.S., B.B.A., B.A.L.S., B.S.B.A., B.S.B.E., B.S.C.J., B.S.E.E., B.S.H.S., B.S.I.E., and B.S.M.E., and B.S.W. degrees. Associate and master's degrees are also awarded. Bachelor's degrees are awarded in BIOLOGICAL SCIENCE (biology/biological science and molecular biology), BUSINESS (accounting, banking and finance, business administration and management, management science, marketing/retailing/merchandising, and sports management), COMMUNICATIONS AND THE ARTS (advertising, communications, and English), COMPUTER AND PHYSICAL SCIENCE (chemistry, computer science, information sciences and systems, and mathematics), EDUCATION (elementary and secondary), ENGINEERING AND ENVIRONMENTAL DESIGN (bioengineering, biomedical engineering, computer engineering, electrical/electronics engineering, industrial engineering, and mechanical engineering), SOCIAL SCIENCE (criminal justice, economics, forensic studies, history, international studies, liberal arts/general studies, philosophy, political science/government, psychology, social work, and sociology). Criminal justice, management, and psychology are the largest.

Required: To graduate, students must complete 122 credit hours, with a minimum GPA of 2.0. Requirements include 2 courses each in English, math, lab science, and phys ed, and 1 course each in history, culture, and computers. A first-year seminar is also required for freshmen. Other requirements vary according to the major.

Special: Students may cross-register with cooperating colleges of Greater Springfield. The college offers internships, study abroad, a Washington semester, work-study programs, B.A.-B.S. degrees, an accelerated degree program, and dual and student-designed majors. The 3+3 law program offers qualified students the opportunity to earn a J.D. in 6 years. There are 6 national honor societies and a freshman honors program.

Faculty/Classroom: 68% of faculty are male; 32%, female. No introductory courses are taught by graduate students. The average class size in an introductory lecture is 23; in a laboratory, 20; and in a regular course, 20.

Admissions: The SAT scores for the 2005-2006 freshman class were: Verbal--33% below 500, 51% between 500 and 599, 15% between 600 and 700, and 1% above 700; Math--29% below 500, 43% between 500 and 599, 26% between 600 and 700, and 2% above 700. 25% of the current freshmen were in the top fifth of their class; 59% were in the top two fifths. 1 freshman graduated first in their class.

Requirements: The SAT is required. In addition, applicants must be graduates of an approved secondary school and must have completed 4 years of high school English, 2 or more years of math, 1 or more years of science, and 1 year of history and social science. An interview is recommended. ACT is accepted in lieu of SAT. A GPA of 2.2 is required. AP and CLEP credits are accepted. Important factors in the admissions decision are advanced placement or honor courses, extracurricular activities record, and recommendations by school officials.

Procedure: Freshmen are admitted fall and spring. Entrance exams should be taken in the spring of the junior year or fall of the senior year. There is a deferred admissions plan. Application deadlines are open. Applications are accepted on-line.

Transfer: 110 transfer students enrolled in 2004-2005. Applicants must have a minimum GPA of 2.3. Grades of C or better transfer for credit. The college admits transfer students in the fall and spring. 30 of 122 credits required for the bachelor's degree must be completed at WNEC.

Visiting: There are regularly scheduled orientations for prospective students, including multiple open houses. There are guides for informal visits and visitors may sit in on classes and stay overnight. To schedule a visit, contact the Undergraduate Admissions Office.

Financial Aid: In 2005-2006, 93% of all full-time freshmen received some form of financial aid. 74% of full-time freshmen received need-based aid. The average freshman award was $13,133. WNEC is a member of CSS. The FAFSA and federal tax returns and W-2s are required. The priority date for freshman financial aid applications for fall entry is April 1. The deadline for filing freshman financial aid applications for fall entry is rolling.

International Students: There are 6 international students enrolled. They must take the TOEFL or the SAT ot ACT.

Computers: Wireless access is available. All students may access the system at varying hours from campus labs; 24 hours a day from residence halls. There are no time limits and no fees.

Graduates: From July 1, 2004 to June 30, 2005, 727 bachelor's degrees were awarded. The most popular majors were accounting (7%), criminal justice (7%), and psychology (7%). In an average class, 4% graduate in 3 years, 56% graduate in 4 years, 56% graduate in 5 years, and 60% graduate in 6 years. Of the 2004 graduating class, 14% were enrolled in graduate school within 6 months of graduation and 87% were employed.

Admissions Contact: Dr. Charles R. Pollock, Vice President for Enrollment Management. A video is available. E-mail: *ugradmis@wnec.edu* Web: *www.wnec.edu*

WESTFIELD STATE COLLEGE B-3

Westfield, MA 01086-1630　　　**(413) 572-5218**
(800) 322-8401; Fax: (413) 572-0520

Full-time: 1650 men, 2070 women	Faculty: 171; IIA, av$
Part-time: 260 men, 325 women	Ph.D.s: 85%
Graduate: 200 men, 450 women	Student/Faculty: 22 to 1
Year: semesters, summer session	Tuition: $4900 ($11,000)
Application Deadline: see profile	Room & Board: $5300
Freshman Class: n/av	
SAT Verbal/Math: required	ACT: not required **COMPETITIVE**

Westfield State College, founded in 1838, is a public college with liberal arts and teacher preparation programs and professional training. There is 1 graduate school. Figures in the above capsule and profile are approximate. In addition to regional accreditation, 577 Westfield State has baccalaureate program accreditation with CAAHEP and CSWE. The library contains 124,363 volumes, 547,002 microform items, and 2379 audio/video tapes/CDs/DVDs, and subscribes to 819 periodicals including electronic. Computerized library services include the card catalog, interlibrary loans, and database searching. Special learning facilities include a learning resource center, art gallery, radio station, TV station, and a geology museum. The 257-acre campus is in a rural area 15 miles west of Springfield. Including any residence halls, there are 14 buildings.

Student Life: 93% of undergraduates are from Massachusetts. Others are from 20 states, 1 foreign country, and Canada. 78% are white. The average age of freshmen is 18; all undergraduates, 20. 26% do not continue beyond their first year.

Housing: 2114 students can be accommodated in college housing, which includes coed dormitories, on-campus apartments, and a living/

learning unit, and special housing for international students. On-campus housing is guaranteed for all 4 years. 59% of students live on campus; of those, 70% remain on campus on weekends. Upperclassmen may keep cars.

Activities: There are no fraternities or sororities. There are 50 groups on campus, including art, band, chess, choir, chorale, chorus, drama, ethnic, gay, honors, jazz band, literary magazine, musical theater, newspaper, orchestra, pep band, photography, political, professional, radio and TV, religious, social service, student government, and yearbook. Popular campus events include Halloween Dance, Spring Weekend, and Comedy Night.

Sports: There are 6 intercollegiate sports for men and 8 for women, and 11 intramural sports for men and 11 for women. Facilities include a track, baseball and softball fields, tennis courts, a 400-seat gym, and a 5000-seat stadium.

Disabled Students: 60% of the campus is accessible. Wheelchair ramps, elevators, special parking, specially equipped rest rooms, special class scheduling, lowered telephones, and special housing are available.

Services: Counseling and information services are available, as is tutoring in every subject. There is a reader service for the blind, and remedial math, reading, and writing.

Campus Safety and Security: Measures include 24-hour foot and vehicle patrol, security escort services, shuttle buses, and pamphlets/posters/films. There are emergency telephones and lighted pathways/sidewalks.

Programs of Study: Westfield State confers B.A., B.S., and B.S.E degrees. Master's degrees are also awarded. Bachelor's degrees are awarded in BIOLOGICAL SCIENCE (biology/biological science), BUSINESS (business administration and management), COMMUNICATIONS AND THE ARTS (communications, dramatic arts, English, fine arts, and music), COMPUTER AND PHYSICAL SCIENCE (computer science, information sciences and systems, and mathematics), EDUCATION (art, business, early childhood, elementary, middle school, music, science, secondary, and special), ENGINEERING AND ENVIRONMENTAL DESIGN (environmental science), SOCIAL SCIENCE (criminal justice, economics, history, interdisciplinary studies, physical fitness/movement, political science/government, psychology, social work, sociology, and urban studies). Computer science, English, and psychology are the strongest academically. Criminal justice, education, and business are the largest.

Required: Students must complete a total of 120 credit hours, with 43 or more credits in 8 specified areas and 30 to 40 hours in the major. The college requires a 2.0 GPA overall and 2.0 in major courses. U.S. history or government and diversity awareness courses are required.

Special: Students may cross-register through College Academic Program Sharing, National Student Exchange, and Cooperating Colleges of Greater Springfield. Internships are for credit only in conjunction with all major programs. The college offers study abroad in 36 countries, a Washington semester for political science, criminal justice, and psychology majors, dual majors, student-designed majors, and some credit for military experience. There are 8 national honor societies and a freshman honors program.

Faculty/Classroom: 63% of faculty are male; 37%, female. All teach undergraduates. No introductory courses are taught by graduate students. The average class size in an introductory lecture is 28; in a laboratory, 15; and in a regular course, 25.

Requirements: The SAT is required. In addition, applicants must achieve between a 2.0 and 3.0 cumulative average in academic subjects, contingent upon the SAT scores. They must be graduates of an accredited secondary school and must have completed 4 years of college preparatory level English, 3 years of math (algebra I and II and geometry), 2 years of social sciences (including 1 year of U.S history), 3 sciences, including 2 with lab, 2 foreign language, and 2 years of electives. The GED is accepted. A portfolio is required for admission to the art program, and an audition is necessary for admission to the music program. A GPA of 2.0 is required. AP and CLEP credits are accepted. Important factors in the admissions decision are advanced placement or honor courses, leadership record, and evidence of special talent.

Procedure: Freshmen are admitted fall and spring. Entrance exams should be taken in the spring of the junior year and fall of the senior year. There are deferred admissions and rollijng admissions plans. Check with the school for application deadlines. Notification is sent on a rolling basis. Applications are accepted on-line. The fall 2005 application fee was $25.

Transfer: 284 transfer students enrolled in a recent year. Transfer students must have 24 transferable credits with a minimum cumulative GPA of 2.0 (higher for some majors). A grade of C- or better with a 2.0 GPA will transfer for credit. Of the 120 credits required for a bachelor's degree, a minimum of 30 credits must be completed at the college. Transfer students are admitted in the fall and spring. 30 of 120 credits required for the bachelor's degree must be completed at Westfield State.

Visiting: There are regularly scheduled orientations for prospective students, including a campus tour, classroom observation, academic department presentations, lunch with faculty, staff, and students, and a question-and-answer session moderated by a panel of administrators. There are guides for informal visits. To schedule a visit, contact the Admission Office.

Financial Aid: In a recent year, 58% of all full-time freshmen and 62% of continuing full-time students received some form of financial aid. 44% of full-time freshmen and 45% of continuing full-time students received need-based aid. The average freshman award was $4878. Need-based scholarships or need-based grants averaged $3764; and need-based self-help aid (loans and jobs) averaged $2330. 21% of undergraduates worked part time. The average financial indebtedness of a recent graduate was $12,347. Westfield State is a member of CSS. The FAFSA is required. Check with the school for application deadlines.

International Students: They must score satisfactorily on the written TOEFL and also take the SAT.

Computers: All students may access the system. There are no time limits and no fees.

Admissions Contact: Michelle Mattie, Director of Student Admin. Service Center. A video is available. E-mail: *admission@wsc.ma.edu* Web: *www.wsc.ma.edu*

WHEATON COLLEGE   D-3
Norton, MA 02766   (508) 286-8251
                              (800) 394-6003; Fax: (508) 286-8271

Full-time: 589 men, 969 women	Faculty: 121; IIB, +$
Part-time: 1 man, 9 women	Ph.D.s: 98%
Graduate: none	Student/Faculty: 13 to 1
Year: semesters	Tuition: $32,350
Application Deadline: January 15	Room & Board: $7830
Freshman Class: 3697 applied, 1638 accepted, 466 enrolled	
SAT Verbal/Math: 640/620*	ACT: 28

HIGHLY COMPETITIVE+

Wheaton College, established in 1834, is an independent liberal arts institution. The library contains 371,675 volumes, 86,184 microform items, and 14,686 audio/video tapes/CDs/DVDs, and subscribes to 7692 periodicals including electronic. Computerized library services include the card catalog, interlibrary loans, database searching, and Internet access. Special learning facilities include a learning resource center, art gallery, planetarium, radio station, and TV station. The 385-acre campus is in a suburban area 35 miles southeast of Boston and 15 miles north of Providence. Including any residence halls, there are 87 buildings.

Student Life: 65% of undergraduates are from out of state, mostly the Northeast. Students are from 46 states, 42 foreign countries, and Canada. 63% are from public schools. 79% are white. The average age of freshmen is 18; all undergraduates, 20. 14% do not continue beyond their first year; 74% remain to graduate.

Housing: 1568 students can be accommodated in college housing, which includes single-sex and coed dormitories. In addition, there are language houses and special-interest houses, including among others, House of Living Arts, Women Empowering Women, Global Awareness, and Outdoor Education. On-campus housing is guaranteed for all 4 years. 96% of students live on campus; of those, 75% remain on campus on weekends. All students may keep cars.

Activities: There are no fraternities or sororities. There are 69 groups on campus, including art, BACCHUS, band, choir, chorale, chorus, dance, debate, drama, ethnic, film, gay, Habitat for Humanity, honors, international, jazz band, literary magazine, musical theater, newspaper, photography, political, radio and TV, religious, social, social service, student government, symphony, Visions (gospel choir), yearbook, and Zen club. Popular campus events include Otis Social Justice Symposium and Award and Spring Weekend.

Sports: There are 9 intercollegiate sports for men and 12 for women, and 7 intramural sports for men and 7 for women. Facilities include an 8-lane stretch pool, a field house with 5 tennis courts, 1 outdoor and 3 indoor basketball courts, a 200-meter track, a golf/archery range and batting cage, an 850-seat gym, 7 lighted outdoor tennis courts, a running course, a baseball stadium, 2 athletic fields, an aerobics/dance studio, and a fitness center.

Disabled Students: 50% of the campus is accessible. Wheelchair ramps, elevators, special parking, specially equipped rest rooms, special class scheduling, and lowered telephones are available.

Services: Counseling and information services are available, as is tutoring in most subjects. There is a reader service for the blind and remedial writing. Peer tutoring and note takers for hearing-impaired students are available.

Campus Safety and Security: Measures include 24-hour foot and vehicle patrol, self-defense education, security escort services, and informal discussions. There are pamphlets/posters/films, emergency telephones, and lighted pathways/sidewalks.

Programs of Study: Wheaton confers the A.B. degree. Bachelor's degrees are awarded in BIOLOGICAL SCIENCE (biochemistry and biology/biological science), COMMUNICATIONS AND THE ARTS (art history and appreciation, classics, creative writing, dramatic arts, English, fine arts, French, German, Greek, Latin, literature, music, Russian, and studio art), COMPUTER AND PHYSICAL SCIENCE (astronomy, chemistry, computer mathematics, computer science, mathematics, and physics), ENGINEERING AND ENVIRONMENTAL DESIGN (environmental science), SOCIAL SCIENCE (American studies, anthropology, Asian/Oriental studies, classical/ancient civilization, economics, German area studies, Hispanic American studies, history, international relations, Italian studies, philosophy, political science/government, psychobiology, psychology, religion, Russian and Slavic studies, sociology, and women's studies). Arts and sciences are the strongest academically. English, psychology, and economics are the largest.

Required: Among the requirements for graduation are 32 course credits (4 semester hours each), with a minimum of 10 courses in the major, at least 3 of which are at the 300 level or above. The core classes consist of English, quantitative skills, foreign language, natural science, and non-Western history. Students must maintain a minimum GPA of 2.0 (C-) in all courses to remain in good academic standing.

Special: Students may cross-register with Brown University as well as with colleges in the Southeastern Association for Cooperation in Higher Education in Massachusetts and with schools participating in the 12 College Exchange Program. Wheaton offers study abroad in 54 countries, internship programs, nondegree study, dual majors, student-designed majors, a Washington semester at American University, and interdisciplinary majors, including math and economics, math and computer science, physics and astronomy, and theater and English dramatic literature. A 3-2 engineering degree is offered with George Washington University, Dartmouth College, and Worcester Polytechnic Institute. Pass/fail options are possible. There are 8 national honor societies, including Phi Beta Kappa, a freshman honors program, and all departments have honors programs.

Faculty/Classroom: 50% of faculty are male; 50%, female. All teach undergraduates and 100% do research. The average class size in an introductory lecture is 40; in a laboratory, 20; and in a regular course, 19.

Admissions: 44% of the 2005-2006 applicants were accepted. The SAT scores for the 2005-2006 freshman class were: Verbal--4% below 500, 21% between 500 and 599, 55% between 600 and 700, and 20% above 700; Math--1% below 500, 33% between 500 and 599, 52% between 600 and 700, and 14% above 700. The ACT scores were 35% between 24 and 26, 28% between 27 and 28, and 37% above 28. 78% of the current freshmen were in the top fifth of their class; 95% were in the top two fifths. 6 freshmen graduated first in their class.

Requirements: Submission of SAT or ACT scores is optional. Applicants must be graduates of an accredited secondary school. Recommended courses include English with emphasis on composition skills, 4 years; foreign language and math, 3 to 4 years each; social studies, 3 years; and lab science, 2 to 3 years. Wheaton requires an essay and a graded writing sample and strongly recommends an interview. AP credits are accepted. Important factors in the admissions decision are advanced placement or honor courses, extracurricular activities record, and leadership record.

Procedure: Freshmen are admitted fall and spring. Entrance exams should be taken in October and/or November. There are early decision and deferred admissions plans. Early decision applications should be filed by November 15; regular applications, by January 15 for fall entry and November 1 for spring entry. Notification of early decision is sent December 15; regular decision, April 1. The fall 2005 application fee was $55. 196 early decision candidates were accepted for the 2005-2006 class. 736 applicants were on the 2005 waiting list; 2 were admitted. Applications are accepted on-line.

Transfer: 6 transfer students enrolled in 2004-2005. Transfer students are encouraged to present a strong B average in their college work to date. Preference will be given to college over high school work. The college transcript is evaluated. High school and college transcripts, essay or personal statement, statement of good standing, 2 instructor recommendations, and a mid-term evaluation are required. 16 of 32 credits required for the bachelor's degree must be completed at Wheaton.

Visiting: There are regularly scheduled orientations for prospective students, including class visits, tours, panels on financial aid, student life, and athletics, lunch with faculty, and department open houses. There are guides for informal visits and visitors may sit in on classes and stay overnight. To schedule a visit, contact the Admissions Office at *admission@wheatoncollege.edu*.

Financial Aid: In 2005-2006, 63% of all full-time freshmen and 61% of continuing full-time students received some form of financial aid. 49% of full-time freshmen and 50% of continuing full-time students received need-based aid. The average freshman award was $20,257. 43% of undergraduates work part time. Average annual earnings from campus work are $800. The average financial indebtedness of the 2005 graduate was $22,380. Wheaton is a member of CSS. The CSS/Profile or FAFSA and parents' and student's federal tax returns, and if applicable, noncustodial profile are required. The deadline for filing freshman financial aid applications for fall entry is February 1.

International Students: There are 40 international students enrolled. The school actively recruits these students. They must score satisfactorily on the written TOEF.

Computers: Wireless access is available. Roughly one-fourth of Wheaton courses rely on Blackboard, a course management software system allowing instructors to make syllabi, reading lists, assignments, announcements, electronic discussions, and quizzes available on the Web. Beyond the approximately 285 publicly available PCs, all residence halls rooms and academic buildings support wired Inernet access. Wireless Internet access is available in select locations, including the library, portions of the some academic buildings, the student center, dining halls, and the newest residence hall. All students may access the system 24 hours a day, 7 days a week. There are no time limits and no fees. It is strongly recommended that all students have a personal computer.

Graduates: From July 1, 2004 to June 30, 2005, 410 bachelor's degrees were awarded. The most popular majors were English (68%), psychology (64%), and economics (49%). In an average class, 74% graduate in 5 years or less, and 75% graduate in 6 years or less. 22 companies recruited on campus in 2004-2005. Of the 2004 graduating class, 29% were enrolled in graduate school within 6 months of graduation and 50% were employed.

Admissions Contact: Gail Berson, Vice President for Enrollment and Dean of Admission and Student.
E-mail: *admission@wheatoncollege.edu*
Web: *www.wheatoncollege.edu*

WHEELOCK COLLEGE   E-2
Boston, MA 02215-4176

(617) 879-2206
(800) 734-5212; Fax: (617) 879-2449

Full-time: 39 men, 596 women	**Faculty:** 65; IIA, av$
Part-time: 3 men, 37 women	**Ph.D.s:** 89%
Graduate: 23 men, 330 women	**Student/Faculty:** 10 to 1
Year: semesters	**Tuition:** $23,625
Application Deadline: March 1	**Room & Board:** $9450
Freshman Class: 703 applied, 535 accepted, 181 enrolled	
SAT Verbal/Math: 509/485*	**COMPETITIVE**

Wheelock College, established in 1888, is a private institution with programs in education, child life and family studies, social work, juvenile justice and youth advocacy, and human services. In addition to regional accreditation, Wheelock College has baccalaureate program accreditation with CSWE and NCATE. The library contains 83,573 volumes, 483,257 microform items, and 3633 audio/video tapes/CDs/DVDs, and subscribes to 12,629 periodicals including electronic. Computerized library services include the card catalog, interlibrary loans, database searching, Internet access, and laptop Internet portals. Special learning facilities include a learning resource center, art gallery, and the Wheelock Family Theater. The 7-acre campus is in an urban area in Boston. Including any residence halls, there are 12 buildings.

Student Life: 63% of undergraduates are from Massachusetts. Others are from 22 states and 2 foreign countries. 90% are from public schools. 85% are white. The average age of freshmen is 18; all undergraduates, 20. 29% do not continue beyond their first year; 73% remain to graduate.

Housing: 500 students can be accommodated in college housing, which includes single-sex and coed dorms. In addition, there is a cooperative living house, nonsmoking floors and a wellness floor. On-campus housing is guaranteed for all 4 years. 73% of students live on campus; of those, 50% remain on campus on weekends. Upperclassmen may keep cars.

Activities: There are no fraternities or sororities. There are 25 groups on campus, including Best Buddies, choir, chorale, chorus, dance, drama, ethnic, gay, honors, international, professional, religious, sign choir, social, social service, student government, and women's center. Popular campus events include Kids Day, Family Weekend, and COF Concerts and carnivals.

Sports: There are 5 intercollegiate sports for women, and 9 intramural sports for men and 9 for women. Facilities include a sports complex at a neighboring college with a pool and diving board, racquetball courts, a weight room, an indoor track, a basketball court, crew tanks, and cardiovascular equipment.

Disabled Students: 67% of the campus is accessible. Wheelchair ramps, elevators, special parking, specially equipped rest rooms, special class scheduling, lowered drinking fountains, lowered telephones, and assistive technology in the learning center are available.

Services: Counseling and information services are available, as is tutoring in every subject. There is a reader service for the blind, and remedial math, reading, and writing. Academic support services provide individualized assistance upon request.

Campus Safety and Security: Measures include 24-hour foot and vehicle patrol, security escort services, informal discussions, and emergency telephones. There are lighted pathways/sidewalks.

Programs of Study: Wheelock College confers B.A., B.S., and B.S.W. degrees. Associate and master's degrees are also awarded. Bachelor's degrees are awarded in EDUCATION (early childhood, elementary, and special), SOCIAL SCIENCE (child care/child and family studies, human development, and social work). Teaching, social work, and child life are the strongest academically and have the largest enrollments.

Required: To graduate, students must complete between 134 and 140 credit hours, with a minimum GPA of 2.0. Wheelock requires at least a 32-credit major combined with a 36-credit professional studies program. Students must earn 26 credits in English composition, math, human growth and development, children and their environments, first-year seminar, visual and performing arts, and 1 course in first aid.

Special: Wheelock offers cross-registration with all colleges in the Colleges of the Fenway and internships that include student teaching and social work practice. Dual majors, study-abroad programs, and pass/fail options are available. Students may receive credit for life and work experience. Students begin practical fieldwork their freshman year and continue for all 4 years. There is 1 national honor society.

Faculty/Classroom: 13% of faculty are male; 87%, female. 70% teach undergraduates. No introductory courses are taught by graduate students. The average class size in an introductory lecture is 20; in a laboratory, 17; and in a regular course, 15.

Admissions: 76% of the 2005-2006 applicants were accepted. The SAT scores for the 2005-2006 freshman class were: Verbal--44% below 500, 43% between 500 and 599, 12% between 600 and 700, and 1% above 700; Math--54% below 500, 38% between 500 and 599, 8% between 600 and 700, and 1% above 700. The ACT scores were 56% below 21, 11% between 21 and 23, and 33% between 24 and 26. 28% of the current freshmen were in the top fifth of their class; 54% were in the top two fifths.

Requirements: The SAT is required. In addition, applicants must be graduates of an accredited secondary school and must have completed 4 years of English, 3 years of math, and 2 years each of science and history. The GED is accepted. The college requires a graded writing sample and recommends an interview. A GPA of 2.0 is required. AP and CLEP credits are accepted. Important factors in the admissions decision are advanced placement or honor courses, evidence of special talent, and personality/intangible qualities.

Procedure: Freshmen are admitted fall and spring. Entrance exams should be taken in the spring of the junior year and/or fall of the senior year. There are early decision, deferred admissions, and rolling admissions plans. Early decision applications should be filed by December 1; regular applications, by March 1 for fall entry and December 1 for spring entry, along with a $35 fee. Notification of early decision is sent December 15; regular decision, on a rolling basis. 41 early decision candidates were accepted for the 2005-2006 class. Applications are accepted online.

Transfer: 75 transfer students enrolled in 2004-2005. Transfer students must have a minimum GPA of 2.0 and must present 1 letter of recommendation. Grades of C- or better transfer for credit. Applicants must submit all official high school and college transcripts. 67 of 134 credits required for the bachelor's degree must be completed at Wheelock College.

Visiting: There are regularly scheduled orientations for prospective students. Information sessions are held on select Saturdays in the fall and spring. Students hear a presentation from a counselor, have a tour, and may speak to a counselor individually. There are guides for informal visits and visitors may sit in on classes and stay overnight. To schedule a visit, contact the Undergraduate Admissions Office.

Financial Aid: In 2005-2006, 94% of all full-time freshmen and 82% of continuing full-time students received some form of financial aid. 63% of full-time freshmen and 70% of continuing full-time students received need-based aid. The average freshman award was $23,709. Need-based scholarships or need-based grants averaged $6821 ($19,200 maximum); need-based self-help aid (loans and jobs) averaged $4425 ($8425 maximum); and other non-need-based awards and non-need-based scholarships averaged $18,026 ($23,600 maximum). 33% of undergraduates work part time. Average annual earnings from campus work are $1800. The average financial indebtedness of the 2005 graduate was $21,125. The FAFSA is required. The priority date for freshman financial aid applications for fall entry is February 15.

International Students: There were 5 international students enrolled in a recent year. Satisfactory scores are required on the written TOEFL and the SAT or ACT. They should submit SAT or ACT scores or TOEFL scores if English is not their official language.

Computers: All students may access the system 24 hours a day any time school is in session. There are no time limits and no fees.

Graduates: From July 1, 2004 to June 30, 2005, 81 bachelor's degrees were awarded. The most popular majors were teacher education (68%), child life (16%), and social work (16%). In an average class, 48% graduate in 4 years or less, 52% graduate in 5 years or less, and 53% graduate in 6 years or less. 35 companies recruited on campus in 2004-2005. Of the 2004 graduating class, 22% were enrolled in graduate school within 6 months of graduation and 95% were employed.

Admissions Contact: Lynne Harding, Dean of Admissions.
E-mail: *undergrad@wheelock.edu* Web: *www.wheelock.edu*

WILLIAMS COLLEGE
A-1
Williamstown, MA 01267 (413) 597-2211

Full-time: 1022 men, 1099 women	**Faculty:** 247; IIB, ++$
Part-time: 13 men, 20 women	**Ph.Ds:** 96%
Graduate: 20 men, 33 women	**Student/Faculty:** 9 to 1
Year: 4-1-4	**Tuition:** $31,760
Application Deadline: January 1	**Room & Board:** $8551

Freshman Class: 5822 applied, 1095 accepted, 536 enrolled
SAT Verbal/Math: 710/710* ACT: 31 **MOST COMPETITIVE**

Williams College, founded in 1793, is a private institution offering undergraduate degrees in liberal arts and graduate degrees in art history and development economics. The 11 libraries contain 948,365 volumes, 492,374 microform items, and 39,133 audio/video tapes/CDs/DVDs, and subscribe to 13,493 periodicals including electronic. Computerized library services include the card catalog, interlibrary loans, database searching, and Internet access. Special learning facilities include a learning resource center, art gallery, planetarium, radio station, a 2500-acre experimental forest, an environmental studies center, a center for foreign languages, literatures, and cultures, a rare book library, a studio art center, and a 3 Stage center for the performing arts. The 450-acre campus is in a small town 150 miles north of New York City and west of Boston. Including any residence halls, there are 97 buildings.

Student Life: 84% of undergraduates are from out of state, mostly the Northeast. Students are from 46 states, 46 foreign countries, and Canada. 55% are from public schools. 68% are white. The average age of freshmen is 18; all undergraduates, 20. 2% do not continue beyond their first year; 96% remain to graduate.

Housing: 1972 students can be accommodated in college housing, which includes single-sex and coed dorms and on-campus apartments. In addition, there is cooperative housing, in which students prepare their own meals. On-campus housing is guaranteed for all 4 years. Upperclassmen may keep cars.

Activities: There are no fraternities or sororities. There are 115 groups on campus, including a capella, art, band, chess, choir, chorale, chorus, comedt, computers, dance, debate, drama, ethnic, film, gay, handbell choir, honors, international, jazz band, literary magazine, marching band, musical theater, newspaper, orchestra, pep band, photography, political, radio and TV, religious, social service, student government, symphony, and yearbook. Popular campus events include Winter Carnival, Mountain Day, and Multicultural Center-sponsored activities.

Sports: There are 16 intercollegiate sports for men and 15 for women, and 17 intramural sports for men and 17 for women. Facilities include 2 gyms, a 50-meter pool, a dance studio, a weight room, rowing tanks, a boathouse, a golf course, playing fields, artificial turf field, indoor and outdoor tracks, and courts for tennis, squash, and paddle tennis.

Disabled Students: Wheelchair ramps, elevators, special parking, specially equipped rest rooms, special class scheduling, lowered drinking fountains, lowered telephones, wheelchair lifts, and special laundry and kitchen facilities are available.

Services: Counseling and information services are available, as is tutoring in every subject. There is a reader service for the blind, and remedial math, reading, and writing. Other services include a peer health program, rape and sexual assault hotline, and 10-1 counseling service.

Campus Safety and Security: Measures include 24-hour foot and vehicle patrol, self-defense education, security escort services, and informal discussions. There are pamphlets/posters/films, emergency telephones, and lighted pathways/sidewalks.

Programs of Study: Williams confers the B.A. degree. Master's degrees are also awarded. Bachelor's degrees are awarded in BIOLOGICAL SCIENCE (biology/biological science), COMMUNICATIONS AND THE ARTS (art, art history and appreciation, classics, dramatic arts, English, fine arts, French, German, literature, music, Russian, and Spanish), COMPUTER AND PHYSICAL SCIENCE (astronomy, astrophysics, chemistry, computer science, geology, mathematics, and physics), SOCIAL SCIENCE (American studies, anthropology, Asian/Oriental studies, economics, history, philosophy, political science/government, psychology, religion, sociology, and women's studies). Economics, English, and political science are the largest.

Required: All students must complete 4 winter studies and 32 courses, 9 of which are in the major field, with a C- or higher. Requirements include 3 semester-long courses in each of 3 academic divisions: languages and arts, social sciences, and science and math. Also required are 1 course in cultural pluralism and 4 semesters of phys ed.

Special: Students may cross-register at Bennington or Massachusetts College of Liberal Arts and study abroad in Madrid, Oxford, Cairo, Beijing, and Kyoto, or any approved program with another college or university. Teaching and medical field experiences, dual and student-designed majors, internships, and a 3-2 engineering program with Columbia University and Washington University are offered. There are pass/fail options during the winter term. Each department offers at least 1 Oxford-model tutorial every year. There are 2 national honor societies, including Phi Beta Kappa.

Faculty/Classroom: 60% of faculty are male; 40%, female. All both teach and do research. No introductory courses are taught by graduate students. The average class size in an introductory lecture is 31; in a laboratory, 14; and in a regular course, 22.

Admissions: 19% of the 2005-2006 applicants were accepted. The SAT scores for the 2005-2006 freshman class were: Verbal--11% between 500 and 599, 35% between 600 and 700, and 54% above 700; Math--9% between 500 and 599, 36% between 600 and 700, and 56% above 700. The ACT scores were 1% below 21, 1% between 21 and 23, 13% between 24 and 26, 13% between 27 and 28, and 72% above 28.

Requirements: The SAT or ACT is required. In addition, SAT Subject Tests in 3 subjects are required. Secondary preparation should include 4 years each of English and math, 3 to 4 years of foreign language, and at least 2 years each of science and social studies. A personal essay must be submitted. AP credits are accepted. Important factors in the admissions decision are advanced placement or honor courses, recommendations by school officials, and evidence of special talent.

Procedure: Freshmen are admitted in the fall. There are early decision and deferred admissions plans. Early decision applications should be filed by November 10; regular applications, by January 1 for fall entry. The fall 2005 application fee was $60. Notification of early decision is sent December 15; regular decision April 10. A waiting list is an active part of the admissions procedure.Applications are accepted on-line.

Transfer: Transfer applicants should present a 3.5 GPA in previous college work and must submit either SAT or ACT scores.

Visiting: There are regularly scheduled orientations for prospective students, consisting of panels, forums, class visits, and campus tours. There are guides for informal visits and visitors may sit in on classes and stay overnight. To schedule a visit, contact the Purple Key Society office at (413) 597-3148.

Financial Aid: In 2005-2006, 49% of all full-time freshmen and 44% of continuing full-time students received some form of financial aid. The average freshman award was $31,419. 60% of undergraduates work part time. Average annual earnings from campus work are $800. The CSS/Profile or FAFSA and the college's own financial statement are required. Check with the school for current deadlines.

International Students: There are 108 international students enrolled. The school actively recruits these students. A satisfactory score on the TOEFL is required if English is not the applicant's first language. The SAT or the ACT is also required. Students must take SAT Subject Tests in English and 2 other subjects.

Computers: Every student dorm room is wired for high-speed Internet access. Many public spaces on campus have wireless Internet availability. Numerous public computer terminals are located in the Computer Center and library as well as in other student spaces around campus. All students may access the system. There are no time limits and no fees.

Graduates: From July 1, 2004 to June 30, 2005, 531 bachelor's degrees were awarded. The most popular majors were economics (17%), political science (14%), and English (12%). In an average class, 92% graduate in 4 years or less, 95% graduate in 5 years or less, and 96% graduate in 6 years or less. 100 companies recruited on campus in 2004-2005.

Admissions Contact: Richard Nesbitt, Director of Admission.
E-mail: *admission@williams.edu* Web: *www.williams.edu/admission/*

WORCESTER POLYTECHNIC INSTITUTE
C-2
Worcester, MA 01609-2280 (508) 831-5286; Fax: (508) 831-5875

Full-time: 2113 men, 693 women	**Faculty:** IIA, ++$
Part-time: none	**Ph.Ds:** 98%
Graduate: 337 men, 130 women	**Student/Faculty:** 13 to 1
Year: quarters, summer session	**Tuition:** $30,990
Application Deadline: February 1	**Room & Board:** $9460

Freshman Class: n/av
SAT Verbal/Math: 620/670* ACT: 27 **VERY COMPETITIVE+**

Worcester Polytechnic Institute, founded in 1865, is a private institution with a unique, project-enriched curriculum of study primarily in engineering and other technical fields. WPI also offers a program in humanities and arts. In addition to regional accreditation, WPI has baccalaureate program accreditation with ABET and NEASC. The library contains 268,718 volumes, 111,000 microform items, and 1654 audio/video tapes/CDs/DVDs, and subscribes to 25,000 periodicals including electronic. Computerized library services include the card catalog, interlibrary loans, database searching, Internet access, and laptop Internet portals. Special learning facilities include a learning resource center, art gallery, radio station, TV station, a robotics lab, a wind tunnel, and a greenhouse. The 80-acre campus is in a suburban area 40 miles west of Boston. Including any residence halls, there are 32 buildings.

Student Life: 52% of undergraduates are from out of state, mostly the Northeast. Students are from 42 states, 70 foreign countries, and Canada. 74% are from public schools. 80% are white. The average age of freshmen is 18; all undergraduates, 20. 8% do not continue beyond their first year; 80% remain to graduate.

Housing: 1247 students can be accommodated in college housing, which includes coed dorms, on-campus apartments, fraternity houses, and sorority houses. In addition, there are special-interest houses. On-campus housing is guaranteed for the freshman year only and is available on a lottery system for upperclassmen. 60% of students live on campus; of those, 75% remain on campus on weekends. Upperclassmen may keep cars.

Activities: 29% of men belong to 11 national fraternities; 28% of women belong to 2 national sororities. There are more than 200 groups on campus, including art, band, cheerleading, chess, choir, chorale, chorus, computers, dance, debate, drama, ethnic, forensics, gay, honors, international, jazz band, literary magazine, marching band, musical theater, newspaper, orchestra, pep band, photography, political, professional, radio and TV, religious, social, social service, student government, symphony, and yearbook. Popular campus events include Traditions Day, New Voices Festival, and Winter Carnival.

Sports: There are 10 intercollegiate sports for men and 10 for women, and 11 intramural sports for men and 11 for women. Facilities include an aerobics area, baseball and softball fields, bowling alleys, an 8-lane synthetic surface track, a fitness center, a crew center, a playing field with artificial turf, a pool, basketball, tennis, racquetball and squash courts, and a 2,800-seat gym.

Disabled Students: 90% of the campus is accessible. Wheelchair ramps, elevators, special parking, specially equipped rest rooms, special class scheduling, and lowered drinking fountains are available.

Services: Counseling and information services are available, as is tutoring in every subject.

Campus Safety and Security: Measures include 24-hour foot and vehicle patrol, self-defense education, security escort services, and shuttle buses. There are informal discussions, pamphlets/posters/films, emergency telephones, lighted pathways/sidewalks, and and a student-run emergency medical service supervised by the campus police department.

Programs of Study: WPI confers the B.S. degree. Master's and doctoral degrees are also awarded. Bachelor's degrees are awarded in AGRICULTURE (environmental studies), BIOLOGICAL SCIENCE (biochemistry and biotechnology), BUSINESS (business administration and management, management engineering, and management information systems), COMMUNICATIONS AND THE ARTS (technical and business writing), COMPUTER AND PHYSICAL SCIENCE (actuarial science, chemistry, computer science, mathematics, and physics), ENGINEERING AND ENVIRONMENTAL DESIGN (aeronautical engineering, biomedical engineering, chemical engineering, civil engineering, electrical/electronics engineering, engineering physics, environmental engineering, industrial engineering, manufacturing engineering, materials engineering, mechanical engineering, and technology and public affairs), SOCIAL SCIENCE (economics, fire protection, humanities, interdisciplinary studies, social science, and systems science). Engineering and computer science are the largest.

Required: For a B.S. degree, WPI requires that students in science and engineering complete an individual project in the humanities. Students must also complete 2 major team projects. Distribution requirements vary according to the major, and all students must take courses in social sciences and phys ed.

Special: Students may cross-register with 9 other colleges in the Colleges of Worcester Consortium. Co-op programs in all majors, internships, work-study programs, dual majors in every subject, student-designed majors, 3-2 engineering degrees, a Washington semester, non-degree study, and pass/fail options are all available. There is an accelerated degree program in fire protection engineering and math. There are 24 special project centers in 16 countries. There are 10 national honor societies.

Faculty/Classroom: 79% of faculty are male; 21%, female. No introductory courses are taught by graduate students. The average class size in a laboratory is 24 and in a regular course, 25.

Admissions: The SAT scores for the 2005-2006 freshman class were: Verbal--6% below 500, 34% between 500 and 599, 44% between 600 and 700, and 16% above 700; Math--13% between 500 and 599, 53% between 600 and 700, and 34% above 700. The ACT scores were 5% below 21, 11% between 21 and 23, 31% between 24 and 26, 24% between 27 and 28, and 28% above 28. 68% of the current freshmen were in the top fifth of their class; 92% were in the top two fifths. There were 21 National Merit finalists. 20 freshmen graduated first in their class.

Requirements: The SAT or ACT is required. In addition, applicants must have completed 4 years of math, precalculus, and 2 lab sciences. An essay is required, as well as a letter of recommendation from either a math or a science teacher, along with the recommendation from the guidence counselor. AP credits are accepted. Important factors in the admissions decision are advanced placement or honor courses, recommendations by school officials, and extracurricular activities record.

Procedure: Freshmen are admitted fall and spring. Entrance exams should be taken between April and December. There are early admissions and deferred admissions plans. Applications should be filed by February 1 for fall entry and November 15 for spring entry, along with a $60 fee. Notification is sent April 1. 74 early decision candidates were accepted for the 2005-2006 class. 110 applicants were on the 2005 waiting list; 14 were admitted. Applications are accepted on-line.

Transfer: 49 transfer students enrolled in 2004-2005. Grades of C or better transfer for credit. A high school transcript or GED, is requried. Students who have been out of school for a year or more must present a resume or personal biography, and a professional recommendation. 25 of 45 units required for the bachelor's degree must be completed at WPI.

Visiting: There are regularly scheduled orientations for prospective students, consisting of meetings and presentations from various academic and extracurricular groups. There are guides for informal visits and visitors may sit in on classes and stay overnight. To schedule a visit, contact the Admissions Office.

Financial Aid: In 2005-2006, 92% of all full-time freshmen and 86% of continuing full-time students received some form of financial aid. 79% of full-time freshmen and 75% of continuing full-time students received need-based aid. The average freshman award was $21,545. The average financial indebtedness of the 2005 graduate was $26,411. WPI is a member of CSS. The CSS/Profile or FAFSA and CSS Non Custodial Profile are required. The deadline for filing freshman financial aid applications for fall entry is February 1.

International Students: There are 170 international students enrolled. The school actively recruits these students. They must score satisfactory on the written TOEFL or on the electronic version or take the MELAB, or the college's own test. They must also take the SAT or the ACT.

Computers: Wireless access is available. There are 31 PC labs/classrooms available to students, each with an average of 19 PCs. There is a wireless connectivity between student laptops and the Internet. All students may access the system 24 hours daily. There are no time limits and no fees.

Graduates: From July 1, 2004 to June 30, 2005, 616 bachelor's degrees were awarded. The most popular majors were electrical and computer engineering (21%), mechanical engineering (20%), and computer science (15%). In an average class, 65% graduate in 4 years or less, and 74% graduate in 5 years or less. 112 companies recruited on campus in 2004-2005.

Admissions Contact: Edward J. Connor, Director of Admissions. A video is available. E-mail: *admissions@wpi.edu* Web: *www.wpi.edu*

WORCESTER STATE COLLEGE   C-2

Worcester, MA 01602-2597   (508) 929-8040; Fax: (508) 929-8131

Full-time: 1345 men, 1897 women	**Faculty:** 167
Part-time: 482 men, 874 women	**Ph.D.s:** 76%
Graduate: 202 men, 671 women	**Student/Faculty:** 19 to 1
Year: semesters, summer session	**Tuition:** $5079 ($11,159)
Application Deadline: open	**Room & Board:** $7420
Freshman Class: 3113 applied, 1841 accepted, 648 enrolled	
SAT Verbal/Math: 504/510*	**ACT:** 20 **COMPETITIVE**

Worcester State College, established in 1874, is part of the Massachusetts public higher education system and offers undergraduate and graduate programs. A liberal arts core is emphasized, as are selected areas of science, the health professions, education, business and management. In addition to regional accreditation, WSC has baccalaureate program accreditation with ACOTE, ASLA, JRCERT, and NLN. The library contains 193,112 volumes, 16,159 microform items, and 5017 audio/video tapes/CDs/DVDs, and subscribes to 1982 periodicals including electronic. Computerized library services include the card catalog, interlibrary loans, database searching, and Internet access. Special learning facilities include a learning resource center, radio station, TV station, photographic labs, audiovisual center, multimedia classrooms with satellite connectivity, discipline-specific computer labs, and a speech, language, and hearing clinic. The 53-acre campus is in an urban area 40 miles west of Boston. Including any residence halls, there are 8 buildings.

Student Life: 97% of undergraduates are from Massachusetts. Students are from 19 states, 27 foreign countries, and Canada. 77% are white. The average age of freshmen is 18; all undergraduates, 25. 25% do not continue beyond their first year; 45% remain to graduate.

Housing: 1000 students can be accommodated in college housing, which includes coed dorms and on-campus apartments. On-campus housing is available on a first-come, first-served basis. Priority is given to out-of-town students. 85% of students commute. Alcohol is not permitted. Upperclassmen may keep cars.

Activities: There are no fraternities or sororities. There are 52 groups on campus, including cheerleading, chorale, drama, ethnic, gay, honors, international, jazz band, newspaper, professional, radio and TV, religious, social, social service, and student government. Popular campus events include Winter Carnival, Senior Week, and a lecture series.

Sports: There are 9 intercollegiate sports for men and 10 for women, and 13 intramural sports for men and 13 for women. Facilities include an auditorium, a gym, a fitness center, tennis courts, a track, baseball and softball diamonds, and football, field hockey, and all-purpose fields.

Disabled Students: All of the campus is accessible. Wheelchair ramps, elevators, special parking, specially equipped rest rooms, lowered drinking fountains, lowered telephones, special housing, and priority registration are available.

Services: Counseling and information services are available, as is tutoring in most subjects. There is a reader service for the blind, in conjunction with Quinsigamond Community College courses and WSC instructors.

Campus Safety and Security: Measures include 24-hour foot and vehicle patrol, self-defense education, informal discussions, and pamphlets/posters/films. There are emergency telephones, and lighted pathways/sidewalks. The dormitory is protected by a security system. An escort service is available on request.

Programs of Study: WSC confers B.A. and B.S. degrees. Master's degrees are also awarded. Bachelor's degrees are awarded in BIOLOGICAL SCIENCE (biology/biological science and biotechnology), BUSINESS (business administration and management), COMMUNICATIONS AND THE ARTS (communications, English, and Spanish), COMPUTER AND PHYSICAL SCIENCE (chemistry, computer science, mathematics, and natural sciences), EDUCATION (early childhood and elementary), HEALTH PROFESSIONS (health, health science, nursing, occupational therapy, and speech pathology/audiology), SOCIAL SCIENCE (criminal justice, economics, geography, history, psychology, sociology, and urban studies). Occupational therapy and nursing are the strongest academically. Business administration, psychology, and communications are the largest.

Required: To graduate, students must complete a foundation requirement, including English composition, math, and the study of the U.S. and Massachusetts constitutions. Distribution requirements include 12 credits each in humanities, behavioral and social sciences, and natural sciences and math; 9 in fine arts; and 3 in health or phys ed. Students must complete 120 credits, 30 to 48 in the major, with a minimum 2.0 GPA overall and in the major.

Special: Cross-registration with the Worcester Consortium for Higher Education is available, as are co-op programs, internships, study abroad, a Washington semester, work-study, B.A.-B.S. degrees, dual majors, a 3-2 engineering degree with Worcester Polytechnic Institute and the Universities of Massachusetts at Dartmouth and Lowell, nondegree study, and a pass/fail option. There are 17 national honor societies, a freshman honors program, and 15 departmental honors programs.

Faculty/Classroom: 49% of faculty are male; 51%, female. 86% teach undergraduates. No introductory courses are taught by graduate students.

Admissions: 59% of the 2005-2006 applicants were accepted. The SAT scores for the 2005-2006 freshman class were: Verbal--47% below 500, 41% between 500 and 599, and 12% between 600 and 700; Math--42% below 500, 50% between 500 and 599, and 8% between 600 and 700. The ACT scores were 60% below 21, 30% between 21 and 23, 4% between 24 and 26, 6% between 27 and 28, and 2% above 28.

Requirements: The SAT is required. In addition, for students with a GPA of 2.9 or above, a minimum SAT or ACT score may be required.

For students whose GPA is below 2.9, a minimum SAT or ACT score is applied according to a scale established by WSC. Applicants must graduate from an accredited secondary school. They should have completed 4 years of English, 3 of math, 2 each of a foreign language, a lab science, and social studies, including 1 year of U.S. history and government, and 2 electives. The College Board Student Descriptive questionnaire must be submitted.

Procedure: Freshmen are admitted fall, spring, and summer. Entrance exams should be taken in spring of the junior year or fall of the senior year. There is a deferred admissions and a rolling admissions plan. Application deadlines are open. Application fee is $20. Applications are accepted on-line. Notification is sent on a rolling basis.

Transfer: 541 transfer students enrolled in 2005-2006. Transfer applicants must have earned a minimum of 12 college credits with a minimum 2.5 GPA or 13 to 23 credits with a minimum 2.0 GPA. Students with fewer than 23 transfer credits may be admitted under the same criteria as first-time freshmen. 30 of 120 credits required for the bachelor's degree must be completed at WSC.

Visiting: There are regularly scheduled orientations for prospective students, including a campus tour and review of campus life and organizations, success in college, special opportunities, and available services. There are guides for informal visits and visitors may sit in on classes and stay overnight. To schedule a visit, contact Dean of Enrollment Management.

Financial Aid: In a recent year, 86% of all full-time freshmen and 58% of continuing full-time students received some form of financial aid. 60% of full-time freshmen and 38% of continuing full-time students received need-based aid. The average freshman award was $6539. The average financial indebtedness of a recent years graduate was $11,843. WSC is a member of CSS. The FAFSA is required. The deadline for filing freshman financial aid applications for fall entry is March 1.

International Students: There are 99 international students enrolled. A satisfactory score is required. Students must also take the SAT or the ACT.

Computers: Wireless access is available. All students may access the system. There are no time limits and no fees. All students are required to have PCs. WSC recommends Dell PCs.

Graduates: From July 1, 2004 to June 30, 2005, 705 bachelor's degrees were awarded. The most popular majors were psychology (21%), business administration (20%), and communications (9%). In an average class, 2% graduate in 3 years or less, 37% graduate in 4 years or less, 50% graduate in 5 years or less, and 54% graduate in 6 years or less.

Admissions Contact: Jay Tierney, Admissions Director, Interim. A video is available. E-mail: *admissions@worcester.edu* Web: *http://www.worcester.edu/*

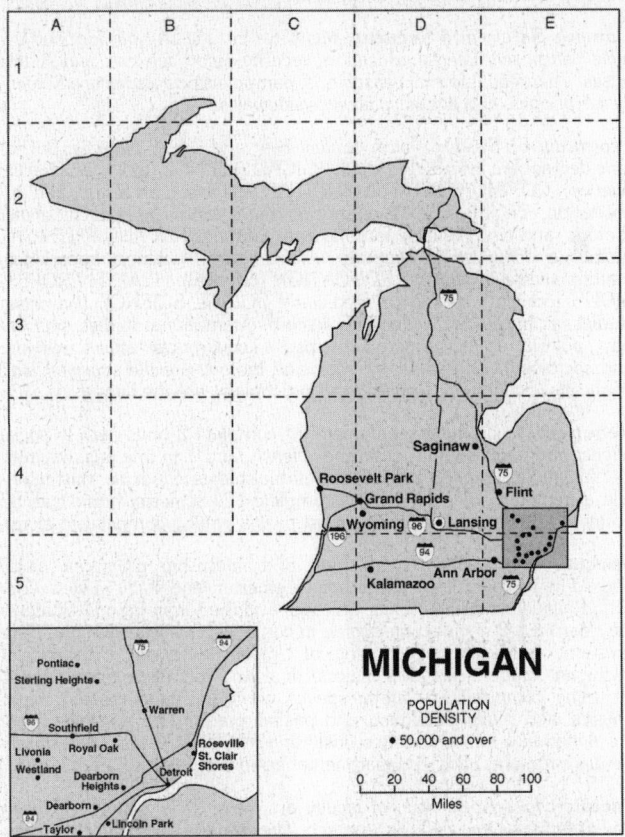

MICHIGAN

POPULATION
DENSITY

• 50,000 and over

0 20 40 60 80 100
Miles

ADRIAN COLLEGE
E-5

Adrian, MI 49221-2575

(517) 265-5161, ext. 4326
(800) 877-2246; Fax: (517) 264-3331

Full-time: 400 men, 500 women	Faculty: 65
Part-time: 20 men, 30 women	Ph.D.s: 85%
Graduate: none	Student/Faculty: 15 to 1
Year: semesters, summer session	Tuition: $17,000
Application Deadline: see profile	Room & Board: $6000
Freshman Class: n.av	
SAT or ACT: required	COMPETITIVE

Adrian College, founded in 1859, is a private liberal arts institution affiliated with the United Methodist Church. Figures in the above capsule and in this profile are approximate.The library contains 146,200 volumes, 47,500 microform items, and 1500 audio/video tapes/CDs/DVDs, and subscribes to 600 periodicals including electronic. Computerized library services include the card catalog, interlibrary loans, database searching, and Internet access. Special learning facilities include a learning resource center, art gallery, planetarium, radio station, solar greenhouse, and observatory. The 100-acre campus is in a suburban area 35 miles southwest of Ann Arbor. Including any residence halls, there are 30 buildings.

Student Life: 80% of undergraduates are from Michigan. Others are from 14 states and 7 foreign countries. 76% are white. 40% claim no religious affiliation; 20% are Catholic; 18% Protestant. The average age of freshmen is 18; all undergraduates, 19. 28% do not continue beyond their first year; 49% remain to graduate.

Housing: 1117 students can be accommodated in college housing, which includes single-sex and coed dorms, fraternity houses, and sorority houses. In additiion, there are substance-free, smoke f-free, extended-quiet-hours, and upperclassman-only residence halls. On-campus housing is guaranteed for all 4 years. 75% of students live on campus. All students may keep cars.

Activities: 30% of men belong to 4 national fraternities; 30% of women belong to 3 national sororities. There are 60 groups on campus, including art, band, cheerleading, choir, chorale, chorus, computers, dance, drama, ethnic, gay, honors, international, jazz band, literary magazine, musical theater, orchestra, photography, political, professional, radio and TV, religious, social, social service, student government, symphony,

and yearbook. Popular campus events include Greek Week, Family Weekend, and International Week.

Sports: There are 8 intercollegiate sports for men and 8 for women, and 10 intramural sports for men and 10 for women. Facilities include a sport and fitness center featuring a multipurpose forum with 3 courts for basketball, volleyball, and tennis, and an indoor track, racquetball courts, a weight room, and a 1350-seat performance gym; a 5000-seat football stadium; baseball and softball fields; 2 soccer fields; 6 tennis courts; a 400-meter track; and numerous intramural fields.

Disabled Students: 80% of the campus is accessible. Wheelchair ramps, elevators, special parking, specially equipped rest rooms, lowered drinking fountains, lowered telephones, special housing, readers, scribes and note takers, and test accommodations are available.

Services: Counseling and information services are available, as is tutoring in most subjects. There is a reader service for the blind, and remedial math, reading, and writing.

Campus Safety and Security: Measures include 24-hour foot and vehicle patrol, self-defense education, security escort services, and informal discussions. There are pamphlets/posters/films, emergency telephones, and lighted pathways/sidewalks.

Programs of Study: Adrian confers B.A., B.S., B.B.A., B.F.A., B.M., and B.M.E. degrees. Associate degrees are also awarded. Bachelor's degrees are awarded in BIOLOGICAL SCIENCE (biology/biological science), BUSINESS (accounting, business administration and management, and international business management), COMMUNICATIONS AND THE ARTS (art, arts administration/management, communications, dramatic arts, English, French, German, music, musical theater, and Spanish), COMPUTER AND PHYSICAL SCIENCE (chemistry, earth science, mathematics, and physics), EDUCATION (elementary, physical, and secondary), ENGINEERING AND ENVIRONMENTAL DESIGN (environmental science and interior design), SOCIAL SCIENCE (criminal justice, economics, history, human services, international studies, philosophy, political science/government, psychology, religion, and sociology). Social sciences, art and design, and teacher education are the largest.

Required: To graduate, students must maintain a 2.0 average over 124 credit hours, 30 of which must be in upper-division courses. 19 hours of distribution requirements and 25 of basic educational proficiency are required, including 2 semesters of foreign language and 1 each of communication, English, fine arts, fitness, humanities, math, natural or physical science, religion or philosophy, and social science.

Special: Adrian offers preprofessional programs in engineering, health sciences, law, ministry, and art therapy; study abroad in 16 countries and a Washington Semester; student-designed majors and a dual philosophy/religion program; internships in more than 650 locations; and a 3-2 engineering degree with Washington University in St. Louis and the University of Detroit Mercy. There are 14 national honor societies and a freshman honors program.

Faculty/Classroom: 65% of faculty are male; 35%, female. All teach undergraduates. The average class size in an introductory lecture is 20; in a laboratory, 13; and in a regular course, 15.

Admissions: 88% of recent applicants were accepted. The ACT scores for a recent freshman class were: 46% below 21, 25% between 21 and 23, 20% between 24 and 26, 7% between 27 and 28, and 2% above 28. 41% of recent freshmen were in the top fifth of their class; 72% were in the top two fifths.

Requirements: The SAT or ACT is required. In addition, applicants must be graduates of an accredited secondary school. The GED is accepted. Each student is reviewed individually based on several criteria. An interview is recommended. Adrian requires applicants to be in the upper 50% of their class. A GPA of 2.5 is required. AP and CLEP credits are accepted. Important factors in the admissions decision are advanced placement or honor courses, leadership record, and extracurricular activities record.

Procedure: Freshmen are admitted in the fall. Entrance exams should be taken during the spring of the junior year or fall of the senior year. There is a deferred admissions plan. Check with the school for current application deadlines. The fall 2005 application fee was $20. Notification is sent on a rolling basis. Applications are accepted on-line.

Transfer: 38 transfer students enrolled in a recent year. Applicants must have an above-average GPA and provide final high school transcripts. If the student has completed fewer than 24 semester hours, ACT or SAT I test scores are also required. Grades of 2.0 and above transfer for credit. The college admits transfer students every semester. 34 of 124 credits required for the bachelor's degree must be completed at Adrian.

Visiting: There are regularly scheduled orientations for prospective students, including a student-guided campus tour and visits with an admissions counselor, professors from the student's area of interest, and an athletics coach, if applicable. Visitors may sit in on classes and stay overnight. To schedule a visit, contact the Admissions Office.

Financial Aid: In a recent year, 79% of all full-time freshmen and 71% of continuing full-time students received some form of financial aid. 79% of full-time freshmen and 75% of continuing full-time students received need-based aid. The average freshman award was $16,684. Need-based scholarships or need-based grants averaged $10,344; and need-based self-help aid (loans and jobs) averaged $4786. 50% of undergraduates work part time. Average annual earnings from campus work are $757. The average financial indebtedness of a recent graduate was $13,970. The FAFSA is required. Check with the school for current deadlines.

International Students: There were 20 international students enrolled in a recent year. The school actively recruits these students. They must score satisfactorily on the written TOEFL or on the electronic version and also take the SAT or the ACT.

Computers: All students may access the system 24 hours a day. There are no time limits and no fees. It is strongly recommended that all students have a personal computer.

Graduates: In a recent year, 192 bachelor's degrees were awarded. The most popular majors were social sciences/history (20%), business (17%), and visual and performing arts (14%). In an average class, 28% graduate in 4 years or less, 39% graduate in 5 years or less, and 41% graduate in 6 years or less. 22 companies recruited on campus in a recent year.

Admissions Contact: Director of Admissions.
E-mail: *admissions@adrian.edu* Web: *www.adrian.edu*

ALBION COLLEGE D-5
Albion, MI 49224

(517) 629-0321
(800) 858-6770; Fax: (517) 629-0569

Full-time: 700 men, 900 women	**Faculty:** 121; IIB, av$
Part-time: 10 man, and women	**Ph.D.s:** 92%
Graduate: none	**Student/Faculty:** 13 to 1
Year: semesters, summer session	**Tuition:** $20,000
Application Deadline: open	**Room & Board:** $6000
Freshman Class: n/av	
SAT or ACT: required	**VERY COMPETITIVE**

Albion College, established in 1835, is a private institution affiliated with the United Methodist Church and offering undergraduate degrees in liberal arts curricula. Figures in the above capsule and in this profile are approximate. In addition to regional accreditation, Albion has baccalaureate program accreditation with NASM. The library contains 355,000 volumes, 67,200 microform items, and 6000 audio/video tapes/CDs/DVDs, and subscribes to 1000 periodicals including electronic. Computerized library services include the card catalog, interlibrary loans, and database searching. Special learning facilities include a learning resource center, art gallery, radio station, nature center, women's center, observatory, and honors program center. The 225-acre campus is in a small town 90 miles west of Detroit and 175 miles east of Chicago. Including any residence halls, there are 30 buildings.

Student Life: 89% of undergraduates are from Michigan. Others are from 28 states, 19 foreign countries, and Canada. 84% are from public schools. 86% are white. 28% are Catholic; 26% claim no religious affiliation. The average age of freshmen is 18; all undergraduates, 20. 15% do not continue beyond their first year.

Housing: 1600 students can be accommodated in college housing, which includes single-sex and coed dorms, on-campus apartments, off-campus apartments, married-student housing, and fraternity houses. In addition, there are language houses and special-interest houses and annexes. On-campus housing is guaranteed for all 4 years. 99% of students live on campus; of those, 70% remain on campus on weekends. All students may keep cars.

Activities: 40% of men belong to 5 national fraternities; 40% of women belong to 6 national sororities. There are 122 groups on campus, including art, band, cheerleading, chess, choir, chorale, chorus, computers, dance, drama, ethnic, film, gay, honors, international, jazz band, literary magazine, marching band, medieval society, musical theater, newspaper, opera, orchestra, pep band, political, professional, radio and TV, religious, social, social service, sports club association, student government, symphony, and yearbook. Popular campus events include International Week, Briton Bash, and Albion Performing Arts and Lecture Series.

Sports: There are 9 intercollegiate sports for men and 9 for women, and 19 intramural sports for men and 18 for women. Facilities include a stadium, an aquatic center, a gym, baseball, soccer, and football fields, tennis courts, an archery range, a surfaced track, a field events area, outdoor basketball courts, practice fields, and a canoeing facility. There is also a recreation and wellness center with intramural basketball, volleyball, badminton, racquetball, and tennis courts, a track, a weight training room, a human performance lab, and a training/rehabilitation unit.

Disabled Students: 90% of the campus is accessible. Wheelchair ramps, elevators, special parking, specially equipped rest rooms, special class scheduling, lowered drinking fountains, and lowered telephones are available.

Services: Counseling and information services are available, as is tutoring in most subjects and assistance for the deaf. There is a reader service for the blind. The Developing Skills Center offers individual assistance to students for study skills enhancement.

Campus Safety and Security: Measures include 24-hour foot and vehicle patrol, self-defense education, security escort services, and shuttle buses. There are informal discussions, pamphlets/posters/films, emergency telephones, and lighted pathways/sidewalks.

Programs of Study: Albion confers B.A. and B.F.A. degrees. Bachelor's degrees are awarded in BIOLOGICAL SCIENCE (biology/biological science), COMMUNICATIONS AND THE ARTS (art, art history and appreciation, English, French, German, music, Spanish, speech/debate/rhetoric, and visual and performing arts), COMPUTER AND PHYSICAL SCIENCE (chemistry, computer science, earth science, geoscience, mathematics, and physics), EDUCATION (physical), HEALTH PROFESSIONS (predentistry and premedicine), SOCIAL SCIENCE (American studies, anthropology, economics, history, international studies, philosophy, political science/government, psychology, public affairs, religion, and sociology). English, economics, and biology are the strongest academically. Economics, English, and psychology are the largest.

Required: To graduate, students must complete 2 units each in social science, humanities, and math and science, and 1 in fine arts, environmental studies, gender studies, and ethnic studies. Students must maintain a minimum GPA of 2.0 and complete 124 semester hours with 32 hours in the major. All students must pass a writing competence exam.

Special: Albion offers work-study and internship programs, study abroad in 19 countries, a Washington semester, and study in New York City, Philadelphia, Oak Ridge, Chicago, and the Virgin Islands. Students may earn a 3-2 engineering degree in conjunction with Columbia, Case Western, or Michigan Technological Universities or the University of Michigan. Student-designed majors, dual and interdisciplinary majors, including computational math, speech communication theater, math/physics, and math/economics, and pas/fail grading are possible. There are 4 national honor societies, including Phi Beta Kappa, a freshman honors program, and 18 departmental honors programs.

Faculty/Classroom: 70% of faculty are male; 30%, female. All teach undergraduates and 94% do research. The average class size in an introductory lecture is 27; in a laboratory, 16; and in a regular course, 17.

Requirements: The SAT or ACT is required. In addition, applicants must graduate from an accredited secondary school or earn a GED. Completion of 15 Carnegie credits is required. A strong background in English, math, and the lab and social sciences is recommended. Albion requires applicants to be in the upper 50% of their class. A GPA of 2.5 is required. AP and CLEP credits are accepted. Important factors in the admissions decision are advanced placement or honor courses, extracurricular activities record, and personality/intangible qualities.

Procedure: Freshmen are admitted fall and spring. Entrance exams should be taken in April or June of the junior year. There are early decision, early admissions, and deferred admissions plans. Check with the school for the current deadlines for early decision applications. Deadlines are open for regular applications. The fall 2005 application fee was $20. Notification of regular decision is sent on a rolling basis. Applications are accepted on-line.

Transfer: Transfer applicants must submit official college transcripts. Grades of 2.0 or better are considered for transfer credit. Albion evaluates the applicant's course work before conferring transfer credit. 12 of 124 credits required for the bachelor's degree must be completed at Albion.

Visiting: There are regularly scheduled orientations for prospective students, consisting of 5 SOAR programs for students and parents: 1 1/2-day events held from early May to late August. There are guides for informal visits and visitors may sit in on classes and stay overnight. To schedule a visit, contact the Admissions Office.

Financial Aid: Albion is a member of CSS. The FAFSA is required. Check with the school for current deadlines.

International Students: The school actively recruits these students. They must score satisfactorily on the written TOEFL and also take the SAT or the ACT.

Computers: All students may access the system most days and evening hours. There are no time limits and no fees. It is strongly recommended that all students have a personal computer.

Admissions Contact: Doug Kellar, Associate Vice President for Enrollment. A video is available. E-mail: *dkellar@albion.edu* Web: *www.albion.edu*

ALMA COLLEGE
Alma, MI 48801-1599

D-4

(989) 463-7139
(800) 321-ALMA; Fax: (989) 463-7057

Full-time: 517 men, 725 women	Faculty: 82; IIB, av$
Part-time: 11 men, 31 women	Ph.D.s: 88%
Graduate: none	Student/Faculty: 15 to 1
Year: n/av	Tuition: $21,134
Application Deadline: open	Room & Board: $7410
Freshman Class: 1471 applied, 1189 accepted, 336 enrolled	
SAT Verbal/Math: 586/574*	ACT: 25 VERY COMPETITIVE

Alma College, established in 1886, is a residential private, liberal arts and sciences college affiliated with the Presbyterian Church (U.S.A.). In addition to regional accreditation, Alma has baccalaureate program accreditation with ACS and NASM. The library contains 266,554 volumes, 244,591 microform items, and 8400 audio/video tapes/CDs/DVDs, and subscribes to 1583 periodicals including electronic. Computerized library services include the card catalog, interlibrary loans, database searching, and Internet access. Special learning facilities include a learning resource center, art gallery, planetarium, radio station, an audio-visual center, and a writing lab. The 125-acre campus is in a small town 50 miles north of Lansing. Including any residence halls, there are 26 buildings.

Student Life: 94% of undergraduates are from Michigan. Others are from 21 states, 9 foreign countries, and Canada. 93% are from public schools. 93% are white. 30% claim no religious affiliation; 24% Protestant; 22% Catholic; 14% more than 15 other denominations. The average age of freshmen is 18; all undergraduates, 20. 20% do not continue beyond their first year; 71% remain to graduate.

Housing: 1109 students can be accommodated in college housing, which includes single-sex and coed dormitories, on-campus apartments, fraternity houses, and sorority houses. In addition, there are special-interest houses and academis-themed houses. On-campus housing is guaranteed for all 4 years and is available on a first-come, first-served basis. 83% of students live on campus; of those, 65% remain on campus on weekends. All students may keep cars.

Activities: 17% of men belong to 1 local and 4 national fraternities; 26% of women belong to 1 local and 4 national sororities. There are 96 groups on campus, including art, band, cheerleading, chess, choir, chorale, chorus, computers, dance, drama, ethnic, gay, honors, international, jazz band, literary magazine, marching band, newspaper, orchestra, political, professional, radio and TV, religious, social, social service, student government, symphony, and yearbook. Popular campus events include All nighter and Song Fest.

Sports: There are 9 intercollegiate sports for men and 9 for women, and 10 intramural sports for men and 10 for women. Facilities include a recreation center with a climbing wall, fitness center, 4 courts and suspended 3-lane track; an indoor gym and pool; an outdoor sports complex with an artificial turf playing field, an 8-lane track, a baseball, soccer and softball fields; a weight training room; and racquetball and tennis courts.

Disabled Students: 75% of the campus is accessible. Wheelchair ramps, elevators, special parking, specially equipped rest rooms, special class scheduling, lowered drinking fountains, 2 residence halls with private baths, and several small housing units are available.

Services: Counseling and information services are available, as is tutoring in every subject. Both individual and group tutoring are available. There is a reader service for the blind.

Campus Safety and Security: Measures include informal discussions, pamphlets/posters/films, emergency telephones, and lighted pathways/sidewalks, and 24-hour foot patrol.

Programs of Study: Alma confers B.A., B.S., B.F.A. and B.M. degrees. Bachelor's degrees are awarded in BIOLOGICAL SCIENCE (biochemistry and biology/biological science), BUSINESS (business administration and management and international business management), COMMUNICATIONS AND THE ARTS (art, communications, design, dramatic arts, English, French, German, music, and Spanish), COMPUTER AND PHYSICAL SCIENCE (chemistry, computer science, mathematics, and physics), EDUCATION (elementary and secondary), HEALTH PROFESSIONS (health science), SOCIAL SCIENCE (anthropology, economics, history, philosophy, political science/government, psychology, religion, and sociology). Education, business administration, and exercise and health science are the strongest academically and have the largest enrollments.

Required: Degree requirements include completion of a minimum of 136 credit hours; 148 hours are required for the B.F.A. degree, 136 to 156 for the B.M. degree. Students must attain a minimum GPA of 2.0, or 3.0 for fine arts majors. All students must demonstrate proficiency in English, communication, and computation, and they must complete distribution requirements, which include 16 fine arts and humanities credits (4 credits in each of creative or performing arts, literature, philosophy, or religious studies, and humanities), and 16 each of social science and life and physical science credits. The total number of program credits is 36 for a departmental major, 56 for an interdepartmental major, and 56 to 58 for self-designed majors.

Special: Alma offers internships in many fields, study abroad in 15 countries, experiential learning program at the Philadelphia Center, and a Washington semester at American University. There are work-study programs, dual majors, B.A.-B.S. degrees, and student-designed majors in a wide variety of subjects. The college confers 3-2 engineering degrees in conjunction with the University of Michigan and Michigan Technological University. Nondegree study may be pursued, and students have a pass/fail grading option. A 4-week spring term provides intensive study in 1 course, often combined with travel. There are 5 national honor societies, including Phi Beta Kappa, a freshman honors program, and 17 departmental honors programs.

Faculty/Classroom: 62% of faculty are male; 38%, female. All teach undergraduates and 80% do research. The average class size in an introductory lecture is 21; in a laboratory, 14; and in a regular course, 16.

Admissions: 81% of the 2005-2006 applicants were accepted. The SAT scores for the 2005-2006 freshman class were: Verbal--17% below 500, 35% between 500 and 599, 26% between 600 and 700, and 22% above 700; Math--22% below 500, 22% between 500 and 599, 39% between 600 and 700, and 15% above 700. The ACT scores were 19% below 21, 25% between 21 and 23, 28% between 24 and 26, 14% between 27 and 28, and 14% above 28. 53% of the current freshmen were in the top fifth of their class; 81% were in the top two fifths. There were 3 National Merit finalists. 24 freshmen graduated first in their class.

Requirements: The SAT or ACT is required. The ACT is preferred. Applicants must have graduated from an accredited secondary school and have earned 16 Carnegie units, including 4 years of English and 3 each of math, science, and social studies, with 2 of a foreign language recommended. Alma prefers applicants in the upper 25% of their class. Portfolio and audition are required for performing arts scholarships. A GPA of 3.0 is required. AP credits are accepted. Important factors in the admissions decision are advanced placement or honor courses, leadership record, and recommendations by school officials.

Procedure: Freshmen are admitted fall, winter, and spring. Entrance exams should be taken in the spring of the junior year or as late as the winter of the senior year. There is a deferred admissions and a rolling admission plan. Application deadlines are open. Application fee is $25. Applications are accepted on-line.

Transfer: 36 transfer students enrolled in 2004-2005. Students wishing to transfer to Alma must have a minimum GPA of 2.0 from other colleges attended. 34 of 136 credits required for the bachelor's degree must be completed at Alma.

Visiting: There are regularly scheduled orientations for prospective students, consisting of faculty talks, tours, a meal on campus, financial aid information, and admissions sessions. There are guides for informal visits and visitors may sit in on classes and stay overnight. To schedule a visit, contact the Admissions Office.

Financial Aid: In 2005-2006, 99% of all full-time students received some form of financial aid. 75% of full-time freshmen and 76% of continuing full-time students received need-based aid. The average freshman award was $18,976. Need-based scholarships or need-based grants averaged $18,976 ($20,934 maximum); need-based self-help aid (loans and jobs) averaged $4672 ($5000 maximum); and other non-need-based awards and non-need-based scholarships averaged $2998. Other aid includes external and restricted awards, plus employee dependent tuition grants. 46% of undergraduates work part time. Average annual earnings from campus work are $800. The average financial indebtedness of the 2005 graduate was $18,947. The FAFSA is required. The priority date for freshman financial aid applications for fall entry is March 1.

International Students: There are 19 international students enrolled. The school actively recruits these students. They must score satisfactorily on the written TOEFL or on the electronic version. The SAT or ACT is required if the TOEFL is not submitted.

Computers: Wireless access is available. Alma has 266 PCs acessible by students located in general, departmental, and residence hall labs. All students may access the system all hours. There are no time limits and no fees. It is strongly recommended that all students have a personal computer.

Graduates: From July 1, 2004 to June 30, 2005, 232 bachelor's degrees were awarded. The most popular majors were business administration (17%), biology (14%), and exercise and health science (12%). In an average class, 1% graduate in 3 years or less, 52% graduate in 4 years or less, 69% graduate in 5 years or less, and 71% graduate in 6 years or less. 9 companies recruited on campus in 2004-2005. Of the 2004 graduating class, 25% were enrolled in graduate school within 6 months of graduation and 75% were employed.

Admissions Contact: Karen Klumpp, Vice President for Enrollment. E-mail: *admissions@alma.edu* Web: *www.alma.edu*

ANDREWS UNIVERSITY
C-5

Berrien Springs, MI 49104-0740
(616) 471-6343
(800) 253-2874; Fax: (616) 471-3228

Full-time: 666 men, 823 women	**Faculty:** 110
Part-time: 107 men, 130 women	**Ph.D.s:** 72%
Graduate: 871 men, 490 women	**Student/Faculty:** 14 to 1
Year: semesters, summer session	**Tuition:** $16,506
Application Deadline: open	**Room & Board:** $5280
Freshman Class: 1324 applied, 762 accepted, 305 enrolled	
SAT Verbal/Math: 540/520*	**ACT:** 23	**COMPETITIVE**

Andrews University, established in 1874, is a private institution affiliated with the Seventh-day Adventist Church that offers undergraduate degrees in business, education, arts and sciences, architecture, and technology. There are 5 undergraduate and 6 graduate schools. In addition to regional accreditation, Andrews has baccalaureate program accreditation with AACSB, ADA, AHEA, APTA, CAHEA, CSWE, NAAB, NASM, NCATE, and NLN. The library contains 928,829 volumes, 85,520 microform items, and 15,332 audio/video tapes/CDs/DVDs, and subscribes to 2874 periodicals including electronic. Computerized library services include the card catalog, interlibrary loans, database searching, and Internet access. Special learning facilities include an art gallery, natural history museum, radio station, and an archeological museum. The 1600-acre campus is in a rural area 10 miles south of Benton Harbor. Including any residence halls, there are 51 buildings.

Student Life: 59% of undergraduates are from out of state, mostly the Middle Atlantic. Others are from 46 states, 51 foreign countries, and Canada. 22% are from public schools. 50% are white; 19% African American; 12% foreign nationals; 10% Hispanic. 88% are Protestant; 12% unknown. The average age of freshmen is 18; all undergraduates, 22. 20% do not continue beyond their first year; 48% remain to graduate.

Housing: 1500 students can be accommodated in college housing, which includes single-sex dorms, on-campus apartments, and married-student housing. On-campus housing is available on a first-come, first-served basis. 54% of students live on campus. Alcohol is not permitted. All students may keep cars.

Activities: There is 1 national fraternity and 1 national sorority. There are 30 groups on campus, including band, choir, chorale, chorus, computers, drama, ethnic, honors, international, newspaper, professional, religious, social, social service, and student government. Popular campus events include Alumni Weekend and International Food Fair.

Sports: There are 6 intramural sports for men and 4 for women. Facilities include a gym, a pool, racquetball courts, and health clubs in 2 of 3 dorms.

Disabled Students: 50% of the campus is accessible. Wheelchair ramps, elevators, special parking, specially equipped rest rooms, special class scheduling, lowered drinking fountains, lowered telephones,and special housing. A special committee deals with needs as they arise.

Services: Counseling and information services are available, as is tutoring in most subjects. There are math, writing, and reading, learning, and assessment centers.

Campus Safety and Security: Measures include 24-hour foot and vehicle patrol, security escort services, informal discussions, and pamphlets/posters/films. There are lighted pathways/sidewalks and CPR training.

Programs of Study: Andrews confers B.A., B.S., B.B.A., B.F.A., B.Mus., B.S.D., B.S.Educ., B.S.El.Ed., B.S.W., and B.T. degrees. Associate, master's, and doctoral degrees are also awarded. Bachelor's degrees are awarded in AGRICULTURE (agriculture, animal science, and horticulture), BIOLOGICAL SCIENCE (anatomy, biochemistry, biology/ biological science, biophysics, botany, molecular biology, nutrition, and zoology), BUSINESS (accounting, banking and finance, business administration and management, business economics, management information systems, and marketing/retailing/merchandising), COMMUNICATIONS AND THE ARTS (art, ceramic art and design, communications, creative writing, design, English, French, graphic design, journalism, literature, music, music performance, painting, photography, public relations, Spanish, and visual and performing arts), COMPUTER AND PHYSICAL SCIENCE (applied mathematics, chemistry, computer science, information sciences and systems, mathematics, and physics), EDUCATION (art, elementary, English, mathematics, music, science, secondary, social studies, and teaching English as a second/foreign language (TESOL/TEFOL)), ENGINEERING AND ENVIRONMENTAL DESIGN (aeronautical technology, aircraft mechanics, architecture, aviation administration/management, aviation computer technology, biomedical equipment technology, computer graphics, computer technology, electrical/electronics engineering, engineering, environmental science, graphic arts technology, and landscape architecture/design), HEALTH PROFESSIONS (allied health, art therapy, biomedical science, medical laboratory technology, nursing, preveterinary science, public health, and speech pathology/audiology), SOCIAL SCIENCE (anthropology, behavioral science, crosscultural studies, dietetics, economics, family/consumer studies, history, human development, interdisciplinary

studies, pastoral studies, political science/government, psychology, religion, religious education, social studies, social work, sociology, theological studies, and youth ministry). Health sciences, business, and architecture are the largest.

Required: Students must complete a minimum of 124 semester credits. Specific course requirements include religion, English, behavioral sciences, fine arts, and phys ed.

Special: Students may pursue a second major in business administration. Study abroad, student-designed majors, nondegree study, and pass/fail options are available. There is a freshman honors program.

Faculty/Classroom: 68% of faculty are male; 32%, female. The average class size in a laboratory is 16 and in a regular course, 18.

Admissions: 58% of the 2005-2006 applicants were accepted. The SAT scores for the 2005-2006 freshman class were: Verbal--37% below 500, 42% between 500 and 599, 23% between 600 and 700, and 4% above 700; Math--41% below 500, 35% between 500 and 599, 20% between 600 and 700, and 4% above 700. The ACT scores were 28% below 21, 31% between 21 and 23, 21% between 24 and 26, 7% between 27 and 28, and 13% above 28. 29% of the current freshmen were in the top fifth of their class; 61% were in the top two fifths. There were 2 National Merit finalists.

Requirements: The SAT or ACT is required. In addition, candidates for admission must graduate from an accredited secondary school or earn a GED. Ten Carnegie units are required, and students must have completed 4 courses in English and 2 courses each in history, math, and science. Interviews are recommended for all applicants. A GPA of 2.25 is required. CLEP credit is accepted. Important factors in the admissions decision are advanced placement or honor courses, recommendations by school officials, and evidence of special talent.

Procedure: Freshmen are admitted fall, spring, and summer. Entrance exams should be taken as early as possible. There are deferred admissions and rolling admissions plans. Application deadlines are open. Application fee is $30.

Transfer: 131 transfer students enrolled in 2004-2005. Transfer applicants must submit a high school transcript and transcripts from all colleges attended. A maximum of 70 semester credits from a 2-year school or 90 semester credits from a 4-year school may be transferred toward a bachelor's degree. Credits should be relevant to the student's major at Andrews University. The minimum GPA is 2.25, and the ACT is preferred. Students must meet freshman entrance requirements if they are tranferring with less than sophomore standing from an accredited college. 30 of 124 credits required for the bachelor's degree must be completed at Andrews.

Visiting: There are regularly scheduled orientations for prospective students, tours, meetings with faculty, and social activities. There are guides for informal visits and visitors may sit in on classes and stay overnight. To schedule a visit, contact the Admissions Office at visit@andrews.edu.

Financial Aid: The FAFSA is required. The priority date for freshman financial aid applications for fall entry is open.

International Students: There are 186 international students enrolled. The school actively recruits these students. A satisfactory score is required on the written TOEFL.

Computers: Most campus buildings are wireless; dorms have wired internet access, several PC labs at various campus locations are available for student use. All students may access the system. There are no time limits and no fees. It is strongly recommended that all students have personal computers. Students in architecture are require to have personal computers. A Dell is recommended.

Graduates: From July 1, 2004 to June 30, 2005, 293 bachelor's degrees were awarded. The most popular majors were health professions (15%), business (11%), and architecture (9%). In an average class, 28% graduate in 4 years or less, 42% graduate in 5 years or less, and 48% graduate in 6 years or less.

Admissions Contact: Delmus Pinkston, Undergraduate Admissions Supervisor. E-mail: undergraduate@andrews.edu
Web: www.andrews.edu

AQUINAS COLLEGE
D-4

Grand Rapids, MI 49506-1799
(616) 732-4460
(800) 678-9593; Fax: (616) 732-4469

Full-time: 514 men, 955 women	**Faculty:** 94; IIB, --$
Part-time: 113 men, 200 women	**Ph.D.s:** 60%
Graduate: 125 men, 286 women	**Student/Faculty:** 16 to 1
Year: semesters, summer session	**Tuition:** $17,926
Application Deadline: open	**Room & Board:** $5824
Freshman Class: 1726 applied, 1409 accepted, 364 enrolled	
ACT: 22	**COMPETITIVE**

Aquinas College, established in 1866, is a private liberal arts institution affiliated with the Roman Catholic Church and offers undergraduate and graduate degrees through day and evening programs. There are 3 undergraduate and 2 graduate schools. The library contains 112,252 volumes, 227,444 microform items, and 5890 audio/video tapes/CDs/DVDs, and subscribes to 792 periodicals including electronic. Computerized library services include the card catalog, interlibrary loans, database searching, and Internet access. Special learning facilities include a learning resource center, art gallery, radio station, greenhouses, and an observatory. The 107-acre campus is in a suburban area in Grand Rapids. Including any residence halls, there are 30 buildings.

Student Life: 95% of undergraduates are from Michigan. Others are from 24 states and 7 foreign countries. 79% are from public schools. 88% are white. 52% are Catholic; 14% Protestant. The average age of freshmen is 18; all undergraduates, 21. 21% do not continue beyond their first year; 51% remain to graduate.

Housing: 700 students can be accommodated in college housing, which includes single-sex and coed dormitories and on-campus apartments. In addition, there are special-interest houses and service learning houses. On-campus housing is guaranteed for all 4 years. 75% of students live on campus; of those, 70% remain on campus on weekends. All students may keep cars.

Activities: There are no fraternities or sororities. There are 45 groups on campus, including cheerleading, choir, chorus, computers, dance, drama, ethnic, honors, international, jazz band, literary magazine, newspaper, photography, political, radio and TV, religious, social, social service, and student government. Popular campus events include Spring Fling, Activities @ Moose Cafe, and a jazz festival.

Sports: There are 9 intercollegiate sports for men and 10 for women, and 6 intramural sports for men and 6 for women. Facilities include a gym, a weight room, a recreation room, an indoor track, softball and soccer fields, and indoor tennis courts.

Disabled Students: 95% of the campus is accessible. Wheelchair ramps, elevators, special parking, specially equipped rest rooms, special class scheduling, lowered drinking fountains, and lowered telephones are available.

Services: Counseling and information services are available, as is tutoring in most subjects. There is a reader service for the blind, and remedial math, reading, and writing.

Campus Safety and Security: Measures include 24-hour foot and vehicle patrol, self-defense education, security escort services, and informal discussions. There are pamphlets/posters/films, emergency telephones, and lighted pathways/sidewalks.

Programs of Study: Aquinas confers B.A., B.S., B.A.G.E., B.F.A., B.S.B.A., and B.S.I.B. degrees. Associate and master's degrees are also awarded. Bachelor's degrees are awarded in AGRICULTURE (environmental studies), BIOLOGICAL SCIENCE (biology/biological science), BUSINESS (accounting, business administration and management, business economics, international business management, and management information systems), COMMUNICATIONS AND THE ARTS (art, art history and appreciation, ceramic art and design, communications, drawing, English, fine arts, French, German, language arts, music, painting, performing arts, photography, printmaking, sculpture, and Spanish), COMPUTER AND PHYSICAL SCIENCE (applied science, chemistry, information sciences and systems, and mathematics), EDUCATION (education, education of the physically handicapped, music, physical, and special), ENGINEERING AND ENVIRONMENTAL DESIGN (environmental science), HEALTH PROFESSIONS (health and medical technology), SOCIAL SCIENCE (community services, economics, geography, history, interdisciplinary studies, international studies, philosophy, political science/government, psychology, religious music, social science, social studies, sociology, and theological studies). Business administration and education are the strongest academically and have the largest enrollments.

Required: To graduate, students must complete 124 semester hours, with 30 to 48 in the major, and maintain a minimum GPA of 2.0. The general education program consists of a core of 18 to 30 hours, which includes, from the first to the fourth year, foreign language and a year-long integrated skills course, and courses in the humanities, religion, and global perspectives; and distribution requirements of 30 to 33 hours, which include courses in cultural diversity, mythology and spirituality, natural sciences, the fine arts, and quantitative reasoning and technology.

Special: Students may cross-register with the Dominican Consortium and may study abroad in Ireland, Germany, France, Spain, Costa Rica, Peru, or Japan. Co-op programs and internships are available in all majors, and work-study programs are also available. Students may pursue dual majors in business administration and accounting, sports management, communication arts, or art and B.A.-B.S. degrees in business, geography, or psychology. Student-designed majors can be arranged. There is a 3-1 program in nuclear medicine technology with St. Louis University, as well as preengineering, prehealth, and teacher certification programs. Aquinas offers a general studies degree and may confer credit for life, military, and work experience. A pass/fail grading option is available. There are 5 national honor societies, a freshman honors program, and 5 departmental honors programs.

Faculty/Classroom: 54% of faculty are male; 46%, female. All teach undergraduates. No introductory courses are taught by graduate students. The average class size in an introductory lecture is 20; in a laboratory, 20; and in a regular course, 16.

Admissions: 82% of the 2005-2006 applicants were accepted. The ACT scores for the 2005-2006 freshman class were: 35% below 21, 25% between 21 and 23, 24% between 24 and 26, 9% between 27 and 28, and 7% above 28. 35% of the current freshmen were in the top fifth of their class; 65% were in the top two fifths. 10 freshmen graduated first in their class.

Requirements: The SAT or ACT is recommended. In addition, candidates for admission must graduate from an accredited secondary school. Students must have completed 15 Carnegie units and 4 years of English and social studies and 3 to 4 years each of math and science. Auditions are recommended in appropriate instances. A GPA of 2.5 is required. AP and CLEP credits are accepted. Important factors in the admissions decision are advanced placement or honor courses, leadership record, and extracurricular activities record.

Procedure: Freshmen are admitted fall and winter. There is a rolling admissions plan. Entrance exams should be taken during the spring of the junior year. Application deadlines are open. Applications are accepted on-line.

Transfer: 75 transfer students enrolled in 2004-2005. Transfer applicants must have earned at least 12 credits in academic course work from an accredited junior or 4-year college with a minimum GPA of 2.0. Interviews are recommended. 30 of 124 credits required for the bachelor's degree must be completed at Aquinas.

Visiting: There are regularly scheduled orientations for prospective students, consisting of a tour of the campus and presentations by financial aid personnel, program directors, coaches, and faculty. There are guides for informal visits and visitors may sit in on classes and stay overnight. To schedule a visit, contact Erica Davis, Admissions at (616) 632-2900.

Financial Aid: In 2005-2006, 76% of all full-time freshmen and 72% of continuing full-time students received some form of financial aid. 76% of full-time freshmen and 72% of continuing full-time students received need-based aid. The average freshman award was $14,446. Need-based scholarships or need-based grants averaged $12,518; need-based self-help aid (loans and jobs) averaged $1928; non-need-based athletic scholarships averaged $2335; and other non-need-based awards and non-need-based scholarships averaged $8785. 17% of undergraduates work part time. Average annual earnings from campus work are $2748. The average financial indebtedness of the 2005 graduate was $14,645. The FAFSA is required. The deadline for filing freshman financial aid applications for fall entry is June 1.

International Students: There are 12 international students enrolled. They must score satidfactorily on the written TOEFL.

Computers: Wireless access is available. Students may connect to the network from dorm rooms and various locations around campus. Computer labs are available in the residence halls, student center, library, and academic center. Classrooms are wired for network access with multimedia technology available for faculty and student use. There is a 24-hour online knowledge center and online help desk system. All students may access the system 91 hours per week during open lab times. There are no time limits and no fees. It is strongly recommended that all students have a personal computer.

Graduates: From July 1, 2004 to June 30, 2005, 381 bachelor's degrees were awarded. The most popular majors were education (22%), business administration (21%), and social science (9%). In an average class, 22% graduate in 4 years or less, 46% graduate in 5 years or less, and 51% graduate in 6 years or less. 30 companies recruited on campus in a recent year. Of the 2004 graduating class, 13% were enrolled in graduate school within 6 months of graduation and 83% were employed.

Admissions Contact: Thomas Mikowski, Director of Admissions. E-mail: *mikowtho@aquinas.edu* Web: *www.aquinas.edu/admissions*

BAKER COLLEGE OF FLINT
E-4

Flint, MI 48507-5508

(810) 766-4000
(800) 822-2537; Fax: (810) 766-4049

Full-time: 800 men, 1600 women	**Faculty:** 23
Part-time: 600 men, 1400 women	**Ph.D.s:** 13%
Graduate: none	**Student/Faculty:** 41 to 1
Year: quarters, summer session	**Tuition:** $7000
Application Deadline: open	**Room & Board:** $800
Freshman Class: n/av	
SAT or ACT: not required	**NONCOMPETITIVE**

Baker College, established in 1911, is an independent institution offering undergraduate degrees in business, health science, and technical curricula. It is part of the Baker College System. Figures in the above capsule and in this profile are approximate. In addition to regional accreditation, Baker has baccalaureate program accreditation with CAHEA. The library contains 60,000 volumes, 1200 microform items, and 500 audio/video tapes/CDs/DVDs, and subscribes to 200 periodicals including electronic. Computerized library services include the card catalog, interlibrary loans, and database searching. Special learning facilities include a learning resource center. The 30-acre campus is in an urban area 60 miles northwest of Detroit. Including any residence halls, there are 6 buildings.

Student Life: 92% of undergraduates are from Michigan. Others are from 4 foreign countries and Canada. 72% are white; 22% African American. The average age of all undergraduates is 28.

Housing: 189 students can be accommodated in college housing, which includes single-sex and coed dorms, on-campus apartments, and off-campus apartments. On-campus housing is available on a first-come, first-served basis. Priority is given to out-of-town students. 98% of students commute. Alcohol is not permitted. All students may keep cars.

Activities: There are no fraternities or sororities. There are 15 groups on campus, including computers, literary magazine, professional, and social. Popular campus events include Baker College Spirit Day and Martin Luther King Jr. Day.

Sports: There is no sports program at Baker. Facilities include a gym and a weight room.

Disabled Students: All of the campus is accessible. Wheelchair ramps, elevators, special parking, specially equipped rest rooms, lowered drinking fountains, and lowered telephones are available.

Services: Counseling and information services are available, as is tutoring in most subjects.

Campus Safety and Security: Measures include 24-hour foot and vehicle patrol, self-defense education, security escort services, and informal discussions. There are pamphlets/posters/films and lighted pathways/sidewalks, and high-traffic areas of the college are monitored by video camera.

Programs of Study: Baker confers B.B.A., B.B.L., and B.I.M. degrees. Associate degrees are also awarded. Bachelor's degrees are awarded in BUSINESS (accounting, business administration and management, marketing management, and office supervision and management), COMPUTER AND PHYSICAL SCIENCE (computer programming), ENGINEERING AND ENVIRONMENTAL DESIGN (aviation administration/management, drafting and design technology, electrical/electronics engineering technology, and interior design), HEALTH PROFESSIONS (health care administration and occupational therapy). Business administration and health information management are the largest.

Required: Degree requirements include completion of 180 to 208 quarter hours with a minimum GPA of 2.0. All students must complete math and computer courses and an employment course.

Special: Co-op programs, work study internships, and dual and interdisciplinary majors are available. An accelerated degree program is possible in business administration.

Faculty/Classroom: 46% of faculty are male; 54%, female. All teach undergraduates.

Requirements: There are no entrance requirements to Baker College. Students without either a high school diploma or a GED may still be admitted on the basis of Baker College test results.

Procedure: Freshmen are admitted to all sessions. There is a rolling admissions plan Application deadlines are open. The fall 2005 application fee was $20.

Transfer: Transcripts from all previous colleges must be submitted. Grades of C or better are eligible for transfer credit. 48 of 180 quarter credits required for the bachelor's degree must be completed at Baker.

Visiting: There are regularly scheduled orientations for prospective students, including orientation and testing. There are guides for informal visits and visitors may sit in on classes. To schedule a visit, contact the Admissions Office.

Financial Aid: The FAFSA and the college's own financial statement are required. Check with the school for current deadlines.

Computers: All students may access the system during school hours. There are no time limits and no fees.

Admissions Contact: Vice President of Admissions.
E-mail: heaton_m@flint.baker.edu

CALVIN COLLEGE   D-4
Grand Rapids, MI 49546

	(616) 526-6106
	(800) 688-0122; Fax: (616) 526-6777
Full-time: 1818 men, 2150 women	**Faculty:** 309; IIB, av$
Part-time: 81 men, 76 women	**Ph.D.s:** 82%
Graduate: 11 men, 41 women	**Student/Faculty:** 13 to 1
Year: 4-1-4, summer session	**Tuition:** $19,150
Application Deadline: August 15	**Room & Board:** $6585
Freshman Class: 2156 applied, 2104 accepted, 1007 enrolled	
SAT Verbal/Math: 610/610*	**ACT:** 26 **NONCOMPETITIVE**

Calvin College, established in 1876, is a private institution affiliated with the Christian Reformed Church, offering undergraduate and graduate degrees in liberal arts and in some professional programs. In addition to regional accreditation, Calvin has baccalaureate program accreditation with ABET, ACCE, CSWE, NASM, NCATE, and NLN. The library contains 479,600 volumes, 790,800 microform items, and 2853 audio/video tapes/CDs/DVDs, and subscribes to 15,000 periodicals including electronic. Computerized library services include the card catalog, interlibrary loans, database searching, and Internet access. Special learning facilities include a learning resource center, art gallery, and TV Studio,

ecosystem preserve and interpretive center, electron microscope lav, an observatory with a 16-inch telescope, a greenhouse, and an audiology and speech pathology clinic. The 390-acre campus is in a suburban area 7 miles southeast of downtown Grand Rapids. Including any residence halls, there are 40 buildings.

Student Life: 52% of undergraduates are from Michigan. Others are from 49 states, 45 foreign countries, and Canada. 42% are from public schools. 85% are white. Most are Protestant. The average age of freshmen is 18; all undergraduates, 20. 12% do not continue beyond their first year; 72% remain to graduate.

Housing: 2397 students can be accommodated in college housing, which includes single-sex dormitories and on-campus apartments. In addition, there are language houses, special-interest houses, a residence hall wing designated as a multicultural community, and 3 urban houses designated as residential living with a community/urban focus. 58% of students live on campus; of those, 90% remain on campus on weekends. Alcohol is not permitted. All students may keep cars.

Activities: There are no fraternities or sororities. There are 54 groups on campus, including art, band, chess, choir, chorale, chorus, computers, dance, drama, ethnic, film, honors, international, jazz band, literary magazine, musical theater, newspaper, orchestra, pep band, political, professional, radio and TV, religious, social, social service, student government, symphony, and yearbook. Popular campus events include Family Weekend, the spring and fall music and art festivals, and the January lecture series.

Sports: There are 8 intercollegiate sports for men and 9 for women, and 18 intramural sports for men and 14 for women. Facilities include a 4500-seat field house, a soccer facility, baseball and softball diamonds, an 8K cross country course, an 8-lane, 400-meter polyurethane track, a weight-training/exercise room, a natatorium that contains a diving pool, 6 tennis courts, 2 sand beach volleyball courts, and a paved recreational trail around campus.

Disabled Students: 85% of the campus is accessible. Wheelchair ramps, elevators, special parking, specially equipped rest rooms, special class scheduling, lowered drinking fountains, lowered telephones, special housing, electric door openers, and reserved classroom seating are available.

Services: Counseling and information services are available, as is tutoring in most subjects. There is a reader service for the blind, and remedial math, reading, and writing. There is a Braille print service for the blind, books on tape, note taking, interpreting, diagnostic testing, special advising, and early registration.

Campus Safety and Security: Measures include 24-hour foot and vehicle patrol, self-defense education, security escort services, and informal discussions. There are pamphlets/posters/films, emergency telephones, lighted pathways/sidewalks, a crime alert bulletin, and reports in the school newspaper.

Programs of Study: Calvin confers B.A., B.S.,B.A.S.P.A., B.C.S., B.F.A., B.M.E., B.S.A., B.S.C.D., B.S.E., B.S.N., B.S.P.A., B.S.R., and B.S.W. degrees. Master's degrees are also awarded. Bachelor's degrees are awarded in BIOLOGICAL SCIENCE (biochemistry, biology/biological science, and biotechnology), BUSINESS (accounting, business administration and management, business communications, and recreation and leisure services), COMMUNICATIONS AND THE ARTS (art, art history and appreciation, classical languages, classics, communications, dramatic arts, Dutch, English, film arts, French, German, Greek, Latin, media arts, music, Spanish, and voice), COMPUTER AND PHYSICAL SCIENCE (chemistry, computer science, digital arts/technology, geology, information sciences and systems, mathematics, and physics), EDUCATION (art, elementary, music, physical, secondary, and special), ENGINEERING AND ENVIRONMENTAL DESIGN (chemical engineering, civil engineering, electrical/electronics engineering, engineering, environmental science, and mechanical engineering), HEALTH PROFESSIONS (nursing, occupational therapy, predentistry, premedicine, prepharmacy, preveterinary science, and speech pathology/audiology), SOCIAL SCIENCE (area studies, Asian/Oriental studies, economics, geography, history, international studies, philosophy, political science/government, prelaw, psychology, religion, social work, and sociology). Natural sciences, history, and English are the strongest academically. Education, engineering, and business are the largest.

Required: Degree requirements include completion of 124 credit hours, with 28 credits in the major. All students must complete specific course work in English, religion, history, science, math, communication, fine arts, psychology or sociology, economics or political science, philosophy, phys ed, research and information technology, and cross-cultural engagement. A minimum GPA of 2.0 is required.

Special: A variety of dual majors and student-designed majors is available, as well as combined curriculum programs in occupational therapy, and speech pathology. Students may study abroad in 16 countries and enroll in a Washington semester. Cooperative programs include Los Angeles film studies, the Au Sable Institute, the Chicago Metropolitan program, Oregon extension, Latin American, Middle East, Chinese, and Russian studies, and in business. Internships, work-study programs, and cross-registration at Grand Valley State University in special education, at Michigan State in communications disorders, in occupational therapy at Washington University, and in religion at Reformed Bible College are also available. There are 6 national honor societies, a freshman honors program, and 25 departmental honors programs.

Faculty/Classroom: 70% of faculty are male; 30%, female. All both teach and do research. No introductory courses are taught by graduate students. The average class size in an introductory lecture is 26; in a laboratory, 17; and in a regular course, 20.

Admissions: 98% of the 2005-2006 applicants were accepted. The SAT scores for the 2005-2006 freshman class were: Verbal--12% below 500, 34% between 500 and 599, 38% between 600 and 700, and 16% above 700; Math--9% below 500, 33% between 500 and 599, 41% between 600 and 700, and 17% above 700. The ACT scores were 9% below 21, 20% between 21 and 23, 26% between 24 and 26, 21% between 27 and 28, and 24% above 28. 47% of the current freshmen were in the top fifth of their class; 72% were in the top two fifths. There were 21 National Merit finalists and 21 semifinalists. 52 freshmen graduated first in their class.

Requirements: The ACT is required. In addition, in selecting students for admission, Calvin College looks for evidence of Christian commitment and for the capacity and desire to learn. Students who are interested in the Christian perspective and curriculum of Calvin, and who show interest in its aims, are eligible for consideration. Although the prospect of academic success is of primary consideration, the aspirations of the applicant, the recommendation of a high school counselor, teacher, or principal, and the ability of Calvin to be of service, will also be considered in admission decisions. A GPA of 2.5 is required. AP and CLEP credits are accepted. Important factors in the admissions decision are recommendations by school officials, leadership record, and extracurricular activities record.

Procedure: Freshmen are admitted to all sessions. Entrance exams should be taken during the spring of the junior year or fall of the senior year. There is a deferred admissions and a rolling admissions plan. Applications should be filed by August 15 for fall entry, January 15 for spring entry, and open for summer entry, along with a $35 fee, which is waived if submitted before December 1. Notification is sent on a rolling basis. Applications are accepted on-line.

Transfer: 101 transfer students enrolled in 2004-2005. Applicants from 4-year colleges are required to have a minimum GPA of 2.0; from 2-year colleges, 2.5. Students must have a satisfactory score on the SAT. A minimum score of 20 is required on the ACT. 31 of 124 credits required for the bachelor's degree must be completed at Calvin.

Visiting: There are regularly scheduled orientations for prospective students. Prospective students and their families are invited to explore Calvin firsthand by scheduling an individual visit or through the "Fridays at Calvin" campus visitation program, which offers sectionals, class visits, lunch with professors, campus tours, and an overnight stay at the residence halls. There are guides for informal visits and visitors may sit in on classes and stay overnight. To schedule a visit, contact the Admissions Office.

Financial Aid: In 2005-2006, 92% of all full-time freshmen and 90% of continuing full-time students received some form of financial aid. 63% of full-time freshmen and 62% of continuing full-time students received need-based aid. The average freshman award was $13,605. Need-based scholarships or need-based grants averaged $9325; need-based self-help aid (loans and jobs) averaged $5100; and other non-need-based awards and non-need-based scholarships averaged $4115. 80% of undergraduates work part time. Average annual earnings from campus work are $1200. The average financial indebtedness of the 2005 graduate was $18,000. The FAFSA and the college's own financial statement are required. The priority date for freshman financial aid applications for fall entry is February 15. The deadline for filing freshman financial aid applications for fall entry is August 1.

International Students: There are 294 international students enrolled. The school actively recruits these students. They must score satisfactorily on the written TOEFL or on the electronic version or take the MELAB if the student scored low on the TOEFL. Students must also take the SAT or ACT, with a satisfactory score on the SAT or a score of 20 on the ACT. Exceptions are made for strong students without access to standardized exams.

Computers: Calvin provides resident students with high-speed Internet connections, telephones, cable television, access to fax machines, and HelpDesk support services. All students enjoy access to more than 800 PC's in campus labs and classrooms. All students may access the system at any time. There are no time limits and no fees.

Graduates: From July 1, 2004 to June 30, 2005, 913 bachelor's degrees were awarded. The most popular majors were business (10%), elementary education (8%), and English (7%). In an average class, 1% graduate in 3 years or less, 56% graduate in 4 years or less, 72% graduate in 5 years or less, and 74% graduate in 6 years or less. 275 companies recruited on campus in 2004-2005. Of the 2004 graduating class, 19% were enrolled in graduate school within 6 months of graduation and 80% were employed.

Admissions Contact: Dale D. Kuiper, Director of Admissions.
E-mail: *admissions@calvin.edu* Web: *www.calvin.edu*

CENTRAL MICHIGAN UNIVERSITY   D-4

Mount Pleasant, MI 48859
(989) 774-3076
(888) 292-5366; Fax: (989) 774-7267

Full-time: 7344 men, 9712 women	**Faculty:** 692; I, --$
Part-time: 478 men, 566 women	**Ph.D.s:** 82%
Graduate: 703 men, 1114 women	**Student/Faculty:** 25 to 1
Year: semesters, summer session	**Tuition:** $5868 ($13,632)
Application Deadline: open	**Room & Board:** $6376
Freshman Class: 13,550 applied, 10,198 accepted, 3718 enrolled	
SAT Verbal/Math: 510/520*	**ACT:** 22 COMPETITIVE

Central Michigan University, founded in 1892, is a public university offering programs in liberal arts, business, health, education, and human services. There are 6 undergraduate schools and 1 graduate school. In addition to regional accreditation, CMU has baccalaureate program accreditation with AACSB, ACCE, ACEJMC, ASC, CAAHEP, CADE, CSWE, NASM, NCATE, and NRPA. The library contains 1,012,774 volumes, 1,342,550 microform items, and 28,008 audio/video tapes/CDs/DVDs, and subscribes to 3330 periodicals including electronic. Computerized library services include the card catalog, interlibrary loans, database searching, and Internet access. Special learning facilities include a learning resource center, art gallery, natural history museum, radio station, TV station, Museum of Cultural and Natural History, Clarke Historical Library, Gerald L. Poor School Museum, Brooks Astronomical Observatory, leadership institute, and a multicultural education center. The 837-acre campus is in a small town 70 miles north of Lansing. Including any residence halls, there are 54 buildings.

Student Life: 98% of undergraduates are from Michigan. Others are from 48 states, 61 foreign countries, and Canada. 89% are from public schools. 84% are white. The average age of freshmen is 18; all undergraduates, 21. 23% do not continue beyond their first year; 49% remain to graduate.

Housing: 6635 students can be accommodated in college housing, which includes single-sex and coed dormitories, on-campus apartments, and married-student housing. In addition, there are honors houses and residential colleges. On-campus housing is guaranteed for all 4 years. 67% of students commute. Alcohol is not permitted. All students may keep cars.

Activities: 6% of men belong to 14 national fraternities; 6% of women belong to 11 national sororities. There are 279 groups on campus, including art, band, cheerleading, choir, chorus, computers, dance, debate, drama, ethnic, film, forensics, gay, honors, international, jazz band, literary magazine, marching band, musical theater, newspaper, orchestra, pep band, photography, political, professional, radio and TV, religious, social, social service, student government, symphony, and yearbook. Popular campus events include Michigan Story Festival, Native American Pow Wow, and Lem Tucker Journalism Scholarship and Speaker Series Event.

Sports: There are 6 intercollegiate sports for men and 8 for women, and 21 intramural sports for men and 21 for women. Facilities include a football stadium, softball fields, field hockey complex, indoor athletic complex, indoor and outdoor track, soccer field, baseball stadium, arena, and student activity center.

Disabled Students: 95% of the campus is accessible. Wheelchair ramps, elevators, special parking, specially equipped rest rooms, special class scheduling, lowered drinking fountains, lowered telephones, special housing, and Student Disability Services office are available.

Services: Counseling and information services are available, as is tutoring in most subjects. There is a reader service for the blind, and remedial math, reading, and writing.

Campus Safety and Security: Measures include security escort services, shuttle buses, informal discussions, and pamphlets/posters/films. There are emergency telephones, lighted pathways/sidewalks, and a blue light phone system.

Programs of Study: CMU confers B.A., B.S., B.A.A., B.F.A., B.S., B.M, B.M.E., B.S.B.A., B.S.E., B.S.E.E., B.S.E.T., B.S.M.E. and B.S.W. degrees. Master's and doctoral degrees are also awarded. Bachelor's degrees are awarded in AGRICULTURE (environmental studies, and natural resource management), BIOLOGICAL SCIENCE (biology/biological science, microbiology, and neurosciences), BUSINESS (accounting, banking and finance, business administration and management, business economics, entrepreneurial studies, fashion merchandising, hospitality management services, human resources, international business management, investments and securities, logistics, management information systems, management science, marketing and distribution, marketing/retailing/merchandising, purchasing/inventory management, and retailing), COMMUNICATIONS AND THE ARTS (apparel design, art, broadcasting, communications, creative writing, dramatic arts, English, English literature, fine arts, French, German, graphic design, journalism, language arts, literature, music, music history and appreciation, music performance, music theory and composition, musical theater, photography, piano/organ, public relations, Spanish, speech/debate/rhetoric, theater design, visual and performing arts, and voice), COMPUTER AND PHYSICAL SCIENCE (actuarial science, astronomy, chemistry, computer science, earth science, geology, mathematics, physical sciences, physics, and statistics), EDUCATION (art, athletic training, business, education, education of the emotionally handicapped, education of the mentally handicapped, elementary, English, foreign languages, mathematics, music, physical, social studies, special, and trade and industrial), ENGINEERING AND ENVIRONMENTAL DESIGN (computer technology, electrical/electronics engineering, engineering technology, interior design, land use management and reclamation, manufacturing technology, mechanical engineering, and mechanical engineering technology), HEALTH PROFESSIONS (biomedical science, health care administration, medical technology, predentistry, premedicine, preoptometry, preosteopathy, prepharmacy, preventive/wellness health care, public health, recreation therapy, speech pathology/audiology, and sports medicine), SOCIAL SCIENCE (anthropology, child psychology/development, cognitive science, community services, criminal justice, dietetics, early childhood studies, economics, European studies, family/consumer studies, food production/management/services, history, interdisciplinary studies, parks and recreation management, philosophy, political science/government, psychology, religion, social science, social studies, social work, sociology, and women's studies). Physical therapy and education are the strongest academically. Science and technology, humanities and social and behavioral sciences, and business administration are the largest.

Required: Students must complete 124 credit hours, including 30 in the major, with a GPA of 2.0. They must fulfill the requirements in the University Program (27 to 30 semester hours of coursework in humanities, natural sciences social studies, and integrative and area studies), and fulfill competency requirements in written English (Freshman and Advanced Composition), oral English, and math.

Special: CMU offers internships in business administration, study abroad in 41 countries, and dual majors in chemistry/physics and computer science/math. Student-designed majors are available for a individualized studies degree and there is credit for life, military, and work experience. Students may take up to 25 hours for pass/fail grades. CMU off-campus programs offer external degree programs in which students can get degrees without attending classes on campus. There are 13 national honor societies, a freshman honors program, and 21 departmental honors programs.

Faculty/Classroom: 61% of faculty are male; 39%, female. All teach undergraduates. Graduate students teach 2% of introductory courses. The average class size in an introductory lecture is 40; in a laboratory, 17; and in a regular course, 32.

Admissions: 75% of the 2005-2006 applicants were accepted. The SAT scores for the 2005-2006 freshman class were: Verbal--45% below 500, 34% between 500 and 599, 18% between 600 and 700, and 4% above 700; Math--37% below 500, 42% between 500 and 599, 14% between 600 and 700, and 8% above 700. The ACT scores were 39% below 21, 30% between 21 and 23, 21% between 24 and 26, 7% between 27 and 28, and 3% above 28. 28% of the current freshmen were in the top fifth of their class; 53% were in the top two fifths.

Requirements: The ACT is recommended. In addition, applicants must be high school graduates or hold a GED. The university strongly recommends 4 years each of English and math, 3 each of science and social studies, and 2 of foreign language, as well as 1 course each in computer science and fine arts. AP and CLEP credits are accepted.

Procedure: Freshmen are admitted to all sessions. Entrance exams should be taken during the junior or senior year of high school. There is a deferred admissions plan and a rolling admissions plan. Application deadlines are open. 398 applicants were on the 2005 waiting list; 304 were admitted. Applications are accepted on-line. The fall 2005 application fee was $35.

Transfer: 1101 transfer students enrolled in 2004-2005. Transfer students must have a GPA of 2.5. 30 of 124 credits required for the bachelor's degree must be completed at CMU.

Visiting: There are guides for informal visits and visitors may sit in on classes and stay overnight. To schedule a visit, contact Admissions at *cmuadmit@cmich.edu.*

Financial Aid: In 2005-2006, 93% of all full-time freshmen and 90% of continuing full-time students received some form of financial aid. 49% of full-time freshmen and 42% of continuing full-time students received need-based aid. The average freshman award was $8346. Need-based scholarships or need-based grants averaged $4154; need-based self-help aid (loans and jobs) averaged $3707; non-need-based athletic scholarships averaged $7009; and other non-need-based awards and non-need-based scholarships averaged $2486. 22% of undergraduates work part time. Average annual earnings from campus work are $1800. The average financial indebtedness of the 2005 graduate was $16,312. The FAFSA is required.

International Students: There are 129 international students enrolled. The school actively recruits these students. They must take the TOEFL.

Computers: Wireless access is available. CMU has a wide variety of technology resources and technology support available for students. Visit the school's web site for further information. All students may access the system at any time. There are no time limits and no fees.

Graduates: From July 1, 2004 to June 30, 2005, 3555 bachelor's degrees were awarded. The most popular majors were business/marketing (27%), education (11%), and social sciences (8%). In an average class, 1% graduate in 3 years or less, 19% graduate in 4 years or less, 47% graduate in 5 years or less, and 55% graduate in 6 years or less. 325 companies recruited on campus in 2004-2005. Of the 2004 graduating class, 17% were enrolled in graduate school within 6 months of graduation and within 1 year 88% were employed.

Admissions Contact: Betty Wagner, Director of Admissions.
E-mail: *cmeadmit@cmich.edu* Web: *www.cmich.edu*

CLEARY COLLEGE
E-5

Ann Arbor, MI 48197
(517) 548-3670 (Howell)
(800) 589-1979; Fax: (517) 548-2170

Full-time: 200 men, 200 women	**Faculty:** 11; III, --$
Part-time: 100 men, 200 women	**Ph.D.s:** 12%
Graduate: none	**Student/Faculty:** 35 to 1
Year: quarters, summer session	**Tuition:** $11,000
Application Deadline: open	**Room & Board:** n/app
Freshman Class: n/av	
ACT: recommended	**LESS COMPETITIVE**

Cleary University, formerly Cleary College and founded in 1883, is a private institution offering bachelor's and associate degrees in business. Figures in the above capsule and in this profile are approximate. The university serves an entirely commuter student body. A second campus, similar in size and programs, is located in Howell, and there are extension sites throughout southeastern Michigan. The library contains 7900 volumes and 200 audio/video tapes/CDs/DVDs, and subscribes to 30 periodicals including electronic. Computerized library services include the card catalog, interlibrary loans, and database searching. Special learning facilities include a learning resource center. The 27-acre campus is in a suburban area 25 miles east of Lansing and 40 miles west of Detroit. There is 1 building.

Student Life: 99% of undergraduates are from Michigan. Others are from 2 states, 1 foreign country, and Canada. 90% are from public schools. 91% are white. The average age of all undergraduates is 36.

Housing: There are no residence halls. All of students commute. Alcohol is not permitted. All students may keep cars.

Activities: There are no fraternities or sororities. Popular campus events include picnics.

Sports: There is no sports program at Cleary.

Disabled Students: All of the campus is accessible. Wheelchair ramps, special parking, specially equipped rest rooms, lowered drinking fountains, and lowered telephones are available.

Services: Counseling and information services are available, as is tutoring in some subjects, including English, math, and computers. There is remedial math and writing.

Campus Safety and Security: Measures include informal discussions, pamphlets/posters/films, and lighted pathways/sidewalks.

Programs of Study: Cleary confers the B.B.A. degree. Associate degrees are also awarded. Bachelor's degrees are awarded in BUSINESS (accounting, banking and finance, business administration and management, human resources, and marketing management), COMPUTER AND PHYSICAL SCIENCE (information sciences and systems), HEALTH PROFESSIONS (health care administration). Accounting is the strongest academically. Business administration is the largest.

Required: Core requirements include 90 quarter credits of business courses in economics, management, basic accounting, communication, and ethics. To graduate, students must complete a senior project and at least 180 quarter credit hours with a minimum GPA of 2.5

Special: Cleary offers internships, work study, and co-op programs in all majors, accelerated degree programs in accounting, marketing, finance, management information technology, quality management, human resource management, health services management, corporate and public accounting, and business management. Cleary also offers credit for prior learning experiences and opportunities for individualized study. Nondegree study is possible.

Faculty/Classroom: 45% of faculty are male; 55%, female. All teach undergraduates. The average class size in an introductory lecture is 15; in a laboratory, 12; and in a regular course, 12.

Requirements: The ACT is recommended. In addition, applicants must be graduates of an accredited secondary school or have earned a GED. A GPA of 2.5 is required. AP and CLEP credits are accepted.

Procedure: Freshmen are admitted to all sessions. There are early decision, early admissions, and deferred admissions plans. There is a rolling admissions plan. Application deadlines are open. The fall 2005 application fee was $25.

Transfer: Applicants must submit official transcripts from all institutions previously attended and have a minimum GPA of 2.5. 45 of 180 quarter credits required for the bachelor's degree must be completed at Cleary.

Visiting: There are regularly scheduled orientations for prospective students. There are guides for informal visits and visitors may sit in on classes. To schedule a visit, contact Admissions.

Financial Aid: In a recent year, 1% of undergraduates worked part time. Average annual earnings from campus work were $2500. Cleary is a member of CSS. The FAFSA is required. Check with the school for current deadlines.

International Students: They must score satisfactorily on the written TOEFL or take the MELAB.

Computers: All students may access the system. There are no time limits and no fees. All students are required to have personal computers.

Admissions Contact: Admissions Officer. Web: *www.cleary.edu*

COLLEGE FOR CREATIVE STUDIES E-5

Detroit, MI 48202-4034

(313) 664-7425
(800) 952-ARTS; Fax: (313) 872-2739

Full-time: 600 men, 400 women	**Faculty:** 43
Part-time: 100 men, 100 women	**Ph.Ds:** 78%
Graduate: none	**Student/Faculty:** 24 to 1
Year: semesters, summer session	**Tuition:** $20,000
Application Deadline: see profile	**Room & Board:** $4000
Freshman Class: n/av	
SAT or ACT: required	**SPECIAL**

The College for Creative Studies, established in 1906, is a private, independent institution offering comprehensive 4-year B.F.A programs in animation and digital media, crafts, fine arts, communication design, industrial design, interior design, and photography, as well as teacher certification in art education. Figures in the above capsule and in this profile are approximate. There is 1 undergraduate school. In addition to regional accreditation, CCS has baccalaureate program accreditation with NASAD. The library contains 21,000 volumes and subscribes to 100 periodicals including electronic. Special learning facilities include a learning resource center and art gallery. The 11-acre campus is in an urban area 3 miles from downtown Detroit in the University Cultural Center, which includes the Detroit Institute of Art. Including any residence halls, there are 6 buildings.

Student Life: 83% of undergraduates are from Michigan. Others are from 35 states, 18 foreign countries, and Canada. 66% are white. The average age of freshmen is 18; all undergraduates, 23. 26% do not continue beyond their first year; 56% remain to graduate.

Housing: 263 students can be accommodated in college housing, which includes coed on-campus apartments. On-campus housing is available on a first-come, first-served basis. Priority is given to out-of-town students. 79% of students commute. Alcohol is not permitted. All students may keep cars.

Activities: There are no fraternities or sororities. There are 6 groups on campus, including ethnic, professional, and student government. Popular campus events include an annual student exhibition, Noel Night, and Detroit Festival of the Arts.

Sports: There is no sports program at CCS.

Disabled Students: All of the campus is accessible. Wheelchair ramps, elevators, special parking, specially equipped rest rooms, and lowered telephones are available.

Services: Counseling and information services are available, as is tutoring in every subject. There is remedial reading and writing.

Campus Safety and Security: Measures include 24-hour foot and vehicle patrol, security escort services, informal discussions, and pamphlets/posters/films. There are lighted pathways/sidewalks.

Programs of Study: CCS confers the B.F.A degree. Bachelor's degrees are awarded in COMMUNICATIONS AND THE ARTS (advertising, animation, ceramic art and design, fine arts, glass, graphic design, illustration, industrial design, metal/jewelry, painting, photography, printmaking, and sculpture), COMPUTER AND PHYSICAL SCIENCE (digital arts/technology), EDUCATION (art), ENGINEERING AND ENVIRONMENTAL DESIGN (interior design), SOCIAL SCIENCE (textiles and clothing). Industrial design and communication design are the strongest academically. Animation and digital media are the largest.

Required: Degree requirements include work in English, behavioral science, art history, history, speech, philosophy, and art and design. Students must complete 42 credits in liberal arts. A minimum GPA of 2.0 is required, and students must complete 126 credits with 63 in the major to graduate.

Special: Internships are available within the student's departmental major. Credit for internships and dual majors are available. Study abroad is possible.

Faculty/Classroom: 62% of faculty are male; 38%, female. All teach undergraduates. The average class size in an introductory lecture is 20; in a laboratory, 15; and in a regular course, 18.

Admissions: 77% of recent applicants were accepted.

Requirements: The SAT or ACT is required. In addition, applicants must graduate from an accredited secondary school or earn a GED. A portfolio of representative work and an essay are required. A GPA of 2.5 is required. AP and CLEP credits are accepted. Important factors in the admissions decision are evidence of special talent and advanced placement or honor courses.

Procedure: Freshmen are admitted fall and winter. There is a deferred admissions plan. Check with the school for current application deadlines. The fall 2005 application fee was $35. Notification is sent on a rolling basis. Applications are accepted on-line.

Transfer: 155 transfer students enrolled in a recent year. Transfer applicants should submit a portfolio that includes artwork done at the previous college. Transcripts and portfolio review will determine how many credits may transfer. The approval of the chairperson of the department to which the student is applying is required for transfer of studio credit. The minimum GPA is 2.0. 33 of 126 credits required for the bachelor's degree must be completed at CCS.

Visiting: There are regularly scheduled orientations for prospective students, including an introduction to the college by an admission professional, a digital presentation of student work, application/financial aid information, and a campus tour. The orientations are scheduled every other week from September through April. There are guides for informal visits and visitors may sit in on classes. To schedule a visit, contact the Admission Office.

Financial Aid: The FAFSA is required. Check with the school for current deadlines.

International Students: The school actively recruits these students. They must score satisfactorily on the written TOEFL or on the electronic version and also take the SAT or the ACT.

Computers: All students may access the system. There are no time limits and no fees. It is strongly recommended that all students have a personal computer.

Graduates: In a recent year, 190 bachelor's degrees were awarded. The most popular majors were industrial design (28%), animation and digital media (16%), and communication design (15%). In an average class, 56% graduate in 6 years or less. 35 companies recruited on campus in a recent year.

Admissions Contact: Admissions Officer.
E-mail: *admissions@ccscad.edu* Web: *www.ccscad.edu*

CONCORDIA UNIVERSITY, ANN ARBOR E-5

Ann Arbor, MI 48105

(734) 995-7311
(800) 253-0680; Fax: (734) 995-4610

Full-time: 221 men, 285 women	**Faculty:** 35
Part-time: 23 men, 30 women	**Ph.Ds:** 60%
Graduate: 16 men, 25 women	**Student/Faculty:** 14 to 1
Year: semesters, summer session	**Tuition:** $18,205
Application Deadline: open	**Room & Board:** $6948
Freshman Class: 550 applied, 451 accepted, 115 enrolled	
SAT Verbal/Math: 570/575*	**ACT:** 22 **COMPETITIVE+**

Concordia University, established in 1963, is a private institution affiliated with the Missouri Synod of the Lutheran Church, offering undergraduate and graduate degrees in the arts and sciences, business, education, and human services. There are 4 undergraduate schools and 1 graduate school. In addition to regional accreditation, Concordia has baccalaureate program accreditation with NCATE. The library contains 110,680 volumes, 36,020 microform items, and 6510 audio/video tapes/CDs/DVDs, and subscribes to 18,780 periodicals including electronic. Computerized library services include the card catalog, interlibrary loans, database searching, Internet access, and laptop Internet portals. Special learning facilities include a learning resource center and an art gallery. The 187-acre campus is in a suburban area 40 miles west of Detroit. Including any residence halls, there are 30 buildings.

Student Life: 83% of undergraduates are from Michigan. Others are from 18 states, 5 foreign countries, and Canada. 84% are white; 10% African American. 83% are Protestant; 9% Catholic; 8% claim no religious affiliation. The average age of freshmen is 18; all undergraduates, 24. 31% do not continue beyond their first year; 43% remain to graduate.

Housing: 446 students can be accommodated in college housing, which includes single-sex dorms and married-student housing. On-campus housing is guaranteed for all 4 years. 61% of students live on campus; of those, 55% remain on campus on weekends. Alcohol is not permitted. All students may keep cars.

Activities: There are no fraternities or sororities. There are 21 groups on campus, including band, choir, chorale, computers, dance, debate, drama, ethnic, jazz band, musical theater, newspaper, pep band, religious, social, social service, student government, and yearbook. Popular campus events include Boar's Head Festival, Servant Events, and a Fall carnival.

Sports: There are 5 intercollegiate sports for men and 5 for women, and 10 intramural sports for men and 10 for women. Facilities include a soccer field, baseball and softball diamonds, sand volleyball courts, a phys ed building (gymnasium), and an open field for intramurals.

Disabled Students: 90% of the campus is accessible. Wheelchair ramps, elevators, special parking, specially equipped rest rooms, and lowered drinking fountains are available.

Services: Counseling and information services are available, as is tutoring in every subject. There is also a writing lab with consultants.

Campus Safety and Security: Measures include 24-hour foot and vehicle patrol, security escort services, informal discussions, and pamphlets/posters/films. There are lighted pathways/sidewalks.

Programs of Study: Concordia confers the B.A. degree. Associate and master's degrees are also awarded. Bachelor's degrees are awarded in BIOLOGICAL SCIENCE (biology/biological science), BUSINESS (business administration and management), COMMUNICATIONS AND THE ARTS (art, communications, dramatic arts, English, and music), COMPUTER AND PHYSICAL SCIENCE (information sciences and systems, mathematics, physical sciences, and science), EDUCATION (elementary, physical, and secondary), HEALTH PROFESSIONS (predentistry, and premedicine), SOCIAL SCIENCE (biblical languages, criminal justice, family/consumer studies, history, psychology, religion, religious music, and social studies). Education and business are the strongest academically. Business administration, teacher education, and English are the largest.

Required: Degree requirements include completion of 128 credit hours, with more than 30 in the major, and up to 49 credit hours of general studies, and a minimum GPA of 2.0. The student must also demonstrate proficiency in foreign language, writing, speech, and math. Required courses include upper-level general studies, writing-intensive, physical activities, computer applications, religion, humanities, social science, language/communication, and science. A senior project is required. Education students must take the Michigan Test for Teacher Certification.

Special: Internships are available in most academic majors. Cross-registration is available with Eastern Michigan and Kettering Universities, and Walsh and Schoolcraft Colleges. Students may study abroad in 6 countries. Accelerated degree programs are available in business administration and criminal justice administration. The college confers credit for life, military, and work experience through the School of Adult and Continuing Education. Nondegree study, dual majors in many combinations, student-designed majors, a 3-2 engineering degree with Kettering University, and a pass/fail grading option are available.

Faculty/Classroom: 48% of faculty are male; 52%, female. All teach undergraduates. No introductory courses are taught by graduate students. The average class size in an introductory lecture is 20; in a laboratory, 13; and in a regular course, 14.

Admissions: 82% of the 2005-2006 applicants were accepted. The SAT scores for the 2005-2006 freshman class were: Verbal--38% below 500, 25% between 500 and 599, 33% between 600 and 700, and 4% above 700; Math--21% below 500, 38% between 500 and 599, 33% between 600 and 700, and 8% above 700. The ACT scores were 37% below 21, 24% between 21 and 23, 20% between 24 and 26, 9% between 27 and 28, and 10% above 28.

Requirements: The SAT or ACT is required, the ACT is preferred. Applicants must graduate from an accredited secondary school or have the GED. 20 Carnegie units are recommended, including 4 units in English, 3 each in math, and 2 each in science, social studies, and foreign language. AP and CLEP credits are accepted. Important factors in the admissions decision are evidence of special talent, advanced placement or honor courses, and leadership record.

Procedure: Freshmen are admitted fall and spring. There is a deferred admissions plan and a rolling admissions plan. Application deadlines are open. The fall 2005 application fee was $25. Notification is sent on a rolling basis. Applications are accepted on-line.

Transfer: 76 transfer students enrolled in 2004-2005. A GPA of 2.0 is required for transfer students; a GPA of 2.5 is required for admittance to the teacher education program. Transfer students who have earned 12 or more credits are not required to take the ACT. Interviews are recommended. 30 of 128 credits required for the bachelor's degree must be completed at Concordia.

Visiting: There are regularly scheduled orientations for prospective students, including 3 Discover Concordia days, Teacher Education Information Day, Senior Day, Junior Day, Art Day, Music Day, and Theatre Day. Individual tours are arranged by appointment. There are guides for informal visits and visitors may sit in on classes and stay overnight. To schedule a visit, contact the Admissions Office at (734) 995-7322 or *admissions@cuaa.edu.*

Financial Aid: In 2005-2006, 99% of all full-time students received some form of financial aid. 80% of full-time freshmen and 83% of continuing full-time students received need-based aid. The average freshman award was $16,979. Need-based scholarships or need-based grants averaged $3859 ($16,400 maximum); need-based self-help aid (loans and jobs) averaged $4397 ($8175 maximum); non-need-based athletic scholarships averaged $2519 ($18,035 maximum); and other non-need-based awards and non-need-based scholarships averaged $6204 ($19,365 maximum). 42% of undergraduates work part time. Average annual earnings from campus work are $845. The average financial indebtedness of the 2005 graduate was $23,567. The FAFSA and the college's own financial statement are required. The deadline for filing freshman financial aid applications for fall entry is March 1.

International Students: There are 7 international students enrolled. Satisfactory scores are required on the written TOEFL, the MELAB, and the SAT or the ACT.

Computers: Wireless access is available. Every student living on campus has access to the University's network. Virus protection and firewall protection are required. Access is from the dorm room, library, or computer lab. All students may access the system 8 A.M. to midnight, with 24-hour access from dorm rooms. There are no time limits and no fees. It is strongly recommended that all students have a personal computer.

Graduates: From July 1, 2004 to June 30, 2005, 86 bachelor's degrees were awarded. The most popular majors were teacher education (26%), business (14%), and criminal justice (13%). In an average class, 1% graduate in 3 years or less, 18% graduate in 4 years or less, 34% graduate in 5 years or less, and 36% graduate in 6 years or less.

Admissions Contact: Gary Neuman, Director of Admissions. A video is available. E-mail: *neumag@cuaa.edu* Web: *www.cuaa.edu*

CORNERSTONE UNIVERSITY AND GRAND RAPIDS THEOLOGICAL SEMINARY   D-4

Grand Rapids, MI 49525

(616) 222-1426
(800) 787-9778; Fax: (616) 222-1418

Full-time: 808 men, 752 women	**Faculty:** 65; IIB, --$
Part-time: 243 men, 374 women	**Ph.D.s:** 60%
Graduate: 218 men, 165 women	**Student/Faculty:** 24 to 1
Year: semesters, summer session	**Tuition:** $15,550
Application Deadline: open	**Room & Board:** $5800
Freshman Class: 840 applied, 815 accepted, 339 enrolled	
ACT: 23	**NONCOMPETITIVE**

Cornerstone University and Grand RapidsTheological Seminary, founded in 1941, is a private liberal arts college and graduate seminary educating students from a Christian perspective. Major undergraduate programs include business, teacher education, music, and ministry. In addition to regional accreditation, Cornerstone has baccalaureate program accreditation with NASM and ATS. The library contains 152,951 volumes, 288,342 microform items, and 4249 audio/video tapes/CDs/DVDs, and subscribes to 1329 periodicals including electronic. Computerized library services include the card catalog, interlibrary loans, database searching, Internet access, and laptop Internet portals. Special learning facilities include a learning resource center, radio station, and the Center for Guitar/Center for Antiquities. The 132-acre campus is in a suburban area on the northeast side of Grand Rapids. Including any residence halls, there are 25 buildings.

Student Life: 88% of undergraduates are from Michigan. Others are from 34 states, 10 foreign countries, and Canada. 62% are from public schools. 76% are white; 18% African American. Most are Protestant. The average age of freshmen is 18; all undergraduates, 22. 22% do not continue beyond their first year; 47% remain to graduate.

Housing: 852 students can be accommodated in college housing, which includes single-sex dorms, on-campus apartments, and married-student housing. In addition, there are honors houses. On-campus housing is guaranteed for all 4 years. 54% of students live on campus; of those, 50% remain on campus on weekends. Alcohol is not permitted. All students may keep cars.

Activities: There are no fraternities or sororities. There are 22 groups on campus, including band, cheerleading, choir, chorale, chorus, dance, drama, ethnic, film, honors, international, jazz band, musical theater, newspaper, orchestra, pep band, photography, political, professional, religious, social, social service, student government, symphony, and yearbook. Popular campus events include Sibling Weekends, Friends Weekend, and Variety Show.

Sports: There are 6 intercollegiate sports for men and 7 for women, and 4 intramural sports for men and 4 for women. Facilities include a 2700-seat basketball/volleyball arena, a field house servicing tennis, volleyball, basketball, soccer, and softball, a baseball diamond, 2 soccer fields/intramural fields, a softball field, a sand volleyball court, a fitness center, human performance labs, 6 locker rooms, a training room, and racquetball courts.

Disabled Students: All of the campus is accessible. Wheelchair ramps, elevators, special parking, specially equipped rest rooms, special class scheduling, special housing, large computer monitors for the visually impaired, and soundproof rooms for using tape recorders that read books-on-tape are available.

Services: Counseling and information services are available, as is tutoring in every subject. There is a Learning Center with a computer lab and special adaptive software that specialize in writing and math, tutoring by appointment in the residence halls, test-taking assistance, and readers and typists as needed. There is a reader service for the blind and remedial math and writing.

Campus Safety and Security: Measures include 24-hour foot and vehicle patrol, self-defense education, security escort services, and informal discussions. There are pamphlets/posters/films, emergency telephones, and lighted pathways/sidewalks.

Programs of Study: Cornerstone confers B.A., B.S., and B.Mus. degrees. Associate and master's degrees are also awarded. Bachelor's degrees are awarded in BIOLOGICAL SCIENCE (biology/biological science), BUSINESS (accounting, business administration and management, international business management, and marketing/retailing/merchandising), COMMUNICATIONS AND THE ARTS (communications, English, fine arts, music, music performance, music theory and composition, and speech/debate/rhetoric), COMPUTER AND PHYSICAL SCIENCE (computer science), EDUCATION (elementary, middle school, music, physical, science, and secondary), HEALTH PROFESSIONS (predentistry, premedicine, and preveterinary science), SOCIAL SCIENCE (biblical languages, biblical studies, family/consumer studies, history, interdisciplinary studies, philosophy, political science/government, prelaw, psychology, religion, religious education, social work, sociology, and youth ministry). English, music, and education are the strongest academically. Education, business, and youth ministry are the largest.

Required: To graduate, the student must complete 120 to 129 credit hours depending on degree, including 58 in the liberal arts core consisting of the humanities, math, social sciences, science, Bible/religion, foreign language, and phys ed. Specific courses include 2 phys ed courses, freshman rhetoric, biology, math, psychology or sociology, world civilization, fine arts, philosophy, Old Testament, and inductive Bible study. The number of hours in the major varies. The student must have an overall GPA of 2.0, 2.5 in the major, 2.0 in the minor, and pass a comprehensive exam, in most majors, exceot Bible and communication.

Special: All students choose a student-ministries assignment each semester. Cornerstone requires internships in all areas of study. Study abroad in 8 countries, a co-op program in political science, cross-registration with Calvin College, accelerated degrees in organizational leadership, management, business administration, ministry leadership, and education, a Washington semester, and an interdisciplinary major in missionary aviation, are available. There is 1 national honor society, and a freshman honors program.

Faculty/Classroom: 73% of faculty are male; 27%, female. All teach undergraduates, 50% do research, and 50% do both. The average class size in an introductory lecture is 75; in a laboratory, 30; and in a regular course, 21.

Admissions: 97% of the 2005-2006 applicants were accepted. 34% of the current freshmen were in the top fifth of their class; 56% were in the top two fifths. There were 2 National Merit semifinalists. 17 freshmen graduated first in their class.

Requirements: The ACT is required. The ACT Optional Writing test is also required. The university requires a high school transcript or GED certificate, and recommends 15 Carnegie units, including 4 years of English, 3 each of math and social sciences, 2 of science, as well as 10 semesters of electives. The university recommends that the student appear for an interview, and requires auditions for music scholarships. A pastoral reference is required. A GPA of 2.5 is required. AP and CLEP credits are accepted. Important factors in the admissions decision are personality/intangible qualities, extracurricular activities record, and leadership record.

Procedure: Freshmen are admitted to all sessions. Entrance exams should be taken during the junior or senior year. There is a deferred admissions plan. Application deadlines are open. Application fee is $25. Applications are accepted on-line.

Transfer: 104 transfer students enrolled in 2004-2005. The college requires high school and college transcripts from students, as well as a pastor's reference. The applicant must have taken the ACT if under 25 years of age with fewer than 30 hours of college credit. 32 of 120 to 129 credits required for the bachelor's degree must be completed at Cornerstone.

Visiting: There are regularly scheduled orientations for prospective students, including admissions and financial aid presentations, class visits, and course preregistration. There are guides for informal visits and visitors may sit in on classes and stay overnight. To schedule a visit, contact the Admissions Office at admissions@cornerstone.edu.

Financial Aid: In 2005-2006, 98% of all full-time freshmen and 97% of continuing full-time students received some form of financial aid. 78% of full-time freshmen and 76% of continuing full-time students received need-based aid. The average freshman award was $12,763. Need-based scholarships or need-based grants averaged $7562 ($20,646 maximum); need-based self-help aid (loans and jobs) averaged $6106 ($19,169 maximum); non-need-based athletic scholarships averaged $4115 ($14,369 maximum); and other non-need-based awards and non-need-based scholarships averaged $4376 ($17,977 maximum). 34% of undergraduates work part time. Average annual earnings from campus work are $938. The average financial indebtedness of the 2005 graduate was $19,173. The FAFSA is required. The priority date for freshman financial aid applications for fall entry is February 20.

International Students: There are 25 international students enrolled. They must take the TOEFL and also take the SAT or the ACT.

Computers: Wireless access is available. All students may access the system year-round; 24 hours a day. There are no time limits and no fees. All students are required to have personal computers. All traditional undergrads are in the laptop program. The school chooses a new model each year.

Graduates: From July 1, 2004 to June 30, 2005, 333 bachelor's degrees were awarded. The most popular majors were business (39%), ed-

ucation (26%), and psychology (6%). In an average class, 1% graduate in 3 years or less, 26% graduate in 4 years or less, 35% graduate in 5 years or less, and 39% graduate in 6 years or less. 10 companies recruited on campus in 2004-2005.

Admissions Contact: Brent Rudin, Associate Dean of Marketing and Admissions. A video is available. E-mail: admissions@cornerstone.edu Web: www.cornerstone.edu

DAVENPORT UNIVERSITY   D-4
Grand Rapids, MI 49503

(616) 698-7111
(866) 925-3884; Fax: (616) 698-0333

Full-time: 1020 men, 2083 women	**Faculty:** 110
Part-time: 1924 men, 7035 women	**Ph.D.s:** 24%
Graduate: 274 men, 482 women	**Student/Faculty:** 28 to 1
Year: semesters, summer session	**Tuition:** $8905
Application Deadline: September	**Room & Board:** $6300
Freshman Class: 3283 applied, 3283 accepted, 1754 enrolled	
ACT: n/av	**NONCOMPETITIVE**

Davenport University, founded in 1866, is a private, independent institution specializing in business education. It serves 13,500 students at 24 campuses throughout Michigan and northern Indiana. Davenport offers business-focused degrees.The university also offers online courses. There are 4 undergraduate schools and 1 graduate school. In addition to regional accreditation, Davenport has baccalaureate program accreditation with CAAHEP. The library contains 127,424 volumes, 346 microform items, and 13,695 audio/video tapes/CDs/DVDs, and subscribes to 1914 periodicals including electronic. Computerized library services include interlibrary loans, database searching, and Internet access. Special learning facilities include a learning resource center. The 43-acre campus is in an urban area in Grand Rapids. Including any residence halls, there are 2 buildings.

Student Life: 92% of undergraduates are from Michigan. Others are from 11 states, 29 foreign countries, and Canada. 97% are from public schools. 58% are white; 23% African American. The average age of freshmen is 29; all undergraduates, 31.

Housing: 75 students can be accommodated in college housing, which includes coed dorms and on-campus apartments. On-campus housing is guaranteed for all 4 years. Alcohol is not permitted. All students may keep cars.

Activities: There are no fraternities or sororities. There are 4 groups on campus, including ethnic, professional, religious, and student government. Popular campus events include Diversity Book Club.

Sports: There are 4 intercollegiate sports for men and 3 for women.

Disabled Students: All of the campus is accessible. Wheelchair ramps, elevators, special parking, specially equipped rest rooms, special class scheduling, lowered drinking fountains, and lowered telephones are available.

Services: Counseling and information services are available, as is tutoring in most subjects. There are tutoring labs for math, English, and computers, and a learning assistance center. There is remedial math, reading, and writing.

Campus Safety and Security: Measures include security escort services, emergency telephones, lighted pathways/sidewalks, and and 24-hour foot patrols.

Programs of Study: Davenport confers B.S., B.A.S., and B.B.A. degrees. Associate and master's degrees are also awarded. Bachelor's degrees are awarded in BUSINESS (accounting, banking and finance, electronic business, entrepreneurial studies, human resources, international business management, management science, and marketing management), COMMUNICATIONS AND THE ARTS (advertising), COMPUTER AND PHYSICAL SCIENCE (information sciences and systems and web technology), HEALTH PROFESSIONS (medical records administration/services and nursing), SOCIAL SCIENCE (paralegal studies). Business is the strongest academically. Accounting and management are the largest.

Required: Davenport requires all students to complete 120 credit hours, 37 in the major, with a minimum GPA of 2.0 overall and in career courses. The general education core consists of 42 credits, and the business core of 26 credits. At least 18 credits must be completed on campus in the classroom.

Special: Davenport offers co-op programs in administrative services, sales and marketing, and paralegal studies. There are internships in most disciplines. Study abroad is available through C.I.E.E. and A.I.F.S.

Faculty/Classroom: 46% of faculty are male; 54%, female. 99% teach undergraduates. The average class size in an introductory lecture is 13 and in a regular course, 13.

Admissions: 100% of the 2005-2006 applicants were accepted.

Requirements: In addition, graduation from an accredited secondary school or a GED is accepted. An interview is recommended. CLEP credit is accepted. Important factors in the admissions decision are ability to finance college education, recommendations by school officials, and personality/intangible qualities.

Procedure: Freshmen are admitted to all sessions. Entrance exams should be taken . There are early decision and rolling admissions plans. Early decision applications should be filed by August; regular applications, by September for fall entry, January for winter entry, March for spring entry, and June for summer entry, along with a $25 fee. The college accepts all applicants. Notification is sent on a rolling basis. Applications are accepted on-line.

Transfer: 1240 transfer students enrolled in 2004-2005. C is the minimum grade accepted for transfer. There is a 75% maximum credit transfer for the bachelor's degree. 30 of 120 credits required for the bachelor's degree must be completed at Davenport.

Visiting: There are regularly scheduled orientations for prospective students, consisting of an appointment, set up in advance. There are guides for informal visits and visitors may sit in on classes and stay overnight. To schedule a visit, contact Admissions at gr_admiss@davenport.edu.

Financial Aid: The FAFSA is required.

International Students: There are 177 international students enrolled. The school actively recruits these students. A satisfactory score is required on the written TOEFL. Applicants must and also take the Comprehensive English Language Test or the college's own test.

Computers: Wireless access is available. All students may access the system 8 A.M. to midnight on weekdays, and noon to 6 P.M. on weekends. There are no time limits and no fees.

Graduates: From July 1, 2004 to June 30, 2005, 1262 bachelor's degrees were awarded. The most popular majors were management (23%), information management (13%), and applied business (7%).

Admissions Contact: Mailbox, Admissions.
E-mail: Gradmiss@davenport.edu Web: www.davenport.edu

EASTERN MICHIGAN UNIVERSITY   E-5
Ypsilanti, MI 48197

	(734) 487-0193
	(800) GO TO EMU; Fax: (734) 487-1484
Full-time: 5152 men, 7846 women	**Faculty:** 740; IIA, av$
Part-time: 2297 men, 3283 women	**Ph.D.s:** 82%
Graduate: 1605 men, 3057 women	**Student/Faculty:** 18 to 1
Year: semesters, summer session	**Tuition:** $6541 ($17,896)
Application Deadline: July 31	**Room & Board:** $6356
Freshman Class: 10,151 applied, 8041 accepted, 2386 enrolled	
SAT Verbal/Math: 520/510*	**ACT:** 21 **COMPETITIVE**

Eastern Michigan University, founded in 1849, is a public institution offering programs in arts and sciences, business, education, health and human services, and technology. There are 5 undergraduate schools and 1 graduate school. In addition to regional accreditation, EMU has baccalaureate program accreditation with AACN, AACSB, ABET, ACCE, ACS, ADA, AHEA, AOTA, ASLA, ASLHA, CACREP, CAHEA, CED, CSWE, FIDER, NAACLS, NASM, NCATE, NLN, and NRPA. The library contains 939,660 volumes, 984,301 microform items, and 14,023 audio/video tapes/CDs/DVDs, and subscribes to 4000 periodicals including electronic. Computerized library services include the card catalog, interlibrary loans, and database searching. Special learning facilities include a learning resource center, art gallery, and radio station. The 460-acre campus is in a suburban area 8 miles east of Ann Arbor. Including any residence halls, there are 112 buildings.

Student Life: 93% of undergraduates are from Michigan. Others are from 46 states, 58 foreign countries, and Canada. 90% are from public schools. 74% are white; 19% African American. The average age of freshmen is 18; all undergraduates, 24. 25% do not continue beyond their first year; 41% remain to graduate.

Housing: 3308 students can be accommodated in college housing, which includes single-sex and coed dormitories, on-campus apartments, married-student housing, and sorority houses. In addition, there are honors houses, special-interest houses, special housing known as Community of scholars, upper-class halls, and a first-year center. On-campus housing is available on a first-come, first-served basis and is available on a lottery system for upperclassmen. 83% of students commute. All students may keep cars.

Activities: 4% of men belong to 2 local and 13 national fraternities; 4% of women belong to 1 local and 14 national sororities. There are 190 groups on campus, including art, band, cheerleading, chess, choir, chorale, chorus, computers, dance, debate, drama, drill team, ethnic, film, forensics, gay, honors, international, jazz band, literary magazine, marching band, musical theater, opera, orchestra, pep band, photography, political, professional, radio and TV, religious, social, social service, student government, and symphony. Popular campus events include Martin Luther King Birthday Celebration and Family Weekend.

Sports: There are 9 intercollegiate sports for men and 12 for women, and 25 intramural sports for men and 25 for women. Facilities include a 30,000-seat stadium, outdoor playing fields, a field house, a student recreation and intramural center, and an outdoor park including a lake, amphitheater, lighted basketball courts, volleyball courts, and lake house. There are 2 pools, a whirlpool/sauna, softball and soccer fields, 4 weight rooms, an aerobic studio, and a pro shop.

Disabled Students: 93% of the campus is accessible. Wheelchair ramps, elevators, special parking, specially equipped rest rooms, special class scheduling, lowered drinking fountains, lowered telephones, and special housing are available.

Services: Counseling and information services are available, as is tutoring in every subject. There is a reader service for the blind, and remedial math, reading, and writing. Notetakers and interpreters are provided for the handicapped.

Campus Safety and Security: Measures include 24-hour foot and vehicle patrol, self-defense education, security escort services, and shuttle buses. There are informal discussions, pamphlets/posters/films, emergency telephones, lighted pathways/sidewalks, bicycle patrols, a crime prevention officer, area police officers in dorms, an anonymous tip line, Operation Identification, vehicle glass etching, a bike lock lease program, and surveillance cameras.

Programs of Study: EMU confers B.A., B.S., B.A.E., B.A. in Language and World Business, B.B.A., B.B.E., B.F.A., B.M.E., B.M.T., B.M.U., and B.S.N. degrees. Master's and doctoral degrees are also awarded. Bachelor's degrees are awarded in AGRICULTURE (forestry and related sciences), BIOLOGICAL SCIENCE (biochemistry, biology/biological science, botany, microbiology, and zoology), BUSINESS (accounting, banking and finance, business administration and management, business data processing, business economics, business systems analysis, fashion merchandising, hospitality management services, insurance and risk management, international business management, labor studies, management information systems, management science, marketing/retailing/merchandising, office supervision and management, personnel management, real estate, recreation and leisure services, secretarial studies/office management, and tourism), COMMUNICATIONS AND THE ARTS (advertising, American literature, applied music, art, arts administration/management, classical languages, communications, communications technology, dance, design, dramatic arts, English, English as a second/foreign language, English literature, film arts, fine arts, French, German, graphic design, historic preservation, Japanese, journalism, linguistics, literature, music, music performance, performing arts, piano/organ, Spanish, speech/debate/rhetoric, and telecommunications), COMPUTER AND PHYSICAL SCIENCE (actuarial science, applied mathematics, astronomy, chemistry, computer programming, computer science, earth science, geology, information sciences and systems, mathematics, physics, polymer science, and statistics), EDUCATION (art, bilingual/bicultural, business, computer, drama, early childhood, education, education of the deaf and hearing impaired, education of the emotionally handicapped, education of the mentally handicapped, education of the multiply handicapped, education of the physically handicapped, education of the visually handicapped, educational media, elementary, English, foreign languages, health, industrial arts, mathematics, middle school, music, physical, psychology, reading, school psychology, science, secondary, social foundations, social science, special, and teaching English as a second/foreign language (TESOL/TEFOL)), ENGINEERING AND ENVIRONMENTAL DESIGN (aviation administration/management, city/community/regional planning, computer graphics, computer technology, construction management, interior design, land use management and reclamation, manufacturing technology, military science, plastics technology, preengineering, and urban planning technology), HEALTH PROFESSIONS (allied health, health care administration, medical laboratory technology, music therapy, nursing, occupational therapy, predentistry, premedicine, preoptometry, prepharmacy, recreation therapy, speech pathology/audiology, and sports medicine), SOCIAL SCIENCE (African American studies, anthropology, area studies, clothing and textiles management/production/services, counseling/psychology, criminal justice, dietetics, economics, family/consumer studies, geography, gerontology, history, interdisciplinary studies, international relations, liberal arts/general studies, paralegal studies, parks and recreation management, philosophy, political science/government, prelaw, psychology, public administration, social science, social work, sociology, and women's studies). Education, business, and health/nursing are the strongest academically. Elementary education, arts/sciences, and business are the largest.

Required: To graduate, students must have a GPA of 2.0, and complete a minimum of 124 semester hours, including usually 30 in the major, and 40 or more of basic studies. Required courses include English composition, political science, computer literacy, and phys ed.

Special: EMU offers internships, work-study programs, a Washington semester in public administration, and co-op programs and cross-registration with the University of Michigan at Ann Arbor, Concordia College, and Washtenaw Community College. Students may study abroad in more than 23 countries. EMU allows dual majors, nondegree study, B.A.-B.S. degrees in all majors and student-designed majors, accelerated degree programs, and confers a general studies degree, as well as a B.A.-B.BBA. degree in language and world business. Students may receive credit for life, military, and work experience, and pass/fail options are open. There are 9 national honor societies, a freshman honors program, and 36 departmental honors programs.

Faculty/Classroom: 52% of faculty are male; 48%, female. 70% teach undergraduates. Graduate students teach 2% of introductory courses. The average class size in a laboratory is 15 and in a regular course, 27.

Admissions: 79% of the 2005-2006 applicants were accepted. The SAT scores for the 2005-2006 freshman class were: Verbal--39% below 500, 43% between 500 and 599, 16% between 600 and 700, and 2% above 700; Math--41% below 500, 41% between 500 and 599, 15% between 600 and 700, and 3% above 700. The ACT scores were 49% below 21, 24% between 21 and 23, 17% between 24 and 26, 5% between 27 and 28, and 4% above 28.

Requirements: The SAT or ACT is required. Applicants should be high school graduates or hold a GED. The university recommends that students complete 19 academic credits in high school, consisting of 4 in English, 3 each in math, science, and social studies, 2 each in foreign language and history, and 2 to 3 in other traditional college-preparatory courses. A portfolio is required for applicants to the art program, and an audition is required for music students. A GPA of 2.0 is required. AP and CLEP credits are accepted.

Procedure: Freshmen are admitted to all sessions. Entrance exams should be taken by November of the senior year of high school. There are early admissions and rolling admissions plans. Applications should be filed by July 31 for fall entry, December 9 for winter entry, April 15 for spring entry, and June 6 for summer entry. Notification is sent on a rolling basis. Applications are accepted on-line. The fall 2005 application fee was $20.

Transfer: 1771 transfer students enrolled in 2004-2005. Transfer students must have at least 12 semester hours of college credit, with a GPA of 2.0. 30 of 124 credits required for the bachelor's degree must be completed at EMU.

Visiting: There are regularly scheduled orientations for prospective students, including tours scheduled every morning and afternoon, as well as Saturday morning, with trained student tour guides. There are guides for informal visits and visitors may sit in on classes and stay overnight. To schedule a visit, contact the admissions On-Campus Programs at (734) 487-1111.

Financial Aid: In 2005-2006, 87% of all full-time freshmen and 47% of continuing full-time students received some form of financial aid. 47% of full-time freshmen received need-based aid. The average freshman award was $8558. Need-based scholarships or need-based grants averaged $3430 ($13,825 maximum); need-based self-help aid (loans and jobs) averaged $3290 ($9080 maximum); non-need-based athletic scholarships averaged $10,608 ($27,460 maximum); and other non-need-based awards and non-need-based scholarships averaged $2824 ($15,507 maximum). 16% of undergraduates work part time. Average annual earnings from campus work are $3400. The average financial indebtedness of the 2005 graduate was $21,397. EMU is a member of CSS. The FAFSA is required. The deadline for filing freshman financial aid applications for fall entry is December 21.

International Students: There are 199 international students enrolled. The school actively recruits these students. They must score satisfactorily on the written TOEFL or on the electronic version. The IELTS is also required.

Computers: All students may access the system at all times. Dial-in access is limited to 1 to 2 hours per session if using a modem. On campus there is no limit. There is network connection.

Graduates: From July 1, 2004 to June 30, 2005, 2923 bachelor's degrees were awarded. The most popular majors were elementary education (9%), psychology (5%), and communications (5%). In an average class, 11% graduate in 4 years or less, 29% graduate in 5 years or less, and 38% graduate in 6 years or less. 885 companies recruited on campus in 2004-2005. Of the 2004 graduating class, 14% were enrolled in graduate school within 6 months of graduation and 81% were employed.

Admissions Contact: Judy Benfield-Tatum, Director of Admissions. Web: *www.emich.edu/public/admissions/admissions.html*

FERRIS STATE UNIVERSITY D-4

Big Rapids, MI 49307

(231) 591-2100
(800) 433-7747; Fax: (231) 591-3944

Full-time: 4837 men, 3999 women	Faculty: 545; IIA, av$
Part-time: 1039 men, 1176 women	Ph.D.s: 51%
Graduate: none	Student/Faculty: 16 to 1
Year: semesters, summer session	Tuition: $6882 ($13,622)
Application Deadline: August 4	Room & Board: $6816
Freshman Class: 12,877 applied, 6021 accepted, 2417 enrolled	
ACT: 21	COMPETITIVE

Ferris State University, established in 1884, is a public institution offering day and evening courses through its Schools of Arts and Sciences, Education, Allied Health, Technology, Business, and Pharmacy, College of Optometry, University College, and Kendall College of Art and Design. There are 9 undergraduate and 3 graduate schools. In addition to regional accreditation, Ferris State has baccalaureate program accreditation with ABET, ACPE, ADA, AHEA, CAHEA, CSWE, and NLN. The li-

brary contains 339,891 volumes, 3,630,677 microform items, and 4125 audio/video tapes/CDs/DVDs, and subscribes to 3294 periodicals including electronic. Computerized library services include the card catalog, interlibrary loans, database searching, Internet access, and laptop Internet portals. Special learning facilities include a learning resource center, art gallery, natural history museum, planetarium, and TV station. The 880-acre campus is in a small town 55 miles north of Grand Rapids. Including any residence halls, there are 98 buildings.

Student Life: 96% of undergraduates are from Michigan. Others are from 43 states, 55 foreign countries, and Canada. 79% are white. The average age of freshmen is 19; all undergraduates, 21. 30% do not continue beyond their first year.

Housing: 4333 students can be accommodated in college housing, which includes single-sex and coed dormitories, on-campus apartments, and married-student housing. In addition, there are honors houses. On-campus housing is guaranteed for all 4 years. 57% of students commute. All students may keep cars.

Activities: 6% of men belong to 30 national fraternities; 2% of women belong to 8 national sororities. There are 220 groups on campus, including art, band, cheerleading, chess, choir, chorale, chorus, computers, dance, drama, drill team, drum and bugle corps, ethnic, film, gay, honors, international, jazz band, literary magazine, newspaper, orchestra, pep band, photography, political, professional, radio and TV, religious, social, social service, student government, and symphony. Popular campus events include January Jams Concert, Ferris Fest, and Autumn a LIVE Concert.

Sports: There are 7 intercollegiate sports for men and 8 for women, and 21 intramural sports for men and 19 for women. Facilities include a golf course, a racquetball and fitness club, an ice arena, a 10,000-seat stadium, a student recreation center with a pool, and tennis courts.

Disabled Students: All of the campus is accessible. Wheelchair ramps, elevators, special parking, specially equipped rest rooms, special class scheduling, lowered drinking fountains, lowered telephones, and special housing are available.

Services: Counseling and information services are available, as is tutoring in most subjects. There is a reader service for the blind, and remedial math, reading, and writing.

Campus Safety and Security: Measures include 24-hour foot and vehicle patrol, self-defense education, security escort services, and informal discussions. There are pamphlets/posters/films, emergency telephones, and lighted pathways/sidewalks.

Programs of Study: Ferris State confers B.A., B.S., B.F.A., B.S.N., and B.S.W. degrees. Associate and master's degrees are also awarded. Bachelor's degrees are awarded in BIOLOGICAL SCIENCE (biology/ biological science), BUSINESS (accounting, banking and finance, business administration and management, hospitality management services, human resources, insurance, international business management, marketing/retailing/merchandising, and small business management), COMMUNICATIONS AND THE ARTS (advertising and public relations), COMPUTER AND PHYSICAL SCIENCE (applied mathematics and computer programming), EDUCATION (business, mathematics, and technical), ENGINEERING AND ENVIRONMENTAL DESIGN (construction management, engineering technology, plastics engineering, and surveying engineering), HEALTH PROFESSIONS (health care administration, nuclear medical technology, nursing, optometry, and pharmacy), SOCIAL SCIENCE (criminal justice and social work). Pharmacy and optometry are the strongest academically. Business administration and marketing are the largest.

Required: Degree requirements include a minimum 2.0 GPA, 12 semester credit hours in English and speech communications, 9 each in the humanities and social sciences, and 7 to 8 in natural sciences. The number of credits students must earn in the major and the total required for graduation vary by course of study. Other required courses include math and cultural enrichment.

Special: Ferris State offers co-op programs in automotive service technology with GM, Chrysler, and Ford, cross registration, an external degree, independent study, internships, study abroad, work-study programs, accelerated degrees, dual and student-designed majors, credit for life, military, and work experience, and a pass/fail grading option. There are 8 national honor societies and a freshman honors program.

Faculty/Classroom: 58% of faculty are male; 42%, female. All teach undergraduates. The average class size in an introductory lecture is 23; in a laboratory, 17; and in a regular course, 21.

Admissions: 47% of the 2005-2006 applicants were accepted. The ACT scores for the 2005-2006 freshman class were: 50% below 21, 25% between 21 and 23, 16% between 24 and 26, 5% between 27 and 28, and 3% above 28.

Requirements: The SAT or ACT is required. In addition, applicants must graduate from an accredited secondary school or earn a GED. 4 years each of English, science, (2 lab) and math, 3 years each of foreign language, and academic electives, and 2 years each of social studies and history are advised. Interviews are recommended. A GPA of 2.35 is required. AP and CLEP credits are accepted. Important factors in the admissions decision are personality/intangible qualities, recommendations by school officials, and extracurricular activities record.

Procedure: Freshmen are admitted to all sessions. Entrance exams should be taken before course registration. Applications should be filed by August 4 for fall entry. There is a rolling admissions plan. Notification is sent on a rolling basis. The fall 2005 application fee was $30.

Transfer: 1381 transfer students enrolled in 2004-2005. A GPA of at least 2.0 is required, as are college transcripts, and a statement of good standing from previously attended institutions. Some students may need to submit high school transcripts and test scores. 30 credits required for the bachelor's degree must be completed at Ferris State.

Visiting: There are regularly scheduled orientations for prospective students. There are guides for informal visits and visitors may sit in on classes and stay overnight. To schedule a visit, contact the Admissions Office.

Financial Aid: In 2005-2006, 64% of all full-time freshmen and 66% of continuing full-time students received some form of financial aid. Atleast 55% of full-time freshmen and atleast 58% of continuing full-time students received need-based aid. The average freshman award was $7100. Need-based scholarships or need-based grants averaged $3000; need-based self-help aid (loans and jobs) averaged $2400; non-need-based athletic scholarships averaged $4000; and other non-need-based awards and non-need-based institutional scholarships averaged $2000. 49% of undergraduates work part time. Average annual earnings from campus work are $1654. The average financial indebtedness of the 2005 graduate was $14,750. Ferris State is a member of CSS. The FAFSA is required. The priority date for freshman financial aid applications for fall entry is March 1. The deadline for filing freshman financial aid applications for fall entry is rolling.

International Students: In a recent year there were 274 international students enrolled. The school actively recruits these students. They must score satisfactorily on the written TOEFL and also take the SAT or ACT or a supplemental math exam, scoring 15.

Computers: All students may access the system at any time; labs are open 16 hours daily. Students may access the system 6 A.M. to 10 P.M. There are no fees.

Graduates: From July 1, 2004 to June 30, 2005, 1403 bachelor's degrees were awarded. The most popular majors were business/marketing (24%), engineering technologies (17%), and visual and performing arts (10%). In an average class, 9% graduate in 4 years or less, 31% graduate in 5 years or less, and 29% graduate in 6 years or less. 378 companies recruited on campus in a recent year.

Admissions Contact: Admissions Officer. A video is available.
E-mail: *admissions@ferris.edu*
Web: *www.ferris.edu/admissions/appprocess.htm*

GRACE BIBLE COLLEGE   D-4
Grand Rapids, MI 49509

	(616) 538-2330
	(800) 968-1887; Fax: (616) 538-2330
Full-time: 78 men, 72 women	**Faculty:** 8
Part-time: 6 men, 5 women	**Ph.D.s:** 22%
Graduate: none	**Student/Faculty:** 19 to 1
Year: semesters	**Tuition:** $10,950
Application Deadline: open	**Room & Board:** $6860
Freshman Class: 133 applied, 85 accepted, 33 enrolled	
SAT Verbal/Math: 584/534*	**ACT:** 20 COMPETITIVE

Grace Bible College, founded in 1939, is a private institution affiliated with the Grace Gospel Fellowship. Its mission is to provide a curriculum that integrates general education and biblical studies and prepares students for service in their career, church, and society. In addition to regional accreditation, GBC has baccalaureate program accreditation with AABC. The library contains 40,760 volumes and 2711 audio/video tapes/CDs/DVDs, and subscribes to 234 periodicals including electronic. Computerized library services include the card catalog, interlibrary loans, database searching, Internet access, and laptop Internet portals. Special learning facilities include a recording studio. The 21-acre campus is in a suburban area on the southwest side of Grand Rapids. Including any residence halls, there are 12 buildings.

Student Life: 70% of undergraduates are from Michigan. Others are from 14 states and 4 foreign countries. 93% are white. Most are Protestant. The average age of freshmen is 19; all undergraduates, 22. 39% do not continue beyond their first year; 50% remain to graduate.

Housing: 80 students can be accommodated in college housing, which includes single-sex dorms, on-campus apartments, off-campus apartments, and married-student housing. On-campus housing is guaranteed for all 4 years. 54% of students live on campus; of those, 60% remain on campus on weekends. Alcohol is not permitted. All students may keep cars.

Activities: There are no fraternities or sororities. There are some groups and organizations on campus, including cheerleading, choir, drama, jazz band, musical theater, religious, student government, and yearbook. Popular campus events include Opera Dinner Theater, Winter Formal, and Missions Conference.

Sports: There are 2 intercollegiate sports for men and 2 for women. Facilities include a 500-seat soccer field and an athletic center with a 500-seat gym for basketball and volleyball, a racquetball court, and an exercise and weight room.

Disabled Students: 85% of the campus is accessible. Wheelchair ramps, elevators, special parking, specially equipped rest rooms, and lowered drinking fountains are available.

Services: Counseling and information services are available, as is tutoring in most subjects. There is remedial writing.

Campus Safety and Security: Measures include informal discussions, pamphlets/posters/films, lighted pathways/sidewalks, and an evening and overnight foot patrol.

Programs of Study: GBC confers B.S., B.Mus., B.R.E., and B.Th. degrees. Associate degrees are also awarded. Bachelor's degrees are awarded in BUSINESS (business administration and management), COMMUNICATIONS AND THE ARTS (music), COMPUTER AND PHYSICAL SCIENCE (digital arts/technology), EDUCATION (elementary and secondary), SOCIAL SCIENCE (early childhood studies, human services, interdisciplinary studies, missions, pastoral studies, religion, religious education, and youth ministry). Elementary/secondary education, digital communication/media/multimedia, and human services are the largest.

Required: To graduate, students must complete 126 to 158 credits, depending on the major, with a minimum GPA of 2.0 and must be considered worthy in character and conduct by the faculty. Course work is required in arts and sciences, ministry studies, Bible/theology, math/computer science, lab science, and phys ed. Attendance is expected at worship services twice a week.

Special: Cross-registration is available with Cornerstone and Davenport Universities. GBC offers 6-month internships for theology majors.

Faculty/Classroom: 61% of faculty are male; 39%, female. All teach undergraduates. The average class size in an introductory lecture is 30 and in a regular course, 25.

Admissions: 64% of the 2005-2006 applicants were accepted. The SAT scores for the 2005-2006 freshman class were: Verbal--57% between 500 and 599, and 43% between 600 and 700; Math--29% below 500, 43% between 500 and 599, and 28% between 600 and 700. The ACT scores were 63% below 21, 21% between 21 and 23, 8% between 24 and 26, and 8% between 27 and 28. 19% of the current freshmen were in the top fifth of their class; 50% were in the top two fifths.

Requirements: The ACT is required. In addition, applicants must be graduates of accredited secondary schools or have earned a GED. The application must show involvement in Christian activities and personal salvation through Jesus Christ. GBC requires applicants to be in the upper 57% of their class. A GPA of 2.5 is required. AP and CLEP credits are accepted.

Procedure: Freshmen are admitted fall and spring. There is a rolling admissions plan. Application deadlines are open.

Transfer: 17 transfer students enrolled in 2004-2005. Applicants must present a GPA of 2.0 and be in good standing at their previous school. Those with fewer than 24 college credit hours must submit high school records. 63 of 126 credits required for the bachelor's degree must be completed at GBC.

Visiting: There are regularly scheduled orientations for prospective students, consisting of 7 Friday programs a year that include workshops, class visits, and campus tours. There are guides for informal visits and visitors may sit in on classes and stay overnight. To schedule a visit, contact Kevin Gilliam, Director of Enrollment.

Financial Aid: In 2005-2006, 93% of all full-time freshmen and 94% of continuing full-time students received some form of financial aid. 69% of full-time freshmen and 79% of continuing full-time students received need-based aid. The average freshman award was $5107. Need-based scholarships or need-based grants averaged $3175 ($5000 maximum); need-based self-help aid (loans and jobs) averaged $2625 ($2625 maximum); and other non-need-based awards and non-need-based scholarships averaged $686 ($1000 maximum). 68% of undergraduates work part time. Average annual earnings from campus work are $1578. The average financial indebtedness of the 2005 graduate was $14,081. The FAFSA is required. The priority date for freshman financial aid applications for fall entry is March 1.

International Students: There are 2 international students enrolled. They must score satisfactorily on the written TOEFL or on the electronic version.

Graduates: From July 1, 2004 to June 30, 2005, 40 bachelor's degrees were awarded. The most popular majors were liberal arts/biblical (74%), philosophy, religion, theology (13%), and visual performing arts (13%). In an average class, 33% graduate in 3 years or less, 14% graduate in 4 years or less, 38% graduate in 5 years or less, and 15% graduate in 6 years or less.

Admissions Contact: Kevin Gilliam, Director of Enrollment.
E-mail: *enrollment@gbcol.edu* Web: *www.gbcol.edu*

GRAND VALLEY STATE UNIVERSITY D-4
Allendale, MI 49401-9403 (616) 331-2025
(800) 331-0246; Fax: (616) 895-2000

Full-time: 6000 men, 9000 women	Faculty: 839; IIA, av$
Part-time: 1100 men, 1700 women	Ph.D.s: 80%
Graduate: 1200 men, 2400 women	Student/Faculty: 18 to 1
Year: semesters, summer session	Tuition: $6000 ($13,000)
Application Deadline: see profile	Room & Board: $6000
Freshman Class: n/av	
ACT: required	VERY COMPETITIVE

Grand Valley State University, founded in 1960, is a comprehensive public institution offering graduate and undergraduate liberal arts and professional education. There are 12 undergraduate and 9 graduate schools. Figures in the above capsule and in this profile are approximate. In addition to regional accreditation, Grand Valley has baccalaureate program accreditation with AACSB, ABET, APTA, CSWE, NASAD, NASM, NCATE, and NLN. The 2 libraries contain 672,000 volumes, 577,800 microform items, and 9800 audio/video tapes/CDs/DVDs, and subscribe to 3700 periodicals including electronic. Computerized library services include the card catalog, interlibrary loans, database searching, and Internet access. Special learning facilities include a learning resource center, art gallery, radio station, TV station, cadaver lab, 2 Great Lakes research vessels, a performance auditorium, and dance studios. The 900-acre campus is in a small town 12 miles west of Grand Rapids. Including any residence halls, there are 64 buildings.

Student Life: 96% of undergraduates are from Michigan. Others are from 43 states, 52 foreign countries, and Canada. 75% are from public schools. 88% are white. The average age of freshmen is 18; all undergraduates, 22. 22% do not continue beyond their first year; 48% remain to graduate.

Housing: 4832 students can be accommodated in college housing, which includes coed dorms, on-campus apartments, off-campus apartments, and married-student housing. In addition, there are honors houses, language houses, and special-interest houses. On-campus housing is guaranteed for the freshman year only, is available on a first-come, first-served basis, and is available on a lottery system for upperclassmen. Priority is given to out-of-town students. 71% of students commute. Alcohol is not permitted. All students may keep cars.

Activities: 3% of men belong to 2 local and 8 national fraternities; 3% of women belong to 2 local and 9 national sororities. There are 130 groups on campus, including art, band, cheerleading, chess, choir, chorale, chorus, computers, dance, drama, ethnic, film, gay, honors, international, jazz band, literary magazine, marching band, newspaper, orchestra, pep band, photography, political, professional, radio and TV, religious, social, social service, student government, and symphony. Popular campus events include Family Day, Hispanic Awareness Week, and Black History Month.

Sports: There are 9 intercollegiate sports for men and 10 for women, and 22 intramural sports for men and 21 for women. Facilities include a football stadium, a baseball field, a basketball arena, swimming and diving pools, an indoor track, a weight room, a fitness building/intramural center, and an outdoor cross-country track.

Disabled Students: 98% of the campus is accessible. Wheelchair ramps, elevators, special parking, specially equipped rest rooms, special class scheduling, lowered drinking fountains, and lowered telephones are available.

Services: Counseling and information services are available, as is tutoring in most subjects. There is a reader service for the blind, and remedial math, reading, and writing.

Campus Safety and Security: Measures include 24-hour foot and vehicle patrol, self-defense education, security escort services, and shuttle buses. There are informal discussions, pamphlets/posters/films, emergency telephones, and lighted pathways/sidewalks.

Programs of Study: Grand Valley confers B.A., B.S., B.B.A., B.F.A., B.M., B.M.E., B.S.E., B.S.N., and B.S.W. degrees. Master's degrees are also awarded. Bachelor's degrees are awarded in BIOLOGICAL SCIENCE (biology/biological science), BUSINESS (accounting, banking and finance, business administration and management, business economics, hotel/motel and restaurant management, international business management, management science, marketing/retailing/merchandising, and personnel management), COMMUNICATIONS AND THE ARTS (advertising, broadcasting, communications, design, dramatic arts, English, film arts, fine arts, journalism, languages, music, and photography), COMPUTER AND PHYSICAL SCIENCE (chemistry, computer science, geology, mathematics, and physics), EDUCATION (art, elementary, foreign languages, middle school, music, science, and secondary), ENGINEERING AND ENVIRONMENTAL DESIGN (engineering and industrial engineering technology), HEALTH PROFESSIONS (health science, medical laboratory technology, nursing, physical therapy, physician's assistant, predentistry, and premedicine), SOCIAL SCIENCE (anthropology, criminal justice, economics, geography, history, international relations, philosophy, political science/government, prelaw, psychology, public adminis-

tration, social science, social work, and sociology). Health sciences, English, and psychology are the largest.

Required: To graduate, students must have earned 30 credits in general education, comprised of 10 courses selected from specific groups, and have completed the university's required courses in English and math, as well as the upper-division writing course. A total of 120 credits, with 36 to 60 in the major and a GPA of 2.0, are required to graduate.

Special: Many programs offer dual majors and internships, and most majors qualify for B.A.-B.S. degrees. There is an engineering cooperative program, a student-designed major in liberal studies, and many work-study programs. Outside opportunities include study abroad in 10 countries and a Washington semester. There are 14 national honor societies, a freshman honors program, and 12 departmental honors programs.

Faculty/Classroom: 56% of faculty are male; 44%, female. 94% teach undergraduates. No introductory courses are taught by graduate students. The average class size in an introductory lecture is 47; in a laboratory, 18; and in a regular course, 27.

Admissions: 73% of recent applicants were accepted. The ACT scores for a recent freshman class were: 19% below 21, 34% between 21 and 23, 28% between 24 and 26, 10% between 27 and 28, and 9% above 28. 41% of recent freshmen were in the top fifth of their class; 74% were in the top two fifths. 10 freshmen graduated first in their class.

Requirements: Michigan residents must submit ACT test scores, non-residents either ACT or SAT scores. In addition, high school transcripts should indicate 4 years of English with 1 composition course, 2 of a foreign language, and 3 each of history, math (including 2 years of algebra), science, and social studies. Applicants who graduated from high school more than 3 years ago need not show test results. The GED is accepted. A GPA of 3.0 is required. AP and CLEP credits are accepted.

Procedure: Freshmen are admitted to all sessions. Entrance exams should be taken during the junior year. Check with the school for current application deadlines. The fall 2005 application fee was $30. Notification is sent on a rolling basis. A waiting list is an active part of the admissions procedure. Applications are accepted on-line.

Transfer: 1772 transfer students enrolled in a recent year. Transfer students must have a minimum of 30 college credits with a 2.0 GPA. 30 of 120 credits required for the bachelor's degree must be completed at Grand Valley.

Visiting: There are regularly scheduled orientations for prospective students, including registration activities. There are guides for informal visits and visitors may sit in on classes and stay overnight. To schedule a visit, contact the Admissions Office.

Financial Aid: In a recent year, 81% of all full-time freshmen and 69% of continuing full-time students received some form of financial aid. 54% of full-time freshmen and 51% of continuing full-time students received need-based aid. The average freshman award was $6614. Need-based scholarships or need-based grants averaged $2645 ($6725 maximum); need-based self-help aid (loans and jobs) averaged $2941 ($6825 maximum); non-need-based athletic scholarships averaged $120 ($10,521 maximum); and other non-need-based awards and non-need-based scholarships averaged $908 ($9200 maximum). 72% of undergraduates work part time. Average annual earnings from campus work are $1800. The average financial indebtedness of a recent graduate was $8928. Grand Valley is a member of CSS. The FAFSA is required. Check with the school for current deadlines.

International Students: There were 98 international students enrolled in a recent year. The school actively recruits these students. They must score satisfactorily on the written TOEFL or take the MELAB or the Comprehensive English Language Test.

Computers: All students may access the system. There are no time limits and no fees. It is strongly recommended that all students have a personal computer.

Graduates: In a recent year, 2024 bachelor's degrees were awarded. The most popular majors were business (20%), health sciences (18%), and psychology (10%). In an average class, 48% graduate in 6 years or less.

Admissions Contact: Jodi Chycinski, Director of Admissions. A video is available. E-mail: go2gvsu@gvsu.edu Web: www.gvsu.edu

HILLSDALE COLLEGE D-5
Hillsdale, MI 49242 (517) 607-2327; Fax: (517) 607-2223

Full-time: 618 men, 644 women	Faculty: 100
Part-time: 8 men, 34 women	Ph.D.s: 90%
Graduate: none	Student/Faculty: 13 to 1
Year: semesters, summer session	Tuition: $17,410
Application Deadline: February 15	Room & Board: $6750
Freshman Class: 1090 applied, 890 accepted, 355 enrolled	
SAT Verbal/Math: 660/620*	ACT: 27 HIGHLY COMPETITIVE

Hillsdale College, founded in 1844, is a private liberal arts college emphasizing classical liberal arts, preprofessional, business, education, science and humanities. The 3 libraries contain 35,000 volumes, 57,000 microform items, and 12,000 audio/video tapes/CDs/DVDs, and subscribe to 1600 periodicals including electronic. Computerized library services include the card catalog, interlibrary loans, database searching, and Internet access. Special learning facilities include a learning resource center and a media center, an early childhood education lab, an arboretum, a 3000-book economics library, and a rare books room. The 250-acre campus is in a small town 120 miles southwest of Detroit. Including any residence halls, there are 60 buildings.

Student Life: 51% of undergraduates are from out of state, mostly the Midwest. Students are from 47 states, 14 foreign countries, and Canada. 40% are from public schools. 96% are white. 47% claim no religious affiliation; 35% Protestant; 17% Catholic. The average age of freshmen is 18; all undergraduates, 20. 13% do not continue beyond their first year; 72% remain to graduate.

Housing: 1000 students can be accommodated in college housing, which includes single-sex dormitories, on-campus apartments, fraternity houses, and sorority houses. In addition, there are honors houses and special-interest houses. On-campus housing is guaranteed for all 4 years. 80% of students live on campus; of those, 85% remain on campus on weekends. Alcohol is not permitted. All students may keep cars.

Activities: 35% of men belong to 34 national fraternities; 45% of women belong to 34 national sororities. There are 60 groups on campus, including art, bagpipe band, cheerleading, choir, chorale, chorus, computers, dance, debate, drama, drill team, drum and bagpipe coprs, equestrian, ethnic, forensics, honors, international intrevarsity, jazz band, literary magazine, musical theater, newspaper, orchestra, pep band, photography, political, professional, religious, social, student government, yearbook and young life. Popular campus events include Parents Weekend, President's Ball, and Greek Week.

Sports: There are 6 intercollegiate sports for men and 7 for women, and 7 intramural sports for men and 7 for women. Facilities include an athletic complex with a prescription turf football field, a swimming pool, a 200-meter indoor track, a basketball arena, a weight room, an outdoor Olympic track, an exercise/physiology room, and volleyball, handball, racquetball, wallyball, and indoor tennis courts. The campus stadium seats 8000; the gym 2600.

Disabled Students: 85% of the campus is accessible. Wheelchair ramps, elevators, special parking, specially equipped rest rooms, and lowered drinking fountains are available.

Services: Counseling and information services are available, as is tutoring in every subject. A writing center on campus and a peer tutoring program are administered by current students.

Campus Safety and Security: Measures include 24-hour foot and vehicle patrol, informal discussions, pamphlets/posters/films, and emergency telephones. There are lighted pathways/sidewalks.

Programs of Study: Hillsdale confers B.A. and B.S. degrees. Bachelor's degrees are awarded in BIOLOGICAL SCIENCE (biology/biological science), BUSINESS (accounting, banking and finance, business administration and management, international business management, and marketing/retailing/merchandising), COMMUNICATIONS AND THE ARTS (classics, comparative literature, dramatic arts, English, fine arts, French, German, music, Spanish, and speech/debate/rhetoric), COMPUTER AND PHYSICAL SCIENCE (chemistry, mathematics, and physics), EDUCATION (art, early childhood, elementary, foreign languages, middle school, music, physical, science, and secondary), HEALTH PROFESSIONS (predentistry, premedicine, and preveterinary science), SOCIAL SCIENCE (American studies, Christian studies, economics, European studies, history, political science/government, prelaw, psychology, religion, social science, and sociology). History, economics, and biology are the strongest academically. Business, history, and English are the largest.

Required: To graduate, the student must complete 124 semester hours with a GPA of 2.0. Required courses include 1 year of English, 1 year of science, 1 semester of Western Heritage and 1 semester of American Heritage, 1 semester of political science, 15 hours of the humanities, 12 of the natural sciences and math, 12 of the social sciences, and 2 of phys ed. Students must also enroll in 2 seminars at the school's Center for Constructive Alternatives. 12 credit hours in a foreign language for a B.A. degree and 36 credit hours in math and science for a B.S. degree are also required.

Special: Special academic programs include the Washington Journalism Internship at the National Journalism Center and the Washington-Hillsdale Intern Program (WHIP), which places students in congressional or government offices. Students may study abroad in France, Germany, or Spain, and qualified students are chosen to attend Oxford University for a year. A business internship is offered in London at Regents College. The Thomas Professional Sales Intern program is also available. The college offers an accelerated degree; interdisciplinary majors, including political economy combining economics, history, and political science; 3-2 and 2-2 engineering degrees; and work-study programs at the city radio station WCSR and the city newspaper, the Hillsdale Daily News. There are 20 national honor societies, a freshman honors program, and all departments have honors programs.

Faculty/Classroom: 80% of faculty are male; 20%, female. All teach undergraduates and 1% both teach and do research. The average class size in an introductory lecture is 24; in a laboratory, 7; and in a regular course, 21.

Admissions: 82% of the 2005-2006 applicants were accepted. The ACT scores for the 2005-2006 freshman class were: 4% below 21, 15% between 21 and 23, 28% between 24 and 26, 20% between 27 and 28, and 32% above 28. 75% of the current freshmen were in the top fifth of their class; 92% were in the top two fifths. There were 12 National Merit finalists and 72 semifinalists. 32 freshmen graduated first in their class.

Requirements: The SAT or ACT is required. In addition, the student must be a high school graduate or have earned a GED, and must have completed 4 years of English, 3 each of math and science, and 2 each of history, social studies, and foreign language. The college requires a letter of recommendation and an essay. An interview is also recommended. For music majors, an audition is required. The school recommends taking SAT: Subject tests. Hillsdale requires applicants to be in the upper 50% of their class. A GPA of 3.1 is required. AP and CLEP credits are accepted. Important factors in the admissions decision are advanced placement or honor courses, leadership record, and extracurricular activities record.

Procedure: Freshmen are admitted fall, spring, and summer. Entrance exams should be taken in the spring of the junior year and/or the fall of the senior year. There is a deferred admissions plan. Early decision applications should be filed by November 15; regular applications, by February 15 for fall entry, December 15 for spring entry, and May 1 for summer entry, along with a $35 fee. Notification of early decision is sent November 15; regular decision, April 1. Applications are accepted online.

Transfer: 33 transfer students enrolled in 2004-2005. Transfer students must have a GPA of 3.0, and have a transfer evaluation form completed by the dean of students of their school. Hillsdale also requires high school and college transcripts. 24 of 124 credits required for the bachelor's degree must be completed at Hillsdale.

Visiting: There are regularly scheduled orientations for prospective students, including a spring orientation and a formal junior and senior visitation program. There are guides for informal visits and visitors may sit in on classes and stay overnight. To schedule a visit, contact Margaret Bramany at the Admissions Office at (517) 607-2327.

Financial Aid: In 2005-2006, 84% of all full-time freshmen and 87% of continuing full-time students received some form of financial aid. 77% of full-time freshmen and 85% of continuing full-time students received need-based aid. The average freshman award was $11,500. 65% of undergraduates work part time. Average annual earnings from campus work are $1300. The average financial indebtedness of the 2005 graduate was $15,000. Hillsdale is a member of CSS. The CSS/Profile or FAFSA and the college's own financial statement are required. The priority date for freshman financial aid applications for fall entry is February 1. The deadline for filing freshman financial aid applications for fall entry is April 1.

International Students: There are 24 international students enrolled. The school actively recruits these students. They must score satisfactorily on the written TOEFL or on the electronic version. Applicants can also complete ESL level 108, with a minimum score of 15 in the motivational and proficiency categories.

Computers: Wireless access is available. All students may access the system at any time. There are no time limits and no fees.

Graduates: From July 1, 2004 to June 30, 2005, 243 bachelor's degrees were awarded. The most popular majors were business (24%), biology (14%), and history (13%). In an average class, 1% graduate in 3 years or less, 68% graduate in 4 years or less, 71% graduate in 5 years or less, and 72% graduate in 6 years or less. 50 companies recruited on campus in 2004-2005. Of the 2004 graduating class, 25% were enrolled in graduate school within 6 months of graduation and 74% were employed.

Admissions Contact: Jeffrey S. Lantis, Director of Admissions. A video is available. E-mail: *jeff.lantis@hillsdale.edu* Web: *www.hillsdale.edu*

HOPE COLLEGE   C-4
Holland, MI 49423

(616) 395-7850
(800) 968-7850; Fax: (616) 395-7130

Full-time: 1174 men, 1855 women	**Faculty:** 215; IIB, av$
Part-time: 49 men, 63 women	**Ph.D.s:** 77%
Graduate: none	**Student/Faculty:** 14 to 1
Year: semesters, summer session	**Tuition:** $21,540
Application Deadline: open	**Room & Board:** $6668

Freshman Class: 2328 applied, 2071 accepted, 760 enrolled
SAT Verbal/Math: 614/618*   **ACT:** 26   **VERY COMPETITIVE+**

Hope College, founded by Dutch pioneers in 1866, is a private liberal arts institution affiliated with the Reformed Church in America. In addition to regional accreditation, Hope has baccalaureate program accreditation with ABET, ACS, CSWE, NASAD, NASM, NCATE, and NLN. The 2 libraries contain 361,632 volumes, 389,996 microform items, and

11,955 audio/video tapes/CDs/DVDs, and subscribe to 8500 periodicals including electronic. Computerized library services include the card catalog, interlibrary loans, database searching, Internet access, and laptop Internet portals. Special learning facilities include a learning resource center, art gallery, planetarium, radio station, TV station, an academic support center, and a modern and classical language lab. The 120-acre campus is in a suburban area 26 miles southwest of Grand Rapids and 5 miles east of Lake Michigan. Including any residence halls, there are 106 buildings.

Student Life: 72% of undergraduates are from Michigan. Others are from 42 states, 32 foreign countries, and Canada. 86% are from public schools. 92% are white. 68% are Protestant; 11% Catholic. The average age of freshmen is 18; all undergraduates, 19. 11% do not continue beyond their first year; 75% remain to graduate.

Housing: 2200 students can be accommodated in college housing, which includes single-sex and coed dormitories, on-campus apartments, married-student housing, fraternity houses, and sorority houses. In addition, there are language houses and student cottages. On-campus housing is guaranteed for all 4 years. 81% of students live on campus; of those, 75% remain on campus on weekends. Alcohol is not permitted. All students may keep cars.

Activities: 6% of men belong to 5 local and 1 national fraternity; 15% of women belong to 6 local and 1 national sorority. There are 67 groups on campus, including art, band, cheerleading, choir, chorale, chorus, computers, dance, drama, ethnic, film, honors, international, jazz band, literary magazine, musical theater, newspaper, orchestra, pep band, photography, political, professional, radio and TV, religious, social, social service, student government, and yearbook. Popular campus events include Winter Fantasia, Spring Festival, and Nykerk Cup Competition.

Sports: There are 9 intercollegiate sports for men and 9 for women, and 16 intramural sports for men and 13 for women. Facilities include athletic fields, a field house, a tennis center, and a health and phys ed center that contains gyms, a running track, a swimming and diving pool, exercise rooms, a dance studio, racquetball courts, gymnastics rooms, and health-fitness equipment. The athletic arena includes a 6000-square foot weight room.

Disabled Students: 95% of the campus is accessible. Wheelchair ramps, elevators, special parking, specially equipped rest rooms, special class scheduling, lowered drinking fountains, and special housing are available.

Services: Counseling and information services are available, as is tutoring in every subject. There is a reader service for the blind.

Campus Safety and Security: Measures include 24-hour foot and vehicle patrol, security escort services, shuttle buses, and informal discussions. There are pamphlets/posters/films, emergency telephones, and lighted pathways/sidewalks.

Programs of Study: Hope confers B.A., B.S., B.Mus., and B.S.N. degrees. Bachelor's degrees are awarded in BIOLOGICAL SCIENCE (biochemistry and biology/biological science), BUSINESS (accounting and business administration and management), COMMUNICATIONS AND THE ARTS (communications, dance, dramatic arts, English, fine arts, French, German, Latin, music, and Spanish), COMPUTER AND PHYSICAL SCIENCE (chemistry, computer science, geology, mathematics, and physics), EDUCATION (art, elementary, foreign languages, music, science, secondary, and special), ENGINEERING AND ENVIRONMENTAL DESIGN (engineering), HEALTH PROFESSIONS (nursing), SOCIAL SCIENCE (economics, history, international studies, philosophy, physical fitness/movement, political science/government, psychology, religion, social work, and sociology). Chemistry, biological sciences, and phsycology are the strongest academically. Management and English are the largest.

Required: To graduate, students must complete 126 semester hours with a 2.0 GPA. All students must take 56 hours of the general education program, including a first-year seminar, 10 hours of math and natural science, 8 of cultural heritage, 6 each of social science, performing and fine arts, and religion, 4 each of a language and writing, 4 in a senior seminar, 4 credits of cultural diversity courses, and 2 hours of health dynamics.

Special: The college offers internships in all academic areas as well as on-campus work-study programs, student designed majors, study abroad in more than 57 countries, and Washington, Chicago, New York, and Philadelphia semesters. Students may take dual majors. There are 20 national honor societies, including Phi Beta Kappa, and 1 departmental honors program.

Faculty/Classroom: 59% of faculty are male; 41%, female. All teach undergraduates. The average class size in an introductory lecture is 25; in a laboratory, 25; and in a regular course, 25.

Admissions: 89% of the 2005-2006 applicants were accepted. The SAT scores for the 2005-2006 freshman class were: Verbal--8% below 500, 36% between 500 and 599, 37% between 600 and 700, and 20% above 700. Math--6% below 500, 34% between 500 and 599, 40% between 600 and 700, and 20% above 700. The ACT scores were 7% below 21, 19% between 21 and 23, 28% between 24 and 26, 18% between 27 and 28, and 28% above 28. 54% of the current freshmen were

in the top fifth of their class; 77% were in the top two fifths. There were 17 National Merit finalists.

Requirements: The SAT or ACT is required. In addition, the college requires a high school transcript, which must include 4 years of English, 2 each of math, a foreign language, and social science, and 1 year of a lab science, as well as 5 other academic courses. The college requires submission of an essay and recommends an interview. A portfolio or audition is required for certain majors. The GED is considered. AP and CLEP credits are accepted. Important factors in the admissions decision are leadership record, evidence of special talent, and advanced placement or honor courses.

Procedure: Freshmen are admitted fall, winter, and spring. Entrance exams should be taken during spring of the junior year or fall of the senior year. There is a deferred admissions and a rolling admissions plan. Application deadlines are open. 4 applicants were on the 2005 waiting list; 4 were admitted. Applications are accepted on-line. The fall 2005 application fee was $35.

Transfer: 66 transfer students enrolled in 2004-2005. Transfer students must have a GPA of 2.0 in at least 1 year of liberal arts courses. 32 of 126 credits required for the bachelor's degree must be completed at Hope.

Visiting: There are regularly scheduled orientations for prospective students, including tours, classes, lunch with a current student, and appointments with professors. There are guides for informal visits and visitors may sit in on classes and stay overnight. To schedule a visit, contact the Admissions Office.

Financial Aid: In 2005-2006, 96% of all full-time freshmen and 89% of continuing full-time students received some form of financial aid. 60% of full-time freshmen and 57% of continuing full-time students received need-based aid. The average freshman award was $17,727. Need-based scholarships or need-based grants averaged $13,809; need-based self-help aid (loans and jobs) averaged $3917; and other non-need-based awards and non-need-based scholarships averaged $6616. 40% of undergraduates work part time. Average annual earnings from campus work are $1515. The average financial indebtedness of the 2005 graduate was $16,618. Hope is a member of CSS. The FAFSA and the college's own financial statement are required. The priority date for freshman financial aid applications for fall entry is March 1.

International Students: In a recent year there were 47 international students enrolled. The school actively recruits these students. They must score satisfactorily on the written TOEFL.

Computers: All students may access the system 24 hours a day. There are no time limits and no fees.

Graduates: From July 1, 2004 to June 30, 2005, 652 bachelor's degrees were awarded. The most popular majors were management (12%), psychology (11%), and English/language arts teacher (7%). In an average class, 1% graduate in 3 years or less, 64% graduate in 4 years or less, 74% graduate in 5 years or less, and 75% graduate in 6 years or less. 39 companies recruited on campus in 2004-2005. Of the 2004 graduating class, 24% were enrolled in graduate school within 6 months of graduation and 64% were employed.

Admissions Contact: James R. Bekkering, Vice President for Admissions. E-mail: *admissions@hope.edu* Web: *www.hope.edu*

KALAMAZOO COLLEGE D-5

Kalamazoo, MI 49006-3295

(616) 337-7166
(800) 253-3602; Fax: (616) 337-7390

Full-time: 546 men, 717 women	Faculty: 97; IIB, av$
Part-time: none	Ph.D.s: 90%
Graduate: none	Student/Faculty: 13 to 1
Year: 4-1-4	Tuition: $25,734
Application Deadline: February 15	Room & Board: $6708
Freshman Class: 1669 applied, 1133 accepted, 367 enrolled	
SAT Verbal/Math: 631/630*	ACT: 28 **VERY COMPETITIVE+**

Kalamazoo College is a liberal arts and sciences institution founded in 1833. The library contains 346,648 volumes, 54,055 microform items, and 8938 audio/video tapes/CDs/DVDs, and subscribes to 1250 periodicals including electronic. Computerized library services include the card catalog, interlibrary loans, and database searching. Special learning facilities include a learning resource center, art gallery, and radio station. The 60-acre campus is in a suburban area 140 miles from Detroit and Chicago, IL. Including any residence halls, there are 30 buildings.

Student Life: 76% of undergraduates are from Michigan. Students are from 42 states, 16 foreign countries, and Canada. 85% are from public schools. 83% are white. 40% are claim no religious affiliation; 34% Protestant; 22% Catholic. The average age of freshmen is 18; all undergraduates, 20. 12% do not continue beyond their first year; 71% remain to graduate.

Housing: 868 students can be accommodated in college housing, which includes coed dorms. In addition, there are special-interest houses. On-campus housing is guaranteed for all 4 years. 75% of students live on campus; of those, 85% remain on campus on weekends. Upperclassmen may keep cars.

Activities: There are no fraternities or sororities. There are 50 groups on campus, including art, band, cheerleading, choir, chorale, chorus, computers, dance, drama, ethnic, film, gay, honors, international, jazz band, literary magazine, musical theater, newspaper, orchestra, photography, political, professional, radio and TV, religious, social, social service, student government, symphony, and yearbook. Popular campus events include Monte Carlo Night, Quadstock, and Day of Gracious Living.

Sports: There are 8 intercollegiate sports for men and 8 for women, and 12 intramural sports for men and 11 for women. Facilities include a field house that houses a 2000-seat gym, basketball and volleyball courts, weight-training rooms, and a dance studio; a 1500-seat, 11-court tennis stadium; a racquet center with 4 tennis courts, 3 racquetball courts, and a squash court; a natatorium; a 4000-seat football stadium; and soccer and baseball fields.

Disabled Students: 25% of the campus is accessible. Wheelchair ramps, elevators, special parking, specially equipped rest rooms, and special class scheduling are available.

Services: Counseling and information services are available, as is tutoring in most subjects. A writing center, language labs, and supplemental instruction are also available.

Campus Safety and Security: Measures include 24-hour foot and vehicle patrol, self-defense education, security escort services, and informal discussions. There are pamphlets/posters/films, emergency telephones, lighted pathways/sidewalks, and secured residence halls with an electronic entry system.

Programs of Study: Kalamazoo confers the B.A. degree. Bachelor's degrees are awarded in BIOLOGICAL SCIENCE (biology/biological science), BUSINESS (business economics), COMMUNICATIONS AND THE ARTS (art, art history and appreciation, dramatic arts, English, French, German, music, and Spanish), COMPUTER AND PHYSICAL SCIENCE (chemistry, computer science, mathematics, and physics), HEALTH PROFESSIONS (health science), SOCIAL SCIENCE (anthropology, classical/ancient civilization, history, human development, interdisciplinary studies, international relations, international studies, philosophy, political science/government, psychology, religion, and sociology). Foreign languages, international studies and commerce, and health sciences are the strongest academically. Economics, English, and political science are the largest.

Required: To graduate, students must complete 38 academic units, including 8 units in the major, with a minimum 2.0 GPA. Required courses include 4 units in social science, 3 in natural science, computer science, or math, 2 each in literature and philosophy/religion, and 1 in fine arts. The college further requires completion of a senior individualized project, a credit from the liberal arts colloquium, and a passing grade on a comprehensive exam in the major. The student must also take 5 non-credit courses in phys ed and show proficiency in writing as well as in a foreign language.

Special: Students may study abroad in more than 12 countries and choose from among 900 career internships in the United States, Europe, Asia, and Africa. The school offers a Washington semester, allows dual and interdisciplinary majors, and has cross-registration with Western Michigan University. A 3-2 engineering degree is offered with Washington University and the University of Michigan. There are accelerated 3-year programs in predentistry, premedicine, and preveterinary medicine. There are 3 national honor societies, including Phi Beta Kappa.

Faculty/Classroom: 52% of faculty are male; 48%, female. All teach undergraduates. The average class size in an introductory lecture is 18; in a laboratory, 24; and in a regular course, 18.

Admissions: 68% of the 2005-2006 applicants were accepted. The SAT scores for the 2005-2006 freshman class were: Verbal--1% below 500, 13% between 500 and 599, 60% between 600 and 700, and 26% above 700; Math--1% below 500, 22% between 500 and 599, 51% between 600 and 700, and 26% above 700. The ACT scores were 10% between 21 and 23, 60% between 24 and 26, and 30% above 28. 43% of the current freshmen were in the top fifth of their class; 77% were in the top two fifths. There were 11 National Merit finalists. 43 freshmen graduated first in their class.

Requirements: The SAT or ACT is required. In addition, the college also requires a high school transcript, an essay, and teacher and counselor recommendations; an interview is recommended. Applications are accepted on computer disk. AP credits are accepted. Important factors in the admissions decision are advanced placement or honor courses, evidence of special talent, and leadership record.

Procedure: Freshmen are admitted in the fall. Entrance exams should be taken by December of the senior year. There are early decision, early admissions, and deferred admissions plans. Early decision applications should be filed by November 15; regular applications, by February 15 for fall entry. The fall 2005 application fee was $35. Notification of early decision is sent December 1; regular decision, April 1. 11 early decision candidates were accepted for the 2005-2006 class; 31 were admitted.

Transfer: 6 transfer students enrolled in 2004-2005. A 3.0 GPA from previous institution(s) is required. 18 of 38 credits required for the bachelor's degree must be completed at Kalamazoo.

Visiting: There are regularly scheduled orientations for prospective students, including interviews, tours, and class visits as requested. Special preview events include formal presentation of the unique curriculum and financial aid seminars. There are guides for informal visits and visitors may sit in on classes and stay overnight. To schedule a visit, contact the visit coordinator, Pat Marcinkowski.

Financial Aid: The CSS/Profile or FAFSA is required. Check with school for current deadlines.

International Students: The school actively recruits these students. A satisfactory score is required on the written TOEFL or the MELAB.

Computers: All students may access the system. There are no time limits and no fees. It is strongly recommended that all students have a PC.

Admissions Contact: John M. Carroll, Director of Admission. A video is available. E-mail: *admissions@kzoo.edu* Web: *www.kzoo.edu*

KENDALL COLLEGE OF ART AND DESIGN OF FERRIS STATE UNIVERSITY   D-4

Grand Rapids, MI 49503-3002

(616) 451-2787
(800) 676-2787; Fax: (616) 831-9689

Full-time and Part-time: 1036 men and women	**Faculty:** 46
	Ph.D.s: 89%
Part-time: none	**Student/Faculty:** n/av
Graduate: n/av none	**Tuition:** $11,870 ($17,606)
Year: semesters, summer session	**Room & Board:** n/app
Application Deadline: open	
Freshman Class: n/av	
SAT or ACT: required	**SPECIAL**

The Kendall College of Art and Design of Ferris State University, founded in 1928, is a commuter institution specializing in design studies and the fine arts. In addition to regional accreditation, Kendall has baccalaureate program accreditation with FIDER and NASAD. The library contains 23,000 volumes, 1000 microform items, and 3500 audio/video tapes/CDs/DVDs, and subscribes to 150 periodicals including electronic. Computerized library services include the card catalog, interlibrary loans, and Internet access. Special learning facilities include a learning resource center, art gallery, a model and wood shop, a photography lab, a print-making lab, fine art studios, and a student gallery. The 1-acre campus is in an urban area in downtown Grand Rapids. There are 2 buildings.

Student Life: 91% of undergraduates are from Michigan. 90% are from public schools. 81% are white. The average age of all undergraduates is 24.

Housing: There are no residence halls. All of students commute. Alcohol is not permitted.

Activities: There are no fraternities or sororities. There are 17 groups on campus, including art, ethnic, film, gay, international, literary magazine, newspaper, photography, professional, religious, and student government. Popular campus events include Advising Day and an all-campus picnic.

Sports: There is no sports program at Kendall. Facilities include Grand Rapids Community College's pool, track, and sports facilities, which students may use upon payment of an annual fee.

Disabled Students: All of the campus is accessible. Wheelchair ramps, elevators, special parking, specially equipped rest rooms, lowered drinking fountains, lowered telephones, and special drawing tables are available.

Services: Counseling and information services are available, as is tutoring in every subject. There is a reader service for the blind.

Campus Safety and Security: Measures include security escort services, informal discussions, pamphlets/posters/films, and emergency telephones. There are lighted pathways/sidewalks.

Programs of Study: Kendall confers B.S. and B.F.A. degrees. Master's degrees are also awarded. Bachelor's degrees are awarded in COMMUNICATIONS AND THE ARTS (art history and appreciation, drawing, fine arts, graphic design, illustration, industrial design, media arts, metal/jewelry, multimedia, painting, photography, printmaking, and sculpture), COMPUTER AND PHYSICAL SCIENCE (digital arts/technology), EDUCATION (art), ENGINEERING AND ENVIRONMENTAL DESIGN (furniture design, interior design, and woodworking). Illustration, graphic design, and digital media are the largest.

Required: To graduate, students must complete 120 credit hours, including 45 to 69 in the major, 30 to 45 of liberal arts and sciences, 12 to 18 of a foundation studio core, 12 to 15 of art history, and 12 to 15 of studio electives. All students must complete a graduation portfolio. A minimum GPA of 2.0 is required, with a minimum GPA of 2.25 in the student's major studio core courses.

Special: Study abroad may be arranged by the student and approved by the college; trips to Perugia, Italy, and London, England, are offered each year. Dual majors are possible.

Faculty/Classroom: 56% of faculty are male; 44%, female. All teach undergraduates. The average class size in an introductory lecture is 35; in a laboratory, 15; and in a regular course, 20.

Requirements: The SAT or ACT is required. ACT or SAT scores are not required of applicants who are 23 years or older. In addition, a high school transcript is required. The GED certificate is accepted. Students must submit an essay with their application, and most majors require a portfolio review. An interview is recommended. Prospective students are encouraged to take courses in drawing, painting, and design in high school. A GPA of 2.25 is required. AP and CLEP credits are accepted. Important factors in the admissions decision are leadership record, personality/intangible qualities, and evidence of special talent.

Procedure: Freshmen are admitted to all sessions. There are early decision, deferred admissions and rolling admissions plans. Application deadlines are open. Application fee is $30. Applications are accepted on-line.

Transfer: Applicants must have a GPA of 2.25 and pass a portfolio review. An interview is recommended. 30 of 120 credits required for the bachelor's degree must be completed at Kendall.

Visiting: There are regularly scheduled orientations for prospective students, consisting of "Connect to Kendall" events several times a year, during which prospective students may see student work, visit studios and classrooms, and talk with staff, faculty, and students. There are guides for informal visits and visitors may sit in on classes. To schedule a visit, contact the Admissions Office at (616) 451-2787 or (800) 676-2787.

Financial Aid: 7% of undergraduates work part time. Average annual earnings from campus work are $2000. The FAFSA is required. The priority date for freshman financial aid applications for fall entry is February 1.

International Students: There are 10 international students enrolled. The school actively recruits these students. They must score satisfactorily on the written TOEFL or on the electronic version and also take the SAT or the ACT.

Computers: All students may access the system. There are no time limits. The fee is $205 per semester.

Admissions Contact: Sandy Britton, Director of Enrollment Management. E-mail: *brittons@ferris.edu* Web: *www.kcad.edu*

KETTERING UNIVERSITY
E-4
Flint, MI 48504-4898

(810) 762-7865
(800) 955-4464; Fax: (810) 762-9837

Full-time: 2008 men, 368 women	**Faculty:** 140; IIB, +$
Part-time: none	**Ph.D.s:** 93%
Graduate: 379 men, 140 women	**Student/Faculty:** 17 to 1
Year: semesters, summer session	**Tuition:** $23,898
Application Deadline: open	**Room & Board:** $5440
Freshman Class: 2140 applied, 1558 accepted, 495 enrolled	
SAT Verbal/Math: 580/650*	**ACT: 26 HIGHLY COMPETITIVE**

Kettering University is a private college founded in 1919. In the 4.5-year undergraduate program students alternate 11-week terms of full-time classes with 12-week terms of full-time paid professional cooperative education (co-op) work experience in industry. Students typically begin co-op during their freshman year and co-op in 43 states and several countries. There are 3 undergraduate schools and 1 graduate school. In addition to regional accreditation, Kettering has baccalaureate program accreditation with ABET and ACBSP. The library contains 128,500 volumes, 35,000 microform items, and 780 audio/video tapes/CDs/DVDs, and subscribes to 550 periodicals including electronic. Computerized library services include interlibrary loans, database searching, and Internet access. Special learning facilities include a learning resource center, art gallery, radio station, and Industrial History Archives. The 85-acre campus is in a suburban area 60 miles north of Detroit. Including any residence halls, there are 10 buildings.

Student Life: 63% of undergraduates are from Michigan. Students are from 50 states, 24 foreign countries, and Canada. 85% are from public schools. 74% are white. The average age of freshmen is 18; all undergraduates, 20. 12% do not continue beyond their first year; 65% remain to graduate.

Housing: 623 students can be accommodated in university housing, which includes single-sex and coed dorms, on-campus apartments, fraternity houses, and sorority houses. On-campus housing is guaranteed for the freshman year only and is available on a lottery system for upperclassmen. Priority is given to out-of-town students. 50% of students live on campus. Alcohol is not permitted. All students may keep cars.

Activities: 40% of men belong to 13 national fraternities; 35% of women belong to 6 national sororities. There are 40 groups on campus, including art, chorus, computers, dance, drama, ethnic, gay, honors, international, jazz band, literary magazine, newspaper, pep band, photography, political, professional, radio and TV, religious, social, social service, student government, and yearbook. Popular campus events include Greek Week, Diversity Week, and Student and Alumni Industry Speaker Series.

Sports: There are 22 intramural sports for men and 22 for women. Facilities include a recreation center with 2 basketball and 2 tennis/basketball courts; 4 racquetball and squash courts; a one-eighth mile track; an Olympic-size pool, free weight, Nautilus, and group exercise

rooms. A 25-acre sports and recreation complex includes 4 softball and 2 soccer fields, a golf green, a 1 km outdoor track, and a picnic pavilion.

Disabled Students: All of the campus is accessible. Wheelchair ramps, elevators, special parking, specially equipped rest rooms, special class scheduling, lowered drinking fountains, and lowered telephones are available.

Services: Counseling and information services are available. Tutoring is routinely available for most subjects in the Academic Support Center, in the residence hall, and with faculty. Supplemental tutoring is coordinated through the Academic Services Department. Math and writing labs are available. A Strategies for Academic Success program is available.

Campus Safety and Security: Measures include 24-hour foot and vehicle patrol, self-defense education, security escort services, and informal discussions. There are pamphlets/posters/films, emergency telephones, lighted pathways/sidewalks, and after-hours access (e.g., to the academic building) is secure via the tunnel from the residence hall and campus center.

Programs of Study: Kettering confers B.S.A.M., B.S.A.P., B.S.C., B.S.C.E, B.S.C.S., B.S.E.E., B.S.I.E., B.S.M.G., and B.S.M.E. degrees. Master's degrees are also awarded. Bachelor's degrees are awarded in BUSINESS (business administration and management), COMPUTER AND PHYSICAL SCIENCE (applied mathematics, applied physics, chemistry, and computer science), ENGINEERING AND ENVIRONMENTAL DESIGN (computer engineering, electrical/electronics engineering, industrial engineering, and mechanical engineering). Mechanical engineering, electrical engineering, and computer engineering are the largest.

Required: Degree requirements include completion of 160 credit hours, with 60 in the major. All students must take specific courses in math, chemistry, physics, written and oral communication, humanities, and economics, and complete at least 5 terms of co-op experience in industry plus 2 work terms designated for a senior thesis project. A minimum grade average of 80 on a scale of 100 is required for graduation. The GPA is determined by a formula combining the numerical grades achieved and the number of credits attempted. Students must complete a thesis.

Special: All undergraduate students participate in paid professional co-operative education work experience. Students may pursue a dual major in any degree combination. Accelerated degree programs in engineering are available in most majors, as is study abroad in 3 countries. There are 8 national honor societies.

Faculty/Classroom: 80% of faculty are male; 20%, female. 98% teach undergraduates, 16% do research, and 16% do both. Graduate students teach 1% of introductory courses. The average class size in an introductory lecture is 40; in a laboratory, 14; and in a regular course, 20.

Admissions: 73% of the 2005-2006 applicants were accepted. The SAT scores for the 2005-2006 freshman class were: Verbal--10% below 500, 46% between 500 and 599, 34% between 600 and 700, and 10% above 700; Math--1% below 500, 20% between 500 and 599, 56% between 600 and 700, and 23% above 700. The ACT scores were 5% below 21, 20% between 21 and 23, 29% between 24 and 26, 24% between 27 and 28, and 23% above 28. 52% of the current freshmen were in the top fifth of their class; 84% were in the top two fifths. 17 freshmen graduated first in their class.

Requirements: The SAT or ACT is required. In addition, applicants must graduate from an accredited secondary school with a minimum of 16 academic credits. Applicants must have completed 3 years of English, 3 1/2 years of math, including trigonometry, and 2 years of lab science, 1 of which must be chemistry or physics (both are strongly recommended). AP credits are accepted. Important factors in the admissions decision are leadership record, advanced placement or honor courses, and extracurricular activities record.

Procedure: Freshmen are admitted fall, winter, and summer. Entrance exams should be taken during the spring of the junior year and fall of the senior year. There is a deferred admissions plan. Application deadlines are open. Application fee is $35. Applications are accepted on-line.

Transfer: 72 transfer students enrolled in 2004-2005. Transfer applicants must present the same minimum preparation as freshmen in math and science and must submit both high school and college transcripts and SAT or ACT scores. Required courses can be taken in high school or college. A minimum GPA of 3.0 in English, math, and science is expected. Transfers who present less than 30 credits of full-time study will be judged on both their college and high school record and test scores. 85 of 160 credits required for the bachelor's degree must be completed at Kettering.

Visiting: There are regularly scheduled orientations for prospective students, including 3 open house programs for prospective students. There are guides for informal visits and visitors may sit in on classes and stay overnight. To schedule a visit, contact the Admissions Office at (800) 955-4464, ext. 7865 or *admissions@kettering.edu*.

Financial Aid: In 2005-2006, 90% of all full-time freshmen and 85% of continuing full-time students received some form of financial aid. 74% of full-time freshmen and 62% of continuing full-time students received need-based aid. The average freshman award was $14,977. Need-based

scholarships or need-based grants averaged $3992; need-based self-help aid (loans and jobs) averaged $3723 ($3845 maximum); and other non-need-based awards and non-need-based scholarships averaged $8718. 13% of undergraduates work part time. Average annual earnings from campus work are $754. The average financial indebtedness of the 2005 graduate was $30,903. The FAFSA, and the university's own financial statement are required. The priority date for freshman financial aid applications for fall entry is February 14.

International Students: There are 61 international students enrolled. The school actively recruits these students. They must take the TOEFL or the MELAB.

Computers: All students may access the system 24 hours per day, 7 days per week. There are no time limits and no fees. It is strongly recommended that all students have a personal computer.

Graduates: From July 1, 2004 to June 30, 2005, 441 bachelor's degrees were awarded. The most popular majors were mechanical engineering (48%), electrical engineering (13%), and industrial and manufacturing engineering (5%). In an average class, 3% graduate in 4 years or less, 52% graduate in 5 years or less, and 61% graduate in 6 years or less. 100 companies recruited on campus in 2004-2005. Of the 2004 graduating class, 20% were enrolled in graduate school within 6 months of graduation and 98% were employed.

Admissions Contact: Barbara Sosin, Director of Admissions.
E-mail: *admissions@kettering.edu* Web: *www.kettering.edu*

LAKE SUPERIOR STATE UNIVERSITY D-2

Sault Sainte Marie, MI 49783-1699 (906) 635-2231
(888) 800-5778; Fax: (906) 635-6669

Full-time: 1189 men, 1126 women	**Faculty:** 112
Part-time: 235 men, 338 women	**Ph.D.s:** 73%
Graduate: none	**Student/Faculty:** 21 to 1
Year: semesters, summer session	**Tuition:** $6306 ($12,294)
Application Deadline: open	**Room & Board:** $6536
Freshman Class: 1566 applied, 1328 accepted, 546 enrolled	
ACT: required	**LESS COMPETITIVE**

Lake Superior State University, founded in 1946, is a public university offering degrees in sciences, business, and liberal arts. There are 12 undergraduate schools and 1 graduate school. In addition to regional accreditation, LSSU or Lake State has baccalaureate program accreditation with ABET, CAAHEP, and NLN. The library contains 106,618 volumes and 810 audio/video tapes/CDs/DVDs, and subscribes to 950 periodicals including electronic. Computerized library services include the card catalog, interlibrary loans, and database searching. Special learning facilities include a learning resource center, natural history museum, planetarium, radio station, fish hatchery and aquatics lab, and interactive television for distance education. The 115-acre campus is in a small town 280 miles north of Lansing. Including any residence halls, there are 37 buildings.

Student Life: 75% of undergraduates are from Michigan. Others are from 30 states, 7 foreign countries, and Canada. 94% are from public schools. 69% are white. The average age of freshmen is 19; all undergraduates, 22. 33% do not continue beyond their first year; 45% remain to graduate.

Housing: 1198 students can be accommodated in college housing, which includes single-sex and coed dorms, on-campus apartments, married-student housing, fraternity houses, and sorority houses. In addition, there are honors houses. On-campus housing is guaranteed for the freshman year only, is available on a first-come, first-served basis, and is available on a lottery system for upperclassmen. 76% of students commute. All students may keep cars.

Activities: There is 1 local and 4 national fraternities; 10% of women belong to 4 national sororities. There are more than 60 groups on campus, including band, cheerleading, chess, chorale, computers, dance, drama, ethnic, film, gay, honors, jazz band, newspaper, pep band, political, professional, radio and TV, religious, social, social service, and student government. Popular campus events include Winter Carnival, Spring Fling, and Beach Party.

Sports: There are 5 intercollegiate sports for men and 5 for women, and 17 intramural sports for men and 15 for women. Facilities include a 2800-seat gym, a 4100-seat ice arena, basketball and racquetball courts, indoor and outdoor tennis courts, an indoor pool, weight rooms, a dance studio, a 16-lane indoor track, and 4 multipurpose courts for basketball, volleyball, and tennis.

Disabled Students: 90% of the campus is accessible. Wheelchair ramps, elevators, special parking, specially equipped rest rooms, special class scheduling, lowered drinking fountains, and lowered telephones are available.

Services: Counseling and information services are available, as is tutoring in most subjects, on request and free of charge. There is a reader service for the blind, and remedial math, reading, and writing. There are also math, reading, and writing labs.

Campus Safety and Security: Measures include 24-hour foot and vehicle patrol, self-defense education, security escort services, and informal discussions. There are pamphlets/posters/films and lighted pathways/sidewalks.

Programs of Study: LSSU, or Lake State confers B.A. and B.S. degrees. Associate and master's degrees are also awarded. Bachelor's degrees are awarded in AGRICULTURE (fish and game management, and wildlife management), BIOLOGICAL SCIENCE (biology/biological science), BUSINESS (accounting, business administration and management, and marketing/retailing/merchandising), COMMUNICATIONS AND THE ARTS (English, and fine arts), COMPUTER AND PHYSICAL SCIENCE (computer science, geology, and mathematics), EDUCATION (athletic training, early childhood, elementary, and secondary), ENGINEERING AND ENVIRONMENTAL DESIGN (electrical/electronics engineering, engineering, engineering management, engineering technology, environmental engineering technology, environmental science, manufacturing technology, and mechanical engineering), HEALTH PROFESSIONS (exercise science, medical laboratory technology, nursing, predentistry, premedicine, and recreation therapy), SOCIAL SCIENCE (criminal justice, economics, fire science, history, human services, paralegal studies, parks and recreation management, political science/government, prelaw, psychology, social science, and sociology). Engineering technology, nursing, and biology are the strongest academically. Business and criminal justice are the largest.

Required: To graduate, students must complete 124 semester hours with a GPA of 2.0. The core curriculum includes course work in computer literacy, English, oral communications, aesthetics, critical thinking, humanities, math, science, social science, ethics, and cultural diversity. At least 32 of the final credits, and 50% of all upper-level courses, must be taken in residence at Lake State. Math and English competency must be met.

Special: Lake State offers internships in criminal justice, medical technology, human services, legal assistance studies, and natural resources technology, work-study programs, co-op programs in engineering technology, and cross-registration with the Canadian Colleges of Sault and Algoma and Bridge International Consortium. Study abroad, and student-designed majors are available. Distance learning and weekend college study formats are offered. There is a freshman honors program.

Faculty/Classroom: 53% of faculty are male; 47%, female. All teach undergraduates and 20% both teach and do research. The average class size in an introductory lecture is 25; in a laboratory, 15; and in a regular course, 30.

Admissions: 85% of the 2005-2006 applicants were accepted.

Requirements: The ACT is required. In addition, applicants should be high school graduates with 4 years of English, 3 each of math and science, 2 each of a foreign language and social studies, and 1 of history, and should have a GPA of 2.0. The GED is accepted. A GPA of 2.0 is required. AP and CLEP credits are accepted. Important factors in the admissions decision are advanced placement or honor courses, recommendations by school officials, and recommendations by alumni.

Procedure: Freshmen are admitted to all sessions. There is a deferred admissions plan and a rolling plan. Application deadlines are open. The fall 2005 application fee was $20. Applications are accepted on-line.

Transfer: 251 transfer students enrolled in 2004-2005. Applicants must be eligible to return to the last institution attended, and must have an overall college GPA of 2.0. An interview is recommended. ACT scores are required if high school graduation was within 26 months of the semester of entry. High school transcripts and GED scores are required if transferring with fewer than 19 semester hours of credit. 32 of 124 credits required for the bachelor's degree must be completed at LSSU.

Visiting: There are regularly scheduled orientations for prospective students. There are guides for informal visits and visitors may sit in on classes. To schedule a visit, contact the Admissions Office at *admissions@lssu.edu*.

Financial Aid: In 2005-2006, 83% of all full-time students received some form of financial aid. Average annual earnings from campus work are $2500. The FAFSA and OSAP are required. The deadline for filing freshman financial aid applications for fall entry is March 1.

International Students: The school actively recruits these students. They must take the TOEFL.

Computers: Wireless access is available. There are 450 workstations for general student use. PC labs are in the library and various locations around campus. Residence halls are wired for high-speed Internet connection and for access to the campus network. Wireless capabilities exist in the library, student center, and most of the main academic buildings. All students may access the system during lab hours. There are no time limits and no fees.

Graduates: From July 1, 2004 to June 30, 2005, 514 bachelor's degrees were awarded. Of the 2004 graduating class, 86% were enrolled in graduate school or employed within 6 months of graduation.

Admissions Contact: Susan Camp, Director of Admissions.
E-mail: *admissions@lssu.edu* Web: *www.lssu.edu*

LAWRENCE TECHNOLOGICAL UNIVERSITY E-5

Southfield, MI 48075
(248) 204-3160
(800) CALL-LTU; Fax: (248) 204-3188

Full-time: 1111 men, 370 women	**Faculty:** 113
Part-time: 1138 men, 287 women	**Ph.D.s:** 78%
Graduate: 824 men, 418 women	**Student/Faculty:** 13 to 1
Year: semesters, summer session	**Tuition:** $18,248
Application Deadline: open	**Room & Board:** $7227
Freshman Class: 998 applied, 521 accepted, 372 enrolled	
SAT Verbal/Math: 530/560*	**ACT:** 22 **VERY COMPETITIVE**

Lawrence Technological University, founded in 1932 as the Lawrence Institute of Technology, is a private institution housing colleges of engineering, management, arts and sciences, and architecture and design. There are 4 undergraduate and 4 graduate schools. In addition to regional accreditation, Lawrence Tech has baccalaureate program accreditation with ABET, ACBSP, FIDER, NAAB, and NASAD. The library contains 118,000 volumes, 28,265 microform items, and 423 audio/video tapes/CDs/DVDs, and subscribes to 1100 periodicals including electronic. Computerized library services include the card catalog, interlibrary loans, database searching, and Internet access. Special learning facilities include a learning resource center, a Frank Lloyd Wright-designed home used as an academic resource, and the personal library of the late architect Albert Kahn. The 120-acre campus is in a suburban area 30 minutes north of downtown Detroit. Including any residence halls, there are 11 buildings.

Student Life: 92% of undergraduates are from Michigan. Others are from 16 states, 16 foreign countries, and Canada. 61% are white; 11% African American. The average age of freshmen is 19; all undergraduates, 23. 29% do not continue beyond their first year; 48% remain to graduate.

Housing: 516 students can be accommodated in college housing, which includes coed on-campus apartments. On-campus housing is available on a first-come, first-served basis. 85% of students commute. All students may keep cars.

Activities: 5% of men belong to 1 local fraternity and 6 national fraternities; 7% of women belong to 2 local and 2 national sororities. There are 43 groups on campus, including art, chess, computers, ethnic, honors, political, professional, religious, social, student government, and yearbook. Popular campus events include Open House, Reunion Weekend, and Greek Week.

Sports: There are 10 intramural sports for men and 7 for women. Facilities include a field house with 4 racquetball courts, a weight room, a track, a sauna, and a gym. The gym seats 1500; an arena 350.

Disabled Students: 97% of the campus is accessible. Wheelchair ramps, elevators, special parking, specially equipped rest rooms, special class scheduling, lowered drinking fountains, lowered telephones, and special housing are available.

Services: Counseling and information services are available, as is tutoring in some subjects, including math, computers, science, and English. There is a reader service for the blind, and remedial math, reading, and writing. There is also an Academic Achievement Center.

Campus Safety and Security: Measures include 24-hour foot and vehicle patrol, security escort services, pamphlets/posters/films, and emergency telephones. There are lighted pathways/sidewalks and closed-circuit camera monitoring.

Programs of Study: Lawrence Tech confers B.S., B.F.A., and B.F.M. degrees. Associate, master's, and doctoral degrees are also awarded. Bachelor's degrees are awarded in BIOLOGICAL SCIENCE (biochemistry), BUSINESS (business administration and management), COMMUNICATIONS AND THE ARTS (illustration and technical and business writing), COMPUTER AND PHYSICAL SCIENCE (chemistry, computer science, information sciences and systems, mathematics, and physics), ENGINEERING AND ENVIRONMENTAL DESIGN (architecture, biomedical engineering, civil engineering, computer engineering, construction management, electrical/electronics engineering, engineering technology, environmental science, industrial administration/management, interior design, mechanical engineering, and technological management), SOCIAL SCIENCE (humanities and psychology). Mathematics, computer science, and engineering are the strongest academically. Engineering and architecture are the largest.

Required: To graduate, students must have completed, depending on the major, 120 to 131 semester credit hours, with a GPA no lower than 2.0. Senior projects are required in most degree programs.

Special: There are co-op programs in a number of majors, internships, dual majors, and work-study programs. There are 7 national honor societies and 6 departmental honors programs.

Faculty/Classroom: 75% of faculty are male; 25%, female. No introductory courses are taught by graduate students. The average class size in an introductory lecture is 19; in a laboratory, 18; and in a regular course, 19.

Admissions: 52% of the 2005-2006 applicants were accepted. The SAT scores for the 2005-2006 freshman class were: Verbal--38% below 500, 28% between 500 and 599, 30% between 600 and 700, and 4% above 700; Math--26% below 500, 28% between 500 and 599, 40% between 600 and 700, and 6% above 700. The ACT scores were 35% below 21, 25% between 21 and 23, 20% between 24 and 26, 10% between 27 and 28, and 10% above 28. 41% of the current freshmen were in the top fifth of their class; 73% were in the top two fifths. 9 freshmen graduated first in their class.

Requirements: The ACT is required and the SAT is recommended. In addition, students must have a high school diploma and a GPA no lower than 2.5, at least 2.0 in each subject area pertaining to their major. Applicants should have taken 4 years each of math, science, and English and 3 years of social science. The GED is accepted. An interview is recommended. AP and CLEP credits are accepted. Important factors in the admissions decision are advanced placement or honor courses, personality/intangible qualities, and leadership record.

Procedure: Freshmen are admitted to all sessions. Entrance exams should be taken in the semester preceding entry. There are early admissions and deferred admissions plans. There is a rolling admissions plan. Application deadlines are open. The fall 2005 application fee was $30. Notification is sent on a rolling basis. Applications are accepted on-line.

Transfer: 256 transfer students enrolled in 2004-2005. Admission is based on the college GPA, which must be 2.0 or higher, with 30 or more semester hours. If less than 30 hours have been completed, admission is based on high school transcripts. 28 of 120 to 131 credits required for the bachelor's degree must be completed at Lawrence Tech.

Visiting: There are regularly scheduled orientations for prospective students. There are guides for informal visits and visitors may sit in on classes and stay overnight. To schedule a visit, contact the Admissions Office.

Financial Aid: In 2005-2006, 94% of all full-time freshmen and 96% of continuing full-time students received some form of financial aid. 62% of full-time freshmen and 57% of continuing full-time students received need-based aid. The average freshman award was $11,874. Need-based scholarships or need-based grants averaged $7303 ($9050 maximum); need-based self-help aid (loans and jobs) averaged $4552 ($8625 maximum); and other non-need-based awards and non-need-based scholarships averaged $7221 ($27,000 maximum). 85% of undergraduates work part time. Average annual earnings from campus work are $2100. The average financial indebtedness of the 2005 graduate was $24,495. Lawrence Tech is a member of CSS. The FAFSA is required. The deadline for filing freshman financial aid applications for fall entry is April 1.

International Students: There are 282 international students enrolled. The school actively recruits these students. A satisfacory score on the TOEFL is required; students applying to LTU as freshmen only must take the SAT or ACT.

Computers: Wireless access is available from any campus location. The LTU network is available to all students all day. There are 35000 PC systems on campus, each with network access, including the Internet. All students may access the system 24 hours daily. There are no time limits and no fees. LTU provides notebook computers to all undergraduates. These systems are custom configured to the requirements of students' declared majors. Students are discouraged from providing their own systems.

Graduates: From July 1, 2004 to June 30, 2005, 435 bachelor's degrees were awarded. The most popular majors were architecture (24%), mechanical engineering (20%), and engineering technology (14%). In an average class, 27% graduate in 4 years or less, 42% graduate in 5 years or less, and 48% graduate in 6 years or less. 175 companies recruited on campus in 2004-2005.

Admissions Contact: Jane Rohrback, Admissions Director. A video is available. E-mail: *admissions@ltu.edu* Web: *http://www.ltu.edu*

MADONNA UNIVERSITY E-5

Livonia, MI 48150-1173
(734) 432-5317
(800) 852-4951; Fax: (734) 432-5424

Full-time: 406 men, 1273 women	**Faculty:** 209; IIB, -$
Part-time: 429 men, 1268 women	**Ph.D.s:** 55%
Graduate: 269 men, 663 women	**Student/Faculty:** 8 to 1
Year: summer session	**Tuition:** $10,300
Application Deadline: open	**Room & Board:** $5768
Freshman Class: 295 accepted, 165 enrolled	
SAT Verbal/Math: 533/518*	**ACT:** 23 **VERY COMPETITIVE**

Madonna University, founded in 1947, is a liberal arts institution affiliated with the Roman Catholic Church. There are 8 undergraduate schools and 1 graduate school. In addition to regional accreditation, MU has baccalaureate program accreditation with ADA, CSWE, NCATE, and NLN. The 2 libraries contain 112,400 volumes, 453,180 microform items, and 1872 audio/video tapes/CDs/DVDs, and subscribe to 14,109 periodicals including electronic. Computerized library services include interlibrary loans, database searching, Internet access, and laptop Internet portals. Special learning facilities include a learning resource center, art gallery, radio station, TV station, computerized writing lab, the Center for Personalized Instruction, Office of Disability Resources, and Office of

Service Learning. The 49-acre campus is in a suburban area 25 miles west of Detroit. Including any residence halls, there are 4 buildings.

Student Life: 99% of undergraduates are from Michigan. Others are from 15 states, 39 foreign countries, and Canada. 83% are from public schools. 74% are white; 12% African American. 40% are Catholic; 19% Protestant. The average age of freshmen is 28; all undergraduates, 30. 21% do not continue beyond their first year; 36% remain to graduate.

Housing: 250 students can be accommodated in college housing, which includes single-sex dorms. On-campus housing is guaranteed for all 4 years. 93% of students commute. Alcohol is not permitted. All students may keep cars.

Activities: There are no fraternities or sororities. There are 23 groups on campus, including art, chorale, computers, environmental, ethnic, honors, international, newspaper, orchestra, peace and justice, photography, political, professional, radio and TV, religious, social, social service, and student government. Popular campus events include Peace & Justice Week, Alternative Spring Breaks, and International Festival.

Sports: There are 5 intercollegiate sports for men and 6 for women. Facilities include an activities center, a weight training room, a 700-seat gym, and an outdoor softball arena.

Disabled Students: All of the campus is accessible. Wheelchair ramps, elevators, special parking, specially equipped rest rooms, special class scheduling, lowered drinking fountains, lowered telephones, telecommunication devices and visible fire alarms for hearing-impaired students, talking books, tape recorders, diagnostic testing service, early syllabus, recorded exams, a Learning Center, oral exams, proofreading service, reading machine, take-home exams, and software for vision impaired students are available.

Services: Counseling and information services are available, as is tutoring in most subjects. There is a reader service for the blind, and remedial math, reading, and writing. Interpreters and note takers for hearing-impaired and visually impaired students, controlled dormitory access, and student patrols are available.

Campus Safety and Security: Measures include 24-hour foot and vehicle patrol, security escort services, informal discussions, and pamphlets/posters/films. There are emergency telephones, lighted pathways/sidewalks, and an emergency car service.

Programs of Study: MU confers B.A., B.S., B.A.S., B.S.M.T., B.S.N., and B.S.W. degrees. Associate and master's degrees are also awarded. Bachelor's degrees are awarded in BIOLOGICAL SCIENCE (biochemistry, biology/biological science, and nutrition), BUSINESS (accounting, business administration and management, hospitality management services, international business management, management science, and marketing/retailing/merchandising), COMMUNICATIONS AND THE ARTS (art, communications, English, fine arts, graphic design, journalism, music, Spanish, speech/debate/rhetoric, technical and business writing, and video), COMPUTER AND PHYSICAL SCIENCE (applied science, chemistry, computer science, information sciences and systems, mathematics, natural sciences, and science), EDUCATION (art, music, and secondary), ENGINEERING AND ENVIRONMENTAL DESIGN (commercial art and occupational safety and health), HEALTH PROFESSIONS (allied health, hospice care, medical laboratory technology, and nursing), SOCIAL SCIENCE (child psychology/development, criminal justice, dietetics, family/consumer studies, fire science, food science, gerontology, history, interpreter for the deaf, Japanese studies, liberal arts/general studies, pastoral studies, psychology, religion, religious music, safety and security technology, social science, social work, and sociology). Nursing is the strongest academically. Nursing and criminal justice are the largest.

Required: To graduate, students must complete at least 120 semester hours with a 2.0 GPA; required hours in the major vary from 30 to 62. A minimum of 52 hours of general education courses are required, including 25 hours in humanities, 15 in social science, and 12 in math and science. All students are required to take English 101 and 102 or ESL 423 and a senior seminar, which includes a comprehensive exam.

Special: MU offers cross-registration with Marygrove and St. Mary of Orchard Lake Colleges, Sacred Heart Seminary, and the University of Detroit Mercy. Students may pursue co-op programs in 30 majors, internships, a B.A.-B.S. degree in gerontology and may receive credit for life, military, or work experience. Work-study at MU and study abroad in 13 countries are also possible. There are 9 national honor societies, and 8 departmental honors programs.

Faculty/Classroom: 38% of faculty are male; 62%, female. All teach undergraduates. No introductory courses are taught by graduate students. The average class size in an introductory lecture is 19; in a laboratory, 16; and in a regular course, 16.

Admissions: The ACT scores for the 2005-2006 freshman class were: 22% below 21, 35% between 21 and 23, 24% between 24 and 26, 8% between 27 and 28, and 11% above 28.

Requirements: The ACT is required. The ACT Optional Writing test is also recommended. In addition, students should have completed 4 years of English, 3 of math, 2 of science, and 1 of history. The school accepts the GED. An essay is required. For some majors, students are asked to submit a portfolio or to appear for an interview or audition. A GPA of

2.75 is required. AP and CLEP credits are accepted. Important factors in the admissions decision are advanced placement or honor courses, recommendations by school officials, and leadership record.

Procedure: Freshmen are admitted to all sessions. Entrance exams should be taken during either the junior or senior year. There are early admissions and rolling admissions plans. Application deadlines are open. Application fee is $25. Notification is sent on a rolling basis. Applications are accepted on-line.

Transfer: Applicants must be in good academic and personal standing at their previous colleges and must submit official transcripts of college and high school work. Courses completed at an accredited institution with a grade of C or better will be considered for transfer credit. 30 of 120 credits required for the bachelor's degree must be completed at MU.

Visiting: There are regularly scheduled orientations for prospective students, including an interview and a tour of the campus. There are guides for informal visits and visitors may sit in on classes and stay overnight. To schedule a visit, contact the Office of Undergraduate Admissions at (734) 432-5339 or admis@madonna.edu.

Financial Aid: In 2005-2006, 82% of all full-time freshmen and 74% of continuing full-time students received some form of financial aid. 49% of full-time freshmen and 53% of continuing full-time students received need-based aid. The average freshman award was $7616. Need-based scholarships or need-based grants averaged $3220 ($6850 maximum); need-based self-help aid (loans and jobs) averaged $2625 ($2625 maximum); non-need-based athletic scholarships averaged $2512 ($8000 maximum); and other non-need-based awards and non-need-based scholarships averaged $2592 ($8250 maximum). 23% of undergraduates work part time. The average financial indebtedness of the 2005 graduate was $19,252. The FAFSA is required. The deadline for filing freshman financial aid applications for fall entry is February 21.

International Students: There are 89 international students enrolled. The school actively recruits these students. A satisfactory score is required on the written TOEFL or the MELAB, or an equivalent English Proficiency test (IELTS). Applicants must also take the SAT or the ACT.

Computers: Wireless access is available. All students may access the system 9 A.M. to 10 P.M. daily, 9 A.M. to 5 P.M. Saturday, and 1 P.M. to 5 P.M. Sunday. Students may access the system 1 hour per day if others are waiting. There are no fees.

Graduates: From July 1, 2004 to June 30, 2005, 509 bachelor's degrees were awarded. The most popular majors were nursing (10%), business (5%), and criminal justice (5%). In an average class, 26% graduate in 3 years or less, 32% graduate in 4 years or less, 38% graduate in 5 years or less, and 41% graduate in 6 years or less. 11 companies recruited on campus in 2004-2005. Of the 2004 graduating class, 7% were enrolled in graduate school within 6 months of graduation and 50% were employed.

Admissions Contact: Frank Hribar, Director for Enrollment Management. A video is available. E-mail: fhribar@madonna.edu
Web: www.madonna.edu

MARYGROVE COLLEGE E-5

Detroit, MI 48221-2599   **(313) 927-1240**
(866) 313-1927; Fax: (313) 927-1345

Full-time: 113 men, 285 women	**Faculty:** 65; IIA, --$
Part-time: 54 men, 280 women	**Ph.D.s:** 70%
Graduate: 641 men, 2215 women	**Student/Faculty:** 6 to 1
Year: semesters, summer session	**Tuition:** $13,110
Application Deadline: August 15	**Room & Board:** $6200
Freshman Class: 414 applied, 173 accepted, 80 enrolled	
ACT: 18	**COMPETITIVE+**

Founded in 1927 and grounded in the liberal arts, Marygrove College is a private comprehensive institution affiliated with the Catholic Church. In addition to regional accreditation, Marygrove College has baccalaureate program accreditation with ADA, CAHEA, CSWE, and NCATE. The library contains 76,689 volumes, 68,750 microform items, and 2834 audio/video tapes/CDs/DVDs, and subscribes to 447 periodicals including electronic. Computerized library services include the card catalog, interlibrary loans, and database searching. Special learning facilities include a learning resource center, art gallery, and a writing center, a learning clinic, and a theater. The 50-acre campus is in an urban area 11 miles from downtown Detroit. Including any residence halls, there are 4 buildings.

Student Life: 99% of undergraduates are from Michigan. Others are from 5 states and 14 foreign countries. 64% are African American. The average age of freshmen is 20; all undergraduates, 32. 29% do not continue beyond their first year; 27% remain to graduate.

Housing: 110 students can be accommodated in college housing, which includes coed dorms. 89% of students commute. Alcohol is not permitted. All students may keep cars.

Activities: There are no fraternities or sororities. There are 18 groups on campus, including art, choir, chorale, computers, dance, honors, religious, social service, and student government. Popular campus events include Honors Day, Martin Luther King Day, and contemporary American authors lecture series.

Sports: There is 1 intercollegiate sport for men and 1 for women. Facilities include a fitness center and a gym.

Disabled Students: 90% of the campus is accessible. Wheelchair ramps, elevators, special parking, specially equipped rest rooms, lowered drinking fountains, and portable wheelchair ramps are available.

Services: Counseling and information services are available, as is tutoring in most subjects. There is remedial math, reading, and writing.

Campus Safety and Security: Measures include 24-hour foot and vehicle patrol, self-defense education, security escort services, and informal discussions. There are pamphlets/posters/films, emergency telephones, and lighted pathways/sidewalks.

Programs of Study: Marygrove College confers B.A., B.S., B.A.S., B.B.A., B.F.A., B.M., and B.S.W. degrees. Associate and master's degrees are also awarded. Bachelor's degrees are awarded in BIOLOGICAL SCIENCE (biology/biological science), BUSINESS (business administration and management), COMMUNICATIONS AND THE ARTS (art, dance, English, language arts, and music), COMPUTER AND PHYSICAL SCIENCE (chemistry, information sciences and systems, mathematics, and science), EDUCATION (early childhood, social studies, and special), ENGINEERING AND ENVIRONMENTAL DESIGN (environmental science), HEALTH PROFESSIONS (art therapy), SOCIAL SCIENCE (child psychology/development, history, political science/government, psychology, religion, social science, and social work). English, education, and social work are the strongest academically. Business, computer science, and social work are the largest.

Required: To graduate, students must complete 128 semester hours with a minimum GPA of 2.0. The required core program includes 28 credit hours with a minimum of one 3 to 4 hour course in the following nine areas: historical and cultural traditions, literature and languages, scientific inquiry (lab science), identity and reason, social environment, religious and philosophical traditions, creative expression, local and national perspectives, and global awareness. Common Experience requirements include: liberal arts seminar (for freshmen only), communication, writing-intensive course in major, and senior seminar. The required number of hours in the major varies.

Special: A consortium program is offered with the University of Detroit Mercy, Sacared Heart Seminary, and Madonna University. Also available are nondegree study, student-designed and dual majors, study abroad in 5 countries, internships, pass/fail options, and work-study programs. Students may acquire credit for life experience by documenting their achievements in a portfolio. There are 4 national honor societies, a freshman honors program, and 1 departmental honors program.

Faculty/Classroom: 38% of faculty are male; 62%, female. All teach undergraduates. No introductory courses are taught by graduate students. The average class size in an introductory lecture is 17 and in a laboratory, 10.

Admissions: 42% of the 2005-2006 applicants were accepted. The ACT scores for the 2005-2006 freshman class were: 86% below 21, 9% between 21 and 23, 1% between 24 and 26, and 4% between 27 and 28.

Requirements: The ACT is required. In addition, the applicant must be a graduate of an accredited high school. An interview is recommended. The student's average, class rank, recommendations, and special talents are important factors in admission. Entering students must take the College Placement Examinations. A GPA of 2.0 is required. AP and CLEP credits are accepted. Important factors in the admissions decision are recommendations by school officials, evidence of special talent, and advanced placement or honor courses.

Procedure: Freshmen are admitted to all sessions. There are deferred admissions and rolling admissions plans. Applications should be filed by August 15 for fall entry. Notification of early decision is sent on a rolling basis; regular decision, on a rolling basis. The fall 2005 application fee was $25. Applications are accepted on-line.

Transfer: 90 transfer students enrolled in 2004-2005. Transfer students must have a minimum 2.0 GPA. An associate degree or 24 completed credit hours and an interview are recommended. 30 of 128 credits required for the bachelor's degree must be completed at Marygrove College.

Visiting: There are regularly scheduled orientations for prospective students, including a tour of the campus followed by college workshops, first-year-student panels, and a college financial planning seminar. There are guides for informal visits and visitors may sit in on classes. To schedule a visit, contact the Admissions Office at *info@marygrove.edu*.

Financial Aid: In 2005-2006, 98% of continuing full-time students received some form of financial aid. 90% of full-time freshmen and 98% of continuing full-time students received need-based aid. Marygrove College is a member of CSS. The CSS/Profile or FAFSA and the college's own financial statement are required. The deadline for filing freshman financial aid applications for fall entry is March 15.

International Students: There are 17 international students enrolled. Satisfactory scores are required on the TOEFL and the college's own test. Students must also take a placement test in reading, writing, and math after admission.

Computers: All students may access the system. There are no time limits and no fees.

Graduates: From July 1, 2004 to June 30, 2005, 101 bachelor's degrees were awarded. The most popular majors were social work (16%), education (14%), and business and management (13%). In an average class, 17% graduate in 5 years or less, and 27% graduate in 6 years or less.

Admissions Contact: John Ambrose, Director of Admission. A video is available. E-mail: *jambrose@marygrove.edu* Web: *www.marygrove.edu*

MICHIGAN STATE UNIVERSITY — D-4

East Lansing, MI 48824   (517) 355-8332; Fax: (517) 353-1647

Full-time: 14,855 men, 17,345 women	Faculty: 2411; I, av$
Part-time: 1705 men, 1773 women	Ph.D.s: 90%
Graduate: 4017 men, 5471 women	Student/Faculty: 13 to 1
Year: semesters, summer session	Tuition: $7945 ($19,697)
Application Deadline: July 25	Room & Board: $5744
Freshman Class: 21,844 applied, 16,686 accepted, 7266 enrolled	
SAT Verbal/Math: 560/590*	ACT: 24 VERY COMPETITIVE

Michigan State University, a pioneer land-grant institution, was founded in 1855. Its 14 colleges and more than 100 departments offer 200 undergraduate and 250 graduate fields of study. The university's Honors College offers students an alternative education program. There are 12 undergraduate and 13 graduate schools. In addition to regional accreditation, MSU has baccalaureate program accreditation with AACSB, ABET, ACEJMC, ADA, ASLA, CAHEA, CSWE, FIDER, NASM, NCATE, NLN, and SAF. The 10 libraries contain 4,503,950 volumes, 5,601,101 microform items, and 299,287 audio/video tapes/CDs/DVDs, and subscribe to 33,760 periodicals including electronic. Computerized library services include the card catalog, interlibrary loans, database searching, and Internet access. Special learning facilities include a learning resource center, art gallery, natural history museum, planetarium, radio station, TV station, botanical garden, superconducting cyclotron lab, environmental toxicology center, pesticide research center, and center for computer-aided and engineering and manufacturing. The 5239-acre campus is in a suburban area 80 miles northwest of Detroit. Including any residence halls, there are 564 buildings.

Student Life: 89% of undergraduates are from Michigan. Others are from 49 states, 120 foreign countries, and Canada. 78% are white. The average age of freshmen is 18; all undergraduates, 20. 9% do not continue beyond their first year; 71% remain to graduate.

Housing: 17,000 students can be accommodated in college housing, which includes coed dorms, on-campus apartments, and married-student housing. In addition, there are honors houses and special-interest houses. On-campus housing is guaranteed for all 4 years. 58% of students commute. Upperclassmen may keep cars.

Activities: There are 33 national fraternities and 16 national sororities. There are 525 groups on campus, including art, band, cheerleading, chess, choir, chorale, chorus, computers, dance, debate, drama, ethnic, film, gay, honors, international, jazz band, marching band, musical theater, newspaper, opera, orchestra, pep band, photography, political, professional, radio and TV, religious, social, social service, student government, symphony, and yearbook. Popular campus events include home football games, Spartan basketball, and Welcome Days.

Sports: There are 12 intercollegiate sports for men and 13 for women, and 22 intramural sports for men and 22 for women. Facilities include a 76,000-seat stadium, a 4000-seat gym and field house, an ice arena, and a multipurpose 15,500-seat student events center. The university also has an indoor football practice facility, 3 intramural facilities, indoor and outdoor tennis courts, ball fields, a running track, 2 golf courses, and 4 swimming pools, including 1 Olympic-size outdoor pool.

Disabled Students: 75% of the campus is accessible. Wheelchair ramps, elevators, special parking, specially equipped rest rooms, special class scheduling, lowered drinking fountains, lowered telephones, tape recorders, videotaped classes, reading machines, readers, and note takers are available.

Services: Counseling and information services are available, as is tutoring in most subjects. There is a reader service for the blind and remedial math and writing.

Campus Safety and Security: Measures include 24-hour foot and vehicle patrol, self-defense education, security escort services, and shuttle buses. There are informal discussions, pamphlets/posters/films, emergency telephones, lighted pathways/sidewalks, and regional/campus bus service.

Programs of Study: MSU confers B.A., B.S., B.F.A., B.Land.Arch., B.Mus., and B.S. in Nursing degrees. Master's and doctoral degrees are also awarded. Bachelor's degrees are awarded in AGRICULTURE (agriculture, animal science, environmental studies, fishing and fisheries, forestry and related sciences, horticulture, natural resource management, soil science, and wildlife management), BIOLOGICAL SCIENCE (biochemistry, bioinformatics, biology/biological science, biotechnology, botany, entomology, environmental biology, microbiology, nutrition, physiology, plant pathology, and zoology), BUSINESS (accounting, banking and finance, business administration and management, hospitality management services, human resources, marketing management, marketing/retailing/merchandising, personnel management, and tourism), COMMUNICATIONS AND THE ARTS (advertising, art history and appreciation, communications, dramatic arts, East Asian languages and literature, English, French, German, jazz, journalism, Latin, linguistics, music, music performance, music theory and composition, Russian, Spanish, studio art, and telecommunications), COMPUTER AND PHYSICAL SCIENCE (astrophysics, chemical physics, chemistry, computer science, earth science, geology, geophysics and seismology, geoscience, information sciences and systems, mathematics, physical sciences, physics, and statistics), EDUCATION (agricultural, art, education, music, physical, and special), ENGINEERING AND ENVIRONMENTAL DESIGN (chemical engineering, city/community/regional planning, civil engineering, computational sciences, computer engineering, construction management, electrical/electronics engineering, engineering, engineering mechanics, interior design, landscape architecture/design, manufacturing engineering, materials engineering, mechanical engineering, textile technology, and urban planning technology), HEALTH PROFESSIONS (clinical science, medical laboratory technology, music therapy, nursing, speech pathology/audiology, and veterinary science), SOCIAL SCIENCE (American studies, anthropology, child psychology/development, classical/ancient civilization, criminal justice, dietetics, economics, family and community services, family/consumer resource management, family/consumer studies, food production/management/services, food science, geography, history, humanities, interdisciplinary studies, parks and recreation management, philosophy, political science/government, prelaw, psychology, public administration, religion, social science, social work, sociology, and women's studies). Engineering, education, and business are the strongest academically. Business, communications, and social science are the largest.

Required: To graduate, students must complete a freshman writing course and a writing course specified by the major and degree program. Students must complete the 26-credit University Integrative Studies requirement consisting of 8 credits of arts and humanitites, 8 of social, behavioral, and economic sciences, 8 of general science, and 3 of a transcollegiate course. Students must also complete a math requirement determined by each undergraduate college (minimum of college algebra plus trigonometry/finite math/statistics.) A minimum 2.0 GPA and 120 semester hours are required.

Special: Special academic programs include an engineering co-op program with business and industry; internships in business, education, political science, agriculture, and communication arts; study abroad in more than 62 countries; on-campus work-study programs; and a sea semester. An accelerated degree program in all majors and student-designed majors are offered at the Honors College. Nondegree study, pass/fail options in some courses, and dual majors are possible. Educationally disadvantaged students may avail themselves of the College Achievement Admissions Program (CAAP). Cross-registration with the Committee on Institutional Cooperation schools is available. There are 48 national honor societies, including Phi Beta Kappa, and a freshman honors program.

Faculty/Classroom: 63% of faculty are male; 37%, female. The average class size in an introductory lecture is 100; in a laboratory, 30; and in a regular course, 30.

Admissions: 76% of the 2005-2006 applicants were accepted. The SAT scores for the 2005-2006 freshman class were: Verbal--26% below 500, 39% between 500 and 599, 26% between 600 and 700, and 9% above 700; Math--16% below 500, 36% between 500 and 599, 35% between 600 and 700, and 13% above 700. The ACT scores were 14% below 21, 26% between 21 and 23, 32% between 24 and 26, 14% between 27 and 28, and 14% above 28. 52% of the current freshmen were in the top fifth of their class; 89% were in the top two fifths.

Requirements: The SAT or ACT is required. In addition, applicants must be graduates of an accredited secondary school and have completed 4 years of English, 3 years each of math and social studies, 2 years of science, and 2 years of a single foreign language. A personal statement is strongly recommended. The GED is accepted. Music majors must audition. AP and CLEP credits are accepted. Important factors in the admissions decision are advanced placement or honor courses, recommendations by school officials, and evidence of special talent.

Procedure: Freshmen are admitted fall, spring, and summer. Entrance exams should be taken during the junior year of high school. There is a deferred admissions and a rolling admissions plan. Applications should be filed by July 25 for fall entry, December 1 for spring entry, and April 15 for summer entry. Notification is sent on a rolling basis. 1524 applicants were on the 2005 waiting list; 228 were admitted. Applications are accepted on-line. The fall 2005 application fee waas $35.

Transfer: 2150 transfer students enrolled in a recent year. To transfer, a minimum GPA of 2.0 is required, (prefer 3.0 overall GPA). MSU Integrative Studies requirement should be fulfilled (28 general graduation credits), and college algebra completed. 30 of 120 credits required for the bachelor's degree must be completed at MSU.

Visiting: There are regularly scheduled orientations for prospective students, including a presentation and a tour of the campus. There are

guides for informal visits and visitors may sit in on classes and stay overnight. To schedule a visit, contact the Admissions office.

Financial Aid: In a recent year, 93% of all full-time freshmen and 68% of continuing full-time students received some form of financial aid. 28% of full-time freshmen and 22% of continuing full-time students received need-based aid. The average freshman award was $7148. The average financial indebtedness of a recent year's graduate was $18,121. The FAFSA is required. The priority date for freshman financial aid applications for fall entry is March 1. The deadline for filing freshman financial aid applications for fall entry is June 30.

International Students: There were 1046 international students enrolled in a recent year. The school actively recruits these students. They must score satisfactorily on the TOEFL or take the MELAB, the Comprehensive English Language Test, or the college's own test.

Computers: All students may access the system 24 hours per day, 7 days per week. There are no time limits and no fees. All students are required to have personal computers.

Graduates: From July 1, 2004 to June 30, 2005, 7733 bachelor's degrees were awarded. The most popular majors were business (19%), communications (14%), and social science (10%). In an average class, 36% graduate in 4 years or less, 66% graduate in 5 years or less, and 71% graduate in 6 years or less.

Admissions Contact: Pamela T. Horne, Director of Admissions and Scholarships. A video is available. E-mail: *admis@msu.edu* Web: *admissions.msu.edu*

MICHIGAN TECHNOLOGICAL UNIVERSITY B-1

Houghton, MI 49931-1295 (906) 487-2335
(888) MTU-1885; Fax: (906) 487-2125

Full-time: 4063 men, 1096 women	**Faculty:** 349; I, --$
Part-time: 323 men, 132 women	**Ph.D.s:** 83%
Graduate: 601 men, 295 women	**Student/Faculty:** 15 to 1
Year: semesters, summer session	**Tuition:** $8194 ($19,384)
Application Deadline: open	**Room & Board:** $6375
Freshman Class: 3928 applied, 3326 accepted, 1327 enrolled	
SAT Verbal/Math: 587/630*	**VERY COMPETITIVE**

Michigan Technological University, founded in 1885, is a state-supported institution offering degrees in engineering, liberal arts, sciences, forestry, business, and technology. There are 5 undergraduate schools and 1 graduate school. In addition to regional accreditation, Michigan Tech has baccalaureate program accreditation with AACSB, ABET, and SAF. The library contains 821,263 volumes, 546,199 microform items, and 5228 audio/video tapes/CDs/DVDs, and subscribes to 2891 periodicals including electronic. Computerized library services include the card catalog, interlibrary loans, database searching, Internet access, and laptop Internet portals. Special learning facilities include a learning resource center, radio station, the A.E. Seaman Mineral Museum, the Rozsa Center for the Performing Arts, the Ford Forestry Center and Researh Forest, cosmic ray observatory, x-ray fluorescence spectrometer, process simulation and control center, remote sensing institute, computer-aided engineering lab, microfabrication lab, and subsurface visualization lab. The 925-acre campus is in a small town 325 miles northwest of Milwaukee, Wisconsin. Including any residence halls, there are 42 buildings.

Student Life: 72% of undergraduates are from Michigan. Others are from 46 states, 71 foreign countries, and Canada. 81% are white. The average age of freshmen is 19; all undergraduates, 21. 20% do not continue beyond their first year; 62% remain to graduate.

Housing: 3159 students can be accommodated in college housing, which includes coed dormitories, on-campus apartments, and married-student housing. Each dorm has smoke-free rooms for inter national students, the first year experience program, the health living house, and the computer science learning center. On-campus housing is guaranteed for the freshman year only and is available on a first-come, first-served basis. 60% of students commute. All students may keep cars.

Activities: 9% of men belong to 5 local and 10 national fraternities; 15% of women belong to 4 local and 4 national sororities. There are 269 groups on campus, including art, band, cheerleading, chess, choir, chorale, chorus, computers, dance, drama, drill team, ethnic, film, gay, honors, international, jazz band, literary magazine, musical theater, newspaper, orchestra, pep band, photography, political, professional, radio and TV, religious, social, social service, student government, and symphony. Popular campus events include Winter Carnival, K-Day, and Spring Fling.

Sports: There are 7 intercollegiate sports for men and 6 for women, and 41 intramural sports for men and 41 for women. Facilities include a complex with a 4200-seat ice arena and a 3200-seat gym, a lakeside golf course, football and softball fields, a tennis center, Mont Ripley Ski Hill and a cross-country ski trail, a multipurpose room, a pool, a fitness center, racquetball/squash courts, a dance room, and a gymnastics room.

Disabled Students: 90% of the campus is accessible. Wheelchair ramps, elevators, special parking, specially equipped rest rooms, special class scheduling, lowered drinking fountains, and special housing are available.

Services: Counseling and information services are available, as is tutoring in some subjects. There is a reader service for the blind, and remedial math, reading, and writing. Learning centers for English, math, chemistry, physics, biology, computer science, and engineering are available.

Campus Safety and Security: Measures include 24-hour foot and vehicle patrol, self-defense education, security escort services, and shuttle buses. There are informal discussions, pamphlets/posters/films, emergency telephones, and lighted pathways/sidewalks.

Programs of Study: Michigan Tech confers B.A. and B.S. degrees. Associate, master's, and doctoral degrees are also awarded. Bachelor's degrees are awarded in AGRICULTURE (forestry and related sciences and wildlife management), BIOLOGICAL SCIENCE (bioinformatics, biology/biological science, and ecology), BUSINESS (business administration and management), COMMUNICATIONS AND THE ARTS (audio technology, communications, technical and business writing, and theater design), COMPUTER AND PHYSICAL SCIENCE (applied physics, chemistry, computer science, geology, geophysics and seismology, mathematics, physics, and software engineering), ENGINEERING AND ENVIRONMENTAL DESIGN (biomedical engineering, chemical engineering, civil engineering, computer engineering, construction management, electrical/electronics engineering, electrical/electronics engineering technology, engineering, environmental engineering, geological engineering, materials engineering, mechanical engineering, mechanical engineering technology, and surveying engineering), HEALTH PROFESSIONS (clinical science), SOCIAL SCIENCE (economics, history, liberal arts/general studies, psychology, and social science). Engineering, forestry, and physical science are the strongest academically. Mechanical, civil, and electrical engineering are the largest.

Required: To graduate, students must complete 120 to 145 credit hours, maintain a minimum GPA of 2.0, and fulfill basic general education requirements. The basic general education curriculum consists of 4 core courses to be taken by every baccalaureate student, a 15 credit distribution requirement, physical education, and a science/math requirement. In general, 30 of the last 36 credit hours and 30 hours of advanced-level courses must be completed at MTU.

Special: Michigan Tech offers co-op programs in almost all majors, internships in medical technology and secondary teacher education, work-study programs, study abroad in more than 100 countries, dual majors, and a B.A.-B.S. degree in scientific and technical communication. There are interinstitutional programs with Northwestern Michigan, Gogebic Community, and Delta Colleges. A 3-2 engineering degree is possible in conjunction with the University of Wisconsin/Superior, the College of St. Scholastica, and Adrian, Albion, Augsburg, Northland, and Olivet Colleges. There are 16 national honor societies.

Faculty/Classroom: 74% of faculty are male; 26%, female. All teach undergraduates, 84% do research, and 84% do both. Graduate students teach 6% of introductory courses. The average class size in an introductory lecture is 76; in a laboratory, 23; and in a regular course, 30.

Admissions: 85% of the 2005-2006 applicants were accepted. The SAT scores for the 2005-2006 freshman class were: Verbal--15% below 500, 36% between 500 and 599, 40% between 600 and 700, and 9% above 700; Math--6% below 500, 26% between 500 and 599, 49% between 600 and 700, and 19% above 700. The ACT scores were 12% below 21, 22% between 21 and 23, 29% between 24 and 26, 17% between 27 and 28, and 20% above 28. 47% of the current freshmen were in the top fifth of their class; 76% were in the top two fifths. There were 8 National Merit finalists. 50 freshmen graduated first in their class.

Requirements: The SAT or ACT is required. Scores are used for admission and placement. Admissions requirements include graduation from an accredited secondary school, with 15 academic credits. These must include 3 credits in English, 1 credit of chemistry or physics, and 3 credits in math for engineering and science curricula; credits in social studies and foreign language are recommended. The GED is accepted. AP and CLEP credits are accepted. Important factors in the admissions decision are advanced placement or honor courses, leadership record, and recommendations by school officials.

Procedure: Freshmen are admitted to all sessions. Entrance exams should be taken in the junior year or fall of their senior year. There are deferred admissions and rolling admissions plans. Application deadlines are open. Applications are accepted on-line. The fall 2005 application fee was $40.

Transfer: 198 transfer students enrolled in 2004-2005. Transfer students must have a minimum GPA of 2.5 on a 4.0 scale; grades of B or better are expected in math and science courses (some programs require a 2.75 or higher). 30 of 120 credits required for the bachelor's degree must be completed at Michigan Tech.

Visiting: There are regularly scheduled orientations for prospective students, including campus tours 10 A.M. and 2 P.M. Monday through Friday. Separate interviews are available with academic department advisors, admissions counselors, and the financial aid department. There are guides for informal visits and visitors may sit in on classes and stay overnight. To schedule a visit, contact the Admissions Office at (906) 487-2334.

Financial Aid: In 2005-2006, 91% of all full-time freshmen and 83% of continuing full-time students received some form of financial aid. 53% of full-time freshmen and 51% of continuing full-time students received need-based aid. The average freshman award was $9452. Need-based scholarships or need-based grants averaged $3486 ($18,750 maximum); need-based self-help aid (loans and jobs) averaged $8271 ($2300 maximum); non-need-based athletic scholarships averaged $7995 ($18,750 maximum); and other non-need-based awards and non-need-based scholarships averaged $3148 ($18,750 maximum). 25% of undergraduates work part time. Average annual earnings from campus work are $6292. The average financial indebtedness of the 2005 graduate was $13,344. Michigan Tech is a member of CSS. The FAFSA is required. The priority date for freshman financial aid applications for fall entry is February 21.

International Students: There are 203 international students enrolled. The school actively recruits these students. They must score satisfactorily on the written TOEFL or on the electronic version.

Computers: PC workstations are located in departmental labs, classrooms, the campus library, and the student union. Wireless hotspots are located throughout campus. Workstations and hotspots are accessible to any enrolled student provided that they have a calid network login. There are approximately 1,300 workstations on campus and all have access to the internet. All students may access the system 24 hours a day. There are no time limits. The fee varies with major.

Graduates: From July 1, 2004 to June 30, 2005, 1048 bachelor's degrees were awarded. The most popular majors were mechanical engineering (19%), civil engineering (12%), and electrical engineering (11%). In an average class, 28% graduate in 4 years or less, 56% graduate in 5 years or less, and 62% graduate in 6 years or less. 241 companies recruited on campus in 2004-2005. Of the 2004 graduating class, 15% were enrolled in graduate school within 6 months of graduation and 94% were employed.

Admissions Contact: Allison Carter, Interim.
E-mail: *mtu4u@mtu.edu* Web: *www.mtu.edu/apply/*

NORTHERN MICHIGAN UNIVERSITY
Marquette, MI 49855

C-2

(906) 227-2650
(800) 682-9797; Fax: (906) 227-1747

Full-time: 3712 men, 4129 women	Faculty: 294; IIA, -$
Part-time: 376 men, 497 women	Ph.D.s: 65%
Graduate: 255 men, 410 women	Student/Faculty: 27 to 1
Year: semesters, summer session	Tuition: $5858 ($9602)
Application Deadline: open	Room & Board: $6482
Freshman Class: n/av	
SAT or ACT: required	LESS COMPETITIVE

Northern Michigan University, founded in 1899, is a public institution offering undergraduate programs in the arts and sciences, business, education, health science, human services, nursing, and technology. There are 4 undergraduate schools and 1 graduate school. In addition to regional accreditation, NMU has baccalaureate program accreditation with AACSB, ADA, CSWE, NASM, NCATE, and NLN. The library contains 592,689 volumes, 830,197 microform items, and 7369 audio/video tapes/CDs/DVDs. Computerized library services include the card catalog, interlibrary loans, database searching, and Internet access. Special learning facilities include a learning resource center, art gallery, radio station, TV station, and an observatory. The 320-acre campus is in an urban area on the southern shores of Lake Superior. Including any residence halls, there are 55 buildings.

Student Life: 81% of undergraduates are from Michigan. Students are from 49 states, 36 foreign countries, and Canada. 90% are white. The average age of freshmen is 20; all undergraduates, 24. 31% do not continue beyond their first year.

Housing: 2500 students can be accommodated in college housing, which includes coed dorms, on-campus apartments, and married-student housing. In addition, there are honors houses and special-interest houses, and smoke-free and chemical-free houses. On-campus housing is guaranteed for all 4 years. 66% of students commute. All students may keep cars.

Activities: 1% of men and about 1% of women belong to 2 national fraternities; 1% of women belong to 3 national sororities. There are 200 groups on campus, including art, band, cheerleading, chess, choir, chorale, chorus, computers, dance, drama, drill team, ethnic, film, gay, health, honors, international, international dance club, jazz band, literary magazine, marching band, musical theater, orchestra, pep band, philosophy, photography, political, professional, radio and TV, religious, social, social service, student government, symphony, and yearbook. Popular campus events include Winterfest, Be a Part from the Start, and U.P. 200 Dog Sled Race.

Sports: There are 5 intercollegiate sports for men and 7 for women, and 9 intramural sports for men and 8 for women. Facilities include indoor and outdoor playing fields, an aerobic and fitness training area, an ice rink, a swimming pool, a diving tank, a field house, an 8000-seat stadium, a 4000-seat basketball and hockey arena, a rock-climbing wall, racquetball courts, the neighboring forests and rivers, and Lake Superior.

Disabled Students: 90% of the campus is accessible. Wheelchair ramps, elevators, special parking, specially equipped rest rooms, lowered drinking fountains, lowered telephones, and special housing are available.

Services: Counseling and information services are available, as is tutoring in every subject. There is a reader service for the blind, and remedial math, reading, and writing.

Campus Safety and Security: Measures include 24-hour foot and vehicle patrol, self-defense education, security escort services, and shuttle buses. There are informal discussions, pamphlets/posters/films, emergency telephones, lighted pathways/sidewalks, and a crime prevention program with a full-time staff.

Programs of Study: NMU confers B.A., B.S., B.F.A., B.M.Ed., B.S.N., and B.S.W. degrees. Associate and master's degrees are also awarded. Bachelor's degrees are awarded in BIOLOGICAL SCIENCE (biochemistry, biology/biological science, botany, ecology, microbiology, physiology, and zoology), BUSINESS (accounting, banking and finance, business administration and management, entrepreneurial studies, and marketing/retailing/merchandising), COMMUNICATIONS AND THE ARTS (broadcasting, communications, design, dramatic arts, English, fine arts, French, music, public relations, Spanish, and speech/debate/rhetoric), COMPUTER AND PHYSICAL SCIENCE (chemistry, computer programming, computer science, earth science, information sciences and systems, mathematics, and physics), EDUCATION (art, business, computer, education of the mentally handicapped, elementary, health, industrial arts, music, physical, science, and secondary), ENGINEERING AND ENVIRONMENTAL DESIGN (construction management, electrical/electronics engineering technology, industrial engineering technology, and manufacturing technology), HEALTH PROFESSIONS (clinical science, cytotechnology, medical laboratory technology, nursing, predentistry, premedicine, preveterinary science, and speech pathology/audiology), SOCIAL SCIENCE (criminal justice, economics, geography, history, international studies, parks and recreation management, philosophy, physical fitness/movement, political science/government, prelaw, psychology, public administration, social work, sociology, and water resources). Biology, chemistry, and education are the strongest academically. Business, education, and biology are the largest.

Required: Students must earn 40 semester credits in liberal studies requirements, including courses in humanities, composition, natural sciences/math, social sciences, communications, and visual and performing arts. Graduation requirements vary by degree program; at the minimum, students must earn 124 semester credits, including 32 in a major field, with a GPA of 2.0. Courses in phys ed/health and world culture are also required.

Special: Cross-registration is available with other Michigan universities and colleges. Students may study abroad in Europe, Latin America, and Japan. NMU also offers internships, a co-op program in business, accelerated degree programs, a combined accounting/computer information systems major, dual and student-designed majors, limited pass/fail options, and nondegree study. There are 9 national honor societies, a freshman honors program, and 5 departmental honors programs.

Faculty/Classroom: 63% of faculty are male; 37%, female. All teach undergraduates. Graduate students teach 1% of introductory courses. The average class size in an introductory lecture is 23; in a laboratory, 16; and in a regular course, 23.

Requirements: The SAT or ACT is required, with a satisfactory score for the SAT and for the ACT. Applicants must be graduates of accredited secondary schools or have earned a GED. NMU requires 12 to 16 Carnegie units; recommended secondary school preparation includes 4 years of English, 3 each of math, history, social studies, foreign language, and science, 2 of fine arts or performing arts, and 1 of computer instruction. Students seeking art scholarships must submit a portfolio; those seeking music and theater scholarships must audition. A GPA of 2.25 is required. AP and CLEP credits are accepted. Important factors in the admissions decision are advanced placement or honor courses, evidence of special talent, and recommendations by school officials.

Procedure: Freshmen are admitted to all sessions. Entrance exams should be taken during the year prior to enrollment. There are deferred admissions and rolling admissions plans. Application deadlines are open. Application fee is $30. Applications are accepted on-line.

Transfer: 514 transfer students enrolled in 2004-2005. Applicants must present a minimum GPA of 2.0 in at least 12 semester credits of college-level work. 32 of 124 credits required for the bachelor's degree must be completed at NMU.

Visiting: There are regularly scheduled orientations for prospective students, including an admissions interview, a tour, and a faculty visit. Visitors may sit in on classes and stay overnight. To schedule a visit, contact the Campus Visit Office at (906) 227-1709.

Financial Aid: In 2005-2006, 86% of all full-time freshmen and 83% of continuing full-time students received some form of financial aid. 36% of full-time freshmen and 34% of continuing full-time students received need-based aid. Need-based scholarships or need-based grants averaged $3928 ($5450 maximum); need-based self-help aid (loans and jobs) averaged $3337 ($9025 maximum); non-need-based athletic scholarships averaged $6445 ($16,634 maximum); and other non-need-based awards and non-need-based scholarships averaged $3322 ($16,234 maximum). 24% of undergraduates work part time. The average financial indebtedness of the 2005 graduate was $19,200. The FAFSA is required. The priority date for freshman financial aid applications for fall entry is March 1.

International Students: In a recent year, there were 107 international students enrolled. The school actively recruits these students. They must score satisfactory on the written TOEFL or on the electronic version.

Computers: Wireless access is available. All students may access the system. There are no time limits and no fees. All students are required to have personal computers. An IBM Thinkpad or iBook is provided as part of tuition and fees.

Admissions Contact: Gerri Daniels, Director of Admissions. A video is available. E-mail: *admiss@nmu.edu* Web: *www.nmu.edu*

NORTHWOOD UNIVERSITY

D-4

Midland, MI 48640

(989) 837-4273
(800) 457-7878; Fax: (989) 837-4104

Full-time: 1100 men, 600 women	**Faculty:** 44
Part-time: 20 men, 30 women	**Ph.D.s:** 23%
Graduate: 200 men, 100 women	**Student/Faculty:** 39 to 1
Year: quarters, summer session	**Tuition:** $14,000
Application Deadline: see profile	**Room & Board:** $7000
Freshman Class: n/av	
SAT or ACT: required	**LESS COMPETITIVE**

Northwood University, founded in 1959, is a private, nonprofit college offering undergraduate and graduate programs in business management. Campuses are located in Florida, Michigan, and Texas. Figures in the above capsule and in this profile are approximate. The library contains 41,000 volumes, 46,500 microform items, and 70 audio/video tapes/CDs/DVDs, and subscribes to 300 periodicals including electronic. Computerized library services include the card catalog, interlibrary loans, and database searching. Special learning facilities include a learning resource center, art gallery, and creativity center. The 270-acre campus is in a suburban area 135 miles north of Detroit. Including any residence halls, there are 29 buildings.

Student Life: 75% of undergraduates are from Michigan. Others are from 35 states, 27 foreign countries, and Canada. 70% are from public schools. 71% are white; 15% African American; 10% foreign nationals. The average age of freshmen is 19; all undergraduates, 21. 28% do not continue beyond their first year; 56% remain to graduate.

Housing: 868 students can be accommodated in college housing, which includes single-sex dorms and on-campus apartments. On-campus housing is guaranteed for the freshman year only and is available on a first-come, first-served basis. 63% of students commute. All students may keep cars.

Activities: 30% of men belong to 3 local and 4 national fraternities; 20% of women belong to 1 local and 3 national sororities. There are 35 groups on campus, including cheerleading, chorale, computers, dance, drama, ethnic, forensics, honors, international, investment, newspaper, pep band, political, professional, religious, social, social service, student government, and yearbook. Popular campus events include Auto Show Weekend, Greek Week, and Values Emphasis Week.

Sports: There are 8 intercollegiate sports for men and 9 for women, and 10 intramural sports for men and 10 for women. Facilities include a 1500-seat indoor gym, a 3500-seat stadium, 3 multipurpose courts, a 4-lane track and a fitness center.

Disabled Students: 95% of the campus is accessible. Wheelchair ramps, elevators, special parking, specially equipped rest rooms, special class scheduling, and lowered drinking fountains are available.

Services: Counseling and information services are available, as is tutoring in most subjects. There is remedial math, reading, and writing.

Campus Safety and Security: Measures include 24-hour foot and vehicle patrol, informal discussions, pamphlets/posters/films, and lighted pathways/sidewalks. There is a professional security force.

Programs of Study: Northwood confers the B.B.A. degree. Associate and master's degrees are also awarded. Bachelor's degrees are awarded in BUSINESS (accounting, banking and finance, business administration and management, business economics, fashion merchandising, hotel/motel and restaurant management, international business management, management information systems, marketing management, sports management, and transportation and travel marketing), COMMUNICATIONS AND THE ARTS (advertising), COMPUTER AND PHYSICAL SCIENCE (computer management). Accounting is the strongest academically. Marketing/management are the largest.

Required: To graduate, all students must complete a minimum of 180 credit hours, with 36 credit hours in the major. A minimum GPA of 2.0 must be maintained, and 6 credits of computer science management and 2 credits of executive fitness must be completed. Internships for 1 to 6 credits are required in some majors.

Special: Northwood offers on- and off-campus work-study and a competitive study-abroad program in 20 countries. Dual majors with management are available in all majors. Credit for life military and work experience is possible through a plan of study. Nondegree study, accelerated degree programs, externships in most majors, and pass/fail options are offered. There is a freshman honors program.

Faculty/Classroom: 59% of faculty are male; 41%, female. All teach undergraduates. No introductory courses are taught by graduate students. The average class size in an introductory lecture is 21; in a laboratory, 14; and in a regular course, 22.

Admissions: 87% of recent applicants were accepted. The SAT scores for a recent freshman class were: Verbal--81% below 500, 15% between 500 and 599, and 4% between 600 and 700; Math--57% below 500, 32% between 500 and 599, and 11% between 600 and 700. The ACT scores were 55% below 21, 23% between 21 and 23, 16% between 24 and 26, 4% between 27 and 28, and 2% above 28. 24% of recent freshmen were in the top fifth of their class; 45% were in the top two fifths. 3 freshmen graduated first in their class.

Requirements: The SAT or ACT is required. In addition, graduation from an accredited secondary school is required. The GED is accepted. A GPA of 2.0 is required. AP and CLEP credits are accepted. Important factors in the admissions decision are advanced placement or honor courses, evidence of special talent, and leadership record.

Procedure: Freshmen are admitted to all sessions. Entrance exams should be taken in the spring of the junior year. There are early admissions and deferred admissions plans. Check with the school for current application deadlines. The fall 2005 application fee was $25. Notification is sent on a rolling basis. Applications are accepted on-line.

Transfer: 217 transfer students enrolled in a recent year. Transfer students must have a minimum of 12 credit hours and a minimum GPA of 2.0. An associate's degree and an interview are recommended. 45 of 180 quarter credits required for the bachelor's degree must be completed at Northwood.

Visiting: There are regularly scheduled orientations for prospective students, including academic and social seminars and presentations. There are guides for informal visits and visitors may sit in on classes and stay overnight. To schedule a visit, contact the Admissions Department.

Financial Aid: In a recent year, 93% of all full-time freshmen and 94% of continuing full-time students received some form of financial aid. 68% of full-time freshmen and 74% of continuing full-time students received need-based aid. The average freshman award was $12,757. Need-based scholarships or need-based grants averaged $7607 ($11,640 maximum); need-based self-help aid (loans and jobs) averaged $4296 ($10,724 maximum); non-need-based athletic scholarships averaged $4567 ($20,565 maximum); and other non-need-based awards and non-need-based scholarships averaged $5036 ($14,495 maximum). 16% of undergraduates work part time. Average annual earnings from campus work are $1715. The average financial indebtedness of a recent graduate was $10,770. The FAFSA is required. The deadline for filing freshman financial aid applications for fall entry is open.

International Students: There were 160 international students enrolled in a recent year. The school actively recruits these students. They must score satisfactorily on the written TOEFL or on the electronic version.

Computers: All students may access the system any time.

Graduates: In a recent year, 787 bachelor's degrees were awarded. The most popular majors were management (29%), marketing management (24%), and international business (11%). In an average class, 41% graduate in 4 years or less, and 56% graduate in 6 years or less. 33 companies recruited on campus in a recent year. Of a recent graduating class, 3% were enrolled in graduate school within 6 months of graduation and 84% were employed.

Admissions Contact: Dan Toland, Director of Admissions. A video is available. E-mail: *admissions@northwood.edu*
Web: *www.northwood.edu*

OAKLAND UNIVERSITY — E-4

Rochester, MI 48309-4401 (248) 370-3570; Fax: (800) OAK-UNIV

Full-time: 3729 men, 6031 women	Faculty: 449; IIA, av$
Part-time: 1441 men, 2247 women	Ph.D.s: 92%
Graduate: 1343 men, 2548 women	Student/Faculty: 22 to 1
Year: semesters, summer session	Tuition: $5856 ($13,056)
Application Deadline: see profile	Room & Board: $6080
Freshman Class: 5948 applied, 4890 accepted, 2213 enrolled	
ACT: 22	COMPETITIVE

Oakland University, established in 1957, is a comprehensive state-supported institution serving a primarily commuter student body. There are 6 undergraduate schools and 1 graduate school. In addition to regional accreditation, Oakland has baccalaureate program accreditation with AACSB, ABET, APTA, CSAB, NASM, NCATE, NLN, NASPAA, NAST,, NASD, ACS,, and CCNE. The 2 libraries contain 853,874 volumes, 1,178,512 microform items, and 18,886 audio/video tapes/CDs/DVDs, and subscribe to 2995 periodicals including electronic. Computerized library services include the card catalog, interlibrary loans, database searching, Internet access, and laptop Internet portals. Special learning facilities include a learning resource center, art gallery, radio sta-

tion, TV station, and the Product Development and Manufacturing Center, the Historical House Museum, and the Lean-Learning Institute. The 1444-acre campus is in a suburban area 25 miles north of Detroit. Including any residence halls, there are 46 buildings.

Student Life: 98% of undergraduates are from Michigan. Others are from 34 states, 50 foreign countries, and Canada. 83% are white; 10% African American. The average age of freshmen is 19; all undergraduates, 23. 29% do not continue beyond their first year.

Housing: 1870 students can be accommodated in college housing, which includes single-sex and coed dorms, on-campus apartments, married-student housing, and sorority houses. In addition, there are honors houses, special-interest houses, Community outreach, international culture, and wellness communities. On-campus housing is guaranteed for all 4 years. Priority is given to out-of-town students. 87% of students commute. All students may keep cars.

Activities: 1% of men belong to 3 national fraternities; 1% of women belong to 7 national sororities. There are 117 groups on campus, including art, band, cheerleading, choir, chorale, chorus, computers, dance, drama, ethnic, film, forensics, gay, honors, international, jazz band, musical theater, newspaper, orchestra, pep band, political, professional, radio and TV, religious, social, social service, student government, symphony, and yearbook. Popular campus events include Welcome Week, Hispanic Celebration, and Week of Champion at OU.

Sports: There are 7 intercollegiate sports for men and 9 for women, and 15 intramural sports for men and 14 for women. Facilities include a 250,000-square-foot student recreation and athletic center that includes softball and baseball diamonds, an indoor track, soccer and touch football fields, and facilities for swimming, basketball, weight training, dance, fencing, handball, squash, racquetball, and golf.

Disabled Students: 90% of the campus is accessible. Wheelchair ramps, elevators, special parking, specially equipped rest rooms, special class scheduling, lowered drinking fountains, lowered telephones, special housing, and automatic door openers are available.

Services: Counseling and information services are available, as is tutoring in every subject. There is a reader service for the blind and remedial math and writing. There is a mentorship program.

Campus Safety and Security: Measures include 24-hour foot and vehicle patrol, self-defense education, security escort services, and informal discussions. There are pamphlets/posters/films, emergency telephones, and lighted pathways/sidewalks.

Programs of Study: Oakland confers B.A., B.S., B.G.S., B.Mus., B.S.E., and B.S.N. degrees. Master's and doctoral degrees are also awarded. Bachelor's degrees are awarded in BIOLOGICAL SCIENCE (biochemistry, and biology/biological science), BUSINESS (accounting, banking and finance, business administration and management, human resources, management information systems, marketing/retailing/merchandising, and personnel management), COMMUNICATIONS AND THE ARTS (art history and appreciation, Chinese, communications, English, fine arts, French, German, Japanese, journalism, linguistics, music, performing arts, Russian, Spanish, and studio art), COMPUTER AND PHYSICAL SCIENCE (chemistry, computer science, information sciences and systems, mathematics, medical physics, physics, and statistics), EDUCATION (elementary, and music), ENGINEERING AND ENVIRONMENTAL DESIGN (chemical engineering, computer engineering, electrical/electronics engineering, engineering chemistry, engineering physics, mechanical engineering, and systems engineering), HEALTH PROFESSIONS (environmental health science, health science, industrial hygiene, medical laboratory science, nursing, physical therapy, and preventive/wellness health care), SOCIAL SCIENCE (African American studies, anthropology, Asian/Oriental studies, East Asian studies, economics, history, Latin American studies, liberal arts/general studies, philosophy, political science/government, psychology, public administration, Russian and Slavic studies, sociology, South Asian studies, and women's studies). Physical sciences, biological sciences, and engineering are the strongest academically. Psychology, elementary education, and communications are the largest.

Required: To graduate, students must complete 124 credit hours (153 to 161 for the B.Mus.degree or 128 for the B.S., Env. Health). All students must complete 40 credits of general education requirements, including at least 1 course (3 or more credits) from the list of approved courses in each of the 10 knowledge areas: writing, formal reasoning, arts, foreign language, and culture, global perspective, literature, natural science and technology, social science, western civilization, and knowledge application. A GPA of 2.0 is required. The number of hours in the major varies from 32 to 36.

Special: Special academic programs include internships, cooperative programs for most disciplines, and many work-study opportunities. There are organized programs for study abroad in 7 countries; independent programs can be arranged. Oakland also offers a B.A.-B.S. degree in biology and economics, a general studies program, dual majors, a student-designed major, cross-regiatration with Macomb Community College, and preprofessional studies in medicine, dentistry, optometry, and veterinary medicine. There are 5 national honor societies, a freshman honors program, and 39 departmental honors programs.

Faculty/Classroom: 52% of faculty are male; 48%, female. No introductory courses are taught by graduate students.

Admissions: 82% of the 2005-2006 applicants were accepted. The ACT scores for the 2005-2006 freshman class were: 40% below 21, 30% between 21 and 23, 20% between 24 and 26, 6% between 27 and 28, and 4% above 28.

Requirements: The ACT is required. In addition, admissions requirements include graduation from an accredited secondary school and high school level college preparatory work, including 4 years of English and 3 years each of math, science, and social studies. 2 years of foreign language and 1 semester of computer science are recommended as well. Music and dance majors must audition. A GPA of 2.5 is required. AP and CLEP credits are accepted. Important factors in the admissions decision are advanced placement or honor courses, leadership record, and evidence of special talent.

Procedure: Freshmen are admitted to all sessions. Entrance exams should be taken during the spring of the junior year or early fall of the senior year. There are deferred admissions and rolling admissions plans. Contact the school for current application deadlines. The fall 2005 application fee was $35. Notification is sent on a rolling basis.

Transfer: 1294 transfer students enrolled in a recent year. Applicants must have at least a 2.5 GPA; a higher GPA is required in some majors. 32 of 124 credits required for the bachelor's degree must be completed at Oakland.

Visiting: There are regularly scheduled orientations for prospective students, including a review of services, academic advising, and course registration. There are guides for informal visits and visitors may sit in on classes and stay overnight. To schedule a visit, contact the Admissions Office.

Financial Aid: The FAFSA and the college's own financial statement are required. The deadline for filing freshman financial aid applications for fall entry is April 1.

International Students: There are 97 international students enrolled. Satisfactory scores are required on the written TOEFL and the ACT.

Computers: All students may access the system. There are no time limits and no fees.

Graduates: From July 1, 2004 to June 30, 2005, 2012 bachelor's degrees were awarded. The most popular majors were elementary education (15%), communications (9%), and psychology (6%). In an average class, 13% graduate in 4 years or less, 37% graduate in 5 years or less, and 49% graduate in 6 years or less.

Admissions Contact: Eleanor Reynolds, Int. Asst VP Student Affairs. A video is available. E-mail: *ouinfo@oakland.edu* Web: *www.oakland.edu*

OLIVET COLLEGE D-4

Olivet, MI 49076

Full-time: 533 men, 407 women	(800) 456-7189; Fax: (616) 749-3821
Part-time: 58 men, 44 women	Faculty: 55; IIB, --$
Graduate: 10 men, 18 women	Ph.D.s: 36%
Year: semesters, summer session	Student/Faculty: 17 to 1
Application Deadline: open	Tuition: $15,182
Freshman Class: 1200 applied, 545 accepted, 285 enrolled	Room & Board: $4802
ACT: 19	COMPETITIVE+

Olivet College, founded in 1844, is a private liberal arts institution affiliated with both the United Church of Christ and the Congregational Christian Churches. The library contains 85,000 volumes and 117 microform items, and subscribes to 450 periodicals including electronic. Computerized library services include the card catalog, interlibrary loans, database searching, and Internet access. Special learning facilities include a learning resource center, art gallery, planetarium, radio station, an observatory, and a nature preserve. The 92-acre campus is in a small town 30 miles south of Lansing and 120 miles west of Detroit. Including any residence halls, there are 24 buildings.

Student Life: 82% of undergraduates are from Michigan. Others are from 15 states, 12 foreign countries, and Canada. 92% are from public schools. 72% are white; 16% African American. 21% are Catholic; 18% claim no religious affiliation; 6% Protestant. The average age of freshmen is 19; all undergraduates, 23. 35% do not continue beyond their first year; 40% remain to graduate.

Housing: 700 students can be accommodated in college housing, which includes single-sex and coed dormitories, fraternity houses, and sorority houses. In addition, there are honors houses, special-interest houses. A global cultural center, and an African American cultural center. On-campus housing is guaranteed for all 4 years, is available on a first-come, first-served basis, and is available on a lottery system for upperclassmen. Priority is given to out-of-town students. 72% of students live on campus; of those, 45% remain on campus on weekends. All students may keep cars.

Activities: 9% of men and about 2% of women belong to 6 local fraternities; 7% of women belong to 4 local sororities. There are 27 groups on campus, including art, band, cheerleading, choir, chorale, chorus, computers, drama, drill team, drum and bugle corps, ethnic, gay, honors, in-

ternational, literary magazine, musical theater, newspaper, pep band, photography, professional, radio and TV, religious, social, social service, student government, and yearbook. Popular campus events include Diversity Week, Community Service Week, and Honors Convocation.

Sports: There are 9 intercollegiate sports for men and 9 for women, and 6 intramural sports for men and 6 for women. Facilities include an athletic center, football field, gym, fitness center, soccer fields, softball and baseball fields, tennis courts, a student center, and a pool.

Disabled Students: 25% of the campus is accessible. Wheelchair ramps, elevators, special parking, and specially equipped rest rooms are available.

Services: Counseling and information services are available, as is tutoring in most subjects. There is a reader service for the blind, and remedial math, reading, and writing.

Campus Safety and Security: Measures include 24-hour foot and vehicle patrol, self-defense education, security escort services, and informal discussions. There are pamphlets/posters/films, emergency telephones, and lighted pathways/sidewalks.

Programs of Study: Fighting Comets confers the B.A. degree. Master's degrees are also awarded. Bachelor's degrees are awarded in BIOLOGICAL SCIENCE (biochemistry and biology/biological science), BUSINESS (accounting, business administration and management, insurance, international business management, and marketing management), COMMUNICATIONS AND THE ARTS (communications, design, English, fine arts, illustration, and journalism), COMPUTER AND PHYSICAL SCIENCE (chemistry, computer science, and mathematics), EDUCATION (athletic training, elementary, physical, and secondary), ENGINEERING AND ENVIRONMENTAL DESIGN (environmental science), HEALTH PROFESSIONS (health, predentistry, premedicine, and preveterinary science), SOCIAL SCIENCE (anthropology, criminal justice, economics, history, prelaw, psychology, social studies, and sociology). Business administration, teacher education, and criminal justice are the strongest academically.

Required: To graduate, students must complete 120 semester hours, with 36 to 60 in the major. Their minimum GPA must be 2.0; those seeking certification must maintain a minimum 2.5 GPA in all education courses and in all courses in their major and minor fields. Students must demonstrate competency in 16 areas and complete a 33-hour general education program. In addition, a 40-hour service learning course and senior experience class are required. Distribution requirements include arts, exploration, creative experience, and math proficiency. Specific courses required include self and community, writing and rhetoric, civilization, liberal arts, and natural world.

Special: Olivet offers internships, cooperative education opportunities, and both student-designed and dual majors. There are 2 national honor societies, a freshman honors program, and 4 departmental honors programs.

Faculty/Classroom: 55% of faculty are male; 45%, female. All teach undergraduates. No introductory courses are taught by graduate students. The average class size in an introductory lecture is 20; in a laboratory, 14; and in a regular course, 16.

Admissions: 45% of the 2005-2006 applicants were accepted. The ACT scores for the 2005-2006 freshman class were: 25% below 21, 40% between 21 and 23, 15% between 24 and 26, 15% between 27 and 28, and 5% above 28. 25% of the current freshmen were in the top fifth of their class; 50% were in the top two fifths. 6 freshmen graduated first in their class.

Requirements: The SAT or ACT is recommended, with satisfactory scores. Students must be graduates of an accredited secondary school, with a scholastic GPA of at least 2.6 and completion of college-preparatory courses. The GED is accepted. Individual consideration is given to applicants not meeting these criteria but demonstrating other potential. A GPA of 2.6 is required. AP and CLEP credits are accepted. Important factors in the admissions decision are evidence of special talent, extracurricular activities record, and recommendations by school officials.

Procedure: Freshmen are admitted fall, spring, and summer. There are deferred admissions and rolling admissions plans. Application deadlines are open. Application fee is $25. Applications are accepted on-line.

Transfer: 105 transfer students enrolled in a recent year. Transcripts of college work completed elsewhere must show a 2.0 GPA. Transfer applicants must be high school graduates or the equivalent. 30 of 120 credits required for the bachelor's degree must be completed at Fighting Comets.

Visiting: There are regularly scheduled orientations for prospective students, consisting of a day and a half of orientation. There are guides for informal visits and visitors may sit in on classes and stay overnight. To schedule a visit, contact the Admissions Office.

Financial Aid: In a recent year, 94% of all full-time freshmen and 95% of continuing full-time students received some form of financial aid. 88% of full-time freshmen and 92% of continuing full-time students received need-based aid. The average freshman award was $6500. 45% of undergraduates worked part time. Average annual earnings from campus work were $1200. The average financial indebtedness of a recent graduate was $18,000. The FAFSA is required. Check with the school for current application deadlines.

International Students: In a recent year, there are 42 international students enrolled. The school actively recruits these students. A satisfactory score is required on the written TOEFL.

Computers: All students may access the system 24 hours a day, 7 days per week during the academic year. There are no time limits and no fees.

Graduates: In a recent year, 147 bachelor's degrees were awarded. The most popular majors were business administration (17%), psychology (11%), and biology (11%). 9 companies recruited on campus in a recent year .

Admissions Contact: Bernie McConnel, Assistant Vice President for Enrollment Management. E-mail: *admissions@olivetcollege.edu*
Web: *olivetcollege.edu*

ROCHESTER COLLEGE
E-4

Rochester Hills, MI 48307
(248) 218-2031
(800) 521-6010; Fax: (248) 218-2035

Full-time: 272 men, 418 women	**Faculty:** 41
Part-time: 133 men, 228 women	**Ph.D.s:** 39%
Graduate: 5 men, 3 women	**Student/Faculty:** 17 to 1
Year: semesters	**Tuition:** $12,356
Application Deadline: August 30	**Room & Board:** $3280
Freshman Class: 375 applied, 307 accepted, 194 enrolled	
SAT Verbal/Math: 620/570*	**ACT:** 21 **COMPETITIVE+**

Rochester College, founded in 1959, is a private institution affiliated with the Churches of Christ. It offers undergraduate programs in business, behavioral sciences, Christian studies, English, interdisciplinary studies, history, music, communication, and general science. There are 3 undergraduate schools and 1 graduate school. The library contains 70,111 volumes, 16,725 microform items, and 2242 audio/video tapes/CDs/DVDs, and subscribes to 247 periodicals including electronic. Computerized library services include interlibrary loans, database searching, Internet access, and laptop Internet portals. Special learning facilities include a learning resource center. The 83-acre campus is in a suburban area 25 miles north of Detroit. Including any residence halls, there are 12 buildings.

Student Life: 93% of undergraduates are from Michigan. Others are from 22 states, 6 foreign countries, and Canada. 75% are white; 19% African American. 89% are Protestant; 11% Catholic. The average age of freshmen is 18; all undergraduates, 23. 41% do not continue beyond their first year; 36% remain to graduate.

Housing: 366 students can be accommodated in college housing, which includes single-sex dorms and married-student housing. On-campus housing is available on a first-come, first-served basis. 50% of students live on campus; of those, 55% remain on campus on weekends. Alcohol is not permitted. All students may keep cars.

Activities: 10% of men belong to 3 local fraternities; 10% of women belong to 3 local sororities. There are 22 groups on campus, including band, cheerleading, chorale, chorus, dance, drama, jazz band, newspaper, professional, religious, social, social service, student government, and yearbook. Popular campus events include Celebration.

Sports: There are 3 intercollegiate sports for men and 4 for women, and 16 intramural sports for men and 16 for women. Facilities include a gym, plus soccer and baseball fields.

Disabled Students: 65% of the campus is accessible. Wheelchair ramps, elevators, special parking, specially equipped rest rooms, special class scheduling, and special housing are available.

Services: Counseling and information services are available, as is tutoring in some subjects, including Bible. There is remedial math, reading, and writing.

Campus Safety and Security: Measures include lighted pathways/sidewalks and evening security guards.

Programs of Study: RC confers B.A., B.S., and B.B.A. degrees. Associate and master's degrees are also awarded. Bachelor's degrees are awarded in BUSINESS (accounting, marketing management, and sports management), COMMUNICATIONS AND THE ARTS (communications, English, and music), COMPUTER AND PHYSICAL SCIENCE (computer management), EDUCATION (technical), SOCIAL SCIENCE (behavioral science, biblical studies, counseling/psychology, early childhood studies, history, interdisciplinary studies, ministries, psychology, and youth ministry). Management, education and psychology are the largest.

Required: All students must follow a core curriculum that includes courses in religion, communication, humanities, phys ed, science, math, and social science. To graduate, students must complete 128 credits with a minimum GPA of 2.0.

Special: A co-op program in education is available. Cross-registration with Oakland University, Madonna University, Oakland Community College, Mott Community College, Specs Howard School of Broadcast Arts and Macomb Community College is offered. Internships, which are required for many majors, study abroad, student-designed majors and

work-study programs are also offered. There are 2 national honor societies, and 1 departmental honors program.

Faculty/Classroom: 58% of faculty are male; 42%, female. All teach undergraduates, 25% do research, and 25% do both. The average class size in an introductory lecture is 35; in a laboratory, 20; and in a regular course, 20.

Admissions: 82% of the 2005-2006 applicants were accepted. The SAT scores for the 2005-2006 freshman class were: Verbal--21% below 500, 21% between 500 and 599, 43% between 600 and 700, and 15% above 700; Math--29% below 500, 43% between 500 and 599, 21% between 600 and 700, and 7% above 700. The ACT scores were 45% below 21, 25% between 21 and 23, 17% between 24 and 26, 6% between 27 and 28, and 7% above 28. 22% of the current freshmen were in the top fifth of their class; 50% were in the top two fifths.

Requirements: The SAT or ACT is required for some programs. A GPA of 2.25 is required. AP and CLEP credits are accepted. Important factors in the admissions decision are leadership record, personality/intangible qualities, and extracurricular activities record.

Procedure: Freshmen are admitted to all sessions. Entrance exams should be taken as early as possible. There are early admissions, deferred admissions and rolling admissions plans. Applications should be filed by August 30 for fall entry and January 17 for spring entry, along with a $25 fee. Notification is sent on a rolling basis. Applications are accepted on-line.

Transfer: 51 transfer students enrolled in 2004-2005. A 2.0 college GPA is required. 32 of 128 credits required for the bachelor's degree must be completed at RC.

Visiting: There are regularly scheduled orientations for prospective students, including several College Life Preview Days in fall and winter and Celebration Saturday in March. There are guides for informal visits and visitors may sit in on classes and stay overnight. To schedule a visit, contact Enrollment Services Office at *admissions@rc.edu*.

Financial Aid: In a recent year, 98% of all full-time freshmen and 96% of continuing full-time students received some form of financial aid. 69% of full-time freshmen and 79% of continuing full-time students received need-based aid. The average freshman award was $7747. Need-based scholarships or need-based grants averaged $3343 ($7250 maximum); need-based self-help aid (loans and jobs) averaged $1550 ($8125 maximum); non-need-based athletic scholarships averaged $2000 ($3500 maximum); and other non-need-based awards and non-need-based scholarships averaged $3278 ($8217 maximum). 25% of undergraduates work part time. Average annual earnings from campus work are $994. The average financial indebtedness of the 2005 graduate was $10,416. The CSS/Profile, FAFSA, FFS or SFS and the college's own financial statement are required.

International Students: There are 16 international students enrolled. The school actively recruits these students. A satisfactory score is required on the written TOEFL.

Computers: Wireless access is available. Students may use a total of 84 computers as well as wireless hot spots across the campus. All students may access the system. Schedules for computer use vary. There are no time limits and no fees.

Graduates: From July 1, 2004 to June 30, 2005, 297 bachelor's degrees were awarded. The most popular majors were business communication (20%), early childhood education (17%), and couseling/psychology (15%). In an average class, 13% graduate in 4 years, 14% graduate in 5 years, and 5% graduate in 6 years. Of the 2004 graduating class, 10% were enrolled in graduate school within 6 months of graduation and 80% were employed.

Admissions Contact: Kelvin Brown, Vice President for Enrollment Service and Dean of Admissions. E-mail: *admissions@rc.edu*
Web: *www.rc.edu*

SAGINAW VALLEY STATE UNIVERSITY
D-4

University Center, MI 48710-0001
(989) 964-4200
(800) 968-9500; Fax: (989) 790-0180

Full-time: 2420 men, 3624 women	**Faculty:** 260
Part-time: 745 men, 1140 women	**Ph.D.s:** 79%
Graduate: 410 men, 1230 women	**Student/Faculty:** 23 to 1
Year: semesters, summer session	**Tuition:** $5282 ($11,891)
Application Deadline: open	**Room & Board:** $6150
Freshman Class: 3785 applied, 3387 accepted, 1263 enrolled	
ACT: 21	**COMPETITIVE**

Saginaw Valley State University, founded in 1963, is a state-supported institution offering undergraduate and graduate degrees in arts and behavioral sciences, business and management, education, nursing and health sciences, science, engineering, and technology. There are 5 undergraduate and 5 graduate schools. In addition to regional accreditation, SVSU has baccalaureate program accreditation with AACSB, ACOTE, ABET, ACS, AMA, ACSP, CSWE, NCATE, and NLN. The library contains 636,202 volumes, 370,156 microform items, and 24,853 audio/video tapes/CDs/DVDs, and subscribes to 10,009 periodicals including electronic. Computerized library services include the card catalog, interlibrary loans, database searching, Internet access, and laptop Internet portals. Special learning facilities include a learning resource center, art gallery, and an observatory. The 782-acre campus is in a suburban area 5 miles north of Saginaw. Including any residence halls, there are 61 buildings.

Student Life: 97% of undergraduates are from Michigan. Others are from 18 states, 16 foreign countries, and Canada. 97% are from public schools. 84% are white. The average age of freshmen is 18; all undergraduates, 22. 29% do not continue beyond their first year; 36% remain to graduate.

Housing: 1900 students can be accommodated in college housing, which includes coed dorms, on-campus apartments, married-student housing healthy lifestyle floors and buildings, and first-year suites. On-campus housing is guaranteed for all 4 years. 70% of students commute. Alcohol is not permitted. All students may keep cars.

Activities: 3% of men and 2% of women belong to 4 national fraternities; 2% of women belong to 1 local and 4 national sororities. There are 75 groups on campus, including art, band, cheerleading, choir, chorus, computers, dance, drama, ethnic, film, gay, honors, international, jazz band, literary magazine, marching band, musical theater, newspaper, orchestra, pep band, photography, political, professional, religious, social, social service, and student government. Popular campus events include Coming Home, Cards Party, and International Food Festival.

Sports: There are 9 intercollegiate sports for men and 8 for women, and 19 intramural sports for men and 19 for women. Facilities include a health and phys ed complex with an Olympic-size pool, indoor track, basketball courts, badmitton courts, volleyball courts, racquetball courts, and fitness center; tennis courts; intramural, baseball, softball, and soccer fields; an archery range; a fitness trail; a football stadium; a golf driving range and putting green; and horse shoe pits.

Disabled Students: 99% of the campus is accessible. Wheelchair ramps, elevators, special parking, specially equipped rest rooms, special class scheduling, lowered drinking fountains, lowered telephones, special housing, electronically opened doors, and special access to the library are available. All buildings are interconnected on the second floor.

Services: Counseling and information services are available, as is tutoring in most subjects, including most 100- and 200-level classes. There is a reader service for the blind, and remedial math, reading, and writing.

Campus Safety and Security: Measures include 24-hour foot and vehicle patrol, self-defense education, security escort services, and informal discussions. There are pamphlets/posters/films, emergency telephones, and lighted pathways/sidewalks. The SVSU public safety department has commissioned police officers providing police services.

Programs of Study: SVSU confers B.A., B.S., B.A.S., B.B.A., B.F.A., B.P.A., B.S.E.E., B.S.M.E., B.S.N., and B.S.W. degrees. Master's degrees are also awarded. Bachelor's degrees are awarded in BIOLOGICAL SCIENCE (biochemistry and biology/biological science), BUSINESS (accounting, banking and finance, business administration and management, business economics, business law, international business management, and marketing management), COMMUNICATIONS AND THE ARTS (art, communications, design, dramatic arts, English, fine arts, French, music, and Spanish), COMPUTER AND PHYSICAL SCIENCE (applied mathematics, applied physics, chemical physics, chemistry, computer mathematics, computer science, information sciences and systems, mathematics, optics, and physics), EDUCATION (art, athletic training, elementary, English, foreign languages, mathematics, music, physical, science, social studies, and special), ENGINEERING AND ENVIRONMENTAL DESIGN (electrical/electronics engineering, engineering technology, environmental science, industrial administration/management, and mechanical engineering), HEALTH PROFESSIONS (allied health, exercise science, medical technology, nursing, and occupational therapy), SOCIAL SCIENCE (criminal justice, economics, history, interdisciplinary studies, international studies, political science/government, psychology, public administration, social work, and sociology). Elementary education, secondary education, and nursing are the largest.

Required: Students must complete a minimum of 124 credits, satisfy basic skills and general education requirements, maintain a minimum GPA of 2.0, complete at least 31 credits at SVSU, and be enrolled on campus the last semester.

Special: Opportunities are provided for student-designed majors, work-study, internships, co-op education, credit by exam, nondegree study, pass/fail options, and study abroad in 17 countries. There are 3 national honor societies.

Faculty/Classroom: 58% of faculty are male; 42%, female. All teach undergraduates. No introductory courses are taught by graduate students.

Admissions: 89% of the 2005-2006 applicants were accepted. The ACT scores for the 2005-2006 freshman class were: 48% below 21, 25% between 21 and 23, 17% between 24 and 26, 5% between 27 and 28, and 5% above 28.

Requirements: The ACT is required. In addition, graduation from an accredited secondary school or a GED is required. Applicants should submit records of successful completion of 4 years each of English and

math, 3 each of social science and science, 2 each of a foreign language and fine arts, and 1 course in computer literacy. A GPA of 2.5 is required. AP and CLEP credits are accepted.

Procedure: Freshmen are admitted to all sessions. Application deadlines are open. There is a rolling admissions plan. Application fee is $25. Applications are accepted on-line.

Transfer: 572 transfer students enrolled in a recent year. Transfer students with fewer than 45 credits from a previous college must submit high school and college transcripts. A minimum GPA of 2.0 is needed. An interview may be required. 31 of 124 minimum credits required for the bachelor's degree must be completed at SVSU.

Visiting: There are regularly scheduled orientations for prospective students, including tours, help with schedules, basic information, and counseling. There are guides for informal visits. To schedule a visit, contact the Office of Admissions.

Financial Aid: In 2005-2006, 59% of all full-time freshmen and 56% of continuing full-time students received some form of financial aid. 42% of full-time freshmen and 41% of continuing full-time students received need-based aid. Need-based scholarships or need-based grants averaged $2885; need-based self-help aid (loans and jobs) averaged $2236; non-need-based athletic scholarships averaged $2997; and other non-need-based awards and non-need-based scholarships averaged $3229. Average annual earnings from campus work are $1500. The average financial indebtedness of the 2005 graduate was $19,333. The FAFSA is required. Check with the school for current application deadlines.

International Students: There are 191 international students enrolled. The school actively recruits these students. Satisfactory scores are required on the written TOEFL.

Computers: Wireless access is available. All students may access the system. There are no time limits and no fees.

Graduates: From July 1, 2004 to June 30, 2005, 1084 bachelor's degrees were awarded. The most popular majors were elementary education (21%), criminal justice (8%), and nursing (5%). In an average class, 8% graduate in 4 years or less, 27% graduate in 5 years or less, and 36% graduate in 6 years or less. 167 companies recruited on campus in 2004-2005. Of the 2004 graduating class, 23% were enrolled in graduate school within 6 months of graduation and 87% were employed.

Admissions Contact: James Dwyer, Director of Admissions.
E-mail: *admissions@svsu.edu* Web: *www.svsu.edu*

SIENA HEIGHTS UNIVERSITY
(Formerly Siena Height College)

E-5

Adrian, MI 49221

(517) 264-7183
(800) 521-0009; Fax: (517) 264-7745

Full-time: 300 men, 500 women	**Faculty:** 53; IIB, -$
Part-time: 100 men, 200 women	**Ph.D:s:** 64%
Graduate: 50 men, 100 women	**Student/Faculty:** 14 to 1
Year: semesters, summer session	**Tuition:** $12,000
Application Deadline: open	**Room & Board:** $5000
Freshman Class: n/av	
ACT: required	**LESS COMPETITIVE**

Siena Heights University, founded in 1919, is a private liberal arts institution affiliated with the Roman Catholic Church. There is 1 graduate school. Figures in the above capsule and in this profile are approximate. In addition to regional accreditation, Siena has baccalaureate program accreditation with NASAD. The library contains 112,000 volumes, 24,200 microform items, and 4700 audio/video tapes/CDs/DVDs, and subscribes to 500 periodicals including electronic. Computerized library services include the card catalog, interlibrary loans, and database searching. Special learning facilities include an art gallery. The 140-acre campus is in a small town 75 miles southwest of Detroit. Including any residence halls, there are 12 buildings.

Student Life: 80% are from public schools. 84% are white. The average age of freshmen is 18; all undergraduates, 25. 45% do not continue beyond their first year.

Housing: 450 students can be accommodated in college housing, which includes coed dorms. On-campus housing is available on a first-come, first-served basis and is available on a lottery system for upperclassmen. Priority is given to out-of-town students. 69% of students commute. All students may keep cars.

Activities: 10% of men belong to 2 national fraternities; 10% of women belong to 2 national sororities. There are 30 groups on campus, including art, cheerleading, choir, chorale, chorus, computers, drama, ethnic, international, jazz band, literary magazine, musical theater, newspaper, professional, religious, social, social service, student government, and symphony. Popular campus events include Alumni/Family Weekend, International Dinner, and athletic banquets.

Sports: There are 6 intercollegiate sports for men and 6 for women, and 4 intramural sports for men and 6 for women. Facilities include a 57,000-square-foot student activity center, which houses 5 basketball, 4 volleyball, and 2 tennis courts, a 200-meter, 4-lane track, a baseball batting cage, training and exercise rooms, ballrooms, and the Sage Union.

The indoor gym seats 4000. There is also a soccer field and a sand volleyball pit.

Disabled Students: 70% of the campus is accessible. Wheelchair ramps, elevators, special parking, specially equipped rest rooms, and lowered drinking fountains are available.

Services: Counseling and information services are available, as is tutoring in most subjects. There is remedial math, reading, and writing.

Campus Safety and Security: Measures include 24-hour foot and vehicle patrol, self-defense education, security escort services, and informal discussions. There are pamphlets/posters/films and lighted pathways/sidewalks.

Programs of Study: Siena confers B.A., B.S., B.A.S., and B.F.A. degrees. Associate and master's degrees are also awarded. Bachelor's degrees are awarded in BIOLOGICAL SCIENCE (biology/biological science), BUSINESS (accounting, business administration and management, hotel/motel and restaurant management, and retailing), COMMUNICATIONS AND THE ARTS (art history and appreciation, communications, English, fine arts, music, and Spanish), COMPUTER AND PHYSICAL SCIENCE (chemistry, information sciences and systems, mathematics, and natural sciences), EDUCATION (business, elementary, and music), HEALTH PROFESSIONS (premedicine), SOCIAL SCIENCE (American studies, child psychology/development, criminal justice, history, human services, humanities, liberal arts/general studies, philosophy, psychology, public administration, religion, social science, and social work). Art, business, and biology are the strongest academically. Business, art, and education are the largest.

Required: To graduate, students must complete 120 semester hours, including 30 hours in the major, and maintain at least a 2.0 GPA. A core curriculum of 33 to 35 semester hours is required, including 2 courses in English composition and 1 each in literature, math, science, fine/performing arts, social science, history, philosophy, and religious studies. A seminar in education is also required.

Special: Special academic programs include 2-2 engineering co-op programs with the University of Detroit and the University of Michigan, a 2-2 business administration program at Lake Michigan College, internships in a student's major, study abroad in Mexico for various majors and Siena, Italy, for art students, and on-and off-campus work-study. Also offered are dual and inverted majors, B.A.-B.S. degrees, a general studies degree, and student-designed majors. 3-year bachelor's degrees may be earned, and a directed student-teaching program is available for education majors. Flexible learning formats include weekend and evening courses. There is 1 national honor society.

Faculty/Classroom: 52% of faculty are male; 48%, female. 95% teach undergraduates. No introductory courses are taught by graduate students. The average class size in a regular course is 15.

Requirements: The ACT is required. Admissions requirements include graduation from an accredited secondary school. The GED is accepted. A GPA of 2.3 is required. AP and CLEP credits are accepted. Important factors in the admissions decision are recommendations by school officials, parents or siblings attending the school, and recommendations by alumni.

Procedure: Freshmen are admitted to all sessions. SAT or ACT scores should be available when the application is filed. There is a deferred admissions plan.There is a rolling admissions plan. Application deadlines are open. The fall 2005 application fee was $25. Applications are accepted on-line.

Transfer: Applicants must have a 2.0 GPA. High school and college transcripts must be submitted. 30 of 120 credits required for the bachelor's degree must be completed at Siena.

Visiting: There are regularly scheduled orientations for prospective students. There are guides for informal visits and visitors may sit in on classes and stay overnight. To schedule a visit, contact the Admissions Office at (517) 264-7180 or (800) 521-0009, ext. 7180.

Financial Aid: Siena is a member of CSS. The FAFSA is required. Check with the school for current deadlines.

International Students: The school actively recruits these students. They must score satisfactorily on the written TOEFL and also take the ACT, scoring 17.

Computers: All students may access the system from 8 A.M. to 11 P.M., except when classes are in session. There are no time limits and no fees.

Admissions Contact: Kevin C. Kucera, Dean of Admissions and Enrollment Services. E-mail: *admissions@sienahts.edu*
Web: *www.sienahts.edu*

SPRING ARBOR UNIVERSITY · D-5
Spring Arbor, MI 49283-9799

(517) 750-6468
(800) 968-0011; Fax: (517) 750-6620

Full-time: 515 men, 846 women	**Faculty:** 76; IIB, --$
Part-time: 74 men, 153 women	**Ph.D.s:** 60%
Graduate: 279 men, 812 women	**Student/Faculty:** 18 to 1
Year: semesters, summer session	**Tuition:** $16,666
Application Deadline: open	**Room & Board:** $5810
Freshman Class: n/av	
ACT: recommended	COMPETITIVE

Spring Arbor University, founded in 1873, is a private institution affiliated with the Free Methodist Church. It offers undergraduate programs in fine arts, humanities, philosophy, religion, natural science, social science, and education. Graduate programs in business and education are also offered. There are 3 undergraduate and 6 graduate schools. In addition to regional accreditation, SAU has baccalaureate program accreditation with CCNE, CSWE, and NCATE. The library contains 101,940 volumes, 358,801 microform items, and 6379 audio/video tapes/CDs/DVDs, and subscribes to 659 periodicals including electronic. Computerized library services include the card catalog, interlibrary loans, database searching, and Internet access. Special learning facilities include a learning resource center, radio station and TV production facilities and equipment. The 123-acre campus is in a small town 8 miles west of Jackson. Including any residence halls, there are 36 buildings.

Student Life: 88% of undergraduates are from Michigan. Students are from 28 states, 7 foreign countries, and Canada. 88% are white. 66% are Protestant; 23% claim no religious affiliation; 13% independent/nondenominations. 22% do not continue beyond their first year; 57% remain to graduate.

Housing: 984 students can be accommodated in college housing, which includes single-sex dorms, on-campus apartments, and married-student housing. On-campus housing is guaranteed for all 4 years. 60% of students live on campus; of those, 60% remain on campus on weekends. Alcohol is not permitted. Upperclassmen may keep cars.

Activities: There are no fraternities or sororities. There are 38 groups on campus, including band, choir, chorale, drama, ethnic, honors, international, jazz band, literary magazine, musical theater, newspaper, pep band, radio and TV, religious, social, social service, student government, symphony, and yearbook. Popular campus events include Blu Butta Caf'e, Culture Fest, and Arbor Games.

Sports: There are 7 intercollegiate sports for men and 7 for women, and 7 intramural sports for men and 6 for women. Facilities include a 500-seat stadium, a 2600-seat gym, all-weather and indoor tracks, tennis courts, a basketball court, an Olympic pool, a weight-training room with cardiovascular equipment, and baseball, softball, and soccer fields.

Disabled Students: 80% of the campus is accessible. Wheelchair ramps, elevators, special parking, specially equipped rest rooms, lowered drinking fountains, lowered telephones and special housing are available.

Services: Counseling and information services are available, as is tutoring in most subjects. There is a reader service for the blind, and remedial math, reading, and writing. Religious counseling and health services are also available.

Campus Safety and Security: Measures include 24-hour foot and vehicle patrol, self-defense education, security escort services, and informal discussions. There are lighted pathways/sidewalks, a night security guard, and bike patrol.

Programs of Study: SAU confers B.A. and B.S.W. degrees. Associate and master's degrees are also awarded. Bachelor's degrees are awarded in BIOLOGICAL SCIENCE (biochemistry and biology/biological science), BUSINESS (accounting, business administration and management, and management information systems), COMMUNICATIONS AND THE ARTS (advertising, art, communications, contemporary Christian music, English, film arts, language arts, music, Spanish, and visual and performing arts), COMPUTER AND PHYSICAL SCIENCE (chemistry, computer science, mathematics, and physics), EDUCATION (Christian, music, and special), HEALTH PROFESSIONS (exercise science, health, and nursing), SOCIAL SCIENCE (behavioral science, history, philosophy, philosophy and religion, physical fitness/movement, psychology, social science, social studies, social work, sociology, and youth ministry). Business, teacher education, and social science are the strongest academically. Business, English, and education are the largest.

Required: Students must complete 4 Christian perspective courses, cross-cultural studies, writing skills, speech, and physical fitness. Liberal arts requirements are in fine arts, humanities, natural science/math, philosophy/religion, and social science. To graduate, at least 124 semester hours, 30 to 60 in the major, with a minimum GPA of 2.0 overall and 2.2 in the major, are needed.

Special: Each student participates in a cross-cultural experience, which includes travel to a foreign country. Additional study-abroad opportunities can be arranged. A washington semester is available through the American Studies Program. The university also offers cross-registration with Jackson Community College, work-study, a dual major in physics/

math, student-designed majors, pass/fail options, and nondegree study. Alternative programs for adult learners provide field-based study and assign credit for life experience. An accelerated B.A. program for such students is also offered. A 3-2 engineering degree is offered with the University of Michigan, and Michigan State, Western Michigan, and Tri-State Universities. There are 3 national honor societies and a freshman honors program.

Faculty/Classroom: 60% of faculty are male; 40%, female. 91% teach undergraduates. No introductory courses are taught by graduate students.

Admissions: The SAT scores for the 2005-2006 freshman class were: Verbal--27% below 500, 35% between 500 and 599, 33% between 600 and 700, and 4% above 700; Math--27% below 500, 48% between 500 and 599, 17% between 600 and 700, and 8% above 700. The ACT scores were 36% below 21, 27% between 21 and 23, 22% between 24 and 26, 10% between 27 and 28, and 6% above 28. 37% of the current freshmen were in the top fifth of their class; 63% were in the top two fifths. 11 freshmen graduated first in their class.

Requirements: The ACT is recommended. In addition, applicants must be graduates of accredited secondary schools or have a GED. An interview is advised for those who do not meet the requirements. Homeschooled applicants must take the ACT or the SAT, provide transcripts of course work, and submit a 2- to 3-page paper. A GPA of 2.6 is required. AP and CLEP credits are accepted. Important factors in the admissions decision are personality/intangible qualities, parents or siblings attending the school, and leadership record.

Procedure: Freshmen are admitted to all sessions. Entrance exams should be taken in the spring of the junior year or fall of the senior year. There is a deferred admissions and a rolling admissions plan. Application deadlines are open. Applications are accepted on-line. The fall 2005 application fee was $30.

Transfer: 137 transfer students enrolled in 2004-2005. Applicants should have a minimum GPA of 2.0 and are encouraged to arrange an interview. A release of information form is required from the previous college attended. 30 of 124 credits required for the bachelor's degree must be completed at SAU.

Visiting: There are regularly scheduled orientations for prospective students, including a tour, class and chapel attendance, lunch, and a student panel discussion. There are guides for informal visits and visitors may sit in on classes and stay overnight. To schedule a visit, contact the Admissions Office.

Financial Aid: In 2005-2006, 100% of all full-time freshmen and 78% of continuing full-time students received some form of financial aid. 85% of full-time freshmen and 74% of continuing full-time students received need-based aid. The average freshman award was $16,177. Need-based scholarships or need-based grants averaged $9661; need-based self-help aid (loans and jobs) averaged $3371; and non-need-based athletic scholarships averaged $3006. 35% of undergraduates work part time. Average annual earnings from campus work are $1000. The average financial indebtedness of the 2005 graduate was $11,989. The FAFSA is required. The deadline for filing freshman financial aid applications for fall entry is May 1.

International Students: There are 22 international students enrolled. They must score satisfactorily on the written TOEFL or on the electronic version and also take the MELAB.

Computers: Wireless access is available. SAU has 10 computer labs with 171 PC located in various locations on campus for students to access. There are also 800 wireless network connections available for students. All students may access the system. There are no time limits. The fee is $180 per year. It is strongly recommended that all students have a personal computer. A windows XP Professional or a Mac 10.3 05 is recommended.

Graduates: From July 1, 2004 to June 30, 2005, 768 bachelor's degrees were awarded. The most popular majors were business (35%), family life (22%), and education (11%). In an average class, 36% graduate in 4 years or less, 52% graduate in 5 years or less, and 57% graduate in 6 years or less. Of the 2004 graduating class, 20% were enrolled in graduate school within 6 months of graduation and 60% were employed.

Admissions Contact: Randy Comfort, Director of Admissions. A video is available. E-mail: admissions@arbor.edu Web: www.arbor.edu

---

UNIVERSITY OF DETROIT MERCY   E-5
Detroit, MI 48219-0900   (313) 993-1245
                                         (800) 635-5020; Fax: (313) 993-3317

Full-time: 800 men, 1100 women	**Faculty:** n/av
Part-time: 400 men, 1100 women	**Ph.D.s:** 85%
Graduate: 1100 men, 1100 women	**Student/Faculty:** n/av
Year: semesters, summer session	**Tuition:** $20,000
Application Deadline: see profile	**Room & Board:** $7000
Freshman Class: n/av	
SAT or ACT: required	**COMPETITIVE**

University of Detroit Mercy, founded in 1877, is a private, independent institution affiliated with the Jesuits and Sisters of Mercy. It offers undergraduate programs in liberal arts, education and human services, business administration, engineering and science, architecture, and nursing and health sciences. There are 7 undergraduate and 5 graduate schools. Figures in the above capsule and in this profile are approximate. In addition to regional accreditation, U of DM has baccalaureate program accreditation with AACSB, ABET, ADA, CSWE, NAAB, and NLN. The 3 libraries contain 733,000 volumes, 1,007,500 microform items, and 33,200 audio/video tapes/CDs/DVDs, and subscribe to 4000 periodicals including electronic. Computerized library services include the card catalog, interlibrary loans, database searching, and Internet access. Special learning facilities include a learning resource center and radio station. The 70-acre campus is in an urban area 7 miles north of downtown Detroit.

Student Life: 93% of undergraduates are from Michigan. Others are from 27 states, 19 foreign countries, and Canada. 50% are white; 33% African American. 32% are Catholic; 32% a variety of denominations and religions; 26% claim no religious affiliation; 11% are Protestant. The average age of freshmen is 18; all undergraduates, 29. 12% do not continue beyond their first year.

Housing: 955 students can be accommodated in college housing, which includes coed dorms and married-student housing. In addition, there are a freshman residence program, honors floors, and a peace and justice floor. On-campus housing is guaranteed for all 4 years. 79% of students commute. All students may keep cars.

Activities: There are 3 national fraternities and 3 national sororities. There are 50 groups on campus, including cheerleading, chorale, computers, drama, ethnic, honors, international, literary magazine, newspaper, pep band, political, professional, radio and TV, religious, social, social service, and student government. Popular campus events include Engineering and Architecture Week, Ethics Bowl, and Alternative Spring Break.

Sports: There are 7 intercollegiate sports for men and 8 for women, and 7 intramural sports for men and 7 for women. Facilities include a fitness center, a gym, racquetball/handball courts, an indoor track, a game room in the Student Union, and soccer, softball, and baseball fields.

Disabled Students: 80% of the campus is accessible. Wheelchair ramps, elevators, special parking, and special class scheduling are available.

Services: Counseling and information services are available, as is tutoring in most subjects, including all freshman courses and many other courses. There is remedial math, reading, and writing.

Campus Safety and Security: Measures include 24-hour foot and vehicle patrol, self-defense education, security escort services, and informal discussions. There are pamphlets/posters/films, emergency telephones, and lighted pathways/sidewalks.

Programs of Study: U of DM confers B.A., B.S., B.Arch., B.B.A., B.C.E., B.E.E., B.En., B.F.A., B.M.E., B.S.C.S., B.S.Ed., B.S.N., and B.S.W. degrees. Associate, master's, and doctoral degrees are also awarded. Bachelor's degrees are awarded in BIOLOGICAL SCIENCE (biochemistry and biology/biological science), BUSINESS (accounting and business administration and management), COMMUNICATIONS AND THE ARTS (communications, dramatic arts, and English), COMPUTER AND PHYSICAL SCIENCE (chemistry, computer science, information sciences and systems, and mathematics), EDUCATION (early childhood, elementary, middle school, secondary, and special), ENGINEERING AND ENVIRONMENTAL DESIGN (architecture, civil engineering, electrical/electronics engineering, engineering, manufacturing engineering, and mechanical engineering), HEALTH PROFESSIONS (dental hygiene, health care administration, nursing, predentistry, premedicine, and sports medicine), SOCIAL SCIENCE (addiction studies, criminal justice, economics, history, human services, liberal arts/general studies, paralegal studies, philosophy, political science/government, prelaw, psychology, religion, social work, and sociology). Engineering, nursing, and business administration are the strongest academically. Business administration, nursing, and mechanical engineering are the largest.

Required: Students must successfully complete at least 126 credit hours, including a core curriculum, and maintain a minimum GPA of 2.0. Required courses include English composition, religion, philosophy, speech fundamentals, math, and a computer course.

Special: Cooperative education is mandatory for engineering, architecture, and nursing majors and is optional for others. Cross-registration is available with a consortium of Catholic colleges in the Detroit area. There are internships, and a B.A.-B.S. degree is available for math, chemistry, and biology majors. An accelerated 6-year degree program in dentistry is provided. Study abroad is available in England, China, Canada, Mexico, Italy, Poland, Israel, and Greece. Academic exploration courses are provided to help students who are undecided about a future vocation. There are 3 national honor societies and a freshman honors program.

Admissions: 69% of recent applicants were accepted. The ACT scores for a recent freshman class were: 37% below 21, 29% between 21 and 23, 18% between 24 and 26, 11% between 27 and 28, and 5% above 28. 22% of recent freshmen were in the top fifth of their class; 33% were in the top two fifths.

Requirements: The SAT or ACT is required. In addition, graduation from an accredited secondary school is required; a GED will be accepted. Students must submit 16 academic credits, which should include, as a minimum, 4 units of English, 3 of math, and 2 each of history or social studies and natural science, including a lab course. Remaining credits should be distributed in a foreign language, speech, music, art, and other college preparatory electives. An interview is recommended. A GPA of 2.5 is required. AP and CLEP credits are accepted. Advanced placement or honor courses is an important factor in the admission decision.

Procedure: Freshmen are admitted to all sessions. Entrance exams should be taken during the junior or senior year. There is an early admissions plan. Check with the school for current application deadlines. The fall 2005 application fee was $25. Notification is sent on a rolling basis. Applications are accepted on-line.

Transfer: Transfer applicants with fewer than 24 semester hours of credit at an accredited institution must submit SAT or ACT scores and have maintained a minimum GPA of 2.0. If the student is older than 23 years of age, SAT or ACT scores need not be submitted. 32 of 126 credits required for the bachelor's degree must be completed at U of DM.

Visiting: There are regularly scheduled orientations for prospective students, including a look at student life, testing and advising, and registration. There are guides for informal visits and visitors may sit in on classes and stay overnight. To schedule a visit, contact the Admissions Office.

Financial Aid: In a recent year, All of all full-time students received some form of financial aid. 81% of full-time freshmen and 65% of continuing full-time students received need-based aid. The average freshman award was $22,851. Need-based scholarships or need-based grants averaged $5711 ($7650 maximum); need-based self-help aid (loans and jobs) averaged $6308 ($10,025 maximum); non-need-based athletic scholarships averaged $8323 ($26,182 maximum); and other non-need-based awards and non-need-based scholarships averaged $12,017 ($19,590 maximum). 22% of undergraduates work part time. Average annual earnings from campus work are $2500. U of DM is a member of CSS. The FAFSA is required. Check with the school for current deadlines.

International Students: There were 79 international students enrolled in a recent year. The school actively recruits these students. They must take the university's own test.

Computers: All students may access the system. There are no time limits and no fees.

Admissions Contact: Admissions Counselors.
E-mail: *admissions@udmercy.edu* Web: *www.udmercy.edu*

UNIVERSITY OF MICHIGAN/ANN ARBOR E-5

Ann Arbor, MI 48109 (734) 764-7433; Fax: (734) 936-0740

Full-time: 12,074 men, 12,372 women	**Faculty:** I, av$
Part-time: 513 men, 508 women	**Ph.D.s:** 91%
Graduate: 8098 men, 6428 women	**Student/Faculty:** n/av
Year: trimesters, summer session	**Tuition:** $9213 ($27,601)
Application Deadline: February 1	**Room & Board:** $7374
Freshman Class: 23,882 applied, 13,610 accepted, 6115 enrolled	
SAT Verbal/Math: 640/690*	**ACT:** 28
	HIGHLY COMPETITIVE+

The University of Michigan/Ann Arbor, founded in 1817, is the main campus of the University of Michigan. The public institution offers undergraduate programs in the arts and sciences, architecture, business administration, education, engineering, fine arts, kinesiology, natural resources, nursing, and professional studies, as well as a wide range of graduate and professional programs. There are 12 undergraduate and 19 graduate schools. In addition to regional accreditation, UM has baccalaureate program accreditation with AACSB, ABET, ACEJMC, ACPE, ADA, ASLA, CSWE, NAAB, NASAD, NASM, NCATE, NLN, and SAF. The 24 libraries contain 7,958,145 volumes, 8,218,665 microform items, and 87,705 audio/video tapes/CDs/DVDs, and subscribe to 67,554 periodicals including electronic. Computerized library services include the card catalog, interlibrary loans, database searching, Internet access, and laptop Internet portals. Special learning facilities include a learning resource center, art gallery, natural history museum, planetarium, radio station, TV station, archeology museum, botanical gardens, and 2 historical museums. The 3177-acre campus is in a suburban area

38 miles west of Detroit. Including any residence halls, there are 538 buildings.

Student Life: 69% of undergraduates are from Michigan. Others are from 49 states, 90 foreign countries, and Canada. 64% are white; 13% Asian American. The average age of freshmen is 18; all undergraduates, 20. 4% do not continue beyond their first year.

Housing: 12,562 students can be accommodated in college housing, which includes single-sex and coed dormitories, on-campus apartments, married-student housing, fraternity houses, and sorority houses. In addition, there are honors houses, language houses, special-interest houses, substance-free dorm rooms, women-in-science housing, and cooperative housing. On-campus housing is guaranteed for the freshman year only, is available on a first-come, first-served basis, and is available on a lottery system for upperclassmen. 63% of students commute. All students may keep cars.

Activities: 12% of men belong to 1 local and 30 national fraternities; 15% of women belong to 22 national sororities. There are more than 900 groups on campus, including art, band, cheerleading, chess, choir, chorale, chorus, computers, dance, debate, drama, ethnic, film, forensics, gay, honors, international, jazz band, literary magazine, marching band, musical theater, newspaper, opera, orchestra, pep band, photography, political, professional, radio and TV, religious, social, social service, student government, symphony, and yearbook. Popular campus events include Martin Luther King Day, Native American Powwow, and Holocaust conference.

Sports: There are 12 intercollegiate sports for men and 13 for women, and 25 intramural sports for men and 25 for women. Facilities include a 107,501-seat stadium, a 1000-seat gym, an indoor track and tennis complex, an indoor practice center, 3 recreational buildings, 2 golf courses, a natatorium and separate swimming pools, an ice arena, and several other athletic arenas, the largest of which seats 13,000.

Disabled Students: 97% of the campus is accessible. Wheelchair ramps, elevators, special parking, specially equipped rest rooms, special class scheduling, lowered drinking fountains, lowered telephones, special housing, para-transit service, specially equipped vans, talking calculators, telecommunication devices for the deaf, and an adaptive technology computing site that includes a high-speed scanner, voice input and voice output, braille display and large-print screens, and a braille printer are available.

Services: Counseling and information services are available, as is tutoring in some subjects, including introductory English and math. There is a reader service for the blind.

Campus Safety and Security: Measures include 24-hour foot and vehicle patrol, self-defense education, security escort services, and shuttle buses. There are informal discussions, pamphlets/posters/films, emergency telephones, lighted pathways/sidewalks, a nite-owl bus service, officer bicycle patrols, and a taxi service.

Programs of Study: UM confers A.B., B.S., A.B.E.D., B.B.A., B.D.A., B.F.A., B.F.A.D., B.F.A.M.T., B.F.A.(T), B.G.S., B.Mus., B.Mus.A., B.S.A.O.S., B.S.Chem., B.S.D.Hyg., B.S.E.AET., B.S.E.C.E., B.S.E.Ch., B.S.E.Civ., B.S.E.Comp., B.S.Ed., B.S.E.E.E., B.S.E.E.P., B.S.E.E.S., B.S.E.I.O., B.S.E.I.S., B.S.E.M.A., B.S.E.M.E., B.S.E.Met., B.S.E.M.S., B.S.Eng., B.S.M.C., B.S.MET., B.S.N., B.S.(NRE), B.S.P.O., and B.S.P.S. degrees. Master's and doctoral degrees are also awarded. Bachelor's degrees are awarded in AGRICULTURE (natural resource management), BIOLOGICAL SCIENCE (biochemistry, biology/biological science, biophysics, botany, cell biology, microbiology, and zoology), BUSINESS (business administration and management, recreation and leisure services, and sports management), COMMUNICATIONS AND THE ARTS (applied music, art history and appreciation, ceramic art and design, Chinese, classical languages, communications, comparative literature, creative writing, dance, design, English, fiber/textiles/weaving, film arts, French, German, graphic design, Greek, Greek (modern), Hebrew, industrial design, Italian, Japanese, jazz, Latin, linguistics, literature, media arts, metal/jewelry, music, music history and appreciation, music performance, music theory and composition, musical theater, painting, percussion, performing arts, photography, piano/organ, printmaking, romance languages and literature, Russian, sculpture, Spanish, speech/debate/rhetoric, strings, voice, and winds), COMPUTER AND PHYSICAL SCIENCE (astronomy, astrophysics, atmospheric sciences and meteorology, chemistry, computer science, geoscience, mathematics, oceanography, physics, and statistics), EDUCATION (art, elementary, music, physical, and secondary), ENGINEERING AND ENVIRONMENTAL DESIGN (aeronautical engineering, architecture, chemical engineering, civil engineering, computer engineering, electrical/electronics engineering, engineering and applied science, engineering physics, industrial engineering, interior design, landscape architecture/design, materials engineering, materials science, mechanical engineering, naval architecture and marine engineering, and nuclear engineering), HEALTH PROFESSIONS (biomedical science, dental hygiene, medical technology, nursing, and pharmacy), SOCIAL SCIENCE (African American studies, African studies, American studies, anthropology, archeology, biblical studies, biopsychology, classical/ancient civilization, economics, geography, history, humanities, Islamic studies, Judaic studies, Latin American studies, liberal arts/general studies, medieval studies, Middle

Eastern studies, Near Eastern studies, philosophy, physical fitness/movement, political science/government, psychology, religion, Russian and Slavic studies, Scandinavian studies, social science, sociology, and women's studies). Psychology, engineering, and business administration are the largest.

Required: Academic requirements vary by program. For the College of Literature, Science, and the Arts, most students must fulfill requirements in English (including composition), race and ethnicity (1 course), and foreign language, and must complete 9 semester hours each of humanities, social science, and natural science/math. Students must also meet the quantitative reasoning requirement, designed to ensure proficiency in using and analyzing quantitative information. To graduate, students must complete 120 to 128 semester hours, including 24 to 30 in a major field, with a minimum GPA of 2.0.

Special: A co-op program in engineering and cross-registration with Big Ten institutions and the University of Chicago are available, as are internships, study abroad in some 35 countries, and a Washington semester. B.A.-B.S. degrees, dual and student-designed majors, and a 3-2 engineering degree with several colleges and universities are possible. Interdisciplinary majors are offered in anthropology and zoology, music and technology, natural resources and biometry, materials and metallurgical engineering, materials science and engineering, biopsychology and cognitive science, and social anthropology. Interdisciplinary liberal arts programs offering small group living/learning environments are available in the Residential College and the Lloyd Scholars Program. Also available are Honors College preferred admission to professional programs and a Women in Science Program. There are 21 national honor societies, including Phi Beta Kappa, and a freshman honors program.

Faculty/Classroom: 62% of faculty are male; 38%, female. All both teach and do research. The average class size in a regular course is 29.

Admissions: 57% of the 2005-2006 applicants were accepted. The SAT scores for the 2005-2006 freshman class were: Verbal--3% below 500, 24% between 500 and 599, 47% between 600 and 700, and 26% above 700; Math--2% below 500, 12% between 500 and 599, 42% between 600 and 700, and 44% above 700. The ACT scores were 3% below 21. 88% of the current freshmen were in the top fifth of their class; 98% were in the top two fifths. There were 47 National Merit finalists.

Requirements: The SAT or ACT is required. In addition, applicants must be graduates of accredited secondary schools or have earned a GED. The university requires 15 academic credits or 20 Carnegie units, including 4 in English, 3 in math (4 for engineering majors), 3 in history and social studies, 2 in foreign language, and 2 in science. The following are recommended electives: 1 unit of hands-on computer study and 1 unit of fine or performing arts. An essay is required for all applicants. Students applying to the School of Art must submit a portfolio; those applying to the School of Music must present an audition. AP and CLEP credits are accepted.

Procedure: Freshmen are admitted to all sessions. Entrance exams should be taken at the end of the junior year or the beginning of the senior year. There are deferred admissions and rolling admissions plans. Applications should be filed by February 1 for fall entry, November 1 for winter entry, February 1 for spring entry, and February 1 for summer entry. Notification is sent on a rolling basis. 4836 applicants were on the 2005 waiting list. Applications are accepted on-line. The fall 2005 application fee was $40.

Transfer: 909 transfer students enrolled in 2004-2005. A minimum college GPA of 3.0 is required for junior-level transfers. 60 of 120 credits required for the bachelor's degree must be completed at UM.

Visiting: There are regularly scheduled orientations for prospective students, including placement testing, academic counseling, course registration, social activities, and informational programs on student life, computing resources, campus safety, and career planning. There are guides for informal visits and visitors may sit in on classes.

Financial Aid: In 2003-2004, 73% of all full-time freshmen and 63% of continuing full-time students received some form of financial aid. 50% of full-time freshmen and 44% of continuing full-time students received need-based aid. Need-based scholarships or need-based grants averaged $7813; need-based self-help aid (loans and jobs) averaged $5588; non-need-based athletic scholarships averaged $22,690; and other non-need-based awards and non-need-based scholarships averaged $4081. The average financial indebtedness of the 2003 graduate was $21,326. The FAFSA and tax returns are required. The deadline for filing freshman financial aid applications for fall entry is September 30.

International Students: There are 1228 international students enrolled. They must score satisfactorily on the written TOEFL or on the electronic version or take the MELAB. Thet must also take the SAT or the ACT.

Computers: Wireless access is available. Wireless access is available in libraries, classroom buildings, labs, office buildings, and student unions. U of M provides an interactive map to help identify where wireless access is available. All students may access the system at any time. There are no time limits and no fees.

Graduates: From July 1, 2004 to June 30, 2005, 5939 bachelor's degrees were awarded. The most popular majors were engineering (21%),

psychology (11%), and business (6%). In an average class, 2% graduate in 3 years or less, 62% graduate in 4 years or less, 80% graduate in 5 years or less, and 82% graduate in 6 years or less. More than 1000 companies recruited on campus in 2004-2005.

Admissions Contact: Theodore L. Spencer, Director of Admissions. A video is available. E-mail: *ugadmiss@umich.edu*
Web: *www.admissions.umich.edu*

UNIVERSITY OF MICHIGAN/DEARBORN   E-5

Dearborn, MI 48128-1491   (313) 593-5100; Fax: (313) 436-9167

Full-time: 1800 men, 1900 women	**Faculty:** IIA, +$
Part-time: 1200 men, 1500 women	**Ph.D.s:** 88%
Graduate: 1200 men, 1000 women	**Student/Faculty:** n/av
Year: semesters, summer session	**Tuition:** $7000 ($16,000)
Application Deadline: open	**Room & Board:** n/app
Freshman Class: n/av	
SAT or ACT: required	**VERY COMPETITIVE**

The University of Michigan/Dearborn, founded in 1959, is a public, comprehensive commuter institution that is part of the University of Michigan system. The emphasis of its degree programs is on the liberal arts, management, engineering, and education. There are 4 undergraduate and 4 graduate schools. Figures in the above capsule and in this profile are approximate. In addition to regional accreditation, University of Michigan/Dearborn has baccalaureate program accreditation with ABET and NCATE. The library contains 335,000 volumes, 548,000 microform items, and 4600 audio/video tapes/CDs/DVDs, and subscribes to 1100 periodicals including electronic. Computerized library services include the card catalog, interlibrary loans, and database searching. Special learning facilities include a learning resource center, an art gallery, a natural history museum, a radio station, a TV station, a nature preserve, an Armenian research center, a child development center, an engineering education and practice center, and the Henry Ford Estate, a National Historic Landmark. The 196-acre campus is in a suburban area 10 miles from Detroit. There are 20 buildings.

Student Life: 96% of undergraduates are from Michigan. Others are from 16 states, 22 foreign countries, and Canada. 77% are from public schools. 73% are white. The average age of freshmen is 18; all undergraduates, 22.

Housing: There are no residence halls. All of students commute. Alcohol is not permitted. All students may keep cars.

Activities: 2% of men and about 1% of women belong to 7 national fraternities; 2% of women belong to 4 national sororities. There are 92 groups on campus, including art, cheerleading, chess, choir, computers, debate, drama, ethnic, film, gay, honors, international, literary magazine, newspaper, pep band, photography, political, professional, radio and TV, religious, social, social service, and student government. Popular campus events include Martin Luther King Diversity Celebration, Native American Pow Wow, and Fallfest.

Sports: There is 1 intercollegiate sport for men and 2 for women, and 21 intramural sports for men and 20 for women. Facilities include a 1200-seat gym, an ice rink, an indoor/outdoor track, a playing field, sand volleyball courts, weight and exercise rooms, and outdoor tennis courts.

Disabled Students: All of the campus is accessible. Wheelchair ramps, elevators, special parking, specially equipped rest rooms, lowered drinking fountains, and lowered telephones are available.

Services: Counseling and information services are available, as is tutoring in most subjects, including science, computer classes, composition, and math. There is a reader service for the blind, and remedial math, reading, and writing.

Campus Safety and Security: Measures include 24-hour foot and vehicle patrol, self-defense education, security escort services, and informal discussions. There are pamphlets/posters/films, emergency telephones, lighted pathways/sidewalks, vehicle etching, Crime Prevention Day, CPR training, and a rape awareness seminar.

Programs of Study: University of Michigan/Dearborn confers B.A., B.S., B.B.A., B.G.S., B.S.A., and B.S.E. degrees. Master's degrees are also awarded. Bachelor's degrees are awarded in BIOLOGICAL SCIENCE (biochemistry, biology/biological science, and microbiology), BUSINESS (business administration and management), COMMUNICATIONS AND THE ARTS (art history and appreciation, arts administration/management, English, languages, and music history and appreciation), COMPUTER AND PHYSICAL SCIENCE (chemistry, computer science, mathematics, physics, and science), EDUCATION (early childhood, elementary, science, secondary, and social studies), ENGINEERING AND ENVIRONMENTAL DESIGN (computer engineering, electrical/electronics engineering, environmental science, industrial engineering, manufacturing engineering, and mechanical engineering), SOCIAL SCIENCE (American studies, anthropology, behavioral science, economics, history, humanities, international studies, liberal arts/general studies, philosophy, political science/government, psychology, social science, and sociology). Electrical engineering and business administration are the strongest academically. Mechanical engineering, prebusiness, and business administration are the largest.

Required: Each college within the university has its own unique requirements. To graduate, students must complete 120 to 128 credit hours.

Special: UMD offers internships, study abroad, work-study and accelerated degree programs, a general studies degree, a dual major in engineering mathematics, student-designed majors, and co-op programs in engineering, business administration, and arts and sciences. Nondegree study and pass/fail options are possible. There is a freshman honors program.

Faculty/Classroom: 68% of faculty are male; 32%, female. The average class size in an introductory lecture is 43 and in a regular course, 28.

Admissions: 67% of recent applicants were accepted.

Requirements: The SAT or ACT is required. Other admissions requirements normally include graduation from an accredited secondary school; recommended high school units include 4 years each in math, English, and history, 3 each in science and foreign language, and 1 each in art and information technology. The GED is accepted with a minimum score of 55. An essay and interview are recommended. A GPA of 3.0 is required. AP credits are accepted. Important factors in the admissions decision are advanced placement or honor courses, recommendations by school officials, and leadership record.

Procedure: Freshmen are admitted to all sessions. Entrance exams should be taken in the spring of the junior year or the fall of the senior year. There is a deferred admissions plan. There is a rolling admissions plan. Application deadlines are open. The fall 2005 application fee was $30.

Transfer: 721 transfer students enrolled in a recent year. Applicants are required to have 25 to 30 transferable semester/credit hours; if they have fewer than 25, the SAT or ACT is mandatory. The required minimum GPA ranges from 2.5 to 3.0, depending on the intended major. 60 of 120 to 128 credits required for the bachelor's degree must be completed at University of Michigan/Dearborn.

Visiting: There are regularly scheduled orientations for prospective students, consisting of a tour, a student panel, academic unit introduction, and campus life sessions. There are guides for informal visits and visitors may sit in on classes. To schedule a visit, contact the Admissions Office.

Financial Aid: In a recent year, 38% of all full-time freshmen and 39% of continuing full-time students received some form of financial aid. 24% of full-time freshmen and 35% of continuing full-time students received need-based aid. The average freshman award was $6173. Need-based scholarships or need-based grants averaged $3604; need-based self-help aid (loans and jobs) averaged $2104; non-need-based athletic scholarships averaged $1133; and other non-need-based awards and non-need-based scholarships averaged $2014. 85% of undergraduates work part time. Average annual earnings from campus work are $2000. The average financial indebtedness of a recent graduate was $23,753. The FAFSA is required. Check with the school for current deadlines.

International Students: They must score satisfactorily on the written TOEFL or on the electronic version or take the MELAB or the APIEL exam.

Computers: All students may access the system. There are no time limits and no fees.

Graduates: In a recent year, 1141 bachelor's degrees were awarded. The most popular majors were business/marketing (21%), engineering/engineering technologies (20%), and education (11%). In an average class, 14% graduate in 4 years or less, 42% graduate in 5 years or less, and 54% graduate in 6 years or less.

Admissions Contact: Gabrielle Williams, Assistant Director of Admissions and Orientation. E-mail: *admissions@umd.umich.edu* Web: *www.umd.umich.edu*

UNIVERSITY OF MICHIGAN/FLINT	E-4
Flint, MI 48502-1950	(810) 762-3300; Fax: (810) 762-3272
Full-time: 1292 men, 2166 women	**Faculty:** IIA, -$
Part-time: 784 men, 1429 women	**Ph.D.s:** n/av
Graduate: 267 men, 484 women	**Student/Faculty:** n/av
Year: semesters, summer session	**Tuition:** $6398 ($12,150)
Application Deadline: September 15	**Room & Board:** n/app
Freshman Class: 1651 applied, 1396 accepted, 579 enrolled	
SAT Verbal/Math: 495/475*	**ACT:** 21 **COMPETITIVE**

The University of Michigan/Flint, established in 1956, is a public institution offering programs in the liberal arts and sciences, education, health professions, and business. There are 4 undergraduate and 6 graduate schools. In addition to regional accreditation, UM-Flint has baccalaureate program accreditation with AACN, AACSB, ACS, APTA, CCNE, CSWE, IAME, JRCERT, NASM, and NLN. The library contains 301,854 volumes, 676,427 microform items, and 18,366 audio/video tapes/CDs/DVDs, and subscribes to 900 periodicals including electronic. Computerized library services include the card catalog, interlibrary loans, and database searching. Special learning facilities include a learning resource center, art gallery, and TV station. The 72-acre campus is in an urban area

60 miles northwest of Detroit, 50 miles east of Lansing, and 55 miles north of Ann Arbor. There are 9 buildings.

Student Life: 98% of undergraduates are from Michigan. Others are from 32 states, 22 foreign countries, and Canada. 99% are from public schools. 76% are white; 11% African American. The average age of freshmen is 18; all undergraduates, 26. 20% do not continue beyond their first year; 37% remain to graduate.

Housing: There are no residence halls. All of students commute. Alcohol is not permitted. All students may keep cars.

Activities: 1% of men belong to 1 local and 2 national fraternities; 1% of women belong to 1 local and 4 national sororities. There are 58 groups on campus, including art, band, choir, chorale, chorus, computers, dance, drama, ethnic, gay, honors, jazz band, literary magazine, musical theater, newspaper, political, professional, radio and TV, religious, social, social service, and student government. Popular campus events include Welcome Back Week.

Sports: There are 8 intramural sports for men and 8 for women. Facilities include a recreation building housing a multipurpose gym, racquetball courts, a weight training area, and a swimming pool.

Disabled Students: 97% of the campus is accessible. Wheelchair ramps, elevators, special parking, specially equipped rest rooms, special class scheduling, lowered drinking fountains, lowered telephones, and a telephone for the hearing impaired. Reasonable accommodations may be made for students with documented disabilities.

Services: Counseling and information services are available, as is tutoring in every subject. There is a reader service for the blind, and remedial math, reading, and writing.

Campus Safety and Security: Measures include 24-hour foot and vehicle patrol, self-defense education, security escort services, and informal discussions. There are pamphlets/posters/films, emergency telephones, and lighted pathways/sidewalks.

Programs of Study: UM-Flint confers B.A., B.S., B.A.S., B.B.A., B.F.A., B.G.S., B.Mus.Ed., and B.S.N. degrees. Master's degrees are also awarded. Bachelor's degrees are awarded in BIOLOGICAL SCIENCE (biology/biological science and ecology), BUSINESS (accounting, banking and finance, business administration and management, human resources, and marketing/retailing/merchandising), COMMUNICATIONS AND THE ARTS (art, communications, dramatic arts, English, French, music, and Spanish), COMPUTER AND PHYSICAL SCIENCE (applied science, chemistry, computer science, mathematics, physical sciences, physics, and science), EDUCATION (early childhood, education, elementary, foreign languages, music, and secondary), ENGINEERING AND ENVIRONMENTAL DESIGN (engineering), HEALTH PROFESSIONS (environmental health science, health care administration, health science, medical laboratory technology, nursing, physical therapy, and radiation therapy), SOCIAL SCIENCE (anthropology, community psychology, criminal justice, economics, geography, history, philosophy, political science/government, psychology, public administration, social science, social work, sociology, and urban studies). Business and nursing are the strongest academically. Business, education, and health sciences are the largest.

Required: To graduate, all students must complete at least 120 credits, including 30 to 70 in the major along with satisfying all major requirements, and maintain a GPA of 2.0. Distribution requirements total 50 credits in English composition, humanities, fine arts, social science, and natural science.

Special: Special arrangements include co-op programs and dual majors, student-designed majors, cross-registration with Mott Community College, internships, study abroad, work-study, a 3-2 engineering program, an accelerated business degree, a general studies degree, nondegree study, and pass/fail options. There is a chapter of Phi Beta Kappa and a freshman honors program.

Faculty/Classroom: 51% of faculty are male; 49%, female. All both teach and do research. No introductory courses are taught by graduate students. The average class size in an introductory lecture is 24; in a laboratory, 19; and in a regular course, 22.

Admissions: 85% of the 2005-2006 applicants were accepted. The SAT scores for the 2005-2006 freshman class were: Verbal--58% below 500, 21% between 500 and 599, 16% between 600 and 700, and 5% above 700; Math--58% below 500, 32% between 500 and 599, and 10% between 600 and 700. The ACT scores were 43% below 21, 26% between 21 and 23, 21% between 24 and 26, 5% between 27 and 28, and 5% above 28. 2 freshmen graduated first in their class.

Requirements: The SAT or ACT is required; the ACT is preferred, the ACT is preferred. Graduation from secondary school is required, with 4 years of English, 3 each of math and social studies, and 2 of science. The GED is accepted. SAT: Subject tests and an interview are recommended. Applied music students must audition. A GPA of 2.7 is required. AP and CLEP credits are accepted. Important factors in the admissions decision are advanced placement or honor courses, evidence of special talent, and leadership record.

Procedure: Freshmen are admitted to all sessions. Entrance exams should be taken in the spring of the junior year or fall of the senior year. There is a deferred admissions and a rolling admissions plan. Applications should be filed by September 15 for fall entry and December 15 for winter entry. The fall 2005 application fee was $30. Notification is sent on a rolling basis. Applications are accepted on-line.

Transfer: 1149 transfer students enrolled in a recent year. Applicants must have at least 12 college credits and a minimum GPA of 2.0 in transferable courses. An associate degree and an interview are recommended. 45 of 120 credits required for the bachelor's degree must be completed at UM-Flint.

Visiting: There are regularly scheduled orientations for prospective students. There are guides for informal visits and visitors may sit in on classes. To schedule a visit, contact the Admissions Office at *admissions@umflint.edu.*

Financial Aid: In a recent year, 46% of all full-time freshmen and 54% of continuing full-time students received some form of financial aid. 26% of full-time freshmen and 34% of continuing full-time students received need-based aid. The average freshman award was $6325. The FAFSA is required. The deadline for filing freshman financial aid applications for fall entry is March 1.

International Students: There are 43 international students enrolled. Satisfactory scores are required on the written TOEFL and the MELAB.

Computers: Wireless access is available. All students may access the system. There are no fees.

Graduates: From July 1, 2004 to June 30, 2005, 907 bachelor's degrees were awarded. In a recent year, the most popular majors were elementary education (21%), business (16%), and health professions (12%). In an average class, 1% graduate in 3 years or less, 10% graduate in 4 years or less, 29% graduate in 5 years or less, and 38% graduate in 6 years or less. 125 companies recruited on campus in 2004-2005. Of the 2004 graduating class, 9% were enrolled in graduate school within 6 months of graduation.

Admissions Contact: Kimberly Buster Williams, Director of Admissions. E-mail: *admissions@list.umich.edu*
Web: *www.umflint.edu/resources/office/admissions/index.php*

WAYNE STATE UNIVERSITY

E-5

Detroit, MI 48202

(313) 577-3577; Fax: (313) 577-7536

Full-time: 11,010 men and women	**Faculty:** 1689; I, av$
Part-time: 9145 men and women	**Ph.D.s:** 85%
Graduate: 12,945 men and women	**Student/Faculty:** 7 to 1
Year: semesters, summer session	**Tuition:** $5280 ($11,300)
Application Deadline: see profile	**Room & Board:** $6525
Freshman Class: n/av	
SAT or ACT: required	**COMPETITIVE**

Wayne State University, founded in 1868, is a state-supported, nonprofit institution. Primarily a commuter college, it offers a variety of academic and professional programs. Figures in this profile and capsule are approximate. There are 11 undergraduate and 13 graduate schools. In addition to regional accreditation, Wayne State has baccalaureate program accreditation with AACSB, ABET, ABFSE, ACPE, ACS, ADA, AOTA, APTA, ASHLA, CAHEA, CCNE, CSWE, NAACLS, NASM, NCATE, and NLN. The 6 libraries contain 3,323,580 volumes, 3,816,051 microform items, and 71,715 audio/video tapes/CDs/DVDs, and subscribe to 18,643 periodicals including electronic. Computerized library services include the card catalog, database searching, and Internet access. Special learning facilities include a learning resource center, art gallery, natural history museum, planetarium, and TV station. The 203-acre campus is in an urban area 2 miles north of downtown Detroit in the New Center area. There are 97 buildings.

Student Life: 89% of undergraduates are from Michigan. Others are from 42 states, 107 foreign countries, and Canada. 87% are from public schools. 50% are white; 26% African American; 10% foreign nationals. The average age of freshmen is 22; all undergraduates, 26.

Housing: There are no residence halls, but there coed on-campus apartments. On-campus housing is available on a first-come, first-served basis. 95% of students commute. All students may keep cars.

Activities: 2% of men belong to 8 national fraternities; 2% of women belong to 10 national sororities. There are 114 groups on campus, including band, chess, choir, computers, dance, ethnic, film, forensics, gay, honors, international, jazz band, marching band, newspaper, orchestra, pep band, political, professional, radio and TV, religious, social, social service, student government, symphony, and yearbook. Popular campus events include Student Organization Day, the International Fair, and Detroit Festival of the Arts.

Sports: There are 9 intercollegiate sports for men and 8 for women, and 6 intramural sports for men and 6 for women. Facilities include a phys ed building, a recreation and fitness center, various swimming pools, courts, and soccer and softball fields.

Disabled Students: All of the campus is accessible. Wheelchair ramps, elevators, special parking, specially equipped rest rooms, lowered drinking fountains, lowered telephones, and educational accessibility services are available.

Services: Counseling and information services are available, as is tutoring in every subject. There is a reader service for the blind, and remedial math, reading, and writing. Tutorial services are available through centralized counseling or academic departments.

Campus Safety and Security: Measures include 24-hour foot and vehicle patrol, self-defense education, security escort services, and informal discussions. There are pamphlets/posters/films, emergency telephones, and lighted pathways/sidewalks.

Programs of Study: Wayne State confers B.A., B.S., B.A.S., B.F.A., B.I.S., B.Mus., B.P.A., B.S.A.H.S., B.S.C.T., B.S.E.T., B.S.M.S., B.S.N., B.S.W., and B.T.I.S. degrees. Master's and doctoral degrees are also awarded. Bachelor's degrees are awarded in BIOLOGICAL SCIENCE (biology/biological science), BUSINESS (accounting, banking and finance, business economics, funeral home services, labor studies, management information systems, management science, and marketing/retailing/merchandising), COMMUNICATIONS AND THE ARTS (Arabic, art, art history and appreciation, broadcasting, classics, communications, dance, design, dramatic arts, English, film arts, fine arts, German, Italian, journalism, linguistics, music, public relations, Russian, Slavic languages, and Spanish), COMPUTER AND PHYSICAL SCIENCE (chemistry, computer science, geology, information sciences and systems, mathematics, and physics), EDUCATION (art, business, elementary, mathematics, physical, science, special, and technical), ENGINEERING AND ENVIRONMENTAL DESIGN (chemical engineering, civil engineering, computer technology, electrical/electronics engineering, industrial engineering technology, manufacturing technology, mechanical engineering, and mechanical engineering technology), HEALTH PROFESSIONS (nursing, occupational therapy, pharmacy, radiation therapy, and speech pathology/audiology), SOCIAL SCIENCE (African studies, American studies, anthropology, criminal justice, dietetics, economics, food science, French studies, geography, history, international studies, liberal arts/general studies, Mexican-American/Chicano studies, Near Eastern studies, parks and recreation management, peace studies, philosophy, political science/government, psychology, public affairs, social work, sociology, urban studies, and women's studies). Chemistry, biology, and pharmacy are the strongest academically. Elementary education, art, and psychology are the largest.

Required: To graduate, students must complete at least 120 credit hours and have a minimum GPA of 2.0. General Education has 2 components. Students must complete competencies in written communication, math, oral communication, and computer literacy. In addition, students must complete group requirements in natural science, social science, American society and institutions, foreign culture, humanities, and the university and its libraries.

Special: Special academic programs include cross-registration with Macomb University Center, the University of Michigan, and the University of Windsor; internships in business, industry, or communications; study abroad in Germany, Japan, or England; on-campus work-study programs; accelerated degree programs in liberal arts, science, engineering, and nursing; a general studies degree; co-op programs; nondegree study; and limited pass/fail options. The College of Lifelong Learning offers televised, weekend, and evening courses. There is 1 national honor society, including Phi Beta Kappa, a freshman honors program, and 23 departmental honors program.

Faculty/Classroom: 61% of faculty are male; 39%, female. 62% teach undergraduates, 92% do research, and 54% do both. Graduate students teach 13% of introductory courses. The average class size in an introductory lecture is 100; in a laboratory, 20; and in a regular course, 30.

Requirements: The SAT or ACT is required, with the ACT preferred. If the GPA is below 2.75, the applicant must have a satisfactory SAT score or an ACT score of 21. Admissions requirements include graduation from an accredited secondary school; the GED with an acceptable SAT or ACT score is also allowable. A GPA of 2.75 is required. AP and CLEP credits are accepted.

Procedure: Freshmen are admitted to all sessions. If necessary, the ACT should be taken in the junior year or the SAT in the senior year. There are deferred admissions and rolling admissions plans. Check with the school for application deadlines. Notification is sent on a rolling basis. Applications are accepted on-line.

Transfer: 2551 transfer students enrolled in a recent year. Applicants must have 30 transferable credit hours with a 3.0 GPA, and an overall minimum GPA of 2.0. 30 of 120 credits required for the bachelor's degree must be completed at Wayne State.

Visiting: There are guides for informal visits and visitors may sit in on classes. To schedule a visit, contact the Office of Admissions.

Financial Aid: In a recent year, 58% of all full-time freshmen and 49% of continuing full-time students received some form of financial aid. 40% of full-time freshmen and 34% of continuing full-time students received need-based aid. The average freshman award was $6473. Need-based scholarships or need-based grants averaged $3833; need-based self-help aid (loans and jobs) averaged $2993; non-need-based athletic scholarships averaged $4659; and other non-need-based awards and non-need-based scholarships averaged $4720. 11% of undergraduates worked part time. Average annual earnings from campus work were $2786. The average financial indebtedness of a recent graduate was $15,457. Wayne State is a member of CSS. The FAFSA, federal tax returns, and W-2s are required. Check with the school for application deadlines.

International Students: In a recent year, there were 1074 international students enrolled. The school actively recruits these students. They must score satisfactorily on the written TOEFL or on the electronic version or take the MELAB.

Computers: All students may access the system 24 hours a day. There are no time limits and no fees.

Graduates: In a recent year, 2249 bachelor's degrees were awarded. The most popular majors were elementary education (9%), psychology (7%), and nursing (6%). In an average class, 12% graduate in 3 years or less, 27% graduate in 4 years or less, 37% graduate in 5 years or less, and 42% graduate in 6 years or less. 93 companies recruited on campus in a recent year. Of a recent graduating class, 36% were enrolled in graduate school within 6 months of graduation and 98% were employed.

Admissions Contact: Susan A. Zwieg, Director of Admissions. E-mail: *admissions@wayne.edu* Web: *www.wayne.edu*

WESTERN MICHIGAN UNIVERSITY   D-5

Kalamazoo, MI 49008   (269) 387-2380
(800) 400-4968; Fax: (269) 387-2096

Full-time: 9240 men, 9520 women	Faculty: 729; I, --$
Part-time: 1312 men, 1362 women	Ph.D.s: 82%
Graduate: 1952 men, 2853 women	Student/Faculty: 26 to 1
Year: semesters, summer session	Tuition: $6478 ($15,856)
Application Deadline: open	Room & Board: $6821
Freshman Class: 13,074 applied, 11,173 accepted, 3837 enrolled	
ACT: 22	COMPETITIVE

Western Michigan University, founded in 1903, is a public institution offering 252 degree programs in the liberal arts and sciences, aviation, business, education, engineering, fine arts, health and human services, and preprofessional studies. There are 7 undergraduate schools and 1 graduate school. In addition to regional accreditation, WMU has baccalaureate program accreditation with AACSB, ABET, ACOTE, ADA, ARC-PA, ACS, CAA, CSAB, CSWE, FIDER, NASAD, NASM, NASPE, NCATE, and NLN. The 5 libraries contain 2,069,948 volumes, 1,965,298 microform items, and 26,547 audio/video tapes/CDs/DVDs, and subscribe to 10,033 periodicals including electronic. Computerized library services include the card catalog, interlibrary loans, and database searching. Special learning facilities include a learning resource center, art gallery, radio station, aviation flight simulators, an electron microscope, a particle accelerator, a paper manufacturing and fiber recovery pilot plant, a business technology and research park, a health education facility, a fleet of Cirrus aircraft and Imaging Center, and numerous specialized labs in the academic departments. The 1200-acre campus is in an urban area 140 miles west of Detroit and 140 miles east of Chicago. Including any residence halls, there are 151 buildings.

Student Life: 93% of undergraduates are from Michigan. Students are from 48 states, 98 foreign countries, and Canada. 86% are white. The average age of freshmen is 18; all undergraduates, 21. 27% do not continue beyond their first year; 55% remain to graduate.

Housing: 6200 students can be accommodated in college housing, which includes single-sex and coed dorms, on-campus apartments, off-campus apartments, married-student housing, fraternity houses, and sorority houses. In addition, there are honors houses, special-interest houses, a health and wellness house, and an international house. On-campus housing is guaranteed for the freshman year only and is available on a first-come, first-served basis. 57% of students commute. All students may keep cars.

Activities: There are 14 local and national fraternities; 8% of women belong to 12 local and national sororities. There are 300 groups on campus, including art, band, cheerleading, chess, choir, chorale, chorus, computers, dance, drama, ethnic, film, gay, honors, international, jazz band, literary magazine, marching band, musical theater, newspaper, orchestra, pep band, photography, political, professional, radio and TV, religious, social, social service, student government, and symphony. Popular campus events include Family Weekend, Into the Streets, and Campus Classic races.

Sports: There are 6 intercollegiate sports for men and 10 for women, and 18 intramural sports for men and 18 for women. Facilities include a recreation center designed as a sports village, which includes a recreational swimming pool, a swirl pool, a weight and fitness room with more than 100 stations, facilities for basketball, floor hockey, and indoor soccer, a climbing wall, baseball/softball infields, a golf driving range, an elevated track for jogging, and facilities for aerobics, archery, badminton, tennis, and volleyball. The field house includes a 5800-seat arena for basketball and volleyball competition and facilities for gymnasts. There is also a 400-meter Olympic model Martin-surface track, a cross-country course, bowling lanes, a video game area, tennis courts, a 30,000-seat stadium, a competition swimming pool, and an ice arena.

Disabled Students: 85% of the campus is accessible. Wheelchair ramps, elevators, special parking, specially equipped rest rooms, special class scheduling, lowered drinking fountains, lowered telephones, and special housing. A lift-equipped van to take disabled students to classes and adaptive computer equipment are also available.

Services: Counseling and information services are available, as is tutoring in most subjects. There is a reader service for the blind, and remedial math, reading, and writing.

Campus Safety and Security: Measures include 24-hour foot and vehicle patrol, self-defense education, security escort services, and shuttle buses. There are informal discussions, pamphlets/posters/films, emergency telephones, and lighted pathways/sidewalks. There is also a student watch program, Operation Identification, an enhanced telephone system, and a residence hall security system.

Programs of Study: WMU confers B.A., B.S., B.B.A., B.F.A., B.Mus., B.S., B.S.E., B.S.N., and B.S.W. degrees. Master's and doctoral degrees are also awarded. Bachelor's degrees are awarded in AGRICULTURE (environmental studies), BIOLOGICAL SCIENCE (biochemistry and biology/biological science), BUSINESS (accounting, banking and finance, business administration and management, business communications, business economics, human resources, management information systems, management science, marketing/retailing/merchandising, recreation and leisure services, and tourism), COMMUNICATIONS AND THE ARTS (advertising, art, art history and appreciation, broadcasting, communications, dance, dramatic arts, English, French, German, graphic design, industrial design, jazz, journalism, Latin, media arts, music, music history and appreciation, music performance, music theory and composition, musical theater, public relations, Spanish, telecommunications, and theater design), COMPUTER AND PHYSICAL SCIENCE (chemistry, computer science, digital arts/technology, earth science, geochemistry, geology, geophysics and seismology, hydrogeology, mathematics, physics, and statistics), EDUCATION (art, athletic training, business, elementary, health, home economics, marketing and distribution, music, physical, secondary, special, and vocational), ENGINEERING AND ENVIRONMENTAL DESIGN (aeronautical engineering, aeronautical science, aircraft mechanics, airline piloting and navigation, aviation administration/management, chemical engineering, civil engineering, computer engineering, construction engineering, drafting and design technology, electrical/electronics engineering, engineering management, graphic arts technology, industrial engineering, industrial engineering technology, interior design, manufacturing engineering, manufacturing technology, mechanical engineering, paper and pulp science, and paper engineering), HEALTH PROFESSIONS (biomedical science, community health work, exercise science, health, music therapy, nursing, occupational therapy, predentistry, premedicine, and speech pathology/audiology), SOCIAL SCIENCE (African studies, American studies, anthropology, criminal justice, dietetics, economics, family/consumer studies, food production/management/services, geography, gerontology, history, interdisciplinary studies, international studies, philosophy, political science/government, prelaw, psychology, public administration, religion, social work, sociology, textiles and clothing, and women's studies). Marketing, finance and commercial law, and education are the largest.

Required: Students must complete 122 semester hours, including 35 of general education courses and a minimum of 24 in the major. A minimum GPA of 2.0 is required. Students must complete courses in science, social science, humanities, and fine arts, and 1 course in non-Western world study. Comprehensive exams are required in some departments. All students must complete 2 semester hours of phys ed and demonstrate computer literacy.

Special: Cross-registration is available through the Kalamazoo Consortium. Opportunities are provided for internships in occupational and music therapy, teaching, business, history, and engineering. Also available are work-study programs, student-designed majors, pass/fail options, and credit by exam. Students may study abroad in more than 65 countries on 4 continents. There are 9 national honor societies, including Phi Beta Kappa, a freshman honors program, and 33 departmental honors programs.

Faculty/Classroom: 56% of faculty are male; 44%, female. Graduate students teach 31% of introductory courses. The average class size in an introductory lecture is 113; in a laboratory, 20; and in a regular course, 36.

Admissions: 85% of the 2005-2006 applicants were accepted. The ACT scores for the 2005-2006 freshman class were: 37% below 21, 30% between 21 and 23, 21% between 24 and 26, 7% between 27 and 28, and 5% above 28. 27% of the current freshmen were in the top fifth of their class; 56% were in the top two fifths. 57 freshmen graduated first in their class.

Requirements: The ACT is required. In addition, applicants must submit an official high school transcript. An audition is required for music majors. An interview may be recommended. The College of Fine Arts requires an audition, portfolio, or interview of all applicants. A GPA of 2.0 is required. AP and CLEP credits are accepted. Important factors in the admissions decision are advanced placement or honor courses, extracurricular activities record, and recommendations by school officials.

Procedure: Freshmen are admitted to all sessions. Entrance exams should be taken late in the junior year or early in the senior year. There is a deferred admissions and a rolling admissions plan. Application deadlines are open. Application fee is $35. Applications are accepted on-line.

Transfer: 2406 transfer students enrolled in 2004-2005. Applicants must have a minimum GPA of 2.0 in transferable college courses. Consideration will also be given to the trend of grades and recent course work. 30 of 122 credits required for the bachelor's degree must be completed at WMU.

Visiting: There are regularly scheduled orientations for prospective students, including an admission presentation, departmental advising, lunch, and a campus tour. Visitors may sit in on classes and stay overnight. To schedule a visit, contact the campus visit coordinator at (269) 387-2289.

Financial Aid: 25% of undergraduates work part time. Average annual earnings from campus work are $4000. The FAFSA is required. Check with the school for specific financial aid information.

International Students: There are 429 international students enrolled. The school actively recruits these students. They must score satisfactory on the written TOEFL.

Computers: Wireless access is available. The wireless system is available throughout the entire campus including, wired Internet access in residence halls, campus apartments, computer labs, classrooms, offices, in all academic and administrative buildings, and 2000 PCs are available to students across campus in labs, libraries, and dorms. All students may access the system 24 hours a day. There are no fees. It is strongly recommended that all students have a personal computer.

Graduates: From July 1, 2004 to June 30, 2005, 4291 bachelor's degrees were awarded. The most popular majors were education (17%), marketing (10%), and management (5%). In an average class, 20% graduate in 4 years or less, 47% graduate in 5 years or less, and 12% graduate in 6 years or less. 510 companies recruited on campus in 2004-2005.

Admissions Contact: John E. Beacon, Vice Provost for Enrollment Management. E-mail: ask-wmu@wmich.edu
Web: http://www.wmich.edu/

WILLIAM TYNDALE COLLEGE — E-5

Farmington Hills, MI 48331-3147
(248) 553-7200
(800) 483-0707; Fax: (248) 553-5963

Full-time: 60 men, 60 women	**Faculty:** 6
Part-time: 90 men, 80 women	**Ph.D.s:** 40%
Graduate: none	**Student/Faculty:** 20 to 1
Year: semesters, summer session	**Tuition:** $9000
Application Deadline: open	**Room & Board:** $4000
Freshman Class: n/av	
ACT: required	**NONCOMPETITIVE**

William Tyndale College, established in 1945, is a Christian liberal arts college offering undergraduate degrees in Christian studies, humanities and social sciences, math and natural sciences, and professional studies. Figures in the above capsule and in this profile are approximate. The library contains 50,000 volumes and 300 audio/video tapes/CDs/DVDs, and subscribes to 230 periodicals including electronic. Computerized library services include the card catalog, interlibrary loans, database searching, and Internet access. The 28-acre campus is in a suburban area 15 miles west of Detroit. Including any residence halls, there are 2 buildings.

Student Life: 96% of undergraduates are from Michigan. Others are from 5 states, 10 foreign countries, and Canada. 73% are from public schools. 64% are white; 32% African American. 76% are Protestant; 22% claim no religious affiliation. The average age of freshmen is 28; all undergraduates, 32. 34% do not continue beyond their first year.

Housing: 54 students can be accommodated in college housing, which includes coed dorms. On-campus housing is available on a first-come, first-served basis. Priority is given to out-of-town students. 85% of students commute. Alcohol is not permitted. All students may keep cars.

Activities: There are no fraternities or sororities. There are 9 groups on campus, including choir, drama, honors, international, newspaper, religious, social, social service, and student government. Popular campus events include New Student Retreat, Senior Banquet, and Billy T's Coffeehouse.

Sports: There are 1 intramural sports for men and 1 for women. Facilities include a soccer field and access to local school gyms.

Disabled Students: All of the campus is accessible. Wheelchair ramps, elevators, special parking, specially equipped rest rooms, lowered drinking fountains, and lowered telephones are available.

Services: Counseling and information services are available, as is tutoring in every subject. There is remedial math, reading, and writing.

Campus Safety and Security: Measures include lighted pathways/sidewalks.

Programs of Study: Tyndale confers B.A., B.B.A., B.Mus., and B.R.E. degrees. Associate degrees are also awarded. Bachelor's degrees are awarded in BUSINESS (business administration and management), COMMUNICATIONS AND THE ARTS (communications, English, music, and music performance), SOCIAL SCIENCE (biblical studies, Christian studies, history, pastoral studies, psychology, religious music, social science, theological studies, and youth ministry). Business administration, Christian thought, and psychology are the largest.

Required: Students must complete 120 credits, with at least 30 in the major, and maintain a minimum GPA of 2.0. Special curriculum requirements include 28 hours of social and natural sciences, 27 of humanities, and 24 of Christian thought.

Special: Internships in youth studies and pastoral studies majors are available. An accelerated degree program in business administration allows students to complete a B.B.A. degree in 19 months attending class once a week. Dual majors in music/youth are offered. There are 2 national honor societies.

Faculty/Classroom: 59% of faculty are male; 41%, female. All teach undergraduates. The average class size in an introductory lecture is 18.

Admissions: All of a recent year's applicants were accepted. The ACT scores for a recent freshman class were: 33% below 21, 33% between 21 and 23, 17% between 24 and 26, and 17% above 28. 60% of recent freshmen were in the top fifth of their class; 80% were in the top two fifths.

Requirements: The ACT is required. Graduation from an accredited secondary school is required; the GED is accepted. Music majors must audition. In addition home-schooled students must provide writing samples, a recommendation, and an interview; business administration students must submit an essay. A GPA of 2.0 is required. AP and CLEP credits are accepted. Important factors in the admissions decision are advanced placement or honor courses, leadership record, and parents or siblings attending the school.

Procedure: Freshmen are admitted to all sessions. Entrance exams should be taken in the senior year. There is a deferred admissions plan. There is a rolling admissions plan. Application deadlines are open. Applications are accepted on-line.

Transfer: Transfer students must have a GPA of 2.0 for college work. A high school transcript is required if they have fewer than 30 college credits. 45 of 120 credits required for the bachelor's degree must be completed at Tyndale.

Visiting: There are regularly scheduled orientations for prospective students, including an overview of academic programs, student life, campus activities, and financial aid, registration, and advising. There are guides for informal visits and visitors may sit in on classes and stay overnight. To schedule a visit, contact the Admissions Counselor, Office of Admissions at admissions@williamtyndale.edu.

Financial Aid: In a recent year, 83% of all full-time freshmen and 80% of continuing full-time students received some form of financial aid. 63% of full-time freshmen and 60% of continuing full-time students received need-based aid. The average freshman award was $5177. Need-based scholarships or need-based grants averaged $3941 ($8196 maximum); need-based self-help aid (loans and jobs) averaged $3905 ($6939 maximum); and other non-need-based awards and non-need-based scholarships averaged $2794 ($6000 maximum). 5% of undergraduates work part time. Average annual earnings from campus work are $1963. Tyndale is a member of CSS. The FAFSA and the college's own financial statement are required. Check with the school for current deadlines.

International Students: The school actively recruits these students. They must score satisfactorily on the written TOEFL.

Computers: All students may access the system 7 A.M. to 10 P.M. Monday through Saturday. There are no time limits and no fees. It is strongly recommended that all students have a personal computer.

Graduates: In a recent year, 151 bachelor's degrees were awarded.

Admissions Contact: Fred A. Schebor, Vice President for Enrollment Management. E-mail: faschebor@williamtyndale.edu
Web: www.williamtyndale.edu

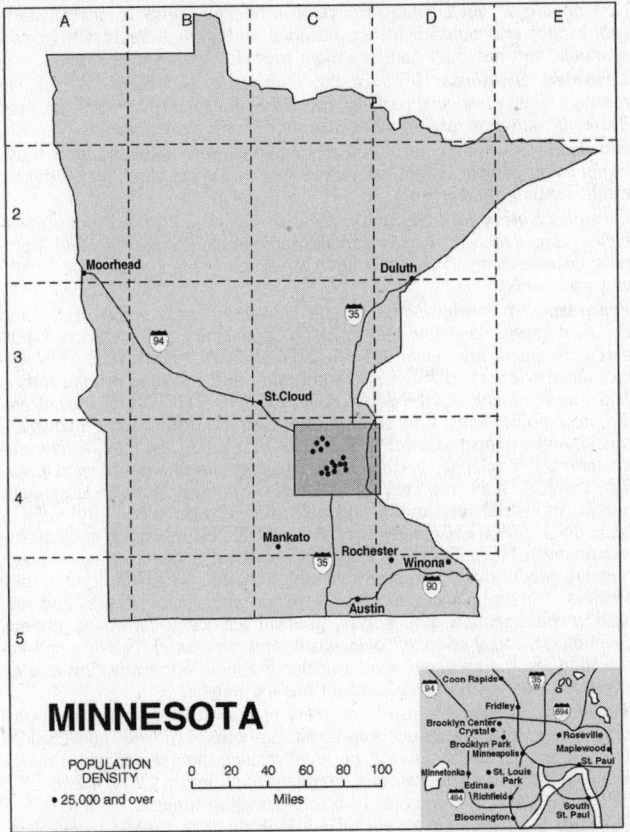

MINNESOTA

POPULATION
DENSITY

• 25,000 and over

0   20   40   60   80   100

Miles

AUGSBURG COLLEGE   C-4

Minneapolis, MN 55454

(612) 330-1001
(800) 788-5678; Fax: (612) 330-1590

Full-time: 1008 men, 1234 women   **Faculty:** IIB, -$
Part-time: 178 men, 388 women   **Ph.D.s:** n/av
Graduate: 224 men, 450 women   **Student/Faculty:** n/av
Year: trimesters, summer session   **Tuition:** $21,960
Application Deadline: May 1   **Room & Board:** $6340
Freshman Class: 980 applied, 743 accepted, 323 enrolled
SAT Verbal/Math: 541/542*   **ACT:** 23   **COMPETITIVE**

Augsburg College, established in 1869, is a private liberal arts institution affiliated with the Evangelical Lutheran Church in America. In addition to regional accreditation, Augsburg has baccalaureate program accreditation with CSWE, NASM, NCATE, and NLN. The library contains 182,289 volumes, 21,355 microform items, and 3477 audio/video tapes/ CDs/DVDs, and subscribes to 686 periodicals including electronic. Computerized library services include the card catalog, interlibrary loans, database searching, Internet access, and laptop Internet portals. Special learning facilities include a learning resource center, art gallery, radio station, and TV station. The 23-acre campus is in an urban area in Minneapolis. Including any residence halls, there are 25 buildings.

Student Life: 89% of undergraduates are from Minnesota. Others are from 39 states, 31 foreign countries, and Canada. 67% are white. 51% are Protestant; 18% claim no religious affiliation; 16% Catholic. The average age of freshmen is 19; all undergraduates, 26. 20% do not continue beyond their first year.

Housing: 949 students can be accommodated in college housing, which includes coed dorms, on-campus apartments, and married-student housing. In addition, there are special-interest houses. On-campus housing is guaranteed for the freshman year only, is available on a first-come, first-served basis, and is available on a lottery system for upperclassmen. Priority is given to out-of-town students. 55% of students live on campus; of those, 60% remain on campus on weekends. All students may keep cars.

Activities: There are no fraternities or sororities. There are 40 groups on campus, including art, band, cheerleading, choir, chorus, dance, drama, ethnic, gay, honors, international, jazz band, literary magazine, newspaper, orchestra, pep band, political, professional, radio and TV,

religious, social, social service, student government, and yearbook. Popular campus events include Days in May, Spring Affair, and Advent Vespers.

Sports: There are 9 intercollegiate sports for men and 7 for women, and 4 intramural sports for men and 4 for women. Facilities include a 1500-seat sports field, a 2800-seat gym, tennis courts, a double-rink ice arena, and a domed field facility for winter.

Disabled Students: 92% of the campus is accessible. Wheelchair ramps, elevators, special parking, specially equipped rest rooms, special class scheduling, lowered drinking fountains, and lowered telephones are available.

Services: Counseling and information services are available, as is tutoring in every subject. There is a reader service for the blind and remedial math and writing. Taped textbooks and adaptive computer technology, including a text scanner, speaking software, a touch tablet, and text magnification software are available.

Campus Safety and Security: Measures include 24-hour foot and vehicle patrol, self-defense education, security escort services, and informal discussions. There are pamphlets/posters/films, emergency telephones, and lighted pathways/sidewalks.

Programs of Study: Augsburg confers B.A., B.S., and B.M. degrees. Master's degrees are also awarded. Bachelor's degrees are awarded in BIOLOGICAL SCIENCE (biology/biological science), BUSINESS (accounting, business administration and management, international business management, management information systems, and marketing/ retailing/merchandising), COMMUNICATIONS AND THE ARTS (art history and appreciation, communications, dramatic arts, English, French, German, music, Scandinavian languages, Spanish, speech/debate/ rhetoric, and studio art), COMPUTER AND PHYSICAL SCIENCE (chemistry, computer science, mathematics, and physics), EDUCATION (elementary, health, music, physical, and secondary), HEALTH PROFESSIONS (music therapy), SOCIAL SCIENCE (East Asian studies, economics, history, international relations, philosophy, political science/ government, psychology, religion, Russian and Slavic studies, Scandinavian studies, social work, sociology, urban studies, and women's studies). Physics, chemistry, and English are the strongest academically. Business, communication, and education are the largest.

Required: To graduate, all students must have a minimum GPA of 2.0 and a total of 32 courses, with 10 to 15 in the major. They must complete 15 courses from 8 perspective areas, and first-year fall orientation and seminar. Students must also satisfy entry-level and graduation skills requirements in writing, critical thinking, math, quantitative reasoning, and speaking and demonstrate proficiency in 2 sports.

Special: Special academic programs include internships and co-op programs in business, government, and nonprofit and community-based organizations, a Washington semester, and study abroad in Europe, Latin America, and Africa. There are student-designed majors, cross-registration through the Associated Colleges of the Twin Cities (ACTC), dual and 3-2 engineering degrees with Washington University, Michigan Technological University, and the University of Minnesota, and pre-professional programs in dentistry, law, medicine, physical therapy, pharmacy, theology, and veterinary medicine. Credit for previous learning experience may be granted, and pass/fail options are possible. There is 1 national honor society, and a freshman honors program.

Faculty/Classroom: 50% of faculty are male; 50%, female. 99% teach undergraduates. No introductory courses are taught by graduate students. The average class size in an introductory lecture is 20; in a laboratory, 16; and in a regular course, 16.

Admissions: 76% of the 2005-2006 applicants were accepted. The SAT scores for the 2005-2006 freshman class were: Verbal--18% below 500, 42% between 500 and 599, 35% between 600 and 700, and 5% above 700; Math--15% below 500, 55% between 500 and 599, 25% between 600 and 700, and 5% above 700. The ACT scores were 26% below 21, 25% between 21 and 23, 28% between 24 and 26, 11% between 27 and 28, and 9% above 28. 32% of the current freshmen were in the top fifth of their class; 58% were in the top two fifths. 4 freshmen graduated first in their class.

Requirements: A satisfactory score in the SAT or ACT is required. Admissions requirements include graduation from an accredited secondary school, with 4 years of English. The GED is also accepted. An essay is required and an interview is recommended. Augsburg requires applicants to be in the upper 50% of their class. A GPA of 2.5 is required. AP and CLEP credits are accepted. Important factors in the admissions decision are advanced placement or honor courses, leadership record, and recommendations by school officials.

Procedure: Freshmen are admitted fall and spring. Entrance exams should be taken during the fall of the senior year in high school. There are early decision, deferred admissions, and rolling admissions plans. Early decision applications should be filed by December 15; regular applications, by May 1 for fall entry and December 1 for spring entry, along with a $25 fee. Notification is sent on a rolling basis. Applications are accepted on-line.

Transfer: 215 transfer students enrolled in 2004-2005. Applicants must have a minimum GPA of 2.2 in college course work. 9 of 32 courses required for the bachelor's degree must be completed at Augsburg.

Visiting: There are regularly scheduled orientations for prospective students, including admissions interviews and campus tours. Students may also arrange to meet with professors and coaches and to attend lectures. There are guides for informal visits and visitors may sit in on classes and stay overnight. To schedule a visit, contact the Admissions Office at (612) 330-1001 or (800) 788-5678 or admissions@augsburg.edu.

Financial Aid: In 2005-2006, 89% of all full-time freshmen and 75% of continuing full-time students received some form of financial aid. 77% of full-time freshmen and 64% of continuing full-time students received need-based aid. The average freshman award was $12,883. Need-based scholarships or need-based grants averaged $11,308 ($27,892 maximum); and other non-need-based awards and non-need-based scholarships averaged $1631 ($21,460 maximum). 44% of undergraduates work part time. Average annual earnings from campus work are $1710. In a recent year, the average financial indebtedness of graduates was $24,546. The FAFSA and the college's own financial statement are required. The priority date for freshman financial aid applications for fall entry is April 15. The deadline for filing freshman financial aid applications for fall entry is August 1.

International Students: There are 58 international students enrolled. The school actively recruits these students. A satisfactory score is required on the written TOEFL. Applicants must also take the SAT or the ACT, scoring 17.

Computers: Wireless access is available. More than 210 PCs, Macs, and web kiosks are available for student use throughout the campus. Additionally, printers, scanners, and specialty software are accessible. Laptops may be checked out in the library by students, faculty, and staff. All students may access the system. There are no time limits and no fees. It is strongly recommended that all students have a personal computer.

Graduates: From July 1, 2004 to June 30, 2005, 543 bachelor's degrees were awarded. The most popular majors were business management (10%), accounting/ public accounting (6%), and elementary education (6%). In an average class, 7% graduate in 3 years or less, 38% graduate in 4 years or less, 53% graduate in 5 years or less, and 55% graduate in 6 years or less. 66 companies recruited on campus in 2004-2005. Of the 2004 graduating class, 25% were enrolled in graduate school within 6 months of graduation and 75% were employed.

Admissions Contact: Carrie Carroll, Director of Admissions. E-mail: carrollc@augsburg.edu Web: www.augsburg.edu

BEMIDJI STATE UNIVERSITY — B-2

Bemidji, MN 56601-2699

(218) 755-2040
(800) 475-2001; Fax: (218) 755-2074

Full-time: 1612 men, 1628 women	**Faculty:** 246; IIB, +$
Part-time: 448 men, 834 women	**Ph.D.s:** 79%
Graduate: 180 men, 325 women	**Student/Faculty:** 13 to 1
Year: semesters, summer session	**Tuition:** $6014
Application Deadline: open	**Room & Board:** $5166
Freshman Class: n/av	
ACT: required	**LESS COMPETITIVE**

Bemidji State University, founded in 1919, is a public liberal arts university. There are 3 undergraduate schools and 1 graduate school. In addition to regional accreditation, Bemidji State University has baccalaureate program accreditation with CSWE, NASM, and NLN. The library contains 190,000 volumes, 721,255 microform items, and 2500 audio/video tapes/CDs/DVDs, and subscribes to 907 periodicals including electronic. Computerized library services include the card catalog, interlibrary loans, and database searching. Special learning facilities include a learning resource center, art gallery, radio station, and TV station. The 89-acre campus is in a small town 220 miles northwest of Minneapolis. Including any residence halls, there are 21 buildings.

Student Life: 88% of undergraduates are from Minnesota. Others are from 46 states, 34 foreign countries, and Canada. 95% are from public schools. 89% are white. The average age of freshmen is 20; all undergraduates, 25. 29% do not continue beyond their first year; 43% remain to graduate.

Housing: 1700 students can be accommodated in college housing, which includes single-sex and coed dorms and on-campus apartments. In addition, there are special-interest houses and single-parent apartments. On-campus housing is available on a first-come, first-served basis. 68% of students commute. Alcohol is not permitted. All students may keep cars.

Activities: 2% of men belong to 2 national fraternities; 1% of women belong to 1 national sorority. There are 80 groups on campus, including art, band, cheerleading, choir, chorus, computers, dance, drama, ethnic, gay, honors, international, jazz band, literary magazine, musical theater, newspaper, opera, orchestra, pep band, political, professional, radio and TV, religious, social, social service, and student government. Popular campus events include Funtastic Dance Follies, madrigal music, and plays and concerts.

Sports: There are 7 intercollegiate sports for men and 7 for women, and 7 intramural sports for men and 4 for women. Facilities include a basketball gym, an Olympic-size pool, a hockey arena, a football stadium, indoor and outdoor tracks, baseball and softball fields, tennis, racquetball, and handball courts, weight rooms, and a dance studio.

Disabled Students: 95% of the campus is accessible. Wheelchair ramps, elevators, special parking, specially equipped rest rooms, lowered drinking fountains, and lowered telephones are available.

Services: Counseling and information services are available, as is tutoring in every subject. There is a reader service for the blind, and remedial math, reading, and writing.

Campus Safety and Security: Measures include 24-hour foot and vehicle patrol, security escort services, informal discussions, and pamphlets/posters/films. There are emergency telephones and lighted pathways/sidewalks.

Programs of Study: Bemidji State University confers B.A., B.S., and B.F.A. degrees. Associate and master's degrees are also awarded. Bachelor's degrees are awarded in BIOLOGICAL SCIENCE (biology/biological science), BUSINESS (accounting and business administration and management), COMMUNICATIONS AND THE ARTS (broadcasting, communications, English, fine arts, German, journalism, languages, music, and Spanish), COMPUTER AND PHYSICAL SCIENCE (chemistry, computer science, earth science, geology, mathematics, and physics), EDUCATION (art, early childhood, elementary, foreign languages, health, industrial arts, middle school, science, and secondary), ENGINEERING AND ENVIRONMENTAL DESIGN (industrial engineering technology), HEALTH PROFESSIONS (medical laboratory technology, nursing, predentistry, and premedicine), SOCIAL SCIENCE (community services, criminal justice, economics, geography, history, parks and recreation management, philosophy, political science/government, prelaw, psychology, social science, social work, and sociology). Nursing and accounting are the strongest academically. Business administration and elementary and secondary education are the largest.

Required: All students must complete at least 128 semester hours, of which 42 are general education, including courses in freshman English, the humanities, social science, physical science, liberal education activities, and phys ed. Students must maintain a minimum GPA of 2.0; a 2.3 GPA is required in the major (2.5 for education majors).

Special: Students may attend other schools within the Minnesota State University system. Students may study abroad in England, China, Japan, and Malaysia. Paid internships and work-study programs are available in many fields. Students may receive credit for life, military, and work experience. Student-designed dual majors, nondegree study, and pass/fail options are offered. There are 2 national honor societies and a freshman honors program.

Faculty/Classroom: 59% of faculty are male; 41%, female. Graduate students teach 1% of introductory courses. The average class size in an introductory lecture is 35; in a laboratory, 20; and in a regular course, 23.

Requirements: The ACT is required. Applicants must have a minimum high school rank of 50% or a composite score of 21 on the ACT. They should have had 4 years of English and 3 years each of math, science, and social studies. AP and CLEP credits are accepted. Important factors in the admissions decision are recommendations by school officials, advanced placement or honor courses, and extracurricular activities record.

Procedure: Freshmen are admitted to all sessions. Entrance exams should be taken during the junior year. There is a deferred admissions plan and a rolling admissions plan. Application deadlines are open. Application fee is $20.

Transfer: 450 transfer students enrolled in a recent year. Applicants must have a minimum GPA of 2.0. 32 of 128 credits required for the bachelor's degree must be completed at Bemidji State University.

Visiting: There are regularly scheduled orientations for prospective students, including an interview with an admissions counselor, a tour of the campus, and visits with faculty. There are guides for informal visits and visitors may sit in on classes and stay overnight. To schedule a visit, contact the Admissions Office at (888) 345-1721.

Financial Aid: In a recent year, 78% of all full-time freshmen and 79% of continuing full-time students received some form of financial aid. 68% of full-time freshmen and 72% of continuing full-time students received need-based aid. The average freshman award was $6944. 35% of undergraduates work part time. Average annual earnings from campus work are $1950. The average financial indebtedness of the 2005 graduate was $16,045. The FAFSA and the college's own financial statement are required. The priority date for freshman financial aid applications for fall entry is May 15.

International Students: There were 150 international students enrolled in a recent year. The school actively recruits these students. They must score satisfactorily on the written TOEFL.

Computers: All students may access the system 24 hours a day on campus; 18 hours a day in other locations. There are no time limits. The fee is $1 per credit.

Graduates: In a recent year, 741 bachelor's degrees were awarded. In an average class, 41% graduate in 6 years or less. 45 companies recruited on campus in a recent year.

Admissions Contact: Paul Muller, Associate Director, Admissions. A video is available. E-mail: *admissions@bemidjistate.edu* Web: *www.bemidjistate.edu*

BETHEL UNIVERSITY
(Formerly Bethel College)   C-4

St. Paul, MN 55112

(651) 638-6242
(800) 255-8706; Fax: (651) 635-1490

Full-time: 1137 men, 1737 women	**Faculty:** 172; IIB, av$
Part-time: 84 men, 326 women	**Ph.D.s:** 74%
Graduate: 207 men, 453 women	**Student/Faculty:** 17 to 1
Year: 4-1-4, summer session	**Tuition:** $22,700
Application Deadline: December 1	**Room & Board:** $7140
Freshman Class: 1496 applied, 1427 accepted, 731 enrolled	
SAT Verbal/Math: 580/580*	**ACT:** 25 **VERY COMPETITIVE**

Bethel University, formely Bethel College, established in 1871, is a private liberal arts university affiliated with the Baptist General Conference. There are 2 undergraduate schools and 1 graduate school. In addition to regional accreditation, Bethel has baccalaureate program accreditation with CSWE, NCATE, and NLN. The library contains 152,603 volumes, 180,142 microform items, and 11,356 audio/video tapes/CDs/DVDs, and subscribes to 26,637 periodicals including electronic. Computerized library services include the card catalog, interlibrary loans, database searching, and Internet access. Special learning facilities include a learning resource center, art gallery, radio station, and TV station. The 231-acre campus is in a suburban area 10 miles north of Minneapolis/St. Paul. Including any residence halls, there are 14 buildings.

Student Life: 78% of undergraduates are from Minnesota. Students are from 36 states, 18 foreign countries, and Canada. 92% are white. Most are Protestant. The average age of freshmen is 18; all undergraduates, 22. 16% do not continue beyond their first year; 68% remain to graduate.

Housing: 2085 students can be accommodated in college housing, which includes single-sex dorms, on-campus apartments, off-campus apartments, and townhouses. On-campus housing is available on a first-come, first-served basis and is available on a lottery system for upperclassmen. 70% of students live on campus; of those, 60% remain on campus on weekends. Alcohol is not permitted. Upperclassmen may keep cars.

Activities: There are no fraternities or sororities. There are 102 groups on campus, including art, band, cheerleading, choir, chorale, chorus, debate, drama, ethnic, film, forensics, honors, international, jazz band, literary magazine, musical theater, orchestra, pep band, political, professional, radio and TV, religious, social, social service, student government, and yearbook. Popular campus events include Nik Dag, Gad Kin, and Festival of Christmas.

Sports: There are 9 intercollegiate sports for men and 8 for women, and 12 intramural sports for men and 12 for women. Facilities include a gym, an indoor recreation center with 1/8-mile track and 4 multipurpose courts, weight room, and racqetball courts, soccer fields, tennis courts and a football, baseball, and softball stadium.

Disabled Students: 99% of the campus is accessible. Wheelchair ramps, elevators, special parking, specially equipped rest rooms, special class scheduling, lowered drinking fountains, and lowered telephones are available.

Services: Counseling and information services are available, as is tutoring in most subjects. There is a reader service for the blind. An academic enrichment and support center offers tutoring, a writing lab, and time management and study skills workshops.

Campus Safety and Security: Measures include 24-hour foot and vehicle patrol, security escort services, shuttle buses, and pamphlets/posters/films. There are emergency telephones and lighted pathways/sidewalks.

Programs of Study: Bethel confers B.A., B.S., B.Mus., and B.Mus.Ed degrees. Associate and master's degrees are also awarded. Bachelor's degrees are awarded in BIOLOGICAL SCIENCE (biochemistry and biology/biological science), BUSINESS (accounting, banking and finance, business administration and management, and marketing/retailing/merchandising), COMMUNICATIONS AND THE ARTS (communications, dramatic arts, English, fine arts, multimedia, music, Spanish, and speech/debate/rhetoric), COMPUTER AND PHYSICAL SCIENCE (chemistry, computer science, mathematics, and physics), EDUCATION (art, athletic training, business, early childhood, elementary, foreign languages, health, mathematics, music, physical, science, and secondary), ENGINEERING AND ENVIRONMENTAL DESIGN (engineering and applied science and environmental science), HEALTH PROFESSIONS (nursing), SOCIAL SCIENCE (economics, ethnic studies, history, international relations, philosophy, political science/government, psychology, religion, social work, and youth ministry). Physical sciences, life sciences,

and computer science are the strongest academically. Business, education, and nursing are the largest.

Required: Students must complete a minimum of 122 semester credit hours, with 30 to 60 in the major and 50 to 51 in general education. Specific general education courses include introduction to the Bible, Christianity and Western culture, college writing, creativity in fine arts, and physical wellness. An overall GPA of 2.0 and a GPA of 2.25 in the major are needed.

Special: Students may arrange internships, study abroad in various countries, and select various work-study programs. Dual majors in cross-cultural studies are available. Students may design their own majors, earn a 3-2 engineering degree, and select limited pass/fail options. An adult degree completion program is offered. There are 2 national honor societies, a freshman honors program, and 100 departmental honors programs.

Faculty/Classroom: 54% of faculty are male; 46%, female. All teach undergraduates. No introductory courses are taught by graduate students. The average class size in an introductory lecture is 33; in a laboratory, 17; and in a regular course, 23.

Admissions: 95% of the 2005-2006 applicants were accepted. The SAT scores for the 2005-2006 freshman class were: Verbal--15% below 500, 36% between 500 and 599, 33% between 600 and 700, and 16% above 700; Math--15% below 500, 35% between 500 and 599, 35% between 600 and 700, and 10% above 700. The ACT scores were 14% below 21, 26% between 21 and 23, 24% between 24 and 26, 18% between 27 and 28, and 18% above 28. 57% of the current freshmen were in the top fifth of their class; 79% were in the top two fifths. There were 9 National Merit finalists and 3 semifinalists. 42 freshmen graduated first in their class.

Requirements: The SAT or ACT is required. In addition, the PSAT is accepted. In addition, applicants must be graduates of an accredited secondary school or have a GED. An interview is recommended. Bethel requires applicants to be in the upper 50% of their class. AP and CLEP credits are accepted. Important factors in the admissions decision are advanced placement or honor courses, extracurricular activities record, and personality/intangible qualities.

Procedure: Freshmen are admitted fall and spring. Entrance exams should be taken in the spring of the junior year. There is an early admissions plan. Applications should be filed by December 1 for fall entry, November 1 for winter entry, and December 1 for spring entry, along with a $25 fee. Notification is sent January 15. 25 applicants were on the 2005 waiting list; 2 were admitted. Applications are accepted on-line.

Transfer: 146 transfer students enrolled in 2004-2005. Applicants must have a minimum GPA of 2.5 and must submit all college transcripts. 28 of 122 credits required for the bachelor's degree must be completed at Bethel.

Visiting: There are regularly scheduled orientations for prospective students throughout the school year. There are guides for informal visits and visitors may sit in on classes and stay overnight. To schedule a visit, contact the Admissions Office.

Financial Aid: In 2005-2006, 92% of all full-time freshmen and 95% of continuing full-time students received some form of financial aid. 64% of full-time freshmen and 66% of continuing full-time students received need-based aid. The average freshman award was $13,135. Need-based scholarships or need-based grants averaged $6750 ($20,862 maximum); need-based self-help aid (loans and jobs) averaged $5880 ($7225 maximum); and other non-need-based awards and non-need-based scholarships averaged $5144 ($14,350 maximum). 55% of undergraduates work part time. Average annual earnings from campus work are $1408. The average financial indebtedness of the 2005 graduate was $21,000. Bethel is a member of CSS. The FAFSA, the college's own financial statement and the students' and parents' most recent federal tax returns are required. The deadline for filing freshman financial aid applications for fall entry is April 15.

International Students: There are 14 international students enrolled. A satisfactory score is required on the written TOEFL.

Computers: Wireless access is available. All students may access the system 24 hours a day. There are no time limits and no fees.

Graduates: From July 1, 2004 to June 30, 2005, 765 bachelor's degrees were awarded. The most popular majors were business (19%), elementary education (10%), and nursing (8%). In an average class, 62% graduate in 4 years or less, 72% graduate in 5 years or less, and 73% graduate in 6 years or less.

Admissions Contact: Jay T. Fedje, Director of Admissions. E-mail: *buadmissions-cas@bethel.edu* Web: *http://www.bethel.edu*

CARLETON COLLEGE

C-4

Northfield, MN 55057

(507) 646-4190
(800) 995-CARL; Fax: (507) 646-4526

Full-time: 931 men, 1005 women	**Faculty:** 198; IIB, ++$
Part-time: 9 men, 14 women	**Ph.D.s:** 92%
Graduate: none	**Student/Faculty:** 10 to 1
Year: trimesters	**Tuition:** $32,649
Application Deadline: January 15	**Room & Board:** $7818
Freshman Class: 5036 applied, 1471 accepted, 542 enrolled	
SAT or ACT: required	**MOST COMPETITIVE**

Carleton College, founded in 1866, is a private liberal arts college. The library contains 957,655 volumes, 203,313 microform items, and 792 audio/video tapes/CDs/DVDs, and subscribes to 14,435 periodicals including electronic. Computerized library services include the card catalog, interlibrary loans, database searching, and Internet access. Special learning facilities include a learning resource center, art gallery, radio station, observatory, and 850-acre arboretum. The 955-acre campus is in a small town 35 miles south of Minneapolis-St. Paul. Including any residence halls, there are 46 buildings.

Student Life: 73% of undergraduates are from out of state, mostly the Midwest. Students are from 50 states, 36 foreign countries, and Canada. 74% are from public schools. 73% are white; 10% Asian American. 38% are claim no religious affiliation; 31% Protestant; 13% Catholic; 11% Muslim, Hindu, Buddhist, Unitarian Universalist, other; 7% Jewish. The average age of freshmen is 18; all undergraduates, 20. 3% do not continue beyond their first year; 87% remain to graduate.

Housing: 1627 students can be accommodated in college housing, which includes single-sex and coed dorms, on-campus apartments, and off-campus apartments. In addition, there are language houses and special-interest houses. On-campus housing is guaranteed for all 4 years. 90% of students live on campus; of those, 97% remain on campus on weekends. No one may keep cars.

Activities: There are no fraternities or sororities. There are 132 groups on campus, including art, band, chess, choir, chorale, chorus, computers, dance, debate, drama, educational, environmental/outdoor, ethnic, film, gay, hobby, honors, international, jazz band, literary magazine, musical theater, newspaper, orchestra, photography, political, professional, radio and TV, religious, social, social service, student government, symphony, and yearbook. Popular campus events include Mai Fete, spring concert, and mid-Winter Ball.

Sports: There are 23 intercollegiate sports for men and 24 for women, and 8 intramural sports for men and 8 for women. Facilities include a gym with a 1220-seat arena, 6-lane swimming pool, and wrestling room; a recreation center with a gym, dance studio, indoor tennis court, sauna, and 5-lane swimming pool; a 7000-seat stadium complex with handball and racquetball courts, a 200-meter indoor track, a baseball batting cage, a weight room; and an additional recreation center with a 200-meter indoor track, sport courts, weight room, dance studio, and climbing wall. In addition, there are fields for baseball, softball, soccer, ultimate Frisbee, lacrosse, rugby, and field hockey; 12 outdoor tennis courts; and 16 miles of running, biking, hiking, and cross-country skiing trails in Carleton's 800-acre arboretum.

Disabled Students: 28% of the campus is accessible. Wheelchair ramps, elevators, special parking, specially equipped rest rooms, special class scheduling, lowered drinking fountains, and lowered telephones are available.

Services: Counseling and information services are available, as is tutoring in every subject There are also writing and math skills assistance centers. There is a reader service for the blind.

Campus Safety and Security: Measures include 24-hour foot and vehicle patrol, self-defense education, security escort services, and informal discussions. There are pamphlets/posters/films, emergency telephones, lighted pathways/sidewalks, and nighttime transport service.

Programs of Study: Carleton confers the B.A. degree. Bachelor's degrees are awarded in BIOLOGICAL SCIENCE (biology/biological science), COMMUNICATIONS AND THE ARTS (art history and appreciation, classics, English, French, German, Greek, Latin, media arts, music, romance languages and literature, Russian, Spanish, and studio art), COMPUTER AND PHYSICAL SCIENCE (chemistry, computer science, geology, mathematics, and physics), SOCIAL SCIENCE (African American studies, African studies, American studies, anthropology, Asian/Oriental studies, classical/ancient civilization, economics, history, international relations, Latin American studies, philosophy, political science/government, psychology, religion, sociology, and women's studies). Social sciences and history, physical sciences, and biological life sciences are the largest.

Required: Students are required to demonstrate proficiency in English composition and in a foreign language, and to take 1 course centrally concerned with another culture. 4 terms of phys ed are required. Students must complete 210 credits, or 117 semester hours, including 12 credits each from arts and literature and humanities, and 18 credits each from social sciences and math and science. Students must maintain a minimum GPA of 2.0. The total number of hours required for the major

varies by department (72 is the norm). All seniors must complete a senior integrative exercise in their major, which may consist of a comprehensive exam, an extensive research project or paper, a public lecture, or a combination of these.

Special: Students may cross-register with Saint Olaf College and pursue a variety of internships. The college offers study abroad in 44 countries. Dual majors in all areas and student-designed majors are available. Students may earn a 3-2 engineering degree with Washington or Columbia Universities, a 3-2 degree in nursing, and a 3-3 degree in law. Pass/fail options are offered. There are 3 national honor societies, including Phi Beta Kappa.

Faculty/Classroom: 58% of faculty are male; 42%, female. All both teach and do research. The average class size in an introductory lecture is 21; in a laboratory, 14; and in a regular course, 15.

Admissions: 29% of the 2005-2006 applicants were accepted. The SAT scores for the 2005-2006 freshman class were: Verbal--1% below 500, 8% between 500 and 599, 32% between 600 and 700, and 60% above 700; Math--1% below 500, 7% between 500 and 599, 39% between 600 and 700, and 54% above 700. The ACT scores were 8% below 21, 34% between 21 and 23, and 58% between 24 and 26. 91% of the current freshmen were in the top quarter of their class; 100% were in the top half. There were 78 National Merit finalists. 65 freshmen graduated first in their class.

Requirements: The SAT or ACT is required. The ACT Optional Writing test is also required. There are no secondary school requirements, but it is recommended that applicants have completed 4 years of English, 3 years each of math and a foreign language, 2 years each of history and science, and 1 year of social studies. An essay and 2 teacher recommendations are required. AP credits are accepted. Important factors in the admissions decision are advanced placement or honor courses, personality/intangible qualities, and evidence of special talent.

Procedure: Freshmen are admitted in the fall. Entrance exams should be taken before March 1. There are early decision and deferred admissions plans. Early decision applications should be filed by November 15; regular applications, by January 15 for fall entry, along with a $30 fee. Notification of early decision is sent December 15; regular decision, by April 15. 200 early decision candidates were accepted for the 2005-2006 class. 310 applicants were on the 2005 waiting list. Applications are accepted on-line.

Transfer: 7 transfer students enrolled in 2004-2005. Transfers are usually accepted for sophomore and junior classes. A 3.0 GPA is recommended. 108 of 210 credits required for the bachelor's degree must be completed at Carleton.

Visiting: There are regularly scheduled orientations for prospective students, including an open house in October. There are guides for informal visits and visitors may sit in on classes and stay overnight. To schedule a visit, contact the Admissions Office.

Financial Aid: In 2005-2006, 68% of all full-time freshmen and 58% of continuing full-time students received some form of financial aid. 65% of full-time freshmen and 58% of continuing full-time students received need-based aid. The average freshman award was $25,462. Need-based scholarships or need-based grants averaged $21,611; need-based self-help aid (loans and jobs) averaged $3782; and other non-need-based awards and non-need-based scholarships averaged $3803. 86% of undergraduates work part time. Average annual earnings from campus work was $2147. The average financial indebtedness of the 2005 graduate was $17,842. Carleton is a member of CSS. The CSS/Profile or FAFSA is required. The deadline for filing freshman financial aid applications for fall entry is February 15.

International Students: There are 109 international students enrolled. The school actively recruits these students. They must score satisfactorily on the TOEFL and also take the SAT or ACT.

Computers: Wireless access is available. Dorms offer hard-wired or wireless hookups. There are 32 computer labs, with 247 general purpose computers available in 14 general purpose labs. All students may access the system 24 hours a day. There are no time limits and no fees.

Graduates: From July 1, 2004 to June 30, 2005, 500 bachelor's degrees were awarded. The most popular majors were social science and history (28%), biological and life sciences (13%), and physical sciences (9%). In an average class, 80% graduate in 4 years or less, 86% graduate in 5 years or less, and 87% graduate in 6 years or less. 32 companies recruited on campus in 2004-2005. Of the 2004 graduating class, 22% were enrolled in graduate school within 6 months of graduation and 64% were employed.

Admissions Contact: Paul Thiboutot, Dean of Admissions. A video is available. E-mail: admissions@acs.carleton.edu Web: www.carleton.edu

COLLEGE OF SAINT BENEDICT
C-3

St. Joseph, MN 56374-2099

(320) 363-2196
(800) 544-1489; Fax: (320) 363-2750

Full-time: 1993 women	**Faculty:** 148; IIB, av$
Part-time: 52 women	**Ph.D.s:** 80%
Graduate: none	**Student/Faculty:** 13 to 1
Year: semesters	**Tuition:** $23,454
Application Deadline: December 1	**Room & Board:** $6637
Freshman Class: 1472 applied, 1267 accepted, 576 enrolled	
SAT Verbal/Math: 580/570*	**ACT:** 25 **VERY COMPETITIVE**

The College of Saint Benedict, established in 1887, is a private, Benedictine Catholic institution offering undergraduate liberal arts study for women in partnership with St. John's University, a Benedictine Catholic institution for men. The coordinate institutions share an academic calendar, academic curriculum, and many combined extracurricular activities. In addition to regional accreditation, St. Benedict has baccalaureate program accreditation with ACS ADA, CCNE, CSWE, NASM, and NCATE. The 2 libraries contain 716,202 volumes, 120,432 microform items, and 38,396 audio/video tapes/CDs/DVDs, and subscribe to 14,863 periodicals including electronic. Computerized library services include the card catalog, interlibrary loans, database searching, Internet access, and laptop Internet portals. Special learning facilities include a learning resource center, art gallery, radio station, a pottery studio, an arboretum, an observatory, a greenhouse and labyrinth, and Hill Monastic Manuscript library and natural history museum at St. John's University. The 315-acre campus is in a small town 70 miles northwest of Minneapolis and 10 miles west of St. Cloud. Including any residence halls, there are 33 buildings.

Student Life: 83% of undergraduates are from Minnesota. Others are from 31 states, 23 foreign countries, and Canada. 76% are from public schools. 92% are white. 67% are Catholic; 26% Protestant; 6% claim no religious affiliation. The average age of freshmen is 18; all undergraduates, 20. 12% do not continue beyond their first year; 82% remain to graduate.

Housing: 1527 students can be accommodated in college housing, which includes dorms, on-campus apartments, off-campus apartments, and 3 college houses. In addition, there are special-interest houses. Freshmen and sophomores must live in on-camus housing. On-campus housing is available on a first-come, first-served basis and is available on a lottery system for upperclassmen. 82% of students live on campus. All students may keep cars.

Activities: There are no sororities. There are 80 groups on campus, including art, band, choir, chorale, chorus, computers, dance, debate, drama, ethnic, gay, honors, international, jazz band, literary magazine, musical theater, newspaper, opera, orchestra, pep band, political, professional, radio and TV, religious, social, social service, student government, symphony, and yearbook. Popular campus events include Festival of Cultures, Asian New Year, and Li'l Sibs Weekend.

Sports: Facilities include a 1000-seat volleyball and basketball arena, racquetball and indoor and outdoor tennis courts, a weight room, an indoor pool, a field house with indoor running track, an aerobics studio, a fitness center with exercise and weight-training equipment, a softball diamond, soccer fields, lakes, and 30 miles of cross-country ski trails. Students have access to St. John's University facilities as well, including a 4-story climbing wall and a fitness center.

Disabled Students: 90% of the campus is accessible. Wheelchair ramps, elevators, special parking, specially equipped rest rooms, special class scheduling, lowered drinking fountains, lowered telephones, and special housing are available.

Services: Counseling and information services are available, as is tutoring in most subjects, a writing center, a math skills center, and test-taking skills instruction. Various academic accommodations are made for students with documented disabilities.

Campus Safety and Security: Measures include 24-hour foot and vehicle patrol, self-defense education, security escort services, and shuttle buses. There are informal discussions, pamphlets/posters/films, emergency telephones, and lighted pathways/sidewalks.

Programs of Study: St. Benedict confers B.A. and B.S.N. degrees. Bachelor's degrees are awarded in AGRICULTURE (environmental studies and forestry and related sciences), BIOLOGICAL SCIENCE (biochemistry, biology/biological science, and nutrition), BUSINESS (accounting and management science), COMMUNICATIONS AND THE ARTS (art, classics, communications, dramatic arts, English, fine arts, French, German, music, and Spanish), COMPUTER AND PHYSICAL SCIENCE (chemistry, computer science, mathematics, natural sciences, and physics), EDUCATION (elementary), ENGINEERING AND ENVIRONMENTAL DESIGN (preengineering), HEALTH PROFESSIONS (nursing, occupational therapy, physical therapy, predentistry, premedicine, prepharmacy, and preveterinary science), SOCIAL SCIENCE (dietetics, economics, history, humanities, liberal arts/general studies, ministries, pastoral studies, peace studies, philosophy, political science/government, prelaw, psychology, social science, social work, sociology, and theological studies). Chemistry, economics, and music are the strongest academically. Nursing, psychology, and communication are the largest.

Required: To graduate, students must complete the core curriculum of writing, discussion, quantitative reasoning, and gender and global perspectives. Distribution requirements include 6 credits in fine arts, 5 in humanities, 2 each in natural science and social science, and 1 in math. All students must prove math and foreign language proficiency. A total of 124 credits must be earned, with 40 credits in upper-division courses and an overall GPA of 2.0. Students must complete a first-year symposium and a senior seminar.

Special: Students may cross-register with St. Cloud State University. There are study-abroad programs in Australia, Austria, Chile, China, England, France, Guatemala, Greece, Ireland, Italy, Japan, South Africa, and Spain. Internships, student-designed majors, preprofessional programs, and liberal studies degrees may be pursued. A 3-2 engineering program is offered through University of Minnesota. Nondegree study and a pass/fail grading option are also available. There is 1 national honor society, and a freshman honors program. All departments have honors programs.

Faculty/Classroom: 44% of faculty are male; 56%, female. All both teach and do research. The average class size in an introductory lecture is 25; in a laboratory, 18; and in a regular course, 22.

Admissions: 86% of the 2005-2006 applicants were accepted. The SAT scores for the 2005-2006 freshman class were: Verbal--18% below 500, 39% between 500 and 599, 39% between 600 and 700, and 4% above 700; Math--15% below 500, 44% between 500 and 599, 35% between 600 and 700, and 6% above 700. The ACT scores were 8% below 21, 25% between 21 and 23, 36% between 24 and 26, 14% between 27 and 28, and 17% above 28. 70% of the current freshmen were in the top fifth of their class; 92% were in the top two fifths. There was 1 National Merit finalist. 36 freshmen graduated first in their class.

Requirements: The SAT or ACT is required. In addition, students should be graduates of an accredited secondary school. Academic preparation should include 17 units, including 4 of English, 3 of math, 2 each of a laboratory science and social studies, and 6 electives. A foreign language is recommended. The GED is accepted. An essay is required. Homeschooled applicants are not required to have a high school diploma but are required to provide appropriate documentation of college preparatory curriculum. St. Benedict requires applicants to be in the upper 50% of their class. A GPA of 3.0 is required. AP and CLEP credits are accepted. Important factors in the admissions decision are geographic diversity, advanced placement or honor courses, and parents or siblings attending the school.

Procedure: Freshmen are admitted fall and spring. Entrance exams should be taken during the spring of the junior year or fall of the senior year. There is a deferred admissions plan. There is a rolling admissions plan. The priority deadline for fall entry is December 1. Notification is sent on a rolling basis beginning January 15. 35 applicants were on the 2005 waiting list; 15 were admitted. Applications are accepted on-line.

Transfer: 42 transfer students enrolled in 2004-2005. Transfer applicants must have a minimum college GPA of 2.75. An essay or personal statement, high school and college transcripts, and a transfer student evaluation form are required. Standardized test scores may be required of some. 45 of 124 credits required for the bachelor's degree must be completed at St. Benedict.

Visiting: There are regularly scheduled orientations for prospective students. A variety of programs are offered throughout the year. Information can be found at the web site. There are guides for informal visits and visitors may sit in on classes and stay overnight. To schedule a visit, contact the Admissions Office.

Financial Aid: In 2005-2006, 97% of all full-time freshmen and 95% of continuing full-time students received some form of financial aid. 68% of full-time freshmen and 66% of continuing full-time students received need-based aid. The average freshman award was $20,417. Need-based scholarships or need-based grants averaged $14,435; need-based self-help aid (loans and jobs) averaged $6021; and other non-need-based awards and non-need-based scholarships averaged $9605. 45% of undergraduates work part time. Average annual earnings from campus work are $2100. The average financial indebtedness of the 2005 graduate was $24,764. St. Benedict is a member of CSS. The FAFSA and the college's own financial statement are required. The priority date for freshman financial aid applications for fall entry is March 15.

International Students: There are 82 international students enrolled. The school actively recruits these students. A satisfactory score on the TOEFL is required. The SAT is recommended.

Computers: Students are not required to own a computer, but network connections are available for all students in their residence hall. Students can access computers in computer labs, libraries, student centers, and residence halls. All students may access the system 24 hours per day. There are no time limits. The fee is $190.

Graduates: From July 1, 2004 to June 30, 2005, 504 bachelor's degrees were awarded. The most popular majors were psychology (11%), communication (10%), and biology (10%). In an average class, 1% graduate in 3 years or less, 76% graduate in 4 years or less, 81% graduate in 5 years or less, and 82% graduate in 6 years or less. 102 companies recruited on campus in 2004-2005. Of the 2004 graduating class, 16% were enrolled in graduate school within 6 months of graduation and 80% were employed.

Admissions Contact: Mary Milbert, Dean of Admission.
E-mail: *admissions@csbsju.edu* Web: *www.csbsju.edu*

COLLEGE OF SAINT CATHERINE — C-4

St. Paul, MN 55105

(651) 690-8850
(800) 656-KATE; Fax: (651) 690-8824

Full-time: 11 men, 2347 women	**Faculty:** 246
Part-time: 86 men, 1067 women	**Ph.D.s:** n/av
Graduate: 146 men, 1156 women	**Student/Faculty:** 10 to 1
Year: 4-1-4, summer session	**Tuition:** $21,385
Application Deadline: open	**Room & Board:** $6120
Freshman Class: 1415 applied, 1157 accepted, 413 enrolled	
SAT or ACT: required	**VERY COMPETITIVE**

The College of Saint Catherine, founded in 1905, is a private, comprehensive women's college affiliated with the Roman Catholic Church. In addition to regional accreditation, CSC has baccalaureate program accreditation with ADA, APTA, NASM, and NLN. The 2 libraries contain 390,613 volumes, 169,236 microform items, and 13,627 audio/video tapes/CDs/DVDs, and subscribe to 2166 periodicals including electronic. Computerized library services include the card catalog, interlibrary loans, and database searching. Special learning facilities include a learning resource center, art gallery, and observatory. The 110-acre campus is in an urban area 6 miles southwest of downtown St. Paul. Including any residence halls, there are 19 buildings.

Student Life: 90% of undergraduates are from Minnesota. Students are from 29 states, 30 foreign countries, and Canada. 80% are from public schools. 74% are white. 50% are Catholic; 20% Protestant. The average age of freshmen is 18; all undergraduates, 22. 19% do not continue beyond their first year; 58% remain to graduate.

Housing: 700 students can be accommodated in college housing, which includes single-sex dorms and on-campus apartments. There are also apartments for student-parents. On-campus housing is guaranteed for all 4 years. 63% of students commute. All students may keep cars.

Activities: There are no fraternities. There are 42 groups on campus, including art, band, choir, chorale, chorus, dance, drama, ethnic, gay, honors, international, jazz band, literary magazine, musical theater, newspaper, orchestra, photography, political, professional, religious, social, social service, and student government. Popular campus events include Student Life Week, Dew Drop Bop, and opening convocation and picnic.

Sports: Facilities include a fitness facility, a gym, a weight room, a swimming pool, an outdoor fitness course, tennis courts, a soccer field, and a softball field.

Disabled Students: 90% of the campus is accessible. Wheelchair ramps, elevators, special parking, specially equipped rest rooms, special class scheduling, lowered drinking fountains, and lowered telephones are available.

Services: Counseling and information services are available, as is tutoring in most subjects. There is a reader service for the blind, and remedial math, reading, and writing.

Campus Safety and Security: Measures include 24-hour foot and vehicle patrol, self-defense education, security escort services, and informal discussions. There are pamphlets/posters/films, emergency telephones, and lighted pathways/sidewalks.

Programs of Study: CSC confers B.A. and B.S. degrees. Associate and master's degrees are also awarded. Bachelor's degrees are awarded in BIOLOGICAL SCIENCE (biochemistry, biology/biological science, and nutrition), BUSINESS (accounting, business administration and management, fashion merchandising, international economics, management information systems, and marketing/retailing/merchandising), COMMUNICATIONS AND THE ARTS (American Sign Language, art, communications, dramatic arts, English, fine arts, French, media arts, music, Spanish, and speech/debate/rhetoric), COMPUTER AND PHYSICAL SCIENCE (chemistry, information sciences and systems, and mathematics), EDUCATION (art, early childhood, elementary, home economics, music, and physical), HEALTH PROFESSIONS (health care administration, medical records administration/services, nursing, occupational therapy, rehabilitation therapy, and respiratory therapy), SOCIAL SCIENCE (dietetics, economics, ethnic studies, family/consumer studies, fashion design and technology, history, international relations, philosophy, physical fitness/movement, political science/government, psychology, social studies, social work, sociology, theological studies, and women's studies). Nursing, business administration, and elementary education are the largest.

Required: To graduate, students must complete 130 semester credits, including a liberal arts core with courses in history, foreign language, philosophy, math, fine arts, literature, and theology, and 80 credits outside the major. Required courses are The Reflective Woman and The Global Search for Justice. At least 36 hours are required in the major. Students

must have a minimum 2.0 GPA and demonstrate proficiency in composition, math, and computer literacy.

Special: CSC offers co-op programs with Carondolet College, the University of Minnesota, and George Washington University, and cross-registration with the Associated Colleges of the Twin Cities and other colleges sponsored by the Sisters of St. Joseph. Students may arrange internships, a Washington semester, and study abroad. Dual majors are available in the sciences and engineering. Students may receive credit for life, military, or work experience. Student-designed majors, nondegree study, and pass/fail options are available. The Weekend College offers a B.A. degree. There are 24 national honor societies, including Phi Beta Kappa and a freshman honors program.

Faculty/Classroom: 21% of faculty are male; 79%, female. All teach undergraduates. No introductory courses are taught by graduate students. The average class size in an introductory lecture is 16; in a laboratory, 14; and in a regular course, 13.

Admissions: 78% of the 2005-2006 applicants were accepted. 47% of the current freshmen were in the top fifth of their class; 80% were in the top two fifths.

Requirements: The SAT or ACT is required. In addition, applicants must have completed a college preparatory program including 4 courses in English, 3 in math, and 2 each in a foreign language, science, and social studies. CSC requires applicants to be in the upper 50% of their class. A GPA of 2.5 is required. AP and CLEP credits are accepted. Important factors in the admissions decision are advanced placement or honor courses, recommendations by school officials, and extracurricular activities record.

Procedure: Freshmen are admitted to all sessions. Entrance exams should be taken during the senior year. There is a deferred admissions and a rolling admissions plan. Application deadlines are open. Applications are accepted on-line.

Transfer: 723 transfer students enrolled in 2004-2005. Transfer applicants must submit high school and college transcripts. 48 of 130 credits required for the bachelor's degree must be completed at CSC.

Visiting: There are regularly scheduled orientations for prospective students, including a tour, an admissions interview, and an appointment with a faculty member. There are guides for informal visits and visitors may sit in on classes and stay overnight. To schedule a visit, contact the Admissions Office.

Financial Aid: In 2005-2006, 72% of all full-time freshmen and 69% of continuing full-time students received some form of financial aid. At least 56% of full-time freshmen and 60% of continuing full-time students received need-based aid. The average freshman award was $24,647. Need-based scholarships or need-based grants averaged $7991; and need-based self-help aid (loans and jobs) averaged $5308. 93% of undergraduates work part time. Average annual earnings from campus work are $1800. The average financial indebtedness of a recent graduate was $24,537. CSC is a member of CSS. The FAFSA and the college's own financial statement are required. The deadline for filing freshman financial aid applications for fall entry is April 1.

International Students: There were 85 international students enrolled in a recent year. The school actively recruits these students. They must score satisfactorily on the TOEFL or take the MELAB or the college's own test. The SAT is required only if the student attended a U.S. high school, whether in this country or overseas.

Computers: All students may access the system 24 hours a day. There are no time limits and no fees.

Graduates: From July 1, 2004 to June 30, 2005, 518 bachelor's degrees were awarded. The most popular majors were nursing (17%), occupational therapy (10%), and elementary education (9%). In an average class, 40% graduate in 4 years or less, 55% graduate in 5 years or less, and 58% graduate in 6 years or less. 9 companies recruited on campus in 2004-2005. Of a recent graduating class, 12% were enrolled in graduate school within 6 months of graduation and 90% were employed.

Admissions Contact: Marlene Mohs, Senior Associate Director of Admission. E-mail: *admissions@stkate.edu* Web: *www.stkate.edu*

COLLEGE OF SAINT SCHOLASTICA — D-3

Duluth, MN 55811

(218) 723-6046
(800) 447-5444; Fax: (218) 723-5991

Full-time: 693 men, 1603 women	**Faculty:** 138; IIB, -$
Part-time: 93 men, 224 women	**Ph.D.s:** 63%
Graduate: 148 men, 477 women	**Student/Faculty:** 16 to 1
Year: semesters, summer session	**Tuition:** $22,240
Application Deadline: open	**Room & Board:** $6216
Freshman Class: 1459 applied, 1268 accepted, 490 enrolled	
SAT Verbal/Math: 560/570*	**ACT:** 23 COMPETITIVE+

The College of St. Scholastica, founded in 1912, is an independent private college affiliated with the Roman Catholic Church. The College offers a variety of graduate and undergraduate programs. In addition to regional accreditation, Saints has baccalaureate program accreditation with ACOTE, APTA, CCNE, CSWE, and NLN. The library contains

126,835 volumes, 1845 microform items, and 14,131 audio/video tapes/CDs/DVDs, and subscribes to 19,123 periodicals including electronic. Computerized library services include the card catalog, interlibrary loans, database searching, Internet access, and laptop Internet portals. Special learning facilities include a music library. The 186-acre campus is in a suburban area 150 miles north of Minneapolis and St. Paul. Including any residence halls, there are 18 buildings.

Student Life: 85% of undergraduates are from Minnesota. Others are from 28 states, 23 foreign countries, and Canada. 86% are white. 32% are Catholic; 28% claim no religious affiliation; 24% Protestant. The average age of freshmen is 22; all undergraduates, 24. 19% do not continue beyond their first year; 64% remain to graduate.

Housing: 1046 students can be accommodated in college housing, which includes coed dorms and on-campus apartments. Single-parent housing space is available. On-campus housing is available on a first-come, first-served basis and is available on a lottery system for upperclassmen. 51% of students live on campus; of those, 65% remain on campus on weekends. All students may keep cars.

Activities: There are no fraternities or sororities. There are 70 groups on campus, including band, cheerleading, choir, chorale, chorus, computers, dance, drama, ethnic, gay, honors, international, jazz band, literary magazine, newspaper, outdoor, pep band, photography, political, professional, radio and TV, religious, social, social service, student government, and yearbook. Popular campus events include Mayfest Week, Fall Fest, and International Week.

Sports: There are 8 intercollegiate sports for men and 8 for women, and 10 intramural sports for men and 9 for women. Facilities include a 63,000 square-foot wellness center, which includes a 6-lane 200 meter track, aerobic studio, free weight room, complete machine fitness space, athletic trainer's room, and climbing wall.

Disabled Students: 95% of the campus is accessible. Wheelchair ramps, elevators, special parking, specially equipped rest rooms, special class scheduling, lowered drinking fountains, lowered telephones, and special housing are available.

Services: Counseling and information services are available, as is tutoring in most subjects. There is a reader service for the blind and remedial writing. Sign language interpreters, a note-taking service, tape recorders, voice input computers, and remedial study skills are also available.

Campus Safety and Security: Measures include 24-hour foot and vehicle patrol, self-defense education, security escort services, and informal discussions. There are pamphlets/posters/films, emergency telephones, lighted pathways/sidewalks, electronically operated dorm entrances, and student door monitors in the evening and at night.

Programs of Study: Saints confers the B.A. degree. Master's and doctoral degrees are also awarded. Bachelor's degrees are awarded in BIOLOGICAL SCIENCE (biochemistry and biology/biological science), BUSINESS (accounting, business administration and management, marketing management, and organizational behavior), COMMUNICATIONS AND THE ARTS (advertising, communications, English, languages, music, and theater management), COMPUTER AND PHYSICAL SCIENCE (chemistry, computer science, mathematics, and natural sciences), EDUCATION (education, educational media, and social science), HEALTH PROFESSIONS (exercise science, health care administration, health science, and nursing), SOCIAL SCIENCE (behavioral science, economics, history, humanities, Native American studies, psychology, religion, and social work). Education, nursing, and management are the largest.

Required: To graduate, students must complete 128 semester credits, with a 2.0 GPA. Approximately 52 credits of general education courses are required, including 4 credits each of English composition, social science, natural science, oral communication, literature, history, fine arts, philosophy, religious studies, math, and cultural diversity and 2 to 8 credits in a foreign language. The hours required in the major vary. Some majors require an internship for graduation. A senior project may be required.

Special: Students may cross-register with the University of Minnesota at Duluth and the University of Wisconsin at Superior. Self-designed majors, a Washington semester with American University, internships, study abroad in several countries, accelerated degrees, nondegree study, pass/fail options, and credit for life, military, or work experience are available. There is a 3-2 engineering degree with the Institute of Technology of the University of Minnesota. There are 2 national honor societies.

Faculty/Classroom: 39% of faculty are male; 61%, female. No introductory courses are taught by graduate students. The average class size in an introductory lecture is 18; in a laboratory, 15; and in a regular course, 20.

Admissions: 87% of the 2005-2006 applicants were accepted. The SAT scores for the 2005-2006 freshman class were: Verbal--25% below 500, 47% between 500 and 599, 12% between 600 and 700, and 16% above 700; Math--12% below 500, 47% between 500 and 599, 28% between 600 and 700, and 13% above 700. The ACT scores were 22% below 21, 30% between 21 and 23, 28% between 24 and 26, 13% between 27 and 28, and 7% above 28. 40% of the current freshmen were in the top fifth of their class; 64% were in the top two fifths. 16 freshmen graduated first in their class.

Requirements: The SAT or ACT is required. In addition, students are also required to send official high school transcripts. AP and CLEP credits are accepted. Important factors in the admissions decision are personality/intangible qualities, advanced placement or honor courses, and recommendations by school officials.

Procedure: Freshmen are admitted to all sessions. Entrance exams should be taken by January of the senior year of high school. There are early admissions and deferred admissions plans. Application deadlines are open. Application fee is $25. Applications are accepted on-line.

Transfer: 169 transfer students enrolled in 2004-2005. Applicants must have a GPA of 2.0. 32 of 128 credits required for the bachelor's degree must be completed at Saints.

Visiting: There are regularly scheduled orientations for prospective students, including a class placement survey, peer and academic advisement, and registration. There are guides for informal visits and visitors may sit in on classes and stay overnight. To schedule a visit, contact the Admissions Office at 218-723-6046 or admissions@css.edu.

Financial Aid: In 2005-2006, 98% of all full-time freshmen and 97% of continuing full-time students received some form of financial aid. 85% of all full-time students received need-based aid. The average freshman award was $21,042. Need-based scholarships or need-based grants averaged $5608; need-based self-help aid (loans and jobs) averaged $3915; other non-need-based awards and non-need-based scholarships averaged $9137; and other awards averaged $9708. 20% of undergraduates work part time. Average annual earnings from campus work are $2139. The average financial indebtedness of the 2005 graduate was $29,942. The FAFSA, and the college's own financial statement are required. The deadline for filing freshman financial aid applications for fall entry is March 15.

International Students: There are 69 international students enrolled. The school actively recruits these students. They must score satisfactorily on the written TOEFL or on the electronic version.

Computers: All students may access the system. There are no time limits and no fees.

Graduates: From July 1, 2004 to June 30, 2005, 568 bachelor's degrees were awarded. The most popular majors were management (21%), nursing (20%), and computer science info systems (9%). In an average class, 55% graduate in 4 years or less, 63% graduate in 5 years or less, and 64% graduate in 6 years or less. 24 companies recruited on campus in 2004-2005. Of the 2004 graduating class, 22% were enrolled in graduate school within 6 months of graduation and 74% were employed.

Admissions Contact: Brian Dalton, Vice President for Enrollment Management. A video is available. E-mail: bdalton@css.edu Web: www.css.edu

COLLEGE OF VISUAL ARTS C-4

St. Paul, MN 55102   (651) 224-3416
(800) 224-1536; Fax: (651) 224-8854

Full-time: 71 men, 104 women	Faculty: n/av
Part-time: 5 men, 14 women	Ph.Ds: 58%
Graduate: none	Student/Faculty: 16 to 1
Year: semesters, summer session	Tuition: $18,040
Application Deadline: March 1	Room & Board: n/app
Freshman Class: 84 applied, 55 enrolled	
ACT: 21*	SPECIAL

Founded in 1924, the College of Visual Arts is a fully accredited private college of art and design, offering degrees in communication design, photography, illustration, and fine arts (painting, drawing, sculpture, and printmaking). The library contains 7465 volumes and 50 audio/video tapes/CDs/DVDs, and subscribes to 38 periodicals including electronic. Computerized library services include the card catalog, interlibrary loans, database searching, Internet access, and laptop Internet portals. Special learning facilities include a learning resource center and art gallery. The 3-acre campus is in an urban area in a historic residential area near downtown St. Paul. There are 5 buildings.

Student Life: 88% of undergraduates are from Minnesota. Others are from 11 states and 3 foreign countries. 91% are white. The average age of freshmen is 20; all undergraduates, 22.

Housing: There are no residence halls. Housing assistance is offered. Off-campus apartments are available. All students commute. Alcohol is not permitted. All students may keep cars.

Activities: There are no fraternities or sororities. There are 8 groups on campus including American Institute of Graphic Arts (AIGA), Student Chapter, Anime Club, art, film, mentorship program, photography, professional, and student government. Popular campus events include a symposium series with theatre events and art and design panel discussions; monthly gallery openings; and roundtable discussions/gallery talks and artist talks.

Sports: There is no sports program at CVA.

Disabled Students: 65% of the campus is accessible. Elevators, special parking, specially equipped rest rooms, and lowered drinking fountains are available.

Services: Counseling and information services are available, as is tutoring in most subjects. There is a technology tutor available, and remedial math, reading, and writing.

Campus Safety and Security: Measures include security escort services, informal discussions, pamphlets/posters/films, and emergency telephones. There is a security guard for evenings and weekends. Informational visits and discussions with police are also available.

Programs of Study: CVA confers the B.F.A. degree. Bachelor's degrees are awarded in COMMUNICATIONS AND THE ARTS (drawing, fine arts, graphic design, illustration, painting, photography, printmaking, and sculpture), SOCIAL SCIENCE (liberal arts/general studies).

Required: All students must complete 126 semester hours, including an 18-credit first-year foundation program, 48 hours of liberal arts requirements, 33 to 39 hours in the major, 9 to 12 hours of supportive art/design requirements, and 18 hours of studio electives. A minimum GPA of 2.0 is needed, and projects in art and design must be completed.

Special: Juniors and seniors will be required to take internships in various area organizations and businesses. CVA also offers study abroad in France, Italy, and England and a German exchange program. All departments have honors programs.

Faculty/Classroom: 51% of faculty are male; 49%, female. All teach undergraduates. The average class size in an introductory lecture is 24 and in a laboratory, 16.

Admissions: The ACT scores for the 2005-2006 freshman class were: 55% below 21, 24% between 21 and 23, 12% between 24 and 26, and 9% between 27 and 28.

Requirements: The SAT or ACT is required. In addition, applicants must submit an admissions application, a personal statement of interest, and a portfolio. An interview and a visit to the college are highly recommended. A GPA of 2.7 is required. AP credits are accepted. Important factors in the admissions decision are personality/intangible qualities, evidence of special talent, and recommendations by school officials.

Procedure: Freshmen are admitted fall and spring. Entrance exams should be taken in fall or spring of the junior year or fall of the senior year. There is a deferred admissions plan. Applications should be filed by March 1 for fall entry and December 1 for spring entry, along with a $40 fee. There is a rolling admissions plan. Notification is sent on a rolling basis. Applications are accepted on-line.

Transfer: 23 transfer students enrolled in 2004-2005. Required are a personal statement, an interview, transcripts from all postsecondary institutions attended, ACT or SAT scores, and a faculty review of work done in studio art classes at other postsecondary institutions. 66 of 126 credits required for the bachelor's degree must be completed at CVA.

Visiting: There are regularly scheduled orientations for prospective students, consisting of annual open house events, including student artwork, financial aid discussion, a tour of facilities, a student panel, drawing and, portfolio workshops, and a parent and student session. There are guides for informal visits and visitors may sit in on classes. To schedule a visit, contact the Admissions Office at admissions@cva.edu.

Financial Aid: In 2005-2006, 85% of all full-time freshmen and 94% of continuing full-time students received some form of financial aid. 80% of full-time freshmen and 74% of continuing full-time students received need-based aid. The average freshman award was $13,566. Need-based scholarships or need-based grants averaged $4017 ($9750 maximum); need-based self-help aid (loans and jobs) averaged $2509 ($4600 maximum); and other non-need-based awards and non-need-based scholarships averaged $1900 ($3000 maximum). CVA Scholarships are also available. 35% of undergraduates work part time. Average annual earnings from campus work are $4000. The average financial indebtedness of the 2005 graduate was $30,000. The FAFSA and the college's own financial statement are required. The priority date for freshman financial aid applications for fall entry is March 1. The deadline for filing freshman financial aid applications for fall entry is April 1.

International Students: The school actively recruits these students. They must take the TOEFL and also take the SAT or the college's own entrance exam.

Computers: The college has a full T1 Internet connection. There are 40 PCs in 3 computer labs in the main building; 5 in the library lab. The library also has 8 wired connections for laptops. All students may access the system during open building hours. The fee is $75. It is strongly recommended that all students have a personal computer.

Graduates: From July 1, 2004 to June 30, 2005, 48 bachelor's degrees were awarded. The most popular majors were communication design (42%), photography (19%), and fine arts (8%). In an average class, 50% graduate in 4 years or less, 83% graduate in 5 years or less, and 100% graduate in 6 years or less. Of the 2004 graduating class, 75% were employed within 6 months of graduation.

Admissions Contact: Jane Nordhorn, Director of Admissions. A video is available. E-mail: info@cva.edu Web: www.cva.edu

CONCORDIA COLLEGE: MOORHEAD

A-2

Moorhead, MN 56562

(218) 299-3004 (collect)
(800) 699-9897; Fax: (218) 299-3947

Full-time: 988 men, 1667 women	**Faculty:** 190; IIB, -$
Part-time: 13 men, 18 women	**Ph.D.s:** 72%
Graduate: none	**Student/Faculty:** 9 to 1
Year: semesters, summer session	**Tuition:** $17,775
Application Deadline: open	**Room & Board:** $4700
Freshman Class: n/av	
SAT Verbal/Math: 570/545*	**ACT:** 24 **VERY COMPETITIVE**

Concordia College, founded in 1891, is a private, liberal arts institution affiliated with the Evangelical Lutheran Church in America. Tuition figures in this capsule and profile are approximate. In addition to regional accreditation, Concordia has baccalaureate program accreditation with ADA, CSWE, NASM, NCATE, and NLN. The library contains 300,000 volumes, 43,296 microform items, and 11,048 audio/video tapes/CDs/DVDs, and subscribes to 1463 periodicals including electronic. Computerized library services include the card catalog, interlibrary loans, and database searching. Special learning facilities include a learning resource center, art gallery, radio station, TV station, and observatory. The 120-acre campus is in an urban area 240 miles northwest of Minneapolis and St. Paul. Including any residence halls, there are 36 buildings.

Student Life: 71% of undergraduates are from Minnesota. Others are from 37 states, 34 foreign countries, and Canada. 96% are from public schools. 91% are white. 81% are Protestant; 13% Catholic; 6% claim no religious affiliation. The average age of freshmen is 19; all undergraduates, 20. 21% do not continue beyond their first year; 63% remain to graduate.

Housing: 1850 students can be accommodated in college housing, which includes single-sex dormitories and on-campus apartments. In addition, there are language houses and townhouses. On-campus housing is guaranteed for the freshman year only, is available on a first-come, first-served basis, and is available on a lottery system for upperclassmen. Priority is given to out-of-town students. 65% of students live on campus; of those, 75% remain on campus on weekends. Alcohol is not permitted. All students may keep cars.

Activities: There are no fraternities or sororities. There are 150 groups on campus, including art, band, cheerleading, choir, chorale, chorus, dance, debate, drama, drill team, ethnic, film, forensics, gay, honors, international, jazz band, literary magazine, musical theater, newspaper, orchestra, pep band, photography, political, professional, radio and TV, religious, social, social service, student government, symphony, and yearbook. Popular campus events include Family Weekend, Winter Meltdown, and Black History Week.

Sports: There are 10 intercollegiate sports for men and 10 for women, and 9 intramural sports for men and 10 for women. Facilities include a health club, a 200-meter indoor track with 4 multipurpose basketball/tennis courts, an indoor swimming pool and sauna, a 7000-seat stadium with an all-weather track, a field house with a 4500-seat auditorium, 2 more basketball courts, 2 auxiliary gyms and a weight room, 6 outdoor tennis courts, softball and soccer competition fields, a baseball complex, and soccer practice fields.

Disabled Students: 95% of the campus is accessible. Wheelchair ramps, elevators, special parking, specially equipped rest rooms, special class scheduling, lowered drinking fountains, and automatic doors are available.

Services: Counseling and information services are available, as is tutoring in most subjects. There is a reader service for the blind and an interpreter service for the deaf.

Campus Safety and Security: Measures include 24-hour foot and vehicle patrol, security escort services, informal discussions, and pamphlets/posters/films. There are lighted pathways/sidewalks.

Programs of Study: Concordia confers B.A. and B.M. degrees. Master's degrees are also awarded. Bachelor's degrees are awarded in BIOLOGICAL SCIENCE (biology/biological science), BUSINESS (accounting, business administration and management, international business management, and office supervision and management), COMMUNICATIONS AND THE ARTS (advertising, apparel design, art history and appreciation, classical languages, communications, creative writing, dramatic arts, English, French, German, journalism, Latin, literature, music, music performance, public relations, Spanish, speech/debate/rhetoric, and studio art), COMPUTER AND PHYSICAL SCIENCE (chemistry, computer science, mathematics, and physics), EDUCATION (art, business, elementary, foreign languages, health, home economics, middle school, music, physical, science, secondary, and social studies), ENGINEERING AND ENVIRONMENTAL DESIGN (environmental science and preengineering), HEALTH PROFESSIONS (health, health care administration, medical laboratory technology, nursing, predentistry, premedicine, and preveterinary science), SOCIAL SCIENCE (dietetics, economics, family/consumer studies, history, humanities, international relations, ministries, philosophy, political science/government, prelaw, psychology, religion, Russian and Slavic studies, Scandinavian studies, social work, and sociology). Premedicine, prelaw, and math are the strongest academically. Business administration, communications, and biology are the largest.

Required: All students must maintain a minimum GPA of 2.0 while taking 126 semester hours, including at least 32 in the major. Required courses include freshman English, oral communication, an introduction to liberal arts, an integration course, and 2 courses each in phys ed and religion. Distribution requirements include 7 courses taken from 5 areas: science and math, social science, foreign language, foundation/premises of civilization, and literature/fine arts.

Special: Cross-registration is offered through the Tri-College University Consortium. Co-op programs and internships are available in most majors, and accelerated degree programs and dual majors are available in all majors. There is a Washington semester and an urban studies semester in Chicago. Study abroad in more than 30 countries, on- and off-campus work-study, a B.A.-B.M. degree in music, and 3-2 and 2-2 engineering degrees with Washington and North Dakota State Universities and the University of Minnesota are possible. Nondegree study for special students and pass/fail options are also available. There are 10 national honor societies, a freshman honors program, and 11 departmental honors programs.

Faculty/Classroom: 52% of faculty are male; 48%, female. All teach undergraduates. The average class size in an introductory lecture is 25; in a laboratory, 18; and in a regular course, 19.

Admissions: The SAT scores for the 2005-2006 freshman class were: Verbal--21% below 500, 39% between 500 and 599, 28% between 600 and 700, and 11% above 700; Math--23% below 500, 43% between 500 and 599, 19% between 600 and 700, and 15% above 700. The ACT scores were 19% below 21, 28% between 21 and 23, 29% between 24 and 26, 13% between 27 and 28, and 11% above 28. 51% of the current freshmen were in the top fifth of their class; 78% were in the top two fifths.

Requirements: The SAT or ACT is required. In addition, 2 character references are required, and an interview is recommended. The GED is accepted. Academic performance and preparation, as evidenced in a high school transcript, is the single most important factor in the admissions decision. AP and CLEP credits are accepted. Important factors in the admissions decision are recommendations by school officials, advanced placement or honor courses, and personality/intangible qualities.

Procedure: Freshmen are admitted to all sessions. Entrance exams should be taken by the first semester of the senior year. There are early admissions, deferred admissions, and rolling admissions plans. Application deadlines are open. Applications are accepted on-line. The fall 2005 application fee was $20.

Transfer: Transfer applicants must have a minimum 2.0 GPA, and provide official transcripts from previously attended schools. 32 of 126 credits required for the bachelor's degree must be completed at Concordia.

Visiting: There are regularly scheduled orientations for prospective students, including an extensive campus tour and meetings with admissions counselors and faculty members. There are guides for informal visits and visitors may sit in on classes and stay overnight. To schedule a visit, contact the Office of Admissions.

Financial Aid: In a recent year, 90% of all full-time freshmen and 78% of continuing full-time students received some form of financial aid. 57% of full-time freshmen and 53% of continuing full-time students received need-based aid. Need-based scholarships or need-based grants averaged $4998 ($15,635 maximum); need-based self-help aid (loans and jobs) averaged $4612 ($11,834 maximum); and other non-need-based awards and non-need-based scholarships averaged $8160 ($21,640 maximum). 52% of undergraduates worked part time. Average annual earnings from campus work were $1058. Concordia is a member of CSS. The FAFSA and the college's own financial statement are required.

International Students: The school actively recruits these students. They must score satisfactorily on the written TOEFL.

Computers: All students may access the system 20 to 24 hours per day. There are no time limits and no fees.

Graduates: From July 1, 2004 to June 30, 2005, 625 bachelor's degrees were awarded. In an average class, 56% graduate in 4 years or less, 62% graduate in 5 years or less, and 62% graduate in 6 years or less.

Admissions Contact: Office of Admissions, Concordia College: Moorhead. E-mail: *admissions@gloria.cord.edu* Web: *www.cord.edu*

CONCORDIA UNIVERSITY SAINT PAUL · C-4

St. Paul, MN 55104-5494 · (651) 641-8230
(800) 333-4705; Fax: (651)603-6320

Full-time: 581 men, 891 women	**Faculty:** 85
Part-time: 91 men, 173 women	**Ph.D.s:** 67%
Graduate: 107 men, 226 women	**Student/Faculty:** 17 to 1
Year: semesters, summer session	**Tuition:** $21,312
Application Deadline: August 1	**Room & Board:** $6464
Freshman Class: 651 applied, 415 accepted, 165 enrolled	
SAT Verbal/Math: 490/550*	**ACT:** 22 · COMPETITIVE

Concordia University St. Paul, founded in 1893 and a unit of the Concordia University system, is a private institution affiliated with the Lutheran Church Missouri Synod and offering programs in teacher education, business, church vocations, and the liberal arts. Master's programs and bachelor's degree completion programs for adult learners are also available. There are 4 undergraduate schools and 1 graduate school. In addition to regional accreditation, CSP has baccalaureate program accreditation with NCATE. The library contains 136,216 volumes, 10,266 microform items, and 6847 audio/video tapes/CDs/DVDs, and subscribes to 355 periodicals including electronic. Computerized library services include the card catalog, interlibrary loans, and database searching. Special learning facilities include a learning resource center, art gallery, natural history museum, and TV station. The 37-acre campus is in an urban area in the Midway area of St. Paul. Including any residence halls, there are 29 buildings.

Student Life: 77% of undergraduates are from Minnesota. Others are from 44 states, 4 foreign countries, and Canada. 63% are white. 43% are Protestant; 17% Catholic. The average age of freshmen is 18; all undergraduates, 24. 30% do not continue beyond their first year; 45% remain to graduate.

Housing: 481 students can be accommodated in college housing, which includes single-sex and coed dorms, on-campus apartments, and married-student housing. On-campus housing is guaranteed for the freshman year only and is available on a first-come, first-served basis. Priority is given to out-of-town students. 50% of students live on campus. Alcohol is not permitted. All students may keep cars.

Activities: There are no fraternities or sororities. There are 40 groups on campus, including art, band, cheerleading, choir, drama, ethnic, jazz band, musical theater, newspaper, pep band, radio and TV, religious, social, student government, and yearbook.

Sports: There are 6 intercollegiate sports for men and 7 for women, and 5 intramural sports for men and 5 for women. Facilities include a 4500-seat stadium, a 1200-seat gym, a health and wellness center, a rock-climbing wall, a 200-meter track, and several playing fields for various sports.

Disabled Students: 75% of the campus is accessible. Wheelchair ramps, elevators, special parking, specially equipped rest rooms, special class scheduling, lowered drinking fountains, lowered telephones, and touch-pad doors are available.

Services: Counseling and information services are available, as is tutoring in every subject. There is remedial math, reading, and writing.

Campus Safety and Security: Measures include 24-hour foot and vehicle patrol, self-defense education, security escort services, and informal discussions. There are pamphlets/posters/films, emergency telephones, and lighted pathways/sidewalks.

Programs of Study: CSP confers B.A. and B.B.A. degrees. Associate and master's degrees are also awarded. Bachelor's degrees are awarded in BIOLOGICAL SCIENCE (biology/biological science), BUSINESS (accounting, banking and finance, business administration and management, management information systems, marketing management, and organizational behavior), COMMUNICATIONS AND THE ARTS (art, communications, dramatic arts, English, music, and studio art), COMPUTER AND PHYSICAL SCIENCE (natural sciences), EDUCATION (early childhood, elementary, English, mathematics, middle school, music, physical, science, secondary, and social studies), ENGINEERING AND ENVIRONMENTAL DESIGN (environmental science), SOCIAL SCIENCE (child care/child and family studies, criminal justice, history, psychology, religion, religious education, religious music, sociology, and theological studies). Business, education, and psychology are the largest.

Required: To graduate, students must complete 128 credit hours in the form of 1 major or 2 minors. GPA varies from 2.0 to 2.75 and required hours in the major vary from 32 to 44, depending on the program. The core curriculum consists of 48 hours of liberal arts courses.

Special: CSP offers cross-registration with other area colleges and other members of the Concordia University system, internships in most programs, and study abroad in England, India, and Mexico. Accelerated degree programs, and interdisciplinary majors are also available. Credit for life experience, nondegree study, and pass/fail options are possible. Degree completion programs designed for working adults are offered in cohort-delivered format via face-to-face or on-line learning. There is 1 national honor society and 1 departmental honors program.

Faculty/Classroom: 58% of faculty are male; 42%, female. 85% teach undergraduates. No introductory courses are taught by graduate stu-

dents. The average class size in an introductory lecture is 20; in a laboratory, 20; and in a regular course, 15.

Admissions: 64% of the 2005-2006 applicants were accepted. The SAT scores for the 2005-2006 freshman class were: Verbal--50% below 500, 16% between 500 and 599, 17% between 600 and 700, and 17% above 700; Math--42% below 500, 16% between 500 and 599, and 42% between 600 and 700. The ACT scores were 43% below 21, 24% between 21 and 23, 17% between 24 and 26, 10% between 27 and 28, and 6% above 28. 27% of the current freshmen were in the top fifth of their class; 49% were in the top two fifths. 2 freshmen graduated first in their class.

Requirements: The ACT is required for some programs. In addition, applicants are required to have 4 years of English, 2 each of math, science, fine arts, and history/social studies, and 1 of health or phys ed. 2 letters of recommendation are required. An interview and essay are recommended. The GED is accepted. CSP requires applicants to be in the upper 50% of their class. A GPA of 2.0 is required. AP and CLEP credits are accepted.

Procedure: Freshmen are admitted fall and spring. Entrance exams should be taken during the senior year. There is a deferred admissions plan. There is a rolling admissions plan. Applications should be filed by August 1 for fall entry and December 1 for spring entry. The application fee is $30. Notification is sent on a rolling basis. Applications are accepted on-line.

Transfer: 83 transfer students enrolled in 2004-2005. Applicants must have a 2.0 GPA and submit 2 letters of recommendation. Students with fewer than 1 year of college credits must also submit ACT scores and an official high school transcript. 32 of 128 credits required for the bachelor's degree must be completed at CSP.

Visiting: There are regularly scheduled orientations for prospective students, including a 3-day program before classes begin, with class visits, lunch, and meetings with professors. There are guides for informal visits and visitors may sit in on classes and stay overnight. To schedule a visit, contact the Director of Undergraduate Admission.

Financial Aid: In 2005-2006, 98% of all full-time freshmen and 65% of continuing full-time students received some form of financial aid. 84% of full-time freshmen and 55% of continuing full-time students received need-based aid. The average freshman award was $24,620. The average financial indebtedness of the 2005 graduate was $14,200. The FAFSA, the college's own financial statement, and the federal tax return are required. The priority date for freshman financial aid applications for fall entry is March 1.

International Students: There are 6 international students enrolled. They must achieve a satisfactory score on the TOEFL or take the MELAB, the Comprehensive English Language Test, the college's own test, or Level 109 of ELS.

Computers: Wireless access is available. CSP is a laptop university. Students may access the network from a variety of campus locations and via dial-in from off campus. All students may access the system 24 hours a day. There are no time limits and no fees. All students are required to have personal computers.

Graduates: From July 1, 2004 to June 30, 2005, 543 bachelor's degrees were awarded. The most popular majors were organizational management (28%), marketing (16%), and teacher education (11%). In an average class, 45% graduate in 6 years or less.

Admissions Contact: Director of Undergraduate Admission.
E-mail: *admiss@csp.edu* Web: *www.csp.edu*

GUSTAVUS ADOLPHUS COLLEGE

C-4

St. Peter, MN 56082-1498

(507) 933-7676
(800) GUSTAVU; Fax: (507) 933-6270

Full-time: 1095 men, 1451 women	**Faculty:** 187; IIB, av$
Part-time: 11 men, 14 women	**Ph.D.s:** 94%
Graduate: none	**Student/Faculty:** 14 to 1
Year: 4-1-4	**Tuition:** $24,865
Application Deadline: April 1	**Room & Board:** $6055
Freshman Class: 2689 applied, 2135 accepted, 705 enrolled	
SAT Verbal/Math: 625/615*	**ACT:** 26 HIGHLY COMPETITIVE

Gustavus Adolphus College, founded in 1862, is a private liberal arts college affiliated with the Lutheran Church. In addition to regional accreditation, Gustavus has baccalaureate program accreditation with NASM, NCATE, and NLN. The library contains 294,053 volumes, 36,013 microform items, and 17,026 audio/video tapes/CDs/DVDs, and subscribes to 999 periodicals including electronic. Computerized library services include the card catalog, interlibrary loans, database searching, Internet access, and laptop Internet portals. Special learning facilities include a learning resource center, art gallery, radio station, TV station, and an arboretum. The 340-acre campus is in a small town 65 miles southwest of Minneapolis. Including any residence halls, there are 55 buildings.

Student Life: 77% of undergraduates are from Minnesota. Others are from 40 states, 19 foreign countries, and Canada. 93% are from public schools. 91% are white. 72% are Protestant; 18% Catholic. The average

age of freshmen is 18; all undergraduates, 20. 11% do not continue beyond their first year; 81% remain to graduate.

Housing: 1960 students can be accommodated in college housing, which includes coed dormitories and on-campus apartments. In addition, there are language houses and special-interest houses. On-campus housing is guaranteed for all 4 years. 80% of students live on campus; of those, 75% remain on campus on weekends. All students may keep cars.

Activities: 20% of men belong to 6 local fraternities; 17% of women belong to 4 local and 1 national sorority. There are 110 groups on campus, including art, band, cheerleading, choir, chorus, computers, dance, debate, drama, ethnic, forensics, gay, honors, international, jazz band, literary magazine, musical theater, newspaper, orchestra, pep band, political, professional, radio and TV, religious, social, social service, student government, symphony, and yearbook. Popular campus events include Christmas in Christ Chapel, Earth Jam All-Day Music Festival, and Frost Week.

Sports: There are 12 intercollegiate sports for men and 13 for women, and 17 intramural sports for men and 10 for women. Facilities include an ice arena, an Olympic-size pool, a gymnastics area, an indoor tennis center, an arena, playing fields, racquetball and tennis courts, a weight room, an indoor and an outdoor running track, and varsity and intramural fields for soccer, softball, baseball, lacrosse, rugby, and ultimate frisbee.

Disabled Students: 90% of the campus is accessible. Wheelchair ramps, elevators, special parking, specially equipped rest rooms, special class scheduling, lowered drinking fountains, and special housing are available.

Services: Counseling and information services are available, as is tutoring in most subjects. A writing lab is available.

Campus Safety and Security: Measures include 24-hour foot and vehicle patrol, security escort services, shuttle buses, and informal discussions. There are pamphlets/posters/films, emergency telephones, and lighted pathways/sidewalks.

Programs of Study: Gustavus confers the B.A. degree. Bachelor's degrees are awarded in AGRICULTURE (environmental studies), BIOLOGICAL SCIENCE (biochemistry and biology/biological science), BUSINESS (accounting, business administration and management, business economics, and international business management), COMMUNICATIONS AND THE ARTS (classics, communications, dance, dramatic arts, English, fine arts, French, German, music, Russian, Scandinavian languages, Spanish, and speech/debate/rhetoric), COMPUTER AND PHYSICAL SCIENCE (chemistry, computer science, geology, mathematics, and physics), EDUCATION (art, business, elementary, foreign languages, health, middle school, music, science, and secondary), HEALTH PROFESSIONS (nursing, physical therapy, predentistry, and premedicine), SOCIAL SCIENCE (anthropology, criminal justice, economics, geography, history, philosophy, political science/government, prelaw, psychology, religion, social science, sociology, and women's studies). Physical science and social science are the strongest academically. Business, biology, and social science are the largest.

Required: All students are required to complete 35 courses totaling 140 semester hours, including 3 January-term courses and 1 course in phys ed. Core and distribution requirements include a first-term seminar and 2 additional writing classes, 4 courses in language and humanities, 2 each in fine arts, math/science, and social science, and foreign culture, and 1 in religion. A minimum GPA of 2.0 is necessary for graduation. A total of 7 to 11 courses is required in the major.

Special: Co-op programs in nursing with St. Olaf College and cross-registration with Minnesota State University are available. The college offers internships, a Washington semester, study abroad in 22 countries, student-designed majors, nondegree study, and pass/fail options for some courses. A 3-2 engineering degree program with the University of Minnesota and Minnesota State University, Mankato is offered. The Curriculum II core offers a 12-course interdisciplinary program. There are 16 national honor societies, including Phi Beta Kappa, and 12 departmental honors programs.

Faculty/Classroom: 60% of faculty are male; 40%, female. 97% both teach and do research. The average class size in an introductory lecture is 25; in a laboratory, 15; and in a regular course, 15.

Admissions: 79% of the 2005-2006 applicants were accepted. The SAT scores for the 2005-2006 freshman class were: Verbal--6% below 500, 29% between 500 and 599, 47% between 600 and 700, and 18% above 700; Math--7% below 500, 33% between 500 and 599, 46% between 600 and 700, and 14% above 700. The ACT scores were 8% below 21, 22% between 21 and 23, 28% between 24 and 26, 18% between 27 and 28, and 24% above 28. 63% of the current freshmen were in the top fifth of their class; 88% were in the top two fifths. There were 12 National Merit finalists. 62 freshmen graduated first in their class.

Requirements: The SAT or ACT is required. In addition, applicants must have completed 4 years of English, 3 each of math and science, and 2 each of a foreign language, history, and social studies. AP credits are accepted. Important factors in the admissions decision are advanced placement or honor courses, evidence of special talent, and parents or siblings attending the school.

Procedure: Freshmen are admitted fall, winter, and spring. Entrance exams should be taken in the fall of the senior year. There are deferred admissions and rolling admissions plans. Applications should be filed by April 1 for fall entry, December 15 for winter entry, and January 15 for spring entry. Notification is sent on a rolling basis. 125 applicants were on the 2005 waiting list; 11 were admitted. Applications are accepted on-line.

Transfer: 44 transfer students enrolled in 2004-2005. Transfer applicants must have earned a 2.4 GPA at their previous college. 72 of 140 credits required for the bachelor's degree must be completed at Gustavus.

Visiting: There are regularly scheduled orientations for prospective students, consisting of an interview, a tour, and meetings with faculty and students. There are guides for informal visits and visitors may sit in on classes and stay overnight. To schedule a visit, contact the Admissions Office.

Financial Aid: In a recent year, 93% of all full-time freshmen and 92% of continuing full-time students received some form of financial aid. 68% of full-time freshmen and 65% of continuing full-time students received need-based aid. The average freshman award was $11,698. Need-based scholarships or need-based grants averaged $13,311 ($28,355 maximum); and need-based self-help aid (loans and jobs) averaged $5200 ($6800 maximum). 71% of undergraduates work part time. Average annual earnings from campus work are $1600. The average financial indebtedness of the 2005 graduate was $17,900. Gustavus is a member of CSS. The FAFSA, the college's own financial statement and the the CSS Profile for early aid decisions are required. The priority date for freshman financial aid applications for fall entry is December 1. The deadline for filing freshman financial aid applications for fall entry is April 1.

International Students: There are 51 international students enrolled. The school actively recruits these students. They must score satisfactorily on the written TOEFL or on the electronic version.

Computers: Wireless access is available. All residence halls and most acdemic buildings are wireless-capable. Computer labs (containing approximately 400 PCs) are in every residence hall and academic building. In addition to wireless, Internet access is available via Ethernet connection in every dorm room. All students may access the system. There are no time limits and no fees. It is strongly recommended that all students have a personal computer.

Graduates: From July 1, 2004 to June 30, 2005, 581 bachelor's degrees were awarded. The most popular majors were communication studies (12%), psychology (10%), and biology (7%). In an average class, 2% graduate in 3 years or less, 79% graduate in 4 years or less, 82% graduate in 5 years or less, and 82% graduate in 6 years or less. 40 companies recruited on campus in a recent year. Of a recent graduating class, 30% were enrolled in graduate school within 6 months of graduation and 65% were employed.

Admissions Contact: Mark H. Anderson, Dean of Admission. A video is available. E-mail: *admission@gustavus.edu* Web: *www.gustavus.edu*

HAMLINE UNIVERSITY — C-4

St. Paul, MN 55105

(651) 523-2207
(800) 753-9753; Fax: (651) 523-2458

Full-time: 761 men, 1142 women	Faculty: 147; IIA, --$
Part-time: 18 men, 23 women	Ph.D.s: 34%
Graduate: 431 men, 1073 women	Student/Faculty: 13 to 1
Year: 4-1-4, summer session	Tuition: $20,850
Application Deadline: open	Room & Board: $6220
Freshman Class: 1806 applied, 1417 accepted, 194 enrolled	
SAT Verbal/Math: 598/589*	ACT: 24 VERY COMPETITIVE

Hamline University, founded in 1854, is a private liberal arts and sciences university affiliated with the United Methodist Church. Graduate enrollment figures in the above capsule include the law school. The tuition fees in the above capsule are approximate. In addition to regional accreditation, Hamline has baccalaureate program accreditation with NASM and NCATE. The 2 libraries contain 292,178 volumes, 931,602 microform items, and 2642 audio/video tapes/CDs/DVDs, and subscribe to 4041 periodicals including electronic. Computerized library services include the card catalog, interlibrary loans, database searching, Internet access, and laptop Internet portals. Special learning facilities include a learning resource center, art gallery, radio station, centers for environmental education and applied research, the Jewish History Society Archives, and the Center for Exellence in Urban Teaching. The 57-acre campus is in an urban area between the downtowns of Minneapolis and St. Paul. Including any residence halls, there are 27 buildings.

Student Life: 85% of undergraduates are from Minnesota. Others are from Canada. 82% are white. 21% are Catholic; 10% claim no religious affiliation. The average age of freshmen is 18; all undergraduates, 21. 16% do not continue beyond their first year; 71% remain to graduate.

Housing: 922 students can be accommodated in college housing, which includes coed dorms, on-campus apartments, married-student housing, fraternity houses, and sorority houses. In addition, there are

language houses, special-interest houses. PRIDE (African-American) house, Spectrum (gay/lesbian) house, Hmong Student Association house, foreign language house, and theme housing. On-campus housing is guaranteed for all 4 years. 59% of students commute. All students may keep cars.

Activities: 55% of women belong to 1 local sorority. There are no fraternities. There are 80 groups on campus, including art, band, cheerleading, chess, choir, chorale, chorus, computers, dance, drama, ethnic, film, gay, honors, international, jazz band, literary magazine, musical theater, newspaper, orchestra, pep band, political, professional, radio and TV, religious, social, social service, student government, symphony, and yearbook. Popular campus events include World Fest, Community Service Week, and Fall Fair.

Sports: There are 9 intercollegiate sports for men and 9 for women, and 8 intramural sports for men and 10 for women. Facilities include a stadium, a field house and swimming pool, a playing field, and an athletic center.

Disabled Students: 75% of the campus is accessible. Wheelchair ramps, elevators, special parking, specially equipped rest rooms, special class scheduling, lowered drinking fountains, and lowered telephones are available.

Services: Counseling and information services are available, as is tutoring in every subject. There is a reader service for the blind, and remedial math, reading, and writing.

Campus Safety and Security: Measures include 24-hour foot and vehicle patrol, self-defense education, security escort services, and informal discussions. There are pamphlets/posters/films, emergency telephones, and lighted pathways/sidewalks.

Programs of Study: Hamline confers the B.A. degree. Master's and doctoral degrees are also awarded. Bachelor's degrees are awarded in BIOLOGICAL SCIENCE (biology/biological science), BUSINESS (business administration and management and international business management), COMMUNICATIONS AND THE ARTS (art, art history and appreciation, communications, dramatic arts, English, fine arts, French, German, music, and Spanish), COMPUTER AND PHYSICAL SCIENCE (chemistry, mathematics, and physics), EDUCATION (athletic training, elementary, foreign languages, physical, science, and secondary), ENGINEERING AND ENVIRONMENTAL DESIGN (environmental science), HEALTH PROFESSIONS (predentistry and premedicine), SOCIAL SCIENCE (anthropology, criminal justice, East Asian studies, economics, European studies, history, international relations, Latin American studies, paralegal studies, peace studies, philosophy, political science/government, prelaw, psychology, religion, social science, sociology, urban studies, and women's studies). Prelaw, premedicine, and international relations are the strongest academically. Psychology, English, and political science are the largest.

Required: To graduate, students must complete 32 course credits (128 semester hours) with a minimum overall GPA of 2.0. 63 course credits must be outside the major. In their first year, all students are required to take a freshman seminar and freshman English and demonstrate computer literacy. All students must also take 3 writing-intensive courses, 1 each year following, and 3 courses on human or cultural diversity; 2 speaking-intensive courses and 2 courses each in fine arts, humanities, natural sciences, and social sciences; and 1 course each in computer utilization and formal reasoning. An independent study project and an internship are also required.

Special: Cross-registration with Augsburg, Macalester, and Saint Catherine Colleges, and the University of Saint Thomas is possible. Students may select cooperative programs, study abroad, a Washington semester with American University, dual majors, student-designed majors, and pass/fail options. Students may earn a 3-2 or 4-2 engineering degree at the University of Minnesota or Washington University. On-campus work-study is available, as are extensive internship opportunities on and off campus. There are 18 national honor societies, including Phi Beta Kappa, a freshman honors program, and 10 departmental honors programs.

Faculty/Classroom: 45% of faculty are male; 55%, female. All teach undergraduates. No introductory courses are taught by graduate students. The average class size in an introductory lecture is 27; in a laboratory, 14; and in a regular course, 19.

Admissions: 78% of the 2005-2006 applicants were accepted. 58% of the current freshmen were in the top fifth of their class; 79% were in the top two fifths. There were 3 National Merit finalists and 7 semifinalists. 22 freshmen graduated first in their class.

Requirements: The SAT or ACT is required. In addition, it is recommended that candidates for admission complete 4 years of English with 1 year of college preparatory writing, 4 years of social studies, and 4 of academic electives, 3 years each of math, lab science, and social science, and 2 years of a foreign language. The GED is accepted. AP and CLEP credits are accepted. Important factors in the admissions decision are advanced placement or honor courses, recommendations by school officials, and leadership record.

Procedure: Freshmen are admitted in the fall. Entrance exams should be taken by February of the senior year. There are early admissions, deferred admissions, and rolling admissions plans. Applications should be filed by December 1 for early action; regular decision application deadlines are open. 25 applicants were on the 2005 waiting list; 10 were admitted. Notification of early action is sent December 15; regular decision, on a rolling basis. Applications are accepted on-line.

Transfer: 124 transfer students enrolled in 2004-2005. Transfer applicants must submit the application form, transcript copies, teacher/advisor recommendation, and a secondary school transcript, if fewer than 32 semester hours have been competed. Applicants must submit an essay or personal statement. A minimum college grade point average of 2.00 is required. 56 of 128 credits required for the bachelor's degree must be completed at Hamline.

Visiting: There are guides for informal visits and visitors may sit in on classes and stay overnight. To schedule a visit, contact the Admissions Office.

Financial Aid: In 2005-2006, 77% of all full-time freshmen and 73% of continuing full-time students received some form of financial aid. At least 56% of full-time freshmen and 63% of continuing full-time students received need-based aid. The average freshman award was $21,868. Need-based scholarships or need-based grants averaged $7413; need-based self-help aid (loans and jobs) averaged $1767; and other institutional non-need-based awards and non-need-based scholarships averaged $13,382. 100% of undergraduates work part time. Average annual earnings from campus work are $2100. The average financial indebtedness of the 2005 graduate was $23,197. The FAFSA is required. The priority date for freshman financial aid applications for fall entry is March 1.

International Students: There were 71 international students enrolled in a recent year. The school actively recruits these students. A satisfactory score is required on the written TOEFL or the MELAB. Students must also take the ACT.

Computers: All students may access the system 24 hours a day, year-round. There are no time limits and no fees. It is strongly recommended that all students have a PC.

Graduates: From July 1, 2004 to June 30, 2005, 432 bachelor's degrees were awarded. The most popular majors were social sciences (25%), psychology (11%), and business/marketing (8%). In an average class, 1% graduate in 3 years or less, 63% graduate in 4 years or less, 67% graduate in 5 years or less, and 68% graduate in 6 years or less. 18 companies recruited on campus in 2004-2005. Of the 2004 graduating class, 35% were enrolled in graduate school within 6 months of graduation and 91% were employed.

Admissions Contact: Steven Bjork, Director of Admissions.
E-mail: cla-admis@gw.hamline.edu Web: www.hamline.edu

MACALESTER COLLEGE   C-4
St. Paul, MN 55105

	(651) 696-6357
	(800) 231-7974; Fax: (651) 696-6724
Full-time: 766 men, 1061 women	**Faculty:** 151; IIB, +$
Part-time: 17 men, 25 women	**Ph.D.s:** 95%
Graduate: none	**Student/Faculty:** 12 to 1
Year: semesters	**Tuition:** $28,642
Application Deadline: January 15	**Room & Board:** $7858
Freshman Class: 4317 applied, 1893 accepted, 491 enrolled	
SAT Verbal/Math: 700/670*	**ACT:** 30 **MOST COMPETITIVE**

Macalester College, founded in 1874, is a nonsectarian liberal arts and sciences institution affiliated with the United Presbyterian Church. In addition to regional accreditation, Macalester has baccalaureate program accreditation with NASM. The library contains 455,554 volumes, 78,180 microform items, and 10,507 audio/video tapes/CDs/DVDs, and subscribes to 2647 periodicals including electronic. Computerized library services include the card catalog, interlibrary loans, database searching, and Internet access. Special learning facilities include a learning resource center, art gallery, radio station, and a 280-acre natural history study area 25 miles from campus. The 53-acre campus is in an urban area midway between downtown St. Paul and Minneapolis. Including any residence halls, there are 39 buildings.

Student Life: 62% of undergraduates are from out of state, mostly the Midwest. Students are from 50 states, 80 foreign countries, and Canada. 71% are from public schools. 72% are white; 12% foreign nationals. The average age of freshmen is 18; all undergraduates, 20. 7% do not continue beyond their first year; 85% remain to graduate.

Housing: 1300 students can be accommodated in college housing, which includes single-sex and coed dorms and on-campus apartments. In addition, there are language houses, special-interest houses, a vegetarian co-op, and a Hebrew house. On-campus housing is available on a lottery system for upperclassmen. 70% of students live on campus; of those, 99% remain on campus on weekends. Upperclassmen may keep cars.

Activities: There are no fraternities or sororities. There are more than 80 groups on campus, including art, bagpipe band, band, chess, choir, chorale, chorus, computers, dance, debate, drama, ethnic, forensics, gay, honors, international, jazz band, literary magazine, newspaper, orchestra, photography, political, professional, radio and TV, religious, so-cial, social service, student government, and symphony. Popular campus events include Volunteer Service Week, Fall Festival, and Midnight Breakfast.

Sports: There are 10 intercollegiate sports for men and 11 for women, and 20 intramural sports for men and 20 for women. Facilities include a field house, a 650-seat gym, a 4000-seat stadium, a swimming pool, 2 racquetball courts, 6 tennis courts, a dance studio, a track, 2 weight rooms, and baseball and softball diamonds.

Disabled Students: 80% of the campus is accessible. Wheelchair ramps, elevators, special parking, specially equipped rest rooms, special class scheduling, lowered drinking fountains, and lowered telephones are available.

Services: Counseling and information services are available, as is tutoring in most subjects. There is remedial math, reading, and writing.

Campus Safety and Security: Measures include 24-hour foot and vehicle patrol, self-defense education, security escort services, and informal discussions. There are pamphlets/posters/films, emergency telephones, lighted pathways/sidewalks, and a security site on the school's web site.

Programs of Study: Macalester confers the B.A. degree. Bachelor's degrees are awarded in AGRICULTURE (environmental studies), BIOLOGICAL SCIENCE (biology/biological science and neurosciences), COMMUNICATIONS AND THE ARTS (art, classics, dramatic arts, English, French, Japanese, linguistics, music, Russian, and Spanish), COMPUTER AND PHYSICAL SCIENCE (chemistry, computer science, geology, mathematics, and physics), SOCIAL SCIENCE (American studies, anthropology, Asian/Oriental studies, economics, geography, German area studies, history, international studies, Latin American studies, philosophy, political science/government, psychology, religion, Russian and Slavic studies, sociology, urban studies, and women's studies). International studies, economics, and biology/chemistry are the strongest academically. Economics, political science, and English are the largest.

Required: All students are required to complete 128 semester hours, with 32 to 44 in the major, and an overall minimum GPA of 2.0. Required courses include 12 hours in humanities and fine arts, 8 hours in natural science and/or math, 8 hours in social science, 4 hours each in domestic diversity and international diversity, and a first-year course. Second language proficiency equivalent to 2 years of college-level language must be shown, and every major requires a capstone experience.

Special: Cross-registration at Minneapolis College of Art and Design is offered; in addition, the college belongs to several consortiums, including the Associated Colleges of the Twin Cities. There also are cooperative programs in liberal arts and architecture with Washington University in St. Louis, engineering with the same school and the University of Minnesota, and nursing with Rush-Presbyterian-St. Luke's Medical Center in Chicago. Internships are available in government, financial services, law, medicine, research, the arts, and other fields. Students study abroad in more than 45 countries. Credit by exam under supervision of individual instructors, nondegree study, student-designed majors, and pass/fail options for no more than 1 course per semester also are available. There are 13 national honor societies, including Phi Beta Kappa, and 30 departmental honors programs.

Faculty/Classroom: 52% of faculty are male; 48%, female. All teach undergraduates and 90% both teach and do research. The average class size in an introductory lecture is 20; in a laboratory, 12; and in a regular course, 17.

Admissions: 44% of the 2005-2006 applicants were accepted. The SAT scores for the 2005-2006 freshman class were: Verbal--3% below 500, 12% between 500 and 599, 35% between 600 and 700, and 50% above 700; Math--12% between 500 and 599, 51% between 600 and 700, and 37% above 700. The ACT scores were 3% between 21 and 23, 41% between 27 and 28, and 56% above 28. 88% of the current freshmen were in the top fifth of their class; 99% were in the top two fifths. There were 25 National Merit finalists and 53 semifinalists. 50 freshmen graduated first in their class.

Requirements: The SAT or ACT is required. In addition, applicants should have earned at least 16 academic credits, including 4 years of English and 3 each in math, laboratory science, foreign language, and social studies/history. The college also expects applicants to have taken honors, AP, or IB courses where available. An essay is required, and an interview is recommended. AP credits are accepted. Important factors in the admissions decision are advanced placement or honor courses, extracurricular activities record, and recommendations by school officials.

Procedure: Freshmen are admitted in the fall. Entrance exams should be taken in the fall of the senior year. There are early decision and deferred admissions plans. Early decision applications should be filed by November 15 or January 3; regular applications, by January 15 for fall entry, along with a $40 fee. Notification of early decision is sent December 15 or February 3; regular decision, April 1. 115 early decision candidates were accepted for the 2005-2006 class. 139 applicants were on the 2005 waiting list; 18 were admitted. Applications are accepted on-line.

Transfer: 23 transfer students enrolled in 2004-2005. Transfer students usually must present a GPA of 3.33 (B+), a secondary school transcript, and recommendations from 2 teachers and from the dean of students. In addition, the SAT or ACT is required, and an interview is recommended. Transferable grades are evaluated on the basis of the nature and quality of work. Generally, a grade of C or better is accepted. 64 of 128 credits required for the bachelor's degree must be completed at Macalester.

Visiting: There are regularly scheduled orientations for prospective students, including interviews, information sessions, a class visit, and a tour of campus. There are guides for informal visits and visitors may sit in on classes and stay overnight. To schedule a visit, contact the Admissions Office.

Financial Aid: In 2005-2006, 77% of all full-time freshmen and 74% of continuing full-time students received some form of financial aid. 71% of full-time freshmen and 68% of continuing full-time students received need-based aid. The average freshman award was $23,862, with $19,090 from need-based scholarships or need-based grants and $4,772 from need-based self-help aid (loans and jobs). 65% of undergraduates work part time. Average annual earnings from campus work are $1500. The average financial indebtedness of the 2005 graduate was $15,000. Macalester is a member of CSS. The CSS/Profile or FAFSA, parent W-2 and tax forms, and student tax forms are required. The deadline for filing freshman financial aid applications for fall entry is February 8.

International Students: There are 229 international students enrolled. The school actively recruits these students. They must take the TOEFL, the MELAB, the Comprehensive English Language test, or the college's own test.

Computers: Wireless access is available. All students may access the system 24 hours a day. There are no time limits and no fees. It is strongly recommended that all students have a personal computer.

Graduates: From July 1, 2004 to June 30, 2005, 455 bachelor's degrees were awarded. The most popular majors were economics (11%), political science (8%), and psychology (7%). In an average class, 86% graduate in 4 years, 84% graduate in 5 years, and 85% graduate in 6 years. 54 companies recruited on campus in 2004-2005. Of the 2004 graduating class, 29% were enrolled in graduate school within 6 months of graduation and 67% were employed.

Admissions Contact: Lorne T. Robinson, Dean of Admissions and Financial Aid. E-mail: *admissions@macalester.edu*
Web: *www.macalester.edu*

METROPOLITAN STATE UNIVERSITY   C-4

St. Paul, MN 55106   **(651) 793-1305; Fax: (651) 793-1310**

Full-time: 893 men, 1203 women	Faculty: 123; IIA, av$
Part-time: 1447 men, 2416 women	Ph.D.s: 81%
Graduate: 227 men, 322 women	Student/Faculty: 17 to 1
Year: varies by program, summer session	Tuition: $4682 ($9111)
	Room & Board: n/app

Application Deadline: June 15
Freshman Class: 541 applied, 438 accepted, 193 enrolled
SAT or ACT: recommended   **SPECIAL**

Metropolitan State University, founded in 1971, is a public institution primarily serving working adults through a variety of majors and individually designed degree programs. There are 6 undergraduate and 2 graduate schools. In addition to regional accreditation, Metro State has baccalaureate program accreditation with NLN. The 2 libraries contain 33,655 volumes and 5112 audio/video tapes/CDs/DVDs, and subscribe to 242 periodicals including electronic. Computerized library services include the card catalog, interlibrary loans, database searching, Internet access, and laptop Internet portals. Special learning facilities include a learning resource center and art gallery. The campus is in an urban area The campus is composed of several small dispersed sites throughout the Twin Cities Metro area. There are 7 buildings.

Student Life: 98% of undergraduates are from Minnesota. Others are from 21 states, 53 foreign countries, and Canada. 95% are from public schools. 72% are white; 12% African American. The average age of freshmen is 26; all undergraduates, 31.

Housing: There are no residence halls. 100% of students commute. Alcohol is not permitted.

Activities: There are no fraternities or sororities. There are 18 groups on campus, including drama, ethnic, gay, honors, international, literary magazine, newspaper, professional, religious, social, and student government.

Sports: There is no sports program at Metro State.

Disabled Students: All of the campus is accessible. Elevators, special parking, specially equipped rest rooms, lowered drinking fountains, and lowered telephones are available.

Services: Counseling and information services are available, as is tutoring in some subjects, including accounting, finance, economics, writing, math, and ESL.

Campus Safety and Security: Measures include security escort services, pamphlets/posters/films, and surveillance cameras.

Programs of Study: Metro State confers B.A., B.S., B.A.S., and B.S.N. degrees. Master's degrees are also awarded. Bachelor's degrees are awarded in BIOLOGICAL SCIENCE (biology/biological science), BUSINESS (accounting, banking and finance, business administration and management, hospitality management services, human resources, international business management, management information systems, marketing and distribution, marketing management, operations management, and trade and industrial supervision and management), COMMUNICATIONS AND THE ARTS (advertising, communications, dramatic arts, English, playwriting/screenwriting, and technical and business writing), COMPUTER AND PHYSICAL SCIENCE (applied mathematics, computer science, computer security and information assurance, and information sciences and systems), EDUCATION (early childhood), HEALTH PROFESSIONS (nursing), SOCIAL SCIENCE (addiction studies, child psychology/development, criminal justice, developmental psychology, early childhood studies, economics, ethnic studies, food production/management/services, history, human services, law enforcement and corrections, liberal arts/general studies, philosophy, psychology, public administration, social science, social work, and women's studies). Nursing is the strongest academically. Accounting and business administration are the largest.

Required: To graduate, all students must complete 120 to 124 semester credits, with a varying number of hours required in the major, 48 credits in a core curriculum, and a 2.0 GPA. Other requirements include natural/physical science; math/logic; global awareness; humanities and fine arts.

Special: Internships, co-op programs in many areas, study abroad, dual majors, and student-designed programs are offered.

Faculty/Classroom: 55% of faculty are male; 45%, female. All teach undergraduates. The average class size in an introductory lecture is 24; in a laboratory, 24; and in a regular course, 19.

Admissions: 81% of the 2005-2006 applicants were accepted.

Requirements: The SAT or ACT is recommended. In addition, Metro State requires applicants to be in the upper 50% of their class or have ACT, PSAT, or SAT scores at or above the national median. Applicants not meeting these requirements will be considered in the alternative admissions process. The GED is accepted. AP and CLEP credits are accepted.

Procedure: Freshmen are admitted to all sessions. There is a deferred admissions plan. Applications should be filed by June 15 for fall entry, November 15 for spring entry, and March 15 for summer entry, along with a $20 fee. Notification is rolling. Applications are accepted on-line.

Transfer: 902 transfer students enrolled in 2004-2005. Applicants must have at least a C average. 30 of 120 to 124 credits required for the bachelor's degree must be completed at Metro State.

Visiting: There are regularly scheduled orientations for prospective students, including a campus tour, meetings with a financial aid adviser, faculty, and students, and a general information session. To schedule a visit, contact the Admissions Office at (651) 793-1300 or *www.metrostate.edu*.

Financial Aid: In a recent year, 63% of all full-time freshmen and 71% of continuing full-time students received some form of financial aid. 63% of full-time freshmen and 71% of continuing full-time students received need-based aid. The average freshman award was $3000. Need-based scholarships or need-based grants averaged $1500 ($4050 maximum); need-based self-help aid (loans and jobs) averaged $4000 ($10,500 maximum); and other non-need-based awards and non-need-based scholarships averaged $500 ($3000 maximum). 94% of undergraduates work part time. Average annual earnings from campus work are $3000. The average financial indebtedness of the recent graduate was $12,125. Metro State is a member of CSS. The FAFSA is required. The priority date for freshman financial aid applications for fall entry is August 1. The deadline for filing freshman financial aid applications for fall entry is August 1.

International Students: There are 182 international students enrolled. They must take the TOEFL.

Computers: Wireless access is available. All students may access the system Monday through Thursday 8:30 A.M. to 10 P.M.; Friday and Saturday 8:30 A.M. to 5 P.M. There are no time limits. The fee is $5 per credit hour.

Graduates: From July 1, 2004 to June 30, 2005, 1175 bachelor's degrees were awarded. The most popular majors were individualized (16%), business (11%), and accounting (7%). In an average class, 22% graduate in 4 years or less. 30 companies recruited on campus in 2004-2005.

Admissions Contact: Bruce Holzschuh, Admissions Counselor.
E-mail: *bruce.holzschul@metrostate.edu* Web: *www.metrostate.edu*

MINNEAPOLIS COLLEGE OF ART AND DESIGN   C-4

Minneapolis, MN 55404   **(612) 874-3760**
(800) 874-6223; Fax: (612) 874-3701

Full-time: 319 men, 302 women	**Faculty:** 39; IIB, -$
Part-time: 15 men, 20 women	**Ph.D.s:** 67%
Graduate: 17 men, 30 women	**Student/Faculty:** 16 to 1
Year: semesters, summer session	**Tuition:** $25,140
Application Deadline: February 15	**Room & Board:** $5970
Freshman Class: 462 applied, 355 accepted, 177 enrolled	
SAT Verbal/Math: 550/525*	**ACT:** 23 **SPECIAL**

The Minneapolis College of Art and Design, founded in 1886, is a private college of art. In addition to regional accreditation, MCAD has baccalaureate program accreditation with NASAD. The library contains 60,000 volumes, 9 microform items, and 2103 audio/video tapes/CDs/DVDs, and subscribes to 180 periodicals including electronic. Computerized library services include interlibrary loans, database searching, and Internet access. Special learning facilities include a learning resource center, art gallery, and on-line radio. The 7-acre campus is in an urban area 1 mile south of downtown Minneapolis. Including any residence halls, there are 9 buildings.

Student Life: 64% of undergraduates are from Minnesota. Others are from 36 states, 21 foreign countries, and Canada. 78% are from public schools. 86% are white. The average age of freshmen is 19; all undergraduates, 22. 9% do not continue beyond their first year; 72% remain to graduate.

Housing: 285 students can be accommodated in college housing, which includes coed on-campus apartments. On-campus housing is available on a first-come, first-served basis and is available on a lottery system for upperclassmen. Priority is given to out-of-town students. 53% of students commute. All students may keep cars.

Activities: There are no fraternities or sororities. There are 25 groups on campus, including art, computers, drama, film, gay, photography, professional, and student government. Popular campus events include Senior Show, Thanksgiving Dinner, and Art Sale.

Sports: There are 2 intramural sports for men and 2 for women. Facilities include off-campus facilities.

Disabled Students: 95% of the campus is accessible. Wheelchair ramps, elevators, special parking, specially equipped rest rooms, and special class scheduling are available.

Services: Counseling and information services are available, as is tutoring in most subjects. There is remedial reading and writing.

Campus Safety and Security: Measures include 24-hour foot and vehicle patrol, self-defense education, security escort services, and informal discussions. There are pamphlets/posters/films, emergency telephones, lighted pathways/sidewalks, and a taxi service.

Programs of Study: MCAD confers B.S. and B.F.A degrees. Master's degrees are also awarded. Bachelor's degrees are awarded in COMMUNICATIONS AND THE ARTS (advertising, animation, design, drawing, film arts, graphic design, illustration, painting, photography, printmaking, sculpture, studio art, and video), COMPUTER AND PHYSICAL SCIENCE (digital arts/technology), ENGINEERING AND ENVIRONMENTAL DESIGN (furniture design). Graphic design, illustration, and photography are the largest.

Required: All B.F.A. students must satisfactorily complete 120 semester credits, including 38 in foundation studies and 27 to 42 in the major. A 2.0 minimum GPA must be maintained. A senior project is required.

Special: MCAD offers cross-registration with Macalester College, internships, study abroad in 8 countries and mobility programs with many other art and design colleges in the U.S. and Canada. Work-study is possible, as are student-designed majors.

Faculty/Classroom: 55% of faculty are male; 45%, female. All teach undergraduates. No introductory courses are taught by graduate students. The average class size in an introductory lecture is 25; in a laboratory, 14; and in a regular course, 12.

Admissions: 77% of the 2005-2006 applicants were accepted. The SAT scores for the 2005-2006 freshman class were: Verbal--20% below 500, 40% between 500 and 599, 30% between 600 and 700, and 10% above 700; Math--30% below 500, 35% between 500 and 599, 25% between 600 and 700, and 10% above 700. The ACT scores were 10% below 21, 40% between 21 and 23, 40% between 24 and 26, 7% between 27 and 28, and 3% above 28. 40% of the current freshmen were in the top fifth of their class; 70% were in the top two fifths.

Requirements: The SAT or ACT is required. In addition, applicants must submit a personal statement of interest, an essay, a letter of recommendation, transcripts, and a portfolio (B.F.A.). An interview is strongly encouraged. The GED is accepted. A GPA of 2.5 is required. AP credits are accepted. Important factors in the admissions decision are evidence of special talent, personality/intangible qualities, and recommendations by school officials.

Procedure: Freshmen are admitted fall and spring. Entrance exams should be taken in the spring of the junior year in high school or early fall senior year. There are deferred admissions and rolling admissions

plans. There are application deadlines to quailfy for merit scholarships. Applications should be filed by February 15 for fall entry and October 1 for spring entry. Notification is sent on a rolling basis. Applications are accepted on-line.

Transfer: 88 transfer students enrolled in 2004-2005. B.F.A. applicants must submit a portfolio for the transfer of studio credit and an official transcript from all postsecondary schools. 45 of 120 credits required for the bachelor's degree must be completed at MCAD.

Visiting: There are regularly scheduled orientations for prospective students, consisting of tours, a program about putting a portfolio together, and career and financial aid information. There are guides for informal visits and visitors may sit in on classes and stay overnight. To schedule a visit, contact the Admissions Office at (800) 874-6223, ext. 1.

Financial Aid: In 2005-2006, 95% of all full-time freshmen received some form of financial aid. 71% of full-time freshmen received need-based aid. Need-based scholarships or need-based grants averaged $7884; and need-based self-help aid (loans and jobs) averaged $3506. 25% of undergraduates work part time. Average annual earnings from campus work are $1300. The average financial indebtedness of the 2005 graduate was $38,980. MCAD is a member of CSS. The FAFSA and parent and student federal income tax forms are required. The priority date for freshman financial aid applications for fall entry is March 15. The deadline for filing freshman financial aid applications for fall entry is August 1.

International Students: There are 12 international students enrolled. They must score satisfactorily on the written TOEFL or on the electronic version.

Computers: Wireless access is available. All academic buildings and dorms have wireless access. 5 computer labs are available for student use 24/7. All students may access the system. There are no time limits. All students are required to have a computer. A Mac laptop is required.

Graduates: From July 1, 2004 to June 30, 2005, 121 bachelor's degrees were awarded. The most popular majors were graphic design (23%), illustration (15%), and animation (9%). In an average class, 29% graduate in 4 years or less, 34% graduate in 5 years or less, and 35% graduate in 6 years or less. Of the 2004 graduating class, 10% were enrolled in graduate school within 6 months of graduation and 94% were employed.

Admissions Contact: William Mullen, Director of Admissions and Recruitment. E-mail: *admissions@mcad.edu* Web: *www.mcad.edu*

MINNESOTA STATE UNIVERSITY, MANKATO   C-4

Mankato, MN 56001   **(507) 389-1822**
(800) 722-0544; Fax: (507) 389-1511

Full-time: 5422 men, 5915 women	**Faculty:** 491; IIA, av$
Part-time: 594 men, 753 women	**Ph.D.s:** 79%
Graduate: 612 men, 739 women	**Student/Faculty:** 23 to 1
Year: semesters, summer session	**Tuition:** $5402 ($10,750)
Application Deadline: open	**Room & Board:** $4874
Freshman Class: 5605 applied, 5035 accepted, 2257 enrolled	
ACT: 21	**LESS COMPETITIVE**

Minnesota State University, Mankato, founded in 1868 and a unit of Minnesota State Colleges and Universities, offers programs in the liberal arts and sciences, as well as business, education, engineering and technology, and nursing. There are 6 undergraduate schools and 1 graduate school. In addition to regional accreditation, Minnesota State or MSU has baccalaureate program accreditation with AACSB, ABET, ADA, CSWE, NASAD, NASM, NCATE, NLN, and NRPA. The library contains 1,107,354 volumes, 253,560 microform items, and 30,686 audio/video tapes/CDs/DVDs, and subscribes to 3126 periodicals including electronic. Computerized library services include the card catalog, interlibrary loans, database searching, Internet access, and laptop Internet portals. Special learning facilities include a learning resource center, art gallery, radio station, and 2 observatories. The 354-acre campus is in a rural area 85 miles southwest of Minneapolis-St. Paul. Including any residence halls, there are 18 buildings.

Student Life: 84% of undergraduates are from Minnesota. Others are from 47 states, 68 foreign countries, and Canada. 94% are from public schools. 71% are white. The average age of freshmen is 19; all undergraduates, 22. 22% do not continue beyond their first year; 49% remain to graduate.

Housing: 3100 students can be accommodated in college housing, which includes coed dorms. There are special-interest floors including freshman quiet-study floors, upper class floors, engineering floors and computer science floors. On-campus housing is guaranteed for the freshman year only, is available on a first-come, first-served basis, and is available on a lottery system for upperclassmen. 78% of students commute. Alcohol is not permitted. All students may keep cars.

Activities: 1% of men belong to 7 national fraternities; 1% of women belong to 4 national sororities. There are 114 groups on campus, including art, band, cheerleading, choir, chorale, chorus, computers, dance, debate, drama, ethnic, film, forensics, gay, honors, international, jazz band, literary magazine, marching band, musical theater, newspaper, opera, orchestra, pep band, photography, political, professional, radio and TV, religious, social, social service, and student government. Popular campus events include Greek Week, multicultural activities and celebrations, and homecoming.

Sports: There are 10 intercollegiate sports for men and 10 for women, and 35 intramural sports for men and 35 for women. Facilities include a 7000-seat stadium, a field house, a recreation center including an indoor swimming pool, racquetball courts, a walking jogging track, multipurpose rooms, weights, and workout machines; 2 gyms, an indoor track, tennis courts, and a 5000 seat ice hockey arena (city owned).

Disabled Students: 90% of the campus is accessible. Wheelchair ramps, elevators, special parking, specially equipped rest rooms, special class scheduling, lowered drinking fountains, lowered telephones, and assistive technology are available.

Services: Counseling and information services are available, as is tutoring in most subjects. There is a reader service for the blind, and remedial math, reading, and writing. Also available are alternative testing accommodations, note taking, sign language interpreting, and taped texts.

Campus Safety and Security: Measures include 24-hour foot and vehicle patrol, self-defense education, security escort services, and shuttle buses. There are informal discussions, pamphlets/posters/films, emergency telephones, lighted pathways/sidewalks, closed-circuit parking lot cameras, and motion-sensitive lights in low traffic areas.

Programs of Study: Minnesota State or MSU confers B.A., B.S., B.F.A., B.Mus., B.S.E.E., and B.S.M.E. degrees. Associate and master's degrees are also awarded. Bachelor's degrees are awarded in BIOLOGICAL SCIENCE (avian sciences, biochemistry, biology/biological science, biotechnology, and life science), BUSINESS (accounting, banking and finance, business administration and management, international business management, management science, and marketing/retailing/merchandising), COMMUNICATIONS AND THE ARTS (applied art, art, communications, dance, dramatic arts, English, French, German, journalism, music, music business management, Spanish, and speech/debate/rhetoric), COMPUTER AND PHYSICAL SCIENCE (astronomy, chemistry, computer security and information assurance, earth science, information sciences and systems, mathematics, and physics), EDUCATION (art, athletic training, early childhood, elementary, foreign languages, health, industrial arts, music, physical, science, and secondary), ENGINEERING AND ENVIRONMENTAL DESIGN (automotive technology, aviation administration/management, civil engineering, computer engineering, computer technology, construction management, electrical/electronics engineering, electrical/electronics engineering technology, engineering technology, environmental science, interior design, manufacturing technology, mechanical engineering, and preengineering), HEALTH PROFESSIONS (clinical science, dental hygiene, health science, medical laboratory technology, nursing, predentistry, premedicine, preosteopathy, prepharmacy, prepodiatry, preveterinary science, public health, and speech pathology/audiology), SOCIAL SCIENCE (anthropology, corrections, dietetics, economics, ethnic studies, family/consumer studies, food science, geography, history, human development, humanities, law enforcement and corrections, parks and recreation management, philosophy, political science/government, prelaw, psychology, Scandinavian studies, social studies, social work, sociology, theological studies, urban studies, and women's studies). Engineering, nursing, and sciences are the strongest academically. Business, nursing, and education are the largest.

Required: To graduate, students must complete 128 semester hours of credit, with a minimum GPA of 2.0 and at least 45 hours in the major. Most programs require 44 hours of general education, including courses in English, speech, science, math, social/behavioral science, arts and humanities, cultural diversity, global perspective, ethnic/civic responsibility, and people and the environment.

Special: The university offers cross-registration within the Minnesota State University System and with Gustavus Adolphus College. Students may serve internships, study abroad, or participate in an accelerated degree program. B.A.-B.S. degrees, dual and student-designed majors, nondegree study, and pass/fail options also are available. There are 11 national honor societies, a freshman honors program, and 1 departmental honors program.

Faculty/Classroom: 55% of faculty are male; 45%, female. 96% teach undergraduates and 51% do research. Graduate students teach 4% of introductory courses. The average class size in an introductory lecture is 43; in a laboratory, 11; and in a regular course, 21.

Admissions: 90% of the 2005-2006 applicants were accepted. The ACT scores for the 2005-2006 freshman class were: 40% below 21, 36% between 21 and 23, 18% between 24 and 26, 5% between 27 and 28, and 2% above 28. 21% of the current freshmen were in the top fifth of their class; 54% were in the top two fifths. 20 freshmen graduated first in their class.

Requirements: The ACT is required. In addition, applicants must be graduates of an accredited secondary school and rank in the top 50% of their high school class or have an ACT composite score of 21 or higher along with a satisfactory class rank. AP and CLEP credits are accepted.

Procedure: Freshmen are admitted to all sessions. Entrance exams should be taken in the spring of the junior year or the fall of the senior

year. There are deferred admissions and rolling admissions plans. Application deadlines are open. Application fee is $20. Applications are accepted on-line.

Transfer: 1097 transfer students enrolled in 2004-2005. Transfer applicants must have a minimum GPA of 2.0 and have completed at least 75% of all college-level courses attempted. 30 of 128 credits required for the bachelor's degree must be completed at Minnesota State or MSU.

Visiting: There are regularly scheduled orientations for prospective students, consisting of overview presentations, campus tours, and academic information fairs. There are guides for informal visits and visitors may sit in on classes. To schedule a visit, contact the Admissions Office.

Financial Aid: In 2005-2006, 45% of all full-time freshmen and 46% of continuing full-time students received some form of financial aid. 45% of full-time freshmen and 46% of continuing full-time students received need-based aid. The average freshman award was $6365. Need-based scholarships or need-based grants averaged $3750; need-based self-help aid (loans and jobs) averaged $3703; and non-need-based athletic scholarships averaged $4773. 21% of undergraduates work part time. Average annual earnings from campus work are $1960. The FAFSA is required. The deadline for filing freshman financial aid applications for fall entry is March 15.

International Students: In recent year, there were 460 international students enrolled. A satisfactory score is required on the written TOEFL oron the electronic version and also take an English placement test at matriculation.

Computers: Wireless access is available. There are computer labs and workstations throughout campus; wireless computer access; residence hall high speed internet hook-up is included. All students may access the system. There are no time limits. The fee is $3.11 per semester credit. For the College of Business, a laptop PC is required. Dell is recommended.

Graduates: In a recent year, 1819 bachelor's degrees were awarded. The most popular majors were management (8%), elementary education (6%), and marketing (4%). 260 companies recruited on campus in a recent year.

Admissions Contact: Walt Wolff, Director of Admissions.
E-mail: *admissions@mankato.msus.edu* Web: *mnsu.edu*

MINNESOTA STATE UNIVERSITY, MOORHEAD   A-2

Moorhead, MN 56563   (218) 236-2161
(800) 593-7246; Fax: (218) 236-2168

Full-time: 1805 men, 3005 women	**Faculty:** 255
Part-time: 305 men, 805 women	**Ph.Ds:** 75%
Graduate: 75 men, 235 women	**Student/Faculty:** 19 to 1
Year: semesters, summer session	**Tuition:** $3550 ($6550)
Application Deadline: see profile	**Room & Board:** $3550
Freshman Class: n/av	
SAT or ACT: n/av	**LESS COMPETITIVE**

Moorhead State University, founded in 1885, is a public liberal arts institution. Figures in above capsule and in this profile are approximate. In addition to regional accreditation, Moorhead State has baccalaureate program accreditation with CSWE, NASAD, NASM, NCATE, and NLN. The library contains 365,000 volumes, 45,000 microform items, and 7000 audio/video tapes/CDs/DVDs, and subscribes to 1626 periodicals including electronic. Computerized library services include the card catalog, interlibrary loans, and database searching. Special learning facilities include an art gallery, planetarium, radio station, TV station, and a science center. The 104-acre campus is in a suburban area 240 miles northwest of Minneapolis-St. Paul and across the river from Fargo, North Dakota. Including any residence halls, there are 23 buildings.

Student Life: 96% are white. The average age of freshmen is 18; all undergraduates, 24.

Housing: 2164 students can be accommodated in college housing, which includes single-sex and coed dormitories. On-campus housing is available on a first-come, first-served basis. 67% of students commute. Alcohol is not permitted. All students may keep cars.

Activities: 2% of men belong to 1 local and 1 national fraternity; 1% of women belong to 3 national sororities. There are 150 groups on campus, including art, band, cheerleading, choir, chorus, computers, dance, drama, drill team, ethnic, film, gay, honors, international, jazz band, literary magazine, musical theater, newspaper, orchestra, pep band, photography, political, professional, radio and TV, religious, social, social service, and student government. Popular campus events include Parents Day, Straw Hat Summer Theatre, and Meltdown Concert.

Sports: There are 5 intercollegiate sports for men and 9 for women, and 18 intramural sports for men and 18 for women. Facilities include 4 gyms, racquetball and volleyball courts, 2 swimming pools, indoor and outdoor tennis courts, weight and wrestling rooms, a running track, and 3 softball diamonds.

Disabled Students: Wheelchair ramps, elevators, special parking, specially equipped rest rooms, lowered drinking fountains, and lowered telephones are available.

Services: Counseling and information services are available, as is tutoring in every subject. There is a reader service for the blind, and remedial math, reading, and writing.

Campus Safety and Security: Measures include 24-hour foot and vehicle patrol, self-defense education, security escort services, and informal discussions. There are pamphlets/posters/films, emergency telephones, and lighted pathways/sidewalks.

Programs of Study: Moorhead State confers B.A., B.S., B.F.A., B.M., B.S.N., and B.S.W. degrees. Associate and master's degrees are also awarded. Bachelor's degrees are awarded in BIOLOGICAL SCIENCE (biology/biological science), BUSINESS (accounting, banking and finance, business administration and management, hotel/motel and restaurant management, international business management, marketing/retailing/merchandising, and trade and industrial supervision and management), COMMUNICATIONS AND THE ARTS (advertising, broadcasting, communications, dramatic arts, English, fine arts, French, German, journalism, music, public relations, Spanish, and speech/debate/rhetoric), COMPUTER AND PHYSICAL SCIENCE (chemistry, computer science, mathematics, and physics), EDUCATION (art, early childhood, elementary, foreign languages, health, industrial arts, music, science, secondary, social studies, and special), ENGINEERING AND ENVIRONMENTAL DESIGN (construction engineering), HEALTH PROFESSIONS (medical laboratory technology, nursing, predentistry, premedicine, prepharmacy, preveterinary science, and speech pathology/audiology), SOCIAL SCIENCE (American studies, anthropology, criminal justice, economics, history, paralegal studies, philosophy, political science/government, prelaw, psychology, social science, social work, and sociology). Music and speech/theater are the strongest academically. Business, education, and mass communications are the largest.

Required: To graduate students must have a 2.0 GPA and complete 128 semester hours, including a liberal arts core of 45 credits and 43 semester hours in upper-division courses. Required courses include 6 hours each of natural science, social science, humanities, and communications, language, or symbolic systems, and 5 credits in cultural diversity. All students must complete an upper-level writing requirement.

Special: Internships are available in most disciplines. The university offers cross-registration with North Dakota State University and Concordia College, and is a member of the National Student Exchange. Students may study abroad in more than 60 countries. Student-designed and dual majors, credit for military experience, nondegree study, and pass/fail options are possible. There are 7 national honor societies, a freshman honors program, and 1 departmental honors program.

Requirements: A high school diploma is required and the GED is accepted. A satisfactorily SAT score or ACT score is required for applicants whose high school rank is below the top half. Moorhead State requires applicants to be in the upper 50% of their class. AP and CLEP credits are accepted.

Procedure: Freshmen are admitted to all sessions. There is a rolling admission plan. Entrance exams should be taken in the junior or senior year of high school. Check with the school for application deadlines. Notification is sent on a rolling basis.

Transfer: Applicants must submit a high school transcript or GED score and all other transcripts for post-secondary schools attended. A minimum GPA of 2.0 (higher for entry in some departments) is necessary for transfer credit. 30 of 128 credits required for the bachelor's degree must be completed at Moorhead State.

Visiting: There are regularly scheduled orientations for prospective students, including a campus tour, lunch, and meetings with faculty and an admissions officer. There are guides for informal visits. To schedule a visit, contact the Admissions Office.

Financial Aid: The average financial. The FAFSA anf the college's own financial statement are required. Check with the school for application deadlines.

International Students: The school actively recruits these students. They must score satisfactorily on the written TOEFL.

Computers: All students may access the system 24 hours a day, 7 days a week. There are no time limits.

Admissions Contact: Director of Admissions.

NORTH CENTRAL UNIVERSITY
C-4

Minneapolis, MN 55404

(612) 343-4460
(800) 289-6222; Fax: (612) 343-4146

Full-time: 483 men, 652 women	Faculty: 40
Part-time: 47 men, 43 women	Ph.D.s: 50%
Graduate: none	Student/Faculty: 31 to 1
Year: semesters, summer session	Tuition: $12,166
Application Deadline: June 1	Room & Board: $4480
Freshman Class: 800 applied, 770 accepted, 500 enrolled	
SAT Verbal/Math: 555/370*	ACT: 21 LESS COMPETITIVE

North Central University, founded in 1930 and affiliated with the Assemblies of God, is a Christian university that emphasizes rigorous academic training and spiritual passion. The library contains 70,041 volumes, 29 microform items, and 200 audio/video tapes/CDs/DVDs, and subscribes

to 325 periodicals including electronic. Computerized library services include the card catalog, interlibrary loans, database searching, and Internet access. Special learning facilities include a learning resource center, radio station, and TV station. The 8-acre campus is in an urban area in downtown Minneapolis. Including any residence halls, there are 12 buildings.

Student Life: 65% of undergraduates are from out of state, mostly the Midwest. Others are from 42 states, 7 foreign countries, and Canada. 88% are from public schools. 94% are white. Most are Protestant. The average age of freshmen is 18; all undergraduates, 20. 25% do not continue beyond their first year; 50% remain to graduate.

Housing: 950 students can be accommodated in college housing, which includes single-sex dorms and on-campus apartments. In addition, there are honors houses. 78% of students live on campus. Alcohol is not permitted. Upperclassmen may keep cars.

Activities: There are no fraternities or sororities. There are 28 groups on campus, including art, band, choir, chorale, chorus, drama, jazz band, literary magazine, musical theater, newspaper, orchestra, photography, political, radio and TV, religious, social, student government, and yearbook. Popular campus events include All-College Picnic, Community Outreach Day, and Spring Banquet.

Sports: There are 6 intercollegiate sports for men and 6 for women, and 4 intramural sports for men and 4 for women. Facilities include Elliot Park, the Clark-Danielson College Life Center gym, and the National Sports Complex.

Disabled Students: All of the campus is accessible. Wheelchair ramps, elevators, special parking, specially equipped rest rooms, special class scheduling, lowered drinking fountains, and lowered telephones are available.

Services: Counseling and information services are available, as is tutoring in every subject.

Campus Safety and Security: Measures include 24-hour foot and vehicle patrol, security escort services, pamphlets/posters/films, and lighted pathways/sidewalks.

Programs of Study: NCU confers B.A. and B.S. degrees. Associate degrees are also awarded. Bachelor's degrees are awarded in COMMUNICATIONS AND THE ARTS (communications), EDUCATION (elementary), SOCIAL SCIENCE (behavioral science, biblical languages, ministries, pastoral studies, religion, religious education, and religious music). Elementry education, English, and business are the strongest academically. Music, elementry education, and youth ministries are the largest.

Required: Students must complete 129 to 144 credits for their particular bachelor's degree. Each program has specific requirements, including general education and biblical studies core classes. Internships are required for all programs. Students must take 60 or more total hours in their major, with a minimum overall GPA of 2.0 (2.2 for teacher education).

Special: Students may pursue co-op programs in nursing or secondary education, study abroad in 6 countries, or nondegree study, or receive credit for life, military, or work experience. Work-study, dual majors, and student-designed majors are available.

Faculty/Classroom: 63% of faculty are male; 37%, female. All teach undergraduates. The average class size in an introductory lecture is 80; in a laboratory, 15; and in a regular course, 25.

Admissions: 96% of the 2005-2006 applicants were accepted. The SAT scores for the 2005-2006 freshman class were: Verbal--25% below 500, 50% between 500 and 599, and 25% between 600 and 700; Math--25% below 500, 50% between 500 and 599, and 25% between 600 and 700. The ACT scores were 25% below 21, 50% between 21 and 23, 10% between 24 and 26, 10% between 27 and 28, and 5% above 28. 11% of the current freshmen were in the top fifth of their class; 32% were in the top two fifths.

Requirements: The University requires a minimum ACT score of 18, high school transcripts, and academic and pastoral references. A GPA of 2.2 is required. AP and CLEP credits are accepted.

Procedure: Freshmen are admitted fall and spring. Entrance exams should be taken during junior or senior of high school. Applications should be filed by June 1 for fall entry and December 31 for spring entry, along with a $25 fee. Notification is sent on a rolling basis.

Transfer: 146 transfer students enrolled in a recent year. Transfer applicants must submit a completed application, a pastor's reference, a high school transcript or the GED, and college transcripts. Applicants with less than a year of college credit must also submit ACT or SAT scores and academic references. 27 of 129 credits required for the bachelor's degree must be completed at NCU.

Visiting: There are regularly scheduled orientations for prospective students. There are guides for informal visits and visitors may sit in on classes and stay overnight. To schedule a visit, contact the Admissions Office at (800) 289-6222 or admissions@northcentral.edu.

Financial Aid: In a recent year, 90% of all full-time students received some form of financial aid. 90% of all full-time students received need-based aid. The average freshman award was $6000. 100% of undergraduates work part time. Average annual earnings from campus work were $3500. The average financial indebtedness of the recent graduate was $13,369. The FAFSA or FFS and the college's own financial statement are required. The priority date for freshman financial aid applications for fall entry is May 1. The deadline for filing freshman financial aid applications for fall entry is May 1.

International Students: There are 18 international students enrolled. They must take the TOEFL and also take the SAT or the ACT.

Computers: All students may access the system. There are no time limits. The fee is $42.

Graduates: The most popular majors were music (10%), elementry education (10%), and youth ministries (10%). In an average class, 40% graduate in 4 years or less, and 50% graduate in 5 years or less. Of the 2004 graduating class, 10% were enrolled in graduate school within 6 months of graduation and 90% were employed.

Admissions Contact: Joe Kessler, Admissions Director. A video is available. E-mail: jmkesslet@northcentral.edu
Web: www.northcentral.edu

NORTHWESTERN COLLEGE   C-4

St. Paul, MN 55113-1598

(651) 631-5209
(800) 827-6827; Fax: (651) 631-5680

Full-time: 693 men, 1033 women	Faculty: 85; IIB, -$
Part-time: 18 men, 23 women	Ph.D.s: 67%
Graduate: 9 men, 9 women	Student/Faculty: n/av
Year: semesters, summer session	Tuition: $19,100
Application Deadline: August 1	Room & Board: $6120
Freshman Class: 918 applied, 904 accepted, 468 enrolled	
ACT: 23	NONCOMPETITIVE

Northwestern College, founded in 1902, is a Christian college offering traditional undergraduate programs in Bible, liberal arts, and professional studies and providing nontraditional educational opportunities through its degree completion, and distance education divisions. In addition to regional accreditation, Northwestern has baccalaureate program accreditation with NASM. The library contains 112,298 volumes, 152 microform items, and 4432 audio/video tapes/CDs/DVDs, and subscribes to 965 periodicals including electronic. Computerized library services include the card catalog, interlibrary loans, database searching, Internet access, and laptop Internet portals. Special learning facilities include a learning resource center, art gallery, radio station, and language labs. The 100-acre campus is in a suburban area 7 miles north of downtown St. Paul. Including any residence halls, there are 13 buildings.

Student Life: 67% of undergraduates are from Minnesota. Students are from 35 states, 14 foreign countries, and Canada. 90% are white. Most are Protestant. The average age of freshmen is 18; all undergraduates, 20. 21% do not continue beyond their first year; 57% remain to graduate.

Housing: 1061 students can be accommodated in college housing, which includes single-sex and coed dorms, on-campus apartments, and off-campus apartments. On-campus housing is guaranteed for the freshman year only and is available on a first-come, first-served basis. Priority is given to out-of-town students. 61% of students live on campus; of those, 70% remain on campus on weekends. Alcohol is not permitted. Upperclassmen may keep cars.

Activities: There are no fraternities or sororities. There are 25 groups on campus, including band, cheerleading, choir, chorale, chorus, drama, ethnic, forensics, honors, international, jazz band, literary magazine, musical theater, newspaper, opera, orchestra, pep band, political, professional, radio and TV, religious, social, social service, student government, and yearbook. Popular campus events include Spiritual Emphasis Week, Residence Hall Open House, and Spring Variety Show.

Sports: There are 9 intercollegiate sports for men and 8 for women, and 9 intramural sports for men and 9 for women. Facilities include softball, baseball, and football/soccer fields, outdoor tennis courts, and a waterfront for aquatic sports in summer and broomball in winter. There is a health and phys ed center, with a full basketball court, 2 racquetball courts, an elevated jogging surface, a fitness center, and an athletic training room. The student center has a small swimming pool.

Disabled Students: 80% of the campus is accessible. Wheelchair ramps, elevators, special parking, specially equipped rest rooms, special class scheduling, lowered drinking fountains, and special housing are available.

Services: Counseling and information services are available, as is tutoring in some subjects, including including math, English, Greek, accounting, and statistics for psychology. There is remedial math, reading, and writing.

Campus Safety and Security: Measures include 24-hour foot and vehicle patrol, security escort services, shuttle buses, and informal discussions. There are pamphlets/posters/films, emergency telephones, and lighted pathways/sidewalks.

Programs of Study: Northwestern confers B.A., B.S., B.M.E. (music education), and B.Mus. degrees. Associate degrees are also awarded. Bachelor's degrees are awarded in BIOLOGICAL SCIENCE (biology/biological science), BUSINESS (accounting, banking and finance, business administration and management, international business management, management information systems, and marketing management), COMMUNICATIONS AND THE ARTS (broadcasting, communications, English, English as a second/foreign language, graphic design, music, music performance, and studio art), COMPUTER AND PHYSICAL SCIENCE (digital arts/technology and mathematics), EDUCATION (art, Christian, early childhood, elementary, English, mathematics, music, physical, and social studies), HEALTH PROFESSIONS (exercise science), SOCIAL SCIENCE (biblical studies, crosscultural studies, history, interdisciplinary studies, ministries, pastoral studies, psychology, social science, and youth ministry). Elementary education, business, and music are the strongest academically. Education, psychology, communications, and general business are the largest.

Required: To graduate, students must complete 125-167 semester credits (depends on specific major) with a 2.0 GPA. The number of credits required in the major varies from 36 to 100 (average of 57). Core courses include 3 credits of Bible, 10 credits of compostion/speech/computer literacy, 7 to 8 credits of Western Civilization, social science, and foreign language/cross-cultural course, 6 to 8 credits of math and science, 6 credits each of fine arts/literature/philosophy, Western civilization/social science, and foreign language/cross-cultural courses, and 1 credit of phys ed.

Special: The college offers 7 study-abroad programs and 4 U.S. off-campus programs through the Council for Christian Colleges and Universities. International business majors are placed in overseas internships. A 3-2 engineering degree with the University of Minnesota-Twin Cities is offered. There are 2 national honor societies, a freshman honors program, and 2 departmental honors programs.

Faculty/Classroom: 59% of faculty are male; 41%, female. All teach undergraduates. The average class size in a laboratory is 17 and in a regular course, 25.

Admissions: 98% of the 2005-2006 applicants were accepted. The ACT scores for the 2005-2006 freshman class were: 35% below 21, 23% between 21 and 23, 23% between 24 and 26, 12% between 27 and 28, and 7% above 28. 44% of the current freshmen were in the top fifth of their class; 70% were in the top two fifths. 13 freshmen graduated first in their class.

Requirements: The ACT is required. The ACT Optional Writing test is also recommended. In addition, the ACTis preferred but the SAT is accepted. A high school diploma is required; the GED is accepted. The minimum high school GPA is 2.0, but a 3.0 or higher is recommended. Applicants are expected to have completed the following Carnegie units: 4 in English, 3 each in math, science, and social studies, and 2 Carnegie units. 2 in foreign language are recommended. A statement of Christian faith and an assent to a lifestyle agreement are required. 2 letters of reference must be submitted, 1 from the applicant's pastor. A personal interview is required for some students. Northwestern requires applicants to be in the upper 50% of their class. A GPA of 2.0 is required. AP and CLEP credits are accepted. Important factors in the admissions decision are personality/intangible qualities, recommendations by school officials, and leadership record.

Procedure: Freshmen are admitted to all sessions. Entrance exams should be taken Fall of the senior year of high school. There are early admissions, deferred admissions, and rolling admisssionsplans. Applications should be filed by August 1 for fall entry, December 15 for spring entry, and May 1 for summer entry, along with a $30 fee. Notification is sent on a rolling basis.

Transfer: 136 transfer students enrolled in 2004-2005. Applicants must have an average of C or better from an accredited institution. 30 of 125 tp 167 credits required for the bachelor's degree must be completed at Northwestern.

Visiting: There are regularly scheduled orientations for prospective students. There are guides for informal visits and visitors may sit in on classes and stay overnight. To schedule a visit, contact the Admissions Office at (651) 631-5111 or admissions@bwc.edu.

Financial Aid: In 2005-2006, 99% of all full-time freshmen and 96% of continuing full-time students received some form of financial aid. 82% of full-time freshmen and 80% of continuing full-time students received need-based aid. The average freshman award was $14,364. Need-based scholarships or need-based grants averaged $6875; need-based self-help aid (loans and jobs) averaged $2461; and other non-need-based awards and non-need-based scholarships averaged $7084. 29% of undergraduates work part time. Average annual earnings from campus work are $1900. The average financial indebtedness of the 2005 graduate was $16,656. The FAFSA and the college's own financial statement are required. The priority date for freshman financial aid applications for fall entry is March 1. The deadline for filing freshman financial aid applications for fall entry is June 1.

International Students: There are 22 international students enrolled. A satisfactory score is required on the written TOEFL Students must also take the SAT or the ACT.

Computers: Wireless access is available. There is full wireless access in all academic buildings. Dorms are fully wired ("port to pillow"). All students may access the system anytime. There are no time limits and no fees. All students are required to have personal computers. A laptop is recommended.

Graduates: From July 1, 2004 to June 30, 2005, 374 bachelor's degrees were awarded. The most popular majors were psychology (10%), elementary education (10%), and communication (6%). In an average class, 5% graduate in 3 years or less, 46% graduate in 4 years or less, 57% graduate in 5 years or less, and 58% graduate in 6 years or less. 156 companies recruited on campus in 2004-2005. Of the 2004 graduating class, 8% were enrolled in graduate school within 6 months of graduation and 74% were employed.

Admissions Contact: Kenneth K. Faffler, Director of Admissions. A video is available. E-mail: *kkfaffler@nwc.edu* Web: *www.nwc.edu*

SAINT CLOUD STATE UNIVERSITY
St. Cloud, MN 56301-4498

C-3

(320) 308-2244
(800) 369-4260; Fax: (320) 308-2243

Full-time: 5381 men, 6230 women	Faculty: 650; IIA, av$
Part-time: 1190 men, 1685 women	Ph.D.s: n/av
Graduate: 554 men, 924 women	Student/Faculty: 18 to 1
Year: semesters, summer session	Tuition: $5322 ($10,894)
Application Deadline: open	Room & Board: $4688
Freshman Class: 5912 applied, 4622 accepted, 2152 enrolled	
ACT: 22	**COMPETITIVE**

Saint Cloud State University, founded in 1869, is a comprehensive university with 5 colleges plus 5 graduate schools offering programs that include the liberal arts and career preparation with emphasis on diversity, hands-on learning, and service to the community. There are 5 undergraduate and 5 graduate schools. In addition to regional accreditation, SCSU has baccalaureate program accreditation with AACSB, ABET, ACEJMC, ASLA, CSWE, NASAD, NASM, and NCATE. The library contains 887,462 volumes, 1,810,866 microform items, and 24,244 audio/video tapes/CDs/DVDs, and subscribes to 1762 periodicals including electronic. Computerized library services include the card catalog, interlibrary loans, database searching, and Internet access. Special learning facilities include a learning resource center, art gallery, natural history museum, planetarium, radio station, TV station, and a National Hockey Center. The 922-acre campus is in a suburban area 60 miles northwest of Minneapolis. Including any residence halls, there are 35 buildings.

Student Life: 92% of undergraduates are from Minnesota. Students are from 50 states, 85 foreign countries, and Canada. 77% are white. The average age of freshmen is 19; all undergraduates, 22. 29% do not continue beyond their first year.

Housing: 3000 students can be accommodated in college housing, which includes single-sex and coed dorms and special housing for international students. 82% of students commute. Alcohol is not permitted. All students may keep cars.

Activities: There are 5 national fraternities and 4 national sororities. There are 240 groups on campus, including art, band, cheerleading, chess, choir, chorale, chorus, computers, dance, drama, entrepreneurial, ethnic, film, gay, hobby, honors, international, jazz band, literary magazine, marching band, musical theater, opera, orchestra, pep band, photography, political, professional, radio and TV, religious, social, social service, sports, student government, symphony, travel, and yearbook. Popular campus events include Music Festival, Ethnic Awareness Week, and major speakers and workshops.

Disabled Students: 86% of the campus is accessible. Wheelchair ramps, elevators, special parking, specially equipped rest rooms, special class scheduling, lowered drinking fountains, and lowered telephones are available.

Services: Counseling and information services are available, as is tutoring in every subject. There is a reader service for the blind, and remedial math, reading, and writing.

Campus Safety and Security: Measures include 24-hour foot and vehicle patrol, security escort services, shuttle buses, and informal discussions. There are pamphlets/posters/films, emergency telephones, lighted pathways/sidewalks, and a required short safety course.

Programs of Study: SCSU confers B.A., B.S., B.E.S., B.F.A., and B.Mus. degrees. Associate, master's, and doctoral degrees are also awarded. Bachelor's degrees are awarded in BIOLOGICAL SCIENCE (biology/biological science), BUSINESS (accounting, banking and finance, business administration and management, business economics, international business management, marketing/retailing/merchandising, and personnel management), COMMUNICATIONS AND THE ARTS (advertising, broadcasting, communications, dramatic arts, English, fine arts, journalism, languages, music, and speech/debate/rhetoric), COMPUTER AND PHYSICAL SCIENCE (atmospheric sciences and meteorology, chemistry, computer science, earth science, geology, mathematics, physics, and statistics), EDUCATION (art, early childhood, elementary, foreign languages, guidance, health, industrial arts, music, science, and secondary), ENGINEERING AND ENVIRONMENTAL DESIGN (aviation administration/management, electrical/electronics engineering, engineering technology, and manufacturing engineering), HEALTH PROFESSIONS (predentistry, premedicine, public health, and

speech pathology/audiology), SOCIAL SCIENCE (anthropology, criminal justice, economics, geography, history, international relations, philosophy, political science/government, prelaw, psychology, public administration, social science, social work, sociology, and urban studies). Mass communication, elementary education, and special education are the largest.

Required: Students must complete a minimum of 120 semester credit hours, including 40 hours of general education requirements, and 60 to 180 hours in the major, and must maintain at least a 2.0 GPA, higher for many majors. Students must complete English 191, English 192, Speech 192, 2 credits in phys ed, and 24 credits in philosophy/humanities/fine arts, natural science and math, social and behavioral science, and diversity courses.

Special: The university offers cross-registration, internships in almost all majors, work-study programs, and study abroad in 25 countries. Students may take dual majors, design their own majors for a Bachelor of Elective Studies degree, and earn a general degree or a B.A.-B.S. degree in all majors, including meteorology and photographic technology. The university gives credit for military experience and allows nondegree study and pass/fail options. There are 4 national honor societies and a freshman honors program.

Faculty/Classroom: 56% of faculty are male; 44%, female. All teach undergraduates.

Admissions: 78% of the 2005-2006 applicants were accepted.

Requirements: The ACT is required. SCSU requires applicants to be in the upper 50% of their class. AP and CLEP credits are accepted.

Procedure: Freshmen are admitted fall, spring, and summer. Entrance exams should be taken in the junior or senior year. Application deadlines are open. The fall 2005 application fee was $20. Notification is sent on a rolling basis.

Transfer: 1238 transfer students enrolled in 2004-2005. Applicants must have a minimum 2.0 GPA from their previous college if they transfer with 12 or more credits. If they have fewer than 12 credits, they are treated as entering freshmen. 30 of 120 credits required for the bachelor's degree must be completed at SCSU.

Visiting: There are regularly scheduled orientations for prospective students. There are guides for informal visits and visitors may sit in on classes. To schedule a visit, contact the Admissions Office.

Financial Aid: The FAFSA and the college's own financial statement are required.

International Students: There are 633 international students enrolled. The school actively recruits these students. A satisfactory score is required on the written TOEFL.

Computers: Wireless access is available. All students may access the system any time. There are no time limits and no fees.

Graduates: From July 1, 2004 to June 30, 2005, 2379 bachelor's degrees were awarded. The most popular majors were business marketing (23%), education (18%), and social science and history (9%). In an average class, 14% graduate in 4 years or less, 34% graduate in 5 years or less, and 43% graduate in 6 years or less.

Admissions Contact: Pat Krueger, Associate Director of Admissions. A video is available. E-mail: *scsu4u@stcloud.state.edu* Web: *www.stcloudstate.edu*

SAINT JOHN'S UNIVERSITY
Collegeville, MN 56321-7155

B-3

(320) 363-2196
(800) 544-1489; Fax: (320) 363-2750

Full-time: 1845 men	Faculty: 147; IIB, av$
Part-time: 30 men	Ph.D.s: 88%
Graduate: 58 men, 63 women	Student/Faculty: 13 to 1
Year: semesters	Tuition: $23,474
Application Deadline: open	Room & Board: $6275
Freshman Class: 1167 applied, 1017 accepted, 447 enrolled	
SAT Verbal/Math: 590/610*	ACT: 25 **VERY COMPETITIVE**

St. John's University, founded in 1857, is a private, Benedictine Catholic institution offering undergraduate liberal arts study for men in partnership with the College of Saint Benedict, a Benedicitne institution for women. In addition to regional accreditation, St. John's has baccalaureate program accreditation with ACS, ADA, ATS, CCNE, CSWE, NASM, and NCATE. The 2 libraries contain 716,202 volumes, 120,432 microform items, and 38,396 audio/video tapes/CDs/DVDs, and subscribe to 14,863 periodicals including electronic. Computerized library services include the card catalog, interlibrary loans, database searching, Internet access, and laptop Internet portals. Special learning facilities include a learning resource center, art gallery, natural history museum, radio station, an observatory, a greenhouse, an arboretum, an herbarium, a pottery studio, and Hill Manuscript Museum and Library. The 2400-acre campus is in a rural area 15 miles west of St. Cloud and 70 miles northwest of Minneapolis and St. Paul. Including any residence halls, there are 35 buildings.

Student Life: 82% of undergraduates are from Minnesota. Others are from 36 states, 24 foreign countries, and Canada. 78% are from public schools. 92% are white. 67% are Catholic; 23% Protestant; 8% claim no religious affiliation. The average age of freshmen is 19; all undergraduates, 20. 12% do not continue beyond their first year; 82% remain to graduate.

Housing: 1468 students can be accommodated in college housing, which includes single-sex dorms and on-campus apartments. In addition, there are special-interest houses, a health and wellness floor, ROTC,and international housing. On-campus housing is available on a first-come, first-served basis and is available on a lottery system for upperclassmen. 82% of students live on campus. All students may keep cars.

Activities: There are no sororities. There are 80 groups on campus, including academic, art, band, choir, chorale, chorus, computers, dance, debate, drama, ethnic, gay, honors, international, jazz band, literary magazine, musical theater, newspaper, opera, orchestra, outdoor ledearship center, pep band, political, professional, radio and TV, religious, social, social service, student government, symphony, and yearbook. Popular campus events include Pinestock, Asian New Year, Li'l Sibs Weekend.

Sports: Facilities include basketball and racquetball courts, soccer, baseball, and rugby fields, indoor and outdoor tennis courts, indoor and outdoor tracks, aerobics studio, a fitness center, a swimming pool, a climbing wall, 5 lakes for canoeing, fishing, swimming, rowing, and kayaking, and access to facilities at the College of Saint Benedict.

Disabled Students: 90% of the campus is accessible. Wheelchair ramps, elevators, special parking, specially equipped rest rooms, special class scheduling, lowered drinking fountains, lowered telephones, and special housing are available.

Services: Counseling and information services are available, as is tutoring in most subjects. There are centers for writing and math skills, test-taking skills instruction, and various academic accomodations for students with documented disabilities.

Campus Safety and Security: Measures include 24-hour foot and vehicle patrol, self-defense education, security escort services, and shuttle buses. There are informal discussions, pamphlets/posters/films, emergency telephones, and lighted pathways/sidewalks.

Programs of Study: St. John's confers B.A. and B.S.N. degrees. Master's degrees are also awarded. Bachelor's degrees are awarded in AGRICULTURE (environmental studies and forestry and related sciences), BIOLOGICAL SCIENCE (biochemistry, biology/biological science, and nutrition), BUSINESS (accounting and management science), COMMUNICATIONS AND THE ARTS (art, classics, communications, dramatic arts, English, fine arts, French, German, music, and Spanish), COMPUTER AND PHYSICAL SCIENCE (chemistry, computer science, mathematics, natural sciences, and physics), EDUCATION (elementary), ENGINEERING AND ENVIRONMENTAL DESIGN (preengineering), HEALTH PROFESSIONS (nursing, occupational therapy, physical therapy, predentistry, premedicine, prepharmacy, and preveterinary science), SOCIAL SCIENCE (dietetics, economics, history, humanities, liberal arts/general studies, pastoral studies, peace studies, philosophy, political science/government, prelaw, psychology, social science, social work, sociology, and theological studies). Chemistry, economics, and music are the strongest academically. Management, biology, and political science are the largest.

Required: To graduate, students must complete the core curriculum of writing, discussion, quantitative reasoning, and gender and global perspectives. Distribution requirements include 6 credits in fine arts, 5 in humanities, 2 each in natural science and social science, and 1 in math. All students must prove proficiency in math and foreign language. A total of 124 credits must be earned, with 40 credits in upper-division courses and an overall GPA of 2.0. Students must complete a first-year symposium and senior seminar.

Special: Students may cross-register with the Saint Cloud State University. There are study-abroad programs in Australia, Austria, Chile, China, England, France, Guatemala, Greece, Ireland, Itlay, Japan, South Africa, and Spain. Internships, student-designed majors, preprofessional programs, and liberal studies degrees may be pursued. A 3-2 engineering program is offered with the University of Minnesota. Nondegree study and a pass/fail grading option are also available. There is, a freshman honors program. All departments have honor programs.

Faculty/Classroom: 71% of faculty are male; 29%, female. 100% both teach and do research. No introductory courses are taught by graduate students. The average class size in an introductory lecture is 25; in a laboratory, 18; and in a regular course, 22.

Admissions: 87% of the 2005-2006 applicants were accepted. The SAT scores for the 2005-2006 freshman class were: Verbal--12% below 500, 39% between 500 and 599, 36% between 600 and 700, and 13% above 700; Math--14% below 500, 26% between 500 and 599, 51% between 600 and 700, and 9% above 700. The ACT scores were 7% below 21, 25% between 21 and 23, 31% between 24 and 26, 18% between 27 and 28, and 19% above 28. 42% of the current freshmen were in the top fifth of their class; 77% were in the top two fifths. There were 5 National Merit finalists. 7 freshmen graduated first in their class.

Requirements: The SAT or ACT is required. In addition, students should be graduates of an accredited secondary school. Academic prep-

aration should include 17 units, including 4 of English, 3 of math, 2 each of a laboratory science and social studies, and 6 electives. A foreign language is recommended. The GED is accepted. An essay is required. Home-schooled applicants are not required to have a high school diploma but are required to provide appropriate documentation of college preparatory curriculum. St. John's requires applicants to be in the upper 50% of their class. A GPA of 3.0 is required. AP and CLEP credits are accepted. Important factors in the admissions decision are geographic diversity, advanced placement or honor courses, and parents or siblings attending the school.

Procedure: Freshmen are admitted fall and spring. Entrance exams should be taken by the fall of the senior year. There are deferred admissions and rolling admissions plans. Application deadlines are open. The priority date for fallentry is December 1. Notification for regular decision is sent on a rolling basis beginning October 1. A waiting list is an active part of the admissions procedure. Applications are accepted on-line.

Transfer: 61 transfer students enrolled in 2004-2005. Transfer applicants must have a minimum college GPA of 2.75. An essay or personal statement, high school and college transcripts, and a transfer student evaluation form are also required. Standardized test scores may be required. 45 of 124 credits required for the bachelor's degree must be completed at St. John's.

Visiting: There are regularly scheduled orientations for prospective students, including a variety of programs that are offered throughout the year. Information can be found at the College's web site. There are guides for informal visits and visitors may sit in on classes. Admitted students may stay overnight. To schedule a visit, contact the Admissions Office at *admissions@csbsju.edu*.

Financial Aid: In 2005-2006, 96% of all full-time freshmen and 93% of continuing full-time students received some form of financial aid. 61% of full-time freshmen and 58% of continuing full-time students received need-based aid. The average freshman award was $19,044. Need-based scholarships or need-based grants averaged $14,142; need-based self-help aid (loans and jobs) averaged $4993; and other non-need-based awards and non-need-based scholarships averaged $8584. 63% of undergraduates work part time. Average annual earnings from campus work are $2100. The average financial indebtedness of the 2005 graduate was $24,663. St. John's is a member of CSS. The FAFSA, the college's own financial statement, federal tax returns, and W-2s are required. The priority date for freshman financial aid applications for fall entry is March 15.

International Students: There are 73 international students enrolled. The school actively recruits these students. A satisfactory score is required on the written TOEFL.

Computers: Students are not required to own a compute, but network connections are available for all students in their residence hall. Students can access computers in the computer labs, libraries, student centers, and residence halls. Information Technology services provide help desk services, software support, and training workshops in a wide variety of software applications. All students may access the system 24 hours a day. There are no time limits. The fee is $190.

Graduates: From July 1, 2004 to June 30, 2005, 424 bachelor's degrees were awarded. The most popular majors were business and management (16%), biology (10%), and political science and economics (9%). In an average class, 1% graduate in 3 years or less, 74% graduate in 4 years or less, 81% graduate in 5 years or less, and 82% graduate in 6 years or less. 102 companies recruited on campus in 2004-2005. Of the 2004 graduating class, 21% were enrolled in graduate school within 6 months of graduation and 75% were employed.

Admissions Contact: Mary Milbert, Dean of Admissions.
E-mail: *admissions@csbsju.edu* Web: *www.csbsju.edu*

SAINT MARY'S UNIVERSITY OF MINNESOTA   D-5
Winona, MN 55987-1399   (507) 457-1700
(800) 635-5987; Fax: (507) 457-1722

Full-time: 547 men, 661 women	**Faculty:** 94; IIA, --$
Part-time: 16 men, 27 women	**Ph.Ds:** 66%
Graduate: 1184 men, 2358 women	**Student/Faculty:** 13 to 1
Year: semesters	**Tuition:** $18,137
Application Deadline: May 1	**Room & Board:** $5720
Freshman Class: 1048 applied, 873 accepted, 311 enrolled	
SAT Verbal/Math: 570/580*	**ACT:** 22 **VERY COMPETITIVE**

Saint Mary's University of Minnesota, founded in 1912, is a private liberal arts college affiliated with the Catholic Church, offering a traditional liberal arts and sciences curriculum combined with career preparation. There are 4 undergraduate schools and 1 graduate school. In addition to regional accreditation, SMU has baccalaureate program accreditation with IACBE and NASM. The library contains 176,236 volumes, 140,000 microform items, and 8419 audio/video tapes/CDs/DVDs, and subscribes to 14,447 periodicals including electronic. Computerized library services include the card catalog, interlibrary loans, database searching, and Internet access. Special learning facilities include a learning resource center, art gallery, radio station, observatory, and natural resource center. The 400-acre campus is in a small town 110 miles southeast of the Twin Cities, and 275 miles northwest of Chicago. Including any residence halls, there are 55 buildings.

Student Life: 60% of undergraduates are from Minnesota. Others are from 26 states and 8 foreign countries. 70% are from public schools. 84% are white. 61% are Catholic; 24% Muslim, Buddhist, and other Christian; 14% Protestant. The average age of freshmen is 19; all undergraduates, 20. 25% do not continue beyond their first year; 63% remain to graduate.

Housing: 1103 students can be accommodated in college housing, which includes single-sex and coed dorms and on-campus apartments. In addition there are first year and substance-free residence halls. On-campus housing is guaranteed for all 4 years and is available on a lottery system for upperclassmen. 82% of students live on campus. All students may keep cars.

Activities: 6% of men belong to 2 national fraternities; 3% of women belong to 1 national sorority. There are 80 groups on campus, including art, band, choir, chorale, chorus, dance, drama, ethnic, gay, honors, international, jazz band, literary magazine, musical theater, newspaper, political, professional, radio and TV, religious, social, social service, sports, student government, and yearbook. Popular campus events include Cardinal Days, Family Weekend, and Finals Breakfast.

Sports: There are 10 intercollegiate sports for men and 11 for women, and 17 intramural sports for men and 15 for women. Facilities include 7 basketball courts, indoor tennis courts, an indoor ice arena, 4 racquetball courts, exercise and weight rooms, baseball, softball, and soccer fields, nordic ski trails, running trails, an indoor track, an indoor swimming pool, and a dance studio.

Disabled Students: 75% of the campus is accessible. Wheelchair ramps, elevators, special parking, specially equipped rest rooms, lowered drinking fountains, lowered telephones, special housing, and TDD phones are available.

Services: Counseling and information services are available, as is tutoring in most subjects. There is a reader service for the blind, and remedial math, reading, and writing.

Campus Safety and Security: Measures include 24-hour foot and vehicle patrol, self-defense education, security escort services, and informal discussions. There are pamphlets/posters/films, emergency telephones, and lighted pathways/sidewalks.

Programs of Study: SMU confers the B.A. degree. Master's and doctoral degrees are also awarded. Bachelor's degrees are awarded in BIOLOGICAL SCIENCE (biochemistry, biology/biological science, biophysics, and environmental biology), BUSINESS (accounting, electronic business, human resources, international business management, and marketing management), COMMUNICATIONS AND THE ARTS (art, French, literature, music business management, music performance, music technology, public relations, Spanish, theater design, and theater management), COMPUTER AND PHYSICAL SCIENCE (chemistry, computer science, and mathematics), EDUCATION (English, foreign languages, music, science, and social science), ENGINEERING AND ENVIRONMENTAL DESIGN (computer engineering and engineering physics), HEALTH PROFESSIONS (cytotechnology, medical technology, and nuclear medical technology), SOCIAL SCIENCE (early childhood studies, history, human services, law enforcement and corrections, pastoral studies, philosophy, political science/government, psychology, public administration, religious education, social science, sociology, theological studies, and youth ministry). Physics, theology, and education are the strongest academically. Business, social science, and biology are the largest.

Required: Students must have a 2.0 cumulative major GPA and complete a minimum of 122 semester credits, including at least 45 at the upper-division level. Students must complete a major program and the general education program.

Special: Students may cross-register with Winona State University. Internships, co-op programs, student teaching and study abroad, work-study programs, and a Washington semester are available. The university also offers dual and student-designed majors, nondegree study, pass/fail options, credit for life, military, and work experience, and an honors program that also serves as an alternative general education program. There are 13 national honor societies.

Faculty/Classroom: 60% of faculty are male; 40%, female. All both teach and do research. No introductory courses are taught by graduate students. The average class size in an introductory lecture is 20; in a laboratory, 13; and in a regular course, 15.

Admissions: 83% of the 2005-2006 applicants were accepted. The SAT scores for the 2005-2006 freshman class were: Verbal--11% below 500, 63% between 500 and 599, 16% between 600 and 700, and 11% above 700; Math--16% below 500, 37% between 500 and 599, 42% between 600 and 700, and 5% above 700. The ACT scores were 34% below 21, 27% between 21 and 23, 21% between 24 and 26, 10% between 27 and 28, and 8% above 28. 41% of the current freshmen were in the top fifth of their class; 61% were in the top two fifths. 9 freshmen graduated first in their class.

Requirements: The SAT or ACT is required. In addition, candidates for admission should have completed 4 units of English, 3 of natural sci-

ence, 3 of math, 2 of social studies, and 6 academic electives. Completion of 2 units of foreign language is recommended. SMU requires applicants to be in the upper 50% of their class. A GPA of 2.5 is required. AP and CLEP credits are accepted. Important factors in the admissions decision are advanced placement or honor courses, leadership record, and extracurricular activities record.

Procedure: Freshmen are admitted fall and spring. Entrance exams should be taken by the fall of the senior year. There are early admissions and deferred admissions plans. Applications should be filed by May 1 for fall entry and December 1 for spring entry, along with a $25 fee. Notification is sent on a rolling basis. Applications are accepted on-line.

Transfer: 60 transfer students enrolled in 2004-2005. Applicants must have a 2.0 GPA with at least 12 credits. 60 of 122 credits required for the bachelor's degree must be completed at SMU.

Visiting: There are regularly scheduled orientations for prospective students, including an interview, a tour, class visits, and lunch. There are guides for informal visits and visitors may sit in on classes and stay overnight. To schedule a visit, contact the Office of Admissions at (800) 635-8987, ext. 1700 or admissions@smumn.edu.

Financial Aid: In 2005-2006, 94% of all full-time freshmen and 88% of continuing full-time students received some form of financial aid. 59% of full-time freshmen and 58% of continuing full-time students received need-based aid. The average freshman award was $15,752. Need-based scholarships or need-based grants averaged $6789 ($20,704 maximum); need-based self-help aid (loans and jobs) averaged $3197 ($7925 maximum); and other non-need-based awards and non-need-based scholarships averaged $5678 ($15,000 maximum). 45% of undergraduates work part time. Average annual earnings from campus work are $1286. The average financial indebtedness of the 2005 graduate was $27,130. The FAFSA and the college's own financial statement are required. The priority date for freshman financial aid applications for fall entry is March 15. The deadline for filing freshman financial aid applications for fall entry is open.

International Students: There are 16 international students enrolled. The school actively recruits these students. They must score satisfactorily on the written TOEFL.

Computers: Wireless access is available. There are approximately 305 public computers available to the undergrad student population, spread among centrally located labs, library labs, residential hall public areas, and classrooms. All students may access the system any time. There are no time limits. The fee is $275.

Graduates: From July 1, 2004 to June 30, 2005, 242 bachelor's degrees were awarded. The most popular majors were marketing (9%), public relations (7%), and psychology (7%). In an average class, 1% graduate in 3 years or less, 52% graduate in 4 years or less, 62% graduate in 5 years or less, and 63% graduate in 6 years or less. 113 companies recruited on campus in 2004-2005. Of the 2004 graduating class, 14% were enrolled in graduate school within 1 year of graduation and 60% were employed.

Admissions Contact: Anthony M. Piscitiello, Vice President for Admission. A video is available. E-mail: admissions@smumn.edu Web: http://www.smumn.edu

SAINT OLAF COLLEGE
C-4

Northfield, MN 55057-1098
(507) 646-3025
(800) 800-3025; Fax: (507) 646-3832

Full-time: 1256 men, 1749 women	**Faculty:** 196; IIB, av$
Part-time: 30 men, 23 women	**Ph.D.s:** 93%
Graduate: none	**Student/Faculty:** 15 to 1
Year: 4-1-4, summer session	**Tuition:** $26,500
Application Deadline: February 1	**Room & Board:** $6300
Freshman Class: 2991 applied, 2183 accepted, 764 enrolled	
SAT Verbal/Math: 644/635*	**ACT:** 27 HIGHLY COMPETITIVE

St. Olaf College, founded in 1874, is a private liberal arts institution affiliated with the Evangelical Lutheran Church in America. In addition to regional accreditation, St. Olaf has baccalaureate program accreditation with CSWE, NASD, NASM, NAST, NCATE, and NLN. The 4 libraries contain 707,351 volumes, 9193 microform items, and 13,239 audio/video tapes/CDs/DVDs, and subscribe to 2538 periodicals including electronic. Computerized library services include the card catalog, interlibrary loans, database searching, Internet access, and laptop Internet portals. Special learning facilities include a learning resource center, art gallery, radio station, and 700 acres of land dedicated to natural habitat, sustainable agriculture, and conventional agriculture. The 300-acre campus is in a small town 35 miles south of Minneapolis/St. Paul. Including any residence halls, there are 57 buildings.

Student Life: 57% of undergraduates are from Minnesota. Others are from 48 states, 20 foreign countries, and Canada. 85% are from public schools. 85% are white. 67% are Protestant; 18% various and unknown; 13% Catholic. The average age of freshmen is 18; all undergraduates, 20. 8% do not continue beyond their first year; 78% remain to graduate.

Housing: 2688 students can be accommodated in college housing, which includes coed dorms. In addition, there are honors houses, language houses, and special-interest houses. On-campus housing is guaranteed for all 4 years. 96% of students live on campus; of those, 80% remain on campus on weekends. Alcohol is not permitted. No one may keep cars.

Activities: There are no fraternities or sororities. There are 117 groups on campus, including art, band, chess, choir, chorus, computers, dance, drama, drill team, ethnic, film, gay, honors, international, jazz band, literary magazine, musical theater, newspaper, opera, orchestra, pep band, photography, political, professional, radio and TV, religious, social, social service, student government, symphony, and yearbook. Popular campus events include Christmas Festival, Wellstock, and President's Ball.

Sports: There are 14 intercollegiate sports for men and 13 for women, and 16 intramural sports for men and 16 for women. Facilities include 2 athletic complexes, a field house with batting cages, a long jump pit, 5 indoor tennis courts, and a 6-lane indoor track, plus an upper level walking/running track, a fitness center, 45-foot climbing wall, a soccer pitch, and baseball diamonds, 2 weight rooms, a football field, an 8-lane all-weather track and field, a 9-hole Frisbee golf course, and practice and recreation space.

Disabled Students: 75% of the campus is accessible. Wheelchair ramps, elevators, special parking, specially equipped rest rooms, special class scheduling, lowered drinking fountains, lowered telephones, special housing, electric door openers, curb cuts, and a sling for swimming pool entry are available.

Services: Counseling and information services are available, as is tutoring in every subject. There is a reader service for the blind. Study sessions are available.

Campus Safety and Security: Measures include 24-hour foot and vehicle patrol, self-defense education, security escort services, and informal discussions. There are pamphlets/posters/films, emergency telephones, and lighted pathways/sidewalks. All residence halls are card access.

Programs of Study: St. Olaf confers B.A. and B.Mus. degrees. Bachelor's degrees are awarded in AGRICULTURE (environmental studies), BIOLOGICAL SCIENCE (biology/biological science), COMMUNICATIONS AND THE ARTS (art, art history and appreciation, classics, dance, dramatic arts, English, French, German, Greek, Latin, music, music performance, music theory and composition, Norwegian, Russian, Slavic languages, Spanish, and studio art), COMPUTER AND PHYSICAL SCIENCE (chemistry, computer science, mathematics, and physics), EDUCATION (music and social studies), HEALTH PROFESSIONS (exercise science and nursing), SOCIAL SCIENCE (American studies, Asian/American studies, classical/ancient civilization, economics, ethnic studies, family/consumer studies, Hispanic American studies, history, interdisciplinary studies, medieval studies, philosophy, political science/government, psychology, religion, religious music, Russian and Slavic studies, social work, sociology, and women's studies). English, psychology, and biology are the largest.

Required: In addition to the distribution requirements, students are required to demonstrate skills at an intermediate level in a foreign language, proficiency in English composition, to complete the phys ed requirement, and to have taken a 1/4-credit oral communication course and a 1-credit mathematical reasoning course. A first-year writing course is also required. Distribution requirements include courses in history, literature, art, science, human behavior, Bible and theology, multicultural studies, and ethical issues. A minimum of 24 full-course credits out of 35 must be graded, 18 must be upper-division. A minimum of 8 full-credit courses in a disciplinary or interdisciplinary major are required. All majors include writing requirements. Students must complete 35 credits and maintain a minimum GPA of 2.0.

Special: St. Olaf offers cross-registration with Carleton College, study abroad in 42 countries, a Washington semester, preprofessional programs, internships, and a 3-2 B.A.-B.S.E. degree in engineering with Washington University in St. Louis or the University of Minnesota. There are dual majors, nondegree study, on-campus work-study, and pass/fail options. The Center for Integrative Studies allows students to design individual majors with an emphasis on tutorials and seminars. There are 18 national honor societies, including Phi Beta Kappa.

Faculty/Classroom: 55% of faculty are male; 45%, female. All both teach and do research. The average class size in an introductory lecture is 27; in a laboratory, 19; and in a regular course, 24.

Admissions: 73% of the 2005-2006 applicants were accepted. The mean SAT scores for the 2005-2006 freshman class were: Verbal--4% below 500, 24% between 500 and 599, 42% between 600 and 700, and 30% above 700; Math--5% below 500, 27% between 500 and 599, 44% between 600 and 700, and 24% above 700. The ACT scores were 2% below 18, 14% between 18 and 23, 56% between 24 and 29, and 28% above 29. 71% of the current freshmen were in the top fifth of their class; 91% were in the top two fifths. There were 40 National Merit finalists and 53 semifinalists. 88 freshmen graduated first in their class.

Requirements: The SAT or ACT is required. In addition, it is recommended that applicants completed 4 years of English, 3 to 4 of math and social studies/history, and 2 to 3 of science (2 labs) and a foreign language. A GPA of 3.0 is required. AP credits are accepted.

Procedure: Freshmen are admitted fall, winter, and spring. Entrance exams should be taken in the spring of the junior year or the fall of the senior year. There are early action, early admissions, and deferred admissions plans. There is a rolling admissions plan. Early decision applications should be filed by November 15; regular applications, by February 1 for fall entry, along with a $35 fee. Notification of early decision is sent December 6; regular decision, on a rolling basis. 85 early action candidates were accepted for the 2005-2006 class. 88 applicants were on the 2005 waiting list; 17 were admitted. Applications are accepted on-line.

Transfer: 44 transfer students enrolled in 2004-2005. Applicants must have a 3.0 GPA at their previous institution. 17 of 35 credits required for the bachelor's degree must be completed at St. Olaf.

Visiting: There are regularly scheduled orientations for prospective students, consisting of information sessions in an open house format. There are guides for informal visits and visitors may sit in on classes and stay overnight. To schedule a visit, contact Anne Donahue, Visit Coordinator at *admissions@stolaf.edu.*

Financial Aid: In 2005-2006, 79% of all full-time freshmen and 73% of continuing full-time students received some form of financial aid. 62% of all full-time students received need-based aid. Need-based scholarships or need-based grants averaged $15,105 ($31,100 maximum), and need-based self-help aid (loans and jobs) averaged $5572 ($15,500 maximum). 61% of undergraduates work part time. Average annual earnings from campus work are $1151. The average financial indebtedness of the 2005 graduate was $19,410. St. Olaf is a member of CSS. The CSS/Profile or FAFSA and St. Olaf noncustodial parent's statement are required. The priority date for freshman financial aid applications for fall entry is December 1. The deadline for filing freshman financial aid applications for fall entry is February 1.

International Students: There are 35 international students enrolled. The school actively recruits these students. They must score satisfactorily on the TOEFL.

Computers: Wireless access is available. St. Olaf students may access the college network, the Internet, and Internet 2 (a high-speed research network) from more than 800 student-accessible computers or from their own PCs in residence hall rooms. Students can also connect labtops to the campus wireless network at numerous locations on campus, including some residence halls, the library, student commons, and academic buildings. All students may access the system. There are no time limits and no fees.

Graduates: From July 1, 2004 to June 30, 2005, 689 bachelor's degrees were awarded. The most popular majors were English (10%), psychology (9%), and biology (8%). In an average class, 78% graduate in 4 years or less, 83% graduate in 5 years or less, and 84% graduate in 6 years or less. 107 companies recruited on campus in 2004-2005. Of the 2004 graduating class, 29% were enrolled in graduate school within 6 months of graduation and 56% were employed.

Admissions Contact: Michael Kyle, Director of Admissions.
E-mail: *admissions@stolaf.edu* Web: *http://www.stolaf.edu/admissions/*

SOUTHWEST MINNESOTA STATE UNIVERSITY B-4
Marshall, MN 56258
(507) 537-6286
(800) 642-0684; Fax: (507) 537-7154

Full-time: 1060 men, 1249 women	**Faculty:** 127; IIB, av$
Part-time: 148 men, 235 women	**Ph.D.s:** 76%
Graduate: 156 men, 365 women	**Student/Faculty:** 18 to 1
Year: semesters, summer session	**Tuition:** $5855
Application Deadline: August 15	**Room & Board:** $5120
Freshman Class: n/av	
ACT: 22	**COMPETITIVE**

Southwest Minnesota State University, founded in 1963, is a public institution offering programs in liberal arts, technology, and preprofessional training. In addition to regional accreditation, SMSU has baccalaureate program accreditation with ACS and CSWE. The library contains 168,000 volumes, 228,000 microform items, and 12,000 audio/video tapes/CDs/DVDs, and subscribes to 950 periodicals including electronic. Computerized library services include the card catalog, interlibrary loans, database searching, Internet access, and laptop Internet portals. Special learning facilities include a learning resource center, art gallery, natural history museum, planetarium, radio station, and TV station. The 216-acre campus is in a rural area 150 miles southwest of Minneapolis. Including any residence halls, there are 24 buildings.

Student Life: 75% of undergraduates are from Minnesota. Others are from 29 states, 33 foreign countries, and Canada. 95% are from public schools. 85% are white. The average age of freshmen is 19; all undergraduates, 22. 25% do not continue beyond their first year; 35% remain to graduate.

Housing: 1182 students can be accommodated in college housing, which includes single-sex and coed dorms and on-campus apartments. In addition, there are special-interest houses, a quiet house, a reduced quiet house, and a weekend programming house. On-campus housing is guaranteed for the freshman year only. Alcohol is not permitted. All students may keep cars.

Activities: There are no fraternities or sororities. There are 100 groups on campus, including art, band, cheerleading, chess, choir, chorus, computers, dance, debate, drama, ethnic, forensics, honors, international, jazz band, literary magazine, marching band, musical theater, newspaper, orchestra, pep band, political, professional, radio and TV, religious, social, social service, student government, and symphony. Popular campus events include Martin Luther King Celebration, Cinco de Mayo, and Dakota Indigenous Nations Studies Conference.

Sports: There are 5 intercollegiate sports for men and 6 for women, and 14 intramural sports for men and 13 for women. Facilities include a 2,000-seat gym, a baseball complex, softball facilities, racquetball courts, a football stadium, wrestling rooms, a weight room, an Olympic-size pool, a 3800-seat mulitipurpose facility, a soccer field, and a fitness center.

Disabled Students: 98% of the campus is accessible. Wheelchair ramps, elevators, special parking, specially equipped rest rooms, special class scheduling, lowered drinking fountains, lowered telephones, and special housing are available.

Services: Counseling and information services are available, as is tutoring in most subjects. There is a reader service for the blind, and remedial math, reading, and writing.

Campus Safety and Security: Measures include 24-hour foot and vehicle patrol, self-defense education, security escort services, and informal discussions. There are pamphlets/posters/films, emergency telephones, and lighted pathways/sidewalks.

Programs of Study: SMSU confers B.A., B.S., and B.A.S. degrees. Associate and master's degrees are also awarded. Bachelor's degrees are awarded in AGRICULTURE (agricultural business management), BIOLOGICAL SCIENCE (biology/biological science), BUSINESS (accounting, business administration and management, hotel/motel and restaurant management, and marketing/retailing/merchandising), COMMUNICATIONS AND THE ARTS (art, communications, creative writing, dramatic arts, literature, music, and Spanish), COMPUTER AND PHYSICAL SCIENCE (applied science, chemistry, computer science, and mathematics), EDUCATION (art, early childhood, elementary, foreign languages, health, mathematics, music, physical, and science), ENGINEERING AND ENVIRONMENTAL DESIGN (environmental science), HEALTH PROFESSIONS (dental laboratory technology and medical technology), SOCIAL SCIENCE (history, interdisciplinary studies, law enforcement and corrections, political science/government, psychology, public administration, social work, and sociology). Education, business administration, and psychology are the largest.

Required: To graduate, students must complete at least 128 semester credit hours, a minimum of 27 of which must be at the 300 or 400 level, and a liberal arts core curriculum, with a minimum GPA of 2.0.

Special: SMSU has cooperative programs with various local colleges, cross-registration with several state universities, and an accelerated degree. SMSU also offers internships in every discipline, work-study programs, student-designed and interdisciplinary majors including speech communication and theater arts, nondegree study, pass/fail options, and credit for life, military, and work experience. There are 2 national honor societies and a freshman honors program.

Faculty/Classroom: 56% of faculty are male; 44%, female. All teach undergraduates. The average class size in an introductory lecture is 26; in a laboratory, 19; and in a regular course, 21.

Admissions: 82% of the 2005-2006 applicants were accepted. The ACT scores for the 2005-2006 freshman class were: 49% below 21, 28% between 21 and 23, 15% between 24 and 26, 4% between 27 and 28, and 4% above 28. 3 freshmen graduated first in their class.

Requirements: The ACT is required and the SAT is recommended. The ACT is preferred, with a composite score of 21. Admission is based on class rank or ACT/SAT composite. Students should be graduates of an accredited secondary school or have a GED certificate. An interview is recommended. SMSU requires applicants to be in the upper 50% of their class. AP and CLEP credits are accepted. Important factors in the admissions decision are recommendations by school officials, leadership record, and personality/intangible qualities.

Procedure: Freshmen are admitted to all sessions. Entrance exams should be taken during the junior or senior year. There are deferred admissions and rolling admissions plans. Applications should be filed by August 15 for fall entry and January 10 for spring entry, along with a $20 fee. Notification is sent on a rolling basis. Applications are accepted on-line.

Transfer: 230 transfer students enrolled in 2004-2005. Applicants need a minimum GPA of 2.0 in previous college-level work at an accredited institution. High school transcripts are required if students are transferring with fewer than 24 semester credits. 48 of 128 credits required for the bachelor's degree must be completed at SMSU.

Visiting: There are regularly scheduled orientations for prospective students. There are guides for informal visits and visitors may sit in on classes and stay overnight. To schedule a visit, contact the Admissions Office.

Financial Aid: In 2005-2006, 83% of all full-time students received some form of financial aid. 54% of full-time freshmen and 58% of continuing full-time students received need-based aid. The average freshman award was $8502. Need-based scholarships or need-based grants averaged $4710; need-based self-help aid (loans and jobs) averaged $2834 ($7125 maximum); non-need-based athletic scholarships averaged $2291 ($14,180 maximum); and other non-need-based awards and non-need-based scholarships averaged $4184 ($14,180 maximum). 30% of undergraduates work part time. Average annual earnings from campus work are $1415. The average financial indebtedness of the 2005 graduate was $16,202. The FAFSA and the college's own financial statement are required. The priority date for freshman financial aid applications for fall entry is March 1. The deadline for filing freshman financial aid applications for fall entry is May 1.

International Students: There are 188 international students enrolled. The school actively recruits these students. A satisfactory score is required on the written TOEFL.

Computers: Wireless access is available. The library has 2 classroom/labs with computer workstations for each student and projection-ready instruction stations. All students may access the system 24 hours per day. There are no time limits. The fee is $7 per credit.

Graduates: From July 1, 2004 to June 30, 2005, 414 bachelor's degrees were awarded. The most popular majors were business and public affairs (34%), education (28%), and social science (16%). In an average class, 64% graduate in 4 years, 86% graduate in 5 years, and 25% graduate in 6 years. 15 companies recruited on campus in 2004-2005. Of the 2004 graduating class, 10% were enrolled in graduate school within 6 months of graduation and 96% were employed.

Admissions Contact: Richard Shearer, Director of Enrollment.
E-mail: *shearerr@southwestmsu.edu* Web: *www.southwestmsu.edu*

UNIVERSITY OF MINNESOTA SYSTEM

The University of Minnesota System, established in 1851, is a public system in Minnesota. It is governed by a board of regents, whose chief administrator is the President. The primary goal of the system is teaching, research, and public service. The main priorities are undergraduate education, basic and applied research, and graduate education. The total enrollment is usually about 73,000, with 3400 faculty members. Altogether there are some 236 baccalaureate, 191 master's, and 123 doctoral programs offered in University of Minnesota System. 4-year campuses are located in Duluth,, Morris,, and Twin Cities. Profiles of the 4-year campuses are included in this section.

UNIVERSITY OF MINNESOTA/CROOKSTON   A-2
Crookston, MN 56716-5001   (218) 281-8569
(800) 232-6466; Fax: (218) 281-8050

Full-time: 966 men and women	Faculty: 51; IIB, av$
Part-time: 1168 men and women	Ph.Ds: 51%
Graduate: none	Student/Faculty: 19 to 1
Year: semesters	Tuition: $8119
Application Deadline: open	Room & Board: $5038
Freshman Class: 415 applied, 365 accepted, 198 enrolled	
SAT Verbal/Math: 475/460*	ACT: 21 LESS COMPETITIVE

University of Minnesota/Crookston, founded in 1965, is a public institution offering undergraduate degrees in agriculture, business, education, health, and hotel, restaurant, and institutional management. In addition to regional accreditation, UMC has baccalaureate program accreditation with AACSB and ADA. The library contains 33,366 volumes, 4639 microform items, and 1498 audio/video tapes/CDs/DVDs, and subscribes to 16,513 periodicals including electronic. Computerized library services include the card catalog, interlibrary loans, database searching, Internet access, and laptop Internet portals. Special learning facilities include a learning resource center. The 237-acre campus is in a small town 25 miles from Grand Forks, North Dakota. Including any residence halls, there are 32 buildings.

Student Life: 67% of undergraduates are from Minnesota. Others are from 12 states, 6 foreign countries, and Canada. 90% are white. The average age of freshmen is 18; all undergraduates, 24. 37% do not continue beyond their first year; 36% remain to graduate.

Housing: 436 students can be accommodated in college housing, which includes coed dorms and on-campus apartments. On-campus housing is available on a first-come, first-served basis. Priority is given to out-of-town students. 64% of students commute. Alcohol is not permitted. All students may keep cars.

Activities: 1% of men belong to 1 national fraternity; 1% of women belong to 1 national sorority. There are 45 groups on campus, including cheerleading, chess, choir, chorale, chorus, computers, drama, ethnic, gay, honors, international, newspaper, opera, pep band, political, religious, social, social service, student government, and yearbook.

Sports: There are 5 intercollegiate sports for men and 7 for women, and 8 intramural sports for men and 8 for women. Facilities include a 3200-seat gym; and indoor complex with basketball/volleyball and racquetball courts, a training room with a sauna, and a fitness center; a lit football field surrounded by an all-weather track; tennis courts; and soccer, baseball, and softball fields.

Disabled Students: 95% of the campus is accessible. Wheelchair ramps, elevators, special parking, specially equipped rest rooms, special class scheduling, lowered drinking fountains, lowered telephones, and special housing are available.

Services: Counseling and information services are available, as is tutoring in most subjects. There is a reader service for the blind, and remedial math, reading, and writing. The Academic Assistance Center also provides help with study strategies and English as a second language, and federally funded Student Support Services are available to those who are eligible.

Campus Safety and Security: Measures include self-defense education, security escort services, informal discussions, and pamphlets/posters/films. There are emergency telephones and lighted pathways/sidewalks.

Programs of Study: UMC confers B.S., B.A.H., B.M.M. degrees. Associate degrees are also awarded. Bachelor's degrees are awarded in AGRICULTURE (agricultural business management, animal science, equine science, natural resource management, plant protection (pest management), and plant science), BUSINESS (accounting, business administration and management, hotel/motel and restaurant management, and sports management), COMMUNICATIONS AND THE ARTS (communications), COMPUTER AND PHYSICAL SCIENCE (information sciences and systems and software engineering), EDUCATION (agricultural and early childhood), ENGINEERING AND ENVIRONMENTAL DESIGN (applied aviation and industrial administration/management), HEALTH PROFESSIONS (health care administration, health science, physical therapy, predentistry, premedicine, prepharmacy, and preveterinary science). Business management, natural resources, and equine industries management are the largest.

Special: UMC offers cross-registration with other University of Minnesota campuses, study abroad through more than 300 study, work, and internship programs in 67 countries, and student-designed majors, through the applied studies bachelor of science degree program. There is 1 national honor society and a freshman honors program.

Faculty/Classroom: 64% of faculty are male; 36%, female. All teach undergraduates. The average class size in an introductory lecture is 25; in a laboratory, 18; in a regular course, 25.

Admissions: 88% of the 2005-2006 applicants were accepted. The SAT scores for the 2005-2006 freshman class were: Verbal--50% below 500, 10% between 500 and 599, and 40% between 600 and 700; Math--56% below 500, 33% between 500 and 599, and 11% between 600 and 700. The ACT scores were 46% below 21, 29% between 21 and 23, 17% between 24 and 26, 4% between 27 and 28, and 4% above 28. 25% of the current freshmen were in the top fifth of their class; 49% were in the top two fifths.

Requirements: The ACT is required. Students must be in the upper half of their graduating class or have a satisfactory score on the ACT. Students who do not meet either of these requirements are considered using a combination of high school rank, GPA, test scores, high school curriculum, and other indicators of academic potential. AP and CLEP credits are accepted.

Procedure: Freshmen are admitted fall and spring. Entrance exams should be taken by July 15 for all admission. There is a rolling admissions and deferred admissions plan. Application deadlines are open notification is sent beginning October 15. The application fee is $30. Applications are accepted on-line.

Transfer: 107 transfer students enrolled in 2004-2005. Students who have attempted 26 or more semester credits of college work are eligible for admission with advanced standing. Students are eligible for admission if they have a cumulative GPA of 2.0 in their previous college work. Students who do not meet this standard are considered through an individual review process. 30 of 120 credits required for the bachelor's degree must be completed at UMC.

Visiting: There are regularly scheduled orientations for prospective students including twice-daily tours. There are guides for informal visits and visitors may sit in on classes and stay overnight. To schedule a visit, contact the Admissions Office.

Financial Aid: In 2005-2006, 73% of all full-time freshmen and 70% of continuing full-time students received some form of financial aid. 65% of full-time freshmen and 58% of continuing full-time students received need-based aid. Need-based scholarships or need-based grants averaged $4802; and other non-need-based awards and non-need-based scholarships averaged $3052. Average annual earnings from campus work was $900. The average financial indebtedness of the 2005 graduate was $14,521. The FAFSA is required. The priority date for freshman financial aid applications for fall entry is March 31.

International Students: There are 30 international students enrolled. The school actively recruits these students. They must score satisfactorily on the TOEFL.

Computers: Wireless access is available. Every UMC student is provided with a labtop computer for his or her use 24 hours a day, 7 days a week, in or out of the classroom. Students use their computer to manage their schedules, conduct and analyze research, study, communicate with professionals on and off campus, and develop and deliver multimedia

presentations. All students may access the system. There are no time limits and no fees.

Graduates: From July 1, 2004 to June 30, 2005, 231 bachelor's degrees were awarded. The most popular majors were business management (19%), natural resources (15%), and information technology management (10%). In an average class, 4% graduate in 3 years or less, 22% graduate in 4 years or less, 35% graduate in 5 years or less, and 39% graduate in 6 years or less. 33 companies recruited on campus in 2004-2005. Of the 2004 graduating class, 4% were enrolled in graduate school within 6 months of graduation and 77% were employed.

Admissions Contact: Rick Eber, Director of Admissions.
E-mail: *Info@UMCrookston.edu*
Web: *http://www.umcrookston.edu/people/admissions/*

UNIVERSITY OF MINNESOTA/DULUTH   D-3
Duluth, MN 55812-2496   (218) 726-7171
                                    (800) 232-1339; Fax: (218) 726-6394

Full-time: 4280 men, 4113 women	**Faculty:** 407; IIA, av$
Part-time: 584 men, 561 women	**Ph.D.s:** 76%
Graduate: 489 men, 469 women	**Student/Faculty:** 21 to 1
Year: semesters, summer session	**Tuition:** $8428 ($19,628)
Application Deadline: August 1	**Room & Board:** $5546
Freshman Class: 6989 applied, 5522 accepted, 2164 enrolled	
ACT: 23	**COMPETITIVE**

The University of Minnesota Duluth, founded in 1947, is a liberal arts institution offering undergraduate and graduate programs as a campus of the University of Minnesota. There are 5 undergraduate and 2 graduate schools. In addition to regional accreditation, UMD has baccalaureate program accreditation with ABET, ASLA, CSAB, CSWE, NASM, and NCATE. The library contains 705,000 volumes, 750,000 microform items, and 14,000 audio/video tapes/CDs/DVDs, and subscribes to 2737 periodicals including electronic. Computerized library services include the card catalog, interlibrary loans, database searching, Internet access, and laptop Internet portals. Special learning facilities include a learning resource center, art gallery, planetarium, radio station, TV station, and performing arts centers (theatre and music). The 244-acre campus is in a suburban area 150 miles north of Minneapolis and St. Paul. Including any residence halls, there are 52 buildings.

Student Life: 87% of undergraduates are from Minnesota. Others are from 28 states, 31 foreign countries, and Canada. 95% are from public schools. 89% are white. The average age of freshmen is 18; all undergraduates, 22. 25% do not continue beyond their first year; 38% remain to graduate.

Housing: 3081 students can be accommodated in college housing, which includes single-sex and coed dormitories and on-campus apartments. On-campus housing is available on a first-come, first-served basis and is available on a lottery system for upperclassmen. 70% of students commute. Alcohol is not permitted. All students may keep cars.

Activities: 1% of men belong to 2 local and 2 national fraternities; 1% of women belong to 2 local and 1 national sorority. There are 150 groups on campus, including band, chamber orchestra, cheerleading, chess, choir, chorale, chorus, dance, drama, ethnic, gay, honors, international, jazz band, jazz chior, jazz ensemble, musical theater, opera, orchestra, pep band, political, professional, radio and TV, religious, social, social service, student government, and wind ensemble. Popular campus events include Winter Festival, Black History Month, and Hispanic Heritage Month.

Sports: There are 7 intercollegiate sports for men and 8 for women, and 16 intramural sports for men and 16 for women. Facilities include a multipurpose ice center, a football and track-and-field stadium, a baseball park, softball and soccer fields, a field house for track and tennis, and a gym for basketball and volleyball, as well as a nearby country club for cross-country and golf.

Disabled Students: All of the campus is accessible. Wheelchair ramps, elevators, special parking, specially equipped rest rooms, lowered drinking fountains, lowered telephones, and special housing are available.

Services: Counseling and information services are available, as is tutoring in some subjects, including math, business, economics, sciences, accounting, computer science, and writing. There is a reader service for the blind and remedial math and writing. Workshops and seminars are also offered on study skills, note taking, time management, test-taking strategies, and goal setting.

Campus Safety and Security: Measures include 24-hour foot and vehicle patrol, self-defense education, security escort services, informal discussions, and pamphlets/posters/films. There are emergency telephones and lighted pathways/sidewalks.

Programs of Study: UMD confers B.A., B.S., B.A.A., B.Ac., B.A.S., B.B.A., B.Ch.E., B.E.C.E., B.F.A., B.I.E., B.M., B.S.CH.E., B.S.E.C.E, and B.S.I.E. degrees. Master's degrees are also awarded. Bachelor's degrees are awarded in BIOLOGICAL SCIENCE (biology/biological science), BUSINESS (business administration and management), COMMUNICATIONS AND THE ARTS (art, communications, dramatic arts, English, graphic design, jazz, music, music performance, and Spanish),

COMPUTER AND PHYSICAL SCIENCE (chemistry, computer science, earth science, geology, mathematics, and physics), EDUCATION (art, athletic training, elementary, English, foreign languages, health, mathematics, music, physical, recreation, science, and social studies), ENGINEERING AND ENVIRONMENTAL DESIGN (chemical engineering, computer engineering, electrical/electronics engineering, environmental science, and industrial engineering), HEALTH PROFESSIONS (speech pathology/audiology), SOCIAL SCIENCE (anthropology, criminology, early childhood studies, economics, geography, history, interdisciplinary studies, international studies, Native American studies, philosophy, political science/government, psychology, sociology, urban studies, and women's studies). Business, sciences, and engineering are the strongest academically. Business administration, communication, and biology are the largest.

Required: To graduate, students must complete 120 to 136 semester credits, including 2 courses in college writing and a liberal education distribution of at least 35 credits in 10 academic areas. At least 4 credits of course work must emphasize cultural diversity, and 4 should emphasize an international perspective.

Special: Students may study abroad in England, Sweden, Finland, and Australia. UMD also offers a 3-2 engineering degree with the University of Minnesota Twin Cities, cross-registration with the College of St. Scholastica and the University of Wisconsin/Superior, internships, work-study programs, a B.A.-B.S. degree in several fields, dual degrees such as biochemistry and molecular biology, student-designed majors, and nondegree study. There are 6 national honor societies, including Phi Beta Kappa, a freshman honors program, and 17 departmental honors programs.

Faculty/Classroom: 57% of faculty are male; 43%, female. All teach undergraduates. No introductory courses are taught by graduate students.

Admissions: 79% of the 2005-2006 applicants were accepted. The ACT scores for the 2005-2006 freshman class were: 12% below 21, 48% between 21 and 23, 24% between 24 and 26, 13% between 27 and 28, and 3% above 28. 29% of the current freshmen were in the top fifth of their class; 66% were in the top two fifths. 70 freshmen graduated first in their class.

Requirements: The ACT is required and the SAT is recommended. The ACT Optional Writing test is also required. In addition, applicants must have completed 4 years in English, 3 each in math and sciences, and 2 each in a single second language and social studies. Course work in the visual and performing arts and computer skills is recommended. Students with a GED certificate will be admitted selectively as space permits. UMD requires applicants to be in the upper 60% of their class. AP and CLEP credits are accepted. Important factors in the admissions decision are advanced placement or honor courses, recommendations by school officials, and evidence of special talent.

Procedure: Freshmen are admitted to all sessions. Entrance exams should be taken at the end of the junior year or the beginning of the senior year. There is a rolling admissions plan. Applications should be filed by August 1 for fall entry and November 15 for spring entry. Notification is sent on a rolling basis. The fall 2005 application fee was $35.

Transfer: 409 transfer students enrolled in a recent year. Applicants who have completed 26 or more semester credits must have a minimum 2.0 GPA and a 75% completion ratio; applicants who have attempted fewer than 26 semester credits must have a high school rank at or above the 50th percentile, a 1.8 GPA in their previous college work, and a 75% completion ratio. 30 of 120 credits required for the bachelor's degree must be completed at UMD.

Visiting: There are regularly scheduled orientations for prospective students, including a campus tour and an appointment with admissions counselors, faculty, or coaches, if requested. There are guides for informal visits and visitors may sit in on classes. To schedule a visit, contact the Admissions Office.

Financial Aid: In 2005-2006, 81% of all full-time freshmen received some form of financial aid. 7% of undergraduates work part time. The FAFSA is required. The deadline for filing freshman financial aid applications for fall entry is March 31.

International Students: The school actively recruits these students. They must score satisfactorily on the written TOEFL.

Computers: All students may access the system 8 A.M. to 12 P.M. weekdays; Saturday and Sunday hours are also available. There are no time limits. The fee is $2 per credit.

Graduates: The most popular majors were business administration (18%), communication (18%), and criminology (10%). In an average class, 5% graduate in 3 years or less, 19% graduate in 4 years or less, 17% graduate in 5 years or less, and 5% graduate in 6 years or less. 60 companies recruited on campus in 2004-2005.

Admissions Contact: Beth Esselstrom, Director of Admissions.
E-mail: *umdadmis@d.umn.edu* Web: *http://www.d.umn.edu*

UNIVERSITY OF MINNESOTA/MORRIS — B-3

Morris, MN 56267-2199 (320) 589-6035
(888) UMM-EDUC; Fax: (320) 589-1673

Full-time: 722 men, 1121 women	Faculty: 145; IIB, -$
Part-time: none	Ph.D.s: 97%
Graduate: none	Student/Faculty: 13 to 1
Year: semesters, summer session	Tuition: $9722
Application Deadline: February 1	Room & Board: $5750
Freshman Class: 1106 applied, 863 accepted, 388 enrolled	
SAT Verbal/Math: 600/600*	ACT: 25 VERY COMPETITIVE

The University of Minnesota/Morris, founded in 1959, is a public liberal arts institution within the University of Minnesota system. In addition to regional accreditation, UMM has baccalaureate program accreditation with NCATE. The library contains 197,220 volumes, 221,216 microform items, and 2140 audio/video tapes/CDs/DVDs, and subscribes to 885 periodicals including electronic. Computerized library services include the card catalog, interlibrary loans, and database searching. Special learning facilities include a learning resource center, art gallery, radio station, TV station, language lab, observatory, and agricultural experiment station. The 130-acre campus is in a small town 150 miles northwest of Minneapolis. Including any residence halls, there are 36 buildings.

Student Life: 86% of undergraduates are from Minnesota. Others are from 27 states, 17 foreign countries, and Canada. 95% are from public schools. 79% are white. The average age of freshmen is 18; all undergraduates, 21. 18% do not continue beyond their first year; 60% remain to graduate.

Housing: 1032 students can be accommodated in college housing, which includes coed dorms and on-campus apartments. On-campus housing is guaranteed for all 4 years, is available on a first-come, first-served basis, and is available on a lottery system for upperclassmen. 60% of students live on campus; of those, 80% remain on campus on weekends. Alcohol is not permitted. All students may keep cars.

Activities: There are no fraternities or sororities. There are 100 groups on campus, including art, band, cheerleading, chess, choir, chorus, computers, dance, debate, drama, ethnic, forensics, gay, honors, international, jazz band, literary magazine, musical theater, newspaper, orchestra, photography, political, professional, radio and TV, religious, social, social service, student government, and yearbook. Popular campus events include Cultural Heritage Week, Diversity Jam, and Jazz Fest.

Sports: There are 6 intercollegiate sports for men and 10 for women, and 12 intramural sports for men and 12 for women. Facilities include a 4500-seat stadium, a phys ed center, 5 gyms, wrestling, exercise, and weight rooms, an Olympic-size pool, handball and racquetball courts, a track, fields for softball, baseball, soccer, and football, a diving well, a warm-water pool and slide, an indoor track, and a cardiovascular fitness room.

Disabled Students: 70% of the campus is accessible. Wheelchair ramps, elevators, special parking, specially equipped rest rooms, special class scheduling, lowered drinking fountains, a disability services coordinator, and special learning equipment and services through the academic assistance center are available.

Services: Counseling and information services are available, as is tutoring in every subject. There is a reader service for the blind, and remedial math, reading, and writing.

Campus Safety and Security: Measures include 24-hour foot and vehicle patrol, self-defense education, security escort services, and shuttle buses. There are informal discussions, pamphlets/posters/films, emergency telephones, and lighted pathways/sidewalks.

Programs of Study: UMM confers the B.A. degree. Bachelor's degrees are awarded in BIOLOGICAL SCIENCE (biology/biological science), BUSINESS (management science), COMMUNICATIONS AND THE ARTS (art history and appreciation, dramatic arts, English, French, German, music, Spanish, speech/debate/rhetoric, and studio art), COMPUTER AND PHYSICAL SCIENCE (chemistry, computer science, geology, mathematics, physics, and statistics), EDUCATION (elementary and secondary), HEALTH PROFESSIONS (premedicine), SOCIAL SCIENCE (anthropology, economics, European studies, history, Latin American studies, liberal arts/general studies, philosophy, political science/government, prelaw, psychology, social science, sociology, and women's studies). Psychology and sciences are the strongest academically. Education, English, and biology are the largest.

Required: In addition to 40 semester hours in the major, students are required to complete 60 credits of a general education curriculum, including courses in writing, computing, foreign language or equivalent, and advanced study, as well as courses focusing on the arts, the physical and abstract worlds, and the self and others. All first-year students participate in a freshman seminar and the cumulative of their major work is presented in the senior seminar, which is a requirement for all seniors.

Special: UMM offers work-study programs, internships, study abroad, dual majors, student-designed majors, nondegree study, pass/fail options, and credit for life, military, and work experience. There is a 3-2 engineering degree with the University of Minnesota at Twin Cities. A competitive, merit-based program that pairs students and professors in order to undertake creative projects is available. There is a freshman honors program. All department have honors programs.

Faculty/Classroom: 58% of faculty are male; 42%, female. All teach undergraduates and 89% both teach and do research. The average class size in an introductory lecture is 16; in a laboratory, 16; and in a regular course, 16.

Admissions: 78% of the 2005-2006 applicants were accepted. The SAT scores for the 2005-2006 freshman class were: Verbal--15% below 500, 35% between 500 and 599, 35% between 600 and 700, and 15% above 700; Math--12% below 500, 35% between 500 and 599, 40% between 600 and 700, and 13% above 700. The ACT scores were 10% below 21, 25% between 21 and 23, 36% between 24 and 26, 15% between 27 and 28, and 14% above 28. 59% of the current freshmen were in the top fifth of their class; 92% were in the top two fifths. In a recent year, there were 2 National Merit finalists and 7 semifinalists. 29 freshmen graduated first in their class.

Requirements: The SAT or ACT is required. The ACT Optional Writing test is also required. In addition, applicants should be graduates of an accredited secondary school or have a GED certificate. They must have completed 4 years of English, 3 each of math and science, 2 of a single foreign language, and 1 each of social studies and American history. A GPA of 3.0 is required. AP and CLEP credits are accepted. Important factors in the admissions decision are leadership record, extracurricular activities record, and advanced placement or honor courses.

Procedure: Freshmen are admitted fall and spring. Entrance exams should be taken before December 1 of the senior year. There is a deferred admissions and a rolling admissions plan. Early decision applications should be filed by December 1; regular applications, by February 1 for fall entry and March 15 for winter entry, along with a $35 fee. Notification of early decision is sent December 15; regular decision, on a rolling basis. Applications are accepted on-line.

Transfer: 82 transfer students enrolled in a recent year. Applicants must complete the application for admission, all college transcripts, and have maintained a minimum GPA of 2.5. 30 of 120 credits required for the bachelor's degree must be completed at UMM.

Visiting: There are regularly scheduled orientations for prospective students, including a campus tour, lunch with faculty, a session with admissions staff, and a student panel. There are guides for informal visits and visitors may sit in on classes and stay overnight. To schedule a visit, contact the Admissions Office at or *admissions@morris.umn.edu.*

Financial Aid: In a recent year, 61% of all full-time freshmen and 74% of continuing full-time students received some form of financial aid. 59% of full-time freshmen and 61% of continuing full-time students received need-based aid. The average freshman award was $9477. Need-based scholarships or need-based grants averaged $5669; need-based self-help aid (loans and jobs) averaged $4853; and other non-need-based awards and non-need-based scholarships averaged $2719. 78% of undergraduates work part time. Average annual earnings from campus work are $1065. The average financial indebtedness of the 2005 graduate was $15,194. The FAFSA is required. The priority date for freshman financial aid applications for fall entry is March 1.

International Students: There are 23 international students enrolled in a recent year. They must score satisfactorily on the TOEFL or take the SAT.

Computers: All students may access the system 24 hours per day. There are no time limits and no fees.

Graduates: In a recent year, 339 bachelor's degrees were awarded. The most popular majors were biology (12%), English (12%), and elementary education (10%). In an average class, 44% graduate in 4 years or less, 60% graduate in 5 years or less, and 67% graduate in 6 years or less. 72 companies recruited on campus in 2004-2005. Of the 2004 graduating class, 29% were enrolled in graduate school within 6 months of graduation and 71% were employed.

Admissions Contact: Jaime Moquin, Director of Admissions.
E-mail: *admissions@morris.umn.edu* Web: *http://www.morris.umn.edu*

UNIVERSITY OF MINNESOTA/TWIN CITIES C-4
Minneapolis, MN 55455

(612) 625-2008
(800) 752-1000; Fax: (612) 625-1693

Full-time: 12,277 men, 13,912 women	Faculty: 1680; 1, av$
Part-time: 1364 men, 1404 women	Ph.D.s: 90%
Graduate: 6870 men, 6823 women	Student/Faculty: 16 to 1
Year: semesters, summer session	Tuition: $7120 ($18,750)
Application Deadline: open	Room & Board: $6045
Freshman Class: 20,641 applied, 14,708 accepted, 5305 enrolled	
SAT Verbal/Math: 600/600*	ACT: 25 HIGHLY COMPETITIVE

University of Minnesota/Twin Cities, founded in 1851, is a land-grant institution offering programs in liberal and fine arts, physical and biological sciences, health sciences, education, natural resources, human ecology, business, agriculture, engineering, and professional training in law, medicine, dentistry, pharmacy, and veterinary medicine. The tuition figures in the above capsule are approximate. There are 18 undergraduate schools and 1 graduate school. In addition to regional accreditation, the universi-

ty has baccalaureate program accreditation with AACSB, ABET, ABFSE, ACEJMC, ADA, APTA, ASLA, CSWE, FIDER, NAAB, NASM, NCATE, NLN, and SAF. The 17 libraries contain 5.6 million volumes, 5.4 million microform items, and 500,000 audio/video tapes/CDs/DVDs, and subscribe to 48,105 periodicals including electronic. Computerized library services include the card catalog, interlibrary loans, and database searching. Special learning facilities include a learning resource center, art gallery, natural history museum, planetarium, radio station, and TV station. The 2000-acre campus is in an urban area within both Minneapolis and St. Paul. Including any residence halls, there are 205 buildings.

Student Life: 74% of undergraduates are from Minnesota. Others are from 50 states, 110 foreign countries, and Canada. 85% are from public schools. 54% are white. The average age of freshmen is 18; all undergraduates, 21. 13% do not continue beyond their first year; 61% remain to graduate.

Housing: 5636 students can be accommodated in college housing, which includes single-sex and coed dorms, on-campus apartments, off-campus apartments, married-student housing, fraternity houses, and sorority houses. In addition, there are honors houses, special-interest houses and cooperative housing. On-campus housing is guaranteed for the freshman year only, is available on a first-come, first-served basis, and is available on a lottery system for upperclassmen. 78% of students commute. Alcohol is not permitted. All students may keep cars.

Activities: There are 33 local fraternities and 18 local sororities. There are 525 groups on campus, including art, band, cheerleading, chess, choir, chorale, chorus, computers, dance, debate, drama, ethnic, film, gay, honors, international, jazz band, literary magazine, marching band, musical theater, newspaper, orchestra, pep band, photography, political, professional, radio and TV, religious, social, social service, student government, and symphony. Popular campus events include Campus Carnival.

Sports: There are 12 intercollegiate sports for men and 11 for women, and 16 intramural sports for men and 16 for women. Facilities include a domed stadium, 3 gyms, 2 field houses, a hockey rink, an Olympic-size aquatic center, and a student recreation center.

Disabled Students: 75% of the campus is accessible. Wheelchair ramps, elevators, special parking, specially equipped rest rooms, special class scheduling, lowered drinking fountains, lowered telephones, special housing, listening devices, TTY and volume-control phones, print enlargers, and adaptive computers are available. In addition, support groups and counselors provide assistance with all areas of university life and career planning.

Services: Counseling and information services are available, as is tutoring in every subject. There is a reader service for the blind, and remedial math, reading, and writing. There is also test proctoring, and sign language interpreters.

Campus Safety and Security: Measures include 24-hour foot and vehicle patrol, self-defense education, security escort services, and shuttle buses. There are informal discussions, pamphlets/posters/films, emergency telephones, lighted pathways/sidewalks, a 20-member university police force, and blue light phone centers.

Programs of Study: The university confers B.A., B.S., B.Aerospace Eng., B.Agr.Eng., B.C.E., B.Ch., B.Ch.E., B.Comp.Sci., B.E.E., B.F.A., B.G.E., B.I.S., B.M., B.Materials Sci., B.Mathematics, B.M.E., B.Pcs., B.S.Bus., B.S.G., B.S. in Astrophysics, B.S. in Geophysics, B.S.N., and B.Statistics degrees. Master's and doctoral degrees are also awarded. Bachelor's degrees are awarded in AGRICULTURE (agricultural business management, agricultural economics, fishing and fisheries, forestry and related sciences, forestry production and processing, and natural resource management), BIOLOGICAL SCIENCE (biochemistry, biology/biological science, botany, cell biology, ecology, evolutionary biology, genetics, microbiology, nutrition, physiology, and wildlife biology), BUSINESS (accounting, business administration and management, management science, marketing/retailing/merchandising, recreation and leisure services, recreational facilities management, and retailing), COMMUNICATIONS AND THE ARTS (art history and appreciation, Chinese, classical languages, dance, English, film arts, French, German, Greek, Hebrew, Italian, Japanese, languages, Latin, linguistics, music, Russian, Scandinavian languages, Spanish, speech/debate/rhetoric, and studio art), COMPUTER AND PHYSICAL SCIENCE (actuarial science, astronomy, astrophysics, chemistry, computer science, geology, geophysics and seismology, mathematics, physics, and statistics), EDUCATION (agricultural, art, bilingual/bicultural, business, early childhood, elementary, English, home economics, industrial arts, mathematics, music, physical, science, social studies, and teaching English as a second/foreign language (TESOL/TEFOL)), ENGINEERING AND ENVIRONMENTAL DESIGN (aeronautical engineering, agricultural engineering, architecture, chemical engineering, civil engineering, electrical/electronics engineering, environmental design, geological engineering, industrial engineering, interior design, landscape architecture/design, materials engineering, materials science, mechanical engineering, and metallurgical engineering), HEALTH PROFESSIONS (dental hygiene, medical laboratory technology, music therapy, nursing, occupational therapy, pharmacy, physical therapy, predentistry, premedicine, prepharmacy, preveterinary science, and speech pathology/audiology), SOCIAL SCIENCE (African American studies, African studies, American Indian studies, American studies, anthropology, child psychology/development, East Asian studies, economics, food science, geography, history, humanities, international relations, Mexican-American/Chicano studies, Middle Eastern studies, philosophy, political science/government, prelaw, psychology, Russian and Slavic studies, sociology, South Asian studies, textiles and clothing, urban studies, and women's studies). Chemical engineering, psychology, and economics are the strongest academically. Mechanical engineering, psychology, and electrical engineering are the largest.

Required: To graduate, students must complete 120 to 130 semester credits, including 45 in the major, with a minimum GPA of 2.0. Distribution requirements include course work in the 4 areas of communication, language, and symbolic systems, physical and biological sciences, the individual and society, and artistic expression. Other requirements vary by program.

Special: The university offers cooperative programs, cross-registration with the Minnesota Community College system, internships, study abroad in 65 countries, work-study programs both on and off campus, a B.A.-B.S. degree in all majors, a general studies degree, and dual and student-designed majors. Pass/fail options and credit for life, military, or work experience are available. There are 21 national honor societies, including Phi Beta Kappa, a freshman honors program, and 8 departmental honors programs.

Faculty/Classroom: 70% of faculty are male; 30%, female. All both teach and do research. The average class size in an introductory lecture is 29.

Admissions: 71% of the 2005-2006 applicants were accepted. The SAT scores for the 2005-2006 freshman class were: Verbal--12% below 500, 34% between 500 and 599, 41% between 600 and 700, and 13% above 700; Math--8% below 500, 28% between 500 and 599, 47% between 600 and 700, and 17% above 700. The ACT scores were 13% below 21, 20% between 21 and 23, 29% between 24 and 26, 17% between 27 and 28, and 21% above 28. 61% of the current freshmen were in the top fifth of their class; 91% were in the top two fifths.

Requirements: The SAT or ACT is required. In addition, the university uses a formula index in evaluating high school rank and ACT test scores. A portfolio is required for studio arts and architecture, an audition for music, and an interview for architecture and education. A high school diploma is required; the GED is accepted. AP and CLEP credits are accepted. Important factors in the admissions decision are advanced placement or honor courses, evidence of special talent, and leadership record.

Procedure: Freshmen are admitted to all sessions. Entrance exams should be taken by the end of the junior year or October/November/ December of the senior year. There are early admissions and deferred admissions plans. There is a rolling admissions plan. Application deadlines are open. Notificatin is sent on a rolling basis. Application fee is $45. Applications are accepted on-line.

Transfer: 1882 transfer students enrolled in 2004-2005. Admission requirements vary by major/program, with a minimum 2.2 GPA needed for consideration. College transcripts are required. 30 of 120 credits required for the bachelor's degree must be completed at the university.

Visiting: There are regularly scheduled orientations for prospective students. There are guides for informal visits and visitors may sit in on classes and stay overnight. To schedule a visit, contact The Visit Line at (612) 625-0000.

Financial Aid: In 2005-2006, 48% of all full-time students received some form of financial aid. At least 36% of full-time freshmen and 34% of continuing full-time students received need-based aid. The average freshman award was $11,075. Need-based scholarships or need-based grants averaged $6842; need-based self-help aid (loans and jobs) averaged $7159; and institutional non-need-based athletic scholarships averaged $3981. The FAFSA and the college's own financial statement are required.

International Students: Students must take the TOEFL or the MELAB, the college's own test, the Minnesota Battery, and the Institutional TOEFL. Residents of Minnesota and neighboring states must take the ACT, residents of other states must take the SAT.

Computers: All students may access the system 24 hours a day, 7 days a week. Students may access the system 2 hours per session if there are others waiting or signed on. The fee is $45 per quarter. It is strongly recommended that all students have a personal computer.

Graduates: From July 1, 2004 to June 30, 2005, 6088 bachelor's degrees were awarded. The most popular majors were business/marketing (35%), education (28%), and foreign languages and literature (18%). In an average class, 32% graduate in 4 years or less, 56% graduate in 5 years or less, and 61% graduate in 6 years or less.

Admissions Contact: Dr. Wayne Sigler, Director of Admissions. A video is available. E-mail: *admissions@tc.umn.edu.* Web: *www.umn.edu*

UNIVERSITY OF SAINT THOMAS C-4

St. Paul, MN 55105 (651) 962-6150
(800) 328-6819, ext. 2-6150; Fax: (651) 962-6160

Full-time: 2300 men, 2300 women	**Faculty:** 243; I, --$
Part-time: 300 men, 300 women	**Ph.D.s:** 84%
Graduate: 2800 men, 3000 women	**Student/Faculty:** 19 to 1
Year: 4-1-4, summer session	**Tuition:** $21,000
Application Deadline: open	**Room & Board:** $7000
Freshman Class: n/av	
SAT or ACT: required	**VERY COMPETITIVE**

The University of Saint Thomas, founded in 1885, is a private liberal arts institution affiliated with the Roman Catholic Church. There are 4 undergraduate and 9 graduate schools. Figures in the above capsule and in this profile are approximate. In addition to regional accreditation, Saint Thomas has baccalaureate program accreditation with ABET, ACS, CSWE, NASM, and NCATE. The 3 libraries contain 541,600 volumes, 980,800 microform items, and 5100 audio/video tapes/CDs/DVDs, and subscribe to 4800 periodicals including electronic. Computerized library services include the card catalog, interlibrary loans, and database searching. Special learning facilities include a learning resource center. The 78-acre campus is in an urban area 5 miles west of St. Paul and 5 miles east of Minneapolis. Including any residence halls, there are 74 buildings.

Student Life: 82% of undergraduates are from Minnesota. Others are from 44 states, 54 foreign countries, and Canada. 73% are from public schools. 89% are white. 53% are Catholic; 23% Protestant; 16% Muslim, Orthodox, Buddhist, Hindu, and other denominations. The average age of freshmen is 18; all undergraduates, 21. 15% do not continue beyond their first year; 85% remain to graduate.

Housing: 2000 students can be accommodated in college housing, which includes single-sex dorms, on-campus apartments, and off-campus apartments. In addition, there are special-interest houses and chemical-free, first-year experience, and women in science housing. On-campus housing is available on a first-come, first-served basis and is available on a lottery system for upperclassmen. 60% of students commute. All students may keep cars.

Activities: There are no fraternities or sororities. There are 94 groups on campus, including art, band, cheerleading, chess, choir, chorus, computers, dance, debate, drama, drill team, ethnic, gay, honors, international, jazz band, lecture committee, literary magazine, musical theater, newspaper, pep band, photography, political, professional, radio and TV, religious, social, social service, student government, student programming board, and yearbook. Popular campus events include Spring Fling, Taste of St. Thomas, and Senior Send-off.

Sports: There are 10 intercollegiate sports for men and 10 for women, and 10 intramural sports for men and 10 for women. Facilities include a field house with a 1/10-mile track, 5 volleyball courts, a 2000-seat gym, 4 basketball courts, 4 tennis courts, 6 racquetball courts, a fitness center, weight training and aerobics rooms, 2 swimming pools, 2 squash courts, a 5000-seat football and track stadium that includes an 8-lane Olympic caliber track, a baseball diamond, soccer, softball, and other playing fields, and 6 outdoor tennis courts.

Disabled Students: 80% of the campus is accessible. Wheelchair ramps, elevators, special parking, specially equipped rest rooms, special class scheduling, lowered drinking fountains, and lowered telephones are available.

Services: Counseling and information services are available, as is tutoring in most subjects. There is a reader service for the blind.

Campus Safety and Security: Measures include 24-hour foot and vehicle patrol, security escort services, shuttle buses, and informal discussions. There are pamphlets/posters/films, emergency telephones, and lighted pathways/sidewalks.

Programs of Study: Saint Thomas confers B.A., B.S., B.S.E., and B.S.M.E. degrees. Master's and doctoral degrees are also awarded. Bachelor's degrees are awarded in AGRICULTURE (environmental studies), BIOLOGICAL SCIENCE (biochemistry, biology/biological science, and neurosciences), BUSINESS (accounting, banking and finance, business administration and management, entrepreneurial studies, international business management, marketing management, personnel management, and real estate), COMMUNICATIONS AND THE ARTS (art history and appreciation, classical languages, communications, dramatic arts, English, French, German, journalism, Latin, literature, music, music business management, Russian, and Spanish), COMPUTER AND PHYSICAL SCIENCE (actuarial science, chemistry, computer science, geology, mathematics, and physics), EDUCATION (elementary, health, music, physical, science, and secondary), ENGINEERING AND ENVIRONMENTAL DESIGN (electrical/electronics engineering, environmental science, and mechanical engineering), HEALTH PROFESSIONS (community health work), SOCIAL SCIENCE (Christian studies, classical/ancient civilization, criminal justice, East Asian studies, economics, geography, history, international studies, peace studies, philosophy, political science/government, psychology, Russian and Slavic studies, social science, social studies, social work, sociology, theological studies, and women's studies). Business is the largest.

Required: All students must maintain a minimum GPA of 2.0 and complete at least 33 courses, or 132 semester credits, plus 1 in phys ed for no credit. Core curriculum requirements include 3 courses each in language and culture, faith and Catholic tradition, and natural science and mathematical and quantitative reasoning, 2 courses each in moral and philosophical reasoning and literature and writing, and 1 course each in fine arts, historical studies, social analysis, and human diversity. Students must complete 84 credits outside their major and demonstrate proficiency in operating a computer.

Special: Students may cross-register with Augsburg and Macalester Colleges, the College of Saint Catherine, and Hamline University. Study abroad is available in more than 40 countries, and there are several work-study programs. There are formal 3-2 engineering degree arrangements with Washington and Notre Dame Universities and the University of Minnesota, and 3-2 engineering degrees can also be arranged with many other accredited engineering programs. Nondegree study and pass/fail options also are available. There are 14 national honor societies and a freshman honors program.

Faculty/Classroom: 64% of faculty are male; 36%, female. 80% teach undergraduates and 20% do research. No introductory courses are taught by graduate students. The average class size in an introductory lecture is 24; in a laboratory, 15; and in a regular course, 21.

Admissions: 87% of recent applicants were accepted. The SAT scores for the 2005-2006 freshman class were: Verbal--15% below 500, 47% between 500 and 599, 27% between 600 and 700, and 10% above 700; Math--11% below 500, 46% between 500 and 599, 34% between 600 and 700, and 9% above 700. The ACT scores were 12% below 21, 32% between 21 and 23, 32% between 24 and 26, 12% between 27 and 28, and 12% above 28. 55% of recent freshmen were in the top fifth of their class; 75% were in the top two fifths. There were 11 National Merit finalists in a recent year. 41 freshmen graduated first in their class in a recent year.

Requirements: The SAT or ACT is required. In addition, saint Thomas recommends 4 units each of English, math (3 units of math required), and foreign language and 2 each of science and history or social sciences. An essay is required. The GED is accepted. AP and CLEP credits are accepted. Important factors in the admissions decision are recommendations by school officials, geographic diversity, and parents or siblings attending the school.

Procedure: Freshmen are admitted fall and spring. Entrance exams should be taken by the fall of the senior year. There is a deferred admissions plan. There is a rolling admissions plan. Application deadlines are open. Check eith the school for the current fee. Applications are accepted on-line.

Transfer: 246 transfer students enrolled in a recent year. Transfer applicants must have a minimum GPA of 2.3 in transferable college credits. 32 of 132 credits required for the bachelor's degree must be completed at Saint Thomas.

Visiting: There are regularly scheduled orientations for prospective students, consisting of an open house in fall and spring that includes an admissions counselor presentation, a tour, a faculty fair, lunch, and a financial aid presentation. Other smaller orientations are also available. There are guides for informal visits and visitors may sit in on classes and stay overnight. To schedule a visit, contact the Visit Coordinator at (651) 962-6154 or admvisit@stthomas.edu.

Financial Aid: In a recent year, 95% of all full-time freshmen and 87% of continuing full-time students received some form of financial aid. 48% of full-time freshmen and 49% of continuing full-time students received need-based aid. The average freshman award was $13,963. Need-based scholarships or need-based grants averaged $5527 ($30,698 maximum); need-based self-help aid (loans and jobs) averaged $2538 ($12,925 maximum); and other non-need-based awards and non-need-based scholarships averaged $2729 ($29,625 maximum). 53% of undergraduates work part time. Average annual earnings from campus work are $2460. The average financial indebtedness of a recent graduate was $23,084. The FAFSA is required. Check with the school for current deadlines.

International Students: They must score satisfactorily on the written TOEFL or take the MELAB.

Computers: All students may access the system any time. There are no time limits and no fees.

Graduates: In a recent year, 1151 bachelor's degrees were awarded. The most popular majors were business administration/marketing (43%), journalism/communications (9%), and social science/history (9%). In an average class, 1% graduate in 3 years or less, 62% graduate in 4 years or less, 74% graduate in 5 years or less, and 76% graduate in 6 years or less. 70 companies recruited on campus in a recent year. Of a recent graduating class, 20% were enrolled in graduate school within 6 months of graduation and 92% were employed.

Admissions Contact: Marla Friederichs, Associate Vice President for Enrollment Management. E-mail: admissions@stthomas.edu
Web: www.stthomas.edu

WINONA STATE UNIVERSITY D-5
Winona, MN 55987-5838 (507) 457-5100
(800) DIAL-WSU; Fax: (507) 457-5620

Full-time: 2574 men, 4221 women	**Faculty:** IIA, av$
Part-time: 240 men, 412 women	**Ph.D.s:** 80%
Graduate: 157 men, 413 women	**Student/Faculty:** n/av
Year: semesters, summer session	**Tuition:** $5877 ($10,297)
Application Deadline: January 30	**Room & Board:** $5456
Freshman Class: 5107 applied, 4243 accepted, 1721 enrolled	
SAT Verbal/Math: 524/540*	**ACT:** 23 **COMPETITIVE**

Winona State University, founded in 1858, is a public liberal arts institution and part of the Minnesota State Colleges and Universities system. There are 5 undergraduate schools and 1 graduate school. In addition to regional accreditation, WSU has baccalaureate program accreditation with ABET, ACCE, CSWE, NCATE, and NLN. The library contains 245,000 volumes and 831,000 microform items, and subscribes to 1400 periodicals including electronic. Computerized library services include interlibrary loans and database searching. Special learning facilities include a learning resource center, art gallery, and radio station. The 47-acre campus is in a small town 100 miles southeast of Minneapolis and St. Paul. Including any residence halls, there are 29 buildings.

Student Life: 55% of undergraduates are from Minnesota. Students are from 40 states, 51 foreign countries, and Canada. 80% are from public schools. 94% are white. 40% are Catholic; 40% Protestant. The average age of freshmen is 18; all undergraduates, 23. 25% do not continue beyond their first year; 55% remain to graduate.

Housing: 2500 students can be accommodated in college housing, which includes single-sex and coed dorms and on-campus apartments. On-campus housing is guaranteed for the freshman year only, is available on a first-come, first-served basis, and is available on a lottery system for upperclassmen. Alcohol is not permitted. All students may keep cars.

Activities: 3% of men belong to 3 national fraternities; 3% of women belong to 3 national sororities. There are 155 groups on campus, including art, band, cheerleading, chess, choir, chorale, chorus, computers, dance, debate, drama, ethnic, forensics, gay, honors, international, jazz band, literary magazine, musical theater, newspaper, orchestra, pep band, photography, political, professional, radio and TV, religious, social, social service, student government, and symphony.

Sports: There are 6 intercollegiate sports for men and 9 for women, and 15 intramural sports for men and 15 for women. Facilities include a 4000-seat stadium, 8 outdoor tennis courts, and a field house with 10 gyms, 3 weight rooms, a swimming pool, indoor track and tennis facilities, handball/racquetball courts, and a wellness center.

Disabled Students: Wheelchair ramps, elevators, special parking, specially equipped rest rooms, special class scheduling, lowered drinking fountains, lowered telephones, and special housing are available.

Services: Counseling and information services are available, as is tutoring in most subjects.

Campus Safety and Security: Measures include 24-hour foot and vehicle patrol, self-defense education, security escort services, and shuttle buses. There are informal discussions, pamphlets/posters/films, emergency telephones, and lighted pathways/sidewalks.

Programs of Study: WSU confers B.A., B.S., B.S.E., B.S.N., and B.S.W. degrees. Associate and master's degrees are also awarded. Bachelor's degrees are awarded in BIOLOGICAL SCIENCE (biology/biological science), BUSINESS (accounting, banking and finance, business administration and management, business economics, human resources, management information systems, marketing/retailing/merchandising, personnel management, and recreation and leisure services), COMMUNICATIONS AND THE ARTS (advertising, broadcasting, communications, dramatic arts, English, fine arts, French, German, graphic design, journalism, music, Spanish, and speech/debate/rhetoric), COMPUTER AND PHYSICAL SCIENCE (chemistry, computer science, earth science, geology, mathematics, physics, and statistics), EDUCATION (art, business, early childhood, elementary, foreign languages, health, music, physical, science, secondary, and special), ENGINEERING AND ENVIRONMENTAL DESIGN (materials engineering), HEALTH PROFESSIONS (cytotechnology, exercise science, medical laboratory technology, nursing, physical therapy, predentistry, premedicine, preveterinary science, and public health), SOCIAL SCIENCE (community services, criminal justice, economics, history, international relations, liberal arts/general studies, paralegal studies, parks and recreation management, physical fitness/movement, political science/government, prelaw, psychology, public administration, social science, social work, and sociology). Engineering, nursing, and education are the strongest academically. Business administration, mass communication, and education are the largest.

Required: To graduate, students must complete 128 credit hours with a minimum GPA of 2.5 in most majors. General education requirements include 6 credits each in humanities, science/math, social science, and a different culture, 4 in English, 3 each in speech and math, and 2 in phys ed. Majors average 46 credits, and some require a capstone experience.

Special: WSU offers cross-registration with St. Mary's University, study abroad in 25 countries, internships, work-study programs, student-designed majors, dual majors, pass/fail options, and credit for life, military, and work experience. Students may earn accelerated degrees in all majors and a general studies degree. There are 12 national honor societies, including Phi Beta Kappa, and 8 departmental honors programs.

Faculty/Classroom: 60% of faculty are male; 40%, female. 90% teach undergraduates, 10% do research, and 25% do both. No introductory courses are taught by graduate students. The average class size in an introductory lecture is 40; in a laboratory, 20; and in a regular course, 30.

Admissions: 83% of the 2005-2006 applicants were accepted. The SAT scores for the 2005-2006 freshman class were: Verbal--27% below 500, 18% between 500 and 599, 18% between 600 and 700, and 4% above 700; Math--27% below 500, 40% between 500 and 599, 20% between 600 and 700, and 7% above 700. The ACT scores were 27% below 21, 41% between 21 and 23, 22% between 24 and 26, 6% between 27 and 28, and 3% above 28. 27% of the current freshmen were in the top fifth of their class; 62% were in the top two fifths. There were 4 National Merit finalists and 48 semifinalists. 48 freshmen graduated first in their class.

Requirements: The ACT is required. In addition, candidates should have completed 4 units of English, 1 of which may be speech; 3 each of math, social studies, and science; 2 of a world language; and 1 elective, preferably in world culture, the arts, or computer science. AP and CLEP credits are accepted. Important factors in the admissions decision are advanced placement or honor courses, leadership record, and evidence of special talent.

Procedure: Freshmen are admitted fall, spring, and summer. Entrance exams should be taken in the junior year. There are early admissions, deferred admissions and rolling admissions plans. Applications should be filed by January 30 for fall entry and open for spring entry, along with a $20 fee. Notification is sent on a rolling basis. 190 applicants were on a recent waiting list. Applications are accepted on-line.

Transfer: 476 transfer students enrolled in 2004-2005. Applicants must have completed 24 semester hours of credit with a minimum GPA of 2.4. 32 of 128 credits required for the bachelor's degree must be completed at WSU.

Visiting: There are regularly scheduled orientations for prospective students, including daily tours and admissions visits from October through January on select Saturday mornings. There are guides for informal visits and visitors may sit in on classes. To schedule a visit, contact the Office of Admissions.

Financial Aid: In a recent year, 73% of all full-time freshmen and 70% of continuing full-time students received some form of financial aid. 50% of full-time freshmen received need-based aid. The average freshman award was $3700. 40% of undergraduates worked part time. Average annual earnings from campus work were $1800. The average financial indebtedness of a recent graduate was $7500. The FAFSA is required. Check with the school for current application deadlines.

International Students: In a recent year, there were 325 international students enrolled. The school actively recruits these students. They must score satisfactory on the written TOEFL or on the electronic version.

Computers: Wireless access is available. All students lease laptops from the university. All students may access the system 24 hours a day. There are no time limits. There is a $1000 a year lease fee. All students are required to have personal computers.

Admissions Contact: Carl T. Stange, Director of Admissions. A video is available. E-mail: *admissions@winona.edu* Web: *www.winona.edu*

Sports: There are 8 intercollegiate sports for men and 10 for women, and 9 intramural sports for men and 9 for women. Facilities include a 10,000-seat stadium and a 5000-seat gym.

Disabled Students: 15% of the campus is accessible. Wheelchair ramps, elevators, special parking, specially equipped rest rooms, and lowered drinking fountains are available.

Services: Counseling and information services are available, as is tutoring in most subjects. There is remedial math, reading, English, and writing.

Campus Safety and Security: Measures include 24-hour foot and vehicle patrol, pamphlets/posters/films, and lighted pathways/sidewalks.

Programs of Study: Alcorn State University confers B.A., B.S., B.M., B.M.E., and B.S.N. degrees. Associate and master's degrees are also awarded. Bachelor's degrees are awarded in AGRICULTURE (agricultural economics, agriculture, animal science, and plant science), BIOLOGICAL SCIENCE (biology/biological science and nutrition), BUSINESS (accounting, business administration and management, and office supervision and management), COMMUNICATIONS AND THE ARTS (communications and English), COMPUTER AND PHYSICAL SCIENCE (chemistry, computer science, and mathematics), EDUCATION (elementary, industrial arts, music, physical, recreation, science, and special), ENGINEERING AND ENVIRONMENTAL DESIGN (industrial administration/management), HEALTH PROFESSIONS (health science and nursing), SOCIAL SCIENCE (child care/child and family studies, criminal justice, economics, family/consumer studies, history, liberal arts/general studies, political science/government, psychology, and sociology). General studies, biology, and elementary education are the largest.

Required: To graduate, students must complete at least 128 semester hours with a minimum GPA of 2.0. Core requirements include 12 hours of social science, 9 each of natural science and creative arts, 6 of English, 4 of phys ed or military science, and 3 each of math and oral communications, as well as 1 of student adjustment.

Special: The university offers cooperative programs in medical technology and physical therapy, internships, and work-study programs. There is 1 national honor society Phi Beta Kappa, a freshman honors program, and 5 departmental honors program.

Faculty/Classroom: 56% of faculty are male; 44%, female. 95% teach undergraduates.

Requirements: The SAT or ACT is required. In addition, students must have graduated from an accredited high school with at least a C average and have completed 15 1/2 units of a college prep curriculum. A GPA of 2.0 is required. AP and CLEP credits are accepted.

Procedure: Freshmen are admitted to all sessions. Entrance exams should be taken so that scores may be submitted at the time application is made. There are early decision and deferred admissions plans. Application deadlines are open.

Transfer: 254 transfer students enrolled in 2004-2005. Applicants must have at least 6 hours each of composition and lab sciences, 3 hours of college algebra or above, and 9 other transferable elective hours, and have maintained an overall minimum GPA of 2.0. 104 of 128 credits required for the bachelor's degree must be completed at Alcorn State University.

Visiting: There are regularly scheduled orientations for prospective students. There are guides for informal visits and visitors may sit in on classes and stay overnight. To schedule a visit, contact Emanuel F. Barnes.

Financial Aid: In a recent year, 70% of all full-time freshmen and 74% of continuing full-time students received some form of financial aid. 36% of full-time freshmen received need-based aid. The average freshman award was $6600. Need-based scholarships or need-based grants averaged $1200 ($2400 maximum); need-based self-help aid (loans and jobs) averaged $2578 ($4685 maximum); and non-need-based athletic scholarships averaged $7280 ($11,786 maximum). 65% of undergraduates work part time. Average annual earnings from campus work were $2060. The average financial indebtedness of the recent graduate was $6500. Alcorn State University is a member of CSS. The FAFSA and the college's own financial statement are required. The deadline for filing freshman financial aid applications for fall entry is April 1.

International Students: There were 30 international students enrolled in a recent year. The school actively recruits these students. They must take the TOEFL and also take the SAT or the ACT.

Computers: All students may access the system. There are no time limits and no fees.

Graduates: From July 1, 2004 to June 30, 2005, 397 bachelor's degrees were awarded. The most popular majors were general studies (21%), elementary education (8%), and biology (8%). In an average class, 44% graduate in 6 years or less. 224 companies recruited on campus in 2004-2005.

Admissions Contact: Emanuel F. Barnes, Director of Admissions.
E-mail: *ebarnes@lorman.alcorn.edu* Web: *www.alcorn.edu*

ALCORN STATE UNIVERSITY   B-4
Alcorn State, MS 39096-7500

(601) 877-6147
(800) 222-6790; Fax: (601) 877-6347

Full-time: 1042 men, 1634 women	**Faculty:** 186; IIB, --$
Part-time: 60 men, 226 women	**Ph.D.s:** 66%
Graduate: 153 men, 429 women	**Student/Faculty:** 14 to 1
Year: semesters, summer session	**Tuition:** $3918 ($8886)
Application Deadline: open	**Room & Board:** $4272
Freshman Class: n/av	
SAT: required	**LESS COMPETITIVE**

Alcorn State University, founded in 1871, is a public institution offering programs in agriculture, the arts and sciences, business, engineering, and nursing. There are 6 undergraduate schools and 1 graduate school. In addition to regional accreditation, Alcorn State University has baccalaureate program accreditation with AACSB, AAFCS, ADA, AHEA, NAIT, NASM, NCATE, and NLN. The library contains 220,393 volumes, 577,874 microform items, and 17,152 audio/video tapes/CDs/DVDs, and subscribes to 1046 periodicals including electronic. Computerized library services include the card catalog, interlibrary loans, database searching, and Internet access. Special learning facilities include a learning resource center and radio station. The 1756-acre campus is in a rural area 45 miles south of Vicksburg and 7 miles west of Lorman. Including any residence halls, there are 128 buildings.

Student Life: 82% of undergraduates are from Mississippi. Others are from 34 states, 11 foreign countries, and Canada. 95% are from public schools. 92% are African American. The average age of freshmen is 22; all undergraduates, 23. 26% do not continue beyond their first year; 44% remain to graduate.

Housing: 2411 students can be accommodated in college housing, which includes single-sex dorms. In addition, there are honors houses. On-campus housing is guaranteed for all 4 years. 52% of students live on campus; of those, 45% remain on campus on weekends. Alcohol is not permitted. All students may keep cars.

Activities: 7% of men belong to 4 local and 4 national fraternities; 10% of women belong to 4 local and 4 national sororities. There are 79 groups on campus, including band, cheerleading, choir, chorus, dance, drama, honors, jazz band, marching band, newspaper, photography, radio and TV, religious, student government, and yearbook. Popular campus events include High School Day and Career Development Day.

BELHAVEN COLLEGE   C-4
Jackson, MS 39202   (601) 968-5940
(800) 960-5940; Fax: (601) 968-8946

Full-time: 557 men, 1085 women	**Faculty:** 68
Part-time: 21 men, 51 women	**Ph.D.s:** 84%
Graduate: 68 men, 187 women	**Student/Faculty:** 24 to 1
Year: semesters, summer session	**Tuition:** $14,100
Application Deadline: February 1	**Room & Board:** $5430
Freshman Class: 426 applied, 425 accepted, 208 enrolled	
SAT Verbal/Math: 560/560*	**ACT:** 23 NONCOMPETITIVE

Belhaven College, founded in 1883, is a private liberal arts institution with a Presbyterian heritage. There is 1 graduate school. In addition to regional accreditation, Belhaven has baccalaureate program accreditation with NASAD and NASM. The library contains 118,374 volumes, 11,867 microform items, and 3815 audio/video tapes/CDs/DVDs, and subscribes to 15,117 periodicals including electronic. Computerized library services include the card catalog, interlibrary loans, database searching, Internet access, and laptop Internet portals. Special learning facilities include a learning resource center and art gallery. The 42-acre campus is in an urban area in Jackson. Including any residence halls, there are 17 buildings.

Student Life: 73% of undergraduates are from Mississippi. Others are from 29 states, 21 foreign countries, and Canada. 49% are white; 38% African American. Most are Protestant. The average age of freshmen is 18; all undergraduates, 29. 31% do not continue beyond their first year; 39% remain to graduate.

Housing: 537 students can be accommodated in college housing, which includes single-sex dorms. On-campus housing is guaranteed for all 4 years. 69% of students commute. Alcohol is not permitted. All students may keep cars.

Activities: There are no fraternities or sororities. There are 24 groups on campus, including art, cheerleading, choir, chorus, dance, drama, ethnic, honors, literary magazine, musical theater, newspaper, political, professional, religious, social service, student government, and yearbook. Popular campus events include Singing Christmas Tree, concert and lecture series, and Lake Day.

Sports: There are 7 intercollegiate sports for men and 7 for women, and 6 intramural sports for men and 6 for women. Facilities include a gym, 5 tennis courts, a lake, an intramural and soccer field, a baseball field, a football/soccer practice field, an athletic training facility, and an exercise, weight, and conditioning complex.

Disabled Students: 25% of the campus is accessible. Wheelchair ramps, elevators, special parking, specially equipped rest rooms, special class scheduling, lowered drinking fountains, and special housing are available.

Services: There is remedial math, reading, and writing and study halls for athletes.

Campus Safety and Security: Measures include 24-hour foot and vehicle patrol, security escort services, informal discussions, and lighted pathways/sidewalks.

Programs of Study: Belhaven confers B.A., B.S., B.A.A., B.B.A., B.F.A., B.H.A., and B.S.M. degrees. Associate and master's degrees are also awarded. Bachelor's degrees are awarded in BIOLOGICAL SCIENCE (biology/biological science), BUSINESS (accounting and business administration and management), COMMUNICATIONS AND THE ARTS (art, ballet, communications, creative writing, dance, dramatic arts, English, and music), COMPUTER AND PHYSICAL SCIENCE (chemistry, computer science, information sciences and systems, and mathematics), EDUCATION (athletic training and elementary), HEALTH PROFESSIONS (exercise science), SOCIAL SCIENCE (biblical studies, history, humanities, international studies, philosophy, political science/government, psychology, religious music, and social work). Biology and chemistry are the strongest academically. Business administration and education are the largest.

Required: Requirements for graduation vary by degree, but students must complete at least 124 semester hours, including 25 hours of World View Curriculum courses, with a minimum 2.0 GPA.

Special: Students may participate in various internships, including one in Washington, D.C., or in 6 countries through the study-travel program. Belhaven also offers accelerated degree programs, dual majors, student-designed majors, nondegree study, pass/fail options, a 3-2 engineering degree with Mississippi State University, and work-study. 2 1-month summer sessions and 2 2-week minisessions offer additional opportunities for credit. There are 7 national honor societies, a freshman honors program, and 17 departmental honors programs.

Faculty/Classroom: 62% of faculty are male; 38%, female. All teach undergraduates. No introductory courses are taught by graduate students. The average class size in an introductory lecture is 24; in a laboratory, 16; and in a regular course, 18.

Admissions: The SAT scores for the 2005-2006 freshman class were: Verbal--10% below 500, 32% between 500 and 599, 32% between 600 and 700, and 26% above 700; Math--8% below 500, 45% between 500

and 599, 39% between 600 and 700, and 8% above 700. The ACT scores were 9% below 21, 29% between 21 and 23, 27% between 24 and 26, 10% between 27 and 28, and 25% above 28. There were 4 National Merit finalists.

Requirements: The SAT or ACT is required. In addition, applicants should be graduates of an accredited secondary school, with 16 academic units, including 4 of English, 2 of math, a recommended 2 of a foreign language, 1 each of history and natural science, and 6 of electives. A personal recommendation and essay are also required. A GPA of 2.0 is required. AP and CLEP credits are accepted.

Procedure: Freshmen are admitted to all sessions. Entrance exams should be taken in the junior year. Notification is sent on a rolling basis. Applications are accepted on-line.

Transfer: 140 transfer students enrolled in 2004-2005. Transfer applicants must have a minimum 2.0 GPA and submit all college transcripts. 31 of 124 credits required for the bachelor's degree must be completed at Belhaven.

Visiting: There are regularly scheduled orientations for prospective students, including Preview Days, which allow students to see the campus, meet students, interview with faculty and admissions, and attend classes. There are guides for informal visits and visitors may sit in on classes and stay overnight. To schedule a visit, contact the Admissions Office.

Financial Aid: In 2005-2006, 94% of all full-time freshmen and 93% of continuing full-time students received some form of financial aid. 72% of all full-time students received need-based aid. Need-based scholarships or need-based grants averaged $3217 ($5050 maximum); need-based self-help aid (loans and jobs) averaged $6222 ($6625 maximum); non-need-based athletic scholarships averaged $5074 ($14,000 maximum); and other non-need-based awards and non-need-based scholarships averaged $8848 ($14,000 maximum). 12% of undergraduates work part time. Average annual earnings from campus work are $1545. The average financial indebtedness of the 2005 graduate was $17,800. The FAFSA is required. The priority date for freshman financial aid applications for fall entry is March 1.

International Students: There are 36 international students enrolled. A satisfactory score on the TOEFL is required.

Computers: All students may access the system. There are no time limits and no fees.

Graduates: From July 1, 2004 to June 30, 2005, 403 bachelor's degrees were awarded. The most popular majors were business administration (65%), elementary education (6%), and biblical studies (5%). In an average class, 31% graduate in 4 years or less, 39% graduate in 5 years or less, and 39% graduate in 6 years or less. 15 companies recruited on campus in 2004-2005.

Admissions Contact: Suzanne Sullivan, Director of Admission. A video is available. E-mail: *admissions@belhaven.edu* Web: *www.belhaven.edu*

BLUE MOUNTAIN COLLEGE   D-1
Blue Mountain, MS 38610-0160   (662) 685-4161
(800) 235-0136; Fax: (662) 685-4776

Full-time: 77 men, 206 women	**Faculty:** 24
Part-time: 7 men, 75 women	**Ph.D.s:** 50%
Graduate: none	**Student/Faculty:** 12 to 1
Year: semesters, summer session	**Tuition:** $7320
Application Deadline: open	**Room & Board:** $3766
Freshman Class: 172 applied, 95 accepted, 47 enrolled	
ACT: required	COMPETITIVE

Blue Mountain College, founded in 1873 and affiliated with the Mississippi Baptist Convention, is a private liberal arts college for women that also admits men who are preparing for a church-related vocation. The 3 libraries contain 65,267 volumes, 375 microform items, and 3645 audio/video tapes/CDs/DVDs, and subscribe to 4883 periodicals including electronic. Computerized library services include the card catalog, database searching, Internet access, and laptop Internet portals. Special learning facilities include a learning resource center. The 44-acre campus is in a rural area 65 miles southeast of Memphis. Including any residence halls, there are 14 buildings.

Student Life: 90% of undergraduates are from Mississippi. Students are from 8 states and 1 foreign countries. 87% are from public schools. 84% are white; 14% African American. Most are Protestant. The average age of freshmen is 20; all undergraduates, 25. 28% do not continue beyond their first year; 45% remain to graduate.

Housing: 232 students can be accommodated in college housing, which includes single-sex dorms. In addition, there are special-interest houses. On-campus housing is available on a first-come, first-served basis. 66% of students commute. Alcohol is not permitted. All students may keep cars.

Activities: There are no fraternities or sororities. There are 30 groups on campus, including art, choir, chorale, chorus, drama, honors, literary magazine, musical theater, pep band, professional, religious, social, student government, and yearbook. Popular campus events include High School Weekend, Field Day, and formal dinners and plays.

Sports: There are 2 intercollegiate sports for women, and 4 intramural sports for men and 8 for women. Facilities include a gym, a swimming pool, and a softball field, and a fitness center.

Disabled Students: 50% of the campus is accessible. Wheelchair ramps, elevators, special parking, specially equipped rest rooms, special class scheduling, and lowered drinking fountains are available.

Services: There is remedial math, reading, and writing.

Campus Safety and Security: Measures include 24-hour foot and vehicle patrol, self-defense education, informal discussions, and pamphlets/posters/films. There are lighted pathways/sidewalks.

Programs of Study: BMC confers B.A., B.S., and B.S.Ed. degrees. Bachelor's degrees are awarded in BIOLOGICAL SCIENCE (biology/biological science), BUSINESS (business administration and management), COMMUNICATIONS AND THE ARTS (dramatic arts, English, music, piano/organ, Spanish, and speech/debate/rhetoric), COMPUTER AND PHYSICAL SCIENCE (chemistry, and mathematics), EDUCATION (business, elementary, English, foreign languages, mathematics, music, physical, science, secondary, and social science), HEALTH PROFESSIONS (medical technology), SOCIAL SCIENCE (biblical studies, history, psychology, and social science). Education is the strongest academically. Education and biblical studies are the largest.

Required: All students must take a minimum of 120 semester hours, with a minimum of 40 hours on junior-senior level; 25% of total degree hours required must be earned at Blue Mountain. No more than 42 hours of course work carrying the same prefix must be credited toward the degree. Core curriculum requirements include 12 semester hours of English, 6 hours each of history and biblical studies, 4 of biological science, 3 each of psychology, fine arts, math, physical science, computer applications, electives, and 2 of phys ed. A 2.0 GPA overall and in the major is required ; 2.5 for teacher education.

Special: The college offers dual majors and internships (maximum 6 credits). A 3-2 nursing degree with Union University is possible. There is 1 national honor society, and 7 departmental honors program.

Faculty/Classroom: 39% of faculty are male; 61%, female. 88% teach undergraduates. The average class size in an introductory lecture is 17; in a laboratory, 12; and in a regular course, 11.

Admissions: 55% of the 2005-2006 applicants were accepted. 45% of the current freshmen were in the top fifth of their class; 67% were in the top two fifths. 2 freshmen graduated first in their class.

Requirements: The ACT is required. In addition, BMC recommends that applicants for admission have completed 4 units of English, 3 each of math, science, and social studies, and 2 of a foreign language. A GPA of 2.0 is required. AP and CLEP credits are accepted. Important factors in the admissions decision are ability to finance college education, recommendations by alumni, and recommendations by school officials.

Procedure: Freshmen are admitted fall, spring, and summer. Entrance exams should be taken starting in the junior year (ACT). Application deadlines are open. Application fee is $10. Applications are accepted on-line.

Transfer: 63 transfer students enrolled in 2004-2005. Transfer students who have been enrolled in other colleges must submit official transcripts from each college attended and must be eligible to re-enter tha last college attended. A maximum of 64 semester hours of credit mya be transferred from a community or junior college to Blue Mountain. 30 of 120 credits required for the bachelor's degree must be completed at BMC.

Visiting: There are regularly scheduled orientations for prospective students. There are guides for informal visits and visitors may sit in on classes and stay overnight. To schedule a visit, contact the Office of Admissions at admissions@bmc.edu.

Financial Aid: In 2005-2006, 95% of all full-time freshmen and 96% of continuing full-time students received some form of financial aid. 67% of full-time freshmen and 69% of continuing full-time students received need-based aid. The average freshman award was $9258. Need-based scholarships or need-based grants averaged $2375 ($4850 maximum); need-based self-help aid (loans and jobs) averaged $1455 ($5400 maximum); non-need-based athletic scholarships averaged $10,070 ($11,126 maximum); and other non-need-based awards and non-need-based scholarships averaged $5626 ($13,868 maximum). 41% of undergraduates work part time. Average annual earnings from campus work are $1400. The average financial indebtedness of the 2005 graduate was $11,000. The FAFSA and the college's own financial statement are required. The priority date for freshman financial aid applications for fall entry is March 1. The deadline for filing freshman financial aid applications for fall entry is July 15.

International Students: There is 1 international student enrolled. A satisfactoy score 500 on the written TOEFL is required. Students must and also take the ACT.

Computers: Wireless access is available. Students may access the Internet on a wireless system in the library, with provided labtops. Computers are provided in each dorm, the library, and the curriculum lab. All students may access the system during regular library hours. There are no time limits and no fees. It is strongly recommended that all students have a personal computer.

Graduates: From July 1, 2004 to June 30, 2005, 84 bachelor's degrees were awarded. The most popular majors were elementary education

(48%), biblical studies (13%), and social science (10%). In an average class, 1% graduate in 3 years or less, 33% graduate in 4 years or less, 43% graduate in 5 years or less, and 43% graduate in 6 years or less. 7 companies recruited on campus in 2004-2005. Of the 2004 graduating class, 13% were enrolled in graduate school within 6 months of graduation and 22% were employed.

Admissions Contact: Maria Teel, Director of Admissions.
E-mail: mteel@bmc.edu Web: www.bmc.edu

DELTA STATE UNIVERSITY   C-2
Cleveland, MS 38733   (662) 846-4655
(800) 468-6378; Fax: (662) 846-4683

Full-time: 1161 men, 1591 women	**Faculty:** 165
Part-time: 145 men, 360 women	**Ph.D.s:** 55%
Graduate: 207 men, 534 women	**Student/Faculty:** 17 to 1
Year: semesters, summer session	**Tuition:** $3762 ($8702)
Application Deadline: August 1	**Room & Board:** $3947
Freshman Class: 398 enrolled	
ACT: 20	**COMPETITIVE**

Delta State University, founded in 1924, is a public liberal arts institution offering degrees in arts and sciences, business, education, health science, and nursing. There are 4 undergraduate and 4 graduate schools. In addition to regional accreditation, DSU has baccalaureate program accreditation with AAFCS, ACBSP, ACEJMC, ACS, AHEA, CAAHEP, CCNE, CSWE, NASAD, NASM, NCATE, and NLN. The library contains 345,565 volumes, 828,979 microform items, and 18,493 audio/video tapes/CDs/DVDs, and subscribes to 1268 periodicals including electronic. Computerized library services include the card catalog, interlibrary loans, database searching, and Internet access. Special learning facilities include a learning resource center, art gallery, natural history museum, planetarium, and a performing arts center. The 332-acre campus is in a small town 110 miles south of Memphis, and 130 miles north of Jackson. Including any residence halls, there are 46 buildings.

Student Life: 91% of undergraduates are from Mississippi. Others are from 33 states, 17 foreign countries, and Canada. 60% are white; 38% African American. The average age of freshmen is 18; all undergraduates, 25. 28% do not continue beyond their first year.

Housing: 1347 students can be accommodated in college housing, which includes single-sex dormitories and married-student housing. On-campus housing is guaranteed for all 4 years. 69% of students commute. Alcohol is not permitted. All students may keep cars.

Activities: 18% of men belong to 8 national fraternities; 13% of women belong to 6 national sororities. There are 118 groups on campus, including art, band, cheerleading, choir, chorale, chorus, computers, dance, drama, drill team, ethnic, honors, jazz band, literary magazine, marching band, musical theater, newspaper, opera, orchestra, pep band, photography, political, professional, religious, social, social service, student government, and yearbook. Popular campus events include Springfest, Christmas Madrigal Feast, and Pig Pickin.

Sports: There are 8 intercollegiate sports for men and 7 for women, and 22 intramural sports for men and 22 for women. Facilities include a coliseum, an indoor pool, a gym, a baseball field, a softball field, a football stadium, a 9-hole golf course, outdoor tennis courts, 2 intramural fields, an outdoor walking facility, and a fitness center.

Disabled Students: 95% of the campus is accessible. Wheelchair ramps, elevators, special parking, specially equipped rest rooms, special class scheduling, lowered drinking fountains, and lowered telephones are available.

Services: Counseling and information services are available, as is tutoring in every subject. There is remedial math, reading, and writing.

Campus Safety and Security: Measures include 24-hour foot and vehicle patrol, self-defense education, security escort services, and informal discussions. There are pamphlets/posters/films, emergency telephones, and lighted pathways/sidewalks.

Programs of Study: DSU confers B.A., B.S., B.B.A., B.C.A., B.F.A., B.M., B.M.E., B.S.C.J., B.S.E., B.S.G.S., B.S.N., and B.S.W. degrees. Master's and doctoral degrees are also awarded. Bachelor's degrees are awarded in BIOLOGICAL SCIENCE (biology/biological science), BUSINESS (accounting, business administration and management, fashion merchandising, hospitality management services, insurance, management science, marketing/retailing/merchandising, and secretarial studies/office management), COMMUNICATIONS AND THE ARTS (art, English, journalism, music, and music performance), COMPUTER AND PHYSICAL SCIENCE (chemistry, information sciences and systems, and mathematics), EDUCATION (athletic training, business, elementary, English, foreign languages, health, mathematics, music, science, secondary, social science, social studies, and special), ENGINEERING AND ENVIRONMENTAL DESIGN (aviation administration/management and environmental science), HEALTH PROFESSIONS (nursing, predentistry, premedicine, and speech pathology/audiology), SOCIAL SCIENCE (criminal justice, family/consumer studies, history, political science/government, psychology, social science, social work, and sociology). Elementary education, biology, and computer information systems are the largest.

Required: To graduate, students must complete 124 semester hours, including 30 to 54 in the major, depending on the program, with a minimum GPA of 2.0. General education requirements include 6 hours each of English composition, English literature, history, lab science, and social science; 3 hours each of fine arts, math, psychology, and speech; and 2 hours of personal development.

Special: DSU offers internships in several majors. A general studies degree and nondegree study are also available. There are 28 national honor societies, a freshman honors program, and 7 departmental honors programs.

Faculty/Classroom: 51% of faculty are male; 48%, female. No introductory courses are taught by graduate students.

Admissions: The ACT scores for the 2005-2006 freshman class were: 62% below 21, 22% between 21 and 23, 9% between 24 and 26, 5% between 27 and 28, and 2% above 28. 34% of the current freshmen were in the top fifth of their class; 63% were in the top two fifths.

Requirements: The SAT or ACT is required. In addition, students may gain admission by completing the college prep curriculum with a minimum 3.2 GPA; by completing the college prep curriculum with a minimum of 2.5 GPA and scoring at least 16 on the ACT (similarly on the SAT), by ranking in the upper 50% of the class and scoring at least 16 on the ACT (similarly on the SAT); or by completing the college prep curriculum with a minimum 2.0 GPA and scoring 18 or higher on the ACT (similarly on the SAT). The Nelson Denny Reading Test and Math Placement Test must also be taken. Applicants must be graduates of an accredited secondary school or have the GED. They should have completed 4 courses in English; 3 each in math, science, and social studies; 2 in a foreign language, world geography, or additional science/math; and 1/2 in computer applications. A GPA of 2.0 is required. AP credits are accepted.

Procedure: Freshmen are admitted to all sessions. Entrance exams should be taken as early as possible. There is a rolling admissions plan. Applications should be filed by August 1 for fall entry and January 1 for spring entry. Notification is sent on a rolling basis. Applications are accepted on-line. The fall 2005 application fee was $15.

Transfer: 469 transfer students enrolled in 2004-2005. A minimum GPA of 2.0 is required, as is an associate degree and ACT or SAT scores; students must be in good standing with last college or university attended. 30 of 124 credits required for the bachelor's degree must be completed at DSU.

Visiting: There are regularly scheduled orientations for prospective students, including campus tours and introduction to faculty and staff. There are guides for informal visits and visitors may sit in on classes and stay overnight. To schedule a visit, contact School Relations and Recruitment at (662) 846-4018.

Financial Aid: In 2005-2006, 75% of all full-time freshmen and 80% of continuing full-time students received some form of financial aid. 70% of full-time freshmen and 75% of continuing full-time students received need-based aid. Need-based scholarships or need-based grants averaged $3235 ($4050 maximum); need-based self-help aid (loans and jobs) averaged $2938 ($4275 maximum); and non-need-based athletic scholarships averaged $3935 ($7825 maximum). 9% of undergraduates work part time. The average financial indebtedness of the 2005 graduate was $16,800. The FAFSA is required. The deadline for filing freshman financial aid applications for fall entry is March 1.

International Students: There are 40 international students enrolled. They must score satisfactorily on the written TOEFL or on the electronic version and also take the SAT or the ACT.

Computers: Wireless access is available. All students may access the system from 8 A.M. to 11 P.M. daily. There are no time limits and no fees. It is recommended that students in the executive MBA program have personal computers.

Graduates: From July 1, 2004 to June 30, 2005, 584 bachelor's degrees were awarded. The most popular majors were health physical education and recreation (8%), elementary education (8%), and management (7%). In an average class, 2% graduate in 3 years or less, 23% graduate in 4 years or less, 41% graduate in 5 years or less, and 45% graduate in 6 years or less. 75 companies recruited on campus in 2004-2005.

Admissions Contact: Debbie Heslep, Associate Dean of Enrollment Management. E-mail: dheslep@deltastate.edu
Web: http://deltastate.edu

JACKSON STATE UNIVERSITY   C-4
Jackson, MS 39217

(601) 979-2100
(800) 848-6817; Fax: (601) 973-3445

Full-time: 2200 men, 3250 women	**Faculty:** 356; IIA, --$
Part-time: 260 men, 600 women	**Ph.D.s:** 70%
Graduate: 450 men, 1095 women	**Student/Faculty:** 15 to 1
Year: semesters, summer session	**Tuition:** $3700 ($8200)
Application Deadline: open	**Room & Board:** $4800
Freshman Class: n/av	
SAT or ACT: required	**COMPETITIVE**

Jackson State University, founded in 1877, is a public institution with an emphasis on liberal arts, business, music, and teacher preparation. There are 5 undergraduate schools and 1 graduate school. Figures in the above capsule and profile are approximate. In addition to regional accreditation, JSU has baccalaureate program accreditation with AACSB, CSWE, NASAD, NASM, and NCATE. The library contains 486,478 volumes, 675,035 microform items, and 2104 audio/video tapes/CDs/DVDs, and subscribes to 1736 periodicals including electronic. Computerized library services include the card catalog, interlibrary loans, database searching, and Internet access. Special learning facilities include a learning resource center and radio station. The 150-acre campus is in an urban area 190 miles north of New Orleans. Including any residence halls, there are 40 buildings.

Student Life: 80% of undergraduates are from Mississippi. Students are from 40 states and 38 foreign countries. 94% are African American. The average age of freshmen is 21; all undergraduates, 23. 24% do not continue beyond their first year; 37% remain to graduate.

Housing: 2454 students can be accommodated in college housing, which includes single-sex dorms. In addition, there are honors houses. On-campus housing is available on a first-come, first-served basis. 53% of students commute. Alcohol is not permitted. All students may keep cars.

Activities: 5% of men belong to 4 national fraternities; 5% of women belong to 4 national sororities. There are many groups and organizations on campus, including art, band, cheerleading, choir, dance, drama, drill team, ethnic, honors, jazz band, marching band, musical theater, newspaper, opera, orchestra, pep band, photography, political, radio and TV, religious, social service, student government, symphony, and yearbook.

Sports: There are 7 intercollegiate sports for men and 4 for women, and 2 intramural sports for men and 2 for women. Facilities include an Olympic-size swimming pool, a gym with 2 basketball courts, indoor and outdoor tennis courts, badminton and volleyball courts, a dance studio, a baseball diamond, soccer and athletic fields, an archery range, a track, and a bowling alley.

Disabled Students: All of the campus is accessible. Wheelchair ramps, elevators, special parking, specially equipped rest rooms, lowered drinking fountains, and lowered telephones are available.

Services: Counseling and information services are available, as is tutoring in every subject. There is remedial math, reading, and writing.

Campus Safety and Security: Measures include 24-hour foot and vehicle patrol, self-defense education, shuttle buses, and informal discussions. There are pamphlets/posters/films and emergency telephones.

Programs of Study: JSU confers B.A., B.S., B.B.A, B.M., B.M.E., B.S.Ed., and B.S.W. degrees. Master's and doctoral degrees are also awarded. Bachelor's degrees are awarded in BIOLOGICAL SCIENCE (biology/biological science), BUSINESS (accounting, banking and finance, business administration and management, marketing/retailing/merchandising, and office supervision and management), COMMUNICATIONS AND THE ARTS (art, communications, English, languages, piano/organ, and speech/debate/rhetoric), COMPUTER AND PHYSICAL SCIENCE (atmospheric sciences and meteorology, chemistry, computer science, mathematics, and physics), EDUCATION (business, elementary, health, industrial arts, mathematics, music, social science, and special), HEALTH PROFESSIONS (premedicine), SOCIAL SCIENCE (child care/child and family studies, corrections, criminal justice, economics, history, political science/government, psychology, social work, sociology, and urban studies). Computer science, biology, and accounting are the strongest academically. Biology, elementary education, and business administration are the largest.

Required: To graduate, students must complete at least 128 semester hours with a minimum GPA of 2.0. At least 30 upper-division hours must be earned in the major. Distribution requirements include a total of 49 to 59 hours in communications, humanities and fine arts, social and behavioral sciences, natural sciences, health and physical education, and concepts for success in college.

Special: Internships with various corporations, nondegree study, work-study programs, a cooperative education program, accelerated degrees, combined B.A.-B.S. degrees, and a student-exchange program are available. There are 4 national honor societies, a freshman honors program, and 14 departmental honors programs.

Faculty/Classroom: 55% of faculty are male; 45%, female.

Requirements: The SAT or ACT is required. In addition, applicants must be graduates of an accredited secondary school or have a GED certificate. They must have earned 15½ Carnegie units, including 4 of English, 3 each of math, social studies, and sciences, ½ of computer applications, and 2 of advanced electives. A composite ACT score of 20 or above, or a satisfactory SAT score or exempts students from the specific high school unit requirements. An interview is recommended. A GPA of 2.0 is required. AP and CLEP credits are accepted. Important factors in the admissions decision are recommendations by school officials, leadership record, and extracurricular activities record.

Procedure: Freshmen are admitted to all sessions. Entrance exams should be taken during the first semester of the senior year. There are early admissions, deferred admissions, and rolling admissions plans. Application deadlines are open. Applications are accepted on-line.

Transfer: 379 transfer students enrolled in a recent year. Applicants should submit an official transcript from each institution attended, be in good standing at the last college or university attended, and have a minimum cumulative GPA of 2.0. 30 of 128 credits required for the bachelor's degree must be completed at JSU.

Visiting: There are regularly scheduled orientations for prospective students. There are guides for informal visits and visitors may sit in on classes and stay overnight. To schedule a visit, contact the Office of Marketing and Recruitment at (601) 979-2911.

Financial Aid: In a recent year, 97% of all full-time freshmen and 93% of continuing full-time students received some form of financial aid. 84% of full-time freshmen and 83% of continuing full-time students received need-based aid. The average freshman award was $8812. Need-based scholarships or need-based grants averaged $2866 ($4050 maximum); need-based self-help aid (loans and jobs) averaged $3906 ($8500 maximum); non-need-based athletic scholarships averaged $5561 ($8308 maximum); other non-need-based awards and non-need-based scholarships averaged $2662 ($16,552 maximum); and other awards averaged $3768 ($17,824 maximum). Average annual earnings from campus work were $2200. The average financial indebtedness of a recent graduate was $18,000. JSU is a member of CSS. The FAFSA is required. Check with the school for application deadlines.

International Students: The school actively recruits these students. They must score satisfactorily on the written TOEFL and also take a placement test and the SAT or the ACT, scoring 20 on the ACT.

Computers: All students may access the system 7 A.M. to 12 A.M., with access to PCs during business hours. There are no time limits and no fees.

Graduates: In a recent year, 760 bachelor's degrees were awarded. The most popular majors were biology (8%), child care and family education (8%), and business administration (7%). In an average class, 37% graduate in 6 years or less.

Admissions Contact: Stephanie Chatman, Associate Director of Admissions. E-mail: *schatman@ccaix.jsums.edu* Web: *www.jsums.edu*

MILLSAPS COLLEGE   C-4
Jackson, MS 39210

(601) 974-1050
(800) 352-1050; Fax: (601) 974-1059

Full-time: 526 men, 513 women	**Faculty:** 92; IIB, -$
Part-time: 25 men, 21 women	**Ph.D.s:** 97%
Graduate: 38 men, 31 women	**Student/Faculty:** 11 to 1
Year: semesters, summer session	**Tuition:** $20,690
Application Deadline: February 1	**Room & Board:** $7566
Freshman Class: 1008 applied, 829 accepted, 258 enrolled	
SAT Verbal/Math: 610/585*	**ACT:** 27 **VERY COMPETITIVE+**

Millsaps College, founded in 1890, is an independent liberal arts institution affiliated with the United Methodist Church. In addition to regional accreditation, Millsaps has baccalaureate program accreditation with AACSB, ACS, and NCATE. The library contains 193,040 volumes, 79,858 microform items, and 8470 audio/video tapes/CDs/DVDs, and subscribes to 874 periodicals including electronic. Computerized library services include the card catalog, interlibrary loans, database searching, Internet access, and laptop Internet portals. Special learning facilities include an art gallery, an observatory, and many types of equipment in teaching labs. The 100-acre campus is in an urban area in the capital city of Jackson. Including any residence halls, there are 30 buildings.

Student Life: 51% of undergraduates are from out of state, mostly the South. Students are from 32 states, 15 foreign countries, and Canada. 67% are from public schools. 82% are white; 12% African American. 52% are Protestant; 27% claim no religious affiliation; 17% Catholic. The average age of freshmen is 18; all undergraduates, 20. 17% do not continue beyond their first year.

Housing: 1003 students can be accommodated in college housing, which includes single-sex and coed dorms and fraternity houses. In addition, there are special-interest houses, designated housing for freshmen, and an alcohol-and drug-free hall in a dorm. On-campus housing is guaranteed for the freshman year only, is available on a first-come, first-served basis, and is available on a lottery system for upperclassmen. The selection process for campus housing for upperclassmen awards points based on years enrolled and GPA. 81% of students live on campus; of those, 75% remain on campus on weekends. All students may keep cars.

Activities: 54% of men belong to 6 national fraternities; 52% of women belong to 6 national sororities. There are 75 groups on campus, including art, band, cheerleading, choir, chorale, chorus, computers, dance, debate, drama, ethnic, gay, honors, instrumental performance, international, literary magazine, musical theater, newspaper, pep band, photography, political, professional, religious, social, social service, student government, and yearbook. Popular campus events include Major Madness (spring music festival), Project Midtown (semiannual Saturday of service), and Purple Pride Day (athletics).

Sports: There are 7 intercollegiate sports for men and 7 for women, and 20 intramural sports for men and 20 for women. Facilities include a 63,300-square-foot activities center containing a fitness center with basketball and volleyball courts, a cardio theater, an aerobics room, fitness and weight-training equipment, a free-weight room, an outdoor pool, racquetball and handball courts, and a squash court. Outdoor areas include 6 tennis courts, a sand volleyball court, and softball, baseball, football, soccer, and multipurpose fields.

Disabled Students: 90% of the campus is accessible. Wheelchair ramps, elevators, special parking, specially equipped rest rooms, special class scheduling, lowered drinking fountains, and lowered telephones are available. Other needs can be addressed through the ADA coordinator on an individual basis.

Services: Counseling and information services are available, as is tutoring in most subjects by request, as needed. A writing center, a language lab, and a math lab are available for assistance.

Campus Safety and Security: Measures include 24-hour foot and vehicle patrol, self-defense education, security escort services, and informal discussions. There are pamphlets/posters/films, emergency telephones, lighted pathways/sidewalks, and key card access to buildings. Entrances to campus are staffed at night.

Programs of Study: Millsaps confers B.A., B.S., and B.B.A. degrees. Master's degrees are also awarded. Bachelor's degrees are awarded in BIOLOGICAL SCIENCE (biology/biological science), BUSINESS (accounting and business administration and management), COMMUNICATIONS AND THE ARTS (art, classics, dramatic arts, English, French, German, music, and Spanish), COMPUTER AND PHYSICAL SCIENCE (chemistry, computer science, geology, mathematics, and physics), EDUCATION (elementary), SOCIAL SCIENCE (anthropology, economics, European studies, history, philosophy, political science/government, psychology, religion, and sociology). Biology/chemistry/premed, geology, and sociology/anthropology are the strongest academically. Business administration, biology, and psychology are the largest.

Required: To graduate, students must complete 128 credit hours with 32 to 48 hours in the major and a minimum GPA of 2.0. The core curriculum includes 4 interdisciplinary courses in humanities and 4 in the sciences and math. Students must also take Introduction to Liberal Studies during the freshman year and Reflections on Liberal Studies during the senior year. Other requirements include satisfactory completion of a 7-paper writing proficiency portfolio and a comprehensive exam in the specific field of study.

Special: Millsaps College offers programs abroad in China, Costa Rica, England, Ireland, France, Germany, Greece, Italy, Mexico (Yucatan), Albania, Japan, Tanzania, and Ghana, a Washington semester, internships and research opportunities, dual majors, and dual degree programs in conjunction with other schools in business, nursing, math, engineering, computer science, and other applied sciences. There are 3-2 degree programs in engineering with Auburn, Columbia, Vanderbilt, and Washington Universities. There are 25 national honor societies, including Phi Beta Kappa, and 25 departmental honors programs.

Faculty/Classroom: 56% of faculty are male; 44%, female. All teach undergraduates and 90% both teach and do research. No introductory courses are taught by graduate students. The average class size in an introductory lecture is 21; in a laboratory, 19; and in a regular course, 14.

Admissions: 82% of the 2005-2006 applicants were accepted. The SAT scores for the 2005-2006 freshman class were: Verbal--11% below 500, 33% between 500 and 599, 42% between 600 and 700, and 14% above 700; Math--15% below 500, 41% between 500 and 599, 35% between 600 and 700, and 9% above 700. The ACT scores were 9% below 21, 19% between 21 and 23, 18% between 24 and 26, 19% between 27 and 28, and 33% above 28. 56% of the current freshmen were in the top fifth of their class; 79% were in the top two fifths. There was 1 National Merit finalist and 6 semifinalists. 12 freshmen graduated first in their class.

Requirements: The SAT or ACT is required. In addition, applicants should be graduates of an accredited secondary school or have a GED certificate, and have completed at least 14 academic units, including 4 in English, 3 in math, 2 in social studies, and 2 in history. An essay is required. A GPA of 2.5 is required. AP and CLEP credits are accepted. Important factors in the admissions decision are advanced placement or honor courses, extracurricular activities record, and recommendations by school officials.

Procedure: Freshmen are admitted fall and spring. Entrance exams should be taken in the spring of the junior year or fall of the senior year. There are early actions and deferred admissions plans. There is a rolling admissions plan. Early action applications should be filed by December

1; regular applications, by February 1 for fall entry, along with a $25 fee. Notification of early action is sent December 15; regular decision, on a rolling basis. Applications are accepted on-line.

Transfer: 68 transfer students enrolled in 2004-2005. Applicants must have a minimum GPA of 2.75 and be in good standing at their previous school. Requirements include high school and college transcripts, an essay or personal statement, and standardized test scores. 32 of 128 credits required for the bachelor's degree must be completed at Millsaps.

Visiting: There are regularly scheduled orientations for prospective students, including meetings with faculty and student services personnel. There are guides for informal visits and visitors may sit in on classes and stay overnight. To schedule a visit, contact the Admissions Office.

Financial Aid: In 2005-2006, 97% of all full-time freshmen and 94% of continuing full-time students received some form of financial aid. 60% of full-time freshmen and 57% of continuing full-time students received need-based aid. The average freshman award was $18,185. Need-based scholarships or need-based grants averaged $7354 ($10,275 maximum); need-based self-help aid (loans and jobs) averaged $4825; and other non-need-based awards and non-need-based scholarships averaged $10,758 ($28,000 maximum). 80% of undergraduates work part time. Average annual earnings from campus work are $1029. The average financial indebtedness of the 2005 graduate was $22,285. The FAFSA and the college's own financial statement are required. The priority date for freshman financial aid applications for fall entry is March 1.

International Students: There are 19 international students enrolled. A satisfactory score on the TOEFL is required; the SAT or ACT is required in lieu of the TOEFL.

Computers: Wireless access is available in the library, the College Center, the central outdoor areas, and the top 2 floors of Murrah Hall in the first phase of a project that will eventually cover the entire campus. Students have acess to 120 computers across campus. Student residential consultants (ResCons) in each residence hall and fraternity house are trained in network connectivity, software support, and troubleshooting and provide support to students. All students may access the system at any time. There are no time limits and no fees. It is strongly recommended that all students have a personal computer. Millsaps partners with Dell Computer Corporation to offer discounts on Dell models and peripherals and on-site technical support.

Graduates: From July 1, 2004 to June 30, 2005, 276 bachelor's degrees were awarded. The most popular majors were psychology (14%), business administration (13%), and biology (8%). In an average class, 63% graduate in 4 years or less, 69% graduate in 5 years or less, and 71% graduate in 6 years or less. 54 companies recruited on campus in 2004-2005. Of the 2004 graduating class, 50% were enrolled in graduate school within 6 months of graduation and all graduates no in graduate school were employed.

Admissions Contact: Matthew Cox, Dean of Enrollment Management. E-mail: *admissions@millsaps.edu* Web: *http://www.millsaps.edu/admiss/*

MISSISSIPPI COLLEGE — C-4
Clinton, MS 39058

(601) 925-3800
(800) 738-1236; Fax: (601) 925-3950

Full-time: 945 men, 1266 women	Faculty: 143
Part-time: 94 men, 248 women	Ph.D.s: 67%
Graduate: 558 men, 794 women	Student/Faculty: 15 to 1
Year: semesters, summer session	Tuition: $10,150 ($12,058)
Application Deadline: open	Room & Board: $4424 ($5694)
Freshman Class: 2038 applied, 1164 accepted, 396 enrolled	
SAT Verbal/Math: 571/563*	ACT: 23 VERY COMPETITIVE

Mississippi College, founded in 1826 and affiliated with the Southern Baptist Church, is a private institution offering degrees in liberal arts, business, education, and health sciences. There are 4 undergraduate and 2 graduate schools. In addition to regional accreditation, MC has baccalaureate program accreditation with ACBSP, CSWE, NASM, NCATE, and NLN. The 2 libraries contain 235,000 volumes, 265,000 microform items, and 13,000 audio/video tapes/CDs/DVDs, and subscribe to 750 periodicals including electronic. Computerized library services include the card catalog, interlibrary loans, and database searching. Special learning facilities include a learning resource center, art gallery, radio station, and TV station. The 320-acre campus is in a suburban area 5 miles west of Jackson. Including any residence halls, there are 30 buildings.

Student Life: 82% of undergraduates are from Mississippi. Students are from 31 states and 5 foreign countries. 87% are white; 11% African American. Most are Protestant. The average age of freshmen is 18; all undergraduates, 22. 21% do not continue beyond their first year.

Housing: 1599 students can be accommodated in college housing, which includes single-sex dorms and married-student housing. On-campus housing is available on a first-come, first-served basis. 61% of students live on campus. Alcohol is not permitted. All students may keep cars.

Activities: There are no fraternities or sororities. There are 55 groups on campus, including art, band, cheerleading, choir, chorale, chorus, computers, debate, drama, ethnic, forensics, honors, international, jazz band, literary magazine, marching band, musical theater, newspaper, opera, pep band, political, professional, radio and TV, religious, social, social service, student government, and yearbook. Popular campus events include I Love America Day, Derby Day, and Spring Fever Week.

Sports: There are 6 intercollegiate sports for men and 6 for women, and 6 intramural sports for men and 6 for women. Facilities include a coliseum, an 8300-seat stadium, tennis courts, soccer and softball fields, a swimming pool, a 4000-seat gym, a fitness facility, and a campus weight training facility.

Disabled Students: 95% of the campus is accessible. Wheelchair ramps, elevators, special parking, specially equipped rest rooms, special class scheduling, lowered drinking fountains, lowered telephones, and wide doors and special dorm rooms equipped for the physically disabled are available.

Services: Counseling and information services are available, as is tutoring in most subjects, including study skills classes. There is remedial math, reading, and writing.

Campus Safety and Security: Measures include 24-hour foot and vehicle patrol, security escort services, informal discussions, and emergency telephones. There are lighted pathways/sidewalks.

Programs of Study: MC confers B.A., B.S., B.M., B.M.Ed., B.S.B.A., B.S.Ed., B.S.N., and B.S.W. degrees. Master's degrees are also awarded. Bachelor's degrees are awarded in BIOLOGICAL SCIENCE (biochemistry and biology/biological science), BUSINESS (accounting, business administration and management, and marketing/retailing/merchandising), COMMUNICATIONS AND THE ARTS (applied music, art, communications, English, French, graphic design, languages, modern language, music, music theory and composition, piano/organ, Spanish, voice, and winds), COMPUTER AND PHYSICAL SCIENCE (chemistry, computer science, mathematics, and physics), EDUCATION (art, business, elementary, music, and special), ENGINEERING AND ENVIRONMENTAL DESIGN (engineering physics and interior design), HEALTH PROFESSIONS (nursing), SOCIAL SCIENCE (American studies, Christian studies, criminal justice, family/consumer studies, history, paralegal studies, political science/government, psychology, religious music, social studies, social work, and sociology). Premedicine, nursing, and business are the strongest academically. Business, education, and biology are the largest.

Required: To graduate, students must complete 130 credit hours, with an average of C or better in the major. The core curriculum includes English, history, economics, computer science, religion, math, art, social science, phys ed, and chapel. 30 hours are usually required in the major; some majors require 36 to 45. Students must pass a writing proficiency exam. B.A. candidates and English majors must take 12 hours of a foreign language.

Special: Cooperative programs, including a 3-2 engineering degree and a program in agriculture, are offered with the University of Mississippi, Mississippi State University, and Auburn University. MC also offers study abroad in up to 10 contries, a 3-3 law school program with the School of Law, work-study programs, internships, B.A.-B.S. degrees, and credit for military experience and by exam. There are 18 national honor societies and a freshman honors program.

Faculty/Classroom: 62% of faculty are male; 38%, female. 82% teach undergraduates. Graduate students teach 19% of introductory courses. The average class size in an introductory lecture is 30; in a laboratory, 25; and in a regular course, 25.

Admissions: 57% of the 2005-2006 applicants were accepted. The SAT scores for the 2005-2006 freshman class were: Verbal--17% below 500, 49% between 500 and 599, 30% between 600 and 700, and 7% above 700; Math--23% below 500, 40% between 500 and 599, 28% between 600 and 700, and 9% above 700. The ACT scores were 31% below 21, 26% between 21 and 23, 25% between 24 and 26, 7% between 27 and 28, and 11% above 28. 56% of the current freshmen were in the top fifth of their class; 80% were in the top two fifths. There was 1 National Merit semifinalist. 79 freshmen graduated first in their class.

Requirements: In addition to the application for admission, students must submit a 250-word essay, at least one letter of recommendation (3 are recommended for scholarship consideration), and a transcript from all schools previously attended. For freshmen, SAT or ACT scores must be submitted (ACT is preferred). A satisfactory ACT or SAT composite score is required for regular admission. Students scoring below these levels may be considered for acceptance into the developmental program. A well-rounded high school program is advisable. An interview is recommended, as is a portfolio or audition for some majors. A GPA of 2.0 is required. AP and CLEP credits are accepted. Important factors in the admissions decision are personality/intangible qualities, extracurricular activities record, and leadership record.

Procedure: Freshmen are admitted fall, spring, and summer. Entrance exams should be taken by December of the senior year. There are early decision, early admissions, deferred admissions and rolling admissions plans. Application deadlines are open. Notification is sent on a rolling basis. 184 early decision candidates were accepted for the 2005-2006 class.

Transfer: 371 transfer students enrolled in 2004-2005. Applicants must be junior college graduates or students in good academic standing with the college they last attended. They must have a minimum GPA of 2.0. Transfer students will be considered as freshmen if fewer than 12 semester hours or 16 quarter hours have been completed. Applicants must submit transcripts from all schools previously attended. 33 of 130 credits required for the bachelor's degree must be completed at MC.

Visiting: There are regularly scheduled orientations for prospective students, including attending classes, touring the campus, and meeting with administrators and departmental advisers. There are guides for informal visits and visitors may sit in on classes and stay overnight. To schedule a visit, contact Chad Phillips, Director of Admissions.

Financial Aid: In 2005-2006, 82% of all full-time freshmen and 74% of continuing full-time students received some form of financial aid. 35% of full-time freshmen and 44% of continuing full-time students received need-based aid. The average freshman award was $13,578. The FAFSA is required. Check with the school for current deadlines.

International Students: A satisfactory score is required on the written TOEFL.

Computers: Students who have been assigned an account may access the system. There are no time limits and no fees.

Admissions Contact: Chad Phillips, Director of Admissions.
E-mail: *enrollment-services@mc.edu* Web: *www.mc.edu*

MISSISSIPPI STATE UNIVERSITY
E-3

Mississippi State, MS 39762

(662) 325-2224
Fax: (662) 325-7360

Full-time: 5840 men, 5258 women	Faculty: 1043; I, --$
Part-time: 716 men, 741 women	Ph.D.s: 80%
Graduate: 1644 men, 1645 women	Student/Faculty: 11 to 1
Year: semesters, summer session	Tuition: $4312 ($9772)
Application Deadline: August 1	Room & Board: $5265
Freshman Class: 1454 applied, 1205 accepted, 1189 enrolled	
ACT: 23	COMPETITIVE

Mississippi State University, founded in 1878 as a land-grant institution, offers degree programs in the arts and sciences, agriculture, business and industry, education, engineering, forest resources, architecture, accounting, and professional training in veterinary medicine. There are 9 undergraduate schools and 1 graduate school. In addition to regional accreditation, State has baccalaureate program accreditation with AACSB, ABET, ACCE, ACS, ADA, AHEA, APA, ASLA, CAERP, CSWE, FIDER, NAAB, NASAD, NASM, NASPPA, NCATE, and SAF. The 3 libraries contain 205,138 volumes, 2,903,393 microform items, and 19,456 audio/video tapes/CDs/DVDs, and subscribe to 18,104 periodicals including electronic. Computerized library services include the card catalog, interlibrary loans, database searching, and Internet access. Special learning facilities include a learning resource center, art gallery, natural history museum, planetarium, radio station, TV station, a music museum, an archeology museum, and an entomology museum. The 4200-acre campus is in a small town 125 miles northeast of Jackson. Including any residence halls, there are 164 buildings.

Student Life: 80% of undergraduates are from Mississippi. Others are from 49 states, 66 foreign countries, and Canada. 75% are white; 18% African American. The average age of freshmen is 21; all undergraduates, 23. 19% do not continue beyond their first year; 81% remain to graduate.

Housing: 4000 students can be accommodated in college housing, which includes single-sex and coed dormitories, on-campus apartments, married-student housing, fraternity houses, and sorority houses. In addition, there are honors houses. On-campus housing is available on a first-come, first-served basis. 80% of students commute. Alcohol is not permitted. All students may keep cars.

Activities: 17% of men belong to 17 national fraternities; 18% of women belong to 1 local and 11 national sororities. There are 302 groups on campus, including art, band, cheerleading, chess, choir, chorale, chorus, computers, dance, drama, drill team, ethnic, gay, honors, international, jazz band, literary magazine, marching band, musical theater, newspaper, orchestra, pep band, political, professional, radio and TV, religious, social, social service, student government, and symphony. Popular campus events include pep rallies, concerts, and Lyceum Series.

Sports: There are 7 intercollegiate sports for men and 9 for women, and 16 intramural sports for men and 16 for women. Facilities include a 52,000-seat football stadium, a 6,700-seat baseball park, a 9,200-seat multipurpose coliseum, a physical fitness complex, an all-weather track, 4 practice football fields, a 6-court tennis complex, an 18-hole golf course, 5 lighted tennis courts, the Sanderson Center, which consists of 7 basketball courts, 6 volleyball courts, 8 racquetball courts, 10,000 square feet for strength and aerobic conditioning, 3 full size dance studios, an indoor rock climbing wall, a 1/8 mile walking track, and Rec-Plex, which is a multipurpose field complex with 4 softball, 2 soccer, and 6 flag football fields.

Disabled Students: 90% of the campus is accessible. Wheelchair ramps, elevators, special parking, specially equipped rest rooms, special class scheduling, lowered drinking fountains, lowered telephones, special housing, and phones equipped with TTY in the union and library are available.

Services: Counseling and information services are available, as is tutoring in some subjects, including math, English, chemistry, physics, and study skills. There is a reader service for the blind, and remedial math, reading, and writing. Writing effectiveness, study assistance, preparation for professional exams and credit courses in reading and study skills are also available.

Campus Safety and Security: Measures include 24-hour foot and vehicle patrol, self-defense education, security escort services, and shuttle buses. There are informal discussions, pamphlets/posters/films, emergency telephones, and lighted pathways/sidewalks.

Programs of Study: State confers B.A., B.S., B.Accy., B.Arch., B.B.A., B.F.A., B.G.S., B.Land.Arch., B.Mus.Ed., and B.S.W. degrees. Master's and doctoral degrees are also awarded. Bachelor's degrees are awarded in AGRICULTURE (agricultural business management, agricultural economics, agriculture, agronomy, animal science, fishing and fisheries, forestry production and processing, horticulture, plant protection (pest management), poultry science, and wildlife management), BIOLOGICAL SCIENCE (biochemistry, biology/biological science, and microbiology), BUSINESS (accounting, banking and finance, business administration and management, insurance, marketing/retailing/merchandising, real estate, and trade and industrial supervision and management), COMMUNICATIONS AND THE ARTS (art, communications, English, and languages), COMPUTER AND PHYSICAL SCIENCE (chemistry, computer science, geoscience, information sciences and systems, mathematics, physics, and science), EDUCATION (agricultural, business, education, elementary, music, physical, secondary, special, and technical), ENGINEERING AND ENVIRONMENTAL DESIGN (aerospace studies, agricultural engineering technology, architecture, bioengineering, chemical engineering, civil engineering, computer engineering, electrical/electronics engineering, industrial engineering, industrial engineering technology, landscape architecture/design, and mechanical engineering), HEALTH PROFESSIONS (medical technology), SOCIAL SCIENCE (anthropology, economics, food science, history, interdisciplinary studies, liberal arts/general studies, philosophy, political science/government, psychology, social work, and sociology). Accounting, biochemistry, and physics are the strongest academically. General business administration, elementary education, and biology are the largest.

Required: The core curriculum includes 6 to 9 hours of math and natural science, 6 each of humanities, English composition, and social behavior, and 3 each of public speaking, computer literacy, and fine arts, and junior/senior-level writing. The total number of hours required for graduation and in the major varies. A minimum GPA of 2.0 must be maintained.

Special: Cooperative education, cross-registration with the Academic Common Market, internships, and study abroad in 15 countries are offered. Work-study programs, a Washington semester, accelerated degree programs, a general studies degree, nondegree study, student-designed majors, B.A.-B.S. degrees, and pass/fail options for some courses are available. There are 40 national honor societies, a freshman honors program, and 14 departmental honors programs.

Faculty/Classroom: 65% of faculty are male; 35%, female.

Admissions: 121% of the 2005-2006 applicants were accepted. The ACT scores for the 2005-2006 freshman class were: 33% below 21, 21% between 21 and 23, 20% between 24 and 26, 10% between 27 and 28, and 16% above 28. 30% of the current freshmen were in the top fifth of their class; 55% were in the top two fifths. There were 22 National Merit finalists. 51 freshmen graduated first in their class.

Requirements: The SAT or ACT is required. In addition, applicants should have completed 15 1/2 high school academic credits, including 4 in English, 3 each in math, science, and social science, 2 advanced electives (foreign language, world geography, 4th year lab-based science, or 4th year math), and 1/2 credit in the computer as a productivity tool (not keyboarding). Full admission is granted with all of the above and one of the following: minimum 3.2 GPA on required high school courses; 2.5 GPA on required high school classes or class standing in top 50% with ACT score of 16 or higher, a satisfactory score on SAT; 2.0 GPA on required high school classes with ACT score of 18 or higher, a similar score on the SAT; or satisfy National Collegiate Athletic Association standards for student-athletes who are full qualifiers under Division I guidelines. Students with a GED are accepted with the required ACT/SAT score. A GPA of 2.0 is required. AP and CLEP credits are accepted.

Procedure: Freshmen are admitted fall, spring, and summer. Entrance exams should be taken in the spring semester of junior year or fall semester of senior year. There are deferred admissions and rolling admissions plans. Applications should be filed by August 1 for fall entry, November 15 for spring entry, and May 15 for summer entry. Notification is sent on a rolling basis. Applications are accepted on-line. The fall 2005 application fee was $25.

Transfer: 1593 transfer students enrolled in a recent year. Applicants must submit an official college transcript from each college attended, indicating a minimum GPA of 2.0 (some departents require 2.5), and must be in good standing at their previous school. 32 of 136 credits required for the bachelor's degree must be completed at State.

Visiting: There are regularly scheduled orientations for prospective students, including 2 day sessions for freshmen, and 1-day session for transfers. There are guides for informal visits and visitors may sit in on classes and stay overnight. To schedule a visit, contact John Dickerson, Director of Enrollment Services at (662) 325-3076.

Financial Aid: In a recent year, 75% of all full-time freshmen and 76% of continuing full-time students received some form of financial aid. 35% of full-time freshmen and 40% of continuing full-time students received need-based aid. The average freshman award was $5230. Need-based scholarships or need-based grants averaged $3505 ($5550 maximum); need-based self-help aid (loans and jobs) averaged $3022 ($5785 maximum); non-need-based athletic scholarships averaged $3611 ($6855 maximum); and other non-need-based awards and non-need-based scholarships averaged $3506 ($17,970 maximum). 39% of undergraduates worked part time. Average annual earnings from campus work were $1996. The average financial indebtedness of a recent graduate was $16,996. The FAFSA is required. The deadline for filing freshman financial aid applications for fall entry is April 1.

International Students: There are 126 international students enrolled. They must score satisfactorily on the written TOEFL or on the electronic version and also take the SAT.

Computers: All students may access the system 24 hours a day. There are no time limits and no fees.

Graduates: In a recent year, 2698 bachelor's degrees were awarded. The most popular majors were elementary education (9%), marketing (8%), and business administration (6%). In an average class, 25% graduate in 4 years or less, 48% graduate in 5 years or less, and 56% graduate in 6 years or less. 285 companies recruited on campus in a recent year.

Admissions Contact: Diane Wolfe, Director of Admissions.
E-mail: *admit@admissions.msstate.edu*
Web: *http://www.msstate.edu/dept/admissions*

MISSISSIPPI UNIVERSITY FOR WOMEN   E-2
Columbus, MS 39701

	(662) 329-7106
	(877) 462-8439; Fax: (662) 241-7481
Full-time: 300 men, 1600 women	**Faculty:** 116; IIB, --$
Part-time: 300 men, 1000 women	**Ph.D.s:** 68%
Graduate: 20 men, 100 women	**Student/Faculty:** 16 to 1
Year: semesters, summer session	**Tuition:** $3000 ($7000)
Application Deadline: open	**Room & Board:** $3000
Freshman Class: n/av	
SAT or ACT: recommended	**LESS COMPETITIVE**

Mississippi University for Women, founded in 1884, is a public institution offering degrees in liberal arts, education, business and communications, nursing, human sciences, science and math, health and kinesiology, and culinary arts. There are 8 undergraduate and 2 graduate schools. Figures in the above capsule and in this profile are approximate. In addition to regional accreditation, MUW has baccalaureate program accreditation with AHEA, NASAD, NASM, NCATE, and NLN. The library contains 232,600 volumes, 569,400 microform items, and 100 audio/video tapes/CDs/DVDs, and subscribes to 1600 periodicals including electronic. Computerized library services include the card catalog, interlibrary loans, and database searching. Special learning facilities include a learning resource center, art gallery, radio station, TV station, and distance learning studio. The 110-acre campus is in a small town 120 miles west of Birmingham, Alabama. Including any residence halls, there are 53 buildings.

Student Life: 89% of undergraduates are from Mississippi. Others are from 20 states, 25 foreign countries, and Canada. 84% are from public schools. 70% are white; 27% African American. The average age of freshmen is 19; all undergraduates, 29. 30% do not continue beyond their first year; 43% remain to graduate.

Housing: 1100 students can be accommodated in college housing, which includes single-sex dorms, on-campus apartments, and married-student housing. On-campus housing is available on a first-come, first-served basis. 77% of students commute. Alcohol is not permitted. All students may keep cars.

Activities: 10% of men belong to 1 national and 2 local fraternities; 20% of women belong to 12 local and 3 national sororities. There are 84 groups on campus, including art, band, choir, chorale, chorus, computers, dance, drama, ethnic, film, honors, international, jazz band, literary magazine, musical theater, newspaper, orchestra, photography, political, professional, radio and TV, religious, social, social service, student government, and yearbook. Popular campus events include Mardi Gras, Oktoberfest, and Nutcracker.

Sports: There are 4 intercollegiate sports for women, and 5 intramural sports for men and 5 for women. Facilities include 3 gyms, a softball field, tennis and racquetball courts, indoor and outdoor swimming pools,

a gymnastics room, a weight room, a dance studio, a 3-hole pitch-and-putt golf course, a soccer and flag football field, and a Vita course.

Disabled Students: 95% of the campus is accessible. Wheelchair ramps, elevators, special parking, specially equipped rest rooms, special class scheduling, lowered drinking fountains, and lowered telephones are available.

Services: Counseling and information services are available, as is tutoring in most subjects. There is remedial math, reading, and writing.

Campus Safety and Security: Measures include 24-hour foot and vehicle patrol, security escort services, informal discussions, and pamphlets/posters/films. There are lighted pathways/sidewalks, guard gates, and a freshman orientation class.

Programs of Study: MUW confers B.A., B.S., B.F.A., B.M., and B.S.N. degrees. Associate and master's degrees are also awarded. Bachelor's degrees are awarded in BIOLOGICAL SCIENCE (biology/biological science and microbiology), BUSINESS (accounting, business administration and management, fashion merchandising, and sports management), COMMUNICATIONS AND THE ARTS (communications, English, fine arts, music, and Spanish), COMPUTER AND PHYSICAL SCIENCE (chemistry, mathematics, and physical sciences), EDUCATION (art, elementary, and music), HEALTH PROFESSIONS (nursing and speech pathology/audiology), SOCIAL SCIENCE (clothing and textiles management/production/services, food production/management/services, history, human development, paralegal studies, physical fitness/movement, political science/government, psychology, and social science). Biology, chemistry, and English are the strongest academically. Business, nursing, and elementary education are the largest.

Required: To graduate, students must complete 128 credit hours, including 30 to 39 in a major, with a minimum GPA of 2.0. The core curriculum requires 12 hours of English, 8 of lab-based science, 6 each of history and social sciences, 3 each of speech or philosophy, fine arts, and math, 2 of phys ed, and 1 of a freshman seminar. Students must also pass a comprehensive exam.

Special: Cross-registration and a 3-2 engineering degree are available with Mississippi State University. MUW also offers internships in all divisions, co-op and work-study programs, several combinations of dual majors, study abroad in 5 countries, credit for experience, nondegree study, and a pass/fail option. There are 15 national honor societies, a freshman honors program, and 3 departmental honors programs.

Faculty/Classroom: 39% of faculty are male; 61%, female. 94% teach undergraduates. No introductory courses are taught by graduate students. The average class size in an introductory lecture is 35; in a laboratory, 23; and in a regular course, 25.

Requirements: The SAT or ACT is recommended. In addition, prospective students should have completed 4 units of English; 3 each of math, science, and social studies courses in U.S. history, world history, government, and economics or geography; 2 of advanced electives, including foreign language or geography; and a course in computer applications. A GPA of 2.0 is required. AP and CLEP credits are accepted. Important factors in the admissions decision are recommendations by school officials, leadership record, and advanced placement or honor courses.

Procedure: Freshmen are admitted to all sessions. Entrance exams should be taken as early as possible. There are early decision and early admissions plans. Application deadlines are open. The fall 2005 application fee was $25.

Transfer: Applicants must have a GPA of 2.0 in 6 semester hours of both English composition and a lab science, 3 of college algebra or above, and 9 of transferable electives. High school and college transcripts are required. 32 of 128 credits required for the bachelor's degree must be completed at MUW.

Visiting: There are regularly scheduled orientations for prospective students, including talks with various student services officers and preregistering. There are guides for informal visits and visitors may sit in on classes and stay overnight. To schedule a visit, contact the Director of Admissions.

Financial Aid: MUW is a member of CSS. The FAFSA is required. Check with the school for current deadlines.

International Students: The school actively recruits these students. They must score satisfactorily on the written TOEFL and also take the SAT or the ACT, scoring 16 on the ACT.

Computers: All students may access the system 8 A.M. to 12 A.M. Monday through Friday. There are no time limits and no fees. It is strongly recommended that all students have a personal computer.

Admissions Contact: Director of Admissions.
E-mail: *admissions@muw.edu* Web: *www.muw.edu*

MISSISSIPPI VALLEY STATE UNIVERSITY C-2

Itta Bena, MS 38941-1400 (662) 254-3347; Fax: (662) 254-7900

Full-time: 800 men, 1634 women	**Faculty:** 116; IIB, --$
Part-time: 65 men, 249 women	**Ph.D.s:** 61%
Graduate: 77 men, 340 women	**Student/Faculty:** 21 to 1
Year: semesters, summer session	**Tuition:** $4024 ($9283)
Application Deadline: August 10	**Room & Board:** $3946
Freshman Class: 4832 applied, 1226 accepted, 407 enrolled	
ACT: 17	**COMPETITIVE**

Mississippi Valley State University, founded in 1946, offers programs in the arts and sciences, business, and education. There are 5 undergraduate schools and 1 graduate school. In addition to regional accreditation, MVSU has baccalaureate program accreditation with AACSB, NASAD, NASM, and NCATE. The library contains 127,109 volumes, 295,500 microform items, and 853 audio/video tapes/CDs/DVDs, and subscribes to 350 periodicals including electronic. Computerized library services include the card catalog, interlibrary loans, database searching, and Internet access. Special learning facilities include a learning resource center, art gallery, radio station, TV station, and a campus nursery/preschool. The 450-acre campus is in a small town 8 miles from Greenwood and 100 miles north of Jackson. Including any residence halls, there are 35 buildings.

Student Life: 92% of undergraduates are from Mississippi. Others are from 26 states, 4 foreign countries, and Canada. 92% are from public schools. 94% are African American. The average age of freshmen is 18; all undergraduates, 20. 25% do not continue beyond their first year; 40% remain to graduate.

Housing: 1914 students can be accommodated in college housing, which includes single-sex dorms. In addition, there are honors houses. On-campus housing is available on a first-come, first-served basis. 72% of students commute. Alcohol is not permitted. All students may keep cars.

Activities: There are 5 local and 4 national fraternities and 5 local and 4 national sororities. There are 44 groups on campus, including art, band, cheerleading, choir, chorus, computers, dance, drama, drill team, honors, international, jazz band, literary magazine, marching band, newspaper, performing, political, professional, radio and TV, religious, social, social service, student government, and yearbook. Popular campus events include Founders Day, Pride Day, and Black History Month.

Sports: There are 8 intercollegiate sports for men and 6 for women, and 10 intramural sports for men and 9 for women. Facilities include a stadium for football and track, a gymnastics room, a dance studio, an indoor pool, a 2200-seat gym, a basketball arena, a weight-training room, and handball, squash, and paddleball courts.

Disabled Students: 99% of the campus is accessible. Wheelchair ramps, elevators, special parking, specially equipped rest rooms, and lowered drinking fountains are available.

Services: Counseling and information services are available, as is tutoring in most subjects. There is remedial math, reading, and writing.

Campus Safety and Security: Measures include 24-hour foot and vehicle patrol, informal discussions, pamphlets/posters/films, and emergency telephones. There are lighted pathways/sidewalks.

Programs of Study: MVSU confers B.A., B.S., B.M.E., B.S.E, and B.S.W. degrees. Master's degrees are also awarded. Bachelor's degrees are awarded in BIOLOGICAL SCIENCE (biology/biological science), BUSINESS (accounting, business administration and management, and office supervision and management), COMMUNICATIONS AND THE ARTS (art, communications, English, fine arts, and speech/debate/rhetoric), COMPUTER AND PHYSICAL SCIENCE (chemistry, computer science, and mathematics), EDUCATION (early childhood, elementary, English, mathematics, music, physical, science, and social science), ENGINEERING AND ENVIRONMENTAL DESIGN (industrial engineering technology), HEALTH PROFESSIONS (environmental health science), SOCIAL SCIENCE (criminal justice, history, political science/government, public administration, social work, and sociology). Education, business, and early childhood education are the largest.

Required: General education requirements include 12 semester hours in English, 6 each in social studies and lab science, 3 each in college algebra, speech, fine arts, psychology, and health ed, and 2 in phys ed. To graduate, students must complete at least 124 credit hours with a minimum GPA of 2.0 overall and in the major.

Special: MVSU offers a special cooperative education program, B.A.-B.S. degrees, internships in social work and environmental health, an accelerated degree program, work-study, and nondegree study. Credit may be granted for military experience. A pass/fail option is possible. There are 4 national honor societies, and a freshman honors program.

Faculty/Classroom: 57% of faculty are male; 43%, female. All teach undergraduates. No introductory courses are taught by graduate students. The average class size in an introductory lecture is 30; in a laboratory, 25; and in a regular course, 30.

Admissions: 25% of the 2005-2006 applicants were accepted. The ACT scores for the 2005-2006 freshman class were: 91% below 21, 6% between 21 and 23, and 3% between 24 and 26.

Requirements: The ACT is required for Mississippi residents. Out-of-state students may submit SAT scores. Applicants must be graduates of a secondary school or have a GED and have completed 4 credits in English, 3 each in math and natural sciences, 2 1/2 in social sciences, and 1 in a foreign language. Recommendations are considered important. A GPA of 2.0 is required. AP and CLEP credits are accepted.

Procedure: Freshmen are admitted fall, spring, and summer. There is an early admissions plan. There is a rolling admissions plan. Applications should be filed by August 10 for fall entry, January for spring entry, and May for summer entry. Notification is sent on a rolling basis. Applications are accepted on-line.

Transfer: 221 transfer students enrolled in 2004-2005. Transfers must have a minimum 2.0 GPA in at least 24 specified credit hours. A minimum of 30 of 124 credits required for the bachelor's degree must be completed at MVSU.

Visiting: There are regularly scheduled orientations for prospective students, including campus tours with a student guide. Visitors may sit in on classes. To schedule a visit, contact the Dean of Students.

Financial Aid: The CSS/Profile or FAFSA and the college's own financial statement are required. The deadline for filing freshman financial aid applications for fall entry is June 1.

International Students: There are 23 international students enrolled. The school actively recruits these students. They must achieve a satisfactory score on the TOEFL and also take the SAT or the ACT, scoring 16 on the ACT.

Computers: All students may access the system at various times depending on location. There are no time limits and no fees. It is strongly recommended that all students have a personal computer.

Graduates: From July 1, 2004 to June 30, 2005, 346 bachelor's degrees were awarded. The most popular majors were early childhood education (14%), social work (14%), and criminal justice (9%). In an average class, 19% graduate in 4 years, 15% graduate in 5 years, and 6% graduate in 6 years.

Admissions Contact: Nora Taylor, Director.
E-mail: *nbtaylor@mvsu.edu* Web: *http://www.mvsu.edu*

RUST COLLEGE D-1

Holly Springs, MS 38635 (662) 252-8000, ext. 4059
(888) 886-8492, ext. 4059; Fax: (662) 252-8895

Full-time: 293 men, 546 women	**Faculty:** 45
Part-time: 58 men, 104 women	**Ph.D.s:** 47%
Graduate: none	**Student/Faculty:** 19 to 1
Year: semesters, summer session	**Tuition:** $6000
Application Deadline: July 15	**Room & Board:** $2600
Freshman Class: 4271 applied, 1586 accepted, 530 enrolled	
SAT or ACT: required	**COMPETITIVE+**

Rust College, founded in 1866, is a private liberal arts college affiliated with the United Methodist Church. The academic year consists of semesters, each divided into two 8-week modules, plus a summer term. The library contains 123,055 volumes and 106 audio/video tapes/CDs/DVDs, and subscribes to 340 periodicals including electronic. Computerized library services include the card catalog, interlibrary loans, database searching, and Internet access. Special learning facilities include a learning resource center, radio station, TV station, and the Dr. Ron Trojak collection of African tribal art. The 126-acre campus is in a small town 35 miles southeast of Memphis, Tennessee. Including any residence halls, there are 23 buildings.

Student Life: 55% of undergraduates are from Mississippi. Others are from 24 states and 6 foreign countries. 90% are from public schools. 93% are African American. 60% are Protestant; 29% claim no religious affiliation. The average age of freshmen is 19; all undergraduates, 22. 57% do not continue beyond their first year.

Housing: 856 students can be accommodated in college housing, which includes single-sex dormitories. In addition, there are honors houses. On-campus housing is guaranteed for all 4 years. 65% of students live on campus; of those, 50% remain on campus on weekends. Alcohol is not permitted. All students may keep cars.

Activities: 2% of men belong to 3 local and 3 national fraternities; 6% of women belong to 4 local and 4 national sororities. There are 32 groups on campus, including band, cheerleading, choir, chorale, computers, drama, ethnic, honors, international, marching band, newspaper, political, radio and TV, religious, social, social service, and student government. Popular campus events include Career Day, Religious Emphasis Week and African American Student Leadership Conference.

Sports: There are 7 intercollegiate sports for men and 7 for women. Facilities include a 2500-seat gym, a swimming pool, tennis courts, a track, a 2000-seat stadium, a bowling alley, pool tables, and the Magic Johnson Sports Arena.

Disabled Students: All of the campus is accessible. Wheelchair ramps, elevators, special parking, specially equipped rest rooms, and lowered drinking fountains are available.

Services: Counseling and information services are available, as is tutoring in most subjects. There is remedial math, reading, and writing.

Campus Safety and Security: Measures include 24-hour foot and vehicle patrol, security escort services, informal discussions, and pamphlets/posters/films. There are lighted pathways/sidewalks.

Programs of Study: Rust confers B.A., B.S., and B.S.W. degrees. Associate degrees are also awarded. Bachelor's degrees are awarded in BIOLOGICAL SCIENCE (biology/biological science), BUSINESS (business administration and management), COMMUNICATIONS AND THE ARTS (communications, English, journalism, and music), COMPUTER AND PHYSICAL SCIENCE (chemistry, computer science, and mathematics), EDUCATION (business, elementary, English, mathematics, science, secondary, and social science), HEALTH PROFESSIONS (health), SOCIAL SCIENCE (political science/government, social work, and sociology). Business administration and management are the strongest academically. Biology, computer science, and social work are the largest.

Required: All students must earn a minimum of 124 semester hours while maintaining a cumulative GPA of 2.0. Distribution requirements include 59 1/2 general education credits in the fields of education, humanities, science, and math, and a required freshman program. A minimum of 50 credits constitutes a major, and comprehensive exams are given in all programs. Required courses in addition to the freshman program include math, biology, physical science, computer science, English, foreign language, literature, speech, social science, and history.

Special: Internships are available in all areas and may be required for some majors. On-campus work-study, study abroad, credit by examination, independent study, B.A.-B.S. degrees, and dual majors in a variety of programs are available. There are 3-2 degrees in preprofessional programs and medical technology, and a 3-2 engineering degree with the student's school of choice. There are 3 national honor societies, a freshman honors program, and 5 departmental honors programs.

Faculty/Classroom: 67% of faculty are male; 33%, female. All teach undergraduates. The average class size in an introductory lecture is 10; in a laboratory, 10; and in a regular course, 25.

Admissions: 37% of the 2005-2006 applicants were accepted. The ACT scores for the 2005-2006 freshman class were: 47% below 21, 22% between 21 and 23, and 3% between 27 and 28.

Requirements: The SAT or ACT is required. In addition, students must submit 19 academic credits, including 4 in English, 3 each in math, science, and social studies, and 6 electives. An audition, an interview, and 2 letters of recommendation are required. The GED is accepted. An essay and portfolio are recommended. A GPA of 2.0 is required. AP and CLEP credits are accepted. Important factors in the admissions decision are evidence of special talent, extracurricular activities record, and recommendations by school officials.

Procedure: Freshmen are admitted fall, spring, and summer. Entrance exams should be taken prior to the first semester of the freshman year. There is a rolling admissions plan. Applications should be filed by July 15 for fall entry and December 15 for spring entry, along with a $10 fee. Notification is sent on a rolling basis. Applications are accepted on-line.

Transfer: 45 transfer students enrolled in 2004-2005. Transfer applicants with at least 15 semester hours of credit need not take the ACT or SAT. No credits below C in any course and no credits for any course which are not in keeping with the college's catalog will be accepted. 30 of 124 credits required for the bachelor's degree must be completed at Rust.

Visiting: There are regularly scheduled orientations for prospective students, including a campus tour, departmental visits, introduction to the application process, financial aid orientation, and question-and-answer session. There are guides for informal visits and visitors may sit in on classes and stay overnight. To schedule a visit, contact Johnny McDonald, Enrollment Services.

Financial Aid: In 2004-2005, 96% of all full-time students received some form of financial aid. 88% of full-time freshmen and 74% of continuing full-time students received need-based aid. The average freshman award was $7210. Need-based scholarships or need-based grants averaged $3460 ($6550 maximum); need-based self-help aid (loans and jobs) averaged $2613 ($3625 maximum); other non-need-based awards and non-need-based scholarships averaged $2064 ($8400 maximum); and non-need based jobs averaged $650 ($1100 maximum). 64% of undergraduates work part time. Average annual earnings from campus work are $1100. The average financial indebtedness of the 2004 graduate was $9314. The FFS and the college's own financial statement are required. The deadline for filing freshman financial aid applications for fall entry is July 15.

International Students: In a recent year there were 74 international students enrolled. They must score satisfactorily on the written TOEFL.

Computers: All students may access the system. There are no time limits and no fees.

Graduates: From July 1, 2004 to June 30, 2005, 102 bachelor's degrees were awarded. The most popular majors were computer science (17%), biology (14%), and business administration (12%). In an average class, 14% graduate in 4 years or less, 12% graduate in 5 years or less, and 3% graduate in 6 years or less. 42 companies recruited on campus in a recent year. Of the 2004 graduating class, 19% were enrolled in graduate school within 6 months of graduation and 52% were employed.

Admissions Contact: Johnny McDonald, Director Enrollment Services. E-mail: *jbmcdonald@rustcollege.edu* Web: *rustcollege.edu*

TOUGALOO COLLEGE
C-4
Tougaloo, MS 39174

(601) 977-7764
(888) 424-2566; Fax: (601) 977-6185

Full-time: 270 men, 600 women	**Faculty:** 66
Part-time: 20 men, 50 women	**Ph.D.s:** 52%
Graduate: none	**Student/Faculty:** 15 to 1
Year: semesters, summer session	**Tuition:** $9755
Application Deadline: open	**Room & Board:** $6220
Freshman Class: n/av	
SAT or ACT: required	**NONCOMPETITIVE**

Tougaloo College, founded in 1869, is a private arts and sciences institution with an affiliation with the United Church of Christ. Enrollment figures in the above capsule are approximate. There are 5 undergraduate schools. In addition to regional accreditation, Tougaloo has baccalaureate program accreditation with NCATE. The library contains 117,000 volumes, 7371 microform items, and 3600 audio/video tapes/CDs/DVDs, and subscribes to 126,934 periodicals including electronic. Computerized library services include the card catalog, interlibrary loans, database searching, Internet access, and laptop Internet portals. Special learning facilities include a learning resource center, art gallery, and manuscripts and archival materials, and the largest collection of civil rights archives in the South. The 500-acre campus is in a suburban area 1 mile north of Jackson. Including any residence halls, there are 35 buildings.

Student Life: 87% of undergraduates are from Mississippi. Others are from 23 states and 2 foreign countries. 98% are from public schools. 97% are African American. 80% are Protestant; 20% Catholic. The average age of freshmen is 18; all undergraduates, 20. 18% do not continue beyond their first year; 68% remain to graduate.

Housing: 800 students can be accommodated in college housing, which includes single-sex dorms. On-campus housing is available on a first-come, first-served basis. 60% of students live on campus; of those, 80% remain on campus on weekends. Alcohol is not permitted. All students may keep cars.

Activities: 35% of men belong to 4 national fraternities; 40% of women belong to 4 national sororities. There are many groups and organizations on campus, including art, cheerleading, choir, chorus, computers, dance, debate, drama, film, honors, international, jazz band, literary magazine, newspaper, photography, political, professional, radio and TV, religious, social, social service, student government, and yearbook. Popular campus events include Founders Week, Humanities Festival, and Mr. and Miss UNCF.

Sports: There are 5 intercollegiate sports for men and 5 for women, and 2 intramural sports for men and 2 for women. Facilities include a gym, tennis courts, a baseball diamond, an outdoor swimming pool, and access to a bowling alley and a golf course.

Disabled Students: 80% of the campus is accessible. Wheelchair ramps, elevators, special parking, specially equipped rest rooms, and special housing are available.

Services: Counseling and information services are available, as is tutoring in every subject. There is remedial math, reading, and writing.

Campus Safety and Security: Measures include 24-hour foot and vehicle patrol, self-defense education, security escort services, and informal discussions. There are pamphlets/posters/films, emergency telephones, and lighted pathways/sidewalks.

Programs of Study: Tougaloo confers B.A. and B.S. degrees. Associate degrees are also awarded. Bachelor's degrees are awarded in BIOLOGICAL SCIENCE (biology/biological science), BUSINESS (hospitality management services and recreation and leisure services), COMMUNICATIONS AND THE ARTS (art, communications, English, journalism, and music performance), COMPUTER AND PHYSICAL SCIENCE (chemistry, computer science, mathematics, and physics), EDUCATION (elementary, English, mathematics, music, physical, science, and special), SOCIAL SCIENCE (child psychology/development, economics, history, humanities, political science/government, psychology, religion, and sociology). Biology, chemistry and economics are the strongest academically. Biology, economics and psychology are the largest.

Required: To graduate, students must complete a minimum 124 credit hours, including 27 to 48 in the major, with a minimum GPA of 2.0 Students must fulfill about 56 hours of general education requirements, take computer science and phys ed courses, complete a senior paper, pass an English/writing proficiency exam, and complete 60 hours of community service.

Special: Tougaloo offers domestic exchange programs with Brown, Boston and New York Universities, and Smith and Bowdoin Colleges. Study abroad in African, European, South American, and Caribbean countries, a Washington semester in conjunction with American University, an internship in a congressman's office, other internships, work-study programs, credit for military service, and pass/fail options are available. There are 3 national honor societies, a freshman honors program, and 2 departmental honors programs.

Faculty/Classroom: 55% of faculty are male; 45%, female. All teach undergraduates, 20% do research, and 20% do both. The average class size in an introductory lecture is 30; in a laboratory, 15; and in a regular course, 15.

Admissions: 25% of the current freshmen were in the top fifth of their class; 45% were in the top two fifths. There were 5 National Merit semifinalists. 54 freshmen graduated first in their class.

Requirements: The SAT or ACT is required. The ACT Optional Writing test is also recommended. In addition, candidates should be graduates of an accredited secondary school or have a GED certificate. They should have completed 3 credits of English, 2 each of math and science, and 1 each of history and social studies. An interview is recommended. A GPA of 2.0 is required. AP and CLEP credits are accepted. Important factors in the admissions decision are advanced placement or honor courses, evidence of special talent, and leadership record.

Procedure: Freshmen are admitted fall and spring. Entrance exams should be taken by March of the senior year. There is a rolling admissions plan. Application deadlines are open. Application fee is $25. Applications are accepted on-line.

Transfer: 41 transfer students enrolled in 2005-2006. Applicants must submit transcripts of all college course work and have a minimum GPA of 2.0. 30 of 124 credits required for the bachelor's degree must be completed at Tougaloo.

Visiting: There are regularly scheduled orientations for prospective students, consisting of information on the admission process and financial aid a campus tour, an interview with departmental faculty if previously scheduled, and for music majors, auditions. There are guides for informal visits and visitors may sit in on classes and stay overnight. To schedule a visit, contact the Office of Enrollment Management at (601) 977-7765 or jjacobs@tougaloo.edu ssmith@tougaloo.edu.

Financial Aid: In 2005-2006, 90% of all full-time freshmen and 89% of continuing full-time students received some form of financial aid. 80% of all full-time students received need-based aid. Need-based scholarships or need-based grants averaged $3182; need-based self-help aid (loans and jobs) averaged $6682; non-need-based athletic scholarships averaged $7530; other non-need-based awards and non-need-based scholarships averaged $6145; and endowed scholarships averaged $2525. 13% of undergraduates work part time. Average annual earnings from campus work are $1841. The average financial indebtedness of the 2005 graduate was $20,000. Tougaloo is a member of CSS. The CSS Profile, FAFSA, FFS, or SFS is required.

International Students: There are 5 international students enrolled. They must take the TOEFL and also take the SAT or the ACT.

Computers: Wireless access is available. PCs are located in the math, reading, and writing labs, the computer labs, residential halls, and in the Coleman Library. Roughly 300 computers are available for student use 24 hours a day. All students may access the system. There are no time limits and no fees. It is strongly recommended that all students have a personal computer. A Dell is recommended.

Graduates: From July 1, 2004 to June 30, 2005, 168 bachelor's degrees were awarded. The most popular majors were psychology (14%), English (13%), and biology (8%). 46 companies recruited on campus in 2004-2005. Of the 2004 graduating class, 68% were enrolled in graduate school within 6 months of graduation and 31% were employed.

Admissions Contact: Steve Smith, Assistant Vice President for Enrollment Management. A video is available. E-mail: ssmith@tougaloo.edu Web: www.tougaloo.edu

UNIVERSITY OF MISSISSIPPI   D-2
University, MS 38677

(662) 915-7226
(800) OLE-MISS; Fax: (662) 915-5869

Full-time: 4500 men, 4700 women	Faculty: 495; I, --$
Part-time: 300 men, 300 women	Ph.D.s: 83%
Graduate: 1000 men, 1000 women	Student/Faculty: 17 to 1
Year: semesters, summer session	Tuition: $4000 ($9000)
Application Deadline: see profile	Room & Board: $5000
Freshman Class: n/av	
SAT or ACT: required	COMPETITIVE

The University of Mississippi, founded in 1844, is a public institution offering undergraduate and graduate programs in the liberal arts, business, pharmacy, engineering, accountancy, and education. There are 6 undergraduate and 2 graduate schools. Figures in the above capsule and in this profile are approximate. In addition to regional accreditation, Ole Miss has baccalaureate program accreditation with AACSB, ABET, ACE-JMC, CSAB, CSWE, NASAD, NASM, and NCATE. The 3 libraries contain 1 million volumes and 42,000 audio/video tapes/CDs/DVDs, and subscribe to 6400 periodicals including electronic. Computerized library services include the card catalog, interlibrary loans, and database searching. Special learning facilities include a learning resource center, an art gallery, a radio station, a TV station, a museum, the Center for the Study of Southern Culture, the National Center for Physical Acoustics, Rowan Oak, the home of William Faulkner, the National Center for Development of Natural Products, the National Food Service Management Institute, and the Croft Institute for International Studies. The 2000-acre campus is in a small town 70 miles southeast of Memphis, Tennessee. Including any residence halls, there are 193 buildings.

Student Life: 65% of undergraduates are from Mississippi. Others are from 47 states, 70 foreign countries, and Canada. 70% are from public schools. 82% are white; 12% African American. The average age of all undergraduates is 21. 26% do not continue beyond their first year; 54% remain to graduate.

Housing: 4513 students can be accommodated in college housing, which includes single-sex dorms, on-campus apartments, married-student housing, fraternity houses, and sorority houses. In addition, there are honors floors and special interest floors in serveral dorms. On-campus housing is guaranteed for the freshman year only, is available on a first-come, first-served basis, and is available on a lottery system for upperclassmen. Alcohol is not permitted. All students may keep cars.

Activities: 35% of men belong to 19 national fraternities; 40% of women belong to 13 national sororities. There are 200 groups on campus, including art, band, cheerleading, chess, choir, chorale, chorus, computers, dance, drama, drill team, ethnic, gay, honors, international, jazz band, literary magazine, marching band, musical theater, newspaper, orchestra, pep band, political, professional, radio and TV, religious, social, social service, student government, symphony, and yearbook. Popular campus events include Faulkner and Yoknapatawpha Conference, Red and Blue Week, and Oxford Conference for the Book.

Sports: There are 8 intercollegiate sports for men and 10 for women, and 35 intramural sports for men and 35 for women. Facilities include a 50,577-seat football stadium, an 8800-seat gym, a baseball diamond, an indoor pool, 10 racquetball courts, 23 outdoor tennis courts, 3 playing fields, women's soccer and softball fields, volleyball, an indoor tennis facility, and a fitness center.

Disabled Students: 25% of the campus is accessible. Wheelchair ramps, elevators, special parking, specially equipped rest rooms, special class scheduling, lowered drinking fountains, and lowered telephones are available.

Services: Counseling and information services are available, as is tutoring in every subject. There is a reader service for the blind and remedial math and reading.

Campus Safety and Security: Measures include 24-hour foot and vehicle patrol, self-defense education, security escort services, and informal discussions. There are pamphlets/posters/films, emergency telephones, lighted pathways/sidewalks, and a full-time campus safety officer.

Programs of Study: Ole Miss confers B.A., B.S., B.Ac., B.A.E., B.A.Ed., B.A.L.M., B.B.A., B.C.R., B.E., B.F.A., B.Mus., B.P.A., B.S.C.E., B.S.Ch.E., B.S.C.S., B.S.E.E., B.S.E.S., B.S.F.C.S., B.S.G.E., B.S.J., B.S.M.E., B.S.Pharm., and B.S.W. degrees. Master's and doctoral degrees are also awarded. Bachelor's degrees are awarded in BIOLOGICAL SCIENCE (biology/biological science), BUSINESS (accounting, banking and finance, business administration and management, business economics, court reporting, insurance, international business management, investments and securities, management information systems, management science, marketing/retailing/merchandising, real estate, recreation and leisure services, and recreational facilities management), COMMUNICATIONS AND THE ARTS (advertising, art, art history and appreciation, broadcasting, design, dramatic arts, English, French, German, journalism, linguistics, music, radio/television technology, and Spanish), COMPUTER AND PHYSICAL SCIENCE (chemistry, computer science, geology, and physics), EDUCATION (elementary, English, foreign languages, home economics, mathematics, science, social science, and special), ENGINEERING AND ENVIRONMENTAL DESIGN (chemical engineering, civil engineering, electrical/electronics engineering, engineering, geological engineering, and mechanical engineering), HEALTH PROFESSIONS (biomedical science, exercise science, medical laboratory technology, medical technology, pharmacy, speech pathology/audiology, and speech therapy), SOCIAL SCIENCE (anthropology, area studies, classical/ancient civilization, economics, family/consumer studies, forensic studies, history, international studies, liberal arts/general studies, philosophy, political science/government, psychology, public administration, social work, and sociology). General business, accountancy, and biological sciences are the largest.

Required: Students must maintain a minimum GPA of 2.0 (2.5 in teacher education) while taking 126 to 139 semester hours, including 24 to 42 in the major. Other requirements include 6 hours each of English composition and lab science and 3 each of college algebra and humanities and fine arts.

Special: Internships in journalism, accounting, and engineering, study abroad in numerous countries, and work-study programs within the college are offered. Dual majors, a general studies degree, credit by exam, special testing in music and languages, credit for military experience, and limited pass/fail options also are available. There are 24 national honor societies and a freshman honors program.

Faculty/Classroom: 69% of faculty are male; 31%, female.

Requirements: The SAT or ACT is required, with a minimum composite score of 18 on the ACT or a comparable SAT score. Applicants need

15 academic credits, including 4 units in English, 3 each in math, science lab courses, and social studies, 2 in foreign language or world geography, and 1/2 in computer applications. A portfolio for art majors and an audition for theater and music majors are required. The GED is not accepted. A GPA of 2.0 is required. AP and CLEP credits are accepted.
Procedure: Freshmen are admitted to all sessions. There are early admissions and deferred admissions plans. Check with the school for current application dealines and fee. Notification is sent on a rolling basis. Aplications are accepted on-line.
Transfer: Transfer students must have earned a minimum 2.0 GPA on previous college work. The SAT or ACT may be required depending on credits earned. 30 of 126 to 139 credits required for the bachelor's degree must be completed at Ole Miss.
Visiting: There are regularly scheduled orientations for prospective students, including academic information/student life discussions and tours. Class attendance and academic appointments can be arranged. There are guides for informal visits and visitors may stay overnight. To schedule a visit, contact the Office of Admissions.
Financial Aid: Ole Miss is a member of CSS. The FAFSA is required. Check with the school for curent deadlines.
International Students: The school actively recruits these students. They must score satisfactorily on the written TOEFL or on the electronic version or take the college's own test and also take the SAT or the ACT.
Computers: All students may access the system 24 hours daily. There are no time limits and no fees. It is strongly recommended that all students have a personal computer.
Admissions Contact: Admissions Officer. A video is available. E-mail: *admissions@olemiss.edu* Web: *www.olemiss.edu*

UNIVERSITY OF SOUTHERN MISSISSIPPI   D-5
Hattiesburg, MS 39406-1000
(601) 266-5000
Fax: (601) 266-5148

Full-time: 4248 men, 6479 women	Faculty: 708; I, --$
Part-time: 646 men, 1095 women	Ph.D.s: 80%
Graduate: 972 men, 1590 women	Student/Faculty: 15 to 1
Year: semesters, summer session	Tuition: $4312 ($9742)
Application Deadline: see profile	Room & Board: $5800
Freshman Class: 5153 applied, 3151 accepted, 1346 enrolled	
SAT Verbal/Math: 520/520*	ACT: 21 COMPETITIVE

The University of Southern Mississippi, founded in 1910, is a public institution offering comprehensive undergraduate and graduate programs. There are 5 undergraduate schools and 1 graduate school. In addition to regional accreditation, Southern Miss has baccalaureate program accreditation with AACSB, ABET, ACEJMC, ADA, AHEA, ASLA, CAHEA, CSAB, CSWE, FIDER, NASAD, NASM, NCATE, NLN, and NRPA. The 2 libraries contain 1,319,836 volumes, 4,813,531 microform items, and 19,082 audio/video tapes/CDs/DVDs, and subscribe to 19,759 periodicals including electronic. Computerized library services include the card catalog, interlibrary loans, database searching, and Internet access. Special learning facilities include a learning resource center, art gallery, natural history museum, radio station, TV station, TV production studios, the Museum of Natural Science, and a music resource center. The 1090-acre campus is in a suburban area 90 miles southeast of Jackson and 105 miles north of New Orleans. Including any residence halls, there are 185 buildings.
Student Life: 90% of undergraduates are from Mississippi. Others are from 47 states, 41 foreign countries, and Canada. 67% are white; 28% African American. The average age of freshmen is 18; all undergraduates, 24. 25% do not continue beyond their first year; 46% remain to graduate.
Housing: 3488 students can be accommodated in college housing, which includes single-sex dorms, married-student housing, fraternity houses, and sorority houses. In addition, there are special-interest houses and a section of 1 dorm reserved for honor students. Freshmen are housed togueter. On-campus housing is available on a first-come, first-served basis. 69% of students commute. Alcohol is not permitted. All students may keep cars.
Activities: 20% of men belong to 16 local and 16 national fraternities; 17% of women belong to 12 local and 12 national sororities. There are 239 groups on campus, including art, band, cheerleading, choir, chorale, chorus, computers, dance, drama, drum and bugle corps, ethnic, film, gay, honors, international, jazz band, literary magazine, marching band, musical theater, newspaper, opera, orchestra, pep band, photography, political, professional, radio and TV, religious, social, social service, student government, and symphony.
Sports: There are 7 intercollegiate sports for men and 9 for women, and 41 intramural sports for men and 41 for women. Facilities include a recreational lake, a football stadium, a basketball coliseum, a baseball park, a golf course, a softball stadium, a track and field stadium, a fitness institute, a natatorium, and playing fields for softball, flag football, and soccer.
Disabled Students: 80% of the campus is accessible. Wheelchair ramps, elevators, special parking, specially equipped rest rooms, special

class scheduling, lowered drinking fountains, lowered telephones, special housing, and an Office of Support Services for students with disabilities are available.
Services: Counseling and information services are available, as is tutoring in most subjects. There is a reader service for the blind, and remedial math, reading, and writing.
Campus Safety and Security: Measures include 24-hour foot and vehicle patrol, self-defense education, security escort services, and shuttle buses. There are informal discussions, pamphlets/posters/films, emergency telephones, and lighted pathways/sidewalks.
Programs of Study: Southern Miss confers B.A., B.S., B.F.A., B.M., B.M.E., and B.S.B.A degrees. Master's and doctoral degrees are also awarded. Bachelor's degrees are awarded in BIOLOGICAL SCIENCE (biology/biological science), BUSINESS (accounting, banking and finance, business administration and management, business economics, hotel/motel and restaurant management, international business management, marketing/retailing/merchandising, and personnel management), COMMUNICATIONS AND THE ARTS (advertising, communications, dance, design, dramatic arts, English, fine arts, journalism, languages, music, radio/television technology, and speech/debate/rhetoric), COMPUTER AND PHYSICAL SCIENCE (chemistry, computer science, geology, information sciences and systems, mathematics, physics, polymer science, and statistics), EDUCATION (art, business, early childhood, elementary, foreign languages, guidance, health, home economics, industrial arts, middle school, music, science, and secondary), ENGINEERING AND ENVIRONMENTAL DESIGN (architectural technology, computer technology, construction technology, electrical/electronics engineering technology, engineering technology, and mechanical engineering technology), HEALTH PROFESSIONS (medical laboratory technology, nursing, predentistry, premedicine, and speech pathology/audiology), SOCIAL SCIENCE (anthropology, criminal justice, economics, geography, history, international studies, parks and recreation management, philosophy, political science/government, prelaw, psychology, social science, social work, and sociology). Polymer science and accounting are the strongest academically. Accounting is the largest.
Required: To graduate, students must complete at least 128 semester hours, including 64 at the senior college level, with a minimum GPA of 2.0. Core requirements include courses in reasoning and communication skills, English, including composition, history, humanities and fine arts, social and behavioral sciences, human wellness, and natural and applied sciences.
Special: Southern Miss offers many cooperative programs, internships, dual majors, nondegree study, limited pass/fail options, credit for life experience, and study abroad in England, Germany, Austria, and Italy. The university also participates in the Title IV College Work-Study Program. Accelerated degrees, distance learning, ESL, independent study, and a teacher certification program are also available. There are 27 national honor societies and a freshman honors program.
Faculty/Classroom: 56% of faculty are male; 44%, female. 91% teach undergraduates and 75% do research. The average class size in an introductory lecture is 37; in a laboratory, 32; and in a regular course, 29.
Admissions: 61% of the 2005-2006 applicants were accepted. The SAT scores for the 2005-2006 freshman class were: Verbal--40% below 500, 41% between 500 and 599, 15% between 600 and 700, and 4% above 700; Math--34% below 500, 48% between 500 and 599, 14% between 600 and 700, and 4% above 700. The ACT scores were 47% below 21, 26% between 21 and 23, 14% between 24 and 26, 6% between 27 and 28, and 7% above 28. 29% of the current freshmen were in the top fifth of their class; 69% were in the top two fifths. There were 3 National Merit semifinalists.
Requirements: A satisfactory score is required on the ACT. Applicants must be graduates of an accredited secondary school or have a GED certificate. They should have completed 4 units of English, 3 each of math and lab science, 2 each of history and advanced electives, and 1 each of social studies and computer applications. A GPA of 2.0 is required. AP and CLEP credits are accepted. Important factors in the admissions decision are evidence of special talent and parents or siblings attending the school.
Procedure: Freshmen are admitted to all sessions. Entrance exams should be taken in the fall of the senior year. There are early action, and deferred admissions plans. Check with the school for current deadlines. There is no application fee. Notification is sent on a rolling basis. Applications are accepted on-line.
Transfer: 1634 transfer students enrolled in 2004-2005. Applicants must be eligible to return to their previous institution and present a statement of good standing from those institutions, along with college transcripts showing a 2.0 GPA. 32 of 128 credits required for the bachelor's degree must be completed at Southern Miss.
Visiting: There are regularly scheduled orientations for prospective students, including campus tours and general session orientations. There are guides for informal visits and visitors may sit in on classes. To schedule a visit, contact the Office of Admission.
Financial Aid: In 2005-2006, 62% of all full-time freshmen and 64% of continuing full-time students received some form of financial aid. At

least 49% of full-time freshmen and 53% of continuing full-time students received need-based aid. The average freshman award was $6156. Need-based scholarships or need-based grants averaged $3296; institutional need-based self-help aid (loans and jobs) averaged $2959; non-need-based athletic scholarships averaged $5296; and other non-need-based awards and non-need-based scholarships averaged $2910. The average financial indebtedness of the 2005 graduate is $15,776. The FAFSA and the college's own financial statement are required. The priority date for freshman financial aid applications for fall entry is March 15.

International Students: In a recent year, there were 114 international students enrolled. The school actively recruits these students. A satisfactory score is required on the written TOEFL. Students must also take the ACT, scoring 18.

Computers: All students may access the system at any time labs are open (departmental labs are for the department only). There are no time limits and no fees.

Graduates: From July 1, 2004 to June 30, 2005, 2300 bachelor's degrees were awarded. The most popular majors were business/marketing (20%), education (11%), and health professions and related sciences (10%). In an average class, 23% graduate in 4 years or less, 41% graduate in 5 years or less, and 46% graduate in 6 years or less. 918 companies recruited on campus in 2004-2005.

Admissions Contact: Matthew Cox, Admissions Office. A video is available. E-mail: *admissions@usm.edu* Web: *www.usm.edu*

WILLIAM CAREY COLLEGE   D-5

Hattiesburg, MS 39401-5499   **(601) 582-6103**
                                    (800) 962-5991; Fax: (601) 582-6454

Full-time: 500 men, 900 women	**Faculty:** 80
Part-time: 150 men, 300 women	**Ph.D.s:** 57%
Graduate: none	**Student/Faculty:** 17 to 1
Year: trimesters, summer session	**Tuition:** $8000
Application Deadline: see profile	**Room & Board:** $3000
Freshman Class: n/av	
ACT: required	**LESS COMPETITIVE**

William Carey College, founded in 1906, is a private liberal arts college affiliated with the Mississippi Baptist Convention. There are 4 undergraduate and 2 graduate schools. Figures in the above capsule and in this profile are approximate. In addition to regional accreditation, Carey has baccalaureate program accreditation with NASDTEC, NASM, and NLN. The 4 libraries contain 135,000 volumes, 30,000 microform items, and 3000 audio/video tapes/CDs/DVDs, and subscribe to 600 periodicals including electronic. Computerized library services include the card catalog, interlibrary loans, and database searching. Special learning facilities include a learning resource center and art gallery. The 120-acre campus is in a small town 100 miles from New Orleans, Louisiana. Including any residence halls, there are 15 buildings.

Student Life: The average age of freshmen is 18.

Housing: 428 students can be accommodated in college housing, which includes single-sex dorms and on-campus apartments. 50% of students live on campus. Alcohol is not permitted. All students may keep cars.

Activities: There is 1 national fraternity and 1 national and 2 local sororities. There are 20 groups on campus, including art, cheerleading, choir, chorale, drama, ethnic, honors, international, literary magazine, newspaper, pep band, professional, religious, social, social service, student government, and yearbook. Popular campus events include Hydromania and Mudbowl, Spring Fling Week, and Crawfish Boil.

Sports: There are 4 intercollegiate sports for men and 4 for women, and 3 intramural sports for men and 3 for women. Facilities include a gym, a baseball field, an intramural field, and tennis courts.

Disabled Students: 80% of the campus is accessible. Wheelchair ramps, special parking, specially equipped rest rooms, and special class scheduling are available.

Services: Counseling and information services are available, as is tutoring in every subject. There is remedial math, reading, and writing.

Campus Safety and Security: Measures include 24-hour foot and vehicle patrol, security escort services, informal discussions, and pamphlets/posters/films. There are emergency telephones, lighted pathways/sidewalks, and campus security personnel are on duty 24 hours a day.

Programs of Study: Carey confers B.A., B.S., B.F.A., B.G.S., B.L.S., B.M., B.S.B., and B.S.N. degrees. Master's degrees are also awarded. Bachelor's degrees are awarded in BIOLOGICAL SCIENCE (biology/biological science), BUSINESS (business administration and management), COMMUNICATIONS AND THE ARTS (art, communications, dramatic arts, English, music, music performance, and Spanish), COMPUTER AND PHYSICAL SCIENCE (chemistry, mathematics, and radiological technology), EDUCATION (elementary, music, and physical), HEALTH PROFESSIONS (medical laboratory technology, music therapy, and nursing), SOCIAL SCIENCE (history, liberal arts/general studies, psychology, religion, religious music, and social science). Education, music, and nursing are the strongest academically. Education and nursing are the largest.

Required: Students must complete a core curriculum, including 6 credits each in religion, English, history, and social and behavioral science; 4 in lab science; 3 each in math, fine arts, communication, and literature; and 2 in phys ed. A total of 128 trimester hours, with a minimum 2.0 GPA overall and in the major, is needed to graduate.

Special: Internships are available in some disciplines, and nondegree study, a 3-2 program in forestry, and a 3-1 program in medical technology are also available. 2-year professional programs are possible in engineering, physical therapy, medical records administration, radiological technology, optometry, and pharmacy. Upperclassmen may choose 1 pass/fail option per trimester. There are 7 national honor societies and a freshman honors program.

Requirements: The ACT is required. In addition, applicants must have earned 16 Carnegie units, including courses in English, foreign language, social studies, science, and math. The admissions committee also considers special skills or aptitudes and other evidence of academic potential. Recommendations from high school officials and college alumni, extracurricular activities, honors courses, leadership potential, and ability to pay also are considered. Carey requires applicants to be in the upper 50% of their class. A GPA of 2.0 is required. AP and CLEP credits are accepted.

Procedure: Freshmen are admitted to all sessions. There are early admissions and deferred admissions plans. Check with the school for current application deadlines. The fall 2005 applicatin fee was $20. Notification is sent on a rolling basis.

Transfer: Transfer students must have a minimum GPA of 1.4 for freshmen, 1.7 for sophomores, and 2.0 for juniors. 30 of 128 credits required for the bachelor's degree must be completed at Carey.

Visiting: There are regularly scheduled orientations for prospective students, including panel discussions, campus tours, faculty advising, and financial aid seminars. There are guides for informal visits and visitors may sit in on classes and stay overnight. To schedule a visit, contact the Admissions Office.

Financial Aid: The FAFSA is required. Check with the school for current deadlines.

International Students: They must score satisfactorily on the written TOEFL or take the MELAB or the college's own test, and must also take the SAT or the ACT.

Computers: All students may access the system. There are no time limits and no fees.

Admissions Contact: Admissions Officer.
E-mail: *admiss@wmcarey.edu* Web: *www.wmcarey.edu*

MISSOURI

POPULATION DENSITY
● 25,000 and over

0   20   40   60   80   100
Miles

AVILA UNIVERSITY
A-2

Kansas City, MO 64145

(816) 501-2400
(800) GO-AVILA; Fax: (816) 501-2453

Full-time: 317 men, 593 women	**Faculty:** 64; IIB, --$
Part-time: 95 men, 209 women	**Ph.D.s:** 77%
Graduate: 146 men, 337 women	**Student/Faculty:** 14 to 1
Year: semesters, summer session	**Tuition:** $16,700
Application Deadline: open	**Room & Board:** $5400
Freshman Class: 920 applied, 516 accepted, 173 enrolled	
SAT Verbal/Math: 490/490*	**ACT:** 21 **COMPETITIVE**

Avila University, founded in 1916, is a comprehensive liberal arts institution sponsored by the Sisters of St. Joseph of Carondelet. In addition to regional accreditation, Avila has baccalaureate program accreditation with CAHEA, CCNE, and CSWE. The library contains 77,000 volumes, 493,706 microform items, and 3094 audio/video tapes/CDs/DVDs, and subscribes to 551 periodicals including electronic. Computerized library services include the card catalog, interlibrary loans, database searching, and Internet access. Special learning facilities include a learning resource center, art gallery, TV station, a 500-seat theater, an interactive video library, and video production facilities. The 48-acre campus is in a suburban area in Kansas City, Missouri. Including any residence halls, there are 11 buildings.

Student Life: 65% of undergraduates are from Missouri. Others are from 26 states, 24 foreign countries, and Canada. 88% are from public schools. 74% are white; 15% African American. 25% are Catholic; 9% Protestant. The average age of freshmen is 18; all undergraduates, 27. 29% do not continue beyond their first year; 41% remain to graduate.

Housing: 230 students can be accommodated in college housing, which includes coed dorms. On-campus housing is guaranteed for all 4 years. 77% of students commute. Alcohol is not permitted. All students may keep cars.

Activities: There are no fraternities or sororities. There are 36 groups on campus, including art, cheerleading, choir, chorale, chorus, computers, dance, drama, ethnic, film, gay, honors, international, literary magazine, musical theater, newspaper, photography, political, professional, radio and TV, religious, social, social service, and student government. Popular campus events include sports and theatrical events, Family Day, and International Festival.

Sports: There are 4 intercollegiate sports for men and 7 for women, and 6 intramural sports for men and 6 for women. Facilities include a field house with basketball and volleyball courts, a training room, and weight and fitness equipment. There is also an athletic complex with baseball, softball, and soccer fields, tennis courts, and practice fields.

Disabled Students: 95% of the campus is accessible. Wheelchair ramps, elevators, special parking, specially equipped rest rooms, special class scheduling, lowered drinking fountains, and lowered telephones are available.

Services: Counseling and information services are available, as is tutoring in most subjects. There is a reader service for the blind, and remedial math, reading, and writing.

Campus Safety and Security: Measures include self-defense education, security escort services, informal discussions, and pamphlets/posters/films. There are lighted pathways/sidewalks. There are evening and night security patrols and 24-hour closed-circuit television in residence hall entryways, computer labs, and the student lounge. Another closed circuit system monitors gym areas.

Programs of Study: Avila confers B.A., B.S., B.F.A., B.S.B.A., B.S.N., and B.S.W. degrees. Master's degrees are also awarded. Bachelor's degrees are awarded in BIOLOGICAL SCIENCE (biology/biological science), BUSINESS (accounting, banking and finance, business administration and management, international business management, management science, and marketing/retailing/merchandising), COMMUNICATIONS AND THE ARTS (art, communications, dramatic arts, English, and music), COMPUTER AND PHYSICAL SCIENCE (chemistry, computer science, information sciences and systems, mathematics, natural sciences, and radiological technology), EDUCATION (business, elementary, middle school, and special), HEALTH PROFESSIONS (medical laboratory technology, nursing, premedicine, and sports medicine), SOCIAL SCIENCE (history, liberal arts/general studies, paralegal studies, political science/government, psychology, social work, sociology, and theological studies). Nursing, education, and communications are the strongest academically. Nursing, education, and radiologic technology are the largest.

Required: To graduate, students must complete at least 128 semester hours with a minimum 2.0 GPA. The 41 to 46 hour core curriculum consists of courses in composition, communication, math, history, literature, theology, philosophy, the arts, the sciences, and social institutions.

Special: Students may cross-register with the Kansas City Area Student Exchange, the Sisters of Saint Joseph College Consortium, and the Council of Independent Colleges Student Exchange. Avila also offers internships in business, communication, graphic design, paralegal, and other majors, work-study, a Washington center program, dual majors in science, math, and health professions, and accelerated degree programs in business administration and psychology. There are 4 national honor societies.

Faculty/Classroom: 38% of faculty are male; 62%, female. All both teach and do research. No introductory courses are taught by graduate students. The average class size in an introductory lecture is 22; in a laboratory, 25; and in a regular course, 16.

Admissions: 56% of the 2005-2006 applicants were accepted. The SAT scores for the 2005-2006 freshman class were: Verbal--55% below 500, 18% between 500 and 599, and 27% between 600 and 700; Math--55% below 500, 18% between 500 and 599, 18% between 600 and 700, and 9% above 700. The ACT scores were 53% below 21, 25% between 21 and 23, 16% between 24 and 26, 3% between 27 and 28, and 4% above 28. 27% of the current freshmen were in the top fifth of their class; 53% were in the top two fifths.

Requirements: The SAT or ACT is required. Applicants must be graduates of an accredited secondary school or have a GED certificate. They should have completed 16 academic units, including 4 in English, 3 in math, 2 to 4 in foreign language, 2 to 3 in natural and social sciences, and 1 to 2 in fine arts. A GPA of 2.5 is required. AP and CLEP credits are accepted. Important factors in the admissions decision are recommendations by school officials, extracurricular activities record, and leadership record.

Procedure: Freshmen are admitted to all sessions. There is a rolling admissions plan. Entrance exams should be taken in the spring or summer of the junior year. Application deadlines are open.

Transfer: 207 transfer students enrolled in 2004-2005. Applicants must have a minimum GPA of 2.0. 30 of 128 credits required for the bachelor's degree must be completed at Avila.

Visiting: There are regularly scheduled orientations for prospective students, including a visit with admissions and a faculty member and a campus tour. There are guides for informal visits and visitors may sit in on classes and stay overnight. To schedule a visit, contact the Campus Visit Coordinator at (816) 501-3603.

Financial Aid: In 2005-2006, 97% of all full-time freshmen and 87% of continuing full-time students received some form of financial aid. 76% of full-time freshmen and 74% of continuing full-time students received

need-based aid. The average freshman award was $8550. Need-based scholarships or need-based grants averaged $6393 ($6638 maximum); need-based self-help aid (loans and jobs) averaged $3353 ($4957 maximum); and non-need-based athletic scholarships averaged $3260 ($3212 maximum). 92% of undergraduates work part time. Average annual earnings from campus work are $1200. The average financial indebtedness of the 2005 graduate was $16,625. The FAFSA is required. The priority date for freshman financial aid applications for fall entry is March 1. The deadline for filing freshman financial aid applications for fall entry is April 1.

International Students: There are 73 international students enrolled. The school actively recruits these students. They must score satisfactorily on the written TOEFL.

Computers: Computers provided for student use include 84 PCs and 30 Macs in classrooms, plus 35 in the library and 10 in residence halls. Internet access is available on Avila-owned computers and inresidence hall rooms. There is no wireless access currently available on campus. All students may access the system. There are no time limits and no fees.

Graduates: From July 1, 2004 to June 30, 2005, 226 bachelor's degrees were awarded. The most popular majors were business (15%), psychology (12%), and education (9%). In an average class, 35% graduate in 4 years or less, 39% graduate in 5 years or less, and 41% graduate in 6 years or less. Of the 2004 graduating class, 20% were enrolled in graduate school within 6 months of graduation and 97% were employed.

Admissions Contact: Patti Harper, Director of Admissions.
E-mail: *admissions@mail.avila.edu* Web: *www.avila.edu*

CENTRAL METHODIST UNIVERSITY C-2
Fayette, MO 65248

(660) 248-6247
(877) CMU-1854; Fax: (660) 248-1872

Full-time: 400 men, 400 women	**Faculty:** 64
Part-time: 20 men, 30 women	**Ph.D.s:** 50%
Graduate: 10 men, 50 women	**Student/Faculty:** 12 to 1
Year: semesters, summer session	**Tuition:** $13,000
Application Deadline: open	**Room & Board:** $5000
Freshman Class: n/av	
ACT: required	**COMPETITIVE**

Central Methodist University, formerly Central Methodist College and founded in 1854, is a private liberal arts institution affiliated with the Methodist Church. Figures in the above capsule and in this profile are approximate. In addition to regional accreditation, CMC has baccalaureate program accreditation with NASM. The library contains 102,700 volumes, 140,800 microform items, and 3700 audio/video tapes/CDs/DVDs, and subscribes to 450 periodicals including electronic. Computerized library services include the card catalog, interlibrary loans, and database searching. Special learning facilities include a learning resource center, art gallery, natural history museum, radio station, TV station, and an observatory. The 2-acre campus is in a small town 30 miles northwest of Columbia. Including any residence halls, there are 22 buildings.

Student Life: 90% of undergraduates are from Missouri. Others are from 20 states, 8 foreign countries, and Canada. 96% are from public schools. 87% are white. 77% are Protestant; 20% Catholic. The average age of freshmen is 18; all undergraduates, 21. 39% do not continue beyond their first year.

Housing: 667 students can be accommodated in college housing, which includes single-sex and coed dorms, off-campus apartments, and married-student housing. On-campus housing is guaranteed for all 4 years. 70% of students live on campus; of those, 60% remain on campus on weekends. Alcohol is not permitted. All students may keep cars.

Activities: 40% of men belong to 6 local fraternities; 40% of women belong to 5 local sororities. There are 30 groups on campus, including band, cheerleading, choir, chorale, chorus, computers, debate, drama, drill team, honors, jazz band, literary magazine, marching band, newspaper, pep band, photography, political, professional, radio and TV, religious, social, social service, student government, and yearbook. Popular campus events include the Music Festival.

Sports: There are 7 intercollegiate sports for men and 7 for women, and 10 intramural sports for men and 10 for women. Facilities include a field house with a 2000-seat gym, playing fields, and a recreation center.

Disabled Students: 65% of the campus is accessible. Wheelchair ramps, elevators, special parking, specially equipped rest rooms, special class scheduling, and lowered drinking fountains are available.

Services: Counseling and information services are available, as is tutoring in some subjects. There is remedial math, reading, and writing.

Campus Safety and Security: Measures include 24-hour foot and vehicle patrol, security escort services, informal discussions, and pamphlets/posters/films. There are emergency telephones and lighted pathways/sidewalks.

Programs of Study: CMC confers B.A., B.S., B.M., B.M.E., B.S.E., and B.S.N. degrees. Associate degrees are also awarded. Bachelor's degrees are awarded in BIOLOGICAL SCIENCE (biology/biological science), BUSINESS (accounting, business administration and management, and recreational facilities management), COMMUNICATIONS AND THE ARTS (broadcasting, communications, dramatic arts, English, French, music, and Spanish), COMPUTER AND PHYSICAL SCIENCE (chemistry, computer science, mathematics, and physics), EDUCATION (athletic training, early childhood, elementary, foreign languages, music, physical, science, and social science), ENGINEERING AND ENVIRONMENTAL DESIGN (environmental science), HEALTH PROFESSIONS (nursing), SOCIAL SCIENCE (criminal justice, economics, history, interdisciplinary studies, philosophy, political science/government, psychology, public administration, religion, and sociology). Sciences, music, and preprofessional programs are the strongest academically. Business and education are the largest.

Required: To graduate, students must complete 124 to 131 credit hours, including at least 24 in the major, depending on the degree sought. A minimum GPA of 2.0 is required for all but the athletic training and education programs, which require a 2.5. Students must complete 53 hours of a distribution curriculum, including computer literacy, phys ed or a competency exam, religion, philosophy, freshman orientation to college life, and a senior capstone.

Special: CMC offers cooperative programs in medical technology and physical therapy, and 3-2 engineering degrees with the University of Missouri at Rolla, the University of Evansville, Stanford University, and Washington University at St. Louis. Work-study programs, internships, study abroad in France, Germany, and Spain, dual majors, a general studies degree, and nondegree study are also available. There are 10 national honor societies, and a freshman honors program.

Faculty/Classroom: 60% of faculty are male; 40%, female. All teach undergraduates. No introductory courses are taught by graduate students. The average class size in a laboratory is 9 and in a regular course, 14.

Requirements: The ACT is required, with a minimum score of 18. Those students with a GPA lower than 2.0 may write a letter of appeal and have an interview. Applicants should be graduates of an accredited secondary school or have a GED certificate. Recommended preparatory courses include 4 units of English, 3 of math, and 2 each of science, social studies, and humanities. AP and CLEP credits are accepted. Important factors in the admissions decision are advanced placement or honor courses, evidence of special talent, and extracurricular activities record.

Procedure: Freshmen are admitted fall, winter, and summer. There are early decision and early admissions plans. There is a rolling admissions plan. Application deadlines are open. The fall application fee is $20. Applications are accepted on-line.

Transfer: Transfer applicants must be in good academic standing at their previous college. 30 of 124 credits required for the bachelor's degree must be completed at CMC.

Visiting: There are regularly scheduled orientations for prospective students, including a campus tour and visits with faculty members. There are guides for informal visits and visitors may sit in on classes and stay overnight. To schedule a visit, contact Admissions/Student Affairs at (660) 248-2242.

Financial Aid: The FAFSA is required. Check with the school for current deadlines.

International Students: The school actively recruits these students. They must score satisfactorily on the written TOEFL or take the MELAB.

Computers: All students may access the system during lab hours for up to an hour at a time. There are no time limits.

Admissions Contact: Office of Admissions. A video is available.
E-mail: *admissions@centralmethodist.edu*
Web: *wwwcentralmethodist.edu*

CENTRAL MISSOURI STATE UNIVERSITY B-2
Warrensburg, MO 64093

(660) 543-4290
(800) 956-0177; Fax: (660) 543-8517

Full-time: 3300 men, 3800 women	**Faculty:** 428; IIA, --$
Part-time: 700 men, 900 women	**Ph.D.s:** 67%
Graduate: 700 men, 900 women	**Student/Faculty:** 17 to 1
Year: semesters, summer session	**Tuition:** $5000 ($10,000)
Application Deadline: open	**Room & Board:** $5000
Freshman Class: n/av	
ACT: required	**COMPETITIVE**

Central Missouri State University, founded in 1871, is a public liberal arts institution offering a comprehensive range of degree programs. There are 5 undergraduate schools and 1 graduate school. Figures in the above capsule and in this profile are approximate. In addition to regional accreditation, Central has baccalaureate program accreditation with AACSB, ABET, ACCE, ACS, ADA, ADDA, ASLA, CAA, CSWE, NAIT, NASAD, NASM, NASPE, NCATE, NLN, and SOA. The library contains 2,503,000 volumes, 1,601,700 microform items, and 23,900 audio/video tapes/CDs/DVDs, and subscribes to 3500 periodicals including electronic. Computerized library services include the card catalog, interlibrary loans, and database searching. Special learning facilities include a learning resource center, an art gallery, a natural history museum, a radio station, a TV station, an instructional airport, a 200-acre farm, a driving/safety range, a speech and hearing clinic, a child development lab, and an English Language Center. The 1561-acre campus is in a small town 50 miles southeast of Kansas City. Including any residence halls, there are 50 buildings.

Student Life: 90% of undergraduates are from Missouri. Others are from 43 states, 59 foreign countries, and Canada. 92% are from public schools. 88% are white. 62% are Protestant; 23% Catholic. The average age of freshmen is 18; all undergraduates, 21. 28% do not continue beyond their first year; 46% remain to graduate.

Housing: 3545 students can be accommodated in college housing, which includes single-sex and coed dormitories, on-campus apartments, off-campus apartments, married-student housing, fraternity houses, and sorority houses. In addition, there are honors houses, special-interest houses and quiet dorms. On-campus housing is available on a first-come, first-served basis. 68% of students commute. All students may keep cars.

Activities: 12% of men belong to 13 national fraternities; 10% of women belong to 10 national sororities. There are 200 groups on campus, including art, band, cheerleading, chess, choir, chorale, chorus, computers, dance, debate, drama, drill team, ethnic, film, forensics, gay, honors, international, jazz band, literary magazine, marching band, musical theater, newspaper, opera, orchestra, pep band, photography, political, professional, radio and TV, religious, social, social service, student government, symphony, and yearbook. Popular campus events include Performing Arts Series, Technology Fair, and Repertory Theater.

Sports: There are 7 intercollegiate sports for men and 7 for women, and 45 intramural sports for men and 45 for women. Facilities include a stadium seating more than 12,000, 3 gyms, baseball, softball, women's soccer, and practice fields, a bowling alley, tennis courts, and a multipurpose building that contains a swimming pool, weight rooms, and courts for basketball, racquetball, and volleyball. A nearby outdoor recreation area has an 18-hole golf course and facilities for swimming and other activities.

Disabled Students: 95% of the campus is accessible. Wheelchair ramps, elevators, special parking, specially equipped rest rooms, special class scheduling, lowered drinking fountains, lowered telephones, and special housing are available.

Services: Counseling and information services are available, as is tutoring in some subjects, including math, chemistry, physics, biology, accounting, economics, and business. There is a reader service for the blind and remedial math. Writing and learning labs are available for all students. Tutoring is available through TRIO Student Support Services.

Campus Safety and Security: Measures include 24-hour foot and vehicle patrol, self-defense education, security escort services, and informal discussions. There are pamphlets/posters/films, emergency telephones, lighted pathways/sidewalks, a bike patrol, and a canine patrol.

Programs of Study: Central confers B.A., B.S., B.F.A., B.M., B.M.E., B.S.B.A., B.S.Ed., and B.S.W. degrees. Associate and master's degrees are also awarded. Bachelor's degrees are awarded in AGRICULTURE (agricultural business management, agricultural economics, and conservation and regulation), BIOLOGICAL SCIENCE (biology/biological science), BUSINESS (accounting, banking and finance, business administration and management, hotel/motel and restaurant management, human resources, management science, marketing/retailing/merchandising, organizational behavior, recreation and leisure services, and tourism), COMMUNICATIONS AND THE ARTS (broadcasting, communications, English, French, German, journalism, music, photography, public relations, Spanish, speech/debate/rhetoric, studio art, and theater design), COMPUTER AND PHYSICAL SCIENCE (actuarial science, chemistry, computer science, earth science, geology, information sciences and systems, mathematics, and physics), EDUCATION (agricultural, art, business, early childhood, elementary, English, foreign languages, home economics, industrial arts, mathematics, middle school, music, physical, science, secondary, social studies, and special), ENGINEERING AND ENVIRONMENTAL DESIGN (agricultural engineering technology, automotive technology, aviation computer technology, commercial art, construction management, drafting and design technology, electrical/electronics engineering, electrical/electronics engineering technology, engineering, engineering technology, graphic arts technology, industrial engineering technology, interior design, manufacturing technology, and occupational safety and health), HEALTH PROFESSIONS (medical laboratory technology, nursing, predentistry, premedicine, and speech pathology/audiology), SOCIAL SCIENCE (child care/child and family studies, criminal justice, dietetics, economics, geography, history, political science/government, prelaw, psychology, safety management, social work, sociology, and textiles and clothing). Curriculum and instruction, criminal justice, and business management are the largest.

Required: To graduate, students must complete a minimum of 124 hours, including 35 to 64 in the major, and have a minimum GPA of 2.0; several majors require a higher cumulative GPA. General education requirements include a total of 39 to 45 hours in humanities, social sciences, multicultural studies, technology, English and oral communications, math, science, and individual development. A comprehensive exam may be part of the exit assessment in selected majors.

Special: Central offers cross-registration with the Midwest Student Exchange Program, credit and noncredit internships, study abroad in more than 15 countries, a B.A.-B.S. degree, dual and student-designed majors, credit for military service, pass/fail options, nondegree study, and a 3-2 engineering degree with the University of Missouri at Columbia and at Rolla and with the University of Indiana. There are 25 national honor societies and a freshman honors program.

Faculty/Classroom: 62% of faculty are male; 38%, female. The average class size in an introductory lecture is 30.

Admissions: 76% of recent applicants were accepted. The ACT scores for a recent freshman class were: 41% below 21, 31% between 21 and 23, 15% between 24 and 26, 7% between 27 and 28, and 6% above 28. 32% of recent freshmen were in the top fifth of their class; 58% were in the top two fifths. There was 1 National Merit finalist, and 32 freshmen graduated first in their class in a recent year.

Requirements: The ACT is required. In addition, applicants must have completed 16 academic credits, including 4 in English with a writing emphasis, and 3 each in math (algebra and beyond) and social science, 2 in natural sciences, and 1 in fine or performing arts, as well as 3 in academic electives. A foreign language is recommended. The GED is accepted. Central requires applicants to be in the upper 50% of their class. AP and CLEP credits are accepted.

Procedure: Freshmen are admitted to all sessions. Entrance exams should be taken in the junior year. Application deadlines are open. The fall 2005 application fee was $25. Notification is sent on a rolling basis. Applications are accepted on-line.

Transfer: 752 transfer students enrolled in a recent year. Applicants must have a minimum GPA of 2.0, as indicated by an official college transcript. 30 of 124 credits required for the bachelor's degree must be completed at Central.

Visiting: There are regularly scheduled orientations for prospective students, including orientation sessions on housing, general education requirements, and enrollment for fall classes. There are guides for informal visits and visitors may sit in on classes and stay overnight. To schedule a visit, contact the Office of Admissions.

Financial Aid: In a recent year, 82% of all full-time freshmen and 81% of continuing full-time students received some form of financial aid. 75% of all full-time students received need-based aid. The average freshman award was $6752. Need-based scholarships or need-based grants averaged $3754 ($7350 maximum); need-based self-help aid (loans and jobs) averaged $2308 ($3597 maximum); non-need-based athletic scholarships averaged $3616 ($12,975 maximum); and other non-need-based awards and non-need-based scholarships averaged $2643 ($19,491 maximum). 39% of undergraduates work part time. Average annual earnings from campus work are $1900. The average financial indebtedness of a recent graduate was $9300. Central is a member of CSS. The FAFSA is required. Check with the school for current deadlines.

International Students: There were 309 international students enrolled in a recent year. The school actively recruits these students. They must score satisfactorily on the written TOEFL and also participate in institutional assessment.

Computers: All students may access the system 24 hours a day. There are no time limits and no fees.

Graduates: In a recent year, 1643 bachelor's degrees were awarded. The most popular majors were curriculum and instruction (66%), criminal justice (37%), and computer infomation systems and business (34%). In an average class, 1% graduate in 3 years or less, 20% graduate in 4 years or less, 39% graduate in 5 years or less, and 49% graduate in 6 years or less. 322 companies recruited on campus in a recent year. Of a recent graduating class, 12% were enrolled in graduate school within 6 months of graduation and 94% were employed.

Admissions Contact: Dr. Matt Melvin, Assistant Provost of Enrollment Management. A video is available. E-mail: *admit@cmsu1.cmsu.edu* Web: *cmsu.edu*

COLLEGE OF THE OZARKS
Point Lookout, MO 65726

B-4

(417) 334-6411, ext. 4219
(800) 222-0525; Fax: (417) 335-2618

Full-time: 585 men, 719 women	Faculty: 71; IIB, --$
Part-time: 18 men, 26 women	Ph.D.s: 58%
Graduate: none	Student/Faculty: 18 to 1
Year: semesters	Tuition: $330
Application Deadline: February 1	Room & Board: $3800
Freshman Class: 2137 applied, 290 accepted, 254 enrolled	
ACT: 22	VERY COMPETITIVE+

College of the Ozarks, founded in 1906, is a private liberal arts college affiliated with the Presbyterian Church (U.S.A.). Instead of paying tuition, students work a total of 560 hours in campus jobs and are responsible only for room and board, books, personal expenses, and an incidental fee of $280. Students may also elect to work in a summer program, which will cover their room and board costs as well. There is 1 undergraduate school. In addition to regional accreditation, C of O has baccalaureate program accreditation with ADA. The library contains 121,507 volumes, 31,186 microform items, and 5549 audio/video tapes/CDs/DVDs, and subscribes to 6952 periodicals including electronic. Computerized library services include the card catalog, interlibrary loans, database searching, and Internet access. Special learning facilities include a learning resource center, art gallery, radio station, museum, grist mill, weaving studio, firehouse, print shop, orchid greenhouses, fruit-cake/jelly kitchens, day care center, and 3 farm operations. The 1000-acre campus is in a small town 40 miles south of Springfield, adjacent to the resort town of Branson. Including any residence halls, there are 82 buildings.

Student Life: 62% of undergraduates are from Missouri. Others are from 40 states and 15 foreign countries. 85% are from public schools. 94% are white. 74% are Protestant; 20% claim no religious affiliation; 6% Catholic. The average age of freshmen is 19; all undergraduates, 21. 24% do not continue beyond their first year; 70% remain to graduate.

Housing: 1031 students can be accommodated in college housing, which includes single-sex dorms. On-campus housing is guaranteed for all 4 years. 68% of students live on campus; of those, 80% remain on campus on weekends. Alcohol is not permitted. All students may keep cars.

Activities: There are no fraternities or sororities. There are 49 groups on campus, including art, band, cheerleading, choir, chorale, computers, dance, departmental academic major clubs, drama, film, honors, international, jazz band, literary magazine, musical theater, newspaper, orchestra, pep band, photography, political, professional, radio and TV, religious, social service, student government, and yearbook. Popular campus events include Fourth of July, lectures, and concerts.

Sports: There are 2 intercollegiate sports for men and 2 for women, and 12 intramural sports for men and 12 for women. Facilities include an all-weather track, an indoor walking track, horseshoe pit, softball and baseball fields, tennis courts, handball courts, volleyball and sand volleyball, badminton and table tennis facilities, an aerobics room and rehabilitation training room, and a field house with a 4500-seat gym, 3 basketball courts, an Olympic-size pool, a weight training room, racquetball courts, and a dance studio.

Disabled Students: 95% of the campus is accessible. Wheelchair ramps, elevators, special parking, and specially equipped rest rooms are available.

Services: Counseling and information services are available, as is tutoring in some subjects, including math and foreign language. There is also a center for writing and thinking. There is remedial math.

Campus Safety and Security: Measures include 24-hour foot and vehicle patrol, informal discussions, pamphlets/posters/films, and emergency telephones. There are lighted pathways/sidewalks, a parking lot security system, and a 24-hour paramedic service on campus. The front gate is locked at 1 A.M. daily and women's dorms are locked at closing hours.

Programs of Study: C of O confers B.A. and B.S. degrees. Bachelor's degrees are awarded in AGRICULTURE (agricultural business management, agriculture, agronomy, animal science, conservation and regulation, and horticulture), BIOLOGICAL SCIENCE (biology/biological science), BUSINESS (accounting, business administration and management, business economics, hotel/motel and restaurant management, international business management, and marketing management), COMMUNICATIONS AND THE ARTS (art, broadcasting, communications, dramatic arts, English, journalism, media arts, music, music business management, musical theater, performing arts, public relations, Spanish, studio art, and theater design), COMPUTER AND PHYSICAL SCIENCE (chemistry, computer science, information sciences and systems, and mathematics), EDUCATION (agricultural, art, business, early childhood, elementary, English, foreign languages, mathematics, music, physical, recreation, secondary, social studies, and vocational), ENGINEERING AND ENVIRONMENTAL DESIGN (graphic arts technology and preengineering), HEALTH PROFESSIONS (health, medical technology, premedicine, prepharmacy, and preveterinary science), SOCIAL SCIENCE (child psychology/development, clothing and textiles management/production/services, corrections, criminal justice, criminology, dietetics, family/consumer studies, food science, forensic studies, gerontology, history, home economics, interdisciplinary studies, law enforcement and corrections, philosophy, political science/government, prelaw, psychology, religion, religious music, social work, and sociology). Sciences, history, and education are the strongest academically. Business administration and education are the largest.

Required: 55 to 58 hours of general education requirements include specific courses in English, speech, religion, history and political science, math, and phys ed. Students must also select courses from an arts and letters, social science, and physical science distribution. B.A. candidates must complete 8 credit hours of foreign language, and B.S. candidates must complete 6 to 8 credit hours of additional physical science, biology, or math. To graduate, all students must complete at least 124 credit hours, including 36 upper level and 30 in a major field, with a minimum GPA of 2.0 in the major as well as overall. A portfolio is required.

Special: The college offers co-op programs, internships, a 3-2 engineering degree program, and independent study/practicum courses,. There are 4 national honor societies and 6 departmental honors programs.

Faculty/Classroom: 73% of faculty are male; 27%, female. All teach undergraduates. The average class size in an introductory lecture is 35; in a laboratory, 20; and in a regular course, 21.

Admissions: 14% of the 2005-2006 applicants were accepted. The ACT scores for the 2005-2006 freshman class were: 40% below 21, 33% between 21 and 23, 18% between 24 and 26, 5% between 27 and 28, and 4% above 28. 33% of the current freshmen were in the top fifth of their class; 61% were in the top two fifths. 8 freshmen graduated first in their class.

Requirements: The ACT is required. In addition, applicants must be graduates of accredited secondary schools or have earned a GED or have an ACT score of 19 or better. A physical exam, financial aid application, 2 recommendations (preferably from school personnel) and an interview are required. C of O requires applicants to be in the upper 3% of their class. A GPA of 3.0 is required. AP and CLEP credits are accepted. Important factors in the admissions decision are ability to finance college education, advanced placement or honor courses, and leadership record.

Procedure: Freshmen are admitted fall and spring. Entrance exams should be taken in October or December of the senior year. There is a rolling admissions plan. Early decision applications should be filed by February 15; regular applications, by February 1 for fall entry and March 15 for winter entry. Notification of early decision is sent February 15; regular decision, March 15. 340 applicants were on the 2005 waiting list; 111 were admitted. Applications are accepted on-line.

Transfer: 51 transfer students enrolled in 2004-2005. Transfer applicants must present a minimum GPA of 2.0 and may not have a previous disciplinary or loan default record. The ACT or the SAT is required if the applicant has completed fewer than 48 credit hours. An interview is required. The dean of students at the transfer college must complete a form attesting to the positive character of the applicant. All transfer students must submit a financial aid transcript. 45 of 125 credits required for the bachelor's degree must be completed at C of O.

Visiting: There are regularly scheduled orientations for prospective students, Mondays through Fridays. There are guides for informal visits and visitors may sit in on classes. To schedule a visit, contact the Admissions Office at (417) 334-6411 or *admiss4@cofo.edu*.

Financial Aid: In 2005-2006, 100% of all full-time students received some form of financial aid. 90% of all full-time students received need-based aid. The average freshman award was $14,900. Need-based scholarships or need-based grants averaged $12,161 ($12,161 maximum); need-based self-help aid (loans and jobs) averaged $2884 ($2884 maximum); and non-need-based athletic scholarships averaged $2662 ($2662 maximum). 100% of undergraduates work part time. Average annual earnings from campus work are $2884. The average financial indebtedness of the 2005 graduate was $4079. The FAFSA and student and parent federal tax returns are required. The priority date for freshman financial aid applications for fall entry is February 15. The deadline for filing freshman financial aid applications for fall entry is March 15.

International Students: There are 24 international students enrolled. A satisfactory score, is required on the written TOEFL and it is recommended that they also take the ACT or the SAT.

Computers: Computer labs and dorm rooms have Internet access. All students may access the system from 8 A.M. to 11 P.M. There are no time limits and no fees.

Graduates: From July 1, 2004 to June 30, 2005, 251 bachelor's degrees were awarded. The most popular majors were education (19%), business (15%), and psychology (8%). In an average class, 21% graduate in 4 years or less, 39% graduate in 5 years or less, and 44% graduate in 6 years or less. 152 companies recruited on campus in 2004-2005.

Admissions Contact: Marci Linson, Dean of Admissions.
E-mail: *admiss4@cofo.edu* Web: *http://www.cofo.edu*

COLUMBIA COLLEGE C-2
Columbia, MO 65216
(573) 875-7352
(800) 231-2391; Fax: (573) 875-7506

Full-time: 315 men, 442 women	Faculty: 56; IIB, --$
Part-time: 97 men, 155 women	Ph.D.s: 86%
Graduate: 51 men, 89 women	Student/Faculty: 14 to 1
Year: semesters, summer session	Tuition: $11,994
Application Deadline: open	Room & Board: $4906
Freshman Class: 819 applied, 509 accepted, 163 enrolled	
SAT Verbal/Math: 530/520*	ACT: 22 COMPETITIVE

Columbia College, founded in 1851, is a private liberal arts and sciences institution affiliated with the Christian Church (Disciples of Christ). In addition to regional accreditation, Columbia has baccalaureate program accreditation with CSWE. The library contains 80,000 volumes, 12,860 microform items, and 2100 audio/video tapes/CDs/DVDs, and subscribes to 10,706 periodicals including electronic. Computerized library services include the card catalog, interlibrary loans, database searching, and Internet access. Special learning facilities include a learning resource center and art gallery. The 30-acre campus is in an urban area 120 miles east of Kansas City and 120 miles west of St. Louis. Including any residence halls, there are 18 buildings.

Student Life: 89% of undergraduates are from Missouri. Others are from 25 states, 12 foreign countries, and Canada. 93% are from public schools. 78% are white. 80% are claim no religious affiliation; 12% are Protestant; 6% Catholic. The average age of freshmen is 19; all undergraduates, 23. 31% do not continue beyond their first year; 46% remain to graduate.

Housing: 360 students can be accommodated in college housing, which includes single-sex and coed dorms. In addition, there is a wellness floor. On-campus housing is guaranteed for all 4 years. 65% of students commute. Alcohol is not permitted. All students may keep cars.

Activities: There are no fraternities or sororities. There are 35 groups on campus, including art, choir, chorale, ethnic, honors, international, literary magazine, newspaper, photography, political, professional, religious, social, social service, student government, and yearbook. Popular campus events include Ivy Chain, Holiday Lighting Ceremony, and Schiffman Ethics Lectures.

Sports: There are 2 intercollegiate sports for men and 3 for women, and 16 intramural sports for men and 16 for women. Facilities include softball and soccer fields, a dance studio, indoor tennis courts, an exercise/weight room, and a gym and sports complex.

Disabled Students: 97% of the campus is accessible. Wheelchair ramps, elevators, special parking, specially equipped rest rooms, special class scheduling, lowered drinking fountains, and lowered telephones are available.

Services: Counseling and information services are available, as is tutoring in most subjects, including accounting, English composition, geography, math, history, and psychology, as well as in study skills. There is remedial math and writing.

Campus Safety and Security: Measures include 24-hour foot and vehicle patrol, security escort services, informal discussions, and pamphlets/posters/films. There are emergency telephones and lighted pathways/sidewalks.

Programs of Study: Columbia confers B.A., B.S., B.A.I.S, and B.F.A. degrees. Associate and master's degrees are also awarded. Bachelor's degrees are awarded in AGRICULTURE (environmental studies), BIOLOGICAL SCIENCE (biology/biological science), BUSINESS (accounting, banking and finance, business administration and management, and marketing/retailing/merchandising), COMMUNICATIONS AND THE ARTS (art, English, and fine arts), COMPUTER AND PHYSICAL SCIENCE (chemistry, computer science, and information sciences and systems), EDUCATION (elementary, middle school, and secondary), SOCIAL SCIENCE (criminal justice, forensic studies, history, interdisciplinary studies, philosophy, political science/government, psychology, social work, and sociology). Art, psychology, and biology are the strongest academically. Business administration is the largest.

Required: To graduate, students must complete 120 semester hours and with a minimum GPA of 2.0. Distribution requirements include 12 hours in basic skills such as English composition and computers, 6 each in humanities, history, math and science, and social science, and 3 in ethics. All majors require students to complete a capstone course.

Special: Columbia offers cross-registration with the University of Missouri/Columbia and Stephens College, internships, study abroad in more than 20 countries, B.A.-B.S. degrees in most disciplines, an interdisciplinary studies degree, student-designed and dual majors, nondegree study, and pass/fail options. Select students who complete a special 2-semester project earn a bachelor's degree with distinction (B.A.D.). There are 15 national honor societies, a freshman honors program, and all departments have honors programs.

Faculty/Classroom: 57% of faculty are male; 43%, female. All teach undergraduates and 50% do research. No introductory courses are taught by graduate students. The average class size in an introductory lecture is 24; in a laboratory, 14; and in a regular course, 16.

Admissions: 62% of the 2005-2006 applicants were accepted. The SAT scores for the 2005-2006 freshman class were: Verbal--20% below 500, 50% between 500 and 599, and 30% between 600 and 700; Math--20% below 500, 60% between 500 and 599, and 20% between 600 and 700. The ACT scores were 41% below 21, 22% between 21 and 23, 20% between 24 and 26, 10% between 27 and 28, and 7% above 28. 17% of the current freshmen were in the top fifth of their class; 49% were in the top two fifths. 1 freshman graduated first in the class.

Requirements: The ACT or SAT is required. In addition, applicants must be graduates of an accredited secondary school or have a GED certificate. Students should have completed 4 units of English, 3 of math including 2 of algebra and 1 of geometry, and 2 each of natural science and social studies. Columbia requires applicants to be in the upper 50% of their class. A GPA of 2.5 is required. AP and CLEP credits are accepted.

Procedure: Freshmen are admitted to all sessions. Entrance exams should be taken in spring of the junior year or fall of the senior year. There are rolling admissions and a deferred admissions plan. Application deadlines are open. The fall 2005 application fee was $25, but is waived prior to January 1 for day program fall applicants and October 1 for day program spring applicants. Applications are accepted on-line.

Transfer: 142 transfer students enrolled in 2004-2005. Applicants must have a minimum GPA of 2.0 overall and in the last semester attended and must submit a high school transcript and SAT or ACT scores. 24 of 120 credits required for the bachelor's degree must be completed at Columbia.

Visiting: There are regularly scheduled orientations for prospective students, including a campus tour, a workshop in financial aid, an academic/organization fair, and a luncheon. There are guides for informal visits and visitors may sit in on classes and stay overnight. To schedule a visit, contact the Admissions Office at (800) 231-2391, ext. 7352, or *admissions@ccis.edu*.

Financial Aid: In 2005-2006, 89% of all full-time freshmen and 68% of continuing full-time students received some form of financial aid. 64% of full-time freshmen and 46% of continuing full-time students received need-based aid. The average freshman award was $11,366. Need-based scholarships or need-based grants averaged $2855 ($8050 maximum); need-based self-help aid (loans and jobs) averaged $4432 ($5625 maximum); non-need-based athletic scholarships averaged $12,351 ($17,006 maximum); and other non-need-based awards and non-need-based scholarships averaged $8128 ($14,622 maximum). 14% of undergraduates work part time. Average annual earnings from campus work are $2400. The average financial indebtedness of the 2005 graduate was $14,879. The FAFSA and the college's own financial statement are required. The priority date for freshman financial aid applications for fall entry is March 15. The deadline for filing freshman financial aid applications for fall entry is April 30.

International Students: There are 62 international students enrolled. The school actively recruits these students. They must score satisfactorily on the written TOEFL or on the electronic version or take the MELAB, the Comprehensive English Language Test, or the college's own test and also take the ACT.

Computers: PCs with Internet access are located in student computing labs, the library, the administration building, and the student commons. Wireless access is available throughout the campus, including residence halls. All students may access the system from 8 A.M. to 10 P.M. in the computer lab. There are no time limits and no fees. It is strongly recommended that all students have a personal computer. It is recommended that students in computer science (B.S.) are required to have personal computers. An IBM ThinkPad laptop is recommended.

Graduates: From July 1, 2004 to June 30, 2005, 134 bachelor's degrees were awarded. The most popular majors were business administration (34%), education (7%), and psychology (7%). In an average class, 43% graduate in 4 years or less, 48% graduate in 5 years or less, and 49% graduate in 6 years or less.

Admissions Contact: Regina Morin, Director of Admissions. E-mail: *admissions@ccis.edu* Web: *www.ccis.edu*

CULVER-STOCKTON COLLEGE   C-1
Canton, MO 63435-1299   (217) 231-6331
(800) 537-1883; Fax: (217) 231-6618

Full-time: 330 men, 436 women	Faculty: 44; IIB, --$
Part-time: 25 men, 49 women	Ph.D.s: 68%
Graduate: none	Student/Faculty: 17 to 1
Year: semesters, summer session	Tuition: $14,450
Application Deadline: open	Room & Board: $6175
Freshman Class: 959 applied, 727 accepted, 155 enrolled	
ACT: 22	COMPETITIVE

Culver-Stockton College, established in 1853, is a private liberal arts institution affiliated with the Disciples of Christ. In addition to regional accreditation, C-SC has baccalaureate program accreditation with CAAHEP, IACBE, and NLN. The library contains 165,402 volumes, 5211 microform items, and 4485 audio/video tapes/CDs/DVDs, and subscribes to 10,257 periodicals including electronic. Computerized library services include the card catalog, interlibrary loans, and database searching. Special learning facilities include a learning resource center, art gallery, radio station, rare books collection, performing arts center, publications lab, and tutorial center. The 143-acre campus is in a rural area 125 miles north of St. Louis. Including any residence halls, there are 19 buildings.

Student Life: 56% of undergraduates are from Missouri. Others are from 24 states and 4 foreign countries. 93% are from public schools. 88% are white. 55% are Protestant; 21% claim no religious affiliation; 16% Catholic. The average age of freshmen is 18; all undergraduates, 19. 32% do not continue beyond their first year; 51% remain to graduate.

Housing: 723 students can be accommodated in college housing, which includes single-sex and coed dorms, fraternity houses, and sorority houses. On-campus housing is guaranteed for all 4 years. 75% of students live on campus; of those, 50% remain on campus on weekends. Alcohol is not permitted. All students may keep cars.

Activities: 23% of men belong to 4 national fraternities; 27% of women belong to 3 national sororities. There are 40 groups on campus, including art, band, cheerleading, choir, chorus, dance, drama, ethnic, forensics, honors, international, jazz band, literary magazine, musical theater, newspaper, opera, pep band, photography, political, professional, religious, radio, social, social service, and student government. Popular campus events include National Collegiate Alcohol Awareness Week and Spring Fling.

Sports: There are 5 intercollegiate sports for men and 5 for women, and 9 intramural sports for men and 9 for women. Facilities include a 2000-seat football stadium, a soccer field, a baseball field, intramural fields, a swimming pool, a dance studio, a weight room, and a field house with basketball, volleyball, tennis, and racquetball courts.

Disabled Students: 40% of the campus is accessible. Wheelchair ramps, elevators, special parking, and specially equipped rest rooms are available.

Services: Counseling and information services are available, as is tutoring in most subjects. There is remedial math and writing.

Campus Safety and Security: Measures include self-defense education, security escort services, informal discussions, and pamphlets/posters/films. There are emergency telephones, lighted pathways/sidewalks, and a nighttime security patrol.

Programs of Study: C-SC confers B.A., B.S., B.F.A., B.M.E., and B.S.N. degrees. Bachelor's degrees are awarded in BIOLOGICAL SCIENCE (biology/biological science), BUSINESS (accounting, banking and finance, business administration and management, management science, and recreational facilities management), COMMUNICATIONS AND THE ARTS (art, arts administration/management, communications, dramatic arts, English, and music), COMPUTER AND PHYSICAL SCIENCE (information sciences and systems and mathematics), EDUCATION (art, athletic training, drama, elementary, music, and physical), HEALTH PROFESSIONS (nursing), SOCIAL SCIENCE (criminal justice, history, psychology, and religion). Education and nursing are the strongest academically. Education, business, and nursing are the largest.

Required: To graduate, students must complete 124 credit hours, including 24 to 64 in the major, with a minimum GPA of 2.0. Distribution requirements include 1 course in Western Culture, religion, creativity and arts, non-Western culture, and technology, and 2 courses in individual and society, natural science, and math. English composition, speech, phys ed., technology, religion, and service learning are required.

Special: Culver-Stockton offers a joint-degree program in nursing in conjunction with Blessing-Rieman College of Nursing, and a 3-2 occupational therapy degree with Washington University at St.Louis. Study abroad, internships, and dual and individualized majors are also available. A course entitled Decades of Destiny is presented in nontraditional 5-week modules. There are 6 national honor societies, a freshman honors program, and 18 departmental honors programs.

Faculty/Classroom: 55% of faculty are male; 45%, female. All teach undergraduates. The average class size in an introductory lecture is 22; in a laboratory, 15; and in a regular course, 17.

Admissions: 76% of the 2005-2006 applicants were accepted. The ACT scores for the 2005-2006 freshman class were: 45% below 21, 27% between 21 and 23, 16% between 24 and 26, 9% between 27 and 28, and 3% above 28. 31% of the current freshmen were in the top fifth of their class; 60% were in the top two fifths. 6 freshmen graduated first in their class.

Requirements: The SAT or ACT is required, with the ACT preferred. Secondary school preparation should include 4 years of English, 2 to 4 of science, and 2 of math. The GED is accepted. C-SC requires applicants to be in the upper 50% of their class. A GPA of 2.0 is required. AP and CLEP credits are accepted. Important factors in the admissions decision are advanced placement or honor courses, recommendations by school officials, and evidence of special talent.

Procedure: Freshmen are admitted fall and spring. Entrance exams should be taken by April of the entering school year. There is a deferred admissions plan and a rolling admissions plan. Application deadlines are open. Application fee is $25. Applications are accepted on-line.

Transfer: 78 transfer students enrolled in 2004-2005. Transfer applicants must submit college transcripts and must have a minimum college GPA of 2.0. 30 of 124 credits required for the bachelor's degree must be completed at C-SC.

Visiting: There are regularly scheduled orientations for prospective students, including meetings with professors, students, coaches, and extracurricular advisers, financial aid information, a student life panel, and campus tours. There are guides for informal visits and visitors may sit in on classes and stay overnight. To schedule a visit, contact Enrollment Services.

Financial Aid: In 2005-2006, 98% of all full-time freshmen and all of continuing full-time students received some form of financial aid. 91% of full-time freshmen and 89% of continuing full-time students received need-based aid. The average freshman award was $12,226. Need-based scholarships or need-based grants averaged $9537; need-based self-help aid (loans and jobs) averaged $3239; non-need-based athletic scholarships averaged $2580; and other non-need-based awards and non-need-based scholarships averaged $14,200. 34% of undergraduates work part time. Average annual earnings from campus work are $548. The average financial indebtedness of the 2005 graduate was $18,429.

C-SC is a member of CSS. The FAFSA is required. The deadline for filing freshman financial aid applications for fall entry is June 15.

International Students: There are 18 international students enrolled. The school actively recruits these students. They must score satisfactorily on the TOEFL and also take the SAT or the ACT International students are not required to take the TOEFL if they have resided in this country for 1 semester or submit SAT or ACT scores.

Computers: Wireless access is available. Students have 24/7 access in all residence hall rooms. They are wired on a port-per-pillow basis. In addition, there are cluster (house PCs) in each residence hall. Students have access to 4 public computer labs, 1 open 24 hours per day, as well as 3 specialty computer labs. There are writing PCs available in the library. All students may access the system days, evenings, and weekends. There are no time limits and no fees.

Graduates: From July 1, 2004 to June 30, 2005, 172 bachelor's degrees were awarded. The most popular majors were business administration (20%), nursing (18%), and education (11%). In an average class, 36% graduate in 4 years or less, 43% graduate in 5 years or less, and 43% graduate in 6 years or less. 50 companies recruited on campus in 2004-2005. Of the 2004 graduating class, 12% were enrolled in graduate school within 6 months of graduation and 84% were employed.

Admissions Contact: Betty Smith, Director of Enrollment Services. A video is available. E-mail: *enrollment@culver.edu*
Web: *www.culver.edu*

DEACONESS COLLEGE OF NURSING — D-2

St. Louis, MO 63139
(314) 768-3179
(800) 942-4310; Fax: (314) 768-5673

Full-and part time: 400 men and women	**Faculty:** 16
	Ph.D.s: 15%
Graduate: none	**Student/Faculty:** n/av
Year: semesters, summer session	**Tuition:** $12,000
Application Deadline: open	**Room & Board:** $5000
Freshman Class: n/av	
SAT or ACT: required	**SPECIAL**

Deaconess College of Nursing, established in 1889 and affiliated with the United Church of Christ, is a private college offering undergraduate programs in nursing. Figures in the above capsule and in this profile are approximate. In addition to regional accreditation, Deaconess has baccalaureate program accreditation with NLN. The library contains 8000 volumes and 130 audio/video tapes/CDs/DVDs, and subscribes to 230 periodicals including electronic. Computerized library services include interlibrary loans and database searching. Special learning facilities include a learning resource center nursing archives, and nursing arts lab. The 15-acre campus is in an urban area 4 miles west of downtown St. Louis. Including any residence halls, there are 10 buildings.

Student Life: 72% of undergraduates are from Missouri. Others are from 6 states and 2 foreign countries. 78% are from public schools. 87% are white; 10% African American. 46% are Catholic; 40% Protestant; 14% claim no religious affiliation. The average age of freshmen is 21; all undergraduates, 23. 13% do not continue beyond their first year; 65% remain to graduate.

Housing: 98 students can be accommodated in college housing, which includes coed dorms. On-campus housing is available on a first-come, first-served basis. Priority is given to out-of-town students. 72% of students commute. Alcohol is not permitted. Upperclassmen may keep cars.

Activities: There are no fraternities or sororities. There are 7 groups on campus, including newspaper, professional, religious, social, and student government. Popular campus events include Dedication Ceremony, Christmas Tea, and Welcome Week.

Sports: There is no sports program at Deaconess. Facilities include a weight room.

Disabled Students: 90% of the campus is accessible. Wheelchair ramps, elevators, special parking, and specially equipped rest rooms are available.

Services: Counseling and information services are available, as is tutoring in some subjects, including sciences and statistics. There is remedial math, reading, and writing. Each student is assigned an academic adviser.

Campus Safety and Security: Measures include 24-hour foot and vehicle patrol, self-defense education, security escort services, and shuttle buses. There are informal discussions, pamphlets/posters/films, emergency telephones, lighted pathways/sidewalks, and and a card reader security system.

Programs of Study: Deaconess confers the B.S.N. degree. Associate degrees are also awarded. Bachelor's degrees are awarded in HEALTH PROFESSIONS (nursing).

Required: To graduate, students must complete 128 credit hours, including 62 in nursing courses, with a minimum GPA of 2.0. General education requirements include 30 hours of math and science, 24 of liberal arts and humanities, and 12 of social science.

Special: Students may opt for credit by exam. A work-study program with Deaconess Hospital and cross-registration with Fontbonne University are available.

Faculty/Classroom: All faculty are female. All teach undergraduates and 2% do research. The average class size in an introductory lecture is 30; in a laboratory, 20; and in a regular course, 25.

Admissions: 71% of recent applicants were accepted. The ACT scores for a recent freshman class were: 70% between 21 and 23, and 30% between 24 and 26. All recent freshmen were in the top two fifths of their class.

Requirements: The SAT or ACT is required, with the ACT is preferred. Applicants must be graduates of an accredited secondary school or have a GED certificate. They should have completed 3 years each of math and science and 4 years of English. An essay must be submitted. Academic ranking in the upper third of the high school graduating class is preferred. A GPA of 3.5 is required. AP and CLEP credits are accepted. Important factors in the admissions decision are advanced placement or honor courses, recommendations by school officials, and recommendations by alumni.

Procedure: Freshmen are admitted in the fall. Entrance exams should be taken by December of the senior year. There is a rolling admissiions plan. Application deadlines are open. The fall 2005 application fee was $30. Applications are accepted on-line.

Transfer: Academic ranking in the top third of the high school graduating class is preferred. Applicants should have a cumulative GPA of 2.5 in postsecondary work. 44 of 128 credits required for the bachelor's degree must be completed at Deaconess.

Visiting: There are regularly scheduled orientations for prospective students, consisting of an introduction to the school and its program, a review of the curriculum, admissions procedures, and financial aid, and tours. There are guides for informal visits and visitors may sit in on classes and stay overnight. To schedule a visit, contact the Admissions Office.

Financial Aid: The FAFSA is required. Check with the school for current deadlines.

International Students: They must score satisfactorily on the written TOEFL.

Computers: All students may access the system. There are no time limits and no fees.

Graduates: In an average class, 65% graduate in 4 years or less, and 70% graduate in 5 years or less.

Admissions Contact: Michelle McGrail, Dean of Enrollment.
Web: *www.deaconess,edu*

DEVRY UNIVERSITY/KANSAS CITY — A-2

Kansas City, MO 64131-3626
(816) 941-2810
(800) 821-3766; Fax: (816) 941-0896

Full-time: 1000 men, 300 women	Faculty: n/av
Part-time: 400 men, 200 women	Ph.D.s: n/av
Graduate: none	Student/Faculty: n/av
Year: semesters, summer session	Tuition: $11,000
Application Deadline: open	Room & Board: n/app
Freshman Class: n/av	
SAT or ACT: see profile	LESS COMPETITIVE

DeVry University/Kansas City, a private institution founded in 1931, joined the DeVry schools in 1969. One of 67 DeVry University locations in the United States and Canada, the school offers undergraduate programs in business administration, electronics, engineering, telecommunications, computer information systems, technical management, information technology, and computer engineering technology. Figures in the above capsule and in this profile are approximate. In addition to regional accreditation, DeVry has baccalaureate program accreditation with ABET. The library contains 16,800 volumes, 28,700 microform items, and 500 audio/video tapes/CDs/DVDs, and subscribes to 70 periodicals including electronic. Computerized library services include the card catalog, interlibrary loans, and database searching. Special learning facilities include a learning resource center and electronics and other labs. The 11-acre campus is in an urban area. There is one building.

Student Life: 76% are white; 16% African American. The average age of all undergraduates is 28.

Housing: There are no residence halls. Housing referrals may be obtained through the Student Housing Ofice. There are private apartments, student-plan housing, and private rooms. All of students commute. Alcohol is not permitted. All students may keep cars.

Activities: There are no fraternities or sororities. There are 9 groups on campus, including ethnic, honors, international, newspaper, paintball, professional, religious, social, and student government. Popular campus events include Try-Athalon, Student Picnic, and Casino Night.

Sports: There are 3 intramural sports for men and 3 for women.

Disabled Students: All of the campus is accessible. Wheelchair ramps, elevators, special parking, specially equipped rest rooms, special class scheduling, lowered drinking fountains, and lowered telephones are available.

Services: Counseling and information services are available, as is tutoring in every subject.

Campus Safety and Security: Measures include 24-hour foot and vehicle patrol and lighted pathways/sidewalks, and A security detection system is deployed when the facility is closed.

Programs of Study: DeVry confers the B.S. degree. Associate degrees are also awarded. Bachelor's degrees are awarded in BIOLOGICAL SCIENCE (bioinformatics), BUSINESS (business administration and management), COMMUNICATIONS AND THE ARTS (telecommunications), COMPUTER AND PHYSICAL SCIENCE (information sciences and systems), ENGINEERING AND ENVIRONMENTAL DESIGN (biomedical engineering, computer engineering, electrical/electronics engineering technology, and technological management). Telecommunications and computer information systems are the largest.

Required: To graduate, students must achieve a GPA of at least 2.0 and satisfactorily complete all curriculum requirements. Course requirements vary according to program. All first-semester students take courses in business organization, computer applications, algebra, psychology, and student success strategies.

Special: Nondegree study, co-op programs, accelerated degree programs, distance learning, and evening and weekend classes are possible. There are 2 national honor societies.

Faculty/Classroom: All teach undergraduates.

Requirements: Admissions requirements include graduation from a secondary school; the GED is also accepted. Applicants must pass the DeVry entrance exam or present satisfactory ACT or SAT scores. An interview is required. CLEP credit is accepted.

Procedure: Freshmen are admitted fall, spring, and summer. There are early admissions and deferred admissions plans. There is a rolling admission plan. Application deadlines are open. The fall of 2005 application fee was $25. Applications are accepted on-line.

Transfer: Applicants must present passing grades in all completed college course work, demonstrate language skills proficiency with at least 24 completed semester credits, and evidence math proficiency by appropriate college-level credits. A minimum GPA of 2.0 is required. 25% of 48 to 154 credits required for the bachelor's degree must be completed at DeVry.

Visiting: There are regularly scheduled orientations for prospective students. There are guides for informal visits. To schedule a visit, contact the New Student Coordinator at (816) 941-0430.

Financial Aid: In a recent year, 50% of all full-time freshmen and 73% of continuing full-time students received some form of financial aid. 49% of full-time freshmen and 72% of continuing full-time students received need-based aid. The average freshman award was $6588. Need-based scholarships or need-based grants averaged $3801; need-based self-help aid (loans and jobs) averaged $4220; and non-need-based athletic scholarships averaged $7554. The FAFSA is required. Check with the school for current deadlines.

International Students: They must score satisfactorily on the written TOEFL or on the electronic version.

Computers: Students in the computer information systems program may access the system during published lab hours. There are no fees.

Graduates: In a recent year, 471 bachelor's degrees were awarded. The most popular majors were computer information systems (78%), business (14%), and electronics engineering technology (8%).

Admissions Contact: Shane Smeed, Director of Admissions.
E-mail: *ssmeed@kc.devry.edu* Web: *www.kc.devry.edu*

DRURY UNIVERSITY — B-3

Springfield, MO 65802
(417) 873-7205
(800) 922-2274; Fax: (417) 866-3873

Full-time: 669 men, 872 women	Faculty: 123; II B, --$
Part-time: 27 men, 12 women	Ph.D.s: 88%
Graduate: 91 men, 290 women	Student/Faculty: 13 to 1
Year: semesters, summer session	Tuition: $14,687
Application Deadline: August 1	Room & Board: $5430
Freshman Class: 1106 applied, 858 accepted, 378 enrolled	
SAT Verbal/Math: 580/590*	ACT: 25 VERY COMPETITIVE

Drury University, founded in 1873, is a private university with degree programs emphasizing the liberal arts, architecture, business, communications, economics, education, and health sciences. There are 3 undergraduate and 5 graduate schools. In addition to regional accreditation, Drury has baccalaureate program accreditation with ACBSP, NAAB, NASM, and NCATE. The library contains 177,794 volumes, 119,683 microform items, and 60,098 audio/video tapes/CDs/DVDs, and subscribes to 868 periodicals including electronic. Computerized library services include the card catalog, interlibrary loans, database searching, Internet access, and laptop Internet portals. Special learning facilities include an art gallery, radio station, TV station, astronomical observatory, greenhouse, teleconference facility, art and architecture slide collection, speech communication center, and writing center. The 80-acre campus is in an urban area 200 miles southwest of St. Louis and 150 miles southeast of Kansas City. Including any residence halls, there are 38 buildings.

Student Life: 81% of undergraduates are from Missouri. Others are from 34 states, 22 foreign countries, and Canada. 85% are from public schools. 91% are white. The average age of freshmen is 19; all undergraduates, 22. 22% do not continue beyond their first year; 63% remain to graduate.

Housing: 948 students can be accommodated in college housing, which includes single-sex and coed dorms, on-campus apartments, off-campus apartments, married-student housing, and fraternity houses. There are also leadership, community service, and living-learning communities. On-campus housing is guaranteed for all 4 years. 52% of students live on campus; of those, 80% remain on campus on weekends. All students may keep cars.

Activities: 32% of men belong to 4 national fraternities; 24% of women belong to 4 national sororities. There are 50 groups on campus, including academic interests, art, band, cheerleading, chess, choir, chorale, chorus, computers, dance, debate, drama, ethnic, film, forensics, gay, honors, international, jazz band, leadership, literary magazine, minority students, musical theater, newspaper, opera, orchestra, pep band, photography, political, professional, radio and TV, religious, social, social service, student life, student government, and symphony. Popular campus events include Fall Festival, Beaux Arts Ball, and Christmas Vespers.

Sports: There are 7 intercollegiate sports for men and 7 for women, and 6 intramural sports for men and 6 for women. Facilities include a gym, lighted tennis and racquetball courts, a soccer stadium also used for intramurals, a practice field for soccer, a baseball field (off campus), a tennis stadium (off campus), an Olympic-size pool, a fitness center, a running track, and a 2200-seat indoor stadium for basketball and volleyball.

Disabled Students: 95% of the campus is accessible. Wheelchair ramps, elevators, special parking, specially equipped rest rooms, special class scheduling, lowered drinking fountains, and lowered telephones are available.

Services: Counseling and information services are available, as is tutoring in every subject. There is a reader service for the blind. There is a math and reading learning center, a writing center, and a communications center.

Campus Safety and Security: Measures include 24-hour foot and vehicle patrol, self-defense education, security escort services, and informal discussions. There are pamphlets/posters/films, emergency telephones, lighted pathways/sidewalks, and lighted parking lots with security cameras.

Programs of Study: Drury confers B.A., B.Arch., and B.M.E., B.M.T. degrees. Master's degrees are also awarded. Bachelor's degrees are awarded in BIOLOGICAL SCIENCE (biology/biological science), BUSINESS (accounting, business administration and management, international business management, and sports management), COMMUNICATIONS AND THE ARTS (advertising, art history and appreciation, arts administration/management, broadcasting, communications, dramatic arts, English, fine arts, French, German, journalism, music, public relations, Spanish, and speech/debate/rhetoric), COMPUTER AND PHYSICAL SCIENCE (chemistry, computer science, information sciences and systems, mathematics, and physics), EDUCATION (elementary, music, physical, and secondary), ENGINEERING AND ENVIRONMENTAL DESIGN (architecture and environmental science), HEALTH PROFESSIONS (exercise science, predentistry, premedicine, and preveterinary science), SOCIAL SCIENCE (criminology, economics, history, international studies, philosophy, political science/government, prelaw, psychology, and sociology). Premedicine, business, and architecture are the strongest academically. Business administration, biology, and communication are the largest.

Required: To graduate, students must complete 124 credit hours (150 for accounting and 170 for B.Arch.). They must also maintain a minimum GPA of 2.0 and complete 26 to 32 credit hours in the major (99 for architecture). Students pursue a broad curriculum called Global Perspectives that includes requirements in science, math, humanities, fine arts, fitness, foreign language, and social science, with specific classes in Alpha Seminar, Math and Science Inquiry, Global Awareness, Global Futures, and Values Analysis. All students who complete the curriculum are awarded a minor in global studies.

Special: Drury offers study abroad in Volos, Greece and 19 other countries as well as cross-registration with colleges in England, Australia, France, Spain, Germany, Denmark, Senegal, and China; 40% of students study abroad. Premedical early admission arrangements with St. Louis University, the University of Missouri, and Kirksville College of Osteopathic Medicine, a 3-2 engineering dual-degree program in conjunction with the University of Missouri, and Washington University in St. Louis, and a 3-z dual-degree occupational therapy degree in cooperation with Washington University are available. Co-op programs include computer information systems and arts administration. 75% of students complete a professional internship; options include public and private sectors and a Washington semester. Work-study, credit by exam, nondegree study, dual majors in most majors, and satisfactory/unsatisfactory op-

tions are also possible. There are 17 national honor societies, a freshman honors program, and 19 departmental honors programs.

Faculty/Classroom: 60% of faculty are male; 40%, female. All teach undergraduates and 40% both teach and do research. No introductory courses are taught by graduate students. The average class size in an introductory lecture is 21; in a laboratory, 21; and in a regular course, 18.

Admissions: 78% of the 2005-2006 applicants were accepted. The SAT scores for the 2005-2006 freshman class were: Verbal--19% below 500, 38% between 500 and 599, 36% between 600 and 700, and 7% above 700; Math--13% below 500, 44% between 500 and 599, 33% between 600 and 700, and 10% above 700. The ACT scores were 11% below 21, 24% between 21 and 23, 29% between 24 and 26, 13% between 27 and 28, and 23% above 28. 61% of the current freshmen were in the top fifth of their class; 84% were in the top two fifths. There were 2 National Merit finalists and 4 semifinalists in a recent year.

Requirements: The SAT or ACT is required. In addition, applicants must be graduates of an accredited secondary school or have a GED certificate. Recommended high school credits include 4 units of English and at least 3 each of math through algebra II, natural science, and social studies. An essay and a reference from the high school counselor or principal are required. A GPA of 2.7 is required. AP and CLEP credits are accepted. Important factors in the admissions decision are advanced placement or honor courses, extracurricular activities record, and leadership record.

Procedure: Freshmen are admitted to all sessions. Entrance exams should be taken in the spring of the junior year or fall of the senior year. There is a deferred admissions plan and a rolling admissions plan. Applications should be filed by August 1 for fall entry and December 1 for spring entry, along with a $25 fee. Notification is sent October 1. Applications are accepted on-line.

Transfer: 95 transfer students enrolled in 2004-2005. Applicants must have a minimum GPA of 2.0 in all college work completed, and supply an essay or writing sample. 30 of 124 credits required for the bachelor's degree must be completed at Drury.

Visiting: There are regularly scheduled orientations for prospective students, including visit days for all students as well as visit days specialized for premed, architecture, preengineering, math, physics, computer sciences, arts and sciences, and social sciences students. There are guides for informal visits and visitors may sit in on classes and stay overnight. To schedule a visit, contact the Admissions Office at *campusvisit@drury.edu.*

Financial Aid: In 2005-2006, 92% of all full-time freshmen and 89% of continuing full-time students received some form of financial aid. 91% of full-time freshmen and 86% of continuing full-time students received need-based aid. The average freshman award was $7168. Need-based scholarships or need-based grants averaged $6102 ($12,995 maximum); need-based self-help aid (loans and jobs) averaged $4096 ($12,000 maximum); non-need-based athletic scholarships averaged $6287 ($12,995 maximum); and other non-need-based awards and non-need-based scholarships averaged $3962 ($13,411 maximum). 87% of undergraduates work part time. Average annual earnings from campus work are $2250. The average financial indebtedness of the 2005 graduate was $15,450. Drury is a member of CSS. The FAFSA and the college's own financial statement are required. The deadline for filing freshman financial aid applications for fall entry is March 15.

International Students: There are 56 international students enrolled. The school actively recruits these students. They must take the TOEFL and also take the SAT or the ACT.

Computers: Wireless access is available. Wireless access is available in all academic buildings, most other buildings, and 80% of campus overall, including some outdoor spaces. 389 PCs are available in labs. Residence halls are equipped with one network port per student. All students may access the system 24 hours a day, 7 days a week in technology centers. There are no time limits and no fees.

Graduates: From July 1, 2004 to June 30, 2005, 308 bachelor's degrees were awarded. The most popular majors were business administration (18%), biology (13%), and communication (10%). In an average class, 1% graduate in 3 years or less, 47% graduate in 4 years or less, and 63% graduate in 5 or 6 years or less. 15 companies recruited on campus in 2004-2005. Of the 2004 graduating class, 33% were enrolled in graduate school within 6 months of graduation and 59% were employed.

Admissions Contact: Chip Parker, Director of Admission.
E-mail: *druryad@drury.edu* Web: *www.drury.edu*

EVANGEL UNIVERSITY
B-3

Springfield, MO 65802
(417) 865-2811
(800) EVANGEL; Fax: (417) 865-9599

Full-time: 650 men, 1022 women	**Faculty:** 103
Part-time: 29 men, 34 women	**Ph.D.s:** 74%
Graduate: 27 men, 48 women	**Student/Faculty:** 16 to 1
Year: semesters, summer session	**Tuition:** $12,760
Application Deadline: see profile	**Room & Board:** $4620
Freshman Class: 881 applied, 713 accepted, 423 enrolled	
ACT: 21	**COMPETITIVE**

Evangel University, established in 1955, is a private facility affiliated with the Assemblies of God. In addition to regional accreditation, Evangel has baccalaureate program accreditation with CSWE, NASM, and NCATE. The library contains 96,487 volumes, 11,386 microform items, and 6801 audio/video tapes/CDs/DVDs, and subscribes to 748 periodicals including electronic. Computerized library services include interlibrary loans. Special learning facilities include a learning resource center, art gallery, radio station, and TV station. The 80-acre campus is in an urban area 225 miles west of St. Louis. Including any residence halls, there are 14 buildings.
Student Life: 61% of undergraduates are from out of state, mostly the Midwest. Others are from 48 states, 5 foreign countries, and Canada. 81% are from public schools. 86% are white. Most are Protestant. The average age of freshmen is 18; all undergraduates, 20. 25% do not continue beyond their first year; 71% remain to graduate.
Housing: 1460 students can be accommodated in college housing, which includes single-sex and coed dorms and married-student housing. There are also honors floors. On-campus housing is guaranteed for all 4 years. 84% of students live on campus; of those, 100% remain on campus on weekends. Alcohol is not permitted. All students may keep cars.
Activities: There are no fraternities or sororities. There are 19 groups on campus, including band, cheerleading, choir, chorale, chorus, drama, forensics, honors, jazz band, musical theater, newspaper, orchestra, pep band, photography, political, professional, radio and TV, religious, student government, and yearbook. Popular campus events include College Weekend.
Sports: There are 5 intercollegiate sports for men and 6 for women, and 4 intramural sports for men and 4 for women. Facilities include a student activities center and a 2000-seat gym.
Disabled Students: All of the campus is accessible. Wheelchair ramps, elevators, special parking, specially equipped rest rooms, lowered drinking fountains, and lowered telephones are available.
Services: Counseling and information services are available, as is tutoring in every subject. There is a reader service for the blind, and remedial math, reading, and writing.
Campus Safety and Security: Measures include 24-hour foot and vehicle patrol, security escort services, emergency telephones, and lighted pathways/sidewalks.
Programs of Study: Evangel confers B.A., B.S., B.B.A., B.F.A., B.M., and B.S.W. degrees. Associate and master's degrees are also awarded. Bachelor's degrees are awarded in BIOLOGICAL SCIENCE (biology/biological science), BUSINESS (accounting, management science, and marketing/retailing/merchandising), COMMUNICATIONS AND THE ARTS (art, broadcasting, communications, design, dramatic arts, English, journalism, music, music performance, Spanish, and speech/debate/rhetoric), COMPUTER AND PHYSICAL SCIENCE (chemistry, computer science, and mathematics), EDUCATION (business, early childhood, elementary, foreign languages, music, physical, science, secondary, and special), HEALTH PROFESSIONS (medical laboratory technology), SOCIAL SCIENCE (biblical studies, criminal justice, history, international studies, missions, parks and recreation management, political science/government, psychology, public administration, religion, religious music, social science, social work, and sociology). Science and technology and behavioral science are the strongest academically. Business is the largest.
Required: All students must complete 50 to 53 general education hours, including courses in phys ed, computer literacy, English composition, English literature, and Bible study. A minimum GPA of 2.0 is required for graduation. Students must complete 124 credit hours, 36 of which are upper division level, with approximately 30 credit hours in the major.
Special: There are 3-2 engineering degrees available in conjunction with Washington University and University of Missouri at Columbia. Other options include work-study, credit by exam, and a Washington semester. There are 9 national honor societies and 8 departmental honors programs.
Faculty/Classroom: 62% of faculty are male; 38%, female. All teach undergraduates. No introductory courses are taught by graduate students. The average class size in an introductory lecture is 40 and in a regular course, 20.
Admissions: 81% of the 2005-2006 applicants were accepted. The ACT scores for the 2005-2006 freshman class were: 37% below 21, 29%

between 21 and 23, 18% between 24 and 26, 9% between 27 and 28, and 7% above 28.
Requirements: The SAT or ACT is recommended. In addition, the recommended preparatory curriculum includes 3 credits in English, 2 each in math and social studies, and 1 in lab science. The GED is accepted. A GPA of 2.0 is required. AP and CLEP credits are accepted.
Procedure: Freshmen are admitted to all sessions. Entrance exams should be taken before high school graduation. There is a rolling admissions plan. Notification is sent on a rolling basis. The application fee is $25. Applications are accepted on-line.
Transfer: 143 transfer students enrolled in 2004-2005. Transfer applicants must be in good standing with their previous institutions and have a cumulative GPA of 2.0. 30 of 124 credits required for the bachelor's degree must be completed at Evangel.
Visiting: There are regularly scheduled orientations for prospective students, consisting of scheduled visits every Friday and by appointment. There are guides for informal visits and visitors may sit in on classes and stay overnight. To schedule a visit, contact Office of Admissions at *fahlstromc@evangel.edu*.
Financial Aid: In 2005-2006, 92% of all full-time freshmen and 93% of continuing full-time students received some form of financial aid. 81% of full-time freshmen and 69% of continuing full-time students received need-based aid. The average freshman award was $5912. 26% of undergraduates work part time. Average annual earnings from campus work are $1875. The FAFSA is required. The deadline for filing freshman financial aid applications for fall entry is August 1.
International Students: There are 9 international students enrolled. Satisfactory scores are required on the written TOEFL and the SAT or the ACT.
Computers: All students may access the system during hours of operation. There are no limits and no fees. It is strongly recommended that all students have a personal computer.
Graduates: From July 1, 2004 to June 30, 2005, 411 bachelor's degrees were awarded. The most popular majors were behavioral science (13%), business (12%), and education (11%). In an average class, 84% graduate in 4 years and 2% graduate in 5 years. 88 companies recruited on campus in 2004-2005.
Admissions Contact: Charity Fahlstrom, Director of Admissions. A video is available. E-mail: *admissions@evangel.edu*
Web: *http://www.evangel.edu/*

FONTBONNE UNIVERSITY
D-2

St. Louis, MO 63105
(314) 889-1413; Fax: (314) 889-1451

Full-time: 372 men, 1175 women	**Faculty:** 72
Part-time: 140 men, 391 women	**Ph.D.s:** 69%
Graduate: 189 men, 569 women	**Student/Faculty:** 21 to 1
Year: semesters, summer session	**Tuition:** $16,320
Application Deadline: August 1	**Room & Board:** $6988
Freshman Class: 618 applied, 456 accepted, 185 enrolled	
ACT: 21	**COMPETITIVE**

Fontbonne University, founded in 1917, is a private institution affiliated with the Catholic Church. It offers undergraduate degree programs in education, natural sciences, human environmental sciences, business, and communication and fine arts. In addition to regional accreditation, Fontbonne has baccalaureate program accreditation with ADA and ASLA. The library contains 90,000 volumes and 4141 audio/video tapes/CDs/DVDs, and subscribes to 310 periodicals including electronic. Computerized library services include the card catalog, interlibrary loans, and database searching. Special learning facilities include a learning resource center, art gallery, radio station, a biological field station, a broadcast center, and a communications disorder clinic. The 13-acre campus is in a suburban area 1 mile west of St. Louis. Including any residence halls, there are 10 buildings.
Student Life: 89% of undergraduates are from Missouri. Others are from 18 states and 19 foreign countries. 55% are from public schools. 60% are white; 33% African American. 55% are Catholic; 23% Protestant; 10% claim no religious affiliation. The average age of freshmen is 19; all undergraduates, 30. 34% do not continue beyond their first year; 51% remain to graduate.
Housing: 288 students can be accommodated in college housing, which includes single-sex and coed dormitories and on-campus apartments. On-campus housing is guaranteed for the freshman year only and is available on a first-come, first-served basis. Priority is given to out-of-town students. 90% of students commute. All students may keep cars.
Activities: There is 1 local fraternity. There are no sororities. There are 36 groups on campus, including cheerleading, choir, chorus, computers, drama, drill team, ethnic, gay, honors, international, literary magazine, musical theater, photography, political, professional, radio and TV, religious, social, social service, student government, and yearbook. Popular campus events include Spring Fest, art shows, and musical performances.
Sports: There are 6 intercollegiate sports for men and 7 for women, and 4 intramural sports for men and 7 for women. Facilities include stu-

dent activity center that houses a 2000-seat gym, weight room, track, aerobics room, and cafe.

Disabled Students: 70% of the campus is accessible. Wheelchair ramps, elevators, special parking, specially equipped rest rooms, special class scheduling, lowered drinking fountains, and lowered telephones are available.

Services: Counseling and information services are available, as is tutoring in most subjects. There is remedial math, reading, and writing.

Campus Safety and Security: Measures include self-defense education, shuttle buses, informal discussions, and pamphlets/posters/films. There are emergency telephones, lighted pathways/sidewalks, and security personnel as needed.

Programs of Study: Fontbonne confers B.A., B.S., B.B.A., and B.F.A. degrees. Master's degrees are also awarded. Bachelor's degrees are awarded in BIOLOGICAL SCIENCE (biology/biological science and biotechnology), BUSINESS (business administration and management, fashion merchandising, and sports management), COMMUNICATIONS AND THE ARTS (advertising, art, broadcasting, communications, English, fine arts, and performing arts), COMPUTER AND PHYSICAL SCIENCE (computer science, information sciences and systems, and mathematics), EDUCATION (art, early childhood, education of the deaf and hearing impaired, elementary, middle school, and special), HEALTH PROFESSIONS (speech pathology/audiology), SOCIAL SCIENCE (dietetics, family/consumer studies, history, human services, liberal arts/general studies, and prelaw). Education, computer science, and math are the strongest academically. Business administration, organizational studies, and education are the largest.

Required: To graduate, students must complete 128 credit hours, including 44 in general education requirements, with a minimum GPA of 2.0. The number of hours required for the major varies.

Special: Fontbonne offers cross-registration with several area colleges and a student exchange program with the Sisters of St. Joseph Consortium. There are also cooperative programs in all majors except education, internships with major companies, study abroad in 2 countries, work-study programs, student-designed and dual majors, credit by exam, nondegree study, pass/fail options, and B.A.-B.S. degrees. In addition, an accelerated degree program in business is available, as are 3-2 degrees in engineering and social work with Washington University. There are 4 national honor societies and a freshman honors program.

Faculty/Classroom: 91% teach undergraduates, 2% do research, and 2% do both. The average class size in an introductory lecture is 21; in a laboratory, 12; and in a regular course, 13.

Admissions: 74% of the 2005-2006 applicants were accepted. The ACT scores for the 2005-2006 freshman class were: 42% below 21, 31% between 21 and 23, 18% between 24 and 26, 7% between 27 and 28, and 2% above 28. 40% of the current freshmen were in the top fifth of their class; 83% were in the top two fifths.

Requirements: The SAT or ACT is required. Applicants must be graduates of an accredited secondary school or have a GED certificate. They must have completed 16 academic credits, including 4 in English, 3 in math, 2 each in science and social studies, and 1 in history. An audition or portfolio may be required. Fontbonne requires applicants to be in the upper 50% of their class. A GPA of 2.5 is required. AP and CLEP credits are accepted. Important factors in the admissions decision are advanced placement or honor courses, extracurricular activities record, and leadership record.

Procedure: Freshmen are admitted to all sessions. Entrance exams should be taken prior to registration. There are early admissions, deferred admissions, and rolling admissions plans. Applications should be filed by August 1 for fall entry and January 1 for spring entry. Notification is sent on a rolling basis. Applications are accepted on-line. The fall 2005 application fee was $25.

Transfer: 240 transfer students enrolled in 2004-2005. Applicants must have a minimum GPA of 2.0 and either submit the ACT or the SAT scores or take a placement test. Students with fewer than 30 credits must submit a high school transcript. An interview is recommended. 32 of 128 credits required for the bachelor's degree must be completed at Fontbonne.

Visiting: There are regularly scheduled orientations for prospective students, including a campus tour, a financial aid presentation, and visits with faculty and current students. There are guides for informal visits and visitors may sit in on classes and stay overnight. To schedule a visit, contact the Admissions Office at 314-889-1400 or 1-800-205-5862.

Financial Aid: In a recent year, 92% of all full-time freshmen and 99% of continuing full-time students received some form of financial aid. 62% of full-time freshmen and 79% of continuing full-time students received need-based aid. The average freshman award was $11,830. 22% of undergraduates worked part time. Average annual earnings from campus work were $1243. The average financial indebtedness of a recent graduate was $22,000. The CSS/Profile, FAFSA, or FFS and the college's own financial statement are required. The deadline for filing freshman financial aid applications for fall entry is April 1.

International Students: In a recent year there were 13 international students enrolled. The school actively recruits these students. They must score satisfactorily on the written TOEFL.

Computers: Wireless access is available. There are 133 PCs available for use across campus. Students can sign on to the wireless network after their PC is registered with Information Technology. All students may access the system 24 hour access. There are no time limits and no fees.

Graduates: From July 1, 2004 to June 30, 2005, 362 bachelor's degrees were awarded. The most popular majors were business administration (45%), special education (8%), and organizational behavior studies (6%). In an average class, 33% graduate in 4 years or less, 51% graduate in 5 years or less, and 54% graduate in 6 years or less. 25 companies recruited on campus in 2004-2005. Of the 2004 graduating class, 23% were enrolled in graduate school within 6 months of graduation and 74% were employed.

Admissions Contact: Ketih Quigley, Director of Freshman Recruitment. E-mail: *kquigley@fontbonne.edu* Web: *www.fontbonne.edu*

HANNIBAL-LAGRANGE COLLEGE   D-2
Hannibal, MO 63401   (573) 221-3113
(800) HLG-1119; Fax: (573) 221-6594

Full-time: 781 men and women	**Faculty:** 59
Part-time: 275 men and women	**Ph.D.s:** 32%
Graduate: none	**Student/Faculty:** 13 to 1
Year: semesters, summer session	**Tuition:** $11,780
Application Deadline: August 29	**Room & Board:** $4610
Freshman Class: 146 enrolled	
SAT or ACT: required	**COMPETITIVE**

Hannibal-LaGrange College, founded in 1858, is a private facility affiliated with the Southern Baptist Church. The library contains 137,392 volumes, 26,390 microform items, and 7001 audio/video tapes/CDs/DVDs, and subscribes to 321 periodicals including electronic. Computerized library services include the card catalog, interlibrary loans, database searching, and Internet access. Special learning facilities include a learning resource center, art gallery, and a nature trail. The 110-acre campus is in a small town 100 miles north of St. Louis. Including any residence halls, there are 18 buildings.

Student Life: 77% of undergraduates are from Missouri. Students are from 37 states, 7 foreign countries, and Canada. 98% are from public schools. 91% are white. The average age of freshmen is 18; all undergraduates, 23. 53% of freshmen remain to graduate.

Housing: 457 students can be accommodated in college housing, which includes single-sex dorms and on-campus apartments. In addition, there are honors houses. On-campus housing is available on a first-come, first-served basis. 59% of students commute. Alcohol is not permitted. All students may keep cars.

Activities: There are no fraternities or sororities. There are 22 groups on campus, including art, band, cheerleading, choir, chorus, drama, honors, jazz band, musical theater, newspaper, political, professional, religious, science, social, social service, student government and women students. Popular campus events include Campus Visitation Days, Encounter Visitation Days, and Spring Gala.

Sports: There are 4 intercollegiate sports for men and 5 for women, and 6 intramural sports for men and 6 for women. Facilities include baseball, softball, and soccer fields and a 41,000-square foot sports complex that contains a gym, weight and aerobics rooms, and volleyball, tennis, and racquetball courts.

Disabled Students: 65% of the campus is accessible. Wheelchair ramps, elevators, special parking, specially equipped rest rooms, special class scheduling, and special housing are available.

Services: Counseling and information services are available, as is tutoring in some subjects, including math and business/accounting. There is a reader service for the blind, remedial math and writing and sign language for hearing-impaired students.

Campus Safety and Security: Measures include 24-hour foot and vehicle patrol, security escort services, pamphlets/posters/films, and emergency telephones. There are lighted pathways/sidewalks.

Programs of Study: HLG confers B.A., B.S., B.A.S., B.S.E., and B.S.N. degrees. Associate degrees are also awarded. Bachelor's degrees are awarded in BIOLOGICAL SCIENCE (biology/biological science), BUSINESS (accounting, business administration and management, organizational behavior, and recreation and leisure services), COMMUNICATIONS AND THE ARTS (art, communications, dramatic arts, English, music, music performance, piano/organ, and speech/debate/rhetoric), COMPUTER AND PHYSICAL SCIENCE (computer programming, information sciences and systems, and mathematics), EDUCATION (Christian, early childhood, elementary, music, and secondary), HEALTH PROFESSIONS (nursing), SOCIAL SCIENCE (biblical studies, criminal justice, history, human services, liberal arts/general studies, psychology, religious music, and sociology). Accounting and business administration are the strongest academically. Education, business, and organizational management are the largest.

Required: All students must complete a minimum of 124 credit hours with a 2.0 GPA to graduate. The major usually requires 36 or more credit hours of study. General education requirements include 8 hours in natural science; 6 hours each in Bible, composition, literature, foreign language, history, fine arts, and social science; 3 hours each in speech and algebra; 2 hours in phys ed; and 1 hour in Success in Education. Different core requirements pertain to education and nursing students.

Special: Internships are available for students taking courses in human services, data processing, criminal justice, and Bible studies, and work-study is possible with local non-profit organizations. Study abroad in England is also available. There are accelerated degree programs in administration of justice and organizational management and a 3-2 engineering degree with the University of Missouri/Rolla. Credit by exam and nondegree study are possible. There is 1 national honor society, Phi Beta Kappa and a freshman honors program.

Faculty/Classroom: 48% of faculty are male; 52%, female. All teach undergraduates. The average class size in an introductory lecture is 17; in a laboratory, 18; and in a regular course, 16.

Admissions: The ACT scores for the 2005-2006 freshman class were: 20% below 21, 43% between 21 and 23, 27% between 24 and 26, 4% between 27 and 28, and 6% above 28. 27% of the current freshmen were in the top fifth of their class; 47% were in the top two fifths. 21 freshmen graduated first in their class.

Requirements: The SAT or ACT is required. In addition, applicants must be graduates of an accredited secondary school or have the GED. An interview is required. A GPA of 2.0 is required. AP and CLEP credits are accepted.

Procedure: Freshmen are admitted to all sessions. Entrance exams should be taken before registration. There is a rolling admissions plan. Applications should be filed by August 29 for fall entry and January 8 for spring entry, along with a $150 fee. Notification is sent on a rolling basis. Applications are accepted on-line.

Transfer: 167 transfer students enrolled in 2004-2005. Applicants must submit transcripts from all colleges attended. Students applying with fewer than 30 credit hours must also submit a high school transcript along with ACT or SAT scores. 32 of 124 credits required for the bachelor's degree must be completed at HLG.

Visiting: There are regularly scheduled orientations for prospective students, consisting of Encounter Days, which are organized tours of the campus covering financial aid, student affairs, and academic areas and which include lunch in the cafeteria. There are guides for informal visits and visitors may sit in on classes and stay overnight. To schedule a visit, contact the Admissions Office at (800) HLG-1119 or jjohnson@hlg.edu.

Financial Aid: In 2005-2006, 93% of all full-time freshmen and 92% of continuing full-time students received some form of financial aid. 52% of full-time freshmen and 62% of continuing full-time students received need-based aid. The average freshman award was $11,862. 70% of undergraduates work part time. Average annual earnings from campus work are $1100. The average financial indebtedness of the 2005 graduate was $16,689. The FAFSA is required. The deadline for filing freshman financial aid applications for fall entry is July 1.

International Students: There are 27 international students enrolled. The school actively recruits these students. A satisfactory score on the TOEFL is required.

Computers: All students may access the system. There are no time limits.

Graduates: From July 1, 2004 to June 30, 2005, 172 bachelor's degrees were awarded. The most popular majors were education (23%), organizational management (20%), and business administration (12%). In an average year, 53% graduate in 6 years or less. 12 companies recruited on campus in 2004-2005. Of the 2004 graduating class, 27% were enrolled in graduate school within 6 months of graduation and 65% were employed.

Admissions Contact: Ray Carty, Vice President of Enrollment Management. E-mail: rcarty@hlg.edu Web: www.hlg.edu

HARRIS-STOWE STATE COLLEGE   D-2

St. Louis, MO 63103	(314) 340-3300; Fax: (314) 340-3555
Full-time: 190 men, 385 women	Faculty: 55
Part-time: 120 men, 560 women	Ph.D.s: 65%
Graduate: none	Student/Faculty: 10 to 1
Year: semesters, summer session	Tuition: $3250 ($6250)
Application Deadline: open	Room & Board: n/app
Freshman Class: n/av	
SAT or ACT: required	SPECIAL

Harris-Stowe State College, founded in 1857, is a state-supported, commuter institution offering undergraduate programs in business administration, teacher, and urban education. Figures in the above capsule and profile are approximate. In addition to regional accreditation, Harris-Stowe has baccalaureate program accreditation with ACBSP, NCATE, and IACBE. The library contains 99,000 volumes and 32,124 microform items, and subscribes to 352 periodicals including electronic. Computerized library services include the card catalog, interlibrary loans, database searching, and Internet access. Special learning facilities include a learning resource center and Jazz Institute. The 22-acre campus is in an urban area in metropolitan St. Louis. There are 3 buildings.

Student Life: 99% of undergraduates are from Missouri. Others are from 3 states, 13 foreign countries, and Canada. 84% are African American; 13% white. The average age of freshmen is 24; all undergraduates, 28. 38% do not continue beyond their first year; 62% remain to graduate.

Housing: There are no residence halls. All of students commute. Alcohol is not permitted. All students may keep cars.

Activities: 1% of men belong to 5 local and 5 national fraternities; 1% of women belong to 4 local and 4 national sororities. There are 43 groups on campus, including art, cheerleading, choir, chorale, dance, drama, ethnic, honors, international, literary magazine, newspaper, professional, religious, social, student government, and yearbook. Popular campus events include President's Tailgate Party.

Sports: There are 3 intercollegiate sports for men and 4 for women.

Disabled Students: All of the campus is accessible. Wheelchair ramps, elevators, special parking, specially equipped rest rooms, special class scheduling, lowered drinking fountains, and lowered telephones are available.

Services: Counseling and information services are available, as is tutoring in most subjects. There is remedial math, reading, and writing.

Campus Safety and Security: Measures include 24-hour foot and vehicle patrol, security escort services, shuttle buses, and pamphlets/posters/films. There are lighted pathways/sidewalks.

Programs of Study: Harris-Stowe confers B.S.B.A., B.S.T.E., and B.S.U.E. degrees. Bachelor's degrees are awarded in BUSINESS (business administration and management), EDUCATION (early childhood, education, elementary, and middle school). Teacher education is the strongest academically. Teacher education and business administration are the largest.

Required: Students are required to complete 120 to 149 semester hours, including a 42-hour core curriculum of general education courses, and must maintain a minimum GPA of 2.5 (2.0 for nonteaching majors).

Special: Opportunities are provided for internships as part of the degree in urban education, credit by examination, and pass/fail options in developmental courses. Cross-registration with the University of Missouri-St. Louis and St. Louis University and student-designed majors are possible. There are 3 national honor societies.

Faculty/Classroom: 52% of faculty are male; 48%, female. All teach undergraduates. The average class size in an introductory lecture is 30; in a laboratory, 25; and in a regular course, 30.

Requirements: The SAT or ACT is required. In addition, applicants should have completed 16 academic units at an accredited secondary school or hold a GED. A GPA of 2.0 is required. AP and CLEP credits are accepted.

Procedure: Freshmen are admitted to all sessions. Entrance exams should be taken before the close of registration. There are deferred admissions and rolling admissions plans. Application deadlines are open. Application fee is $15.

Transfer: 206 transfer students enrolled in a recent year. Students must have completed 24 college-level credit hours. 30 of 120 credits required for the bachelor's degree must be completed at Harris-Stowe.

Visiting: There are guides for informal visits and visitors may sit in on classes. To schedule a visit, contact the Director of Admissions/Academic Advisement.

Financial Aid: In a recent year, 88% of all full-time freshmen and 81% of continuing full-time students received some form of financial aid. 86% of full-time freshmen and 65% of continuing full-time students received need-based aid. Need-based scholarships or need-based grants averaged $2890 ($3120 maximum); need-based self-help aid (loans and jobs) averaged $1779 ($3120 maximum); and non-need-based athletic scholarships averaged $1782 ($3120 maximum). Average annual earnings from campus work were $3000. The average financial indebtedness of a recent graduate was $14,000. The FAFSA and the college's own financial statement are required. Check with the school for application deadlines.

International Students: In a recent year, there were 18 international students enrolled. They must score satisfactorily on the written TOEFL or on the electronic version and also take the SAT or the ACT, or Harris-Stowe's own examination if ACT/SAT scores are not high enough.

Computers: There are no time limits and no fees.

Graduates: In a recent year, 147 bachelor's degrees were awarded. The most popular majors were professional interdisciplinary studies (21%), elementary education (20%), and information science and computer technol (8%). 80 companies recruited on campus in a recent year.

Admissions Contact: LaShanda Boone, Director of Admissions. A video is available. E-mail: boonel@hssc.edu Web: www.hssc.edu

JEWISH HOSPITAL COLLEGE OF NURSING AND ALLIED HEALTH · D-2

St. Louis, MO 63110-1091

(314) 454-7057
(800) 832-9009; Fax: (314) 454-5239

Full-time: 20 men, 200 women	**Faculty:** n/av
Part-time: 50 men, 400 women	**Ph.D.s:** n/av
Graduate: 10 men, 90 women	**Student/Faculty:** 9 to 1
Year: 8-week terms, summer session	**Tuition:** $9000
Application Deadline: open	**Room & Board:** $3000
Freshman Class: n/av	
SAT or ACT: required	**SPECIAL**

Jewish Hospital College of Nursing and Allied Health, founded in 1993, is a small private college located within the Washington University Medical Center. Figures in the above capsule and in this profile are approximate. In addition to regional accreditation, Jewish Hospital College has baccalaureate program accreditation with NLN. The library contains 3200 volumes and 450 audio/video tapes/CDs/DVDs, and subscribes to 123 periodicals including electronic. Computerized library services include the card catalog, interlibrary loans, database searching, and Internet access. The 4-acre campus is in an urban area in the central west end of the city of St. Louis. Including any residence halls, there is 1 building.
Student Life: 60% of undergraduates are from Missouri. Others are from 10 states. 68% are white; 20% African American. The average age of freshmen is 26; all undergraduates, 29. 10% do not continue beyond their first year; 85% remain to graduate.
Housing: 82 students can be accommodated in college housing, which includes coed dorms. On-campus housing is available on a first-come, first-served basis. 92% of students commute. All students may keep cars.
Activities: There are no fraternities or sororities. There are 3 groups on campus, including computers, professional, and student government. Popular campus events include Holiday Party, Lobby Day, and walkathons.
Sports: There is no sports program at Jewish Hospital College.
Disabled Students: 60% of the campus is accessible. Wheelchair ramps, elevators, special parking, specially equipped rest rooms, and lowered drinking fountains are available.
Services: Counseling and information services are available, as is tutoring in most subjects.
Campus Safety and Security: Measures include 24-hour foot and vehicle patrol, security escort services, shuttle buses, and informal discussions. There are pamphlets/posters/films and lighted pathways/sidewalks.
Programs of Study: Jewish Hospital College confers B.S. and B.S.N. degrees. Associate and master's degrees are also awarded. Bachelor's degrees are awarded in HEALTH PROFESSIONS (clinical science, cytotechnology, nursing, and radiological science). Nursing is the largest.
Required: To graduate, 121 credit hours are required with a minimum GPA of 2.0.
Special: Study abroad in 1 country is offered.
Admissions: All recent applicants were accepted.
Requirements: The SAT or ACT is required. Jewish Hospital College requires applicants to be in the upper 50% of their class. A GPA of 2.5 is required. CLEP credit is accepted. Advanced placement or honor courses is an important factor in the admission decision.
Procedure: Freshmen are admitted fall and spring. There are early decision and deferred admissions plans.There is a rolling admissions plan. Application deadlines are open. The fall 2005 application fee was $25. A waiting list is an active part of the admissions procedure.
Transfer: Applicants should be high school graduates in the upper half of their class, with a 2.5 GPA in high school and college and with a composite score of 21 on the ACT or a comparable SATscore. 30 of 121 credits required for the bachelor's degree must be completed at Jewish Hospital College.
Visiting: There are regularly scheduled orientations for prospective students, including an overview of the college and programs offered, tours given by current students, and a question-and-answer period. There are guides for informal visits and visitors may sit in on classes. To schedule a visit, contact the recruiter.
Financial Aid: In a recent year, 75% of all full-time students received need-based aid. The average freshman award was $7000. Need-based scholarships or need-based grants averaged $2000 ($8500 maximum); need-based self-help aid (loans and jobs) averaged $2625 ($10,000 maximum); and other non-need-based awards and non-need-based scholarships averaged $500 ($1200 maximum). 88% of undergraduates work part time. Average annual earnings from campus work are $1000. The average financial indebtedness of a recent graduate was $15,000. The FAFSA and the college's own financial statement are required. Check with the school for current deadlines.
International Students: There were 10 international students enrolled in a recent year. They must score satisfactorily on the written TOEFL and also take the SAT or the ACT.
Computers: All students may access the system. There are no time limits and no fees.

Graduates: In a reent year, 34 bachelor's degrees were awarded. The most popular majors were nursing (97%), cytotechnology (2%), and allied health (1%). In an average class, 85% graduate in 3 years or less, and 5% graduate in 4 years or less. 5 companies recruited on campus in a recent year. Of a recent graduating class, 10% were enrolled in graduate school within 6 months of graduation and 96% were employed.
Admissions Contact: Christie Schneider Admissions Contact-Dorman, Admissions Director. E-mail: *jhcollegeinquiry@bjc.org* Web: *www.barnesjewishcollege.edu*

KANSAS CITY ART INSTITUTE · A-2

Kansas City, MO 64111

(816) 474-5224
(800) 522-5224; Fax: (816) 802-3309

Full-time: 260 men, 334 women	**Faculty:** 46; IIB, --$
Part-time: 5 men, 2 women	**Ph.D.s:** 82%
Graduate: none	**Student/Faculty:** 13 to 1
Year: semesters, summer session	**Tuition:** $22,392
Application Deadline: rolling	**Room & Board:** $7150
Freshman Class: 414 applied, 108 accepted, 174 enrolled	
SAT Verbal/Math: 559/523*	**ACT:** 22 **SPECIAL**

The Kansas City Art Institute, founded in 1885, is an independent professional college of art and design. In addition to regional accreditation, KCAI has baccalaureate program accreditation with NASAD. The library contains 32,000 volumes and 38 audio/video tapes/CDs/DVDs, and subscribes to 96 periodicals including electronic. Computerized library services include the card catalog, interlibrary loans, database searching, Internet access, and laptop Internet portals. Special learning facilities include a learning resource center and art gallery. The 17-acre campus is in an urban area. Including any residence halls, there are 14 buildings.
Student Life: 61% of undergraduates are from out of state, mostly the Midwest. Students are from 37 states, 12 foreign countries, and Canada. 90% are from public schools. 82% are white. The average age of freshmen is 18; all undergraduates, 21. 21% do not continue beyond their first year; 57% remain to graduate.
Housing: 180 students can be accommodated in college housing, which includes single-sex and coed dorms and off-campus apartments. The Student Affairs Office offers assistance finding off-campus housing. On-campus housing is guaranteed for the freshman year only and is available on a first-come, first-served basis. 75% of students commute. Alcohol is not permitted. All students may keep cars.
Activities: There are no fraternities or sororities. There are 2 groups on campus, including literary magazine and newspaper. Popular campus events include dances, film series, and poetry readings.
Sports: There is no sports program at KCAI.
Disabled Students: 50% of the campus is accessible. Wheelchair ramps, elevators, specially equipped rest rooms, and, sign language interpreters are available.
Services: Counseling and information services are available, as is tutoring in every subject. There is remedial reading and writing.
Campus Safety and Security: Measures include 24-hour foot and vehicle patrol, security escort services, informal discussions, and pamphlets/posters/films. There are emergency telephones, lighted pathways/sidewalks, and a free taxi service.
Programs of Study: KCAI confers the B.F.A. degree. Bachelor's degrees are awarded in COMMUNICATIONS AND THE ARTS (animation, art history and appreciation, ceramic art and design, creative writing, design, fiber/textiles/weaving, media arts, painting, photography, printmaking, sculpture, and video). Painting, printmaking, and sculpture are the strongest academically. Painting, design, and fiber are the largest.
Required: Students must maintain a minimum GPA of 2.0 overall and within their studio major. A total of 129 credit hours is needed, including 81 in studio classes; 45 distributed among courses in history of Western thought, art history, literature, humanities, and other liberal arts; and 3 in electives.
Special: KCAI offers internships with major corporations such as Hallmark and Disney, independent study, work-study programs, study abroad in 7 countries, cross-registration, an exchange program, and nondegree study.
Faculty/Classroom: 27% of faculty are male; 43%, female. All teach undergraduates. The average class size in an introductory lecture is 31; in a laboratory, 15; and in a regular course, 22.
Admissions: 26% of the 2005-2006 applicants were accepted. The SAT scores for the 2005-2006 freshman class were: Verbal--27% below 500, 41% between 500 and 599, 27% between 600 and 700, and 6% above 700; Math--35% below 500, 43% between 500 and 599, 19% between 600 and 700, and 3% above 700. The ACT scores were 24% below 21, 39% between 21 and 23, 24% between 24 and 26, 8% between 27 and 28, and 5% above 28. 20% of the current freshmen were in the top fifth of their class; 51% were in the top two fifths.
Requirements: The SAT or ACT is required. In addition, applicants must submit a portfolio consisting of 10 to 20 pieces of artwork, 2 letters of recommendation, and high school transcripts. The GED is accepted.

A statement of purpose and an interview are required. A GPA of 2.5 is required. AP and CLEP credits are accepted. Important factors in the admissions decision are evidence of special talent, advanced placement or honor courses, and recommendations by school officials.

Procedure: Freshmen are admitted fall and spring. Entrance exams should be taken in spring of the junior year or fall of the senior year. There is a deferred admissions plan and a rolling admissions plan. Application deadlines for fall entry, are rolling. There is a $35 fee. Notification is sent on a rolling basis.

Transfer: 62 transfer students enrolled in 2005-2006. Transfer applicants must submit official transcripts and a portfolio. A minimum GPA of 2.0 is required. 72 of 129 credits required for the bachelor's degree must be completed at KCAI.

Visiting: There are regularly scheduled orientations for prospective students, consisting of information sessions offered every other Friday. There are guides for informal visits and visitors may sit in on classes and stay overnight. To schedule a visit, contact the Admissions Office at (816) 802-3300 or *admiss@kcai.edu*.

Financial Aid: In 2005-2006, 98% of all full-time students received some form of financial aid. 90% of full-time freshmen and 80% of continuing full-time students received need-based aid. The average freshman award was $12,489. Need-based scholarships or need-based grants averaged $12,692 ($21,446 maximum); need-based self-help aid (loans and jobs) averaged $4996 ($9625 maximum); and other non-need-based awards and non-need-based scholarships averaged $9872 ($21,446 maximum). 65% of undergraduates work part time. Average annual earnings from campus work are $1000. The average financial indebtedness of the 2005 graduate was $17,125. The FAFSA and student and parent IRS tax forms, if requested. are required. The deadline for filing freshman financial aid applications for fall entry is March 15.

International Students: There were 14 international students enrolled in a recent year. They must take the TOEFL.

Computers: All students may access the system. There are no time limits and no fees. It is strongly recommended that all students have personal computers, especially students in design and animation majors.

Graduates: From July 1, 2004 to June 30, 2005, 102 bachelor's degrees were awarded. The most popular majors were painting (16%), sculpture (16%), and illustration and ceramics (16%). In an average class, 43% graduate in 4 years or less, and 52% graduate in 5 or 6 years or less. Of the 2004 graduating class, 11% were enrolled in graduate school within 6 months of graduation and 50% were employed.

Admissions Contact: Larry Stone, Vice President for Enrollment Management. E-mail: *admiss@kcai.edu* Web: *www.kcai.edu*

LESTER L. COX COLLEGE OF NURSING AND HEALTH SCIENCES
B-3

Springfield, MO 65802

(417) 269-3038
(866) 898-5355; Fax: (417) 269-3586

Full-time: 21 men, 258 women	**Faculty:** n/av
Part-time: 27 men, 286 women	**Ph.D.s:** n/av
Graduate: none	**Student/Faculty:** 12 to 1
Year: semesters, summer session	**Tuition:** $10,290
Application Deadline: February 1	**Room & Board:** $2000
Freshman Class: n/av	
ACT: recommended	**SPECIAL**

Lester L. Cox College of Nursing and Health Sciences, founded in 1994, is a private institution providing comprehensive educational programs that prepare graduates for a changing health care enviornment. Some information in this profile is approximate. In addition to regional accreditation, Cox College has baccalaureate program accreditation with CCNE and NLN. The library contains 7000 volumes, and subscribes to 440 periodicals including electronic. Computerized library services include the card catalog, interlibrary loans, database searching, and Internet access. Special learning facilities include a learning resource center, a nursing skills lab, and an audiovisual learning center. The campus is in an urban area adjacent to the Cox Health North Campus. Including any residence halls, there is 1 building.

Student Life: 99% of undergraduates are from Missouri. 96% are white. The average age of all undergraduates is 27.

Housing: 60 students can be accommodated in college housing, which includes coed dorms. On-campus housing is available on a first-come, first-served basis. 90% of students commute. Alcohol is not permitted. All students may keep cars.

Activities: There are no fraternities or sororities. There are 3 groups on campus, including professional, religious, and student government. Popular campus events include Fall Fling, Wellness Days, and Diversity Day.

Sports: There is no sports program at Cox College.

Disabled Students: Wheelchair ramps, elevators, and special parking are available.

Services: Counseling and information services are available, as is tutoring in some subjects, including math and writing. There is remedial math, reading, and writing. Peer tutoring is available for most science courses.

Campus Safety and Security: Measures include 24-hour foot and vehicle patrol, security escort services, pamphlets/posters/films, and emergency telephones. There are lighted pathways/sidewalks.

Programs of Study: Cox College confers the B.S.N. degree. Associate degrees are also awarded. Bachelor's degrees are awarded in HEALTH PROFESSIONS (nursing).

Required: A total of 122 credit hours and a minimum 2.5 GPA is required for the B.S.N.

Special: Cox College offers cross-registration with Evangel University, work-study programs, and an accelerated degree program in nursing.

Faculty/Classroom: All teach undergraduates. The average class size in an introductory lecture is 25; in a laboratory, 33; and in a regular course, 25.

Requirements: The ACT is recommended. A GPA of 2.5 is required. AP and CLEP credits are accepted.

Procedure: Freshmen are admitted fall, spring, and summer. Entrance exams should be taken after admission, prior to registration. There is an early decision plan. Early decision applications should be filed by November 1; regular applications, by February 1 for fall entry, September 1 for spring entry, and February 1 for summer entry. The college accepts all applicants. Notification of early decision is sent December 1; regular decision, March 1. The fall 2005 application fee was $30.

Transfer: A GPA of 2.5 or better is required, with 12 or more hours of credit. Only courses with a grade of C or better will be considered for transfer. Transfer applicants are not required to submit an ACT score. 30 of 122 credits required for the bachelor's degree must be completed at Cox College.

Visiting: There are guides for informal visits and visitors may sit in on classes.

Financial Aid: In 2005-2006, 85% of all full-time freshmen and 78% of continuing full-time students received some form of financial aid. 4% of undergraduates work part time. The FAFSA is required. Check with the school for current application deadlines.

International Students: They must score satisfactorily on the written TOEFL or on the electronic version and also take the ACT or Asset, scoring 22 on the ACT.

Computers: There are no time limits and no fees.

Graduates: The most popular major was nursing (100%). Of a recent graduating class, all were employed within 6 months of graduation.

Admissions Contact: Stacy Danaher, Admissions Coordinator. A video is available. E-mail: *admissions@coxcollege.edu* Web: *coxcollege.edu*

LINCOLN UNIVERSITY
C-2

Jefferson City, MO 65102-0029

(573) 681-5599
(800) 521-5052; Fax: (573) 681-5889

Full-time: 900 men, 1100 women	**Faculty:** 141; IIA, --$
Part-time: 400 men, 700 women	**Ph.D.s:** 30%
Graduate: 70 men, 200 women	**Student/Faculty:** 14 to 1
Year: semesters, summer session	**Tuition:** $4000 ($7000)
Application Deadline: see profile	**Room & Board:** $4000
Freshman Class: n/av	
ACT: required	**NONCOMPETITIVE**

Lincoln University, established in 1866, is a land-grant institution offering degree programs in agriculture, arts and sciences, business, applied technology, and education. There are 3 undergraduate schools and 1 graduate school. Figures in the above capsule and in this profile are approximate. In addition to regional accreditation, LU has baccalaureate program accreditation with NASM and NCATE. The library contains 340,000 volumes, 100,000 microform items, and 3000 audio/video tapes/CDs/DVDs, and subscribes to 1000 periodicals including electronic. Computerized library services include the card catalog, interlibrary loans, and database searching. Special learning facilities include a learning resource center, radio station, TV station, and ethnic studies center. The 155-acre campus is in a small town 130 miles west of St. Louis. Including any residence halls, there are 36 buildings.

Student Life: 89% of undergraduates are from Missouri. Others are from 28 states, 29 foreign countries, and Canada. 63% are white; 30% African American. The average age of freshmen is 18; all undergraduates, 22.

Housing: 630 students can be accommodated in college housing, which includes single-sex dorms. On-campus housing is available on a first-come, first-served basis. 82% of students commute. Alcohol is not permitted. All students may keep cars.

Activities: 3% of men belong to 4 national fraternities. There are 4 national sororities. There are 28 groups on campus, including art, band, cheerleading, choir, dance, drama, honors, international, jazz band, marching band, newspaper, opera, professional, radio and TV, religious, student government, and yearbook. Popular campus events include Black History Week and Unity Awards in Media.

Sports: There are 6 intercollegiate sports for men and 4 for women, and 2 intramural sports for men. Facilities include a 5600-seat stadium and a 2500-seat gym.

Disabled Students: Wheelchair ramps, elevators, special parking, specially equipped rest rooms, special class scheduling, lowered drinking fountains, and lowered telephones are available.

Services: Counseling and information services are available, as is tutoring in most subjects. There is a reader service for the blind, and remedial math, reading, and writing.

Campus Safety and Security: Measures include 24-hour foot and vehicle patrol, self-defense education, security escort services, and informal discussions. There are pamphlets/posters/films, emergency telephones, and lighted pathways/sidewalks.

Programs of Study: LU confers B.A., B.S., B.M.E., and B.S.Ed. degrees. Associate and master's degrees are also awarded. Bachelor's degrees are awarded in AGRICULTURE (agriculture), BIOLOGICAL SCIENCE (biology/biological science), BUSINESS (accounting, business administration and management, marketing/retailing/merchandising, and office supervision and management), COMMUNICATIONS AND THE ARTS (art, English, French, journalism, and Spanish), COMPUTER AND PHYSICAL SCIENCE (chemistry, information sciences and systems, mathematics, and physics), EDUCATION (art, business, elementary, home economics, music, physical, social science, and special), ENGINEERING AND ENVIRONMENTAL DESIGN (civil engineering technology, engineering, and mechanical design technology), HEALTH PROFESSIONS (medical technology and nursing), SOCIAL SCIENCE (criminal justice, economics, history, liberal arts/general studies, philosophy, political science/government, psychology, public administration, and sociology). Business administration, nursing, and education are the largest.

Required: To graduate, students must complete 121 semester hours including at least 30 in the major, with 18 hours in upper-division courses. Students must maintain a minimum GPA of 2.0. Course work is required in math, English, speech, humanities, history, social science, cultural diversity, and phys ed. Seniors must pass a major field exit exam.

Special: LU offers cross-registration with the University of Missouri/Columbia and William Woods, Westminster, and Columbia Colleges; federal, state, local, and private internships; co-op programs, and a 3-2 engineering degree with the University of Missouri Rolla. Credit by exam, student-designed majors, and a continuing education program are available. There is a freshman honors program.

Faculty/Classroom: 61% of faculty are male; 39%, female. All teach undergraduates and 14% do research. No introductory courses are taught by graduate students. The average class size in an introductory lecture is 50; in a laboratory, 13; and in a regular course, 25.

Requirements: The ACT is required. In addition, students must be graduates of an accredited secondary school or have the GED. A GPA of 2.0 is required. CLEP credit is accepted.

Procedure: Freshmen are admitted to all sessions. Entrance exams should be taken prior to registration. There is an early admissions plan. Check with the school for current application deadlines. The fall 2005 application fee was $17. The college accepts all in-state residents. Notification is sent on a rolling basis.

Transfer: All applicants must submit a college transcript from each institution previously attended; those students transferring fewer than 30 hours must also submit the high school transcript and ACT scores. 30 of 121 credits required for the bachelor's degree must be completed at LU.

Visiting: There are regularly scheduled orientations for prospective students, consisting of a freshman orientation held each July. There are guides for informal visits and visitors may sit in on classes and stay overnight. To schedule a visit, contact the Enrollment Services Office at (573) 681-5022.

Financial Aid: LU is a member of CSS. The FAFSA is required. Check with the school for current deadlines.

International Students: They must score satisfactorily on the written TOEFL or take the MELAB and also take the ACT or placement tests.

Computers: All students may access the system 8 A.M. to 10 P.M. Monday through Friday, 8 A.M. to 7 P.M. Saturday, and 9 A.M. to 2 P.M. Sunday. There are no time limits and no fees.

Admissions Contact: Constance Williams, Vice President, Student Affairs. Web: *www.lincolnu.edu*

LINDENWOOD UNIVERSITY   D-2
St. Charles, MO 63301-1695

	(636) 949-4949
	Fax: (636) 949-4989

Full-time: 2223 men, 2869 women	**Faculty:** 208
Part-time: 219 men, 417 women	**Ph.D.s:** 60%
Graduate: 955 men, 2383 women	**Student/Faculty:** 24 to 1
Year: 4-1-4, summer session	**Tuition:** $12,600
Application Deadline: open	**Room & Board:** $6000
Freshman Class: 2906 applied, 1249 accepted, 773 enrolled	
ACT: 23	**VERY COMPETITIVE**

Lindenwood University, founded in 1827, is a private institution offering undergraduate and graduate degree programs in the arts and sciences, business, education, and preprofessional fields. There are 6 undergraduate and 5 graduate schools. In addition to regional accreditation, Lindenwood has baccalaureate program accreditation with CAAHEP and TEAC. The library contains 171,562 volumes, 26,128 microform items, and 1763 audio/video tapes/CDs/DVDs, and subscribes to 793 periodicals including electronic. Computerized library services include the card catalog, interlibrary loans, database searching, Internet access, and laptop Internet portals. Special learning facilities include a learning resource center, art gallery, radio station, TV station, a greenhouse, a wetlands program facility, a success center, and the Boone Home historic site. The 500-acre campus is in a suburban area 25 miles west of St. Louis. Including any residence halls, there are 30 buildings.

Student Life: 83% of undergraduates are from Missouri. Students are from 43 states, 60 foreign countries, and Canada. 77% are white; 13% African American. 49% are Catholic; 45% Protestant. The average age of freshmen is 19; all undergraduates, 25. 31% do not continue beyond their first year; 46% remain to graduate.

Housing: 3256 students can be accommodated in college housing, which includes single-sex dorms, on-campus apartments, married-student housing, and sorority houses. In addition, there are honors houses. On-campus housing is guaranteed for all 4 years. 70% of students live on campus; of those, 67% remain on campus on weekends. Alcohol is not permitted. All students may keep cars.

Activities: 2% of men belong to 2 national fraternities; 2% of women belong to 1 national sorority. There are 69 groups on campus, including art, band, cheerleading, chess, choir, chorale, chorus, computers, dance, debate, drama, drill team, film, forensics, honors, international, jazz band, literary magazine, marching band, musical theater, newspaper, pep band, photography, political, professional, radio and TV, religious, social, social service, and student government. Popular campus events include Spring Fling, Alumni Weekend, and Christmas Walk.

Sports: There are 20 intercollegiate sports for men and 18 for women, and 6 intramural sports for men and 6 for women. Facilities include an indoor pool, a gym, weight rooms, a 5000-seat stadium, a 3000-seat performance arena, a sand volleyball court, tennis courts, softball, baseball, and soccer fields, and a state-of-the art all-weather track, and dual ice rinks. Students may use the local golf course and bowling alley for a discounted fee.

Disabled Students: 50% of the campus is accessible. Wheelchair ramps, elevators, special parking, specially equipped rest rooms, special class scheduling, lowered drinking fountains, lowered telephones, and curb cuts are available.

Services: Counseling and information services are available, as is tutoring in every subject. There is a reader service for the blind, and remedial math, reading, and writing.

Campus Safety and Security: Measures include 24-hour foot and vehicle patrol, self-defense education, security escort services, and informal discussions. There are pamphlets/posters/films, emergency telephones, and lighted pathways/sidewalks.

Programs of Study: Lindenwood confers B.A., B.S., and B.F.A. degrees. Master's degrees are also awarded. Bachelor's degrees are awarded in AGRICULTURE (agricultural business management), BIOLOGICAL SCIENCE (biology/biological science), BUSINESS (accounting, banking and finance, business administration and management, human resources, management information systems, marketing/retailing/merchandising, and sports management), COMMUNICATIONS AND THE ARTS (art history and appreciation, communications, creative writing, dance, dramatic arts, English, French, music, performing arts, Spanish, and studio art), COMPUTER AND PHYSICAL SCIENCE (chemistry, computer science, and mathematics), EDUCATION (art, athletic training, business, early childhood, elementary, music, physical, science, and secondary), ENGINEERING AND ENVIRONMENTAL DESIGN (engineering), HEALTH PROFESSIONS (medical technology), SOCIAL SCIENCE (criminal justice, fashion design and technology, history, human services, international studies, liberal arts/general studies, ministries, political science/government, prelaw, psychology, public administration, religion, social work, and sociology). Biology, education, and mass communications are the strongest academically. Business, education, and mass communications are the largest.

Required: In order to graduate, students must complete a minimum of 128 credit hours, including at least 36 in the major and 42 in upper-division courses, with a minimum GPA of 2.0. Core curriculum courses include 10 hours of math and science, 9 each of social sciences, humanities, and civilization, 6 of English, and 3 each of fine arts and communications. They must score at proficiency level on a writing assessment.

Special: The university offers internships in most majors, a co-op program in computer science, study abroad and a Washington semester for juniors, and cross-registration through a consortium of Greater St. Louis College and universities. Dual and student-designed majors, accelerated degree programs, 3-2 degrees in engineering with Washington University in St. Louis and the University of Missouri-Columbia, work-study programs, and nondegree study are also available. Lindenwood is also designed to meet the needs of working adults; there are evening and weekend classes and 5-year bachelor's programs. There are 9 national honor societies, a freshman honors program, and 6 departmental honors programs.

Faculty/Classroom: 56% of faculty are male; 44%, female. 75% teach undergraduates. No introductory courses are taught by graduate students. The average class size in an introductory lecture is 30; in a laboratory, 25; and in a regular course, 25.

Admissions: 43% of the 2005-2006 applicants were accepted. The ACT scores for the 2005-2006 freshman class were: 21% below 21, 47% between 21 and 23, 16% between 24 and 26, 10% between 27 and 28, and 6% above 28. 29% of the current freshmen were in the top fifth of their class; 53% were in the top two fifths. 14 freshmen graduated first in their class.

Requirements: The SAT or ACT is required. Applicants must be graduates of an accredited secondary school or have a GED. High school preparation should include at least 16 academic units, including 4 years of English, 2 to 3 each of math, science, and social studies, 2 of a foreign language, and some study of fine or performing arts. An essay and an interview are recommended. Lindenwood requires applicants to be in the upper 50% of their class. A GPA of 2.25 is required. AP and CLEP credits are accepted. Important factors in the admissions decision are leadership record, evidence of special talent, and advanced placement or honor courses.

Procedure: Freshmen are admitted to all sessions. There are deferred admissions and rolling admissions plans. Application deadlines are open. Application fee is $25.

Transfer: 676 transfer students enrolled in a recent year. Applicants must have a minimum GPA of 2.0 and should submit official college transcripts in order to transfer credits. 38 of 128 credits required for the bachelor's degree must be completed at Lindenwood.

Visiting: There are regularly scheduled orientations for prospective students, including an admissions interview, a campus tour, and advising. There are guides for informal visits and visitors may sit in on classes and stay overnight. To schedule a visit, contact the Office of Undergraduate Admissions.

Financial Aid: In 2005-2006, 95% of all full-time students received some form of financial aid. 46% of all full-time students received need-based aid. Need-based scholarships or need-based grants averaged $3636; and need-based self-help aid (loans and jobs) averaged $2671. 91% of undergraduates work part time. Average annual earnings from campus work are $2400. The average financial indebtedness of the 2005 graduate was $14,000. The FAFSA is required. The priority date for freshman financial aid applications for fall entry is April 1.

International Students: There are 450 international students enrolled. The school actively recruits these students. They must score satisfactorily on the written TOEFL or on the electronic version.

Computers: Wireless access is available. Every dorm room is wired capable for 10/100MB connection to the Internet, usually 2 drops. Wireless is currently available at 2 locations on campus, the Loft (student lounge) and Butler Library. There are PCs for student use in several locations. The Internet is provided for student use for the purpose of study. The dorm rooms have limited access to the Internet. The Loft has unlimited access to the Internet. The public use computers, in lab areas, have a more limited Internet access. All students may access the system 8 A.M. to 12 A.M. There are no time limits and no fees.

Graduates: In a recent year, 872 bachelor's degrees were awarded. The most popular majors were business administration (23%), education (7%), and information technology (3%). In an average class, 5% graduate in 3 years or less, 27% graduate in 4 years or less, 42% graduate in 5 years or less, and 46% graduate in 6 years or less. 77 companies recruited on campus in a recent year. Of a recent graduating class, 14% were enrolled in graduate school within 6 months of graduation and 94% were employed.

Admissions Contact: Joe Parisi, Associate Dean of Admissions. A video is available. E-mail: *admissions@lindenwood.edu*
Web: *www.lindenwood.edu*

MARYVILLE UNIVERSITY OF SAINT LOUIS   D-2
St. Louis, MO 63141-7299   (314) 529-9350
1-(800) 627-9855, ext.9350; Fax: (314) 529-9927

Full-time: 400 men, 1100 women	Faculty: 82; IIA, --$
Part-time: 300 men, 900 women	Ph.D.s: 90%
Graduate: 100 men, 500 women	Student/Faculty: 19 to 1
Year: semesters, summer session	Tuition: $16,000
Application Deadline: see profile	Room & Board: $7000
Freshman Class: n/av	
SAT or ACT: required	VERY COMPETITIVE

Maryville University of Saint Louis, established in 1872, is an independent institution offering undergraduate programs in arts, sciences, business, education, and health-related fields and graduate programs in business administration, education, health administration, nursing, occupational therapy, physical therapy, and rehabilitation counseling. There are 4 undergraduate and 3 graduate schools. Figures in the above capsule and in this profile are approximate. In addition to regional accreditation, Maryville has baccalaureate program accreditation with AC-BSP, AOTA, APTA, CCNE, CORE, FIDER, NASAD, NASM, NCATE,

and NLN. The library contains 205,500 volumes, 487,800 microform items, and 10,900 audio/video tapes/CDs/DVDs, and subscribes to 9000 periodicals including electronic. Computerized library services include the card catalog, interlibrary loans, database searching, and Internet access. Special learning facilities include a learning resource center, an art gallery, an observatory, a teaching lab, art and design labs, clinical labs for nursing, occupational therapy, and physical therapy, a communications lab, video conferencing facilities on all campuses, 4 multimedia-ready classrooms, and residence hall computer labs. The 130-acre campus is in a suburban area 20 miles west of downtown St. Louis. Including any residence halls, there are 18 buildings.

Student Life: 92% of undergraduates are from Missouri. Others are from 18 states, 23 foreign countries, and Canada. 80% are from public schools. 72% are white. 62% claim no religious affiliation; 16% are Catholic; 7% Protestant. The average age of freshmen is 18; all undergraduates, 27. 26% do not continue beyond their first year; 69% remain to graduate.

Housing: 450 students can be accommodated in college housing, which includes single-sex and coed dorms and on-campus apartments. On-campus housing is available on a first-come, first-served basis. 70% of students commute. All students may keep cars.

Activities: There are no fraternities or sororities. There are 33 groups on campus, including art, band, cheerleading, chorale, dance, departmental drama, ethnic, honors, international, jazz band, literary magazine, newspaper, political, professional, religious, social, social service, and student government. Popular campus events include Christmas tree-lighting ceremony, Fall Festival, and Cram Jam.

Sports: There are 6 intercollegiate sports for men and 6 for women, and 8 intramural sports for men and 8 for women. Facilities include an outdoor swimming pool, tennis courts, soccer, softball, and baseball fields, a gym, outdoor and indoor basketball hoops, an expanded fitness center, a student center with table tennis and billiards, a sand volleyball court, and outdoor walking and hiking trails.

Disabled Students: 90% of the campus is accessible. Wheelchair ramps, elevators, special parking, specially equipped rest rooms, special class scheduling, lowered drinking fountains, lowered telephones, electronic doors, note takers, and interpreters for the hearing impaired are available.

Services: Counseling and information services are available, as is tutoring in every subject. There is a reader service for the blind. There also is a writing center, learning styles inventorying, and help with time management and test-taking skills, and there are study skills materials, workshops, and individual consultations.

Campus Safety and Security: Measures include 24-hour foot and vehicle patrol, self-defense education, security escort services, and pamphlets/posters/films. There are emergency telephones, lighted pathways/sidewalks, video security systems in residence halls, and security key operated dorm entrances.

Programs of Study: Maryville confers B.A., B.S., B.F.A., B.S.C.L.S., B.S.M.T., and B.S.N. degrees. Master's degrees are also awarded. Bachelor's degrees are awarded in AGRICULTURE (environmental studies), BIOLOGICAL SCIENCE (biology/biological science), BUSINESS (accounting, business administration and management, electronic business, marketing/retailing/merchandising, and organizational behavior), COMMUNICATIONS AND THE ARTS (communications, English, graphic design, and studio art), COMPUTER AND PHYSICAL SCIENCE (actuarial science, chemistry, computer science, information sciences and systems, mathematics, and science), EDUCATION (art, early childhood, elementary, middle school, and secondary), ENGINEERING AND ENVIRONMENTAL DESIGN (environmental science and interior design), HEALTH PROFESSIONS (clinical science, health care administration, health science, music therapy, and nursing), SOCIAL SCIENCE (criminology, history, liberal arts/general studies, paralegal studies, psychology, and sociology). Actuarial science, education and physical therapy are the strongest academically. Nursing, business administration, and accounting are the largest.

Required: To graduate, all students must complete a minimum of 128 credit hours, with a minimum GPA of 2.0. The core curriculum consists of 12 credit hours each of humanities, math and science, and social and behavioral science, and 8 credit hours each of communication skills and fine arts. 48 upper-division credits must be completed.

Special: There is cross-registration with Missouri Baptist College and Fontbonne, Webster, and Lindenwood Universities. Students may choose internships in various fields, and cooperative programs are available with such employers as Edward Jones, Daimler Chrysler, Smith Barney, Verizon Wireless, Gateway, the U.S. Army Corps of Engineers, IBM, Citimortgage, Northwestern Mutual, and Walgreens. Other options include dual and student-designed majors, study abroad in England, Japan, Korea, China, and other countries, a Washington semester, nondegree study, and pass-fail grading. A 3-2 engineering degree is available in conjunction with Washington University. There are 8 national honor societies, and a freshman honors program.

Faculty/Classroom: 37% of faculty are male; 63%, female. 71% teach undergraduates. No introductory courses are taught by graduate stu-

dents. The average class size in an introductory lecture is 17; in a laboratory, 15; and in a regular course, 16.

Admissions: The ACT scores for a recent freshman class were: 22% below 21, 28% between 21 and 23, 31% between 24 and 26, 10% between 27 and 28, and 9% above 28. 49% of recent freshmen were in the top fifth of their class; 76% were in the top two fifths. 4 freshmen graduated first in their class in a recent year.

Requirements: The SAT or ACT is required. In addition, students must have graduated from an accredited secondary school with 22 academic credits or have the GED. Expected preparatory courses include 4 units of English, 3 of math, and 2 each of science and social studies, plus 3 additional units in any of the perceding areas or in a foreign language. Some majors have additional admission requirements. A GPA of 2.5 is required. AP and CLEP credits are accepted. Important factors in the admissions decision are recommendations by school officials, advanced placement or honor courses, and leadership record.

Procedure: Freshmen are admitted to all sessions. Entrance exams should be taken during the junior year. Check with the school for current application deadlines. The fall 2005 application fee was $25. Notification is sent on a rolling basis. Applications are accepted on-line.

Transfer: 403 transfer students enrolled in a recent year . A minimum GPA of 2.0, or higher for some majors, is required. Some majors may require ACT or SAT scores. 30 of 128 credits required for the bachelor's degree must be completed at Maryville.

Visiting: There are regularly scheduled orientations for prospective students, including visiting the campus and arranging a personal interview with an admissions counselor. There are guides for informal visits and visitors may sit in on classes and stay overnight. To schedule a visit, contact the Admissions Office.

Financial Aid: In a recent year, 98% of all full-time freshmen and 76% of continuing full-time students received some form of financial aid. 76% of full-time freshmen and 68% of continuing full-time students received need-based aid. The average freshman award was $12,409. Need-based scholarships or need-based grants averaged $12,106 ($18,800 maximum); need-based self-help aid (loans and jobs) averaged $8489 ($21,960 maximum); other non-need-based awards and non-need-based scholarships averaged $5549 ($21,850 maximum); and parental loans averaged $17,085 ($20,400 maximum). 17% of undergraduates work part time. Average annual earnings from campus work are $1655. The average financial indebtedness of a recent graduate was $11,167. Maryville is a member of CSS. The FAFSA is required. Check with the school for current deadlines.

International Students: There were 45 international students enrolled in a recent year. The school actively recruits these students. They must score satisfactorily on the written TOEFL or on the electronic version.

Computers: All students may access the system in the computer center lab from 8 A.M. to 10 P.M.; 24-hour access is available from 2 residence halls. There are no time limits and no fees.

Graduates: In a recent year, 558 bachelor's degrees were awarded. The most popular majors were information systems (10%), business administration (8%), and nursing (8%). In an average class, 55% graduate in 4 years or less, 67% graduate in 5 years or less, and 69% graduate in 6 years or less. 62 companies recruited on campus in a recent year.

Admissions Contact: Director of Admissions. A video is available. E-mail: *admissions@maryville.edu* Web: *www.maryville.edu*

MISSOURI BAPTIST UNIVERSITY D-2

St. Louis, MO 63141-8660

(314) 392-2296
(877) 434-1115; Fax: (314) 434-7596

Full-time: 546 men, 665 women	**Faculty:** 48; IIB, --$
Part-time: 898 men, 1375 women	**Ph.D.s:** 56%
Graduate: 228 men, 747 women	**Student/Faculty:** 25 to 1
Year: semesters, summer session	**Tuition:** $13,840
Application Deadline: open	**Room & Board:** $5800
Freshman Class: 551 applied, 288 accepted, 221 enrolled	
ACT: 20	**COMPETITIVE**

Missouri Baptist Univesity, established in 1964, is a private liberal arts institution. There are 8 undergraduate schools and 1 graduate school. In addition to regional accreditation, MBU has baccalaureate program accreditation with NASM and NCATE. The library contains 72,744 volumes, 48,132 microform items, and 1999 audio/video tapes/CDs/DVDs, and subscribes to 425 periodicals including electronic. Computerized library services include the card catalog, interlibrary loans, database searching, Internet access, and laptop Internet portals. Special learning facilities include a radio station and an audiovisual production lab. The 63-acre campus is in a suburban area 15 miles west of St. Louis. Including any residence halls, there are 6 buildings.

Student Life: 93% of undergraduates are from Missouri. Others are from 25 states, 28 foreign countries, and Canada. 78% are white. 39% claim no religious affiliation; 39% Protestant; 16% Catholic. The average age of freshmen is 19; all undergraduates, 25.

Housing: 239 students can be accommodated in college housing, which includes single-sex dorms and off-campus apartments. In addition,

there are honors houses. On-campus housing is available on a first-come, first-served basis. 85% of students commute. Alcohol is not permitted. All students may keep cars.

Activities: There are no fraternities or sororities. There are 31 groups on campus, including band, business, cheerleading, choir, chorale, chorus, computers, drama, film, honors, international, jazz band, literary magazine, musical theater, opera, political, professional, radio and TV, religious, student government, and yearbook. Popular campus events include Spring Musical, Christmas Concert, and Hanging of the Green.

Sports: There are 14 intercollegiate sports for men and 14 for women, and 4 intramural sports for men and 4 for women. Facilities include a gym, weight-training rooms, a game room, and baseball, softball, and soccer fields.

Disabled Students: 71% of the campus is accessible. Wheelchair ramps, elevators, special parking, specially equipped rest rooms, and lowered drinking fountains are available.

Services: Counseling and information services are available, as is tutoring in some subjects, by arrangement. There is a reader service for the blind and remedial math and writing.

Campus Safety and Security: Measures include 24-hour foot and vehicle patrol, self-defense education, and lighted pathways/sidewalks.

Programs of Study: MBU confers B.A., B.S., B.M., B.P.S., and B.S.E. degrees. Associate and master's degrees are also awarded. Bachelor's degrees are awarded in BIOLOGICAL SCIENCE (biology/biological science), BUSINESS (accounting, business administration and management, management science, and sports management), COMMUNICATIONS AND THE ARTS (communications, English, and music performance), COMPUTER AND PHYSICAL SCIENCE (chemistry, information sciences and systems, mathematics, and science), EDUCATION (athletic training, early childhood, elementary, middle school, and music), HEALTH PROFESSIONS (health science, nursing, and sports medicine), SOCIAL SCIENCE (behavioral science, child psychology/development, criminal justice, history, human services, ministries, physical fitness/movement, psychology, religion, religious education, religious music, and social science). Education, business, and psychology are the strongest academically and have the largest enrollments.

Required: All students must take courses in the humanities/fine arts, social and behavorial sciences, natural sciences, phys ed, computer literacy, and Old and New Testament history. A minimum GPA of 2.0 is required (some majors require a GPA of 2.5 or better). To graduate, students must complete at least 128 credit hours, with a minimum of 30 hours in the major and 45 hours of upper-division courses; pass a general education exam and an exit exam or other assessment in the major; and complete a capstone project.

Special: There is cross-registration with Fontbonne College and Maryville, Lindenwood, and Webster Universities. Students may opt for credit by exam, nondegree study, and student-designed majors. A 3-2 engineering degree with the University of Missouri/Columbia or a 2-2 engineering degree with the University of Missouri/Rolla is available. Study abroad is possible at Harlaxton College in England and at Hong Kong Baptist University. MBC also offers internships in various disciplines and dual majors in some business and education fields. There are 5 national honor societies.

Faculty/Classroom: 60% of faculty are male; 40%, female. 94% teach undergraduates. No introductory courses are taught by graduate students. The average class size in an introductory lecture is 30; in a laboratory, 20; and in a regular course, 15.

Admissions: 52% of the 2005-2006 applicants were accepted. The ACT scores for the 2005-2006 freshman class were: 55% below 21, 20% between 21 and 23, 15% between 24 and 26, 4% between 27 and 28, and 6% above 28. 19% of the current freshmen were in the top fifth of their class; 43% were in the top two fifths.

Requirements: The SAT or ACT is required. Applicants must be graduates of an accredited secondary school. GED and homeschooled students are accepted. MBU requires applicants to be in the upper 50% of their class. A GPA of 2.0 is required. AP and CLEP credits are accepted. Important factors in the admissions decision are advanced placement or honor courses, leadership record, and evidence of special talent.

Procedure: Freshmen are admitted to all sessions. Entrance exams should be taken in the junior year. There is a rolling admissions plan. Application deadlines are open. Application fee is $25. Applications are accepted on-line.

Transfer: 301 transfer students enrolled in 2004-2005. Applicants must have a 2.0 GPA, with some programs requiring 2.5 or better. Students must submit official transcripts from all previous colleges attended, along with a character reference. 24 of 128 credits required for the bachelor's degree must be completed at MBU.

Visiting: There are regularly scheduled orientations for prospective students, consisting of Welcome Weekend, open houses, and campus tours. There are guides for informal visits and visitors may sit in on classes and stay overnight. To schedule a visit, contact the Admissions Office.

Financial Aid: In a recent year, 88% of all full-time freshmen and 83% of continuing full-time students received some form of financial aid. 50% of full-time freshmen and 67% of continuing full-time students received

need-based aid. The average freshman award was $5634. 6% of undergraduates work part time. Average annual earnings from campus work are $1133. MBU is a member of CSS. The FAFSA and the college's own financial statement are required.

International Students: There are 83 international students enrolled. A satisfactory score on the TOEFL is required for students from a non-English-speaking country.

Computers: Wireless access is available. All students may access the system. There are no time limits. The fee is $10 per credit hour.

Graduates: From July 1, 2004 to June 30, 2005, 255 bachelor's degrees were awarded. The most popular majors were elementary education (23%), business administration (14%), and psychology (9%). In an average class, 37% graduate in 4 years or less, 49% graduate in 5 years or less, and 57% graduate in 6 years or less. 63 companies recruited on campus in 2004-2005.

Admissions Contact: Terry Dale Cruse, Director of Admissions.
E-mail: *admissions@mobap.edu* Web: *www.mobap.edu*

MISSOURI SOUTHERN STATE UNIVERSITY A-4

Joplin, MO 64801-1595

(417) 782-6772
(866) 818-6778; Fax: (417) 659-4429

Full-time: 1607 men, 2242 women	**Faculty:** 206; IIB, -$
Part-time: 595 men, 1029 women	**Ph.D.s:** 96%
Graduate: none	**Student/Faculty:** 18 to 1
Year: semesters, summer session	**Tuition:** $3916 ($7666)
Application Deadline: August 21	**Room & Board:** $4480
Freshman Class: 1576 applied, 1560 accepted, 897 enrolled	
ACT: 22	**NONCOMPETITIVE**

Missouri Southern State University, founded in 1937, is a public, primarily commuter institution offering undergraduate degree programs in the arts and sciences, business, education, psychology, and technology. International or global education is a distinctive theme of the college mission. There are 4 undergraduate schools. In addition to regional accreditation, Missouri Southern has baccalaureate program accreditation with ABET, ACBSP, ADA, NAACLS, NCATE, and NLN. The library contains 234,291 volumes, 754,023 microform items, and 7704 audio/video tapes/CDs/DVDs, and subscribes to 18,117 periodicals including electronic. Computerized library services include the card catalog, interlibrary loans, database searching, and Internet access. Special learning facilities include a learning resource center, art gallery, radio station, TV station, a biology pond, child development center, a crime lab, a small business development center, a performing arts center, a greenhouse, and an international trade and quality center. The 365-acre campus is in a small town in the southwest corner of the state, 138 miles south of Kansas City. Including any residence halls, there are 41 buildings.

Student Life: 90% of undergraduates are from Missouri. Others are from 30 states and 27 foreign countries. 90% are white. The average age of freshmen is 22; all undergraduates, 26. 36% do not continue beyond their first year; 29% remain to graduate.

Housing: 700 students can be accommodated in college housing, which includes single-sex dormitories and on-campus apartments. On-campus housing is available on a first-come, first-served basis. 88% of students commute. Alcohol is not permitted. All students may keep cars.

Activities: 1% of men belong to 2 national fraternities; 1% of women belong to 2 national sororities. There are 95 groups on campus, including art, band, cheerleading, chess, choir, chorale, chorus, computers, dance, debate, drama, ethnic, film, forensics, honors, international, jazz band, literary magazine, marching band, musical theater, newspaper, orchestra, pep band, photography, political, professional, radio and TV, religious, social, social service, student government, and symphony. Popular campus events include Spring Fling, Natural High, and International Semesters.

Sports: There are 7 intercollegiate sports for men and 7 for women, and 14 intramural sports for men and 14 for women. Facilities include a 10,000-seat Astroturf football stadium, a 4000-seat gym, a 4000-seat auditorium, a natatorium, a student life center, a black-box theater, a 3240-seat gym with a basketball court, a 6-lane 200-meter indoor track, a training and weight room, cross-country course and soccer, softball, and baseball fields.

Disabled Students: 99% of the campus is accessible. Wheelchair ramps, elevators, special parking, specially equipped rest rooms, special class scheduling, lowered drinking fountains, lowered telephones, and special housing are available.

Services: There is a reader service for the blind, and remedial math, reading, and writing. Assistance is also provided for improving time management and test-taking skills.

Campus Safety and Security: Measures include 24-hour foot and vehicle patrol, security escort services, informal discussions, and pamphlets/posters/films. There are lighted pathways/sidewalks and courtesy services such as unlocking cars, and providing jump starts are provided.

Programs of Study: Missouri Southern confers B.A., B.S., B.G.S., B.S.B.A., and B.S.E. degrees. Associate and master's degrees are also awarded. Bachelor's degrees are awarded in BIOLOGICAL SCIENCE (biology/biological science, biotechnology, ecology, genetics, marine biology, and microbiology), BUSINESS (accounting, banking and finance, business administration and management, business economics, international business management, management information systems, management science, and marketing/retailing/merchandising), COMMUNICATIONS AND THE ARTS (art, communications, dramatic arts, English, fine arts, French, German, graphic design, music, Spanish, and speech/debate/rhetoric), COMPUTER AND PHYSICAL SCIENCE (chemistry, computer mathematics, computer science, information sciences and systems, mathematics, and physics), EDUCATION (art, business, drama, early childhood, elementary, English, foreign languages, health, mathematics, middle school, music, physical, reading, science, secondary, social science, social studies, special, teaching English as a second/foreign language (TESOL/TEFOL), and trade and industrial), ENGINEERING AND ENVIRONMENTAL DESIGN (computer technology and manufacturing technology), HEALTH PROFESSIONS (environmental health science, medical laboratory technology, nursing, physical therapy, predentistry, premedicine, preoptometry, prepharmacy, and preveterinary science), SOCIAL SCIENCE (criminal justice, economics, history, international studies, liberal arts/general studies, political science/government, psychology, social science, social studies, and sociology). Biology, pre-engineering and economics and finance are the strongest academically. Business, education, and criminal justice are the largest.

Required: General education requirements include a total of 51 credit hours, with 15 in basic studies, 12 each in science and cultural studies, 9 in humanities, and 3 in international studies. Students must also demonstrate proficiency in computer skills and writing. To graduate, students must complete at least 124 credit hours, including a minimum of 40 in the major, and present a minimum GPA of 2.0, 2.75 for the B.S.E.

Special: There are co-op programs in radiological and medical technology, respiratory therapy, paramedical studies, aviation, and engineering. Students may study abroad at Oxford or Cambridge and in 100 countries through ISEP. Missouri Southern also offers internships in many majors, accelerated degree programs in all majors, a 3-2 engineering degree with the University of Missouri-Rolla, a general studies degree, and credit for life experience. Nondegree study is possible. There are 14 national honor societies, a freshman honors program, and 1 departmental honors program.

Faculty/Classroom: 62% of faculty are male; 38%, female. All teach undergraduates.

Admissions: 99% of the 2005-2006 applicants were accepted. The ACT scores for the 2005-2006 freshman class were: 37% below 21, 30% between 21 and 23, 22% between 24 and 26, 6% between 27 and 28, and 5% above 28. 35% of the current freshmen were in the top fifth of their class; 63% were in the top two fifths. 23 freshmen graduated first in their class.

Requirements: The ACT is required. Applicants must be graduates of accredited secondary schools or have earned a GED. The college requires completion of 16 Carnegie units in core courses for high school graduates. Missouri Southern requires applicants to be in the upper 50% of their class. A GPA of 2.25 is required. AP and CLEP credits are accepted. Advanced placement or honor courses is an important factor in the admission decision.

Procedure: Freshmen are admitted to all sessions. Entrance exams should be taken during the junior or senior year of high school. There are deferred admissions and rolling admissions plans. Applications should be filed by August 21 for fall entry, January 15 for spring entry, and June 5 for summer entry. Notification is sent on a rolling basis. Applications are accepted on-line. The fall 2005 application fee was $15.

Transfer: 426 transfer students enrolled in 2004-2005. Applicants must have a GPA of 2.0. They must be able to return to their previous college. 30 of 124 credits required for the bachelor's degree must be completed at Missouri Southern.

Visiting: There are regularly scheduled orientations for prospective students, including a preenrollment tour during the summer. There are guides for informal visits and visitors may sit in on classes and stay overnight. To schedule a visit, contact the Admissions Office at (866) 818-6778.

Financial Aid: In 2005-2006, 75% of all full-time freshmen and 80% of continuing full-time students received some form of financial aid. 70% of full-time freshmen and 69% of continuing full-time students received need-based aid. Need-based scholarships or need-based grants averaged $3699; need-based self-help aid (loans and jobs) averaged $1946; non-need-based athletic scholarships averaged $5666; and other non-need-based awards and non-need-based scholarships averaged $2209. 32% of undergraduates work part time. Average annual earnings from campus work are $3600. The average financial indebtedness of the 2005 graduate was $16,137. The FAFSA is required. The deadline for filing freshman financial aid applications for fall entry is August 1.

International Students: There are 73 international students enrolled. The school actively recruits these students. They must score satisfactorily on the written TOEFL and also take the ACT, scoring 18 but can have less than 18 if they ranked in the top half of their class or have a cumlative GPA of 225.

Computers: All students may access the system. There are no time limits. The fee $20.

Graduates: From July 1, 2004 to June 30, 2005, 706 bachelor's degrees were awarded. The most popular majors were business (21%), education (18%), and criminal justice (9%). In an average class, 10% graduate in 4 years or less, 24% graduate in 5 years or less, and 29% graduate in 6 years or less. 150 companies recruited on campus in 2004-2005. Of the 2004 graduating class, 8% were enrolled in graduate school within 6 months of graduation and 51% were employed.

Admissions Contact: Derek S. Skaggs, Director of Enrollment Services. E-mail: *admissions@mssu.edu* Web: *http://www.mssu.edu*

MISSOURI STATE UNIVERSITY
(Formerly Southwest Missouri State University)

B-3

Springfield, MO 65897

(417) 836-5521
(800) 492-7900; Fax: (417) 836-6334

Full-time: 5594 men, 7014 women
Part-time: 826 men, 1029 women
Graduate: 894 men, 1436 women
Year: semesters, summer session
Application Deadline: July 20
Freshman Class: 6866 applied, 5257 accepted, 2621 enrolled
ACT: 24

Faculty: IIA, --$
Ph.D.s: 61%
Student/Faculty: n/av
Tuition: $5454 ($10,374)
Room & Board: $5294

COMPETITIVE+

Missouri State University, formerly Southwest Missouri State University, founded in 1905, is a public institution offering undergraduate programs in arts and letters, business administration, humanities and social sciences, education and psychology, health and applied sciences, and science and math. There are 7 undergraduate schools and 1 graduate school. In addition to regional accreditation, MSU has baccalaureate program accreditation with AACSB, ADA, AHEA, ASLA, CSAB, CSWE, NASM, NCATE, NLN, and NRPA. The library contains 675,000 volumes, 900,000 microform items, and 30,000 audio/video tapes/CDs/DVDs, and subscribes to 5000 periodicals including electronic. Computerized library services include the card catalog, interlibrary loans, and database searching. Special learning facilities include a learning resource center, art gallery, and radio station. The 225-acre campus is in a suburban area 220 miles southwest of St. Louis. Including any residence halls, there are 60 buildings.

Student Life: 93% of undergraduates are from Missouri. Others are from 47 states, 66 foreign countries, and Canada. 90% are from public schools. 88% are white. The average age of freshmen is 18; all undergraduates, 22. 27% do not continue beyond their first year; 51% remain to graduate.

Housing: 4170 students can be accommodated in college housing, which includes coed dorms, on-campus apartments, married-student housing, fraternity houses, and sorority houses. In addition, there are honors houses, wellness house, and housing for international students, nontraditional students (age 23 and older), upperclassmen, and families. On-campus housing is guaranteed for all 4 years. 76% of students commute. Alcohol is not permitted. All students may keep cars.

Activities: There are 15 national fraternities and 10 national sororities. There are 252 groups on campus, including art, band, cheerleading, chess, choir, chorale, chorus, computers, dance, drama, drill team, ethnic, gay, honors, international, jazz band, literary magazine, marching band, musical theater, newspaper, orchestra, pep band, political, professional, radio and TV, religious, social, social service, student government, and symphony. Popular campus events include Tent Theater, Spring Fling, and Leadership Conference.

Sports: There are 10 intercollegiate sports for men and 9 for women, and 19 intramural sports for men and 19 for women. Facilities include a 16,600-seat stadium, a 9000-seat arena, a 9000-seat gym, a student center, an athletic center, a swimming pool, softball and practice fields, tennis courts, and bowling lanes.

Disabled Students: 95% of the campus is accessible. Wheelchair ramps, elevators, special parking, specially equipped rest rooms, special class scheduling, lowered drinking fountains, lowered telephones, special housing, TDD terminals, and automatic door openers are available.

Services: Counseling and information services are available, as is tutoring in some subjects. There is a reader service for the blind, and remedial math, reading, and writing. A math center and a writing center are available for student use. Proctors are available for tests given to those with disabilities.

Campus Safety and Security: Measures include 24-hour foot and vehicle patrol, self-defense education, security escort services, and shuttle buses. There are informal discussions, pamphlets/posters/films, emergency telephones, and lighted pathways/sidewalks.

Programs of Study: MSU confers B.A., B.S., B.F.A., B.M., B.S.E., B.S.N., and B.S.W. degrees. Master's and doctoral degrees are also awarded. Bachelor's degrees are awarded in AGRICULTURE (agriculture, agronomy, animal science, conservation and regulation, horticulture, and wildlife management), BIOLOGICAL SCIENCE (biology/biological science, cell biology, and nutrition), BUSINESS (accounting,

banking and finance, business administration and management, hotel/motel and restaurant management, institutional management, insurance, marketing/retailing/merchandising, and recreation and leisure services), COMMUNICATIONS AND THE ARTS (art, broadcasting, communications, dance, design, dramatic arts, English, film arts, French, German, Latin, music, music performance, Spanish, speech/debate/rhetoric, and technical and business writing), COMPUTER AND PHYSICAL SCIENCE (chemistry, computer science, earth science, geology, information sciences and systems, mathematics, and physics), EDUCATION (agricultural, art, athletic training, business, early childhood, elementary, foreign languages, health, home economics, industrial arts, middle school, music, physical, science, secondary, and special), ENGINEERING AND ENVIRONMENTAL DESIGN (cartography, construction management, drafting and design, electrical/electronics engineering technology, engineering physics, industrial administration/management, interior design, manufacturing technology, mechanical design technology, printing technology, and urban planning technology), HEALTH PROFESSIONS (medical laboratory technology, nursing, predentistry, radiograph medical technology, respiratory therapy, and speech pathology/audiology), SOCIAL SCIENCE (anthropology, child care/child and family studies, clothing and textiles management/production/services, dietetics, economics, geography, gerontology, history, parks and recreation management, philosophy, political science/government, psychology, public administration, religion, social science, social work, and sociology). Education and business are the largest.

Required: A total of 125 to 130 semester hours, including 30 to 60 in the major, and a minimum GPA of 2.0 are required. 45 general education semester hours are required, to include 8 in natural sciences, 6 to 9 each in social sciences and humanities, 6 in American studies, 4 in phys ed, 3 to 6 in English composition, 3 each in math and speech, and 1 in freshman orientation.

Special: MSU offers co-op programs, internships, study abroad in 40 countries, and work-study programs. Also available are B.A.-B.S. degrees in 12 majors, preprofessional programs in law and medicine, accelerated degree programs and student-designed and interdisciplinary majors, including antiquities, agriculture business and agriculture education, chemistry/biochemistry, communication management, and finance/real estate. A 3-2 engineering degree is available through the University of Missouri-Rolla. Credit for military experience and pass/not-pass options are offered. There are 31 national honor societies and a freshman honors program.

Faculty/Classroom: 57% of faculty are male; 43%, female. 97% teach undergraduates. Graduate students teach 4% of introductory courses. The average class size in a regular course is 23.

Admissions: 77% of the 2005-2006 applicants were accepted. The ACT scores for the 2005-2006 freshman class were: 19% below 21, 32% between 21 and 23, 25% between 24 and 26, 12% between 27 and 28, and 11% above 28. 44% of the current freshmen were in the top fifth of their class; 73% were in the top two fifths.

Requirements: The SAT or ACT is required; the ACT is preferred. Admission is based on a sliding scale of rank or GPA and test score. Freshmen must also have a 16-unit high school core curriculum, including 4 in English, 3 each in math and social studies, 2 in science, 1 in visual and performing arts, and 3 electives. AP and CLEP credits are accepted. Important factors in the admissions decision are advanced placement or honor courses, extracurricular activities record, and personality/intangible qualities.

Procedure: Freshmen are admitted to all sessions. Entrance exams should be taken as early as possible. There is a rolling admissions plan. Applications for priority admissions should be filed by March 1 for fall entry; regular admissions, by July 20 for fall entry. The fall 2005 application fee was $30. Notification is sent on a rolling basis.

Transfer: 1119 transfer students enrolled in 2004-2005. Applicants must present a minimum GPA of 2.0 on transferable courses. If they have completed less than 24 semester hours, they are also required to meet freshman admission requirements. 30 of 125 credits required for the bachelor's degree must be completed at MSU.

Visiting: There are regularly scheduled orientations for prospective students, including academic advising and enrollment for classes. There are guides for informal visits. To schedule a visit, contact the Admissions Office.

Financial Aid: In 2005-2006, 53% of all full-time freshmen and 56% of continuing full-time students received some form of financial aid. At least 42% of full-time freshmen and 50% of continuing full-time students received need-based aid. The average freshman award was $5748. Need-based scholarships or need-based grants averaged $4595; need-based self-help aid (loans and jobs) averaged $2849; institutional non-need-based athletic scholarships averaged $7636; and other institutional non-need-based awards and non-need-based scholarships averaged $9341. 51% of undergraduates work part time. Average annual earnings from campus work are $1500. The average financial indebtedness of the 2005 graduate was $12,997. MSU is a member of CSS. The FAFSA is required. The priority date for freshman financial aid applications for fall entry is March 30.

International Students: The school actively recruits these students. A satisfactory score is required on the written TOEFL.

Computers: All students may access the system. There are no time limits and no fees.

Graduates: From July 1, 2004 to June 30, 2005, 2546 bachelor's degrees were awarded. In an average class, 22% graduate in 4 years or less, 45% graduate in 5 years or less, and 51% graduate in 6 years or less.

Admissions Contact: Donald E. Simpson, Director of Admissions. A video is available. E-mail: info@missouristate.edu
Web: www.missouristate.edu

MISSOURI VALLEY COLLEGE — B-2

Marshall, MO 65340 (660) 831-4157; Fax: (660) 831-4039

Full-time: 800 men, 500 women	Faculty: 57
Part-time: 100 men, 200 women	Ph.D.s: 58%
Graduate: none	Student/Faculty: 23 to 1
Year: 4-1-4, summer session	Tuition: $14,000
Application Deadline: open	Room & Board: $6000
Freshman Class: n/av	
SAT or ACT: required	COMPETITIVE

Missouri Valley College, founded in 1889, is a private liberal arts college affiliated with the Presbyterian Church (U.S.A.) offering 25 majors. Figures in the above capsule and in this profile are approximate. The library contains 71,000 volumes, 1700 microform items, and 1100 audio/video tapes/CDs/DVDs, and subscribes to 400 periodicals including electronic. Computerized library services include interlibrary loans and database searching. Special learning facilities include a learning resource center, radio station, and TV station. The 140-acre campus is in a small town 80 miles from Kansas City and 150 miles from St. Louis. Including any residence halls, there are 17 buildings.

Student Life: 66% of undergraduates are from Missouri. Others are from 43 states, 9 foreign countries, and Canada. 75% are from public schools. 79% are white; 13% African American. 73% are Protestant; 20% Catholic. The average age of freshmen is 19; all undergraduates, 21. 25% do not continue beyond their first year; 20% remain to graduate.

Housing: 1100 students can be accommodated in college housing, which includes single-sex dorms, on-campus apartments, married-student housing, fraternity houses, and sorority houses. In addition, there are honors houses and special-interest houses. On-campus housing is guaranteed for all 4 years. 81% of students live on campus; of those, 50% remain on campus on weekends. Alcohol is not permitted. All students may keep cars.

Activities: 30% of men belong to 4 national fraternities; 20% of women belong to 3 national sororities. There are 40 groups on campus, including art, band, cheerleading, choir, chorale, chorus, computers, dance, drama, drill team, ethnic, film, honors, international, jazz band, literary magazine, musical theater, newspaper, orchestra, pep band, photography, radio and TV, religious, social, social service, SAAD, student government, symphony, and yearbook. Popular campus events include Springfest and Parents Weekend.

Sports: There are 8 intercollegiate sports for men and 7 for women, and 7 intramural sports for men and 7 for women. Facilities include a 2000-seat gym, tennis and basketball courts, football and soccer fields, a 1000-seat stadium, and horse stables.

Disabled Students: 20% of the campus is accessible. Wheelchair ramps, elevators, special parking, specially equipped rest rooms, special class scheduling, and lowered drinking fountains are available.

Services: Counseling and information services are available, as is tutoring in most subjects. There is remedial math, reading, and writing.

Campus Safety and Security: Measures include security escort services, informal discussions, pamphlets/posters/films, and emergency telephones. There are lighted pathways/sidewalks and 5 P.M. to 3 A.M. foot and vehicle patrol.

Programs of Study: MVC confers B.A. and B.S. degrees. Associate degrees are also awarded. Bachelor's degrees are awarded in AGRICULTURE (agricultural business management), BIOLOGICAL SCIENCE (biology/biological science), BUSINESS (accounting, business administration and management, and recreational facilities management), COMMUNICATIONS AND THE ARTS (art, communications, dramatic arts, English, and speech/debate/rhetoric), COMPUTER AND PHYSICAL SCIENCE (actuarial science, information sciences and systems, and mathematics), EDUCATION (elementary, physical, and social studies), HEALTH PROFESSIONS (exercise science), SOCIAL SCIENCE (addiction studies, criminal justice, economics, history, human services, liberal arts/general studies, philosophy, political science/government, psychology, public administration, religion, and sociology). Education is the strongest academically. Business administration, phys ed, and psychology are the largest.

Required: All students must complete 128 credit hours, including 35 to 40 hours in their major, with a GPA of at least 2.0. Distribution requirements include the 40-hour core curriculum of English, phys ed, math,

fine arts, and science. A computer course is strongly recommended. All students must complete a senior assessment.

Special: Accelerated degree programs, internships, work-study, co-op programs, nondegree study, and pass/fail options are available. There are 3 national honor societies, and 3 departmental honors programs.

Faculty/Classroom: 73% of faculty are male; 27%, female. All teach undergraduates. The average class size in an introductory lecture is 30; in a laboratory, 25; and in a regular course, 28.

Admissions: 66% of recent applicants were accepted. There were 5 National Merit semifinalists in a recent year.

Requirements: The SAT or ACT is required. In addition, students must have graduated from an accredited secondary school or have the GED. A GPA of 2.0 is required. AP and CLEP credits are accepted. Important factors in the admissions decision are advanced placement or honor courses, evidence of special talent, and extracurricular activities record.

Procedure: Freshmen are admitted to all sessions. Entrance exams should be taken as early as possible. Application deadlines are open. The fall 2005 application fee was $15. Applications are accepted on-line.

Transfer: A minimum GPA of 2.0 is recommended; D grades do not transfer. 30 of 128 credits required for the bachelor's degree must be completed at MVC.

Visiting: There are regularly scheduled orientations for prospective students, including jump-start days in the summer and registration days during the school year. There are guides for informal visits and visitors may sit in on classes and stay overnight. To schedule a visit, contact the Admission Coordinator at (660) 831-4114.

Financial Aid: MVC is a member of CSS. The FAFSA is required. Check with the school for current deadlines.

International Students: The school actively recruits these students. They must take the TOEFL and also take the SAT or the ACT.

Computers: All students may access the system. There are no time limits and no fees. It is strongly recommended that all students have a personal computer.

Admissions Contact: Director of Admissions.
E-mail: admissions@moval.edu Web: www.moval.edu

MISSOURI WESTERN STATE COLLEGE
(See Missouri Western State University)

MISSOURI WESTERN STATE UNIVERSITY — A-2
(Formerly Missouri Western State College)

St. Joseph, MO 64507 (816) 271-4266
(800) 662-7041; Fax: (816) 271-5833

Full-time: 1545 men, 2255 women	Faculty: 180; IIB, --$
Part-time: 543 men, 905 women	Ph.D.s: 81%
Graduate: none	Student/Faculty: 21 to 1
Year: semesters, summer session	Tuition: $4778 ($8408)
Application Deadline: May 1	Room & Board: $4756
Freshman Class: 2789 applied, 2789 accepted, 1079 enrolled	
ACT: 19	NONCOMPETITIVE

Missouri Western State University, formerly Missouri Western State College, founded in 1915, is a public institution offering undergraduate degrees in the arts and sciences, business administration, education, nursing, technology, and social work. There are 2 undergraduate schools. In addition to regional accreditation, Western has baccalaureate program accreditation with ABET, CSWE, NASM, NCATE, and NLN. The library contains 210,000 volumes, 112,000 microform items, and 16,000 audio/video tapes/CDs/DVDs, and subscribes to 1500 periodicals including electronic. Computerized library services include the card catalog, interlibrary loans, and database searching. Special learning facilities include a learning resource center, planetarium, and a biology nature study area. The 740-acre campus is in a suburban area 50 miles north of Kansas City. Including any residence halls, there are 15 buildings.

Student Life: 91% of undergraduates are from Missouri. Students are from 35 states, 10 foreign countries, and Canada. 86% are white; 11% African American. The average age of freshmen is 20; all undergraduates, 24. 44% do not continue beyond their first year; 29% remain to graduate.

Housing: 1050 students can be accommodated in college housing, which includes single-sex and coed dorms and on-campus apartments. On-campus housing is available on a first-come, first-served basis. 80% of students commute. Alcohol is not permitted. All students may keep cars.

Activities: 7% of men belong to 5 national fraternities; 3% of women belong to 7 national sororities. There are 51 groups on campus, including art, band, cheerleading, choir, dance, drama, drill team, ethnic, honors, international, jazz band, marching band, musical theater, newspaper, pep band, political, professional, religious, social, social service, student government, symphony, and yearbook. Popular campus events include Spring Fest, Fall Convocation, and Family Day.

Sports: There are 4 intercollegiate sports for men and 5 for women, and 20 intramural sports for men and 20 for women. Facilities include

tennis and racquetball courts, a 6000-seat football stadium, a 468-seat auditorium, a swimming pool, a jogging/walking trail, a fitness center, baseball and softball fields, a trapshooting range, a volleyball area, a track, and 2 gyms, the larger seating 4000.

Disabled Students: 99% of the campus is accessible. Wheelchair ramps, elevators, special parking, specially equipped rest rooms, lowered drinking fountains, and lowered telephones are available.

Services: Counseling and information services are available, as is tutoring in some subjects. There is a reader service for the blind, and remedial math, reading, and writing.

Campus Safety and Security: Measures include 24-hour foot and vehicle patrol, self-defense education, security escort services, and informal discussions. There are pamphlets/posters/films, emergency telephones, and lighted pathways/sidewalks.

Programs of Study: Western confers B.A., B.S., B.I.S., B.S.B.A., B.S.E., B.S.N., B.S.T., and B.S.W. degrees. Associate degrees are also awarded. Bachelor's degrees are awarded in BIOLOGICAL SCIENCE (biology/biological science), BUSINESS (accounting, business administration and management, and marketing/retailing/merchandising), COMMUNICATIONS AND THE ARTS (communications, English, fine arts, French, graphic design, music, Spanish, and speech/debate/rhetoric), COMPUTER AND PHYSICAL SCIENCE (chemistry, computer programming, computer science, information sciences and systems, mathematics, and natural sciences), EDUCATION (art, early childhood, elementary, foreign languages, music, and secondary), ENGINEERING AND ENVIRONMENTAL DESIGN (engineering technology), HEALTH PROFESSIONS (medical laboratory technology and nursing), SOCIAL SCIENCE (criminal justice, economics, history, parks and recreation management, political science/government, psychology, and social work). Physical sciences is the strongest academically. Education, nursing, and criminal justice are the largest.

Required: The core curriculum consists of 12 credit hours of basic skills (English composition, algebra, and speech), 9 to 10 of humanities, 9 of social sciences, 8 to 10 of natural sciences, and 4 of physical health. To graduate, students must complete at least 124 credit hours, including 45 to 71 in the major, with a minimum GPA of 2.0.

Special: MWSC offers internships, work-study programs with local employers, dual majors, a 3-2 engineering degree program with the University of Missouri/Rolla, credit for life experience, pass/fail options, and nondegree study. There are 6 national honor societies, a freshman honors program, and 12 departmental honors programs.

Faculty/Classroom: 60% of faculty are male; 40%, female. All teach undergraduates. The average class size in an introductory lecture is 35; in a laboratory, 25; and in a regular course, 25.

Admissions: All of the 2005-2006 applicants were accepted. The ACT scores for the 2005-2006 freshman class were: 63% below 21, 20% between 21 and 23, 11% between 24 and 26, 4% between 27 and 28, and 2% above 28. 20% of the current freshmen were in the top fifth of their class; 45% were in the top two fifths. 14 freshmen graduated first in their class.

Requirements: The ACT is required. In addition, applicants must be graduates of an accredited secondary school or have earned a GED. AP and CLEP credits are accepted.

Procedure: Freshmen are admitted to all sessions. Entrance exams should be taken at least 6 months prior to enrollment. Applications should be filed by May 1 for fall entry, November 1 for spring entry, and April 15 for summer entry, along with a $15 fee. The college accepts all applicants.

Transfer: 431 transfer students enrolled in 2004-2005. The required GPA depends on the number of credit hours completed, but a minimum of 2.0 is standard. 30 of 124 credits required for the bachelor's degree must be completed at Western.

Visiting: There are regularly scheduled orientations for prospective students. There are guides for informal visits. To schedule a visit, contact the Admissions Office.

Financial Aid: In 2005-2006, 85% of all full-time students received some form of financial aid. 70% of full-time freshmen and 80% of continuing full-time students received need-based aid. The average freshman award was $4488. 69% of undergraduates work part time. The FAFSA is required. Check with the school for current application deadlines.

International Students: In a recent year, there were 17 international students enrolled. They must score satisfactorily on the written TOEFL and also take the ACT.

Computers: All students may access the system. There are no time limits. The fee is $4 per credit hour. This fee is included in the required fees.

Graduates: In a recent year, 758 bachelor's degrees were awarded. The most popular majors were management (15%), criminal justice (15%), and elementary education (7%). In an average class, 12% graduate in 4 years or less, 24% graduate in 5 years or less, and 29% graduate in 6 years or less. Of a recent graduating class, 20% were enrolled in graduate school within 6 months of graduation and 90% were employed.

Admissions Contact: Howard McCauley, Director of Admissions. A video is available. E-mail: *admissn@missouriwestern.edu* Web: *www.missouriwesternc.edu*

NORTHWEST MISSOURI STATE UNIVERSITY A-1
Maryville, MO 64468 (660) 562-1722
(800) 633-1175; Fax: (660) 562-1121

Full-time: 2200 men, 2800 women	**Faculty:** 244; IIA, --$
Part-time: 300 men, 400 women	**Ph.D.s:** 71%
Graduate: 300 men, 700 women	**Student/Faculty:** 20 to 1
Year: trimesters, summer session	**Tuition:** $5000 ($8000)
Application Deadline: open	**Room & Board:** $5000
Freshman Class: n/av	
SAT or ACT: required	**COMPETITIVE**

Northwest Missouri State University, founded in 1905, is a public institution offering undergraduate courses in agriculture, science, arts and humanities, business, government, computer science, and education. There are 3 undergraduate schools and 1 graduate school. Figures in the above capsule and in this profile are approximate. In addition to regional accreditation, Northwest has baccalaureate program accreditation with ADA, AHEA, NASM, and NCATE. The library contains 286,300 volumes, 15,900 microform items, and 1900 audio/video tapes/CDs/DVDs, and subscribes to 3400 periodicals including electronic. Computerized library services include the card catalog, interlibrary loans, and database searching. Special learning facilities include a learning resource center, art gallery, radio station, TV station, and model elementary library collection with curriculum materials for grades K-6. The 240-acre campus is in a rural area 90 miles north of Kansas City. Including any residence halls, there are 33 buildings.

Student Life: 66% of undergraduates are from Missouri. Others are from 41 states, 23 foreign countries, and Canada. 95% are from public schools. 93% are white. The average age of freshmen is 19; all undergraduates, 21. 35% do not continue beyond their first year; 40% remain to graduate.

Housing: 2800 students can be accommodated in college housing, which includes single-sex and coed dorms and sorority houses. On-campus housing is guaranteed for all 4 years. 51% of students live on campus; of those, 65% remain on campus on weekends. Alcohol is not permitted. All students may keep cars.

Activities: 10% of men belong to 9 national fraternities; 10% of women belong to 5 national sororities. There are 162 groups on campus, including band, cheerleading, choir, chorale, chorus, computers, drama, drill team, drum and bugle corps, ethnic, international, jazz band, literary magazine, marching band, newspaper, pep band, photography, political, professional, radio and TV, religious, social, student government, and yearbook. Popular campus events include Tower Dance, Black Awareness Week, and Greek Week.

Sports: There are 6 intercollegiate sports for men and 5 for women, and 35 intramural sports for men and 35 for women. Facilities include a 7000-seat stadium, a 3000-seat basketball arena, 3 gyms, 4 racquetball courts, a weight-lifting area, volleyball and tennis courts, dance areas, and an aquatic center with 2 pools.

Disabled Students: 90% of the campus is accessible. Wheelchair ramps, elevators, special parking, specially equipped rest rooms, special class scheduling, lowered drinking fountains, and lowered telephones are available.

Services: Counseling and information services are available, as is tutoring in most subjects. There is a reader service for the blind, and remedial math, reading, and writing.

Campus Safety and Security: Measures include 24-hour foot and vehicle patrol, security escort services, informal discussions, and pamphlets/posters/films. There are lighted pathways/sidewalks.

Programs of Study: Northwest confers B.A., B.S., B.F.A., B.S.Ed., B.S.Med.Tech., and B.Tech. degrees. Master's degrees are also awarded. Bachelor's degrees are awarded in AGRICULTURE (agricultural business management, agricultural mechanics, agriculture, agronomy, animal science, conservation and regulation, forestry and related sciences, horticulture, and wildlife management), BIOLOGICAL SCIENCE (biology/biological science, botany, and zoology), BUSINESS (accounting, banking and finance, business administration and management, business economics, international business management, marketing/retailing/merchandising, personnel management, and recreation and leisure services), COMMUNICATIONS AND THE ARTS (advertising, art, broadcasting, communications, dramatic arts, English, fine arts, French, journalism, music, public relations, Spanish, and speech/debate/rhetoric), COMPUTER AND PHYSICAL SCIENCE (chemistry, computer management, computer science, earth science, geology, information sciences and systems, mathematics, physics, science, and statistics), EDUCATION (agricultural, art, business, early childhood, education of the mentally handicapped, elementary, mathematics, middle school, music, physical, recreation, science, secondary, special, and specific learning disabilities), ENGINEERING AND ENVIRONMENTAL DESIGN (preengineering), HEALTH PROFESSIONS (predentistry, premedicine, prepharmacy, and preveterinary science), SOCIAL SCIENCE (child care/ child and family studies, clothing and textiles management/production/ services, economics, family/consumer resource management, food science, geography, history, home economics, humanities, industrial and organizational psychology, philosophy, political science/government, prelaw, psychology, public administration, social science, sociology, and textiles and clothing). Education, mass communications, and agriculture are the strongest academically.

Required: All students must maintain a minimum GPA of 2.0 while taking at least 124 credit hours. Distribution requirements include 9 hours each in social science and humanities, 8 in natural science, 6 in composition, 4 each in math and phys ed, 3 each in oral communications and behavioral sciences, and 1 in the freshman seminar.

Special: Co-op programs with the University of Missouri/Rolla, cross-registration with Missouri Western State College, campuswide internships, study abroad in England and Mexico, and a Washington semester are available. Work-study programs, student-designed majors, a 3-2 engineering degree with the University of Missouri/Rolla, credit for military experience, nondegree study, and pass/fail options are possible. There are 3 national honor societies.

Faculty/Classroom: 61% of faculty are male; 39%, female. All teach undergraduates. No introductory courses are taught by graduate students. The average class size in an introductory lecture is 40; in a laboratory, 20; and in a regular course, 24.

Admissions: 89% of recent applicants were accepted. 43% of recent freshmen were in the top fifth of their class; 78% were in the top two fifths.

Requirements: The SAT or ACT is required; if scores are below minimum levels, a combined percentile index obtained from the SAT or ACT score and high school rank will be used. Northwest requires applicants to be in the upper 50% of their class. A GPA of 2.0 is required. AP and CLEP credits are accepted. Important factors in the admissions decision are evidence of special talent, leadership record, and recommendations by alumni.

Procedure: Freshmen are admitted fall, spring, and summer. Entrance exams should be taken in the fall of the senior year. There is a rolling admissions plan. Application deadlines are open. The fall 2005 application fee was $15. Applications are accepted on-line.

Transfer: Applicants must present a minimum GPA of 2.0. 30 of 124 credits required for the bachelor's degree must be completed at Northwest.

Visiting: There are regularly scheduled orientations for prospective students. There are guides for informal visits and visitors may sit in on classes and stay overnight. To schedule a visit, contact the Mable Cook Admissions and Visitors Center at (660) 562-1562.

Financial Aid: The FAFSA is required. Check with the school for current deadlines.

International Students: They must score satisfactorily on the written TOEFL.

Computers: All students may access the system 24 hours daily. There are no time limits and no fees. It is strongly recommended that all students have a personal computer.

Admissions Contact: Jeremy Waldeier, Associate Director, Admissions. A video is available. E-mail: *jeremyw@mail.nwmissouri.edu* Web: *www.nwmissouri.edu*

PARK UNIVERSITY   A-2

Parkville, MO 64152-9974

(816) 584-6215
(800) 745-7275; Fax: (816) 741-4462

Full-time: 385 men, 617 women	**Faculty:** 107
Part-time: 6238 men, 5448 women	**Ph.Ds:** 63%
Graduate: 210 men, 355 women	**Student/Faculty:** 9 to 1
Year: semesters, summer session	**Tuition:** $6412
Application Deadline: August 15	**Room & Board:** $5180
Freshman Class: 352 applied, 260 accepted, 142 enrolled	
ACT: 20	**COMPETITIVE**

Park University, founded in 1875, is a private institution offering degree programs in the humanities, performing arts, natural and life sciences, and social and administrative sciences. There are 2 undergraduate and 3 graduate schools. In addition to regional accreditation, Park has baccalaureate program accreditation with NLN. The library contains 141,870 volumes, 195,530 microform items, and 670 audio/video tapes/CDs/ DVDs, and subscribes to 775 periodicals including electronic. Computerized library services include the card catalog, interlibrary loans, and database searching. Special learning facilities include a learning resource center, art gallery, radio station, and TV station. The 700-acre campus is in a suburban area 12 miles north of Kansas City. Including any residence halls, there are 17 buildings.

Student Life: 80% of undergraduates are from Missouri. Students are from 49 states, 106 foreign countries, and Canada. 80% are from public schools. 58% are white; 21% African American; 15% Hispanic. 88% are claim no religious affiliation; 6% Protestant. The average age of fresh-

men is 18; all undergraduates, 32. 34% do not continue beyond their first year; 43% remain to graduate.

Housing: 226 students can be accommodated in college housing, which includes coed dorms and on-campus apartments. In addition, there are honors houses. On-campus housing is guaranteed for all 4 years. 98% of students commute. Alcohol is not permitted. All students may keep cars.

Activities: There are no fraternities or sororities. There are 30 groups on campus, including cheerleading, computers, drama, ethnic, honors, international, literary magazine, newspaper, outdoor, photography, political, professional, radio and TV, religious, social, social service, student government, and yearbook. Popular campus events include Fall Harvest Festival, Spring Fling, and International Week.

Sports: There are 6 intercollegiate sports for men and 7 for women, and 3 intramural sports for men and 3 for women. Facilities include 2 indoor gyms with basketball and volleyball courts, one with 800 and one with 350 seats, an all-weather outdoor track, soccer and softball fields, a sports medicine room, 4 tennis courts, and an outdoor sand volleyball and basketball court.

Disabled Students: 95% of the campus is accessible. Wheelchair ramps, elevators, special parking, specially equipped rest rooms, special class scheduling, and lowered drinking fountains are available.

Services: Counseling and information services are available, as is tutoring in most subjects. There is a reader service for the blind, and remedial math, reading, and writing.

Campus Safety and Security: Measures include 24-hour foot and vehicle patrol, security escort services, informal discussions, and pamphlets/posters/films. There are lighted pathways/sidewalks.

Programs of Study: Park confers B.A., B.S., and B.P.A. degrees. Associate and master's degrees are also awarded. Bachelor's degrees are awarded in BIOLOGICAL SCIENCE (biology/biological science), BUSINESS (accounting, business administration and management, business economics, human resources, management information systems, and marketing management), COMMUNICATIONS AND THE ARTS (communications, dramatic arts, English, fine arts, graphic design, music, public relations, and Spanish), COMPUTER AND PHYSICAL SCIENCE (chemistry, computer science, information sciences and systems, mathematics, and natural sciences), EDUCATION (athletic training, early childhood, and elementary), ENGINEERING AND ENVIRONMENTAL DESIGN (aviation administration/management, computational sciences, engineering management, and interior design), HEALTH PROFESSIONS (health care administration), SOCIAL SCIENCE (child care/child and family studies, criminal justice, economics, fire protection, fire services administration, history, human services, law, liberal arts/general studies, political science/government, psychology, public administration, social psychology, social work, and sociology). Management, management/computer information systems, and management/human resources are the largest.

Required: All students must complete core requirements, including 3 semesters of English composition, and 1 of algebra, as well as 1 science course. They must also complete 24 to 27 hours of general education courses and 9 hours of liberal learning courses. Of the 120 credit hours needed for the bachelor's degree, 45 must be completed in upper-division work and 30 to 60 in the major, with a minimum GPA of 2.0.

Special: Cross-registration is available through a Kansas City consortium, and study abroad is possible through other schools. The university also offers internships in most majors, work-study programs with local companies, a Washington semester, credit for life and military experience, pass/fail options, and nondegree study. An accelerated degree program is offered in some majors. There are 2 national honor societies and a freshman honors program.

Faculty/Classroom: 52% of faculty are male; 48%, female. All teach undergraduates and 80% do research. No introductory courses are taught by graduate students. The average class size in an introductory lecture is 20; in a laboratory, 10; and in a regular course, 15.

Admissions: 74% of the 2005-2006 applicants were accepted. The ACT scores for the 2005-2006 freshman class were: 52% below 21, 24% between 21 and 23, 13% between 24 and 26, 6% between 27 and 28, and 4% above 28. 27% of the current freshmen were in the top fifth of their class; 57% were in the top two fifths. 3 freshmen graduated first in their class.

Requirements: The SAT or ACT is required. In addition, the GED is accepted with a minimum total score of 225 and no area less than 35. Park requires applicants to be in the upper 50% of their class. A GPA of 2.0 is required. AP and CLEP credits are accepted. Important factors in the admissions decision are advanced placement or honor courses, leadership record, and extracurricular activities record.

Procedure: Freshmen are admitted fall, spring, and summer. Entrance exams should be taken during the junior year or early in the senior year. There are early admissions and rolling admissions plans. Applications should be filed by August 15 for fall entry and December 15 for spring entry. The fall 2005 application fee was $25. Notification is sent on a rolling basis. Applications are accepted on-line.

Transfer: The college requires a GPA of at least 2.0. A minimum ACT composite score of 20 is recommended, but is waived for students age

25 or older. 24 of 120 credits required for the bachelor's degree must be completed at Park.

Visiting: There are regularly scheduled orientations for prospective students, including a campus tour, lunch, an information session with a student panel, sessions on admissions, scholarships, and financial aid, and a chance to attend a class and meet with a faculty member. There are guides for informal visits and visitors may sit in on classes and stay overnight. To schedule a visit, contact Cathy Colapietro, Director of Admissions and Student Financial Services.

Financial Aid: 85% of undergraduates work part time. Average annual earnings from campus work are $1000. The average financial indebtedness of the 2005 graduate was $10,000. The FAFSA and the college's own financial statement are required. The deadline for filing freshman financial aid applications for fall entry is April 1.

International Students: The school actively recruits these students. A satisfactory score is required on the written TOEFL.

Computers: Wireless access is available. All students may access the system Monday through Thursday, 8 A.M. to 11 P.M.; Friday, 8 A.M. to 5 p.m; Saturday, 10 A.M. to 5 P.M.; Sunday, 12 noon to 5 P.M. There are no time limits and no fees.

Graduates: From July 1, 2004 to June 30, 2005, 3054 bachelor's degrees were awarded. The most popular majors were management (21%), human resources (15%), and management information systems (13%). In an average class, 2% graduate in 3 years or less, 20% graduate in 4 years or less, 36% graduate in 5 years or less, and 43% graduate in 6 years or less. 15 companies recruited on campus in 2004-2005. Of the 2004 graduating class, 9% were enrolled in graduate school within 6 months of graduation and 94% were employed.

Admissions Contact: Cathy Colapietro, Director of Admissions.
E-mail: *admissions@park.edu* Web: *www.park.edu*

RESEARCH COLLEGE OF NURSING — A-2

Kansas City, MO 64132

(816) 501-4000
(800) 842-6776; Fax: (816) 501-4241

Full-time: 33 men, 210 women	**Faculty:** 33
Part-time: 1 man, 2 women	**Ph.D.s:** 23%
Graduate: 4 men, 37 women	**Student/Faculty:** 7 to 1
Year: semesters, summer session	**Tuition:** $19,540
Application Deadline: June 30	**Room & Board:** $6100
Freshman Class: 192 applied, 123 accepted, 48 enrolled	
ACT: 23	SPECIAL

Research College of Nursing, founded in 1980, is a private college of nursing affiliated with Rockhurst University of Kansas City, a Jesuit-run, 25-acre liberal arts college with an enrollment of about 1500 undergraduates. Located on the campus of the Research Medical Center, the Research College of Nursing offers classes on its home campus, on the Rockhurst campus, and in a variety of health-related settings in the Kansas City area. There is 1 graduate school. In addition to regional accreditation, Research College has baccalaureate program accreditation with CCNE and NLN. The library contains 109,000 volumes, 150,000 microform items, and 1100 audio/video tapes/CDs/DVDs, and subscribes to 700 periodicals including electronic. Computerized library services include the card catalog, interlibrary loans, database searching, and Internet access. Special learning facilities include a learning resource center, art gallery, and radio station. The campus is in an urban area in Kansas City. Including any residence halls, there are 3 buildings.

Student Life: 90% of undergraduates are from Missouri. Others are from 6 states and 1 foreign country. 55% are from public schools. 79% are white. 45% are Catholic; 17% Protestant. The average age of freshmen is 18; all undergraduates, 22. 30% do not continue beyond their first year; 63% remain to graduate.

Housing: 815 students can be accommodated in college housing, which includes single-sex and coed dorms, on-campus apartments, married-student housing, and fraternity houses. On-campus housing is guaranteed for all 4 years. 65% of students live on campus; of those, 60% remain on campus on weekends. All students may keep cars.

Activities: 27% of men belong to 3 national fraternities; 12% of women belong to 3 national sororities. There are 35 groups on campus, including art, cheerleading, chess, choir, chorus, computers, drama, drill team, ethnic, honors, international, literary magazine, musical theater, newspaper, political, professional, radio and TV, religious, social, social service, student government, and yearbook. Popular campus events include the Mass of the Holy Spirit.

Sports: There are 6 intercollegiate sports for men and 5 for women, and 30 intramural sports for men and 30 for women. Facilities include a gym, an exercise facility, a fitness center, and racquetball courts.

Disabled Students: 80% of the campus is accessible. Wheelchair ramps, elevators, special parking, specially equipped rest rooms, lowered drinking fountains, and lowered telephones are available.

Services: Counseling and information services are available, as is tutoring in some subjects, including primarily freshman- and sophomore-level courses. There is remedial writing. The learning center offers assistance with college writing tasks and study strategies.

Campus Safety and Security: Measures include 24-hour foot and vehicle patrol, security escort services, informal discussions, and emergency telephones. There are lighted pathways/sidewalks.

Programs of Study: Research College confers the B.S.N. degree. Master's degrees are also awarded. Bachelor's degrees are awarded in HEALTH PROFESSIONS (nursing).

Required: To earn the B.S.N., students must complete a total of 128 semester hours, with 66 in liberal arts and sciences and 62 in the nursing major. A 2.0 GPA overall and in all nursing course work is required to graduate.

Special: Work-study, co-op, and accelerated degree programs, study abroad in 7 countries, and a Washington semester are available. There is a chapter of Phi Beta Kappa and a freshman honors program.

Faculty/Classroom: All of faculty are female. All teach undergraduates. No introductory courses are taught by graduate students. The average class size in an introductory lecture is 55 and in a laboratory, 8.

Admissions: 64% of the 2005-2006 applicants were accepted. The ACT scores for the 2005-2006 freshman class were: 25% below 21, 25% between 21 and 23, 38% between 24 and 26, 5% between 27 and 28, and 7% above 28. 33% of the current freshmen were in the top fifth of their class; 67% were in the top two fifths.

Requirements: A satisfactory score on the ACT is required. A satisfactory score on the SAT may be substituted. Applicants should graduate from an accredited secondary school or have the GED. An interview is recommended. Applicants should have completed 3 years of high school math, including algebra II, 3 years of English, and 2 years of science, including chemistry. Research College requires applicants to be in the upper 50% of their class. A GPA of 2.5 is required. AP and CLEP credits are accepted. Important factors in the admissions decision are advanced placement or honor courses, recommendations by school officials, and leadership record.

Procedure: Freshmen are admitted to all sessions. Entrance exams should be taken during the junior or senior year of high school. There is a deferred admissions plan. There is a rolling admissions plan. Applications should be filed by June 30 for fall entry, along with a $25 fee. Notification is sent on a rolling basis.

Transfer: 25 transfer students enrolled in 2004-2005. A minimum GPA of 2.7 is required to interview for the Research/Rockhurst Joint B.S.N. Program. Students must complete the sophomore-level nursing course before entering the junior-level clinical; this course is offered only in the spring. Admission requires an interview along with all official transcripts. Admission for transfers is very limited. 30 of 128 credits required for the bachelor's degree must be completed at Research College.

Visiting: There are regularly scheduled orientations for prospective students, consisting of 5 weekend programs for students and their parents. There are guides for informal visits and visitors may sit in on classes and stay overnight. To schedule a visit, contact the Rockhurst Admission and Financial Aid Office at (816) 502-4100 or *amy.johnson@rockhurst.edu*.

Financial Aid: 29% of undergraduates work part time. Average annual earnings from campus work are $1500. The FAFSA is required.

International Students: There is 1 international student enrolled. A satisfactory score on the TOEFL is required. A satisfactory score on the ACT is also required; the school will accept the SAT but prefers the ACT.

Computers: Wireless access is available to all students, faculty, and staff as well as 24/7 access to 2 computer labs. All students may access the system. There are no time limits and no fees. It is strongly recommended that all students have a personal computer.

Graduates: In a recent year 40 bachelor's degrees were awarded. The most popular major was nursing (100%). Of a recent graduating class, 95% were employed within 6 months of graduation.

Admissions Contact: Nathan Elliott, Admission Counselor.
E-mail: *nathan.elliott@rockhurst.edu* Web: *www.researchcollege.edu*

ROCKHURST UNIVERSITY — A-2

Kansas City, MO 64110-2561

(816) 501-4100
(800) 842-6776; Fax: (816) 501-4241

Full-time: 564 men, 697 women	**Faculty:** 113; IIA, --$
Part-time: 304 men, 526 women	**Ph.D.s:** 84%
Graduate: 364 men, 489 women	**Student/Faculty:** 11 to 1
Year: semesters, summer session	**Tuition:** $19,540
Application Deadline: June 30	**Room & Board:** $5900
Freshman Class: 1775 applied, 1314 accepted, 370 enrolled	
SAT Verbal/Math: 570/570*	**ACT:** 25 VERY COMPETITIVE

Rockhurst University, founded in 1910, is a private comprehensive, Catholic Jesuit institution that offers undergraduate programs in the arts and sciences, education, nursing, and business. There are 4 undergraduate and 2 graduate schools. In addition to regional accreditation, Rockhurst has baccalaureate program accreditation with AACTE, APTA, CAHEA, NLN and TEAC. The library contains 375,000 volumes, 250,000 microform items, and 4000 audio/video tapes/CDs/DVDs, and subscribes to 6000 periodicals including electronic. Computerized library services include the card catalog, interlibrary loans, database searching, Internet access, and laptop Internet portals. Special learning facilities include a learning resource center, art gallery, and multimedia classrooms. The 55-acre campus is in an urban area in Kansas City. Including any residence halls, there are 19 buildings.

Student Life: 60% of undergraduates are from Missouri. Others are from 30 states, 10 foreign countries, and Canada. 54% are from public schools. 80% are white. 64% are Catholic; 17% Protestant; 10% claim no religious affiliation; 9% Buddhist, Hindu, Muslim/Islamic, and other. The average age of freshmen is 18; all undergraduates, 21. 11% do not continue beyond their first year; 66% remain to graduate.

Housing: 815 students can be accommodated in college housing, which includes single-sex and coed dormitories and on-campus apartments. In addition, there are honors houses and special-interest houses. On-campus housing is available on a first-come, first-served basis. Priority is given to out-of-town students. 61% of students live on campus; of those, 45% remain on campus on weekends. All students may keep cars.

Activities: 7% of men belong to 4 national fraternities; 7% of women belong to 2 national sororities. There are 55 groups on campus, including art, cheerleading, choir, chorale, chorus, computers, drama, ethnic, honors, international, literary magazine, musical theater, newspaper, photography, political, professional, radio and TV, religious, social, social service, student government, and yearbook. Popular campus events include fraternity socials, coffee house events, and Rockstock (live bands).

Sports: There are 5 intercollegiate sports for men and 5 for women, and 12 intramural sports for men and 12 for women. Facilities include athletic and soccer fields; tennis, handball, racquetball, badminton, basketball, and volleyball courts; a weight and exercise room, gymnastics facilities, and a NCAA baseball field.

Disabled Students: 90% of the campus is accessible. Wheelchair ramps, elevators, special parking, specially equipped rest rooms, lowered drinking fountains, and lowered telephones are available.

Services: Counseling and information services are available, as is tutoring in some subjects, including primarily freshman- and sophomore-level courses. The Learning Center offers tutoring in many subjects, assistance with any college writing task, and study strategies.

Campus Safety and Security: Measures include 24-hour foot and vehicle patrol, self-defense education, security escort services, and shuttle buses. There are informal discussions, pamphlets/posters/films, emergency telephones, lighted pathways/sidewalks, and formal presentations, and a full in-house security program geared toward integration of security into the overall campus operation.

Programs of Study: Rockhurst confers B.A., B.S., B.S.B.A., and B.S.N. degrees. Master's and doctoral degrees are also awarded. Bachelor's degrees are awarded in BIOLOGICAL SCIENCE (biochemistry, bioinformatics, and biology/biological science), BUSINESS (business administration and management, business communications, business economics, and nonprofit/public organization management), COMMUNICATIONS AND THE ARTS (communications, English, French, and Spanish), COMPUTER AND PHYSICAL SCIENCE (chemistry, computer science, mathematics, and physics), EDUCATION (elementary, foreign languages, and secondary), ENGINEERING AND ENVIRONMENTAL DESIGN (computer technology), HEALTH PROFESSIONS (clinical science, nursing, and speech pathology/audiology), SOCIAL SCIENCE (economics, history, international relations, philosophy, political science/government, psychology, sociology, and theological studies). Chemistry, psychology, and philosophy are the strongest academically. Biology, nursing, and psychology are the largest.

Required: Students must complete 128 credit hours with a minimum of 18 in the major, with at least a 2.0 GPA. 52 prescribed semester hours in philosophy, theology, history, literature, science, social studies, and the arts are required. Students must also demonstrate proficiency in oral and written communication and math.

Special: Students may obtain career-related work experience through the Cooperative Education Program. Internships for credit and salary are available. Students are encouraged to study abroad in 1 of 5 countries for a semester, to take a semester in New York at Fordham University, or to participate in a congressional intern/study program in Washington, D.C., through Marquette University. B.A.-B.S. degrees are available in business administration. Work-study and an accelerated degree in nursing are also available. Students may pursue dual majors, a 3-2 engineering degree, and interdisciplinary majors. There are 7 national honor societies, including Phi Beta Kappa, a freshman honors program, and 12 departmental honors programs.

Faculty/Classroom: 57% of faculty are male; 43%, female. 89% teach undergraduates. No introductory courses are taught by graduate students. The average class size in an introductory lecture is 20; in a laboratory, 14; and in a regular course, 21.

Admissions: 74% of the 2005-2006 applicants were accepted. The SAT scores for the 2005-2006 freshman class were: Verbal--14% below 500, 41% between 500 and 599, 43% between 600 and 700, and 1% above 700; Math--12% below 500, 43% between 500 and 599, 41% between 600 and 700, and 4% above 700. The ACT scores were 14% below 21, 25% between 21 and 23, 26% between 24 and 26, 15% between 27 and 28, and 20% above 28. 57% of the current freshmen were

in the top fifth of their class; 82% were in the top two fifths. 7 freshmen graduated first in their class.

Requirements: The ACT is required and the SAT is recommended. In addition, the applicant must be a graduate of an accredited secondary school or have earned a GED. The university requires completion of 15 academic credits, including 4 years of English, 3 to 4 of history/social science, 3 of math, 2 to 4 of a foreign language, and 1 of visual or performing arts. An interview is recommended, and a recommendation is required. Rockhurst requires applicants to be in the upper 50% of their class. A GPA of 2.0 is required. AP and CLEP credits are accepted. Important factors in the admissions decision are advanced placement or honor courses, recommendations by school officials, and leadership record.

Procedure: Freshmen are admitted to all sessions. Entrance exams should be taken in April or June of the junior year or October, December, or February of the senior year. There is a deferred admissions and a rolling admissions plan. Early decision applications should be filed by May 1; regular applications, by June 30 for fall entry, along with a $25 fee. Notification of early decision is sent July 1; regular decision, on a rolling basis. Applications are accepted on-line.

Transfer: 120 transfer students enrolled in 2004-2005. Transfer applicants must have a GPA of at least 2.25. An interview is recommended. All college transcripts must be submitted; a high school transcript and test scores are required if the applicant has completed fewer than 24 college semester hours. 30 of 128 credits required for the bachelor's degree must be completed at Rockhurst. The fee is $25 or free on-line.

Visiting: There are regularly scheduled orientations for prospective students, including a campus tour, an interview with an admissions counselor, and a classroom visit or meeting with a faculty member. There are guides for informal visits and visitors may sit in on classes and stay overnight. To schedule a visit, contact Amy Johnson in Admissions at (816) 501-4256.

Financial Aid: In a recent year, 93% of all full-time freshmen and 85% of continuing full-time students received some form of financial aid. 76% of full-time freshmen and 67% of continuing full-time students received need-based aid. The average freshman award was $17,169. Need-based scholarships or need-based grants averaged $4946 ($25,966 maximum); need-based self-help aid (loans and jobs) averaged $3129 ($5975 maximum); non-need-based athletic scholarships averaged $10,242 ($23,930 maximum); and other non-need-based awards and non-need-based scholarships averaged $9202 ($16,950 maximum). 22% of undergraduates work part time. Average annual earnings from campus work were $1500. The average financial indebtedness of a recent graduate was $14,556. The FAFSA is required. The priority date for freshman financial aid applications for fall entry is March 1. The deadline for filing freshman financial aid applications for fall entry is June 1.

International Students: There are 17 international students enrolled. The school actively recruits these students. They must score satisfactorily on the written TOEFL and also take the SAT or the ACT, scoring 20 on the ACT.

Computers: All students may access the system 24 hours a day. There are no time limits. The fee is $50 per semester.

Graduates: From July 1, 2004 to June 30, 2005, 372 bachelor's degrees were awarded. The most popular majors were business (35%), nursing/health professions (21%), and psychology/social science/history (13%). In an average class, 51% graduate in 4 years or less, 63% graduate in 5 years or less, and 66% graduate in 6 years or less. 63 companies recruited on campus in a recent year.

Admissions Contact: Phil Gebauer, Associate Vice President for Enrollment. E-mail: *admission@rockhurst.edu* Web: *rockhurst.edu*

SAINT LOUIS UNIVERSITY   D-2
St. Louis, MO 63103-2097

(314) 977-2500
(800) SLUFORU; Fax: (314) 977-7136

Full-time: 2952 men, 3865 women	**Faculty:** 507; I, --$
Part-time: 238 men, 366 women	**Ph.D.s:** 95%
Graduate: 1847 men, 2555 women	**Student/Faculty:** 13 to 1
Year: semesters, summer session	**Tuition:** $24,958
Application Deadline: August 1	**Room & Board:** $8200
Freshman Class: 8105 applied, 6310 accepted, 1521 enrolled	
ACT: 26	**VERY COMPETITIVE+**

Saint Louis University, founded in 1818, is a private institution affiliated with the Jesuit Order of the Roman Catholic Church. There are 7 undergraduate and 3 graduate schools. In addition to regional accreditation, SLU has baccalaureate program accreditation with AACSB, ABET, ACS, ADA, AHIMA, AOTA, APTA, ASHKA, CAA, CCNE, JRCNMT, CSWE, NAACLS, NCATE, and NLN.. The 3 libraries contain 1,893,063 volumes, 2,605,155 microform items, and 195,435 audio/video tapes/CDs/DVDs, and subscribe to 15,597 periodicals including electronic. Computerized library services include the card catalog, interlibrary loans, database searching, Internet access, and laptop Internet portals. Special learning facilities include a learning resource center, art gallery, radio station, and TV station. The 244-acre campus is in an urban area in the

Midtown Arts District of St. Louis. Including any residence halls, there are 124 buildings.

Student Life: 54% of undergraduates are from Missouri. Others are from 46 states, 55 foreign countries, and Canada. 75% are white. 42% are Catholic; 31% claim no religious affiliation; 21% Protestant. The average age of freshmen is 18; all undergraduates, 20. 14% do not continue beyond their first year; 75% remain to graduate.

Housing: 3407 students can be accommodated in college housing, which includes single-sex and coed dormitories, on-campus apartments, and married-student housing. In addition, there are honors houses, language houses, and special-interest houses. On-campus housing is available on a first-come, first-served basis. 57% of students commute. All students may keep cars.

Activities: 18% of men belong to 12 national fraternities; 23% of women belong to 6 national sororities. There are more than 100 groups on campus, including cheerleading, chorale, chorus, computers, dance, debate, drama, drill team, ethnic, film, gay, honors, international, musical theater, newspaper, pep band, political, professional, radio and TV, religious, social, social service, student government, and yearbook. Popular campus events include comedians, major concerts, and Make a Difference Day.

Sports: There are 7 intercollegiate sports for men and 9 for women, and 20 intramural sports for men and 19 for women. Facilities include a 2000-seat gym, a 6050-seat outdoor sports center, a 19,000-seat off-campus arena, a recreation center with multipurpose courts, a swimming pool, a diving well, track facilities, a weight-training room, and a natural grass soccer facility.

Disabled Students: 95% of the campus is accessible. Wheelchair ramps, elevators, special parking, specially equipped rest rooms, special class scheduling, lowered drinking fountains, lowered telephones, and special housing are available.

Services: Counseling and information services are available, as is tutoring in most subjects, including math, English, history, economics, and natural sciences. There are also books on tape, academic success seminars, time management help, and test-taking techniques dealing with test anxiety and study skills available.

Campus Safety and Security: Measures include 24-hour foot and vehicle patrol, security escort services, shuttle buses, and informal discussions. There are pamphlets/posters/films, emergency telephones, lighted pathways/sidewalks, metrolink field trips, residence hall presentations, community building programs, 24-hour emergency telephone/alarm devices, and electronically operated dorm entrances.

Programs of Study: SLU confers B.A. and B.S. degrees. Master's and doctoral degrees are also awarded. Bachelor's degrees are awarded in BIOLOGICAL SCIENCE (biochemistry, biology/biological science, and nutrition), BUSINESS (business administration and management, human resources, and organizational behavior), COMMUNICATIONS AND THE ARTS (art history and appreciation, classical languages, communications, dramatic arts, English, French, Greek, Latin, music, Spanish, and studio art), COMPUTER AND PHYSICAL SCIENCE (applied mathematics, atmospheric sciences and meteorology, chemistry, computer programming, computer science, earth science, geology, geophysics and seismology, information sciences and systems, mathematics, and physics), EDUCATION (education), ENGINEERING AND ENVIRONMENTAL DESIGN (aeronautical engineering, aeronautical science, aeronautical technology, aerospace studies, aircraft mechanics, aviation administration/management, biomedical engineering, computer technology, electrical/electronics engineering, environmental science, and mechanical engineering), HEALTH PROFESSIONS (clinical science, exercise science, health care administration, nuclear medical technology, nursing, and speech pathology/audiology), SOCIAL SCIENCE (American studies, classical/ancient civilization, criminal justice, economics, forensic studies, German area studies, history, humanities, philosophy, political science/government, psychology, Russian and Slavic studies, social work, sociology, theological studies, urban studies, and women's studies). Aerospace engineering, psychology, and philosophy are the strongest academically. Biology, business administration and nurisng are the largest.

Required: Students must maintain a 2.0 GPA while completing a minimum of 120 credit hours. The core curriculum includes courses in philosophy, theology, math, English, science, and social/behavioral science.

Special: Students may study abroad in Spain, France, Germany, and Belgium. Cross-registration with Washington University and the University of Missouri at St. Louis, internships, work-study programs on campus, an accelerated degree program in nursing, a 3-2 engineering degree program with Washington University in St. Louis, dual majors, student-designed majors, a Washington semester, and pass/fail options are also possible. Students may also participate in university-sponsored mission trips. There are 3 national honor societies, including Phi Beta Kappa, and a freshman honors program.

Faculty/Classroom: 63% of faculty are male; 37%, female. 76% teach undergraduates. All do research, and 76% do both. The average class size in an introductory lecture is 28; in a laboratory, 18; and in a regular course, 24.

Admissions: 78% of the 2005-2006 applicants were accepted. The SAT scores for the 2005-2006 freshman class were: Verbal--8% below 500, 39% between 500 and 599, 44% between 600 and 700, and 9% above 700; Math--9% below 500, 34% between 500 and 599, 43% between 600 and 700, and 14% above 700. The ACT scores were 7% below 21, 18% between 21 and 23, 29% between 24 and 26, 18% between 27 and 28, and 29% above 28. 57% of the current freshmen were in the top fifth of their class; 83% were in the top two fifths. There were 9 National Merit finalists.

Requirements: The ACT is required. In addition, a complete application is required which consists of an application, esssay, high school transcript, test scores, and counselor recommendation. A GPA of 2.5 is required. AP and CLEP credits are accepted. Important factors in the admissions decision are advanced placement or honor courses, leadership record, and recommendations by school officials.

Procedure: Freshmen are admitted fall, spring, and summer. Entrance exams should be taken in the junior or senior year. There are deferred admissions and rolling admissions plans. Applications should be filed by August 1 for fall entry, along with a $25 fee. Notification is sent on a rolling basis. Applications are accepted on-line.

Transfer: 432 transfer students enrolled in 2004-2005. The university recommends that transfer applicants have a GPA of at least 2.0. 30 of 120 credits required for the bachelor's degree must be completed at SLU.

Visiting: There are regularly scheduled orientations for prospective students, consisting of a campus tour, individual and group visits to a class or an academic department, and admissions and financial aid counseling. There are guides for informal visits and visitors may sit in on classes and stay overnight. To schedule a visit, contact Admissions.

Financial Aid: In 2005-2006, 99% of all full-time students received some form of financial aid. 51% of full-time freshmen and 61% of continuing full-time students received need-based aid. The average freshman award was $20,751. Need-based scholarships or need-based grants averaged $12,644 ($44,288 maximum); need-based self-help aid (loans and jobs) averaged $8941 ($41,125 maximum); and other non-need-based awards and non-need-based scholarships averaged $22,568 ($24,760 maximum). 19% of undergraduates work part time. Average annual earnings from campus work are $1663. The average financial indebtedness of the 2005 graduate was $18,164. The priority date for freshman financial aid applications for fall entry is March 1.

International Students: There are 150 international students enrolled. The school actively recruits these students. They must score satisfactorily on the written TOEFL or on the electronic version or take the MELAB, or the Comprehensive English Language Test, or the college's own test, or a writing test.

Computers: Wireless access is available. The campus-wide network allows students to access their own information system, enroll for classes, and access Web-based information provided by faculty, administrators, and other students. All students may access the system. There are no time limits and no fees. It is strongly recommended that all students have a personal computer.

Graduates: From July 1, 2004 to June 30, 2005, 1710 bachelor's degrees were awarded. The most popular majors were biology (7%), business administration (6%), and nursing (6%). In an average class, 61% graduate in 4 years or less, 74% graduate in 5 years or less, and 75% graduate in 6 years or less. 271 companies recruited on campus in 2004-2005. Of the 2004 graduating class, 30% were enrolled in graduate school within 6 months of graduation and 61% were employed.

Admissions Contact: Kalith Smith, Interim Director of Undergraduate Admissions. A video is available. E-mail: *admitme@slu.edu* Web: *www.slu.edu*

SOUTHEAST MISSOURI STATE UNIVERSITY   E-3

Cape Girardeau, MO 63701   (573) 651-2590; Fax: (573) 651-5936

Full-time: 2846 men, 3952 women	**Faculty:** 388; IIA, --$
Part-time: 816 men, 1354 women	**Ph.D.s:** 81%
Graduate: 300 men, 1024 women	**Student/Faculty:** 18 to 1
Year: semesters, summer session	**Tuition:** $5145 ($9000)
Application Deadline: August 1	**Room & Board:** $5451
Freshman Class: 4060 applied, 3619 accepted, 1679 enrolled	
ACT: 22	**COMPETITIVE**

Southeast Missouri State University, founded in 1873, is a public institution offering undergraduate and graduate programs in arts and sciences, business, agriculture, education, and health. It includes a school of polytechnic studies. There are 7 undergraduate schools and 1 graduate school. In addition to regional accreditation, Southeast has baccalaureate program accreditation with AACSB, ACS, ADA, ASLA, CSWE, NASM, NCATE, NLN, and NRPA. The library contains 431,942 volumes, 11,359 microform items, and 15,909 audio/video tapes/CDs/DVDs, and subscribes to 4776 periodicals including electronic. Computerized library services include the card catalog, interlibrary loans, database searching, Internet access, and laptop Internet portals. Special learning facilities include a learning resource center, radio station, and a museum of archeological items and artworks. The 60-acre campus is in a small town 120 miles south of St. Louis. Including any residence halls, there are 55 buildings.

Student Life: 86% of undergraduates are from Missouri. Others are from 19 states, 37 foreign countries, and Canada. 88% are white. 60% are Protestant; 30% Catholic. The average age of freshmen is 20; all undergraduates, 23. 30% do not continue beyond their first year; 49% remain to graduate.

Housing: 2748 students can be accommodated in college housing, which includes single-sex and coed dorms, on-campus apartments, fraternity houses, and sorority houses. In addition, there are honors houses and special-interest houses. On-campus housing is guaranteed for the freshman year only and is available on a first-come, first-served basis. 73% of students commute. Alcohol is not permitted. All students may keep cars.

Activities: 14% of men belong to 11 national fraternities; 8% of women belong to 8 national sororities. There are 135 groups on campus, including art, band, cheerleading, choir, chorus, dance, drama, drill team, ethnic, honors, international, jazz band, literary magazine, marching band, musical theater, newspaper, opera, orchestra, pep band, political, professional, radio and TV, religious, social, social service, student government, symphony, and yearbook. Popular campus events include Family Weekends, Spring Fling, and International Week.

Sports: There are 6 intercollegiate sports for men and 9 for women, and 24 intramural sports for men and 24 for women. Facilities include 2 student recreation centers housing indoor tracks, a climbing wall, 6 racquetball courts, indoor basketball courts, a weight room, volleyball courts, bicycle and rowing machines, strength-training equipment, stair climbers, and ellipticals.

Disabled Students: All of the campus is accessible. Wheelchair ramps, elevators, special parking, specially equipped rest rooms, special class scheduling, lowered drinking fountains, lowered telephones, special housing, and priority enrollment are available.

Services: Counseling and information services are available, as is tutoring in most subjects. There is a reader service for the blind, and remedial math, reading, and writing.

Campus Safety and Security: Measures include 24-hour foot and vehicle patrol, self-defense education, security escort services, and shuttle buses. There are informal discussions, pamphlets/posters/films, emergency telephones, and lighted pathways/sidewalks.

Programs of Study: Southeast confers B.A., B.S., B.F.A., B.F.C.S.Ed., B.G.S., B.S.B.A., B.S.Ed., B.S.M., B.S.Mus.Ed., and B.S.N. degrees. Associate and master's degrees are also awarded. Bachelor's degrees are awarded in AGRICULTURE (agricultural business management, agriculture, agronomy, animal science, horticulture, plant science, and soil science), BIOLOGICAL SCIENCE (biology/biological science), BUSINESS (accounting, banking and finance, business economics, fashion merchandising, human resources, management information systems, marketing management, office supervision and management, recreation and leisure services, and sports management), COMMUNICATIONS AND THE ARTS (advertising, art, communications, dramatic arts, English, fine arts, French, German, historic preservation, journalism, literature, music, music performance, public relations, radio/television technology, Spanish, video, and voice), COMPUTER AND PHYSICAL SCIENCE (chemistry, computer science, earth science, mathematics, and physics), EDUCATION (art, athletic training, business, early childhood, education of the exceptional child, elementary, English, foreign languages, industrial arts, mathematics, middle school, music, physical, science, secondary, and social studies), ENGINEERING AND ENVIRONMENTAL DESIGN (engineering physics, environmental science, graphic arts technology, industrial administration/management, industrial engineering technology, and preengineering), HEALTH PROFESSIONS (medical technology, nursing, predentistry, premedicine, preoptometry, prepharmacy, preventive/wellness health care, preveterinary science, speech pathology/audiology, and sports medicine), SOCIAL SCIENCE (anthropology, child care/child and family studies, child psychology/development, corrections, criminal justice, criminology, economics, family/consumer studies, history, interdisciplinary studies, law enforcement and corrections, liberal arts/general studies, philosophy, political science/government, prelaw, psychology, social work, and sociology). Teacher education is the strongest academically. Elementary education is the largest.

Required: Students must complete 124 credit hours, up to 64 in the major. The core curriculum includes 48 credit hours in the University Studies program, as well as interdisciplinary studies, English, and math. Minimum GPAs (at least 2.0) and other graduation requirements vary by program. A writing exam must also be passed.

Special: Southeast offers a Cooperative Doctor of Education in Educational Leadership with the University of Missouri/Columbia. Opportunities are provided for individually arranged internships and work-study, study abroad in 48 countries, a general studies degree, dual and student-designed majors (interdisciplinary studies), credit by exam, nondegree study, and pass/fail options. A 3-2 engineering degree is possible in conjunction with the University of Missouri at Rolla or at Columbia. There are preprofessional programs in architecture, chiropractic, dentistry, engineering, law, medicine, optometry, pharmacy, physical therapy, and veterinary medicine. There are 8 national honor societies, a freshman honors program, and 9 departmental honors programs.

Faculty/Classroom: 52% of faculty are male; 48%, female. All teach undergraduates. The average class size in an introductory lecture is 23; in a laboratory, 10; and in a regular course, 19.

Admissions: 89% of the 2005-2006 applicants were accepted. The ACT scores for the 2005-2006 freshman class were: 40% below 21, 26% between 21 and 23, 20% between 24 and 26, 7% between 27 and 28, and 7% above 28. 30% of the current freshmen were in the top fifth of their class; 56% were in the top two fifths. There was 1 National Merit semifinalist. 39 freshmen graduated first in their class.

Requirements: The ACT is required. In addition, graduation from an accredited secondary school is required; the GED is accepted. Applicants should submit an academic record with 4 credits in English, 3 in social studies, 3 in algebra or higher math, 3 in science, 3 additional credits in English, math, science, social studies, speech, or a foreign language, and 1 unit in visual/performing arts. A GPA of 2.0 is required. AP and CLEP credits are accepted.

Procedure: Freshmen are admitted fall, spring, and summer. Entrance exams should be taken in the spring of the junior year or fall of the senior year. There is a rolling admissions plan. Applications should be filed by August 1 for fall entry, December 1 for spring entry, and May 15 for summer entry. The fall 2005 application fee was $20. Notification is sent on a rolling basis. Applications are accepted on-line.

Transfer: 558 transfer students enrolled in 2004-2005. Transcripts from the student's previous college must be submitted, listing at least 24 credits earned and a minimum GPA of 2.0. The ACT is required for those students who have less than 24 credit hours. 30 of 124 credits required for the bachelor's degree must be completed at Southeast.

Visiting: There are regularly scheduled orientations for prospective students, including academic advising and other university information. There are guides for informal visits and visitors may sit in on classes and stay overnight. To schedule a visit, contact the Admissions Office.

Financial Aid: In 2005-2006, 86% of all full-time freshmen and 74% of continuing full-time students received some form of financial aid. 52% of full-time freshmen and 47% of continuing full-time students received need-based aid. The average freshman award was $5614. Need-based scholarships or need-based grants averaged $2548 ($3312 maximum); need-based self-help aid (loans and jobs) averaged $1505 ($4625 maximum); non-need-based athletic scholarships averaged $4395 ($7789 maximum); other non-need-based awards and non-need-based scholarships averaged $2329 ($9108 maximum); and fee waivers averaged $1161 ($2377 maximum). 15% of undergraduates work part time. Average annual earnings from campus work are $1606. The average financial indebtedness of the 2005 graduate was $16,274. The FAFSA is required. The priority date for freshman financial aid applications for fall entry is March 1.

International Students: There are 151 international students enrolled. The school actively recruits these students. They must achieve a satisfactory score on the TOEFL.

Computers: Wireless access is available. Students are granted access to the university network for Internet, e-mail, and web publishing. There are 1311 PCs on campus for student use. For more information, visit www6.semo.edu/infotech/student/index.asp. All students may access the system. There are no time limits and no fees.

Graduates: From July 1, 2004 to June 30, 2005, 1402 bachelor's degrees were awarded. The most popular majors were elementary education (9%), general studies (7%), and business administration management (6%). In an average class, 24% graduate in 4 years or less, 46% graduate in 5 years or less, and 50% graduate in 6 years or less. 14 companies recruited on campus in 2004-2005.

Admissions Contact: Deborah Below, Director of Admissions. A video is available. E-mail: *admissions@semo.edu* Web: *www.semo.edu/admissions/index.htm*

SOUTHWEST BAPTIST UNIVERSITY   B-3
Bolivar, MO 65613
(417) 328-1817
(800) 526-5859; Fax: (417) 328-1514

Full-time: 686 men, 1085 women	**Faculty:** 94
Part-time: 127 men, 551 women	**Ph.Ds:** 66%
Graduate: 183 men, 556 women	**Student/Faculty:** 19 to 1
Year: 4-1-4, summer session	**Tuition:** $14,100
Application Deadline: open	**Room & Board:** $4200
Freshman Class: 720 applied, 614 accepted, 364 enrolled	
SAT Verbal/Math: 536/533*	**ACT:** 23 COMPETITIVE

Southwest Baptist University, founded in 1878, is a private liberal arts institution affiliated with the Southern Baptist Convention. There are 6 undergraduate and 3 graduate schools. In addition to regional accreditation, SBU has baccalaureate program accreditation with ACBSP, ADA, NASM, NLN, and CAPTE, CAAHEP. The 4 libraries contain 196,425 volumes, 482,073 microform items, and 11,339 audio/video tapes/CDs/DVDs, and subscribe to 19,600 periodicals including electronic. Computerized library services include the card catalog, interlibrary loans, database searching, Internet access, and laptop Internet portals. Special learning facilities include a learning resource center and art gallery. The 180-acre campus is in a small town 28 miles north of Springfield. Including any residence halls, there are 26 buildings.

Student Life: 69% of undergraduates are from Missouri. Others are from 45 states and 16 foreign countries. 92% are white. Most are Protestant. The average age of freshmen is 18; all undergraduates, 21. 32% do not continue beyond their first year; 68% remain to graduate.

Housing: 1071 students can be accommodated in college housing, which includes single-sex dormitories and on-campus apartments. On-campus housing is guaranteed for all 4 years. 63% of students live on campus; of those, 70% remain on campus on weekends. Alcohol is not permitted. All students may keep cars.

Activities: There are no fraternities or sororities. There are 34 groups on campus, including art, band, cheerleading, choir, chorale, chorus, computers, debate, drama, forensics, honors, international, jazz band, musical theater, newspaper, opera, orchestra, pep band, photography, political, professional, radio and TV, religious, social service, and student government. Popular campus events include Welcoe Week, concerts and Courtwarming.

Sports: There are 9 intercollegiate sports for men and 8 for women, and 6 intramural sports for men and 6 for women. Facilities include the Jane and Ken Meyer Wellness and Sports Center, which houses intramural basketball courts, racquetball courts, a rock climbing wall, weight rooms, an aerobics room, an indoor walking/jogging track, health and phys ed classrooms, and an Olympic-size swimming pool. The sports arena has seating for 2800 people.

Disabled Students: 95% of the campus is accessible. Wheelchair ramps, elevators, special parking, specially equipped rest rooms, special class scheduling, and lowered drinking fountains are available.

Services: Counseling and information services are available, as is tutoring in every subject. There is remedial math, reading, and writing.

Campus Safety and Security: Measures include 24-hour foot and vehicle patrol, informal discussions, pamphlets/posters/films, and emergency telephones. There are lighted pathways/sidewalks.

Programs of Study: SBU confers B.A., B.S., B.A.S., B.M., and B.S.N. degrees. Associate, master's, and doctoral degrees are also awarded. Bachelor's degrees are awarded in BIOLOGICAL SCIENCE (biology/biological science), BUSINESS (accounting, business administration and management, recreation and leisure services, and sports management), COMMUNICATIONS AND THE ARTS (art, communications, dramatic arts, English, music, and Spanish), COMPUTER AND PHYSICAL SCIENCE (chemistry, computer science, information sciences and systems, and mathematics), EDUCATION (art, athletic training, early childhood, elementary, middle school, music, physical, and social science), ENGINEERING AND ENVIRONMENTAL DESIGN (commercial art, and occupational safety and health), HEALTH PROFESSIONS (medical technology, and nursing), SOCIAL SCIENCE (biblical studies, criminal justice, history, human services, ministries, political science/government, psychology, religion, religious education, religious music, and sociology). Education, psychology, and business administration are the largest.

Required: To graduate, students must complete 128 credit hours, with 40 in upper-division courses, and 52 in general education requirements, and maintain a 2.0 GPA. The number of hours in the major varies.

Special: SBU offers internships, study abroad in 80 countries, an Oxford honors program, a Washington Semester, work-study programs, dual majors, and a 3-2 engineering degree with the University of Missouri-Rolla. There are also American Studies, contemporary music, family failm, and journalism programs. There are 4 national honor societies, and 4 departmental honors programs.

Faculty/Classroom: No introductory courses are taught by graduate students. The average class size in an introductory lecture is 40; in a laboratory, 25; and in a regular course, 20.

Admissions: 85% of the 2005-2006 applicants were accepted. The SAT scores for the 2005-2006 freshman class were: Verbal--38% below 500, 34% between 500 and 599, 26% between 600 and 700, and 2% above 700; Math--32% below 500, 43% between 500 and 599, 21% between 600 and 700, and 4% above 700. The ACT scores were 32% below 21, 26% between 21 and 23, 22% between 24 and 26, 9% between 27 and 28, and 11% above 28. 35% of the current freshmen were in the top fifth of their class; 62% were in the top two fifths.

Requirements: The SAT or ACT is required. In addition, an SBU applicant must present one of the following: proof of graduation from an accredited or approved high school or a homeschool transcript. Additionally, students must meet two of these three qualifiers: 2.5 high school GPA on a 4.0 scale; 21 ACT or satisfactory SAT composite score; or top 50% of high school rank. Applicants are recommended to have 13 academic credits, including a recommended 4 credits in English, 3 in math, 2 each in natural science and history or social science, and 2 elective units. AP and CLEP credits are accepted.

Procedure: Freshmen are admitted to all sessions. Entrance exams should be taken at any time prior to admission. There are deferred admissions and rolling admissions plans. Application deadlines are open. The fall 2005 application fee was $30. Applications are accepted on-line.

Transfer: 138 transfer students enrolled in 2004-2005. Applicants must submit official college and high school transcripts and have a minimum GPA of 2.0. An interview is encouraged. Students who have not yet met SBU's English and math requirements must present scores from the ACT, SAT, or other approved placement test. Only 6 hours of D credit can be transferred in. 30 of 128 credits required for the bachelor's degree must be completed at SBU.

Visiting: There are regularly scheduled orientations for prospective students, including fall and spring visitation days. There are guides for informal visits and visitors may sit in on classes and stay overnight. To schedule a visit, contact Darren Crowder, Director of Admissions at *dcrowder@sbuniv.edu*.

Financial Aid: In 2005-2006, 97% of all full-time freshmen and 73% of continuing full-time students received some form of financial aid. The average freshman award was $6354. Need-based scholarships or need-based grants averaged $3866; need-based self-help aid (loans and jobs) averaged $4307; non-need-based athletic scholarships averaged $7661; and other non-need-based awards and non-need-based scholarships averaged $5192. Average annual earnings from campus work are $1080. The average financial indebtedness of the 2005 graduate was $11,268. The FAFSA and the college's own financial statement are required. The priority date for freshman financial aid applications for fall entry is March 15.

International Students: There are 20 international students enrolled. Satisfactory scores are required on the written TOEFL and the SAT or the ACT.

Computers: Wireless access is available. All students may access the system. Dorm and wireless access is available any time. Computer labs are open from 8 A.M. to 1:30 A.M. daily. There are no time limits. The fee is $260.

Graduates: From July 1, 2004 to June 30, 2005, 794 bachelor's degrees were awarded. The most popular majors were education (20%), psychology (16%), and business (11%). In an average class, 50% graduate in 6 years or less. 74 companies recruited on campus in 2004-2005.

Admissions Contact: Darren Crowder, Director of Admissions. A video is available. E-mail: *dcrowder@sbuniv.edu* Web: *www.sbuniv.edu*

SOUTHWEST MISSOURI STATE UNIVERSITY
(See Missouri State University)

STEPHENS COLLEGE   C-2
Columbia, MO 65215
(573) 876-7207
(800) 876-7207; Fax: (573) 876-7237

Full-time: 13 men, 561 women	**Faculty:** 43
Part-time: 11 men, 169 women	**Ph.D.s:** 83%
Graduate: 7 men, 65 women	**Student/Faculty:** 13 to 1
Year: semesters, summer session	**Tuition:** $19,300
Application Deadline: open	**Room & Board:** $7630
Freshman Class: n/av	
SAT Verbal/Math: 580/530*	**ACT:** 23 **VERY COMPETITIVE**

Stephens College, founded in 1833, is a private college primorily for women, offering undergraduate programs in the arts and sciences, business, education, and fine arts. There are 2 undergraduate and 2 graduate schools. The library contains 129,915 volumes, 11,322 microform items, and 1254 audio/video tapes/CDs/DVDs, and subscribes to 9836 periodicals including electronic. Computerized library services include interlibrary loans, database searching, and Internet access. Special learning facilities include a learning resource center, art gallery, radio station, and TV station. The 86-acre campus is in an urban area 120 miles west of St. Louis. Including any residence halls, there are 35 buildings.

Student Life: 55% of undergraduates are from out of state, mostly the Midwest. Students are from 44 states and 3 foreign countries. 80% are from public schools. 87% are white. The average age of freshmen is 18; all undergraduates, 20. 27% do not continue beyond their first year; 58% remain to graduate.

Housing: 842 students can be accommodated in college housing, which includes single-sex dorm and on-campus apartments. In addition, there are honors houses, special-interest houses intercultural scholars and fine arts majors and houses with designated academic floors, nonsmoking floors, and pet floors. On-campus housing is guaranteed for all 4 years. 75% of students live on campus; of those, 90% remain on campus on weekends. All students may keep cars.

Activities: 88% of women belong to 2 national sororitie. There are 45 groups on campus, including art, choir, chorale, chorus, dance, drama, ethnic, gay, honors, international, literary magazine, musical theater, newspaper, photography, political, professional, radio and TV, religious, social, social service, student government, and yearbook. Popular campus events include the opening convocation, Honors Convocation, and performing arts events.

Sports: There are 4 intercollegiate sports for women. Facilities include a 300-seat gym, an Olympic-size pool, and tennis courts.

Disabled Students: 80% of the campus is accessible. Wheelchair ramps, elevators, special parking, specially equipped rest rooms, special

class scheduling, lowered drinking fountains, and special housing are available.

Services: Counseling and information services are available, as is tutoring in most subjects, including English and courses with written expectations. There is remedial writing.

Campus Safety and Security: Measures include 24-hour foot and vehicle patrol, self-defense education, security escort services, and informal discussions. There are pamphlets/posters/films, emergency telephones, and lighted pathways/sidewalks.

Programs of Study: Stephens confers B.A., B.S., and B.F.A. degrees. Associate and master's degrees are also awarded. Bachelor's degrees are awarded in AGRICULTURE (equine science), BIOLOGICAL SCIENCE (biology/biological science), BUSINESS (accounting, business administration and management, and fashion merchandising), COMMUNICATIONS AND THE ARTS (creative writing, dance, dramatic arts, English, film arts, graphic design, public relations, and theater design), EDUCATION (early childhood and elementary), ENGINEERING AND ENVIRONMENTAL DESIGN (interior design), SOCIAL SCIENCE (fashion design and technology, liberal arts/general studies, and prelaw). Education and biology are the strongest academically. Performing arts, fashion, and biology are the largest.

Required: All students must complete 6 hours of English and a distribution of 9 courses in lower-division work, including 6 hours of social sciences and 3 hours each of math, science, literary studies, history, cultural studies, and ethics. The bachelor's degree requires completion of at least 120 semester hours, including 30 to 72 in a major field, with a minimum GPA of 2.0.

Special: Students may study abroad in England, Italy, Mexico, France, Ecuador, and South Korea. Stephens also offers cross-registration with the Mid-Missouri Association of Colleges and Universities, many internships, a Washington semester, dual and student-designed majors, a 3-2 occupational therapy degree program with Washington University, accelerated degree programs in dance and theater arts, and pass/fail options for electives. There are 8 national honor societies and a freshman honors program.

Faculty/Classroom: 40% of faculty are male; 60%, female. 92% teach undergraduates. The average class size in an introductory lecture is 30; in a laboratory, 12; and in a regular course, 20.

Admissions: The SAT scores for the 2005-2006 freshman class were: Verbal--12% below 500, 54% between 500 and 599, 32% between 600 and 700, and 2% above 700; Math--28% below 500, 50% between 500 and 599, 20% between 600 and 700, and 2% above 700. The ACT scores were 12% below 21, 33% between 21 and 23, 39% between 24 and 26, 10% between 27 and 28, and 6% above 28. 45% of the current freshmen were in the top fifth of their class; 77% were in the top two fifths. 5 freshmen graduated first in their class.

Requirements: The SAT or ACT is required. In addition, applicants must be graduates of accredited secondary schools or have earned a GED. An essay is also required, and an interview is recommended. A GPA of 2.5 is required. AP and CLEP credits are accepted. Important factors in the admissions decision are advanced placement or honor courses, leadership record, and recommendations by school officials.

Procedure: Freshmen are admitted fall and spring. There is a deferred admissions plan and a rolling admissions plan. Application deadlines are open. Application fee is $25. Applications are accepted on-line.

Transfer: 47 transfer students enrolled in 2004-2005. Applicants must submit official transcripts from all college work attempted or completed as well as a recommendation from an academic college instructor. Transfers must submit an official high school transcript. 36 of 120 credits required for the bachelor's degree must be completed at Stephens.

Visiting: There are regularly scheduled orientations for prospective students, consisting of attendance at classes, a campus tour, an appointment with instructors, and an interview. There are guides for informal visits and visitors may sit in on classes and stay overnight. To schedule a visit, contact the campus visit coordinator at (800) 876-7207 or apply@stephens.edu.

Financial Aid: In 2005-2006, 97% of all full-time students received some form of financial aid. 62% of full-time freshmen and 54% of continuing full-time students received need-based aid. The average freshman award was $16,866. Need-based scholarships or need-based grants averaged $6868 ($19,160 maximum); need-based self-help aid (loans and jobs) averaged $3670 ($8025 maximum); non-need-based athletic scholarships averaged $3500 ($6000 maximum); and other non-need-based awards and non-need-based scholarships averaged $9203 ($19,300 maximum). 42% of undergraduates work part time. Average annual earnings from campus work are $1020. The average financial indebtedness of the 2005 graduate was $12,775. The FAFSA is required. The priority date for freshman financial aid applications for fall entry is March 15.

International Students: There are 3 international students enrolled. The school actively recruits these students. They must take the TOEFL.

Computers: Wireless access is available. There are wireless computer labs, and wireless access is available in residence halls and academic buildings. All students may access the system. There are no time limits and no fees.

Graduates: From July 1, 2004 to June 30, 2005, 111 bachelor's degrees were awarded. The most popular majors were theater arts (21%), fashion design (11%), and fashion marketing (7%). In an average class, 13% graduate in 3 years or less, 43% graduate in 4 years or less, 50% graduate in 5 years or less, and 53% graduate in 6 years or less. 15 companies recruited on campus in 2004-2005.

Admissions Contact: David Adams, Director of Enrollment.
E-mail: dadams@stephens.edu Web: www.stephens.edu

TRUMAN STATE UNIVERSITY   C-1
Kirksville, MO 63501   (660) 785-4114
                                 (800) 892-7792; Fax: (660) 785-7456

Full-time: 2281 men, 3175 women	**Faculty:** 346; IIA, --$
Part-time: 61 men, 50 women	**Ph.D.s:** 83%
Graduate: 74 men, 158 women	**Student/Faculty:** 16 to 1
Year: semesters, summer session	**Tuition:** $5862 ($10,042)
Application Deadline: March 1	**Room & Board:** $5380
Freshman Class: 4912 applied, 4035 accepted, 1444 enrolled	
SAT Verbal/Math: 630/610*	**ACT:** 27 **HIGHLY COMPETITIVE**

Truman State University, founded in 1867, is a public liberal arts institution offering undergraduate and graduate degree programs in business and accountancy, education, fine arts, human potential and performance, language and literature, mathematics and computer science, science, and social science. There are 7 undergraduate and 6 graduate schools. In addition to regional accreditation, Truman has baccalaureate program accreditation with AACSB, ACS, ASLA, CAAHEP, CACREP, NASM, NCATE, and NLN. The library contains 460,116 volumes, 1,537,884 microform items, and 40,527 audio/video tapes/CDs/DVDs, and subscribes to 3396 periodicals including electronic. Computerized library services include the card catalog, interlibrary loans, database searching, Internet access, and laptop Internet portals. Special learning facilities include a learning resource center, art gallery, radio station, TV studio, a biofeedback lab, an independent learning center for nursing students, an observatory, a greenhouse chamber, and a speech and hearing clinic. The 140-acre campus is in a small town 170 miles northeast of Kansas City and 200 miles north of St. Louis. Including any residence halls, there are 40 buildings.

Student Life: 73% of undergraduates are from Missouri. Others are from 40 states and 46 foreign countries. 80% are from public schools. 85% are white. 52% are Protestant; 28% Catholic; 19% no affiliation or other religious affiliation. The average age of freshmen is 18; all undergraduates, 20. 14% do not continue beyond their first year; 66% remain to graduate.

Housing: 2981 students can be accommodated in university housing, which includes single-sex and coed dorms, on-campus apartments, and married-student housing. On-campus housing is guaranteed for the freshman year only, is available on a first-come, first-served basis, and is available on a lottery system for upperclassmen. 51% of students live on campus. Alcohol is not permitted. All students may keep cars.

Activities: 31% of men belong to 18 national fraternities; 22% of women belong to 1 local sorority and 10 national sororities. There are 230 groups on campus, including art, band, cheerleading, chess, choir, chorale, chorus, computers, dance, debate, drama, drill team, ethnic, film, forensics, gay, honors, international, jazz band, literary magazine, marching band, musical theater, newspaper, orchestra, pep band, political, professional, radio and TV, religious, social, social service, student government, and yearbook. Popular campus events include Dog Days (Spring Carnival), Family Day, and International Week.

Sports: There are 11 intercollegiate sports for men and 10 for women, and 21 intramural sports for men and 21 for women. Facilities include a 5000-seat football stadium, a soccer field, tennis and racquetball courts, a softball diamond, a baseball diamond, a 3000-seat arena with 3 basketball courts, an Olympic-size pool, weight training rooms, indoor and outdoor track facilities, and a 60,000-square-foot student recreation center.

Disabled Students: 90% of the campus is accessible. Wheelchair ramps, elevators, special parking, specially equipped rest rooms, special class scheduling, lowered drinking fountains, lowered telephones, and special housing, are available. The swimming pool is equipped with a lift to assist physically disabled swimmers.

Services: Counseling and information services are available, as is tutoring in most subjects. There are services for the hearing impaired and a braille scanner and printer. There is a reader service for the blind. Services for Individuals with Disabilities provides recording, note-taking, test-taking, and advising services.

Campus Safety and Security: Measures include 24-hour foot and vehicle patrol, self-defense education, security escort services, and informal discussions. There are pamphlets/posters/films, emergency telephones, lighted pathways/sidewalks, and personal body alarms, available on a limited basis.

Programs of Study: Truman confers B.A., B.S., B.F.A., B.M., and B.S.N. degrees. Master's degrees are also awarded. Bachelor's degrees are awarded in AGRICULTURE (agricultural economics, agriculture, agronomy, animal science, and equine science), BIOLOGICAL SCIENCE (biology/biological science), BUSINESS (accounting and business administration and management), COMMUNICATIONS AND THE ARTS (art, art history and appreciation, classics, communications, dramatic arts, English, fine arts, French, German, journalism, music, music performance, Russian, Spanish, and speech/debate/rhetoric), COMPUTER AND PHYSICAL SCIENCE (chemistry, computer science, mathematics, and physics), ENGINEERING AND ENVIRONMENTAL DESIGN (preengineering), HEALTH PROFESSIONS (health science, nursing, physical therapy, predentistry, premedicine, preoptometry, prepharmacy, preveterinary science, and speech pathology/audiology), SOCIAL SCIENCE (anthropology, criminal justice, economics, history, interdisciplinary studies, philosophy, physical fitness/movement, political science/government, prelaw, psychology, religion, and sociology). Chemistry, political science, and business are the strongest academically. Business administration, biology, and English are the largest.

Required: All students must complete 63 hours of course work in the liberal arts, 16 of which must be in written and oral communication, math and statistics, computer literacy, and personal well-being, and 23 of which must be in history, science, social science, philosophy/religion, and aesthetics. The B.A., B.F.A., and B.M. degree require intermediate proficiency in one foreign language, and the B.S. and B.S.N. require additional course work in science, math, statistics, computer science, social sciences, or logic. Skills such as writing, quantitative analysis, problem solving, and critical thinking are reinforced throughout the curriculum, and all seniors end their studies with a capstone, or culminating experience, in their majors. Students must also complete a nationally normed exam in their subject area as part of Truman's assessment program.

Special: Study abroad in 47 countries is offered through Truman's own programs and those of the College Consortium for International Studies, the Council on International Educational Exchange, and the International Student Exchange Program. The university requires internships in education and health and exercise science. Voluntary legislative internships are offered to all students at the state capitol, and internships through the Washington Center. There is a 3-2 engineering program with the University of Missouri-Rolla. Work-study programs, B.A.-B.S. degrees, dual majors, student-designed majors in health and exercise science, biology, history, and agricultural science, credit for military experience, pass/fail options for internships, and nondegree study are available. There are 36 national honor societies, including Phi Beta Kappa, a freshman honors program, and 23 departmental honors programs.

Faculty/Classroom: 61% of faculty are male; 39%, female. 98% teach undergraduates. Graduate students teach 1% of introductory courses. The average class size in an introductory lecture is 24; in a laboratory, 19; and in a regular course, 23.

Admissions: 82% of the 2005-2006 applicants were accepted. The SAT scores for the 2005-2006 freshman class were: Verbal--5% below 500, 29% between 500 and 599, 50% between 600 and 700, and 16% above 700; Math--7% below 500, 33% between 500 and 599, 48% between 600 and 700, and 12% above 700. The ACT scores were 1% below 21, 12% between 21 and 23, 27% between 24 and 26, 22% between 27 and 28, and 38% above 28. 73% of the current freshmen were in the top fifth of their class; 94% were in the top two fifths. There were 20 National Merit finalists. 144 freshmen graduated first in their class in a recent year.

Requirements: The SAT or ACT is required; the University prefers the ACT, with a recommended minimum score of 22. Applicants should have completed 4 units of English, 3 each of science and social studies, 2 of foreign language, and 1 of art or music. 4 units of math are strongly recommended. An essay is required and an interview or visit is recommended. AP and CLEP credits are accepted. Important factors in the admissions decision are leadership record, advanced placement or honor courses, and extracurricular activities record.

Procedure: Freshmen are admitted to all sessions. Entrance exams should be taken during the spring or summer following the junior year. There are early admissions and deferred admissions plans. Early decision applications should be filed by November 15; regular applications, by March 1 for fall entry. Notification of early decision is sent December 15; regular decision, on a rolling basis. Applications are accepted online.

Transfer: 113 transfer students enrolled in 2004-2005. Transfer applicants should present a minimum 2.75 GPA on transferable hours and must meet minimum criteria for entering freshmen. 45 of 124 credits required for the bachelor's degree must be completed at Truman.

Visiting: There are regularly scheduled orientations for prospective students, including an interview with an admission counselor, a student-led campus tour, an appointment with a faculty member in the student's major, appointments in any areas of special interest, and the opportunity to observe a class. There are guides for informal visits and visitors may sit in on classes and stay overnight. To schedule a visit, contact the Admissions Office at (660) 785-4135 or admissions@truman.edu.

Financial Aid: In a recent year, 98% of all full-time freshmen and 92% of continuing full-time students received some form of financial aid. 32% of full-time freshmen and 30% of continuing full-time students received need-based aid. The average freshman award was $6872. Need-based

scholarships or need-based grants averaged $3188 ($4600 maximum); need-based self-help aid (loans and jobs) averaged $2875 ($10,500 maximum); non-need-based athletic scholarships averaged $3523 ($12,622 maximum); and other non-need-based awards and non-need-based scholarships averaged $3326 ($16,946 maximum). 21% of undergraduates work part time. Average annual earnings from campus work are $1696. The average financial indebtedness of the 2005 graduate was $16,546. Truman is a member of CSS. The FAFSA and the college's own financial statement are required. The deadline for filing freshman financial aid applications for fall entry is April 1.

International Students: There are 213 international students enrolled. The school actively recruits these students. They must take the TOEFL and the Comprehensive English Language Test.

Computers: Truman has 417 PCs available for general student use in 89 computer labs and classrooms in the residence halls, library, student union, and academic buildings. Student areas are wireless. On-campus students have free high-speed Internet access, and off-campus students have free dial-up service through Truman's server. All students may access the system. Labs are open until 1 A.M. in the academic buildings, and 7:30 A.M. to 1 A.M. in the library. Residence hall labs are always open. An individual time limit of 30 minutes is imposed only when other students are waiting. There are no fees.

Graduates: From July 1, 2004 to June 30, 2005, 1215 bachelor's degrees were awarded. The most popular majors were business administration (14%), biology (10%), and psychology (9%). In an average class, 2% graduate in 3 years or less, 40% graduate in 4 years or less, 64% graduate in 5 years or less, and 66% graduate in 6 years or less. Of the 2004 graduating class, 45% were enrolled in graduate school within 6 months of graduation and 54% were employed.

Admissions Contact: Brad Chambers, Co-Director of Admission. E-mail: admissions@truman.edu Web: admissions.truman.edu

---

UNIVERSITY OF MISSOURI SYSTEM

The University of Missouri System, established in 1966, is a public system in Missouri. It is governed by a board of curators, whose chief administrator is the President. The primary goal of the system is teaching, research, extension, and other public service. The main priorities are to provide the highest quality of instructional and research programs, to provide educational access to qualified students who demonstrate likelihood of academic success, and to operate in an effective and cost-efficient manner. The total enrollment of all 4 campuses is usually about 57,100; with 4800 faculty members. Altogether there are some 214 baccalaureate, 228 master's, and 106 doctoral programs offered in University of Missouri System. 4-year campuses are located in Columbia, Kansas City, Rolla, and and St. Louis. Profiles of the 4-year campuses are included in this section.

UNIVERSITY OF MISSOURI/COLUMBIA   C-2

Columbia, MO 65211   (573) 882-7786
                                  (800) 225-6075; Fax: (573) 882-7887

Full-time: 9631 men, 10,348 women	**Faculty:** 1255; I, -$
Part-time: 696 men, 700 women	**Ph.D:s:** 92%
Graduate: 2311 men, 3216 women	**Student/Faculty:** 16 to 1
Year: semesters, summer session	**Tuition:** $6960 ($16,085)
Application Deadline: May 1	**Room & Board:** $6540
Freshman Class: n/av	
ACT: 25	**VERY COMPETITIVE**

The University of Missouri/Columbia, established in 1839, offers a comprehensive array of undergraduate and graduate programs as well as professional training in law, medicine, and veterinary medicine. There are 10 undergraduate and 14 graduate schools. In addition to regional accreditation, Mizzou has baccalaureate program accreditation with AACSB, ABET, ACEJMC, ADA, APTA, CAHEA, CSWE, FIDER, NASAD, NASM, NCATE, NRPA, and SAF. The 11 libraries contain 3,256,756 volumes and 6,896,250 microform items, and subscribe to 26,886 periodicals including electronic. Computerized library services include the card catalog, interlibrary loans, database searching, Internet access, and laptop Internet portals. Special learning facilities include a learning resource center, art gallery, natural history museum, radio station, TV station, an astronomy observatory, freedom of information center, herbarium, and anthropology, fishery, and wildlife collections. The 1358-acre campus is in a suburban area 120 miles west of St. Louis and 120 miles east of Kansas City. Including any residence halls, there are 355 buildings.

Student Life: 81% of undergraduates are from Missouri. Others are from 50 states, 101 foreign countries, and Canada. 81% are white. The average age of freshmen is 18; all undergraduates, 20. 16% do not continue beyond their first year; 66% remain to graduate.

Housing: 9032 students can be accommodated in college housing, which includes single-sex and coed dorms, off-campus apartments, married-student housing, fraternity houses, and sorority houses. In addition, there are honors houses, language houses, and special-interest houses. On-campus housing is guaranteed for all 4 years. 58% of students commute. Alcohol is not permitted. All students may keep cars.

Activities: 20% of men belong to 32 national fraternities; 25% of women belong to 25 national sororities. There are 442 groups on campus, including art, band, cheerleading, chess, choir, chorale, chorus, computers, dance, debate, drama, drill team, drum and bugle corps, ethnic, film, gay, honors, international, jazz band, literary magazine, marching band, musical theater, newspaper, orchestra, pep band, photography, political, professional, radio and TV, religious, social, social service, student government, symphony, and yearbook. Popular campus events include Big Twelve athletics, academic weeks, and Meet Mizzou Day.

Sports: There are 8 intercollegiate sports for men and 10 for women, and 26 intramural sports for men and 26 for women. Facilities include a recreation complex with a 50-meter competitive pool and diving well, club pool, high-tech fitness club, heavy-lifting gym, a climbing and bouldering wall, multicourts, raquetball courts, and an indoor track. There is a 62,000-seat stadium, a 1,300-seat indoor gym, and an 18,000-seat auditorium.

Disabled Students: All of the campus is accessible. Wheelchair ramps, elevators, special parking, specially equipped rest rooms, special class scheduling, lowered drinking fountains, and lowered telephones are available.

Services: Counseling and information services are available, as is tutoring in some subjects. There is a reader service for the blind.

Campus Safety and Security: Measures include 24-hour foot and vehicle patrol, self-defense education, security escort services, and shuttle buses. There are informal discussions, pamphlets/posters/films, emergency telephones, lighted pathways/sidewalks, and a 24-hour bicycle patrol.

Programs of Study: Mizzou confers B.A., B.S., B.E.S., B.F.A., B.G.S., B.H.S., B.J., B.M., B.S.Acc., B.S.B.A., B.S.B.E., B.S.ChE., B.S.CiE., B.S.C.E., B.S.CoE, B.S.E.E., B.S.Ed., B.S.F., B.S.F.W., B.S.H.E.S., B.S.I.E., B.S.M.E., degrees. Master's and doctoral degrees are also awarded. Bachelor's degrees are awarded in AGRICULTURE (agricultural business management, agricultural economics, agriculture, animal science, plant science, and soil science), BIOLOGICAL SCIENCE (biochemistry, biology/biological science, microbiology, and nutrition), BUSINESS (accounting, banking and finance, business administration and management, business economics, hotel/motel and restaurant management, marketing/retailing/merchandising, real estate, and tourism), COMMUNICATIONS AND THE ARTS (advertising, art history and appreciation, broadcasting, classics, communications, design, dramatic arts, English, French, German, journalism, linguistics, music, Russian, and Spanish), COMPUTER AND PHYSICAL SCIENCE (atmospheric sciences and meteorology, chemistry, computer science, geology, mathematics, physics, and statistics), EDUCATION (art, early childhood, education, elementary, middle school, music, and secondary), ENGINEERING AND ENVIRONMENTAL DESIGN (biomedical engineering, chemical engineering, civil engineering, computer engineering, electrical/electronics engineering, industrial engineering, and mechanical engineering), HEALTH PROFESSIONS (nursing, occupational therapy, physical therapy, radiological science, and respiratory therapy), SOCIAL SCIENCE (anthropology, archeology, economics, family/consumer resource management, food science, geography, history, human development, international studies, liberal arts/general studies, parks and recreation management, philosophy, political science/government, psychology, religion, social science, social work, sociology, and textiles and clothing). Biological sciences, business administration, and psychology are the strongest academically. Business, journalism, and engineering are the largest.

Required: To graduate, students must maintain a minimum 2.0 GPA and complete at least 120 credits, of which at least 30 must be in their major, although credit requirements can vary by degree program. All students must take English, plus 2 additional writing-intensive courses, demonstrate competency in college algebra, take 1 additional course in development math and reasoning skills, and complete a course in American history or government. Students must complete 9 hours in social and behavioral sciences, 9 in physical and biological sciences (including 1 lab course), and 9 in humanities and fine arts. A capstone experience is also required.

Special: Available academic programs include co-op programs and cross-registration with other schools, internships, study abroad, a Washington semester, and work-study programs. Special degrees or studies include an accelerated degree, dual majors, a general studies degree, and student-designed majors. For highly motivated students there is an honors college and the possibility of early admission to the schools of law and medicine. There are 24 national honor societies, including Phi Beta Kappa, and freshman honors program.

Faculty/Classroom: 68% of faculty are male; 32%, female.

Admissions: The ACT scores for the 2005-2006 freshman class were: 6% below 21, 24% between 21 and 23, 30% between 24 and 26, 18% between 27 and 28, and 22% above 28. 48% of the current freshmen were in the top fifth of their class; 88% were in the top two fifths. There were 19 National Merit finalists.

Requirements: The ACT is required. In addition, students may gain probationary admission with sufficient GED scores. The usual requirements are completion of 17 Carnegie units, including 4 each in English and math, 3 each in social studies and science, 2 in a foreign language, and 1 in fine arts. Admission is determined by these units and a combination of class rank and ACT score. AP and CLEP credits are accepted. Important factors in the admissions decision are advanced placement or honor courses and evidence of special talent.

Procedure: Freshmen are admitted to all sessions. Entrance exams should be taken late in the junior year or in the senior year. There are deferred admissions and rolling admissions plans. Applications should be filed by May 1 for fall entry, along with a $35 fee. Notification is sent on a rolling basis. Applications are accepted on-line.

Transfer: 1336 transfer students enrolled in 2004-2005. Transfer students must present 24 hours of completed college-level course work with a minimum 2.0 GPA, and show a C average in all course work attempted. An interview is recommended. The last 30 of 120 credits required for the bachelor's degree must be completed at Mizzou. The number of credits required for the bachelor's degree varies by division.

Visiting: There are regularly scheduled orientations for prospective students, consisting of a campus tour, a visit with an admissions representative, and a visit with an academic representative on request. There are guides for informal visits and visitors may sit in on classes. To schedule a visit, contact the Admissions Office.

Financial Aid: In 2005-2006, 44% of all full-time freshmen and 42% of continuing full-time students received some form of financial aid. 39% of full-time freshmen and 36% of continuing full-time students received need-based aid. Need-based scholarships or need-based grants averaged $6110; need-based self-help aid (loans and jobs) averaged $3939; and non-need-based athletic scholarships averaged $9023. 6% of undergraduates work part time. The average financial indebtedness of the 2005 graduate was $17,907. The FAFSA is required. The deadline for filing freshman financial aid applications for fall entry is March 1.

International Students: There are 279 international students enrolled. A satisfatoty score is required on the written TOEFL.

Computers: Wireless access is available. The majority of the campus is wireless and residence hall rooms are wired for access as are numerous computer labs across campus. Network is easily accessible with username and password, which students receive upon arriving. All students may access the system 24 hours daily by modem; lab hours vary, but they are open 7 days a week. There are no time limits and no fees.

Graduates: From July 1, 2004 to June 30, 2005, 4259 bachelor's degrees were awarded. The most popular majors were business (17%), journalism (10%), and sociology (9%). In an average class, 1% graduate in 3 years or less, 37% graduate in 4 years or less, 63% graduate in 5 years or less, and 67% graduate in 6 years or less. 1500 companies recruited on campus in a recent year.

Admissions Contact: Barbara Rupp, Director Undergraduate Admissions. E-mail: *MU4U@missouri.edu* Web: *www.missouri.edu*

UNIVERSITY OF MISSOURI/KANSAS CITY
A-2

Kansas City, MO 64110	(816) 235-1111; Fax: (816) 235-5544
Full-time: 2000 men, 3100 women	**Faculty:** 615; 1, --$
Part-time: 1700 men, 2400 women	**Ph.D.s:** 84%
Graduate: 2100 men, 3000 women	**Student/Faculty:** 8 to 1
Year: semesters, summer session	**Tuition:** $7000 ($15,000)
Application Deadline: open	**Room & Board:** $8000
Freshman Class: n/av	
ACT: required	**VERY COMPETITIVE**

The University of Missouri/Kansas City, which opened in 1933, is a public institution offering undergraduate and graduate programs in the arts and sciences, engineering, business, education, health fields, preprofessional, and professional studies. There are 9 undergraduate and 13 graduate schools. Figures in the above capsule and in this profile are approximate. In addition to regional accreditation, UMKC has baccalaureate program accreditation with AACSB, ABET, ACPE, ADA, NASM, NCATE, and NLN. The 4 libraries contain 1,265,100 volumes, 2,377,500 microform items, and 451,600 audio/video tapes/CDs/DVDs, and subscribe to 7200 periodicals including electronic. Computerized library services include the card catalog, interlibrary loans, and database searching. Special learning facilities include a learning resource center, art gallery, natural history museum, planetarium, and radio station. The 262-acre campus is in an urban area in Kansas City. Including any residence halls, there are 42 buildings.

Student Life: 79% of undergraduates are from Missouri. Others are from 42 states, 81 foreign countries, and Canada. 63% are white; 14% African American. The average age of freshmen is 19; all undergraduates, 23. 28% do not continue beyond their first year; 76% remain to graduate.

Housing: 1300 students can be accommodated in college housing, which includes coed dorms and on-campus apartments. On-campus housing is available on a first-come, first-served basis. 90% of students commute. Alcohol is not permitted. All students may keep cars.

Activities: 3% of men belong to 6 national fraternities; 5% of women belong to 2 local and 7 national sororities. There are 202 groups on campus, including art, band, cheerleading, chess, choir, chorale, chorus, computers, dance, debate, drama, ethnic, gay, honors, international, jazz band, literary magazine, newspaper, opera, orchestra, photography, political, professional, radio and TV, religious, social, social service, student government, and yearbook. Popular campus events include International Food and Culture Night, Welcome Back Week, and Spring Fling.

Sports: There are 6 intercollegiate sports for men and 7 for women, and 13 intramural sports for men and 13 for women. Facilities include a recreation center with 5 gyms, an indoor/outdoor pool, indoor and outdoor tracks, a fitness center, and handball, racquetball, and squash courts. There are also recreation facilities at the University Center.

Disabled Students: 95% of the campus is accessible. Wheelchair ramps, elevators, special parking, specially equipped rest rooms, special class scheduling, lowered drinking fountains, and lowered telephones are available.

Services: There is a reader service for the blind.

Campus Safety and Security: Measures include 24-hour foot and vehicle patrol, self-defense education, security escort services, and shuttle buses. There are informal discussions, pamphlets/posters/films, emergency telephones, and lighted pathways/sidewalks.

Programs of Study: UMKC confers B.A., B.S., B.B.A., B.F.A., B.I.T., B.L.A., B.M., B.M.E., B.S.C.I.E., B.S.D.H., B.S.E.E., B.S.M.E., and B.S.N. degrees. Master's and doctoral degrees are also awarded. Bachelor's degrees are awarded in BIOLOGICAL SCIENCE (biology/biological science), BUSINESS (accounting, and business administration and management), COMMUNICATIONS AND THE ARTS (art, art history and appreciation, communications, dance, dramatic arts, English, fine arts, French, German, music, music performance, music theory and composition, performing arts, Spanish, speech/debate/rhetoric, and studio art), COMPUTER AND PHYSICAL SCIENCE (chemistry, computer science, geology, information sciences and systems, mathematics, and physics), EDUCATION (elementary, health, music, physical, and secondary), ENGINEERING AND ENVIRONMENTAL DESIGN (civil engineering, electrical/electronics engineering, environmental science, and mechanical engineering), HEALTH PROFESSIONS (dental hygiene, medical technology, music therapy, and nursing), SOCIAL SCIENCE (American studies, criminal justice, economics, geography, history, Judaic studies, liberal arts/general studies, philosophy, political science/government, psychology, sociology, and urban studies). Health sciences and performing arts are the strongest academically. Liberal arts is the largest.

Required: Most candidates for the B.A. and B.S. degrees must complete a core curriculum that consists of courses in English, a foreign language, math, philosophy, fine arts, history, literature, natural sciences, and social sciences. They must complete 120 credit hours, including 36 in their major, with a 2.0 GPA.

Special: Special academic programs include co-op programs and internships in several majors, study abroad in 8 countries, an accelerated degree program, dual majors, and numerous work-study opportunities in the Kansas City area. Special degrees include a B.A.-B.S. degree in the computer science program and a liberal arts degree offered by the adult program. The pass/fail option is available in some courses. Freshmen may enter 6-year medical and dental programs. There are 4 national honor societies, a freshman honors program, and 1 departmental honors program.

Faculty/Classroom: 57% of faculty are male; 43%, female. The average class size in an introductory lecture is 30; in a laboratory, 16; and in a regular course, 24.

Admissions: 93% of recent applicants were accepted. The SAT scores for a recent freshman class were: Verbal--19% below 500, 29% between 500 and 599, 40% between 600 and 700, and 11% above 700; Math--11% below 500, 38% between 500 and 599, 36% between 600 and 700, and 15% above 700. The ACT scores were 25% below 21, 22% between 21 and 23, 24% between 24 and 26, 12% between 27 and 28, and 16% above 28. 60% of recent freshmen were in the top fifth of their class; 85% were in the top two fifths.

Requirements: The ACT or SAT is required. A combination of the student's test score and class rank determines admissibility. Graduation from an accredited secondary school is a requirement for admission; the GED is also accepted. Required high school subjects include 4 units of English, 3 each of math and social studies, 2 of science, 1 of arts, and 3 more units selected from the above subjects or from a foreign language. A portfolio is required for art majors, an audition for music majors, and an interview for only those students applying for the pharmacy degree or the 6-year medical and dental programs. AP and CLEP credits are accepted.

Procedure: Freshmen are admitted to all sessions. Entrance exams should be taken by March of the senior year. There is a rolling admissions plan. Application deadlines are open. The fall 2005 application fee was $35.

Transfer: 1477 transfer students enrolled in a recent year. A maximum of 60 semester hours from community colleges or 30 hours earned within the University of Missouri System will be accepted. Transfer students must have maintained a 2.0 GPA. The SAT or ACT is recommended. 30 of 120 credits required for the bachelor's degree must be completed at UMKC.

Visiting: There are regularly scheduled orientations for prospective students, consisting of a 1-day program for new freshmen or a half-day optional program for transfer students. There are guides for informal visits. To schedule a visit, contact the UMKC Welcome Center at (816) 235-8652.

Financial Aid: In a recent year, 61% of all full-time students received some form of financial aid. 50% of full-time freshmen and 40% of continuing full-time students received need-based aid. The average freshman award was $16,206. Need-based scholarships or need-based grants averaged $4597; need-based self-help aid (loans and jobs) averaged $6195; non-need-based athletic scholarships averaged $11,577; and other non-need-based awards and non-need-based scholarships averaged $4989. 6% of undergraduates work part time. Average annual earnings from campus work are $2930. The average financial indebtedness of a recent graduate was $15,714. The FAFSA is required. Check with the school for current deadlines.

International Students: There were 290 international students enrolled in a recent year. The school actively recruits these students. They must score satisfactorily on the written TOEFL.

Computers: All students may access the system 24 hours, 7 days a week. Students may access the system There is a dial-up limit of 15 hours; no limit for lab use. The fee is approximately $10 per credit hour.

Graduates: In a recent year, 1138 bachelor's degrees were awarded. The most popular majors were liberal arts (21%), business/marketing (11%), and education, social sciences, history (8%). In an average class, 11% graduate in 4 years or less, 24% graduate in 5 years or less, and 42% graduate in 6 years or less. 475 companies recruited on campus in a recent year.

Admissions Contact: Director of Admissions.
E-mail: *admit@umkc.edu* Web: *http://www.umkc.edu*

UNIVERSITY OF MISSOURI/ROLLA   C-3

Rolla, MO 65409-   (573) 341-4164
                              (800) 522-0938; Fax: (573) 341-4082

Full-time: 2900 men, 800 women	**Faculty:** 275; I, -$
Part-time: 300 men, 100 women	**Ph.D.s:** 91%
Graduate: 1100 men, 300 women	**Student/Faculty:** 13 to 1
Year: semesters, summer session	**Tuition:** $7492 ($16,617)
Application Deadline: July 1	**Room & Board:** $5840
Freshman Class: n/av	
SAT or ACT: required	**HIGHLY COMPETITIVE**

The University of Missouri/Rolla, founded in 1870, is part of the University of Missouri system. A public institution, it offers comprehensive undergraduate and graduate programs and confers degrees in arts and sciences, engineering, mines and metallurgy, and management and information systems. There are 4 undergraduate and 4 graduate schools. Figures in the above capsule and in this profile are approximate. In addition to regional accreditation, UMR has baccalaureate program accreditation with ABET and CSAB. The library contains 435,000 volumes, 51,400 microform items, and 6300 audio/video tapes/CDs/DVDs, and subscribes to 1600 periodicals including electronic. Computerized library services include the card catalog, interlibrary loans, database searching, and Internet access. Special learning facilities include a learning resource center, radio station, writing center, student design center, nuclear reactor, observatory, explosives testing labs, and underground mine. The 284-acre campus is in a small town 90 miles southwest of St. Louis. Including any residence halls, there are 71 buildings.

Student Life: 78% of undergraduates are from Missouri. Students are from 43 states, 34 foreign countries, and Canada. 85% are from public schools. 83% are white. 37% are Protestant; 34% claim no religious affiliation; 22% are Catholic. The average age of freshmen is 18; all undergraduates, 21. 17% do not continue beyond their first year; 60% remain to graduate.

Housing: 1365 students can be accommodated in college housing, which includes single-sex and coed dorms, on-campus apartments, married-student housing, fraternity houses, and sorority houses. In addition, there are community learning centers and the Voyageur Program. On-campus housing is guaranteed for the freshman year only and is available on a first-come, first-served basis. 53% of students live on campus; of those, 65% remain on campus on weekends. Alcohol is not permitted. All students may keep cars.

Activities: 27% of men belong to 20 national fraternities; 24% of women belong to 1 local and 5 national sororities. There are 200 groups on campus, including bagpipe band, band, cheerleading, chess, choir, chorale, chorus, computers, drama, drill team, ethnic, gay, honors, international, jazz band, literary magazine, marching band, musical theater, newspaper, orchestra, pep band, political, professional, radio and TV, religious, social, social service, student government, and yearbook. Popular campus events include St. Patrick's Day, Black Culture Month, and Hispanic Culture Month.

Sports: There are 7 intercollegiate sports for men and 5 for women, and 19 intramural sports for men and 19 for women. Facilities include a gym, a weight room, a pool, a golf course, a track, racquetball and tennis courts, ball and soccer fields, and a 5000-seat stadium.

Disabled Students: 95% of the campus is accessible. Wheelchair ramps, elevators, special parking, specially equipped rest rooms, special class scheduling, lowered drinking fountains, lowered telephones, special housing, assistive listening devices, closed-circuit TV, wheelchairs, signers, aides, and specialized testing accommodations are available.

Services: Counseling and information services are available, as is tutoring in most subjects. There is a reader service for the blind.

Campus Safety and Security: Measures include 24-hour foot and vehicle patrol, self-defense education, security escort services, and informal discussions. There are pamphlets/posters/films, emergency telephones, lighted pathways/sidewalks, and crime prevention and rape/sexual assault programs.

Programs of Study: UMR confers B.A. and B.S. degrees. Master's and doctoral degrees are also awarded. Bachelor's degrees are awarded in BIOLOGICAL SCIENCE (biology/biological science, environmental biology, and life science), BUSINESS (business administration and management, electronic business, and management information systems), COMMUNICATIONS AND THE ARTS (English, and technical and business writing), COMPUTER AND PHYSICAL SCIENCE (applied mathematics, chemistry, computer science, geology, geophysics and seismology, information sciences and systems, mathematics, physics, polymer science, and statistics), EDUCATION (secondary), ENGINEERING AND ENVIRONMENTAL DESIGN (aeronautical engineering, architectural engineering, ceramic engineering, chemical engineering, civil engineering, computer engineering, electrical/electronics engineering, engineering, engineering management, engineering mechanics, environmental engineering, geological engineering, industrial engineering, manufacturing engineering, materials engineering, mechanical engineering, metallurgical engineering, mining and mineral engineering, nuclear engineering, petroleum/natural gas engineering, plastics engineering, and systems engineering), HEALTH PROFESSIONS (environmental health science, predentistry, and premedicine), SOCIAL SCIENCE (economics, history, philosophy, prelaw, and psychology). Engineering, science and technology are the strongest academically. Engineering, arts, and sciences are the largest.

Required: Candidates for graduation must maintain at least a 2.0 GPA. A total of 120 to 132 credits, depending on the degree, is required. An assessment exam is required.

Special: UMR offers internships in business and government, co-op programs in which students work and attend school on alternating schedules, and study abroad in 20 countries. Accelerated degrees in science and engineering, dual majors, B.A.-B.S. degrees, a 3-2 engineering degree, work-study programs, a 5 year masters' degree program, credit for life/military/work experience, and pass/fail options in certain courses are also available. There are 23 national honor societies, a freshman honors program, and 24 departmental honors programs.

Faculty/Classroom: 86% of faculty are male; 14%, female. 88% teach undergraduates. Graduate students teach 25% of introductory courses. The average class size in an introductory lecture is 36; in a laboratory, 18; and in a regular course, 25.

Admissions: 79% of recent applicants were accepted. The ACT scores for a recent freshman class were: 5% below 21, 11% between 21 and 23, 25% between 24 and 26, 20% between 27 and 28, and 39% above 28. 61% of recent freshmen were in the top fifth of their class; 88% were in the top two fifths.

Requirements: The SAT or ACT is required. The sum of the high school student's class rank percentile and aptitude exam percentile must be 120 or higher. Candidates must be graduates of an accredited secondary school or have the GED. The applicant must have completed 16 academic credit units, including 4 each in English and math, 3 each in science and social studies, and 2 in a foreign language. AP and CLEP credits are accepted. Important factors in the admissions decision are leadership record, extracurricular activities record, and advanced placement or honor courses.

Procedure: Freshmen are admitted fall, winter, and summer. Entrance exams should be taken late in the junior year or early in the senior year. Applications should be filed by July 1 for fall entry, December 1 for spring entry, and May 1 for summer entry, along with a $35 fee. Notification is sent on a rolling basis. A waiting list is an active part of the admissions procedure. Applications are accepted on-line.

Transfer: 254 transfer students enrolled in a recent year. Applicants with fewer than 24 semester hours of college-level work must apply as freshmen; those with 24 or more must have attained at least a 2.0 GPA in all college-level courses. 60 of 120 credits required for the bachelor's degree must be completed at UMR.

Visiting: There are regularly scheduled orientations for prospective students, including a tour with a student, admissions and financial aid counseling, special interest contact, and a departmental visit with a faculty member. There are guides for informal visits and visitors may sit in on classes and stay overnight. To schedule a visit, contact UMR Visitor's Center at (573) 341-4165.

Financial Aid: UMR is a member of CSS. The FAFSA is required. Check with the school for current deadlines.

International Students: There were 107 international students enrolled in a recent year. They must score 550 on the written TOEFL or 213 on the electronic version or take the MELAB, the Comprehensive English Language Test, or the university's own test.

Computers: All students may access the system. There are no time limits and no fees.

Graduates: In a recent year, 743 bachelor's degrees were awarded. The most popular majors were mechanical engineering (17%), electrical engineering (11%), and civil engineering (10%). In an average class, 14% graduate in 4 years or less, 43% graduate in 5 years or less, and 57% graduate in 6 years or less. 561 companies recruited on campus in a recent year. Of a recent graduating class, 17% were enrolled in graduate school within 6 months of graduation and 79% were employed.

Admissions Contact: Lynn Stichnote, Director of Admissions. A video is available. E-mail: *admissions@umr.edu*
Web: *http://www.umr.edu/admissions*

UNIVERSITY OF MISSOURI/ST. LOUIS   D-2
St. Louis, MO 63121-4400   **(314) 516-UMSL**
888 GO-2-UMSL; Fax: (314) 516-5310

Full-time: 2403 men, 3484 women	**Faculty:** 391; I, --$
Part-time: 2524 men, 4208 women	**Ph.D.s:** 81%
Graduate: 999 men, 1779 women	**Student/Faculty:** 15 to 1
Year: semesters, summer session	**Tuition:** $7618 ($17,395)
Application Deadline: July 1	**Room & Board:** $6428
Freshman Class: 2227 applied, 1182 accepted, 542 enrolled	
SAT Verbal/Math: 550/540*	**ACT:** 24 **VERY COMPETITIVE**

The University of Missouri/St. Louis, founded in 1963, is a public institution offering undergraduate and graduate programs and conferring degrees in arts and sciences, business, nursing, education, engineering, and optometry. There are 7 undergraduate and 7 graduate schools. In addition to regional accreditation, UMSL has baccalaureate program accreditation with AACSB, ABET, CSWE, NASM, NCATE, and NLN. The 3 libraries contain 1,050,458 volumes, 1,249,971 microform items, and 3902 audio/video tapes/CDs/DVDs, and subscribe to 3199 periodicals including electronic. Computerized library services include interlibrary loans, database searching, Internet access, and laptop Internet portals. Special learning facilities include a learning resource center, art gallery, and planetarium. The Mercantile Library Collection is housed in the Thomas Jefferson Library. The 350-acre campus is in an urban area 10 miles north of downtown St. Louis. Including any residence halls, there are 44 buildings.

Student Life: 91% of undergraduates are from Missouri. Others are from 44 states, 81 foreign countries, and Canada. 68% are white; 15% African American. The average age of freshmen is 18; all undergraduates, 26. 27% do not continue beyond their first year; 73% remain to graduate.

Housing: 983 students can be accommodated in college housing, which includes coed dorms, on-campus apartments, off-campus apartments, married-student housing, and sorority houses. In addition, there are honors houses. On-campus housing is available on a first-come, first-served basis. Priority is given to out-of-town students. 92% of students commute. Alcohol is not permitted. All students may keep cars.

Activities: 1% of men belong to 3 national fraternities; 1% of women belong to 3 national sororities. There are 96 groups on campus, including art, band, cheerleading, chess, choir, chorale, chorus, computers, dance, debate, drama, ethnic, forensics, gay, honors, international, jazz band, literary magazine, newspaper, pep band, photography, political, professional, religious, social, social service, and student government. Popular campus events include Mirthday, Expo, and Welcome Week.

Sports: There are 5 intercollegiate sports for men and 6 for women, and 12 intramural sports for men and 12 for women. Facilities include indoor handball/racquetball, basketball, volleyball, and badminton courts, wrestling, dance, and conditioning rooms, and a swimming pool; outdoors, there are intramural fields and facilities for baseball, soccer, handball, racquetball, and tennis.

Disabled Students: All of the campus is accessible. Wheelchair ramps, elevators, special parking, specially equipped rest rooms, special class scheduling, lowered drinking fountains, lowered telephones, and special housing are available.

Services: Counseling and information services are available, as is tutoring in most subjects, including math and writing labs. There is remedial math.

Campus Safety and Security: Measures include 24-hour foot and vehicle patrol, self-defense education, security escort services, and shuttle buses. There are informal discussions, pamphlets/posters/films, emergency telephones, lighted pathways/sidewalks, and criminal investigations.

Programs of Study: UMSL confers B.A., B.S., B.E.S., B.F.A., B.G.S., B.L.S., B.M., B.M.E., B.S.Acc., B.S.B.A., B.S.C.I.E., B.S.Ed., B.S.E.E., B.S.M.E., B.S.MIS., B.S.N., B.S.P.P.A., and B.S.W. degrees. Master's and doctoral degrees are also awarded. Bachelor's degrees are awarded in BIOLOGICAL SCIENCE (biology/biological science), BUSINESS (accounting, business administration and management, and management information systems), COMMUNICATIONS AND THE ARTS (art history and appreciation, communications, dance, dramatic arts, English, French, German, music, Spanish, and studio art), COMPUTER AND PHYSICAL SCIENCE (chemistry, computer science, mathematics, and physics), EDUCATION (early childhood, education, elementary, music, physical, secondary, and special), ENGINEERING AND ENVIRONMENTAL DESIGN (civil engineering, electrical/electronics engineering, and mechanical engineering), HEALTH PROFESSIONS (nursing), SOCIAL SCIENCE (anthropology, criminal justice, economics, history, liberal arts/general studies, philosophy, political science/government, psychology, social work, and sociology). Business, chemistry, and education are the strongest academically. Business, education, and nursing are the largest.

Required: To graduate, students must complete 120 credit hours, 42 of which must be in the area of general education. They must maintain a 2.0 GPA. The number of hours required for the major varies.

Special: Cross-registration with Washington University, St. Louis University, and St. Louis Community College and cooperative programs in all majors are offered. Study abroad in 32 countries, including England, France, and Germany, is available. Most degree programs are available through the Evening Courses. Some work-study is available. There is an accelerated nursing degree program and student-designed majors for the B.L.S. There are 24 national honor societies, a freshman honors program, and 16 departmental honors programs.

Faculty/Classroom: 54% of faculty are male; 46%, female. The average class size in an introductory lecture is 47; in a laboratory, 19; and in a regular course, 17.

Admissions: 53% of the 2005-2006 applicants were accepted. The SAT scores for the 2005-2006 freshman class were: Verbal--36% below 500, 32% between 500 and 599, 26% between 600 and 700, and 6% above 700; Math--32% below 500, 38% between 500 and 599, 28% between 600 and 700, and 2% above 700. The ACT scores were 22% below 21, 31% between 21 and 23, 27% between 24 and 26, 10% between 27 and 28, and 10% above 28. 41% of the current freshmen were in the top fifth of their class; 74% were in the top two fifths. 11 freshmen graduated first in their class.

Requirements: The SAT or ACT is required. In addition, applicants are required to have a total of 17 units, including 4 each in English and math, 3 each in social studies and science, 2 in the same foreign language, and 1 in fine arts. Class rank and test scores are used to determine eligibility for admission. AP and CLEP credits are accepted.

Procedure: Freshmen are admitted fall, spring, and summer. Entrance exams should be taken in the junior year. There is an early admissions plan. There is a rolling admissions plan. Applications should be filed by July 1 for fall entry, December 1 for winter entry, and May 1 for summer entry, along with a $35 fee. Notification is sent on a rolling basis. Applications are accepted on-line.

Transfer: 1911 transfer students enrolled in 2004-2005. Transfer students must have earned a minimum of 24 credit hours and maintained a minimum 2.0 GPA. 30 of 120 credits required for the bachelor's degree must be completed at UMSL.

Visiting: There are regularly scheduled orientations for prospective students, including a 20-minute information session, special appointments if needed, and a campus walking tour. There are guides for informal visits and visitors may sit in on classes and stay overnight. To schedule a visit, contact Yolanda Weathersby at (314) 516-5460 or *weathersby@umsl.edu.*

Financial Aid: The FAFSA is required.

International Students: The school actively recruits these students. They must achieve a satisfactory score on the TOEFL and also take the college's own test.

Computers: Wireless access is available. There are more than 1000 PCs on campus in classroom and open lab facilities for student usage. All students have access to the campus wireless network. Both types are acessed by student Single Sign On (SSO) ID and password. All students may access the system. There are no time limits. The fee is $11 per credit hour. It is strongly recommended that all students have a personal computer.

Graduates: From July 1, 2004 to June 30, 2005, 1902 bachelor's degrees were awarded. The most popular majors were business (28%), education (15%), and social science/history (11%). In an average class, 21% graduate in 4 years, 17% graduate in 5 years, and 6% graduate in 6 years. 328 companies recruited on campus in 2004-2005. Of the 2004 graduating class, 8% were enrolled in graduate school within 6 months of graduation and 85% were employed.

Admissions Contact: Jerry D. Hoffman, Associate Director of Undergraduate Admissions. E-mail: *admissionsu@msx.umsl.edu* Web: *www.umsl.edu*

WASHINGTON UNIVERSITY IN SAINT LOUIS   D-2

St. Louis, MO 63130-4899   (314) 935-6000
(800) 638-0700; Fax: (314) 935-4290

Full-time: 3023 men, 3146 women	**Faculty:** I, ++$
Part-time: 530 men, 767 women	**Ph.D.s:** n/av
Graduate: 3136 men, 2781 women	**Student/Faculty:** n/av
Year: semesters, summer session	**Tuition:** $32,042
Application Deadline: January 15	**Room & Board:** $10,064
Freshman Class: 21,515 applied, 4044 accepted, 1388 enrolled	
SAT or ACT: required	**MOST COMPETITIVE**

Washington University, founded in 1853, is a private, independent institution offering undergraduate and graduate programs in arts and sciences, business, architecture, engineering, art, and professional programs in law, medicine (including physical therapy and occupational therapy), and social work. There are 5 undergraduate and 8 graduate schools. In addition to regional accreditation, Washington U. has baccalaureate program accreditation with AACSB, ABET, and NASAD. The 14 libraries contain 3,694,504 volumes, 3,355,312 microform items, and 74,196 audio/video tapes/CDs/DVDs, and subscribe to 44,806 periodicals including electronic. Computerized library services include the card catalog, interlibrary loans, database searching, Internet access, and laptop Internet portals. Special learning facilities include a learning resource center, art gallery, planetarium, radio station, TV station, dance studio, professional theater, observatory, and studio theater. The 169-acre campus is in a suburban area 7 miles west of downtown St. Louis. Including any residence halls, there are 108 buildings.

Student Life: 88% of undergraduates are from out of state, mostly the Midwest. Students are from 50 states, 64 foreign countries, and Canada. 63% are from public schools. 64% are white; 10% Asian American. 25% claim no religious affiliation; 20% Catholic; 20% Jewish. The average age of freshmen is 18; all undergraduates, 21. 4% do not continue beyond their first year; 91% remain to graduate.

Housing: 4580 students can be accommodated in college housing, which includes single-sex and coed dorms, on-campus apartments, off-campus apartments, married-student housing, and fraternity houses. In addition, there are special-interest, sprcial-interest suites within residence halls, upper-class housing, single-sex floors in coed buildings, on-campus, transfer-specific housing , and small group housing for students who share common interests and goals. On-campus housing is guaranteed for the freshman year only and is available on a lottery system for upperclassmen. 63% of students live on campus; of those, 97% remain on campus on weekends. Upperclassmen may keep cars.

Activities: 25% of men belong to 12 national fraternities; 25% of women belong to 6 national sororities. There are 200 groups on campus, including art, band, cheerleading, chess, choir, chorale, chorus, computers, dance, debate, drama, ethnic, film, forensics, gay, honors, international, jazz band, literary magazine, musical theater, newspaper, opera, orchestra, pep band, photography, political, professional, radio and TV, religious, social, social service, student government, symphony, and yearbook. Popular campus events include multicultural celebrations, College Bowl, and student-run carnival.

Sports: There are 9 intercollegiate sports for men and 9 for women, and 31 intramural sports for men and 30 for women. Facilities include gyms, a swimming pool, tracks, a weight room, saunas, recreational playing fields, a football stadium, a fitness center, and racquetball, tennis, handball, wallyball, and squash courts.

Disabled Students: 95% of the campus is accessible. Wheelchair ramps, elevators, special parking, specially equipped rest rooms, special class scheduling, lowered drinking fountains, lowered telephones, and magnification devices and hearing-assist devices are available.

Services: Counseling and information services are available, as is tutoring in every subject. There is a reader service for the blind.

Campus Safety and Security: Measures include 24-hour foot and vehicle patrol, self-defense education, security escort services, and shuttle buses. There are informal discussions, pamphlets/posters/films, emergency telephones, and lighted pathways/sidewalks.

Programs of Study: Washington U. confers B.A., B.S., B.F.A., B.M., B.S.B.A, B.S.B.M.E., B.S.C.E., B.S.Ch.E., B.S.C.S., B.S.Co.E., B.S.E.E., B.S.I.M., B.S.M.E., and B.S.S.E. degrees. Master's and doctoral degrees are also awarded. Bachelor's degrees are awarded in AGRICULTURE (environmental studies and plant science), BIOLOGICAL SCIENCE (biochemistry, biology/biological science, biophysics, and neurosciences), BUSINESS (accounting, banking and finance, business administration and management, business economics, entrepreneurial studies, human resources, international business management, international economics, marketing management, marketing/retailing/merchandising, and trade and industrial supervision and management), COMMUNICATIONS AND THE ARTS (advertising, American literature, Arabic, art history and appreciation, ceramic art and design, Chinese, classical languages, classics, communications, comparative literature, creative writing, dance, design, dramatic arts, drawing, East Asian languages and literature, English, English literature, film arts, fine arts, French, German, Germanic languages and literature, graphic design,

Greek (classical), Hebrew, illustration, Italian, Japanese, journalism, languages, Latin, literature, music, music theory and composition, painting, performing arts, photography, printmaking, romance languages and literature, Russian, sculpture, Spanish, studio art, and visual and performing arts), COMPUTER AND PHYSICAL SCIENCE (applied mathematics, chemistry, computer programming, computer science, earth science, geology, information sciences and systems, mathematics, physical sciences, physics, and statistics), EDUCATION (art, education, elementary, foreign languages, mathematics, middle school, science, secondary, social science, and social studies), ENGINEERING AND ENVIRONMENTAL DESIGN (aerospace studies, architectural technology, architecture, bioengineering, biomedical engineering, chemical engineering, civil engineering, commercial art, computer engineering, electrical/electronics engineering, engineering, engineering mechanics, engineering physics, environmental science, mechanical engineering, systems engineering, and technology and public affairs), HEALTH PROFESSIONS (pharmacy, predentistry, premedicine, prepharmacy, and preveterinary science), SOCIAL SCIENCE (African American studies, African studies, American studies, anthropology, archeology, area studies, Asian/Oriental studies, biopsychology, East Asian studies, Eastern European studies, economics, ethnic studies, European studies, fashion design and technology, history, humanities, industrial and organizational psychology, interdisciplinary studies, international relations, international studies, Islamic studies, Judaic studies, Latin American studies, medieval studies, Middle Eastern studies, Near Eastern studies, philosophy, political science/government, psychology, religion, Russian and Slavic studies, social science, South Asian studies, systems science, urban studies, Western European studies, and women's studies). Natural sciences and engineering are the strongest academically. Natural sciences, engineering, and social sciences are the largest.

Required: Students must complete 120 credits and maintain a minimum GPA of 2.0. In addition, all students must complete a course in English composition and 3 courses in the major liberal arts disciplines.

Special: Opportunities are provided for cooperative programs with other schools, internships, work-study programs, study abroad, a Washington (D.C.) semester, accelerated degree programs, a B.A.-B.S. engineering degree, credit by examination, nondegree study, pass/fail options, and dual and student-designed majors. There are 18 national honor societies, including Phi Beta Kappa.

Faculty/Classroom: 69% of faculty are male; 31%, female. The average class size in an introductory lecture is 24; in a laboratory, 16; and in a regular course, 20.

Admissions: 19% of the 2005-2006 applicants were accepted. The SAT scores for the 2005-2006 freshman class were: Verbal--3% between 500 and 599, 38% between 600 and 700, and 59% above 700; Math--1% between 500 and 599, 26% between 600 and 700, and 73% above 700. The ACT scores were 3% between 24 and 26, 9% between 27 and 28, and 88% above 28. There were 237 National Merit finalists. 141 freshmen graduated first in their class.

Requirements: The SAT or ACT is required. The ACT Optional Writing test is also required. In addition, an essay is required from all applicants. Fine arts students may submit portfolios. 4 years of English, math, science, and social science/history, and 2 of a foreign language are recommended. Also required are recommendations from a teacher and a counselor. AP credits are accepted. Important factors in the admissions decision are advanced placement or honor courses, evidence of special talent, and extracurricular activities record.

Procedure: Freshmen are admitted in the fall. Entrance exams should be taken by December of the senior year. There are early decision and deferred admissions plans. Early decision applications should be filed by November 15; regular applications, by January 15 for fall entry, along with a $55 fee. Notification of early decision is sent December 15; regular decision, April 1. 144 applicants were on the 2005 waiting list; 29 were admitted. Applications are accepted on-line.

Transfer: 147 transfer students enrolled in 2004-2005. Students less than 5 years out of high school must submit an official transcript from secondary schools previously attended. A minimum GPA of 3.0 is required. An interview is recommended. If the student has taken the SAT or the ACT in the last 5 years, results must be submitted. College transcript(s) and recommendations from a professor and dean/adviser are required. 36 of 120 credits required for the bachelor's degree must be completed at Washington U.

Visiting: There are regularly scheduled orientations for prospective students, consisting of group presentations followed by a campus tour, as well as visits to classes and meetings with current students and faculty. There are guides for informal visits and visitors may sit in on classes and stay overnight. To schedule a visit, contact the Office of Undergraduate Admissions at *admissions@wustl.edu*.

Financial Aid: In a recent year, 58% of all full-time freshmen and 60% of continuing full-time students received some form of financial aid. 42% of full-time freshmen and 46% of continuing full-time students received need-based aid. 50% of undergraduates work part time. Average annual earnings from campus work are $2000. Washington U. is a member of CSS. The CSS/Profile or FAFSA, noncustodial parent's statement, student and parent 1040 tax return, or signed wavier if there is no tax re-

turn are required. The deadline for filing freshman financial aid applications for fall entry is February 15.

International Students: There are 288 international students enrolled. The school actively recruits these students. They must score satisfactorily on the TOEFL and also take the SAT, ACT, or the ACT Optional Writing.

Computers: Wireless access is available. Specialized computing resources are available to students. The Center for Engineering Computing provides access to about 100 computing stations accessible from the campus-wide network. The School of Business provides a student lab with more than 65 PCs. In addition, Residental Technology Services provides 11 computer clusters throughout the residence halls that are available 24 hours a day. All rooms in the residence halls have Internet connections. The Olin Library provides wireless access to the Internet, e-mail, and a variety of other specialized software. All students may access the system 24 hours per day, 7 days per week. There are no time limits and no fees.

Graduates: From July 1, 2004 to June 30, 2005, 1529 bachelor's degrees were awarded. The most popular majors were biology and psychology (20%), engineering (14%), and business (11%). In an average class, 1% graduate in 3 years or less, 82% graduate in 4 years or less, 90% graduate in 5 years or less, and 91% graduate in 6 years or less. 400 companies recruited on campus in 2004-2005. Of the 2004 graduating class, 33% were enrolled in graduate school within 6 months of graduation and 62% were employed.

Admissions Contact: Office of Undergraduate Admissions. A video is available. E-mail: *admissions@wustl.edu*.
Web: *http://admissions.wustl.edu*

WEBSTER UNIVERSITY   D-2
St. Louis, MO 63119-3194

(314) 968-6991
(800) 75-ENROL; Fax: (314) 968-7115

Full-time: 1482 men, 1915 women	**Faculty:** 170; IIA, av$
Part-time: 566 men, 936 women	**Ph.D.s:** 80%
Graduate: 6522 men, 8875 women	**Student/Faculty:** 19 to 1
Year: semesters, summer session	**Tuition:** $17,210
Application Deadline: March 1	**Room & Board:** $7070
Freshman Class: 1368 applied, 807 accepted, 407 enrolled	
SAT Verbal/Math: 610/540*	**ACT:** 24 **VERY COMPETITIVE**

Webster University, founded in 1915, is an independent institution with programs in fine and performing arts, liberal arts and sciences, education, nursing, and business. There are 5 undergraduate and 5 graduate schools. In addition to regional accreditation, Webster has baccalaureate program accreditation with NASM and NLN. The library contains 299,339 volumes, 137,000 microform items, and 17,355 audio/video tapes/CDs/DVDs, and subscribes to 15,603 periodicals including electronic. Computerized library services include the card catalog, interlibrary loans, database searching, and Internet access. Special learning facilities include a learning resource center, art gallery, radio station, a media center, a writing center, and a theater. The 47-acre campus is in a suburban area 12 miles southwest of St. Louis. Including any residence halls, there are 45 buildings.

Student Life: 58% of undergraduates are from Missouri. Others are from 43 states, 102 foreign countries, and Canada. 67% are from public schools. 57% are white; 19% foreign nationals; 10% African American. The average age of freshmen is 20; all undergraduates, 25. 20% do not continue beyond their first year; 57% remain to graduate.

Housing: 500 students can be accommodated in college housing, which includes single-sex and coed dorms and on-campus apartments. In addition, there are special-interest houses, on-campus houses, and substance-free housing. On-campus housing is guaranteed for the freshman year only, is available on a first-come, first-served basis, and is available on a lottery system for upperclassmen. Priority is given to out-of-town students. 85% of students commute. All students may keep cars.

Activities: There are no fraternities or sororities. There are 48 groups on campus, including amnesty, art, band, cheerleading, chess, choir, chorale, chorus, computers, dance, debate, departmental, drama, ethnic, film, forensics, gay, honors, international, jazz band, literary magazine, musical theater, newspaper, opera, orchestra, outdoor, photography, political, professional, radio and TV, religious, social, social service, student government, symphony, and women. Popular campus events include Spring Fest, Back-to-School Dance, and Multicultural Week.

Sports: There are 6 intercollegiate sports for men and 7 for women, and 4 intramural sports for men and 4 for women. Facilities include a gym, an athletic training center, a sauna, a fitness center, a 25-yard, 6-lane indoor swiming pool, and a chipping and putting green.

Disabled Students: 75% of the campus is accessible. Wheelchair ramps, elevators, special parking, specially equipped rest rooms, special class scheduling, lowered drinking fountains, lowered telephones, special housing, telephones for the hearing impaired, automatic door openers, a reading machine, computer for paraplegic students, reading and writing software, deaf interpreters, note takers, and textbooks on tape. All TV monitors in classrooms have closed caption capabilities.

Services: Counseling and information services are available, as is tutoring in most subjects. There is a reader service for the blind. Peer tutoring and study skills training are available.

Campus Safety and Security: Measures include 24-hour foot and vehicle patrol, self-defense education, security escort services, and informal discussions. There are pamphlets/posters/films, emergency telephones, and lighted pathways/sidewalks.

Programs of Study: Webster confers B.A., B.S., B.B.A., B.F.A., B.M., B.M.Ed., and B.S.N. degrees. Master's and doctoral degrees are also awarded. Bachelor's degrees are awarded in BIOLOGICAL SCIENCE (biology/biological science), BUSINESS (accounting, business administration and management, and management science), COMMUNICATIONS AND THE ARTS (advertising, art, audio technology, broadcasting, communications, dance, dramatic arts, English, film arts, French, German, journalism, literature, media arts, music, musical theater, photography, public relations, Spanish, theater design, and video), COMPUTER AND PHYSICAL SCIENCE (computer science, information sciences and systems, and mathematics), EDUCATION (education and music), ENGINEERING AND ENVIRONMENTAL DESIGN (environmental science), HEALTH PROFESSIONS (nursing), SOCIAL SCIENCE (anthropology, economics, history, international relations, international studies, law, philosophy, political science/government, psychology, religion, social science, and sociology). Liberal arts is the strongest academically. Business is the largest.

Required: To graduate, students must complete at least 128 semester hours, with a minimum GPA of 2.0. A freshman seminar is required; otherwise, the curriculum requires specific courses within the major field of study only, as well as successful completion of an approved major, and successful completion of 9 general education goals, usually by taking a 3-credit hour course in each area. At least 30 semester credits of a student's final 36 credits must be earned at Webster.

Special: Students may cross-register with Washington University and the University of Missouri/Columbia, and with Fontbonne, Maryville, Lindenwood, and Missouri Baptist Colleges and Eden Seminary. The university offers co-op programs, work-study programs, internships, dual majors, student-designed majors, B.A.-B.S. degrees, a 3-2 engineering degree with the University of Missouri/Columbia and Washington University, and a 3-4 architecture program with Washington University. Study abroad, nondegree study, pass/fail options, and credit for life, military, and work experience are available. There is 1 national honor society.

Faculty/Classroom: 57% of faculty are male; 43%, female. 99% teach undergraduates. No introductory courses are taught by graduate students. The average class size in an introductory lecture is 15; in a laboratory, 10; and in a regular course, 15.

Admissions: 59% of the 2005-2006 applicants were accepted. The SAT scores for the 2005-2006 freshman class were: Verbal--10% below 500, 38% between 500 and 599, 45% between 600 and 700, and 7% above 700; Math--22% below 500, 44% between 500 and 599, 28% between 600 and 700, and 6% above 700. The ACT scores were 18% below 21, 30% between 21 and 23, 27% between 24 and 26, 12% between 27 and 28, and 13% above 28. 43% of the current freshmen were in the top fifth of their class; 71% were in the top two fifths. There were 2 National Merit semifinalists. 11 freshmen graduated first in their class.

Requirements: The SAT or ACT is required. The ACT Optional Writing test is also required for some programs. In addition, applicants must be graduates of an accredited secondary school. The GED is accepted. Webster recommends that students complete 16 high school academic units, including 4 units of English, 3 each of social studies/history and math, and 2 each of foreign language, science, and electives. An essay is required of all students, and a portfolio or audition is required for art, dance, music, musical theater, and film. Webster requires applicants to be in the upper 50% of their class. A GPA of 2.5 is required. AP and CLEP credits are accepted. Important factors in the admissions decision are advanced placement or honor courses, leadership record, and recommendations by school officials.

Procedure: Freshmen are admitted fall and spring. Entrance exams should be taken in the spring of the junior year. There are early admissions, deferred admissions, and rolling admissions plans. Applications should be filed by March 1 for fall entry and December 1 for spring entry, along with a $25 fee. Notification is sent on a rolling basis. Applications are accepted on-line.

Transfer: 507 transfer students enrolled in 2004-2005. Applicants for transfer must have a minimum GPA of 2.5. for college credit completed. If they have fewer than 30 transferable hours, they must submit high school transcripts. 30 of 128 credits required for the bachelor's degree must be completed at Webster.

Visiting: There are regularly scheduled orientations for prospective students, consisting of an open house, which includes classes, meetings with faculty, a financial aid workshop, a tour of the university, and a student activities overview. There are guides for informal visits and visitors may sit in on classes and stay overnight. To schedule a visit, contact Visit Coordinator at (800) 753-6765 or *admit@webster.edu*.

Financial Aid: In 2005-2006, 92% of all full-time freshmen and 64% of continuing full-time students received some form of financial aid. 76% of full-time freshmen and 45% of continuing full-time students received need-based aid. The average freshman award was $17,176. Need-based scholarships or need-based grants averaged $5335; need-based self-help aid (loans and jobs) averaged $3972 ($4625 maximum); and other non-need-based awards and non-need-based scholarships averaged $6142. 9% of undergraduates work part time. Average annual earnings from campus work are $1992. The average financial indebtedness of the 2005 graduate was $17,279. The FAFSA and the college's own financial statement are required. The deadline for filing freshman financial aid applications for fall entry is April 1.

International Students: There are 142 international students enrolled. The school actively recruits these students. A satisfactory score is required on the written TOEFL. Applicants must also take the Comprehensive English Language Test, written and oral/listening tests, IELTS and also take SAT or ACT if they are graduates of U.S. high schools or international secondary schools that use English as the language of instruction.

Computers: Wireless access is available. There are 450 PCs on campus in the library, labs, and classrooms. There are no time limits and no fees.

Graduates: From July 1, 2004 to June 30, 2005, 1234 bachelor's degrees were awarded. The most popular majors were management (19%), computer science (9%), and business (7%). In an average class, 1% graduate in 3 years or less, 42% graduate in 4 years or less, 53% graduate in 5 years or less, and 57% graduate in 6 years or less. 60 companies recruited on campus in 2004-2005. Of the 2004 graduating class, 10% were enrolled in graduate school within 6 months of graduation and 84% were employed.

Admissions Contact: Niel DeVasto, Director, Undergraduate Admissions. A video is available. E-mail: *admit@websteruniv.edu* Web: *www.webster.edu*

WESTMINSTER COLLEGE C-2

Fulton, MO 65251

(573) 592-5251
(800) 475-3361; Fax: (573) 592-5255

Full-time: 513 men, 375 women	**Faculty:** 58; IIB, -$
Part-time: 3 men	**Ph.D.s:** 80%
Graduate: none	**Student/Faculty:** 15 to 1
Year: semesters, summer session	**Tuition:** $13,410
Application Deadline: open	**Room & Board:** $5650
Freshman Class: 1155 applied, 908 accepted, 270 enrolled	
SAT Verbal/Math: 530/560*	**ACT:** 24 **VERY COMPETITIVE**

Westminster College, founded in 1851, is a private liberal arts and sciences college affiliated with the Presbyterian Church (U.S.A.). The 2 libraries contain 97,177 volumes, 19,049 microform items, and 9199 audio/video tapes/CDs/DVDs, and subscribe to 16,685 periodicals including electronic. Computerized library services include the card catalog, interlibrary loans, database searching, Internet access, and laptop Internet portals. Special learning facilities include a learning resource center, a photospectrometer lab, a multimedia language and learning lab, a multimedia classroom, and the Winston Churchill Memorial Museum. The 65-acre campus is in a small town 20 miles east of Columbia. Including any residence halls, there are 26 buildings.

Student Life: 64% of undergraduates are from Missouri. Others are from 24 states, 42 foreign countries, and Canada. 75% are from public schools. 81% are white; 10% foreign nationals. 56% are Protestant; 20% Catholic; 15% claim no religious affiliation. The average age of freshmen is 18; all undergraduates, 20. 24% do not continue beyond their first year; 55% remain to graduate.

Housing: 455 students can be accommodated in college housing, which includes single-sex and coed dormitories, off-campus apartments, and fraternity houses. In addition, there are special-interest houses. On-campus housing is guaranteed for all 4 years. 85% of students live on campus; of those, 95% remain on campus on weekends. All students may keep cars.

Activities: 56% of men belong to 6 national fraternities; 49% of women belong to 3 national sororities. There are 56 groups on campus, including art, Blue Blazers Investment Club, cheerleading, choir, chorale, chorus, drama, ethnic, honors, international, literary magazine, Multicultural Club, musical theater, newspaper, pep band, photography, political, professional, religious, social, social service, student government, and yearbook. Popular campus events include Alumni Weekend, College Bowl, and Fulton Jazz Festival.

Sports: There are 6 intercollegiate sports for men and 6 for women, and 16 intramural sports for men and 10 for women. Facilities include an 800-seat gym, an aerobic training center, weight room and training room, football, baseball, softball, and soccer fields, a field sports area, tennis, racquetball, and sand volleyball courts, a swimming pool, an indoor rifle range, and a 1500-seat auditorium/arena.

Disabled Students: 80% of the campus is accessible. Wheelchair ramps, elevators, special parking, specially equipped rest rooms, special class scheduling, lowered drinking fountains, and lowered telephones are available.

Services: Counseling and information services are available, as is tutoring in most subjects. There is remedial math and reading.

Campus Safety and Security: Measures include 24-hour foot and vehicle patrol, self-defense education, security escort services, and informal discussions. There are pamphlets/posters/films, emergency telephones, and lighted pathways/sidewalks.

Programs of Study: Westminster confers the B.A. degree. Bachelor's degrees are awarded in BIOLOGICAL SCIENCE (biology/biological science), BUSINESS (accounting, business administration and management, international business management, and management information systems), COMMUNICATIONS AND THE ARTS (English, French, and Spanish), COMPUTER AND PHYSICAL SCIENCE (chemistry, computer science, mathematics, and physics), EDUCATION (elementary, middle school, physical, and secondary), ENGINEERING AND ENVIRONMENTAL DESIGN (environmental science), SOCIAL SCIENCE (anthropology, economics, history, international studies, philosophy, political science/government, psychology, religion, and sociology). English, biology, and psychology are the strongest academically. Business administration, biology, and psychology are the largest.

Required: To graduate, students must complete 122 credit hours, including a maximum of 40 hours in their major, with a minimum GPA of 2.0. All students are required to take Westminster seminar, academic writing, statistics or calculus, 4 hours of foreign language, and 1 hour of phys ed. Students must also take 6 to 10 hours (37 to 42 total) in scientific inquiry, historical awareness, fundamental questions, artistic expression, human behaviors and institutions, cultural diversity, and global interdependence. In addition, an integrative upper-level course, 2 writing intensive courses, and an upper-level course from a non-major academic division are required.

Special: Westminster offers co-op programs with colleges of the Mid-Missouri Associated Colleges and Universities, cross-registration with William Woods University, internships in all areas, study abroad in 15 countries, a Washington semester, a United Nations semester, and an urban studies program in Chicago. Student-designed majors are available as well as a 3-2 engineering degree with Washington University in St. Louis. The pass/fail option and dual majors are available. There are 15 national honor societies, a freshman honors program, and 8 departmental honors programs.

Faculty/Classroom: 66% of faculty are male; 34%, female. All teach undergraduates, 75% do research, and 75% do both. The average class size in an introductory lecture is 19; in a laboratory, 20; and in a regular course, 15.

Admissions: 79% of the 2005-2006 applicants were accepted. The SAT scores for the 2005-2006 freshman class were: Verbal--37% below 500, 38% between 500 and 599, 21% between 600 and 700, and 4% above 700; Math--28% below 500, 32% between 500 and 599, 35% between 600 and 700, and 5% above 700. The ACT scores were 13% below 21, 27% between 21 and 23, 37% between 24 and 26, 10% between 27 and 28, and 13% above 28. 40% of the current freshmen were in the top fifth of their class; 71% were in the top two fifths. There were 2 National Merit finalists and 3 semifinalists. 5 freshmen graduated first in their class.

Requirements: The SAT or ACT is required. In addition, applicants must be graduates of an accredited secondary school. The GED is also accepted. Students must have completed 4 years each of social studies and English, 3 years each of math and science, and 2 years each of a foreign language and history. An essay is required and an interview is recommended. Westminster requires applicants to be in the upper 50% of their class. A GPA of 2.5 is required. AP and CLEP credits are accepted. Important factors in the admissions decision are advanced placement or honor courses, leadership record, and extracurricular activities record.

Procedure: Freshmen are admitted to all sessions. Entrance exams should be taken in the junior year of high school. There are early decision, deferred admissions and a rolling admissions plans. Application deadlines are open. Applications are accepted on-line.

Transfer: 55 transfer students enrolled in 2004-2005. Applicants must have taken either the ACT or the SAT and must complete at least 4 semesters at Westminster as full-time students. 60 of 122 credits required for the bachelor's degree must be completed at Westminster.

Visiting: There are regularly scheduled orientations for prospective students, including 1-day summer programs with a general orientation and class registration. There are guides for informal visits and visitors may sit in on classes and stay overnight. To schedule a visit, contact Kelle Silvey, Officer of Enrollment Services at (573) 592-5195.

Financial Aid: In 2005-2006, 99% of all full-time students received some form of financial aid. 53% of full-time freshmen and 51% of continuing full-time students received need-based aid. The average freshman award was $11,700, with $2700 ($8000) maximum from need-based scholarships or need-based grants $16000 (2625 maximum) from need-based self-help aid (loans and jobs); and $7400 ($12,300) maximum from other non-need-based awards and non-need-based scholarships. 35% of undergraduates work part time. Average annual earnings from campus work are $1467. The average financial indebtedness of the 2005 graduate was $9100. The FAFSA is required. The priority date for freshman financial aid applications for fall entry is February 15.

International Students: There are 91 international students enrolled. The school actively recruits these students. They must score satisfactorily on the written TOEFL or on the electronic version.

Computers: Wireless access is available. All students may access the system. There are no time limits and no fees.

Graduates: From July 1, 2004 to June 30, 2005, 158 bachelor's degrees were awarded. The most popular majors were business administration (20%), management information/computer science (8%), and biology and psychology (8%). In an average class, 42% graduate in 4 years or less, 54% graduate in 5 years or less, and 55% graduate in 6 years or less. 71 companies recruited on campus in 2004-2005. Of the 2004 graduating class, 24% were enrolled in graduate school within 6 months of graduation and 90% were employed.

Admissions Contact: Patrick Kirby, Dean of Enrollment Services. E-mail: *kirbypt@jaynet.wcmo.edu* Web: *http://www.wcmo.edu*

WILLIAM JEWELL COLLEGE   B-2
Liberty, MO 64068

(816) 781-7700, ext. 5137
(800) 753-7009; Fax: (816) 415-5027

Full-time: 529 men, 756 women	**Faculty:** 76; IIB, -$
Part-time: 18 men, 28 women	**Ph.Ds:** 65%
Graduate: none	**Student/Faculty:** 17 to 1
Year: semesters, summer session	**Tuition:** $21,150
Application Deadline: August 15	**Room & Board:** $3190
Freshman Class: n/av	
SAT or ACT: required	**COMPETITIVE**

William Jewell College, founded in 1849, is an academically selective Christian liberal arts college and offers undergraduate programs in the arts and sciences, business, education, and health fields. In addition to regional accreditation, Jewell has baccalaureate program accreditation with NASM and CCNE. The library contains 271,275 volumes, 219,574 microform items, and 29,437 audio/video tapes/CDs/DVDs, and subscribes to 780 periodicals including electronic. Computerized library services include the card catalog, interlibrary loans, database searching, and Internet access. Special learning facilities include a learning resource center, art gallery, planetarium, and radio station. The 200-acre campus is in a suburban area 15 miles northeast of Kansas City. Including any residence halls, there are 23 buildings.

Student Life: 75% of undergraduates are from Missouri. Others are from 28 states, 12 foreign countries, and Canada. 90% are from public schools. 71% are white. 75% are Protestant; 20% Catholic. The average age of freshmen is 18; all undergraduates, 22. 19% do not continue beyond their first year.

Housing: 906 students can be accommodated in college housing, which includes single-sex and coed dorms, fraternity houses, and sorority houses. In addition, there are honors houses and language houses. On-campus housing is guaranteed for all 4 years. 63% of students live on campus; of those, 60% remain on campus on weekends. Alcohol is not permitted. All students may keep cars.

Activities: 33% of men belong to 3 national fraternities; 31% of women belong to 4 national sororities. There are 47 groups on campus, including cheerleading, choir, chorale, chorus, computers, dance, debate, drama, drill team, ethnic, honors, international, jazz band, ministries, musical theater, newspaper, orchestra, pep band, photography, political, professional, radio and TV, religious, social, social service, student government, symphony, and yearbook. Popular campus events include Parents/Grandparents Day, Hanging of the Green/Lighting of the Quad, and Undergraduate Research Colloquium.

Sports: There are 9 intercollegiate sports for men and 9 for women, and 12 intramural sports for men and 12 for women. Facilities include a football and soccer stadium, a complex for baseball and softball, a phys ed center with an indoor track, a dance room, and facilities for basketball, racquetball, swimming, indoor tennis, volleyball, and weight lifting. The total seating capacity of the stadium is 3200 and that of the indoor gym is 1000.

Disabled Students: 30% of the campus is accessible. Wheelchair ramps, elevators, special parking, specially equipped rest rooms, special class scheduling, lowered drinking fountains, and special housing are available.

Services: Counseling and information services are available, as is tutoring in most subjects.

Campus Safety and Security: Measures include 24-hour foot and vehicle patrol, self-defense education, informal discussions, and pamphlets/posters/films. There are emergency telephones and lighted pathways/sidewalks.

Programs of Study: Jewell confers B.A. and B.S. degrees. Bachelor's degrees are awarded in BIOLOGICAL SCIENCE (biochemistry and biology/biological science), BUSINESS (accounting, business administration and management, business economics, and international business management), COMMUNICATIONS AND THE ARTS (art, communications, dramatic arts, English, French, music, and Spanish), COMPUTER AND PHYSICAL SCIENCE (chemistry, computer science, information sciences and systems, mathematics, and physics), EDUCATION (elementary, music, and secondary), HEALTH PROFESSIONS (medical laboratory technology and nursing), SOCIAL SCIENCE (history, international relations, Japanese studies, philosophy, political science/government, psychology, and religion). Business is the largest.

Required: To graduate, students must complete a minimum of 124 credits with a minimum 2.0 GPA, fulfilling the proper core requirements for their major and degree. All students must take The Responsible Self in their first semester, and must also take courses in oral and written communication, phys ed, math, and foreign language, interdisciplinary courses in 4 categories, and a general education capstone course. Comprehensive exams in most majors are required.

Special: Internships for juniors or seniors, study abroad in Europe, Japan, Mexico, Australia, and Hong Kong, and a Washington semester are offered. B.A.-B.S. degrees, dual majors of any combination, an accelerated degree in nursing, student-designed majors, and 3-2 engineering degrees with Washington University and the Universities of Missouri and Kansas are available. The Oxbridge Honors Program for major study is patterned after the teaching methods of Oxford and Cambridge and includes a year at either Oxford or Cambridge. Leadership and service learning programs are offered. There are 13 national honor societies, a freshman honors program, and 13 departmental honors programs.

Faculty/Classroom: 51% of faculty are male; 49%, female. All teach undergraduates. The average class size in an introductory lecture is 30; in a laboratory, 20; and in a regular course, 15.

Admissions: 47% of the current freshmen were in the top fifth of their class; 84% were in the top two fifths. There were 3 National Merit finalists and 6 semifinalists. 18 freshmen graduated first in their class.

Requirements: The SAT or ACT is required. In addition, students must be graduates of an accredited secondary school; the GED is also accepted. The college recommends that applicants have taken 4 English courses and 4 academic electives, 3 courses each in math, social studies, and science, (of these, 1 must be a lab), and 2 in foreign language and in fine arts. An interview is recommended. An audition is advised for music applicants. AP and CLEP credits are accepted. Important factors in the admissions decision are advanced placement or honor courses, extracurricular activities record, and leadership record.

Procedure: Freshmen are admitted fall, spring, and summer. Entrance exams should be taken in the junior year. There are early admissions and deferred admissions plans. Applications should be filed by August 15 for fall entry, along with a $25 fee. The college accepts all in-state residents. Notification is sent on a rolling basis. Applications are accepted on-line.

Transfer: 74 transfer students enrolled in 2004-2005. Transfer students must have maintained a 2.0 GPA and be in good academic standing with their former schools and submit all college transcripts. Education majors must take the ACT, achieving a minimum score of 20. An interview is recommended for all students. 30 of 124 credits required for the bachelor's degree must be completed at Jewell.

Visiting: There are regularly scheduled orientations for prospective students, and personalized visits can be arranged upon request. There are guides for informal visits and visitors may sit in on classes and stay overnight. To schedule a visit, contact the Admission Office.

Financial Aid: In 2005-2006, 56% of all full-time freshmen and 57% of continuing full-time students received some form of financial aid. At least 47% of full-time freshmen and 50% of continuing full-time students received need-based aid. The average freshman award was $16,295. Need-based scholarships or need-based grants averaged $12,773; and need-based self-help aid (loans and jobs) averaged $4780. The average financial indebtedness of the 2005 graduate was $17,133. Jewell is a member of CSS. The FAFSA is required. The priority date for freshman financial aid applications for fall entry is March 1.

International Students: There were 13 international students enrolled in a recent year. The school actively recruits these students. They must take the TOEFL or the MELAB.

Computers: All students may access the system. There are no time limits and no fees. It is strongly recommended that all students have a personal computer.

Graduates: From July 1, 2004 to June 30, 2005, 291 bachelor's degrees were awarded. The most popular majors were business/marketing (25%), health professions and related sciences (18%), and psychology (9%). 36 companies recruited on campus in a recent year. Of the 2004 graduating class, 32% were enrolled in graduate school within 6 months of graduation and 77% were employed.

Admissions Contact: Chad Jolly, Dean of Enrollment Development. E-mail: *admission@william.jewell.edu* Web: *www.jewell.edu*

WILLIAM WOODS UNIVERSITY
Fulton, MO 65251

C-2

(573) 592-4221
(800) 995-3159; Fax: (573) 592-1146

Full-time: 197 men, 617 women	**Faculty:** 50
Part-time: 94 men, 243 women	**Ph.D.s:** 66%
Graduate: 670 men, 1096 women	**Student/Faculty:** 16 to 1
Year: semesters, summer session	**Tuition:** $15,120
Application Deadline: open	**Room & Board:** $5900
Freshman Class: 806 applied, 636 accepted, 308 enrolled	
SAT Verbal/Math: 529/501*	**ACT:** 22	**COMPETITIVE**

William Woods University, founded in 1870, is an independent professions-oriented, liberal arts institution affiliated with the Christian Church (Disciples of Christ). Unique programs of study include an equestrian studies program and a four-year American Sign Language Interpreting program. There is 1 graduate school. In addition to regional accreditation, William Woods has baccalaureate program accreditation with ABA, CAAHEP, and CSWE. The library contains 134,338 volumes, 11,072 microform items, and 28,711 audio/video tapes/CDs/DVDs, and subscribes to 15,796 periodicals including electronic. Computerized library services include the card catalog, interlibrary loans, database searching, and Internet access. Special learning facilities include a learning resource center, art gallery, radio station, 12 'smart classrooms' equipped with Smartboards and networked computers, labs for photography, foreign languages, and art, equestrian studies stables, a model courtroom, an American Sign Language interpreting lab, and an observatory. The 170-acre campus is in a small town 100 miles west of St. Louis. Including any residence halls, there are 35 buildings.

Student Life: 72% of undergraduates are from Missouri. Others are from 44 states, 14 foreign countries, and Canada. 88% are white. 50% are Baptist, Christian, Methodist, Lutheran, Presbyterian, Pentecostal, Episcopalian, or United Church of Christ; 25% Catholic; 20% claim no religious affiliation. The average age of freshmen is 18; all undergraduates, 25. 24% do not continue beyond their first year; 55% remain to graduate.

Housing: 712 students can be accommodated in college housing, which includes single-sex and coed dorms, on-campus apartments, fraternity houses, and sorority houses. In addition, there are special-interest houses. On-campus housing is guaranteed for all 4 years. 80% of students live on campus; of those, 50% remain on campus on weekends. All students may keep cars.

Activities: 43% of men belong to 2 national fraternities; 38% of women belong to 4 national sororities. There are 40 groups on campus, including art, choir, drama, honors, international, musical theater, newspaper, professional, radio and TV, religious, social, social service, student government, and yearbook. Popular campus events include Salute to the Arts, Campus Involvement and Activities Fair, and Autumn at the Woods.

Sports: There are 5 intercollegiate sports for men and 6 for women, and 7 intramural sports for men and 7 for women. Facilities include a gym, a fitness center, a sand volleyball court, tennis courts, soccer, baseball, and softball fields, a weight room, a lake with a sand beach, table tennis and pool tables, a cross-country trail equipped with FitTrail stations, and a sauna.

Disabled Students: 66% of the campus is accessible. Wheelchair ramps, elevators, special parking, specially equipped rest rooms, special class scheduling, lowered telephones, and campus access to TTY phones are available.

Services: Counseling and information services are available, as is tutoring in most subjects. There is a reader service for the blind and remedial math and writing. Interpreting is provided for the deaf upon request and receipt of supporting documentation.

Campus Safety and Security: Measures include 24-hour foot and vehicle patrol, self-defense education, security escort services, and informal discussions. There are pamphlets/posters/films, and lighted pathways/sidewalks. A student hotline allows students to call H-E-L-P from any phone on campus and be directly connected to the security dispatch office or on-call security officer.

Programs of Study: William Woods confers B.A., B.S., B.F.A., and B.S.W. degrees. Associate and master's degrees are also awarded. Bachelor's degrees are awarded in AGRICULTURE (equine science), BIOLOGICAL SCIENCE (biology/biological science), BUSINESS (accounting and business administration and management), COMMUNICATIONS AND THE ARTS (art, communications, dramatic arts, English, graphic design, journalism, and studio art), COMPUTER AND PHYSICAL SCIENCE (computer science, information sciences and systems, mathematics, and science), EDUCATION (athletic training, early childhood, elementary, middle school, physical, and special), SOCIAL SCIENCE (family/juvenile justice, history, interdisciplinary studies, international studies, interpreter for the deaf, paralegal studies, political science/government, psychology, and social work). Business, equestrian studies, and political/legal studies are the strongest academically. Business, equestrian studies, and ASL/English interpreting are the largest.

Required: Students must complete a minimum of 122 credits to graduate, including at least 30 in the major and 52 in Common Studies, with 7 in the natural sciences, 6 each in English, the humanities, and behavioral and social sciences, 3 each in oral communication, math, and fine or performing arts, and 2 in freshman seminar. They must have maintained a minimum GPA of 2.0.

Special: William Woods University offers cross-registration with schools in the Mid-Missouri Association of Colleges and Universities, internships in various fields, including equestrian studies and computer information systems, study abroad, a Washington semester, and work-study. An accelerated degree program in most majors, B.A.-B.S. degrees, and student-designed and dual majors are possible. Credit for life, military, and work experience and pass/fail are available. The LEAD (Leading, Educating, Achieving, and Developing) program provides awards ($5000 to residential students) to any incoming student who makes a commitment to attend a minimum number of campus activities and participate within the surrounding community. There are 12 national honor societies, and a freshman honors program.

Faculty/Classroom: 46% of faculty are male; 54%, female. All teach undergraduates. No introductory courses are taught by graduate students. The average class size in an introductory lecture is 25; in a laboratory, 15; and in a regular course, 25.

Admissions: 79% of the 2005-2006 applicants were accepted. The SAT scores for the 2005-2006 freshman class were: Verbal--36% below 500, 41% between 500 and 599, 14% between 600 and 700, and 9% above 700; Math--48% below 500, 38% between 500 and 599, and 14% between 600 and 700. The ACT scores were 39% below 21, 26% between 21 and 23, 21% between 24 and 26, 7% between 27 and 28, and 7% above 28. 27% of the current freshmen were in the top fifth of their class; 58% were in the top two fifths. 5 freshmen graduated first in their class.

Requirements: The SAT or ACT is required. Students must graduate within the top 50% of an accredited high school class to be admitted. The GED is also accepted. They must have completed 16 course units, 11 of which must be distributed among English, a foreign language, math, natural sciences, and social sciences. 2 references and an interview is recommended. A GPA of 2.5 is required. AP and CLEP credits are accepted. Important factors in the admissions decision are personality/intangible qualities, leadership record, and recommendations by school officials.

Procedure: Freshmen are admitted to all sessions. Entrance exams should be taken in the spring of the junior year or the fall of the senior year. There is a deferred admissions plan, and a rolling admissions plan. Application deadlines are open. Application fee is $25. Applications are accepted on-line.

Transfer: 55 transfer students enrolled in 2004-2005. Transfer students must submit high school transcripts or GED and all college transcripts. They must also provide 2 references and be in good standing with their previous institution. 30 of 122 credits required for the bachelor's degree must be completed at William Woods.

Visiting: There are regularly scheduled orientations for prospective students, including the opportunity to talk with an academic adviser and an extensive student development-directed orientation to campus life. There are guides for informal visits and visitors may sit in on classes and stay overnight. To schedule a visit, contact the Office of Enrollment Services at (800) 995-3159, ext. 4221 or admissions@williamwoods.edu.

Financial Aid: In 2005-2006, all full-time freshmen and 95% of continuing full-time students received some form of financial aid. The average freshman award was $12,863. Need-based scholarships or need-based grants averaged $9876; need-based self-help aid (loans and jobs) averaged $4058; and non-need-based athletic scholarships averaged $4592. 41% of undergraduates work part time. Average annual earnings from campus work are $1200. The average financial indebtedness of the 2005 graduate was $14,129. The FAFSA and the college's own financial statement are required. The deadline for filing freshman financial aid applications for fall entry is March 1.

International Students: There are 58 international students enrolled. The school actively recruits these students. They must score satisfactorily on the written TOEFL.

Computers: Wireless access is available. Students can access campus network resources through wired residence hall connections, a dedicated student computer lab, and wireless access points located in key buildings throughout the campus. All semester students receive an e-mail address and space on the campus network to store files. All students may access the system 7 days a week. There are no time limits. The fee is $70 per semester.

Graduates: From July 1, 2004 to June 30, 2005, 272 bachelor's degrees were awarded. The most popular majors were business (43%), computer information science (12%), and equestrian studies/equestrian administration (11%). In an average class, 43% graduate in 4 years or less, and 55% graduate in 6 years or less.

Admissions Contact: Jimmy Clay, Executive Director of Enrollment Services. E-mail: admissions@williamwoods.edu
Web: www.williamwoods.edu

MONTANA

POPULATION DENSITY
• 10,000 and over

0 20 40 60 80 100
Miles

CARROLL COLLEGE   C-2
Helena, MT 59625-0002
(406) 447-4384
(800) 992-3648; Fax: (406) 447-4533

Full-time: 550 men, 733 women | **Faculty:** 82
Part-time: 91 men, 125 women | **Ph.D.s:** 70%
Graduate: none | **Student/Faculty:** 16 to 1
Year: semesters, summer session | **Tuition:** $17,078
Application Deadline: June 1 | **Room & Board:** $6246
Freshman Class: 1002 applied, 798 accepted, 289 enrolled
SAT Verbal/Math: 534/540* | **ACT:** 24 | **COMPETITIVE+**

Carroll College, founded in 1909, is a small liberal arts college affiliated with the Roman Catholic Church. It offers undergraduate programs in arts and sciences, business, engineering, nursing, education, religion, and selected preprofessional training. In addition to regional accreditation, Carroll has baccalaureate program accreditation with CAHEA, CSWE, NLN, and NRPA. The library contains 89,003 volumes, 64,500 microform items, and 3890 audio/video tapes/CDs/DVDs, and subscribes to 504 periodicals including electronic. Computerized library services include the card catalog, interlibrary loans, database searching, and Internet access. Special learning facilities include a learning resource center, radio station, civil engineering lab, nursing lab (SimMan), performing arts theatre, and astronomical observatory. The 64-acre campus is in a small town 110 miles east of Missoula and 100 miles west of Bozeman. Including any residence halls, there are 16 buildings.

Student Life: 64% of undergraduates are from Montana. Students are from 30 states, 11 foreign countries, and Canada. 81% are from public schools. 67% are white. 67% are Catholic; 31% Lutheran, Methodist, Baptist. The average age of freshmen is 18; all undergraduates, 21. 21% do not continue beyond their first year; 60% remain to graduate.

Housing: 830 students can be accommodated in college housing, which includes single-sex and coed dorms, on-campus apartments, and a freshman dorm. On-campus housing is guaranteed for all 4 years. 54% of students live on campus; of those, 95% remain on campus on weekends. All students may keep cars.

Activities: There are no fraternities or sororities. There are 35 groups on campus, including art, cheerleading, choir, dance, drama, drill team, ethnic, film, forensics, honors, international, jazz band, literary magazine, musical theater, newspaper, pep band, political, professional, radio and TV, religious, social, social service, student government, and yearbook. Popular campus events include theme dances, Casino night, and softball tournament.

Sports: There are 3 intercollegiate sports for men and 5 for women, and 10 intramural sports for men and 10 for women. Facilities include basketball, tennis, and racquetball courts, weight-lifting, aerobics, and dance rooms, a swimming pool, football stadium, soccer field, fitness center, and a 4200-seat gym.

Disabled Students: 90% of the campus is accessible. Wheelchair ramps, elevators, special parking, specially equipped rest rooms, special class scheduling, and lowered drinking fountains are available.

Services: Counseling and information services are available, as is tutoring in most subjects, including writing, math, statistics, economics, chemistry, accounting, and anatomy and physiology. There is remedial math, reading, and writing.

Campus Safety and Security: Measures include security escort services, informal discussions, and lighted pathways/sidewalks.

Programs of Study: Carroll confers the B.A. degree. Associate degrees are also awarded. Bachelor's degrees are awarded in BIOLOGICAL SCIENCE (biology/biological science), BUSINESS (accounting and business administration and management), COMMUNICATIONS AND THE ARTS (classical languages, communications, creative writing, dramatic arts, English, French, performing arts, public relations, and Spanish), COMPUTER AND PHYSICAL SCIENCE (chemistry, computer science, and mathematics), EDUCATION (elementary, foreign languages, physical, secondary, and teaching English as a second/foreign language (TESOL/TEFOL)), ENGINEERING AND ENVIRONMENTAL DESIGN (civil engineering and environmental science), HEALTH PROFESSIONS (clinical science, health care administration, nursing, predentistry, premedicine, preoptometry, prepharmacy, and preveterinary science), SOCIAL SCIENCE (history, international relations, philosophy, political science/government, prelaw, psychology, public administration, religion, social science, and sociology). Business, nursing, and biology are the largest.

Required: To graduate, students must complete 122 semester hours and maintain the specific GPA and credit concentration required by their major. The college's general liberal arts requirements include courses in writing, communications, history, math, natural and social sciences, philosophy, theology, and fine arts.

Special: Carroll College offers a 3-2 engineering program leading to acceptance to any of 6 cooperating universities. In addition, internships, study abroad in Paris, Japan, Spain, Germany, Korea, and many other countries through a consortium for international studies, and work-study programs in certain fields are available. Students may take a dual major in any two fields of study, select an interdisciplinary major such as health information management, earn credit for life, military, and work experience, or pursue nondegree study. A pass/fail option is available. There are 6 national honor societies, including Phi Beta Kappa, a freshman honors program, and 5 departmental honors programs.

Faculty/Classroom: 62% of faculty are male; 38%, female. All teach undergraduates. The average class size in an introductory lecture is 22; in a laboratory, 13; and in a regular course, 17.

Admissions: 80% of the 2005-2006 applicants were accepted. The SAT scores for the 2005-2006 freshman class were: Verbal--30% below 500, 45% between 500 and 599, 22% between 600 and 700, and 3% above 700; Math--28% below 500, 44% between 500 and 599, 27% between 600 and 700, and 1% above 700. The ACT scores were 23% below 21, 25% between 21 and 23, 35% between 24 and 26, 9% between 27 and 28, and 7% above 28. 37% of the current freshmen were in the top fifth of their class; 69% were in the top two fifths. 22 freshmen graduated first in their class.

Requirements: The SAT or ACT is required. Students must be graduates of an accredited secondary school or have a GED. An essay is required. A GPA of 2.5 is required. AP and CLEP credits are accepted. Important factors in the admissions decision are advanced placement or honor courses, recommendations by school officials, and leadership record.

Procedure: Freshmen are admitted fall and spring. Entrance exams should be taken in the fall of the senior year. There are deferred admissions and rolling admissions plans. Applications should be filed by June 1 for fall entry, along with a $35 fee. Notification is sent on a rolling basis. Applications are accepted on-line.

Transfer: 72 transfer students enrolled in 2004-2005. Transfer students need a 2.5 GPA and must submit ACT or SAT scores if fewer than 30 college credits have been completed. Letters of recommendation are required. 30 of 122 credits required for the bachelor's degree must be completed at Carroll.

Visiting: There are regularly scheduled orientations for prospective students, consisting of several "Super Saturdays" and 3 visiting sessions in the summer, which include a tour of the campus, overnight housing, social activities, and preregistration for classes. Orientation takes place Thursday through Monday before the start of fall classes. There are guides for informal visits and visitors may sit in on classes and stay overnight. To schedule a visit, contact the Admissions Office at *cthornqu@carroll.edu*.

Financial Aid: In a recent year, 71% of all full-time freshmen and 68% of continuing full-time students received some form of financial aid. 61% of full-time freshmen and 60% of continuing full-time students received need-based aid. The average freshman award was $14,377. The average financial indebtedness of the recent year's graduate was $22,868. The FAFSA is required. The deadline for filing freshman financial aid applications for fall entry is March 1.

International Students: The school actively recruits these students. A satisfactory score is required on the written TOEFL. English-speaking students must submit SAT or ACT scores.

Computers: Wireless access is available. All students may access the system. There are no time limits and no fees.

Graduates: From July 1, 2004 to June 30, 2005, 229 bachelor's degrees were awarded. The most popular majors were business (21%), education (14%), and biology (12%). In an average class, 43% graduate in 4 years or less, 56% graduate in 5 years or less, and 57% graduate in 6 years or less.

Admissions Contact: Candace Cain, Dean of Enrollment Services. A video is available. E-mail: *enroll@caroll.edu* Web: *www.carroll.edu*

MONTANA STATE UNIVERSITY-BILLINGS D-3
Billings, MT 59101-0298

(406) 657-2158
(800) 565-MSUB; Fax: (406) 657-2302

Full-time: 1197 men, 1973 women	**Faculty:** 156; IIA, --$
Part-time: 375 men, 862 women	**Ph.D.s:** 87%
Graduate: 120 men, 345 women	**Student/Faculty:** 20 to 1
Year: semesters, summer session	**Tuition:** $4856 ($13,096)
Application Deadline: open	**Room & Board:** $4050
Freshman Class: 949 applied, 911 accepted, 602 enrolled	
SAT Verbal/Math: 500/513*	**ACT:** 21 COMPETITIVE

Montana State University-Billings, founded in 1927, is a comprehensive, regional, public university offering instructional and learning opportunities in the arts and sciences as well as professional programs in business, technology, human services, rehabilitation, and education. There are 6 undergraduate schools and 1 graduate school. In addition to regional ac-

creditation, MSU-Billings has baccalaureate program accreditation with CORE, NASAD, NASM, and NCATE. The 2 libraries contain 294,562 volumes, 530,891 microform items, and 3667 audio/video tapes/CDs/DVDs, and subscribe to 790 periodicals including electronic. Computerized library services include the card catalog, interlibrary loans, database searching, and Internet access. Special learning facilities include a learning resource center, art gallery, radio station, a scientific field station, a small business institute, an urban institute, a special education learning center, a disabilities center, a center for business enterprise, and a center for applied economic research. The 92-acre campus is in an urban area in Billings. Including any residence halls, there are 21 buildings.

Student Life: 93% of undergraduates are from Montana. Others are from 37 states, 17 foreign countries, and Canada. 97% are from public schools. 85% are white. The average age of freshmen is 21; all undergraduates, 25. 37% do not continue beyond their first year; 26% remain to graduate.

Housing: 558 students can be accommodated in college housing, which includes single-sex and coed dorms and married-student housing. On-campus housing is available on a first-come, first-served basis. 83% of students commute. All students may keep cars.

Activities: There are no fraternities or sororities. There are 53 groups on campus, including art, band, cheerleading, choir, chorale, chorus, computers, drama, ethnic, honors, international, jazz band, literary magazine, newspaper, orchestra, pep band, political, professional, radio and TV, religious, social, social service, and student government. Popular campus events include Powwow and Native American Day.

Sports: There are 6 intercollegiate sports for men and 7 for women, and 6 intramural sports for men and 5 for women. Facilities include a phys ed building with an Olympic-size pool, 2 gyms, a running track, weight-training equipment, 6 racquetball courts, and a soccer/softball field.

Disabled Students: All of the campus is accessible. Wheelchair ramps, elevators, special parking, specially equipped rest rooms, special class scheduling, lowered drinking fountains, lowered telephones, and a Disability Support Services Office are available.

Services: Counseling and information services are available, as is tutoring in most subjects. There is a reader service for the blind, and remedial math, reading, and writing. There is an academic support center.

Campus Safety and Security: Measures include 24-hour foot and vehicle patrol, security escort services, informal discussions, and pamphlets/posters/films. There are emergency telephones and lighted pathways/sidewalks.

Programs of Study: MSU-Billings confers B.A., B.S., B.A. or B.S. in Business Administration, B.A.S., B.S.Ed., B.S.H.S., B.S. in Rehabilitation and Related Services, B.S.L.S. degrees. Associate and master's degrees are also awarded. Bachelor's degrees are awarded in BIOLOGICAL SCIENCE (biology/biological science), BUSINESS (business administration and management), COMMUNICATIONS AND THE ARTS (art, communications, dramatic arts, English, music, music performance, and public relations), COMPUTER AND PHYSICAL SCIENCE (chemistry, information sciences and systems, and mathematics), EDUCATION (art, early childhood, education, elementary, health, mathematics, middle school, music, physical, science, secondary, social science, social studies, and special), ENGINEERING AND ENVIRONMENTAL DESIGN (environmental science), HEALTH PROFESSIONS (health care administration and rehabilitation therapy), SOCIAL SCIENCE (history, liberal arts/general studies, psychology, sociology, and Spanish studies). The sciences, business, and education are the strongest academically. Education and business are the largest.

Required: To graduate, students must have earned a minimum of 120 semester credits, including 30 in their major. They must maintain a minimum 2.0 GPA; education and human services majors must maintain a minimum 2.7 GPA. General education requirements must also be fulfilled.

Special: MSU-Billings offers co-op programs in business, human services, and liberal arts, internships, work-study programs, B.A.-B.S. degrees, dual majors, nondegree study, and pass/fail options. There are 10 national honor societies, a freshman honors program, and 1 departmental honors program.

Faculty/Classroom: 60% of faculty are male; 40%, female. All teach undergraduates. Graduate students teach 1% of introductory courses. The average class size in an introductory lecture is 30 and in a laboratory, 20.

Admissions: 96% of the 2005-2006 applicants were accepted. The SAT scores for the 2005-2006 freshman class were: Verbal--44% below 500, 46% between 500 and 599, 9% between 600 and 700, and 1% above 700; Math--43% below 500, 41% between 500 and 599, and 16% between 600 and 700. The ACT scores were 57% below 21, 20% between 21 and 23, 15% between 24 and 26, 5% between 27 and 28, and 3% above 28. 30% of the current freshmen were in the top fifth of their class; 66% were in the top two fifths. 10 freshmen graduated first in their class.

Requirements: The SAT or ACT is required. In addition, applicants must be graduates of an accredited secondary school; the GED is also accepted. The applicant must have taken 4 years of English, 3 each of social science and math, and 2 each of science, foreign languages, or humanities. Students need to meet 1 of 3 criteria: be in the upper 50% of their class; have a GPA of 2.0 or better; or have a score of 22 on the ACT or satisfactory scores on the SAT. MSU-Billings requires applicants to be in the upper 50% of their class. A GPA of 2.5 is required. AP and CLEP credits are accepted. Important factors in the admissions decision are advanced placement or honor courses, geographic diversity, and evidence of special talent.

Procedure: Freshmen are admitted to all sessions. Entrance exams should be taken in the senior year of high school. There is a deferred admissions plan and a rolling admissions plan. Application deadlines are open. Notification is sent on a rolling basis. The fall 2005 application fee was $30. Applications are accepted on-line.

Transfer: 431 transfer students enrolled in 2004-2005. Out-of-state transfer students must have earned a 2.0 GPA; in-state transfer students must be in good academic standing. 32 of 120 credits required for the bachelor's degree must be completed at MSU-Billings.

Visiting: There are regularly scheduled orientations for prospective students. There are guides for informal visits and visitors may sit in on classes and stay overnight. To schedule a visit, contact Shelly Andersen at *sandersen@msubillings.edu.*

Financial Aid: In a recent year, 58% of all full-time freshmen and 61% of continuing full-time students received some form of financial aid. 46% of full-time freshmen and 56% of continuing full-time students received need-based aid. The average freshman award was $4325. Average annual earnings from campus work are $1600. The average financial indebtedness of a recent graduate was $16,000. The FAFSA and the college's own financial statement are required. The priority date for freshman financial aid applications for fall entry is March 1.

International Students: There are 42 international students enrolled. The school actively recruits these students. They must take the TOEFL and the ACT.

Computers: Wireless access is available. There are 650 computers in campus buildings. All students may access the system 24 hours a day. There are no time limits. The fee is $2.65 per credit hour. It is strongly recommended that all students have a personal computer.

Graduates: From July 1, 2004 to June 30, 2005, 525 bachelor's degrees were awarded. The most popular majors were arts and sciences (44%), education (30%), and business (18%). In an average class, 12% graduate in 4 years or less, 23% graduate in 5 years or less, and 26% graduate in 6 years or less. 100 companies recruited on campus in 2004-2005. Of the 2004 graduating class, 7% were enrolled in graduate school within 6 months of graduation and 90% were employed.

Admissions Contact: Cheri Johanenes, Director of Admissions and Records and Registrar. E-mail: *cjohannes@msubillings.edu*
Web: *www.msubillings.edu*

MONTANA STATE UNIVERSITY-BOZEMAN   C-3

Bozeman, MT 59717	(406) 994-2452; Fax: (406) 994-1923
Full-time: 5023 men, 4262 women	Faculty: 553; I, --$
Part-time: 768 men, 789 women	Ph.D.s: 83%
Graduate: 739 men, 669 women	Student/Faculty: 16 to 1
Year: semesters, summer session	Tuition: $5221 ($14,945)
Application Deadline: open	Room & Board: $6150
Freshman Class: 5124 applied, 3784 accepted, 2236 enrolled	
SAT Verbal/Math: 550/570*	ACT: 23 COMPETITIVE

Montana State University-Bozeman, founded in 1893, is a public, land-grant institution offering programs in agriculture, business, arts and architecture, education, engineering, health and human development, nursing, and letters and science. There are 7 undergraduate schools and 1 graduate school. In addition to regional accreditation, MSU has baccalaureate program accreditation with AACSB, AAFCS, ABET, ADA, CACREP, CCNE, CSAB, NAAB, NASAD, NASM, NCATE, and NLN. The 2 libraries contain 670,407 volumes, 2,107,544 microform items, and 5386 audio/video tapes/CDs/DVDs, and subscribe to 6643 periodicals including electronic. Computerized library services include the card catalog, interlibrary loans, and database searching. Special learning facilities include a learning resource center, art gallery, natural history museum, planetarium, radio station, TV station, Center for Biofilm Engineering, Burns Telecommunication Center, and a geographic information and analysis center. The 1170-acre campus is in a small town 140 miles west of Billings and 90 miles north of Yellowstone National Park. Including any residence halls, there are 83 buildings.

Student Life: 69% of undergraduates are from Montana. Students are from 49 states, 59 foreign countries, and Canada. 88% are white. The average age of freshmen is 19; all undergraduates, 22. 29% do not continue beyond their first year; 47% remain to graduate.

Housing: 5400 students can be accommodated in college housing, which includes coed dorms and married-student housing. In addition, there are honors houses, floors for older students, nonsmoking floors, and wellness floors. On-campus housing is guaranteed for the freshman year only and is available on a first-come, first-served basis. 78% of students commute. All students may keep cars.

Activities: 2% of men belong to 9 national fraternities. There are 4 national sororities. There are 150 groups on campus, including art, band, cheerleading, chess, choir, chorale, chorus, computers, dance, drama, drill team, ethnic, film, gay, honors, international, jazz band, marching band, musical theater, newspaper, orchestra, pep band, photography, political, professional, radio and TV, religious, social, social service, student government, and symphony. Popular campus events include International Food Bazaar and Native American Pow-Wow.

Sports: There are 6 intercollegiate sports for men and 7 for women, and 38 intramural sports for men and 40 for women. Facilities include a 10,000-seat stadium, numerous gyms, handball courts, weight rooms, and 2 pools.

Disabled Students: 90% of the campus is accessible. Wheelchair ramps, elevators, special parking, specially equipped rest rooms, special class scheduling, lowered drinking fountains, lowered telephones, services through the resource center, and a taping service for the blind are available.

Services: Counseling and information services are available, as is tutoring in most subjects. There is a reader service for the blind, and remedial math, reading, and writing.

Campus Safety and Security: Measures include 24-hour foot and vehicle patrol, self-defense education, security escort services, and informal discussions. There are pamphlets/posters/films, emergency telephones, and lighted pathways/sidewalks.

Programs of Study: MSU confers B.A., B.S., B.F.A., and B.Mus.Ed. degrees. Master's and doctoral degrees are also awarded. Bachelor's degrees are awarded in AGRICULTURE (agricultural business management, animal science, horticulture, natural resource management, plant science, and range/farm management), BIOLOGICAL SCIENCE (biology/biological science, biotechnology, cell biology, microbiology, and neurosciences), BUSINESS (business administration and management), COMMUNICATIONS AND THE ARTS (art, English, fine arts, media arts, modern language, and music), COMPUTER AND PHYSICAL SCIENCE (chemistry, computer science, earth science, mathematics, and physics), EDUCATION (agricultural, elementary, music, secondary, and technical), ENGINEERING AND ENVIRONMENTAL DESIGN (agricultural engineering technology, chemical engineering, civil engineering, computer engineering, construction engineering, electrical/electronics engineering, environmental design, environmental science, industrial engineering, land use management and reclamation, mechanical engineering, and mechanical engineering technology), HEALTH PROFESSIONS (health and nursing), SOCIAL SCIENCE (anthropology, economics, history, human development, philosophy, political science/government, psychology, and sociology). Engineering, physical science, and architecture are the strongest academically. Business, education, and nursing are the largest.

Required: To graduate, students must complete a core curriculum of 8 credits of natural sciences, 6 credits each of multicultural studies, humanities, social science, and communications, and 3 credits each of fine arts and math. The total number of credits required varies by program, with 120 being the minimum; at least one third must be in upper-division courses. A minimum 2.0 GPA is needed. Students must be officially registered in their chosen curriculum for at least 2 semesters before graduation.

Special: MSU-Bozeman offers internships in selected majors, study aboard in 40 countries, cross-registration in selected programs, B.A.-B.S. degrees, dual and interdisciplinary majors, nondegree study, and pass/fail options. There are 23 national honor societies and a freshman honors program.

Faculty/Classroom: 60% of faculty are male; 40%, female. All both teach and do research. Graduate students teach 21% of introductory courses. The average class size in an introductory lecture is 66; in a laboratory, 18; and in a regular course, 22.

Admissions: 74% of the 2005-2006 applicants were accepted. The SAT scores for the 2005-2006 freshman class were: Verbal--27% below 500, 42% between 500 and 599, 26% between 600 and 700, and 5% above 700; Math--22% below 500, 39% between 500 and 599, 32% between 600 and 700, and 7% above 700. The ACT scores were 27% below 21, 28% between 21 and 23, 22% between 24 and 26, 12% between 27 and 28, and 11% above 28. 33% of the current freshmen were in the top fifth of their class; 48% were in the top two fifths. There were 17 National Merit finalists and 3 semifinalists. 102 freshmen graduated first in their class.

Requirements: The SAT or ACT is required. In addition, MSU-Bozeman requires applicants to have a minimum GPA of 2.5, rank in the upper 50% of their graduating class or have minimum composite scores of 22 on the ACT or a satisfactory score on the SAT. They must be graduates of an accredited secondary school. The GED is accepted. Students should have completed 4 years of English, 3 years each of social studies and math, 2 years of lab science, and 2 years of language, computer science, visual and performing arts, or vocational education. MSU requires applicants to be in the upper 50% of their class. A GPA of 2.5 is required. AP and CLEP credits are accepted.

Procedure: Freshmen are admitted fall, spring, and summer. Entrance exams should be taken in the fall of the senior year. There are early admissions, deferred admissions and rolling admissions plans. Application deadlines are open. The fall 2005 application fee was $30. Notication is sent on a rolling basis. Applications are accepted on-line.

Transfer: 730 transfer students enrolled in 2004-2005. Applicants must have a minimum GPA of 2.0; grades of D or better transfer for credit. 30 of 120 credits required for the bachelor's degree must be completed at MSU.

Visiting: There are regularly scheduled orientations for prospective students, including program overviews, a tour, and meetings with assistant deans. There are guides for informal visits and visitors may sit in on classes and stay overnight. To schedule a visit, contact the Office of New Student Services at (888) MSU-CATS or *admissions@montana.edu*.

Financial Aid: In a recent year, 50% of all full-time freshmen and 52% of continuing full-time students received some form of financial aid. 40% of full-time freshmen and 45% of continuing full-time students received need-based aid. The average freshman award was $6869. Need-based scholarships or need-based grants averaged $3939; need-based self-help aid (loans and jobs) averaged $3554; non-need-based athletic scholarships averaged $5224; and other non-need-based awards and non-need-based scholarships averaged $2536. 20% of undergraduates work part time. Average annual earnings from campus work are $3000. The average financial indebtedness of the recent year's graduate was $18,081. The FAFSA is required. The deadline for filing freshman financial aid applications for fall entry is March 1.

International Students: In a recent year, there were 164 international students enrolled. The school actively recruits these students. A satisfactory score is required on the written TOEFL. Students must also submit proof of American Cultural Exchange Language Institute Level 6 (available at MSU).

Computers: All students may access the system. There are no time limits. The fee is included in the mandatory fees. It is recommended that students in environmental design have personal computers.

Graduates: From July 1, 2004 to June 30, 2005, 1805 bachelor's degrees were awarded. The most popular majors were business (13%), health and human development (13%), and engineering (11%). In an average class, 19% graduate in 4 years or less, 40% graduate in 5 years or less, and 47% graduate in 6 years or less. 100 companies recruited on campus in 2004-2005. Of the 2004 graduating class, 15% were enrolled in graduate school within 6 months of graduation and 95% were employed.

Admissions Contact: Ronda Russell, Director, Office of New Student Services. A video is available. E-mail: *admissions@montana.edu* Web: *http://www.montana.edu/wwwnss/*

MONTANA STATE UNIVERSITY-NORTHERN · D-1

Havre, MT 59501-7751

(406) 265-3704
(800) 662-6132; Fax: (406) 265-3792

Full-time: 600 men, 500 women	**Faculty:** 71; IIA, --$
Part-time: 100 men, 200 women	**Ph.Ds:** 47%
Graduate: 50 men, 100 women	**Student/Faculty:** 16 to 1
Year: semesters, summer session	**Tuition:** $4000 ($9000)
Application Deadline: open	**Room & Board:** $6000
Freshman Class: n/av	
SAT or ACT: required	NONCOMPETITIVE

Montana State University-Northern, founded in 1929, is part of the Montana University System and offers programs in the liberal arts, teacher education, business, and technology. There is 1 graduate school. Figures in the above capsule and in this profile are approximate. In addition to regional accreditation, MSU-Northern has baccalaureate program accreditation with NLN. The library contains 100,000 volumes and 600,000 microform items, and subscribes to 650 periodicals including electronic. Computerized library services include the card catalog, interlibrary loans, and database searching. Special learning facilities include a learning resource center and radio station. The 105-acre campus is in a small town 115 miles north of Great Falls. Including any residence halls, there are 21 buildings.

Student Life: The average age of freshmen is 21; all undergraduates, 28.

Housing: 450 students can be accommodated in college housing, which includes single-sex and coed dorms, on-campus apartments, and married-student housing. On-campus housing is guaranteed for all 4 years. 60% of students live on campus. All students may keep cars.

Activities: There are no fraternities or sororities. There are 30 groups on campus, including dance, ethnic, musical theater, newspaper, pep band, religious, social service, student government, and yearbook. Popular campus events include concerts, dances, and theatrical productions.

Sports: There are 3 intercollegiate sports for men and 3 for women, and 11 intramural sports for men and 9 for women. Facilities include tennis courts, a swimming pool, weight and wrestling rooms, and 2 gyms, the larger seating 2500. Nearby Glacier National Park offers outdoor facilities.

Disabled Students: Wheelchair ramps, elevators, special parking, and specially equipped rest rooms are available.

Services: Counseling and information services are available, as is tutoring in every subject. There is remedial math, reading, and writing.

Campus Safety and Security: Measures include lighted pathways/sidewalks.

Programs of Study: MSU-Northern confers B.A., B.S., B.S.Ed., and B.T. degrees. Associate and master's degrees are also awarded. Bachelor's degrees are awarded in AGRICULTURE (agricultural mechanics), BIOLOGICAL SCIENCE (biology/biological science and ecology), COMMUNICATIONS AND THE ARTS (communications, dramatic arts, English, fine arts, French, and music), COMPUTER AND PHYSICAL SCIENCE (chemistry), EDUCATION (business, elementary, industrial arts, physical, science, secondary, and social science), ENGINEERING AND ENVIRONMENTAL DESIGN (automotive technology, civil engineering technology, construction technology, drafting and design technology, electrical/electronics engineering technology, engineering technology, environmental science, and manufacturing technology), HEALTH PROFESSIONS (nursing), SOCIAL SCIENCE (history, humanities, interdisciplinary studies, Native American studies, and social science). Business technology, nursing, and education are the largest.

Required: To graduate, students must complete at least 128 credits with a minimum GPA of 2.0 overall and 2.25 in their major and minor. Distribution requirements include 12 credits each of humanities, social science, math/science, and technology/applied arts. Students also must demonstrate proficiency in computing and in written and oral communication.

Special: B.A.-B.S. and other dual-degree programs, pass/fail options, cooperative programs in most disciplines, independent study, dual majors, and work-study programs are available.

Faculty/Classroom: All teach undergraduates. No introductory courses are taught by graduate students.

Requirements: The SAT or ACT is required. Applicants must be graduates of an accredited high school or have a GED certificate. They should have completed 4 years of English, 3 each of math, social science, and history, including global studies and U.S. history, and 2 each of lab science and electives. MSU-Northern requires applicants to be in the upper 50% of their class. A GPA of 2.5 is required. CLEP credit is accepted.

Procedure: Freshmen are admitted to all sessions. There is an early admissions plan. There is a rolling admissions plan. Application deadlines are open. The fall 2005 application fee was $30.

Transfer: Nonresidents must have a minimum GPA of 2.0. Any applicant with fewer than 12 transfer credits must submit a transcript of college work completed and meet standard freshman requirements. 36 of 128 credits required for the bachelor's degree must be completed at MSU-Northern.

Visiting: There are regularly scheduled orientations for prospective students. There are guides for informal visits and visitors may sit in on classes and stay overnight. To schedule a visit, contact the Admissions Office.

Financial Aid: The college's own financial statement is required.

International Students: The school actively recruits these students. They must score satisfactorily on the written TOEFL.

Computers: All students may access the system when the buildings are open. There are no time limits.

Admissions Contact: Stacey Gonsalez, Admissions Counselor. E-mail: *admissions@msun.edu* Web: *www.msun.edu*

MONTANA TECH OF THE UNIVERSITY OF MONTANA · C-3

Butte, MT 59701-8997

(406) 496-4632
(800) 445-TECH; Fax: (406) 496-4710

Full-time: 1026 men, 684 women	**Faculty:** IIB, -$
Part-time: 138 men, 246 women	**Ph.Ds:** n/av
Graduate: 51 men, 42 women	**Student/Faculty:** n/av
Year: semesters, summer session	**Tuition:** $5078 ($14,070)
Application Deadline: open	**Room & Board:** $5356
Freshman Class: 400 accepted, 394 enrolled	
SAT Verbal/Math: 530/549*	**ACT:** 22 COMPETITIVE

Founded in 1893 as the Montana School of Mines, Montana Tech still focuses on its original programs in minerals and energy engineering and has expanded its offerings to include science, engineering, business, computer science, technical communications, health care, and related programs. There are 4 undergraduate schools and 1 graduate school. In addition to regional accreditation, Montana Tech has baccalaureate program accreditation with ABET, ACS, CSAB, NIASE, and NLNAC. The library contains 167,262 volumes, 259,581 microform items, and 2947 audio/video tapes/CDs/DVDs, and subscribes to 394 periodicals including electronic. Computerized library services include the card catalog, interlibrary loans, database searching, Internet access, and laptop Internet portals. Special learning facilities include a learning resource center, radio station, a mineral museum, and METNET 2-way interactive communication studio. The 56-acre campus is in a small town. Including any residence halls, there are 19 buildings.

Student Life: 86% of undergraduates are from Montana. Others are from 11 states and Canada. 90% are from public schools. 92% are white. The average age of freshmen is 19; all undergraduates, 22. 39% do not continue beyond their first year; 58% remain to graduate.

Housing: 526 students can be accommodated in college housing, which includes coed dorms, off-campus apartments, and married-student housing. On-campus housing is guaranteed for the freshman year only and is available on a first-come, first-served basis. Priority is given to out-of-town students. 87% of students commute. All students may keep cars.

Activities: There are no fraternities or sororities. There are 33 groups on campus, including band, cheerleading, chess, choir, chorale, computers, ethnic, international, newspaper, pep band, photography, professional, radio and TV, religious, social, social service, student government, symphony, and yearbook. Popular campus events include M-Day, International Dinner, and Bed Races.

Sports: There are 3 intercollegiate sports for men and 3 for women, and 10 intramural sports for men and 10 for women. Facilities include an athletic/recreational complex housing 3 basketball courts, a 25-meter swimming pool, volleyball courts, a weight-lifting room, 6 handball/racquetball courts, tennis courts, a stadium with skybox seating, 3 classrooms and 2 practice fields, and a baseball facility.

Disabled Students: 75% of the campus is accessible. Wheelchair ramps, elevators, special parking, specially equipped rest rooms, special class scheduling, lowered drinking fountains, and lowered telephones are available.

Services: Counseling and information services are available, as is tutoring in most subjects, including math, physics, chemistry, biology, engineering science, and business and computer science. There is a reader service for the blind and remedial math. Tutoring in additional subject areas is available upon request.

Campus Safety and Security: Measures include 24-hour foot and vehicle patrol, self-defense education, security escort services, and informal discussions. There are pamphlets/posters/films, emergency telephones, and lighted pathways/sidewalks.

Programs of Study: Montana Tech confers B.S. and B.A.S. degrees. Associate and master's degrees are also awarded. Bachelor's degrees are awarded in BIOLOGICAL SCIENCE (biology/biological science), BUSINESS (business systems analysis), COMMUNICATIONS AND THE ARTS (communications and communications technology), COMPUTER AND PHYSICAL SCIENCE (chemistry, computer programming, computer science, mathematics, and science), ENGINEERING AND ENVIRONMENTAL DESIGN (computer engineering, engineering, environmental engineering, geological engineering, geophysical engineering, metallurgical engineering, mining and mineral engineering, occupational safety and health, and petroleum/natural gas engineering), SOCIAL SCIENCE (humanities and social science and liberal arts/general studies). Engineering and science are the strongest programs academically and have the largest enrollments.

Required: For graduation, students must complete at least 120 semester credits (more for engineering degrees) and maintain a minimum 2.0 GPA. Requirements include 6 to 7 hours of physical and life sciences and 6 hours each of communications, humanities, mathematical sciences, and social sciences. Engineering students must satisfy specific requirements within the individual curriculum.

Special: Montana Tech has cooperative programs in all areas with 7 other institutions and cross-registration with Flathead Valley Community College, Montana State University, and the University of Montana. Internships are available in all degree programs, and there is a student-faculty exchange program with the People's Republic of China and a mining exchange program with Peru. Work-study, accelerated degree programs, 3-2 engineering degrees, student-designed majors, nondegree study, and credit for military experience are available. There are 3 national honor societies.

Faculty/Classroom: 81% of faculty are male; 20%, female. All teach undergraduates; 25% also do research. The average class size in an introductory lecture is 34; in a laboratory, 15; and in a regular course, 21.

Admissions: The SAT scores for the 2005-2006 freshman class were: Verbal--34% below 500, 40% between 500 and 599, 23% between 600 and 700, and 2% above 700. The ACT scores were 25% below 21, 37% between 21 and 23, 12% between 24 and 26, and 25% between 27 and 28. 35% of the current freshmen were in the top fifth of their class; 66% were in the top two fifths. 19 freshmen graduated first in their class.

Requirements: The SAT or ACT is required. In addition, applicants must be graduates of an accredited secondary school. The GED is accepted. 14 academic credits are required, including English, 4 years; math and social studies, 3 years each; science, 2 years; plus 2 years chosen from foreign language, computer science, visual and performing arts, or vocational education. Applicants must have a minimum composite score of 22 on the ACT or satisfactory scores on the SAT, or a 2.5 GPA, or be in the top half of their graduating class. Other factors regarding admissions are considered only if the preceding standards are not met. Montana Tech requires applicants to be in the upper 50% of their class. A GPA of 2.5 is required. AP and CLEP credits are accepted.

Procedure: Freshmen are admitted to all sessions. Entrance exams should be taken in the senior year. There is a deferred admissions plan and a rolling admissions plan. Application deadlines are open. Notification is on a rolling basis. Application fee is $30. Applications are accepted on-line.

Transfer: 211 transfer students enrolled in 2004-2005. Transfer applicants must have a minimum GPA of 2.0. Grades of C and above transfer for credit. 30 of 120 credits required for the bachelor's degree must be completed at Montana Tech.

Visiting: There are regularly scheduled orientations for prospective students, including an official fall orientation, though visits are welcome any time. There are guides for informal visits and visitors may sit in on classes and stay overnight. To schedule a visit, contact the Admissions Office at *admissions@mtech.edu*.

Financial Aid: In 2005-2006, 80% of all full-time students received some form of financial aid, including need-based aid. The average freshman award was $5000. Need-based scholarships or need-based grants averaged $2000 ($4050 maximum); need-based self-help aid (loans and jobs) averaged $4000 ($4625 maximum); non-need-based athletic scholarships averaged $3236; and other non-need-based awards and non-need-based scholarships averaged $2000 ($6000 maximum). The FAFSA and the college's own financial statement are required. The priority date for freshman financial aid applications for fall entry is March 1.

International Students: There are 70 international students enrolled. The school actively recruits these students. They must take the TOEFL and also take the SAT or the ACT.

Computers: Wireless access is available. There are over 500 computers available for student use. These are located in a number of computer labs and public areas. Wireless access is available in all buildings. All students may access the system any time. There are no time limits. The fee is $36 per student.

Graduates: The most popular majors were general engineering (17%), petroleum engineering (14%), and business and information technology (12%). In an average class, 1% graduate in 3 years or less, 40% graduate in 4 years or less, 60% graduate in 5 years or less, and 67% graduate in 6 years or less.

Admissions Contact: Tony Campeau, Director of Admissions. A video is available. E-mail: *admissions@mtech.edu* Web: *www.mtech.edu*

MONTANA UNIVERSITY SYSTEM

The Montana University System, established in 1972, is a public system. It is governed by a Board of Regents whose chief administrator is the Commissioner of Higher Education. The primary goal of the system is teaching first, then research and public service. The main priorities are funding, system structure, and transfer articulation. The total enrollment of all six 4-year campuses is approximately 32,059, with about 1100 faculty members. There are 148 baccalaureate, 107 master's, and 33 doctoral programs offered in the system. Profiles of the 4-year campuses are included in this section.

ROCKY MOUNTAIN COLLEGE D-3

Billings, MT 59102
(406) 657-1000 or 657-1026
(800) 877-6259; Fax: (406) 657-1189

Full-time: 413 men, 483 women	**Faculty:** 53
Part-time: 26 men, 42 women	**Ph.D.s:** 62%
Graduate: 15 men, 30 women	**Student/Faculty:** 17 to 1
Year: semesters, summer session	**Tuition:** $15,325
Application Deadline: August 1	**Room & Board:** $5480
Freshman Class: 728 applied, 565 accepted, 218 enrolled	
SAT Verbal/Math: 525/527*	**ACT:** 22 COMPETITIVE

Rocky Mountain College, established in 1878, is a private liberal arts institution affiliated with the United Church of Christ, the United Methodist Church, and the Presbyterian Church (U.S.A.). In addition to regional accreditation, Rocky has baccalaureate program accreditation with ARC-PA and IACBE. The library contains 99,194 volumes, 1200 microform items, and 1032 audio/video tapes/CDs/DVDs, and subscribes to 387 periodicals including electronic. Computerized library services include the card catalog, interlibrary loans, database searching, Internet access, and laptop Internet portals. Special learning facilities include a learning resource center, art gallery, flight school, and equestrian facilities. The 60-acre campus is in a small town 550 miles north of Denver, Colorado, in south-central Montana. Including any residence halls, there are 16 buildings.

Student Life: 68% of undergraduates are from Montana. Others are from 37 states, 13 foreign countries, and Canada. 83% are white. 45% are Protestant; 35% claim no religious affiliation; 18% Catholic. The average age of freshmen is 18; all undergraduates, 23. 28% do not continue beyond their first year; 39% remain to graduate.

Housing: 477 students can be accommodated in college housing, which includes coed dorms, on-campus apartments, and married-student housing. On-campus housing is guaranteed for the freshman year only and is available on a first-come, first-served basis. 53% of students commute. Alcohol is not permitted. All students may keep cars.

Activities: There are no fraternities or sororities. There are 26 groups on campus, including aviation band, cheerleading, choir, chorale, chorus, computers, drama, equestrian forensics, honors, international, jazz band, literary magazine, marching band, musical theater, newspaper, pep band, photography, professional, religious, social, social service, student government, and yearbook. Popular campus events include convocations, intercollegiate athletics, and Woodrow Wilson Visiting Fellow.

Sports: There are 4 intercollegiate sports for men and 4 for women, and 12 intramural sports for men and 12 for women. Activities include skiing trips; river rafting, kayaking, and canoeing on the Yellowstone River; and climbing in the Beartooth Mountains. There is a health club facility on campus.

Disabled Students: 60% of the campus is accessible. Wheelchair ramps, elevators, special parking, specially equipped rest rooms, special class scheduling, lowered drinking fountains, and special housing are available.

Services: Counseling and information services are available, as is tutoring in most subjects. There is a reader service for the blind, and remedial math, reading, and writing. Note taking is available for qualified students.

Campus Safety and Security: Measures include self-defense education, security escort services, informal discussions, and pamphlets/posters/films. There are lighted pathways/sidewalks, security cameras, and eletronic access systems.

Programs of Study: Rocky confers B.A. and B.S. degrees. Associate and master's degrees are also awarded. Bachelor's degrees are awarded in AGRICULTURE (environmental studies and equine science), BIOLOGICAL SCIENCE (biochemistry and biology/biological science), BUSINESS (accounting, business administration and management, and business economics), COMMUNICATIONS AND THE ARTS (art, communications, dramatic arts, literature, and music performance), COMPUTER AND PHYSICAL SCIENCE (chemistry, computer science, geology, mathematics, and natural sciences), EDUCATION (art, education, elementary, English, mathematics, music, physical, psychology, science, social science, and social studies), ENGINEERING AND ENVIRONMENTAL DESIGN (aeronautical science, aviation administration/management, and environmental science), SOCIAL SCIENCE (anthropology, history, philosophy, political science/government, psychology, religion, and sociology). Education, business and economics, and aviation are the strongest academicaly and are the largest.

Required: To graduate, students must complete a minimum of 124 credit hours, complete all major requirements with a minimum overall GPA of 2.0 and 2.25 in the major. If a minor area is chosen, a minimum of 18 hours is required. There are general education requirements in humanities, the natural and social sciences, fine arts, and religious thought, as well as writing, speech, math, experiential learning, and health requirements.

Special: The college offers internships, study abroad in 20 countries, dual majors, individualized programs of study, and credit for life, military, and work experience. Juniors and seniors may elect to take 1 course on a pass/fail basis each semester. There are 3 national honor societies, a freshman honors program, and 2 departmental honors programs.

Faculty/Classroom: 56% of faculty are male; 44%, female. All teach undergraduates and 5% do research. No introductory courses are taught by graduate students. The average class size in an introductory lecture is 22; in a laboratory, 10; and in a regular course, 14.

Admissions: 78% of the 2005-2006 applicants were accepted. The SAT scores for the 2005-2006 freshman class were: Verbal--37% below 500, 41% between 500 and 599, 15% between 600 and 700, and 7% above 700; Math--32% below 500, 47% between 500 and 599, 19% between 600 and 700, and 2% above 700. The ACT scores were 34% below 21, 29% between 21 and 23, 27% between 24 and 26, 8% between 27 and 28, and 2% above 28. 32% of the current freshmen were in the top fifth of their class; 61% were in the top two fifths. 13 freshmen graduated first in their class.

Requirements: The SAT or ACT is required. The ACT Optional Writing test is also required for some programs. In addition, applicants must be graduates of an accredited secondary school; the GED is accepted. Students must have completed 4 units of English, 1 unit of history, and 2 units each in 3 of the following: foreign language, math, natural sciences, and social sciences. The school recommends a portfolio for admission to the art program, an audition for admission to the music or theatre program, and an interview for academically challenged students. A GPA of 2.5 is required. AP and CLEP credits are accepted. Important factors in the admissions decision are ability to finance college education, parents or siblings attending the school, and recommendations by school officials.

Procedure: Freshmen are admitted fall, spring, and summer. Entrance exams should be taken during the first half of the senior year, if not before. There are early admissions and deferred admissions plans. There

is a rolling admissions plan. Applications should be filed by August 1 for fall entry, along with a $25 fee. Notification is sent on a rolling basis. Applications are accepted on-line.

Transfer: 96 transfer students enrolled in 2004-2005. Transfer students must have a minimum GPA of 2.0; grades of 2.0 and higher transfer for credit. Transfers are admitted every term. 30 of 124 credits required for the bachelor's degree must be completed at Rocky.

Visiting: There are regularly scheduled orientations for prospective students, in late spring and summer. There are guides for informal visits and visitors may sit in on classes and stay overnight. To schedule a visit, contact the Director of Admissions at admissions@rocky.edu.

Financial Aid: In 2005-2006, 88% of all full-time freshmen and 86% of continuing full-time students received some form of financial aid. 69% of full-time freshmen and 73% of continuing full-time students received need-based aid. The average freshman award was $13,644. Need-based scholarships or need-based grants averaged $9195; need-based self-help aid (loans and jobs) averaged $4447; non-need-based athletic scholarships averaged $11,299; and other non-need-based awards and non-need-based scholarships averaged $8806. Average annual earnings from campus work are $1200. The average financial indebtedness of the 2005 graduate was $18,653. The FAFSA and the college's own financial statement are required. The deadline for filing freshman financial aid applications for fall entry is March 1.

International Students: There are 55 international students enrolled. The school actively recruits these students. They must score satisfactorily on the TOEFL or take the MELAB or IELTS.

Computers: Wireless access is available. There are 11 computer labs that house 104 PCs for student use. Wireless access points include the student center, the library, and in the residence halls. All students may access the system. There are no time limits and no fees.

Graduates: From July 1, 2004 to June 30, 2005, 159 bachelor's degrees were awarded. The most popular majors were business/marketing (18%), education (11%), and physician assistant (10%). In an average class, 26% graduate in 4 years or less, 39% graduate in 5 years or less, and 39% graduate in 6 years or less. 30 companies recruited on campus in 2004-2005. Of the 2004 graduating class, 22% were enrolled in graduate school within 6 months of graduation and 99% were employed.

Admissions Contact: Bonnie Knapp, Director of Admissions. E-mail: admissions@rocky.edu Web: www.rocky.edu

UNIVERSITY OF GREAT FALLS   C-2
Great Falls, MT 59405   (406) 791-5200
                              (800) 856-9544; Fax: (406) 791-5209

Full-time: 200 men, 300 women	Faculty: 41
Part-time: 100 men, 200 women	Ph.D.s: 54%
Graduate: 30 men, 100 women	Student/Faculty: 12 to 1
Year: semesters, summer session	Tuition: $11,000
Application Deadline: see profile	Room & Board: $6000
Freshman Class: n/av	
SAT: recommended	COMPETITIVE

The University of Great Falls, established in 1932, is a private, liberal arts institution affiliated with the Roman Catholic Church. There are 2 undergraduate schools and 1 graduate school. Figures in the above capsule and in this profile are approximate. The library contains 106,135 volumes, 124,608 microform items, and 3894 audio/video tapes/CDs/DVDs, and subscribes to 587 periodicals including electronic. Computerized library services include the card catalog, interlibrary loans, and database searching. Special learning facilities include a learning resource center and art gallery. The 40-acre campus is in an urban area. Including any residence halls, there are 13 buildings.

Student Life: 93% of undergraduates are from Montana. Others are from 20 states and Canada. 99% are from public schools. 80% are white. 28% are Catholic; 22% claim no religious affiliation; 19% Protestant. The average age of freshmen is 26; all undergraduates, 33. 46% do not continue beyond their first year; 20% remain to graduate.

Housing: 189 students can be accommodated in college housing, which includes single-sex and coed dormitories, off-campus apartments, and married-student housing. On-campus housing is guaranteed for the freshman year only and is available on a first-come, first-served basis. Priority is given to out-of-town students. 88% of students commute. Alcohol is not permitted. All students may keep cars.

Activities: There are no fraternities or sororities. There are 15 groups on campus, including art, cheerleading, chess, choir, chorus, computers, drama, ethnic, forensics, honors, literary magazine, musical theater, newspaper, orchestra, photography, professional, religious, social, social service, student government, and symphony. Popular campus events include Orientation Barbecue, Halloween Dance, and Intramural Festival.

Sports: There are 1 intercollegiate sports for men and 2 for women, and 7 intramural sports for men and 7 for women. Facilities include a gym, Olympic-size pool, game room, and workout room.

Disabled Students: All of the campus is accessible. Wheelchair ramps, elevators, special parking, specially equipped rest rooms, special class scheduling, and lowered drinking fountains are available.

Services: Counseling and information services are available, as is tutoring in some subjects, including 100-level courses, 200-level courses, and selected 300-level courses. There is a reader service for the blind, and remedial math, reading, and writing. and tutoring in basic skills.

Campus Safety and Security: Measures include 24-hour foot and vehicle patrol, self-defense education, security escort services, and informal discussions. There are pamphlets/posters/films, emergency telephones, and lighted pathways/sidewalks.

Programs of Study: UGF confers B.A. and B.S. degrees. Associate and master's degrees are also awarded. Bachelor's degrees are awarded in BIOLOGICAL SCIENCE (biology/biological science, botany, microbiology, molecular biology, and physiology), BUSINESS (accounting, business administration and management, management science, and marketing/retailing/merchandising), COMMUNICATIONS AND THE ARTS (art, English, and fine arts), COMPUTER AND PHYSICAL SCIENCE (computer management, computer programming, computer science, mathematics, physical sciences, and science), EDUCATION (education of the exceptional child, elementary, health, mathematics, middle school, physical, reading, science, secondary, social studies, and special), ENGINEERING AND ENVIRONMENTAL DESIGN (computer graphics), HEALTH PROFESSIONS (health care administration, predentistry, and premedicine), SOCIAL SCIENCE (counseling/psychology, criminal justice, history, human services, law enforcement and corrections, paralegal studies, political science/government, prelaw, psychology, religion, social science, sociology, and theological studies). Biology, paralegal studies, and computer science are the strongest academically. Education, criminal justice, and business are the largest.

Required: Students must complete 128 credit hours, including 30 to 65 in the major, plus 15 to 21 minor credits, maintaining a minimum GPA of 2.0. The 52-credit-hour core curriculum includes math, computer science, art, behavioral science, history, literature, philosophy, science, writing, theology, and religion. Specific disciplines required include human nature, intellectual inquiry, and religious dimension.

Special: Internships are offered in sociology, criminal justice, paralegal studies, health care administration, and chemical-dependency counseling. Opportunities are provided for work-study programs, B.A.-B.S. degrees in most majors, dual majors, a general studies degree, credit by exam or for military service, and nondegree study. A 3-2 engineering degree for applied computer science and applied math majors is offered with Montana State University-Bozeman. Specialized instruction is available through the use of videotape and telephone discussions in 14 locations throughout Montana and Canada. There is 1 national honor society.

Faculty/Classroom: 59% of faculty are male; 42%, female. All teach undergraduates. No introductory courses are taught by graduate students. The average class size in an introductory lecture is 15; in a laboratory, 10; and in a regular course, 14.

Requirements: The SAT or ACT is recommended. In addition, graduation from an accredited secondary school is required; the GED is accepted. Applicants should have 4 years of English, 3 of math, and 2 each of social studies, science, and electives, including foreign language, art, music, and vocational education. An interview is recommended. A GPA of 2.0 is required. AP and CLEP credits are accepted.

Procedure: Freshmen are admitted fall, spring, and summer. Entrance exams should be taken prior to registration. Notification is sent on a rolling basis.

Transfer: 98 transfer students enrolled in 2004-2005. Transfer applicants must be in good academic standing from another accredited college or university, and must submit official transcripts from all colleges or universities attended. Those without a bachelor's degree must also submit an official high school transcript. 30 of 128 credits required for the bachelor's degree must be completed at UGF.

Visiting: There are regularly scheduled orientations for prospective students, including meeting with prospective advisers and staff, financial aid presentation, campus tour, and lunch. There are guides for informal visits and visitors may sit in on classes and stay overnight. To schedule a visit, contact the Office of Admissions.

Financial Aid: In 2005-2006, 81% of all full-time freshmen and 83% of continuing full-time students received some form of financial aid. 82% of full-time freshmen and 61% of continuing full-time students received need-based aid. The average freshman award was $9578. 39% of undergraduates work part time. Average annual earnings from campus work are $3000. The average financial indebtedness of the 2005 graduate was $20,470. UGF is a member of CSS. The FAFSA is required.

International Students: There are 19 international students enrolled. The school actively recruits these students. They must score satisfactorily on the written TOEFL.

Computers: All students may access the system 7 days a week. There are no time limits and no fees. It is strongly recommended that all students have a personal computer.

Graduates: From July 1, 2004 to June 30, 2005, 180 bachelor's degrees were awarded. The most popular majors were education (29%), criminal justice (13%), and business (11%). In an average class, 6% graduate in 3 years or less, 6% graduate in 4 years or less, 14% graduate in 5 years or less, and 20% graduate in 6 years or less. 70 companies recruited on campus in 2004-2005. Of the 2004 graduating class, 18% were employed within 6 months of graduation.

Admissions Contact: Cathy Day, Director of Admissions.
E-mail: *adminrec@ugf.edu* Web: *www.ugf.edu*

UNIVERSITY OF MONTANA — B-2

Missoula, MT 59812

(406) 243-6266
(800) 462-8636; Fax: (406) 243-5711

Full-time: 4470 men, 5150 women	**Faculty:** 439; I, --$
Part-time: 853 men, 1031 women	**Ph.D.s:** 86%
Graduate: 922 men, 1176 women	**Student/Faculty:** 21 to 1
Year: semesters, summer session	**Tuition:** $4944 ($13,932)
Application Deadline: March 1	**Room & Board:** $5658
Freshman Class: n/av	
SAT or ACT: required	**COMPETITIVE**

The University of Montana, founded in 1893, is a public institution with programs in arts and sciences, business administration, fine arts, education, forestry, journalism, and pharmacy and allied health sciences. It is part of the Montana University System. Some figures in the above capsule and in this profile are approximate. There are 8 undergraduate and 2 graduate schools. In addition to regional accreditation, U of M has baccalaureate program accreditation with AACSB, ACCE, ACPE, APTA, CAHEA, CSAB, CSWE, NASAD, NASDTEC, NASM, NCATE, and SAF. The 4 libraries contain 100,000,000 volumes, 2,000,000 microform items, and 28,000 audio/video tapes/CDs/DVDs, and subscribe to 4700 periodicals including electronic. Computerized library services include the card catalog, interlibrary loans, and database searching. Special learning facilities include an art gallery, radio station, TV station, and experimental forest, biological station, ranch, Center for People and Forests, geology field camp, international language lab, wilderness institute, observatory, and freshwater research center. The 220-acre campus is in an urban area 200 miles east of Spokane. Including any residence halls, there are 57 buildings.

Student Life: 70% of undergraduates are from Montana. Students are from 50 states, 67 foreign countries, and Canada. 80% are from public schools. 93% are white. The average age of freshmen is 19; all undergraduates, 25. 22% do not continue beyond their first year; 39% remain to graduate.

Housing: 2600 students can be accommodated in college housing, which includes single-sex and coed dorms, off-campus apartments, and married-student housing. In addition, there are honors houses and special-interest houses. On-campus housing is guaranteed for the freshman year only. 75% of students commute. All students may keep cars.

Activities: 10% of men belong to 9 national fraternities; 8% of women belong to 4 national sororities. There are 130 groups on campus, including art, band, cheerleading, chess, choir, chorale, chorus, computers, dance, drill team, ethnic, gay, honors, international, jazz band, literary magazine, marching band, newspaper, opera, orchestra, pep band, political, professional, radio and TV, religious, social, social service, student government, and symphony. Popular campus events include Foresters Day, Founders Day, and International Week.

Sports: There are 6 intercollegiate sports for men and 8 for women, and 16 intramural sports for men and 12 for women. Facilities include a field house, a 10,000-seat gym, an 18,000-seat stadium, a fitness center, a golf course, soccer and rugby fields, an Olympic-size pool, a game room, a climbing wall, weight rooms, and mountain trails.

Disabled Students: 75% of the campus is accessible. Wheelchair ramps, elevators, special parking, specially equipped rest rooms, special class scheduling, lowered drinking fountains, lowered telephones, special housing, and stadium access are available.

Services: Counseling and information services are available, as is tutoring in every subject. There is a reader service for the blind, and remedial math, reading, and writing. Mentors and note takers are available, as are books on tape for LD students.

Campus Safety and Security: Measures include 24-hour foot and vehicle patrol, self-defense education, security escort services, and informal discussions. There are pamphlets/posters/films, emergency telephones, and lighted pathways/sidewalks.

Programs of Study: U of M confers B.A., B.S., B.A.E., B.S.H.P.E., and B.S.M. degrees. Associate, master's, and doctoral degrees are also awarded. Bachelor's degrees are awarded in AGRICULTURE (environmental studies and forestry and related sciences), BIOLOGICAL SCIENCE (biology/biological science, botany, microbiology, wildlife biology, and zoology), BUSINESS (accounting, banking and finance, business administration and management, marketing/retailing/merchandising, personnel management, and small business management), COMMUNICATIONS AND THE ARTS (classics, communications, dramatic arts, English, fine arts, French, German, Japanese, journalism, music, music performance, radio/television technology, Russian, and Spanish), COMPUTER AND PHYSICAL SCIENCE (chemistry, computer science, geology, mathematics, and physics), EDUCATION (elementary, music, physical, science, and secondary), HEALTH PROFESSIONS (medical technology and pharmacy), SOCIAL SCIENCE (anthropology, economics, geography, history, liberal arts/general studies, Native American studies, philosophy, political science/government, psychology, social work, sociology, and women's studies). Journalism, forestry, and liberal arts are the strongest academically. Business, forestry, and education are the largest.

Required: A total of 120 credits is required for graduation in most majors. The number of hours in the major varies; some majors require a thesis. There are competency requirements in writing, math, and foreign language or symbolic systems. Juniors must pass writing exams. Distribution requirements include courses in expressive arts, literary and artistic studies, historical and cultural studies, social sciences, ethical and human values, and natural sciences. A minimum GPA of 2.0 must be maintained.

Special: Students may cross-register with Montana Tech and Western Montana College. Co-op programs exist in business, communications, economics, management, and liberal studies; internships in most majors, work-study programs with nonprofit organizations, and study abroad in 12 countries are available. The school offers a B.A.-B.S. degree in chemistry, pass/fail options in classes other than major requirements, and dual majors in physics and computer science as well as history and political science. There are 7 national honor societies, including Phi Beta Kappa, a freshman honors program, and 5 departmental honors programs.

Faculty/Classroom: 67% of faculty are male; 33%, female. All both teach and do research. Graduate students teach 2% of introductory courses. The average class size in an introductory lecture is 35; in a laboratory, 25; and in a regular course, 35.

Admissions: The SAT scores for the 2005-2006 freshman class were: Verbal--26% below 500, 42% between 500 and 599, 25% between 600 and 700, and 6% above 700; Math--28% below 500, 47% between 500 and 599, 22% between 600 and 700, and 4% above 700. 17% of the current freshmen were in the top tentfh of their class; 41% were in the top quarter; 71% were in the top half.

Requirements: The SAT or ACT is required, with a minimum composite ACT score of 22 or a satisfactory SAT verbal-math-writing composite score. Applicants must be graduates of an accredited secondary school. The GED is accepted. Students should have completed 4 years of English, 3 of math, 3 of social studies, 2 of lab science, and 2 from foreign language, computer science, visual arts, or vocational educattion. U of M requires applicants to be in the upper 50% of their class. A GPA of 2.5 is required. AP and CLEP credits are accepted. Important factors in the admissions decision are advanced placement or honor courses, evidence of special talent, and geographic diversity.

Procedure: Freshmen are admitted to all sessions. There are deferred admissions and rolling admissions plans. Applications should be filed by March 1 for fall entry and November 15 for spring entry, along with a $30 fee. Notification is sent on a rolling basis. Applications are accepted on-line.

Transfer: 1373 transfer students enrolled in 2004-2005. Applicants must have a minimum GPA of 2.0. Grades of 2.0 or better transfer for credit. 30 of 120 credits required for the bachelor's degree must be completed at U of M.

Visiting: There are regularly scheduled orientations for prospective students, including placement testing, advising, workshops, and social events. There are guides for informal visits and visitors may sit in on classes. To schedule a visit, contact the Office of Admissions and New Student Services.

Financial Aid: In a recent year, 79% of all full-time freshmen and 83% of continuing full-time students received some form of financial aid. 79% of full-time freshmen and 83% of continuing full-time students received need-based aid. The average freshman award in a recent year was $8000. Need-based scholarships or need-based grants averaged $3069; need-based self-help aid (loans and jobs) averaged $7961; non-need-based athletic scholarships averaged $2297; and other non-need-based awards and non-need-based scholarships averaged $3000. U of M is a member of CSS. The FAFSA is required. Check with the school for current deadlines.

International Students: The school actively recruits these students. A satisfactory score is required on the written TOEFL.

Computers: All students may access the system any time. There are no time limits. The fee is $3 per credit. It is strongly recommended that all students have a PC.

Admissions Contact: Jed Liston, Assistant VP for Enrollment. A video is available. E-mail: admiss@umontana.edu Web: http://admissions.umt.edu

UNIVERSITY OF MONTANA--WESTERN   B-3
Dillon, MT 59725   (406) 683-7331
                              (866) UMW-MONT; Fax: (406) 683-7493

Full-time: 441 men, 500 women	**Faculty:** 47; IIB, --$
Part-time: 32 men, 186 women	**Ph.D.s:** 75%
Graduate: none	**Student/Faculty:** 20 to 1
Year: semesters, summer session	**Tuition:** $3506 ($12,300)
Application Deadline: July 1	**Room & Board:** $4900
Freshman Class: n/av	
SAT or ACT: required	**NONCOMPETITIVE**

The University of Montana-Western College, established in 1893, is a public institution, part of the University of Montana system. The college emphasizes teacher education and liberal studies. There are 2 undergraduate schools. In addition to regional accreditation, Western has baccalaureate program accreditation with NCATE. The library contains 90,431 volumes, 5792 microform items, and 3718 audio/video tapes/CDs/DVDs, and subscribes to 7127 periodicals including electronic. Computerized library services include the card catalog, interlibrary loans, database searching, and Internet access. Special learning facilities include a learning resource center, art gallery, radio station, and a humanities resource center. The 34-acre campus is in a small town 60 miles south of Butte and 150 miles from Yellowstone National Park. Including any residence halls, there are 29 buildings.

Student Life: 85% of undergraduates are from Montana. Students are from 12 states, 2 foreign countries, and Canada. 90% are from public schools. 86% are white. The average age of freshmen is 22; all undergraduates, 22. 30% do not continue beyond their first year.

Housing: 485 students can be accommodated in college housing, which includes single-sex and coed dorms, on-campus apartments, and married-student housing. On-campus housing is guaranteed for all 4 years, is available on a first-come, first-served basis, and is available on a lottery system for upperclassmen. 75% of students commute. Alcohol is not permitted. All students may keep cars.

Activities: There are no fraternities or sororities. There are 24 groups on campus, including art, band, cheerleading, choir, chorale, drama, ethnic, honors, musical theater, newspaper, pep band, political, radio and TV, religious, social, social service, student government, and yearbook. Popular campus events include Alumni Weekend and International Week.

Sports: There are 4 intercollegiate sports for men and 4 for women, and 7 intramural sports for men and 7 for women. Facilities include a 5000-seat gym, 3 basketball and 4 racquetball courts, a dance floor, tennis courts, 2 weight rooms, an aerobics room, circuit training, an indoor arena, and a 3000-seat stadium.

Disabled Students: 98% of the campus is accessible. Wheelchair ramps, elevators, special parking, specially equipped rest rooms, special class scheduling, lowered drinking fountains, and lowered telephones are available.

Services: Counseling and information services are available, as is tutoring in most subjects, including . There is a reader service for the blind and remedial math.

Campus Safety and Security: Measures include 24-hour foot and vehicle patrol, security escort services, informal discussions, and pamphlets/posters/films. There are emergency telephones and lighted pathways/sidewalks.

Programs of Study: Western confers B.A., B.S. Business, B.Applied Sc., and B.S.Ed. degrees. Associate degrees are also awarded. Bachelor's degrees are awarded in COMMUNICATIONS AND THE ARTS (art, communications, creative writing, English literature, and technical and business writing), EDUCATION (art, business, elementary, industrial arts, middle school, music, science, and secondary), ENGINEERING AND ENVIRONMENTAL DESIGN (environmental science), SOCIAL SCIENCE (liberal arts/general studies and social science). Elementary education is the largest.

Required: For graduation, students must complete 120 credit hours (128 for education) and maintain a minimum GPA of 2.0. Other requirements vary by major.

Special: The college offers co-op programs, work-study programs, B.A.-B.S. degrees, dual majors, and pass/fail options. The Rural Education Program is designed to prepare students for teaching in smaller rural school settings. There are 2 national honor societies and a freshman honors program.

Faculty/Classroom: 56% of faculty are male; 44%, female. All teach undergraduates. The average class size in an introductory lecture is 35; in a laboratory, 20; and in a regular course, 19.

Admissions: 3 freshmen graduated first in their class in a recent year.

Requirements: The SAT or ACT is required. In addition, new students who have not taken the ACT or SAT must complete it during their first semester of attendance. Applicants must be graduates of an accredited secondary school. The GED is accepted. Students should have completed 4 years of English, 3 each of social studies and math and 2 years each of lab science, and science, and electives. Western requires applicants to be in the upper 50% of their class. A GPA of 2.5 is required. AP and CLEP credits are accepted.

Procedure: Freshmen are admitted to all sessions. There are deferred admissions and rolling admissions plans. Applications should be filed by July 1 for fall entry, December 1 for spring entry, and May 1 for summer entry, along with a $30 fee. The college accepts all applicants. Notification is sent on a rolling basis. Applications are accepted on-line.

Transfer: 153 transfer students enrolled in 2004-2005. Transfers must have attempted a minimum of 12 credit hours and have a cumulative GPA of 2.0. Credits earned at any accredited college can be used to satisfy curriculum or degree requirements only after evaluation. 30 of 120 credits required for the bachelor's degree must be completed at Western.

Visiting: There are regularly scheduled orientations for prospective students, including Sunday through Monday overnight stays. There are guides for informal visits and visitors may sit in on classes and stay overnight. To schedule a visit, contact the Admissions Office.

Financial Aid: In 2005-2006, 76% of all full-time freshmen and 80% of continuing full-time students received some form of financial aid. 68% of full-time freshmen and 43% of continuing full-time students received need-based aid. The average freshman award was $4743. 96% of undergraduates work part time. Average annual earnings from campus work are $1500. The average financial indebtedness of the 2005 graduate was $17,750. The FAFSA is required. The priority date for freshman financial aid applications for fall entry is March 1.

International Students: There were 3 international students enrolled in a recent year. A satisfactory score is required on the written TOEFL. The ACT or SAT is required for Canadian high school students.

Computers: All students may access the system from 8 A.M. to 10 P.M. There are no time limits. The fee is $36. It is strongly recommended that all students have a PC.

Graduates: From July 1, 2004 to June 30, 2005, 147 bachelor's degrees were awarded. The most popular majors were elementary education (27%), liberal arts and sciences (27%), and secondary education (22%). In an average class, 10% graduate in 4 years or less, 22% graduate in 5 years or less, and 28% graduate in 6 years or less. Of the 2004 graduating class, 94% were employed within 6 months of graduation.

Admissions Contact: Eric Murray, Dean of Student Affairs. E-mail: *admissions@umwestern.edu* Web: *www.umwestern.edu*

NEBRASKA

NEBRASKA

POPULATION DENSITY
• 10,000 and over

0 20 40 60 80 100
Miles

BELLEVUE UNIVERSITY   F-3
Bellevue, NE 68005

(402) 293-3702
(800) 756-7920; Fax: (402) 293-3730

Full-time: 1282 men, 1140 women	**Faculty:** 48; IIA, --$
Part-time: 590 men, 654 women	**Ph.D.s:** 56%
Graduate: 534 men, 643 women	**Student/Faculty:** 50 to 1
Year: semesters, summer session	**Tuition:** $4440
Application Deadline: open	**Room & Board:** n/app
Freshman Class: n/av	
SAT or ACT: required	**NONCOMPETITIVE**

Bellevue University, established in 1966, is a private commuter institution offering undergraduate degrees in arts and sciences, professional studies, and business. Figures in the above capsule and in this profile are approximate. There are 3 undergraduate schools and 1 graduate school. The library contains 122,000 volumes and 6700 microform items, and subscribes to 500 periodicals including electronic. Computerized library services include the card catalog, interlibrary loans, and database searching. Special learning facilities include a learning resource center and art gallery. The 19-acre campus is in a suburban area 5 miles south of Omaha. There are 6 buildings.

Student Life: 95% of undergraduates are from Nebraska. Others are from 66 foreign countries. 90% are from public schools. 86% are white. The average age of all undergraduates is 25. 12% do not continue beyond their first year; 40% remain to graduate.

Housing: There are no residence halls. All students commute. Alcohol is not permitted.

Activities: There are no fraternities or sororities. There are 3 groups on campus, including cheerleading, newspaper, and professional. Popular campus events include Halloween and Christmas parties, Black History Month, and Spring Bash.

Sports: There are 2 intercollegiate sports for men and 1 for women. Facilities include racquetball, basketball, and volleyball courts and weight-lifting equipment.

Disabled Students: All of the campus is accessible. Wheelchair ramps, special parking, specially equipped rest rooms, and lowered drinking fountains are available.

Services: Counseling and information services are available, as is tutoring in most subjects.

Campus Safety and Security: Measures include self-defense education, informal discussions, pamphlets/posters/films, and lighted pathways/sidewalks.

Programs of Study: Bellevue University confers B.A., B.S., and B.F.A. degrees. Master's degrees are also awarded. Bachelor's degrees are awarded in BUSINESS (accounting, business administration and management, and personnel management), COMMUNICATIONS AND THE ARTS (communications, English, fine arts, and photography), COMPUTER AND PHYSICAL SCIENCE (information sciences and systems), EDUCATION (physical), SOCIAL SCIENCE (criminal justice, geography, history, philosophy, political science/government, psychology, social science, sociology, and urban studies). Business administration is the strongest academically.

Required: To graduate, students must complete the core curriculum, with course work in communicative arts, a foreign language, art, English literature, foreign language literature, culture, civilization, music, philosophy, biology, chemistry, geology, math, geography, physics, psychology, sociology, economics, history, and political science. The required distribution of core credits varies by degree program from 63 to 66, and the total number of hours in the major varies by major. Students must earn 127 to 132 credits, depending on the degree. The minimum required GPA is 2.0 overall and 2.5 in the major.

Special: Bellevue University offers co-op programs with Buena Vista Colleges and Grace College of the Bible, internships, and work-study. Students may earn B.A.-B.S. degrees, and an accelerated degree program is possible in professional studies. The university permits dual majors, and composite, interdisciplinary majors are available in the social sciences and urban studies. Credit may be conferred for military experience. Nondegree study is possible. The Lockstep Degree Competition Program offers an alternative to the traditional academic structure. The School of Arts and Sciences operates on a 4-day academic week to provide flexibility. There is 1 national honor society.

Faculty/Classroom: 91% teach undergraduates. No introductory courses are taught by graduate students. The average class size in an introductory lecture is 35; in a laboratory, 25; and in a regular course, 25.

Requirements: The ACT, or the SAT is required for those entering college within 2 years after high school graduation; submission of ACT or SAT scores is recommended for all others. Applicants must be graduates of an accredited secondary school or have a GED. Interviews are recommended. AP and CLEP credits are accepted.

Procedure: Freshmen are admitted to all sessions. Entrance exams should be taken in April. There are early decision and early admissions plans. There is a rolling admissions plan. Application deadlines are open. The fall 2005 application fee was $10.

Transfer: 30 of 127 to 132 credits required for the bachelor's degree must be completed at Bellevue University.

Visiting: There are regularly scheduled orientations for prospective students. There are guides for informal visits and visitors may sit in on classes. To schedule a visit, contact the Admissions Office.

Financial Aid: The FAFSA is required.

International Students: The school actively recruits these students. They must score satisfactorily on the written TOEFL or take the MELAB and must also take the ACT or SAT.

Computers: Students enrolled in classes where a computer fee is charged may access the system. There are no time limits.

Admissions Contact: Elizabeth Wall, Director of Admissions. E-mail: eaw@scholars.bellevue.edu Web: http://www.bellevue.edu

CHADRON STATE COLLEGE   B-1
Chadron, NE 69337

(308) 432-6263
(800) CHADRON; Fax: (308) 432-6229

Full-time: 755 men, 1015 women	**Faculty:** 98; IIA, --$
Part-time: 175 men, 360 women	**Ph.D.s:** 74%
Graduate: 120 men, 305 women	**Student/Faculty:** 18 to 1
Year: semesters, summer session	**Tuition:** $2450 ($4550)
Application Deadline: open	**Room & Board:** $3900
Freshman Class: n/av	
SAT or ACT: recommended	**NONCOMPETITIVE**

Chadron State College, founded in 1911, is a public college offering programs in liberal arts and professional training. There are 2 undergraduate schools and 1 graduate school. Figures in the above capsule and profile are approximate. In addition to regional accreditation, CSC has baccalaureate program accreditation with CSWE and NCATE. The library contains 205,398 volumes, 361,342 microform items, and 4160 audio/video tapes/CDs/DVDs, and subscribes to 720 periodicals including electronic. Computerized library services include the card catalog, interlibrary loans, and database searching. Special learning facilities include a learning resource center, natural history museum, planetarium, and radio station. The 281-acre campus is in a small town 100 miles south of Rapid City, South Dakota. Including any residence halls, there are 27 buildings.

Student Life: 72% of undergraduates are from Nebraska. Others are from 6 foreign countries and Canada. 97% are from public schools. 90% are white. 45% are Protestant; 40% Catholic; 13% claim no religious affiliation. The average age of freshmen is 18; all undergraduates, 22. 35% do not continue beyond their first year; 33% remain to graduate.

Housing: 1200 students can be accommodated in college housing, which includes single-sex and coed dormitories and married-student housing. In addition, there are honors houses. On-campus housing is guaranteed for all 4 years. 65% of students commute. Alcohol is not permitted. All students may keep cars.

Activities: There are no fraternities or sororities. There are 71 groups on campus, including art, band, cheerleading, choir, dance, ethnic, gay, honors, international, jazz band, musical theater, newspaper, orchestra, pep band, photography, political, radio and TV, science fiction, student government, symphony and video. Popular campus events include Spring Daze.

Sports: There are 5 intercollegiate sports for men and 5 for women, and 46 intramural sports for men and 46 for women. Facilities include a 3000-seat stadium, a gym, a swimming pool, and an activity center.

Disabled Students: All of the campus is accessible. Wheelchair ramps, elevators, special parking, specially equipped rest rooms, special class scheduling, lowered drinking fountains, and special housing are available.

Services: Counseling and information services are available, as is tutoring in most subjects. There is a reader service for the blind, and remedial math, reading, and writing.

Campus Safety and Security: Measures include 24-hour foot and vehicle patrol, self-defense education, informal discussions, and pamphlets/posters/films. There are emergency telephones and lighted pathways/sidewalks.

Programs of Study: CSC confers B.A., B.S., and B.S.E. degrees. Master's degrees are also awarded. Bachelor's degrees are awarded in BIOLOGICAL SCIENCE (biology/biological science), BUSINESS (business administration and management), COMMUNICATIONS AND THE ARTS (art, dramatic arts, English, music, and speech/debate/rhetoric), COMPUTER AND PHYSICAL SCIENCE (chemistry, mathematics, and physics), EDUCATION (early childhood, elementary, health, science, and secondary), ENGINEERING AND ENVIRONMENTAL DESIGN (industrial engineering technology), HEALTH PROFESSIONS (predentistry and premedicine), SOCIAL SCIENCE (criminal justice, history, political science/government, prelaw, psychology, social science, social work, and sociology). Education, business, and health professions are the strongest academically. Education, business, and justice studies are the largest.

Required: For graduation, students must complete 125 credit hours, including 47 hours of general education courses, and maintain a 2.0 GPA for the B.A. and a 2.5 GPA for the B.S.E. Other requirements vary by major.

Special: The college offers internships, a Washington semester, and work-study programs. Dual majors, co-op programs, and credit for life, military, and work experience are possible. There are 12 national honor societies, and a freshman honors program.

Faculty/Classroom: 72% of faculty are male; 28%, female. All teach undergraduates. Graduate students teach 2% of introductory courses. The average class size in an introductory lecture is 36; in a laboratory, 19; and in a regular course, 25.

Requirements: The SAT or ACT is recommended unless the applicant has been out of high school for more than 5 years. Applicants need not be graduates of an accredited secondary school. The GED is accepted. High school work should include a minimum of 15 academic units, with at least 3 units in English, and others in math, science, social studies, and foreign language. AP and CLEP credits are accepted. Important factors in the admissions decision are advanced placement or honor courses, evidence of special talent, and leadership record.

Procedure: Freshmen are admitted to all sessions. There is a rolling admissions plan. Entrance exams should be taken . Application deadlines are open. Applications are accepted on-line. The fall 2005 application fee was $15.

Transfer: A maximum of 66 semester credits earned at an accredited 2-year college may be transferred. The registrar will evaluate credit earned at a 3- or 4-year college to determine the student's classification. All passing credit obtained from an institution is accepted in programs offered by Chadron State. Transfers are admitted every term. 30 of 125 credits required for the bachelor's degree must be completed at CSC.

Visiting: There are regularly scheduled orientations for prospective students, including visits with faculty, tours of the campus, meetings with financial aid and housing advisers, and complimentary meals. There are guides for informal visits and visitors may sit in on classes and stay overnight. To schedule a visit, contact the Admissions Office.

Financial Aid: Check with the school for application deadlines.

International Students: They must score satisfactorily on the written TOEFL and also take the SAT or the ACT.

Computers: All students may access the system 7:30 A.M. to 10:30 P.M.

Graduates: In a recent year, 499 bachelor's degrees were awarded. The most popular majors were education (27%), business (25%), and justice studies (15%). In an average class, 1% graduate in 3 years or less, 12% graduate in 4 years or less, 30% graduate in 5 years or less, and 34% graduate in 6 years or less. 7 companies recruited on campus in a recent year.

Admissions Contact: Tena Cook Gould, Director of Admissions. E-mail: tgould@csc.edu Web: www.csc.edu

CLARKSON COLLEGE   F-3
Omaha, NE 68131

(402) 552-3041
(800) 647-5500; Fax: (402) 552-6057

Full-time: 10 men, 200 women	**Faculty:** 43; IIB, --$
Part-time: 20 men, 100 women	**Ph.D.s:** 36%
Graduate: 10 men, 100 women	**Student/Faculty:** 4 to 1
Year: semesters, summer session	**Tuition:** $10,000
Application Deadline: open	**Room & Board:** $3000
Freshman Class: n/av	
SAT or ACT: required	**COMPETITIVE**

Clarkson College, established in 1888 and affiliated with the Episcopal Church, offers undergraduate and graduate degrees in the health care professions and business. There are 3 undergraduate and 2 graduate schools.Figures in the above capsule and in this profile are approximate. In addition to regional accreditation, Clarkson has baccalaureate program accreditation with NLN. The library contains 8100 volumes, 100 microform items, and 600 audio/video tapes/CDs/DVDs, and subscribes to 300 periodicals including electronic. Computerized library services include the card catalog, interlibrary loans, and database searching. Special learning facilities include a learning resource center, art gallery, and regional medical center. The 29-acre campus is in an urban area in Omaha. Including any residence halls, there are 13 buildings.

Student Life: 61% of undergraduates are from Nebraska. Others are from 13 states and 1 foreign country. 90% are from public schools. 90% are white. 50% are Catholic; 45% Protestant. The average age of freshmen is 23; all undergraduates, 27. 10% do not continue beyond their first year; 87% remain to graduate.

Housing: 54 students can be accommodated in college housing, which includes coed on-campus apartments. On-campus housing is available on a first-come, first-served basis. Priority is given to out-of-town students. 90% of students commute. Alcohol is not permitted. All students may keep cars.

Activities: There are no fraternities or sororities. There are 12 groups on campus, including chorus, newspaper, professional, social, social service, and student government. Popular campus events include holiday dances and parties.

Sports: There is no sports program at Clarkson. Facilities are available at the adjacent University of Nebraska Medical Center and include basketball and volleyball courts, exercise equipment, and a weight room.

Disabled Students: 95% of the campus is accessible. Wheelchair ramps, elevators, special parking, specially equipped rest rooms, special class scheduling, lowered drinking fountains, and lowered telephones are available.

Services: Counseling and information services are available, as is tutoring in every subject.

Campus Safety and Security: Measures include 24-hour foot and vehicle patrol, self-defense education, security escort services, and informal discussions. There are pamphlets/posters/films, emergency telephones, and lighted pathways/sidewalks.

Programs of Study: Clarkson confers B.S. and B.S.N. degrees. Associate and master's degrees are also awarded. Bachelor's degrees are awarded in BUSINESS (business administration and management), COMPUTER AND PHYSICAL SCIENCE (radiological technology), HEALTH PROFESSIONS (nursing and radiograph medical technology). Radiological technology and nursing are the strongest academically. Nursing is the largest.

Required: To graduate, students must complete 128 credit hours, including 68 in the major, and maintain a minimum GPA of 2.0. General education requirements include courses in the humanities, English, behavioral and social sciences, science and math, and phys ed. A 9-hour core curriculum is also required.

Special: A co-op program in nursing, study abroad in England, work-study programs, and dual majors are available. Credit is given for military experience, and nondegree study is possible. The distance education option allows advanced placement students living a distance from the campus to complete their studies at home. There is 1 national honor society.

Faculty/Classroom: 21% of faculty are male; 79%, female. All teach undergraduates. No introductory courses are taught by graduate students. The average class size in an introductory lecture is 45; in a laboratory, 10; and in a regular course, 35.

Requirements: The SAT or ACT is required. The ACT is preferred. Tests are not required for applicants more than 2 years out of high school. Applicants must be graduates of an accredited secondary school, with 3 years of English and 2 each of social science, algebra, and science (including lab science). The GED is accepted. Clarkson requires applicants to be in the upper 50% of their class. A GPA of 2.0 is required. AP and CLEP credits are accepted. Important factors in the admissions decision are advanced placement or honor courses, extracurricular activities record, and evidence of special talent.

Procedure: Freshmen are admitted to all sessions. Entrance exams should be taken during the junior year or first semester of the senior year. There is a deferred admissions plan. Application deadlines are open. The fall 2005 application fee was $15. A waiting list is an active part of the admissions procedure.

Transfer: Transfer students must have a minimum GPA of 2.5. Grades of C or better transfer for credit. Transfers are admitted for fall and spring. An interview is sometimes required. 64 of 128 credits required for the bachelor's degree must be completed at Clarkson.

Visiting: There are regularly scheduled orientations for prospective students. There are guides for informal visits and visitors may sit in on classes. To schedule a visit, contact the Admissions Office.

Financial Aid: Clarkson is a member of CSS. The FAFSA and the college's own financial statement are required. Check with the school for current deadlines.

International Students: They must score satisfactorily on the written TOEFL, 85 on the MELAB, or 5 on the TWE and also take the SAT or the ACT.

Computers: All students may access the system 7 A.M. to 8:30 P.M. There are no time limits and no fees.

Admissions Contact: Director of Admissions.
E-mail: *admiss@clarksoncollege.edu* Web: *www.clarksoncollege.edu*

COLLEGE OF SAINT MARY   F-2
Omaha, NE 68106

	(402) 399-2425
	(800) 926-5534; Fax: (402) 399-2412
Full-time: 641 women	Faculty: 53; IIB, --$
Part-time: 298 women	Ph.D.s: 43%
Graduate: 16 women	Student/Faculty: 12 to 1
Year: semesters, summer session	Tuition: $18,038
Application Deadline: open	Room & Board: $5900
Freshman Class: 239 applied, 233 accepted, 82 enrolled	
ACT: 20	COMPETITIVE

College of Saint Mary, founded in 1923, is a private Roman Catholic women's college offering a program that combines training for professional careers with a liberal arts component. In addition to regional accreditation, CSM has baccalaureate program accreditation with ACOTE,

AHIMA, CAHEA, and NLN. The library contains 149,126 volumes and 2276 audio/video tapes/CDs/DVDs, and subscribes to 277 periodicals including electronic. Computerized library services include the card catalog, interlibrary loans, database searching, Internet access, and laptop Internet portals. Special learning facilities include a learning resource center and art gallery. The 25-acre campus is in a suburban area 5 miles west of downtown Omaha. Including any residence halls, there are 8 buildings.

Student Life: 90% of undergraduates are from Nebraska. Others are from 17 states and 7 foreign countries. 82% are from public schools. 87% are white. Most are Catholic. The average age of freshmen is 27; all undergraduates, 28. 29% do not continue beyond their first year; 47% remain to graduate.

Housing: 274 students can be accommodated in college housing, which includes dorms. In addition, here is a residential program for single mothers. On-campus housing is guaranteed for all 4 years. 85% of students commute. All students may keep cars.

Activities: There are 20 groups on campus, including cheerleading, ethnic, honors, international, professional, religious, social, social service, and student government. Popular campus events include Fine Arts Festival, the Queen of Hearts Dance, and Casino Nite.

Sports: Facilities include a gym, a 6-lane swimming pool, a weight room, an elevated running track, an exercise room, a training room, 4 outdoor tennis courts, 2 soccer fields, and 2 softball fields.

Disabled Students: 85% of the campus is accessible. Wheelchair ramps, elevators, special parking, specially equipped rest rooms, special class scheduling, lowered drinking fountains, special housing, and electric door openers are available.

Services: Counseling and information services are available, as is tutoring in most subjects. There is a reader service for the blind, and remedial math, reading, and writing. There are also study groups.

Campus Safety and Security: Measures include 24-hour foot and vehicle patrol, self-defense education, security escort services, and informal discussions. There are pamphlets/posters/films, lighted pathways/sidewalks, and camera-monitored and coded entrances to residence halls.

Programs of Study: CSM confers B.A., B.S., B.B.L., and B.G.S. degrees. Associate and master's degrees are also awarded. Bachelor's degrees are awarded in BIOLOGICAL SCIENCE (biology/biological science), BUSINESS (business administration and management), COMMUNICATIONS AND THE ARTS (art and English), COMPUTER AND PHYSICAL SCIENCE (chemistry, computer management, mathematics, and natural sciences), EDUCATION (early childhood, education, elementary, and special), HEALTH PROFESSIONS (medical laboratory technology, nursing, and occupational therapy), SOCIAL SCIENCE (human services, humanities, liberal arts/general studies, paralegal studies, and psychology). Preprofessional studies and occupational therapy are the strongest academically. Nursing, business, and education are the largest.

Required: To graduate, students must complete 128 semester hours, with a minimum of 30 hours in the major and a 2.0 GPA in the major and overall. Required core education courses total 47 hours, with 9 in math and science, 6 in English, 3 each in communications, computer, ethics, fine arts, liberal arts, history, philosophy, social science, and theology, and 1 each in phys ed and a core seminar. Students must demonstrate competency in math and English.

Special: Students may pursue internships in any major, including research courses in the sciences. CSM also offers dual majors, study abroad in 11 countries, nondegree study, pass/fail options, an accelerated degree program in business leadership, and credit for life, military, and work experience. There are 2 national honor societies.

Faculty/Classroom: 20% of faculty are male; 80%, female. 98% teach undergraduates. The average class size in an introductory lecture is 19; in a laboratory, 20; and in a regular course, 11.

Admissions: 97% of the 2005-2006 applicants were accepted. The ACT scores for the 2005-2006 freshman class were: 54% below 21, 34% between 21 and 23, 8% between 24 and 26, 3% between 27 and 28, and 1% above 28. 30% of the current freshmen were in the top fifth of their class; 71% were in the top two fifths. 2 freshmen graduated first in their class.

Requirements: The SAT or ACT is required. In addition, students must meet 2 out of 3 criteria: a satisfactory score on the ACT, a GPA of at least 2.0, and rank in the upper 50% of their class. Applicants must be graduates of an accredited secondary school. The GED is accepted. Students should have completed 16 academic units, including 4 years of English and 2 each of math, social studies, and science, with biology and chemistry required for the various health profession majors. An interview is recommended. AP and CLEP credits are accepted.

Procedure: Freshmen are admitted to all sessions. Entrance exams should be taken in the junior or senior year. There are rolling admissions and a deferred admissions plan. Application deadlines are open. Application fee is $30. Notification is sent within 2 weeks of receipt of an application. Applications are accepted on-line.

Transfer: 248 transfer students enrolled in 2004-2005. Applicants should have a minimum GPA of 2.0 and submit official transcripts from previous colleges attended. Students with fewer than 12 credit hours must also submit ACT or SAT scores. Grades of C or better transfer for credit. Students are admitted every term. 30 of 128 credits required for the bachelor's degree must be completed at CSM.

Visiting: There are regularly scheduled orientations for prospective students, consisting of touring the campus, attending financial aid and student-life presentations, and sitting in on classes of a student's choice. Visitors are CSM's guests for lunch or overnight. There are guides for informal visits. To schedule a visit, contact the Office of Enrollment Services at (402) 399-2405 or *enroll@csm.edu.*

Financial Aid: In 2005-2006, 80% of all full-time freshmen and 86% of continuing full-time students received some form of financial aid. 68% of full-time freshmen and 75% of continuing full-time students received need-based aid. The average freshman award was $15,284. Need-based scholarships or need-based grants averaged $504; need-based self-help aid (loans and jobs) averaged $1796; non-need-based athletic scholarships averaged $3373; and other non-need-based awards and non-need-based scholarships averaged $10,504. 17% of undergraduates work part time. Average annual earnings from campus work are $1176. The average financial indebtedness of the 2005 graduate was $16,000. The FAFSA is required. The priority date for freshman financial aid applications for fall entry is March 1. The deadline for filing freshman financial aid applications for fall entry is April 1.

International Students: There are 8 international students enrolled. The school actively recruits these students. They must score satisfactorily on the written TOEFL.

Computers: Students can access campus resources from 100 PCs spread across 5 PC labs. Wired connections allow access to file and print resources. 2 wireless zones, 1 in the library and 1 in the main auditorium, provide connectivity for students' laptops. 8 wireless laptops are available in the library. All students may access the system 8 A.M. to midnight Monday through Thursday, 8 A.M. to 5 P.M. Friday, 10 A.M. to 5 P.M. Saturday, and 1 P.M. to midnight Sunday. There are no time limits and no fees.

Graduates: From July 1, 2004 to June 30, 2005, 116 bachelor's degrees were awarded. The most popular majors were nursing (45%), business (14%), and education (10%). In an average class, 39% graduate in 4 years or less, 46% graduate in 5 years or less, and 47% graduate in 6 years or less. 86 companies recruited on campus in 2004-2005. Of the 2004 graduating class, 3% were enrolled in graduate school within 6 months of graduation and 85% were employed.

Admissions Contact: Sue Kropf, Enrollment Director.
E-mail: *enroll@csm.edu* Web: *www.csm.edu*

CONCORDIA UNIVERSITY NEBRASKA E-3

Seward, NE 68434

(402) 643-7233
(800) 535-5494; Fax: (402) 643-4073

Full-time: 500 men, 600 women	**Faculty:** 66; IIB, --$
Part-time: 30 men, 50 women	**Ph.D.s:** 85%
Graduate: 40 men, 80 women	**Student/Faculty:** 17 to 1
Year: semesters, summer session	**Tuition:** $16,000
Application Deadline: see profile	**Room & Board:** $4500
Freshman Class: n/av	
SAT or ACT: required	**COMPETITIVE+**

Concordia University Nebraska, founded in 1894, is a private university owned and operated by the Lutheran Church-Missouri Synod, with degree programs in professional education and liberal arts. Figures in the above capsule and in this profile are approximate. Among Concordia's major programs are those for professional work in the Lutheran Church: teacher education, director of Christian education, preseminary pastoral training, and church music. In addition to regional accreditation, Concordia has baccalaureate program accreditation with NCATE. The 3 libraries contain 177,700 volumes, 10,700 microform items, and 13,200 audio/video tapes/CDs/DVDs, and subscribe to 550 periodicals including electronic. Computerized library services include the card catalog and database searching. Special learning facilities include a learning resource center, art gallery, natural history museum, and observatory. The 120-acre campus is in a small town 25 miles west of Lincoln. Including any residence halls, there are 25 buildings.

Student Life: 59% of undergraduates are from out of state, mostly the Midwest. Students are from 37 states and 9 foreign countries. 95% are white. Most are Protestant. The average age of freshmen is 18; all undergraduates, 21. 48% of freshmen remain to graduate.

Housing: 815 students can be accommodated in college housing, which includes single-sex dorms, off-campus apartments, and married-student housing. On-campus housing is guaranteed for all 4 years. 90% of students live on campus; of those, 90% remain on campus on weekends. Alcohol is not permitted. All students may keep cars.

Activities: There are no fraternities or sororities. There are 35 groups on campus, including band, cheerleading, choir, chorale, chorus, computers, dance, debate, drama, drill team, ethnic, forensics, honors, international, jazz band, literary magazine, musical theater, newspaper, orchestra, pep band, photography, professional, religious, social, social

service, student government, and yearbook. Popular campus events include Spring Weekend and Multicultural Awareness Week.

Sports: There are 8 intercollegiate sports for men and 8 for women, and 7 intramural sports for men and 7 for women. Facilities include a gym, a weight-training room, an indoor pool, football, baseball, and soccer fields, and a track and field stadium.

Disabled Students: 35% of the campus is accessible. Wheelchair ramps, elevators, special parking, specially equipped rest rooms, lowered drinking fountains, and lowered telephones are available.

Services: Counseling and information services are available, as is tutoring in every subject. There is a reader service for the blind, and there are talking books and tape recorders.

Campus Safety and Security: Measures include 24-hour foot and vehicle patrol, self-defense education, security escort services, and informal discussions. There are pamphlets/posters/films, emergency telephones, lighted pathways/sidewalks,vehicle and bicycle registration, and a possession ID engraving program.

Programs of Study: Concordia confers B.A., B.S., B.F.A., B.S.Med.Tech., B.Mus., and B. Sacred Music degrees. Master's degrees are also awarded. Bachelor's degrees are awarded in BIOLOGICAL SCIENCE (biology/biological science), BUSINESS (accounting, business administration and management, and sports management), COMMUNICATIONS AND THE ARTS (communications, dramatic arts, English, fine arts, music, speech/debate/rhetoric, and studio art), COMPUTER AND PHYSICAL SCIENCE (chemistry, computer science, mathematics, natural sciences, and physical sciences), EDUCATION (business, Christian, early childhood, elementary, home economics, industrial arts, middle school, music, physical, science, secondary, and special), HEALTH PROFESSIONS (exercise science, health, medical laboratory technology, predentistry, and premedicine), SOCIAL SCIENCE (behavioral science, geography, history, physical fitness/movement, prelaw, psychology, and theological studies). Education, business, and art are the strongest academically. Education is the largest.

Required: To graduate, students must complete a minimum of 128 credits with a GPA of at least 2.0. Required general education courses include 12 hours of theology, 9 hours each of English/speech, social science, and science, 6 of fine arts, 3 each of math and health and phys ed, 2 to 3 of electives, and 1 hour minimum of computer literacy.

Special: Concordia offers cross-registration with the University of Nebraska in Lincoln. Internships are available in education, business, and Christian education. B.A.-B.S. degrees, student-designed majors, dual majors, study abroad in England and China, nondegree studies, and pass/fail options are available. There is an accelerated degree program in organizational management. There is a freshman honors program.

Faculty/Classroom: 71% of faculty are male; 29%, female. All teach undergraduates. Graduate students teach 1% of introductory courses. The average class size in an introductory lecture is 20; in a laboratory, 15; and in a regular course, 15.

Admissions: 89% of recent applicants were accepted. The SAT scores for a recent freshman class were: Verbal--29% below 500, 48% between 500 and 599, 14% between 600 and 700, and 10% above 700; Math--36% below 500, 33% between 500 and 599, 21% between 600 and 700, and 10% above 700. 43% of recent freshmen were in the top fifth of their class.

Requirements: The SAT or ACT is required. Applicants need not be graduates of an accredited secondary school. The GED is accepted. The school strongly encourages high school courses in art, English, foreign language, history, math, music, phys ed, science, and social studies. An interview is recommended. Concordia requires applicants to be in the upper 50% of their class. A GPA of 2.0 is required. AP and CLEP credits are accepted. Important factors in the admissions decision are ability to finance college education, leadership record, and recommendations by alumni.

Procedure: Freshmen are admitted to all sessions. Entrance exams should be taken in the junior or senior year. Check with the school for current application deadlines. The fall 2005 application fee was $15. Notification is sent on a rolling basis. Applications are accepted on-line.

Transfer: Applicants should have a minimum GPA of 2.0 and a minimum ACT score of 18. An interview is recommended. Passing grades transfer for credit. Transfers are admitted every term. 30 of 128 credits required for the bachelor's degree must be completed at Concordia.

Visiting: There are regularly scheduled orientations for prospective students, including a campus tour, sitting in on classes, visits with professors/coaches, and an admission interview. There are guides for informal visits and visitors may stay overnight. To schedule a visit, contact the Office of Admission.

Financial Aid: The FAFSA and the university's own financial statement are required. Check with the school for current deadlines.

International Students: The school actively recruits these students. They must score satisfactorily on the written TOEFL and also take the SAT or the ACT.

Computers: All students may access the system. There are no time limits and no fees.

Admissions Contact: Office of Admission. A video is available.
E-mail: *admiss@cune.edu* Web: *www.cune.edu/*

CREIGHTON UNIVERSITY
F-3

Omaha, NE 68178-0001

(402) 280-2703
(800) 282-5835; Fax: (402) 280-2685

Full-time: 1526 men, 2205 women	Faculty: 271; IIA, av$
Part-time: 109 men, 148 women	Ph.D.s: 85%
Graduate: 1287 men, 1516 women	Student/Faculty: 14 to 1
Year: semesters, summer session	Tuition: $22,378
Application Deadline: August 1	Room & Board: $7540
Freshman Class: 3435 applied, 2985 accepted, 972 enrolled	
SAT Verbal/Math: 600/610*	ACT: 26 VERY COMPETITIVE+

Creighton University, founded in 1878, is a private Jesuit Catholic institution offering undergraduate programs in arts and sciences, business administration, and nursing as well as graduate, dental, medical, law, pharmacy, physical therapy, and occupational therapy programs. There are 3 undergraduate and 5 graduate schools. In addition to regional accreditation, Creighton has baccalaureate program accreditation with AACSB, ACPE, CCNE, NCATE, and NLN. The 3 libraries contain 854,217 volumes, 1,106,051 microform items, and 18,266 audio/video tapes/CDs/DVDs, and subscribe to 23,230 periodicals including electronic. Computerized library services include the card catalog, interlibrary loans, database searching, Internet access, and laptop Internet portals. Special learning facilities include a learning resource center and art gallery. The 108-acre campus is in an urban area near downtown Omaha. Including any residence halls, there are 49 buildings.

Student Life: 55% of undergraduates are from out of state, mostly the Midwest. Students are from 49 states, 40 foreign countries, and Canada. 63% are from public schools. 82% are white. Most are claim no religious affiliation. The average age of freshmen is 18; all undergraduates, 23. 13% do not continue beyond their first year; 75% remain to graduate.

Housing: 2174 students can be accommodated in college housing, which includes single-sex and coed dorms, on-campus apartments, and married-student housing. In addition, there are honors houses, special-interest houses and a Cortina Community and freshman leadership program. On-campus housing is guaranteed for all 4 years. 59% of students live on campus; of those, 90% remain on campus on weekends. All students may keep cars.

Activities: 21% of men belong to 5 national fraternities; 28% of women belong to 6 national sororities. There are 171 groups on campus, including art, band, cheerleading, chess, choir, chorale, chorus, computers, dance, debate, drama, drill team, ethnic, film, forensics, gay, honors, international, jazz band, literary magazine, musical theater, newspaper, orchestra, pep band, photography, political, professional, radio and TV, religious, social, social service, student government, and yearbook. Popular campus events include Diversity Week, JayJam and Carnival, and Spring Fling Week.

Sports: There are 6 intercollegiate sports for men and 8 for women, and 21 intramural sports for men and 19 for women. Facilities include a sports complex, an outdoor artificial turf area with baseball, softball, and soccer fields, an intercollegiate soccer facility, and a physical fitness center with courts for basketball, volleyball, badminton, or gymnastics, a pool, a weight room, and a jogging track; another center offers practice courts and training rooms for all intercollegiate sports.

Disabled Students: 90% of the campus is accessible. Wheelchair ramps, elevators, special parking, specially equipped rest rooms, special class scheduling, lowered drinking fountains, lowered telephones, and special housing are available.

Services: Counseling and information services are available, as is tutoring in most subjects. There is a reader service for the blind, and remedial math, reading, and writing.

Campus Safety and Security: Measures include 24-hour foot and vehicle patrol, self-defense education, security escort services, and shuttle buses. There are informal discussions, pamphlets/posters/films, emergency telephones, and lighted pathways/sidewalks.

Programs of Study: Creighton confers B.A., B.S., B.F.A., B.S. Atmospheric Science, B.S.B.A., B.S.Chem., B.S. Computer Science, B.S. Environmental Science, B.S. Mathematics, B.S.N., B.S. Physics, B.S.Soc., and B.S.W. degrees. Associate, master's, and doctoral degrees are also awarded. Bachelor's degrees are awarded in BIOLOGICAL SCIENCE (biology/biological science), BUSINESS (accounting, banking and finance, business administration and management, international business management, management information systems, management science, and marketing/retailing/merchandising), COMMUNICATIONS AND THE ARTS (art, communications, dance, dramatic arts, English, fine arts, French, German, Greek, journalism, Latin, music, Spanish, speech/debate/rhetoric, and theater design), COMPUTER AND PHYSICAL SCIENCE (atmospheric sciences and meteorology, chemistry, computer science, mathematics, and physics), EDUCATION (athletic training, elementary, secondary, and special), ENGINEERING AND ENVIRONMENTAL DESIGN (environmental science), HEALTH PROFESSIONS (emergency medical technologies, exercise science, health care administration, and nursing), SOCIAL SCIENCE (African studies, American studies, anthropology, classical/ancient civilization, economics, history, ministries, Native American studies, peace studies, philosophy,

political science/government, prelaw, psychology, social work, sociology, and theological studies). Business, science/health science, and nursing are the strongest academically, and have the largest enrollments.

Required: For graduation, students must complete a minimum of 128 credit hours and maintain a GPA of 2.0. Each school has general education requirements. Total number of hours required in major varies by major.

Special: The university offers study abroad at more than 110 partner institutions in 41 countries, a Washington semester, and numerous internship opportunities. Nursing students may take an accelerated degree program, and B.A.-B.S. degrees are possible. Dual majors, non-degree study, pass/fail options, and credit for life, military, and work experience are available. There is also a 2-2 engineering degree with the University of Detroit Mercy and Marquette University. There are 14 national honor societies, a freshman honors program, and 100 departmental honors program and the honors program is university wide.

Faculty/Classroom: 57% of faculty are male; 43%, female. 59% teach undergraduates. No introductory courses are taught by graduate students. The average class size in an introductory lecture is 29; in a laboratory, 22; and in a regular course, 25.

Admissions: 87% of the 2005-2006 applicants were accepted. The SAT scores for the 2005-2006 freshman class were: Verbal--12% below 500, 37% between 500 and 599, 44% between 600 and 700, and 8% above 700; Math--9% below 500, 33% between 500 and 599, 47% between 600 and 700, and 11% above 700. The ACT scores were 7% below 21, 19% between 21 and 23, 29% between 24 and 26, 19% between 27 and 28, and 25% above 28. 65% of the current freshmen were in the top fifth of their class; 91% were in the top two fifths. There were 10 National Merit finalists and 10 semifinalists. 92 freshmen graduated first in their class.

Requirements: The SAT or ACT is required. In addition, applicants must be graduates of an accredited secondary school. The GED is accepted. Students should have completed 16 credits, including 4 credits in English, 3 each in math and electives, and 2 each in foreign language, science, and social studies. Home-schooled students are welcome. Creighton requires applicants to be in the upper 50% of their class. A GPA of 2.5 is required. AP and CLEP credits are accepted. Important factors in the admissions decision are recommendations by school officials, advanced placement or honor courses, and leadership record.

Procedure: Freshmen are admitted to all sessions. Entrance exams should be taken prior to May 1 of the senior year. Applications should be filed by August 1 for fall entry and January 1 for spring entry, along with a $40 fee. There is deferred admissions plan and a rolling admissions plan. Notification is sent on a rolling basis. 75 applicants were on the 2005 waiting list; 10 were admitted. Applications are accepted online.

Transfer: 103 transfer students enrolled in 2004-2005. Applicants must have a 2.0 minimum GPA in a regionally accredited school. A minimum score of 21 on the ACT or 990 on the SAT is recommended. Grades of C or better transfer for credit. Transfers are admitted every semester. 48 of 128 credits required for the bachelor's degree must be completed at Creighton.

Visiting: There are regularly scheduled orientations for prospective students, consisting of an open house program with various presentations and campus tours. There are guides for informal visits and visitors may sit in on classes and stay overnight. To schedule a visit, contact the Admissions Office.

Financial Aid: In 2005-2006, 86% of all full-time freshmen and 67% of continuing full-time students received some form of financial aid. 59% of full-time freshmen and 41% of continuing full-time students received need-based aid. The average freshman award was $16,898. Need-based scholarships or need-based grants averaged $15,096; need-based self-help aid (loans and jobs) averaged $5188; non-need-based athletic scholarships averaged $18,577; and other non-need-based awards and non-need-based scholarships averaged $8752. 52% of undergraduates work part time. Average annual earnings from campus work are $1493. The average financial indebtedness of the 2005 graduate was $26,013. The FAFSA and the college's own financial statement are required. The deadline for filing freshman financial aid applications for fall entry is April 1.

International Students: In a recent year, there were 48 international students enrolled. The school actively recruits these students. They must score satisfactorily on the written TOEFL or on the electronic version.

Computers: Wireless access is available. All residence halls offer student connectivity 24/7. Additionally, other areas of the campus, including some classrooms, offer wireless and hard-wire connectivity. All students may access the system any time. There are no time limits and no fees. It is strongly recommended that all students have a personal computer. Computers are provided to pharmacy students.

Graduates: From July 1, 2004 to June 30, 2005, 772 bachelor's degrees were awarded. The most popular majors were health professions and related sciences (26%), business/marketing (21%), and biological/life sciences (8%). In an average class, 1% graduate in 3 years or less, 63% graduate in 4 years or less, 73% graduate in 5 years or less, and

75% graduate in 6 years or less. 200 companies recruited on campus in 2004-2005. Of the 2004 graduating class, 39% were enrolled in graduate school within 6 months of graduation and 59% were employed.

Admissions Contact: Mary Chase, Director of Admissions. A video is available. E-mail: *admissions@creighton.edu*
Web: *admission@creighton.edu*

DANA COLLEGE   F-2
Blair, NE 68008-1099

(402) 426-7222
(800) 444-3262; Fax: (402) 426-7386

Full-time: 361 men, 292 women	**Faculty:** 42
Part-time: 8 men, 15 women	**Ph.D.s:** 69%
Graduate: none	**Student/Faculty:** 16 to 1
Year: 4-1-4, summer session	**Tuition:** $17,450
Application Deadline: August 1	**Room & Board:** $4940
Freshman Class: 901 applied, 686 accepted, 208 enrolled	
SAT Verbal/Math: 480/475*	**ACT:** 22 **COMPETITIVE**

Dana College, established in 1884, is a private liberal arts institution affiliated with the Evangelical Lutheran Church in America. In addition to regional accreditation, Dana has baccalaureate program accreditation with ACBSP, CSWE, and NCATE. The library contains 158,752 volumes, 14,200 microform items, and 5260 audio/video tapes/CDs/DVDs, and subscribes to 6155 periodicals including electronic. Computerized library services include the card catalog, interlibrary loans, database searching, and Internet access. Special learning facilities include a learning resource center, art gallery, radio station, TV station, a theater, and Danish immigrant archives. The 150-acre campus is in a small town 20 miles north of Omaha. Including any residence halls, there are 17 buildings.

Student Life: 55% of undergraduates are from Nebraska. Others are from 32 states, 2 foreign countries, and Canada. 92% are white. Most are Catholic. The average age of freshmen is 18; all undergraduates, 20. 42% do not continue beyond their first year; 51% remain to graduate.

Housing: 650 students can be accommodated in college housing, which includes single-sex and coed dorms, on-campus apartments, and married-student housing. On-campus housing is guaranteed for all 4 years. 63% of students live on campus; of those, 50% remain on campus on weekends. Alcohol is not permitted. All students may keep cars.

Activities: There are no fraternities or sororities. There are 35 groups on campus, including art, band, cheerleading, choir, chorale, chorus, computers, dance, drama, drill team, enviromental, ethnic, honors, international, jazz band, literary magazine, musical theater, newspaper, orchestra, pep band, photography, political, professional, radio and TV, religious, social, social service, student government, and yearbook. Popular campus events include Sights and Sounds of Christmas, Spring Fling, and Winterfest.

Sports: There are 7 intercollegiate sports for men and 7 for women, and 14 intramural sports for men and 14 for women. Facilities include fields for socccer, cross country, football/track, softball, and baseball, and a coliseum for basketball, swimming, tennis, volleyball, wrestling, and weight training.

Disabled Students: 70% of the campus is accessible. Wheelchair ramps, elevators, special parking, specially equipped rest rooms, special class scheduling, and lowered drinking fountains are available.

Services: Counseling and information services are available, as is tutoring in some subjects, including most 100- and 200-level general education courses. There is a reader service for the blind and remedial math and writing. A study skills course and study sessions for individual courses are available.

Campus Safety and Security: Measures include 24-hour foot and vehicle patrol, self-defense education, security escort services, and informal discussions. There are pamphlets/posters/films, emergency telephones, and lighted pathways/sidewalks.

Programs of Study: Dana confers the B.A. degree. Bachelor's degrees are awarded in BIOLOGICAL SCIENCE (biology/biological science), BUSINESS (accounting, business administration and management, and management information systems), COMMUNICATIONS AND THE ARTS (art, communications, English, German, graphic design, music, and Spanish), COMPUTER AND PHYSICAL SCIENCE (chemistry, computer science, and mathematics), EDUCATION (art, business, drama, elementary, English, foreign languages, mathematics, music, physical, science, secondary, social science, social studies, and special), ENGINEERING AND ENVIRONMENTAL DESIGN (environmental science), SOCIAL SCIENCE (criminal justice, history, interdisciplinary studies, international relations, liberal arts/general studies, psychology, religion, social work, and sociology). Social work, education, and business are the strongest academically. Elementary education, biology, and business administration are the largest.

Required: To graduate, students must complete 128 credit hours, including at least 30 in the major and 40 at the 300 or 400 level, with a minimum GPA of 2.0. Other requirements include demonstrated competency in verbal and written communication skills, 15 core hours in liberal arts, 2 credits in wellness, and 1 religion course. Also required are 18 distributive hours in 3 of 4 areas of study: human culture, human scientific inquiry, human development and organizations, and human aesthetic expression.

Special: Dana offers cross-registration with Midland Lutheran College, internships in most majors, study abroad, and work-study programs. Integrated studies, credit for life, military, and work experience, nondegree study, and pass/fail options are available. There are preprofessional programs in prechiropractic, preoccupational therapy, prephysician's assistant, preseminary, and prelaw. Students in the medical arts major, leading to a degree or certification in a medical technology field, spend senior year in a hospital-based program. There are 3 national honor societies, a freshman honors program, and 1 departmental honors program.

Faculty/Classroom: 50% of faculty are male; 50%, female. All teach undergraduates and 60% do research. The average class size in an introductory lecture is 35; in a laboratory, 10; and in a regular course, 24.

Admissions: 76% of the 2005-2006 applicants were accepted. The SAT scores for the 2005-2006 freshman class were: Verbal--61% below 500, 22% between 500 and 599, 11% between 600 and 700, and 6% above 700; Math--58% below 500, 28% between 500 and 599, 8% between 600 and 700, and 6% above 700. The ACT scores were 51% below 21, 25% between 21 and 23, 21% between 24 and 26, 3% between 27 and 28, and 2% above 28. 33% of the current freshmen were in the top fifth of their class; 64% were in the top two fifths. 9 freshmen graduated first in their class in a recent year.

Requirements: The SAT or ACT is required. The ACT Optional Writing test is also recommrnded. Applicants must be graduates of an accredited secondary school. The GED is accepted. Prospective students are encouraged to take college-preparatory courses, including 4 years each of English and social science, 3 each of science and math, and 2 of a foreign language. An interview is recommended. A GPA of 2.0 is required. AP and CLEP credits are accepted. Important factors in the admissions decision are advanced placement or honor courses, recommendations by school officials, and leadership record.

Procedure: Freshmen are admitted to all sessions. Entrance exams should be taken in the spring of the junior year or fall of the senior year. There are early admissions and deferred admissions plans. There is a rolling admissions plan. Applications should be filed by August 1 for fall entry and January 10 for spring entry. Notification is sent on a rolling basis. Applications are accepted on-line.

Transfer: 59 transfer students enrolled in 2004-2005. Applicants with an associate degree and a minimum college GPA of 2.0 will be considered, those with less than a 2.0 GPA will be evaluated on the basis of high school performance and an interview with the admissions committee. Grades of C or better transfer for credit. Students are admitted every term. 32 of 128 credits required for the bachelor's degree must be completed at Dana.

Visiting: There are regularly scheduled orientations for prospective students, including appointments with faculty, coaches, and activity directors, a campus tour, a financial aid session, an admissions session, and lunch. Overnight lodging is available at no charge. There are guides for informal visits and visitors may sit in on classes and stay overnight. To schedule a visit, contact the Admissions Office at *tblair@dana.edu*.

Financial Aid: In 2005-2006, all full-time freshmen received some form of financial aid. 83% of full-time freshmen and 81% of continuing full-time students received need-based aid. The average freshman award was $15,665. Need-based scholarships or need-based grants averaged $4320; need-based self-help aid (loans and jobs) averaged $4440; and non-need-based athletic scholarships averaged $7046. 53% of undergraduates work part time. Average annual earnings from campus work are $495. The average financial indebtedness of the 2005 graduate was $17,773. Dana is a member of CSS. The FAFSA and the college's own financial statement are required. The priority date for freshman financial aid applications for fall entry is March 15. The deadline for filing freshman financial aid applications for fall entry is April 1.

International Students: There are 3 international students enrolled. The school actively recruits these students. They must score satisfactorily on the TOEFL some applicants may be accepted into a program supported by ESL courses.

Computers: Wireless access is available. There are about 110 computers on campus, located in residence halls, classroom buildings, and the library. Students also have wireless access in their residence hall rooms. All students may access the system 24 hours a day. There are no time limits and no fees. It is recommended that students in interactive media major have personal computers by junior year.

Graduates: From July 1, 2004 to June 30, 2005, 116 bachelor's degrees were awarded. The most popular majors were education (35%), business (33%), and biology (7%). In an average class, 1% graduate in 3 years or less, 74% graduate in 4 years or less, and 99% graduate in 5 years or less. 19 companies recruited on campus in 2004-2005. Of the 2004 graduating class, 7% were enrolled in graduate school within 6 months of graduation and 97% were employed.

Admissions Contact: James Lynes, Dean of Enrollment.
E-mail: *admissions@dana.edu* Web: *www.dana.edu*

DOANE COLLEGE
E-3

Crete, NE 68333

(402) 826-8222

(800) 333-6263; Fax: (402) 826-8600

Full-time: 447 men, 516 women	**Faculty:** 76; IIA, --$
Part-time: 4 men, 6 women	**Ph.D.s:** 63%
Graduate: none	**Student/Faculty:** 13 to 1
Year: 4-1-4	**Tuition:** $17,536
Application Deadline: August 15	**Room & Board:** $4922
Freshman Class: n/av	
ACT: 23	**COMPETITIVE**

Doane College, founded in 1872, is a private liberal arts and science college. In addition to regional accreditation, Doane has baccalaureate program accreditation with NCATE. The library contains 314,795 volumes, 6841 microform items, and 9074 audio/video tapes/CDs/DVDs. Computerized library services include the card catalog, interlibrary loans, database searching, and Internet access. Special learning facilities include a learning resource center, art gallery, radio station, TV station, and an observatory. The 300-acre campus is in a small town 25 miles southwest of Lincoln. Including any residence halls, there are 27 buildings.

Student Life: 85% of undergraduates are from Nebraska. Students are from 22 states and 1 foreign country. 80% are from public schools. 93% are white. 34% are Protestant; 23% Catholic. The average age of freshmen is 18; all undergraduates, 21. 29% do not continue beyond their first year; 62% remain to graduate.

Housing: 875 students can be accommodated in college housing, which includes single-sex and coed dorms, on-campus apartments, and married-student housing. In addition, there are honors houses and special-interest houses. On-campus housing is guaranteed for all 4 years. 74% of students live on campus. All students may keep cars.

Activities: 48% of men belong to 5 local fraternities; 40% of women belong to 4 local sororities. There are 50 groups on campus, including alternative spring break, art, band, cheerleading, choir, chorale, chorus, computers, dance, drama, ethnic, forensics, gay, hanson leadership program, honors, international, investment, jazz band, literary magazine, marching band, musical theater, newspaper, pep band, photography, political, professional, radio and TV, religious, social, social service, speech team, student government, and wildlife/conservation. Popular campus events include Parents Day, Stop Day, and Christmas festival and concert.

Sports: There are 8 intercollegiate sports for men and 8 for women, and 4 intramural sports for men and 4 for women. Facilities include a phys ed building, a field house, a sports field, a fitness center, a gym, a pool, nature and cross-country trails, a challenge course, and indoor and outdoor tracks.

Disabled Students: 60% of the campus is accessible. Wheelchair ramps, elevators, special parking, specially equipped rest rooms, and special class scheduling are available.

Services: Counseling and information services are available, as is tutoring in every subject. There is remedial math, reading, and writing.

Campus Safety and Security: Measures include security escort services, informal discussions, pamphlets/posters/films, and emergency telephones. There are lighted pathways/sidewalks and evening patrols by trained security personnel.

Programs of Study: Doane confers B.A. and B.S. degrees. Master's degrees are also awarded. Bachelor's degrees are awarded in BIOLOGICAL SCIENCE (biology/biological science), BUSINESS (accounting and business administration and management), COMMUNICATIONS AND THE ARTS (art, communications, dramatic arts, English, English as a second/foreign language, French, German, language arts, music, Spanish, and speech/debate/rhetoric), COMPUTER AND PHYSICAL SCIENCE (chemistry, computer science, mathematics, physical sciences, and physics), EDUCATION (elementary, physical, and special), ENGINEERING AND ENVIRONMENTAL DESIGN (environmental science), SOCIAL SCIENCE (economics, history, international studies, philosophy, political science/government, psychology, public administration, religion, and sociology). Biology and economics (emphasis business management) are the strongest academically and the largest. Biology and economics are the strongest academically and the largest.

Required: The Doane Plan requires students to complete 60 to 70 credits in heritage studies, contemporary issues, international/multicultural perspective, natural science, quantitative reasoning, communication, aesthetic perspective, health and well-being, and community and leadership. Students are also required to complete 2 hours of phys ed, demonstrate computer skills in word processing, and in most disciplines, complete a senior seminar. Students must complete 132 credit hours and have a minimum GPA of 2.0 in the major to graduate.

Special: Internships for sophomores through seniors, a Washington semester, and study abroad in numerous countries are possible. A 3-2 engineering program in conjunction with Washington at St. Louis and Columbia Universities, work-study, student-designed and interdisciplinary majors, dual majors and accelerated degrees in all areas, credit by exam, nondegree study, and pass/fail options are available. Doane also offers

the HELPS program, designed for Doane College graduates who wish to return as full-time students to seek further education in preparation for career advancement. Students may pursue a 3-2 environmental studies/forestry degree in conjunction with Duke University. Doane's Lincoln campus, designed for adults, offers intensive 8-week classes in the evening and on weekends in both undergraduate and graduate programs. Doane offers an honors program, leadership development program, and the opportunity to conduct summer research projects with faculty. There are 7 national honor societies, a freshman honors program, and 2 departmental honors programs.

Faculty/Classroom: 61% of faculty are male; 39%, female. All teach undergraduates. The average class size in an introductory lecture is 24; in a laboratory, 16; and in a regular course, 18.

Admissions: The ACT scores for the 2005-2006 freshman class were: 30% below 21, 25% between 21 and 23, 19% between 24 and 26, 13% between 27 and 28, and 13% above 28. 45% of the current freshmen were in the top fifth of their class; 80% were in the top two fifths.

Requirements: The ACT is required for some programs. In addition, applicants must be graduates of an accredited secondary school. The GED is accepted. It is recommended that 4 units of English and 3 units each of math, science, and the social sciences be completed. An interview is recommended. Art students must submit a portfolio, and music and drama students must audition. AP and CLEP credits are accepted. Important factors in the admissions decision are advanced placement or honor courses, recommendations by school officials, and ability to finance college education.

Procedure: Freshmen are admitted fall, winter, and spring. Entrance exams should be taken by spring of the junior year or early senior year. There is a deferred admissions and a rolling admissions plan. Applications should be filed by August 15 for fall entry. Notification is sent on a rolling basis. The fall 2005 application fee was $15. Applications are accepted on-line.

Transfer: 24 transfer students enrolled in 2004-2005. Transfer students must submit a transcript from previously attended colleges and have been in good standing. The SAT or ACT is usually required. Grades of 2.0 or higher generally transfer for credit. 30 of 132 credits required for the bachelor's degree must be completed at Doane.

Visiting: There are regularly scheduled orientations for prospective students, including 4 scheduled half-day visits that incorporate a parents program. There are guides for informal visits and visitors may sit in on classes and stay overnight. To schedule a visit, contact the Admissions Office at kim.jacobs@doane.edu.

Financial Aid: In 2005-2006, 87% of all full-time freshmen and 75% of continuing full-time students received some form of financial aid. 87% of full-time freshmen and 78% of continuing full-time students received need-based aid. The average freshman award was $14,636. 48% of undergraduates work part time. Average annual earnings from campus work are $766. The average financial indebtedness of the 2005 graduate was $14,915. The FAFSA is required. The deadline for filing freshman financial aid applications for fall entry is March 1.

International Students: There are 3 international students enrolled. The school actively recruits these students. A satisfactory score is required on the written TOEFL. Students must also take the SAT or the ACT.

Computers: Wireless access is available. All students may access the system any time. There are no time limits and no fees.

Graduates: From July 1, 2004 to June 30, 2005, 181 bachelor's degrees were awarded. The most popular majors were biology (15%), economics (12%), and elementary education (10%). In an average class, 1% graduate in 3 years or less, 55% graduate in 4 years or less, 65% graduate in 5 years or less, and 68% graduate in 6 years or less. 45 companies recruited on campus in 2004-2005. Of the 2004 graduating class, 22% were enrolled in graduate school within 6 months of graduation and 78% were employed.

Admissions Contact: Kim Jacobs, Acting Vice President of Admissions. A video is available. E-mail: admissions@doane.edu Web: www.doane.edu

HASTINGS COLLEGE
D-3

Hastings, NE 68901

(402) 461-7403

(800) 532-7642; Fax: (402) 461-7490

Full-time: 574 men, 547 women	**Faculty:** 79; IIB, --$
Part-time: 11 men, 12 women	**Ph.D.s:** 71%
Graduate: 19 men, 26 women	**Student/Faculty:** 14 to 1
Year: 4-1-4, summer session	**Tuition:** $17,268
Application Deadline: August 1	**Room & Board:** $4950
Freshman Class: 1413 applied, 1115 accepted, 311 enrolled	
ACT: 23	**VERY COMPETITIVE**

Hastings College, founded in 1882 and affiliated with the Presbyterian Church (U.S.A.) offers programs in the liberal arts and sciences, education, business, and pre-health professions. In addition to regional accreditation, Hastings College has baccalaureate program accreditation with NASM and NCATE. The library contains 140,000 volumes, 21,000 microform items, and 955 audio/video tapes/CDs/DVDs, and subscribes to 935 periodicals including electronic. Computerized library services include the card catalog, interlibrary loans, database searching, Internet access, and laptop Internet portals. Special learning facilities include a learning resource center, art gallery, radio station, TV station, and an observatory, and a glass blowing studio. The 109-acre campus is in a rural area 150 miles west of Omaha. Including any residence halls, there are 40 buildings.

Student Life: 77% of undergraduates are from Nebraska. Others are from 23 states, 5 foreign countries, and Canada. 88% are from public schools. 93% are white. 39% are claim no religious affiliation; 38% Protestant; 22% Catholic. The average age of freshmen is 19; all undergraduates, 21. 22% do not continue beyond their first year; 62% remain to graduate.

Housing: 859 students can be accommodated in college housing, which includes single-sex and coed dorms and on-campus apartments. In addition, there are honors houses. On-campus housing is guaranteed for the freshman year only and is available on a first-come, first-served basis. Priority is given to out-of-town students. 75% of students live on campus; of those, 60% remain on campus on weekends. All students may keep cars.

Activities: 20% of men belong to 4 local fraternities; 30% of women belong to 4 local sororities. There are 80 groups on campus, including art, band, cheerleading, choir, chorus, dance, debate, drama, ethnic, flag team, forensics, gay, health advisory council, honors, jazz band, literary magazine, marching band, musical theater, newspaper, nontraditional students, orchestra, peer educators, pep band, photography, political, professional public relations, radio and TV, religious, social, social service, student government, symphony, and yearbook. Popular campus events include May Fete, Festival of Lessons and Carols, and Artist Lecture Series.

Sports: There are 9 intercollegiate sports for men and 9 for women, and 9 intramural sports for men and 9 for women. Facilities include a physical fitness center, a pool, a weight room, indoor and outdoor tennis courts, a 3000-seat stadium, a 2500-seat gym, a wellness center, and an all-weather track.

Disabled Students: 90% of the campus is accessible. Wheelchair ramps, elevators, special parking, specially equipped rest rooms, special class scheduling, lowered drinking fountains, and lowered telephones are available.

Services: Counseling and information services are available, as is tutoring in most subjects, including all core subjects and most lower-division courses.

Campus Safety and Security: Measures include security escort services, pamphlets/posters/films, emergency telephones, and lighted pathways/sidewalks. There is a night security patrol.

Programs of Study: Hastings College confers B.A. and B.M. degrees. Master's degrees are also awarded. Bachelor's degrees are awarded in BIOLOGICAL SCIENCE (biology/biological science), BUSINESS (accounting and business administration and management), COMMUNICATIONS AND THE ARTS (broadcasting, communications, dramatic arts, English, fine arts, German, music, Spanish, and speech/debate/rhetoric), COMPUTER AND PHYSICAL SCIENCE (chemistry, computer science, mathematics, and physics), EDUCATION (art, business, elementary, foreign languages, music, science, secondary, and special), HEALTH PROFESSIONS (health care administration), SOCIAL SCIENCE (economics, history, human services, philosophy, political science/government, psychology, religion, social science, and sociology). Physics is the strongest academically. Business administration and education are the largest.

Required: Students are required to take courses in written and oral communication, physical and life science, foreign language, history, social and political science, literature, philosophy, religion, health/wellness, computer science, the fine arts, and phys ed. A minimum 2.0 GPA and 127 credit hours, with 30 to 36 in the major, are required to graduate.

Special: There is a co-op nursing program with Creighton University, programs in construction management and agribusiness in cooperation with Central Community College, a 3-2 engineering program with Columbia and Washington Universities and Georgia Institute of Technology, and a 3-2 degree in occupational therapy with Boston and Washington Universities. Internships, study abroad in England, Spain, Russia, Ireland, Holland, Germany, or Thailand, work-study, dual majors in all areas, and student-designed majors are possible. Credit by exam, credit for military experience, and pass/fail options are available. There are 12 national honor societies.

Faculty/Classroom: 67% of faculty are male; 33%, female. All teach undergraduates and 25% both teach and do research. No introductory courses are taught by graduate students. The average class size in an introductory lecture is 25; in a laboratory, 24; and in a regular course, 23.

Admissions: 79% of the 2005-2006 applicants were accepted. The SAT scores for the 2005-2006 freshman class were: Verbal--13% below 500, 43% between 500 and 599, 28% between 600 and 700, and 16% above 700; Math--19% below 500, 36% between 500 and 599, 26% between 600 and 700, and 19% above 700. The ACT scores were 11% below 21, 27% between 21 and 23, 28% between 24 and 26, 19% between 27 and 28, and 15% above 28. 55% of the current freshmen were in the top fifth of their class; 88% were in the top two fifths. 14 freshmen graduated first in their class.

Requirements: The SAT or ACT is required. In addition, applicants should graduate from an accredited secondary school with a minimum of 4 academic credits in English and 2 each in math, science, social studies, and a foreign language. Generally, placement in the upper half of the graduating class, a minimum GPA of 2.0, or a satisfactory score on the enhanced ACT, is a minimal requirement for consideration for admission. Hastings College requires applicants to be in the upper 50% of their class. A GPA of 2.0 is required. AP and CLEP credits are accepted. Important factors in the admissions decision are advanced placement or honor courses, leadership record, and personality/intangible qualities.

Procedure: Freshmen are admitted to all sessions. Entrance exams should be taken before November. There is a rolling admissions plan. Applications should be filed by August 1 for fall entry, December 1 for winter entry, January 1 for spring entry, and May 15 for summer entry. Notification of early decision is sent on a rolling basis; regular decision on a rolling basis. The fall 2005 application fee was $20. Applications are accepted on-line.

Transfer: 26 transfer students enrolled in 2004-2005. Transfer students must have completed course work equivalent by description to that of Hastings and have earned grades of C or better. 30 of 127 credits required for the bachelor's degree must be completed at Hastings College.

Visiting: There are regularly scheduled orientations for prospective students, including academic department presentations, a financial aid session, a student panel discussion, a student guided tour, and an activities fair. There are guides for informal visits and visitors may sit in on classes and stay overnight. To schedule a visit, contact the Admissions Office at (402) 461-7315 or kjones@hastings.edu.

Financial Aid: In a recent year, 99% of all full-time freshmen and 98% of continuing full-time students received some form of financial aid. 79% of full-time freshmen and 71% of continuing full-time students received need-based aid. The average freshman award was $12,552. Need-based scholarships or need-based grants averaged $9643; need-based self-help aid (loans and jobs) averaged $3868; and non-need-based athletic scholarships averaged $4957. 54% of undergraduates work part time. Average annual earnings from campus work are $775. The average financial indebtedness of the 2005 graduate was $14,598. Hastings College is a member of CSS. The FAFSA is required. The deadline for filing freshman financial aid applications for fall entry is May 1.

International Students: There are 15 international students enrolled. The school actively recruits these students. A satisfactory score is required on the written TOEFL. International athletes should take a standardized test for athletic eligibility.

Computers: Wireless access is available. There are more than 180 PCs (including nearly 30 Macs) in computer labs across campus. Most labs are open until 2 A.M. Limited wireless spots are offered on campus, and they can handle approximately 100 users at one time. All students may access the system. There are no time limits and no fees.

Graduates: From July 1, 2004 to June 30, 2005, 221 bachelor's degrees were awarded. The most popular majors were education (23%), business administration (19%), and biology (13%). In an average class, 51% graduate in 4 years or less, 61% graduate in 5 years or less, and 62% graduate in 6 years or less. 35 companies recruited on campus in 2004-2005.

Admissions Contact: Mary Molliconi, Director of Admissions. A video is available. E-mail: mmolliconi@hastings.edu Web: www.hastings.edu

MIDLAND LUTHERAN COLLEGE
Fremont, NE 68025

E-2

(402) 941-6501
(800) 642-8382; Fax: (402)-721-2050

Full-time: 400 men, 500 women	**Faculty:** 69; IIB, --$
Part-time: 20 men, 30 women	**Ph.D.s:** 45%
Graduate: none	**Student/Faculty:** 14 to 1
Year: 4-1-4, summer session	**Tuition:** $15,000
Application Deadline: see profile	**Room & Board:** $4000
Freshman Class: n/av	
SAT or ACT: recommended	**COMPETITIVE**

Midland Lutheran College, established in 1883, is a private liberal arts institution affiliated with the Evangelical Lutheran Church in America. Figures in the above capsule and in this profile are approximate. In addition to regional accreditation, Midland has baccalaureate program accreditation with NLN. The library contains 105,000 volumes and 1000 audio/video tapes/CDs/DVDs, and subscribes to 900 periodicals including electronic. Computerized library services include interlibrary loans and database searching. Special learning facilities include a learning resource center and planetarium. The 27-acre campus is in a small town 30 miles northwest of Omaha. Including any residence halls, there are 18 buildings.

Student Life: 75% of undergraduates are from Nebraska. Others are from 23 states, 10 foreign countries, and Canada. 94% are from public schools. 91% are white. 57% are Protestant; 32% Catholic; 10% claim no religious affiliation. The average age of freshmen is 18; all undergraduates, 20. 16% do not continue beyond their first year; 56% remain to graduate.

Housing: 575 students can be accommodated in college housing, which includes single-sex and coed dorms and off-campus apartments. On-campus housing is guaranteed for all 4 years, is available on a first-come, first-served basis, and is available on a lottery system for upperclassmen. 52% of students live on campus; of those, 50% remain on campus on weekends. Alcohol is not permitted. All students may keep cars.

Activities: 20% of men belong to 4 local fraternities; 20% of women belong to 4 local sororities. There are 36 groups on campus, including art, band, cheerleading, choir, chorale, chorus, computers, drama, drill team, ethnic, film, forensics, honors, jazz band, literary magazine, musical theater, newspaper, pep band, photography, political, professional, radio and TV, religious, social, social service, student government, and yearbook. Popular campus events include Journalism Day, Greek Games, and Snow Week.

Sports: There are 9 intercollegiate sports for men and 9 for women, and 6 intramural sports for men and 6 for women. Facilities include a phys ed center, an athletic practice field, an indoor pool, an indoor track, and a weight room.

Disabled Students: 90% of the campus is accessible. Wheelchair ramps, elevators, special parking, specially equipped rest rooms, special class scheduling, lowered drinking fountains, and lowered telephones are available.

Services: Counseling and information services are available, as is tutoring in every subject. There is remedial reading and writing.

Campus Safety and Security: Measures include 24-hour foot and vehicle patrol, security escort services, informal discussions, and pamphlets/posters/films. There are lighted pathways/sidewalks.

Programs of Study: Midland confers B.A., B.S., B.S.B.A., and B.S.N. degrees. Associate degrees are also awarded. Bachelor's degrees are awarded in BIOLOGICAL SCIENCE (biology/biological science), BUSINESS (accounting, business administration and management, business economics, management information systems, and marketing/retailing/merchandising), COMMUNICATIONS AND THE ARTS (advertising, communications, English, fine arts, journalism, and music), COMPUTER AND PHYSICAL SCIENCE (chemistry, computer programming, computer science, and mathematics), EDUCATION (art, business, early childhood, elementary, middle school, music, science, and secondary), HEALTH PROFESSIONS (nursing, predentistry, and premedicine), SOCIAL SCIENCE (community services, economics, history, parks and recreation management, prelaw, psychology, religion, social science, and sociology). Business, journalism, and education are the strongest academically. Business, education, and nursing are the largest.

Required: To graduate, students need a total of 128 credit hours, with 33 of these in distribution requirements of the student's selection. English, speech, and math courses are required, as well as 1 year of foreign language on the high school or college level. The total number of hours in the major varies from 34 to 48, and students must maintain a GPA of at least 2.0 overall and 2.25 in the major, with some departments requiring a higher minimum GPA.

Special: There is cross-registration with Dana College in Blair, internships in business, public relations, journalism, and art, study abroad in 3 countries, student-designed majors, work-study programs, and a 3-2 engineering degree with Washington University. Other options include dual majors, independent study, directed study, and the pass/no credit grading system. There are 2 national honor societies.

Faculty/Classroom: 60% of faculty are male; 40%, female. All teach undergraduates. The average class size in a laboratory is 20 and in a regular course, 20.

Requirements: The SAT or ACT is recommended. In addition, applicants should be graduates of an accredited secondary school. The GED is accepted. Recommended preparation includes 3 units of English, 2 each of math and foreign language, and 10 of electives. An interview is recommended. Midland requires applicants to be in the upper 50% of their class. AP and CLEP credits are accepted. Important factors in the admissions decision are leadership record, extracurricular activities record, and evidence of special talent.

Procedure: Freshmen are admitted fall and winter. Entrance exams should be taken during the fall of the senior year. There are early decision, early admissions, and deferred admissions plans. Check with the school for current application deadlines. The fall 2005 application fee was $20. Notification of regular decision is sent, on a rolling basis. Applications are accepted on-line.

Transfer: Applicants must be in good standing at their previous college and generally have a 2.0 minimum GPA. Grades of C or higher transfer for credit. 30 of 128 credits required for the bachelor's degree must be completed at Midland.

Visiting: There are regularly scheduled orientations for prospective students. Campus visits are scheduled on an individual basis and as much as possible include visits with faculty, students, and financial aid counsel-

ors. There are guides for informal visits and visitors may sit in on classes and stay overnight. To schedule a visit, contact the Admissions Office.

Financial Aid: Midland is a member of CSS. The FAFSA or FFS is required. Check with the school for current deadlines.

International Students: The school actively recruits these students. They must score satisfactorily on the written TOEFL.

Computers: All students may access the system. There are no time limits and no fees. It is recommended that students in business and education have personal computers.

Admissions Contact: Admissions Officer.
E-mail: *admissions@mlc.edu* Web: *www.mlc.edu*

NEBRASKA METHODIST COLLEGE OF NURSING AND ALLIED HEALTH F-3

Omaha, NE 68114
(402) 354-4879
(800) 335-5510; Fax: (402) 354-8875

Full-time: 47 men, 453 women	Faculty: n/av
Part-time: none	Ph.D.s: n/av
Graduate: 1 man, 64 women	Student/Faculty: n/av
Year: semesters, summer session	Tuition: $11,250
Application Deadline: March 1	Room & Board: $1700
Freshman Class: 119 applied, 60 accepted, 41 enrolled	
ACT: 20	SPECIAL

Nebraska Methodist College, founded in 1891, is a private institution offering education opportunities in health care careers. The College enrolls more than 500 students in short term certificate programs, AS and BS degrees, as well as online master's degree programs. In addition to regional accreditation, Nebraska Methodist College has baccalaureate program accreditation with CAHEA and CCNE. The library contains 13,059 volumes, 1722 microform items, and 500 audio/video tapes/CDs/DVDs, and subscribes to 598 periodicals including electronic. Computerized library services include the card catalog, interlibrary loans, and database searching. Special learning facilities include a learning resource center and assessment labs for nursing and allied health students, and a human cadaver lab. The 5-acre campus is in an urban area in the center of Omaha. Including any residence halls, there are 3 buildings.

Student Life: 95% of undergraduates are from Nebraska. Students are from 10 states and 2 foreign countries. 95% are from public schools. 95% are white. The average age of freshmen is 18; all undergraduates, 27. 10% do not continue beyond their first year; 74% remain to graduate.

Housing: 80 students can be accommodated in college housing, which includes coed dorms. On-campus housing is available on a first-come, first-served basis. Priority is given to out-of-town students. 80% of students commute. Alcohol is not permitted. All students may keep cars.

Activities: 55% of women belong to 1 local sorority. There are no fraternities. There are 10 groups on campus, including ethnic, professional, social, social service, and student government. Popular campus events include Honors Convocation and pledging ceremonies.

Sports: There is no sports program at Nebraska Methodist College. Facilities include a fitness center.

Disabled Students: 75% of the campus is accessible. Elevators, special parking, and specially equipped rest rooms are available.

Services: Counseling and information services are available, as is tutoring in most subjects. There is remedial math, reading, and writing. A reader service for the blind is available in the metropolitan area.

Campus Safety and Security: Measures include self-defense education, informal discussions, pamphlets/posters/films, and lighted pathways/sidewalks.

Programs of Study: Nebraska Methodist College confers B.S. and B.S.N. degrees. Associate and master's degrees are also awarded. Bachelor's degrees are awarded in HEALTH PROFESSIONS (health, nursing, and respiratory therapy). Nursing has the largest enrollment.

Required: All students must complete 45 credit hours of core curriculum courses in the humanities, social and behavioral sciences, and natural and applied sciences. A total of 127 credit hours is required, 55 of these in the major. Students must maintain a minimum GPA of 2.0.

Special: There is nondegree study and credit by exam. Credit by correspondence may be considered. An accelerated degree in nursing is offered. There is 1 national honor society and 2 departmental honors program.

Faculty/Classroom: 15% of faculty are male; 85%, female. All teach undergraduates. No introductory courses are taught by graduate students. The average class size in an introductory lecture is 35; in a laboratory, 10; and in a regular course, 20.

Admissions: 50% of the 2005-2006 applicants were accepted. The ACT scores for the 2005-2006 freshman class were: 55% below 21, 25% between 21 and 23, and 20% between 24 and 26. 35% of the current freshmen were in the top fifth of their class; 80% were in the top two fifths. 1 freshman graduated first in the class.

Requirements: The ACT is required. In addition, students must be graduates of an accredited secondary school with the number of academic credits required under Nebraska state law. The GED is accepted. Students should have completed 4 years of English and 2 years each of math (including algebra), science (including biology and chemistry), and social science. An essay and an interview are required for admissions consideration. Nebraska Methodist College requires applicants to be in the upper 75% of their class. A GPA of 2.0 is required. AP and CLEP credits are accepted. Important factors in the admissions decision are personality/intangible qualities, advanced placement or honor courses, and leadership record.

Procedure: Freshmen are admitted fall and spring. Entrance exams should be taken as early as possible. There is a rolling admissions plan. Applications should be filed by March 1 for fall entry and October 1 for spring entry, along with a $25 fee. Notification is sent by April 15. Applications are accepted on-line.

Transfer: 119 transfer students enrolled in 2004-2005. Applicants must have a GPA above 2.0. Grades of C and above can be transferred for credit. An interview is required. 30 of 127 credits required for the bachelor's degree must be completed at Nebraska Methodist College.

Visiting: There are regularly scheduled orientations for prospective students. There are guides for informal visits and visitors may sit in on classes. To schedule a visit, contact the Admissions Office at *admissions@methodistcollege.edu.*

Financial Aid: 66% of undergraduates work part time. The FAFSA and the college's own financial statement are required. The deadline for filing freshman financial aid applications for fall entry is May 1.

International Students: In a recent year, there are 2 international students enrolled. Satisfactory score is required on the written TOEFL and the ACT.

Computers: All students may access the system. There are no time limits and no fees.

Graduates: In a recent year, 74 bachelor's degrees were awarded. The most popular majors were nursing (85%), sonography (10%), and respiratory care (5%). In an average class, 72% graduate in 4 years or less. 4 companies recruited on campus in 2004-2005. Of the 2004 graduating class, 90% were employed within 6 months of graduation.

Admissions Contact: Admissions Officer.
E-mail: *admissions@methodistcollege.edu*
Web: *www.methodistcollege.edu*

NEBRASKA WESLEYAN UNIVERSITY
Lincoln, NE 68504

E-3

(402) 465-2218
(800) 541-3818; Fax: (402) 465-2179

Full-time: 705 men, 901 women	Faculty: 101; IIB, --$
Part-time: 75 men, 158 women	Ph.D.s: 89%
Graduate: 26 men, 148 women	Student/Faculty: 16 to 1
Year: semesters, summer session	Tuition: $18,400
Application Deadline: May 1	Room & Board: $5015
Freshman Class: 1296 applied, 1262 accepted, 406 enrolled	
ACT: 24	COMPETITIVE+

Nebraska Wesleyan University, founded in 1887, is a private liberal arts institution affiliated with the United Methodist Church. There are 18 departments and 2 programs. In addition to regional accreditation, NWU has baccalaureate program accreditation with ACBSP, CSWE, NASM, NCATE, and NLN. The library contains 207,278 volumes, 4678 microform items, and 6938 audio/video tapes/CDs/DVDs, and subscribes to 708 periodicals including electronic. Computerized library services include the card catalog, interlibrary loans, and database searching. Special learning facilities include a learning resource center, art gallery, planetarium, laboratory theater, sleep lab, greenhouse, herbarium, and nuclear magnetic resonance lab. The 50-acre campus is in a suburban area 50 miles west of Omaha. Including any residence halls, there are 23 buildings.

Student Life: 92% of undergraduates are from Nebraska. Others are from 25 states and 11 foreign countries. 95% are white. 59% are Protestant; 23% Catholic; 10% claim no religious affiliation. The average age of freshmen is 18; all undergraduates, 21. 18% do not continue beyond their first year; 69% remain to graduate.

Housing: 847 students can be accommodated in college housing, which includes single-sex and coed dorms, on-campus apartments, off-campus apartments, fraternity houses, and sorority houses. On-campus housing is guaranteed for all 4 years. 63% of students live on campus; of those, 70% remain on campus on weekends. All students may keep cars.

Activities: 24% of men belong to 1 local and 3 national fraternities; 22% of women belong to 2 local and 2 national sororities. There are 80 groups on campus, including art, band, cheerleading, choir, chorus, computers, debate, drama, drill team, ethnic, forensics, gay, honors, international, jazz band, literary magazine, musical theater, newspaper, opera, orchestra, pep band, political, professional, religious, social, social service, student government, and yearbook. Popular campus events include international dinners, Mosaic Week (week emphasizing multicultural activities), and Visions and Ventures Symposium.

Sports: There are 8 intercollegiate sports for men and 8 for women, and 10 intramural sports for men and 10 for women. Facilities include a recreation and fitness center, a field house and gym, a football/soccer stadium, a swimming pool, an outdoor track, football and baseball fields, and tennis courts.

Disabled Students: 85% of the campus is accessible. Wheelchair ramps, elevators, special parking, specially equipped rest rooms, special class scheduling, lowered drinking fountains, lowered telephones, and special housing, are available. All academic programs can be moved or adapted as needed to accommodate students.

Services: Counseling and information services are available, as is tutoring in some subjects, including sciences, social sciences, humanities, and math.

Campus Safety and Security: Measures include security escort services, informal discussions, emergency telephones, lighted pathways/sidewalks and nighttime foot patrol.

Programs of Study: NWU confers B.A., B.S., B.F.A., B.M., and B.S.N. degrees. Master's degrees are also awarded. Bachelor's degrees are awarded in BIOLOGICAL SCIENCE (biochemistry, biology/biological science, and molecular biology), BUSINESS (accounting, business administration and management, international business management, and sports management), COMMUNICATIONS AND THE ARTS (applied music, art, communications, dramatic arts, English, French, German, language arts, music, Spanish, and studio art), COMPUTER AND PHYSICAL SCIENCE (chemistry, computer programming, computer science, information sciences and systems, mathematics, and physics), EDUCATION (athletic training, elementary, English, middle school, music, physical, science, social science, and special), HEALTH PROFESSIONS (exercise science, health, and nursing), SOCIAL SCIENCE (biopsychology, economics, history, international studies, paralegal studies, philosophy, political science/government, psychology, religion, social work, sociology, and women's studies). Business administration, biology, and psychology are the largest.

Required: To graduate, students must complete approximately 42 to 48 hours of general education requirements, including 9 hours in First-year Experience, 8 in Developing Foundations courses, 7 in Scientific Inquiry, 6 in U.S. Culture and Society, 3 to 11 in Global Perspectives, 3 in Western Intellectual and Religious Traditions, and 3 in Fine Arts. At least 126 credit hours, including 30 in the major, must be completed with a minimum GPA of 2.0. A senior comprehensive is also needed, consisting of a comprehensive exam in the major discipline, a thesis or independent study, or an internship, presentation, or performance.

Special: NWU offers the Capitol Hill Internship Program, study abroad in 35 countries, a global studies major, and many other interdisciplinary studies majors and minors. Internships are available in most departments and required in many. Natural sciences majors can complete summer research fellowships at labs, universities, and agencies naitionwide and internationally. Other options include pass/fail options, dual majors, credit by exam, and a 3-2 engineering degree in conjunction with Washington and Columbia Universities. There are 20 national honor societies.

Faculty/Classroom: 48% of faculty are male; 52%, female. 96% teach undergraduates. No introductory courses are taught by graduate students. The average class size in an introductory lecture is 21; in a laboratory, 15; and in a regular course, 19.

Admissions: 97% of the 2005-2006 applicants were accepted. The ACT scores for the 2005-2006 freshman class were: 19% below 21, 30% between 21 and 23, 28% between 24 and 26, 12% between 27 and 28, and 12% above 28. 48% of the current freshmen were in the top fifth of their class; 80% were in the top two fifths. 28 freshmen graduated first in their class.

Requirements: The SAT or ACT is required. Freshmen must be graduates of an accredited secondary school or submit the GED. A campus visit is recommended. NWU requires applicants to be in the upper 50% of their class. AP and CLEP credits are accepted.

Procedure: Freshmen are admitted fall and spring. Entrance exams should be taken no later than December of the senior year. There are early decision and deferred admissions plans. Early decision applications should be filed by November 15; regular applications, by May 1 for fall entry, December 15 for spring entry, and April 15 for summer entry. The fall 2005 aplication fee was $20 (waived for on-line applications). Notification of early decision is sent December 15; regular decision, January 15. 307 early decision candidates were accepted for the 2005-2006 class. Applications are accepted on-line.

Transfer: 86 transfer students enrolled in 2004-2005. Applicants must be in good standing at their previous school and have a 2.0 GPA or higher. Grades of C- or better transfer for credit. 30 of 126 credits required for the bachelor's degree must be completed at NWU.

Visiting: There are regularly scheduled orientations for prospective students, consisting of a tour, classroom visits, and meetings with faculty, financial aid and admissions personnel, and current students. There are guides for informal visits and visitors may sit in on classes and stay overnight. To schedule a visit, contact the Admissions Office.

Financial Aid: In 2005-2006, 97% of all full-time freshmen and 94% of continuing full-time students received some form of financial aid. 70%

of full-time freshmen and 67% of continuing full-time students received need-based aid. The average freshman award was $11,274. Need-based scholarships or need-based grants averaged $6806 ($2019 maximum); need-based self-help aid (loans and jobs) averaged $2370 ($8459 maximum); and other non-need-based awards and non-need-based scholarships averaged $2098 ($21,900 maximum). 91% of undergraduates work part time. Average annual earnings from campus work are $1300. The average financial indebtedness of the 2005 graduate was $17,100. The FAFSA is required. The deadline for filing freshman financial aid applications for fall entry is August 15.

International Students: There are 16 international students enrolled. The school actively recruits these students. They must score satisfactorily on the TOEFL. The SAT or ACT is recommended.

Computers: Wireless access is available. Computer labs are available in classroom buildings as well as in residence facilities. All students may access the system at anytime.

Graduates: From July 1, 2004 to June 30, 2005, 394 bachelor's degrees were awarded. The most popular majors were business administration (17%), education (14%), and nursing (10%). In an average class, 1% graduate in 3 years or less, 56% graduate in 4 years or less, 67% graduate in 5 years or less, and 68% graduate in 6 years or less. 81 companies recruited on campus in 2004-2005.

Admissions Contact: Patty Karthauser, Vice President for Enrollment and Marketing. A video is available.
E-mail: admissions@nebrwesleyan.edu
Web: http://www.nebrwesleyan.edu

PERU STATE COLLEGE   F-3
Peru, NE 68421-0010

(402) 872-2221
(800) 742-4412; Fax: (402) 872-2296

Full-time: 420 men, 460 women	**Faculty:** 39; IIB, --$
Part-time: 245 men, 330 women	**Ph.D.s:** 64%
Graduate: 45 men, 135 women	**Student/Faculty:** 23 to 1
Year: semesters, summer session	**Tuition:** $2550 ($4650)
Application Deadline: open	**Room & Board:** $3800
Freshman Class: n/av	
ACT: recommended	**NONCOMPETITIVE**

Peru State College, established in 1867 and a part of the Nebraska State College System, is a public institution offering curricula in the arts, business, military studies, teacher preparation, and technical studies. Figures in the above capsule and profile are approximate. In addition to regional accreditation, Bobcats has baccalaureate program accreditation with NCATE. The library contains 102,432 volumes, 494,101 microform items, and 10,403 audio/video tapes/CDs/DVDs, and subscribes to 313 periodicals including electronic. Computerized library services include the card catalog, interlibrary loans, and database searching. Special learning facilities include a learning resource center and art gallery. The 103-acre campus is in a rural area 60 miles south of Omaha. Including any residence halls, there are 21 buildings.

Student Life: Students are from 12 states, 8 foreign countries, and Canada. 98% are from public schools. 87% are white. The average age of freshmen is 18; all undergraduates, 22. 28% do not continue beyond their first year; 35% remain to graduate.

Housing: 590 students can be accommodated in college housing, which includes single-sex dormitories, on-campus apartments, married-student housing, and substance-free facilities.. On-campus housing is guaranteed for all 4 years. 65% of students live on campus; of those, 27% remain on campus on weekends. Alcohol is not permitted. All students may keep cars.

Activities: There are no fraternities or sororities. There are 27 groups on campus, including art, band, cheerleading, choir, chorus, computers, drama, ethnic, gay, honors, jazz band, pep band, photography, professional, religious, social, social service, student government, and yearbook. Popular campus events include Spring Break Trip.

Sports: There are 3 intercollegiate sports for men and 3 for women, and 7 intramural sports for men and 7 for women. Facilities include a playing field, an activity trail, a 2500-seat stadium, and a health and recreation complex containing basketball and tennis courts, an indoor track, and an Olympic-sized swimming pool.

Disabled Students: 80% of the campus is accessible. Wheelchair ramps, elevators, special parking, specially equipped rest rooms, special class scheduling, lowered drinking fountains, and lowered telephones are available.

Services: Counseling and information services are available, as is tutoring in most subjects. There is a reader service for the blind, and remedial math, reading, and writing. Tutoring is available in writing and other subjects.

Campus Safety and Security: Measures include 24-hour foot and vehicle patrol, security escort services, informal discussions, and pamphlets/posters/films. There are lighted pathways/sidewalks.

Programs of Study: Bobcats confers B.A., B.S., and B.T. degrees. Master's degrees are also awarded. Bachelor's degrees are awarded in AGRICULTURE (wildlife management), BIOLOGICAL SCIENCE (biolo-

gy/biological science), BUSINESS (accounting, business administration and management, marketing/retailing/merchandising, and sports management), COMMUNICATIONS AND THE ARTS (English, music, and music business management), COMPUTER AND PHYSICAL SCIENCE (computer management, computer programming, computer science, mathematics, nuclear technology, and physical sciences), EDUCATION (art, elementary, music, physical, science, secondary, and special), ENGINEERING AND ENVIRONMENTAL DESIGN (preengineering), HEALTH PROFESSIONS (premedicine, prepharmacy, and preveterinary science), SOCIAL SCIENCE (history, prelaw, psychology, social science, and sociology).

Required: To graduate, students must complete 45 to 53 hours of general education requirements in literature, communications, fine arts, social and behavioral sciences, health and hygiene, computer science, and natural sciences, as well as a phys ed requirement. Teacher education majors must have a GPA of 2.5; all others must have a GPA of 2.0. The college requires 125 credit hours for graduation.

Special: The college offers cooperative programs, internships, B.A.-B.S. degrees, dual majors, work-study programs, and nondegree study. Credit may be granted for military experience. There are 2 national honor societies, and a freshman honors program.

Faculty/Classroom: 79% of faculty are male; 21%, female. All teach undergraduates. No introductory courses are taught by graduate students. The average class size in an introductory lecture is 40; in a laboratory, 25; and in a regular course, 25.

Requirements: The ACT is recommended. Applicants who have graduated from an accredited Nebraska secondary school will be admitted; holders of the GED will be considered. Out-of-state applicants should have earned 16 Carnegie units. A GPA of 2.0 is required. AP and CLEP credits are accepted.

Procedure: Freshmen are admitted to all sessions. Entrance exams should be taken . There are deferred admissions and rolling admissions plans. Application deadlines are open. Applications are accepted on-line. The fall 2005 application fee was $20.

Transfer: Transfer students must be in good standing with the previously attended institution. 30 of 125 credits required for the bachelor's degree must be completed at Bobcats.

Visiting: There are regularly scheduled orientations for prospective students. There are guides for informal visits and visitors may sit in on classes and stay overnight. To schedule a visit, contact the Admissions Office.

Financial Aid: The FAFSA is required. Check with the school for application deadlines.

International Students: They must score satisfactorily on the written TOEFL or on the electronic version.

Computers: There are no time limits and no fees.

Admissions Contact: Janelle Moran, Director of Admission and Recruitment. E-mail: jmoran@oakmail.peru.edu
Web: http://www.peru.edu

UNION COLLEGE   E-3
Lincoln, NE 68506

(402) 486-2504
(800) 228-4600; Fax: (402) 486-2895

Full-time: 338 men, 419 women	**Faculty:** 58
Part-time: 59 men, 69 women	**Ph.D.s:** 45%
Graduate: 12 men, 33 women	**Student/Faculty:** 14 to 1
Year: semesters, summer session	**Tuition:** $13,990
Application Deadline: open	**Room & Board:** $4720
Freshman Class: 173 enrolled	
ACT: 22	**COMPETITIVE**

Union College, established in 1891, is a private liberal arts institution affiliated with the Seventh-day Adventist Church. In addition to regional accreditation, Union College has baccalaureate program accreditation with CSWE and NCATE. The library contains 157,725 volumes, 1785 microform items, and 1933 audio/video tapes/CDs/DVDs, and subscribes to 573 periodicals including electronic. Computerized library services include the card catalog, interlibrary loans, database searching, and Internet access. Special learning facilities include a learning resource center, art gallery, and a state-run natural arboretum. The 26-acre campus is in a suburban area in southeast Lincoln. Including any residence halls, there are 11 buildings.

Student Life: 78% of undergraduates are from out of state, mostly the Midwest. Others are from 44 states, 26 foreign countries, and Canada. 78% are white; 11% foreign nationals. The average age of freshmen is 18; all undergraduates, 22. 28% do not continue beyond their first year; 54% remain to graduate.

Housing: 635 students can be accommodated in college housing, which includes single-sex dorms, on-campus apartments, and married-student housing. On-campus housing is guaranteed for the freshman year only and is available on a first-come, first-served basis. 58% of students live on campus; of those, 67% remain on campus on weekends. Alcohol is not permitted. All students may keep cars.

Activities: There are no fraternities or sororities. There are 18 groups on campus, including art, band, choir, chorale, chorus, computers, drama, ethnic, honors, international, literary magazine, newspaper, orchestra, photography, religious, social, student government, and yearbook.

Sports: There are 2 intercollegiate sports for men and 3 for women, and 8 intramural sports for men and 8 for women. Facilities include an Olympic-size indoor swimming pool, a weight room, tennis courts, and a sandlot volleyball court.

Disabled Students: 75% of the campus is accessible. Wheelchair ramps, elevators, special parking, specially equipped rest rooms, and lowered telephones are available.

Services: Counseling and information services are available, as is tutoring in most subjects. There is a reader service for the blind, and remedial math, reading, and writing. Tutoring is available upon request.

Campus Safety and Security: Measures include 24-hour foot and vehicle patrol, security escort services, emergency telephones, and lighted pathways/sidewalks.

Programs of Study: Union College confers B.A., B.S., B.A.T., B.Ed., B.M., B.S.W., and B.T. degrees. Associate degrees are also awarded. Bachelor's degrees are awarded in BIOLOGICAL SCIENCE (biology/biological science), BUSINESS (accounting, banking and finance, business administration and management, management science, marketing and distribution, and small business management), COMMUNICATIONS AND THE ARTS (communications, English, French, German, graphic design, journalism, literature, music, music performance, public relations, Spanish, and studio art), COMPUTER AND PHYSICAL SCIENCE (chemistry, computer science, mathematics, physics, and science), EDUCATION (art, business, computer, elementary, English, mathematics, music, physical, secondary, and social science), HEALTH PROFESSIONS (medical laboratory technology, nursing, and physician's assistant), SOCIAL SCIENCE (history, international studies, pastoral studies, physical fitness/movement, psychology, religion, religious education, social science, social work, and theological studies). Physician's assistant and physical science are the strongest academically. Business administration and nursing are the largest.

Required: Students must complete 128 semester hours, with fulfillment of a major, and maintain a minimum GPA of 2.0. There are 56 hours of core classes, including those in art/fine arts, computer science, English, history, math, science, and philosophy/religion. Courses in phy ed are also required.

Special: Special academic programs include study abroad in 7 countries, co-op programs with 9 Adventist institutions abroad, and cross-registration with the University of Nebraska, Nebraska Wesleyan University, and Southeast Community College. Student-designed majors are available through the Personalized Bachelor's Degree Program. There are pass/fail options in electives for upperclassmen with a minimum cumulative GPA of 2.0. Some internships are available. There is a freshman honors program.

Faculty/Classroom: 52% of faculty are male; 48%, female. The average class size in an introductory lecture is 21 and in a regular course, 16.

Admissions: The ACT scores for the 2005-2006 freshman class were: 40% below 21, 30% between 21 and 23, 17% between 24 and 26, 8% between 27 and 28, and 5% above 28. 31% of the current freshmen were in the top fifth of their class; 57% were in the top two fifths.

Requirements: The ACT is required. In addition, freshmen with a high school GPA below 2.5 and/or an ACT composite score below the 20th percentile will be enrolled in the freshman development program. Applicants must have graduated from an accredited secondary school with 18 academic credits, including 3 units of English and 1 unit each of math, science, and history. For math and science programs, 2 units of algebra and 1 unit each of geometry and trigonometry are recommended. For majors in nursing, biology, chemistry, physics, or engineering, applicants should complete physics and chemistry courses. The GED is also accepted. An essay and interview are advised, and music students should audition. A GPA of 2.5 is required. AP and CLEP credits are accepted.

Procedure: Freshmen are admitted fall and spring. Entrance exams should be taken by fall of the senior year. There is a rolling admissions plan. Application deadlines are open.

Transfer: Transfer students must have a minimum GPA of 2.0. The ACT is required, and high school and college transcripts must be submitted. 30 of 128 credits required for the bachelor's degree must be completed at Union College.

Visiting: There are regularly scheduled orientations for prospective students. There are guides for informal visits and visitors may sit in on classes and stay overnight. To schedule a visit, contact the Admissions Office Campus Hostess. at ucenroll@ucollege.edu.

Financial Aid: In 2005-2006, 99% of all full-time freshmen and 91% of continuing full-time students received some form of financial aid. 97% of full-time freshmen and 79% of continuing full-time students received need-based aid. The average freshman award was $10,130. 53% of undergraduates work part time. Average annual earnings from campus work are $2250. The average financial indebtedness of the 2005 graduate was $18,809. The FAFSA is required.

International Students: There were 87 international students enrolled in a recent year. The school actively recruits these students. A satisfactory score is required on the written TOEFL.

Computers: Wireless access is available. All students are assigned a user code and can access a variety of labs on campus with that code. They can also register their own computer and have the same access and services. All students may access the system. There are no time limits and no fees. It is strongly recommended that all students have a personal computer.

Graduates: From July 1, 2004 to June 30, 2005, 200 bachelor's degrees were awarded. The most popular majors were physician's assistant (16%), business administration (13%), and nursing (11%). In an average class, 35% graduate in 4 years or less, and 54% graduate in 6 years or less. 32 companies recruited on campus in 2004-2005. Of the 2004 graduating class, 13% were enrolled in graduate school within 6 months of graduation and 69% were employed.

Admissions Contact: Huda McClelland, Director of Admissions. E-mail: ucenrol@ucollege.edu Web: www.ucollege.edu

UNIVERSITY OF NEBRASKA SYSTEM

The University of Nebraska System, established in 1869, is a public system in Nebraska. It is governed by a board of regents and a central administration, whose chief administrator is the president. The primary goal of the system is The primary mission and priorities of the system are teaching, research, and service. The total enrollment is usually about 32,000; with 3200 faculty members. Altogether there are 263 baccalaureate, 137 master's, and 40 doctoral programs offered in University of Nebraska System. There is a 4-year campus located in Kearney, Lincoln and Omaha. Profiles of the 4-year campuses are included in this section.

UNIVERSITY OF NEBRASKA AT KEARNEY   D-3

Kearney, NE 68849

(308) 865-8526
(800) KEARNEY; Fax: (308) 865-8987

Full-time: 2400 men, 3000 women	**Faculty:** 305; IIA, -$
Part-time: 300 men, 400 women	**Ph.D.s:** 74%
Graduate: 600 men, 1200 women	**Student/Faculty:** 18 to 1
Year: semesters, summer session	**Tuition:** $4000 ($8000)
Application Deadline: open	**Room & Board:** $5000
Freshman Class: n/av	
SAT or ACT: required	**NONCOMPETITIVE**

The University of Nebraska at Kearney, founded in 1903, is a public facility. There are 4 undergraduate schools and 1 graduate school. Figures in the above capsule and in this profile are approximate. In addition to regional accreditation, UNK has baccalaureate program accreditation with ADA, CSWE, NASM, NCATE, and NLN. The library contains 287,000 volumes, 985,000 microform items, and 1300 audio/video tapes/CDs/DVDs, and subscribes to 1650 periodicals including electronic. Computerized library services include the card catalog, interlibrary loans, database searching, and Internet access. Special learning facilities include a learning resource center, art gallery, planetarium, radio station, TV station, and writing center. The 235-acre campus is in a small town 180 miles west of Omaha. Including any residence halls, there are 36 buildings.

Student Life: 91% of undergraduates are from Nebraska. Others are from 39 states, 46 foreign countries, and Canada. 93% are white. The average age of freshmen is 19; all undergraduates, 21. 20% do not continue beyond their first year; 47% remain to graduate.

Housing: 2600 students can be accommodated in college housing, which includes single-sex and coed dorms, off-campus apartments, married-student housing, fraternity houses, and sorority houses. In addition, there are honors houses and special-interest houses. On-campus housing is guaranteed for the freshman year only and is available on a first-come, first-served basis. 60% of students commute. Alcohol is not permitted. All students may keep cars.

Activities: 11% of men belong to 16 national fraternities; 10% of women belong to 4 national sororities. There are 160 groups on campus, including art, band, cheerleading, choir, chorale, chorus, computers, dance, debate, drama, drill team, ethnic, forensics, gay, honors, international, jazz band, marching band, musical theater, newspaper, opera, orchestra, pep band, photography, political, professional, radio and TV, religious, social, social service, student government, symphony, and yearbook. Popular campus events include Welcome Week, Bike Bowl, and the Midwest Conference on World Affairs.

Sports: There are 8 intercollegiate sports for men and 8 for women, and 14 intramural sports for men and 14 for women. Facilities include a field, tennis courts, and a health and sports facility.

Disabled Students: Wheelchair ramps, elevators, special parking, specially equipped rest rooms, and lowered drinking fountains are available.

Services: Counseling and information services are available, as is tutoring in most subjects. There is a reader service for the blind, and remedial math, reading, and writing.

Campus Safety and Security: Measures include 24-hour foot and vehicle patrol, security escort services, informal discussions, and pamphlets/posters/films. There are emergency telephones and lighted pathways/sidewalks.

Programs of Study: UNK confers B.A., B.S., B.A.Ed., B.F.A., B.G.S., and B.S.Ed. degrees. Master's degrees are also awarded. Bachelor's degrees are awarded in BIOLOGICAL SCIENCE (biology/biological science), BUSINESS (accounting, banking and finance, business administration and management, business economics, marketing/retailing/merchandising, personnel management, and tourism), COMMUNICATIONS AND THE ARTS (advertising, broadcasting, communications, dramatic arts, English, fine arts, French, German, journalism, music, Spanish, speech/debate/rhetoric, and telecommunications), COMPUTER AND PHYSICAL SCIENCE (chemistry, computer programming, computer science, information sciences and systems, mathematics, physics, and statistics), EDUCATION (art, business, early childhood, elementary, foreign languages, health, middle school, music, physical, science, secondary, special, and teaching English as a second/foreign language (TESOL/TEFOL)), HEALTH PROFESSIONS (nursing, predentistry, and premedicine), SOCIAL SCIENCE (criminal justice, economics, family/consumer studies, geography, history, human development, international studies, political science/government, prelaw, psychology, social science, social work, and sociology). Business, communication, and psychology are the strongest academically. Business administration, elementary education, and special education are the largest.

Required: To graduate, all students must complete courses in humanities, communications, civilization, math, natural sciences, and social and behavioral sciences. A minimum of 125 credit hours is required, with approximately 60 in the major. Students must maintain a GPA of 2.0 or higher.

Special: Special arrangements include internships, work-study programs, study at other U.S. colleges and universities under the auspices of the National Student Exchange Program, and study abroad in more than 40 countries through the International Student Exchange Program. Cooperative programs in some health science majors, an international studies degree, and a credit/no credit grading option are available. There is a chapter of Phi Beta Kappa and a freshman honors program.

Faculty/Classroom: 66% of faculty are male; 34%, female. 99% teach undergraduates. The average class size in an introductory lecture is 32; in a laboratory, 25; and in a regular course, 20.

Requirements: The SAT or ACT is required. In addition, applicants must be graduates of an accredited secondary school. The GED is accepted. They should have completed 4 years of high school English, 3 years each of math, science, and social studies, 2 years of the same foreign language, and 1 year of an academic elective. They should score 20 or above on the ACT or achieve a comparable score on the SAT or be in the top half of their graduating class. AP and CLEP credits are accepted. Important factors in the admissions decision are recommendations by school officials, evidence of special talent, and advanced placement or honor courses.

Procedure: Freshmen are admitted fall, spring, and summer. Entrance exams should be taken at the end of the junior year or beginning of the senior year. There is a rolling admissions plan. Application deadlines are open. The fall 2005 application fee was $45. Applications are accepted on-line.

Transfer: Transfer students must supply transcripts from previous institutions. If the GPA from the previous school is lower than 2.0, students will be evaluated by the Admissions Director. Transfers must show proof of honorable dismissal from the last institution attended. Grades of C and above transfer for credit. 45 of 125 credits required for the bachelor's degree must be completed at UNK.

Visiting: There are regularly scheduled orientations for prospective students, including registration for classes and campus orientation. There are guides for informal visits and visitors may sit in on classes and stay overnight. To schedule a visit, contact the Admissions Office.

Financial Aid: 80% of undergraduates work part time. The FAFSA and the college's own financial statement are required. Check with the school for current deadlines.

International Students: There were 295 international students enrolled in a recent year. The school actively recruits these students. They must score satisfactorily on the written TOEFL or 173 on the electronic version.

Computers: All students may access the system. There are no time limits. It is strongly recommended that all students have a personal computer.

Graduates: In a recent year, 1058 bachelor's degrees were awarded.

Admissions Contact: Admissions Officer.
E-mail: *admissionsug@unk.edu* Web: *www.unk.edu*

UNIVERSITY OF NEBRASKA AT LINCOLN E-3

Lincoln, NE 68588-0417

(402) 472-2023
(800) 742-8800; Fax: (402) 472-0670

Full-time: 8339 men, 7429 women	**Faculty:** I, -$
Part-time: 731 men, 538 women	**Ph.D.s:** 97%
Graduate: 2265 men, 2373 women	**Student/Faculty:** n/av
Year: semesters, summer session	**Tuition:** $5540 ($14,450)
Application Deadline: June 30	**Room & Board:** $5861
Freshman Class: 7474 applied, 5633 accepted, 3560 enrolled	
SAT Verbal/Math: 590/610*	**ACT:** 25 **VERY COMPETITIVE**

University of Nebraska-Lincoln, part of the University of Nebraska system, was founded in 1869 as a land-grant facility. There are 8 undergraduate schools and 1 graduate school. In addition to regional accreditation, UNL has baccalaureate program accreditation with AACSB, ABET, ACCE, ACEJMC, ADA, FIDER, NAAB, NASAD, NASM, and NCATE. The 8 libraries contain 2,922,720 volumes, 3,603,325 microform items, and 41,699 audio/video tapes/CDs/DVDs, and subscribe to 45,228 periodicals including electronic. Computerized library services include the card catalog, interlibrary loans, database searching, Internet access, and laptop Internet portals. Special learning facilities include a learning resource center, art gallery, natural history museum, planetarium, radio station, TV station, a center for mass spectrometry, an observatory, the Buros Institute of Mental Measurements, an animal sciences complex, and a center for performing arts. The 609-acre campus is in an urban area 55 miles southwest of Omaha. Including any residence halls, there are 238 buildings.

Student Life: 80% of undergraduates are from Nebraska. Students are from 50 states, 112 foreign countries, and Canada. 89% are from public schools. 82% are white. The average age of freshmen is 18; all undergraduates, 21. 16% do not continue beyond their first year; 63% remain to graduate.

Housing: 6125 students can be accommodated in university housing, which includes single-sex and coed dormitories, on-campus apartments, off-campus apartments, married-student housing, fraternity houses, and sorority houses. In addition, there are honors houses, language houses, an international house, and special-interest houses, as well as floors for modern languages, scholars, engineering, business, and journalism. On-campus housing is guaranteed for the freshman year only and is available on a first-come, first-served basis. 76% of students commute. Alcohol is not permitted. All students may keep cars.

Activities: 11% of men belong to 1 local fraternity and 26 national fraternities; 14% of women belong to 18 national sororities. There are 335 groups on campus, including art, band, cheerleading, chess, choir, chorale, chorus, computers, dance, debate, drama, ethnic, film, forensics, gay, honors, international, jazz band, literary magazine, marching band, musical theater, newspaper, opera, orchestra, pep band, photography, political, professional, radio and TV, religious, social, social service, student government, symphony, and yearbook. Popular campus events include Cornstock, Parents Weekend, and Freshmen Friday.

Sports: There are 9 intercollegiate sports for men and 12 for women, and 65 intramural sports for men and 45 for women. Facilities include a recreation center and 34 acres of outdoor recreational space.

Disabled Students: 80% of the campus is accessible. Wheelchair ramps, elevators, special parking, specially equipped rest rooms, special class scheduling, lowered drinking fountains, lowered telephones, special housing, and assistance from the Office of Handicapped Services are available.

Services: Counseling and information services are available, as is tutoring in most subjects. There is a reader service for the blind.

Campus Safety and Security: Measures include 24-hour foot and vehicle patrol, self-defense education, security escort services, and shuttle buses. There are informal discussions, pamphlets/posters/films, emergency telephones, and lighted pathways/sidewalks.

Programs of Study: UNL confers B.A., B.S., B.A.Ed., B.B.A., B.F.A., B.F.A.Ed., B.J., B.M., B.M.Ed., B.S.A.E., B.S.Agr., B.S.Arch., B.S.B.A., B.S.B.S.E., B.S.C., B.S.C.E., B.S.C.M., B.S.C.S., B.S.Ch.E., B.S.E.E., B.S.E.T., B.S.Ed., B.S.H.E., B.S.H.R.E.S., B.S.I.C.E., B.S.I.E., B.S.I.T., B.S.M.E., and B.S.N.R. degrees. Associate, master's, and doctoral degrees are also awarded. Bachelor's degrees are awarded in AGRICULTURE (agricultural business management, agricultural communications, agricultural economics, agricultural mechanics, agriculture, agronomy, animal science, environmental studies, fish and game management, horticulture, natural resource management, plant protection (pest management), range/farm management, and soil science), BIOLOGICAL SCIENCE (biochemistry and biology/biological science), BUSINESS (accounting, banking and finance, business administration and management, business economics, international business management, management science, marketing/retailing/merchandising, and recreational facilities management), COMMUNICATIONS AND THE ARTS (advertising, art, art history and appreciation, broadcasting, classics, communications, dance, design, dramatic arts, English, English as a second/foreign language, film arts, fine arts, French, German, Greek, journalism, language arts, languages, Latin, music, Russian, Spanish, and speech/debate/

rhetoric), COMPUTER AND PHYSICAL SCIENCE (actuarial science, atmospheric sciences and meteorology, chemistry, computer science, earth science, geology, information sciences and systems, mathematics, natural sciences, and physics), EDUCATION (agricultural, art, athletic training, business, early childhood, education, education of the deaf and hearing impaired, elementary, foreign languages, guidance, health, home economics, industrial arts, journalism, middle school, music, nutrition, physical, reading, science, secondary, special, technical, and trade and industrial), ENGINEERING AND ENVIRONMENTAL DESIGN (agricultural engineering, architectural engineering, architecture, bioengineering, chemical engineering, civil engineering, computer engineering, construction management, construction technology, electrical/electronics engineering, electrical/electronics engineering technology, environmental design, environmental science, fire protection engineering, industrial engineering, industrial engineering technology, interior design, manufacturing technology, and mechanical engineering), HEALTH PROFESSIONS (community health work, exercise science, medical laboratory technology, predentistry, premedicine, prepharmacy, speech pathology/audiology, and veterinary science), SOCIAL SCIENCE (anthropology, area studies, dietetics, economics, ethnic studies, European studies, family/consumer studies, food science, geography, history, human development, interdisciplinary studies, international relations, international studies, Latin American studies, law, medieval studies, philosophy, political science/government, prelaw, psychology, religion, sociology, textiles and clothing, water resources, and women's studies). Biochemistry, engineering, and journalism are the strongest academically. Psychology, business administration, and education are the largest.

Required: Distribution requirements include 9 courses across 8 areas of essential studies and 10 courses from the integrative studies area. A minimum GPA of 2.0 is required. Each college and major has its own requirements; there are few graduation requirements that apply to all students.

Special: There is cross-registration with many schools, and co-op programs are available in the Colleges of Engineering and Technology and Agriculture. Through membership in the International Student Exchange Program, the university can place students in more than 90 universities around the world. Internship opportunities abound, as do work-study programs. Accelerated degree programs, a Washington semester, B.A.-B.S. degrees, dual majors, combined pre-professional programs, student-designed majors, credit by exam, nondegree study, and pass/fail options are also available. There are 51 national honor societies, including Phi Beta Kappa, a freshman honors program, and 18 departmental honors programs.

Faculty/Classroom: 74% of faculty are male; 26%, female. Graduate students teach 14% of introductory courses. The average class size in an introductory lecture is 41; in a laboratory, 13; and in a regular course, 34.

Admissions: 75% of the 2005-2006 applicants were accepted. The SAT scores for the 2005-2006 freshman class were: Verbal--16% below 500, 35% between 500 and 599, 36% between 600 and 700, and 13% above 700; Math--13% below 500, 30% between 500 and 599, 39% between 600 and 700, and 17% above 700. The ACT scores were 14% below 21, 18% between 21 and 23, 26% between 24 and 26, 25% between 27 and 28, and 17% above 28. 47% of the current freshmen were in the top fifth of their class; 74% were in the top two fifths. There were 60 National Merit finalists and 6 semifinalists.

Requirements: The SAT or ACT is recommended. In addition, applicants must be graduates of an accredited secondary school. The GED is accepted. Students must have completed 3 years of English, 2 years each of math, science, and social studies, and an additional year of language arts. UNL requires applicants to be in the upper 50% of their class. AP and CLEP credits are accepted. Important factors in the admissions decision are advanced placement or honor courses, recommendations by school officials, and evidence of special talent.

Procedure: Freshmen are admitted to all sessions. Entrance exams should be taken in April of the junior year. Applications should be filed by June 30 for fall entry and December 15 for spring entry, along with a $25 fee. Notification is sent on a rolling basis. Applications are accepted on-line.

Transfer: 877 transfer students enrolled in 2004-2005. Transfer students must have a 2.0 GPA for both the cumulative average of all postsecondary facilities attended and for the most recent term of attendance. In certain majors, a higher GPA and/or extra course work may be required. 30 credits required for the bachelor's degree must be completed at UNL.

Visiting: There are regularly scheduled orientations for prospective students, including an information session, a campus tour, a visit to areas of academic interest, and a meeting with a department representative. There are guides for informal visits and visitors may sit in on classes and stay overnight. To schedule a visit, contact High School and College Relations at (402) 472-4887.

Financial Aid: In 2005-2006, 68% of all full-time freshmen and 77% of continuing full-time students received some form of financial aid. 44% of full-time freshmen and 55% of continuing full-time students received need-based aid. The average freshman award was $12,270. Need-based scholarships or need-based grants averaged $5560; need-based self-help aid (loans and jobs) averaged $3751; non-need-based athletic scholarships averaged $8958; and other non-need-based awards and non-need-based scholarships averaged $10,661. 100% of undergraduates work part time. Average annual earnings from campus work are $1200. The average financial indebtedness of the 2005 graduate was $17,020. The FAFSA is required. The priority date for freshman financial aid applications for fall entry is April 1. The deadline for filing freshman financial aid applications for fall entry is rolling.

International Students: There are 421 international students enrolled. The school actively recruits these students. They must take the written TOEFL.

Computers: Wireless access is available. There are 650 computer stations available. All students may access the system 24 hours a day, 7 days per week. There are no time limits and no fees. It is recommended that students in architecture and community and regional planning have personal computers.

Graduates: From July 1, 2004 to June 30, 2005, 3267 bachelor's degrees were awarded. The most popular majors were psychology (5%), business adminstration (5%), and management (4%). In an average class, 23% graduate in 4 years or less, 55% graduate in 5 years or less, and 63% graduate in 6 years or less. 261 companies recruited on campus in 2004-2005.

Admissions Contact: Alan Cerveney, Dean of Admissions. E-mail: *nuhusker@unl.edu* Web: *http://www.unl.edu*

UNIVERSITY OF NEBRASKA AT OMAHA   F-3
Omaha, NE 68182

(402) 554-2393
(800) 858-8648; Fax: (402) 554-3472

Full-time: 3972 men, 4560 women	**Faculty:** 482; IIA, av$
Part-time: 1299 men, 1498 women	**Ph.D.s:** 85%
Graduate: 1074 men, 1690 women	**Student/Faculty:** 18 to 1
Year: semesters, summer session	**Tuition:** $4825 ($12,872)
Application Deadline: August 1	**Room & Board:** $6410
Freshman Class: 3732 applied, 3310 accepted, 1758 enrolled	
SAT Verbal/Math: 552/548*	**ACT:** 23 **COMPETITIVE**

The University of Nebraska at Omaha, established in 1908, is a public institution and part of the University of Nebraska system. There are 9 undergraduate schools and 1 graduate school. In addition to regional accreditation, UNOmaha has baccalaureate program accreditation with AACSB, ABET, ACS, CAA, CAAHEP, CACREP, CSWE, NASAD, NASM, NASPAA, and NCATE. The library contains 700,000 volumes, 2,000,000 microform items, and 7000 audio/video tapes/CDs/DVDs, and subscribes to 3000 periodicals including electronic. Computerized library services include the card catalog, interlibrary loans, database searching, and Internet access. Special learning facilities include an art gallery, radio station, and TV station. The 158-acre campus is in a suburban area within the Omaha city limits. Including any residence halls, there are 46 buildings.

Student Life: 93% of undergraduates are from Nebraska. Others are from 34 states, 78 foreign countries, and Canada. 86% are from public schools. 82% are white. The average age of freshmen is 18; all undergraduates, 23. 29% do not continue beyond their first year; 39% remain to graduate.

Housing: 1212 students can be accommodated in college housing, which includes single-sex and coed dorms and on-campus apartments. In addition, there are honors houses. On-campus housing is available on a first-come, first-served basis. 91% of students commute. Alcohol is not permitted. All students may keep cars.

Activities: 2% of men belong to 7 national fraternities; 2% of women belong to 9 national sororities. There are 112 groups on campus, including band, cheerleading, chess, choir, chorale, chorus, dance, drama, drill team, ethnic, film, gay, honors, international, jazz band, literary magazine, marching band, musical theater, newspaper, opera, orchestra, pep band, political, professional, radio and TV, religious, social, social service, student government, and symphony. Popular campus events include Celebrate UNO, International Week, and Black History Month.

Sports: There are 5 intercollegiate sports for men and 8 for women, and 16 intramural sports for men and 16 for women. Facilities include a football field, a field house, and a recreation building housing basketball and volleyball courts, weight rooms, and a swimming pool.

Disabled Students: 99% of the campus is accessible. Wheelchair ramps, elevators, special parking, specially equipped rest rooms, special class scheduling, lowered drinking fountains, and lowered telephones are available.

Services: Counseling and information services are available, as is tutoring in some subjects, including math and psychology. There is a reader service for the blind.

Campus Safety and Security: Measures include 24-hour foot and vehicle patrol, self-defense education, security escort services, and shuttle buses. There are informal discussions, pamphlets/posters/films, emergency telephones, and lighted pathways/sidewalks.

Programs of Study: UNOmaha confers B.A., B.S., B.A.A.H., B.A.S.A., B.A.T.H., B.F.A., B.I.S., B.G.S., B.M., B.S.B.A., B.S.C.N., B.S.C.S., B.S.E.D., B.S.P.A., and B.S.S.W. degrees. Master's and doctoral degrees are also awarded. Bachelor's degrees are awarded in AGRICULTURE (environmental studies), BIOLOGICAL SCIENCE (bioinformatics, biology/biological science, and biotechnology), BUSINESS (accounting, banking and finance, business communications, management information systems, management science, marketing/retailing/merchandising, real estate, and recreation and leisure services), COMMUNICATIONS AND THE ARTS (art, art history and appreciation, broadcasting, communications, creative writing, dramatic arts, English, fine arts, French, German, journalism, music, Spanish, and speech/debate/rhetoric), COMPUTER AND PHYSICAL SCIENCE (chemistry, computer science, geology, information sciences and systems, mathematics, and physics), EDUCATION (elementary, library science, physical, and secondary), ENGINEERING AND ENVIRONMENTAL DESIGN (aviation administration/management, and engineering physics), HEALTH PROFESSIONS (community health work and health care administration), SOCIAL SCIENCE (African American studies, criminal justice, economics, geography, history, interdisciplinary studies, international studies, Latin American studies, liberal arts/general studies, philosophy, political science/government, psychology, public administration, social work, sociology, and women's studies). Elementary education, criminal justice, and marketing management are the largest.

Required: To graduate, students must complete 30 hours of distribution requirements in natural and physical sciences, humanities and fine arts, and social and behavioral sciences; 15 hours in fundamental academic skills in English writing, math, and public speaking; and 6 hours in cultural diversity.

Special: UNOmaha offers internships for business students, cooperative programs, and credit by examination. Students may study abroad in various European countries. There are 15 national honor societies, a freshman honors program, and 10 departmental honors programs.

Faculty/Classroom: 59% of faculty are male; 41%, female. 97% teach undergraduates. Graduate students teach 4% of introductory courses. The average class size in an introductory lecture is 38; in a laboratory, 12; and in a regular course, 21.

Admissions: 89% of the 2005-2006 applicants were accepted. The SAT scores for the 2005-2006 freshman class were: Verbal--30% below 500, 33% between 500 and 599, 31% between 600 and 700, and 6% above 700; Math--27% below 500, 46% between 500 and 599, 20% between 600 and 700, and 7% above 700. The ACT scores were 34% below 21, 27% between 21 and 23, 21% between 24 and 26, 7% between 27 and 28, and 10% above 28. 27% of the current freshmen were in the top fifth of their class; 55% were in the top two fifths. 27 freshmen graduated first in their class.

Requirements: The SAT or ACT is required. In addition, students must be graduates of an accredited secondary school. The GED is accepted. Students must have completed 4 units of English and 2 each of math, social sciences, and sciences. UNOmaha requires applicants to be in the upper 50% of their class. A GPA of 2.0 is required. AP and CLEP credits are accepted. Important factors in the admissions decision are recommendations by school officials, evidence of special talent, and personality/intangible qualities.

Procedure: Freshmen are admitted fall, spring, and summer. Entrance exams should be taken by the senior year. There is a rolling admissions plan. Applications should be filed by August 1 for fall entry, December 1 for spring entry, and June 1 for summer entry, along with a $45 fee. Notification is sent on a rolling basis. Applications are accepted on-line.

Transfer: 1068 transfer students enrolled in 2004-2005. Applicants must present evidence of good standing at the last institution they attended. Grades of C or better transfer for credit. A minimum GPA of 2.0 is required. 30 of 125 credits required for the bachelor's degree must be completed at UNOmaha.

Visiting: There are regularly scheduled orientations for prospective students. There are guides for informal visits and visitors may sit in on classes. To schedule a visit, contact Office of Orientation at (402) 554-2677.

Financial Aid: In a recent year, 44% of all full-time freshmen and 45% of continuing full-time students received some form of financial aid. 42% of full-time freshmen and 43% of continuing full-time students received need-based aid. The average freshman award was $4900. 6% of undergraduates work part time. Average annual earnings from campus work are $3800. The average financial indebtedness of the 2005 graduate was $16,900. The FAFSA is required. The deadline for filing freshman financial aid applications for fall entry is March 1.

International Students: There are 199 international students enrolled. The school actively recruits these students. A satisfactory score is required on the written TOEFL. Students must also take the college's own entrance exam.

Computers: Wireless access is available. 65% of classrooms allow wireless connectivity. UNO has 88 computer labs, classrooms, and other locations accessible by students with 2,200 PCs available. All students may access the system at any time. There are no time limits. There is a technology fee which is included in the admission fee ($8 per credit hour).

Graduates: From July 1, 2004 to June 30, 2005, 1648 bachelor's degrees were awarded. The most popular majors were criminal justice (10%), elementary education (8%), and marketing management (6%). In an average class, 10% graduate in 4 years or less, 28% graduate in 5 years or less, and 39% graduate in 6 years or less. 138 companies recruited on campus in 2004-2005. Of the 2004 graduating class, 17% were enrolled in graduate school within 6 months of graduation.

Admissions Contact: Jolene Adams, Director of Admissions. E-mail: *unoadm@unomaha.edu* Web: *www.unomaha.edu*

WAYNE STATE COLLEGE   E-2

Wayne, NE 68787 (402) 375-7000
(800) 228-9972; Fax: (402) 375-7204

Full-time: 1126 men, 1357 women	**Faculty:** 124; IIA, --$
Part-time: 71 men, 152 women	**Ph.D.s:** 75%
Graduate: 167 men, 449 women	**Student/Faculty:** 20 to 1
Year: semesters, summer session	**Tuition:** $3803 ($6735)
Application Deadline: open	**Room & Board:** $4230
Freshman Class: 1202 applied, 1202 accepted, 593 enrolled	
ACT: 21	**NONCOMPETITIVE**

Wayne State College, founded in 1910, is a public liberal arts facility. There are 4 undergraduate and 2 graduate schools. In addition to regional accreditation, Wayne State has baccalaureate program accreditation with NCATE. The library contains 270,371 volumes, 94,531 microform items, and 14,952 audio/video tapes/CDs/DVDs, and subscribes to 16,000 periodicals including electronic. Computerized library services include the card catalog, interlibrary loans, database searching, and Internet access. Special learning facilities include a learning resource center, art gallery, natural history museum, planetarium, radio station, TV station, and an arboretum. The 128-acre campus is in a rural area 45 miles southwest of Sioux City, Iowa. Including any residence halls, there are 25 buildings.

Student Life: 86% of undergraduates are from Nebraska. Others are from 31 states, 14 foreign countries, and Canada. 90% are from public schools. 89% are white. 47% are Protestant; 31% Catholic; 18% claim no religious affiliation. The average age of freshmen is 18; all undergraduates, 22. 33% do not continue beyond their first year; 46% remain to graduate.

Housing: 1587 students can be accommodated in college housing, which includes single-sex and coed dorms. On-campus housing is guaranteed for the freshman year only and is available on a first-come, first-served basis. 56% of students commute. Alcohol is not permitted. All students may keep cars.

Activities: There is 1 national fraternity and 2 local and 1 national sororities. There are 92 groups on campus, including art, band, cheerleading, choir, chorale, chorus, computers, dance, drama, drill team, ethnic, forensics, gay, honors, international, jazz band, literary magazine, marching band, musical theater, newspaper, orchestra, pep band, political, professional, radio and TV, religious, social, student government, symphony, and yearbook. Popular campus events include International Dinner, Elizabethan Dinners, and Greek Olympics.

Sports: There are 6 intercollegiate sports for men and 7 for women, and 40 intramural sports for men and 38 for women. Facilities include tennis courts, softball, flag football and soccer fields, a gym, a 33,000-square-foot recreation center, which has an indoor track, weight room, pool, and handball, volleyball, basketball, and tennis courts, a football stadium, an outdoor track, and a baseball/softball complex.

Disabled Students: 90% of the campus is accessible. Wheelchair ramps, elevators, special parking, specially equipped rest rooms, special class scheduling, lowered drinking fountains, lowered telephones, special housing, and a pool equipped with special steps are available.

Services: Counseling and information services are available, as is tutoring in most subjects. There is a reader service for the blind.

Campus Safety and Security: Measures include 24-hour foot and vehicle patrol, security escort services, pamphlets/posters/films, and emergency telephones. There are lighted pathways/sidewalks and In addition, there are articles in the campus newspaper relating to safety and security.

Programs of Study: Wayne State confers B.A. and B.S. degrees. Master's degrees are also awarded. Bachelor's degrees are awarded in BIOLOGICAL SCIENCE (biology/biological science and life science), BUSINESS (business administration and management and sports management), COMMUNICATIONS AND THE ARTS (art, communications, dramatic arts, English, graphic design, modern language, music, Spanish, and speech/debate/rhetoric), COMPUTER AND PHYSICAL SCIENCE (chemistry, computer science, and mathematics), EDUCATION (elementary, foreign languages, health, home economics, industrial arts, music, science, and special), ENGINEERING AND ENVIRONMENTAL DESIGN (technological management), SOCIAL SCIENCE (counseling/psychology, criminal justice, early childhood studies, family/consumer studies, food production/management/services, geography, history, interdisciplinary studies, parks and recreation management, political science/government, psychology, social science, and sociology). Business, education, and social sciences are the largest.

Required: Students must complete a specified 46-credit general education curriculum. A minimum of 125 credit hours is required for graduation, with 30 to 66 in the major and 40 in upper-division courses. Students must maintain at least a 2.0 GPA.

Special: There are co-op programs and cross-registration with Northeast Community College. Also offered are pass/fail options, internships, credit by exam, any combination of dual majors, a B.A.-B.S. degree in certain instances, and some student-designed majors. There is also a Regional Health Opportunities Program. There are 17 national honor societies, a freshman honors program, and 9 departmental honors programs.

Faculty/Classroom: 54% of faculty are male; 46%, female. All teach undergraduates. Graduate students teach 7% of introductory courses. The average class size in an introductory lecture is 18 and in a laboratory, 25.

Admissions: 100% of the 2005-2006 applicants were accepted. The ACT scores for the 2005-2006 freshman class were: 45% below 21, 23% between 21 and 23, 20% between 24 and 26, 7% between 27 and 28, and 5% above 28. 26% of the current freshmen were in the top fifth of their class; 50% were in the top two fifths. 21 freshmen graduated first in their class.

Requirements: In addition, applicants must be graduates of an accredited secondary school. The GED is accepted. Entering freshmen must have completed 12 credits, with a recommended 4 units of English, 3 each of math and social studies, and 2 of science. Additional units in foreign language, fine and performing arts, and computer literacy are recommended. AP and CLEP credits are accepted.

Procedure: Freshmen are admitted to all sessions. Entrance exams should be taken in the spring of the junior year or fall of the senior year. There are deferred admissions and rolling admissions plans. Application deadlines are open. Application fee is $30. Applications are accepted on-line.

Transfer: 187 transfer students enrolled in 2004-2005. Transfer students must have a minimum GPA of 2.0. Grades of C and above transfer for credit. 40 of 125 credits required for the bachelor's degree must be completed at Wayne State.

Visiting: There are guides for informal visits and visitors may sit in on classes and stay overnight. To schedule a visit, contact the Admissions Office at (402) 375-7234.

Financial Aid: In a recent year, 77% of all full-time freshmen and 79% of continuing full-time students received some form of financial aid. 59% of all full-time students received need-based aid. The average freshman award was $3470. Need-based scholarships or need-based grants averaged $1385; and need-based self-help aid (loans and jobs) averaged $1530. The FAFSA and the college's own financial statement are required. The priority date for freshman financial aid applications for fall entry is May 1. The deadline for filing freshman financial aid applications for fall entry is open.

International Students: There are 22 international students enrolled. A satisfactory score is required on the written TOEFL.

Computers: All students may access the system any time. There are no time limits and no fees.

Graduates: From July 1, 2004 to June 30, 2005, 552 bachelor's degrees were awarded. The most popular majors were business (22%), elementary education (14%), and criminal justice (5%). In an average class, 25% graduate in 4 years or less, 44% graduate in 5 years or less, and 46% graduate in 6 years or less.

Admissions Contact: R. Lincoln Morris, Director of Admissions. E-mail: admit1@wsc.edu Web: www.wsc.edu

YORK COLLEGE
E-3

York, NE 68467-2699

(402) 363-5608
(800) 950-YORK (9675); Fax: (402) 363-5623

Full-time: 207 men, 208 women	**Faculty:** 35
Part-time: 16 men, 21 women	**Ph.D.s:** 41%
Graduate: none	**Student/Faculty:** 12 to 1
Year: semesters, summer session	**Tuition:** $12,430
Application Deadline: open	**Room & Board:** $3900
Freshman Class: 206 applied, 203 accepted, 117 enrolled	
SAT Verbal/Math: 520/490*	**ACT:** 21 **NONCOMPETITIVE**

York College, founded in 1890, is an independent undergraduate college affiliated with the Churches of Christ. The library contains 126,086 volumes, 21,578 microform items, and 7017 audio/video tapes/CDs/DVDs, and subscribes to 301 periodicals including electronic. Computerized library services include the card catalog, interlibrary loans, and database searching. The 40-acre campus is in a small town 45 miles west of Lincoln. Including any residence halls, there are 18 buildings.

Student Life: 67% of undergraduates are from out of state, mostly the Midwest. Others are from 28 states, 10 foreign countries, and Canada. 90% are from public schools. 87% are white. 22% are Protestant; 9% claim no religious affiliation; 7% Catholic. The average age of freshmen is 18; all undergraduates, 20. 15% do not continue beyond their first year; 45% remain to graduate.

Housing: 472 students can be accommodated in college housing, which includes single-sex dormitories and on-campus apartments. On-campus housing is guaranteed for all 4 years. 72% of students live on campus; of those, 85% remain on campus on weekends. Alcohol is not permitted. All students may keep cars.

Activities: 57% of men belong to 4 local fraternities; 62% of women belong to 4 local sororities. There are 25 groups on campus, including art, choir, chorus, computers, drama, honors, international, literary magazine, musical theater, newspaper, pep band, photography, political, professional, religious, social, social service, student government, and yearbook. Popular campus events include High School Days, Fall Musical, and All School Banquet.

Sports: There are 7 intercollegiate sports for men and 7 for women, and 6 intramural sports for men and 6 for women. Facilities include basketball and volleyball courts, a gym, soccer, baseball, and intramural fields, a weight room, and an indoor track.

Disabled Students: 50% of the campus is accessible. Wheelchair ramps, elevators, special parking, specially equipped rest rooms, lowered drinking fountains, and lowered telephones are available.

Services: Counseling and information services are available, as is tutoring in most subjects. There is remedial math, reading, and writing. and a peer tutoring program.

Campus Safety and Security: Measures include self-defense education, pamphlets/posters/films, emergency telephones, lighted pathways/sidewalks, and an evening/night foot patrol.

Programs of Study: York confers B.A., B.S., B.B.A., and B.Mus. degrees. Associate degrees are also awarded. Bachelor's degrees are awarded in BIOLOGICAL SCIENCE (biology/biological science), BUSINESS (accounting, business administration and management, and human resources), COMMUNICATIONS AND THE ARTS (communications, English, music performance, and voice), COMPUTER AND PHYSICAL SCIENCE (natural sciences), EDUCATION (drama, education, elementary, English, middle school, music, psychology, science, secondary, social science, and special), SOCIAL SCIENCE (biblical studies, biopsychology, history, human services, liberal arts/general studies, psychology, and youth ministry). Education, natural science, and psychology are the strongest academically. Education and business are the largest.

Required: To graduate, students must complete a minimum of 128 credits with a 2.0 GPA. Course work includes a general education requirement of 18 hours of humanities, 16 of Bible, 12 of social science, 6 of science, and 3 of math or computer science. The major requirements vary according to concentration; typically, 40 hours or more are required. Some majors and minors require a 2.5 GPA.

Special: Summer internships are required in biblical studies and psychology, and work-study is available on campus. Honors and independent study are available as adjuncts to a normal course load. There are 2 national honor societies, a freshman honors program, and 2 departmental honors programs.

Faculty/Classroom: 73% of faculty are male; 27%, female. All teach undergraduates. The average class size in an introductory lecture is 30; in a laboratory, 20; and in a regular course, 25.

Admissions: 99% of the 2005-2006 applicants were accepted. The SAT scores for the 2005-2006 freshman class were: Verbal--41% below 500, 42% between 500 and 599, and 17% between 600 and 700; Math--59% below 500, 25% between 500 and 599, 8% between 600 and 700, and 8% above 700. The ACT scores were 45% below 21, 24% between 21 and 23, 20% between 24 and 26, 7% between 27 and 28, and 4% above 28. 22% of the current freshmen were in the top fifth of their class; 44% were in the top two fifths. 5 freshmen graduated first in their class.

Requirements: The ACT is recommended. In addition, for regular acceptance, students must meet 2 of the following 3 requirements: a 2.0 cumulative GPA; graduate in the top half of their graduating class; satisfactory scores on the ACT or SAT. York requires applicants to be in the upper 50% of their class. AP and CLEP credits are accepted. Important factors in the admissions decision are ability to finance college education, personality/intangible qualities, and evidence of special talent.

Procedure: Freshmen are admitted to all sessions. Entrance exams should be taken before April. Application deadlines are open. Application fee is $20.

Transfer: 38 transfer students enrolled in 2004-2005. Transfer students with less than 24 semester hours must have a high school transcript, ACT scores, college transcripts, and 1 reference. Transfers with 24 to 60 hours must have proof of high school graduation (diploma or final), a college transcript, and 1 reference. Transfers with more than 60 hours must have a college transcript and 1 reference letter. 30 of 128 credits required for the bachelor's degree must be completed at York.

Visiting: There are regularly scheduled orientations for prospective students, including a campus tour visit with financial aid and admissions representatives, and a visit with the registrar and possibly with a faculty member within the student's major area of concentration. There are guides for informal visits and visitors may sit in on classes and stay overnight. To schedule a visit, contact Joy Colwell at (402) 363-5627 or jcolwell@york.edu.

Financial Aid: In 2005-2006, 98% of all full-time freshmen and 99% of continuing full-time students received some form of financial aid. 98% of full-time freshmen and 99% of continuing full-time students received need-based aid. The average freshman award was $11,964. Need-based scholarships or need-based grants averaged $4176; need-based self-help aid (loans and jobs) averaged $3223; non-need-based athletic scholarships averaged $2361; and other non-need-based awards and non-need-based scholarships averaged $2203. 72% of undergraduates work part time. Average annual earnings from campus work are $825. The average financial indebtedness of the 2005 graduate was $18,798. The FAFSA is required. The priority date for freshman financial aid applications for fall entry is April 1.

International Students: There are 18 international students enrolled. They must score satisfactorily on the written TOEFL or on the electronic version and also take the SAT or the ACT.

Computers: All students may access the system 8 A.M. to 10:30 P.M. weekdays and various times on weekends. There are no time limits and no fees.

Graduates: From July 1, 2004 to June 30, 2005, 75 bachelor's degrees were awarded. The most popular majors were education (37%), business (18%), and psychology (10%). In an average class, 2% graduate in 3 years or less, 17% graduate in 4 years or less, and 38% graduate in 5 years or less. Of the 2004 graduating class, 6% were enrolled in graduate school within 6 months of graduation and 90% were employed.

Admissions Contact: Tod Martin, Director of Admissions.
E-mail: *tjmartin@york.edu* Web: *www.york.edu*

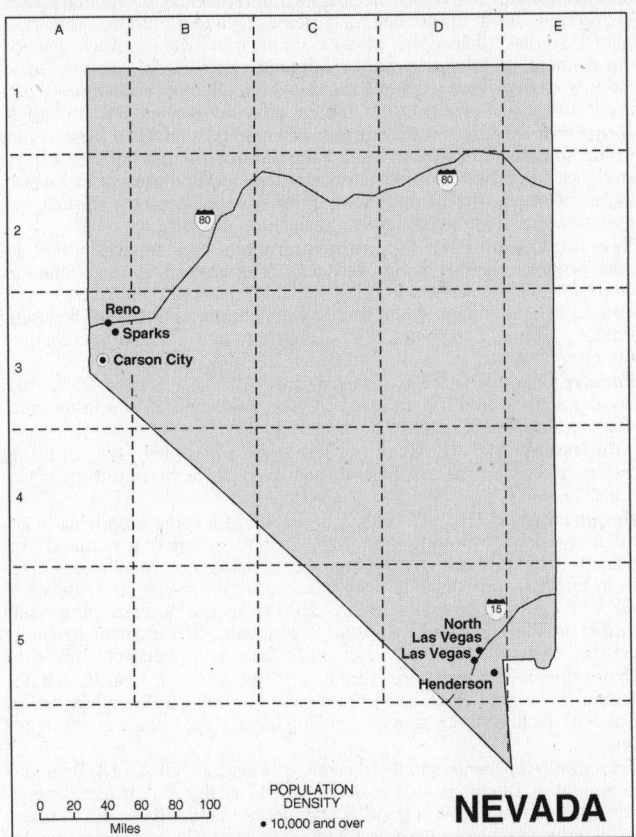

POPULATION
DENSITY
• 10,000 and over

0 20 40 60 80 100
Miles

NEVADA

SIERRA NEVADA COLLEGE   A-3
Incline Village, NV 89451
(775) 831-1314
(866) 412-4636; Fax: (775) 831-6223

Full-time: 141 men, 150 women	**Faculty:** 20
Part-time: 21 men, 8 women	**Ph.D.s:** n/av
Graduate: 89 men, 242 women	**Student/Faculty:** 15 to 1
Year: semesters, summer session	**Tuition:** $19,500
Application Deadline: February 15	**Room & Board:** $7450
Freshman Class: 359 applied, 237 accepted, 104 enrolled	
SAT Verbal/Math: 500/490*	**COMPETITIVE**

Sierra Nevada College, founded in 1969, is a private institution offering programs in liberal arts, fine arts, business, hotel resort management, ski business management, environmental science, and teacher education. There are 7 undergraduate schools. The library contains 20,000 volumes and 10,000 microform items, and subscribes to 100 periodicals including electronic. Computerized library services include interlibrary loans. Special learning facilities include an art gallery, an observatory, and a recording studio. The 35-acre campus is in a rural area 25 miles west of Reno. Including any residence halls, there are 7 buildings.

Student Life: 70% of undergraduates are from out of state, mostly the West. Students are from 30 states, 8 foreign countries, and Canada. 60% are from public schools. 95% are white. The average age of freshmen is 19; all undergraduates, 22. 20% do not continue beyond their first year; 50% remain to graduate.

Housing: 120 students can be accommodated in college housing, which includes single-sex dorms and on-campus apartments. On-campus housing is guaranteed for all 4 years. 50% of students commute. Alcohol is not permitted. All students may keep cars.

Activities: There are no fraternities or sororities. There are many groups and organizations on campus, including art, choir, chorale, chorus, dance, honors, international, musical theater, newspaper, political, student government, and yearbook. Popular campus events include Bohemia Night, Nevada Day, and a faculty-student softball game.

Sports: There is 1 intercollegiate sport for men and 1 for women, and 2 intramural sports for men and 2 for women. Facilities include nearby ski areas, hiking and mountain biking trails, volleyball and softball areas, community tennis courts and golf courses, and sites for water sports and beach volleyball.

Disabled Students: Wheelchair ramps, specially equipped rest rooms, and special class scheduling are available.

Services: Counseling and information services are available, as is tutoring in most subjects. There is remedial math, reading, and writing.

Campus Safety and Security: Measures include informal discussions.

Programs of Study: SNC confers B.A., B.S., and B.F.A. degrees. Bachelor's degrees are awarded in BUSINESS (business administration and management and recreational facilities management), COMMUNICATIONS AND THE ARTS (fine arts and music), COMPUTER AND PHYSICAL SCIENCE (science), ENGINEERING AND ENVIRONMENTAL DESIGN (environmental science), SOCIAL SCIENCE (humanities). Environmental science/ecology is the strongest academically. Business administration is the largest.

Required: All students must complete at least 120 semester hours, including 40 in upper-division courses with a minimum GPA of 2.0. Students also must pass the writing proficiency exam and meet distribution requirements in 4 interdisciplinary themes: symbols, relationships with nature and humans, memberships in groups and institutions, and ethics, values, and beliefs.

Special: Business administration concentrations are offered in ski business and resort management and in hotel, restaurant, and resort management. Student-designed majors, work-study programs, internships, credit for life experiences and volunteer community work, and nondegree study are available.

Faculty/Classroom: 60% of faculty are male; 40%, female. All teach undergraduates. The average class size in an introductory lecture is 15; in a laboratory, 8; and in a regular course, 15.

Admissions: 66% of the 2005-2006 applicants were accepted.

Requirements: The SAT or ACT is required. The ACT Optional Writing test is also required. In addition, all applicants are reviewed individually. Official transcripts, an essay, and 2 letters of recommendation are required, and an interview is recommended. AP and CLEP credits are accepted. Important factors in the admissions decision are advanced placement or honor courses, recommendations by school officials, and personality/intangible qualities.

Procedure: Freshmen are admitted to all sessions. Entrance exams should be taken in the spring of junior year or fall of senior year. There is a deferred admissions plan. There is a rolling admissions plan. Applications should be filed by February 15 for fall entry. Notification is sent on a rolling basis. Applications are accepted on-line.

Transfer: 46 transfer students enrolled in 2005-2006. The college accepts applications from students who have completed course work at an accredited postsecondary institution. If fewer than 15 credits have been earned, the high school transcript and standardized test scores are also required. Transfer applicants are expeced to be in good academic standing at their college or university. 96 of 120 credits required for the bachelor's degree must be completed at SNC.

Visiting: There are regularly scheduled orientations for prospective students, including a student-led campus tour that is available by appointment and 1-night overnight stays. There are guides for informal visits and visitors may sit in on classes and stay overnight. To schedule a visit, contact the Office of Admissions at (775) 831-1314, ext. 7445 or *admissions@sierranevada.edu*.

Financial Aid: In 2005-2006, 80% of all full-time students received some form of financial aid, including need-based aid. The average freshman award was $15,000. Need-based scholarships or need-based grants averaged $7000 ($16,000 maximum); need-based self-help aid (loans and jobs) averaged $3800 ($7500 maximum); and other non-need-based awards and non-need-based scholarships averaged $3000 ($10,000 maximum). The FAFSA and the college's own financial statement are required.

International Students: The school actively recruits these students. They must achieve a satisfactory score on the TOEFL or take any other English proficiency test.

Computers: All students may access the system 8 A.M. to 9 P.M. daily. There are no time limits and no fees. It is strongly recommended that all students have a personal computer.

Admissions Contact: Patricia Coleman, Dean of Admission and Financial Aid. E-mail: *admissions@sierranevada.edu*
Web: *www.sierranevada.edu*

UNIVERSITY AND COMMUNITY COLLEGE SYSTEM OF NEVADA

The University and Community College System of Nevada, established in 1865, is a public system in Nevada. It is governed by a board of regents, whose chief administrator is the chancellor. The primary goal of the system is teaching, research, and public service. The main priorities are to provide all public programs of postsecondary instruction in Nevada, to sponsor programs of basic and applied research that contribute to the cultural, economic, and social development of Nevada, and to sponsor programs of public service for citizens of the state. The total enrollment of all 7 campuses is usually about 65,000; with 1800 faculty members. Altogether there are 135 baccalaureate, 97 master's, and 34 doctoral programs offered in University and Community College System of Nevada. There is a 4-year campus located in Las Vegas and Reno. Profiles of the 4-year campuses are included in this section.

UNIVERSITY OF NEVADA/LAS VEGAS   D-5
Las Vegas, NV 89154-1021

(702) 774-UNLV
Fax: (702) 774-8008

Full-time: 6300 men, 8100 women	Faculty: 676; I, av$
Part-time: 2900 men, 3400 women	Ph.D.s: 87%
Graduate: 1800 men, 2600 women	Student/Faculty: 21 to 1
Year: semesters, summer session	Tuition: $3000 ($12,000)
Application Deadline: see profile	Room & Board: $9000
Freshman Class: n/av	
SAT or ACT: required for some programs	COMPETITIVE

University of Nevada/Las Vegas, established in 1957, is a state-supported institution offering undergraduate and graduate programs in business, education, health science, engineering, science and math, hotel administration, fine arts, liberal arts, urban affairs, and honors. There are 10 undergraduate schools and 1 graduate school. Figures in the above capsule and in this profile are approximate. In addition to regional accreditation, UNLV has baccalaureate program accreditation with AACSB, ABET, CSWE, NASM, NCATE, and NLN. The 4 libraries contain 888,200 volumes, 1,705,000 microform items, and 20,100 audio/video tapes/CDs/DVDs, and subscribe to 6380 periodicals including electronic. Computerized library services include the card catalog and interlibrary loans. Special learning facilities include a learning resource center, art gallery, natural history museum, and radio station. The 335-acre campus is in an urban area. Including any residence halls, there are 60 buildings.

Student Life: 77% of undergraduates are from Nevada. Others are from 49 states, 77 foreign countries, and Canada. 74% are white; 10% Asian American. The average age of freshmen is 18; all undergraduates, 25. 25% do not continue beyond their first year; 74% remain to graduate.

Housing: 1500 students can be accommodated in college housing, which includes single-sex and coed dorms. In addition, there are special-interest house and substance-free and study-intensive recess housing. On-campus housing is guaranteed for the freshman year only and is available on a first-come, first-served basis. Priority is given to out-of-town students. 94% of students commute. All students may keep cars.

Activities: 5% of men belong to 15 national fraternities; 5% of women belong to 1 local and 7 national sororities. There are 160 groups on campus, including band, cheerleading, choir, chorus, computers, dance, drama, drill team, ethnic, gay, honors, international, jazz band, marching band, musical theater, newspaper, orchestra, pep band, political, professional, radio and TV, religious, social, student government, and symphony. Popular campus events include Unityfest, Majors Exploration Fair, and Career Day.

Sports: There are 7 intercollegiate sports for men and 8 for women, and 8 intramural sports for men and 8 for women. Facilities include an arena, a football stadium, tennis courts, softball and soccer fields, racquetball courts, a weight room, 2 gyms, and separate athletic/training facilities for intercollegiate athletes.

Disabled Students: All of the campus is accessible. Wheelchair ramps, elevators, special parking, specially equipped rest rooms, special class scheduling, lowered drinking fountains, lowered telephones, and priority class registration are available.

Services: Counseling and information services are available, as is tutoring in every subject. There is a reader service for the blind, and remedial math, reading, and writing.

Campus Safety and Security: Measures include 24-hour foot and vehicle patrol, self-defense education, security escort services, and shuttle buses. There are emergency telephones and lighted pathways/sidewalks.

Programs of Study: UNLV confers B.A., B.S., and B.F.A. degrees. Master's and doctoral degrees are also awarded. Bachelor's degrees are awarded in BIOLOGICAL SCIENCE (biology/biological science), BUSINESS (accounting, banking and finance, hotel/motel and restaurant management, human resources, international business management, management information systems, management science, marketing/retailing/merchandising, real estate, and recreational facilities management), COMMUNICATIONS AND THE ARTS (art history and appreciation, communications, dance, dramatic arts, English, film arts, fine arts, French, German, music, romance languages and literature, and Spanish), COMPUTER AND PHYSICAL SCIENCE (applied physics, chemistry, computer science, earth science, geology, mathematics, physics, and radiological technology), EDUCATION (elementary, health, physical, recreation, secondary, special, and trade and industrial), ENGINEERING AND ENVIRONMENTAL DESIGN (architectural engineering, civil engineering, computer engineering, construction management, electrical/electronics engineering, environmental science, interior design, land-

scape architecture/design, mechanical engineering, and urban planning technology), HEALTH PROFESSIONS (clinical science, exercise science, health care administration, nuclear medical technology, nursing, and sports medicine), SOCIAL SCIENCE (anthropology, criminal justice, economics, food production/management/services, history, interdisciplinary studies, philosophy, physical fitness/movement, political science/government, psychology, public administration, social science, social work, sociology, and women's studies). Hotel administration and dance are the strongest academically. Liberal arts and business are the largest.

Required: Students must complete 124 credits, with 45 of these credits in the student's major, and must maintain a minimum GPA of 2.0. All students must meet core requirements that include courses in English, logic and math, the Constitution, social science, fine arts, science, humanities, and international and multicultural diversity.

Special: Opportunities are provided for internships, an accelerated degree program, B.A.-B.S. degrees, dual majors, credit by examination, credit for military service, nondegree study, pass/fail options, and study abroad in 8 countries. There are 16 national honor societies, including Phi Beta Kappa, a freshman honors program, and 11 departmental honors programs.

Faculty/Classroom: 63% of faculty are male; 37%, female. 95% teach undergraduates and 5% do research. The average class size in an introductory lecture is 21 and in a laboratory, 20.

Admissions: 80% of recent applicants were accepted. 47% of recent freshmen were in the top fifth of their class; 83% were in the top two fifths.

Requirements: The SAT or ACT is required for some programs. In addition, graduation from an accredited secondary school is required. Applicants should submit an academic record distributed as follows: 4 credits in English, and 3 each in history, social studies, math, and science. A GPA of 2.5 is required. AP and CLEP credits are accepted. Important factors in the admissions decision are advanced placement or honor courses, recommendations by school officials, and geographic diversity.

Procedure: Freshmen are admitted to all sessions. Check with the school for current application deadlines. The fall 2005 application fee was $40. Notification is sent on a rolling basis. Applications are accepted on-line.

Transfer: Applicants should present a minimum GPA of 2.0. and a minimum of 12 credits for transfer. The SAT or the ACT is recommended. Applicants must be in good academic standing and eligible to return to the educational institution last attended. 30 of 124 credits required for the bachelor's degree must be completed at UNLV.

Visiting: There are regularly scheduled orientations for prospective students, consisting of a complete introduction to the campus, student services, and parent orientation. There are guides for informal visits and visitors may sit in on classes. To schedule a visit, contact the Admissions Office.

Financial Aid: In a recent year, 42% of all full-time freshmen and 60% of continuing full-time students received some form of financial aid. 68% of full-time freshmen and 74% of continuing full-time students received need-based aid. The average freshman award was $5681. Need-based scholarships or need-based grants averaged $2913; and need-based self-help aid (loans and jobs) averaged $4640. 75% of undergraduates work part time. UNLV is a member of CSS. The CSS/Profile, FAFSA, FFS or SFS, the university's own financial statement and the Singlefile Form are required. Check with the school for current deadlines.

International Students: The school actively recruits these students. They must score satisfactorily on the written TOEFL or take the MELAB, or prove English proficiency by other means.

Computers: All students may access the system 24 hours a day, 7 days a week. There are no time limits.

Admissions Contact: Kristi Rodriguez, Assistant Director of Admissions. Web: http://www.unlv.edu

UNIVERSITY OF NEVADA/RENO   A-3
Reno, NV 89557

(775) 784-1110
(800) 622-4867; Fax: (775) 784-4283

Full-time: 4600 men, 5657 women	Faculty: 560; I, -$
Part-time: 1024 men, 1123 women	Ph.D.s: 88%
Graduate: 1322 men, 1862 women	Student/Faculty: 18 to 1
Year: semesters, summer session	Tuition: $3270 ($12,737)
Application Deadline: February 1	Room & Board: $8885
Freshman Class: 4309 applied, 3752 accepted, 2174 enrolled	
SAT Verbal/Math: 526/533*	ACT: 22 NONCOMPETITIVE

The University of Nevada/Reno, established in 1874, is a land-grant institution and part of the University and Community College System of Nevada. It offers programs in agriculture, arts and science, business administration, education, engineering, human and community sciences, journalism, medicine, and mining, as well as interdisciplinary studies. There are 10 undergraduate schools and 1 graduate school. In addition to regional accreditation, Nevada has baccalaureate program accreditation with AACSB, ABET, ACEJMC, AHEA, CSWE, NASM, NCATE, and NLN. The 6 libraries contain 1,149,824 volumes, 3,353,220 microform items, and 66,087 audio/video tapes/CDs/DVDs, and subscribe to 15,906 periodicals including electronic. Computerized library services include the card catalog, interlibrary loans, database searching, and Internet access. Special learning facilities include a learning resource center, art gallery, planetarium, radio station, TV station, and the Nevada Historical Society Museum. The 200-acre campus is in an urban area 200 miles east of San Francisco. Including any residence halls, there are 86 buildings.

Student Life: 82% of undergraduates are from Nevada. Others are from 49 states, 74 foreign countries, and Canada. 70% are white. The average age of freshmen is 18; all undergraduates, 22. 25% do not continue beyond their first year.

Housing: 1759 students can be accommodated in college housing, which includes single-sex and coed dorms, on-campus apartments, off-campus apartments, and married-student housing. In addition, there are honors houses. On-campus housing is available on a first-come, first-served basis. 86% of students commute. All students may keep cars.

Activities: 7% of men belong to 2 local and 11 national fraternities; 6% of women belong to 4 national sororities. There are 100 groups on campus, including art, band, cheerleading, chess, choir, chorale, chorus, computers, dance, debate, drama, drill team, ethnic, film, gay, honors, international, jazz band, literary magazine, marching band, musical theater, newspaper, orchestra, pep band, photography, political, professional, radio and TV, religious, social, social service, student government, symphony, and yearbook. Popular campus events include Mackay Week and Winter Carnival.

Sports: There are 7 intercollegiate sports for men and 8 for women, and 14 intramural sports for men and 11 for women. Facilities include a recreation center, a 30,000-seat stadium, a 6000-seat gym, a 12,500-seat auditorium, and an 11,600-seat indoor events center.

Disabled Students: 99% of the campus is accessible. Wheelchair ramps, elevators, special parking, specially equipped rest rooms, special class scheduling, lowered drinking fountains, lowered telephones, special housing, and automatic door openers are available.

Services: Counseling and information services are available, as is tutoring in most subjects. There is a reader service for the blind, and remedial math, reading, and writing. Students are mainstreamed with special services for the disabled.

Campus Safety and Security: Measures include 24-hour foot and vehicle patrol, self-defense education, security escort services, and shuttle buses. There are pamphlets/posters/films, emergency telephones, and lighted pathways/sidewalks.

Programs of Study: Nevada confers B.A., B.S., B.A.C.J., B.A.Ed., B.F.A., B.G.S., B.M., B.S.Bus.Ad., B.S.C.E., B.S.Chem., B.S.Chem.E.,B.S.C.S., B.S.Ed., B.S.E.E., B.S.E.P., B.S.Geog., B.S.Geol., B.S.Geol.E., B.S.Geophys., B.S.M.E., B.S.Met.E., B.S.Min.E., B.S.Nurs., and B.S.Vet.Sc. degrees. Master's and doctoral degrees are also awarded. Bachelor's degrees are awarded in AGRICULTURE (agricultural economics, animal science, and natural resource management), BIOLOGICAL SCIENCE (biochemistry, biology/biological science, and nutrition), BUSINESS (accounting, banking and finance, business economics, management science, and marketing/retailing/merchandising), COMMUNICATIONS AND THE ARTS (applied music, art, dramatic arts, English, French, German, journalism, music, Spanish, and speech/debate/rhetoric), COMPUTER AND PHYSICAL SCIENCE (chemistry, computer science, geology, geophysics and seismology, hydrology, information sciences and systems, mathematics, and physics), EDUCATION (elementary, music, secondary, and special), ENGINEERING AND ENVIRONMENTAL DESIGN (chemical engineering, civil engineering, electrical/electronics engineering, engineering physics, environmental science, geological engineering, interior design, mechanical engineering, metallurgical engineering, and mining and mineral engineering), HEALTH PROFESSIONS (nursing and speech pathology/audiology), SOCIAL SCIENCE (anthropology, child care/child and family studies, criminal justice, geography, history, human ecology, international relations, liberal arts/general studies, philosophy, political science/government, psychology, social work, and sociology). Psychology, biology, and computer science are the largest.

Required: To graduate, all students must complete 124 to 138 semester credits and earn a GPA of 2.0. The core curriculum includes 9 credits of Western Traditions, 6 each of capstone courses and natural science, 3 to 6 of writing, 3 each of math, social science, and fine arts, and fulfillment of the diversity requirement.

Special: Students may study abroad in 24 countries, pursue internships, and complete dual majors in many subject areas. There is a freshman honors program.

Faculty/Classroom: 63% of faculty are male; 37%, female. All both teach and do research. Graduate students teach 8% of introductory courses. The average class size in an introductory lecture is 39; in a laboratory, 19; and in a regular course, 31.

Admissions: 87% of the 2005-2006 applicants were accepted. The SAT scores for the 2005-2006 freshman class were: Verbal--36% below 500, 44% between 500 and 599, 18% between 600 and 700, and 2% above 700; Math--32% below 500, 44% between 500 and 599, 22% between 600 and 700, and 2% above 700. The ACT scores were 31% below 21, 32% between 21 and 23, 27% between 24 and 26, 8% between 27 and 28, and 2% above 28.

Requirements: The SAT or ACT is required; however, test scores are used for placement purposes only. Applicants should have completed 13 1/2 academic credits, including 4 in English, 3 each in math, science, and social studies/history, and a half credit in computer literacy. The GED is not accepted. A GPA of 2.5 is required. AP and CLEP credits are accepted. Important factors in the admissions decision are advanced placement or honor courses, recommendations by school officials, and leadership record.

Procedure: Freshmen are admitted fall and spring. Entrance exams should be taken in October of the senior year. There are early admissions and deferred admissions plans. There is a rolling admissions plan. Applications should be filed by February 1 for fall entry and November 1 for spring entry. The fall 2005 application fee was $60. Notification is sent on a rolling basis.

Transfer: 1564 transfer students enrolled in 2004-2005. Applicants should have a 2.0 GPA and 12 transferable credits. College transcripts are required. 32 of 124 credits required for the bachelor's degree must be completed at Nevada.

Visiting: There are regularly scheduled orientations for prospective students. There are guides for informal visits and visitors may sit in on classes. To schedule a visit, contact the Office of Outreach Services/the Office for Prospective Students.

Financial Aid: In 2005-2006, 29% of all full-time freshmen and 32% of continuing full-time students received some form of financial aid. 15% of full-time freshmen and 22% of continuing full-time students received need-based aid. Need-based scholarships or need-based grants averaged $2805; need-based self-help aid (loans and jobs) averaged $2718; non-need-based athletic scholarships averaged $10,950; and other non-need-based awards and non-need-based scholarships averaged $2797. The average financial indebtedness of the 2005 graduate was $16,273. The FAFSA is required. Check with the school for current application deadlines.

International Students: There are 273 international students enrolled. The school actively recruits these students. A satisfactory score on the TOEFL is required. The SAT or ACT may also be submitted.

Computers: Wireless access is available. All students may access the system. There are no time limits. The fee varies per class laboratory session.

Graduates: From July 1, 2004 to June 30, 2005, 1815 bachelor's degrees were awarded. The most popular majors were general studies (7%), elementary education (5%), and psychology (5%). In an average class, 15% graduate in 4 years or less, 39% graduate in 5 years or less, and 49% graduate in 6 years or less.

Admissions Contact: Dr. Melisa N. Choroszy, Assistant Vice President, Records/Enrollment Services. E-mail: *asknevada@unr.edu* Web: *www.unr.edu*

NEW HAMPSHIRE

POPULATION
DENSITY
● 10,000 and over

0 10 20 30 40 50
Miles

COLBY-SAWYER COLLEGE   C-5
New London, NH 03257

(603) 526-3700
(800) 272-1015; Fax: (603) 526-3452

Full-time: 300 men, 600 women	**Faculty:** 49; IIB, -$
Part-time: 10 men, 20 women	**Ph.D.s:** 78%
Graduate: none	**Student/Faculty:** 18 to 1
Year: semesters	**Tuition:** $21,000
Application Deadline: open	**Room & Board:** $8000
Freshman Class: n/av	
SAT or ACT: required	**LESS COMPETITIVE**

Colby-Sawyer College, established in 1837, is an independent institution offering a variety of undergraduate majors, including fine arts, nursing, business, and communications, as well as education certification. Figures in the above capsule and in this profile are approximate. In addition to regional accreditation, Colby-Sawyer has baccalaureate program accreditation with CAAHEP and NLN. The library contains 92,100 volumes, 197,600 microform items, and 2100 audio/video tapes/CDs/DVDs, and subscribes to 4100 periodicals including electronic. Computerized library services include the card catalog, interlibrary loans, and database searching. Special learning facilities include a learning resource center, art gallery, radio station, academic development center, and laboratory school (K-3). The 200-acre campus is in a small town 100 miles northwest of Boston. Including any residence halls, there are 28 buildings.

Student Life: 69% of undergraduates are from out of state, mostly the Northeast. Students are from 27 states and 9 foreign countries. 79% are from public schools. 95% are white. 39% are claim no religious affiliation; 35% are Catholic; 18% Protestant. The average age of freshmen is 18; all undergraduates, 20. 19% do not continue beyond their first year; 58% remain to graduate.

Housing: 835 students can be accommodated in college housing, which includes single-sex and coed dorms. In addition, there is a substance-free residence hall. On-campus housing is guaranteed for all 4 years. 88% of students live on campus; of those, 70% remain on campus on weekends. All students may keep cars.

Activities: There are no fraternities or sororities. There are 40 groups on campus, including academic couseling, art, chorus, dance, drama, environmental, film, honors, international, literary magazine, musical theater, newspaper, outing, photography, professional, radio and TV, religious, social, social service, student government, tour guides and year-

book. Popular campus events include Fall and Spring Weekends and Mountain Day.

Sports: There are 8 intercollegiate sports for men and 9 for women, and 15 intramural sports for men and 15 for women. Facilities include 6 outdoor and 3 indoor tennis courts, a fitness center, an NCAA-approved swimming pool, a suspended track, squash and racquetball courts, 4 outdoor competitive fields, and nearby golf courses, ski and biking trails, and an indoor riding arena.

Disabled Students: 50% of the campus is accessible. Wheelchair ramps, elevators, special parking, specially equipped rest rooms, special class scheduling, and handicap accessible residence hall suites are available.

Services: Counseling and information services are available, as is tutoring in every subject. There is a reader service for the blind, and remedial math, reading, and writing.

Campus Safety and Security: Measures include 24-hour foot and vehicle patrol, self-defense education, security escort services, and shuttle buses. There are informal discussions, pamphlets/posters/films, emergency telephones, lighted pathways/sidewalks, and monthly meetings between students and campus safety personnel.

Programs of Study: Colby-Sawyer confers B.A., B.S., and B.F.A. degrees. Associate degrees are also awarded. Bachelor's degrees are awarded in AGRICULTURE (environmental studies), BIOLOGICAL SCIENCE (biology/biological science), BUSINESS (business administration and management and sports management), COMMUNICATIONS AND THE ARTS (art, communications, design, English, and graphic design), EDUCATION (art, athletic training, early childhood, English, science, and social studies), HEALTH PROFESSIONS (exercise science and nursing), SOCIAL SCIENCE (child psychology/development, history, and psychology). Exercise and sport sciences, business administration, and child development are the largest.

Required: Required courses include writing, math, and computer literacy. Four required interdisciplinary core courses are Creative Expression, Process of Discovery, Social Analysis, and Judgment and Belief. Required electives include 1 each in fine and performing arts and natural sciences, and 2 each in social sciences and humanities. Most majors must also complete an internship or a senior research project. A total of 120 credit hours, with a minimum GPA of 2.0, is needed for graduation.

Special: There is cross-registration through the New Hampshire College and University Council. Students may choose internships (required in some majors) and may study abroad in Australia, Canada, and several European countries. A Washington semester with American University is available. Other options include student-designed majors, education certification, credit by exam, a general studies degree, and interdisciplinary majors such as history, society, and culture. There is 1 national honor society, a freshman honors program, and 2 departmental honors program.

Faculty/Classroom: 45% of faculty are male; 55%, female. All teach undergraduates. The average class size in a regular course is 18.

Requirements: The SAT or ACT is required. The GED is accepted. A minimum of 15 college preparatory credits is recommended for admission, including 4 years of English, 3 or more of social studies, 3 of math, 2 of the same foreign language, and 2 or more of lab science. An essay is required, as are 2 letters of recommendation. Interviews are strongly recommended. A GPA of 2.0 is required. AP and CLEP credits are accepted. Important factors in the admissions decision are advanced placement or honor courses, recommendations by school officials, and leadership record.

Procedure: Freshmen are admitted fall and spring. Entrance exams should be taken in the fall of the senior year. There is a deferred admissions plan. There is a rolling admissions plan. Application deadlines are open. The fall 2005 application fee was $40.

Transfer: College-level work will be emphasized. College transcripts, course descriptions, and a dean's form are required in addition to the standard requirements. 60 of 120 credits required for the bachelor's degree must be completed at Colby-Sawyer.

Visiting: There are regularly scheduled orientations for prospective students, including tours and interviews. 2 open house programs offer tours as well as academic, athletic, campus life, career development, and academic development presentations; several visiting-day programs offer tours, interviews, and class visits. There are guides for informal visits and visitors stay overnight. To schedule a visit, contact the Admissions Office.

Financial Aid: Colby-Sawyer is a member of CSS. The FAFSA and the college's own financial statement are required. Check with the school for current deadlines.

International Students: The school actively recruits these students. They must score satisfactorily on the written TOEFL.

Computers: All students may access the system. There are no time limits and no fees.

Admissions Contact: Office of Admissions and Financial Aid.
E-mail: *csadmiss@colby-sawyer.edu* Web: *http://www.colby-sawyer.edu*

COLLEGE FOR LIFELONG LEARNING
(See Granite State College)

DANIEL WEBSTER COLLEGE
D-6

Nashua, NH 03063-1300

(603) 577-6600
(800) 325-6876; Fax: (603) 577-6001

Full-time: 400 men, 100 women	**Faculty:** 33
Part-time: 62 men, 8 women	**Ph.D.s:** 43%
Graduate: none	**Student/Faculty:** 15 to 1
Year: semesters, summer session	**Tuition:** $18,000
Application Deadline: open	**Room & Board:** $7000
Freshman Class: n/av	
SAT: required	**COMPETITIVE**

Daniel Webster College, founded in 1965, is a private college offering study in the fields of aviation, business, computer sciences, engineering, sports management, and social sciences. There are 5 undergraduate schools. Figures in the above capsule and in this profile are approximate. The library contains 32,000 volumes, 55,294 microform items, and 1457 audio/video tapes/CDs/DVDs, and subscribes to 390 periodicals including electronic. Computerized library services include the card catalog, interlibrary loans, and database searching. Special learning facilities include a learning resource center, a flight center, a flight tower, air traffic control labs, flight simulators, a hangar, and a fleet of airplanes. The 54-acre campus is in a suburban area 35 miles northwest of Boston. Including any residence halls, there are 13 buildings.

Student Life: 72% of undergraduates are from out of state, mostly the Middle Atlantic. Others are from 27 states, 18 foreign countries, and Canada. 79% are from public schools. 91% are white. The average age of freshmen is 18; all undergraduates, 20. 35% do not continue beyond their first year; 51% remain to graduate.

Housing: 500 students can be accommodated in college housing, which includes single-sex and coed dormitories and on-campus apartments. In addition, there are suites, quiet floors, smoke-free areas, and a substance free, 10-month housing option. On-campus housing is guaranteed for all 4 years. 72% of students live on campus; of those, 80% remain on campus on weekends. All students may keep cars.

Activities: There are no fraternities or sororities. There are 16 groups on campus, including computers, drama, film, flight team honors, jazz band, newspaper, professional, religious, social, social service, student government, and yearbook. Popular campus events include Ski Day, Family Weekend, and a whitewater rafting trip.

Sports: There are 7 intercollegiate sports for men and 5 for women, and 6 intramural sports for men and 5 for women. Facilities include an indoor basketball/volleyball court, a weight room, tennis courts, soccer, lacrosse, and softball fields, and cross-country trails.

Disabled Students: 75% of the campus is accessible. Wheelchair ramps, elevators, special parking, specially equipped rest rooms, special class scheduling, and lowered drinking fountains are available.

Services: Counseling and information services are available, as is tutoring in every subject. There is remedial math and writing, and there are study skills and test skills workshops, study groups, a math-science center, a writing center, and accommodations for students with learning disabilities.

Campus Safety and Security: Measures include 24-hour foot and vehicle patrol, self-defense education, security escort services, and informal discussions. There are pamphlets/posters/films, emergency telephones, and lighted pathways/sidewalks.

Programs of Study: DWC confers the B.S. degree. Associate degrees are also awarded. Bachelor's degrees are awarded in BUSINESS (business administration and management, management information systems, and sports management), COMPUTER AND PHYSICAL SCIENCE (computer science and information sciences and systems), ENGINEERING AND ENVIRONMENTAL DESIGN (air traffic control, airline piloting and navigation, aviation administration/management, and computer technology), SOCIAL SCIENCE (social science). Aviation, computer science, and information systems are the strongest academically. Aviation is the largest.

Required: Students must complete general education courses in communication, computer literacy, math, natural science, the humanities, and the social sciences. At least 120 credits, with 45 to 58 in the major, are required for graduation. Students must maintain a minimum overall GPA of 2.0 and grades of C or better in their major.

Special: There is cross-registration with the New Hampshire College and University Council. All programs offer credit by exam. Interdisciplinary majors, including aviation flight operations and aviation management/air traffic management are available. Study abroad, internships in aviation, business management, computer sciences, and sports management, a general studies degree, and a 2-2 engineering program with the Universities of New Hampshire and Massachusetts at Lowell and Kettering and Clarkson Universities are additional options. There is 1 national honor society.

Faculty/Classroom: 76% of faculty are male; 24%, female. All both teach and do research. The average class size in an introductory lecture is 17; in a laboratory, 12; and in a regular course, 20.

Requirements: The SAT is required. In addition, applicants must be graduates of an accredited secondary school or submit the GED. Students should have taken 4 years of English, 3 of math, 2 each of social studies and science, and 1 of history. An essay and an interview are recommended. AP and CLEP credits are accepted. Important factors in the admissions decision are advanced placement or honor courses, recommendations by school officials, and leadership record.

Procedure: Freshmen are admitted to all sessions. There are early admissions and deferred admissions plans. Application deadlines are open. The fall 2005 application fee was $35. Notification is sent on a rolling basis. Applications are accepted on-line.

Transfer: Transfer students must have a minimum college GPA of 2.0. The SAT is required. Grades of C or better transfer for credit. 30 of 120 credits required for the bachelor's degree must be completed at DWC.

Visiting: There are regularly scheduled orientations for prospective students, including a tour and an admissions interview; also available are meetings with faculty and coaches and an aerial tour of the campus. There are guides for informal visits and visitors may sit in on classes and stay overnight. To schedule a visit, contact the Office of Admissions.

Financial Aid: The FAFSA and the college's own financial statement are required. Check with the school for current deadlines.

International Students: They must score satisfactorily on the written TOEFL.

Computers: All students may access the system when the computer center is open. There are no time limits. The fee one-time technology fee is $120. It is strongly recommended that all students have a personal computer.

Admissions Contact: Jim Thatcher, Enrollment Services.
E-mail: admissions@dwc.edu Web: www.dwc.edu

DARTMOUTH COLLEGE
B-4

Hanover, NH 03755

(603) 646-2875; Fax: (603) 646-1216

Full-time: 2024 men, 2003 women	**Faculty:** 406; I, +$
Part-time: 22 men, 30 women	**Ph.D.s:** 93%
Graduate: 1012 men, 613 women	**Student/Faculty:** 10 to 1
Year: quarters, summer session	**Tuition:** $30,465
Application Deadline: January 1	**Room & Board:** $9000
Freshman Class: 11,734 applied, 2173 accepted, 1077 enrolled	
SAT Verbal/Math: 713/719*	**MOST COMPETITIVE**

Dartmouth College, chartered in 1769, is a private liberal arts institution offering a wide range of graduate and undergraduate programs. There is a year-round academic calendar of 4 10-week terms. The 10 libraries contain 2,429,070 volumes, 2,583,499 microform items, and 752,243 audio/video tapes/CDs/DVDs, and subscribe to 20,931 periodicals including electronic. Computerized library services include the card catalog, interlibrary loans, database searching, and Internet access. Special learning facilities include a learning resource center, art gallery, radio station, creative and performing arts center, life sciences lab, physical and social sciences centers, and observatory. The 265-acre campus is in a rural area 140 miles northwest of Boston. Including any residence halls, there are 100 buildings.

Student Life: 96% of undergraduates are from out of state, mostly the Middle Atlantic. Students are from 50 states, 80 foreign countries, and Canada. 63% are from public schools. 57% are white; 13% Asian American. 30% are Protestant; 28% claim no religious affiliation; 23% Catholic; 11% Jewish. The average age of freshmen is 18; all undergraduates, 20. 2% do not continue beyond their first year; 95% remain to graduate.

Housing: 3500 students can be accommodated in college housing, which includes coed dorms, on-campus apartments, married-student housing, fraternity houses, and sorority houses. In addition, there are language houses, special-interest houses,substances-free and smoke-free residence halls,and faculty-in-reidence and academic affinity programs. On-campus housing is guaranteed for the freshman year only, is available on a first-come, first-served basis, and is available on a lottery system for upperclassmen. 83% of students live on campus. Upperclassmen may keep cars.

Activities: 39% of men belong to 8 local and 7 national fraternities; 34% of women belong to 3 local and 6 national sororities. There are more than 300 groups on campus, including art, band, cheerleading, chess, choir, chorale, chorus, computers, dance, debate, drama, ethnic, film, forensics, gay, honors, international, jazz band, literary magazine, marching band, musical theater, newspaper, opera, orchestra, outing, pep band, photography, political, professional, radio and TV, religious, social, social service, student government, symphony, and yearbook. Popular campus events include Dartmouth Night, Winter and Summer Carnivals, and Green Key Service Weekend.

Sports: There are 17 intercollegiate sports for men and 17 for women, and 25 intramural sports for men and 25 for women. Facilities include a 2100-seat stadium, a fitness center, squash and racquetball courts, a dance studio, a 5000-seat arena, a gym, a 21,000-seat football stadium, a boathouse, a tennis center with indoor and outdoor courts, a golf course, a ski slope with 3 chairlifts, and a riding farm.

Disabled Students: All of the campus is accessible. Wheelchair ramps, elevators, special parking, specially equipped rest rooms, special class scheduling, lowered drinking fountains, lowered telephones, and special housing are available.

Services: Counseling and information services are available, as is tutoring in every subject. There is a reader service for the blind. There is an academic skills center for all students. Readers, note takers, tape recorders, and support for learning-disabled students are available.

Campus Safety and Security: Measures include 24-hour foot and vehicle patrol, self-defense education, security escort services, and shuttle buses. There are informal discussions, pamphlets/posters/films, emergency telephones, and lighted pathways/sidewalks.

Programs of Study: Dartmouth confers B.A. and B.Eng. degrees. Master's and doctoral degrees are also awarded. Bachelor's degrees are awarded in BIOLOGICAL SCIENCE (biochemistry, biology/biological science, evolutionary biology, and genetics), COMMUNICATIONS AND THE ARTS (Arabic, art history and appreciation, Chinese, classics, comparative literature, creative writing, dramatic arts, English, English literature, film arts, French, German, Italian, linguistics, music, romance languages and literature, Russian, and Spanish), COMPUTER AND PHYSICAL SCIENCE (chemistry, computer science, earth science, mathematics, and physics), ENGINEERING AND ENVIRONMENTAL DESIGN (engineering and applied science, engineering physics, and environmental science), SOCIAL SCIENCE (African American studies, African studies, anthropology, Asian/Oriental studies, classical/ancient civilization, cognitive science, economics, geography, German area studies, history, Latin American studies, Middle Eastern studies, Native American studies, philosophy, political science/government, psychology, religion, Russian and Slavic studies, social science, sociology, Spanish studies, and women's studies). Economics, psychology, and government are the largest.

Required: All students must pass 35 courses, 10 of which must be distributed in the following fields: arts; social analysis; literature; quantitative or deductive science; philosophical, religious, or historical analysis; natural science; technology or applied science; and international or comparative study. 3 world culture courses are required from the U.S., Europe, and at least 1 non-Western society. A multidisciplinary or interdisciplinary course, a freshman seminar, a senior project, and foreign language proficiency are also required.

Special: Students may design programs using the college's unique Dartmouth Plan, which divides the academic calendar into 4 10-week terms, based on the seasons. The plan permits greater flexibility for vacations and for the 39 study-abroad programs in 22 countries, including Italy, France, Scotland, Russia, and Brazil. Cross-registration is offered through the Twelve College Exchange Network, which includes Amherst and Mount Holyoke. Exchange programs also exist with the University of California at San Diego, McGill University in Montreal, selected German universities, Keio University in Tokyo, and Beijing Normal University in China. There are special academic programs in Washington, D.C., and Tucson, Arizona. Students may design their own interdisciplinary majors, involving multiple departments if desired, take dual majors in all fields, or satisfy a modified major involving 2 departments, with emphasis in 1. Hands-on computer science education, internships, combined B.A.-B.S. degrees, and work-study programs also are available. A 3-2 engineering degree is offered with Dartmouth's Thayer School of Engineering. There are 3 national honor societies, including Phi Beta Kappa.

Faculty/Classroom: 65% of faculty are male; 35%, female. All both teach and do research. No introductory courses are taught by graduate students. The average class size in an introductory lecture is 34; in a laboratory, 16; and in a regular course, 23.

Admissions: 19% of the 2005-2006 applicants were accepted. The SAT scores for the 2005-2006 freshman class were: Verbal--7% between 500 and 599, 27% between 600 and 700, and 65% above 700; Math--1% below 500, 5% between 500 and 599, 25% between 600 and 700, and 70% above 700. 95% of the current freshmen were in the top fifth of their class; all were in the top two fifths. 149 freshmen graduated first in their class.

Requirements: The SAT or ACT is required. The ACT Optional Writing test is also required, as are 2 SAT Subject Tests. Evidence of intellectual capacity, motivation, and personal integrity are prime considerations in the highly competitive admissions process, which also considers talent, accomplishment, and involvement in nonacademic areas. Course requirements are flexible, but students are urged to take English, foreign language, math, lab science, and history. The GED is accepted. AP credits are accepted.

Procedure: Freshmen are admitted in the fall. Entrance exams should be taken no later than January of the senior year. There are early decision and deferred admissions plans. Early decision applications should be filed by November 1; regular applications, by January 1 for fall entry. The fall 2005 application fee was $70. Notification of early decision is sent December 15; regular decision, April 1. 384 early decision candidates were accepted for the 2005-2006 class. Applications are accepted on-line.

Transfer: 13 transfer students enrolled in 2004-2005. Applicants must demonstrate high achievement and intellectual motivation through college transcripts as well as standardized test scores and high school transcripts. 18 of 35 courses required for the bachelor's degree must be completed at Dartmouth.

Visiting: There are regularly scheduled orientations for prospective students, including tours, group information sessions, and interviews. There are guides for informal visits and visitors may sit in on classes and stay overnight. To schedule a visit, contact the Office of Admissions at *admissions.office@dartmouth.edu*.

Financial Aid: In 2005-2006, 48% of all full-time freshmen and 50% of continuing full-time students received some form of financial aid. 47% of all full-time students received need-based aid. The average freshman award was $28,113. Need-based scholarships or need-based grants averaged $24,375; and need-based self-help aid (loans and jobs) averaged $4847. The average financial indebtedness of the 2005 graduate was $18,095. Dartmouth is a member of CSS. The CSS/Profile or FAFSA and parent and student federal income tax returns are required. In addition, a Noncustodial Parents' statement, W-2s, and a Business/Farm Supplement may be required. The deadline for filing freshman financial aid applications for fall entry is February 1.

International Students: There are 219 international students enrolled. The school actively recruits these students. They must take the TOEFL and the SAT or the ACT. They must also take SAT Subject Tests in any 2 subjects.

Computers: Wireless access is available. All students may access the system 24 hours daily. There are no time limits and no fees. All students are required to have personal computers.

Graduates: In a recent year, 1101 bachelor's degrees were awarded. The most popular majors were economics (12%), psychology and brain sciences (11%), and government and history (10%). In an average class, 88% graduate in 4 years or less, 95% graduate in 5 years or less, and 95% graduate in 6 years or less. 300 companies recruited on campus in 2004-2005. Of a recent graduating class, 19% were enrolled in graduate school within 6 months of graduation and 65% were employed.

Admissions Contact: Karl Furstenberg, Dean of Admissions.
E-mail: *undergraduate.admissions@dartmouth.edu*
Web: *www.dartmouth.edu*

FRANKLIN PIERCE COLLEGE C-8
Rindge, NH 03461-0060 (603) 899-4050
(800) 437-0048; Fax: (603) 899-4394

Full-time: 820 men, 776 women	**Faculty:** 59; IIB, -$
Part-time: 13 men, 26 women	**Ph.D.s:** 75%
Graduate: none	**Student/Faculty:** 23 to 1
Year: semesters, summer session	**Tuition:** $23,710
Application Deadline: open	**Room & Board:** $7990
Freshman Class: 4076 applied, 3025 accepted, 523 enrolled	
SAT or ACT: required	**COMPETITIVE**

Franklin Pierce College, founded in 1962, is a private liberal arts institution that also has an extensive continuing education program, which offers undergraduate and graduate degrees at locations in Concord, Keene, Lebanon, Manchester, Nashua, and Portsmouth in New Hampshire. The library contains 123,004 volumes, 5409 microform items, and 13,368 audio/video tapes/CDs/DVDs, and subscribes to 10,275 periodicals including electronic. Computerized library services include the card catalog, interlibrary loans, database searching, Internet access, and laptop Internet portals. Special learning facilities include a learning resource center, art gallery, radio station, TV station, computer labs, theaters, and studios. The 1200-acre campus is in a rural area 65 miles northwest of Boston. Including any residence halls, there are 30 buildings.

Student Life: 83% of undergraduates are from out of state, mostly the Northeast. Students are from 34 states, 17 foreign countries, and Canada. 81% are white. The average age of freshmen is 18; all undergraduates, 20. 34% do not continue beyond their first year; 48% remain to graduate.

Housing: 1380 students can be accommodated in college housing, which includes single-sex and coed dorms, on-campus apartments, and off-campus apartments. On-campus housing is guaranteed for all 4 years. 85% of students live on campus; of those, 70% remain on campus on weekends. All students may keep cars.

Activities: There are no fraternities or sororities. There are 35 groups on campus, including art, cheerleading, chess, choir, chorale, chorus, computers, dance, drama, ethnic, forensics, gay, honors, international, jazz band, literary magazine, musical theater, newspaper, outing photography, political, professional, radio and TV, religious, social, social service, student government, and yearbook. Popular campus events include Winter Carnival, Spring and Fall Weekends, and Up All Night Mardi Gras.

Sports: There are 9 intercollegiate sports for men and 11 for women, and 32 intramural sports for men and 32 for women. Facilities include a 72,000-square-foot airframe activity center (with tennis courts, indoor turf soccer field, basketball courts, track, fitness center, and volleyball courts), a field house, a fitness center, an 800-seat gym, an athletic training facility, playing fields including an artificial turf baseball field, an artificial turf soccer/lacrosse and field hockey field, a softball field, and another all-purpose field, a lake with a beach, a fleet of sailboats and kayaks, cross-country and hiking trails, and courts for tennis, basketball, and volleyball.

Disabled Students: 70% of the campus is accessible. Wheelchair ramps, elevators, special parking, specially equipped rest rooms, special class scheduling, and special housing are available.

Services: Counseling and information services are available, as is tutoring in every subject. There is a reader service for the blind, remedial math, reading, and writing, note takers, a professional reading specialist, alternative testing, reduced course loads, study skills workshops, and content-area study skills courses.

Campus Safety and Security: Measures include 24-hour foot and vehicle patrol, self-defense education, security escort services, and shuttle buses. There are informal discussions, pamphlets/posters/films, emergency telephones, and lighted pathways/sidewalks.

Programs of Study: FPC confers B.A. and B.S. degrees. Master's degrees are also awarded. Bachelor's degrees are awarded in BIOLOGICAL SCIENCE (biology/biological science), BUSINESS (accounting, banking and finance, business administration and management, business economics, management science, marketing/retailing/merchandising, and sports management), COMMUNICATIONS AND THE ARTS (arts administration/management, communications, dramatic arts, English, fine arts, graphic design, and music), COMPUTER AND PHYSICAL SCIENCE (information sciences and systems), EDUCATION (education, elementary, and secondary), ENGINEERING AND ENVIRONMENTAL DESIGN (environmental science), SOCIAL SCIENCE (American studies, anthropology, criminal justice, history, political science/government, psychology, and social work). Anthropology, biology, and history are the strongest academically. Criminal justice, mass communication, and English are the largest.

Required: Students must complete 120 semester hours with a cumulative GPA of at least 2.0 and pass exams for writing and math competency. Individual and Community core requirements total 11 courses, including Individual and Community, College Writing, Integrated Science, American Experience, Challenge of Business in Society, Twentieth Century, Mathematics, Experiencing the Arts or Music in Our World, Ancient and Medieval Worlds or Reason and Romanticism, Science of Society, and a senior liberal arts seminar.

Special: Cross-registration is offered in nearly every subject through the New Hampshire College and University Council, a 13-member consortium of area institutions. Study abroad in 6 countries, internships in most majors on or off campus, a Washington semester, and work-study through the college are possible. In addition, accelerated degree programs in all majors, dual majors in most fields, student-designed majors, credit for life experience, and nondegree study are available. There are 7 national honor societies and a freshman honors program.

Faculty/Classroom: 61% of faculty are male; 39%, female. All teach undergraduates and 50% both teach and do research. The average class size in an introductory lecture is 60; in a laboratory, 16; and in a regular course, 19.

Admissions: 74% of the 2005-2006 applicants were accepted. The SAT scores for the 2005-2006 freshman class were: Verbal--52% below 500, 39% between 500 and 599, 8% between 600 and 700, and 1% above 700; Math--56% below 500, 37% between 500 and 599, 6% between 600 and 700, and 1% above 700. 12% of the current freshmen were in the top fifth of their class; 38% were in the top two fifths.

Requirements: The SAT or ACT is required. In addition, applicants must have earned 10 academic units or 16 Carnegie units in high school, including 4 years of English, 3 each in math and social studies, and 2 in science. An interview is recommended. The GED is accepted. AP and CLEP credits are accepted. Important factors in the admissions decision are recommendations by school officials, advanced placement or honor courses, and extracurricular activities record.

Procedure: Freshmen are admitted to all sessions. Entrance exams should be taken in the spring of junior year or the fall of the senior year. There are early admissions and deferred admissions plans. There is a rolling admissions plan. Application deadlines are open. Notification is sent on a rolling basis. Applications are accepted on-line.

Transfer: 32 transfer students enrolled in 2004-2005. A minimum 2.0 GPA in college work is required. Students with fewer than 30 credits must submit SAT results (no minimum score) and official high school transcripts. A personal recommendation is necessary, and an interview is recommended. 30 of 120 credits required for the bachelor's degree must be completed at FPC.

Visiting: There are regularly scheduled orientations for prospective students, including open houses held each spring and fall and interviews and tours available weekdays and most Saturdays. There are guides for informal visits and visitors may sit in on classes and stay overnight. To schedule a visit, contact the Admissions Office.

Financial Aid: In 2005-2006, 90% of all full-time freshmen and 82% of continuing full-time students received some form of financial aid. 68%

of full-time freshmen and 79% of continuing full-time students received need-based aid. The average freshman award was $15,177. Need-based scholarships or need-based grants averaged $12,025; need-based self-help aid (loans and jobs) averaged $3584; non-need-based athletic scholarships averaged $12,839; and other non-need-based awards and non-need-based scholarships averaged $7944. 43% of undergraduates work part time. Average annual earnings from campus work are $618. The average financial indebtedness of the 2005 graduate was $22,417. The FAFSA is required. Check with the school for current application deadlines.

International Students: There are 42 international students enrolled. The school actively recruits these students. They must either take the TOEFL, the SAT, or the ACT.

Computers: Wireless access is available. There is 1 PC lab always available for general use by any student, and there are 2 PC labs available during the day if not in use by classes and always available in evenings. There is 1 Mac lab available in the evenings. Students can save important documents to their personal folder on the network and can access the Internet and the college's intranet. All students may access the system 24 hours a day, 7 days a week. There are no time limits. The fee is $350 a year. It is strongly recommended that all students have a personal computer.

Graduates: From July 1, 2004 to June 30, 2005, 280 bachelor's degrees were awarded. The most popular majors were mass communication (10%), English (8%), and criminal justice (7%). In an average class, 2% graduate in 3 years or less, 43% graduate in 4 years or less, 46% graduate in 5 years or less, and 47% graduate in 6 years or less. 30 companies recruited on campus in 2004-2005. Of the 2004 graduating class, 19% were enrolled in graduate school within 6 months of graduation and 79% were employed.

Admissions Contact: Lucy C. Shonk, Dean of Admissions. A video is available. E-mail: *admissions@fpc.edu* Web: *www.fpc.edu*

GRANITE STATE COLLEGE
(Formerly College for Lifelong Learning)

Concord, NH 03301-7317

(603) 513-1320
(888) 228-3000; Fax: (603) 513-1387

Full-time: 131 men, 360 women	**Faculty:** n/av
Part-time: 190 men, 683 women	**Ph.D.s:** n/av
Graduate: 40 men, 126 women	**Student/Faculty:** n/av
Year: trimesters, summer session	**Tuition:** $4800 ($5280)
Application Deadline: open	**Room & Board:** n/app
Freshman Class: n/av	
SAT or ACT: not required	**SPECIAL**

Granite State College, formerly the College for Lifelong Learning and established as part of the University System of New Hampshire in 1972, offers statewide and on-line access to undergraduate prgrams in a variety of general and professional majors for adults of all ages. Computerized library services include interlibrary loans and database searching. Special learning facilities include a learning resource center and a virtual library that serves all 9 local Centers throughout the state, as well as on-line students. The campus is in a small town.

Student Life: 92% of undergraduates are from New Hampshire. Others are from 4 states and 1 foreign country. 96% are white. The average age of all undergraduates is 38.

Housing: There are no residence halls. All students commute. Alcohol is not permitted.

Activities: There are no fraternities or sororities.

Sports: There is no sports program at GSC.

Disabled Students: All of the campus is accessible. Wheelchair ramps, special parking, and specially equipped rest rooms are available.

Services: There is remedial math, reading, and writing.

Campus Safety and Security: Measures include informal discussions and pamphlets/posters/films.

Programs of Study: GSC confers B.A. and B.S. degrees. Associate degrees are also awarded. Bachelor's degrees are awarded in BUSINESS (management science), COMPUTER AND PHYSICAL SCIENCE (information sciences and systems), SOCIAL SCIENCE (behavioral science, criminal justice, and liberal arts/general studies). Self-designed majors and management are the largest.

Required: Students must complete 124 credits, at least 32 to 39 in the major, and must maintain a minimum GPA of 2.0. All students are required to complete courses in computer competency, critical thinking/problem solving, mathematical reasoning, written and oral communications, and self-directed learning. General education requirements include courses in humanities/arts, science and technology, and social science.

Special: Opportunities are provided for internships, cross-registration with all USNH schools, student-designed and dual majors, credit by exam, nondegree study, and pass/fail options (for degree students only). GSC offers programs throughout the state through a network of 9 local Centers, as well as on-line. There is 1 national honor society.

Faculty/Classroom: 45% of faculty are male; 55%, female. All teach undergraduates. The average class size in a regular course is 10.

Requirements: Applicants must pass the College Board Accuplacer computerized placement series, unless they have graduated with a degree from a regionally accredited institution within the past 5 years. A GED will be considered if submitted for admissions evaluation. An interview is required. AP and CLEP credits are accepted.

Procedure: Freshmen are admitted to all sessions. There is a rolling admission plan. Application deadlines are open. The fall 2005 application fee was $45. Notification is sent on a rolling basis. Applications are accepted on-line.

Transfer: Transfer credits will be accepted via transcript if they are from a regionally accredited institution and will be evaluated to determine whether they contribute toward meeting GSC degree requirements. Minimum grade for transferred course credits is a C. There is no time limit on past college credits. 30 of 124 credits required for the bachelor's degree must be completed at GSC.

Visiting: There are regularly scheduled orientations for prospective students, consisting of an overview of college programs, financial aid, services, and transfer policies. Visitors may sit in on classes. To schedule a visit, contact a local Center.

Financial Aid: The average financial indebtedness of the 2005 graduate was $13,801. The FAFSA is required.

International Students: A satisfacory score is required on the written TOEFL. Students must also take the College Board Accuplacer computerized placement series.

Computers: Wireless access is available. Computer labs (average of 16 PCs each), along with designated computers in resource rooms, are available for student use at all local Centers. Wireless routers are also available at each Center. All provide access to the Internet. All students may access the system during regular operating hours. There are no time limits and no fees.

Graduates: From July 1, 2004 to June 30, 2005, 237 bachelor's degrees were awarded. The most popular majors were self-designed studies (40%), behavioral science (24%), and management (23%).

Admissions Contact: Ruth Nawn, Director of Admissions. A video is available. E-mail: *ruth.nawn@granite.edu* Web: *www.granite.edu*

HESSER COLLEGE
Manchester, NH 03101

(603) 668-6660
(800) 526-9231; Fax: (603) 666-4722

Full-time: 300 men, 400 women	**Faculty:** 29
Part-time: 22 men, 50 women	**Ph.D.s:** 1%
Graduate: none	**Student/Faculty:** 26 to 1
Year: semesters, summer session	**Tuition:** $11,500
Application Deadline: see profile	**Room & Board:** $6200
Freshman Class: n/av	
SAT or ACT: not required	**LESS COMPETITIVE**

Hesser College, founded in 1900, is a small, private institution affiliated with the Kaplan Education Corporation and offering more than 30 associate and 2+2 bachelor degree programs. Students must have an associate degree from Hesser in order to pursue a bachelor's degree. Figures in the above capsule and in this profile are approximate. The library contains 26,000 volumes and 2000 audio/video tapes/CDs/DVDs, and subscribes to 170 periodicals including electronic. Computerized library services include the card catalog, interlibrary loans, database searching, and Internet access. Special learning facilities include a learning resource center, radio station, TV station, and medical labs, G4 graphic design lab, and massage therapy lab. The 2-acre campus is in a medium-size city. Including any residence halls, there are 2 buildings.

Student Life: 64% of undergraduates are from New Hampshire. Others are from 13 states and 8 foreign countries. The average age of freshmen is 19; all undergraduates, 19.

Housing: 500 students can be accommodated in college housing, which includes single-sex dorms. On-campus housing is guaranteed for the freshman year only and is available on a lottery system for upperclassmen. 50% of students live on campus; of those, 50% remain on campus on weekends. Alcohol is not permitted. All students may keep cars.

Activities: There are no fraternities or sororities. There are some groups and organizations on campus, including cheerleading, honors, international, newspaper, professional, radio and TV, social, and student government.

Sports: There are 4 intercollegiate sports for men and 4 for women, and 5 intramural sports for men and 4 for women. Basketball, volleyball, soccer, and softball programs are available.

Disabled Students: Elevators and special parking are available.

Services: Counseling and information services are available, as is tutoring in every subject. There is remedial math, reading, and writing. There is a center for teaching, learning, and assessment.

Campus Safety and Security: Measures include 24-hour foot and vehicle patrol and security escort services.

Programs of Study: Hesser College confers B.B.A. and B.C.J. degrees. Associate degrees are also awarded. Bachelor's degrees are awarded in

BUSINESS (accounting and business administration and management), SOCIAL SCIENCE (criminal justice). Criminal justice is the largest.

Required: A minimum 2.0 GPA is required. Contact the school for specific program information.

Special: Internships and work-study programs are available. The college offers a J.D. degree through an articulation agreement with the Massachusetts School of Law, Andover. There is 1 national honor society, Phi Beta Kappa, and a freshman honors program.

Faculty/Classroom: 54% of faculty are male; 46%, female. The average class size in a regular course is 20.

Admissions: 25% of recent freshmen were in the top fifth of their class; 60% were in the top two fifths.

Requirements: Applicants must be high school graduates. The GED is accepted. An interview is required. A GPA of 2.0 is required. Important factors in the admissions decision are personality/intangible qualities, recommendations by school officials, and leadership record.

Procedure: Freshmen are admitted fall and spring. Entrance exams should be taken at orientation. Check with the school for current application deadlines. The fall 2005 application fee was $10. Notification is sent on a rolling basis. Applications are accepted on-line.

Visiting: There are regularly scheduled orientations for prospective students, including campus tours Monday through Friday during the school year and Monday through Thursday during the summer. Open house and Saturday tour days are also available. There are guides for informal visits and visitors may sit in on classes. To schedule a visit, contact Kevin Wilkinson, Director of Admissions at (603) 668-6660, ext. 2110.

Financial Aid: The FAFSA and the college's own financial statement are required. Check with the school for current deadlines.

International Students: The school actively recruits these students. They must score satisfactorily on the written TOEFL or take the MELAB or the Kaplan English Language Proficiency Test.

Admissions Contact: Kevin Wilkinson, Director of Admissions. A video is available. E-mail: *kwilkinson@hesser.edu* Web: *www.hesser.edu*

KEENE STATE COLLEGE
Keene, NH 03435

B-6

(603) 358-2276
(800) KSC-1909; Fax: (603) 358-2767

Full-time: 1781 men, 2350 women	**Faculty:** 184; IIA, av$
Part-time: 97 men, 142 women	**Ph.D.s:** 91%
Graduate: 22 men, 68 women	**Student/Faculty:** 22 to 1
Year: semesters, summer session	**Tuition:** $7352 ($14,192)
Application Deadline: April 1	**Room & Board:** $6484
Freshman Class: 3527 applied, 2693 accepted, 1008 enrolled	
SAT Verbal/Math: 500/500*	**ACT:** 20 **COMPETITIVE**

Keene State College, founded in 1909, is part of the public University System of New Hampshire and offers a liberal arts program that includes teacher preparation, art, and business emphases. There are 3 undergraduate schools and 1 graduate school. In addition to regional accreditation, KSC has baccalaureate program accreditation with CAAHEP, NASM, and NCATE. The library contains 301,741 volumes, 757,561 microform items, and 6630 audio/video tapes/CDs/DVDs, and subscribes to 1083 periodicals including electronic. Computerized library services include the card catalog, interlibrary loans, database searching, and Internet access. Special learning facilities include a learning resource center, art gallery, radio station, TV station, and the Holocaust Resource Center. The 150-acre campus is in a suburban area 90 miles northwest of Boston. Including any residence halls, there are 70 buildings.

Student Life: 53% of undergraduates are from out of state, mostly the Northeast. Students are from 28 states and 9 foreign countries. 90% are white. The average age of freshmen is 18; all undergraduates, 21. 24% do not continue beyond their first year; 61% remain to graduate.

Housing: 2362 students can be accommodated in college housing, which includes single-sex and coed dorms, on-campus apartments, married-student housing, fraternity houses, and sorority houses. In addition, there are special-interest houses. On-campus housing is guaranteed for the freshman year only and is available on a lottery system for upperclassmen. 54% of students live on campus; of those, 65% remain on campus on weekends. Upperclassmen may keep cars.

Activities: 2% of men and about 1% of women belong to 3 local fraternities; 4% of women belong to 5 local sororities. There are 80 groups on campus, including art, band, cheerleading, choir, chorale, chorus, computers, dance, drama, ethnic, film, gay, honors, international, jazz band, literary magazine, musical theater, newspaper, orchestra, photography, political, professional, radio and TV, religious, social, social service, student government, and yearbook. Popular campus events include Spring Weekend, Pumpkin Festival, and Alternative Spring Break.

Sports: There are 7 intercollegiate sports for men and 9 for women, and 17 intramural sports for men and 17 for women. Facilities include a 4600-square-foot recreational center, a 1500-seat gym, a 1000-seat stadium for soccer and field hockey, an indoor pool, a fitness center, racquetball, tennis, squash, basketball, volleyball, and indoor soccer courts, a jogging track, and a training room.

Disabled Students: 90% of the campus is accessible. Wheelchair ramps, elevators, special parking, specially equipped rest rooms, lowered drinking fountains, and lowered telephones are available.

Services: Counseling and information services are available, as is tutoring in most subjects. There is a writing process center, a reading center, and a math center. There is a reader service for the blind, and remedial math, reading, and writing.

Campus Safety and Security: Measures include 24-hour foot and vehicle patrol, self-defense education, security escort services, and shuttle buses. There are informal discussions, pamphlets/posters/films, emergency telephones, and lighted pathways/sidewalks.

Programs of Study: KSC confers B.A., B.S., B.F.A., and B.M. degrees. Associate and master's degrees are also awarded. Bachelor's degrees are awarded in BIOLOGICAL SCIENCE (biology/biological science), BUSINESS (management science), COMMUNICATIONS AND THE ARTS (art, communications, dance, English, film arts, fine arts, French, graphic design, journalism, music, music performance, Spanish, and theater design), COMPUTER AND PHYSICAL SCIENCE (chemistry, computer mathematics, computer science, geology, mathematics, and physical sciences), EDUCATION (early childhood, education, elementary, foreign languages, mathematics, music, physical, science, secondary, and special), ENGINEERING AND ENVIRONMENTAL DESIGN (architectural technology and environmental science), HEALTH PROFESSIONS (health science), SOCIAL SCIENCE (American studies, dietetics, economics, geography, history, psychology, safety management, social science, and sociology). Education, management, and safety studies are the largest.

Required: All students must take 120 to 142 credits, with 36 to 50 hours in their major, while maintaining a 2.0 GPA. Distribution requirements include 5 courses in the arts and humanities, 4 each in the social sciences, math, and sciences, and 1 in English composition. Students also must demonstrate proficiency in math.

Special: Internships and co-op programs in all areas of study, study abroad anywhere in the world, and work-study at the college are available. Student teaching is required for education majors. Students also may pursue dual majors, a general studies degree, individualized majors, accelerated degrees in the psychology honors program, and a 3-2 engineering degree with Clarkson University or the University of New Hampshire. In addition, there are pass/fail options and credit for life experience. There are 21 national honor societies and 1 departmental honors program.

Faculty/Classroom: 55% of faculty are male; 45%, female. All teach undergraduates. No introductory courses are taught by graduate students. The average class size in an introductory lecture is 21; in a laboratory, 14; and in a regular course, 13.

Admissions: 76% of the 2005-2006 applicants were accepted. The SAT scores for the 2005-2006 freshman class were: Verbal--46% below 500, 42% between 500 and 599, 11% between 600 and 700, and 1% above 700; Math--48% below 500, 40% between 500 and 599, 11% between 600 and 700, and 1% above 700. The ACT scores were 100% below 21. 9% of the current freshmen were in the top fifth of their class; 33% were in the top two fifths. 1 freshman graduated first in the class.

Requirements: The SAT or ACT is required. The ACT Optional Writing test is also required. In addition, applicants must submit an official high school transcript, an essay, and a letter of recommendation. Applicants need at least 14 academic credits, including 4 years of English, 3 each of math and science, and 2 each of social studies and academic electives. A portfolio or an audition is required for certain programs, and an interview is recommended. A GPA of 2.5 is required. AP and CLEP credits are accepted. Important factors in the admissions decision are advanced placement or honor courses, recommendations by school officials, and evidence of special talent.

Procedure: Freshmen are admitted fall and spring. Entrance exams should be taken during the spring of the junior year or fall of the senior year. There is a deferred admissions plan. There is a rolling admissions plan. Applications should be filed by April 1 for fall entry and December 1 for spring entry. The fall 2005 application fee was $35. Applications are accepted on-line.

Transfer: 209 transfer students enrolled in 2004-2005. Transfer students must have a 2.0 cumulative GPA, and transcripts must be submitted. An interview is recommended. 30 of 120 credits required for the bachelor's degree must be completed at KSC.

Visiting: There are regularly scheduled orientations for prospective students, consisting of a personal interview with the professional staff and a tour. There are guides for informal visits and visitors may sit in on classes. To schedule a visit, contact the Admissions Office.

Financial Aid: In 2005-2006, 56% of all full-time freshmen and 53% of continuing full-time students received some form of financial aid. 50% of full-time freshmen and 49% of continuing full-time students received need-based aid. The average freshman award was $7385. Need-based scholarships or need-based grants averaged $4458; and need-based self-help aid (loans and jobs) averaged $3101. 14% of undergraduates work part time. Average annual earnings from campus work are $844. The average financial indebtedness of the 2005 graduate was $20,065. The

FAFSA and IRS tax returns are required. The deadline for filing freshman financial aid applications for fall entry is March 1.

International Students: There are 21 international students enrolled. A satisfactory score on the TOEFL is required.

Computers: The wireless network is available in the library and some classrooms. Laptop computers with wireless access cards are available at the library. All residence halls are wired for high speed Internet access, and there are 750 open, wired network connections on campus including all classrooms. The wireless network can accommodate 200 simultaneous users. All students may access the system 24 hours per day. There are no time limits and no fees.

Graduates: From July 1, 2004 to June 30, 2005, 855 bachelor's degrees were awarded. The most popular majors were education (14%), psychology (12%), and management (8%). In an average class, 28% graduate in 4 years or less, 50% graduate in 5 years or less, and 53% graduate in 6 years or less. 20 companies recruited on campus in 2004-2005. Of the 2004 graduating class, 13% were enrolled in graduate school within 6 months of graduation.

Admissions Contact: Peggy Richmond, Director of Admissions. A video is available. E-mail: *admissions@keene.edu* Web: *www.keene.edu*

NEW ENGLAND COLLEGE   C-5

Henniker, NH 03242

(603) 428-2223
(800) 521-7642; Fax: (608) 428-3155

Full-time: 463 men, 484 women	**Faculty:** 58
Part-time: 25 men, 48 women	**Ph.D.s:** 75%
Graduate: 92 men, 213 women	**Student/Faculty:** 16 to 1
Year: semesters, summer session	**Tuition:** $23,010
Application Deadline: open	**Room & Board:** $8456
Freshman Class: 1817 applied, 1512 accepted, 342 enrolled	
SAT Verbal/Math: 450/440*	**COMPETITIVE**

New England College, founded in 1946, is an independent liberal arts institution emphasizing small classes and a cocurricular leadership program. The library contains 104,000 volumes, 36,000 microform items, and 2000 audio/video tapes/CDs/DVDs, and subscribes to 650 periodicals including electronic. Computerized library services include the card catalog, interlibrary loans, database searching, Internet access, and laptop Internet portals. Special learning facilities include a learning resource center, art gallery, radio station, and the Center for Educational Innovation, with a high-tech classroom building. The 225-acre campus is in a small town 17 miles west of Concord and 80 miles north of Boston, Massachusetts. Including any residence halls, there are 31 buildings.

Student Life: 67% of undergraduates are from out of state, mostly the Northeast. Students are from 34 states, 15 foreign countries, and Canada. 73% are from public schools. 89% are white. The average age of freshmen is 18; all undergraduates, 20. 37% do not continue beyond their first year; 48% remain to graduate.

Housing: 685 students can be accommodated in college housing, which includes coed dormitories, on-campus apartments, fraternity houses, and sorority houses. In addition, there are special-interest houses and students may choose to live in cooperative substance-free housing. On-campus housing is guaranteed for all 4 years. 65% of students live on campus; of those, 80% remain on campus on weekends. All students may keep cars.

Activities: 8% of men belong to 3 local fraternities; 6% of women belong to 1 local and 1 national sorority. There are 30 groups on campus, including chorus, dance, drama, ethnic, film, gay, honors, international, literary magazine, newspaper, photography, political, professional, radio and TV, religious, social, social service, student government, and yearbook. Popular campus events include International Week and Spring Weekend.

Sports: There are 6 intercollegiate sports for men and 7 for women, and 7 intramural sports for men and 7 for women. Facilities include a gym, a field house, 26 acres of playing fields, indoor and outdoor basketball and tennis courts, cross-country ski trails, Alpine skiing at a local ski area, and a fitness center.

Disabled Students: 80% of the campus is accessible. Wheelchair ramps, elevators, special parking, specially equipped rest rooms, and special class scheduling are available.

Services: Counseling and information services are available, as is tutoring in most subjects. There is remedial math and writing. The mentor program provides both academic and social advising.

Campus Safety and Security: Measures include 24-hour foot and vehicle patrol, security escort services, shuttle buses, and informal discussions. There are pamphlets/posters/films, emergency telephones, and lighted pathways/sidewalks.

Programs of Study: NEC confers B.A. and B.S. degrees. Associate and master's degrees are also awarded. Bachelor's degrees are awarded in BIOLOGICAL SCIENCE (biology/biological science), BUSINESS (business administration and management, recreation and leisure services, and sports management), COMMUNICATIONS AND THE ARTS (art history and appreciation, communications, comparative literature, creative writing, dramatic arts, English literature, and fine arts), COMPUT-

ER AND PHYSICAL SCIENCE (mathematics), EDUCATION (elementary, physical, secondary, and special), ENGINEERING AND ENVIRONMENTAL DESIGN (environmental science), HEALTH PROFESSIONS (health science), SOCIAL SCIENCE (criminal justice, philosophy, physical fitness/movement, political science/government, psychology, sociology, and women's studies). Business, education, and psychology are the strongest academically. Business, education, and kinesiology are the largest.

Required: All students must earn a minimum GPA of 2.0 and take 120 credit hours, including an average of 40 in their major. Distribution requirements cover 5 general education areas, including science, humanities, social science, math, and world culture and human rights. Specific requirements include College Writing I and II, a math course (or a passing grade on a placement test), computer science, and science courses.

Special: Cross-registration is available with the New Hampshire College and University Council. Also available are internships for juniors and seniors with a GPA of 2.5, study abroad in most countries, work-study programs, dual majors, student-designed majors, interdisciplinary majors, nondegree study, pass/fail options, and a 3-2 engineering degree with Clarkson University. A 4+1 MBA Union University; 3+3 Law program New York Law School are also offered. There is 1 national honor society, a freshman honors program, and all departments have honors programs.

Faculty/Classroom: 45% of faculty are male; 55%, female. All teach undergraduates and 20% both teach and do research. No introductory courses are taught by graduate students. The average class size in an introductory lecture is 20; in a laboratory, 14; and in a regular course, 16.

Admissions: 83% of the 2005-2006 applicants were accepted. The SAT scores for the 2005-2006 freshman class were: Verbal--72% below 500, 24% between 500 and 599, 3% between 600 and 700, and 1% above 700; Math--77% below 500, 18% between 500 and 599, and 5% between 600 and 700. 22% of the current freshmen were in the top fifth of their class; 56% were in the top two fifths.

Requirements: 4 years of English, 3 years each of math and social studies, and 2 years each of science and electives are recommended. An essay is required and an interview is recommended. A GPA of 2.0 is required. AP and CLEP credits are accepted. Important factors in the admissions decision are personality/intangible qualities, extracurricular activities record, and leadership record.

Procedure: Freshmen are admitted fall, spring, and summer. There is a deferred admission and a rolling admissions plan. Application deadlines are open. Application fee is $30. Applications are accepted on-line.

Transfer: 63 transfer students enrolled in 2004-2005. Transfer students should have a 2.0 minimum GPA from the previous college. A recommendation from the dean of students is required. An interview is recommended. 30 of 120 credits required for the bachelor's degree must be completed at NEC.

Visiting: There are regularly scheduled orientations for prospective students, including class registration and meeting faculty and other students. There are guides for informal visits and visitors may sit in on classes and stay overnight. To schedule a visit, contact Muriel Schlosser in the Admissions Office at (603) 428-2223.

Financial Aid: In 2005-2006, 95% of all full-time freshmen and 91% of continuing full-time students received some form of financial aid. 83% of full-time freshmen and 76% of continuing full-time students received need-based aid. The average freshman award was $25,247. Need-based scholarships or need-based grants averaged $11,410; need-based self-help aid (loans and jobs) averaged $7849; and other non-need-based awards and non-need-based scholarships averaged $10,360. 50% of undergraduates work part time. Average annual earnings from campus work are $1500. The average financial indebtedness of the 2005 graduate was $28,167. The FAFSA and the college's own financial statement are required. The priority date for freshman financial aid applications for fall entry is March 15. The deadline for filing freshman financial aid applications for fall entry is September 3.

International Students: There are 56 international students enrolled. The school actively recruits these students. They must score satisfactorily on the written TOEFL or on the electronic version.

Computers: Wireless access is available at most locations across campus. PCs are located in several computer labs, the library, and the writing lab. All students may access the system 24 hours a day, 7 days a week. There are no time limits and no fees. It is strongly recommended that all students have a personal computer. An IBM Thinkpad laptop is recommended.

Graduates: From July 1, 2004 to June 30, 2005, 146 bachelor's degrees were awarded. The most popular majors were business (30%), psychology (12%), and communications (8%). In an average class, 45% graduate in 4 years or less, 46% graduate in 5 years or less, and 49% graduate in 6 years or less. 20 companies recruited on campus in 2004-2005. Of the 2004 graduating class, 18% were enrolled in graduate school within 6 months of graduation and 95% were employed.

Admissions Contact: Office of Admission. A video is available.
E-mail: *admission@necl.nec.edu* Web: *www.nec.edu*

PLYMOUTH STATE UNIVERSITY D-4

Plymouth, NH 03264-1595 (603) 535-2237
(800) 842-6900; Fax: (603) 535-2714

Full-time: 1830 men, 1890 women	**Faculty:** 156; IIA, +$
Part-time: 130 men, 130 women	**Ph.D.s:** 87%
Graduate: 235 men, 710 women	**Student/Faculty:** 24 to 1
Year: semesters, summer session	**Tuition:** $6250 ($12,366)
Application Deadline: see profile	**Room & Board:** $6060
Freshman Class: n/av	
SAT or ACT: required	**LESS COMPETITIVE**

Plymouth State University, formerly Plymouth State College, founded in 1871, is a public institution offering programs in business, education, and liberal arts and sciences. Figures in the above capsule and profile are approximate. In addition to regional accreditation, PSU has baccalaureate program accreditation with ACBSP, CAAHEP, CSWE, and NCATE. The library contains 306,314 volumes, 796,924 microform items, and 23,095 audio/video tapes/CDs/DVDs, and subscribes to 1043 periodicals including electronic. Computerized library services include the card catalog, interlibrary loans, and database searching. Special learning facilities include a learning resource center, art gallery, planetarium, radio station, a major performing arts center, an NAEYC-accredited lab school for children ages 2 to 6, geographic information systems lab, meteorology lab, graphic design, computer lab, MIDI lab, and weather technology evaluation center. The 170-acre campus is in a small town 2 hours north of Boston. Including any residence halls, there are 66 buildings.

Student Life: 58% of undergraduates are from New Hampshire. Others are from 27 states, 9 foreign countries, and Canada. 96% are from public schools. 90% are white. The average age of freshmen is 18; all undergraduates, 21. 26% do not continue beyond their first year; 53% remain to graduate.

Housing: 2107 students can be accommodated in college housing, which includes coed dormitories, on-campus apartments, married-student housing, and sorority houses. In addition, there are special-interest houses, a wellness residence hall and special interest areas in the residence halls for skiing, snowboarding, biking, hiking, music/theater, fine arts, community service, and fitness. On-campus housing is guaranteed for the freshman year only. 54% of students live on campus; of those, 70% remain on campus on weekends. All students may keep cars.

Activities: 4% of men belong to 2 national fraternities; 7% of women belong to 2 local and 2 national sororities. There are 100 groups on campus, including Alliance for Women's Awareness, art, band, cheerleading, choir, chorale, computers, dance, debate, drama, ethnic, gay, honors, international, jazz band, Leadership Effectiveness and Development Seminar, literary magazine, musical theater, newspaper, OS-SIPEE, professional, radio and TV, religious, social, social service, Students in Adventure Growth Experiences, student government, student wellness organization, and yearbook. Popular campus events include Spring Fling, Family Weekend, and Winter Carnival.

Sports: There are 8 intercollegiate sports for men and 9 for women, and 30 intramural sports for men and 30 for women. Facilities include a 2500-seat stadium, a 2000-seat gym, playing fields, and facilities for basketball, racquetball, indoor soccer, swimming, tennis, volleyball, softball, and lacrosse. There is also a 75,000-square-foot recreation student center separate from athletics, as well as a ropes course.

Disabled Students: 75% of the campus is accessible. Wheelchair ramps, elevators, special parking, specially equipped rest rooms, lowered drinking fountains, and lowered telephones. The shuttle service is wheelchair-accessible, and there are handicap-accessible student apartment units, ADA compliant alarm systems, and TDD/TTY.

Services: Counseling and information services are available, as is tutoring in some subjects, including 100-and 200-level courses and some upper-level courses. Peer tutoring is available.

Campus Safety and Security: Measures include 24-hour foot and vehicle patrol, self-defense education, security escort services, and shuttle buses. There are informal discussions, pamphlets/posters/films, emergency telephones, and lighted pathways/sidewalks. There are also programs in defensive driving, alcohol awareness, drug identification, and personal safety.

Programs of Study: PSU confers B.A., B.S., and B.F.A. degrees. Master's degrees are also awarded. Bachelor's degrees are awarded in BIOLOGICAL SCIENCE (biology/biological science, biotechnology, and environmental biology), BUSINESS (accounting, business administration and management, marketing management, and recreation and leisure services), COMMUNICATIONS AND THE ARTS (art, communications, English, French, graphic design, music, performing arts, and Spanish), COMPUTER AND PHYSICAL SCIENCE (atmospheric sciences and meteorology, chemistry, computer science, information sciences and systems, and mathematics), EDUCATION (art, athletic training, health, music, physical, recreation, and science), ENGINEERING AND ENVIRONMENTAL DESIGN (city/community/regional planning), SOCIAL SCIENCE (anthropology, child care/child and family studies, criminal justice, early childhood studies, economics, geography, history, humanities, interdisciplinary studies, medieval studies, philosophy, political science/government, psychology, public administration, social science, and social work). Meteorology, computer science, and graphic design are the strongest academically. Childhood studies, management, and phys ed are the largest.

Required: All students must maintain a minimum GPA of 2.0 while enrolled in 122 semester hours, including 2 credits in psys ed, 1 credit of introduction to the academic community, and 1 course each in composition and math foundations. Distribution requirements are part of the general education program, which requires 7 credits in scientific and science lab, 6 credits in social and psychological, 3 credits in technological, and 3 credits each in the following perspectives: fine and performing arts, global, historical, literary, philosophical, and quantitative reasoning. Some majors have a higher GPA and total credit requirement.

Special: Cross-registration with the New Hampshire College and University Council is available. Internships, study abroad in 3 countries, and college work-study programs are available. Dual majors, an accelerated degree program, offering an undergraduate business and M.B.A. degree in 5 years, and student-designed majors are possible. There are 9 national honor societies, a freshman honors program, and 2 departmental honors programs.

Faculty/Classroom: 57% of faculty are male; 43%, female. 85% teach undergraduates. The average class size in an introductory lecture is 25; in a laboratory, 17; and in a regular course, 20.

Requirements: The SAT or ACT is required. In addition, PSU requires that applicants have completed 4 units of English, 3 each of math, social studies and science, 2 of history, and recommends 2 in foreign language. An audition for certain programs is required, and an essay is required. The GED is accepted. AP and CLEP credits are accepted. Important factors in the admissions decision are advanced placement or honor courses, recommendations by school officials, and leadership record.

Procedure: Freshmen are admitted fall and spring. Entrance exams should be taken in November of the senior year. There are deferred admissions and rolling admissions plans. Check with the school for application deadlines. Notification is sent on a rolling basis. Applications are accepted on-line.

Transfer: 232 transfer students enrolled in a recent year. Transfer students must have a minimum GPA of 2.0 on prior work to be considered. 30 of 122 credits required for the bachelor's degree must be completed at PSU.

Visiting: There are regularly scheduled orientations for prospective students, including an admission presentation, a tour of the campus, and a meal in the dining hall. There are guides for informal visits and visitors may sit in on classes. To schedule a visit, contact the Admission Office.

Financial Aid: In a recent year, 61% of all full-time freshmen and 58% of continuing full-time students received some form of financial aid. 58% of full-time freshmen and 56% of continuing full-time students received need-based aid. The average freshman award was $6562. Need-based scholarships or need-based grants averaged $4248; need-based self-help aid (loans and jobs) averaged $4029; and other non-need-based awards and non-need-based scholarships averaged $1930. 14% of undergraduates worked part time. Average annual earnings from campus work were $850. The FAFSA is required. Check with the school for application deadlines.

International Students: In a recent year, there were 13 international students enrolled. The school actively recruits these students. They must score satisfactorily on the written TOEFL or on the electronic version.

Computers: All students may access the system. There are no time limits. The fee is $330 annual tech fee. It is strongly recommended that all students have a personal computer.

Graduates: In a recent year, 559 bachelor's degrees were awarded. The most popular majors were childhood studies (14%), management (11%), and communications studies (9%). In an average class, 26% graduate in 4 years or less, 45% graduate in 5 years or less, and 48% graduate in 6 years or less. 68 companies recruited on campus in a recent year.

Admissions Contact: Eugene D. Fahey, Senior Associate Director of Admission. E-mail: *plymouthadmit@plymouth.edu*
Web: *www.plymouth.edu*

RIVIER COLLEGE
D-6

Nashua, NH 03060-5086

(603) 897-8507
(800) 44-RIVIER; Fax: (603) 891-1799

Full-time: 300 men, 600 women	**Faculty:** 63; IIA, --$
Part-time: 200 men, 500women	**Ph.Ds:** 88%
Graduate: 200 men, 600 women	**Student/Faculty:** 13 to 1
Year: semesters, summer session	**Tuition:** $19,500
Application Deadline: open	**Room & Board:** $7100
Freshman Class: n/av	
SAT: required	**COMPETITIVE**

Rivier College, founded in 1933 by the Sisters of the Presentation of Mary, is a private Roman Catholic college offering a liberal arts and professional curriculum. Figures in the above capsule and in this profile are approximate. In addition to regional accreditation, Rivier has baccalau-

reate program accreditation with NLN. The library contains 107,200 volumes, 89,572 microform items, and 29,094 audio/video tapes/CDs/DVDs, and subscribes to 480 periodicals including electronic. Computerized library services include the card catalog, interlibrary loans, and database searching. Special learning facilities include a learning resource center, art gallery, radio station, TV station, education curriculum resources center, legal reference center, early childhood center/laboratory school, and language lab. The 68-acre campus is in a suburban area 45 miles north of Boston. Including any residence halls, there are 44 buildings.

Student Life: 68% of undergraduates are from New Hampshire. Others are from 13 states, 13 foreign countries, and Canada. 80% are from public schools. 93% are white. Most are Catholic. The average age of freshmen is 18; all undergraduates, 28. 29% do not continue beyond their first year.

Housing: 425 students can be accommodated in college housing, which includes coed dorms. In addition, there is a substance-free/wellness hall. On-campus housing is guaranteed for all 4 years and is available on a first-come, first-served basis. 56% of students commute. All students may keep cars.

Activities: There are no fraternities or sororities. There are 32 groups on campus, including art, behavioral sciences, chorus, computers, debate, drama, ethnic, history, honors, international, literary magazine, newspaper, nursing, paralegal, political, professional, religious, social, social sciences, social service, student government, and yearbook. Popular campus events include Spirit Week, Black History Month, and Women's History Month.

Sports: There are 5 intercollegiate sports for men and 5 for women, and 7 intramural sports for men and 7 for women. Facilities include a 300-seat gym, a weight room, and soccer and softball fields.

Disabled Students: 75% of the campus is accessible. Wheelchair ramps, elevators, special parking, specially equipped rest rooms, and lowered drinking fountains are available.

Services: Counseling and information services are available, as is tutoring in some subjects, including math, English, business, and languages. There is remedial math and writing. There is a full-service writing center.

Campus Safety and Security: Measures include 24-hour foot and vehicle patrol, security escort services, informal discussions, and pamphlets/posters/films. There are emergency telephones, lighted pathways/sidewalks, 24-hour access by telephone or walkie-talkie, and electronically operated dorm entrances using security cards.

Programs of Study: Rivier confers B.A., B.S., and B.F.A. degrees. Associate and master's degrees are also awarded. Bachelor's degrees are awarded in BIOLOGICAL SCIENCE (biology/biological science), BUSINESS (business administration and management, management information systems, and management science), COMMUNICATIONS AND THE ARTS (communications, English, graphic design, illustration, and studio art), COMPUTER AND PHYSICAL SCIENCE (computer science and mathematics), EDUCATION (art, early childhood, elementary, English, mathematics, secondary, and social studies), HEALTH PROFESSIONS (nursing, predentistry, premedicine, and preveterinary science), SOCIAL SCIENCE (history, human development, liberal arts/general studies, political science/government, prelaw, psychology, and sociology). Art, education, and nursing are the strongest academically. Education, psychology, and business are the largest.

Required: A writing sample is required at entry, and a demonstration of writing proficiency must be shown prior to graduation. Students must complete at least 120 credit hours, ordinarily consisting of 40 3-credit courses with 35 to 60 credits in the student's major, and they must maintain a minimum GPA of 2.0. Distribution requirements include 17 core courses in basic skills of writing and math, the humanities, and the sciences. These courses include religious studies, philosophy, physical and life sciences, fine arts, modern languages, literature, behavioral and social sciences, and Western civilization.

Special: Rivier offers cross-registration through the New Hampshire College and University Council, internships in most majors, an accelerated master's program in English, dual majors, a liberal studies degree, credit by challenge exam, nondegree study, and pass/fail options. There is 1 national honor society and a freshman honors program.

Faculty/Classroom: 38% of faculty are male; 62%, female. 88% teach undergraduates. No introductory courses are taught by graduate students. The average class size in an introductory lecture is 25; in a laboratory, 20; and in a regular course, 17.

Admissions: 77% of recent applicants were accepted. The SAT scores for a recent freshman class were: Verbal--50% below 500, 35% between 500 and 599, and 15% between 600 and 700; Math--50% below 500, 35% between 500 and 599, and 15% between 600 and 700. 24% of a recent freshmen were in the top fifth of their class; 70% were in the top two fifths.

Requirements: The SAT is required. In addition, applicants must be high school graduates or hold the GED. The recommended college preparatory curriculum includes 4 years of English, 3 of math, 2 or more each of foreign language and social studies, 1 of lab science, and 4 academic electives. An essay and 1 or 2 letters of recommendation are required, and an interview is highly recommended. Prospective art majors must submit a portfolio. Rivier requires applicants to be in the upper 50% of their class. A GPA of 2.5 is required. AP and CLEP credits are accepted. Important factors in the admissions decision are advanced placement or honor courses, recommendations by school officials, and extracurricular activities record.

Procedure: Freshmen are admitted fall and spring. Entrance exams should be taken in the junior or senior year. There is a deferred admissions plan. Application deadlines are open. The fall 2005 application fee was $25. Notification is sent on a rolling basis. Applications are accepted on-line.

Transfer: 160 transfer students enrolled in a recent year. Transfer applicants should have a minimum GPA of 2.5 and submit SAT I or ACT scores if they have earned fewer than 12 credits at the previous institution. Official college transcripts are required and an interview is recommended. 60 of 120 credits required for the bachelor's degree must be completed at Rivier.

Visiting: There are regularly scheduled orientations for prospective students, including an opportunity to interview, a tour, class visits, and opportunities to meet with faculty, coaches, and current students. There are guides for informal visits and visitors may sit in on classes and stay overnight. To schedule a visit, contact the Office of Undergraduate Admissions.

Financial Aid: 35% of undergraduates work part time. Average annual earnings from campus work are $546. The average financial indebtedness of a recent graduate was $17,500. Rivier is a member of CSS. The FAFSA is required. Check with the school for current deadlines.

International Students: The school actively recruits these students. They must score satisfactorily on the written TOEFL and also take the college's own test.

Computers: All students may access the system 24 hours a day. There are no time limits. The fee varies.

Admissions Contact: David A. Boisvert, Director of Undergraduate Admissions. E-mail: *rivadmit@rivier.edu* Web: *www.rivier.edu*

SAINT ANSELM COLLEGE
Manchester, NH 03102

D-6

(603) 641-7500
(888)-4-ANSELM; Fax: (603) 641-7550

Full-time: 827 men, 1119 women	Faculty: IIB, av$
Part-time: 17 men, 24 women	Ph.D.s: 91%
Graduate: none	Student/Faculty: n/av
Year: semesters, summer session	Tuition: $24,740
Application Deadline: March 1	Room & Board: $9070
Freshman Class: 3252 applied, 2326 accepted, 511 enrolled	
SAT Verbal/Math: 560/560*	COMPETITIVE

Saint Anselm College, founded in 1889, is a private Roman Catholic institution offering a liberal arts education. In addition to regional accreditation, Saint Anselm has baccalaureate program accreditation with NLN. The library contains 219,000 volumes, 65,000 microform items, and 8000 audio/video tapes/CDs/DVDs, and subscribes to 3900 periodicals including electronic. Computerized library services include the card catalog, interlibrary loans, database searching, and Internet access. Special learning facilities include a learning resource center, art gallery, planetarium, and TV station. The 404-acre campus is in a suburban area 50 miles north of Boston. Including any residence halls, there are 63 buildings.

Student Life: 76% of undergraduates are from out of state, mostly the Northeast. Others are from 28 states, 16 foreign countries, and Canada. 67% are from public schools. 93% are white. 78% are Catholic; 9% Protestant; 8% claim no religious affiliation. The average age of freshmen is 18; all undergraduates, 20. 16% do not continue beyond their first year; 77% remain to graduate.

Housing: 1644 students can be accommodated in college housing, which includes single-sex and coed dorms and on-campus apartments. In addition, there are special-interest houses and substance-free housing. On-campus housing is guaranteed for all 4 years. 87% of students live on campus; of those, 85% remain on campus on weekends. All students may keep cars.

Activities: There are no fraternities or sororities. There are 64 groups on campus, including art, cheerleading, chess, choir, chorale, chorus, computers, dance, debate, drama, ethnic, honors, international, jazz band, literary magazine, newspaper, orchestra, pep band, photography, political, professional, radio and TV, religious, social, social service, student government, and yearbook. Popular campus events include Winter Weekend, Family Weekend, and Road for Hope.

Sports: There are 10 intercollegiate sports for men and 10 for women, and 13 intramural sports for men and 13 for women. Facilities include a 1500-seat gym, an ice hockey arena, an activity center that houses basketball, volleyball, tennis, and racquetball courts, and weight and training rooms; a 2500-seat football stadium; a 500-seat baseball stadium; and athletic fields.

Disabled Students: 60% of the campus is accessible. Wheelchair ramps, elevators, special parking, specially equipped rest rooms, special class scheduling, and lowered drinking fountains are available.

Services: Counseling and information services are available, as is tutoring in most subjects. There is a reader service for the blind.

Campus Safety and Security: Measures include 24-hour foot and vehicle patrol, informal discussions, pamphlets/posters/films, and emergency telephones. There are lighted pathways/sidewalks and security escort upon request.

Programs of Study: Saint Anselm confers B.A. and B.S.N. degrees. Bachelor's degrees are awarded in BIOLOGICAL SCIENCE (biochemistry and biology/biological science), BUSINESS (accounting, banking and finance, and business administration and management), COMMUNICATIONS AND THE ARTS (classics, English, fine arts, French, and Spanish), COMPUTER AND PHYSICAL SCIENCE (chemistry, computer science, mathematics, and natural sciences), EDUCATION (secondary), ENGINEERING AND ENVIRONMENTAL DESIGN (engineering and environmental science), HEALTH PROFESSIONS (nursing, predentistry, and premedicine), SOCIAL SCIENCE (criminal justice, economics, history, liberal arts/general studies, philosophy, political science/government, prelaw, psychology, sociology, and theological studies). Business, English, and psychology are the largest.

Required: All students must maintain a GPA of 2.0 in the major while completing at least 40 semester courses, including 4 semesters in the humanities, 3 each in philosophy and theology, 2 each in English and lab science, and 2 to 4 in foreign language; 10 to 13 courses are required in the major area of study.

Special: Saint Anselm offers a 5-year liberal arts and a 3-2 engineering program in cooperation with Manhattan College, University of Notre Dame, University of Massachusetts Lowell, and Catholic University of America. Cross-registration is possible. In addition, internships, work-study, a Washington semester, a New York City semseter, study abroad, and nondegree study are available. There are 11 national honor societies, a freshman honors program, and 20 departmental honors programs.

Faculty/Classroom: 60% of faculty are male; 40%, female. All teach undergraduates. The average class size in an introductory lecture is 20; in a laboratory, 14; and in a regular course, 24.

Admissions: 72% of the 2005-2006 applicants were accepted. The SAT scores for the 2005-2006 freshman class were: Verbal--18% below 500, 54% between 500 and 599, 26% between 600 and 700, and 2% above 700; Math--17% below 500, 57% between 500 and 599, 24% between 600 and 700, and 2% above 700. 37% of the current freshmen were in the top fifth of their class; 72% were in the top two fifths. 7 freshmen graduated first in their class in a recent year.

Requirements: The SAT is required. In addition, applicants must have 16 academic credits and 16 Carnegie units, including 4 years of English, 3 each of math and science, 2 of foreign language, and 1 each of history and social studies. An essay is required, and an interview is recommended. The GED is accepted. A GPA of 2.0 is required. AP and CLEP credits are accepted. Important factors in the admissions decision are advanced placement or honor courses, leadership record, and recommendations by school officials.

Procedure: Freshmen are admitted fall and spring. Entrance exams should be taken during the spring of the junior year or fall of the senior year. There are early decision, deferred admissions and rolling admissions plans. Early decision applications should be filed by November 15; regular applications, by March 1 for fall entry and December 1 for spring entry, along with a $55 fee. Notification of early decision is sent December 1; regular decision, on a rolling basis. 76 early decision candidates were accepted for the 2005-2006 class. A waiting list is an active part of the admissions procedure. Applications are accepted on-line.

Transfer: 25 transfer students enrolled in 2004-2005. Transfer students must have a minimum GPA of 2.5 after earning at least 30 college credits. The SAT is required and an interview is recommended. In addition, 2 letters of recommendation are necessary. 20 of 40 courses required for the bachelor's degree must be completed at Saint Anselm.

Visiting: There are regularly scheduled orientations for prospective students, consisting of daily individual interviews and/or group information sessions followed by a campus tour. There are guides for informal visits and visitors may sit in on classes and stay overnight. To schedule a visit, contact the Office of Admission.

Financial Aid: In 2004-2005, 74% of all full-time freshmen and 71% of continuing full-time students received some form of financial aid. At least 74% of full-time freshmen and 70% of continuing full-time students received need-based aid. The average freshman award was $18,025. Need-based scholarships or need-based grants averaged $13,349; need-based self-help aid (loans and jobs) averaged $4323; non-need-based athletic scholarships averaged $13,283; and other non-need-based awards and non-need-based scholarships averaged $12,085. The average financial indebtedness of the 2005 graduate was $23,437. Saint Anselm is a member of CSS. The CSS Profile or FAFSA is required. The deadline for filing freshman financial aid applications for fall entry is March 15.

International Students: The school actively recruits International students. Satisfactory scores are required on the written TOEFL, the SAT or the ACT.

Computers: All students may access the system 8:30 A.M. to 12 a.m, Monday through Friday; 10 A.M. to 6 P.M. Saturday; 1 P.M. to 12 A.M. Sunday. There are no time limits and no fees.

Graduates: From July 1, 2003 to June 30, 2004, 408 bachelor's degrees were awarded. The most popular majors were business/marketing (22%), social sciences and history (21%), and protective services/ public administrati (13%). In an average class, 66% graduate in 4 years or less, 70% graduate in 5 years or less, and 70% graduate in 6 years or less.

Admissions Contact: Nancy Griffin, Director of Admission.
E-mail: admission@anselm.edu Web: www.anselm.edu

SOUTHERN NEW HAMPSHIRE UNIVERSITY   D-6

Manchester, NH 03106-1045   (603) 645-9611
                                (800) 642-4968; Fax: (603) 645-9693

Full-time: 748 men, 914 women	Faculty: 114; IIA, av$
Part-time: 17 men, 27 women	Ph.D.s: 75%
Graduate: 4506 men, 5031 women	Student/Faculty: 15 to 1
Year: semesters, summer session	Tuition: $20,514
Application Deadline: March 15	Room & Board: $8250
Freshman Class: 2294 applied, 1648 accepted, 479 enrolled	
SAT Verbal/Math: 495/498*	COMPETITIVE

Southern New Hampshire University, founded in 1932, is a private university offering academic programs in business, education, liberal arts, culinary arts, and hospitality, and community economic development. There are 4 undergraduate and 5 graduate schools. In addition to regional accreditation, SNHU has baccalaureate program accreditation with ACBSP and ACF. The library contains 89,349 volumes, 378,160 microform items, and 2200 audio/video tapes/CDs/DVDs, and subscribes to 738 periodicals including electronic. Computerized library services include the card catalog, interlibrary loans, database searching, Internet access, and laptop Internet portals. Special learning facilities include a learning resource center, art gallery, radio station, a center for financial studies, an advertising agency (on campus), an audiovisual studio, a psychology observation lab, a career development center, and an iMAC graphics lab. The 280-acre campus is in a suburban area 55 miles north of Boston. Including any residence halls, there are 28 buildings.

Student Life: 54% of undergraduates are from out of state, mostly the Northeast. Student are from 23 states, 21 foreign countries, and Canada. 83% are from public schools. 80% are white. 41% are Catholic; 28% claim no religious affiliation; 24% Protestant. The average age of freshmen is 19; all undergraduates, 20. 29% do not continue beyond their first year; 52% remain to graduate.

Housing: 1430 students can be accommodated in college housing, which includes single-sex and coed dormitories and on-campus apartments. In addition, there are special-interest houses and a wellness housing area. On-campus housing is guaranteed for all 4 years and is available on a first-come, first-served basis. 74% of students live on campus; of those, 65% remain on campus on weekends. All students may keep cars.

Activities: 4% of men belong to 3 national fraternities; 5% of women belong to 3 local and 1 national sorority. There are 52 groups on campus, including cheerleading, chess, choir, chorus, crew club, dance, debate, drama, ethnic, field hocky, honors, international, model UN, musical theater, newspaper, political, professional, radio and TV, religious, social, social service, student government, and yearbook. Popular campus events include Fall, Winter, and Spring Weekends, International Night, and trips to Italy and Greece.

Sports: There are 8 intercollegiate sports for men and 7 for women, and 18 intramural sports for men and 14 for women. Facilities include 2 gyms, a swimming pool, 4 lighted tennis courts, an artificial surface game field, a fitness room, baseball and softball fields, a natural grass practice field, a racquetball court, and an aerobic room.

Disabled Students: 80% of the campus is accessible. Wheelchair ramps, elevators, special parking, specially equipped rest rooms, special class scheduling, lowered drinking fountains, lowered telephones, special housing, and automatic door openers are available.

Services: Counseling and information services are available, as is tutoring in every subject. There is a reader service for the blind and remedial math and writing. Peer mentoring and structured learning assistance services are also available.

Campus Safety and Security: Measures include 24-hour foot and vehicle patrol, security escort services, informal discussions, and pamphlets/posters/films. There are emergency telephones, lighted pathways/sidewalks, winter driving seminars for international students, and public safety officers.

Programs of Study: SNHU confers B.A., B.S., and B.A.S.H.A. degrees. Associate, master's, and doctoral degrees are also awarded. Bachelor's degrees are awarded in AGRICULTURE (environmental studies), BUSINESS (accounting, business administration and management, fashion merchandising, hospitality management services, hotel/motel and restaurant management, international business management, marketing management, marketing/retailing/merchandising, retailing, sports management, and tourism), COMMUNICATIONS AND THE ARTS (adver-

tising, communications, creative writing, English, English literature, and graphic design), COMPUTER AND PHYSICAL SCIENCE (computer science, digital arts/technology, and information sciences and systems), EDUCATION (business, early childhood, education, elementary, English, marketing and distribution, secondary, social studies, and special), SOCIAL SCIENCE (child psychology/development, culinary arts, history, liberal arts/general studies, political science/government, psychology, public affairs, and social science). Business administration is the strongest academically. Business administration, sports management, and culinary arts are the largest.

Required: To graduate, students must complete a minimum of 120 credit hours, including 39 in their major, with a GPA of 2.0. Distribution requirements total 45 credits from the college core, including 2 to 3 courses in writing, 2 in economics, and 1 in math, information technology, public speaking, statistics, and social science, electives in fine arts, literature, and the social and natural sciences.

Special: Co-op programs and study abroad in England and the Netherlands are strongly promoted. A general business studies degree with 14 different concentrations, work-study programs, dual majors, a 3 year bachelor's degree and an accelerated degree program in business administration are available. There are 5 national honor societies, a freshman honors program, and 1 departmental honors program.

Faculty/Classroom: 59% of faculty are male; 41%, female. 90% teach undergraduates, 78% do research, and 73% do both. No introductory courses are taught by graduate students. The average class size in an introductory lecture is 20; in a laboratory, 15; and in a regular course, 21.

Admissions: 72% of the 2005-2006 applicants were accepted. The SAT scores for the 2005-2006 freshman class were: Verbal--52% below 500, 39% between 500 and 599, 8% between 600 and 700, and 1% above 700; Math--50% below 500, 40% between 500 and 599, and 11% between 600 and 700. The ACT scores were 63% below 21, 14% between 21 and 23, 14% between 24 and 26, 4% between 27 and 28, and 4% above 28. 19% of the current freshmen were in the top fifth of their class; 52% were in the top two fifths.

Requirements: The SAT or ACT is required. The ACT Optional Writing test is also required. In addition, students must have completed 4 years of English and 3 of math. An essay, high school transcript, SAT or ACT (with writing) and a letter of recommendation from a guidance counselor or 2 teachers are required. An interview is strongly recommended. The GED is accepted. A GPA of 2.0 is required. AP and CLEP credits are accepted.

Procedure: Freshmen are admitted fall and spring. There are early admissions, deferred admissions, and rolling admissions plans. Early decision applications should be filed by November 15; regular applications, by March 15 for fall entry and December 1 for spring entry, along with a $35 fee. Notification is sent on a rolling basis. Applications are accepted on-line.

Transfer: 151 transfer students enrolled in 2004-2005. Transfer applicants must submit a completed application, essay, official high school transcript, official college transcripts, supplemental transfer form, and a letter of recommendation. An interview is also highly recommended. Most successful applicants for transfer admission have a cumulative GPA of 2.5 or higher. 30 of 120 credits required for the bachelor's degree must be completed at SNHU.

Visiting: There are regularly scheduled orientations for prospective students, including a greeting from college administrators, campus tours with students, and informal presentation/discussions with faculty, staff, and students. There are guides for informal visits and visitors may sit in on classes. To schedule a visit, contact the Admission Office..

Financial Aid: In 2005-2006, 93% of all full-time freshmen and 92% of continuing full-time students received some form of financial aid. 74% of full-time freshmen and 70% of continuing full-time students received need-based aid. Need-based scholarships or need-based grants averaged $8008 ($16,450 maximum); need-based self-help (loans and jobs) averaged $4555 ($6025 maximum); non-need-based athletic scholarships averaged $11,626 ($30,464 maximum); and other non-need-based awards and non-need-based scholarships averaged $12,406 ($30,199 maximum). The average financial indebtedness of the 2005 graduate was $21,138. SNHU is a member of CSS. The FAFSA is required. The deadline for filing freshman financial aid applications for fall entry is March 15.

International Students: There are 77 international students enrolled. The school actively recruits these students. They must score satisfactorily on the written TOEFL or on the electronic version and also take the MELAB, the Comprehensive English Language Test, or the college's own test.

Computers: Wireless access is available. The university provides over 500 publicly accessible PCs around the main campus and at the continuing education centers, located in general computer labs, specialty computer labs, and in classrooms. All students may use these PCs for Internet and e-mail access. All students may access the system 8 A.M. to 12 P.M. daily; extended hours during final exams. There are no time limits and no fees. It is strongly recommended that all students have a personal computer. It is recommended that students in the School of Business have personal computers. Dell Latitude D610 or D810 are recommended.

Graduates: From July 1, 2004 to June 30, 2005, 985 bachelor's degrees were awarded. The most popular majors were business administration (47%), hotel and restaurant management (9%), and accounting (8%). In an average class, 34% graduate in 4 years or less, 49% graduate in 5 years or less, and 52% graduate in 6 years or less. 75 companies recruited on campus in 2004-2005. Of the 2004 graduating class, 88% were employed within 6 months of graduation.

Admissions Contact: Steven Soba, Director of Admission. A video is available. E-mail: *admission@snhu.edu* Web: *www.snhu.edu*

THOMAS MORE COLLEGE OF LIBERAL ARTS   D-6

Merrimack, NH 03054   (603) 880-8308
                                        (800) 880-8308; Fax: (603) 880-9280

Full-time: 40 men, 30 women	**Faculty:** 5
Part-time: none	**Ph.D.s:** 100%
Graduate: none	**Student/Faculty:** 14 to 1
Year: semesters	**Tuition:** $10,000
Application Deadline: open	**Room & Board:** $7700
Freshman Class: n/av	
SAT or ACT: required	**COMPETITIVE**

Thomas More College of Liberal Arts, founded in 1978 by Roman Catholic educators, is an undergraduate institution. Figures in the above capsule and in this profile are approximate. In addition to regional accreditation, TMC has baccalaureate program accreditation with AALE. The library contains 50,000 volumes and subscribes to 20 periodicals including electronic. The 12-acre campus is in a suburban area between Nashua and Manchester, 40 miles north of Boston. Including any residence halls, there are 5 buildings.

Student Life: 81% of undergraduates are from out of state, mostly the Northeast. Students are from 20 states, 2 foreign countries, and Canada. 84% are white. The average age of freshmen is 18; all undergraduates, 20. 9% do not continue beyond their first year.

Housing: College housing includes single-sex dormitories. On-campus housing is guaranteed for all 4 years. All of students commute. Alcohol is not permitted. All students may keep cars.

Activities: There are no fraternities or sororities.

Disabled Students: 70% of the campus is accessible. Wheelchair ramps, special parking, and specially equipped rest rooms are available.

Services: Informal tutoring is available by request.

Campus Safety and Security: Measures include security escort services, informal discussions, and lighted pathways/sidewalks.

Programs of Study: TMC confers the B.A. degree. Bachelor's degrees are awarded in BIOLOGICAL SCIENCE (biology/biological science), COMMUNICATIONS AND THE ARTS (literature), SOCIAL SCIENCE (philosophy and political science/government).

Required: To graduate, students must complete 120 credit hours (125 for biology majors), including 48 in humanities, 12 in writing workshop, 12 in classical languages, 12 in math and science, 6 in theology, and 3 in fine arts. At least 24 hours (32 for biology majors) in the major are required. In addition, students must complete a junior project of independent study and a senior thesis.

Special: A semester in Rome for sophomores is required unless waived.

Faculty/Classroom: 80% of faculty are male; 20%, female. All teach undergraduates, and 80% do research.

Requirements: The SAT or ACT is required. In addition, applicants should be high school graduates with 4 college preparatory units of English, 3 of math, and 2 each of foreign language, social science, and lab science. The GED is accepted. An essay and 2 letters of recommendation are required. An interview is strongly recommended. Important factors in the admissions decision are personality/intangible qualities, evidence of special talent, and leadership record.

Procedure: Freshmen are admitted fall and spring. There is a rolling admissions plan. Application deadlines are open. The fall 2005 application fee was$25. Applications are accepted on-line.

Transfer: Applicants must submit a transcript from all higher institutions attended.

Visiting: There are guides for informal visits and visitors may sit in on classes and stay overnight. To schedule a visit, contact Kristen S. Kelly, Director of Admissions.

Financial Aid: In a recent year, 80% of all full-time freshmen and 90% of continuing full-time students received some form of financial aid. 65% of full-time freshmen and 77% of continuing full-time students received need-based aid. The average freshman award was $8768. 59% of undergraduates work part time. Average annual earnings from campus work are $1960. The average financial indebtedness of a recent graduate was $13,056. TMC is a member of CSS. The FAFSA is required. Check with the school for current deadlines.

International Students: There were 2 international students enrolled in a recent year. The school actively recruits these students. .

Computers: All students may access the system durning library hours. There are no time limits and no fees.

Admissions Contact: Kristen S. Kelly, Director of Admissions.
E-mail: *admissions@thomasmorecolege.edu*
Web: *www.thomasmorecolege.edu*

UNIVERSITY OF NEW HAMPSHIRE   E-5

Durham, NH 03824   (603) 862-1360; Fax: (603) 862-0077

Full-time: 4677 men, 6131 women	**Faculty:** 503; I, av$
Part-time: 110 men, 165 women	**Ph.D.s:** 91%
Graduate: 992 men, 1489 women	**Student/Faculty:** 21 to 1
Year: semesters, summer session	**Tuition:** $9778 ($21,498)
Application Deadline: February 1	**Room & Board:** $7032
Freshman Class: 12,310 applied, 8804 accepted, 2624 enrolled	
SAT Verbal/Math: 560/570*	**VERY COMPETITIVE**

The University of New Hampshire, founded in 1866, is part of the public university system of New Hampshire and offers degree programs in liberal arts, engineering, physical sciences, business, economics, life sciences, agriculture, and health and human services. There are 6 undergraduate schools and 1 graduate school. In addition to regional accreditation, UNH has baccalaureate program accreditation with AACSB, ABET, ADA, AHEA, CAAHEP, CAHEA, CCNE, CSAB, CSWE, NASM, NLN, NRPA, and SAF. The 5 libraries contain 1,795,812 volumes, 3,009,753 microform items, and 38,601 audio/video tapes/CDs/DVDs, and subscribe to 33,924 periodicals including electronic. Computerized library services include the card catalog, interlibrary loans, database searching, and Internet access. Special learning facilities include a learning resource center, art gallery, radio station, TV station, optical observatory, marine research laboratory, experiential learning center, electron microscope, child development center, journalism laboratory, various agricultural and equine facilities, sawmill, and language lab. The 2600-acre campus is in a rural area 50 miles north of Boston. Including any residence halls, there are 150 buildings.

Student Life: 57% of undergraduates are from New Hampshire. Others are from 44 states, 26 foreign countries, and Canada. 75% are from public schools. 86% are white. 33% are Catholic; 31% claim no religious affiliation; 22% Protestant. The average age of freshmen is 18; all undergraduates, 20. 14% do not continue beyond their first year; 72% remain to graduate.

Housing: 5900 students can be accommodated in college housing, which includes single-sex and coed dormitories, on-campus apartments, and married-student housing. In addition, there are honors houses, language houses, special-interest houses, and international and substance-free residence halls. On-campus housing is available on a first-come, first-served basis. 57% of students live on campus; of those, 65% remain on campus on weekends. Upperclassmen may keep cars.

Activities: 4% of men belong to 1 local and 8 national fraternities; 5% of women belong to 5 national sororities. There are 200 groups on campus, including art, band, cheerleading, chess, choir, chorale, chorus, computers, dance, debate, drama, ethnic, film, gay, honors, international, jazz band, literary magazine, marching band, musical theater, newspaper, orchestra, pep band, photography, political, professional, radio and TV, religious, social, social service, student government, and symphony. Popular campus events include International Day, concert and lecture series, and Winter Carnival.

Sports: There are 10 intercollegiate sports for men and 14 for women, and 22 intramural sports for men and 23 for women. Facilities include indoor and outdoor swimming pools, tracks, tennis courts, gyms, wrestling and gymnastics rooms, a dance studio, playing fields, an indoor ice rink, and cross-country ski trails. A 3-story recreation and sports complex which seats 6500 for hockey and 7500 for basketball games and special events, includes a fitness center, jogging track, a weight room, racquetball courts, an international squash court, aerobics and martial arts studios, multipurpose courts, and basketball courts.

Disabled Students: 80% of the campus is accessible. Wheelchair ramps, elevators, special parking, specially equipped rest rooms, special class scheduling, lowered drinking fountains, lowered telephones and special housing are available. Accommodations made on a case-by-case basis include sign language interpreters, reduced course loads, extended exam time, accessible transportation, academic modifications, note takers, text on tape, and note takers are available.

Services: Counseling and information services are available.. Instruction in learning strategies, study skills, time management, and organizational skills is available. The university writing center offers free assistance by trained consultants.

Campus Safety and Security: Measures include 24-hour foot and vehicle patrol, self-defense education, security escort services, and shuttle buses. There are informal discussions, pamphlets/posters/films, emergency telephones, lighted pathways/sidewalks, and limited access to dorms, and prevention awareness programs.

Programs of Study: UNH confers B.A., B.S., B.F.A., B.M., and B.S.F. degrees. Associate, master's, and doctoral degrees are also awarded. Bachelor's degrees are awarded in AGRICULTURE (animal science, dairy science, environmental studies, forestry and related sciences, horticulture, plant science, soil science, and wildlife management), BIOLOGI-

CAL SCIENCE (biochemistry, biology/biological science, microbiology, nutrition, and zoology), BUSINESS (business administration and management, hospitality management services, hotel/motel and restaurant management, recreation and leisure services, and tourism), COMMUNICATIONS AND THE ARTS (art history and appreciation, classics, communications, dramatic arts, English, English literature, fine arts, French, German, Greek, Latin, linguistics, music, music history and appreciation, music performance, music theory and composition, Russian, Spanish, studio art, and voice), COMPUTER AND PHYSICAL SCIENCE (chemistry, computer science, earth science, geology, mathematics, and physics), EDUCATION (athletic training, English, environmental, mathematics, music, physical, recreation, and science), ENGINEERING AND ENVIRONMENTAL DESIGN (chemical engineering, city/community/regional planning, civil engineering, computer engineering, electrical/electronics engineering, environmental engineering, environmental science, and mechanical engineering), HEALTH PROFESSIONS (health care administration, medical laboratory science, nursing, occupational therapy, preveterinary science, and speech pathology/audiology), SOCIAL SCIENCE (anthropology, economics, European studies, family/consumer studies, French studies, geography, history, humanities, law enforcement and corrections, philosophy, physical fitness/movement, political science/government, psychology, social work, sociology, water resources, and women's studies). College of Engineering and Physical Science are the strongest academically. Business administration, English, and psychology are the largest.

Required: To graduate, all students must maintain a GPA of 2.0 and complete at least 128 credits, with a minimum of 36 credits and 10 classes in the major. General education requirements include 4 writing-intensive courses, including freshman composition; 3 courses each in quantitative reasoning and science; and 1 course each in historical perspectives, social science, fine arts, foreign culture, and philosophy/literature. Honors students and most seniors write a thesis or complete a project.

Special: Joint programs with Cornell University in marine science are available. Extensive cross-registration is possible through the New Hampshire College and University Council Consortium. There also is nationwide study through the National Student Exchange and worldwide study through the Center for International Education. Internships, study abroad throughout the world, a Washington semester, work-study, and B.A.-B.S. degrees, dual majors, a general studies degree, student-designed majors, extensive 3-2 B.S./M.B.A. programs and other bachelor's/graduate degree plans, nondegree study, and pass/fail options are also available. A 3-2 engineering degree is offered with the New Hampshire Technical Institute, Vermont Technical College, and Keene State College, and other institutions. There are 18 national honor societies, including Phi Beta Kappa, a freshman honors program, and 41 departmental honors programs.

Faculty/Classroom: 62% of faculty are male; 38%, female. All both teach and do research. Graduate students teach 2% of introductory courses. The average class size in an introductory lecture is 39; in a laboratory, 18; and in a regular course, 16.

Admissions: 72% of the 2005-2006 applicants were accepted. The SAT scores for the 2005-2006 freshman class were: Verbal--21% below 500, 51% between 500 and 599, 25% between 600 and 700, and 3% above 700; Math--18% below 500, 49% between 500 and 599, 29% between 600 and 700, and 4% above 700. 47% of the current freshmen were in the top fifth of their class; 89% were in the top two fifths. 40 freshmen graduated first in their class.

Requirements: The SAT or ACT is required. The ACT Optional Writing test is also required. In addition, applicants should have 18 academic credits, including 4 each in English and math, 3 each in science and foreign language and 2 in social studies. An essay is required for all students. An audition is required for music students. AP and CLEP credits are accepted. Important factors in the admissions decision are advanced placement or honor courses, recommendations by school officials, and evidence of special talent.

Procedure: Freshmen are admitted fall and spring. Entrance exams should be taken before February 1 of the senior year. There is a deferred admissions plan. Applications should be filed by February 1 for fall entry and November 1 for spring entry, along with a $45 fee. Notification is sent April 15. Applications are accepted on-line.

Transfer: 439 transfer students enrolled in 2004-2005. Applicants must submit an overall minimum GPA of 2.8 and 3.0 in a general education curriculum. The SAT or the ACT is required unless waived. An essay is required. A letter of recommendation is optional. 32 of 128 credits required for the bachelor's degree must be completed at UNH.

Visiting: There are regularly scheduled orientations for prospective students, including campus tours, a group information session, and open house programs. Visitors may sit in on classes. To schedule a visit, contact the Admissions Office .

Financial Aid: In 2004-2005, 84% of all full-time freshmen and 76% of continuing full-time students received some form of financial aid. 57% of full-time freshmen and 64% of continuing full-time students received need-based aid. The average freshman award was $15,275. Need-based scholarships or need-based grants averaged $2708 ($8656 maximum); need-based self-help aid (loans and jobs) averaged $2163 ($6625 maximum); non-need-based athletic scholarships averaged $7381 ($28,462 maximum); and other non-need-based awards and non-need-based scholarships averaged $4164. 31% of undergraduates work part time. Average annual earnings from campus work are $1763. The average financial indebtedness of the 2005 graduate was $21,459. The FAFSA and are required. The priority date for freshman financial aid applications for fall entry is March 1.

International Students: There are 66 international students enrolled. The school actively recruits these students. They must score satisfactorily on the written TOEFL or on the electronic version and also take the SAT, or the ACT.

Computers: Wireless access is available. Students can access the system from residence halls, PC clusters, and classrooms, as well as the student union. All students may access the system. There are no time limits and no fees.

Graduates: From July 1, 2004 to June 30, 2005, 2293 bachelor's degrees were awarded. The most popular majors were business administration (10%), psychology (8%), and english (6%). In an average class, 54% graduate in 4 years or less, 68% graduate in 5 years or less, and 71% graduate in 6 years or less. More than 250 companies recruited on campus in 2004-2005.

Admissions Contact: Robert McGann, Director, Admissions.
E-mail: admissions@unh.edu Web: www.unh.edu/admissions/

UNIVERSITY SYSTEM OF NEW HAMPSHIRE

The University System of New Hampshire (USNH), established in 1963, is a public system in New Hampshire. It is governed by a board of trustees, whose chief administrator is the chancellor. The system includes the University of New Hampshire, Plymouth State University, Keene State College, and Granite State College. The primary goal of USNH is to serve the higher educational needs of the people of New Hampshire. The main priorities are to provide a well-coordinated system of higher education, student access and diversity, and quality programs through a commitment to excellence. The total enrollment of all 4 institutions is just under 30,000; there are more than 1080 faculty members. Altogether there are 181 baccalaureate, 80 master's, and 21 doctoral programs offered through USNH institutions. 4-year residential campuses are located in Durham, Keene, and Plymouth. Profiles of the 4-year campuses are included in this section. USNH can be found online at www.usnh.unh.edu.

NEW JERSEY

POPULATION DENSITY

• 10,000 and over

0 10 20 30 40
Miles

and cultural events (including musical events, lectures, speakers, film festivals, and theatrical events).

Sports: There are 4 intercollegiate sports for men and 4 for women, and 3 intramural sports for men and 3 for women. Facilities include a 500-seat gym, weight-lifting facilities, and a basketball and volleyball court.

Disabled Students: 39% of the campus is accessible. Wheelchair ramps, elevators, special parking, specially equipped rest rooms, lowered drinking fountains, lowered telephones, lower fire stations, ADA signage, and lever handles for classroom access are available.

Services: Counseling and information services are available, as is tutoring in most subjects. There is a reader service for the blind, and remedial math, reading, and writing.

Campus Safety and Security: Measures include 24-hour foot and vehicle patrol, security escort services, informal discussions, and pamphlets/posters/films. There are emergency telephones, and lighted pathways/sidewalks. Security cameras are installed in all high-traffic areas.

Programs of Study: Bloomfield confers B.A. and B.S. degrees. Bachelor's degrees are awarded in BIOLOGICAL SCIENCE (biology/biological science), BUSINESS (accounting and business administration and management), COMMUNICATIONS AND THE ARTS (English and fine arts), COMPUTER AND PHYSICAL SCIENCE (applied mathematics, chemistry, and information sciences and systems), EDUCATION (education), ENGINEERING AND ENVIRONMENTAL DESIGN (graphic arts technology), HEALTH PROFESSIONS (allied health, clinical science, and nursing), SOCIAL SCIENCE (history, philosophy, political science/government, psychology, religion, and sociology). Nursing is the strongest academically. Business, education, and sociology are the largest.

Required: All students must complete a common core, meet general education requirements, and maintain a 2.0 GPA. At least 33 course units are required for graduation.

Special: Co-op programs, internships, study abroad, and work-study programs are available. Double majors and contract majors are also possible. There are 4 national honor societies and a freshman honors program. All departments have honors programs.

Faculty/Classroom: 44% of faculty are male; 56%, female. All teach undergraduates. The average class size in an introductory lecture is 15; in a laboratory, 14; and in a regular course, 15.

Admissions: 5% of the current freshmen were in the top fifth of their class; 25% were in the top two fifths.

Requirements: The SAT or ACT is required. In addition, the college requires at least 14 academic units, which should include English, math, history, and lab science. An essay and 2 personal recommendations are required. A GPA of 2.8 is required. AP and CLEP credits are accepted. Important factors in the admissions decision are advanced placement or honor courses, recommendations by school officials, and extracurricular activities record.

Procedure: Freshmen are admitted to all sessions. Entrance exams should be taken during the senior year. There is a deferred admissions plan and a rolling admissions plan. Applications should be filed by March 14 for fall entry and December 1 for spring entry. Notification is sent on a rolling basis. Applications are accepted on-line. The fall 2004 application fee was $35.

Transfer: 362 transfer students enrolled in 2004-2005. Applicants must present a minimum GPA of 2.0 from an accredited institution and submit official transcripts from all previously attended colleges. 32 of 132 credits required for the bachelor's degree must be completed at Bloomfield.

Visiting: There are regularly scheduled orientations for prospective students, consisting of a campus tour, an admissions interview, and other activities by request. There are guides for informal visits and visitors may sit in on classes. To schedule a visit, contact the Office of Admissions at (973) 748-9000, ext. 230.

Financial Aid: In 2005-2006, 96% of all full-time freshmen and 80% of continuing full-time students received some form of financial aid. 93% of full-time freshmen and 79% of continuing full-time students received need-based aid. The average freshman award was $16,368. Need-based scholarships or need-based grants averaged $11,706 ($18,550 maximum); need-based self-help aid (loans and jobs) averaged $5558 ($21,848 maximum); non-need-based athletic scholarships averaged $6470 ($23,000 maximum); and other non-need-based awards and non-need-based scholarships averaged $4605 ($17,303 maximum). 8% of undergraduates work part time. Average annual earnings from campus work are $1800. The FAFSA is required. The priority date for freshman financial aid applications for fall entry is March 15. The deadline for filing freshman financial aid applications for fall entry is October 1.

International Students: There are 43 international students enrolled. The school actively recruits these students. They must take the TOEFL and also take the SAT.

BLOOMFIELD COLLEGE | E-2

Bloomfield, NJ 07003

(973) 748-9000, ext. 392
(800) 848-4555; Fax: (973) 748-0916

Full-time: 580 men, 1141 women	**Faculty:** 62; IIB, +$
Part-time: 110 men, 381 women	**Ph.D.s:** 77%
Graduate: none	**Student/Faculty:** 28 to 1
Year: semesters, summer session	**Tuition:** $15,100
Application Deadline: March 14	**Room & Board:** $7400
Freshman Class: n/av	
SAT or ACT: required	**LESS COMPETITIVE**

Bloomfield College, founded in 1868 and affiliated with the Presbyterian Church (U.S.A.), is an independent institution offering programs in liberal arts and sciences, creative arts and technology, professional studies, and the clinical and health sciences. In addition to regional accreditation, Bloomfield has baccalaureate program accreditation with CCNE and NLN. The library contains 64,700 volumes, 59 microform items, and 1437 audio/video tapes/CDs/DVDs. Computerized library services include interlibrary loans, database searching, Internet access, and laptop Internet portals. Special learning facilities include a learning resource center, art gallery, electronic classrooms, and Web-based radio station. The 12-acre campus is in a suburban area 15 miles from New York City. Including any residence halls, there are 52 buildings.

Student Life: 96% of undergraduates are from New Jersey. Others are from 15 states and 3 foreign countries. 67% are from public schools. 52% are African American; 18% Hispanic; 16% white. The average age of freshmen is 20; all undergraduates, 26. 36% do not continue beyond their first year; 27% remain to graduate.

Housing: 346 students can be accommodated in college housing, which includes single-sex and coed dorms, fraternity houses, and sorority houses. In addition, there are honors houses and special-interest houses. On-campus housing is available on a first-come, first-served basis. Priority is given to out-of-town students. 88% of students commute. All students may keep cars.

Activities: 1% of men belong to 2 national fraternities; 1% of women belong to 3 national sororities. There are 35 groups on campus, including art, choir, dance, DEEP retreat, drama, ethnic, film, gay, honors, international, literary magazine, musical theater, professional, religious, social, social service, STEP retreat, student government, and yearbook. Popular campus events include formal dinners, multicultural festivals,

Computers: Wireless access is available through labs, dorms, and the library. All students may access the system. There are no time limits and no fees.

Graduates: From July 1, 2004 to June 30, 2005, 144 bachelor's degrees were awarded. The most popular majors were business administration (26%), sociology (15%), and nursing (15%). In an average class, 9% graduate in 4 years or less, 24% graduate in 5 years or less, and 27% graduate in 6 years or less. 37 companies recruited on campus in 2004-2005. Of the 2004 graduating class, 12% were enrolled in graduate school within 6 months of graduation and 63% were employed.

Admissions Contact: Lourdes Delgado, Dean of Admissions. E-mail: *admission@bloomfield.edu* Web: *http://www.bloomfield.edu*

CALDWELL COLLEGE   E-2

Caldwell, NJ 07006   **(973) 618-3000**
                                        (888) 864-9516; Fax: (973) 618-3600

Full-time: 373 men, 692 women	**Faculty:** 79; IIB, av$
Part-time: 161 men, 458 women	**Ph.D.s:** 81%
Graduate: 108 men, 450 women	**Student/Faculty:** 13 to 1
Year: semesters, summer session	**Tuition:** $18,800
Application Deadline: open	**Room & Board:** $7650
Freshman Class: 1234 applied, 960 accepted, 298 enrolled	
SAT Verbal/Math: 460/450*	**LESS COMPETITIVE**

Caldwell College, founded in 1939, is a private school offering programs in liberal arts, science, business, fine arts, and education. It is affiliated with the Roman Catholic Church. In addition to regional accreditation, Caldwell has baccalaureate program accreditation with TEAC. The library contains 144,909 volumes, 6228 microform items, and 2112 audio/video tapes/CDs/DVDs, and subscribes to 370 periodicals including electronic. Computerized library services include the card catalog, interlibrary loans, database searching, and Internet access. Special learning facilities include a learning resource center and art gallery. The 80-acre campus is in a suburban area 20 miles west of New York City. Including any residence halls, there are 9 buildings.

Student Life: 87% of undergraduates are from New Jersey. Others are from 14 states, 31 foreign countries, and Canada. 75% are from public schools. 68% are white; 13% African American. The average age of freshmen is 18; all undergraduates, 34. 27% do not continue beyond their first year; 56% remain to graduate.

Housing: 380 students can be accommodated in college housing, which includes coed dorms. On-campus housing is guaranteed for all 4 years. 61% of students commute. All students may keep cars.

Activities: There are no fraternities or sororities. There are 21 groups on campus, including art, band, cheerleading, choir, ethnic, honors, international, literary magazine, newspaper, orchestra, professional, religious, social, social service, student government, and yearbook. Popular campus events include Founders Day, Freshman Investiture, and Fall Festival.

Sports: There are 5 intercollegiate sports for men and 5 for women, and 4 intramural sports for men and 4 for women. Facilities include a multipurpose gym, a training room, tennis courts, weight rooms, playing fields, and a pool.

Disabled Students: 85% of the campus is accessible. Wheelchair ramps, elevators, special parking, specially equipped rest rooms, special class scheduling, lowered drinking fountains, and lowered telephones are available.

Services: Counseling and information services are available, as is tutoring in most subjects. There is a reader service for the blind, and remedial math, reading, and writing, and a writing lab.

Campus Safety and Security: Measures include 24-hour foot and vehicle patrol, self-defense education, security escort services, and informal discussions. There are pamphlets/posters/films, emergency telephones, and lighted pathways/sidewalks.

Programs of Study: Caldwell confers B.A., B.S., and B.F.A. degrees. Master's degrees are also awarded. Bachelor's degrees are awarded in BIOLOGICAL SCIENCE (biology/biological science), BUSINESS (accounting, business administration and management, international business management, management science, and marketing and distribution), COMMUNICATIONS AND THE ARTS (art, communications, English, fine arts, French, music, Spanish, and studio art), COMPUTER AND PHYSICAL SCIENCE (chemistry, computer management, computer science, information sciences and systems, and mathematics), EDUCATION (elementary), HEALTH PROFESSIONS (medical laboratory technology), SOCIAL SCIENCE (criminal justice, history, political science/government, psychology, social studies, sociology, and theological studies). Liberal arts, education, and sciences are the strongest academically. Business, education, and psychology are the largest.

Required: Students must maintain a minimum GPA of 2.0 while taking 120 credit hours, including a minimum of 30 in the major. The 55-credit core includes 15 credits in religion/philosophy, 6 each in history, English, language, social science, math and computer science, and fine arts, and 2 in communication arts. Students must participate in an outcome as-

sessment that is unique for each department. It is a comprehensive exam for some.

Special: Caldwell offers co-op and internship programs in all majors; study abroad in 6 countries; a Washington semester; 1-semester internships; and work-study with Dominican Adult Day Care, Hill Top Day Care, and Family and Child Services of North Essex. B.A.-B.S. degrees in 29 fields, dual majors in all majors, credit for life experience in adult education, nondegree study, student-designed majors, and pass/fail options are possible. The Continuing Education Program offers adults (23 years or older) a chance to complete degree requirements in the evening and Saturdays, and the External Degree Program gives adults an opportunity to earn a degree without attending on-campus classes. There are 15 national honor societies, a freshman honors program.

Faculty/Classroom: 49% of faculty are male; 51%, female. 89% teach undergraduates. No introductory courses are taught by graduate students. The average class size in an introductory lecture is 15; in a laboratory, 13; and in a regular course, 12.

Admissions: 78% of the 2005-2006 applicants were accepted. The SAT scores for the 2005-2006 freshman class were: Verbal--65% below 500, 27% between 500 and 599, and 8% between 600 and 700; Math--67% below 500, 23% between 500 and 599, 9% between 600 and 700, and 1% above 700.

Requirements: The SAT is required. In addition, applicants need 16 academic credits or 16 Carnegie units, including 4 years in English, 2 each in foreign language, math, and science, and 1 in history. A written recommendation from a high school counselor is required. A portfolio, audition, and interview are recommended, depending on the field of study. The GED is accepted. A GPA of 2.0 is required. AP and CLEP credits are accepted. Important factors in the admissions decision are advanced placement or honor courses, leadership record, and recommendations by school officials.

Procedure: Freshmen are admitted to all sessions. Entrance exams should be taken in fall of the senior year. There are early admissions and rolling admissions plans. Application deadlines are open. Application fee is $40. Applications are accepted on-line.

Transfer: 28 transfer students enrolled in 2004-2005. Transfer students must have a minimum GPA of 2.0 (2.5 in teacher education) and 12 transferable credits. 45 of 120 credits required for the bachelor's degree must be completed at Caldwell.

Visiting: There are regularly scheduled orientations for prospective students, including a brief presentation by faculty and students, followed by a tour. There are guides for informal visits and visitors may sit in on classes and stay overnight. To schedule a visit, contact the Admissions Office.

Financial Aid: In 2005-2006, 83% of all full-time freshmen and 79% of continuing full-time students received some form of financial aid. 65% of full-time freshmen and 60% of continuing full-time students received need-based aid. The average freshman award was $13,750. Need-based scholarships or need-based grants averaged $3279 ($8820 maximum); need-based self-help aid (loans and jobs) averaged $2123 ($3500 maximum); non-need-based athletic scholarships averaged $5383 ($14,000 maximum); and other non-need-based awards and non-need-based scholarships averaged $6281 ($26,500 maximum). 36% of undergraduates work part time. Average annual earnings from campus work were $850. The average financial indebtedness of the 2005 graduate was $13,500. The FAFSA and the college's own financial statement are required. The priority date for freshman financial aid applications for fall entry is June 1.

International Students: There are 80 international students enrolled. The school actively recruits these students. A satisfactory score is required on the written TOEFL.

Computers: All students may access the system Monday to Thursday 9 A.M. to 9:30 P.M., Friday 10:30 A.M. to 4 P.M., and weekends, 12 P.M. to 5 P.M. There are no time limits and no fees.

Graduates: From July 1, 2004 to June 30, 2005, 322 bachelor's degrees were awarded. The most popular majors were psychology (20%), business administration (13%), and criminal justice (9%). In an average class, 1% graduate in 3 years, 35% graduate in 4 years, 51% graduate in 5 years, and 47% graduate in 6 years.

Admissions Contact: Kathryn Reilly, Director of Admissions. A video is available. E-mail: *admissions@caldwell.edu* Web: *www.caldwell.edu*

CENTENARY COLLEGE
Hackettstown, NJ 07840

C-2

(908) 852-1400
(800) 236-8679; Fax: (908) 852-3454

Full-time: 593 men, 1024 women	Faculty: 63
Part-time: 92 men, 178 women	Ph.D.s: 67%
Graduate: 214 men, 371 women	Student/Faculty: 26 to 1
Year: semesters, summer session	Tuition: $20,970
Application Deadline: open	Room & Board: $7900
Freshman Class: 652 applied, 564 accepted, 266 enrolled	
SAT Verbal/Math: 460/460*	ACT: 19 LESS COMPETITIVE

Centenary College, founded in 1867, is a private institution affiliated with the United Methodist Church. The college offers undergraduate and graduate programs in liberal arts, business, international studies, education, equine studies, fashion, and fine arts. In addition to regional accreditation, Centenary has baccalaureate program accreditation with NASDTEC. The library contains 68,000 volumes, 20,000 microform items, and 5000 audio/video tapes/CDs/DVDs, and subscribes to 375 periodicals including electronic. Computerized library services include the card catalog, interlibrary loans, database searching, and Internet access. Special learning facilities include a learning resource center, art gallery, radio station, TV station, an equestrian center, a CAD lab, and a wireless network. The 42-acre campus is in a suburban area 55 miles west of New York City. Including any residence halls, there are 14 buildings.

Student Life: 85% of undergraduates are from New Jersey. Students are from 19 states, 14 foreign countries, and Canada. 78% are from public schools. 53% are white. The average age of freshmen is 18; all undergraduates, 24. 27% do not continue beyond their first year; 33% remain to graduate.

Housing: 620 students can be accommodated in college housing, which includes single-sex and coed dorms and on-campus apartments. On-campus housing is available on a first-come, first-served basis and is available on a lottery system for upperclassmen. 59% of students live on campus; of those, 50% remain on campus on weekends. All students may keep cars.

Activities: 20% of men belong to 1 local fraternity; 60% of women belong to 3 local sororities. There are 27 groups on campus, including art, cheerleading, chorus, dance, drama, ethnic, honors, international, literary magazine, newspaper, photography, professional, radio and TV, religious, social, social service, student government, and yearbook. Popular campus events include Presidents Ball and Community Plunge.

Sports: There are 7 intercollegiate sports for men and 7 for women. Facilities include a gym, a fitness center and indoor pool, tennis courts, playing fields, and an equine center and stables.

Disabled Students: 50% of the campus is accessible. Wheelchair ramps, special parking, specially equipped rest rooms, special class scheduling, and lowered telephones are available.

Services: Counseling and information services are available, as is tutoring in some subjects, including as requested. There is remedial math, reading, and writing. Learning associates provide personalized subject matter support.

Campus Safety and Security: Measures include security escort services, informal discussions, pamphlets/posters/films, and lighted pathways/sidewalks.

Programs of Study: Centenary confers B.A., B.S., and B.F.A. degrees. Associate and master's degrees are also awarded. Bachelor's degrees are awarded in AGRICULTURE (equine science), BIOLOGICAL SCIENCE (biology/biological science), BUSINESS (accounting and business administration and management), COMMUNICATIONS AND THE ARTS (applied art, communications, dramatic arts, and English), COMPUTER AND PHYSICAL SCIENCE (mathematics), EDUCATION (elementary and secondary), SOCIAL SCIENCE (criminal justice, fashion design and technology, history, interdisciplinary studies, international studies, political science/government, psychology, and sociology). Equine studies, business, and education certification are the strongest academically.

Required: Students must complete a distribution of 40 to 46 semester hours in core courses, including college seminars, and 9 credits in liberal arts studies, as well as the required number of credits, usually 48, for their major. At least 128 semester hours and a minimum GPA of 2.0 are needed to earn the bachelor's degree.

Special: Centenary offers internships in every major. The college offers study abroad in England and other countries, dual majors, as long as they are covered under the same degree, an accelerated degree program in liberal arts and bsuiness administration, student-designed majors, work-study on-campus, and a pass/fail option. Students aged 25 or older may earn life experience credits. There is 1 national honor society and a freshman honors program.

Faculty/Classroom: 58% of faculty are male; 42%, female. All both teach and do research. No introductory courses are taught by graduate students. The average class size in an introductory lecture is 25; in a laboratory, 20; and in a regular course, 15.

Admissions: 87% of the 2005-2006 applicants were accepted. The SAT scores for the 2005-2006 freshman class were: Verbal--68% below 500, 28% between 500 and 599, 3% between 600 and 700, and 1% above 700; Math--86% below 500, 13% between 500 and 599, and 1% between 600 and 700. The ACT scores were 10% below 21. 30% of the current freshmen were in the top fifth of their class; 53% were in the top two fifths. 1 freshman graduated first in the class.

Requirements: A satisfactory score on the SAT or ACT is required. Applicants must be graduates of accredited secondary schools or have earned a GED. Centenary requires 16 academic credits or Carnegie units, based on 4 years of English, math, and science, and 2 years each of foreign language and history. An essay is required for freshmen, and an interview is recommended. Applicants to specific fine arts programs must also submit a portfolio. AP and CLEP credits are accepted. Important factors in the admissions decision are advanced placement or honor courses, leadership record, and ability to finance college education.

Procedure: Freshmen are admitted fall and spring. Entrance exams should be taken as early as possible in the senior year. There are early admissions, deferred admissions, and rolling admissions plans. Application deadlines are open. Application fee is $30. Notification is sent on a rolling basis. Applications are accepted on-line.

Transfer: 114 transfer students enrolled in a recent year. Applicants must have a minimum college GPA of 2.0 and submit proof of high school graduation or the equivalent. 32 of 128 credits required for the bachelor's degree must be completed at Centenary.

Visiting: There are regularly scheduled orientations for prospective students, including basic skills testing, advising, registration, and social events. Visitors may sit in on classes and stay overnight. To schedule a visit, contact the Admissions Office.

Financial Aid: In a recent year, 89% of all full-time freshmen and 86% of continuing full-time students received some form of financial aid. 66% of full-time freshmen and 68% of continuing full-time students received need-based aid. The average freshman award was $15,817. 75% of undergraduates work part time. Average annual earnings from campus work are $1200. The average financial indebtedness of the 2005 graduate was $20,383. The FAFSA and other forms as requested are required. The priority date for freshman financial aid applications for fall entry is March 15. The deadline for filing freshman financial aid applications for fall entry is September 1.

International Students: There were 90 international students enrolled in a recent year. The school actively recruits these students. A satisfactory score is required on the written TOEFL. Students must also take the SAT or the ACT.

Computers: All students may access the system. Computer and CAD lab use depends on lab hours. The fee is $400 annually.

Graduates: From July 1, 2004 to June 30, 2005, 322 bachelor's degrees were awarded. The most popular majors were business administration (54%), social sciences (11%), and equine (9%). In an average class, 32% graduate in 6 years or less. 35 companies recruited on campus in 2004-2005. Of the 2004 graduating class, 11% were enrolled in graduate school within 6 months of graduation and 72% were employed.

Admissions Contact: Glenna Warren, Dean of Admissions.
E-mail: *admissions@centenarycollege.edu* Web: *centenarycollege.edu*

COLLEGE OF NEW JERSEY, THE
Ewing, NJ 08628-0718

D-3

(609) 771-2131
(800) 624-0967; Fax: (609) 637-5174

Full-time: 2432 men, 3293 women	Faculty: 331; IIA, +$
Part-time: 63 men, 107 women	Ph.D.s: 90%
Graduate: 180 men, 693 women	Student/Faculty: 17 to 1
Year: semesters	Tuition: $9857 ($15,120)
Application Deadline: February 15	Room & Board: $8458
Freshman Class: 7300 applied, 3289 accepted, 1236 enrolled	
SAT Verbal/Math: 630/650*	MOST COMPETITIVE

The College of New Jersey, founded in 1855, is a public institution offering programs in the liberal arts, sciences, business, engineering, nursing, and education. There are 7 undergraduate schools and 1 graduate school. In addition to regional accreditation, TCNJ has baccalaureate program accreditation with AACSB, ABET, CSAB, NASDTEC, NASM, NCATE, and NLN. The library contains 572,582 volumes, 397,104 microform items, and 24,084 audio/video tapes/CDs/DVDs, and subscribes to 19,450 periodicals including electronic. Computerized library services include interlibrary loans, database searching, Internet access, and laptop Internet portals. Special learning facilities include a learning resource center, art gallery, planetarium, radio station, TV station, an electron microscopy lab, a nuclear magnetic resonance lab, and a greenhouse. The 289-acre campus is in a suburban area between Princeton and Trenton, NJ. Including any residence halls, there are 38 buildings.

Student Life: 95% of undergraduates are from New Jersey. Others are from 6 states, 15 foreign countries, and Canada. 65% are from public schools. 77% are white. 50% are Catholic; 20% Protestant; 14% claim no religious affiliation; 12% Eastern Orthodox, Buddhist, Muslim, Islamic, Quaker. The average age of freshmen is 18; all undergraduates, 20. 5% do not continue beyond their first year; 81% remain to graduate.

Housing: 3586 students can be accommodated in college housing, which includes single-sex and coed dormitories, on-campus apartments, and off-campus apartments. In addition, there are honors houses, special-interest houses, study floors with extended quiet hours, and a living-learning center for the First-Year Experience taken by all entering students. On-campus housing is guaranteed for the freshman year only and is available on a lottery system for upperclassmen. 61% of students live on campus; of those, 70% remain on campus on weekends. Upperclassmen may keep cars.

Activities: 12% of men belong to 2 local and 9 national fraternities; 14% of women belong to 14 national sororities. There are 195 groups on campus, including art, band, cheerleading, chess, choir, chorale, chorus, computers, dance, drama, ethnic, film, foreign language, gay, honors, international, jazz band, literary magazine, musical theater, newspaper, opera, orchestra, pep band, photography, political, professional, radio and TV, recreational, religious, social, social service, student government, symphony, and yearbook. Popular campus events include Community Fest, Heritage Day, and Spirit Week Competition.

Sports: There are 11 intercollegiate sports for men and 10 for women, and 9 intramural sports for men and 9 for women. Facilities include a 5000-seat stadium with an Astroturf field, an aquatic center, baseball and softball diamonds, a Sportexe-surface soccer/multipurpose field, an all-weather track, a sand volleyball court, 5 grass playing fields, a 1200-seat gym, a physical enhancement center, a student recreation center, tennis, racquetball, and basketball/volleyball courts, and a free weight room.

Disabled Students: 90% of the campus is accessible. Wheelchair ramps, elevators, special parking, specially equipped rest rooms, special class scheduling, lowered drinking fountains, lowered telephones, assistive technology equipment in the library for those who are hard of hearing, are blind or visually challenged, or use wheelchairs, automatic doors and proximity card readers on many buildings, and TDD machines for person who are deaf are available.

Services: Counseling and information services are available, as is tutoring in most subjects. There is a reader service for the blind, and remedial math, reading, and writing.

Campus Safety and Security: Measures include 24-hour foot and vehicle patrol, self-defense education, security escort services, and informal discussions. There are pamphlets/posters/films, emergency telephones, and lighted pathways/sidewalks.

Programs of Study: TCNJ confers B.A., B.S., B.A.B.M., B.F.A., B.Mus., B.S.Co.E., B.S.E.E., B.S.M.E., and B.S.N. degrees. Master's degrees are also awarded. Bachelor's degrees are awarded in BIOLOGICAL SCIENCE (biology/biological science), BUSINESS (accounting, banking and finance, business administration and management, international business management, management science, and marketing/retailing/merchandising), COMMUNICATIONS AND THE ARTS (art, communications, English, fine arts, graphic design, journalism, music, and Spanish), COMPUTER AND PHYSICAL SCIENCE (chemistry, computer science, digital arts/technology, mathematics, physics, and statistics), EDUCATION (art, early childhood, education of the deaf and hearing impaired, elementary, English, foreign languages, health, mathematics, music, physical, science, social studies, special, technical, and vocational), ENGINEERING AND ENVIRONMENTAL DESIGN (biomedical engineering, civil engineering, computer engineering, electrical/electronics engineering, engineering and applied science, and mechanical engineering), HEALTH PROFESSIONS (exercise science, and nursing), SOCIAL SCIENCE (criminal justice, economics, history, international studies, philosophy, political science/government, psychology, sociology, and women's studies). Biology, English, and accounting are the strongest academically. Biology, elementary education, and psychology are the largest.

Required: To graduate, students must earn 120 semester hours, with a minimum GPA of 2.0. Students must complete a liberal learning curriculum of 32 to 34 course units that include diversity and community engagement and major-area proficiencies, as well as student-designed interdisciplinary concentrations in the natural, physical, and social sciences, humanities, and arts. Students must also complete a first-year seminar, which is discipline-based and thematically relevant to important social and cultural issues. The credits required in the major vary by program.

Special: TCNJ offers cross-registration with the New Jersey Marine Science Consortium, numerous internships in the public and private sectors, and study abroad in more than a dozen countries through the International Student Exchange program (ISEP). Pass/fail options and some dual majors are possible. Specially designed research courses allow students to participate in collaborative scholarly projects with members of the faculty. Combined advanced and accelerated degree programs are offered in law and justice, medicine, and optometry with other area schools. There are 19 national honor societies, a freshman honors program, and 8 departmental honors programs.

Faculty/Classroom: 53% of faculty are male; 47%, female. All teach undergraduates and 50% both teach and do research. No introductory courses are taught by graduate students. The average class size in an introductory lecture is 23; in a laboratory, 20; and in a regular course, 21.

Admissions: 45% of the 2005-2006 applicants were accepted. The SAT scores for the 2005-2006 freshman class were: Verbal--8% below 500, 25% between 500 and 599, 53% between 600 and 700, and 14% above 700; Math--5% below 500, 18% between 500 and 599, 54% between 600 and 700, and 23% above 700. 90% of the current freshmen were in the top fifth of their class; 98% were in the top two fifths. There were 14 National Merit finalists and 1 semifinalist. 20 freshmen graduated first in their class.

Requirements: The SAT is required. In addition, applicants must have earned 16 academic credits in high school, consisting of 4 in English, 2 each in math, science, and social studies, and 6 others distributed among math, science, social studies, and a foreign language. An essay is required. Art majors must submit a portfolio, and music majors must audition. The GED is accepted. AP and CLEP credits are accepted. Important factors in the admissions decision are advanced placement or honor courses, leadership record, and evidence of special talent.

Procedure: Freshmen are admitted fall and spring. Entrance exams should be taken by the end of the junior year or early in the senior year. There are early decision and early admissions plans. Early decision applications should be filed by November 15; regular applications, by February 15 for fall entry and November 15 for January entry, along with a $50 fee. Notification of early decision is sent December 15; regular decision, on a rolling basis. 200 early decision candidates were accepted for the 2005-2006 class. 426 applicants were on the 2005 waiting list; 113 were admitted. Applications are accepted on-line.

Transfer: 379 transfer students enrolled in 2004-2005. Transfer students must have a minimum GPA of 2.5, and those with fewer than 33 credits must submit SAT scores. An associate degree is recommended. All transfer students must submit high school transcripts. 48 of 128 credits required for the bachelor's degree must be completed at TCNJ.

Visiting: There are regularly scheduled orientations for prospective students, consisting of an admissions presentation and a tour of campus. Reservations are required. There are guides for informal visits and visitors may sit in on classes and stay overnight. To schedule a visit, contact the Admissions Office at *tcnjinfo@tcnj.edu.*

Financial Aid: In 2005-2006, 78% of all full-time freshmen and 69% of continuing full-time students received some form of financial aid. 31% of full-time freshmen and 32% of continuing full-time students received need-based aid. The average freshman award was $9483. Need-based scholarships or need-based grants averaged $12,033 ($16,607 maximum); need-based self-help aid (loans and jobs) averaged $2906 ($3000 maximum); and other non-need-based awards and non-need-based scholarships averaged $7267 ($22,327 maximum). 77% of undergraduates work part time. Average annual earnings from campus work are $1764. The average financial indebtedness of the 2005 graduate was $18,524. TCNJ is a member of CSS. The FAFSA and copies of students' and parents' tax returns as applicable are required. The priority date for freshman financial aid applications for fall entry is March 1. The deadline for filing freshman financial aid applications for fall entry is October 15.

International Students: There are 23 international students enrolled. They must score satisfactorily on the written TOEFL and also take the SATor ACT. The SAT is required for merit scholarship consideration.

Computers: There are 581 computers in 30 computer labs on campus; all classrooms are connected to the college network. Most of the campus is wireless. All residence hall rooms have access to the college network. All students may access the system. There are no time limits. The fee is $149. It is strongly recommended that all students have a personal computer.

Graduates: From July 1, 2004 to June 30, 2005, 1415 bachelor's degrees were awarded. The most popular majors were business administration (14%), psychology (11%), and elementary/early childhood education (9%). In an average class, 1% graduate in 3 years or less, 61% graduate in 4 years or less, 79% graduate in 5 years or less, and 81% graduate in 6 years or less. 800 companies recruited on campus in 2004-2005. Of the 2004 graduating class, 13% were enrolled in graduate school within 6 months of graduation and 85% were employed.

Admissions Contact: Lisa Angeloni, Director of Admissions.
E-mail: *admiss@tcnj.edu* Web: *www.tcnj.edu*

COLLEGE OF SAINT ELIZABETH
E-2
Morristown, NJ 07960-6989
(973) 290-4700
(800) 210-7900; Fax: (973) 290-4710

Full-time: 12 men, 659 women	**Faculty:** 60
Part-time: 79 men, 455 women	**Ph.D.s:** 82%
Graduate: 82 men, 571 women	**Student/Faculty:** 11 to 1
Year: semesters, summer session	**Tuition:** $19,520
Application Deadline: August 15	**Room & Board:** $8975
Freshman Class: 422 applied, 335 accepted, 130 enrolled	
SAT Verbal/Math: 480/460	**COMPETITIVE**

The College of St. Elizabeth, founded in 1899, is a private Roman Catholic college primarily for women. Undergraduate programs are offered in the arts and sciences, business administration, education, foods and nutrition, and upper-level nursing. There are graduate programs in education, management, health care management, nutrition, psychology, and theology. Adult undergraduate degree programs and graduate programs are coeducational.There is 1graduate school. In addition to regional accreditation, CSE has baccalaureate program accreditation with ADA and NLN. The library contains 110,272 volumes, 104,965 microform items, and 1612 audio/video tapes/CDs/DVDs, and subscribes to 633 periodicals including electronic. Computerized library services include the card catalog, interlibrary loans, database searching, and Internet access. Special learning facilities include a learning resource center, art gallery, and a television studio. The 188-acre campus is in a suburban area 40 miles west of New York City. Including any residence halls, there are 11 buildings.

Student Life: 94% of undergraduates are from New Jersey. Others are from 15 states and 10 foreign countries. 62% are from public schools. 46% are white; 20% Hispanic; 17% African American. 48% are Catholic; 14% Protestant; 7% claim no religious affiliation. The average age of freshmen is 18; all undergraduates, 20. 18% do not continue beyond their first year; 62% remain to graduate.

Housing: 402 students can be accommodated in college housing, which includes single-sex dormitories and off-campus apartments. On-campus housing is guaranteed for all 4 years, is available on a first-come, first-served basis, and is available on a lottery system for upperclassmen. 65% of students live on campus; of those, 22% remain on campus on weekends. All students may keep cars.

Activities: There are no fraternities or sororities. There are 28 groups on campus, including chorale, drama, ethnic, honors, international, literary magazine, newspaper, professional, religious, social, social service, and student government. Popular campus events include Oktoberfest, International Night, and Christmas celebrations.

Sports: There are 8 intercollegiate sports for women. Facilities include a student center that houses a swimming pool, a weight room, an archery range, and a gym. Tennis courts are also available, as is a bike and fitness trail.

Disabled Students: 75% of the campus is accessible. Wheelchair ramps, elevators, special parking, specially equipped rest rooms, special class scheduling, and handrails are available.

Services: Counseling and information services are available, as is tutoring in most subjects. There is remedial math, reading, and writing. Other services include books on tape, large monitor computers, and notetakers.

Campus Safety and Security: Measures include 24-hour foot and vehicle patrol, security escort services, informal discussions, and pamphlets/posters/films. There are emergency telephones and lighted pathways/sidewalks.

Programs of Study: CSE confers B.A., B.S., and B.S.N. degrees. Master's degrees are also awarded. Bachelor's degrees are awarded in BIOLOGICAL SCIENCE (biochemistry, biology/biological science, nutrition, and toxicology), BUSINESS (business administration and management), COMMUNICATIONS AND THE ARTS (art, communications, English, fine arts, music, and Spanish), COMPUTER AND PHYSICAL SCIENCE (chemistry, computer science, and mathematics), EDUCATION (early childhood, elementary, and special), HEALTH PROFESSIONS (nursing and premedicine), SOCIAL SCIENCE (American studies, economics, history, international studies, philosophy, prelaw, psychology, sociology, and theological studies). Math, chemistry, and education are the strongest academically. Business administration, education, and psychology are the largest.

Required: To graduate, students must complete 128 semester hours, with a minimum of 32 in the major, while maintaining a GPA of 2.0, or 2.75 for education majors. Core requirements include 27 credits in specific humanities courses focusing on theology, philosophy, literature, history, foreign language, and fine arts, 6 to 8 in math and science, and 6 in social science. In addition, 2 credits in fitness/wellness and an interdisciplinary course are required. Students must also demonstrate proficiency in writing and complete a comprehensive or capstone experience.

Special: There is cross-registration with Drew and Fairleigh Dickinson Universities. CSE also offers internships in business, law, technology, health, government, sports, and television. On-campus work-study, accelerated degree programs, dual majors, student-designed majors, study abroad, credit for life experience, pass/fail options, and nondegree study are also available. Continuing studies programs are geared to the working student. There are 10 national honor societies and a freshman honors program.

Faculty/Classroom: 36% of faculty are male; 64%, female. 80% teach undergraduates, 5% do research, and 5% do both. The average class size in an introductory lecture is 15; in a laboratory, 12; and in a regular course, 13.

Admissions: 79% of the 2005-2006 applicants were accepted. The SAT scores for the 2005-2006 freshman class were: Verbal--59% below 500, 30% between 500 and 599, 8% between 600 and 700, and 3% above 700; Math--61% below 500, 32% between 500 and 599, 6% between 600 and 700, and 1% above 700. 26% of the current freshmen were in the top fifth of their class; 57% were in the top two fifths.

Requirements: The SAT is required, with a satisfactory score. Applicants must be graduates of accredited secondary schools or have earned a GED. The college requires 16 academic units, including 3 each in English and math/science, 2 each in foreign language, and 1 in history. An essay and 2 letters of recommendaiton are required and an interview is recommended. CSE requires applicants to be in the upper 50% of their class. A GPA of 2.0 is required. AP and CLEP credits are accepted. Important factors in the admissions decision are advanced placement or honor courses, recommendations by school officials, and leadership record.

Procedure: Freshmen are admitted fall and spring. Entrance exams should be taken early in the senior year. There are deferred admissions and rolling admissions plans. Applications should be filed by August 15 for fall entry and December 15 for spring entry, along with a $35 fee. Notification is sent on a rolling basis. Applications are accepted on-line.

Transfer: 112 transfer students enrolled in 2004-2005. Applicants must present a minimum GPA of 2.0 in course work from an accredited college. SAT or ACT scores, an associate degree, and an interview are also recommended. 56 of 128 credits required for the bachelor's degree must be completed at CSE.

Visiting: There are regularly scheduled orientations for prospective students, including interviews, tours, and class visitation. There are guides for informal visits and visitors may sit in on classes and stay overnight. To schedule a visit, contact Donna Tartarka, Dean of Admission.

Financial Aid: In 2005-2006, all full-time freshmen and 91% of continuing full-time students received some form of financial aid. 75% of full-time freshmen and 72% of continuing full-time students received need-based aid. The average freshman award was $20,676. Need-based scholarships or need-based grants averaged $14,858; need-based self-help aid (loans and jobs) averaged $2871; and non-need-based athletic scholarships averaged $10,695. 93% of undergraduates work part time. Average annual earnings from campus work are $2000. The average financial indebtedness of the 2005 graduate was $17,288. CSE is a member of CSS. The FAFSA is required. The priority date for freshman financial aid applications for fall entry is March 1. The deadline for filing freshman financial aid applications for fall entry is September 1.

International Students: There are 36 international students enrolled. The school actively recruits these students. They must take the TOEFL or other approved assessment tests. Applicants from English-speaking countries may submit scores from either the TOEFL or the SAT.

Computers: All students may access the system. There are no time limits and no fees.

Graduates: From July 1, 2004 to June 30, 2005, 263 bachelor's degrees were awarded. The most popular majors were business (25%), communication (20%), and education (14%). In an average class, 1% graduate in 3 years or less, 56% graduate in 4 years or less, 61% graduate in 5 years or less, and 62% graduate in 6 years or less. 3 companies recruited on campus in 2004-2005. Of the 2004 graduating class, 21% were enrolled in graduate school within 6 months of graduation and 66% were employed.

Admissions Contact: Donna Tartarka, Dean of Admission. A video is available. E-mail: *apply@www.cse.edu* Web: *www.cse.edu*

DEVRY COLLEGE OF TECHNOLOGY/NORTH BRUNSWICK

D-3

North Brunswick, NJ 08902

(732) 435-4850
(800) 33-DEVRY; Fax: (732) 435-4856

Full-time: 1300 men, 300 women	**Faculty:** n/av
Part-time: 700 men, 200 women	**Ph.D.s:** n/av
Graduate: none	**Student/Faculty:** n/av
Year: semesters, summer session	**Tuition:** $10,500
Application Deadline: open	**Room & Board:** n/app
Freshman Class: n/av	
SAT or ACT: see profile	**LESS COMPETITIVE**

DeVry College of Technology/North Brunswick, founded in 1969, is a private institution offering hands-on programs in electronics, business administration, computer information systems, and information technology. The school is 1 of 67 DeVry University locations throughout the United States and Canada. Figures in the above capsule and in this profile are approximate. In addition to regional accreditation, DeVry has baccalaureate program accreditation with ABET. The library contains 32,201 volumes and 1870 audio/video tapes/CDs/DVDs, and subscribes to 210 periodicals including electronic. Computerized library services include the card catalog, interlibrary loans, and database searching. Special learning facilities include a learning resource center. The 15-acre campus is in a small town. There is one building.

Student Life: 43% are white; 25% African American; 19% Hispanic. The average age of all undergraduates is 24.

Housing: There are no residence halls. Housing referrals may be obtained through the student housing office. There are private apartments, student-plan housing, and private rooms. All of students commute. Alcohol is not permitted. All students may keep cars.

Activities: There are no fraternities or sororities. There are 11 groups on campus, including ethnic, honors, and professional. Popular campus events include Student Appreciation Day.

Sports: There is no sports program at DeVry.

Disabled Students: All of the campus is accessible. Wheelchair ramps, elevators, special parking, specially equipped rest rooms, special class scheduling, lowered drinking fountains, and lowered telephones are available.

Services: Counseling and information services are available, as is tutoring in every subject.

Programs of Study: DeVry confers the B.S. degree. Associate degrees are also awarded. Bachelor's degrees are awarded in COMMUNICATIONS AND THE ARTS (telecommunications), COMPUTER AND PHYSICAL SCIENCE (information sciences and systems), ENGINEERING AND ENVIRONMENTAL DESIGN (electrical/electronics engineering technology). Telecommunications is the largest.

Required: To graduate, students must achieve a GPA of at least 2.0, complete 48 to 154 credit hours, and satisfactorily complete all curriculum requirements. Course requirements vary according to program. All first-semester students take courses in business organization, computer applications, algebra, psychology, and student success strategies.

Special: Evening and weekend classes, distance learning, co-op programs, and an accelerated degree program are offered. There are 2 national honor societies, including Phi Beta Kappa.

Faculty/Classroom: All teach undergraduates.

Requirements: Admissions requirements include graduation from a secondary school; the GED is also accepted. Applicants must pass the DeVry entrance exam or present satisfactory ACT or SAT scores. An interview is required. CLEP credit is accepted.

Procedure: Freshmen are admitted fall, spring, and summer. There are early admissions and deferred admissions plans. Application deadlines are open. The fall 2005 application fee was $50. Notification is sent on a rolling basis. Applications are accepted on-line.

Transfer: Applicants must present passing grades in all completed college course work, demonstrate language skills proficiency with at least 24 completed semester hours, and present evidence of math proficiency by appropriate college-level credits. A minimum GPA of 2.0 is required. 25 of 48 credits required for the bachelor's degree must be completed at DeVry.

Visiting: There are regularly scheduled orientations for prospective students. There are guides for informal visits and visitors may sit in on classes. To schedule a visit, contact Danielle DiNapoli, Dean of Admissions.

Financial Aid: In a recent year, 49% of all full-time freshmen and 63% of continuing full-time students received some form of financial aid. 48% of full-time freshmen and 61% of continuing full-time students received need-based aid. The average freshman award was $6840. Need-based scholarships or need-based grants averaged $5175; need-based self-help aid (loans and jobs) averaged $3542; and other non-need-based awards and non-need-based scholarships averaged $9018. The FAFSA is required.

International Students: They must score satisfactorily on the written TOEFL or 173 on the electronic version and also take the college's own entrance exam.

Computers: Computer information students may access the system during published lab hours. There are no fees. Students in the information technology program have DeVry-issued laptop computers.

Graduates: In a recent year, 259 bachelor's degrees were awarded. The most popular majors were computer information systems (95%) and electronics engineering technology (5%).

Admissions Contact: Danielle DiNapoli, Dean of Admissions.
E-mail: *admissions@devry.edu* Web: *www.nj.devry.edu*

DREW UNIVERSITY/COLLEGE OF LIBERAL ARTS   D-2

Madison, NJ 07940	(973) 408-DREW; Fax: (973) 408-3068
Full-time: 669 men, 892 women	Faculty: 148; IIA, +$
Part-time: 17 men, 35 women	Ph.D.s: 94%
Graduate: 381 men, 405 women	Student/Faculty: 11 to 1
Year: semesters, summer session	Tuition: $31,286
Application Deadline: February 15	Room & Board: $8412
Freshman Class: 3436 applied, 2831 accepted, 395 enrolled	
SAT Verbal/Math: 608/596*	ACT: 25 VERY COMPETITIVE

The College of Liberal Arts was added to Drew University in 1928 and is part of an educational complex that includes a theological school and a graduate school. Drew is a private, independent institution affiliated with the United Methodist Church. The library contains 571,850 volumes, 485,288 microform items, and 2611 audio/video tapes/CDs/DVDs, and subscribes to 21,997 periodicals including electronic. Computerized library services include the card catalog, interlibrary loans, database searching, Internet access, and laptop Internet portals. Special learning facilities include a learning resource center, art gallery, radio station, TV station, observatory, and photography gallery. The 186-acre campus is in a small town 30 miles west of New York City. Including any residence halls, there are 57 buildings.

Student Life: 57% of undergraduates are from New Jersey. Others are from 45 states and 11 foreign countries. 65% are from public schools.

66% are white. The average age of freshmen is 18; all undergraduates, 20. 84% of freshmen remain to graduate.

Housing: 1354 students can be accommodated in college housing, which includes single-sex and coed dorms, on-campus apartments, and married-student housing. In addition, there are language houses and special-interest houses. On-campus housing is guaranteed for all 4 years. 85% of students live on campus; of those, 70% remain on campus on weekends. Upperclassmen may keep cars.

Activities: There are no fraternities or sororities. There are 80 groups on campus, including art, cheerleading, choir, chorale, computers, dance, drama, ecology, ethnic, film, gay, honors, international, jazz band, literary magazine, newspaper, orchestra, pep band, photography, political, professional, radio and TV, religious, social, social service, student government, women's and yearbook. Popular campus events include Holiday Semiformal, Annual Picnic, and Multicultural Awareness Day.

Sports: There are 11 intercollegiate sports for men and 12 for women, and 12 intramural sports for men and 12 for women. Facilities include an artificial turf athletic field with a 1000-seat gym, a 1000-seat auditorium, a swimming pool, a lighted tennis complex, a weight training room, a game room, an indoor track, a forest preserve, and an arboretum.

Disabled Students: Wheelchair ramps, elevators, special parking, specially equipped rest rooms, special class scheduling, lowered drinking fountains, and lowered telephones are available.The main dining facility, the student center and commons, and the ground floor of every dorm and classroom building are accessible to students with physical disabilities are available.

Services: Counseling and information services are available, as is tutoring in most subjects. There is a reader service for the blind.

Campus Safety and Security: Measures include 24-hour foot and vehicle patrol, self-defense education, security escort services, and informal discussions. There are pamphlets/posters/films, emergency telephones, and lighted pathways/sidewalks.

Programs of Study: Drew confers the B.A. degree. Master's and doctoral degrees are also awarded. Bachelor's degrees are awarded in BIOLOGICAL SCIENCE (biochemistry, biology/biological science, and neurosciences), COMMUNICATIONS AND THE ARTS (art, art history and appreciation, Chinese, classics, dramatic arts, English, French, German, music, and Spanish), COMPUTER AND PHYSICAL SCIENCE (chemistry, computer science, mathematics, and physics), SOCIAL SCIENCE (African studies, anthropology, behavioral science, economics, history, philosophy, political science/government, psychology, religion, sociology, and women's studies). Psychology, political science, and English are the largest.

Required: To graduate, students must earn at least 128 credits, of which at least 64 must be beyond the lower level and at least 32 must be at the upper level. All students must fulfill the requirements of a major and those of the general education program. For graduation, the cumulative GPA, both overall and in the major, must be at least 2.0. General education requirements include a first-year seminar, demonstration of writing competency, at least 8 credits in foreign language and fulfillment of a language-in-context requirement, and completion of at least 4 credits in each of 2 different departments in the following 4 divisions: natural and mathematical sciences, social sciences, humanities, and arts and literature. Each student must also complete a minor.

Special: Drew offers co-op programs with Duke University, as well as cross-registration with the College of Saint Elizabeth and Fairleigh Dickinson University. There are also dual majors, study abroad, a Wall Street semester, a Washington semester, student-designed majors, internships, 3-2 engineering programs with Washington University in St. Louis, the Stevens Institute of Technology, and Columbia University in New York City, and a 7-year B.A.-M.D. program in medicine with UMDNJ. There are 11 national honor societies, including Phi Beta Kappa, and 12 departmental honors programs.

Faculty/Classroom: 52% of faculty are male; 48%, female. All both teach and do research. Graduate students teach 1% of introductory courses. The average class size in an introductory lecture is 25; in a laboratory, 20; and in a regular course, 18.

Admissions: 82% of the 2005-2006 applicants were accepted. The SAT scores for the 2005-2006 freshman class were: Verbal--8% below 500, 35% between 500 and 599, 42% between 600 and 700, and 15% above 700; Math--8% below 500, 44% between 500 and 599, 38% between 600 and 700, and 10% above 700. The ACT scores were 14% below 21, 21% between 21 and 23, 27% between 24 and 26, 17% between 27 and 28, and 22% above 28. 65% of the current freshmen were in the top fifth of their class; 90% were in the top two fifths. 8 freshmen graduated first in their class.

Requirements: The SAT or ACT is required. In addition, the university strongly recommends 18 academic credits or Carnegie units, including 4 in English, 3 in math, and 2 each in foreign language, science, social studies, and history, with the remaining 3 in additional academic courses. An essay is also required, and an interview is recommended. AP and CLEP credits are accepted. Important factors in the admissions decision are advanced placement or honor courses, ability to finance college education, and extracurricular activities record.

Procedure: Freshmen are admitted fall and spring. Entrance exams should be taken by January of the senior year. There are early decision, early admissions, and deferred admissions plans. Early decision applications should be filed by December 1; regular applications, by February 15 for fall entry and December 1 for spring entry, along with a $50 fee. Notification of early decision is sent December 24; regular decision, March 15. 413 applicants were on the 2005 waiting list; 363 were admitted. Applications are accepted on-line.

Transfer: 33 transfer students enrolled in 2004-2005. Applicants must submit satisfactory high school and college academic records, a personal essay, and a statement of good standing from previous schools attended. An interview also may be required. Students with fewer then 12 credits must apply as entering freshman. 64 of 128 credits required for the bachelor's degree must be completed at Drew.

Visiting: There are regularly scheduled orientations for prospective students. There are guides for informal visits and visitors may sit in on classes and stay overnight. To schedule a visit, contact the Admissions Office at (973) 408-3739 or cadm@drew.edu.

Financial Aid: In 2005-2006, 53% of all full-time freshmen and 76% of continuing full-time students received some form of financial aid. The average freshman award was $21,339. Need-based scholarships or need-based grants averaged $17,024; and need-based self-help aid (loans and jobs) averaged $3842. 29% of undergraduates work part time. Average annual earnings from campus work are $1200. The average financial indebtedness of the 2005 graduate was $17,586. Drew is a member of CSS. The CSS/Profile or FAFSA is required. The deadline for filing freshman financial aid applications for fall entry is February 15.

International Students: There are 15 international students enrolled. The school actively recruits these students. They must score satisfactorily on the TOEFL.

Computers: Wireless access is available. All students may access the system. There are no time limits and no fees. The college strongly recommends students own an IBM Thinkpad.

Graduates: From July 1, 2004 to June 30, 2005, 323 bachelor's degrees were awarded. The most popular majors were political science (16%), psychology (12%), and economics (12%). In an average class, 66% graduate in 4 years or less, 74% graduate in 5 years or less, and 73% graduate in 6 years or less. 78 companies recruited on campus in 2004-2005. Of the 2004 graduating class, 22% were enrolled in graduate school within 6 months of graduation and 49% were employed.

Admissions Contact: Mary Beth Carey, Dean of Admissions and Financial Assistance. E-mail: cadm@drew.edu
Web: http://www.drew.edu

FAIRLEIGH DICKINSON UNIVERSITY SYSTEM

The Fairleigh Dickinson University System, established in 1942, is a private system in New Jersey. It is governed by Board of Trustees, whose chief administrator is President. The primary goal of the system is Teaching/Research. The main priorities are To provide an academically challenging learning experience to prepare students for employment or enrollment in graduate and professional schools; To promote independent thinking and collaborative learning in students as part of the educational process; and To cultivate a holistic, integrated living-learning experience as part of the educational process, and to foster the ideals of good citizenship and community service. The total enrollment of both campuses usually exceeds 11,000; there were about 670 faculty members. Altogether there are 38 baccalaureate, 51 master's, and 1 doctoral programs offered in Fairleigh Dickinson University System. There is a 4-year campus located in Florham Park/Madison Campus. Profiles of the 4-year campuses are included in this section.

FAIRLEIGH DICKINSON UNIVERSITY/COLLEGE AT FLORHAM · D-3

Madison, NJ 07940

(973) 443-8900
(800) 338-8803; Fax: (973) 443-8088

Full-time: 1060 men, 1200 women	**Faculty:** 113; IIA, av$
Part-time: 170 men, 230 women	**Ph.D.s:** 76%
Graduate: 410 men, 700 women	**Student/Faculty:** 20 to 1
Year: semesters, summer session	**Tuition:** $21,880
Application Deadline: March 1	**Room & Board:** $8250
Freshman Class: 2829 applied, 2030 accepted, 616 enrolled	
SAT Verbal/Math: 517/515*	COMPETITIVE

Fairleigh Dickinson University/College at Florham, founded in 1942, is an independent university with 40 acadmeic majors and 35 graduate programs. Studies are rooted in the liberal arts, but they also offer hands-on opportunities in business and professional internships, cooperative education, and global studies abroad. Figures in the above capsule are approximate. There are 2 undergraduate and 2 graduate schools. In addition to regional accreditation, College at Florham has baccalaureate program accreditation with AACSB, ACS, and APTA. The library contains 150,669 volumes, 108,000 microform items, and 681 audio/video

tapes/CDs/DVDs, and subscribes to 643 periodicals including electronic. Computerized library services include the card catalog, interlibrary loans, database searching, and Internet access. Special learning facilities include a learning resource center, art gallery, radio station, web-lab, ITV multimedia classrooms, and theaters. The 178-acre campus is in a suburban area 27 miles west of New York City, in Morris County. Including any residence halls, there are 33 buildings.

Student Life: 86 % of undergraduated are from New Jersey. Students are from 27 states and 21 foreign countries. 73% are white. The average age of freshmen is 18; all undergraduates, 20. 23% do not continue beyond their first year; 51% remain to graduate.

Housing: 1530 students can be accommodated in college housing, which includes coed dorms, on-campus apartments, fraternity houses, and sorority houses. In addition, there are honors houses and special-interest houses. On-campus housing is guaranteed for the freshman year only and is available on a first-come, first-served basis. 59% of students live on campus; of those, 40% remain on campus on weekends. Upperclassmen may keep cars.

Activities: 20% of men belong to 6 national fraternities; 30% of women belong to 4 national sororities. There are 35 groups on campus, including art, cheerleading, computers, debate, drama, ethnic, film, gay, honors, international, jazz band, literary magazine, musical theater, newspaper, pep band, photography, political, professional, radio and TV, religious, social, social service, student government, and yearbook. Popular campus events include Welcome Week, Softball Marathon, and Senior Days.

Sports: There are 9 intercollegiate sports for men and 9 for women, and 11 intramural sports for men and 10 for women. Facilities include a state-of-the-art synthetic turf field for football, field hockey, soccer, and lacrosse.

Disabled Students: 40% of the campus is accessible. Wheelchair ramps, elevators, special parking, specially equipped rest rooms, special class scheduling, lowered drinking fountains, lowered telephones, special housing, and oral interpretation for the hearing impaired are available.

Services: Counseling and information services are available, as is tutoring in most subjects. There is a reader service for the blind, and remedial math, reading, and writing. Workshops also offer assistance with study skills and time management, and support services for basic skills students and freshmen are available. There is a Regional Center for College Students with Learning Disabilities that offers comprehensive support to students admitted to the program.

Campus Safety and Security: Measures include 24-hour foot and vehicle patrol, self-defense education, security escort services, and shuttle buses. There are informal discussions, pamphlets/posters/films, emergency telephones, lighted pathways/sidewalks, an active crime prevention program, and a bike patrol.

Programs of Study: College at Florham confers B.A., B.S., B.S.A.H.T., B.S.C.L.S., and B.S.N. degrees. Associate and master's degrees are also awarded. Bachelor's degrees are awarded in BIOLOGICAL SCIENCE (biology/biological science and marine biology), BUSINESS (accounting, business administration and management, entrepreneurial studies, hotel/motel and restaurant management, and marketing/retailing/merchandising), COMMUNICATIONS AND THE ARTS (communications, creative writing, dramatic arts, fine arts, literature, and video), COMPUTER AND PHYSICAL SCIENCE (chemistry, computer science, mathematics, and radiological technology), HEALTH PROFESSIONS (allied health, clinical science, and medical laboratory technology), SOCIAL SCIENCE (economics, French studies, history, humanities, liberal arts/general studies, philosophy, political science/government, psychology, sociology, and Spanish studies). Psychology, business management, and communications are the largest.

Required: To graduate, students must complete a minimum of 128 credits, including 30 to 44 in the major, with an overall minimum 2.0 GPA (2.5 in the major). Distribution requirements include courses in English, communications, math, phys ed, foreign language, humanities, social and behavioral sciences, lab and computer science, an integrated, interdisciplinary university core sequence, and freshman seminar.

Special: The college offers co-op programs in all majors, internships, and study abroad. A Washington semester, work-study, accelerated degrees, and student-designed majors in the humanities and general studies are possible. A prepharmacy program, as well as joint baccalaureate dental programs, are available. There are 17 national honor societies, a freshman honors program, and 19 departmental honors programs.

Faculty/Classroom: 62% of faculty are male; 38%, female. All teach undergraduates.

Admissions: 72% of the 2005-2006 applicants were accepted. The SAT scores for the 2005-2006 freshman class were: Verbal--40% below 500, 44% between 500 and 599, 14% between 600 and 700, and 1% above 700; Math--41% below 500, 43% between 500 and 599, 15% between 600 and 700, and 1% above 700. 22% of the current freshmen were in the top fifth of their class; 50% were in the top two fifths. 1 freshman graduated first in the class in a recent year.

Requirements: The SAT or ACT is required. In addition, applicants should be graduates of an accredited high school or have a GED certificate. They should have completed a minimum of 16 academic units, including 4 in English, 3 in math, 2 each in history, foreign language, and lab science (3 are recommended), and 3 in electives. Those students applying to science and health sciences programs must meet additional requirements. An interview may be requested by the university. A GPA of 3.0 is required. AP and CLEP credits are accepted. Important factors in the admissions decision are leadership record, recommendations by school officials, and extracurricular activities record.

Procedure: Freshmen are admitted to all sessions. Entrance exams should be taken in May of the junior year. There are early admissions and deferred admissions plans. There is a rolling admissions plan. Applications should be filed by March 1 for fall entry, along with a $40 fee. Notification is sent on a rolling basis. Applications are accepted on-line.

Transfer: 132 transfer students enrolled in 2004-2005. All transfer applicants must submit official transcripts for all college work taken. Those students with fewer than 24 credits must also submit a high school transcript or a copy of their state department of education's equivalency score, and SAT scores. 60 of 128 credits required for the bachelor's degree must be completed at College at Florham.

Visiting: There are regularly scheduled orientations for prospective students, including standardized placement testing, faculty advisement, class registration, and educational and social activities to prepare students for entrance in the fall. There are guides for informal visits and visitors may sit in on classes and stay overnight. To schedule a visit, contact the Admissions Office.

Financial Aid: In 2005-2006, 88% of all full-time freshmen and 83% of continuing full-time students received some form of financial aid. 75% of full-time freshmen and 72% of continuing full-time students received need-based aid. The average freshman award was $17,365. Need-based scholarships or need-based grants averaged $10,712; need-based self-help aid (loans and jobs) averaged $2856; and other non-need-based awards and non-need-based scholarships averaged $7449. College at Florham is a member of CSS. The FAFSA and the college's own financial statement are required. The priority date for freshman financial aid applications for fall entry is February 15. The deadline for filing freshman financial aid applications for fall entry is rolling.

International Students: There are 38 international students enrolled. The school actively recruits these students. They must take the TOEFL, achieving a satisfactory score, or take the MELAB, the Comprehensive English Language Test, the college's own test, or the IELTS. The SAT or ACT is highly recommended.

Computers: All students may access the system. There are no time limits. The fee is $480. It is strongly recommended that all students have a personal computer.

Graduates: From July 1, 2004 to June 30, 2005, 461 bachelor's degrees were awarded. The most popular majors were business/marketing (30%), psychology (16%), and liberal arts/general studies (13%). In an average class, 32% graduate in 4 years or less, 48% graduate in 5 years or less, and 52% graduate in 6 years or less. 101 companies recruited on campus in 2004-2005.

Admissions Contact: Bernetta Millonde, University Director of Admissions. E-mail: *globaleducation@fdu.edu* Web: *www.fdu.edu*

FAIRLEIGH DICKINSON UNIVERSITY/METROPOLITAN CAMPUS   E-2

Teaneck, NJ 07666 (201) 692-2553
(800) 338-8803; Fax: (201)692-7319

Full-time: 850 men, 1283 women	**Faculty:** 182
Part-time: 1682 men, 1929 women	**Ph.D.s:** 77%
Graduate: 1137 men, 1356 women	**Student/Faculty:** 12 to 1
Year: semesters, summer session	**Tuition:** $20,340
Application Deadline: March 15	**Room & Board:** $8250
Freshman Class: 2775 applied, 1792 accepted, 499 enrolled	
SAT Verbal/Math: 498/507*	**COMPETITIVE**

Farleigh Dickinson University/Metropolitan Campus, founded in 1942, is an independent university offering undergraduate and graduate degrees in business, arts and sciences, professional studies, public administration, and hotel, restaurant, and tourism management. Tuition figures in the above capsule are approximate. There are 3 undergraduate and 3 graduate schools. In addition to regional accreditation, FDU has baccalaureate program accreditation with AACSB, ABET, APTA, CSAB, NASDTEC, and NLN. The 3 libraries contain 268,865 volumes, 230,266 microform items, and 1884 audio/video tapes/CDs/DVDs, and subscribe to 1420 periodicals including electronic. Computerized library services include the card catalog, interlibrary loans, database searching, and Internet access. Special learning facilities include a learning resource center, radio station, computer labs, ITV multimedia classrooms, photonics lab, theater, art galleries, web-lab, and Center for Psychological Sevices. The 88-acre campus is in a suburban area 13 miles from midtown Manhattan, New York City. Including any residence halls, there are 53 buildings.

Student Life: 87% of undergraduates are from New Jersey. Others are from 22 states, 51 foreign countries, and Canada. 43% are white; 19%

African American; 17% Hispanic. The average age of freshmen is 18; all undergraduates, 22. 30% do not continue beyond their first year; 48% remain to graduate.

Housing: 1013 students can be accommodated in college housing, which includes single-sex and coed dorms. In addition, there are special-interest houses, international houses, and Honors and Global Scholar houses. On-campus housing is available on a first-come, first-served basis and is available on a lottery system for upperclassmen. 84% of students commute. Alcohol is not permitted. All students may keep cars.

Activities: 2% of men belong to 5 national fraternities; 8% of women belong to 7 national sororities. There are 62 groups on campus, including art, cheerleading, choir, computers, dance, drama, ethnic, film, gay, honors, international, literary magazine, musical theater, newspaper, pep band, photography, political, professional, radio and TV, religious, social, social service, student government, student programming board, and yearbook. Popular campus events include Welcome Back Week, Spring Fest, and dances.

Sports: There are 8 intercollegiate sports for men and 10 for women, and 15 intramural sports for men and 15 for women. Facilities include a 5000-seat facility with a 6-lane, 200-meter track, 4 full basketball courts, 2 volleyball courts, 4 racquetball courts, and a fully equipped weight room, a 6 outdoor tennis courts, a baseball field and soccer field with bleachers, 2 training room facilities, a softball field, and a state-of-the-art fitness center with an aerobics room, a selectorized weight room, and a cardio room.

Disabled Students: 35% of the campus is accessible. Wheelchair ramps, elevators, special parking, specially equipped rest rooms, special class scheduling, lowered drinking fountains, lowered telephones, special housing, and oral interpretation for the hearing impaired are available.

Services: Counseling and information services are available, as is tutoring in every subject. There is a reader service for the blind, and remedial math, reading, and writing. Workshops offer assistance with academic study skills, time management, and advanced reading and writing. Support services for basic skills students and freshmen are available. There is also a Regional Center for College Students with Learning Disabilities that offers comprehensive support to students admitted to the program.

Campus Safety and Security: Measures include 24-hour foot and vehicle patrol, self-defense education, security escort services, and informal discussions. There are pamphlets/posters/films, emergency telephones, lighted pathways/sidewalks, an active crime prevention program, and a bike patrol.

Programs of Study: FDU confers B.A., B.S., B.S.Civ.E.T., B.S.C.L.S., B.S.Con.E.T., B.S.E.E., B.S.E.E.T., B.S.M.E.T., and B.S.N. degrees. Associate, master's, and doctoral degrees are also awarded. Bachelor's degrees are awarded in BIOLOGICAL SCIENCE (biochemistry, biology/biological science, and marine biology), BUSINESS (accounting, business administration and management, entrepreneurial studies, hotel/motel and restaurant management, and marketing/retailing/merchandising), COMMUNICATIONS AND THE ARTS (communications, dramatic arts, English literature, and fine arts), COMPUTER AND PHYSICAL SCIENCE (chemistry, computer science, information sciences and systems, mathematics, radiological technology, and science), ENGINEERING AND ENVIRONMENTAL DESIGN (civil engineering technology, construction engineering, electrical/electronics engineering, electrical/electronics engineering technology, environmental science, and mechanical engineering technology), HEALTH PROFESSIONS (allied health, clinical science, medical laboratory technology, and nursing), SOCIAL SCIENCE (criminal justice, economics, French studies, history, humanities, interdisciplinary studies, international studies, liberal arts/general studies, philosophy, political science/government, psychology, sociology, and Spanish studies). Individualized studies, business management, and psychology are the largest.

Required: To graduate, students must complete 120 to 128 credits, including 30 to 44 in the major, with an overall minimum 2. GPA. Students must complete a 4-semester interdisciplinary sequence and 1 course in freshman seminar. Core curriculum includes 12 credits in university core, 6 in English, and 3 each in math and computer science.

Special: FDU offers co-op programs in all majors, cross-registration, internships, and study abroad in England. A Washington semester, work-study, accelerated degrees, and student-designed majors in the humanities and general studies are possible. A 7-year medical program is available with Karol Marcinkowski School of Medicine in Poland, as is an accelerated chiropractic program with New York Chiropractic College and Logan Chiropractic College. There are 14 national honor societies, a freshman honors program, and 19 departmental honors programs.

Faculty/Classroom: 57% of faculty are male; 43%, female. All teach undergraduates. No introductory courses are taught by graduate students.

Admissions: 65% of the 2005-2006 applicants were accepted. The SAT scores for the 2005-2006 freshman class were: Verbal--51% below 500, 39% between 500 and 599, 9% between 600 and 700, and 1% above 700; Math--46% below 500, 41% between 500 and 599, 12% between 600 and 700, and 1% above 700. 21% of the current freshmen were in the top fifth of their class; 57% were in the top two fifths. 5 freshmen graduated first in their class.

Requirements: The SAT or ACT is required. In addition, applicants should be graduates of an accredited high school or have a GED certificate. They should have completed a minimum of 16 academic units, including 4 in English, 3 in math, 2 each in history, foreign language, and lab science (3 are recommended), and 3 in electives. Those students applying to science, engineering, and health sciences programs must meet additional requirements. An interview may be requested by the university. A GPA of 3.0 is required. AP and CLEP credits are accepted. Important factors in the admissions decision are leadership record, recommendations by school officials, and extracurricular activities record.

Procedure: Freshmen are admitted to all sessions. Entrance exams should be taken May of the junior year. There are early admissions and deferred admissions plans. Applications should be filed by March 15 for fall entry, along with a $40 fee. Notification is sent on a rolling basis. Applications are accepted on-line.

Transfer: 427 transfer students enrolled in 2004-2005. All applicants must submit official transcripts for all college work taken. Those students with fewer than 24 credits must also submit a high school transcript or a copy of their state department of education's equivalency score, and SAT scores. 60 of 128 credits required for the bachelor's degree must be completed at FDU.

Visiting: There are regularly scheduled orientations for prospective students, including standardized placement testing, faculty advisement, class registration, and educational and social activities to prepare students for entrance in the fall. There are guides for informal visits and visitors may sit in on classes and stay overnight. To schedule a visit, contact the Admissions Office.

Financial Aid: In 2005-2006, 13% of all full-time freshmen and 41% of continuing full-time students received some form of financial aid. 12% of full-time freshmen and 35% of continuing full-time students received need-based aid. The average freshman award was $19,618. Need-based scholarships or need-based grants averaged $10,390; need-based self-help aid (loans and jobs) averaged $2781; non-need-based athletic scholarships averaged $14,533; and other non-need-based awards and non-need-based scholarships averaged $4572. FDU is a member of CSS. The FAFSA and the college's own financial statement are required. The priority date for freshman financial aid applications for fall entry is February 15. The deadline for filing freshman financial aid applications for fall entry is rolling.

International Students: There are 243 international students enrolled. The school actively recruits these students. They must take the TOEFL, achieving a satisfactory score, or take the MELAB, the Comprehensive English Language Test, the college's own test, or the IELTS. The SAT or ACT is highly recommended.

Computers: All students may access the system. There are no time limits. The fee is $480 per year. It is strongly recommended that all students have a personal computer.

Graduates: From July 1, 2004 to June 30, 2005, 545 bachelor's degrees were awarded. The most popular majors were liberal arts/general studies (41%), business/marketing (15%), and communications (8%). In an average class, 26% graduate in 4 years or less, 38% graduate in 5 years or less, and 40% graduate in 6 years or less. 200 companies recruited on campus in 2004-2005.

Admissions Contact: Bernetta Millonde, University Director of Admissions. E-mail: *globaleducation@fdu.edu* Web: *www.fdu.edu*

FELICIAN COLLEGE | E-2

Lodi, NJ 07644   **(201) 559-6131; Fax: (201) 559-6188**

Full-time: 250 men, 700 women	**Faculty:** 66
Part-time: 80 men, 350 women	**Ph.Ds:** 55%
Graduate: 15 men, 100 women	**Student/Faculty:** 15 to 1
Year: semesters, summer session	**Tuition:** $18,000
Application Deadline: open	**Room & Board:** $8,000
Freshman Class: n/av	
SAT: required	**COMPETITIVE**

Felician College, founded in 1942, is a private, Roman Catholic, liberal arts school with concentrations in health science, teacher education, and arts and sciences. There are 3 undergraduate and 3 graduate schools. Figures in the above capsule in this profile are approximate. In addition to regional accreditation, Felician has baccalaureate program accreditation with CAHEA and NLN. The library contains 104,000 volumes, 78,039 microform items, and 4202 audio/video tapes/CDs/DVDs, and subscribes to 401 periodicals including electronic. Computerized library services include interlibrary loans and database searching. Special learning facilities include a learning resource center and a nursing clinical lab. The 32-acre campus is in a suburban area 10 miles west of New York City. Including any residence halls, there are 5 buildings.

Student Life: 94% of undergraduates are from New Jersey. Students are from 8 states, 6 foreign countries, and Canada. 65% are from public schools. 52% are white; 15% Hispanic; 11% African American. The average age of freshmen is 19; all undergraduates, 26. 10% do not continue beyond their first year; 35% remain to graduate.

Housing: 700 students can be accommodated in college housing, which includes single-sex and coed dorms. On-campus housing is guar-

anteed for all 4 years. Alcohol is not permitted. Upperclassmen may keep cars.

Activities: There are no fraternities or sororities. There are 18 groups on campus, including art, cheerleading, chess, choir, computers, drama, education, ethnic, free enterprise, honors, international, karate, literary magazine, professional, religious, science, social service, and student government. Popular campus events include College festival, springfest, and sibling weekend.

Sports: There are 4 intercollegiate sports for men and 4 for women. Facilities include 2 fitness centers and a gym.

Disabled Students: 90% of the campus is accessible. Wheelchair ramps, elevators, special parking, specially equipped rest rooms, lowered drinking fountains, lowered telephones, special housing, and wheelchair lifts are available.

Services: Counseling and information services are available, as is tutoring in most subjects. There is remedial math, reading, and writing.

Campus Safety and Security: Measures include 24-hour foot and vehicle patrol and lighted pathways/sidewalks.

Programs of Study: Felician confers B.A., B.S., and B.S.N. degrees. Associate and master's degrees are also awarded. Bachelor's degrees are awarded in BIOLOGICAL SCIENCE (biology/biological science), BUSINESS (business administration and management and institutional management), COMMUNICATIONS AND THE ARTS (art and English), COMPUTER AND PHYSICAL SCIENCE (computer science, and mathematics), EDUCATION (elementary and special), HEALTH PROFESSIONS (clinical science and nursing), SOCIAL SCIENCE (history, humanities, philosophy, psychology, and religion). Education and nursing are the strongest academically.

Required: All students must earn a minimum GPA of 2.0 (2.5 in medical lab technology, 2.75 in nursing, and 3.0 in education), while taking 120 credit hours (128 to 130 in education), with 39 to 57 hours in their majors. Distribution requirements include 45 to 47 hours from a core curriculum, including courses in English, philosophy, religious studies, humanities, historical tradition, science, and social-cultural studies.

Special: Co-op programs are available in clinical lab sciences with the University of Medicine and Dentistry of New Jersey. In addition, internships for credit, work-study at the college, dual majors in education, an interdisciplinary studies degree, an accelerated degree in organizational management, student-designed majors within humanities and social and behavioral sciences, weekend college, and pass/fail options are possible. There is a freshman honors program.

Faculty/Classroom: 51% of faculty are male; 49%, female. The average class size in an introductory lecture is 25; in a laboratory, 20; and in a regular course, 15.

Admissions: 24% of recent applicants were accepted.

Requirements: The SAT is required. The college also recommends that applicants have 16 academic c, and 3 to 6 in academic electives, including foreign languages and studies. An interview is recommended. The GED is accepted. A GPA of 2.0 is required. AP and CLEP credits are accepted. Important factors in the admissions decision are recommendations by school officials, advanced placement or honor courses, and extracurricular activities record.

Procedure: Freshmen are admitted fall, spring, and summer. There is a rolling admissions plan. Application deadlines are open. Check with the school for current application deadlines and fee. Applications are accepted on-line. Notification is sent on a rolling basis.

Transfer: 155 transfer students enrolled in a recent year. Applicants must have maintained a minimum GPA of 2.5 (2.75 in nursing and 3.0 in education). An interview is recommended. Nursing majors require previous college-level lab science. 30 of 120 credits required for the bachelor's degree must be completed at Felician.

Visiting: There are guides for informal visits and visitors may sit in on classes. To schedule a visit, contact the Admissions Office.

Financial Aid: In a recent year, 100% of all full-time students received some form of financial aid. 48% of full-time freshmen and 50% of continuing full-time students received need-based aid. The average freshman award was $11,130. Need-based scholarships or need-based grants averaged $6000; need-based self-help aid (loans and jobs) averaged $3800; non-need-based athletic scholarships averaged $7626; and other non-need-based awards and non-need-based scholarships averaged $7626. 97% of undergraduates work part time. Average annual earnings from campus work are $3000. The average financial indebtedness of a recent graduate was $40,000. The FAFSA and the college's own financial statement are required. Check with the school for current deadlines.

International Students: The school actively recruits these students. They must take the TOEFL.

Computers: All students may access the system. There are no time limits and no fees.

Graduates: In a recent year, 171 bachelor's degrees were awarded. The most popular majors were business/marketing (43%), education (30%), and psychology (12%). In an average class, 20% graduate in 4 years or less, 10% graduate in 5 years or less, and 2% graduate in 6 years or less.

Admissions Contact: Cynthia Sievewright, Director of Admissions. E-mail: *admissions@inet.felician.edu* Web: *www.felician.edu*

GEORGIAN COURT COLLEGE — E-4
Lakewood, NJ 08701-2697

Full-time: 50 men, 1000 women	**Faculty:** 82; IIA, --$
Part-time: 100 men, 400 women	**Ph.D.s:** 72%
Graduate: 160 men, 700 women	**Student/Faculty:** 13 to 1
Year: semesters, summer session	**Tuition:** $14,000
Application Deadline: see profile	**Room & Board:** $6000
Freshman Class: n/av	
SAT or ACT required	**LESS COMPETITIVE**

(732) 364-2200, ext. 760
(800) 458-8422; Fax: (732) 364-4442

Georgian Court College, founded in 1908, is an independent Roman Catholic college. The day division matriculates only women; the evening and graduate divisions are coeducational. Undergraduate programs are offered in the arts and sciences, business administration, religion, social work, and teacher preparation. Figures in the above capsule and in this profile are approximate. In addition to regional accreditation, The Court has baccalaureate program accreditation with ACBSP and NASDTEC. The library contains 130,000 volumes, 620,000 microform items, and 2000 audio/video tapes/CDs/DVDs, and subscribes to 1400 periodicals including electronic. Computerized library services include the card catalog, interlibrary loans, and database searching. Special learning facilities include a learning resource center, art gallery, and and an arboretum. The 150-acre campus is in a suburban area 60 miles south of New York City and 60 miles east of Philadelphia. Including any residence halls, there are 17 buildings.

Student Life: 99% of undergraduates are from New Jersey. Students are from 5 states and 3 foreign countries. 83% are from public schools. 78% are white. 48% are Catholic; 9% Protestant. The average age of freshmen is 18; all undergraduates, 26. 1% do not continue beyond their first year; 84% remain to graduate.

Housing: 356 students can be accommodated in college housing, which includes single-sex dorms. On-campus housing is guaranteed for all 4 years. 74% of students commute. All students may keep cars.

Activities: There are no fraternities or sororities. There are 38 groups on campus, including art, band, choir, chorale, ethnic, honors, international, literary magazine, newspaper, professional, religious, social, social service, student government, and yearbook. Popular campus events include Irish Afternoon, Family Day, and Christmas Reception.

Sports: There are 4 intercollegiate sports for women. Facilities include a porcelain-faced swimming pool, basketball and volleyball courts, a 300-seat gym, a fitness center, athletic fields, and a tennis court.

Disabled Students: 73% of the campus is accessible. Wheelchair ramps, elevators, special parking, specially equipped rest rooms, special class scheduling, lowered drinking fountains, lowered telephones, and special equipment for the visually and hearing impaired are available.

Services: Counseling and information services are available, as is tutoring in most subjects. There is remedial math, reading, and writing.

Campus Safety and Security: Measures include 24-hour foot and vehicle patrol, security escort services, informal discussions, and pamphlets/posters/films. There are lighted pathways/sidewalks.

Programs of Study: The Court confers B.A., B.S., B.F.A., and B.S.W. degrees. Master's degrees are also awarded. Bachelor's degrees are awarded in BIOLOGICAL SCIENCE (biochemistry and biology/ biological science), BUSINESS (accounting and business administration and management), COMMUNICATIONS AND THE ARTS (art, art history and appreciation, English, French, music, and Spanish), COMPUTER AND PHYSICAL SCIENCE (chemistry, mathematics, and physics), EDUCATION (elementary and special), SOCIAL SCIENCE (history, humanities, psychology, religion, social work, and sociology). Education, psychology, and business administration are the largest.

Required: General education requirements include 9 semester courses in humanities, 5 in social science, and 3 in natural science/math. Students under 25 also must complete a semester course in phys ed. The bachelor's degree requires completion of at least 132 credit hours, including a minimum of 30 in a major field. Students must maintain a GPA of at least 2.0 overall and 2.5 in all majors but social work, which requires a 3.0.

Special: Business administration majors may participate in cooperative programs and work-study programs with various employers. Georgian Court also offers study abroad through the College Consortium for International Studies, internships in history, social work, and political science, dual majors in education, a general studies degree in humanities, field experience externships in art, psychology, education, and social work, credit for life experience, and pass/fail options. Nondegree study is possible. There are 15 national honor societies and 13 departmental honors programs.

Faculty/Classroom: 47% of faculty are male; 53%, female. 79% teach undergraduates. No introductory courses are taught by graduate students. The average class size in an introductory lecture is 19; in a laboratory, 7; and in a regular course, 13.

Requirements: The SAT or ACT is required. In addition, applicants must be graduates of accredited secondary schools or have earned a GED. The college requires 16 academic credits or Carnegie units, based on 6 years of academic electives, 4 of English, 2 each of foreign language and math, and 1 each of history and a lab science. An interview is recommended for all students, and an audition is required for applied music majors. The Court requires applicants to be in the upper 50% of their class. AP and CLEP credits are accepted.

Procedure: Freshmen are admitted fall and spring. Entrance exams should be taken by January of the senior year. There is an early admissions plan and a rolling admissions plan. Check with the school for current application deadlines and fee. Notification is sent on a rolling basis.

Transfer: Applicants with fewer than 24 credits must fulfill freshman requirements. 50 of 132 credits required for the bachelor's degree must be completed at The Court.

Visiting: There are regularly scheduled orientations for prospective students, including visits with faculty and students and a tour of facilities. There are guides for informal visits and visitors may sit in on classes and stay overnight. To schedule a visit, contact the Director of Admissions.

Financial Aid: The Court is a member of CSS. The FAFSA, the college's own financial statement, and parent and student 1040 tax forms are required. Check with the school for current deadlines.

International Students: The school actively recruits these students. They must take the TOEFL.

Computers: All students may access the system from 8 A.M. to 10 P.M. daily. There are no time limits and no fees.

Admissions Contact: Director of Admissions.
E-mail: *admissions-ugrad@georgian.edu* Web: *www.georgian.edu*

KEAN UNIVERSITY — E-2
Union, NJ 07083-0411

Full-time: 2946 men, 4645 women	**Faculty:** 382; IIA, ++$
Part-time: 716 men, 1728 women	**Ph.D.s:** 90%
Graduate: 660 men, 2263 women	**Student/Faculty:** 20 to 1
Year: semesters, summer session	**Tuition:** $7506 ($10,139)
Application Deadline: May 31	**Room & Board:** $8374
Freshman Class: 4289 applied, 3039 accepted, 1432 enrolled	
SAT Verbal/Math: 490/500*	**COMPETITIVE**

(908) 737-7100; Fax: (908) 737-7105

Kean University, founded in 1855, is a public institution offering undergraduate and graduate programs in the arts and sciences, business, education, government, nursing, and technology. Kean is primarily a metropolitan commuter university. There are 5 undergraduate schools and 1 graduate school. In addition to regional accreditation, Kean has baccalaureate program accreditation with CAHEA, CSWE, FIDER, NASAD, NASDTEC, NASM, NCATE, and NLN. The library contains 27,800 volumes, 792,000 microform items, and 6000 audio/video tapes/CDs/ DVDs, and subscribes to 25,000 periodicals including electronic. Computerized library services include the card catalog, interlibrary loans, database searching, and Internet access. Special learning facilities include a learning resource center, art gallery, radio station, TV station, and Holocaust Resource Center. The 151-acre campus is in a suburban area 12 miles west of New York City. Including any residence halls, there are 36 buildings.

Student Life: 96% of undergraduates are from New Jersey. Others are from 20 states, 65 foreign countries, and Canada. 48% are white; 21% African American; 20% Hispanic. The average age of freshmen is 21; all undergraduates, 25. 21% do not continue beyond their first year; 45% remain to graduate.

Housing: 1310 students can be accommodated in college housing, which includes coed dorms, on-campus apartments, and freshman housing. On-campus housing is guaranteed for all 4 years. 86% of students commute. Alcohol is not permitted. Upperclassmen may keep cars.

Activities: There are 13 local and 10 national fraternities and 6 local and 10 national sororities. There are 141 groups on campus, including art, cheerleading, choir, chorale, chorus, computers, dance, drama, ethnic, gay, honors, international, jazz band, leadership institute, literary magazine, musical theater, newspaper, orchestra, pep band, photography, political, professional, radio and TV, religious, social, social service, student government, and yearbook. Popular campus events include Campus Awareness Festival, Food Bank Luncheon, and Culturefest.

Sports: There are 8 intercollegiate sports for men and 10 for women, and 15 intramural sports for men and 5 for women. Facilities include a 3000-seat stadium, an 8-lane track, 7 playing fields, 4 gyms, basketball courts, 22 tennis courts, swimming pools, a track, a weight training room, pool tables, and pinball and video machines.

Disabled Students: All of the campus is accessible. Wheelchair ramps, elevators, special parking, specially equipped rest rooms, lowered drinking fountains, lowered telephones, and special housing are available.

Services: Counseling and information services are available, as is tutoring in most subjects. There is a reader service for the blind, remedial math, reading, and writing. and a full program for learning-disabled students.

Campus Safety and Security: Measures include 24-hour foot and vehicle patrol, self-defense education, security escort services, and shuttle buses. There are informal discussions, pamphlets/posters/films, emergency telephones, and lighted pathways/sidewalks.

Programs of Study: Kean confers B.A., B.S., B.F.A., B.I.D., B.S.N., and B.S.W. degrees. Master's degrees are also awarded. Bachelor's degrees are awarded in BIOLOGICAL SCIENCE (biology/biological science), BUSINESS (accounting, banking and finance, business administration and management, management science, marketing/retailing/merchandising, and recreation and leisure services), COMMUNICATIONS AND THE ARTS (art history and appreciation, communications, dramatic arts, English, fine arts, graphic design, industrial design, music, Spanish, and studio art), COMPUTER AND PHYSICAL SCIENCE (chemistry, computer science, earth science, and mathematics), EDUCATION (drama, early childhood, elementary, industrial arts, music, physical, special, and technical), ENGINEERING AND ENVIRONMENTAL DESIGN (graphic arts technology, industrial engineering technology, and interior design), HEALTH PROFESSIONS (health care administration, medical technology, nursing, rehabilitation therapy, and speech pathology/audiology), SOCIAL SCIENCE (criminal justice, economics, history, philosophy, political science/government, psychology, public administration, social work, and sociology). Allied health and education are the strongest academically. Business and education are the largest.

Required: Students must complete a freshman seminar, 18 credits of core requirements, 2 upper-level writing courses, and at least 30 credits in a major field. The bachelor's degree requires completion of 124 to 129 semester hours with a minimum GPA of 2.0.

Special: Students may study abroad in over 50 countries, and Kean offers cooperative programs and cross-registration with other members of the Consortium of East New Jersey. There are also dual majors in elementary education, a B.A. or B.S. degree in biology, chemistry, or earth science internships in many majors, a Washington semester, credit for life experience, and pass/fail options. There are 9 national honor societies, a freshman honors program, and 20 departmental honors programs.

Faculty/Classroom: 55% of faculty are male; 45%, female. All teach undergraduates. No introductory courses are taught by graduate students. The average class size in a laboratory is 16 and in a regular course, 20.

Admissions: 71% of the 2005-2006 applicants were accepted. The SAT scores for the 2005-2006 freshman class were: Verbal--57% below 500, 37% between 500 and 599, and 6% between 600 and 700; Math--45% below 500, 46% between 500 and 599, and 9% between 600 and 700. 18% of the current freshmen were in the top fifth of their class; 45% were in the top two fifths.

Requirements: The SAT is required. In addition, applicants must be graduates of accredited secondary schools or have earned a GED. College preparatory study includes 4 courses in English, 3 in math, 2 each in lab science and social studies, and 5 in academic electives. An essay is also required. Kean requires applicants to be in the upper 50% of their class. A GPA of 2.0 is required. AP and CLEP credits are accepted. Important factors in the admissions decision are leadership record, advanced placement or honor courses, and recommendations by school officials.

Procedure: Freshmen are admitted fall and spring. Applications should be filed by May 31 for fall entry and December 1 for spring entry, along with a $50 fee. There is a rolling admissions plan. Notification is sent on a rolling basis. Applications are accepted on-line.

Transfer: 992 transfer students enrolled in 2004-2005. Applicants must present a minimum GPA of 2.0. Those students tranferring fewer than 15 credits must also submit SAT scores. 32 of 124 credits required for the bachelor's degree must be completed at Kean.

Visiting: There are regularly scheduled orientations for prospective students. There are guides for informal visits. To schedule a visit, contact the Admissions Office at *admitme@KEAN.EDU*.

Financial Aid: In 2005-2006, 73% of all full-time freshmen and 64% of continuing full-time students received some form of financial aid. 66% of full-time freshmen and 56% of continuing full-time students received need-based aid. The average freshman award was $7022. Need-based scholarships or need-based grants averaged $4741; need-based self-help aid (loans and jobs) averaged $2066; and other non-need-based awards and non-need-based scholarships averaged $1079. 9% of undergraduates work part time. Average annual earnings from campus work are $1989. The average financial indebtedness of the 2005 graduate was $16,363. The FAFSA is required. The priority date for freshman financial aid applications for fall entry is March 15.

International Students: There are 238 international students enrolled. The school actively recruits these students. A satisfactory score is required on the SAT or the ACT.

Computers: All students may access the system. There are no time limits and no fees.

Graduates: From July 1, 2004 to June 30, 2005, 1802 bachelor's degrees were awarded. The most popular majors were management science (10%), psychology (8%), and elementary education (7%). In an average class, 14% graduate in 4 years or less, 38% graduate in 5 years or less, and 45% graduate in 6 years or less.

Admissions Contact: Audley Bridges, Director of Admissions. A video is available. E-mail: *admitme@kean.edu* Web: *www.kean.edu*

MONMOUTH UNIVERSITY
West Long Branch, NJ 07764-1898

E-3

(732) 571-3456
(800) 543-9671; Fax: (732) 263-5166

Full-time: 1768 men, 2348 women	**Faculty:** 212; IIA, av$
Part-time: 139 men, 300 women	**Ph.D.s:** 76%
Graduate: 476 men, 1319 women	**Student/Faculty:** 19 to 1
Year: semesters, summer session	**Tuition:** $20,686
Application Deadline: March 1	**Room & Board:** $8270
Freshman Class: 5089 applied, 3504 accepted, 943 enrolled	
SAT Verbal/Math: 528/548*	**ACT:** 23 **COMPETITIVE**

Monmouth University, founded in 1933, is a private comprehensive institution offering both undergraduate and graduate programs in the arts and sciences, business, education, upper-level nursing, technology, and professional training. There are 6 undergraduate schools and 1 graduate school. In addition to regional accreditation, Monmouth has baccalaureate program accreditation with AACSB, ABET, ACS, CCNNE, CSWE, and NLN. The library contains 248,000 volumes, and subscribes to 22,500 periodicals including electronic. Computerized library services include the card catalog, interlibrary loans, database searching, Internet access, and laptop Internet portals. Special learning facilities include a learning resource center, art gallery, radio station, TV station, theater, and greenhouse. The 155-acre campus is in a suburban area 60 miles south of New York City. Including any residence halls, there are 54 buildings.

Student Life: 92% of undergraduates are from New Jersey. Others are from 22 states, 10 foreign countries, and Canada. 78% are white. The average age of freshmen is 18; all undergraduates, 22. 25% do not continue beyond their first year; 55% remain to graduate.

Housing: 1740 students can be accommodated in college housing, which includes coed dormitories, on-campus apartments, and off-campus apartments. In addition, there are honors houses. On-campus housing is available on a first-come, first-served basis and is available on a lottery system for upperclassmen. Priority is given to out-of-town students. 58% of students commute. All students may keep cars.

Activities: 8% of men belong to 7 national fraternities; 9% of women belong to 6 national sororities. There are 62 groups on campus, including band, cheerleading, choir, chorus, computers, dance, drama, ethnic, gay, honors, international, jazz band, literary magazine, musical theater, newspaper, pep band, political, professional, radio and TV, religious, social service, student government, and yearbook. Popular campus events include Springfest, Ebony Night, and Winter Ball.

Sports: There are 8 intercollegiate sports for men and 9 for women, and 8 intramural sports for men and 9 for women. Facilities include a 2500-seat gym, a 4600-seat football field, outdoor tennis courts, 3 basketball courts, an 8-lane all-weather track, an indoor Olympic-size pool, exercise and weight rooms, and baseball, softball, soccer, and field hockey fields.

Disabled Students: 90% of the campus is accessible. Wheelchair ramps, elevators, special parking, specially equipped rest rooms, special class scheduling, lowered drinking fountains, special housing, and academic assistance provided within the classroom are available.

Services: Counseling and information services are available, as is tutoring in every subject. There is a reader service for the blind, and remedial math, reading, and writing.

Campus Safety and Security: Measures include 24-hour foot and vehicle patrol, self-defense education, security escort services, and informal discussions. There are pamphlets/posters/films, emergency telephones, and lighted pathways/sidewalks. There is an official Monmouth University police force and a student watch organization.

Programs of Study: Monmouth confers B.A., B.S., B.F.A., B.S.N., and B.S.W. degrees. Associate and master's degrees are also awarded. Bachelor's degrees are awarded in BIOLOGICAL SCIENCE (biology/biological science and marine biology), BUSINESS (accounting, banking and finance, business administration and management, business economics, and marketing management), COMMUNICATIONS AND THE ARTS (art, art history and appreciation, communications, English, modern language, music, and music business management), COMPUTER AND PHYSICAL SCIENCE (chemistry, computer science, mathematics, and software engineering), EDUCATION (art, English, foreign languages, mathematics, music, science, secondary, and special), ENGINEERING AND ENVIRONMENTAL DESIGN (computer graphics), HEALTH PROFESSIONS (clinical science, medical laboratory technology, nursing, and premedicine), SOCIAL SCIENCE (anthropology, criminal justice, history, political science/government, prelaw, psychology, and social work). Business, education, and communication are the largest.

Required: General education requirements include 6 credits each of English composition, literature, history, natural science, social sciences, and cross-cultural studies; 3 each of math, computer science, critical discourse, and global issues; and 1 of phys ed. Students must also pass a writing proficiency examination. To graduate, students must earn at least 128 credits, including 30 to 81 in a major, with a minimum GPA of 2.0 overall and 2.1 in the major.

Special: Students may study abroad. There are cooperative and internship programs and a Washington semester. Monmouth also offers work-study programs, dual majors, flexible studies programs, and credit for life experience. Nondegree study is possible. There are 13 national honor societies and a freshman honors program.

Faculty/Classroom: 52% of faculty are male; 48%, female. 92% teach undergraduates. No introductory courses are taught by graduate students. The average class size in an introductory lecture is 26; in a laboratory, 10; and in a regular course, 22.

Admissions: 69% of the 2005-2006 applicants were accepted. The SAT scores for the 2005-2006 freshman class were: Verbal--30% below 500, 56% between 500 and 599, and 13% between 600 and 700; Math--21% below 500, 56% between 500 and 599, 22% between 600 and 700, and 1% above 700. The ACT scores were 33% below 21, 25% between 21 and 23, 25% between 24 and 26, 13% between 27 and 28, and 4% above 28. 26% of the current freshmen were in the top fifth of their class; 58% were in the top two fifths.

Requirements: The SAT or ACT is required. The ACT Optional Writing test is also required. Applicants must be graduates of accredited secondary schools or have earned a GED. The college requires 16 Carnegie units, based on 4 years of English, 3 of math, and 2 each of history and science, with the remaining 5 units in academic electives. An essay and an interview are also recommended. A GPA of 2.25 is required. AP and CLEP credits are accepted. Important factors in the admissions decision are advanced placement or honor courses, extracurricular activities record, and leadership record.

Procedure: Freshmen are admitted fall, spring, and summer. Entrance exams should be taken by December of the senior year. There are early decision and deferred admissions plans. Early decision applications should be filed by December 1; regular applications, by March 1 for fall entry and January 1 for spring entry, along with a $35 fee. Notification of early decision is sent January 1; regular decision, April 1. 150 early decision candidates were accepted for the 2005-2006 class. 760 applicants were on the 2005 waiting list; 22 were admitted. Applications are accepted on-line.

Transfer: 581 transfer students enrolled in 2004-2005. Transfers with fewer than 24 transferable college credits must provide a high school transcript and SAT scores. All transfer applicants must submit college transcripts and a statement of good standing. A minimum college GPA of 2.0 is required. 32 of 128 credits required for the bachelor's degree must be completed at Monmouth.

Visiting: There are regularly scheduled orientations for prospective students, including campus tours and interviews. There are guides for informal visits and visitors may sit in on classes. To schedule a visit, contact the Admissions Office at (800) 543-9671.

Financial Aid: In 2005-2006, 97% of all full-time freshmen and 94% of continuing full-time students received some form of financial aid. 84% of full-time freshmen and 77% of continuing full-time students received need-based aid. Need-based scholarships or need-based grants averaged $3084 ($9026 maximum); need-based self-help aid (loans and jobs) averaged $4100 ($5500 maximum); non-need-based athletic scholarships averaged $9993 ($23,274 maximum); and other non-need-based awards and non-need-based scholarships averaged $4091 ($15,000 maximum). Average annual earnings from campus work are $1500. The FAFSA is required.

International Students: There are 14 international students enrolled. The school actively recruits these students. They must score satisfactorily on the written TOEFL or on the electronic version or take the MELAB. They must also take the IELTS, or the Cambridge ESOL (CAE). Students from English speaking countries must take the SAT or ACT.

Computers: Wireless access is available. There are more than 670 PCs available for students use in computer labs on campus in academic buildings, the library, the student center, and residence halls, and 2 of these labs are open 24 hours. There is wireless network service in the library, academic buildings, the student center, the resident dining hall, the administration building, and outside locations. Students are provided with campus-wide network connectivity, controlled Internet access, access to personal e-mail accounts, and to network servers. All students may access the system 24 hours a day, 7 days a week. There are no time limits and no fees.

Graduates: From July 1, 2004 to June 30, 2005, 904 bachelor's degrees were awarded. The most popular majors were business (29%), education (18%), and communication (17%). In an average class, 37% graduate in 4 years or less, 53% graduate in 5 years or less, and 54% graduate in 6 years or less. 205 companies recruited on campus in 2004-2005.

Admissions Contact: Lauren Vento Cifelli, Director of Undergraduate Admission. E-mail: admission@monmouth.edu Web: www.monmouth.edu

MONTCLAIR STATE UNIVERSITY   E-2
Upper Montclair, NJ 07043-1624   (973) 655-4444
(800) 331-9205; Fax: (973) 655-7700

Full-time: 3927 men, 5982 women	**Faculty:** 477; IIA, ++$
Part-time: 812 men, 1453 women	**Ph.D.s:** 94%
Graduate: 1052 men, 2837 women	**Student/Faculty:** 21 to 1
Year: semesters, summer session	**Tuition:** $7709 ($12,157)
Application Deadline: March 1	**Room & Board:** $8618
Freshman Class: 8843 applied, 4773 accepted, 1907 enrolled	
SAT Verbal/Math: 537/548*	**COMPETITIVE**

Montclair State University, established in 1908, is a public institution offering programs in liberal arts and sciences, business administration, fine and performing arts, and professional studies. There are 5 undergraduate schools and 1 graduate school. In addition to regional accreditation, Montclair has baccalaureate program accreditation with AACSB, ABET, ADA, ASHA, CAAHEP, CSAB, NASAD, NASD, NASDTEC, NASM, NAST, NCATE, and NRPA. The library contains 430,968 volumes, 1,132,237 microform items, and 21,145 audio/video tapes/CDs/DVDs, and subscribes to 18,000 periodicals including electronic. Computerized library services include the card catalog, interlibrary loans, database searching, and Internet access. Special learning facilities include a learning resource center, art gallery, radio station, TV station, psychoeducational center, and Academic Success Center. The 275-acre campus is in a suburban area 14 miles west of New York City. Including any residence halls, there are 55 buildings.

Student Life: 95% of undergraduates are from New Jersey. Others are from 37 states, 92 foreign countries, and Canada. 80% are from public schools. 56% are white; 17% Hispanic; 10% African American. 47% are Catholic; 33% Muslim 3%, Hindu 1%, Buddhist 1%, no preference 14%, unknown 14%; Protestant 17%. The average age of freshmen is 18; all undergraduates, 23. 18% do not continue beyond their first year; 58% remain to graduate.

Housing: 3300 students can be accommodated in college housing, which includes single-sex and coed dorms and on-campus apartments. In addition, there are honors houses and special-interest houses. On-campus housing is available on a first-come, first-served basis. Priority is given to out-of-town students. 67% of students commute. Alcohol is not permitted. All students may keep cars.

Activities: 4% of men belong to 1 local and 14 national fraternities; 4% of women belong to 4 local and 12 national sororities. There are 115 groups on campus, including band, cheerleading, choir, chorus, dance, drama, ethnic, gay, honors, international, jazz band, literary magazine, marching band, musical theater, newspaper, orchestra, professional, radio and TV, religious, social, social service, and student government. Popular campus events include Welcome Week, Montclairfest, and Spring Week.

Sports: There are 8 intercollegiate sports for men and 8 for women, and 10 intramural sports for men and 10 for women. Facilities include a gym complex with competitive pool, 2 basketball courts, an auxiliary gym, wrestling room, a 6000-seat Astroturf stadium, a baseball stadium, a softball stadium, soccer park, all-weather track, tennis courts, and a fitness center.

Disabled Students: 90% of the campus is accessible. Wheelchair ramps, elevators, special parking, specially equipped rest rooms, special class scheduling, lowered drinking fountains, lowered telephones, special housing, curb cuts, speaker phones, special building signs, TDDs, and priority registration are available. An office for students with disabilities has been established.

Services: Counseling and information services are available, as is tutoring in most subjects. There is a reader service for the blind, and remedial math, reading, and writing. Audio textbooks are available.

Campus Safety and Security: Measures include 24-hour foot and vehicle patrol, self-defense education, security escort services, and shuttle buses. There are informal discussions, pamphlets/posters/films, emergency telephones, lighted pathways/sidewalks, a full-time campus police force, a crime prevention officer, and crime prevention programs.

Programs of Study: Montclair confers B.A., B.S., B.F.A., and B.Mus. degrees. Master's degrees are also awarded. Bachelor's degrees are awarded in BIOLOGICAL SCIENCE (biochemistry, biology/biological science, environmental biology, and molecular biology), BUSINESS (accounting, banking and finance, business administration and management, business economics, hospitality management services, international business management, management information systems, marketing management, recreation and leisure services, retailing, and tourism), COMMUNICATIONS AND THE ARTS (art, art history and appreciation, broadcasting, classics, communications, communications technology, creative writing, dance, dramatic arts, English, film arts, fine arts, French, Italian, Latin, linguistics, music, music performance, music theory and composition, musical theater, public relations, Spanish, speech/debate/rhetoric, studio art, and theater design), COMPUTER AND PHYSICAL SCIENCE (applied mathematics, astronomy, chemistry, computer science, geoscience, information sciences and systems, mathematics, and physics), EDUCATION (art, athletic training, business, early childhood, health, home economics, music, and physical), HEALTH PROFESSIONS (allied health, community health work, music therapy, predentistry, premedicine, and prepharmacy), SOCIAL SCIENCE (anthropology, criminal justice, economics, food production/management/services, geography, gerontology, history, home economics, human ecology, humanities, law, paralegal studies, parks and recreation management, philosophy, political science/government, psychology, religion, sociology, and women's studies). Business administration, family, and child studies, and psychology are the largest.

Required: Students must successfully complete a minimum of 120 semester hours, with 33 to 82 in the major, while maintaining a minimum GPA of 2.0. General education requirements include courses in communications, contemporary issues, art appreciation, a foreign language, humanities, math, natural/physical science, social sciences, and multicultural awareness, as well as 1 semester hour in phys ed and 3 semester hours in computer science.

Special: Internships, co-op programs in all majors, credit by exam, pass/fail options, work-study, credit for life experience, independent study, and study abroad in 50 countries are offered. Joint-degree programs are offered in practical anthropology and applied economics, and a 5-year B.A.-B.Mus. program in music is available, as is an articulated medical, dental, physical therapy, and physician assistant program with the University of Medicine and Dentistry of New Jersey and an articulated program leading to a Pharm.D. with Rutgers University. There are 28 national honor societies, a freshman honors program, and 3 departmental honors programs.

Faculty/Classroom: 56% of faculty are male; 44%, female. All teach undergraduates. The average class size in an introductory lecture is 24 and in a regular course, 24.

Admissions: 54% of the 2005-2006 applicants were accepted. The SAT scores for the 2005-2006 freshman class were: Verbal--25% below 500, 58% between 500 and 599, 14% between 600 and 700, and 3% above 700; Math--18% below 500, 60% between 500 and 599, 21% between 600 and 700, and 2% above 700. 37% of the current freshmen were in the top fifth of their class; 73% were in the top two fifths. 25 freshmen graduated first in their class.

Requirements: The SAT is required. In addition, applicants must submit 16 Carnegie units, including 4 in English, 3 to 4 in math (including algebra I and II and geometry), 2 each in lab science, social studies, and a foreign language, and the remainder in additional courses in these fields. The GED is accepted. A portfolio, audition, or interview is required for students planning to major in fine arts, music, speech, or theater. Admission to computer science requires 4 years of math, including trigonometry. AP and CLEP credits are accepted. Important factors in the admissions decision are advanced placement or honor courses, recommendations by school officials, and leadership record.

Procedure: Freshmen are admitted fall and spring. Entrance exams should be taken in October, November, or December of the senior year. There is a rolling admissions plan. Applications should be filed by March 1 for fall entry and November 1 for spring entry. Notification is sent on a rolling basis. Applications are accepted on-line.The fall 2005 application fee waas $55.

Transfer: 1801 transfer students enrolled in 2004-2005. Applicants must have completed a minimum of 15 credits from an accredited college. A cumulative GPA of 2.5 is required for most majors, with higher required in select programs. Applicants must have completed English composition. High school and college transcripts are required. 32 of 120 semester hours required for the bachelor's degree must be completed at Montclair.

Visiting: There are regularly scheduled orientations for prospective students. There are guides for informal visits. To schedule a visit, contact the Admissions Office at (973) 655-5322 or *www.montclair.edu/admissions/visit.html*.

Financial Aid: In 2005-2006, 73% of all full-time freshmen and 57% of continuing full-time students received some form of financial aid. 53% of full-time freshmen and 44% of continuing full-time students received need-based aid. The average freshman award was $9682. Need-based scholarships or need-based grants averaged $6557 ($11,784 maximum); need-based self-help aid (loans and jobs) averaged $3108 ($6525 maximum); and other non-need-based awards and non-need-based scholarships averaged $4384 ($17,540 maximum). 48% of undergraduates work part time. Average annual earnings from campus work are $1795. The average financial indebtedness of the 2005 graduate was $16,654. The FAFSA is required. The priority date for freshman financial aid applications for fall entry is March 1.

International Students: There are 422 international students enrolled. The school actively recruits these students. They must score satisfactorily on the TOEFL.

Computers: Wireless access is available. PC and Mac labs are located throughout the campus, with about 250 computers and PC printers. A network of Sun workstations is also available. A wide variety of general and discipline-specific software is offered. Residence hall rooms are wired for network connections and Internet access is available. All students may access the system. There are no time limits and no fees. It is

recommended that students in Business Administration have personal computers.

Graduates: From July 1, 2004 to June 30, 2005, 2206 bachelor's degrees were awarded. The most popular majors were business administration (22%), psychology (12%), and human ecology (10%). In an average class, 1% graduate in 3 years or less, 24% graduate in 4 years or less, 52% graduate in 5 years or less, and 58% graduate in 6 years or less. 150 companies recruited on campus in 2004-2005. Of the 2004 graduating class, 18% were enrolled in graduate school within 6 months of graduation and 88% were employed.

Admissions Contact: Dennis Craig, Director of Admissions. E-mail: *msuadm@mail.montclair.edu* Web: *www.montclair.edu*

NEW JERSEY CITY UNIVERSITY   E-2

Jersey City, NJ 07305   (201) 200-3234
                                     (888) 441-NJCU; Fax: (201) 200-2044

Full-time: 1760 men, 2809 women	**Faculty:** 251
Part-time: 475 men, 925 women	**Ph.Ds:** 79%
Graduate: none	**Student/Faculty:** 18 to 1
Year: semesters, summer session	**Tuition:** $6389 ($11,429)
Application Deadline: April 1	**Room & Board:** $7306
Freshman Class: 2722 applied, 1469 accepted, 691 enrolled	
SAT Verbal/Math: 440/440*	**LESS COMPETITIVE**

New Jersey City University, founded in 1927, is a public institution offering undergraduate and graduate programs in the arts and sciences, business administration, education, health science, upper-level nursing, and other professional fields. There are 3 undergraduate schools and 1 graduate school. In addition to regional accreditation, NJCU has baccalaureate program accreditation with AACSB, NASAD, NASM, NCATE, and NLN. The library contains 255,780 volumes, 499,237 microform items, and 2470 audio/video tapes/CDs/DVDs, and subscribes to 24,377 periodicals including electronic. Computerized library services include the card catalog, interlibrary loans, database searching, and Internet access. Special learning facilities include a learning resource center, art gallery, radio station, a media arts center, and a lab school for special education instruction. The 17-acre campus is in an urban area 10 miles west of New York City. Including any residence halls, there are 15 buildings.

Student Life: 99% of undergraduates are from New Jersey. Others are from 18 states and 47 foreign countries. 32% are white; 24% Hispanic; 15% African American. The average age of freshmen is 18; all undergraduates, 23. 24% do not continue beyond their first year; 37% remain to graduate.

Housing: 276 students can be accommodated in college housing, which includes coed dorms. On-campus housing is guaranteed for all 4 years. 95% of students commute. Alcohol is not permitted. All students may keep cars.

Activities: 1% of men belong to 4 local and 14 national fraternities; 1% of women belong to 4 local and 3 national sororities. There are 30 groups on campus, including art, band, choir, chorale, chorus, computers, dance, drama, ethnic, film, gay, honors, international, jazz band, literary magazine, musical theater, newspaper, opera, orchestra, photography, political, professional, radio and TV, religious, social, social service, student government, symphony, and yearbook. Popular campus events include President's Picnic, Town and Gown Concert, and lecture series.

Sports: There are 6 intercollegiate sports for men and 7 for women, and 14 intramural sports for men and 14 for women. Facilities include an athletic and fitness center with a 2000-seat arena, jogging track, fitness facilities, 6-lane pool, sauna, racquetball courts, and soccer, tennis, baseball, and softball facilities.

Disabled Students: All of the campus is accessible. Wheelchair ramps, elevators, special parking, specially equipped rest rooms, special class scheduling, lowered drinking fountains, and lowered telephones are available.

Services: Counseling and information services are available, as is tutoring in most subjects. There is remedial math, reading, and writing.

Campus Safety and Security: Measures include 24-hour foot and vehicle patrol, security escort services, shuttle buses, and informal discussions. There are pamphlets/posters/films, emergency telephones, and lighted pathways/sidewalks.

Programs of Study: NJCU confers B.A., B.S., B.F.A., and B.S.N. degrees. Master's degrees are also awarded. Bachelor's degrees are awarded in BIOLOGICAL SCIENCE (biology/biological science), BUSINESS (business administration and management and retailing), COMMUNICATIONS AND THE ARTS (design, English, fine arts, media arts, music, photography, and Spanish), COMPUTER AND PHYSICAL SCIENCE (chemistry, computer science, geology, mathematics, and physics), EDUCATION (art, early childhood, elementary, health, music, secondary, and special), HEALTH PROFESSIONS (medical laboratory technology, nuclear medical technology, nursing, and public health), SOCIAL SCIENCE (criminal justice, economics, geography, history, philosophy, political science/government, psychology, and sociology). Business, computer science, and criminal justice are the largest.

Required: Students must complete 66 semester hours in general education courses, satisfy college requirements in English, communication, and math, and complete the introductory career exploration and computer usage courses. The bachelor's degree requires completion of at least 128 semester hours, including 36 to 54 in a major field, with a minimum GPA of 2.0. Distribution requirements include 9 credits each in natural science, social science, humanities, and fine and performing arts and 6 credits in communications and contemporary world.

Special: Co-op programs and internships in all majors are available. NJCU also offers study abroad, work-study programs, numerous health science programs, and some programs affiliated with New Jersey College of Medicine and Dentistry in Newark. Nondegree study and dual majors are possible. There are 4 national honor societies, a freshman honors program, and 1 departmental honors program.

Faculty/Classroom: 52% of faculty are male; 48%, female. All teach undergraduates. The average class size in an introductory lecture is 25; in a laboratory, 15; and in a regular course, 16.

Admissions: 54% of the 2005-2006 applicants were accepted. The SAT scores for the 2005-2006 freshman class were: Verbal--79% below 500, 16% between 500 and 599, and 4% between 600 and 700; Math--74% below 500, 23% between 500 and 599, and 3% between 600 and 700. 27% of the current freshmen were in the top fifth of their class; 35% were in the top two fifths.

Requirements: The SAT is required. In addition, applicants must be graduates of accredited secondary schools or have earned a GED. The college requires 16 Carnegie units, including 4 in English, 3 in math, and 2 each in social studies and a lab science, with the remaining 5 units in a foreign language and additional academic courses. An essay is also required, and an interview is recommended. NJCU requires applicants to be in the upper 50% of their class. A GPA of 2.5 is required. AP and CLEP credits are accepted. Important factors in the admissions decision are advanced placement or honor courses, evidence of special talent, and recommendations by school officials.

Procedure: Freshmen are admitted fall and spring. Entrance exams should be taken in the spring of the junior year or fall of the senior year. There is a deferred admissions plan and a rolling admissions plan. Applications should be filed by April 1 for fall entry, along with a $35 fee. Notification is sent on a rolling basis. A waiting list is an active part of the admissions procedure. Applications are accepted on-line.

Transfer: 761 transfer students enrolled in 2004-2005. Applicants must present a minimum GPA of 2.0 in at least 12 credit hours completed at the college level. Students transferring fewer than 12 credits must also submit satisfactory SAT scores. An interview is recommended for all transfers. A basic skills test is required for transfers who have fewer than 30 credits or have not taken English or math at their previous school. 36 of 128 credits required for the bachelor's degree must be completed at NJCU.

Visiting: There are regularly scheduled orientations for prospective students, including a financial aid workshop, guided tours, and open house. There is a summer orientation. There are guides for informal visits and visitors may sit in on classes. To schedule a visit, contact the Admissions Office.

Financial Aid: The FAFSA is required.

International Students: There was 100 international students enrolled in a recent year. They must score satisfactorily on the TOEFL and or the SAT.

Computers: All students may access the system 24 hours a day. There are no time limits and no fees.

Graduates: From July 1, 2004 to June 30, 2005, 879 bachelor's degrees were awarded. The most popular majors were business administration (23%), computer science (10%), and criminal justice (10%). In an average class, 4% graduate in 4 years or less, 20% graduate in 5 years or less, and 37% graduate in 6 years or less. 350 companies recruited on campus in 2004-2005.

Admissions Contact: Carmen Panlilio, Assistant Vice President for Admissions and Financial Aid. E-mail: *admissions@njcu.edu* Web: *www.njcu.edu*

NEW JERSEY INSTITUTE OF TECHNOLOGY   E-2

Newark, NJ 07102-1982

(973) 596-3300
(800) 222-NJIT; Fax: (973) 596-6085

Full-time: 3400 men, 900 women	**Faculty:** 301; I, +$
Part-time: 1200 men, 300 women	**Ph.D.s:** 98%
Graduate: 2100 men, 1000 women	**Student/Faculty:** 14 to 1
Year: semesters, summer session	**Tuition:** $9000 ($14,000)
Application Deadline: see profile	**Room & Board:** $8000
Freshman Class: n/av	
SAT: required	**VERY COMPETITIVE**

New Jersey Institute of Technology is a public research university providing instruction, research, and public service in engineering, computer science, management, architecture, engineering technology, applied sciences, and related fields. Figures in the above capsule and in this profile are approximate. There are 6 undergraduate schools and 1 graduate school. In addition to regional accreditation, NJIT has baccalaureate program accreditation with AACSB, ABET, and NAAB. The 2 libraries contain 220,000 volumes, 7325 microform items, and 73,807 audio/video tapes/CDs/DVDs, and subscribe to 2500 periodicals including electronic. Computerized library services include the card catalog, interlibrary loans, and database searching. Special learning facilities include a learning resource center, art gallery, radio station, and 3 TV studios. NJIT is home to many government- and industry-sponsored labs and research centers, including the EPA Northeast Hazardous Substance Research Center, the National Center for Transportation and Industrial Productivity, the Center for Manufacturing Systems, the Emission Reduction Research Center, the Microelectronics Research Center, the Center for Microwave and Lightwave Engineering, and the Multi-Lifecycle Engineering Center. The 45-acre campus is in an urban area 10 miles west of New York City. Including any residence halls, there are 25 buildings.

Student Life: 94% of undergraduates are from New Jersey. Students are from 36 states, 109 foreign countries, and Canada. 80% are from public schools. 31% are white; 22% Asian American; 14% foreign nationals. The average age of freshmen is 18; all undergraduates, 23. 15% do not continue beyond their first year; 49% remain to graduate.

Housing: 1434 students can be accommodated in college housing, which includes coed dorms. On-campus housing is available on a first-come, first-served basis and is available on a lottery system for upperclassmen. Priority is given to out-of-town students. 75% of students commute. All students may keep cars.

Activities: 7% of men belong to 4 local and 10 national fraternities; 5% of women belong to 4 local and 5 national sororities. There are 92 groups on campus, including art, chess, computers, drama, drum and bugle corps, ethnic, gay, honors, international, musical theater, newspaper, photography, professional, radio and TV, religious, social, social service, student government, and yearbook. Popular campus events include Miniversity, International Students Food Festival, and Leadership Training Weekend.

Sports: There are 9 intercollegiate sports for men and 6 for women, and 13 intramural sports for men and 7 for women. Facilities include a 1000-seat stadium, a fitness center with an indoor track, a 6-lane swimming pool, 4 tennis courts, 4 racquet sport courts, playing fields, bowling lanes, a table tennis and billiards area, and 3 gyms, the largest of which seats 1200.

Disabled Students: 95% of the campus is accessible. Wheelchair ramps, elevators, special parking, specially equipped rest rooms, special class scheduling, lowered drinking fountains, and lowered telephones are available.

Services: Counseling and information services are available, as is tutoring in most subjects. There is a reader service for the blind, and remedial math, reading, and writing.

Campus Safety and Security: Measures include 24-hour foot and vehicle patrol, self-defense education, security escort services, and shuttle buses. There are informal discussions, pamphlets/posters/films, emergency telephones, and lighted pathways/sidewalks.

Programs of Study: NJIT confers B.A., B.S., and B.Arch. degrees. Master's and doctoral degrees are also awarded. Bachelor's degrees are awarded in BIOLOGICAL SCIENCE (biology/biological science), BUSINESS (management science), COMMUNICATIONS AND THE ARTS (communications and technical and business writing), COMPUTER AND PHYSICAL SCIENCE (applied mathematics, applied physics, chemistry, computer management, computer science, information sciences and systems, and mathematics), ENGINEERING AND ENVIRONMENTAL DESIGN (architecture, biomedical engineering, chemical engineering, civil engineering, computer engineering, computer technology, electrical/electronics engineering, engineering and applied science, engineering technology, environmental engineering, environmental science, geophysical engineering, industrial engineering, manufacturing engineering, mechanical engineering, technological management, and technology and public affairs), SOCIAL SCIENCE (history). Engineering, computer science, and architecture are the strongest academically. Engineering is the largest.

Required: General university requirements include 9 credits of humanities and social science electives, 7 of natural sciences, 6 each of math, cultural history, basic social sciences, and engineering technology, 3 each of English and management, and 2 of computer science. Students must also complete 2 courses in phys ed. To graduate, students must earn between 124 and 164 credits, depending on the program, including 50 in the major, with a minimum GPA of 2.0 in upper-level major courses.

Special: Cross-registration is offered in conjunction with Essex County College, Rutgers University's Newark campus, and the University of Medicine and Dentistry of New Jersey. Cooperative programs, available in all majors, include two 6-month internships. There are 3-2 engineering degree programs with Stockton State College and Lincoln and Seton Hall Universities. NJIT also offers work-study programs, study abroad in 18 countries, dual and interdisciplinary majors, accelerated degree programs, distance learning, and nondegree study. There is 1 national honor society and a freshman honors program.

Faculty/Classroom: 84% of faculty are male; 16%, female. 74% teach undergraduates. All do research, and 74% do both. Graduate students teach 10% of introductory courses. The average class size in an introductory lecture is 30; in a laboratory, 27; and in a regular course, 25.

Admissions: 68% of recent applicants were accepted. 1% of recent freshmen were in the top fifth of their class; 7% were in the top two fifths.

Requirements: The SAT is required. In addition, the SAT: Subject Test in Math I or II is also required. Applicants should have completed 16 secondary school units, including 4 each in English and math, 2 in a lab science, and 6 in a distribution of social studies, foreign language, math, and science courses. AP and CLEP credits are accepted. Important factors in the admissions decision are advanced placement or honor courses, recommendations by school officials, and geographic diversity.

Procedure: Freshmen are admitted fall and spring. Entrance exams should be taken in May of the junior year or November of the senior year. Check with the school for current application and deadlines and fee. There is a rolling admissions plan.11 applicants were on a recent waiting list; 11 were admitted. Applications are accepted on-line.

Transfer: 494 transfer students enrolled in a recent year. A minimum college GPA of 2.0 is required, but 2.5 or higher is recommended. Students must submit transcripts of all attempted postsecondary academic work. Applicants with fewer than 30 credits may be asked to provide scores on the SAT and the SAT: Subject Test in Math, as well as high school transcripts. Engineering technology students must present an associate degree. Admission to the School of Architecture is very competitive for transfer students. 33 of 124 credits required for the bachelor's degree must be completed at NJIT.

Visiting: There are regularly scheduled orientations for prospective students, including tours and meetings with admissions personnel, students, and faculty. There are guides for informal visits and visitors may sit in on classes and stay overnight. To schedule a visit, contact Kathy Kelly, Director of Admissions.

Financial Aid: In a recent year, 70% of all full-time students received some form of financial aid. 65% of all full-time students received need-based aid. Need-based scholarships or need-based grants averaged $4200; need-based self-help aid (loans and jobs) averaged $2800; and other non-need-based awards and non-need-based scholarships averaged $2420. 70% of undergraduates work part time. Average annual earnings from campus work are $2150. The average financial indebtedness of a recent graduate was $11,000. The FAFSA and the college's own financial statement are required. The priority date for freshman financial aid applications for fall entry is March 15. The deadline for filing freshman financial aid applications for fall entry is May 15. Check with the school for current deadlines.

International Students: There were 289 international students enrolled in a recent year. The school actively recruits these students. They must take the TOEFL and also take the SAT. Students must also take SAT: Subject Tests in Math I or II.

Computers: All students may access the system. There are no time limits and no fees. All students are required to have personal computers.

Graduates: In a recent year, 894 bachelor's degrees were awarded. The most popular majors were computer science (20%), computer engineering (13%), and engineering technology (12%). In an average class, 16% graduate in 4 years or less, 39% graduate in 5 years or less, and 49% graduate in 6 years or less. 200 companies recruited on campus in a recent year. Of a recent graduating class, 20% were enrolled in graduate school within 6 months of graduation.

Admissions Contact: Kathy Kelly, Director of Admissions.
E-mail: *admissions@admin.njit.edu*

PRINCETON UNIVERSITY

D-3

Princeton, NJ 08544-0430   (609) 258-3060; Fax: (609) 258-6743

Full-time: 2510 men, 2200 women	**Faculty:** 840; I, ++$
Part-time: none	**Ph.D.s:** 94%
Graduate: 1240 men, 779 women	**Student/Faculty:** 6 to 1
Year: semesters	**Tuition:** $31,450
Application Deadline: January 2	**Room & Board:** $8763
Freshman Class: 16,529 applied, 1826 accepted, 1230 enrolled	
SAT: required	**MOST COMPETITIVE**

Princeton University, established in 1746, is a private institution offering degrees in the liberal arts and sciences, engineering, applied science, architecture, public and international affairs, interdisciplinary and regional studies, and the creative arts. In addition to regional accreditation, Princeton has baccalaureate program accreditation with ABET and NAAB. The 16 libraries contain 6.2 million volumes, 6.3 million microform items, and 60,000 audio/video tapes/CDs/DVDs, and subscribe to 15,000 periodicals including electronic. Computerized library services include the card catalog, interlibrary loans, and Internet access. Special learning facilities include an art gallery, natural history museum, radio station, a music center, a visual and performing arts center, several theaters, an observatory, a plasma physics lab, and a center for environmental and energy studies. The 500-acre campus is in a small town 50 miles south of New York City. Including any residence halls, there are 160 buildings.

Student Life: 85% of undergraduates are from out of state, mostly the Middle Atlantic. Students are from 50 states, 70 foreign countries, and Canada. 64% are white; 13% Asian American. The average age of freshmen is 18; all undergraduates, 20. 2% do not continue beyond their first year; 97% remain to graduate.

Housing: 6729 students can be accommodated in college housing, which includes coed dorms, on-campus apartments, and married-student housing. Freshman and sophomores are assigned to 1 of 5 residential colleges; most juniors and seniors live in upper-class dorms and select from among such dining options as co-ops and private clubs. On-campus housing is guaranteed for all 4 years. 98% of students live on campus; of those, 100% remain on campus on weekends. Upperclassmen may keep cars.

Activities: There are no fraternities or sororities. There are more than 200 groups on campus, including art, band, cheerleading, chess, choir, chorale, chorus, computers, dance, debate, drama, ethnic, film, forensics, gay, honors, international, jazz band, literary magazine, marching band, musical theater, newspaper, opera, orchestra, pep band, photography, political, professional, radio and TV, religious, social, social service, student government, and symphony.

Sports: There are 20 intercollegiate sports for men and 18 for women, and 35 intramural sports for men and 35 for women. Facilities include a 30,000-seat football and track stadium, an 18-hole golf course, 2 gyms, an Olympic swimming and diving complex, playing fields, a boathouse and Olympic-level racing course for crew and sailing, a health fitness center, an ice rink, dance studios, and tennis, squash, and volleyball courts.

Disabled Students: Wheelchair ramps, elevators, special parking, specially equipped rest rooms, lowered drinking fountains, lowered telephones, and special housing are available.

Services: Counseling and information services are available, as is tutoring in every subject. There is a reader service for the blind.

Campus Safety and Security: Measures include 24-hour foot and vehicle patrol, self-defense education, security escort services, and shuttle buses. There are informal discussions, pamphlets/posters/films, emergency telephones, and lighted pathways/sidewalks.

Programs of Study: Princeton confers A.B. and B.S.E. degrees. Master's and doctoral degrees are also awarded. Bachelor's degrees are awarded in BIOLOGICAL SCIENCE (ecology, evolutionary biology, and molecular biology), BUSINESS (operations research), COMMUNICATIONS AND THE ARTS (classics, comparative literature, English, French, German, Italian, music, Portuguese, Slavic languages, and Spanish), COMPUTER AND PHYSICAL SCIENCE (astrophysics, chemistry, computer science, geoscience, mathematics, and physics), ENGINEERING AND ENVIRONMENTAL DESIGN (aeronautical engineering, architectural engineering, architecture, chemical engineering, civil engineering, electrical/electronics engineering, and mechanical engineering), SOCIAL SCIENCE (anthropology, archeology, East Asian studies, economics, history, international relations, Near Eastern studies, philosophy, political science/government, psychology, religion, and sociology).

Required: To graduate, students must complete 8 semesters, or academic units. Candidates for the A.B. degree must demonstrate proficiency in English composition and a foreign language and complete distribution requirements in 7 academic areas. Candidates for the B.S.E. must satisfy the English composition requirement and complete a minimum of 7 courses in the humanities and social sciences spread over 4 distribution areas. A junior project and senior thesis are required of virtually all students.

Special: Princeton offers independent study, preceptorials, accelerated degree programs, a program in teacher preparation, student-proposed courses and majors, field study, study abroad, seminars, and internships in public affairs. The university operates on an honor code whereby exams are not proctored by faculty members. There are 2 national honor societies, including Phi Beta Kappa, and All departments have honors programs.

Faculty/Classroom: 73% of faculty are male; 28%, female. All both teach and do research. No introductory courses are taught by graduate students.

Admissions: 11% of the 2005-2006 applicants were accepted. The SAT scores for the 2005-2006 freshman class were: Verbal--4% between 500 and 599, 23% between 600 and 700, and 73% above 700; Math--2% between 500 and 599, 24% between 600 and 700, and 74% above 700. 99% of the current freshmen were in the top fifth of their class.

Requirements: The SAT is required. The ACT is accepted in lieu of the SAT when every other school to which the student applies requires only the ACT. 3 SAT Subject Tests are also required for all applicants. Recommended college preparatory courses include 4 years each of English, math, and a foreign language, 2 years each of lab science and history, and some study of art and music. Essays are required as part of the application and an interview is recommended. Students with special talent in visual or performing arts may submit supplementary tapes, CDs, or DVDs. AP credits are accepted.

Procedure: Freshmen are admitted in the fall. Entrance exams should be taken by January of the senior year at the latest. There are early decision, early admissions, and deferred admissions plans. Early decision applications should be filed by November 1; regular applications, by January 1 for fall entry, along with a $65 fee. Notification of early decision is sent in December; regular decision, in April. 593 early decision candidates were accepted for the 2005-2006 class. Applications are accepted on-line.

Transfer: Princeton does not have a transfer admissions option.

Visiting: There are regularly scheduled orientations for prospective students, including daily tours conducted by student guides, general information sessions, and student sessions with admissions staff. There are guides for informal visits and visitors may sit in on classes.

Financial Aid: In 2005-2006, 75% of all full-time students received some form of financial aid. 55% of full-time freshmen and 51% of continuing full-time students received need-based aid. The average freshman award was $29,750. 67% of undergraduates work part time. Average annual earnings from campus work are $1500. The average financial indebtedness of the 2005 graduate was $2310. Princeton is a member of CSS. The FAFSA and the college's own financial statement are required. The deadline for filing freshman financial aid applications for fall entry is February 1.

International Students: There are 377 international students enrolled. The school actively recruits these students. They must take the TOEFL. The SAT Subject Test in writing many be substituted for the TOEFL. Students must also take the SAT and 3 SAT Subject Tests.

Computers: Wireless access is available. All students may access the system. There are no time limits and no fees. It is strongly recommended that all students have a personal computer.

Graduates: From July 1, 2004 to June 30, 2005, 946 bachelor's degrees were awarded. In an average class, 91% graduate in 4 years or less, and 97% graduate in 6 years or less. 310 companies recruited on campus in 2004-2005.

Admissions Contact: Janet L. Rapelye, Dean of Admissions. Web: *www.princeton.edu*

RAMAPO COLLEGE OF NEW JERSEY D-2

Mahwah, NJ 07430

(201) 684-7300
(800) 9-RAMAPO; Fax: (201) 684-7964

Full-time: 1718 men, 2555 women	**Faculty:** 190; IIB, +$
Part-time: 376 men, 584 women	**Ph.D.s:** 94%
Graduate: 60 men, 245 women	**Student/Faculty:** 22 to 1
Year: semesters, summer session	**Tuition:** $8792 ($13,709)
Application Deadline: March 1	**Room & Board:** $7838
Freshman Class: n/av	
SAT: required	**VERY COMPETITIVE**

Ramapo College, founded in 1969, is a public institution offering undergraduate programs in the arts and sciences, American and international studies, business administration, and human services. Personal interaction is incorporated throughout the curriculum as is an international, multicultural component including telecommunications and computer technology. There are 5 undergraduate and 4 graduate schools. In addition to regional accreditation, Ramapo has baccalaureate program accreditation with NLN. The library contains 162,399 volumes, 20,819 microform items, and 3291 audio/video tapes/CDs/DVDs, and subscribes to 803 periodicals including electronic. Computerized library services include the card catalog, interlibrary loans, database searching, Internet access, and laptop Internet portals. Special learning facilities include a learning resource center, art gallery, radio station, TV station, and an international telecommunications satellite center, and an alternative energy center. The 314-acre campus is in a suburban area 25 miles northwest of New York City. Including any residence halls, there are 54 buildings.

Student Life: 92% of undergraduates are from New Jersey. Others are from 19 states and 57 foreign countries. 79% are white. The average age of freshmen is 18; all undergraduates, 23.

Housing: 2553 students can be accommodated in college housing, which includes coed dormitories and on-campus apartments. In addition, there are honors houses, special-interest houses, and blocks at rooms are reserved for scholars and honer students. On-campus housing is available on a first-come, first-served basis. 60% of students live on campus. All students may keep cars.

Activities: 18% of men belong to 10 national fraternities; 11% of women belong to 7 national sororities. There are 100 groups on campus, including cheerleading, choir, chorale, chorus, computers, debate, drama, ethnic, film, gay, honors, international, jazz band, literary magazine, musical theater, newspaper, pep band, photography, political, professional, radio and TV, religious, social, social service, student government, and yearbook. Popular campus events include the Annual Step Show, Spring Conert, and Fashion Show.

Sports: There are 8 intercollegiate sports for men and 8 for women. Facilities include a 1200-seat stadium, which includes a 6-lane track and grass field, 12 lighted tennis courts, and baseball, softball, field hockey, and soccer fields. A 1457-seat competition arena houses basketball and volleyball courts. An auxiliary gym for intramurals and recreation in-

cludes basketball, volleyball, and tennis courts. A 5000-square-foot fitness center includes a recreation and game room, an athletic training room, a 6-lane swimming pool, and multiple locker rooms.

Disabled Students: All of the campus is accessible. Wheelchair ramps, elevators, special parking, specially equipped rest rooms, special class scheduling, lowered drinking fountains, lowered telephones, and special housing are available.

Services: Counseling and information services are available, as is tutoring in every subject. There is a reader service for the blind, and remedial math, reading, and writing.

Campus Safety and Security: Measures include 24-hour foot and vehicle patrol, security escort services, shuttle buses, and informal discussions. There are pamphlets/posters/films, emergency telephones, lighted pathways/sidewalks, and surveillance cameras.

Programs of Study: Ramapo confers B.A., B.S., B.S.N., and B.S.W. degrees. Master's degrees are also awarded. Bachelor's degrees are awarded in AGRICULTURE (environmental studies), BIOLOGICAL SCIENCE (biochemistry and biology/biological science), BUSINESS (accounting, business administration and management, and international business management), COMMUNICATIONS AND THE ARTS (art, communications, literature, music, and visual and performing arts), COMPUTER AND PHYSICAL SCIENCE (chemistry, computer science, information sciences and systems, mathematics, and physics), ENGINEERING AND ENVIRONMENTAL DESIGN (environmental science), HEALTH PROFESSIONS (allied health, clinical science, and nursing), SOCIAL SCIENCE (American studies, economics, history, international studies, law, political science/government, psychology, social science, social work, and sociology). Physics, biochemistry, and chemistry are the strongest academically. Business administration, psychology, communication arts are the largest.

Required: Students must complete general education requirements of approximately 50 credits in science, social science, humanities, and English composition, as well as core requirements in their school of study and their particular major. A senior seminar is also required. To graduate, students must earn at least 128 credits with a minimum GPA of 2.0.

Special: Ramapo's curriculum emphasizes the interdependence of global society and includes an international dimension in all academic programs. Students may study abroad in 7 countries. Cooperative programs are available with various corporations and in 12 foreign countries. Cross-registration is possible with local state colleges. Ramapo offers accelerated degree programs, dual, student-designed, and interdisciplinary majors including law and society, credit for life experience, pass/fail options, interships, work-study programs, and certificate programs in gerontology and substance abuse. A program of study is offered for teachers education. There are 13 national honor societies, and a freshman honors program.

Faculty/Classroom: 59% of faculty are male; 41%, female. All teach undergraduates. The average class size in an introductory lecture is 26; in a laboratory, 15; and in a regular course, 21.

Admissions: 64% of the current freshmen were in the top fifth of their class; 95% were in the top two fifths.

Requirements: The SAT is required. In addition, applicants must be graduates of accredited secondary schools or have earned a GED. The college requires 16 academic credits, including 4 in English, 3 in math, 2 each in science and social studies, and the remaining 5 in academic electives. Students are encouraged to take 2 years of a foreign language. Students must also submit an essay. An interview is recommended. A GPA of 3.0 is required. AP and CLEP credits are accepted. Important factors in the admissions decision are advanced placement or honor courses, recommendations by school officials, and evidence of special talent.

Procedure: Freshmen are admitted fall and spring. Entrance exams should be taken during the senior year. There are early decision, deferred admissions and rolling admissions plans. Applications should be filed by March 1 for fall entry and December 1 for spring entry. Notification is sent on a rolling basis. 321 applicants were on the 2005 waiting list; 22 were admitted. Applications are accepted on-line. The fall 2005 application fee was $55.

Transfer: 498 transfer students enrolled in a recent year. Applicants must supply a completed admission application, official transcripts from all previously attended colleges, official high school transcript (if fewer than 60 credits from another college attempted), and a non-refundable application fee. Visit the school's website for further information. 45 of 128 credits required for the bachelor's degree must be completed at Ramapo.

Visiting: There are regularly scheduled orientations for prospective students, including orientation, advisement, registration, and immediate decision days. There are guides for informal visits and visitors may sit in on classes. To schedule a visit, contact the Admissions Office at (201) 684-7300 or *admissions@ramapo.edu*.

Financial Aid: In 2004-2005, 72% of all full-time freshmen and 76% of continuing full-time students received some form of financial aid. 49% of all full-time students received need-based aid. The average freshman award was $10,835. Need-based scholarships or need-based grants averaged $8890; and need-based self-help aid (loans and jobs) averaged $2780. 15% of undergraduates work part time. Average annual earnings from campus work are $1177. The average financial indebtedness of the 2005 graduate was $15,666. The FAFSA is required. The priority date for freshman financial aid applications for fall entry is March 1. The deadline for filing freshman financial aid applications for fall entry is March 15.

International Students: There are 129 international students enrolled. The school actively recruits these students. They must score satisfactorily on the written TOEFL or on the electronic version and also take the SAT.

Computers: Wireless access is available. All residential halls are wired for Internet access. All students have access to computers on campus. More than 650 computers are networked in labs, and academic cores and the student center have wireless access. All students may access the system according to a posted schedules for lab times. There are no time limits and no fees.

Graduates: From July 1, 2004 to June 30, 2005, 1046 bachelor's degrees were awarded. The most popular majors were communication arts (16%), psychology (15%), and business administration (13%). In an average class, 29% graduate in 4 years or less, 49% graduate in 5 years or less, and 54% graduate in 6 years or less. 122 companies recruited on campus in 2004-2005.

Admissions Contact: Nancy E. Jaeger, Director of Admissions. A video is available. E-mail: admissions@ramapo.edu
Web: www.ramapo.edu

RICHARD STOCKTON COLLEGE OF NEW JERSEY   D-5

Pomona, NJ 08240-0195   **(609) 652-4261; Fax: (609) 748-5541**

Full-time: 2300 men, 3150 women	**Faculty:** 196; IIB, ++$
Part-time: 400 men, 700 women	**Ph.D.s:** 98%
Graduate: 100 men, 230 women	**Student/Faculty:** 28 to 1
Year: semesters, summer session	**Tuition:** $7000 ($10,000)
Application Deadline: see profile	**Room & Board:** $7000
Freshman Class: 3795 applied, 1624 accepted, 825 enrolled	
SAT or ACT: required	**VERY COMPETITIVE**

Richard Stockton College of New Jersey, founded in 1969, is a public liberal arts college with 28 undergraduate programs and 6 graduate specialty areas. There is and 1 graduate school. Figures in the above capsule and in this profile are approximate. In addition to regional accreditation, Stockton has baccalaureate program accreditation with APTA, CSWE, NASDTEC, NCATE, and NLN. The library contains 574,754 volumes, 703,045 microform items, and 14,227 audio/video tapes/CDs/DVDs, and subscribes to 1333 periodicals including electronic. Computerized library services include the card catalog, interlibrary loans, and database searching. Special learning facilities include a learning resource center, art gallery, radio station, TV station, astronomical observatory, marine science field lab, marina with a fleet of small boats, Holocaust resource center, and educational technology training center. The 1600-acre campus is in a suburban area 12 miles northwest of Atlantic City. Including any residence halls, there are 55 buildings.

Student Life: 98% of undergraduates are from New Jersey. Students are from 23 states, 24 foreign countries, and Canada. 74% are from public schools. 82% are white. The average age of freshmen is 18; all undergraduates, 22. 15% do not continue beyond their first year; 65% remain to graduate.

Housing: 2081 students can be accommodated in college housing, which includes coed dorms and on-campus apartments. In addition, there are special-interest houses, and wellness, substance-free academis and smoke-free housing. On-campus housing is guaranteed for the freshman year only, is available on a first-come, first-served basis, and is available on a lottery system for upperclassmen. 68% of students commute. All students may keep cars.

Activities: 5% of men belong to 9 national fraternities; 9% of women belong to 10 national sororities. There are 75 groups on campus, including art, band, cheerleading, chess, choir, chorale, chorus, computers, dance, drama, ethnic, honors, international, jazz band, literary magazine, newspaper, orchestra, pep band, photography, political, professional, radio and TV, religious, social, social service, student government, and yearbook. Popular campus events include Spring Concert, Spring Fling, and Black History Month.

Sports: There are 7 intercollegiate sports for men and 10 for women, and 10 intramural sports for men and 10 for women. Facilities include an indoor 6-lane swimming pool, an outdoor track, a weight-lifting gym, 2 multipurpose gyms, a sauna, steam baths, and dance studios, as well as playing fields, a 60-acre lake for fishing and canoeing, cross-country courses, bike trails, an all-weather track, and tennis, racquetball, and basketball courts. There are 9 club sports in addition to intramurals.

Disabled Students: 99% of the campus is accessible. Wheelchair ramps, elevators, special parking, specially equipped rest rooms, special class scheduling, lowered drinking fountains, lowered telephones, and electric doors are available.

Services: Counseling and information services are available, as is tutoring in most subjects. There is a reader service for the blind, and remedial

math, reading, and writing. In addition, there is a skills center and a learning access program for learning-disabled students.

Campus Safety and Security: Measures include 24-hour foot and vehicle patrol, self-defense education, security escort services, and informal discussions. There are pamphlets/posters/films, emergency telephones, lighted pathways/sidewalks, and a fully commissioned police department.

Programs of Study: Stockton confers B.A., B.S., and B.S.N. degrees. Master's degrees are also awarded. Bachelor's degrees are awarded in BIOLOGICAL SCIENCE (biochemistry, biology/biological science, and marine science), BUSINESS (accounting, banking and finance, business administration and management, and management science), COMMUNICATIONS AND THE ARTS (dance, dramatic arts, fine arts, and music), COMPUTER AND PHYSICAL SCIENCE (chemistry, computer science, information sciences and systems, mathematics, and physics), ENGINEERING AND ENVIRONMENTAL DESIGN (environmental science and preengineering), HEALTH PROFESSIONS (nursing, physical therapy, public health, and speech pathology/audiology), SOCIAL SCIENCE (anthropology, criminal justice, economics, history, liberal arts/general studies, philosophy, political science/government, psychology, religion, and social work). Sciences are the strongest academically. Business, psychology, and criminal justice are the largest.

Required: To graduate, students must earn 128 credit hours, with 32 in the general studies curriculum and maintain a minumum GPA of 2.0. 3 quantitative reasoning and 4 writing courses as well as freshman seminar are required.

Special: Stockton offers internships in all fields with a wide variety of companies, work-study with various government agencies and corporations, a Washington semester, independent study, and study abroad in 10 countries. Dual majors in all programs, student-designed majors, an accelerated degree in medicine, 3-2 engineering degrees with the New Jersey Institute of Technology and Rutgers University, and general studies degrees are also offered. Nondegree study, pass/fail options, and credit for life, military, and work experience are possible. There are 5 national honor societies.

Faculty/Classroom: 56% of faculty are male; 44%, female. 91% teach undergraduates and 95% both teach and do research. The average class size in an introductory lecture is 30; in a laboratory, 12; and in a regular course, 17.

Admissions: 43% of recent applicants were accepted. 50% of recent freshmen were in the top fifth of their class; 80% were in the top two fifths.

Requirements: The SAT or ACT is required. In addition, applicants must be high school graduates; the GED is accepted. 16 academic credits are required, including 4 years in English, 3 each in math and social studies, 2 in science, and 4 additional years of any of the above or a foreign language, or both. An essay and an interview are recommended, and a portfolio or audition is necessary where appropriate. Stockton requires applicants to be in the upper 50% of their class. A GPA of 2.5 is required. AP and CLEP credits are accepted. Important factors in the admissions decision are advanced placement or honor courses, leadership record, and evidence of special talent.

Procedure: Freshmen are admitted fall and spring. Entrance exams should be taken once in the junior year and again before January in the senior year. There is an early admissions plan and a rolling admissions plan. Notification is sent on a rolling basis. Check with the school for current application deadlines and fee. A waiting list is an active part of the admissions procedure. Applications are accepted on-line.

Transfer: 913 transfer students enrolled in a recent year. Transfer students must have earned at least 16 credits at other colleges and must submit college and high school transcripts as well as SAT scores. 32 of 128 credits required for the bachelor's degree must be completed at Stockton.

Visiting: There are regularly scheduled orientations for prospective students, including academic advising and orientation. There are guides for informal visits and visitors may sit in on classes. To schedule a visit, contact Enrollment Management at (609) 652-4251 or heather.medina@stockton.edu.

Financial Aid: In a recent year, 78% of all full-time freshmen and 71% of continuing full-time students received some form of financial aid. 48% of full-time freshmen and 49% of continuing full-time students received need-based aid. The average freshman award was $8462. Need-based scholarships or need-based grants averaged $5814 ($12,372 maximum); need-based self-help aid (loans and jobs) averaged $2288 ($6425 maximum); and other non-need-based awards and non-need-based scholarships averaged $1935 ($11,926 maximum). 23% of undergraduates work part time. Average annual earnings from campus work are $1073. The average financial indebtedness of a recent graduate was $14,372. The FAFSA is required. Check with the school for current deadlines.

International Students: There were 35 international students enrolled in a recent year. They must take the TOEFL.

Computers: All students may access the system 24 hours a day. There are no time limits and no fees.

Admissions Contact: Sal Catalfamo, Dean, Enrollment Management. E-mail: admissions@stockton.edu Web: www.stockton.edu

RIDER UNIVERSITY | D-3

Lawrenceville, NJ 08648-3099 (609) 896-5042
(800) 257-9026; Fax: (609) 895-6645

Full-time: 1396 men, 1886 women	**Faculty:** 234; IIA, ++$
Part-time: 278 men, 489 women	**Ph.D.s:** 92%
Graduate: 314 men, 746 women	**Student/Faculty:** 14 to 1
Year: semesters, summer session	**Tuition:** $23,720
Application Deadline: open	**Room & Board:** $8840
Freshman Class: 4257 applied, 3473 accepted, 861 enrolled	
SAT Verbal/Math: 530/540*	**ACT:** 22	**COMPETITIVE**

Rider University, founded in 1865, is a private institution offering undergraduate programs in the areas of business administration, liberal arts, education, sciences, and continuing studies. Westminster Choir College, located in nearby Princeton, is Rider's fourth college. There are 4 undergraduate and 2 graduate schools. In addition to regional accreditation, Rider has baccalaureate program accreditation with AACSB and NCATE. The library contains 455,809 volumes, 874,019 microform items, and 20,890 audio/video tapes/CDs/DVDs, and subscribes to 21,931 periodicals including electronic. Computerized library services include the card catalog, interlibrary loans, database searching, Internet access, and laptop Internet portals. Special learning facilities include a learning resource center, art gallery, radio station, TV station, journalism and sociology labs, and a holocaust/genocide center. The 340-acre campus is in a suburban area 3 miles north of Trenton and 7 miles south of Princeton. Including any residence halls, there are 37 buildings.

Student Life: 76% of undergraduates are from New Jersey. Others are from 35 states, 31 foreign countries, and Canada. 81% are white. 39% are Catholic; 30% claim no religious affiliation; 11% Protestant. The average age of freshmen is 18; all undergraduates, 22. 21% do not continue beyond their first year; 58% remain to graduate.

Housing: 2342 students can be accommodated in college housing, which includes single-sex and coed dorms, on-campus apartments, fraternity houses, and sorority houses. In addition, there are special-interest, and learning community, wellness, science area, and first-year experience housing. On-campus housing is guaranteed for all 4 years. 61% of students live on campus; of those, 50% remain on campus on weekends. All students may keep cars.

Activities: 17% of men belong to 7 national fraternities; 16% of women belong to 7 national sororities. There are 110 groups on campus, including art, band, cheerleading, choir, chorale, chorus, computers, dance, drama, ethnic, film, gay, honors, international, jazz band, literary magazine, musical theater, newspaper, opera, orchestra, pep band, photography, political, professional, radio and TV, religious, social, social service, student government, symphony, and yearbook. Popular campus events include Cranberry Fest, Family Day, and Unity Day.

Sports: There are 10 intercollegiate sports for men and 10 for women, and 10 intramural sports for men and 6 for women. Facilities include a recreation center with basketball, volleyball, and tennis courts, and an elevated jogging/walking track, and a fitness center with cardio equipment, weight room machines, and free weights.

Disabled Students: 63% of the campus is accessible. Wheelchair ramps, elevators, special parking, specially equipped rest rooms, special class scheduling, lowered drinking fountains, and lowered telephones are available.

Services: Counseling and information services are available, as is tutoring in most subjects. There is remedial math, reading, and writing.

Campus Safety and Security: Measures include 24-hour foot and vehicle patrol, self-defense education, security escort services, and informal discussions. There are pamphlets/posters/films, emergency telephones, lighted pathways/sidewalks, a shuttle car, a staffed kiosk at the entrance, a security system in residence halls, video camera surveillance, bike patrol, and a property ID program.

Programs of Study: Rider confers B.A., B.S., and B.S.B.A. degrees. Associate and master's degrees are also awarded. Bachelor's degrees are awarded in BIOLOGICAL SCIENCE (biochemistry, biology/biological science and marine science), BUSINESS (accounting, banking and finance, business administration and management, business economics, human resources, international business management, management science, marketing/retailing/merchandising, and office supervision and management), COMMUNICATIONS AND THE ARTS (advertising, art, broadcasting, communications, dance, dramatic arts, English, English literature, fine arts, French, German, journalism, multimedia, music, piano/organ, public relations, Russian, Spanish, and voice), COMPUTER AND PHYSICAL SCIENCE (actuarial science, chemistry, geoscience, information sciences and systems, mathematics, and physics), EDUCATION (business, early childhood, elementary, English, foreign languages, marketing and distribution, mathematics, music, science, secondary, and social studies), ENGINEERING AND ENVIRONMENTAL DESIGN (environmental science), HEALTH PROFESSIONS (premedicine), SOCIAL SCIENCE (American studies, biopsychology, economics, history, liberal arts/general studies, philosophy, political science/government, prelaw, psychology, and sociology). Accounting and biology are the strongest

academically. Accounting, elementary education, and business administration are the largest.

Required: To graduate, all students must maintain a minimum GPA of 2.0 while taking 120 semester hours. Students also must fulfill core curriculum requirements, including 9 hours in humanities, 7 to 8 in science, 6 each in English writing and foreign language (may be waived if proficiency is demonstrated), social sciences/communications, and history, and 3 in math. 30 to 76 credits are required in the major. A thesis is required in the honors program and some science majors.

Special: Internships in many programs, a co-op program in retail marketing, work-study, study abroad in 7 countries, a B.A.-B.S. degree in all liberal arts and sciences, dual majors in education, a liberal studies degree, and nondegree study are possible. There are 28 national honor societies, a freshman honors program, and 19 departmental honors programs.

Faculty/Classroom: 61% of faculty are male; 39%, female. All teach undergraduates. No introductory courses are taught by graduate students. The average class size in an introductory lecture is 26; in a laboratory, 14; and in a regular course, 20.

Admissions: 82% of the 2005-2006 applicants were accepted. The SAT scores for the 2005-2006 freshman class were: Verbal--28% below 500, 53% between 500 and 599, 17% between 600 and 700, and 3% above 700; Math--22% below 500, 53% between 500 and 599, 23% between 600 and 700, and 2% above 700. The ACT scores were 50% below 21, and 50% between 21 and 23. 27% of the current freshmen were in the top fifth of their class; 60% were in the top two fifths.

Requirements: The SAT or ACT is required. In addition, applicants need 16 Carnegie units, including 4 years of English and 2 of math. 3 units of math are required for prospective math, science, and business majors. An essay is recommended. An audition is required for theater scholarships. The GED is accepted. Rider requires applicants to be in the upper 50% of their class. A GPA of 2.0 is required. AP and CLEP credits are accepted. Important factors in the admissions decision are advanced placement or honor courses, extracurricular activities record, and leadership record.

Procedure: Freshmen are admitted fall and spring. Entrance exams should be taken by January of the senior year. There are early admissions, deferred admissions and rolling admissions plans. Early decision application should be filed by November 15; regular application deadlines are open. Application fee is $45. Applications are accepted on-line.

Transfer: 186 transfer students enrolled in 2004-2005. A GPA of 2.5 or better is required for applicants. If students have fewer than 30 credits, they also must submit high school transcripts and SAT scores. An essay or personal statement is required, and an interview is recommended. 30 of 120 credits required for the bachelor's degree must be completed at Rider.

Visiting: There are regularly scheduled orientations for prospective students, including 4 open houses, Saturday information sessions and other programs that consist of a welcome, a campus tour, and a variety of formal and informal activities to meet faculty, staff, current students, and alumni. There are guides for informal visits and visitors may sit in on classes. To schedule a visit, contact the Office of Admissions.

Financial Aid: In 2005-2006, 93% of all full-time freshmen and 90% of continuing full-time students received some form of financial aid. 70% of full-time freshmen and 68% of continuing full-time students received need-based aid. The average freshman award was $23,078. Need-based scholarships or need-based grants averaged $8916 ($12,500 maximum); need-based self-help aid (loans and jobs) averaged $5856 ($7325 maximum); and non-need-based athletic scholarships averaged $11,874 ($33,029 maximum). 21% of undergraduates work part time. Average annual earnings from campus work are $9161. The average financial indebtedness of the 2005 graduate was $28,800. The FAFSA is required. The priority date for freshman financial aid applications for fall entry is March 1. The deadline for filing freshman financial aid applications for fall entry is June 30.

International Students: There are 74 international students enrolled. The school actively recruits these students. Satisfactory scores are required on the written TOEFL and the SAT.

Computers: Wireless access is available. Wireless is available in various campus hot spots. All students may access the system during regular lab hours and at any time in residence halls. There are no time limits. Rider has special pricing available for students with Dell. All business must provide PCs.

Graduates: From July 1, 2004 to June 30, 2005, 851 bachelor's degrees were awarded. The most popular majors were elementary education (14%), speech and rhetorical studies (12%), and business administration (7%). In an average class, 44% graduate in 4 years or less, 56% graduate in 5 years or less, and 58% graduate in 6 years or less. 155 companies recruited on campus in 2004-2005. Of the 2004 graduating class, 16% were enrolled in graduate school within 6 months of graduation and 90% were employed.

Admissions Contact: Susan C. Christian, Director of Admissions. A video is available. E-mail: *admissions@rider.edu* Web: *www.rider.edu*

ROWAN UNIVERSITY

Glassboro, NJ 08028

C-4

(856) 256-4200
(800) 447-1165; Fax: (856) 256-4430

Full-time: 3000 men, 3800 women	**Faculty:** 380
Part-time: 400 men, 800 women	**Ph.D.s:** 82%
Graduate: 700 men, 300 women	**Student/Faculty:** 18 to 1
Year: semesters, summer session	**Tuition:** $8000 ($13,000)
Application Deadline: see profile	**Room & Board:** $8000
Freshman Class: n/av	
SAT: required	**VERY COMPETITIVE**

Rowan University was founded in 1923 as a public institution offering undergraduate programs in the arts and sciences, business administration, communication, education, fine and performing arts, and engineering. There are 6 undergraduate schools and 1 graduate school. Figures in the above capsule and in this profile are approximate. In addition to regional accreditation, Rowan has baccalaureate program accreditation with AACSB, ABET, CSAB, NASAD, NASDTEC, NASM, NAST, and NCATE. The library contains 345,926 volumes, 497,842 microform items, and 47,525 audio/video tapes/CDs/DVDs, and subscribes to 5789 periodicals including electronic. Computerized library services include the card catalog, interlibrary loans, database searching, and Internet access. Special learning facilities include a learning resource center, art gallery, planetarium, radio station, TV station, and an observatory. The 200-acre campus is in a suburban area 20 miles southeast of Philadelphia. Including any residence halls, there are 40 buildings.

Student Life: 95% of undergraduates are from New Jersey. Students are from 11 states, 25 foreign countries, and Canada. 65% are from public schools. 79% are white. The average age of freshmen is 19; all undergraduates, 21. 14% do not continue beyond their first year; 62% remain to graduate.

Housing: 2300 students can be accommodated in college housing, which includes coed dorms, on-campus apartments, off-campus apartments, and married-student housing. In addition, there are honors houses, language houses, special-interest houses, and healthy living facilities. On-campus housing is guaranteed for all 4 years. 60% of students live on campus; of those, 85% remain on campus on weekends. Alcohol is not permitted. Upperclassmen may keep cars.

Activities: 10% of men belong to 1 local and 12 national fraternities; 10% of women belong to 5 local and 8 national sororities. There are 150 groups on campus, including art, band, cheerleading, chess, choir, chorale, chorus, computers, concert band, dance, drama, ethnic, film, gay, honors, international, jazz band, literary magazine, music ensembles, musical theater, newspaper, opera, orchestra, pep band, photography, political, professional, radio and TV, religious, social, social service, student government, symphony, and yearbook. Popular campus events include Spring Fling, Unity Day, and The Big Event.

Sports: There are 8 intercollegiate sports for men and 10 for women, and 7 intramural sports for men and 6 for women. Facilities include a 3000-seat stadium, an 1800-seat gym, a 1000-seat auditorium, a swimming pool, tennis courts, and playing fields.

Disabled Students: 95% of the campus is accessible. Wheelchair ramps, elevators, special parking, specially equipped rest rooms, special class scheduling, lowered drinking fountains, lowered telephones, and special housing are available.

Services: Counseling and information services are available, as is tutoring in every subject. There is remedial math, reading, and writing.

Campus Safety and Security: Measures include 24-hour foot and vehicle patrol, self-defense education, security escort services, and shuttle buses. There are informal discussions, pamphlets/posters/films, emergency telephones, and lighted pathways/sidewalks.

Programs of Study: Rowan confers B.A., B.S., B.F.A., and B.M. degrees. Master's and doctoral degrees are also awarded. Bachelor's degrees are awarded in BIOLOGICAL SCIENCE (biology/biological science), BUSINESS (accounting, business administration and management, marketing/retailing/merchandising, personnel management, and small business management), COMMUNICATIONS AND THE ARTS (art, broadcasting, communications, dramatic arts, English, fine arts, journalism, music, Spanish, and speech/debate/rhetoric), COMPUTER AND PHYSICAL SCIENCE (chemistry, computer science, mathematics, and physics), EDUCATION (early childhood, elementary, foreign languages, music, and science), ENGINEERING AND ENVIRONMENTAL DESIGN (civil engineering and engineering), HEALTH PROFESSIONS (health), SOCIAL SCIENCE (criminal justice, economics, geography, history, liberal arts/general studies, political science/government, psychology, and sociology). Communications, business administration, and elementary education are the strongest academically and the largest.

Required: General education requirements include 12 to 18 semester hours of social and behavioral sciences, 12 to 16 of science and math, 6 to 9 of communications, 6 of fine and performing arts, and 3 to 6 of history/humanities/languages/arts. Students must also complete 6 semester hours of writing, and 3 of phys ed, lab science, computer literacy, and math. Students also must attend the Roman Seminar. The bachelor's degree requires completion of 120 to 132 semester hours, including 30 to 39 in a major field, with a minimum GPA of 2.0.

Special: Students may study abroad in 51 countries. Internships are available in all majors both with and without pay. Rowan also offers accelerated degree programs and 3-2 degrees in optometry, podiatry, and pharmacy. There are dual majors, pass/fail options, and credit for military experience. There are 12 national honor societies, a freshman honors program, and 100 departmental honors programs.

Faculty/Classroom: 58% of faculty are male; 42%, female. All teach undergraduates. No introductory courses are taught by graduate students. The average class size in an introductory lecture is 22; in a laboratory, 16; and in a regular course, 22.

Admissions: 46% of recent applicants were accepted. 46% of recent freshmen were in the top fifth of their class; 74% were in the top two fifths.

Requirements: The SAT is required. Applicants must be graduates of accredited secondary schools or have earned a GED. Rowan requires 16 academic credits or Carnegie units, including 4 in English, 3 each in math and college preparatory electives, and 2 each in foreign language, history, and lab science. A portfolio or audition is required for specific majors. Rowan requires applicants to be in the upper 75% of their class. A GPA of 3.0 is required. AP and CLEP credits are accepted. Important factors in the admissions decision are advanced placement or honor courses, evidence of special talent, and leadership record.

Procedure: Freshmen are admitted fall and spring. Entrance exams should be taken in May or June of the junior year, or by December of the senior year. There is a deferred admissions plan. Check with the school for current application deadlines and fee. 100 applicants were on a recent waiting list; 40 were admitted. Applications are accepted online.

Transfer: 791 transfer students enrolled in a recent year. Applicants must have a minimum GPA of 2.0, but should present a GPA of 2.5 to be competitive. An associate degree is recommended. Students who have earned fewer than 24 semester hours must also submit a high school transcript and SAT results. 30 of 120 credits required for the bachelor's degree must be completed at Rowan.

Visiting: There are regularly scheduled orientations for prospective students, consisting of a 2-day summer program providing schedule confirmation/adjustment, student activities updates, and workshops for students and parents. There are guides for informal visits and visitors may sit in on classes and stay overnight. To schedule a visit, contact the Admissions Office at admissions@rowan.edu.

Financial Aid: In a recent year, 70% of all full-time students received some form of financial aid, including need-based aid. The average freshman award was $9093. 10% of undergraduates work part time. Average annual earnings from campus work are $1200. The FAFSA is required. Check with the school for current deadlines.

International Students: The school actively recruits these students. They must take the TOEFL and also take the SAT or ACT. Applicants from English-speaking countries must submit an SAT score.

Computers: All students may access the system 24 hours a day. There are no time limits and no fees. It is recommended that students in engineering have personal computers.

Admissions Contact: Marvin G. Sills, Director of Admissions. E-mail: admissions@rowan.edu Web: rowan.edu/admissions

RUTGERS, THE STATE UNIVERSITY OF NEW JERSEY

The Rutgers, the State University of New Jersey, established in 1766, is a public system in New Jersey. It is governed by a board of governors, whose chief administrator is the president. The primary goal of the system is instruction, research, and service. The main priorities are to continue development as a distinguished comprehensive public university, to enhance undergraduate education, to strengthen graduate education and research, and to develop and improve programs to serve society New Jersey's needs. The total enrollment of all 3 campuses is usually about 50,000, with 2000 faculty members. Altogether there are more than 100 baccalaureate, 100 master's, and 80 doctoral programs offered in Rutgers, the State University of New Jersey. 4-year campuses are located in New Brunswick, Newark, and and Camden. Profiles of the 4-year campuses are included in this section.

RUTGERS, THE STATE UNIVERSITY OF NEW JERSEY/CAMDEN CAMPUS

C-4

Camden, NJ 08102-1461   (856) 225-1766; Fax: (856) 225-6498

Full-time: 1253 men, 1678 women	Faculty: 229; IIA, ++$
Part-time: 324 men, 519 women	Ph.D.s: 99%
Graduate: 314 men, 289 women	Student/Faculty: 13 to 1
Year: semesters, summer session	Tuition: $7600 ($14,110)
Application Deadline: open	Room & Board: $7400
Freshman Class: 6153 applied, 3284 accepted, 353 enrolled	
SAT Verbal/Math: 560/560*	ACT: required

VERY COMPETITIVE

Rutgers, The State University of New Jersey/Camden Campus, founded in 1927, is comprised of 3 undergraduate, degree-granting schools: College of the Arts and Sciences, University College--Camden, and the School of Business--Camden. Each school has individual requirements, policies, and fees. Cost figures in the above capsule are approximate. Applicants should contact the particular school for the most current information. There are 3 undergraduate and 3 graduate schools. In addition to regional accreditation, Camden has baccalaureate program accreditation with AACSB, CSWE, CCNE, and NAACLS. The 2 libraries contain 703,308 volumes, 924,818 microform items, and 260 audio/video tapes/CDs/DVDs, and subscribe to 4309 periodicals including electronic. Computerized library services include the card catalog, interlibrary loans, database searching, and Internet access. Special learning facilities include a learning resource center, art gallery, and radio station. The 40-acre campus is in an urban area 1 mile east of Philadelphia.

Student Life: 97% of undergraduates are from New Jersey. Others are from 5 states. 57% are white; 13% African American. The average age of freshmen is 23; all undergraduates, 24. 16% do not continue beyond their first year; 54% remain to graduate.

Housing: College housing which includes coed dorms and on-campus apartments. 88% of students commute. Alcohol is not permitted.

Activities: There are no fraternities or sororities. There are 70 groups on campus, including computers, drama, ethnic, gay, honors, international, literary magazine, political, professional, radio and TV, religious, social, social service, student government, and yearbook. Popular campus events include Raptor Day, Springfest, and Bill Maher Lecture.

Sports: There is no sports program at Camden.

Disabled Students: 95% of the campus is accessible. Wheelchair ramps, elevators, special parking, specially equipped rest rooms, special class scheduling, lowered drinking fountains, lowered telephones, and special housing are available. Facilities vary from building to building. However, all classes are scheduled in accessible locations for disabled students.

Services: Counseling and information services are available, as is tutoring in some subjects, including introductory classes. There is a reader service for the blind, and remedial math, reading, and writing.

Campus Safety and Security: Measures include 24-hour foot and vehicle patrol, self-defense education, security escort services, and shuttle buses. There are informal discussions, pamphlets/posters/films, emergency telephones, and lighted pathways/sidewalks. The police department is supplemented by security guards.

Programs of Study: Camden confers B.A., B.S., and B.H.M. degrees. Master's degrees are also awarded. Bachelor's degrees are awarded in BIOLOGICAL SCIENCE (biochemistry and biology/biological science), BUSINESS (accounting, banking and finance, hospitality management services, management science, and marketing/retailing/merchandising), COMMUNICATIONS AND THE ARTS (art, art history and appreciation, dramatic arts, English, French, German, music, and Spanish), COMPUTER AND PHYSICAL SCIENCE (chemistry, computer science, mathematics, physics, and science), HEALTH PROFESSIONS (medical laboratory technology and nursing), SOCIAL SCIENCE (African American studies, criminal justice, economics, history, liberal arts/general studies, philosophy, political science/government, psychology, religion, social work, sociology, and urban studies). Psychology, computer science, and economics are the largest.

Required: To graduate, students must complete 120 credits, with 30 to 48 in the major, and maintain a minimum GPA of 2.0. A core curriculum of 60 credits is required, including 3 credits each in literary masterpieces, art, music or theater arts, and a foreign language, with an additional 3 credits in English or a foreign language; and 3 credits in math, with an additional 3 credits in math, computer science, or statistics. 1 interdisciplinary course is required, as are 9 credits from social science disciplines, 6 credits in English composition, 6 credits in history, 6 credits in the natural science disciplines, and an additional 9 credits in courses offered outside the major department.

Special: The university offers co-op programs, cross-registration, internships, accelerated degrees, student-designed majors, dual majors, non-degree study, and pass/fail options. Students may study abroad in numerous countries. In addition, there is an 8-year B.A./M.D. program with U.M.D.N.J., and many combined bachelor's and master's programs. There are distance learning, English as a Second Language, honors, and independent study programs. There is a freshman honors program.

Faculty/Classroom: 61% of faculty are male; 39%, female.

Admissions: 53% of the 2005-2006 applicants were accepted. The SAT scores for the 2005-2006 freshman class were: Verbal--18% below 500, 51% between 500 and 599, 28% between 600 and 700, and 3% above 700; Math--17% below 500, 49% between 500 and 599, 28% between 600 and 700, and 6% above 700. 30% of the current freshmen were in the top fifth of their class; 89% were in the top two fifths.

Requirements: The SAT or ACT is required, but not for students who have been out of high school for 2 years or more. SAT Subject tests are required of students without a high school diploma from an accredited high school and from some GED holders. A high school diploma is required; the GED is accepted. Students must have completed a general college-preparatory program, including 16 academic credits or Carnegie units, with 4 years of English, 3 years of math (4 recommended), and 2 years each of a foreign language and science, plus 5 in electives. AP and CLEP credits are accepted. Important factors in the admissions decision are advanced placement or honor courses, evidence of special talent, and leadership record.

Procedure: Freshmen are admitted in the fall. It is recommended that entrance exams be taken by December of senior year. There is an early admissions plan. Application deadlines are open. Application fee is $50. A waiting list is an active part of the admissions procedure. Applications are accepted on-line.

Transfer: 417 transfer students enrolled in 2004-2005. Applicants must have a minimum of 12 credit hours. Grades of C or better in courses that correspond in content and credit to those offered by the college transfer for credit. Transfer students are admitted in the fall and spring semesters. All high school and previous college transcripts are required. 30 of 120 credits required for the bachelor's degree must be completed at Camden.

Visiting: There are regularly scheduled orientations for prospective students, including an information session with an admissions officer and a campus tour. Visitors may sit in on classes. To schedule a visit, contact the Admissions Office (Camden).

Financial Aid: In 2005-2006, 58% of all full-time freshmen and 62% of continuing full-time students received some form of financial aid. At least 41% of full-time freshmen and 44% of continuing full-time students received need-based aid. The average freshman award was $10,174. Need-based scholarships or need-based grants averaged $7404; need-based self-help aid (loans and jobs) averaged $3364; non-need-based athletic scholarships averaged $4869; and other non-need-based awards and institutional scholarships averaged $4869. The average financial indebtedness of the 2005 graduate was $17,378. The FAFSA is required. The deadline for filing freshman financial aid applications for fall entry is open.

International Students: They must take the TOEFL and also take the SAT or the ACT.

Computers: All students may access the system. Public labs are open whenever the building housing the lab is open. There are no time limits. The fee is $200.

Graduates: From July 1, 2004 to June 30, 2005, 831 bachelor's degrees were awarded. The most popular majors were business/marketing (27%), science technologies (16%), and social sciences (13%). In an average class, 22% graduate in 4 years or less, 43% graduate in 5 years or less, and 54% graduate in 6 years or less.

Admissions Contact: Dr. Deborah Bowles, Associate Provost for Enrollment Management. Web: admissions.rutgers.edu

RUTGERS, THE STATE UNIVERSITY OF NEW JERSEY/NEW BRUNSWICK/PISCATAWAY CAMPUS

D-3

Piscataway, NJ 08854   (732) 932-1766; Fax: (732) 445-0237

Full-time: 11,920 men, 12,322 women	Faculty: 1535; I, +$
Part-time: 917 men, 1013 women	Ph.D.s: 98%
Graduate: 2435 men, 3889 women	Student/Faculty: 16 to 1
Year: semesters, summer session	Tuition: $7600 ($14,110)
Application Deadline: open	Room & Board: $8210
Freshman Class: 25,462 applied, 15,437 accepted, 5230 enrolled	
SAT Verbal/Math: 590/620*	ACT: required

HIGHLY COMPETITIVE

Rutgers, The State University of New Jersey, New Brunswick/Piscataway Campus, founded in 1766, is comprised of 12 undergraduate degree-granting colleges. Students in New Brunswick/Piscataway enroll in 1 of 4 liberal arts colleges: Douglass College, Livingston College, Rutgers College, or University College-New Brunswick, or in 1 of 8 professional schools: Cook College, Mason Gross School of the Arts, Ernest Mario School of Pharmacy, Rutgers Business School: Undergraduate-New Brunswick, School of Communication, Information, and Library Studies, School of Engineering, Edward J. Bloustein School of Planning and Public Policy, or the School of Management and Labor Relations. Each school within the New Brunswick campus has individual requirements, policies, and fees. Cost figures in the above capsule are approximate. Applicants should contact the particular school for the most current information. There are 12 undergraduate and 10 graduate schools. In addition to regional accreditation, New Brunswick has baccalaureate program accreditation with AACSB, ABET, ASLA, CSWE, NASM, and NASD. The 13 libraries contain 3,362,820 volumes, 4,459,329 microform items, and 133,009 audio/video tapes/CDs/DVDs, and subscribe to 20,833 periodicals including electronic. Computerized library services include the card catalog, interlibrary loans, database searching, and Internet access. Special learning facilities include a learning resource center, art gallery, radio station, TV station, geology museum, and various research centers. The campus is in a small town 33 miles south of New York City. Including any residence halls, there are 109 buildings.

Student Life: 91% of undergraduates are from New Jersey. Others are from 19 states. 45% are white; 17% Asian American. The average age of freshmen is 18; all undergraduates, 21. 11% do not continue beyond their first year; 71% remain to graduate.

Housing: College housing which includes single-sex and coed dorms, married-student housing, fraternity houses, and sorority houses. In addition, there are language houses, special-interest houses, a substance-free house, a math/science/engineering house for women, a first year residence and a residence for single mothers and children. 51% of students commute. Alcohol is not permitted.

Activities: 9% of men belong to 27 national fraternities and 15 national sororities. There are 400 groups on campus, including art, band, cheerleading, chess, choir, chorale, chorus, computers, dance, drama, drill team, ethnic, film, gay, honors, international, jazz band, literary magazine, marching band, newspaper, opera, orchestra, pep band, photography, political, professional, radio and TV, religious, social, social service, student government, symphony, and yearbook. Popular campus events include UC Festival, theater trips, and annual picnic.

Sports: There are 15 intercollegiate sports for men and 15 for women.

Disabled Students: Wheelchair ramps, elevators, special parking, specially equipped rest rooms, special class scheduling, lowered drinking fountains, lowered telephones, and special housing are available. Facilities vary from building to building. However, all classes are scheduled in accessible locations for disabled students.

Services: Counseling and information services are available, as is tutoring in most subjects, with specific assistance in difficult first- and second-level courses, as well as reading assistance. There is remedial math, reading, and writing. There is computer software with aids, library technology, and assistance.

Campus Safety and Security: Measures include 24-hour foot and vehicle patrol, self-defense education, security escort services, and shuttle buses. There are informal discussions, pamphlets/posters/films, emergency telephones, and lighted pathways/sidewalks. The police department is supplemented by security guards and student safety officers.

Programs of Study: New Brunswick confers B.A., B.S., B.F.A., and B.Mus. degrees. Master's and doctoral degrees are also awarded. Bachelor's degrees are awarded in AGRICULTURE (agriculture, animal science, natural resource management, and plant science), BIOLOGICAL SCIENCE (biochemistry, biology/biological science, biomathematics, biotechnology, botany, cell biology, ecology, evolutionary biology, genetics, marine science, microbiology, molecular biology, nutrition, and physiology), BUSINESS (accounting, banking and finance, business administration and management, labor studies, management information systems, management science, and marketing/retailing/merchandising), COMMUNICATIONS AND THE ARTS (art, art history and appreciation, Chinese, classics, communications, comparative literature, dance, dramatic arts, East Asian languages and literature, English, French, German, Italian, journalism, Latin, linguistics, music, Portuguese, Russian, Spanish, and visual and performing arts), COMPUTER AND PHYSICAL SCIENCE (astrophysics, chemistry, computer science, geology, information sciences and systems, mathematics, physics, and statistics), ENGINEERING AND ENVIRONMENTAL DESIGN (bioresource engineering, ceramic engineering, chemical engineering, civil engineering, electrical/electronics engineering, engineering and applied science, environmental science, industrial engineering, and mechanical engineering), HEALTH PROFESSIONS (biomedical science, exercise science, medical technology, pharmacy, and public health), SOCIAL SCIENCE (African American studies, American studies, anthropology, Asian/Oriental studies, criminal justice, economics, food science, geography, Hispanic American studies, history, humanities, Judaic studies, Latin American studies, medieval studies, Middle Eastern studies, philosophy, political science/government, psychology, religion, Russian and Slavic studies, social work, sociology, urban studies, and women's studies). Biological sciences, psychology, and English are the largest.

Required: To graduate, students must complete 120 credits, with a minimum GPA of 2.0. A liberal arts core requirement includes 12 credits each of humanities, social sciences, math, and science and 6 credits of English composition. Check with the indivdual college for specific program requirements.

Special: The college offers co-op programs, cross registration, and study abroad in numerous countries. A Washington semester, work-study and accelerated degree programs, B.A.-B.S. degrees, student-designed majors, nondegree study, and pass/fail options are available. There is an 8-year B.A.- or B.S./M.D. program with UMDNJ and several

dual degree (5 year and 6 year) programs. There are 2 national honor societies, including Phi Beta Kappa, and a freshman honors program.

Faculty/Classroom: 64% of faculty are male; 36%, female.

Admissions: 61% of the 2005-2006 applicants were accepted. The SAT scores for the 2005-2006 freshman class were: Verbal--9% below 500, 44% between 500 and 599, 37% between 600 and 700, and 9% above 700; Math--5% below 500, 32% between 500 and 599, 43% between 600 and 700, and 19% above 700. 69% of the current freshmen were in the top fifth of their class; 95% were in the top two fifths.

Requirements: The SAT or ACT is required. In addition, a high school diploma is required. The GED is accepted. Students must have completed a general college-preparatory program, including 16 academic credits or Carnegie units, with 4 years of English, 3 years of math 4 recommended, including (algebra I and II, and geometry), 2 years each of a foreign language and science, and 5 in electives. Engineering students need 4 years of math and must take chemistry and physics for sciences; nursing and pharmacy students must take biology and chemistry. SAT Subject tests are required for students without a high school diploma from an accredited high school and from some GED holders. AP and CLEP credits are accepted. Important factors in the admissions decision are evidence of special talent, extracurricular activities record, and ability to finance college education.

Procedure: Freshmen are admitted in the fall. It is recommended that entrance exams be taken December of senior year. There is an early admissions plan. Application deadlines are open. Application fee is $50. A waiting list is an active part of the admissions procedure. Applications are accepted on-line.

Transfer: 1028 transfer students enrolled in 2004-2005. Applicant must have a minimum of 12 credit hours earned. High school and college transcripts are required. Transfers are admitted in the fall or spring. 30 of 120 credits required for the bachelor's degree must be completed at New Brunswick.

Visiting: There are regularly scheduled orientations for prospective students, including a preadmission orientation for prospective students. To schedule a visit, contact University Undergraduate Admissions.

Financial Aid: In 2005-2006, 51% of all full-time freshmen and 50% of continuing full-time students received some form of financial aid. 32% of full-time freshmen and 33% of continuing full-time students received need-based aid. The average freshman award was $11,555. Need-based scholarships or need-based grants averaged $8379; need-based self-help aid (loans and jobs) averaged $3810; non-need-based athletic scholarships averaged $6365; and other non-need-based awards and institutional scholarships averaged $5641. The average financial indebtedness of the 2005 graduate was $15,362. The FAFSA is required. The deadline for filing freshman financial aid applications for fall entry is open.

International Students: They must take the TOEFL.

Computers: All students may access the system 24 hours per day. There are no time limits. The fee is $200.

Graduates: From July 1, 2004 to June 30, 2005, 5948 bachelor's degrees were awarded. The most popular majors were social sciences (20%), psychology (10%), and biological/life sciences (8%). In an average class, 46% graduate in 4 years or less, 66% graduate in 5 years or less, and 71% graduate in 6 years or less.

Admissions Contact: Office of University Undergraduate Admissions. Web: *admissions.rutgers.edu*

RUTGERS, THE STATE UNIVERSITY OF NEW JERSEY/NEWARK CAMPUS

E-2

Newark, NJ 07102-1897	(973) 353-1766; Fax: (973) 353-1440
Full-time: 2060 men, 2834 women	Faculty: 422; I, +$
Part-time: 421 men, 648 women	Ph.D.s: 96%
Graduate: 1426 men, 1194 women	Student/Faculty: 12 to 1
Year: semesters, summer session	Tuition: $7600 ($14,110)
Application Deadline: open	Room & Board: $8040
Freshman Class: 9927 applied, 4653 accepted, 702 enrolled	
SAT Verbal/Math: 540/570*	ACT: required
	VERY COMPETITIVE

Rutgers, The State University of New Jersey/Newark Campus, founded in 1930, is comprised of 4 undergraduate, degree-granting schools: Newark College of Arts and Sciences, University College-Newark, Rutgers Business School: Undergraduate-Newark, and College of Nursing. Each school has individual requirements, policies, and fees. Cost figures in the above capsule are approximate. Applicants should contact the particular school for the most current information. There are 4 undergraduate and 4 graduate schools. In addition to regional accreditation, Newark has baccalaureate program accreditation with AACSB, CCNE, CSWE, and NASM. The 4 libraries contain 1,014,684 volumes, 1,487,235 microform items, and 37,084 audio/video tapes/CDs/DVDs, and subscribe to 6593 periodicals including electronic. Computerized library services include the card catalog, interlibrary loans, database searching, and Internet access. Special learning facilities include a learning resource center, art gallery, radio station, molecular and behavioral neuroscience center, and institutes of jazz and animal behavior. The 34-acre campus is in an urban area 7 miles west of New York City.

Student Life: 94% of undergraduates are from New Jersey. Others are from 9 states and 6 foreign countries. 19% are white; 16% Asian American; 14% African American; 13% Hispanic. The average age of freshmen is 20; all undergraduates, 22. 14% do not continue beyond their first year; 54% remain to graduate.

Housing: College housing includes coed dorms, on-campus apartments, fraternity houses, and sorority houses. 85% of students commute. Alcohol is not permitted.

Activities: There are no fraternities or sororities. There are 85 groups on campus, including chess, chorale, chorus, drama, newspaper, outreach, radio and TV, student government, and yearbook. Popular campus events include Black History month, Honors convocation, and Alpha Sigma Lambda.

Disabled Students: 80% of the campus is accessible. Wheelchair ramps, elevators, special parking, specially equipped rest rooms, special class scheduling, lowered drinking fountains, lowered telephones, and special housing are available. Facilities vary from building to building. However, all classes are scheduled in accessible locations for disabled students.

Services: Counseling and information services are available, as is tutoring in most subjects. There is a reader service for the blind, and remedial math, reading, and writing.

Campus Safety and Security: Measures include 24-hour foot and vehicle patrol, self-defense education, security escort services, and shuttle buses. There are informal discussions, pamphlets/posters/films, emergency telephones, and lighted pathways/sidewalks. Security guards assist Rutgers police in providing public safety services. There is also a student marshal program.

Programs of Study: Newark confers B.A., B.S., and B.F.A. degrees. Master's and doctoral degrees are also awarded. Bachelor's degrees are awarded in BIOLOGICAL SCIENCE (biology/biological science, botany, and zoology), BUSINESS (accounting, banking and finance, business administration and management, management science, and marketing/retailing/merchandising), COMMUNICATIONS AND THE ARTS (art, dramatic arts, English, French, German, journalism, music, Portuguese, Spanish, and visual and performing arts), COMPUTER AND PHYSICAL SCIENCE (applied mathematics, applied physics, chemistry, computer science, geology, geoscience, information sciences and systems, mathematics, and physics), ENGINEERING AND ENVIRONMENTAL DESIGN (environmental science), HEALTH PROFESSIONS (allied health, clinical science, and nursing), SOCIAL SCIENCE (African American studies, American studies, anthropology, criminal justice, Eastern European studies, economics, history, medieval studies, philosophy, political science/government, psychology, Puerto Rican studies, science and society, social work, sociology, and women's studies). Accounting, management, and psychology are the largest.

Required: To graduate, students must complete 124 credits with a minimum GPA of 2.0. Distribution requirements include 8 credits in natural science/math or 3 courses in nonlab science, math, or computer science; 6 credits each in history, literature, social sciences, humanities, and fine arts; 1 course in critical thinking; and 15 credits of electives. All students must take English composition and demonstrate math proficiency either by exam or by successfully completing a college algebra course or any other advanced course in math, a college calculus course (with a grade of C or better), or a precalculus course (with a grade of B or better).

Special: Students may cross-register with the New Jersey Institute of Technology and the University of Medicine and Dentistry of New Jersey. Internships are available. The school offers study abroad, accelerated degree programs in business administration and criminal justice, co-op programs, independent study, distance learning, English as a Second Language, dual majors, student-designed majors, nondegree study, and pass/fail options. Contact the school for information on the Honors College. There are 12 national honor societies, including Phi Beta Kappa, and a freshman honors program.

Faculty/Classroom: 60% of faculty are male; 40%, female. 100% both teach and do research. The average class size in an introductory lecture is 30; in a laboratory, 20; and in a regular course, 30.

Admissions: 47% of the 2005-2006 applicants were accepted. The SAT scores for the 2005-2006 freshman class were: Verbal--22% below 500, 54% between 500 and 599, 21% between 600 and 700, and 4% above 700; Math--15% below 500, 47% between 500 and 599, 31% between 600 and 700, and 7% above 700. 61% of the current freshmen were in the top fifth of their class; 91% were in the top two fifths.

Requirements: The SAT or ACT is required. In addition, a high school diploma is required; the GED is accepted. SAT: Subject tests are required of students without a high school diploma from an accredited high school and from some GED holders. Students should have completed 16 high school academic credits or Carnegie units, with 4 years of English, 3 years of math (4 recommended), 2 years each of science, a general college-preparatory program, including a foreign language and 5 electives. Biology and chemistry are required for nursing students. AP and CLEP credits are accepted. Important factors in the admissions decision are advanced placement or honor courses, evidence of special talent, and leadership record.

Procedure: Freshmen are admitted in the fall. It is recommended that entrance exams be taken by December of senior year. There is an early admissions plan. Application deadlines are open. Application fee is $50. A waiting list is an active part of the admissions procedure. Applications are accepted on-line.

Transfer: 464 transfer students enrolled in 2004-2005. Students who have completed at least 12 credit hours at another college with a cumulative GPA of 2.0 are considered for admission as transfer students. Transfers are admitted in the fall and spring. High school and college transcripts are required. 30 of 124 credits required for the bachelor's degree must be completed at Newark.

Visiting: There are regularly scheduled orientations for prospective students, including an information session with an admissions counselor and a tour of the campus. There are guides for informal visits and visitors may sit in on classes. To schedule a visit, contact the Admissions Office (Newark).

Financial Aid: In 2005-2006, 61% of all full-time freshmen and 64% of continuing full-time students received some form of financial aid. At least 43% of full-time freshmen and 49% of continuing full-time students received need-based aid. The average freshman award was $10,615. Need-based scholarships or need-based grants averaged $8210; need-based self-help aid (loans and jobs) averaged $3168; non-need-based athletic scholarships averaged $6975; and other non-need-based awards and institutional scholarships averaged $6922. Average annual earnings from campus work are $1365. The average financial indebtedness of the 2005 graduate was $16,553. The FAFSA is required. The deadline for filing freshman financial aid applications for fall entry is open.

International Students: International students must take the TOEFL and the college's own test.

Computers: All students may access the system. Access to accounts, e-mail, and the Internet is available from the campus labs from 8:30 A.M. to midnight, and 24 hours a day from dial-up lines. There are no time limits. The fee is $200. All students are required to have personal computers.

Graduates: From July 1, 2004 to June 30, 2005, 1164 bachelor's degrees were awarded. The most popular majors were business/marketing (28%), health professions and related sciences (11%), and computer and information science (9%). In an average class, 24% graduate in 4 years or less, 48% graduate in 5 years or less, and 54% graduate in 6 years or less.

Admissions Contact: Bruce Neimeyer, Director of Admissions-Newark. Web: *admissions.rutgers.edu*

SAINT PETER'S COLLEGE
E-2

Jersey City, NJ 07306-5997

(201) 915-9213
(888) SPC-9933; Fax: (201) 432-5860

Full-time: 2200 men and women	**Faculty:** 110; IIA, --$
Part-time: 600 men and women	**Ph.D.s:** 78%
Graduate: none	**Student/Faculty:** 20 to 1
Year: semesters, summer session	**Tuition:** $21,390
Application Deadline: open	**Room & Board:** $8770
Freshman Class: n/av	
SAT or ACT: required	**LESS COMPETITIVE**

Saint Peter's College, founded in 1872, is a private liberal arts and business college affiliated with the Roman Catholic Church and known as New Jersey's Jesuit College. Enrollment figures in the above capsule are approximate. There are 2 undergraduate and 3 graduate schools. In addition to regional accreditation, SPC has baccalaureate program accreditation with NLN. The 2 libraries contain 285,000 volumes, 70,000 microform items, and 3800 audio/video tapes/CDs/DVDs, and subscribe to 1800 periodicals including electronic. Computerized library services include the card catalog, interlibrary loans, and database searching. Special learning facilities include a learning resource center, art gallery, radio station, and TV station. The 15-acre campus is in an urban area 2 miles west of New York City. Including any residence halls, there are 29 buildings.

Student Life: 87% of undergraduates are from New Jersey. Others are from 26 states and 10 foreign countries. 56% are from public schools. 44% are white; 27% Hispanic; 21% African American. 68% are Catholic; 8% claim no religious affiliation; 6% Protestant. The average age of freshmen is 18; all undergraduates, 24. 23% do not continue beyond their first year; 51% remain to graduate.

Housing: 863 students can be accommodated in college housing, which includes single-sex and coed dorms and on-campus apartments. In addition, there are community service houses. On-campus housing is guaranteed for all 4 years. 50% of students live on campus; of those, 50% remain on campus on weekends. Upperclassmen may keep cars.

Activities: There are no fraternities or sororities. There are 50 groups on campus, including cheerleading, chess, chorus, computers, debate, drama, ethnic, forensics, honors, international, literary magazine, newspaper, pep band, political, professional, radio and TV, religious, social,

social service, and student government. Popular campus events include International Day, career fairs, and SpringFest.

Sports: There are 10 intercollegiate sports for men and 8 for women, and 20 intramural sports for men and 18 for women. Facilities include a recreational center, a 2000-seat gym, and an athletic field.

Disabled Students: 80% of the campus is accessible. Wheelchair ramps, elevators, special parking, specially equipped rest rooms, special class scheduling, lowered drinking fountains, lowered telephones, and specially equipped rooms in residence halls are available.

Services: Counseling and information services are available, as is tutoring in every subject. There is a reader service for the blind, and remedial math, reading, and writing.

Campus Safety and Security: Measures include 24-hour foot and vehicle patrol, self-defense education, security escort services, and shuttle buses. There are informal discussions, pamphlets/posters/films, emergency telephones, and security desk monitoring of access to residence halls.

Programs of Study: SPC confers B.A., B.S., and B.S.N. degrees. Associate and master's degrees are also awarded. Bachelor's degrees are awarded in BIOLOGICAL SCIENCE (biochemistry and biology/biological science), BUSINESS (accounting, business administration and management, international business management, and marketing/retailing/merchandising), COMMUNICATIONS AND THE ARTS (art history and appreciation, classical languages, communications, English, fine arts, graphic design, modern language, Spanish, and visual and performing arts), COMPUTER AND PHYSICAL SCIENCE (chemistry, computer science, mathematics, natural sciences, and physics), EDUCATION (elementary and secondary), HEALTH PROFESSIONS (biomedical science, health care administration, medical laboratory technology, nursing, predentistry, and premedicine), SOCIAL SCIENCE (African American studies, American studies, classical/ancient civilization, criminal justice, economics, history, humanities, interdisciplinary studies, international studies, Latin American studies, philosophy, political science/government, prelaw, psychology, social science, sociology, theological studies, and urban studies). Natural sciences and accounting are the strongest academically. Business management, accounting, and computer sciences are the largest.

Required: To graduate, students must complete 129 credit hours, including 57 in the core curriculum, 12 in core electives, between 30 and 45 in the major, and the rest in subjects related to the major. The core curriculum requires 9 credits of natural sciences, 6 to 8 of math, and 3 each of social science, philosophy, history, literature, a modern language, fine arts, and communication. Students must earn a GPA of 2.0.

Special: There are co-op programs with local companies, as well as departmental programs, and many internships available in Jersey City and nearby New York City. A Washington semester and study abroad in any of 60 countries are offered. There are preprofessional programs in dentistry, pharmacy, physician assistant, and physical therapy. The college also offers dual majors and student-designed majors, credit for life, military, and work experience, nondegree study, and pass/fail options. There are 9 national honor societies, a freshman honors program, and 1 departmental honors program.

Faculty/Classroom: 64% of faculty are male; 36%, female. All teach undergraduates. The average class size in an introductory lecture is 23; in a laboratory, 14; and in a regular course, 16.

Requirements: The SAT or ACT is required. In addition, applicants must be high school graduates or submit the GED certificate. Students should have completed 16 Carnegie units of high school study, including 4 years of English, 3 of math, 2 each of science, history, and a foreign language, and another 3 of additional work in any of these subjects. An essay and 2 letters of recommendation are required, and an interview is recommended. AP and CLEP credits are accepted. Important factors in the admissions decision are advanced placement or honor courses, extracurricular activities record, and recommendations by school officials.

Procedure: Freshmen are admitted fall and spring. Entrance exams should be taken by the fall of the senior year. There are early admissions, deferred admissions, and rolling admissions plans. Application deadlines are open. Check with the school for current fee. Notification is sent on a rolling basis. Applications are accepted on-line.

Transfer: 93 transfer students enrolled in 2004-2005. The school requires a 2.0 college GPA of transfer students, as well as a high school transcript and a satisfactory composite SAT score for students less than 2 years out of high school. An interview is recommended. 30 of 129 credits required for the bachelor's degree must be completed at SPC.

Visiting: There are regularly scheduled orientations for prospective students, including open houses, weekend and weekday visit days with a tour and class and information sessions, as well as tours and interviews by appointment. There are guides for informal visits and visitors may sit in on classes and stay overnight. To schedule a visit, contact the Admissions Office.

Financial Aid: In 2005-2006, 91% of all full-time freshmen received some form of financial aid. SPC is a member of CSS. The FAFSA is required. The deadline for filing freshman financial aid applications for fall entry is March 1.

International Students: The school actively recruits these students. A satisfactory score is required on the written TOEFL.

Computers: All students may access the system. The system may be used for remote access 24 hours a day; for local access, about 94 hours a week. There are no time limits and no fees.

Admissions Contact: Joseph Giglio, Director of Admissions.
E-mail: *admissions@spc.edu* Web: *www.spc.edu*

SETON HALL UNIVERSITY E-2

South Orange, NJ 07079-2691   (973) 761-9332
(800) THE-HALL; Fax: (973) 275-2040

Full-time: 2243 men, 2558 women	**Faculty:** 275; I, -$
Part-time: 229 men, 305 women	**Ph.D.s:** 92%
Graduate: 1986 men, 2316 women	**Student/Faculty:** 17 to 1
Year: semesters, summer session	**Tuition:** $23,460
Application Deadline: March 1	**Room & Board:** $10,162
Freshman Class: 4982 applied, 4160 accepted, 1120 enrolled	
SAT Verbal/Math: 550/560*	**ACT:** required
	VERY COMPETITIVE

Seton Hall University, founded in 1856, is affiliated with the Roman Catholic Church, and offers programs in business, communications, diplomacy, education, health, and law. The University comprises nine schools and colleges. There are 5 undergraduate and 8 graduate schools. In addition to regional accreditation, Seton Hall has baccalaureate program accreditation with AACSB, CCNN, CSWE, NCATE, and NLN. The 2 libraries contain 523,000 volumes, 500,000 microform items, and 4800 audio/video tapes/CDs/DVDs, and subscribe to 1875 periodicals including electronic. Computerized library services include the card catalog, interlibrary loans, database searching, Internet access, and laptop Internet portals. Special learning facilities include a learning resource center, art gallery, natural history museum, radio station, TV station, and various institutes, and centers for learning and research. The 58-acre campus is in a suburban area 14 miles west of New York City. Including any residence halls, there are 33 buildings.

Student Life: 73% of undergraduates are from New Jersey. Others are from 44 states, 53 foreign countries, and Canada. 69% are from public schools. 51% are white; 11% African American. 65% are Catholic; 11% Protestant. The average age of freshmen is 18; all undergraduates, 22. 17% do not continue beyond their first year; 57% remain to graduate.

Housing: 2290 students can be accommodated in college housing, which includes single-sex and coed dorms and off-campus apartments. In addition, there are special-interest houses, a freshman interest-group floor, first-year residence halls, and alcohol-free buildings. On-campus housing is available on a lottery system for upperclassmen. Priority is given to out-of-town students. 58% of students commute. Upperclassmen may keep cars.

Activities: 5% of men belong to 3 local and 12 national fraternities; 3% of women belong to 4 local and 8 national sororities. There are 100 groups on campus, including art, cheerleading, chess, choir, commuter council, computers, drama, drill team, ethnic, forensics, honors, international, literary magazine, musical theater, newspaper, pep band, photography, political, professional, radio and TV, recreation, religious, social, social service, student ambassador society, student government, and volunteer. Popular campus events include University Day, Theatre-in-the-Round, and Career Day.

Sports: There are 8 intercollegiate sports for men and 9 for women, and 20 intramural sports for men and 20 for women. Facilities include A 2000-seat on-campus arena, recreational field house, indoor track, indoor pool, fitness and aerobics rooms, a soccer and baseball field, a softball field, and tennis and racquetball courts. Men's basketball also uses the Continental Arena, which seats 19,759.

Disabled Students: 75% of the campus is accessible. Wheelchair ramps, elevators, special parking, specially equipped rest rooms, special class scheduling, and lowered drinking fountains are available.

Services: Counseling and information services are available, as is tutoring in most subjects. There is a reader service for the blind, and remedial math, reading, and writing. There is also tutorial assistance for disabled students.

Campus Safety and Security: Measures include 24-hour foot and vehicle patrol, self-defense education, security escort services, and shuttle buses. There are informal discussions, pamphlets/posters/films, emergency telephones, and lighted pathways/sidewalks. Paid student security attendants are posted at residence hall entrances.

Programs of Study: Seton Hall confers B.A., B.S., B.A.BA., B.S.BA., B.S.Ed., and B.S.N. degrees. Master's and doctoral degrees are also awarded. Bachelor's degrees are awarded in BIOLOGICAL SCIENCE (biochemistry and biology/biological science), BUSINESS (accounting, banking and finance, business administration and management, business economics, management information systems, marketing/retailing/merchandising, and sports management), COMMUNICATIONS AND THE ARTS (art, broadcasting, communications, English, fine arts, French, Italian, journalism, modern language, music, and Spanish), COMPUTER AND PHYSICAL SCIENCE (chemistry, computer science, mathematics, and physics), EDUCATION (elementary, secondary, and special), HEALTH PROFESSIONS (nursing), SOCIAL SCIENCE (African American studies, anthropology, Asian/Oriental studies, Christian studies, classical/ancient civilization, criminal justice, economics, history, international relations, liberal arts/general studies, philosophy, political science/government, psychology, religion, social science, social work, and sociology). Business, biology, and diplomacy are the strongest academically. Communication, nursing and criminal justice are the largest.

Required: To graduate, students must complete at least 128 to 130 hours, including a minimum of 36 hours in the major, both varying by major. Students must take freshman composition as well as courses in English, math, social science, natural sciences, religious studies, and philosophy, earning a minimum GPA of 2.0 (2.5 in the College of Education and Human Services).

Special: Co-op and work-study are possible through the College of Arts and Sciences and the School of Business; internships are available through the college of arts and sciences and school of diplomacy. Education majors go into the field during their sophomore year. Cross-registration is available in engineering, including 3-2 engineering degrees, with the New Jersey Institute of Technology. Political science majors may take a Washington semester or study abroad in more than 15 countries. An accelerated B.S.N. degree, a 5-year B.A.-M.A. in diplomacy, a 5-year B.A.-M.B.A., a 5-year B.A.-M.P.A., a 5-year B.A.-B.S. degree in engineering, a 6-year B.S.-M.S. in athletic training, physician assistant, and occupational therapy, and a 7-year B.S.-Doctor of Physical Therapy are offered. Nondegree study is permitted, as are pass/fail options in electives. There are 21 national honor societies, a freshman honors program, and 3 departmental honors programs.

Faculty/Classroom: 54% of faculty are male; 46%, female. 70% teach undergraduates. Graduate students teach 3% of introductory courses. The average class size in an introductory lecture is 30; in a laboratory, 10; and in a regular course, 20.

Admissions: 84% of the 2005-2006 applicants were accepted. The SAT scores for the 2005-2006 freshman class were: Verbal--21% below 500, 48% between 500 and 599, 26% between 600 and 700, and 5% above 700; Math--16% below 500, 50% between 500 and 599, 31% between 600 and 700, and 3% above 700. 44% of the current freshmen were in the top fifth of their class; 75% were in the top two fifths. 3 freshmen graduated first in their class.

Requirements: Satisfactory scores are required on the SAT or ACT. Applicants must supply high school transcripts or a GED certificate. Students should have completed 16 Carnegie units of high school study, including 4 years of English, 3 of math, 2 each of a foreign language and either history or social studies, 1 of science, and 4 academic electives. An essay is optional and an interview is recommended. A GPA of 2.5 is required. AP and CLEP credits are accepted. Important factors in the admissions decision are advanced placement or honor courses, leadership record, and parents or siblings attending the school.

Procedure: Freshmen are admitted fall and spring. Entrance exams should be taken by January of the senior year. There is a deferred admissions plan. Applications should be filed by March 1 for fall entry and December 1 for spring entry, along with a $55 fee for paper applications. Notification is sent on a rolling basis. 935 applicants were on the 2005 waiting list; 631 were admitted. Applications are accepted on-line. The online application is $45.

Transfer: 275 transfer students enrolled in 2004-2005. Applicants should have earned 30 hours of college credit, with a minimum GPA of 2.5, or 2.8 for the business and science schools. The SAT is required for students with fewer than 30 credits of college-level work at the time of application, and an interview is recommended. 30 of 128 credits required for the bachelor's degree must be completed at Seton Hall.

Visiting: There are regularly scheduled orientations for prospective students, including campus tours weekdays and Saturdays during the academic year and on weekdays during the summer. Open houses for prospective applicants are available each fall. Visitors may sit in on classes. To schedule a visit, contact the Enrollment Services Office at (973) 761-9332 or thehall@shu.edu.

Financial Aid: In 2005-2006, 91% of all full-time freshmen and 86% of continuing full-time students received some form of financial aid. 60% of full-time freshmen and 53% of continuing full-time students received need-based aid. The average freshman award was $19,253. Need-based scholarships or need-based grants averaged $6947 ($27,434 maximum); need-based self-help aid (loans and jobs) averaged $3109 ($18,094 maximum); non-need-based athletic scholarships averaged $22,069 ($35,533 maximum); other non-need-based awards and non-need-based scholarships averaged $11,124 ($30,779 maximum); and institutional jobs, PLUS loans, NJ Class, and private parent loans averaged $8472 ($18,963 maximum). 14% of undergraduates work part time. Average annual earnings from campus work are $2688. The average financial indebtedness of the 2005 graduate was $16,461. The FAFSA is required. The priority date for freshman financial aid applications for fall entry is February 15. The deadline for filing freshman financial aid applications for fall entry is open.

International Students: There are 141 international students enrolled. The school actively recruits these students. Satisfactory scores are required on the written TOEFL and the SAT.

Computers: Wireless access is available. All undergraduate students are issued laptops that automatically work with the University's wireless network. Graduate students can bring their laptops to a computer help desk and have their computers configured for the wireless network. In addition, there are computer labs. All students may access the system. Public labs are available until 11 P.M.; there is 24-hour remote network access. There are no time limits and no fees. All students are required to have personal computers. All full-time under graduate students are required to participate in the Mobile Computing Program. Pentium-based IBM laptops are recommended.

Graduates: From July 1, 2004 to June 30, 2005, 1027 bachelor's degrees were awarded. The most popular majors were communications (13%), nursing (12%), and finance (9%). In an average class, 40% graduate in 4 years or less, 55% graduate in 5 years or less, and 58% graduate in 6 years or less. More than 300 companies recruited on campus in 2004-2005. Of the 2004 graduating class, 25% were enrolled in graduate school within 6 months of graduation and 70% were employed.

Admissions Contact: Robert Herr, Director of Admissions. A video is available. E-mail: thehall@shu.edu Web: www.shu.edu

STEVENS INSTITUTE OF TECHNOLOGY
E-2

Hoboken, NJ 07030

(201) 216-5194
(800) 458-5323; Fax: (201) 216-8348

Full-time: 1349 men, 439 women	**Faculty:** 222
Part-time: 1 man	**Ph.D.s:** 81%
Graduate: 2150 men, 734 women	**Student/Faculty:** 8 to 1
Year: semesters, summer session	**Tuition:** $31,435
Application Deadline: February 15	**Room & Board:** $9500
Freshman Class: n/av	
SAT or ACT: required	**HIGHLY COMPETITIVE**

Stevens Institute of Technology, founded in 1870, is a private institution offering programs of study in science, computer science, engineering, business, and humanities. There are 3 undergraduate schools and 1 graduate school. In addition to regional accreditation, Stevens has baccalaureate program accreditation with ABET and CSAB. The library contains 13,176 microform items, and subscribes to more than 31,000 periodicals including electronic. Computerized library services include the card catalog, interlibrary loans, and database searching. Special learning facilities include a radio station, TV station, lab for ocean and coastal engineering, environmental lab, design and manufacturing institute, technology center, telecommunications institute, computer vision lab, ultrafast laser spectroscopy and high-speed communications lab, and wireless network security center. The 55-acre campus is in an urban area 1 mile west of New York City.

Student Life: 65% of undergraduates are from New Jersey. Others are from 38 states, 30 foreign countries, and Canada. 53% are white; 15% Asian American. The average age of freshmen is 18; all undergraduates, 20. 12% do not continue beyond their first year; 75% remain to graduate.

Housing: 1114 students can be accommodated in college housing, which includes single-sex and coed dormitories, on-campus apartments, off-campus apartments, married-student housing, fraternity houses, and sorority houses. In addition, there are special-interest houses and special-interest floors. On-campus housing is guaranteed for all 4 years. 85% of students live on campus; of those, 70% remain on campus on weekends. Alcohol is not permitted. Upperclassmen may keep cars.

Activities: 34% of men belong to 10 national fraternities; 31% of women belong to 5 national sororities. There are 71 groups on campus, including art, band, chess, choir, chorus, computers, dance, drama, ethnic, film, honors, international, jazz band, literary magazine, musical theater, newspaper, pep band, photography, political, professional, radio and TV, religious, social, social service, student government, and yearbook. Popular campus events include Fall Tech Fest, Spring Boken Festival, and Midnight Breakfast.

Sports: There are 12 intercollegiate sports for men and 12 for women, and 12 intramural sports for men and 12 for women. Facilities include a 6000-square-foot complex with an NCAA regulation swimming pool convertible to international size, a 1000-seat basketball arena, fitness rooms, racquetball/squash courts, a playing field, a student union, and several outdoor courts.

Disabled Students: All of the campus is accessible. Wheelchair ramps, elevators, special parking, specially equipped rest rooms, and lowered drinking fountains are available.

Services: Counseling and information services are available, as is tutoring in every subject.

Campus Safety and Security: Measures include 24-hour foot and vehicle patrol, self-defense education, security escort services, and informal discussions. There are pamphlets/posters/films, emergency telephones, and lighted pathways/sidewalks.

Programs of Study: Stevens confers B.A., B.S., and B.E. degrees. Master's and doctoral degrees are also awarded. Bachelor's degrees are awarded in BIOLOGICAL SCIENCE (biochemistry and bioinformatics), BUSINESS (business administration and management), COMMUNICA-

TIONS AND THE ARTS (literature and music technology), COMPUTER AND PHYSICAL SCIENCE (chemistry, computer science, computer security and information assurance, digital arts/technology, information sciences and systems, mathematics, physics, and science technology), ENGINEERING AND ENVIRONMENTAL DESIGN (biomedical engineering, chemical engineering, civil engineering, computational sciences, computer engineering, electrical/electronics engineering, engineering management, engineering physics, environmental engineering, mechanical engineering, naval architecture and marine engineering, and systems engineering), SOCIAL SCIENCE (history, Middle Eastern studies, and philosophy). Engineering is the strongest academically as well the largest.

Required: To graduate, the student must have earned 120 to 150 credit hours (dependent on program) with a minimum 2.0 GPA; the total hours in the major vary by program. The core curriculum includes courses in engineering, science, computer science, math, liberal arts, and phys ed.

Special: Stevens offers cross-registration and a 3-2 engineering degree with New York University, a work-study program within the school, co-op programs, corporate and research internships through the Undergraduate Projects in Technology and Medicine, study abroad in 7 countries, and pass/fail options for extra courses. Students may undertake dual majors as well as accelerated degree programs in medicine, dentistry, and law and can receive a B.A.-B.E. degree or a B.A.-B.S. degree in all majors. Undergraduates may take graduate courses. There are 9 national honor societies and a freshman honors program.

Faculty/Classroom: 85% of faculty are male; 15%, female. 80% both teach and do research. No introductory courses are taught by graduate students. The average class size in an introductory lecture is 100; in a laboratory, 50; and in a regular course, 20.

Admissions: 71% of the current freshmen were in the top fifth of their class; 93% were in the top two fifths. 6 freshmen graduated first in their class.

Requirements: The SAT or ACT is required; the SAT is preferred. Stevens recommends a minimum of 2 SAT Subject Tests, depending on the intended major. In addition, applicants must provide official high school transcripts. Students should have taken 4 years of English, math, and science. An interview is required. AP credits are accepted. Important factors in the admissions decision are advanced placement or honor courses, extracurricular activities record, and personality/intangible qualities.

Procedure: Freshmen are admitted in the fall. Entrance exams should be taken by February of the senior year. There are early decision, early admissions, and deferred admissions plans. Early decision applications should be filed by November 15; regular applications, by February 15 for fall entry and December 1 for spring entry, along with a $55 fee. Notification of early decision is sent December 15; regular decision, March 15. 166 early decision candidates were accepted for the 2005-2006 class. 269 applicants were on the 2005 waiting list; 27 were admitted. Applications are accepted on-line.

Transfer: 37 transfer students enrolled in 2005-2006. Applicants should have a minimum GPA of 3.0. They must submit all college transcripts, including course descriptions; SAT or ACT scores are required of those students with fewer than 30 hours of college credit. 50 credits required for the bachelor's degree must be completed at Stevens.

Visiting: There are regularly scheduled orientations for prospective students, including interviews and campus tours. There are guides for informal visits and visitors may sit in on classes and stay overnight. To schedule a visit, contact the Admissions Office.

Financial Aid: In 2005-2006, 94% of all full-time freshmen and 92% of continuing full-time students received some form of financial aid. 82% of full-time freshmen and 81% of continuing full-time students received need-based aid. The average freshman award was $24,380. Need-based scholarships or need-based grants averaged $15,021; need-based self-help aid (loans and jobs) averaged $4613; and other non-need-based awards and non-need-based scholarships averaged $7878. 40% of undergraduates work part time. Average annual earnings from campus work are $800. The average financial indebtedness of the 2005 graduate was $14,113. The FAFSA is required. The priority date for freshman financial aid applications for fall entry is February 15.

International Students: There are 86 international students enrolled. The school actively recruits these students. They must score satisfactorily on the written TOEFL and also take the SAT.

Computers: Wireless access is available. All undergraduates get laptops as part of their admission to the institution. These laptops are all wireless enabled, and wireless access is available all over the campus. All students may access the system at all times. There are no time limits and no fees.

Graduates: From July 1, 2004 to June 30, 2005, 367 bachelor's degrees were awarded. The most popular majors were computer engineering (21%), computer science (18%), and electrical engineering (12%). In an average class, 25% graduate in 4 years or less, 68% graduate in 5 years or less, and 75% graduate in 6 years or less. 175 companies recruited on campus in 2004-2005. Of the 2004 graduating class, 12% were enrolled in graduate school within 6 months of graduation and 95% were employed.

Admissions Contact: Daniel Gallagher, Dean of University Admissions. E-mail: *admissions@stevens.edu* Web: *www.stevens.edu*

THOMAS EDISON STATE COLLEGE D-3

Trenton, NJ 08608-1176	**(888) 442-8372; Fax: (609) 984-8447**
Full-time: none	**Faculty:** n/av
Part-time: 6110 men, 4794 women	**Ph.D.s:** n/av
Graduate: 157 men, 163 women	**Student/Faculty:** n/av
Year: n/app	**Tuition:** $3780 ($5400)
Application Deadline: open	**Room & Board:** n/app
Freshman Class: n/av	
SAT or ACT: not required	**SPECIAL**

Thomas Edison State College, founded in 1972, is a public institution of higher education. The college provides many ways to complete a degree in more than 100 areas of study, including credit by exam, assessment of experiential learning, guided independent study, and credit for corporate and military training. The College offers 2 tuition plans, a comprehensive tuition plan and a per-service tuition plan. There are 5 undergraduate schools and 1 graduate school. In addition to regional accreditation, Thomas Edison State College has baccalaureate program accreditation with NLN. Special learning facilities include the New Jersey State Library, an affiliate of the college. The 2-acre campus is in an urban area 40 miles north of Philadelphia. There are 4 buildings.

Student Life: 54% of undergraduates are from New Jersey. Others are from 50 states, 79 foreign countries, and Canada. 67% are white; 12% African American. The average age of all undergraduates is 36.

Housing: There are no residence halls. Alcohol is not permitted.

Activities: There are no fraternities or sororities.

Sports: There is no sports program at Thomas Edison State College.

Disabled Students: 97% of the campus is accessible. Wheelchair ramps, elevators, special parking, specially equipped rest rooms, and lowered drinking fountains, are available. Visually impaired students may make use of "Talking Books", and Braille service is available if needed. An interpreter is available for hearing-impaired students, and exams can be recorded on cassette tapes. Other services are provided as needed.

Campus Safety and Security: Measures include lighted pathways/sidewalks. There is a guard on the premises 7 A.M. to 11 P.M.; the outside is patrolled by the New Jersey State Police.

Programs of Study: Thomas Edison State College confers B.A., B.S., B.S.A.S.T., B.S.B.A., B.S.H.S., and B.S.N. degrees. Associate and master's degrees are also awarded. Bachelor's degrees are awarded in AGRICULTURE (animal science, environmental studies, forestry and related sciences, and horticulture), BIOLOGICAL SCIENCE (biology/biological science), BUSINESS (accounting, banking and finance, hotel/motel and restaurant management, human resources, institutional management, insurance, international business management, labor studies, logistics, management science, marketing and distribution, office supervision and management, operations management, purchasing/inventory management, real estate, recreation and leisure services, retailing, small business management, and transportation management), COMMUNICATIONS AND THE ARTS (advertising, art, communications, dramatic arts, English, journalism, music, and photography), COMPUTER AND PHYSICAL SCIENCE (computer science, information sciences and systems, mathematics, and natural sciences), EDUCATION (foreign languages and health), ENGINEERING AND ENVIRONMENTAL DESIGN (air traffic control, architecture, aviation computer technology, aviation maintenance management, biomedical equipment technology, civil engineering technology, computer technology, construction engineering, drafting and design, electrical/electronics engineering technology, emergency/disaster science, environmental science, manufacturing technology, marine engineering, mechanical engineering technology, nuclear engineering technology, and survey and mapping technology), HEALTH PROFESSIONS (clinical science, cytotechnology, dental hygiene, health, health care administration, hospital administration, medical technology, mental health/human services, nuclear medical technology, nursing, radiation therapy, and respiratory therapy), SOCIAL SCIENCE (anthropology, child psychology/development, community services, criminal justice, economics, fire protection, gerontology, history, humanities, liberal arts/general studies, philosophy, political science/government, psychology, public administration, religion, social science, social work, and sociology). Nuclear engineering technology, liberal studies, and general management are the largest.

Required: The baccalaureate student must complete a general education requirement that includes courses in English composition, humanities, social science, natural sciences, and math, for a total of approximately 60 general education credits. To graduate, 120 semester hours are required, with a minimum GPA of 2.0.

Special: Students may take dual majors in all degree programs except nursing. The B.S. in health sciences is available as a joint degree with the University of Medicine and Dentistry of New Jersey. Credit for college-level knowledge gained through life, military, and work experience is an option. Students work on their own, proceeding at their own pace, depending on the option selected for earning credit. Thomas Edison State College has a 12-semester calendar. There is 1 national honor society.

Requirements: Applicants must have a high school diploma or the equivalent and be at least 21 years old. Certain health-related and other areas of study are limited to persons holding appropriate certification. Admission to the bachelor's degree nursing program is limited to registered nurses (RNs) who are currently licensed in the U.S. AP and CLEP credits are accepted.

Procedure: Freshmen are admitted to all sessions. Application deadlines are open. There is a rolling admissions plan. Applications are accepted on-line. The fall 2005 application fee was $75.

Transfer: Transfers, like other students, must be at least 21 and be high school graduates or the equivalent. The granting of credit for course work successfully completed elsewhere is an intrinsic part of the school's system. Transfer credits are awarded with the grades earned.

Visiting: To schedule a visit, contact the Director of Admissions at *admissions@tesc.edu*.

Financial Aid: Thomas Edison State College is a member of CSS. The FAFSA and the college's own financial statement are required.

International Students: There were 276 international students enrolled in a recent year. They must take the TOEFL.

Computers: Wireless access is available. There is an on-line course management system that utilizes the blackboard platform. The system provides students an opportunity to communicate with fellow students and mentors directly through MyEdison. All students may access the system. There are no time limits. The fee is $90.

Graduates: From July 1, 2004 to June 30, 2005, 1799 bachelor's degrees were awarded. The most popular majors were liberal studies (27%), nuclear engineering technology (15%), and humanities (5%).

Admissions Contact: Renee San Giacomo, Director of Admissions. E-mail: *admissions@tesc.edu* Web: *http://www.tesc.edu*

WESTMINSTER CHOIR COLLEGE   D-3

Princeton, NJ 08540   **(609) 921-7100; (800) 962-4647**

Full-time: 115 men, 209 women	Faculty: n/av
Part-time: 6 men, 4 women	Ph.D.s: n/av
Graduate: 37 men, 82 women	Student/Faculty: n/av
Year: semesters, summer session	Tuition: $23,470
Application Deadline: open	Room & Board: $9200
Freshman Class: 206 applied, 156 accepted, 88 enrolled	
SAT Verbal/Math: 550/540*	SPECIAL

Westminster Choir College is a residential college of music located on a 23 acre campus in Princeton, N.J. offering a Bachelors in Music, a Bachelor of Arts in Music, and a Master's of Music. WCC also offers two summer study degree programs: Master's of Music Education and Voice Pedagogy. In addition to regional accreditation, Westminster Choir College has baccalaureate program accreditation with NASDTEC, NASM, and NCATE. The library contains 455,809 volumes, 874,019 microform items, and 20,890 audio/video tapes/CDs/DVDs, and subscribes to 21,931 periodicals including electronic. Computerized library services include the card catalog. Special learning facilities include a TV station. The 23-acre campus is in a suburban area 50 miles south of New York City. Including any residence halls, there are 13 buildings.

Student Life: 56% of undergraduates are from out of state, mostly the Middle Atlantic. Students are from 26 states and 10 foreign countries. 80% are white. The average age of freshmen is 19. 21% do not continue beyond their first year.

Housing: College-sponsored housing is single-sex and coed. There are special-interest houses. On-campus housing is available on a first-come, first-served basis and is available on a lottery system for upperclassmen. 57% of students live on campus. Upperclassmen may keep cars.

Activities: There are many groups and organizations on campus, including choir, chorale, chorus, ethnic, gay, honors, international, musical theater, newspaper, opera, professional, religious, social, social service, and student government. Popular campus events include Family Day and Spring Fling.

Disabled Students: 43% of the campus is accessible. Elevators, special parking, and specially equipped rest rooms are available.

Services: Counseling and information services are available, as is tutoring in most subjects, Including math, reading, writing. music theory, and music history.

Campus Safety and Security: Measures include 24-hour foot and vehicle patrol, self-defense education, security escort services, and informal discussions. There are pamphlets/posters/films, emergency telephones, and lighted pathways/sidewalks.

Programs of Study: Westminster Choir College confers B.A.M. and B.M. degrees. Master's degrees are also awarded. Bachelor's degrees are awarded in COMMUNICATIONS AND THE ARTS (music, music theory and composition, musical theater, piano/organ, and voice), and EDUCATION (music).

Required: To graduate,all students must maintain a minimum GPA of 2.0 while taking 120 semester hours.

Special: Internships in many programs, work study, summer study in Europe, and dual majors are available. There is a freshman honors program.

Admissions: 76% of the 2005-2006 applicants were accepted. The SAT scores for the 2005-2006 freshman class were: Verbal--25% below 500, 39% between 500 and 599, 26% between 600 and 700, and 10% above 700; Math--26% below 500, 43% between 500 and 599, 29% between 600 and 700, and 2% above 700. 35% of the current freshmen were in the top fifth of their class; 66% were in the top two fifths.

Requirements: All undergradute students must submit official high school transcripts and official SAT or ACT scores. All undergraduate applicants must complete an academic course of study in high school. The GED is accepted. Two letters of recommendation, at least one of which must be from a music reference, are required, as is a personal essay. Graduate students must submit official college transcripts showing proof of graduation. All applicants must audition.

Visiting: There are guides for informal visits. To schedule a visit, contact the Office of Admissions at (800)-962-4647 or *wccadmission@rider.educ*.

Admissions Contact: Katherine Shields, Director of Admissions. E-mail: *wccadmission@rider.edu* Web: *www.rider.edu/Westminister*

WILLIAM PATERSON UNIVERSITY OF NEW JERSEY   E-2

Wayne, NJ 07470   **(973) 720-2125**
(877) WOU EXCEL; Fax: (973) 720-2910

Full-time: 3244 men, 4228 women	Faculty: IIA, ++$
Part-time: 610 men, 1028 women	Ph.D.s: 92%
Graduate: 421 men, 1439 women	Student/Faculty: n/av
Year: semesters, summer session	Tuition: $8740 ($13,856)
Application Deadline: May 1	Room & Board: $9070
Freshman Class: 6793 applied, 3188 accepted, 1302 enrolled	
SAT or ACT: required	COMPETITIVE+

William Paterson University of New Jersey, founded in 1855 as a college, is a public institution comprised of the colleges of Arts and Communication; Education; Humanities and Social Sciences; Science and Health; and Business. There are 5 undergraduate and 5 graduate schools. In addition to regional accreditation, WPUNJ has baccalaureate program accreditation with ASLA, NASM, NCATE, and NLN. The library contains 300,000 volumes, 1,000,000 microform items, and 20,000 audio/video tapes/CDs/DVDs, and subscribes to 5000 periodicals including electronic. Computerized library services include the card catalog, interlibrary loans, and database searching. Special learning facilities include an art gallery, radio station, TV station, a speech and hearing clinic, an academic support center, a computerized writing center, and a teleconference center. The 320-acre campus is in a suburban area 25 miles west of New York City. Including any residence halls, there are 35 buildings.

Student Life: 98% of undergraduates are from New Jersey. Students are from 22 states, 58 foreign countries, and Canada. 75% are from public schools. 63% are white; 15% Hispanic; 12% African American. The average age of freshmen is 18; all undergraduates, 24.

Housing: Housing includes coed dorms, on-campus apartments, and honors houses. On-campus housing is guaranteed for all 4 years. 76% of students commute. Upperclassmen may keep cars.

Activities: 2% of men belong to 3 local and 8 national fraternities; 3% of women belong to 3 local and 11 national sororities. There are 50 groups on campus, including art, cheerleading, chorus, computers, dance, drama, ethnic, film, gay, honors, international, jazz band, literary magazine, musical theater, newspaper, opera, orchestra, photography, political, professional, radio and TV, religious, student government, and yearbook. Popular campus events include Midday Artist Series, Puerto Rican Heritage Month, and Latin American Week.

Sports: There are 7 intercollegiate sports for men and 7 for women, and 24 intramural sports for men and 24 for women. Facilities include a recreation center with courts for basketball, tennis, racquetball, volleyball, and badminton, weight and exercise rooms, saunas and whirlpools, and a 4000-seat auditorium. The university also offers an Olympic-size pool, 8 additional tennis courts, and an athletic complex with fields for baseball, field hockey, football, soccer, softball, and track.

Disabled Students: Wheelchair ramps, elevators, special parking, specially equipped rest rooms, special class scheduling, lowered drinking fountains, lowered telephones, and special housing are available.

Services: Counseling and information services are available, as is tutoring in most subjects. There is remedial math, reading, and writing. There is a science enrichment center, a writing center, and a business tutorial lab.

Campus Safety and Security: Measures include 24-hour foot and vehicle patrol, security escort services, shuttle buses, and informal discussions. There are pamphlets/posters/films, emergency telephones, and lighted pathways/sidewalks.

Programs of Study: WPUNJ confers B.A., B.S., B.F.A., and B.M. degrees. Master's degrees are also awarded. Bachelor's degrees are awarded in BIOLOGICAL SCIENCE (biology/biological science and biotechnology), BUSINESS (accounting, banking and finance, and business administration and management), COMMUNICATIONS AND THE ARTS (art history and appreciation, communications, dramatic arts, English, fine arts, music, Spanish, and studio art), COMPUTER AND PHYSICAL SCIENCE (chemistry, computer science, and mathematics), EDUCATION (health, music, physical, and special), ENGINEERING AND ENVIRONMENTAL DESIGN (environmental science), HEALTH PROFESSIONS (community health work, health science, and nursing), SOCIAL SCIENCE (African American studies, anthropology, economics, geography, history, philosophy, political science/government, psychology, and sociology). Biology/biotechnology, computer science, and English are the strongest academically. Management, communications, and education are the largest.

Required: All students must maintain a cumulative GPA of at least 2.0 and take 128 credit hours, typically including 30 to 40 in their major. General education requirements include 21 credits in the humanities, 11 or 12 in science, 9 in the social sciences, and 6 in art and communication. Also required are 1 course in health or movement science, 1 course dealing with racism or sexism, and 1 course in non-Western culture. Students also complete 6 credits of general education electives and a minimum of 9 credits of upper-level elective courses.

Special: Study abroad in 33 countries, cross-registration, internships, work-study programs on campus, accelerated degree programs, dual majors, individual curriculum design, and credit for military experience are available. Nondegree study and some pass/fail options are also possible. In the Learning Clusters Project, students experience how 3 general education courses, taken together, reinforce and better integrate each other. There is a professional program in teacher education leading to certification in early childhood, elementary, middle, and secondary education. There are 6 national honor societies and 4 departmental honors programs.

Faculty/Classroom: 52% of faculty are male; 48%, female. All teach undergraduates and 40% do research. No introductory courses are taught by graduate students. The average class size in an introductory lecture is 32; in a laboratory, 24; and in a regular course, 19.

Admissions: 47% of the 2005-2006 applicants were accepted. The SAT scores for the 2005-2006 freshman class were: Verbal--36% below 500, 51% between 500 and 599, 12% between 600 and 700, and 1% above 700; Math--30% below 500, 55% between 500 and 599, 14% between 600 and 700, and 1% above 700. 31% of the current freshmen were in the top fifth of their class; 61% were in the top two fifths.

Requirements: The SAT or ACT is required. In addition, applicants must have 16 academic credits or Carnegie units, including 4 in English, 3 in math, 2 each in science lab and social studies, and 5 electives such as foreign language and history. An essay and interview are recommended for some applicants, as are a portfolio and audition. The GED is accepted. AP and CLEP credits are accepted. Important factors in the admissions decision are advanced placement or honor courses, recommendations by school officials, and evidence of special talent.

Procedure: Freshmen are admitted fall and spring. Entrance exams should be taken by January 31. There are early admissions, deferred admissions,and rolling admissions plans. Early decision applications should be filed by April 1; regular applications, by May 1 for fall entry. The fall 2005 application fee was $50. Notification is sent on a rolling basis. A waiting list is an active part of the admissions procedure.Applications are accepted on-line.

Transfer: 758 transfer students enrolled in 2004-2005. Transfer students need a minimum GPA of 2.0 (business, nursing, computer science, and education students need a 2.5 GPA) and at least 12 credit hours earned. 38 of 128 credits required for the bachelor's degree must be completed at WPUNJ.

Visiting: There are regularly scheduled orientations for prospective students, including a campus tour, guest speakers, and dissemination of printed information. There are guides for informal visits and visitors may sit in on classes. To schedule a visit, contact the Admissions Office.

Financial Aid: In 2005-2006, 54% of all full-time freshmen and 49% of continuing full-time students received some form of financial aid. 41% of full-time freshmen and 39% of continuing full-time students received need-based aid. The average freshman award was $9845. Need-based scholarships or need-based grants averaged $6412; need-based self-help aid (loans and jobs) averaged $2645; and other non-need-based awards and non-need-based scholarships averaged $5790. The average financial indebtedness of the 2005 graduate was $9981. WPUNJ is a member of CSS. The FAFSA and parent and student federal income tax forms are required. Check with the school for current deadlines.

International Students: A satisfactory score is required on the written TOEFL.

Computers: All students may access the system at all times. There are no time limits. The fee is $30.

Graduates: In a recent year, 1449 bachelor's degrees were awarded. The most popular majors ina recent year were Social studies/history (19%), business and marketing (18%), and communications/communicatons technologies (14%).

Admissions Contact: Director of Admissions.
E-mail: *admissions@wpunj.edu* Web: *www.wpunj.edu*

NEW MEXICO

POPULATION
DENSITY
● 25,000 and over

0 20 40 60 80 100
Miles

COLLEGE OF SANTA FE   C-2
Santa Fe, NM 87505-7634

(505) 473-6133
(800) 456-2673; Fax: (505) 473-6129

Full-time: 284 men, 356 women	**Faculty:** 76; IIB, av$
Part-time: 283 men, 419 women	**Ph.D.s:** 81%
Graduate: 84 men, 235 women	**Student/Faculty:** 8 to 1
Year: semesters, summer session	**Tuition:** $22,276
Application Deadline: rolling	**Room & Board:** $6702
Freshman Class: 641 applied, 527 accepted, 129 enrolled	
SAT Verbal/Math: 580/520*	**ACT:** 23 COMPETITIVE

The College of Santa Fe, founded in 1874, is a private (not for profit) comprehensive institution grounded in a strong liberal arts curriculum and distinguished by its programs in the creative arts. There are 8 undergraduate and 2 graduate schools. In addition to regional accreditation, CSF has baccalaureate program accreditation with IACBE and NCATE. The 3 libraries contain 170,566 volumes, 89,807 microform items, and 13,533 audio/video tapes/CDs/DVDs, and subscribe to 460 periodicals including electronic. Computerized library services include the card catalog, interlibrary loans, database searching, Internet access, and laptop Internet portals. Special learning facilities include a learning resource center, art gallery, a professional sound stage for film and video, a visual arts center, a theater center, and a digital center. The 98-acre campus is in a suburban area 60 miles north of Albuquerque. Including any residence halls, there are 100 buildings.

Student Life: 67% of undergraduates are from out of state, mostly the Southwest. Students are from 46 states and 5 foreign countries. 68% are from public schools. 75% are white; 12% Hispanic. Most claim no religious affiliation. The average age of freshmen is 19; all undergraduates, 22. 25% do not continue beyond their first year; 45% remain to graduate.

Housing: 499 students can be accommodated in college housing, which includes single-sex and coed dorms and on-campus apartments. On-campus housing is guaranteed for the freshman year only and is available on a lottery system for upperclassmen. 62% of students live on campus; of those, 75% remain on campus on weekends. All students may keep cars.

Activities: There are no fraternities or sororities. There are 29 groups on campus, including Amnesty International, Anime Club, art, bowling,

chorale, composting, Crafty Progressives, dance, drama, ethnic, film, gay, honors, international, literary magazine, martial arts, musical theater, newspaper, outdoor, photography, political, professional, radio and TV, religious, rugby, Sierra Club, social, social service, and student government. Popular campus events include Day of Service, Fiesta de Santa Fe, and the semiformal.

Sports: There is 1 intercollegiate sport for men and 1 for women, and 4 intramural sports for men and 4 for women. Facilities include a fitness center housing a gym, racquetball/squash courts, a weight room, and a multipurpose exercise room, and an international-class tennis facility with indoor and outdoor courts.

Disabled Students: 95% of the campus is accessible. Wheelchair ramps, elevators, special parking, specially equipped rest rooms, special class scheduling, lowered drinking fountains, lowered telephones, special housing, and lowered light switches and controls in dorms are available.

Services: Counseling and information services are available, as is tutoring in every subject. There is a reader service for the blind. Deaf interpreting, extended time on testing, note takers, books on tape, and special tutors for students with writing-related disabilities are available.

Campus Safety and Security: Measures include 24-hour foot and vehicle patrol, self-defense education, security escort services, and informal discussions. There are pamphlets/posters/films, emergency telephones, and lighted pathways/sidewalks.

Programs of Study: CSF confers B.A., B.S., B.B.A., and B.F.A. degrees. Associate and master's degrees are also awarded. Bachelor's degrees are awarded in AGRICULTURE (environmental studies), BIOLOGICAL SCIENCE (environmental biology), BUSINESS (accounting, business administration and management, international business management, management information systems, and organizational behavior), COMMUNICATIONS AND THE ARTS (art history and appreciation, arts administration/management, communications, creative writing, dramatic arts, English, film arts, multimedia, music, musical theater, painting, performing arts, photography, sculpture, studio art, technical and business writing, theater design, and theater management), COMPUTER AND PHYSICAL SCIENCE (computer science), EDUCATION (elementary and secondary), ENGINEERING AND ENVIRONMENTAL DESIGN (environmental science), SOCIAL SCIENCE (applied psychology, counseling/psychology, criminal justice, humanities, interdisciplinary studies, political science/government, psychology, public administration, religion, and Southwest American studies). Social sciences, humanities, and film are the strongest academically. Performing arts, moving image arts, and studio arts are the largest.

Required: Students must successfully complete 128 credit hours with a minimum GPA of 2.0 The 39-credit core curriculum includes courses in sciences, social sciences, humanities, creative expression, cultural diversity, ethical responsibility, and a capstone experience. Freshmen are required to complete a 9-credit learning community course.

Special: CSF offers co-op programs in business, studio art, and film, internships in all areas of study, study abroad in 11 countries, work-study programs, dual majors, student-designed majors, a pass/fail option, credit by exam and credit for life and work experience. There is 1 national honor society, a freshman honors program, and 8 departmental honors program.

Faculty/Classroom: 64% of faculty are male; 36%, female. All teach undergraduates. The average class size in an introductory lecture is 13; in a laboratory, 10; and in a regular course, 13.

Admissions: 82% of the 2005-2006 applicants were accepted. The SAT scores for the 2005-2006 freshman class were: Verbal--16% below 500, 46% between 500 and 599, 31% between 600 and 700, and 7% above 700; Math--33% below 500, 51% between 500 and 599, 15% between 600 and 700, and 1% above 700. The ACT scores were 36% below 21, 22% between 21 and 23, 24% between 24 and 26, 9% between 27 and 28, and 9% above 28. 27% of the current freshmen were in the top fifth of their class; 51% were in the top two fifths.

Requirements: The SAT or ACT is required. In addition, graduation from an accreditied secondary school is required. The GED is accepted. Applicants must have 18 academic credits, including 4 years of English, 2 each of math, science, and social studies, and the remainder in college-prep courses. An essay, an interview, and a letter of recommendation from a teacher and a counselor are required. A portfolio or audition is required for specific majors. AP and CLEP credits are accepted. Important factors in the admissions decision are evidence of special talent, recommendations by school officials, and advanced placement or honor courses.

Procedure: Freshmen are admitted to all sessions. Entrance exams should be taken in the junior year of high school. There are early decision and deferred admissions plans. There is a rolling admissions plan. Early decision applications should be filed by November 15; the deadline for regular applications is rolling for fall entry. The fall 2005 application fee was $35. Notification of early decision is sent December 15; regular decision, on a rolling basis. 13 early decision candidates were accepted for the 2005-2006 class. Applications are accepted on-line.

Transfer: 74 transfer students enrolled in 2004-2005. Applicants must submit an official high school transcript, official transcripts from all previous colleges, and SAT or ACT scores. An interview is recommended. 30 of 128 credits required for the bachelor's degree must be completed at CSF.

Visiting: There are regularly scheduled orientations for prospective students, including campus tours, departmental receptions, a meeting with an admissions counselor, a campus event, and an outdoor activity. Students are housed with current students and eat in the campus dining room. There are guides for informal visits and visitors may sit in on classes and stay overnight. To schedule a visit, contact the Office of Admissions.

Financial Aid: In 2005-2006, 64% of all full-time freshmen and 67% of continuing full-time students received some form of financial aid. 55% of full-time freshmen and 60% of continuing full-time students received need-based aid. The average freshman award was $18,101. Need-based scholarships or need-based grants averaged $7782; need-based self-help aid (loans and jobs) averaged $4894; and other non-need-based awards and non-need-based scholarships averaged $6133. 41% of undergraduates work part time. Average annual earnings from campus work are $2000. The average financial indebtedness of the 2005 graduate was $17,540. The FAFSA is required. The priority date for freshman financial aid applications for fall entry is March 15. The deadline for filing freshman financial aid applications for fall entry is November 3.

International Students: There are 5 international students enrolled. The school actively recruits these students. They must achieve a satisfactory score on the TOEFL and also take the SAT or the ACT.

Computers: Wireless access is available. There are 84 networked computers distributed throughout the campus at 7 labs. All dorm rooms have cable modems. All students may access the system. There are no time limits and no fees.

Graduates: From July 1, 2004 to June 30, 2005, 304 bachelor's degrees were awarded. The most popular majors were studio art (19%), film (17%), and psychology (11%). In an average class, 26% graduate in 4 years or less, 37% graduate in 5 years or less, and 45% graduate in 6 years or less. Of the 2004 graduating class, 21% were enrolled in graduate school within 6 months of graduation and 84% were employed.

Admissions Contact: Jeff Miller, Dean of Enrollment. A video is available. E-mail: *admissions@csf.edu* Web: *www.csf.edu*

COLLEGE OF THE SOUTHWEST
Hobbs, NM 88240-9987

E-4

(505) 392-6563
(800) 530-4400; Fax: (505) 392-6006

Full-time: 169 men, 223 women	**Faculty:** 24
Part-time: 39 men, 97 women	**Ph.D.s:** 62%
Graduate: 14 men, 81 women	**Student/Faculty:** 16 to 1
Year: semesters, summer session	**Tuition:** $9920
Application Deadline: open	**Room & Board:** $2500
Freshman Class: 592 applied, 93 accepted, 64 enrolled	
SAT Verbal/Math: 431/456*	**ACT:** 19	COMPETITIVE+

College of the Southwest, founded in 1962, is an independent college offering undergraduate programs in arts and sciences, business, education, psychology, and criminal justice. Graduate programs are offered in education. The library contains 74,049 volumes, 23,209 microform items, and 1538 audio/video tapes/CDs/DVDs, and subscribes to 302 periodicals including electronic. Computerized library services include the card catalog, interlibrary loans, database searching, and Internet access. Special learning facilities include a learning resource center. The 162-acre campus is in a small town 110 miles southwest of Lubbock, Texas. Including any residence halls, there are 10 buildings.

Student Life: 65% of undergraduates are from New Mexico. Others are from 12 states, 11 foreign countries, and Canada. 57% are white; 30% Hispanic. The average age of freshmen is 20; all undergraduates, 26. 40% do not continue beyond their first year; 30% remain to graduate.

Housing: 172 students can be accommodated in college housing, which includes single-sex and coed dorms and on-campus apartments. On-campus housing is available on a first-come, first-served basis. Priority is given to out-of-town students. 70% of students commute. Alcohol is not permitted. All students may keep cars.

Activities: There are no fraternities or sororities. There are 7 groups on campus, including chorus, debate, drama, honors, international, newspaper, professional, religious, student government, and yearbook. Popular campus events include Annual Students in Free Enterprise Dinner and Award Presentation, Family Week, and speakers' presentations.

Sports: There are 4 intercollegiate sports for men and 6 for women, and 5 intramural sports for men and 5 for women. Facilities include soccer and baseball fields, a game room, and a physical fitness center with a multipurpose gym, racquetball courts, and physiology lab.

Disabled Students: All of the campus is accessible. Wheelchair ramps, special parking, and specially equipped rest rooms are available.

Services: Counseling and information services are available, as is tutoring in most subjects. There is remedial math and writing.

Campus Safety and Security: Measures include 24-hour foot and vehicle patrol, informal discussions, and pamphlets/posters/films.

Programs of Study: CSW confers B.S., B.A.S., and B.B.A. degrees. Master's degrees are also awarded. Bachelor's degrees are awarded in BIOLOGICAL SCIENCE (biology/biological science), BUSINESS (accounting, business administration and management, and marketing/retailing/merchandising), COMMUNICATIONS AND THE ARTS (English, fine arts, and sports media), COMPUTER AND PHYSICAL SCIENCE (mathematics), EDUCATION (elementary, secondary, and special), SOCIAL SCIENCE (criminal justice, history, humanities, psychology, and sociology). Education and business are the strongest academically. Education, business, and criminal justice are the largest.

Required: To graduate, students must complete 128 semester hours with a minimum GPA of 2.0 (2.5 for education majors). General education requirements include 12 semester hours each of social science and math/science, 9 each of humanities/fine arts and communications, 6 of religion, and 3 of economics, as well as a course in free enterprise and a senior seminar in leadership and ethics.

Special: The school offers co-op programs in early childhood education. Internships are available for students majoring in business, psychology, and education. CSW also offers nondegree study and credit for military experience. There are 2 national honor societies and 1 departmental honors program.

Faculty/Classroom: 51% of faculty are male; 49%, female. 99% teach undergraduates. No introductory courses are taught by graduate students. The average class size in an introductory lecture is 15; in a laboratory, 7; and in a regular course, 12.

Admissions: 16% of the 2005-2006 applicants were accepted. The SAT scores for the 2005-2006 freshman class were: Verbal--77% below 500, and 23% between 500 and 599; Math--61% below 500, 35% between 500 and 599, and 3% between 600 and 700. The ACT scores were 76% below 21, 20% between 21 and 23, 2% between 24 and 26, and 2% above 28. 33% of the current freshmen were in the top fifth of their class; 67% were in the top two fifths.

Requirements: A satisfactory score on the SAT or ACT is required. Applicants must be graduates of an accredited secondary school or have a GED certificate. CSW requires applicants to be in the upper 50% of their class. A GPA of 2.0 is required. AP and CLEP credits are accepted. Important factors in the admissions decision are advanced placement or honor courses, extracurricular activities record, and ability to finance college education.

Procedure: Freshmen are admitted to all sessions. There is a rolling admissions plan. Application deadlines are open. Application fee is $25. Applications are accepted on-line.

Transfer: 135 transfer students enrolled in 2004-2005. Applicants must present a minimum GPA of 2.0 and official transcripts from all colleges attended. 30 of 128 credits required for the bachelor's degree must be completed at CSW.

Visiting: There are guides for informal visits and visitors may sit in on classes and stay overnight. To schedule a visit, contact Karen Workentin, Dean of Admissions at (800) 530-4400, ext. 1005 or *kworkentin@csw.edu*.

Financial Aid: 17% of undergraduates work part time. Average annual earnings from campus work are $2000. The FAFSA and the college's own financial statement are required. The deadline for filing freshman financial aid applications for fall entry is June 15.

International Students: There are 19 international students enrolled. They must score satisfactorily on the TOEFL and also take the SAT or the ACT.

Computers: Internet connections are in the dorms, and the library has computers with Internet access. Students have unlimited hours, but some sites are blocked from viewing. Students sign a form stating they will not misuse this privilege. There are no time limits and no fees. It is strongly recommended that all students have a personal computer.

Graduates: From July 1, 2004 to June 30, 2005, 122 bachelor's degrees were awarded. The most popular majors were education (40%), psychology (11%), and accounting (8%). In an average class, 19% graduate in 5 years or less. 10 companies recruited on campus in 2004-2005. Of the 2004 graduating class, 5% were enrolled in graduate school within 6 months of graduation.

Admissions Contact: Karen Workentin, Dean of Admissions. E-mail: *kworkentin@csw.edu* Web: *www.csw.edu*

EASTERN NEW MEXICO UNIVERSITY   E-3
Portales, NM 88130

(505) 562-2178
(800) 367-3668; Fax: (505) 562-2118

Full-time: 1188 men, 1322 women	**Faculty:** 140; IIA, --$
Part-time: 256 men, 537 women	**Ph.D.s:** 78%
Graduate: 202 men, 547 women	**Student/Faculty:** 18 to 1
Year: semesters, summer session	**Tuition:** $2784 ($8340)
Application Deadline: open	**Room & Board:** $4480
Freshman Class: 1804 applied, 1167 accepted, 567 enrolled	
SAT Verbal/Math: 475/479*	**ACT:** 19 COMPETITIVE

Eastern New Mexico University, founded in 1934, is a public institution offering programs in the liberal arts and sciences, as well as education, business, fine arts, and vocational and technical fields. There are 4 undergraduate schools and 1 graduate school. In addition to regional accreditation, Eastern has baccalaureate program accreditation with ACBSP, ASLA, NASM, NCATE, and NLN. The library contains 539,010 volumes, 704,842 microform items, and 24,343 audio/video tapes/CDs/DVDs, and subscribes to 17,200 periodicals including electronic. Computerized library services include the card catalog, interlibrary loans, and database searching. Special learning facilities include a learning resource center, art gallery, natural history museum, radio station, TV station, and nearby important archeological sites. The 400-acre campus is in a small town 120 miles northeast of Lubbock, Texas. Including any residence halls, there are 50 buildings.

Student Life: 81% of undergraduates are from New Mexico. Others are from 44 states, 16 foreign countries, and Canada. 58% are white; 27% Hispanic. 37% are Protestant; 24% Catholic; 11% claim no religious affiliation. The average age of freshmen is 18; all undergraduates, 23. 41% do not continue beyond their first year.

Housing: 1366 students can be accommodated in college housing, which includes single-sex and coed dorms, on-campus apartments, and married-student housing. In addition, there are freshmen-only living areas. On-campus housing is guaranteed for all 4 years. 73% of students commute. Alcohol is not permitted. All students may keep cars.

Activities: There are 8 national fraternities and 2 national sororities. There are 55 groups on campus, including art, band, cheerleading, choir, chorus, computers, dance, debate, drama, drill team, ethnic, forensics, gay, honors, international, jazz band, literary magazine, marching band, musical theater, newspaper, orchestra, pep band, photography, political, professional, radio and TV, religious, social, social service, steel drum band, student government, and yearbook. Popular campus events include Green and Silver Breakthrough, Peanut Valley Festival, and Fiesta International.

Sports: There are 6 intercollegiate sports for men and 7 for women, and 15 intramural sports for men and 15 for women. Facilities include a 5200-seat arena, tennis courts, an indoor pool, a 5300-seat stadium, and handball and racquetball courts.

Disabled Students: All of the campus is accessible. Wheelchair ramps, elevators, special parking, specially equipped rest rooms, special class scheduling, lowered drinking fountains, special housing, automatic door openers, and curb cuts are available.

Services: Counseling and information services are available, as is tutoring in every subject. There is a reader service for the blind, and remedial math, reading, and writing.

Campus Safety and Security: Measures include 24-hour foot and vehicle patrol, self-defense education, security escort services, and pamphlets/posters/films. There are emergency telephones and lighted pathways/sidewalks.

Programs of Study: Eastern confers B.A., B.S., B.A.E., B.B.A., B.F.A., B.M., B.M.E., B.S.E., and B.U.S. degrees. Associate and master's degrees are also awarded. Bachelor's degrees are awarded in AGRICULTURE (agricultural business management, agriculture, and wildlife management), BIOLOGICAL SCIENCE (biology/biological science), BUSINESS (accounting, banking and finance, business administration and management, business economics, marketing/retailing/merchandising, and personnel management), COMMUNICATIONS AND THE ARTS (art, communications, dramatic arts, English, fine arts, journalism, music, music performance, Spanish, and speech/debate/rhetoric), COMPUTER AND PHYSICAL SCIENCE (chemistry, computer science, geology, information sciences and systems, mathematics, physics, and statistics), EDUCATION (agricultural, business, elementary, home economics, music, physical, and special), ENGINEERING AND ENVIRONMENTAL DESIGN (electrical/electronics engineering technology), HEALTH PROFESSIONS (medical laboratory technology, nursing, and speech pathology/audiology), SOCIAL SCIENCE (anthropology, criminal justice, economics, history, human services, political science/government, psychology, religion, social studies, and sociology). Business is the strongest academically. Education, biology, and business administration are the largest.

Required: To graduate, students must earn 128 credit hours, 36 in the major, with a minimum GPA of 2.0. Required courses include those in English, science, math, social studies, humanities, fine arts, and phys ed.

Special: The school offers co-op programs in wildlife and fisheries and communication, internships, study abroad in 3 countries, work-study programs, student-designed majors, a general studies degree, credit for life, military, and work experience, nondegree study, and pass/fail options. There are 2 national honor societies and a freshman honors program.

Faculty/Classroom: 53% of faculty are male; 47%, female. 95% teach undergraduates. Graduate students teach 13% of introductory courses.

Admissions: 65% of the 2005-2006 applicants were accepted. The SAT scores for the 2005-2006 freshman class were: Verbal--62% below 500, 23% between 500 and 599, 13% between 600 and 700, and 2% above 700; Math--56% below 500, 33% between 500 and 599, 9% between 600 and 700, and 2% above 700. The ACT scores were 68% below 21, 20% between 21 and 23, 10% between 24 and 26, 2% between 27 and 28, and 1% above 28. 27% of the current freshmen were in the top fifth of their class; 54% were in the top two fifths. 10 freshmen graduated first in their class.

Requirements: A satisfactory score on the SAT or ACT. Applicants must be high school graduates or have the GED, having earned 20 units, including 4 in English, 3 in math, 2 in science, and 1 each in history, music, and social studies. Provisional and special admissions are available. A GPA of 2.25 is required. AP and CLEP credits are accepted.

Procedure: Freshmen are admitted to all sessions. Entrance exams should be taken in the junior or senior year. There is a rolling admissions plan. Application deadlines are open. Applications are accepted on-line.

Transfer: 310 transfer students enrolled in 2004-2005. Transfer students must have a minimum GPA of 2.0. 32 of 128 credits required for the bachelor's degree must be completed at Eastern.

Visiting: There are regularly scheduled orientations for prospective students, including meetings with admissions, financial aid, and faculty, a tour of campus, and a meal in the dining hall. There are guides for informal visits and visitors may sit in on classes and stay overnight. To schedule a visit, contact the Admissions Office.

Financial Aid: In 2005-2006, 74% of all full-time freshmen and 61% of continuing full-time students received some form of financial aid. 64% of full-time freshmen and 68% of continuing full-time students received need-based aid. The average freshman award was $7054. Average annual earnings from campus work are $2800. The average financial indebtedness of the 2005 graduate was $10,861. The FAFSA, the college's own financial statement, and an institutional scholarship form are required. The deadline for filing freshman financial aid applications for fall entry is March 1.

International Students: There are 28 international students enrolled. The school actively recruits these students. They must achieve a satisfactory sore on the TOEFL as well as on the SAT or ACT.

Computers: All students may access the system. There are no time limits and no fees.

Graduates: From July 1, 2004 to June 30, 2005, 449 bachelor's degrees were awarded. The most popular majors were elementary education (13%), university studies (8%), and criminal justice (6%). In an average class, 10% graduate in 4 years or less, 27% graduate in 5 years or less, and 34% graduate in 6 years or less. 91 companies recruited on campus in 2004-2005.

Admissions Contact: Donna Kittrell, Admissions.
E-mail: *donna.kittrell@enmu.edu* Web: *www.enmu.edu*

NEW MEXICO HIGHLANDS UNIVERSITY   D-2
Las Vegas, NM 87701

(505) 454-3434
(800) 338-6648; Fax: (505) 454-3552

Full-time: 459 men, 652 women	**Faculty:** 77
Part-time: 308 men, 573 women	**Ph.D.s:** 75%
Graduate: 508 men, 1207 women	**Student/Faculty:** 14 to 1
Year: semesters, summer session	**Tuition:** $2280 ($3420)
Application Deadline: open	**Room & Board:** $3992
Freshman Class: 1775 applied, 1324 accepted, 590 enrolled	
SAT Verbal/Math: 447/442*	**ACT:** 18 NONCOMPETITIVE

New Mexico Highlands University, founded in 1893, is a state-supported institution offering undergraduate programs in liberal and fine arts, science and engineering, and professional studies. There are 4 undergraduate and 4 graduate schools. In addition to regional accreditation, Highlands University has baccalaureate program accreditation with ACBSP, CSWE, and NCATE. The library contains 616,364 volumes, 184,454 microform items, and 139 audio/video tapes/CDs/DVDs, and subscribes to 747 periodicals including electronic. Computerized library services include the card catalog, interlibrary loans, database searching, and Internet access. Special learning facilities include a learning resource center, art gallery, radio station, TV station, and a video production studio. The 248-acre campus is in a small town 65 miles northeast of Santa Fe. Including any residence halls, there are 45 buildings.

Student Life: 92% of undergraduates are from New Mexico. Others are from 31 states, 10 foreign countries, and Canada. 98% are from public schools. 51% are Hispanic; 32% white. The average age of freshmen is 21; all undergraduates, 28. 24% of freshmen remain to graduate.

Housing: 480 students can be accommodated in college housing, which includes single-sex and coed dorms, on-campus apartments, and married-student housing. On-campus housing is guaranteed for the freshman year only and is available on a first-come, first-served basis. All students may keep cars.

Activities: There are no fraternities or sororities. There are 45 groups on campus, including art, band, cheerleading, choir, chorale, chorus, dance, departmental, drama, ethnic, film, gay, honors, international, jazz band, marching band, musical theater, newspaper, pep band, photography, political, professional, radio and TV, religious, social, social service, student government, and yearbook. Popular campus events include Multicultural Week, Career Day, and Welcome Back Weeks.

Sports: There are 4 intercollegiate sports for men and 3 for women, and 8 intramural sports for men and 8 for women. Facilities include a 5000-seat football stadium, a 3600-seat arena, an indoor swimming pool, a weight room, athletic fields, a 9-hole golf course, and tennis, racquetball, and basketball courts. Hiking and skiing are nearby.

Disabled Students: All of the campus is accessible. Wheelchair ramps, elevators, special parking, specially equipped rest rooms, special class scheduling, lowered drinking fountains, lowered telephones, special housing, and accessible technology are available.

Services: Counseling and information services are available, as is tutoring in most subjects. There is remedial math, reading, and writing.

Campus Safety and Security: Measures include 24-hour foot and vehicle patrol, self-defense education, security escort services, and informal discussions. There are pamphlets/posters/films.

Programs of Study: Highlands University confers B.A., B.S., B.B.A., B.F.A., B.S.E., and B.S.W. degrees. Associate and master's degrees are also awarded. Bachelor's degrees are awarded in AGRICULTURE (natural resource management), BIOLOGICAL SCIENCE (biology/biological science), BUSINESS (accounting, banking and finance, business administration and management, management information systems, marketing and distribution, and marketing/retailing/merchandising), COMMUNICATIONS AND THE ARTS (art, communications, English, graphic design, music, and Spanish), COMPUTER AND PHYSICAL SCIENCE (chemistry, computer science, mathematics, and physics), EDUCATION (early childhood, elementary, science, and special), ENGINEERING AND ENVIRONMENTAL DESIGN (engineering, and environmental science), HEALTH PROFESSIONS (health), SOCIAL SCIENCE (anthropology, history, physical fitness/movement, political science/government, psychology, social work, and sociology). Physical sciences and psychology are the strongest academically. Education, business administration, and social work are the largest.

Required: Students must complete 40 to 51 credits of core curriculum requirements, including courses in English, history, science, social environment, thought and critical analysis, fine arts, literature, communicating skills, and phys ed. Proficiency in language and math must be demonstrated. A minimum of 128 credits, including at least 30 in the major, with a GPA of at least 2.0 is required to graduate.

Special: Highlands offers practicum, internship, study abroad in 2 countries, and field-study courses; cooperative programs in most majors; internships in education; minors in geology, physics, secondary education, philosophy, and theater; and credit for military training. There are 5 national honor societies, a freshman honors program, and 3 departmental honors programs.

Faculty/Classroom: 54% of faculty are male; 46%, female. All teach undergraduates and 20% both teach and do research. No introductory courses are taught by graduate students. The average class size in an introductory lecture is 42; in a laboratory, 15; and in a regular course, 18.

Admissions: 75% of the 2005-2006 applicants were accepted. The SAT scores for the 2005-2006 freshman class were: Verbal--76% below 500, and 24% between 500 and 599; Math--76% below 500, 12% between 500 and 599, and 12% between 600 and 700. The ACT scores were 82% below 21, 12% between 21 and 23, 5% between 24 and 26, and 1% between 27 and 28. 22% of the current freshmen were in the top fifth of their class; 47% were in the top two fifths.

Requirements: The ACT is required. SAT scores may be substituted. Scores are used for placement purposes. Applicants should be graduates of an accredited secondary school; the GED is accepted. A GPA of 2.0 is required. AP and CLEP credits are accepted. Important factors in the admissions decision are advanced placement or honor courses, evidence of special talent, and recommendations by school officials.

Procedure: Freshmen are admitted to all sessions. There are early decision, deferred admissions, and rolling admissions plans. Application deadlines are open. The fall 2005 application fee was $15. Applications are accepted on-line.

Transfer: Transfer applicants with 16 or more semester credit hours must have at least a 2.0 GPA. 32 of 128 credits required for the bachelor's degree must be completed at Highlands University.

Visiting: There are regularly scheduled orientations for prospective students, available on a call-in basis. There are guides for informal visits and visitors may sit in on classes and stay overnight. To schedule a visit, contact the Admissions Office at (505) 454-3593.

Financial Aid: In 2005-2006, 94% of all full-time freshmen and 75% of continuing full-time students received some form of financial aid. 63%

of full-time freshmen and 60% of continuing full-time students received need-based aid. Need-based scholarships or need-based grants averaged $1895 ($5250 maximum); need-based self-help aid (loans and jobs) averaged $2549 ($5505 maximum); non-need-based athletic scholarships averaged $1532 ($2500 maximum); and other non-need-based awards and non-need-based scholarships averaged $959 ($5736 maximum). 30% of undergraduates work part time. Average annual earnings from campus work are $2298. The average financial indebtedness of the 2005 graduate was $9625. The FAFSA is required. The priority date for freshman financial aid applications for fall entry is March 1. The deadline for filing freshman financial aid applications for fall entry is October 1.

International Students: There are 9 international students enrolled. They must score satisfactorily on the TOEFL and also take IELTS.

Computers: Wireless access is available. The student center has 53 computers. All students may access the system 24 hours daily. There are no time limits and no fees. It is strongly recommended that all students have a personal computer.

Graduates: From July 1, 2004 to June 30, 2005, 224 bachelor's degrees were awarded. The most popular majors were social work (53%), education (22%), and business administration (10%). In an average class, 24% graduate in 6 years or less. 16 companies recruited on campus in a recent year.

Admissions Contact: John Coca, Director of Admissions. A video is available. E-mail: *admissions@nmhu.edu* Web: *www.nmhu.edu*

NEW MEXICO INSTITUTE OF MINING AND TECHNOLOGY   C-3

Socorro, NM 87801   (505) 835-5424
(800) 428-TECH; Fax: (505) 835-5989

Full-time: 826 men, 297 women	Faculty: 120
Part-time: 115 men, 148 women	Ph.D.s: 86%
Graduate: 288 men, 215 women	Student/Faculty: 9 to 1
Year: semesters, summer session	Tuition: $3644 ($10,463)
Application Deadline: August 1	Room & Board: $4866
Freshman Class: 428 applied, 346 accepted, 281 enrolled	
SAT : not required	ACT: 26 VERY COMPETITIVE+

New Mexico Institute of Mining and Technology, founded in 1889 as the New Mexico School of Mines, is a science and engineering university. It has 4 research-associated divisions: the New Mexico Bureau of Geology and Mineral Resources, the Energetic Materials Research and Testing Center, the Petroleum Recovery Research Center, and the Langmuir Laboratory for Atmospheric Research. In addition to regional accreditation, New Mexico Tech has baccalaureate program accreditation with ABET. The library contains 321,829 volumes, 217,540 microform items, and 2526 audio/video tapes/CDs/DVDs, and subscribes to 884 periodicals including electronic. Computerized library services include the card catalog, interlibrary loans, database searching, and Internet access. Special learning facilities include a radio station, mineral museum, seismic research mine, and campus astronomical observatory. The 320-acre campus is in a small town 75 miles south of Albuquerque. Including any residence halls, there are 28 buildings.

Student Life: 86% of undergraduates are from New Mexico. Others are from 49 states, 38 foreign countries, and Canada. 70% are white; 20% Hispanic. The average age of freshmen is 18; all undergraduates, 21. 26% do not continue beyond their first year; 40% remain to graduate.

Housing: 700 students can be accommodated in college housing, which includes single-sex and coed dorms, on-campus apartments, off-campus apartments, and married-student housing. On-campus housing is available on a first-come, first-served basis. 56% of students commute. Alcohol is not permitted. All students may keep cars.

Activities: There are no fraternities or sororities. There are 55 groups on campus, including art, band, chess, chorus, computers, drama, ethnic, gay, honors, international, jazz band, musical theater, orchestra, political, professional, radio and TV, religious, social, social service, student government, and yearbook. Popular campus events include 49ers, Spring Fling, and International Student Exhibit.

Sports: There are 9 intramural sports for men and 9 for women. Facilities include 2 gyms, a swimming pool, an 18-hole golf course, an athletic field, a climbing wall, a weight/fitness room, racquetball/squash, tennis, and sand volleyball courts, a Ping-Pong area, and a martial arts/combatives room.

Disabled Students: Most of the campus is wheelchair accessible. Wheelchair ramps, elevators, special parking, specially equipped rest rooms, lowered drinking fountains, and lowered telephones are available.

Services: Counseling and information services are available, as is tutoring in most subjects. There is a reader service for the blind.

Campus Safety and Security: Measures include 24-hour foot and vehicle patrol, self-defense education, security escort services, and informal discussions. There are pamphlets/posters/films, emergency telephones, and lighted pathways/sidewalks.

Programs of Study

New Mexico Tech confers B.S. and B.G.S. degrees. Associate, master's, and doctoral degrees are also awarded. Bachelor's degrees are awarded in BIOLOGICAL SCIENCE (biology/biological science), BUSINESS (business administration and management), COMMUNICATIONS AND THE ARTS (technical and business writing), COMPUTER AND PHYSICAL SCIENCE (chemistry, computer science, earth science, information sciences and systems, mathematics, and physics), ENGINEERING AND ENVIRONMENTAL DESIGN (chemical engineering, civil engineering, electrical/electronics engineering, engineering mechanics, environmental engineering, environmental science, materials engineering, mechanical engineering, mining and mineral engineering, and petroleum/natural gas engineering), SOCIAL SCIENCE (liberal arts/general studies and psychology). Physics and electrical engineering are the strongest academically. Electrical engineering, computer science, and physics are the largest.

Required: The student must earn at least 130 credit hours to graduate, including 42 hours of basic science, consisting in part of 10 hours of physics and 8 each of chemistry, calculus, and biology/geology/engineering. Additional distribution requirements include 18 hours of literature, philosophy, the arts, and social science, 9 hours each of written and spoken English, and a senior seminar or senior design project. The credit hours required in the major vary by program. The student must also maintain a cumulative GPA of 2.0.

Special: New Mexico Tech offers co-op programs in computer science and all engineering majors, internships in technical communications, and cross-registration with New Mexico State, University of New Mexico, and Los Alamos National Laboratories in the WERC consortium. Dual majors are offered in engineering, computer science, physics, and math. Student-designed majors in environmental science, general studies, and basic science, work-study, nondegree study, and pass/fail options are also available. There are 4 national honor societies.

Faculty/Classroom: 77% of faculty are male; 23%, female. 95% both teach and do research. Graduate students teach 12% of introductory courses. The average class size in an introductory lecture is 18; in a laboratory, 12; and in a regular course, 18.

Admissions: 81% of the 2005-2006 applicants were accepted. The SAT scores for the 2005-2006 freshman class were: Verbal--10% below 500, 25% between 500 and 599, 48% between 600 and 700, and 17% above 700; Math--6% below 500, 31% between 500 and 599, 44% between 600 and 700, and 20% above 700. The ACT scores were 1% between 21 and 23, 30% between 24 and 26, 52% between 27 and 28, and 17% above 28.

Requirements: A satisfactory score is required on the ACT. Applicants must be high school graduates or present a GED certificate. Students should have earned 15 academic credits, consisting of 4 units of English, 3 each of social science and math (2 beyond general math), and 2 of science (including 1 of lab science), and electives. A GPA of 2.5 is required. AP credits are accepted. Important factors in the admissions decision are advanced placement or honor courses, evidence of special talent, and extracurricular activities record.

Procedure: Freshmen are admitted to all sessions. Entrance exams should be taken by December of the senior year. There are early decision and deferred admissions plans. There is a rolling admissions plan. Applications should be filed by August 1 for fall entry and December 1 for spring entry. The fall 2005 application fee was $15. Notification is sent on a rolling basis.

Transfer: 40 transfer students enrolled in 2004-2005. Transfer students must have a GPA of 2.0 and have completed 30 semester hours of transferable credit. Those who have fewer than 30 credit hours, or who have not completed freshman English, must present a satisfactory score on the ACT, as well as high school transcripts. 30 of 130 credits required for the bachelor's degree must be completed at New Mexico Tech.

Visiting: There are regularly scheduled orientations for prospective students, including 2 days of get-acquainted social activities, information sessions for parents and students, and transition sessions for parents. There are guides for informal visits and visitors may sit in on classes and stay overnight. To schedule a visit, contact the Admission Office.

Financial Aid: The FAFSA is required. The priority date for freshman financial aid applications for fall entry is March 1. The deadline for filing freshman financial aid applications for fall entry is June 1.

International Students: There were 28 international students enrolled in a recent year. A satisfactory score on the written TOEFL is required.

Computers: All students may access the system 16 1/2 hours a day on site and 24 hours a day via network. There are no time limits. The fee is $2 per semester. It is strongly recommended that all students have a personal computer.

Graduates: From July 1, 2004 to June 30, 2005, 177 bachelor's degrees were awarded. The most popular majors were electrical engineering (16%), math (10%), and computer science (10%). In an average class, 33% graduate in 5 years or less, and 40% graduate in 6 years or less.

Admissions Contact: Mike Kloeppel, Director of Admission.
E-mail: *admission@admin.nmt.edu* Web: *http://www.nmt.edu*

NEW MEXICO STATE UNIVERSITY   C-4
Las Cruces, NM 88003-8001   (505) 646-3121
                          (800) 662-6678; Fax: (505) 646-6330

Full-time: 4362 men, 5237 women	**Faculty:** 692; I, --$
Part-time: 1251 men, 1806 women	**Ph.D.s:** 81%
Graduate: 1418 men, 2098 women	**Student/Faculty:** 14 to 1
Year: semesters, summer session	**Tuition:** $3918 ($13,206)
Application Deadline: open	**Room & Board:** $5332
Freshman Class: 5522 applied, 4483 accepted, 2019 enrolled	
ACT: 21	**COMPETITIVE**

New Mexico State University, founded in 1888, is a public institution offering undergraduate and graduate programs that include study in liberal arts, agriculture, business, engineering, health science, education, and visual and performing arts. There are 6 undergraduate schools and 1 graduate school. In addition to regional accreditation, NMSU has baccalaureate program accreditation with AACSB, ABET, ADA, AHEA, APA,CACREP,CAHEA,CCNE, CSWE, NASM, and NCATE. The 2 libraries contain 1,692,035 volumes and 1,463,677 microform items, and subscribe to 5975 periodicals including electronic. Computerized library services include the card catalog, interlibrary loans, database searching, Internet access, and laptop Internet portals. Special learning facilities include a learning resource center, art gallery, natural history museum, radio station, TV station, a 289-acre experimental farm and orchard, a 61,760-acre cattle and experimental ranch, and a 2160-acre recreational area in the Organ Mountains. The 900-acre campus is in an urban area 40 miles north of El Paso. Including any residence halls, there are 287 buildings.

Student Life: 83% of undergraduates are from New Mexico. Others are from 50 states, 77 foreign countries, and Canada. 48% are white; 41% Hispanic. The average age of freshmen is 18; all undergraduates, 23.

Housing: 3080 students can be accommodated in college housing, which includes single-sex and coed dorm, on-campus apartments, married-student housing, fraternity houses, and sorority houses. In addition, there are honors houses. On-campus housing is guaranteed for all 4 years. 85% of students commute. All students may keep cars.

Activities: There are 12 national fraternities and 6 national sororities. There are 217 groups on campus, including art, band, cheerleading, chess, choir, chorale, chorus, computers, dance, drama, drill team, drum and bugle corps, ethnic, gay, honors, international, jazz band, literary magazine, marching band, musical theater, newspaper, opera, orchestra, pep band, photography, political, professional, radio and TV, religious, social, social service, student government, and symphony. Popular campus events include Chicano Week, American Indian Week, and Black Week.

Sports: There are 6 intercollegiate sports for men and 9 for women, and 29 intramural sports for men and 27 for women. Facilities include a game room, a natatorium, tennis courts, playing fields, a gym, and rodeo grounds. One campus stadium seats 30,342 while the other seats more than 13,000.

Disabled Students: 95% of the campus is accessible. Wheelchair ramps, elevators, special parking, specially equipped rest rooms, lowered drinking fountains, lowered telephones, and priority registration are available.

Services: Counseling and information services are available, as is tutoring in most subjects. There is a reader service for the blind. Remedial classes are offered at the Dona Ana Branch Community College. There is also an interpreter for the hearing impaired.

Campus Safety and Security: Measures include 24-hour foot and vehicle patrol, self-defense education, security escort services, and shuttle buses. There are informal discussions, pamphlets/posters/films, emergency telephones, and lighted pathways/sidewalks.

Programs of Study: NMSU confers B.A., B.S., B.S.N., and B.S.W. degrees. Associate, master's, and doctoral degrees are also awarded. Bachelor's degrees are awarded in AGRICULTURE (agricultural business management, agricultural economics, agriculture, agronomy, animal science, horticulture, range/farm management, and soil science), BIOLOGICAL SCIENCE (biochemistry, biology/biological science, ecology, microbiology, nutrition, and wildlife biology), BUSINESS (accounting, banking and finance, business administration and management, business economics, fashion merchandising, hotel/motel and restaurant management, international business management, management information systems, marketing/retailing/merchandising, recreational facilities management, and tourism), COMMUNICATIONS AND THE ARTS (art, communications, dance, dramatic arts, English, fine arts, journalism, languages, and music), COMPUTER AND PHYSICAL SCIENCE (chemistry, computer science, geology, information sciences and systems, mathematics, and physics), EDUCATION (agricultural, athletic training, early childhood, elementary, home economics, music, physical, secondary, and special), ENGINEERING AND ENVIRONMENTAL DESIGN (chemical engineering, city/community/regional planning, civil engineering, electrical/electronics engineering, engineering physics, engineering technology, environmental engineering, environmental science, industrial engineering, mechanical engineering, and surveying engineering),

HEALTH PROFESSIONS (community health work, environmental health science, nursing, and speech pathology/audiology), SOCIAL SCIENCE (anthropology, child psychology/development, criminal justice, economics, family/consumer studies, geography, history, philosophy, physical fitness/movement, political science/government, psychology, social work, sociology, and women's studies). Elementary education, business administration, and criminal justice are the largest.

Required: All students must complete a minimum of 128 credits, including at least 50 upper-division credits. A minimum GPA of 2.0 is needed. Distribution requirements include communications, humanities, math, natural sciences, and social sciences.

Special: Internships, cooperative programs in engineering, math, science, teacher education, business, and other majors, dual majors, study abroad in 39 countries, work-study, nondegree study, and B.A.-B.S. degrees are available. There is cross-registration with the Dona Ana Branch Community College. There are 22 national honor societies, a freshman honors program, and 17 departmental honors programs.

Faculty/Classroom: 61% of faculty are male; 39%, female. All both teach and do research. Graduate students teach 10% of introductory courses. The average class size in an introductory lecture is 37; in a laboratory, 16; and in a regular course, 30.

Admissions: 81% of the 2005-2006 applicants were accepted. The ACT scores for the 2005-2006 freshman class were: 50% below 21, 26% between 21 and 23, 16% between 24 and 26, 5% between 27 and 28, and 3% above 28. 40% of the current freshmen were in the top fifth of their class; 82% were in the top two fifths. 41 freshmen graduated first in their class.

Requirements: The ACT is required. Applicants must score 20 on the ACT or may take the SAT (accepted, but not recommended). The GED is accepted. Minimum high school preparation of 4 units of English, 3 of math, 2 beyond general science, and 1 foreign language/fine arts is required. A GPA of 2.0 is required. AP and CLEP credits are accepted.

Procedure: Freshmen are admitted to all sessions. There is a rolling admissions plan. Entrance exams should be taken during the high school junior or senior year. Application deadlines are open. Notification is sent on a rolling basis. Application fee is $15. Applications are accepted online.

Transfer: 684 transfer students enrolled in 2004-2005. Applicants must have a minimum GPA of 2.0. They need 30 credits to avoid freshman admission requirements. If the applicant has earned 30 academic credit hours or more, the ACT score will be waived. If the applicant has earned 48 academic credit hours or more, the high school transcript will be waived. 30 of 128 credits required for the bachelor's degree must be completed at NMSU.

Visiting: There are regularly scheduled orientations for prospective students, including meetings with admissions counselors, faculty members, and financial aid advisers and a tour of the campus. There are guides for informal visits and visitors may sit in on classes and stay overnight. To schedule a visit, contact the Office of Admissions.

Financial Aid: In 2005-2006, 90% of all full-time freshmen and 82% of continuing full-time students received some form of financial aid. 57% of full-time freshmen and 56% of continuing full-time students received need-based aid. Need-based scholarships or need-based grants averaged $6185 ($23,290 maximum); need-based self-help aid (loans and jobs) averaged $2745 ($19,274 maximum); non-need-based athletic scholarships averaged $10,291 ($18,740 maximum); and other non-need-based awards and non-need-based scholarships including tuition waivers, averaged $3874 ($19,719 maximum). 6% of undergraduates work part time. The FAFSA is required. The deadline for filing freshman financial aid applications for fall entry is March 1.

International Students: There are 125 international students enrolled. They must take the TOEFL.

Computers: All students may access the system at any time. There are no time limits and no fees.

Graduates: From July 1, 2004 to June 30, 2005, 2122 bachelor's degrees were awarded. The most popular majors were elementary education (7%), criminal justice (5%), and accounting (5%). In an average class, 12% graduate in 4 years or less, 37% graduate in 5 years or less, and 42% graduate in 6 years or less. 636 companies recruited on campus in 2004-2005.

Admissions Contact: Angela Mora-Riley, Director of Admissions. A video is available. E-mail: *admissions@nmsu.edu* Web: *www.nmsu.edu/admissions.html*

SAINT JOHN'S COLLEGE C-2

Santa Fe, NM 87505 (505) 984-6060
(800) 331-5232; Fax: (505) 984-6162

Full-time: 240 men, 200 women	**Faculty:** IIB, +$
Part-time: 1 man, 1 woman	**Ph.D.s:** n/av
Graduate: 60 men, 40 women	**Student/Faculty:** 6 to 1
Year: semesters, summer session	**Tuition:** $30,000
Application Deadline: open	**Room & Board:** $8000
Freshman Class: n/av	
SAT or ACT: not required	**COMPETITIVE**

St. John's College, founded in 1696, offers a curriculum based on the Great Books Program in which students and faculty work together in small discussion classes without lecture courses, written finals, or emphasis on grades. The program is a rigorous interdisciplinary curriculum based on great books -- literature, math, philosophy, theology, sciences, political theory, music, history, economics -- from Homer to Freud, Euclid to Einstein. Some figures in the above capsule and in this profile are approximate. Figures in the above capsule and in this profile are approximate. The library contains 65,000 volumes and 8205 audio/video tapes/CDs/DVDs, and subscribes to 135 periodicals including electronic. Computerized library services include the card catalog, interlibrary loans, and database searching. Special learning facilities include an art gallery, a music library, a search and rescue headquarters, and music practice rooms. The 250-acre campus is in a suburban area in Santa Fe. Including any residence halls, there are 31 buildings.

Student Life: 90% of undergraduates are from out of state, mostly the Southwest. Students are from 46 states, 8 foreign countries, and Canada. 58% are from public schools. 88% are white. The average age of freshmen is 19; all undergraduates, 20. 10% do not continue beyond their first year; 60% remain to graduate.

Housing: 329 students can be accommodated in college housing, which includes single-sex and coed dorms and on-campus apartments. In addition, there are smoke-free and alcohol-free residences. On-campus housing is guaranteed for the freshman year only and is available on a lottery system for upperclassmen. 75% of students live on campus; of those, All remain on campus on weekends. All students may keep cars.

Activities: There are no fraternities or sororities. There are 32 groups on campus, including art, chess, choir, chorale, chorus, computers, dance, drama, fencing, film, gay, jazz band, literary magazine, newspaper, orchestra, photography, search and rescue, social service, student government, and yearbook. Popular campus events include Oktoberfest, Halloween and Christmas parties, and Reality weekend.

Sports: There are 5 intramural sports for men and 5 for women. Facilities include a soccer field, a track, tennis courts, an outdoor basketball court, a gym with weight room, racquetball, squash, and basketball courts, nearby mountains, and a ski mountain 30 minutes from campus.

Disabled Students: 75% of the campus is accessible. Wheelchair ramps, elevators, special parking, specially equipped rest rooms, and special class scheduling are available.

Services: Counseling and information services are available, as is tutoring in every subject.

Campus Safety and Security: Measures include 24-hour foot and vehicle patrol, self-defense education, security escort services, and shuttle buses. There are informal discussions, pamphlets/posters/films, emergency telephones, and lighted pathways/sidewalks.

Programs of Study: St. John's confers the B.A. degree. Master's degrees are also awarded. Bachelor's degrees are awarded in SOCIAL SCIENCE (liberal arts/general studies).

Required: The college has 1 curriculum, based on the Great Books program, for a total of 135 credits. Students attend seminars, preceptorials on specific works or topics, language, music, and math tutorials, and a 3-year science lab. Students take oral exams each semester and write annual essays. Sophomores take a math exam and seniors take a final essay and oral exam.

Special: Internships with alumni in a wide range of fields are available and students may transfer between the Santa Fe and Annapolis campuses. Work study programs are available with the state government, museums, galleries, Santa Fe Institute, businesses, and schools. Premedical studies at universities around the country and 4-1 teaching certification through the University of New Mexico are possible.

Faculty/Classroom: 71% of faculty are male; 29%, female. All teach undergraduates. No introductory courses are taught by graduate students. The average class size in an introductory lecture is 15; in a laboratory, 15; and in a regular course, 15.

Admissions: 81% of recent applicants were accepted. 37% of recent freshmen were in the top fifth of their class; 64% were in the top two fifths. There were 4 National Merit finalists and 12 semifinalists in a recent year.

Requirements: Applicants must write 3 personal essays and submit 2 teacher references, a secondary school report including a reference from a school official, and transcripts of all academic work in high school and

College. A campus visit and interview are recommended. 3 years of math and 2 years of foreign language are required; 4 years each of math, foreign language, English, and science are recommended. The GED is accepted for early admission candidates. The SAT or ACT is required of early admission candidates. Important factors in the admissions decision are advanced placement or honor courses, evidence of special talent, and recommendations by school officials.

Procedure: Freshmen are admitted fall and spring. There are early admissions, deferred admissions, and rolling admissions plans. Application deadlines are open. Check with the school for current application deadlines and fee.

Transfer: 35 transfer students enrolled in a recent year. St. John's accepts transfers only for its freshman class; no previous college credit is recognized. Admission requirements are the same as for freshmen. All credits required for the bachelor's degree must be completed at St. John's.

Visiting: There are regularly scheduled orientations for prospective students, including a tour of the campus and housing, class visits, and an interview. There are guides for informal visits and visitors may sit in on classes and stay overnight. To schedule a visit, contact the Admissions Office.

Financial Aid: In a recent year, 69% of all full-time students received some form of financial aid. 66% of full-time freshmen and 68% of continuing full-time students received need-based aid. The average freshman award was $23,160. Need-based scholarships or need-based grants averaged $15,960 ($28,937 maximum); and need-based self-help aid (loans and jobs) averaged $7200 ($10,500 maximum). 63% of undergraduates work part time. Average annual earnings from campus work are $2400. The average financial indebtedness of the recent year's graduate was $22,140. St. John's is a member of CSS. The CSS/Profile, FAFSA, the Business/FARM Supplement, and non-custodial parent statement are required. Check with the school for current deadlines.

International Students: There were 12 international students enrolled in a recent year. The school actively recruits these students. A satisfactory score is required on the TOEFL and the SAT.

Computers: All students may access the system. There are no time limits and no fees.

Graduates: In a recent year, 80 bachelor's degrees were awarded. The most popular major was liberal arts (100%). In an average class, 53% graduate in 4 years or less, 63% graduate in 5 years or less, and 64% graduate in 6 years or less. 10 companies recruited on campus in a recent year. Of a recent graduating class, 9% were enrolled in graduate school within 6 months of graduation and 91% were employed.

Admissions Contact: Larry Clendenin, Director of Admissions.
E-mail: *admissions@sjcsf.edu* Web: *http://www.sjcsf.edu*

UNIVERSITY OF NEW MEXICO   C-2
Albuquerque, NM 87131
(505) 277-2446
(800) 225-5866; Fax: (505) 277-6686

Full-time: 6099 men, 8305 women	Faculty: 874; I, --$
Part-time: 2371 men, 3583 women	Ph.D.s: 87%
Graduate: 2550 men, 3372 women	Student/Faculty: 16 to 1
Year: semesters, summer session	Tuition: $4735 ($14,064)
Application Deadline: June 15	Room & Board: $6518
Freshman Class: 7134 applied, 5254 accepted, 3021 enrolled	
SAT Verbal/Math: 550/540*	ACT: 21 COMPETITIVE

The University of New Mexico, founded in 1889, is a public university offering instruction in liberal and fine arts, business, engineering, health science, teacher preparation, law, and technology. In addition to the main campuses, there are 4 branch campuses and 2 graduate centers. There are 11 undergraduate and 5 graduate schools. In addition to regional accreditation, UNM has baccalaureate program accreditation with AACSB, ABET, ACCE, ACPE, ADA, APTA, ASLA, CAHEA, CSAB, NAAB, NASM, NCATE, NLN, and NRPA. The 10 libraries contain 2,730,993 volumes, 3,790,332 microform items, and 58,405 audio/video tapes/CDs/DVDs, and subscribe to 17,607 periodicals including electronic. Computerized library services include the card catalog, interlibrary loans, database searching, and Internet access. Special learning facilities include a learning resource center, art gallery, planetarium, radio station, TV station, robotics lab, photo-history collection, lithography and meteoritic institutes, observatory, and museums of geology, anthropology, biology, and art. The 875-acre campus is in an urban area within the city of Albuquerque. Including any residence halls, there are 195 buildings.

Student Life: 88% of undergraduates are from New Mexico. Students are from 50 states, 90 foreign countries, and Canada. 47% are white; 33% Hispanic. The average age of freshmen is 18; all undergraduates, 23. 24% do not continue beyond their first year; 44% remain to graduate.

Housing: 2183 students can be accommodated in college housing, which includes single-sex and coed dorms, on-campus apartments, married-student housing, fraternity houses, and sorority houses. In addition, there are honors houses, special-interest houses, freshman living learning communities, scholar's wing, wellness unit, and a global learning community. 89% of students commute. Alcohol is not permitted. All students may keep cars.

Activities: 3% of men belong to 2 local and 9 national fraternities; 3% of women belong to 2 local and 9 national sororities. There are 356 groups on campus, including art, band, cheerleading, chess, choir, chorale, chorus, computers, dance, debate, drama, drill team, ethnic, film, forensics, gay, honors, international, jazz band, literary magazine, marching band, musical theater, newspaper, opera, orchestra, pep band, photography, political, professional, radio and TV, religious, social, social service, student government, and symphony. Popular campus events include Spring Fiesta, Welcome Back Days, and Hanging of the Greens.

Sports: There are 10 intercollegiate sports for men and 11 for women, and 6 intramural sports for men and 17 for women. Facilities include 2 gyms, a football field, 2 pools, weights, and racquetball, basketball, and tennis courts. The stadium seats 30,000, the gym 7000, and the largest arena 20,000.

Disabled Students: All of the campus is accessible. Wheelchair ramps, elevators, special parking, specially equipped rest rooms, special class scheduling, lowered drinking fountains, and lowered telephones are available.

Services: Counseling and information services are available, as is tutoring in most subjects. There is a reader service for the blind, and remedial math, reading, and writing.

Campus Safety and Security: Measures include 24-hour foot and vehicle patrol, self-defense education, security escort services, and shuttle buses. There are informal discussions, pamphlets/posters/films, emergency telephones, lighted pathways/sidewalks, and Crime Stoppers, Operation ID, bicycle registraion, and a 911 emergency system.

Programs of Study: UNM confers B.A., B.S., B.A.Ed., B.B.A., B.E., B.F.A., B.M., B.S. Ed., and B.U.S. degrees. Associate, master's, and doctoral degrees are also awarded. Bachelor's degrees are awarded in BIOLOGICAL SCIENCE (biochemistry, biology/biological science, life science, and nutrition), BUSINESS (accounting, banking and finance, business administration and management, human resources, international business management, marketing/retailing/merchandising, personnel management, and recreation and leisure services), COMMUNICATIONS AND THE ARTS (American Sign Language, art, art history and appreciation, classics, communications, comparative literature, dance, English, fine arts, French, German, journalism, languages, linguistics, media arts, music, Portuguese, Russian, Spanish, studio art, and technical and business writing), COMPUTER AND PHYSICAL SCIENCE (astrophysics, chemistry, computer science, earth science, mathematics, physics, and statistics), EDUCATION (art, athletic training, bilingual/bicultural, early childhood, elementary, health, mathematics, music, physical, social studies, special, and teaching English as a second/foreign language (TESOL/TEFOL)), ENGINEERING AND ENVIRONMENTAL DESIGN (architecture, chemical engineering, civil engineering, computer engineering, construction engineering, construction management, electrical/electronics engineering, environmental design, environmental science, manufacturing engineering, mechanical engineering, and nuclear engineering), HEALTH PROFESSIONS (dental hygiene, emergency medical technologies, exercise science, medical laboratory technology, nursing, occupational therapy, pharmacy, physician's assistant, radiological science, and speech pathology/audiology), SOCIAL SCIENCE (African American studies, American studies, anthropology, Asian/Oriental studies, child care/child and family studies, criminal justice, economics, European studies, family/consumer studies, geography, history, human development, human services, interdisciplinary studies, Latin American studies, Native American studies, philosophy, political science/government, psychology, religion, and sociology). Biology, elementary education, and psychology are the largest.

Required: All students must take 2 English courses, including English composition, and complete the University Core Curriculum. A minimum of 128 credit hours is required, along with a GPA of 2.0.

Special: There is a 3-2 engineering program with the Anderson School of Management. Study abroad is available in 25 countries. The university offers cooperative programs in arts and sciences, management, and engineering, a Washington semester, work-study, dual and student-designed majors, a general studies degree, credit for military experience, nondegree study, and pass/fail options. There are 20 national honor societies, including Phi Beta Kappa and a freshman honors program. All departments have honors programs.

Faculty/Classroom: 56% of faculty are male; 44%, female.

Admissions: 74% of the 2005-2006 applicants were accepted. The SAT scores for the 2005-2006 freshman class were: Verbal--31% below 500, 40% between 500 and 599, 24% between 600 and 700, and 4% above 700; Math--33% below 500, 40% between 500 and 599, 24% between 600 and 700, and 3% above 700. The ACT scores were 40% below 21, 28% between 21 and 23, 19% between 24 and 26, 8% between 27 and 28, and 2% above 28. 36% of the current freshmen were in the top fifth of their class; 67% were in the top two fifths.

Requirements: The SAT or ACT is required. In addition, a total of 13 academic credits is required, including 4 years of English, 3 years of math, and 2 years each of foreign language, natural science (1 lab), and social science (1 U.S. history). A GED is accepted. A GPA of 2.25 is required. AP and CLEP credits are accepted. Important factors in the admissions decision are leadership record, evidence of special talent, and advanced placement or honor courses.

Procedure: Freshmen are admitted fall, spring, and summer. Entrance exams should be taken late in the junior or early in the senior year. There are early admissions, deferred admissions, and rolling admissions plans. The fall 2005 application fee was $20. Early decision applications are filed on a rolling basis; regular applications, by June 15 for fall entry, November 15 for spring entry, and May 1 for summer entry, along with a. notification of early decision is sent on a rolling basis; regular decision, on a rolling basis. Applications are accepted on-line.

Transfer: 1087 transfer students enrolled in 2004-2005. Applicants must have at least a 2.0 GPA in all transferable courses. 30 of 128 credits required for the bachelor's degree must be completed at UNM.

Visiting: There are regularly scheduled orientations for prospective students, including academic advisement, admissions and financial aid counseling, and a tour of the campus and housing. There are guides for informal visits and visitors may sit in on classes and stay overnight. To schedule a visit, contact Recruitment Services at (505) 277-2260 or www.unmlobos.edu.

Financial Aid: The FAFSA is required. The deadline for filing freshman financial aid applications for fall entry is March 1.

International Students: There are 160 international students enrolled. The school actively recruits these students. A satisfactory score on the written TOEFL or the MELAB is required, as is the University of Cambridge English Examination (CPE or CAE), and the International English Language Testing System (IELTS).

Computers: Wireless access is available. All students have access to 5 computer pods and 10 computer classrooms. Wireless access is available. All students may access the system. There are no time limits and no fees.

Graduates: From July 1, 2004 to June 30, 2005, 2818 bachelor's degrees were awarded. The most popular majors were university studies (7%), elementary education (7%), and biology (6%). In an average class, 42% graduate in 6 years or less. 109 companies recruited on campus in 2004-2005.

Admissions Contact: Terry Babbitt, Interim Director of Admissions and Director of Recruitment Services. A video is available.
E-mail: apply@unm.edu Web: http://www.unm.edu

WESTERN NEW MEXICO UNIVERSITY   B-4
Silver City, NM 88061

	(505) 538-6106
	(800) 222-9668; Fax: (505) 538-6127
Full-time: 200 men, 300 women	**Faculty:** n/av
Part-time: 40 men, 80 women	**Ph.D.s:** n/av
Graduate: 70 men, 130 women	**Student/Faculty:** 7 to 1
Year: semesters, summer session	**Tuition:** $2863 ($8127)
Application Deadline: July 21	**Room & Board:** $4370
Freshman Class: n/av	
SAT or ACT: required	**LESS COMPETITIVE**

Western New Mexico University, founded in 1893, is a public institution offering vocational, liberal arts, science, and professional programs. Some figures given in above capsule and in this profile are approximate. There are 2 undergraduate and 3 graduate schools. The library contains 120,000 volumes, 500,000 microform items, and 500 audio/video tapes/CDs/DVDs, and subscribes to 950 periodicals including electronic. Computerized library services include the card catalog, interlibrary loans, and database searching. Special learning facilities include a learning resource center, art gallery, natural history museum, and instrumental-vocal music center with individual practice rooms. The 80-acre campus is in a small town 113 miles northwest of Las Cruces and a few minutes from the Gila National Forest. Including any residence halls, there are 40 buildings.

Housing: 285 students can be accommodated in college housing, which includes single-sex and coed dormitories, on-campus apartments, and married-student housing. All students may keep cars.

Activities: There is 1 local fraternities and 1 local sorority. There are many groups and organizations on campus, including academic, band,

cheerleading, choir, chorus, dance, drama, ethnic, honors, international, jazz band, marching band, musical theater, newspaper, orchestra, pep band, political, professional, religious, social, social service, and student government.

Sports: There are 4 intercollegiate sports for men and 5 for women. We have an indoor swimming pool, locker rooms for public use, intramural gym, two athletic gyms (1 specifically for spectator sports), athletics only locker rooms, football stadium with attatched free-weight/cardio facility and locker rooms, circuit training room, and an athletic traning facility for athletics use.

Disabled Students: Wheelchair ramps, elevators, special parking, specially equipped rest rooms, lowered drinking fountains, and special housing are available.

Services: Counseling and information services are available, as is tutoring in most subjects. There is a reader service for the blind, and remedial math, reading, and writing. Two tutoring facilities exist on campus for free student use.

Campus Safety and Security: Measures include 24-hour foot and vehicle patrol.

Programs of Study: WNMU confers B.A., B.S., B.B.A., B.S.V.T., and B.S.W. degrees. Associate and master's degrees are also awarded. Bachelor's degrees are awarded in AGRICULTURE (forestry and related sciences), BIOLOGICAL SCIENCE (biology/biological science, botany, and zoology), BUSINESS (accounting, business administration and management, international business management, management information systems, and marketing/retailing/merchandising), COMMUNICATIONS AND THE ARTS (English, fine arts, music, and Spanish), COMPUTER AND PHYSICAL SCIENCE (chemistry, computer science, mathematics, and science), EDUCATION (art, business, elementary, physical, science, secondary, special, and vocational), HEALTH PROFESSIONS (medical laboratory technology, predentistry, premedicine, prepharmacy, and public health), SOCIAL SCIENCE (Hispanic American studies, history, human services, humanities, law enforcement and corrections, psychology, public administration, social science, social work, and sociology). The School of Education is the strongest academically and has the largest enrollment.

Required: To graduate, students must earn at least 128 credit hours, including 30 to 54 in the major, with a minimum GPA of 2.0, and complete 51 hours of general education requirements.

Special: WNMU offers internships, dual and student-designed majors, and work-study programs. There is a freshman honors program.

Requirements: The SAT or ACT is required. In addition, applicants should be graduates of an accredited secondary school or present a GED. Students should have completed at least 3 units of English, and 2 of social studies, including U.S. history, as well as 2 each of science and math. Intermediate algebra and plane geometry are advised for students planning to enter certain fields. WNMU recommends a 2.0 GPA, but lower averages will be considered if applicants' test scores and personal recommendations are strong. CLEP credit is accepted.

Procedure: Freshmen are admitted to all sessions. Entrance exams should be taken before registration, preferably in the senior year. There ia a rolling admissions plan. Applications should be filed by July 21 for fall entry. Notification is sent on a rolling basis.

Transfer: Transfer students must have a GPA of 2.0. Those with fewer than 32 hours of college credit must supply ACT or SAT scores and a high school transcript. 30 of 128 credits required for the bachelor's degree must be completed at WNMU.

Visiting: There are regularly scheduled orientations for prospective students. There are guides for informal visits and visitors may sit in on classes and stay overnight. To schedule a visit, contact the Admissions Office at 505-538-6108.

Financial Aid: The FAFSA is required. Check with the school for current deadlines.

International Students: The school actively recruits these students. A satisfactory score is required. on the written TOEFL and also take the SAT or the ACT.

Computers: There are no time limits and no fees.

Admissions Contact: Dan Tressler, Director of Admissions.
Web: www.wnmu.edu

NEW YORK

POPULATION DENSITY

• 50,000 and over

0 20 40 60 80 100
Miles

ADELPHI UNIVERSITY
Garden City, NY 11530

D-5

(516) 877-3050
(800) ADELPHI; Fax: (516) 877-3039

Full-time: 1000 men, 2400 women	**Faculty:** 228; I, -$
Part-time: 170 men, 560 women	**Ph.D.s:** 87%
Graduate: 660 men, 2500 women	**Student/Faculty:** 15 to 1
Year: semesters, summer session	**Tuition:** $18,000
Application Deadline: open	**Room & Board:** $9000
Freshman Class: n/av	
SAT or ACT: required	**VERY COMPETITIVE**

Adelphi University, founded in 1896, is a private liberal arts institution. There are 7 undergraduate and 6 graduate schools. Figures in the above capsule and in this profile are approximate. In addition to regional accreditation, Adelphi has baccalaureate program accreditation with CCNE, CSWE, and NLN. The 2 libraries contain 856,909 volumes, 788,698 microform items, and 44,531 audio/video tapes/CDs/DVDs, and subscribe to 850 periodicals including electronic. Computerized library services include the card catalog, interlibrary loans, database searching, and Internet access. Special learning facilities include a learning resource center, art gallery, radio station, observatory, theater, sculpture and ceramics studios, a bronze casting foundry, and language labs. The 75-acre campus is in a suburban area 20 miles east of New York City. Including any residence halls, there are 24 buildings.

Student Life: 89% of undergraduates are from New York. Students are from 37 states, 51 foreign countries, and Canada. 70% are from public schools. 63% are white; 16% African American; 12% Hispanic. 57% are Catholic; 21% Protestant; 9% claim no religious affiliation; 6% Jewish; 6% Greek Orthodox, Hindu, and Muslim. The average age of freshmen is 19; all undergraduates, 25. 21% do not continue beyond their first year; 53% remain to graduate.

Housing: 1086 students can be accommodated in college housing, which includes coed dorms. On-campus housing is available on a first-come, first-served basis and is available on a lottery system for upperclassmen. Priority is given to out-of-town students. 75% of students commute. Alcohol is not permitted. All students may keep cars.

Activities: 2% of men belong to 1 local and 3 national fraternities; 4% of women belong to 1 local and 6 national sororities. There are 76 groups on campus, including art, band, cheerleading, chorale, chorus, computers, dance, drama, ethnic, film, gay, honors, international, jazz band, literary magazine, musical theater, newspaper, orchestra, political, professional, radio and TV, religious, social, social service, student government, and yearbook. Popular campus events include Senior Week, Halloween Party, and Fall Fest.

Sports: There are 9 intercollegiate sports for men and 9 for women, and 16 intramural sports for men and 16 for women. Facilities include a 3000-seat stadium, a 600-seat gym, a swimming pool, racquetball, squash, tennis, and handball courts, exercise rooms, a dance studio, a track, and playing fields for baseball, softball, and soccer.

Disabled Students: 95% of the campus is accessible. Wheelchair ramps, elevators, special parking, specially equipped rest rooms, special class scheduling, lowered drinking fountains, lowered telephones, and special housing are available.

Services: Counseling and information services are available, as is tutoring in most subjects. A learning center offers tutoring in writing, and quantitative skills, and help with class assignments. There is a reader service for the blind. A writing center is also available.

Campus Safety and Security: Measures include 24-hour foot and vehicle patrol, self-defense education, security escort services, and shuttle buses. There are informal discussions, pamphlets/posters/films, emergency telephones and lighted pathways/sidewalks, and Dorm main entrances are videotaped and dorm doors are locked 24 hours a day.

Programs of Study: Adelphi confers B.A., B.S., B.B.A., B.F.A., B.S.Ed., and B.S.S.W. degrees. Associate, master's, and doctoral degrees are also awarded. Bachelor's degrees are awarded in AGRICULTURE (environmental studies), BIOLOGICAL SCIENCE (biochemistry and biology/biological science), BUSINESS (accounting, banking and finance, business administration and management, and management information systems), COMMUNICATIONS AND THE ARTS (art history and appreciation, communications, dance, design, dramatic arts, English, fine arts, languages, music, performing arts, theater design, and visual and performing arts), COMPUTER AND PHYSICAL SCIENCE (chemistry, computer science, earth science, mathematics, natural sciences, and physics), EDUCATION (art, education of the deaf and hearing impaired, elementary, English, foreign languages, mathematics, music, physical, science, secondary, and social studies), HEALTH PROFESSIONS (nursing and speech pathology/audiology), SOCIAL SCIENCE (anthropology, economics, history, Latin American studies, liberal arts/general studies, philosophy, physical fitness/movement, political science/government, psychology, social science, social work, and sociology). Business management, psychology, and social studies are the largest.

Required: To graduate, students need at least a 2.0 cumulative GPA (higher in some programs) and 120 credit hours with a minimum of 27 in the major. 6 credits each are required in the arts, humanities, and languages, natural sciences and math, and social sciences. Other course requirements include English composition, freshman seminar, (3 credits each), and a 1-credit freshman orientation experience. Cross-registration with Tufts credit for life experience for adult students, nondegree study in special cases, and pass/fail options are possible. A 3-2 engineering degree is offered with Rensselaer Polytechnic, Columbia, Polytechnic, and Stevens Institute of Tech, and joint degree programs are offered in computer science, dentistry, engineering, environmental studies, law, optometry, and physical therapy with other universities and technical institutions.

Special: Internships are available in accounting, banking and money management, and communications, among others. Study abroad is available in more than 20 countries, including Spain, France, Denmark, and England. A 5-year bachelor's/masters degree in a number of fields, including biology, social work, and education is offered. In addition, work-study programs, double majors, the B.A.-B.S. degree, an accelerated degree program, student-designed majors, and a Washington semester are available. There are 19 national honor societies and a freshman honors program.

Faculty/Classroom: 52% of faculty are male; 48%, female. All teach undergraduates. No introductory courses are taught by graduate students. The average class size in a laboratory is 16 and in a regular course, 23.

Admissions: 71% of a recent applicants were accepted. 39% of recent freshmen were in the top fifth of their class; 74% were in the top two fifths. 4 freshmen graduated first in their class in a recent year.

Requirements: The SAT or ACT is required. Applicants should have 16 academic credits, including a recommended 4 units of English, history, and social studies, 3 each of math and science, and 2 or 3 of foreign language. An essay is required and an interview recommended for all applicants. A portfolio for art and technical theater candidates, an audition for music, dance, and theater candidates, and an interview for nursing, social work, and honors candidates are required. The SAT is recommended for the general studies and learning disabilities programs. A GPA of 2.5 is required. AP credits are accepted. Important factors in the admissions decision are advanced placement or honor courses, leadership record, and personality/intangible qualities.

Procedure: Freshmen are admitted fall and spring. Entrance exams should be taken in October of the senior year, or May of the junior year. There are early admissions and deferred admissions plans. There is a rolling admissions plan. Application deadlines are open. Applications are accepted on-line. Check with the school for current application deadlines and fee,

Transfer: 646 transfer students enrolled in a recent year. A GPA of 2.5 is recommended in addition to an essay, an official high school transcript, and official records of all work completed or in progress from previous colleges and universities. An interview is required for students in social work and nursing, while an audition is needed for music, dance, and theater students, and a portfolio for art and technical theater students. 30 of 120 credits required for the bachelor's degree must be completed at Adelphi.

Visiting: There are regularly scheduled orientations for prospective students, including a campus tour, an interview, and information sessions. There are guides for informal visits and visitors may sit in on classes. To schedule a visit, contact Undergraduate Admissions.

Financial Aid: In a recent year, 93% of all full-time freshmen and 88% of continuing full-time students received some form of financial aid. 71% of full-time freshmen and 68% of continuing full-time students received need-based aid. The average freshman award was $13,500. Need-based scholarships or need-based grants averaged $5256 ($7500 maximum); need-based self-help aid (loans and jobs) averaged $4693 ($8000 maximum); and non-need-based athletic scholarships averaged $14,588 ($26,300 maximum). 30% of undergraduates work part time. Average annual earnings from campus work are $1400. The average financial indebtedness of a recent graduate was $22,500. Adelphi is a member of CSS. The FAFSA is required. Check with the school for current deadlines.

International Students: There were 125 international students enrolled in a recent year. The school actively recruits these students. They must take the TOEFL and also take the SAT or the ACT.

Computers: All students may access the system. There are no time limits. The fee is $100 (full-time), $50 (part-time).

Graduates: In a recent year, 837 bachelor's degrees were awarded. The most popular majors were business (23%), social science (19%), and health professions (10%). In an average class, 3% graduate in 3 years or less, 45% graduate in 4 years or less and 53% graduate in 5 or 6 years or less. 247 companies recruited on campus in a recent year. Of a recent year graduating class, 41% were enrolled in graduate school within 6 months of graduation and 87% were employed.

Admissions Contact: Christine Murphy, Director, Office of University Admissions. E-mail: *admissions@adelphi.edu* Web: *www.adelphi.edu*

ALBANY COLLEGE OF PHARMACY   D-3
Albany, NY 12208   **(518) 694-7221**
    (888) 203-8010; Fax: (518) 694-7202

Full-time: 380 men, 483 women	**Faculty:** 63
Part-time: 2 men, 1 woman	**Ph.D.s:** 75%
Graduate: 98 men, 184 women	**Student/Faculty:** 14 to 1
Year: semesters, summer session	**Tuition:** $18,890
Application Deadline: February 1	**Room & Board:** $6200
Freshman Class: n/av	
SAT Verbal/Math: 560/600*	**ACT:** 26 **SPECIAL**

Albany College of Pharmacy, founded in 1881, is a private, 6-year institution and a division of Union University. In addition to regional accreditation, Albany College of Pharmacy has baccalaureate program accreditation with ACPE. The library contains 12,314 volumes, 28,388 microform items, and 2676 audio/video tapes/CDs/DVDs, and subscribes to 1399 periodicals including electronic. Computerized library services include the card catalog, interlibrary loans, database searching, and Internet access. Special learning facilities include a learning resource center and a pharmacy museum. The 1-acre campus is in an urban area in the University Heights area of Albany. Including any residence halls, there are 6 buildings.

Student Life: 80% of undergraduates are from New York. Students are from 27 states, 6 foreign countries, and Canada. 75% are from public schools. 79% are white; 10% Asian American. The average age of freshmen is 18; all undergraduates, 21. 24% do not continue beyond their first year; 71% remain to graduate.

Housing: 335 students can be accommodated in college housing, which includes coed dorms and off-campus apartments. Priority for on-campus housing is given to out-of-town students. 52% of students commute. Alcohol is not permitted. All students may keep cars.

Activities: 45% of men belong to 6 national fraternities. 43 % of women belong to sororities.There are 18 groups on campus, including bowling choir, chorus, cross country, dance, ethnic, honors, international, literary magazine, multicultural, newspaper, outdoors, photography, professional, ski, social service, student government, and yearbook. Popular campus events include Parents Weekend, Interview Day and Springfest.

Sports: There are 2 intercollegiate sports for men and 2 for women, and 3 intramural sports for men and 3 for women. Facilities include a gym, a fitness center, a outdoor track, and a soccer field.

Disabled Students: 98% of the campus is accessible. Wheelchair ramps, elevators, special parking, and specially equipped rest rooms are available.

Services: Counseling and information services are available, as is tutoring in most subjects.

Campus Safety and Security: Measures include 24-hour foot and vehicle patrol, self-defense education, informal discussions, and pamphlets/posters/films. There are emergency telephones and lighted pathways/sidewalks.

Programs of Study: Albany College of Pharmacy confers B.S Med. Tech., and B.S. Pharm. Science degrees. Master's and doctoral degrees are also awarded. Bachelor's degrees are awarded in HEALTH PROFESSIONS (biomedical science and pharmaceutical science). Pharmacy is the strongest academically.

Required: To graduate, students must complete between 129 and 162 credits, depending on the degree program, including core curriculum courses, with a minimum GPA of 2.0.

Special: The college offers cross-registration with other area colleges, dual majors leading to master's and doctoral degrees, an accelerated degree, and work-study programs. There is 1 national honor society.

Faculty/Classroom: 54% of faculty are male; 46%, female. No introductory courses are taught by graduate students. The average class size in an introductory lecture is 130; in a laboratory, 23; and in a regular course, 50.

Admissions: The SAT scores for the 2005-2006 freshman class were: Verbal--11% below 500, 57% between 500 and 599, 28% between 600 and 700, and 4% above 700; Math--5% below 500, 44% between 500 and 599, 44% between 600 and 700, and 7% above 700. 10 freshmen graduated first in their class.

Requirements: The SAT or ACT is required. In addition, applicants must be graduates of an accredited high school with at least 17 credits, including 4 each of English and math through precalculus and 3 of science, including chemistry. The GED is accepted. Albany College of Pharmacy requires applicants to be in the upper 50% of their class. A GPA of 3.0 is required. AP and CLEP credits are accepted. Important factors in the admissions decision are advanced placement or honor courses, extracurricular activities record, and recommendations by alumni.

Procedure: Freshmen are admitted in the fall. Entrance exams should be taken in the junior year. There is an early decision plan. Early decision applications should be filed by November 1; regular applications, by February 1 for fall entry. Notification of early decision is sent December 15; regular decision, March 1. 100 applicants were on the 2005 waiting list; 39 were admitted. Applications are accepted on-line.

Transfer: Applicants must have a GPA of 3.2.

Visiting: There are regularly scheduled orientations for prospective students, including a tour of the school and residence halls and a discussion of admissions requirements, financial aid, and student activities. There are guides for informal visits and visitors may sit in on classes and stay overnight. To schedule a visit, contact the Office of Admissions at (518) 694-7221 or *admissions@acp.edu*.

Financial Aid: In 2005-2006, 81% of all full-time freshmen and 85% of continuing full-time students received some form of financial aid. 64% of full-time freshmen and 70% of continuing full-time students received need-based aid. 95% of undergraduates work part time. Average annual earnings from campus work are $800. The FAFSA is required. The priority date for freshman financial aid applications for fall entry is February 1.

International Students: There are 77 international students enrolled. A satisfactory score is required on the written TOEFL. Students must also take the TSE and the SAT or the ACT.

Computers: Wireless access is available. All students may access the system 24 hours a day. There are no time limits and no fees. All students are required to have personal computers.

Graduates: In an average class, 76% graduate in 5 years or less, and 76% graduate in 6 years or less. 50 companies recruited on campus in 2004-2005.

Admissions Contact: Michael Green, Assistant Director of Admissions. A video is available. E-mail: *greenmi@acp.edu* Web: *www.acp.edu*

ALBERT A. LIST COLLEGE OF JEWISH STUDIES   D-5

New York, NY 10027-4649   (212) 678-8832; Fax: (212) 678-8947

Full-time: 80 men, 80 women

Part-time: 10 men,10 women

Graduate: none

Year: semesters, summer session

Application Deadline: see profile

Freshman Class: n/av

SATor ACT: required

Faculty: 40

Ph.D.s: 98%

Student/Faculty: 4 to 1

Tuition: $11,000

Room & Board: $9000

HIGHLY COMPETITIVE+

Albert A. List College of Jewish Studies, the undergraduate division of the Jewish Theological Seminary, founded in 1886, is a private institution affiliated with the Conservative branch of the Jewish faith. List College offers programs in all aspects of Judaism, including Bible, rabbinics, literature, history, philosophy, education, and communal service. There is also a combined liberal arts program with Columbia University and Barnard College. Figures in the above capsule and in this profile are approximate. The library contains 320,000 volumes and 3500 microform items, and subscribes to 750 periodicals including electronic. Computerized library services include the card catalog, interlibrary loans, and database searching. Special learning facilities include a learning resource center, art gallery, a music center, a Jewish education, research center, and the Jewish Museum Archives Center. The 1-acre campus is in an urban area on the upper west side of Manhattan. Including any residence halls, there are 6 buildings.

Student Life: 75% of undergraduates are from out of state, mostly the Middle Atlantic.Students are from 12 states, 3 foreign countries, and Canada. 70% are from public schools. All are white. Most are Jewish. The average age of freshmen is 18; all undergraduates, 20. 96% of freshmen remain to graduate.

Housing: 212 students can be accommodated in college housing, which includes coed dorms, on-campus apartments, off-campus apartments, and married-student housing. There is also a Kosher housing. On-campus housing is guaranteed for all 4 years. 93% of students live on campus; of those, 95% remain on campus on weekends. Alcohol is not permitted. All students may keep cars.

Activities: Through Columbis University, 12% of men belong to fraternities; 4% of women belong to sororities. There are many groups and organizations on campus, including art, band, choir, chorus, computers, dance, drama, ethnic, film, gay, honors, international, literary magazine, musical theater, newspaper, orchestra, photography, political, professional, radio and TV, religious, social, social service, student government, and yearbook. List College students have access to all clubs and organizations at Columbia and Barnard. Popular campus events include Purim, Simchat Torah, and Orientation.

Sports: There are 3 intramural sports for men and 3 for women. List College students may use the facilities at Columbia University.

Disabled Students: All of the campus is accessible. Wheelchair ramps, elevators, special parking, specially equipped rest rooms, lowered drinking fountains, lowered telephones, and elevators with braille panels are available.

Services: Counseling and information services are available, as is tutoring in most subjects.

Campus Safety and Security: Measures include 24-hour foot and vehicle patrol, security escort services, informal discussions, and pamphlets/posters/films. There are emergency telephones and lighted pathways/sidewalks.

Programs of Study: List College confers the B.A. degree. Bachelor's degrees are awarded in SOCIAL SCIENCE (biblical studies and Judaic studies).

Required: Students must take a Hebrew language requirement, 24 credits in Jewish history, 9 in literature, and 6 each in Bible, Jewish philosophy, and Talmud. In addition, there are 60 required credits in liberal arts, including 6 credits each in English, history/philosophy/social science, and math or lab science to be completed at another college or university. A total of 156 credits (96 taken at List College) is required for graduation, with 21 in a major field.

Special: There is a joint program with Columbia University and a double-degree program with Barnard College, which enable students to earn 2 B.A. degrees in 4 to 4 1/2 years. Study abroad is available in Israel, England, France, and Spain. Student-designed majors, credit by exam, and nondegree study are also offered. There is a chapter of Phi Beta Kappa and a freshman honors program.

Faculty/Classroom: 68% of faculty are male; 32%, female. All both teach and do research. The average class size in an introductory lecture is 30 and in a regular course, 10.

Requirements: The SAT or ACT is required, as are SAT: Subject Tests. Applicants must be graduates of an accredited secondary school or have the GED. An essay and 2 recommendations are required; an interview is strongly recommended. Students can print on-line applications and submit them by mail. AP credits are accepted. Important factors in the admissions decision are advanced placement or honor courses, extracurricular activities record, and personality/intangible qualities.

Procedure: Freshmen are admitted fall and spring. Entrance exams should be taken in the spring of the junior year. There are early decision, early admissions, and deferred admissions plans. Check with the school for urrent application and fee.

Transfer: Applicants must submit SATor ACT scores, an essay, high school and college transcripts, and 2 academic recommendations. A minimum college GPA of 2.5 is required. An interview is recommended. 48 of 156 credits required for the bachelor's degree must be completed at List College.

Visiting: There are regularly scheduled orientations for prospective students, including a tour of the campus and of Columbia University, an interview with the dean, and an overnight dorm stay. There are guides for informal visits and visitors may sit in on classes and stay overnight. To schedule a visit, contact Reena Kamins, Admissions Director at lcadmissions@jtsa.edu.

Financial Aid: List College is a member of CSS. The CSS Profile, the college's own financial statement and 1040 tax forms are required. Check with the school for current deadlines.

International Students: They must take the TOEFL the college's own test, the American Language English Placement Test and also take the SAT or the ACT.

Computers: All students may access the system.

Admissions Contact: Reena Kamins, Director of Admissions.

E-mail: lcadmissions@jtsa.edu Web: www.jtsa.edu

ALFRED UNIVERSITY   B-4

Alfred, NY 14802-1205   (607) 871-2115

(800) 541-9229; Fax: (607) 871-2198

Full-time: 945 men, 918 women

Part-time: 40 men, 58 women

Graduate: 104 men, 170 women

Year: semesters, summer session

Application Deadline: February 1

Freshman Class: 2135 applied, 1640 accepted, 428 enrolled

SAT Verbal/Math: 562/570*

Faculty: 170; IIA, av$

Ph.D.s: 93%

Student/Faculty: 11 to 1

Tuition: $20,960

Room & Board: $9746

VERY COMPETITIVE

Alfred University, founded in 1836, is composed of the privately endowed College of Business, College of Liberal Arts and Sciences, and New York State College of Ceramics (School of Engineering and School of Art and Design). The above tuition figures are for incoming freshmen at the College of Business and the College of Liberal Arts and Sciences. There are 4 undergraduate schools and 1 graduate school. In addition to regional accreditation, AU has baccalaureate program accreditation with AACSB, ABET, and NASAD. The 2 libraries contain 323,944 volumes and 94,298 microform items, and subscribe to 6467 periodicals including electronic. Computerized library services include the card catalog, interlibrary loans, database searching, and Internet access. Special learning facilities include a learning resource center, art gallery, radio station, TV station, and observatory. The 232-acre campus is in a rural area 70 miles south of Rochester. Including any residence halls, there are 54 buildings.

Student Life: 69% of undergraduates are from New York. Others are from 38 states, 10 foreign countries, and Canada. 90% are from public schools. 86% are white. The average age of freshmen is 18; all undergraduates, 20. 21% do not continue beyond their first year; 65% remain to graduate.

Housing: 1350 students can be accommodated in college housing, which includes coed dorms, on-campus apartments, fraternity houses, and sorority houses. In addition, there are honors houses, language houses, and special-interest houses. On-campus housing is guaranteed for the freshman year only, is available on a first-come, first-served basis, and is available on a lottery system for upperclassmen. 65% of students live on campus; of those, 90% remain on campus on weekends. All students may keep cars.

Activities: There are no fraternities or sororities. There are more than 100 groups and organizations on campus, including art, band, cheerleading, chess, chorale, chorus, computers, dance, drama, ethnic, film, gay, honors, international, jazz band, literary magazine, musical theater, newspaper, orchestra, pep band, photography, political, professional, radio and TV, religious, social, social service, student activities board, student government, and yearbook. Popular campus events include Alumni Weekend, Hot Dog Day, and Family Weekend.

Sports: There are 9 intercollegiate sports for men and 10 for women, and 14 intramural sports for men and 13 for women. Facilities include an omniturf football surface, a soccer and lacrosse field, an Olympic-size pool, tennis courts, racquetball and squash courts, a weight room, and a dance and exercise studio. The campus stadium seats 4200, the indoor gym, 3000. There is also a fitness center, an equestrian center, many hiking trails, and easy access to cross-country skiing.

Disabled Students: 50% of the campus is accessible. Wheelchair ramps, elevators, special parking, specially equipped rest rooms, special class scheduling, and lowered drinking fountains are available.

Services: Counseling and information services are available, as is tutoring in most subjects. There is a reader service for the blind, and remedial

math, reading, and writing. Time management and study skills workshops and advocacy and support for students with learning and physical disabilities are available.

Campus Safety and Security: Measures include security escort services, informal discussions, pamphlets/posters/films, and emergency telephones. There are lighted pathways/sidewalks and vehicle and foot patrol.

Programs of Study: AU confers B.A., B.S., and B.F.A. degrees. Certificates of advanced study an master's and doctoral degrees are also awarded. Bachelor's degrees are awarded in BIOLOGICAL SCIENCE (biology/biological science), BUSINESS (accounting, banking and finance, business administration and management, management science, and marketing/retailing/merchandising), COMMUNICATIONS AND THE ARTS (ceramic art and design, communications, dramatic arts, English, fine arts, French, German, glass, performing arts, and Spanish), COMPUTER AND PHYSICAL SCIENCE (chemistry, geology, mathematics, physics, and science), EDUCATION (art, athletic training, business, early childhood, mathematics, science, secondary, and social studies), ENGINEERING AND ENVIRONMENTAL DESIGN (ceramic engineering, electrical/electronics engineering, environmental science, materials engineering, and mechanical engineering), SOCIAL SCIENCE (criminal justice, crosscultural studies, early childhood studies, economics, gerontology, history, interdisciplinary studies, philosophy, political science/government, psychology, public administration, and sociology). Ceramic engineering, electrical engineering, and mechanical engineering are the strongest academically. Art and design, business administration, and ceramic engineering are the largest.

Required: To graduate, students must complete 120 to 137 credits, depending on the major, with 36 to 48 credits in the major. Students must demonstrate basic competencies in writing, oral communication, math, and computers. Freshmen must attend 10 freshman forums and complete a phys ed course. Distribution requirements include 8 credits each of social studies and natural science and 4 credits each of philosophy or religion, literature, art, and history. A minimum GPA of 2.0 is required.

Special: There are cooperative programs in engineering and business with Duke, Clarkson, and Columbia Universities and SUNY/Brockport. There is cross-registration with the SUNY College of Technology and a 5-year program in environmental management/forestry with Duke. Alfred offers internships in all programs, extensive study abroad, Washington and Albany semesters, work-study, a general studies degree, student-designed majors, dual majors, credit by exam, and pass/fail options. There are 12 national honor societies, including Phi Beta Kappa, a freshman honors program, and 42 departmental honors programs.

Faculty/Classroom: 65% of faculty are male; 35%, female. 90% both teach and do research. No introductory courses are taught by graduate students. The average class size in an introductory lecture is 25; in a laboratory, 15; and in a regular course, 18.

Admissions: 77% of the 2005-2006 applicants were accepted. The SAT scores for the 2005-2006 freshman class were: Verbal--20% below 500, 47% between 500 and 599, 27% between 600 and 700, and 6% above 700; Math--15% below 500, 48% between 500 and 599, 32% between 600 and 700, and 5% above 700. The ACT scores were 18% below 21, 30% between 21 and 23, 24% between 24 and 26, 16% between 27 and 28, and 12% above 28. There were 7 National Merit finalists. 10 freshmen graduated first in their class.

Requirements: The SAT or ACT is required. The ACT Optional Writing test is also required for some programs. A GED is accepted. A minimum of 16 Carnegie units is required, including 4 years of English and 2 to 3 years each of math, history/social studies, and science. The remaining units may be in either a foreign language or any of the previously mentioned fields. An essay is required, and applicants to B.F.A. programs must submit a portfolio. Interviews are encouraged. AP credits are accepted. Important factors in the admissions decision are advanced placement or honor courses, personality/intangible qualities, and extracurricular activities record.

Procedure: Freshmen are admitted fall and spring. Entrance exams should be taken in the junior year. There are early decision, early admissions, and deferred admissions plans. Early decision applications should be filed by December 1; regular applications, by February 1 for fall entry and December 1 for spring entry, along with a $40 fee. Notification of early decision is sent December 15; regular decision, on a rolling basis. 38 early decision candidates were accepted for the 2005-2006 class. Applications are accepted on-line.

Transfer: 84 transfer students enrolled in 2004-2005. Transfer applicants must have a GPA of at least 2.5. They must submit at least 1 letter of recommendation and official high school and college transcripts. Art students must submit a portfolio. 30 of 120 credits required for the bachelor's degree must be completed at AU.

Visiting: There are regularly scheduled orientations for prospective students, including a campus tour, a social activities panel, a financial aid presentation, faculty discussions, and on-campus interviews. There are guides for informal visits and visitors may sit in on classes and stay overnight. To schedule a visit, contact the Admissions Office at *campusvisits@alfred.edu.*

Financial Aid: 50% of undergraduates work part time. Average annual earnings from campus work are $1000. AU is a member of CSS. The FAFSA, the college's own financial statement, the business/farm supplement, and the noncustodial parent statement are required. The deadline for filing freshman financial aid applications for fall entry is May 1.

International Students: There are 45 international students enrolled. The school actively recruits these students. If they do not submit an SAT or ACT, they must submit the TOEFL, achieving a satisfactory score.

Computers: Wireless access is available. Each dorm room is wired and also has a small computer lab; wireless is available in libraries, the campus center, and in some classrooms. There are approximately 400 PCs available across campus for student use. All students may access the system 24 hours a day, 7 days a week. There are no time limits and no fees.

Graduates: From July 1, 2004 to June 30, 2005, 430 bachelor's degrees were awarded. The most popular majors were art and design (26%), business administration (9%), and ceramic engineering (7%). In an average class, 1% graduate in 3 years or less, 50% graduate in 4 years or less, 65% graduate in 5 years or less, and 66% graduate in 6 years or less. 79 companies recruited on campus in 2004-2005. Of the 2004 graduating class, 28% were enrolled in graduate school within 6 months of graduation and 68% were employed.

Admissions Contact: Jeremy Spencer, Director of Admissions. A video is available. E-mail: *spencer@alfred.edu or admissions@alfred.edu* Web: *http://www.alfred.edu*

AUDREY COHEN COLLEGE
(See Metropolitan College of New York)

BARD COLLEGE D-4
Annandale-on-Hudson, NY 12504-5000   (845) 758-7472
Fax: (845) 758-5208

Full-time: 655 men, 866 women	Faculty: 130; IIB, ++$
Part-time: 31 men, 33 women	Ph.D.s: 80%
Graduate: 94 men, 179 women	Student/Faculty: 12 to 1
Year: 4-1-4	Tuition: $32,490
Application Deadline: January 15	Room & Board: $9310
Freshman Class: 4142 applied, 1325 accepted, 515 enrolled	
SAT or ACT: not required	HIGHLY COMPETITIVE+

Bard College, founded in 1860, is an independent liberal arts and sciences institution affiliated historically with the Association of Episcopal Colleges. Discussion-oriented seminars and independent study are encouraged, tutorials are on a one-to-one basis, and most classes are kept small, with fewer than 15 students. The library contains 287,000 volumes, 9250 microform items, and 5900 audio/video tapes/CDs/DVDs, and subscribes to 18,000 periodicals including electronic. Computerized library services include the card catalog, interlibrary loans, database searching, and Internet access. Special learning facilities include a learning resource center, art gallery, radio station, an ecology field station, the Levy Economics Institute, the Institute for Writing and Thinking, the Institute for Advanced Theology, the Center for Curatorial Studies and Art in Contemporary Culture, and an archeological field school. The 600-acre campus is in a rural area 100 miles north of New York City. Including any residence halls, there are 70 buildings.

Student Life: 69% of undergraduates are from out of state, mostly the Middle Atlantic. Students are from 47 states, 46 foreign countries, and Canada. 64% are from public schools. 72% are white. The average age of freshmen is 18; all undergraduates, 20. 12% do not continue beyond their first year; 71% remain to graduate.

Housing: 1200 students can be accommodated in college housing, which includes single-sex and coed dorms. In addition, there are special-interest houses, a single-sex dorm, and quiet dorms. On-campus housing is guaranteed for the freshman year only and is available on a lottery system for upperclassmen. 99% of students live on campus; of those, 72% remain on campus on weekends. All students may keep cars.

Activities: There are no fraternities or sororities. There are 60 groups on campus, including art, band, chamber groups, chess, choir, chorus, computers, dance, drama, ethnic, film, gay, international, jazz band, literary magazine, model UN, newspaper, opera, orchestra, photography, political, radio and TV, religious, social, social service, student government, and yearbook. Popular campus events include Winter Carnival, Spring Festival, and International Students Cultural Show.

Sports: There are 6 intercollegiate sports for men and 5 for women, and 11 intramural sports for men and 11 for women. Facilities include a gym and pool, soccer and softball fields, squash and tennis courts, cross-country trails, bike paths, and the Tivoli bays of the Hudson River.

Disabled Students: 70% of the campus is accessible. Wheelchair ramps, elevators, special parking, specially equipped rest rooms, lowered drinking fountains, and lowered telephones are available.

Services: Counseling and information services are available, as is tutoring in every subject. There is a reader service for the blind.

Campus Safety and Security: Measures include 24-hour foot and vehicle patrol, self-defense education, security escort services, and shuttle

buses. There are informal discussions, pamphlets/posters/films, emergency telephones, lighted pathways/sidewalks, volunteer emergency medical technicians on call 24 hours a day, and Bard Response to Rape and Associated Violence Education (BRAVE).

Programs of Study: Bard confers B.A. and B.S. degrees. Associate, master's, and doctoral degrees are also awarded. Bachelor's degrees are awarded in BIOLOGICAL SCIENCE (biochemistry, biology/biological science, cell biology, ecology, microbiology, and molecular biology), COMMUNICATIONS AND THE ARTS (American literature, art history and appreciation, Chinese, classical languages, classics, creative writing, dance, dramatic arts, drawing, English, English literature, film arts, French, German, Germanic languages and literature, Italian, music history and appreciation, music performance, music theory and composition, painting, photography, Russian, sculpture, and Spanish), COMPUTER AND PHYSICAL SCIENCE (chemistry, mathematics, natural sciences, and physics), ENGINEERING AND ENVIRONMENTAL DESIGN (environmental science), HEALTH PROFESSIONS (predentistry and premedicine), SOCIAL SCIENCE (African studies, American studies, anthropology, archeology, area studies, Asian/Oriental studies, British studies, Celtic studies, clinical psychology, developmental psychology, Eastern European studies, economics, European studies, French studies, history, history of philosophy, history of science, human development, interdisciplinary studies, Italian studies, Judaic studies, Latin American studies, medieval studies, philosophy, political science/government, prelaw, religion, Russian and Slavic studies, social psychology, social science, sociology, and Spanish studies). Languages and literature, the arts, and social studies are the largest.

Required: All students must complete a 3-week workshop in language and thinking, a first year seminar, and a senior project. A conference in the junior year is required, and through a moderation process in the sophomore year, the student chooses a concentration in an academic department. A distribution of at least 1 course in each of the 8 academic areas is required, with a maximum of 84 hours in the student's major and a total of 124 credit hours needed to graduate. "Rethinking Differences," a course fulfilling the diversity requirement, is also required.

Special: Bard offers opportunities for study abroad, internships (no academic credit), Washington and New York semesters, dual majors, student-designed majors, accelerated degree programs and pass/fail options. A 3-2 engineering degree is available with the Columbia Univesity, Washington University (St. Louis.), and Dartmouth College-Schools of Engineering. Other 3-2 degrees are available in forestry and environmental studies, social work, architecture, city and regional planning, public health, and business administration. There are also opportunities for independent study, multicultural and ethnic studies, area studies, human rights, and globalization and international affairs.

Faculty/Classroom: 55% of faculty are male; 45%, female. All both teach and do research. No introductory courses are taught by graduate students.

Admissions: 32% of the 2005-2006 applicants were accepted. The SAT scores for the 2005-2006 freshman class were: Verbal--9% between 500 and 599, 44% between 600 and 700, and 47% above 700; Math--23% between 500 and 599, 50% between 600 and 700, and 27% above 700. 86% of the current freshmen were in the top fifth of their class; 98% were in the top two fifths. 20 freshmen graduated first in their class.

Requirements: In addition, Bard places strong emphasis on the academic background and intellectual curiosity of applicants, as well as indications of the student's commitment to social and environmental concerns, independent research, volunteer work, and other important extracurricular activities. Students applying for admission are expected to have graduated from an accredited secondary school (the GED is accepted) and must submit written essays with the application. The high school record should include a full complement of college-preparatory courses. Honors and advanced placement courses are also considered. An interview is recommended. Bard requires applicants to be in the upper 50% of their class. A GPA of 3.0 is required. AP credits are accepted. Important factors in the admissions decision are advanced placement or honor courses, evidence of special talent, and extracurricular activities record.

Procedure: Freshmen are admitted in the fall. There are early admissions and deferred admissions plans. Early decision applications should be filed by November 1; regular applications, by January 15 for fall entry and November 1 for spring entry, along with a $50 fee. Notification of early decision is sent January 1; regular decision, April 1. 311 applicants were on the 2005 waiting list. Applications are accepted on-line.

Transfer: 15 transfer students enrolled in 2004-2005. Admission requirements are the same as for regular applicants. A minimum GPA of 3.0 and an interview are recommended. 60 of 124 credits required for the bachelor's degree must be completed at Bard.

Visiting: There are regularly scheduled orientations for prospective students, consisting of regularly scheduled daily tours and information sessions, which are strongly recommended. Visitors may sit in on classes. To schedule a visit, contact the Admissions Office.

Financial Aid: In 2005-2006, 69% of all full-time freshmen and 67% of continuing full-time students received some form of financial aid. 69%

of full-time freshmen and 67% of continuing full-time students received need-based aid. The average freshman award was $25,265. Need-based scholarships or need-based grants averaged $24,046 ($35,900 maximum); and need-based self-help aid (loans and jobs) averaged $3167 ($5775 maximum). 34% of undergraduates work part time. Average annual earnings from campus work are $1200. The average financial indebtedness of the 2005 graduate was $18,345. The CSS/Profile or FAFSA and the state aid form are required. The deadline for filing freshman financial aid applications for fall entry is February 15.

International Students: There are 131 international students enrolled. The school actively recruits these students. A satisfactory score is required on the written TOEFL.

Computers: All students may access the system. There are no time limits and no fees.

Graduates: From July 1, 2004 to June 30, 2005, 330 bachelor's degrees were awarded. The most popular majors were visual and performing arts (38%), social studies (35%), and language and literature (19%). In an average class, 71% graduate in 4 years, 77% graduate in 5 years, and 74% graduate in 6 years. 100 companies recruited on campus in 2004-2005. Of a recent year's graduating class, 45% were enrolled in graduate school within 6 months of graduation and 50% were employed.

Admissions Contact: Mary Backlund, Director of Admissions. A video is available. E-mail: *admissions@bard.edu* Web: *www.bard.edu*

BERKELEY COLLEGE OF NEW YORK CITY   D-5

New York, NY 10017   (212) 986-4343
                                        (800)446-5400; Fax: (212) 697-3371

Full-time: 659 men, 1479 women	**Faculty:** n/av
Part-time: 48 men, 135 women	**Ph.D.s:** 51%
Graduate: none	**Student/Faculty:** 53 to 1
Year: quarters	**Tuition:** $16,950
Application Deadline: open	**Room & Board:** n/app
Freshman Class: n/av	
SAT or ACT: required	**LESS COMPETITIVE**

Berkeley College of New York City, founded in 1931, is a private institution offering undergraduate programs in business. Figures in the above capsule are approximate. The library contains 11,000 volumes, and subscribes to 130 periodicals including electronic. Computerized library services include the card catalog, interlibrary loans, and database searching. Special learning facilities include a learning resource center. The campus is in an urban area in midtown Manhattan, a short walk from Grand Central Station. There are 2 buildings.

Student Life: 75% of undergraduates are from New York. Others are from 24 states, 34 foreign countries, and Canada. 23% are Hispanic; 22% African American; 17% white; 15% foreign nationals.

Housing: There are no residence halls. All of students commute.

Services: Counseling and information services are available, as is tutoring in most subjects. There is remedial math, reading, and writing.

Programs of Study: Berkeley College of New York City confers the B.B.A. degree. Associate degrees are also awarded. Bachelor's degrees are awarded in BUSINESS (accounting, business administration and management, international business management, and marketing/retailing/merchandising).

Faculty/Classroom: All teach undergraduates.

Requirements: The SAT or ACT is required. In addition, graduation from an accredited high school or the GED, and an entrance exam or SAT or ACT scores are basic requirements for admission. A personal interview is strongly recommended. AP and CLEP credits are accepted.

Procedure: Freshmen are admitted to all sessions. Entrance exams should be taken any time. There is a deferred admissions and a rolling admissions plan. Application deadlines are open. Application fee is $50. Notification is sent on a rolling basis. Applications are accepted on-line.

Transfer: A transcript from each college or university attended must be submitted to receive credit. 60 of 180 credits required for the bachelor's degree must be completed at Berkeley College of New York City.

Visiting: There are guides for informal visits.

Financial Aid: In 2005-2006, 90% of all full-time freshmen received some form of financial aid. The FAFSA, the college's own financial statement and the state income tax form are required. Check with the school for current deadlines.

International Students: There are 130 international students enrolled. The school actively recruits these students. .

Computers: All students may access the system. There are no time limits and no fees.

Graduates: From July 1, 2004 to June 30, 2005, 308 bachelor's degrees were awarded. The most popular majors were management (29%), international business (20%), and marketing (19%). Of the 2004 graduating class, 94% were employed within 6 months of graduation.

Admissions Contact: Admissions Officer.
E-mail: *info@berkeleycollege.edu* Web: *www.berkeleycollege.edu*

BERKELEY COLLEGE-WESTCHESTER CAMPUS   D-5

White Plains, NY 10601

(914) 694-1122
(800) 446-5400; Fax: (914) 328-9469

Full-time: 164 men, 400 women	**Faculty:** n/av
Part-time: 8 men, 38 women	**Ph.D.s:** 54%
Graduate: none	**Student/Faculty:** n/av
Year: quarters, summer session	**Tuition:** $17,700
Application Deadline: open	**Room & Board:** $9000
Freshman Class: n/av	
SAT or ACT: required	**LESS COMPETITIVE**

Berkeley College, established in 1945, is a private institution with 5 campuses in New York and New Jersey. Its programs are designed to prepare students for careers in business by providing an education that balances academic studies, professional training, and hands-on experience. The informaton in this profile refers to the Westchester campus. The library contains 9500 volumes and 800 audio/video tapes/CDs/DVDs, and subscribes to 80 periodicals including electronic. Computerized library services include the card catalog, interlibrary loans, and database searching. Special learning facilities include a learning resource center. The 10-acre campus is in a suburban area. Including any residence halls, there are 3 buildings.

Student Life: 80% of undergraduates are from New York. Others are from 8 states and 14 foreign countries. 66% are white; 16% African American; 11% Hispanic. The average age of freshmen is 19; all undergraduates, 20.

Housing: 96 students can be accommodated in college housing, which includes coed dorms. Priority for on-campus housing is given to out-of-town students. 86% of students commute. Alcohol is not permitted. All students may keep cars.

Activities: There are no fraternities or sororities. There are 6 groups on campus, including international, newspaper, professional, social, social service, and student government. Popular campus events include Multicultural Month and Commuter Appreciation Day.

Sports: There is no sports program at Berkeley College-Westchester Campus. Students have access to the sports and exercise facilities at nearby Manhattanville College.

Disabled Students: Wheelchair ramps, elevators, and special parking are available.

Services: Counseling and information services are available, as is tutoring in every subject. There is remedial math, reading, and writing.

Campus Safety and Security: Measures include lighted pathways/sidewalks and night patrols by trained security personnel.

Programs of Study: Berkeley College-Westchester Campus confers the B.B.A. degree. Associate degrees are also awarded. Bachelor's degrees are awarded in BUSINESS (accounting, business administration and management, international business management, and marketing/retailing/merchandising).

Requirements: Graduation from an accredited high school or the equivalent (GED) and an entrance exam or SAT or ACT scores are basic requirements for admission. A personal interview is strongly recommended. AP and CLEP credits are accepted.

Procedure: Freshmen are admitted to all sessions. Entrance exams should be taken as soon as the application is submitted, if possible. There is a deferred admissions plan and a rolling admissions plan. Application deadlines are open. The fall 2005 application fee was $35. Notification is sent on a rolling basis. Applications are accepted on-line.

Transfer: Applicants must submit a transcript from each college attended and a high school transcript or equivalent (GED). 60 of 180 credits required for the bachelor's degree must be completed at Berkeley College-Westchester Campus.

Visiting: There are guides for informal visits.

Financial Aid: The FAFSA, the college's own financial statement, and the state income tax return are required. Check with the school for current deadlines.

International Students: The school actively recruits these students.

Computers: All students may access the system. There are no time limits and no fees.

Admissions Contact: Admissions Officer.
E-mail: *info@berkeleycollege.edu* Web: *www.berkeleycollege.edu*

BORICUA COLLEGE   D-5

New York, NY 10032

(212) 694-1000 or (718) 782-2200
Fax: (212) 694-1015 or (718) 782-2050

Full-time: 250 men, 900 women	**Faculty:** n/av
Part-time: none	**Ph.D.s:** n/av
Graduate: none	**Student/Faculty:** n/av
Year: semsters, summer session	**Tuition:** $8000
Application Deadline: open	**Room & Board:** n/app
Freshman Class: n/av	
SAT or ACT: not required	**COMPETITIVE**

Boricua College, founded in 1974, is a private college for bilingual students, designed to meet the needs of a Spanish-speaking population. Figures in the above capsule and in this profile are approximate. There are 2 graduate schools. The library contains 128,727 volumes and 3000 audio/video tapes/CDs/DVDs, and subscribes to 227 periodicals including electronic. Computerized library services include the card catalog and database searching. Special learning facilities include a learning resource center and art gallery. The campus is in an urban area in Manhattan and Brooklyn and Brooklyn. There are 4 buildings.

Student Life: 70% of students are from public schools. 85% are Hispanic; 10% African American. The average age of freshmen is 29; all undergraduates, 32. 12% do not continue beyond their first year; 80% remain to graduate.

Housing: There are no residence halls. Alcohol is not permitted. No one may keep cars.

Activities: There are no fraternities or sororities. There are 5 groups on campus, including art, chorus, drama, newspaper, and student government. Popular campus events include cultural programs, Puerto Rican Discovery Day and Christmas and Spring concerts with chorus and orchestra.

Sports: Facilities include a gym.

Disabled Students: Elevators and specially equipped rest rooms are available.

Services: Counseling and information services are available, as is tutoring in most subjects.

Campus Safety and Security: Measures include shuttle buses, informal discussions, pamphlets/posters/films, and emergency telephones. There are lighted pathways/sidewalks.

Programs of Study: Bachelor's degrees are awarded in BUSINESS (business administration and management), EDUCATION (elementary), SOCIAL SCIENCE (human services and liberal arts/general studies).

Required: A total of 124 credits is required for the bachelor's degree.

Requirements: Boricua administers its own tests to prospective students, although either the SAT or ACT is accepted. Applicants must be graduates of an accredited secondary school or have a GED. 2 letters of recommendation and an admissions interview are required. Applicants must demonstrate a working knowledge of English and Spanish to a faculty panel. CLEP credit is accepted. Important factors in the admissions decision are leadership record, personality/intangible qualities, and recommendations by school officials.

Procedure: Freshmen are admitted fall, spring, and summer. Entrance exams should be taken when called by the admissions staff. There is an early decision plan and a rolling admissions plan. Application deadlines are open. Check with the school for current application deadlines and fee.

Transfer: Applicants with associate degrees may transfer up to 60 credits. All college credits passed with grade C and above are accepted. 80 of 124 credits required for the bachelor's degree must be completed at Boricua.

Visiting: There are regularly scheduled orientations for prospective students. Letters are sent to prospective students advising them of scheduled orientations. To schedule a visit, contact Abraham Cruz at or Miriam Prefferat.

Financial Aid: Boricua is a member of CSS. The FAFSA and income tax forms are required. Check with the school for current deadlines.

Computers: All students may access the system. There are no time limits and no fees.

Admissions Contact: Abraham Cruz (Manhattan) or Miriam Pfeffer, Director of Student Services. E-mail: *acruz@boricuacollege.edu* or *mpfeffer@boricuacolleg*

CANISIUS COLLEGE
A-3

Buffalo, NY 14208

(716) 888-2200
(800) 843-1517; Fax: (716) 888-3230

Full-time: 1431 men, 1879 women	**Faculty:** 205; IIA, av$
Part-time: 116 men, 165 women	**Ph.D.s:** 94%
Graduate: 523 men, 865 women	**Student/Faculty:** 16 to 1
Year: semesters, summer session	**Tuition:** $23,297
Application Deadline: May 1	**Room & Board:** $8960
Freshman Class: 4114 applied, 2962 accepted, 774 enrolled	
SAT Verbal/Math: 550/561*	**ACT:** 24 **VERY COMPETITIVE**

Canisius College, founded in 1870, is a private Roman Catholic college in the Jesuit tradition. It offers undergraduate programs in the liberal arts and sciences, business, education, and human services. There are 3 undergraduate and 3 graduate schools. In addition to regional accreditation, Canisius has baccalaureate program accreditation with AACSB, ACS, CAHEA, CED, and NCATE. The library contains 336,449 volumes, 598,068 microform items, and 8443 audio/video tapes/CDs/DVDs, and subscribes to 16,935 periodicals including electronic. Computerized library services include the card catalog, interlibrary loans, database searching, and Internet access. Special learning facilities include a learning resource center, art gallery, radio station, a television studio, foreign language lab, 87 media-assisted classrooms, digital media lab, and musical instrument digital interface classroom. The 36-acre campus is in an urban area in Buffalo. Including any residence halls, there are 51 buildings.

Student Life: 88% of undergraduates are from New York. Students are from 32 states, 14 foreign countries, and Canada. 70% are from public schools. 75% are white. The average age of freshmen is 18; all undergraduates, 20. 16% do not continue beyond their first year; 66% remain to graduate.

Housing: 1599 students can be accommodated in college housing, which includes single-sex and coed dorms, on-campus apartments, and off-campus apartments. In addition, there are honors houses, special-interest houses, an intercultural hall, and townhouse. On-campus housing is guaranteed for all 4 years. 58% of students commute. Alcohol is not permitted. All students may keep cars.

Activities: 1% of men belong to 1 national fraternity; 1% of women belong to 1 national sorority. There are 100 groups on campus, including art, band, cheerleading, chess, choir, chorale, computers, dance, drama, drill team, ethnic, gay, honors, international, jazz band, literary magazine, musical theater, newspaper, orchestra, pep band, political, professional, radio and TV, religious, social, social service, student government, and yearbook. Popular campus events include Fall Semiformal, Senior Week, and Springfest.

Sports: There are 8 intercollegiate sports for men and 8 for women, and 12 intramural sports for men and 12 for women. Facilities include an 1800-seat athletic center with a 25-yard pool, racquetball courts, and training rooms, a 1000-seat sports complex with Astroturf playing fields, a rifle range, and a mirrored dance studio.

Disabled Students: 90% of the campus is accessible. Wheelchair ramps, elevators, special parking, specially equipped rest rooms, special class scheduling, lowered drinking fountains, lowered telephones, automatic doors, TDD, a shuttle service for students with disabilities, distraction-free testing spaces, and adjustable classroom desks are available.

Services: Counseling and information services are available, as is tutoring in every subject. There is a reader service for the blind, and remedial math, reading, and writing.

Campus Safety and Security: Measures include 24-hour foot and vehicle patrol, self-defense education, security escort services, and shuttle buses. There are informal discussions, pamphlets/posters/films, emergency telephones, lighted pathways/sidewalks, a crime prevention officer, bicycle patrols, and crime prevention programs.

Programs of Study: Canisius confers B.A. and B.S. degrees. Master's degrees are also awarded. Bachelor's degrees are awarded in BIOLOGICAL SCIENCE (biochemistry, bioinformatics, and biology/biological science), BUSINESS (accounting, banking and finance, business administration and management, business economics, business systems analysis, entrepreneurial studies, international business management, management information systems, and marketing/retailing/merchandising), COMMUNICATIONS AND THE ARTS (art history and appreciation, communications, English, French, German, music, and Spanish), COMPUTER AND PHYSICAL SCIENCE (chemistry, computer science, digital arts/technology, mathematics, and physics), EDUCATION (athletic training, early childhood, mathematics, middle school, physical, secondary, and special), ENGINEERING AND ENVIRONMENTAL DESIGN (environmental science and preengineering), HEALTH PROFESSIONS (clinical science), SOCIAL SCIENCE (anthropology, criminal justice, economics, European studies, history, international relations, philosophy, political science/government, psychology, religion, sociology, and urban studies). Accounting, biology, and chemistry are the strongest academically. Psychology, management, and education are the largest.

Required: All students must complete a core curriculum consisting of 4 courses in general studies (literature, writing, philosophy, and religion) and 14 courses in area studies (natural sciences, social studies, art and literature, history, philosophy, religious studies, math, and languages). In addition, students must take 10 3-credit courses in the major. A minimum of 120 credit hours and a minimum GPA of 2.0 are required for graduation.

Special: Canisius offers internships, credit by exam, pass/fail options, nondegree studies, dual majors in all majors, a Washington semester, work-study programs, and study abroad in 10 countries. Cooperative programs are available with the Fashion Institute of Technology in New York City and the SUNY College of Environmental Science and Forestry in Syracuse. Cross-registration is permitted with 14 schools in the Western New York Consortium of Higher Education. Canisius also offers early assurance and joint degree programs with SUNY health professions schools in Buffalo and Syracuse, and a 3-2 MBA. There are 9 national honor societies, a freshman honors program, and 2 departmental honors programs.

Faculty/Classroom: 68% of faculty are male; 32%, female. 94% teach undergraduates, 75% do research, and 65% do both. No introductory courses are taught by graduate students. The average class size in an introductory lecture is 23; in a laboratory, 18; and in a regular course, 20.

Admissions: 72% of the 2005-2006 applicants were accepted. The SAT scores for the 2005-2006 freshman class were: Verbal--23% below 500, 50% between 500 and 599, 23% between 600 and 700, and 3% above 700; Math--19% below 500, 50% between 500 and 599, 27% between 600 and 700, and 4% above 700. The ACT scores were 19% below 21, 33% between 21 and 23, 25% between 24 and 26, 11% between 27 and 28, and 11% above 28. 43% of the current freshmen were in the top fifth of their class; 72% were in the top two fifths. 6 freshmen graduated first in their class.

Requirements: The SAT or ACT is required. In addition, all students must submit official high school transcript (or GED). College preparatory course work should include 4 units each of English and social science and 3 units each of math, science, and foreign language. Students with a B+ average and satisfactory SAT results are most competitive. An essay and an interview are recommended. A GPA of 2.0 is required. AP and CLEP credits are accepted. Important factors in the admissions decision are advanced placement or honor courses, recommendations by school officials, and leadership record.

Procedure: Freshmen are admitted fall, spring, and summer. Entrance exams should be taken during the junior or senior year. There is a deferred admissions plan and a rolling admissions plan. Applications should be filed by May 1 for fall entry, along with a $40 fee. Notification is sent on a rolling basis. Applications are accepted on-line.

Transfer: 202 transfer students enrolled in 2004-2005. Applicants must present a minimum GPA of 2.0 and a transfer recommendation form. 30 of 120 credits required for the bachelor's degree must be completed at Canisius.

Visiting: There are regularly scheduled orientations for prospective students, including campus overnights and single-day visits. Also available are summer visitations for families, an open house in the fall and spring, and a financial aid workshop in January. There are guides for informal visits and visitors may sit in on classes and stay overnight. To schedule a visit, contact the Admissions Office at admissions@canisius.edu.

Financial Aid: In 2005-2006, 98% of all full-time freshmen and 95% of continuing full-time students received some form of financial aid. 80% of full-time freshmen and 76% of continuing full-time students received need-based aid. The average freshman award was $20,925. Need-based scholarships or need-based grants averaged $5348 ($26,781 maximum); need-based self-help aid (loans and jobs) averaged $4601 ($6625 maximum); non-need-based athletic scholarships averaged $14,132 ($32,257 maximum); and other non-need-based awards and non-need-based scholarships averaged $10,155 ($22,500 maximum). 21% of undergraduates work part time. Average annual earnings from campus work are $1458. The average financial indebtedness of the 2005 graduate was $21,801. Canisius is a member of CSS. The FAFSA and the college's own financial statement are required. The priority date for freshman financial aid applications for fall entry is February 15.

International Students: There are 78 international students enrolled. The school actively recruits these students. They must take the TOEFL and also take the SAT or the ACT.

Computers: Wireless access is available. Students amy access more than 490 PCs throughout campus. All computers are connected to the Internet and have access to extensive on-line research databases provided by the library. Laptops with wireless access are available for use in the library. All students may access the system. The Web can be accessed at any time. There are no time limits. The fee is $225. It is strongly recommended that all students have a personal computer.

Graduates: From July 1, 2004 to June 30, 2005, 671 bachelor's degrees were awarded. The most popular majors were education (10%), communication studies (9%), and psychology (7%). In an average class, 51% graduate in 4 years or less, 66% graduate in 5 years or less, and 67% graduate in 6 years or less. 29 companies recruited on campus in 2004-2005. Of the 2004 graduating class, 26% were enrolled in graduate school within 6 months of graduation and 63% were employed.

Admissions Contact: Jill Marie Atkins and Ann Marie Moscovic, Co-Director of Admissions. E-mail: *admissions@canisius.edu* Web: *http://www.canisius.edu*

CAZENOVIA COLLEGE — C-3

Cazenovia, NY 13035
(315) 655-7208
(800) 654-3210; Fax: (315) 655-2190

Full-time: 210 men, 600 women	Faculty: 50
Part-time: 38 men, 141 women	Ph.D.s: 63%
Graduate: none	Student/Faculty: 16 to 1
Year: semesters, summer session	Tuition: $19,190
Application Deadline: open	Room & Board: $7710
Freshman Class: n/av	
SAT or ACT: recommended	COMPETITIVE

Cazenovia College, founded in 1824, is a private institution offering degree programs in applied arts and sciences and preprofessional studies. The library contains 64,000 volumes, 13,000 microform items, and 3000 audio/video tapes/CDs/DVDs, and subscribes to 456 periodicals including electronic. Computerized library services include interlibrary loans, database searching, and Internet access. Special learning facilities include a learning resource center, art gallery, radio station, and a nearby campus farm with equine center. The 40-acre campus is in a small town 18 miles southeast of Syracuse. Including any residence halls, there are 24 buildings.

Student Life: 80% of undergraduates are from New York. Others are from 24 states, 4 foreign countries, and Canada. 90% are from public schools. 85% are white. The average age of freshmen is 18. 30% do not continue beyond their first year; 50% remain to graduate.

Housing: 700 students can be accommodated in college housing, which includes single-sex and coed dorms and on-campus apartments. In addition, there is a quiet building, a wellness center, a global awarness cluster, and all-female residence hall, and an upperclass-only section. On-campus housing is guaranteed for all 4 years. 83% of students live on campus; of those, 75% remain on campus on weekends. Alcohol is not permitted. Upperclassmen may keep cars.

Activities: There are no fraternities or sororities. There are many groups and organizations on campus, including art, band, cheerleading, choir, chorale, computers, debate, drama, ethnic, gay, honors, literary magazine, musical theater, newspaper, political, professional, social service, student government, and yearbook. Popular campus events include Spring Day, and athletic events.

Sports: There are 6 intercollegiate sports for men and 7 for women, and 9 intramural sports for men and 9 for women. Facilities include an athletic center with a pool, 2 gyms, a weight room, 2 racquetball courts, outdoor tennis courts, and athletic fields.

Disabled Students: 86% of the campus is accessible. Wheelchair ramps, elevators, special parking, specially equipped rest rooms, special class scheduling, lowered telephones, and special housing are available.

Services: Counseling and information services are available, as is tutoring in every subject. There is a reader service for the blind, and remedial math, reading, and writing.

Campus Safety and Security: Measures include 24-hour foot and vehicle patrol, security escort services, informal discussions, and pamphlets/posters/films. There are emergency telephones and lighted pathways/sidewalks.

Programs of Study: Cazenovia confers B.A., B.S., B.F.A., and B.P.S. degrees. Bachelor's degrees are awarded in AGRICULTURE (environmental studies), BUSINESS (business administration and management and management science), COMMUNICATIONS AND THE ARTS (communications, English, studio art, and visual design), EDUCATION (early childhood and elementary), ENGINEERING AND ENVIRONMENTAL DESIGN (commercial art and interior design), SOCIAL SCIENCE (criminology, fashion design and technology, human services, liberal arts/general studies, psychology, and social science). Interior design, liberal arts, and human services are the strongest academically. Management is the largest.

Required: A total of 120 semester credits and a GPA of 2.0 are required for the bachelor's degree. Students must take courses in speech, academic writing, diversity and social consciousness, science or math, visual literacy, communications, ethics, cultural literacy, and research methods. They must also demonstrate math proficiency and complete a senior capstone course.

Special: Cazenovia offers internships, a Washington semester, work-study, B.A.-B.S. degrees in liberal studies and liberal and professional studies. There is a study-abroad program at Canterbury Christ Church University in the United Kingdom. There are 3 national honor societies, a freshman honors program, and 2 departmental honors programs.

Faculty/Classroom: 39% of faculty are male; 61%, female. All teach undergraduates and 1 do research. The average class size in an introductory lecture is 20; in a laboratory, 15; and in a regular course, 16.

Admissions: 79% of the 2005-2006 applicants were accepted. 30% of the current freshmen were in the top fifth of their class; 65% were in the top two fifths. 4 freshmen graduated first in their class.

Requirements: The SAT or ACT is recommended. In addition, applicants should be graduates of an accredited secondary school or the equivalent. A recommendation from a guidance counselor or teacher is required. A GPA of 2.5 is required. AP and CLEP credits are accepted. Important factors in the admissions decision are advanced placement or honor courses and leadership record.

Procedure: Freshmen are admitted fall and spring. Entrance exams should be taken by the fall of the senior year. There are deferred admissions and rolling admissions plans. Application deadlines are open. Application fee is $30. A waiting list is an active part of the admissions procedure. Applications are accepted on-line.

Transfer: 48 transfer students enrolled in 2004-2005. Applicants must present at least 12 college credits, with a minimum GPA of 2.0, and official transcripts from previous colleges attended. Students with fewer than 24 credits must also submit a high school transcript. 30 of 120 credits required for the bachelor's degree must be completed at Cazenovia.

Visiting: There are regularly scheduled orientations for prospective students, consisting of a welcome by the president and deans, financial aid sessions, placement testing, academic advising, and registration. There are guides for informal visits and visitors may sit in on classes and stay overnight. To schedule a visit, contact the Admissions and Financial Aid Office.

Financial Aid: Cazenovia is a member of CSS. The FAFSA and Express TAP are required. The deadline for filing freshman financial aid applications for fall entry is March 15.

International Students: There are 4 international students enrolled. The school actively recruits these students. A satisfactory score is required on the written TOEFL.

Computers: Wireless access is available. All students may access the system daily from 8 A.M. to midnight. There are no time limits. The fee is $100.

Graduates: From July 1, 2004 to June 30, 2005, 150 bachelor's degrees were awarded. The most popular majors were management (39%), human services (25%), and visual communications (19%). In an average class, 35% graduate in 5 years or less. 23 companies recruited on campus in 2004-2005.

Admissions Contact: Robert A. Croot, Dean for Admissions and Financial Aid. E-mail: *admission@cazcollege.edu* Web: *www.cazenovia.edu*

CITY UNIVERSITY OF NEW YORK

The City University of New York, established in 1847, is a public system in New York. It is governed by a Board of Trustees, whose chief administrator is Chancellor. The primary goal of the system is To maintain and expand its commitment to academic excellence, and to the provision of equal access and opportunity. The main priorities are Providing access for all students who seek to enroll, Insuring student success. Enhancing instructional and research excellence. The total enrollment is usually about 200,000; with 7000 faculty members. Altogether there are some 600 baccalaureate, 300 master's, and 50 doctoral programs offered in City University of New York. Profiles of the 4-year campuses are included in this section.

CITY UNIVERSITY OF NEW YORK/BARUCH COLLEGE — D-5

New York, NY 10010-5585
(646) 312-1400; Fax: (646) 312-1361

Full-time: 4602 men, 5151 women	Faculty: 405; IIA, ++$
Part-time: 1209 men, 1882 women	Ph.D.s: 87%
Graduate: 1456 men, 1456 women	Student/Faculty: 24 to 1
Year: semesters, summer session	Tuition: $4320 (8960)
Application Deadline: February 1	Room & Board: n/app
Freshman Class: 14,917 applied, 4962 accepted, 1641 enrolled	
SAT Verbal/Math: 520/580*	VERY COMPETITIVE+

Baruch College was founded in 1919 and became a separate unit of the City University of New York in 1968. It offers undergraduate programs in business and public administration and liberal arts and sciences. There are 3 undergraduate and 3 graduate schools. Figures in the above capsule and in this profile are approximate. In addition to regional accreditation, Baruch has baccalaureate program accreditation with AACSB. The library contains 456,132 volumes, 2,066,108 microform items, and 1017 audio/video tapes/CDs/DVDs, and subscribes to 4548 periodicals including electronic. Computerized library services include the card catalog, interlibrary loans, database searching, Internet access, and laptop Internet portals. Special learning facilities include an art gallery and radio station. The 39-acre campus is in Manhattan. There are 6 buildings.

Student Life: 98% of undergraduates are from New York. Students are from 15 states, 144 foreign countries, and Canada. 70% are from public schools. 32% are white; 28% Asian American; 17% Hispanic; 13% African American; 11% foreign nationals. The average age of freshmen is 18; all undergraduates, 25. 13% do not continue beyond their first year.

Housing: There are no residence halls. All of students commute. Alcohol is not permitted. No one may keep cars.

Activities: 1% of men belong to 1 local and 3 national fraternities; 1% of women belong to 1 local and 3 national sororities. There are 165 groups on campus, including cheerleading, chess, choir, chorus, computers, dance, drama, ethnic, gay, honors, international, literary magazine, newspaper, photography, political, professional, radio and TV, religious, social, social service, student government, and yearbook. Popular campus events include club fairs, street fairs, and Caribbean Week.

Sports: There are 7 intercollegiate sports for men and 7 for women, and 5 intramural sports for men and 5 for women. Facilities include a gym, a swimming pool, a weight room, an exercise room, and racquetball courts.

Disabled Students: All of the campus is accessible. Wheelchair ramps, elevators, specially equipped rest rooms, and special class scheduling are available.

Services: Counseling and information services are available, as is tutoring in most subjects. There is a reader service for the blind and remedial math and writing. Note takers large-print computer screens and interpreters for the deaf are available.

Campus Safety and Security: Measures include 24-hour foot and vehicle patrol, self-defense education, security escort services, and informal discussions. There are pamphlets/posters/films, lighted pathways/sidewalks, intercollege phones in buildings used as emergency phones, fire safety directors, and an ID system that uses card swipe in turnstiles for entry.

Programs of Study: Baruch confers B.A., B.S., and B.B.A. degrees. Master's and doctoral degrees are also awarded. Bachelor's degrees are awarded in BUSINESS (accounting, investments and securities, management science, marketing management, marketing/retailing/merchandising, operations research, personnel management, and real estate), COMMUNICATIONS AND THE ARTS (advertising, communications, English, journalism, music, and Spanish), COMPUTER AND PHYSICAL SCIENCE (actuarial science, information sciences and systems, mathematics, and statistics), SOCIAL SCIENCE (economics, history, industrial and organizational psychology, philosophy, political science/government, psychology, public affairs, and sociology). Economics, English, and math are the strongest academically. Accounting, finance, and computer information systems are the largest.

Required: Students must complete a minimum of 120 credits for the B.A. or B.S. and 124 for the B.B.A., with at least 24 hours in the major, and maintain a GPA of 2.0 overall in the major. Students' core curriculum should include courses in English, literature, communications, history, philosophy, psychology, microeconomics, and fine and performing arts.

Special: Students may take courses at all CUNY schools. The college offers internships and study abroad in Great Britain, France, Germany, Mexico, and Israel. Students may design their own liberal arts major. A federal work-study program is available, and pass/fail options are permitted for liberal arts majors. Students may combine any undergraduate major with a master's in accountancy. There are 7 national honor societies, a freshman honors program, and a freshman honors programs.

Faculty/Classroom: 64% of faculty are male; 36%, female. 93% teach undergraduates and 89% do research. Graduate students teach 4% of introductory courses. The average class size in an introductory lecture is 275; in a laboratory, 20; and in a regular course, 35.

Requirements: The SAT or ACT is required. In addition, applicants must present an official high school transcript (a GED will be accepted) indicating a minimum grade average of 82% in academic subjects (minimum of 14 credits). AP and CLEP credits are accepted.

Procedure: Freshmen are admitted fall and spring. Entrance exams should be taken by March 1. There is an early decision plan. Check with the school for current application deadlines and fee. The fall 2005 application fee was $65. Admissions processing takes about 6 to 8 weeks.

Transfer: Applicants must have a minimum GPA of 2.5 for 12 to 34.9 credits submitted, a minimum GPA of 2.25 for 35 to 59.9 credits, and a minimum GPA of 2.0 for 60 or more credits. Business applicants must have a 2.75 GPA. Students applying for transfer with fewer than 12 credits earned must have a minimum GPA of 2.5 and a minimum high school average of 80%. 32 of 128 credits required for the bachelor's degree must be completed at Baruch.

Visiting: There are regularly scheduled orientations for prospective students, including a meeting with an admissions counselor. There are guides for informal visits. To schedule a visit, contact the Admissions Office.

Financial Aid: Baruch is a member of CSS. The FAFSA is required. Check with the school for current deadlines.

International Students: There are 1480 international students enrolled. A satisfactory score is required on the written TOEFL.

Computers: All students may access the system. There are no time limits and no fees.

Admissions Contact: James Murphy, Director of Undergraduate Admissions and Financial Aid. A video is available.
E-mail: *james_murphy@baruch.cuny.edu*

CITY UNIVERSITY OF NEW YORK/BROOKLYN COLLEGE D-5

Brooklyn, NY 11210-2889	(718) 951-5001; Fax: (718) 951-4506
Full-time: 3329 men, 4780 women	**Faculty:** 517; IIA, +$
Part-time: 1222 men, 2033 women	**Ph.D.s:** 90%
Graduate: 1235 men, 2682 women	**Student/Faculty:** 16 to 1
Year: semesters, summer session	**Tuition:** $4377 ($9017)
Application Deadline: open	**Room & Board:** n/app
Freshman Class: 13,494 applied, 6273 accepted, 1413 enrolled	
SAT or ACT: required	**COMPETITIVE+**

Brooklyn College, established in 1930, is a publicly supported college of liberal arts, sciences, preprofessional, and professional studies. It is part of the City University of New York and serves the commuter student. There are 2 undergraduate schools and 1 graduate school. In addition to regional accreditation, Brooklyn College has baccalaureate program accreditation with ADA, ASHLA, and NCATE. The library contains 1,312,942 volumes, 1,679,403 microform items, and 22,806 audio/video tapes/CDs/DVDs, and subscribes to 18,750 periodicals including electronic. Computerized library services include the card catalog, interlibrary loans, database searching, and Internet access. Special learning facilities include a learning resource center, art gallery, radio station, TV station, 3 color studios, and a speech and hearing clinic. The 26-acre campus is in an urban area in Brooklyn, New York. There are 10 buildings.

Student Life: 91% of undergraduates are from New York. Others are from 21 states, 86 foreign countries, and Canada. 77% are from public schools. 42% are white; 28% African American; 12% Hispanic; 11% Asian American. The average age of freshmen is 18; all undergraduates, 24. 24% do not continue beyond their first year; 76% remain to graduate.

Housing: There are no residence halls. All of students commute. Alcohol is not permitted. No one may keep cars.

Activities: 3% of men belong to 1 local and 6 national fraternities; 3% of women belong to 4 local and 3 national sororities. There are 150 groups on campus, including academic, art, chess, choir, chorus, computers, dance, drama, ethnic, film, forensics, gay, honors, international, literary magazine, musical theater, newspaper, orchestra, photography, political, professional, radio and TV, religious, social, social service, student government, symphony, and yearbook. Popular campus events include Country Fair, Fall Festival, and Black Solidarity Day.

Sports: There are 8 intercollegiate sports for men and 8 for women, and 17 intramural sports for men and 17 for women. Facilities include swimming pools, a soccer field, volleyball, racquetball, squash, tennis, and basketball courts, a weight-training room, and a jogging track.

Disabled Students: All of the campus is accessible. Wheelchair ramps, elevators, special parking, specially equipped rest rooms, special class scheduling, lowered drinking fountains, and lowered telephones are available.

Services: Counseling and information services are available, as is tutoring in every subject. There is a reader service for the blind.

Campus Safety and Security: Measures include 24-hour foot and vehicle patrol, security escort services, shuttle buses, and informal discussions. There are pamphlets/posters/films, emergency telephones, lighted pathways/sidewalks, CCTV cameras, and informational assistants.

Programs of Study: Brooklyn College confers B.A., B.S., B.F.A., and B.Mus. degrees. Master's degrees are also awarded. Bachelor's degrees are awarded in BIOLOGICAL SCIENCE (biology/biological science), BUSINESS (accounting, banking and finance, and business administration and management), COMMUNICATIONS AND THE ARTS (art, art history and appreciation, broadcasting, classics, comparative literature, creative writing, English, film arts, French, German, Greek, Hebrew, Italian, journalism, languages, Latin, linguistics, music, music performance, music theory and composition, radio/television technology, Russian, Spanish, theater management, and visual and performing arts), COMPUTER AND PHYSICAL SCIENCE (chemistry, computer science, geology, information sciences and systems, mathematics, and physics), EDUCATION (art, bilingual/bicultural, early childhood, education of the deaf and hearing impaired, elementary, English, foreign languages, health, mathematics, music, physical, science, secondary, and social studies), HEALTH PROFESSIONS (health science and speech pathology/audiology), SOCIAL SCIENCE (African studies, American studies, anthropology, archeology, Caribbean studies, economics, Hispanic American studies, history, Judaic studies, Latin American studies, philosophy, political science/government, psychology, religion, sociology, and women's studies). Education, business, and psychology and have the largest enrollments and are the strongest academically.

Required: 10 required, interrelated courses cover the following core curriculum areas: classics, art, music, political science, sociology, history, literature, math, computer science, chemistry, physics, biology, geology, philosophy, and comparative cultures. There are basic skills requirements in reading, composition, speech, and math, as well as a foreign language requirement. A 2.0 GPA and a minimum of 120 credit hours, with 31 to 36 in the major (67 to 70 for chemistry), are required to graduate.

Special: There are numerous cross-registration programs with colleges and universities in the area. Many internships and work-study programs are available. Study abroad is possible in more than 50 countries. A B.A.-M.D., B.S.-M.P.S., and accelerated B.A.-M.A. programs are available. A number of B.A.-B.S. degrees, dual majors, a 3-2 engineering degree, and student-designed majors are possible. Credit by exam, credit for life experience, nondegree study, and pass/fail options are offered. There is a Latin and Greek Institute offered during the summer through the graduate center. There are 13 national honor societies, including Phi Beta Kappa, a freshman honors program, and 26 departmental honors programs.

Faculty/Classroom: 56% of faculty are male; 44%, female. 80% teach undergraduates and 80% do research. The average class size in a laboratory is 15 and in a regular course, 35.

Admissions: 37% of the current freshmen were in the top fifth of their class; 69% were in the top two fifths.

Requirements: A satisfactory score on the SAT or ACT is required. The GED, with a score of 3000 or higher, is accepted. Requirements are higher for B.A.-M.D. entrants and for the scholars program. Applicants not meeting the standard requirements are eligible for admission to the City University's community colleges. AP and CLEP credits are accepted.

Procedure: Freshmen are admitted fall and spring. Entrance exams should be taken prior to admission. There is an early admissions plan for the CUNY Honors Program and a rolling admissions plan for regular programs. Application deadlines are open. Application fee is $65. Notification is sent on a rolling basis. Applications are accepted on-line.

Transfer: 1521 transfer students enrolled in 2004-2005. Transfer students must have a minimum 2.0 GPA with 24 or more credits; 2.25 with 15 to 23 credits; and 2.5 with 7 to 14 credits. Students with less than 7 credits must have an acceptable high school average and a 2.0 college GPA. 30 of 120 credits required for the bachelor's degree must be completed at Brooklyn College.

Visiting: There are regularly scheduled orientations for prospective students, including campus tours, presentations, and meetings with faculty. There are guides for informal visits. To schedule a visit, contact Lawrence Bosket, Admissions at (718) 951-4355 or *Lbosket@brooklyn.cuny.edu.*

Financial Aid: In a recent year, 66% of all full-time freshmen and 62% of continuing full-time students received some form of financial aid. 64% of full-time freshmen and 65% of continuing full-time students received need-based aid. The average freshman award was $5470. 71% of undergraduates work part time. Average annual earnings from campus work are $1200. The average financial indebtedness of the recent year's graduate was $9700. The FAFSA is required. The priority date for freshman financial aid applications for fall entry is April 1.

International Students: There are 793 international students enrolled. The school actively recruits these students. A satisfactory score is required on the written TOEFL. Students must also take the college's own test.

Computers: All students may access the system. Students may access the system 1 hour, when other students are waiting. There are no fees.

Graduates: From July 1, 2004 to June 30, 2005, 1688 bachelor's degrees were awarded. The most popular majors were business (30%), psychology (13%), and education (8%). In an average class, 15% graduate in 4 years or less, 32% graduate in 5 years or less, and 39% graduate in 6 years or less. 68 companies recruited on campus in a recent year. Of the 2004 graduating class, 39% were enrolled in graduate school within 6 months of graduation and 90% were employed.

Admissions Contact: Marianne Booufall Tynan, Director of Admissions. E-mail: *adminqry@brooklyn.cuny.edu* Web: *www.brooklyn.cuny.edu*

CITY UNIVERSITY OF NEW YORK/CITY COLLEGE   D-5

New York, NY 10031-9101 (212) 650-6977; Fax: (212) 650-6417

Full-time: 3488 men, 3252 women	Faculty: 490; IIA, ++$
Part-time: 1343 men, 1411 women	Ph.D.s: 85%
Graduate: 1307 men, 1639 women	Student/Faculty: 14 to 1
Year: semesters, summer session	Tuition: $4280 ($360/credit)
Application Deadline: December 1	Room & Board: n/app
Freshman Class: 1311 accepted, 1169 enrolled	
SAT Verbal/Math: 471/514*	COMPETITIVE

City College, founded in 1847, is a public liberal arts college that is part of the City University of New York. The college offers programs through 4 undergraduate and 4 graduate schools and 2 professional centers. In addition to regional accreditation, CCNY has baccalaureate program accreditation with ABET, ABFSE, NAAB, and NCATE. The 4 libraries contain 1,444,400 volumes, 887,471 microform items, and 38,300 audio/video tapes/CDs/DVDs, and subscribe to 5000 periodicals including electronic. Computerized library services include the card catalog, interlibrary loans, database searching, Internet access, and laptop Inter-

net portals. Special learning facilities include a learning resource center, art gallery, planetarium, radio station, TV station, weather station, laser labs, microwave labs, and Structural Biology Lab. The 34-acre campus is in an urban area in New York City. There are 14 buildings.

Student Life: Students are from 36 states, 153 foreign countries, and Canada. 91% are from public schools. 32% are Hispanic; 24% African American; 17% Asian American; 15% foreign nationals; 12% white. The average age of freshmen is 18; all undergraduates, 24. 12% do not continue beyond their first year; 34% remain to graduate.

Housing: There are no residence halls. All of students commute. Alcohol is not permitted. All students may keep cars.

Activities: There are no fraternities or sororities. There are 100 groups on campus, including art, band, cheerleading, chess, chorus, computers, drama, ethnic, gay, honors, international, jazz band, literary magazine, newspaper, orchestra, political, professional, radio and TV, religious, social, social service, and student government. Popular campus events include Langston Hughes Poetry Contest, Dance Theater of Harlem performances at Davis Center, and Architecture Lecture Series.

Sports: There are 7 intercollegiate sports for men and 7 for women. Facilities include swimming pools, 2 gyms, a weight room, and an outdoor track and field stadium.

Disabled Students: 92% of the campus is accessible. Wheelchair ramps, elevators, special parking, specially equipped rest rooms, special class scheduling, lowered drinking fountains, and lowered telephones are available.

Services: Counseling and information services are available, as is tutoring in most subjects. There is a reader service for the blind.

Campus Safety and Security: Measures include 24-hour foot and vehicle patrol, security escort services, shuttle buses, and informal discussions. There are pamphlets/posters/films, emergency telephones, lighted pathways/sidewalks, bicycle patrols, IDs, criminal investigations, and security systems.

Programs of Study: CCNY confers B.A., B.S., B.Arch., B.E., B.F.A., B.M.E., and B.S.Ed. degrees. Master's degrees are also awarded. Bachelor's degrees are awarded in BIOLOGICAL SCIENCE (biology/biological science), BUSINESS (business administration and management), COMMUNICATIONS AND THE ARTS (art, communications, comparative literature, dramatic arts, English, film arts, fine arts, French, multimedia, music, performing arts, romance languages and literature, Spanish, and video), COMPUTER AND PHYSICAL SCIENCE (atmospheric sciences and meteorology, chemistry, computer science, earth science, geology, mathematics, physics, and quantitative methods), EDUCATION (art, bilingual/bicultural, early childhood, education of the emotionally handicapped, education of the mentally handicapped, elementary, English, foreign languages, mathematics, secondary, social studies, and special), ENGINEERING AND ENVIRONMENTAL DESIGN (architecture, biomedical engineering, chemical engineering, civil engineering, computer engineering, electrical/electronics engineering, landscape architecture/design, and mechanical engineering), HEALTH PROFESSIONS (biomedical science, physician's assistant, predentistry, and premedicine), SOCIAL SCIENCE (American studies, anthropology, area studies, Asian/Oriental studies, economics, ethnic studies, history, international studies, Latin American studies, philosophy, political science/government, prelaw, psychology, sociology, and urban studies). Engineering, architecture, and sciences are the strongest academically. Engineering, architecture, and psychology are the largest.

Required: Students must successfully complete 120 credits, with 32 to 48 in the major, and maintain a minimum GPA of 2.0. A core curriculum must be met, and students must complete a college proficiency exam and courses in basic writing, world humanities, world civilizations, computer literacy, world arts, and U.S. society.

Special: Cross-registration is permitted with other City University colleges. A 6-year urban legal studies degree and a 7-year biomedical education degree are available. Opportunities are provided for a co-op program in engineering, a B.A.-B.S. degree in biomedical engineering, internships, a Washington semester, work-study programs, a wide variety of accelerated degree programs, dual majors, credit by exam, credit for life experience, and study abroad in Germany, Austria, England, Morocco, and Romania. There are 2 national honor societies, including Phi Beta Kappa, a freshman honors program, and 100 departmental honors programs.

Faculty/Classroom: 62% of faculty are male; 38%, female. 69% teach undergraduates, 59% do research, and 41% do both. No introductory courses are taught by graduate students. The average class size in an introductory lecture is 28; in a laboratory, 15; and in a regular course, 19.

Admissions: The SAT scores for the 2005-2006 freshman class were: Verbal--63% below 500, 22% between 500 and 599, 11% between 600 and 700, and 4% above 700; Math--45% below 500, 31% between 500 and 599, 20% between 600 and 700, and 4% above 700. 57% of the current freshmen were in the top fifth of their class; 79% were in the top two fifths.

Requirements: A satisfactory score on the SAT is required. Graduation from an accredited secondary school is generally required, but a GED will be accepted. 14 academic credits should be presented, with a minimum grade average of 80. AP credits are accepted.

Procedure: Freshmen are admitted fall and spring. Entrance exams should be taken prior to registration. There is a rolling admissions plan. Applications should be filed by December 1 for fall entry and October 15 for spring entry. The fall 2005 application fee was $40.Notification is sent on a rolling basis. Applications are accepted on-line.

Transfer: 1070 transfer students enrolled in a recent year. Transfer applicants must have earned a minimum of 24 credit hours and maintained a GPA of 2.0. Selected programs have more competitive requirements. 32 of 120 credits required for the bachelor's degree must be completed at CCNY.

Visiting: There are regularly scheduled orientations for prospective students. There are guides for informal visits and visitors may sit in on classes. To schedule a visit, contact the Admissions Office at (212) 650-6476.

Financial Aid: In 2005-2006, 70% of all full-time freshmen and 75% of continuing full-time students received some form of financial aid. 64% of full-time freshmen and 73% of continuing full-time students received need-based aid. 65% of undergraduates work part time. The average financial indebtedness of a recent graduate was $18,408. The FAFSA and the state aid form are required. The priority date for freshman financial aid applications for fall entry is April 1. The deadline for filing freshman financial aid applications for fall entry is rolling.

International Students: There are 1089 international students enrolled. They must take the TOEFL or and also the CUNY Placement Exam.

Computers: Wireless access is available. All students may access the system. There are no time limits and no fees.

Graduates: From July 1, 2004 to June 30, 2005, 1010 bachelor's degrees were awarded. The most popular majors were psychology (13%), liberal arts (10%), and computer science (6%). In an average class, 4% graduate in 4 years or less, and 31% graduate in 6 years or less. 1100 companies recruited on campus in 2004-2005.

Admissions Contact: Acting Director of Admissions. A video is available. E-mail: *admissions@admin.ccny.cuny.edu* Web: *www.ccny.cuny.edu*

CITY UNIVERSITY OF NEW YORK/COLLEGE OF STATEN ISLAND
D-5

Staten Island, NY 10314	**(718) 982-2010; Fax: (718) 982-2500**
Full-time: 3170 men, 4123 women	**Faculty:** IIA, +$
Part-time: 1216 men, 2411 women	**Ph.D.s:** n/av
Graduate: 262 men, 901 women	**Student/Faculty:** n/av
Year: semesters, summer session	**Tuition:** $4328 ($8968)
Application Deadline: open	**Room & Board:** n/app
Freshman Class: 7366 applied, 7366 accepted, 2197 enrolled	
SAT Verbal/Math: 516/532*	**NONCOMPETITIVE**

The College of Staten Island, a public institution founded in 1955, offers associate, baccalaureate, and master degrees and Ph.D.s in conjunction with CUNY Graduate Center. In addition to regional accreditation, CSI has baccalaureate program accreditation with ABET, CAAHEP, CAPTE, CSAB, NAACLS, NCATE, and NLN. The library contains 229,345 volumes, 605,465 microform items, and 8123 audio/video tapes/CDs/DVDs, and subscribes to 15,000 periodicals including electronic. Computerized library services include the card catalog, interlibrary loans, database searching, Internet access, and laptop Internet portals. Special learning facilities include an art gallery, radio station, and an astrophysical observatory. The 204-acre campus is in an urban area in New York City's borough of Staten Island. There are 19 buildings.

Student Life: 99% of undergraduates are from New York. Others are from 8 states, 78 foreign countries, and Canada. 44% are white. The average age of freshmen is 22; all undergraduates, 25. 19% do not continue beyond their first year; 45% remain to graduate.

Housing: There are no residence halls. All students commute. Alcohol is not permitted. All students may keep cars.

Activities: There are no fraternities or sororities. There are 50 groups on campus, including art, chorus, computers, dance, drama, ethnic, film, gay, honors, international, jazz band, literary magazine, newspaper, photography, political, professional, radio and TV, religious, social, social service, and student government. Popular campus events include Kwanzaa, Spring Festival, and cultural dances.

Sports: There are 5 intercollegiate sports for men and 5 for women, and 7 intramural sports for men and 7 for women. Facilities include a 1200-seat gymnasium, a 25 meter indoor pool, a 2500 seat baseball stadium, softball, and soccer fields, with state of the art Field Turf playing surfaces, 6 outdoor and 6 bubbled tennis courts, outdoor recreational basketball courts, outdoor track and field facilities, 4 volleyball fields, 5 raquetball courts, 2 fitness centers and an ancillary gymnasium.

Disabled Students: 95% of the campus is accessible. Wheelchair ramps, elevators, special parking, specially equipped rest rooms, special class scheduling, lowered drinking fountains, lowered telephones, wheelchair accessible campus bus, assistance with registration, and special accommodations in the computer lab are available.

Services: Counseling and information services are available, as is tutoring in most subjects. There is a reader service for the blind, and remedial math, reading, and writing.

Campus Safety and Security: Measures include 24-hour foot and vehicle patrol, security escort services, shuttle buses, and informal discussions. There are pamphlets/posters/films, emergency telephones, lighted pathways/sidewalks, an emergency "blue light" system, radar-controlled traffic monitoring, bicycle patrol and an emergency broadcast system.

Programs of Study: CSI confers B.A., B.S. degrees. Associate, master's, and doctoral degrees are also awarded. Bachelor's degrees are awarded in BIOLOGICAL SCIENCE (biochemistry and biology/biological science), BUSINESS (accounting and business administration and management), COMMUNICATIONS AND THE ARTS (art, communications, dramatic arts, English, film arts, music, and Spanish), COMPUTER AND PHYSICAL SCIENCE (chemistry, computer science, information sciences and systems, mathematics, and physics), EDUCATION (education), ENGINEERING AND ENVIRONMENTAL DESIGN (engineering and applied science), HEALTH PROFESSIONS (medical technology, nursing, physical therapy, and physician's assistant), SOCIAL SCIENCE (African American studies, American studies, economics, history, international studies, philosophy, political science/government, psychology, social work, sociology, and women's studies). Business, Education, and Biological/Life Sciences are the largest.

Required: The curriculum varies for each degree, but phys ed and English are required for all majors as well as courses from each of three areas: science/technology/math, social sciences/history/philosophy, and humanities. A minimum 2.0 GPA and 120 credit hours are required to graduate.

Special: Cross-registration is available with any other CUNY college. Internships are available in most fields. Study abroad is possible in more than 30 countries, including Italy, Ecuador, England, China, Greece, Denmark, and Spain. There are student-designed majors and interdisciplinary majors, including computer science-math, sociology-anthropology, and science, letters, and society. Credit by exam, credit for life experience, dual majors, and nondegree study are available. There are 7 national honor societies, a freshman honors program, and 19 departmental honors programs.

Faculty/Classroom: 57% of faculty are male; 43%, female. No introductory courses are taught by graduate students.

Admissions: 100% of the 2005-2006 applicants were accepted. The SAT scores for the 2005-2006 freshman class were: Verbal--36% below 500, 50% between 500 and 599, 14% between 600 and 700, and 1% above 700; Math--29% below 500, 52% between 500 and 599, 16% between 600 and 700, and 2% above 700.

Requirements: The SAT is required. The ACT Optional Writing test is also required for some programs. All graduates of an accredited secondary school, or students holding a GED equivalent, are accepted for admission. Applicants must have an 80 grade average or graduate in the upper two thirds of their class to be eligible for admission to the 4-year programs. AP and CLEP credits are accepted.

Procedure: Freshmen are admitted fall and spring. Entrance exams should be taken before registration as a matriculated student. Application deadlines are open. Application fee is $65. Applications are accepted on-line.

Transfer: 693 transfer students enrolled in 2004-2005. Applicants must have a minimum 2.0 GPA and official transcripts. 30 of 120 credits required for the bachelor's degree must be completed at CSI.

Visiting: There are regularly scheduled orientations for prospective students, including campus tours, presentations, and lunch every Thursday at 3:30 P.M. There are guides for informal visits and visitors may sit in on classes. To schedule a visit, contact the Office of Recruitment/Admissions at (718) 982-2259 or *topple@mail.csi.cuny.edu.*

Financial Aid: 61% of full-time freshmen and 16% of continuing full-time students received need-based aid. Need-based scholarships or need-based grants averaged $5968; and need-based self-help aid (loans and jobs) averaged $1820. CSI is a member of CSS. The FAFSA, the state aid form, and TAP/APTS are required. The priority date for freshman financial aid applications for fall entry is March 31. The deadline for filing freshman financial aid applications for fall entry is November 30.

International Students: There are 205 international students enrolled. The school actively recruits these students. They must take the TOEFL and also take the SAT for the Bachelor's program and the college's own entrance exam for the Associate program.

Computers: Wireless access is available. Access points are available in essentially all academic areas and locations where students gather to do their work, including the library, computer center, and selected locations in the recreation center and outdoors. All students may access the system 8 A.M. to midnight Monday through Thursday, 8 A.M. to 11 P.M. Friday. There are no time limits. The fee is $75/semester. It is strongly recommended that all students have a personal computer.

Graduates: From July 1, 2004 to June 30, 2005, 1024 bachelor's degrees were awarded. The most popular majors were business (18%), education (10%), and accounting (9%). In an average class, 12% graduate in 4 years or less, 33% graduate in 5 years or less, and 41% graduate in 6 years or less. 83 companies recruited on campus in 2004-2005.

Admissions Contact: Mary Beth Riley, Director of Recruitment and Admissions. E-mail: *reilly@postbox.csi.cuny.edu* Web: *www.csi.cuny.edu*

CITY UNIVERSITY OF NEW YORK/HERBERT H. LEHMAN COLLEGE
D-5

Bronx, NY 10468

(718) 960-8700
(877) LEHMAN-1; Fax: (718) 960-8712

Full-time: 4200 men and women	**Faculty:** 296
Part-time: 3000 men and women	**Ph.D.s:** 89%
Graduate: 1860 men and women	**Student/Faculty:** 14 to 1
Year: semesters, summer session	**Tuition:** $4000 ($7000)
Application Deadline: see profile	**Room & Board:** n/app
Freshman Class: n/av	
SAT or ACT: recommended	**LESS COMPETITIVE**

Lehman College, established in 1968 as an independent unit of the City University of New York, is a commuter institution offering programs in the arts and humanities, natural and social sciences, nursing, and professional studies. There are 5 undergraduate and 4 graduate schools. Figures in the above capsule and in this profile are approximate. In addition to regional accreditation, Lehman has baccalaureate program accreditation with ADA, CSWE, NCATE, and NLN. The library contains 556,275 volumes, 620,660 microform items, and 1832 audio/video tapes/CDs/DVDs, and subscribes to 1513 periodicals including electronic. Computerized library services include the card catalog and database searching. Special learning facilities include a learning resource center, art gallery, radio station, TV station, and center for performing arts. The 37-acre campus is in an urban area in the Bronx, New York City. There are 15 buildings.

Student Life: 98% of undergraduate are from New York. Students are from 90 foreign countries. 74% are from public schools. 44% are Hispanic; 33% African American; 16% white. 54% are Catholic; 14% claim no religious affiliation. The average age of freshmen is 20; all undergraduates, 29.

Housing: There are no residence halls. All of students commute. Alcohol is not permitted. All students may keep cars.

Activities: There are no fraternities. There are 54 groups on campus, including art, band, chess, choir, chorus, computers, dance, drama, ethnic, film, honors, international, literary magazine, musical theater, newspaper, professional, radio and TV, religious, social, social service, student government, and yearbook.

Sports: There are 9 intercollegiate sports for men and 7 for women, and 9 intramural sports for men and 9 for women. Facilities include 3 gyms, an exercise room, a swimming pool, outdoor tennis courts, soccer and baseball fields, and a dance studio.

Disabled Students: 90% of the campus is accessible. Wheelchair ramps, elevators, special parking, specially equipped rest rooms, and special class scheduling are available.

Services: Counseling and information services are available, as is tutoring in every subject. There is a reader service for the blind, and remedial math, reading, and writing. A writing center offers individual and small group tutorials and workshops.

Campus Safety and Security: Measures include 24-hour foot and vehicle patrol, pamphlets/posters/films, emergency telephones, and lighted pathways/sidewalks.

Programs of Study: Lehman confers B.A., B.S., and B.F.A. degrees. Master's degrees are also awarded. Bachelor's degrees are awarded in BIOLOGICAL SCIENCE (biology/biological science), BUSINESS (accounting, business administration and management, and management science), COMMUNICATIONS AND THE ARTS (communications, comparative literature, dance, English, fine arts, French, German, Greek, Hebrew, Italian, languages, Latin, linguistics, music, Russian, Spanish, and speech/debate/rhetoric), COMPUTER AND PHYSICAL SCIENCE (chemistry, computer science, geology, mathematics, and physics), EDUCATION (art, business, early childhood, elementary, foreign languages, health, science, and secondary), HEALTH PROFESSIONS (health care administration, nursing, predentistry, premedicine, and speech pathology/audiology), SOCIAL SCIENCE (African American studies, American studies, anthropology, dietetics, economics, geography, history, international relations, philosophy, political science/government, prelaw, psychology, social work, and sociology). Economics and accounting, education and nursing are the largest.

Required: To graduate, students must successfully complete 120 credits, including 64 in the major, with a minimum GPA of 2.0. Requirements include 17 credits of core courses, 8 of English composition, 3 to 10 of a foreign language, and 3 of oral communication, as well as 22 credits distributed among courses in comparative culture, historical studies, social science, natural science, literature, art, and knowledge, self, and values. Students must demonstrate proficiency in basic reading, writing, and math skills before entering the upper division.

Special: Lehman offers internships, study abroad, work-study programs, dual and student-designed majors, nondegree study, pass/fail options, and credit for life experience. A 3-2 social work degree is offered

in conjunction with the senior college of CUNY, Bard, and Sarah Lawrence Colleges. Transfer programs in preengineering, prepharmacy, and preenvironmental science and forestry allow students to complete their degrees at specialized colleges of other New York universities. There are 21 national honor societies, including Phi Beta Kappa, a freshman honors program, and 60 departmental honors programs.

Faculty/Classroom: 53% of faculty are male; 47%, female. No introductory courses are taught by graduate students. The average class size in an introductory lecture is 25 and in a laboratory, 12.

Requirements: The SAT or ACT is recommended, with satisfactory SAT scores. Graduation from an accredited secondary school is required; a GED will be accepted. A grade average of 80% is required. AP and CLEP credits are accepted.

Procedure: Freshmen are admitted fall and spring. Entrance exams should be taken before registration. There are early decision, early admissions, and deferred admissions plans. There is a rolling admissions plan. Notification is sent on a rolling basis. Check with the school for current application deadlines and fee.

Transfer: Applicants must submit all educational records and show a minimum GPA of 2.0 in previous college work. Applicants with fewer than 13 college credits must also have a high school average of 80 in academic subjects. 38 of 120 credits required for the bachelor's degree must be completed at Lehman.

Visiting: There are regularly scheduled orientations for prospective students. There are guides for informal visits and visitors may sit in on classes. To schedule a visit, contact the Office of Student Recruitment at (718) 960-8713.

Financial Aid: The college's own financial statement is required. Check with the school for current deadlines.

International Students: They must take the TOEFL and also take the college's own test.

Computers: All students may access the system. There are no time limits and no fees.

Admissions Contact: Clarence A. Wilkes, Director of Admissions. A video is available. E-mail: *enroll@alpha.lehman.cuny.edu* Web: *www.lehman.cuny.edu*

CITY UNIVERSITY OF NEW YORK/HUNTER COLLEGE
D-5

New York, NY 10021

(212) 772-4490; (800) 772-4000

Full-time: 3200 men, 7300 women	**Faculty:** 552; IIA, ++$
Part-time: 1600 men, 3800 women	**Ph.D.s:** 85%
Graduate: 1100 men, 3800 women	**Student/Faculty:** 19 to 1
Year: semesters, summer session	**Tuition:** $5000 ($12,000)
Application Deadline: open	**Room & Board:** $3000
Freshman Class: n/av	
SAT : required	**COMPETITIVE+**

Hunter College, a comprehensive, nonprofit institution established in 1870, is part of the City University of New York and is both city- and state-supported. Primarily a commuter college, it emphasizes liberal arts in its undergraduate and graduate programs. Figures in the above capsule and in this profile are approximate. There are 3 undergraduate and 4 graduate schools. In addition to regional accreditation, Hunter has baccalaureate program accreditation with ADA, APTA, ASLA, CSWE, NCATE, and NLN. The library contains 775,000 volumes, 1,186,000 microform items, and 13,300 audio/video tapes/CDs/DVDs, and subscribes to 2477 periodicals including electronic. Computerized library services include the card catalog and database searching. Special learning facilities include a learning resource center, art gallery, radio station, a geography/geology lab, on-campus elementary and secondary schools, and a theater. The 3-acre campus is in an urban area in New York City. Including any residence halls, there are 6 buildings.

Student Life: 98% of undergraduates are from New York. Students are from 35 states, 149 foreign countries, and Canada. 87% are from public schools. 40% are white; 21% Hispanic; 17% African American; 15% Asian American. The average age of freshmen is 18; all undergraduates, 25. 20% do not continue beyond their first year.

Housing: 500 students can be accommodated in college housing, which includes coed dorms. On -campus housing is available on a first-come, first-served basis and is available on a lottery system for upperclassmen. 99% of students commute. No one may keep cars.

Activities: 2% of men belong to 1 local and 1 national fraternity; 1% of women belong to sororities. There are 130 groups on campus, including art, band, cheerleading, choir, chorale, chorus, drama, ethnic, film, gay, honors, international, jazz band, literary magazine, musical theater, newspaper, orchestra, political, professional, radio and TV, religious, social, social service, student government, symphony, and yearbook. Popular campus events include Major Day Fair.

Sports: There are 9 intercollegiate sports for men and 11 for women. Facilities include fencing, dance, and weight rooms, racquetball courts, a pool, outdoor tennis courts, and a gym.

Disabled Students: All of the campus is accessible. Wheelchair ramps, elevators, special parking, specially equipped rest rooms, special class scheduling, lowered drinking fountains, lowered telephones, special advisement office, and a student organization are available.

Services: Counseling and information services are available, as is tutoring in every subject. There is a reader service for the blind, and remedial math, reading, and writing. Review of graduate-level papers through the writing center and a math tutoring center are available.

Campus Safety and Security: Measures include self-defense education, shuttle buses, pamphlets/posters/films, and emergency telephones. There is a 24-hour foot patrol.

Programs of Study: Hunter confers B.A., B.S., B.F.A., B.Mus., and B.S.Ed degrees. Master's degrees are also awarded. Bachelor's degrees are awarded in BIOLOGICAL SCIENCE (biology/biological science and nutrition), BUSINESS (accounting), COMMUNICATIONS AND THE ARTS (Chinese, classics, comparative literature, creative writing, dance, dramatic arts, English, English literature, film arts, fine arts, French, German, Greek, Hebrew, Italian, languages, Latin, media arts, music, Russian, and Spanish), COMPUTER AND PHYSICAL SCIENCE (chemistry, computer science, mathematics, physics, and statistics), EDUCATION (art, early childhood, elementary, foreign languages, health, middle school, music, science, and secondary), ENGINEERING AND ENVIRONMENTAL DESIGN (energy management technology, environmental science, and preengineering), HEALTH PROFESSIONS (medical laboratory technology, nursing, physical therapy, predentistry, premedicine, and public health), SOCIAL SCIENCE (African American studies, anthropology, archeology, economics, geography, Hispanic American studies, history, international relations, Judaic studies, Latin American studies, philosophy, political science/government, prelaw, psychology, religion, social science, sociology, urban studies, and women's studies). Nursing is the strongest academically. Psychology is the largest.

Required: To graduate, students must complete 120 credits. The total number of hours in a major varies from 24 credits for a liberal arts major to 63 credits for a professional concentration; a minimum GPA of 2.0 is needed overall and in the major. Distribution requirements include 12 credits of social sciences, up to 12 credits of a foreign language, 10 or more of math and science, 9 of humanities and the arts, 6 of literature, and 3 of English composition.

Special: Special academic programs include internships, student-designed majors, work-study, study abroad in 20 countries, and dual majors. There is cross-registration with the Brooklyn School of Law, Marymount Manhattan College, and the YIVO Institute. Through the National Student Exchange Program, Hunter students can study for 1 or 2 semesters at any of 150 U.S. campuses. Accelerated degree programs are offered in anthropology, biopharmacology, economics, English, history, math, physics, sociology, and social research. Exchange programs in Paris or Puerto Rico are possible. There are 2 national honor societies, including Phi Beta Kappa, a freshman honors program, and 19 departmental honors programs.

Faculty/Classroom: The average class size in a laboratory is 19 and in a regular course, 30.

Admissions: 36% of recent applicants were accepted.

Requirements: The SAT is required. Admission is based on a combination of high school grade average, high school academic credits, including English and math, and SAT scores. AP and CLEP credits are accepted.

Procedure: Freshmen are admitted fall and spring. Entrance exams should be taken by October of their junior year. There are early admissions and deferred admissions plans. There ia a rolling admissions plan. Application deadlines are open. Check with the school for current application deadlines and fee. 4 early decision candidates were accepted for a recent class. Applications are accepted on-line.

Transfer: 2678 transfer students enrolled in a recent year. Applicants must have at least a 2.0 GPA. All students must complete 30 of the 120 credits required for a bachelor's degree at the college, including half of those needed for both the major and the minor.

Visiting: There are regularly scheduled orientations for prospective students, including presentations and tours every Friday. Please call (212) 772-4490 for details. There are guides for informal visits and visitors may sit in on classes. To schedule a visit, contact the Office of Admissions at *admissions@hunter.cuny.edu.*

Financial Aid: 25% of undergraduates work part time. The college's own financial statement is required. Check with the school for current deadlines.

International Students: There were 1238 international students enrolled in a recent year. They must take the TOEFL and also take the college's own test.

Computers: All students may access the system 24 hours a day. There are no time limits and no fees.

Graduates: In a recent year, 2052 bachelor's degrees were awarded. The most popular majors were psychology (15%), English (11%), and sociology (10%). In an average class, 36% graduate in 6 years or less.

Admissions Contact: Office of Admissions.
E-mail: *admissions@hunter.cuny.edu* Web: *www.hunter.cuny.edu*

CITY UNIVERSITY OF NEW YORK/JOHN JAY COLLEGE OF CRIMINAL JUSTICE   D-5

New York, NY 10019	(212) 237-8878; Fax: (212) 237-8777
Full-time: 3200 men, 5200 women	Faculty: 322; IIA, +$
Part-time: 1300 men, 1700 women	Ph.D.s: 85%
Graduate: 500 men, 1000 women	Student/Faculty: 26 to 1
Year: semesters, summer session	Tuition: $5000 ($9000)
Application Deadline: open	Room & Board: n/app
Freshman Class: n/av	
SAT : recommended	COMPETITIVE

John Jay College of Criminal Justice, established in 1964, is a liberal arts college and part of the City University of New York, with special emphasis in the fields of criminology, forensic science, correction administration, and other areas of the criminal justice system. Figures in the above and in this profile are approximate. The library contains 215,609 volumes, 198,832 microform items, and 3000 audio/video tapes/CDs/DVDs, and subscribes to 10,335 periodicals including electronic. Computerized library services include the card catalog, interlibrary loans, and database searching. Special learning facilities include a learning resource center, art gallery, radio station, TV station, a fire science lab, a security technology lab, and an explosion-proof forensic science/toxicology lab. The 1-acre campus is in an urban area in midtown Manhattan. There are 3 buildings.

Student Life: 95% of undergraduates are from New York. 80% are from public schools. 35% are Hispanic; 25% African American; 23% white. The average age of freshmen is 19; all undergraduates, 23. 26% do not continue beyond their first year; 40% remain to graduate.

Housing: There are no residence halls. All students commute. All students may keep cars.

Activities: There are no fraternities or sororities. There are 26 groups on campus, including art, cheerleading, chess, choir, chorale, chorus, computers, dance, drama, ethnic, film, gay, honors, international, literary magazine, musical theater, newspaper, photography, political, professional, radio and TV, religious, social, social service, student government, and yearbook.

Sports: There are 5 intercollegiate sports for men and 5 for women, and 15 intramural sports for men and 15 for women. Facilities include 2 gyms, 2 racquetball courts, a fitness center, a swimming pool, a strength training center, and a rooftop outdoor tennis court and jogging track.

Disabled Students: 99% of the campus is accessible. Wheelchair ramps, elevators, special parking, specially equipped rest rooms, special class scheduling, lowered drinking fountains, and lowered telephones are available.

Services: Counseling and information services are available, as is tutoring in most subjects, including English, math, and reading. There is a reader service for the blind, and remedial math, reading, and writing.

Campus Safety and Security: Measures include 24-hour foot and vehicle patrol, self-defense education, informal discussions, and pamphlets/posters/films. There are emergency telephones and lighted pathways/sidewalks.

Programs of Study: John Jay confers B.A. and B.S. degrees. Associate and master's degrees are also awarded. Bachelor's degrees are awarded in BIOLOGICAL SCIENCE (toxicology), COMPUTER AND PHYSICAL SCIENCE (information sciences and systems), SOCIAL SCIENCE (corrections, criminal justice, criminology, fire science, forensic studies, law enforcement and corrections, political science/government, public administration, and safety management). Forensic science is the strongest academically. Criminal justice, forensic psychology, and police science are the largest.

Required: Students are required to complete 128 credit hours, with 36 to 42 of these hours in the student's major, and must maintain a minimum GPA of 2.0. 1 credit in phys ed is required of all students.

Special: The school offers co-op programs, and cross-registration with other schools in the City University of New York. Internships are available with the Manhattan District Attorney, the Queens Supreme Court, the New York City Police Department, the United States Marshal's Service, and the New York City Corrections Department. Opportunities are provided for work-study programs, a Washington semester in public administration, interdisciplinary and student-designed majors, including forensic psychology, pass/fail options, nondegree study, credit for life experience, B.A.-M.A. programs in forensic psychology, criminal justice, and public administration, and study abroad in 5 countries, including England, Barbados, and Israel. There is 1 national honor society and a freshman honors program.

Faculty/Classroom: 54% of faculty are male; 46%, female. 94% teach undergraduates and 80% both teach and do research. Graduate students teach 5% of introductory courses. The average class size in an introductory lecture is 25; in a laboratory, 15; and in a regular course, 20.

Admissions: 72% of recent applicants were accepted.

Requirements: The SAT is recommended. In addition, applicants must have graduated from an accredited secondary school or a GED certificate will be accepted. Admission to associate degree programs requires satisfactory SAT score of, a high school average of 72, or a GED score of 300. Admission to baccalaureate degree programs requires satisfactory SAT scores or a high school average of 80, and 12 academic units, with 4 units in English and math and 1 unit in each discipline. John Jay requires applicants to be in the upper 50% of their class. A grade average of 80 is required. AP and CLEP credits are accepted.

Procedure: Freshmen are admitted fall and spring. There is an early admissions plan. And a rolling admissions plan. Application deadlines are open. Check with the school for current application deadlines and fee.

Transfer: 2031 transfer students enrolled in a recent year. Applicants must have completed 24 credits with a cumulative GPA of 2.0. If fewer than 24 credits are presented, a high school transcript should be presented. Half of the credits required for the major must be completed at John Jay.

Visiting: There are regularly scheduled orientations for prospective students, consisting of a freshman/transfer workshop. There are guides for informal visits and visitors may sit in on classes.

Financial Aid: In a recent year, 70% of all full-time students received some form of financial aid. 85% of full-time freshmen and 75% of continuing full-time students received need-based aid. The average freshman award was $4800. Need-based scholarships or need-based grants averaged $5100; need-based self-help aid (loans and jobs), averaged $2500; and other non-need-based awards and non-need-based scholarships averaged $500. 5% of undergraduates work part time. Average annual earnings from campus work are $1000. The average financial indebtedness of a recent graduate was $10,000. The FAFSA is required. Check with school for current deadlines.

International Students: There were 185 international students enrolled in a recent year. They must take the TOEFL.

Computers: All students may access the system. There are no time limits and no fees.

Graduates: In a recent year, 1347 bachelor's degrees were awarded. The most popular majors were criminal justice (30%), forensic psychology (26%), and legal studies (7%). In an average class, 2% graduate in 3 years or less, 8% graduate in 4 years or less, 21% graduate in 5 years or less, and 39% graduate in 6 years or less. 75 companies recruited on campus in a recent year. Of a recent graduating class, 30% were enrolled in graduate school within 6 months of graduation and 88% were employed.

Admissions Contact: Richard Saulnier, Dean of Admissions and Registration. E-mail: *rsaulnier@jjay.cuny.edu*

CITY UNIVERSITY OF NEW YORK/MEDGAR EVERS COLLEGE   D-5

Brooklyn, NY 11225-2201   **(718) 270-6021; Fax: (718) 270-6198**

Full-time: 790 men, 2344 women	Faculty: 150; IIB
Part-time: 434 men, 1644 women	Ph.D.s: 72%
Graduate: none	Student/Faculty: 21 to 1
Year: semesters, summer session	Tuition: $4250 ($360 per credit)
Application Deadline: open	Room & Board: n/app
Freshman Class: 4069 applied, 3918 accepted, 787 enrolled	
SAT Verbal/Math: 340/430*	NONCOMPETITIVE

Medgar Evers College, established in 1969 as part of the City University of New York, is an undergraduate commuter institution offering programs in business, education, natural sciences and math, nursing, and social sciences. There are 4 undergraduate schools. The library contains 118,000 volumes, 40,000 microform items, and 20,000 audio/video tapes/CDs/DVDs, and subscribes to 420 periodicals including electronic. Computerized library services include the card catalog, interlibrary loans, database searching, and Internet access. Special learning facilities include a learning resource center, radio station, TV station, and a TV lab. The 4-acre campus is in an urban area located in the Crown Heights section of Brooklyn. There are 2 buildings.

Student Life: 88% of undergraduates are from New York. Others are from 3 states and 37 foreign countries. 99% are from public schools. 88% are African American. 50% are Islamic 2%, Buddhist 1%, others 47%; 22% Catholic; 14% Protestant; 12% claim no religious affiliation. The average age of freshmen is 22; all undergraduates, 29. 46% do not continue beyond their first year; 28% remain to graduate.

Housing: There are no residence halls . All of students commute. No one may keep cars.

Activities: 2% of men belong to 2 national fraternities and 1 national sorority. There are 5 groups on campus, including choir, dance, ethnic, newspaper, political, radio and TV, religious, social service, and student government. Popular campus events include Kwaanza and Black Solidarity Day.

Sports: There are 4 intercollegiate sports for men and 3 for women, and 5 intramural sports for men and 3 for women. Facilities include a swimming pool, a gym, and an exercise room.

Disabled Students: All of the campus is accessible. Wheelchair ramps, elevators, special parking, specially equipped rest rooms, lowered drinking fountains, and lowered telephones are available.

Services: Counseling and information services are available, as is tutoring in every subject. There is a reader service for the blind, and remedial math, reading, and writing.

Campus Safety and Security: Measures include 24-hour foot and vehicle patrol.

Programs of Study: MEC confers B.A. and B.S. degrees. Associate degrees are also awarded. Bachelor's degrees are awarded in BIOLOGICAL SCIENCE (biology/biological science), BUSINESS (accounting, business administration and management, and management information systems), COMMUNICATIONS AND THE ARTS (English), COMPUTER AND PHYSICAL SCIENCE (computer science and mathematics), EDUCATION (elementary and special), ENGINEERING AND ENVIRONMENTAL DESIGN (environmental science), HEALTH PROFESSIONS (nursing), SOCIAL SCIENCE (liberal arts/general studies, psychology, and public administration). Nursing is the strongest academically. Education is the largest.

Required: To graduate, students must complete 120 credits (depending on program) with a minimum GPA of 2.0. The core curriculum requires a total of 42 credits in English, philosophy, speech, math, liberal arts, career planning, and phys ed. Students must demonstrate proficiency in basic reading, writing, and math skills prior to entering their junior year.

Special: MEC offers exchange programs with other CUNY institutions, evening and weekend classes, credit for military and prior learning experience, pass/fail options, and nondegree study. Study abroad in 3 countries is also possible. There is 1 national honor society, a freshman honors program, and 11 departmental honors programs.

Faculty/Classroom: 62% of faculty are male; 38%, female. All teach undergraduates and 8% both teach and do research. The average class size in an introductory lecture is 25; in a laboratory, 23; and in a regular course, 19.

Admissions: 96% of the 2005-2006 applicants were accepted. The SAT scores for the 2005-2006 freshman class were: Verbal--96% below 500, 3% between 500 and 599, and 1% between 600 and 700; Math--92% below 500, 7% between 500 and 599, and 1% between 600 and 700.

Requirements: The SAT is recommended. In addition, MEC accepts all applicants who either are graduates of an accredited secondary school or have earned a GED with a score of 225 or higher. Students must meet the university's health standards. CLEP credit is accepted.

Procedure: Freshmen are admitted fall and spring. There is a rolling admissions plan. Entrance exams should be taken during the last year of high school. Application deadlines are open. The fall 2005 application fee was $65.

Transfer: 413 transfer students enrolled in a recent year. Applicants must have a minimum GPA of 2.0. Those students with fewer than 24 college credits must also submit a high school transcript. 32 of 120 credits required for the bachelor's degree must be completed at MEC.

Financial Aid: In a recent year, 75% of all full-time students received some form of financial aid. 75% of all full-time students received need-based aid. The average freshman award was $3200. Need-based scholarships or need-based grants averaged $3863 ($7200 maximum); and need-based self-help aid (loans and jobs) averaged $1368 ($3700 maximum). 80% of undergraduates worked part time. Average annual earnings from campus work were $1500. The FAFSA and CUNY Student Aid Form (CSAF) are required. Check with the school for current application deadlines.

International Students: There are 174 international students enrolled. The school actively recruits these students. They must score satisfactorily on the written TOEFL and also take the ACT or the college's own entrance exam.

Computers: All students may access the system. There are no time limits. The fee is $75 per semester.

Graduates: In a recent year, 234 bachelor's degrees were awarded. The most popular majors were business (22%), psychology (14%), and nursing (10%). In an average class, 5% graduate in 4 years or less, 11% graduate in 5 years or less, and 19% graduate in 6 years or less. 15 companies recruited on campus in a recent year.

Admissions Contact: Warren Heusner, Director of Admissions. Web: *www.mec.cuny.edu*

CITY UNIVERSITY OF NEW YORK/NEW YORK CITY COLLEGE OF TECHNOLOGY D-5

Brooklyn, NY 11201-2983   (718) 260-5500; Fax: (718) 260-5504

Full-time: 3805 men, 3301 women	Faculty: 304
Part-time: 2466 men, 2871 women	Ph.D.s: n/av
Graduate: none	Student/Faculty: 23 to 1
Year: semesters, summer session	Tuition: $4269 ($8909)
Application Deadline: open	Room & Board: n/app
Freshman Class: n/av	
SAT: required for some programs	NONCOMPETITIVE

New York City College of Technology, founded in 1946 and made part of the City University of New York system in 1964, is an undergraduate commuter college offering day and evening programs in technology. There are 3 undergraduate schools. In addition to regional accreditation, City Tech has baccalaureate program accreditation with ABET, ADA, NCATE, and NLN. The library contains 183,104 volumes, 13,941 microform items, and 6155 audio/video tapes/CDs/DVDs, and subscribes to 23,235 periodicals including electronic. Computerized library services include the card catalog, interlibrary loans, and database searching. Special learning facilities include a learning resource center and art gallery. The campus is in an urban area. There are 9 buildings.

Student Life: 99% of students are from New York. Others are from 7 states and Canada. 41% are African American; 30% Hispanic; 17% Asian American; 12% white. The average age of freshmen is 19; all undergraduates, 25. 35% do not continue beyond their first year.

Housing: There are no residence halls. All students commute. Alcohol is not permitted. All students may keep cars.

Activities: There are no fraternities or sororities. There are 57 groups on campus, including computers, drama, ethnic, gay, honors, international, musical theater, newspaper, professional, religious, social, social service, and student government. Popular campus events include Latino Heritage, Women's History Month, and Multicultural Week.

Sports: There are 5 intercollegiate sports for men and 5 for women. Facilities include a gym, basketball courts, and a weight room.

Disabled Students: Wheelchair ramps, elevators, and specially equipped rest rooms are available.

Services: Counseling and information services are available, as is tutoring in most subjects. There is a reader service for the blind, and remedial math, reading, and writing.

Campus Safety and Security: Measures include 24-hour foot and vehicle patrol, security escort services, informal discussions, and pamphlets/posters/films. There are emergency telephones and lighted pathways/sidewalks.

Programs of Study: City Tech confers B.S., B.S. ED, and B.T. degrees. Associate degrees are also awarded. Bachelor's degrees are awarded in BUSINESS (hospitality management services and institutional management), COMMUNICATIONS AND THE ARTS (communications and telecommunications), COMPUTER AND PHYSICAL SCIENCE (applied mathematics and information sciences and systems), EDUCATION (technical and vocational), ENGINEERING AND ENVIRONMENTAL DESIGN (architectural technology, computer engineering, electromechanical technology, and graphic and printing production), HEALTH PROFESSIONS (health care administration), SOCIAL SCIENCE (human services, interdisciplinary studies, and paralegal studies). Computer system technology is the largest.

Required: Students must receive CUNY certification in reading, writing, and math and complete associate degree requirements. General education requirements include selections from African-American, Puerto Rican, and Latin American studies, sciences, humanities, and social sciences. A total of 120 credits is required for the B.S., B.S.Ed. or B.T. degree.

Special: B.A. and B.S. degrees are offered through CUNY's university-wide bachelor's exchange credits program. An alternative format program for adults offers credit for life/work experience. Nondegree study is possible. Internships are required in most majors. There is a college-wide honors program.

Faculty/Classroom: 55% of faculty are male; 45%, female. All teach undergraduates. The average class size in an introductory lecture is 27; in a laboratory, 14; and in a regular course, 24.

Requirements: The SAT is required for some programs. In addition, applicants should be graduates of an accredited secondary school or have the GED equivalent and meet the university's immunization requirements. A GPA of 2.0 is required. AP and CLEP credits are accepted.

Procedure: Freshmen are admitted fall, spring, and summer. Entrance exams should be taken during the spring or summer prior to fall entrance. Application deadlines are open.

Transfer: 848 transfer students enrolled in 2004-2005. Candidates must have a 2.0 GPA. They must meet CUNY requirements in reading, writing, and math. 34 of 120 credits required for the bachelor's degree must be completed at City Tech.

Visiting: To schedule a visit, contact Joseph Lento at (718) 260-5250 or Jlento@citytech.cuny.edu.

Financial Aid: In 2005-2006, 80% of all full-time freshmen and 65% of continuing full-time students received some form of financial aid. 60% of undergraduates work part time. The average financial indebtedness of the 2005 graduate was $9100. The FAFSA and CUNY Student Aid Form (CSAF) are required.

International Students: There are 285 international students enrolled. The school actively recruits these students. They must take the college's own entrance exam.

Computers: Wireless access is available. All students may access the system. There are no time limits and no fees.

Graduates: From July 1, 2004 to June 30, 2005, 528 bachelor's degrees were awarded. The most popular majors were computer information systems (36%), human services (14%), and hospitality management (13%). In an average class, 3% graduate in 4 years or less, 17% graduate in 5 years or less, and 31% graduate in 6 years or less.

Admissions Contact: Joseph Lento, Director of Admissions. A video is available. E-mail: jlento@citytech.cuny.edu
Web: www.citytech.cuny.edu

CITY UNIVERSITY OF NEW YORK/NEW YORK CITY TECHNICAL COLLEGE
(See City University of New York/New York City College of Technology)

CITY UNIVERSITY OF NEW YORK/QUEENS COLLEGE D-5

Flushing, NY 11367-1597   (718) 997-5608; Fax: (718) 997-5617

Full-time: 3490 men, 5326 women	Faculty: 464; IIA
Part-time: 1488 men, 2714 women	Ph.D.s: 95%
Graduate: 1324 men, 3296 women	Student/Faculty: 19 to 1
Year: semesters, summer session	Tuition: $4356 ($11,156)
Application Deadline: January 1	Room & Board: n/app
Freshman Class: 12,023 applied, 5217 accepted, 1509 enrolled	
SAT Verbal/Math: 509/545*	COMPETITIVE

Queens College, founded in 1937, is a public commuter institution within the City University of New York system. In addition to regional accreditation, Queens has baccalaureate program accreditation with ACS, ADA, APA, ASLHA, and NCATE. The 2 libraries contain 1,013,740 volumes, 937,606 microform items, and 104,250 audio/video tapes/CDs/DVDs, and subscribe to 2689 periodicals including electronic. Computerized library services include the card catalog, interlibrary loans, database searching, Internet access, and laptop Internet portals. Special learning facilities include a learning resource center, art gallery, radio station, a center for the performing arts, and a center for environmental teaching and research located on Long Island. The 76-acre campus is in an urban area 10 miles from Manhattan. There are 20 buildings.

Student Life: 99% of undergraduates are from New York. Others are from 15 states, 116 foreign countries, and Canada. 55% are from public schools. 48% are white; 18% Asian American; 17% Hispanic. 44% are Catholic; 23% Jewish; 11% Protestant; 11% Muslim, Hindu, Buddhist, Taoist. The average age of freshmen is 19; all undergraduates, 26. 14% do not continue beyond their first year; 53% remain to graduate.

Housing: There are no residence halls. All students commute. Alcohol is not permitted. All students may keep cars.

Activities: 1% of men belong to 3 national fraternities; 1% of women belong to 3 national sororities. There are 140 groups on campus, including band, choir, chorus, debate, drama, ethnic, gay, honors, international, jazz band, literary magazine, musical theater, newspaper, orchestra, political, radio and TV, religious, social, social service, student government, symphony, and yearbook. Popular campus events include fall and spring campus fests and a spring job fair.

Sports: There are 10 intercollegiate sports for men and 12 for women, and 10 intramural sports for men and 7 for women. Facilities include a gym complex, a swimming pool, dance studios, weight rooms, an outdoor quarter-mile track, soccer, lacrosse, and baseball fields, and 18 tennis courts.

Disabled Students: 90% of the campus is accessible. Wheelchair ramps, elevators, special parking, specially equipped rest rooms, special class scheduling, lowered drinking fountains, and lowered telephones are available.

Services: Counseling and information services are available, as is tutoring in most subjects. There is a reader service for the blind.

Campus Safety and Security: Measures include 24-hour foot and vehicle patrol, pamphlets/posters/films, emergency telephones, and lighted pathways/sidewalks.

Programs of Study: Queens confers B.A., B.S., B.B.A., B.F.A., and B.Mus. degrees. Master's degrees are also awarded. Bachelor's degrees are awarded in AGRICULTURE (environmental studies), BIOLOGICAL SCIENCE (biochemistry, biology/biological science, and environmental biology), BUSINESS (accounting, business administration and management, and labor studies), COMMUNICATIONS AND THE ARTS (art, art history and appreciation, communications, comparative literature, dance, dramatic arts, English, film arts, French, German, Greek, Greek (modern), Hebrew, Italian, Latin, linguistics, media arts, music, music performance, Russian, Spanish, and studio art), COMPUTER AND PHYSICAL SCIENCE (actuarial science, chemistry, computer science, geology, mathematics, and physics), EDUCATION (art, early childhood, elementary, home economics, music, and physical), ENGINEERING AND ENVIRONMENTAL DESIGN (environmental science), SOCIAL SCIENCE (African studies, American studies, anthropology, classical/ancient civilization, East Asian studies, economics, family/consumer studies, history, home economics, interdisciplinary studies, Judaic studies, Latin American studies, philosophy, political science/government, psychology, religion, sociology, urban studies, and women's studies). Music, English, and linguistics are the strongest academically. Accounting, computer science, and psychology are the largest.

Required: To graduate, students must complete 120 credits with a minimum GPA of 2.0. They must fulfill requirements in the major and 35 to 40 credits of a liberal arts core curriculum.

Special: Queens offers co-op programs, cross-registration with other CUNY campuses, internships in business, liberal arts, journalism, and social sciences, study abroad, work-study, accelerated degrees, dual and student-designed majors, pass/fail options, and nondegree study. There are preprofessional programs in engineering, law, and pre-health. The SEEK program provides financial and educational resources for underprepared freshmen. There are 15 national honor societies, including Phi Beta Kappa, and a freshman honors program.

Faculty/Classroom: 58% of faculty are male; 42%, female. 60% teach undergraduates, 20% do research, and 80% do both. Graduate students teach 1% of introductory courses. The average class size in an introductory lecture is 35; in a laboratory, 20; and in a regular course, 27.

Admissions: 43% of the 2005-2006 applicants were accepted. The SAT scores for the 2005-2006 freshman class were: Verbal--50% below 500, 37% between 500 and 599, 11% between 600 and 700, and 3% above 700; Math--33% below 500, 45% between 500 and 599, 18% between 600 and 700, and 3% above 700.

Requirements: The SAT is required. In addition, high school preparation should include 4 years each of English and social studies, 3 each of math and foreign language, and 2 of lab science. A GPA of 3.0 is required. AP and CLEP credits are accepted.

Procedure: Freshmen are admitted fall and spring. Entrance exams should be taken in the spring of the junior year or the fall of the senior year. There is an early admissions plan and a rolling admissions plan. Applications should be filed by January 1 for fall entry and October 15 for spring entry, along with a $65 fee. Notification of regular decision is sent February 1.

Transfer: 1812 transfer students enrolled in 2004-2005. First-year transfers should have a minimum GPA of 2.5 and must meet freshman criteria; most others need a 2.25 for consideration. 45 of 120 credits required for the bachelor's degree must be completed at Queens.

Visiting: There are regularly scheduled orientations for prospective students, including information sessions and a campus tour. Visitors may sit in on classes. To schedule a visit, contact the Admissions Office at (718) 997-5614.

Financial Aid: In 2005-2006, 80% of all full-time freshmen and 55% of continuing full-time students received some form of financial aid. 76% of full-time freshmen and 44% of continuing full-time students received need-based aid. The average freshman award was $6500. Need-based scholarships or need-based grants averaged $6500 ($9000 maximum); and need-based self-help aid (loans and jobs) averaged $1900 ($4125 maximum). 3% of undergraduates work part time. Average annual earnings from campus work are $1900. The average financial indebtedness of the 2005 graduate was $12,000. The FAFSA and the state aid form are required. The priority date for freshman financial aid applications for fall entry is March 15. The deadline for filing freshman financial aid applications for fall entry is May 1.

International Students: There are 983 international students enrolled. Satisfactory scores are required on the written TOEFL and the SAT or the CUNY Skills Assessment Test. Honors students should take SAT: Subject tests.

Computers: Wireless access is available. Access to computers and the Internet is available in the library and computer labs across the campus. All students may access the system during day and evening hours, 7 days a week. There are no time limits. The fee is $75 per semester.

Graduates: From July 1, 2004 to June 30, 2005, 2151 bachelor's degrees were awarded. The most popular majors were accounting (17%), psychology (12%), and sociology (8%). In an average class, 3% graduate in 3 years or less, 23% graduate in 4 years or less, 45% graduate in 5 years or less, and 53% graduate in 6 years or less. 100 companies recruited on campus in 2004-2005. Of the 2004 graduating class, 21% were enrolled in graduate school within 6 months of graduation and 70% were employed.

Admissions Contact: Dr. Vincent J. Angrisani, Executive Director of Admissions, Marketing, and Sholarship. A video is available. Web: *www.qc.edu*

CITY UNIVERSITY OF NEW YORK/YORK COLLEGE D-5

Jamaica, NY 11451

(718) 262-2165; Fax: (718) 262-2601

Full-time: 1300 men, 2579 women	**Faculty:** 180; IIB
Part-time: 568 men, 1453 women	**Ph.Ds:** 71%
Graduate: none	**Student/Faculty:** 22 to 1
Year: semesters, summer session	**Tuition:** $4242 ($8882)
Application Deadline: open	**Room & Board:** n/app
Freshman Class: n/av	
SAT or ACT: required	**NONCOMPETITIVE**

York College, established in 1966, is a public liberal arts commuter college and part of the City University of New York system. In addition to regional accreditation, York has baccalaureate program accreditation with ACOTE, CAHEA, CSWE, and NLN. The library contains 180,000 volumes, 154,000 microform items, and 4613 audio/video tapes/CDs/DVDs, and subscribes to 1100 periodicals including electronic. Computerized library services include the card catalog, interlibrary loans, and database searching. Special learning facilities include a learning resource center, art gallery, TV station, Cardio-pneumo simulator, and theater. The 50-acre campus is in an urban area in New York City. There are 5 buildings.

Student Life: 96% of undergraduates are from New York. Others are from 4 states, 82 foreign countries, and Canada. 48% are African American; 15% Hispanic; 10% Asian American. The average age of freshmen is 20; all undergraduates, 24. 31% do not continue beyond their first year; 69% remain to graduate.

Housing: There are no residence halls . All of students commute. Alcohol is not permitted. All students may keep cars.

Activities: There are no fraternities or sororities. There are 50 groups on campus, including art, cheerleading, choir, chorus, computers, drama, ethnic, honors, international, jazz band, literary magazine, musical theater, newspaper, political, professional, radio and TV, religious, social, social service, and student government. Popular campus events include club fairs, talent shows, and ethnic fairs.

Sports: There are 9 intercollegiate sports for men and 10 for women, and 9 intramural sports for men and 10 for women. Facilities include a 1200-seat gym, a 25-meter, 6-lane swimming pool with diving boards, a health risk appraisal center, an exercise therapy room, outdoor track; tennis courts, soccer field, indoor walking/jogging track, weight room, aerobics room, handball courts, and multipurpose room.

Disabled Students: All of the campus is accessible. Wheelchair ramps, elevators, special parking, specially equipped rest rooms, special class scheduling, lowered drinking fountains, and lowered telephones are available.

Services: Counseling and information services are available, as is tutoring in every subject. There is a reader service for the blind, and remedial math, reading, and writing.

Campus Safety and Security: Measures include 24-hour foot and vehicle patrol, security escort services, informal discussions, and pamphlets/posters/films. There are emergency telephones and lighted pathways/sidewalks.

Programs of Study: York confers B.A. and B.S. degrees. Bachelor's degrees are awarded in BIOLOGICAL SCIENCE (biology/biological science and biotechnology), BUSINESS (accounting, business administration and management, and marketing/retailing/merchandising), COMMUNICATIONS AND THE ARTS (art history and appreciation, dramatic arts, English, French, music, Spanish, speech/debate/rhetoric, and studio art), COMPUTER AND PHYSICAL SCIENCE (chemistry, geology, information sciences and systems, mathematics, and physics), EDUCATION (physical), HEALTH PROFESSIONS (community health work, environmental health science, exercise science, medical laboratory technology, nursing, and occupational therapy), SOCIAL SCIENCE (African American studies, anthropology, economics, gerontology, history, liberal arts/general studies, philosophy, political science/government, psychology, social work, and sociology). Business, psychology, and social work are the largest.

Required: All students are required to complete 120 credits and maintain a minimum GPA of 2.0. The core curriculum of 61 credits includes courses in humanities, behavioral science, cultural diversity, math, natural science, and junior level writing. Students must also take a 2-credit phys ed course and complete 2 semesters of English.

Special: Cross-registration with all schools in the City University of New York system is permitted. Also provided are work-study programs, credit by exam, dual majors in physics and math, nondegree study, pass/fail options, credit for life experience, internships, cooperative programs with other schools, and student-designed majors. There are 6 national honor societies and 4 departmental honors programs.

Faculty/Classroom: 56% of faculty are male; 44%, female. 93% teach undergraduates and 7% both teach and do research.

Requirements: A satisfactory score on the SAT or ACT is required. Applicants must have graduated from an accredited secondary school or present a GED certificate. An audition is recommended for music majors. AP and CLEP credits are accepted.

Procedure: Freshmen are admitted fall and spring. There are early admissions and deferred admissions plans. There is a rolling admissions plan. Application deadlines are open.

Transfer: 304 transfer students enrolled in 2004-2005. Students must present a minimum GPA of 2.0. 40 of 120 credits required for the bachelor's degree must be completed at York.

Visiting: There are regularly scheduled orientations for prospective students, including workshops and group meetings with faculty and staff on matriculation, registration, financial aid, and degree requirements, and advisement for classes. Visitors may sit in on classes. To schedule a visit, contact the Director of Admissions or Admissions counselor.

Financial Aid: The FAFSA and the college's own financial statement are required. Check with the school for current deadlines.

International Students: They must score satisfactorily on the written TOEFL and also take the SAT or ACT and a Math placement test if student comes from non-English-speaking country.

Computers: All students may access the system during hours of operation of college facilities. There are no time limits and no fees.

Graduates: From July 1, 2004 to June 30, 2005, 823 bachelor's degrees were awarded. The most popular majors were business administration (16%), psychology (13%), and information systems (11%). In an average class, 1% graduate in 3 years or less, 4% graduate in 4 years or less, 15% graduate in 5 years or less, and 24% graduate in 6 years or less. 100 companies recruited on campus in 2004-2005.

Admissions Contact: Diane Warmsley, Director of Admissions and Enrollment. A video is available. E-mail: *admissions@york.cuny.edu* Web: *http://www.york.cuny.edu*

CLARKSON UNIVERSITY D-2
Potsdam, NY 13699

(315) 268-6479
(800) 527-6577; Fax: (315) 268-7647

Full-time: 1988 men, 645 women	Faculty: 153; I, -$
Part-time: 7 men, 8 women	Ph.D.s: 93%
Graduate: 297 men, 100 women	Student/Faculty: 17 to 1
Year: semesters, summer session	Tuition: $25,586
Application Deadline: March 1	Room & Board: $9344
Freshman Class: 2405 applied, 2073 accepted, 630 enrolled	
SAT Verbal/Math: 570/620*	**VERY COMPETITIVE**

Clarkson University, founded in 1896, is a private nationally ranked research institute offering undergraduate programs in engineering, business, science, and the humanities, and graduate programs in engineering, business, science, and health sciences. There are 3 undergraduate and 4 graduate schools. In addition to regional accreditation, Clarkson has baccalaureate program accreditation with AACSB, ABET, and APTA. The 2 libraries contain 298,044 volumes, 271,541 microform items, and 2081 audio/video tapes/CDs/DVDs, and subscribe to 2124 periodicals including electronic. Computerized library services include the card catalog, interlibrary loans, database searching, Internet access, and laptop Internet portals. Special learning facilities include a learning resource center, radio station, and TV station. The 640-acre campus is in a rural area 70 miles north of Watertown and 75 miles south of Ottawa, Canada. Including any residence halls, there are 43 buildings.

Student Life: 73% of undergraduates are from New York. Others are from 32 states, 21 foreign countries, and Canada. 81% are from public schools. 88% are white. 63% claim no religious affiliation; 22% Catholic; 10% Buddhist, Hindu, Muslim, Mormon, Orthodox, and others. The average age of freshmen is 18; all undergraduates, 20. 13% do not continue beyond their first year; 74% remain to graduate.

Housing: 2179 students can be accommodated in college housing, which includes single-sex and coed dorms, on-campus apartments, married-student housing, and fraternity houses. In addition, there are special-interest houses. On-campus housing is guaranteed for all 4 years. 83% of students live on campus; of those, 90% remain on campus on weekends. All students may keep cars.

Activities: 15% of men belong to 3 local and 7 national fraternities; 13% of women belong to 3 national sororities. There are 57 groups on campus, including cheerleading, chess, chorus, computers, drama, ethnic, honors, international, jazz band, literary magazine, musical theater, newspaper, orchestra, pep band, photography, professional, radio and TV, religious, social, social service, student government, and yearbook. Popular campus events include Culture Night, Greek Week, and Senior Week.

Sports: There are 10 intercollegiate sports for men and 8 for women. Facilities include a 3000-seat multipurpose ice arena, a fitness center, a gym, a swimming pool, a weight room, a field house, and racquetball, paddleball, and tennis courts.

Disabled Students: 85% of the campus is accessible. Wheelchair ramps, elevators, special parking, specially equipped rest rooms, special class scheduling, lowered drinking fountains, lowered telephones, and special housing are available.

Services: Counseling and information services are available, as is tutoring in most subjects, including all freshman- and sophomore-level courses and some junior-level courses.

Campus Safety and Security: Measures include 24-hour foot and vehicle patrol, security escort services, shuttle buses, and informal discussions. There are pamphlets/posters/films, emergency telephones, and lighted pathways/sidewalks.

Programs of Study: Clarkson confers B.S. and B.P.S. degrees. Master's and doctoral degrees are also awarded. Bachelor's degrees are awarded in BIOLOGICAL SCIENCE (biology/biological science and molecular biology), BUSINESS (accounting, business administration and management, business systems analysis, electronic business, management information systems, and marketing/retailing/merchandising), COMMUNICATIONS AND THE ARTS (technical and business writing), COMPUTER AND PHYSICAL SCIENCE (applied mathematics, chemistry, computer science, digital arts/technology, information sciences and systems, mathematics, physics, science, and software engineering), ENGINEERING AND ENVIRONMENTAL DESIGN (aeronautical engineering, chemical engineering, civil engineering, computer engineering, electrical/electronics engineering, engineering management, environmental engineering, environmental science, and mechanical engineering), HEALTH PROFESSIONS (industrial hygiene), SOCIAL SCIENCE (history, humanities, interdisciplinary studies, political science/government, psychology, social science, and sociology). Engineering, business, and interdisciplinary English and management are the strongest academically and are the largest.

Required: Students must complete at least 120 credit hours, with 30 in the major and a minimum GPA of 2.0 to graduate. Students must meet a foundation curriculum requirement. All students entering as first-year students must take the First-Year Seminar or an equivalent course that may be offered by the University.

Special: Clarkson offers cross-registration with the Associate Colleges of the St. Lawrence Valley: St. Lawrence University and Potsdam and Canton Colleges. Co-op programs in all academic areas, dual majors in business and liberal arts, interdisciplinary majors, internships, accelerated degree programs, student-designed majors in the B.P.S. degree program, and study abroad in England, Italy, New Zealand, Sweden, Germany, Australia, France, Austria, China, Korea, Mexico, Slovenia, Croatia, Spain, Hong Kong, and Canada are possible. There are 3-2 engineering programs with many institutions in the Northeast; students who participate take the first 3 years of the prescribed program at a 4-year liberal arts institution and then transfer with junior standing into one of Clarkson's 4-year engineering curricula. There are interdisciplinary programs in biomolecular science, environmental science and policy, environmental and occupational health, and software engineering. There are 9 national honor societies, including Phi Beta Kappa, a freshman honors program, and 12 departmental honors programs.

Faculty/Classroom: 77% of faculty are male; 23%, female. 90% teach undergraduates, 69% do research, and 69% do both. No introductory courses are taught by graduate students. The average class size in an introductory lecture is 38; in a laboratory, 27; and in a regular course, 37.

Admissions: 86% of the 2005-2006 applicants were accepted. The SAT scores for the 2005-2006 freshman class were: Verbal--15% below 500, 47% between 500 and 599, 32% between 600 and 700, and 6% above 700; Math--4% below 500, 32% between 500 and 599, 49% between 600 and 700, and 15% above 700. 62% of the current freshmen were in the top fifth of their class; 90% were in the top two fifths. 21 freshmen graduated first in their class.

Requirements: The SAT or ACT is required. SAT Subject tests are also recommended. Applicants must have graduated from an accredited secondary school or have the GED. A campus visit and interview are also recommended. AP and CLEP credits are accepted. Important factors in the admissions decision are advanced placement or honor courses, recommendations by school officials, and extracurricular activities record.

Procedure: Freshmen are admitted fall and spring. Entrance exams should be taken by November. There are early decision and deferred admissions plans. Early decision applications should be filed by December 1; regular applications, by March 1 for fall entry and December 1 for spring entry, along with a $50 fee. Notification of early decision is sent January 1; regular decision, February. 139 early decision candidates were accepted for the 2005-2006 class. 16 applicants were on the 2005 waiting list; 1 was admitted. Applications are accepted on-line.

Transfer: 78 transfer students enrolled in 2004-2005. Transfer students should submit transcripts from all colleges attended and 2 letters of recommendation, including 1 from an academic professsor or instructor. An associate degree will be considered, and an interview is recommended. 30 of 120 credits required for the bachelor's degree must be completed at Clarkson.

Visiting: There are regularly scheduled orientations for prospective students, including meetings with administration and faculty. There are guides for informal visits and visitors may sit in on classes and stay overnight. To schedule a visit, contact the Admissions Office.

Financial Aid: In 2005-2006, 95% of all full-time freshmen and 92% of continuing full-time students received some form of financial aid. 86% of full-time freshmen and 84% of continuing full-time students received need-based aid. The average freshman award was $20,539. Need-based scholarships or need-based grants averaged $8154 ($23,518 maximum); need-based self-help aid (loans and jobs) averaged $9838 ($11,825 maximum); non-need-based athletic scholarships averaged $33,503 ($35,837 maximum); other non-need-based awards and non-need-based scholarships averaged $8409 ($12,000 maximum); and state awards averaged $2451 ($5000 maximum). 35% of undergraduates work part time. Average annual earnings from campus work are $900. The average financial indebtedness of the 2005 graduate was $19,942. The FAFSA is required. The deadline for filing freshman financial aid applications for fall entry is February 15.

International Students: There are 71 international students enrolled. They must score satisfactorily on the written TOEFL or on the electronic version and also take SAT Reasoning test if first year students.

Computers: Wireless access is available. All students may access the system. There are no time limits and no fees. It is strongly recommended that all students have a personal computer. Students are allowed to bring their own computers.

Graduates: From July 1, 2004 to June 30, 2005, 637 bachelor's degrees were awarded. The most popular majors were engineering (47%), business (19%), and engineering and management (12%). In an average class, 61% graduate in 4 years or less, 73% graduate in 5 years or less, and 74% graduate in 6 years or less. 88 companies recruited on campus in 2004-2005. Of the 2004 graduating class, 24% were enrolled in graduate school within 6 months of graduation and 67% were employed.

Admissions Contact: Brian T. Grant, Director of Admission. E-mail: *grantbt@clarkson.edu* Web: *http://www.clarkson.edu*

COLGATE UNIVERSITY C-3

Hamilton, NY 13346	**(315) 228-7401; Fax: (315) 228-7544**
Full-time: 1345 men, 1402 women	**Faculty:** 245; IIB, ++$
Part-time: 14 men, 10 women	**Ph.D.s:** 97%
Graduate: 3 men, 5 women	**Student/Faculty:** 11 to 1
Year: semesters	**Tuition:** $33,105
Application Deadline: January 15	**Room & Board:** $8065
Freshman Class: 8008 applied, 2168 accepted, 729 enrolled	
SAT Verbal/Math: 666/681*	**ACT:** 31 **MOST COMPETITIVE**

Colgate University, founded in 1819, is a private liberal arts institution. The 2 libraries contain 1,272,089 volumes, 684,687 microform items, and 35,987 audio/video tapes/CDs/DVDs, and subscribe to 3229 periodicals including electronic. Computerized library services include the card catalog, interlibrary loans, database searching, and Internet access. Special learning facilities include an art gallery, radio station, TV station, an anthropology museum, and an observatory. The 515-acre campus is in a rural area 45 miles southeast of Syracuse and 35 miles southwest of Utica. Including any residence halls, there are 87 buildings.

Student Life: 69% of undergraduates are from out of state, mostly the Northeast. Students are from 44 states, 29 foreign countries, and Canada. 71% are from public schools. 76% are white. The average age of freshmen is 19; all undergraduates, 20. 4% do not continue beyond their first year; 91% remain to graduate.

Housing: 2400 students can be accommodated in college housing, which includes coed dorms, on-campus apartments, fraternity houses, and sorority houses. In addition, there are language houses and special-interest houses. 89% of students live on campus; of those, 96% remain on campus on weekends. All students may keep cars.

Activities: 33% of men belong to 6 national fraternities; 29% of women belong to 4 national sororities. There are 125 groups on campus, including art, band, cheerleading, chess, choir, chorale, chorus, computers, dance, debate, drama, ethnic, film, forensics, gay, honors, international, jazz band, literary magazine, musical theater, newspaper, orchestra, pep band, photography, political, professional, radio and TV, religious, social, social service, student government, symphony, and yearbook. Popular campus events include Family Weekend, Colgate versus Cornell men's hockey game, and Winter Olympics.

Sports: There are 11 intercollegiate sports for men and 12 for women, and 19 intramural sports for men and 19 for women. Facilities include numerous athletic fields, a softball diamond, an outdoor artificial surface field, a football stadium, an athletic center, a 3000-seat gym, a golf course, a field house, a ski center, a 50-meter pool, a bowling center, a hockey rink, a 9000-square-foot fitness center, running trails, a trap range, and courts for basketball, tennis, squash, handball, and racquetball.

Disabled Students: 20% of the campus is accessible. Wheelchair ramps, elevators, special parking, specially equipped rest rooms, special class scheduling, and lowered drinking fountains are available.

Services: Counseling and information services are available, as is tutoring in every subject. There is a reader service for the blind and remedial writing. There is a note-taker service for students with learning and sensory disabilities, and a writing center.

Campus Safety and Security: Measures include 24-hour foot and vehicle patrol, self-defense education, security escort services, and shuttle buses. There are informal discussions, pamphlets/posters/films, emergency telephones, and lighted pathways/sidewalks.

Programs of Study: Colgate confers the B.A. degree. Master's degrees are also awarded. Bachelor's degrees are awarded in BIOLOGICAL SCI-

ENCE (biochemistry, biology/biological science, molecular biology, and neurosciences), COMMUNICATIONS AND THE ARTS (art history and appreciation, Chinese, classics, dramatic arts, English, French, German, Greek, Japanese, Latin, music, Russian, Spanish, and studio art), COMPUTER AND PHYSICAL SCIENCE (astronomy, astrophysics, chemistry, computer science, geology, geophysics and seismology, mathematics, natural sciences, physical sciences, and physics), EDUCATION (education), ENGINEERING AND ENVIRONMENTAL DESIGN (environmental science), SOCIAL SCIENCE (African studies, Asian/Oriental studies, economics, geography, history, humanities, international relations, Latin American studies, Native American studies, peace studies, philosophy, political science/government, psychology, religion, Russian and Slavic studies, social science, sociology, and women's studies). English, economics, and history are the largest.

Required: To graduate, students must complete a First-Year Seminar course and the core curriculum, including 4 general education courses and 2 courses each in the natural sciences, social sciences, and humanities. A total of 32 courses is required, with 8 to 12 courses in the major. Study in a foreign language, phys ed, and a swimming test are also required. Students need a minimum 2.0 GPA.

Special: Colgate offers various internships, semester and summer research opportunities with faculty, work-study, study abroad in 14 countries, accelerated degree programs, dual majors, and student-designed majors. A 3-2 engineering degree with Columbia and Washington Universities and Rensselaer Polytechnic Institute, an early assurance medical program with George Washington University, credit by exam, and pass/fail options are available. There are 12 national honor societies, including Phi Beta Kappa, and 10 departmental honors programs.

Faculty/Classroom: 58% of faculty are male; 42%, female. All both teach and do research. No introductory courses are taught by graduate students. The average class size in an introductory lecture is 21; in a laboratory, 17; and in a regular course, 18.

Admissions: 27% of the 2005-2006 applicants were accepted. The SAT scores for the 2005-2006 freshman class were: Verbal--2% below 500, 12% between 500 and 599, 49% between 600 and 700, and 37% above 700; Math--10% between 500 and 599, 46% between 600 and 700, and 44% above 700. The ACT scores were 3% between 21 and 23, 4% between 24 and 26, 10% between 27 and 28, and 83% above 28. 86% of the current freshmen were in the top fifth of their class; 97% were in the top two fifths. 29 freshmen graduated first in their class in a recent year.

Requirements: The SAT or ACT is required. In addition, 2 teacher recommendations and a counselor's report are required. An interview, though not evaluated, is recommended. Students should present 16 or more Carnegie credits, based on 4 years each of English and math and at least 3 of lab science, social science, and a foreign language, with electives in the arts. AP and CLEP credits are accepted. Important factors in the admissions decision are advanced placement or honor courses, recommendations by school officials, and leadership record.

Procedure: Freshmen are admitted in the fall. Entrance exams should be taken in time for score reports to reach the university by January 15. There are early decision and deferred admissions plans. Early decision applications should be filed by November 15; regular applications, by January 15 for fall entry, along with a $55 fee. Notification of early decision is sent December 15; regular decision, April 1. 312 early decision candidates were accepted for the 2005-2006 class. 503 applicants were on the 2005 waiting list; 34 were admitted. Applications are accepted on-line.

Transfer: 17 transfer students enrolled in 2004-2005. Either the SAT or the ACT is required, as well as college and high school transcripts, a dean's report, and faculty recommendations. 16 of 32 courses required for the bachelor's degree must be completed at Colgate.

Visiting: There are regularly scheduled orientations for prospective students, including nonevaluative interviews, group information sessions, and student-led tours. There are guides for informal visits and visitors may sit in on classes and stay overnight. To schedule a visit, contact the Office of Admission.

Financial Aid: In 2005-2006, 35% of all full-time freshmen and 47% of continuing full-time students received some form of financial aid, including need-based aid. The average freshman award was $31,901. Need-based scholarships or need-based grants averaged $27,326; need-based self-help aid (loans and jobs) averaged $3924; and non-need-based athletic scholarships averaged $29,825. 50% of undergraduates work part time. Average annual earnings from campus work are $890. The average financial indebtedness of the 2005 graduate was $13,452. Colgate is a member of CSS. The CSS/Profile or FAFSA is required. International students need the Financial Aid Application and the International Student Certification of Finances. The deadline for filing freshman financial aid applications for fall entry is January 15.

International Students: There are 142 international students enrolled. The school actively recruits these students. They must achieve a satisfactory score on the TOEFL and also take the SAT or the ACT.

Computers: Wireless access is available. A general appropriate use policy exist for students using the university's network. Colgate provides 53 computer labs for students with an average of 16 computers in each lab.

All classrooms allow for both wired and wireless connectivity to the Internet. All students may access the system. There are no time limits and no fees. It is strongly recommended that all students have a personal computer.

Graduates: From July 1, 2004 to June 30, 2005, 690 bachelor's degrees were awarded. The most popular majors were economics (12%), English (10%), and history (10%). In an average class, 1% graduate in 3 years or less, 88% graduate in 4 years or less, 90% graduate in 5 years or less, and 91% graduate in 6 years or less. 200 companies recruited on campus in 2004-2005. Of the 2004 graduating class, 15% were enrolled in graduate school within 6 months of graduation and 81% were employed.

Admissions Contact: Gary L. Ross, Dean of Admission.
E-mail: *admission@mail.colgate.edu* Web: *www.colgate.edu*

COLLEGE OF AERONAUTICS
(See Vaughn College of Aeronautics and Technology)

COLLEGE OF MOUNT SAINT VINCENT   D-5
Riverdale, NY 10471

	(718) 405-3267
	(800) 665-CMSV; Fax: (718) 549-7945
Full-time: 250 men, 900 women	**Faculty:** 71
Part-time: 25 men, 150 women	**Ph.D.s:** 87%
Graduate: 100 men, 300 women	**Student/Faculty:** 16 to 1
Year: semesters, summer session	**Tuition:** $20,000
Application Deadline: see profile	**Room & Board:** $8000
Freshman Class: n/av	
SAT or ACT: required	**COMPETITIVE**

The College of Mount Saint Vincent, founded as an academy in 1847 and chartered as a college in 1911, is a private liberal arts institution in the Catholic tradition. Figures in the above capsule and in this profile are approximate. In addition to regional accreditation, The Mount has baccalaureate program accreditation with ACBSP and NLN. The library contains 129,000 volumes, 7000 microform items, and 6500 audio/video tapes/CDs/DVDs, and subscribes to 234 periodicals including electronic. Computerized library services include the card catalog, interlibrary loans, database searching, and Internet access. Special learning facilities include a learning resource center, radio station, and TV station. The 70-acre campus is in an urban area 11 miles north of midtown Manhattan. Including any residence halls, there are 11 buildings.

Student Life: 89% of undergraduates are from New York. Others are from 19 states and 4 foreign countries. 46% are from public schools. 38% are white; 32% Hispanic; 14% African American; 10% Asian American. Most are Catholic. The average age of freshmen is 18; all undergraduates, 22. 25% do not continue beyond their first year; 62% remain to graduate.

Housing: 540 students can be accommodated in college housing, which includes coed dorms. On-campus housing is guaranteed for all 4 years. 53% of students commute. All students may keep cars.

Activities: There are no fraternities or sororities. There are 30 groups on campus, including art, cheerleading, chess, choir, chorus, computers, dance, debate, drama, ethnic, film, gay, honors, international, literary magazine, musical theater, newspaper, photography, professional, radio and TV, religious, social, social service, student government, and yearbook. Popular campus events include Annual Block Party, Bachelor Auction, and Battle of the Dorms.

Sports: There are 7 intercollegiate sports for men and 8 for women, and 6 intramural sports for men and 6 for women. Facilities include a gym, a swimming pool, a weight room, a dance studio, a recreation room, a fitness center with aerobic and Nautilus facilities, and basketball, squash, and tennis courts.

Disabled Students: 90% of the campus is accessible. Wheelchair ramps, elevators, special parking, specially equipped rest rooms, lowered drinking fountains, and lowered telephones are available.

Services: Counseling and information services are available, as is tutoring in most subjects, including computer science, math, chemistry, biology, languages, psychology, sociology, writing, and economics. There is a reader service for the blind, and remedial math, reading, and writing.

Campus Safety and Security: Measures include 24-hour foot and vehicle patrol, security escort services, shuttle buses, and informal discussions. There are pamphlets/posters/films, emergency telephones, lighted pathways/sidewalks, and a college committee on safety and security on campus.

Programs of Study: The Mount confers B.A. and B.S. degrees. Associate and master's degrees are also awarded. Bachelor's degrees are awarded in BIOLOGICAL SCIENCE (biochemistry and biology/biological science), BUSINESS (business administration and management), COMMUNICATIONS AND THE ARTS (communications, English, French, modern language, and Spanish), COMPUTER AND PHYSICAL SCIENCE (chemistry, computer science, mathematics, and physics), EDUCATION (health, physical, and special), HEALTH PROFESSIONS (allied health and nursing), SOCIAL SCIENCE (economics,

history, liberal arts/general studies, philosophy, psychology, religion, sociology, and urban studies). Nursing and biology are the strongest academically. Nursing, psychology, and business are the largest.

Required: All students must complete a 56-credit core curriculum with courses in humanities, social sciences, math and computers, and natural sciences. A total of 120 credits for a B.A. or 126 credits for a B.S., with a minimum of 30 credits in the major, and a minimum GPA of 2.0 are required.

Special: Cross-registration with Manhattan College offers cooperative B.A. programs in international studies, philosophy, phys ed, physics, religious studies, and urban affairs. Internships, work-study, study abroad in 6 countries, a 3-2 engineering degree with Manhattan College, dual majors, and student-designed majors in liberal arts are available. B.A.-B.S. degrees in computer science, health education, math, and psychology, and teacher dual certification programs with special education and elementary, middle school, and secondary education are possible. There are 15 national honor societies, a freshman honors program, and 5 departmental honors programs.

Faculty/Classroom: 39% of faculty are male; 61%, female. All teach undergraduates and 80% both teach and do research. No introductory courses are taught by graduate students. The average class size in an introductory lecture is 25; in a laboratory, 15; and in a regular course, 15.

Admissions: 75% of recent applicants were accepted.

Requirements: The SAT or ACT is required. In addition, applicants should have completed 4 high school academic units of English, 3 of science, and 2 each of math, foreign language, and social sciences, as well as electives. An essay is required, and an interview is recommended. 1 letter of recommendation is required, and additional letters are encouraged. A grade average of 80 is required. AP and CLEP credits are accepted. Important factors in the admissions decision are advanced placement or honor courses, recommendations by school officials, and extracurricular activities record.

Procedure: Freshmen are admitted fall and spring. Entrance exams should be taken during the junior year and/or fall of the senior year. There is an early admissions plan and a rolling admissions plan. Notification is sent on a rolling basis. Applications are accepted on-line. Check with the school for current application deadlines and fee.

Transfer: 113 transfer students enrolled in a recent year. Transfer applicants should have a minimum GPA of 2.0. Those majoring in nursing, the sciences, math, or computer science need at least a 2.5 GPA. An interview is recommended. 45 of 120 credits required for the bachelor's degree must be completed at The Mount.

Visiting: There are regularly scheduled orientations for prospective students. Upon request, students may have an interview with an admissions counselor, sit in on classes, and tour the campus. All students are invited to an open house. Accepted students may have a one-on-one meeting with a student on campus. There are guides for informal visits and visitors may sit in on classes and stay overnight. To schedule a visit, contact the Admissions Office.

Financial Aid: In a recent year, 90% of all full-time freshmen and 75% of continuing full-time students received some form of financial aid. 80% of full-time freshmen and 75% of continuing full-time students received need-based aid. The average freshman award was $9600. 50% of undergraduates work part time. Average annual earnings from campus work are $500. The average financial indebtedness of a recent graduate was $17,000. The Mount is a member of CSS. The FAFSA and the TAP application for New York state residents are required. Check with the school for current deadlines.

International Students: The school actively recruits these students. They must take the TOEFL or complete ELS Level 109, available on campus, and also take the SAT with satisfactory scores or the ACT.

Computers: All students may access the system 9 A.M. to 10 P.M. Monday through Thursday and 9 A.M. to 4 P.M. Friday, Saturday, and Sunday. There are no time limits. The fee is $150.

Graduates: In a recent year, 188 bachelor's degrees were awarded. The most popular majors were nursing (24%), communications (14%), and business (11%). In an average class, 46% graduate in 4 years or less, 60% graduate in 5 years or less, and 62% graduate in 6 years or less. 80 companies recruited on campus in a recent year.

Admissions Contact: Timothy P. Nash, Dean of Admission and Financial Aid. A video is available.
E-mail: *admissns@mountsaintvincent.edu* Web: *www.cmsv.edu*

COLLEGE OF NEW ROCHELLE   D-5

New Rochelle, NY 10805-2339   **(914) 654-5452**
(800) 933-5923; Fax: (914) 654-5464

Full-time: 16 men, 694 women	**Faculty:** 62; IIA, av$
Part-time: 52 men, 344 women	**Ph.D.s:** 84%
Graduate: 178 men, 1022 women	**Student/Faculty:** 11 to 1
Year: semesters, summer session	**Tuition:** $20,596
Application Deadline: August 15	**Room & Board:** $7800
Freshman Class: 1430 applied, 710 accepted, 195 enrolled	
SAT Verbal/Math: 500/480*	**ACT:** 18 **COMPETITIVE+**

The College of New Rochelle was founded in 1904 by the Ursuline order as the first Catholic college for women in New York State. Now independent, there are 3 undergraduate schools. The School of Arts and Sciences offers liberal arts baccalaureate education for women only; the School of Nursing is coeducational. The School of New Resources is described in a separate profile. There are 3 undergraduate schools and 1 graduate school. In addition to regional accreditation, CNR has baccalaureate program accreditation with CCNE, CSWE, and NLN. The library contains 224,000 volumes, 277 microform items, and 5700 audio/video tapes/CDs/DVDs, and subscribes to 1432 periodicals including electronic. Computerized library services include the card catalog, interlibrary loans, database searching, and Internet access. Special learning facilities include a learning resource center, an art gallery, and the Learning Center for Nursing. The 20-acre campus is in a suburban area 12 miles north of New York City. Including any residence halls, there are 20 buildings.

Student Life: 82% of undergraduates are from New York. Students are from 16 states and 10 foreign countries. 73% are from public schools. 52% are African American; 20% white; 18% Hispanic. 77% are Catholic; 18% Protestant. The average age of freshmen is 19; all undergraduates, 27. 29% do not continue beyond their first year; 71% remain to graduate.

Housing: 430 students can be accommodated in college housing, which includes single-sex dorms. On-campus housing is guaranteed for all 4 years. 56% of students live on campus; of those, 50% remain on campus on weekends. All students may keep cars.

Activities: There are no fraternities or sororities. There are 18 groups on campus, including art, cheerleading, choir, chorus, drama, ethnic, film, honors, international, literary magazine, musical theater, newspaper, photography, political, professional, religious, social, social service, and student government. Popular campus events include Junior Celebration, Family Weekend, and Strawberry Festival.

Sports: There are 6 intercollegiate sports for women. Facilities include a fitness center and tennis courts.

Disabled Students: 50% of the campus is accessible. Wheelchair ramps, elevators, special parking, specially equipped rest rooms, and special class scheduling are available.

Services: Counseling and information services are available, as is tutoring in some subjects, including science and languages. There is remedial math, reading, and writing. Individual counseling and educational workshops about self-development and personal concerns are available, as are self-help materials.

Campus Safety and Security: Measures include 24-hour foot and vehicle patrol, self-defense education, security escort services, and shuttle buses. There are informal discussions, pamphlets/posters/films, emergency telephones, lighted pathways/sidewalks, card access to dorms, and surveillance cameras.

Programs of Study: CNR confers B.A., B.S., B.F.A., and B.S.N. degrees. Master's degrees are also awarded. Bachelor's degrees are awarded in AGRICULTURE (environmental studies), BIOLOGICAL SCIENCE (biology/biological science), BUSINESS (business administration and management), COMMUNICATIONS AND THE ARTS (art history and appreciation, classics, communications, English, French, and Spanish), COMPUTER AND PHYSICAL SCIENCE (chemistry and mathematics), EDUCATION (art), HEALTH PROFESSIONS (art therapy and nursing), SOCIAL SCIENCE (economics, history, international studies, philosophy, political science/government, psychology, religion, social work, sociology, and women's studies). Nursing, art, and psychology are the largest.

Required: Students must complete 120 credit hours, 60 to 90 in liberal arts courses, depending on the major, meet specific course distribution requirements, and maintain a minimum GPA of 2.0 to graduate. 4 phys ed courses are also required.

Special: CNR provides cooperative programs in all disciplines, work-study programs, dual majors in all majors, interdisciplinary studies, an accelerated degree program in nursing, a Washington semester, internships, study abroad in 9 countries, nondegree study, pass/fail options, student-designed majors, and a general studies degree. There is 1 national honor society and a freshman honors program.

Faculty/Classroom: 27% of faculty are male; 73%, female. All both teach and do research. No introductory courses are taught by graduate students. The average class size in an introductory lecture is 25; in a laboratory, 10; and in a regular course, 15.

Admissions: 50% of the 2005-2006 applicants were accepted. The SAT scores for the 2005-2006 freshman class were: Verbal--37% below 500, 51% between 500 and 599, 9% between 600 and 700, and 3% above 700; Math--43% below 500, 46% between 500 and 599, 10% between 600 and 700, and 1% above 700. 35% of the current freshmen were in the top fifth of their class; 66% were in the top two fifths.

Requirements: The SAT is required. In addition, graduation from an accredited secondary school is required; the GED is accepted. Applicants must have completed 15 academic credits, with 4 in English, 3 each in math, science, and social studies, and 2 in a foreign language. A portfolio is required for art majors. An essay and interview are recommended. AP and CLEP credits are accepted. Important factors in the admissions decision are advanced placement or honor courses, recommendations by school officials, and leadership record.

Procedure: Freshmen are admitted to all sessions. Entrance exams should be taken in the junior year or fall of the senior year. There are early decision, early admissions, deferred admissions, and rolling admissions plans. Early decision applications should be filed by November 1; regular applications, by August 15 for fall entry and January 10 for spring entry. Notification of early decision is sent December 15; regular decision, on a rolling basis. The fall 2005 application fee was $20.

Transfer: 52 transfer students enrolled in 2004-2005. Transfer students must submit a transcript from their previous college showing courses completed and a minimum GPA of 2.0. High school records and SAT scores are required. An interview is recommended. 30 of 120 credits required for the bachelor's degree must be completed at CNR.

Visiting: There are regularly scheduled orientations for prospective students, including several open houses providing information on admission. There are guides for informal visits and visitors may sit in on classes and stay overnight. To schedule a visit, contact the Office of Admissions at admission@cnr.edu.

Financial Aid: In 2005-2006, 86% of all full-time freshmen and 80% of continuing full-time students received some form of financial aid. 88% of full-time freshmen and 76% of continuing full-time students received need-based aid. The average freshman award was $20,980. Need-based scholarships or need-based grants averaged $11,882; and need-based self-help aid (loans and jobs) averaged $10,484. 60% of undergraduates work part time. Average annual earnings from campus work are $1200. The average financial indebtedness of the 2005 graduate was $17,978. The CSS/Profile, FAFSA, FFS or SFS, the college's own financial statement, and income documentation are required. The deadline for filing freshman financial aid applications for fall entry is open.

International Students: A satisfactory score is required on the written TOEFL or the ESL Language Test. Students must also also take the SAT or ACT, the SAT is preferred.

Computers: All students may access the system 24 hours per day. There are no time limits and no fees. It is strongly recommended that all students have a PC. Dell notebook computers are provided free of charge to all entering full-time freshmen.

Graduates: From July 1, 2004 to June 30, 2005, 244 bachelor's degrees were awarded. In an average class, 43% graduate in 4 years or less, 52% graduate in 5 years or less, and 54% graduate in 6 years or less. 27 companies recruited on campus in a recent year. Of the recent year's graduating class, 20% were enrolled in graduate school within 6 months of graduation and 60% were employed.

Admissions Contact: Stephanie Decker, Director of Admission. A video is available. E-mail: sdecker@cnr.edu Web: www.cnr.edu

COLLEGE OF NEW ROCHELLE - SCHOOL OF NEW RESOURCES   D-5

New Rochelle, NY 10805-2339   **(914) 654-5526**
(800) 288-4767; Fax: (914) 654-5664

Full-time: 397 men, 3508 women	**Faculty:** 25
Part-time: 48 men, 391 women	**Ph.D.s:** 27%
Graduate: none	**Student/Faculty:** 156 to 1
Year: semesters, summer session	**Tuition:** $7700
Application Deadline: August 15	**Room & Board:** n/app
Freshman Class: n/av	
SAT or ACT: n/av	**SPECIAL**

The College of New Rochelle's School of New Resources is a liberal arts institution serving adult baccalaureate students. The library contains 224,000 volumes, 277 microform items, and 5700 audio/video tapes/CDs/DVDs, and subscribes to 1432 periodicals including electronic. Computerized library services include the card catalog, interlibrary loans, database searching, and Internet access. Special learning facilities include a learning resource center, art gallery, TV station, and Access Centers to assist students in improving writing, reading, and math skills. The campus is in an urban area 12 miles north of New York City. Five additional campuses are located within the city. There are 20 buildings.

Student Life: 98% of undergraduates are from New York. Students are from 3 states and 3 foreign countries. 82% are African American; 14% Hispanic. The average age of freshmen is 33; all undergraduates, 36. 35% do not continue beyond their first year; 65% remain to graduate.

Housing: There are no residence halls. All students commute. Alcohol is not permitted. All students may keep cars.

Activities: There are no fraternities or sororities. There are some groups and organizations on campus, including drama, musical theater, religious, and student government. Popular campus events include Founders Day, College Bowl, and numerous women's and ethnic activities.

Sports: There is no sports program at SNR.

Services: Counseling and information services are available, as is tutoring in some subjects, including communication skills, problem solving, and math skills. There is remedial math, reading, and writing.

Campus Safety and Security: Measures include 24-hour foot and vehicle patrol, self-defense education, security escort services, and shuttle buses. There are informal discussions, pamphlets/posters/films, emergency telephones, lighted pathways/sidewalks, and surveillance cameras.

Programs of Study: SNR confers the B.A. degree. Bachelor's degrees are awarded in SOCIAL SCIENCE (liberal arts/general studies).

Required: Students must complete 120 credit hours, meet specific course distribution requirements, and maintain a minimum GPA of 2.0 to graduate. Entrance, core, and exit seminars are required, as are degree-planning courses.

Special: SNR provides a voluntary work-study program. Student-designed internships, courses, and degree plans are available. Credit for prior learning may be obtained.

Faculty/Classroom: 54% of faculty are male; 46%, female. All teach undergraduates. The average class size in an introductory lecture is 15; in a laboratory, 10; and in a regular course, 15.

Requirements: Enrolling students must be age 21 or older, have a high school diploma or its equivalent, and have successfully completed an English assessment. Test scores are not required. New students are expected to attend an orientation workshop. AP and CLEP credits are accepted.

Procedure: Freshmen are admitted to all sessions. Entrance exams should be taken in the junior year or fall of the senior year. There is a rolling admissions plan. Early decision applications should be filed by November 1; regular applications, by August 15 for fall entry and January 10 for spring entry. Notification of early decision is sent December 15; regular decision, on a rolling basis.

Transfer: Transfer students must obtain a transcript from their previous college. With some restrictions, course grades of C- or better will be accepted. 30 of 120 credits required for the bachelor's degree must be completed at SNR.

Financial Aid: 6% of undergraduates work part time. Average annual earnings from campus work are $2000. The FAFSA, the college's own financial statement and the income documentation are required. The deadline for filing freshman financial aid applications for fall entry is open.

Computers: All students may access the system from 8:30 A.M. to 11 P.M. daily. Students may access the system 2 hours during peak usage. There are no fees.

Graduates: From July 1, 2004 to June 30, 2005, 781 bachelor's degrees were awarded. The most popular major was liberal arts/general studies (100%). In an average class, 17% graduate in 4 years or less, 28% graduate in 5 years or less, and 31% graduate in 6 years or less.

Admissions Contact: Donna Tyler, Associate Dean. A video is available.

COLLEGE OF SAINT ROSE   D-3

Albany, NY 12203

(518) 454-5150
(800) 637-8556; Fax: (518) 454-2013

Full-time: 742 men, 2052 women	**Faculty:** IIA, --$
Part-time: 58 men, 152 women	**Ph.D.s:** 77%
Graduate: 488 men, 1507 women	**Student/Faculty:** n/av
Year: semesters, summer session	**Tuition:** $17,954
Application Deadline: February 1	**Room & Board:** $7730
Freshman Class: 3133 applied, 2218 accepted, 598 enrolled	
SAT or ACT: required	**COMPETITIVE**

The College of Saint Rose, established in 1920, is an independent liberal arts institution sponsored by the Sisters of St. Joseph of Carondelet. There are 4 undergraduate schools and 1 graduate school. In addition to regional accreditation, CSR has baccalaureate program accreditation with ACBSP, ASLA, and NASAD. The library contains 206,692 volumes, 307,904 microform items, and 1510 audio/video tapes/CDs/DVDs, and subscribes to 902 periodicals including electronic. Computerized library services include the card catalog, interlibrary loans, database searching, and Internet access. Special learning facilities include a learning resource center, art gallery, and TV station. The 28-acre campus is in a suburban area in a residential section, 1 1/2 miles from downtown Albany. Including any residence halls, there are 77 buildings.

Student Life: 92% of undergraduates are from New York. Students are from 20 states, 9 foreign countries, and Canada. 80% are white. The average age of freshmen is 18; all undergraduates, 22. 15% do not continue beyond their first year; 65% remain to graduate.

Housing: 1102 students can be accommodated in college housing, which includes single-sex and coed dorms, on-campus apartments, and married-student housing. On-campus housing is available on a first-come, first-served basis and is available on a lottery system for upperclassmen. 62% of students commute. All students may keep cars.

Activities: There are no fraternities or sororities. There are 37 groups on campus, including cheerleading, chorale, circle K commuter, computers, dance, departmental, disabled, drama, ethnic, international, jazz band, literary magazine, newspaper, political, professional, religious, social, social service, student government, womens, and yearbook. Popular campus events include Harvest Fest, Rose Rock, and Land and Water Olympics.

Sports: There are 6 intercollegiate sports for men and 6 for women, and 5 intramural sports for men and 5 for women. Facilities include a gym with basketball and volleyball courts, a weight room, an indoor swimming pool, and access to city soccer, baseball, and softball fields.

Disabled Students: 98% of the campus is accessible. Wheelchair ramps, elevators, special parking, specially equipped rest rooms, lowered drinking fountains, lowered telephones, and some automatic-open doors are available.

Services: Counseling and information services are available, as is tutoring in most subjects, including writing, math, accounting, computer science, and others as needed. There is a reader service for the blind, and remedial math, reading, and writing. There is also a full-time assistant director of disabled student services.

Campus Safety and Security: Measures include 24-hour foot and vehicle patrol, security escort services, shuttle buses, and informal discussions. There are pamphlets/posters/films, emergency telephones, lighted pathways/sidewalks, a student volunteer escort service, and fire drills.

Programs of Study: CSR confers B.A., B.S., and B.F.A. degrees. Master's degrees are also awarded. Bachelor's degrees are awarded in BIOLOGICAL SCIENCE (biochemistry and biology/biological science), BUSINESS (accounting and business administration and management), COMMUNICATIONS AND THE ARTS (communications, English, graphic design, music, Spanish, and studio art), COMPUTER AND PHYSICAL SCIENCE (chemistry, information sciences and systems, and mathematics), EDUCATION (art, early childhood, elementary, English, foreign languages, mathematics, music, science, social studies, special, and technical), ENGINEERING AND ENVIRONMENTAL DESIGN (environmental science), HEALTH PROFESSIONS (cytotechnology, medical technology, and speech pathology/audiology), SOCIAL SCIENCE (American studies, criminal justice, history, interdisciplinary studies, political science/government, psychology, religion, social work, and sociology). Education, art, and music are the strongest academically. Business, special education, and elementary education are the largest.

Required: To graduate, students must complete 122 credits with a minimum GPA of 2.0 overall and in the major; these requirements are higher for certain majors. Liberal education requirements consist of 6 credits in college writing and speech and 30 credits in the humanities, science and math, social science and business, and the arts. Students must also complete 2 credits in phys ed.

Special: CSR offers cross-registration with the Hudson-Mohawk Association and the CSI Consortium, internships, work-study programs, study abroad in several countries, dual and student-designed majors, nondegree study, and pass/fail options. There are 3-2 engineering degree programs with Alfred and Clarkson Universities, Union College, and Rensselaer Polytechnic University, as well as a 6-year law program with Albany Law School. There are 6 national honor societies and 5 departmental honors programs.

Faculty/Classroom: 41% of faculty are male; 59%, female. No introductory courses are taught by graduate students. The average class size in a laboratory is 14 and in a regular course, 25.

Admissions: 71% of the 2005-2006 applicants were accepted.

Requirements: The SAT or ACT is required. The ACT Optional Writing test is also recommended. In addition, applicants must be graduates of an accredited secondary school or have a GED certificate. They should have completed college preparatory programs including 4 years of English, social studies, and history, and 3 years of math, science, and foreign language. All students must submit a letter of recommendation. Art students must submit portfolios, and music students must audition. AP and CLEP credits are accepted. Important factors in the admissions decision are advanced placement or honor courses, leadership record, and recommendations by school officials.

Procedure: Freshmen are admitted fall and spring. Entrance exams should be taken during spring of junior year or fall of senior year. There are early admissions, deferred admissions, and rolling admissions plans. Priority date for fall entry applications is December 1. Applications should be filed by February 1 for fall entry and November 1 for spring entry, along with a $35 fee. Notification is sent on a rolling basis beginning October 1. Applications are accepted on-line. There is no fee for on-line applications.

Transfer: 299 transfer students enrolled in 2004-2005. Applicants must submit official transcripts, a letter of recommendation, and a personal statement of the reasons for seeking transfer. An interview is recommended. Art majors must submit a portfolio, and music majors must audition. 60 of 122 credits required for the bachelor's degree must be completed at CSR.

Visiting: There are regularly scheduled orientations for prospective students, including visits with admissions and financial aid representatives, an overnight program hosted by students, Saturday information sessions in the fall, open house, and Accepted Student Day in April. There are guides for informal visits and visitors may sit in on classes and stay overnight. To schedule a visit, contact the Admissions Office at *admit@mail.strose.edu.*

Financial Aid: 1% of undergraduates work part time. CSR is a member of CSS. The FAFSA is required. Check with the school for current deadlines.

International Students: There were 7 international students enrolled in a recent year. A satisfactory score is required on the written TOEFL.

Computers: All students may access the system 24 hours a day Monday through Saturday, and additional hours on Sunday. There are no time limits. The fee is $100 per semester.

Graduates: In a recent year, 596 bachelor's degrees were awarded. The most popular majors were education (48%), communication (9%), and visual and performing arts (8%). In an average class, 50% graduate in 4 years or less, 64% graduate in 5 years or less, and 65% graduate in 6 years or less. 45 companies recruited on campus in 2004-2005. Of the 2004 graduating class, 43% were enrolled in graduate school within 6 months of graduation and 89% were employed.

Admissions Contact: Mary Grondahl, Associate Vice President for Undergraduate Admissions. A video is available.
E-mail: *admit@rosnet.strose.edu* Web: *www.strose.edu*

COLUMBIA UNIVERSITY SYSTEM

The Columbia University System, established in 1754, is a public system in New York. It is governed by a board of trustees, whose chief administrator is president. The primary goal of the system is teaching and research. The main priorities are providing outstanding undergraduate instruction; conducting research to develop new knowledge and methods; and training of professionals in law, business, social work, and medicine. The total enrollment is usually about 19,000; with 2100 faculty members. Altogether there are some 110 baccalaureate, 160 master's, and 80 doctoral programs offered in Columbia University System. Profiles of the 4-year campuses are included in this section.

COLUMBIA UNIVERSITY/BARNARD COLLEGE   D-5

New York, NY 10027-6598   (212) 854-2014; Fax: (212) 854-6220

Full-time: 2300 women	Faculty: 186; IIB, ++$
Part-time: 50 women	Ph.D.s: 93%
Graduate: none	Student/Faculty: 12 to 1
Year: semesters	Tuition: $27,000
Application Deadline: see profile	Room & Board: $11,000
Freshman Class: n/av	
SAT or ACT: required	MOST COMPETITIVE

Barnard College, founded in 1889, is an independent affiliate of Columbia University. It is an undergraduate women's liberal arts college. Figures in the capsule and in this profile are approximate. The library contains 204,906 volumes, 17,705 microform items, and 17,448 audio/video tapes/CDs/DVDs, and subscribes to 543 periodicals including electronic. Computerized library services include the card catalog, interlibrary loans, database searching, and Internet access. Special learning facilities include a learning resource center, art gallery, radio station, TV station, a greenhouse, history of physics lab, child development research and study center, dance studio, modern theater, women's research archives within a women's center, and multimedia labs and classrooms. The 4-acre campus is in an urban area occupying 4 city blocks of Manhattan's Upper West Side. Including any residence halls, there are 15 buildings.

Student Life: 65% of undergraduates are from out of state, mostly the Middle Atlantic. Students are from 48 states, 35 foreign countries, and Canada. 53% are from public schools. 66% are white; 19% Asian American. The average age of freshmen is 18; all undergraduates, 20. 7% do not continue beyond their first year; 84% remain to graduate.

Housing: 2057 students can be accommodated in college housing, which includes single-sex and coed dorms, on-campus apartments, and off-campus apartments. In addition, there are special-interest houses. On-campus housing is guaranteed for all 4 years. 89% of students live on campus; of those, 75% remain on campus on weekends. Alcohol is not permitted. All students may keep cars.

Activities: There are no fraternities. There are 100 groups on campus, including art, band, cheerleading, choir, chorale, chorus, dance, debate, drama, ethnic, film, gay, international, jazz band, literary magazine, marching band, musical theater, newspaper, opera, orchestra, photography, political, professional, radio and TV, religious, social, social service, student government, symphony, and yearbook. Popular campus events

include Spring and Winter Festivals, Founders Day, and Take Back the Night.

Sports: Facilities include pools, weight rooms, gyms, tennis courts, an indoor track, and a boat slip.

Disabled Students: 90% of the campus is accessible. Wheelchair ramps, elevators, special parking, specially equipped rest rooms, special class scheduling, lowered drinking fountains, lowered telephones, and special housing, are available. The Office of Disability Services provides a variety of support services to students with permanent and temporary disabilities.

Services: Counseling and information services are available, as is tutoring in every subject. There is a reader service for the blind. A student-staffed writing room is available for students of all levels of writing ability, and a math help room is also available to students in all math courses.

Campus Safety and Security: Measures include 24-hour foot and vehicle patrol, security escort services, shuttle buses, and informal discussions. There are pamphlets/posters/films, emergency telephones, lighted pathways/sidewalks, and safety and security education programs.

Programs of Study: Barnard College confers the B.A. degree. Bachelor's degrees are awarded in BIOLOGICAL SCIENCE (biochemistry and biology/biological science), COMMUNICATIONS AND THE ARTS (art history and appreciation, classics, comparative literature, dance, dramatic arts, English, film arts, French, German, Greek, Italian, Latin, linguistics, music, Russian, and Spanish), COMPUTER AND PHYSICAL SCIENCE (astronomy, chemistry, computer science, mathematics, physics, and statistics), ENGINEERING AND ENVIRONMENTAL DESIGN (architecture and environmental science), SOCIAL SCIENCE (American studies, anthropology, biopsychology, classical/ancient civilization, East Asian studies, economics, European studies, history, international studies, medieval studies, Middle Eastern studies, philosophy, political science/government, psychology, religion, sociology, urban studies, and women's studies). English, psychology, and economics are the strongest academically and the largest.

Required: A total of 120 credits is required, with a minimum GPA of 2.0. All students must take 4 semesters each of a foreign language, humanities, or social sciences outside the major, geographic and cultural diversity courses that may satisfy the major or other requirements, 2 semesters each of lab science and phys ed, and 1 semester each in first-year seminar, first-year English, and quantitative reasoning.

Special: Barnard offers cross-registration with Columbia University, more than 2500 internships with New York City firms and institutions, and study abroad worldwide. A 3-2 engineering program with the Columbia School of Engineering and double-degree programs with the Columbia University Schools of International and Public Affairs, Law, and Dentistry, the Juilliard School, and the Jewish Theological Seminary are possible. The college offers dual and student-designed majors and multidisciplinary majors, including economic history. There is 1 national honor society, Phi Beta Kappa.

Faculty/Classroom: 38% of faculty are male; 62%, female. All both teach and do research. The average class size in an introductory lecture is 30; in a laboratory, 11; and in a regular course, 13.

Admissions: 96% of recent freshmen were in the top fifth of their class; 99% were in the top two fifths. There were 21 National Merit finalists in a recent year. 20 freshmen graduated first in their class in a recent year.

Requirements: The SAT or ACT is required. In addition, if taking the SAT, an applicant must also take 3 SAT: Subject Tests, one of which must be in writing or literature. A GED is accepted. Applicants should prepare with 4 years of English, 3 or 4 of a foreign language, 3 of math, 2 of a lab science, and 1 of history. An interview is recommended. AP credits are accepted. Important factors in the admissions decision are advanced placement or honor courses, evidence of special talent, and extracurricular activities record.

Procedure: Freshmen are admitted fall and spring. Entrance exams should be taken by January of the senior year. There are early decision and deferred admissions plans. Check with the school for current application deadlines and fee. 153 early decision candidates were accepted for a recent class. 766 applicants were on a recent waiting list; 36 were admitted. Applications are accepted on-line.

Transfer: 81 transfer students enrolled in a recent year. Applicants must complete at least 1 college course. The SAT or ACT is required. Check with the school for current deadlines. 60 of 120 credits required for the bachelor's degree must be completed at Barnard College.

Visiting: There are regularly scheduled orientations for prospective students, consisting of open house programs regularly scheduled throughout the fall. There are guides for informal visits and visitors may sit in on classes and stay overnight. To schedule a visit, contact the Office of Admissions at *admissions@barnard.edu.*

Financial Aid: In a recent year, 53% of all full-time students received some form of financial aid. 39% of all full-time students received need-based aid. The average freshman award was $25,424. Need-based scholarships or need-based grants averaged $23,436 ($39,090 maximum); and need-based self-help aid (loans and jobs) averaged $3287 ($4400 maximum). 46% of undergraduates work part time. The average financial indebtedness of a recent graduate was $16,275. Barnard College is a member of CSS. The CSS Profile, FAFSA, the college's own financial statement parent's and student's federal tax returns, and the business and/or noncustodial parent statement, if applicable are required. Check with the school for current deadlines.

International Students: There were 68 international students enrolled in a recent year. The school actively recruits these students. They must take the TOEFL and also take the SAT or ACT. Applicants who take the SAT must also take SAT: Subject Tests in writing or literature and 2 others.

Computers: All students may access the system. There are no time limits and no fees. It is strongly recommended that all students have a personal computer.

Graduates: In a recent years, 597 bachelor's degrees were awarded. The most popular majors were psychology (13%), English (13%), and economics (12%). In an average class, 2% graduate in 3 years or less, 82% graduate in 4 years or less, 88% graduate in 5 years or less, and 84% graduate in 6 years. 90 companies recruited on campus in a recent year. Of a recent graduating class, 24% were enrolled in graduate school within 6 months of graduation and 70% were employed.

Admissions Contact: Jennifer Fondiller, Dean of Admissions.
E-mail: *admissions@barnard.edu* Web: *http://www.barnard.edu*

COLUMBIA UNIVERSITY/COLUMBIA COLLEGE   D-5

New York, NY 10027	**(212) 854-2522; Fax: (212) 854-1209**
Full-time: 2030 men, 2195 women	**Faculty:** 692; I, ++$
Part-time: none	**Ph.Ds:** 100%
Graduate: none	**Student/Faculty:** 6 to 1
Year: semesters, summer session	**Tuition:** $33,246
Application Deadline: January 2	**Room & Board:** $9338
Freshman Class: 15,793 applied, 1693 accepted, 1024 enrolled	
SAT Verbal/Math: 720/710*	**ACT:** 30 **MOST COMPETITIVE**

Columbia College of Columbia University, founded in 1754, is a private college offering programs in the liberal arts and sciences. The 25 libraries contain 8.7 million volumes. Computerized library services include the card catalog, interlibrary loans, and database searching. Special learning facilities include an art gallery, planetarium, radio station, TV station, and an observatory. The 36-acre campus is in an urban area in New York City. Including any residence halls, there are 50 buildings.

Student Life: 75% of undergraduates are from out of state, mostly the Middle Atlantic. Students are from 50 states, 55 foreign countries, and Canada. 51% are from public schools. 49% are white; 13% Asian American. The average age of freshmen is 18; all undergraduates, 20. 2% do not continue beyond their first year; 94% remain to graduate.

Housing: All students can be accommodated in college housing, which includes single-sex and coed dorms, on-campus apartments, and fraternity houses. In addition, there are language houses and special-interest houses. On-campus housing is guaranteed for all 4 years. 93% of students live on campus. All students may keep cars.

Activities: 10% of men belong to 20 national fraternities; 6% of women belong to 12 national sororities. There are 300 groups on campus, including art, band, cheerleading, chess, choir, chorale, chorus, computers, dance, debate, drama, ethnic, film, gay, honors, international, jazz band, literary magazine, marching band, musical theater, newspaper, opera, orchestra, outdoor, pep band, photography, political, professional, radio and TV, religious, social, social service, student government, and symphony. Popular campus events include Columbia Fest, United Minorities Board Ethnic Festival, and Holiday Lighting Ceremony/Yule Log.

Sports: There are 14 intercollegiate sports for men and 15 for women, and 13 intramural sports for men and 13 for women. Facilities include a football stadium, indoor and outdoor track and field facilities, a baseball field, a soccer stadium, a recreational gym with a swimming pool, basketball/volleyball courts, aerobic, fencing, wrestling, martial arts, and weight rooms, a boathouse, and tennis, squash, handball, and racquetball courts.

Disabled Students: All of the campus is accessible. Wheelchair ramps, elevators, special parking, specially equipped rest rooms, special class scheduling, lowered drinking fountains, lowered telephones, special housing, and chairlifts are available.

Services: Counseling and information services are available, as is tutoring in every subject. There is a reader service for the blind.

Campus Safety and Security: Measures include 24-hour foot and vehicle patrol, self-defense education, security escort services, and shuttle buses. There are informal discussions, pamphlets/posters/films, emergency telephones, and lighted pathways/sidewalks.

Programs of Study: Columbia confers the A.B. degree. Bachelor's degrees are awarded in BIOLOGICAL SCIENCE (biochemistry, biology/biological science, biophysics, environmental biology, and neurosciences), COMMUNICATIONS AND THE ARTS (art history and appreciation, classics, comparative literature, dance, dramatic arts, English, film arts, French, German, Germanic languages and literature, Greek, Latin, linguistics, music, Russian, Spanish, and visual and performing arts), COMPUTER AND PHYSICAL SCIENCE (astronomy, astrophys-

ics, chemistry, computer science, earth science, geochemistry, geology, geophysics and seismology, mathematics, physics, and statistics), EDUCATION (education), ENGINEERING AND ENVIRONMENTAL DESIGN (architecture and environmental science), SOCIAL SCIENCE (African American studies, American studies, anthropology, archeology, area studies, Asian/American studies, Asian/Oriental studies, classical/ancient civilization, East Asian studies, economics, Hispanic American studies, history, Italian studies, Latin American studies, medieval studies, Middle Eastern studies, philosophy, political science/government, psychology, religion, Russian and Slavic studies, sociology, urban studies, and women's studies). Political science, economics, and history are the largest.

Required: All students complete a core curriculum consisting of classes in Western and non-Western cultures, literature and philosophy, history, social science, art, sculpture and architecture, and music of the Western tradition; 2 courses in non-Western areas are also required. Distribution requirements include 2 years of foreign language (unless competency can be demonstrated), 3 semesters of science, 1 year of phys ed, and 1 semester of writing. Courses in logic and rhetoric are also required. A thesis may be required for departmental honors in certain departments. A total of 124 credit hours is required; usually 30 to 40 of these are in the major. The minimum required GPA is 2.0.

Special: There is a study-abroad program at more than 100 locations, including France, Oxford and Cambridge Universities in England, and the Kyoto Center for Japanese Studies in Japan. Cross-registration is possible with the Juilliard School and Barnard College. Combined B.A.-B.S. degrees are offered via 3-2 or 4-1 engineering programs. A 3-2 engineering degree is offered with Columbia's Fu Foundation School of Engineering and Applied Science. There is also a 5-year B.A./M.I.A. with Columbia's School of International and Public Affairs. The college offers work-study, internships, credit by exam, pass/fail options, and dual, student-designed, and interdisciplinary majors, including regional studies and ancient studies. There is a chapter of Phi Beta Kappa.

Faculty/Classroom: 68% of faculty are male; 32%, female. All both teach and do research. The average class size in an introductory lecture is 70; in a laboratory, 15; and in a regular course, 25.

Admissions: 11% of the 2005-2006 applicants were accepted. The SAT scores for the 2005-2006 freshman class were: Verbal--1% below 500, 7% between 500 and 599, 26% between 600 and 700, and 67% above 700; Math--5% between 500 and 599, 35% between 600 and 700, and 60% above 700. The ACT scores were 1% below 21, 5% between 21 and 23, 14% between 24 and 26, 17% between 27 and 28, and 64% above 28. 95% of the current freshmen were in the top fifth of their class; 99% were in the top two fifths.

Requirements: The SAT or ACT is required. In addition, and 2 SAT Subject Tests, are also required. A GED is accepted. Students should prepare with 4 years of English and 3 or 4 years each of foreign language, social studies/history, math, and lab science. An essay is required; interviews are not required. 2 academic faculty recommendations and a written evaluation or recommendation from a school official are also required. AP credits are accepted. Important factors in the admissions decision are advanced placement or honor courses, recommendations by school officials, and leadership record.

Procedure: Freshmen are admitted in the fall. The college prefers that entrance exams be taken no later than October or November of the senior year. There are early decision, early admissions, and deferred admissions plans. Early decision applications should be filed by November 1; regular applications, by January 2 for fall entry. The fall 2005 application fee was $65. Notification of early decision is sent December 15; regular decision, April 1. 446 early decision candidates were accepted for the 2005-2006 class. 795 applicants were on the 2005 waiting list; 57 were admitted. Applications are accepted on-line.

Transfer: 57 transfer students enrolled in 2004-2005. Applicants must have completed 1 full year of college (24 credits) with a GPA of at least 3.0. They must submit high school and college transcripts. 60 of 124 credits required for the bachelor's degree must be completed at Columbia.

Visiting: There are regularly scheduled orientations for prospective students, consisting of group information sessions and student-led tours. There are guides for informal visits and visitors may sit in on classes and stay overnight. To schedule a visit, contact the Visitors Center at (212) 854-4900.

Financial Aid: In 2005-2006, 53% of all full-time freshmen and 41% of continuing full-time students received some form of financial aid. 44% of full-time freshmen and 36% of continuing full-time students received need-based aid. The average freshman award was $26,931. The average financial indebtedness of the 2005 graduate was $13,870. Columbia is a member of CSS. The CSS/Profile or FAFSA, the college's own financial statement, federal tax returns, the business/farm supplement, and/or the divorced/separated parents statement, if applicable, are required. The deadline for filing freshman financial aid applications for fall entry is February 10.

International Students: There are 242 international students enrolled. The school actively recruits these students. They must receive a satisfactory score on the TOEFL and also take the SAT or the ACT. Students must take 2 SAT Subject tests.

Computers: There are computer labs and stand-alone terminals throughout the campus and computer clusters in residence halls. Every dorm room has an Ethernet connection. All students may access the system 24 hours a day, 7 days a week. There are no time limits.

Graduates: From July 1, 2004 to June 30, 2005, 970 bachelor's degrees were awarded. The most popular majors were political science (12%), English (12%), and economics (10%). 370 companies recruited on campus in 2004-2005.

Admissions Contact: Admissions Officer, Office of Undergraduate Admissions. A video is available.
Web: *http://www.studentaffairs.columbia.edu/admissions*

COLUMBIA UNIVERSITY/FU FOUNDATION SCHOOL OF ENGINEERING AND APPLIED SCIENCE   D-5

New York, NY 10027	**(212) 854-2521; Fax: (212) 854-1209**
Full-time: 1048 men, 388 women	**Faculty:** 142
Part-time: none	**Ph.D.s:** 100%
Graduate: none	**Student/Faculty:** 10 to 1
Year: semesters, summer session	**Tuition:** $33,246
Application Deadline: January 2	**Room & Board:** $9338
Freshman Class: 2332 applied, 1040 accepted, 315 enrolled	
SAT Verbal/Math: 700/760*	**ACT:** 34 **MOST COMPETITIVE**

The Fu Foundation School of Engineering and Applied Science of Columbia University, founded in 1754, offers undergraduate and graduate degree programs in engineering and applied science. In addition to regional accreditation, Columbia Engineering has baccalaureate program accreditation with ABET. The 25 libraries contain 8.7 million volumes and 48,000 microform items. Computerized library services include the card catalog, interlibrary loans, and database searching. Special learning facilities include an art gallery, radio station, TV station, and an observatory. The 36-acre campus is in an urban area in New York City. Including any residence halls, there are 50 buildings.

Student Life: 63% of undergraduates are from out of state, mostly the Middle Atlantic. Students are from 42 states, 39 foreign countries, and Canada. 60% are from public schools. 35% are white; 32% Asian American; 12% foreign nationals. The average age of freshmen is 18; all undergraduates, 20. 2% do not continue beyond their first year; 88% remain to graduate.

Housing: University housing, includes single-sex and coed dorms, on-campus apartments, fraternity houses, and sorority houses. In addition, there are language houses and special-interest houses. On-campus housing is guaranteed for all 4 years. 95% of students live on campus. All students may keep cars.

Activities: 10% of men belong to 20 national fraternities; 6% of women belong to 12 national sororities. There are 300 groups on campus, including art, band, cheerleading, chess, choir, chorus, computers, dance, debate, drama, ethnic, film, gay, honors, international, jazz band, literary magazine, marching band, musical theater, newspaper, opera, orchestra, pep band, photography, political, professional, radio and TV, religious, social, social service, student government, and symphony. Popular campus events include Columbia Fest, Holiday Lighting Ceremony/Yule Log, and Ethnic Festival.

Sports: There are 14 intercollegiate sports for men and 15 for women, and 13 intramural sports for men and 13 for women. Facilities include a football stadium, indoor and outdoor track-and-field facilities, a baseball field, a soccer stadium, a recreational gym with a swimming pool, basketball/volleyball courts, and aerobic exercise, fencing, wrestling, martial arts, and weight rooms, a boathouse, and tennis, squash, handball, and racquetball courts.

Disabled Students: All of the campus is accessible. Wheelchair ramps, elevators, special parking, specially equipped rest rooms, special class scheduling, lowered drinking fountains, lowered telephones, special housing, and chair lifts are available.

Services: Counseling and information services are available, as is tutoring in every subject. There is a reader service for the blind.

Campus Safety and Security: Measures include 24-hour foot and vehicle patrol, self-defense education, security escort services, and shuttle buses. There are pamphlets/posters/films, emergency telephones, and lighted pathways/sidewalks.

Programs of Study: Columbia Engineering confers the B.S. degree. Master's and doctoral degrees are also awarded. Bachelor's degrees are awarded in BUSINESS (operations research), COMPUTER AND PHYSICAL SCIENCE (applied mathematics, applied physics, and computer science), ENGINEERING AND ENVIRONMENTAL DESIGN (biomedical engineering, chemical engineering, civil engineering, computer engineering, electrical/electronics engineering, engineering management, engineering mechanics, geological engineering, industrial engineering technology, materials science, mechanical engineering, metallurgical engineering, and mining and mineral engineering). Biomedical engineering, mechanical engineering, and engineering are the largest.

Required: All students must complete 128 semester hours, including 38 hours of technical course work in math, physics, chemistry, and computer science, and 27 hours in nontechnical courses covering the humanities and economics. Courses in logic and rhetoric, economics, and 1 year of phys ed are required. They must take 66 hours in the major and maintain a 2.5 GPA.

Special: Students may study at Columbia College or any of more than 90 other liberal arts colleges throughout the country in a 5-year program leading to the combined B.A.-B.S. degree or a 3-2 engineering degree. There is cross-registration with Barnard College, Teacher's College, and The Juilliard School. The school offers study abroad in more than 100 locations, including Paris, Kyoto, and Oxford and Cambridge Universities in England, internships, work-study, and pass/fail options. There is a chapter of Phi Beta Kappa.

Faculty/Classroom: 92% of faculty are male; 8%, female. All both teach and do research. The average class size in an introductory lecture is 50; in a laboratory, 15; and in a regular course, 25.

Admissions: 45% of the 2005-2006 applicants were accepted. The SAT scores for the 2005-2006 freshman class were: Verbal--1% below 500, 6% between 500 and 599, 35% between 600 and 700, and 58% above 700; Math--1% between 500 and 599, 8% between 600 and 700, and 91% above 700. The ACT scores were 6% between 24 and 26, 11% between 27 and 28, and 83% above 28. 94% of the current freshmen were in the top fifth of their class; 99% were in the top two fifths.

Requirements: The SAT or ACT is required, as are 3 SAT: Subject tests in mathematics, Level I or II, chemistry or physics, and writing. Applicants must be graduates of an accredited secondary school with a recommended 4 years of English, 3 or 4 of history and social studies, 2 or 3 of a foreign language, 1 each of physics and chemistry, and math courses through calculus. Also required are a written evaluation or recommendation from a college adviser or guidance counselor and 2 recommendations from teachers of academic classroom subjects (1 from a teacher of math). An essay is required and an interview is recommended. AP credits are accepted. Important factors in the admissions decision are advanced placement or honor courses, evidence of special talent, and recommendations by alumni.

Procedure: Freshmen are admitted in the fall. All testing must be completed by November of the senior year of high school (October for early decision applicants). There are early decision, early admissions, and deferred admissions plans. Early decision applications should be filed by November 1; regular applications, by January 2 for fall entry, along with a $65 fee. Notification of early decision is sent December 15; regular decision, April 1. 132 early decision candidates were accepted for the 2005-2006 class. 161 applicants were on the 2005 waiting list; 11 were admitted. Applications are accepted on-line.

Transfer: 15 transfer students enrolled in a recent year. Applicants should have completed 1 year each of calculus, physics, and chemistry with lab, in addition to appropriate liberal arts courses. 60 of 128 credits required for the bachelor's degree must be completed at Columbia Engineering.

Visiting: There are regularly scheduled orientations for prospective students, consisting of group information sessions and student-led tours. There are guides for informal visits and visitors may sit in on classes and stay overnight. To schedule a visit, contact the Visitor Center at (212) 854-4900.

Financial Aid: In 2005-2006, 48% of all full-time students received some form of financial aid. 59% of full-time freshmen and 53% of continuing full-time students received need-based aid. The average freshman award was $24,180. The average financial indebtedness of the 2005 graduate was $14,227. The CSS/Profile or FAFSA and the college's own financial statement are required. The deadline for filing freshman financial aid applications for fall entry is February 10.

International Students: There are 177 international students enrolled. The school actively recruits these students. They must score 600 on the written TOEFL or 250 on the electronic version and also take the college's own test and SAT: Subject tests in writing, mathematics Level I or II, and physics or chemistry.

Computers: All students may access the system 24 hours a day, 7 days a week. There are no time limits. The fee is included in the graduate fee.

Graduates: From July 1, 2004 to June 30, 2005, 340 bachelor's degrees were awarded. The most popular majors were biomedical engineering (17%), engineering and management systems (13%), and computer science (12%). 370 companies recruited on campus in 2004-2005.

Admissions Contact: Admissions Officer.
Web: *http://www.studentaffairs.columbia.edu/admissions*

COLUMBIA UNIVERSITY/SCHOOL OF GENERAL STUDIES
D-5

New York, NY 10027

(212) 854-2772
(800) 895-1169; Fax: (212) 854-6316

Full-time: 350 men, 297 women
Part-time: 224 men, 275 women
Graduate: none
Year: semesters, summer session
Application Deadline: June 1
Freshman Class: n/av
SAT or ACT: recommended

Faculty: n/av
Ph.D.s: 99%
Student/Faculty: n/av
Tuition: $32,176
Room & Board: $9340

COMPETITIVE

The School of General Studies of Columbia University, founded in 1947, offers liberal arts degree programs and postgraduate studies for adult men and women whose post-high school education has been interrupted or postponed by at least 1 year. Computerized library services include the card catalog, interlibrary loans, database searching, and Internet access. Special learning facilities include a learning resource center, art gallery, radio station, and TV station. The 36-acre campus is in an urban area on the upper west side of Manhattan in New York City.

Student Life: 42% of undergraduates are from out of state, mostly the Northeast. 56% are white; 11% Asian American. The average age of all undergraduates is 28.

Housing: 229 students can be accommodated in college housing, which includes single-sex and coed off-campus apartments, married-student housing, fraternity houses, and an international house. On-campus housing is available on a first-come, first-served basis. Priority is given to out-of-town students. 80% of students commute. Alcohol is not permitted. No one may keep cars.

Activities: Less than 1% of men belong to fraternities; less than 1% of women belong to sororities. There are more than 250 groups on campus, including art, band, cheerleading, chess, choir, chorale, computers, dance, debate, drama, ethnic, film, gay, international, jazz band, literary magazine, marching band, musical theater, newspaper, opera, orchestra, photography, political, professional, radio and TV, religious, social, social service, student government, symphony, womens, writers, and yearbook.

Sports: There are 14 intercollegiate sports for men and 13 for women, and 10 intramural sports for men and 10 for women. Facilities include 2 gyms, a swimming pool, tennis, squash, and racquetball courts, a training center, 2 dance/martial arts studios, a fencing room, a wrestling room, and an indoor track.

Disabled Students: Wheelchair ramps, elevators, specially equipped rest rooms, lowered drinking fountains, and lowered telephones are available.

Services: Counseling and information services are available, as is tutoring in some subjects, including English composition, math, languages, and sciences.

Campus Safety and Security: Measures include 24-hour foot and vehicle patrol, security escort services, shuttle buses, and pamphlets/posters/films. There are emergency telephones and lighted pathways/sidewalks.

Programs of Study: GS confers B.A. and B.S. degrees. Master's and doctoral degrees are also awarded. Bachelor's degrees are awarded in BIOLOGICAL SCIENCE (biology/biological science), COMMUNICATIONS AND THE ARTS (art history and appreciation, classics, comparative literature, dance, dramatic arts, English literature, film arts, French, German, Italian, literature, music, Slavic languages, Spanish, and visual and performing arts), COMPUTER AND PHYSICAL SCIENCE (applied mathematics, astronomy, chemistry, computer science, geoscience, mathematics, physics, and statistics), ENGINEERING AND ENVIRONMENTAL DESIGN (architecture and environmental science), SOCIAL SCIENCE (African American studies, anthropology, archeology, classical/ancient civilization, East Asian studies, economics, French studies, German area studies, Hispanic American studies, history, Italian studies, Latin American studies, Middle Eastern studies, philosophy, political science/government, psychology, religion, sociology, urban studies, and women's studies).

Required: All students must complete 124 credit hours, including 56 distribution requirement credits in literature, humanities, foreign language or literature, social science, science, and cultural diversity. Proficiency in English composition and math is required. A GPA of 2.0 is necessary to graduate.

Special: Preprofessional studies in allied health and medical fields and interdisciplinary majors, minors, and concentrations are offered. Internships in New York City, work-study programs on campus, study abroad, a 3-2 engineering degree at Columbia University School of Engineering and Applied Science, B.A.-B.S. degrees, and dual majors are available. There is a chapter of Phi Beta Kappa.

Faculty/Classroom: 68% of faculty are male; 32%, female.

Requirements: The SAT or ACT is recommended. SAT, ACT, or Columbia's General Studies Admissions Exam scores should be submitted along with high school and all college transcripts. An autobiographical statement is required. An interview is encouraged. A GPA of 2.5 is required. AP credits are accepted. Important factors in the admissions decision are personality/intangible qualities, extracurricular activities record, and evidence of special talent.

Procedure: Freshmen are admitted to all sessions. Entrance exams should be taken as early as possible. There is a deferred admissions plan. Early decision applications should be filed by March 1; regular applications, by June 1 for fall entry, October 15 for spring entry, and April 1 for summer entry, along with a $65 fee. Notification for early decision is sent 4 to 6 weeks after application is received; regular decision, 6 weeks after application is required. Applications are accepted on-line.

Transfer: 216 transfer students enrolled in 2004-2005. Most students come to GS with some college credit. 64 of 124 credits required for the bachelor's degree must be completed at GS.

Visiting: There are regularly scheduled orientations for prospective students, consisting of an admissions information session every other Wednesday, preceeded by a campus tour. For information call (212) 854-5109. There are guides for informal visits.

Financial Aid: 75% of undergraduates work part time. Average annual earnings from campus work are $2500. GS is a member of CSS. The FAFSA and the college's own financial statement are required. Check with the school for current application deadlines.

International Students: There are 104 international students enrolled. The school actively recruits these students. They must score satisfactorily on the written TOEFL or on the electronic version and also take the college's own test. Submission of recent SAT scores is encouraged. Students who have not taken the SAT must take Columbia's General Studies Admissions Exam.

Computers: Wireless access is available. There are computer facilities in over 65 buildings. All students may access the system. Students may access the system 1 hour. There are no fees. It is strongly recommended that all students have a personal computer.

Graduates: From July 1, 2004 to June 30, 2005, 243 bachelor's degrees were awarded. The most popular majors were economics (11%), political science (10%), and literature-writing (10%). 300 companies recruited on campus in 2004-2005.

Admissions Contact: Curtis Rodgers, Dean of Admissions.
E-mail: *gs-admit@columbia.edu* Web: *www.gs.columbia.edu*

CONCORDIA COLLEGE-NEW YORK
D-5

Bronxville, NY 10708

(914) 337-9300
(800) 937-2655; Fax: (914) 395-4636

Full-time: 269 men, 348 women
Part-time: 30 men, 66 women
Graduate: none
Year: semesters
Application Deadline: March 15
Freshman Class: 612 applied, 455 accepted, 142 enrolled
SAT Verbal/Math: 480/470*

Faculty: 29
Ph.D.s: 72%
Student/Faculty: 21 to 1
Tuition: $19,800
Room & Board: $7940

ACT: 18

COMPETITIVE

Concordia College, founded in 1881, is a Christian liberal arts college offering undergraduate majors, including business, education, music, social work, and professional training in ministry. In addition to regional accreditation, Concordia has baccalaureate program accreditation with CSWE and NCATE. The library contains 85,000 volumes, 25,000 microform items, and 8750 audio/video tapes/CDs/DVDs, and subscribes to 350 periodicals including electronic. Computerized library services include the card catalog, interlibrary loans, database searching, Internet access, and laptop Internet portals. Special learning facilities include a learning resource center, art gallery, education center, family center, and Lutheran education service. The 33-acre campus is in a suburban area 15 miles north of New York City. Including any residence halls, there are 21 buildings.

Student Life: 66% of undergraduates are from New York. Others are from 27 states and 34 foreign countries. 54% are white; 11% African American. 40% are Protestant; 32% Catholic; 19% Unknown; 8% claim no religious affiliation. The average age of freshmen is 18; all undergraduates, 24. 24% do not continue beyond their first year; 45% remain to graduate.

Housing: 424 students can be accommodated in college housing, which includes single-sex dorms. In addition, there are special-interest houses. On-campus housing is guaranteed for all 4 years. 66% of students live on campus; of those, 75% remain on campus on weekends. All students may keep cars.

Activities: 10% of men belong to 2 national fraternities; 10% of women belong to 2 national sororities. There are 25 groups on campus, including art, chamber and jazz ensembles, cheerleading, choir, chorus, drama, ethnic, honors, international, jazz band, literary magazine, musical theater, newspaper, orchestra, organist guild, photography, professional, religious, social, social service, student government, symphony, and yearbook. Popular campus events include guest lectures, dramatic presentations, and spring and fall festivals.

Sports: There are 5 intercollegiate sports for men and 6 for women, and 10 intramural sports for men and 10 for women. Facilities include

an athletic center, a field house, indoor and outdoor tennis courts, squash and racquetball courts, a weight room, a fitness center, and 3 athletic fields.

Disabled Students: 50% of the campus is accessible. Wheelchair ramps, elevators, special parking, specially equipped rest rooms, lowered drinking fountains, and lowered telephones are available.

Services: Counseling and information services are available, as is tutoring in most subjects. There is remedial math, reading, and writing.

Campus Safety and Security: Measures include 24-hour foot and vehicle patrol, security escort services, informal discussions, and emergency telephones. There are lighted pathways/sidewalks.

Programs of Study: Concordia confers B.A., B.S. degrees. Associate degrees are also awarded. Bachelor's degrees are awarded in BIOLOGICAL SCIENCE (biology/biological science), BUSINESS (business administration and management), COMMUNICATIONS AND THE ARTS (applied music, arts administration/management, English, and music), COMPUTER AND PHYSICAL SCIENCE (mathematics), EDUCATION (early childhood, education, elementary, mathematics, music, and social studies), ENGINEERING AND ENVIRONMENTAL DESIGN (environmental science), SOCIAL SCIENCE (behavioral science, history, interdisciplinary studies, international studies, religion, religious music, and social work). Education, behavioral sciences, and social work are the strongest academically. Education, business administration, and behavioral sciences are the largest.

Required: To graduate, students must complete 122 semester hours with a minimum GPA of 2.0. General education requirements include 21 hours of integrated learning courses and 18 credits of discipline support courses. Students are required to take 3 credits each of phys ed. A thesis is required in some majors.

Special: A registered professional nurse program is offered in cooperation with Mount Vernon Hospital School of Nursing. Concordia also offers co-op programs in social work and education, cross-registration with a consortium of nearby colleges, internships, study abroad in England, B.A.- B.S. degrees, an interdisciplinary studies degree, and credit for life experience. Accelerated degree programs are available in business administration and behavioral sciences. There is 1 national honor society, a freshman honors program, and 10 departmental honors program.

Faculty/Classroom: 55% of faculty are male; 45%, female. All teach undergraduates. The average class size in an introductory lecture is 19; in a laboratory, 12; and in a regular course, 12.

Admissions: 74% of the 2005-2006 applicants were accepted. The SAT scores for the 2005-2006 freshman class were: Verbal--57% below 500, 36% between 500 and 599, and 7% between 600 and 700; Math--65% below 500, 27% between 500 and 599, and 8% between 600 and 700. The ACT scores were 90% below 21, and 10% between 21 and 23. 18% of the current freshmen were in the top fifth of their class; 48% were in the top two fifths.

Requirements: The SAT or ACT is required. In addition, applicants should be graduates of an accredited secondary school or have a GED certificate. Concordia prefers completion of 4 years of English, 3 of math,and 2 each of social studies, laboratory, science, and a foreign language. An interview is recommended, and those students applying to the music program must audition. A GPA of 2.5 is required. AP and CLEP credits are accepted. Important factors in the admissions decision are advanced placement or honor courses, evidence of special talent, and extracurricular activities record.

Procedure: Freshmen are admitted fall and spring. Entrance exams should be taken in the fall of the senior year. There are early decision, early admissions, and rolling admissions plans. Early decision applications should be filed by November 15; regular applications, by March 15 for fall entry and December 30 for spring entry, along with a $40 fee. Notification of early decision is sent December 1; regular decision, on a rolling basis. 12 early decision candidates were accepted for the 2005-2006 class. Applications are accepted on-line.

Transfer: 58 transfer students enrolled in 2004-2005. A 2.0 GPA is recommended. Applicants must submit official transcripts from previous colleges attended. Students must complete the last 30 credits at Concordia College. 30 of 122 credits required for the bachelor's degree must be completed at Concordia.

Visiting: There are regularly scheduled orientations for prospective students, which include opportunities to interact with faculty, tour the campus, learn about admission and financial aid, and discover academic and student life opportunities. There are guides for informal visits and visitors may sit in on classes and stay overnight. To schedule a visit, contact the Admissions Office.

Financial Aid: In 2005-2006, 94% of all full-time freshmen and 93% of continuing full-time students received some form of financial aid. 79% of full-time freshmen and 70% of continuing full-time students received need-based aid. The average freshman award was $14,565. 36% of undergraduates work part time. Average annual earnings from campus work are $1275. The average financial indebtedness of the 2005 graduate was $14,350. The FAFSA is required. The priority date for freshman financial aid applications for fall entry is February 15. The deadline for filing freshman financial aid applications for fall entry is April 1.

International Students: There are 55 international students enrolled. The school actively recruits these students. They must score satisfactorily on the written TOEFL or on the electronic version and or take the SAT.

Computers: Wireless access is available. Concordia provides high-speed Internet access, e-mail services, individual disk storage file services, and access to library services and the college intranet. A total of 40 PCs are available for student use in the library, the Writing Center, and two computer labs. Resident students can also use their PCs for access to the local network from their dorm rooms. All students may access the system any time. There are no time limits and no fees.

Graduates: From July 1, 2004 to June 30, 2005, 124 bachelor's degrees were awarded. The most popular majors were business administration (32%), elementary education (18%), and social work (6%). In an average class, 2% graduate in 3 years or less, 41% graduate in 4 years or less, 45% graduate in 5 years or less, and 51% graduate in 6 years or less. Of the 2004 graduating class, 18% were enrolled in graduate school within 6 months of graduation and 79% were employed.

Admissions Contact: Donna Hoyt, Director of Admission.
E-mail: *admissions@concordia-ny.edu* Web: *www.concordia-ny.edu*

COOPER UNION FOR THE ADVANCEMENT OF SCIENCE AND ART   D-5

New York, NY 10003-7120	(212) 353-4120; Fax: (212) 353-4342
Full-time: 593 men, 326 women	**Faculty:** 53; II B, ++$
Part-time: 3 men, 2 women	**Ph.D.s:** 82%
Graduate: 48 men, 6 women	**Student/Faculty:** 17 to 1
Year: semesters, summer session	**Tuition:** $27,500
Application Deadline: January 1	**Room & Board:** $11,000
Freshman Class: 2301 applied, 308 accepted, 228 enrolled	
SAT Verbal/Math: 670/700*	**MOST COMPETITIVE**

The Cooper Union for the Advancement of Science and Art is an all honors college that provides full-tuition scholarships (estimated value $27,500) to all undergraduates accepted. It offers degrees in architecture, art, and engineering. There are 3 undergraduate schools and 1 graduate school. In addition to regional accreditation, Cooper Union has baccalaureate program accreditation with ABET, NAAB, and NASAD. The library contains 100,000 volumes, 50,000 microform items, and 300 audio/video tapes/CDs/DVDs, and subscribes to 350 periodicals including electronic. Computerized library services include the card catalog, interlibrary loans, database searching, and Internet access. Special learning facilities include a learning resource center, art gallery, a center for speaking and writing, an electronic resources center, and a visual resources center. The campus is in an urban area located in the heart of lower Manhattan. Including any residence halls, there are 5 buildings.

Student Life: 60% of undergraduates are from New York. Students are from 40 states, 14 foreign countries, and Canada. 75% are from public schools. 50% are white; 25% Asian American; 10% foreign nationals. The average age of freshmen is 18; all undergraduates, 20. 3% do not continue beyond their first year; 82% remain to graduate.

Housing: 183 students can be accommodated in college housing, which includes coed on-campus apartments. 78% of students commute. All students may keep cars.

Activities: 20% of men belong to 2 national fraternities; 10% of women belong to 1 local sorority. There are 95 groups on campus, including chess, chorale, computers, drama, environmental, ethnic, film, gay, honors, international, literary magazine, newspaper, orchestra, political, professional, religious, social, social service, student government, and yearbook. Popular campus events include an end-of-the-year student art, architecture, and engineering exhibit and ongoing events in the Great Hall.

Sports: There are 5 intercollegiate sports for men and 2 for women, and 12 intramural sports for men and 12 for women. Facilities include a cardio/weight room, martial arts, fencing rooms, a nearby swimming pool, and basketball courts.

Disabled Students: 80% of the campus is accessible. Wheelchair ramps, elevators, specially equipped rest rooms, and special class scheduling are available.

Services: Counseling and information services are available, as is tutoring in some subjects, including math, physics, speech, and writing.

Campus Safety and Security: Measures include informal discussions, pamphlets/posters/films, emergency telephones, lighted pathways/sidewalks and community security and police.

Programs of Study: Cooper Union confers B.S., B.Arch., B.E., and B.F.A. degrees. Master's degrees are also awarded. Bachelor's degrees are awarded in COMMUNICATIONS AND THE ARTS (fine arts and graphic design), ENGINEERING AND ENVIRONMENTAL DESIGN (architecture, chemical engineering, civil engineering, electrical/electronics engineering, engineering, and mechanical engineering). Engineering is the strongest academically and has the largest enrollment.

Required: The 5-year architecture program requires 160 credits, including 30 in liberal arts and electives, for graduation. Art students must complete 128 credits, including 38 in liberal arts and electives, with a minimum overall GPA of 2.0 to graduate. A 2.5 GPA is expected in studio work. Engineering students are required to complete a minimum of 135 credits, including a computer literacy course and 24 credits in humanities and social sciences, with a minimum GPA of 2.0.

Special: Cross-registration with New School University, internships, study abroad for art students in 8 countries and for engineering students in 6 countries, and some pass/fail options are available. Nondegree study is possible. An accelerated degree in engineering is also available. There are 4 national honor societies and 1 departmental honors program.

Faculty/Classroom: 74% of faculty are male; 26%, female. All both teach and do research. No introductory courses are taught by graduate students. The average class size in an introductory lecture is 28; in a laboratory, 20; and in a regular course, 20.

Admissions: 13% of the 2005-2006 applicants were accepted. The SAT scores for the 2005-2006 freshman class were: Verbal--4% below 500, 16% between 500 and 599, 50% between 600 and 700, and 30% above 700; Math--5% below 500, 12% between 500 and 599, 25% between 600 and 700, and 58% above 700. 80% of the current freshmen were in the top fifth of their class; 95% were in the top two fifths. There were 4 National Merit finalists and 25 semifinalists. 10 freshmen graduated first in their class.

Requirements: The SAT is required. In addition, engineering applicants must take SAT Subject Tests in mathematics I or II and physics or chemistry. Graduation from an approved secondary school is required. Applicants should have completed 16 to 18 high school academic credits, depending on their major. An essay is part of the application process. Art students must submit a portfolio. Art and architecture applicants must complete a project called the hometest. AP credits are accepted. Important factors in the admissions decision are evidence of special talent, advanced placement or honor courses, and personality/intangible qualities.

Procedure: Freshmen are admitted in the fall. Entrance exams should be taken before February 1. There are early decision and deferred admissions plans. Early decision applications should be filed by December 1; regular applications, by January 1 for fall entry, along with a $50 fee. Notification of early decision is sent February 1; regular decision, April 1. 80 early decision candidates were accepted for the 2005-2006 class. 30 applicants were on the 2005 waiting list; 2 were admitted. Applications are accepted on-line.

Transfer: 45 transfer students enrolled in 2004-2005. Art and architecture transfer applicants must present a portfolio and a minimum of 24 credits in studio classes. Engineering transfer applicants must submit a transcript with grades of B or better in at least 24 credits of appropriate courses.

Visiting: There are regularly scheduled orientations for prospective students, consisting of open house and portfolio review days for art and open house for engineering; architecture tours are by appointment. There are guides for informal visits and visitors may sit in on classes. To schedule a visit, contact the Office of Admissions and Records.

Financial Aid: In 2005-2006, all full-time students received some form of financial aid. 32% of full-time freshmen and 33% of continuing full-time students received need-based aid. Need-based scholarships or need-based grants for freshman averaged $2680 ($4050 maximum); need-based self-help aid (loans and jobs) averaged $2515 ($3000 maximum); and other non-need-based awards and non-need-based scholarships averaged $27,500 maximum. 44% of undergraduates work part time. Average annual earnings from campus work are $1126. The average financial indebtedness of the 2005 graduate was $11,617. Cooper Union is a member of CSS. The CSS/Profile or FAFSA is required. The priority date for freshman financial aid applications for fall entry is May 1.

International Students: There are 80 international students enrolled. A satisfactory score on thee TOEFL is required. All freshman applicants must take the SAT; art and architecture students must also take the hometest.Students must take SAT Subject tests in Engineering students must take SAT: Subject Tests in math and physics or chemistry.

Computers: Wireless access is available. All students may access the system whenever the engineering building is open. There are no time limits and no fees.

Graduates: From July 1, 2004 to June 30, 2005, 223 bachelor's degrees were awarded. The most popular majors were fine arts (30%), electrical engineering (15%), and architecture (14%). In an average class, 1% graduate in 3 years or less, 70% graduate in 4 years or less, and 82% graduate in 5 years or less. 110 companies recruited on campus in 2004-2005. Of the 2004 graduating class, 56% were enrolled in graduate school within 6 months of graduation and 40% were employed.

Admissions Contact: Mitchell Lipton, Dean of Admissions and Records and Registrar. A video is available.
E-mail: *admissions@cooper.edu* Web: *www.cooper.edu*

CORNELL UNIVERSITY — C-3

Ithaca, NY 14850 (607) 255-5241

Full-time: 6884 men, 6800 women	**Faculty:** 1675; I, +$
Part-time: none	**Ph.D.s:** 90%
Graduate: 3447 men, 2511 women	**Student/Faculty:** 8 to 1
Year: semesters, summer session	**Tuition:** $31,467
Application Deadline: January 1	**Room & Board:** $10,250

Freshman Class: 24,452 applied, 6621 accepted, 3108 enrolled
SAT Verbal/Math: 680/710* **ACT:** 30 **MOST COMPETITIVE**

Cornell University was founded in 1865 as a land-grant institution. Privately supported undergraduate divisions include the College of Architecture, Art, and Planning; the College of Arts and Sciences; the College of Engineering; and the School of Hotel Administration. State-assisted undergraduate divisions include the College of Agriculture and Life Sciences, the College of Human Ecology, and the School of Industrial and Labor Relations. There are 7 undergraduate and 4 graduate schools. In addition to regional accreditation, Cornell has baccalaureate program accreditation with AACSB, ABET, ADA, ASLA, AVMA, CSWE, FIDER, LCME, and NAAB. The 18 libraries contain 7,403,263 volumes, 8,204,567 microform items, and 440,676 audio/video tapes/CDs/DVDs, and subscribe to 72,788 periodicals including electronic. Computerized library services include the card catalog, interlibrary loans, database searching, Internet access, and laptop Internet portals. Special learning facilities include a learning resource center, art gallery, planetarium, radio station, a bird sanctuary, 4 designated national resource centers, 2 local optical observatories, Africana Studies center, Cornell Platations, particle accelerator, supercomputer, national resource centers, national research centers, performing arts center, observatories, and marine laboratory. The 745-acre campus is in a rural area 60 miles south of Syracuse. Including any residence halls, there are 770 buildings.

Student Life: 64% of undergraduates are from out of state, mostly the Middle Atlantic. Students are from 50 states, 120 foreign countries, and Canada. 56% are white; 16% Asian American. The average age of freshmen is 18; all undergraduates, 20. 4% do not continue beyond their first year; 92% remain to graduate.

Housing: 8168 students can be accommodated in college housing, which includes single-sex and coed dorms, on-campus apartments, married-student housing, fraternity houses, and sorority houses. In addition, there are language houses and special-interest houses. On-campus housing is guaranteed for the freshman year only and is available on a lottery system for upperclassmen. 54% of students live on campus; of those, 90% remain on campus on weekends. All students may keep cars.

Activities: 28% of men belong to 1 local and 43 national fraternities; 22% of women belong to 22 national sororities. There are 754 groups on campus, including art, band, cheerleading, chess, choir, chorale, chorus, computers, dance, debate, drama, drill team, drum and bugle corps, ethnic, film, forensics, gay, honors, international, literary magazine, marching band, musical theater, newspaper, orchestra, pep band, photography, political, professional, radio and TV, religious, social, social service, student government, symphony, and yearbook. Popular campus events include Dragon Day, New Student Reading Project, and Third World Festival of the Arts.

Sports: There are 18 intercollegiate sports for men and 18 for women, and 27 intramural sports for men and 27 for women. Facilities include indoor and outdoor tracks, a 5000-seat indoor gym, 3 swimming pools, a 25,000-seat stadium, 16 intercollegiate fields, a bowling alley, intramural fields, a boat house, indoor and outdoor tennis courts, and the Lindseth climbing wall.

Disabled Students: 90% of the campus is accessible. Wheelchair ramps, elevators, special parking, specially equipped rest rooms, special class scheduling, lowered drinking fountains, lowered telephones, alternative test arrangements, and bus passes or van transportation are available.

Services: Counseling and information services are available, as is tutoring in most subjects. There is a reader service for the blind. Note takers, biology and math student support centers, and writing workshops are also available.

Campus Safety and Security: Measures include 24-hour foot and vehicle patrol, self-defense education, security escort services, and shuttle buses. There are informal discussions, pamphlets/posters/films, emergency telephones, and lighted pathways/sidewalks.

Programs of Study: Cornell confers B.A., B.S., B.Arch., and B.F.A. degrees. Master's and doctoral degrees are also awarded. Bachelor's degrees are awarded in AGRICULTURE (agricultural business management, agricultural economics, agriculture, agronomy, animal science, horticulture, international agriculture, natural resource management, plant science, and soil science), BIOLOGICAL SCIENCE (biochemistry, biology/biological science, biometrics and biostatistics, biotechnology, botany, ecology, entomology, evolutionary biology, genetics, microbiology, neurosciences, and nutrition), BUSINESS (hotel/motel and restaurant management, labor studies, and operations research), COMMUNICATIONS AND THE ARTS (art history and appreciation, classics, communications, comparative literature, dance, design, dramatic arts,

English, film arts, fine arts, French, German, Greek, Italian, languages, Latin, linguistics, music, Russian, and Spanish), COMPUTER AND PHYSICAL SCIENCE (astronomy, atmospheric sciences and meteorology, chemistry, computer science, earth science, geology, information sciences and systems, mathematics, physics, science technology, and statistics), EDUCATION (education), ENGINEERING AND ENVIRONMENTAL DESIGN (aerospace studies, agricultural engineering, architectural history, architecture, bioengineering, chemical engineering, city/community/regional planning, civil engineering, computer engineering, electrical/electronics engineering, engineering physics, environmental engineering technology, landscape architecture/design, materials science, and mechanical engineering), SOCIAL SCIENCE (African studies, American studies, anthropology, archeology, Asian/Oriental studies, classical/ancient civilization, consumer services, economics, family/consumer studies, food production/management/services, food science, German area studies, history, human development, Near Eastern studies, philosophy, political science/government, psychology, public affairs, religion, rural sociology, Russian and Slavic studies, sociology, textiles and clothing, urban studies, and women's studies). Biology, hotel administration, and industrial and labor relations are the largest.

Required: Entering freshmen must meet basic swimming and water safety competency requirements. All undergraduates must take 2 semesters each of freshman writing seminar and phys ed. Graduation requirements vary by program, including a minimum of 120 credits.

Special: Co-op programs are offered in the College of Engineering and the School of Industrial and Labor Relations. Cross-registration is available with Ithaca College. Public-policy internships are available in Washington, D.C., Albany, and New York City. Cornell also offers study abroad in more than 50 countries, B.A.-B.S. and B.A.-B.F.A. degrees, other dual degrees, interdisciplinary/intercollegiate options, student-designed and dual majors, work-study programs, a Washington semester, accelerated degree programs, pass/fail options, and limited nondegree study. A 6-year B.S./M.B.A/M.Eng. program is offered. There are 24 national honor societies, including Phi Beta Kappa, and all departments have honors programs.

Faculty/Classroom: 70% of faculty are male; 30%, female. All both teach and do research. Graduate students teach 1% of introductory courses. The average class size in an introductory lecture is 45; in a laboratory, 21; and in a regular course, 29.

Admissions: 27% of the 2005-2006 applicants were accepted. The SAT scores for the 2005-2006 freshman class were: Verbal--1% below 500, 13% between 500 and 599, 50% between 600 and 700, and 34% above 700; Math--1% below 500, 6% between 500 and 599, 41% between 600 and 700, and 53% above 700. The ACT scores were 4% between 21 and 23, 14% between 24 and 26, 14% between 27 and 28, and 68% above 28. 93% of the current freshmen were in the top fifth of their class; 98% were in the top two fifths. There were 166 National Merit finalists. 234 freshmen graduated first in their class.

Requirements: The SAT or ACT is required. The ACT Optional Writing test is also required. In addition, an essay is required as part of the application process. Other requirements vary by division or program, including specific SAT Subject tests and selection of courses within the minimum 16 secondary-school academic units needed. An interview and/or portfolio is required for specific majors. AP credits are accepted. Important factors in the admissions decision are advanced placement or honor courses, evidence of special talent, and leadership record.

Procedure: Freshmen are admitted fall and spring. Entrance exams should be taken by December of the senior year. There are early decision and deferred admissions plans. Early decision applications should be filed by November 10; regular applications, by January 1 for fall entry and November 10 for spring entry. Notification of early decision is sent mid-December; regular decision, mid-April. 1052 early decision candidates were accepted for the 2005-2006 class. 1544 applicants were on the 2005 waiting list; 209 were admitted. Applications are accepted online. The fall 2005 application fee was $65.

Transfer: 481 transfer students enrolled in 2004-2005. All applicants must submit high school and college transcripts, as well as scores from the SAT or ACT if taken previously. Other admission requirements vary by program, including the number of credits that must be completed at Cornell. 60 of 120 credits required for the bachelor's degree must be completed at Cornell.

Visiting: There are regularly scheduled orientations for prospective students, including campus tours and information sessions. There are guides for informal visits and visitors may sit in on classes and stay overnight. To schedule a visit, contact the Red Carpet Society at (607) 255-3447.

Financial Aid: In 2005-2006, 49% of all full-time freshmen and 47% of continuing full-time students received some form of financial aid. 46% of full-time freshmen and 44% of continuing full-time students received need-based aid. The average freshman award was $26,900. Need-based scholarships or need-based grants averaged $21,000; and non-need-based athletic scholarships averaged $7900. 45% of undergraduates work part time. The average financial indebtedness of the 2005 graduate was $23,450. Cornell is a member of CSS. The CSS/Profile or FAFSA

is required. The IRS form is required after enrollment. The deadline for filing freshman financial aid applications for fall entry is February 11.

International Students: There are 1014 international students enrolled. The school actively recruits these students. They must score 600 on the written TOEFL and also take the SAT or the ACT. Some divisions require SAT: Subject tests.

Computers: Wireless access is available. Students have access to campuswide PC centers and more than 30 departmental facilities with more than 1350 Pcs, as well as networks in residence halls. Wireless connections are available in many campus locations. All networks are connected to the Internet. All students may access the system. There are no time limits and no fees. It is strongly recommended that all students have a personal computer.

Graduates: From July 1, 2004 to June 30, 2005, 3474 bachelor's degrees were awarded. The most popular majors were engineering (18%), social sciences and history (12%), and biological sciences/life sciences (12%). In an average class, 3% graduate in 3 years or less, 84% graduate in 4 years or less, 91% graduate in 5 years or less, and 92% graduate in 6 years or less. 468 companies recruited on campus in 2004-2005. Of the 2004 graduating class, 34% were enrolled in graduate school within 6 months of graduation and 40% were employed.

Admissions Contact: Jason Locke, Director of Undergraduate Admissions. A video is available. E-mail: *admissions@cornell.edu*
Web: *http://admissions.cornell.edu*

DAEMEN COLLEGE

A-3

Amherst, NY 14226-3592

(716) 839-8225
(800) 462-7652; Fax: (716) 839-8370

Full-time: 302 men, 969 women	**Faculty:** 63; IIB, -$
Part-time: 69 men, 263 women	**Ph.Ds:** 74%
Graduate: 157 men, 555 women	**Student/Faculty:** 20 to 1
Year: semesters, summer session	**Tuition:** $16,800
Application Deadline: open	**Room & Board:** $7780
Freshman Class: n/av	
SAT Verbal/Math: 520/520*	**ACT:** 22 COMPETITIVE

Daemen College, founded in 1947, is a private institution offering undergraduate and graduate programs in the liberal and fine arts, business, education, allied health professions, and natural sciences. In addition to regional accreditation, Daemen has baccalaureate program accreditation with APTA, ARC-PA, CSWE, and NLN. The library contains 140,176 volumes, 23,778 microform items, and 5045 audio/video tapes/CDs/DVDs, and subscribes to 945 periodicals including electronic. Computerized library services include the card catalog, interlibrary loans, database searching, and Internet access. Special learning facilities include a learning resource center, art gallery, and a video conference center. The 35-acre campus is in a suburban area 9 miles northeast of downtown Buffalo. Including any residence halls, there are 18 buildings.

Student Life: 95% of undergraduates are from New York. Others are from 20 states, 7 foreign countries, and Canada. 79% are white; 15% African American. 46% are Catholic; 19% Protestant. The average age of freshmen is 19; all undergraduates, 23. 28% do not continue beyond their first year; 40% remain to graduate.

Housing: 524 students can be accommodated in college housing, which includes coed dorms and on-campus apartments. There is a quiet dorm. On-campus housing is guaranteed for all 4 years. 58% of students commute. All students may keep cars.

Activities: 6% of men belong to 1 local fraternity; 4% of women belong to 4 local sororities. There are 42 groups on campus, including art, cheerleading, choir, dance, drama, ethnic, gay, honors, literary magazine, multicultural, musical theater, newspaper, professional, social, social service, student government, and yearbook. Popular campus events include Welcome Back Week, Springfest, and Battle of the Bands.

Sports: There are 4 intercollegiate sports for men and 4 for women, and 4 intramural sports for men and 2 for women. Facilities include a gym, weight and exercise rooms, saunas, and a volleyball sand court.

Disabled Students: 83% of the campus is accessible. Wheelchair ramps, elevators, special parking, specially equipped rest rooms, lowered drinking fountains, and lowered telephones are available.

Services: Counseling and information services are available, as is tutoring in every subject. There is remedial math, reading, and writing.

Campus Safety and Security: Measures include 24-hour foot and vehicle patrol, security escort services, informal discussions, and pamphlets/posters/films. There are emergency telephones, lighted pathways/sidewalks, and video monitors.

Programs of Study: Daemen confers B.A., B.S., and B.F.A. degrees. Master's and doctoral degrees are also awarded. Bachelor's degrees are awarded in BIOLOGICAL SCIENCE (biochemistry and biology/biological science), BUSINESS (accounting and business administration and management), COMMUNICATIONS AND THE ARTS (applied art, art, English, fine arts, French, graphic design, and Spanish), COMPUTER AND PHYSICAL SCIENCE (mathematics and natural sciences), EDUCATION (art, early childhood, elementary, English, foreign languages, health, mathematics, science, social studies, and special), HEALTH

PROFESSIONS (health science, nursing, and physician's assistant), SOCIAL SCIENCE (history, political science/government, psychology, religion, and social work). Physical therapy, physician's assistant, and natural science are the strongest academically. Education, physical therapy, and natural science are the largest.

Required: To graduate, students must complete 120 to 199 hours (depending on the degree program) with a minimum GPA of 2.0. Students are required to complete a minimum of 30 credit hours of course work in residence. The final semester's course work must be taken in residence.

Special: Daemen offers cooperative programs in all majors, internships, cross-registration within the Western New York Consortium of Colleges and Universities, student-designed majors, work-study programs, an accelerated degree program in nursing, dual majors, a Washington semester, and study abroad in 6 countries. There is an International Studies Program that leads to a minor in international studies. There are 9 national honor societies, a freshman honors program, and 20 departmental honors programs.

Faculty/Classroom: 39% of faculty are male; 61%, female. 64% teach undergraduates and 1% both teach and do research. No introductory courses are taught by graduate students. The average class size in an introductory lecture is 18; in a laboratory, 10; and in a regular course, 15.

Admissions: The SAT scores for the 2005-2006 freshman class were: Verbal--36% below 500, 53% between 500 and 599, and 11% between 600 and 700; Math--27% below 500, 57% between 500 and 599, 15% between 600 and 700, and 1% above 700. The ACT scores were 35% below 21, 32% between 21 and 23, 22% between 24 and 26, 7% between 27 and 28, and 4% above 28. 40% of the current freshmen were in the top fifth of their class; 74% were in the top two fifths. 3 freshmen graduated first in their class.

Requirements: The SAT or ACT is required. In addition, applicants must be graduates of an accredited secondary school or have the GED equivalent. Some departments have further admissions requirements, including a portfolio review for art majors, 3-year sequences of math and science for all natural science programs, and 2 essays, 3 letters of recommendation, and a supplemental application for the physician's assistant program. A GPA of 2.0 is required. AP and CLEP credits are accepted. Important factors in the admissions decision are advanced placement or honor courses, leadership record, and evidence of special talent.

Procedure: Freshmen are admitted fall, spring, and summer. Entrance exams should be taken by the summer following the senior year. There are early admissions and deferred admissions plans. There is a rolling admissions plan. Application deadlines are open. Notification is sent on a rolling-basis. Applications are accepted on-line. The fall 2005 application fee was $25 (fee is waived for on-line applications).

Transfer: 163 transfer students enrolled in 2004-2005. Applicants must present college transcripts an indication of good standing from the last institution attended, and a minimum GPA of 2.0 to 2.8. Physician's assistant applicants should submit essays, 3 letters of recommendation, and supplemental applications. 30 of 120 credits required for the bachelor's degree must be completed at Daemen.

Visiting: There are regularly scheduled orientations for prospective students, consisting of a 5-day orientation during July and August that includes a campus tour, an interview, and placement testing in math and English. There are guides for informal visits and visitors may sit in on classes and stay overnight. To schedule a visit, contact the Admissions Office.

Financial Aid: In 2004-2005, 80% of all full-time freshmen and 95% of continuing full-time students received some form of financial aid. 74% of full-time freshmen and 88% of continuing full-time students received need-based aid. The average freshman award was $14,228. Need-based scholarships or need-based grants averaged $7484; need-based self-help aid (loans and jobs) averaged $3932; non-need-based athletic scholarships averaged $3389; and other non-need-based awards and non-need-based scholarships averaged $5035. 20% of undergraduates work part time. Average annual earnings from campus work are $1077. The average financial indebtedness of the 2005 graduate was $13,323. The FAFSA, the state aid form, and foreign student certification of finances are required. The priority date for freshman financial aid applications for fall entry is March 15. There is a rolling deadline for filing freshman financial aid applications for fall entry.

International Students: There are 19 international students enrolled. They must take the TOEFL.

Computers: All students may access the system. There are no time limits and no fees.

Graduates: From July 1, 2004 to June 30, 2005, 284 bachelor's degrees were awarded. The most popular majors were nursing (27%), education (14%), and natural science (12%). In an average class, 23% graduate in 4 years or less, 37% graduate in 5 years or less, and 40% graduate in 6 years or less. 80 companies recruited on campus in 2004-2005. Of the 2004 graduating class, 19% were enrolled in graduate school within 6 months of graduation and 90% were employed.

Admissions Contact: Donna Shaffner, Director of Undergraduate Admissions. A video is available. E-mail: *admissions@daemen.edu* Web: *http://www.daemen.edu/admissions/*

DEVRY INSTITUTE OF TECHNOLOGY/NEW YORK   D-5

Long Island City, NY 11101-3051   (718) 472-2728
(888) 713-3879; Fax: (718) 361-0004

Full-time: 1000 men, 300 women	**Faculty:** n/av
Part-time: 400 men, 140 women	**Ph.D.s:** n/av
Graduate: none	**Student/Faculty:** n/av
Year: semesters, summer session	**Tuition:** $12,000
Application Deadline: open	**Room & Board:** n/app
Freshman Class: n/av	
SAT or ACT: n/av	**LESS COMPETITIVE**

DeVry Institute of Technology/New York, founded in 1998, is a private institution offering hands-on programs in electronics, business administration, computer information systems, telecommunications, and computer technology. The school is 1 of 67 DeVry University locations throughout the United States and Canada. Figures in the above and in this profile are approximate. The library contains 9752 volumes and 708 audio/video tapes/CDs/DVDs, and subscribes to 120 periodicals including electronic. Computerized library services include the card catalog, interlibrary loans, and database searching. Special learning facilities include a learning resource center and electronics and other labs. The 2-acre campus is in an urban area. There is 1 building.

Student Life: 40% are African American; 23% Hispanic; 10% white. The average age of all undergraduates is 24.

Housing: There are no residence halls. There are private apartments, student-plan housing; and private rooms. All students commute. Alcohol is not permitted. All students may keep cars.

Activities: There are no fraternities or sororities. There are 7 groups on campus, including chess, international, professional, social, and yearbook. Popular campus events include DSA Time Out, End of Semester Bashment, and Post Ramadan Celebration.

Sports: There is no sports program at DeVry.

Disabled Students: All of the campus is accessible. Elevators, special parking, specially equipped rest rooms, special class scheduling, lowered drinking fountains, and lowered telephones are available.

Services: Counseling and information services are available, as is tutoring in every subject.

Campus Safety and Security: Measures include 24-hour foot and vehicle patrol, security escort services, informal discussions, and pamphlets/posters/films. There are emergency telephones and lighted pathways/sidewalks.

Programs of Study: DeVry confers the B.S. degree. Associate and master's degrees are also awarded. Bachelor's degrees are awarded in BUSINESS (business administration and management), COMMUNICATIONS AND THE ARTS (telecommunications), COMPUTER AND PHYSICAL SCIENCE (information sciences and systems), ENGINEERING AND ENVIRONMENTAL DESIGN (computer technology and electrical/electronics engineering technology). Electronics, computer information systems, and business administration are the largest.

Required: To graduate, students must complete 48 to 154 credit hours with a 2.0 minimum GPA. Course requirements vary according to program. All first-semester students take courses in algebra, psychology, and student success strategies.

Special: Evening and weekend classes, co-op programs, distance learning, and an accelerated degree program are offered.

Faculty/Classroom: All teach undergraduates.

Requirements: Admissions requirements include graduation from a secondary school; the GED is also accepted. Applicants must pass the DeVry entrance exam or present satisfactory ACT or SAT scores. An interview is required. CLEP credit is accepted.

Procedure: Freshmen are admitted fall, spring, and summer. There are early admissions and deferred admissions plans. There is a rolling admissions plan. Application deadlines are open. Notification is sent on a rolling basis. Applications are accepted on-line. Check with the school for current application deadlines. The fall 2005 application fee was $50.

Transfer: Applicants must present passing grades in all completed college course work, demonstrate language skills proficiency with at least 24 completed semester hours, and present evidence of math proficiency by appropriate college-level credits. A minimum GPA of 2.0 is required. 25 of 48 credits required for the bachelor's degree must be completed at DeVry.

Visiting: There are regularly scheduled orientations for prospective students. There are guides for informal visits and visitors may sit in on classes. To schedule a visit, contact the Director of Admissions.

Financial Aid: In a recent year, 66% of all full-time freshmen and 76% of continuing full-time students received some form of financial aid. 64% of full-time freshmen and 74% of continuing full-time students received need-based aid. The average freshman award was $8821. Need-based scholarships or need-based grants averaged $6115; need-based self-help aid (loans and jobs) averaged $3326; and other non-need-based awards and non-need-based scholarships averaged $6490. The FAFSA is required.

International Students: International students must take the TOEFL and also take the college's own entrance exam.

Computers: Computer information systems students may access the system during lab hours. Students may access the system. There are no fees.

Graduates: In a recent year, 204 bachelor's degrees were awarded. The most popular majors were computer information systems (57%), business (25%), and electronics engineering technology (17%).

Admissions Contact: Director of Admissions.
E-mail: *nyemailleads@ny.devry.edu* Web: *www.ny.devry.edu*

DOMINICAN COLLEGE
Orangeburg, NY 10962
D-5

(845) 359-3533 ext. 15
(866) 432-4636; Fax: (845) 365-3150

Full-time: 383 men, 693 women	**Faculty:** 53; IIB, --$
Part-time: 71 men, 236 women	**Ph.D.s:** n/av
Graduate: 25 men, 87 women	**Student/Faculty:** 20 to 1
Year: semesters, summer session	**Tuition:** $17,910
Application Deadline: open	**Room & Board:** $8720
Freshman Class: 1229 applied, 1015 accepted, 294 enrolled	
SAT Verbal/Math: 440/450*	**LESS COMPETITIVE**

Dominican College, founded in 1952, is a private Catholic institution offering undergraduate programs in business, biology, education, liberal arts, nursing, premedicine, occupational therapy, and social sciences. In addition to regional accreditation, DC has baccalaureate program accreditation with CSWE, CCNE, and TEAC. The library contains 103,000 volumes, 15,000 microform items, and 1000 audio/video tapes/CDs/DVDs, and subscribes to 10,000 periodicals including electronic. Computerized library services include interlibrary loans, database searching, and Internet access. Special learning facilities include a learning resource center. The 24-acre campus is in a suburban area 17 miles north of New York City. Including any residence halls, there are 8 buildings.

Student Life: 80% of undergraduates are from New York. Others are from 15 states. 70% are from public schools. 51% are white; 18% African American; 15% Hispanic. The average age of freshmen is 19; all undergraduates, 25. 33% do not continue beyond their first year; 50% remain to graduate.

Housing: 485 students can be accommodated in college housing, which includes coed dorms. On-campus housing is guaranteed for all 4 years. 78% of students commute. Alcohol is not permitted. All students may keep cars.

Activities: There are no fraternities or sororities. There are 17 groups on campus, including chorus, computers, drama, honors, literary magazine, musical theater, newspaper, professional, religious, social service, student government, and yearbook. Popular campus events include Family Day, Springfest, and Fall Festival.

Sports: There are 6 intercollegiate sports for men and 6 for women, and 3 intramural sports for men and 3 for women. Facilities include a soccer and lacrosse field, a softball field, a gym, a track, and a fitness center.

Disabled Students: All of the campus is accessible. Wheelchair ramps, special parking, specially equipped rest rooms, lowered drinking fountains, and lowered telephones are available.

Services: Counseling and information services are available, as is tutoring in some subjects, including English and math. There is remedial math, reading, and writing.

Campus Safety and Security: Measures include 24-hour foot and vehicle patrol, security escort services, shuttle buses, and informal discussions. There are pamphlets/posters/films and lighted pathways/sidewalks.

Programs of Study: DC confers B.A., B.S., B.S.Ed., B.S.N., and B.S.W. degrees. Associate and master's degrees are also awarded. Bachelor's degrees are awarded in BIOLOGICAL SCIENCE (biology/biological science), BUSINESS (accounting, banking and finance, business administration and management, business economics, human resources, international business management, and marketing/retailing/merchandising), COMMUNICATIONS AND THE ARTS (English and Spanish), COMPUTER AND PHYSICAL SCIENCE (computer science, information sciences and systems, and mathematics), EDUCATION (athletic training, elementary, mathematics, science, secondary, and special), HEALTH PROFESSIONS (health care administration, nursing, and occupational therapy), SOCIAL SCIENCE (history, humanities, psychology, social science, and social work). Nursing and occupational therapy are the largest.

Required: All students must complete courses in English and speech. Computer courses are required for business majors. In order to graduate, all students must complete 120 semester hours, including a general education curriculum of 36 to 39 credits. Distribution requirements include 12 to 15 credits in general skills, and 12 credits each in Roots of Contemporary Life and Culture,and Issues in Contemporary Life and Culture. A minimum GPA of 2.7 must be maintained by nursing majors; 3.0 for occupational therapy majors. All other majors require a minimum of 2.0.

Special: There are internship opportunities available in various fields. A 3-2 engineering degree with Manhattan College is also offered. Dual teacher certification in elementary or secondary education and special education is available. Credit for life experience is granted through sub-

mission of a portfolio. An accelerated B.S.N. degree is available. Weekend College, offered on a trimester basis, is designed to meet the needs of working adults. There are 5 national honor societies, and a freshman honors program.

Faculty/Classroom: 30% of faculty are male; 70%, female. 94% teach undergraduates. No introductory courses are taught by graduate students. The average class size in a regular course is 16.

Admissions: 83% of the 2005-2006 applicants were accepted. The SAT scores for the 2005-2006 freshman class were: Verbal--75% below 500, 22% between 500 and 599, and 3% between 600 and 700; Math--75% below 500, 21% between 500 and 599, and 4% between 600 and 700.

Requirements: The SAT is required. In addition, applicants should be graduates of an accredited secondary school or possess a GED equivalent. An interview and an essay are required for some professional programs. Recommended preparation includes 16 academic units of study distributed among English, math, natural sciences, and foreign language. AP and CLEP credits are accepted. Important factors in the admissions decision are advanced placement or honor courses, leadership record, and extracurricular activities record.

Procedure: Freshmen are admitted to all sessions. Entrance exams should be taken by November of the senior year. There are early admissions and deferred admissions plans. There is a rolling admissions plan. Application deadlines are open. Notification is sent on a rolling basis. Application fee is $35. Applications are accepted on-line.

Transfer: 89 transfer students enrolled in 2004-2005. Applicants must submit a transcript from their previous school. A minimum GPA of 2.0 is required. An interview might be required. 30 of 120 credits required for the bachelor's degree must be completed at DC.

Visiting: There are regularly scheduled orientations for prospective students. There are guides for informal visits and visitors may sit in on classes. To schedule a visit, contact Joyce Elbe, Director of Admissions at *joyce.elbe@dc.edu.*

Financial Aid: In a recent year, 97% of all full-time freshmen and 84% of continuing full-time students received some form of financial aid. 86% of full-time freshmen and 75% of continuing full-time students received need-based aid. The average freshman award was $10,215. Need-based scholarships or need-based grants averaged $10,199 ($15,000 maximum); need-based self-help aid (loans and jobs) averaged $3652 ($4625 maximum); non-need-based athletic scholarships averaged $3178 ($10,000 maximum); and other non-need-based awards and non-need-based scholarships averaged $4695 ($24,000 maximum). 85% of undergraduates work part time. Average annual earnings from campus work are $1500. The average financial indebtedness ofa recent graduate was $22,318. DC is a member of CSS. The FAFSA and the state aid form are required. The priority date for freshman financial aid applications for fall entry is February 15. The deadline for filing freshman financial aid applications for fall entry is June 15.

International Students: They must take the TOEFL or and also take the SAT or the ACT.

Computers: There are 3 computer labs. The library provides an Internet-based circulation/card system that can be accessed using PCs. The main residence hall has a network connection in every room. All students may access the system. There are no time limits and no fees.

Graduates: From July 1, 2004 to June 30, 2005, 264 bachelor's degrees were awarded. The most popular majors were nursing (17%), occupational therapy/social sciences (10%), and elementary education (8%). In an average class, 49% graduate in 4 years or less, 77% graduate in 5 years or less, and 88% graduate in 6 years or less. 21 companies recruited on campus in 2004-2005.

Admissions Contact: Joyce Elbe, Director of Admissions.
E-mail: *admissions@dc.edu* Web: *www.dc.edu*

DOWLING COLLEGE
Oakdale, NY 11769-1999
E-5

(631) 244-3436
(800) DOWLING; Fax: (631) 563-3827

Full-time: 903 men, 1395 women	**Faculty:** 89
Part-time: 529 men, 800 women	**Ph.D.s:** 90%
Graduate: 944 men, 1808 women	**Student/Faculty:** 26 to 1
Year: 4-1-4, summer session	**Tuition:** $13,800
Application Deadline: open	**Room & Board:** $8310
Freshman Class: 2399 applied, 2082 accepted, 465 enrolled	
SAT Verbal/Math: 460/470*	**LESS COMPETITIVE**

Dowling College, founded in 1955, is an independent (not for profit) comprehensive institution offering programs in the arts and sciences, aviation and transportation, business, and education. There are 4 undergraduate and 3 graduate schools. In addition to regional accreditation, Dowling has baccalaureate program accreditation with NCATE. The 2 libraries contain 217,466 volumes, 394,000 microform items, and 2626 audio/video tapes/CDs/DVDs, and subscribe to 955 periodicals including electronic. Computerized library services include the card catalog, interlibrary loans, database searching, Internet access, and laptop Internet portals. Special learning facilities include a learning resource center, art gallery, radio station, government documents, and the Federal Aviation Administration (FAA) Aviation Education Resource Center. The 156-acre campus is in a suburban area 50 miles east of New York City. Including any residence halls, there are 10 buildings.

Student Life: 90% of undergraduates are from New York. Others are from 25 states, 45 foreign countries, and Canada. 89% are from public schools. 59% are white. The average age of freshmen is 19; all undergraduates, 23. 30% do not continue beyond their first year; 34% remain to graduate.

Housing: 481 students can be accommodated in college housing, which includes coed on-campus apartments. On-campus housing is available on a first-come, first-served basis. Priority is given to out-of-town students. 83% of students commute. Alcohol is not permitted. All students may keep cars.

Activities: There are no fraternities or sororities. There are 39 groups on campus, including aeronautics, art, cheerleading, choir, chorus, computers, drama, ethnic, gay, gospel choir, honors, international, literary magazine, martial arts, newspaper, orchestra, photography, professional, psychology, radio and TV, religious, social, student government, and yearbook. Popular campus events include Freshman Mixer, Holiday Party, and Spring Cotillion.

Sports: There are 7 intercollegiate sports for men and 6 for women, and 3 intramural sports for men and 3 for women. Facilities include a basketball court, a weight room, tennis courts, and a fitness center.

Disabled Students: All of the campus is accessible. Wheelchair ramps, elevators, special parking, specially equipped rest rooms, special class scheduling, lowered drinking fountains, and lowered telephones are available.

Services: Counseling and information services are available, as is tutoring in most subjects. There is remedial math, reading, and writing.

Campus Safety and Security: Measures include 24-hour foot and vehicle patrol, security escort services, shuttle buses, and informal discussions. There are pamphlets/posters/films, emergency telephones, and lighted pathways/sidewalks.

Programs of Study: Dowling confers B.A., B.S., and B.B.A. degrees. Master's and doctoral degrees are also awarded. Bachelor's degrees are awarded in BIOLOGICAL SCIENCE (biology/biological science and marine biology), BUSINESS (accounting, banking and finance, business administration and management, international business management, marketing/retailing/merchandising, sports management, tourism, and transportation management), COMMUNICATIONS AND THE ARTS (communications, English, fine arts, languages, music, romance languages and literature, speech/debate/rhetoric, and visual and performing arts), COMPUTER AND PHYSICAL SCIENCE (applied mathematics, computer science, information sciences and systems, mathematics, and natural sciences), EDUCATION (art, elementary, music, secondary, and special), ENGINEERING AND ENVIRONMENTAL DESIGN (aeronautical science, aeronautical technology, and aviation administration/management), SOCIAL SCIENCE (economics, history, humanities, liberal arts/general studies, philosophy, political science/government, psychology, social science, and sociology). Business, education, and computer sciences are the largest.

Required: To graduate, students must complete 122 credits with a minimum GPA of 2.0. The required 36-credit general education core includes a senior seminar.

Special: Dowling offers a B.S. in professional and liberal studies, internships, independent study, work-study, and nondegree study. There are cooperative programs in several majors, including aeronautics and airway science majors, with the FAA. There are 10 national honor societies, a freshman honors program, and 3 departmental honors programs.

Faculty/Classroom: 57% of faculty are male; 43%, female. 64% teach undergraduates. No introductory courses are taught by graduate students. The average class size in an introductory lecture is 20; in a laboratory, 15; and in a regular course, 17.

Admissions: 87% of the 2005-2006 applicants were accepted. The SAT scores for the 2005-2006 freshman class were: Verbal--63% below 500, 28% between 500 and 599, 8% between 600 and 700, and 1% above 700; Math--57% below 500, 31% between 500 and 599, 9% between 600 and 700, and 1% above 700. 25% of the current freshmen were in the top fifth of their class; 50% were in the top two fifths.

Requirements: The SAT or ACT is recommended. In addition, applicants should be graduates of an accredited secondary school and have completed at least 16 Carnegie units, including 4 in English. An interview is strongly recommended. AP and CLEP credits are accepted. Important factors in the admissions decision are advanced placement or honor courses, evidence of special talent, and recommendations by school officials.

Procedure: Freshmen are admitted to all sessions. Entrance exams should be taken by January of the senior year. There are deferred admissions and rolling admissions plans. Application deadlines are open. Application fee is $25. Applications are accepted on-line.

Transfer: 410 transfer students enrolled in 2004-2005. Applicants must submit official transcripts from all colleges attended. Courses completed with a grade of C or better may transfer. 30 of 122 credits required for the bachelor's degree must be completed at Dowling.

Visiting: There are regularly scheduled orientations for prospective students, including a campus tour and meetings with enrollment services members, staff, and faculty. There are guides for informal visits and visitors may sit in on classes and stay overnight. To schedule a visit, contact the Enrollment Services Office at (631) 244-3426.

Financial Aid: In 2005-2006, 87% of all full-time freshmen and 73% of continuing full-time students received some form of financial aid. 79% of full-time freshmen and 70% of continuing full-time students received need-based aid. The average freshman award was $10,411. Need-based scholarships or need-based grants averaged $7600 ($14,600 maximum); need-based self-help aid (loans and jobs) averaged $4300 ($6625 maximum); non-need-based athletic scholarships averaged $4900 ($20,000 maximum); and other non-need-based awards and non-need-based scholarships averaged $3500 ($13,350 maximum). 100% of undergraduates work part time. Average annual earnings from campus work are $1265. The average financial indebtedness of the 2005 graduate was $5091. Dowling is a member of CSS. The FAFSA and the college's own financial statement are required. The deadline for filing freshman financial aid applications for fall entry is May 1.

International Students: There are 135 international students enrolled. The school actively recruits these students. A satisfactory score is required on the written TOEFL.

Computers: All students may access the system 7 A.M. to 10:45 P.M. Monday through Thursday and 7 A.M. to 5 P.M. Friday through Sunday. There are no time limits and no fees.

Graduates: From July 1, 2004 to June 30, 2005, 531 bachelor's degrees were awarded. The most popular majors were education (18%), liberal arts/general studies (10%), and social science (8%). In an average class, 3% graduate in 3 years or less, 20% graduate in 4 years or less, 31% graduate in 5 years or less, and 34% graduate in 6 years or less. 100 companies recruited on campus in 2004-2005.

Admissions Contact: Bridget Masturzo, Director of Enrollment Services. A video is available. E-mail: *masturzb@dowling.edu* Web: *www.dowling.edu*

D'YOUVILLE COLLEGE   A-3
Buffalo, NY 14201

(716) 829-7600
(800) 777-3921; Fax: (716) 829-7900

Full-time: 316 men, 905 women	**Faculty:** 105
Part-time: 57 men, 200 women	**Ph.D.s:** 57%
Graduate: 373 men, 1050 women	**Student/Faculty:** 12 to 1
Year: semesters, summer session	**Tuition:** $15,800
Application Deadline: open	**Room & Board:** $7860
Freshman Class: 1408 applied, 1024 accepted, 242 enrolled	
SAT Verbal/Math: 490/500*	**ACT:** 21 COMPETITIVE

D'Youville College, founded in 1908, is a private nonsectarian liberal arts institution. In addition to regional accreditation, D'Youville has baccalaureate program accreditation with ADA, APTA, CAHEA, CCNE, and CSWE. The library contains 102,000 volumes, 200,480 microform items, and 3283 audio/video tapes/CDs/DVDs, and subscribes to 680 periodicals including electronic. Computerized library services include the card catalog, database searching, and Internet access. Special learning facilities include a learning resource center and a professional theater. The 10-acre campus is in an urban area 1 mile north of downtown Buffalo. Including any residence halls, there are 10 buildings.

Student Life: 89% of undergraduates are from New York. Students are from 26 states, 29 foreign countries, and Canada. 80% are from public schools. 66% are white; 19% African American. The average age of freshmen is 19; all undergraduates, 25. 30% do not continue beyond their first year; 59% remain to graduate.

Housing: 478 students can be accommodated in college housing, which includes single-sex and coed dorms and on-campus apartments. There are also quiet floors and 21 and older floors. On-campus housing is guaranteed for all 4 years. 79% of students commute. All students may keep cars.

Activities: There are no fraternities or sororities. There are 35 groups on campus, including cheerleading, chorus, computers, dance, drama, drill team, ethnic, gay, honors, international, literary magazine, newspaper, professional, religious, social, social service and student government. Popular campus events include Moving Up Days, Family and Friends, and Honors Convocation.

Sports: There are 5 intercollegiate sports for men and 5 for women, and 9 intramural sports for men and 9 for women. Facilities include a 500-seat gym that houses basketball and volleyball courts and an indoor batting cage, and a fitness facility with aerobic and free weights, swimming pool, and dance studio.

Disabled Students: 95% of the campus is accessible. Wheelchair ramps, elevators, special parking, specially equipped rest rooms, lowered drinking fountains, lowered telephones, and special housing are available.

Services: Counseling and information services are available, as is tutoring in some subjects, based on tutor accessibility. There is a reader service for the blind, and remedial math, reading, and writing.

Campus Safety and Security: Measures include 24-hour foot and vehicle patrol, self-defense education, security escort services, and informal discussions. There are pamphlets/posters/films, emergency telephones, lighted pathways/sidewalks, a special focus program, and a security committee.

Programs of Study: D'Youville confers B.A., B.S., and B.S.N. degrees. Master's and doctoral degrees are also awarded. Bachelor's degrees are awarded in BIOLOGICAL SCIENCE (biology/biological science), BUSINESS (accounting, business administration and management, and international business management), COMMUNICATIONS AND THE ARTS (English), COMPUTER AND PHYSICAL SCIENCE (information sciences and systems and mathematics), EDUCATION (business, elementary, and special), HEALTH PROFESSIONS (exercise science, health care administration, nursing, occupational therapy, physical therapy, and physician's assistant), SOCIAL SCIENCE (dietetics, history, interdisciplinary studies, international studies, philosophy, psychology, and sociology). Education and health professions are the strongest academically. Health professions, business, and nursing are the largest.

Required: All students must complete general program and core curriculum requirements, including 5 courses in humanities, 2 each in English and natural sciences, and 1 each in ethics, philosophy or religion, history, sociology, psychology, economics or political science, math, and computer science. A minimum of 120 to 144 credit hours, varying by major, with a minimum GPA of 2.0, is required to graduate.

Special: D'Youville has cross-registration with member colleges of the Western New York Consortium. Internships, work-study programs, dual majors, study abroad in 5 countries, and pass/fail options are available. Accelerated 5-year B.S.-M.S. programs in occupational therapy, international business, elementary education, nursing, and dietetics are offered. For freshmen with undecided majors, the Career Discovery Program offers special courses, internships, and faculty advisers. There are 2 national honor societies.

Faculty/Classroom: 44% of faculty are male; 56%, female. All both teach and do research. No introductory courses are taught by graduate students. The average class size in an introductory lecture is 30; in a laboratory, 12; and in a regular course, 23.

Admissions: 73% of the 2005-2006 applicants were accepted. The SAT scores for the 2005-2006 freshman class were: Verbal--52% below 500, 38% between 500 and 599, 9% between 600 and 700, and 1% above 700; Math--49% below 500, 40% between 500 and 599, 10% between 600 and 700, and 1% above 700. The ACT scores were 35% below 21, 35% between 21 and 23, 26% between 24 and 26, 1% between 27 and 28, and 3% above 28.

Requirements: The SAT or ACT is required. In addition, applicants should have completed 16 Carnegie units, including 4 years of high school English, 3 of social studies, and 1 each of math and science; some majors require additional years of math and science. The GED is accepted. An interview is recommended. A GPA of 2.0 is required. AP and CLEP credits are accepted.

Procedure: Freshmen are admitted fall and spring. Entrance exams should be taken by the end of the junior year. There is a deferred admissions plan and a rolling admission plan. Application deadlines are open. Application fee is $25. Applications are accepted on-line.

Transfer: 207 transfer students enrolled in 2004-2005. Applicants need a minimum GPA of 2.0, or 2.5 for some programs. An interview is recommended. There are very few openings for transfers seeking part-time studies. 30 of 120 to 144 credits required for the bachelor's degree must be completed at D'Youville.

Visiting: There are regularly scheduled orientations for prospective students. There are guides for informal visits and visitors may sit in on classes and stay overnight. To schedule a visit, contact the Admissions Office at admiss@dyc.edu.

Financial Aid: In 2005-2006, 99% of all full-time freshmen and 86% of continuing full-time students received some form of financial aid. 90% of full-time freshmen and 94% of continuing full-time students received need-based aid. The average freshman award was $15,309. Need-based scholarships or need-based grants averaged $11,038 ($12,550 maximum); need-based self-help aid (loans and jobs) averaged $7666 ($8425 maximum); and other non-need-based awards and non-need-based scholarships averaged $6759 ($7800 maximum). 54% of undergraduates work part time. Average annual earnings from campus work are $922. The average financial indebtedness of the 2005 graduate was $16,643. The FAFSA and the state aid form are required. The deadline for filing freshman financial aid applications for fall entry is April 15.

International Students: There are 73 international students enrolled. The school actively recruits these students. They must take the TOEFL and also take the SAT or the ACT.

Computers: Wireless access is available. There are 2 general use PC labs, 2 classroom labs, a PC lab in each dorm, a lab in the library, and 10 wireless access areas on campus. All students may access the system. There are no time limits and no fees. It is strongly recommended that all students have a personal computer.

Graduates: From July 1, 2004 to June 30, 2005, 194 bachelor's degrees were awarded. The most popular majors were physical/

occupational therapy (20%), physician assistant (15%), and nursing (11%). In an average class, 59% graduate in 6 years or less. 92 companies recruited on campus in 2004-2005. Of the 2004 graduating class, 10% were enrolled in graduate school within 6 months of graduation and 96% were employed.

Admissions Contact: Ron H. Dannecker, Director of Undergraduate Admissions. E-mail: admiss@dyc.edu Web: www.dyc.edu

EASTMAN SCHOOL OF MUSIC   B-3
Rochester, NY 14604   (585) 274-1060
(800) 388-9695; Fax: (585) 232-8601

Full-time: 250 men, 250 women	**Faculty:** 89
Part-time: 5 men	**Ph.D.s:** 55%
Graduate: 200 men, 200 women	**Student/Faculty:** 5 to 1
Year: semesters	**Tuition:** $25,000
Application Deadline: see profile	**Room & Board:** $10,000
Freshman Class: n/av	
SAT or ACT: recommended	**SPECIAL**

Eastman School of Music, founded in 1921, is a private professional school of music within the University of Rochester. Figures in the above and in this profile are approximate. In addition to regional accreditation, Eastman has baccalaureate program accreditation with NASM. The library contains 333,014 volumes, 14,116 microform items, and 78,154 audio/video tapes/CDs/DVDs, and subscribes to 620 periodicals including electronic. Computerized library services include the card catalog, interlibrary loans, database searching, and Internet access. Special learning facilities include a learning resource center, art gallery, recording studios, a music library, a theater, and 3 recital halls. The 3-acre campus is in an urban area in downtown Rochester. Including any residence halls, there are 5 buildings.

Student Life: 82% of undergraduates are from out of state, mostly the Middle Atlantic. Students are from 48 states, 32 foreign countries, and Canada. 90% are from public schools. 62% are white; 21% foreign nationals. The average age of freshmen is 18; all undergraduates, 20. 11% do not continue beyond their first year; 78% remain to graduate.

Housing: 360 students can be accommodated in college housing, which includes single-sex and coed dorms, fraternity houses, and sorority houses. The Student Living Center is divided into separate 'houses' that can be organized by special interest upon student request. In addition, there are special-interest houses. On-campus housing is guaranteed for all 4 years. 72% of students live on campus; of those, all remain on campus on weekends. All students may keep cars.

Activities: 5% of men and about 2% of women belong to 2 national fraternities; 4% of women belong to 1 national sorority. There are 20 groups on campus, including Association for injury prevention, band, choir, chorale, chorus, computers, dance, gay, international, jazz band, literary magazine, newspaper, opera, orchestra, professional, religious, social, social service, student government, symphony, and yearbook. Popular campus events include Holiday Sing and Boo Blast.

Sports: There is no sports program at Eastman. All athletic facilities of the University of Rochester, as well as a nearby YMCA, are available to students.

Disabled Students: 95% of the campus is accessible. Wheelchair ramps, elevators, special parking, specially equipped rest rooms, lowered drinking fountains, and lowered telephones are available.

Services: Counseling and information services are available, as is tutoring in every subject. There is a reader service for the blind and remedial writing. English tutoring for nonnative English speakers is available.

Campus Safety and Security: Measures include 24-hour foot and vehicle patrol, self-defense education, security escort services, and shuttle buses. There are informal discussions, pamphlets/posters/films, emergency telephones, lighted pathways/sidewalks, and security cameras.

Programs of Study: Eastman confers the B.M. degree. Master's and doctoral degrees are also awarded. Bachelor's degrees are awarded in COMMUNICATIONS AND THE ARTS (jazz, music, music performance, and music theory and composition), EDUCATION (music). Performance is the largest.

Required: All students must complete core requirements in a major instrument or voice, music theory, music history, and Western cultural tradition, as well as English and humanities electives. A total of 120 to 148 credit hours, varying by program, with a minimum GPA of 2.0, is required to graduate.

Special: The school and the University of Rochester cooperatively offer the B.A. degree with a music concentration. All the facilities of the university are open to Eastman students. Cross-registration is also available with colleges in the Rochester Consortium. Dual majors are available in all areas of study. Internships, work-study, and study abroad in 7 countries are also possible. There is 1 national honor society.

Faculty/Classroom: 60% of faculty are male; 40%, female. All both teach and do research. Graduate students teach 10% of introductory courses. The average class size in an introductory lecture is 30 and in a regular course, 15.

Admissions: 32% of recent applicants were accepted.

Requirements: The SAT or ACT is recommended, but is required of home-schooled applicants. Applicants should be graduates of an accredited secondary school with 16 academic credits, including 4 years of English. The GED is accepted. An audition and an interview are required, as are 3 letters of recommendation. Some majors have other specific requirements. AP credits are accepted. Important factors in the admissions decision are evidence of special talent, recommendations by alumni, and personality/intangible qualities.

Procedure: Freshmen are admitted fall and spring. There is a deferred admissions plan and a rolling admissions plan. Check with the school for current application deadlines and fee. Notification is sent on a rolling basis. 72 applicants were on a recent waiting list; 3 were admitted. Applications are accepted on-line.

Transfer: 8 transfer students enrolled ina recent year. Requirements include satisfactory academic standing at the previous institution, a successful audition, and an interview.

Visiting: There are regularly scheduled orientations for prospective students, including group information sessions and a tour of the facilities. To schedule a visit, contact the Admissions Office at *admissions@esm.edu.*

Financial Aid: In a recent year, 99% of all full-time freshmen and 98% of continuing full-time students received some form of financial aid. 80% of full-time freshmen and 83% of continuing full-time students received need-based aid. The average freshman award was $22,150. Need-based scholarships or need-based grants averaged $7925 ($10,550 maximum); need-based self-help aid (loans and jobs) averaged $2725 ($3500 maximum); and other non-need-based awards and non-need-based scholarships averaged $11,500 ($17,500 maximum). 52% of undergraduates work part time. Average annual earnings from campus work are $900. The average financial indebtedness of a recent graduate was $14,725. Eastman is a member of CSS. The CSS/Profile, FAFSA, the state aid form, and the college's own financial statement are required. Check with the school for current deadlines.

International Students: There were 50 international students enrolled in a recent year. The school actively recruits these students. They must take the TOEFL.

Computers: All students may access the system. There are no time limits. The fee is $125. It is strongly recommended that all students have a personal computer.

Graduates: In a recent year, 117 bachelor's degrees were awarded. The most popular majors were music performance (73%), music education (12%), and jazz studies and contemporary media (9%). In an average class, 70% graduate in 4 years or less, and 79% graduate in 5 years or less. 35 companies recruited on campus in a recent year. Of a recent graduating class, 70% were enrolled in graduate school within 6 months of graduation and 16% were employed.

Admissions Contact: Adrian Daly, Director of Admissions.
E-mail: *admissions@esm.rochester.edu*
Web: *http://www.rochester.edu/Eastman*

ELMIRA COLLEGE   C-4

Elmira, NY 14901
(607) 735-1724
(800) 935-6472; Fax: (607) 735-1718

Full-time: 364 men, 819 women	**Faculty:** 82; IIB, -$
Part-time: 74 men, 240 women	**Ph.Ds:** 100%
Graduate: 94 men, 275 women	**Student/Faculty:** 14 to 1
Year: terms, summer session	**Tuition:** $28,500
Application Deadline: open	**Room & Board:** $8700
Freshman Class: 1968 applied, 1266 accepted, 305 enrolled	
SAT Verbal/Math: 580/560*	**ACT:** 25 **VERY COMPETITIVE**

Elmira College, founded in 1855, is a private liberal arts institution offering general and preprofessional programs. In addition to regional accreditation, Elmira has baccalaureate program accreditation with NLN. The library contains 389,000 volumes, 1,320,000 microform items, and 8059 audio/video tapes/CDs/DVDs, and subscribes to 859 periodicals including electronic. Computerized library services include the card catalog, interlibrary loans, database searching, and Internet access. Special learning facilities include a learning resource center, art gallery, radio station, speech and hearing clinic, and Mark Twain's study. The 50-acre campus is in a suburban area 90 miles southwest of Syracuse. Including any residence halls, there are 25 buildings.

Student Life: 54% of undergraduates are from out of state, mostly the Northeast. Students are from 35 states, 23 foreign countries, and Canada. 59% are from public schools. 89% are white. The average age of freshmen is 18; all undergraduates, 20. 16% do not continue beyond their first year; 60% remain to graduate.

Housing: 1083 students can be accommodated in college housing, which includes single-sex and coed dorms and on-campus apartments. In addition, there are honors floors and alcohol-free and tobacco-free floors. On-campus housing is guaranteed for all 4 years. 92% of students live on campus; of those, 90% remain on campus on weekends. All students may keep cars.

Activities: There are no fraternities or sororities. There are 91 groups on campus, including art, band, cheerleading, chorale, chorus, dance, drama, honors, international, literary magazine, musical theater, newspaper, orchestra, pep band, political, professional, radio, religious, social, social service, student government, and yearbook. Popular campus events include Mountain Day, Midnight Breakfast, and Spring Weekend.

Sports: There are 6 intercollegiate sports for men and 10 for women, and 21 intramural sports for men and 21 for women. Facilities include 2500-seat and 950-seat gyms, indoor tennis facilities, a 3500-seat hockey arena, racquetball courts, a fitness center, a dance studio, and a swimming pool.

Disabled Students: 25% of the campus is accessible. Wheelchair ramps, elevators, special parking, specially equipped rest rooms, special class scheduling, and special housing are available.

Services: Counseling and information services are available, as is tutoring in most subjects. There is a reader service for the blind. Tutoring in math and freshman English is available in each freshman dorm.

Campus Safety and Security: Measures include 24-hour foot and vehicle patrol, security escort services, informal discussions, and pamphlets/posters/films. There are emergency telephones and lighted pathways/sidewalks.

Programs of Study: Elmira confers B.A. and B.S. degrees. Associate and master's degrees are also awarded. Bachelor's degrees are awarded in BIOLOGICAL SCIENCE (biochemistry and biology/biological science), BUSINESS (accounting, business administration and management, business economics, international business management, and marketing/retailing/merchandising), COMMUNICATIONS AND THE ARTS (art, classics, dramatic arts, English literature, fine arts, French, languages, music, and Spanish), COMPUTER AND PHYSICAL SCIENCE (chemistry and mathematics), EDUCATION (art, elementary, foreign languages, science, and secondary), ENGINEERING AND ENVIRONMENTAL DESIGN (environmental science), HEALTH PROFESSIONS (medical laboratory technology, nursing, predentistry, premedicine, and speech pathology/audiology), SOCIAL SCIENCE (American studies, anthropology, criminal justice, history, human services, international studies, philosophy, political science/government, prelaw, psychology, and sociology). History, theater, and premedicine are the strongest academically. Psychology, management, and education are the largest.

Required: All students must complete general degree requirements, including communication skills, writing courses, math competency, and a core curriculum; distribution requirements in culture and civilization, contemporary social institutions, the scientific method, the creative process, and phys ed; and a field experience program. A total of 120 credit hours with a minimum GPA of 2.0 overall and in the major is required to graduate.

Special: The required field experience program provides a career-related internship as well as community service. A junior year abroad program, a Washington semester, an accelerated degree program, a general studies degree, student-designed majors, and pass/fail options are available. A 3-2 chemical engineering degree is offered with Clarkson University. B.A.-B.S. degrees are offered in biochemistry, biology, chemistry, economics, education, environmental studies, history, math, political science, and psychology. Elmira is a member of the Spring Term Consortium, enabling students to take 6-week courses at participating institutions. There are 10 national honor societies, including Phi Beta Kappa.

Faculty/Classroom: 57% of faculty are male; 43%, female. All both teach and do research. No introductory courses are taught by graduate students. The average class size in an introductory lecture is 24; in a laboratory, 10; and in a regular course, 16.

Admissions: 64% of the 2005-2006 applicants were accepted. The SAT scores for the 2005-2006 freshman class were: Verbal--23% below 500, 51% between 500 and 599, 22% between 600 and 700, and 4% above 700; Math--25% below 500, 51% between 500 and 599, 20% between 600 and 700, and 4% above 700. The ACT scores were 2% below 21, 29% between 21 and 23, 42% between 24 and 26, 20% between 27 and 28, and 7% above 28. 70% of the current freshmen were in the top fifth of their class; 90% were in the top two fifths. There were 2 National Merit finalists and 11 semifinalists. 20 freshmen graduated first in their class.

Requirements: The SAT or ACT is required. In addition, applicants should have completed 4 years of high school English, 3 of math, and 2 of science. An essay is part of the application process. An interview is strongly recommended. A GPA of 2.0 is required. AP and CLEP credits are accepted. Important factors in the admissions decision are advanced placement or honor courses, extracurricular activities record, and recommendations by school officials.

Procedure: Freshmen are admitted fall, winter, and spring. Entrance exams should be taken by January of the entry year. There are early decision and deferred admissions plans. There is a rolling admissions plan. Early decision applications should be filed by November 15 and January 15; regular application deadline is open for fall entry. Application fee is $50. Notification of early decision is sent December 15 and January 31; regular decision, on a rolling basis. 71 early decision candidates were accepted for the 2005-2006 class. 73 applicants were on the 2005 waiting list; 9 were admitted. Applications are accepted on-line.

Transfer: 55 transfer students enrolled in 2004-2005. Applicants should have a minimum GPA of 2.0. An interview is strongly recommended. 30 of 120 credits required for the bachelor's degree must be completed at Elmira.

Visiting: There are regularly scheduled orientations for prospective students, consisting of an open house format and overview, a tour, lunch, a student panel, a faculty panel, general admissions and scholarship information, and an optional interview. Individual visits for interviews and tours are available year-round, including Saturday mornings. There are guides for informal visits and visitors may sit in on classes and stay overnight. To schedule a visit, contact the Office of Admissions.

Financial Aid: In 2005-2006, 82% of all full-time freshmen and 80% of continuing full-time students received some form of financial aid. 81% of full-time freshmen and 77% of continuing full-time students received need-based aid. The average freshman award was $21,877. Need-based scholarships or need-based grants averaged $16,130; and need-based self-help aid (loans and jobs) averaged $5292. 50% of undergraduates work part time. Average annual earnings from campus work are $1200. The average financial indebtedness of the 2005 graduate was $19,875. The FAFSA and the state aid form are required. The priority date for freshman financial aid applications for fall entry is February 15. The deadline for filing freshman financial aid applications for fall entry is March 15.

International Students: There were 65 international students enrolled in a recent year. The school actively recruits these students. A satisfactory score on the TOEFL is required.

Computers: All students may access the system weekdays 15 hours per day and weekends 8 to 10 hours per day and any time from residence halls. There are no time limits and no fees. It is strongly recommended that all students have a personal computer.

Graduates: From July 1, 2004 to June 30, 2005, 325 bachelor's degrees were awarded. The most popular majors were business (24%), psychology (13%), and education (10%). In an average class, 1% graduate in 3 years or less, 68% graduate in 4 years or less, 98% graduate in 5 years or less, and 100% graduate in 6 years or less. 60 companies recruited on campus in 2004-2005. Of the 2004 graduating class, 45% were enrolled in graduate school within 6 months of graduation and 52% were employed.

Admissions Contact: Garry Fallis, Dean of Admissions.
E-mail: *admissions@elmira.edu* Web: *elmira.edu*

EUGENE LANG COLLEGE NEW SCHOOL FOR LIBERAL ARTS   D-3
(Formerly Eugene Lang College-New School University)

New York, NY 10011-8963 (212) 229-5665; Fax: (212) 229-5166

Full-time: 293 men, 674 women	Faculty: 78
Part-time: 8 men, 10 women	Ph.D.s: 100%
Graduate: none	Student/Faculty: 13 to 1
Year: semesters	Tuition: $27,050
Application Deadline: February 1	Room & Board: $11,750
Freshman Class: 862 applied, 760 accepted, 232 enrolled	
SAT Verbal/Math: 617/570*	ACT: 25	COMPETITIVE+

Eugene Lang College, established in 1978, is the liberal arts undergraduate division of the New School . There are 4 undergraduate and 3 graduate schools. The 4 libraries contain 413,722 volumes, 4,656,818 microform items, and 52,188 audio/video tapes/CDs/DVDs, and subscribe to 22,041 periodicals including electronic. Computerized library services include the card catalog, interlibrary loans, and database searching. Special learning facilities include an art gallery and writing center. The 5-acre campus is in an urban area in the heart of Greenwich Village. Including any residence halls, there are 14 buildings.

Student Life: 55% of undergraduates are from out of state, mostly the Northeast. Others are from 43 states, 13 foreign countries, and Canada. 66% are from public schools. 52% are white. The average age of freshmen is 18; all undergraduates, 20. 15% do not continue beyond their first year; 85% remain to graduate.

Housing: 1100 students can be accommodated in college housing, which includes single-sex and coed dorms and off-campus apartments. On-campus housing is guaranteed for the freshman year only; is available on a first-come, first-served basis, and is available on a lottery system for upperclassmen. Priority is given to out-of-town students. 57% of students commute. Alcohol is not permitted. All students may keep cars.

Activities: There are no fraternities or sororities. There are 15 groups on campus, including choir, chorus, computers, drama, ethnic, gay, international, jazz band, literary magazine, newspaper, photography, political, social, social service, and student government. Popular campus events include Lang in the City, a program that makes cultural events available to students.

Sports: Students receive discounted rates at area gyms and city recreation facilities.

Disabled Students: Wheelchair ramps, elevators, specially equipped rest rooms, lowered telephones, and special housing are available.

Services: Counseling and information services are available, as is tutoring in some subjects, including writing at the writing center. There is remedial writing.

Campus Safety and Security: Measures include self-defense education, informal discussions, pamphlets/posters/films, and 24-hour dorm security.

Programs of Study: Eugene Lang College confers the B.A. degree. Bachelor's degrees are awarded in COMMUNICATIONS AND THE ARTS (creative writing, dramatic arts, and English), EDUCATION (education), SOCIAL SCIENCE (crosscultural studies, economics, history, political science/government, prelaw, psychology, social science, sociology, urban studies, and women's studies). Creative writing, history, urban studies, and education are the strongest academically. Writing and cultural studies are the largest.

Required: To graduate, students must complete 120 credit hours, with a GPA of 2.0 and a minimum of 36 hours in 1 of 11paths of study: writing, literature, the arts (includes dance and theatre); urban studies; social and historical inquiry; cultural studies and media; philosophy; religious studies; psychology; education studies; science, technology and society. Also required are 88 credit hours in Lang College courses and 4 credits of senior work. Required courses include a first-year writing seminar and a freshman peer advising workshop program.

Special: Lang College offers a concentration rather than a traditional major; there is no core curriculum and students are instructed in small seminars. Students may cross-register with other New School divisions. A large variety of internships for credit, study abroad, B.A./M.A. and B.A./M.S.T. options, a B.A./B.F.A. degree with Parsons The New School for Design and the New School for Jazz and Contemporary Music, student-designed majors, and nondegree study are available.

Faculty/Classroom: 51% of faculty are male; 49%, female. All teach undergraduates. The average class size in a laboratory is 15 and in a regular course, 18.

Admissions: 88% of the 2005-2006 applicants were accepted.

Requirements: The SAT or ACT is required. In addition, 4 SAT: Subject tests may be substituted for either test. Applicants must be enrolled in a strong college preparatory program. The GED is accepted. An essay and an interview are required. Art students must present a portfolio and complete a home exam. Jazz students are required to audition. AP credits are accepted. Important factors in the admissions decision are personality/intangible qualities, advanced placement or honor courses, and recommendations by school officials.

Procedure: Freshmen are admitted fall and spring. Entrance exams should be taken in May of the junior year or October of the senior year. There are early decision, early admissions, and deferred admissions plans. Early decision applications should be filed by November 15; regular applications, by February 1 for fall entry and November 15 for spring entry, along with a $50 fee. Notification of early decision is sent December 15; regular decision, April 1. 45 early decision candidates were accepted for the 2005-2006 class. 70 applicants were on the 2005 waiting list; 21 were admitted. Applications are accepted on-line.

Transfer: 95 transfer students enrolled in 2004-2005. Applicants must have a minimum college GPA of 2.5 and must submit high school transcripts, ACT or SAT scores (if taken in the last 5 years), and 2 recommendations. An interview is required. Grades of C or better transfer for credit. 60 of 120 credits required for the bachelor's degree must be completed at Eugene Lang College.

Visiting: There are regularly scheduled orientations for prospective students, including a campus tour, visits to classes, and panel discussions. There are guides for informal visits and visitors may sit in on classes and stay overnight. To schedule a visit, contact the Office of Admissions at *lang@newschool.edu*.

Financial Aid: In 2005-2006, 68% of all full-time students received some form of financial aid. 66% of all full-time students received need-based aid. The average freshman award was $17,000. Need-based scholarships or need-based grants averaged $13,910; need-based self-help aid (loans and jobs) averaged $3412; and other non-need-based awards and non-need-based scholarships averaged $5443. The average financial indebtedness of the 2005 graduate was $22,000. The FAFSA is required. The priority date for freshman financial aid applications for fall entry is March 1.

International Students: The school actively recruits these students. Satisfactory scores are required on the written TOEFL and the SAT or the ACT.

Computers: Wireless access is available. Students can arrange for access for statistical course work and dissertation research. There are no time limits and no fees. It is strongly recommended that all students have a personal computer.

Graduates: In a recent year, 133 bachelor's degrees were awarded. The most popular major was liberal arts/general studies (100%). In an average class, 33% graduate in 4 years or less, 42% graduate in 5 years or less, and 48% graduate in 6 years or less.

Admissions Contact: Nicole Curvin, Director of Admissions.
E-mail: *lang@newschool.edu* Web: *www.lang.edu*

EXCELSIOR COLLEGE   D-3
Albany, NY 12203-5159   (518) 464-8500
                                    (888) 674-2388; Fax: (518) 464-8777

Full-time: none	Faculty: n/av
Part-time: 11,144 men, 15,133 women	Ph.D.s: n/av
Graduate: 188 men, 346 women	Student/Faculty: n/av
Year: n/app	Tuition: $995
Application Deadline: open	Room & Board: n/app
Freshman Class: n/av	
SAT or ACT: not required	**SPECIAL**

Excelsior College, founded in 1971, offers 34 degree programs designed to meet the needs of working adults, of which approximately 6200 are members of the U.S. armed forces. The college is home to a competency-based nursing program and the largest school of nursing in the United States. The college offers nondegree certificate programs as well as a series of ACE evaluated college-level proficiency exams that students can use to earn credit toward a degree at hundreds of colleges around the country. There are 4 undergraduate and 3 graduate schools. In addition to regional accreditation, Excelsior has baccalaureate program accreditation with ABET and NLN. Computerized library services include the card catalog, interlibrary loans, database searching, and Internet access. Special learning facilities include an electronic peer network available on the Internet. The campus is in a suburban area in Albany. There are 3 buildings.

Student Life: 90% of undergraduates are from out of state. Students are from 50 states, 52 foreign countries, and Canada. 64% are white; 16% African American. The average age of all undergraduates is 40.

Housing: There are no residence halls.

Activities: There are no fraternities or sororities. Popular campus events include commencement.

Disabled Students: All of the campus is accessible. Wheelchair ramps, elevators, special parking, specially equipped rest rooms, and lowered drinking fountains are available.

Services: Counseling and information services are available, as is tutoring in some subjects, including statistics and writing.

Programs of Study: Excelsior confers B.A., B.S., B.S.Comp.Tech, B.S.Elect.Tech, B.S.N., B.S.Nuc.T, and B.S.T. degrees. Associate and master's degrees are also awarded. Bachelor's degrees are awarded in BIOLOGICAL SCIENCE (biology/biological science), BUSINESS (accounting, banking and finance, business administration and management, human resources, insurance and risk management, international business management, management information systems, and marketing/retailing/merchandising), COMMUNICATIONS AND THE ARTS (communications, English literature, languages, and music), COMPUTER AND PHYSICAL SCIENCE (chemistry, geology, information sciences and systems, mathematics, nuclear technology, and physics), ENGINEERING AND ENVIRONMENTAL DESIGN (computer technology, electrical/electronics engineering technology, and technological management), HEALTH PROFESSIONS (nursing), SOCIAL SCIENCE (criminal justice, economics, geography, history, liberal arts/general studies, philosophy, political science/government, psychology, and sociology). Nursing and liberal studies are the largest.

Required: To graduate, students must complete 120 credits with 30 in the major and a minimum 2.0 GPA. At least 50% of course work must be in the arts and sciences. The required core courses include 6 to 12 credits each in humanities, math/science, and social science/history and 1 credit in information literacy. The nursing program requires a different set of core courses as well as the nursing performance exams. All students must fulfill a written English requirement.

Special: B.A. or B.S. candidates may major in liberal studies or in most traditional academic disciplines. Faculty consultants design curricula, approve sources of credit, create exams, and assess student learning. Students receive academic advising by telephone, letter, computer, or in person. The flexibility of this alternate program enables adults to pursue an undergraduate degree independently. Exams are available. Pass/fail options are possible. There is 1 national honor society.

Faculty/Classroom: 30% of faculty are male; 70%, female.

Requirements: There are no admissions requirements except for nursing students. Applicants need not be residents of New York State. Students without a high school diploma or equivalent are admitted as special students. Nursing enrollment is available only to students with certain health care backgrounds. AP and CLEP credits are accepted.

Procedure: Freshmen are admitted to all sessions. There is a rolling admissions plan. Application deadlines are open. Applications are accepted on-line. The fall 2005 application fee was $75.

Transfer: 10714 transfer students enrolled in 2004-2005.

Financial Aid: The college's own financial statement is required.

International Students: There are 355 international students enrolled. The school actively recruits these students.

Computers: All students may access the system 24 hours a day, 7 days a week, via the Internet. There are no time limits and no fees.

Graduates: From July 1, 2004 to June 30, 2005, 2333 bachelor's degrees were awarded. The most popular majors were liberal arts (68%), business (9%), and nursing (8%).

Admissions Contact: Prospective Student Adviser.
E-mail: *info@excelsior.edu* Web: *www.excelsior.edu*

FARMINGDALE STATE UNIVERSITY OF NEW YORK E-5
(Formerly SUNY/College of Technology at Farmingdale)
Farmingdale, NY 11735   (631) 420-2200; Fax: (631) 420-2633

Full-time: 2559 men, 1461 women	Faculty: 151
Part-time: 1189 men, 1252 women	Ph.D.s: 60%
Graduate: none	Student/Faculty: 24 to 1
Year: semesters, summer session	Tuition: $5231 ($11,181)
Application Deadline: open	Room & Board: $8290
Freshman Class: 4115 applied, 2517 accepted, 1053 enrolled	
SAT Verbal/Math: 478/494*	**COMPETITIVE**

Farmingdale State University of New York, formerly State University of New York/College of Technology at Farmingdale, founded in 1912, is a public institution offering associate and bachelor's degrees in the applied sciences and technology. There are 4 undergraduate schools. In addition to regional accreditation, SUNY Farmingdale has baccalaureate program accreditation with ABET and CAHEA. The library contains 150,000 volumes, 63,000 microform items, and 3100 audio/video tapes/CDs/DVDs, and subscribes to 900 periodicals including electronic. Computerized library services include the card catalog, interlibrary loans, database searching, and Internet access. Special learning facilities include a learning resource center, art gallery, radio station, dental hygiene clinic, CAD/CAM and CIM labs, a fleet of multi- and single-engine airplanes, and a greenhouse complex. The 380-acre campus is in a suburban area on Long Island, about 35 miles east of New York City. Including any residence halls, there are 40 buildings.

Student Life: 99% of undergraduates are from New York. Students are from 12 states and 11 foreign countries. 92% are from public schools. 60% are white; 12% African American. The average age of freshmen is 22; all undergraduates, 26. 35% do not continue beyond their first year; 36% remain to graduate.

Housing: 500 students can be accommodated in college housing, which includes coed dorms. On-campus housing is available on a first-come, first-served basis and is available on a lottery system for upperclassmen. Priority is given to out-of-town students. 91% of students commute. Alcohol is not permitted. All students may keep cars.

Activities: There are no fraternities or sororities. There are 32 groups on campus, including art, cheerleading, computers, drama, ethnic, honors, literary magazine, musical theater, newspaper, professional, radio and TV, religious, social, student government, and yearbook. Popular campus events include Comedy Nights, Spring Fling, and black, Hispanic, and women's history months.

Sports: There are 7 intercollegiate sports for men and 5 for women, and 11 intramural sports for men and 11 for women. Facilities include basketball, badminton, volleyball, racquetball, handball, squash, and tennis courts, a swimming pool, a wrestling room, bowling alleys, weight training rooms, indoor and outdoor tracks, a golf driving range and 3-hole golf layout, and baseball, softball, soccer/lacrosse, and multipurpose fields.

Disabled Students: 90% of the campus is accessible. Wheelchair ramps, elevators, special parking, specially equipped rest rooms, lowered drinking fountains, and lowered telephones are available.

Services: Counseling and information services are available, as is tutoring in most subjects. There is a reader service for the blind, and remedial math, reading, and writing. There is a learning disabilities specialist counselor available.

Campus Safety and Security: Measures include 24-hour foot and vehicle patrol, security escort services, informal discussions, and pamphlets/posters/films. There are emergency telephones and lighted pathways/sidewalks.

Programs of Study: SUNY Farmingdale confers B.S. and B.Tech. degrees. Associate degrees are also awarded. Bachelor's degrees are awarded in BIOLOGICAL SCIENCE (biology/biological science), ENGINEERING AND ENVIRONMENTAL DESIGN (aeronautical science, automotive technology, aviation administration/management, computer technology, construction management, electrical/electronics engineering technology, graphic arts technology, industrial administration/management, industrial engineering technology, and manufacturing technology), SOCIAL SCIENCE (safety and security technology). Electrical engineering technology and bioscience are the strongest academically. Management of technology and computer programming are the largest.

Required: To graduate, students must complete 124 to 141 credits, including 60 to 70 in the major, with a minimum GPA of 2.0. The core curriculum includes 4 courses each in social science, math/science, and English/humanities, including English composition.

Special: Study abroad in 3 countries is available. There are 3 national honor societies and 1 departmental honors program.

Faculty/Classroom: 59% of faculty are male; 41%, female. All teach undergraduates. The average class size in an introductory lecture is 30; in a laboratory, 15; and in a regular course, 21.

Admissions: 61% of the 2005-2006 applicants were accepted. The SAT scores for the 2005-2006 freshman class were: Verbal--62% below 500, 33% between 500 and 599, 4% between 600 and 700, and 1% above 700; Math--49% below 500, 42% between 500 and 599, 8% between 600 and 700, and 1% above 700. 6% of the current freshmen were in the top fifth of their class; 36% were in the top two fifths.

Requirements: The SAT is required. In addition, applicants must be graduates of an accredited secondary school or have earned a GED. Specific entrance requirements vary by program, but recommended preparation includes 4 units of English and 3 each of math, science, and social science. Art programs require a portfolio and an interview. A GPA of 2.0 is required. AP and CLEP credits are accepted.

Procedure: Freshmen are admitted fall and spring. There are early admissions, deferred admissions and rolling admissions plans. Application deadlines are open. Application fee is $40. Notification is sent on a rolling basis.

Transfer: 944 transfer students enrolled in 2004-2005. Applicants must have a minimum GPA of 2.0 and be eligible to return to their previous college. 90 of 124 credits required for the bachelor's degree must be completed at SUNY Farmingdale.

Visiting: There are regularly scheduled orientations for prospective students, including a tour of the campus and general information about the college, admissions, financial aid, and residence life. There are guides for informal visits. To schedule a visit, contact the Admissions Office at *admissions@farmingdale.edu.*

Financial Aid: The FAFSA, the state aid form and the college's own financial statement are required. Check with the school for current deadlines.

International Students: A satisfactory score is required on the written TOEFL.

Computers: All students may access the system during lab hours of Monday through Friday, 8 A.M. to 10:30 P.M., and Saturday, 9 A.M. to 4 P.M., or through dial-in access. There are no time limits and no fees. It is strongly recommended that all students have a PC. It is recommended that students in computer programming have PC.

Graduates: In a recent year, 291 bachelor's degrees were awarded. The most popular majors in a recent year were management of technology (27%), aviation technology (15%), and visual communications (14%). In an average class, 17% graduate in 4 years or less, and 17% graduate in 5 years or less. 72 companies recruited on campus in a recent year. Of the recent years graduating class, 30% were employed within 6 months of graduation.

Admissions Contact: Jim Hall, Admissions Director. A CD is available. E-mail: *jim.hall@farmingdale.edu* Web: *farmingdale.edu*

FASHION INSTITUTE OF TECHNOLOGY/STATE UNIVERSITY OF NEW YORK

D-5

New York, NY 10001-5992

(212) 217-7675
(800) Go-To-FIT; Fax: (212) 217-7481

Full-time: 1000 men, 5600 women	**Faculty:** 208
Part-time: 800 men, 3300 women	**Ph.D.s:** n/av
Graduate: 10 men, 100 women	**Student/Faculty:** 32 to 1
Year: 4-1-4, summer session	**Tuition:** $5000 ($11,000)
Application Deadline: see profile	**Room & Board:** $6600
Freshman Class: n/av	
SAT or ACT: not required	**COMPETITIVE+**

The Fashion Institute of Technology, founded in 1944 as part of the State University of New York, is an art and design, business, and technology college that prepares students for careers in fashion and related design professions and industries. Figures in the above and in this profile are approximate. In addition to regional accreditation, FIT has baccalaureate program accreditation with FIDER and NASAD. The library contains 168,879 volumes, 4712 microform items, and 244,335 audio/video tapes/CDs/DVDs, and subscribes to 502 periodicals including electronic. Computerized library services include the card catalog, interlibrary loans, and database searching. Special learning facilities include an art gallery, radio station, design lab, lighting lab, quick response center, computer-aided design and communications facility, and the Annette Green Fragrance Foundation Studio Collections of the Museum at FIT. The 5-acre campus is in an urban area in Manhattan. Including any residence halls, there are 8 buildings.

Student Life: 63% of undergraduates are from New York. Others are from 50 states, 80 foreign countries, and Canada. 43% are white; 12% foreign nationals; 10% Asian American; 10% Hispanic. The average age of freshmen is 22; all undergraduates, 29. 81% do not continue beyond their first year; 51% remain to graduate.

Housing: 1250 students can be accommodated in college housing, which includes single-sex and coed dorms and on-campus apartments. On-campus housing is available on a lottery system for upperclassmen.

Priority is given to out-of-town students. 83% of students commute. Alcohol is not permitted. No one may keep cars.

Activities: There are no fraternities or sororities. There are 70 groups on campus, including art, cheerleading, choir, dance, drama, ethnic, gay, honors, literary magazine, musical theater, newspaper, photography, political, professional, radio and TV, religious, social, social service, student government, and yearbook. Popular campus events include fashion shows, a lecture series, and craft center events.

Sports: There are 4 intercollegiate sports for men and 4 for women, and 4 intramural sports for men and 4 for women. Facilities include 2 gyms, a dance studio, and a weight room.

Disabled Students: 95% of the campus is accessible. Wheelchair ramps, elevators, special parking, specially equipped rest rooms, lowered drinking fountains, lowered telephones, services/facilities for the hearing impaired, and library tapes are available.

Services: Counseling and information services are available, as is tutoring in every subject. There is remedial math, reading, and writing. The school has a special program for the learning disabled.

Campus Safety and Security: Measures include 24-hour foot and vehicle patrol, self-defense education, informal discussions, and pamphlets/posters/films. There are emergency telephones, lighted pathways/sidewalks, and lectures by the New York City Police Department.

Programs of Study: FIT confers B.S. and B.F.A. degrees. Associate and master's degrees are also awarded. Bachelor's degrees are awarded in BUSINESS (apparel and accessories marketing, fashion merchandising, and marketing/retailing/merchandising), COMMUNICATIONS AND THE ARTS (advertising, design, fiber/textiles/weaving, graphic design, illustration, and toy design), ENGINEERING AND ENVIRONMENTAL DESIGN (computer graphics, interior design, and textile technology), SOCIAL SCIENCE (fashion design and technology, home furnishings and equipment management/production/services, and textiles and clothing). Fashion merchandising management, fashion design, and communication design are the largest.

Required: To graduate, students must complete the credit and course requirements for their majors with a 2.0 GPA. Students may qualify for a degree in 2 ways: by earning 60 credits, with half in the major while in residence at the upper-division level, or by earning 30 credits at the upper-division level in addition to an FIT associate degree. There is a 2-credit phys ed requirement.

Special: Internships are offered, and students may study abroad in 8 countries. Nondegree study is available.

Faculty/Classroom: 48% of faculty are male; 52%, female. All teach undergraduates. No introductory courses are taught by graduate students. The average class size in an introductory lecture is 25; in a laboratory, 18; and in a regular course, 25.

Admissions: 46% of recent applicants were accepted. 36% of recent freshmen were in the top fifth of their class; 72% were in the top two fifths.

Requirements: Applicants must be high school graduates or have a GED certificate. An essay and, when appropriate, a portfolio are required. FIT requires applicants to be in the upper 50% of their class. A GPA of 2.0 is required. AP and CLEP credits are accepted. Important factors in the admissions decision are personality/intangible qualities, leadership record, and evidence of special talent.

Procedure: Freshmen are admitted fall and spring. There is an early decision plan and rolling admissions plan. Check with school for current application deadlines and fee. Notification is sent on a rolling basis. 381 early decision candidates were accepted for a recent class. A waiting list is an active part of the admissions procedure. Applications are accepted on-line.

Transfer: 1029 transfer students enrolled in a recent year. Applicants must have a GPA of 2.0 and at least 30 college credits. An interview is required for art and design applicants, as well as a portfolio when appropriate. 30 of 60 credits required for the bachelor's degree must be completed at FIT.

Visiting: There are regularly scheduled orientations for prospective students, including a presentation and group information session with a counselor. To schedule a visit, contact the Admissions Office at *fitinfo@fitnyc.edu.*

Financial Aid: In a recent year, 70% of all full-time freshmen and 51% of continuing full-time students received some form of financial aid. 51% of full-time freshmen and 40% of continuing full-time students received need-based aid. The average freshman award was $5858. Need-based scholarships or need-based grants averaged $3457 ($9450 maximum); need-based self-help aid (loans and jobs) averaged $3008 ($2625 maximum); and other non-need-based awards and non-need-based scholarships averaged $1447 ($1500 maximum). The average financial indebtedness of a recent year graduate was $9395. FIT is a member of CSS. The FAFSA and the state aid form are required. Check with the school for current deadlines.

International Students: There were 905 international students enrolled in a recent year. They must take the TOEFL.

Computers: All students may access the system. There are no time limits and no fees.

Graduates: In a recent year, 937 bachelor's degrees were awarded. The most popular majors were fashion merchandising management (32%), advertising, marketing, and communication (12%), and fashion design (12%). 90 companies recruited on campus in a recent year.

Admissions Contact: Dolores Lombardi, Director of Admissions. A video is available. E-mail: *fitinfo@fitnyc.edu* Web: *www.fitnyc.edu*

FIVE TOWNS COLLEGE   E-5
Dix Hills, NY 11746

(631) 424-7000, ext. 2110
Fax: (631) 656-2172

Full-time: 648 men, 394 women	**Faculty:** n/av
Part-time: 17 men, 29 women	**Ph.Ds:** 51%
Graduate: 39 men, 35 women	**Student/Faculty:** n/av
Year: semesters, summer session	**Tuition:** $14,350
Application Deadline: March	**Room & Board:** $10,250
Freshman Class: 1162 applied, 598 accepted, 363 enrolled	
SAT Verbal/Math: 484/470*	**ACT:** 21	**SPECIAL**

Five Towns College, founded in 1972, is a private institution offering undergraduate programs in music, music business, business, liberal arts, theater, elementary education, and mass communication (broadcasting, journalism). The library contains 28,000 volumes, 50 microform items, and 9575 audio/video tapes/CDs/DVDs, and subscribes to 550 periodicals including electronic. Computerized library services include interlibrary loans, database searching, and Internet access. Special learning facilities include a learning resource center, radio station, 72-, 48-, and 24-track recording studios, a MIDI studio, and a film video/TV studio. The 40-acre campus is in a suburban area 48 miles east of New York City. Including any residence halls, there are 3 buildings.

Student Life: 95% of undergraduates are from New York. Others are from 20 states and 7 foreign countries. 91% are from public schools. 62% are white; 15% African American; 14% Hispanic. The average age of freshmen is 19; all undergraduates, 21. 30% do not continue beyond their first year; 58% remain to graduate.

Housing: 180 students can be accommodated in college housing, which includes coed dorms and off-campus apartments. Priority for on-campus housing is given to out-of-town students. 90% of students commute. Alcohol is not permitted. All students may keep cars.

Activities: There are no fraternities or sororities. There are many groups and organizations on campus, including art, band, barber shop quartets, broadcasting, choir, chorale, chorus, drama, film, hiphop, honors, international, jazz band, live audio, music business, musical theater, newspaper, orchestra, photography, professional, radio and TV, readers theater, social, student government, symphony, theatrical concert, and yearbook. Popular campus events include the Cultural Hour, the Annual Picnic, and spring and fall festivals.

Sports: There are 2 intramural sports for men and 2 for women. Facilities include a gym with basketball and volleyball courts, an outdoor baseball/soccer field, and a fitness center.

Disabled Students: All of the campus is accessible. Wheelchair ramps, special parking, specially equipped rest rooms, special class scheduling, lowered drinking fountains, lowered telephones, and special housing are available.

Services: Counseling and information services are available, as is tutoring in most subjects. There is remedial math, reading, and writing.

Campus Safety and Security: Measures include 24-hour foot and vehicle patrol, shuttle buses, informal discussions, and pamphlets/posters/films. There are lighted pathways/sidewalks.

Programs of Study: FTC confers B.S., B.F.A., B.P.S., and Mus.B. degrees. Associate, master's, and doctoral degrees are also awarded. Bachelor's degrees are awarded in COMMUNICATIONS AND THE ARTS (audio technology, communications, dramatic arts, jazz, music business management, music performance, music theory and composition, and video), EDUCATION (elementary and music). Music and childhood education are the strongest academically. Audio recording technology is the largest.

Required: To graduate, all students must complete a total of 128 credits for a Mus.B. or B.F.A. degree, 120 for a B.P.S. degree, or 130 for a B.S. degree. Students must maintain at least a C average in their major concentration and have a minimum GPA of 2.0 to graduate. Distribution requirements include 45 credits in core courses in liberal arts. The core curriculum consists of English Composition 101 and 102, Speech 101, 3 credits each of either psychology or sociology, and various upper-division liberal arts and social science courses. All music students must pass a jury exam. Music majors and elementary education majors must take a comprehensive exam.

Special: Cross-registration is available with schools in the Long Island Regional Advisory Council on Higher Education. Co-op programs in audio recording technology, music business, film/video arts, and broadcasting are available, and internships are possible. Work-study programs are offered on campus, and B.A./B.S. degrees are possible. Students can have dual majors in music, audio recording technology, business, music business, and video production. There is 1 national honor society and 4 departmental honors program.

Faculty/Classroom: 66% of faculty are male; 34%, female. All both teach and do research. The average class size in an introductory lecture is 30 and in a laboratory, 24.

Admissions: 51% of the 2005-2006 applicants were accepted. The SAT scores for the 2005-2006 freshman class were: Verbal--74% below 500, 24% between 500 and 599, and 2% between 600 and 700; Math--73% below 500, 25% between 500 and 599, and 2% between 600 and 700. The ACT scores were 99% below 21, and 1% between 21 and 23. 8% of the current freshmen were in the top fifth of their class; 28% were in the top two fifths.

Requirements: The SAT or ACT is required. The ACT Optional Writing test is also required. In addition, a minimum high school average of 80 is required. A GED with a minimum score of 2500 is accepted. An audition is required for students in music and theater. A GPA of 2.0 is required. AP and CLEP credits are accepted. Important factors in the admissions decision are advanced placement or honor courses, evidence of special talent, and parents or siblings attending the school.

Procedure: Freshmen are admitted fall, spring, and summer. Entrance exams should be taken prior to admission. There are early decision, deferred admissions and rolling admissions plans. Applications should be filed by mid March for fall entry and mid December for spring entry. Notification is sent on a rolling basis. The fall 2005 application fee was $25.

Transfer: 285 transfer students enrolled in 2004-2005. Students must be in good academic standing at their former school and have a minimum GPA of 2.0. 45 of 120 credits required for the bachelor's degree must be completed at FTC.

Visiting: There are regularly scheduled orientations for prospective students, including a campus tour, academic counseling, and financial aid counseling. There are guides for informal visits and visitors may sit in on classes. To schedule a visit, contact the Admissions Office at (631) 656-2110.

Financial Aid: In a recent year, 77% of all full-time freshmen and 98% of continuing full-time students received some form of financial aid. 70% of full-time freshmen and 68% of continuing full-time students received need-based aid. The average freshman award was $4500. 74% of undergraduates worked part time. Average annual earnings from campus work were $2000. The average financial indebtedness of a recent graduate was $18,000. The FAFSA and the college's own financial statement are required. Check with the school for current application deadlines.

International Students: In a recent year there were 14 international students enrolled. They must score satisfactorily on the written TOEFL or on the electronic version and also take the college's own test the SAT or the ACT.

Computers: All students may access the system during school hours.

Graduates: In a recent year, 115 bachelor's degrees were awarded. The most popular majors were business (48%), music education and music performance (25%), and film/video and theater (21%). In an average class, 54% graduate in 4 years or less, 44% graduate in 5 years or less, and 2% graduate in 6 years or less. 64 companies recruited on campus in a recent year. Of a recent graduating class, 3% were enrolled in graduate school within 6 months of graduation and 88% were employed.

Admissions Contact: Jerry Cohen, Director of Admissions. A video is available. E-mail: *admissions@ftc.edu* Web: *www.ftc.edu*

FORDHAM UNIVERSITY SYSTEM

The Fordham University, established in 1841, is a private university in the Jesuit tradition. It is governed by a board of trustees whose chief administrator is the president. The primary goal of the university is to educate talented men and women in the liberal arts, sciences, business, and performing arts. The main priorities are excellence in undergraduate and selected graduate/professional programs, and commitment to teaching, research, and service. The total undergraduate enrollment of all 3 campuses is about 8,000, with more than 600 faculty members. There are 69 baccalaureate, 71 master's, and 25 doctoral programs through Fordham University. Profiles of the 4-year campuses are included in this section.

FORDHAM UNIVERSITY   D-5
Bronx, NY 10458

(718) 817-4000
(800) FORDHAM; Fax: (718) 367-3426

Full-time: 3000 men, 4000 women	**Faculty:** 447; I, +$
Part-time: 250 men, 500 women	**Ph.Ds:** 95%
Graduate: 2800 men, 4500 women	**Student/Faculty:** 15 to 1
Year: semesters, summer session	**Tuition:** $26,000
Application Deadline: see profile	**Room & Board:** $10,000
Freshman Class: n/av	
SAT or ACT required	**HIGHLY COMPETITIVE**

Fordham University, founded in 1841, is a private institution offering an education based on the Jesuit tradition, with 3 campuses in New York: 1 in the Bronx, 1 in Manhattan near Lincoln Center, and 1 in Tarrytown.

There are 5 undergraduate and 6 graduate schools. Figures in the above and in this profile are approximate. In addition to regional accreditation, Fordham University has baccalaureate program accreditation with AACSB and NCATE. The 4 libraries contain 2,033,124 volumes, 3,080,449 microform items, and 19,295 audio/video tapes/CDs/DVDs, and subscribe to 15,940 periodicals including electronic. Computerized library services include the card catalog, interlibrary loans, database searching, and Internet access. Special learning facilities include a learning resource center, radio station, a seismic station, an archeological site, and a biological field station. The 85-acre campus is in an urban area adjacent to the Bronx Zoo and New York Botanical Garden. Including any residence halls, there are 32 buildings.

Student Life: 59% of undergraduates are from New York. Others are from 50 states, 50 foreign countries, and Canada. 40% are from public schools. 58% are white; 11% Hispanic. 66% are Catholic; 13% describe themselves as Buddhist, Greek Orthodox, Hindu, Muslim/Islam; 10% claim no religious affiliation; 9% Protestant. The average age of freshmen is 19; all undergraduates, 20. 10% do not continue beyond their first year; 74% remain to graduate.

Housing: 3947 students can be accommodated in college housing, which includes coed dorms, on-campus apartments, and off-campus apartments. On-campus housing is guaranteed for all 4 years. 59% of students live on campus; of those, 90% remain on campus on weekends. All students may keep cars.

Activities: There are no fraternities or sororities. There are 133 groups on campus, including art, band, cheerleading, choir, chorale, chorus, computers, dance, drama, ethnic, film, gay, honors, international, jazz band, literary magazine, marching band, musical theater, newspaper, orchestra, pep band, photography, political, professional, radio and TV, religious, social, social service, student admission ambassador, student government, symphony, and yearbook. Popular campus events include Spring Weekend, Spring Semiformal, and Senior Week.

Sports: There are 19 intercollegiate sports for men and 17 for women, and 22 intramural sports for men and 22 for women. Facilities include a 6000-seat football stadium, an Olympic-size pool with a separate diving area, an indoor track, a 3200-seat gym, and tennis, squash, and racquetball courts.

Disabled Students: 80% of the campus is accessible. Wheelchair ramps, elevators, special parking, specially equipped rest rooms, special class scheduling, and lowered drinking fountains are available.

Services: Counseling and information services are available, as is tutoring in most subjects.

Campus Safety and Security: Measures include 24-hour foot and vehicle patrol, security escort services, shuttle buses, and informal discussions. There are pamphlets/posters/films, emergency telephones, and lighted pathways/sidewalks.

Programs of Study: Fordham University confers B.A., B.S., and B.F.A. degrees. Master's and doctoral degrees are also awarded. Bachelor's degrees are awarded in BIOLOGICAL SCIENCE (biology/biological science), BUSINESS (accounting, business administration and management, business economics, international business management, and marketing management), COMMUNICATIONS AND THE ARTS (art history and appreciation, broadcasting, classical languages, communications, comparative literature, dance, dramatic arts, English, film arts, fine arts, French, German, Italian, journalism, music, performing arts, Spanish, and visual and performing arts), COMPUTER AND PHYSICAL SCIENCE (chemistry, computer science, information sciences and systems, mathematics, physics, and science), SOCIAL SCIENCE (African American studies, African studies, American studies, anthropology, classical/ancient civilization, economics, French studies, German area studies, history, international studies, Italian studies, Latin American studies, medieval studies, Middle Eastern studies, philosophy, political science/government, psychology, religion, social science, social work, sociology, Spanish studies, theological studies, urban studies, and women's studies). Communications, social sciences, and English are the strongest academically. Business, psychology, and history are the largest.

Required: All students must complete a core curriculum, including 2 courses each in English literature, history, philosophy, theology, natural sciences, social sciences, and foreign language competency and 1 each in math, English composition, and fine arts. A total of 124 credits with 30 in the major and a 2.0 minimum GPA are required. A thesis is required for the honors program.

Special: Fordham University offers career-oriented internships in communications and other majors during the junior or senior year with New York City companies and institutions. A combined 3-2 engineering program is available with Columbia and Case Western Reserve Universities. Study abroad, a Washington semester, accelerated degrees, dual and student-designed majors, and pass/fail options are available. There are 6 national honor societies, including Phi Beta Kappa, and a freshman honors program.

Faculty/Classroom: 64% of faculty are male; 36%, female. 74% both teach and do research. No introductory courses are taught by graduate students. The average class size in an introductory lecture is 21; in a laboratory, 11; and in a regular course, 17.

Admissions: 54% of recent applicants were accepted.

Requirements: The SAT or ACT is required. In addition, applicants should have completed 4 years of high school English and 3 each of math, science, social studies, history, and foreign language. An essay is part of the application process. An interview is recommended. Auditions are required for theater and dance majors. A GED is accepted (minimum 3,000 on new scale; 300 on old scale). AP credits are accepted. Important factors in the admissions decision are leadership record, parents or siblings attending the school, and recommendations by school officials.

Procedure: Freshmen are admitted fall and spring. Entrance exams should be taken by December of the senior year. There is a deferred admissions plan. Check with the school for current application deadlines and fee. 129 early decision candidates were accepted for a recent class. 700 applicants were on a recent waiting list; 151 were admitted. Applications are accepted on-line.

Transfer: 246 transfer students enrolled in a recent year. A 3.0 minimum GPA is recommended. Applicants with less than 1 full year of full-time course work at a postsecondary institution should submit SAT or ACT scores. An interview is recommended. 64 of 124 credits required for the bachelor's degree must be completed at Fordham University.

Visiting: There are regularly scheduled orientations for prospective students. There are guides for informal visits and visitors may sit in on classes and stay overnight. To schedule a visit, contact the Admissions Office at *enroll@fordham.edu*.

Financial Aid: In a recent year, 68% of all full-time freshmen and 65% of continuing full-time students received some form of financial aid. 63% of full-time freshmen and 61% of continuing full-time students received need-based aid. The average freshman award was $17,591. Need-based scholarships or need-based grants averaged $14,812; need-based self-help aid (loans and jobs) averaged $3780; non-need-based athletic scholarships averaged $13,259; and other non-need-based awards and non-need-based scholarships averaged $6954. 95% of undergraduates work part time. Average annual earnings from campus work are $1600. The average financial indebtedness of the 2005 graduate was $16,274. Fordham University is a member of CSS. The CSS/Profile and FAFSA are required. Check with the school for current deadlines.

International Students: There were 89 international students enrolled in a recent year. The school actively recruits these students. They must take the TOEFL, the college's own test, and the SAT or the ACT.

Computers: All students may access the system. There are no time limits and no fees.

Graduates: In a recent year, 1487 bachelor's degrees were awarded. The most popular majors were business administration/marketing (24%), social sciences/history (22%), and communications (14%). In an average class, 1% graduate in 3 years or less, 68% graduate in 4 years or less, 72% graduate in 5 years or less, and 73% graduate in 6 years or less. 500 companies recruited on campus in a recent year. Of a recent graduating class, 25% were enrolled in graduate school within 6 months of graduation and 90% were employed.

Admissions Contact: John W. Buckley, Dean of Admission.
E-mail: *enroll@fordham.edu* Web: *www.fordham.edu*

HAMILTON COLLEGE C-3

Clinton, NY 13323
(315) 859-4421
(800) 843-2655; Fax: (315) 859-4457

Full-time: 904 men, 898 women	**Faculty:** 206; IIB, +$
Part-time: 12 men and women	**Ph.D.s:** 92%
Graduate: none	**Student/Faculty:** 9 to 1
Year: semesters	**Tuition:** $33,350
Application Deadline: January 1	**Room & Board:** $8310
Freshman Class: 4189 applied, 1502 accepted, 498 enrolled	
SAT Verbal/Math: 690/680*	**MOST COMPETITIVE**

Hamilton College, founded in 1793, is a private, nonsectarian, liberal arts school offering undergraduate programs in the arts and sciences. The 3 libraries contain 577,031 volumes, 416,230 microform items, and 57,096 audio/video tapes/CDs/DVDs, and subscribe to 3645 periodicals including electronic. Computerized library services include the card catalog and database searching. Special learning facilities include an art gallery, radio station, and an observatory. The 1200-acre campus is in a rural area 9 miles southwest of Utica. Including any residence halls, there are 51 buildings.

Student Life: 66% of undergraduates are from out of state, mostly the Northeast. Students are from 44 states, 38 foreign countries, and Canada. 60% are from public schools. 73% are white. 31% are Catholic; 30% Protestant; 25% claim no religious affiliation; 8% Jewish. The average age of freshmen is 18; all undergraduates, 20. 7% do not continue beyond their first year; 88% remain to graduate.

Housing: 1750 students can be accommodated in college housing, which includes coed dorms, on-campus apartments, and married-student housing. In addition, there are language houses, special-interest houses, quiet floors, and substance-free areas. On-campus housing is guaranteed for all 4 years. 98% of students live on campus; of those, 95% remain on campus on weekends. Upperclassmen may keep cars.

Activities: 34% of men belong to 8 national fraternities; 20% of women belong to 3 local sororities. There are 60 groups on campus, including art, chess, choir, chorale, chorus, computers, dance, drama, ethnic, film, gay, honors, international, jazz band, literary magazine, musical theater, newspaper, pep band, photography, political, professional, radio, religious, social, social service, student government, and yearbook. Popular campus events include Class and Charter Day, February Fest (Winter Carnival), and Springfest.

Sports: There are 12 intercollegiate sports for men and 12 for women, and 26 intramural sports for men and 29 for women. Facilities include a gym, a field house, squash and racquetball courts, indoor and outdoor tennis courts, a football stadium, a 9-hole golf course, a swimming pool, indoor and outdoor tracks, numerous grass fields, an artificial turf field, paddle tennis courts, and an ice rink.

Disabled Students: Wheelchair ramps, elevators, special parking, specially equipped rest rooms, and special class scheduling are available.

Services: Counseling and information services are available, as is tutoring in some subjects through the New York State Higher Education Opportunity Program (HEOP).

Campus Safety and Security: Measures include 24-hour foot and vehicle patrol, self-defense education, security escort services, and shuttle buses. There are informal discussions, pamphlets/posters/films, emergency telephones, and lighted pathways/sidewalks.

Programs of Study: Hamilton confers the B.A. degree. Bachelor's degrees are awarded in BIOLOGICAL SCIENCE (biochemistry, biology/biological science, and neurosciences), COMMUNICATIONS AND THE ARTS (art, art history and appreciation, classics, communications, comparative literature, creative writing, dance, dramatic arts, English, French, German, languages, music, Spanish, and studio art), COMPUTER AND PHYSICAL SCIENCE (chemistry, computer science, geology, mathematics, and physics), SOCIAL SCIENCE (African studies, American studies, anthropology, archeology, Asian/Oriental studies, classical/ancient civilization, economics, history, international relations, philosophy, political science/government, psychobiology, psychology, public affairs, religion, Russian and Slavic studies, sociology, and women's studies). Government, economics, and psychology are the largest.

Required: Students must successfully complete 128 credits, with 32 to 40 of these in the student's major, and must maintain at least a 72 average in half the courses taken. Students are required to take 3 courses designated as writing intensive, as well as 2 semesters of phys ed. A senior project in the student's major is also required.

Special: Cross-registration is permitted with Colgate University and Utica College of Syracuse University. Opportunities are provided for internships, a cooperative program through the Williams College Mystic Seaport Program in Connecticut, and a Washington semester. Accelerated degree programs, dual majors, nondegree study, pass/fail options, student-designed majors, a program for early assurance of acceptance to medical school, and study abroad in many countries are available. 3-2 engineering degrees are offered with Washington University, Rensselaer Polytechnic Institute, and Columbia University. There are 4 national honor societies, including Phi Beta Kappa.

Faculty/Classroom: 59% of faculty are male; 41%, female. All teach undergraduates.

Admissions: 36% of the 2005-2006 applicants were accepted. The SAT scores for the 2005-2006 freshman class were: Verbal--2% below 500, 14% between 500 and 599, 49% between 600 and 700, and 35% above 700; Math--1% below 500, 9% between 500 and 599, 59% between 600 and 700, and 31% above 700. 87% of the current freshmen were in the top fifth of their class; 98% were in the top two fifths.

Requirements: The SAT or ACT is required. Although graduation from an accredited secondary school or a GED is desirable, and a full complement of college-preparatory courses is recommended, Hamilton will consider all highly recommended candidates who demonstrate an ability and desire to perform at intellectually demanding levels. An essay is required, and an interview is recommended. AP credits are accepted. Important factors in the admissions decision are advanced placement or honor courses, recommendations by school officials, and parents or siblings attending the school.

Procedure: Freshmen are admitted in the fall. Entrance exams should be taken prior to February of the senior year. There are early decision, early admissions, and deferred admissions plans. Early decision applications should be filed by November 15; regular applications, by January 1 for fall entry. Notification of early decision is sent December 15; regular decision, April 1. 246 early decision candidates were accepted for the 2005-2006 class. 15 were admitted. Applications are accepted on-line. The fall 2005 application fee was $50.

Transfer: 23 transfer students enrolled in 2004-2005. Transfer applicants must submit high school and college transcripts, an essay or personal statement, and standardized test scores, and must present a minimum GPA of 3.0 in all college-level work. 64 of 128 credits required for the bachelor's degree must be completed at Hamilton.

Visiting: There are regularly scheduled orientations for prospective students, consisting of an interview, tour, class visit, and open house program. There are guides for informal visits and visitors may sit in on classes and stay overnight. To schedule a visit, contact the Admissions Office at 800-843-2655.

Financial Aid: In 2005-2006, 60% of all full-time students received some form of financial aid. 55% of all full-time students received need-based aid. The average freshman award was $26,760. 48% of undergraduates work part time. Average annual earnings from campus work are $1400. The average financial indebtedness of the 2005 graduate was $16,776. The CSS/Profile or FAFSA is required. The deadline for filing freshman financial aid applications for fall entry is February 1.

International Students: There are 95 international students enrolled. The school actively recruits these students. They must take the TOEFL and also take the SAT or the ACT.

Computers: All students may access the system. There are no time limits and no fees.

Graduates: From July 1, 2004 to June 30, 2005, 423 bachelor's degrees were awarded. The most popular majors were economics (12%), government (10%), and psychology (7%). In an average class, 1% graduate in 3 years or less, 83% graduate in 4 years or less, 86% graduate in 5 years or less, and 88% graduate in 6 years or less.

Admissions Contact: Monica Inzer, Dean of Admissions and Financial Aid. E-mail: *admission@hamilton.edu* Web: *www.hamilton.edu*

HARTWICK COLLEGE   D-3

Oneonta, NY 13820-4020   (607) 431-4150
(888) HARTWICK; Fax: (607) 431-4102

Full-time: 613 men, 792 women	**Faculty:** 109; IIB, av$
Part-time: 25 men, 33 women	**Ph.Ds:** 94%
Graduate: none	**Student/Faculty:** 13 to 1
Year: 4-1-4	**Tuition:** $28,585
Application Deadline: February 15	**Room & Board:** $7480
Freshman Class: 2211 applied, 1928 accepted, 409 enrolled	
SAT Verbal/Math: 570/565*	**ACT:** 24 **COMPETITIVE+**

Hartwick College, founded in 1797, is a private undergraduate liberal arts and sciences college. In addition to regional accreditation, Hartwick has baccalaureate program accreditation with CCNE, NASAD, NASM, and NLN. The library contains 348,699 volumes, 56,817 microform items, and 1400 audio/video tapes/CDs/DVDs. Computerized library services include the card catalog, interlibrary loans, database searching, Internet access, and laptop Internet portals. Special learning facilities include an art gallery, radio station, TV station, a museum, a 914-acre environmental study center, an observatory, and an environmental field station. The 425-acre campus is in a small town 75 miles southwest of Albany. Including any residence halls, there are 28 buildings.

Student Life: 61% of undergraduates are from New York. Others are from 38 states, 29 foreign countries, and Canada. 84% are from public schools. 63% are white. The average age of freshmen is 18; all undergraduates, 20. 24% do not continue beyond their first year; 58% remain to graduate.

Housing: 1259 students can be accommodated in college housing, which includes single-sex and coed dorms, on-campus apartments, fraternity houses, and sorority houses. In addition, there are special-interest houses. On-campus housing is guaranteed for all 4 years. 88% of students live on campus; of those, 90% remain on campus on weekends. All students may keep cars.

Activities: 15% of men belong to 1 local and 4 national fraternities; 17% of women belong to 3 local and 1 national sorority. There are 60 groups on campus, including academic, art, band, cheerleading, choir, chorale, chorus, computers, dance, drama, ethnic, film, gay, honors, international, jazz band, literary magazine, musical theater, newspaper, orchestra, outing, pep band, photography, political, professional, radio and TV, religious, social, social service, and student government. Popular campus events include Holiday Ball, Earth Day, and Multicultural Month.

Sports: There are 11 intercollegiate sports for men and 13 for women, and 9 intramural sports for men and 9 for women. Facilities include 2 gyms, an indoor pool, a dance room, athletic and training facilities, a track, a Nautilus exercise gym, a fitness center, a lighted all-weather playing field, a lighted soccer field, a minor league field for baseball, an equestrian complex, and courts for handball, racquetball, squash, and tennis.

Disabled Students: 50% of the campus is accessible. Wheelchair ramps, elevators, special parking, specially equipped rest rooms, special class scheduling, lowered drinking fountains, and lowered telephones are available.

Services: Counseling and information services are available, as is tutoring in every subject. There is a reader service for the blind. There are writing and math centers and an academic center for excellence.

Campus Safety and Security: Measures include 24-hour foot and vehicle patrol, self-defense education, security escort services, and shuttle buses. There are informal discussions, pamphlets/posters/films, emergency telephones, and lighted pathways/sidewalks.

Programs of Study: Hartwick confers B.A. and B.S. degrees. Bachelor's degrees are awarded in BIOLOGICAL SCIENCE (biochemistry and biology/biological science), BUSINESS (accounting and business administration and management), COMMUNICATIONS AND THE ARTS (art,

art history and appreciation, dramatic arts, English, French, German, languages, music, and Spanish), COMPUTER AND PHYSICAL SCIENCE (chemistry, computer science, geology, information sciences and systems, mathematics, and physics), EDUCATION (music), ENGINEERING AND ENVIRONMENTAL DESIGN (environmental science), HEALTH PROFESSIONS (medical technology and nursing), SOCIAL SCIENCE (anthropology, economics, history, philosophy, political science/government, psychology, religion, and sociology). Anthropology, biology, and English are the strongest academically. Psychology, management, and nursing are the largest.

Required: Students must complete 120 credit hours with at least a 2.0 GPA. Core requirements are in the study areas of continuity, interdependence, science and technology, critical thinking, effective communication, and electives. Courses are chosen from offerings in humanities, science and math, social and behavioral sciences, foreign language, and phys ed. A first-year seminar and a contemporary issues seminar for juniors and seniors are required. Students are strongly urged to include an off-campus learning experience.

Special: Students may design their own majors and choose independent study. Cross-registration with SUNY College at Oneonta is possible and local and international internships are available. There is a January thematic term, a Washington semester, and study abroad in 30 countries. First-year students may participate in specially designated off-campus programs. Experiential programs include Outward Bound and the National Outdoor Leadership School. All departments offer dual majors and accelerated degree options. There is a 3-2 engineering program with Clarkson University or Columbia University, and a 3-3 program with Albany Law School. There are 10 national honor societies and a freshman honors program.

Faculty/Classroom: 61% of faculty are male; 39%, female. All teach undergraduates. The average class size in an introductory lecture is 20; in a laboratory, 20; and in a regular course, 30.

Admissions: 87% of recent applicants were accepted. 36% of recent freshmen were in the top fifth of their class; 71% were in the top two fifths. 5 freshmen graduated first in a recent class.

Requirements: Reporting of SAT and ACT scores is optional. The recommended secondary course of study includes 4 years of English, and 3 years each of math, a foreign language, history, and lab science. Hartwick strongly recommends that applicants plan a campus visit and interview. Prospective art majors should submit a portfolio, and music majors must audition. AP and CLEP credits are accepted. Important factors in the admissions decision are advanced placement or honor courses, recommendations by school officials, and ability to finance college education.

Procedure: Freshmen are admitted to all sessions. Entrance exams should be taken in the spring of the junior year and/or the fall of the senior year. There are early decision and deferred admissions plans. Check with the school for current application deadlines and fee. 75 early decision candidates were accepted for a recent class class. A waiting list is an active part of the admissions procedure. Applications are accepted online. The fall 2005 aplication fee was $35.

Transfer: Applicants should present a minimum GPA of 2.0. 60 of 120 credits required for the bachelor's degree must be completed at Hartwick.

Visiting: There are regularly scheduled orientations for prospective students, consisting of an interview and tour, lunch, departmental open houses, presentations on student life, off-campus programs, and a career planning process. There are guides for informal visits and visitors may sit in on classes and stay overnight. To schedule a visit, contact the Admissions Office.

Financial Aid: In Check with the school for current deadlines. Hartwick is a member of CSS. The FAFSA and the college's own financial statement are required.

International Students: There were 58 international students enrolled in a recent year. The school actively recruits these students. They must score satisfactorily on the written TOEFL.

Computers: Wireless access is available. All students are required to have notebook computers; wired and wireless access is available in all buildings. All students may access the system 24 hours per day, 7 days per week. There are no time limits and no fees.

Graduates: In a recent year, 270 bachelor's degrees were awarded. The most popular majors were management (18%), psychology (11%), and history (8%). In an average class, 48% graduate in 4 years or less, 55% graduate in 5 years or less, and 57% graduate in 6 years or less. 20 companies recruited on campus in a recent year.

Admissions Contact: Patricia Maben, Director.
E-mail: *admissions@hartwick.edu* Web: *http://www.hartwick.edu*

HILBERT COLLEGE   A-3

Hamburg, NY 14075-1597   (716) 649-7900, ext. 211
                                   (800) 649-8003; Fax: (716) 649-0702

Full-time: 296 men, 438 women	**Faculty:** 39; IIB, --$
Part-time: 113 men, 258 women	**Ph.Ds:** 51%
Graduate: none	**Student/Faculty:** 19 to 1
Year: semesters, summer session	**Tuition:** $14,900
Application Deadline: open	**Room & Board:** $5580
Freshman Class: n/av	
SAT or ACT: recommended	**LESS COMPETITIVE**

Hilbert College, founded in 1957, is a private institution offering degree programs in business, criminal justice, and social sciences. The library contains 36,076 volumes, 3616 microform items, and 1165 audio/video tapes/CDs/DVDs, and subscribes to 23,190 periodicals including electronic. Computerized library services include the card catalog, interlibrary loans, database searching, Internet access, and laptop Internet portals. Special learning facilities include a learning resource center film studies lab and undergraduate psychology research lab. The 44-acre campus is in an urban area about 15 miles south of Buffalo. Including any residence halls, there are 11 buildings.

Student Life: 99% of undergraduates are from New York. Students are from 4 states, 2 foreign countries, and Canada. 86% are from public schools. 88% are white. The average age of freshmen is 24; all undergraduates, 26. 26% do not continue beyond their first year; 74% remain to graduate.

Housing: 134 students can be accommodated in college housing, which includes coed dorms, on-campus apartments, and off-campus apartments. On-campus housing is guaranteed for all 4 years. 88% of students commute. All students may keep cars.

Activities: There are no fraternities or sororities. There are 20 groups on campus, including academic, cheerleading, chorus, ethnic, film, honors, literary magazine, newspaper, professional, religious, social, social service, and student government. Popular campus events include Quad Party, Welcome Back Picnic, and Fall Family Weekend.

Sports: There are 5 intercollegiate sports for men and 6 for women, and 4 intramural sports for men and 4 for women. Facilities include a soccer/lacrosse field, baseball and softball diamonds, a practice field, a weight room, and a 900-seat NCAA regulation indoor athletic facility.

Disabled Students: 95% of the campus is accessible. Wheelchair ramps, elevators, special parking, specially equipped rest rooms, special class scheduling, lowered drinking fountains, and lowered telephones are available.

Services: Counseling and information services are available, as is tutoring in some subjects, including writing, accounting, and math. There is remedial math and writing.

Campus Safety and Security: Measures include 24-hour foot and vehicle patrol, self-defense education, security escort services, and informal discussions. There are pamphlets/posters/films, emergency telephones, and lighted pathways/sidewalks.

Programs of Study: Hilbert confers B.A. and B.S. degrees. Associate degrees are also awarded. Bachelor's degrees are awarded in BUSINESS (accounting and business administration and management), COMMUNICATIONS AND THE ARTS (English), HEALTH PROFESSIONS (rehabilitation therapy), SOCIAL SCIENCE (criminal justice, criminology, forensic studies, human services, liberal arts/general studies, paralegal studies, political science/government, and psychology). Economic crime investigation, paralegal studies, and accounting are the strongest academically. Criminal justice, economic crime investigation, and business administration are the largest.

Required: To graduate, students must complete 120 credit hours, including at least 36 in the major and 60 in liberal arts, with a minimum 2.0 GPA. Students must fulfill requirements in English, math, philosophy, social sciences, and senior seminar.

Special: Hilbert offers study abroad, cross-registration with other members of the Western New York College Consortium, internships in most majors, and work-study programs. The college maintains articulation agreements with New York State community colleges. There are 4 national honor societies, a freshman honors program, and 3 departmental honors programs.

Faculty/Classroom: 60% of faculty are male; 40%, female. All teach undergraduates and 10% do research. The average class size in an introductory lecture is 20; in a laboratory, 4; and in a regular course, 15.

Requirements: The SAT or ACT is recommended. A grade average of 70% is required. AP and CLEP credits are accepted. Important factors in the admissions decision are leadership record, advanced placement or honor courses, and recommendations by school officials.

Procedure: Freshmen are admitted to all sessions. There is a deferred admissions plan and a rolling admissions plan. Application deadlines are open. The fall 2005 application fee was $20. Applications are accepted on-line.

Transfer: 145 transfer students enrolled in a recent year. Applicants must submit official transcripts from all colleges attended and, in somes cases, the high school transcript. 30 of 120 credits required for the bachelor's degree must be completed at Hilbert.

Visiting: There are regularly scheduled orientations for prospective students, consisting of a campus tour, a student panel, and admissions, financial aid, and academic information sessions. There are guides for informal visits and visitors may sit in on classes and stay overnight. To schedule a visit, contact the Office of Admissions.

Financial Aid: In a recent year, 91% of all full-time freshmen and 89% of continuing full-time students received some form of financial aid. All of full-time freshmen and 98% of continuing full-time students received need-based aid. The average freshman award was $10,552. Need-based scholarships or need-based grants averaged $2570 ($5000 maximum); need-based self-help aid (loans and jobs) averaged $3642 ($5500 maximum); and other non-need-based awards and non-need-based scholarships averaged $2855 ($5000 maximum). 7% of undergraduates work part time. Average annual earnings from campus work are $1735. The average financial indebtedness of a recent graduate was $16,295. Hilbert is a member of CSS. The FAFSA is required. The priority date for freshman financial aid applications for fall entry is April 1. The deadline for filing freshman financial aid applications for fall entry is December 1.

International Students: Students must take the TOEFL.

Computers: All students may access the system. There are no time limits. The fee is $25 per semester.

Graduates: In a recent year, 179 bachelor's degrees were awarded. The most popular majors were criminal justice (25%), business administration (18%), and paralegal studies (17%). In an average class, 34% graduate in 3 years, 24% graduate in 4 years, and 4% graduate in 5 years. 40 companies recruited on campus in a recent year. Of a recent graduating class, 8% were enrolled in graduate school within 6 months of graduation and 69% were employed.

Admissions Contact: Director of Admissions. A video is available.
E-mail: *admissions@hilbert.edu* Web: *www.hilbert.edu*

HOBART AND WILLIAM SMITH COLLEGES   C-3

Geneva, NY 14456-3397

H: (315) 781-3622
H: (800) 852-2256; Fax: (315) 781-3471

Full-time: 860 men, 1005 women	**Faculty:** IIB, +$
Part-time: 3 men and women	**Ph.D.s:** n/av
Graduate: none	**Student/Faculty:** 12 to 1
Year: semesters	**Tuition:** $32,737
Application Deadline: February 1	**Room & Board:** $8386
Freshman Class: 3410 applied, 2209 accepted, 545 enrolled	
SAT Verbal/Math: 585/590*	**VERY COMPETITIVE**

Hobart College, a men's college founded in 1822, shares campus, classes, and faculty with William Smith College, a women's college founded in 1908. Together, these coordinate colleges offer degree programs in the liberal arts. Some figures in the above capsule and in this profile are approximate. The library contains 375,762 volumes, 77,396 microform items, and 9600 audio/video tapes/CDs/DVDs, and subscribes to 1926 periodicals including electronic. Computerized library services include the card catalog, interlibrary loans, database searching, and Internet access. Special learning facilities include a learning resource center, art gallery, radio station, a 100-acre natural preserve, and a 70-foot research vessel. The 170-acre campus is in a small town 50 miles west of Syracuse and 50 miles east of Rochester, on the north shore of Seneca Lake. Including any residence halls, there are 95 buildings.

Student Life: 51% of undergraduates are from out of state, mostly the Northeast. Students are from 40 states, 19 foreign countries, and Canada. 65% are from public schools. 86% are white. 30% are Catholic; 30% Protestant; 20% claim no religious affiliation; 15% Jewish. The average age of freshmen is 18; all undergraduates, 20. 15% do not continue beyond their first year; 75% remain to graduate.

Housing: 1500 students can be accommodated in college housing, which includes single-sex and coed dorms, on-campus apartments, and fraternity houses. In addition, there are honors houses, language houses, special-interest houses, Cooperative houses in which students plan and prepare their own meals, and town houses for upperclassman. On-campus housing is guaranteed for all 4 years. 90% of students live on campus; of those, 93% remain on campus on weekends. All students may keep cars.

Activities: 15% of men belong to 5 national fraternities. There are no sororities. There are 70 groups on campus, including art, chess, choir, chorale, chorus, computers, dance, debate, drama, ethnic, film, forensics, gay, honors, international, jazz band, literary magazine, musical theater, newspaper, orchestra, photography, political, professional, radio and TV, religious, social, social service, student government, symphony, and yearbook. Popular campus events include Folk Festival, Charter Day, and Moving Up Day.

Sports: There are 11 intercollegiate sports for men and 11 for women, and 23 intramural sports for men and 23 for women. Facilities include a sport and recreation center, 2 gyms, numerous athletic fields, a swimming pool, 5 indoor tennis courts, 3 weight rooms, basketball and rac-

quetball courts, an indoor track, international squash courts, a boathouse, and a crew facility.

Disabled Students: Wheelchair ramps, elevators, special parking, specially equipped rest rooms, special class scheduling, and lowered drinking fountains are available.

Services: Counseling and information services are available, as is tutoring in every subject. There is a reader service for the blind, and remedial math, reading, and writing. There is a counseling center staffed by 5 therapists/counselors as well as various support groups and educational workshops.

Campus Safety and Security: Measures include 24-hour foot and vehicle patrol, self-defense education, security escort services, and shuttle buses. There are informal discussions, pamphlets/posters/films, emergency telephones, and lighted pathways/sidewalks.

Programs of Study: HWS confers B.A. and B.S. degrees. Master's degrees are also awarded. Bachelor's degrees are awarded in BIOLOGICAL SCIENCE (biology/biological science), COMMUNICATIONS AND THE ARTS (art history and appreciation, classics, comparative literature, dance, English, fine arts, French, modern language, music, and studio art), COMPUTER AND PHYSICAL SCIENCE (chemistry, computer science, geoscience, mathematics, and physics), ENGINEERING AND ENVIRONMENTAL DESIGN (architecture and environmental science), SOCIAL SCIENCE (African studies, American studies, anthropology, Asian/Oriental studies, economics, European studies, history, international relations, Latin American studies, philosophy, political science/government, psychology, religion, Russian and Slavic studies, sociology, Spanish studies, urban studies, and women's studies). Natural sciences, environmental studies, and creative writing are the strongest academically. English, economics, and political science are the largest.

Required: All first-year students must take a seminar. Students should complete a major of 14 to 18 courses and a minor of 6 to 8 courses, or a second major. Of the major or the minor (or second major), one must be disciplinary and the other interdisciplinary. Minimum grade and GPA standards apply. In addition, all students must meet the 8 goals established by the faculty to ensure breadth across the disciplines as well as depth in the major.

Special: Students are encouraged to spend at least 1 term in a study-abroad program, offered in more than 29 countries and locales within the United States. Options include a United Nations term, a Washington semester, an urban semester, and prearchitecture semesters in New York, Paris, Florence, or Copenhagen. HWS offers dual and student-designed majors, internships, credit for life/military/work experience, nondegree study, and pass/fail options. There are also advanced business degree programs with Clarkson University and Rochester Institute of Technology and 3-2 engineering degrees with Columbia University, Rensselaer Polytechnic Institute, and Dartmouth College. There are 9 national honor societies, including Phi Beta Kappa, and all departments have honors programs.

Faculty/Classroom: 60% of faculty are male; 40%, female. All both teach and do research. The average class size in an introductory lecture is 40; in a laboratory, 18; and in a regular course, 18.

Admissions: 65% of the 2005-2006 applicants were accepted. The SAT scores for the 2005-2006 freshman class were: Verbal--10% below 500, 49% between 500 and 599, 35% between 600 and 700, and 6% above 700; Math--8% below 500, 47% between 500 and 599, 42% between 600 and 700, and 4% above 700. 57% of the current freshmen were in the top fifth of their class; 87% were in the top two fifths. 5 freshmen graduated first in their class.

Requirements: The SAT or ACT is required. SAT: Subject tests are not required but will be considered if taken. A GED may be is accepted. A total of 19 academic credits is required, including 4 years of English, 3 of math, and at least 3 each of lab science, foreign language, and history. An essay is required; an interview is recommended. AP credits are accepted. Important factors in the admissions decision are advanced placement or honor courses, evidence of special talent, and leadership record.

Procedure: Freshmen are admitted in the fall. Entrance exams should be taken no later than December of the senior year. There are early decision, early admissions, and deferred admissions plans. Early decision applications should be filed by November 15; regular applications, by February 1 for fall entry, along with a $45 fee. Notification of early decision is sent December 15; regular decision, March. 123 early decision candidates were accepted for the 2005-2006 class. 381 applicants were on the 2005 waiting list; 28 were admitted. Applications are accepted on-line.

Transfer: 38 transfer students enrolled in 2004-2005. Applicants must have a 2.5 GPA and have completed 1 year of college study. They are required to take the SAT I or ACT. An interview is recommended. 16 of 32 courses required for the bachelor's degree must be completed at HWS.

Visiting: There are regularly scheduled orientations for prospective students, including 7 open houses in the spring, summer, and fall and daily tours and personal interviews year round. Information sessions are offered February through April and on Saturdays in the summer. There are guides for informal visits and visitors may sit in on classes and stay overnight. To schedule a visit, contact the Office of Admissions.

Financial Aid: In 2005-2006, 68% of all full-time students received some form of financial aid. 58% of full-time freshmen and 62% of continuing full-time students received need-based aid. The average freshman award was $24,825. Need-based scholarships or need-based grants averaged $22,193 ($26,000 maximum); need-based self-help aid (loans and jobs) averaged $3276 ($8425 maximum); and other non-need-based awards and non-need-based scholarships averaged $11,795 ($28,400 maximum). In a recent year, 52% of undergraduates worked part time. Average annual earnings from campus work were $677. The average financial indebtedness of a recent graduate was $20,508. HWS is a member of CSS. The CSS/Profile or FAFSA is required. Check with the school for current application deadlines.

International Students: In a recent year there were 43 international students enrolled. The school actively recruits these students. They must score satisfactorily on the written TOEFL or on the electronic version and also take the SAT or the ACT.

Computers: All students may access the system from 8 A.M. to 1 A.M., 7 days a week. There are no time limits and no fees. It is strongly recommended that all students have a personal computer.

Graduates: In a recent year, 365 bachelor's degrees were awarded. The most popular majors were English (10%), economics (9%), and history (8%). In an average class, 65% graduate in 4 years or less, 70% graduate in 5 years or less, and 72% graduate in 6 years or less. Of a recent graduating class, 27% were enrolled in graduate school within 6 months of graduation and 82% were employed.

Admissions Contact: John W. Young, Director of Admissions. E-mail: *jyoung@hws.edu* Web: *www.hws.edu*

HOFSTRA UNIVERSITY   D-5
Hempstead, NY 11549

                                     (516) 463-6700
                    (800) HOFSTRA; Fax: (516) 560-7660

Full-time: 3702 men, 4329 women	**Faculty:** 430; I, av$
Part-time: 435 men, 418 women	**Ph.D.s:** 91%
Graduate: 1472 men, 2534 women	**Student/Faculty:** 19 to 1
Year: 4-1-4, summer session	**Tuition:** $23,130
Application Deadline: n/av	**Room & Board:** $9500
Freshman Class: 15,981 applied, 9953 accepted, 1774 enrolled	
SAT Verbal/Math: 570/580*	**ACT:** 23 **VERY COMPETITIVE**

Hofstra University, founded in 1935, is an independent institution offering programs in liberal arts and sciences, business, communications, and education. There are 8 undergraduate and 6 graduate schools. In addition to regional accreditation, Hofstra has baccalaureate program accreditation with AACSB, ABA, ABET, ACEJMC, ACS, APA, ASHA, CAAHEP, CORE, and NCATE. The 3 libraries contain 1,200,000 volumes, 3,481,190 microform items, and 14,197 audio/video tapes/CDs/DVDs, and subscribe to 9070 periodicals including electronic. Computerized library services include the card catalog, interlibrary loans, database searching, Internet access, and laptop Internet portals. Special learning facilities include a learning resource center, art gallery, radio station, TV station, financial trading room, comprehensive media production facility, career center, writing center, linux beowolf cluster, digital language lab, technology, science and engineering labs, a rooftop observatory, 7 theaters, assessment centers for child observation and counseling, child care institute, cultural center, museum, arboretum, and bird sanctuary. The 240-acre campus is in a suburban area 25 miles east of New York City. Including any residence halls, there are 113 buildings.

Student Life: 70% of undergraduates are from New York. Students are from 45 states, 48 foreign countries, and Canada. 61% are white. The average age of freshmen is 18; all undergraduates, 21. 22% do not continue beyond their first year; 55% remain to graduate.

Housing: 4200 students can be accommodated in college housing, which includes single-sex and coed dorms, off-campus apartments, and married-student housing. In addition, there are honors houses, special-interest houses, and living for learning and quiet floors. There is also international student housing, freshman housing, and apartmnet-style housing. On-campus housing is guaranteed for all 4 years, is available on a first-come, first-served basis, and is available on a lottery system for upperclassmen. Priority is given to out-of-town students. 51% of students commute. All students may keep cars.

Activities: 6% of men belong to 15 national fraternities; 7% of women belong to 3 local and 11 national sororities. There are about 150 groups on campus, including art, band, cheerleading, chess, choir, chorale, chorus, commuter, computers, dance, debate, drama, drum and bugle corps, ethnic, film, forensics, gay, honors, international, jazz band, literary magazine, musical theater, newspaper, opera, orchestra, pep band, photography, political, professional, radio and TV, religious, resident students, social, social service, student government, symphony, and yearbook. Popular campus events include New Student Convocation, Kick-Off Weekend, and Great Writers/Great Readings.

Sports: There are 9 intercollegiate sports for men and 9 for women, and 7 intramural sports for men and 7 for women. Facilities include a 15,000-seat stadium, a 5000-seat arena, a 1600-seat soccer stadium, a physical fitness center, a swim center with an Olympic-size swimming

pool and high-dive area, a softball stadium, intramurals field, a recreation center with a multipurpose gym, an indoor track, a weight room, a lounge area, and a cardio area.

Disabled Students: All of the campus is accessible. Wheelchair ramps, elevators, special parking, specially equipped rest rooms, special class scheduling, lowered drinking fountains, lowered telephones, special housing, automated door openings, and TTY visual telephones are available.

Services: Counseling and information services are available, as is tutoring in most subjects. There is a reader service for the blind, and remedial math, reading, and writing.

Campus Safety and Security: Measures include 24-hour foot and vehicle patrol, self-defense education, security escort services, and shuttle buses. There are informal discussions, pamphlets/posters/films, emergency telephones, lighted pathways/sidewalks, security cameras in residence halls, and a motorist assistance program.

Programs of Study: Hofstra confers B.A., B.S., B.B.A., B.E., B.F.A., and B.S.Ed. degrees. Master's and doctoral degrees are also awarded. Bachelor's degrees are awarded in AGRICULTURE (environmental studies), BIOLOGICAL SCIENCE (biochemistry and biology/biological science), BUSINESS (accounting, banking and finance, business administration and management, business law, entrepreneurial studies, international business management, labor studies, management information systems, and marketing management), COMMUNICATIONS AND THE ARTS (American literature, art history and appreciation, audio technology, ceramic art and design, classics, comparative literature, creative writing, dance, design, dramatic arts, English literature, film arts, fine arts, French, German, Hebrew, Italian, jazz, journalism, linguistics, media arts, metal/jewelry, music, music business management, music history and appreciation, music performance, music theory and composition, painting, photography, public relations, publishing, radio/television technology, Russian, Spanish, speech/debate/rhetoric, theater design, theater management, video, and visual and performing arts), COMPUTER AND PHYSICAL SCIENCE (applied mathematics, applied physics, chemistry, computer science, geology, mathematics, natural sciences, and physics), EDUCATION (art, athletic training, business, early childhood, elementary, English, foreign languages, health, mathematics, music, physical, science, secondary, and social studies), ENGINEERING AND ENVIRONMENTAL DESIGN (biomedical engineering, civil engineering, computer engineering, electrical/electronics engineering, environmental engineering, industrial engineering, manufacturing engineering, and mechanical engineering), HEALTH PROFESSIONS (allied health, community health work, exercise science, physician's assistant, predentistry, premedicine, preoptometry, preosteopathy, prepodiatry, preveterinary science, and speech pathology/audiology), SOCIAL SCIENCE (African studies, American studies, anthropology, Asian/Oriental studies, Caribbean studies, economics, geography, Hispanic American studies, history, humanities, interdisciplinary studies, Judaic studies, Latin American studies, liberal arts/general studies, philosophy, political science/government, psychology, social science, and sociology). Accounting, audio/video/film, and biology are the strongest academically. Psychology, accounting, and education are the largest.

Required: A total of 120 to 147 credit hours is required for graduation, with approximately 30 to 36 in the major depending on degree program and a minimum GPA of 2.0. Students must pass English 1 and 2 and pass a writing proficiency exam. A minimum of 6 semester hours each is required in humanities, natural sciences, math, computer science, and social science. Foreign language study is required for the B.A. the B.B.A., in international business, and some B.S. programs.

Special: Internships in numerous career fields, a Washington semester, and an Albany State Assembly internship, study abroad in 19 countries, and dual and student-designed majors are offered. Credit for military and work experience and credit by exam are given. Hofstra offers non-degree study and pass/fail options. There are 30 national honor societies, including Phi Beta Kappa, a freshman honors program, and 30 departmental honors programs.

Faculty/Classroom: 54% of faculty are male; 46%, female. 85% teach undergraduates, 100% do research, and 85% do both. No introductory courses are taught by graduate students. The average class size in an introductory lecture is 29; in a laboratory, 15; and in a regular course, 22.

Admissions: 62% of the 2005-2006 applicants were accepted. The SAT scores for the 2005-2006 freshman class were: Verbal--11% below 500, 54% between 500 and 599, 34% between 600 and 700, and 2% above 700; Math--8% below 500, 52% between 500 and 599, 38% between 600 and 700, and 3% above 700. The ACT scores were 22% below 21, 29% between 21 and 23, 28% between 24 and 26, 11% between 27 and 28, and 11% above 28. 46% of the current freshmen were in the top fifth of their class; 73% were in the top two fifths. 9 freshmen graduated first in their class.

Requirements: The SAT or ACT is required for some programs. In addition, applicants should graduate from an accredited secondary school or have a GED. Preparatory work should include 4 years of English, 3 each of history and social studies, math, and science, and 2 of foreign language. Engineering students are required to have 4 years of math and 1 each of chemistry and physics. An essay is required. Interviews are recommended. One counselor or teacher recommendation is also recommended. AP and CLEP credits are accepted. Important factors in the admissions decision are advanced placement or honor courses, recommendations by school officials, and leadership record.

Procedure: Freshmen are admitted fall and spring. Entrance exams should be taken in the junior or senior year. There are early admissions and deferred admissions plans. Early decision applications should be filed by November 15, along with a $50 fee. Notification of early decision is sent December 15; regular decision, on a rolling basis. 3578 early decision candidates were accepted for the 2005-2006 class. 677 applicants were on the 2005 waiting list; 227 were admitted. Applications are accepted on-line.

Transfer: 702 transfer students enrolled in 2004-2005. Admission is based primarily on prior college work. A maximum of 64 credits from a 2-year school or 94 credits from a 4-year school is accepted. The minimum GPA is 2.5. 30 of 120 credits required for the bachelor's degree must be completed at Hofstra.

Visiting: There are regularly scheduled orientations for prospective students, including an open house, a campus tour, and a program in which a prospective student spends the day with a current student in a similar major. There are guides for informal visits and visitors may sit in on classes and stay overnight. To schedule a visit, contact the Ambassador Program at (516) 463-6798.

Financial Aid: In 2005-2006, 90% of all full-time freshmen and 82% of continuing full-time students received some form of financial aid. 62% of full-time freshmen and 58% of continuing full-time students received need-based aid. The average freshman award was $12,950. Need-based scholarships or need-based grants averaged $10,100 ($26,478 maximum); need-based self-help aid (loans and jobs) averaged $3425 ($30,894 maximum); non-need-based athletic scholarships averaged $24,525 ($37,022 maximum); and other non-need-based awards and non-need-based scholarships averaged $9800 ($41,444 maximum). 35% of undergraduates work part time. Average annual earnings from campus work are $1520. The average financial indebtedness of the 2005 graduate was $20,500. The FAFSA and the state aid form are required. The priority date for freshman financial aid applications for fall entry is February 15.

International Students: There are 133 international students enrolled. The school actively recruits these students. They must take the TOEFL and some must also take the SAT or the ACT.

Computers: Wireless access is available. Students have access to 1600 Pcs in labs and classrooms. These computers are all connected to the campus network and have access to the Internet and to Internet2. Students can use the extensive network of wireless hotspots or plug into public ports to gain access to the campus network and the Internet using their laptops. Residence hall rooms have a high-speed port per student for access to the network. All students may access the system. There are no time limits. The fee is $105 per semester. It is strongly recommended that all students have a personal computer.

Graduates: From July 1, 2004 to June 30, 2005, 1822 bachelor's degrees were awarded. The most popular majors were psychology (12%), marketing (9%), and education (8%). In an average class, 36% graduate in 4 years or less, 52% graduate in 5 years or less, and 55% graduate in 6 years or less. 390 companies recruited on campus in 2004-2005. Of the 2004 graduating class, 27% were enrolled in graduate school within 6 months of graduation and 71% were employed.

Admissions Contact: Sunil Samuel, Senior Associate Dean of Admissions. A video is available. E-mail: *hofstra@hofstra.edu*
Web: *www.hofstra.edu*

HOUGHTON COLLEGE   B-3
Houghton, NY 14744   (585) 567-9353
                              (800) 777-2556; Fax: (585) 567-9522

Full-time: 444 men, 893 women	Faculty: 83; IIB, -$
Part-time: 28 men, 36 women	Ph.D.s: 84%
Graduate: 7 men, 6 women	Student/Faculty: 16 to 1
Year: 4-1-4	Tuition: $19,420
Application Deadline: open	Room & Board: $6560
Freshman Class: 968 applied, 908 accepted, 323 enrolled	
SAT Verbal/Math: 593/574*	ACT: 26 VERY COMPETITIVE+

Houghton College, founded in 1883, is a Christian liberal arts college with more than 40 majors and programs. In addition to regional accreditation, Houghton has baccalaureate program accreditation with NASM. The library contains 237,020 volumes, 47,148 microform items, and 10,769 audio/video tapes/CDs/DVDs, and subscribes to 4090 periodicals including electronic. Computerized library services include the card catalog, interlibrary loans, database searching, Internet access, and laptop Internet portals. Special learning facilities include an art gallery, radio station, and an equestrian center. The 1300-acre campus is in a rural area 65 miles southeast of Buffalo and 70 miles southwest of Rochester. Including any residence halls, there are 20 buildings.

Student Life: 60% of undergraduates are from New York. Students are from 37 states, 19 foreign countries, and Canada. 70% are from public

schools. 90% are white. 69% are Protestant; 21% nondenominational; 6% Catholic. The average age of freshmen is 18; all undergraduates, 21. 15% do not continue beyond their first year; 70% remain to graduate.

Housing: 1052 students can be accommodated in college housing, which includes single-sex dorms, on-campus apartments, and married-student housing. Equestrian students have the opportunity to live on-site. On-campus housing is guaranteed for the freshman year only and is available on a lottery system for upperclassmen. Priority is given to out-of-town students. 80% of students live on campus; of those, 65% remain on campus on weekends. Alcohol is not permitted. All students may keep cars.

Activities: There are no fraternities or sororities. There are 40 groups on campus, including art, bagpipe band, band, cheerleading, choir, chorale, chorus, drama, ethnic, honors, international, jazz band, literary magazine, mission, musical theater, newspaper, opera, orchestra, outreach, political, professional, radio and TV, religious, social service, student government, and yearbook. Popular campus events include Christian Life Emphasis Week, and Winter Weekend.

Sports: There are 4 intercollegiate sports for men and 6 for women, and 8 intramural sports for men and 6 for women. Facilities include 3 basketball and 4 racquetball courts, a swimming pool, an indoor track, a downhill ski slope, cross-country ski trails, 6 tennis courts, a climbing wall, an 8-lane all weather track, a ropes course, and a 386-acre equestrian center with an indoor riding ring. The gym seats 1800; the auditorium, 1300.

Disabled Students: 85% of the campus is accessible. Wheelchair ramps, elevators, special parking, specially equipped rest rooms, special class scheduling, lowered drinking fountains, lowered telephones, and special housing are available.

Services: Counseling and information services are available, as is tutoring in some subjects, including general education courses. There is a reader service for the blind. There is support for learning-disabled students.

Campus Safety and Security: Measures include 24-hour foot and vehicle patrol, security escort services, shuttle buses, and informal discussions. There are pamphlets/posters/films, emergency telephones, and lighted pathways/sidewalks.

Programs of Study: Houghton confers B.A., B.S., and B.M. degrees. Associate and master's degrees are also awarded. Bachelor's degrees are awarded in BIOLOGICAL SCIENCE (biology/biological science), BUSINESS (accounting, business administration and management, and recreation and leisure services), COMMUNICATIONS AND THE ARTS (art, communications, English, French, music performance, music theory and composition, and Spanish), COMPUTER AND PHYSICAL SCIENCE (chemistry, computer science, information sciences and systems, mathematics, physics, and science), EDUCATION (elementary, music, physical, science, and secondary), ENGINEERING AND ENVIRONMENTAL DESIGN (environmental science), HEALTH PROFESSIONS (medical technology), SOCIAL SCIENCE (biblical studies, crosscultural studies, history, humanities, international relations, ministries, philosophy, political science/government, psychology, religion, and sociology). Biology, religion, and music are the strongest academically. Education, biology, and psychology are the largest.

Required: Required courses include 10 hours of math and science, 9 of religion, 6 of social science, 4 each of philosophy, and Western civilization, 3 each of writing, literature, humanities, intermediate language, and fine arts, 2 to 3 of communication, and 2 of phys ed. A total of between 124 and 129 credits, with at least 24 in the major, and a minimum GPA of 2.0 are required to graduate.

Special: Students may cross-register with members of the Western New York Consortium. Internships are available in psychology (at West Seneca campus), social work, business, accounting, educational ministries, physical fitness, political science, graphic design, communication, athletic training, recreation, English, and Christian education. Study abroad in 25 countries, a Washington semester, dual majors, and a 3-2 engineering degree with Clarkson and Washington Universities are available. Credit for military experience and nondegree study are possible. There are 2 national honor societies and a freshman honors program.

Faculty/Classroom: 78% of faculty are male; 22%, female. All teach undergraduates, 15% do research, and 5% do both. No introductory courses are taught by graduate students. The average class size in an introductory lecture is 23; in a laboratory, 15; and in a regular course, 17.

Admissions: 94% of the 2005-2006 applicants were accepted. The SAT scores for the 2005-2006 freshman class were: Verbal--13% below 500, 39% between 500 and 599, 33% between 600 and 700, and 14% above 700; Math--19% below 500, 38% between 500 and 599, 36% between 600 and 700, and 7% above 700. The ACT scores were 9% below 21, 23% between 21 and 23, 29% between 24 and 26, 17% between 27 and 28, and 22% above 28. 57% of the current freshmen were in the top fifth of their class; 81% were in the top two fifths. There were 5 National Merit finalists and 4 semifinalists. 16 freshmen graduated first in their class.

Requirements: A satisfactory score is required on the SAT or ACT. Applicants must graduate from an accredited secondary school or have a

GED. A total of 16 academic credits is recommended, including 4 of English, 3 of social studies, and 2 each of foreign language, math, and science. An essay is required. Music students must audition. An interview is recommended. Houghton requires applicants to be in the upper 50% of their class. A GPA of 2.5 is required. AP and CLEP credits are accepted. Important factors in the admissions decision are personality/intangible qualities, recommendations by school officials, and advanced placement or honor courses.

Procedure: Freshmen are admitted fall and spring. Entrance exams should be taken in the spring of the junior year or fall of the senior year. There is a deferred admissions plan. Application deadlines are open. Applications are accepted on-line.

Transfer: 67 transfer students enrolled in 2004-2005. Applicants should have a 2.75 or better GPA. A pastor's recommendation and high school transcripts must be submitted. The SAT or ACT and an interview are recommended. 30 of 124 credits required for the bachelor's degree must be completed at Houghton.

Visiting: There are regularly scheduled orientations for prospective students, including a tour, an admissions interview, a financial aid session, a class visit, and academic program sessions. There are guides for informal visits and visitors may sit in on classes and stay overnight.

Financial Aid: In 2005-2006, 97% of all full-time freshmen and 98% of continuing full-time students received some form of financial aid. 79% of full-time freshmen and 80% of continuing full-time students received need-based aid. The average freshman award was $13,350. Need-based scholarships or need-based grants averaged $10,214 ($26,730 maximum); need-based self-help aid (loans and jobs) averaged $5078 ($12,300 maximum); non-need-based athletic scholarships averaged $7177 ($9710 maximum); and other non-need-based awards and non-need-based scholarships averaged $7303 ($24,424 maximum). 50% of undergraduates work part time. Average annual earnings from campus work are $744. The average financial indebtedness of the 2005 graduate was $16,028. Houghton is a member of CSS. The FAFSA is required. The priority date for freshman financial aid applications for fall entry is March 1.

International Students: There are 42 international students enrolled. The school actively recruits these students. They must score 550 on the written TOEFL or the electronic version and the SAT or the ACT.

Computers: Wireless access is available. All students are provided with a laptop computer upon enrollment. The campus is fully wired and has wireless capabilities. All students are provided with network access. There are no time limits and no fees.

Graduates: From July 1, 2004 to June 30, 2005, 404 bachelor's degrees were awarded. The most popular majors were psychology (11%), business administration (11%), and childhood education (11%). In an average class, 3% graduate in 3 years or less, 56% graduate in 4 years or less, and 65% graduate in 5 years or less. 33 companies recruited on campus in 2004-2005. Of the 2004 graduating class, 36% were enrolled in graduate school within 6 months of graduation and 78% were employed.

Admissions Contact: Tim Fuller, Vice President for Enrollment Management. E-mail: *admission@houghton.edu* Web: *www.houghton.edu*

IONA COLLEGE

D-5

New Rochelle, NY 10801-1890

(914) 633-2503
(800) 231-IONA; Fax: (914) 633-2096

Full-time: 1421 men, 1701 women	**Faculty:** 176; IIA, +$
Part-time: 123 men, 120 women	**Ph.D.s:** 92%
Graduate: 295 men, 524 women	**Student/Faculty:** 18 to 1
Year: semesters, summer session	**Tuition:** $20,980
Application Deadline: February 15	**Room & Board:** $9898
Freshman Class: 4802 applied, 3217 accepted, 779 enrolled	
SAT Verbal/Math: 550/540*	**ACT:** 21 **VERY COMPETITIVE**

Iona College, founded in 1940, is a private, largely commuter college offering programs through schools of general studies, arts and science, and business. It has a campus in Rockland County in addition to the main campus in New Rochelle. There are 2 undergraduate and 2 graduate schools. In addition to regional accreditation, Iona has baccalaureate program accreditation with AACSB, ABET, ACEJMC, CSWE, NCATE, and NLN. The 2 libraries contain 271,371 volumes, 510,186 microform items, and 3110 audio/video tapes/CDs/DVDs, and subscribe to 763 periodicals including electronic. Computerized library services include the card catalog, interlibrary loans, database searching, Internet access, and laptop Internet portals. Special learning facilities include a learning resource center, art gallery, radio station, TV station, an electron microscope, and a speech and hearing clinic. The 35-acre campus is in a suburban area 20 miles northeast of New York City. Including any residence halls, there are 37 buildings.

Student Life: 79% of undergraduates are from New York. Others are from 37 states, 42 foreign countries, and Canada. 76% are white; 12% Hispanic. The average age of freshmen is 18; all undergraduates, 19. 24% do not continue beyond their first year; 55% remain to graduate.

Housing: 968 students can be accommodated in college housing, which includes single-sex and coed dorms and off-campus apartments. On-campus housing is available on a first-come, first-served basis and is available on a lottery system for upperclassmen. Priority is given to out-of-town students. 69% of students commute. Upperclassmen may keep cars.

Activities: 4% of men belong to 3 local and 1 national fraternity; 6% of women belong to 5 local and 1 national sorority. There are 65 groups on campus, including bagpipe band, cheerleading, choir, chorale, computers, dance, debate, drama, ethnic, film, gay, honors, international, literary magazine, musical theater, newspaper, pep band, photography, political, professional, radio and TV, religious, social, social service, student government, and yearbook. Popular campus events include Spring Concert, and Involvement Fair.

Sports: There are 10 intercollegiate sports for men and 11 for women, and 2 intramural sports for men and 3 for women. Facilities include an all-weather football-soccer/lacrosse field and an athletic center with a Nautilus, weight, and aerobics rooms, and a swimming pool. The campus stadium seats 1200 and the indoor gym, 3,000.

Disabled Students: 90% of the campus is accessible. Wheelchair ramps, elevators, special parking, specially equipped rest rooms, special class scheduling, lowered drinking fountains, lowered telephones and special housing are available. All classes are on the first floor.

Services: Counseling and information services are available, as is tutoring in every subject. There is a reader service for the blind.

Campus Safety and Security: Measures include 24-hour foot and vehicle patrol, security escort services, shuttle buses, and informal discussions. There are pamphlets/posters/films, emergency telephones, and lighted pathways/sidewalks.

Programs of Study: Iona confers B.A., B.S., B.B.A., and B.P.S. degrees. Master's degrees are also awarded. Bachelor's degrees are awarded in BIOLOGICAL SCIENCE (biochemistry, biology/biological science, and ecology), BUSINESS (accounting, banking and finance, business administration and management, international business management, management information systems, management science, marketing management, and marketing/retailing/merchandising), COMMUNICATIONS AND THE ARTS (advertising, communications, dramatic arts, English, French, Italian, Spanish, and speech/debate/rhetoric), COMPUTER AND PHYSICAL SCIENCE (chemistry, computer science, mathematics, and physics), EDUCATION (early childhood, elementary, foreign languages, middle school, science, and secondary), HEALTH PROFESSIONS (health care administration, medical laboratory technology, medical technology, predentistry, premedicine, prepharmacy, preveterinary science, and speech pathology/audiology), SOCIAL SCIENCE (behavioral science, criminal justice, economics, history, international studies, liberal arts/general studies, philosophy, political science/government, psychology, religion, social science, social work, and sociology). Accounting, computer science, and mass communications are the strongest academically. Mass communications, psychology, and criminal justice are the largest.

Required: The core curriculum includes 24 credits of humanities, 12 credits of natural and symbolic languages, and 6 credits each of communications, social science, and science and technology. There is an arts core, a science core, and a business core. Computer literacy is required. The total number of credits required to graduate is at least 120, depending on the major, with at least 30 in the major. The minimum GPA is 2.0.

Special: There are internships for upperclassmen. Study abroad is available in Australia, Ireland, France, Spain, Italy, and England. There is work-study in Iona offices and academic departments. Students may earn a combined B.A.-B.S. degree in economics, psychology, childhood education, early adolescence education, and math education. There is a joint B.S./M.S. program with New York Medical College in physical therapy. 5-year programs are offered in computer science, psychology, history, and English. There are 23 national honor societies, a freshman honors program, and collegewide departmental honors programs.

Faculty/Classroom: 62% of faculty are male; 38%, female. 93% teach undergraduates. No introductory courses are taught by graduate students. The average class size in an introductory lecture is 22; in a laboratory, 16; and in a regular course, 21.

Admissions: 67% of the 2005-2006 applicants were accepted. The SAT scores for the 2005-2006 freshman class were: Verbal--26% below 500, 45% between 500 and 599, 28% between 600 and 700, and 1% above 700; Math--25% below 500, 47% between 500 and 599, 27% between 600 and 700, and 1% above 700. The ACT scores were 10% below 21, 36% between 21 and 23, 33% between 24 and 26, and 21% between 27 and 28. 46% of the current freshmen were in the top fifth of their class; 85% were in the top two fifths.

Requirements: The SAT is required and the ACT is recommended. In addition, applicants must complete 16 academic credits, including 4 units of English, 3 of math, 2 of foreign language, and 1 each of history, science, and social studies. A GED is accepted. An essay is required, and an interview is recommended. A GPA of 2.5 is required. AP and CLEP credits are accepted. Important factors in the admissions decision are recommendations by school officials, leadership record, and advanced placement or honor courses.

Procedure: Freshmen are admitted fall and spring. Entrance exams should be taken in the spring of the senior year. There are early admissions and deferred admissions plans. Applications should be filed by February 15 for fall entry and January 1 for spring entry. Notification is sent March 20. 179 applicants were on the 2005 waiting list; 78 were admitted. Applications are accepted on-line. The fall 2005 application fee was $50.

Transfer: 263 transfer students enrolled in 2004-2005. Transfer applicants must have a GPA of at least 2.5 and must submit high school transcripts if they have earned fewer than 30 college credits. An interview is recommended. 30 of 120 credits required for the bachelor's degree must be completed at Iona.

Visiting: There are regularly scheduled orientations for prospective students, including a meeting with an admissions counselor, a campus tour, and a variety of on-campus programs during the summer and fall. There are guides for informal visits and visitors may sit in on classes. To schedule a visit, contact Elizabeth English at (914) 633-2622.

Financial Aid: In 2005-2006, 96% of all full-time freshmen and 93% of continuing full-time students received some form of financial aid. 56% of full-time freshmen and 52% of continuing full-time students received need-based aid. The average freshman award was $18,495. Need-based scholarships or need-based grants averaged $3628 ($8050 maximum); need-based self-help aid (loans and jobs) averaged $3476 ($8625 maximum); non-need-based athletic scholarships averaged $9353 ($32,099 maximum); and other non-need-based awards and non-need-based scholarships averaged $15,278 ($36,680 maximum). 16% of undergraduates work part time. Average annual earnings from campus work are $1772. The average financial indebtedness of the 2005 graduate was $21,491. Iona is a member of CSS. The FAFSA, the college's own financial statement and the TAP (Tuition Assistance Program) form are required. The deadline for filing freshman financial aid applications for fall entry is February 15.

International Students: There are 62 international students enrolled. The school actively recruits these students. They must score satisfactorily on the written TOEFL and also take the SAT or the ACT.

Computers: Wireless access is available. The campus WAN consists of 60 servers (43 NT, 15 LINUX, and 2 UNIX). There are 1500 college - and student owned, high-end, wired and wireless Pentium systems available in computing labs, classrooms, residence halls, libraries, and the student center for student use. All students may access the system There is unlimited access to PC software, the Internet, and computing facilities. PeopleSoft Web Access to student information is also available 24 hours. There are no time limits. The fee is $85 per semester. It is strongly recommended that all students have a personal computer.

Graduates: From July 1, 2004 to June 30, 2005, 649 bachelor's degrees were awarded. The most popular majors were business (38%), mass communications (13%), and education (10%). In an average class, 37% graduate in 4 years or less, 52% graduate in 5 years or less, and 55% graduate in 6 years or less. 104 companies recruited on campus in 2004-2005. Of the 2004 graduating class, 53% were enrolled in graduate school within 6 months of graduation and 72% were employed.

Admissions Contact: Thomas Weede, Director of Admissions.
E-mail: *icad@iona.edu* Web: *http://www.iona.edu*

ITHACA COLLEGE C-3

Ithaca, NY 14850-7020

(607) 274-3124
(800) 429-4274; Fax: (607) 274-1900

Full-time: 2657 men, 3304 women	Faculty: 441; IIA, av$
Part-time: 46 men, 91 women	Ph.D.s: 90%
Graduate: 85 men, 229 women	Student/Faculty: 14 to 1
Year: semesters, summer session	Tuition: $25,194
Application Deadline: February 1	Room & Board: $9950

Freshman Class: 11,087 applied, 7870 accepted, 1680 enrolled
SAT Verbal/Math: 590/590*   **VERY COMPETITIVE**

Ithaca College, founded in 1892, is a private college offering undergraduate and graduate programs in business, communications, health science and human performance, humanities and sciences, music, and interdisciplinary and international studies. There are 6 undergraduate schools and 1 graduate school. In addition to regional accreditation, Ithaca has baccalaureate program accreditation with AACSB, ACTA, APTA, CAAHEP, CAPTE, NASM, and NRPA. The library contains 355,000 volumes, 251,300 microform items, and 32,000 audio/video tapes/CDs/DVDs, and subscribes to 2500 periodicals including electronic. Computerized library services include the card catalog, interlibrary loans, database searching and Internet access. Special learning facilities include an art gallery, radio station, TV station, digital audio and video labs, speech, hearing, wellness, and physical therapy clinics, a greenhouse, a financial "trading room"; an observatory and electroacoustic music studios. The 757-acre campus is in a small town 250 miles northwest of New York City. Including any residence halls, there are 85 buildings.

Student Life: 54% of undergraduates are from out of state, mostly the Middle Atlantic. Students are from 47 states, 70 foreign countries, and Canada. 75% are from public schools. 86% are white. The average age of freshmen is 18; all undergraduates, 20. 14% do not continue beyond their first year; 73% remain to graduate.

Housing: 4300 students can be accommodated in college housing, which includes single-sex and coed dorms and on-campus apartments. There is also first-year students only housing, a quiet study residence hall, service and music honor fraternities, smoke-free buildings and floors, coed by door building, multi-cultural housing, and several freshman seminar groups housed together. On-campus housing is guaranteed for all 4 years. 70% of students live on campus; of those, 95% remain on campus on weekends. All students may keep cars.

Activities: 1% of men belong to 4 national fraternities; 1% of women belong to 1 local sorority. There are 170 groups on campus, including academic, art, band, cheerleading, chess, choir, chorale, chorus, computers, cultural, dance, drama, drum and bugle corps, ethnic, film, gay, honors, international, jazz band, literary magazine, musical theater, newspaper, opera, orchestra, pep band, photography, political, professional, radio and TV, religious, social, social service, sports, student government, and symphony. Popular campus events include Pep rally, Student Involvement Fair, and various multicultural awareness events.

Sports: There are 11 intercollegiate sports for men and 12 for women, and 27 intramural sports for men and 27 for women. Facilities include 5 gyms, 2 dance studios, a student union, indoor and outdoor pools, a fitness center and wellness clinic, tennis courts, and baseball, football, lacrosse, field hockey, and soccer fields.

Disabled Students: Wheelchair ramps, elevators, special parking, specially equipped rest rooms, special class scheduling, lowered drinking fountains, and lowered telephones are available.

Services: Nonremedial tutoring is available.

Campus Safety and Security: Measures include 24-hour foot and vehicle patrol, security escort services, pamphlets/posters/films, and emergency telephones. There are lighted pathways/sidewalks and crime prevention programs.

Programs of Study: Ithaca confers B.A., B.S., B.F.A., and Mus.B. degrees. Master's degrees are also awarded. Bachelor's degrees are awarded in BIOLOGICAL SCIENCE (biochemistry and biology/biological science), BUSINESS (accounting, banking and finance, business administration and management, business economics, electronic business, human resources, international business management, management science, marketing management, marketing/retailing/merchandising, organizational behavior, personnel management, recreation and leisure services, and sports management), COMMUNICATIONS AND THE ARTS (art, art history and appreciation, audio technology, broadcasting, communications, creative writing, dramatic arts, English, film arts, fine arts, French, German, jazz, journalism, languages, media arts, modern language, music, music performance, music theory and composition, musical theater, performing arts, photography, public relations, Spanish, speech/debate/rhetoric, sports media, studio art, telecommunications, theater design, theater management, video, and visual and performing arts), COMPUTER AND PHYSICAL SCIENCE (chemistry, computer mathematics, computer science, information sciences and systems, mathematics, and physics), EDUCATION (art, athletic training, education, education of the deaf and hearing impaired, educational media, English, foreign languages, health, mathematics, middle school, music, physical, secondary, social studies, speech correction, and sports studies), ENGINEERING AND ENVIRONMENTAL DESIGN (environmental science), HEALTH PROFESSIONS (allied health, clinical science, community health work, exercise science, health, health science, hospital administration, occupational therapy, physical therapy, predentistry, premedicine, public health, recreation therapy, rehabilitation therapy, speech pathology/audiology, speech therapy, and sports medicine), SOCIAL SCIENCE (anthropology, economics, German area studies, gerontology, history, industrial and organizational psychology, interdisciplinary studies, Italian studies, liberal arts/general studies, philosophy, physical fitness/movement, political science/government, prelaw, psychology, social studies, and sociology). Physical therapy, theater, and music are the strongest academically. Music, business administration, and television-radio are the largest.

Required: Students must successfully complete a minimum of 120 credit hours. In addition, each student must meet the requirements of a core curriculum, which varies with each school within the college and includes courses in the liberal arts and professional courses outside the student's major.

Special: Cross-registration is available with Cornell University and Wells College. Opportunities are also provided for internships, work-study programs, dual majors, accelerated degree programs, nondegree study, pass/fail options, student-designed majors, a 3-2 engineering degree with Cornell University, Clarkson University, Rensselaer Polytechnic Institute, and SUNY Binghamton, and study abroad in London, Valencia, and other foreign cities. A 4-1 advanced business degree program, a 3-1 optometry program, and a semester program in marine biology with Duke University are also available. There are 24 national honor societies, a freshman honors program, and 16 departmental honors programs.

Faculty/Classroom: 55% of faculty are male; 45%, female. All teach undergraduates. Graduate students teach 6% of introductory courses. The average class size in an introductory lecture is 20 and in a regular course, 16.

Admissions: 71% of the 2005-2006 applicants were accepted. The SAT scores for the 2005-2006 freshman class were: Verbal--9% below 500, 45% between 500 and 599, 39% between 600 and 700, and 7% above 700; Math--7% below 500, 46% between 500 and 599, 41% between 600 and 700, and 6% above 700. 54% of the current freshmen were in the top fifth of their class; 87% were in the top two fifths. There were 3 National Merit finalists. 15 freshmen graduated first in their class.

Requirements: The SAT or ACT is required. In addition, applicants should be graduates of an accredited secondary school with a minimum of 16 Carnegie units, including 4 years of English, 3 each of math, science, and social studies, 2 of foreign language, and other college-preparatory electives. The GED is accepted. An essay is required, as is an audition for music and theater students. In some majors, a portfolio and an interview are recommended. Ithaca requires applicants to be in the upper 25% of their class. AP and CLEP credits are accepted.

Procedure: Freshmen are admitted fall and spring. Entrance exams should be taken in spring of the junior year or fall of the senior year. There are early decision and deferred admissions plans. There is a rolling admissions plan. Early decision applications should be filed by November 1; regular applications, by February 1 for fall entry and December 1 for spring entry, along with a $55 fee. Notification of early decision is sent December 15; regular decision, on a rolling basis. Beginning April 15, 207 early decision candidates were accepted for the 2005-2006 class. Applications are accepted on-line.

Transfer: 171 transfer students enrolled in 2004-2005. Transfer applicants must submit SAT or ACT scores, a high school transcript, transcripts from previously attended colleges, and a personal recommendation from their adviser or Dean of Students. A minimum college GPA of 2.75 is recommended. 30 of 120 credits required for the bachelor's degree must be completed at Ithaca.

Visiting: There are regularly scheduled orientations for prospective students, including a campus tour and an interview with an admissions counselor. Fall open house programs offering personal meetings with faculty are available by appointment. There are guides for informal visits and visitors may sit in on classes and stay overnight. To schedule a visit, contact the Director of Admission at *admissions@ithaca.edu*.

Financial Aid: In 2005-2006, 86% of all full-time freshmen and 85% of continuing full-time students received some form of financial aid. 74% of full-time freshmen and 68% of continuing full-time students received need-based aid. The average freshman award was $25,444. Need-based scholarships or need-based grants averaged $14,710 ($34,470 maximum); need-based self-help aid (loans and jobs) averaged $8133 ($24,825 maximum); and other non-need-based awards and non-need-based scholarships averaged $8411 ($37,414 maximum). 42% of undergraduates work part time. Average annual earnings from campus work are $2200. Ithaca is a member of CSS. The FAFSA is required. The CSS/Profile is required for early decision applicants only and must be filed by Novemeber 1. The deadline for filing freshman financial aid applications for fall entry is February 1.

International Students: There are 187 international students enrolled. The school actively recruits these students. They must take the TOEFL and also take the SAT or the ACT.

Computers: Wireless access is available. Students may access Ithaca College's network from any of the approximately 640 computers available for general student use in labs, classrooms, and the library as well as via wireless networks in several areas on campus. All students may access the system 24 hours a day. There are no time limits and no fees.

Graduates: From July 1, 2004 to June 30, 2005, 1541 bachelor's degrees were awarded. The most popular majors were television-radio (10%), business administration (10%), and music (5%). In an average class, 2% graduate in 3 years or less, 70% graduate in 4 years or less, 72% graduate in 5 years or less, and 73% graduate in 6 years or less. 117 companies recruited on campus in 2004-2005. Of the 2004 graduating class, 33% were enrolled in graduate school within 6 months of graduation and 83% were employed.

Admissions Contact: Paula Mitchell, Director of Admission. A video is available. E-mail: *admission@ithaca.edu* Web: *www.ithaca.edu*

JULLIARD SCHOOL   D-5
New York, NY 10023-6588   (212) 799-5000, ext. 223
                                                         Fax: (212) 724-6420

Full-time: 248 men, 230 women	**Faculty:** n/av
Part-time: none	**Ph.D.s:** n/av
Graduate: 171 men, 156 women	**Student/Faculty:** 4 to 1
Year: semesters	**Tuition:** $28,050
Application Deadline: December 1	**Room & Board:** $9570
Freshman Class: 2523 applied, 136 accepted, 96 enrolled	
SAT or ACT: not required	**SPECIAL**

The Juilliard School, founded in 1905, is a private conservatory for dance, drama, and music. The library contains 96,013 volumes, 1399 microform items, and 25,960 audio/video tapes/CDs/DVDs, and subscribes to 230 periodicals including electronic. Computerized library services include the card catalog, interlibrary loans, database searching, Internet access, and laptop Internet portals. Special learning facilities include 200 practice rooms, 5 theaters, scenery and costume shops, and dance studios. The campus is in an urban area at Lincoln Center in New York City. Including any residence halls, there are 2 buildings.

Student Life: 84% of undergraduates are from out of state, mostly the Northeast. Others are from 45 states, 44 foreign countries, and Canada. 59% are white; 29% foreign nationals; 28% Asian American; 10% African American. The average age of freshmen is 18; all undergraduates, 20. 6% do not continue beyond their first year; 81% remain to graduate.

Housing: 350 students can be accommodated in college housing, which includes single-sex dorms. In addition, there are special-interest houses, quiet, alcohol-free, and single-sex (all female) floors. All floors are smoke free. On-campus housing is guaranteed for the freshman year only, is available on a first-come, first-served basis, and is available on a lottery system for upperclassmen. 60% of students live on campus.

Activities: There are no fraternities or sororities. There are 15 groups on campus, including band, book discussion, choir, chorale, chorus, community service, dance, drama, environmental consciousness, ethnic, gay, international, jazz band, marching band, opera, orchestra, professional, recreation, religious, social, social service, student government, and symphony. Popular campus events include performances by the Juilliard orchestras at Lincoln Center, dance concerts, and drama and opera productions.

Sports: There is no sports program at Juilliard. Facilities include a fitness center in the residence hall.

Disabled Students: All of the campus is accessible. Wheelchair ramps, elevators, specially equipped rest rooms, lowered drinking fountains, and lowered telephones are available.

Services: Counseling and information services are available, as is tutoring in some subjects, including ear training, literature and materials of music, and English.

Campus Safety and Security: Measures include 24-hour foot and vehicle patrol, self-defense education, informal discussions, and pamphlets/posters/films. There are emergency telephones, lighted pathways/sidewalks, video cameras, and turnstiles with ID card access.

Programs of Study: Juilliard confers B.Mus. and B.F.A. degrees. Master's and doctoral degrees are also awarded. Bachelor's degrees are awarded in COMMUNICATIONS AND THE ARTS (dance, dramatic arts, and music). Piano, voice, and violin are the largest.

Required: Each division has its own requirements for graduation.

Special: A joint program with Columbia College and Barnard College (at Columbia University) allows students to obtain a 5-year B.A.-B.Mus. degree. Internships are available with cultural organizations in New York City. There is study abroad in music academies in England, Israel, and Russia. Work-study programs, accelerated degrees and dual majors in music, a combined B.Mus.-M.Mus. degree, nondegree study, and pass/fail options are available.

Faculty/Classroom: 67% of faculty are male; 33%, female.

Admissions: 5% of the 2005-2006 applicants were accepted.

Requirements: A high school diploma or GED is required. Students are accepted primarily on the basis of personal auditions rather than tests. Evidence of special talent is an important factor in the admission decision.

Procedure: Freshmen are admitted in the fall. Personal auditions should be completed in December for opera, January & February for drama; February & March for dance; March for music; February & March for jazz. See www.juilliard.edu/admissions/deadlines.html. Applications should be filed by December 1 for fall entry, along with a $100 fee. Notification is sent April 1. 43 applicants were on the 2005 waiting list; 11 were admitted.

Transfer: 17 transfer students enrolled in 2004-2005. Transfer applicants must audition in person. 2 years required for the bachelor's degree must be completed at Juilliard.

Visiting: There are regularly scheduled orientations for prospective students, including guided tours and question-and-answer sessions, Monday to Friday at noon. Visitors may sit in on classes and stay overnight. To schedule a visit, contact Sarah J. Adriance in the Admissions Office at *sadriance@juilliard.edu*.

Financial Aid: In 2005-2006, 97% of all full-time freshmen and 88% of continuing full-time students received some form of financial aid. 91% of full-time freshmen and 82% of continuing full-time students received need-based aid. The average freshman award was $24,274. Need-based scholarships or need-based grants averaged $18,071 ($29,330 maximum); need-based self-help aid (loans and jobs) averaged $8415 ($12,000 maximum); and other non-need-based awards and non-need-based scholarships averaged $2234 ($5000 maximum). 67% of undergraduates work part time. Average annual earnings from campus work are $1179. The average financial indebtedness of the 2005 graduate was $24,695. The FAFSA and the college's own financial statement are required. The priority date for freshman financial aid applications for fall entry is March 1. The deadline for filing freshman financial aid applications for fall entry is March 1.

International Students: There are 118 international students enrolled. Satisfactory scores are required on the TOEFL and the college's own test, TWE. All students must audition in person.

Computers: All students may access the system. Students may access the system during lab hours. There are no fees.

Graduates: From July 1, 2004 to June 30, 2005, 102 bachelor's degrees were awarded. The most popular majors were music (76%), dance (15%), and drama (10%). In an average class, 73% graduate in 4 years or less, 81% graduate in 5 years or less, and 82% graduate in 6 years or less.

Admissions Contact: Office of Admissions.
E-mail: *admissions@juilliard.edu* Web: *www.juilliard.edu*

KEUKA COLLEGE B-3

Keuka Park, NY 14478

(315) 536-5254, ext. 254
(800) 33-KEUKA; Fax: (315) 536-5386

Full-time: 344 men, 771 women	**Faculty:** 56; IIB, --$
Part-time: 22 men, 130 women	**Ph.Ds:** 80%
Graduate: none	**Student/Faculty:** 20 to 1
Year: 4-1-4, summer session	**Tuition:** $18,070
Application Deadline: see profile	**Room & Board:** $7980
Freshman Class: 659 accepted, 268 enrolled	
SAT Verbal/Math: 483/487*	**ACT:** 20 **COMPETITIVE**

Keuka College, founded in 1890, is an independent college affiliated with American Baptist Churches and offers instruction in the liberal arts. In addition to regional accreditation, Keuka has baccalaureate program accreditation with AHEA, CSWE, and NLN. The library contains 87,263 volumes, 4190 microform items, and 4190 audio/video tapes/CDs/DVDs, and subscribes to 18,151 periodicals including electronic. Computerized library services include the card catalog, interlibrary loans, and database searching. Special learning facilities include a learning resource center, art gallery, and radio station. The 203-acre campus is in a rural area 60 miles south of Rochester. Including any residence halls, there are 19 buildings.

Student Life: 94% of undergraduates are from New York. Others are from 26 states, 2 foreign countries, and Canada. 80% are from public schools. 90% are white. The average age of freshmen is 18; all undergraduates, 23. 27% do not continue beyond their first year; 52% remain to graduate.

Housing: 719 students can be accommodated in college housing, which includes single-sex and coed dorms. In addition, there are honors houses, special-interest houses, cooperative living, and leadership and wellness housing. On-campus housing is guaranteed for all 4 years. 55% of students live on campus; of those, 60% remain on campus on weekends. Alcohol is not permitted. Upperclassmen may keep cars.

Activities: There are no fraternities or sororities. There are 45 groups on campus, including art, cheerleading, choir, chorale, community service, dance, drama, ethnic, honors, international, leadership, literary magazine, newspaper, political, professional, religious, social, social service, student government, and yearbook. Popular campus events include Spring Weekend, May Day, and Family Weekend.

Sports: There are 7 intercollegiate sports for men and 8 for women, and 8 intramural sports for men and 8 for women. Facilities include an Olympic-size pool, a gym, a fitness center, a weight room, and an outdoor athletic facility.

Disabled Students: 65% of the campus is accessible. Wheelchair ramps, elevators, special parking, specially equipped rest rooms, special class scheduling, lowered drinking fountains, and special housing are available.

Services: Counseling and information services are available, as is tutoring in every subject. There is a reader service for the blind, and remedial math, reading, and writing. Individual and group tutoring is available free through the college's academic support services.

Campus Safety and Security: Measures include 24-hour foot and vehicle patrol, self-defense education, shuttle buses, and informal discussions. There are pamphlets/posters/films, emergency telephones, and lighted pathways/sidewalks.

Programs of Study: Keuka confers B.A. and B.S. degrees. Master's degrees are also awarded. Bachelor's degrees are awarded in BIOLOGI-

CAL SCIENCE (biochemistry, and biology/biological science), BUSINESS (accounting, business administration and management, hotel/motel and restaurant management, and marketing/retailing/merchandising), COMMUNICATIONS AND THE ARTS (American Sign Language, communications, and English), EDUCATION (elementary, and secondary), ENGINEERING AND ENVIRONMENTAL DESIGN (environmental science), HEALTH PROFESSIONS (medical laboratory technology, nursing, occupational therapy, predentistry, premedicine, and preveterinary science), SOCIAL SCIENCE (criminal justice, political science/government, prelaw, psychology, social work, and sociology). Occupational therapy, biology, and education are the strongest academically. Occupational therapy, education, and management are the largest.

Required: Students must complete 1 field period combining academic study and professional experience for each year of enrollment. The core curriculum consists of 43 to 46 credits, including but not limited to required courses in phys ed, computer science, and integrative studies. A total of 120 credit hours is required for graduation with a minimum of 30 credits in the major and a major and cumulative GPA of 2.0.

Special: There are co-op programs with other members of the Rochester Area Colleges Consortium. The college offers internships, study abroad, a Washington semester, dual majors, and student-designed majors. Credit is also given by exam and for work experience. There are 16 national honor societies.

Faculty/Classroom: 42% of faculty are male; 58%, female. All teach undergraduates. The average class size in an introductory lecture is 20; in a laboratory, 15; and in a regular course, 20.

Admissions: The SAT scores for the 2005-2006 freshman class were: Verbal--56% below 500, 35% between 500 and 599, 8% between 600 and 700, and 1% above 700; Math--56% below 500, 38% between 500 and 599, 6% between 600 and 700, and 1% above 700. The ACT scores were 31% below 21, 29% between 21 and 23, 23% between 24 and 26, 16% between 27 and 28, and 1% above 28. 27% of the current freshmen were in the top fifth of their class; 62% were in the top two fifths.

Requirements: The SAT or ACT is required. In addition, students should graduate from an accredited secondary school with a minimum GPA of 2.8. The GED is accepted. A minimum of 15 Carnegie units is required, including 4 years of English, 3 of history, 2 to 3 of math and science, 2 of foreign language, and 1 of social studies. An essay is required, and an interview is recommended. AP and CLEP credits are accepted. Important factors in the admissions decision are recommendations by school officials, extracurricular activities record, and leadership record.

Procedure: Freshmen are admitted fall and spring. Entrance exams should be taken in the spring of the junior year or the fall of the senior year. There are early decision and deferred admissions plans. There is a rolling admission plan. Check with the school for current application deadlines. The fall 2005 application fee was $30. Notification is sent on a rolling basis. Applications are accepted on-line.

Transfer: Applicants must take the SAT or ACT and submit transcripts. An interview is recommended. A minimum GPA of 2.5 is required in college work. 30 of 120 credits required for the bachelor's degree must be completed at Keuka.

Visiting: There are regularly scheduled orientations for prospective students, including open houses held in October and April, when students can speak with faculty, student affairs and financial aid representatives, and current students. There are guides for informal visits and visitors may sit in on classes and stay overnight. To schedule a visit, contact the Admissions Office at (315) 279-4411.

Financial Aid: In 2005-2006, 95% of all full-time freshmen and 93% of continuing full-time students received some form of financial aid. 93% of full-time freshmen and 90% of continuing full-time students received need-based aid. The average freshman award was $18,249. Need-based scholarships or need-based grants averaged $12,809 ($6282 maximum). 65% of undergraduates work part time. Average annual earnings from campus work are $1000. The average financial indebtedness of the 2005 graduate was $13,041. The FAFSA and the college's own financial statement are required. The deadline for filing freshman financial aid applications for fall entry is March 15.

International Students: A satisfactory score on the TOEFL is required.

Computers: All students may access the system. There are no time limits and no fees. It is strongly recommended that all students have a personal computer.

Graduates: From July 1, 2004 to June 30, 2005, 258 bachelor's degrees were awarded. The most popular majors were unified elementary/special education (13%), nursing (10%), and management (9%). In an average class, 35% graduate in 4 years or less, 52% graduate in 5 years or less, and 52% graduate in 6 years or less.

Admissions Contact: Claudine Ninestine, Director of Admissions. A video is available. E-mail: *admissions@mail.keuka.edu* Web: *www.keuka.edu*

LABORATORY INSTITUTE OF MERCHANDISING   D-5
New York, NY 10022-5268   (212) 752-1530
                                 (800) 677-1323; Fax: (212) 317-8602

Full-time: 18 men, 467 women	**Faculty:** 9
Part-time: 8 women	**Ph.D.s:** n/av
Graduate: none	**Student/Faculty:** 54 to 1
Year: semesters, summer session	**Tuition:** $15,150
Application Deadline: open	**Room & Board:** $10,000
Freshman Class: n/av	
SAT or ACT: required	**SPECIAL**

The Laboratory Institute of Merchandising, founded in 1939, is a private college offering programs in fashion merchandising, marketing, and visual merchandising. In addition to regional accreditation, LIM has baccalaureate program accreditation with IACBE. The library contains 8600 volumes and 200 audio/video tapes/CDs/DVDs, and subscribes to 80 periodicals including electronic. Computerized library services include database searching. Special learning facilities include a learning resource center and a temporary art gallery. The campus is in an urban area. Including any residence halls, there are 2 buildings.

Student Life: 50% of undergraduates are from out of state, mostly the Middle Atlantic. Students are from 27 states and 7 foreign countries. 58% are from public schools. 64% are white; 18% Hispanic; 11% African American. The average age of freshmen is 18; all undergraduates, 20. 30% do not continue beyond their first year.

Housing: 50 students can be accommodated in college housing, which includes coed dormitories. On-campus housing is available on a first-come, first-served basis. 92% of students commute. Alcohol is not permitted. No one may keep cars.

Activities: There are no fraternities or sororities. There are 10 groups on campus, including art, ethnic, fashion club, film, honors, newspaper, professional, religious, social service, and student government. Popular campus events include an annual fashion show, a ski trip, and a Halloween costume party.

Sports: There is no sports program at LIM.

Disabled Students: Elevators and specially equipped rest rooms are available.

Services: Counseling and information services are available, as is tutoring in most subjects. There is remedial math, reading, and writing.

Campus Safety and Security: Measures include informal discussions and pamphlets/posters/films.

Programs of Study: LIM confers B.B.A. and B.P.S. degrees. Associate degrees are also awarded. Bachelor's degrees are awarded in BUSINESS (fashion merchandising and marketing/retailing/merchandising).

Required: Students must complete 34 credits in the liberal arts and a minimum of 72 in fashion/business courses. Freshmen and sophomores must successfully complete a 3-credit work project each year. Seniors must complete a 13-credit, semester-long co-op program. A total of 126 credits and a GPA of 2.0 are required to graduate.

Special: Internships are required in the first, second, and fourth years. Study abroad is available in China, Italy, Spain, France, and England. There are co-op programs as well as work-study programs with major department stores and specialty shops, manufacturers, showrooms, magazine publishers, and cosmetics companies. There is 1 national honor society.

Faculty/Classroom: 41% of faculty are male; 59%, female. The average class size in an introductory lecture is 19 and in a regular course, 22.

Requirements: The SAT or ACT is required. In addition, an essay and an interview are required. Applicants should be high school graduates or hold the GED. AP and CLEP credits are accepted. Important factors in the admissions decision are recommendations by school officials, leadership record, and personality/intangible qualities.

Procedure: Freshmen are admitted fall and spring. There is a rolling admissions plan. Application deadlines are open. Application fee is $40.

Transfer: 75 transfer students enrolled in a recent year. Applicants must submit their official high school and college transcripts. Students with fewer than 30 college credits must submit SAT or ACT scores. Interviews are required of all applicants, and recommendation letters are encouraged but not required. 46 of 126 credits required for the bachelor's degree must be completed at LIM.

Visiting: There are regularly scheduled orientations for prospective students, consisting of the open house program, which includes a tour, 3 presentations, a financial aid overview, breakfast, and interviews. There are guides for informal visits and visitors may sit in on classes. To schedule a visit, contact the Admissions Office.

Financial Aid: The FAFSA and the college's own financial statement are required. Check with the school for current application deadlines.

International Students: In a recent year, there were 4 international students enrolled. They must score satisfactorily on the written TOEFL or on the electronic version and also take the SAT or the ACT.

Computers: All students may access the system. There are no time limits and no fees.

Graduates: In a recent year, 68 bachelor's degrees were awarded. Of a recent graduating class, 10% were employed within 6 months of graduation.

Admissions Contact: Karen Hamill Iglio, Director of Admissions. E-mail: *admissions@limcollege.edu* Web: *www.limcollege.edu*

LE MOYNE COLLEGE   C-3
Syracuse, NY 13214-1301   (315) 445-4300
                                 (800) 333-4733; Fax: (315) 445-4711

Full-time: 915 men, 1403 women	**Faculty:** 153; IIA, av$
Part-time: 113 men, 358 women	**Ph.D.s:** 92%
Graduate: 251 men, 540 women	**Student/Faculty:** 15 to 1
Year: semesters, summer session	**Tuition:** $21,280
Application Deadline: February 1	**Room & Board:** $8290
Freshman Class: 2946 applied, 2133 accepted, 520 enrolled	
SAT Verbal/Math: 550/570*	**ACT:** 23 **VERY COMPETITIVE**

Le Moyne College founded in 1946, strives for academic excellence in the Catholic and Jesuit tradition through programs rooted in the liberal arts and sciences. Its emphasis is on education of the whole person and on the search for meaning and value as integral parts of the intellectual life. The library contains 251,561 volumes, 597,719 microform items, and 9036 audio/video tapes/CDs/DVDs, and subscribes to 35,534 periodicals including electronic. Computerized library services include the card catalog, interlibrary loans, database searching, internet access and laptop Internet portals. Special learning facilities include a learning resource center, art gallery, and radio station. The 151-acre campus is in a suburban area on the eastern edge of Syracuse. Including any residence halls, there are 36 buildings.

Student Life: 93% of undergraduates are from New York. Students are from 24 states, 19 foreign countries, and Canada. 82% are from public schools. 83% are white. 48% are unknown, Buddhist, or Muslim; 45% Catholic; 6% Protestant. The average age of freshmen is 18; all undergraduates, 20. 13% do not continue beyond their first year; 74% remain to graduate.

Housing: 1519 students can be accommodated in college housing, which includes single-sex and coed dorms, on-campus apartments, and off-campus apartments. In addition, there are special-interest houses, and living learning communities. On-campus housing is available on a first-come, first-served basis, and is available on a lottery system for upperclassmen. Priority is given to out-of-town students. 64% of students live on campus; of those, 85% remain on campus on weekends. All students may keep cars.

Activities: There are no fraternities or sororities. There are 70 groups on campus, including art, band, cheerleading, chess, choir, chorale, chorus, computers, dance, drama, ethnic, honors, international, jazz band, literary magazine, musical theater, newspaper, pep band, political, professional, radio and TV, religious, social, social service, and student government. Popular campus events include Spring Olympics, Halloween Dance, and Snow Ball Holiday Party.

Sports: There are 8 intercollegiate sports for men and 8 for women, and 9 intramural sports for men and 8 for women. Facilities include a 2500-seat gym, indoor batting cages, team rooms, a 25-yard lap pool with diving capabilities, a whirlpool, a fitness center, an athletic training room, a jogging track, racquetball courts, a recreational gym, and locker rooms. Outdoor facilities include fields for intercollegiate baseball, softball, soccer, and lacrosse, tennis courts, a cross-country trail, and several intramural and club sports fields.

Disabled Students: 95% of the campus is accessible. Wheelchair ramps, elevators, special parking, specially equipped rest rooms, lowered drinking fountains, lowered telephones, special housing, automatic door openers, and a strobe fire alarm system are available.

Services: Counseling and information services are available, as is tutoring in some subjects, including math, biology, chemistry, physics, economics, philosophy, Spanish, French, German, and Latin. There is a reader service for the blind and remedial math and writing. Study groups are available for selected courses, and there is writing tutor support for all subjects.

Campus Safety and Security: Measures include 24-hour foot and vehicle patrol, self-defense education, security escort services, and shuttle buses. There are informal discussions, pamphlets/posters/films, emergency telephones, lighted pathways/sidewalks, 6 blue light security phones, 39 stationary closed-circuit security cameras, AT&T campuswide card access, and 7 pan-tilt-zoom closed-circuit security cameras.

Programs of Study: Le Moyne confers B.A. and B.S. degrees. Master's degrees are also awarded. Bachelor's degrees are awarded in BIOLOGICAL SCIENCE (biochemistry and biology/biological science), BUSINESS (accounting, business administration and management, human resources, labor studies, management information systems, and marketing management), COMMUNICATIONS AND THE ARTS (communications, creative writing, dramatic arts, English, French, and Spanish), COMPUTER AND PHYSICAL SCIENCE (applied mathematics, chemistry, information sciences and systems, mathematics, physical sciences, physics, and science), EDUCATION (education administration, elementary, English, foreign languages, mathematics, science, secondary, and social studies), HEALTH PROFESSIONS (nursing, physician's assistant, predentistry, premedicine, preoptometry, prepharmacy, prepodiatry, and preveterinary science), SOCIAL SCIENCE (criminology, economics, history, international studies, peace studies, philosophy, political science/government, prelaw, psychology, religion, and sociology). Business, psychology, and biology are the largest.

Required: A core curriculum of 14 courses in the humanities, natural sciences, and social sciences is required. Students must earn a GPA of 2.0, 30 hours in the major, and 120 total credit hours to graduate.

Special: Internships are available to students in all majors. A campus work-study program, study abroad in 9 countries, dual majors, and a Washington semester are offered. A 3-2 engineering degree is available with Manhattan College, Clarkson University, and University of Detroit Mercy, and there are early assurance medical and dental programs and a physician assistant program. Some pass/fail options are offered. There are 14 national honor societies, a freshman honors program, and 11 departmental honors programs.

Faculty/Classroom: 58% of faculty are male; 42%, female. All both teach and do research. No introductory courses are taught by graduate students. The average class size in an introductory lecture is 25; in a laboratory, 14; and in a regular course, 22.

Admissions: 72% of the 2005-2006 applicants were accepted. The SAT scores for the 2005-2006 freshman class were: Verbal--23% below 500, 50% between 500 and 599, 25% between 600 and 700, and 2% above 700; Math--16% below 500, 51% between 500 and 599, 31% between 600 and 700, and 2% above 700. The ACT scores were 17% below 21, 34% between 21 and 23, 31% between 24 and 26, 10% between 27 and 28, and 8% above 28. 43% of the current freshmen were in the top fifth of their class; 73% were in the top two fifths. In a recent year, 3 freshmen graduated first in their class.

Requirements: The SAT or ACT is required. In addition, students should graduate from an accredited high school, having completed 17 academic units that include 4 in English and social studies, 3 to 4 each in math and science, and 3 in foreign language. A personal statement and letters of recommendation from a teacher and a counselor are required. AP and CLEP credits are accepted. Important factors in the admissions decision are recommendations by school officials, advanced placement or honor courses, and extracurricular activities record.

Procedure: Freshmen are admitted fall and spring. Entrance exams should be taken in the spring of the junior year or fall of the senior year. There are early decision, early admissions, and deferred admissions and rolling admission plans. Early decision applications should be filed by December 1; regular applications, by February 1 for fall entry and December 1 for spring entry, along with a $35 fee. Notification of early decision is sent December 15; regular decision, on a rolling basis. 91 applicants were on the 2005 waiting list; 23 were admitted. Applications are accepted on-line.

Transfer: 226 transfer students enrolled in 2004-2005. A 2.6 GPA is required for admission to most programs. Official college transcripts, a letter of recommendation from an academic official at the last college attended, and a personal statement must be submitted. Official high school transcripts and SAT or ACT scores are needed for students with fewer than 24 completed college credits at the time of application. 30 of 120 credits required for the bachelor's degree must be completed at Le Moyne.

Visiting: There are regularly scheduled orientations for prospective students, including a campus tour and an interview with admissions counselors. Accepted students are invited to attend class and stay overnight in a residence hall. There are guides for informal visits, and visitors may sit in on classes and stay overnight. To schedule a visit, contact the Admission Office.

Financial Aid: In 2004-2005, 92% of all full-time students received some form of financial aid. 82% of full-time freshmen and 83% of continuing full-time students received need-based aid. The average freshman award was $18,335. Need-based scholarships or need-based grants averaged $14,765 ($28,875 maximum); need-based self-help aid (loans and jobs) averaged $3968 ($5625 maximum); non-need-based athletic scholarships averaged $7088 ($28,710 maximum); and other non-need-based awards and non-need-based scholarships averaged $9133 ($17,500 maximum). 93% of undergraduates work part time. Average annual earnings from campus work are $1037. The average financial indebtedness of the 2004 graduate was $19,137. Le Moyne is a member of CSS. The FAFSA and the college's own financial statement are required. Check with the school for current deadlines.

International Students: There are 19 international students enrolled. The school actively recruits these students. A satisfactory score is required on the written TOEFL. Students must also take the SAT or the ACT.

Computers: Connected to the campus network are about 325 PCs and Macs in public and departmental labs across campus, providing access to the library system, the Internet, and Novell servers with a multitude of applications. There is access to personal space on these servers. Access from residence hall rooms includes the library system, personal space, and the Internet. Wireless is available throughout most of the campus,

including all academic areas. All students may access the system 24 hours a day. There are no time limits and no fees.

Graduates: From July 1, 2004 to June 30, 2005, 537 bachelor's degrees were awarded. The most popular majors were business (22%), psychology (17%), and English (10%). In an average class, 61% graduate in 4 years or less, 71% graduate in 5 years or less, and 74% graduate in 6 years or less. 78 companies recruited on campus in 2004-2005. Of the 2004 graduating class, 32% were enrolled in graduate school within 6 months of graduation and 61% were employed.

Admissions Contact: Dennis J. Nicholson, Director of Admission. A video is available. E-mail: *admission@lemoyne.edu*
Web: *www.lemoyne.edu*

LONG ISLAND UNIVERSITY SYSTEM

The Long Island University System, established in 1886, is a private system in New York. It is governed by a board of trustees, whose chief administrator is the president. The primary goal of the system is to provide Long Island's communities with high-quality, humane higher education. The main priorities are teaching in the liberal arts and professions, extending higher education to underrepresented populations, and providing every student with opportunities for cooperative education placements in a field related to his or her major. The total enrollment is usually about 18,000 with 1500 faculty members. Altogether there are some 180 baccalaureate, 150 master's, and 2 doctoral programs offered in Long Island University System. 4-year campuses are located in Brooklyn, Brookville, and, and Southampton. Profiles of the 4-year campuses are included in this section.

LONG ISLAND UNIVERSITY/BROOKLYN CAMPUS D-5

Brooklyn, NY 11201   (718) 488-1292
(800) LIU-PLAN; Fax: (718) 797-2399

Full-time: 1300 men, 3100 women	**Faculty:** 211; IIA, ++$
Part-time: 250 men, 800 women	**Ph.Ds:** 76%
Graduate: 900 men, 1200 women	**Student/Faculty:** 21 to 1
Year: semesters, summer session	**Tuition:** $18,000
Application Deadline: open	**Room & Board:** $7,000
Freshman Class: n/av	
SAT or ACT: recommended	**COMPETITIVE**

Long Island University/Brooklyn Campus, founded in 1926, is part of the Long Island University system. It is a private institution offering programs in liberal arts and sciences, pharmacy, health professions, education, business, nursing, and special programs. It is largely a commuter school. Some figures in the above capsule and in this profile are approximate. There are 6 undergraduate and 5 graduate schools. In addition to regional accreditation, LIU has baccalaureate program accreditation with ACPE and NLN. The library contains 2,100,000 volumes, 813,544 microform items, and 7902 audio/video tapes/CDs/DVDs, and subscribes to 8042 periodicals including electronic. Computerized library services include the card catalog and interlibrary loans. Special learning facilities include a learning resource center, art gallery, radio station, and TV station. The 10-acre campus is in an urban area. Including any residence halls, there are 11 buildings.

Student Life: 86% of undergraduates are from New York. Others are from 35 states, 21 foreign countries, and Canada. 75% are from public schools. 43% are African American; 27% white; 19% Hispanic; 11% Asian American. The average age of freshmen is 21; all undergraduates, 25. 36% do not continue beyond their first year; 61% remain to graduate.

Housing: 525 students can be accommodated in college housing, which includes single-sex and coed dorms and married-student housing. On-campus housing is available on a first-come, first-served basis. 89% of students commute. Alcohol is not permitted. No one may keep cars.

Activities: There are 75 groups on campus, including band, cheerleading, chess, chorale, computers, dance, ethnic, honors, international, jazz band, literary magazine, newspaper, pep band, photography, political, radio and TV, religious, student government, and yearbook.

Sports: There are 7 intercollegiate sports for men and 6 for women, and 6 intramural sports for men and 6 for women. Facilities include a baseball/soccer field and a basketball gym.

Disabled Students: All of the campus is accessible. Wheelchair ramps, elevators, specially equipped rest rooms, special class scheduling, lowered drinking fountains, and lowered telephones are available.

Services: Counseling and information services are available, as is tutoring in most subjects. There is remedial math, reading, and writing.

Campus Safety and Security: Measures include 24-hour foot and vehicle patrol, pamphlets/posters/films, emergency telephones, and lighted pathways/sidewalks.

Programs of Study: LIU confers B.A., B.S., and B.F.A. degrees. Associate, master's, and doctoral degrees are also awarded. Bachelor's degrees are awarded in BIOLOGICAL SCIENCE (biology/biological science), BUSINESS (accounting, banking and finance, business administration and management, and marketing/retailing/merchandising), COMMUNICATIONS AND THE ARTS (broadcasting, communications, English, fine arts, journalism, languages, music, and speech/debate/rhetoric), COMPUTER AND PHYSICAL SCIENCE (chemistry, computer science, information sciences and systems, and mathematics), EDUCATION (art, business, early childhood, elementary, music, science, secondary, special, and teaching English as a second/foreign language (TESOL/TEFOL)), HEALTH PROFESSIONS (nursing, occupational therapy, pharmacy, physical therapy, physician's assistant, predentistry, and premedicine), SOCIAL SCIENCE (anthropology, economics, history, philosophy, political science/government, prelaw, psychology, social science, social work, and sociology). Health professions, pharmacy, and liberal arts are the strongest academically. Health professions, liberal arts, and business are the largest.

Required: Proficiency courses include basic English and math, English composition, and speech. Distribution requirements are 6 credits each in foreign language, math, and science. Students must complete a core curriculum of 18 credits in the humanities, 12 in social sciences, 8 in natural sciences, and 6 in math. A total of 128 credits (197 for pharmacy) is required for graduation, with 36 credits in the major, and a GPA of 2.0.

Special: Accelerated degree programs are available in all majors. Students may cross-register with other LIU campuses. Internships in career-related jobs provide cooperative education credits. Study abroad, dual-majors, credit for life, military, and work experience, and pass/fail options are also offered. There is a chapter of Phi Beta Kappa and a freshman honors program.

Faculty/Classroom: All teach undergraduates. The average class size in a regular course is 22.

Requirements: The SAT or ACT is recommended. LIU requires applicants to be in the upper 75% of their class. A GPA of 2.0 is required. AP and CLEP credits are accepted. Important factors in the admissions decision are recommendations by school officials, advanced placement or honor courses, and evidence of special talent.

Procedure: Freshmen are admitted to all sessions. Entrance exams should be taken by January of the senior year. There is a deferred admissions plan and rolling admissions plan. Application deadlines are open. Application fee is $30. Applications are accepted on-line. Check with the school for current application deadlines and fee.

Transfer: A GPA of 2.5 is required. 32 of 128 credits required for the bachelor's degree must be completed at LIU.

Visiting: There are regularly scheduled orientations for prospective students. Visitors may sit in on classes. To schedule a visit, contact the Admissions Office at (718) 488-1011.

Financial Aid: In a recent year, 93% of all full-time freshmen received some form of financial aid. The CSS/Profile and the college's own financial statement are required. Check with the school for current deadlines.

International Students: There were 95 international students enrolled in a recent year. The school actively recruits these students. They must take the TOEFL and also take the SAT or the ACT.

Computers: All students may access the system during library hours. There are no time limits and no fees.

Graduates: In a recent year, 552 bachelor's degrees were awarded. The most popular majors were nursing (15%), psychology (9%), and business (8%). In an average class, 30% graduate in 4 years or less, 60% graduate in 5 years or less, and 70% graduate in 6 years or less.

Admissions Contact: Richard Sunday, Acting Dean of Admissions. E-mail: *attend@liu.edu* Web: *www.liu.edu*

LONG ISLAND UNIVERSITY/C.W. POST CAMPUS   D-5

Brookville, NY 11548-1300

(516) 299-2900
(800) LIU-PLAN; Fax: (516) 299-2137

Full-time: 1600 men, 2400 women	**Faculty:** IIA, ++$
Part-time: 1100 men, 1500 women	**Ph.D.s:** n/av
Graduate: 1000 men, 2600 women	**Student/Faculty:** n/av
Year: semesters, summer session	**Tuition:** $21,000
Application Deadline: open	**Room & Board:** $8,000
Freshman Class: n/av	
SAT or ACT required	**COMPETITIVE**

Long Island University/C.W. Post Campus, founded in 1954 as part of the private Long Island University system, offers 100 undergraduate and 63 graduate majors in education, liberal arts and sciences, accountancy, business, public service, health professions and nursing, and information and computer science. There are 6 undergraduate and 6 graduate schools. Figures in the above and in this profile are approximate. In addition to regional accreditation, C.W. Post has baccalaureate program accreditation with AACSB, ADA, ASLA, CAHEA, CSWE, and NLN. The library contains 1,132,318 volumes, 834,413 microform items, and 9606 audio/video tapes/CDs/DVDs, and subscribes to 10,999 periodicals including electronic. Computerized library services include the card catalog, interlibrary loans, and database searching. Special learning facilities include a learning resource center, art gallery, radio station, TV station, an art museum, a tax institute, a speech and hearing center, a center for business research, a federal depository, and a multimedia computer cen-

ter. The 307-acre campus is in a suburban area 25 miles east of New York City, on the former estate of Marjorie Merriweather Post. Including any residence halls, there are 53 buildings.

Student Life: 91% of undergraduates are from New York. Others are from 32 states, 46 foreign countries, and Canada. 71% are from public schools. 13% are white. The average age of freshmen is 18; all undergraduates, 21. 31% do not continue beyond their first year; 37% remain to graduate.

Housing: 1710 students can be accommodated in college housing, which includes single-sex and coed dorms. There is a quiet hall. On-campus housing is guaranteed for all 4 years. 60% of students commute. All students may keep cars.

Activities: 1% of men belong to 4 national fraternities; 3% of women belong to 9 national sororities. There are 80 groups on campus, including art, band, chamber singing, cheerleading, choir, chorale, chorus, dance, drama, equestrian, ethnic, film, gay, honors, international, jazz band, literary magazine, Madrigal, musical theater, newspaper, orchestra, pep band, photography, political, professional, radio and TV, religious, renaissance music, social, social service, student government, vocal jazz, and yearbook. Popular campus events include Theater Festival, Spring Fling, and Cereal Bowl: The Inter-Residential Hall Competition.

Sports: There are 7 intercollegiate sports for men and 10 for women, and 5 intramural sports for men and 5 for women. Facilities include a 5,000-seat football stadium, an equestrian center, tennis courts, 70 acres of baseball, soccer, lacrosse, softball, and practice fields, a recreational center with an 8-lane swimming pool, 3 basketball courts with spectator seating for 3,000, racquetball courts, an indoor track, and weight and aerobic rooms.

Disabled Students: 75% of the campus is accessible. Wheelchair ramps, elevators, special parking, specially equipped rest rooms, special class scheduling, lowered drinking fountains, lowered telephones, special housing, and electric doors are available.

Services: Counseling and information services are available, as is tutoring in most subjects. There is a reader service for the blind, and remedial math, reading, and writing. There is an academic resource center for learning-disabled students.

Campus Safety and Security: Measures include 24-hour foot and vehicle patrol, self-defense education, security escort services, and shuttle buses. There are informal discussions, pamphlets/posters/films, emergency telephones, lighted pathways/sidewalks, and restricted night access to campus, card-access residence entrances, and an electronic keyless locking system for dorm rooms.

Programs of Study: C.W. Post confers B.A., B.S., B.F.A., and B.S.Ed. degrees. Associate, master's, and doctoral degrees are also awarded. Bachelor's degrees are awarded in AGRICULTURE (conservation and regulation), BIOLOGICAL SCIENCE (biology/biological science, molecular biology, and nutrition), BUSINESS (accounting, banking and finance, business administration and management, and marketing/retailing/merchandising), COMMUNICATIONS AND THE ARTS (arts administration/management, broadcasting, communications, dance, dramatic arts, English, film arts, fine arts, French, German, Italian, journalism, music, photography, public relations, and Spanish), COMPUTER AND PHYSICAL SCIENCE (chemistry, computer science, geology, information sciences and systems, mathematics, physics, and radiological technology), EDUCATION (art, early childhood, elementary, English, foreign languages, health, music, science, and secondary), ENGINEERING AND ENVIRONMENTAL DESIGN (preengineering), HEALTH PROFESSIONS (art therapy, biomedical science, health care administration, medical laboratory technology, medical records administration/services, nursing, predentistry, premedicine, prepharmacy, and speech pathology/audiology), SOCIAL SCIENCE (criminal justice, economics, geography, history, international studies, philosophy, political science/government, prelaw, psychology, public administration, and social work). Accounting, radiologic technology, and biology are the strongest academically. Business, education, and media arts are the largest.

Required: Core requirements include 9 credits each of history and philosophy, 8 of lab science, 6 each of language and literature, arts, political science and economics, sociology, psychology, and geography or anthropology, and 3 of math. A minimum of 128 credits is required to graduate. GPA requirements range from 2.0 to 2.5 in most departments, 3.0 in interdisciplinary studies. Students must demonstrate competency in writing, quantitative skills, computer skills, oral communications, and library use.

Special: There is cross-registration with several other Long Island colleges. C.W. Post offers co-op programs in all majors, internships, study abroad in 11 countries, work-study in most departments, accelerated degree programs, and a Washington semester for outstanding criminal justice students. Dual and student-designed majors are available. There is a 3-2 engineering degree with Polytechnic University, Pratt Institute, and Arizona State University, and credit is available for life, military, and work experience. Nondegree study is available, as are pass/fail options. There are 14 national honor societies, a freshman honors program, and 16 departmental honors programs.

Faculty/Classroom: No introductory courses are taught by graduate students. The average class size in an introductory lecture is 26; in a laboratory, 20; and in a regular course, 19.

Admissions: 76% of recent applicants were accepted. The ACT scores for the 2005-2006 freshman class were: 52% below 21, 33% between 21 and 23, 5% between 24 and 26, 6% between 27 and 28, and 4% above 28. 30% of recent freshmen were in the top fifth of their class; 61% were in the top two fifths. There were 4 National Merit finalists.

Requirements: The SAT or ACT is required. Applicants should be graduates of an accredited secondary school with a B average or have a GED. Preparatory work should include 4 years each of English and social science, and 2 each of foreign language, college preparatory math, and lab science. A grade average of 75 is required. AP and CLEP credits are accepted. Important factors in the admissions decision are advanced placement or honor courses, recommendations by school officials, and evidence of special talent.

Procedure: Freshmen are admitted to all sessions. Entrance exams should be taken from May of the junior year through December of the senior year. There are early admissions and deferred admissions plans. There is a rolling admissions plan. Application deadlines are open. Check with the school for current application deadlines and fee. Applications are accepted on-line.

Transfer: Applicants should have appropriate high school credentials and a minimum college GPA of 2.25. 32 of 128 credits required for the bachelor's degree must be completed at C.W. Post.

Visiting: There are regularly scheduled orientations for prospective students, consisting of Post Preview Days, which include meeting the faculty, an admissions and financial aid overview, and a campus tour. There are guides for informal visits and visitors may sit in on classes. To schedule a visit, contact the Office of Admissions.

Financial Aid: In a recent year, 85% of all full-time students received some form of financial aid, including need-based aid. The average freshman award was $9600. Need-based scholarships or need-based grants averaged $8574 ($25,000 maximum); need-based self-help aid (loans and jobs) averaged $3538 ($6625 maximum); non-need-based athletic scholarships averaged $6500 ($27,240 maximum); and other non-need-based awards and non-need-based scholarships averaged $6328 ($16,000 maximum). 31% of undergraduates work part time. Average annual earnings from campus work are $1200. The average financial indebtedness of a recent graduate was $15,000. C.W. Post is a member of CSS. The CSS/Profile and FAFSA are required. Check with the school for current deadlines.

International Students: There were 380 international students enrolled in a recent year. The school actively recruits these students. They must take the TOEFL. SAT or ACT scores are recommended to help evaluate students admissions eligibility and enable students to be considered for scholarships.

Computers: All students may access the system Monday to Thursday 8 A.M. to 11 P.M. and Friday to Sunday 9 A.M. to 10 P.M. Dial-up capacity is available 24 hours a day. There are no time limits and no fees.

Admissions Contact: Beth Carson, Acting Director of Admissions. E-mail: *enroll@cwpost.liu.edu* Web: *www.liu.edu*

MANHATTAN COLLEGE

Riverdale, NY 10471

D-5

(718) 862-7200
(800) 622-9235; Fax: (718) 862-8019

Full-time: 1300 men, 1400 women	**Faculty:** 162
Part-time: 100 men, 100 women	**Ph.D.s:** 94%
Graduate: 200 men, 200 women	**Student/Faculty:** 17 to 1
Year: semesters, summer session	**Tuition:** $20,000
Application Deadline: see profile	**Room & Board:** $9,000
Freshman Class: n/av	
SAT: required	**VERY COMPETITIVE**

Manhattan College, founded in 1853, is a private institution affiliated with the Christian Brothers of the Catholic Church. It offers degree programs in the arts and sciences, education and human services, business, and engineering. There are 5 undergraduate and 3 graduate schools. Figures in the above and in this profile are approximate. In addition to regional accreditation, Manhattan has baccalaureate program accreditation with ABET, AHEA, and CAHEA. The 4 libraries contain 193,100 volumes, 383,480 microform items, and 3244 audio/video tapes/CDs/DVDs, and subscribe to 1527 periodicals including electronic. Computerized library services include the card catalog, interlibrary loans, and database searching. Special learning facilities include a learning resource center, radio station, nuclear reactor lab, and media center. The 26-acre campus is in an urban area 10 miles north of midtown Manhattan. Including any residence halls, there are 28 buildings.

Student Life: 75% of undergraduates are from New York. Others are from 33 states and 10 foreign countries. 60% are from public schools. 67% are white; 14% Hispanic. The average age of freshmen is 18; all undergraduates, 20. 15% do not continue beyond their first year; 68% remain to graduate.

Housing: 1440 students can be accommodated in college housing, which includes coed dorms and off-campus apartments. On-campus housing is guaranteed for all 4 years. 54% of students live on campus; of those, 80% remain on campus on weekends. All students may keep cars.

Activities: 2% of men belong to 3 local and 1 national fraternity; 1% of women belong to 4 local sororities. There are 70 groups on campus, including bagpipe band, cheerleading, choir, chorus, computers, dance, debate, drama, ethnic, honors, international, jazz band, literary magazine, musical theater, newspaper, orchestra, pep band, political, professional, radio and TV, religious, social, social service, student government, and yearbook. Popular campus events include Annual Springfest, Special Olympics, and Jasper Jingle.

Sports: There are 8 intercollegiate sports for men and 8 for women, and 7 intramural sports for men and 7 for women. Facilities include 5 full basketball courts, which can also be used for volleyball and tennis, an indoor track, a weight room, a swimming pool, and a Nautilus center.

Disabled Students: All of the campus is accessible. Wheelchair ramps, elevators, special parking, and specially equipped rest rooms are available.

Services: Counseling and information services are available, as is tutoring in every subject.

Campus Safety and Security: Measures include 24-hour foot and vehicle patrol, security escort services, informal discussions, and pamphlets/posters/films. There are emergency telephones and lighted pathways/sidewalks.

Programs of Study: Manhattan confers B.A., B.S., and B.S.E. degrees. Master's degrees are also awarded. Bachelor's degrees are awarded in BIOLOGICAL SCIENCE (biochemistry and biology/biological science), BUSINESS (accounting, banking and finance, business economics, international business management, and marketing/retailing/merchandising), COMMUNICATIONS AND THE ARTS (communications, English, French, and Spanish), COMPUTER AND PHYSICAL SCIENCE (chemistry, computer science, information sciences and systems, mathematics, and physics), EDUCATION (early childhood, elementary, foreign languages, health, middle school, physical, science, secondary, and special), ENGINEERING AND ENVIRONMENTAL DESIGN (chemical engineering, civil engineering, electrical/electronics engineering, environmental engineering, and mechanical engineering), HEALTH PROFESSIONS (predentistry, premedicine, and radiological science), SOCIAL SCIENCE (economics, history, peace studies, philosophy, political science/government, prelaw, psychology, religion, sociology, and urban studies). Engineering and business are the strongest academically. Arts, business, and education are the largest.

Required: All students must take courses in English composition and literature, religious studies, philosophy, humanities, social science, science, math, and a modern foreign language. About 130 credit hours are required for graduation, with about 36 in the major. The minimum GPA is 2.0.

Special: Manhattan offers co-op programs in 11 majors, cross-registration with the College of Mount St. Vincent, and off-campus internships in business, industry, government, and social or cultural organizations. Students may study abroad in 10 countries and enter work-study programs with major U.S. corporations, in health services, or the arts. A general studies degree, a 3-2 engineering degree, a dual major in international business, credit by exam, and nondegree study are also available. There are 22 national honor societies, including Phi Beta Kappa, a freshman honors program, and 28 departmental honors programs.

Faculty/Classroom: 70% of faculty are male; 30%, female. All teach undergraduates and 80% both teach and do research. No introductory courses are taught by graduate students. The average class size in an introductory lecture is 15 and in a regular course, 22.

Requirements: The SAT is required. In addition, applicants must graduate from an accredited secondary school or have earned a GED. 16 academic units are required, including 4 of English, 3 each of math and social studies, and 2 of foreign language, lab sciences, and electives. An essay is required and an interview is recommended. AP and CLEP credits are accepted. Important factors in the admissions decision are advanced placement or honor courses, leadership record, and recommendations by school officials.

Procedure: Freshmen are admitted fall and spring. Entrance exams should be taken in the spring of the junior year or the fall of the senior year. There are early decision and deferred admissions plans. There is a rolling admissions plan. Check with the school for current application deadlines and fee. 20 early decision candidates were accepted for a recent class. A waiting list is an active part of the admissions procedure. Applications are accepted on-line.

Transfer: 125 transfer students enrolled in 2004-2005. Applicants must have a GPA of 2.5 and meet subject course requirements according to their course of study. They must submit transcripts from colleges and high schools attended. An interview is recommended. 66 of 130 credits required for the bachelor's degree must be completed at Manhattan.

Visiting: There are regularly scheduled orientations for prospective students during 2 days in the summer, which include scheduling, parent workshops, loan seminars, and English and math testing. There are guides for informal visits and visitors may sit in on classes and stay overnight. To schedule a visit, contact the Admission Center at *admit@manhattan.edu.*

Financial Aid: In a recent year, 82% of all full-time freshmen and 71% of continuing full-time students received some form of financial aid. 73% of full-time freshmen and 63% of continuing full-time students received need-based aid. The average freshman award was $12,688. Need-based scholarships or need-based grants averaged $7179; need-based self-help aid (loans and jobs) averaged $3097; non-need-based athletic scholarships averaged $10,750; and other non-need-based awards and non-need-based scholarships averaged $6988. 15% of undergraduates work part time. Average annual earnings from campus work are $600. The average financial indebtedness of a recent graduate was $12,100. The FAFSA and the college's own financial statement are required. Check with the school for current deadlines.

International Students: The school actively recruits these students. They must take the TOEFL and also take the SAT or the ACT.

Computers: All students may access the system 13 hours a day in the labs and 24 hours a day in residence halls or by modem. There are no time limits and no fees.

Graduates: In an average class, 53% graduate in 4 years or less, 64% graduate in 5 years or less, and 68% graduate in 6 years or less. 200 companies recruited on campus in a recent year. Of recent graduating class, 16% were enrolled in graduate school within 6 months of graduation and 61% were employed.

Admissions Contact: William J. Bisset, Jr., Assistant Vice President for Enrollment Management. A video is available.
E-mail: *admit@manhattan.edu* Web: *www.manhattan.edu*

MANHATTAN SCHOOL OF MUSIC   **D-5**
New York, NY 10027-4678   (212) 749-2802, ext. 4501
                                                      Fax: (212) 749-5471

Full-time: 180 men, 190 women	**Faculty:** 35
Part-time: 10 men, 20 women	**Ph.Ds:** 40%
Graduate: 175 men, 270 women	**Student/Faculty:** 11 to 1
Year: semesters	**Tuition:** $22,000
Application Deadline: see profile	**Room & Board:** $11,000
Freshman Class: n/av	
SAT or ACT: recommended	**SPECIAL**

The Manhattan School of Music, founded in 1917, is a private college offering undergraduate and graduate degrees in music performance and composition. Figures in the above and in this profile are approximate. The library contains 73,405 volumes and 21,074 audio/video tapes/CDs/DVDs, and subscribes to 128 periodicals including electronic. Computerized library services include the card catalog, interlibrary loans, and database searching. Special learning facilities include 2 electronic music studios and a recording studio. The 1-acre campus is in an urban area in New York City. Including any residence halls, there are 2 buildings.

Student Life: 77% of undergraduates are from out of state, mostly the Northeast. Students are from 41 states, 46 foreign countries, and Canada. 81% are from public schools. 36% are foreign nationals; 36% white. The average age of freshmen is 18; all undergraduates, 21. 17% do not continue beyond their first year; 54% remain to graduate.

Housing: 380 students can be accommodated in college housing, which includes single-sex and coed dorms. On-campus housing is guaranteed for the freshman year only and is available on a lottery system for upperclassmen. Priority is given to out-of-town students. 50% of students live on campus; of those, 95% remain on campus on weekends. All students may keep cars.

Activities: 10% of men belong to 2 local fraternities; 20% of women belong to 2 local sororities. There are 13 groups on campus, including choir, chorale, chorus, ethnic, gay, international, jazz band, musical theater, opera, orchestra, student government, and symphony. Popular campus events include a Halloween party, a Christmas/Chanukah party, and post-opera party.

Sports: There is no sports program at MSM.

Disabled Students: 70% of the campus is accessible. Wheelchair ramps, elevators, specially equipped rest rooms, special class scheduling, and lowered telephones are available.

Services: Counseling and information services are available, as is tutoring in most subjects. There is a reader service for the blind.

Campus Safety and Security: Measures include 24-hour foot and vehicle patrol, informal discussions, pamphlets/posters/films, and lighted pathways/sidewalks.

Programs of Study: MSM confers the B.Mus. degree. Master's and doctoral degrees are also awarded. Bachelor's degrees are awarded in COMMUNICATIONS AND THE ARTS (jazz, music, music performance, music theory and composition, piano/organ, strings, and voice). Classical piano, classical voice, and jazz are the largest.

Required: All students must take 4 music theory courses, a 4-course core curriculum in the humanities, 4 elective humanities courses, and perform a final, senior-year recital. Composition majors must complete

an original symphonic work. To graduate, students must earn 120 to 130 credit hours, including 90 to 100 in the major, with a minimum GPA of 2.0.

Special: There is cross-registration with Barnard College. Credit by exam in theory and music history is available.

Faculty/Classroom: 69% of faculty are male; 31%, female. All teach undergraduates. Graduate students teach 1% of introductory courses. The average class size in an introductory lecture is 20 and in a regular course, 15.

Requirements: The SAT or ACT is recommended. In addition, applicants should graduate from an accredited high school with a minimum GPA of 2.5. The GED is accepted. Admission is based on a performance audition, evaluation of scholastic achievements, and available openings in the major field. A GPA of 2.9 is required. AP and CLEP credits are accepted. Important factors in the admissions decision are evidence of special talent, personality/intangible qualities, and extracurricular activities record.

Procedure: Freshmen are admitted in the fall. Check with the school for current application deadline and fee.

Transfer: Applicants must audition and submit college transcripts. 60 of 120 credits required for the bachelor's degree must be completed at MSM.

Visiting: There are regularly scheduled orientations for prospective students, consisting of a tour of the facility and a discussion with a counselor. There are guides for informal visits and visitors may sit in on classes. To schedule a visit, contact the Office of Admission and Financial Aid at (212) 749-2802, ext. 2.

Financial Aid: The CSS/Profile, FAFSA, and the college's own financial statement are required. Check with the school for current deadlines.

International Students: The school actively recruits these students. They must take the written TOEFL and also take the International English Language Testing System (IELTS).

Computers: All students may access the system. There are no time limits and no fees.

Admissions Contact: Lee Cioppa, Director of Admission.
E-mail: *admission@msmnyc.edu* Web: *www.msmnyc.edu*

MANHATTANVILLE COLLEGE   **D-5**
Purchase, NY 10577   (914) 323-5464
                                    (800) 32 VILLE; Fax: (914) 694-1732

Full-time: 485 men, 1050 women	**Faculty:** 88; IIA, -$
Part-time: 50 men, 100 women	**Ph.Ds:** 93%
Graduate: 200 men, 725 women	**Student/Faculty:** 17 to 1
Year: semesters, summer session	**Tuition:** $23,100
Application Deadline: open	**Room & Board:** $9400
Freshman Class: n/av	
SAT or ACT required	**COMPETITIVE+**

Manhattanville College, founded in 1841, is an independent liberal arts institution offering more than 45 undergraduate areas of study. There are 2 graduate schools. Figures in the above capsule and profile are approximate. In addition to regional accreditation, M'ville has baccalaureate program accreditation with NASM. The library contains 282,892 volumes, 532,732 microform items, and 3936 audio/video tapes/CDs/DVDs, and subscribes to 14,227 periodicals including electronic. Computerized library services include the card catalog, interlibrary loans, database searching, and Internet access. Special learning facilities include a learning resource center, art gallery, radio station, and TV station. The 100-acre campus is in a suburban area 25 miles north of New York City. Including any residence halls, there are 21 buildings.

Student Life: 66% of undergraduates are from New York. Others are from 35 states, 49 foreign countries, and Canada. 58% are white; 14% Hispanic. The average age of freshmen is 18; all undergraduates, 20. 23% do not continue beyond their first year; 58% remain to graduate.

Housing: 1114 students can be accommodated in college housing, which includes single-sex and coed dormitories. On-campus housing is guaranteed for all 4 years. 73% of students live on campus; of those, 75% remain on campus on weekends. All students may keep cars.

Activities: There are no fraternities or sororities. There are 60 groups on campus, including art, band, cheerleading, chess, choir, chorale, chorus, computers, dance, debate, drama, ethnic, film, gay, honors, international, jazz band, literary magazine, musical theater, newspaper, orchestra, pep band, photography, political, professional, radio and TV, religious, social, social service, student government, and yearbook. Popular campus events include Quad Jam, Fall Jam, and The Global Pot.

Sports: There are 7 intercollegiate sports for men and 7 for women, and 3 intramural sports for men and 3 for women. Facilities include a 1000-seat gym, a 25-yard indoor pool, 6 deco-turf tennis courts, a healthworks-wellness center, baseball, lacrosse, field hockey, and softball fields, and batting cages.

Disabled Students: All of the campus is accessible. Wheelchair ramps, elevators, special parking, specially equipped rest rooms, and special class scheduling are available.

Services: Counseling and information services are available, as is tutoring in every subject. There is a program for students with documented learning disabilities.

Campus Safety and Security: Measures include 24-hour foot and vehicle patrol, security escort services, shuttle buses, and informal discussions. There are pamphlets/posters/films, emergency telephones, and lighted pathways/sidewalks.

Programs of Study: M'ville confers B.A., B.F.A., and B.Mus. degrees. Master's degrees are also awarded. Bachelor's degrees are awarded in BIOLOGICAL SCIENCE (biochemistry and biology/biological science), BUSINESS (banking and finance, and management science), COMMUNICATIONS AND THE ARTS (art, art history and appreciation, classics, dance, English, French, German, music, romance languages and literature, and Spanish), COMPUTER AND PHYSICAL SCIENCE (chemistry, computer science, mathematics, and physics), EDUCATION (education), SOCIAL SCIENCE (American studies, Asian/Oriental studies, economics, history, international studies, philosophy, political science/government, psychology, religion, and sociology). Management, art, and psychology are the strongest academically. Psychology, management, and history are the largest.

Required: Distribution requirements include 18 credits in social sciences and humanities and either a major or minor in foreign language or 18 credits in Western and non-Western courses, 8 credits in math and natural sciences, and 6 in the arts. A yearlong freshman humanities course, courses in library skills, writing, and global perspective, and a preceptorial are required. A total of 120 credit hours and a minimum GPA of 2.0 are needed to graduate.

Special: Manhattanville offers cross-registration with SUNY Purchase, internships in all majors for credit, a Washington semester, and study abroad in 10 countries. Dual, student-designed, and interdisciplinary majors and pass/fail options are also available. Under the portfolio degree plan, students develop an individualized program combining both academic and nonacademic training. There is a freshman honors program.

Faculty/Classroom: 54% of faculty are male; 46%, female. All teach undergraduates. No introductory courses are taught by graduate students. The average class size in an introductory lecture is 15; in a laboratory, 12; and in a regular course, 10.

Requirements: The SAT or ACT is required. In addition, applicants should graduate in the upper 50% of their class with 4 years of English, 3 each of history, math, and science, including 2 of lab science, and one half year each of art and music. The GED is accepted. Interviews are strongly encouraged. Art applicants must submit a portfolio; music applicants must audition. A GPA of 2.0 is required. AP and CLEP credits are accepted. Important factors in the admissions decision are leadership record, recommendations by alumni, and recommendations by school officials.

Procedure: Freshmen are admitted fall and spring. Entrance exams should be taken in the spring of the junior or fall of the senior year. There are early decision, early admissions, deferred admissions, and rolling admissions plans. Application deadlines are open. Application fee is $50. Applications are accepted on-line.

Transfer: 72 transfer students enrolled in a recent year. Applicants must submit college transcripts. A minimum GPA of 2.5 and a statement of good standing are required. Applicants with fewer than 40 credits must submit all high school records and SAT scores. 60 of 120 credits required for the bachelor's degree must be completed at M'ville.

Visiting: There are regularly scheduled orientations for prospective students, including a campus tour, and a meeting in Admissions. There are guides for informal visits and visitors may sit in on classes and stay overnight. To schedule a visit, contact the Office of Admissions.

Financial Aid: In a recent year, 68% of all full-time freshmen and 66% of continuing full-time students received some form of financial aid. 63% of full-time freshmen and 58% of continuing full-time students received need-based aid. The average freshman award was $15,500. 31% of undergraduates worked part time. Average annual earnings from campus work were $1700. The average financial indebtedness of a recent graduate was $21,160. The FAFSA, the state aid form and the college's own financial statement are required. Check with the school for application deadlines.

International Students: In a recent year, there were 131 international students enrolled. The school actively recruits these students. They must score satisfactorily on the written TOEFL or on the electronic version and also take the SAT or the ACT.

Computers: All students may access the system. Internet and intranet are usable 24 hours per day, 7 days a week. Computer labs are open about 64 to 70 hours throughout the week. There are no time limits and no fees.

Graduates: In a recent year, 332 bachelor's degrees were awarded. The most popular majors were management (18%), psychology (13%), and sociology (9%). In an average class, 51% graduate in 4 years or less, 58% graduate in 5 years or less, and 58% graduate in 6 years or less. 34 companies recruited on campus in a recent year. Of a recent graduating class, 18% were enrolled in graduate school within 6 months of graduation and 64% were employed.

Admissions Contact: Jose Flores, Director of Admissions. A video is available. E-mail: *admissions@mville.edu* Web: *www.manhattanville.edu*

MANNES COLLEGE OF MUSIC D-5

New York, NY 10024

(212) 580-0210, ext. 247
(800) 292-3040; Fax: (212) 580-1738

Full-time: 50 men, 80 women	**Faculty:** 23
Part-time: none	**Ph.D.s:** n/av
Graduate: 70 men, 90 women	**Student/Faculty:** 6 to 1
Year: semesters	**Tuition:** $24,000
Application Deadline: see profile	**Room & Board:** $8400
Freshman Class: n/av	
SAT or ACT: not required	**SPECIAL**

Mannes College of Music, founded in 1916 and today part of the New School University, is a private institution offering instruction in music. Figures in the above capsule and in this profile are approximate. There is 1 undergraduate and 1 graduate school. The library contains 36,500 volumes, 3 microform items, and 8800 audio/video tapes/CDs/DVDs, and subscribes to 77 periodicals including electronic. Computerized library services include the card catalog, interlibrary loans, database searching, and Internet access. Special learning facilities include 2 concert/recital halls, recording studio, and electronic music studio. The campus is in an urban area in Manhattan. Including any residence halls, there are 2 buildings.

Student Life: 71% of undergraduates are from out of state, mostly the Northeast. Students are from 18 states, 18 foreign countries, and Canada. The average age of freshmen is 19; all undergraduates, 21. 17% do not continue beyond their first year; 47% remain to graduate.

Housing: 30 students can be accommodated in college housing, which includes coed dorms. On-campus housing is guaranteed for the freshman year only and is available on a first-come, first-served basis. Priority is given to out-of-town students. Alcohol is not permitted.

Activities: There are no fraternities or sororities. There are 6 groups on campus, including choir, chorus, jazz band, opera, orchestra, and symphony. Popular campus events include orchestra/chorus concerts, Christmas parties, and recitals.

Sports: There is no sports program at Mannes.

Disabled Students: All of the campus is accessible. Elevators and specially equipped rest rooms are available.

Services: Counseling and information services are available, as is tutoring in most subjects.

Campus Safety and Security: There is a security guard 24 hours a day at the front entrance of the dorm and from 8 A.M. to 11 P.M. at the front desk of the college lobby.

Programs of Study: Mannes confers B.S. and B.Mus. degrees. Master's degrees are also awarded. Bachelor's degrees are awarded in COMMUNICATIONS AND THE ARTS (music, music performance, music theory and composition, and voice). Voice, piano, and violin are the largest.

Required: The required core curriculum includes courses in English, Western civilization, art history, and literature. Students majoring in instruments and voice must participate in various ensemble classes. Courses are also required in techniques and history of music. To graduate, performance majors must perform before a faculty jury, and composition majors must submit 5 original pieces for juried consideration.

Special: Mannes offers cross-registration with New School University. There are some dual majors by permission.

Faculty/Classroom: No introductory courses are taught by graduate students. The average class size in an introductory lecture is 10 and in a regular course, 6.

Requirements: Applicants must be graduates of an accredited secondary school or have a GED certificate. An audition, an interview, a letter of recommendation, and a written test in music theory and musicianship are required. Important factors in the admissions decision are evidence of special talent, personality/intangible qualities, and recommendations by school officials.

Procedure: Freshmen are admitted in the fall. Entrance exams should be taken at the time of the audition. There is a deferred admissions plan. Check with the school for current application deadlines and fee. Applications are accepted on-line.

Transfer: 27 transfer students enrolled in a recent year. Transfer applicants must complete the same procedures as entering freshmen and submit transcripts from all secondary schools and colleges attended.

Visiting: There are guides for informal visits and visitors may sit in on classes. To schedule a visit, contact the Admissions Office.

Financial Aid: Mannes is a member of CSS. The FAFSA and the college's own financial statement are required. Check with the school for current deadlines.

International Students: There were 75 international students enrolled in a recent year. A satisfactory score is required on the written TOEFL. Students must also take the college's own test and also take the college's own entrance exam.

Computers: All students may access the system. There are no time limits and no fees.

Graduates: In a recent year, 21 bachelor's degrees were awarded. The most popular majors were voice (32%), piano (16%), and composition (16%).

Admissions Contact: Allison Scola, Director of Admissions.
E-mail: *mannesadmissions@mannes.edu* Web: *www.mannes.edu*

MARIST COLLEGE   D-4
Poughkeepsie, NY 12601   (845) 575-3226
                                 (800) 436-5483; Fax: (845) 575-3215

Full-time: 1843 men, 2570 women	**Faculty:** 201; IIA, -$
Part-time: 242 men, 241 women	**Ph.D.s:** 82%
Graduate: 386 men, 462 women	**Student/Faculty:** 22 to 1
Year: semesters, summer session	**Tuition:** $21,202
Application Deadline: February 15	**Room & Board:** $9364
Freshman Class: 7077 applied, 3513 accepted, 1017 enrolled	
SAT Verbal/Math: 580/590*	**ACT:** 25 **VERY COMPETITIVE**

Marist College, founded in 1929, is a private liberal arts college with a Catholic tradition. There are 7 undergraduate and 4 graduate schools. In addition to regional accreditation, Marist has baccalaureate program accreditation with AACSB, CSWE, and NAACLS. The library contains 183,538 volumes, 251,760 microform items, and 5554 audio/video tapes/CDs/DVDs, and subscribes to 18,465 periodicals including electronic. Computerized library services include the card catalog, interlibrary loans, database searching, Internet access, and laptop Internet portals. Special learning facilities include a learning resource center, art gallery, radio station, TV station, a gallery of Lowell Thomas memorabilia, estuarine and environmental studies lab, public opinion institute, and economic research center. The 150-acre campus is in a suburban area 75 miles north of New York City on the Hudson River. Including any residence halls, there are 58 buildings.

Student Life: 60% of undergraduates are from New York. Others are from 36 states, 10 foreign countries, and Canada. 70% are from public schools. 78% are white. The average age of freshmen is 18; all undergraduates, 22. 10% do not continue beyond their first year; 76% remain to graduate.

Housing: 2858 students can be accommodated in college housing, which includes coed dorms, on-campus apartments, and off-campus apartments. In addition, there are special-interest houses, freshman dorms with mentors, and housing for upperclassman 73% of students live on campus; of those, 90% remain on campus on weekends. Alcohol is not permitted. Upperclassmen may keep cars.

Activities: 1% of men belong to 3 national fraternities; 6% of women belong to 1 local sorority and 3 national sororities. There are 76 groups on campus, including art, band, cheerleading, chess, choir, chorale, chorus, computers, dance, debate, drama, ethnic, film, gay, honors, international, jazz band, literary magazine, marching band, musical theater, newspaper, orchestra, pep band, photography, political, professional, radio and TV, religious, social, social service, student government, symphony, and yearbook. Popular campus events include Activities Fair, Foxfest, and Giving Tree Program.

Sports: There are 11 intercollegiate sports for men and 12 for women, and 4 intramural sports for men and 4 for women. Facilities include a boathouse, a 3600-seat basketball arena, a 3000-seat stadium, 30 acres of playing fields, a field house, a swimming pool, a diving well, racquetball courts, a dance and aerobics studio, a weight room, intramural basketball courts, an all-purpose playing space, and a fitness center.

Disabled Students: All of the campus is accessible. Wheelchair ramps, elevators, special parking, specially equipped rest rooms, special class scheduling, lowered drinking fountains, and lowered telephones are available.

Services: Counseling and information services are available, as is tutoring in every subject. There is a reader service for the blind, and remedial math, reading, and writing.

Campus Safety and Security: Measures include 24-hour foot and vehicle patrol, security escort services, informal discussions, and pamphlets/posters/films. There are emergency telephones and lighted pathways/sidewalks.

Programs of Study: Marist confers B.A., B.S., and B.P.S. degrees. Master's degrees are also awarded. Bachelor's degrees are awarded in BIOLOGICAL SCIENCE (biology/biological science), BUSINESS (accounting, business administration and management, and fashion merchandising), COMMUNICATIONS AND THE ARTS (communications, English, fine arts, French, and Spanish), COMPUTER AND PHYSICAL SCIENCE (chemistry, computer mathematics, computer science, digital arts/technology, information sciences and systems, and mathematics), EDUCATION (athletic training and special), ENGINEERING AND ENVIRONMENTAL DESIGN (environmental science), HEALTH PROFESSIONS (medical technology), SOCIAL SCIENCE (American studies, criminal justice, economics, fashion design and technology, history, interdisciplinary studies, philosophy, political science/government, psy-

chology, and social work). Business administration, communications, and psychology are the largest.

Required: To graduate, students must maintain a GPA of 2.0 in the major while taking 120 credits. A 30-credit core curriculum and 30 to 36 credits in a major are required. Distribution requirements include 6 credits each in natural sciences, social sciences, history, literature, and math and 3 credits each in fine arts and philosophy/religious studies. Specific course requirements include English writing skills and foundation courses in those areas defined by major programs.

Special: Marist offers cross-registration with schools in the Mid-Hudson Career Consortium and study abroad in 32 countries. The school also offers a 3-year degree in social work; co-op programs in computer science and computer information systems, inform technology, accounting, and business; work-study programs; and dual and student-designed majors. There are internships available with more than 1100 organizations in the United States and abroad, including New York State Legislature and White House programs. There are 14 national honor societies and a freshman honors program.

Faculty/Classroom: 57% of faculty are male; 43%, female. 98% both teach and do research. No introductory courses are taught by graduate students. The average class size in an introductory lecture is 20; in a laboratory, 20; and in a regular course, 19.

Admissions: 50% of the 2005-2006 applicants were accepted. The SAT scores for the 2005-2006 freshman class were: Verbal--10% below 500, 50% between 500 and 599, 36% between 600 and 700, and 4% above 700; Math--5% below 500, 45% between 500 and 599, 43% between 600 and 700, and 7% above 700. The ACT scores were 7% below 21, 16% between 21 and 23, 44% between 24 and 26, 17% between 27 and 28, and 16% above 28. 55% of the current freshmen were in the top fifth of their class; 92% were in the top two fifths. There were 2 National Merit finalists. 4 freshmen graduated first in their class.

Requirements: The SAT or ACT is required. The ACT Optional Writing test is also required. In addition, applicants should have 17 high school units, including at least 4 years in English, 3 each in math, science, and social studies/history, and 2 in foreign language. An essay and 2 letters of recommendation are also required. Marist requires applicants to be in the upper 50% of their class. A grade average of 83.0 is required. AP and CLEP credits are accepted. Important factors in the admissions decision are advanced placement or honor courses, leadership record, and recommendations by school officials.

Procedure: Freshmen are admitted fall and spring. Entrance exams should be taken during the fall of the senior year. There are early decision and early admissions plans. Early decision applications should be filed by November 15; regular applications, by February 15 for fall entry and November 1 for spring entry, along with a $40 fee. Notification of early decision is sent December 15; regular decision, March 15. Applications are accepted on-line.

Transfer: 193 transfer students enrolled in 2004-2005. Applicants must have at least a 2.8 GPA (depending on the college and major program) in at least 30 college credits. Students with fewer than 25 credits will be treated as freshmen. Grades of C or better transfer. 30 of 120 credits required for the bachelor's degree must be completed at Marist.

Visiting: There are regularly scheduled orientations for prospective students, including 1-day June visits for freshmen and a 1-week welcome program. There are guides for informal visits and visitors may sit in on classes and stay overnight. To schedule a visit, contact the Admissions Office receptionist at *www.marist.edu/admissions*.

Financial Aid: In 2005-2006, 90% of all full-time freshmen and 86% of continuing full-time students received some form of financial aid. 61% of full-time freshmen and 57% of continuing full-time students received need-based aid. The average freshman award was $12,745. Need-based scholarships or need-based grants averaged $10,971 ($32,691 maximum); need-based self-help aid (loans and jobs) averaged $4954 ($7325 maximum); and non-need-based athletic scholarships averaged $7769 ($26,000 maximum). 23% of undergraduates work part time. Average annual earnings from campus work are $1724. The average financial indebtedness of the 2005 graduate was $20,618. The FAFSA is required. The deadline for filing freshman financial aid applications for fall entry is February 15.

International Students: There are 13 international students enrolled. The school actively recruits these students. They must take the TOEFL and also take the college's own test. The IELTS is accepted.

Computers: Wireless access is available. All residence halls and classrooms are connected to the campus network and the Internet. Students can also access Marist's wireless network from their residence halls, as well as the library, dining room, lounges, and laundry rooms. There are 37 computer labs and clusters with a total of 566 for student access. Internet 2 is available to all students to share resources with other Internet 2 institutions. All students may access the system. There are no time limits and no fees. It is strongly recommended that all students have a personal computer.

Graduates: From July 1, 2004 to June 30, 2005, 1084 bachelor's degrees were awarded. The most popular majors were business (21%), communications (17%), and psychology (13%). In an average class,

68% graduate in 4 years or less, 76% graduate in 5 years or less, and 76% graduate in 6 years or less. 200 companies recruited on campus in 2004-2005. Of the 2004 graduating class, 26% were enrolled in graduate school within 6 months of graduation and 77% were employed.

Admissions Contact: Sean P. Kaylor, Vice President of Admissions and Enrollment. E-mail: *admissions@marist.edu* Web: *www.marist.edu*

MARYMOUNT MANHATTAN COLLEGE   D-5

New York, NY 10021
(212) 517-0555
(800) 627-9668; Fax: (212) 517-0448

Full-time: 394 men, 1209 women	**Faculty:** 86; IIB, av$
Part-time: 58 men, 346 women	**Ph.D.s:** 80%
Graduate: none	**Student/Faculty:** 19 to 1
Year: semesters, summer session	**Tuition:** $18,529
Application Deadline: open	**Room & Board:** $11,520
Freshman Class: 2031 applied, 1567 accepted, 432 enrolled	
SAT Verbal/Math: 550/510*	**VERY COMPETITIVE**

Marymount Manhattan College is an urban, independent liberal arts college, offering programs in the arts and sciences for all ages, as well as substantial preprofessional preparation. The library contains 75,000 volumes, 70 microform items, and 4000 audio/video tapes/CDs/DVDs, and subscribes to 2740 periodicals including electronic. Computerized library services include the card catalog, interlibrary loans, database searching, Internet access, and laptop Internet portals. Special learning facilities include a learning resource center, art gallery, radio station, TV station, and communication arts multimedia suite featuring digital editing technology. The 1-acre campus is in an urban area in Manhattan. Including any residence halls, there are 3 buildings.

Student Life: 50% of undergraduates are from New York. Others are from 44 states, 31 foreign countries, and Canada. 57% are from public schools. 61% are white; 12% African American; 11% Hispanic. The average age of freshmen is 18; all undergraduates, 24. 27% do not continue beyond their first year; 45% remain to graduate.

Housing: 717 students can be accommodated in college housing, which includes single-sex and coed dorms and off-campus apartments. On-campus housing is available on a first-come, first-served basis and is available on a lottery system for upperclassmen. Priority is given to out-of-town students. 55% of students commute. Alcohol is not permitted. All students may keep cars.

Activities: Tthere are 2 national sororities. There are no fraternities. There are 29 groups on campus, including academic, art, choir, comedy, computers, dance, drama, ethnic, feminist, film, gay, honors, international, leadership, literary magazine, musical theater, newspaper, photography, political, professional, radio and TV, religious, social, social service, and student government. Popular campus events include Strawberry Festival, honors day, and Holiday Soiree.

Sports: There are 3 intramural sports for men and 3 for women.

Disabled Students: All of the campus is accessible. Wheelchair ramps, elevators, specially equipped rest rooms, special class scheduling, and lowered drinking fountains are available.

Services: Counseling and information services are available, as is tutoring in every subject. There is remedial math, reading, and writing.

Campus Safety and Security: Measures include 24-hour foot and vehicle patrol, self-defense education, shuttle buses, and informal discussions. There are pamphlets/posters/films, lighted pathways/sidewalks, security cameras, and photo ID check-in.

Programs of Study: MMC confers B.A., B.S., and B.F.A. degrees. Associate degrees are also awarded. Bachelor's degrees are awarded in BIOLOGICAL SCIENCE (biology/biological science), BUSINESS (accounting and business administration and management), COMMUNICATIONS AND THE ARTS (communications, dance, dramatic arts, English, and fine arts), COMPUTER AND PHYSICAL SCIENCE (information sciences and systems), EDUCATION (elementary), HEALTH PROFESSIONS (premedicine and speech pathology/audiology), SOCIAL SCIENCE (history, international studies, liberal arts/general studies, political science/government, psychology, and sociology). Theater, communications, and business, are the strongest academically.

Required: To graduate, students must complete 120 credit hours, including 31 to 71 in the major, with a minimum GPA of 2.0. The core plus shared curriculum totals 48 credits in the areas of critical thinking, psychology and philosophy, quantitative reasoning and science, the modern world, communications/language, and the arts.

Special: MMC offers study abroad, interdisciplinary courses, pass/fail options, nondegree study, credit for life experience, and some 250 internships in all majors. Cooperative programs in business and finance, dance, music, languages, nursing, and urban education are offered in conjunction with local colleges and institutes. There is a January minisession, cross-registration with Hunter College and the China Institute, and a 5-year masters in publishing with Pace University. There are 7 national honor societies and 5 departmental honors programs.

Faculty/Classroom: 42% of faculty are male; 58%, female. 65% teach undergraduates and 35% both teach and do research. The average class size in an introductory lecture is 25; in a laboratory, 15; and in a regular course, 20.

Admissions: 77% of the 2005-2006 applicants were accepted. The SAT scores for the 2005-2006 freshman class were: Verbal--26% below 500, 47% between 500 and 599, 23% between 600 and 700, and 4% above 700; Math--40% below 500, 44% between 500 and 599, and 16% between 600 and 700. The ACT scores were 25% below 21, 18% between 21 and 23, 50% between 24 and 26, and 7% between 27 and 28.

Requirements: The SAT or ACT is required. In addition, applicants should be graduates of an accredited secondary school or have a GED certificate. MMC recommends completion of 16 academic units, including 4 each in English and electives, and 3 each in language, math, social science, and science. Recommendations are required, and an interview is strongly advised. Applicants to the dance and acting programs must audition. A GPA of 2.5 is required. AP and CLEP credits are accepted. Important factors in the admissions decision are personality/intangible qualities, evidence of special talent, and leadership record.

Procedure: Freshmen are admitted to all sessions. Entrance exams should be taken as early as possible. There are rolling admissions, early decision, early admissions, and deferred admissions plans. Early decision applications should be filed by November 1; regular applications, by open for fall entry and open for spring entry. Notification of early decision is sent December 15; regular decision, on a rolling basis. 12 early decision candidates were accepted for the 2005-2006 class. Applications are accepted on-line.

Transfer: 129 transfer students enrolled in 2004-2005. Applicants who have graduated from high school less then 5 years ago must meet standard freshman requirements and must submit official transcripts from all colleges attended. 30 of 120 credits required for the bachelor's degree must be completed at MMC.

Visiting: There are regularly scheduled orientations for prospective students, including an interview with an admissions counselor, a tour of the school and dorms, and a meeting with a financial aid adviser. There are guides for informal visits and visitors may sit in on classes. To schedule a visit, contact the Admissions Office.

Financial Aid: In 2005-2006, 87% of all full-time freshmen and 76% of continuing full-time students received some form of financial aid. 67% of full-time freshmen and 60% of continuing full-time students received need-based aid. The average freshman award was $11,697. Need-based scholarships or need-based grants averaged $7998 ($17,550 maximum); need-based self-help aid (loans and jobs) averaged $5534 ($15,625 maximum); and other non-need-based awards and non-need-based scholarships averaged $6715 ($33,149 maximum). 75% of undergraduates work part time. Average annual earnings from campus work are $2940. The average financial indebtedness of the 2005 graduate was $29,706. The FAFSA and TAP (for New York state residents) are required. The deadline for filing freshman financial aid applications for fall entry is March 15.

International Students: There are 39 international students enrolled. The school actively recruits these students. They must score satisfactorily on the written TOEFL or on the electronic version.

Computers: There are 2 PC labs with 22 stations each in the main building, and 1 PC lab for general use in the library. There are specialized computer labs for communications students and arts students. Wireless access is available in the library and in the Nugent building. There are 100 laptops in the library that can be used to access the Internet. All students may access the system. There are no time limits. The fee is $140 per semester.

Graduates: From July 1, 2004 to June 30, 2005, 439 bachelor's degrees were awarded. The most popular majors were communication arts (26%), theater/acting (22%), and business (10%). In an average class, 33% graduate in 4 years or less, 43% graduate in 5 years or less, and 45% graduate in 6 years or less. 37 companies recruited on campus in 2004-2005. Of the 2004 graduating class, 23% were enrolled in graduate school within 6 months of graduation and 63% were employed.

Admissions Contact: James Rogers, Dean of Admissions. E-mail: *admissions@mmm.edu* Web: *www.mmm.edu*

MEDAILLE COLLEGE   C-1

Buffalo, NY 14214
(716) 884-3281
(800) 292-1582; Fax: (716) 884-0291

Full-time: 500 men, 1000 women	**Faculty:** 60; IIB, -$
Part-time: 40 men, 100 women	**Ph.D.s:** 66%
Graduate: 200 men, 400 women	**Student/Faculty:** 25 to 1
Year: semesters, summer session	**Tuition:** $14,000
Application Deadline: see profile	**Room & Board:** $7,000
Freshman Class: n/av	
SAT: required	**COMPETITIVE**

Medaille College, founded in 1875, is a private, nonsectarian institution offering undergraduate programs in liberal arts, education, business, and sciences, and graduate programs in business and education, to a primarily commuter student body. Figures in the above and in this profile are approximate. The library contains 55,950 volumes and 2309 audio/video tapes/CDs/DVDs, and subscribes to 228 periodicals including electronic. Computerized library services include the card catalog, interlibrary loans, and database searching. Special learning facilities include a learning resource center, radio station, TV station, and a media institute. The 13-acre campus is in an urban area 3 miles from downtown Buffalo. Including any residence halls, there are 17 buildings.

Student Life: 91% of undergraduates are from New York. Others are from 12 states, 2 foreign countries, and Canada. 67% are white; 15% foreign nationals; 13% African American. The average age of freshmen is 20; all undergraduates, 26. 30% do not continue beyond their first year; 39% remain to graduate.

Housing: 450 students can be accommodated in college housing, which includes single-sex and coed dorms, on-campus apartments, and off-campus apartments. On-campus housing is guaranteed for all 4 years. 82% of students commute. All students may keep cars.

Activities: There are no fraternities or sororities. There are 16 groups on campus, including academic clubs, art, cheerleading, ethnic, honors, literary magazine, newspaper, photography, professional, radio and TV, social, student government, and yearbook. Popular campus events include Founders Day, Silent Auction, and Honors Convocation.

Sports: There are 5 intercollegiate sports for men and 6 for women, and 3 intramural sports for men and 3 for women. Facilities include an NCAA regulation gym located in the student center, and a softball and soccer field.

Disabled Students: All of the campus is accessible. Wheelchair ramps, elevators, special parking, specially equipped rest rooms, lowered drinking fountains, and lowered telephones are available.

Services: Counseling and information services are available, as is tutoring in most subjects. There is a reader service for the blind, and remedial math, reading, and writing.

Campus Safety and Security: Measures include 24-hour foot and vehicle patrol, self-defense education, security escort services, and shuttle buses. There are informal discussions, pamphlets/posters/films, emergency telephones, and lighted pathways/sidewalks.

Programs of Study: Medaille confers B.A., B.S., B.B.A., and B.S.Ed. degrees. Associate and master's degrees are also awarded. Bachelor's degrees are awarded in BIOLOGICAL SCIENCE (biology/biological science), BUSINESS (banking and finance, business administration and management, human resources, and sports management), COMMUNICATIONS AND THE ARTS (communications and visual and performing arts), COMPUTER AND PHYSICAL SCIENCE (information sciences and systems), EDUCATION (elementary), HEALTH PROFESSIONS (veterinary science), SOCIAL SCIENCE (child care/child and family studies, criminal justice, human services, humanities, liberal arts/general studies, political science/government, psychology, and social science). Psychology and humanities are the strongest academically. Education, business administration, and veterinary technology are the largest.

Required: The bachelor's degree requires successful completion of 120 credit hours or 128 for elementary education and biology majors. In addition to specific course requirements for each major, students must maintain a minimum GPA of 2.0. 5 theme areas must be satisfied: Theme I - Self and Others; Theme II - Global Perspectives; Theme III - Creative Expression; Theme IV - Science, Technology, and Environment; and Theme V - Communication. Students must also complete 6 credits in capstone courses.

Special: Cross-registration is available with colleges in the Western New York Consortium. Most degree programs require internships. Opportunities are provided for student-designed majors, credit by exam, pass/fail options, accelerated degrees, dual majors, and credit for work experience. The 2-year veterinary technology program combined with additional liberal arts and sciences courses leads to the B.S. in liberal studies degree. A modular program of evening courses, as well as Weekend College classes, enable students to maintain full-time status by attending classes either 2 nights a week or on weekends. There are 2 national honor societies, and a freshman honors program.

Faculty/Classroom: 63% of faculty are male; 37%, female. 95% teach undergraduates and 31% both teach and do research. No introductory courses are taught by graduate students. The average class size in an introductory lecture is 20; in a laboratory, 10; and in a regular course, 14.

Admissions: 66% of recent applicants were accepted. 19% of recent freshmen were in the top fifth of their class; 62% were in the top two fifths.

Requirements: The SAT is required. In addition, applicants must be graduates of an accredited secondary school or hold the GED. An essay and an interview are required. A grade average of 70 is required. AP and CLEP credits are accepted. Important factors in the admissions decision are advanced placement or honor courses, personality/intangible qualities, and leadership record.

Procedure: Freshmen are admitted to all sessions. Entrance exams should be taken in May. There is a deferred admissions plan and rolling admissions plan. Check with the school for current application deadlines and fee. Notification is sent on a rolling basis. Applications are accepted on-line.

Transfer: 252 transfer students enrolled in a recent year. Transfer applicants must have a minimum GPA of 2.0 in their previous college work. An interview and recommendations are required. 30 of 120 credits required for the bachelor's degree must be completed at Medaille.

Visiting: There are regularly scheduled orientations for prospective students, including campus tours, academic program meetings, icebreakers, and a review of policies and procedures. There are guides for informal visits and visitors may sit in on classes and stay overnight. To schedule a visit, contact Jacqueline S. Matheny at jmatheny@medaille.edu.

Financial Aid: In a recent year, 95% of all full-time freshmen and 93% of continuing full-time students received some form of financial aid. 85% of all full-time students received need-based aid. The average freshman award was $11,500. 15% of undergraduates work part time. Average annual earnings from campus work are $1500. The average financial indebtedness of a recent graduate was $18,500. Medaille is a member of CSS. The FAFSA and the college's own financial statement are required. Check with school for current deadlines.

International Students: There are 230 international students enrolled in a recent year. They must take the TOEFL and also take the SAT.

Computers: All students may access the system. There are no time limits and no fees.

Graduates: In a recent year, 394 bachelor's degrees were awarded. The most popular majors were elementary teacher education (54%), business administration (25%), and liberal studies (8%). In an average class, 30% graduate in 4 years or less, 38% graduate in 5 years or less, and 39% graduate in 6 years or less. 65 companies recruited on campus in a recent year. Of a recent graduating class, 20% were enrolled in graduate school within 6 months of graduation and 95% were employed.

Admissions Contact: Jacqueline S. Matheny, Director Enrollment Management. E-mail: jmatheny@medaille.edu Web: www.medaille.edu

MERCY COLLEGE
D-5

Dobbs Ferry, NY 10522-1189

(914) 693-7600
(800)MERCY NY; Fax: (914) 674-7382

Full-time: 1300 men, 2900 women	**Faculty:** 125; IIA, +$
Part-time: 600 men, 1700 women	**Ph.D.s:** 75%
Graduate: 800 men, 2200 women	**Student/Faculty:** 33 to 1
Year: semesters, summer session	**Tuition:** $11,000
Application Deadline: open	**Room & Board:** $9000
Freshman Class: n/av	
SAT or ACT: recommended	**NONCOMPETITIVE**

Mercy College, founded in 1950, is a private institution offering programs in liberal arts, business, and health science. Figures in above capsule and in this profile are approximate. In addition to regional accreditation, Mercy has baccalaureate program accreditation with AACSB, ACOTE, CAPTE, CCNE, CSWE, and NLN. The 8 libraries contain 304,212 volumes and 28,105 microform items, and subscribe to 2099 periodicals including electronic. Computerized library services include the card catalog, interlibrary loans, database searching, and Internet access. Special learning facilities include a learning resource center, radio station, TV station, computer lab, reference library, and a digital arts center. The 60-acre campus is in a suburban area 12 miles north of New York City. Including any residence halls, there are 10 buildings.

Student Life: 97% of undergraduates are from New York. Others are from 14 states, 100 foreign countries, and Canada. 95% are from public schools. 29% are white; 25% Hispanic; 24% African American. The average age of freshmen is 19; all undergraduates, 29. 25% do not continue beyond their first year; 60% remain to graduate.

Housing: 165 students can be accommodated in college housing, which includes coed dorms. On-campus housing is guaranteed for all 4 years. 99% of students commute. Alcohol is not permitted. All students may keep cars.

Activities: There are no fraternities or sororities. There are 19 groups on campus, including chess, computers, drama, ethnic, film, gay, honors, international, literary magazine, mentoring program, newspaper, political, professional, radio and TV, religious, social, social service, student government and veterinary club. Popular campus events include Presidential Lecture Series, Hudson Valley Lecture Series, and Open Houses.

Sports: There are 6 intercollegiate sports for men and 5 for women. Facilities include a gym, a soccer/baseball field, 3 swimming pools, 2 tennis courts, a track, and a basketball court.

Disabled Students: 75% of the campus is accessible. Wheelchair ramps, elevators, special parking, specially equipped rest rooms, special class scheduling, and lowered drinking fountains are available.

Services: Counseling and information services are available, as is tutoring in every subject. There is a reader service for the blind, and remedial math, reading, and writing.

Campus Safety and Security: Measures include 24-hour foot and vehicle patrol and lighted pathways/sidewalks.

Programs of Study: Mercy confers B.A. and B.S. degrees. Associate and master's degrees are also awarded. Bachelor's degrees are awarded in BIOLOGICAL SCIENCE (biology/biological science), BUSINESS (accounting and business administration and management), COMMUNICATIONS AND THE ARTS (English, journalism, and music), COMPUTER AND PHYSICAL SCIENCE (computer science, information sciences and systems, and mathematics), EDUCATION (education of the deaf and hearing impaired, elementary, special, and teaching English as a second/foreign language (TESOL/TEFOL)), HEALTH PROFESSIONS (medical laboratory technology, nursing, recreation therapy, and veterinary science), SOCIAL SCIENCE (behavioral science, criminal justice, history, interdisciplinary studies, paralegal studies, political science/government, psychology, social work, and sociology). The health professions programs is the strongest academically. Business and education are the largest.

Required: To graduate, students must complete 120 semester hours with a minimum GPA of 2.0 overall and in the major. Distribution requirements include 12 credits each of math/natural science and philosophy/language/fine arts, 9 of social science, 6 each of English and history, and 3 of speech.

Special: Mercy offers internships in each major, co-op programs in education, work-study programs through the Westchester Employee Association, study abroad, dual majors and degrees, credit for life experience, nondegree study, and pass/fail options. There are 14 national honor societies, including Phi Beta Kappa, a freshman honors program, and 14 departmental honors programs.

Faculty/Classroom: 98% teach undergraduates and 5% do research. No introductory courses are taught by graduate students. The average class size in an introductory lecture is 15; in a laboratory, 12; and in a regular course, 14.

Admissions: All applicants are accepted. There is an open admissions policy.

Requirements: The SAT or ACT is recommended. In addition, applicants must be graduates of an accredited secondary school or have a GED certificate. They should have completed at least 16 academic units. An interview is required and a letter of recommendation from the high school counselor or principal is required. Art students must submit a portfolio; music students must audition. AP and CLEP credits are accepted.

Procedure: Freshmen are admitted to all sessions. Entrance exams should be taken between January and August of the senior year. There are early decision, early admissions, and deferred admissions plans. There is a rolling admissions plan. Application deadlines are open. Check with the school for current application deadlines and fee. Applications are accepted on-line.

Transfer: Applicants must submit official transcripts from all colleges attended. Students with fewer than 15 college credits must also submit their high school transcripts. An interview is required. 30 of 120 credits required for the bachelor's degree must be completed at Mercy.

Visiting: There are regularly scheduled orientations for prospective students, including spring and fall open houses and information sessions. There are guides for informal visits. To schedule a visit, contact the Admissions Office at admissions@mercy.edu.

Financial Aid: Mercy is a member of CSS. The FAFSA is required. Check with the school for current deadlines.

International Students: There were 208 international students enrolled in a recent year. The school actively recruits these students. They must take the TOEFL and also take the college's own entrance exam.

Computers: All students may access the system. There are no time limits. The fee is $75.

Graduates: 150 companies recruited on campus in a recent year.

Admissions Contact: Marie A. Noblitt, Vice President for Enrollment Management. Web: www.mercy.edu

METROPOLITAN COLLEGE OF NEW YORK
(Formerly Audrey Cohen College)

D-5

New York, NY 10013

(212) 343-1234, ext. 5001
(800) 33-THINK; Fax: (212) 343-8470

Full-time: 300 men, 1000 women	Faculty: 36
Part-time: none	Ph.D.s: 70%
Graduate: 60 men, 300 women	Student/Faculty: 36 to 1
Year: trimesters, summer session	Tuition: $16,000
Application Deadline: see profile	Room & Board: n/app
Freshman Class: n/av	
SAT or ACT: not required	COMPETITIVE

Metropolitan College of New York, formerly Audrey Cohen College, founded in 1964, is a private institution offering programs in human services and business management. The college operates on a 3-semester calendar, including a complete summer semester. All bachelor's degree programs involve a combination of class work and field work and may be completed in 2 years and 8 months. Masters degree programs can be completed in 1 year. There are 2 undergraduate and 2 graduate schools. Figures in the above capsule and in this profile are approximate. Figures in the above capsule and in this profile are approximate. The library

contains 32,000 volumes and 1800 microform items, and subscribes to 3300 periodicals including electronic. Computerized library services include the card catalog, interlibrary loans, database searching, and Internet access. Special learning facilities include a learning resource center. The campus is in an urban area in New York City. There is 1 building.

Student Life: 95% of undergraduates are from New York. Students are from 4 states, 9 foreign countries, and Canada. 68% are from public schools. 61% are African American; 21% Hispanic. The average age of freshmen is 32; all undergraduates, 32. 30% do not continue beyond their first year; 41% remain to graduate.

Housing: There are no residence halls. All of students commute. Alcohol is not permitted.

Activities: There are no fraternities or sororities. There are 10 groups on campus, including computers, ethnic, gay, honors, newspaper, professional, social, social service, student government, and yearbook. Popular campus events include career fairs, admissions open house, and dean's list ceremonies.

Sports: There is no sports program at the college.

Disabled Students: All of the campus is accessible. Wheelchair ramps, elevators, specially equipped rest rooms, special class scheduling, lowered drinking fountains, and lowered telephones are available.

Services: Counseling and information services are available, as is tutoring in every subject. There is remedial math, reading, and writing.

Campus Safety and Security: Measures include 24-hour foot and vehicle patrol, pamphlets/posters/films, lighted pathways/sidewalks, fire drills, and a fire escape stairwell.

Programs of Study: The college confers B.B.A. and B.P.S. degrees. Associate and master's degrees are also awarded. Bachelor's degrees are awarded in BUSINESS (business administration and management), EDUCATION (early childhood), HEALTH PROFESSIONS (mental health/human services), SOCIAL SCIENCE (child care/child and family studies, community services, gerontology, human services, prelaw, psychology, and social work). Business management is the strongest academically. Human services is the largest.

Required: To graduate, students must complete 128 credit hours with a minimum GPA of 2.0. The curriculum is prescribed and no electives are featured. A constructive action document based on performance in the field and mastery of course work is required each semester.

Special: Internships, which include required weekly 14-hour field sites, study abroad in 3 countries, work-study programs, B.A.- B.S. degrees and accelerated degree programs in human services and business management, credit by exam, and credit for life experience are offered.

Faculty/Classroom: 72% of faculty are male; 28%, female. 95% teach undergraduates. No introductory courses are taught by graduate students. The average class size in an introductory lecture is 25; in a laboratory, 18; and in a regular course, 20.

Admissions: 71% of recent applicants were accepted.

Requirements: Students must take the Test of Adult Basic Education (TABE) in English, reading, and math; recent high school graduates who have satisfactory composite SAT scores may present the SAT instead. Applicants must have graduated from an accredited secondary school. The GED is accepted. An essay and an interview are required. CLEP credit is accepted. Important factors in the admissions decision are evidence of special talent, leadership record, and personality/intangible qualities.

Procedure: Freshmen are admitted to all sessions. Entrance exams should be taken in the senior year. There is a rolling admissioms plan. Check with the school for current application deadlines and fee. Notification is sent on a rolling basis. Applications are accepted on-line.

Transfer: 90 transfer students enrolled ina recent year. Admission is based on current skills and abilities as measured on the entrance exam and essay. 64 of 128 credits required for the bachelor's degree must be completed at the college.

Visiting: There are regularly scheduled orientations for prospective students. There are guides for informal visits and visitors may sit in on classes. To schedule a visit, contact the Admissions Office admissions@metropolitan.edu.

Financial Aid: In a recent year, 84% of all full-time freshmen and 85% of continuing full-time students received some form of financial aid. The average freshman award was $19,001. The CSS Profile, FAFSA, and the New York State Higher Education Financial statement. are required. Check with the school for current deadlines.

International Students: They must take the TOEFL and also take the TABE.

Computers: All students may access the system whenever the college is open. There are no time limits. The fee is $75. It is strongly recommended that all students have a personal computer.

Graduates: In a recent year,281 bachelor's degrees were awarded. In an average class, 41% graduate in 4 years or less. 55 companies recruited on campus in a recent year. Of a recent graduating class, 50% were enrolled in graduate school within 6 months of graduation and 85% were employed.

Admissions Contact: Sharon Handelsman, Director of Admissions and Recruitment. E-mail: shandelsman@metropolitan.edu
Web: www.metropolitan.edu

MOLLOY COLLEGE   D-5
Rockville Centre, NY 11570   **(516) 678-5000**
                                          (888) 466-5569; Fax: (516) 256-2247

Full-time: 461 men, 1406 women	**Faculty:** IIB, av$
Part-time: 115 men, 607 women	**Ph.Ds:** 28%
Graduate: 131 men, 722 women	**Student/Faculty:** n/av
Year: semesters, summer session	**Tuition:** $16,510
Application Deadline: open	**Room & Board:** n/app
Freshman Class: 1093 applied, 705 accepted, 294 enrolled	
SAT Verbal/Math: 505/518*	**COMPETITIVE**

Molloy College, founded in 1955 in the Catholic and Dominican tradition, is an independent commuter college. It offers programs in liberal arts and sciences, business, nursing and health professions, social work, teacher certification, and preprofessional studies. In addition to regional accreditation, Molloy has baccalaureate program accreditation with CSWE and NLN. The library contains 110,000 volumes, 13,850 microform items, and 3170 audio/video tapes/CDs/DVDs, and subscribes to 720 periodicals including electronic. Computerized library services include the card catalog, interlibrary loans, database searching, and Internet access. Special learning facilities include a learning resource center, art gallery, and TV station. The 30-acre campus is in a suburban area 20 miles east of New York City. There are 4 buildings.

Student Life: 98% of undergraduates are from New York. Others are from 1 state and 9 foreign countries. 66% are from public schools. 65% are white; 20% African American. 66% are Catholic; 7% Protestant; 6% claim no religious affiliation. The average age of freshmen is 18; all undergraduates, 24. 18% do not continue beyond their first year; 57% remain to graduate.

Housing: There are no residence halls. All of students commute. Alcohol is not permitted. All students may keep cars.

Activities: There are no fraternities or sororities. There are 23 groups on campus, including band, cheerleading, choir, chorus, dance, drama, ethnic, honors, international, jazz band, literary magazine, musical theater, newspaper, professional, radio and TV, religious, social, social service, and student government. Popular campus events include Senior 55 Nights Party, Junior Ring Night, and Box Town.

Sports: There are 6 intercollegiate sports for men and 8 for women. Facilities include a gym, a dance studio, a weight room, sports fields, and basketball and tennis courts.

Disabled Students: All of the campus is accessible. Wheelchair ramps, elevators, special parking, specially equipped rest rooms, special class scheduling, lowered drinking fountains, and lowered telephones are available.

Services: Counseling and information services are available, as is tutoring in every subject. There is a reader service for the blind, and remedial math, reading, and writing.

Campus Safety and Security: Measures include 24-hour foot and vehicle patrol, security escort services, pamphlets/posters/films, and emergency telephones. There are lighted pathways/sidewalks and a Campus Concerns Committee.

Programs of Study: Molloy confers B.A., B.S., and B.F.A. degrees. Associate and master's degrees are also awarded. Bachelor's degrees are awarded in BIOLOGICAL SCIENCE (biology/biological science), BUSINESS (accounting and business administration and management), COMMUNICATIONS AND THE ARTS (art, communications, English, music, and Spanish), COMPUTER AND PHYSICAL SCIENCE (computer science, information sciences and systems, and mathematics), EDUCATION (elementary, secondary, and special), ENGINEERING AND ENVIRONMENTAL DESIGN (environmental science), HEALTH PROFESSIONS (music therapy, nursing, and speech pathology/audiology), SOCIAL SCIENCE (criminal justice, gerontology, history, interdisciplinary studies, peace studies, philosophy, political science/government, psychology, social work, sociology, and theological studies). Nursing, education, and social work are the strongest academically. Nursing, business, and psychology are the largest.

Required: General Education requirements consist of 45 to 54 credits. A total of 128 to 137 credit hours is required for graduation.

Special: Students may cross-register with 16 area colleges. The college offers internships, a Washington semester, study abroad, and dual and student-designed majors. Credit by examination and for life, military, and work experience, nondegree study, and pass/fail options are available. There are 15 national honor societies, and a freshman honors program.

Faculty/Classroom: 32% of faculty are male; 68%, female. 91% teach undergraduates and 25% do research. No introductory courses are taught by graduate students. The average class size in an introductory lecture is 27; in a laboratory, 15; and in a regular course, 18.

Admissions: 65% of the 2005-2006 applicants were accepted. The SAT scores for the 2005-2006 freshman class were: Verbal--38% below 500, 47% between 500 and 599, 14% between 600 and 700, and 1% above 700; Math--37% below 500, 46% between 500 and 599, 15% between 600 and 700, and 2% above 700. 48% of the current freshmen were in the top fifth of their class; 65% were in the top two fifths.

Requirements: The SAT or ACT is required, the SAT is preferred. Applicants should be graduates of a secondary school or have a GED. Preparation should include 4 years of English, 3 each of math and history, and 2 each of foreign language and science. An essay is required, and an interview is recommended. Music students must audition and take a theory exam. A GPA of 80.0 is required. AP and CLEP credits are accepted. Important factors in the admissions decision are advanced placement or honor courses, recommendations by school officials, and extracurricular activities record.

Procedure: Freshmen are admitted fall and spring. Entrance exams should be taken in the fall of the senior year. There are early decision and deferred admissions plans. There is a rolling admissions plan. Application deadlines are open. Application fee is $30. Applications are accepted on-line.

Transfer: 499 transfer students enrolled in a recent year. A minimum college GPA of 2.0 is required, with some majors requiring a higher GPA. An interview is recommended. 30 of 128 to 137 credits required for the bachelor's degree must be completed at Molloy.

Visiting: There are regularly scheduled orientations for prospective students, including an address by the president of the college, department presentations, campus tours, and admissions, financial aid, and scholarship information. There are guides for informal visits and visitors may sit in on classes. To schedule a visit, contact the Admissions Office.

Financial Aid: 6% of undergraduates work part time. Molloy is a member of CSS. The FAFSA is required. The priority date for freshman financial aid applications for fall entry is April 15. The deadline for filing freshman financial aid applications for fall entry is May 1.

International Students: There were 19 international students enrolled in a recent year. They must score satisfactorily on the written TOEFL and also take the college's own entrance exam.

Computers: Wireless access is available. All students may access the system. There are no time limits and no fees.

Graduates: 459 bachelor's degrees were awarded in a recent year. The most popular majors were nursing (29%), psychology (15%), and business (8%). In an average class, 42% graduate in 4 years or less, 55% graduate in 5 years or less, and 57% graduate in 6 years or less. 70 companies recruited on campus in a recent year.

Admissions Contact: Marguerite Lane, Director of Admissions. E-mail: *mlane@molloy.edu* Web: *www.molloy.edu*

MONROE COLLEGE   D-5
Bronx, NY 10468   **(718) 933-6700**
                                          (800) 55 MONROE; Fax: (718) 364-3552

Full-time: 1400 men, 3500 women	**Faculty:** 300
Part-time: 150 men, 400 women	**Ph.D.s:** n/av
Graduate: none	**Student/Faculty:** n/av
Year: trimesters, summer session	**Tuition:** $9760
Application Deadline: August 15	**Room & Board:** $6200
Freshman Class: n/av	
SAT: recommended	**LESS COMPETITIVE**

Monroe College, founded in 1933, offers bachelor's degrees in accounting, business management, computer information systems, criminal justice, hospitality management, and health services administration. Enrollment and faculty figures in the above capsule and in this profile are approximate. Computerized library services include interlibrary loans, database searching, Internet access, and laptop Internet portals. Special learning facilities include a learning resource center. The Bronx campus is located in the Fordham Road section of the Bronx. The New Rochelle campus is located on Main Street in New Rochelle. Including any residence halls, there are 5 buildings on the Bronx campus and 16 buildings on the New Rochelle campus.

Student Life: 96% of undergraduates are from New York. 46% are African American (including West Indies); 42% Hispanic. The average age of freshmen is 23; all undergraduates, 26.

Housing: 620 students can be accommodated in college housing, which includes single-sex and coed dormitories and off-campus apartments. In addition, there are honors houses. On-campus housing is guaranteed for all 4 years. 90% of students commute. All students may keep cars.

Activities: There are no fraternities or sororities. There are some groups and organizations on campus, including cheerleading, computers, dance, drama, honors, literary magazine, newspaper, professional, and social service. Popular campus events include talent shows, President's and Deans' List Galas, and cultural trips to New York City.

Sports: There are 4 intercollegiate sports for men and 4 for women.

Disabled Students: All of the campus is accessible. Wheelchair ramps, elevators, special parking, specially equipped rest rooms, special class scheduling, lowered drinking fountains, lowered telephones, and special housing are available.

Services: Counseling and information services are available, as is tutoring in every subject. There is a reader service for the blind, and remedial math, reading, and writing.

Campus Safety and Security: Measures include 24-hour foot and vehicle patrol, self-defense education, security escort services, and shuttle buses. There are informal discussions, pamphlets/posters/films, emergency telephones, and lighted pathways/sidewalks.

Programs of Study: Monroe College confers B.S. and B.B.A. degrees. Associate and master's degrees are also awarded. Bachelor's degrees are awarded in BUSINESS (accounting, business administration and management, and hospitality management services), COMPUTER AND PHYSICAL SCIENCE (information sciences and systems), HEALTH PROFESSIONS (health care administration), SOCIAL SCIENCE (criminal justice). Business management, criminal justice, and health services administration are the largest.

Required: To graduate, students must have 120 credit hours and at least a 2.0 GPA. The core curriculum includes courses in writing/literature, math, liberal arts, and business or technology.

Special: Co-op programs are available in all degree programs. Study abroad is available for culinary students interested in studying in Italy. There is 1 national honor society, a freshman honors program, and 1 departmental honors program.

Faculty/Classroom: All teach undergraduates. The average class size in an introductory lecture is 30.

Requirements: The SAT is recommended. In addition, an application, an essay, and an interview are required. Monroe College requires applicants to be in the upper 50% of their class. A GPA of 70.0 is required. AP and CLEP credits are accepted.

Procedure: Freshmen are admitted fall, winter, and spring. There is an early decision and rolling admissions plans. Early decision applications should be filed by February 1; regular applications, by August 15 for fall entry, January 5 for winter entry, and April 15 for spring entry. Notification is sent on a rolling basis. The fall 2005 application fee was $35.

Transfer: Transfer students must provide an official transcript from any prior institution they have attended in addition to the application and an essay. 30 of 120 credits required for the bachelor's degree must be completed at Monroe College.

Visiting: There are regularly scheduled orientations for prospective students, including a variety of open houses during the semester in which applicants can tour the campus and talk with faculty and/or chairs of individual departments. There are guides for informal visits and visitors may sit in on classes and stay overnight. To schedule a visit, contact Evan Jerome (Bronx) or Emerson Phillips (New Rochelle).

Financial Aid: The FAFSA, the state aid form and the college's own financial statement are required. Check with the school for current application deadlines.

International Students: There are 464 international students enrolled. The school actively recruits these students. They must take the MELAB, the Comprehensive English Language Test, or the college's own test.

Computers: Wireless access is available. There are a number of learning centers, libraries, and classrooms at both the Bronx and New Rochelle campuses where students have free use of more than 300 computers. Most of these computers have Internet access as well as access to the college's network. All students may access the system. There are no time limits and no fees.

Graduates: 70 companies recruited on campus in 2004-2005. Of the 2004 graduating class, 92% were employed within 6 months of graduation.

Admissions Contact: Evan Jerome, Director of Admissions. A video is available. E-mail: *admissions@monroecollege.edu*
Web: *monroecollege.edu*

MOUNT SAINT MARY COLLEGE D-4
Newburgh, NY 12550

(845) 569-3248
(888) YES-MSMC; Fax: (845) 562-6762

Full-time: 426 men, 1189 women	Faculty: 71; IIB, av$
Part-time: 127 men, 297 women	Ph.D.s: 82%
Graduate: 104 men, 431 women	Student/Faculty: 23 to 1
Year: semesters, summer session	Tuition: $16,930
Application Deadline: open	Room & Board: $8320
Freshman Class: 1625 applied, 1285 accepted, 360 enrolled	
SAT: required	ACT: required COMPETITIVE

MSMC founded in 1959, is a private liberal arts college offering undergraduate programs leading to Bachelor of Arts and Bachelor of Science degrees, and graduate programs leading to the masters in education, nursing, and business administration. An accelerated evening program is offered for non-traditional and adult students. In addition to regional accreditation, the Mount has baccalaureate program accreditation with CCNE and NCATE. The 2 libraries contain 113,676 volumes, 713,375 microform items, and 4164 audio/video tapes/CDs/DVDs, and subscribe to 870 periodicals including electronic. Computerized library services include the card catalog, interlibrary loans, database searching, and Internet access. Special learning facilities include a learning resource center, radio station, TV station, an elementary school, an herbarium field station, and an arboretum. The 70-acre campus is in a suburban area 58 miles north of New York City. Including any residence halls, there are 41 buildings.

Student Life: 88% of undergraduates are from New York. Others are from 18 states and 1 foreign countries. 50% are from public schools. 80% are white. 57% are Catholic; 10% claim no religious affiliation. The average age of freshmen is 18; all undergraduates, 24. 30% do not continue beyond their first year; 60% remain to graduate.

Housing: 834 students can be accommodated in college housing, which includes single-sex dormitories and on-campus townhouses. On-campus housing is guaranteed for all 4 years. 63% of students commute. Upperclassmen may keep cars.

Activities: There are no fraternities or sororities. There are 24 groups on campus, including art, choir, computers, dance, drama, ethnic, honors, literary magazine, musical theater, newspaper, photography, political, professional, radio and TV, religious, social, student government, and yearbook. Popular campus events include Octoberfest, Siblings Weekend, and Hoiliday Formal.

Sports: There are 5 intercollegiate sports for men and 6 for women, and 6 intramural sports for men and 6 for women. Facilities include a gym, a weight room, tennis and handball courts, an indoor running track, a swimming pool, a Nautilus room, a game room, and an aerobics/dance studio.

Disabled Students: All of the campus is accessible. Wheelchair ramps, elevators, special parking, specially equipped rest rooms, lowered telephones, and special equipment in the library and computer centers to accommodate students with low vision are available.

Services: Counseling and information services are available, as is tutoring in every subject. There is remedial math, reading, and writing.

Campus Safety and Security: Measures include 24-hour foot and vehicle patrol, self-defense education, security escort services, and shuttle buses. There are informal discussions, pamphlets/posters/films, emergency telephones, and lighted pathways/sidewalks.

Programs of Study: The Mount confers B.A., B.S., B.S.Ed., and B.S.N. degrees. Master's degrees are also awarded. Bachelor's degrees are awarded in BIOLOGICAL SCIENCE (biology/biological science), BUSINESS (accounting and business administration and management), COMMUNICATIONS AND THE ARTS (communications, English, media arts, and public relations), COMPUTER AND PHYSICAL SCIENCE (chemistry, computer science, information sciences and systems, mathematics, and science), EDUCATION (elementary and secondary), HEALTH PROFESSIONS (medical laboratory technology, nursing, physical therapy, premedicine, preveterinary science, and speech pathology/audiology), SOCIAL SCIENCE (criminal justice, Hispanic American studies, history, human services, interdisciplinary studies, international studies, political science/government, prelaw, psychology, social science, social work, and sociology). Education, nursing, and business are the strongest academically and have the largest enrollments.

Required: The required core curriculum includes 39 credits in natural sciences, math, computer science, philosophy and religion, arts and letters, and social sciences. A total of 120 credit hours is required for the B.A. or B.S., with 24 to 40 in the major and a minimum GPA of 2.0. Overall requirements are higher for nursing, medical technology, and education students. All students must achieve computer literacy before graduation.

Special: Co-op programs and internships are available in all majors. There is cross-registration with other mid-Hudson area colleges, as well as accelerated degree programs in business, accounting, nursing, computer science, and public relations among others. There are several collaborative programs. The college also offers study abroad in more than 22 countries, a Washington semester, work-study, and dual and student-designed majors. Credit by exam and for life, military, and work experience is available for a maximum of 30 credits. There are 9 national honor societies and a freshman honors program.

Faculty/Classroom: 44% of faculty are male; 56%, female. All teach undergraduates, 40% do research, and 40% do both. No introductory courses are taught by graduate students. The average class size in an introductory lecture is 21; in a laboratory, 12; and in a regular course, 19.

Admissions: 79% of the 2005-2006 applicants were accepted. The SAT scores for the 2005-2006 freshman class were: Verbal--42% below 500, 45% between 500 and 599, 12% between 600 and 700, and 1% above 700; Math--38% below 500, 49% between 500 and 599, and 13% between 600 and 700. The ACT scores were 53% below 21, 35% between 21 and 23, 8% between 24 and 26, 3% between 27 and 28, and 3% above 28. 25% of the current freshmen were in the top fifth of their class; 55% were in the top two fifths.

Requirements: The SAT or ACT is required. In addition, students should be graduates of an accredited secondary school. The GED is accepted. Applicants should prepare with 4 years each of English and history and at least 3 each of math and science and 2 of foreign language. An essay and an interview are recommended. A GPA of 75.0 is required. AP and CLEP credits are accepted. Important factors in the admissions decision are advanced placement or honor courses, evidence of special talent, and personality/intangible qualities.

Procedure: Freshmen are admitted to all sessions. Entrance exams should be taken as early as possible. There are early admissions, deferred admissions and rolling admissions plans. Application deadlines are open. Applications are accepted on-line. The fall application fee was $35.

Transfer: 194 transfer students enrolled in 2004-2005. Applicants must have a GPA of at least 2.0 in all college work. The SAT or ACT and an interview are recommended. 30 of 120 credits required for the bachelor's degree must be completed at the Mount.

Visiting: There are regularly scheduled orientations for prospective students, including 6 open houses per year, a 4-day fall orientation program, and a Spend a Day with a Current Student program in the spring. There are guides for informal visits and visitors may sit in on classes and stay overnight. To schedule a visit, contact Admissions.

Financial Aid: In 2005-2006, 83% of all full-time freshmen and 78% of continuing full-time students received some form of financial aid. 58% of full-time freshmen and 62% of continuing full-time students received need-based aid. The average freshman award was $11,700. Need-based scholarships or need-based grants averaged $6600 ($23,000 maximum); need-based self-help aid (loans and jobs) averaged $4100 ($4400 maximum); and other non-need-based awards and non-need-based scholarships averaged $1000 ($16,000 maximum). 17% of undergraduates work part time. Average annual earnings from campus work are $1000. The average financial indebtedness of a recent graduate was $20,000. The FAFSA and the college's own financial statement are required. The priority date for freshman financial aid applications for fall entry is February 15. The deadline for filing freshman financial aid applications for fall entry is March 15.

International Students: In a recent year there was 1 international student enrolled. They must score satisfactorily on the written TOEFL and also take the college's own entrance exam. Freshman are required to take a standard placement test.

Computers: Wireless access is available. The college provides students with access to over 300 computer workstations across campus for instruction and open laboratory access. There are 10 computer classrooms/laboratories, as well as computer facilities and clusters in the library, curriculum library, cyber-café, and the two major residence halls. Campus-wide high-speed wireless network provides students with access to college resources and the Internet from virtually anywhere on campus. All students may access the system weekdays from 8 A.M. to 11 P.M., and weekends from 10 A.M. to 5 P.M. or access through the web module 24 hours a day, 7 days a week. There are no time limits and no fees. It is strongly recommended that all students have a personal computer.

Graduates: From July 1, 2004 to June 30, 2005, 415 bachelor's degrees were awarded. The most popular majors were business (21%), English (14%), and history (13%). In an average class, 1% graduate in 3 years or less, 48% graduate in 4 years or less, 57% graduate in 5 years or less, and 60% graduate in 6 years or less. 75 companies recruited on campus in 2004-2005. Of the 2004 graduating class, 35% were enrolled in graduate school within 6 months of graduation and 84% were employed.

Admissions Contact: J. Randall Ognibene, Director of Admissions. A video is available. E-mail: mtstmary@msmc.edu Web: www.msmc.edu

NAZARETH COLLEGE OF ROCHESTER   B-3
Rochester, NY 14618-3790   (585) 389-2860
                                  (800) 462-3944; Fax: (585) 389-2826

Full-time: 449 men, 1415 women	**Faculty:** 135; IIA, -$
Part-time: 46 men, 147 women	**Ph.D.s:** 94%
Graduate: 186 men, 877 women	**Student/Faculty:** 14 to 1
Year: semesters, summer session	**Tuition:** $19,875
Application Deadline: February 15	**Room & Board:** $8300
Freshman Class: 1974 applied, 1561 accepted, 451 enrolled	
SAT Verbal/Math: 576/576*	**ACT:** 25 **VERY COMPETITIVE**

Nazareth College of Rochester, founded in 1924, is an independent institution offering programs in the liberal arts and sciences and preprofessional areas. There are 4 undergraduate schools. In addition to regional accreditation, Nazareth has baccalaureate program accreditation with CSWE, NASM, ACS, and ASHA, CAPTE, CCNE. The library contains 162,593 volumes, 438,204 microform items, and 12,236 audio/video tapes/CDs/DVDs, and subscribes to 1888 periodicals including electronic. Computerized library services include the card catalog, interlibrary loans, database searching, and Internet access. Special learning facilities include a learning resource center, art gallery, and radio station. The 150-acre campus is in a suburban area 7 miles east of Rochester. Including any residence halls, there are 21 buildings.

Student Life: 95% of undergraduates are from New York. Others are from 25 states, 19 foreign countries, and Canada. 90% are from public schools. 84% are white. The average age of freshmen is 18; all undergraduates, 22. 16% do not continue beyond their first year; 74% remain to graduate.

Housing: 1205 students can be accommodated in college housing, which includes single-sex and coed dormitories and on-campus apartments. In addition, there are language houses and special-interest houses. On-campus housing is guaranteed for all 4 years. 63% of students live on campus; of those, 88% remain on campus on weekends. All students may keep cars.

Activities: There are no fraternities or sororities. There are 51 groups on campus, including art, band, cheerleading, choir, chorale, chorus, computers, dance, drama, ethnic, gay, honors, jazz band, literary magazine, musical theater, newspaper, opera, orchestra, political, professional, radio, religious, social, and student government. Popular campus events include Springfest and Siblings Weekend.

Sports: There are 11 intercollegiate sports for men and 13 for women, and 20 intramural sports for men and 20 for women. Facilities include a gym, a 25-meter swimming pool, soccer and lacrosse fields, including an outdoor turf field, tennis and racquetball courts, a fitness center, a sauna, a 2,200-seat stadium, and a 400-meter all-weather track.

Disabled Students: 80% of the campus is accessible. Wheelchair ramps, elevators, special parking, specially equipped rest rooms, special class scheduling, lowered drinking fountains, and special housing are available.

Services: Counseling and information services are available, as is tutoring in every subject.

Campus Safety and Security: Measures include 24-hour foot and vehicle patrol, security escort services, informal discussions, and pamphlets/posters/films. There are emergency telephones, lighted pathways/sidewalks, an alarm system, and security beepers free to all students.

Programs of Study: Nazareth confers B.A., B.S., and B.Mus. degrees. Master's and doctoral degrees are also awarded. Bachelor's degrees are awarded in BIOLOGICAL SCIENCE (biochemistry and biology/biological science), BUSINESS (accounting and business administration and management), COMMUNICATIONS AND THE ARTS (art, art history and appreciation, dramatic arts, English, fine arts, French, German, Italian, music, music history and appreciation, music performance, Spanish, and speech/debate/rhetoric), COMPUTER AND PHYSICAL SCIENCE (chemistry, information sciences and systems, and mathematics), EDUCATION (art, business, elementary, English, foreign languages, mathematics, middle school, music, science, social studies, and special), ENGINEERING AND ENVIRONMENTAL DESIGN (environmental science), HEALTH PROFESSIONS (music therapy, nursing, physical therapy, and speech pathology/audiology), SOCIAL SCIENCE (American studies, anthropology, economics, history, international studies, peace studies, philosophy, political science/government, psychology, religion, social science, social work, and sociology). Physical therapy, math, and English are the strongest academically. Business, psychology, and art are the largest.

Required: All students must take 1 course each in literature, math, lab science, philosophy, social science, history, fine arts, and religious studies. 2 semesters of phys ed, a course in computer literacy, and a writing competency exam in the junior year are required. Other requirements vary according to the major, with a total of 30 to 75 upper-division credits needed. A total of 120 credit hours is required to graduate. The minimum GPA is 2.0.

Special: There is cross-registration with members of the Rochester Area Colleges Consortium. Internships and a Washington semester are offered. There is study abroad in France, Spain, Italy, and Germany, and there are exchange programs in Australia, Japan, Italy, and Wales. There are 20 national honor societies, and 13 departmental honors programs.

Faculty/Classroom: 42% of faculty are male; 58%, female. All teach undergraduates. No introductory courses are taught by graduate students. The average class size in an introductory lecture is 21; in a laboratory, 13; and in a regular course, 19.

Admissions: 79% of the 2005-2006 applicants were accepted. The SAT scores for the 2005-2006 freshman class were: Verbal--12% below 500, 48% between 500 and 599, 34% between 600 and 700, and 5% above 700; Math--13% below 500, 45% between 500 and 599, 38% between 600 and 700, and 3% above 700. The ACT scores were 12% below 21, 26% between 21 and 23, 39% between 24 and 26, 13% between 27 and 28, and 9% above 28. 54% of the current freshmen were in the top fifth of their class; 89% were in the top two fifths. There were 3 National Merit semifinalists. 5 freshmen graduated first in their class.

Requirements: Satisfactory scores are required on the SAT or ACT. Applicants should graduate from an accredited secondary school or have a GED. A minimum of 16 academic credits is required, including 4 years of English and 3 each of social studies, foreign language, math, and science. An essay is required, as are an audition for music and theater students and a portfolio for art students. An interview is recommended. Nazareth requires applicants to be in the upper 50% of their class. A GPA of 2.75 is required. AP and CLEP credits are accepted. Important factors in the admissions decision are geographic diversity, advanced placement or honor courses, and evidence of special talent.

Procedure: Freshmen are admitted fall and spring. Entrance exams should be taken by December of the senior year. There are early decision, early admissions, and deferred admissions plans. Early decision applications should be filed by November 15; regular applications, by February 15 for fall entry and November 15 for spring entry, along with a $40 fee. Notification of early decision is sent December 15; regular decision, March 1. 20 early decision candidates were accepted for a recent class. 84 applicants were on the 2005 waiting list; 26 were admitted. Applications are accepted on-line.

Transfer: 148 transfer students enrolled in 2004-2005. Applicants must have a college GPA of 2.5 (2.75 for education and physical therapy students). Those with fewer than 30 credits must submit high school transcripts. 30 of 120 credits required for the bachelor's degree must be completed at Nazareth.

Visiting: There are regularly scheduled orientations for prospective students, including individual appointments, group sessions, campus tours, open houses, and summer academic orientation. There are guides for informal visits and visitors may sit in on classes and stay overnight. To schedule a visit, contact the Admissions Office at *admissions@naz.edu*.

Financial Aid: In 2005-2006, 98% of all full-time freshmen and 96% of continuing full-time students received some form of financial aid. 77% of full-time freshmen and 78% of continuing full-time students received need-based aid. The average freshman award was $14,219. Need-based scholarships or need-based grants averaged $16,383; need-based self-help aid (loans and jobs) averaged $4286; and other non-need-based awards and non-need-based scholarships averaged $9287. 44% of undergraduates work part time. Average annual earnings from campus work are $1421. The average financial indebtedness of the 2005 graduate was $19,785. Nazareth is a member of CSS. The FAFSA is required and the CSS Profile is required for early decision applicants only. are required. The priority date for freshman financial aid applications for fall entry is February 15. The deadline for filing freshman financial aid applications for fall entry is May 15.

International Students: The school actively recruits these students. They must take the TOEFL and also take the SAT or the ACT.

Computers: Wireless access is available. All students may access the system. There are no time limits and no fees.

Graduates: From July 1, 2004 to June 30, 2005, 467 bachelor's degrees were awarded. The most popular majors were business (15%), English (11%), and psychology (10%). In an average class, 71% graduate in 5 years or less, and 72% graduate in 6 years or less. 35 companies recruited on campus in 2004-2005. Of the 2004 graduating class, 51% were enrolled in graduate school within 6 months of graduation and 71% were employed.

Admissions Contact: Thomas DaRin, Vice President of Enrollment Management. E-mail: *admissions@naz.edu* Web: *ww.naz.edu*

NEW YORK INSTITUTE OF TECHNOLOGY D-5

Old Westbury, NY 11568-8000 (516) 686-7925
(800) 345-NYIT; Fax: (516) 686-7613

Full-time: 2528 men, 1635 women	**Faculty:** n/av
Part-time: 1083 men, 1240 women	**Ph.D.s:** 87%
Graduate: 2376 men, 2279 women	**Student/Faculty:** n/av
Year: semesters, summer session	**Tuition:** $19,236
Application Deadline: February 1	**Room & Board:** $8890
Freshman Class: 3941 applied, 2623 accepted, 882 enrolled	
SAT Verbal/Math: 530/580*	**ACT:** 22 **VERY COMPETITIVE**

The New York Institute of Technology, founded in 1955, is a nonsectarian, institution of higher learning that provides undergraduate, graduate, and professional programs in allied health, architecture, art, business, culinary arts, communication, arts, education, engineering, hospitality management, and medicine and technology. Traditional and accelerated formats in day, evening, and weekend sessions are available, in addition to noncredit and personal enrichment programs and off-campus independent study. NYIT maintains additional campuses on Long Island and in Manhattan. NYIT'S on-line campus is an innovative virtual campus. Students can take courses or acquire a 4-year degree entirely through Web-based computer conferencing with no campus classes required. There are 7 undergraduate and 8 graduate schools. In addition to regional accreditation, NYIT has baccalaureate program accreditation with ABET, ADA, ACOTE, ARC-PA, FIDER, and NAAB. The 5 libraries contain 206,758 volumes, 857,962 microform items, and 48,950 audio/video tapes/CDs/DVDs, and subscribe to 2249 periodicals including electronic. Computerized library services include the card catalog, interlibrary loans, database searching, and Internet access. Special learning facilities include a learning resource center, art gallery, radio station, TV station, and TV studios. The 525-acre campus is in a suburban area. The Old Westbury campus is 25 miles east of New York City, 10 miles from Queens. Including any residence halls, there are 57 buildings.

Student Life: 72% of undergraduates are from New York. Others are from 49 states, 81 foreign countries, and Canada. 32% are white; 11% African American; 10% foreign nationals. The average age of freshmen is 18; all undergraduates, 23. 29% do not continue beyond their first year; 71% remain to graduate.

Housing: 1000 students can be accommodated in college housing, which includes single-sex and coed dormitories, on-campus apartments, and off-campus apartments. In addition, there are special-interest houses, facilities for international, graduate, architecture, first-year students, student leaders, student government executive board members, and Greek Life organizations. On-campus housing is guaranteed for all 4

years. 89% of students commute. Alcohol is not permitted. All students may keep cars.

Activities: 2% of men belong to 1 local and 4 national fraternities; 1% of women belong to 2 local and 1 national sorority. There are 100 groups on campus, including academic, art, cheerleading, chorale, computers, dance, drama, ethnic, film, honors, international, literary magazine, musical theater, newspaper, political, professional, radio and TV, religious, social, social service, special interest, student government, student media, and yearbook. Popular campus events include May Fest, Club Fair Day, and Earth Day.

Sports: There are 7 intercollegiate sports for men and 7 for women, and 9 intramural sports for men and 9 for women. Facilities include a gym, soccer, softball and baseball fields, a track, courts for tennis, handball, and basketball, a fitness center, aquatic facilities, and a weight room.

Disabled Students: All of the campus is accessible. Wheelchair ramps, elevators, special parking, specially equipped rest rooms, lowered drinking fountains, and special housing are available.

Services: Counseling and information services are available, as is tutoring in every subject. There is remedial math, reading, and writing.

Campus Safety and Security: Measures include 24-hour foot and vehicle patrol, security escort services, shuttle buses, and informal discussions. There are pamphlets/posters/films, emergency telephones, and lighted pathways/sidewalks.

Programs of Study: NYIT confers B.A., B.S., B.Arch., B.F.A., B.P.S., and B.Tech. degrees. Associate, master's, and doctoral degrees are also awarded. Bachelor's degrees are awarded in BIOLOGICAL SCIENCE (biology/biological science, life science, and nutrition), BUSINESS (accounting, banking and finance, business administration and management, hospitality management services, marketing and distribution, and marketing/retailing/merchandising), COMMUNICATIONS AND THE ARTS (advertising, communications, English, fine arts, graphic design, technical and business writing, and telecommunications), COMPUTER AND PHYSICAL SCIENCE (chemistry, computer science, mathematics, and physics), EDUCATION (art, business, education, elementary, health, middle school, science, secondary, technical, and trade and industrial), ENGINEERING AND ENVIRONMENTAL DESIGN (aeronautical engineering, architecture, biomedical engineering, computer engineering, computer graphics, electrical/electronics engineering, electrical/electronics engineering technology, engineering technology, environmental design, environmental engineering technology, industrial engineering, interior design, manufacturing engineering, mechanical engineering, and technological management), HEALTH PROFESSIONS (clinical science, nursing, occupational therapy, physical therapy, physician's assistant, and preosteopathy), SOCIAL SCIENCE (behavioral science, interdisciplinary studies, political science/government, prelaw, social studies, and sociology). Architecture, allied health programs, and engineering are the strongest academically. Computer science, business administration, and architectural technology are the largest.

Required: All students take a core curriculum, sequenced over 8 semesters, that includes 42 credits in English, speech, behavioral and natural science, social science, philosophy, economics, and a capstone course in the major field. A total of 120 to 169 credits and a minimum GPA of 2.0, both overall and in the major, are required for graduation.

Special: NYIT offers cooperative programs, summer study abroad, internships, student-designed majors, a B.A.-B.S. degree in interdisciplinary studies, accelerated degree programs in osteopathic medicine, mechanical engineering, physical therapy, occupational therapy, and criminal justice, and nondegree study. There are 7 national honor societies, a freshman honors program, and 2 departmental honors programs.

Faculty/Classroom: 70% of faculty are male; 30%, female. 88% teach undergraduates, 28% do research, and 28% do both. No introductory courses are taught by graduate students. The average class size in an introductory lecture is 20; in a laboratory, 15; and in a regular course, 17.

Admissions: 67% of the 2005-2006 applicants were accepted. The SAT scores for the 2005-2006 freshman class were: Verbal--34% below 500, 42% between 500 and 599, 21% between 600 and 700, and 3% above 700; Math--20% below 500, 33% between 500 and 599, 31% between 600 and 700, and 16% above 700.

Requirements: The SAT or ACT is required for some programs. In addition, all students must present evidence of completion of high school degree or an equivalence. Architecture, engineering, combined baccalaureate/doctor of osteopathic medicine, nursing, occupational therapy, physical therapy, and physician assistant programs requirements include interviews, essays, letters of recommendation, volunteer hours, and Regents units. Recommendations are required for education program applicants. Portfolios are required for fine arts applicants. AP and CLEP credits are accepted. Important factors in the admissions decision are advanced placement or honor courses, recommendations by school officials, and leadership record.

Procedure: Freshmen are admitted fall, spring, and summer. Entrance exams should be taken in spring for fall enrollment. There are deferred admissions and rolling admissions plans. Applications should be filed by February 1 for fall entry. Notification is sent on a rolling basis. Applications are accepted on-line. The fall 2005 application fee was $50.

Transfer: 862 transfer students enrolled in 2004-2005. Applicants must submit official transcripts from all colleges attended. Students with less than 30 credits of previous college work must submit a high school transcript and standardized test scores. Some majors have specific requirements for their programs. 30 of 120 credits required for the bachelor's degree must be completed at NYIT.

Visiting: There are regularly scheduled orientations for prospective students, including open houses in fall and spring, with campus tours, a president's address, financial aid seminars, honors receptions, sessions with faculty advisers, and major-specific receptions. There are guides for informal visits and visitors may sit in on classes. To schedule a visit, contact the Admissions Office at (516) 686-7520.

Financial Aid: 77% of undergraduates work part time. Average annual earnings from campus work are $2000. The FAFSA and NYS TAP form are required. The priority date for freshman financial aid applications for fall entry is February 1.

International Students: In a recent year, there were 474 international students enrolled. The school actively recruits these students. They must score satisfactorily on the written TOEFL or 213 on the electronic version and also take the SAT or the ACT.

Computers: All students may access the system. There are no time limits and no fees. All students are required to have personal computers. It is recommended that students in architecture, engineering, and technology majors have personal computers.

Graduates: In a recent year, 981 bachelor's degrees were awarded. The most popular majors were communication arts (9%), computer science (8%), and architecture (6%). In an average class, 1% graduate in 3 years or less, 15% graduate in 4 years or less, 24% graduate in 5 years or less, and 31% graduate in 6 years or less. 120 companies recruited on campus in a recent year. Of a recent graduating class, 38% were enrolled in graduate school within 6 months of graduation and 88% were employed.

Admissions Contact: Jacquelyn Nealon, Dean of Admissions and Financial Aid. A video is available. E-mail: *admissions@nyit.edu* Web: *www.nyit.edu*

NEW YORK UNIVERSITY D-5

New York, NY 10011 (212) 998-4500; Fax: (212) 995-4902

Full-time: 7369 men, 11,612 women	Faculty: 2043; I, +$
Part-time: 599 men, 986 women	Ph.D.s: 93%
Graduate: 8446 men, 10,992 women	Student/Faculty: 9 to 1
Year: semesters, summer session	Tuition: $31,690
Application Deadline: January 15	Room & Board: $11,480
Freshman Class: 34,509 applied, 12,662 enrolled	
SAT Verbal/Math: 680/690*	ACT: 30 MOST COMPETITIVE

New York University, founded in 1831, is the largest private university in the United States. NYU, which is composed of 14 schools, colleges, and divisions, occupies 5 major centers in Manhattan and operates branch campus and research programs in other parts of the United States and abroad, as well as study-abroad programs in more than 25 countries. There are 8 undergraduate and 11 graduate schools. In addition to regional accreditation, NYU has baccalaureate program accreditation with AACSB, ACEJMC, ACS, ADA, CSWE, and NLN. The 12 libraries contain 4,642,734 volumes, 6,303,499 microform items, and 121,827 audio/video tapes/CDs/DVDs, and subscribe to 49,044 periodicals including electronic. Computerized library services include the card catalog, interlibrary loans, database searching, Internet access, and laptop Internet portals. Special learning facilities include a learning resource center, art gallery, radio station, TV station, speech/language/hearing clinic, center for students with disabilities, and Speaking Freely (free noncredit foreign language classes). The campus is in an urban area in New York City's Greenwich Village. Including any residence halls, there are 150 buildings.

Student Life: 61% of undergraduates are from out of state, mostly the Northeast. Students are from 50 states, 90 foreign countries, and Canada. 68% are white; 16% Asian American. The average age of freshmen is 18; all undergraduates, 21. 7% do not continue beyond their first year; 83% remain to graduate.

Housing: 10,903 students can be accommodated in college housing, which includes coed dorms, on-campus apartments, and fraternity houses. In addition, there are special-interest houses and SAFE (Substance- and Alcohol-Free Environment). On-campus housing is guaranteed for all 4 years. 52% of students live on campus. All students may keep cars.

Activities: 4% of men belong to 13 national fraternities; 2% of women belong to 9 local and 4 national sororities. There are more than 500 groups on campus, including art, bagpipe band, band, cheerleading, chess, choir, chorale, chorus, computers, dance, debate, drama, ethnic, film, forensics, gay, honors, international, jazz band, literary magazine, musical theater, newspaper, orchestra, pep band, photography, political, professional, radio and TV, religious, social, social service, student government, symphony, and yearbook. Popular campus events include Spring Strawberry Festival, Grad Alley, and Career Services Fair.

Sports: There are 15 intercollegiate sports for men and 13 for women, and 13 intramural sports for men and 14 for women. Facilities include 2 state-of-the-art sports and recreation facilities. The sports center houses multipurpose courts for basketball, volleyball, tennis, and badminton, squash courts, handball and racquetball courts, rooftop tennis courts and running track, a 25-meter swimming pool, a diving tank, saunas, weight-training facilities, an aerobic fitness room, rooms for wrestling, judo, fencing, physical fitness, exercise prescription, and dance, and a rock-climbing wall. The athletic center is equipped with a 25-yard swimming pool, basketball/activities courts, a foot aerobic fitness room with cardio equipment, and a 30-foot indoor climbing center.

Disabled Students: 95% of the campus is accessible. Wheelchair ramps, elevators, specially equipped rest rooms, special class scheduling, lowered drinking fountains, lowered telephones, special housing, buses with hydraulic lifts, adaptive computer equipment, CART or C-print services, a CTV enlargement system, a JAWS speech synthesizer, Dragon Dictate Voice Recognition, and Kurzweil Personal Readers are available.

Services: Counseling and information services are available, as is tutoring in every subject. There is a reader service for the blind. Other services include sign language interpreters, scribes, research aides, and note takers for special needs.

Campus Safety and Security: Measures include 24-hour foot and vehicle patrol, self-defense education, security escort services, and shuttle buses. There are informal discussions, pamphlets/posters/films, emergency telephones, lighted pathways/sidewalks, 24-hour security in residence halls, and a neighborhood-merchant emergency help service.

Programs of Study: NYU confers B.A., B.S., B.F.A., B.S./B.E., and Mus.B. degrees. Associate, master's, and doctoral degrees are also awarded. Bachelor's degrees are awarded in BIOLOGICAL SCIENCE (biochemistry, biology/biological science, neurosciences, and nutrition), BUSINESS (accounting, banking and finance, business administration and management, business economics, hotel/motel and restaurant management, international business management, management science, marketing/retailing/merchandising, operations research, organizational behavior, real estate, recreation and leisure services, and sports management), COMMUNICATIONS AND THE ARTS (American literature, art history and appreciation, classics, communications, communications technology, comparative literature, creative writing, dance, design, dramatic arts, English, English literature, film arts, fine arts, French, German, Germanic languages and literature, Greek, Greek (classical), Hebrew, Italian, journalism, Latin, linguistics, media arts, music, music business management, music performance, music technology, music theory and composition, photography, Portuguese, radio/television technology, romance languages and literature, Russian, Spanish, speech/debate/rhetoric, studio art, technical and business writing, and voice), COMPUTER AND PHYSICAL SCIENCE (actuarial science, chemistry, computer mathematics, computer science, digital arts/technology, earth science, information sciences and systems, mathematics, physics, and statistics), EDUCATION (art, early childhood, elementary, English, foreign languages, mathematics, music, science, secondary, social studies, special, and speech correction), ENGINEERING AND ENVIRONMENTAL DESIGN (computer engineering, graphic arts technology, and urban design), HEALTH PROFESSIONS (dental hygiene, health care administration, nursing, predentistry, premedicine, and speech pathology/audiology), SOCIAL SCIENCE (African American studies, African studies, anthropology, applied psychology, area studies, classical/ancient civilization, East Asian studies, economics, ethnic studies, European studies, gender studies, history, humanities, international relations, Judaic studies, Latin American studies, Luso-Brazilian studies, medieval studies, Middle Eastern studies, philosophy, political science/government, psychology, religion, social science, social work, sociology, and urban studies). Theater, individualized studies, and finance are the largest.

Required: All students must complete a minimum of 128 credit hours and maintain a minimum GPA of 2.0. A course in expository writing is required. Students must complete a core liberal arts curriculum in addition to major and elective credit.

Special: A 3-2 engineering degree (B.S./B.E.) is available with the Stevens Institute of Technology in New Jersey. A vast array of internships is available, as well as study worldwide at NYU's 5 sites: Florence, Paris, Ghana, Madrid, Prague, and London. B.A.-B.S. degree options, accelerated degrees in more than 140 majors, dual and student-designed majors, credit by exam, and pass/fail options are also available. A Washington semester is available to political science majors. There are exchange programs with several historically black colleges. There is a chapter of Phi Beta Kappa and a freshman honors program.

Faculty/Classroom: 56% of faculty are male; 44%, female.

Admissions: 25% of the 2005-2006 applicants were accepted. The SAT scores for the 2005-2006 freshman class were: Verbal--1% below 500, 13% between 500 and 599, 53% between 600 and 700, and 33% above 700; Math--1% below 500, 13% between 500 and 599, 51% between 600 and 700, and 35% above 700. The ACT scores were 16% between 24 and 26, 21% between 27 and 28, and 63% above 28. 91% of the current freshmen were in the top fifth of their class; 99% were in the top two fifths. There were 117 National Merit finalists. 98 freshmen graduated first in their class.

Requirements: The SAT or ACT is required. The ACT Optional Writing test is also required. In addition, applicants must graduate from an accredited secondary school. The GED is accepted. Students must present at least 16 Carnegie units, including 4 in English. Some majors require an audition or submission of a creative portfolio. All applicants must submit an essay and 2 letters of recommendation. AP credits are accepted. Important factors in the admissions decision are advanced placement or honor courses, extracurricular activities record, and leadership record.

Procedure: Freshmen are admitted fall, spring, and summer. Entrance exams should be taken by November of the senior year. There is an early decision plan. Early decision applications should be filed by November 1; regular applications, by January 15 for fall entry, December 1 for spring entry, and May 1 for summer entry, along with a $65 fee. Notification of early decision is sent December 15; regular decision, April 1. 1529 early decision candidates were accepted for the 2005-2006 class. 1608 applicants were on the 2005 waiting list; 41 were admitted. Applications are accepted on-line.

Transfer: 847 transfer students enrolled in 2004-2005. Students must submit official college transcripts from all postsecondary institutions attended, a final high school transcript, and SAT scores. 32 of 128 credits required for the bachelor's degree must be completed at NYU.

Visiting: There are regularly scheduled orientations for prospective students, including campus tours and weekday information sessions by appointment. There are also 2 fall open houses. Visitors may sit in on classes. To schedule a visit, contact the Admissions Office at (212) 998-4524 or *admissions@nyu.edu*, or access the university's web site at *http://events.embark.com/event/nyu*.

Financial Aid: In 2005-2006, 63% of all full-time freshmen and 64% of continuing full-time students received some form of financial aid. 53% of full-time freshmen and 54% of continuing full-time students received need-based aid. The average freshman award was $20,047. 26% of undergraduates work part time. The average financial indebtedness of the 2005 graduate was $29,480. The FAFSA and the state aid form are required. The deadline for filing freshman financial aid applications for fall entry is February 15.

International Students: There are 795 international students enrolled. The school actively recruits these students. They must score satisfactorily on the written TOEFL or on the electronic version or take the IELTS or have ESL testing and also take the SAT, ACT or the ACT. 2 SAT Subject tests are recommended.

Computers: Facilities include MACS and PCs at 4 computer labs; more than 100 public terminals for walk-up access to e-mail and the Internet; laptop plug-in ports and circulating laptops at the library; modem connectors from home or while traveling; NYU Roam for wireless network access; and ResNet for in-room Ethernet access in virtually all residence halls. All students may access the system 24 hours a day, 7 days a week. There are no time limits and no fees.

Graduates: From July 1, 2004 to June 30, 2005, 4696 bachelor's degrees were awarded. The most popular majors were finance (10%), drama/theater arts (10%), and individualized major (9%). In an average class, 76% graduate in 4 years or less, 82% graduate in 5 years or less, and 83% graduate in 6 years or less. More than 600 companies recruited on campus in 2004-2005. Of the 2004 graduating class, 22% were enrolled in graduate school within 6 months of graduation and 72% were employed.

Admissions Contact: Office of Undergraduate Admissions. A video is available. Web: *http://admissions.nyu.edu*

NIAGARA UNIVERSITY
A-3

Niagara University, NY 14109
(716) 286-8700
(800) 462-2111; Fax: (716) 286-8710

Full-time: 1100 men, 1716 women	**Faculty:** 137; IIA, -$
Part-time: 41 men, 85 women	**Ph.D.s:** 93%
Graduate: 295 men, 616 women	**Student/Faculty:** 21 to 1
Year: semesters, summer session	**Tuition:** $19,800
Application Deadline: see profile	**Room & Board:** $8450
Freshman Class: 3249 applied, 2556 accepted, 732 enrolled	
SAT Verbal/Math: 523/528*	**ACT:** 23 **COMPETITIVE**

Niagara University, founded in 1856 by the Vincentian fathers and brothers, is a private institution rooted in a Roman Catholic tradition. Programs offered include those in liberal arts, business, education, nursing, and travel, hotel, and restaurant administration. There are 4 undergraduate and 3 graduate schools. In addition to regional accreditation, Niagara has baccalaureate program accreditation with AACSB, ACCE, CSWE, NCATE, and NLN. The library contains 282,702 volumes, 77,047 microform items, and 772 audio/video tapes/CDs/DVDs, and subscribes to 9000 periodicals including electronic. Computerized library services include the card catalog, interlibrary loans, database searching, and Internet access. Special learning facilities include a learning resource center, art gallery, radio station, TV station, and 2 theaters, and a green-

house. The 160-acre campus is in a suburban area 4 miles north of Niagara Falls, overlooking the Niagara River gorge, 20 miles north of Buffalo. Including any residence halls, there are 25 buildings.

Student Life: 87% of undergraduates are from New York. Others are from 31 states, 10 foreign countries, and Canada. 75% are from public schools. 81% are white. 65% are Catholic; 18% Protestant; 6% claim no religious affiliation. The average age of freshmen is 18; all undergraduates, 21. 18% do not continue beyond their first year; 63% remain to graduate.

Housing: 1497 students can be accommodated in college housing, which includes single-sex and coed dorms and on-campus apartments. In addition, there are honors houses, special-interest houses, and international housing. On-campus housing is guaranteed for all 4 years. 53% of students live on campus; of those, 75% remain on campus on weekends. All students may keep cars.

Activities: 2% of men belong to 2 national fraternities. There are no sororities. There are 78 groups on campus, including art, aviation, cheerleading, choir, chorale, computers, drama, drill team, ethnic, film, honors, international, musical theater, newspaper, pep band, political, professional, radio and TV, religious, social, social service, student government, and yearbook. Popular campus events include Orientation, CARE, and Family Weekend.

Sports: There are 8 intercollegiate sports for men and 9 for women, and 25 intramural sports for men and 25 for women. Facilities include a 3400-seat gym, a 6-lane swimming and diving pool, exercise and weight rooms, saunas and dance areas, outdoor tennis courts, baseball and soccer fields, basketball and racquetball courts, a hockey arena, and multipurpose courts with an indoor track. Hiking and biking trails are nearby.

Disabled Students: 75% of the campus is accessible. Wheelchair ramps, elevators, special parking, specially equipped rest rooms, special class scheduling, lowered drinking fountains, and campus accommodation for the vision impaired are available.

Services: Counseling and information services are available, as is tutoring in most subjects. There is a reader service for the blind, and remedial math, reading, and writing. Study skills development, note taking, and escort-assistance services are available, as are educational assistant services for the vision-impaired, educational/classroom assistance and machines for the hearing-impaired, and services for the learning disabled.

Campus Safety and Security: Measures include 24-hour foot and vehicle patrol, self-defense education, security escort services, and informal discussions. There are pamphlets/posters/films, emergency telephones, lighted pathways/sidewalks, and a campus security advisory board.

Programs of Study: Niagara confers B.A., B.S., B.B.A., and B.F.A. degrees. Associate and master's degrees are also awarded. Bachelor's degrees are awarded in BIOLOGICAL SCIENCE (biochemistry, biology/biological science, and life science), BUSINESS (accounting, business administration and management, business economics, hotel/motel and restaurant management, human resources, marketing/retailing/merchandising, tourism, and transportation management), COMMUNICATIONS AND THE ARTS (communications, dramatic arts, English, French, and Spanish), COMPUTER AND PHYSICAL SCIENCE (chemistry, computer science, information sciences and systems, and mathematics), EDUCATION (business, early childhood, elementary, English, foreign languages, mathematics, middle school, science, secondary, social studies, and special), ENGINEERING AND ENVIRONMENTAL DESIGN (preengineering), HEALTH PROFESSIONS (nursing, predentistry, and premedicine), SOCIAL SCIENCE (criminal justice, history, international studies, liberal arts/general studies, philosophy, political science/government, prelaw, psychology, religion, social science, social work, and sociology). Business, social sciences, and biology are the strongest academically. Business administration, travel and tourism, and education are the largest.

Required: To graduate, students must earn 120 to 126 credit hours and a GPA of at least 2.0; 60 to 66 such hours are required in the major, 20 in specific disciplines, and 20 in liberal arts classes. A comprehensive exam is required in some majors; a thesis is required of honor students and some majors.

Special: Niagara offers a Washington semester, a semester at the state capitol in Albany, on-campus work-study, internships in most majors with such companies as the Big 6 accounting firms and Walt Disney World, and co-op programs in all areas except nursing, education, and social work. Students may study abroad in 8 countries and cross-register through the Western New York Consortium. An accelerated degree program in business, B.A.-B.S. degrees, dual majors, a 2-3 engineering program with the University of Detroit, nondegree study, credit for life, military, and work experience, pass/fail options, and research are also available. There is also an academic exploration program for undeclared majors. There are 14 national honor societies and a freshman honors program.

Faculty/Classroom: 64% of faculty are male; 36%, female. 80% teach undergraduates. No introductory courses are taught by graduate students. The average class size in an introductory lecture is 25 and in a regular course, 22.

Admissions: 79% of the 2005-2006 applicants were accepted. The SAT scores for the 2005-2006 freshman class were: Verbal--36% below 500, 49% between 500 and 599, 14% between 600 and 700, and 1% above 700; Math--33% below 500, 49% between 500 and 599, 16% between 600 and 700, and 2% above 700. The ACT scores were 34% below 21, 30% between 21 and 23, 21% between 24 and 26, and 5% between 27 and 28. 31% of the current freshmen were in the top fifth of their class; 65% were in the top two fifths.

Requirements: The SAT or ACT is required. In addition, applicants should be graduates of an accredited high school. The GED is accepted. The high school program should include 16 academic credits, with 4 in English and 2 each in foreign language, history, math, science, and social studies, as well as academic electives. Science, math, and computer majors should have 3 credits each in math and science. A minimun of 80 % grade average is required. AP and CLEP credits are accepted. Important factors in the admissions decision are advanced placement or honor courses, parents or siblings attending the school, and recommendations by school officials.

Procedure: Freshmen are admitted to all sessions. Entrance exams should be taken in the junior year or fall of the senior year. There are early decision, deferred admissions and rolling admissions plans. The fall 2005 application fee was $30. Notification is sent on a rolling basis. Applications are accepted on-line. Check with the school for current application deadlines.

Transfer: 188 transfer students enrolled in 2004-2005. Applicants must have a minimum GPA of 2.0 in travel, hotel, and restaurant administration, arts and sciences, and academic exploration (except for 2.25 in business and 2.5 for nursing and education majors) and submit all high school and college transcripts. The SAT or ACT is recommended. 30 of 120 credits required for the bachelor's degree must be completed at Niagara.

Visiting: There are regularly scheduled orientations for prospective students, including individual interviews and campus tours. Other arrangements can be made individually, such as to attend a class, eat in the student cafeteria, and/or speak with a faculty member. There are guides for informal visits and visitors may sit in on classes and stay overnight. To schedule a visit, contact the Admissions Office appointment desk.

Financial Aid: In a recent year, 99% of all full-time freshmen and 88% of continuing full-time students received some form of financial aid. 82% of full-time freshmen and 88% of continuing full-time students received need-based aid. The average freshman award was $17,310. 21% of undergraduates work part time. Average annual earnings from campus work are $1592. Niagara is a member of CSS. The FAFSA is required. Check with the school for current application deadlines.

International Students: There are 159 international students enrolled. The school actively recruits these students. A satisfactory score is required on the written TOEFL.

Computers: All students may access the system 9 A.M. to 11 P.M. Monday to Thursday, 9 A.M. to 5 P.M. Friday, noon to 5 P.M. Saturday, and 3 P.M. to 10 P.M. Sunday. There are no time limits and no fees.

Graduates: From July 1, 2004 to June 30, 2005, 551 bachelor's degrees were awarded. The most popular majors were education (22%), commerce and accounting (21%), and hospitality/tourism (11%). In an average class, 55% graduate in 4 years or less, 60% graduate in 5 years or less, and 63% graduate in 6 years or less. 139 companies recruited on campus in 2004-2005. Of the 2004 graduating class, 43% were enrolled in graduate school within 6 months of graduation and 85% were employed.

Admissions Contact: Harry Gong, Director of Admissions.
E-mail: *admissions@niagara.edu* Web: *www.niagara.edu*

NYACK COLLEGE   D-5

Nyack, NY 10960   (845) 358-1710
                                      (800) 336-9225; Fax: (845) 358-3047

Full-time: 700 men, 1000 women	**Faculty:** 71
Part-time: 70 men, 100 women	**Ph.D.s:** 62%
Graduate: 300 men, 300 women	**Student/Faculty:** 16 to 1
Year: semesters, summer session	**Tuition:** $13,000
Application Deadline: open	**Room & Board:** $6000
Freshman Class: n/av	
SAT or ACT: required	**COMPETITIVE**

Nyack College, founded in 1882, is a private liberal arts institution affiliated with the Christian and Missionary Alliance.The enrollment figures in the above capsule include the Manhattan Center and Adult Degree Completion Program students. There is 1 graduate school. Figures in the above capsule and in this profile are approximate. In addition to regional accreditation, Nyack has baccalaureate program accreditation with NASM. The 3 libraries contain 99,000 volumes and 208,000 microform items, and subscribe to 871 periodicals including electronic. Computerized library services include the card catalog, interlibrary loans, and database searching. Special learning facilities include a learning resource center and radio station. The 102-acre campus is in a suburban area 20 miles north of New York City. Including any residence halls, there are 22 buildings.

Student Life: 67% of undergraduates are from New York. Others are from 42 states, 58 foreign countries, and Canada. 36% are white; 27% African American; 23% Hispanic. Most are Protestant. The average age of freshmen is 21; all undergraduates, 27. 35% do not continue beyond their first year; 46% remain to graduate.

Housing: 715 students can be accommodated in college housing, which includes single-sex dorms and on-campus apartments. In addition, there are honors houses. On-campus housing is guaranteed for all 4 years. 81% of students live on campus. Alcohol is not permitted. All students may keep cars.

Activities: There are no fraternities or sororities. There are 19 groups on campus, including band, cheerleading, choir, chorale, drama, ethnic, handball choir, honors, ladies glee club, literary magazine, musical theater, newspaper, orchestra, professional, radio and TV, religious, social service, student government, and yearbook. Popular campus events include music festivals and the Cultural Events Series.

Sports: There are 5 intercollegiate sports for men and 5 for women. Facilities include a gym, baseball, softball, and soccer fields, fitness center, training room, tennis courts, and outdoor basketball courts.

Disabled Students: 70% of the campus is accessible. Elevators, special parking, specially equipped rest rooms, and lowered drinking fountains are available.

Services: Counseling and information services are available, as is tutoring in every subject. There is a reader service for the blind.

Campus Safety and Security: Measures include 24-hour foot and vehicle patrol, security escort services, pamphlets/posters/films, and lighted pathways/sidewalks.

Programs of Study: Nyack confers B.A., B.S., B.Mus., and S.M.B. degrees. Associate and master's degrees are also awarded. Bachelor's degrees are awarded in BUSINESS (accounting and business administration and management), COMMUNICATIONS AND THE ARTS (communications, English, music, music performance, music theory and composition, piano/organ, and voice), COMPUTER AND PHYSICAL SCIENCE (computer science and mathematics), EDUCATION (elementary, music, secondary, and teaching English as a second/foreign language (TESOL/TEFOL)), SOCIAL SCIENCE (biblical studies, crosscultural studies, history, interdisciplinary studies, missions, pastoral studies, philosophy, psychology, religion, religious education, religious music, social science, social work, and youth ministry). Psychology, education, ministry-related programs, and business are the largest.

Required: To graduate, students must complete 126 to 130 credits with a minimum GPA of 2.0 or 2.5 for education majors. General education and major requirements vary by degree program. Students must adhere to the college's standards of Christian living and behavior and complete Bible courses.

Special: Nyack offers internships, cooperative programs with other schools, study abroad in 6 countries, a semester in Hollywood for communications majors, dual and student-designed majors, independent study, nondegree study, a Washington semester, and pass/fail options. The business program provides advanced standing for the M.B.A. program at St. Thomas Aquinas College in Sparkill, NY. There is a freshman honors program.

Faculty/Classroom: 60% of faculty are male; 40%, female. 70% teach undergraduates. No introductory courses are taught by graduate students. The average class size in a laboratory is 15 and in a regular course, 20.

Requirements: The SAT or ACT is required. In addition, high school graduation or its equivalent is essential. Completion of 16 academic credits is required; the college recommends 4 units of English, 3 of history or social science, 3 of any combination of math and science, 2 of a foreign language, and 4 of electives. Students must demonstrate sound Christian character through personal testimony and recommendations. An interview may be required. AP and CLEP credits are accepted.

Procedure: Freshmen are admitted fall and spring. There is a rolling admissions plan. Application deadlines are open. Check with the school for current application deadlines and fee.

Transfer: Applicants must provide all transcripts from previous schools attended. 30 of 126 credits required for the bachelor's degree must be completed at Nyack.

Visiting: There are regularly scheduled orientations for prospective students. There are guides for informal visits and visitors may sit in on classes and stay overnight. To schedule a visit, contact the Office of Admissions.

Financial Aid: The FAFSA and parent and student tax returns, if selected for verification, are required. Check with the school for current deadlines.

International Students: The school actively recruits these students. They must take the TOEFL and also take the SAT or the ACT.

Computers: All students may access the system. There are no time limits and no fees.

Admissions Contact: Miguel Sanchez, Director of Admissions. A video is available. E-mail: *enroll@nyack.edu* Web: *www.nyackcollege.edu*

PACE UNIVERSITY
D-5

New York, NY 10038-1508   (212) 346-1225 or (914) 773-3321
(800) 874-PACE; Fax: (212) 346-1040 or (914) 773-3851

Full-time: 2700 men, 4200 women	**Faculty:** 438; I, +$
Part-time: 800 men, 1200 women	**Ph.D.s:** 88%
Graduate: 2300 men, 2800 women	**Student/Faculty:** 16 to 1
Year: semesters, summer session	**Tuition:** $22,000
Application Deadline: open	**Room & Board:** $8000
Freshman Class: n/av	
SAT or ACT: required	**VERY COMPETITIVE**

Pace University, founded in 1906, is a private institution offering programs in arts and sciences, business, nursing, education, and computer and information science on 3 campuses, with undergraduate studies in New York City and Pleasantville and graduate studies in White Plains. There are 5 undergraduate and 5 graduate schools. Figures in the above capsule and in this profile are approximate. In addition to regional accreditation, Pace has baccalaureate program accreditation with AACSB, ABET, and CCNE. The 3 libraries contain 812,286 volumes, 75,285 microform items, and 976 audio/video tapes/CDs/DVDs, and subscribe to 1862 periodicals including electronic. Computerized library services include the card catalog, interlibrary loans, and database searching. Special learning facilities include a learning resource center, art gallery, radio station, TV station, 2 art galleries, a performing arts center, biological research labs, an environmental center, a language lab, and computer labs. There is an urban campus in downtown New York City and a 200-acre suburban campus in Pleasantville/Briarcliff Manor. Including any residence halls, there are 41 buildings.

Student Life: 65% of undergraduates are from New York. Others are from 41 states, 30 foreign countries, and Canada. 70% are from public schools. 44% are white; 12% Asian American; 11% African American; 11% Hispanic. The average age of freshmen is 19; all undergraduates, 23. 24% do not continue beyond their first year; 54% remain to graduate.

Housing: 2049 students can be accommodated in college housing, which includes coed dorms, on-campus apartments, and off-campus apartments. In addition, there are honors houses, special-interest houses, and a wellness floor. 75% of students commute. All students may keep cars.

Activities: 5% of men belong to 2 local and 4 national fraternities; 5% of women belong to 4 local and 3 national sororities. There are 159 groups on campus, including art, cheerleading, chorus, computers, dance, debate, drama, ethnic, film, gay, honors, international, literary magazine, musical theater, newspaper, photography, political, professional, radio and TV, religious, social, social service, student government, and yearbook. Popular campus events include Spring Fling, Springcoming, and Diade Comida.

Sports: There are 9 intercollegiate sports for men and 9 for women, and 6 intramural sports for men and 5 for women. Facilities include the Civic Center Gym in New York City, gyms, tennis courts, playing fields, and the Goldstein Health Fitness and Recreation Center at the Pleasantville/Briarcliff Manor campus.

Disabled Students: 70% of the campus is accessible. Wheelchair ramps, elevators, special parking, special class scheduling, lowered drinking fountains, lowered telephones, and other facilities that vary by campus are available.

Services: Counseling and information services are available, as is tutoring in every subject. There is remedial math, reading, and writing. All services are provided in the University's Center for Academic Excellence.

Campus Safety and Security: Measures include 24-hour foot and vehicle patrol, security escort services, shuttle buses, and informal discussions. There are pamphlets/posters/films, emergency telephones, and lighted pathways/sidewalks.

Programs of Study: Pace confers B.A., B.S., B.B.A., B.F.A., and B.S.N. degrees. Associate, master's, and doctoral degrees are also awarded. Bachelor's degrees are awarded in BIOLOGICAL SCIENCE (biology/biological science), BUSINESS (accounting, banking and finance, business economics, international business management, and marketing/retailing/merchandising), COMMUNICATIONS AND THE ARTS (communications, English, Spanish, and theater design), COMPUTER AND PHYSICAL SCIENCE (chemistry, computer science, information sciences and systems, mathematics, and physics), EDUCATION (business, early childhood, and elementary), HEALTH PROFESSIONS (medical laboratory technology, nursing, and physician's assistant), SOCIAL SCIENCE (criminal justice, economics, history, political science/government, psychology, social science, and sociology). Accounting is the strongest academically. Business and finance are the largest.

Required: To graduate, students must complete 128 to 133 credit hours, including 32 to 50 in the major, with a minimum GPA of 2.0. A core curriculum of 60 credits and an introductory computer science course are required.

Special: Internships, study abroad, a Washington semester, and a cooperative education program in all majors are available. Pace also offers accelerated degree programs, B.A.-B.S. degrees, dual majors, general studies degrees, and 3-2 engineering degrees with Manhattan College and Rensselaer Polytechnic Institute. Credit for life, military, and work experience, nondegree study, and pass/fail options are available. There are 13 national honor societies and a freshman honors program.

Faculty/Classroom: 60% of faculty are male; 40%, female. 84% teach undergraduates and 24% do research. No introductory courses are taught by graduate students. The average class size in an introductory lecture is 35; in a laboratory, 11; and in a regular course, 23.

Admissions: 74% of recent applicants were accepted. 43% of recent freshmen were in the top fifth of their class; 74% were in the top two fifths.

Requirements: The SAT or ACT is required. In addition, applicants should be graduates of an accredited secondary school, with at least 16 academic credits, including 4 in English, 3 to 4 each in math, science, and history, and 2 to 3 in foreign language. The GED is accepted. An essay and an interview are recommended. A GPA of 3.0 is required. AP and CLEP credits are accepted. Important factors in the admissions decision are advanced placement or honor courses, recommendations by school officials, and leadership record.

Procedure: Freshmen are admitted fall and spring. Entrance exams should be taken by December of the student's senior year. There are early admissions and deferred admissions plans. There is a rolling admissions plan. Application deadlines are open. Applications are accepted on-line. Check with the school for current application deadlines and fee.

Transfer: 510 transfer students enrolled in a recent year. Applicants are admitted in the fall or spring. A college GPA of 2.5 is required. Grades of C or better transfer for credit. A maximum of 68 credits will be accepted from a 2-year school. 32 of 128 credits required for the bachelor's degree must be completed at Pace.

Visiting: There are regularly scheduled orientations for prospective students, including student-for-a-day programs and overnight visits by appointment. There are guides for informal visits and visitors may sit in on classes and stay overnight. To schedule a visit, contact the Office of Undergraduate Admission at *ugnyc@pace.edu* or *infoctr@pace.edu*.

Financial Aid: In a recent year, 78% of all full-time freshmen and 87% of continuing full-time students received some form of financial aid. 76% of full-time freshmen and 81% of continuing full-time students received need-based aid. The average freshman award was $10,507. Average annual earnings from campus work are $3600. The average financial indebtedness of a recent graduate was $20,670. The FAFSA is required. Check with the school for current deadlines.

International Students: There were 354 international students enrolled in a recent year. The school actively recruits these students. They must take the TOEFL and also take the college's own test.

Computers: All students may access the system 24 hours a day. There are no time limits and no fees.

Graduates: In a recent year, 1760 bachelor's degrees were awarded. The most popular majors were computer science information systems (18%), finance (15%), and accounting (11%). In an average class, 1% graduate in 3 years or less, 45% graduate in 4 years or less, 52% graduate in 5 years or less, and 56% graduate in 6 years or less. 174 companies recruited on campus in a recent year. Of a recent graduating class, 81% were employed within 6 months of graduation.

Admissions Contact: Alan Young (NYC) and Joanna Broda, Director(s) of Undergraduate Admissions. E-mail: *infoctr@pace.edu* Web: *www.pace.edu*

PARSONS SCHOOL OF DESIGN
D-5

New York, NY 10011   (877) 528-3321
(877) 528-3324; Fax: (212) 229-5166

Full-time: 551 men, 1573 women	**Faculty:** 56
Part-time: 36 men, 151 women	**Ph.D.s:** n/av
Graduate: 142 men, 280 women	**Student/Faculty:** n/av
Year: semesters, summer session	**Tuition:** $22,630
Application Deadline: open	**Room & Board:** $9612
Freshman Class: n/av	
SAT or ACT: required	**SPECIAL**

Parsons School of Design, founded in 1896, is a private professional art school and is part of the New School for Social Research. In addition to regional accreditation, Parsons has baccalaureate program accreditation with NASAD. The 2 libraries contain 177,000 volumes and 5000 audio/video tapes/CDs/DVDs, and subscribe to 230 periodicals including electronic. Computerized library services include the card catalog and database searching. Special learning facilities include an art gallery. The 2-acre campus is in an urban area in Manhattan's Greenwich Village. Including any residence halls, there are 8 buildings.

Student Life: 52% of undergraduates are from New York. Others are from 49 states, 39 foreign countries, and Canada. 80% are from public schools. 32% are white; 29% foreign nationals; 20% Asian American. The average age of freshmen is 19; all undergraduates, 23.

Housing: 700 students can be accommodated in college housing, which includes coed dormitories and off-campus apartments. On-campus housing is available on a first-come, first-served basis and is available on a lottery system for upperclassmen. Priority is given to out-of-town students. Alcohol is not permitted. All students may keep cars.

Activities: There are no fraternities or sororities. There are some groups and organizations on campus, including ethnic, gay, international, literary magazine, political, religious, social, and student government. Popular campus events include the Fashion Critics Award Show and annual senior shows.

Sports: There is no sports program at Parsons.

Disabled Students: 95% of the campus is accessible. Wheelchair ramps, elevators, and specially equipped rest rooms are available.

Services: Counseling and information services are available, as is tutoring in some subjects, including English and art history. There is remedial reading and writing.

Campus Safety and Security: Measures include informal discussions and pamphlets/posters/films.

Programs of Study: Parsons confers B.A.-B.F.A., B.B.A., and B.F.A. degrees. Associate and master's degrees are also awarded. Bachelor's degrees are awarded in BUSINESS (marketing/retailing/merchandising), COMMUNICATIONS AND THE ARTS (advertising, design, fine arts, graphic design, illustration, photography, and studio art), ENGINEERING AND ENVIRONMENTAL DESIGN (architectural engineering, and interior design), SOCIAL SCIENCE (fashion design and technology). Communication design, illustration, and fashion design are the largest.

Required: To graduate, students must complete 134 credit hours, including 97 in the major, with a minimum GPA of 2.0. Parsons requires a minimum of 30 credits in liberal arts and 12 in art history.

Special: Students may cross-register at the New School for Social Research, Cooper Union, and Pratt Institute. Internships are required for some majors. Students may study abroad at the Parsons campus in Paris or in 4 other countries. The 5-year combined B.A.-B.F.A. degree requires 180 credits for graduation. A mobility semester or year at any AICAD school is available, and interdisciplinary majors, including architecture and environmental design and design marketing, are possible.

Faculty/Classroom: 89% teach undergraduates. No introductory courses are taught by graduate students. The average class size in an introductory lecture is 30 and in a regular course, 17.

Requirements: The SAT or ACT is required. In addition, applicants must be graduates of an accredited secondary school. The GED is accepted. Applicants should have completed 4 years each of art, English, history, and social studies. A portfolio and home exam are required, and an interview is recommended. AP credits are accepted. Important factors in the admissions decision are evidence of special talent, advanced placement or honor courses, and personality/intangible qualities.

Procedure: Freshmen are admitted fall and spring. Entrance exams should be taken by spring of the junior year. There is an early admissions plan. Application deadlines are open. Application fee is $40. A waiting list is an active part of the admissions procedure.

Transfer: 420 transfer students enrolled in 2004-2005. Applicants will receive credit for grade C work or better in college courses that are similar in content, purpose, and standards to the courses offered at Parsons. A high school transcript is required for undergraduates, and the SAT I or ACT is recommended. All students must present a portfolio and home exam. Transfers are admitted in the fall or spring. 67 of 134 credits required for the bachelor's degree must be completed at Parsons.

Visiting: There are guides for informal visits. To schedule a visit, contact the Office of Admissions.

Financial Aid: In 2005-2006, 70% of all full-time freshmen and 59% of continuing full-time students received some form of financial aid. 64% of full-time freshmen and 58% of continuing full-time students received need-based aid. The average freshman award was $12,684. The average financial indebtedness of the 2005 graduate was $23,450. Parsons is a member of CSS. The FAFSA and , and international students must file an institutional application. are required. The deadline for filing freshman financial aid applications for fall entry is March 1.

International Students: The school actively recruits these students. They must score 550 on the written TOEFL.

Computers: All students may access the system. There are no time limits and no fees. It is strongly recommended that all students have a personal computer.

Graduates: From July 1, 2004 to June 30, 2005, 198 bachelor's degrees were awarded. The most popular majors were visual and performing arts (94%) and architecture (6%). In an average class, 46% graduate in 4 years or less, 56% graduate in 5 years or less, and 61% graduate in 6 years or less.

Admissions Contact: Nadine M. Bourgeois, Assistant Dean and Director of Admissions. E-mail: *parsadm@newschool.edu*
Web: *www.parsons.edu*

POLYTECHNIC UNIVERSITY/BROOKLYN D-5
Brooklyn, NY 11201-3840

(718) 260-3100
(800) 765-8324; Fax: (718) 260-3446

Full-time: 1187 men, 264 women	**Faculty:** 94; I, -$
Part-time: 55 men, 13 women	**Ph.D.s:** 90%
Graduate: 978 men, 304 women	**Student/Faculty:** 15 to 1
Year: semesters, summer session	**Tuition:** $28,650
Application Deadline: open	**Room & Board:** $8500
Freshman Class: 1240 applied, 860 accepted, 304 enrolled	
SAT Verbal/Math: 540/640*	**VERY COMPETITIVE**

Polytechnic University, founded in 1854, is a private, multicampus university offering undergraduate and graduate programs through the divisions of arts and sciences, engineering, and management. In addition to regional accreditation, Brooklyn Poly has baccalaureate program accreditation with ABET and CSAB. The library contains 212,264 volumes, 60,106 microform items, and 337 audio/video tapes/CDs/DVDs, and subscribes to 1621 periodicals including electronic. Computerized library services include the card catalog, interlibrary loans, and database searching. Special learning facilities include a learning resource center and radio station. The 3-acre campus is in an urban area 5 minutes from downtown Manhattan. Including any residence halls, there are 6 buildings.

Student Life: 88% of undergraduates are from New York. Others are from 16 states, 16 foreign countries, and Canada. 84% are from public schools. 38% are Asian American; 27% white; 10% African American. The average age of freshmen is 19; all undergraduates, 21. 16% do not continue beyond their first year; 54% remain to graduate.

Housing: 400 students can be accommodated in college housing, which includes coed dormitories and fraternity houses. On-campus housing is available on a first-come, first-served basis. Priority is given to out-of-town students. 85% of students commute. Alcohol is not permitted. No one may keep cars.

Activities: 12% of men and about 3% of women belong to 2 local and 3 national fraternities; 3% of women belong to 1 national sorority. There are 60 groups on campus, including arts and music, chess, computers, ethnic, film, honors, international, literary magazine, newspaper, photography, professional, radio and TV, religious, social, social service, student government, and yearbook. Popular campus events include Chinese New Year, film festivals, and International Food Fair.

Sports: There are 7 intercollegiate sports for men and 7 for women, and 7 intramural sports for men and 7 for women. Facilities include soccer, lacrosse, and baseball fields, and 2 student centers.

Disabled Students: 70% of the campus is accessible. Wheelchair ramps, elevators, special parking, specially equipped rest rooms, lowered drinking fountains, and lowered telephones are available.

Services: Counseling and information services are available, as is tutoring in every subject. There is remedial math and writing.

Campus Safety and Security: Measures include 24-hour foot and vehicle patrol, informal discussions, pamphlets/posters/films, and emergency telephones. There are lighted pathways/sidewalks.

Programs of Study: Brooklyn Poly confers the B.S. degree. Master's and doctoral degrees are also awarded. Bachelor's degrees are awarded in COMMUNICATIONS AND THE ARTS (technical and business writing), COMPUTER AND PHYSICAL SCIENCE (chemistry, computer science, information sciences and systems, mathematics, and physics), ENGINEERING AND ENVIRONMENTAL DESIGN (chemical engineering, civil engineering, computer engineering, electrical/electronics engineering, and mechanical engineering), SOCIAL SCIENCE (humanities, liberal arts/general studies, and social science). Engineering, management, and physical sciences are the strongest academically. Electrical engineering, computer engineering, and computer science are the largest.

Required: Students must complete all university and departmental course requirements, including 24 credits in humanities/social science, 16 in math, 12 in chemistry/physics, 4 in computers with Pascal, 4 in engineering design, and 3 in programming methodology. A total of 124 to 128 credits must be earned, with 32 in the major, and a minimum GPA of 2.0, is required to graduate. A senior design project is also required.

Special: Cooperative programs are available in all majors. Opportunities are provided for internships, work-study programs, study abroad, accelerated degree programs in engineering and computer science, dual majors, student-designed majors, and nondegree study. There are 9 national honor societies, a freshman honors program, and 3 departmental honors programs.

Faculty/Classroom: 84% of faculty are male; 16%, female. 75% teach undergraduates. No introductory courses are taught by graduate students. The average class size in an introductory lecture is 25; in a laboratory, 16; and in a regular course, 29.

Admissions: 69% of the 2005-2006 applicants were accepted. The SAT scores for the 2005-2006 freshman class were: Verbal--20% below 500, 52% between 500 and 599, 26% between 600 and 700, and 2% above 700; Math--5% below 500, 31% between 500 and 599, 48% between 600 and 700, and 16% above 700. There is an early admissions plan.

Requirements: The SAT is required. In addition, graduation from an accredited secondary school is required; a GED will be accepted. Applicants must submit a minimum of 16 credit hours, including 4 each in English, math and science, and 1 each in foreign language, art, music, and social studies. SAT Subject tests in writing, math I or II, and chemistry or physics are recommended. An essay and an interview are recommended. AP credits are accepted. Important factors in the admissions decision are advanced placement or honor courses, leadership record, and evidence of special talent.

Procedure: Freshmen are admitted fall, spring, and summer. Entrance exams should be taken by November of the senior year. There is a deferred admissions and a rolling admissions plan. Application deadlines are open. Applications are accepted on-line. The fall 2005 application fee was $60.

Transfer: 60 transfer students enrolled in 2004-2005. Transfer applicants must have a 2.75 cumulative GPA. Students with fewer than 30 credits must submit SAT scores and secondary school transcripts in addition to official college-level transcripts. 36 of 124 credits required for the bachelor's degree must be completed at Brooklyn Poly.

Visiting: There are regularly scheduled orientations for prospective students, including a keynote speaker, major presentations, financial aid and scholarship sessions, and student life and career services sessions. There are guides for informal visits and visitors may stay overnight. To schedule a visit, contact the Dean of Admissions at 718-637-5917.

Financial Aid: In 2005-2006, 98% of all full-time freshmen and 97% of continuing full-time students received some form of financial aid. 84% of full-time freshmen and 82% of continuing full-time students received need-based aid. The average freshman award was $21,685. Need-based scholarships or need-based grants averaged $7346; and need-based self-help aid (loans and jobs) averaged $5299. 25% of undergraduates work part time. Average annual earnings from campus work are $2800. The average financial indebtedness of the 2005 graduate was $22,332. The FAFSA and the college's own financial statement are required. The priority date for freshman financial aid applications for fall entry is January 31. The deadline for filing freshman financial aid applications for fall entry is May 1. Brooklyn Poly is a member of CSS.

International Students: There were 124 international students enrolled in a recent year. The school actively recruits these students. They must score satisfactorily on the written TOEFL or on the electronic version and also take the SAT.

Computers: All students may access the system 24-hour dial-up service. Computer labs are open 13 hours a day. There are no time limits and no fees. All students are required to have personal computers. It is recommended that students have an IBM ThinkPad T40 or its equivalent with XP Professional Operating system.

Graduates: From July 1, 2004 to June 30, 2005, 275 bachelor's degrees were awarded. The most popular majors were computer science (42%), computer engineering (21%), and electrical engineering (15%). In an average class, 1% graduate in 3 years or less, 36% graduate in 4 years or less, 51% graduate in 5 years or less, and 54% graduate in 6 years or less. 150 companies recruited on campus in 2004-2005. Of the recent graduating class, 5% were enrolled in graduate school within 6 months of graduation and 84% were employed.

Admissions Contact: Jonathan Wexler, Dean of Undergraduate Admissions. E-mail: *uadmit@poly.edu* Web: *www.poly.edu*

PRATT INSTITUTE — D-5

Brooklyn, NY 11205

(718) 636-3669
(800) 331-0834; Fax: (718) 636-3670

Full-time: 1155 men, 1743 women	**Faculty:** n/av
Part-time: 76 men, 78 women	**Ph.D.s:** n/av
Graduate: 522 men, 1165 women	**Student/Faculty:** n/av
Year: 4-1-4, summer session	**Tuition:** $27,580
Application Deadline: February 1	**Room & Board:** $8576
Freshman Class: 3794 applied, 1962 accepted, 625 enrolled	
SAT Verbal/Math: 573/561*	**ACT:** 25 SPECIAL

Pratt Institute, founded in 1887, is a private institution offering undergraduate and graduate programs in architecture, art and design education, art history, industrial, interior, and communication design, fine arts, design management, arts and cultural management, writing for publication, performance and media, and professional studies. Some of the figures in the above capsule and this profile are approximate. There are 2 undergraduate and 3 graduate schools. In addition to regional accreditation, Pratt has baccalaureate program accreditation with FIDER, NAAB, and NASAD. The library contains 208,000 volumes, 50,000 microform items, and 3500 audio/video tapes/CDs/DVDs, and subscribes to 700 periodicals including electronic. Computerized library services include the card catalog, database searching, and Internet access. Special learning facilities include a learning resource center, art gallery, radio station, bronze foundry, and metal forge. The 25-acre campus is in an urban area 3 miles east of downtown Manhattan. Including any residence halls, there are 23 buildings.

Student Life: 53% of undergraduates are from New York. Others are from 46 states, 38 foreign countries, and Canada. 81% are from public schools. 62% are white; 13% Asian American; 10% foreign nationals. The average age of freshmen is 19; all undergraduates, 23. 8% do not continue beyond their first year; 65% remain to graduate.

Housing: 1500 students can be accommodated in college housing, which includes single-sex and coed dormitories, on-campus apartments, and married-student housing. In addition, there are honors houses. On-campus housing is guaranteed for the freshman year only, is available on a first-come, first-served basis, and is available on a lottery system for upperclassmen. Priority is given to out-of-town students. 51% of students commute. All students may keep cars.

Activities: 5% of men belong to 1 local and 1 national fraternity; 5% of women belong to 1 local sorority. There are 50 groups on campus, including art, cheerleading, chess, drama, ethnic, film, gay, honors, international, literary magazine, martial arts, musical theater, newspaper, professional, radio and TV, religious, social, student government, and yearbook. Popular campus events include Springfest, International Food Fair, and Holiday Ball.

Sports: There are 6 intercollegiate sports for men and 4 for women, and 3 intramural sports for men and 1 for women. Facilities include an activities resource center containing 5 indoor tennis courts, a 200-meter indoor track, volleyball and basketball courts, a weight room, and 2 dance studios.

Disabled Students: 75% of the campus is accessible. Wheelchair ramps, elevators, special parking, specially equipped rest rooms, lowered drinking fountains, and special housing are available.

Services: Counseling and information services are available, as is tutoring in some subjects, including math, English, science, social science, and art history. There is a reader service for the blind and individual tutoring and testing services are also available.

Campus Safety and Security: Measures include 24-hour foot and vehicle patrol, security escort services, shuttle buses, and informal discussions. There are pamphlets/posters/films, emergency telephones, lighted pathways/sidewalks, and trained security officers.

Programs of Study: Pratt confers B.Arch., B.F.A., B.I.D., and B.P.S. degrees. Associate and master's degrees are also awarded. Bachelor's degrees are awarded in COMMUNICATIONS AND THE ARTS (art history and appreciation, communications, creative writing, film arts, fine arts, industrial design, and photography), EDUCATION (art), ENGINEERING AND ENVIRONMENTAL DESIGN (architecture, computer graphics, construction management, and interior design), SOCIAL SCIENCE (fashion design and technology). Fine arts, industrial design, and communications design are the strongest academically. Architecture and communications design are the largest.

Required: The number of credits needed for graduation varies with the major, but a minimum of 132 is required, one quarter of which must be in liberal arts. Undergraduates must maintain a GPA of 2.0. All students must take 13 credits (15 for architecture majors) of liberal arts electives, 6 credits each of social sciences or philosophy, English, and cultural history, and 3 credits of science.

Special: Pratt offers co-op programs with the East Coast Consortium (art and design schools) and cross-registration with St. John's College and Queen's College. Internships, study abroad in 4 countries, accelerated degree programs, work-study programs, dual majors, credit for work experience, nondegree study, and pass/fail options are available. There are 4 national honor societies.

Faculty/Classroom: 58% of faculty are male; 42%, female. 92% teach undergraduates and 1% do research. No introductory courses are taught by graduate students. The average class size in an introductory lecture is 22; in a laboratory, 20; and in a regular course, 15.

Admissions: 52% of the 2005-2006 applicants were accepted. The SAT scores for the 2005-2006 freshman class were: Verbal--16% below 500, 46% between 500 and 599, 32% between 600 and 700, and 6% above 700; Math--19% below 500, 45% between 500 and 599, 31% between 600 and 700, and 5% above 700. The ACT scores were 2% below 21, 46% between 18 and 23, 39% between 24 and 29, and 13% above 29.

Requirements: The SAT or ACT is required. SAT: Subject tests in writing and mathematics level I or II are recommended for architecture applicants. Applicants must be graduates of an accredited secondary school. The GED is accepted. Students should have completed 4 years of English, 3 of math, and 2 each of science, social studies, and history. A portfolio is required, as is an interview for all applicants who live within 100 miles of Pratt. A GPA of 2.75 is required. AP and CLEP credits are accepted. Important factors in the admissions decision are evidence of special talent, advanced placement or honor courses, and recommendations by school officials.

Procedure: Freshmen are admitted fall and spring. Entrance exams should be taken by November of the senior year. There is an early decision plan. Early decision applications should be filed by December 15; regular applications, by February 1 for fall entry and November 1 for spring entry, along with a $40 fee. Early decision notification is sent December 15. Regular decision notification is continuous until April 11. 165

applicants were on the 2005 waiting list; 15 were admitted. Applications are accepted on-line.

Transfer: 190 transfer students enrolled in 2004-2005. Applicants should present college transcripts and recommendations. Students with fewer than 30 college credits must submit SAT or ACT scores. All transfer applicants without an associate degree must submit high school transcripts as well. A portfolio is required for architecture and art and design students. An interview is recommended. 48 of 132 credits required for the bachelor's degree must be completed at Pratt.

Visiting: There are regularly scheduled orientations for prospective students, including a campus tour, schoolwide presentations, departmental presentations, and financial aid workshops. There are guides for informal visits and visitors may sit in on classes and stay overnight. To schedule a visit, contact Olga Burger, the Office of Admissions at (800) 331-0834.

Financial Aid: In 2005-2006, 78% of continuing full-time students received some form of financial aid. 68% of full-time freshmen and 58% of continuing full-time students received need-based aid. Pratt is a member of CSS. The CSS/Profile or FAFSA, the college's own financial statement, and the parents' and student's tax returns are required. Check with the school for curent application deadlines.

International Students: In a recent year there were 307 international students enrolled. The school actively recruits these students. They must score satisfactorily on the written TOEFL or on the electronic version and also take the college's own test.

Computers: All students may access the system 24 hours a day, 7 days a week. There are no time limits and no fees. It is strongly recommended that all students have a personal computer.

Admissions Contact: Judith Aaron, Vice President for Enrollment. A video is available. E-mail: *jaaron@pratt.edu* Web: *www.pratt.edu/admiss*

RENSSELAER POLYTECHNIC INSTITUTE   D-3

Troy, NY 12180-3590   (518) 276-6216
                                   (800) 448-6562; Fax: (518) 276-4072

Full-time: 3738 men, 1173 women	**Faculty:** 392; I, +$
Part-time: 23 men, 17 women	**Ph.D.s:** 96%
Graduate: 1643 men, 647 women	**Student/Faculty:** 13 to 1
Year: semesters, summer session	**Tuition:** $31,857
Application Deadline: January 1	**Room & Board:** $9431
Freshman Class: 5574 applied, 4340 accepted, 1240 enrolled	
SAT Verbal/Math: 630/690*	**ACT:** 26
	HIGHLY COMPETITIVE+

Rensselaer Polytechnic Institute, founded in 1824, is a private institution that emphasizes technology in its Schools of Engineering, Architecture, Management, Humanities & Social Sciences, Science, and Information Technology. There are 5 undergraduate and 5 graduate schools. In addition to regional accreditation, Rensselaer has baccalaureate program accreditation with AACSB, ABET, and NAAB. The 2 libraries contain 521,165 volumes, 576,215 microform items, and 8932 audio/video tapes/CDs/DVDs, and subscribe to 38,494 periodicals including electronic. Computerized library services include the card catalog, interlibrary loans, database searching, Internet access, and laptop Internet portals. Special learning facilities include a learning resource center, art gallery, radio station, TV station, and an observatory. The 268-acre campus is in a suburban area 10 miles north of Albany. Including any residence halls, there are 178 buildings.

Student Life: 60% of undergraduates are from out of state, mostly the Northeast. Others are from 48 states, 67 foreign countries, and Canada. 80% are from public schools. 75% are white; 10% Asian American. The average age of freshmen is 18; all undergraduates, 20. 8% do not continue beyond their first year; 81% remain to graduate.

Housing: 2933 students can be accommodated in college housing, which includes single-sex and coed dorms, on-campus apartments, married-student housing, fraternity houses, and sorority houses. In addition, there are special-interest houses and a Black cultural center. On-campus housing is guaranteed for the freshman year only, is available on a first-come, first-served basis, and is available on a lottery system for upperclassmen. 55% of students live on campus. Upperclassmen may keep cars.

Activities: 39% of men belong to 1 local and 31 national fraternities; 18% of women belong to 1 local and 4 national sororities. There are 160 groups on campus, including art, astrophysical society, band, biomedical engineering society, cheerleading, chess, choir, chorale, chorus, computers, dance, drama, drill team, entrepreneurship, ethnic, film, finance, gay, honors, international, jazz band, literary magazine, musical theater, newspaper, orchestra, pep band, photography, political, professional, radio and TV, religious, Rensselaer Biotechnology, students association, social, social service, student government, symphony, and yearbook. Popular campus events include Big Red Freakout, Grand Marshal Week, and Performing Arts Series.

Sports: There are 12 intercollegiate sports for men and 11 for women, and 22 intramural sports for men and 21 for women. Facilities include a 5300-seat field house, 2 pools, a stadium, 2 gyms, a sports and recre-

ation center, several playing fields, 2 weight rooms, 6 tennis courts, 7 handball/squash courts, an artificial turf field, an indoor track, an ice hockey rink, and a fitness center.

Disabled Students: 55% of the campus is accessible. Wheelchair ramps, elevators, special parking, specially equipped rest rooms, special class scheduling, lowered drinking fountains, and lowered telephones are available.

Services: Counseling and information services are available, as is tutoring in every subject. There is a reader service for the blind, and remedial math, reading, and writing. There is a writing center and an advising and learning assistance center.

Campus Safety and Security: Measures include 24-hour foot and vehicle patrol, self-defense education, security escort services, and shuttle buses. There are informal discussions, pamphlets/posters/films, emergency telephones, lighted pathways/sidewalks, card-access residence halls, on-campus bicycle patrol, and a student volunteer program.

Programs of Study: Rensselaer confers B.S. and B.Arch. degrees. Master's and doctoral degrees are also awarded. Bachelor's degrees are awarded in BIOLOGICAL SCIENCE (biochemistry, biology/biological science, and biophysics), BUSINESS (management information systems and management science), COMMUNICATIONS AND THE ARTS (communications and media arts), COMPUTER AND PHYSICAL SCIENCE (applied physics, chemistry, computer science, geology, hydrogeology, mathematics, physics, and science technology), ENGINEERING AND ENVIRONMENTAL DESIGN (aeronautical engineering, architecture, biomedical engineering, chemical engineering, civil engineering, computer engineering, construction engineering, electrical/electronics engineering, engineering, engineering physics, environmental engineering, industrial engineering, materials engineering, mechanical engineering, and nuclear engineering), HEALTH PROFESSIONS (premedicine), SOCIAL SCIENCE (economics, interdisciplinary studies, philosophy, prelaw, and psychology). Architecture, engineering, humanitites & social sciences are the strongest academically. General engineering, management, and computer science are the largest.

Required: For graduation, students must earn at least 124 credits in all majors except engineering (128 needed), B.S. building sciences (126 needed), and the B.Arch. program (168 needed). The core curriculum includes 24 credits in physical, life, and engineering sciences and 24 credits in humanities and social sciences. Students must maintain a minimum GPA of 1.8 and must fulfill a writing requirement.

Special: Rensselaer offers an exchange program with Williams and Harvey Mudd Colleges and cross-registration with 16 regional colleges and universities. Co-op programs, internships, study abroad in several countries, and pass/fail options are available. Students may pursue dual and student-designed majors, a 3-2 engineering degree, and accelerated 4-year B.S.-M.S. degrees. There are 14 national honor societies and 8 departmental honors programs.

Faculty/Classroom: 80% of faculty are male; 20%, female. No introductory courses are taught by graduate students. The average class size in an introductory lecture is 35; in a laboratory, 20; and in a regular course, 24.

Admissions: 78% of the 2005-2006 applicants were accepted. The SAT scores for the 2005-2006 freshman class were: Verbal--3% below 500, 26% between 500 and 599, 49% between 600 and 700, and 22% above 700; Math--8% between 500 and 599, 46% between 600 and 700, and 46% above 700. The ACT scores were 2% below 21, 19% between 21 and 23, 35% between 24 and 26, 27% between 27 and 28, and 16% above 28. 95% of the current freshmen were in the top fifth of their class; 98% were in the top two fifths. 62 freshmen graduated first in their class.

Requirements: The SAT or ACT is required. In addition, SAT Subject tests in math and science are required for accelerated-program applicants. Applicants must have completed 4 years each of English and math (through precalculus), 3 years of science (including chemistry and physics), and 2 years of social studies. An essay is required. Architecture and electronic arts applicants must submit a portfolio. AP credits are accepted. Important factors in the admissions decision are advanced placement or honor courses, recommendations by school officials, and leadership record.

Procedure: Freshmen are admitted fall and spring. Entrance exams should be taken in the junior or senior year. There are early decision and deferred admissions plans. Early decision applications should be filed by November 15; regular applications, by January 1 for fall entry and November 1 for spring entry, along with a $70 fee. Notification of early decision is sent December 31; regular decision, April 15. 134 early decision candidates were accepted for the 2005-2006 class. Applications are accepted on-line.

Transfer: 125 transfer students enrolled in 2004-2005. The SAT or ACT is required for applicants with fewer than 30 credits. All students are encouraged to have an interview and must present faculty recommendations; B.Arch. applicants must present a portfolio. Grades of C or better transfer for credit. 48 of 124 credits required for the bachelor's degree must be completed at Rensselaer.

Visiting: There are regularly scheduled orientations for prospective students. There are guides for informal visits and visitors may sit in on classes. To schedule a visit, contact the Admissions Office at (518) 276-6216 or *admissions@rpi.edu*.

Financial Aid: In 2005-2006, 97% of all full-time freshmen and 89% of continuing full-time students received some form of financial aid. 75% of full-time freshmen and 70% of continuing full-time students received need-based aid. The average freshman award was $25,201. Need-based scholarships or need-based grants averaged $22,153; need-based self-help aid (loans and jobs) averaged $5800; non-need-based athletic scholarships averaged $43,010; and other non-need-based awards and non-need-based scholarships averaged $12,000. 28% of undergraduates work part time. Average annual earnings from campus work are $1978. The average financial indebtedness of the 2005 graduate was $27,235. Rensselaer is a member of CSS. The FAFSA and the state aid form are required. The deadline for filing freshman financial aid applications for fall entry is February 15.

International Students: There are 164 international students enrolled. The school actively recruits these students. Satisfactory scores are required on the written TOEFL and the SAT or the ACT.

Computers: Wireless access is available. Services include support for interactive learning (including WebCT courses), electronic information-retrieval services by the libraries, and on-line student and administrative services. All students may access the system. There are no time limits and no fees. All students are required to have personal computers. It is required that all undergraduates have a laptop computer. An IBM Think-Pad T43 is recommended.

Graduates: From July 1, 2004 to June 30, 2005, 1173 bachelor's degrees were awarded. The most popular majors were engineering (47%), computer science (22%), and management (11%). In an average class, 65% graduate in 4 years or less, 80% graduate in 5 years or less, and 81% graduate in 6 years or less. 370 companies recruited on campus in 2004-2005. Of the 2004 graduating class, 27% were enrolled in graduate school within 6 months of graduation and 68% were employed.

Admissions Contact: Karen Long, Acting Dean, Enrollment Management. E-mail: *admissions@rpi.edu* Web: *http://admissions.rpi.edu*

ROBERTS WESLEYAN COLLEGE
B-3

Rochester, NY 14624-1997

(585) 594-6400
(800) 777-4792; Fax: (585) 594-6371

Full-time: 391 men, 874 women	**Faculty:** n/av
Part-time: 46 men, 97 women	**Ph.D.s:** 67%
Graduate: 154 men, 386 women	**Student/Faculty:** n/av
Year: semesters, summer session	**Tuition:** $19,324
Application Deadline: February 1	**Room & Board:** $7054
Freshman Class: 614 applied, 526 accepted, 222 enrolled	
SAT or ACT: required	**COMPETITIVE**

Roberts Wesleyan College, founded in 1866, is a private institution affiliated with the Free Methodist Church. The curriculum offers a liberal arts education in the Christian tradition. In addition to regional accreditation, Roberts has baccalaureate program accreditation with ACBSP, CSWE, NASAD, NASM, and NLN. The library contains 121,032 volumes, 171,113 microform items, and 3781 audio/video tapes/CDs/DVDs, and subscribes to 856 periodicals including electronic. Computerized library services include the card catalog, interlibrary loans, database searching, Internet access, and laptop Internet portals. Special learning facilities include a learning resource center, art gallery, and radio station. The 75-acre campus is in a suburban area 8 miles southwest of Rochester. Including any residence halls, there are 32 buildings.

Student Life: 88% of undergraduates are from New York. Students are from 21 states, 18 foreign countries, and Canada. 79% are white. 67% are Protestant; 17% Catholic. The average age of freshmen is 19; all undergraduates, 22. 19% do not continue beyond their first year; 50% remain to graduate.

Housing: 792 students can be accommodated in college housing, which includes single-sex dorms, on-campus apartments, and off-campus apartments. On-campus housing is guaranteed for all 4 years. 65% of students live on campus; of those, 50% remain on campus on weekends. Alcohol is not permitted. All students may keep cars.

Activities: There are no fraternities or sororities. There are many groups and organizations on campus, including band, choir, chorale, drama, ethnic, honors, international, jazz band, musical theater, newspaper, orchestra, pep band, radio and TV, religious, social, social service, student government, and yearbook. Popular campus events include Winter Weekend and Spring Formal.

Sports: There are 6 intercollegiate sports for men and 7 for women, and 6 intramural sports for men and 6 for women. Facilities include an athletic center with facilities for basketball, volleyball, tennis, badminton, track, soccer, weightlifting, walleyball, racquetball, and swimming.

Disabled Students: 60% of the campus is accessible. Wheelchair ramps, elevators, special parking, specially equipped rest rooms, special class scheduling, lowered drinking fountains, and lowered telephones are available.

Services: Counseling and information services are available, as is tutoring in every subject. Note takers for the hearing impaired are available.

There is a reader service for the blind, and remedial math, reading, and writing.

Campus Safety and Security: Measures include 24-hour foot and vehicle patrol, self-defense education, security escort services, and informal discussions. There are pamphlets/posters/films, emergency telephones, lighted pathways/sidewalks, and personal-safety education programs.

Programs of Study: Roberts confers B.A. and B.S. degrees. Associate and master's degrees are also awarded. Bachelor's degrees are awarded in BIOLOGICAL SCIENCE (biochemistry and biology/biological science), BUSINESS (accounting and business administration and management), COMMUNICATIONS AND THE ARTS (communications, English, fine arts, and music), COMPUTER AND PHYSICAL SCIENCE (chemistry, computer science, mathematics, and physics), EDUCATION (art, elementary, and music), HEALTH PROFESSIONS (nursing, premedicine, prepharmacy, and preveterinary science), SOCIAL SCIENCE (criminal justice, history, prelaw, psychology, social work, and sociology). Music and teacher education are the strongest academically. Elementary education and organizational management are the largest.

Required: To graduate, students must complete a minimum of 124 credit hours, with a minimum of 30 hours in the major. Required courses include first-year experience, phys ed, modern technology, world issues, speech, writing, history, Bible, and philosophy.

Special: Students may cross-register with members of the Rochester Area Colleges consortium. Internships, study abroad in 8 countries, a Washington semester, co-op programs, B.A.-B.S. degrees, dual majors, and 3-2 engineering degrees with Clarkson University, Rensselaer Polytechnic Institute, and Rochester Institute of Technology are available. Nondegree study and credit for life, military, and work experience are also offered. The organizational management program, geared to adults, consists of 4-hour weekly sessions, with reliance on out-of-class work. There is a freshman honors program.

Faculty/Classroom: 59% of faculty are male; 41%, female. 84% teach undergraduates. No introductory courses are taught by graduate students. The average class size in an introductory lecture is 38; in a laboratory, 15; and in a regular course, 23.

Admissions: 86% of the 2005-2006 applicants were accepted. The SAT scores for the 2005-2006 freshman class were: Verbal--29% below 500, 42% between 500 and 599, 27% between 600 and 700, and 2% above 700; Math--26% below 500, 47% between 500 and 599, 25% between 600 and 700, and 2% above 700. 50% of the current freshmen were in the top fifth of their class; 81% were in the top two fifths. 16 freshmen graduated first in their class in a recent year.

Requirements: The SAT or ACT is required. In addition, applicants must be graduates of an accredited secondary school. The GED is accepted. At least 12 academic credits are required, including 4 years of English and 2 years each of math and science. A foreign language and 3 years of social studies are recommended. The chosen major may modify requirements. An essay is required, and an interview is recommended. Roberts requires applicants to be in the upper 50% of their class. A GPA of 2.3 is required. AP and CLEP credits are accepted. Important factors in the admissions decision are advanced placement or honor courses, personality/intangible qualities, and extracurricular activities record.

Procedure: Freshmen are admitted to all sessions. There are early admissions, rolling admissions, and deferred admissions plans. Applications should be filed by February 1 for fall entry and December 1 for spring entry. Notification is sent on a rolling basis. The fall 2005 application fee was $35. Applications are accepted on-line.

Transfer: 100 transfer students enrolled in 2004-2005. Applicants must submit transcripts from all previous institutions attended. Credit is usually accepted for courses with grade C or better. 30 of 124 credits required for the bachelor's degree must be completed at Roberts.

Visiting: There are regularly scheduled orientations for prospective students, including a campus tour, class visits, admissions and departmental interviews, and a financial aid presentation. There are guides for informal visits and visitors may sit in on classes and stay overnight. To schedule a visit, contact the Admissions Office.

Financial Aid: In 2005-2006, 91% of all full-time freshmen and 93% of continuing full-time students received some form of financial aid. 88% of full-time freshmen and 89% of continuing full-time students received need-based aid. The average freshman award was $19,363. Need-based scholarships or need-based grants averaged $11,115; need-based self-help aid (loans and jobs) averaged $8981; and other non-need-based awards and non-need-based scholarships averaged $7383. 35% of undergraduates work part time. Average annual earnings from campus work are $974. Roberts is a member of CSS. The FAFSA and TAP (New York residents only) are required. The priority date for freshman financial aid applications for fall entry is March 15. The deadline for filing freshman financial aid applications for fall entry is rolling.

International Students: There were 55 international students enrolled. They must score satisfactorily on the TOEFL.

Computers: All students may access the system 24 hours a day, 7 days a week. There are no time limits and no fees.

Graduates: In a recent year, 340 bachelor's degrees were awarded. The most popular majors were organizational management (28%), nursing (14%), and elementary education (11%). In an average class, 46% graduate in 4 years or less, 50% graduate in 5 years or less, and 52% graduate in 6 years or less.

Admissions Contact: Linda Kurtz Hoffman, Vice President for Admissions and Marketing. A video is available.
E-mail: *admissions@roberts.edu* Web: *www.roberts.edu*

ROCHESTER INSTITUTE OF TECHNOLOGY   B-3

Rochester, NY 14623   (585) 475-6631; Fax: (585) 475-7424

Full-time: 7986 men, 3454 women	**Faculty:** 879; IIA, +$
Part-time: 984 men, 509 women	**Ph.D.s:** 85%
Graduate: 1400 men, 867 women	**Student/Faculty:** 13 to 1
Year: quarters, summer session	**Tuition:** $23,619
Application Deadline: open	**Room & Board:** $8451
Freshman Class: 9384 applied, 6519 accepted, 2217 enrolled	
SAT Verbal/Math: 590/620*	**ACT:** 26 **VERY COMPETITIVE+**

Rochester Institute of Technology, a private institution founded in 1829, offers programs in art and design, science, computer science, medical sciences, engineering, fine arts, business, hotel management, graphic arts, information technology, and photography, as well as liberal arts, and includes the National Technical Institute for the Deaf. Most programs include a cooperative education component, which provides full-time work experience to complement classroom studies. There are 14 undergraduate and 14 graduate schools. In addition to regional accreditation, RIT has baccalaureate program accreditation with AACSB, ABET, ADA, CAAHEP, CAHEA, CSAB, CSWE, FIDER, and NASAD. The library contains 407,141 volumes, 495,000 microform items, and 63,904 audio/video tapes/CDs/DVDs, and subscribes to 2519 periodicals including electronic. Computerized library services include the card catalog, interlibrary loans, database searching, and Internet access. Special learning facilities include a learning resource center, art gallery, radio station, TV station, a computer chip manufacturing facility, a student-operated restaurant, an electronic prepress lab, an imaging science facility, and an observatory. The 1300-acre campus is in a suburban area 5 miles south of Rochester. Including any residence halls, there are 185 buildings.

Student Life: 55% of undergraduates are from New York. Others are from 50 states, 80 foreign countries, and Canada. 85% are from public schools. 78% are white. The average age of freshmen is 18; all undergraduates, 21. 10% do not continue beyond their first year; 63% remain to graduate.

Housing: 6500 students can be accommodated in college housing, which includes single-sex and coed dorms, on-campus apartments, married-student housing, fraternity houses, and sorority houses. In addition, there are honors houses and special-interest houses. On-campus housing is guaranteed for the freshman year only, is available on a first-come, first-served basis, and is available on a lottery system for upperclassmen. 61% of students live on campus; of those, 90% remain on campus on weekends. All students may keep cars.

Activities: 5% of men belong to 16 national fraternities; 5% of women belong to 9 national sororities. There are 200 groups on campus, including art, band, cheerleading, chess, choir, chorale, chorus, computers, dance, drama, ethnic, film, gay, gospel choir, honors, international, jazz band, literary magazine, newspaper, orchestra, pep band, photography, political, professional, radio and TV, religious, social, social service, student government, and yearbook. Popular campus events include Fall, Spring, and Winter Weekends and Martin Luther King Celebration.

Sports: There are 12 intercollegiate sports for men and 12 for women, and 13 intramural sports for men and 13 for women. Facilities include 3 gyms, an ice rink, 2 swimming pools, 9 tennis courts, a field house, athletic fields, and a student life center with 8 racquetball courts, dance facilities, weight-training facilities, and an indoor track.

Disabled Students: 95% of the campus is accessible. Wheelchair ramps, elevators, special parking, specially equipped rest rooms, special class scheduling, lowered drinking fountains, lowered telephones, special housing, and special fire alarm systems for hearing-impaired students are available.

Services: Counseling and information services are available, as is tutoring in most subjects. There is a reader service for the blind. There are comprehensive support services for students with physical or learning disabilities and for first-generation college students.

Campus Safety and Security: Measures include 24-hour foot and vehicle patrol, self-defense education, security escort services, and shuttle buses. There are informal discussions, pamphlets/posters/films, emergency telephones, and lighted pathways/sidewalks.

Programs of Study: RIT confers B.S. and B.F.A. degrees. Associate, master's, and doctoral degrees are also awarded. Bachelor's degrees are awarded in BIOLOGICAL SCIENCE (biochemistry, bioinformatics, biology/biological science, biotechnology, and nutrition), BUSINESS (accounting, banking and finance, business administration and management, business systems analysis, hotel/motel and restaurant management, international business management, management information systems, management science, marketing management, and

tourism), COMMUNICATIONS AND THE ARTS (animation, applied art, ceramic art and design, communications, communications technology, crafts, design, film arts, fine arts, glass, graphic design, illustration, industrial design, metal/jewelry, painting, photography, publishing, sculpture, studio art, telecommunications, and video), COMPUTER AND PHYSICAL SCIENCE (applied mathematics, chemistry, computer mathematics, computer science, information sciences and systems, mathematics, physics, polymer science, software engineering, statistics, and systems analysis), EDUCATION (education of the deaf and hearing impaired), ENGINEERING AND ENVIRONMENTAL DESIGN (aerospace studies, biomedical engineering, civil engineering technology, computer engineering, computer graphics, computer technology, electrical/electronics engineering, electrical/electronics engineering technology, engineering, engineering technology, environmental engineering technology, environmental science, furniture design, graphic and printing production, graphic arts technology, industrial engineering, interior design, manufacturing engineering, manufacturing technology, materials science, mechanical engineering, mechanical engineering technology, military science, printing technology, and woodworking), HEALTH PROFESSIONS (allied health, physician's assistant, predentistry, premedicine, preveterinary science, and ultrasound technology), SOCIAL SCIENCE (criminal justice, dietetics, economics, experimental psychology, food production/management/services, interpreter for the deaf, prelaw, psychology, and public affairs). Engineering, computer science, and photography are the strongest academically. Engineering, information technology, and photography are the largest.

Required: Students must have a GPA of 2.0 and have completed 180 quarter credit hours to graduate. Distribution requirements include 36 credits in the liberal arts (writing, humanities, and social sciences). B.S. programs also require a minimum of 20 quarter credit hours in science and math. There are no general science or math requirements for the B.F.A. programs in art, design, photography, or film/video.

Special: RIT offers internships in social science and allied health majors and cooperative education programs with 1500 co-op employers. Cooperative education is required or recommended in most programs and provides full-time paid work experience. Cross-registration with Rochester-area colleges is available. There are accelerated degree programs in science, engineering, public policy, math, computer science, materials science, imaging science, and business. Students may study abroad in 15 countries, and student-designed majors are permitted in applied arts and sciences. There is an honors program in general education and home colleges. There are 6 national honor societies, a freshman honors program, and 7 departmental honors programs.

Faculty/Classroom: 67% of faculty are male; 33%, female. 97% teach undergraduates, 3% do research, and 90% do both. No introductory courses are taught by graduate students. The average class size in an introductory lecture is 30; in a laboratory, 16; and in a regular course, 20.

Admissions: 69% of the 2005-2006 applicants were accepted. The SAT scores for the 2005-2006 freshman class were: Verbal--10% below 500, 44% between 500 and 599, 37% between 600 and 700, and 9% above 700; Math--4% below 500, 32% between 500 and 599, 49% between 600 and 700, and 15% above 700. The ACT scores were 10% below 21, 18% between 21 and 23, 28% between 24 and 26, 20% between 27 and 28, and 24% above 28. 50% of the current freshmen were in the top fifth of their class; 81% were in the top two fifths. There were 8 National Merit finalists and 11 semifinalists. 28 freshmen graduated first in their class.

Requirements: The SAT or ACT is required. In addition, applicants must be high school graduates or have a GED certificate. Applicants are required to submit an essay, and an interview is recommended. The School of Art and the School of Design emphasize a required portfolio of artwork. Required high school math and science credits vary by program, with 3 years in each area generally acceptable. RIT requires applicants to be in the upper 50% of their class. A grade average of 85 is required. AP and CLEP credits are accepted. Important factors in the admissions decision are advanced placement or honor courses, recommendations by school officials, and extracurricular activities record.

Procedure: Freshmen are admitted to all sessions. Entrance exams should be taken during the junior or senior year. There are early decision and deferred admissions plans. There is a rolling admissions plan. Early decision applications should be filed by December 1; the deadline for regular applications, for fall entry is open. There is a $50 fee. Notification of early decision is sent January 15; regular decision, on a rolling basis. 697 early decision candidates were accepted for the 2005-2006 class. 100 applicants were on the 2005 waiting list; 25 were admitted. Applications are accepted on-line.

Transfer: 1099 transfer students enrolled in 2004-2005. Transfer students must have a GPA of 2.5 for admission to most programs; those with fewer than 30 college credits must supply a high school transcript. Other requirements vary by program. 45 of 180 credits required for the bachelor's degree must be completed at RIT.

Visiting: There are regularly scheduled orientations for prospective students, including academic advising and information on housing and student services. There are guides for informal visits and visitors may sit in on classes and stay overnight. To schedule a visit, contact the Admissions Receptionist at (585) 475-6736 or *visit.rit.edu.*

Financial Aid: In a recent year, 85% of all full-time freshmen and 75% of continuing full-time students received some form of financial aid. 75% of full-time freshmen and 65% of continuing full-time students received need-based aid. The average freshman award was $17,500. 60% of undergraduates work part time. Average annual earnings from campus work are $1800. The FAFSA is required. The priority date for freshman financial aid applications for fall entry is March 1. The deadline for filing freshman financial aid applications for fall entry is June 1.

International Students: There are 571 international students enrolled. The school actively recruits these students. A satisfactory score on the TOEFL is required.

Computers: Wireless access is available. More than 600 PCs are available for student use in university computer labs. All students may access the system any time. There are no time limits and no fees.

Graduates: From July 1, 2004 to June 30, 2005, 2265 bachelor's degrees were awarded. The most popular majors were engineering (13%), information technology (13%), and photography (9%). In an average class, 62% graduate in 6 years or less. 600 companies recruited on campus in 2004-2005. Of the 2004 graduating class, 8% were enrolled in graduate school within 6 months of graduation and 90% were employed.

Admissions Contact: Daniel Shelley, Executive Director of Admissions. A video is available. E-mail: *admissions@rit.edu*
Web: *http://www.rit.edu*

RUSSELL SAGE COLLEGE D-3

Troy, NY 12180

(518) 244-2217
(888) Very-Sage; Fax: (518) 244-6880

Full-time: 800 women	**Faculty:** 58; IIA, --$
Part-time: 50 women	**Ph.Ds:** 73%
Graduate: none	**Student/Faculty:** 13 to 1
Year: semesters, summer session	**Tuition:** $20,000
Application Deadline: see profile	**Room & Board:** $7000
Freshman Class: n/av	
SAT or ACT: required	**COMPETITIVE**

Russell Sage, a private, comprehensive college, was founded in 1916 to prepare women for successful professional careers. Baccalaureate degrees in the traditional arts and sciences are offered, along with professional programs in nutrition, athletic training, nursing, physical and occupational therapy, theater, musical theater, creative arts in therapy, business, forensic science, communications, and education. Figures in the above capsule and in this profile are approximate. In addition to regional accreditation, Russell Sage has baccalaureate program accreditation with ADA, AOTA, APTA, NASAD, NCATE, and NLN. The library contains 342,021 volumes, 3341 microform items, and 31,968 audio/video tapes/CDs/DVDs, and subscribes to 803 periodicals including electronic. Computerized library services include the card catalog, interlibrary loans, and database searching. Special learning facilities include a learning resource center, the New York State Theatre Institute, Robinson Athletic Center, and Helen Upton Center for Women's Studies. The 14-acre campus is in an urban area 10 miles from Albany and Schenectady. Including any residence halls, there are 38 buildings.

Student Life: 92% of undergraduates are from New York. Others are from 13 states and 2 foreign countries. 77% are white. The average age of freshmen is 18; all undergraduates, 22. 10% do not continue beyond their first year; 68% remain to graduate.

Housing: 738 students can be accommodated in college housing, which includes single-sex dorms and on-campus apartments. In addition, there are language houses, special-interest houses, 24-hour quiet housing, and substance-free/wellness housing. On-campus housing is guaranteed for all 4 years. 55% of students commute. Upperclassmen may keep cars.

Activities: There are no fraternities. There are 26 groups on campus, including academic clubs in each major, choir, chorus, dance, drama, equestrian, ethnic, gay, honors, leadership, literary magazine, musical theater, newspaper, orchestra, political, religious, social, social service, student government, and yearbook. Popular campus events include Rally Day, Sage Fest, and Family Weekend.

Sports: Facilities include a weight and fitness center, a sports medicine facility, swimming pool, 4 tennis courts, a practice field, 2 gyms, and a large multipurpose room for indoor recreation.

Disabled Students: 70% of the campus is accessible. Wheelchair ramps, elevators, special parking, specially equipped rest rooms, special class scheduling, computer center access, electronic access via blackboard for a variety of information and courses, specially equipped science labs and equipment, and visits to administrative offices by arrangement are available.

Services: Counseling and information services are available, as is tutoring in most subjects. There is remedial math, reading, and writing.

Campus Safety and Security: Measures include 24-hour foot and vehicle patrol, self-defense education, security escort services, and informal discussions. There are pamphlets/posters/films, emergency telephones, lighted pathways/sidewalks, an evening escort service, and monitored video cameras.

Programs of Study: Russell Sage confers B.A. and B.S. degrees. Master's degrees are also awarded. Bachelor's degrees are awarded in BIOLOGICAL SCIENCE (biochemistry, biology/biological science, and nutrition), BUSINESS (business administration and management), COMMUNICATIONS AND THE ARTS (communications, English, musical theater, and Spanish), COMPUTER AND PHYSICAL SCIENCE (chemistry, computer science, and mathematics), EDUCATION (athletic training and elementary), ENGINEERING AND ENVIRONMENTAL DESIGN (environmental science), HEALTH PROFESSIONS (art therapy, nursing, occupational therapy, physical therapy, and public health), SOCIAL SCIENCE (applied psychology, biopsychology, criminal justice, forensic studies, history, interdisciplinary studies, international studies, political science/government, psychology, and sociology). Psychology, English, and nursing are the strongest academically. Health and rehabilitative sciences, education and psychology are the largest.

Required: To graduate, students must complete 120 credits with a 2.0 GPA overall and at least 30 credits and a 2.2 GPA in the major. B.A. candidates must earn a minimum of 90 credits in the liberal arts and sciences and B.S. candidates must earn a minimum of 60. A general education requirement of 36 credits focuses on the experiences of women in a multicultural society, understanding technology, writing skills, and a broad exposure to the various arts and sciences. There is a course requiring community service and a writing-intensive course in the major. Students must also complete 6 credits in a single language or show proficiency and take technology-intensive and cross-cultured courses.

Special: Students may cross-register with the 14 area schools of the Hudson-Mohawk Association of Colleges. A theater major is offered in conjunction with NYSTI. Study abroad, internships, and work-study programs are available. There are several accelerated 5-year programs in the health sciences, a 5-year B.S./M.B.A., a 3-3 program with Albany Law School, and a 3-2 engineering degree with nearby Rensselaer Polytechnic Institute. 9 centers for interdisciplinary inquiry draw students from across majors. The college confers credit for life, military, or work experience. Nondegree study, student-designed majors, dual majors, and pass/fail options are also available. There are 14 national honor societies and a freshman honors program.

Faculty/Classroom: 38% of faculty are male; 62%, female. All both teach and do research. The average class size in an introductory lecture is 19; in a laboratory, 9; and in a regular course, 16.

Admissions: 82% of recent applicants were accepted. 52% of recent freshmen were in the top fifth of their class; 83% were in the top two fifths.

Requirements: The SAT or ACT is required. In addition, applicants must be graduates of an accredited secondary school or have a GED. A minimum of 16 academic units are required, including courses in English, social sciences, natural sciences, math, and foreign language. An essay for applicants still in high school is required, and an interview is recommended. A GPA of 2.0 is required. AP and CLEP credits are accepted. Important factors in the admissions decision are advanced placement or honor courses, leadership record, and evidence of special talent.

Procedure: Freshmen are admitted fall and spring. Entrance exams should be taken during spring of the junior year or fall of the senior year. There are early decision, early admissions, and deferred admissions plans. There is a rolling admissions plan. Notification is sent on a rolling basis. 19 early decision candidates were accepted for a recent class. Applications are accepted on-line. Check with the school for current application deadlines and fee.

Transfer: 121 transfer students enrolled in a recent year. Applicants must have a minimum GPA of 2.5. Interviews are strongly encouraged and may be required in some instances. 45 of 120 credits required for the bachelor's degree must be completed at Russell Sage.

Visiting: There are regularly scheduled orientations for prospective students, including meetings with faculty, a campus tour, a financial aid session, and an admissions interview. There are guides for informal visits and visitors may sit in on classes and stay overnight. To schedule a visit, contact the Office of Admission at (518) 244-2218.

Financial Aid: In a recent year, 95% of all full-time freshmen and 97% of continuing full-time students received some form of financial aid. 79% of full-time freshmen and 83% of continuing full-time students received need-based aid. The average freshman award was $22,025. 37% of undergraduates work part time. Average annual earnings from campus work are $840. The average financial indebtedness of a recent graduate was $18,700. The FAFSA is required. Check with the school for current deadlines.

International Students: There were 2 international students enrolled in a recent year. The school actively recruits these students. They must take the TOEFL. International applicants with English as their native language should also take the SAT or ACT.

Computers: All students may access the system. The public computer labs are open 14 hours per day, 7 days a week; dial-in access is available 24 hours a day. There are no time limits and no fees. It is strongly recommended that all students have a personal computer.

Graduates: In a recent year, 251 bachelor's degrees were awarded. The most popular majors were education (18%), physical therapy (16%), and nursing (11%). In an average class, 33% graduate in 4 years or less, and 68% graduate in 5 or 6 years or less. 59 companies recruited on campus in a recent year. Of a recent graduating class, 42% were enrolled in graduate school within 6 months of graduation and 48% were employed.

Admissions Contact: Elizabeth Robertson, Senior Associate Director of Admissions. E-mail: *rscadm@sage.edu* Web: *www.sage.edu*

SAINT BONAVENTURE UNIVERSITY   A-3

St. Bonaventure, NY 14778-2284   (716) 375-2400
                                             (800) 462-5050; Fax: (716) 375-4005

Full-time: 1034 men, 992 women	**Faculty:** 124; IIA, --$
Part-time: 66 men, 49 women	**Ph.D.s:** 79%
Graduate: 161 men, 312 women	**Student/Faculty:** 13 to 1
Year: semesters, summer session	**Tuition:** $21,450
Application Deadline: April 1	**Room & Board:** $7335
Freshman Class: 1564 applied, 1490 accepted, 477 enrolled	
SAT Verbal/Math: 520/520*	**ACT:** 21 **LESS COMPETITIVE**

Saint Bonaventure University, founded in 1858, is a private Roman Catholic institution in the Franciscan tradition, offering programs in the arts and sciences, education, business, and journalism and mass communication. There are 4 undergraduate schools and 1 graduate school. In addition to regional accreditation, SBU has baccalaureate program accreditation with AACSB, AALE, and NCATE. The library contains 241,000 volumes, 97,000 microform items, and 7000 audio/video tapes/CDs/DVDs, and subscribes to 1500 periodicals including electronic. Computerized library services include the card catalog, interlibrary loans, database searching, Internet access, and laptop Internet portals. Special learning facilities include a learning resource center, art gallery, radio station, TV station, and observatory. The 500-acre campus is in a small town 70 miles southeast of Buffalo. Including any residence halls, there are 30 buildings.

Student Life: 77% of undergraduates are from New York. Students are from 38 states, 9 foreign countries, and Canada. 57% are from public schools. 59% are white. The average age of freshmen is 18; all undergraduates, 20. 24% do not continue beyond their first year; 68% remain to graduate.

Housing: 1450 students can be accommodated in college housing, which includes single-sex and coed dorms and on-campus apartments. On-campus housing is guaranteed for all 4 years. 76% of students live on campus; of those, 90% remain on campus on weekends. All students may keep cars.

Activities: There are no fraternities or sororities. There are 74 groups on campus, including academic, art, band, cheerleading, chess, choir, chorale, chorus, computers, dance, drama, ethnic, honors, international, jazz band, literary magazine, newspaper, orchestra, photography, political, professional, radio and TV, religious, social, social service, student government, and yearbook. Popular campus events include Family Weekend, Spring and Winter Weekends, and varsity basketball games.

Sports: There are 7 intercollegiate sports for men and 7 for women, and 11 intramural sports for men and 10 for women. Facilities include a 6000-seat gym with basketball and volleyball courts, an indoor swimming pool, a 9-hole golf course, weight facilities and free weights, a fitness center with state of the art strength, aerobics and conditioning areas, an indoor track, 3 multi-use courts, and a rock climbing wall. There is also a 77-acre area on campus with soccer, baseball, softball, rugby, and intramural fields.

Disabled Students: 90% of the campus is accessible. Wheelchair ramps, elevators, special parking, specially equipped rest rooms, a counseling center staffed by 2 professionals, and a teaching and learning center with a coordinator for disabled services are available.

Services: Counseling and information services are available, as is tutoring in some subjects, including math and English. There is remedial math, reading, and writing.

Campus Safety and Security: Measures include 24-hour foot and vehicle patrol, self-defense education, security escort services, and shuttle buses. There are informal discussions, pamphlets/posters/films, emergency telephones, and lighted pathways/sidewalks.

Programs of Study: SBU confers B.A., B.S., B.B.A., and B.S.Ed. degrees. Master's degrees are also awarded. Bachelor's degrees are awarded in BIOLOGICAL SCIENCE (biochemistry, biology/biological science, and biophysics), BUSINESS (accounting, banking and finance, management science, and marketing/retailing/merchandising), COMMUNICATIONS AND THE ARTS (classical languages, English, French, journalism, music, Spanish, and visual and performing arts), COMPUTER AND PHYSICAL SCIENCE (chemistry, computer science, mathematics, and physics), EDUCATION (elementary and physical), ENGINEERING AND ENVIRONMENTAL DESIGN (engineering physics and environmental science), HEALTH PROFESSIONS (medical laboratory technology and premedicine), SOCIAL SCIENCE (history, philosophy, political science/government, prelaw, psychology, social science, sociology, and theologi-

cal studies). Psychology, accounting, and biology are the strongest academically. Mass communication, management, and elementary education are the largest.

Required: To graduate, students must complete 121 credit hours, 30 of them in the major, with a minimum GPA of 2.0. Students must also demonstrate writing competency through testing or course work.

Special: Cross-registration can be arranged almost anywhere in the United States through the Visiting Student Program. Internships are available in business, mass communication, political science, psychology, and social science. Study abroad in 18 countries, B.A.-B.S. degrees, accelerated degree programs, dual and student-designed majors, a Washington semester with American University, and pass/fail options are offered. Students may complete a 2-2 or 2-3 engineering degree with the University of Detroit or a 2-3 engineering degree with Clarkson University. Dual admissions with George Washington University School of Medicine, Lake Erie College of Osteopathic Medicine, University at Buffalo School of Dental Medicine, Lake Erie College of Osteopathic Medicine School of Pharmacy, and University of Duquesne Law School is also possible. There are 10 national honor societies and a freshman honors program.

Faculty/Classroom: 74% of faculty are male; 30%, female. 92% teach undergraduates and 1% both teach and do research. Graduate students teach 1% of introductory courses. The average class size in an introductory lecture is 25; in a laboratory, 12; and in a regular course, 18.

Admissions: 95% of the 2005-2006 applicants were accepted. The SAT scores for the 2005-2006 freshman class were: Verbal--36% below 500, 48% between 500 and 599, 15% between 600 and 700, and 2% above 700; Math--36% below 500, 47% between 500 and 599, 16% between 600 and 700, and 1% above 700. The ACT scores were 49% below 21, 26% between 21 and 23, 13% between 24 and 26, 6% between 27 and 28, and 7% above 28. 25% of the current freshmen were in the top fifth of their class; 57% were in the top two fifths. 2 freshmen graduated first in their class.

Requirements: A satisfactory score on the SAT is required. The ACT is recommended. Applicants must be graduates of an accredited secondary school or have a GED. 16 academic credits are required, including 4 years each of English and social studies, 3 each of math and science, and 2 of a foreign language. An essay and an interview are recommended. A grade average of 70 is required. AP and CLEP credits are accepted. Important factors in the admissions decision are recommendations by school officials, advanced placement or honor courses, and extracurricular activities record.

Procedure: Freshmen are admitted to all sessions. Entrance exams should be taken during the spring of the junior year or the fall of the senior year. There are early admissions, deferred admissions, and rolling admissions plans. Applications should be filed by April 1 for fall entry and December 1 for spring entry, along with a $30 fee. Notification is sent on a rolling basis. Applications are accepted on-line.

Transfer: 63 transfer students enrolled in 2004-2005. Applicants must have a minimum 2.5 GPA. Grades of C or better transfer for credit. 60 of 121 credits required for the bachelor's degree must be completed at SBU.

Visiting: There are regularly scheduled orientations for prospective students, including interviews, tours, class visits, and meetings with professors. There are guides for informal visits and visitors may sit in on classes and stay overnight. To schedule a visit, contact the Admissions Office.

Financial Aid: In a recent year, the average freshman award was $15,270. Need-based scholarships or need-based grants averaged $10,928; need-based self-help aid (loans and jobs) averaged $4219; non-need-based athletic scholarships averaged $11,292; and other non-need-based awards and non-need-based scholarships averaged $7042. 38% of undergraduates work part time. Average annual earnings from campus work are $700. The FAFSA is required. Check with the school for current deadlines.

International Students: The school actively recruits these students. A satisfactory score is required on the written TOEFL.

Computers: Wireless access is available. The university supports academic and administrative functions through a variety of systems. A combination of wired computer labs (more than 250 networked PCs) and wireless modems throughout campus provide access. All residence halls have Internet access. All students may access the system 24 hours per day via residence hall rooms or at designated lab hours. There are no time limits and no fees. It is recommended that students in computer science and business information systems have PCs.

Graduates: From July 1, 2004 to June 30, 2005, 422 bachelor's degrees were awarded. The most popular majors were business (29%), communications/journalism (18%), and social sciences (14%). In an average class, 2% graduate in 3 years or less, 58% graduate in 4 years or less, 66% graduate in 5 years or less, and 68% graduate in 6 years or less. Of the 2004 graduating class, 39% were enrolled in graduate school within 6 months of graduation and 56% were employed.

Admissions Contact: James Di Risio, Director of Admissions. A video is available. E-mail: *admissions@sbu.edu* Web: *www.sbu.edu*

SAINT FRANCIS COLLEGE — D-5

Brooklyn, NY 11201   (718) 489-5200; Fax: (718) 802-0453

Full-time: 978 men, 1038 women	**Faculty:** 71; IIB, av$
Part-time: 86 men, 107 women	**Ph.D.s:** 79%
Graduate: none	**Student/Faculty:** 28 to 1
Year: semesters, summer session	**Tuition:** $12,970
Application Deadline: April 1	**Room & Board:** $7004
Freshman Class: 1566 applied, 1438 accepted, 497 enrolled	
SAT Verbal/Math: 480/490*	**LESS COMPETITIVE**

Saint Francis College, chartered in 1884 by the Franciscan Brothers, is an independent Catholic institution conferring degrees in the arts, sciences, business, education, and health sciences. The library contains 140,000 volumes, 10,440 microform items, and 2050 audio/video tapes/CDs/DVDs, and subscribes to 14,300 periodicals including electronic. Computerized library services include interlibrary loans, database searching, Internet access, and laptop Internet portals. Special learning facilities include a learning resource center, a greenhouse, and a television studio. The 1-acre campus is in an urban area in Brooklyn Heights. Including any residence halls, there are 6 buildings.

Student Life: 98% of undergraduates are from New York. Others are from 8 states, 50 foreign countries, and Canada. 45% are from public schools. 50% are white; 24% African American; 17% Hispanic. The average age of freshmen is 19; all undergraduates, 22. 24% do not continue beyond their first year; 55% remain to graduate.

Housing: Students may apply for housing in the dorm at Polytechnic University, a short walk from St. Francis College. Alcohol is not permitted. No one may keep cars.

Activities: There are no fraternities or sororities. There are 38 groups on campus, including art, cheerleading, choir, chorus, computers, dance, departmental drama, ethnic, honors, international, literary magazine, newspaper, political, professional, radio and TV, religious, social, social service, student government, and yearbook. Popular campus events include Open House, Terrier Tuesday, and Thomas J. Volpe Lecture.

Sports: There are 8 intercollegiate sports for men and 8 for women, and 6 intramural sports for men and 6 for women. Facilities include a 1100-seat gym, an Olympic-size swimming pool, a weight-training room, a roof recreation area, and the Genovesi Center, which is a 10,000-square-foot multipurpose facility used for athletic, college, and community events.

Disabled Students: All of the campus is accessible. Wheelchair ramps, elevators, specially equipped rest rooms, lowered drinking fountains, and lowered telephones are available.

Services: There is a reader service for the blind, and remedial math, reading, and writing. In addition, there are workshops in academic skills such as note- and test-taking techniques and study skills.

Campus Safety and Security: Measures include informal discussions and pamphlets/posters/films.

Programs of Study: St. Francis confers B.A. and B.S. degrees. Associate and master's degrees are also awarded. Bachelor's degrees are awarded in BIOLOGICAL SCIENCE (biology/biological science), BUSINESS (accounting and management science), COMMUNICATIONS AND THE ARTS (communications, English, and Spanish), COMPUTER AND PHYSICAL SCIENCE (information sciences and systems and mathematics), EDUCATION (elementary, middle school, physical, and secondary), HEALTH PROFESSIONS (health care administration, health science, medical laboratory technology, physician's assistant, and radiological science), SOCIAL SCIENCE (criminal justice, economics, history, international studies, liberal arts/general studies, philosophy, political science/government, psychology, religion, social studies, and sociology). Biology, accounting, and psychology are the strongest academically. Management, communications, and psychology are the largest.

Required: The core curriculum varies according to the major, but all baccalaureate degree programs require courses in communications, English, fine arts, phys ed, history, philosophy, sociology, and science or math. A minimum 2.0 GPA and 128 credit hours are required to graduate.

Special: There are co-op programs in aviation, physical therapy, nursing, and computer science. A variety of internships are available such as New York Hospital Medical Center of Queens, NBC Sports, and J.P. Morgan Chase. Work-study with Methodist Hospital or the borough president's office is possible, and there are preprofessional health programs with the State University of New York Health Science Center at Brooklyn, NY Methodist Hospital, and St. Vincent's Catholic Medical Center. Study abroad in several countries, dual majors, pass/fail options, and credit for life experience are possible. There are 16 national honor societies, and a freshman honors program.

Faculty/Classroom: 55% of faculty are male; 45%, female. All both teach and do research. The average class size in an introductory lecture is 25; in a laboratory, 19; and in a regular course, 20.

Admissions: 92% of the 2005-2006 applicants were accepted. The SAT scores for the 2005-2006 freshman class were: Verbal--60% below 500, 31% between 500 and 599, and 9% between 600 and 700; Math--54% below 500, 37% between 500 and 599, and 9% between 600 and 700.

Requirements: The SAT is required. In addition, applicants should graduate from an accredited secondary school or have a GED. An entrance essay is required and submission of SAT scores. AP and CLEP credits are accepted. Important factors in the admissions decision are advanced placement or honor courses, extracurricular activities record, and recommendations by school officials.

Procedure: Freshmen are admitted to all sessions. Entrance exams should be taken in spring of the junior year and fall of the senior year. There is a deferred admissions plan and a rolling admissions plan. Applications should be filed by April 1 for fall entry and November 1 for winter entry. Notification is sent on a rolling basis. The fall 2005 application fee was $35. Applications are accepted on-line.

Transfer: 218 transfer students enrolled in 2004-2005. A minimum 2.0 GPA is required for transfer students. Official transcripts from previous colleges and high school transcripts, or a graduation certificate, is also required. 30 of 128 credits required for the bachelor's degree must be completed at St. Francis.

Visiting: There are regularly scheduled orientations for prospective students, including meetings with faculty if desired. There are guides for informal visits and visitors may sit in on classes. To schedule a visit, contact the Office of Admissions at *admissions@stfrancis.edu*.

Financial Aid: In 2005-2006, 82% of all full-time freshmen and 83% of continuing full-time students received some form of financial aid. 75% of full-time freshmen and 51% of continuing full-time students received need-based aid. The average freshman award was $10,735. Need-based scholarships or need-based grants averaged $4026 ($9050 maximum); need-based self-help aid (loans and jobs) averaged $5760 ($16,290 maximum); non-need-based athletic scholarships averaged $12,805 ($23,000 maximum); and other non-need-based awards and non-need-based scholarships averaged $10,375 ($13,000 maximum). 8% of undergraduates work part time. Average annual earnings from campus work are $2100. The FAFSA, the college's own financial statement, and the NY State TAP application are required.

International Students: There are 180 international students enrolled. The school actively recruits these students. They must score satisfactorily on the written TOEFL and also take the SAT. The college requires a placement exam.

Computers: Wireless access is available. There are 158 PC workstations and 10 kiosks available to students throughout the day. This includes the lab, library, academic enhancement, and psychology lab. The Internet is accessible to students on all machines, and there are wireless zones in both the Remsen building and Clinton Library. The campuswide network provides access to services such as Blackboard, Terriermail, and library resources that are accessible to students through the Internet from outside the college. All students may access the system. There are no time limits. The fee is $150 per semester.

Graduates: From July 1, 2004 to June 30, 2005, 440 bachelor's degrees were awarded. The most popular majors were management (17%), special studies (12%), and psychology (9%). In an average class, 1% graduate in 3 years or less, 31% graduate in 4 years or less, 51% graduate in 5 years or less, and 53% graduate in 6 years or less. 20 companies recruited on campus in 2004-2005.

Admissions Contact: Brother George Larkin, O.S.F., Admissions Dean. A video is available. E-mail: *glarkin@stfranciscollege.edu* Web: *www.stfranciscollege.edu*

SAINT JOHN FISHER COLLEGE — B-3

Rochester, NY 14618   (585) 385-8412
(800) 444-4640; Fax: (585) 385-8386

Full-time: 1034 men, 1414 women	**Faculty:** 132; IIB, -$
Part-time: 97 men, 151 women	**Ph.D.s:** 81%
Graduate: 216 men, 616 women	**Student/Faculty:** 19 to 1
Year: semesters, summer session	**Tuition:** $19,560
Application Deadline: open	**Room & Board:** $8300
Freshman Class: 2756 applied, 1798 accepted, 553 enrolled	
SAT Verbal/Math: 530/540*	**ACT:** 23 **COMPETITIVE**

St. John Fisher College is an independent, liberal arts institution in the Catholic tradition of American higher education. Guided since its inception in 1948 by the educational philosophy of the Congregation of St. Basil, the college emphasizes liberal learning for students in traditional academic disciplines, as well as for those in more directly career-oriented fields. The college welcomes qualified students, faculty, and staff regardless of religious or cultural background. There are 3 undergraduate schools and 1 graduate school. In addition to regional accreditation, Fisher has baccalaureate program accreditation with AACSB, ACS, and CCNE. The library contains 209,057 volumes, 208,958 microform items, and 31,411 audio/video tapes/CDs/DVDs, and subscribes to 10,400 periodicals including electronic. Computerized library services include the card catalog, interlibrary loans, database searching, and Internet access. Special learning facilities include a learning resource center, radio station, TV station, multimedia center, "wet" and "dry" multidisci-

plinary science labs, animal labs, growth chambers, and dance and fitness facility. The 142-acre campus is in a suburban area 12 miles southeast of Rochester. Including any residence halls, there are 20 buildings.
Student Life: 98% of undergraduates are from New York. Others are from 16 states, 2 foreign countries, and Canada. 65% are from public schools. 87% are white. The average age of freshmen is 18; all undergraduates, 22. 16% do not continue beyond their first year; 62% remain to graduate.
Housing: 1300 students can be accommodated in college housing, which includes single-sex and coed dormitories and off-campus apartments. On-campus housing is guaranteed for the first 3 years. 66% of students live on campus; of those, 85% remain on campus on weekends. Upperclassmen may keep cars.
Activities: There are no fraternities or sororities. There are 60 groups on campus, including cheerleading, choir, chorale, chorus, commuter students, computers, drama, ethnic, gay, honors, international, literary magazine, musical theater, newspaper, pep band, photography, political, professional, radio and TV, religious, residential students, social, social service, student activities, student government, and yearbook. Popular campus events include Senior Week, Winter Olympics, and TEDDI, a 24-hour dance marathon for charity.
Sports: There are 7 intercollegiate sports for men and 6 for women, and 5 intramural sports for men and 4 for women. Facilities include racquetball, squash, and tennis courts, baseball and softball fields, an all-weather playing field for football, soccer, lacrosse, and intramural athletics, a 9-hole golf course, weight/exercise facilities, a varsity gym for intercollegiate basketball, and a multipurpose student life center for indoor tennis, volleyball, and basketball.
Disabled Students: 95% of the campus is accessible. Wheelchair ramps, elevators, special parking, specially equipped rest rooms, special class scheduling, lowered drinking fountains, and lowered telephones are available.
Services: Counseling and information services are available, as is peer tutoring in most subjects. There is a reader service for the blind. Math and writing centers provide help to students at all levels.
Campus Safety and Security: Measures include 24-hour foot and vehicle patrol, security escort services, shuttle buses, and informal discussions. There are pamphlets/posters/films, emergency telephones, and lighted pathways/sidewalks.
Programs of Study: Fisher confers B.A. and B.S. degrees. Master's degrees are also awarded. Bachelor's degrees are awarded in BIOLOGICAL SCIENCE (biology/biological science), BUSINESS (accounting, management science, and sports management), COMMUNICATIONS AND THE ARTS (communications, English, French, and Spanish), COMPUTER AND PHYSICAL SCIENCE (chemistry, computer science, mathematics, physics, and science technology), EDUCATION (early childhood, education, English, mathematics, science, secondary, social studies, and special), HEALTH PROFESSIONS (nursing), SOCIAL SCIENCE (American studies, anthropology, economics, history, interdisciplinary studies, international studies, philosophy, political science/government, psychology, religion, and sociology). Education and management are the largest.
Required: To graduate, students must complete at least 120 credit hours, including at least 30 in the major, and maintain a 2.0 minimum GPA. Core curriculum requirements include 3 to 4 courses each in literature/foreign languages, social sciences, and religious studies/ philosophy, 3 in math/natural science, and up to 3 in arts. Freshmen must participate in one of the intergrative learning communities.
Special: The college has cooperative programs with the Pennsylvania College of Optometry, and cross-registration with Rochester area colleges. The college offers internships in most majors, independent research in 16 majors, study abroad, work-study programs, accelerated degree programs in many areas, Washington semesters, dual and student-designed majors, and degrees in interdisciplinary studies or liberal studies. A 3-2 engineering degree is offered with Columbia and Clarkson Universities, University of Detroit-Mercy, SUNY at Buffalo, Manhattan College. Navy and Marine ROTC is available at the University of Rochester and Air Force and Army ROTC at the Rochester Institute of Technology. There are 10 national honor societies, a freshman honors program, and 8 departmental honors programs.
Faculty/Classroom: 51% of faculty are male; 49%, female. 84% teach undergraduates. No introductory courses are taught by graduate students. The average class size in an introductory lecture is 24; in a laboratory, 12; and in a regular course, 18.
Admissions: 65% of the 2005-2006 applicants were accepted. The SAT scores for the 2005-2006 freshman class were: Verbal--28% below 500, 52% between 500 and 599, 19% between 600 and 700, and 1% above 700; Math--21% below 500, 53% between 500 and 599, 25% between 600 and 700, and 1% above 700. The ACT scores were 27% below 21, 31% between 21 and 23, 30% between 24 and 26, 9% between 27 and 28, and 2% above 28. 48% of the current freshmen were in the top fifth of their class; 84% were in the top two fifths. 2 freshmen graduated first in their class.
Requirements: The SAT or ACT is required. In addition, applicants must be graduates of an accredited secondary school. 16 academic cred-

its are required, including 4 years each in English, history, and social studies, 3 years each in math and science, and 2 years in a foreign language. Interviews are recommended. AP and CLEP credits are accepted. Important factors in the admissions decision are advanced placement or honor courses, extracurricular activities record, and evidence of special talent.
Procedure: Freshmen are admitted to all sessions. There are early decision and deferred admissions plans. Early decision applications should be filed by December 1; deadlines are open for regular applications. Application fee is $30. Notification is sent on a rolling basis. 41 early decision candidates were accepted for the 2005-2006 class. Applications are accepted on-line.
Transfer: 241 transfer students enrolled in 2004-2005. Applicants must have a minimum GPA of 2.0 to be considered (mean GPA is 2.8). A high school transcript is required for students with fewer than 24 college credits. Interviews are recommended. 30 of 120 credits required for the bachelor's degree must be completed at Fisher.
Visiting: There are regularly scheduled orientations for prospective students, including a tour, an interview with a member of the admissions staff, meetings with faculty and coaches, and lunch on campus. There are guides for informal visits and visitors may sit in on classes and stay overnight. To schedule a visit, contact the Admissions Office at (585) 385-8064 or (800) 444-4640 or admissions@sjfc.edu.
Financial Aid: In 2005-2006, 94% of all full-time freshmen and 82% of continuing full-time students received some form of financial aid. 74% of full-time freshmen and 65% of continuing full-time students received need-based aid. The average freshman award was $16,000. Need-based scholarships or need-based grants averaged $11,728 ($19,000 maximum); and need-based self-help aid (loans and jobs) averaged $5765 ($18,500 maximum). 25% of undergraduates work part time. Average annual earnings from campus work are $1000. The average financial indebtedness of the 2005 graduate was $18,400. The FAFSA is required. The deadline for filing freshman financial aid applications for fall entry is February 15.
International Students: There are 9 international students enrolled. They must score satisfactorily on the written TOEFL or on the electronic version and also take the SAT or the ACT.
Computers: Students may access the Internet from any building on campus with no constraints. Wired and wireless access is all one system and treated the same. Computers for students are located in a variety of locations and total 350. Student ownership of a personal system is approximately 90%. All students may access the system 24 hours. There are no time limits and no fees. It is strongly recommended that all students have a personal computer.
Graduates: From July 1, 2004 to June 30, 2005, 617 bachelor's degrees were awarded. The most popular majors were education (22%), business and management (22%), and psychology (9%). In an average class, 61% graduate in 4 years or less, 63% graduate in 5 years or less, and 62% graduate in 6 years or less. 127 companies recruited on campus in 2004-2005. Of the 2004 graduating class, 26% were enrolled in graduate school within 6 months of graduation and 92% were employed.
Admissions Contact: Stacy A. Ledermann, Director of Freshman Admissions. E-mail: admissions@sjfc.edu Web: http://www.sjfc.edu

SAINT JOHN'S UNIVERSITY
Queens, NY 11439

D-5

(718) 990-2000
(888) 785-6467; Fax: (718) 990-2096

Full-time: 5007 men, 6848 women	**Faculty:** 543; I, av$
Part-time: 1274 men, 1963 women	**Ph.D.s:** 91%
Graduate: 1848 men, 3406 women	**Student/Faculty:** 22 to 1
Year: semesters, summer session	**Tuition:** $23,370
Application Deadline: open	**Room & Board:** $11,000
Freshman Class: 20,669 applied, 12,980 accepted, 3159 enrolled	
SAT Verbal/Math: 520/500*	**COMPETITIVE**

Saint John's University, founded in 1870 by the Vincentian Fathers, is a private Roman Catholic institution offering programs in the arts and sciences, education, business, pharmacy and allied health professions, theology, and professional studies. There are 5 undergraduate and 6 graduate schools. In addition to regional accreditation, St. John's has baccalaureate program accreditation with AACSB, ACPE, APA, CACREP, and ESB. The 4 libraries contain 1,000,000 volumes, 3,419,235 microform items, and 17,918 audio/video tapes/CDs/DVDs, and subscribe to 16,794 periodicals including electronic. Computerized library services include the card catalog, interlibrary loans, database searching, and Internet access. Special learning facilities include a learning resource center, art gallery, radio station, TV station, health education resource center, model pharmacy, speech and hearing clinic, instructional materials center, instructional Media Center, and Institute of Asian Studies. The 97-acre campus is in a suburban area in a residential section of Queens. There is also a 16-acre branch campus in Staten Island, a campus in downtown Manhattan, a campus in Rome, Italy, and a 175-acre campus in Oakdale, Long Island. Including any residence halls, there are 25 buildings.

Student Life: 89% of undergraduates are from New York. Others are from 43 states, 103 foreign countries, and Canada. 64% are from public schools. 46% are white; 13% African American; 13% Asian American; 12% Hispanic. 51% are Catholic; 17% Muslim, Hindu, Buddhist, Greek Orthodox, Mormon, Russian Orthodo; 10% Protestant; 6% claim no religious affiliation. The average age of freshmen is 18; all undergraduates, 20. 21% do not continue beyond their first year; 64% remain to graduate.

Housing: 2766 students can be accommodated in college housing, which includes coed dorms and off-campus apartments. On-campus housing is available on a first-come, first-served basis and is available on a lottery system for upperclassmen. 82% of students commute. All students may keep cars.

Activities: 6% of men belong to 8 local and 11 national fraternities; 6% of women belong to 12 local and 11 national sororities. There are 180 groups on campus, including art, cheerleading, choir, chorus, computers, dance, debate, drama, environmental, ethnic, film, honors, human rights, international, jazz band, literary magazine, musical theater, newspaper, pep band, photography, political, professional, radio and TV, religious, social, social service, student government, and yearbook. Popular campus events include International Night, Spring Fling, and Student Activities Fair.

Sports: There are 7 intercollegiate sports for men and 10 for women, and 16 intramural sports for men and 16 for women. Facilities include gyms, a swimming pool, squash and tennis courts, weight and exercise rooms, baseball and softball diamonds, fields for football, lacrosse, and soccer, and basketball and racquetball courts.

Disabled Students: 90% of the campus is accessible. Wheelchair ramps, elevators, special parking, specially equipped rest rooms, special class scheduling, lowered drinking fountains, and lowered telephones are available.

Services: Counseling and information services are available, as is tutoring in most subjects. There is a reader service for the blind, and remedial math, reading, and writing. Note-taking services, tape recorders, assistance in study skills, and a program for at-risk freshmen are available.

Campus Safety and Security: Measures include 24-hour foot and vehicle patrol, security escort services, informal discussions, and pamphlets/posters/films. There are emergency telephones, lighted pathways/sidewalks, and a crime prevention awareness program.

Programs of Study: St. John's confers B.A., B.S., B.F.A., B.S.Ed., and B.S.Med.Tech. degrees. Associate, master's, and doctoral degrees are also awarded. Bachelor's degrees are awarded in BIOLOGICAL SCIENCE (biology/biological science, ecology, and toxicology), BUSINESS (accounting, banking and finance, business administration and management, business economics, funeral home services, hospitality management services, insurance and risk management, management science, marketing and distribution, real estate, sports management, and transportation management), COMMUNICATIONS AND THE ARTS (advertising, communications, English, fine arts, French, graphic design, illustration, Italian, journalism, languages, literature, photography, radio/television technology, Spanish, speech/debate/rhetoric, and telecommunications), COMPUTER AND PHYSICAL SCIENCE (actuarial science, chemistry, computer science, information sciences and systems, mathematics, physical sciences, and physics), EDUCATION (bilingual/bicultural, early childhood, education of the deaf and hearing impaired, elementary, English, foreign languages, mathematics, middle school, science, secondary, social studies, and special), ENGINEERING AND ENVIRONMENTAL DESIGN (environmental science and preengineering), HEALTH PROFESSIONS (health care administration, medical technology, pharmacy, physician's assistant, predentistry, premedicine, and speech pathology/audiology), SOCIAL SCIENCE (anthropology, Asian/Oriental studies, criminal justice, economics, history, human services, liberal arts/general studies, paralegal studies, philosophy, political science/government, prelaw, psychology, public administration, social science, social studies, sociology, and theological studies). Pharmacy, biology, and psychology are the strongest academically. Pharmacy, psychology, and criminal justice are the largest.

Required: To graduate, students must complete at least 126 credit hours, including core courses and distribution requirements, with a minimum GPA of 2.0 overall and in the major. Other requirements vary by program. Core courses include English, theology, philosophy, math/science, Discover NY, history, scientific inquiry, and speech. Distribution requirements include a second language, fine arts, language and culture, math, philosophy, theology, and social science.

Special: St. John's offers internships, cross-registration, study abroad in Europe, Central and South America, Australia, the Caribbean, Africa, and Asia, an accelerated degree program in many majors, B.A.-B.S. degrees, dual majors and combined degree programs, pass/fail options, and some credit for life, military, and work experience. There are cooperative programs in dentistry with Columbia University, in engineering with Manhattan College, in photography with the International Center of Photography, in funeral service administration with the McAllister Institute, and in optometry with SUNY College of Optometry. There is a 6-year doctor of pharmacy program for incoming freshmen. Other combined degree programs are possible. There are 19 national honor societies, a freshman honors program, and 10 departmental honors programs.

Faculty/Classroom: 60% of faculty are male; 40%, female. 87% teach undergraduates, 91% do research, and 78% do both. No introductory courses are taught by graduate students. The average class size in an introductory lecture is 26; in a laboratory, 23; and in a regular course, 27.

Admissions: 63% of the 2005-2006 applicants were accepted. The SAT scores for the 2005-2006 freshman class were: Verbal--38% below 500, 42% between 500 and 599, 17% between 600 and 700, and 3% above 700; Math--34% below 500, 39% between 500 and 599, 21% between 600 and 700, and 6% above 700. 35% of the current freshmen were in the top fifth of their class; 65% were in the top two fifths. 4 freshmen graduated first in their class.

Requirements: The SAT or ACT is required. In addition, admissions decisions are made by committee and are based on several criteria, including standardized test scores, academic curriculum, and high school average. A GPA of 3.0 is required. AP and CLEP credits are accepted. Important factors in the admissions decision are advanced placement or honor courses, recommendations by school officials, and extracurricular activities record.

Procedure: Freshmen are admitted fall, spring, and summer. Entrance exams should be taken late in the junior year or early in the senior year. There are early decision, deferred admissions, and rolling admissions plans. Application deadlines are open. Notification is sent on a rolling basis. The fall 2005 application was $30. The application fee is waived for on-line applications. 91 applicants were on the 2005 waiting list.

Transfer: 569 transfer students enrolled in 2004-2005. Applicants must present official transcripts of high school and college work, as well as a list of courses in progress. If the student has been out of school a semester or more, a letter of explanation is also required. Admissions requirements for transfer students to the 6-year pharmacy program are stricter, and placement is limited. 36 of 126 credits required for the bachelor's degree must be completed at St. John's.

Visiting: There are regularly scheduled orientations for prospective students, including small group presentations and a tour of the campus. There are guides for informal visits and visitors may sit in on classes. To schedule a visit, contact the Office of Admission.

Financial Aid: In 2005-2006, 98% of all full-time freshmen and 85% of continuing full-time students received some form of financial aid. 85% of full-time freshmen and 69% of continuing full-time students received need-based aid. The average freshman award was $18,242. Need-based scholarships or need-based grants averaged $7565 ($23,376 maximum); need-based self-help aid (loans and jobs) averaged $4293 ($8625 maximum); non-need-based athletic scholarships averaged $22,272 ($34,370 maximum); and other non-need-based awards and non-need-based scholarships averaged $8671 ($34,376 maximum). 85% of undergraduates work part time. Average annual earnings from campus work are $5000. The average financial indebtedness of the 2005 graduate was $24,282. The FAFSA is required. The priority date for freshman financial aid applications for fall entry is February 1. The deadline for filing freshman financial aid applications for fall entry is March 1.

International Students: There are 431 international students enrolled. The school actively recruits these students. A satisfactory score is required on the written TOEFL or the college's own test. This requirement may be waived for international students educated outside of the United States.

Computers: There are 748 workstations for general use in classrooms, 114 in the library, and 303 in computer labs; there are 8738 student laptops. Students can also access the Internet (wired and wireless) from any location on campus. All students may access the system. There are no time limits and no fees.

Graduates: From July 1, 2004 to June 30, 2005, 2320 bachelor's degrees were awarded. The most popular majors were communication arts (9%), finance (7%), and criminal justice (7%). In an average class, 1% graduate in 3 years or less, 39% graduate in 4 years or less, 56% graduate in 5 years or less, and 65% graduate in 6 years or less. 242 companies recruited on campus in 2004-2005. Of the 2004 graduating class, 18% were enrolled in graduate school within 6 months of graduation and 72% were employed.

Admissions Contact: Matthew Whalen, Director.
E-mail: *admissions@stjohns.edu* Web: *www.stjohns.edu*

SAINT JOSEPH'S COLLEGE, NEW YORK, BROOKLYN   D-5
CAMPUS

Brooklyn, NY 11205

(718) 636-6868
(866) AT ST JOE; Fax: (718) 636-8303

Full-time: 149 men, 559 women   **Faculty:** n/av
Part-time: 107 men, 307 women   **Ph.D.s:** 80%
Graduate: 42 men, 154 women   **Student/Faculty:** n/av
Year: semesters, summer session   **Tuition:** $12,206
Application Deadline: August 1   **Room & Board:** n/app
Freshman Class: 635 applied, 507 accepted, 150 enrolled
SAT Verbal/Math: 491/502*   COMPETITIVE

Saint Joseph's College, established in 1916, is a private, independent, multicampus, commuter institution offering undergraduate degrees in arts and sciences, child study, business, accounting, health professions, and nursing. There is a branch campus in Patchogue, Long Island. In addition to regional accreditation, Saint Joseph's has baccalaureate program accreditation with NLN. The library contains 75,000 volumes, 4341 microform items, and 4504 audio/video tapes/CDs/DVDs, and subscribes to 434 periodicals including electronic. Computerized library services include interlibrary loans and database searching. Special learning facilities include an on-campus lab preschool. The 3-acre campus is in an urban area 1 mile east of Manhattan. Including any residence halls, there are 5 buildings.

Student Life: 99% of undergraduates are from New York. Others are from 5 states and Canada. 21% are from public schools. 45% are white; 37% African American; 12% Hispanic. The average age of freshmen is 18; all undergraduates, 27. 15% do not continue beyond their first year; 76% remain to graduate.

Housing: Housing consists of off-campus apartments. 98% of students commute. Alcohol is not permitted. All students may keep cars.

Activities: 15% of men belong to 1 local fraternity; 6% of women belong to 1 local sorority. There are 30 groups on campus, including art, cheerleading, chess, chorus, computers, dance, drama, ethnic, honors, jazz band, literary magazine, newspaper, political, professional, religious, social, social service, student government, and yearbook. Popular campus events include the annual dinner dance, Junior Class Night, and holiday party.

Sports: There are 3 intercollegiate sports for men and 4 for women, and 4 intramural sports for men and 4 for women. Facilities include a gym, a handball court, an outdoor mall, recreation rooms, and an exercise/weight room.

Disabled Students: 10% of the campus is accessible. Wheelchair ramps, elevators, and specially equipped rest rooms are available.

Services: Counseling and information services are available, as is tutoring in most subjects. There is remedial writing.

Campus Safety and Security: Measures include self-defense education, security escort services, informal discussions, and pamphlets/posters/films. There are lighted pathways/sidewalks.

Programs of Study: Saint Joseph's confers B.A. and B.S. degrees. Master's degrees are also awarded. Bachelor's degrees are awarded in BIOLOGICAL SCIENCE (biology/biological science), BUSINESS (accounting, business administration and management, and organizational behavior), COMMUNICATIONS AND THE ARTS (English, Spanish, and speech/debate/rhetoric), COMPUTER AND PHYSICAL SCIENCE (chemistry, information sciences and systems, and mathematics), EDUCATION (early childhood, elementary, secondary, and special), HEALTH PROFESSIONS (community health work, health care administration, and nursing), SOCIAL SCIENCE (history, psychology, and social science). Child study, psychology, and speech are the largest.

Required: To graduate, students must complete a 51-credit core curriculum requirement consisting of 8 courses in humanities, 3 in social science and math/science, and 1 English composition course. The minimum GPA is 2.0. Students must earn 128 credits, with 30 to 36 credits in the major. Most majors require a thesis.

Special: The college offers internship programs in English, history, political science, psychology, sociology, speech, and business/accounting, and an interdisciplinary major in human relations. Adult students may pursue a general studies degree in which the college allows credit for life, military, and work experience. Cross-registration with Knowledge Workers Educational Alliance is possible. There are 5 national honor societies and a freshman honors program.

Faculty/Classroom: 44% of faculty are male; 56%, female. All teach undergraduates, 10% do research, and 10% do both. The average class size in an introductory lecture is 16; in a laboratory, 11; and in a regular course, 12.

Admissions: 80% of the 2005-2006 applicants were accepted. The SAT scores for the 2005-2006 freshman class were: Verbal--56% below 500, 38% between 500 and 599, and 6% between 600 and 700; Math--51% below 500, 40% between 500 and 599, and 4% between 600 and 700.

Requirements: The SAT is required. Applicants must graduate from an accredited secondary school or earn a GED. 16 Carnegie units are re-

quired, including 4 units of English and social studies, 3 of math, 2 of languages and science, and 3 elective units. Interviews are recommended. A GPA of 3.0 is required. AP and CLEP credits are accepted. Important factors in the admissions decision are advanced placement or honor courses, recommendations by school officials, and leadership record.

Procedure: Freshmen are admitted fall and spring. Entrance exams should be taken . There are early decision and deferred admissions plans. Applications should be filed by August 1 for fall entry and January 1 for spring entry, along with a $25 fee. Notification is sent on a rolling basis.

Transfer: 24 transfer students enrolled in 2004-2005. Transfer applicants must have a minimum GPA of 2.0. If fewer than 40 credits have been earned, the SAT is required. 48 of 128 credits required for the bachelor's degree must be completed at Saint Joseph's.

Visiting: There are regularly scheduled orientations for prospective students, including meetings with faculty advisers and student-to-student sessions. There are guides for informal visits and visitors may sit in on classes. To schedule a visit, contact the Admissions Office.

Financial Aid: In 2005-2006, 95% of all full-time freshmen and 85% of continuing full-time students received some form of financial aid. 60% of all full-time students received need-based aid. The average freshman award was $10,000. Need-based scholarships or need-based grants averaged $10,000 ($13,000 maximum); need-based self-help aid (loans and jobs) averaged $2500 ($5000 maximum); and academic scholarships averaged $10,000 ($13,000 maximum). 4% of undergraduates work part time. Average annual earnings from campus work are $1500. The average financial indebtedness of the 2005 graduate was $16,680. Saint Joseph's is a member of CSS. The FAFSA, the state aid form, and the college's own financial statement are required. The priority date for freshman financial aid applications for fall entry is February 25. The deadline for filing freshman financial aid applications for fall entry is rolling.

International Students: They must take the TOEFL and the SAT.

Computers: All students may access the system. There are no time limits and no fees.

Graduates: From July 1, 2004 to June 30, 2005, 265 bachelor's degrees were awarded. The most popular majors were organizational management (19%), child study (15%), and community health and human services (15%). In an average class, 67% graduate in 4 years or less and 76% graduate in 5 years or less. 32 companies recruited on campus in 2004-2005. Of the 2004 graduating class, 42% were enrolled in graduate school within 6 months of graduation and 75% were employed.

Admissions Contact: Theresa LaRocca Meyer, Director of Admissions. Web: *www.sjcny.edu*

SAINT JOSEPH'S COLLEGE, NEW YORK, SUFFOLK   E-5
CAMPUS

Patchogue, NY 11772

(631) 447-3219; Fax: (631) 447-1734

Full-time: 660 men, 1830 women   **Faculty:** 95; IIB, av$
Part-time: 20 men, 300 women   **Ph.D.s:** 62%
Graduate: 1 man, 30 women   **Student/Faculty:** 26 to 1
Year: 4-1-4, summer session   **Tuition:** $12,000
Application Deadline: see profile   **Room & Board:** n/app
Freshman Class: n/av
SAT: required   COMPETITIVE

Saint Joseph's College, established in 1916, is a private, independent, multicampus commuter institution offering a wide variety of undergraduate study options, including traditional liberal arts majors, special course offerings, and certificate, affiliated, and preprofessional programs. The school offers 12 Career Readiness Tracks. There is a campus in Brooklyn. There are 2 undergraduate and 2 graduate schools. Figures in the above capsule in this profile are approximate. In addition to regional accreditation, SJC has baccalaureate program accreditation with NLN. The library contains 120,000 volumes, and subscribes to 400 periodicals including electronic. Computerized library services include the card catalog, database searching, and Internet access. Special learning facilities include a learning resource center. The 25-acre campus is in a suburban area 60 miles east of New York City. There are 5 buildings.

Student Life: 99% of undergraduates are from New York. Others are from 4 states and 4 foreign countries. 85% are from public schools. 86% are white. The average age of freshmen is 18; all undergraduates, 20. 14% do not continue beyond their first year; 67% remain to graduate.

Housing: There are no residence halls. All students commute. Alcohol is not permitted. All students may keep cars.

Activities: 1% of men belong to 1 local fraternity; 4% of women belong to 2 local sororities. There are 31 groups on campus, including cheerleading, chorus, computers, dance, drama, ethnic, jazz band, literary magazine, newspaper, political, religious, social, social service, and student government. Popular campus events include Club Fair, Make a Difference Day, and Spring Fling.

Sports: There are 6 intercollegiate sports for men and 8 for women. Facilities include a swimming pool, a fitness center, an aerobics studio, an indoor running track, and a competition-size basketball court.

Disabled Students: All of the campus is accessible. Wheelchair ramps, elevators, special parking, specially equipped rest rooms, and lowered drinking fountains are available.

Services: Counseling and information services are available, as is tutoring in most subjects.

Campus Safety and Security: Measures include 24-hour foot and vehicle patrol, self-defense education, security escort services, and shuttle buses. There are informal discussions, pamphlets/posters/films, and lighted pathways/sidewalks. The school is monitored through closed-circuit screens.

Programs of Study: SJC confers B.A. and B.S. degrees. Master's degrees are also awarded. Bachelor's degrees are awarded in BIOLOGICAL SCIENCE (biology/biological science), BUSINESS (accounting, business administration and management, and recreation and leisure services), COMMUNICATIONS AND THE ARTS (English and speech/debate/rhetoric), COMPUTER AND PHYSICAL SCIENCE (information sciences and systems and mathematics), EDUCATION (secondary), SOCIAL SCIENCE (child care/child and family studies, history, psychology, and social science). Child study, math/computer science, and business/accounting are the strongest academically. Child study and business/accounting are the largest.

Required: To graduate, students must complete a liberal arts core curriculum. A total of 128 credits is needed to graduate, with a minimum of 33 credits in the major. For education majors, a minimum GPA of 2.8 is required; for all other majors, 2.3.

Special: There is study abroad in approximately 10 countries, an interdisciplinary major in human relations, B.A.-B.S. degrees, and a dual major in child study (elementary and special education). There are 7 national honor societies and 6 departmental honors programs.

Faculty/Classroom: 45% of faculty are male; 55%, female. All teach undergraduates. The average class size in an introductory lecture is 18; in a laboratory, 18; and in a regular course, 18.

Admissions: In a recent year, 77% of the applicants were accepted. The SAT scores for the recent freshman class were: Verbal--30% below 500, 53% between 500 and 599, 16% between 600 and 700, and 1% above 700; Math--22% below 500, 53% between 500 and 599, 24% between 600 and 700, and 1% above 700. The ACT scores were 37% below 21, and 63% between 21 and 23. 45% of the freshmen were in the top fifth of their class; 82% were in the top two fifths. 2 freshmen graduated first in their class.

Requirements: The SAT is required. In addition, high school transcripts, 2 letters of recommendation, a personal essay, and an interview are required. A GPA of 3.0 is required. AP and CLEP credits are accepted.

Procedure: Freshmen are admitted fall and spring. Check with the school for current application deadlines and fee. Notification is sent on a rolling basis.

Transfer: 733 transfer students enrolled in a recent year. Child study and education majors need a 2.8 GPA; all others, 2.3. 48 of 128 credits required for the bachelor's degree must be completed at SJC.

Visiting: There are regularly scheduled orientations for prospective students, including open houses in fall and spring. There are guides for informal visits and visitors may sit in on classes. To schedule a visit, contact the Admissions office.

Financial Aid: In a recent year, 69% of all full-time freshmen and 77% of continuing full-time students received some form of financial aid. 46% of full-time freshmen and 63% of continuing full-time students received need-based aid. The average freshman award was $9798. Need-based scholarships or need-based grants averaged $8136; need-based self-help aid (loans and jobs) averaged $1662; and other non-need-based awards and non-need-based scholarships averaged $5085. 5% of undergraduates work part time. Average annual earnings from campus work are $1500. The average financial indebtedness of the recent graduate was $15,086. The FAFSA and the college's own financial statement are required. Check with the school for application deadlines.

International Students: International students must take the TOEFL and also take the SAT or the ACT.

Computers: All students may access the system during school hours. There are no time limits and no fees.

Graduates: In a reent year, 691 bachelor's degrees were awarded. The most popular majors were education (63%), business (13%), and psychology (6%).

Admissions Contact: Marion E. Salgado, Director of Admissions. E-mail: *suffolkas@sjcny.edu* Web: *www.sjcny.edu*

SAINT LAWRENCE UNIVERSITY   C-2
Canton, NY 13617   (315) 229-5261
                                   (800) 285-1856; Fax: (315) 229-5818

Full-time: 1010 men, 1101 women	**Faculty:** 164; IIB, +$
Part-time: 10 men, 10 women	**Ph.D.s:** 99%
Graduate: 57 men, 76 women	**Student/Faculty:** 13 to 1
Year: semesters, summer session	**Tuition:** $32,365
Application Deadline: February 15	**Room & Board:** $8180

Freshman Class: 2989 applied, 1770 accepted, 537 enrolled
SAT Verbal/Math: 570/580*   **VERY COMPETITIVE**

St. Lawrence University, established in 1856, is a private liberal arts institution. In addition to regional accreditation, St. Lawrence has baccalaureate program accreditation with ACS. The 2 libraries contain 565,996 volumes, 596,095 microform items, and 5804 audio/video tapes/CDs/DVDs, and subscribe to 16,773 periodicals including electronic. Computerized library services include the card catalog, interlibrary loans, database searching, and Internet access. Special learning facilities include a learning resource center, art gallery, radio station, TV station, and a science field station. The 1000-acre campus is in a rural area 80 miles south of Ottawa, Canada. Including any residence halls, there are 30 buildings.

Student Life: 55% of undergraduates are from out of state, mostly the Northeast. Students are from 41 states, 30 foreign countries, and Canada. 71% are from public schools. 70% are white. The average age of freshmen is 19; all undergraduates, 20. 10% do not continue beyond their first year; 75% remain to graduate.

Housing: 1929 students can be accommodated in college housing, which includes coed dorms, on-campus apartments, fraternity houses, and sorority houses. In addition, there are language houses, special-interest houses, and theme cottages, such as Habitat for Humanity. On-campus housing is guaranteed for all 4 years. 99% of students live on campus; of those, 90% remain on campus on weekends. All students may keep cars.

Activities: 8% of men belong to 2 national fraternities; 21% of women belong to 1 local sorority and 3 national sororities. There are 100 groups on campus, including art, chess, choir, chorus, dance, drama, ethnic, forensics, gay, honors, international, literary magazine, newspaper, outdoor, photography, political, professional, radio and TV, religious, social, social service, and student government. Popular campus events include St. Lawrence Festival of the Arts, Black History Week, and Holiday Candlelight Service.

Sports: There are 15 intercollegiate sports for men and 16 for women, and 12 intramural sports for men and 9 for women. Facilities include basketball, squash, and tennis courts, a swimming pool, and a 133-station fitness center. There are also 2 field houses, an arena, an artificial ice rink, an 18-hole golf course, riding stables, jogging and cross-country ski trails, indoor and outdoor competition tracks, and soccer, baseball, and softball fields.

Disabled Students: 75% of the campus is accessible. Wheelchair ramps, elevators, special parking, specially equipped rest rooms, special class scheduling, and visual fire alarms are available.

Services: Counseling and information services are available, as is tutoring in every subject. There is a reader service for the blind. a writing center, and science and technology counseling.

Campus Safety and Security: Measures include 24-hour foot and vehicle patrol, self-defense education, security escort services, and informal discussions. There are pamphlets/posters/films, emergency telephones, lighted pathways/sidewalks, and student patrols.

Programs of Study: St. Lawrence confers B.A. and B.S. degrees. Master's degrees are also awarded. Bachelor's degrees are awarded in AGRICULTURE (environmental studies), BIOLOGICAL SCIENCE (biochemistry, biology/biological science, and neurosciences), COMMUNICATIONS AND THE ARTS (art, art history and appreciation, communications, creative writing, dramatic arts, English, fine arts, French, German, languages, music, Spanish, studio art, and visual and performing arts), COMPUTER AND PHYSICAL SCIENCE (chemistry, computer science, geology, mathematics, and physics), ENGINEERING AND ENVIRONMENTAL DESIGN (environmental science), SOCIAL SCIENCE (African studies, anthropology, Asian/Oriental studies, Canadian studies, economics, history, interdisciplinary studies, international studies, philosophy, political science/government, psychology, religion, and sociology). Psychology, English, and government are the largest.

Required: To graduate, students must maintain a minimum GPA of 2.0 and complete 120 course hours, with 29 to 43 in the major. Freshmen must take a first-year program, a 2-semester team-taught course. Requirements also include 1 course in arts/expression, 1 in humanities, 1 in social science, 1 in math or foreign language, 2 in natural science/science studies, and 2 in diversity.

Special: Students may cross-register with the Associated Colleges of the St. Lawrence Valley. Internships are available through the sociology, psychology, and English departments and through a service learning program. Study-abroad in 14 countries and a Washington semester are offered. Dual majors and student-designed majors can be arranged. Students may earn 3-2 engineering degrees in conjunction with 7 engineering schools. Nondegree study and pass/fail options are available. An Adirondack semester and a leadership academy are also offered. There are 20 national honor societies, including Phi Beta Kappa, and 17 departmental honors programs.

Faculty/Classroom: 52% of faculty are male; 48%, female. 99% teach undergraduates and all do research. No introductory courses are taught by graduate students. The average class size in a regular course is 16.

Admissions: 59% of the 2005-2006 applicants were accepted. The SAT scores for the 2005-2006 freshman class were: Verbal--15% below 500, 47% between 500 and 599, 33% between 600 and 700, and 5% above 700; Math--11% below 500, 46% between 500 and 599, 37% between 600 and 700, and 6% above 700. 62% of the current freshmen were in the top fifth of their class; 88% were in the top two fifths. 9 freshmen graduated first in their class.

Requirements: Applicants must be graduates of an accredited high school. 16 or more academic credits are required, including 4 years of English and 3 years each of foreign languages, math, science, and social studies. Essays are required and interviews are recommended for all applicants. Submissions of standardized test scores is optional. AP and CLEP credits are accepted. Important factors in the admissions decision are advanced placement or honor courses, extracurricular activities record, and recommendations by school officials.

Procedure: Freshmen are admitted fall and spring. Entrance exams should be taken during the spring of the junior year or the fall of the senior year. There are early decision and deferred admissions plans. Early decision applications should be filed by November 15; regular applications, by February 15 for fall entry and December 1 for spring entry, along with a $50 fee. Notification of early decision is sent December 15; regular decision, March 15. 169 early decision candidates were accepted for the 2005-2006 class. 227 applicants were on the 2005 waiting list; 43 were admitted. Applications are accepted on-line.

Transfer: 17 transfer students enrolled in 2004-2005. The high school transcript and SAT scores are evaluated, but college work is more important. High school and college recommendations are required. 16 of 120 credits required for the bachelor's degree must be completed at St. Lawrence.

Visiting: There are regularly scheduled orientations for prospective students, including interviews and tours. There are guides for informal visits and visitors may sit in on classes and stay overnight. To schedule a visit, contact the Admissions Office at admissions@stlawu.edu.

Financial Aid: In 2005-2006, 85% of all full-time freshmen and 83% of continuing full-time students received some form of financial aid. 71% of full-time freshmen and 68% of continuing full-time students received need-based aid. The average freshman award was $18,166. 38% of undergraduates work part time. Average annual earnings from campus work are $1100. St. Lawrence is a member of CSS. The CSS/Profile or FAFSA and the college's own financial statement are required. The deadline for filing freshman financial aid applications for fall entry is February 15.

International Students: There are 96 international students enrolled. The school actively recruits these students. They must take the TOEFL or the SAT or ACT.

Computers: Wireless access is available in some buildings on campus. All students may access the system 24 hours per day. There are no time limits and no fees.

Graduates: From July 1, 2004 to June 30, 2005, 434 bachelor's degrees were awarded. The most popular majors were English (12%), psychology (11%), and government (11%). In an average class, 1% graduate in 3 years or less, 69% graduate in 4 years or less, 74% graduate in 5 years or less, and 74% graduate in 6 years or less. 9 companies recruited on campus in 2004-2005. Of the 2004 graduating class, 20% were enrolled in graduate school within 6 months of graduation and 74% were employed.

Admissions Contact: Teresa Cowdrey, Dean of Admissions and Financial Aid. E-mail: admissions@stlawu.edu Web: www.stlawu.ed

SAINT THOMAS AQUINAS COLLEGE   D-5
Sparkill, NY 10976

(914) 398-4100
(800) 999-STAC; Fax: (914) 398-4224

Full-time: 1310 men and women	Faculty: 76; IIB, +$
Part-time: 700 men and women	Ph.D.s: 75%
Graduate: 65 men, 115 women	Student/Faculty: 17 to 1
Year: 4-1-4, summer session	Tuition: $14,000
Application Deadline: see profile	Room & Board: $8000
Freshman Class: n/av	
SAT or ACT: required	LESS COMPETITIVE

Saint Thomas Aquinas College, founded in 1952, is an independent liberal arts institution. Figures in the above capsule and in this profile are approximate. The library contains 102,943 volumes and 45,900 microform items, and subscribes to 108 periodicals including electronic. Computerized library services include the card catalog, interlibrary loans, and database searching. Special learning facilities include a learning resource

center, radio station, and TV station. The 43-acre campus is in a suburban area 15 miles north of New York City. Including any residence halls, there are 12 buildings.

Student Life: 75% of undergraduates are from New York. Others are from 6 states, 8 foreign countries, and Canada. 80% are from public schools. 84% are white. 62% are Catholic; 23% Protestant. The average age of freshmen is 18; all undergraduates, 23. 16% do not continue beyond their first year; 62% remain to graduate.

Housing: 450 students can be accommodated in college housing, which includes single-sex dorms and on-campus apartments. On-campus housing is guaranteed for all 4 years. 65% of students commute. Alcohol is not permitted. All students may keep cars.

Activities: There are no fraternities or sororities. There are 15 groups on campus, including cheerleading, chorus, computers, drama, honors, international, literary magazine, musical theater, newspaper, professional, radio and TV, religious, social service, student government, and yearbook. Popular campus events include trips to Broadway shows and Halloween and Christmas mixers.

Sports: There are 5 intercollegiate sports for men and 4 for women, and 6 intramural sports for men and 5 for women. Facilities include an auditorium, a 750-seat gym, a weight room, and basketball and tennis courts.

Disabled Students: 90% of the campus is accessible. Wheelchair ramps, elevators, special parking, specially equipped rest rooms, special class scheduling, and lowered telephones are available.

Services: Counseling and information services are available, as is tutoring in most subjects. There is remedial math and writing.

Campus Safety and Security: Measures include 24-hour foot and vehicle patrol, security escort services, pamphlets/posters/films, and emergency telephones. There are lighted pathways/sidewalks.

Programs of Study: STAC confers B.A., B.S., and B.S.E. degrees. Associate and master's degrees are also awarded. Bachelor's degrees are awarded in BUSINESS (accounting, banking and finance, business administration and management, marketing/retailing/merchandising, and recreation and leisure services), COMMUNICATIONS AND THE ARTS (communications, English, fine arts, romance languages and literature, and Spanish), EDUCATION (art, bilingual/bicultural, elementary, foreign languages, science, secondary, and special), ENGINEERING AND ENVIRONMENTAL DESIGN (commercial art), HEALTH PROFESSIONS (medical laboratory technology and premedicine), SOCIAL SCIENCE (criminal justice, history, philosophy, prelaw, psychology, religion, and social science). Education, business administration, and natural sciences are the strongest academically. Business administration is the largest.

Required: To graduate, all students must complete a total of 120 credit hours, with 36 to 54 in the major and a minimum GPA of 2.0. A core curriculum of 51 credits in liberal arts courses is required.

Special: The college offers cross-registration with Barry University and Aquinas College and internships in business, criminal justice, commercial design, recreation and leisure, and communications. Study abroad in Europe and Asia, work-study, a 3-2 engineering degree with George Washington University and Manhattan College, and in physical therapy with New York Medical College, are available. Nondegree study and pass/fail options are possible. There are 7 national honor societies, including Phi Beta Kappa, and a freshman honors program.

Faculty/Classroom: 55% of faculty are male; 45%, female. 99% teach undergraduates, 50% do research, and 50% do both. No introductory courses are taught by graduate students. The average class size in an introductory lecture is 35; in a laboratory, 15; and in a regular course, 20.

Requirements: The SAT or ACT is required. In addition, applicants must be graduates of an accredited secondary school or have a GED certificate. 16 Carnegie units are recommended, including 4 years of English, 3 years of social science, 2 years each of math and science, and 1 year each of foreign language and history. An interview is recommended. A GPA of 2.2 is required. AP and CLEP credits are accepted. Important factors in the admissions decision are leadership record, extracurricular activities record, and advanced placement or honor courses.

Procedure: Freshmen are admitted fall and spring. Entrance exams should be taken by the spring of the junior year. There are early decision, early admissions, and deferred admissions plans. There is a rolling admissions plan. Notification is sent on a rolling basis. Applications are accepted on-line. Check with the school for current application deadlines and fee.

Transfer: Applicants must have a 2.0 GPA from the previous school. 30 of 120 credits required for the bachelor's degree must be completed at STAC.

Visiting: There are guides for informal visits and visitors may sit in on classes and stay overnight. To schedule a visit, contact the Admissions Office.

Financial Aid: STAC is a member of CSS. The FAFSA is required. Check with the school for current deadlines.

International Students: The school actively recruits these students. They must take the TOEFL.

Computers: All students may access the system. There are no time limits. The fee is $100.

Admissions Contact: Tracey A. Howard-Ubelhoer, Director of Admissions. A video is available. E-mail: *thoward@stac.edu* Web: *www.stac.edu*

SARAH LAWRENCE COLLEGE — D-5

Bronxville, NY 10708
(914) 395-2510
(800) 888-2858; Fax: (914) 395-2515

Full-time: 300 men, 900 women	Faculty: 180; IIB, ++$
Part-time: 10 men, 60 women	Ph.D.s: n/av
Graduate: 50 men, 300 women	Student/Faculty: 7 to 1
Year: semesters	Tuition: $31,000
Application Deadline: see profile	Room & Board: $11,000
Freshman Class: n/av	
SAT or ACT: not required	HIGHLY COMPETITIVE

Sarah Lawrence College, established in 1926, is an independent institution conferring liberal arts degrees. The academic structure is based on the British don system. Students meet biweekly with professors in tutorials and are enrolled in small seminars. While there are no formal majors, students develop individual concentrations that are usually interdisciplinary. Figures in the above capsule and in this profile are approximate. The 3 libraries contain 282,676 volumes, 24,218 microform items, and 9319 audio/video tapes/CDs/DVDs, and subscribe to 916 periodicals including electronic. Computerized library services include the card catalog, interlibrary loans, database searching, and Internet access. Special learning facilities include an art gallery, radio station, a slide library with 75,000 slides of art and architecture, an early childhood center, an electronic music studio, music library, a student-run theater, and a student-run art gallery. The 41-acre campus is in a suburban area 15 miles north of midtown Manhattan. Including any residence halls, there are 50 buildings.

Student Life: 81% of undergraduates are from out of state, mostly the Middle Atlantic. Students are from 46 states, 25 foreign countries, and Canada. 65% are from public schools. 70% are white. The average age of freshmen is 18; all undergraduates, 20. 7% do not continue beyond their first year; 72% remain to graduate.

Housing: 965 students can be accommodated in college housing, which includes single-sex and coed dorms and on-campus apartments. A French interest house, the Perkins Art Co-Op, and the Good Life House are also available. On-campus housing is guaranteed for all 4 years. 87% of students live on campus; of those, 90% remain on campus on weekends. Upperclassmen may keep cars.

Activities: There are no fraternities or sororities. There are 30 groups on campus, including art, choir, chorale, chorus, computers, dance, drama, ethnic, film, gay, human rights, international, jazz band, literary magazine, musical theater, newspaper, orchestra, philosophy, photography, poetry, political, radio and TV, religious, social, social service, student government, and yearbook. Popular campus events include Mayfair, "Deb Ball," and a student scholarship fundraising auction.

Sports: There are 5 intercollegiate sports for men and 6 for women, and 9 intramural sports for men and 9 for women. Facilities include a sports center with a gym, a jogging track, a 6-lane swimming pool, a rowing tank, a multipurpose studio, and 3 squash courts a fitness center and weight room, tennis courts, and a number of open fields and lawns. Off campus, the college has the use of a boathouse and stables.

Disabled Students: 50% of the campus is accessible. Wheelchair ramps, elevators, special parking, specially equipped rest rooms, special class scheduling, lowered drinking fountains, and lowered telephones are available.

Services: Counseling and information services are available, as is tutoring in some subjects, including writing. There is a reader service for the blind.

Campus Safety and Security: Measures include 24-hour foot and vehicle patrol, self-defense education, security escort services, and shuttle buses. There are informal discussions, pamphlets/posters/films, emergency telephones, and lighted pathways/sidewalks.

Programs of Study: Sarah Lawrence confers the B.A. degree. Master's degrees are also awarded. Bachelor's degrees are awarded in BIOLOGICAL SCIENCE (biology/biological science), COMMUNICATIONS AND THE ARTS (art history and appreciation, classics, creative writing, dance, dramatic arts, English, film arts, fine arts, French, German, Greek, Italian, Latin, literature, music, Russian, Spanish, and visual and performing arts), COMPUTER AND PHYSICAL SCIENCE (chemistry and mathematics), HEALTH PROFESSIONS (premedicine), SOCIAL SCIENCE (anthropology, Asian/Oriental studies, economics, history, liberal arts/general studies, philosophy, political science/government, psychology, religion, Russian and Slavic studies, sociology, and women's studies).

Required: To graduate, students must complete 120 credit hours and meet distribution requirements in 3 of 4 academic areas, including history and social sciences, creative and performing arts, natural science and math, and humanities. Students must fulfill a first-year studies requirement in one of 18 areas and meet a phys ed requirement. Students must also take 2 lecture courses, where the average class size is 40.

Special: Internships are available in a variety of fields, with the school offering proximity to New York City art galleries and agencies. Study abroad in many countries, work-study programs, dual concentrations, a 3-2 engineering degree with Columbia, and a general degree may be pursued. All concentrations are self-designed and can be combined.

Faculty/Classroom: 49% of faculty are male; 51%, female. All both teach and do research. No introductory courses are taught by graduate students. The average class size in a regular course is 11.

Admissions: 41% of recent applicants were accepted. 66% of recent freshmen were in the top fifth of their class; 95% were in the top two fifths. There were 4 National Merit finalists in a recent years.

Requirements: Important academic requirements are secondary school record, teacher recommendation(s), and essay; class rank is considered. Nonacademic requirements include character and personality qualities; extracurricular activities, talent/ability, volunteer work, and work experience. Campus interview, alumnae/i relations, geographical residence, and minority status are considered. AP credits are accepted. Important factors in the admissions decision are recommendations by school officials, personality/intangible qualities, and extracurricular activities record.

Procedure: Freshmen are admitted in the fall. There are early decision, early admissions, and deferred admissions plans. 100 early decision candidates were accepted for a recent class. 150 applicants were on a recent waiting list; 35 were admitted. Applications are accepted on-line. Check with the school for current application deadlines and fee.

Transfer: 50 transfer students enrolled in a recent year. Applicants must submit high school and college transcripts, and a statement of good standing from prior institution(s). A GPA of 3.0 is required and transfer applicants must have a minimum of 30 credits completed, or the equivalent of 2 semesters of full-time college work. Also required are a $50 application fee, Admission Information Form (in-house Form 1), essays, a graded academic paper, and 2 teacher/faculty evaluations. An interview is recommended, but not required. Check with the school for current deadlines. 60 of 120 credits required for the bachelor's degree must be completed at Sarah Lawrence.

Visiting: There are regularly scheduled orientations for prospective students, consisting of a full day of faculty and student panels, lectures, tours, and discussion with admissions officers, offered twice per year during the fall. There are guides for informal visits and visitors may sit in on classes and stay overnight. To schedule a visit, contact Linda Bloom, Receptionist, Admissions Office at *slcadmit@slc.edu*.

Financial Aid: In a recent year, 50% of all full-time freshmen and 49% of continuing full-time students received some form of financial aid, including need-based aid. The average freshman award was $22,815. 43% of undergraduates work part time. Average annual earnings from campus work are $1000. The average financial indebtedness of a recent graduate was $15,023. Sarah Lawrence is a member of CSS. The CSS Profile, FAFSA, and a noncustodial parent statement are required. Check with the school for current deadlines.

International Students: There were 46 international students enrolled in a recent year. The school actively recruits these students. They take the TOEFL or take the SAT: Subject Test in English as a second language test.

Computers: All students may access the system 24 hours a day. There are no time limits and no fees.

Graduates: In a recent year, 256 bachelor's degrees were awarded. In an average class, 61% graduate in 4 years or less, 9% graduate in 5 years, and 1% graduate in 6 years. Of a recent graduating class, 30% were enrolled in graduate school within 6 months of graduation and 70% were employed.

Admissions Contact: Thyra L. Briggs, Dean of Admission. E-mail: *slcadmit@alc.edu* Web: *www.sarahlawrence.edu*

SCHOOL OF VISUAL ARTS — D-5

New York, NY 10010-3994
(212) 592-2100
(800) 436-4204; Fax: (212) 592-2116

Full-time: 1416 men, 1475 women	Faculty: 94
Part-time: 46 men, 66 women	Ph.D.s: 42%
Graduate: 168 men, 243 women	Student/Faculty: 31 to 1
Year: semesters, summer session	Tuition: $20,580
Application Deadline: March 15	Room & Board: $12,000
Freshman Class: 2135 applied, 1495 accepted, 586 enrolled	
SAT Verbal/Math: 530/520*	ACT: 22 SPECIAL

The School of Visual Arts, established in 1947, is a private institution conferring undergraduate and graduate degrees in fine and commercial arts. There are 8 undergraduate and 5 graduate schools. In addition to regional accreditation, SVA has baccalaureate program accreditation with FIDER and NASAD. The library contains 70,000 volumes, 1070 microform items, and 3168 audio/video tapes/CDs/DVDs, and subscribes to 307 periodicals including electronic. Computerized library services include the card catalog, database searching, Internet access, and laptop Internet portals. Special learning facilities include a learning resource center, art gallery, radio station, 5 student galleries, 3 media arts workshops, 3 film and 2 video studios, numerous editing facilities, animation studio with 3 pencil test facilities, digital audio room, tape transfer room, and multimedia facility with digital printing and editing systems. The campus is in an urban area in the middle of Manhattan. Including any residence halls, there are 12 buildings.

Student Life: 52% of undergraduates are from out of state, mostly the Middle Atlantic. Students are from 44 states, 40 foreign countries, and Canada. 80% are from public schools. 58% are white; 13% Asian American; 11% foreign nationals; 11% Hispanic. The average age of freshmen is 18; all undergraduates, 21. 10% do not continue beyond their first year; 62% remain to graduate.

Housing: 1050 students can be accommodated in college housing, which includes single-sex and coed dorms, on-campus apartments, and off-campus apartments. On-campus housing is guaranteed for the freshman year only and is available on a first-come, first-served basis. 70% of students commute. Alcohol is not permitted. All students may keep cars.

Activities: There are no fraternities or sororities. There are many groups and organizations on campus, including art, computers, drama, ethnic, film, gay, honors, international, literary magazine, newspaper, photography, political, professional, radio and TV, religious, social, social service, student government, and yearbook. Popular campus events include an annual ski trip and a Halloween party.

Sports: There is no sports program at SVA.

Disabled Students: All of the campus is accessible. Wheelchair ramps, elevators, specially equipped rest rooms, special class scheduling, and lowered telephones are available.

Services: There is remedial reading and writing.

Campus Safety and Security: Measures include 24-hour foot and vehicle patrol, shuttle buses, informal discussions, and pamphlets/posters/films. There are emergency telephones and lighted pathways/sidewalks.

Programs of Study: SVA confers the B.F.A. degree. Master's degrees are also awarded. Bachelor's degrees are awarded in COMMUNICATIONS AND THE ARTS (advertising, animation, film arts, fine arts, graphic design, illustration, photography, and video), ENGINEERING AND ENVIRONMENTAL DESIGN (computer graphics and interior design). Graphic design and advertising, film/video and animation, and fine arts are the largest.

Required: To graduate, students must complete 120 credits, including at least 72 in the major, with a minimum GPA of 2.0. These credits must include 30 in humanities and sciences, 12 in art history, and 6 in electives. Students must complete 2 introductory courses in literature and writing and must pass a proficiency exam in the first semester.

Special: SVA offers study abroad in 8 countries, accelerated degree programs, and for-credit internships with more than 200 media-related, design, and advertising firms, including DC Comics, MTV, and Pentagram Design. A summer internship with Walt Disney Studios is possible for illustration/cartooning majors. There is a freshman honors program.

Faculty/Classroom: 60% of faculty are male; 40%, female. 86% teach undergraduates and 12% both teach and do research. No introductory courses are taught by graduate students. The average class size in an introductory lecture is 30 and in a regular course, 20.

Admissions: 70% of the 2005-2006 applicants were accepted. The SAT scores for the 2005-2006 freshman class were: Verbal--35% below 500, 40% between 500 and 599, 20% between 600 and 700, and 5% above 700; Math--40% below 500, 36% between 500 and 599, 21% between 600 and 700, and 3% above 700. The ACT scores were 32% below 21, 23% between 21 and 23, 10% between 24 and 26, 33% between 27 and 28, and 1% above 28.

Requirements: The SAT or ACT is required. The ACT Optional Writing test is also required. In addition, applicants must graduate from an accredited secondary school or have a GED. A statement of intent is required of all students. A portfolio is also required, except for film and video applicants, who must submit a 2-part essay. A personal interview and letters of recommendation are considered helpful. A GPA of 2.7 is required. AP and CLEP credits are accepted. Important factors in the admissions decision are leadership record, personality/intangible qualities, and evidence of special talent.

Procedure: Freshmen are admitted fall and spring. There are early decision and deferred admissions plans. There is a rolling admissions plan. Early decision applications should be filed by December 1; regular applications, by March 15 for fall entry and December 1 for spring entry. The fall 2005 application fee was $50. Notification of early decision is sent January 14; regular decision, on a rolling basis. A waiting list is an active part of the admissions procedure. Applications are accepted on-line.

Transfer: College transcripts from all previously attended accredited colleges or univerities, portfolio, admissions essay, and high school transcripts are required. Letters of recommendation are encouraged; an interview is required if the applicant lives within 200 miles of the campus. 60 of 120 credits required for the bachelor's degree must be completed at SVA.

Visiting: There are regularly scheduled orientations for prospective students, including 6 Saturday open house receptions and weekly tours. There are guides for informal visits. To schedule a visit, contact the Office of Admissions at *admissions@sva.edu.*

Financial Aid: In a recent year, 74% of all full-time freshmen and 61% of continuing full-time students received some form of financial aid. 55% of full-time freshmen and 47% of continuing full-time students received need-based aid. The average freshman award was $9400. 7% of undergraduates work part time. Average annual earnings from campus work were $5000. The average financial indebtedness of the 2005 graduate was $18,000. The FAFSA is required. The deadline for filing freshman financial aid applications for fall entry is February 1.

International Students: The school actively recruits these students. They must score satisfactorily on the TOEFL and also take the college's own test, or earn a minimum score of 6 in all categories of the NYU English proficiency exam.

Computers: Wireless access is available. Every student is given a log-in ID to the school's internal network, including Web-based e-mail account. The computer network can be assessed from anywhere. SVA has over 500 PCs and Macs available for student use, including the library, public areas on campus, and the Writing Resource Center. All students may access the system during normal operating hours of the library and the writing resource center. There are no time limits and no fees. It is strongly recommended that all students have a personal computer. A G4 or G5 Macintosh is recommended.

Graduates: The most popular majors were graphic design/advertising (27%), film/video/animation (19%), and photography (16%). In an average class, 58% graduate in 4 years, 60% graduate in 5 years, and 62% graduate in 6 years. 50 companies recruited on campus in 2004-2005. Of the 2004 graduating class, 6% were enrolled in graduate school within 6 months of graduation and 85% were employed.

Admissions Contact: Teresa Nehra, Director of Admissions.
E-mail: *admissions@sva.edu* Web: *www.schoolofvisualarts.edu*

SIENA COLLEGE   D-3

Loudonville, NY 12211-1462

(518) 783-2423
(888) AT SIENA; Fax: (518) 783-2436

Full-time: 1322 men, 1734 women	**Faculty:** 180; IIB, +$
Part-time: 110 men, 170 women	**Ph.D.s:** 91%
Graduate: none	**Student/Faculty:** 17 to 1
Year: semesters, summer session	**Tuition:** $20,275
Application Deadline: March 1	**Room & Board:** $7985
Freshman Class: 4326 applied, 2620 accepted, 765 enrolled	
SAT Verbal/Math: 554/570*	**ACT:** 26 VERY COMPETITIVE+

Siena College, founded in 1937, is an independent, liberal arts college with a Franciscan and Catholic tradition. Siena offers bachelor's programs in the arts, sciences, and business. There are 3 undergraduate schools. In addition to regional accreditation, Siena has baccalaureate program accreditation with ACS and CSWE . The library contains 331,442 volumes, 27,645 microform items, and 4982 audio/video tapes/CDs/DVDs, and subscribes to 5259 periodicals including electronic. Computerized library services include the card catalog, interlibrary loans, database searching, Internet access, and laptop Internet portals. Special learning facilities include a radio station and the Hickey Financial Technology Center, which features a real-time capital market trading room with stock ticker, data screens, workstations, and access to financial information sources and accounting labs. The 164-acre campus is in a suburban area 2 miles north of Albany. Including any residence halls, there are 28 buildings.

Student Life: 87% of undergraduates are from New York. Others are from 26 states, 10 foreign countries, and Canada. 86% are white. The average age of freshmen is 18; all undergraduates, 21. 11% do not continue beyond their first year; 79% remain to graduate.

Housing: 2415 students can be accommodated in college housing, which includes coed dorms and on-campus apartments. In addition, there are special-interest houses. On-campus housing is guaranteed for the freshman year only and is available on a lottery system for upperclassmen. 79% of students live on campus; of those, 90% remain on campus on weekends. Upperclassmen may keep cars.

Activities: There are no fraternities or sororities. There are 68 groups on campus, including cheerleading, choir, chorus, community service, computers, dance, debate, drama, ethnic, film, gay, honors, international, literary magazine, musical theater, newspaper, opera, orchestra, pep band, political, professional, radio and TV, religious, social, social service, student government, symphony, and yearbook. Popular campus events include Family Weekend, Musical Mayhem, and Charity Week Service Auction.

Sports: There are 7 intercollegiate sports for men and 11 for women, and 9 intramural sports for men and 9 for women. Facilities include an athletic complex with free weights, a training facility, an indoor track, an 8-lane, 25-meter pool, fitness equipment, Lifecycles, 4 multipurpose courts, 6 outdoor tennis courts, 5 outdoor fields, 2 squash courts, and racquetball courts.

Disabled Students: 90% of the campus is accessible. Wheelchair ramps, elevators, special parking, specially equipped rest rooms, special class scheduling, special housing, and an office for students with disabilities that provides various resources are available.

Services: Counseling and information services are available, as is tutoring in most subjects. There is a reader service for the blind, remedial math and writing, and a writing center that offers free one-on-one assistance.

Campus Safety and Security: Measures include 24-hour foot and vehicle patrol, security escort services, informal discussions, and pamphlets/posters/films. There are emergency telephones, lighted pathways/sidewalks, a card access system for residence halls, radio dispatch, and a 911 on-campus telephone system.

Programs of Study: Siena confers B.A., B.S., and B.B.A. degrees. Bachelor's degrees are awarded in BIOLOGICAL SCIENCE (biochemistry and biology/biological science), BUSINESS (accounting, banking and finance, business economics, and marketing management), COMMUNICATIONS AND THE ARTS (classical languages, English, French, Spanish, and visual and performing arts), COMPUTER AND PHYSICAL SCIENCE (chemistry, computer science, mathematics, and physics), ENGINEERING AND ENVIRONMENTAL DESIGN (environmental science), SOCIAL SCIENCE (American studies, economics, history, philosophy, political science/government, psychology, religion, social work, and sociology). Marketing/management, accounting, and biology are the largest.

Required: To graduate, students must earn 120 credits, including 30 to 39 in the major, with at least a 2.0 GPA. At least a C-grade must be earned in every major field course used to satisfy the credit hour requirements of the major. The required core curriculum of 42 credits must include 3 math/science courses, 2 foundation courses, 2 social science courses, 1 to 2 courses in English, history, philosophy, and religious studies, and 1 creative arts course.

Special: The college offers a dual degree program in engineering with Rensselaer Polytechnic Institute, Catholic University, SUNY Binghamton, Western New England College, Clarkson College of Technology, and Manhattan College. A cooperative program in environmental science and forestry with a degree awarded by Syracuse University is offered, as are a cooperative business management program with Clarkson University, Lubin School of Business at Pace University, and the Graduate College of Union University, enabling students to earns a B.A. and M.B.A. in 5 years, and a 4/3 law program with Pace University Law School and Western New England College School of Law. Early admissions master's programs in social work are offered with New York, Fordham, and Syracuse Universities. Early assurance programs are offered with SUNY College of Optometry and SUNY College of Medicine (Health Science Center in Syracuse) as are accelerated programs with Temple University College of Podiatric Medicine and Pennsylvania College of Optometry (time-shortened programs). A time-shortened doctoral degree in dentistry is offered with Siena/Georgetown cooperative as is an early assurance program with SUNY Buffalo School of Dental Medicine. A Washington semester is available with American University. There are 15 national honor societies, a freshman honors program, and 4 departmental honors programs.

Faculty/Classroom: 66% of faculty are male; 34%, female. All teach undergraduates. The average class size in an introductory lecture is 20; in a laboratory, 18; and in a regular course, 21.

Admissions: 61% of the 2005-2006 applicants were accepted. The SAT scores for the 2005-2006 freshman class were: Verbal--18% below 500, 55% between 500 and 599, 25% between 600 and 700, and 1% above 700; Math--11% below 500, 54% between 500 and 599, 32% between 600 and 700, and 3% above 700. 48% of the current freshmen were in the top fifth of their class; 84% were in the top two fifths. 123 freshmen graduated first in their class.

Requirements: The SAT is required. In addition, applicants must be graduates of an accredited secondary school or have a GED. 13 academic credits are required, including 4 years of English, 3 to 4 years each of history/social studies, math, and science, and a recommended 3 years of foreign language study. All applicants must submit an essay; an interview is recommended. AP and CLEP credits are accepted. Important factors in the admissions decision are advanced placement or honor courses, personality/intangible qualities, and extracurricular activities record.

Procedure: Freshmen are admitted fall and spring. Entrance exams should be taken during spring of the junior year or fall of the senior year. There are early decision, early admissions, and deferred admissions plans. Early decision applications should be filed by December 1; regular applications, by March 1 for fall entry, December 1 for spring entry, and May 1 for summer entry, along with a $50 fee. Notification of early decision is sent December 15; regular decision, March 15. 59 early decision candidates were accepted for the 2005-2006 class. 203 applicants were on the 2005 waiting list; 53 were admitted. Applications are accepted on-line.

Transfer: 301 transfer students enrolled in 2004-2005. Applicants must have a minimum 2.5 GPA. An interview is recommended. At least half of the major field requirements must be completed at Siena. 30 of 120 credits required for the bachelor's degree must be completed at Siena.

Visiting: There are regularly scheduled orientations for prospective students. Students may interview with an admissions counselor, tour campus, or attend a group information session. There are guides for informal

visits and visitors may sit in on classes and stay overnight. To schedule a visit, contact the Admissions Office.

Financial Aid: In 2005-2006, 92% of all full-time students received some form of financial aid. 71% of full-time freshmen and 70% of continuing full-time students received need-based aid. The average freshman award was $13,768. 19% of undergraduates work part time. Average annual earnings from campus work are $1492. The average financial indebtedness of the 2005 graduate was $17,415. The FAFSA and the state aid form are required. The deadline for filing freshman financial aid applications for fall entry is April 1.

International Students: There are 27 international students enrolled. The school actively recruits these students. They must achieve a satisfactory score on the TOEFL and also take the SAT or the ACT.

Computers: Wireless access is available. All students have accounts established for them prior to arrival. Students may access more than 123 PCs, Macs, and terminals in more than a dozen locations, some of which are open 24 hours a day. Every residential space includes a network connection. A wireless system is available in the student union, parts of the library, and in some classrooms. A total of 235 wired network connections are available. All students may access the system 24 hours per day. There are no time limits and no fees.

Graduates: From July 1, 2004 to June 30, 2005, 769 bachelor's degrees were awarded. The most popular majors were marketing/management (27%), psychology (11%), and accounting (11%). In an average class, 75% graduate in 4 years or less, 76% graduate in 5 years or less, and 79% graduate in 6 years or less. 278 companies recruited on campus in 2004-2005. Of the 2004 graduating class, 76% were employed within 6 months of graduation.

Admissions Contact: Edward Jones, Assistant Vice President for Admissions. E-mail: *admit@siena.edu* Web: *www.siena.edu*

SKIDMORE COLLEGE   D-3

Saratoga Springs, NY 12866-1632   (518) 580-5570
(800) 867-6007; Fax: (518) 580-5584

Full-time: 1001 men, 1523 women	**Faculty:** 228; IIB, +$
Part-time: 87 men, 162 women	**Ph.Ds:** 82%
Graduate: 12 men, 43 women	**Student/Faculty:** 11 to 1
Year: semesters, summer session	**Tuition:** $32,659
Application Deadline: January 15	**Room & Board:** $9120
Freshman Class: 6055 applied, 2642 accepted, 694 enrolled	
SAT Verbal/Math: 630/630*	**ACT:** 27 **HIGHLY COMPETITIVE**

Skidmore College, established in 1903, is an independent institution offering undergraduate programs in liberal arts and sciences, as well as preprofessional programs (business, social work, education, studio art, dance, and theater). In addition to regional accreditation, Skidmore has baccalaureate program accreditation with CSWE and NASAD. The library contains 420,650 volumes, 9259 microform items, and 13,684 audio/video tapes/CDs/DVDs, and subscribes to 936 periodicals including electronic. Computerized library services include the card catalog, interlibrary loans, database searching, and Internet access. Special learning facilities include a learning resource center, art gallery, radio station, TV station, and an electronic music studio, music and art studios, theater teaching facility, anthropology lab, and special biological habitats on campus. The 892-acre campus is in a small town 30 miles north of Albany. Including any residence halls, there are 73 buildings.

Student Life: 70% of undergraduates are from out of state, mostly the northwest and the Middle Atlantic. Students are from 42 states, 32 foreign countries, and Canada. 61% are from public schools. 70% are white. The average age of freshmen is 18; all undergraduates, 20. 8% do not continue beyond their first year; 78% remain to graduate.

Housing: 1900 students can be accommodated in college housing, which includes single-sex and coed dorms and on-campus apartments. In addition, there are honors houses, language houses, and special-interest houses. On-campus housing is guaranteed for all 4 years. 74% of students live on campus. All students may keep cars.

Activities: There are no fraternities or sororities. There are 80 groups on campus, including art, band, chorale, chorus, computers, dance, debate, drama, ethnic, film, gay, honors, international, jazz band, literary magazine, musical theater, newspaper, opera, orchestra, photography, political, professional, radio and TV, religious, social, social service, student government, and yearbook. Popular campus events include Martin Luther King Week, Oktoberfest, and Spring Fling.

Sports: There are 9 intercollegiate sports for men and 10 for women, and 10 intramural sports for men and 9 for women. Facilities include a fitness center, an indoor swimming and diving pool, 2 gyms with 4 basketball courts, an indoor jogging track, a weight room, fields for baseball and other sports, dance studios, cross-country ski trails, a riding center, courts for tennis, handball, racquetball, and squash, and an outdoor facility with a synthetic surface, a soccer/lacrosse field, an all-weather 400-meter track, lights, and permanent stands.

Disabled Students: 75% of the campus is accessible. Wheelchair ramps, elevators, special parking, specially equipped rest rooms, lowered drinking fountains, and special housing are available.

Services: Counseling and information services are available, as is tutoring in most subjects. There is a reader service for the blind. Diagnostic services, note takers, and books on tape are also offered.

Campus Safety and Security: Measures include 24-hour foot and vehicle patrol, security escort services, shuttle buses, and informal discussions. There are pamphlets/posters/films, emergency telephones, lighted pathways/sidewalks, and a special security alert system, rigorous fire response procedures, and a lock system on dorm entrances.

Programs of Study: Skidmore confers B.A. and B.S. degrees. Master's degrees are also awarded. Bachelor's degrees are awarded in AGRICULTURE (environmental studies), BIOLOGICAL SCIENCE (biochemistry, biology/biological science, and neurosciences), BUSINESS (business administration and management and business economics), COMMUNICATIONS AND THE ARTS (art, art history and appreciation, classics, dance, dramatic arts, English, fine arts, French, German, music, and Spanish), COMPUTER AND PHYSICAL SCIENCE (chemistry, computer science, geology, mathematics, and physics), EDUCATION (elementary), HEALTH PROFESSIONS (exercise science), SOCIAL SCIENCE (American studies, anthropology, Asian/Oriental studies, economics, French studies, history, international relations, liberal arts/general studies, philosophy, political science/government, psychology, religion, social science, social work, sociology, and women's studies). Business, English, and art are the largest.

Required: To graduate, students must complete 120 credits, including at least 24 at the 300 level, with a minimum GPA of 2.0 overall and in the major. B.A. candidates require 90 credits in the liberal arts to graduate; B.S. candidates require 60 credits. Students must fulfill all core curriculum, distribution, and major requirements.

Special: Skidmore offers cross-registration with the Hudson-Mohawk Consortium, individually designed internships, various study-abroad programs, a Washington semester in conjunction with American University, dual and student-designed majors, credit for life and experience, and pass/fail options, as well as a nondegree study program for senior citizens. There are cooperative programs in engineering with Dartmouth College and Clarkson University, 4+1 M.B.A. programs with Clarkson and the Graduate College at Union University, an accelerated law program with Cardozo law School at Yeshiva University, and a 4+1 M.A.T. program with Union. There are 9 national honor societies, including Phi Beta Kappa, and a freshman honors program.

Faculty/Classroom: 46% of faculty are male; 54%, female. No introductory courses are taught by graduate students. The average class size in a regular course is 17.

Admissions: 44% of the 2005-2006 applicants were accepted. The SAT scores for the 2005-2006 freshman class were: Verbal--5% below 500, 27% between 500 and 599, 51% between 600 and 700, and 17% above 700; Math--3% below 500, 29% between 500 and 599, 57% between 600 and 700, and 12% above 700. The ACT scores were 2% below 21, 11% between 21 and 23, 31% between 24 and 26, 34% between 27 and 28, and 23% above 28. 71% of the current freshmen were in the top fifth of their class; 95% were in the top two fifths.

Requirements: The SAT or ACT is required. AP and CLEP credits are accepted. Important factors in the admissions decision are advanced placement or honor courses, recommendations by school officials, and evidence of special talent.

Procedure: Freshmen are admitted fall and spring. Entrance exams should be taken by December of the senior year. There are early decision and deferred admissions plans. Early decision applications should be filed by November 15; regular applications, by January 15 for fall entry, along with a $60 fee. Notification of early decision is sent January 1; regular decision, April 1. A waiting list is an active part of the admissions procedure. Applications are accepted on-line.

Transfer: Transfer students must have a GPA of 2.7 and must submit a high school transcript, all college transcripts, an essay or personal statement, test scores, and a statement of good standing from prior institutions. At least one professor recommendation from the current institution and a midterm report are also required. 60 of 120 credits required for the bachelor's degree must be completed at Skidmore.

Visiting: There are regularly scheduled orientations for prospective students, including full-day open-house programs. There are guides for informal visits and visitors may sit in on classes and stay overnight. To schedule a visit, contact the Admissions Office.

Financial Aid: In 2005-2006, 40% of all full-time freshmen and 41% of continuing full-time students received some form of financial aid. 40% of full-time freshmen and 41% of continuing full-time students received need-based aid. The average freshman award was $26,841. Need-based scholarships or need-based grants averaged $23,209 ($37,975 maximum); need-based self-help aid (loans and jobs) averaged $3632 ($4325 maximum); and other non-need-based awards and non-need-based scholarships averaged $10,000 (maximum). 47% of undergraduates work part time. Average annual earnings from campus work are $921. The average financial indebtedness of the 2005 graduate was $15,857. Skidmore is a member of CSS. The CSS/Profile or FAFSA is required. The deadline for filing freshman financial aid applications for fall entry is January 15.

International Students: The school actively recruits these students. They must score satisfactorily on the written TOEFL or on the electronic version and also take the SAT or the ACT.

Computers: Wireless access is available. Computers can be found in several public areas, the library, and labs. High speed connections are in all residential areas. All students may access the system 24 hours per day. There are no time limits and no fees. It is strongly recommended that all students have a personal computer.

Graduates: From July 1, 2004 to June 30, 2005, 578 bachelor's degrees were awarded. The most popular majors were business (12%), English (9%), and art (9%). In an average class, 73% graduate in 4 years or less, and 78% graduate in 5 years or less. Of the 2004 graduating class, 20% were enrolled in graduate school within 6 months of graduation and 92% were employed.

Admissions Contact: Mary Lou Bates, Director of Admissions. A video is available. E-mail: *admissions@skidmore.edu*
Web: *www.skidmore.edu*

STATE UNIVERSITY OF NEW YORK

The State University of New York, established in 1948, is a public system in New York. It is governed by a board of trustees, whose chief administrator is the chancellor. The primary goals of the system are teaching, research, and public service. The main priorities are to educate the largest number of people possible at the highest level, including educationally disadvantaged groups; to provide students with enhanced educational skills and techniques; and to enhance the quality of life for all New Yorkers. The total enrollment of all 64 campuses is nearly 400,000; there were 12,000 faculty members. Altogether there are 1720 baccalaureate, 1073 master's, and 312 doctoral programs offered in State University of New York. 4-year campuses are located in Albany, Binghamton, Buffalo, Stony Brook, Brockport, Cortland, Empire State College, Environmental Science and Forestry, Fredonia, Geneseo, Morrisville State, New Paltz, Old Westbury, Oneonta, Oswego, Plattsburgh, Potsdam, Purchase, Saratoga Springs, and SUNYIT. Profiles of the 4-year campuses are included in this section. SUNY's website for prospective students can be found at *www.suny.edu/student*.

STATE UNIVERSITY OF NEW YORK AT OSWEGO   C-3

Oswego, NY 13126	(315) 312-2250; Fax: (315) 312-3260
Full-time: 3057 men, 3559 women	**Faculty:** 309; IIA, -$
Part-time: 206 men, 312 women	**Ph.D.s:** 83%
Graduate: 402 men, 741 women	**Student/Faculty:** 21 to 1
Year: semesters, summer session	**Tuition:** $5322 ($11,582)
Application Deadline: January 15	**Room & Board:** $8340
Freshman Class: 7560 applied, 4800 accepted, 1350 enrolled	
SAT Verbal/Math: 540/550*	**ACT:** 21 **VERY COMPETITIVE**

State University of New York at Oswego, founded in 1861, is a comprehensive institution offering more than 110 cooperative, preprofessional, and graduate programs in the arts and sciences, business, and education. There are 3 undergraduate and 3 graduate schools. In addition to regional accreditation, Oswego has baccalaureate program accreditation with AACSB, ACS, NASM, NASP, and NCATE. The library contains more than 475,000 volumes, 2,106,494 microform items, and 15,000 audio/video tapes/CDs/DVDs, and subscribes to more than 1800 periodicals including electronic. Computerized library services include the card catalog, interlibrary loans, database searching, Internet access, and laptop Internet portals. Special learning facilities include a learning resource center, art gallery, planetarium, radio station, TV station, and biological field station. The 696-acre campus is in a small town on the southeast shore of Lake Ontario, 35 miles northwest of Syracuse. Including any residence halls, there are 40 buildings.

Student Life: 97% of undergraduates are from New York. Others are from 26 states, 20 foreign countries, and Canada. 90% are from public schools. 88% are white. 42% are Catholic; 41% Protestant; 14% Jewish. The average age of freshmen is 18; all undergraduates, 21. 23% do not continue beyond their first year; 59% remain to graduate.

Housing: 4000 students can be accommodated in university housing, which includes coed dorms, resident hall living and learning communities, a freshmen-only building, and upperclassmen suites. On-campus housing is guaranteed for all 4 years. 57% of students live on campus; of those, 90% remain on campus on weekends. All students may keep cars.

Activities: 7% of men belong to 7 local and 10 national fraternities; 6% of women belong to 5 local and 7 national sororities. There are 131 groups on campus, including art, band, cheerleading, choir, chorale, chorus, computers, dance, drama, ethnic, gay, honors, international, jazz band, literary magazine, musical theater, newspaper, opera, orchestra, pep band, photography, political, professional, radio and TV, religious, social, social service, student government, and yearbook. Popular campus events include Honors Convocations and Quest, Parents Weekend, and College Open House.

Sports: There are 12 intercollegiate sports for men and 12 for women, and more than 25 intramural sports for men and more than 25 for women. Facilities include an ice hockey rink, a field house with an artificial-grass practice area, 18 tennis courts, an outdoor track, 3 soccer and 3 lacrosse fields, baseball and softball fields, numerous basketball courts, racquetball and squash courts, 2 indoor pools, and a diving well. The gym seats 3500. There are also 2 fitness centers and weight rooms, a cross-country ski lodge, and a martial arts studio.

Disabled Students: 85% of the campus is accessible. Wheelchair ramps, elevators, special parking, specially equipped rest rooms, special class scheduling, lowered drinking fountains, lowered telephones, special housing, and a student support group are available.

Services: Counseling and information services are available, as is tutoring in every subject. There is a reader service for the blind, and remedial math, reading, and writing. In addition, the Office of Disablility Services provides general foundation support.

Campus Safety and Security: Measures include 24-hour foot and vehicle patrol, self-defense education, security escort services, and shuttle buses. There are informal discussions, pamphlets/posters/films, emergency telephones, lighted pathways/sidewalks, and an electronic device that locates students and alerts the police when triggered.

Programs of Study: Oswego confers B.A., B.S., and B.F.A. degrees. Master's degrees are also awarded. Bachelor's degrees are awarded in BIOLOGICAL SCIENCE (biochemistry, biology/biological science, and zoology), BUSINESS (accounting, banking and finance, business administration and management, human resources, international economics, management science, marketing/retailing/merchandising, and recreational facilities management), COMMUNICATIONS AND THE ARTS (art, broadcasting, communications, dramatic arts, English, French, German, graphic design, journalism, linguistics, music, public relations, and Spanish), COMPUTER AND PHYSICAL SCIENCE (applied mathematics, atmospheric sciences and meteorology, chemistry, computer science, geochemistry, geology, information sciences and systems, mathematics, and physics), EDUCATION (agricultural, business, elementary, foreign languages, secondary, teaching English as a second/foreign language ITE-SOL/TEFOLù, trade and industrial, and vocational), ENGINEERING AND ENVIRONMENTAL DESIGN (technological management), SOCIAL SCIENCE (American studies, anthropology, cognitive science, criminal justice, economics, history, human development, international studies, philosophy, political science/government, psychology, sociology, and women's studies). Chemistry, computer science, and accounting are the strongest academically. Elementary/secondary education, business administration, and communication studies are the largest.

Required: To graduate, all students must complete 42 to 48 general education credits, including 6 in human diversity and 3 to 6 each in expository writing and math. Students must have a minimum 2.0 GPA and complete 122 total credit hours (127 hours for technology and vocational education students). The total number of hours in the major varies from 30 to 78.

Special: Oswego offers cross-registration with ACUSNY-Visiting Student Program. More than 1000 internships are available with business, social, cultural, and government agencies. The university also offers a Washington semester, study abroad in more than 80 programs, a 5-year accounting B.S./M.B.A. program, dual majors, B.A.-B.S. degrees in several sciences and a B.A.-B.F.A. in art, credit for military experience, non-degree study, and pass/fail options. A 3-2 engineering degree is offered with Clarkson University, SUNY at Binghamton, and Case Western Reserve University. A 3-4 degree in optometry with SUNY College of Optometry, a 3-2 degree in zoo technology with Santa Fe Community College and Niagara County Community College, and 2-2, 2-3, 3-3, and 4-3 degrees in health sciences with SUNY Health Sciences Center are also possible. There are 21 national honor societies, a freshman honors program, and 9 departmental honors programs.

Faculty/Classroom: 58% of faculty are male; 42%, female. 96% teach undergraduates. No introductory courses are taught by graduate students. The average class size in an introductory lecture is 40; in a laboratory, 15; and in a regular course, 24.

Admissions: 63% of the 2005-2006 applicants were accepted. The SAT scores for the 2005-2006 freshman class were: Verbal--24% below 500, 57% between 500 and 599, 18% between 600 and 700, and 1% above 700; Math--21% below 500, 58% between 500 and 599, 20% between 600 and 700, and 1% above 700. The ACT scores were 14% below 21, 50% between 21 and 23, 17% between 24 and 26, 17% between 27 and 28, and 2% above 28.

Requirements: The SAT or ACT is required. In addition, applicants must be graduates of an accredited secondary school or have a GED certificate. 18 academic credits are required, including 4 years each of English and social studies, 3 each of math and science, and 2 of a foreign language. An essay and interview are recommended. A GPA of 80.0 is required. AP and CLEP credits are accepted. Important factors in the admissions decision are advanced placement or honor courses, extracurricular activities record, and evidence of special talent.

Procedure: Freshmen are admitted fall and spring. Entrance exams should be taken during the spring of the junior year or fall of the senior year. There are early decision, early admissions, and deferred admis-

sions plans. Early decision applications should be filed by November 15; the priority date for regular applications is January 15 for fall entry and November 15 for spring entry, along with a $40 fee. Notification of early decision is sent December 15; regular decision, on a rolling basis after January 1. 75 early decision candidates were accepted for the 2005-2006 class. Applications are accepted on-line.

Transfer: 700 transfer students enrolled in a recent year. Applicants must submit official transcripts from previously attended colleges. Students with a minimum GPA of 2.3 are encouraged to apply. SUNY associate degree holders are given preference. Secondary school records may be required for 1-year transfers. 30 of 122 credits required for the bachelor's degree must be completed at Oswego.

Visiting: There are regularly scheduled orientations for prospective students, usually including a campus tour and a meeting with a counselor. There are guides for informal visits and visitors may sit in on classes and stay overnight. To schedule a visit, contact the Office of Admissions.

Financial Aid: In 2005-2006, 61% of all full-time students received some form of financial aid. 61% of all full-time students received need-based aid. The average freshman award was $6627. Need-based scholarships or need-based grants averaged $3950; need-based self-help aid (loans and jobs) averaged $2846; and other non-need-based awards and non-need-based scholarships averaged $3650. 65% of undergraduates work part time. Average annual earnings from campus work are $1500. The average financial indebtedness of the 2005 graduate was $18,751. Oswego is a member of CSS. The FAFSA and the state aid form are required. The priority date for freshman financial aid applications for fall entry is April 1.

International Students: There are 80 international students enrolled. The school actively recruits these students. They must score satisfactorily on the written TOEFL or on the electronic version.

Computers: Wireless access is available. There are 7 open access labs and 40 departmental computer labs with more than 1000 computers available for student use. All residence halls are equipped with high speed Internet, and the library, the school of business, and all cafeterias have wireless Internet. The library is also accessible to all students through their Oswego accounts and offers rentals of labtop computers. All students may access the system anytime. There are no time limits and no fees. It is strongly recommended that all students have a personal computer. It is recommended that School of Business majors have personal computers.

Graduates: From July 1, 2004 to June 30, 2005, 1448 bachelor's degrees were awarded. The most popular majors were education (30%), business (17%), and communications (7%). In an average class, 32% graduate in 4 years or less, 54% graduate in 5 years or less, and 58% graduate in 6 years or less. 135 companies recruited on campus in 2004-2005. Of the 2004 graduating class, 18% were enrolled in graduate school within 6 months of graduation and 80% were employed.

Admissions Contact: Joseph F. Grant, Jr., Dean of Admissions. A video is available. E-mail: *admiss@oswego.edu* Web: *www.oswego.edu*

STATE UNIVERSITY OF NEW YORK AT POTSDAM   C-2

Potsdam, NY 13676   (315) 267-2180
                                   (877) 768-7326; Fax: (315) 267-2163

Full-time: 1466 men, 1999 women	**Faculty:** 255; IIA, --$
Part-time: 50 men, 104 women	**Ph.D.s:** 79%
Graduate: 191 men, 519 women	**Student/Faculty:** 14 to 1
Year: semesters, summer session	**Tuition:** $5289 ($11,549)
Application Deadline: open	**Room & Board:** $7670
Freshman Class: 3423 applied, 2512 accepted, 739 enrolled	
SAT Verbal/Math: 530/530*	**ACT:** 22 COMPETITIVE

The State University of New York at Potsdam, founded in 1816, joined the state university system in 1948. The school offers more than 40 undergraduate degree programs. There are 3 undergraduate schools and 1 graduate school. In addition to regional accreditation, SUNY Potsdam has baccalaureate program accreditation with NASM and NCATE. The 2 libraries contain 408,755 volumes, 770,007 microform items, and 15,570 audio/video tapes/CDs/DVDs, and subscribe to 933 periodicals including electronic. Computerized library services include the card catalog, interlibrary loans, database searching, Internet access, and laptop Internet portals. Special learning facilities include a learning resource center, art gallery, natural history museum, planetarium, radio station, electronic music composition lab, recording studios, and seismograph lab. The 240-acre campus is in a rural area 140 miles northeast of Syracuse. Including any residence halls, there are 36 buildings.

Student Life: 94% of undergraduates are from New York. Others are from 26 states, 23 foreign countries, and Canada. 77% are white. The average age of freshmen is 19; all undergraduates, 23. 24% do not continue beyond their first year; 46% remain to graduate.

Housing: 2400 students can be accommodated in college housing, which includes single-sex and coed dorms and on-campus apartments. In addition, there are honors houses, special-interest houses, substance-free housing, an international house, and first-year experience housing.

On-campus housing is guaranteed for all 4 years. 52% of students live on campus; of those, 85% remain on campus on weekends. All students may keep cars.

Activities: 4% of men belong to 4 local and 2 national fraternities; 6% of women belong to 7 local sororities and 1 national sorority. There are 100 groups on campus, including art, band, cheerleading, choir, chorale, chorus, computers, dance, drama, environmental awareness, ethnic, gay, honors, international, jazz band, literary magazine, musical theater, newspaper, opera, orchestra, pep band, photography, political, professional, radio and TV, social, social service, student government, symphony, and yearbook. Popular campus events include Harvest Ball, Spring Fest, and Kwanza Ball.

Sports: There are 7 intercollegiate sports for men and 10 for women, and 9 intramural sports for men and 8 for women. Facilities include a 2400-seat ice arena, an Olympic-size pool, a 3000-seat gym, an indoor field house, indoor and outdoor tracks, racquetball, tennis, squash, handball, and basketball courts, a weight room, a dance studio, softball field, artificial turf stadium, an in-line roller rink, a recreation softball field, recreational soccer fields, outdoor basketball courts, an indoor climbing wall, a high ropes course, a bouldering cave, and a sand volleyball court.

Disabled Students: 95% of the campus is accessible. Wheelchair ramps, elevators, special parking, specially equipped rest rooms, special class scheduling, lowered drinking fountains, lowered telephones, special housing, and electric doors are available.

Services: Counseling and information services are available, as is tutoring in most subjects. There is a reader service for the blind, math labs, and a writing center.

Campus Safety and Security: Measures include 24-hour foot and vehicle patrol, self-defense education, security escort services, and informal discussions. There are pamphlets/posters/films, emergency telephones, and lighted pathways/sidewalks.

Programs of Study: SUNY Potsdam confers B.A., B.S., B.A. Mus., and B.M. degrees. Master's degrees are also awarded. Bachelor's degrees are awarded in BIOLOGICAL SCIENCE (biochemistry and biology/biological science), BUSINESS (business administration and management and business economics), COMMUNICATIONS AND THE ARTS (dance, dramatic arts, English, French, music, music business management, music performance, music theory and composition, Spanish, speech/debate/rhetoric, and studio art), COMPUTER AND PHYSICAL SCIENCE (chemistry, computer science, geology, mathematics, and physics), EDUCATION (early childhood, elementary, English, foreign languages, mathematics, middle school, music, science, secondary, and social studies), HEALTH PROFESSIONS (community health work), SOCIAL SCIENCE (anthropology, archeology, criminal justice, economics, history, interdisciplinary studies, philosophy, political science/government, psychology, and sociology). Music, anthropology, and geology are the strongest academically. Music education, childhood education, and psychology are the largest.

Required: To graduate, students must earn 124 to 128 credit hours, with 30 to 33 in the major, and a minimum GPA of 2.0. General education requirements include 10 to 11 semester hours of freshman course work in verbal and quantitative skills, 21 of Modes of Inquiry in liberal arts, and 4 of phys ed, as well as 1 course each in written and oral communication above the freshman level and demonstrated foreign language proficiency.

Special: Cross-registration is offered with Clarkson University, St. Lawrence University, and Canton College. Political science internships in Albany and many other internships are possible. SUNY Potsdam also offers work-study opportunities, a 3-2 engineering degree with Clarkson University, study abroad, 3-2 management and accounting degrees, student-designed majors, dual majors in interdisciplinary natural science, nondegree study, and pass/fail options. There are 23 national honor societies, a freshman honors program, and 18 departmental honors programs.

Faculty/Classroom: 54% of faculty are male; 46%, female. All teach undergraduates. No introductory courses are taught by graduate students.

Admissions: 73% of the 2005-2006 applicants were accepted. The SAT scores for the 2005-2006 freshman class were: Verbal--39% below 500, 39% between 500 and 599, 19% between 600 and 700, and 3% above 700; Math--39% below 500, 42% between 500 and 599, 16% between 600 and 700, and 3% above 700. The ACT scores were 48% below 21, 11% between 21 and 23, 20% between 24 and 26, 11% between 27 and 28, and 10% above 28. 17% of the current freshmen were in the top fifth of their class; 38% were in the top two fifths. 5 freshmen graduated first in their class.

Requirements: The SAT or ACT is required. In addition, applicants must be high school graduates in a college preparatory program or hold a GED. 4 years each of English, social studies, math, foreign language, science, and 1 year of art or music is recommended. An interview is recommended; an audition, when appropriate, is required. A grade average of 80 is required. AP and CLEP credits are accepted. Important factors in the admissions decision are extracurricular activities record, recommendations by school officials, and personality/intangible qualities.

Procedure: Freshmen are admitted fall and spring. Entrance exams should be taken in the junior year or early senior year. There are early admissions and deferred admissions plans. There is a rolling admission plan. Application deadlines are open. Application fee is $40. 64 applicants were on the 2005 waiting list; 27 were admitted. Applications are accepted on-line.

Transfer: 363 transfer students enrolled in a recent year. Applicants must have earned 12 hours of college credit. Transfers with fewer than 24 credit hours must submit a high school transcript. 30 of 124 credits required for the bachelor's degree must be completed at SUNY Potsdam.

Visiting: There are regularly scheduled orientations for prospective students, including a meeting with a counselor and faculty member and a tour of campus with a student. There are guides for informal visits and visitors may sit in on classes. To schedule a visit, contact the Admissions Office.

Financial Aid: In 2005-2006, 87% of all full-time freshmen and 83% of continuing full-time students received some form of financial aid. 67% of full-time freshmen and 76% of continuing full-time students received need-based aid. The average freshman award was $11,212. Need-based scholarships or need-based grants averaged $4985 ($11,450 maximum); need-based self-help aid (loans and jobs) averaged $8009 ($15,835 maximum); and other non-need-based awards and non-need-based scholarships averaged $2278 ($14,970 maximum). Average annual earnings from campus work are $1200. The average financial indebtedness of the 2005 graduate was $16,117. The FAFSA and the state aid form are required. The priority date for freshman financial aid applications for fall entry is January 1. The deadline for filing freshman financial aid applications for fall entry is rolling.

International Students: There were 113 international students were enrolled in a recent year. The school actively recruits these students. A satisfactory score is required on the TOEFL.

Computers: There are 515 PCs available on campus for student use. High-speed connection is available in all dorm rooms. There are 30 wireless hot spots across campus for student use. All students may access the system 7 days a week, 24 hours per day. There are no time limits. There is a $125 technology fee per semester for all students.

Graduates: From July 1, 2004 to June 30, 2005, 662 bachelor's degrees were awarded. The most popular majors were childhood education (12%), music education (11%), and psychology (9%). In an average class, 25% graduate in 4 years or less, 43% graduate in 5 years or less, and 46% graduate in 6 years or less. 44 companies recruited on campus in 2004-2005. Of the 2004 graduating class, 34% were enrolled in graduate school within 6 months of graduation and 52% were employed.

Admissions Contact: Thomas Nesbitt, Director of Admissions.
E-mail: *admissions@potsdam.edu* Web: *www.potsdam.edu*

STATE UNIVERSITY OF NEW YORK/COLLEGE AT BROCKPORT
B-3

Brockport, NY 14420	(585) 395-2751; Fax: (585) 395-5452
Full-time: 2713 men, 3465 women	**Faculty:** 321; IIA, av$
Part-time: 309 men, 478 women	**Ph.D.s:** 93%
Graduate: 536 men, 983 women	**Student/Faculty:** 23 to 1
Year: semesters, summer session	**Tuition:** $5293 ($11,243)
Application Deadline: open	**Room & Board:** $7454
Freshman Class: 7816 applied, 3625 accepted, 988 enrolled	
SAT Verbal/Math: 560/540*	**ACT:** 23 VERY COMPETITIVE

The State University of New York/College at Brockport, established in 1867, is a public institution offering undergraduate programs in liberal arts, sciences, business, and teacher preparation. There are 3 undergraduate and 3 graduate schools. In addition to regional accreditation, SUNY Brockport has baccalaureate program accreditation with AACSB, ABET, CSAB, CSWE, NCATE, NLN, and NRPA. The library contains 642,650 volumes, 2,055,867 microform items, and 7678 audio/video tapes/CDs/DVDs, and subscribes to 16,732 periodicals including electronic. Computerized library services include the card catalog, interlibrary loans, database searching, Internet access, and laptop Internet portals. Special learning facilities include a learning resource center, art gallery, planetarium, radio station, and aquaculture ponds, weather information system, high-resolution germanium detector, research vessel on Lake Ontario, electron microscope, low-temperature lab, vacuum deposition lab, computational physics lab, 2 supercomputers, Doppler Radar system, ultramodern dance facilities including green room, hydrotherapy room, student learning center, academic computing center, and theater. The 435-acre campus is in a small town 16 miles west of Rochester. Including any residence halls, there are 68 buildings.

Student Life: 98% of undergraduates are from New York. Others are from 30 states, 20 foreign countries, and Canada. 88% are white. The average age of freshmen is 19; all undergraduates, 23. 17% do not continue beyond their first year; 83% remain to graduate.

Housing: 2450 students can be accommodated in college housing, which includes coed dorms. In addition, there are special-interest houses, special residence hall communities for first-year students, and international, 24-hour quiet, and academic excellence floors. On-campus housing is guaranteed for all 4 years. 66% of students commute. All students may keep cars.

Activities: 1% of men belong to 6 national fraternities; 2% of women belong to 4 national sororities. There are 63 groups on campus, including art, business, cheerleading, chess, choir, chorus, computers, criminal justice, dance, drama, ethnic, film, gay, honors, international, jazz band, literary magazine, musical theater, newspaper, outdoors, photography, political, professional, radio and TV, religious, social, social service, and student government. Popular campus events include Health Week, Honors Convocation, and Scholar's Day.

Sports: There are 10 intercollegiate sports for men and 12 for women, and 25 intramural sports for men and 25 for women. Facilities include field hockey, baseball, and softball fields; a soccer pitch; a swimming pool; 6 gyms; a gymnastics area; wrestling and weight rooms; handball, squash, tennis, and racquetball courts; an ice arena; and a Special Olympics stadium with a football field and track.

Disabled Students: 95% of the campus is accessible. Wheelchair ramps, elevators, special parking, specially equipped rest rooms, special class scheduling, lowered drinking fountains, lowered telephones, and special classroom accommodations are available.

Services: Counseling and information services are available, as is tutoring in some subjects, which vary from semester to semester. There is remedial math and writing. Study skills support is available to all students.

Campus Safety and Security: Measures include 24-hour foot and vehicle patrol, security escort services, shuttle buses, and informal discussions. There are pamphlets/posters/films, emergency telephones, lighted pathways/sidewalks, and a community policing program, bicycle patrols, and 24-hour locked residence halls.

Programs of Study: SUNY Brockport confers B.A., B.S., B.F.A., and B.S.N. degrees. Master's degrees are also awarded. Bachelor's degrees are awarded in BIOLOGICAL SCIENCE (biology/biological science), BUSINESS (accounting, business administration and management, international business management, and recreation and leisure services), COMMUNICATIONS AND THE ARTS (communications, dance, dramatic arts, English, French, journalism, Spanish, and studio art), COMPUTER AND PHYSICAL SCIENCE (atmospheric sciences and meteorology, chemistry, computer science, earth science, geology, mathematics, and physics), EDUCATION (physical), ENGINEERING AND ENVIRONMENTAL DESIGN (computational sciences and environmental science), HEALTH PROFESSIONS (health science, medical technology, and nursing), SOCIAL SCIENCE (African American studies, African studies, anthropology, criminal justice, history, interdisciplinary studies, international studies, philosophy, political science/government, psychology, social work, sociology, water resources, and women's studies). Biological sciences, meteorology, and computer science are the strongest academically. Physical education, business administration, and criminal justice are the largest.

Required: To graduate, students must complete a minimum of 120 credits, including 30 or more credits in the major, with a 2.0 GPA. The core curriculum includes the SUNY-wide General Education Requirements (1 course each in math, natural sciences, social sciences, American history, Western civilization, world (non-Western) civilization, humanities, the arts, foreign language, and basic communication). All students must take courses in contemporary issues, diversity, and perspectives on women and pass the appropriate competency exams. An academic planning seminar is required of entering freshmen.

Special: Co-op programs, internships in most majors, and work-study programs in education are available. Brockport offers cross-registration with Rochester area colleges, a Washington semester, study abroad in 17 countries, accelerated degree programs, and an interdisciplinary major in arts for children, emphasizing art, dance, music, and theater. Credit for military and work experience, nondegree study, and pass/fail grading options are available. An alternative general education program, Delta College, is an interdisciplinary program that emphasizes global issues and provides opportunities for work or study in other countries, as well as locally, regionally, and nationally. There are 24 national honor societies, a freshman honors program, and 3 departmental honors programs.

Faculty/Classroom: 55% of faculty are male; 45%, female. 93% teach undergraduates. No introductory courses are taught by graduate students. The average class size in an introductory lecture is 25; in a laboratory, 18; and in a regular course, 22.

Admissions: 46% of the 2005-2006 applicants were accepted. The SAT scores for the 2005-2006 freshman class were: Verbal--13% below 500, 58% between 500 and 599, 28% between 600 and 700, and 2% above 700; Math--23% below 500, 60% between 500 and 599, 16% between 600 and 700, and 1% above 700. The ACT scores were 18% below 21, 36% between 21 and 23, 32% between 24 and 26, 12% between 27 and 28, and 2% above 28. 42% of the current freshmen were in the top fifth of their class; 83% were in the top two fifths. 13 freshmen graduated first in their class.

Requirements: The SAT or ACT is required. In addition, SUNY Brockport seeks students who have demonstrated academic success and who show persistence. Applicants must have a high school diploma (preferably from the New York State Regents Program) or have completed a

minimum of 18 academic units: 4 each in English and social studies, 4 in academic electives, 3 each in math and science (1 with lab). An essay and letters of recommendation are encouraged. An audition is required for dance and theater applicants. A high school average of 85 % is required. AP and CLEP credits are accepted. Important factors in the admissions decision are advanced placement or honor courses, leadership record, and extracurricular activities record.

Procedure: Freshmen are admitted fall and spring. Entrance exams should be taken during the spring of the junior year and fall of the senior year. There are deferred admissions and rolling admissions plan. Application deadlines are open. Application fee is $40. Notifications are sent on a rolling basis. Applications are accepted on-line.

Transfer: 979 transfer students enrolled in 2004-2005. applicants must have a minimum GPA of 2.25. Many departments specify prerequisite courses and a higher GPA. SUNY Brockport recommends that transfer applicants have an associate degree or 54 credit hours, with preference given to degree holders. 30 of 120 credits required for the bachelor's degree must be completed at SUNY Brockport.

Visiting: There are regularly scheduled orientations for prospective students, including daily admissions information presentations and campus tours. Visits may be arranged on selected Saturdays and holidays. There are guides for informal visits and visitors may sit in on classes and stay overnight. To schedule a visit, contact the Office of Undergraduate Admissions.

Financial Aid: In 2005-2006, 90% of all full-time freshmen and 84% of continuing full-time students received some form of financial aid. 71% of full-time freshmen and 70% of continuing full-time students received need-based aid. The average freshman award was $8343. Need-based scholarships or need-based grants averaged $3765 ($12,573 maximum); need-based self-help aid (loans and jobs) averaged $4690 ($8125 maximum); and other non-need-based awards and non-need-based scholarships averaged $4064 ($17,900 maximum). 71% of undergraduates work part time. Average annual earnings from campus work are $1280. The average financial indebtedness of the 2005 graduate was $19,083. SUNY Brockport is a member of CSS. The FAFSA is required. The deadline for filing freshman financial aid applications for fall entry is February 15.

International Students: There are 75 international students enrolled. The school actively recruits these students. Satisfactory scores are required on the written TOEFL and the SAT or the ACT.

Computers: All students may access the system 24 hours per day. There are no time limits. The fee is $234 per year.

Graduates: In a recent year,1532 bachelor's degrees were awarded. The most popular majors were physical education (12%), business administration (10%), and psychology (10%). In an average class, 1% graduate in 3 years or less, 28% graduate in 4 years or less, 50% graduate in 5 years or less, and 56% graduate in 6 years or less. 140 companies recruited on campus in 2004-2005. Of the 2004 graduating class, 24% were enrolled in graduate school within 6 months of graduation and 85% were employed.

Admissions Contact: Bernard S. Valento, Director of Undergraduate Admissions. E-mail: *admit@brockport.edu* Web: *www.brockport.edu*

STATE UNIVERSITY OF NEW YORK/COLLEGE AT BUFFALO
A-3

Buffalo, NY 14222   (716) 878-4017; Fax: (716) 878-6100

Full-time: 3076 men, 4742 women	**Faculty:** 397; IIA, -$
Part-time: 608 men, 584 women	**Ph.Ds:** 84%
Graduate: 605 men, 1391 women	**Student/Faculty:** 20 to 1
Year: semesters, summer session	**Tuition:** $5231 ($11,491)
Application Deadline: open	**Room & Board:** $6672
Freshman Class: 8563 applied, 3736 accepted, 1250 enrolled	
SAT Verbal/Math: 500/500*	**COMPETITIVE+**

The State University of New York/College at Buffalo, established in 1867, is a public institution conferring undergraduate liberal arts degrees. In addition to regional accreditation, Buffalo State College has baccalaureate program accreditation with ABET, ACS, ADA, ASLA, CSWE, FIDER, IACBE, NAIT, NAST, and NCATE. The library contains 470,176 volumes, 910,297 microform items, and 10,863 audio/video tapes/CDs/DVDs, and subscribes to 2948 periodicals including electronic. Computerized library services include the card catalog, interlibrary loans, database searching, and Internet access. Special learning facilities include a learning resource center, art gallery, planetarium, radio station, TV station, a speech, language, and hearing clinic, and a center for performing arts. The 115-acre campus is in an urban area in Buffalo. Including any residence halls, there are 37 buildings.

Student Life: 99% of undergraduates are from New York. Others are from 33 states, 16 foreign countries, and Canada. 85% are from public schools. 78% are white; 14% African American. The average age of freshmen is 18; all undergraduates, 22. 25% do not continue beyond their first year; 39% remain to graduate.

Housing: 2086 students can be accommodated in college housing, which includes coed dorms, on-campus apartments, married-student housing, honor houses, and an international student dorm. On-campus housing is available on a first-come, first-served basis. 79% of students commute. Alcohol is not permitted. Upperclassmen may keep cars.

Activities: There is 1 local fraternity and 9 national fraternities and 3 local and 7 national sororities. There are 75 groups on campus, including art, cheerleading, chess, choir, chorus, computers, dance, drama, ethnic, gay, honors, international, jazz band, literary magazine, musical theater, newspaper, orchestra, political, professional, radio and TV, religious, social, social service, student government, and yearbook. Popular campus events include Commuter Daze, the Gathering, and Welcome Back Week.

Sports: There are 8 intercollegiate sports for men and 10 for women, and 6 intramural sports for men and 5 for women. Facilities include a gym, an indoor pool, a basketball/volleyball arena, an ice rink, a game field for football, soccer, and lacrosse, a six-lane track, and a softball diamond.

Disabled Students: All of the campus is accessible. Wheelchair ramps, elevators, special parking, specially equipped rest rooms, special class scheduling, lowered drinking fountains, lowered telephones, and special dorm accommodations are available.

Services: Counseling and information services are available, as is tutoring in every subject. There is a reader service for the blind, and remedial math, reading, and writing. Tutors for visually impaired and hearing-impaired students are also available.

Campus Safety and Security: Measures include 24-hour foot and vehicle patrol, self-defense education, security escort services, and shuttle buses. There are informal discussions, pamphlets/posters/films, emergency telephones, lighted pathways/sidewalks, and community policing.

Programs of Study: Buffalo State College confers B.A., B.S., B.F.A., B.S.Ed., B.MUS., and B.Tech degrees. Master's degrees are also awarded. Bachelor's degrees are awarded in BIOLOGICAL SCIENCE (biology/biological science), BUSINESS (business administration and management and hospitality management services), COMMUNICATIONS AND THE ARTS (art, art history and appreciation, broadcasting, communications, design, dramatic arts, English, fine arts, French, Italian, journalism, music, painting, photography, printmaking, sculpture, and Spanish), COMPUTER AND PHYSICAL SCIENCE (chemistry, earth science, geology, information sciences and systems, mathematics, and physics), EDUCATION (art, business, elementary, foreign languages, industrial arts, science, secondary, and special), ENGINEERING AND ENVIRONMENTAL DESIGN (electrical/electronics engineering technology, industrial engineering technology, and mechanical engineering technology), HEALTH PROFESSIONS (health and speech pathology/audiology), SOCIAL SCIENCE (anthropology, criminal justice, dietetics, economics, geography, history, humanities, philosophy, political science/government, psychology, social work, sociology, and urban studies). Elementary education and exceptional education are the strongest academically. Elementary education, psychology, and business studies are the largest.

Required: To graduate, students must complete a 60-hour general education requirement consisting of 42 core credits in applied science and education, arts, humanities, math and science, and social science, and 18 hours of electives. Students must earn 123 credits with a minimum GPA of 2.0. The number of hours in the major varies.

Special: Students may cross-register with the Western New York Consortium and exchange with 160 campus members of the National Student Exchange. Internships, Washington and Albany semesters, study abroad in 5 countries, dual majors, and a general studies degree are offered. Students may earn 3-2 engineeing degrees in association with the State University of New York centers at Buffalo and Binghamton, and Clarkson University. There is a cooperative program with the Fashion Institute of Technology. Credit for life, military, and work experience, nondegree study, and pass/fail grading options are available. There is a chapter of Phi Beta Kappa and a freshman honors program.

Faculty/Classroom: 56% of faculty are male; 44%, female. All teach undergraduates. The average class size in an introductory lecture is 34; in a laboratory, 12; and in a regular course, 18.

Admissions: 44% of the 2005-2006 applicants were accepted. The SAT scores for the 2005-2006 freshman class were: Verbal--52% below 500, 39% between 500 and 599, 8% between 600 and 700, and 1% above 700; Math--46% below 500, 46% between 500 and 599, 7% between 600 and 700, and 1% above 700. 17% of the current freshmen were in the top fifth of their class; 53% were in the top two fifths.

Requirements: The SAT is required. In addition, students must graduate from an accredited secondary school or have a GED. They must complete 4 years of English, 3 years each of math, science, and social studies, and 2 years of a foreign language. A portfolio is required for fine arts applicants. AP and CLEP credits are accepted. Important factors in the admissions decision are advanced placement or honor courses, evidence of special talent, and recommendations by school officials.

Procedure: Freshmen are admitted to all sessions. Entrance exams should be taken during the junior or senior years. There are early decision and deferred admissions plans. Early decision applications should be filed by November 15; regular applications, are open for fall entry, along with a $40 fee. Notification of early decision is sent December 15;

regular decision, on a rolling basis. 28 early decision candidates were accepted for the 2005-2006 class. A waiting list is an active part of the admissions procedure. Applications are accepted on-line.

Transfer: 1081 transfer students enrolled in 2004-2005. Transfer applicants must have a minimum GPA of 2.0. An associate degree is recommended, and a minimum of 15 credit hours must have been earned. 32 of 123 credits required for the bachelor's degree must be completed at Buffalo State College.

Visiting: There are regularly scheduled orientations for prospective students. There are guides for informal visits and visitors may sit in on classes. To schedule a visit, contact the Admissions Office at (716) 878-5713 or admissions@buffalostate.edu.

Financial Aid: In 2005-2006, 58% of all full-time freshmen and 70% of continuing full-time students received some form of financial aid. 58% of full-time freshmen and 70% of continuing full-time students received need-based aid. Need-based scholarships or need-based grants averaged $3262; need-based self-help aid (loans and jobs) averaged $3476; and other non-need-based awards and non-need-based scholarships averaged $1869. The average financial indebtedness of the 2005 graduate was $16,000. Buffalo State College is a member of CSS. The FAFSA and TAP are required. The priority date for freshman financial aid applications for fall entry is March 15. The deadline for filing freshman financial aid applications for fall entry is May 1.

International Students: There are 35 international students enrolled. The school actively recruits these students. They must take on the TOEFL and also take the SAT or the ACT.

Computers: Wireless access is available. Students may use wireless access points in the library and the student union. All students may access the system during site hours. Dial-in access is available 24 hours per day. There are no time limits and no fees.

Graduates: From July 1, 2004 to June 30, 2005, 1551 bachelor's degrees were awarded. The most popular majors were elementary education (11%), business studies (8%), and communication (8%). In an average class, 1% graduate in 3 years or less, 15% graduate in 4 years or less, 33% graduate in 5 years or less, and 39% graduate in 6 years or less. 100 companies recruited on campus in 2004-2005. Of the 2004 graduating class, 23% were enrolled in graduate school within 6 months of graduation and 87% were employed.

Admissions Contact: Lesa Loritts, Admissions Director.
E-mail: admissions@buffalostate.edu Web: www.buffalostate.edu

STATE UNIVERSITY OF NEW YORK/COLLEGE AT CORTLAND   C-3

Cortland, NY 13045	**(607) 753-4711; Fax: (607) 753-5998**
Full-time: 2300 men, 3200 women	**Faculty:** 266; IIA, -$
Part-time: 120 men, 160 women	**Ph.D.s:** 84%
Graduate: 500 men, 1100 women	**Student/Faculty:** 21 to 1
Year: semesters, summer session	**Tuition:** $6000 ($12,000)
Application Deadline: see profile	**Room & Board:** $7000
Freshman Class: n/av	
SAT or ACT: required	**COMPETITIVE**

The State University of New York/College at Cortland, founded in 1868, is a public institution offering academic programs leading to baccalaureate and master's degrees in liberal arts and professional studies. There are 3 undergraduate and 3 graduate schools. Figures in the above capsule and in this profile are approximate. In addition to regional accreditation, SUNY Cortland has baccalaureate program accreditation with CAHEA and NRPA. The library contains 400,000 volumes, 750,000 microform items, and 5000 audio/video tapes/CDs/DVDs, and subscribes to 3000 periodicals including electronic. Computerized library services include the card catalog, interlibrary loans, and database searching. Special learning facilities include a learning resource center, art gallery, natural history museum, planetarium, radio station, TV station, a natural science museum, a greenhouse, a center for speech and hearing disorders, classrooms equipped with integrated technologies (multimedia enhanced instruction), and many specialized labs to support various program offerings. The 191-acre campus is in a small town 18 miles north of Ithaca and 29 miles south of Syracuse. Including any residence halls, there are 37 buildings.

Student Life: 98% of undergraduates are from New York. Others are from 8 states and 2 foreign countries. 91% are from public schools. 89% are white. The average age of freshmen is 18; all undergraduates, 21. 26% do not continue beyond their first year; 53% remain to graduate.

Housing: 2775 students can be accommodated in college housing, which includes coed dorms, off-campus apartments, fraternity houses, and sorority houses. In addition, there are special-interest houses, a wellness floor in a residence hall, a computer residence hall, quiet residence halls, a residence for Americans majoring in international studies and/or studing abroad, a hall for students 21 or older, and a leadership house. 55% of students live on campus. All students may keep cars.

Activities: 4% of men belong to 1 national fraternity; 9% of women belong to 1 local and 4 national sororities. There are 100 groups on campus, including art, band, cheerleading, chess, choir, chorale, chorus, computers, dance, drama, ethnic, film, gay, honors, international, jazz band, literary magazine, musical theater, newspaper, orchestra, political, professional, radio and TV, religious, social, social service, student government, symphony, and yearbook. Popular campus events include the annual Cortland-Ithaca College football game, Winterfest, and Multicultural Festival.

Sports: There are 11 intercollegiate sports for men and 14 for women, and 55 intramural sports for men and 55 for women. Facilities include an outdoor multupurpose 8000-seat stadium complex, an Olympic-size pool, a 3600 seat gym, a ice arena, a gymnastics arena, wrestling and weight rooms, a dance studio, handball/racquetball and squash courts, an athletic training facility, fitness centers, a free-swimming pool, a track, a baseball field, a football/lacrosse/track field seating 4000, a lighted soccer field, a field house, and 50 acres of athletic fields.

Disabled Students: 75% of the campus is accessible. Wheelchair ramps, elevators, special parking, specially equipped rest rooms, special class scheduling, lowered drinking fountains, and lowered telephones are available.

Services: Counseling and information services are available, as is tutoring in some subjects. There is a reader service for the blind. There is a fully staffed Academic Support and Achievement Program for writing, math, study skills, and learning strategies. Specific course tutoring is available with peer tutors.

Campus Safety and Security: Measures include 24-hour foot and vehicle patrol, self-defense education, security escort services, and shuttle buses. There are informal discussions, pamphlets/posters/films, emergency telephones, and lighted pathways/sidewalks. State University police maintain a web site with safety information and links. University police also have a Silent Witness program for reporting crimes anonymously.

Programs of Study: SUNY Cortland confers B.A., B.S., and B.S.E. degrees. Master's degrees are also awarded. Bachelor's degrees are awarded in BIOLOGICAL SCIENCE (biology/biological science), BUSINESS (management science), COMMUNICATIONS AND THE ARTS (art, communications, English, and film arts), COMPUTER AND PHYSICAL SCIENCE (chemistry, geochemistry, geology, geophysics and seismology, mathematics, and physics), EDUCATION (athletic training, foreign languages, health, middle school, physical, recreation, and secondary), ENGINEERING AND ENVIRONMENTAL DESIGN (environmental science), HEALTH PROFESSIONS (health science and speech pathology/audiology), SOCIAL SCIENCE (African American studies, anthropology, economics, geography, history, human services, international studies, philosophy, political science/government, psychology, and sociology). Biology, political science, and speech pathology/audiology are the strongest academically. Elementary education, phys ed, and communication studies are the largest.

Required: To graduate, undergraduates must complete 6 hours in English composition, and at least 6 hours of writing-intensive courses, with 3 of those in the major. 1 course meeting the quantitative skills criteria must also be passed; 28 to 29 hours of courses in the general education program must also be completed, with no more than 2 courses taken in any 1 of the 8 disciplines in the program. A major of 30 to 36 hours, with no more than 45 credits in discipline-specific courses must be completed. Completion of 90 credits of liberal arts and science courses toward a B.A., 75 credits toward a B.S., or 60 credits toward a B.S.E., is required. A 2.0 GPA, both overall and in all minors and concentrations, must be maintained. Special requirements may be designated by each school of the College.

Special: Cortland offers cross-registration with Tompkins Cortland Community College and has cooperative programs with the State University of New York/College of Environmental Science and Forestry, and Centers at Binghamton and Buffalo, and Cornell and Case Western Reserve Universities. Students may study abroad in 11 countries, and they may enroll in a Washington semester. Work-study programs are available. The college confers an individualized studies degree and allows dual majors. Students may pursue a 3-2 engineering degree in conjunction with Alfred, Case Western Reserve, and Clarkson Universities, and the State University of New York Centers at Binghamton, Buffalo, and Stony Brook. Cortland offers nondegree study opportunities. There are 15 national honor societies, including Phi Beta Kappa, a freshman honors program, and 3 departmental honors programs.

Faculty/Classroom: 53% of faculty are male; 48%, female. All teach undergraduates and 15% also do research. No introductory courses are taught by graduate students. The average class size in an introductory lecture is 38; in a laboratory, 26; and in a regular course, 22.

Admissions: 49% of recent applicants were accepted.

Requirements: The SAT or ACT is required. In addition, applicants must graduate from an accredited secondary school or have a GED. They must have earned 16 Carnegie units and 16 to 20 academic credits, including 4 units each in English and history or social studies and 2 (3 units preferred) each in math and science; the other 4 units must be taken in areas listed above or in a foreign language. Essays and recommendations are required, and in some cases auditions as well. Interviews are strongly recommended. AP and CLEP credits are accepted. Important factors in the admissions decision are advanced placement or honor courses, extracurricular activities record, and recommendations by school officials.

Procedure: Freshmen are admitted fall and spring. Entrance exams should be taken during the spring of the junior year or fall of the senior year. There are early decision, early admissions, and deferred admissions plans. There is a rolling admissions plan. 81 early decision candidates were accepted for a recent class. Applications are accepted on-line.

Transfer: Applicants must have a minimum GPA of 2.5. Some programs are more competitive. Interviews are encouraged. 45 of 124 credits required for the bachelor's degree must be completed at SUNY Cortland.

Visiting: There are regularly scheduled orientations for prospective students, consisting of Autumn Preview Days for prospective students as well as Spring Open House for accepted students. There are guides for informal visits and visitors may sit in on classes. To schedule a visit, contact the Admissions Appointment Secretary.

Financial Aid: In a recent years, 61% of all full-time freshmen and 60% of continuing full-time students received some form of financial aid. 56% of full-time freshmen and 54% of continuing full-time students received need-based aid. The average freshman award was $6977. The FAFSA and NYS TAP application are required. Check with the school for current deadlines.

International Students: There were 29 international students enrolled in a recent year. The school actively recruits these students. They must take the TOEFL and also take the SAT. A General Certificate of Education is acceptable in lieu of the TOEFL.

Computers: All students may access the system 24 hours per day in some labs connected to the campus network. There are no time limits and no fees.

Graduates: In a recent year, 1317 bachelor's degrees were awarded. The most popular majors were health science (31%), education (28%), and social science (16%). In an average class, 30% graduate in 4 years or less, 50% graduate in 5 years or less, and 53% graduate in 6 years or less.

Admissions Contact: Gradin Avery, Director of Admissions. A video is available. E-mail: *admissions@cortland.edu* Web: *www.cortland.edu/adm.html*

STATE UNIVERSITY OF NEW YORK/COLLEGE AT FREDONIA

A-4

Fredonia, NY 14063

(716) 673-3251
(800) 252-1212; Fax: (716) 673-3249

Full-time: 2069 men, 2774 women	**Faculty:** 251; IIA, -$
Part-time: 69 men, 131 women	**Ph.D.s:** 83%
Graduate: 105 men, 284 women	**Student/Faculty:** 19 to 1
Year: semesters, summer session	**Tuition:** $5441 ($11,701)
Application Deadline: open	**Room & Board:** $7330
Freshman Class: 5979 applied, 3329 accepted, 1106 enrolled	
SAT Verbal/Math: 560/560*	**ACT:** 24 **VERY COMPETITIVE**

The State University of New York at Fredonia, established in 1826, is a public institution offering undergraduate programs in the arts and sciences, business and professional curricula, teacher preparation, and the fine and performing arts. There are 6 undergraduate schools and 1 graduate school. In addition to regional accreditation, Fredonia has baccalaureate program accreditation with NASAD and NASM. The library contains 391,121 volumes, 1,060,631 microform items, and 26,574 audio/video tapes/CDs/DVDs, and subscribes to 1983 periodicals including electronic. Computerized library services include the card catalog, interlibrary loans, and database searching. Special learning facilities include a learning resource center, art gallery, radio station, TV station, a greenhouse, a day care center, a speech clinic, and an arts center. The 266-acre campus is in a small town 50 miles south of Buffalo and 45 miles north of Erie, Pennsylvania. Including any residence halls, there are 25 buildings.

Student Life: 97% of undergraduates are from New York. Students are from 23 states, 16 foreign countries, and Canada. 65% are from public schools. 94% are white. The average age of freshmen is 19; all undergraduates, 21. 19% do not continue beyond their first year; 61% remain to graduate.

Housing: 2621 students can be accommodated in college housing, which includes single-sex and coed dorms and on-campus apartments. Living space for fraternities and sororities is available in resdidence halls. In additon, there are special-interest houses for computer and athletics students and quiet-hour centers. On-campus housing is guaranteed for all 4 years. 50% of students live on campus; of those, 80% remain on campus on weekends. All students may keep cars.

Activities: 7% of men belong to 4 national fraternities; 4% of women belong to 3 national sororities. There are 120 groups on campus, including art, band, cheerleading, choir, chorale, chorus, computers, dance, drama, drill team, ethnic, gay, honors, international, jazz band, literary magazine, musical theater, newspaper, opera, orchestra, pep band, photography, political, professional, radio and TV, religious, ski, social, social service, student government, symphony, and yearbook. Popular campus events include various Art Center presentations, Spring Fest, and Little Siblings Weekend.

Sports: There are 8 intercollegiate sports for men and 9 for women, and 15 intramural sports for men and 15 for women. Facilities include a basketball arena, an ice rink, a swimming pool, a gym, a weight room, dance studios, soccer fields, indoor and outdoor tracks, and racquetball, tennis, and volleyball courts.

Disabled Students: 85% of the campus is accessible. Wheelchair ramps, elevators, special parking, specially equipped rest rooms, special class scheduling, lowered drinking fountains, and lowered telephones are available.

Services: Counseling and information services are available, as is tutoring in most subjects. There is a reader service for the blind.

Campus Safety and Security: Measures include 24-hour foot and vehicle patrol, security escort services, shuttle buses, and informal discussions. There are pamphlets/posters/films, emergency telephones, lighted pathways/sidewalks, and card swipe access to residence halls.

Programs of Study: Fredonia confers B.A., B.S., B.F.A., B.S.Ed., and Mus.B. degrees. Master's degrees are also awarded. Bachelor's degrees are awarded in BIOLOGICAL SCIENCE (biochemistry and biology/ biological science), BUSINESS (accounting, business administration and management, business economics, and sports management), COMMUNICATIONS AND THE ARTS (audio technology, communications, dramatic arts, English, fine arts, French, graphic design, media arts, music, and Spanish), COMPUTER AND PHYSICAL SCIENCE (chemistry, computer science, earth science, geology, mathematics, and physics), EDUCATION (early childhood, elementary, foreign languages, middle school, music, science, and secondary), HEALTH PROFESSIONS (health care administration, medical laboratory technology, predentistry, premedicine, and speech pathology/audiology), SOCIAL SCIENCE (history, interdisciplinary studies, philosophy, political science/government, psychology, social work, and sociology). Business, communication, and education are the largest.

Required: To graduate, students must complete 120 hours, including 36 to 90 or more in the major, with a 2.0 GPA. Students must take specific courses in English and math and complete 36 hours of general education courses, including writing, statistical/quantitative abilities, oral communication, natural and social sciences, humanities, and arts.

Special: Cooperative programs are available with many other institutions. Students may cross-register with colleges in the Western New York Consortium. Fredonia offers a variety of internships, study-abroad programs in more than 50 countries, and a Washington semester. Accelerated degrees, a general studies degree, dual and student-designed majors, a 3-2 engineering degree program with 14 universities, nondegree study, and pass/fail grading options are available. There are 19 national honor societies, a freshman honors program, and 19 departmental honors programs.

Faculty/Classroom: 57% of faculty are male; 43%, female. All both teach and do research. No introductory courses are taught by graduate students. The average class size in an introductory lecture is 35; in a laboratory, 16; and in a regular course, 20.

Admissions: 56% of the 2005-2006 applicants were accepted. The SAT scores for the 2005-2006 freshman class were: Verbal--21% below 500, 55% between 500 and 599, 21% between 600 and 700, and 2% above 700; Math--16% below 500, 58% between 500 and 599, 24% between 600 and 700, and 1% above 700. The ACT scores were 8% below 21, 38% between 21 and 23, 32% between 24 and 26, 13% between 27 and 28, and 9% above 28. 34% of the current freshmen were in the top fifth of their class; 76% were in the top two fifths. 10 freshmen graduated first in their class in a recent year.

Requirements: A satisfactory score on the SAT or ACT is required. Applicants must possess a high school diploma or have a GED. 16 academic credits are recommended, including 4 credits each in English and social studies and 3 each in math, science, and a foreign language. 4 years of math and science are encouraged. Essays are recommended, and, where applicable, an audition or portfolio is required. A GPA of 2.5 is required. AP and CLEP credits are accepted. Important factors in the admissions decision are advanced placement or honor courses and recommendations by school officials.

Procedure: Freshmen are admitted fall and spring. Entrance exams should be taken during the spring of the junior year or fall of the senior year. There are early decision and deferred admissions plans. There is a rolling admissions plan. Early decision applications should be filed by November 1; the deadline for regular applications for fall entry is open. There is a $40 fee. Notification of early decision is sent November 25; regular decision, on a rolling basis. 52 early decision candidates were accepted for the 2005-2006 class. Applications are accepted on-line.

Transfer: 556 transfer students enrolled in a recent year. Applicants should have a minimum GPA of 2.0. and appropriate academic course work to be considered. An interview is recommended. 45 of 120 credits required for the bachelor's degree must be completed at Fredonia.

Visiting: There are regularly scheduled orientations for prospective students, including various open house programs and information sessions

and tours Monday through Friday, morning and afternoon, and Saturday tours once a month. Visitors may sit in on classes and stay overnight. To schedule a visit, contact the Office of Admissions.

Financial Aid: In a recent year, 80% of all full-time freshmen and 77% of continuing full-time students received some form of financial aid. 62% of full-time freshmen and 61% of continuing full-time students received need-based aid. The average freshman award was $5935. 20% of undergraduates work part time. Average annual earnings from campus work are $1369. The average financial indebtedness of a recent graduate was $12,430. The FAFSA, the state aid form, and Express TAP Application (ETA) are required. The priority date for freshman financial aid applications for fall entry is February 1.

International Students: There were 42 international students enrolled in a recent year. The school actively recruits these students. They must achieve a satisfactory score on the TOEFL and also take the IELTS.

Computers: All students may access the system. There are no time limits and no fees. It is strongly recommended that all students have a personal computer.

Graduates: From July 1, 2004 to June 30, 2005, 1053 bachelor's degrees were awarded. The most popular majors were elementary education (17%), business administration (10%), and psychology (7%). In an average class, 49% graduate in 4 years or less, 61% graduate in 5 years or less, and 63% graduate in 6 years or less. 55 companies recruited on campus in 2004-2005. Of the 2004 graduating class, 29% were enrolled in graduate school within 6 months of graduation and 88% were employed.

Admissions Contact: Michael Bleecher, Director of Admissions. E-mail: *admissions.office@fredonia.edu* Web: *fredonia.edu*

STATE UNIVERSITY OF NEW YORK/COLLEGE AT GENESEO
B-3

Geneseo, NY 14454

(585) 245-5571
(866) 245-5211; Fax: (585) 245-5550

Full-time: 2103 men, 3075 women	Faculty: 242; IIA, -$
Part-time: 49 men, 80 women	Ph.D.s: 84%
Graduate: 30 men, 149 women	Student/Faculty: 21 to 1
Year: semesters, summer session	Tuition: $5520 ($11,780)
Application Deadline: January 15	Room & Board: $7390
Freshman Class: 8664 applied, 3433 accepted, 1025 enrolled	
SAT Verbal/Math: 634/647*	ACT: 28

HIGHLY COMPETITIVE+

The State University of New York/College at Geneseo, founded in 1871, is a public institution offering liberal arts, business, and accounting programs, teaching certification, and training in communicative disorders and sciences. In addition to regional accreditation, Geneseo has baccalaureate program accreditation with ASLA. The library contains 640,786 volumes, 835,593 microform items, and 15,706 audio/video tapes/CDs/ DVDs, and subscribes to 1785 periodicals including electronic. Computerized library services include the card catalog, interlibrary loans, and database searching. Special learning facilities include a learning resource center, art gallery, planetarium, radio station, TV station, and 3 theaters. The 220-acre campus is in a small town 30 miles south of Rochester. Including any residence halls, there are 40 buildings.

Student Life: 96% of undergraduates are from New York. Others are from 22 states, 49 foreign countries, and Canada. 81% are from public schools. 79% are white. 44% are Catholic; 28% Protestant; 23% claim no religious affiliation. The average age of freshmen is 18; all undergraduates, 20. 10% do not continue beyond their first year; 79% remain to graduate.

Housing: 3026 students can be accommodated in college housing, which includes coed dorms. In addition, there are special-interest houses, including science and math houses. On-campus housing is guaranteed for the freshman year only and is available on a first-come, first-served basis. 75% of students live on campus. All students may keep cars.

Activities: 10% of men belong to 7 local and 2 national fraternities; 12% of women belong to 7 local and 6 national sororities. There are 166 groups on campus, including art, band, cheerleading, choir, chorale, chorus, computers, dance, drama, ethnic, gay, honors, international, jazz band, literary magazine, musical theater, newspaper, orchestra, political, professional, radio and TV, religious, social, social service, student government, symphony, and yearbook. Popular campus events include Siblings Weekend, Parents Weekend, and Spring Weekend.

Sports: There are 8 intercollegiate sports for men and 12 for women, and 26 intramural sports for men and 26 for women. Facilities include an ice arena, 2 swimming pools, 3 gyms, 8 squash and 8 tennis courts, an indoor jogging area, Nautilus and weight rooms, a sauna, an outdoor track, and several playing fields. The largest auditorium/arena seats 3000.

Disabled Students: 92% of the campus is accessible. Wheelchair ramps, elevators, special parking, specially equipped rest rooms, special class scheduling, lowered drinking fountains, lowered telephones, and fire alarms for hearing-impaired students are available.

Services: Counseling and information services are available, as is tutoring in every subject. There is a reader service for the blind and remedial math and writing.

Campus Safety and Security: Measures include 24-hour foot and vehicle patrol, self-defense education, security escort services, and informal discussions. There are pamphlets/posters/films, emergency telephones, and lighted pathways/sidewalks.

Programs of Study: Geneseo confers B.A., B.S., and B.S.Ed. degrees. Master's degrees are also awarded. Bachelor's degrees are awarded in BIOLOGICAL SCIENCE (biochemistry, biology/biological science, and biophysics), BUSINESS (accounting and business administration and management), COMMUNICATIONS AND THE ARTS (art history and appreciation, communications, comparative literature, English, French, music, performing arts, Spanish, and studio art), COMPUTER AND PHYSICAL SCIENCE (applied physics, chemistry, computer science, geochemistry, geology, geophysics and seismology, mathematics, natural sciences, and physics), EDUCATION (early childhood, elementary, and special), HEALTH PROFESSIONS (speech pathology/audiology), SOCIAL SCIENCE (African American studies, American studies, anthropology, economics, geography, history, international relations, philosophy, political science/government, psychology, and sociology). Special education, business administration, and biology are the largest.

Required: To graduate, students must complete 120 credit hours with a minimum 2.0 GPA. The total number of hours in the major varies. The required core curriculum includes 2 courses each in humanities, fine arts, social sciences, and natural sciences and 1 course each in non-Western tradition, critical writing, reading, numeric and symbolic reasoning, and U.S. history.

Special: The college offers a cooperative 3-2 engineering degree with Alfred, Case Western Reserve, Clarkson, Columbia, Penn State, and Syracuse Universities, SUNY at Binghamton and Buffalo, and the University of Rochester, as well as a 3-3 degree with Rochester Institute of Technology. There is also a 3-2 M.B.A degree offered with Pace, SUNY/Buffalo or Syracuse; a 4-1 M.B.A with Alfred, Clarkson, RIT, or Union; and 3-4 degrees with SUNY/Buffalo for Dentistry, SUNY College of Optometry, and NYS College of Osteopathic Medicine. Cross-registration is available with the Rochester Area Colleges Consortium. Geneseo offers internships in all majors, study abroad through more than 95 programs, a Washington semester, dual majors, including theater/English, credit for military experience, and pass/fail options. There are 15 national honor societies, including Phi Beta Kappa, a freshman honors program, and 10 departmental honors programs.

Faculty/Classroom: 59% of faculty are male; 41%, female. All teach undergraduates. No introductory courses are taught by graduate students. The average class size in an introductory lecture is 40; in a laboratory, 18; and in a regular course, 22.

Admissions: 40% of the 2005-2006 applicants were accepted. The SAT scores for the 2005-2006 freshman class were: Verbal--1% below 500, 20% between 500 and 599, 65% between 600 and 700, and 14% above 700; Math--13% between 500 and 599, 71% between 600 and 700, and 16% above 700. The ACT scores were 3% below 21, 2% between 21 and 23, 25% between 24 and 26, 47% between 27 and 28, and 23% above 28. 81% of the current freshmen were in the top fifth of their class; 98% were in the top two fifths. 22 freshmen graduated first in their class.

Requirements: The SAT or ACT is required. In addition, applicants must be graduates of an accredited secondary school or have a GED certificate. The academic program must have included 4 years each of English, math, science, and social studies and 3 years of a foreign language. An essay is required. A portfolio or audition for certain programs and an interview are recommended. Geneseo requires applicants to be in the upper 50% of their class. A GPA of 3.0 is required. AP and CLEP credits are accepted. Important factors in the admissions decision are advanced placement or honor courses, recommendations by school officials, and evidence of special talent.

Procedure: Freshmen are admitted fall and spring. Entrance exams should be taken during the spring of the junior year. There are early decision and deferred admissions plans. Early decision applications should be filed by November 15; regular applications, by January 15 for fall entry and September 15 for spring entry, along with a $40 fee. Notification of early decision is sent December 15; regular decision, on a rolling basis after March 1. 165 early decision candidates were accepted for the 2005-2006 class. 957 applicants were on the 2005 waiting list; 14 were admitted. Applications are accepted on-line.

Transfer: 395 transfer students enrolled in 2004-2005. Applicants must provide transcripts from all previously attended colleges. A minimum 2.0 GPA is required. Students with fewer than 24 credit hours must submit SAT or ACT scores. An essay is required, and an interview is recommended. 30 of 120 credits required for the bachelor's degree must be completed at Geneseo.

Visiting: There are regularly scheduled orientations for prospective students, including a day-and-a-half summer program consisting of academic advisement, registration, and adjustment to college life activities. There are guides for informal visits and visitors may sit in on classes and stay overnight. To schedule a visit, contact the Office of Admissions at 585-245-5571.

Financial Aid: In 2005-2006, 64% of all full-time freshmen and 65% of continuing full-time students received some form of financial aid. 71% of full-time freshmen and 83% of continuing full-time students received need-based aid. The average freshman award was $8552. Need-based scholarships or need-based grants averaged $2509 ($8425 maximum); need-based self-help aid (loans and jobs) averaged $3510 ($6125 maximum); and other non-need-based awards and non-need-based scholarships averaged $700 ($4600 maximum). 22% of undergraduates work part time. Average annual earnings from campus work are $2500. The average financial indebtedness of the 2005 graduate was $15,800. Geneseo is a member of CSS. The FAFSA is required. The deadline for filing freshman financial aid applications for fall entry is February 15.

International Students: There are 112 international students enrolled. The school actively recruits these students. They must score satisfactorily on the written TOEFL or on the electronic version.

Computers: Geneseo provides almost 900 PCs for student use. Internet accessible PCs are provided in all academic buildings and residence halls. The college wireless network is partially present in all campus buildings, and full coverage is available in more than half of the buildings on campus. All students may access the system 24 hours a day. There are no time limits. The fee is $139.50. It is strongly recommended that all students have a personal computer.

Graduates: From July 1, 2004 to June 30, 2005, 1257 bachelor's degrees were awarded. The most popular majors were education (20%), business administration (10%), and psychology (9%). In an average class, 2% graduate in 3 years or less, 6% graduate in 4 years or less, 78% graduate in 5 years or less, and 79% graduate in 6 years or less. 46 companies recruited on campus in 2004-2005. Of the 2004 graduating class, 41% were enrolled in graduate school within 6 months of graduation and 46% were employed.

Admissions Contact: Kris Shay, Director of Admissions. A video is available. E-mail: *admissions@geneseo.edu* Web: *www.geneseo.edu*

STATE UNIVERSITY OF NEW YORK/COLLEGE AT OLD WESTBURY   D-5

Old Westbury, NY 11568-0210　　　　**(516) 876-3073**
　　　　　　　　　　　　　　　　　　　Fax: (516) 876-3307

Full-time: 1058 men, 1659 women	**Faculty:** 252; IIB, av$
Part-time: 263 men, 393 women	**Ph.D.s:** 76%
Graduate: 15 men, 10 women	**Student/Faculty:** 11 to 1
Year: semesters, summer session	**Tuition:** $5071 ($11,331)
Application Deadline: open	**Room & Board:** $8083
Freshman Class: 3267 applied, 1941 accepted, 403 enrolled	
SAT Verbal/Math: 480/490*	**ACT:** 19　　　**COMPETITIVE**

The State University of New York/College at Old Westbury, founded in 1965, is a public institution offering degree programs in the arts and sciences, business, education, fine arts, and health science. There are 3 undergraduate schools and 1 graduate school. The library contains 196,000 volumes, 393,519 microform items, and 854 audio/video tapes/CDs/DVDs, and subscribes to 2134 periodicals including electronic. Computerized library services include the card catalog, interlibrary loans, database searching, and Internet access. Special learning facilities include a learning resource center, art gallery, radio station, and TV studio. The 604-acre campus is in a suburban area 20 miles east of New York City. Including any residence halls, there are 22 buildings.

Student Life: 98% of undergraduates are from New York. Others are from 11 states, 27 foreign countries, and Canada. 31% are white; 27% African American; 21% foreign nationals; 16% Hispanic. The average age of freshmen is 18; all undergraduates, 25. 25% do not continue beyond their first year; 35% remain to graduate.

Housing: 1500 students can be accommodated in college housing, which includes coed dorms. In addition, there are honors houses. On-campus housing is available on a first-come, first-served basis. Priority is given to out-of-town students. 73% of students commute. Alcohol is not permitted. All students may keep cars.

Activities: 1% of men belong to 6 national fraternities; 1% of women belong to 4 national sororities. There are 60 groups on campus, including art, cheerleading, choir, chorale, computers, dance, drama, ethnic, film, gay, honors, international, newspaper, photography, political, professional, radio and TV, religious, social, social service, student government, and yearbook. Popular campus events include Welcome Back Festival, Wellness at Old Westbury, and Mayfest.

Sports: There are 5 intercollegiate sports for men and 5 for women, and 7 intramural sports for men and 7 for women. Facilities include a 3000-seat gym, an auxiliary gym, a cross-country course, playing fields, a swimming pool, a fitness center, a weight room, jogging trails, a student union building, and courts for tennis, paddleball, handball, racquetball, and squash.

Disabled Students: 90% of the campus is accessible. Wheelchair ramps, elevators, special parking, specially equipped rest rooms, special

class scheduling, lowered drinking fountains, lowered telephones, and limited volunteer transportation are available.

Services: Counseling and information services are available, as is tutoring in most subjects. There is a reader service for the blind, and remedial math, reading, and writing.

Campus Safety and Security: Measures include 24-hour foot and vehicle patrol, security escort services, shuttle buses, and informal discussions. There are pamphlets/posters/films, emergency telephones, and lighted pathways/sidewalks. An officer dormitory patrols from 6 P.M. to 2 A.M.

Programs of Study: SUNY Old Westbury confers B.A., B.S., and B.P.S. degrees. Master's degrees are also awarded. Bachelor's degrees are awarded in BIOLOGICAL SCIENCE (biochemistry and biology/biological science), BUSINESS (accounting, banking and finance, business administration and management, labor studies, management information systems, and marketing/retailing/merchandising), COMMUNICATIONS AND THE ARTS (communications, media arts, Spanish, and visual and performing arts), COMPUTER AND PHYSICAL SCIENCE (chemistry, computer science, information sciences and systems, and mathematics), EDUCATION (bilingual/bicultural, early childhood, elementary, foreign languages, mathematics, middle school, science, secondary, social studies, and special), HEALTH PROFESSIONS (community health work and health), SOCIAL SCIENCE (American studies, criminology, economics, humanities, international studies, philosophy, political science/government, psychology, religion, and sociology). Teacher education, business, and psychology are the strongest academically and have the largest enrollments.

Required: To graduate, students must maintain a GPA of 2.0 in 120 or 128 semester credits; accounting and special education majors require 128 credits. General education requirements include courses in writing and reasoning skills, creative arts, ideas and ideology, cross-cultural perspectives, U.S. society and history, physical or life science, and foreign language. A senior project or capstone course is required, based on major.

Special: SUNY Old Westbury offers cross-registration with SUNY Empire State, Lirache, and colleges in Nassau and Suffolk counties, internships in teacher education, extensive study-abroad programs, a B.A.-B.S. in biological science, dual majors, and a 3-2 engineering degree with SUNY at Stony Brook and SUNY Maritime College. Credit for military and life experience, nondegree study, and pass/fail options are available. There is a freshman honors program.

Faculty/Classroom: 47% of faculty are male; 53%, female. All teach undergraduates, 12% do research, and 11% do both. The average class size in an introductory lecture is 22; in a laboratory, 19; and in a regular course, 21.

Admissions: 59% of the 2005-2006 applicants were accepted. The SAT scores for the 2005-2006 freshman class were: Verbal--62% below 500, 34% between 500 and 599, 3% between 600 and 700, and 1% above 700; Math--58% below 500, 36% between 500 and 599, 5% between 600 and 700, and 1% above 700. The ACT scores were 74% below 21, 16% between 21 and 23, 5% between 24 and 26, and 5% between 27 and 28. 16% of the current freshmen were in the top fifth of their class; 47% were in the top two fifths.

Requirements: The SAT is required. In addition, applicants must be graduates of an accredited secondary school or have the GED. An essay, portfolio, and interview also are recommended. Students are evaluated according to qualifying categories of academic achievement (80 high school average or satisfactory SAT score), special knowledge and creative ability, paid work experience, and social or personal experience. AP and CLEP credits are accepted. Important factors in the admissions decision are leadership record, recommendations by school officials, and evidence of special talent.

Procedure: Freshmen are admitted fall and spring. There are early decision, deferred admissions, and rolling admissions plans. Application deadlines are open. Application fee is $40. Notification is sent on a rolling basis. 8 early decision candidates were accepted for the 2005-2006 class. Applications are accepted on-line.

Transfer: 986 transfer students enrolled in 2004-2005. Applicants must submit official transcripts from all colleges attended. Those students with fewer than 24 college credits must also submit a high school transcript. The college requires a minimum overall GPA of 2.0. Specific academic majors may require a higher GPA. 48 of 120 credits required for the bachelor's degree must be completed at SUNY Old Westbury.

Visiting: There are regularly scheduled orientations for prospective students. There are guides for informal visits. To schedule a visit, contact Enrollment Services.

Financial Aid: In a recent year, 68% of all full-time freshmen and 59% of continuing full-time students received some form of financial aid. 64% of full-time freshmen and 54% of continuing full-time students received need-based aid. The average freshman award was $7539. Need-based scholarships or need-based grants averaged $6357; need-based self-help aid (loans and jobs) averaged $1919; and other non-need-based awards and non-need-based scholarships averaged $7000. Average annual earnings from campus work are $874. The average financial indebted-

ness of the recent graduate was $22,775. The FAFSA, the college's own financial statement, the IFAA (Institutional application), and previous years' household income are required. The deadline for filing freshman financial aid applications for fall entry is April 19.

International Students: There are 58 international students enrolled. The school actively recruits these students. Satisfactory scores are required on the written TOEFL and the college's own test.

Computers: Wireless access is available. The College supports a 2000 port network spanning the entire campus, including high speed Internet access in dorm rooms. The wireless network is fully accessible in all academic buildings including the library, student union, and administrative building. There are roughly 350 public computers spread among 8 locations split between public access and departmental labs dedicated to specific disciplines. All students receive e-mail and computer accounts and have access to printers. All students may access the system daily. There are no time limits and no fees. It is strongly recommended that all students have a personal computer.

Graduates: From July 1, 2004 to June 30, 2005, 654 bachelor's degrees were awarded. The most popular majors were business and management (12%), accounting (11%), and psychology (10%).

Admissions Contact: Mary Marquez Bell, Vice President for Enrollment Services. A video is available. E-mail: enroll@oldwestbury.edu Web: www.oldwestbury.edu

STATE UNIVERSITY OF NEW YORK/COLLEGE AT ONEONTA   D-3

Oneonta, NY 13820-4015

(607) 436-2524
(800) 786-9123; Fax: (607) 436-3074

Full-time: 2329 men, 3159 women	**Faculty:** 250; IIA, -$
Part-time: 79 men, 82 women	**Ph.D.s:** 78%
Graduate: 55 men, 155 women	**Student/Faculty:** 22 to 1
Year: semesters, summer session	**Tuition:** $5367 ($11,627)
Application Deadline: May 1	**Room & Board:** $7538
Freshman Class: 10,816 applied, 4904 accepted, 1128 enrolled	
SAT Verbal/Math: 552/563*	**ACT:** 23 **VERY COMPETITIVE**

The State University of New York/College at Oneonta, founded in 1889, offers undergraduate and graduate programs in the arts and sciences with a campuswide emphasis on educational technology and community service. In addition to regional accreditation, Oneonta has baccalaureate program accreditation with AAFCS, ACS, ADA, and NCATE. The library contains 556,445 volumes, 1,166,999 microform items, and 30,763 audio/video tapes/CDs/DVDs, and subscribes to 19,391 periodicals including electronic. Computerized library services include the card catalog, interlibrary loans, database searching, Internet access, and laptop Internet portals. Special learning facilities include a learning resource center, art gallery, planetarium, radio station, TV station, observatory, science discovery center, community service center, college camp, children's center, and off-campus biological field station. The 250-acre campus is in a rural area 75 miles southwest of Albany and 55 miles northeast of Binghamton. Including any residence halls, there are 36 buildings.

Student Life: 96% of undergraduates are from New York. Others are from 14 states and 19 foreign countries. 82% are white. The average age of freshmen is 18; all undergraduates, 20. 20% do not continue beyond their first year; 51% remain to graduate.

Housing: 3019 students can be accommodated in college housing, which includes single-sex and coed dorms. In addition, there is a math and science wing, an international wing, all freshman housing, apartment-style housing, and other special-interest groupings within residence halls. On-campus housing is guaranteed for the freshman year only, is available on a first-come, first-served basis, and is available on a lottery system for upperclassmen. 53% of students live on campus; of those, 56% remain on campus on weekends. Alcohol is not permitted. Upperclassmen may keep cars.

Activities: 1% of men belong to 3 national fraternities; 7% of women belong to 5 national sororities. There are 70 groups on campus, including academic, art, band, cheerleading, choir, chorale, chorus, computers,culture enrichment, dance, drama, ethnic, film, gay, honors, international, jazz band, musical theater, newspaper, orchestra, pep band, photography, political, professional, radio and TV, religious, social, social service, special interest, student government, volunteer, and yearbook. Popular campus events include Exploration (campus orientation), Into the Streets (community service day), and Reunion Weekend.

Sports: There are 10 intercollegiate sports for men and 11 for women, and 17 intramural sports for men and 17 for women. Facilities include a gym, a field house, dance studios, weight rooms, a pool, indoor racquetball courts, tennis courts, indoor and outdoor tracks, athletic fields, and an all-weather field.

Disabled Students: 80% of the campus is accessible. Wheelchair ramps, elevators, special parking, specially equipped rest rooms, special class scheduling and lowered drinking fountains are available. All academic buildings and most residence halls are accessible.

Services: Counseling and information services are available, as is tutoring in most subjects. There is a reader service for the blind, and remedial

math, reading, and writing. Tutoring is also available in all introductory-level courses and most upper-level courses.

Campus Safety and Security: Measures include 24-hour foot and vehicle patrol, self-defense education, security escort services, and shuttle buses. There are informal discussions, pamphlets/posters/films, emergency telephones, lighted pathways/sidewalks, and residence hall workshops.

Programs of Study: Oneonta confers B.A. and B.S. degrees. Master's degrees are also awarded. Bachelor's degrees are awarded in BIOLOGICAL SCIENCE (biology/biological science), BUSINESS (accounting, business economics, and fashion merchandising), COMMUNICATIONS AND THE ARTS (art, communications, dramatic arts, English, fine arts, French, music, music business management, Spanish, and speech/debate/rhetoric), COMPUTER AND PHYSICAL SCIENCE (atmospheric sciences and meteorology, chemistry, computer science, earth science, geology, mathematics, physics, and statistics), EDUCATION (business, elementary, English, foreign languages, home economics, mathematics, science, secondary, and social science), ENGINEERING AND ENVIRONMENTAL DESIGN (environmental science), HEALTH PROFESSIONS (predentistry and premedicine), SOCIAL SCIENCE (African studies, anthropology, child care/child and family studies, criminal justice, dietetics, economics, geography, gerontology, Hispanic American studies, history, home economics, interdisciplinary studies, international studies, philosophy, political science/government, prelaw, psychology, sociology, and water resources). Physical and natural sciences, business economics, and education are the strongest academically. Education, communication arts, and music industry are the largest.

Required: Students must complete 122 semester hours, with at least 48 hours in upper-division courses and 30 to 36 hours in the major. A minimum GPA of 2.0 (2.5 for education majors) must be maintained. In addition, students must complete a 36 hour general education requirement including courses in math, natural sciences, social sciences, American history, Western civilization, other world civilizations, humanities, the arts, foreign language, basic communications, writing skills, and oral communication skills. Students must also pass writing and speech proficiency exams.

Special: Oneonta offers limited cross-registration with Hartwick College, internships in most fields, study abroad through SUNY in 50 countries, a Washington semester, work-study programs, interdisciplinary studies, and dual majors. A 3-2 engineering degree and other cooperative programs are offered. Credit for life experience, nondegree study, and pass/fail options are available. There are 14 national honor societies, a freshman honors program, and 10 departmental honors programs.

Faculty/Classroom: 57% of faculty are male; 43%, female. 99% teach undergraduates. The average class size in an introductory lecture is 25; in a laboratory, 24; and in a regular course, 20.

Admissions: 45% of the 2005-2006 applicants were accepted. The SAT scores for the 2005-2006 freshman class were: Verbal--16% below 500, 62% between 500 and 599, 20% between 600 and 700, and 2% above 700; Math--10% below 500, 62% between 500 and 599, 27% between 600 and 700, and 1% above 700. The ACT scores were 8% below 21, 20% between 21 and 23, 39% between 24 and 26, 23% between 27 and 28, and 10% above 28. 48% of the current freshmen were in the top fifth of their class; 94% were in the top two fifths. 10 freshmen graduated first in their class.

Requirements: The SAT or ACT is required. In addition, applicants should be graduates of an accredited secondary school and have 16 academic credits, including 4 years each of English and history, and 8 years combined of foreign language, math, and science, with at least 2 years in each of these 3 broad areas. The GED is accepted. A GPA of 2.0 is required. AP and CLEP credits are accepted. Important factors in the admissions decision are advanced placement or honor courses, evidence of special talent, and leadership record.

Procedure: Freshmen are admitted fall and spring. Entrance exams should be taken in the spring of the junior year or the fall of the senior year. There is a deferred admissions and a rolling admissions plan. Early decision applications should be filed by November 15; regular applications, by May 1 for fall entry and December 15 for spring entry, along with a $40 fee. Notification is sent on a rolling basis. 224 applicants were on the 2005 waiting list; 5 were admitted. Applications are accepted online.

Transfer: 764 transfer students enrolled in 2004-2005. Official transcripts of all previous college work must be submitted. A minimum of 15 semester hours of transferable credit and a GPA of 2.0 are required. 45 of 122 credits required for the bachelor's degree must be completed at Oneonta.

Visiting: There are regularly scheduled orientations for prospective students, including 2 fall open houses, a summer open house, individual appointments, and group information sessions. There are guides for informal visits and visitors may sit in on classes and stay overnight. To schedule a visit, contact the Admissions Office at 1-800-SUNY-123 or *admissions@oneonta.edu.*

Financial Aid: In 2005-2006, 56% of all full-time freshmen and 57% of continuing full-time students received some form of financial aid. 57% of full-time freshmen and 64% of continuing full-time students received

need-based aid. The average freshman award was $7955. Need-based scholarships or need-based grants averaged $3254; need-based self-help aid (loans and jobs) averaged $3608; and other non-need-based awards and non-need-based scholarships averaged $443. 29% of undergraduates work part time. Average annual earnings from campus work are $800. The average financial indebtedness of the 2005 graduate was $8308. The FAFSA and are required. The deadline for filing freshman financial aid applications for fall entry is April 15.

International Students: There are 85 international students enrolled. The school actively recruits these students. They must score satisfactorily on the TOEFL. The SAT or ACT is recommended.

Computers: Wireless access is available. Wireless and high-speed connections are available in all academic and residential buildings; more than 700 computers are available in general, departmental, and residence-hall labs. There is free dial-up access for off-campus students. All students may access the system anytime. There are no time limits and no fees. It is strongly recommended that all students have a personal computer.

Graduates: From July 1, 2004 to June 30, 2005, 1222 bachelor's degrees were awarded. The most popular majors were elementary education (25%), communication arts (11%), and music industry (8%). In an average class, 1% graduate in 3 years or less, 36% graduate in 4 years or less, 49% graduate in 5 years or less, and 51% graduate in 6 years or less. 45 companies recruited on campus in 2004-2005. Of the 2004 graduating class, 47% were enrolled in graduate school within 6 months of graduation and 83% were employed.

Admissions Contact: Karen Brown, Director of Admissions.
E-mail: *admissions@oneonta.edu* Web: *http://www.oneonta.edu*

STATE UNIVERSITY OF NEW YORK/COLLEGE AT PLATTSBURGH   D-2

Plattsburgh, NY 12901-2681   (518) 564-2040
                                    (888) 673-0012; Fax: (518) 564-2045

Full-time: 2141 men, 2883 women	**Faculty:** 252; IIA, -$
Part-time: 148 men, 222 women	**Ph.D.s:** 92%
Graduate: 197 men, 453 women	**Student/Faculty:** 20 to 1
Year: trimesters, summer session	**Tuition:** $5296 ($11,556)
Application Deadline: August 1	**Room & Board:** $7066
Freshman Class: 5321 applied, 3278 accepted, 1040 enrolled	
SAT Verbal/Math: 510/510*	**ACT:** 22 **COMPETITIVE**

The State University of New York/College at Plattsburgh, founded in 1889, is a public institution offering degree programs in the liberal arts and professional programs. There are 3 undergraduate and 2 graduate schools. In addition to regional accreditation, Plattsburgh State has baccalaureate program accreditation with AACSB, ADA, ASLA, CSWE, and NLN. The library contains 299,556 volumes, 926,246 microform items, and 24,139 audio/video tapes/CDs/DVDs, and subscribes to 1453 periodicals including electronic. Computerized library services include the card catalog, interlibrary loans, database searching, and Internet access. Special learning facilities include a learning resource center, art gallery, planetarium, radio station, TV station, an environmental science institute, a child care center, a research institute, a teacher resource center, a speech and hearing clinic, the Alzheimer's Disease Assistance Center, auditory research labs, a virtual reality simulator, and distance learning facilities. The 300-acre campus is in a suburban area 150 miles north of Albany, 25 miles west of Burlington, Vermont, and 65 miles south of Montreal, Canada Including any residence halls, there are 35 buildings.

Student Life: 90% of undergraduates are from New York. Others are from 26 states, 42 foreign countries, and Canada. 98% are from public schools. 76% are white. The average age of freshmen is 18; all undergraduates, 22. 23% do not continue beyond their first year; 54% remain to graduate.

Housing: 2777 students can be accommodated in college housing, which includes single-sex and coed dorm. In addition, there are special-interest houses, adult student halls/floors, wellness-floors, a substance-free building, and vacation housing. On-campus housing is available on a first-come, first-served basis and is available on a lottery system for upperclassmen. 53% of students commute. All students may keep cars.

Activities: 7% of men belong to 3 local and 4 national fraternities; 5% of women belong to 3 local and 4 national sororities. There are 90 groups on campus, including art, band, cheerleading, choir, chorale, chorus, computers, dance, drama, ethnic, film, gay, honors, international, jazz band, literary magazine, musical theater, newspaper, orchestra, photography, political, professional, radio and TV, religious, social, social service, and student government. Popular campus events include Canada Day, Family Weekend, and Arts and Crafts Fair.

Sports: There are 9 intercollegiate sports for men and 10 for women, and 12 intramural sports for men and 9 for women. Facilities include a 3500-seat ice arena, a 1500-seat gym, an indoor track, soccer and volleyball areas, an indoor swimming pool, exercise and weight rooms, an aerobics studio, racquetball courts, lighted tennis courts, softball, lacrosse, and rugby fields, and a fitness center.

Disabled Students: 80% of the campus is accessible. Wheelchair ramps, elevators, special parking, specially equipped rest rooms, special class scheduling, lowered drinking fountains, lowered telephones, curb cuts, and electronic doors are available.

Services: Counseling and information services are available, as is tutoring in every subject. There is a reader service for the blind, and remedial math, reading, and writing.

Campus Safety and Security: Measures include 24-hour foot and vehicle patrol, security escort services, shuttle buses, and informal discussions. There are pamphlets/posters/films, emergency telephones, lighted pathways/sidewalks, and , bicycle patrols, combination locks on student rooms, a computerized keyless entry system for residence hall access, door viewers, and basement and ground-level security windows in residence halls.

Programs of Study: Plattsburgh State confers B.A., B.S., B.F.A., and B.S.Ed. degrees. Master's degrees are also awarded. Bachelor's degrees are awarded in BIOLOGICAL SCIENCE (biochemistry, biology/biological science, and cell biology), BUSINESS (accounting, business administration and management, business economics, and hotel/motel and restaurant management), COMMUNICATIONS AND THE ARTS (communications, dramatic arts, English, French, journalism, music, and Spanish), COMPUTER AND PHYSICAL SCIENCE (chemistry, computer science, geology, mathematics, and physics), EDUCATION (education of the deaf and hearing impaired, elementary, English, mathematics, science, secondary, social studies, and special), ENGINEERING AND ENVIRONMENTAL DESIGN (environmental science), HEALTH PROFESSIONS (medical laboratory technology and nursing), SOCIAL SCIENCE (anthropology, Canadian studies, child care/child and family studies, community services, criminal justice, dietetics, economics, geography, history, home economics, interdisciplinary studies, Latin American studies, philosophy, political science/government, social work, and sociology). Business, accounting, and art are the strongest academically. Psychology, education, and business are the largest.

Required: To graduate, students must have a 2.0 GPA and complete at least 120 semester hours. General education courses total 41 to 46 credits. In addition, all students must demonstrate proficiency in writing by completion of an advanced writing requirement.

Special: The college offers cross-registration with Clinton Community College and Empire State College, internships, study abroad in 6 countries, cooperative programs with a variety of employers, B.A.-B.S. degrees, dual and student-designed majors, and an accelerated degree program in any major except nursing. A 3-2 engineering degree is offered with SUNY Stony Brook and Binghamton, Clarkson, Syracuse, and McGill Universities, and the University of Vermont. Credit for military experience, nondegree study if space permits, and limited pass/fail options are possible. There are 18 national honor societies, a freshman honors program.

Faculty/Classroom: 54% of faculty are male; 46%, female. All both teach and do research. No introductory courses are taught by graduate students. The average class size in an introductory lecture is 25; in a laboratory, 13; and in a regular course, 23.

Admissions: 62% of the 2005-2006 applicants were accepted. The SAT scores for the 2005-2006 freshman class were: Verbal--41% below 500, 47% between 500 and 599, 11% between 600 and 700, and 1% above 700; Math--39% below 500, 48% between 500 and 599, 12% between 600 and 700, and 1% above 700. The ACT scores were 36% below 21, 35% between 21 and 23, 21% between 24 and 26, 7% between 27 and 28, and 1% above 28. 24% of the current freshmen were in the top fifth of their class; 61% were in the top two fifths. 3 freshmen graduated first in their class.

Requirements: The SAT or ACT is required. In addition, applicants must have at least 12 academic credits, including 4 years of English, 5 combined years of math and science, and 3 years of social studies. An essay, portfolio, audition, and interview may be recommended in some programs. The GED is accepted. Plattsburgh State requires applicants to be in the upper 50% of their class. A grade average of 78 is required. AP and CLEP credits are accepted. Important factors in the admissions decision are advanced placement or honor courses, recommendations by school officials, and leadership record.

Procedure: Freshmen are admitted fall and spring. Entrance exams should be taken during the second half of the junior year or the beginning of the senior year. There are early decision, early admissions, and deferred admissions plans. There is a rolling admissions plan. Early decision applications should be filed by November 15; regular applications, by August 1 for fall entry and November 1 for spring entry. The fall 2005 application fee was $400. Notification of early decision is sent December 15; regular decision, on a rolling basis beginning January 15. 41 early decision candidates were accepted for the 2005-2006 class. 249 applicants were on the 2005 waiting list; 14 were admitted. Applications are accepted on-line.

Transfer: 591 transfer students enrolled in 2004-2005. Applicants must have a minimum 2.0 GPA. Most academic programs require a 2.5 GPA or better. 36 of 120 credits required for the bachelor's degree must be completed at Plattsburgh State.

Visiting: There are regularly scheduled orientations for prospective students, including a group, student-led tour, and either a group or individual interview. Special overnight events for accepted freshmen include meals with students and faculty, classroom visits, discussions with faculty, and special workshops. There are guides for informal visits and visitors may sit in on classes and stay overnight. To schedule a visit, contact the Admissions Office at admissions@plattsburgh.edu.

Financial Aid: The average freshman award was $4144. 37% of undergraduates work part time. Average annual earnings from campus work are $1100. The average financial indebtedness of the 2005 graduate was $16,158. The FAFSA is required. In-state students must also file the TAP application. The priority date for freshman financial aid applications for fall entry is March 1. There is a rolling deadline for filing freshman financial aid applications for fall entry.

International Students: There are 305 international students enrolled. The school actively recruits these students. They must take the TOEFL.

Computers: All students may access the system. There are no time limits. The fee is $50 per semester. It is strongly recommended that all students have a personal computer.

Graduates: From July 1, 2004 to June 30, 2005, 1144 bachelor's degrees were awarded. The most popular majors were business/marketing (19%), education (18%), and communications/journalism (8%). In an average class, 1% graduate in 3 years or less, 31% graduate in 4 years or less, 51% graduate in 5 years or less, and 54% graduate in 6 years or less. 120 companies recruited on campus in 2004-2005. Of the 2004 graduating class, 12% were enrolled in graduate school within 6 months of graduation and 79% were employed.

Admissions Contact: Richard Higgins, Director of Admissions. E-mail: higginrj@splavb.cc.plattsburgh.edu Web: www.plattsburgh.edu

STATE UNIVERSITY OF NEW YORK/COLLEGE AT PURCHASE
D-5

Purchase, NY 10577-1400	(914) 251-6300; Fax: (914) 251-6314
Full-time: 1483 men, 1748 women	Faculty: 144; IIB, +$
Part-time: 194 men, 263 women	Ph.D.s: 100%
Graduate: 72 men, 66 women	Student/Faculty: 22 to 1
Year: semesters, summer session	Tuition: $5529 ($11,789)
Application Deadline: August 15	Room & Board: $6460
Freshman Class: 6946 applied, 2162 accepted, 718 enrolled	
SAT Verbal/Math: 570/540*	VERY COMPETITIVE+

State University of New York/College at Purchase, also known as Purchase College, SUNY, founded in 1967, is a public institution that offers programs in visual arts, music, acting, dance, film, theater/stage design technology, natural science, social science, and humanities. There is 1 undergraduate and 1 graduate school. In addition to regional accreditation, Purchase College SUNY has baccalaureate program accreditation with NASAD and NASM. The library contains 274,478 volumes, 253,274 microform items, and 16,682 audio/video tapes/CDs/DVDs, and subscribes to 18,898 periodicals including electronic. Computerized library services include the card catalog, interlibrary loans, database searching, and Internet access. Special learning facilities include a learning resource center, radio station, TV station, and a listening and viewing center, science and photography labs, music practice rooms and instruments, multitrack synthesizers, experimental stage, typesetting and computer graphics labs, a performing arts complex, an electron microscope, and the Children's Center at Purchase College. The 500-acre campus is in a suburban area 35 miles north of midtown Manhattan. Including any residence halls, there are 40 buildings.

Student Life: 82% of undergraduates are from New York. Others are from 39 states and 24 foreign countries. 70% are white; 12% Hispanic; 10% African American. The average age of freshmen is 18; all undergraduates, 23. 22% do not continue beyond their first year; 45% remain to graduate.

Housing: 2200 students can be accommodated in college housing, which includes single-sex and coed dorms and on-campus apartments. In addition, special-interest house, transfer student units, nontraditional-aged student units, wellness halls, presidential scholar halls, sophomore communities, conservatory halls, and learning communities are offered. On-campus housing is guaranteed for all 4 years. 62% of students live on campus; of those, 75% remain on campus on weekends. All students may keep cars.

Activities: There are no fraternities or sororities. There are 40 groups on campus, including art, band, choir, chorale, computers, dance, drama, environmental awareness, ethnic, gay, jazz band, literary magazine, opera, orchestra, photography, political, professional, religious, social, social service, student government, symphony, and visual arts. Popular campus events include Spring Concert, Alcohol Awareness Week, and film programs.

Sports: There are 6 intercollegiate sports for men and 6 for women, and 20 intramural sports for men and 20 for women. Facilities include 3 basketball courts, a fitness center, 6-lane pool, aerobics studio, 4 racquetball courts, 2 squash courts, 10 tennis courts, 6 of which are lighted, an outdoor climbing wall, 5 soccer fields, a baseball field, a softball field, and a 4-lane bowling lane.

Disabled Students: All of the campus is accessible. Wheelchair ramps, elevators, special parking, specially equipped rest rooms, and note takers, extended test times, quiet rooms for tests, interpreters for the hearing impaired, readers for the visually impaired, a reading machine in the library, and special note-taking paper are available.

Services: Counseling and information services are available, as is tutoring in every subject. There is a reader service for the blind, and remedial math, reading, and writing. There are math and writing drop-in sessions, "The P.J. Project," offering tutoring in residence halls in evenings, assistive technology, supplemental instructors, and computer lab study groups.

Campus Safety and Security: Measures include 24-hour foot and vehicle patrol, security escort services, informal discussions, and pamphlets/posters/films. There are emergency telephones and lighted pathways/sidewalks.

Programs of Study: Purchase College SUNY confers B.A., B.S., B.A.LA., B.F.A., and Mus. B. degrees. Master's degrees are also awarded. Bachelor's degrees are awarded in BIOLOGICAL SCIENCE (biology/biological science), COMMUNICATIONS AND THE ARTS (art history and appreciation, creative writing, dance, dramatic arts, film arts, journalism, literature, music, theater design, and visual and performing arts), COMPUTER AND PHYSICAL SCIENCE (chemistry and mathematics), ENGINEERING AND ENVIRONMENTAL DESIGN (environmental science), SOCIAL SCIENCE (anthropology, economics, ethnic studies, history, liberal arts/general studies, philosophy, political science/government, psychology, sociology, and women's studies). Dance, drama, and film are the strongest academically. Visual arts, music, and liberal studies are the largest.

Required: A minimum 2.0 GPA is required with a minimum of 120 credits. Students majoring in the arts complete a minimum of 90 professional credits and the SUNY general education curriculum. Students majoring in the liberal arts and scieces complete the general education curriculum and major requirements, and must complete a senior thesis.

Special: Purchase College offers cross-registration with Empire State colleges, internships with corporations, newspapers, and local agencies, and student-designed majors, dual majors, study abroad, work-study, nondegree study, and pass/fail options. There is also an arts conservatory program.

Faculty/Classroom: 54% of faculty are male; 46%, female. All teach undergraduates. The average class size in an introductory lecture is 27; in a laboratory, 12; and in a regular course, 14.

Admissions: 31% of the 2005-2006 applicants were accepted. The SAT scores for the 2005-2006 freshman class were: Math--28% below 500, 44% between 500 and 599, 25% between 600 and 700, and 3% above 700.

Requirements: The SAT is required and the ACT is recommended. In addition, minimum scores are required on the SAT or on the ACT. Applicants must be graduates of an accredited secondary school and have completed 16 academic credits and 16 Carnegie units. The GED is accepted. Visual arts students must submit an essay and portfolio and have an interview. Film students need an essay and an interview. Design technology students need a portfolio and an interview. Performing arts students must audition. A GPA of 2.0 is required. AP and CLEP credits are accepted. Important factors in the admissions decision are evidence of special talent, recommendations by school officials, and personality/intangible qualities.

Procedure: Freshmen are admitted fall and spring. Entrance exams should be taken by the fall of the senior year. There are early decision, early admissions, rolling admissions and deferred admissions plans. Early decision applications should be filed by November 15; regular applications, by August 15 for fall entry and December 1 for spring entry, along with a $30 fee. Notification of early decision is sent December 15; regular decision, on a rolling basis. 18 early decision candidates were accepted for the 2005-2006 class. A waiting list is an active part of the admissions procedure. Applications are accepted on-line.

Transfer: 373 transfer students enrolled in 2004-2005. Students transferring to the School of Arts (visual or performing arts) must pass an audition or portfolio review. Transfer credit is limited; students can contact the Office of Admission to get a preliminary credit evaluation. Students transferring to programs in liberal arts and sciences must have a minimum 2.0 G.P.A. if they have completed 30 or more semester hours; if they have fewer than 30 semester hours, the high school transcript is also reviewed. Liberal arts and science transfers can transfer a maximum of 90 semester hours from 4 year colleges and 75 semester hours from 2 year colleges. 30 of 120 credits required for the bachelor's degree must be completed at Purchase College SUNY.

Visiting: There are regularly scheduled orientations for prospective students, including group question and answer sessions followed by a tour of the campus. To schedule a visit, contact the Admissions Office.

Financial Aid: In 2005-2006, 85% of all full-time freshmen and 69% of continuing full-time students received some form of financial aid. 54% of full-time freshmen and 47% of continuing full-time students received

need-based aid. The average freshman award was $7067. Need-based scholarships or need-based grants averaged $5343 ($13,450 maximum); need-based self-help aid (loans and jobs) averaged $3252 ($7625 maximum); and other non-need-based awards and non-need-based scholarships averaged $3086 ($17,625 maximum). Other scholarships or grants are available based on merit or another defining characteristic, such a first in household to attend college, what state the student comes from, the affiliation of a parent in an organization, or from the parent's workplace. 12% of undergraduates work part time. Average annual earnings from campus work are $1073. The average financial indebtedness of the 2005 graduate was $16,058. Purchase College SUNY is a member of CSS. The FAFSA is required. The deadline for filing freshman financial aid applications for fall entry is February 15.

International Students: There are 80 international students enrolled. The school actively recruits these students. A satisfactory score is required on the written TOEFL, also a satisfactory score is required on the SAT: Verbal test. If the TOEFL was not taken, a satisfactory score is required on the IFLTS, and the SAT or ACT.

Computers: All students may access the system when the computer center is open. There are no time limits. The fee is $150 per semester. It is strongly recommended that all students have a personal computer.

Graduates: From July 1, 2004 to June 30, 2005, 499 bachelor's degrees were awarded. The most popular majors were liberal studies (28%), visual arts (23%), and music (17%). In an average class, 32% graduate in 4 years or less, 44% graduate in 5 years or less, and 47% graduate in 6 years or less. 20 companies recruited on campus in 2004-2005.

Admissions Contact: Betsy Immergut, Director of Admissions. E-mail: *betsy.immergut@purchase.edu* Web: *admissn@purchase.edu*

STATE UNIVERSITY OF NEW YORK/COLLEGE OF AGRICULTURE AND TECHNOLOGY AT COBLESKILL

D-3

Cobleskill, NY 12043
(518) 255-5525
(800) 295-8988; Fax: (518) 255-6769

Full-time: 1292 men, 1080 women	**Faculty:** 113; III, -$
Part-time: 38 men, 72 women	**Ph.Ds:** 23%
Graduate: none	**Student/Faculty:** 21 to 1
Year: semesters, summer session	**Tuition:** $5345 ($11,605)
Application Deadline: open	**Room & Board:** $7570
Freshman Class: n/av	
SAT or ACT: recommended	**COMPETITIVE**

The State University of New York/College of Agriculture and Technology at Cobleskill, established in 1916, is a comprehensive public institution offering bachelors and associate degree and a certificate program. The library contains 72,188 volumes, 10,202 microform items, and 3980 audio/video tapes/CDs/DVDs, and subscribes to more than 10,000 periodicals including electronic. Computerized library services include the card catalog, interlibrary loans, database searching, Internet access, and laptop Internet portals. Special learning facilities include a learning resource center, art gallery, and an arboretum, greenhouses, and a plant nursery. The 750-acre campus is in a rural area 35 miles south of Albany. Including any residence halls, there are 53 buildings.

Student Life: 90% of undergraduates are from New York. Others are from 17 states and 6 foreign countries. 98% are from public schools. 76% are white. The average age of freshmen is 18; all undergraduates, 20. 24% do not continue beyond their first year; 52% remain to graduate.

Housing: 1893 students can be accommodated in college housing, which includes single-sex and coed dorms and special interest floors. On-campus housing is guaranteed for the freshman and sophomore years, is available on a first-come, first-served basis, and is available on a lottery system for upperclassmen. 66% of students live on campus; of those, 45% remain on campus on weekends. Alcohol is not permitted. All students may keep cars.

Activities: There are no fraternities or sororities. There are 45 groups on campus, including cheerleading, choir, chorus, departmental, drama, ethnic, gay, honors, international, jazz band, musical theater, newspaper, photography, professional, religious, social, social service, student government, and yearbook. Popular campus events include Parents Weekend and Alumni Weekend.

Sports: There are 10 intercollegiate sports for men and 10 for women, and 4 intramural sports for men and 4 for women. Facilities include indoor and outdoor basketball and tennis courts, playing fields, a gym, a fitness center, a swimming pool, bowling lanes, a field house, badminton, volleyball, and handball courts, archery and golf driving areas, a quarter-mile track, a ski center, and a fitness trail.

Disabled Students: 35% of the campus is accessible. Wheelchair ramps, elevators, special parking, specially equipped rest rooms, special class scheduling, lowered drinking fountains, lowered telephones, and special housing are available.

Services: Counseling and information services are available, as is tutoring in most subjects. There is a reader service for the blind, and remedial math, reading, and writing. There is also an academic support center.

Campus Safety and Security: Measures include 24-hour foot and vehicle patrol, self-defense education, security escort services, and informal discussions. There are pamphlets/posters/films, emergency telephones, and lighted pathways/sidewalks.

Programs of Study: SUNY Cobleskill confers B.S., B.B.A., and B.T. in Agriculture degrees. Associate degrees are also awarded. Bachelor's degrees are awarded in AGRICULTURE (agricultural business management, agricultural mechanics, animal science, fishing and fisheries, plant science, and wildlife management), COMPUTER AND PHYSICAL SCIENCE (information sciences and systems), ENGINEERING AND ENVIRONMENTAL DESIGN (technological management), SOCIAL SCIENCE (child care/child and family studies).

Required: Degree requirements include completion of 126 credit hours, with 30 to 32 upper-division credits in the major, 11 credits of technical electives, 7 to 15 credits in other electives, 1 credit of phys. ed., and a 15-credit internship. Students must maintain a minimum 2.0 GPA.

Special: The college sponsors internship programs and cross-registration is possible with the Hudson-Mohawk Area Consortium. Students may study abroad at Thomas Danby and South Fields Colleges in England. There is 1 national honor society, a freshman honors program, and 1 departmental honors program.

Faculty/Classroom: 74% of faculty are male; 36%, female. All teach undergraduates, 10% do research, and 10% do both. The average class size in an introductory lecture is 19; in a laboratory, 15; and in a regular course, 19.

Requirements: The SAT or ACT is required for some programs. In addition, applicants must have graduated from an accredited secondary school or earned a GED, and are encouraged to have completed college-preparatory courses. A GPA of 75.0 is required. AP and CLEP credits are accepted. Important factors in the admissions decision are advanced placement or honor courses, evidence of special talent, and leadership record.

Procedure: Freshmen are admitted fall and spring. There are early admissions and deferred admissions plans. Application deadlines are open. Application fee is $40. Applications are accepted on-line.

Transfer: 195 transfer students enrolled in 2004-2005. Applicants must have a minimum GPA of 2.0. 45 of 126 credits required for the bachelor's degree must be completed at SUNY Cobleskill.

Visiting: There are regularly scheduled orientations for prospective students. There are guides for informal visits and visitors may sit in on classes and stay overnight. To schedule a visit, contact the Office of Admissions at *admissions@cobleskill.edu.*

Financial Aid: In 2005-2006, 75% of all full-time freshmen and 64% of continuing full-time students received some form of financial aid. 61% of full-time freshmen and 59% of continuing full-time students received need-based aid. The average freshman award was $8689. Need-based scholarships or need-based grants averaged $2016 ($10,325 maximum); need-based self-help aid (loans and jobs) averaged $1351 ($6500 maximum); and other non-need-based awards and non-need-based scholarships averaged $801 ($2500 maximum). 16% of undergraduates work part time. Average annual earnings from campus work are $688. The average financial indebtedness of the 2005 graduate was $6000. SUNY Cobleskill is a member of CSS. The FAFSA, the college's own financial statement, and the EOP Financial eligibility form for EOP applicants only are required. The deadline for filing freshman financial aid applications for fall entry is March 15.

International Students: There are 62 international students enrolled. The school actively recruits these students. They must score satisfactorily on the written TOEFL or on the electronic version.

Computers: Wireless access is available. There are 260 college-owned computers for student use available in the library, residence halls, computer center, and open access labs. All resident halls are wired for high-speed Internet connections. Wireless capabilities are in various locations across campus. All students may access the system 24 hours a day/ 7 days a week (where wireless and in residence halls). There are no time limits. The fee is $260 each year. It is recommended that students in travel and resort marketing and all CIS, CS, and IT majors have personal computers. A laptop/notebook is recommended.

Graduates: From July 1, 2004 to June 30, 2005, 153 bachelor's degrees were awarded. The most popular majors were plant science (11%) and animal science (9%). In an average class, 46% graduate in 3 years or less, and 44% graduate in 4 years or less. 56 companies recruited on campus in 2004-2005.

Admissions Contact: Chris Tacea, Director of Admissions.
E-mail: *admissions@cobleskill.edu* Web: *www.cobleskill.edu*

STATE UNIVERSITY OF NEW YORK/COLLEGE OF ENVIRONMENTAL SCIENCE AND FORESTRY   C-3

Syracuse, NY 13210-2779   (315) 470-6600
(800) 777-7373; Fax: (315) 470-6933

Full-time: 700 men, 500 women	**Faculty:** 122; I, -$
Part-time: 150 men, 160 women	**Ph.D.s:** 80%
Graduate: 300 men, 300 women	**Student/Faculty:** 10 to 1
Year: semesters	**Tuition:** $5000 ($11,000)
Application Deadline: see profile	**Room & Board:** $10,000
Freshman Class: n/av	
SAT or ACT: required	**VERY COMPETITIVE**

The College of Environmental Science and Forestry, founded in 1911 and located adjacent to the campus of Syracuse University, is one of the colleges of the State University of New York. The public institution specializes in undergraduate and graduate degrees in agricultural, biological, environmental, health, and physical sciences, landscape architecture, and engineering. Students have access to the academic, cultural, and social life at Syracuse University. Figures in the above capsule and in this profile are approximate. In addition to regional accreditation, ESF has baccalaureate program accreditation with ABET, ASLA, and SAF. The library contains 130,305 volumes, 200,090 microform items, and 1118 audio/video tapes/CDs/DVDs, and subscribes to 2001 periodicals including electronic. Computerized library services include the card catalog, interlibrary loans, and database searching. Special learning facilities include a learning resource center, art gallery, natural history museum, radio station, and TV station. The 12-acre campus is in an urban area in Syracuse. Including any residence halls, there are 7 buildings.

Student Life: 91% of undergraduates are from New York. Others are from 25 states, 9 foreign countries, and Canada. 85% are from public schools. 87% are white. The average age of freshmen is 18; all undergraduates, 21. 3% do not continue beyond their first year; 75% remain to graduate.

Housing: 600 students can be accommodated in college housing, which includes single-sex and coed dorms, on-campus apartments, off-campus apartments, and married-student housing. In addition, there are special-interest houses, substance-free floors, quiet floors, and learning communities. On-campus housing is guaranteed for all 4 years. 50% of students live on campus; of those, 90% remain on campus on weekends. Alcohol is not permitted. Upperclassmen may keep cars.

Activities: 3% of men belong to 20 national fraternities; 3% of women belong to 20 national sororities. There are 300 groups on campus, including art, band, cheerleading, choir, chorale, chorus, computers, dance, debate, drama, drum and bugle corps, ethnic, film, gay, honors, international, jazz band, marching band, musical theater, newspaper, orchestra, pep band, photography, political, professional, radio and TV, religious, social, social service, student government, symphony, and yearbook. Popular campus events include Activities Fair, Earth Day, and Awards Banquet.

Sports: There are 21 intercollegiate sports for men and 21 for women, and 30 intramural sports for men and 30 for women. Athletic and recreational facilities are contracted through Syracuse University.

Disabled Students: 90% of the campus is accessible. Wheelchair ramps, elevators, special parking, specially equipped rest rooms, lowered drinking fountains, and lowered telephones are available.

Services: Counseling and information services are available, as is tutoring in some subjects. There is a reader service for the blind.

Campus Safety and Security: Measures include 24-hour foot and vehicle patrol, security escort services, shuttle buses, and informal discussions. There are pamphlets/posters/films, emergency telephones, and lighted pathways/sidewalks.

Programs of Study: ESF confers B.S. and B.L.A. degrees. Associate, master's, and doctoral degrees are also awarded. Bachelor's degrees are awarded in AGRICULTURE (animal science, environmental studies, forest engineering, forestry and related sciences, natural resource management, plant science, soil science, and wood science), BIOLOGICAL SCIENCE (biology/biological science, botany, ecology, entomology, environmental biology, microbiology, molecular biology, plant genetics, and plant physiology), COMPUTER AND PHYSICAL SCIENCE (chemistry and polymer science), EDUCATION (environmental and science), ENGINEERING AND ENVIRONMENTAL DESIGN (chemical engineering, construction management, environmental design, environmental engineering, landscape architecture/design, paper and pulp science, paper engineering, and survey and mapping technology), HEALTH PROFESSIONS (predentistry, premedicine, and prepharmacy), SOCIAL SCIENCE (prelaw). Engineering, chemistry, and biology are the strongest academically. Environmental and forest biology and environmental studies are the largest.

Required: Students must complete 125 to 130 credit hours for the B.S. (160 for the B.L.A.), including 60 in the major, with a minimum 2.0 GPA. Courses in chemistry, English, math, and botany are required.

Special: Cross-registration is offered with Syracuse University. Co-op programs, internships, and dual options in biology and forestry are available. Study abroad is available in landscape architecture and through Syracuse University. There is a 4+1 engineering program with Syracuse University. There is 1 national honor society and a freshman honors program. All departments have honors programs.

Faculty/Classroom: 82% of faculty are male; 18%, female. All both teach and do research. Graduate students teach 1% of introductory courses. The average class size in a regular course is 25.

Admissions: 63% of recent applicants were accepted.

Requirements: The SAT or ACT is required. In addition, applicants are required to have a minimum of 3 years of math and science, including chemistry, in a college preparatory curriculum. An essay is required and an interview, letters of recommendation, and a personal portfolio or resume are recommended. A grade average of 85 is required. AP and CLEP credits are accepted. Important factors in the admissions decision are advanced placement or honor courses, leadership record, and extra-curricular activities record.

Procedure: Freshmen are admitted fall and spring. Entrance exams should be taken by October of the senior year. There are early decision, early admissions, and deferred admissions plans. There is a rolling admissions plan. A waiting list is an active part of the admissions procedure. Applications are accepted on-line.

Transfer: Transfer requirements vary by major. Students must successfully complete prerequisite course work and must have a 2.0 or higher GPA to be considered. 24 of 125 credits required for the bachelor's degree must be completed at ESF.

Visiting: There are regularly scheduled orientations for prospective students, including a fall open house, which provides campus tours, faculty sessions, an activities fair, and student affairs presentations. There are guides for informal visits and visitors may sit in on classes. To schedule a visit, contact the Admissions Office.

Financial Aid: In a recent year, 80% of all full-time freshmen and 85% of continuing full-time students received some form of financial aid. 80% of all full-time students received need-based aid. The average freshman award was $6425. Need-based scholarships or need-based grants averaged $1400 ($3000 maximum); need-based self-help aid (loans and jobs) averaged $4125 (maximum); and other non-need-based awards and non-need-based scholarships averaged $4350 (maximum). 75% of undergraduates work part time. Average annual earnings from campus work are $1200. The average financial indebtedness of a recent graduate was $18,800. ESF is a member of CSS. The FAFSA is required. Check with the school for current deadlines.

International Students: Students must take the TOEFL and also take the SAT or the ACT.

Computers: All students may access the system any time. There are no time limits and no fees.

Graduates: In a recent year, 281 bachelor's degrees were awarded. The most popular majors were environmental and forest biology (38%), environmental studies (19%), and resource management (9%). In an average class, 1% graduate in 3 years or less, 47% graduate in 4 years or less, 68% graduate in 5 years or less, and 69% graduate in 6 years or less. 40 companies recruited on campus in a recent year. Of a recent graduating class, 25% were enrolled in graduate school within 6 months of graduation and 60% were employed.

Admissions Contact: Susan H. Sanford, Director of Admissions and Inter-Institutional Relations. A video is available.
E-mail: *esfinfo@esf.edu* Web: *www.esf.edu/admissions/htm*

STATE UNIVERSITY OF NEW YORK/COLLEGE OF TECHNOLOGY AT ALFRED — B-4

Alfred, NY 14802

(607) 587-4215
(800) 4-ALFRED; Fax: (607) 587-4299

Full-time: 2200 men, 900 women	Faculty: 161; III, -$
Part-time: 100 men, 300 women	Ph.D.s: 14%
Graduate: none	Student/Faculty: 19 to 1
Year: semesters, summer session	Tuition: $6000 ($12,000)
Application Deadline: open	Room & Board: $8000
Freshman Class: n/av	
SAT or ACT: required	COMPETITIVE

The State University of New York/College of Technology at Alfred, founded in 1908, is a public institution conferring associate and bachelor's degrees. There are 3 undergraduate schools. Figures in the above capsule and in this profile are approximate. In addition to regional accreditation, Alfred State College has baccalaureate program accreditation with ABET. The 2 libraries contain 71,243 volumes, 594 microform items, and 8148 audio/video tapes/CDs/DVDs, and subscribe to 448 periodicals including electronic. Computerized library services include the card catalog, interlibrary loans, and database searching. Special learning facilities include a learning resource center and radio station. The 150-acre campus is in a rural area 15 miles north of Pennsylvania, 75 miles south of Rochester, and 90 miles southeast of Buffalo. Including any residence halls, there are 48 buildings.

Student Life: 99% of undergraduates are from New York. Others are from 7 states, 5 foreign countries, and Canada. 89% are white. 34% are

Catholic; 30% Protestant; 27% claim no religious affiliation; 8% Buddhist, Hindu, and Muslim. The average age of freshmen is 18; all undergraduates, 19. 52% of freshmen remain to graduate.

Housing: 2407 students can be accommodated in college housing, which includes coed dorms. In addition, there are honors houses, special-interest houses, and wellness, computerized, and adult housing. On-campus housing is guaranteed for all 4 years. 70% of students live on campus; of those, 50% remain on campus on weekends. Alcohol is not permitted. All students may keep cars.

Activities: There are 3 local fraternities and 4 local sororities. There are 62 groups on campus, including band, cheerleading, choir, chorale, computers, drama, ethnic, gay, honors, international, jazz band, karate, literary magazine, musical theater, newspaper, peer education network, pep band, professional, radio and TV, rescue and response team, social, social service, student government, and yearbook. Popular campus events include Family Weekend and Hot Dog Day.

Sports: There are 10 intercollegiate sports for men and 8 for women, and 26 intramural sports for men and 23 for women. Facilities include a fitness center/weight room, an indoor swimming pool, a wrestling room, a full gym, tennis courts, an outdoor track, baseball and softball fields, and practice fields.

Disabled Students: All of the campus is accessible. Wheelchair ramps, elevators, special parking, specially equipped rest rooms, special class scheduling, lowered drinking fountains, lowered telephones, and special housing are available.

Services: Counseling and information services are available, as is tutoring in most subjects. There is a reader service for the blind, and remedial math, reading, and writing.

Campus Safety and Security: Measures include 24-hour foot and vehicle patrol, self-defense education, security escort services, and shuttle buses. There are informal discussions, pamphlets/posters/films, emergency telephones, and lighted pathways/sidewalks.

Programs of Study: Alfred State College confers B.S., B.B.A., and B.T. degrees. Associate degrees are also awarded. Bachelor's degrees are awarded in COMPUTER AND PHYSICAL SCIENCE (information sciences and systems and web services), ENGINEERING AND ENVIRONMENTAL DESIGN (architectural technology, computer technology, construction management, electrical/electronics engineering technology, electromechanical technology, mechanical engineering technology, and survey and mapping technology). Engineering programs are the strongest academically and the largest.

Required: To graduate, candidates for a bachelor's degree must complete a total of 120 credits. A core sequence, including courses in math, physical sciences, and liberal studies, and a year-long senior technical project, are required. A phys ed course is also required.

Special: Cross-registration is offered with Alfred University, Houghton College, Rochester area colleges, and the Western New York Consortium. On-campus work-study programs are available, as are summer internships. There are 2 national honor societies, a freshman honors program, and 52 departmental honors programs.

Faculty/Classroom: 66% of faculty are male; 34%, female. All teach undergraduates. The average class size in an introductory lecture is 40; in a laboratory, 20; and in a regular course, 20.

Admissions: 59% of recent applicants were accepted. 10 freshmen graduated first in their class in a recent year.

Requirements: The SAT or ACT is required. In addition, applicants must have graduated from an accredited secondary school or earned a GED. Specific course requirements vary by curriculum. A portfolio is required for applicants interested in computer art and design. A GPA of 3.0 is required. AP and CLEP credits are accepted. Important factors in the admissions decision are recommendations by school officials, advanced placement or honor courses, and leadership record.

Procedure: Freshmen are admitted fall and spring. Application deadlines are open. Check with the school for current application deadlines and fee. Applications are accepted on-line.

Transfer: 226 transfer students enrolled in a recent year. Transfer applicants must have a minimum 2.4 GPA. 30 of 120 credits required for the bachelor's degree must be completed at Alfred State College.

Visiting: There are regularly scheduled orientations for prospective students, including open houses during the fall and spring semesters. All aspects of the campus are open for visitation. There are guides for informal visits and visitors may sit in on classes and stay overnight. To schedule a visit, contact the Admissions Office.

Financial Aid: The FAFSA is required. Check with the school for current deadlines.

International Students: Students must take the TOEFL.

Computers: All students may access the system 24 hours a day. There are no time limits and no fees.

Admissions Contact: Deborah Goodrich, Director of Admissions and Enrollment Management. E-mail: *alfredstate.edu*
Web: *www.alfredstate.edu*

STATE UNIVERSITY OF NEW YORK/EMPIRE STATE COLLEGE D-3

Saratoga Springs, NY 12866-4390   **(518) 587-2100, ext. 2223**
(800) 847-3000, ext. 223; Fax: (518) 580-0105

Full-time: 1021 men, 2168 women	**Faculty:** IIB, -$
Part-time: 2840 men, 3493 women	**Ph.D.s:** 91%
Graduate: 189 men, 285 women	**Student/Faculty:** n/av
Year: trimesters	**Tuition:** $4575 ($10,835)
Application Deadline: see profile	**Room & Board:** n/app
Freshman Class: n/av	
SAT or ACT: not required	**SPECIAL**

Empire State College, founded in 1971, part of the State University of New York, offers degree programs in the arts and science through its statewide network of regional centers and units.The needs of adult learners are met through guided independent study, distance learning, study groups, cross-registration, and credit for lifelong learning. Administration and coordination is based at the center in Saratoga Springs.Web-based on-line library resources are available at ww.esc.edu/Library. Computerized library services include the card catalog, interlibrary loans, and database searching. Special learning facilities include a learning resource center and a technology building.
Student Life: 90% of undergraduates are from New York. Others are from 50 states, 35 foreign countries, and Canada. 62% are white; 12% African American. The average age of all undergraduates is 36.
Housing: There are no residence halls. All students commute. Alcohol is not permitted.
Activities: There are 2 groups on campus, including literary magazine and student government. Regional centers sponsor events and outside speakers throughout the year.
Sports: There is no sports program at Empire State College.
Disabled Students: 85% of the campus is accessible.
Programs of Study: Empire State College confers B.A., B.S., and B.P.S. degrees. Associate and master's degrees are also awarded. Bachelor's degrees are awarded in BUSINESS (business administration and management, labor studies, and management science), COMPUTER AND PHYSICAL SCIENCE (mathematics and science), EDUCATION (education), SOCIAL SCIENCE (community services, economics, history, human development, humanities and social science, interdisciplinary studies, liberal arts/general studies, and sociology). Business, management, and economics are the largest.
Required: Students must earn 128 credits, including 24 in their major and 30 credits that meet SUNY general education requirements, to graduate. Degree programs are customized and will vary in content.
Special: Empire State College offers cross-registration with numerous consortia and institutions in New York, internships in government, business, nonprofits, and academia, and study abroad in Athens, Thessalonika, Prague, Tirana (Albania), Turkey, and Cyprus. Accelerated degrees and dual and student-designed majors are possible in all programs. Nondegree study and credit for life, military, and work experience is possible.
Faculty/Classroom: 50% of faculty are male; 50%, female. 99% teach undergraduates and 1% both teach and do research. No introductory courses are taught by graduate students.
Requirements: In addition, applicants must be high school graduates, have a GED, or show ability to succeed at the college level. Empire State College also considers the ability of a learning location to meet individual needs. AP and CLEP credits are accepted. Important factors in the admissions decision are recommendations by school officials and personality/intangible qualities.
Procedure: Freshmen are admitted to all sessions. There is a rolling admissions plan. Entrance exams should be taken. Check with the school for current deadlines. Notification is sent on a rolling basis. Applications are accepted on-line.
Transfer: 3601 transfer students enrolled in 2004-2005. Empire State College offers maximum flexibility to transfer applicants, who must provide official transcripts from previous colleges attended. 32 of 128 credits required for the bachelor's degree must be completed at Empire State College.
Visiting: There are regularly scheduled orientations for prospective students, by invitation, after students attend an information session. There are guides for informal visits. To schedule a visit, contact Melanie Kaiser at (518) 587-2100, ext. 2447 or Melanie.Kaiser@esc.edu.
Financial Aid: The FAFSA is required.
International Students: There are 17 international students enrolled. They must take the TOEFL.
Computers: Students can access college resources and their student records via the college web site. All students may access the system 24 hours a day. There are no time limits and no fees. It is strongly recommended that all students have a personal computer.
Graduates: From July 1, 2004 to June 30, 2005, 1914 bachelor's degrees were awarded. The most popular majors were business, management, and economics (39%), community and human services (20%),

and interdisciplinary studies (7%). In an average class, 41% graduate in 3 years or less, 48% graduate in 4 years or less, 50% graduate in 5 years or less, and 52% graduate in 6 years or less.
Admissions Contact: Jennifer Riley, Assistant Director of Admissions. A video is available. E-mail: admissions@esc.edu Web: www.esc.edu

STATE UNIVERSITY OF NEW YORK/FASHION INSTITUTE OF TECHNOLOGY
(See Fashion Institute of Technology/State University of New York)

STATE UNIVERSITY OF NEW YORK/INSTITUTE OF TECHNOLOGY

Utica, NY 13504   **(315) 792-7500**
1-866-2SUNYIT; Fax: (315) 792-7837

Full-time: 790 men, 451 women	**Faculty:** n/av
Part-time: 234 men, 544 women	**Ph.D.s:** n/av
Graduate: 289 men, 282 women	**Student/Faculty:** n/av
Year: semesters, summer session	**Tuition:** $5285 ($11,545)
Application Deadline: March 1	**Room & Board:** $7290
Freshman Class: 1015 applied, 428 accepted, 159 enrolled	
SAT Verbal/Math: 535/590*	**ACT:** 23 **VERY COMPETITIVE**

The State University of New York/Institute of Technology, founded in 1966, is a public institution offering programs in technology and professional studies. There are 4 undergraduate schools. In addition to regional accreditation, SUNYIT has baccalaureate program accreditation with ABET, CAAHEP, and CCNE. Computerized library services include interlibrary loans, database searching, Internet access, and laptop Internet portals. Special learning facilities include a learning resource center, art gallery, and TV station. The 850-acre campus is in a suburban area. At the western end of the Mohawk Valley, Utica is the natural gateway to the Adirondack Mountains and the Thous and Islands. Including any residence halls, there are 7 buildings.
Student Life: 98% of undergraduates are from New York. Students are from 7 states, 13 foreign countries, and Canada. 86% are white. The average age of freshmen is 18; all undergraduates, 22. 17% do not continue beyond their first year.
Housing: 584 students can be accommodated in college housing, which includes coed dorms. In addition, there are special-interest houses. On-campus housing is guaranteed for all 4 years. 76% of students commute. All students may keep cars.
Activities: There are no fraternities or sororities. There are more than 30 groups on campus, including computers, ethnic, film, international, jazz band, newspaper, professional, radio and TV, and yearbook.
Sports: There are 5 intercollegiate sports for men and 5 for women, and 10 intramural sports for men and 1 for women. Facilities include indoor and outdoor facilities, fitness center, pool, fitness trail, outside fields, and a gym with indoor track.
Disabled Students: 99% of the campus is accessible. Wheelchair ramps, elevators, special parking, specially equipped rest rooms, lowered drinking fountains, lowered telephones, and special housing are available.
Services: Counseling and information services are available, as is tutoring in most subjects. There is remedial math, reading, and writing.
Campus Safety and Security: Measures include 24-hour foot and vehicle patrol, self-defense education, security escort services, and shuttle buses. There are informal discussions, pamphlets/posters/films, emergency telephones, and lighted pathways/sidewalks.
Programs of Study: SUNYIT confers B.A., B.S., B.B.A., B.P.S. degrees. Master's degrees are also awarded. Bachelor's degrees are awarded in BUSINESS (accounting, banking and finance, and business administration and management), COMMUNICATIONS AND THE ARTS (communications technology and telecommunications), COMPUTER AND PHYSICAL SCIENCE (applied mathematics, computer science, and computer security and information assurance), ENGINEERING AND ENVIRONMENTAL DESIGN (civil engineering technology, computer technology, electrical/electronics engineering, electrical/electronics engineering technology, industrial engineering, and mechanical engineering technology), HEALTH PROFESSIONS (health, health care administration, and nursing), SOCIAL SCIENCE (liberal arts/general studies, psychology, and sociology).
Required: Students must meet general education requirements and complete 124 to 128 credit hours to graduate.
Special: SUNYIT offers cross-registration with the Mohawk Valley Consortium, internships, and work study. An accelerated degree program in nursing and computer information science is possible, and there is a joint program in electrical engineering with Binghamton University. There are 3 national honor societies.
Faculty/Classroom: 65% of faculty are male; 35%, female. The average class size in an introductory lecture is 23 and in a regular course, 18.
Admissions: 42% of the 2005-2006 applicants were accepted. The SAT scores for the 2005-2006 freshman class were: Verbal--24% below

500, 53% between 500 and 599, 23% between 600 and 700, and 1% above 700; Math--5% below 500, 49% between 500 and 599, 42% between 600 and 700, and 4% above 700. The ACT scores were 21% below 21, 60% between 21 and 23, and 40% between 24 and 26.

Requirements: The SAT or ACT is required. The ACT Optional Writing test is also recommended. In addition, test scores, essay and supplemental application are required. AP and CLEP credits are accepted. Important factors in the admissions decision are advanced placement or honor courses, recommendations by school officials, and extracurricular activities record.

Procedure: Freshmen are admitted fall and spring. Entrance exams should be taken prior to applying. There are early decision and rolling admissions plans. Early decision applications should be filed by December 1; regular applications, by March 1 for fall entry, along with a $40 fee. Notification of early decision is sent December 15; regular decision, January 15. 22 early decision candidates were accepted for the 2005-2006 class.

Transfer: 455 transfer students enrolled in 2004-2005. A G.P.A. greater than 2.5 plus G.P.A. is required, but generally students between 2.0 - 2.5 are considered on a case by case basis and may require an interview. 30 of 124 to 128 credits required for the bachelor's degree must be completed at SUNYIT, and students must complete a 30hour residency requirement.

Visiting: There are regularly scheduled orientations for prospective students. There are guides for informal visits and visitors may sit in on classes and stay overnight. To schedule a visit, contact the Admissions Office at 315-792-7500 or 1-866-2SUNYIT or *admissions@sunyit.edu.*

Financial Aid: In 2005-2006, 85% of all full-time freshmen and 63% of continuing full-time students received some form of financial aid. 65% of full-time freshmen and 55% of continuing full-time students received need-based aid. Need-based scholarships or need-based grants averaged $4886 ($9900 maximum); need-based self-help aid (loans and jobs) averaged $1904 ($8125 maximum); and other non-need-based awards and non-need-based scholarships averaged $2900 ($4500 maximum). The average financial indebtedness of the 2005 graduate was $15,900. The FAFSA, the state aid form and the college's own financial statement are required.

International Students: The school actively recruits these students. They must satisfactory score is required on the written TOEFL. First-time, full-time students must take the SAT or the ACT.

Computers: There are 120 computers across 8 labs with Internet access that all students may use. There are 290 PCs across 19 special purpose labs that are available to students of specific majors or enrolled in specific courses. Four of those labs (70 PCs) are not networked by design. All students may access the system. There are no time limits. The technology fee is $125 per semester. SUNTIT recommends the Dell Dimension 4700 (desktop) or the Dell Inspiration 600m (laptop).

Graduates: From July 1, 2004 to June 30, 2005, 457 bachelor's degrees were awarded. The most popular majors were business and public management (18%), computer 7 information systems (13%), and nursing (9%). 72 companies recruited on campus in 2004-2005. Of the 2004 graduating class, 7% were enrolled in graduate school within 6 months of graduation and 86% were employed.

Admissions Contact: Marybeth Lyons, Director of Admissions. E-mail: *admissions@sunyit.edu* Web: *www.sunyit.edu*

STATE UNIVERSITY OF NEW YORK/MARITIME COLLEGE
D-5

Throggs Neck, NY 10465   **(718) 409-7221**
(800) 642-1874 (Northeast only); Fax: (718) 409-7465

Full-time: 985 men, 122 women	Faculty: IIA, -$
Part-time: 37 men, 6 women	Ph.D.s: 41%
Graduate: 121 men, 23 women	Student/Faculty: n/av
Year: semesters, summer session	Tuition: $4475 ($10,735)
Application Deadline: open	Room & Board: $8000
Freshman Class: 1097 applied, 773 accepted, 340 enrolled	
SAT Verbal/Math: 520/560*	ACT: 21 COMPETITIVE

The Maritime College of the State University of New York, founded in 1874, is a public institution that prepares students for the U.S. Merchant Marine officers' license and for bachelor's degrees in engineering, naval architecture, marine environmental science, and marine transportation/business administration. In addition to regional accreditation, New York Maritime has baccalaureate program accreditation with ABET. The library contains 81,386 volumes, 12,923 microform items, and 3025 audio/video tapes/CDs/DVDs, and subscribes to 333 periodicals including electronic. Computerized library services include interlibrary loans and database searching. Special learning facilities include a learning resource center, planetarium, a 17,000-ton training ship, a tug, a barge, and a center for simulated marine operations, which contains bridge, radar, tanker, and oil spill response simulators. The 55-acre campus is in a suburban area on the Throg's Neck peninsula where Long Island Sound meets the East River. Including any residence halls, there are 27 buildings.

Student Life: 72% of undergraduates are from New York. Others are from 23 states and 15 foreign countries. 57% are from public schools. 78% are white. The average age of freshmen is 18; all undergraduates, 20. 12% do not continue beyond their first year; 62% remain to graduate.

Housing: 800 students can be accommodated in college housing, which includes single-sex and coed dorms. On-campus housing is guaranteed for all 4 years. 97% of students live on campus; of those, 65% remain on campus on weekends. Alcohol is not permitted. Upperclassmen may keep cars.

Activities: There are no fraternities or sororities. There are 38 groups on campus, including art, bagpipe band, band, cheerleading, chess, chorus, computers, drill team, ethnic, honors, international, jazz band, marching band, newspaper, photography, political, professional, religious, social, social service, and student government. Popular campus events include spring formal, Friday night mixers, and Admiral's Ball.

Sports: There are 12 intercollegiate sports for men and 8 for women, and 6 intramural sports for men and 4 for women. Facilities include an athletic center containing a 2000-seat gym, a swimming pool, exercise and weight rooms, a rifle and pistol range, and 3 handball/racquetball and squash courts; a sailing center; and football, baseball, lacrosse, and soccer fields.

Disabled Students: 90% of the campus is accessible. Wheelchair ramps, elevators, special parking, and specially equipped rest rooms are available.

Services: Counseling and information services are available, as is tutoring in every subject.

Campus Safety and Security: Measures include 24-hour foot and vehicle patrol, informal discussions, emergency telephones, and lighted pathways/sidewalks.

Programs of Study: New York Maritime confers B.S. and B.E. degrees. Associate and master's degrees are also awarded. Bachelor's degrees are awarded in BIOLOGICAL SCIENCE (marine science), BUSINESS (business administration and management and transportation management), COMPUTER AND PHYSICAL SCIENCE (atmospheric sciences and meteorology), ENGINEERING AND ENVIRONMENTAL DESIGN (electrical/electronics engineering, engineering, environmental science, marine engineering, maritime science, and naval architecture and marine engineering), SOCIAL SCIENCE (humanities). Engineering, naval architecture, and marine transportation/business administration are the strongest academically. Marine transportation/business administration is the largest.

Required: Bachelor's degree candidates must earn 160 credit hours, with a GPA of 2.0. Distribution requirements and the number of hours required in the major varies. If pursuing the U.S. Merchant Marine officers' license, all students must spend 3 summer semesters at sea acquiring hands-on experience aboard the college's training vessel.

Special: The college offers co-op programs in engineering, an accelerated degree program in marine transportation/transportation management, and internships as cadet observers aboard commercial ships. There are 2 national honor societies, and 2 departmental honors programs.

Faculty/Classroom: 94% teach undergraduates, 12% do research, and 12% do both. No introductory courses are taught by graduate students. The average class size in an introductory lecture is 25; in a laboratory, 15; and in a regular course, 20.

Admissions: 70% of the 2005-2006 applicants were accepted. The SAT scores for the 2005-2006 freshman class were: Verbal--30% below 500, 56% between 500 and 599, 13% between 600 and 700, and 1% above 700; Math--13% below 500, 56% between 500 and 599, 27% between 600 and 700, and 3% above 700. The ACT scores were 46% below 21, 40% between 21 and 23, 11% between 24 and 26, and 3% between 27 and 28. 23% of the current freshmen were in the top fifth of their class; 57% were in the top two fifths.

Requirements: The SAT is required. In addition, applicants must be high school graduates or hold a GED. 16 Carnegie units are required, including 4 years of English, 3 of math (4 are preferred), and 1 of physics or chemistry. An essay is required and an interview is recommended. A GPA of 85.0 is required. AP and CLEP credits are accepted. Important factors in the admissions decision are advanced placement or honor courses, extracurricular activities record, and leadership record.

Procedure: Freshmen are admitted in the fall. Entrance exams should be taken during the junior or senior year. There are early decision and deferred admissions plans. Application deadlines are open. Applications are accepted on-line.

Transfer: Transfer students must have a 2.5 GPA. All applicants must complete the Indoctrination Program and fulfill degree and license requirements at New York Maritime. All credits required for the bachelor's degree must be completed at New York Maritime.

Visiting: There are regularly scheduled orientations for prospective students, including a tour of the campus and facilities and meetings with faculty and students. There are guides for informal visits and visitors may sit in on classes and stay overnight. To schedule a visit, contact the Admissions Office at *admissions@sunymaritime.edu.*

Financial Aid: The FAFSA and student and parent federal income tax returns are required.

International Students: The school actively recruits these students. They must score satisfactorily on the TOEFL and also take the SAT or the ACT.

Computers: All students may access the system from 8:30 A.M. to 11 P.M. The computer center stays open after 11 P.M. when there is sufficient demand. There are no time limits and no fees.

Admissions Contact: Tara Fay, Senior Associate Director of Admissions. E-mail: *sunymaritime.edu* Web: *www.sunymaritime.edu*

STATE UNIVERSITY OF NEW YORK/UNIVERSITY AT ALBANY   D-3

Albany, NY 12222	(518) 442-5435; Fax: (518) 442-5383
Full-time: 5570 men, 5641 women	Faculty: 578; I, -$
Part-time: 387 men, 415 women	Ph.D.s: 97%
Graduate: 1922 men, 3105 women	Student/Faculty: 19 to 1
Year: semesters, summer session	Tuition: $5810 ($11,760)
Application Deadline: March 1	Room & Board: $8050
Freshman Class: 16,725 applied, 10,461 accepted, 2560 enrolled	
SAT Verbal/Math: 560/570*	VERY COMPETITIVE

The State University of New York/University at Albany, established in 1844, is a public institution conferring undergraduate degrees in humanities and fine arts, science and math, social and behavioral sciences, business, public policy, education, and social welfare. There are 7 undergraduate and 9 graduate schools. In addition to regional accreditation, University at Albany has baccalaureate program accreditation with AACSB, ALA, APA, and CSWE. The 3 libraries contain 2,064,576 volumes, 2,860,553 microform items, and 15,111 audio/video tapes/CDs/DVDs. Computerized library services include the card catalog, interlibrary loans, database searching, and Internet access. Special learning facilities include a learning resource center, art gallery, radio station, a linear accelerator, a sophisticated weather data system, a national lightning detection system, an interactive media center, extensive art studios, and a state-of-the-art electronic library. The 795-acre campus is in a suburban area about 5 miles west of downtown Albany. Including any residence halls, there are 166 buildings.

Student Life: 94% of undergraduates are from New York. Others are from 37 states, 51 foreign countries, and Canada. 60% are white. The average age of freshmen is 18; all undergraduates, 21. 15% do not continue beyond their first year; 63% remain to graduate.

Housing: 7400 students can be accommodated in college housing, which includes single-sex and coed dorms, on-campus apartments, and married-student housing. In addition, there are honors houses and special-interest houses. On-campus housing is available on a first-come, first-served basis and is available on a lottery system for upperclassmen. Priority is given to out-of-town students. 54% of students live on campus. Alcohol is not permitted. Upperclassmen may keep cars.

Activities: 2% of men belong to 1 local and 10 national fraternities; 5% of women belong to 3 local and 15 national sororities. There are 160 groups on campus, including band, chamber singers, cheerleading, chess, chorale, college-sponsored electronic music ensemble, computers, dance, debate, drama, ethnic, gay, honors, international, jazz band, literary magazine, newspaper, orchestra, pep band, percussion ensemble, photography, political, professional, radio and TV, religious, social, social service, student government, symphony, and yearbook. Popular campus events include outdoor concerts, Springtime Fountain Festival, and fall semester "Clash of the Quads."

Sports: There are 8 intercollegiate sports for men and 11 for women, and 13 intramural sports for men and 9 for women. Facilities include a gym with an Olympic-size pool; an ancillary gym with a quarter-mile track; football, softball, soccer, and practice fields; and a 5000-seat recreation and convocation center.

Disabled Students: 99% of the campus is accessible. Wheelchair ramps, elevators, special parking, specially equipped rest rooms, lowered drinking fountains, and lowered telephones are available. Disabled Student Services provides a broad range of personalized services to people with disabilities including preadmission information and accessible housing information.

Services: Counseling and information services are available, as is tutoring in most subjects. There is a reader service for the blind, and remedial math, reading, and writing. The Excel program provides low-income and first-generation college students with a variety of mentoring, tutorial, and counseling services.

Campus Safety and Security: Measures include 24-hour foot and vehicle patrol, self-defense education, security escort services, and shuttle buses. There are informal discussions, pamphlets/posters/films, emergency telephones, and lighted pathways/sidewalks.

Programs of Study: University at Albany confers B.A. and B.S. degrees. Master's and doctoral degrees are also awarded. Bachelor's degrees are awarded in BIOLOGICAL SCIENCE (biochemistry, biology/ biological science, and molecular biology), BUSINESS (accounting and business administration and management), COMMUNICATIONS AND THE ARTS (art history and appreciation, Chinese, communications, dramatic arts, English, fine arts, French, Hebrew, Italian, Latin, linguistics, music, Russian, and Spanish), COMPUTER AND PHYSICAL SCIENCE (actuarial science, applied mathematics, atmospheric sciences and meteorology, chemistry, computer science, earth science, geology, information sciences and systems, mathematics, and physics), EDUCATION (English, foreign languages, mathematics, science, secondary, and social studies), ENGINEERING AND ENVIRONMENTAL DESIGN (urban design), HEALTH PROFESSIONS (medical laboratory technology, predentistry, and premedicine), SOCIAL SCIENCE (African American studies, anthropology, Asian/Oriental studies, Caribbean studies, classical/ancient civilization, criminal justice, Eastern European studies, economics, geography, Hispanic American studies, history, Latin American studies, medieval studies, philosophy, political science/government, prelaw, psychology, religion, Russian and Slavic studies, social work, sociology, and women's studies). Criminal justice, information technology, and public administration and policy are the strongest academically. Psychology, English, and business are the largest.

Required: To graduate, students must complete a total of 120 credits with a 2.0 GPA in their major and minor, including 30 to 36 credits required in the major for a B.A. degree and 30 to 42 credits for a B.S. degree. B.A. degree candidates must complete 90 credits in liberal arts courses and B.S. candidates must complete 60. The General Education Program at the University at Albany consists of a minimum of 30 credits of coursework in the following areas: disciplinary perspectives, cultural and historical perspectives, and communication and reasoning competencies.

Special: Cross-registration is available with Rensselaer Polytechnic Institute, Albany Law School, and Union, Siena, and Russell Sage Colleges. Internships may be arranged with state government agencies and private organizations. Study abroad in many countries, a Washington semester, B.A.-B.S. degrees, and work-study programs are offered. Dual and student-designed majors, nondegree study, and pass/fail grading options are available. A 3-2 engineering degree with 1 of 4 institutions is also possible. There are 15 national honor societies, including Phi Beta Kappa, and a freshman honors program. All departments have honors programs.

Faculty/Classroom: 60% of faculty are male; 40%, female. 91% teach undergraduates and 75% do research. The average class size in an introductory lecture is 30; in a laboratory, 16; and in a regular course, 30.

Admissions: 63% of the 2005-2006 applicants were accepted. The SAT scores for the 2005-2006 freshman class were: Verbal--12% below 500, 61% between 500 and 599, 24% between 600 and 700, and 3% above 700; Math--4% below 500, 58% between 500 and 599, 35% between 600 and 700, and 3% above 700. 36% of the current freshmen were in the top fifth of their class; 75% were in the top two fifths. 11 freshmen graduated first in their class.

Requirements: The SAT is required. The SAT is preferred, but the ACT accepted. Applicants must be graduates of an accredited secondary school or have a GED. 18 academic credits are required, including 2 to 3 units of math and 2 units of lab sciences. Foreign language study is also recommended. AP and CLEP credits are accepted. Important factors in the admissions decision are advanced placement or honor courses, personality/intangible qualities, and leadership record.

Procedure: Freshmen are admitted fall, spring, and summer. Entrance exams should be taken by November of the senior year. There are early decision, deferred admissions, and rolling admissions plans. Early decision applications should be filed by November 15; regular applications, by March 1 for fall entry, December 1 for spring entry, and May 1 for summer entry, along with a $40 fee. Notification of early decision is sent January 1; regular decision, on a rolling basis. A waiting list is an active part of the admissions procedure. Applications are accepted on-line.

Transfer: 2561 transfer students enrolled in 2004-2005. Admission to certain programs is competitive and based not only on a required GPA, but also on completion of a certain set of prerequisite core courses. A grade average of B or better is required for applicants to the accounting, business administration, criminal justice, and social welfare programs. 30 of 120 credits required for the bachelor's degree must be completed at University at Albany.

Visiting: There are regularly scheduled orientations for prospective students, including a 2-day summer orientation session. There are guides for informal visits and visitors may sit in on classes. To schedule a visit, contact the Undergraduate Admissions Office at *campusvisit@albany.edu.*

Financial Aid: In 2005-2006, 65% of all full-time freshmen and 62% of continuing full-time students received some form of financial aid. 54% of all full-time students received need-based aid. The average freshman award was $8071. Need-based scholarships or need-based grants averaged $4728; need-based self-help aid (loans and jobs) averaged $3999; and non-need-based athletic scholarships averaged $12,862. 25% of undergraduates work part time. The average financial indebtedness of the 2005 graduate was $16,700. The FAFSA is required; NY State residents should apply for TAP on-line at http://www.tapweb.org. The deadline for filing freshman financial aid applications for fall entry is April 15.

International Students: There are 211 international students enrolled. The school actively recruits these students. A satisfactory score is required on the written TOEFL. International students may submit either their SAT or TOEFL results.

Computers: Wireless access is available. High speed Internet connections are available in dorm rooms and wireless connections are available in select locations. Students without a wireless network interface card (NIC) can check one out at the circulation desk for use in the library. All students may access the system. There are no time limits and no fees.

Graduates: From July 1, 2004 to June 30, 2005, 2675 bachelor's degrees were awarded. The most popular majors were psychology (14%), business (14%), and English (10%). In an average class, 52% graduate in 4 years or less, 60% graduate in 5 years or less, and 63% graduate in 6 months or less. 180 companies recruited on campus in 2004-2005. Of the 2004 graduating class, 33% were enrolled in graduate school within 6 months of graduation and 59% were employed.

Admissions Contact: Robert Andrea, Director, Undergraduate Admissions. An on-line tour is available at the University of Albany website. E-mail: *ugadmissions@albany.edu* Web: *www.albany.edu*

STATE UNIVERSITY OF NEW YORK/UNIVERSITY AT BINGHAMTON   C-4

Binghamton, NY 13902-6000

(607) 777-2171
Fax: (607) 777-4445

Full-time: 5584 men, 5150 women	**Faculty:** 537; I, -$
Part-time: 228 men, 212 women	**Ph.Ds:** 93%
Graduate: 1420 men, 1424 women	**Student/Faculty:** 20 to 1
Year: semesters, summer session	**Tuition:** $5838 ($12,098)
Application Deadline: January 15	**Room & Board:** $8150
Freshman Class: 21,658 applied, 9285 accepted, 2079 enrolled	
SAT Verbal/Math: 620/650*	**ACT:** 27 **HIGHLY COMPETITIVE**

State University of New York/University at Binghamton, founded in 1946, is part of the State University of New York System. The public institution offers programs through the Harpur College of Arts and Sciences, the Schools of Education and Human Development, Nursing, and Management, and the Watson School of Engineering and Applied Science. There are 5 undergraduate schools and 1 graduate school. In addition to regional accreditation, Binghamton University has baccalaureate program accreditation with AACSB, ABET, APA, CCNE, CSAB, NASM, and TEAC. . The 2 libraries contain 2,285,885 volumes, 1,859,740 microform items, and 123,451 audio/video tapes/CDs/DVDs, and subscribe to 36,431 periodicals including electronic. Computerized library services include the card catalog, interlibrary loans, database searching, Internet access, and laptop Internet portals. Special learning facilities include a learning resource center, art gallery, radio station, TV station, nature preserve, and 4-climate greenhouse. The 887-acre campus is in a suburban area 1 mile west of Binghamton. Including any residence halls, there are 123 buildings.

Student Life: 92% of undergraduates are from New York. Others are from 38 states, 66 foreign countries, and Canada. 87% are from public schools. 61% are white; 18% Asian American. 29% are Catholic; 24% claim no religious affiliation; 22% Jewish; 19% Protestant. The average age of freshmen is 18; all undergraduates, 20. 10% do not continue beyond their first year; 79% remain to graduate.

Housing: 6504 students can be accommodated in college housing, which includes coed dorms, on-campus apartments, and married-student housing. In addition, there are special-interest houses and chemical-and smoke-free housing. On-campus housing is available on a lottery system for upperclassmen. 58% of students live on campus; of those, 95% remain on campus on weekends. Upperclassmen may keep cars.

Activities: 8% of men belong to 1 local and 19 national fraternities; 9% of women belong to 15 national sororities. There are more than 200 groups on campus, including art, band, cheerleading, chess, choir, chorale, chorus, computers, cultural, dance, debate, drama, ethnic, film, gay, honors, international, jazz band, literary magazine, musical theater, newspaper, opera, orchestra, pep band, photography, political, professional, radio and TV, religious, social, social service, student government, symphony, and yearbook. Popular campus events include Caribbean Carnival, Spring Fling, and University Fest.

Sports: There are 11 intercollegiate sports for men and 10 for women, and 20 intramural sports for men and 18 for women. Facilities include 2 gyms with swimming pools, an indoor track, dance and karate studios, basketball, volleyball, squash, racquetball, and tennis courts, a weight room, batting and driving cages, a cross-country course, a fitness center, a 400-meter track and soccer complex, plus many playing fields. The larger gym seats 2600. An events center contains basketball/tennis courts and a 200-meter indoor track, with seating for 6000 to 8000.

Disabled Students: 90% of the campus is accessible. Wheelchair ramps, elevators, special parking, specially equipped rest rooms, special class scheduling, lowered drinking fountains, lowered telephones, special housing, and a comprehensive array of services for university students with physical, learning, or other disabilities. See (*ssd.Binghamton.edu*).

Services: Counseling and information services are available, as is tutoring in most subjects. There is a reader service for the blind. Some computer-assisted instruction is available, particularly in languages. Peer walk-in tutoring is available 6 days per week.

Campus Safety and Security: Measures include 24-hour foot and vehicle patrol, self-defense education, security escort services, and shuttle buses. There are informal discussions, pamphlets/posters/films, emergency telephones, lighted pathways/sidewalks, police officers, monitored entrance to campus with proper identification between midnight and 5 A.M., keycard entry to residence halls, and formal personal safety programs.

Programs of Study: Binghamton University confers B.A., B.S., B.F.A., and B.Mus. degrees. Master's and doctoral degrees are also awarded. Bachelor's degrees are awarded in BIOLOGICAL SCIENCE (biochemistry and biology/biological science), BUSINESS (accounting and business administration and management), COMMUNICATIONS AND THE ARTS (Arabic, art, art history and appreciation, classics, comparative literature, dramatic arts, English, film arts, fine arts, French, German, Hebrew, Italian, Latin, linguistics, music, music performance, Spanish, speech/debate/rhetoric, and studio art), COMPUTER AND PHYSICAL SCIENCE (actuarial science, chemistry, computer science, geology, information sciences and systems, mathematics, and physics), ENGINEERING AND ENVIRONMENTAL DESIGN (bioengineering, computer engineering, electrical/electronics engineering, environmental science, industrial engineering, mechanical engineering, and systems engineering), HEALTH PROFESSIONS (nursing), SOCIAL SCIENCE (African American studies, anthropology, Asian/American studies, Caribbean studies, classical/ancient civilization, economics, geography, history, human development, interdisciplinary studies, international studies, Judaic studies, Latin American studies, medieval studies, philosophy, political science/government, psychobiology, psychology, and sociology). Accounting and anthropology are the strongest academically. Management, psychology, and English are the largest.

Required: To graduate, all students must complete 120 to 133 credit hours, with 36 to 72 in the major and a minimum GPA of 2.0. General education requirements over the first 2 years include courses in language and communication, global vision, science and math, aesthetic perspective, physical activity/wellness, and identity. Other requirements vary by school.

Special: The university offers innovative study through the Innovational Projects Board, internships, study abroad in more than 100 countries, a Washington semester through American University, on- and off-campus work-study programs, and B.A.-B.S. degrees in 28 departments in arts and sciences and in the professional schools. There are also dual and interdisciplinary majors such as philosophy, politics, and law, student-designed majors, pass/fail options, and independent study. Binghamton is also a member of the National Student Exchange and International Student Exchange. There are 20 national honor societies, including Phi Beta Kappa, a freshman honors program, and 32 departmental honors programs.

Faculty/Classroom: 64% of faculty are male; 36%, female. All both teach and do research. Graduate students teach 16% of introductory courses. The average class size in an introductory lecture is 61; in a laboratory, 17; and in a regular course, 29.

Admissions: 43% of the 2005-2006 applicants were accepted. The SAT scores for the 2005-2006 freshman class were: Verbal--5% below 500, 34% between 500 and 599, 49% between 600 and 700, and 12% above 700; Math--1% below 500, 19% between 500 and 599, 56% between 600 and 700, and 24% above 700. The ACT scores were 3% below 21, 12% between 21 and 23, 26% between 24 and 26, 29% between 27 and 28, and 30% above 28. 78% of the current freshmen were in the top fifth of their class; 97% were in the top two fifths. 11 freshmen graduated first in their class.

Requirements: The SAT or ACT is required. In addition, applicants must be graduates of an accredited secondary school, or have a GED certificate, and complete 16 academic credits. These include 4 units of English, 3 units of 1 foreign language or 2 units each of 2 foreign languages, 2.5 of math, and 2 each of science and social studies. Students may submit slides of artwork, request an audition for music, prepare a videotape for dance or theater, or share athletic achievements. An essay is required. AP and CLEP credits are accepted. Important factors in the admissions decision are advanced placement or honor courses, extracurricular activities record, and evidence of special talent.

Procedure: Freshmen are admitted fall and spring. Entrance exams should be taken in the spring of the junior year or the fall of the senior year. There are early action, early admissions, and deferred admissions plans. There is a rolling admissions plan. Early decision applications should be filed by December 1; regular applications, by January 15 (recommended) for fall entry and November for spring entry. The fall 2005 application fee was $40. Notification of early action is sent January 1; regular decision, on a rolling basis. 826 applicants were on the 2005 waiting list; 9 were admitted. Applications are accepted on-line.

Transfer: 768 transfer students enrolled in 2004-2005. Applicants must submit college transcripts; students who wish to transfer after their first year of college must also submit their high school transcripts. 30 of 120 to 133 credits required for the bachelor's degree must be completed at Binghamton University.

Visiting: There are regularly scheduled orientations for prospective students, including an information session and a tour of campus to be scheduled a week in advance of a visit. Visitors may sit in on classes. To schedule a visit, contact the Office of Undergraduate Admissions.

Financial Aid: In 2005-2006, 80% of all full-time freshmen and 68% of continuing full-time students received some form of financial aid. 79% of full-time freshmen and 67% of continuing full-time students received need-based aid. The average freshman award was $15,338. Need-based scholarships or need-based grants averaged $4061 ($20,940 maximum); need-based self-help aid (loans and jobs) averaged $3810 ($20,940 maximum); non-need-based athletic scholarships averaged $8208 ($20,940 maximum); and other non-need-based awards and non-need-based scholarships averaged $11,049 ($20,940 maximum). 13% of undergraduates work part time. Average annual earnings from campus work are $1200. The average financial indebtedness of the 2005 graduate was $15,041. The FAFSA is required. The deadline for filing freshman financial aid applications for fall entry is March 1.

International Students: There are 742 international students enrolled. The school actively recruits these students. They must score satisfactorily on the written TOEFL, which replaces the SAT or ACT for nonnative speakers of English.

Computers: Wireless access is available. Every residence hall room has an Ethernet port per resident. Wireless access is provided in the dining areas of all residence hall communities, throughout one complete residence hall community, throughout most academic buildings, and in the university union and library. There are approximately 600 computers in labs on campus. All students may access the system 24 hours per day. There are no time limits and no fees.

Graduates: From July 1, 2004 to June 30, 2005, 2702 bachelor's degrees were awarded. The most popular majors were management (10%), psychology (10%), and English (10%). In an average class, 2% graduate in 3 years or less, 67% graduate in 4 years or less, 78% graduate in 5 years or less, and 79% graduate in 6 years or less. 116 companies recruited on campus in 2004-2005. Of the 2004 graduating class, 38% were enrolled in graduate school within 6 months of graduation and 82% were employed.

Admissions Contact: Cheryl Brown, Director, Undergraduate Admissions. E-mail: *admit@binghamton.edu* Web: *www.binghamton.edu*

STATE UNIVERSITY OF NEW YORK/UNIVERSITY AT BUFFALO   A-3

Buffalo, NY 14260   (716) 645-6900
                      (888) 822-3648/888-UB-ADMIT; Fax: (716) 645-6498

Full-time: 9116 men, 7795 women	**Faculty:** 966; I, av$
Part-time: 690 men, 564 women	**Ph.D.s:** 97%
Graduate: 4231 men, 4824 women	**Student/Faculty:** 18 to 1
Year: semesters, summer session	**Tuition:** $6068 ($12,328)
Application Deadline: see profile	**Room & Board:** $7626
Freshman Class: 18,391 applied, 10,466 accepted, 3230 enrolled	
SAT Verbal/Math: 570/610*	**ACT:** 26 **VERY COMPETITIVE**

The State University of New York at Buffalo, established in 1846, is a public institution offering more than 300 bachelor's, master's, and doctoral degree programs in the arts and sciences and the professions. UB ia a comprehensive research-extensive university and a primary center for professional education and training. There are 9 undergraduate and 14 graduate schools. In addition to regional accreditation, UB has baccalaureate program accreditation with AACSB, ABA, ABET, ACOTE, ACPE, ADA, ALA, APA, APTA, ASHA, CCNE, CORE, CSWE, JRCN-MT, LCM, NAAB, NAACLS, NASAD and PAB.The 10 libraries contain 3,390,583 volumes, 5,406,498 microform items, and 190,800 audio/video tapes/CDs/DVDs, and subscribe to 34,965 periodicals including electronic. Computerized library services include the card catalog, interlibrary loans, database searching, and Internet access. Special learning facilities include a learning resource center, art gallery, radio station, an earthquake enginering research center, an arts center, a bioinformatics and life sciences center, a document analysis and recognition center,a concert hall, an anthropology research center, a computational research center, a poetry and rare books collection, a virtual site museum, center for engineering design and industrial innovation, an electronic poetry center, and a archeological center. The 1350-acre campus is in a suburban area 3 miles north of Buffalo. Including any residence halls, there are 214 buildings.

Student Life: 90% of undergraduates are from New York. Others are from 41 states, 84 foreign countries, and Canada. 70% are white. The average age of freshmen is 18; all undergraduates, 21. 12% do not continue beyond their first year; 58% remain to graduate.

Housing: 6776 students can be accommodated in college housing, which includes coed dorms, on-campus apartments, and married-student housing. In addition, there are honors houses, special-interest houses, freshman-only housing, and cultural interest housing. On-

campus housing is guaranteed for all 4 years. 60% of students commute. All students may keep cars.

Activities: 3% of men belong to 4 local and 21 national fraternities; 4% of women belong to 6 local and 16 national sororities. There are more than 300 groups on campus, including art, band, cheerleading, chess, choir, chorale, chorus, computers, dance, drama, ethnic, film, gay, honors, international, jazz band, literary magazine, marching band, musical theater, newspaper, orchestra, pep band, photography, political, professional, radio and TV, religious, social, social service, student government, and symphony. Popular campus events include Fall Fest, Spring Fest, and UB Pride Day.

Sports: There are 9 intercollegiate sports for men and 9 for women, and 9 intramural sports for men and 9 for women. Facilities include racquetball, squash, tennis, basketball, volleyball, badminton, and handball courts; baseball, soccer, hockey, and multipurpose fields; a football and track and field stadium; an indoor jogging track; an Olympic-size pool and diving well; a triple gym; weight training and wrestling rooms; dance studios; and a spinning room.

Disabled Students: 90% of the campus is accessible. Wheelchair ramps, elevators, special parking, specially equipped rest rooms, special class scheduling, lowered drinking fountains, lowered telephones, special housing, accessible on-campus transportation, and specially equipped rooms in residence halls are available.

Services: Counseling and information services are available, as is tutoring in most subjects. There is a reader service for the blind, and remedial math, reading, and writing. Peer tutoring and some computer-assisted instruction are also available.

Campus Safety and Security: Measures include 24-hour foot and vehicle patrol, self-defense education, security escort services, and shuttle buses. There are informal discussions, pamphlets/posters/films, emergency telephones, lighted pathways/sidewalks, and an alarm system, after-hours card access to academic facilities, community patrols, a university-wide safety committee.

Programs of Study: UB confers B.A., B.S., B.F.A., B.P.S., and Mus.B. degrees. Master's and doctoral degrees are also awarded. Bachelor's degrees are awarded in BIOLOGICAL SCIENCE (biochemistry, biology/biological science, biophysics, and biotechnology), BUSINESS (business administration and management), COMMUNICATIONS AND THE ARTS (art history and appreciation, classics, communications, dance, dramatic arts, English, fine arts, French, German, Italian, linguistics, media arts, music, music performance, musical theater, Spanish, and studio art), COMPUTER AND PHYSICAL SCIENCE (chemistry, computer science, geology, mathematics, physics, and statistics), ENGINEERING AND ENVIRONMENTAL DESIGN (aeronautical engineering, architectural technology, architecture, chemical engineering, civil engineering, computer engineering, electrical/electronics engineering, engineering physics, environmental design, environmental engineering, industrial engineering, and mechanical engineering), HEALTH PROFESSIONS (exercise science, medical technology, nuclear medical technology, nursing, occupational therapy, pharmacy, physical therapy, and speech pathology/audiology), SOCIAL SCIENCE (African American studies, American studies, anthropology, Asian/Oriental studies, economics, geography, history, philosophy, political science/government, psychology, social science, sociology, and women's studies). Engineering, business administration, and psychology are the largest.

Required: To graduate, students must complete 120 semester hours with a minimum GPA of 2.0. General education requirements include writing skills, mathematical sciences, library skills, world civilizations, American pluralism, natural sciences, language, literature and art, social and behavioral sciences, and depth requirement, The total number of hours in the major vaires.

Special: Students may cross-register with the Western New York Consortium. Internships are available, and students may study abroad in 29 countries. UB offers a Washington semester, work-study programs, accelerated degree programs, B.A.-B.S. degrees, dual, student-designed, and interdisciplinary majors, including biochemical pharmacology and medicinal chemistry, nondegree study, and credit for military experience. A 3-2 engineering degree can be pursued. Students may choose a successful/unsuccessful (S/U) grading option for selected courses. There is an early assurance of admission program to medical school for undergraduate sophomore students who have completed particular science courses with a science and overall GPA of 3.75. There are 30 national honor societies, including Phi Beta Kappa, and a freshman honors program. All departments have honors programs.

Faculty/Classroom: 64% of faculty are male; 36%, female. 80% teach undergraduates, All do research, and 80% do both. Graduate students teach 19% of introductory courses. The average class size in an introductory lecture is 52; in a laboratory, 27; and in a regular course, 37.

Admissions: 57% of the 2005-2006 applicants were accepted. The SAT scores for the 2005-2006 freshman class were: Verbal--9% below 500, 53% between 500 and 599, 34% between 600 and 700, and 4% above 700; Math--2% below 500, 41% between 500 and 599, 50% between 600 and 700, and 7% above 700. The ACT scores were 16% between 21 and 23, 38% between 24 and 26, 17% between 27 and 28, and 29% above 28. 54% of the current freshmen were in the top fifth of their class; 88% were in the top two fifths. 23 freshmen graduated first in their class.

Requirements: The SAT is required. In addition, freshmen are evaluated based on secondary school performance, strength of curriculum, standardized test scores, and, in some cases, a supplemental application. A high school diploma is required and the GED is accepted. Art applicants must submit a portfolio; music applicants must audition. AP and CLEP credits are accepted. Important factors in the admissions decision are advanced placement or honor courses, recommendations by school officials, and evidence of special talent.

Procedure: Freshmen are admitted fall and spring. Entrance exams should be taken during the spring of the junior year or the fall of the senior year. There are early decision, early admissions, and rolling admissions plans. Early decision applications should be filed by November 1. Notification of early decision is sent December 15; regular decision, in January, application fee is $40. 329 early decision candidates were accepted for the 2005-2006 class. 785 applicants were on the 2005 waiting list; 372 were admitted. Applications are accepted on-line.

Transfer: 1628 transfer students enrolled in 2004-2005. Transfer applicants with fewer than 24 credit hours must supply high school transcripts, SAT and/or ACT test scores, and the previous college academic record. It is recommended that sutdents present a strong record of college study, with a 2.5 GPA. Entry at junior level requires a higher GPA for some programs. Credit may be awarded for military experience and other nontraditional background. 30 of 120 credits required for the bachelor's degree must be completed at UB.

Visiting: There are regularly scheduled orientations for prospective students, including the Visit UB program, in which visitors tour the campus and a residence hall as well as attend an information session to learn about application procedures, admissions criteria, housing, financial aid, and scholarship programs. The program is offered, with some exceptions, Monday through Friday year-round and on selected Saturdays during the academic year. Reservations are required. Visitors may sit in on classes. To schedule a visit, contact the Office of Admissions at http://www.buffalo.edu/vub.

Financial Aid: In 2005-2006, 66% of all full-time freshmen and 72% of continuing full-time students received some form of financial aid. 65% of full-time freshmen and 72% of continuing full-time students received need-based aid. The average freshman award was $5902. Need-based scholarships or need-based grants averaged $3310; need-based self-help aid (loans and jobs) averaged $2594; non-need-based athletic scholarships averaged $7385; and other non-need-based awards and non-need-based scholarships averaged $2772. The average financial indebtedness of the 2005 graduate was $17,833. The FAFSA is required. The priority date for freshman financial aid applications for fall entry is March 1.

International Students: There are 1201 international students enrolled. The school actively recruits these students. A satisfactory score is required on the written TOEFL. The SAT or ACT is strongly recommended.

Computers: Wireless access is available. More than 2400 computers and workstations, as well as printers and software tools, are provided in student labs. Residence halls have high speed Internet access. Free e-mail, Internet access, student web page hosting, and software are provided. Learning spaces in the libraries are equipped with technology to enable group/team work and collaborative learning. All students may access the system any time. There are no time limits and no fees. It is strongly recommended that all students have a personal computer.

Graduates: From July 1, 2004 to June 30, 2005, 3674 bachelor's degrees were awarded. The most popular majors were business administration (19%), engineering (11%), and communications and psychology (10%). In an average class, 1% graduate in 3 years or less, 39% graduate in 4 years or less, 55% graduate in 5 years or less, and 59% graduate in 6 years or less. 250 companies recruited on campus in 2004-2005. Of the 2004 graduating class, 65% were employed within 6 months of graduation.

Admissions Contact: Patricia Armstrong, Director of Admissions. E-mail: ubadmissions@buffalo.edu Web: www.buffalo.edu

STATE UNIVERSITY OF NEW YORK/UNIVERSITY AT NEW PALTZ   D-4

New Paltz, NY 12561-2443   (845) 257-3200
(888) 639-7589; Fax: (845) 257-3209

Full-time: 1892 men, 3823 women	Faculty: 295; IIA, -$
Part-time: 224 men, 482 women	Ph.D.s: 84%
Graduate: 453 men, 951 women	Student/Faculty: 19 to 1
Year: semesters, summer session	Tuition: $5260 ($11,520)
Application Deadline: April 1	Room & Board: $7220
Freshman Class: 11,358 applied, 5024 accepted, 1050 enrolled	
SAT Verbal/Math: 545/550*	VERY COMPETITIVE

State University of New York/University at New Paltz, founded in 1828, is a public institution offering undergraduate and graduate programs in the liberal arts and sciences, business, education, engineering, fine and performing arts, and the health professions. There are 5 undergraduate schools and 1 graduate school. In addition to regional accreditation, SUNY New Paltz has baccalaureate program accreditation with ABET, ASLA, CSAB, NASAD, NASM, and NLN. The library contains 525,296 volumes, 1,152,597 microform items, and 3247 audio/video tapes/CDs/DVDs, and subscribes to 1392 periodicals including electronic. Computerized library services include the card catalog, interlibrary loans, and database searching. Special learning facilities include a learning resource center, planetarium, radio station, TV station, greenhouse, robotics lab, electron microscope facility, speech and hearing clinic, art museum, music therapy training facility, observatory, Fournier transform mass spectrometer, honors center, electronic media center, electronic classroom, and an IBM e-business virtual lab. The 216-acre campus is in a small town 100 miles north of New York City and 65 miles south of Albany. Including any residence halls, there are 57 buildings.

Student Life: 91% of undergraduates are from New York. Others are from 32 states, 51 foreign countries, and Canada. 90% are from public schools. 61% are white; 10% Hispanic. The average age of freshmen is 18; all undergraduates, 20. 16% do not continue beyond their first year; 56% remain to graduate.

Housing: 2541 students can be accommodated in college housing, which includes coed dorms. In addition, there are special-interest houses. On-campus housing is guaranteed for the freshman year only and is available on a first-come, first-served basis. Priority is given to out-of-town students. 51% of students live on campus; of those, 90% remain on campus on weekends. Upperclassmen may keep cars.

Activities: 3% of men belong to 5 local and 5 national fraternities; 2% of women belong to 5 local and 9 national sororities. There are 135 groups on campus, including art, band, cheerleading, chess, choir, chorale, chorus, computers, dance, drama, ethnic, gay, honors, international, jazz band, literary magazine, musical theater, newspaper, orchestra, photography, political, professional, radio and TV, religious, social, social service, and student government. Popular campus events include Spirit Weekend, New Paltz Summer Repertory Theater, and Rainbow Month.

Sports: There are 9 intercollegiate sports for men and 11 for women, and 20 intramural sports for men and 15 for women. Facilities include a gym with a swimming pool, numerous playing fields, a 35,000-square-foot air-supported structure for tennis, jogging, volleyball, and basketball, and 24 outdoor tennis courts.

Disabled Students: 90% of the campus is accessible. Wheelchair ramps, elevators, special parking, specially equipped rest rooms, special class scheduling, lowered drinking fountains, lowered telephones, and special housing are available.

Services: Counseling and information services are available, as is tutoring in most subjects. There is a reader service for the blind, and remedial math, reading, and writing.

Campus Safety and Security: Measures include 24-hour foot and vehicle patrol, self-defense education, security escort services, and informal discussions. There are pamphlets/posters/films, emergency telephones, lighted pathways/sidewalks, a bicycle patrol, locked residence halls, and a campus 911 system.

Programs of Study: SUNY New Paltz confers B.A., B.S., B.F.A., B.S.E.E., and B.S.N. degrees. Master's degrees are also awarded. Bachelor's degrees are awarded in BIOLOGICAL SCIENCE (biology/biological science), BUSINESS (accounting, banking and finance, business administration and management, and marketing/retailing/merchandising), COMMUNICATIONS AND THE ARTS (art history and appreciation, broadcasting, communications, design, dramatic arts, English, fine arts, French, German, journalism, music, photography, Spanish, speech/debate/rhetoric, and visual and performing arts), COMPUTER AND PHYSICAL SCIENCE (chemistry, computer science, geology, mathematics, and physics), EDUCATION (art, early childhood, elementary, foreign languages, middle school, science, and secondary), ENGINEERING AND ENVIRONMENTAL DESIGN (computer engineering and electrical/electronics engineering), HEALTH PROFESSIONS (premedicine and speech pathology/audiology), SOCIAL SCIENCE (anthropology, Asian/Oriental studies, economics, geography, history, international relations, Latin American studies, philosophy, political science/government, psychology, social science, sociology, and women's studies). Business, computer science, and math are the strongest academically. Business, visual arts, and elementary education are the largest.

Required: To graduate, students must complete a minimum of 120 credits with a 2.0 GPA. The core curriculum of 16 to 17 credits includes courses in English composition, math and analytical skills, and modern world studies. The number of credits required in the major varies. Other requirements include 42 to 52 credits in general education (cultures and civilizations, American experience, social sciences, physical and biological sciences, foreign languages, aesthetic expression), 1 writing-intensive course in the major, and 60 credits in upper-division courses. New York State Teacher Competency Exams are required of education majors. A thesis is required of engineering and art majors.

Special: There is cross-registration with the Mid-Hudson Consortium of Colleges. The university offers co-op programs and internships in most majors, work-study programs on campus and at the Children's Center of New Paltz, and opportunities for student-designed or dual majors. Students may study abroad in 18 countries. A 3-2 advanced degree in environmental biology is offered with SUNY Environmental Science and Forestry. There are 7-year medical and optometry accelerated degree programs. B.A.-B.S. degrees are offered in liberal arts and science, education, business, engineering, and fine and performing arts. There are 4 national honor societies, a freshman honors program, and 6 departmental honors programs.

Faculty/Classroom: 46% of faculty are male; 54%, female. 97% both teach and do research. Graduate students teach 1% of introductory courses. The average class size in an introductory lecture is 19; in a laboratory, 10; and in a regular course, 19.

Admissions: 44% of the 2005-2006 applicants were accepted. The SAT scores for the 2005-2006 freshman class were: Verbal--17% below 500, 53% between 500 and 599, 26% between 600 and 700, and 4% above 700; Math--16% below 500, 53% between 500 and 599, 29% between 600 and 700, and 2% above 700. 38% of the current freshmen were in the top fifth of their class; 80% were in the top two fifths. There were 5 National Merit semifinalists. 5 freshmen graduated first in their class.

Requirements: The SAT is required and the ACT is recommended. Graduation from an accredited secondary school is required; a GED will be accepted. The applicant's academic record must include a college preparatory program of 4 years of English and 3 to 4 years each of social studies, a foreign language, math, and lab science. Where required, a portfolio and an audition are used for placement purposes only. SUNY New Paltz requires applicants to be in the upper 50% of their class. A GPA of 3.0 is required. AP and CLEP credits are accepted. Important factors in the admissions decision are advanced placement or honor courses, extracurricular activities record, and evidence of special talent.

Procedure: Freshmen are admitted in the fall. Entrance exams should be taken on or before December 31. There are early admissions and deferred admissions plans. There is a rolling admissions plan. Applications should be filed by April 1 for fall entry. Notification is sent on a rolling basis. The fall 2005 application fee was $400. 300 applicants were on the 2005 waiting list; 3 were admitted. Applications are accepted on-line.

Transfer: 726 transfer students enrolled in 2004-2005. To be considered, applicants must have maintained a minimum GPA of 2.5 in all previous college work at accredited institutions. Some programs require a higher GPA for consideration. 30 of 120 credits required for the bachelor's degree must be completed at SUNY New Paltz.

Visiting: Half-hour information sesions are given by admissions staff followed by a campus tour given by a student ambassador. Visitors may sit in on classes. To schedule a visit, contact the Admissions Office.

Financial Aid: In 2005-2006, 75% of all full-time students received some form of financial aid. 60% of full-time freshmen and 75% of continuing full-time students received need-based aid. The average freshman award was $2092. Need-based scholarships or need-based grants averaged $2324; need-based self-help aid (loans and jobs) averaged $1551; and other non-need-based awards and non-need-based scholarships averaged $1999. 40% of undergraduates work part time. Average annual earnings from campus work are $800. The average financial indebtedness of the 2005 graduate was $18,900. The FAFSA is required. The deadline for filing freshman financial aid applications for fall entry is March 15.

International Students: There are 184 international students enrolled. The school actively recruits these students. They must take the TOEFL. Conditional acceptance is available, but the applicant must take ESL courses until required proficiency is achieved. The SAT is required if the TOEFL has not been taken.

Computers: Wireless access is available. All students may access the system during those hours that the buildings are open; residence hall terminals and personal PCs, 24 hours a day. There are no time limits and no fees. It is strongly recommended that all students have a personal computer.

Graduates: From July 1, 2004 to June 30, 2005, 1481 bachelor's degrees were awarded. The most popular majors were education (20%), business and marketing (14%), and visual and performing arts (11%). In an average class, 31% graduate in 4 years or less, 50% graduate in 5 years or less, and 56% graduate in 6 years or less. 457 companies recruited on campus in 2004-2005.

Admissions Contact: Kimberly Lavoie, Director of Freshman/ International Admissions. E-mail: *admissions@newpaltz.edu* Web: *www.newpaltz.edu*

STATE UNIVERSITY OF NEW YORK/UNIVERSITY AT STONY BROOK   E-5

Stony Brook, NY 11794   (631) 632-6868; Fax: 631) 632-9027

Full-time: 6671 men, 6509 women	Faculty: I, av$
Part-time: 541 men, 566 women	Ph.D.s: n/av
Graduate: 3311 men, 4413 women	Student/Faculty: n/av
Year: semesters, summer session	Tuition: $5575 ($11,835)
Application Deadline: March 1	Room & Board: $8050
Freshman Class: 18,110 applied, 9182 accepted, 2499 enrolled	
SAT Verbal/Math: 580/620*	HIGHLY COMPETITIVE

Stony Brook University, founded in 1957 and part of the State University of New York, is a public institution offering degree programs in arts and sciences, engineering and applied sciences, nursing, health technology and management, and social welfare. Professional programs in medicine and dental medicine are offered on the graduate level. There are 5 undergraduate and 8 graduate schools. In addition to regional accreditation, Stony Brook University has baccalaureate program accreditation with ABET, AOTA, APA, APTA, CAAHEP, CAHEA, CSWE, NAACLS, and NLN. The 7 libraries contain 1,896,697 volumes, 3,770,432 microform items, and 38,926 audio/video tapes/CDs/DVDs, and subscribe to 11,214 periodicals including electronic. Computerized library services include the card catalog, interlibrary loans, and database searching. Special learning facilities include a learning resource center, art gallery, radio station, and the Museum of Long Island Natural Sciences, and the Fine Arts Center, which includes a 1100-seat main theater, a 400-seat recital hall, and 3 experimental theaters. The 1100-acre campus is in a suburban area on Long Island, 60 miles from New York City. Including any residence halls, there are 113 buildings.

Student Life: 91% of undergraduates are from New York. Others are from 45 states, 83 foreign countries, and Canada. 85% are from public schools. 35% are white; 22% Asian American. 35% are Catholic; 26% Buddhist, Islamic, Mormon, Eastern Orthodox, Hindu, Baptist, 16% claim no religious affiliation; 15% Protestant; 8% Jewish. The average age of freshmen is 18; all undergraduates, 22. 13% do not continue beyond their first year; 58% remain to graduate.

Housing: 8358 students can be accommodated in college housing, which includes coed dorms, on-campus apartments, and married-student housing. In addition, there are honors houses and special-interest houses. There is a choice of undergraduate colleges that integrate academic experience with living enviroments. On-campus housing is guaranteed for all 4 years. 57% of students live on campus; of those, 65% remain on campus on weekends. Alcohol is not permitted. Upperclassmen may keep cars. Freshman and sophomores may petition for waivers.

Activities: There are 4 local and 11 national fraternities and 7 local and 10 national sororities. There are 200 groups on campus, including band, cheerleading, choir, chorale, dance, drama, ethnic, film, gay, honors, international, literary magazine, musical theater, newspaper, orchestra, pep band, photography, political, professional, radio and TV, religious, social, and student government. Popular campus events include Fall Fest, Opening Week Activities, and Caribbean Weekend.

Sports: There are 10 intercollegiate sports for men and 10 for women, and 25 intramural sports for men and 25 for women. Facilities include a sports complex housing a 5000-seat arena, a 1900-seat gym, an indoor track, a swimming pool, 6 squash and 8 racquetball courts, 3 multipurpose courts, a dance studio, and exercise and Universal gym rooms. Outdoor facilities include 20 tennis courts, a 3000-seat stadium, a 400-meter track, 2 sand volleyball courts, 2 basketball and 4 handball courts, and separate fields for baseball, soccer, football, lacrosse, and intramural football.

Disabled Students: 75% of the campus is accessible. Wheelchair ramps, elevators, special parking, specially equipped rest rooms, special class scheduling, lowered drinking fountains, lowered telephones, special housing, and automatic door openers are available.

Services: There is a reader service for the blind and remedial math and writing.

Campus Safety and Security: Measures include 24-hour foot and vehicle patrol, self-defense education, security escort services, and shuttle buses. There are informal discussions, pamphlets/posters/films, emergency telephones, lighted pathways/sidewalks, and a campus Crime Stoppers program.

Programs of Study: Stony Brook University confers B.A., B.S., and B.E. degrees. Master's and doctoral degrees are also awarded. Bachelor's degrees are awarded in AGRICULTURE (environmental studies), BIOLOGICAL SCIENCE (biochemistry and biology/biological science), BUSINESS (business administration and management), COMMUNICATIONS AND THE ARTS (art history and appreciation, comparative literature, dramatic arts, English, film arts, Germanic languages and literature, linguistics, music, Russian languages and literature, and studio art), COMPUTER AND PHYSICAL SCIENCE (applied mathematics, astronomy, atmospheric sciences and meteorology, chemistry, computer science, earth science, geology, information sciences and systems, mathematics, and physics), EDUCATION (athletic training), ENGINEERING AND ENVIRONMENTAL DESIGN (biomedical engineering, chemical engineering, computer engineering, electrical/electronics engineering, engineering and applied science, engineering chemistry, and mechanical engineering), HEALTH PROFESSIONS (clinical science, cytotechnology, health science, nursing, pharmacology, physician's assistant, and respiratory therapy), SOCIAL SCIENCE (African studies, American studies, anthropology, economics, ethnic studies, French studies, history, humanities, interdisciplinary studies, Italian studies, philosophy, political science/government, psychology, religion, social science, social work, sociology, Spanish studies, and women's studies). Applied mathematics and statistics, biochemistry, and biology are the strongest academically. Psychology, biology, and business are the largest.

Required: To graduate, students must have a minimum 2.0 GPA in 120 credit hours (B.A. and B.S.) or 128 (B.E.). The required number of hours in the major varies. At least 39 credits must be earned in upper-division courses. Students must take 14 to 16 courses to satisfy general education requirements in writing and quantitative reasoning skills, literary and philosophic analysis, exposure to the arts, disciplinary diversity, the interrelationship of science and society, and 3 culminating multicultural requirements. Arts and sciences majors must fulfill a foreign language requirement, unless completed through advanced high-school study. Other requirements vary by school.

Special: Cross-registration may be arranged through the Long Island Regional Advisory Council for Higher Education. The university offers a Washington semester and internships with a variety of government, legal, and social agencies, with hospitals and clinics, and in business and industry. The URECA Program allows undergraduates to work with faculty on research and creative projects. An accelerated degree program in nursing, dual majors, student-designed majors, a national student exchange program, study abroad in 10 countries, and pass/fail options are available. There are 4 national honor societies, including Phi Beta Kappa, a freshman honors program, and 30 departmental honors programs.

Faculty/Classroom: Graduate students teach 37% of introductory courses. The average class size in an introductory lecture is 84; in a laboratory, 25; and in a regular course, 38.

Admissions: 51% of the 2005-2006 applicants were accepted. The SAT scores for the 2005-2006 freshman class were: Verbal--7% below 500, 51% between 500 and 599, 34% between 600 and 700, and 8% above 700; Math--1% below 500, 34% between 500 and 599, 48% between 600 and 700, and 17% above 700. 58% of the current freshmen were in the top fifth of their class. There were 5 National Merit finalists and 6 semifinalists.

Requirements: The SAT is required. In addition, applicants must be graduates of an accredited secondary school or have a GED certificate. 16 or 17 academic credits are required, including 4 years each of English and social studies, 3 or 4 of math, 3 of science (4 for engineering majors), and 2 or 3 of a foreign language. 3 SAT Subject Tests, an essay, and an interview are recommended. AP and CLEP credits are accepted. Important factors in the admissions decision are advanced placement or honor courses, extracurricular activities record, and evidence of special talent.

Procedure: Freshmen are admitted fall and spring. Entrance exams should be taken during the junior year or in the fall of the senior year. There are early decision, early admissions, and deferred admissions plans. There is a rolling admissions plan. Early decision applications should be filed by November 15; regular applications, by March 1 for fall entry and November 1 for spring entry. Notification of early decision is sent January 1; regular decision, on a rolling basis. The fall 2005 application fee was $40. Applications are accepted on-line.

Transfer: 1621 transfer students enrolled in 2004-2005. Applicants must have a minimum 2.5 GPA. An associate degree and an interview are recommended. Other requirements vary by program. Applicants who have earned fewer than 24 college credits must submit a high school transcript. 36 credits of 120 to 128 required for the bachelor's degree must be completed at Stony Brook University.

Visiting: There are regularly scheduled orientations for prospective students, consisting of informative sessions about campus life. There are guides for informal visits and visitors may sit in on classes and stay overnight. To schedule a visit, contact the Admissions Office.

Financial Aid: In 2004-2005, 58% of all full-time freshmen received some form of financial aid. 53% of full-time freshmen received need-based aid. The average freshman award was $8394. Need-based scholarships or need-based grants averaged $5658; need-based self-help aid (loans and jobs) averaged $2997; and non-need-based athletic scholarships averaged $7157. 10% of undergraduates work part time. The average financial indebtedness of the 2004 graduate was $13,912. Stony Brook University is a member of CSS. The FAFSA and the state aid form are required. The deadline for filing freshman financial aid applications for fall entry is March 1.

International Students: There are 676 international students enrolled. They must take the TOEFL and also take SAT critical reading or IELTS.

Computers: Wireless access is available. Network access is available in dorm rooms and lounges. There are also various sinc sites located throughout the campus for student use. All students may access the system 24 hours a day. There are no time limits and no fees.

Graduates: From July 1, 2004 to June 30, 2005, 2941 bachelor's degrees were awarded. The most popular majors were psychology (12%), health science (9%), and business (9%). In an average class, 57% graduate in 6 years or less. 500 companies recruited on campus in 2004-2005. Of the 2004 graduating class, 47% were enrolled in graduate school within 6 months of graduation and 22% were employed.

Admissions Contact: Judith Burke-Berhanan.
E-mail: *enroll@stonybrook.edu* Web: *www.stonybrook.edu/admissions*

SUNY/COLLEGE OF TECHNOLOGY AT FARMINGDALE (See Farmingdale State University of New York)

SYRACUSE UNIVERSITY   C-3
Syracuse, NY 13244   (315) 443-3611

Full-time: 5006 men, 6368 women	Faculty: 987; I, -$
Part-time: 42 men, 25 women	Ph.D.s: 88%
Graduate: 1887 men, 2161 women	Student/Faculty: 12 to 1
Year: semesters, summer session	Tuition: $28,285
Application Deadline: January 1	Room & Board: $10,370
Freshman Class: 16,260 applied, 10,514 accepted, 3248 enrolled	
SAT or ACT: required	HIGHLY COMPETITIVE

Syracuse University, founded in 1870, is a private institution offering more than 200 undergraduate programs in liberal arts and sciences, architecture, public communications, education, management, human services and health professions, information studies, visual and performing arts, engineering, and computer science. There are 9 undergraduate and 11 graduate schools. In addition to regional accreditation, Syracuse has baccalaureate program accreditation with AACSB, ABET, ACEJMC, ACS, APA, ASHA, CACREP, CSWE, FIDER, NAAB, NASAD, NASM, NASPAA, NCATE, and NLN. The 6 libraries contain 3,136,964 volumes, 7,255,374 microform items, and 409,502 audio/video tapes/CDs/DVDs, and subscribe to 20,981 periodicals including electronic. Computerized library services include the card catalog, interlibrary loans, database searching, and Internet access. Special learning facilities include a learning resource center, art gallery, radio station, TV station, institute for sensory research, center for public and community service, child care and child development laboratory school, English language institute, center for undergraduate research and innovative learning, audio archives, global collaboratory multimedia classroom, center for science and technology, and community darkrooms (photography). The 200-acre campus is in an urban area 250 miles northwest of New York City. Including any residence halls, there are 170 buildings.

Student Life: 56% of undergraduates are from out of state, mostly the Northeast. Others are from 50 states, 64 foreign countries, and Canada. 80% are from public schools. 69% are white. 38% claim no religious affiliation; 28% Catholic; 14% Jewish. More than 20 religion preferences are represented among the student body. The average age of freshmen is 18; all undergraduates, 20. 8% do not continue beyond their first year; 79% remain to graduate.

Housing: 7500 students can be accommodated in college housing, which includes coed dorms, on-campus apartments, married-student housing, fraternity houses, and sorority houses. In addition, there are language houses special-interest houses, and single-sex floors and wings of residence halls. Learning communities and theme/interest housing are available. Housing is guaranteed for freshman and sophomore years. On-campus housing is available on a lottery system for upperclassmen. 75% of students live on campus; of those, 85% remain on campus on weekends. Alcohol is not permitted. Upperclassmen may keep cars.

Activities: 18% of men belong to 1 local and 23 national fraternities; 21% of women belong to 19 national sororities. There are 300 groups on campus, including art, band, cheerleading, chess, choir, chorale, chorus, computers, dance, debate, drama, ethnic, film, gay, honors, international, jazz band, literary magazine, marching band, musical theater, newspaper, orchestra, pep band, photography, political, professional, radio and TV, religious, social, social service, special interest, student government, symphony, and yearbook. Popular campus events include Opening Weekend Activities, Winter Carnival, and Senior Celebration.

Sports: There are 7 intercollegiate sports for men and 10 for women, and 25 intramural sports for men and 25 for women. Facilities include 4 gyms, 2 swimming pools, weight rooms, tennis courts, exercise rooms, a dance studio, courts for racquet sports, an indoor track, grass playing fields, multiple outdoor artificial turf fields, an outdoor track, a soccer stadium, and a softball stadium. The multipurpose domed stadium seats 50,000 for football and 30,000 for basketball.

Disabled Students: 90% of the campus is accessible. Wheelchair ramps, elevators, special parking, specially equipped rest rooms, special class scheduling, lowered drinking fountains, and lowered telephones, are available. There are also special supportive services for the learning disabled: note taking services, oral tests, readers, talking books, a reading machine, tape recorders, learning center, extended-time tests, support group, study circle, and proofreaders.

Services: Counseling and information services are available, as is tutoring in most subjects. There is a reader service for the blind. In addition to tutoring and study-group support, the academic support resource center provides workshops on generic study skills such as time management and test anxiety reduction as well as information on departmental academic support resources.

Campus Safety and Security: Measures include 24-hour foot and vehicle patrol, security escort services, shuttle buses, and informal discussions. There are pamphlets/posters/films, emergency telephones, and lighted pathways/sidewalks. Other services include bicycle registration, a blue light security system placed throughout campus with a direct link to the Department of Public Safety Communications Center in case of an emergency, and a card key access system in all university residence halls.

Programs of Study: Syracuse confers B.A., B.S., B.Arch., B.F.A., B.I.D., and B.Mus. degrees. Master's and doctoral degrees are also awarded. Bachelor's degrees are awarded in BIOLOGICAL SCIENCE (biology/biological science and nutrition), BUSINESS (accounting, banking and finance, business administration and management, entrepreneurial studies, hospitality management services, management information systems, marketing management, marketing/retailing/merchandising, purchasing/inventory management, retailing, and sports management), COMMUNICATIONS AND THE ARTS (advertising, art, art history and appreciation, broadcasting, ceramic art and design, classics, communications, comparative literature, design, dramatic arts, English, English literature, fiber/textiles/weaving, film arts, fine arts, French, Germanic languages and literature, graphic design, illustration, industrial design, journalism, languages, linguistics, media arts, metal/jewelry, modern language, music, music business management, music performance, music theory and composition, musical theater, painting, photography, printmaking, public relations, publishing, Russian, sculpture, Spanish, speech/debate/rhetoric, telecommunications, theater design, theater management, and video), COMPUTER AND PHYSICAL SCIENCE (chemistry, computer science, geology, information sciences and systems, mathematics, physics, and statistics), EDUCATION (art, early childhood, elementary, English, mathematics, middle school, music, physical, science, secondary, social studies, and special), ENGINEERING AND ENVIRONMENTAL DESIGN (aeronautical engineering, architecture, bioengineering, chemical engineering, civil engineering, computer engineering, computer graphics, electrical/electronics engineering, engineering physics, environmental design, environmental engineering, environmental science, interior design, and mechanical engineering), HEALTH PROFESSIONS (exercise science, health, health science, predentistry, premedicine, preveterinary science, and speech pathology/audiology), SOCIAL SCIENCE (African American studies, American studies, anthropology, child care/child and family studies, classical/ancient civilization, consumer services, dietetics, economics, ethics, politics, and social policy, European studies, family/consumer studies, fashion design and technology, food production/management/services, geography, history, international relations, Italian studies, Latin American studies, medieval studies, peace studies, philosophy, political science/government, prelaw, psychology, public affairs, religion, Russian and Slavic studies, social science, social work, sociology, South Asian studies, textiles and clothing, and women's studies). Inclusive education, aerospace engineering, and art are the strongest academically. Psychology, political science, and TV-radio-film are the largest.

Required: A minimum of 120 credits with a minimum GPA of 2.0 is required to graduate. All students must take a freshman writing seminar and fulfill core requirements in writing and literature, sciences and math, social sciences, and humanities. Additional requirements vary by college and major. Most programs require an arts and science core and a capstone experience.

Special: Cooperative education programs are available in engineering, retailing, and information studies. Study abroad is available in 6 university-operated centers and through other special programs, and a Washington semester is offered through the International Relations Program. Syracuse also offers B.A.-B.S. degrees, dual and student-designed majors, accelerated degree programs, work-study programs, a general studies degree, pass/fail options, and non-degree study. There are 36 national honor societies, including Phi Beta Kappa, and a freshman honors program. Many departments have honors programs.

Faculty/Classroom: 61% of faculty are male; 39%, female. 98% teach undergraduates, 2% do research, and 98% do both. The average class size in a laboratory is 16 and in a regular course, 26.

Admissions: 65% of the 2005-2006 applicants were accepted. The SAT scores for the 2005-2006 freshman class were: Verbal--4% below 500, 42% between 500 and 599, 45% between 600 and 700, and 9% above 700; Math--5% below 500, 32% between 500 and 599, 49% between 600 and 700, and 14% above 700. 72% of the current freshmen were in the top fifth of their class; 96% were in the top two fifths.

Requirements: The SAT or ACT is required. The ACT Optional Writing test is also required. In addition, applicants should have a strong college preparatory record from an accredited secondary school or have a GED equivalent. Essays are required. A portfolio is required for art and architecture majors, and an audition is required for music and drama majors. A secondary school counselor evaluation, or 2 academic recommendations, and a high school transcript, are also required. AP and CLEP credits are accepted. Important factors in the admissions decision are advanced placement or honor courses, evidence of special talent, and recommendations by school officials.

Procedure: Freshmen are admitted fall and spring. Entrance exams should be taken before January of the senior year for regular decision, and before November of the senior year for early decision. There are early decision, early admissions, and deferred admissions plans. Early decision applications should be filed by November 15; regular applications, by January 1 for fall entry and November 15 for spring entry, along with a $60 fee. Notification of early decision is sent in December; regular decision, mid-March. 567 early decision candidates were accepted for the 2005-2006 class. A waiting list is an active part of the admissions procedure. Applications are accepted on-line.

Transfer: 300 transfer students enrolled in 2004-2005. Requirements vary by college. The SAT or ACT scores and secondary school transcripts are required for applicants with fewer than 30 credit hours. A portfolio is required for art and architecture majors, and an audition for music and drama majors. College transcripts of all post secondary work are required. 60 of 120 credits required for the bachelor's degree must be completed at Syracuse.

Visiting: There are regularly scheduled orientations for prospective students, including information programs, a campus tour, and personal interviews. There are guides for informal visits and visitors may sit in on classes and stay overnight. To schedule a visit, contact the Admissions Office at 315-443-3611 or *orange@syr.edu.*

Financial Aid: In 2005-2006, 75% of all full-time students received some form of financial aid. 65% of all full-time students received need-based aid. The average freshman award was $21,150. Need-based scholarships or need-based grants averaged $16,600; and need-based self-help aid (loans and jobs) averaged $5800. Average annual earnings from campus work are $1700. The average financial indebtedness of the 2005 graduate was $19,200. Syracuse is a member of CSS. The CSS/Profile or FAFSA is required. The deadline for filing freshman financial aid applications for fall entry is February 1.

International Students: There are 333 international students enrolled. The school actively recruits these students. Satisfactory scores, are required on the written TOEFL or the Internet-based TOEFL and the SAT or ACT.

Computers: Wireless access is available. Wireless access is available in academic buildings wireless and other central locations. All students may access the system 24 hours per day. It is strongly recommended that all students have a personal computer. Freshman will receive information for purshase of PCs after May.

Graduates: From July 1, 2004 to June 30, 2005, 2403 bachelor's degrees were awarded. The most popular majors were management (14%), communications (14%), and social sciences (14%). In an average class, 66% graduate in 4 years or less, 77% graduate in 5 years or less, and 79% graduate in 6 years or less. 300 companies recruited on campus in 2004-2005. Of the 2004 graduating class, 18% were enrolled in graduate school within 6 months of graduation and 80% were employed.

Admissions Contact: Susan E. Donovan, Dean of Admissions. A video is available. E-mail: *orange@syr.edu* Web: *http://www.syracuse.edu*

TOURO COLLEGE D-5

New York, NY 10010 (718) 252-7800, ext. 399
Fax: (718) 253-9455

Full-time: 2800 men, 5100 women	Faculty: 240
Part-time: 900 men, 900 women	Ph.D.s: 65%
Graduate: 2300 men, 4600 women	Student/Faculty: 33 to 1
Year: semesters, summer session	Tuition: $11,000
Application Deadline: open	Room & Board: $6000
Freshman Class: n/av	
SAT or ACT: recommended	ACT: n/av VERY COMPETITIVE

Touro College, founded in 1971, is a private institution offering undergraduate programs primarily through the Lander College of Liberal Arts and Sciences, the School of General Studies, and the School of Health Sciences. Campuses are in midtown Manhattan, Brooklyn, and Queens. There are 6 undergraduate and 7 graduate schools. Figures in the abovr capsule and in this profile are approximate. In addition to regional accreditation, Touro College has baccalaureate program accreditation with AOTA, APTA,and CAHEA. The 11 libraries contain 271,509 volumes, 14,100 microform items, and 4054 audio/video tapes/CDs/DVDs, and subscribe to 3163 periodicals including electronic. Computerized library services include the card catalog, interlibrary loans, and database searching. Special learning facilities include a learning resource center. The campus is in an urban area. Including any residence halls, there are 12 buildings.

Student Life: 95% of undergraduates are from New York. Others are from 25 states, 30 foreign countries, and Canada. 27% do not continue beyond their first year; 47% remain to graduate.

Housing: 200 students can be accommodated in college housing, which includes single-sex dorms, on-campus apartments, and off-campus apartments. On-campus housing is available on a first-come, first-served basis. Priority is given to out-of-town students. Alcohol is not permitted. No one may keep cars.

Activities: There are no fraternities or sororities. There are 10 groups on campus, including computers, debate, literary magazine, newspaper, political, professional, religious, social, student government, and yearbook. Popular campus events include a student-sponsored lecture series and student-faculty social events.

Sports: There is no sports program at Touro College. Facilities include 1 baseball field, 2 tennis courts, and 2 basketball courts.

Disabled Students: All of the campus is accessible. Wheelchair ramps, elevators, specially equipped rest rooms, lowered drinking fountains, and lowered telephones are available.

Services: Counseling and information services are available, as is tutoring in some subjects, including accounting, math, English, and natural sciences. There is remedial math, reading, and writing.

Campus Safety and Security: Measures include 24-hour foot and vehicle patrol and pamphlets/posters/films.

Programs of Study: Touro College confers B.A., B.S., and B.P.S. degrees. Associate, master's, and doctoral degrees are also awarded. Bachelor's degrees are awarded in BIOLOGICAL SCIENCE (biology/biological science), BUSINESS (accounting, banking and finance, business administration and management, management science, and marketing/retailing/merchandising), COMMUNICATIONS AND THE ARTS (English, Hebrew, literature, and speech/debate/rhetoric), COMPUTER AND PHYSICAL SCIENCE (chemistry, computer science, mathematics, and physics), EDUCATION (elementary and special), HEALTH PROFESSIONS (occupational therapy, physical therapy, predentistry, and premedicine), SOCIAL SCIENCE (economics, history, human services, interdisciplinary studies, Judaic studies, liberal arts/general studies, philosophy, political science/government, prelaw, psychology, social science, and sociology). Business/accounting, education, and health sciences are the strongest academically. Psychology, education, and business are the largest.

Required: To graduate, all students must complete at least 120 credit hours (varies by major), with 30 to 70 in the major. A minimum 2.0 GPA is required, with 2.3 in the major. Specific disciplines include Judaic studies or ethnic studies. Required courses include English composition, history, literature, math, and social and natural sciences.

Special: The college offers cross-registration with the Fashion Institute of Technology, internships for juniors and seniors, study abroad in Israel, work-study programs, interdisciplinary majors, an accelerated degree program, credit for life, military, and work experience, pass/fail options, and dual majors. Early and/or preferential admission to professional programs is also possible. There are 2 national honor societies.

Faculty/Classroom: 60% of faculty are male; 40%, female. No introductory courses are taught by graduate students. The average class size in an introductory lecture is 16; in a laboratory, 12; and in a regular course, 15.

Admissions: 56% of applicants were accepted.

Requirements: The SAT or ACT is recommended. In addition, applicants must be graduates of an accredited secondary school with a satisfactory high school average. Satisfactory SAT scores are recommended. A GPA of 3.2 is required. AP and CLEP credits are accepted. Important factors in the admissions decision are advanced placement or honor courses, recommendations by school officials, and extracurricular activities record.

Procedure: Freshmen are admitted fall, spring, and summer. Entrance exams should be taken in May of the junior year or fall of the senior year. There are early admissions and deferred admissions plans. There is a rolling admissions plan. Application deadlines are open. Check with the school for current application deadlines and fee.

Transfer: A 2.5 GPA is required. If the student has fewer than 60 credits, high school documentation is also required. 45 of 120 credits required for the bachelor's degree must be completed at Touro College.

Visiting: There are regularly scheduled orientations for prospective students. There are guides for informal visits and visitors may sit in on classes and stay overnight. To schedule a visit, contact Steven Toplan.

Financial Aid: The CSS Profile is required. Check with the school for current deadline.

International Students: There are 67 international students enrolled. Students must take the TOEFL and also take the college's own test.

Computers: All students may access the system.

Graduates: Of a recent graduating class, 40% were enrolled in graduate school within 6 months of graduation.

Admissions Contact: Steven Toplan, Director of Admissions. E-mail: *lasadmit@admin.touro.edu* Web: *www.touro.edu*

UNION COLLEGE
D-3

Schenectady, NY 12308-2311
(518) 388-6112
(888) 843-6688; Fax: (518) 388-6986

Full-time: 1210 men, 999 women	Faculty: 198; IIB, +$
Part-time: 19 men, 24 women	Ph.D.s: 94%
Graduate: none	Student/Faculty: 11 to 1
Year: trimesters, summer session	Tuition: $41,595
Application Deadline: January 15	Room & Board: Null
Freshman Class: 4230 applied, 1997 accepted, 581 enrolled	
SAT Verbal/Math: 620/640*	ACT: 27 HIGHLY COMPETITIVE

Union College, founded in 1795, is an independent liberal arts and engineering college. In addition to regional accreditation, Union has baccalaureate program accreditation with ABET. The library contains 583,517 volumes, 915,703 microform items, and 9894 audio/video tapes/CDs/DVDs, and subscribes to 3728 periodicals including electronic. Computerized library services include the card catalog, interlibrary loans, database searching, and Internet access. Special learning facilities include a radio station, theater, high-tech classroom, lab center, multimedia auditorium, and an art, science, and history gallery. The 100-acre campus is in an urban area 15 miles west of Albany. Including any residence halls, there are 100 buildings.

Student Life: 56% of undergraduates are from out of state, mostly the Northeast. Students are from 41 states, 19 foreign countries, and Canada. 73% are from public schools. 84% are white. The average age of freshmen is 18; all undergraduates, 20. 9% do not continue beyond their first year; 84% remain to graduate.

Housing: 1916 students can be accommodated in college housing, which includes single-sex and coed dormitories, on-campus apartments, and fraternity houses. In addition, there are language houses, special-interest houses, 12 theme houses that emphasize varius community atmospheres, and a substance-free focused study option. On-campus housing is available on a lottery system for upperclassmen. 87% of students live on campus; of those, 80% remain on campus on weekends. Upperclassmen may keep cars.

Activities: 24% of men belong to 9 national fraternities; 31% of women belong to 4 national sororities. There are 100 groups on campus, including art, band, chess, choir, computers, dance, debate, drama, ethnic, gay, honors, international, jazz band, literary magazine, newspaper, orchestra, photography, political, professional, radio and TV, religious, social, social service, student government, and yearbook. Popular campus events include Commencement, Party in the Garden, and Spring Fest.

Sports: There are 12 intercollegiate sports for men and 13 for women, and 19 intramural sports for men and 16 for women. Facilities include a field house for volleyball, recreational basketball, indoor track, and intramural activities, 2 synthetic grass fields for soccer, football, field hockey, lacrosse, intramurals, and recreation, basketball/volleyball facility, an ice rink, a gym, that includes a weight room, a fitness center, racquetball/squash courts, aerobics room, and swimming pool, 8 outdoor tennis courts, an outdoor basketball/street hockey court, and boathouse and docks.

Disabled Students: 60% of the campus is accessible. Wheelchair ramps, elevators, special parking, specially equipped rest rooms, special class scheduling, lowered drinking fountains, lowered telephones, and special housing are available.

Services: Counseling and information services are available, as is tutoring in most subjects, including science and math. There is a reader service for the blind. A writing center and a language center are available.

Campus Safety and Security: Measures include 24-hour foot and vehicle patrol, self-defense education, security escort services, and shuttle buses. There are informal discussions, pamphlets/posters/films, emergency telephones, lighted pathways/sidewalks, 24-hour locked residence halls, emergency medical assistance, awareness programs, a bicycle patrol, a trolley escort service, and a shuttle van.

Programs of Study: Union confers B.A. and B.S degrees. Bachelor's degrees are awarded in BIOLOGICAL SCIENCE (biochemistry, biology/biological science, and neurosciences), BUSINESS (business economics), COMMUNICATIONS AND THE ARTS (classics, English, fine arts, modern language, and studio art), COMPUTER AND PHYSICAL SCIENCE (astronomy, chemistry, computer science, geology, mathematics, physics, and science), ENGINEERING AND ENVIRONMENTAL DESIGN (computer engineering, electrical/electronics engineering, and mechanical engineering), SOCIAL SCIENCE (American studies, anthropology, economics, history, humanities, philosophy, political science/government, psychology, Russian and Slavic studies, social science, sociology, and women's studies). Biology, French, and philosophy are the strongest academically. Political science, psychology, and economics are the largest.

Required: Students must complete a minimum of 36 courses and must maintain a minimum GPA of 1.8 overall and 2.0 in the major. Students must also meet the requirements of the freshman preceptorial and the general education program, which includes courses distributed in 4 areas: history, literature, and civilization; social or behavioral science; math and natural science; and foreign languages and non-Western studies.

Special: Cross-registration is permitted with the Hudson Mohawk Consortium. Opportunities are provided for legislative internships in Albany and Washington, D.C. Union also offers a co-op program for engineering majors, pass/fail options, B.A.-B.S. degrees, dual and student-designed majors, a Washington semester, accelerated degree programs in law and medicine, and study abroad in 27 countries. There are 14 national honor societies, including Phi Beta Kappa, a freshman honors program, and 15 departmental honors programs.

Faculty/Classroom: 60% of faculty are male; 40%, female. All teach undergraduates and 97% both teach and do research. The average class size in an introductory lecture is 22; in a laboratory, 14; and in a regular course, 18.

Admissions: 47% of the 2005-2006 applicants were accepted. The SAT scores for the 2005-2006 freshman class were: Verbal--2% below 500, 30% between 500 and 599, 55% between 600 and 700, and 26% above 700; Math--1% below 500, 20% between 500 and 599, 55% between 600 and 700, and 26% above 700. The ACT scores were 1% below 21, 9% between 21 and 23, 29% between 24 and 26, 29% between 27 and 28, and 31% above 28. 77% of the current freshmen were in the top fifth of their class; 92% were in the top two fifths.

Requirements: The SAT or ACT is required or 2 SAT Subject Tests. Applicants for the Leadership in Medicine and Law and Public Policy programs are required to submit the SAT and SAT Subject Tests. Graduation from an accredited secondary school is required. Applicants must submit a minimum of 16 full-year credits, distributed as follows: 4 years of English, 2 of a foreign language, 2 1/2 to 3 1/2 years of math, 2 years each of science and social studies, and the remainder in college-preparatory courses. Engineering and math majors are expected to have completed additional math and science courses beyond the minimum requirements. An essay is also required, and an interview is recommended. AP credits are accepted. Important factors in the admissions decision are advanced placement or honor courses, recommendations by school officials, and extracurricular activities record.

Procedure: Freshmen are admitted in the fall. Entrance exams should be taken by January of the senior year.(December for applicants to the Leadership in Medicine and Law and Public Policy programs). There are early decision, early admissions, and deferred admissions plans. An interview is required for the early admissions plan. Early decision applications should be filed by November 15; regular applications, by January 15 for fall entry, along with a $50 fee. Notification of early decision is sent December 15; regular decision, April 1. 199 early decision candidates were accepted for the 2005-2006 class. 759 applicants were on the 2005 waiting list; 26 were admitted. Applications are accepted on-line.

Transfer: 22 transfer students enrolled in 2004-2005. A 3.0 GPA and 1 full year of college academic work are required. Transfer students must study at Union for at least 2 years. 18 of 36 courses required for the bachelor's degree must be completed at Union.

Visiting: There are regularly scheduled orientations for prospective students, including interviews and a tour of the campus. There are guides for informal visits and visitors may sit in on classes and stay overnight. To schedule a visit, contact the Admissions Office, Grant Hall.

Financial Aid: Union is a member of CSS. The CSS/Profile or FAFSA and Non-custodial Profile and the Business/Farm Supplement are required. The deadline for filing freshman financial aid applications for fall entry is February 1.

International Students: There are 40 international students enrolled. The school actively recruits these students. They must score satisfactorily on the written TOEFL or on the electronic version and also take SAT or 2 SAT Subject tests, or the ACT.

Computers: Wireless access is available. There are more than 1,500 Pcs and workstations on campus, including classrooms, labs, offices, and public spaces. The college's network goes to every building on campus, and there are more than 1,900 network connections in residence halls. All residence halls also have wireless networking available in public and study areas. In addition, the college's wireless network extends to all public/study areas on campus, all classrooms, the library, and all academic buildings. There are also 37 electronic classrooms and 4 genreral-use computer labs. All students may access the system at any time. There are no time limits and no fees.

Graduates: From July 1, 2004 to June 30, 2005, 481 bachelor's degrees were awarded. The most popular majors were political science (10%), psychology (10%), and economics (8%). In an average class, 80% graduate in 4 years or less, 83% graduate in 5 years or less, and 84% graduate in 6 years or less.

Admissions Contact: Dianne Crozier, Director of Admissions. A video is available. E-mail: *admissions@union.edu*
Web: *http://www.union.edu*

UNITED STATES MERCHANT MARINE ACADEMY   D-5
Kings Point, NY 11024-1699

(516) 773-5391
(866) 546-4778; Fax: (516) 773-5390

Full-time: 889 men, 132 women	**Faculty:** 87
Part-time: none	**Ph.D.s:** 40%
Graduate: none	**Student/Faculty:** 12 to 1
Year: trimesters	**Tuition:** $6516
Application Deadline: March 1	**Room & Board:** n/app
Freshman Class: 1647 applied, 397 accepted, 285 enrolled	
SAT Verbal/Math: 620/608*	**ACT:** 28

HIGHLY COMPETITIVE+

The United States Merchant Marine Academy, founded in 1943, is a publicly supported institution offering maritime, military, and engineering programs for the purpose of training officers for the U.S. merchant marine and the maritime industry. Students make no conventional tuition and board payments. Required fees for freshmen are approximately $6,516; costs in subsequent years are less. In addition to regional accreditation, Kings Point has baccalaureate program accreditation with ABET. The library contains 182,192 volumes, 18,507 microform items, and 3611 audio/video tapes/CDs/DVDs, and subscribes to 955 periodicals including electronic. Computerized library services include the card catalog, interlibrary loans, database searching, and Internet access. Special learning facilities include a learning resource center, planetarium, and a maritime museum. The 80-acre campus is in a suburban area 19 miles east of midtown New York City. Including any residence halls, there are 28 buildings.

Student Life: 89% of undergraduates are from out of state, mostly the Middle Atlantic. Students are from 48 states, 2 foreign countries, and Canada. 72% are from public schools. 89% are white. 49% are Protestant; 38% Catholic; 9% claim no religious affiliation. The average age of freshmen is 19; all undergraduates, 20. 8% do not continue beyond their first year; 92% remain to graduate.

Housing: All students can be accommodated in college housing, which includes coed dorms. On-campus housing is guaranteed for all 4 years. 100% of students live on campus; of those, 85% remain on campus on weekends. Alcohol is not permitted. Upperclassmen may keep cars.

Activities: There are no fraternities or sororities. There are 26 groups on campus, including band, choir, chorus, computers, debate, drill team, drum and bugle corps, ethnic, marching band, newspaper, pep band, professional, religious, student government, and yearbook.

Sports: There are 14 intercollegiate sports for men and 5 for women, and 5 intramural sports for men. Facilities include a swimming pool and a football field.

Disabled Students: 5% of the campus is accessible. Wheelchair ramps, elevators, special parking, and specially equipped rest rooms are available.

Services: Counseling and information services are available, as is tutoring in most subjects.

Campus Safety and Security: Measures include 24-hour foot and vehicle patrol, self-defense education, informal discussions, and lighted pathways/sidewalks.

Programs of Study: Kings Point confers the B.S. degree. Bachelor's degrees are awarded in BUSINESS (logistics and transportation management), ENGINEERING AND ENVIRONMENTAL DESIGN (engineering, marine engineering, maritime science, naval architecture and marine engineering, and transportation technology). Marine engineering systems is the strongest academically. Logistics and intermodal transportation are the largest.

Required: To graduate, students must complete 160 credit hours with a 2.0 minimum GPA. The required core curriculum includes courses in math, science, English, humanities and history, naval science, phys ed, ship's medicine, and computer science. Students must spend 10 months during their combined sophomore and junior years at sea on U.S. flag merchant ships. All students must pass resident and sea project courses, the U.S. Coast Guard licensing exam and all required certificates, and the academy physical fitness test. Students must apply for and accept, if offered, a commission in the U.S. uniformed services.

Special: The college offers internships in the maritime industry and work-study programs with U.S. shipping companies.

Faculty/Classroom: 90% of faculty are male; 10%, female. All teach undergraduates. The average class size in an introductory lecture is 18; in a laboratory, 16; and in a regular course, 17.

Admissions: 24% of the 2005-2006 applicants were accepted. The SAT scores for the 2005-2006 freshman class were: Verbal--3% below 500, 46% between 500 and 599, 37% between 600 and 700, and 14% above 700. The ACT scores were 37% between 24 and 26, 47% between 27 and 28, and 16% above 28. 38% of the current freshmen were in the top fifth of their class; 80% were in the top two fifths. There were 20 National Merit finalists. 11 freshmen graduated first in their class.

Requirements: The SAT or ACT is required. In addition, candidates for admission to the academy must be nominated by a member of the U.S. Congress. They must be between the ages of 17 and 25, U.S. citizens (except by special arrangement), and in excellent physical condition. Applicants should be graduates of an accredited secondary school or have a GED equivalent. 18 academic credits are required, including 4 in English, 3 in math, 1 credit in physics or chemistry with a lab, and 10 in electives. An essay is required. Kings Point requires applicants to be in the upper 40% of their class. AP credits are accepted. Important factors in the admissions decision are advanced placement or honor courses, leadership record, and extracurricular activities record.

Procedure: Freshmen are admitted in the fall. Entrance exams should be taken by the first test date of the year of requested entry. There is an early decision plan. Applications should be filed by March 1 for fall entry. Notification is sent March 31. 88 applicants were on the 2005 waiting list; 20 were admitted. Applications are accepted on-line.

Transfer: All students must spend 4 years at the academy. All of the 164 credits required for the bachelor's degree must be completed at Kings Point.

Visiting: There are guides for informal visits and visitors may sit in on classes and stay overnight. To schedule a visit, contact the Admissions Office at (866) 546-4778.

Financial Aid: In 2005-2006, 33% of all full-time freshmen received some form of financial aid. 37% of full-time freshmen received need-based aid. The average freshman award was $5442. Need-based scholarships or need-based grants averaged $2375 ($4050 maximum); need-based self-help aid (loans and jobs) averaged $5334 ($8000 maximum); and other non-need-based awards and non-need-based scholarships averaged $967 ($2000 maximum). The average financial indebtedness of the 2005 graduate was $9221. The FAFSA and the college's own financial statement are required. The priority date for freshman financial aid applications for fall entry is March 1. The deadline for filing freshman financial aid applications for fall entry is May 1.

International Students: There are 16 international students enrolled. They must take the TOEFL and also take the SAT or the ACT.

Computers: Wireless access is available. All students may access the system 24 hours per day. There are no time limits and no fees. All students are issued a laptop computer.

Graduates: From July 1, 2004 to June 30, 2005, 218 bachelor's degrees were awarded. The most popular majors were logistics and intermodal transportation (34%), marine engineering systems (29%), and marine engineering and shipyard management (15%). In an average class, 45% graduate in 4 years, 27% graduate in 5 years or less, and 1% graduate in 6 years or less. 70 companies recruited on campus in 2004-2005. Of the 2004 graduating class, 2% were enrolled in graduate school within 6 months of graduation and 89% were employed.

Admissions Contact: CPT. Robert E. Johnson, Director of Admissions and Financial Aid. A video is available.
E-mail: *admissions@usmma.edu* Web: *www.usmma.edu*

UNITED STATES MILITARY ACADEMY   D-4

West Point, NY 10996	(845) 938-4041; Fax: (845) 938-8121
Full-time: 3500 men, 650 women	**Faculty:** 577; IIA, +$
Part-time: none	**Ph.D.s:** 39%
Graduate: none	**Student/Faculty:** 7 to 1
Year: semesters, summer session	**Tuition:** see profile
Application Deadline: see profile	**Room & Board:** n/app
Freshman Class: n/av	
SAT or ACT: required	**MOST COMPETITIVE**

The United States Military Academy, founded in 1802, offers military, engineering, and comprehensive arts and sciences programs leading to a bachelor's degree and a commission as a second lieutenant in the U.S. Army, with a 5-year active duty service obligation. All students receive free tuition and room and board as well as an annual salary. An initial deposit is required. Figures in above capsule and in this profile are approximate. In addition to regional accreditation, West Point has baccalaureate program accreditation with ABET. The library contains 442,169 volumes, 748,443 microform items, and 12,378 audio/video tapes/CDs/DVDs, and subscribes to 1963 periodicals including electronic. Computerized library services include the card catalog, interlibrary loans, and database searching. Special learning facilities include a learning resource center, art gallery, radio station, TV station, and a military museum. Cadets may conduct research in conjunction with the academic departments through the Operations Research Center, the Photonics Research Center, the Mechanical Engineering Research Center, and the Office of Artificial Intelligence, Analysis, and Evaluation. There is also a visiting artist program featuring painting, sculpture, and photography. The 16,080-acre campus is in a small town 56 miles north of New York City. Including any residence halls, there are 902 buildings.

Student Life: 92% of undergraduates are from out of state, mostly the Northeast. Students are from 50 states and 19 foreign countries. 81% are from public schools. 81% are white. 49% are Protestant; 33% Catholic; 15% claim no religious affiliation. The average age of freshmen is 18; all undergraduates, 20. 8% do not continue beyond their first year; 82% remain to graduate.

Housing: 4500 students can be accommodated in college housing. College-sponsored housing is coed. All cadets live in cadet barracks. On-campus housing is guaranteed for all 4 years. All students live on campus. Upperclassmen may keep cars.

Activities: There are no fraternities or sororities. There are 105 groups on campus, including art, astronomy, bagpipe band, band, cheerleading, chess, choir, chorale, chorus, computers, dance, debate, drama, drill team, drum and bugle corps, ethnic, film, flying, forensics, honors, international, languages, literary magazine, marching band, musical theater, newspaper, pep band, photography, professional, radio and TV, religious, social, social service, student government, and yearbook. Popular campus events include Ring Weekend and 100th Night for Seniors, 500th Night for Juniors, and Yearling Winter Weekend for Sophomores.

Sports: There are 15 intercollegiate sports for men and 9 for women, and 18 intramural sports for men and 14 for women. Facilities include a 40,000-seat football stadium, baseball fields, a 2500-seat hockey rink, a 5000-seat basketball arena, 5 gyms for squash, handball, tennis, and racquetball, 3 swimming pools, workout areas, a field house, indoor/outdoor tracks, a golf course, a ski slope; and hunting, fishing, and boating facilities.

Disabled Students: Wheelchair ramps, elevators, special parking, specially equipped rest rooms, lowered drinking fountains, and lowered telephones are available.

Services: Counseling and information services are available, as is tutoring in every subject. The Center for Enhanced Performance offers 2 courses that provide cadets an opportunity to learn and enhance reading, study, and mental skills.

Campus Safety and Security: Measures include 24-hour foot and vehicle patrol, self-defense education, shuttle buses, and lighted pathways/sidewalks.

Programs of Study: West Point confers the B.S. degree. Bachelor's degrees are awarded in BIOLOGICAL SCIENCE (life science), BUSINESS (management science and operations research), COMMUNICATIONS AND THE ARTS (languages and literature), COMPUTER AND PHYSICAL SCIENCE (chemistry, computer science, mathematics, and physics), ENGINEERING AND ENVIRONMENTAL DESIGN (civil engineering, electrical/electronics engineering, engineering management, engineering physics, environmental engineering, mechanical engineering, military science, nuclear engineering, and systems engineering), SOCIAL SCIENCE (behavioral science, economics, geography, history, international studies, law, philosophy, and political science/government). Engineering, behavioral sciences, and history are the largest.

Required: All cadets must complete a core of 31 courses and 9 academic electives pertinent to their field of study. The major requires an additional 1 to 3 electives in the field. In addition, all cadets must complete 4 courses each in phys ed and military science and a senior thesis or design project in the major. A total of 140 credits, including 127 academic, 7 phys: cal, and 6 military, with at least a C average, is required to graduate.

Special: Junior and senior cadets may participate in 3-week summer educational experiences, including Operations Crossroads Africa, research work in technical areas throughout the country, medical internships at Walter Reed Medical Center, workfellow positions with federal and Department of Defense agencies, language training in foreign countries, and study at other military and civilian institutions. There are 7 national honor societies, including Phi Beta Kappa, a freshman honors program, and 5 departmental honors programs.

Faculty/Classroom: 88% of faculty are male; 12%, female. 40% do research and 40% both teach and do research. The average class size in an introductory lecture is 15; in a laboratory, 15; and in a regular course, 15.

Requirements: The SAT or ACT is required. In addition, applicants must be qualified academically, physically, and medically. Candidates must be nominated for admission by members of the U.S. Congress or executive sources. West Point recommends that applicants have 4 years each of English and math, 2 years each of foreign language and lab science, such as chemistry and physics, and 1 year of U.S. history. Courses in geography, government, and economics are also suggested. An essay is required, and an interview is recommended. The GED is accepted. Applicants must be 17 to 22 years old, a U.S. citizen at the time of enrollment (except by agreement with another country), unmarried, and not pregnant or legally obligated to support children. AP credits are accepted. Important factors in the admissions decision are leadership record, extracurricular activities record, and recommendations by school officials.

Procedure: Freshmen are admitted in the summer. Entrance exams should be taken in the spring of the junior year and not later than the fall of the senior year. There are early decision and early admissions plans. There is a rolling admissions plan. Notification is sent on a rolling basis. Check with the school for current application deadlines.

Transfer: All applicants must enter as freshmen. All 140 credits required for the bachelor's degree must be completed at West Point.

Visiting: There are regularly scheduled orientations for prospective students. Candidates will be escorted by a cadet, will attend class, have lunch with the Corps of Cadets, and talk with cadets about all phases of West Point life. There are guides for informal visits and visitors may sit in on classes and stay overnight. To schedule a visit, contact the Admissions Office.

International Students: Students must take the SAT or the ACT.

Computers: All students may access the system 24 hours daily. There are no time limits and no fees. All students are required to have personal computers.

Admissions Contact: Colonel Michael L. Jones, Director of Admissions. A video is available. E-mail: *admissions@usma.edu*
Web: *www.usma.edu*

UNIVERSITY OF ROCHESTER B-3
Rochester, NY 14627-0251

(585) 275-3221
(888) 822-2256; Fax: (585) 461-4595

Full-time: 2301 men, 2134 women	**Faculty:** I, av$
Part-time: 54 men, 207 women	**Ph.Ds:** 88%
Graduate: 1754 men, 1726 women	**Student/Faculty:** n/av
Year: semesters, summer session	**Tuition:** $31,297
Application Deadline: January 15	**Room & Board:** $9838
Freshman Class: n/av	
SAT Verbal/Math: 637/667*	**MOST COMPETITIVE**

The University of Rochester, founded in 1850, is a private institution offering programs in the arts and sciences, engineering and applied science, nursing, medicine and dentistry, business administration, music, and education. There are 4 undergraduate and 7 graduate schools. In addition to regional accreditation, UR has baccalaureate program accreditation with AACSB, ABET, ACPE, NASM, and NLN. The 7 libraries contain 2,922,335 volumes, 4,145,264 microform items, and 71,100 audio/video tapes/CDs/DVDs, and subscribe to 9829 periodicals including electronic. Computerized library services include the card catalog, interlibrary loans, and database searching. Special learning facilities include a learning resource center, radio station, labs for nuclear structure research and laser energetics, a center for visual science, the Strong Memorial Hospital, an art center, an observatory, an institute of optics, a center for electronic imaging systems, and the National Science Foundation Center for Photoinduced Charge Transfer. The 90-acre campus is in a suburban area 2 miles south of downtown Rochester. Including any residence halls, there are 143 buildings.

Student Life: 53% of undergraduates are from out of state. Others are from Canada. 64% are white; 10% Asian American.

Housing: 3022 students can be accommodated in college housing, which includes single-sex and coed dorms, on-campus apartments, married-student housing, and fraternity houses. In addition, there are language houses, special-interest houses, drama and medieval houses, and faculty- in- residence housing. On-campus housing is guaranteed for the freshman year only and is available on a lottery system for upperclassmen. Upperclassmen may keep cars.

Activities: 25% of men belong to 17 national fraternities; 14% of women belong to 11 national sororities. There are 170 groups on campus, including art, band, campus programming cheerleading, chess, choir, chorale, chorus, computers, dance, debate, drama, drill team, ethnic, film, gay, honors, international, jazz band, literary magazine, musical theater, newspaper, opera, orchestra, pep band, photography, political, professional, radio and TV, religious, social, social service, student government, and symphony. Popular campus events include Dandelion Day, Yellowjacket Day, and Boar's Head Dinner.

Sports: There are 11 intercollegiate sports for men and 11 for women, and 17 intramural sports for men and 17 for women. Facilities include a renovated athletic center, a 5000-seat stadium, a 2500-seat gym, a field house, an ice rink, courts for handball, racquetball, squash, and tennis, an indoor track, a fitness center and weight room, a jogging path, and an aquatic center.

Disabled Students: 75% of the campus is accessible. Wheelchair ramps, elevators, special parking, specially equipped rest rooms, special class scheduling, lowered drinking fountains, and lowered telephones are available. Access to screened reading and adaptive software are also available.

Services: Counseling and information services are available, as is tutoring in every subject. There is a reader service for the blind.

Campus Safety and Security: Measures include 24-hour foot and vehicle patrol, self-defense education, security escort services, and shuttle buses. There are informal discussions, pamphlets/posters/films, emergency telephones, and lighted pathways/sidewalks.

Programs of Study: UR confers B.A., B.S., and B.M. degrees. Master's and doctoral degrees are also awarded. Bachelor's degrees are awarded in AGRICULTURE (environmental studies), BIOLOGICAL SCIENCE (biochemistry, biology/biological science, cell biology, ecology, genetics, microbiology, and neurosciences), COMMUNICATIONS AND THE ARTS (American Sign Language, art history and appreciation, classics, comparative literature, English, film arts, fine arts, French, German, Japanese, jazz, linguistics, music, music theory and composition, Russian, Spanish, and studio art), COMPUTER AND PHYSICAL SCIENCE (applied mathematics, chemistry, computer science, geology, mathematics, optics, physics, and statistics), EDUCATION (music), ENGINEERING AND ENVIRONMENTAL DESIGN (biomedical engineering, chemical engineering, electrical/electronics engineering, engineering and applied science, environmental science, geological engineering, and mechanical engineering), HEALTH PROFESSIONS (health, nursing, and public health), SOCIAL SCIENCE (anthropology, cognitive science, economics, history, interpreter for the deaf, philosophy, political science/government, psychology, religion, and women's studies). Psychology, biology, and political science are the largest.

Required: Students focus on the humanities, social sciences, and natural sciences; 1 of the 3 areas will be their major, and they select a 3-course cluster in each of the other 2. A total of 128 credit hours with a minimum GPA of 2.0 is required to graduate. Additionally, all students satisfy a freshman writing requirement and take 2 upper-level courses in their major that are writing intensive.

Special: Cross-registration is offered with other Rochester area colleges. Internships, a Washington semester, B.A.-B.S. degrees, dual and student-designed majors, nondegree study, and pass/fail options are available. Study abroad is possible in 46 university-sponsored programs, including Australia, China, Japan, Egypt, Israel, the former Soviet Union, and in several European countries. Other options include a fifth year of courses tuition free, courses designed to teach first-year students how to learn and how to make learning a lifetime habit, a management studies certificate, and music lessons for credit at the Eastman School of Music. Qualified freshmen may obtain early assurance of admission to the university's medical school through the Rochester Early Medical Scholars program. Internships are available in the United States and abroad. There are 6 national honor societies, including Phi Beta Kappa, and 13 departmental honors programs.

Faculty/Classroom: 65% of faculty are male; 35%, female. Graduate students teach 5% of introductory courses. The average class size in an introductory lecture is 75; in a laboratory, 20; and in a regular course, 20.

Admissions: The SAT scores for the 2005-2006 freshman class were: Verbal--5% below 500, 23% between 500 and 599, 48% between 600 and 700, and 24% above 700; Math--2% below 500, 16% between 500 and 599, 51% between 600 and 700, and 31% above 700.

Requirements: The SAT or ACT is required. In addition, SAT: Subject tests are recommended. Applicants should be graduates of an accredited secondary school or have a GED equivalent. An audition is required for music majors. The school accepts the institutional application through Embark linked to the UR admissions home page. AP credits are accepted. Important factors in the admissions decision are advanced placement or honor courses, recommendations by school officials, and leadership record.

Procedure: Freshmen are admitted fall and spring. Entrance exams should be taken by December of the senior year. There are early decision and deferred admissions plans. Early decision applications should be filed by November 15; regular applications, by January 15 for fall entry and October 1 for spring entry, along with a $50 fee. Notification of early decision is sent December 15; regular decision, April 1. 227 early decision candidates were accepted for the 2005-2006 class. 1091 applicants were on the 2005 waiting list; 29 were admitted. Applications are accepted on-line.

Transfer: 78 transfer students enrolled in 2004-2005. The most important criterion is an applicant's college record. Transfers are accepted on a rolling admissions basis. 32 of 128 credits required for the bachelor's degree must be completed at UR.

Visiting: There are regularly scheduled orientations for prospective students, including campus tours and group information sessions. There are guides for informal visits and visitors may sit in on classes and stay overnight. To schedule a visit, contact the Admissions Office.

Financial Aid: In 2005-2006, 75% of all full-time freshmen and 74% of continuing full-time students received some form of financial aid. 57% of full-time freshmen and 56% of continuing full-time students received need-based aid. Need-based scholarships or need-based grants averaged $21,544; and need-based self-help aid (loans and jobs) averaged $5088 ($7525 maximum). 33% of undergraduates work part time. Average annual earnings from campus work are $2498. The average financial indebtedness of the 2005 graduate was $26,100. UR is a member of CSS. The CSS/Profile or FAFSA is required. The priority date for freshman financial aid applications for fall entry is February 1.

International Students: The school actively recruits these students. A satisfactory score is required on the written TOEFL. Students must also take the SAT or the ACT.

Computers: All students may access the system 24 hours daily. There are no time limits and no fees.

Graduates: From July 1, 2004 to June 30, 2005, 93 bachelor's degrees were awarded.

Admissions Contact: Jonathan Burdick, Dean of Admissions and Financial Aid. A video is available.
E-mail: *admit@admissions.rochester.edu*
Web: *http://www.rochester.edu*

UTICA COLLEGE   C-3

Utica, NY 13502-4892   (315) 792-3006
                                    (800) 782-8884; Fax: (315) 792-3003

Full-time: 854 men, 1176 women	**Faculty:** 119; IIB, -$
Part-time: 145 men, 238 women	**Ph.D.s:** 92%
Graduate: 178 men, 297 women	**Student/Faculty:** 17 to 1
Year: semesters, summer session	**Tuition:** $22,340
Application Deadline: open	**Room & Board:** $9056
Freshman Class: 2497 applied, 1977 accepted, 470 enrolled	
SAT Verbal/Math: 480/500*	**ACT:** 21 **COMPETITIVE**

Utica College, a private liberal arts institution founded by Syracuse University in 1946, confers the Syracuse University undergraduate degree and Utica College master's degrees. In addition to regional accreditation, UC has baccalaureate program accreditation with ACTA, APTA, and NLN. The library contains 184,425 volumes, 57,214 microform items, and 9608 audio/video tapes/CDs/DVDs, and subscribes to 1931 periodicals including electronic. Computerized library services include the card catalog, interlibrary loans, database searching, Internet access, and laptop Internet portals. Special learning facilities include a learning resource center, art gallery, radio station, an early childhood education lab, and a math and writing center. The 128-acre campus is in a suburban area 50 miles east of Syracuse. Including any residence halls, there are 18 buildings.

Student Life: 87% of undergraduates are from New York. Others are from 39 states, 53 foreign countries, and Canada. 80% are from public schools. 63% are white. The average age of freshmen is 18; all undergraduates, 23. 30% do not continue beyond their first year; 57% remain to graduate.

Housing: 1046 students can be accommodated in college housing, which includes single-sex and coed dorms. On-campus housing is guaranteed for all 4 years. 58% of students commute. All students may keep cars.

Activities: 1% of men belong to 2 local and 3 national fraternities; 1% of women belong to 2 local and 3 national sororities. There are 86 groups on campus, including art, band, cheerleading, choir, chorus, computers, drama, ethnic, film, gay, honors, international, jazz band, literary magazine, musical theater, newspaper, pep band, photography, political, professional, radio and TV, religious, social, social service, student government, and yearbook. Popular campus events include outdoor concerts, mock elections, and Winter Weekend.

Sports: There are 9 intercollegiate sports for men and 11 for women, and 28 intramural sports for men and 28 for women. Facilities include a 2200-seat gym, a competition-size swimming pool, tennis, racquetball, handball, and squash courts, a sauna, Nautilus and weight rooms, dance and aerobic rooms, playing fields, a stadium, and hockey facilities.

Disabled Students: 85% of the campus is accessible. Wheelchair ramps, elevators, special parking, specially equipped rest rooms, lowered drinking fountains, and automatic doors are available.

Services: Counseling and information services are available, as is tutoring in most subjects. There is a reader service for the blind, remedial math, reading, and writing, a writing center, and a math center.

Campus Safety and Security: Measures include 24-hour foot and vehicle patrol, security escort services, shuttle buses, and informal discussions. There are pamphlets/posters/films, emergency telephones, and lighted pathways/sidewalks.

Programs of Study: UC confers B.A. and B.S. degrees. Master's and doctoral degrees are also awarded. Bachelor's degrees are awarded in BIOLOGICAL SCIENCE (biology/biological science), BUSINESS (accounting, business administration and management, and business economics), COMMUNICATIONS AND THE ARTS (communications, English, journalism, and public relations), COMPUTER AND PHYSICAL SCIENCE (chemistry, computer science, mathematics, and physics), HEALTH PROFESSIONS (nursing and recreation therapy), SOCIAL SCIENCE (child psychology/development, criminal justice, economics, history, international studies, philosophy, political science/government, psychology, social studies, and sociology). Occupational therapy, psychology, and biology are the strongest academically. Management, psychology, and criminal justice/economic crime investigation are the largest.

Required: To graduate, students must complete a total of 120 to 128 hours with a minimum 2.0 GPA. They must complete a general education requirement, including basic skills and distribution requirements.

Special: UC offers co-op programs, internships, work-study programs in all majors, accelerated degrees, dual majors, and cross-registration with Hamilton College and the Mohawk Valley Consortium. Study abroad may be arranged in 9 countries. There is a 2-2 engineering degree with any engineering school. There are 5 national honor societies, and a freshman honors program.

Faculty/Classroom: 52% of faculty are male; 48%, female. All both teach and do research. The average class size in an introductory lecture is 23; in a laboratory, 10; and in a regular course, 17.

Admissions: 79% of the 2005-2006 applicants were accepted. The SAT scores for the 2005-2006 freshman class were: Verbal--58% below

500, 35% between 500 and 599, and 7% between 600 and 700; Math--50% below 500, 42% between 500 and 599, 8% between 600 and 700, and 1% above 700.

Requirements: The SAT or ACT is recommended. In addition, graduation from an accredited secondary school or satisfactory scores on the GED are required. Recommended high school courses include 4 years of English, 3 years each of math and social studies, and 2 years each of foreign language and science. An essay and an interview are also recommended. AP and CLEP credits are accepted. Important factors in the admissions decision are advanced placement or honor courses, extracurricular activities record, and leadership record.

Procedure: Freshmen are admitted fall and spring. Entrance exams should be taken during the junior year. There is a deferred admissions plan and a rolling admissions plan. Application deadlines are open. The fall 2005 application fee was $40. Applications are accepted on-line.

Transfer: 230 transfer students enrolled in 2004-2005. Applicants must have a minimum GPA of 2.3. 30 of 120 credits required for the bachelor's degree must be completed at UC.

Visiting: There are regularly scheduled orientations for prospective students, including an interview, financial aid information, and a tour of the campus. There are guides for informal visits and visitors may sit in on classes and stay overnight. To schedule a visit, contact the Admissions Office.

Financial Aid: In 2005-2006, 90% of all full-time students received some form of financial aid, need-based aid. The average freshman award was $9871. UC is a member of CSS. The FAFSA is required. The deadline for filing freshman financial aid applications for fall entry is February 15.

International Students: There are 53 international students enrolled. The school actively recruits these students. They must take the TOEFL or take the IELTS, APIEL, or MELAB. The SAT is recommended if the student's primary language is English.

Computers: Wireless access is available in the library, all smart classrooms, and in 1residence hall. There are 146 workstations located in the library, the student center, and in computer labs. There are also 10 laptops available for use in the library only. All students may access the system during posted hours. Time limits are imposed only during peak hours. The fee is $200.

Graduates: From July 1, 2004 to June 30, 2005, 427 bachelor's degrees were awarded. The most popular majors were criminal justice (17%), management/economics (16%), and health studies (15%). In an average class, 1% graduate in 3 years or less, 40% graduate in 4 years or less, 55% graduate in 5 years or less, and 57% graduate in 6 years or less. 168 companies recruited on campus in 2004-2005. Of the 2004 graduating class, 17% were enrolled in graduate school within 6 months of graduation and 78% were employed.

Admissions Contact: Patrick Quinn, Vice President for Enrollment Management. E-mail: *admiss@utica.edu* Web: *www.utica.edu*

VASSAR COLLEGE   D-4

Poughkeepsie, NY 12604   (845) 437-7300
                                    (800) 827-7270; Fax: (845) 437-7063

Full-time: 960 men, 1366 women	**Faculty:** 278; IIB, ++$
Part-time: 14 men, 38 women	**Ph.D.s:** 96%
Graduate: none	**Student/Faculty:** 8 to 1
Year: semesters	**Tuition:** $33,800
Application Deadline: January 1	**Room & Board:** $7900
Freshman Class: 6314 applied, 1803 accepted, 650 enrolled	
SAT Verbal/Math: 700/686*	**ACT:** 30 **MOST COMPETITIVE**

Vassar College, founded in 1861, is a private, independent college of the liberal arts and sciences. The 3 libraries contain 869,088 volumes, 611,076 microform items, and 23,590 audio/video tapes/CDs/DVDs, and subscribe to 4001 periodicals including electronic. Computerized library services include the card catalog, interlibrary loans, database searching, Internet access, and laptop Internet portals. Special learning facilities include a learning resource center, art gallery, radio station, studio art building, geological museum, observatory, 3 theaters, concert hall, environmental field station, intercultural center, and research-oriented lab facilities for natural sciences. The 1000-acre campus is in a suburban area 75 miles north of New York City. Including any residence halls, there are 100 buildings.

Student Life: 74% of undergraduates are from out of state, mostly the Middle Atlantic. Students are from 50 states, 51 foreign countries, and Canada. 57% are from public schools. 74% are white. The average age of freshmen is 18; all undergraduates, 20. 4% do not continue beyond their first year; 89% remain to graduate.

Housing: 2305 students can be accommodated in college housing, which includes single-sex and coed dorms, on-campus apartments, off-campus apartments, and married-student housing. There is 1 all-women residence hall and 1 cooperative living unit. On-campus housing is guaranteed for all 4 years. 98% of students live on campus; of those, 90% remain on campus on weekends. All students may keep cars.

Activities: There are no fraternities or sororities. There are 100 groups on campus, including art, band, chess, choir, chorale, chorus, computers, dance, debate, drama, ethnic, film, gay, honors, international, jazz band, literary magazine, newspaper, opera, orchestra, photography, political, radio and TV, religious, social, social service, student government, and yearbook. Popular campus events include Founders Day, spring and fall formals, and All Parents Weekend.

Sports: There are 12 intercollegiate sports for men and 13 for women, and 18 intramural sports for men and 18 for women. Facilities include a field house with a swimming pool, 5 indoor tennis courts, a weight and conditioning room, a gym with squash and racquetball courts and basketball facilities, a 9-hole golf course, 13 outdoor tennis courts, an all-weather track, 2 soccer fields, a baseball diamond, a rugby field, club and intramural fields, a competition basketball gym, a banked running track, and a 5000-square foot exercise and fitness center.

Disabled Students: 50% of the campus is accessible. Wheelchair ramps, elevators, special parking, specially equipped rest rooms, special class scheduling, and lowered drinking fountains are available. There is an Office of Disability and Support Services, signage in braille, and assisted listening devices.

Services: Counseling and information services are available, as is tutoring in most subjects. There is a reader service for the blind and remedial math and writing.

Campus Safety and Security: Measures include 24-hour foot and vehicle patrol, self-defense education, security escort services, and shuttle buses. There are informal discussions, pamphlets/posters/films, emergency telephones, and lighted pathways/sidewalks.

Programs of Study: Vassar confers the B.A. degree. Master's degrees are also awarded. Bachelor's degrees are awarded in AGRICULTURE (environmental studies), BIOLOGICAL SCIENCE (biochemistry, biology/biological science, and neurosciences), COMMUNICATIONS AND THE ARTS (art, Chinese, dramatic arts, English, film arts, Japanese, languages, media arts, and music), COMPUTER AND PHYSICAL SCIENCE (astronomy, chemistry, computer science, geology, mathematics, and physics), EDUCATION (foreign languages), ENGINEERING AND ENVIRONMENTAL DESIGN (technology and public affairs), HEALTH PROFESSIONS (premedicine), SOCIAL SCIENCE (African studies, American studies, anthropology, Asian/Oriental studies, biopsychology, classical/ancient civilization, cognitive science, economics, geography, history, international studies, Judaic studies, Latin American studies, medieval studies, philosophy, political science/government, prelaw, psychology, religion, social studies, sociology, Spanish studies, urban studies, Victorian studies, and women's studies). English, psychology, and political science are the largest.

Required: To graduate, students must have a total of 34 units equivalent to 120 credit hours, with a minimum GPA of 2.0. Of this total, no more than 17 units may be in a single field of concentration and 8 1/2 units must be outside the major field. Entering freshmen must take the freshman course. All students must meet the foreign language proficiency requirement and must take a quantitative skills course before their third year. A thesis is required in most departments.

Special: The school offers fieldwork in social agencies and schools, dual majors, independent majors, student-designed majors, cross-registration with the 12 College Consortium, and nonrecorded grade options. Vassar runs study-abroad programs in 7 countries and students also may study in other approved programs around the world. A 3-2 engineering degree with Dartmouth College is offered. There is a chapter of Phi Beta Kappa.

Faculty/Classroom: 54% of faculty are male; 46%, female. All both teach and do research. The average class size in an introductory lecture is 21; in a laboratory, 7; and in a regular course, 16.

Admissions: 29% of the 2005-2006 applicants were accepted. The SAT scores for the 2005-2006 freshman class were: Verbal--3% between 500 and 599, 43% between 600 and 700, and 55% above 700; Math--5% between 500 and 599, 53% between 600 and 700, and 42% above 700. 98% of the current freshmen were in the top two fifths of their class. There were 38 National Merit finalists and 38 semifinalists. 30 freshmen graduated first in their class.

Requirements: The SAT is required. In addition, 2 SAT Subject tests, or the ACT, are required. Graduation from an accredited secondary school or satisfactory scores on the GED are required for admission. The high school program should typically include 4 years each of English, social studies, math, foreign language, and science. An essay and a writing sample are required. AP credits are accepted.

Procedure: Freshmen are admitted in the fall. Entrance exams should be taken as early as possible, but no later than December of the senior year. There are early decision and deferred admissions plans. Early decision applications should be filed by November 15; regular applications, by January 1 for fall entry. Notification of early decision is sent December 15; regular decision, April 1. The fall 2005 application fee was $60. 250 early decision candidates were accepted for the 2005-2006 class. 420 applicants were on the 2005 waiting list; 36 were admitted. Applications are accepted on-line.

Transfer: 21 transfer students enrolled in 2004-2005. Applicants must have a high level of achievement in both high school and college work.

17 of 34 units required for the bachelor's degree must be completed at Vassar.

Visiting: There are regularly scheduled orientations for prospective students, including a campus tour, an information session, and a class visit with advance notice. There are guides for informal visits and visitors may sit in on classes and stay overnight. To schedule a visit, contact the Admissions Office at *admissions@vassar.edu*.

Financial Aid: In 2005-2006, 54% of all full-time freshmen and 59% of continuing full-time students received some form of financial aid. 47% of full-time freshmen and 57% of continuing full-time students received need-based aid. The average freshman award was $27,803. Need-based scholarships or need-based grants averaged $23,920 ($35,000 maximum), and need-based self-help aid (loans and jobs) averaged $3883 ($7500 maximum). 54% of undergraduates work part time. Average annual earnings from campus work are $1056. The average financial indebtedness of the 2005 graduate was $19,038. Vassar is a member of CSS. The CSS/Profile, FAFSA, or FFS and the college's own financial statement are required. The deadline for filing freshman financial aid applications for fall entry is February 1.

International Students: There are 130 international students enrolled. The school actively recruits these students. They must score satisfactorily on the TOEFL and also take the SAT or the ACT. Students must take any 2 SAT Subject tests.

Computers: Wireless access is available. All students may access the system 24 hours per day. There are no time limits and no fees.

Graduates: From July 1, 2004 to June 30, 2005, 670 bachelor's degrees were awarded. The most popular majors were English (11%), political science (10%), and psychology (10%). In an average class, 1% graduate in 3 years or less, 86% graduate in 4 years or less, 91% graduate in 5 years or less, and 91% graduate in 6 years or less. 14 companies recruited on campus in 2004-2005. Of the 2004 graduating class, 17% were enrolled in graduate school within 6 months of graduation and 71% were employed.

Admissions Contact: David Borus, Dean of Admission and Financial Aid. E-mail: *admissions@vassar.edu* Web: *www.vassar.edu*

VAUGHN COLLEGE OF AERONAUTICS AND TECHNOLOGY   D-5
(Formerly College of Aeronautics)

Flushing, NY 11369

(718) 429-6600
(800) 776-2376; Fax: (718) 779-2231

Full-time: 732 men, 110 women	**Faculty:** 43; III, +$
Part-time: 254 men, 30 women	**Ph.D.s:** 10%
Graduate: none	**Student/Faculty:** 20 to 1
Year: semesters, summer session	**Tuition:** $13,680
Application Deadline: open	**Room & Board:** n/app
Freshman Class: 287 applied, 272 accepted, 173 enrolled	
SAT Verbal/Math: 470/560*	**SPECIAL**

Vaughn College of Aeronautics and Technology, formerly the College of Aeronautics, founded in 1932, is a private aviation school offering undergraduate degrees in aeronautical engineering technology, computerized design/animated graphics, airport management, avionics, aviation maintenance, and aircraft operations In addition to regional accreditation, Vaughn has baccalaureate program accreditation with ABET. The library contains 62,000 volumes and 10,000 microform items. Computerized library services include the card catalog, interlibrary loans, database searching, and Internet access. Special learning facilities include a learning resource center flight simulator, nondestructive testing labs, and a 5000-square-foot hangar facility. The 6-acre campus is in an urban area at LaGuardia Airport, 4 miles east of Manhattan. There are 2 buildings.

Student Life: 95% of undergraduates are from New York. Others are from 9 states, 19 foreign countries, and Canada. 96% are from public schools. 35% are Hispanic; 19% African American; 17% white; 11% Asian American. The average age of freshmen is 21; all undergraduates, 23. 27% do not continue beyond their first year; 68% remain to graduate.

Housing: There are no residence halls. College-sponsored housing is coed. All of students commute. Alcohol is not permitted. All students may keep cars.

Activities: There are no fraternities or sororities. There are 6 groups on campus, including ethnic, professional, social, and student government. Popular campus events include Open House-Techno Expo, Winter Fest, and Spring Fest.

Sports: There are 3 intramural sports for men and 3 for women. Facilities include nearby areas for softball, flag football, weight lifting, and basketball.

Disabled Students: 95% of the campus is accessible. Wheelchair ramps, elevators, special parking, specially equipped rest rooms, special class scheduling, lowered drinking fountains, and lowered telephones are available.

Services: Counseling and information services are available, as is tutoring in most subjects. There is remedial math, reading, and writing.

Campus Safety and Security: Measures include 24-hour foot and vehicle patrol, informal discussions, and pamphlets/posters/films.

Programs of Study: Vaughn confers the B.S. degree. Associate degrees are also awarded. Bachelor's degrees are awarded in ENGINEERING AND ENVIRONMENTAL DESIGN (aircraft mechanics, airline piloting and navigation, and aviation administration/management). Computerized design, flight operations, and aviation maintenance management are the strongest academically.

Required: All students must satisfy English, math, and science requirements and fulfill appropriate licensing requirements while maintaining a GPA of at least 2.0. Students with advanced credit must complete 30 credits in residency. A total of 134 credits is required to graduate.

Special: Work-study programs are available with Vaughn College, and internships may be arranged through the career development office. B.A.-B.S. degrees are offered.

Faculty/Classroom: 90% of faculty are male; 10%, female. All teach undergraduates. The average class size in an introductory lecture is 25; in a laboratory, 20; and in a regular course, 20.

Admissions: 95% of the 2005-2006 applicants were accepted.

Requirements: The SAT is required. Applicants are required to have 3 years of math and 2 years each of English and science. An interview is also recommended. A GPA of 2.0 is required. AP credits are accepted. Important factors in the admissions decision are evidence of special talent, advanced placement or honor courses, and personality/intangible qualities.

Procedure: Freshmen are admitted fall and spring. There is an early decision plan. There is a rolling admissions plan. Application deadlines are open. 60 early decision candidates were accepted for the 2005-2006 class.

Transfer: 96 transfer students enrolled in 2004-2005. A minimum 2.0 GPA is required. 30 of 134 credits required for the bachelor's degree must be completed at Vaughn.

Visiting: There are regularly scheduled orientations for prospective students, scheduled prior to registration, which include a tour and academic advisement. There are guides for informal visits and visitors may sit in on classes. To schedule a visit, contact the Admissions Office at *admitme.@vaughn.edu*.

Financial Aid: 86% of undergraduates work part time. Average annual earnings from campus work are $2550. The CSS/Profile or FAFSA and the college's own financial statement are required. The deadline for filing freshman financial aid applications for fall entry is April 15.

International Students: The school actively recruits these students. They must score satisfactorily on the written TOEFL and also take English Proficiency Certificate.

Computers: All students may access the system. There are no time limits and no fees.

Graduates: From July 1, 2004 to June 30, 2005, 119 bachelor's degrees were awarded. In an average class, 30% graduate in 3 years or less, 60% graduate in 4 years or less, 80% graduate in 5 years or less, and 100% graduate in 6 years or less. 30 companies recruited on campus in 2004-2005.

Admissions Contact: Vincent Papandrea, Director of Admissions. E-mail: *admitme@vaughn.edu* Web: *www.vaughn.edu*

WAGNER COLLEGE
Staten Island, NY 10301

D-5

(718) 390-3411
(800) 221-1010; Fax: (718) 390-3105

Full-time: 692 men, 1200 women	Faculty: 99; IIA, -$
Part-time: 25 men, 45 women	Ph.Ds: 72%
Graduate: 119 men, 206 women	Student/Faculty: 19 to 1
Year: semesters, summer session	Tuition: $25,350
Application Deadline: February 15	Room & Board: $7950
Freshman Class: 2858 applied, 1751 accepted, 579 enrolled	
SAT Verbal/Math: 560/560*	ACT: 24 **VERY COMPETITIVE**

Wagner College, founded in 1883, is a private liberal arts institution. In addition to regional accreditation, Wagner has baccalaureate program accreditation with ACBSP, NCATE, and NLN. The library contains 140,000 volumes, 754 microform titles, and 3207 audio/video tapes/CDs/DVDs, and subscribes to 1000 periodicals including electronic. Computerized library services include interlibrary loans, database searching, and Internet access. Special learning facilities include an art gallery, planetarium, and radio station. The 105-acre campus is in a suburban area 10 miles from Manhattan. Including any residence halls, there are 18 buildings.

Student Life: 52% of undergraduates are from out of state, mostly the Northeast. Students are from 40 states, 8 foreign countries, and Canada. 63% are from public schools. 80% are white. 53% are claim no religious affiliation; 34% Catholic; 9% Protestant. The average age of freshmen is 18; all undergraduates, 20. 11% do not continue beyond their first year; 68% remain to graduate.

Housing: 1394 students can be accommodated in college housing, which includes coed dorms and off-campus apartments. In addition, there are fraternity/sorority floors and quiet floors in dorms. On-campus housing is guaranteed for all 4 years. 75% of students live on campus; of those, 75% remain on campus on weekends. Alcohol is not permitted. All students may keep cars.

Activities: 11% of men and about 2% of women belong to 3 local and 2 national fraternities; 9% of women belong to 1 local sorority and 3 national sororities. There are 52 groups on campus, including academics, art, band, cheerleading, chess, choir, chorale, computers, dance, drama, ethnic, gay, honors, international, jazz band, literary magazine, musical theater, newspaper, opera, pep band, political, professional, religious, social service, student government, symphony, women's and yearbook. Popular campus events include Songfest, Spring Fling Week, and Family Weekend.

Sports: There are 9 intercollegiate sports for men and 11 for women, and 8 intramural sports for men and 8 for women. Facilities include a football stadium, a gym, a fitness center, a track, and a basketball arena.

Disabled Students: 25% of the campus is accessible. Wheelchair ramps, elevators, special parking, specially equipped rest rooms, special class scheduling, and lowered drinking fountains are available.

Services: Counseling and information services are available, as is tutoring in every subject. There is a reader service for the blind, and remedial math, reading, and writing.

Campus Safety and Security: Measures include 24-hour foot and vehicle patrol, security escort services, shuttle buses, and informal discussions. There are emergency telephones, lighted pathways/sidewalks, and ID card access into residence halls.

Programs of Study: Wagner confers B.A. and B.S. degrees. Master's degrees are also awarded. Bachelor's degrees are awarded in BIOLOGICAL SCIENCE (biology/biological science and microbiology), BUSINESS (accounting and business administration and management), COMMUNICATIONS AND THE ARTS (arts administration/management, dramatic arts, English, fine arts, and music), COMPUTER AND PHYSICAL SCIENCE (chemistry, computer science, mathematics, and physics), EDUCATION (elementary, middle school, and secondary), HEALTH PROFESSIONS (nursing and physician's assistant), SOCIAL SCIENCE (anthropology, history, political science/government, psychology, public administration, and sociology). Natural sciences is the strongest academically. Business, nursing, and psychology are the largest.

Required: To graduate, students must complete 36 units with 12 to 18 in the major and a minimum GPA of 2.0. All students must take courses in English, math, and multidisciplinary studies. In addition, students must fulfill distribution requirements in physical science, life science, math and computers, history, literature, philosophy and religion, foreign culture, aesthetics, and human behavior.

Special: Internships are required for business and English majors and are recommended for all majors. Students may earn a B.A.-B.S. degree in psychology. Student-designed and dual majors, credit for life experience, a Washington semester, nondegree study, and pass/fail options are available. Study abroad in 14 countries is possible. There are 11 national honor societies, and a freshman honors program.

Faculty/Classroom: 51% of faculty are male; 49%, female. All teach undergraduates. No introductory courses are taught by graduate students. The average class size in an introductory lecture is 21; in a laboratory, 13; and in a regular course, 20.

Admissions: 61% of the 2005-2006 applicants were accepted. The SAT scores for the 2005-2006 freshman class were: Verbal--19% below 500, 50% between 500 and 599, 29% between 600 and 700, and 2% above 700; Math--19% below 500, 55% between 500 and 599, 24% between 600 and 700, and 2% above 700. The ACT scores were 9% below 21, 29% between 21 and 23, 42% between 24 and 26, 17% between 27 and 28, and 3% above 28. 31% of the current freshmen were in the top fifth of their class; 83% were in the top two fifths. 8 freshmen graduated first in their class.

Requirements: The SAT or ACT is required. In addition, graduation from an accredited secondary school is required, with 18 academic credits or Carnegie units, including 4 years of English, 3 years each of history and math, 2 years each of foreign language, science, and social studies, and 1 year each of art and music. An essay is required, and an interview is strongly recommended. Auditions are required for music and theater applicants. A GPA of 3.0 is required. AP and CLEP credits are accepted. Important factors in the admissions decision are advanced placement or honor courses, recommendations by school officials, and extracurricular activities record.

Procedure: Freshmen are admitted fall and spring. Entrance exams should be taken by December of the senior year. There are early decision and deferred admissions plans. Early decision applications should be filed by January 1; regular applications, by February 15 for fall entry, along with a $50 fee. Notification of early decision is sent February 1; regular decision, March 1. 92 early decision candidates were accepted for the 2005-2006 class. 73 applicants were on the 2005 waiting list; 3 were admitted. Applications are accepted on-line.

Transfer: 91 transfer students enrolled in 2004-2005. Transfer students should have a minimum of 30 credit hours earned with a GPA of 2.5. Applicants must submit all college and high school transcripts, a letter of recommendation, and a personal statement. An interview is recommended. SAT or ACT scores taken within the past 5 years may be submitted. 9 of 36 units required for the bachelor's degree must be completed at Wagner.

Visiting: There are regularly scheduled orientations for prospective students, including a presentation by the Admissions Office, a tour of the campus, and meetings with faculty and staff. There are guides for informal visits and visitors may sit in on classes and stay overnight. To schedule a visit, contact the Admissions Office.

Financial Aid: In 2005-2006, 88% of all full-time freshmen and 84% of continuing full-time students received some form of financial aid. 61% of full-time freshmen and 46% of continuing full-time students received need-based aid. The average freshman award was $15,158. Need-based scholarships or need-based grants averaged $12,357; need-based self-help aid (loans and jobs) averaged $4088; non-need-based athletic scholarships averaged $8143; and other non-need-based awards and non-need-based scholarships averaged $6000. 25% of undergraduates work part time. Average annual earnings from campus work are $800. The average financial indebtedness of the 2005 graduate was $16,070. Wagner is a member of CSS. The FAFSA, the state aid form, and the college's own financial statement are required. The priority date for freshman financial aid applications for fall entry is February 15.

International Students: There are 13 international students enrolled. The school actively recruits these students. A satisfactory score on the TOEFL is required.

Computers: Wireless access is available. All students may access the system Monday through Thursday, 9 A.M. to 10 P.M.; Friday, 9 A.M. to 5 P.M.; and Saturday and Sunday, 11 A.M. to 5 P.M. There are no time limits and no fees. It is strongly recommended that all students have a personal computer.

Graduates: From July 1, 2004 to June 30, 2005, 391 bachelor's degrees were awarded. The most popular majors were business (25%), visual and performing arts (19%), and health professions/related sciences (14%). In an average class, 64% graduate in 4 years or less, and 68% graduate in 5 years or less. 60 companies recruited on campus in 2004-2005. Of the 2004 graduating class, 20% were enrolled in graduate school within 6 months of graduation and 79% were employed.

Admissions Contact: Leigh-Ann DePascale, Director of Admissions. E-mail: *admissions@wagner.edu* Web: *www.wagner.edu*

WEBB INSTITUTE   D-5

Glen Cove, NY 11542   **(516) 671-2213; Fax: (516) 674-9838**

Full-time: 60 men, 15 women	Faculty: 8
Part-time: none	Ph.D.s: 50%
Graduate: none	Student/Faculty: 10 to 1
Year: semesters	Tuition: see profile
Application Deadline: see profile	Room & Board: $8340
Freshman Class: 110 applied, 33 accepted, 22 enrolled	
SAT Verbal Math: 680/740	**MOST COMPETITIVE**

Webb Institute, founded in 1889, is a private engineering school devoted to professional knowledge of ship construction, design, and motive power. All students receive 4-year, full-tuition scholarships. In addition to regional accreditation, Webb has baccalaureate program accreditation with ABET. The library contains 51,098 volumes, 1665 microform items, and 1901 audio/video tapes/CDs/DVDs, and subscribes to 271 periodicals including electronic. Computerized library services include the card catalog, interlibrary loans, database searching, and Internet access. Special learning facilities include a marine engineering lab and a ship model testing/towing tank. The 26-acre campus is in a suburban area 24 miles east of New York City. Including any residence halls, there are 11 buildings.

Student Life: 76% of undergraduates are from out of state, mostly the Northeast. Students are from 22 states and 1 foreign country. 70% are from public schools. 96% are white. The average age of freshmen is 18; all undergraduates, 20. 4% do not continue beyond their first year; 73% remain to graduate.

Housing: 110 students can be accommodated in college housing, which includes single-sex dorms. On-campus housing is guaranteed for all 4 years. All students live on campus; of those, 60% remain on campus on weekends. All students may keep cars.

Activities: There are no fraternities or sororities. There are some groups and organizations on campus, including chorale, drama, orchestra, professional, social, student government, yachting, and yearbook. Popular campus events include Parents Day and Webbstock.

Sports: There are 6 intercollegiate sports for men and 6 for women, and 2 intramural sports for men and 2 for women. Facilities include a 60-seat gym, tennis courts, an athletic field, a boat house, and a beachfront dock.

Disabled Students: 90% of the campus is accessible. Elevators and special parking are available.

Services: Counseling and information services are available, as is tutoring in most subjects.

Campus Safety and Security: Measures include 24-hour foot and vehicle patrol, informal discussions, pamphlets/posters/films, and emergen-

cy telephones. There are lighted pathways/sidewalks and student and professional security services.

Programs of Study: Webb confers the B.S. degree. Bachelor's degrees are awarded in ENGINEERING AND ENVIRONMENTAL DESIGN (naval architecture and marine engineering).

Required: The curriculum is prescribed, with all students taking the same courses in each of the 4 years. The Webb program has 4 practical 8-week paid work periods: freshman year, a helper mechanic in a shipyard; sophomore year, a cadet in the engine room of a ship; and junior and senior years, a draftsman or junior engineer in a design office. All students must complete a senior seminar, thesis, and technical reports, as well as make engineering inspection visits. A total of 146 credits with a minimum passing grade of 70% is required to graduate.

Special: All students are employed 2 months each year through co-op programs.

Faculty/Classroom: All faculty are male. All teach undergraduates and 40% both teach and do research. The average class size in an introductory lecture is 25; in a laboratory, 9; and in a regular course, 25.

Admissions: 30% of the 2005-2006 applicants were accepted. The SAT scores for the 2005-2006 freshman class were: Verbal--5% between 500 and 599, 60% between 600 and 700, and 35% above 700; Math--30% between 600 and 700, and 70% above 700. 100% of the current freshmen were in the top fifth of their class. 3 freshmen graduated first in their class.

Requirements: The SAT is required. Applicants should be graduates of an accredited secondary school with 16 academic credits completed, including 4 each in English and math, 2 each in history and science, 1 in foreign language, and 3 in electives. 3 SAT. Subject tests in writing, math, and physics or chemistry are required, as is an interview. Candidates must be U.S. citizens. Webb requires applicants to be in the upper 20% of their class. A GPA of 3.2 is required. Important factors in the admissions decision are advanced placement or honor courses, evidence of special talent, and personality/intangible qualities.

Procedure: Freshmen are admitted in the fall. Entrance exams should be taken by January of the senior year. There is an early decision plan. Check with the school for current application deadlines and fee.

Transfer: Transfers must enter as freshmen. A 3.2 GPA is required. SAT scores and an interview are required. All 146 credits required for the bachelor's degree must be completed at Webb.

Visiting: There are regularly scheduled orientations for prospective students, including an open house one weekend each October. There are guides for informal visits and visitors may sit in on classes and stay overnight. To schedule a visit, contact the Associate Director of Admissions at 516-671-2213, ext.108 or *admissions@webb-institute.edu.*

Financial Aid: The aid available is to assist with room and board. The CSS/Profile and the college's own financial statement are required. Check with the school for current deadlines.

International Students: All applicants must be U.S. Citizens.

Computers: Wireless access is available. The school provides laptops for all students. All students may access the system 24 hours per day.

Admissions Contact: Steven P Ostendorff, Director of Admissions. E-mail: *admissions@webb-institute.edu* Web: *http://www.webb-institute.edu*

WELLS COLLEGE   C-3

Aurora, NY 13026   **(315) 364-3264**
(800) 952-9355; Fax: (315) 364-3227

Full-time: 35 men, 370 women	Faculty: IIB, -$
Part-time: 1 man, 11 women	Ph.D.s: 100%
Graduate: none	Student/Faculty: n/av
Year: semesters	Tuition: $15,790
Application Deadline: March 1	Room & Board: $7280
Freshman Class: 850 applied, 648 accepted, 130 enrolled	
SAT Verbal/Math: 580/540*	ACT: 23 **VERY COMPETITIVE**

Wells College is a private liberal arts, founded in 1868. Historically a women's college, Wells became coeducational in 2005. The library contains 218,284 volumes, 14,830 microform items, and 934 audio/video tapes/CDs/DVDs, and subscribes to 387 periodicals including electronic. Computerized library services include the card catalog, interlibrary loans, database searching, Internet access, and laptop Internet portals. Special learning facilities include an art gallery and the Book Arts Center. The 365-acre campus is in a small town on Cayuga Lake, 30 miles north of Ithaca, and 40 miles southwest of Syracuse. Including any residence halls, there are 22 buildings.

Student Life: 66% of undergraduates are from New York. Others are from 34 states, 10 foreign countries, and Canada. 90% are from public schools. 63% are white. The average age of freshmen is 18; all undergraduates, 20. 22% do not continue beyond their first year; 64% remain to graduate.

Housing: 450 students can be accommodated in college housing, which includes single-sex dormitories and off-campus apartments. In addition, there are special-interest houses and housing for nontraditional-age students. On-campus housing is guaranteed for all 4 years. 84% of students live on campus; of those, 65% remain on campus on weekends. All students may keep cars.

Activities: There are no fraternities. There are 39 groups on campus, including bell ringers, choir, chorale, dance, drama, ethnic, forensics, gay, international, jazz band, literary magazine, musical instrument ensemble, musical theater, newspaper, orchestra, photography, political, professional, religious, social, social service, student government, WILL (Women in Life long Learning), Women's resourse center, and yearbook. Popular campus events include the Odd-Even Basketball Game, Spring Weekend, and 100 Days for Seniors.

Sports: Facilities include a competition-size swimming pool, a gymnasium, a fully equipped fitness/weight/cardo center, an athletic training room, 2 indoor tennis courts/practice space, a dance studio, a 9-hole golf course, 4 all-weather tennis courts, soccer fields, and a boat house and dock with canoes and sailboats.

Disabled Students: 51% of the campus is accessible. Wheelchair ramps, elevators, special parking, specially equipped rest rooms, special class scheduling, lowered drinking fountains, lowered telephones, and special housing are available.

Services: Counseling and information services are available, as is tutoring in every subject. Assistance is provided on an individual, as-needed basis. Untimed and extended-time testing options are available.

Campus Safety and Security: Measures include 24-hour foot and vehicle patrol, self-defense education, security escort services, and shuttle buses. There are informal discussions, pamphlets/posters/films, emergency telephones and lighted pathways/sidewalks. All students must escort their guests on campus at all times; blue light phones are provided.

Programs of Study: Wells confers the B.A. degree. Bachelor's degrees are awarded in AGRICULTURE (environmental studies), BIOLOGICAL SCIENCE (biochemistry, biology/biological science, and molecular biology), BUSINESS (business administration and management), COMMUNICATIONS AND THE ARTS (dance, dramatic arts, English, fine arts, French, German, language arts, music, Spanish, and visual and performing arts), COMPUTER AND PHYSICAL SCIENCE (chemistry, computer science, mathematics, and physics), EDUCATION (elementary), SOCIAL SCIENCE (American studies, anthropology, economics, ethics, politics, and social policy, history, international studies, philosophy, political science/government, psychology, public affairs, religion, sociology, and women's studies). Psychology, English, and mathematical and physical sciences are the largest.

Required: To graduate, students must complete a total of 120 credit hours, including 33 to 63 in the major, with a minimum GPA of 2.0 overall and in the major. All students must complete 2 First-Year Experience courses, a comprehensive exam, 3 January intersession internships/courses, and a senior project/thesis. Distribution requirements include 4 courses in phys ed and wellness, 3 each in natural and social sciences, and arts and humanities, 2 in a foreign language, and 1 in formal reasoning.

Special: Wells offers cross-registration with Cornell University, Cayuga Community College, and Ithaca College, a Washington semester with American University, internships, and accelerated degree programs in all majors. Study abroad in 13 countries is permitted. A 3-2 engineering degree is available with Columbia, Clarkson, and Cornell Universities. Students may also earn 3-2 degrees in business and community health with the University of Rochester and a 3-4 degree in veterinary medicine with Cornell University. Student-designed majors and pass-fail options are available. Work-study, B.A.-B.S. degrees, and dual majors are also offered. There are 2 national honor societies, including Phi Beta Kappa.

Faculty/Classroom: 39% of faculty are male; 61%, female. All teach undergraduates. The average class size in an introductory lecture is 22; in a laboratory, 15; and in a regular course, 13.

Admissions: 76% of the 2005-2006 applicants were accepted. The SAT scores for the 2005-2006 freshman class were: Verbal--18% below 500, 41% between 500 and 599, 36% between 600 and 700, and 5% above 700; Math--34% below 500, 45% between 500 and 599, 19% between 600 and 700, and 2% above 700. The ACT scores were 28% below 21, 26% between 21 and 23, 29% between 24 and 26, 11% between 27 and 28, and 6% above 28. 51% of the current freshmen were in the top fifth of their class; 84% were in the top two fifths. 3 freshmen graduated first in their class.

Requirements: The SAT or ACT is required. In addition, graduation from an accredited secondary school should include 20 academic credits or Carnegie units. High school courses must include 4 years of English, 3 each of a foreign language and math, and 2 each of history and lab science. 2 teacher recommendations and an essay/personal statement are required, and an interview is strongly recommended. AP and CLEP credits are accepted. Important factors in the admissions decision are recommendations by school officials, extracurricular activities record, and advanced placement or honor courses.

Procedure: Freshmen are admitted in the fall. Entrance exams should be taken prior to application. There are early decision, early admissions, and deferred admissions plans. Early decision applications should be filed by December 15; regular applications, by March 1 for fall entry, along with a $40 fee. Notification of early decision is sent January 15;

regular decision, April 1. 16 early decision candidates were accepted for the 2005-2006 class. Applications are accepted on-line.

Transfer: 32 transfer students enrolled in 2004-2005. Applicants must be in good standing at the institution last attended. A minimum GPA of 2.0 is required. Wells requires official college and high school transcripts, a personal statement, standardized test scores, and a recommendation from a professor. An interview is strongly recommended. 60 of 120 credits required for the bachelor's degree must be completed at Wells.

Visiting: There are regularly scheduled orientations for prospective students, including tours, interviews, class attendance, presentations, open houses, an overnight hostess program, and meetings with faculty and coaches. There are guides for informal visits and visitors may sit in on classes and stay overnight (accepted applicants only). To schedule a visit, contact the Admissions Office.

Financial Aid: In 2005-2006, 85% of all full-time freshmen and 86% of continuing full-time students received some form of financial aid. 78% of full-time freshmen and 74% of continuing full-time students received need-based aid. The average freshman award was $14,375. 90% of undergraduates work part time. Average annual earnings from campus work are $1200. The average financial indebtedness of the 2005 graduate was $17,125. The FAFSA is required and early decision applicants must submit the CSS Profile. The deadline for filing freshman financial aid applications for fall entry is May 1.

International Students: There are 16 international students enrolled. The school actively recruits these students. They must score satisfactorily on the written TOEFL or on the electronic version and also take the SAT or the ACT.

Computers: Residence hall rooms are Internet connected, with a ratio of 3 students to computer. It is strongly recommended that all students have a personal computer.

Graduates: In a recent year, 120 bachelor's degrees were awarded. The most popular majors were psychology (25%), sociology/anthropology (11%), and visual arts (9%). In an average class, 2% graduate in 3 years or less, 60% graduate in 4 years or less, 62% graduate in 5 years or less, and 64% graduate in 6 years or less. Of a recent graduating class, 15% were enrolled in graduate school within 6 months of graduation and 37% were employed.

Admissions Contact: Susan Sloan, Director of Admissions. A video is available. E-mail: *admissions@wells.edu* Web: *www.wells.edu*

YESHIVA UNIVERSITY D-5

New York, NY 10033-3201 — (212) 960-5277; Fax: (212) 960-0086

Full-time: 1300 men, 1000 women	**Faculty:** 120
Part-time: 40 men, 20 women	**Ph.D.s:** 79%
Graduate: 1300 men, 1700 women	**Student/Faculty:** 19 to 1
Year: semesters, summer session	**Tuition:** $15,000
Application Deadline: see profile	**Room & Board:** $7,000
Freshman Class: n/av	
SAT or ACT: required	**COMPETITIVE**

Yeshiva University, founded in 1886, is an independent liberal arts institution offering undergraduate programs through Yeshiva College, its undergraduate college for men; Stern College for Women; and Sy Syms School of Business. Figures given in the above capsule and in this profile are approximate. There are 7 graduate schools. In addition to regional accreditation, YU has baccalaureate program accreditation with CSWE. The 7 libraries contain 900,000 volumes, 759,000 microform items, and 980 audio/video tapes/CDs/DVDs, and subscribe to 7790 periodicals including electronic. Computerized library services include the card catalog, interlibrary loans, and database searching. Special learning facilities include an art gallery, radio station, and museum. The 26-acre campus is in an urban area.

Student Life: 48% of undergraduates are from New York. Others are from 31 states, 16 foreign countries, and Canada. 14% are from public schools. The average age of freshmen is 17; all undergraduates, 19. 8% do not continue beyond their first year; 90% remain to graduate.

Housing: 1600 students can be accommodated in college housing, which includes single-sex dorms and off-campus apartments. On-campus housing is guaranteed for all 4 years. 85% of students live on campus. Alcohol is not permitted. All students may keep cars.

Activities: There are no fraternities or sororities. There are 70 groups on campus, including art, choir, computers, drama, honors, international, jazz band, literary magazine, musical theater, newspaper, political, professional, radio, religious, social service, special interest, student government, and yearbook. Popular campus events include holiday and dramatic presentations and Parents Day.

Sports: There are 8 intercollegiate sports for men and 2 for women, and 5 intramural sports for men and 4 for women. The athletic center at Yeshiva College houses a variety of facilities, including a 1000-seat gym.

Disabled Students: 95% of the campus is accessible. Wheelchair ramps and elevators are available.

Services: There is remedial reading and writing. There is also a writing center, which helps students with composition and verbal skills.

Campus Safety and Security: Measures include 24-hour foot and vehicle patrol, security escort services, shuttle buses, and informal discussions. There are pamphlets/posters/films, lighted pathways/sidewalks, ID cards, vulnerability surveys, fire drills, alarm systems, emergency telephone numbers, and transportation for routine and special events.

Programs of Study: YU confers B.A. and B.S. degrees. Associate degrees are also awarded. Bachelor's degrees are awarded in BIOLOGICAL SCIENCE (biology/biological science), BUSINESS (accounting, business administration and management, and marketing/retailing/merchandising), COMMUNICATIONS AND THE ARTS (classical languages, communications, English, French, Hebrew, music, and speech/debate/rhetoric), COMPUTER AND PHYSICAL SCIENCE (chemistry, computer science, and mathematics), ENGINEERING AND ENVIRONMENTAL DESIGN (preengineering), HEALTH PROFESSIONS (health science), SOCIAL SCIENCE (economics, history, philosophy, political science/government, psychology, religion, and sociology). The dual program of liberal arts and Jewish studies is the strongest academically. Accounting, psychology, and economics are the largest.

Required: To graduate, students must complete a total of 128 credit hours. Under the dual program, students pursue a liberal arts or business curriculum together with courses in Hebrew language, literature, and culture. Courses in Jewish learning are geared to the student's level of preparation.

Special: YU offers a 3-2 degree in occupational therapy with Columbia and New York Universities; a 3-4 degree in podiatry with the New York College of Podiatric Medicine; and a 3-2 or 4-2 degree in engineering with Columbia University. Stern College students may take courses in advertising, photography, and design at the Fashion Institute of Technology. Study-abroad programs may be arranged in Israel. The school offers independent study options and an optional pass/no credit system. There are 9 national honor societies and 20 departmental honors programs.

Faculty/Classroom: 73% of faculty are male; 27%, female. 58% teach undergraduates, 60% do research, and 28% do both. No introductory courses are taught by graduate students. The average class size in an introductory lecture is 38; in a laboratory, 15; and in a regular course, 18.

Requirements: The SAT or ACT is required. In addition, graduation from an accredited secondary school with 16 academic credits is required for admission. The GED is accepted under limited and specific circumstances. The SAT II: Subject test in Hebrew is recommended for placement purposes. An interview and an essay are required. A GPA of 3.3 is required. AP and CLEP credits are accepted. Important factors in the admissions decision are extracurricular activities record, personality/intangible qualities, and evidence of special talent.

Procedure: Freshmen are admitted to all sessions. There are early admissions and deferred admissions plans. There is a rolling admissions plan. Notification is sent on a rolling basis. A waiting list is an active part of the admissions procedure. Check with the school for current application deadlines and fee.

Transfer: 95 of 128 credits required for the bachelor's degree must be completed at YU.

Visiting: There are regularly scheduled orientations for prospective students including open houses for high school students. There are guides for informal visits and visitors may sit in on classes and stay overnight. To schedule a visit, contact the Office of Admissions.

Financial Aid: YU is a member of CSS. The CSS/Profile and the college's own financial statement are required.

International Students: The school actively recruits these students. They must take the TOEFL and also take the SAT or the ACT.

Computers: All students may access the system 24 hours per day via modem or when buildings are open. There are no time limits and no fees.

Admissions Contact: Michael Kranzler, Director of Undergraduate Admissions. A video is available. E-mail: *yuadmit@ymail.yu.edu* Web: *www.yu.edu*

NORTH CAROLINA

POPULATION
DENSITY
• 50,000 and over

0   20   40   60   80   100
Miles

APPALACHIAN STATE UNIVERSITY

B-2

Boone, NC 28608

(828) 262-2120; Fax: (828) 262-3296

Full-time: 6000 men, 5900 women	**Faculty:** IIA, av$
Part-time: 400 men, 700 women	**Ph.D.s:** n/av
Graduate: 400 men, 1000 women	**Student/Faculty:** n/av
Year: semesters, summer session	**Tuition:** $3000 ($13,000)
Application Deadline: open	**Room & Board:** $5,000
Freshman Class: n/av	
SAT or ACT: required	**VERY COMPETITIVE**

Appalachian State University, founded in 1899 and a member of the University of North Carolina system, is a comprehensive university offering undergraduate and graduate programs in the arts and sciences, business, teacher education, fine and applied arts, and music. There are 5 undergraduate schools and 1 graduate school. Figures in the above capsule and in this profile are approximate. In addition to regional accreditation, App State has baccalaureate program accreditation with AACSB, AAFCS, ADA, ASLA, ASHLA, CAAHEP, CSAB, CSWE, NASAD, NASM, NCATE, and NRPA. The 2 libraries contain 544,299 volumes, 1,481,544 microform items, and 77,899 audio/video tapes/CDs/DVDs, and subscribe to 40,275 periodicals including electronic. Computerized library services include the card catalog, interlibrary loans, and database searching. Special learning facilities include a learning resource center, art gallery, radio station, TV station, an Appalachian cultural center, and the Dark Sky Observatory. The 1337-acre campus is in a rural area in northwest North Carolina. Including any residence halls, there are 86 buildings.

Student Life: 89% of undergraduates are from North Carolina. Others are from 45 states, 54 foreign countries, and Canada. 97% are from public schools. 92% are white. The average age of freshmen is 18; all undergraduates, 21. 18% do not continue beyond their first year; 65% remain to graduate.

Housing: 5081 students can be accommodated in college housing, which includes single-sex and coed dorms, on-campus apartments, and married-student housing. International student housing and a learning community is also available. On-campus housing is guaranteed for the freshman year only and is available on a lottery system for upperclassmen. 62% of students commute. Alcohol is not permitted. All students may keep cars.

Activities: 5% of men belong to 13 national fraternities; 5% of women belong to 9 national sororities. There are 200 groups on campus, including art, band, cheerleading, chess, choir, chorale, chorus, computers, dance, debate, drama, drill team, ethnic, film, forensics, gay, honors, international, jazz band, literary magazine, marching band, musical theater, newspaper, opera, orchestra, pep band, photography, political, professional, radio and TV, religious, social, social service, student government, symphony, and yearbook. Popular campus events include Appalachian Summer, fall and spring open houses, and multicultural student weekend.

Sports: There are 11 intercollegiate sports for men and 11 for women, and 43 intramural sports for men and 43 for women. Facilities include

a 9000-seat convocation center, a 7000-seat varsity gym, an 18,000-seat stadium, an athletic center, facilities for football, soccer, field hockey, basketball, volleyball, wrestling, indoor and outdoor track, golf, baseball, and tennis, a 2000-seat auditorium, and a fitness center.

Disabled Students: All of the campus is accessible. Wheelchair ramps, elevators, special parking, specially equipped rest rooms, special class scheduling, lowered drinking fountains, lowered telephones, and special housing are available.

Services: Counseling and information services are available, as is tutoring in most subjects. There is a reader service for the blind, and remedial math, reading, and writing.

Campus Safety and Security: Measures include 24-hour foot and vehicle patrol, self-defense education, security escort services, and shuttle buses. There are informal discussions, pamphlets/posters/films, emergency telephones, lighted pathways/sidewalks, and bicycle patrol.

Programs of Study: App State confers B.A., B.S., B.F.A., B.M., B.S.B.A., B.S.C.J., and B.S.W. degrees. Master's and doctoral degrees are also awarded. Bachelor's degrees are awarded in BIOLOGICAL SCIENCE (biology/biological science, ecology, and nutrition), BUSINESS (accounting, banking and finance, hospitality management services, insurance and risk management, marketing/retailing/merchandising, and recreational facilities management), COMMUNICATIONS AND THE ARTS (advertising, art, arts administration/management, communications, dramatic arts, English, French, graphic design, journalism, multimedia, music business management, music performance, public relations, Spanish, and studio art), COMPUTER AND PHYSICAL SCIENCE (chemistry, computer science, geology, information sciences and systems, mathematics, physics, and statistics), EDUCATION (art, business, drama, early childhood, elementary, foreign languages, health, industrial arts, middle school, music, physical, science, secondary, social science, and special), ENGINEERING AND ENVIRONMENTAL DESIGN (construction technology, drafting and design, electrical/electronics engineering technology, environmental science, graphic arts technology, industrial engineering technology, and interior design), HEALTH PROFESSIONS (clinical science, exercise science, health care administration, health science, and music therapy), SOCIAL SCIENCE (anthropology, child psychology/development, clothing and textiles management/production/services, criminal justice, economics, family/consumer studies, geography, history, interdisciplinary studies, philosophy, political science/government, psychology, religion, social work, and sociology). Elementary education, management, and information systems are the largest.

Required: To graduate, students must complete 122 credit hours for most programs, including 60 in the major, with a minimum 2.0 GPA. General education requirements include courses in math, science, history, phys ed, English, social sciences, and humanities.

Special: App State offers co-op programs in clinical lab sciences, cross-registration with Auburn University, Wake Forest University, and the University of North Carolina-Greensboro, internships, work-study programs, B.A.-B.S. degrees, dual majors, and study abroad. Student-designed majors are possible in some programs, and a 3-2 engineering degree is possible with Clemson and Auburn Universities. There are 25 national honor societies, a freshman honors program, and 14 departmental honors programs.

Faculty/Classroom: All faculty both teach and do research. Graduate students teach 1% of introductory courses. The average class size in an introductory lecture is 28; in a laboratory, 22; and in a regular course, 23.

Admissions: 66% of the recent applicants were accepted. 39% of recent freshmen were in the top fifth of their class; 79% were in the top two fifths.

Requirements: The SAT or ACT is required. In addition, applicants must be graduates of an accredited secondary school; the GED is also accepted. They must have completed 4 course units in high school English, 3 in math and science, and 2 in social studies. AP and CLEP credits are accepted. Important factors in the admissions decision are advanced placement or honor courses, extracurricular activities record, and evidence of special talent.

Procedure: Freshmen are admitted to all sessions. Entrance exams should be taken by November, if possible. Application deadlines are open. Check with the school for current application deadlines and fee. 507 applicants were on a recent waiting list.

Transfer: 741 transfer students enrolled in a recent year. Transfer students must have earned a minimum 2.0 GPA on collegiate work. Those students who have accumulated fewer than 30 semester credits, or 45 quarter hours, must also meet freshman requirements. 30 of 122 credits required for the bachelor's degree must be completed at App State.

Visiting: There are regularly scheduled orientations for prospective students, beginning in July for all new students. There are guides for informal visits and visitors may sit in on classes. To schedule a visit, contact the Visitors Center at (828) 262-2179.

Financial Aid: The FAFSA is required. Check with the school for current deadlines.

International Students: There were 53 international students enrolled in a recent year. The school actively recruits these students. They must take the TOEFL. The SAT may be accepted in lieu of the TOEFL.

Computers: All students may access the system. There are no time limits and no fees.

Graduates: In a recent year, 2233 bachelor's degrees were awarded. The most popular majors were elementary education (8%), information technology (6%), and management (5%). In an average class, 1% graduate in 3 years or less, 30% graduate in 4 years or less, 56% graduate in 5 years or less, and 60% graduate in 6 years or less. 275 companies recruited on campus in a recent year.

Admissions Contact: Paul Hiatt, Director of Admissions.
E-mail: *admissions@appstate.edu* Web: *appstate.edu*

BARBER-SCOTIA COLLEGE C-3
Concord, NC 28025

(704) 789-2903
(800) 610-0778; Fax: (704) 789-2958

Full-time: 400 men, 300 women	**Faculty:** 34
Part-time: 5 men, 5 women	**Ph.D.s:** 52%
Graduate: none	**Student/Faculty:** 22 to 1
Year: semesters	**Tuition:** $10,000
Application Deadline: open	**Room & Board:** $5,000
Freshman Class: n/av	
SAT or ACT: required	**LESS COMPETITIVE**

Barber-Scotia College, founded in 1867, is a liberal arts institution affiliated with the Presbyterian Church (U.S.A.) Figures in the above capsule and in this profile are approximate. The library contains 44,518 volumes and 90,901 microform items, and subscribes to 180 periodicals including electronic. Computerized library services include the card catalog, interlibrary loans, database searching, and Internet access. Special learning facilities include a learning resource center. The 40-acre campus is in a suburban area 20 miles from Charlotte. Including any residence halls, there are 24 buildings.

Student Life: 64% of undergraduates are from North Carolina. Others are from 24 states. 98% are from public schools. 97% are African American. Most are Protestant. The average age of freshmen is 19; all undergraduates, 23. 45% do not continue beyond their first year; 30% remain to graduate.

Housing: 562 students can be accommodated in college housing, which includes single-sex dorms and an honors complex. On-campus housing is guaranteed for the freshman year only and is available on a first-come, first-served basis. 66% of students live on campus; of those, 65% remain on campus on weekends. Alcohol is not permitted. Upperclassmen may keep cars.

Activities: There are 4 national fraternities and 4 national sororities. There are 35 groups on campus, including cheerleading, chess, choir, computers, debate, honors, international, newspaper, pep band, political, professional, radio and TV, religious, science, social, social service, student government, and yearbook. Popular campus events include Candlelighting Service, Spring Formal, and Fall Convocation.

Sports: There are 4 intercollegiate sports for men and 5 for women. Facilities include a gym, a tennis court, and an athletic field.

Disabled Students: 50% of the campus is accessible. Wheelchair ramps, elevators, special parking, specially equipped rest rooms, and special housing are available.

Services: Counseling and information services are available, as is tutoring in most subjects. There is remedial math, reading, and writing.

Campus Safety and Security: Measures include 24-hour foot and vehicle patrol, informal discussions, pamphlets/posters/films, and lighted pathways/sidewalks.

Programs of Study: Scotia confers B.A. and B.S. degrees. Bachelor's degrees are awarded in BIOLOGICAL SCIENCE (biology/biological science), BUSINESS (business administration and management and recreational facilities management), COMMUNICATIONS AND THE ARTS (communications and English), COMPUTER AND PHYSICAL SCIENCE (mathematics), EDUCATION (early childhood), SOCIAL SCIENCE (political science/government, and sociology). Education and biology are the strongest academically. Sociology, political science, and business are the largest.

Required: To graduate, students must complete 125 credit hours, 36 in the major, with a 55-hour general education requirement that includes religion, English, phys ed, computer science, and 6 other areas. A 2.0 minimum GPA, 2 years of foreign language, a senior seminar, and comprehensive exams are required.

Special: The college offers cross-registration with the Charlotte Area Consortium, minority colleges, and the University Consortium. Each major program requires a semester experience. There are 2 national honor societies.

Faculty/Classroom: 66% of faculty are male; 34%, female. All teach undergraduates. The average class size in an introductory lecture is 20; in a laboratory, 20; and in a regular course, 15.

Admissions: 70% of recent appicants were accepted. 36% of recent freshmen were in the top fifth of their class; 64% were in the top two fifths. 1 freshman graduated first in a recent class.

Requirements: The SAT or ACT is required. AP and CLEP credits are accepted. Important factors in the admissions decision are ability to finance college education, recommendations by school officials, and personality/intangible qualities.

Procedure: Freshmen are admitted fall and spring. There is a deferred admissions plan and a rolling admissions plan. Check with the school for current application deadlies and fee. The college accepts all applicants. Notification is sent on a rolling basis. Applications are accepted on-line.

Transfer: Applicants for transfer should have a 2.0 GPA. 30 of 125 credits required for the bachelor's degree must be completed at Scotia.

Visiting: There are regularly scheduled orientations for prospective students, which give information about the college. There are guides for informal visits and visitors may sit in on classes and stay overnight. To schedule a visit, contact the Admissions Office at (704) 789-2902 or *ealexander@b-sc.edu*.

Financial Aid: In a recent year, 92% of all full-time freshmen and continuing students received some form of financial aid, including need-based aid. The average freshman award was $11,500. Need-based scholarships or need-based grants averaged $2500 ($6050 maximum); need-based self-help aid (loans and jobs) averaged $2600 ($3225 maximum); non-need-based athletic scholarships averaged $4225 ($13,000 maximum); and other non-need-based awards and non-need-based scholarships averaged $4100 ($9000 maximum). 27% of undergraduates work part time. Average annual earnings from campus work are $650. The average financial indebtedness of a recent graduate was $14,000. The FAFSA and the state aid form are required. Check with the school for current deadlines.

International Students: There were 90 international students enrolled in a recent year. The school actively recruits these students.

Computers: All students may access the system 7 A.M. to 9 P.M. Monday through Saturday. There are no time limits and no fees.

Graduates: In a recent year, 108 bachelor's degrees were awarded.

Admissions Contact: Edward Alexander, Interim Director of Admissions. E-mail: *ealexander@b-sc.edu* Web: *www.b-sc.edu*

BARTON COLLEGE E-2
Wilson, NC 27893

(252) 399-6317
(800) 345-4973; Fax: (252) 399-6572

Full-time: 285 men, 632 women	**Faculty:** 79; IIB, --$
Part-time: 41 men, 231 women	**Ph.D.s:** 57%
Graduate: none	**Student/Faculty:** 12 to 1
Year: 4-1-4, summer session	**Tuition:** $16,436
Application Deadline: open	**Room & Board:** $5880
Freshman Class: 1295 applied, 908 accepted, 247 enrolled	
SAT Verbal/Math: 470/480*	**COMPETITIVE**

Barton College, founded in 1902, is a private baccalaureate college affiliated with the Christian Church (Disciples of Christ). There are 5 undergraduate schools. In addition to regional accreditation, Barton has baccalaureate program accreditation with CAAHEP, CED, CSWE, NCATE, and NLN, CED. The library contains 198,700 volumes, 332,805 microform items, and 3651 audio/video tapes/CDs/DVDs, and subscribes to

14,901 periodicals including electronic. Computerized library services include the card catalog, interlibrary loans, database searching, and Internet access. Special learning facilities include a learning resource center, art gallery, TV station, and writing center. The 65-acre campus is in a suburban area 45 miles east of Raleigh. Including any residence halls, there are 28 buildings.

Student Life: 80% of undergraduates are from North Carolina. Others are from 29 states, 16 foreign countries, and Canada. 83% are from public schools. 68% are white; 23% African American. 55% are Protestant; 26% claim no religious affiliation; 8% Catholic. The average age of freshmen is 18; all undergraduates, 24. 40% do not continue beyond their first year; 43% remain to graduate.

Housing: 690 students can be accommodated in college housing, which includes single-sex and coed dormitories, and sorority floors. On-campus housing is guaranteed for the freshman year only and is available on a first-come, first-served basis. 51% of students live on campus; of those, 50% remain on campus on weekends. All students may keep cars. Alcohol is permitted on a limited basis.

Activities: 14% of men belong to 3 national fraternities; 12% of women belong to 3 national sororities. There are 52 groups on campus, including academic, cheerleading, choir, chorus, drama, ethnic, film, honors, international, literary magazine, musical theater, newspaper, orchestra, photography, political, professional, radio and TV, religious, social, social service, student government, and symphony. Popular campus events include Pre-exam Jam, Lighting of the Luminaries Christmas Celebration, and Welcome Back Barton Day.

Sports: There are 6 intercollegiate sports for men and 6 for women, and 10 intramural sports for men and 10 for women. Facilities include a gym, a tennis complex, baseball, softball, and soccer fields, community parks for intramural activities, and an indoor pool and track.

Disabled Students: 90% of the campus is accessible. Wheelchair ramps, elevators, special parking, specially equipped rest rooms, special class scheduling, lowered drinking fountains, and special housing are available.

Services: Counseling and information services are available, as is tutoring in some subjects, including math and English. Other services include interpreting in class for hearing-impaired students upon request and note takers in class for certain circumstances.

Campus Safety and Security: Measures include 24-hour foot and vehicle patrol, self-defense education, security escort services, and informal discussions. There are pamphlets/posters/films, emergency telephones, lighted pathways/sidewalks, campuswide surveillance cameras, peephole doors to residence rooms, and a city police substation on campus.

Programs of Study: Barton confers B.A., B.S., B.F.A., B.L.S., B.S.N., and B.S.W. degrees. Bachelor's degrees are awarded in BIOLOGICAL SCIENCE (biology/biological science), BUSINESS (accounting, business administration and management, human resources, and sports management), COMMUNICATIONS AND THE ARTS (communications, dramatic arts, English, graphic design, painting, and studio art), COMPUTER AND PHYSICAL SCIENCE (chemistry, information sciences and systems, and mathematics), EDUCATION (art, athletic training, education of the deaf and hearing impaired, elementary, middle school, physical, and specific learning disabilities), ENGINEERING AND ENVIRONMENTAL DESIGN (environmental science), HEALTH PROFESSIONS (exercise science and nursing), SOCIAL SCIENCE (criminal justice, economics, gerontology, history, political science/government, psychology, religion, social studies, social work, and Spanish studies). Nursing, education, and fine arts are the strongest academically. Business, nursing, and education are the largest.

Required: All students must complete a minimum of 126 credit hours, including 36 in the major and 45 to 48 in the core curriculum, with a minimum GPA of 2.0. Core requirements include 12 semester hours in humanities and fine arts, 6 to 9 in global and cross-cultural perspective, 7 in natural sciences, 6 in social sciences, 6 in writing proficiency, 3 each in math, computer proficiency, and first-year seminar (for new freshmen), and 2 in sports science.

Special: Barton offers internships, a Washington semester, a general studies degree, dual majors, work study, and credit by exam in entry-level courses. Preprofessional programs are offered in law, engineering, and a variety of health-related fields, as are 3-2 engineering degrees with North Carolina State and North Carolina Agricultural and Technical State Universities and the University of North Carolina at Charlotte. There are 4 national honor societies, a freshman honors program, and 1 departmental honors program.

Faculty/Classroom: 49% of faculty are male; 51%, female. All teach undergraduates. The average class size in an introductory lecture is 30; in a laboratory, 15; and in a regular course, 18.

Admissions: 70% of the 2005-2006 applicants were accepted. The SAT scores for the 2005-2006 freshman class were: Verbal--63% below 500, 28% between 500 and 599, 7% between 600 and 700, and 2% above 700; Math--57% below 500, 30% between 500 and 599, 11% between 600 and 700, and 2% above 700. 25% of the current freshmen were in the top fifth of their class; 49% were in the top two fifths. 1 freshman graduated first in the class.

Requirements: The SAT or ACT is required. In addition, applicants must be high school graduates with at least 13 college preparatory credits. Barton recommends 4 units of English, 3 of social science, 3 of math (including algebra), and 2 of natural science (including lab science). A foreign language is encouraged. Admission criteria vary for adult learners. A GPA of 2.0 is required. AP and CLEP credits are accepted.

Procedure: Freshmen are admitted to all sessions. Entrance exams should be taken in the spring of the junior year and fall of the senior year. Application deadlines are open. There is a rolling admissions plan. Application fee is $25. Applications are accepted on-line.

Transfer: 101 transfer students enrolled in 2004-2005. Applicants must have a college GPA of 2.0 and be eligible to return to the school they last attended. 45 of 126 credits required for the bachelor's degree must be completed at Barton.

Visiting: There are regularly scheduled orientations for prospective students, including visiting classes, financial aid and freshman advising workshops, tours of the campus, and meeting with administrators, faculty, and students. There are guides for informal visits and visitors may sit in on classes and stay overnight. To schedule a visit, contact the Admissions Office.

Financial Aid: In 2005-2006, 93% of all full-time freshmen and 89% of continuing full-time students received some form of financial aid. 78% of full-time freshmen and 71% of continuing full-time students received need-based aid. The average freshman award was $15,226. Need-based scholarships or need-based grants averaged $4790 ($27,140 maximum); need-based self-help aid (loans and jobs) averaged $1183 ($27,140 maximum); non-need-based athletic scholarships averaged $7009 ($22,050 maximum); and other non-need-based awards and non-need-based scholarships averaged $2290 ($27,140 maximum). 22% of undergraduates work part time. Average annual earnings from campus work are $1200. The average financial indebtedness of the 2005 graduate was $16,966. The FAFSA is required. The priority date for freshman financial aid applications for fall entry is March 15. The deadline for filing freshman financial aid applications for fall entry is June 1.

International Students: There are 21 international students enrolled. The school actively recruits these students. They must score satisfactorily on the written TOEFL or on the electronic version.

Computers: Wireless access is available in the library. All students may access the system 24 hours a day, 7 days a week. There are no time limits and no fees.

Graduates: From July 1, 2004 to June 30, 2005, 231 bachelor's degrees were awarded. The most popular majors were business administration (20%), nursing (14%), and social work (8%). In an average class, 2% graduate in 3 years or less, 31% graduate in 4 years or less, 41% graduate in 5 years or less, and 44% graduate in 6 years or less.

Admissions Contact: Amy Denton, Director of Admissions.
E-mail: *enroll@barton.edu* Web: *www.barton.edu*

BELMONT ABBEY COLLEGE   C-3

Belmont, NC 28012   (704) 825-6665
                                    (888) BAC-0110; Fax: (704) 825-6220

Full-time: 372 men, 426 women	**Faculty:** 49
Part-time: 19 men, 70 women	**Ph.D.s:** 70%
Graduate: none	**Student/Faculty:** 16 to 1
Year: semesters, summer session	**Tuition:** $16,726
Application Deadline: see profile	**Room & Board:** $8588
Freshman Class: 901 applied, 691 accepted, 216 enrolled	
SAT Verbal/Math: 510/510*	**COMPETITIVE**

Belmont Abbey College, founded in 1876, is a private, liberal arts college affiliated with the Roman Catholic Church. In addition to regional accreditation, Belmont Abbey has baccalaureate program accreditation with NCATE. The library contains 110,050 volumes, 59,000 microform items, and 2042 audio/video tapes/CDs/DVDs, and subscribes to 609 periodicals including electronic. Computerized library services include the card catalog, interlibrary loans, database searching, and Internet access. Special learning facilities include a learning resource center and radio station. The 650-acre campus is in a suburban area 12 miles southwest of Charlotte. Including any residence halls, there are 20 buildings.

Student Life: 61% of undergraduates are from North Carolina. Others are from 33 states, 20 foreign countries, and Canada. 72% are white; 12% African American. 37% are Catholic; 35% Protestant; 27% claim no religious affiliation. The average age of freshmen is 18; all undergraduates, 23. 40% do not continue beyond their first year; 46% remain to graduate.

Housing: 600 students can be accommodated in college housing, which includes single-sex and coed dorms and on-campus apartments. In addition, there are special-interest houses and a quiet residence hall. Single-occupancy housing is available for all students.. On-campus housing is guaranteed for all 4 years. 55% of students live on campus; of those, 75% remain on campus on weekends. All students may keep cars.

Activities: 40% of men belong to 1 local fraternity and 2 national fraternities; 30% of women belong to 4 local sororities. There are 30 groups on campus, including cheerleading, chess, choir, chorus, computers, drama, honors, international, literary magazine, newspaper, political, professional, religious, social, social service, and student government. Popular campus events include Spring Weekend, Special Olympics, and Greek Week.

Sports: There are 10 intercollegiate sports for men and 8 for women, and 19 intramural sports for men and 19 for women. Facilities include a phys ed center with a 1200-seat gym and a college union with a 225-seat auditorium.

Disabled Students: 60% of the campus is accessible. Wheelchair ramps, elevators, special parking, specially equipped rest rooms, special class scheduling, and lowered drinking fountains are available.

Services: Counseling and information services are available, as is tutoring in some subjects, including math, English, and accounting. There is a reader service for the blind.

Campus Safety and Security: Measures include 24-hour foot and vehicle patrol, self-defense education, security escort services, and informal discussions. There are pamphlets/posters/films and lighted pathways/sidewalks.

Programs of Study: Belmont Abbey confers B.A. and B.S. degrees. Bachelor's degrees are awarded in BIOLOGICAL SCIENCE (biology/biological science), BUSINESS (accounting, business administration and management, international business management, and sports management), COMMUNICATIONS AND THE ARTS (English), COMPUTER AND PHYSICAL SCIENCE (information sciences and systems), EDUCATION (education and elementary), SOCIAL SCIENCE (economics, history, liberal arts/general studies, philosophy, political science/government, psychology, sociology, and theological studies). Natural and physical sciences and English are the strongest academically. Business administration, education, and biology are the largest.

Required: To graduate, all students must complete a minimum of 120 credits, including 60 credits of core curriculum and 30 upper-level credits in the major. Among the core requirements are history, math, natural sciences, theology, philosophy, English, fine arts, and Great Books Seminar. A minimum 2.0 GPA must be maintained. Honors students must submit a thesis.

Special: Cross-registration is offered through the Charlotte Area Educational Consortium. There are internships in many majors, including required internships in educational studies, as well as on-campus work-study, accelerated degree programs, nondegree study, dual majors, and study abroad in Guatemala, Germany, and France. There are 5 national honor societies and a freshman honors program.

Faculty/Classroom: 61% of faculty are male; 39%, female. All teach undergraduates and 60% both teach and do research. The average class size in an introductory lecture is 24; in a laboratory, 17; and in a regular course, 16.

Admissions: 77% of the 2005-2006 applicants were accepted. The SAT scores for the 2005-2006 freshman class were: Verbal--47% below 500, 39% between 500 and 599, 12% between 600 and 700, and 2% above 700; Math--48% below 500, 39% between 500 and 599, 12% between 600 and 700, and 1% above 700. The ACT scores were 55% below 21, 23% between 21 and 23, 14% between 24 and 26, 6% between 27 and 28, and 2% above 28. 11% of the current freshmen were in the top fifth of their class; 30% were in the top two fifths.

Requirements: A satisfactory score on the SAT or ACT. In addition, candidates must be graduates of an accredited secondary school. A minimum of 16 academic credits must be completed, including 4 in English, 3 each in math and electives, and 2 each in foreign language, history, and science. An interview is recommended. A GPA of 2.0 is required. AP and CLEP credits are accepted. Important factors in the admissions decision are advanced placement or honor courses, extracurricular activities record, and leadership record.

Procedure: Freshmen are admitted fall and spring. Entrance exams should be taken by October of the senior year. There is a deferred admissions plan. Check with the school for current application deadlines. The fee is $35. Notification is sent on a rolling basis. Applications are accepted on-line.

Transfer: 158 transfer students enrolled in 2004-2005. Students with 24 or more credit hours must submit all college transcripts, and those with fewer than 24 credit hours must also submit a high school transcript and SAT scores. All candidates must have a minimum 2.0 GPA and must be eligible to return to the last college attended. An interview is recommended. 30 of 120 credits required for the bachelor's degree must be completed at Belmont Abbey.

Visiting: There are regularly scheduled orientations for prospective students, consisting of a campus tour and meetings with a financial aid adviser, faculty, and students. There are guides for informal visits and visitors may sit in on classes and stay overnight. To schedule a visit, contact the Admissions Office at *admissions@bac.edu*.

Financial Aid: In 2005-2006, 73% of all full-time freshmen and 90% of continuing full-time students received some form of financial aid. 73% of full-time freshmen and 85% of continuing full-time students received need-based aid. The average freshman award was $15,350. 17% of undergraduates work part time. Average annual earnings from campus work are $926. The average financial indebtedness of the 2005 graduate

was $17,000. The FAFSA is required. The deadline for filing freshman financial aid applications for fall entry is April 1.

International Students: There are 51 international students enrolled. The school actively recruits these students. They must achieve satisfactory scores on both the TOEFL and the SAT or ACT.

Computers: Wireless access is available. All students may access the system at any time. There are no time limits and no fees.

Graduates: From July 1, 2004 to June 30, 2005, 173 bachelor's degrees were awarded. The most popular majors were business management (38%), education (20%), and accounting (11%). In an average class, 40% graduate in 4 years or less, 45% graduate in 5 years or less, and 46% graduate in 6 years or less. 22 companies recruited on campus in 2004-2005.

Admissions Contact: Michelle Lynch, Director of Admissions.
E-mail: *michellelynch@bac.edu* Web: *www.belmontabbeycollege.edu*

BENNETT COLLEGE   D-2
Greensboro, NC 27401-3239   (336) 370-8624

Full-time: 500 women	**Faculty:** 57; IIB, --$
Part-time: 10 women	**Ph.D.s:** 68%
Graduate: none	**Student/Faculty:** 11 to 1
Year: semesters, summer session	**Tuition:** $8000 ($11,000)
Application Deadline: open	**Room & Board:** $3500 ($5000)
Freshman Class: n/av	
SAT: required	**COMPETITIVE**

Bennett College, founded in 1873, is a private liberal arts women's institution affiliated with the United Methodist Church. Figures given in the above capsule and in this profile are approximate. In addition to regional accreditation, Bennett has baccalaureate program accreditation with ADA, CSWE, and NCATE. The library contains 98,000 volumes, 300 microform items, and 1600 audio/video tapes/CDs/DVDs, and subscribes to 259 periodicals including electronic. Computerized library servcies include the card catalog, interlibrary loans, and database searching. Special learning facilities include a learning resource center and the Women's Leadership Institute. The 55-acre campus is in an urban area 1 mile from downtown Greensboro. Including any residence halls, there are 31 buildings.

Student Life: 76% of undergraduates are from out of state, mostly the Northeast. Students are from 34 states and 6 foreign countries. 86% are from public schools. 99% are African American. 77% are Protestant; 11% Muslim; 7% claim no religious affiliation. The average age of freshmen is 18; all undergraduates, 21. 21% do not continue beyond their first year; 35% remain to graduate.

Housing: 608 students can be accommodated in college housing, which includes dorms. In addition, there are honors houses. On-campus housing is guaranteed for all 4 years. 80% of students live on campus; of those, 50% remain on campus on weekends. Alcohol is not permitted. All students may keep cars.

Activities: 22% of women belong to 4 national sororities. There are no fraternities. There are 34 groups on campus, including cheerleading, choir, computers, dance, drama, film, honors, international, literary magazine, newspaper, orchestra, professional, religious, student government, and yearbook. Popular campus events include Christmas Concert, President's Ball, and Alumnae Weekend.

Sports: Facilities include a gym, a pool, exercise and gymnastic facilities, an athletic field, and basketball and tennis courts.

Disabled Students: 25% of the campus is accessible. Wheelchair ramps, elevators, special parking, specially equipped rest rooms, and special class scheduling are available.

Services: Counseling and information services are available, as is tutoring in every subject. There is remedial math, reading, and writing.

Campus Safety and Security: Measures include 24-hour foot and vehicle patrol, self-defense education, security escort services, and informal discussions. There are pamphlets/posters/films and lighted pathways/sidewalks.

Programs of Study: Bennett confers B.A., B.S., B.A.S.I.S., and B.S.W. degrees. Associate degrees are also awarded. Bachelor's degrees are awarded in BIOLOGICAL SCIENCE (biology/biological science), BUSINESS (accounting, business administration and management, fashion merchandising, and secretarial studies/office management), COMMUNICATIONS AND THE ARTS (arts administration/management, communications, English, music, and visual and performing arts), COMPUTER AND PHYSICAL SCIENCE (chemistry, computer science, and mathematics), EDUCATION (early childhood, elementary, English, mathematics, middle school, music, science, secondary, and special), SOCIAL SCIENCE (dietetics, interdisciplinary studies, political science/government, psychology, social work, and sociology). Biology, math, and education are the strongest academically. Business administration/accounting and biology are the largest.

Required: All students must take 54 to 64 semester hours of general education courses in communication, humanities, math, natural science, reading, history, foreign language, philosophy, phys ed, religion, and women's studies. A total of 124 semester hours, with 60 to 64 in the major, and at least a 2.0 GPA are required for graduation. Comprehensive exams in math and English are required.

Special: Students may cross-register at member colleges of the Greensboro Regional Consortium, study off campus through exchange programs, take a Washington semester, and study abroad. Bennett offers student-designed majors, dual majors in engineering and nursing, nondegree study, a 3-1 nursing program, a B.A.-B.S. degree in interdisciplinary studies, and a 3-2 engineering degree with North Carolina Agricultural and Technical State University. There are 6 national honor societies, and 6 departmental honors programs.

Faculty/Classroom: 38% of faculty are male; 62%, female. All teach undergraduates. The average class size in an introductory lecture is 25; in a laboratory, 30; and in a regular course, 20.

Requirements: The SAT is required. In addition, applicants must be graduates of accredited high schools or have earned the GED. Secondary preparation should include 4 years of English, 2 of math, 1 each of science and social studies, and 4 of other academic courses. A personal essay is required, and an interview is recommended. A GPA of 2.5 is required. CLEP credit is accepted. Important factors in the admissions decision are recommendations by school officials, parents or siblings attending the school, and evidence of special talent.

Procedure: Freshmen are admitted fall and spring. Entrance exams should be taken preferably during the senior year. There is a deferred admissions plan and a rolling admissions plan. Check with the school for current application deadlines and fee.

Transfer: An official transcript and a catalog from each college previously attended, 2 letters of recommendation, a statement of honorable dismissal from previous colleges, and a personal essay are required. 64 of 124 credits required for the bachelor's degree must be completed at Bennett.

Visiting: There are regularly scheduled orientations for prospective students, including a campus tour and meetings with a financial aid officer and an academic program director. There are guides for informal visits and visitors may sit in on classes and stay overnight. To schedule a visit, contact Linda Torrence, Associate Dean for Enrollment Management.

Financial Aid: Bennett is a member of CSS. The FAFSA and FFS are required. Check with the school for current deadlines.

International Students: The school actively recruits these students. They must take the TOEFL and also take the SAT or the ACT.

Computers: All students may access the system 8 A.M. to 11 P.M. There are no time limits. The fee is $150.

Admissions Contact: Linda Torrence, Associate Dean for Enrollment Management. A video is available.
E-mail: *bcinfo@bennett1.bennett.edu*

CABARRUS COLLEGE OF HEALTH SCIENCES   C-3

Concord, NC 28025-2405   **(704) 783-1555; Fax: (704) 783-2077**

Full-time: 10 men, 180 women	Faculty: n/av
Part-time: 5 men, 60 women	Ph.D.s: n/av
Graduate: none	Student/Faculty: n/av
Year: semesters	Tuition: $8000
Application Deadline: see profile	Room & Board: n/app
Freshman Class: n/av	
SAT or ACT: required	SPECIAL

Cabarrus College of Health Sciences, founded in 1942, is a private institution specializing in health science. Figures in the above capsule and in this profile are approximate. The library contains 6370 volumes and 776 audio/video tapes/CDs/DVDs, and subscribes to 263 periodicals including electronic. Computerized library services include the card catalog, database searching, and Internet access. Special learning facilities include a learning resource center. The campus is in a suburban area.

Housing: There are no residence halls.

Activities: There are some groups and organizations on campus, including honors, professional, and student government.

Disabled Students: All of the campus is accessible. Wheelchair ramps, elevators, special parking, specially equipped rest rooms, lowered drinking fountains, and lowered telephones are available.

Campus Safety and Security: Measures include 24-hour foot and vehicle patrol, emergency telephones, and lighted pathways/sidewalks.

Programs of Study: Cabarrus College of Health Sciences confers the B.S. degree. Associate degrees are also awarded. Bachelor's degrees are awarded in HEALTH PROFESSIONS (health care administration and nursing).

Special: There is 1 national honor society.

Faculty/Classroom: All teach undergraduates. The average class size in an introductory lecture is 20; in a laboratory, 15; and in a regular course, 20.

Admissions: 48% of recent applicatns were accepted.

Requirements: The SAT or ACT is required. Cabarrus College of Health Sciences requires applicants to be in the upper 50% of their class. AP and CLEP credits are accepted.

Procedure: Freshmen are admitted fall and spring. Check with the school for current application deadlines and fee. A waiting list is an active part of the admissioins procedure. Applications are accepted on-line.

Visiting: There are regularly scheduled orientations for prospective students.

Admissions Contact: Mark Ellison, Director of Admissions.
E-mail: *mellison@cabarruscollege.edu* Web: *www.cabarruscollege.edu*

CAMPBELL UNIVERSITY   D-3

Buies Creek, NC 27506   **(800) 334-4111, ext. 1320**
    Fax: (910) 893-1288

Full-time: 1096 men, 1425 women	Faculty: 112
Part-time: 76 men, 81 women	Ph.D.s: 90%
Graduate: 637 men, 886 women	Student/Faculty: 23 to 1
Year: semesters, summer session	Tuition: $15,832
Application Deadline: open	Room & Board: $5305
Freshman Class: 2804 applied, 1709 accepted, 730 enrolled	
SAT Verbal/Math: 539/564*	VERY COMPETITIVE

Campbell University, founded in 1887, is a private, nonsectarian institution affiliated with the North Carolina Baptist Convention and offering degree programs in liberal arts and sciences, business, and education. There are 6 undergraduate and 5 graduate schools. In addition to regional accreditation, Campbell has baccalaureate program accreditation with ACPE, ATS, CAAHEP, CSWE, and NCATE. The 5 libraries contain 218,000 volumes, 1,200,000 microform items, and 4719 audio/video tapes/CDs/DVDs, and subscribe to 12,645 periodicals including electronic. Computerized library services include the card catalog, interlibrary loans, database searching, Internet access, and laptop Internet portals. Special learning facilities include a learning resource center, art gallery, radio station, desktop publishing lab, computerized music lab, family and consumer sciences lab, athletic learning resources center, drug information center for the School of Pharmacy, pharmacy research facility, and the Lundy-Fetterman Museum. The 850-acre campus is in a rural area 28 miles south of Raleigh and 30 miles north of Fayetteville. Including any residence halls, there are 84 buildings.

Student Life: 79% of undergraduates are from North Carolina. Others are from 50 states, 42 foreign countries, and Canada. 90% are from public schools. 80% are white; 10% African American. 76% are Protestant; 8% Catholic; 8% Islamic/Muslim, Hindu, Greek Orthodox, Pentecostal; 7% claim no religious affiliation. The average age of freshmen is 18; all undergraduates, 20. 13% do not continue beyond their first year; 46% remain to graduate.

Housing: 1500 students can be accommodated in college housing, which includes single-sex dorms, on-campus apartments, off-campus apartments, and married-student housing. In addition, there are honors houses. On-campus housing is guaranteed for all 4 years. 60% of students live on campus; of those, 85% remain on campus on weekends. Alcohol is not permitted. All students may keep cars.

Activities: There are no fraternities or sororities. There are 49 groups on campus, including art, band, cheerleading, choir, chorale, chorus, computers, debate, drama, ethnic, honors, international, jazz band, literary magazine, musical theater, newspaper, orchestra, pep band, photography, political, professional, radio and TV, religious, social, social service, student government, and yearbook. Popular campus events include the Staley Lecture Series, Spring Fling, and spring and Christmas formals.

Sports: There are 8 intercollegiate sports for men and 9 for women, and 23 intramural sports for men and 23 for women. Facilities include a 1000-seat gym, athletic complex, 2 golf courses, a nature trail, 2 running tracks, 3 workout facilities, tennis courts, baseball, softball, and soccer fields, and an indoor pool.

Disabled Students: 60% of the campus is accessible. Wheelchair ramps, elevators, special parking, specially equipped rest rooms, special class scheduling, lowered drinking fountains, lowered telephones, and special housing are available.

Services: Counseling and information services are available, as is tutoring in most subjects. There is remedial math and writing.

Campus Safety and Security: Measures include 24-hour foot and vehicle patrol, self-defense education, security escort services, and informal discussions. There are pamphlets/posters/films, emergency telephones, and lighted pathways/sidewalks.

Programs of Study: Campbell confers B.A., B.S., B.Applied Sci., B.B.A., B.H.S., and B.S.W. degrees. Associate, master's, and doctoral degrees are also awarded. Bachelor's degrees are awarded in BIOLOGICAL SCIENCE (biochemistry and biology/biological science), BUSINESS (accounting, business administration and management, international business management, investments and securities, and sports management), COMMUNICATIONS AND THE ARTS (advertising, art, broadcasting, communications, dramatic arts, English, French, journalism, music, and Spanish), COMPUTER AND PHYSICAL SCIENCE (chemistry, computer science, information sciences and systems, and mathematics), EDUCATION (athletic training, elementary, and middle school), ENGINEERING AND ENVIRONMENTAL DESIGN (military science and preengineering), HEALTH PROFESSIONS (clinical science and prepharmacy), SOCIAL SCIENCE (criminal justice, economics, family/consumer studies, history, physical fitness/movement, political science/government, prelaw, psychology, religion, and social work). Life and health science, trust management, and teacher education are the strongest academically. Biology and business administration are the largest.

Required: To graduate, students must complete 128 credit hours with a minimum GPA of 2.0 overall and in the major. All students must take a core curriculum of 45 to 65 hours including English, math, science, social science, religion, fine arts, phys ed, and the Cultural Enrichment Program.

Special: Campbell offers co-op programs, internships, study abroad in 7 countries, a Washington semester, numerous apprenticeships, accelerated degrees, dual majors, and a general studies degree. There is credit for military and work experience. Cross-registration with the North Carolina Model Teacher Education Consortium is possible. There are 14 national honor societies and a freshman honors program. All departments have honors programs.

Faculty/Classroom: 70% of faculty are male; 30%, female. 62% teach undergraduates and 40% do research. No introductory courses are taught by graduate students. The average class size in an introductory lecture is 30; in a laboratory, 20; and in a regular course, 25.

Admissions: 61% of the 2005-2006 applicants were accepted. The SAT scores for the 2005-2006 freshman class were: Verbal--29% below 500, 46% between 500 and 599, 21% between 600 and 700, and 4% above 700; Math--23% below 500, 45% between 500 and 599, 29% between 600 and 700, and 3% above 700. 75% of the current freshmen were in the top fifth of their class; 87% were in the top two fifths. 30 freshmen graduated first in their class.

Requirements: The SAT or ACT is required. In addition, students with test scores below the required levels on the math and verbal sections will be eligible for full admission if they also have a respectable high school GPA, but will be monitored. Applicants shoould have completed 12 high school academic credits, including 4 credits of English, 3 of math, and 2 each of history or social studies, science, and foreign language. An essay, an interview, and a portfolio are recommended. An audition is required for some majors. Campbell requires applicants to be in the upper 50% of their class. A GPA of 2.7 is required. AP and CLEP credits are accepted. Important factors in the admissions decision are advanced placement or honor courses, leadership record, and personality/intangible qualities.

Procedure: Freshmen are admitted to all sessions. Entrance exams should be taken during the junior year or the fall of the senior year. There is a deferred admissions plan and a rolling admissions plan. Application deadlines for fall entry are due August 23; for spring entry, January 11. Application fee is $35. Applications are accepted on-line.

Transfer: 256 transfer students enrolled in 2004-2005. Applicants should have a minimum GPA of 2.0 and supply transcripts from previously attended colleges. 36 of 128 credits required for the bachelor's degree must be completed at Campbell.

Visiting: There are regularly scheduled orientations for prospective students, including a campus tour, student panel and department visits. There are guides for informal visits and visitors may sit in on classes and stay overnight. To schedule a visit, contact the Admissions Office at (910) 893-1290 or adm@mailcenter.campbell.edu.

Financial Aid: In 2005-2006, 97% of all full-time freshmen and 89% of continuing full-time students received some form of financial aid. 66% of full-time freshmen and 67% of continuing full-time students received need-based aid. The average freshman award was $20,396. Need-based scholarships or need-based grants averaged $1844; need-based self-help aid (loans and jobs) averaged $2328; non-need-based athletic scholarships averaged $798; other non-need-based awards and non-need-based scholarships averaged $7512; and non-need based loans averaged $7914. 30% of undergraduates work part time. Average annual earnings from campus work are $531. The average financial indebtedness of the 2005 graduate was $18,646. The FAFSA is required. The deadline for filing freshman financial aid applications for fall entry is March 15.

International Students: There are 153 international students enrolled. The school actively recruits these students. Satisfactory scores are required on the written TOEFL and the SAT, ACT, or MTELP.

Computers: Wireless access is available. All students may access the system during posted student hours, generally, Monday through Thursday, 8 A.M. to 11 p.m, with extended hours Friday through Sunday. There are no time limits and no fees. It is strongly recommended that all students have a personal computer.

Graduates: From July 1, 2004 to June 30, 2005, 916 bachelor's degrees were awarded. The most popular majors were business administration (33%), education (14%), and history (4%). In an average class, 38% graduate in 4 years or less, 41% graduate in 5 years or less, and 45% graduate in 6 years or less. 14 companies recruited on campus in a recent year. Of the 2004 graduating class, 16% were enrolled in graduate school within 6 months of graduation and 67% were employed.

Admissions Contact: Herbert V. Kerner, Jr., Dean of Admissions. A video is available. E-mail: adm@mailcenter.campbell.edu Web: www.campbell.edu

CATAWBA COLLEGE   C-2
Salisbury, NC 28144
(704) 637-4402
(800) 228-2922; Fax: (704) 637-4444

Full-time: 587 men, 635 women	**Faculty:** 72; IIB, --$
Part-time: 13 men, 21 women	**Ph.D.s:** 70%
Graduate: 1 man, 31 women	**Student/Faculty:** 17 to 1
Year: semesters, summer session	**Tuition:** $18,750
Application Deadline: March 15	**Room & Board:** $6250
Freshman Class: 724 applied, 492 accepted, 223 enrolled	
SAT Verbal/Math: 510/520*	**ACT:** 22 COMPETITIVE

Catawba College, founded in 1851, is an independent institution affiliated with the United Church of Christ that offers undergraduate programs in the arts and sciences, business, education, performing arts, forestry and environmental science, social and behavioral sciences, physical education, and preprofessional fields. In addition to regional accreditation, Catawba has baccalaureate program accreditation with NCATE. The 2 libraries contain 181,245 volumes, 626,645 microform items, and 29,268 audio/video tapes/CDs/DVDs, and subscribe to 1209 periodicals including electronic. Computerized library services include the card catalog, interlibrary loans, database searching, and Internet access. Special learning facilities include a curriculum materials center, an observatory, and a nature preserve. The 210-acre campus is in a small town 40 miles northeast of Charlotte. Including any residence halls, there are 30 buildings.

Student Life: 70% of undergraduates are from North Carolina. Students are from 33 states, 16 foreign countries, and Canada. 87% are from public schools. 79% are white; 16% African American. 66% are Protestant; 16% Catholic; 16% claim no religious affiliation. The average age of freshmen is 18; all undergraduates, 23. 35% do not continue beyond their first year; 45% remain to graduate.

Housing: 770 students can be accommodated in college housing, which includes single-sex and coed dorms and nonsmoking and alcohol-free dorms. On-campus housing is guaranteed for the freshman year only. 70% of students live on campus; of those, 75% remain on campus on weekends. All students may keep cars.

Activities: There are no fraternities or sororities. There are 26 groups on campus, including art, band, cheerleading, chess, choir, chorale, chorus, computers, dance, drama, ethnic, honors, jazz band, literary magazine, musical theater, newspaper, orchestra, pep band, political, professional, religious, social, social service, student government, symphony, and yearbook. Popular campus events include Winterfest, Inaugural Ball, and Parents Weekend.

Sports: There are 8 intercollegiate sports for men and 9 for women, and 4 intramural sports for men and 4 for women. Facilities include a 5000-seat stadium and a 3500-seat gym, football, baseball, softball, soccer, and field hockey fields, tennis, volleyball, and racquetball courts, weight lifting, a swimming pool, a challenge course, and table tennis and billiards.

Disabled Students: 95% of the campus is accessible. Wheelchair ramps, elevators, special parking, specially equipped rest rooms, lowered drinking fountains, and lowered telephones are available.

Services: Counseling and information services are available, as is tutoring in most subjects.

Campus Safety and Security: Measures include 24-hour foot and vehicle patrol, self-defense education, security escort services, and informal discussions. There are pamphlets/posters/films, emergency telephones, and lighted pathways/sidewalks.

Programs of Study: Catawba confers B.A., B.S., B.B.A, and B.F.A. degrees. Master's degrees are also awarded. Bachelor's degrees are awarded in AGRICULTURE (environmental studies), BIOLOGICAL SCIENCE (biology/biological science), BUSINESS (accounting, business administration and management, international business management, marketing management, recreation and leisure services, and sports management), COMMUNICATIONS AND THE ARTS (communications, dramatic arts, English, French, language arts, music, musical theater, Spanish, and theater management), COMPUTER AND PHYSICAL SCIENCE (chemistry, information sciences and systems, and mathematics), EDUCATION (athletic training, Christian, education, elementary, mathematics, middle school, music, physical, science, and social studies), ENGINEERING AND ENVIRONMENTAL DESIGN (environmental science), HEALTH PROFESSIONS (medical technology and recreation therapy), SOCIAL SCIENCE (history, philosophy, political science/government, prelaw, psychology, public administration, religion, and sociology). Premedicine, predentistry, and prelaw are the strongest academically. Business, education, and theater arts are the largest.

Required: To graduate, students must complete at least 120 credit hours, including up to 54 in their major, with a minimum GPA of 2.0. General education requirements include 9 semester hours in humanities, 7 in natural sciences, 6 each in social sciences, English composition, and fine arts, 4 to 9 in math, and 1 in physical fitness, college orientation, and foreign language through the elementary level. Students must demonstrate proficiency in math, writing, oral communication, and computer technology.

Special: There are cooperative programs in deaf education with Appalachian State University, forestry and environmental science with Duke University, and physician assistant and medical technician training with Wake Forest University. Cross-registration is possible through the Charlotte Area Educational Consortium. Catawba also offers internships, study abroad in London and Costa Rica, a Washington semester, work-study programs, accelerated degree programs, dual majors, a general studies degree, pass/fail options, and student-designed majors. There are 4 national honor societies, a freshman honors program.

Faculty/Classroom: 59% of faculty are male; 41%, female. All teach undergraduates and 40% both teach and do research. No introductory courses are taught by graduate students. The average class size in an introductory lecture is 18; in a laboratory, 16; and in a regular course, 22.

Admissions: 68% of the 2005-2006 applicants were accepted. The SAT scores for the 2005-2006 freshman class were: Verbal--42% below 500, 43% between 500 and 599, 12% between 600 and 700, and 3% above 700; Math--33% below 500, 51% between 500 and 599, 15% between 600 and 700, and 1% above 700. The ACT scores were 35% below 21, 26% between 21 and 23, 30% between 24 and 26, 3% between 27 and 28, and 6% above 28. 31% of the current freshmen were in the top fifth of their class; 62% were in the top two fifths. 1 freshman graduated first in the class.

Requirements: The SAT or ACT is required. Applicants must be graduates of an accredited secondary school or have a GED. They must have completed 16 academic credits, of which 12 must be Carnegie units. An essay is required, and an interview is encouraged for all students. An audition is required for music and drama scholarships. A GPA of 2.5 is required. AP and CLEP credits are accepted. Important factors in the admissions decision are evidence of special talent, recommendations by school officials, and extracurricular activities record.

Procedure: Freshmen are admitted to all sessions. Entrance exams should be taken by December of the senior year. There is a deferred admissions and a rolling admissions plan. Applications should be filed by March 15 for fall entry, along with a $25 fee. Applications received after Mardh 15 will be considered on a space available basis. Notification is sent on a rolling basis. Applications are accepted on-line.

Transfer: 172 transfer students enrolled in 2004-2005. Applicants must present at least 12 semester hours, a GPA of 2.0 or better, and SAT or ACT scores. Students out of high school for 5 or more years are exempt from the SAT or ACT requirement. 30 of 120 credits required for the bachelor's degree must be completed at Catawba.

Visiting: There are regularly scheduled orientations for prospective students, including campus tours, lunches, meetings with faculty, and financial aid and athletic workshops. There are guides for informal visits and visitors may sit in on classes. To schedule a visit, contact the Office of Admissions.

Financial Aid: In 2005-2006, 98% of all full-time freshmen and 94% of continuing full-time students received some form of financial aid. 54% of full-time freshmen and 49% of continuing full-time students received need-based aid. Need-based scholarships or need-based grants averaged $2496 ($5500 maximum); need-based self-help aid (loans and jobs) averaged $2464 ($5500 maximum); non-need-based athletic scholarships averaged $5032 ($19,500 maximum); and other non-need-based awards and non-need-based scholarships averaged $3642 ($17,600 maximum). 49% of undergraduates work part time. Average annual earnings from campus work are $1100. The average financial indebtedness of the 2005 graduate was $23,000. The FAFSA and the college's own financial statement are required. The deadline for filing freshman financial aid applications for fall entry is March 15.

International Students: There are 19 international students enrolled. A satisfactory score is required on the written TOEFL.

Computers: Students have access to the campus LAN from dorm rooms, public computer labs, the library, and several labs with special software specific to the academic disciplines of music, theater, environmental science, and education. More than 100 desktop machines are located in these public areas. Some wireless access to the network is available from the student center and other buildings on campus. All students may access the system. There are no time limits and no fees.

Graduates: From July 1, 2004 to June 30, 2005, 319 bachelor's degrees were awarded. The most popular majors were business administration (40%), computer information systems (18%), and communication (6%). In an average class, 32% graduate in 4 years or less, 43% graduate in 5 years or less, and 45% graduate in 6 years or less. 15 companies recruited on campus in 2004-2005. Of the 2004 graduating class, 7% were enrolled in graduate school within 6 months of graduation.

Admissions Contact: Dr. Russell Watjen, Vice President and Dean of Admissions. A video is available. E-mail: *lrwatjen@catawba.edu* Web: *http://www.catawba.edu*

DAVIDSON COLLEGE	C-3

Davidson, NC 28035-5000

(704) 894-2230
(800) 768-0380; Fax: (704) 894-2016

Full-time: 840 men, 843 women	**Faculty:** 144; IIB, +$
Part-time: none	**Ph.D.s:** 98%
Graduate: none	**Student/Faculty:** 12 to 1
Year: semesters	**Tuition:** $28,667
Application Deadline: January 2	**Room & Board:** $8158
Freshman Class: 4258 applied, 1146 accepted, 463 enrolled	
SAT Verbal/Math: 680/680*	**ACT:** 30 **MOST COMPETITIVE**

Davidson College, founded in 1837, is a private liberal arts institution affiliated with the Presbyterian Church (U.S.A.). In addition to regional accreditation, Davidson has baccalaureate program accreditation with ACS and NCATE. The 3 libraries contain 617,005 volumes, 507,981 microform items, and 12,714 audio/video tapes/CDs/DVDs, and subscribe to 4546 periodicals including electronic. Computerized library services include the card catalog, interlibrary loans, database searching, and Internet access. Special learning facilities include a learning resource center, art gallery, radio station, and arboretum. The 450-acre campus is in a small town 19 miles north of Charlotte. Including any residence halls, there are 98 buildings.

Student Life: 82% of undergraduates are from out of state, mostly the South. Students are from 48 states, 30 foreign countries, and Canada. 53% are from public schools. 78% are white. The average age of freshmen is 18; all undergraduates, 20. 4% do not continue beyond their first year; 90% remain to graduate.

Housing: 1560 students can be accommodated in college housing, which includes single-sex and coed dorms, on-campus apartments, and off-campus apartments. In addition, there is substance-free housing. On-campus housing is guaranteed for the freshman year only and is available on a lottery system for upperclassmen. 92% of students live on campus. All students may keep cars.

Activities: There are 6 national fraternities. There are no sororities. There are 151 groups on campus, including art, cheerleading, choir, chorale, chorus, computers, dance, drama, ethnic, gay, honors, international, jazz band, literary magazine, musical theater, newspaper, opera, orchestra, outing, pep band, political, professional, radio and TV, religious, social, social service, student government, symphony, and yearbook. Popular campus events include Fall Concert, Spring Concert, and convocations.

Sports: There are 11 intercollegiate sports for men and 10 for women, and 16 intramural sports for men and 15 for women. Facilities include indoor and outdoor tennis courts, 3 racquetball courts, a squash court, a natatorium with a diving well, 2 Nautilus rooms, a gym, a wrestling room, a dance studio, a golf course, a cross-country course and trail, a football and soccer stadium, various other playing fields, and facilities for sailing, swimming, waterskiing, and canoeing at the Lake campus.

Disabled Students: 90% of the campus is accessible. Wheelchair ramps, elevators, special parking, specially equipped rest rooms, special class scheduling, lowered drinking fountains, and lowered telephones are available.

Services: Counseling and information services are available, as is tutoring in some subjects. Tutoring is available as needed through the Student Affairs Office. There is a reader service for the blind.

Campus Safety and Security: Measures include 24-hour foot and vehicle patrol, self-defense education, security escort services, and shuttle buses. There are informal discussions, pamphlets/posters/films, emergency telephones, and lighted pathways/sidewalks.

Programs of Study: Davidson confers A.B. and B.S. degrees. Bachelor's degrees are awarded in BIOLOGICAL SCIENCE (biology/biological science), COMMUNICATIONS AND THE ARTS (art, classics, dramatic arts, English, French, German, music, and Spanish), COMPUTER AND PHYSICAL SCIENCE (chemistry, mathematics, and physics), SOCIAL SCIENCE (anthropology, economics, history, interdisciplinary studies, philosophy, political science/government, psychology, religion, and sociology). Biology, English, and history are the largest.

Required: Students must complete 32 courses, including 10 to 12 in the major, with a 2.0 GPA in order to graduate. Core curriculum requirements include courses in literature, fine arts, history, religion and philosophy, natural science, math, and social sciences. In addition, students must meet foreign language, composition, cultural diversity, and phys ed requirements. Comprehensive exams and a thesis are required in some majors.

Special: Davidson offers interdisciplinary international and South Asian studies programs and study abroad in 12 countries as well as through other schools' study-abroad programs. A 3-2 engineering program may be arranged with Georgia Institute of Technology and Columbia, Duke, North Carolina State, and Washington Universities. Students may design their own majors, cross-register with any college in the Charlotte Area Educational Consortium, enroll in a Washington or Philadelphia semester or a semester or monthlong environmental program at the School for Field Studies, or undertake independent study. There are 15 national honor societies, including Phi Beta Kappa, and 20 departmental honors programs.

Faculty/Classroom: 67% of faculty are male; 33%, female. All both teach and do research. The average class size in an introductory lecture is 16; in a laboratory, 13; and in a regular course, 15.

Admissions: 27% of the 2005-2006 applicants were accepted. The SAT scores for the 2005-2006 freshman class were: Verbal--1% below 500, 10% between 500 and 599, 52% between 600 and 700, and 37% above 700; Math--1% below 500, 6% between 500 and 599, 59% between 600 and 700, and 34% above 700. The ACT scores were 1% below 21, 3% between 21 and 23, 10% between 24 and 26, 22% between 27 and 28, and 64% above 28. 92% of the current freshmen were in the top fifth of their class; 99% were in the top two fifths. 24 freshmen graduated first in their class.

Requirements: The SAT or ACT is required. In addition, 2 SAT Subject Tests are strongly recommended; a mathematics test is particularly encouraged. At least 16 high school units are required, although 20 units are recommended. These should include 4 units of English, 3 of math, and 2 units each of the same foreign language, science, and history/social studies. It is strongly recommended that high school students continue for the third and fourth years in science and in the same foreign language, continue math through calculus, and take additional courses in history. AP credits are accepted. Important factors in the admissions decision are advanced placement or honor courses, recommendations by school officials, and leadership record.

Procedure: Freshmen are admitted in the fall. Entrance exams should be taken by the end of the junior year. There is a deferred admissions plan. Early decision applications should be filed by November 15; regular applications, by January 2 for fall entry. The fall 2005 application fee was $50. Notification of early decision is sent December 15; regular decision, April 1. 211 early decision candidates were accepted for the 2005-2006 class. 1531 applicants were on the 2005 waiting list; 41 were admitted. Applications are accepted on-line.

Transfer: 5 transfer students enrolled in 2004-2005. Applicants must have at least 1 full year of college work, generally with a 3.0 GPA. They must submit official college and high school transcripts, as well as required letters of recommendation, and be in good standing at their previous college. 16 of 32 courses required for the bachelor's degree must be completed at Davidson.

Visiting: There are guides for informal visits and visitors may sit in on classes and stay overnight. To schedule a visit, contact the Admissions Office at (704) 894-2679 or *admission@davidson.edu*.

Financial Aid: In 2004-2005, 51% of all full-time freshmen and 57% of continuing full-time students received some form of financial aid. 29% of full-time freshmen and 34% of continuing full-time students received need-based aid. The average freshman award was $18,007. Need-based scholarships or need-based grants averaged $15,749; need-based self-help aid (loans and jobs) averaged $5516; non-need-based athletic scholarships averaged $12,200; and other non-need-based awards and non-need-based scholarships averaged $3843. 30% of undergraduates work part time. The average financial indebtedness of the 2005 graduate was $22,976. The CSS/Profile, the FAFSA, and the college's own financial statement are required. The deadline for filing freshman financial aid applications for fall entry is February 15.

International Students: There are 58 international students enrolled. The school actively recruits these students. They must achieve a satisfactory score on the written TOEFL and also take the SAT or the ACT.

Computers: Wireless access is available. All students may access the system 24 hours per day. There are no time limits and no fees.

Graduates: From July 1, 2004 to June 30, 2005, 451 bachelor's degrees were awarded. The most popular majors were history (13%), English (12%), biology (11%), and political science (11%). In an average class, 87% graduate in 4 years or less, 89% graduate in 5 years or less, and 90% graduate in 6 years or less. 280 companies recruited on campus in 2004-2005. Of the 2004 graduating class, 16% were enrolled in graduate school within 6 months of graduation and 70% were employed.

Admissions Contact: Christopher J. Gruber, Dean of Admission and Financial Aid. E-mail: *admission@davidson.edu*
Web: *www.davidson.edu*

DUKE UNIVERSITY D-2

Durham, NC 27706 | **(919) 684-3214; Fax: (919) 681-8941**

Full-time: 3267 men, 2977 women	Faculty: 767; I, ++$
Part-time: 9 men, 6 women	Ph.Ds: 97%
Graduate: 3842 men, 3376 women	Student/Faculty: 8 to 1
Year: semesters, summer session	Tuition: $32,409
Application Deadline: January 2	Room & Board: $8830
Freshman Class: 18,090 applied, 3995 accepted, 1724 enrolled	
SAT Verbal/Math: 720/740*	ACT: 31 MOST COMPETITIVE

Duke University, founded in 1838, is a private institution affiliated with the United Methodist Church and offering undergraduate programs in arts and sciences and engineering. There are 2 undergraduate and 8 graduate schools. In addition to regional accreditation, Duke has baccalaureate program accreditation with AACSB, ABET, ACPE, AHEA, APTA, NCATE, NLN, and SAF. The 9 libraries contain 5,471,919 volumes, 4,201,792 microform items, and 61,281 audio/video tapes/CDs/DVDs, and subscribe to 33,934 periodicals including electronic. Computerized library services include the card catalog, interlibrary loans, database searching, and Internet access. Special learning facilities include a learning resource center, art gallery, radio station, TV station, marine lab at Beaufort, primate center, center for international studies, nuclear lab, free electron laser, science research center, institutes of the arts, statistics and decision sciences, policy sciences and public affairs, and centers for teaching and learning, community service, geometric computing, culture, and women. The 9727-acre campus is in a suburban area 285 miles southwest of Washington, D.C. Including any residence halls, there are 208 buildings.

Student Life: 86% of undergraduates are from out of state, mostly the South. Students are from 50 states, 55 foreign countries, and Canada. 60% are from public schools. 56% are white; 14% Asian American; 10% African American. 37% are Protestant; 23% Catholic; 16% claim no religious affiliation; 10% Jewish; 7% Muslim and Eastern religions. The average age of freshmen is 18; all undergraduates, 20. 4% do not continue beyond their first year; 94% remain to graduate.

Housing: 5481 students can be accommodated in college housing, which includes single-sex and coed dorms, on-campus apartments, and married-student housing. In addition, there are language houses and special-interest houses. On-campus housing is guaranteed for all 4 years. 82% of students live on campus. All students may keep cars.

Activities: 29% of men belong to 17 national fraternities; 42% of women belong to 10 national sororities. There are about 400 groups on campus, including art, band, cheerleading, chess, choir, chorale, chorus, computers, dance, debate, drama, drill team, ethnic, film, gay, honors, international, jazz band, literary magazine, marching band, musical theater, newspaper, opera, orchestra, pep band, photography, political, professional, radio and TV, religious, social, social service, student government, and symphony. Popular campus events include College Bowl, Oktoberfest, and Springfest.

Sports: There are 12 intercollegiate sports for men and 11 for women, and 21 intramural sports for men and 19 for women. Facilities include stadiums for baseball, basketball/volleyball, football, and soccer/lacrosse; squash, racquetball, and tennis courts; an aquatic center; training and weight rooms; a golf course; cross-country and jogging trails; and practice and intramural sport club fields. The largest stadium seats 33941; the largest arena, 8564.

Disabled Students: Wheelchair ramps, elevators, special parking, specially equipped rest rooms, special class scheduling, lowered drinking fountains, lowered telephones, and special housing are available. In addition, activities such as concerts can be moved to accessible facilities upon request.

Services: Counseling and information services are available, as is tutoring in every subject. There is a reader service for the blind.

Campus Safety and Security: Measures include 24-hour foot and vehicle patrol, self-defense education, security escort services, and shuttle buses. There are informal discussions, pamphlets/posters/films, emergency telephones, lighted pathways/sidewalks, and a crime prevention program.

Programs of Study: Duke confers B.S., A.B., and B.S.E. degrees. Master's and doctoral degrees are also awarded. Bachelor's degrees are awarded in BIOLOGICAL SCIENCE (anatomy and biology/biological science), COMMUNICATIONS AND THE ARTS (African languages, art history and appreciation, classical languages, dramatic arts, English, Germanic languages and literature, linguistics, literature, music, Slavic languages, Spanish, and visual and performing arts), COMPUTER AND PHYSICAL SCIENCE (chemistry, computer science, geology, mathematics, and physics), ENGINEERING AND ENVIRONMENTAL DESIGN (biomedical engineering, civil engineering, electrical/electronics engineering, environmental science, materials science, and mechanical engineering), SOCIAL SCIENCE (African American studies, African studies, anthropology, area studies, Asian/Oriental studies, Canadian studies, classical/ancient civilization, economics, French studies, history, Italian studies, medieval studies, philosophy, political science/government, psychology, public affairs, religion, sociology, and women's studies). Public policy studies, political science, and economics are the strongest academically. Biology, psychology, and history are the largest.

Required: A minimum of 34 course credits is required for graduation, including natural sciences, quantitative reasoning, and social sciences. No more than 17 course credits are allowed in a major for the B.A. and no more than 19 for the B.S. At least 12 courses must be at or above the 100 level. At least 3 courses designated as seminars, tutorials, independent study, or thesis completion are required. Computer proficiency must be demonstrated by engineering students.

Special: Duke offers cross-registration with the University of North Carolina/Chapel Hill and North Carolina State and North Carolina Central Universities. Also available are internships through the Career Development Center, study abroad in 36 countries, and a Washington semester.

An accelerated degree program is possible, achieving graduation in 3 years or combining the senior year with the first graduate year of the law, business, or environment schools. Several 3-2 and 4-1 medical technology programs (degree completed at Duke) are available. Project Calc, an innovative program in calculus, is also offered. Dual majors of any combination, student-designed majors, nondegree study, and pass/fail options are possible. There are 4 national honor societies, including Phi Beta Kappa, and 38 departmental honors programs.

Faculty/Classroom: 76% of faculty are male; 24%, female. All both teach and do research. Graduate students teach 2% of introductory courses. The average class size in an introductory lecture is 39; in a laboratory, 246; and in a regular course, 21.

Admissions: 22% of the 2005-2006 applicants were accepted. The SAT scores for the 2005-2006 freshman class were: Verbal--1% below 500, 5% between 500 and 599, 31% between 600 and 700, and 63% above 700; Math--1% below 500, 4% between 500 and 599, 23% between 600 and 700, and 72% above 700. The ACT scores were 2% between 21 and 23, 40% between 27 and 28, and 58% above 28. 95% of the current freshmen were in the top fifth of their class; 99% were in the top two fifths.

Requirements: The SAT or ACT is required. The ACT Optional Writing test is also required. In addition, 3 SAT Subject Tests, including writing, are required. Applicants must be graduates of an accredited secondary school and have completed 15 academic credits, with 4 in English and 3 each in math, science, and foreign language; an additional 2 in social studies or history are recommended. Engineering students must have 4 credit units in math and 1 in physics or chemistry. An essay is required, and an interview is recommended. A portfolio or audition is advised in appropriate instances. AP credits are accepted. Important factors in the admissions decision are advanced placement or honor courses, recommendations by school officials, and extracurricular activities record.

Procedure: Freshmen are admitted fall and spring. Entrance exams should be taken in October of the junior year for early decision applicants and by January of the senior year for regular decision. There are early decision, early admissions, and deferred admissions plans. Early decision applications should be filed by November 1; regular applications, by January 2 for fall entry and October 15 for spring entry, along with a $70 fee. Notification of early decision is sent December 15; regular decision, April 15. 470 early decision candidates were accepted for the 2005-2006 class. A waiting list is an active part of the admissions procedure.

Transfer: 21 transfer students enrolled in 2005-2006. A minimum 3.6 GPA is recommended. The SAT, plus 3 SAT Subject Tests, or the ACT is required. 17 of 34 course credits required for the bachelor's degree must be completed at Duke.

Visiting: There are regularly scheduled orientations for prospective students, including student-led tours, counselor-led group information sessions, class visits, and lunch with students. There are guides for informal visits and visitors may sit in on classes and stay overnight. To schedule a visit, contact Undergraduate Admissions at *studenth@valhalla.oit.duke.edu.*

Financial Aid: In 2005-2006, 45% of all full-time freshmen and 40% of continuing full-time students received some form of financial aid. 39% of full-time freshmen and 36% of continuing full-time students received need-based aid. The average freshman award was $27,347. Need-based scholarships or need-based grants averaged $24,354; need-based self-help aid (loans and jobs) averaged $4397; and other non-need-based awards and non-need-based scholarships averaged $31,264. 38% of undergraduates work part time. Average annual earnings from campus work are $1866. The average financial indebtedness of the 2005 graduate was $24,391. The CSS/Profile or FAFSA is required. The deadline for filing freshman financial aid applications for fall entry is February 1.

International Students: There are 296 international students enrolled. The school actively recruits these students. They must take the SAT or ACT. Students taking the SAT must submit SAT Subject Tests.

Computers: All students may access the system 24 hours a day. There are no time limits and no fees. It is strongly recommended that all students have a personal computer.

Graduates: From July 1, 2004 to June 30, 2005, 1557 bachelor's degrees were awarded. The most popular majors were economics (12%), psychology (10%), and biology (9%). In an average class, 1% graduate in 3 years or less, 88% graduate in 4 years or less, 93% graduate in 5 years or less, and 94% graduate in 6 years or less. 2009 companies recruited on campus in 2004-2005. Of the 2004 graduating class, 24% were enrolled in graduate school within 6 months of graduation and 38% were employed.

Admissions Contact: Christoph Guttentag, Director, Undergraduate Admissions. A video is available. E-mail: *askduke@admiss.duke.edu* Web: *http://www.duke.edu/*

EAST CAROLINA UNIVERSITY E-2

Greenville, NC 27858-4353   (252) 328-6640; Fax: (252) 328-6945

Full-time: 6200 men, 9000 women	Faculty: 814; IIA, -$
Part-time: 600 men, 1000 women	Ph.D.s: 68%
Graduate: 1700 men, 3000 women	Student/Faculty: 19 to 1
Year: semesters, summer session	Tuition: $4000 ($14,000)
Application Deadline: see profile	Room & Board: $6000
Freshman Class: n/av	
SAT or ACT: required	COMPETITIVE

East Carolina University, founded in 1907, is a state-supported institution offering degree programs in the arts and sciences, business, education, fine arts and communication, health and human performance, human ecology, technology and computer science, medicine, allied health sciences, and nursing. There are 9 undergraduate and 2 graduate schools. Figures in the above capsule and in this profile are approximate. In addition to regional accreditation, ECU has baccalaureate program accreditation with AACSB, ACCE, ADA, APTA, CSWE, FIDER, NASAD, NASM, NCATE, NLN, and NRPA. The 2 libraries contain 1,330,787 volumes, 2,461,178 microform items, and 30,128 audio/video tapes/CDs/DVDs, and subscribe to 4646 periodicals including electronic. Computerized library services include the card catalog, interlibrary loans, and database searching. Special learning facilities include a learning resource center, art gallery, and radio station. The 1000-acre campus is in an urban area 90 miles east of Raleigh. Including any residence halls, there are 206 buildings.

Student Life: 85% of undergraduates are from North Carolina. Others are from 47 states, 40 foreign countries, and Canada. 80% are white; 15% African American. The average age of freshmen is 18; all undergraduates, 22.

Housing: 5303 students can be accommodated in college housing, which includes single-sex and coed dorms. In addition, there are honors houses, a first-year students' floor, a leadership hall, an extended quiet-hours floor, a substance-free hall, a nonsmoking floor, and an academic-ear hall. On-campus housing is guaranteed for the freshman year only and is available on a first-come, first-served basis. 71% of students commute. Alcohol is not permitted. All students may keep cars.

Activities: 1% of men belong to 22 national fraternities; 1% of women belong to 13 national sororities. There are 244 groups on campus, including academic, art, band, cheerleading, choir, chorale, chorus, computers, dance, drama, drill team, ethnic, gay, honors, international, jazz band, literary magazine, marching band, military, musical theater, newspaper, opera, orchestra, pep band, photography, political, professional, radio and TV, recreation, religious, social, social service, student government, symphony, and yearbook. Popular campus events include Barefoot on the Mall, Midnight Madness, and Pirate Palooza.

Sports: There are 9 intercollegiate sports for men and 9 for women, and 23 intramural sports for men and 23 for women. Facilities include a 43,000-seat stadium, an 8000-seat basketball coliseum, a baseball and softball field, a track, and a natatorium. The Student Recreation Center includes a 6-court multipurpose sports area, a cardiovascular and a weight training area, 3 exercise studios, indoor and outdoor pools, an indoor track, a climbing wall, 7 racquetball courts, a squash court, and a fitness assessment center. The Recreational Sports Complex includes 10 football/soccer fields, 5 softball fields, and a ropes challenge course.

Disabled Students: 94% of the campus is accessible. Wheelchair ramps, elevators, special parking, specially equipped rest rooms, special class scheduling, lowered drinking fountains, lowered telephones, automatic doors, and state-of-the-art adaptive equipment are available.

Services: There is a reader service for the blind and remedial math and reading. Tutoring is established on a department-by-department basis.

Campus Safety and Security: Measures include 24-hour foot and vehicle patrol, self-defense education, security escort services, and shuttle buses. There are informal discussions, pamphlets/posters/films, emergency telephones, lighted pathways/sidewalks, bicycle patrols, bicycle registration, motorist assistance, lost and found, operation ID, the Residence Hall Liaison Officer Program, on-and off-campus crime prevention safety tips, Staff and Faculty Eyes (SAFE) Campus Community Watch Program, and alcohol awareness.

Programs of Study: ECU confers B.A., B.S., B.F.A., B.M., B.S.A., B.S.A.P., B.S.B.A., B.S.B.E., B.S.N., B.S.O.T., and B.S.W. degrees. Master's and doctoral degrees are also awarded. Bachelor's degrees are awarded in BIOLOGICAL SCIENCE (biochemistry, biology/biological science, and nutrition), BUSINESS (accounting, banking and finance, business administration and management, hospitality management services, management information systems, marketing management, and recreational facilities management), COMMUNICATIONS AND THE ARTS (art, art history and appreciation, communications, dance, design, dramatic arts, English, French, German, music performance, music theory and composition, and studio art), COMPUTER AND PHYSICAL SCIENCE (applied physics, chemistry, computer science, geology, mathematics, and physics), EDUCATION (art, athletic training, business, dance, drama, early childhood, education of the emotionally handicapped, education of the mentally handicapped, elementary, English, foreign languages, health, home economics, marketing and distribution, mathematics, middle school, music, physical, science, social studies, and special), ENGINEERING AND ENVIRONMENTAL DESIGN (city/community/regional planning, construction management, electrical/electronics engineering technology, environmental engineering technology, industrial engineering technology, interior design, and manufacturing technology), HEALTH PROFESSIONS (environmental health science, exercise science, medical records administration/services, medical technology, music therapy, nursing, occupational therapy, physician's assistant, recreation therapy, rehabilitation therapy, and speech pathology/audiology), SOCIAL SCIENCE (anthropology, child care/child and family studies, clothing and textiles management/production/services, criminal justice, dietetics, economics, family and community services, geography, Hispanic American studies, history, liberal arts/general studies, parks and recreation management, philosophy, physical fitness/movement, political science/government, psychology, social work, sociology, and women's studies). Allied health, art, music, and geology are the strongest academically. Elementary education, nursing, and fine/studio arts are the largest.

Required: To graduate, students must complete 120 to 128 semester hours with a minimum GPA of 2.0 overall and in the major. General education requirements include 12 hours of social science, 10 of humanities and fine arts, 8 of science, 6 of English, 3 of math, and 3 of health and exercise and sport science. The total must include 12 hours of writing-intensive courses and a course in cultural diversity.

Special: ECU offers cooperative programs in most majors, internships, study abroad in 39 countries, dual majors, work-study, and a student-designed major in multidisciplinary studies. There are 19 national honor societies, a freshman honors program, and 39 departmental honors programs.

Faculty/Classroom: 54% of faculty are male; 46%, female. The average class size in an introductory lecture is 52; in a laboratory, 24; and in a regular course, 33.

Admissions: 77% of recent applicants were accepted. 34% of recent freshmen were in the top fifth of their class; 72% were in the top two fifths. 41 freshmen graduated first in a recent class.

Requirements: The SAT or ACT is required. In addition, applicants must be graduates of an accredited secondary school. All degree-seeking students are required to complete 20 academic units, including 4 in English, 3 in math, 3 in science with 1 lab course, 2 in social studies with 1 in U.S. history, and 2 units in a foreign language. 1 unit in fine arts is recommended. 1 unit each in foreign language, natural science, and math should be taken in the senior year. Special circumstances exist for applicants with a GED. A GPA of 2.0 is required. AP and CLEP credits are accepted.

Procedure: Freshmen are admitted to all sessions. Entrance exams should be taken in the spring of the junior year or the fall of the senior year. There is a deferred admissions plan and a rolling admissions plan. Check with the school for current application deadlines and fee. Notification is sent on a rolling basis. Applications are accepted on-line.

Transfer: 1275 transfer students enrolled in a recent year. Applicants must submit official transcripts from high school and all colleges attended and have a satisfactory GPA in courses attempted. Applicants who will have completed fewer than 30 semester hours will also be required to meet the freshman requirements. 30 of 120 credits required for the bachelor's degree must be completed at ECU.

Visiting: There are regularly scheduled orientations for prospective students, including information sessions and campus tours. There are guides for informal visits. To schedule a visit, contact the Admissions Office at *admis@mail.ecu.edu*.

Financial Aid: In a recent year, 64% of all full-time freshmen and 57% of continuing full-time students received some form of financial aid. 39% of full-time freshmen and 27% of continuing full-time students received need-based aid. The average freshman award was $6736. The average financial indebtedness of a recent graduate was $18,318. ECU is a member of CSS. The FAFSA is required. Check with the school for current deadlines.

International Students: There were 69 international students enrolled in a recent year. The school actively recruits these students. They must take the TOEFL. SAT or ACT scores are required if the student will receive an athletic scholarship or if the student will graduate from a U.S. high school.

Computers: All students may access the system at all times. There are no time limits and no fees. It is strongly recommended that all students have a personal computer.

Graduates: In a recent year, 2849 bachelor's degrees were awarded. The most popular majors were elementary education (6%), nursing (6%), and management (5%). In an average class, 25% graduate in 4 years or less, 48% graduate in 5 years or less, and 54% graduate in 6 years or less. 70 companies recruited on campus in a recent year.

Admissions Contact: Thomas E. Powell, Jr., Director of Undergraduate Admissions. E-mail: *admis@mail.ecu.edu*
Web: *www.ecu.ed/admissions*

ELIZABETH CITY STATE UNIVERSITY   F-2
Elizabeth City, NC 27909   (252) 335-3305
(800) 347-ECSU; Fax: (252) 335-3537

Full-time: 685 men, 1090 women	**Faculty:** 113; IIB, av$
Part-time: 50 men, 150 women	**Ph.D.s:** 68%
Graduate: none	**Student/Faculty:** 16 to 1
Year: semesters, summer session	**Tuition:** $1700 ($8100)
Application Deadline: open	**Room & Board:** $4000
Freshman Class: n/av	
SAT or ACT: required	**LESS COMPETITIVE**

Elizabeth City State University, founded in 1891 as part of the University of North Carolina System, is a public institution offering undergraduate programs in liberal arts and sciences, education, and business. Figures in above capsule and in this profile are approximate. The library contains 174,566 volumes, 486,884 microform items, and 1220 audio/video tapes/CDs/DVDs, and subscribes to 1698 periodicals including electronic. Computerized library services include the card catalog and interlibrary loans. Special learning facilities include a learning resource center, art gallery, planetarium, radio station, TV station, a farm, and a 639-acre educational research tract. The 829-acre campus is in a small town 55 miles from Norfolk, Virginia.

Student Life: 90% of undergraduates are from North Carolina. Others are from 20 states and 5 foreign countries. 75% are African American; 23% white. 25% do not continue beyond their first year; 50% remain to graduate.

Housing: 1019 students can be accommodated in college housing, which includes single-sex dormitories and on-campus apartments. In addition, there are honors houses. On-campus housing is guaranteed for all 4 years. 52% of students commute. Alcohol is not permitted. All students may keep cars.

Activities: There are 4 national fraternities and 4 national sororities. There are many groups and organizations on campus, including band, cheerleading, choir, chorus, dance, drama, honors, international, jazz band, literary magazine, marching band, newspaper, pep band, radio and TV, religious, social, student government, and yearbook.

Sports: Facilities include a 4500-seat gym, a 3500-seat stadium, an all-weather track, a golf range, an Olympic pool, a weight room, 8 tennis courts, dance and exercise studios, handball and racquetball courts, and playing fields.

Disabled Students: Wheelchair ramps, elevators, special parking, specially equipped rest rooms, and lowered drinking fountains are available.

Services: In addition to vocational counseling services, tutoring is available.

Campus Safety and Security: Measures include emergency telephones and ECSU has its own police department on campus.

Programs of Study: ECSU confers B.A., B.S., and B.S.Ed. degrees. Bachelor's degrees are awarded in BIOLOGICAL SCIENCE (biology/biological science), BUSINESS (accounting and business administration and management), COMMUNICATIONS AND THE ARTS (art, English, and music), COMPUTER AND PHYSICAL SCIENCE (chemistry, computer science, geology, mathematics, and physics), EDUCATION (business, elementary, industrial arts, middle school, physical, special, and technical), ENGINEERING AND ENVIRONMENTAL DESIGN (industrial engineering technology), SOCIAL SCIENCE (criminal justice, history, political science/government, psychology, social science, social work, and sociology).

Required: Students must have maintained a minimum GPA of 2.0, fulfilled a major, and completed the requirements of general education courses in the fields of grammar, composition, and literature.

Special: Opportunities are provided for internships, dual majors, weekend/evening degree completion programs, work-study, and credit by exam and for military service. There are 5 national honor societies, and a freshman honors program.

Faculty/Classroom: All teach undergraduates.

Requirements: The SAT or ACT is required. In addition, graduation from an accredited secondary school is required; the GED is accepted. Applicants should submit an academic record with 4 courses in English, 3 each in math and science, and 2 in social science; it is recommended that applicants have at least 2 course units in foreign languages. Students must also pass the NC Competency Examination or its equivalent. A GPA of 2.0 is required. AP and CLEP credits are accepted.

Procedure: Freshmen are admitted fall, spring, and summer. Entrance exams should be taken as early as possible. There are early admissions and deferred admissions plans. Application deadlines are open. The fall 2005 application fee was $30.

Transfer: Applicants must have a minimum college GPA of 2.0 and submit high school and college transcripts. Those with fewer than 30 credit hours must meet both freshman and transfer admission requirements. 30 credits required for the bachelor's degree must be completed at ECSU.

Visiting: There are regularly scheduled orientations for prospective students. There are guides for informal visits. To schedule a visit, contact the Admissions Office.

Financial Aid: The FAFSA, the college's own financial statement, and income tax forms are required. Check with the school for application deadlines.

International Students: They must take the TOELF or the MELAB, and also take the SAT or the ACT.

Computers: Students in computer-related courses may access the system. There are no time limits and no fees. It is strongly recommended that all students have a personal computer.

Admissions Contact: Bridgett Golham, Director of Admissions and Recruitment. A video is available. E-mail: *admissions@alpha.ecsu.edu* Web: *www.ecsu.edu*

ELON UNIVERSITY   D-2
Elon, NC 27244-2010

(336) 278-3566
(800) 334-8448; Fax: (336) 278-7699

Full-time: 1801 men, 2806 women   **Faculty:** 279; II A, -$
Part-time: 47 men, 48 women   **Ph.D.s:** 83%
Graduate: 89 men, 165 women   **Student/Faculty:** 17 to 1
Year: 4-1-4, summer session   **Tuition:** $18,949
Application Deadline: January 10   **Room & Board:** $6422
Freshman Class: 9065 applied, 3743 accepted, 1237 enrolled
SAT Verbal/Math: 600/610*   **HIGHLY COMPETITIVE**

Elon University, founded in 1889 by the United Church of Christ, is a private comprehensive institution that offers programs in the liberal arts and sciences in career-oriented fields of study. There are 4 undergraduate and 3 graduate schools. In addition to regional accreditation, Elon has baccalaureate program accreditation with AACSB, CAHEA, CAPTE, and NCATE. The library contains 250,119 volumes, 909,940 microform items, and 17,267 audio/video tapes/CDs/DVDs, and subscribes to 4955 periodicals including electronic. Computerized library services include the card catalog, interlibrary loans, and database searching. Special learning facilities include a learning resource center, art gallery, radio station, TV station, a writing center, a botanical preserve, and an observatory. The 575-acre campus is in a suburban area adjacent to Burlington and 17 miles east of Greensboro. Including any residence halls, there are 108 buildings.

Student Life: 70% of undergraduates are from out of state, mostly the Middle Atlantic. Students are from 44 states, 41 foreign countries, and Canada. 79% are from public schools. 88% are white. 45% are Protestant; 25% Catholic. The average age of freshmen is 18; all undergraduates, 20. 11% do not continue beyond their first year; 76% remain to graduate.

Housing: 2700 students can be accommodated in college housing, which includes single-sex and coed dorms, on-campus apartments, off-campus apartments, fraternity houses, and sorority houses. In addition, there are honors houses, language houses, special-interest houses, theme suites, and academic living-learning communities. On-campus housing is guaranteed for the freshman year only and is available on a lottery system for upperclassmen. 57% of students live on campus; of those, 70% remain on campus on weekends. All students may keep cars.

Activities: 26% of men belong to 11 national fraternities; 43% of women belong to 11 national sororities. There are 150 groups on campus, including art, band, cheerleading, choir, chorale, chorus, computers, dance, drama, drill team, ethnic, film, gay, honors, international, jazz band, literary magazine, marching band, musical theater, newspaper, orchestra, pep band, photography, political, professional, radio and TV, religious, social, social service, student government, symphony, and yearbook. Popular campus events include Family Weekend, Greek Week, and College Coffee.

Sports: There are 7 intercollegiate sports for men and 9 for women, and 20 intramural sports for men and 20 for women. Facilities include an 8250-seat stadium, lighted tennis courts, a baseball stadium, a field house, and 15 athletic fields. The athletic center has racquetball courts, aerobic rooms, a human performance lab, a weight room, a fitness center, 2 gyms, a driving range, and an indoor swimming pool.

Disabled Students: 75% of the campus is accessible. Wheelchair ramps, elevators, special parking, specially equipped rest rooms, special class scheduling, lowered drinking fountains, lowered telephones, special housing, special class locations, and special headphones in auditoriums are available.

Services: Counseling and information services are available, as is tutoring in most subjects, including many lower-level courses. There is remedial math, reading, and writing. Preparatory courses are offered, which count as elective credit toward graduation.

Campus Safety and Security: Measures include 24-hour foot and vehicle patrol, self-defense education, security escort services, and shuttle buses. There are informal discussions, pamphlets/posters/films, emergency telephones, and lighted pathways/sidewalks.

Programs of Study: Elon confers B.A., B.S., and B.F.A. degrees. Master's and doctoral degrees are also awarded. Bachelor's degrees are awarded in BIOLOGICAL SCIENCE (biology/biological science), BUSINESS (accounting, business administration and management, and sports management), COMMUNICATIONS AND THE ARTS (art, broadcast-

ing, communications, dance, dramatic arts, English, film arts, French, journalism, music, music performance, musical theater, and Spanish), COMPUTER AND PHYSICAL SCIENCE (chemistry, computer science, information sciences and systems, mathematics, and physics), EDUCATION (elementary, foreign languages, health, mathematics, middle school, music, physical, science, secondary, social science, and special), ENGINEERING AND ENVIRONMENTAL DESIGN (engineering, environmental science, and military science), HEALTH PROFESSIONS (medical technology and sports medicine), SOCIAL SCIENCE (economics, history, human services, international studies, philosophy, political science/government, psychology, public administration, religion, and sociology). Business, education, and music theater are the strongest academically. Business, education, and journalism and communications are the largest.

Required: To graduate, students must complete 132 semester hours, including 32 to 68 in the major, with a minimum GPA of 2.0. All students must fulfill the requirements of the General Studies program, which includes a first-year core, experiential learning, liberal studies, and advanced studies, for a total of 59 semester hours, and must satisfactorily complete a comprehensive exam in the major.

Special: Elon offers co-op programs in most majors, dual majors, student-designed majors, cross-registration with 6 other colleges and universities in North Carolina, paid and unpaid internships, study abroad in 40 countries, a Washington semester, work-study programs, pass/fail options, and 3-2 dual engineering degree programs. The 3-week January term includes extensive international study opportunities and courses with domestic travel components. There are 25 national honor societies, a freshman honors program, and 18 departmental honors programs.

Faculty/Classroom: 55% of faculty are male; 45%, female. All teach undergraduates and 61% both teach and do research. No introductory courses are taught by graduate students. The average class size in an introductory lecture is 24; in a laboratory, 19; and in a regular course, 22.

Admissions: 41% of the 2005-2006 applicants were accepted. The SAT scores for the 2005-2006 freshman class were: Verbal--6% below 500, 42% between 500 and 599, 46% between 600 and 700, and 6% above 700; Math--5% below 500, 35% between 500 and 599, 54% between 600 and 700, and 7% above 700. 57% of the current freshmen were in the top fifth of their class; 85% were in the top two fifths. There was 1 National Merit finalist and 3 semifinalists. 22 freshmen graduated first in their class.

Requirements: The SAT or ACT is required. In addition, students must be graduates of an accredited secondary school or have a GED certificate. They should have completed 4 credits in English, 3 or more in math, 2 or more in a foreign language, 2 or more in science, including at least 1 lab science, and 2 or more in social studies, including U.S. history. A GPA of 2.6 is required. AP and CLEP credits are accepted. Important factors in the admissions decision are advanced placement or honor courses, evidence of special talent, and leadership record.

Procedure: Freshmen are admitted in the fall. Entrance exams should be taken in the spring of the junior year and the fall of the senior year. There are early decision, early admissions, and deferred admissions plans. Early decision applications should be filed by November 1; regular applications, by January 10 for fall entry, along with a $40 fee. Notification of early decision is sent December 1; regular decision, March 15. 804 early decision candidates were accepted for the 2005-2006 class. 2251 applicants were on the 2005 waiting list; 24 were admitted. Applications are accepted on-line.

Transfer: 79 transfer students enrolled in 2004-2005. Applicants must present a high school transcript and a minimum GPA of 2.5 in college course work from a 4-year college. An interview is recommended. A dean's evaluation form is required from the last college or university attended, and the applicant must be eligible to return to that institution. 60 of 132 credits required for the bachelor's degree must be completed at Elon.

Visiting: There are regularly scheduled orientations for prospective students, consisting of 2 weekends in spring for deposited freshmen and a spring open house for nondeposited students. There are guides for informal visits and visitors may sit in on classes. To schedule a visit, contact the Admissions Office.

Financial Aid: In 2005-2006, 77% of all full-time freshmen and 72% of continuing full-time students received some form of financial aid. 35% of full-time freshmen and 33% of continuing full-time students received need-based aid. The average freshman award was $12,357. Need-based scholarships or need-based grants averaged $3656 ($17,900 maximum); need-based self-help aid (loans and jobs) averaged $3043 ($12,625 maximum); non-need-based athletic scholarships averaged $10,507 ($28,167 maximum); and other non-need-based awards and non-need-based scholarships averaged $2665 ($18,949 maximum). 25% of undergraduates work part time. Average annual earnings from campus work are $1200. The average financial indebtedness of the 2005 graduate was $21,667. Elon is a member of CSS. The CSS/Profile or FAFSA and the college's own financial statement are required. The priority date for freshman financial aid applications for fall entry is February 15.

International Students: There are 86 international students enrolled. The school actively recruits these students. Satisfactory scores are required on the TOEFL as well as the SAT or ACT.

Computers: Wireless access is available. All students may access the system 24 hours a day via modem. It is strongly recommended that all students have a personal computer.

Graduates: From July 1, 2004 to June 30, 2005, 1084 bachelor's degrees were awarded. The most popular majors were business (19%), journalism and communications (17%), and education (6%). In an average class, 66% graduate in 4 years or less, 72% graduate in 5 years or less, and 76% graduate in 6 years or less. 250 companies recruited on campus in 2004-2005. Of the 2004 graduating class, 15% were enrolled in graduate school within 6 months of graduation and 79% were employed.

Admissions Contact: Susan Klopman, Dean of Admissions. A video is available. E-mail: *admissions@elon.edu* Web: *www.elon.edu*

FAYETTEVILLE STATE UNIVERSITY — D-3
Fayetteville, NC 28301-4298   **(910) 672-1371**
(800) 222-2594; Fax: (910) 437-2512

Full-time: 1200 men, 1900 women	**Faculty:** 202; IIA, -$
Part-time: 200 men, 500 women	**Ph.Ds:** n/av
Graduate: 200 men, 500 women	**Student/Faculty:** 15 to 1
Year: semesters, summer session	**Tuition:** $2000 ($10,000)
Application Deadline: see profile	**Room & Board:** $4000
Freshman Class: n/av	
SAT or ACT: required	**LESS COMPETITIVE**

Fayetteville State University, founded in 1867 and today part of the University of North Carolina system, is a public institution offering degree programs in the arts and sciences, business, and teacher preparation. There are 3 undergraduate schools and 1 graduate school. Figures in the above capsule and in this profile are approximate. In addition to regional accreditation, FSU has baccalaureate program accreditation with NCATE. The library contains 241,022 volumes, 936,006 microform items, and 6656 audio/video tapes/CDs/DVDs. Computerized library services include the card catalog, interlibrary loans, and database searching. Special learning facilities include a planetarium and radio station. The 156-acre campus is in an urban area 60 miles south of Raleigh. Including any residence halls, there are 40 buildings.

Student Life: 90% of undergraduates are from North Carolina. 75% are African American; 19% white. The average age of freshmen is 18; all undergraduates, 24. 29% do not continue beyond their first year; 32% remain to graduate.

Housing: 1200 students can be accommodated in college housing, which includes single-sex and coed dorms and on-campus apartments. There is an honors dorm. On-campus housing is available on a first-come, first-served basis. 67% of students commute. Alcohol is not permitted. All students may keep cars.

Activities: 5% of men belong to 5 local and 4 national fraternities; 5% of women belong to 4 national sororities. There are 20 groups on campus, including band, cheerleading, choir, chorus, dance, drama, film, honors, international, jazz band, literary magazine, marching band, newspaper, pep band, political, radio and TV, religious, social service, student government, and yearbook. Popular campus events include The Lyceum, Martin Luther King Day, and Black History Month.

Sports: There are 6 intercollegiate sports for men and 7 for women, and 4 intramural sports for men and 2 for women. Facilities include 2 gyms, a stadium, tennis courts, a bowling alley, a dance studio, a swimming pool, and playing fields.

Disabled Students: 75% of the campus is accessible. Wheelchair ramps, elevators, special parking, specially equipped rest rooms, and lowered drinking fountains are available.

Services: Counseling and information services are available, as is tutoring in some subjects. There is remedial math, reading, and writing.

Campus Safety and Security: Measures include 24-hour foot and vehicle patrol, security escort services, and lighted pathways/sidewalks.

Programs of Study: FSU confers B.A. and B.S. degrees. Master's degrees are also awarded. Bachelor's degrees are awarded in BIOLOGICAL SCIENCE (biology/biological science), BUSINESS (accounting, banking and finance, business administration and management, business economics, and office supervision and management), COMMUNICATIONS AND THE ARTS (dramatic arts, English, Spanish, speech/debate/rhetoric, and visual and performing arts), COMPUTER AND PHYSICAL SCIENCE (chemistry, computer science, and mathematics), EDUCATION (business, early childhood, elementary, health, marketing and distribution, middle school, music, secondary, and social science), HEALTH PROFESSIONS (medical laboratory technology and nursing), SOCIAL SCIENCE (criminal justice, economics, geography, history, political science/government, psychology, public administration, social science, and sociology).

Required: To graduate, students must complete 120 credit hours with a minimum GPA of 2.0 overall and in the major. The core curriculum includes 8 to 11 credits in natural science, 6 to 15 in humanities, 6 to 7

in math, 3 to 9 in social science, 3 each in critical thinking and speech, and 2 each in phys ed/health and university seminar.

Special: FSU offers cooperative programs in business, math, and biological and physical sciences with North Carolina State University, internships, B.A.-B.S. degrees, dual majors, 3-2 engineering degree programs, credit for military experience, and nondegree study. There are 10 national honor societies, a freshman honors program, and 7 departmental honors programs.

Faculty/Classroom: 60% of faculty are male; 40%, female. All both teach and do research. No introductory courses are taught by graduate students. The average class size in an introductory lecture is 30; in a laboratory, 20; and in a regular course, 30.

Requirements: The SAT or ACT is required. In addition, successful scores are also required on the North Carolina Competency Exam. Applicants must be graduates of an accredited secondary school or have the GED. They should have completed 4 academic units of English, 3 each of math and science with 1 lab course, and 2 of social studies; also recommended are 2 units of a foreign language and completion of 1 unit each of foreign language and math in the senior year. A GPA of 2.0 is required. AP and CLEP credits are accepted. Important factors in the admissions decision are advanced placement or honor courses, recommendations by school officials, and leadership record.

Procedure: Freshmen are admitted to all sessions. Entrance exams should be taken in November. There are early decision, early admissions, and deferred admissions plans. There is a rolling admissions plan. Check with the school for current application deadlines and fee. Notification is sent on a rolling basis.

Transfer: Applicants must submit official transcripts from all colleges attended, have a minimum GPA of 2.0, and be eligible to return to their previous institution. 30 of 120 credits required for the bachelor's degree must be completed at FSU.

Visiting: There are regularly scheduled orientations for prospective students, including a campus tour, recreational activity, placement tests, preregistration, and orientation to FSU services. There are guides for informal visits and visitors may sit in on classes and stay overnight. To schedule a visit, contact the Director of Enrollment Management at *cdarlington@uncfsu.edu*.

Financial Aid: FSU is a member of CSS. The FAFSA is required.

International Students: They must take the TOEFL or other English proficiency exam administered in their country, and also take the SAT or the ACT.

Computers: All students may access the system 24 hours a day. There are no time limits and no fees.

Admissions Contact: Charles Darlington, Director of Enrollment Management. A video is available. E-mail: *cdarlington@uncfsu.edu* Web: *www.uncfsu.edu/admissions/index.htm*

GARDNER-WEBB UNIVERSITY — C-3
Boiling Springs, NC 28017-9980   **(704) 406-4491**
(800) 253-6472; Fax: (704) 406-4488

Full-time: 792 men, 1430 women	**Faculty:** 100
Part-time: 103 men, 301 women	**Ph.Ds:** 72%
Graduate: 455 men, 695 women	**Student/Faculty:** 22 to 1
Year: semesters, summer session	**Tuition:** $15,960
Application Deadline: open	**Room & Board:** $5540
Freshman Class: 2042 applied, 1465 accepted, 431 enrolled	
SAT Verbal/Math: 510/510*	**ACT:** 21 **COMPETITIVE**

Gardner-Webb University, founded in 1905, is an independent institution affiliated with the Baptist Convention of North Carolina and offering undergraduate programs in the arts and science, business, education, nursing and professional studies. There are 3 undergraduate and 3 graduate schools. In addition to regional accreditation, Webb has baccalaureate program accreditation with ATS, CAAHEP, NASM, NCATE, and NLN. The library contains 234,651 volumes, 650,231 microform items, and 10,364 audio/video tapes/CDs/DVDs, and subscribes to 13,000 periodicals including electronic. Computerized library services include interlibrary loans, database searching, and laptop Internet portals. Special learning facilities include a learning resource center, art gallery, radio station, TV station, and an observatory. The 250-acre campus is in a small town 50 miles west of Charlotte. Including any residence halls, there are 37 buildings.

Student Life: 77% of undergraduates are from North Carolina. Others are from 25 states, 30 foreign countries, and Canada. 81% are white; 15% African American. Most are Protestant. The average age of freshmen is 19; all undergraduates, 24. 30% do not continue beyond their first year; 50% remain to graduate.

Housing: 1139 students can be accommodated in university housing, which includes single-sex dorms and on-campus apartments. In addition, there are honors houses. On-campus housing is guaranteed for all 4 years. 65% of students live on campus; of those, 50% remain on campus on weekends. Alcohol is not permitted. All students may keep cars.

Activities: There are no fraternities or sororities. There are 43 groups on campus, including art, band, cheerleading, choir, chorale, chorus, dance, debate, drama, drill team, film, honors, international, jazz band, literary magazine, marching band, musical theater, newspaper, opera, orchestra, pep band, photography, political, professional, radio and TV, religious, social, social service, student government, symphony, and yearbook. Popular campus events include Parents weekend, Festival of Lights, and Bulldog Madness.

Sports: There are 10 intercollegiate sports for men and 10 for women, and 16 intramural sports for men and 17 for women. Facilities include an 8,500-seat stadium, 2 gyms, tennis and racquetball courts, a weight room, a swimming pool, playing fields for softball, soccer, football, and baseball, a 5500-seat arena, an aerobics room, and Broyhill Adventure course.

Disabled Students: All of the campus is accessible. Wheelchair ramps, elevators, special parking, specially equipped rest rooms, special class scheduling, lowered drinking fountains, and special housing are available.

Services: Counseling and information services are available, as is tutoring in every subject. There is a reader service for the blind, and remedial math, reading, and writing.

Campus Safety and Security: Measures include 24-hour foot and vehicle patrol, security escort services, informal discussions, and pamphlets/posters/films. There are emergency telephones, lighted pathways/sidewalks, and a foot patrol inside the dorm.

Programs of Study: Webb confers B.A., B.S., B.M., and B.S.N. degrees. Associate, master's, and doctoral degrees are also awarded. Bachelor's degrees are awarded in BIOLOGICAL SCIENCE (biology/biological science), BUSINESS (accounting, business administration and management, international business management, and sports management), COMMUNICATIONS AND THE ARTS (American Sign Language, art, communications, English, French, music, and Spanish), COMPUTER AND PHYSICAL SCIENCE (chemistry, computer science, information sciences and systems, and mathematics), EDUCATION (athletic training, elementary, foreign languages, health, middle school, music, physical, and secondary), ENGINEERING AND ENVIRONMENTAL DESIGN (industrial administration/management), HEALTH PROFESSIONS (medical technology, nursing, and physician's assistant), SOCIAL SCIENCE (history, interpreter for the deaf, psychology, religion, religious music, social science, and sociology). Nursing, fine arts, and education are the strongest academically. Business and nursing are the largest.

Required: To graduate, students must complete 128 credit hours, including 24 to 32 in the major, with a minimum GPA of 2.0. The required core curriculum includes courses in English, history, religion, fine arts, foreign language, natural science, and math.

Special: The university offers work-study programs, internships, study abroad in 18 countries, 3-2 engineering degrees with Auburn University and the University of North Carolina at Charlotte, a 3+1 medical technology degree with the Bowman Gray School of Medicine of Wake Forest University, and a 3+2 physician's assistant program with the Wake Forest University School of Medicine. Independent study is encouraged. There are 2 national honor societies, a freshman honors program, and 3 departmental honors programs.

Faculty/Classroom: 49% of faculty are male; 58%, female. All teach undergraduates. No introductory courses are taught by graduate students. The average class size in an introductory lecture is 35; in a laboratory, 9; and in a regular course, 18.

Admissions: 72% of the 2005-2006 applicants were accepted. The SAT scores for the 2005-2006 freshman class were: Verbal--46% below 500, 35% between 500 and 599, 16% between 600 and 700, and 3% above 700; Math--43% below 500, 41% between 500 and 599, 15% between 600 and 700, and 1% above 700. 41% of the current freshmen were in the top fifth of their class; 67% were in the top two fifths. There was 1 National Merit finalist and 2 semifinalists. 9 freshmen graduated first in their class.

Requirements: The SAT or ACT is required. In addition, candidates should be graduates of an accredited secondary school or have a GED certificate. The recommended preparatory curriculum includes 4 units of English, 3 of math, and 2 each of social science, natural science, a foreign language, and electives. An interview is encouraged. Webb requires applicants to be in the upper 50% of their class. A GPA of 2.5 is required. AP and CLEP credits are accepted. Important factors in the admissions decision are leadership record, extracurricular activities record, and recommendations by school officials.

Procedure: Freshmen are admitted to all sessions. Entrance exams should be taken in the senior year. There is a deferred admissions plan. Application deadlines are open. Application fee is $25. Applications are accepted on-line.

Transfer: 476 transfer students enrolled in 2004-2005. Applicants must submit the standard application and fee, official high school and college transcripts, and SAT or ACT scores. High school transcripts and test scores are waived for applicants with 30 or more semester credits and a GPA of 2.0. 32 of 128 credits required for the bachelor's degree must be completed at Webb.

Visiting: There are regularly scheduled orientations for prospective students. There are guides for informal visits and visitors may sit in on classes and stay overnight. To schedule a visit, contact the Admissions Office.

Financial Aid: In a recent year, 92% of all full-time freshmen and 78% of continuing full-time students received some form of financial aid. The average freshman award was $9804. Average annual earnings from campus work are $1600. The average financial indebtedness of a recent graduate was $11,770. Webb is a member of CSS. The FAFSA and federal tax returns are required. Check with the school for application deadlines.

International Students: There are 45 international students enrolled. The school actively recruits these students. They must take theTOEFL.

Computers: Wireless access is available. There are 5 PC labs and 1 Mac lab. Wireless connection is available throughout the campus. Students must have a wireless-able system with Ethernet card to take advantage of the system. All students may access the system 7 A.M. to 11 P.M. except when a class is in progress. There are no time limits and no fees. It is strongly recommended that all students have a personal computer.

Graduates: From July 1, 2004 to June 30, 2005, 755 bachelor's degrees were awarded. The most popular majors were business administration (27%), social science (21%), and accounting (9%). Of the 2004 graduating class, 38% were enrolled in graduate school within 6 months of graduation.

Admissions Contact: Nathan Alexander, Director of Admissions and Enrollment Management. A video is available.
E-mail: *admissions@gardner-webb.edu* Web: *www.gardner-webb.edu*

GREENSBORO COLLEGE   D-2
Greensboro, NC 27401-1875   (336) 272-7102, ext. 211
                                       (800) 346-8226; Fax: (336) 378-0154

Full-time: 400 men, 450 women	**Faculty:** 57; IIB, av$
Part-time: 100 men, 200 women	**Ph.D.s:** 77%
Graduate: 20 men, 50 women	**Student/Faculty:** 16 to 1
Year: semesters, summer session	**Tuition:** $16,000
Application Deadline: open	**Room & Board:** $7000
Freshman Class: n/av	
SATor ACT: required	**COMPETITIVE**

Greensboro College, founded in 1838, is a private institution affiliated with the United Methodist Church and offering undergraduate programs in the arts and sciences, business, education, health sciences, and pre-professional studies, and graduate programs in education. Figures in the above capsule and in this profile are approximate. In addition to regional accreditation, Greensboro College has baccalaureate program accreditation with NCATE. The library contains 106,530 volumes, 2981 microform items, and 2695 audio/video tapes/CDs/DVDs, and subscribes to 282 periodicals including electronic. Computerized library services include the card catalog, interlibrary loans, database searching, and Internet access. Special learning facilities include a learning resource center, art gallery, and natural history museum. The 46-acre campus is in an urban area bordering downtown Greensboro. Including any residence halls, there are 23 buildings.

Student Life: 74% of undergraduates are from North Carolina. Others are from 27 states, 24 foreign countries, and Canada. 79% are white; 17% African American. 47% are Protestant; 33% claim no religious affiliation; 11% Catholic. The average age of freshmen is 18; all undergraduates, 23. 31% do not continue beyond their first year; 46% remain to graduate.

Housing: 627 students can be accommodated in college housing, which includes single-sex and coed dorms and on-campus apartments. There is an on-campus community service house. On-campus housing is guaranteed for all 4 years. 52% of students commute. All students may keep cars.

Activities: 3% of men belong to 2 local and 1 national fraternity; 4% of women belong to 2 local sororities. There are 49 groups on campus, including art, band, cheerleading, choir, community service, chorale, computers, dance, drama, ethnic, honors, international, jazz band, literary magazine, marching band, musical theater, newspaper, opera, pep band, photography, political, professional, programming, religious, social, social service, and student government. Popular campus events include Winter Rose Formal, Festival of Lessons and Carols, and Spring Fling.

Sports: There are 8 intercollegiate sports for men and 8 for women, and 5 intramural sports for men and 5 for women. Facilities include an athletic field for soccer and lacrosse, and tennis and basketball courts.

Disabled Students: 80% of the campus is accessible. Wheelchair ramps, elevators, special parking, specially equipped rest rooms, and special class scheduling are available.

Services: Counseling and information services are available, as is tutoring in most subjects. There is remedial math and writing. a computerized writing center, and a Writing Across the Curriculum program to strengthen communication skills. Professional math tutors are available.

Campus Safety and Security: Measures include 24-hour foot and vehicle patrol, self-defense education, security escort services, and informal discussions. There are pamphlets/posters/films, emergency telephones, lighted pathways/sidewalks, and security entrances to residence halls.

Programs of Study: Greensboro College confers B.A. and B.S. degrees. Master's degrees are also awarded. Bachelor's degrees are awarded in BIOLOGICAL SCIENCE (biology/biological science), BUSINESS (accounting and business administration and management), COMMUNICATIONS AND THE ARTS (art, dramatic arts, English, French, music, and Spanish), COMPUTER AND PHYSICAL SCIENCE (chemistry and mathematics), EDUCATION (art, athletic training, drama, early childhood, elementary, English, foreign languages, mathematics, middle school, music, physical, science, secondary, social studies, and special), HEALTH PROFESSIONS (exercise science), SOCIAL SCIENCE (history, political science/government, psychology, religion, and sociology). Education and business are the strongest academically.

Required: To graduate, students must complete 124 credit hours, including 30 to 48 in the major. They must take courses in social science, fine arts, lab science, English and literature, religion, history, phys ed, math, and foreign language. They must also take at least 1 course designated as global awareness, and must demonstrate competency in writing, oral communication, and computing.

Special: The college offers cross-registration with members of the Greater Greensboro Consortium and the Piedmont Independent College Association, accelerated degree programs and internships in all majors, B.A.-B.S. degrees, work-study programs, study abroad, dual and student-designed majors, pass/fail options, and credit for life, military, and work experience. Greensboro's Ethics Across the Curriculum program exposes students to ethical issues in a range of disciplines to promote the study and living of ethical principles at the college. There are 12 national honor societies and a freshman honors program.

Faculty/Classroom: 51% of faculty are male; 49%, female. All teach undergraduates, 50% do research, and 50% do both. The average class size in an introductory lecture is 21; in a laboratory, 16; and in a regular course, 14.

Admissions: 74% of recent applicants were accepted. 10% of recent freshmen were in the top fifth of their class; 38% were in the top two fifths.

Requirements: The SAT or ACT is required. In addition, applicants must be graduates of an accredited secondary school or have a GED certificate. An essay is required and an interview is recommended. Selected majors must audition or present a portfolio. AP and CLEP credits are accepted. Important factors in the admissions decision are advanced placement or honor courses, leadership record, and evidence of special talent.

Procedure: Freshmen are admitted to all sessions. Entrance exams should be taken in the spring of the junior year. There are early decision, early admissions, and deferred admissions plan. There is a rolling admissions plan. Check with the school for current application deadlines and fee. Notification of regular decision is sent on a rolling basis. Applications are accepted on-line.

Transfer: Official transcripts from any college attended are required. Standardized test scores and high school records are required of applicants with fewer than 30 semester hours. An essay is required, and an interview is recommended. 31 of 124 credits required for the bachelor's degree must be completed at Greensboro College.

Visiting: There are regularly scheduled orientations for prospective students, including an interview, a campus tour, and meetings with faculty and students. There are guides for informal visits and visitors may sit in on classes and stay overnight. To schedule a visit, contact the Admissions Office.

Financial Aid: in a recent year, 64% of all full-time freshmen and 80% of continuing full-time students received some form of financial aid. 58% of full-time freshmen and 67% of continuing full-time students received need-based aid. The average freshman award was $15,555. Need-based scholarships or need-based grants averaged $4240; and need-based self-help aid (loans and jobs) averaged $6958. 22% of undergraduates work part time. Average annual earnings from campus work are $700. The average financial indebtedness of a recent graduate was $11,802. Greensboro College is a member of CSS. The FAFSA, the state aid form, and the college's own financial statement are required. Check with the school for current deadlines.

International Students: There were 53 international students enrolled in a recent year. They must take the TOEFL.

Computers: All students may access the system 24 hours a day. There are no time limits and no fees. It is strongly recommended that all students have a personal computer.

Graduates: In a recent year, 170 bachelor's degrees were awarded. The most popular majors were business (26%), visual and performing arts (14%), and education (11%). In an average class, 1% graduate in 3 years or less, 30% graduate in 4 years or less, 44% graduate in 5 years or less, and 46% graduate in 6 years or less. 50 companies recruited on campus in a recent year. Of a recent graduating class, 9% were enrolled in graduate school within 6 months of graduation and 85% were employed.

Admissions Contact: Tim Jackson, Director of Admissions. A video is available. E-mail: *admissions@gborocollege.edu* Web: *http://www.gborocollege.edu*

GUILFORD COLLEGE D-2
Greensboro, NC 27410

(336) 316-2100
(800) 992-7759; Fax: (336) 316-2954

Full-time: 711 men, 1023 women	**Faculty:** 92; IIB, --$
Part-time: 103 men, 264 women	**Ph.D.s:** 73%
Graduate: none	**Student/Faculty:** 19 to 1
Year: semesters, summer session	**Tuition:** $21,630
Application Deadline: February 15	**Room & Board:** $6530
Freshman Class: 1647 applied, 1137 accepted, 298 enrolled	
SAT Verbal/Math: 580/560*	**ACT:** 24 COMPETITIVE+

Guilford College, founded in 1837 by the Religious Society of Friends (Quakers), is a private liberal arts and sciences institution. In addition to regional accreditation, Guilford College has baccalaureate program accreditation with NCATE. The library contains 223,674 volumes, 20,670 microform items, and 9805 audio/video tapes/CDs/DVDs, and subscribes to 812 periodicals including electronic. Computerized library services include the card catalog, interlibrary loans, database searching, Internet access, and laptop Internet portals. Special learning facilities include a learning resource center, art gallery, radio station, an observatory, and a multimedia learning center for cultures and languages. The 340-acre campus is in a suburban area in northwest Greensboro. Including any residence halls, there are 31 buildings.

Student Life: 66% of undergraduates are from North Carolina. Others are from 42 states and 21 foreign countries. 68% are from public schools. 70% are white; 19% African American. 43% are Protestant; 42% claim no religious affiliation; 7% Catholic; 6% Religious Society of Friends. The average age of freshmen is 19; all undergraduates, 22. 29% do not continue beyond their first year; 71% remain to graduate.

Housing: 928 students can be accommodated in college housing, which includes single-sex and coed dormitories and on-campus apartments. In addition, there are special-interest houses, and alternative houses with themes and community service project requirement. On-campus housing is guaranteed for all 4 years. 73% of students live on campus; of those, 80% remain on campus on weekends. All students may keep cars.

Activities: There are no fraternities or sororities. There are 43 groups on campus, including art, bowling, cheerleading, chess, choir, chorale, chorus, computers, dance, debate, drama, ethnic, film, gay, honors, international, jazz band, literary magazine, musical theater, newspaper, pep band, photography, political, professional, radio and TV, rugby, religious, social, social service, student government, ultimate frisbee, yachting and yearbook. Popular campus events include Serendipity Spring Festival, Holiday Choir Concert, and International Dinner and Dance.

Sports: There are 8 intercollegiate sports for men and 8 for women, and 3 intramural sports for men and 3 for women. Facilities include a 3500-seat football/track stadium, a 2500-seat gym, a field house, a baseball field, a softball field, basketball courts, a swimming pool, playing fields, courts for tennis, racquetball, badminton, and volleyball, and a weight room.

Disabled Students: 95% of the campus is accessible. Wheelchair ramps, elevators, special parking, specially equipped rest rooms, special class scheduling, lowered drinking fountains, lowered telephones, and an ATM machine are available.

Services: Counseling and information services are available, as is tutoring in every subject. There is a reader service for the blind, and remedial math, reading, and writing. There is faculty tutoring for skills development and student tutoring for course-specific help. Also available are nonremedial writing help, assistance with organizational/time-management skills, and services for students with learning disabilities. Remedial assistance is individually targeted and developmental with a focus on regular assignments.

Campus Safety and Security: Measures include 24-hour foot and vehicle patrol, security escort services, informal discussions, and pamphlets/posters/films. There are emergency telephones, lighted pathways/sidewalks, and a whistle program.

Programs of Study: Guilford College confers A.B., B.S., and B.F.A. degrees. Bachelor's degrees are awarded in AGRICULTURE (environmental studies), BIOLOGICAL SCIENCE (biology/biological science and life science), BUSINESS (accounting, business administration and management, and sports management), COMMUNICATIONS AND THE ARTS (art, dramatic arts, English, French, German, music, and Spanish), COMPUTER AND PHYSICAL SCIENCE (chemistry, earth science, geology, information sciences and systems, mathematics, and physics), EDUCATION (athletic training and education), ENGINEERING AND ENVIRONMENTAL DESIGN (computer technology), HEALTH PROFESSIONS (exercise science and health science), SOCIAL SCIENCE (African American studies, anthropology, community services, criminal justice, economics, forensic studies, German area studies, history, international studies, liberal arts/general studies, peace studies, philosophy, political science/government, psychology, religion, sociology, and women's studies). Psychology, natural sciences, and English are the strongest academically. Business management, psychology, and forensic biology are the largest.

Required: Students must fulfill requirements in fine arts, English, humanities, sciences, social sciences, and foreign language. They must take a first-year experience and an interdisciplinary capstone course, and courses in historical perspectives, intercultural studies, social justice and environmental responsibility, diversity, business and policy studies, and quantitative literacy. A minimum GPA of 2.0 is required. 128 credit hours must be completed with at least 32 in the major.

Special: There are 3-2 degree programs available in forestry and environmental studies with Duke University, and in physician assistant training with Bowman Gray School of Medicine at Wake Forest University. Guilford also offers many internships, a Washington semester, work-study programs, accelerated degree programs in business management, computer information systems, psychology, and biology, dual majors, student-designed majors, study abroad in 7 countries, B.A.-B.S. degrees, and cross-registration with members of the Greater Greensboro Consortium (8 colleges/universities). There are 2 national honor societies, and a freshman honors program.

Faculty/Classroom: 52% of faculty are male; 48%, female. All both teach and do research. The average class size in an introductory lecture is 23; in a laboratory, 19; and in a regular course, 20.

Admissions: 69% of the 2005-2006 applicants were accepted. The SAT scores for the 2005-2006 freshman class were: Verbal--19% below 500, 37% between 500 and 599, 32% between 600 and 700, and 13% above 700; Math--21% below 500, 44% between 500 and 599, 30% between 600 and 700, and 5% above 700. The ACT scores were 21% below 21, 22% between 21 and 23, 33% between 24 and 26, 9% between 27 and 28, and 15% above 28. 28% of the current freshmen were in the top fifth of their class; 64% were in the top two fifths. There were 2 National Merit semifinalists. 5 freshmen graduated first in their class.

Requirements: The SAT or ACT is required. Applicants should have completed 20 Carnegie units, including 4 in English, 2 each in foreign language and science, and 1 each in history and social studies. The GED is accepted. An essay is required and an interview is recommended. A GPA of 2.0 is required. AP and CLEP credits are accepted. Important factors in the admissions decision are advanced placement or honor courses, leadership record, and evidence of special talent.

Procedure: Freshmen are admitted fall and spring. Entrance exams should be taken in spring of the junior year or fall of the senior year. There is a deferred admissions plan. Early decision applications should be filed by January 15; regular applications, by February 15 for fall entry and December 1 for spring entry, along with a $25 fee. Notification of early decision is sent February 15; regular decision, April 1. 38 early decision candidates were accepted for the 2005-2006 class. 7 applicants were on the 2005 waiting list; 1 was admitted. Applications are accepted on-line.

Transfer: 344 transfer students enrolled in a recent year. Applicants must have a minimum GPA of 2.5 in at least 12 credit hours, submit either SAT or ACT scores, and provide a letter from the academic adviser or dean of the previous school. An interview is recommended. 32 of 128 credits required for the bachelor's degree must be completed at Guilford College.

Visiting: There are regularly scheduled orientations for prospective students, including forums, a campus tour, and presentations by faculty, administrators, and students. There are guides for informal visits and visitors may sit in on classes. To schedule a visit, contact the Admission Office.

Financial Aid: In a recent year, 98% of all full-time freshmen and 92% of continuing full-time students received some form of financial aid. 62% of full-time freshmen and 56% of continuing full-time students received need-based aid. The average freshman award was $15,950. Need-based scholarships or need-based grants averaged $3172 ($18,700 maximum); need-based self-help aid (loans and jobs) averaged $4000 ($8425 maximum); and other non-need-based awards and non-need-based scholarships averaged $3066 ($18,700 maximum). 34% of undergraduates work part time. Average annual earnings from campus work are $765. The average financial indebtedness of a recent graduate was $18,500. The FAFSA is required. The deadline for filing freshman financial aid applications for fall entry is March 1.

International Students: In a recent year there were 34 international students enrolled. The school actively recruits these students. They must score satisfactorily on the written TOEFL or on the electronic version.

Computers: All students may access the system 24 hours a day. There are no time limits and no fees.

Graduates: In a recent year, 253 bachelor's degrees were awarded. The most popular majors were business management (13%), English (9%), and psychology (9%). In an average class, 51% graduated in 4 years or less, 55% graduated in 5 years or less, and 57% graduated in 6 years or less. 85 companies recruited on campus in a recent year. Of a recent graduating class, 17% were enrolled in graduate school within 6 months of graduation and 83% were employed.

Admissions Contact: Randy Doss, Vice President of Enrollment and Marketing. E-mail: *admission@guilford.edu* Web: *www.guilford.edu*

HIGH POINT UNIVERSITY · D-2
High Point, NC 27262-3598

(336) 841-9216
(800) 345-6993; Fax: (336) 888-6382

Full-time: 853 men, 1472 women	Faculty: 122; IIB, av$
Part-time: 81 men, 118 women	Ph.Ds: 76%
Graduate: 92 men, 144 women	Student/Faculty: 19 to 1
Year: semesters, summer session	Tuition: $18,130
Application Deadline: August 15	Room & Board: $7590
Freshman Class: 2184 applied, 1453 accepted, 412 enrolled	
SAT Verbal/Math: 510/500*	ACT: 21 · COMPETITIVE

High Point University, founded in 1924, is a private coeducational, liberal arts university related to the United Methodist Church. It offers day and evening undergraduate degree programs and evening graduate degree programs. There are 3 undergraduate schools and 1 graduate school. In addition to regional accreditation, High Point has baccalaureate program accreditation with NCATE and CAAHEP. The library contains 244,000 volumes, 64,400 microform items, and 6700 audio/video tapes/CDs/DVDs, and subscribes to 1522 periodicals including electronic. Computerized library services include the card catalog, interlibrary loans, database searching, and Internet access. Special learning facilities include a learning resource center, art gallery, radio station, and TV studio. The 90-acre campus is in a suburban area 15 miles southeast of Winston-Salem and 12 miles southwest of Greensboro. Including any residence halls, there are 26 buildings.

Student Life: 68% of undergraduates are from North Carolina. Others are from 37 states, 48 foreign countries, and Canada. 86% are from public schools. 69% are white; 23% African American. 58% are Protestant; 21% Catholic; 9% claim no religious affiliation. The average age of freshmen is 18; all undergraduates, 20. 25% do not continue beyond their first year; 51% remain to graduate.

Housing: 1044 students can be accommodated in college housing, which includes single-sex and coed dorms, on-campus apartments, married-student housing, and fraternity houses. In addition, there are special-interest houses and wellness halls. On-campus housing is guaranteed for all 4 years. 75% of students live on campus; of those, 80% remain on campus on weekends. All students may keep cars.

Activities: 15% of men belong to 4 national fraternities; 25% of women belong to 1 local and 4 national sororities. There are 79 groups on campus, including art, band, cheerleading, choir, chorale, chorus, computers, dance, debate, drama, environmental, ethnic, film, honors, international, literary magazine, musical theater, newspaper, orchestra, outdoor, pep band, political, professional, radio and TV, religious, social, social service, student government, and yearbook. Popular campus events include Greek Week, Pantherpalooza, and Winter Festival.

Sports: There are 7 intercollegiate sports for men and 7 for women, and 6 intramural sports for men and 6 for women. Facilities include intramural fields, tennis courts, an intramural gym, a recreation center featuring a swimming pool, racquetball courts, an aerobics center, a weight room, and a 2500-seat arena. There is a 45,000-square-foot student activities center, a soccer stadium and track, a sports center, and a university park with amphitheater.

Disabled Students: 98% of the campus is accessible. Wheelchair ramps, elevators, special parking, specially equipped rest rooms, special class scheduling, and lowered drinking fountains are available.

Services: Counseling and information services are available, as is tutoring in every subject. There is remedial math, reading, and writing.

Campus Safety and Security: Measures include 24-hour foot and vehicle patrol, self-defense education, security escort services, and informal discussions. There are pamphlets/posters/films, emergency telephones, lighted pathways/sidewalks, 24-hour secured residence halls, and student bike patrols.

Programs of Study: High Point confers B.A. and B.S. degrees. Master's degrees are also awarded. Bachelor's degrees are awarded in AGRICULTURE (forestry and related sciences), BIOLOGICAL SCIENCE (biology/biological science), BUSINESS (accounting, business administration and management, international business management, marketing/retailing/merchandising, recreation and leisure services, and sports management), COMMUNICATIONS AND THE ARTS (art, dramatic arts, English, fine arts, French, modern language, and Spanish), COMPUTER AND PHYSICAL SCIENCE (chemistry, computer science, information sciences and systems, and mathematics), EDUCATION (art, athletic training, elementary, middle school, physical, secondary, and special), ENGINEERING AND ENVIRONMENTAL DESIGN (interior design), HEALTH PROFESSIONS (exercise science, medical laboratory technology, and sports medicine), SOCIAL SCIENCE (American studies, criminal justice, history, home furnishings and equipment management/production/services, human services, industrial and organizational psychology, international studies, philosophy, physical fitness/movement, political science/government, psychology, religion, and sociology). Business administration, exercise and sport science, and education are the largest.

Required: To graduate, students must complete 124 credit hours, including up to 60 in the major, with a minimum GPA of 2.0. The core curriculum consists of 2 courses each in English, history, social science, phys ed, and a modern foreign language, as well as 1 course each in math, lab science, religion, fine arts, ethics, global studies, and senior seminar.

Special: There is cross-registration with the University of North Carolina at Greensboro, North Carolina Agricultural and Technical State University, and Greensboro, Elon, Guilford, and Bennett Colleges. High Point also offers co-op programs, study abroad in 7 countries, the Student Career Internship Program, a dual major in chemistry and business, accelerated degree programs, unique programs in home furnishings marketing/management studies, work-study programs, student-designed majors, and 3-2 forestry and environmental management programs with Duke University. There are 2 national honor societies, a freshman honors program, and 2 departmental honors programs.

Faculty/Classroom: 64% of faculty are male; 36%, female. All teach undergraduates. No introductory courses are taught by graduate students. The average class size in an introductory lecture is 25; in a laboratory, 20; and in a regular course, 16.

Admissions: 67% of the 2005-2006 applicants were accepted. The SAT scores for the 2005-2006 freshman class were: Verbal--43% below 500, 41% between 500 and 599, 14% between 600 and 700, and 2% above 700; Math--47% below 500, 39% between 500 and 599, 12% between 600 and 700, and 2% above 700. The ACT scores were 42% below 21, 30% between 21 and 23, 16% between 24 and 26, 10% between 27 and 28, and 2% above 28. 28% of the current freshmen were in the top fifth of their class; 59% were in the top two fifths.

Requirements: The SAT or ACT is required, the SAT is preferred. Applicants should be graduates of an accredited secondary school or have a GED certificate. They should have completed 14 academic units, including 4 in English, 3 in math, 2 each in science, social studies, and history, and 1 elective. A GPA of 2.0 is required. AP and CLEP credits are accepted. Important factors in the admissions decision are advanced placement or honor courses and evidence of special talent.

Procedure: Freshmen are admitted fall, spring, and summer. Entrance exams should be taken prior to high school graduation. There are early admissions and deferred admissions plans. There is a rolling admissions plan. Applications should be filed by August 15 for fall entry, along with a $25 fee. Notification is sent on a rolling basis. A waiting list is an active part of the admissions procedure. Applications are accepted on-line.

Transfer: 146 transfer students enrolled in 2004-2005. Applicants must submit official transcripts from colleges and high schools previously attended, as well as SAT or ACT scores, if available. Generally, a minimum GPA of 2.0 is required. 31 of 124 credits required for the bachelor's degree must be completed at High Point.

Visiting: There are regularly scheduled orientations for prospective students, which are held at the beginning of each term. There are guides for informal visits and visitors may sit in on classes. To schedule a visit, contact the Admissions Office.

Financial Aid: In 2005-2006, 91% of all full-time freshmen and 90% of continuing full-time students received some form of financial aid. 60% of full-time freshmen and 62% of continuing full-time students received need-based aid. The average freshman award was $13,709. Need-based scholarships or need-based grants averaged $3700 ($5847 maximum); need-based self-help aid (loans and jobs) averaged $5125 ($12,125 maximum); non-need-based athletic scholarships averaged $1146 ($23,779 maximum); and other non-need-based awards and non-need-based scholarships averaged $3738 ($16,600 maximum). 67% of undergraduates work part time. Average annual earnings from campus work are $1500. The average financial indebtedness of the 2005 graduate was $25,125. High Point is a member of CSS. The FAFSA and the state aid form and are required. The priority date for freshman financial aid applications for fall entry is March 1.

International Students: There are 119 international students enrolled. They must score satisfactorily on the TOEFL or take the MELAB, the Comprehensive English Language Test, or the college's own test.

Computers: Wireless access is available. General use labs are accessible for any HPU student to access the Internet, e-mail, etc. Computer programs used for certain classes can also be located in a general use lab. Special purpose labs are dedicated to classroom use, and students require password accounts. All students may access the system. There are no time limits. The fee is $100. It is strongly recommended that all students have a personal computer.

Graduates: From July 1, 2004 to June 30, 2005, 548 bachelor's degrees were awarded. The most popular majors were business (30%), computer and information technology (9%), and psychology (6%). In an average class, 40% graduate in 4 years or less, and 50% graduate in 6 years or less. 10 companies recruited on campus in 2004-2005. Of the 2004 graduating class, 19% were enrolled in graduate school within 6 months of graduation and 59% were employed.

Admissions Contact: Jessie Mclrath-Carter, Director of Admissions. E-mail: *admiss@highpoint.edu* Web: *www.highpoint.edu*

JOHNSON AND WALES UNIVERSITY/CHARLOTTE CAMPUS

Charlotte, NC 28202	(866) 598-2427; Fax: (950) 598-1111
Full-time: 1030 men, 1120 women	Faculty: 67
Part-time: 3 men, 3 women	Ph.D.s: 13%
Graduate: none	Student/Faculty: 32 to 1
Year: trimesters	Tuition: $20,826
Application Deadline: open	Room & Board: $8295
Freshman Class: 6226 applied, 4623 accepted, 789 enrolled	
SAT or ACT : required for some programs	LESS COMPETITIVE

Johnson & Wales University/Charlotte Campus, founded in 2004, offers degree programs in its College of Business, College of Culinary Arts, and Hospitality College. There are 3 undergraduate schools. The library contains 20,559 volumes and 1266 audio/video tapes/CDs/DVDs, and subscribes to 199 periodicals including electronic. Computerized library services include interlibrary loans, database searching, Internet access, and laptop Internet portals. The campus is in an urban area. Including any residence halls, there are 6 buildings.

Student Life: 62% of undergraduates are from out of state, mostly the South. Students are from 45 states, 11 foreign countries, and Canada. 64% are white; 27% African American. The average age of freshmen is 19; all undergraduates, 20.

Housing: 752 students can be accommodated in college housing, which includes coed dorms. Housing is available to freshmen on a first-deposited, first-contract received basis. On-campus housing is available on a lottery system for upperclassmen. 69% of students commute. Alcohol is not permitted. All students may keep cars.

Activities: There are no fraternities or sororities. There are 4 groups on campus, including chorale, dance, student government, and yearbook.

Sports: There are 8 coed intramural sports.

Disabled Students: All of the campus is accessible. Wheelchair ramps, elevators, special parking, specially equipped rest rooms, special class scheduling, lowered drinking fountains, lowered telephones, and special housing are available.

Services: Counseling and information services are available, as is tutoring in every subject.

Campus Safety and Security: Measures include 24-hour foot and vehicle patrol, self-defense education, security escort services, and shuttle buses. There are informal discussions, pamphlets/posters/films, emergency telephones, and lighted pathways/sidewalks.

Programs of Study: J&W confers the B.S. degree. Associate degrees are also awarded. Bachelor's degrees are awarded in BUSINESS (accounting, business administration and management, entrepreneurial studies, hospitality management services, hotel/motel and restaurant management, marketing and distribution, marketing management, marketing/retailing/merchandising, sports management, and tourism), ENGINEERING AND ENVIRONMENTAL DESIGN (food services technology), SOCIAL SCIENCE (clothing and textiles management/production/services, food production/management/services, and parks and recreation management). Culinary, baking and pastry, and food service management are the largest.

Required: To graduate, students must complete 180 quarter credits hours, including at least 36 in the major, with a minimum GPA of 2.0. Required classes include English, math, history, economics, science, psychology, sociology, and professional development.

Special: The university offers co-op programs, accelerated degree programs, dual majors, study abroad, and worldwide work-study opportunities in business, hospitality, technology, and culinary arts. Most majors require 11-week internships. There is a chapter of Phi Beta Kappa.

Faculty/Classroom: 57% of faculty are male; 43%, female. All teach undergraduates.

Requirements: The SAT or ACT is required for some programs. In addition, although SAT and ACT scores are required only for students applying for honors admissions, students who have taken these tests are encouraged to submit their scores. AP and CLEP credits are accepted. Important factors in the admissions decision are advanced placement or honor courses, extracurricular activities record, and recommendations by school officials.

Procedure: Freshmen are admitted to all sessions. There is a deferred admissions and a rolling admissions plan. Application deadlines are open. Applications are accepted on-line.

Transfer: 195 transfer students enrolled in 2004-2005. Applicants are required ro submit official high school and college transcripts and must have earned a minimum college GPA of 2.0. 45 of 180 quarter credit hours required for the bachelor's degree must be completed at J&W.

Visiting: There are regularly scheduled orientations for prospective students, including an intoduction to the academic and social aspects of the campus experience through interactive sessions. There are guides for informal visits and visitors may sit in on classes and stay overnight. To schedule a visit, contact the Admissions Office.

Financial Aid: In 2005-2006, 83% of all full-time freshmen and 82% of continuing full-time students received some form of financial aid. 76%

of full-time freshmen and 68% of continuing full-time students received need-based aid. The average freshman award was $15,218. Need-based scholarships or need-based grants averaged $5513; need-based self-help aid (loans and jobs) averaged $7422; and other non-need-based awards and non-need-based scholarships averaged $4429. J&W is a member of CSS. The FAFSA and the college's own financial statement are required.

International Students: There are 13 international students enrolled. The school actively recruits these students. A satisfactory score is required on the written TOEFL.

Computers: Wireless access is available. There are 5 computer labs. 4 are located in the Academic Center, with more than 160 workstations; 1 is located in the library, with 30 workstations. All students may access the system. There are no fees.

Admissions Contact: Brian Stanly, Director of Admissions. A video is available. E-mail: admissions.clt@jwu.edu Web: www.jwu.edu

JOHNSON C. SMITH UNIVERSITY   C-3
Charlotte, NC 28216

(704) 378-1010
(800) 782-7303; Fax: (704) 378-1242

Full-time: 600 men, 800 women	Faculty: 85
Part-time: 30 men, 50 women	Ph.Ds: n/av
Graduate: none	Student/Faculty: 16 to 1
Year: semesters, summer session	Tuition: $14,000
Application Deadline: open	Room & Board: $6000
Freshman Class: n/av	
SAT or ACT: required	COMPETITIVE

Johnson C. Smith University, founded in 1867, is a progressive historically black private institution offering a liberal arts education and affiliated with the Presbyterian Church (U.S.A.). Figures in the above capsule and in this profile are approximate. There are 2 undergraduate schools. In addition to regional accreditation, JCSU has baccalaureate program accreditation with ACBSP, CSWE, and NCATE. The library contains 168,621 microform items and 3000 audio/video tapes/CDs/DVDs, and subscribes to 700 periodicals including electronic. Computerized library services include the card catalog, interlibrary loans, database searching, and Internet access. Special learning facilities include a learning resource center and radio station. The 105-acre campus is in an urban area in Charlotte. Including any residence halls, there are 46 buildings.

Student Life: 70% of undergraduates are from out of state, mostly the Northeast. Students are from 35 states, 5 foreign countries, and Canada. 94% are from public schools. 99% are African American. Most are Protestant. The average age of freshmen is 18; all undergraduates, 22. 28% do not continue beyond their first year; 6% remain to graduate.

Housing: 1151 students can be accommodated in college housing, which includes single-sex and coed dorms. In addition, there are honors houses. On-campus housing is available on a first-come, first-served basis. 70% of students live on campus; of those, 76% remain on campus on weekends. Alcohol is not permitted. Upperclassmen may keep cars.

Activities: 7% of men belong to 4 local and 4 national fraternities; 14% of women belong to 4 local and 4 national sororities. There are 46 groups on campus, including art, band, cheerleading, chess, choir, chorale, chorus, computers, dance, debate, drama, ethnic, film, gay, honors, international, jazz band, literary magazine, marching band, newspaper, orchestra, pep band, photography, political, professional, radio and TV, religious, social, social service, student government, symphony, and yearbook. Popular campus events include Founders Day, West Fest, and Family Day.

Sports: There are 6 intercollegiate sports for men and 7 for women, and 5 intramural sports for men and 5 for women. Facilities include a 3200-seat gym, a pool, tennis and basketball courts, a weight room, a training room, an Olympic-size track, a football field, and an on-campus stadium seating 4500.

Disabled Students: 5% of the campus is accessible. Wheelchair ramps, elevators, special parking, specially equipped rest rooms, special class scheduling, and lowered drinking fountains are available.

Services: Counseling and information services are available, as is tutoring in every subject.

Campus Safety and Security: Measures include 24-hour foot and vehicle patrol, self-defense education, security escort services, and informal discussions. There are pamphlets/posters/films, emergency telephones, lighted pathways/sidewalks, and push-button emergency stations.

Programs of Study: JCSU confers B.A., B.S., and B.S.W. degrees. Bachelor's degrees are awarded in BIOLOGICAL SCIENCE (biology/biological science), BUSINESS (business administration and management and business economics), COMMUNICATIONS AND THE ARTS (communications, English, music business management, and Spanish), COMPUTER AND PHYSICAL SCIENCE (applied mathematics, chemistry, computer science, mathematics, physics, and science), EDUCATION (elementary, English, health, mathematics, middle school, physical, secondary, and social studies), ENGINEERING AND ENVIRONMENTAL DESIGN (computer engineering, engineering, and preengineering), HEALTH PROFESSIONS (nursing, pharmacy, predentistry, and premedicine), SOCIAL SCIENCE (criminal justice, economics, history, liberal arts/general studies, political science/government, prelaw, psychology, religious music, social science, social work, and sociology). Business administration is the strongest academically. Business and computer science/information systems are the largest.

Required: To graduate, students must complete 122 credit hours, including 30 to 59 in the major, with a minimum GPA of 2.0. Distribution requirements include 47 hours of courses in English, composition, the humanities, social science, health and phys ed, math, computer science, activities, and natural science. Students must take a competency exam in the sophomore year, write a senior paper, participate in community service and Lyceum, and take Learning Across the Curriculum.

Special: JCSU offers cooperative programs in all majors, student-designed majors, 3-2 engineering degrees with UNCC and Florida A & M University, cross-registration with the Charlotte Area Educational Consortium, dual majors in engineering, nursing, and pharmacy, internships with local businesses, work-study programs, study abroad in 5 countries, and a B.A.-B.S. degree in all majors. Nondegree study in continuing education and pass/fail options are available. There are 9 national honor societies, a freshman honors program, and 1 departmental honors program.

Faculty/Classroom: 58% of faculty are male; 42%, female. All teach undergraduates, 2% do research, and 2% do both. The average class size in an introductory lecture is 30; in a laboratory, 15; and in a regular course, 25.

Admissions: 73% of recent applicants were accepted. 39% of recent freshmen were in the top fifth of their class; 60% were in the top two fifths. 47 freshmen graduated first in their class in a recent year.

Requirements: The SAT or ACT is required. Applicants should have completed 16 Carnegie units, including 4 in English, 3 each in math, 2 each in social science and science, and 5 in electives. The GED is accepted. An essay and an interview are suggested. JCSU requires applicants to be in the upper 50% of their class. A GPA of 2.2 is required. AP credits are accepted. Important factors in the admissions decision are advanced placement or honor courses, recommendations by school officials, and extracurricular activities record.

Procedure: Freshmen are admitted fall and spring. Entrance exams should be taken prior to application. There are early decision, early admissions, and deferred admissions plans. Application deadlines are open. There is a rolling admissions plan. Check with the school for current application deadlines and fee. 327 early decision candidates were accepted for a recent class.

Transfer: 52 transfer students enrolled in a recent year. Applicants need a minimum GPA of 2.0 in 12 semester hours of transferable course work. 32 of 122 credits required for the bachelor's degree must be completed at JCSU.

Visiting: There are regularly scheduled orientations for prospective students, including a campus tour, a classroom visit, and a financial aid meeting. There are guides for informal visits and visitors may sit in on classes and stay overnight. To schedule a visit, contact the Director of Admissions.

Financial Aid: In a recent year, 91% of all full-time freshmen and 86% of continuing full-time students received some form of financial aid. 92% of full-time freshmen and 86% of continuing full-time students received need-based aid. The average freshman award was $7500. 60% of undergraduates work part time. Average annual earnings from campus work are $1500. The average financial indebtedness of a recent graduate was $21,000. JCSU is a member of CSS. The FAFSA and the state aid form are required. Check with the school for current deadlines.

International Students: There were 7 international students enrolled in a recent year. The school actively recruits these students. They must take the TOEFL and also take the SAT or the ACT.

Computers: All students may access the system any time. There are no time limits and no fees. All students are required to have personal computers.

Graduates: In a recent year, 244 bachelor's degrees were awarded. The most popular majors were business administration (20%), computer science (11%), and communication arts (9%). In an average class, 37% graduate in 4 years or less, 41% graduate in 5 years or less, and 46% graduate in 6 years or less. 117 companies recruited on campus in a recent year. Of a recent graduating class, 23% were enrolled in graduate school within 6 months of graduation and 57% were employed.

Admissions Contact: Jeffrey A. Smith, Director of Admissions. A video is available. E-mail: jasmith@jscu.edu Web: http://www.jcsu.edu/

LEES-MCRAE COLLEGE · B-2
Banner Elk, NC 28604

(828) 898-8829
(800) 280-4562; Fax: (828) 898-8707

Full-time: 388 men, 475 women	Faculty: 49
Part-time: 3 men, 8 women	Ph.D.s: 85%
Graduate: none	Student/Faculty: 18 to 1
Year: semesters, summer session	Tuition: $17,000
Application Deadline: open	Room & Board: $6000
Freshman Class: 1003 applied, 727 accepted, 224 enrolled	
SAT Verbal/Math: 540/530*	ACT: 23 COMPETITIVE

Lees-McRae College, founded in 1900, is an independent liberal arts institution affiliated with the Presbyterian Church (U.S.A). In addition to regional accreditation, Lees-McRae has baccalaureate program accreditation with NCATE. The library contains 96,628 volumes, 256,447 microform items, and 2326 audio/video tapes/CDs/DVDs, and subscribes to 343 periodicals including electronic. Computerized library services include the card catalog, interlibrary loans, and database searching. Special learning facilities include a learning resource center, art gallery, and an academic success center. The 400-acre campus is in a rural area 17 miles south of Boone and 100 miles northwest of Charlotte. Including any residence halls, there are 33 buildings.

Student Life: 61% of undergraduates are from North Carolina. Students are from 30 states, 16 foreign countries, and Canada. 86% are from public schools. 81% are white; 12% African American. 65% are Protestant; 21% claim no religious affiliation; 10% Catholic. The average age of freshmen is 18; all undergraduates, 22. 30% do not continue beyond their first year; 44% remain to graduate.

Housing: 567 students can be accommodated in college housing, which includes single-sex and coed dorms and on-campus apartments. In addition, there are honors houses and substabce-free housing. On-campus housing is guaranteed for all 4 years. 74% of students live on campus; of those, 70% remain on campus on weekends. Alcohol is not permitted. All students may keep cars.

Activities: There are no fraternities or sororities. There are 30 groups on campus, including cheerleading, choir, chorus, dance, drama, ethnic, honors, international, musical theater, pep band, photography, political, professional, religious, social, social service, student government, and yearbook. Popular campus events include Staley Distinguished Lectureship, Spring Fling, and Mountain Day.

Sports: There are 10 intercollegiate sports for men and 10 for women, and 11 intramural sports for men and 11 for women. Facilities include a main gym that seats 2,000 with basketball/volleyball courts, a match field for soccer/lacrosse, 4 practice fields, a softball field with batting cages, 2 indoor tennis courts, 6 outdoor tennis courts, a secondary gym for intramurals, an indoor Olympic-size pool, a fitness center, a weight room facility, an outdoor basketball court, and a beach volleyball court.

Disabled Students: 50% of the campus is accessible. Wheelchair ramps, special parking, specially equipped rest rooms, special class scheduling, and special housing are available.

Services: Counseling and information services are available, as is tutoring in every subject. There is remedial math, reading, and writing.

Campus Safety and Security: Measures include 24-hour foot and vehicle patrol, security escort services, informal discussions, and pamphlets/posters/films. There are emergency telephones and lighted pathways/sidewalks.

Programs of Study: Lees-McRae confers B.A. and B.S. degrees. Bachelor's degrees are awarded in BIOLOGICAL SCIENCE (biology/biological science), BUSINESS (business administration and management), COMMUNICATIONS AND THE ARTS (arts administration/management, communications, dramatic arts, English, and musical theater), COMPUTER AND PHYSICAL SCIENCE (mathematics), EDUCATION (elementary and physical), HEALTH PROFESSIONS (sports medicine), SOCIAL SCIENCE (criminal justice, history, humanities, interdisciplinary studies, international studies, psychology, religion, and sociology). Biology, performing arts, and elementary education are the strongest academically. Business, biology, and performing arts are the largest.

Required: To graduate, students must complete at least 124 credit hours, including 36 to 57 in the major, with a GPA of 2.0 overall. Core requirements include courses in English, religion, history, natural sciences, social and behavioral sciences, math, computer science, phys ed, and senior seminar.

Special: The college has work-study programs, student-designed majors in the interdisciplinary studies program, and study-abroad opportunities in Ireland and Great Britain. Cross-registration is available with the Marine Science Education Consortium. There is 1 national honor society and a freshman honors program.

Faculty/Classroom: 57% of faculty are male; 43%, female. All teach undergraduates. The average class size in an introductory lecture is 21; in a laboratory, 10; and in a regular course, 11.

Admissions: 72% of the 2005-2006 applicants were accepted. The SAT scores for the 2005-2006 freshman class were: Verbal--25% below 500, 55% between 500 and 599, 19% between 600 and 700, and 1% above 700; Math--26% below 500, 56% between 500 and 599, 17% between 600 and 700, and 1% above 700. The ACT scores were 20% below 21, 57% between 21 and 23, 13% between 24 and 26, 8% between 27 and 28, and 2% above 28. 22% of the current freshmen were in the top fifth of their class; 60% were in the top two fifths. 3 freshmen graduated first in their class.

Requirements: The SAT or ACT is required. The ACT Optional Writing test is also required for some programs. In addition, applicants must have completed 18 units of secondary school academic courses, including 6 of academic electives, 4 of English, 3 of math, 2 of science (1 with lab work), and 1 each of social studies and history. Lees-McRae requires applicants to be in the upper 75% of their class. A GPA of 2.5 is required. AP and CLEP credits are accepted. Important factors in the admissions decision are recommendations by school officials, advanced placement or honor courses, and leadership record.

Procedure: Freshmen are admitted to all sessions. Entrance exams should be taken in the fall of the senior year. There are early admissions, deferred admissions, and rolling admissions plans. Application deadlines are open. Application fee is $25. Applications are accepted on-line.

Transfer: 55 transfer students enrolled in 2004-2005. Applicants must submit a college GPA of 2.0 and be in good standing at the previous or current institution. Students who have completed 24 semester hours or more must submit a dean's evaluation form; those with fewer than 24 must also submit high school transcripts and SAT or ACT scores. 32 of 124 credits required for the bachelor's degree must be completed at Lees-McRae.

Visiting: There are regularly scheduled orientations for prospective students; there are 6 yearly open houses. There are guides for informal visits and visitors may sit in on classes and stay overnight. To schedule a visit, contact the Office of Admissions.

Financial Aid: In 2005-2006, 96% of all full-time freshmen and 95% of continuing full-time students received some form of financial aid. 72% of full-time freshmen and 62% of continuing full-time students received need-based aid. The average freshman award was $14,920. 52% of undergraduates work part time. Average annual earnings from campus work are $1340. The average financial indebtedness of the 2005 graduate was $6414. Lees-McRae is a member of CSS. The FAFSA is required. The deadline for filing freshman financial aid applications for fall entry is July 1.

International Students: There are 38 international students enrolled. The school actively recruits these students. A satisafactory score is required on the written TOEFL. Students must also take the SAT or the ACT.

Computers: Wireless access is available. All students may access the system 24 hours a day. There are no time limits and no fees.

Graduates: From July 1, 2004 to June 30, 2005, 145 bachelor's degrees were awarded. The most popular majors were elementary education (23%), business administration (19%), and criminal justice (13%). In an average class, 40% graduate in 4 years or less, 43% graduate in 5 years or less, and 45% graduate in 6 years or less. Of the 2004 graduating class, 25% were enrolled in graduate school within 6 months of graduation and 70% were employed.

Admissions Contact: Walt Crutchfield, Dean of Admissions. A video is available. E-mail: *admissions@lmc.edu* Web: *www.lmc.edu*

LENOIR-RHYNE COLLEGE · C-2
Hickory, NC 28603

(828) 328-7300
(800) 277-5721; Fax: (828) 328-7378

Full-time: 487 men, 818 women	Faculty: 107; IIA, --$
Part-time: 44 men, 77 women	Ph.D.s: 73%
Graduate: 38 men, 97 women	Student/Faculty: 12 to 1
Year: semesters, summer session	Tuition: $18,900
Application Deadline: open	Room & Board: $6680
Freshman Class: 1700 applied, 1413 accepted, 323 enrolled	
SAT Verbal/Math: 522/543*	ACT: 21 COMPETITIVE

Lenoir-Rhyne College, founded in 1891, is a private institution affiliated with the Lutheran Church, offering liberal arts programs that focus on business, education, and allied health sciences. In addition to regional accreditation, Lenoir-Rhyne has baccalaureate program accreditation with NCATE and NLN. The library contains 145,960 volumes, 462,878 microform items, and 40,379 audio/video tapes/CDs/DVDs, and subscribes to 5376 periodicals including electronic. Computerized library services include the card catalog, interlibrary loans, and database searching. Special learning facilities include a learning resource center, radio station, TV station, and observatory. The 100-acre campus is in a suburban area 45 miles northwest of Charlotte. Including any residence halls, there are 30 buildings.

Student Life: 70% of undergraduates are from North Carolina. Others are from 29 states, 9 foreign countries, and Canada. 89% are from public schools. 87% are white. 68% are Protestant; 23% claim no religious affiliation; 9% Catholic. The average age of freshmen is 18; all undergraduates, 22. 23% do not continue beyond their first year; 63% remain to graduate.

Housing: 900 students can be accommodated in college housing, which includes single-sex and coed dorms, on-campus apartments, and fraternity houses. In addition, there is honors housing and housing for the hearing impaired., the first, second, and third years. On-campus housing is guaranteed for all 4 years and is available on a lottery system for upperclassmen. 65% of students live on campus; of those, 70% remain on campus on weekends. All students may keep cars.

Activities: 23% of men belong to 3 national fraternities; 27% of women belong to 4 national sororities. There are 50 groups on campus, including art, band, cheerleading, choir, chorus, computers, dance, debate, drama, ethnic, honors, international, jazz band, literary magazine, marching band, musical theater, newspaper, pep band, photography, political, professional, radio and TV, religious, social, social service, student government, and yearbook. Popular campus events include Spring Fling and Advent Candlelight Service.

Sports: There are 6 intercollegiate sports for men and 6 for women, and 14 intramural sports for men and 14 for women. Facilities include an 8500-seat football stadium, a 3600-seat gym, practice fields, racquetball courts, weight rooms a sauna, a 25-meter swimming pool, 2 intramural fields, and baseball, softball, and soccer fields.

Disabled Students: All of the campus is accessible. Wheelchair ramps, elevators, special parking, specially equipped rest rooms, and lowered drinking fountains are available. Specially equipped residence halls are available.

Services: Counseling and information services are available, as is tutoring in every subject. There is remedial math and writing and interpreters and note takers for hearing-impaired students.

Campus Safety and Security: Measures include 24-hour foot and vehicle patrol, self-defense education, security escort services, and informal discussions. There are pamphlets/posters/films, emergency telephones, and lighted pathways/sidewalks.

Programs of Study: Lenoir-Rhyne confers B.A., B.S., and B.Mus.Ed. degrees. Master's degrees are also awarded. Bachelor's degrees are awarded in BIOLOGICAL SCIENCE (biology/biological science), BUSINESS (accounting, business administration and management, and international business management), COMMUNICATIONS AND THE ARTS (applied music, classics, communications, dramatic arts, English, French, German, music, and Spanish), COMPUTER AND PHYSICAL SCIENCE (chemistry, computer science, mathematics, and physics), EDUCATION (art, business, early childhood, education of the deaf and hearing impaired, elementary, foreign languages, health, middle school, music, science, and secondary), HEALTH PROFESSIONS (medical laboratory technology, nursing, occupational therapy, physician's assistant, and premedicine), SOCIAL SCIENCE (American studies, economics, history, human services, philosophy, political science/government, prelaw, psychology, religious education, religious music, sociology, and theological studies). Business, education, and nursing are the largest.

Required: To graduate, students must complete 128 credit hours, including 56 to 57 in liberal arts courses, with a minimum GPA of 2.0. The total number of hours in a major varies by program.

Special: Lenoir-Rhyne offers cross-registration in design courses at area schools, study abroad in more than 25 countries, a Washington semester at American University and through the Lutheran College Washington Consortium, internships in most majors, dual majors, a general studies degree, work-study programs, 3-2 enginering degrees with North Carolina State, North Carolina Agricultural and Technical, and Clemson Universities and the University of North Carolina at Charlotte, pass/fail options, and auditing for most courses. In addition, the Broyhill Institute for Business Leadership offers programs to promote undestanding of the business community, The college uses the Dartmount method in foreign language and offers an honors program for outstanding students. There are 11 national honor societies, a freshman honors program, and 18 departmental honors programs.

Faculty/Classroom: 55% of faculty are male; 45%, female. All teach undergraduates. No introductory courses are taught by graduate students. The average class size in an introductory lecture is 28; in a laboratory, 20; and in a regular course, 20.

Admissions: 83% of the 2005-2006 applicants were accepted. The SAT scores for the 2005-2006 freshman class were: Verbal--41% below 500, 40% between 500 and 599, 17% between 600 and 700, and 2% above 700; Math--31% below 500, 44% between 500 and 599, 22% between 600 and 700, and 3% above 700. The ACT scores were 43% below 21, 26% between 21 and 23, 20% between 24 and 26, 10% between 27 and 28, and 1% above 28. 41% of the current freshmen were in the top fifth of their class; 70% were in the top two fifths. 8 freshmen graduated first in their class.

Requirements: The SAT or ACT is required. In addition, applicants need 16 academic credits and should have 4 units in English, 3 in math (algebra 1, geometry, and algebra 2), 2 in the same foreign language, and 1 each in American history and a lab science. An interview is recommended for all students. Music majors must also audition. A GPA of 2.5 is required. AP and CLEP credits are accepted. Important factors in the admissions decision are advanced placement or honor courses, personality/intangible qualities, and leadership record.

Procedure: Freshmen are admitted to all sessions. Entrance exams should be taken in the spring of the junior year and thereafter. There are early admissions and deferred admissions plans. There is a rolling admissions plan. Application deadlines are open. Application fee is $35. Applications are accepted on-line.

Transfer: 233 transfer students enrolled in 2004-2005. Applicants with more than 30 semester hours need a 2.0 minimum GPA in general studies programs or a 2.5 minimum GPA in nursing or education programs. Those with fewer than 30 semester hours must meet freshman entrance criteria. 32 of 128 credits required for the bachelor's degree or the last 25% of course work must be completed at Lenoir-Rhyne.

Visiting: There are regularly scheduled orientations for prospective students, including a meeting with an admissions counselor and a student-guided tour of the campus. There are guides for informal visits and visitors may sit in on classes and stay overnight. To schedule a visit, contact the Admissions Office.

Financial Aid: In 2005-2006, 99% of all full-time freshmen and 92% of continuing full-time students received some form of financial aid. 40% of full-time freshmen and 55% of continuing full-time students received need-based aid. 35% of undergraduates work part time. Average annual earnings from campus work are $1000. The average financial indebtedness of the 2005 graduate was $30,000. The FAFSA and the college's own financial statement are required. The deadline for filing freshman financial aid applications for fall entry is March 15.

International Students: The school actively recruits these students. They must score 500 on the written TOEFL. A satisfactory score on the TOEFL is required.

Computers: All students may access the system 24 hours per day via modem; computer lab hours are 8 A.M. to 11:30 P.M. There are no time limits and no fees.

Admissions Contact: Nick Jenkins, Admissions Counselor.
E-mail: *admission@lrc.edu* Web: *http://www.lrc.edu*

LIVINGSTONE COLLEGE C-2

Salisbury, NC 28144

(704) 216-6005
(800) 835-3435; Fax: (704) 216-6215

Full-time: 464 men, 399 women	**Faculty:** 57
Part-time: 25 men, 7 women	**Ph.Ds:** 50%
Graduate: none	**Student/Faculty:** 15 to 1
Year: semesters	**Tuition:** $12,174
Application Deadline: June	**Room & Board:** $5641
Freshman Class: 1757 applied, 1628 accepted, 240 enrolled	
SAT Verbal/Math: 370/375*	**ACT:** 15 **LESS COMPETITIVE**

Livingstone College, founded in 1879 and affiliated with the African Methodist Episcopal Zion Church, is a private institution offering programs in business, engineering, liberal arts, music, and professional and religious training. There are 4 undergraduate schools. In addition to regional accreditation, LC has baccalaureate program accreditation with CSWE. The library contains 80,457 volumes, 1000 microform items, and 1451 audio/video tapes/CDs/DVDs, and subscribes to 423 periodicals including electronic. Computerized library services include the card catalog, interlibrary loans, database searching, Internet access, and laptop Internet portals. Special learning facilities include a learning resource center and natural history museum. The 272-acre campus is in a small town between Greensboro and Charlotte. Including any residence halls, there are 22 buildings.

Student Life: 55% of undergraduates are from North Carolina. Others are from 22 states and 7 foreign countries. 92% are from public schools. 93% are African American. Most are Protestant. The average age of freshmen is 18; all undergraduates, 19. 39% do not continue beyond their first year; 49% remain to graduate.

Housing: 631 students can be accommodated in college housing, which includes single-sex dormitories and off-campus apartments. In addition, there are honors houses. On-campus housing is guaranteed for all 4 years. 59% of students live on campus; of those, 50% remain on campus on weekends. Alcohol is not permitted. All students may keep cars.

Activities: 40% of men belong to 4 national fraternities; 45% of women belong to 4 national sororities. There are 14 groups on campus, including band, cheerleading, choir, chorus, computers, drama, honors, jazz band, marching band, newspaper, pep band, religious, student government, and yearbook. Popular campus events include Open House, Career Day, and Book Fair.

Sports: There are 4 intercollegiate sports for men and 4 for women, and 5 intramural sports for men and 4 for women. Facilities include a gym and a 4000-seat stadium.

Disabled Students: 90% of the campus is accessible. Wheelchair ramps, special parking, specially equipped rest rooms, special class scheduling, and lowered drinking fountains are available.

Services: Counseling and information services are available, as is tutoring in every subject. There is remedial math, reading, and writing.

Campus Safety and Security: Measures include 24-hour foot and vehicle patrol, security escort services, pamphlets/posters/films, and lighted pathways/sidewalks.

Programs of Study: LC confers B.A., B.S., and B.S.W. degrees. Bachelor's degrees are awarded in BIOLOGICAL SCIENCE (biology/biological science), BUSINESS (accounting, business administration and management, and sports management), COMMUNICATIONS AND THE ARTS (dramatic arts, English, and music), COMPUTER AND PHYSICAL SCIENCE (chemistry, computer science, and mathematics), EDUCATION (early childhood, elementary, music, science, and secondary), HEALTH PROFESSIONS (predentistry, and premedicine), SOCIAL SCIENCE (criminal justice, history, political science/government, prelaw, psychology, social work, sociology, and theological studies). Business administration, criminal justice, and education are the largest.

Required: At least 125 semester hours with a minimum GPA of 2.0 are required for graduation. Required courses include freshman English and religion, 2 semesters each of foreign language and phys ed, 8 hours each of natural science, math, and social science, and 9 hours chosen from offerings in art, literature, music, and philosophy. 80 hours of community service are also required.

Special: Upperclassmen are eligible for a cooperative education program. Cross-registration for a dual engineering degree is available with North Carolina Agricultural and Technical State University. There are 6 national honor societies, a freshman honors program.

Faculty/Classroom: 56% of faculty are male; 44%, female. All teach undergraduates. The average class size in an introductory lecture is 28 and in a regular course, 20.

Admissions: 93% of the 2005-2006 applicants were accepted.

Requirements: The SAT or ACT is required. The ACT Optional Writing test is also required. In addition, applicants should be high school graduates or have earned the GED. Secondary preparation should include 4 academic credits in English, 2 each in history, math, and music, and 1 each in social studies, science, and art. A GPA of 2.0 is required. AP and CLEP credits are accepted. Important factors in the admissions decision are evidence of special talent, leadership record, and extracurricular activities record.

Procedure: Freshmen are admitted fall and spring. Entrance exams should be taken by summer orientation. There is an early decision plan. Applications should be filed by June for fall entry and October for spring entry. Notification is sent on a rolling basis beginning in June and October. A waiting list is an active part of the admissions procedure.

Transfer: 13 transfer students enrolled in 2004-2005. Transfers should have at least a 2.0 GPA in 30 hours of previous college work. Those with fewer hours must meet freshman requirements. 45 of 125 credits required for the bachelor's degree must be completed at LC.

Visiting: There are regularly scheduled orientations for prospective students. There are guides for informal visits and visitors may sit in on classes and stay overnight. To schedule a visit, contact Rolanda Burney, Associate Vice President for Enrollment and Strategic Planning.

Financial Aid: In 2005-2006, 94% of all full-time freshmen and 93% of continuing full-time students received some form of financial aid. 82% of all full-time students received need-based aid. The average freshman award was $15,196. Need-based scholarships or need-based grants averaged $8179 ($17,815 maximum); need-based self-help aid (loans and jobs) averaged $6303 ($10,500 maximum); non-need-based athletic scholarships averaged $4206 ($17,815 maximum); and other non-need-based awards and non-need-based scholarships averaged $6513 ($17,815 maximum). 50% of undergraduates work part time. Average annual earnings from campus work were $1200. The average financial indebtedness of the 2005 graduate was $35,125. LC is a member of CSS. The FAFSA or FFS is required. The priority date for freshman financial aid applications for fall entry is July 1. The deadline for filing freshman financial aid applications for fall entry is December 16.

International Students: The school actively recruits these students. They must take the TOEFL and also take the SAT or ACT.

Computers: Wireless access is available. All students may access the system. There are no time limits and no fees.

Graduates: From July 1, 2004 to June 30, 2005, 118 bachelor's degrees were awarded. The most popular majors were busines administration (23%), criminal justice (14%), and computer science (13%). In an average class, 19% graduate in 4 years or less, and 30% graduate in 5 years or less.

Admissions Contact: Rolanda Burney, Associate Vice President for Enrollment Management and Strategic Planning. A video is available. E-mail: *rburney@livingstone.edu* Web: *www.livingstone.edu*

MARS HILL COLLEGE   B-2
Mars Hill, NC 28754   (828) 689-1201
                                          (800) 543-1514; Fax: (828) 689-1473

Full-time: 500 men, 600 women	**Faculty:** 80; IIB, --$
Part-time: 40 men, 100 women	**Ph.D.s:** 70%
Graduate: none	**Student/Faculty:** 13 to 1
Year: semesters, summer session	**Tuition:** $14,000
Application Deadline: open	**Room & Board:** $5000
Freshman Class: n/av	
SAT or ACT: required	**LESS COMPETITIVE**

Mars Hill College, founded in 1856, is a private institution affiliated with the Baptist Church and offers undergraduate programs in the arts and sciences, business, education, and preprofessional studies. Figures in the above capsule and in this profile are approximate. In addition to regional accreditation, Mars Hill has baccalaureate program accreditation with CSWE, NASM, and NCATE. The library contains 98,150 volumes, 1050 microform items, and 6180 audio/video tapes/CDs/DVDs, and subscribes to 650 periodicals including electronic. Computerized library services include the card catalog, interlibrary loans, and database searching. Special learning facilities include an art gallery, radio station, the Southern Appalachian Center of regional history and culture, and the Rural Life Museum. The 180-acre campus is in a rural area 18 miles north of Asheville. Including any residence halls, there are 47 buildings.

Student Life: 60% of undergraduates are from North Carolina. Others are from 19 states, 20 foreign countries, and Canada. 14% are African American. 81% are Protestant; 13% claim no religious affiliation; 7% Catholic. The average age of freshmen is 18; all undergraduates, 21. 20% do not continue beyond their first year; 49% remain to graduate.

Housing: College housing includes single-sex dorms, on-campus apartments, and married-student housing. In addition, there are honors houses. On-campus housing is guaranteed for all 4 years. 80% of students live on campus; of those, 33% remain on campus on weekends. Alcohol is not permitted. All students may keep cars.

Activities: 30% of men belong to 4 local and 2 national fraternities; 12% of women belong to 4 local and 1 national sorority. There are 80 groups on campus, including art, band, cheerleading, choir, chorale, chorus, dance, drama, ethnic, honors, international, jazz band, literary magazine, marching band, musical theater, newspaper, orchestra, photography, political, professional, radio and TV, religious, social, social service, student government, and yearbook. Popular campus events include Culturefest, Spring Fling, and the Bascom Lamar Lunsford Festival.

Sports: There are 7 intercollegiate sports for men and 6 for women, and 5 intramural sports for men and 5 for women. Facilities include a 5000-seat stadium, a 3500-seat gym, an indoor Olympic-size swimming pool, and a 10-acre complex that has a track, baseball diamond, soccer field, all-purpose playing field, and 6 tennis courts.

Disabled Students: 41% of the campus is accessible. Wheelchair ramps, elevators, special parking, and specially equipped rest rooms are available.

Services: Counseling and information services are available, as is tutoring in every subject. There is remedial math, reading, and writing.

Campus Safety and Security: Measures include 24-hour foot and vehicle patrol, self-defense education, security escort services, and informal discussions. There are pamphlets/posters/films, emergency telephones, and lighted pathways/sidewalks.

Programs of Study: Mars Hill confers B.A., B.S., B.F.A., B.M., and B.S.W. degrees. Bachelor's degrees are awarded in BIOLOGICAL SCIENCE (biology/biological science, botany, and zoology), BUSINESS (accounting, business administration and management, fashion merchandising, and recreation and leisure services), COMMUNICATIONS AND THE ARTS (art history and appreciation, communications, dramatic arts, English, music, music performance, musical theater, performing arts, and Spanish), COMPUTER AND PHYSICAL SCIENCE (chemistry, computer science, and mathematics), EDUCATION (art, athletic training, drama, elementary, mathematics, middle school, music, physical, science, and social studies), HEALTH PROFESSIONS (allied health, physician's assistant, predentistry, premedicine, prepharmacy, and preveterinary science), SOCIAL SCIENCE (history, international studies, political science/government, prelaw, psychology, religion, social work, and sociology). Music, education, and science are the strongest academically. Education is the largest.

Required: To graduate, students must complete at least 128 semester hours with a minimum GPA of 2.0. Distribution requirements include courses in fine arts, literature, American culture, foreign culture, math, natural science, social/behavioral science, ethics, and phys ed.

Special: Mars Hill offers cooperative programs with the Bowman Gray School of Medicine at Wake Forest, internships, study abroad, B.A.-B.S. degrees, dual majors, student-designed majors, and credit for life experience. The Community Life program promotes student involvement in culture and community activities. There are 4 national honor societies and a freshman honors program.

Faculty/Classroom: 58% of faculty are male; 42%, female. All teach undergraduates. The average class size in an introductory lecture is 20; in a laboratory, 15; and in a regular course, 15.

Requirements: The SAT or ACT is required. In addition, applicants need at least 18 academic credits, including 4 in English, 3 in math, and 2 each in history, science, and foreign language. The GED is accepted. A GPA of 2.0 is required. AP and CLEP credits are accepted. Important factors in the admissions decision are advanced placement or honor courses, leadership record, and extracurricular activities record.

Procedure: Freshmen are admitted to all sessions. There are early decision and early admissions plans. There is a rolling admissions plan. Application deadlines are open. Check with the school for current application deadlines and fee.

Transfer: Transfer applicants must be eligible to return to their previous college or have been out of school for at least 1 semester. They must have a minimum GPA of 2.0 for at least 30 semester credit hours. Remedial and developmental hours do not apply. 32 of 128 credits accepted for the bachelor's degree must be completed at Mars Hill.

Visiting: There are regularly scheduled orientations for prospective students, consisting of 2 days during which a variety of special programs are offered. Individual students and their families may visit any time throughout the year. There are guides for informal visits and visitors may sit in on classes and stay overnight. To schedule a visit, contact the Admissions Office.

Financial Aid: Mars Hill is a member of CSS. The FAFSA is required. Check with the school for current deadlines.

International Students: The school actively recruits these students. They must take the TOEFL.

Computers: All students may access the system during library hours, for up to 2 hours at a time. There are no fees.

Admissions Contact: Office of Admissions.
E-mail: *admissions@mhc.edu* Web: *www.mhc.edu*

MEREDITH COLLEGE   D-2

Raleigh, NC 27607-5298

(919) 760-8581
(800) MEREDITH; Fax: (919) 760-2348

Full-time: 1645 women	**Faculty:** 130; IIA, --$
Part-time: 14 men, 356 women	**Ph.D.s:** 89%
Graduate: 17 men, 136 women	**Student/Faculty:** 13 to 1
Year: semesters, summer session	**Tuition:** $20,000
Application Deadline: February 15	**Room & Board:** $5600
Freshman Class: 1132 applied, 1073 accepted, 451 enrolled	
SAT or ACT: required	**COMPETITIVE**

Meredith College, founded in 1891, is an independent college for women offering a comprehensive undergraduate program with a strong emphasis on the liberal arts. Graduate programs in business, music, education, and nutrition serve both women and men. There are 6 undergraduate schools and 1 graduate school. In addition to regional accreditation, Meredith has baccalaureate program accreditation with ADA, CSWE, FIDER, NASM, and NCATE. The 2 libraries contain 186,000 volumes, 15,626 microform items, and 19,686 audio/video tapes/CDs/DVDs, and subscribe to 841 periodicals including electronic. Computerized library services include the card catalog, interlibrary loans, database searching, and Internet access. Special learning facilities include a learning resource center, an art gallery, a child - care lab, greenhouse, experimental and clinical psychology labs including one on autism, an electron microscope suite, astronomy observation deck, student/faculty research labs, and a language lab. The 225-acre campus is in an urban area in the city of Raleigh. Including any residence halls, there are 30 buildings.

Student Life: 89% of undergraduates are from North Carolina. Students are from 31 states and 15 foreign countries. 84% are from public schools. 78% are white; 11% African American. The average age of freshmen is 18; all undergraduates, 23. 23% do not continue beyond their first year; 70% remain to graduate.

Housing: 1016 students can be accommodated in college housing, which includes single-sex dorms. On-campus housing is guaranteed for all 4 years. 56% of students commute. Alcohol is not permitted. All students may keep cars.

Activities: There are no sororities. There are 91 groups on campus, including art, chorale, chorus, commuter, computers, dance, drama, environmental, ethnic, foreign language, gay, honors, international, literary magazine, musical theater, newspaper, nutrition and wellness, orchestra, photography, political, professional, religious, social, social service, student government, symphony, and yearbook. Popular campus events include Academics and Leadership Awards Day, White Iris Ball, and Undergraduate Research Conference.

Sports: There are 6 intercollegiate sports for women. Facilities include an indoor swimming pool, a dance studio, a fitness center, a horseshoe pit, a putting green and driving range, a softball diamond, tennis courts, a soccer field, and a gym with basketball, volleyball, and badminton courts.

Disabled Students: 81% of the campus is accessible. Wheelchair ramps, elevators, special parking, specially equipped rest rooms, special class scheduling, lowered drinking fountains, special housing, a handicap lift in the swimming pool, and lowered fire alarms are available.

Services: Counseling and information services are available, as is tutoring in some subjects, including math, writing, computer lab, French, Spanish, biology, chemistry, study skills, German, GRE prep, Praxis prep, and grammar. There is a reader service for the blind.

Campus Safety and Security: Measures include 24 hour foot and vehicle patrol, self-defense education, security escort services, and informal discussions. There are pamphlets/posters/films, emergency telephones, lighted pathways/sidewalks, controlled campus access at night, and 24 hour locked residence halls.

Programs of Study: Meredith confers B.A., B.S., B.M., and B.S.W. degrees. Master's degrees are also awarded. Bachelor's degrees are awarded in AGRICULTURE (environmental studies), BIOLOGICAL SCIENCE (biology/biological science and nutrition), BUSINESS (accounting, business administration and management, fashion merchandising, and international business management), COMMUNICATIONS AND THE ARTS (applied music, art, communications, dance, dramatic arts, English, fine arts, French, music, music performance, musical theater, and Spanish), COMPUTER AND PHYSICAL SCIENCE (chemistry, computer science, information sciences and systems, and mathematics), EDUCATION (music), ENGINEERING AND ENVIRONMENTAL DESIGN (interior design), HEALTH PROFESSIONS (exercise science), SOCIAL SCIENCE (American studies, child psychology/development, economics, family/consumer studies, history, international studies, political science/government, psychology, public affairs, religion, social work, and sociology). Business, psychology, and biology are the largest.

Required: To graduate, students must complete a total of 124 credit hours, including general education requirements, a major field, and electives, with a minimum GPA of 2.0. General Education is comprised of a core curriculum focusing on understanding diverse cultures, fields of knowledge that ensure breadth in the liberal arts, and across-the-curriculum threads and independent learning experiences that build competencies. Some major fields offer or require a concentration, and contract majors are possible. Electives may be used to complete a second major, a minor, or teacher licensure, or to explore areas of personal, career or pre professional interest.

Special: Meredith offers cooperative programs, cross-registration with Cooperating Raleigh Colleges, internships, study abroad in Europe and Asia, a Washington semester at American University, a U.N. semester at Drew University, and work-study programs on campus. Dual majors, interdisciplinary and student-designed majors, preprofessional programs, and pass/fail options are available. Certification in social work and licensure for teaching are possible. Business administration, management, and social work majors can be completed through evening classes. There are 19 national honor societies, and a freshman honors program.

Faculty/Classroom: 34% of faculty are male; 66%, female. All teach undergraduates. No introductory courses are taught by graduate students. The average class size in an introductory lecture is 21; in a laboratory, 13; and in a regular course, 16.

Admissions: 95% of the 2005-2006 applicants were accepted. The SAT scores for the 2005-2006 freshman class were: Verbal--37% below 500, 47% between 500 and 599, 15% between 600 and 700, and 1% above 700; Math--39% below 500, 46% between 500 and 599, 14% between 600 and 700, and 1% above 700. The ACT scores were 54% below 21, 27% between 21 and 23, 10% between 24 and 26, 3% between 27 and 28, and 6% above 28. 37% of the current freshmen were in the top fifth of their class; 68% were in the top two fifths. 5 freshmen graduated first in their class.

Requirements: The SAT or ACT is required. The ACT Optional Writing test is also required. The SAT is preferred. Applicants must have a minimum of 16 units of credit, including 4 in English, 3 each in math, history/social studies, and science, 2 in foreign language, and 1 elective. Students are expected to rank in the top half of their class, and grades in academic subjects are very important. An interview may be requested as part of the evaluation process. A GPA of 2.0 is required. AP and CLEP credits are accepted. Important factors in the admissions decision are recommendations by school officials, advanced placement or honor courses, and evidence of special talent.

Procedure: Freshmen are admitted fall and spring. Entrance exams should be taken by January of the senior year. There are early decision and deferred admissions plans. There is a rolling admissions plan. Early decision applications should be filed by October 15; regular applications, by February 15 for fall entry and December 1 for spring entry, along with a $40 fee. Notification of early decision is sent November 1; regular decision, on a rolling basis. 77 early decision candidates were accepted for the 2005-2006 class. Applications are accepted on-line.

Transfer: 74 transfer students enrolled in 2004-2005. Applicants must have a minimum GPA of 2.0, be eligible to return to the last college attended, and be recommended by college officials. Those students with fewer than 30 hours of credit must also meet freshman admission requirements. 31 of 124 credits required for the bachelor's degree must be completed at Meredith.

Visiting: There are regularly scheduled orientations for prospective students, including Open Days information sessions for senior students and parents, class visitation, informal conversations with students and faculty/staff, and campus tours. Experience Meredith! for accepted students and their parents includes various off-to-college information sessions, an academic fair, a student activities fair, and campus tours. Individual visitors typically have a conference with an admissions counselor and a campus tour. There are also visitation days for juniors and transfers and a Legacy Day when alumnae bring prospective students for a visit. Visitors may stay overnight. To schedule a visit, contact the Admissions Office.

Financial Aid: In 2005-2006, 96% of all full-time freshmen and 99% of continuing full-time students received some form of financial aid. 69% of full-time freshmen and 68% of continuing full-time students received need-based aid. The average freshman award was $16,651. Need-based scholarships or need-based grants averaged $11,719 ($27,950 maximum); need-based self-help aid (loans and jobs) averaged $4963 ($14,928 maximum); and other non-need-based awards and non-need-based scholarships averaged $6230 ($22,250 maximum). 28% of undergraduates work part time. Average annual earnings from campus work are $1259. The average financial indebtedness of the 2005 graduate was $21,266. Meredith is a member of CSS. The FAFSA is required. The priority date for freshman financial aid applications for fall entry is February 15.

International Students: There are 16 international students enrolled. The school actively recruits these students. A satisfactory score on the TOEFL is required. If English is the student's native language or primary language of instruction, the SAT should be taken instead of the TOEFL.

Computers: Wireless access is available. Meredith provides each new full-time first-year student with a laptop computer with printer, software, and wireless card included. All students may access the system 24 hours per day in residence halls and one lab, 7 A.M. to midnight in other labs. All students are required to have personal computers.

Graduates: From July 1, 2004 to June 30, 2005, 454 bachelor's degrees were awarded. The most popular majors were business administration (16%), psychology (11%), and communications (8%). In an average class, 4% graduate in 3 years or less, 59% graduate in 4 years or less, 68% graduate in 5 years or less, and 70% graduate in 6 years or less.

Admissions Contact: Heidi Fletcher, Director of Admissions. A video is available. E-mail: *admissions@meredith.edu*
Web: *www.meredith.edu*

METHODIST COLLEGE	D-3

Fayetteville, NC 28311-1420
(910) 630-7027
(800) 488-7110; Fax: (910) 630-7285

Full-time: 1600 men and women	Faculty: 90; IIB, --$
Part-time: 300 men and women	Ph.D.s: 54%
Graduate: none	Student/Faculty: 19 to 1
Year: semesters, summer session	Tuition: $15,000
Application Deadline: open	Room & Board: $6,000
Freshman Class: n/av	
SAT or ACT: required	COMPETITIVE

Methodist College, founded in 1956, is a private institution affiliated with the United Methodist Church. The college offers programs in the arts and sciences, education, business, and professional training. Figures in the above capsule and in this profile are approximate. There are 2 undergraduate schools and 1 graduate school. In addition to regional accreditation, Methodist has baccalaureate program accreditation with ACBSP, CAAHEP, CSWE, and NCATE. The library contains 181,833 volumes, 57,759 microform items, and 13,412 audio/video tapes/CDs/DVDs, and subscribes to 587 periodicals including electronic. Computerized library services include the card catalog, interlibrary loans, and database searching. Special learning facilities include a learning resource center, art gallery, and professional golf and tennis management facilities. The 600-acre campus is in a suburban area 5 miles north of Fayetteville. Including any residence halls, there are 30 buildings.

Student Life: 60% of undergraduates are from North Carolina. Others are from 48 states, 37 foreign countries, and Canada. 88% are from public schools. 75% are white; 17% African American. 41% are Protestant; 16% Catholic. The average age of freshmen is 18; all undergraduates, 21. 35% do not continue beyond their first year; 36% remain to graduate.

Housing: 823 students can be accommodated in college housing, which includes single-sex and coed dorms and on-campus apartments. In addition, there are honors houses and a health and wellness hall. On-campus housing is guaranteed for all 4 years. 52% of students live on campus; of those, 70% remain on campus on weekends. Alcohol is not permitted. All students may keep cars.

Activities: 1% of men belong to 2 local fraternities; 1% of women belong to 2 local and 1 national sorority. There are 72 groups on campus, including art, band, cheerleading, chess, choir, chorale, chorus, computers, dance, debate, drama, ethnic, honors, international, jazz band, literary magazine, musical theater, newspaper, orchestra, pep band, photography, political, professional, religious, social, social service, student

government, and yearbook. Popular campus events include Show You Care Day, Annual Woodcutting, and Spring Fest.

Sports: There are 9 intercollegiate sports for men and 10 for women, and 7 intramural sports for men and 4 for women. Facilities include a 1200-seat stadium, a 1500-seat gym, a golf course, a track and field area, tennis courts, and fields for baseball, softball, and soccer.

Disabled Students: 90% of the campus is accessible. Wheelchair ramps, special parking, specially equipped rest rooms, and lowered drinking fountains are available.

Services: Counseling and information services are available, as is tutoring in most subjects. There is a reader service for the blind, and remedial math, reading, and writing.

Campus Safety and Security: Measures include 24-hour foot and vehicle patrol, self-defense education, security escort services, and shuttle buses. There are informal discussions, pamphlets/posters/films, emergency telephones, and lighted pathways/sidewalks.

Programs of Study: Methodist confers B.A., B.S., B.H.S., B.M., and B.S.W. degrees. Associate and master's degrees are also awarded. Bachelor's degrees are awarded in BIOLOGICAL SCIENCE (biology/biological science), BUSINESS (accounting, business administration and management, marketing/retailing/merchandising, organizational behavior, and sports management), COMMUNICATIONS AND THE ARTS (art, communications, creative writing, dramatic arts, English, French, music, music performance, and Spanish), COMPUTER AND PHYSICAL SCIENCE (chemistry, computer science, and mathematics), EDUCATION (art, athletic training, elementary, middle school, music, physical, secondary, and special), ENGINEERING AND ENVIRONMENTAL DESIGN (computer technology), HEALTH PROFESSIONS (physician's assistant and predentistry), SOCIAL SCIENCE (criminal justice, economics, history, international studies, political science/government, prelaw, psychology, religion, social studies, social work, and sociology). Business administration, biology, and music are the strongest academically. Business administration, education, and biology are the largest.

Required: To graduate, students must complete at least 124 semester hours, including core requirements, with a minimum GPA of 2.0. A liberal arts core, ranging from 36 to 62 hours, is required in all majors.

Special: Methodist offers internships in political science and social work, study abroad in 2 countries, a Washington semester, a general studies degree, a 3-2 engineering degree with North Carolina State University, pass/fail options, dual majors, and nondegree study. The business administration major offers concentrations in professional golf, tennis, and resort management with specialized facilities and co-op programs. There are 7 national honor societies, a freshman honors program, and 3 departmental honors programs.

Faculty/Classroom: 67% of faculty are male; 33%, female. All teach undergraduates. The average class size in an introductory lecture is 25; in a laboratory, 20; and in a regular course, 20.

Requirements: The SAT or ACT is required. In addition, applicants should be graduates of an accredited secondary school or have a GED certificate. They must have 16 academic credits, including 4 in English and 3 each in history, math, and science. 2 years of foreign language are recommended. An essay and interview are also recommended. Applicants can apply on-line at the school's web site. AP and CLEP credits are accepted. Important factors in the admissions decision are advanced placement or honor courses, evidence of special talent, and recommendations by school officials.

Procedure: Freshmen are admitted fall, spring, and summer. There is a deferred admissions plan and a rolling admissions plan. Application deadlines are open. Check with the school for current application deadlines and fee. Applications are accepted on-line.

Transfer: Applicants must have a minimum GPA of 2.0. They must also submit a high school transcript, college transcripts, and SAT or ACT scores. 30 of 124 credits required for the bachelor's degree must be completed at Methodist.

Visiting: There are regularly scheduled orientations for prospective students, consisting of a 2-day summer orientation in July. There are guides for informal visits and visitors may sit in on classes and stay overnight. To schedule a visit, contact the Admissions Office.

Financial Aid: The FAFSA is required. Check with the school for current deadlines.

International Students: The school actively recruits these students. They must take the TOEFL. The student may take the SAT or ACT in place of the TOEFL if English proficiency is demonstrated.

Computers: All students may access the system during specified hours.

Admissions Contact: Jamie Legg, Director of Admissions. E-mail: *jlegg@methodist.edu* Web: *www.methodist.edu*

MONTREAT COLLEGE
B-2

Montreat, NC 28757-1267

(828) 669-8012, ext. 3784
(800) 622-6968; Fax: (828) 669-0120

Full-time: 350 men, 590 women	**Faculty:** 31; IIB, --$
Part-time: 5 men, 5 women	**Ph.D:s:** 48%
Graduate: 40 men, 60 women	**Student/Faculty:** 30 to 1
Year: semesters	**Tuition:** $16,182
Application Deadline: open	**Room & Board:** $5258
Freshman Class: n/av	
SAT or ACT: required	**COMPETITIVE**

Montreat College, founded in 1916, is a private liberal arts institution affiliated with the Presbyterian Church (U.S.A.) and committed to the integration of faith and learning. Some figures in the above capsule and in this profile are approximate. In addition to regional accreditation, Montreat has baccalaureate program accreditation with NCATE. The library contains 79,165 volumes, 117,155 microform items, and 3119 audio/video tapes/CDs/DVDs, and subscribes to 485 periodicals including electronic. Computerized library services include the card catalog, interlibrary loans, database searching, and Internet access. Special learning facilities include a learning resource center, art gallery, and the Presbyterian Church (U.S.A.) Historical Foundation. The 100-acre campus is in a rural area 15 miles east of Asheville. Including any residence halls, there are 18 buildings.

Student Life: 79% of undergraduates are from North Carolina. Students are from 21 states and 12 foreign countries. 55% are from public schools. 70% are white; 18% African American. The average age of freshmen is 18. 34% do not continue beyond their first year.

Housing: 392 students can be accommodated in college housing, which includes single-sex dorms. On-campus housing is guaranteed for all 4 years. 76% of students live on campus; of those, 50% remain on campus on weekends. Alcohol is not permitted. All students may keep cars.

Activities: There are no fraternities or sororities. There are 25 groups on campus, including adventure, art, choir, chorus, drama, honors, musical theater, newspaper, photography, political, professional, religious, social, social service, student government, and yearbook.

Sports: There are 6 intercollegiate sports for men and 6 for women, and 4 intramural sports for men and 4 for women. Facilities include standard athletic facilities complemented by opportunities for outdoor recreation activities such as skiing, whitewater sports, mountain climbing, and camping.

Disabled Students: 75% of the campus is accessible. Wheelchair ramps, elevators, special parking, specially equipped rest rooms, special class scheduling, and lowered telephones are available.

Services: Counseling and information services are available, as is tutoring in all academic areas. There is remedial math, reading, and writing.

Campus Safety and Security: Measures include 24-hour foot and vehicle patrol, lighted pathways/sidewalks, and a closed campus.

Programs of Study: Montreat confers B.A., B.S., B.B.A., and B.M. degrees. Associate and master's degrees are also awarded. Bachelor's degrees are awarded in BUSINESS (business administration and management), COMMUNICATIONS AND THE ARTS (English, music business management, and music performance), COMPUTER AND PHYSICAL SCIENCE (mathematics), EDUCATION (elementary), ENGINEERING AND ENVIRONMENTAL DESIGN (environmental science), SOCIAL SCIENCE (American studies, biblical studies, history, human services, liberal arts/general studies, and religion). English is the strongest academically. Business is the largest.

Required: To graduate, students must complete 126 credit hours with a minimum GPA of 2.0. They must pass a comprehensive exam covering math, computation, oral expression, reading, and writing. A thesis is required for some majors.

Special: Montreat offers internships in all majors, study abroad, a Washington semester, work-study programs, alternative majors, and dual majors. There are 2 national honor societies, a freshman honors program, and 3 departmental honors programs.

Faculty/Classroom: 58% of faculty are male; 42%, female. All teach undergraduates. No introductory courses are taught by graduate students. The average class size in an introductory lecture is 30; in a laboratory, 15; and in a regular course, 10.

Requirements: The SAT or ACT is required, and is rated on a sliding scale with the GPA, with minimum scores needed. Applicants must be graduates of an accredited secondary school and have completed 4 years of English, 3 each of math, science, and social studies, and 1 of foreign language. The GED is accepted. A counselor or teacher recommendation is required, and a short autobiographical essay is required unless the student has been interviewed. Montreat requires applicants to be in the upper 50% of their class. A GPA of 2.25 is required. CLEP credit is accepted. Important factors in the admissions decision are advanced placement or honor courses, extracurricular activities record, and evidence of special talent.

Procedure: Freshmen are admitted to all sessions. There is a rolling admissions plan. Application deadlines are open. Application fee is $150. Notication is sent on a rolling basis.

Transfer: 52 transfer students enrolled in a recent year. Applicants must submit official college transcripts, be in good standing at their previous institution, and have completed at least 24 semester hours of college credit with a minimum GPA of 2.0. Students with fewer credits must also submit high school transcripts and SAT or ACT scores. 18 of 126 credits required for the bachelor's degree must be completed at Montreat.

Visiting: There are regularly scheduled orientations for prospective students, including a campus tour, faculty introduction, and student program. There are guides for informal visits and visitors may sit in on classes and stay overnight. To schedule a visit, contact the Admissions Office.

Financial Aid: In a recent year, 98% of all full-time students received some form of financial aid. 71% of full-time freshmen and 75% of continuing full-time students received need-based aid. The average freshman award was $12,337. Need-based scholarships or need-based grants averaged $9758 ($19,125 maximum); need-based self-help aid (loans and jobs) averaged $3880 ($8301 maximum); non-need-based athletic scholarships averaged $9396 ($18,562 maximum); and other non-need-based awards and non-need-based scholarships averaged $4236 ($14,120 maximum). 30% of undergraduates work part time. Average annual earnings from campus work are $1700. The average financial indebtedness of a recent graduate was $17,600. Montreat is a member of CSS. The FAFSA and the college's own financial statement are required. Check with the school for current deadlines.

International Students: There were 12 international students enrolled a recent year. The school actively recruits these students. A satisfactory score on the TOEFL is required.

Computers: All students may access the system during computer lab hours or at any time by PC. There are no time limits and no fees. It is strongly recommended that all students have a personal computer.

Graduates: In a recent year, 206 bachelor's degrees were awarded. The most popular majors were business (76%), outdoor education (6%), and human services (3%). In an average class, 26% graduate in 4 years or less, 38% graduate in 5 years or less, and 42% graduate in 6 years or less.

Admissions Contact: Anita F. Darby, Director of Admissions. A video is available. E-mail: *admissions@montreat.edu*
Web: *www.montreat.edu*

MOUNT OLIVE COLLEGE
E-3

Mount Olive, NC 28365

(919) 658-2502
(800) 653-0854; Fax: (919) 658-7180

Full-time: 650 men, 800 women	**Faculty:** 44
Part-time: 150 men, 200 women	**Ph.D:s:** 79%
Graduate: none	**Student/Faculty:** 33 to 1
Year: semesters, summer session	**Tuition:** $11,000
Application Deadline: open	**Room & Board:** $5000
Freshman Class: n/av	
SAT or ACT: required	**LESS COMPETITIVE**

Mount Olive College, founded in 1951, is a private liberal arts institution affiliated with the Original Free Will Baptist Church. Figures in the above capsule and in this profile are approximate. The 2 libraries contain 77,545 volumes, 48,735 microform items, and 2005 audio/video tapes/CDs/DVDs, and subscribe to 5979 periodicals including electronic. Computerized library services include the card catalog, interlibrary loans, and database searching. Special learning facilities include a learning resource center, art gallery, and a church archives collection. The 123-acre campus is in a small town 65 miles southeast of Raleigh. Including any residence halls, there are 16 buildings.

Student Life: 92% of undergraduates are from North Carolina. Others are from 21 states, 7 foreign countries, and Canada. 93% are from public schools. 68% are white; 25% African American. The average age of freshmen is 18; all undergraduates, 29. 40% do not continue beyond their first year; 20% remain to graduate.

Housing: 306 students can be accommodated in college housing, which includes single-sex dorms and on-campus apartments. On-campus housing is guaranteed for the freshman year only. 77% of students commute. Alcohol is not permitted. All students may keep cars.

Activities: There are no fraternities or sororities. There are 20 groups on campus, including art, cheerleading, choir, chorale, chorus, drama, honors, international, literary magazine, newspaper, orchestra, pep band, photography, political, professional, religious, student government, and yearbook. Popular campus events include Founders Day, Pickle Classic Weekend, and the North Carolina Pickle Festival.

Sports: There are 6 intercollegiate sports for men and 6 for women, and 10 intramural sports for men and 8 for women. Facilities include a 2000-seat gym, racquetball and tennis courts, a track, wrestling/gymnastics and weight rooms, an athletic field, outdoor basketball areas, a student center, and baseball, softball, and soccer fields.

Disabled Students: 90% of the campus is accessible. Wheelchair ramps, elevators, special parking, specially equipped rest rooms, and special class scheduling are available.

Services: Counseling and information services are available, as is tutoring in most subjects, including math, English, and science. There is remedial math and reading.

Campus Safety and Security: Measures include informal discussions, pamphlets/posters/films, lighted pathways/sidewalks, and evening and weekend patrols.

Programs of Study: Mount Olive confers B.A., B.S., and B.Applied Sc. degrees. Associate degrees are also awarded. Bachelor's degrees are awarded in BIOLOGICAL SCIENCE (biology/biological science), BUSINESS (accounting, business administration and management, human resources, and recreation and leisure services), COMMUNICATIONS AND THE ARTS (art, communications, English, fine arts, and music), COMPUTER AND PHYSICAL SCIENCE (computer management, information sciences and systems, and mathematics), EDUCATION (middle school and secondary), ENGINEERING AND ENVIRONMENTAL DESIGN (environmental science), SOCIAL SCIENCE (criminal justice, history, human services, liberal arts/general studies, ministries, psychology, and religion). Business, accounting, and psychology are the strongest academically. Business, psychology, and recreation are the largest.

Required: To graduate, students must have completed a total of 126 credit hours, with a minimum 2.0 overall GPA in 63 credit hours for the B.S. or in 53 hours for the B. Applied Sc. Distribution requirements include 30 to 36 hours in humanities, 18 in science/math, and 12 in social science. Specific course work includes 6 hours of religion, 4 of phys ed, 3 hours of computer competency.

Special: Mount Olive offers co-op programs and internships in all majors, work-study, B.A.-B.S. degrees, dual majors, and accelerated degree programs in business, accounting, and criminal justice administration. Cross-registration with James Sprunt Community College and Wayne Community College, study abroad, and credit for life, military, and work experience are also possible. Professional degree completion programs run continuously for 55 to 57 weeks. There is 1 national honor society and a freshman honors program.

Faculty/Classroom: 58% of faculty are male; 42%, female. All teach undergraduates, 14% do research, and 86% do both.

Requirements: The SAT or ACT is required. Applicants must be graduates of an accredited secondary school or have a GED certificate. They must have completed 4 units of English, 3 each of math and science, and 2 of history. An essay and interview are suggested. A GPA of 2.0 is required. AP and CLEP credits are accepted.

Procedure: Freshmen are admitted to all sessions. Entrance exams should be taken in the junior or senior year. There are early admissions and deferred admissions plans. There is a rolling admissions plan. Application deadlines are open. Check with the school for current application deadlines and fee. Applications are accepted on-line.

Transfer: Applicants must have a minimum GPA of 2.0 and submit an official transcript from the previous institution. An interview may be required. 32 of 126 credits required for the bachelor's degree must be completed at Mount Olive.

Visiting: There are regularly scheduled orientations for prospective students, consisting of 2 days of advising, sports, and entertainment. There are guides for informal visits and visitors may sit in on classes. To schedule a visit, contact the Admissions Office at twoodward@moc.edu.

Financial Aid: The FAFSA and the college's own financial statement are required. Check with the school for current deadlines.

International Students: The school actively recruits these students. They must take the TOEFL and also take the SAT or the ACT.

Computers: All students may access the system 8 A.M. to 10 P.M. Monday through Friday and during scheduled hours on weekends. Students may access the system for a reasonable length of time. There are no fees. It is strongly recommended that all students have a personal computer.

Admissions Contact: Tim Woodard, Director of Admissions. A video is available. E-mail: admissions@exchanbge.moc.edu. Web: www.moc.edu

---

NORTH CAROLINA AGRICULTURAL AND TECHNICAL STATE UNIVERSITY   D-2

Greensboro, NC 27411

(336) 334-7946
(800) 443-8964; Fax: (336) 334-7136

Full-time: 2800 men, 3100 women	Faculty: 442; IIA, av$
Part-time: 350 men, 360 women	Ph.D.s: 96%
Graduate: 370 men, 500 women	Student/Faculty: 13 to 1
Year: semesters, summer session	Tuition: $3000 ($10,000)
Application Deadline: see profile	Room & Board: $5000
Freshman Class: n/av	
SAT or ACT: required	LESS COMPETITIVE

North Carolina Agricultural and Technical State University, founded in 1891, is a public institution within the University of North Carolina System. A & T offers programs in arts and sciences, education, business and economics, agriculture, nursing, engineering, and technology. Figures in the above capsule and in this profile are approximate. There are 7 undergraduate schools and 1 graduate school. In addition to regional accreditation, A & T has baccalaureate program accreditation with AACSB, ABET, ACCE, CSWE, NCATE, and NLN. The library contains 507,036 volumes, 1,038,474 microform items, and 34,025 audio/video tapes/CDs/DVDs, and subscribes to 5446 periodicals including electronic. Computerized library services include the card catalog, interlibrary loans, and database searching. Special learning facilities include an art gallery, planetarium, radio station, TV station, and African Heritage Center. The 191-acre campus is in an urban area 90 miles northeast of Charlotte. Including any residence halls, there are 107 buildings.

Student Life: 82% of undergraduates are from North Carolina. Students are from 39 states and 25 foreign countries. 89% are African American. The average age of freshmen is 18; all undergraduates, 22. 25% do not continue beyond their first year; 49% remain to graduate.

Housing: 2959 students can be accommodated in college housing, which includes single-sex and coed dorms. In addition, there are honors houses. On-campus housing is available on a first-come, first-served basis and is available on a lottery system for upperclassmen. 53% of students commute. Alcohol is not permitted. All students may keep cars.

Activities: 1% of men belong to 5 national fraternities; 1% of women belong to 4 national sororities. There are 150 groups on campus, including art, band, cheerleading, choir, chorus, computers, dance, drama, drill team, ethnic, film, honors, international, jazz band, marching band, newspaper, orchestra, pep band, photography, political, professional, radio and TV, religious, social, social service, student government, symphony, and yearbook. Popular campus events include Graduation, Martin Luther King's Birthday, and Ron McNair Commemoration.

Sports: There are 7 intercollegiate sports for men and 9 for women, and 12 intramural sports for men and 12 for women. Facilities include a gym, a sports center, a stadium, tennis courts, a student union, a field house, and softball/baseball facilities.

Disabled Students: 85% of the campus is accessible. Wheelchair ramps, elevators, special parking, specially equipped rest rooms, special class scheduling, lowered drinking fountains, and lowered telephones are available.

Services: Counseling and information services are available, as is tutoring in every subject. There is a reader service for the blind, and remedial math, reading, and writing.

Campus Safety and Security: Measures include 24-hour foot and vehicle patrol, self-defense education, security escort services, and shuttle buses. There are informal discussions, pamphlets/posters/films, emergency telephones, and lighted pathways/sidewalks.

Programs of Study: A & T confers B.A., B.S., B.F.A., B.S.I.E., B.S.M.E., B.S.N., and B.S.W. degrees. Master's and doctoral degrees are also awarded. Bachelor's degrees are awarded in AGRICULTURE (agricultural business management, agricultural economics, and animal science), BIOLOGICAL SCIENCE (biology/biological science), BUSINESS (accounting and business administration and management), COMMUNICATIONS AND THE ARTS (communications, dramatic arts, English, French, music, and speech/debate/rhetoric), COMPUTER AND PHYSICAL SCIENCE (chemistry, computer science, mathematics, and physics), EDUCATION (agricultural, art, business, early childhood, English, home economics, industrial arts, mathematics, music, physical, social science, and special), ENGINEERING AND ENVIRONMENTAL DESIGN (architectural engineering, chemical engineering, civil engineering, electrical/electronics engineering, engineering physics, industrial engineering, landscape architecture/design, mechanical engineering, and occupational safety and health), HEALTH PROFESSIONS (nursing), SOCIAL SCIENCE (child psychology/development, clothing and textiles management/production/services, economics, history, political science/government, psychology, social work, and sociology). Business, accounting, and electronics and computer technology are the strongest academically. Accounting and electronics and computer technology are the largest.

Required: To graduate, students must complete a minimum of 124 credit hours, including at least 80 in the major, with an overall GPA of 2.0 or better. Specific course work is required in English, math, natural science, social science, humanities, and health or phys ed.

Special: A & T offers cross-registration with the Greensboro Regional Consortium, internships, B.A.-B.S. degrees, cooperative programs in most majors, study abroad in 5 countries, work-study programs, and dual majors. There are 3 national honor societies, a freshman honors program, and 13 departmental honors programs.

Faculty/Classroom: 65% of faculty are male; 35%, female. All teach undergraduates. The average class size in an introductory lecture is 26; in a laboratory, 17; and in a regular course, 24.

Requirements: The SAT or ACT is required. Applicants must be graduates of an accredited secondary school or have a GED certificate. They must have completed at least 16 academic credits, including 4 in English, 3 each in math and science, 2 each in music and social sciences, and a foreign language. An audition is required of fine arts majors, and a portfolio is recommended. An interview is suggested for all applicants. A

GPA of 2.0 is required. AP and CLEP credits are accepted. Important factors in the admissions decision are geographic diversity, advanced placement or honor courses, and personality/intangible qualities.

Procedure: Freshmen are admitted to all sessions. Entrance exams should be taken before April 1. There is a deferred admissions plan and a rolling admissions plan. Notification is sent on a rolling basis. Check with the school for current application deadlines and fee.

Transfer: Applicants must have a minimum GPA of 2.0 in at least 24 semester hours and must be in good standing at their previous school. Specifically, 6 hours of English, history, college algebra, and science are required. 62 of 124 credits required for the bachelor's degree must be completed at A & T.

Visiting: There are regularly scheduled orientations for prospective students. There are guides for informal visits and visitors may sit in on classes. To schedule a visit, contact the Admissions Office.

Financial Aid: A & T is a member of CSS. The FAFSA is required. Check with the school for current deadlines.

International Students: Students must take the TOEFL.

Computers: All students may access the system. There are no time limits and no fees.

Admissions Contact: John Smith, Admissions Director. A video is available. E-mail: *uadmit@ncat.edu* Web: *www.ncat.edu*

NORTH CAROLINA CENTRAL UNIVERSITY
D-2

Durham, NC 27707
(919) 560-6298
Fax: (919) 530-7625 or (919) 560-5462

Full-time: 1500 men, 2700 women	**Faculty:** 257; IIA, +$
Part-time: 300 men, 800 women	**Ph.D.s:** 75%
Graduate: 500 men, 1300 women	**Student/Faculty:** 16 to 1
Year: semesters, summer session	**Tuition:** $4000 ($13,000)
Application Deadline: see profile	**Room & Board:** $5000
Freshman Class: n/av	
SAT or ACT: required	LESS COMPETITIVE

North Carolina Central University, founded in 1909, is a publicly funded liberal arts institution in the University of North Carolina system. Figures in the above capsule and in this profile are approximate. There are 3 undergraduate and 2 graduate schools. In addition to regional accreditation, NCCU has baccalaureate program accreditation with NCATE and NLN. The 6 libraries contain 663,913 volumes, 1,217,019 microform items, and 10,991 audio/video tapes/CDs/DVDs, and subscribe to 6688 periodicals including electronic. Computerized library services include the card catalog and database searching. Special learning facilities include a learning resource center and art gallery. The 103-acre campus is in an urban area 2 miles from the center of Durham. Including any residence halls, there are 57 buildings.

Student Life: 89% of undergraduates are from North Carolina. Students are from 39 states and 17 foreign countries. 80% are African American; 14% white. The average age of freshmen is 19; all undergraduates, 24.

Housing: 2377 students can be accommodated in college housing, which includes single-sex and coed dorms and on-campus apartments. In addition, there are honors houses. On-campus housing is available on a first-come, first-served basis and is available on a lottery system for upperclassmen. 63% of students commute. Alcohol is not permitted. All students may keep cars.

Activities: There are 4 national fraternities and 4 national sororities. There are 45 groups on campus, including art, band, cheerleading, chess, choir, computers, dance, drama, drill team, ethnic, honors, international, jazz band, literary magazine, marching band, newspaper, political, professional, radio and TV, religious, social, social service, student government, symphony, and yearbook.

Sports: There are 6 intercollegiate sports for men and 5 for women. Facilities include a 12,000-seat stadium, a 4500-seat gym, a swimming pool, handball and tennis courts, a track, a bowling alley, dance studios, and a weight room.

Disabled Students: 90% of the campus is accessible. Wheelchair ramps, elevators, special parking, specially equipped rest rooms, special class scheduling, lowered drinking fountains, lowered telephones, lowered dorm intercoms, interpreters, automatic door openers, and adaptive technology are available.

Services: Counseling and information services are available. There is a reader service for the blind, remedial math, reading, and writing and assistance for students in obtaining needed documentations, assistance with registration, and appropriate individual accommodations and assistance as needed.

Campus Safety and Security: Measures include 24-hour foot and vehicle patrol, security escort services, informal discussions, and pamphlets/posters/films. There are emergency telephones and lighted pathways/sidewalks.

Programs of Study: NCCU confers B.A., B.S., B.B.A., B.M., B.S.N., and B.S.W. degrees. Master's degrees are also awarded. Bachelor's degrees are awarded in BIOLOGICAL SCIENCE (biology/biological science and nutrition), BUSINESS (accounting and business administration and management), COMMUNICATIONS AND THE ARTS (art, dramatic arts, English, French, jazz, music, and Spanish), COMPUTER AND PHYSICAL SCIENCE (chemistry, computer science, mathematics, and physics), EDUCATION (elementary, health, middle school, and physical), ENGINEERING AND ENVIRONMENTAL DESIGN (environmental science), HEALTH PROFESSIONS (nursing), SOCIAL SCIENCE (child care/child and family studies, child psychology/development, criminal justice, geography, history, human services, political science/government, psychology, social work, and sociology). Criminal justice and business are the strongest academically. Business, biology, and political science are the largest.

Required: To graduate, students must complete 124 semester hours, including 30 in the major, with a minimum GPA of 2.0. Core requirements include courses in communications, math and natural science, social science, humanities, and health and phys ed.

Special: NCCU offers internships, study abroad, a Washington semester, work-study programs, dual majors, and nondegree study. There are 10 national honor societies, a freshman honors program, and 10 departmental honors programs.

Faculty/Classroom: 53% of faculty are male; 47%, female. All teach undergraduates.

Admissions: 87% of recent applicants were accepted. 17% of recent freshmen were in the top fifth of their class; 49% were in the top two fifths.

Requirements: The SAT or ACT is required. In addition, applicants must be graduates of an accredited secondary school or have a GED certificate. They must have completed 11 academic credits based on 4 years of English, 3 each of math and science, and 2 each of a foreign language and social studies. Music applicants must audition. A GPA of 2.0 is required. AP and CLEP credits are accepted. Important factors in the admissions decision are advanced placement or honor courses, leadership record, and evidence of special talent.

Procedure: Entrance exams should be taken in the spring of the junior year. There is a rolling admissions plan. Check with the school for current application deadlines and fee. Notification is sent on a rolling basis. Applications are accepted on-line.

Transfer: 373 transfer students enrolled in a recent year. Applicants must have a minimum GPA of 2.0 in all college-level courses. 30 of 124 credits required for the bachelor's degree must be completed at NCCU.

Visiting: There are regularly scheduled orientations for prospective students. There are guides for informal visits and visitors may sit in on classes and stay overnight. To schedule a visit, contact LuAnn Harris at (919) 530-7349.

Financial Aid: The FAFSA is required. Check with the school for current deadlines.

International Students: They must take the TOEFL and also take the SAT or ACT unless these tests are not administered in their country.

Computers: All students may access the system 9 A.M. to 5 P.M. Monday through Friday. The computing center also has dial-in service. There are no time limits and no fees. It is strongly recommended that all students have a personal computer.

Graduates: In a recent year, 604 bachelor's degrees were awarded. The most popular majors were business administration (21%), education (11%), and criminal justice (9%). 297 companies recruited on campus in a recent year.

Admissions Contact: Ms. Jocelyn L. Foy, Director of Admissions. A video is available.

NORTH CAROLINA SCHOOL OF THE ARTS
C-2

Winston-Salem, NC 27127-2188
(336) 770-3290
Fax: (336) 770-3370

Full-time: 768 men and women	**Faculty:** 123
Part-time: 11 men and women	**Ph.D.s:** 45%
Graduate: 101 men and women	**Student/Faculty:** 6 to 1
Year: trimesters	**Tuition:** $4305 ($15,585)
Application Deadline: March 1	**Room & Board:** $3096
Freshman Class: n/av	
SAT or ACT: required	SPECIAL

North Carolina School of the Arts, founded in 1963 and part of the University of North Carolina system, is a public conservatory offering professional training in the performing arts. There are 5 undergraduate and 2 graduate schools. The library contains 114,050 volumes, 25,053 microform items, and 73,025 audio/video tapes/CDs/DVDs, and subscribes to 490 periodicals including electronic. Computerized library services include the card catalog, interlibrary loans, and database searching. Special learning facilities include a learning resource center, art gallery, and numerous performance theaters, screening rooms, and CAD studios. The 67-acre campus is in an urban area in Winston-Salem. Including any residence halls, there are 65 buildings.

Student Life: 50% of undergraduates are from out of state, mostly the Middle Atlantic. Students are from 44 states, 28 foreign countries, and Canada. 80% are from public schools. 88% are white. The average age of freshmen is 19; all undergraduates, 25. 25% do not continue beyond their first year.

Housing: 300 students can be accommodated in college housing, which includes coed dorms and on-campus apartments. On-campus housing is available on a first-come, first-served basis. Priority is given to out-of-town students. 58% of students live on campus; of those, 90% remain on campus on weekends. Alcohol is not permitted. All students may keep cars.

Activities: There are no fraternities or sororities. There are many groups and organizations on campus, including art, band, choir, chorale, chorus, dance, drama, ethnic, film, gay, international, jazz band, musical theater, newspaper, opera, orchestra, radio and TV, student government, and symphony.

Sports: There is no sports program at NCSA. Facilities include a gym, fitness and weight rooms, a swimming pool, a soccer and touch football field, a golf course, and courts for tennis, basketball, and volleyball.

Disabled Students: 85% of the campus is accessible. Wheelchair ramps, elevators, special parking, specially equipped rest rooms, and lowered drinking fountains are available.

Services: Counseling and information services are available, as is tutoring in every subject. There is remedial math, reading, and writing. Private tutoring is also offered on a fee basis.

Campus Safety and Security: Measures include 24-hour foot and vehicle patrol, emergency telephones, and lighted pathways/sidewalks.

Programs of Study: NCSA confers B.F.A. and B.M. degrees. Master's degrees are also awarded. Bachelor's degrees are awarded in COMMUNICATIONS AND THE ARTS (ballet, dance, dramatic arts, film arts, music, performing arts, and theater design).

Required: To earn a bachelor's degree, students must demonstrate satisfactory skills in reading, writing, oral communication, and math, take courses in foundations of Western thought, complete studies in fine arts and humanities, social and behavioral sciences, and math and natural science, and meet all requirements in their arts major.

Special: NCSA offers work-study programs, a general studies major, independent study, and design and production apprenticeships. An accelerated degree program is available to high school students in dance, drama, music, and visual arts.

Faculty/Classroom: 70% of faculty are male; 30%, female. All teach undergraduates. No introductory courses are taught by graduate students. The average class size in a regular course is 10.

Admissions: 26% of a recent freshmen class were in the top fifth of their class; 60% were in the top two fifths.

Requirements: The SAT or ACT is required. The ACT Optional Writing test is also required. In addition, applicants must be graduates of an accredited secondary school or have a GED certificate. They should have completed 4 units in English, 3 in math, 3 in science with 1 in a lab course, and 2 in social studies with 1 in U.S. history. Also recommended are 2 units in a foreign language and 1 unit each in foreign language and math in the senior year. An audition or interview demonstrating evidence of special talent is the primary admissions criterion. Applicants to the School of Design and Production must submit a portfolio. Filmmaking applicants must submit a creative writing sample. AP and CLEP credits are accepted. Important factors in the admissions decision are recommendations by school officials, evidence of special talent, and recommendations by alumni.

Procedure: Freshmen are admitted fall and winter. There is a rolling admissions plan. Applications should be filed by March 1 for fall entry. The fall 2005 application fee was $50. Notification is sent on a rolling basis. Applications are accepted on-line.

Transfer: Evidence of special talent and good academic standing are required. Placement is based on ability and experience, prior courses, and interviews and auditions.

Visiting: There are regularly scheduled orientations for prospective students, including tours on audition days and question-and-answer sessions with administration and faculty. Visitors may sit in on classes. To schedule a visit, contact the Admissions Office.

Financial Aid: In a recent year, 64% of all full-time freshmen received some form of financial aid. 58% of full-time freshmen received need-based aid. The FAFSA is required. The deadline for filing freshman financial aid applications for fall entry is March 1.

International Students: There are 29 international students enrolled. The school actively recruits these students. They must take the Comprehensive English Language Test.

Computers: All students may access the system. There are no time limits and no fees. It is recommended that students in film have personal computers. An Apple computer is recommended.

Admissions Contact: Sheeler Lawson, Director of Admissions.
E-mail: *admissions@ncarts.edu* Web: *www.ncarts.edu*

NORTH CAROLINA STATE UNIVERSITY D-2

Raleigh, NC 27695-7103	(919) 515-2434; Fax: (919) 515-5039
Full-time: 10,998 men, 8228 women	**Faculty:** 1671; I, -$
Part-time: 2065 men, 1476 women	**Ph.D.s:** 91%
Graduate: 3961 men, 3349 women	**Student/Faculty:** 12 to 1
Year: semesters, summer session	**Tuition:** $4784 ($16,982)
Application Deadline: February 1	**Room & Board:** $7040
Freshman Class: 13,610 applied, 9039 accepted, 4253 enrolled	
SAT Verbal/Math: 580/615*	**ACT:** 25 **HIGHLY COMPETITIVE**

North Carolina State University, founded in 1887, is a member of the University of North Carolina System. Its degree programs emphasize the arts and sciences, agriculture, business, education, engineering, and pre-professional training. There are 10 undergraduate and 10 graduate schools. In addition to regional accreditation, NC State has baccalaureate program accreditation with ABET, CSAB, CSWE, NAAB, NCATE, NRPA, and SAF. The 5 libraries contain 3,244,543 volumes, 5,355,100 microform items, and 142,831 audio/video tapes/CDs/DVDs, and subscribe to 54,799 periodicals including electronic. Computerized library services include the card catalog, interlibrary loans, database searching, and Internet access. Special learning facilities include a learning resource center, art gallery, radio station, TV station, nuclear reactor, phytotron, electron microscope facilities, Materials Research Center, Integrated Manufacturing Systems Engineering Institute, Japan Center, and Precision Engineering Center. The 2110-acre campus is in an urban area in Raleigh. Including any residence halls, there are 150 buildings.

Student Life: 87% of undergraduates are from North Carolina. Students are from 50 states, 110 foreign countries, and Canada. 91% are from public schools. 77% are white; 10% African American. 60% are Protestant; 18% claim no religious affiliation; 14% Catholic. The average age of freshmen is 18; all undergraduates, 21. 10% do not continue beyond their first year; 71% remain to graduate.

Housing: 7300 students can be accommodated in college housing, which includes single-sex and coed dorms, on-campus apartments, married-student housing, fraternity houses, and sorority houses. In addition, there are honors houses, special-interest houses, and international, arts and creative living, computer theme, and first-year-experience halls. On-campus housing is guaranteed for all 4 years. 66% of students commute. Alcohol is not permitted. Upperclassmen may keep cars.

Activities: 8% of men belong to 27 national fraternities; 10% of women belong to 10 national sororities. There are 400 groups on campus, including art, bagpipe band, band, cheerleading, chess, choir, chorale, chorus, computers, dance, drama, drill team, drum and bugle corps, ethnic, film, gay, honors, international, jazz band, literary magazine, marching band, musical theater, newspaper, orchestra, pep band, photography, political, professional, radio and TV, religious, social, social service, student government, symphony, and yearbook. Popular campus events include Pan African Festival, Wolfstock, and Greek Week.

Sports: There are 20 intercollegiate sports for men and 16 for women, and 28 intramural sports for men and 26 for women. Facilities include a 55,000-seat football stadium, a 20,000-seat sports arena, a 5000-seat soccer stadium, a baseball stadium, a 12,500-seat gym, a tennis complex, areas for track, 2 indoor pools, and an indoor rock=climbing wall.

Disabled Students: 78% of the campus is accessible. Wheelchair ramps, elevators, special parking, specially equipped rest rooms, special class scheduling, lowered drinking fountains, lowered telephones, and van transportation are available.

Services: Counseling and information services are available, as is tutoring in most subjects. There is a reader service for the blind and remedial math and writing.

Campus Safety and Security: Measures include 24-hour foot and vehicle patrol, self-defense education, security escort services, and shuttle buses. There are informal discussions, pamphlets/posters/films, emergency telephones, lighted pathways/sidewalks, and bicycle patrol.

Programs of Study: NC State confers B.A., B.S., B.Arch., B.E.D.A., B.L.A., and B.S.W. degrees. Associate, master's, and doctoral degrees are also awarded. Bachelor's degrees are awarded in AGRICULTURE (agricultural business management, agricultural economics, agriculture, agronomy, animal science, conservation and regulation, fishing and fisheries, forestry and related sciences, horticulture, natural resource management, poultry science, soil science, and wood science), BIOLOGICAL SCIENCE (biochemistry, biology/biological science, botany, microbiology, and zoology), BUSINESS (accounting, business administration and management, business economics, and recreation and leisure services), COMMUNICATIONS AND THE ARTS (communications, design, English, French, graphic design, industrial design, and Spanish), COMPUTER AND PHYSICAL SCIENCE (atmospheric sciences and meteorology, chemistry, computer science, earth science, geology, mathematics, physics, and statistics), EDUCATION (agricultural, education, foreign languages, industrial arts, marketing and distribution, mathematics, middle school, science, secondary, social studies, technical, and vocational), ENGINEERING AND ENVIRONMENTAL DESIGN (aeronautical engineering, agricultural engineering, architecture, chemical engineering, civil engineering, computer engineering, construction management, electrical/electronics engineering, engineering, environmental design, environmental engineering, environmental science, furniture design, industrial engineering, landscape architecture/design, materials science, mechanical engineering, nuclear engineering, paper and pulp science, and textile engineering), HEALTH PROFESSIONS (medical laboratory technology, predentistry, premedicine, preveterinary science, and speech pathology/audiology), SOCIAL SCIENCE (clothing and textiles management/production/services, criminal justice, economics, food science, history, interdisciplinary studies, parks and recreation management, philosophy, political science/government, prelaw, psychology, religion, social science, social work, sociology, and textiles and clothing). Electrical engineering, chemical engineering, and architecture are the strongest academically. Business management, mechanical engineering, and electrical engineering are the largest.

Required: To graduate, students must complete 120 to 142 semester hours, including 60 to 70 in the major, with a minimum GPA of 2.0. Distribution requirements include 12 to 18 hours in humanities and social sciences, 6 to 8 each in math and science, 6 in English composition, and 4 in phys ed.

Special: NC State offers cross-registration within the Cooperating Raleigh Colleges network, study abroad in more than 90 countries, internships, work-study programs, an accelerated degree plan, dual majors within any program, a general studies degree in education, a 3-2 engineering degree with the University of North Carolina at Asheville, student-designed multidisciplinary studies majors, credit by exam, nondegree study, and pass/fail options. There are 15 national honor societies, including Phi Beta Kappa, a freshman honors program, and 44 departmental honors programs.

Faculty/Classroom: 71% of faculty are male; 29%, female. All both teach and do research. Graduate students teach 8% of introductory courses. The average class size in an introductory lecture is 35; in a laboratory, 20; and in a regular course, 30.

Admissions: 66% of the 2005-2006 applicants were accepted. The SAT scores for the 2005-2006 freshman class were: Verbal--12% below 500, 50% between 500 and 599, 33% between 600 and 700, and 5% above 700; Math--5% below 500, 35% between 500 and 599, 48% between 600 and 700, and 12% above 700. The ACT scores were 2% below 18, 37% between 18 and 23, 47% between 24 and 29, and 14% between 30 and 36. 78% of the current freshmen were in the top fifth of their class; 98% were in the top two fifths. 87 freshmen graduated first in their class.

Requirements: The SAT or ACT is required. The ACT Optional Writing test is also required. In addition, the SAT Subject Test in math is recommended. Applicants must be graduates of an accredited secondary school or have a GED certificate. They must have completed 20 academic credits, including 4 units of English, 3 each of science and math (4 of math is advised), 2 each of social studies and foreign language, and 1 of history. An essay is recommended for all applicants. A portfolio and interview are required for the School of Design. AP and CLEP credits are accepted. Important factors in the admissions decision are advanced placement or honor courses, leadership record, and evidence of special talent.

Procedure: Freshmen are admitted to all sessions. Entrance exams should be taken in the spring of the junior year and the fall of the senior year. There is a deferred admissions plan and a rolling admissions plan. Early decision applications should be filed by November 1; regular applications, by February 1 for fall entry, November 1 for spring entry, and February 1 for summer entry, along with a $60 fee. Notification of early decision is sent January 31; regular decision, April 1. 758 applicants were on the 2005 waiting list; 130 were admitted. Applications are accepted on-line.

Transfer: 1027 transfer students enrolled in 2005-2006. Applicants must have completed 30 semester hours of college-level work with a minimum GPA of 2.0. Priority is given to students who have completed 60 hours of relevant course work. An associate degree and an interview are recommended. Applicants must have math, English, and foreign language proficiency. 30 of 120 credits required for the bachelor's degree must be completed at NC State.

Visiting: There are regularly scheduled orientations for prospective students, consisting of admissions information sessions. There are guides for informal visits and visitors may sit in on classes. To schedule a visit, contact the Admissions Office.

Financial Aid: In 2005-2006, 98% of all full-time freshmen and 97% of continuing full-time students received some form of financial aid. 96% of full-time freshmen and 94% of continuing full-time students received need-based aid. Need-based scholarships or need-based grants averaged $6216; need-based self-help aid (loans and jobs) averaged $2714; and non-need-based athletic scholarships averaged $13,706. The average financial indebtedness of the 2005 graduate was $14,505. The FAFSA and the college's own financial statement are required. The deadline for filing freshman financial aid applications for fall entry is March 1.

International Students: There are 142 international students enrolled. The school actively recruits these students. A satisfactory score on the TOEFL is required. These students must also take the SAT or ACT if it is available to students in their country.

Computers: Wireless access is available. All students may access the system. Students may access the system Time limits vary by class. The fee is $100.

Graduates: The most popular majors among 2005 graduates were engineering (23%), business/marketing (14%), and biological/life sciences (10%). In an average class, 36% graduate in 4 years, 30% graduate in 5 years, and 5% graduate in 6 years.

Admissions Contact: Thomas Griffin, Director of Admissions.
E-mail: *undergrad_admissions@ncsu.edu*
Web: *http:admissions.ncsu.edu*

NORTH CAROLINA WESLEYAN COLLEGE   E-2

Rocky Mount, NC 27804   (252) 985-5200
                        (800) 488-NCWC; Fax: (252) 985-5295

Full-time: 612 men, 514 women	**Faculty:** IIB, --$
Part-time: 289 men, 337 women	**Ph.D.s:** 45%
Graduate: none	**Student/Faculty:** n/av
Year: semesters, summer session	**Tuition:** $16,000
Application Deadline: open	**Room & Board:** $6670
Freshman Class: 1169 applied, 951 accepted, 288 enrolled	
SAT or ACT: required	**COMPETITIVE**

North Carolina Wesleyan College, founded in 1956, is a private liberal arts institution affiliated with the United Methodist Church. In addition to regional accreditation, NCWC has baccalaureate program accreditation with NCATE. The library contains 65,721 volumes, 2830 microform items, and 4200 audio/video tapes/CDs/DVDs, and subscribes to 4645 periodicals including electronic. Computerized library services include the card catalog, interlibrary loans, and database searching. Special learning facilities include a learning resource center, art gallery, and performing arts center. The 200-acre campus is in a suburban area 57 miles east of Raleigh. Including any residence halls, there are 18 buildings.

Student Life: 85% of undergraduates are from North Carolina. Others are from 24 states and 9 foreign countries. 70% are from public schools. 45% are African American; 43% white. 70% are Protestant; 16% Catholic; 14% claim no religious affiliation. The average age of freshmen is 19; all undergraduates, 26. 36% do not continue beyond their first year; 26% remain to graduate.

Housing: 504 students can be accommodated in college housing, which includes single-sex and coed dormitories and off-campus apartments. In addition, there are single-occupancy residence halls with kitchens on each floor, and smoke/substance-free housing. On-campus housing is guaranteed for all 4 years. 68% of students commute. All students may keep cars.

Activities: 1% of men belong to 3 national fraternities; 1% of women belong to 3 national sororities. There are 23 groups on campus, including cheerleading, chess, choir, chorus, computers, drama, ethnic, gay, honors, international, literary magazine, musical theater, newspaper, political, professional, religious, social, social service, student government, and yearbook. Popular campus events include Spring Fling, Parents Weekend, and Alumni Homecoming.

Sports: There are 5 intercollegiate sports for men and 5 for women, and 13 intramural sports for men and 13 for women. Facilities include a 1200-seat gym with areas for basketball, volleyball, and indoor soccer matches; tennis courts; a skeet range; and fields for intramurals and for varsity baseball, softball, and soccer.

Disabled Students: 90% of the campus is accessible. Wheelchair ramps, elevators, special parking, specially equipped rest rooms, special class scheduling, lowered drinking fountains, lowered telephones, and special housing are available.

Services: Counseling and information services are available, as is tutoring in most subjects. There is remedial math, reading, and writing.

Campus Safety and Security: Measures include 24-hour foot and vehicle patrol, security escort services, informal discussions, and pamphlets/posters/films. There are emergency telephones and lighted pathways/sidewalks.

Programs of Study: NCWC confers B.A. and B.S. degrees. Bachelor's degrees are awarded in BIOLOGICAL SCIENCE (biology/biological science), BUSINESS (accounting, business administration and management, and hotel/motel and restaurant management), COMMUNICATIONS AND THE ARTS (dramatic arts and English), COMPUTER AND PHYSICAL SCIENCE (chemistry, information sciences and systems, and mathematics), EDUCATION (elementary and middle school), ENGINEERING AND ENVIRONMENTAL DESIGN (environmental science), HEALTH PROFESSIONS (exercise science and premedicine), SOCIAL SCIENCE (criminal justice, history, political science/government, psychology, religion, and sociology). Business administration, justice studies, and computer information systems are the largest.

Required: To graduate, students must complete 124 semester hours, including 30 to 54 in the major, with a minimum GPA of 2.0. Distribution requirements consist of 6 semester hours of English composition or demonstrated proficiency; 4 each of biological and physical science; 3 each of ethics, non-Western culture, math, history, social science, psychology or sociology, religion, literature, and fine arts; 2 of phys ed; and 2 of introduction to college life. Some majors require a thesis.

Special: NCWC offers cooperative programs in all majors, internships, work-study programs through the college offices, credit for military experience, nondegree study, and pass/fail options. The B.A.-B.S. degree may be earned in all majors. There are 2 national honor societies and a freshman honors program.

Faculty/Classroom: 62% of faculty are male; 38%, female. All teach undergraduates. The average class size in an introductory lecture is 23; in a laboratory, 15; and in a regular course, 18.

Admissions: 81% of the 2005-2006 applicants were accepted.

Requirements: The SAT or ACT is required. Applicants should be graduates of an accredited secondary school or have a GED. They should have completed at least 13 academic courses, including 4 in English, 3 in math, and 2 each in foreign language, social studies, and lab sciences. An essay and an interview are advised. AP and CLEP credits are accepted. Important factors in the admissions decision are advanced placement or honor courses, extracurricular activities record, and leadership record.

Procedure: Freshmen are admitted fall and spring. Entrance exams should be taken in spring of the junior year or fall or winter of the senior year. There are early admissions and deferred admissions plans. There is a rolling admissions plan. Application deadlines are open. Application fee is $25. Applications are accepted on-line.

Transfer: 71 transfer students enrolled in 2004-2005. Applicants must have a minimum GPA of 2.0 in their college courses. They must submit transcripts of all high school and college work, along with proof of high school graduation. 31 of 124 credits required for the bachelor's degree must be completed at NCWC.

Visiting: There are regularly scheduled orientations for prospective students, including an individual campus tour, an interview, a financial aid session, and meetings with faculty and coaches. There are guides for informal visits and visitors may sit in on classes and stay overnight. To schedule a visit, contact the Admissions Office.

Financial Aid: In 2005-2006, 84% of all full-time students received some form of financial aid. At least 84% of all full-time students received need-based aid. The average freshman award was $19,730. Need-based scholarships or need-based grants averaged $14,650; need-based self-help aid (loans and jobs) averaged $5080; and other institutional non-need-based awards and non-need-based scholarships averaged $7252. The average financial indebtedness of the 2005 graduate was $17,125. NCWC is a member of CSS. The FAFSA is required. The priority date for freshman financial aid applications for fall entry is March 1.

International Students: They must score satisfactorilty on the written TOEFL and also take the SAT.

Computers: All students may access the system on a sign-up basis in the computer lab or as available at other locations. There are no time limits and no fees.

Graduates: From July 1, 2004 to June 30, 2005, 391 bachelor's degrees were awarded. The most popular majors were business/marketing (48%), computer and information sciences (24%), and law/legal studies (10%). In an average class, 15% graduate in 4 years or less, 23% graduate in 5 years or less, and 26% graduate in 6 years or less.

Admissions Contact: Cecelia Summers, Director of Admissions.
E-mail: *adm@ncwc.edu* Web: *www.ncwc.edu*

PFEIFFER UNIVERSITY   C-2

Misenheimer, NC 28109   (704) 463-1360, ext. 2079
                                           (800) 338-2060; Fax: (704) 463-1363

Full-time: 449 men, 596 women	Faculty: 54; IIA, --$
Part-time: 42 men, 109 women	Ph.D.s: 71%
Graduate: 289 men, 674 women	Student/Faculty: 19 to 1
Year: semesters, summer session	Tuition: $15,590
Application Deadline: August 25	Room & Board: $6310
Freshman Class: 505 applied, 373 accepted, 198 enrolled	
SAT Verbal/Math: 490/510*	ACT: 21	COMPETITIVE

Pfeiffer University, founded in 1885, is a private institution of liberal arts and sciences affiliated with the United Methodist Church. There are 2 undergraduate schools and 1 graduate school. In addition to regional accreditation, Pfeiffer has baccalaureate program accreditation with NASM and NCATE. The library contains 121,594 volumes, 33,143 microform items, and 3084 audio/video tapes/CDs/DVDs, and subscribes to 396 periodicals including electronic. Computerized library services include the card catalog, interlibrary loans, database searching, and Internet access. Special learning facilities include a learning resource center and art gallery. The 350-acre campus is in a rural area 35 miles east of Charlotte. Including any residence halls, there are 28 buildings.

Student Life: 82% of undergraduates are from North Carolina. Others are from 33 states, 13 foreign countries, and Canada. 62% are white; 29% African American. 69% are Protestant; 13% Muslim, Hindu; 10% claim no religious affiliation; 8% Catholic. The average age of freshmen is 18; all undergraduates, 22. 30% do not continue beyond their first year; 48% remain to graduate.

Housing: 717 students can be accommodated in college housing, which includes single-sex and coed dorms and married-student housing.

In addition, there are honors houses and substance-free and academic emphasis living. On-campus housing is guaranteed for all 4 years. 55% of students live on campus; of those, 60% remain on campus on weekends. All students may keep cars.

Activities: There are no fraternities or sororities. There are 37 groups on campus, including band, cheerleading, chess, choir, chorale, chorus, drama, ethnic, honors, international, jazz band, literary magazine, newspaper, pep band, photography, political, professional, religious, social, social service, student government, and yearbook. Popular campus events include Winterfest, Aprilfest, and coffee houses.

Sports: There are 7 intercollegiate sports for men and 9 for women, and 21 intramural sports for men and 21 for women. Facilities include an 1800-seat main gym, an indoor pool, exercise rooms, training facilities, and weight rooms. The campus also has 6 tennis courts, fields for baseball, softball, lacrosse, and soccer, areas for golf practice and volleyball, and an indoor batting cage.

Disabled Students: 50% of the campus is accessible. Wheelchair ramps, elevators, special parking, specially equipped rest rooms, and special class scheduling are available.

Services: Counseling and information services are available, as is tutoring in most subjects. There is remedial math, reading, and writing.

Campus Safety and Security: Measures include 24-hour foot and vehicle patrol, self-defense education, security escort services, and informal discussions. There are pamphlets/posters/films and lighted pathways/sidewalks.

Programs of Study: Pfeiffer confers A.B. and B.S. degrees. Master's degrees are also awarded. Bachelor's degrees are awarded in BIOLOGICAL SCIENCE (biology/biological science), BUSINESS (accounting, business administration and management, international business management, and sports management), COMMUNICATIONS AND THE ARTS (arts administration/management, communications, English literature, languages, and music), COMPUTER AND PHYSICAL SCIENCE (chemistry, information sciences and systems, and mathematics), EDUCATION (athletic training, Christian, elementary, music, physical, science, secondary, and special), ENGINEERING AND ENVIRONMENTAL DESIGN (environmental science and preengineering), HEALTH PROFESSIONS (exercise science and premedicine), SOCIAL SCIENCE (American studies, criminal justice, economics, history, human services, missions, political science/government, prelaw, psychology, religion, religious education, religious music, social studies, and sociology). Chemistry, music, and sports management are the strongest academically. Business administration, criminal justice, and elementary education are the largest.

Required: All students must complete 120 to 124 semester hours, including 60 credits in writing, language and literature, history/political science, music/art/theater, natural science, math, economics/psychology/sociology, religion, and phys ed. Students must maintain an overall minimum GPA of 2.0 and complete 42 to 72 hours in the major. A freshman seminar and senior project in the major are required, as well as participation in the cultural program and basic compentency in computer technology.

Special: A 3-2 program in engineering with Auburn University, work-study programs, many internships in business, education, public service, and phys ed, study abroad in 5 countries, and interdisciplinary majors are offered. There are 5 national honor societies, a freshman honors program, and 10 departmental honors programs.

Faculty/Classroom: 65% of faculty are male; 35%, female. 87% teach undergraduates, 25% do research, and 25% do both. No introductory courses are taught by graduate students. The average class size in an introductory lecture is 24; in a laboratory, 18; and in a regular course, 12.

Admissions: 74% of the 2005-2006 applicants were accepted. The SAT scores for the 2005-2006 freshman class were: Verbal--54% below 500, 37% between 500 and 599, and 8% between 600 and 700; Math--42% below 500, 45% between 500 and 599, 12% between 600 and 700, and 1% above 700. The ACT scores were 72% below 21, 14% between 21 and 23, 9% between 24 and 26, and 5% between 27 and 28. 31% of the current freshmen were in the top fifth of their class; 63% were in the top two fifths.

Requirements: The SAT is required and the ACT is recommended. In addition, all applicants are required to have completed 4 years of English and 3 years of math, including algebra I. The GED is accepted. Pfeiffer requires applicants to be in the upper 50% of their class. A GPA of 2.0 is required. AP and CLEP credits are accepted. Important factors in the admissions decision are advanced placement or honor courses, leadership record, and extracurricular activities record.

Procedure: Freshmen are admitted to all sessions. Entrance exams should be taken by January of the senior year. There are early admissions, deferred admissions, and rolling admissions plans. Applications should be filed by August 25 for fall entry and January 20 for spring entry, along with a $25 fee. Notification is sent on a rolling basis. Applications are accepted on-line.

Transfer: 103 transfer students enrolled in 2004-2005. Applicants should be eligible for readmission to the last college attended and have a minimum GPA of 2.0. 45 of 120 credits required for the bachelor's degree must be completed at Pfeiffer.

Visiting: There are regularly scheduled orientations for prospective students, including meetings with faculty/staff, a question-and-answer session, a tour, and a lunch. There are guides for informal visits and visitors may sit in on classes and stay overnight. To schedule a visit, contact the Admissions Office at *admissions@pfeiffer.edu.*

Financial Aid: In 2005-2006, 85% of all full-time freshmen and 90% of continuing full-time students received some form of financial aid. 83% of full-time freshmen and 90% of continuing full-time students received need-based aid. The average freshman award was $14,500. Need-based scholarships or need-based grants averaged $2880 ($8050 maximum); need-based self-help aid (loans and jobs) averaged $2144 ($3625 maximum); and non-need-based athletic scholarships averaged $3880 ($18,100 maximum). 39% of undergraduates work part time. Average annual earnings from campus work are $1080. The average financial indebtedness of the 2005 graduate was $17,125. The FAFSA is required. The priority date for freshman financial aid applications for fall entry is April 15. The deadline for filing freshman financial aid applications for fall entry is open.

International Students: There are 46 international students enrolled. A satisfactory score is required on the written TOEFL. Applicants must also take the SAT or ACT, or show proven success at a U.S. school.

Computers: All students may access the system. There are no time limits and no fees.

Graduates: From July 1, 2004 to June 30, 2005, 276 bachelor's degrees were awarded. The most popular majors were business administration (43%), criminal justice (16%), and education (11%). In an average class, 40% graduate in 4 years or less, 44% graduate in 5 years or less, and 54% graduate in 6 years or less. 62 companies recruited on campus in 2004-2005. Of the 2004 graduating class, 23% were enrolled in graduate school within 6 months of graduation.

Admissions Contact: Steve Cumming, Director of Admissions. E-mail: *admissions@pfeiffer.edu* Web: *www.pfeiffer.edu*

QUEENS COLLEGE
(See Queens University of Charlotte)

QUEENS UNIVERSITY OF CHARLOTTE   C-3
(Formerly Queens College)

Charlotte, NC 28274

704 337-2212
800 849-0202; Fax: 7040337-2403

Full-time: 273 men, 743 women	**Faculty:** 68; IIA, --$
Part-time: 96 men, 511 women	**Ph.Ds:** 79%
Graduate: 160 men, 330 women	**Student/Faculty:** 15 to 1
Year: semesters, summer session	**Tuition:** $18,028
Application Deadline: open	**Room & Board:** $6500
Freshman Class: 919 applied, 678 accepted, 242 enrolled	
SAT or ACT: required	**COMPETITIVE**

Queens University of Charlotte, founded in 1857, is a private liberal arts institution affiliated with the Presbyterian Church (U.S.A.). Undergraduate programs are offered through the College of Arts and Sciences and the Pauline Lewis Hayworth College, a division offering courses in the evening and on Saturday. There are 2 undergraduate schools and 1 graduate school. In addition to regional accreditation, Queens has baccalaureate program accreditation with ACBSP, NASM, NCATE, and NLN. Computerized library services include the card catalog, interlibrary loans, and database searching. Special learning facilities include a learning resource center, art gallery, rare books and archival collection, photographic lab, ceramics studio, and recital hall. The 25-acre campus is in a suburban area 2 miles south of uptown Charlotte. Including any residence halls, there are 29 buildings.

Student Life: 61% of undergraduates are from North Carolina. 74% are from public schools. 73% are white; 17% African American. The average age of freshmen is 18; all undergraduates, 20. 29% do not continue beyond their first year; 64% remain to graduate.

Housing: 600 students can be accommodated in college housing, which includes single-sex and coed dorms. On-campus housing is guaranteed for the freshman year only and is available on a lottery system for upperclassmen. 72% of students live on campus; of those, 60% remain on campus on weekends. All students may keep cars.

Activities: 17% of men belong to 2 national fraternities; 24% of women belong to 5 national sororities. There are 42 groups on campus, including art, cheerleading, choir, chorale, chorus, dance, drama, ethnic, gay, honors, international, literary magazine, musical theater, newspaper, pep band, political, professional, religious, social, social service, student government, and yearbook. Popular campus events include Casino Party, Mardi Gras Festival, and International Symposium.

Sports: There are 6 intercollegiate sports for men and 8 for women. Facilities include an athletic center with a gym, classrooms, dance studios, weight room, training room, and swimming pool. There are also 6 tennis courts (4 lighted) and a soccer/softball complex. In addition, the college center offers various recreational opportunities, and the residence hall has an 8000=square-foot state-of-the-art fitness center.

Disabled Students: 50% of the campus is accessible. Wheelchair ramps, special parking, specially equipped rest rooms, special class scheduling, and elevators in newer buildings are available.

Services: There is remedial math, reading, and writing and tutoring in English.

Campus Safety and Security: Measures include 24-hour foot and vehicle patrol, self-defense education, security escort services, and informal discussions. There are pamphlets/posters/films, emergency telephones, and lighted pathways/sidewalks.

Programs of Study: Queens confers B.A., B.S., B.Mus., and B.S.N. degrees. Associate and master's degrees are also awarded. Bachelor's degrees are awarded in BIOLOGICAL SCIENCE (biochemistry and biology/biological science), BUSINESS (accounting and business administration and management), COMMUNICATIONS AND THE ARTS (communications, dramatic arts, English, fine arts, French, music, and Spanish), COMPUTER AND PHYSICAL SCIENCE (mathematics), EDUCATION (elementary), HEALTH PROFESSIONS (music therapy and nursing), SOCIAL SCIENCE (American studies, history, international studies, philosophy, political science/government, psychology, and religion). Liberal arts and sciences are the strongest academically. Business, nursing, and communications are the largest.

Required: To graduate, students must complete a total of 122 credit hours with a minimum GPA of 2.0. For the B.A., between 30 and 40 hours are required in the student's major. For the B.S., 32 are required. All students must take a sequence of 5 courses in the Core Program in the Liberal Arts. In addition, 2 courses in English composition, 2 in phys ed, and 1 in lab science are required. If entering freshmen do not pass the placement exams given in math and a foreign language, additional courses will be required. Some majors require a thesis or research project.

Special: Internships in all majors, cross-registration with colleges of the Charlotte Area Educational Consortium, dual majors, nondegree study, and pass/fail options are available. The school offers a Washington semester. A study tour in Europe and Asia (included in the cost of tuition) may be arranged through the school's John Belk International Experience Program. There are 5 national honor societies, and a freshman honors program.

Faculty/Classroom: 39% of faculty are male; 61%, female. All teach undergraduates. No introductory courses are taught by graduate students.

Admissions: 74% of the 2005-2006 applicants were accepted. The SAT scores for the 2005-2006 freshman class were: Verbal--39% below 500, 43% between 500 and 599, 15% between 600 and 700, and 3% above 700; Math--36% below 500, 49% between 500 and 599, 14% between 600 and 700, and 1% above 700. The ACT scores were 25% below 21, 39% between 21 and 23, 28% between 24 and 26, 7% between 27 and 28, and 1% above 28. 45% of the current freshmen were in the top fifth of their class; 80% were in the top two fifths. 2 freshmen graduated first in their class.

Requirements: The SAT or ACT is required. The ACT Optional Writing test is also required. In addition, applicants should have a college preparatory background in an accredited secondary school. The GED is accepted. High school courses should include 4 years of English, 3 of math, 2 each of history or social studies and a foreign language, and 2 years of science, including 1 of lab science. An interview is recommended. An audition or portfolio is recommended for art and music students. A GPA of 2.0 is required. AP and CLEP credits are accepted. Important factors in the admissions decision are recommendations by school officials, advanced placement or honor courses, and leadership record.

Procedure: Freshmen are admitted fall, spring, and summer. Entrance exams should be taken in the junior year or as early as possible in the senior year. There is a roling admissions plan. Application deadlines are open. The application fee is $40. Applications are accepted on-line.

Transfer: 45 transfer students enrolled in 2004-2005. Transfer students are accepted in all but the senior class. A GPA of 2.0 is required for all previous college-level work. 45 of 122 credits required for the bachelor's degree must be completed at Queens.

Visiting: There are regularly scheduled orientations for prospective students, includes a sampling of classes, campus tours, a college overview, a question/answer segment, a meet-the-faculty session, and a scholarship/financial aid session. There are guides for informal visits and visitors may sit in on classes and stay overnight. To schedule a visit, contact the Admissions Office at *admissions@queens.edu.*

Financial Aid: In 2005-2006, 60% of all full-time freshmen and 83% of continuing full-time students received some form of financial aid. 59% of full-time freshmen received need-based aid. The average freshman award was $14,886. Average annual earnings from campus work are $1500. The average financial indebtedness of the 2005 graduate was $16,270. Queens is a member of CSS. The FAFSA is required. The deadline for filing freshman financial aid applications for fall entry is March 1.

International Students: There are 30 international students enrolled. The school actively recruits these students. They must score satisfactorily on the TOEFL and also take the SAT or ACT.

Computers: All students may access the system. There are no time limits and no fees.

Graduates: In a recent year, 216 bachelor's degrees were awarded. The most popular majors were business (33%), communications (15%), and nursing (10%). In an average class, 55% graduate in 4 years or less, 62% graduate in 5 years or less, and 64% graduate in 6 years or less. 300 companies recruited on campus in 2004-2005. Of the 2004 graduating class, 23% were enrolled in graduate school within 6 months of graduation.

Admissions Contact: William Lee, Director of Admissions.
E-mail: *admissions@queens.edu* Web: *www.queens.edu/admissions*

SAINT ANDREWS PRESBYTERIAN COLLEGE   D-3
Laurinburg, NC 28352
(910) 277-5555
(800) 763-0198; Fax: (910) 277-5087

Full-time: 278 men, 428 women	**Faculty:** 44; IIB, --$
Part-time: 15 men, 60 women	**Ph.D.s:** 84%
Graduate: none	**Student/Faculty:** 16 to 1
Year: semesters, summer session	**Tuition:** $17,390
Application Deadline: open	**Room & Board:** $6140
Freshman Class: 691 applied, 651 accepted, 191 enrolled	
SAT Verbal/Math: 500/500*	**ACT:** 20 **COMPETITIVE**

St. Andrews Presbyterian College, founded in 1896, is a private liberal arts institution affiliated with the Presbyterian Church (U.S.A.). The library contains 110,105 volumes, 14,204 microform items, and 1676 audio/video tapes/CDs/DVDs, and subscribes to 416 periodicals including electronic. Computerized library services include the card catalog, interlibrary loans, and database searching. Special learning facilities include a learning resource center, art gallery, 20,000-square-foot science lab, artronics lab, and writing lab. The 600-acre campus is in a small town about 100 miles from Charlotte. Including any residence halls, there are 17 buildings.

Student Life: 56% of undergraduates are from out of state, mostly the South. Students are from 43 states, 12 foreign countries, and Canada. 82% are white. 45% are claim no religious affiliation; 41% Protestant; 9% Catholic. The average age of freshmen is 18; all undergraduates, 20. 32% do not continue beyond their first year; 67% remain to graduate.

Housing: 776 students can be accommodated in college housing, which includes single-sex and coed dorms. On-campus housing is guaranteed for all 4 years. 75% of students live on campus; of those, 90% remain on campus on weekends. All students may keep cars.

Activities: There are no fraternities or sororities. There are 32 groups on campus, including art, bagpipe band, cheerleading, chess, chorale, computers, debate, drama, ethnic, film, gay, honors, international, literary magazine, musical theater, newspaper, political, professional, religious, social, social service, and student government. Popular campus events include Writers' Forum, Extravaganza Weekend, and Springfest.

Sports: There are 8 intercollegiate sports for men and 9 for women, and 6 intramural sports for men and 6 for women. Facilities include a basketball and volleyball arena, equestrian facilities, a pool, and soccer, baseball, and softball fields.

Disabled Students: 90% of the campus is accessible. Wheelchair ramps, elevators, special parking, specially equipped rest rooms, lowered drinking fountains, lowered telephones, and personal aides are available.

Services: Counseling and information services are available, as is tutoring in most subjects.

Campus Safety and Security: Measures include 24-hour foot and vehicle patrol, security escort services, informal discussions, and pamphlets/posters/films. There are emergency telephones and lighted pathways/sidewalks.

Programs of Study: St. Andrews confers B.A, B.S., and B.F.A. degrees. Bachelor's degrees are awarded in BIOLOGICAL SCIENCE (biology/biological science and neurosciences), BUSINESS (business administration and management), COMMUNICATIONS AND THE ARTS (communications, creative writing, English, and visual and performing arts), COMPUTER AND PHYSICAL SCIENCE (chemistry and mathematics), EDUCATION (elementary and physical), SOCIAL SCIENCE (Asian/Oriental studies, forensic studies, history, liberal arts/general studies, philosophy, political science/government, psychology, public history/archives, religion, and therapeutic riding). Business and economics, equine studies, and biology are the strongest academically. Business and economics, elementary education, and phys ed are the largest.

Required: To graduate, students must complete a total of 120 hours with a minimum GPA of 2.0. Between 10 and 15 courses are required in the student's major. All students must complete 15 hours in the interdisciplinary St. Andrews general education core program. In addition, students must satisfy breadth requirements in the creative arts, humanities, lab sciences, social and behavioral sciences, phys ed, and international studies.

Special: St. Andrew's offers disciplinary and student-designed majors for contract and thematic majors, a Washington semester, nondegree study, on-campus work-study, and pass/fail options. Students may study abroad in 11 countries. There are 3-2 engineering and computer science

degree programs with North Carolina State University and there are year-long, semester-long, and summer-term internships in all majors. There are 4 national honor societies, a freshman honors program, and 8 departmental honors programs.

Faculty/Classroom: 66% of faculty are male; 34%, female. All teach undergraduates and 50% do research. The average class size in an introductory lecture is 15; in a laboratory, 15; and in a regular course, 15.

Admissions: 94% of the 2005-2006 applicants were accepted. The SAT scores for the 2005-2006 freshman class were: Verbal--47% below 500, 27% between 500 and 599, 23% between 600 and 700, and 3% above 700; Math--42% below 500, 45% between 500 and 599, and 13% between 600 and 700. The ACT scores were 51% below 21, 31% between 21 and 23, 3% between 24 and 26, 11% between 27 and 28, and 4% above 28.

Requirements: The SAT or ACT is required, with a satisfactory score on the SAT or ACT. Graduation from an accredited secondary school or the GED is required for admission. High school courses should include 4 units of English, 3 each of science and math, and 2 each of a foreign language, social studies, and electives. An essay is required. A GPA of 2.5 is required. AP and CLEP credits are accepted. Important factors in the admissions decision are personality/intangible qualities, recommendations by school officials, and evidence of special talent.

Procedure: Freshmen are admitted to all sessions. Entrance exams should be taken as early as possible. There is a deferred admissions plan and a rolling admissions plan. Application deadlines are open. Application fee is $30. Applications are accepted on-line.

Transfer: 56 transfer students enrolled in 2004-2005. Transfer students must have a minimum GPA of 2.0. Up to 65 semester or 97 quarter hours may be transferred from a 2-year college and 90 semester or 135 quarter hours from a 4-year college. 30 of 120 credits required for the bachelor's degree must be completed at St. Andrews.

Visiting: There are regularly scheduled orientations for prospective students, including activities, fairs, information sessions, summer orientation sessions with activities, and preregistration. There are guides for informal visits and visitors may sit in on classes. To schedule a visit, contact the Admissions Office.

Financial Aid: In 2005-2006, 98% of all full-time freshmen and 93% of continuing full-time students received some form of financial aid. 70% of full-time freshmen and 75% of continuing full-time students received need-based aid. The average freshman award was $8140. 61% of undergraduates work part time. Average annual earnings from campus work are $1800. The average financial indebtedness of the 2005 graduate was $12,325. The FAFSA is required.

International Students: There are 34 international students enrolled. The school actively recruits these students. They must score satisfactorily on the written TOEFL.

Computers: Wireless access is available in some areas. There are 80 PCs in classrooms and labs which provide access to the college's network and the Internet. Internet access and e-mail are available from dorm rooms. All students may access the system every day, 24 hours a day. There are no time limits and no fees.

Graduates: From July 1, 2004 to June 30, 2005, 127 bachelor's degrees were awarded. The most popular majors were business administration (25%), education (15%), and English (6%). In an average class, 1% graduate in 3 years or less, 37% graduate in 4 years or less, and 43% graduate in 5 years or less. Of the 2004 graduating class, 25% were enrolled in graduate school within 6 months of graduation and 50% were employed.

Admissions Contact: Glenn Batten, Vice President for Enrollment and Student Services. A video is available. E-mail: *admissions@sapc.edu* Web: *www.sapc.edu*

SAINT AUGUSTINE'S COLLEGE   D-2
Raleigh, NC 27610-2298
(919) 516-4000
(800) 948-1126; Fax: (919) 516-5805

Full-time: 500 men, 700 women	**Faculty:** 87
Part-time: 50 men, 80 women	**Ph.D.s:** 59%
Graduate: none	**Student/Faculty:** 16 to 1
Year: semesters, summer session	**Tuition:** $9000
Application Deadline: see profile	**Room & Board:** $5000
Freshman Class: n/av	
SAT or ACT: required	**LESS COMPETITIVE**

Saint Augustine's College, founded in 1867, is a historically black liberal arts institution affiliated with the Episcopal Church. Figures in the above capsule and in this profile are approximate. The library contains 70,200 volumes and 500 microform items, and subscribes to 300 periodicals including electronic. Computerized library services include database searching. Special learning facilities include a learning resource center, radio station, and TV station. The 110-acre campus is in an urban area 1 mile northeast of downtown Raleigh. Including any residence halls, there are 37 buildings.

Student Life: 51% of undergraduates are from North Carolina. Students are from 34 states, 16 foreign countries, and Canada. 99% are from public schools. 90% are African American. 58% are Protestant; 39% claim no religious affiliation. The average age of freshmen is 18; all undergraduates, 22. 38% do not continue beyond their first year; 27% remain to graduate.

Housing: 1143 students can be accommodated in college housing, which includes single-sex dorms. In addition, there are honors houses. On-campus housing is guaranteed for all 4 years. 62% of students live on campus; of those, 75% remain on campus on weekends. Alcohol is not permitted. All students may keep cars.

Activities: 6% of men belong to 5 national fraternities; 12% of women belong to 4 national sororities. There are 20 groups on campus, including band, cheerleading, chorale, chorus, dance, drama, ethnic, honors, international, newspaper, photography, professional, radio and TV, religious, social service, student government, and yearbook. Popular campus events include opening convocation each semester, CIAA tournament, and career/job fairs.

Sports: There are 5 intercollegiate sports for men and 4 for women, and 4 intramural sports for men and 3 for women. Facilities include a 1700-seat gym, a track, baseball fields, and tennis and basketball courts.

Disabled Students: 64% of the campus is accessible. Wheelchair ramps, elevators, special parking, and specially equipped rest rooms are available.

Services: There is remedial math, reading, and writing. Help with writing and test-taking skills is available.

Campus Safety and Security: Measures include 24-hour foot and vehicle patrol, informal discussions, pamphlets/posters/films, and emergency telephones. There are lighted pathways/sidewalks.

Programs of Study: Saint Augustine's College confers B.A. and B.S. degrees. Bachelor's degrees are awarded in BIOLOGICAL SCIENCE (biology/biological science), BUSINESS (accounting, business administration and management, and international business management), COMMUNICATIONS AND THE ARTS (communications, English, fine arts, French, music, music business management, Spanish, and visual and performing arts), COMPUTER AND PHYSICAL SCIENCE (applied mathematics, chemistry, computer science, information sciences and systems, and mathematics), EDUCATION (business, education of the exceptional child, elementary, English, mathematics, music, physical, science, and social studies), ENGINEERING AND ENVIRONMENTAL DESIGN (industrial administration/management and industrial engineering), HEALTH PROFESSIONS (industrial hygiene, medical laboratory technology, and premedicine), SOCIAL SCIENCE (African American studies, criminal justice, history, physical fitness/movement, political science/government, prelaw, psychology, sociology, and urban studies). Engineering, math, premedicine, and chemistry are the strongest academically. Computer science, business administration and communications are the largest.

Required: Students must complete at least 120 hours with a minimum 2.0 GPA for graduation. All students must complete a 50 to 55 credit core curriculum that includes courses in reading and communication, foreign language, science, math, philosophy, ethics, humanities, world civilization, psychology, and phys ed. Seniors must pass written and oral exams in their major fields. Total credit hours required for a degree in offered majors range from 124 to 154.

Special: Students may cross-register at any of 5 area colleges, study abroad, or pursue a 3-2 engineering program with North Carolina State University. There is an accelerated degree program in organizational management for adult learners. Field experience programs, nondegree study, internships, work-study, cooperative programs, and credit for military service are offered. There is 1 national honor society and a freshman honors program.

Faculty/Classroom: 60% of faculty are male; 40%, female. All teach undergraduates. The average class size in an introductory lecture is 22; in a laboratory, 13; and in a regular course, 14.

Requirements: The SAT or ACT is required, applicants must be graduates of an accredited secondary school with a C+ average in at least 18 academic units, including 4 in English, 3 in math, and 2 each in social studies and science. A GPA of 2.0 is required. AP credits are accepted. Important factors in the admissions decision are geographic diversity, evidence of special talent, and leadership record.

Procedure: Freshmen are admitted to all sessions. There is a deferred admissions plan and a rolling admissions plan. Notification is sent on a rolling basis. Check with the school for current application deadlines and fee.

Transfer: Transfers must submit high school and college transcripts and must be eligible to reenter the last institution attended. 30 of 124 credits required for the bachelor's degree must be completed at Saint Augustine's College.

Visiting: There are guides for informal visits and visitors may sit in on classes. To schedule a visit, contact the Admissions Office at (919) 516-4016.

Financial Aid: Saint Augustine's College is a member of CSS. The FAFSA is required. Check with the school for current deadlines.

International Students: The school actively recruits these students. They must take on the TOEFL and also take the SAT or the ACT.

Computers: All students may access the system. The system may be used during the operating hours of the library and the science and business buildings. There are no time limits and no fees.

Admissions Contact: Tim Chapman, Interim Director of Admissions. E-mail: *admissions@es.st.aug.edu* Web: *www.st-aug.edu*

SALEM COLLEGE
Winston-Salem, NC 27101

C-2

(336) 721-2621
(800) 327-2536; Fax: (336) 917-5572

Full-time: 8 men, 694 women	**Faculty:** 58; IIB, --$
Part-time: 12 men, 154 women	**Ph.D.s:** 86%
Graduate: 15 men, 226 women	**Student/Faculty:** 12 to 1
Year: 4-1-4, summer session	**Tuition:** $16,975
Application Deadline: open	**Room & Board:** $9251
Freshman Class: 387 applied, 267 accepted, 127 enrolled	
SAT Verbal/Math: 570/550*	**ACT:** 28 **VERY COMPETITIVE+**

Salem College, traces its roots back to 1772, when it was begun as a school for girls by the Moravians, an early Protestant denomination. Today the private college, which retains a historical relationship with the church, offers a liberal arts education primarily for women. In addition to regional accreditation, Salem has baccalaureate program accreditation with NASM and NCATE. The 2 libraries contain 135,000 volumes, 302,534 microform items, and 13,553 audio/video tapes/CDs/DVDs, and subscribe to 15,000 periodicals including electronic. Computerized library services include the card catalog, interlibrary loans, and database searching. Special learning facilities include a learning resource center, art gallery, radio station, and a learning lab (computer lab with multimedia capability). The 64-acre campus is in an urban area in the center of Old Salem, a restored 18th-century village. Including any residence halls, there are 17 buildings.

Student Life: 51% of undergraduates are from North Carolina. Others are from 23 states and 17 foreign countries. 80% are from public schools. 65% are white; 18% African American. The average age of freshmen is 18; all undergraduates, 27. 25% do not continue beyond their first year; 55% remain to graduate.

Housing: 488 students can be accommodated in college housing, which includes single-sex dormitories, on-campus apartments, and off-campus apartments. On-campus housing is guaranteed for all 4 years. 86% of students live on campus; of those, 55% remain on campus on weekends. All students may keep cars.

Activities: There are no fraternities or sororities. There are 41 groups on campus, including chorale, chorus, dance, drama, ethnic, gay, honors, international, literary magazine, marching band, musical theater, newspaper, orchestra, political, professional, radio and TV, religious, social, social service, student government, and yearbook. Students may also participate in band, marching band, and orchestra at Wake Forest University. Popular campus events include Fall Fest, April Arts, and dance weekends.

Sports: There are 7 intercollegiate sports for women and 7 intramural sports for women. Facilities include multiple athletic fields, a swimming pool, 2 gyms (1 practice, 1 regular), tennis courts, a dance studio, a softball field, and a universal weight room.

Disabled Students: 75% of the campus is accessible. Special parking, specially equipped rest rooms, special class scheduling, and lowered drinking fountains are available. Many buildings are historic, so disability access is limited to individual areas that have had recent renovations or were already accessible.

Services: Counseling and information services are available, as is tutoring in every subject. A writing center is also available.

Campus Safety and Security: Measures include 24-hour foot and vehicle patrol, security escort services, informal discussions, and pamphlets/posters/films. There are emergency telephones and lighted pathways/sidewalks.

Programs of Study: Salem confers B.A., B.S., B.M., and B.S.B.A. degrees. Master's degrees are also awarded. Bachelor's degrees are awarded in BIOLOGICAL SCIENCE (biology/biological science), BUSINESS (accounting, business administration and management, and international business management), COMMUNICATIONS AND THE ARTS (art history and appreciation, arts administration/management, communications, English, French, German, music, Spanish, and studio art), COMPUTER AND PHYSICAL SCIENCE (chemistry and mathematics), ENGINEERING AND ENVIRONMENTAL DESIGN (interior design), HEALTH PROFESSIONS (medical laboratory technology), SOCIAL SCIENCE (American studies, economics, history, international relations, philosophy, psychology, religion, and sociology). Sociology, business, and communication are the largest.

Required: To graduate, students must complete a total of 36 courses, or 144 semester hours, with a minimum GPA of 2.0 both cumulative and in the major. All traditional students must complete 4 January-term courses and 2 terms of phys ed. Bachelor of arts degree students must complete the following general ed courses: 3 in a modern foreign language, 3 in math/science (including at least 1 math and at least 1 lab science), 2 each in English, social science, and history, and 1 each in fine arts and philosophy/religion.

Special: Salem offers an extensive internship program in all majors, cross-registration with Wake Forest University, and study abroad at various locations, including a summer program in Oxford, England. A Washington semester, student-designed and interdisciplinary majors, B.A.-B.S. degrees, nondegree study, and pass/fail options during the January term are available. A 3-2 engineering degree is available with Duke and Vanderbilt Universities. Students may participate in a model U.N. program directed by Drew University in Madison, New Jersey. Interdisciplinary majors are offered in American studies, arts management, and international relations. There are 9 national honor societies and a freshman honors program.

Faculty/Classroom: 47% of faculty are male; 53%, female. All both teach and do research. No introductory courses are taught by graduate students. The average class size in an introductory lecture is 18; in a laboratory, 15; and in a regular course, 15.

Admissions: 69% of the 2005-2006 applicants were accepted. The SAT scores for the 2005-2006 freshman class were: Verbal--18% below 500, 41% between 500 and 599, 32% between 600 and 700, and 9% above 700; Math--25% below 500, 37% between 500 and 599, 35% between 600 and 700, and 3% above 700. 2 freshmen graduated first in their class.

Requirements: The SAT or ACT is required. The ACT Optional Writing test is also required for some programs. Graduation from an accredited secondary school or the GED is needed. Students must have 12 academic credits plus electives, including 4 years of high school English, 3 each of math and science, and 2 each of a foreign language and history. An essay is required for all students. Music students must audition. A GPA of 2.0 is required. AP and CLEP credits are accepted. Important factors in the admissions decision are advanced placement or honor courses, leadership record, and evidence of special talent.

Procedure: Freshmen are admitted fall and spring. Entrance exams should be taken by January of the senior year. There are early admissions, deferred admissions, and rolling admissions plans. Application deadlines are open. Application fee is $30. Applications are accepted on-line.

Transfer: 17 transfer students enrolled in a recent year. Applicants must have a minimum GPA of 2.0 in all previous college work and must submit a statement of good standing from the Dean of Students of the college previously attended, 2 letters of recommendation from teachers, a high school transcript, and a transcript and catalog from each college attended. SAT or ACT scores may be required on an individual basis. An interview is recommended. 36 of 144 credits required for the bachelor's degree must be completed at Salem.

Visiting: There are regularly scheduled orientations for prospective students. There are guides for informal visits and visitors may sit in on classes and stay overnight. To schedule a visit, contact the Admissions Office.

Financial Aid: The average freshman award was $14,500. 66% of undergraduates work part time. Average annual earnings from campus work are $1600. The average financial indebtedness of the 2005 graduate was $14,500. The FAFSA and the college's own financial statement are required. The deadline for filing freshman financial aid applications for fall entry is March 15.

International Students: There are 70 international students enrolled. The school actively recruits these students. They must score satisfactorily on the written TOEFL or on the electronic version and also take the SAT or the ACT.

Computers: Wireless access is available in various locations on campus; computers are available in 2 labs and in the library. All residence hall rooms and classrooms have Internet access ports. All students may access the system when school is in session 24 hours a day. There are no time limits and no fees.

Graduates: From July 1, 2004 to June 30, 2005, 189 bachelor's degrees were awarded. The most popular majors were business (13%), sociology (13%), and communication (13%). In an average class, 1% graduate in 3 years or less, 52% graduate in 4 years or less, 55% graduate in 5 years or less, and 56% graduate in 6 years or less. Of the 2004 graduating class, 18% were enrolled in graduate school within 6 months of graduation and 77% were employed.

Admissions Contact: Dama E. Evans, Dean of Admissions and Financial Aid. E-mail: *admissions@salem.edu* Web: *www.salem.edu*

SHAW UNIVERSITY

Raleigh, NC 27601

D-2

(919) 546-8275
(800) 214-6683; Fax: (919) 546-8271

Full-time: 865 men, 1418 women	**Faculty:** n/av
Part-time: 93 men, 189 women	**Ph.D.s:** n/av
Graduate: 94 men, 103 women	**Student/Faculty:** 26 to 1
Year: semesters, summer session	**Tuition:** $9438
Application Deadline: July 30	**Room & Board:** $6050
Freshman Class: 4226 applied, 2728 accepted, 601 enrolled	
SAT or ACT: required	**LESS COMPETITIVE**

Shaw University, founded in 1865, is a private liberal arts university affiliated with the Baptist Church. Some information in this profile is approximate. In addition to regional accreditation, Shaw has baccalaureate program accreditation with CAAHEP and NCATE. The library contains 153,304 volumes, 138,950 microform items, and 1306 audio/video tapes/CDs/DVDs, and subscribes to 15,357 periodicals including electronic. Computerized library services include the card catalog, interlibrary loans, database searching, and Internet access. Special learning facilities include a learning resource center, radio station, a praxis lab, an Academic Assessment and Achievement Center (AAA), and a kinesiotherapy clinic. The 30-acre campus is in an urban area in downtown Raleigh. Including any residence halls, there are 23 buildings.

Student Life: 73% of undergraduates are from North Carolina. Students are from 32 states and 10 foreign countries. 94% are African American. The average age of freshmen is 24; all undergraduates, 28.

Housing: 1293 students can be accommodated in college housing, which includes single-sex dorms. On-campus housing is available on a first-come, first-served basis. 62% of students commute. Alcohol is not permitted. Upperclassmen may keep cars.

Activities: 4% of men belong to 4 national fraternities; 5% of women belong to 4 national sororities. There are 30 groups on campus, including band, business, cheerleading, choir, chorus, criminal justice, dance, drama, ethnic, honors, international, jazz band, marching band, musical theater, newspaper, pep band, professional, radio and TV, religious, social, social service, student government, and yearbook. Popular campus events include Career Day, Awards Day, and Religious Emphasis Week.

Sports: There are 7 intercollegiate sports for men and 7 for women, and 5 intramural sports for men and 4 for women.

Disabled Students: Wheelchair ramps, elevators, special parking, specially equipped rest rooms, lowered drinking fountains, and labels in braille are available.

Services: Counseling and information services are available, as is tutoring in some subjects, including English, math, biology, chemistry, physical science, statistics, and social science. There is remedial math, reading, and writing. There is peer tutoring in accounting.

Campus Safety and Security: Measures include 24-hour foot and vehicle patrol, self-defense education, security escort services, and informal discussions. There are pamphlets/posters/films, lighted pathways/sidewalks, and 24-hour electronic surveillance.

Programs of Study: Shaw confers B.A. and B.S. degrees. Associate and master's degrees are also awarded. Bachelor's degrees are awarded in BIOLOGICAL SCIENCE (biology/biological science), BUSINESS (accounting, business administration and management, and recreation and leisure services), COMMUNICATIONS AND THE ARTS (broadcasting, English, and visual and performing arts), COMPUTER AND PHYSICAL SCIENCE (chemistry, computer science, mathematics, and physics), EDUCATION (athletic training, elementary, English, mathematics, physical, science, secondary, social studies, and special), ENGINEERING AND ENVIRONMENTAL DESIGN (environmental science and preengineering), HEALTH PROFESSIONS (recreation therapy, rehabilitation therapy, and speech pathology/audiology), SOCIAL SCIENCE (African studies, criminal justice, gerontology, international relations, international studies, liberal arts/general studies, political science/government, psychology, public administration, religion, social work, and sociology). Business administration/management, criminal justice, and sociology are the largest.

Required: To graduate (in most majors), students must earn 120 credits, maintain a minimum GPA of 2.0, and successfully complete competency exams in math and English. The general core curriculum includes a total of 54 credits in college orientation, English, math, ethics, humanities, natural sciences, and social sciences.

Special: Shaw offers cross-registration with 4 other North Carolina colleges, internships, a work-study program, a 3-2 engineering degree with North Carolina State University and North Carolina Agrigultural and Technical State University, dual and student-designed majors, independent study, and an external degree program for working adults. There are 4 national honor societies, a freshman honors program.

Faculty/Classroom: 94% teach undergraduates. The average class size in a laboratory is 8 and in a regular course, 13.

Admissions: 65% of the 2005-2006 applicants were accepted.

Requirements: The SAT or ACT is required. In addition, applicants must be graduates of an accredited secondary school or have a GED certificate. They should have completed 3 units of English, 2 each of math, natural science (with 1 in a lab course), and social science, and 4 of academic electives. Admission to the Teacher Education Program follows separate guidelines. A GPA of 2.0 is required. AP and CLEP credits are accepted. Important factors in the admissions decision are advanced placement or honor courses, personality/intangible qualities, and recommendations by school officials.

Procedure: Freshmen are admitted to all sessions. Entrance exams should be taken prior to enrollment. There are deferred admissions and rolling admissions plans. Applications should be filed by July 30 for fall entry and November 30 for spring entry. Notification is sent on a rolling basis. Applications are accepted on-line. The fall 2005 application fee was $25.

Transfer: 246 transfer students enrolled in 2004-2005. Applicants must submit official transcripts from all colleges attended. Transfer credit is given only for course work of grade C or better completed at an accredited degree-granting institution. 30 of 120 credits required for the bachelor's degree must be completed at Shaw.

Visiting: There are regularly scheduled orientations for prospective students, consisting of parent visitation, tours, general administration, and registration. There are guides for informal visits and visitors may sit in on classes. To schedule a visit, contact the Admissions Office at (919) 546-8275 or (919) 546-8276.

Financial Aid: The FAFSA is required. The deadline for filing freshman financial aid applications for fall entry is open.

International Students: In a recent year, there were 73 international students enrolled. The school actively recruits these students. They must take the SAT or the ACT.

Computers: All students may access the system. There are no time limits. It is strongly recommended that all students have a personal computer.

Graduates: In a recent year, 367 bachelor's degrees were awarded. The most popular majors were business (24%), criminal justice (14%), and sociology (11%). In an average class, 26% graduate in 4 years or less, 34% graduate in 5 years or less, and 38% graduate in 6 years or less.

Admissions Contact: Sandy Clifton, Interim Director of Admissions and Recruitment. E-mail: *sclifton@shaw.edu* Web: *www.shawuniversity.edu*

UNIVERSITY OF NORTH CAROLINA SYSTEM

The University of North Carolina system, established in 1931, is a public system in North Carolina. It is governed by UNC Board of Governors, whose chief administrator is president. The primary goal of the system is to discover, create, transmit, and apply knowledge to address the needs of North Carolina and its people. The main priorities are teaching/ instruction, research/scholarship/creative activities, public service (solving societal problems and enriching quality of life). The total enrollment of all 16 campuses is about 196,000; there are about 12,000 faculty members. Altogether there are 1,042 baccalaureate, 697 master's, and 199 doctoral programs offered in University of North Carolina system. Profiles of the 4-year campuses are included in this section.

UNIVERSITY OF NORTH CAROLINA AT ASHEVILLE B-2
Asheville, NC 28804-8510

(828) 251-6481
(800) 531-9842; Fax: (828) 251-6482

Full-time: 1179 men, 1641 women	**Faculty:** 199; IIB, av$
Part-time: 280 men, 376 women	**Ph.D.s:** 84%
Graduate: 14 men, 23 women	**Student/Faculty:** 14 to 1
Year: semesters, summer session	**Tuition:** $3525 ($13,325)
Application Deadline: March 1	**Room & Board:** $5712
Freshman Class: 2362 applied, 1482 accepted, 472 enrolled	
SAT Verbal/Math: 600/590*	**ACT:** 24 **VERY COMPETITIVE**

The University of North Carolina at Asheville is the designated public liberal arts university in the 16-campus UNC system. In addition to regional accreditation, UNCA has baccalaureate program accreditation with NCATE. The library contains 262,283 volumes, 861,742 microform items, and 11,374 audio/video tapes/CDs/DVDs, and subscribes to 4810 periodicals including electronic. Computerized library services include the card catalog, interlibrary loans, database searching, Internet access, and laptop Internet portals. Special learning facilities include a learning resource center, art gallery, distance learning facility, center for creative retirement, undergraduate research center, botanical gardens, music recording center, and the Environmental Quality Institute. The 265-acre campus is in a suburban area 130 miles west of Charlotte. Including any residence halls, there are 27 buildings.

Student Life: 86% of undergraduates are from North Carolina. Others are from 44 states, 21 foreign countries, and Canada. 85% are from public schools. 90% are white. The average age of freshmen is 18; all undergraduates, 22. 24% do not continue beyond their first year; 54% remain to graduate.

Housing: 1171 students can be accommodated in college housing, which includes single-sex and coed dorms and off-campus apartments. In addition, there are honors houses, quiet dorms, and substance-free housing. On-campus housing is guaranteed for all 4 years. 66% of students commute. All students may keep cars.

Activities: 3% of men belong to 3 national fraternities; 2% of women belong to 2 national sororities. There are 70 groups on campus, including art, band, cheerleading, choir, chorus, computers, dance, departmental, drama, ethnic, gay, honors, international, jazz band, literary magazine, newspaper, pep band, political, professional, religious, social, social service, and student government. Popular campus events include Spring Lawn Party and Summer Concerts on the Quad.

Sports: There are 7 intercollegiate sports for men and 7 for women, and 15 intramural sports for men and 15 for women. Facilities include a sports and health center with a state-of-the-art weight room, 4 basketball courts, volleyball and racquetball courts, a dance studio, an indoor swimming pool, indoor and outdoor tracks, outdoor tennis courts, and soccer and baseball fields.

Disabled Students: 95% of the campus is accessible. Wheelchair ramps, elevators, special parking, specially equipped rest rooms, special class scheduling, lowered drinking fountains, and lowered telephones are available.

Services: Counseling and information services are available, as is tutoring in most subjects. There is a reader service for the blind, and remedial math, reading, and writing.

Campus Safety and Security: Measures include 24-hour foot and vehicle patrol, self-defense education, security escort services, and informal discussions. There are pamphlets/posters/films, emergency telephones, and lighted pathways/sidewalks.

Programs of Study: UNCA confers B.A., B.S., and B.F.A. degrees. Master's degrees are also awarded. Bachelor's degrees are awarded in BIOLOGICAL SCIENCE (biology/biological science), BUSINESS (accounting and business administration and management), COMMUNICATIONS AND THE ARTS (art, classics, communications, dramatic arts, French, German, literature, media arts, multimedia, music, music technology, and Spanish), COMPUTER AND PHYSICAL SCIENCE (atmospheric sciences and meteorology, chemistry, computer science, mathematics, and physics), ENGINEERING AND ENVIRONMENTAL DESIGN (environmental science and industrial administration/ management), HEALTH PROFESSIONS (health), SOCIAL SCIENCE (economics, fire control and safety technology, history, liberal arts/ general studies, philosophy, political science/government, psychology, sociology, and women's studies). Psychology, management, and literature are the largest.

Required: To graduate, students must complete a minimum of 120 credit hours, including 27 to 40 in the major, with a senior capstone experience consisting of undergraduate research, an exam, or a seminar. The core curriculim requires a 3 hour Liberal Studies Introductory Colloquium; 12 hours of humanities; 3 hours of interdisciplinary arts; a minimum of 7 hours of natural science including lab; 3 hours of social science; up to 6 hours of foreign language; 4 hours of math; 4 hours of academic writing; 2 hours of health and wellness; and a 3 credit hour Liberal Studies Senior Colloquium. Students take their non-lab natural science and social science courses with an additional liberal arts elective, within an integrative topical cluster. In addition, students are required to do intensive course work in writing, information literacy, quantitative reasoning, and diversity: these courses can be taken in the major, in general education, or in electives, and need not add credit hours to the student's program.

Special: Students may participate in cooperative programs in nursing, forestry, and textile chemistry. UNCA participates in a consortium with Warren Wilson and Mars Hill Colleges, and there is cross-registration with a number of North Carolina universities and colleges. Study-abroad programs are available in 35 countries. The school offers internships, dual majors, student-designed interdisciplinary majors, and a 2-2 engineering degree and joint engineering degree with North Carolina State University. Nondegree study is available. There are 13 national honor societies, a freshman honors program, and 11 departmental honors programs.

Faculty/Classroom: 60% of faculty are male; 40%, female. All teach undergraduates. No introductory courses are taught by graduate students. The average class size in an introductory lecture is 21; in a laboratory, 16; and in a regular course, 18.

Admissions: 63% of the 2005-2006 applicants were accepted. The SAT scores for the 2005-2006 freshman class were: Verbal--13% below 500, 35% between 500 and 599, 39% between 600 and 700, and 13% above 700; Math--10% below 500, 46% between 500 and 599, 38% between 600 and 700, and 6% above 700. The ACT scores were 15% below 21, 26% between 21 and 23, 32% between 24 and 26, 11% between 27 and 28, and 16% above 28. 55% of the current freshmen were in the top fifth of their class; 93% were in the top two fifths. 1 freshman graduated first in their class.

Requirements: The SAT or ACT is required. In addition, graduation from an accredited secondary school is required. UNCA requires a minimum of 16 high school academic units, including 4 of English, 4 of math (algebra I, geometry, algebra II) and 1 math with algebra II as pre-req, 3 of science (biology, physical science, and a lab course), 2 of social studies/history, and 2 of a foreign language. Applicants are evaluated primarily on their academic achievement record, extracurricular activities that support academic achievement, and SAT or ACT scores. AP and CLEP credits are accepted. Important factors in the admissions decision are advanced placement or honor courses, leadership record, and evidence of special talent.

Procedure: Freshmen are admitted fall and spring. Entrance exams should be taken at the end of the junior year or the beginning of the senior year. There are early action and deferred admissions plans. Early decision applications should be filed by November 28; regular applications, by March 1 for fall entry and November 1 for spring entry. Notification is sent monthly. The fall 2005 application fee was $50. Applications are accepted on-line.

Transfer: 370 transfer students enrolled in 2004-2005. Applicants under 24 years of age or with fewer than 24 semester or 36 quarter credit hours must submit high school transcripts and SAT or ACT scores. 30 of 120 credits required for the bachelor's degree must be completed at UNCA.

Visiting: There are regularly scheduled orientations for prospective students, including meetings with faculty or other departments, an information session for students and families, and a campus tour. Pre-registration is prior to fall enrollment during the summer months. There are guides for informal visits and visitors may sit in on classes and stay overnight. To schedule a visit, contact the Office of Admissions at *admissions@unca.edu*.

Financial Aid: In 2005-2006, 62% of all full-time freshmen and 58% of continuing full-time students received some form of financial aid. 36% of full-time freshmen and 41% of continuing full-time students received need-based aid. The average freshman award was $5578. Need-based scholarships or need-based grants averaged $2776 ($9675 maximum); need-based self-help aid (loans and jobs) averaged $2741 ($8673 maximum); non-need-based athletic scholarships averaged $5167 ($19,446 maximum); and other non-need-based awards and non-need-based scholarships averaged $3209 ($11,625 maximum). 20% of undergraduates work part time. Average annual earnings from campus work are $1531. The average financial indebtedness of the 2005 graduate was $15,309. The FAFSA is required. The priority date for freshman financial aid applications for fall entry is March 1.

International Students: There are 41 international students enrolled. The school actively recruits these students. They must score satisfactorily on the TOEFL. The SAT or ACT is required for international athletes.

Computers: Wireless access is available. UNC Asheville students can access the college's network from more than 375 PCs located in computer labs, classrooms, library carrels, and dorm labs. All dorm rooms are wired with a high-speed Internet connection for each occupant. Wireless Internet access is available in the library, student center, and some classrooms. All students may access the system 24 hours a day. There are no time limits and no fees.

Graduates: From July 1, 2004 to June 30, 2005, 576 bachelor's degrees were awarded. The most popular majors were psychology (13%), management (11%), and literature (9%). In an average class, 1% graduate in 3 years or less, 33% graduate in 4 years or less, 50% graduate in 5 years or less, and 54% graduate in 6 years or less. 150 companies recruited on campus in 2004-2005. Of the 2004 graduating class, 21% were enrolled in graduate school within 6 months of graduation and 96% were employed.

Admissions Contact: Scot Schaeffer, Director of Admissions and Financial Aid. A video is available. E-mail: *admissions@unca.edu* Web: *www.unca.edu/admissions*

UNIVERSITY OF NORTH CAROLINA AT CHAPEL HILL D-2
Chapel Hill, NC 27599-2200

(919) 966-3621
Fax: (919) 962-3045

Full-time: 6589 men, 9322 women	Faculty: I, av$
Part-time: 393 men, 460 women	Ph.D.s: 82%
Graduate: 3341 men, 4834 women	Student/Faculty: n/av
Year: semesters, summer session	Tuition: $4613 ($18,411)
Application Deadline: January 15	Room & Board: $6516
Freshman Class: 18,414 applied, 6736 accepted, 3751 enrolled	
SAT Verbal/Math: 643/656*	ACT: 28 MOST COMPETITIVE

The University of North Carolina at Chapel Hill, chartered in 1789 and the nation's first public university, offers academic programs leading to 69 bachelor's, 112 master's, and 77 doctoral degrees, as well as 4 professional degrees. There are 9 undergraduate and 12 graduate schools. The 14 libraries contain 5,366,141 volumes, 4,734,753 microform items, and 32,920 audio/video tapes/CDs/DVDs, and subscribe to 42,238 periodicals including electronic. Computerized library services include the card catalog, interlibrary loans, and database searching. Special learning facilities include a learning resource center, art gallery, planetarium, radio station, TV station, botanical garden, and theater. The 729-acre campus is in a suburban area 25 miles west of Raleigh. Including any residence halls, there are 292 buildings.

Student Life: 82% of undergraduates are from North Carolina. Students are from 50 states, 105 foreign countries, and Canada. 84% are from public schools. 76% are white; 11% African American. The average age of freshmen is 18; all undergraduates, 20. 5% do not continue beyond their first year; 80% remain to graduate.

Housing: 9715 students can be accommodated in college housing, which includes single-sex and coed dorms, married-student housing, fraternity houses, and sorority houses. In addition, there are language houses, special-interest houses and substance-free housing. 56% of students commute. Upperclassmen may keep cars.

Activities: 12% of men belong to 29 national fraternities; 12% of women belong to 1 local sorority and 20 national sororities. There are 565 groups on campus, including art, band, cheerleading, chess, choir, chorus, dance, drama, drill team, ethnic, film, gay, honors, international, jazz band, literary magazine, marching band, musical theater, newspaper, orchestra, pep band, photography, political, professional, radio and TV, religious, social, social service, student government, symphony, and yearbook. Popular campus events include Black Greek Council Stepshow, Apple Chill, and Carolina Jazz Festival.

Sports: There are 12 intercollegiate sports for men and 14 for women, and 40 intramural sports for men and 35 for women. Facilities include a 60,000-seat football stadium, 3 swimming pools, a 21,000-seat sports and student activities center, tennis courts, lacrosse and soccer fields, a golf course, a boathouse, gym facilities, softball fields, and a student recreation center with aerobics, weights, and wellness programs.

Disabled Students: 94% of the campus is accessible. Wheelchair ramps, elevators, special parking, specially equipped rest rooms, special class scheduling, lowered drinking fountains, lowered telephones, and special housing are available.

Services: Counseling and information services are available, as is tutoring in every subject. There is a reader service for the blind and remedial math and writing.

Campus Safety and Security: Measures include 24-hour foot and vehicle patrol, self-defense education, security escort services, and shuttle buses. There are informal discussions, pamphlets/posters/films, emergency telephones, lighted pathways/sidewalks, and building security surveys.

Programs of Study: UNC-Chapel Hill confers B.A., B.S., A.B.J., B.A.Ed., B.F.A., B.M., B.M.Ed., B.S.Applied Sc., and B.S.B.A. degrees. Master's and doctoral degrees are also awarded. Bachelor's degrees are awarded in AGRICULTURE (environmental studies), BIOLOGICAL SCIENCE (biology/biological science, biometrics and biostatistics, and nutrition), BUSINESS (accounting, business administration and management, and recreational facilities management), COMMUNICATIONS AND THE ARTS (art history and appreciation, classics, communications, comparative literature, dramatic arts, English, German, journalism, linguistics, music, music performance, romance languages and literature, Russian, speech/debate/rhetoric, and studio art), COMPUTER AND PHYSICAL SCIENCE (applied science, chemistry, computer science, geology, information sciences and systems, mathematics, and physics), EDUCATION (education, elementary, English, foreign languages, health, mathematics, middle school, music, physical, secondary, and social studies), ENGINEERING AND ENVIRONMENTAL DESIGN (environmental engineering, environmental science, and industrial administration/management), HEALTH PROFESSIONS (clinical science, dental hygiene, exercise science, health care administration, medical laboratory technology, nursing, public health, and radiological science), SOCIAL SCIENCE (African American studies, African studies, American studies, anthropology, Asian/Oriental studies, child care/child and family studies, economics, geography, history, interdisciplinary studies, international studies, Latin American studies, peace studies, philosophy, political science/government, psychology, public affairs, religion, Russian and Slavic studies, sociology, and women's studies). Sociology and journalism are the strongest academically. Biology, psychology, and journalism are the largest.

Required: To graduate, students must complete 120 credits (more for some B.S. degrees) with a 2.0 GPA. The general education requirements fall under 2 headings: Basic Skills (English composition, foreign languages, and mathematical sciences) and Perspectives (Aesthetic, Natural Sciences, Philosophical, Social Sciences, and Western Historical/Non-Western/Comparative). The Basic Skills requirements apply to all students. The Perspectives requirements fall into 2 categories: 9 courses are required of all freshmen and sophomores. 4 more courses, selected from 4 of the 5 perspective areas, are required of juniors and seniors seeking a B.A. degree in the College of Arts and Sciences. 2 phys ed courses are also required.

Special: Students may participate in joint programs with Duke University and North Carolina State University. Internships, study abroad in 64 countries, B.A.-B.S. degrees, and student-designed majors are available. There are pass/fail options and nondegree study. There are 7 national honor societies, including Phi Beta Kappa, and a freshman honors program.

Faculty/Classroom: 62% of faculty are male; 38%, female. All teach undergraduates. Graduate students teach 46% of introductory courses. The average class size in an introductory lecture is 41; in a laboratory, 18; and in a regular course, 28.

Admissions: 37% of the 2005-2006 applicants were accepted. The SAT scores for the 2005-2006 freshman class were: Verbal--3% below 500, 22% between 500 and 599, 55% between 600 and 700, and 20% above 700; Math--2% below 500, 16% between 500 and 599, 58% between 600 and 700, and 24% above 700. The ACT scores were 4% below 21, 10% between 21 and 23, 24% between 24 and 26, 20% between 27 and 28, and 41% above 28. 92% of the current freshmen were in the top fifth of their class; 99% were in the top two fifths. There were 136 National Merit finalists in a recent year. 190 freshmen graduated first in their class.

Requirements: The SAT or ACT is required. The ACT Optional Writing test is also required. In addition, applicants must be graduates of an accredited secondary school. They should complete 16 high school academic credits, including 4 in English, 3 each in math (2 in algebra and 1 in geometry) and science (including at least 1 physical science and 1 lab course), and 2 each in a single foreign language, history, and social studies. A portfolio and an audition are recommended for art and music majors. AP and CLEP credits are accepted.

Procedure: Freshmen are admitted in the fall. Entrance exams should be taken in the junior and senior years. There are early admissions and deferred admissions plans. Applications should be filed by January 15 for fall entry, along with a $70 fee. Notification is sent March 31. 1585 applicants were on the 2005 waiting list; 7 were admitted. Applications are accepted on-line.

Transfer: 827 transfer students enrolled in 2004-2005. Sophomore transfers need at least 24 credit hours and a minimum GPA of 2.0; junior transfers need at least 51 credit hours and a minimum GPA of 2.0. 45 of 120 credits required for the bachelor's degree must be completed at UNC-Chapel Hill.

Visiting: There are regularly scheduled orientations for prospective students, including campus tours and information sessions, offered twice each weekday. There are guides for informal visits and visitors may sit in on classes. To schedule a visit, contact the Office of Undergraduate Admissions at www.admissions.unc.edu/visit/visit.html.

Financial Aid: In 2005-2006, 60% of all full-time freshmen and 52% of continuing full-time students received some form of financial aid. 33% of all full-time students received need-based aid. The average freshman award was $8693. Need-based scholarships or need-based grants averaged $8158 ($27,525 maximum); need-based self-help aid (loans and jobs) averaged $2296 ($8040 maximum); non-need-based athletic scholarships averaged $11,648 ($24,230 maximum); and other non-need-based awards and non-need-based scholarships averaged $4170 ($27,898 maximum). The average financial indebtedness of the 2005 graduate was $12,300. UNC-Chapel Hill is a member of CSS. The CSS/Profile or FAFSA is required. The deadline for filing freshman financial aid applications for fall entry is March 1.

International Students: There are 184 international students enrolled in a recent year. The school actively recruits these students. They must achieve a satisfactory score on the TOEFL and also take the SAT or ACT.

Computers: All students may access the system 24 hours a day. There are no time limits and no fees. All students are required to have personal computers.

Graduates: In a recent year, 3741 bachelor's degrees were awarded. The most popular majors were journalism and mass communication (18%), social sciences and history (18%), and business/marketing (10%). In an average class, 1% graduate in 3 years or less, 67% graduate in 4 years or less, 78% graduate in 5 years or less, and 80% graduate in 6 years or less. 162 companies recruited on campus in a recent year. Of a recent graduating class, 26% were enrolled in graduate school within 6 months of graduation and 59% were employed.

Admissions Contact: Office of Undergraduate Admissions.
E-mail: uadm@email.unc.edu Web: www.unc.edu

UNIVERSITY OF NORTH CAROLINA AT CHARLOTTE C-3

Charlotte, NC 28223-0001 (704) 687-2213; Fax: (704) 687-6483

Full-time: 6450 men, 7190 women	Faculty: IIA, av$
Part-time: 1287 men, 1628 women	Ph.D.s: 85%
Graduate: 1552 men, 2665 women	Student/Faculty: n/av
Year: semesters, summer session	Tuition: $3551 ($13,963)
Application Deadline: July 1	Room & Board: $5550
Freshman Class: 8665 applied, 6738 accepted, 2890 enrolled	
SAT Verbal/Math: 520/550*	ACT: 21 COMPETITIVE

The University of North Carolina at Charlotte, founded in 1946, is a publicly funded institution in the University of North Carolina system. There are 8 undergraduate schools and 1 graduate school. In addition to regional accreditation, UNC-Charlotte has baccalaureate program accreditation with AACSB, ABET, CAAHEP, CCNE, CSWE, NAAB, and NCATE. The library contains 969,680 volumes, 2,137,734 microform items, and 764,103 audio/video tapes/CDs/DVDs, and subscribes to 32,486 periodicals including electronic. Computerized library services include the card catalog, interlibrary loans, database searching, Internet access, and laptop Internet portals. Special learning facilities include a learning resource center, art gallery, on-line teleconferencing facility, high-tech research center in engineering, and botanical garden and greenhouse complex that includes a tropical rain forest. The 1000-acre campus is in a suburban area 8 miles northeast of the center of Charlotte. Including any residence halls, there are 102 buildings.

Student Life: 90% of undergraduates are from North Carolina. Others are from 48 states, 78 foreign countries, and Canada. 75% are white; 15% African American. 67% claim no religious affiliation; 26% Protestant. The average age of freshmen is 18; all undergraduates, 23. 23% do not continue beyond their first year; 43% remain to graduate.

Housing: 4467 students can be accommodated in college housing, which includes single-sex and coed dorms and on-campus apartments. In addition, there are honors houses, special-interest houses an international floor, 5 sorority floors, and 1 fraternity floor. On-campus housing is available on a first-come, first-served basis. 79% of students commute. All students may keep cars.

Activities: 8% of men belong to 14 national fraternities; 6% of women belong to 9 national sororities. There are more than 200 groups on campus, including art, cheerleading, chess, choir, chorale, chorus, computers, dance, debate, drama, ethnic, fashion club, film, gay, honors, international, jazz band, literary magazine, newspaper, nontraditional students, opera, pep band, photography, political, professional, radio and TV, religious, science fiction and fantasy guild social, social service, student government, and yearbook. Popular campus events include Greek Week, Miss 49er Pageant, and International Festival.

Sports: There are 8 intercollegiate sports for men and 8 for women, and 41 intramural sports for men and 41 for women. Facilities include a gym, an Olympic-size pool, basketball, tennis, and racquetball courts, a fitness trail, a track, and a training room. There is also a 9100-seat arena, 2 weight rooms, an aerobics studio, an indoor track, indoor basketball/volleyball courts, an indoor climbing wall, and a 7000-square-foot game room.

Disabled Students: 90% of the campus is accessible. Wheelchair ramps, elevators, special parking, specially equipped rest rooms, special class scheduling, lowered drinking fountains, lowered telephones, and special housing. The Disability Services Office assists students with all academic and physical accommodations.

Services: Counseling and information services are available, as is tutoring in some subjects, including math, science, foreign language, and introductory courses. There is a reader service for the blind.

Campus Safety and Security: Measures include 24-hour foot and vehicle patrol, self-defense education, security escort services, and shuttle buses. There are informal discussions, pamphlets/posters/films, emergency telephones, and lighted pathways/sidewalks.

Programs of Study: UNC-Charlotte confers B.A., B.S., B.Arch., B.F.A., B.M., B.S.B.A., B.S.C.E., B.S.E.E., B.S.E.T., B.S.M.E., B.S.N., and B.S.W. degrees. Master's and doctoral degrees are also awarded. Bachelor's degrees are awarded in BIOLOGICAL SCIENCE (biology/biological science), BUSINESS (accounting, banking and finance, business administration and management, business economics, international business management, management information systems, and marketing/retailing/merchandising), COMMUNICATIONS AND THE ARTS (art, communications, dance, dramatic arts, English, fine arts, French, German, music, music performance, and Spanish), COMPUTER AND PHYSICAL SCIENCE (atmospheric sciences and meteorology, chemistry, computer science, earth science, geology, mathematics, and physics), EDUCATION (art, athletic training, dance, drama, education of the mentally handicapped, elementary, English, foreign languages, mathematics, middle school, music, science, and social studies), ENGINEERING AND ENVIRONMENTAL DESIGN (architecture, civil engineering, civil engineering technology, computer engineering, electrical/electronics engineering, electrical/electronics engineering technology, industrial administration/management, mechanical engineering, and mechanical engineering technology), HEALTH PROFESSIONS (medical technology and nursing), SOCIAL SCIENCE (African American studies, anthropology, child care/child and family studies, criminal justice, economics, fire control and safety technology, geography, history, international studies, Latin American studies, philosophy, physical fitness/movement, political science/government, psychology, religion, social work, and sociology). Architecture, business administration, and computer science are the strongest academically. Business administration, biology, and mechanical engineering are the largest.

Required: To graduate, students must complete a minimum of 120 credit hours with an overall minimum GPA of 2.0. Between 30 and 42 hours are required in the major, with a minimum GPA of 2.0 in major and minor courses. All students must complete core requirements in the 6 interrelated areas of communication, problem solving, values, science and technology, arts, literature and ideas, and the individual, society, and culture.

Special: Cross-registration is available through the Charlotte Area Educational Consortium. Also available are cooperative programs in numerous majors and internships of 1 semester arranged with public and private community organizations. Study abroad in 41 countries, a Washington semester, work-study, B.A.-B.S. degrees, dual majors, and nondegree study are available. Pass/fail options are limited to 1 course per academic year. There are 46 national honor societies, a freshman honors program, and 13 departmental honors programs.

Faculty/Classroom: 62% of faculty are male; 38%, female. Graduate students teach 3% of introductory courses. The average class size in a laboratory is 18 and in a regular course, 30.

Admissions: 78% of the 2005-2006 applicants were accepted. The SAT scores for the 2005-2006 freshman class were: Verbal--34% below 500, 50% between 500 and 599, 14% between 600 and 700, and 2% above 700; Math--21% below 500, 53% between 500 and 599, 24% between 600 and 700, and 2% above 700. The ACT scores were 42% below 21, 32% between 21 and 23, 19% between 24 and 26, 5% between 27 and 28, and 2% above 28. 28% of the current freshmen were in the top fifth of their class; 80% were in the top two fifths. 24 freshmen graduated first in their class.

Requirements: The SAT or ACT is required. In addition, graduation from an accredited secondary school or the GED is required. The school requires 14 academic credits, including 4 years each of English and math, 3 of science (including 1 of physical science), 2 of a foreign language, and 2 of social studies, including 1 of U.S. history. Seniors should select a challenging academic schedule that includes English, math, science, social studies or history, and foreign language. A portfolio and interview are required for art and architecture students only. Admission of students is based on overall performance in a select group of academic courses (80%) and SAT scores (20%). UNC-Charlotte requires applicants to be in the upper 50% of their class. A GPA of 2.0 is required. AP and CLEP credits are accepted. Important factors in the admissions decision are advanced placement or honor courses, leadership record, and recommendations by school officials.

Procedure: Freshmen are admitted fall, spring, and summer. Entrance exams should be taken at the end of the junior year or by December of the senior year. There are early admissions and deferred admissions plans. There is a rolling admissions plan. Applications should be filed by July 1 for fall entry, November 15 for spring entry, and May 1 for summer entry or January 31 for architecture or nursing. The fall 2005 application fee was $50. Notification is sent on a rolling basis. Applications are accepted on-line.

Transfer: 1919 transfer students enrolled in 2004-2005. Transfer students must have a minimum GPA of 2.0 on all college courses attempted. Certain majors have limited space and require a higher GPA and/or prerequisites. Applicants with fewer than 24 hours of transferable credit must meet both transfer and freshman admissions requirements. An interview is required only for architecture students. 30 of 120 credits required for the bachelor's degree must be completed at UNC-Charlotte.

Visiting: There are regularly scheduled orientations for prospective students, including tours. There are guides for informal visits and visitors may sit in on classes and stay overnight. To schedule a visit, contact the Admissions Office.

Financial Aid: In 2005-2006, 62% of all full-time freshmen and 58% of continuing full-time students received some form of financial aid. 47% of all full-time students received need-based aid. The average freshman award was $6108. Need-based scholarships or need-based grants averaged $4191 ($7250 maximum); need-based self-help aid (loans and jobs) averaged $2747 ($7500 maximum); non-need-based athletic scholarships averaged $6237 ($21,000 maximum); and other non-need-based awards and non-need-based scholarships averaged $2020 ($5500 maximum). 86% of undergraduates work part time. Average annual earnings from campus work are $2027. The average financial indebtedness of the 2005 graduate was $18,402. The FAFSA is required. The priority date for freshman financial aid applications for fall entry is April 1.

International Students: There are 205 international students enrolled. They must score satisfactorily on the TOEFL or take the MELAB or IELTS. Students with a satisfactory score on the verbal part of the SAT are not required to take the TOEFL or other English Proficiency exam.

Computers: All students may access the system 24 hours per day. There are no time limits. The fee is $27 per semester.

Graduates: From July 1, 2004 to June 30, 2005, 2843 bachelor's degrees were awarded. The most popular majors were business administration (21%), psychology (8%), and education (7%). In an average class, 26% graduate in 4 years or less, 43% graduate in 5 years or less, and 47% graduate in 6 years or less. 97 companies recruited on campus in a recent year. Of the 2004 graduating class, 15% were enrolled in graduate school within 6 months of graduation and 64% were employed.

Admissions Contact: Craig Fulton, Director of Admissions. A video is available. E-mail: unccadm@email.uncc.edu Web: http://www.uncc.edu/admissions

---

UNIVERSITY OF NORTH CAROLINA AT GREENSBORO

D-2

Greensboro, NC 27412

(336) 334-5243; Fax: (336) 334-4180

Full-time: 3373 men, 7211 women	Faculty: I, --$
Part-time: 575 men, 1132 women	Ph.D.s: 81%
Graduate: 1208 men, 2561 women	Student/Faculty: n/av
Year: semesters, summer session	Tuition: $3467 ($14,735)
Application Deadline: August 1	Room & Board: $5526
Freshman Class: 8093 applied, 6302 accepted, 2424 enrolled	
SAT Verbal/Math: 530/530*	COMPETITIVE

The University of North Carolina at Greensboro, founded in 1891, is a publicly funded liberal arts institution in the University of North Carolina system. There are 7 undergraduate and 7 graduate schools. In addition to regional accreditation, UNCG has baccalaureate program accreditation with AACSB, ABET, ADA, AHEA, CSWE, FIDER, NASM, NCATE, and NLN. The library contains 844,448 volumes, 1,400,761 microform items, and 59,027 audio/video tapes/CDs/DVDs, and subscribes to 8714 periodicals including electronic. Computerized library services include the card catalog, interlibrary loans, database searching, and Internet access. Special learning facilities include a learning resource center, art gallery, radio station, and a cooperative observatory-planetarium (off campus). The 210-acre campus is in an urban area in central Greensboro. Including any residence halls, there are 93 buildings.

Student Life: 93% of undergraduates are from North Carolina. Others are from 49 states, 27 foreign countries, and Canada. 71% are white; 18% African American. The average age of freshmen is 18; all undergraduates, 22. 19% do not continue beyond their first year; 51% remain to graduate.

Housing: 4000 students can be accommodated in college housing, which includes single-sex and coed dorms and on-campus apartments. In addition, there are special-interest houses, an international house, and a residential college program. On-campus housing is guaranteed for all 4 years. 68% of students commute. Alcohol is not permitted. All students may keep cars.

Activities: 8% of men belong to 8 national fraternities; 6% of women belong to 8 national sororities. There are 170 groups on campus, including art, band, choir, chorale, chorus, dance, drama, ethnic, film, gay, honors, international, jazz band, literary magazine, musical theater, newspaper, opera, orchestra, pep band, photography, political, professional, radio and TV, religious, social, social service, student government, symphony, and yearbook. Popular campus events include Spring Fling, Fall Kickoff, and Founders Day.

Sports: There are 7 intercollegiate sports for men and 7 for women, and 25 intramural sports for men and 25 for women. Facilities include a physical activities complex and the 44-acre Piney Lake Field Campus, which includes 2 lakes for swimming, boating, and fishing.

Disabled Students: 80% of the campus is accessible. Wheelchair ramps, elevators, special parking, specially equipped rest rooms, special class scheduling, lowered drinking fountains, lowered telephones, and lifts are available.

Services: Counseling and information services are available, as is tutoring in every subject. There is a reader service for the blind and remedial math.

Campus Safety and Security: Measures include 24-hour foot and vehicle patrol, self-defense education, security escort services, and shuttle buses. There are informal discussions, pamphlets/posters/films, emergency telephones, and lighted pathways/sidewalks.

Programs of Study: UNCG confers B.A., B.S., B.F.A., B.M., B.S.M.T., B.S.N., and B.S.W. degrees. Master's and doctoral degrees are also awarded. Bachelor's degrees are awarded in BIOLOGICAL SCIENCE (biochemistry, biology/biological science, and nutrition), BUSINESS (accounting, banking and finance, business administration and management, international business management, management information systems, and tourism), COMMUNICATIONS AND THE ARTS (art, classics, communications, dance, dramatic arts, English, French, German, jazz, media arts, music, and Spanish), COMPUTER AND PHYSICAL SCIENCE (chemistry, computer science, information sciences and systems, mathematics, and physics), EDUCATION (dance, drama, education of the deaf and hearing impaired, elementary, middle school, music, and special), ENGINEERING AND ENVIRONMENTAL DESIGN (architecture and engineering), HEALTH PROFESSIONS (exercise science, medical laboratory technology, nursing, physical therapy, predentistry, premedicine, prepharmacy, preveterinary science, public health, and speech pathology/audiology), SOCIAL SCIENCE (African American studies, anthropology, economics, geography, history, human development, liberal arts/general studies, parks and recreation management, philosophy, political science/government, prelaw, psychology, religious education, social studies, social work, sociology, and women's studies). Nursing, business administration, and elementary education are the largest.

Required: In order to graduate, students must complete a minimum of 122 credit hours with a GPA of at least 2.0. Major requirements vary from a minimum of 27 credit hours. The liberal education curriculum for all students requires 45 credit hours chosen from specified courses in the humanities, math and physical sciences, social and behavioral sciences, and a foreign language. Students must take 36 hours at the upper-division level and earn 31 hours of resident credit.

Special: Cooperative programs, internships, and accelerated degree programs can be arranged in all majors. Cross-registration is offered with the Greater Greensboro Consortium. Students may study abroad in more than 30 countries, including Spain, where UNCG sponsors a semester of study in Madrid. A Washington semester and student-designed majors are also available. The Residential College, a 2-year program for freshmen and sophomores, offers an interdisciplinary curriculum, with faculty and students living in the same residence. Students in this program participate in independent study, community work, and workshops. There are 18 national honor societies, including Phi Beta Kappa, a freshman honors program, and 14 departmental honors programs.

Faculty/Classroom: 47% of faculty are male; 53%, female. 97% teach undergraduates and 3% do research. The average class size in an introductory lecture is 30; in a laboratory, 19; and in a regular course, 21.

Admissions: 78% of the 2005-2006 applicants were accepted. The SAT scores for the 2005-2006 freshman class were: Verbal--38% below 500, 41% between 500 and 599, 16% between 600 and 700, and 5% above 700; Math--34% below 500, 46% between 500 and 599, 16% between 600 and 700, and 4% above 700. 30% of the current freshmen were in the top fifth of their class; 65% were in the top two fifths.

Requirements: The SAT is required. In addition, graduation from an accredited secondary school or the GED is required. High school courses must include 4 credits of English, 3 each of math and science, 2 of a foreign language, 1 of U.S. history, and 1 of social studies and an elective. A portfolio or audition is required of art and music students. AP and CLEP credits are accepted. Important factors in the admissions decision are advanced placement or honor courses, leadership record, and evidence of special talent.

Procedure: Freshmen are admitted to all sessions. Entrance exams should be taken in June of the junior year or fall of the senior year. There is a rolling admissions plan. Applications should be filed by August 1 for fall entry and December 1 for spring entry. The fall 2005 application fee was $50. Notification is sent on a rolling basis. Applications are accepted on-line.

Transfer: 1249 transfer students enrolled in 2004-2005. Transfer students must have a minimum GPA of 2.0. Students having fewer than 24 semester hours must meet the freshman entrance requirements, including satisfactory scores on the SAT. 31 of 122 credits required for the bachelor's degree must be completed at UNCG.

Visiting: There are regularly scheduled orientations for prospective students. There are guides for informal visits and visitors may sit in on classes and stay overnight. To schedule a visit, contact the Office of Undergraduate Admissions.

Financial Aid: In 2005-2006, 65% of all full-time freshmen and 72% of continuing full-time students received some form of financial aid. 60% of full-time freshmen and 65% of continuing full-time students received need-based aid. The average freshman award was $4282. Need-based scholarships or need-based grants averaged $2143; need-based self-help aid (loans and jobs) averaged $3154; and other non-need-based awards and non-need-based scholarships averaged $2730. The average financial indebtedness of the 2005 graduate was $20,766. The FAFSA is required. The deadline for filing freshman financial aid applications for fall entry is March 1.

International Students: There were 103 international students enrolled in a recent year. A satisfactory score on the TOEFL is required.

Computers: All students may access the system until late-night hours in labs and 24 hours a day via personal modem. There are no time limits and no fees.

Graduates: From July 1, 2004 to June 30, 2005, 2044 bachelor's degrees were awarded. The most popular majors were business administration (10%), nursing (8%), and English (4%). In an average class, 1% graduate in 3 years or less, 27% graduate in 4 years or less, 48% graduate in 5 years or less, and 51% graduate in 6 years or less.

Admissions Contact: Lise Keller, Director, Undergraduate Admissions. E-mail: *admissions@uncg.edu* Web: *http://www.uncg.edu/adm/*

UNIVERSITY OF NORTH CAROLINA AT PEMBROKE   D-3

Pembroke, NC 28372-1510   **(910) 521-6262**
(800) 949-UNCP; Fax: (910) 521-6497

Full-time: 1470 men, 2232 women	Faculty: 233
Part-time: 286 men, 975 women	Ph.D.s: n/av
Graduate: 192 men, 477 women	Student/Faculty: 16 to 1
Year: semesters, summer session	Tuition: $2980 ($12,420)
Application Deadline: July 15	Room & Board: $4960
Freshman Class: 2374 applied, 2036 accepted, 984 enrolled	
SAT Verbal/Math: 462/476*	ACT: 18 LESS COMPETITIVE

UNC Pembroke, founded in 1887, is part of the University of North Carolina state-supported system. It provides a liberal arts education that in-

cludes art, business, health sciences, music, teacher preparation, and preprofessional studies. There are 3 undergraduate schools and 1 graduate school. In addition to regional accreditation, UNCP has baccalaureate program accreditation with CSWE, NASM, and NCATE. The library contains 335,176 volumes, 698,009 microform items, and 2744 audio/video tapes/CDs/DVDs, and subscribes to 1574 periodicals including electronic. Computerized library services include the card catalog, interlibrary loans, database searching, and Internet access. Special learning facilities include an art gallery, TV station, and a Native American resource center. The 152-acre campus is in a small town 30 miles south of Fayetteville, 100 miles south of Raleigh, and 120 miles east of Charlotte. Including any residence halls, there are 41 buildings.

Student Life: 96% of undergraduates are from North Carolina. Students are from 34 states, 24 foreign countries, and Canada. 90% are from public schools. 48% are white; 25% African American; 22% Native American/Eskimo. The average age of freshmen is 19; all undergraduates, 25. 29% do not continue beyond their first year; 71% remain to graduate.

Housing: 1344 students can be accommodated in college housing, which includes single-sex and coed dorms and on-campus apartments. On-campus housing is guaranteed for the freshman year only, is available on a first-come, first-served basis, and is available on a lottery system for upperclassmen. 68% of students commute. All students may keep cars.

Activities: There are 2 local and 6 national fraternities and 1 local sorority and 7 national sororities. There are 97 groups on campus, including art, band, cheerleading, choir, chorale, chorus, dance, drama, ethnic, gay, honors, international, jazz band, literary magazine, musical theater, newspaper, pep band, political, professional, radio and TV, religious, social, social service, and student government. Popular campus events include the Performing Arts Cultural Series, Miss UNCP Scholarship Pageant, and Pembroke Day.

Sports: Facilities include a 3200-seat gym, an auxiliary gym, a track, tennis courts, a natatorium, weight rooms, a bowling alley, a 1700-seat auditorium, fields for soccer, baseball, and softball, 2 swimming pools, and a wellness center.

Disabled Students: 98% of the campus is accessible. Wheelchair ramps, elevators, special parking, specially equipped rest rooms, special class scheduling, lowered drinking fountains, and lowered telephones are available.

Services: Counseling and information services are available, as is tutoring in every subject. There is a reader service for the blind, remedial math, reading, and writing as well as Americans with Disabilities services.

Campus Safety and Security: Measures include 24-hour foot and vehicle patrol, self-defense education, security escort services, and shuttle buses. There are informal discussions, pamphlets/posters/films, emergency telephones, and lighted pathways/sidewalks.

Programs of Study: UNCP confers B.A., B.S., B.M., B.S.A.S., B.S.N., and B.S.W. degrees. Master's degrees are also awarded. Bachelor's degrees are awarded in BIOLOGICAL SCIENCE (biology/biological science and biotechnology), BUSINESS (accounting and business administration and management), COMMUNICATIONS AND THE ARTS (art, communications, dramatic arts, English, music, musical theater, and Spanish), COMPUTER AND PHYSICAL SCIENCE (chemistry, computer science, mathematics, and physics), EDUCATION (art, athletic training, early childhood, elementary, English, health, mathematics, middle school, music, physical, science, social studies, and special), ENGINEERING AND ENVIRONMENTAL DESIGN (environmental science), HEALTH PROFESSIONS (community health work and nursing), SOCIAL SCIENCE (American Indian studies, criminal justice, history, parks and recreation management, philosophy, physical fitness/movement, political science/government, psychology, religion, social work, and sociology). Education, business administration, and physical sciences are the strongest academically. Education, business, and social science are the largest.

Required: All students are required to complete 120 to 128 total credits, which include 44 semester hours of general education courses, 39 to 69 hours in a major, and a university orientation class before entrance. A minimum GPA of 2.0 must be maintained.

Special: Co-op programs, cross-registration, internships, study abroad in Sweden, a Washington semester, and work-study programs are available. A 3-1 degree program is offered in medical technology. The B.A.-B.S. degree is available in American Indian studies or with the B.S.A.S. degree. In addition, dual majors, credit for military experience, and non-degree study are offered. There are 6 national honor societies, including Phi Beta Kappa, a freshman honors program, and 5 departmental honors programs.

Faculty/Classroom: 95% teach undergraduates. Graduate students teach 2% of introductory courses. The average class size in an introductory lecture is 20; in a laboratory, 14; and in a regular course, 16.

Admissions: 86% of the 2005-2006 applicants were accepted. The SAT scores for the 2005-2006 freshman class were: Verbal--75% below 500, 23% between 500 and 599, and 2% between 600 and 700; Math--69% below 500, 27% between 500 and 599, and 4% between 600 and

700. The ACT scores were 80% below 21, 14% between 21 and 23, 3% between 24 and 26, and 3% between 27 and 28. 23% of the current freshmen were in the top fifth of their class; 49% were in the top two fifths.

Requirements: The SAT or ACT is required. In addition, applicants must be graduates of an accredited secondary school with 20 academic credits, including 4 courses in English, 3 each in math and science, and 2 in history. An essay and an interview are recommended. Students also must submit an official high school transcript that shows their class rank and GPA. The College Opportunity Program is designed to admit a limited number of students who meet most, but not all, of the regular admissions standards. Students who receive the GED should consult an admissions counselor. UNCP requires applicants to be in the upper 50% of their class. A GPA of 2.0 is required. AP and CLEP credits are accepted. Important factors in the admissions decision are advanced placement or honor courses, recommendations by school officials, and evidence of special talent.

Procedure: Freshmen are admitted to all sessions. Entrance exams should be taken during the junior and senior years. There is a deferred admissions plan and a rolling admissins plan. Applications should be filed by July 15 for fall entry, December 1 for spring entry, and May 15 for summer entry. The fall 2005 application fee was $40. Notification is sent on a rolling basis.

Transfer: 502 transfer students enrolled in 2004-2005. Applicants must have a minimum GPA of 2.0, submit transcripts from high school and from all previous colleges, and be eligible to return to the last institution attended. The SAT and an interview are recommended. 30 of 128 credits required for the bachelor's degree must be completed at UNCP.

Visiting: There are regularly scheduled orientations for prospective students, including open houses in the fall, spring, and winter. There are guides for informal visits and visitors may sit in on classes and stay overnight. To schedule a visit, contact the Office of Admissions.

Financial Aid: In 2005-2006, 84% of all full-time freshmen and 82% of continuing full-time students received some form of financial aid. 74% of all full-time students received need-based aid. The average freshman award was $7237. Need-based scholarships or need-based grants averaged $4006 ($18,560 maximum); need-based self-help aid (loans and jobs) averaged $2724 ($8125 maximum); and other non-need-based awards and non-need-based scholarships averaged $4809 ($21,625 maximum). 8% of undergraduates work part time. Average annual earnings from campus work are $1500. The average financial indebtedness of the 2005 graduate was $14,783. The FAFSA is required. The deadline for filing freshman financial aid applications for fall entry is March 15.

International Students: There are 47 international students enrolled. They must take the TOEFL.

Computers: Wireless access is available. All students may access the system. Students may access the system 1 hour at a time. There are no fees.

Graduates: From July 1, 2004 to June 30, 2005, 581 bachelor's degrees were awarded. The most popular majors were education (17%), business (15%), and social science (13%). In an average class, 20% graduate in 4 years, 12% graduate in 5 years, and 4% graduate in 6 years. 175 companies recruited on campus in 2004-2005.

Admissions Contact: Jacqueline Clark, VC for Enrollment Management. A video is available. E-mail: *admissions@papa.uncp.edu* Web: *www.uncp.edu*

UNIVERSITY OF NORTH CAROLINA AT WILMINGTON E-4
Wilmington, NC 28403-5904

(910) 962-3243
Fax: (910) 962-3038

Full-time: 4028 men, 5563 women	**Faculty:** 492; IIA, -$
Part-time: 338 men, 652 women	**Ph.D.s:** 87%
Graduate: 378 men, 694 women	**Student/Faculty:** 19 to 1
Year: semesters, summer session	**Tuition:** $3695 ($13,630)
Application Deadline: February 1	**Room & Board:** $6412 ($5578)
Freshman Class: 8820 applied, 5377 accepted, 1943 enrolled	
SAT Verbal/Math: 560/574*	**ACT:** 23 **VERY COMPETITIVE**

The University of North Carolina at Wilmington, founded in 1947, is a publicly funded institution offering programs in the liberal arts and sciences, education, and business. It is a part of the University of North Carolina System. There are 4 undergraduate schools and 1 graduate school. In addition to regional accreditation, UNC at Wilmington has baccalaureate program accreditation with NCATE and NLN. The library contains 542,399 volumes, 230,800 microform items, and 69,682 audio/video tapes/CDs/DVDs, and subscribes to 13,683 periodicals including electronic. Computerized library services include the card catalog, interlibrary loans, database searching, Internet access, and laptop Internet portals. Special learning facilities include a radio station, TV station, wildflower preserve, nature preserve, museum of world cultures, and the research vessel Seahawk, used for a marine biology lab and for research. The 661-acre campus is in a suburban area 125 miles southeast of Raleigh. Including any residence halls, there are 84 buildings.

Student Life: 87% of undergraduates are from North Carolina. Others are from 48 states, 36 foreign countries, and Canada. 89% are white. The average age of freshmen is 18; all undergraduates, 22. 14% do not continue beyond their first year; 43% remain to graduate.

Housing: 2364 students can be accommodated in college housing, which includes single-sex and coed dorms, on-campus apartments, and an international student dorm. In addition, there are honors houses. On-campus housing is available on a first-come, first-served basis. 80% of students commute. All students living outside a 1 mile radius from campus may keep cars.

Activities: 7% of men belong to 1 local fraternity and 11 national fraternities; 8% of women belong to 11 national sororities. There are 163 groups on campus, including academic, art, cheerleading, chorale, computers, dance, drama, ethnic, film, gay, honors, international, jazz band, literary magazine, musical theater, newspaper, pep band, political, radio and TV, reader's theater, religious, social, social service, student government, symphony, and team. Popular campus events include Business Week, Greek Week, and Spring Week.

Sports: There are 10 intercollegiate sports for men and 11 for women, and 9 intramural sports for men and 9 for women. Facilities include a 6000-seat coliseum, an Olympic-size swimming pool and separate diving tank, a track and field complex, and basketball, tennis, and racquetball courts.

Disabled Students: 98% of the campus is accessible. Wheelchair ramps, elevators, special parking, specially equipped rest rooms, special class scheduling, lowered drinking fountains, and lowered telephones are available.

Services: Counseling and information services are available, as is tutoring in most subjects. There is a reader service for the blind, and remedial math, reading, and writing.

Campus Safety and Security: Measures include 24-hour foot and vehicle patrol, self-defense education, security escort services, and shuttle buses. There are informal discussions, pamphlets/posters/films, emergency telephones, lighted pathways/sidewalks, Rape Awareness Defense (RAD) training, and counseling; the University police services are available.

Programs of Study: UNC at Wilmington confers B.A., B.S., B.F.A., and B.S.W. degrees. Master's degrees are also awarded. Bachelor's degrees are awarded in BIOLOGICAL SCIENCE (biology/biological science, marine biology, and marine science), BUSINESS (accounting, banking and finance, business administration and management, business economics, business systems analysis, and marketing/retailing/merchandising), COMMUNICATIONS AND THE ARTS (art history and appreciation, creative writing, dramatic arts, English, film arts, French, music, music performance, Spanish, speech/debate/rhetoric, and studio art), COMPUTER AND PHYSICAL SCIENCE (chemistry, computer science, geology, mathematics, physics, and statistics), EDUCATION (athletic training, early childhood, elementary, middle school, music, physical, secondary, and special), ENGINEERING AND ENVIRONMENTAL DESIGN (environmental science), HEALTH PROFESSIONS (clinical science and nursing), SOCIAL SCIENCE (anthropology, criminal justice, economics, geography, German area studies, history, parks and recreation management, philosophy, political science/government, psychology, religion, social work, sociology, and therapeutic riding). Psychology is the largest.

Required: Students may qualify for the bachelor's degree by successfully completing the basic studies requirements, an approved course of study in an academic major, a minimum of 124 semester hours of credit, and a minimum quality point average of 2.0. The final 31 semester hours of course credit, including the final 15 semester hours in the major, must be completed at the University of North Carolina at Wilmington.

Special: UNC at Wilmington offers short-term internships, study abroad in several countries, and work-study programs. Dual majors may be pursued if requirements are met, and credit is given for military experience. There are 13 national honor societies, a freshman honors program, and 31 departmental honors programs.

Faculty/Classroom: 57% of faculty are male; 43%, female. 8% do research. The average class size in a regular course is 35.

Admissions: 61% of the 2005-2006 applicants were accepted. The SAT scores for the 2005-2006 freshman class were: Verbal--19% below 500, 57% between 500 and 599, 22% between 600 and 700, and 2% above 700; Math--11% below 500, 59% between 500 and 599, 28% between 600 and 700, and 2% above 700. The ACT scores were 20% below 21, 40% between 21 and 23, 27% between 24 and 26, 9% between 27 and 28, and 4% above 28. 49% of the current freshmen were in the top fifth of their class; 85% were in the top two fifths.

Requirements: The SAT or ACT is required; the SAT is preferred. The ACT Optional Writing test is also required. In addition, graduation from an accredited secondary school or the GED is required for admission. High school courses must include 4 years of English, 4 years of math (algebra I, II, and geometry),and a math beyond Algebra II, 3 units of science (1 year each of biology, physical science, and a lab course), 2 years of social studies including 1 year of U.S. history and 2 years of a foreign language. A GPA of 2.0 is required. AP and CLEP credits are accepted.

Procedure: Freshmen are admitted fall and summer. Entrance exams should be taken during the junior or senior year. There is an early admissions plan. Early decision applications should be filed by November 1; regular applications, by February 1 for fall entry and May 1 for summer entry, along with a $45 fee. Notification of early decision is sent January 20; regular decision, April 1. A waiting list is an active part of the admissions procedure.Applications are accepted on-line.

Transfer: 1228 transfer students enrolled in 2004-2005. Transfer students must have a minimum GPA of 2.2 and be eligible to return to the institution last attended. Prior to admission, transfer applicants must have successfully completed 1 year of freshman-level English, 1 unit of college-level math and have completed at least 24 semester hours or 36 quarter hours of credit. 31 of 124 credits required for the bachelor's degree must be completed at UNC at Wilmington.

Visiting: There are regularly scheduled orientations for prospective students. There are guides for informal visits. To schedule a visit, contact the Admissions Office at *admissions@uncw.edu.*

Financial Aid: In 2005-2006, 54% of all full-time freshmen and 59% of continuing full-time students received some form of financial aid. 30% of all full-time students received need-based aid. The average freshman award was $10,002. Need-based scholarships or need-based grants averaged $3761 ($14,291 maximum); need-based self-help aid (loans and jobs) averaged $3159 ($9125 maximum); and non-need-based athletic scholarships averaged $5488 ($20,420 maximum). 3% of undergraduates work part time. Average annual earnings from campus work are $1594. The average financial indebtedness of the 2005 graduate was $15,620. The FAFSA is required. The priority date for freshman financial aid applications for fall entry is March 1. The deadline for filing freshman financial aid applications for fall entry is December 31.

International Students: There are 56 international students enrolled. The school actively recruits these students. They must take the TOEFL. The SAT (with acceptable socres) is accepted if the TOEFL is not available.

Computers: UNCW has a laptop program that provides students with access to 35 laptops equipped with wireless cards. These are available in distributed locations such as the library, the union, and the technology support center. Students' personal computers are signed onto the network in their freshman year. Students who live off of campus also have access to wireless and network services. All students may access the system from 8 A.M. to 11 P.M. at on-campus clusters and 24-hours daily via the Internet. There are no time limits and no fees. It is strongly recommended that all students have a personal computer.

Graduates: From July 1, 2004 to June 30, 2005, 2206 bachelor's degrees were awarded. The most popular majors were speech communication (7%), psychology (7%), and biology (5%). In an average class, 42% graduate in 4 years or less, 62% graduate in 5 years or less, and 64% graduate in 6 years or less. 153 companies recruited on campus in 2004-2005. Of the 2004 graduating class, 16% were enrolled in graduate school within 6 months of graduation.

Admissions Contact: Terrence M. Curran, Associate Provost of Academic Affairs. A video is available. Web: *uncw.edu*

WAKE FOREST UNIVERSITY   C-2
Winston-Salem, NC 27109-7305   (336) 758-5201

Full-time: 2026 men, 2112 women	Faculty: 372; IIA, ++$
Part-time: 71 men, 54 women	Ph.D.s: 90%
Graduate: 1325 men, 1128 women	Student/Faculty: 11 to 1
Year: semesters, summer session	Tuition: $30,210
Application Deadline: January 15	Room & Board: $8080
Freshman Class: 7484 applied, 2882 accepted, 1120 enrolled	
SAT: required	**MOST COMPETITIVE**

Wake Forest University, established in 1834, is a private institution offering undergraduate programs in the liberal arts and sciences, education, and preprofessional fields. There are 2 undergraduate and 5 graduate schools. In addition to regional accreditation, Wake Forest has baccalaureate program accreditation with AACSB and NCATE. The 3 libraries contain 1,788,033 volumes, 2,390,965 microform items, and 28,238 audio/video tapes/CDs/DVDs, and subscribe to 15,071 periodicals including electronic. Computerized library services include the card catalog, interlibrary loans, database searching, and Internet access. Special learning facilities include a learning resource center, art gallery, radio station, TV station, and fine arts center, anthropology museum, and laser research facility. The 340-acre campus is in a suburban area 4 miles northwest of Winston-Salem. Including any residence halls, there are 43 buildings.

Student Life: 72% of undergraduates are from out of state, mostly the South. Others are from 48 states, 26 foreign countries, and Canada. 69% are from public schools. 85% are white. 60% are Protestant; 21% Catholic; 14% Muslim, Hindu, Buddhist, Mormon, and Greek Orthodox. The average age of freshmen is 18; all undergraduates, 21. 7% do not continue beyond their first year; 88% remain to graduate.

Housing: 3024 students can be accommodated in college housing, which includes coed dormitories and on-campus apartments. In addition, there are honors houses, language houses, and special-interest

houses. On-campus housing is guaranteed for all 4 years. 71% of students live on campus; of those, 75% remain on campus on weekends. All students may keep cars.

Activities: 33% of men belong to 14 national fraternities; 53% of women belong to 9 national sororities. There are 125 groups on campus, including art, band, cheerleading, choir, chorale, chorus, computers, dance, debate, drama, drill team, environmental, ethnic, film, gay, honors, international, jazz band, literary magazine, marching band, musical theater, newspaper, orchestra, pep band, photography, political, professional, radio and TV, religious, social, social service, student government, symphony, women's, and yearbook. Popular campus events include Convocation, Moravian Christmas Love Feast, and Family Weekend.

Sports: There are 8 intercollegiate sports for men and 8 for women, and 20 intramural sports for men and 16 for women. Facilities include 7 playing fields, 4 indoor basketball courts, a swimming pool, a track, racquetball and tennis courts, an exercise room and weight room, an indoor tennis center, a fitness center, a soccer complex, a golf practice complex, and a cross-country course.

Disabled Students: 85% of the campus is accessible. Wheelchair ramps, elevators, special parking, specially equipped rest rooms, special class scheduling, lowered drinking fountains, and lowered telephones are available.

Services: Counseling and information services are available, as is tutoring in some subjects, including primarily in the sciences, math, and foreign languages. There is a reader service for the blind. The Learning Assistance Center offers instructional support and skill development in writing, reading, and study strategies.

Campus Safety and Security: Measures include 24-hour foot and vehicle patrol, self-defense education, security escort services, and shuttle buses. There are informal discussions, pamphlets/posters/films, emergency telephones, lighted pathways/sidewalks, and There are gatehouses at 2 of the university's 3 entrances that operate from 10 P.M. to 6 A.M. During those hours, the third entrance is closed.

Programs of Study: Wake Forest confers B.A. and B.S. degrees. Master's and doctoral degrees are also awarded. Bachelor's degrees are awarded in BIOLOGICAL SCIENCE (biology/biological science), BUSINESS (accounting, banking and finance, and business administration and management), COMMUNICATIONS AND THE ARTS (art, classics, communications, dramatic arts, English, French, German, Greek, Latin, music, and Spanish), COMPUTER AND PHYSICAL SCIENCE (chemistry, computer science, mathematics, and physics), EDUCATION (education), HEALTH PROFESSIONS (exercise science), SOCIAL SCIENCE (anthropology, economics, history, philosophy, political science/government, psychology, religion, and sociology). Business, communication, and political science are the largest.

Required: To graduate, students must complete a total of 120 credits with a minimum GPA of 2.0. The number of hours required in the major varies. All students must take 1 semester of a writing seminar, a first-year seminar, and 1 course in foreign language literature. In addition, students must complete 3 courses each in natural sciences and math, social and behavioral sciences, and history, religion, and philosophy; 2 courses in literature; and 1 course in fine arts.

Special: Wake Forest offers cooperative programs in engineering with any other schools of engineering accredited by ABET; political science majors who minor in Latin American studies have the opportunity to pursue a 5-year cooperative B.A./M.A. program with Georgetown University. Cross-registration with Salem College is available for full-time students. Wake Forest sponsors study-abroad semester programs in 7 countries. Other special opportunities include internships, work-study programs, dual majors, and a minor in entrepreneurship and social enterprise. Students can also be certified in Spanish language translation and interpreting. An accerlerated degree program may be arranged in medical technology. Interdisciplinary honors courses and the Open Curriculum program are available for selected students. Wake Forest owns residences in London, Venice, and Vienna where students and professors attend semester-long courses in a variety of disciplines. There are 11 national honor societies, including Phi Beta Kappa, a freshman honors program, and 23 departmental honors programs.

Faculty/Classroom: 66% of faculty are male; 34%, female. All teach undergraduates. No introductory courses are taught by graduate students. The average class size in a regular course is 19.

Admissions: 39% of the 2005-2006 applicants were accepted. The SAT scores for the 2005-2006 freshman class were: Verbal--2% below 500, 13% between 500 and 599, 57% between 600 and 700, and 29% above 700; Math--2% below 500, 11% between 500 and 599, 50% between 600 and 700, and 38% above 700. 83% of the current freshmen were in the top fifth of their class; 97% were in the top two fifths.

Requirements: The SAT is required. In addition, SAT Subject Tests are considered if submitted. Graduation from an accredited secondary school or the GED is required. The school requires 16 academic credits, including 4 credits of English, 3 of math, 2 each of a foreign language, history, and social studies, and 1 of science. 1 credit each of art and music is recommended. All students must submit an essay. AP and CLEP credits are accepted. Important factors in the admissions decision are recommendations by school officials, leadership record, and advanced placement or honor courses.

Procedure: Freshmen are admitted fall and spring. Entrance exams should be taken during the junior year, and at least 1 SAT should be taken during the senior year. There are early decision, early admissions, and deferred admissions plans. Early decision applications should be filed by November 15; regular applications, by January 15 for fall entry and November 15 for spring entry. Notification of early decision is sent December 15; regular decision, April 1. 382 early decision candidates were accepted for the 2005-2006 class. A waiting list is an active part of the admissions procedure. Applications are accepted on-line.

Transfer: 51 transfer students enrolled in 2004-2005. Transfer students must have a minimum GPA of 2.0 on all college work attempted. The SAT is required. 60 of 120 credits required for the bachelor's degree must be completed at Wake Forest.

Visiting: There are regularly scheduled orientations for prospective students, including group information sessions and tours by appointment. There are guides for informal visits and visitors may sit in on classes and stay overnight. To schedule a visit, contact the Admissions Office.

Financial Aid: In 2005-2006, 38% of all full-time freshmen and 35% of continuing full-time students received some form of financial aid. At least 37% of full-time freshmen and 32% of continuing full-time students received need-based aid. The average freshman award was $22,516. Need-based scholarships or need-based grants averaged $17,826; need-based self-help aid (loans and jobs) averaged $7077; institutional non-need-based athletic scholarships averaged $25,426; and other institutional non-need-based awards and non-need-based scholarships averaged $8621. 30% of undergraduates work part time. Average annual earnings from campus work are $2400. The average financial indebtedness of the 2005 graduate was $22,831. Wake Forest is a member of CSS. The CSS/Profile, FAFSA, the state aid form, and noncustodial Profile are required. The priority date for freshman financial aid applications for fall entry is February 1. The priority date for filing freshman financial aid applications for fall entry is February 1; regular freshman applications, March 1.

International Students: In a recent year, there were 43 international students enrolled. Satisfactory scores are required on the written TOEFL and a the SAT.

Computers: Wireless access is available. All new students receive as part of tuition an IBM ThinkPad laptop computer and an all-in-one color printer/scanner/copier. All ThinkPads are equipped with wireless connectivity, which alows students access to the campus high-speed wired and wireless network from all residence hall rooms, classrooms, the campus library, and all common areas. At the beginning of their junior year, students exchange their ThinkPad for an upgraded model and keep the new unit as well as the printer after they graduate. All students have wireless access to the campus network at all times. All students may access the system 24 hours per day. There are no time limits and no fees. All students are required to have PCs. Wake Forest requires an IBM R52 ThinkPad (model for 2005).

Graduates: From July 1, 2004 to June 30, 2005, 953 bachelor's degrees were awarded. The most popular majors were business (12%), political science (11%), and communication (10%). In an average class, 88% graduate in 5 years or less, and 88% graduate in 6 years or less. 160 companies recruited on campus in 2004-2005. Of the 2004 graduating class, 30% were enrolled in graduate school within 6 months of graduation and 60% were employed.

Admissions Contact: Martha B. Allman, Director of Admissions. A video is available. E-mail: *admissions@wfu.edu* Web: *www.wfu.edu*

WARREN WILSON COLLEGE   B-2
Asheville, NC 28815-9000

	(828) 771-2073
	(800) 934-3536; Fax: (828) 298-1440
Full-time: 322 men, 498 women	**Faculty:** 62; IIB, --$
Part-time: 8 men, 4 women	**Ph.D.s:** 92%
Graduate: 21 men, 48 women	**Student/Faculty:** 13 to 1
Year: semesters	**Tuition:** $18,916
Application Deadline: March 15	**Room & Board:** $5466
Freshman Class: 857 applied, 664 accepted, 245 enrolled	
SAT Verbal/Math: 616/567*	**ACT:** 24 **VERY COMPETITIVE**

Warren Wilson College, founded in 1894, is a liberal arts institution affiliated with the Presbyterian Church (U.S.A.) and known for its triad of academics, work, and service. All students work 15 hours per week in jobs related to the operation and maintenance of the college. In exchange, room and board is provided at a low rate. In addition to regional accreditation, Warren Wilson College has baccalaureate program accreditation with CSWE and NCATE. The library contains 107,747 volumes, 33,706 microform items, and 2872 audio/video tapes/CDs/DVDs, and subscribes to 11,076 periodicals including electronic. Computerized library services include the card catalog, interlibrary loans, database searching, and Internet access. Special learning facilities include a learning resource center, art gallery, radio station, and outdoor adventure learning lab.

The 1135-acre campus is in a small town 5 miles east of Asheville. Including any residence halls, there are 62 buildings.

Student Life: 84% of undergraduates are from out of state, mostly the Northeast and middle Atlantic. Students are from 44 states and 8 foreign countries. 74% are from public schools. 91% are white. Most claim no religious affiliation. The average age of freshmen is 18; all undergraduates, 20. 34% do not continue beyond their first year; 46% remain to graduate.

Housing: 700 students can be accommodated in college housing, which includes single-sex and coed dormitories. On-campus housing is guaranteed for all 4 years. 91% of students live on campus; of those, 95% remain on campus on weekends. Upperclassmen may keep cars.

Activities: There are no fraternities or sororities. There are many groups and organizations on campus, including art, chess, choir, chorus, computers, dance, drama, environmental, ethnic, film, gay, honors, international, jazz band, literary magazine, musical theater, newspaper, orchestra, outdoor activities, photography, political, professional, radio and TV, religious, social, socail justice, social service, student government, and yearbook. Popular campus events include International Fair, Work Day, and Service Day.

Sports: There are 6 intercollegiate sports for men and 6 for women, and 5 intramural sports for men and 5 for women. Facilities include 2 gyms, an aquatic center, weight and fitness rooms, tennis courts, playing fields, 25 miles of hiking/biking trails, kayak slalom gates, indoor climbing wall, alpine tower, mountain bike skills area, and outdoor basketball court.

Disabled Students: 90% of the campus is accessible. Wheelchair ramps, elevators, special parking, specially equipped rest rooms, special class scheduling, lowered drinking fountains, lowered telephones, and special housing are available.

Services: Counseling and information services are available, as is tutoring in most subjects. Tutoring is available through the Peer Assistance Center and the Writing Center. ESL tutoring is also available.

Campus Safety and Security: Measures include 24-hour foot and vehicle patrol, security escort services, informal discussions, and pamphlets/posters/films. There are emergency telephones and lighted pathways/sidewalks.

Programs of Study: Warren Wilson College confers B.A. and B.S. degrees. Master's degrees are also awarded. Bachelor's degrees are awarded in AGRICULTURE (environmental studies), BIOLOGICAL SCIENCE (biology/biological science), BUSINESS (business economics), COMMUNICATIONS AND THE ARTS (art, creative writing, English, and Spanish), COMPUTER AND PHYSICAL SCIENCE (chemistry and mathematics), EDUCATION (elementary, English, middle school, and recreation), SOCIAL SCIENCE (anthropology, behavioral science, history, humanities, international studies, philosophy, psychology, social work, sociology, and women's studies). Biology is the strongest academically. Environmental studies, biology, and English are the largest.

Required: To graduate, students must complete a total of 128 semester hours with a minimum GPA of 2.0. Between 32 and 40 hours are required in the student's major. All students must complete 36 hours in the core curriculum. All students must also complete 100 hours of community service over four years. A first-year seminar and college composition are required.

Special: Cross-registration is offered with Mars Hill College and the University of North Carolina at Asheville. Internships related to the major may be arranged. Study-abroad programs in South America, Europe, Japan, and India are available. The college offers an accelerated degree program in education, student-designed majors, nondegree study, and pass/fail options. There are dual majors in history/political science and English/theater arts. Cooperative programs are available in engineering with Washington University in St. Louis and with Duke University.

Faculty/Classroom: 53% of faculty are male; 47%, female. All both teach and do research. No introductory courses are taught by graduate students. The average class size in an introductory lecture is 16; in a laboratory, 15; and in a regular course, 11.

Admissions: 77% of the 2005-2006 applicants were accepted. The SAT scores for the 2005-2006 freshman class were: Verbal--5% below 500, 36% between 500 and 599, 39% between 600 and 700, and 20% above 700; Math--18% below 500, 41% between 500 and 599, 37% between 600 and 700, and 4% above 700. 23% of the current freshmen were in the top fifth of their class; 79% were in the top two fifths. There were 5 National Merit finalists. 2 freshmen graduated first in their class.

Requirements: The SAT or ACT is required, with a satisfactory score on each section of the SAT or a satisfactory score on the ACT. Graduation from an accredited secondary school or the GED is required. Applicants should have a total of 12 academic credits. An essay and an interview are recommended. A GPA of 2.75 is required. AP credits are accepted. Important factors in the admissions decision are advanced placement or honor courses, evidence of special talent, and recommendations by school officials.

Procedure: Freshmen are admitted fall and winter. Entrance exams should be taken by January 20 of the senior year. There are early decision, early admissions, and deferred admissions plans. Early decision applications should be filed by November 15; regular applications, by March 15 for fall entry and November 1 for winter entry. Notification of early decision is sent December 1; regular decision, April 1. 86 early decision candidates were accepted for the 2005-2006 class.

Transfer: 68 transfer students enrolled in 2004-2005. Applicants must have a minimum GPA of 2.75. A year of residence at Warren Wilson is required for graduation. Applicants must be eligible to return to their previous institutions. 32 of 128 credits required for the bachelor's degree must be completed at Warren Wilson College.

Visiting: There are guides for informal visits and visitors may sit in on classes and stay overnight. To schedule a visit, contact the campus visit coordinator.

Financial Aid: In 2005-2006, 95% of all full-time freshmen and 80% of continuing full-time students received some form of financial aid. 64% of full-time freshmen and 56% of continuing full-time students received need-based aid. The average freshman award was $11,344. Need-based scholarships or need-based grants averaged $9045 ($17,050 maximum); need-based self-help aid (loans and jobs) averaged $3224 ($5097 maximum); other non-need-based awards and non-need-based scholarships averaged $3178 ($17,322 maximum); and non-need based loans and work averaged $2983 ($13,400 maximum). 89% of undergraduates work part time. Average annual earnings from campus work are $2472. The average financial indebtedness of the 2005 graduate was $16,211. The FAFSA and the college's own financial statement are required. The priority date for freshman financial aid applications for fall entry is April 1.

International Students: There are 38 international students enrolled. The school actively recruits these students. They must score satisfactorily on the written TOEFL or on the electronic version.

Computers: Wireless access is available. PCs are located in one 30-seat lab and 4 smaller teaching labs. There is wireless access in 3 dorms, the library, and a computer lab. All students may access the system. There are no time limits and no fees. It is strongly recommended that all students have a personal computer.

Graduates: From July 1, 2004 to June 30, 2005, 153 bachelor's degrees were awarded. The most popular majors were environmental studies (16%), biology (12%), and psychology (6%). 40 companies recruited on campus in 2004-2005.

Admissions Contact: Richard Blomgren, Dean of Admission. A video is available. E-mail: rickb@warren-wilson.edu
Web: www.warren-wilson.edu

WESTERN CAROLINA UNIVERSITY   B-3
Cullowhee, NC 28723

	(828) 227-7317
	1-877-WCU4YOU; Fax: (828) 227-7319
Full-time: 2700 men, 2700 women	**Faculty:** 323; IIA, -$
Part-time: 300 men, 500 women	**Ph.D.s:** 80%
Graduate: 600 men, 900 women	**Student/Faculty:** 16 to 1
Year: semesters, summer session	**Tuition:** $3000 ($12,000)
Application Deadline: see profile	**Room & Board:** $4000
Freshman Class: n/av	
SAT: required	**COMPETITIVE**

Western Carolina University, founded in 1889, is a publicly funded institution in the University of North Carolina system. There are 5 undergraduate schools and 1 graduate school. Figures in the above capsule and in this profile are approximate. In addition to regional accreditation, Western has baccalaureate program accreditation with AACSB, ABET, ADA, CSWE, FIDER, NASM, NCATE, and NLN. The library contains 583,694 volumes, 1,352,489 microform items, and 6300 audio/video tapes/CDs/DVDs, and subscribes to 2928 periodicals including electronic. Computerized library services include the card catalog, interlibrary loans, database searching, and Internet access. Special learning facilities include a learning resource center, art gallery, natural history museum, radio station, and a mountain heritage center. The 265-acre campus is in a rural area 160 miles northeast of Atlanta, and 50 miles west of Asheville. Including any residence halls, there are 89 buildings.

Student Life: 91% of undergraduates are from North Carolina. Students are from 40 states, 39 foreign countries, and Canada. 95% are from public schools. 88% are white. The average age of freshmen is 17; all undergraduates, 22. 29% do not continue beyond their first year; 46% remain to graduate.

Housing: 3100 students can be accommodated in college housing, which includes single-sex and coed dorms, on-campus apartments, and married-student housing. In addition, there are honors houses. On-campus housing is guaranteed for all 4 years. 55% of students commute. All students may keep cars.

Activities: 13% of men belong to 12 national fraternities; 11% of women belong to 8 national sororities. There are 91 groups on campus, including art, band, cheerleading, choir, chorale, chorus, computers, dance, drama, drill team, ethnic, film, gay, honors, international, literary magazine, marching band, musical theater, newspaper, pep band, photography, political, professional, radio and TV, religious, social, social service, student government, and yearbook. Popular campus events in-

clude Mountain Heritage Day, Greek Week, and Madrigal Christmas Dinners.

Sports: There are 6 intercollegiate sports for men and 7 for women, and 38 intramural sports for men and 39 for women. Facilities include a football stadium, a baseball diamond, a track/tennis complex, 6 intramural softball and football fields, a soccer field, 5 gyms, a field house, jogging trails, picnic areas, game rooms, a weight training room, a swimming pool, an archery range, a golf driving range, and a golf putting green.

Disabled Students: 90% of the campus is accessible. Wheelchair ramps, elevators, special parking, specially equipped rest rooms, special class scheduling, lowered drinking fountains, and lowered telephones are available.

Services: Counseling and information services are available, as is tutoring in most subjects. There is a reader service for the blind, and remedial math, reading, and writing.

Campus Safety and Security: Measures include 24-hour foot and vehicle patrol, shuttle buses, informal discussions, and pamphlets/posters/films. There are emergency telephones, lighted pathways/sidewalks, and crime-prevention education programs.

Programs of Study: Western confers B.A., B.S., B.F.A., B.S.B.A., B.S.Ed., and B.S.N. degrees. Master's and doctoral degrees are also awarded. Bachelor's degrees are awarded in AGRICULTURE (natural resource management), BIOLOGICAL SCIENCE (biology/biological science, environmental biology, and nutrition), BUSINESS (accounting, banking and finance, business law, entrepreneurial studies, hospitality management services, international business management, management science, marketing and distribution, marketing management, and sports management), COMMUNICATIONS AND THE ARTS (art, communications, dramatic arts, English, French, German, music, Spanish, speech/debate/rhetoric, and studio art), COMPUTER AND PHYSICAL SCIENCE (chemistry, computer science, geology, information sciences and systems, and mathematics), EDUCATION (art, early childhood, elementary, English, foreign languages, mathematics, middle school, music, physical, science, secondary, social science, special, and speech correction), ENGINEERING AND ENVIRONMENTAL DESIGN (construction management, electrical/electronics engineering technology, emergency/disaster science, engineering technology, industrial engineering technology, interior design, manufacturing technology, and preengineering), HEALTH PROFESSIONS (clinical science, emergency medical technologies, environmental health science, medical records administration/services, nursing, predentistry, premedicine, preoptometry, prepharmacy, preveterinary science, and recreation therapy), SOCIAL SCIENCE (anthropology, criminal justice, dietetics, geography, history, liberal arts/general studies, parks and recreation management, philosophy, political science/government, prelaw, psychology, social science, social work, and sociology). Elementary education, nursing, and criminal justice are the largest.

Required: In order to graduate, students must complete a total of 120 to 128 credit hours with a minimum GPA of 2.0. Between 30 and 64 hours are required in the major. All students must fulfill liberal studies requirements in writing, oral communication, wellness, social sciences, physical and biological sciences, math, humanities, history, fine and performing arts, world cultures, the freshman seminar, and 1 course in upper level perspectives outside the major.

Special: WCU offers cooperative education programs in most majors, extensive internship opportunities, work-study programs, accelerated degree programs, B.A.-B.S. degrees, dual majors, a special studies degree, nondegree study, pass/fail options in designated courses, and credit for life experience. Study-abroad programs may be arranged in 38 countries. A joint degree program in electrical engineering with the University of North Carolina-Charlotte is possible. There are 15 national honor societies and a freshman honors program.

Faculty/Classroom: 58% of faculty are male; 42%, female. All teach undergraduates. Graduate students teach 5% of introductory courses. The average class size in an introductory lecture is 27; in a laboratory, 15; and in a regular course, 19.

Admissions: 74% of recent applicants were accepted. 21% of recent freshmen were in the top fifth of their class; 51% were in the top two fifths. There were 4 National Merit finalists and 1 semifinalist in a recent year. 2 freshmen graduated first in their class in a recent year.

Requirements: The SAT is required. Graduation from an accredited secondary school or the GED is required. High school courses must include 4 units of English, 3 each of math and science, 2 of social studies, including 1 of U.S. history, and 2 units of a foreign language. Western requires applicants to be in the upper 25% of their class. A GPA of 2.5 is required. AP and CLEP credits are accepted. Important factors in the admissions decision are advanced placement or honor courses, recommendations by school officials, and evidence of special talent.

Procedure: Freshmen are admitted to all sessions. Entrance exams should be taken during the spring of the junior year or the fall of the senior year. There is an early admissions plan and a rolling admissions plan. Notification is sent on a rolling basis. Applications are accepted online. Check with the school for current application deadlines and fee.

Transfer: 598 transfer students enrolled in a recent year. Tranfer students must have a minimum GPA of 2.0 and meet freshman admissions requirements. 30 of 120 credits required for the bachelor's degree must be completed at Western.

Visiting: There are regularly scheduled orientations for prospective students, consisting of open houses, 2 in fall, 2 in spring, which include registration, a visit to the department of choice, a campus tour, and an athletic event. There are guides for informal visits and visitors may sit in on classes and stay overnight. To schedule a visit, contact the Admissions Office at admiss@email.wcu.edu.

Financial Aid: In a recent year, 71% of all full-time students received some form of financial aid. 47% of all full-time students received need-based aid. The average freshman award was $7493. Need-based scholarships or need-based grants averaged $2620 ($6844 maximum); need-based self-help aid (loans and jobs) averaged $3065 ($8025 maximum); non-need-based athletic scholarships averaged $6576 ($16,173 maximum); other non-need-based awards and non-need-based scholarships averaged $2218 ($14,594 maximum); and non-need based loans including PLUS loans. averaged $5724 ($20,211 maximum). 15% of undergraduates work part time. Average annual earnings from campus work are $1400. The average financial indebtedness of a recent graduate was $16,238. The FAFSA is required. Check with the school for current application deadlines.

International Students: There are 58 international students enrolled a recent year. The school actively recruits these students. They must take the TOEFL or and also take the SAT.

Computers: All students may access the system 24 hours a day. There are no time limits and no fees. All students are required to have personal computers. The school provides required specifications.

Graduates: In a recent year, 1093 bachelor's degrees were awarded. The most popular majors were marketing (7%), criminal justice (7%), and nursing (6%). In an average class, 1% graduate in 3 years or less, 23% graduate in 4 years or less, 46% graduate in 5 years or less, and 46% graduate in 6 years or less. 270 companies recruited on campus in a recent year.

Admissions Contact: Phil Cauley, Admissions Officer.
E-mail: admiss@email.wcu.edu Web: http://www.poweryourmind.com/

WINGATE UNIVERSITY   C-3
Wingate, NC 28174

	(704) 233-8200
	(800) 755-5550; Fax: (704) 233-8110
Full-time: 628 men, 683 women	**Faculty:** 81; IIB, --$
Part-time: 14 men, 16 women	**Ph.D.s:** 93%
Graduate: 113 men, 178 women	**Student/Faculty:** 13 to 1
Year: semesters, summer session	**Tuition:** $16,850
Application Deadline: open	**Room & Board:** $6450
Freshman Class: 1247 applied, 1050 accepted, 371 enrolled	
SAT Verbal/Math: 510/520*	**ACT:** 20 **COMPETITIVE**

Wingate University, founded in 1896, is a private liberal arts institution affiliated with the Baptist State Convention of North Carolina. There are 3 undergraduate and 2 graduate schools. In addition to regional accreditation, Wingate has baccalaureate program accreditation with ACBSP, NASM, and NCATE. The library contains 110,000 volumes, 14,000 microform items, and 5750 audio/video tapes/CDs/DVDs, and subscribes to 560 periodicals including electronic. Computerized library services include the card catalog, interlibrary loans, database searching, and Internet access. Special learning facilities include a learning resource center, art gallery, TV station, student newspaper, and the Center for the Performing Arts. The 330-acre campus is in a small town 25 miles east of Charlotte. Including any residence halls, there are 35 buildings.

Student Life: 58% of undergraduates are from North Carolina. Others are from 35 states, 18 foreign countries, and Canada. 90% are from public schools. 81% are white; 11% African American. 67% are Protestant; 15% Catholic; 12% claim no religious affiliation. The average age of freshmen is 18; all undergraduates, 20. 30% do not continue beyond their first year; 48% remain to graduate.

Housing: 1114 students can be accommodated in college housing, which includes single-sex dorms, on-campus apartments, and married-student housing. On-campus housing is guaranteed for all 4 years. 81% of students live on campus; of those, 60% remain on campus on weekends. Alcohol is not permitted. All students may keep cars.

Activities: 9% of men belong to 4 national fraternities; 10% of women belong to 3 national sororities. There are 45 groups on campus, including academic, art, band, cheerleading, choir, chorale, chorus, computers, dance, drama, ethnic, honors, international, jazz band, literary magazine, musical theater, newspaper, pep band, photography, political, professional, radio and TV, religious, running, social, social service, student government, swimming, and yearbook. Popular campus events include Spring Fling and Fall Festival at campus lake, name-band concerts, and Home Coming.

Sports: There are 8 intercollegiate sports for men and 8 for women, and 17 intramural sports for men and 17 for women. Facilities include an athletic complex with a gym, swimming pool, racquetball courts,

weight room, and tennis courts. The student center has an exercise room, table tennis, pool, and a game room. The University also has a football field and additional practice fields.

Disabled Students: 95% of the campus is accessible. Wheelchair ramps, elevators, special parking, specially equipped rest rooms, special class scheduling, and lowered drinking fountains are available.

Services: Counseling and information services are available, as is tutoring in every subject, and additional academic support is available for students with learning disabilities.

Campus Safety and Security: Measures include 24-hour foot and vehicle patrol, self-defense education, security escort services, and informal discussions. There are pamphlets/posters/films, emergency telephones, and lighted pathways/sidewalks.

Programs of Study: Wingate confers B.A., B.S., B.F.A., B.L.S., and B.M.Ed. degrees. Master's degrees are also awarded. Bachelor's degrees are awarded in BIOLOGICAL SCIENCE (biology/biological science and environmental biology), BUSINESS (accounting, banking and finance, business administration and management, business economics, management information systems, marketing/retailing/merchandising, and sports management), COMMUNICATIONS AND THE ARTS (art, communications, English, fine arts, journalism, media arts, music, music business management, public relations, and Spanish), COMPUTER AND PHYSICAL SCIENCE (applied mathematics, chemistry, computer mathematics, computer science, and mathematics), EDUCATION (art, athletic training, elementary, English, mathematics, middle school, music, physical, reading, and science), ENGINEERING AND ENVIRONMENTAL DESIGN (preengineering), HEALTH PROFESSIONS (predentistry, premedicine, prepharmacy, preveterinary science, and sports medicine), SOCIAL SCIENCE (American studies, history, human services, law, liberal arts/general studies, parks and recreation management, philosophy, prelaw, psychology, religion, and sociology). Biological sciences, history, and English are the strongest academically. Business, athletic training, and communications are the largest.

Required: To graduate, students must complete a minimum of 125 credit hours with a GPA of 2.0. At least 30 hours must be completed in the student's major. All students must take core courses in English composition, literature, religion, fine arts, history, social sciences, foreign language, math, lab science, fitness and wellness, phys ed, and freshman experience.

Special: Cross-registration through the Charlotte Area Education Consortium and Army and Air Force ROTC programs, internships, a liberal studies degree, B.A.-B.S. degrees, and nondegree study are available. Wingate conducts foreign study semesters in London, Denmark, and China. The school also sponsors Winternational, a semester seminar with a 10-day trip to a foreign country for which students earn academic credit at little personal cost. Dual majors are offered in biology and education, history and education, art and education, English and education, math and education, and chemistry and business. There are 9 national honor societies and a freshman honors program.

Faculty/Classroom: 61% of faculty are male; 39%, female. All teach undergraduates. No introductory courses are taught by graduate students. The average class size in an introductory lecture is 26; in a laboratory, 15; and in a regular course, 13.

Admissions: 84% of the 2005-2006 applicants were accepted. The SAT scores for the 2005-2006 freshman class were: Verbal--50% below 500, 37% between 500 and 599, 13% between 600 and 700, and 1% above 700; Math--38% below 500, 42% between 500 and 599, 19% between 600 and 700, and 1% above 700. The ACT scores were 38% below 21, 23% between 21 and 23, 23% between 24 and 26, 10% between 27 and 28, and 7% above 28. 25% of the current freshmen were in the top fifth of their class; 41% were in the top two fifths.

Requirements: The SAT or ACT is required. In addition, graduation from an accredited secondary school or the GED is required. High school curriculum must include 4 courses in English, 3 in math, 2 each in history and science, and 1 in social studies. 2 courses in a foreign language are recommended. An essay is required of all applicants, and an interview is recommended in some cases. A GPA of 2.7 is required. AP and CLEP credits are accepted. Important factors in the admissions decision are advanced placement or honor courses, leadership record, and recommendations by school officials.

Procedure: Freshmen are admitted fall, spring, and summer. Entrance exams should be taken in spring of the junior year or fall of the senior year. Application deadlines are open. The fall 2005 application fee was $30. Applications are accepted on-line.

Transfer: 78 transfer students enrolled in 2004-2005. Applicants must have a minimum GPA of 2.0 and must be eligible to return to the institution last attended. The SAT or ACT is required if a student has been out of high school for less than 5 years or has fewer than 24 transferable hours. An interview may be recommended in some cases. 30 of 125 credits required for the bachelor's degree must be completed at Wingate.

Visiting: There are regularly scheduled orientations for prospective students, including Saturday Preview Day 4 times a year, campus tours, and presentations of travel programs, academic life, athletics, and student life. New student orientation occurs 4 days prior to opening of school each fall. There are guides for informal visits and visitors may sit in on classes and stay overnight. To schedule a visit, contact the Admissions Office at (704) 233-8201 or *admit@wingate.edu*.

Financial Aid: In 2005-2006, 97% of all full-time freshmen and 96% of continuing full-time students received some form of financial aid. 56% of full-time freshmen and 49% of continuing full-time students received need-based aid. The average freshman award was $11,582. Need-based scholarships or need-based grants averaged $3021; need-based self-help aid (loans and jobs) averaged $863; non-need-based athletic scholarships averaged $5330; and other non-need-based awards and non-need-based scholarships averaged $4881. 22% of undergraduates work part time. Average annual earnings from campus work are $1200. The average financial indebtedness of the 2005 graduate was $18,759. The FAFSA is required. The deadline for filing freshman financial aid applications for fall entry was May 1.

International Students: There are 40 international students enrolled. They must take the TOEFL and also take the SAT or the ACT.

Computers: Wireless access is available. The library, the student center, and student housing are wired with DSL for web access, some areas also have a wireless environment. All students may access the system. Student portal is not available from 10:00pm to 12:00pm. Internet access 24 hrs 7 days a week. There are no time limits. The fee is $100.00 per term for residential students--$50.00 per term for commuters.

Graduates: From July 1, 2004 to June 30, 2005, 247 bachelor's degrees were awarded. The most popular majors were business administration (22%), sport management (8%), and athletic training (6%). In an average class, 34% graduate in 4 years or less, 15% graduate in 5 years or less, and 51% graduate in 6 years or less. 45 companies recruited on campus in 2004-2005. Of the 2004 graduating class, 20% were enrolled in graduate school within 6 months of graduation and 80% were employed.

Admissions Contact: Rhett Brown, Dean of Admissions. A video is available. E-mail: *admit@wingate.edu* Web: *www.wingate.edu*

WINSTON-SALEM STATE UNIVERSITY   C-2

Winston-Salem, NC 27110

(336) 750-2070
(800) 257-4052; Fax: (336) 750-2079

Full-time: 1075 men, 2240 women	**Faculty:** 194; IIB, +$
Part-time: 180 men, 440 women	**Ph.D.s:** 64%
Graduate: 45 men, 130 women	**Student/Faculty:** 17 to 1
Year: semesters, summer session	**Tuition:** $3650 ($11,900)
Application Deadline: open	**Room & Board:** $5310
Freshman Class: n/av	
SAT or ACT: required	**LESS COMPETITIVE**

Winston-Salem State University, founded in 1892, is a state-supported liberal arts institution offering undergraduate programs through divisions of arts and sciences, business and economics, education, and nursing and allied health. Figures in the above capsule and profile are approximate. In addition to regional accreditation, WSSU has baccalaureate program accreditation with NASM, NCATE, and NLN. The library contains 196,168 volumes, 246,029 microform items, and 2198 audio/video tapes/CDs/DVDs, and subscribes to 1010 periodicals including electronic. Computerized library services include the card catalog, interlibrary loans, and database searching. Special learning facilities include a learning resource center, art gallery, radio station, TV station, a PLATO lab, and an enrichment center. The 94-acre campus is in a suburban area in Winston-Salem. Including any residence halls, there are 36 buildings.

Student Life: 92% of undergraduates are from North Carolina. Others are from 34 states and 7 foreign countries. 82% are African American; 16% white. The average age of freshmen is 19; all undergraduates, 24. 23% do not continue beyond their first year; 10% remain to graduate.

Housing: 1228 students can be accommodated in college housing, which includes single-sex and coed dormitories. On-campus housing is guaranteed for the freshman year only and is available on a first-come, first-served basis. 59% of students commute. Alcohol is not permitted. All students may keep cars.

Activities: There are 70 groups on campus, including art, band, cheerleading, choir, computers, dance, drama, drill team, ethnic, honors, international, jazz band, marching band, newspaper, photography, political, radio and TV, social, student government, and yearbook.

Sports: There are 4 intercollegiate sports for men and 5 for women. Facilities include 2 gyms, tennis courts, an indoor swimming pool, and a track.

Disabled Students: 90% of the campus is accessible. Wheelchair ramps, elevators, special parking, specially equipped rest rooms, lowered drinking fountains, and lowered telephones are available.

Services: Counseling and information services are available, as is tutoring in most subjects. There is remedial math, reading, and writing.

Campus Safety and Security: Measures include 24-hour foot and vehicle patrol, informal discussions, pamphlets/posters/films, and emergency telephones. There are lighted pathways/sidewalks.

Programs of Study: WSSU confers B.A., B.S., B.S.App.Sci., B.S.Med.Tech., B.S.N., and B.S.P.T. degrees. Master's degrees are also awarded. Bachelor's degrees are awarded in BIOLOGICAL SCIENCE (biology/biological science), BUSINESS (accounting, business administration and management, management information systems, and sports management), COMMUNICATIONS AND THE ARTS (art, communications, English, music business management, and Spanish), COMPUTER AND PHYSICAL SCIENCE (chemistry, computer science, and mathematics), EDUCATION (elementary, music, physical, and special), HEALTH PROFESSIONS (medical technology, nursing, physical therapy, and recreation therapy), SOCIAL SCIENCE (economics, history, political science/government, psychology, public administration, and sociology). Phys ed, computer science, and math are the strongest academically. Nursing, business administration, and education are the largest.

Required: Students must complete a minimum of 121 semester hours, with 40 of these hours in upper-level courses, and must maintain an overall minimum GPA of 2.0. All students must also complete the general education core requirement, which includes courses in English composition, social sciences, math and natural sciences, humanities, and phys ed or military science.

Special: Opportunities are provided for cooperative programs, internships, work-study programs, a B.A.-B.S. degree, a general studies degree, and credit for military experience. The nursing division offers flexible scheduling for employed RNs. There is a freshman honors program.

Faculty/Classroom: 44% of faculty are male; 56%, female. All teach undergraduates. The average class size in an introductory lecture is 60; in a laboratory, 25; and in a regular course, 43.

Admissions: 77% of the 2005-2006 applicants were accepted.

Requirements: The SAT or ACT is required. Graduation from an accredited secondary school is required; a GED will be accepted. Applicants should submit an academic record including 4 credits in English, 3 each in math and science, 2 in a foreign language, and 1 each in U.S. history, social studies, and phys ed and health. A GPA of 2.0 is required. AP and CLEP credits are accepted. Important factors in the admissions decision are advanced placement or honor courses, leadership record, and recommendations by school officials.

Procedure: Freshmen are admitted to all sessions. Entrance exams should be taken in the summer or early fall of the senior year in high school. There are early admissions, deferred admissions, and rolling admissions plans. Application deadlines are open. Applications are accepted on-line. The fall 2005 application fee was $30.

Transfer: 335 transfer students enrolled in a recent year. Transfer applicants must submit official transcripts from all colleges previously attended, showing no grade lower than C. No more than 64 semester hours (96 quarter hours) will be accepted for transfer. Those applicants transferring fewer than 29 credits will be admitted as freshmen and must meet all freshman admission requirements. 30 of 121 credits required for the bachelor's degree must be completed at WSSU.

Visiting: There are regularly scheduled orientations for prospective students, including summer and fall orientation. There are guides for informal visits and visitors may sit in on classes. To schedule a visit, contact Gilbert Wright in the Admissions Office.

Financial Aid: In a recent year, 81% of all full-time freshmen and 80% of continuing full-time students received some form of financial aid. 63% of full-time freshmen and 86% of continuing full-time students received need-based aid. Need-based scholarships or need-based grants averaged $2381; need-based self-help aid (loans and jobs) averaged $1260; non-need-based athletic scholarships averaged $3562; and other non-need-based awards and non-need-based scholarships averaged $2125. The average financial indebtedness of a recent graduate was $10,600. WSSU is a member of CSS. The CSS/Profile or FFS and the college's own financial statement are required. Check with the school for application deadlines.

International Students: They must score satisfactorily on the written TOEFL.

Computers: All students may access the system. There are no time limits. The $20 fee is included in tuition.

Graduates: In a recent year, 496 bachelor's degrees were awarded. The most popular majors were nursing (24%), business administration (17%), and psychology (6%). In an average class, 20% graduate in 4 years or less, 38% graduate in 5 years or less, and 80% graduate in 6 years or less.

Admissions Contact: Daniel Lovette, Vice Chancellor of Enrollment Management. A video is available. E-mail: *lovetted@wssu.edu* Web: *www.wssu.edu*

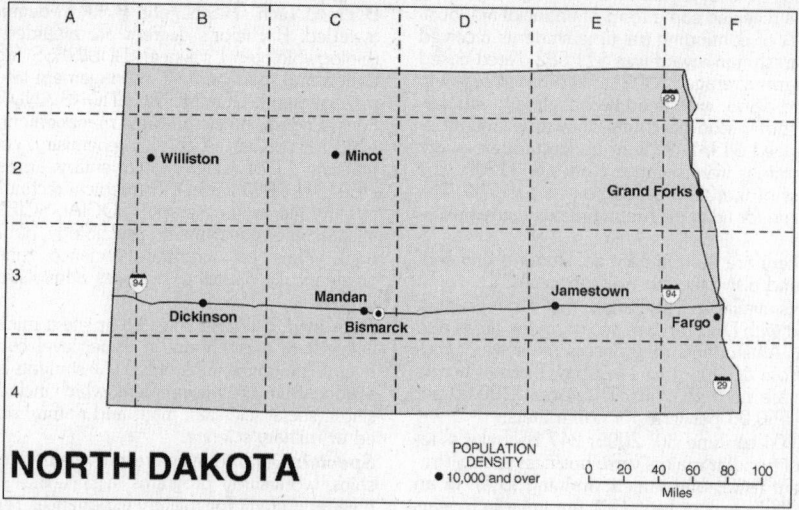

NORTH DAKOTA

POPULATION DENSITY
● 10,000 and over

0 20 40 60 80 100
Miles

DICKINSON STATE UNIVERSITY

B-3

Dickinson, ND 58601-4896

(701) 483-2175
(800) 279-4295; Fax: (701) 483-2409

Full-time: 782 men, 973 women
Part-time: 279 men, 482 women
Graduate: none
Year: semesters, summer session
Application Deadline: August 15
Freshman Class: n/av
SAT Verbal/Math: 460/490*

Faculty: 79
Ph.D.s: 55%
Student/Faculty: 22 to 1
Tuition: $4153 ($9683)
Room & Board: $3694

ACT: 22   **NONCOMPETITIVE**

Dickinson State University is a public, regional institution offering undergraduate programs in teacher education, the liberal arts, business, health sciences, agriculture, and computer science. There is opportunity for pre-professional study and vocational training in selected areas. There are 2 undergraduate schools. In addition to regional accreditation, DSU has baccalaureate program accreditation with NCATE and NLN. The library contains 91,870 volumes, 8941 microform items, and 5493 audio/video tapes/CDs/DVDs, and subscribes to 1748 periodicals including electronic. Computerized library services include the card catalog, interlibrary loans, and database searching. Special learning facilities include a learning resource center and art gallery. The 100-acre campus is in a rural area 100 miles west of Bismarck. Including any residence halls, there are 15 buildings.

Student Life: 70% of undergraduates are from North Dakota. Others are from 34 states, 20 foreign countries, and Canada. 95% are from public schools. 76% are white. 50% are Catholic; 50% Protestant. The average age of freshmen is 19; all undergraduates, 22. 2% do not continue beyond their first year; 25% remain to graduate.

Housing: 478 students can be accommodated in college housing, which includes single-sex and coed dorms and married-student housing. In addition, there are honors houses. On-campus housing is guaranteed for the freshman year only and is available on a first-come, first-served basis. 70% of students commute. Alcohol is not permitted. All students may keep cars.

Activities: There are no fraternities or sororities. There are 38 groups on campus, including art, band, cheerleading, choir, chorale, chorus, computers, dance, drama, drill team, ethnic, forensics, honors, international, jazz band, literary magazine, marching band, musical theater, newspaper, pep band, political, professional, religious, social, and student government. Popular campus events include Winter, Spring, and Back to School Weeks, and Family Weekend.

Sports: There are 9 intercollegiate sports for men and 8 for women, and 5 intramural sports for men and 3 for women. Facilities include a gym, an outdoor stadium, an indoor/outdoor rodeo arena, and an indoor track.

Disabled Students: 90% of the campus is accessible. Wheelchair ramps, elevators, special parking, specially equipped rest rooms, special class scheduling, lowered drinking fountains, and lowered telephones are available.

Services: Counseling and information services are available, as is tutoring in every subject. There is a reader service for the blind, and remedial math, reading, and writing.

Campus Safety and Security: Measures include pamphlets/posters/films, lighted pathways/sidewalks, and 10-hour-a-day security.

Programs of Study: DSU confers B.A., B.S., B.A.S.T., B.S.E., B.S.N., and B.U.S. degrees. Associate degrees are also awarded. Bachelor's degrees are awarded in AGRICULTURE (agricultural business management), BIOLOGICAL SCIENCE (biology/biological science), BUSINESS (accounting, business administration and management, and personnel management), COMMUNICATIONS AND THE ARTS (communications, English, fine arts, journalism, music, Spanish, and speech/debate/rhetoric), COMPUTER AND PHYSICAL SCIENCE (chemistry, computer programming, computer science, earth science, and mathematics), EDUCATION (art, business, early childhood, elementary, middle school, music, science, and secondary), HEALTH PROFESSIONS (nursing), SOCIAL SCIENCE (geography, history, political science/government, social work, and sociology). Elementary education, math, and business are the strongest academically. Education, business, and nursing are the largest.

Required: To graduate, students must complete 128 semester hours, 36 in the major, with a minimum GPA of 2.0. General education requirements include 10 hours in scientific inquiry, including 9 hours each in expressions of human civilizations, understanding human civilization, and communication, 2 hours in phys ed, and 1 computer science course.

Special: DSU offers a co-op program in social work with the University of North Dakota and in agriculture with North Dakota State University. An additional co-op program exists with Bismarck State College and Williston State College. Cross-registration is available within the North Dakota University System. Internships in business and social work, study abroad in 3 countries, credit for life experience, and pass/fail options are available. Student-designed majors are possible through the Bachelor of University Studies program. There are 5 national honor societies, including Phi Beta Kappa, and a freshman honors program.

Faculty/Classroom: 70% of faculty are male; 30%, female. All teach undergraduates and 5% do research. The average class size in an introductory lecture is 40; in a laboratory, 25; and in a regular course, 20.

Admissions: The SAT scores for the 2005-2006 freshman class were: Verbal--48% below 500, 45% between 500 and 599, and 6% between 600 and 700; Math--51% below 500, 39% between 500 and 599, and 9% between 600 and 700. The ACT scores were 51% below 21, 25% between 21 and 23, 15% between 24 and 26, 3% between 27 and 28, and 3% above 28. 17% of the current freshmen were in the top fifth of their class; 42% were in the top two fifths.

Requirements: The SAT or ACT is required; the ACT is preferred. Graduation from an accredited secondary school is recommended. The GED is accepted. Students must have 20 academic credits. An essay is not required. AP and CLEP credits are accepted.

Procedure: Freshmen are admitted to all sessions. Entrance exams should be taken in the spring before fall entrance. There is an early admissions plan and a rolling admissions plan. Applications should be filed by August 15 for fall entry, January 1 for spring entry, and May 15 for summer entry, along with a $35 fee. The college accepts all applicants. Notification is sent on a rolling basis. Applications are accepted on-line.

Transfer: 299 transfer students enrolled in a recent year. Transfer students must have a minimum GPA of 2.0. The ACT is preferred, but applicants may submit SAT scores. 32 of 128 credits required for the bachelor's degree must be completed at DSU.

Visiting: There are regularly scheduled orientations for prospective students, consisting of two 2-day orientations and two 1-day sessions in July and August. There are guides for informal visits and visitors may sit in on classes and stay overnight. To schedule a visit, contact the Office of Admissions and Academic Records at *dsu.hawks@dsu.nodak.edu.*

Financial Aid: 63% of all full-time students received need-based aid. The average freshman award was $8726. Need-based scholarships or need-based grants averaged $3480; need-based self-help aid (loans and jobs) averaged $3664; and other non-need-based awards and non-need-based scholarships averaged $1582. 56% of undergraduates work part time. Average annual earnings from campus work are $1164. The average financial indebtedness of the 2005 graduate was $17,125. The FAFSA is required. The priority date for freshman financial aid applications for fall entry is March 15. The deadline for filing freshman financial aid applications for fall entry is open.

International Students: There are 143 international students enrolled. The school actively recruits these students. A satisfactory score is required on the written TOEFL.

Computers: Wireless access is available. All students may access the system. There are no time limits and no fees.

Graduates: From July 1, 2004 to June 30, 2005, 329 bachelor's degrees were awarded. In an average class, 8% graduate in 4 years or less, 19% graduate in 5 years or less, and 25% graduate in 6 years or less. 55 companies recruited on campus in 2004-2005.

Admissions Contact: Marshall Melbye, Director of Admissions and Academic Records. E-mail: *dsu.hawk@dsu.nodak.edu*
Web: *www.dickinsonstate.com*

JAMESTOWN COLLEGE   E-3

Jamestown, ND 58405

(701) 252-3467, ext. 2548
(800) 336-2554; Fax: (701) 253-4318

Full-time: 428 men, 532 women	Faculty: 58; IIB, --$
Part-time: 28 men, 38 women	Ph.D.s: 56%
Graduate: none	Student/Faculty: 17 to 1
Year: semesters, summer session	Tuition: $10,000
Application Deadline: open	Room & Board: $4130
Freshman Class: 937 applied, 907 accepted, 270 enrolled	
ACT: 22	NONCOMPETITIVE

Jamestown College, founded in 1883, is a private, nonprofit institution affiliated with the Presbyterian Church (U.S.A.) Its emphases are on the liberal arts, business, arts, health science, music, religious studies, and teacher preparation. In addition to regional accreditation, Jamestown College has baccalaureate program accreditation with IACBE and NLN. The library contains 112,169 volumes, 9000 microform items, and 5518 audio/video tapes/CDs/DVDs, and subscribes to 18,610 periodicals including electronic. Computerized library services include the card catalog, interlibrary loans, database searching, and Internet access. Special learning facilities include a learning resource center and art gallery. The 110-acre campus is in a small town The campus is located, 100 miles west of Fargo, 350 miles west of Minneapolis. Including any residence halls, there are 25 buildings.

Student Life: 58% of undergraduates are from North Dakota. Others are from 28 states, 10 foreign countries, and Canada. 92% are white. 53% are Protestant; 22% Catholic; 19% claim no religious affiliation. The average age of freshmen is 18; all undergraduates, 21. 32% do not continue beyond their first year; 59% remain to graduate.

Housing: 704 students can be accommodated in college housing, which includes coed dorms and on-campus apartments. On-campus housing is guaranteed for the freshman year only, is available on a first-come, first-served basis, and is available on a lottery system for upperclassmen. 65% of students live on campus; of those, 65% remain on campus on weekends. Alcohol is not permitted. All students may keep cars.

Activities: There are no fraternities or sororities. There are 35 groups on campus, including art, band, choir, chorale, chorus, computers, dance, drama, drill team, honors, international, jazz band, literary magazine, musical theater, newspaper, orchestra, pep band, political, professional, religious, social, social service, and student government. Popular campus events include Family Weekend and Jimmie Jive Week.

Sports: There are 7 intercollegiate sports for men and 7 for women, and 6 intramural sports for men and 6 for women. Facilities include an athletics center with a basketball court and wrestling and volleyball practice and composition area; a football stadium with an all-weather track; a soccer field; and a sports center with a swimming pool, weight room, running track, YMCA, and basketball, handball, and racquetball courts. Nearby facilities include a civic arena, softball field, baseball stadium, swimming pool, tennis courts, municipal golf course, and winter sports complex.

Disabled Students: 38% of the campus is accessible. Wheelchair ramps, elevators, special parking, specially equipped rest rooms, special class scheduling, lowered drinking fountains, lowered telephones, and special housing are available.

Services: Counseling and information services are available, as is tutoring in most subjects. There is remedial math, reading, and writing.

Campus Safety and Security: Measures include security escort services, informal discussions, pamphlets/posters/films, and lighted pathways/sidewalks.

Programs of Study: Jamestown College confers B.A., B.S., and B.S.N. degrees. Bachelor's degrees are awarded in BIOLOGICAL SCIENCE (biochemistry and biology/biological science), BUSINESS (accounting and business administration and management), COMMUNICATIONS AND THE ARTS (communications, English, fine arts, French, German, music, and Spanish), COMPUTER AND PHYSICAL SCIENCE (chemistry, computer science, information sciences and systems, mathematics, and radiological technology), EDUCATION (elementary and physical), HEALTH PROFESSIONS (clinical science, health care administration, and nursing), SOCIAL SCIENCE (criminal justice, economics, history, philosophy, political science/government, psychology, and religion). Business, nursing, and physical sciences are the strongest academically. Business, nursing, and education are the largest.

Required: To graduate, students must have a minimum of 128 semester credits, at least 48 of which must be at the upper-division level, with an average of 48 semester credits in the major, and maintain at least a 2.0 GPA. General education requirements include 47 to 56 credits, based on degree sought, in the areas of moral and civic education, communication skills, cultural and social heritage, natural science and quantitative reasoning, and phys ed.

Special: Special academic options include co-op programs in business, nursing, computer science, and criminal justice, on-campus work-study, internships, study abroad, dual majors within any of the concentrations, student-designed majors, nondegree study, pass/fail options, and credit for life, military, and work experience. Directed study is also possible. There are preprofessional programs in law, health-related fields, and engineering, including a 3-2 engineering program with North Dakota State University and the University of North Dakota. Teacher certification may be earned in secondary education. There are 5 national honor societies, and 10 departmental honors programs.

Faculty/Classroom: 54% of faculty are male; 46%, female. All teach undergraduates. The average class size in an introductory lecture is 26; in a laboratory, 15; and in a regular course, 20.

Admissions: 97% of the 2005-2006 applicants were accepted. The ACT scores for the 2005-2006 freshman class were: 35% below 21, 29% between 21 and 23, 20% between 24 and 26, 8% between 27 and 28, and 8% above 28. 29% of the current freshmen were in the top fifth of their class; 57% were in the top two fifths.

Requirements: The ACT is recommended. In addition, other admissions requirements include graduation from an accredited secondary school; the GED is also accepted. An interview is highly recommended. Jamestown College requires applicants to be in the upper 50% of their class. A GPA of 2.5 is required. AP and CLEP credits are accepted. Important factors in the admissions decision are evidence of special talent, extracurricular activities record, and leadership record.

Procedure: Freshmen are admitted to all sessions. Entrance exams should be taken before or during the fall of the senior year. There are deferred admissions and rolling admissions plans. Application deadlines are open. Application fee is $20. Applications are accepted on-line.

Transfer: 61 transfer students enrolled in 2004-2005. Applicants must have at least a 2.5 GPA and be in good standing with their previous college; if suspended, the student must allow 1 semester to elapse before applying for probationary admission. 35 of 128 credits required for the bachelor's degree must be completed at Jamestown College.

Visiting: There are regularly scheduled orientations for prospective students, including a campus tour and faculty visits. There are guides for informal visits and visitors may sit in on classes and stay overnight. To schedule a visit, contact the Admissions Office at *admissions@jc.edu.*

Financial Aid: In 2005-2006, 100% of all full-time freshmen and 99% of continuing full-time students received some form of financial aid. 79% of full-time freshmen and 82% of continuing full-time students received need-based aid. The average freshman award was $8728. Need-based scholarships or need-based grants averaged $6245 ($16,700 maximum); need-based self-help aid (loans and jobs) averaged $3540 ($6625 maximum); non-need-based athletic scholarships averaged $1559 ($10,000 maximum); and other non-need-based awards and non-need-based scholarships averaged $7371 ($15,230 maximum). 33% of undergraduates work part time. Average annual earnings from campus work are $933. The average financial indebtedness of the 2005 graduate was $19,732. The FAFSA is required.

International Students: There are 36 international students enrolled. The school actively recruits these students. Satisfactory scores are required on the written TOEFL and the MELAB.

Computers: Wireless access is available. All students may access the system 24 hours a day. There are no time limits and no fees.

Graduates: From July 1, 2004 to June 30, 2005, 189 bachelor's degrees were awarded. The most popular majors were business (23%), nursing (13%), and elementry education (9%). In an average class, 41% graduate in 4 years or less, 59% graduate in 5 years or less, and 60% graduate in 6 years or less. 25 companies recruited on campus in 2004-2005. Of the 2004 graduating class, 13% were enrolled in graduate school within 6 months of graduation and 80% were employed.

Admissions Contact: Judy Erickson, Director of Admissions.
E-mail: admissions@jc.edu Web: www.jc.edu

MAYVILLE STATE UNIVERSITY E-3

Mayville, ND 58257-1299

(701) 788-5222
(800) 437-4104; Fax: (701) 788-4748

Full-time: 318 men, 307 women	Faculty: 37
Part-time: 98 men, 189 women	Ph.D.s: 51%
Graduate: none	Student/Faculty: 17 to 1
Year: semesters, summer session	Tuition: $4943 ($10,454)
Application Deadline: open	Room & Board: $3724
Freshman Class: 250 applied, 150 accepted, 144 enrolled	
ACT: 19	NONCOMPETITIVE

Mayville State University, founded in 1889, is a public institution that emphasizes teacher education, business, and information technology. There are 5 undergraduate schools. In addition to regional accreditation, Mayville State has baccalaureate program accreditation with NCATE. The library contains 93,685 volumes, 15,224 microform items, and 9057 audio/video tapes/CDs/DVDs, and subscribes to 505 periodicals including electronic. Computerized library services include the card catalog, interlibrary loans, database searching, and Internet access. Special learning facilities include a learning resource center, art gallery, and a learning services center. The 55-acre campus is in a rural area 58 miles north of Fargo and 42 miles south of Grand Forks. Including any residence halls, there are 19 buildings.

Student Life: 66% of undergraduates are from North Dakota. Others are from 35 states, 9 foreign countries, and Canada. 95% are from public schools. 85% are white. 70% are Protestant; 29% Catholic. The average age of freshmen is 18. 42% do not continue beyond their first year; 35% remain to graduate.

Housing: 408 students can be accommodated in college housing, which includes single-sex and coed dormitories, on-campus apartments, and married-student housing. On-campus housing is guaranteed for the freshman year only and is available on a first-come, first-served basis. 70% of students commute. Alcohol is not permitted. All students may keep cars.

Activities: There are no fraternities or sororities. There are 21 groups on campus, including bagpipe band, cheerleading, choir, chorus, computers, debate, drama, ethnic, forensics, international, literary magazine, musical theater, newspaper, pep band, political, professional, religious, social service, student government, and yearbook. Popular campus events include Spring Fling.

Sports: There are 4 intercollegiate sports for men and 4 for women, and 10 intramural sports for men and 9 for women. Facilities include a 4500-seat football stadium, a track and practice field, a baseball diamond, tennis courts, a swimming pool, a soccer field, a fitness center, and handball and racquetball courts.

Disabled Students: 75% of the campus is accessible. Elevators, special parking, special class scheduling, lowered drinking fountains, and lowered telephones are available.

Services: Counseling and information services are available, as is tutoring in some subjects, including writing, math, reading, and study skills. There is remedial math and writing.

Campus Safety and Security: Measures include informal discussions, pamphlets/posters/films, lighted pathways/sidewalks, and a nighttime foot patrol.

Programs of Study: Mayville State confers B.A., B.S., B.A.S., B.G.S., and B.S.Ed. degrees. Associate degrees are also awarded. Bachelor's degrees are awarded in BIOLOGICAL SCIENCE (biology/biological science), BUSINESS (business administration and management and office supervision and management), COMMUNICATIONS AND THE ARTS (English), COMPUTER AND PHYSICAL SCIENCE (chemistry, computer programming, mathematics, physical sciences, and science), EDUCATION (business, early childhood, elementary, health, physical, science, and secondary), SOCIAL SCIENCE (liberal arts/general studies and social science). Business administration, computer information science, and elementary education are the strongest academically. Business administration and elementary education are the largest.

Required: To graduate, students must complete 120 semester hours with a minimum overall GPA of 2.0 in most programs and 2.75 in education. General requirements include 8 semester hours of science, 6 each of humanities and social science, 6 of English, up to 3 of math, and 3 each of computer information systems, psychology, speech, and phys ed.

Special: Through a special tuition waiver program, residents of all contiguous states, and Canadian provinces, and selected states in the MHEC and WUE consortiums pay a considerably reduced out-of-state tuition. Mayville State also offers preprofessional programs, internships, work-study programs, B.A.-B.S. degrees, dual majors, a general studies degree, credit for life experience, nondegree study, and pass/fail options. Co-op programs are available, including a certified education program for all subject areas. There is also a 4-year major in early childhood edu-

cation. There is 1 national honor society and a freshman honors program.

Faculty/Classroom: 54% of faculty are male; 46%, female. All teach undergraduates. The average class size in an introductory lecture is 25; in a laboratory, 15; and in a regular course, 20.

Admissions: 60% of the 2005-2006 applicants were accepted. The ACT scores for the 2005-2006 freshman class were: 71% below 21, 17% between 21 and 23, 6% between 24 and 26, and 7% between 27 and 28. 30% of the current freshmen were in the top fifth of their class; 60% were in the top two fifths.

Requirements: The ACT is required. In addition, applicants must be graduates of an accredited secondary school or have a GED certificate. Required core courses include 4 in English and 3 each in math (algebra I or higher), sciences, and social sciences. A GPA of 2.0 is required. AP and CLEP credits are accepted.

Procedure: Freshmen are admitted to all sessions. Entrance exams should be taken during the senior year. There is an early admissions and a rolling admissions plan. Application deadlines are open. Application fee is $35. Applications are accepted on-line.

Transfer: 143 transfer students enrolled in 2004-2005. Applicants must submit official transcripts from all colleges attended and should have a minimum GPA of 2.0. Scores on the SAT or ACT are also recommended. 30 of 120 credits required for the bachelor's degree must be completed at Mayville State.

Visiting: There are regularly scheduled orientations for prospective students, including a campus tour, meetings with faculty in fields of interest, and meetings with the financial aid director if needed. There are guides for informal visits and visitors may sit in on classes and stay overnight. To schedule a visit, contact the Office of Enrollment Services at (701) 786-4842.

Financial Aid: In 2005-2006, 58% of all full-time freshmen and 52% of continuing full-time students received some form of financial aid. 54% of full-time freshmen and 46% of continuing full-time students received need-based aid. The average freshman award was $5438. Need-based scholarships or need-based grants averaged $2752; need-based self-help aid (loans and jobs) averaged $2900; non-need-based athletic scholarships averaged $739; and other non-need-based awards and non-need-based scholarships averaged $849. 25% of undergraduates work part time. Average annual earnings from campus work are $1200. The average financial indebtedness of the 2005 graduate was $18,190. The FAFSA is required. The priority date for freshman financial aid applications for fall entry is February 15. The deadline for filing freshman financial aid applications for fall entry is March 15.

International Students: There are 55 international students enrolled. The school actively recruits these students. They must score satisfactorily on the written TOEFL or on the electronic version. The SAT or ACT is recommended.

Computers: Wireless access is available. Every full-time student receives a tablet PC and has wireless access in most classrooms, the library, campus center, and other public areas. All residence hall rooms have Internet and local area network access. All students may access the system. There are no time limits and no fees. All students are required to have personal computers.

Graduates: From July 1, 2004 to June 30, 2005, 106 bachelor's degrees were awarded. The most popular majors were elementary education (33%), business administration (25%), and computer information systems (9%). In an average class, 22% graduate in 4 years or less, 31% graduate in 5 years or less, and 35% graduate in 6 years or less. 3 companies recruited on campus in 2004-2005. Of the 2004 graduating class, 6% were enrolled in graduate school within 6 months of graduation and 98% were employed.

Admissions Contact: Cherine Heckman, Vice Presdient for Enrollment Management. A video is available.
E-mail: admit@mayvillestate.edu Web: www.mayvillestate.edu

MINOT STATE UNIVERSITY C-2

Minot, ND 58707

(701) 858-4347
(800) 777-0750; Fax: (701) 839-6933

Full-time: 945 men, 1570 women	Faculty: 159; IIA, --$
Part-time: 430 men, 655 women	Ph.D.s: 60%
Graduate: 55 men, 180 women	Student/Faculty: 16 to 1
Year: semesters, summer session	Tuition: $3300 ($7800)
Application Deadline: open	Room & Board: $3400
Freshman Class: n/av	
SAT or ACT: required	LESS COMPETITIVE

Minot State University, founded in 1913, is a public institution offering undergraduate and graduate programs in arts and sciences, education, business, nursing, and human services. There are 3 undergraduate schools and 1 graduate school. Figures above capsule and profile are approximate. In addition to regional accreditation, MSU has baccalaureate program accreditation with CSWE, NASM, NCATE, and NLN. The library contains 411,678 volumes, 687,708 microform items, and 12,722 audio/video tapes/CDs/DVDs, and subscribes to 802 periodicals including electronic. Computerized library services include the card catalog, interlibrary loans, and database searching. Special learning facilities include a learning resource center, art gallery, natural history museum, radio station, and TV station. The 103-acre campus is in a small town. Including any residence halls, there are 21 buildings.

Student Life: 83% of undergraduates are from North Dakota. Others are from 44 states, 18 foreign countries, and Canada. 95% are from public schools. 84% are white. The average age of freshmen is 19; all undergraduates, 21. 36% do not continue beyond their first year; 32% remain to graduate.

Housing: 643 students can be accommodated in college housing, which includes single-sex and coed dormitories, on-campus apartments, and married-student housing. In addition, there are special-interest houses. On-campus housing is guaranteed for the freshman year only, is available on a first-come, first-served basis, and is available on a lottery system for upperclassmen. 88% of students commute. Alcohol is not permitted. All students may keep cars.

Activities: There are no fraternities or sororities. There are 60 groups on campus, including art, band, cheerleading, choir, chorale, chorus, drama, ethnic, honors, international, jazz band, literary magazine, musical theater, newspaper, orchestra, pep band, political, professional, radio and TV, religious, social service, student government, symphony, and yearbook. Popular campus events include Welcome Week, Final Frenzy, and Native American Awareness Week.

Sports: There are 6 intercollegiate sports for men and 6 for women, and 4 intramural sports for men and 4 for women. Facilities include a 10,000-seat field house, a 2800-seat football stadium, and a 3000-seat gym.

Disabled Students: 99% of the campus is accessible. Wheelchair ramps, elevators, special parking, specially equipped rest rooms, special class scheduling, lowered drinking fountains, lowered telephones, and special housing are available.

Services: Counseling and information services are available, as is tutoring in most subjects. Special services are offered for disabled students on request.

Campus Safety and Security: Measures include self-defense education, informal discussions, pamphlets/posters/films, and emergency telephones. There are lighted pathways/sidewalks.

Programs of Study: MSU confers B.A., B.S., B.A.S., B.G.S., B.S. Ed., B.S.N., and B.S.W. degrees. Associate and master's degrees are also awarded. Bachelor's degrees are awarded in BIOLOGICAL SCIENCE (biology/biological science), BUSINESS (accounting, banking and finance, international business management, management information systems, management science, and marketing/retailing/merchandising), COMMUNICATIONS AND THE ARTS (art, broadcasting, communications, English, French, German, multimedia, music, and Spanish), COMPUTER AND PHYSICAL SCIENCE (chemistry, computer science, earth science, geology, mathematics, physical sciences, physics, and radiological technology), EDUCATION (business, drama, education of the deaf and hearing impaired, education of the exceptional child, education of the mentally handicapped, elementary, English, foreign languages, mathematics, music, physical, and science), HEALTH PROFESSIONS (dental laboratory technology, nursing, and speech pathology/audiology), SOCIAL SCIENCE (addiction studies, criminal justice, economics, history, liberal arts/general studies, physical fitness/movement, psychology, social science, social work, and sociology). Communication disorders, special education, and elementary education are the strongest academically. Business, criminal justice, and education are the largest.

Required: Students must take a number of general education courses in humanities, history, communication, math, natural sciences, social and behavioral sciences, and leisure-time education. They must complete at least 128 semester hours, with 30 to 37 in the major and a minimum GPA of 2.0.

Special: A general studies degree, independent research, internships, work-study, and unique programs of study, including student-designed majors, are available. Cross-registration through the North Dakota University System, co-op programs in all majors, including student-designed majors and study, abroad in 3 countries also are offered. Preliminary programs are available in dental hygiene, dentistry, engineering, law, medicine, and many other areas. There is a freshman honors program.

Faculty/Classroom: 49% of faculty are male; 51%, female. All teach undergraduates and 20% do research. No introductory courses are taught by graduate students. The average class size in an introductory lecture is 60; in a laboratory, 20; and in a regular course, 16.

Requirements: The SAT or ACT is required. In addition, applicants must submit a high school diploma or GED certificate. Core course requirements include 4 years of English and 3 each of math, social studies, and science. AP and CLEP credits are accepted.

Procedure: Freshmen are admitted to all sessions. Entrance exams should be taken any time. There are deferred admissions and rolling admissions plans. Application deadlines are open. Application fee is $35. Applications are accepted on-line.

Transfer: 449 transfer students enrolled in a recent year. Transfers must submit transcripts from each college attended. 30 of 128 credits required for the bachelor's degree must be completed at MSU.

Visiting: There are regularly scheduled orientations for prospective students, prior to the beginning of the fall term. There are guides for informal visits and visitors may sit in on classes. To schedule a visit, contact Enrollment Services at (701) 858-3350.

Financial Aid: In a recent year, 67% of all full-time students received some form of financial aid. 64% of full-time freshmen and 67% of continuing full-time students received need-based aid. The average freshman award was $5802. 1% of undergraduates worked part time. Average annual earnings from campus work were $1260. The average financial indebtedness of a recent graduate was $12,900. The FAFSA is required. Check with school for current application deadlines.

International Students: In a recent year there were 41 international students enrolled. The school actively recruits these students. They must score satisfactorily on the written TOEFL or on the electronic version.

Computers: All students may access the system 24 hours daily. There are no time limits and no fees.

Graduates: In a recent year, 488 bachelor's degrees were awarded. The most popular majors were elementary education (15%), nursing (10%), and criminal justice (9%). In an average class, 37% graduate in 6 years or less. 105 companies recruited on campus in a recent year. Of a recent graduating class, 11% were enrolled in graduate school within 6 months of graduation and 89% were employed.

Admissions Contact: Alexis Hendricks, Enrollment Services Representative. E-mail: *alexis@minotstateu.edu* Web: *www.minotstateu.edu*

NORTH DAKOTA STATE UNIVERSITY F-3
Fargo, ND 58105-5454
(701) 231-8643
(800) 488-NDSU; Fax: (701) 231-8802

Full-time: 5140 men, 3850 women	**Faculty:** 468; I, --$
Part-time: 525 men, 645 women	**Ph.D.s:** 91%
Graduate: 820 men, 660 women	**Student/Faculty:** 19 to 1
Year: semesters, summer session	**Tuition:** $4000 ($9650)
Application Deadline: see profile	**Room & Board:** $4500
Freshman Class: n/av	
SAT or ACT: required	**COMPETITIVE**

North Dakota State University, founded in 1890, is a comprehensive, public, land-grant institution. Its undergraduate and graduate programs emphasize the liberal arts and sciences, agricultural and technical studies, architecture, business, engineering, teacher preparation, and pharmaceutical studies. There are 8 undergraduate schools and 1 graduate school. Figures in the above capsule and profile are approximate. In addition to regional accreditation, NDSU has baccalaureate program accreditation with ABET, ACCE, ACPE, ACS, ADA, AHEA, CSAB, FIDER, NAAB, NASM, NCATE, and NLN. The 4 libraries contain 784,978 volumes, 444,951 microform items, and 2873 audio/video tapes/CDs/DVDs, and subscribe to 5090 periodicals including electronic. Computerized library services include the card catalog, interlibrary loans, database searching, and Internet access. Special learning facilities include a learning resource center, art gallery, and radio station. The 258-acre campus is in an urban area 229 miles northwest of Minneapolis-St. Paul. Including any residence halls, there are 97 buildings.

Student Life: 60% of undergraduates are from North Dakota. Others are from 36 states, 62 foreign countries, and Canada. 95% are white. The average age of freshmen is 18; all undergraduates, 27. 28% do not continue beyond their first year; 41% remain to graduate.

Housing: 3550 students can be accommodated in college housing, which includes single-sex and coed dormitories, on-campus apartments, married-student housing, learning communities, an engineering/architecture floor, and first year student halls. On-campus housing is guaranteed for all 4 years. 72% of students commute. Alcohol is not permitted. All students may keep cars.

Activities: 10% of men belong to 10 national fraternities; 5% of women belong to 5 national sororities. There are 200 groups on campus, including academic, art, band, cheerleading, choir, chorus, computers, dance, debate, drama, drill team, ethnic, forensics, gay, honors, international, jazz band, leisure learning opportunities, marching band, musical theater, newspaper, pep band, political, professional, radio and TV, recreational, religious, social, social service, and student government. Popular campus events include International Students' Week, Spring Blast, and multicultural activities.

Sports: There are 8 intercollegiate sports for men and 8 for women, and 5 intramural sports for men and 6 for women. Facilities include a sports arena, indoor and outdoor tracks, baseball and softball fields, a pool, wrestling and weight rooms, a multipurpose fitness room, and volleyball, tennis, basketball, and racquetball courts, and a wellness center.

Disabled Students: 50% of the campus is accessible. Wheelchair ramps, elevators, special parking, specially equipped rest rooms, special class scheduling, lowered drinking fountains, lowered telephones, and special transportation are available.

Services: Counseling and information services are available, as is tutoring in most subjects. There is a reader service for the blind, and remedial math, reading, and writing, and note takers.

Campus Safety and Security: Measures include 24-hour foot and vehicle patrol, self-defense education, security escort services, and shuttle buses. There are informal discussions, pamphlets/posters/films, emergency telephones, and lighted pathways/sidewalks.

Programs of Study: NDSU confers B.A., B.S., B.Arch., B.F.A. in Theater Arts, B.L.A., B.Mus., and B.Univ.Studies degrees. Master's and doctoral degrees are also awarded. Bachelor's degrees are awarded in AGRICULTURE (agricultural business management, agricultural economics, agricultural mechanics, agriculture, animal science, equine science, horticulture, natural resource management, plant protection (pest management), plant science, range/farm management, and soil science), BIOLOGICAL SCIENCE (biology/biological science, biotechnology, botany, microbiology, nutrition, and zoology), BUSINESS (accounting, business administration and management, hotel/motel and restaurant management, institutional management, management information systems, recreation and leisure services, and sports management), COMMUNICATIONS AND THE ARTS (art, communications, dramatic arts, English, French, music, performing arts, and Spanish), COMPUTER AND PHYSICAL SCIENCE (actuarial science, chemistry, computer science, earth science, geology, mathematics, physics, radiological technology, and statistics), EDUCATION (agricultural, athletic training, elementary, health, home economics, music, physical, and secondary), ENGINEERING AND ENVIRONMENTAL DESIGN (agricultural engineering, architecture, civil engineering, computer engineering, construction engineering, construction management, electrical/electronics engineering, engineering management, environmental design, industrial engineering, interior design, landscape architecture/design, manufacturing engineering, and mechanical engineering), HEALTH PROFESSIONS (clinical science, nursing, pharmacy, preveterinary science, respiratory therapy, and veterinary science), SOCIAL SCIENCE (anthropology, child care/child and family studies, criminal justice, economics, food science, history, humanities, international studies, physical fitness/movement, political science/government, psychology, social science, sociology, and textiles and clothing). Biotechnology, polymers and coatings science, and pharmacy are the strongest academically. Sciences, engineering, and human development and education are the largest.

Required: Students must complete at least 122 semester credits, with at least 24 in the major, and maintain at least a 2.0 GPA. General education requirements include: 10 credits in science and technology, including a 1 credit lab course, 9 credits in communication, which includes freshman English and public speaking, 6 credits each in humanities and fine arts, and in social and behavioral science, 3 credits in quantitative reasoning, at least 2 credits in a wellness course, and a first year experience course. Included in these courses must be 1 course designated as a cultural diversity course and 1 designated as a global perspectives course.

Special: Special academic programs include cooperative work programs and internships. There is cross-registration with the Tri-college Consortium and all North Dakota State institutions. Student-designed and dual majors, study abroad, a B.A.-B.S. degree, credit for life, military, and work experience, nondegree study, and pass/fail options are possible. There are 22 national honor societies and a freshman honors program.

Faculty/Classroom: 72% of faculty are male; 28%, female. 97% both teach and do research. Graduate students teach 20% of introductory courses. The average class size in a laboratory is 26 and in a regular course, 42.

Requirements: The SAT or ACT is required. In addition, applicants must have completed 4 units of English, and 3 each of math (Algebra I or above), laboratory science, and social science. The GED is accepted, with a minimum score of 45 and no subject score lower than 40. A GPA of 2.5 is required. AP and CLEP credits are accepted.

Procedure: Freshmen are admitted to all sessions. Entrance exams should be taken in the spring of the junior year or in the fall of the senior year. There are deferred admissions and rolling admissions plans. Check with the school for application deadlines. Notification is sent on a rolling basis. Applications are accepted on-line. The fall 2005 application fee was $35.

Transfer: 798 transfer students enrolled in a recent year. Transfer students must have a minimum GPA of 2.0; ACT or SAT I scores are required if the applicant has less than 24 semester credits. 36 of 122 credits required for the bachelor's degree must be completed at NDSU.

Visiting: There are regularly scheduled orientations for prospective students, including tours of the campus, academic appointments, and meetings with admissions counselors and financial aid counselors. There are guides for informal visits and visitors may sit in on classes. To schedule a visit, contact the Office of Admission.

Financial Aid: In a recent year, 80% of all full-time freshmen and 77% of continuing full-time students received some form of financial aid. 55% of full-time freshmen and 54% of continuing full-time students received need-based aid. The average freshman award was $5462. Need-based scholarships or need-based grants averaged $3736; need-based self-help aid (loans and jobs) averaged $3396; non-need-based athletic scholarships averaged $3177; and other non-need-based awards and non-need-based scholarships averaged $2039. 60% of undergraduates

worked part time. Average annual earnings from campus work were $885. The average financial indebtedness of a recent graduate was $20,498. The FAFSA is required. Check with the school for application deadlines.

International Students: In a recent year, there were 112 international students enrolled. The school actively recruits these students. They must score satisfactorily on the written TOEFL.

Computers: All students may access the system 24 hours a day or as posted. There are no time limits and no fees. It is recommended that students in architecture and landscape architecture (sophomore level) have personal computers.

Graduates: In a recent year, 1525 bachelor's degrees were awarded. The most popular majors were engineering (20%), business (13%), and health and related sciences (9%). In an average class, 16% graduate in 4 years or less, 25% graduate in 5 years or less, and 40% graduate in 6 years or less. 93 companies recruited on campus in a recent year. Of a recent graduating class, 18% were enrolled in graduate school within 6 months of graduation and 91% were employed.

Admissions Contact: Dr. Kate Haugen, Associate Dean/Enrollment Management. E-mail: *ndsu.admission@ndsu.nodak.edu* Web: *www.ndsu.edu*

UNIVERSITY OF MARY   C-3
Bismarck, ND 58504-9652
(701) 355-8190
(800) 288-6279; Fax: (701) 255-7687

Full-time: 807 men, 1237 women	**Faculty:** 95
Part-time: 56 men, 97 women	**Ph.D.s:** 36%
Graduate: 202 men, 359 women	**Student/Faculty:** 22 to 1
Year: semesters, summer session	**Tuition:** $11,324
Application Deadline: August 15	**Room & Board:** $4050
Freshman Class: 1040 applied, 897 accepted, 352 enrolled	
SAT or ACT: recommended	**COMPETITIVE**

The University of Mary, founded in 1959, is a private institution affiliated with the Roman Catholic Church. Undergraduate and graduate programs emphasize liberal arts, humanities, social sciences, business, health science, music, professional training, philosophy and religious studies, and teacher preparation. There are 8 undergraduate and 4 graduate schools. In addition to regional accreditation, Mary has baccalaureate program accreditation with CAHEA, CSWE, NLN, and CCNE. The library contains 55,000 volumes and 2500 audio/video tapes/CDs/DVDs, and subscribes to 550 periodicals including electronic. Computerized library services include the card catalog, interlibrary loans, and database searching. Special learning facilities include a learning resource center, art gallery, radio station, and TV station. The 107-acre campus is in a suburban area 7 miles south of Bismarck. Including any residence halls, there are 8 buildings.

Student Life: 71% of undergraduates are from North Dakota. Others are from 28 states, 22 foreign countries, and Canada. 95% are from public schools. 89% are white. 60% are Catholic; 30% Protestant. The average age of freshmen is 18; all undergraduates, 27. 29% do not continue beyond their first year; 57% remain to graduate.

Housing: 791 students can be accommodated in college housing, which includes single-sex dorms and on-campus apartments. On-campus housing is guaranteed for all 4 years. 66% of students commute. Alcohol is not permitted. All students may keep cars.

Activities: There are no fraternities or sororities. There are 22 groups on campus, including band, cheerleading, choir, chorale, chorus, computers, drama, ethnic, forensics, jazz band, musical theater, newspaper, orchestra, pep band, photography, political, professional, radio and TV, religious, social, social service, student government, and symphony. Popular campus events include intramural sports and the Convocation Series.

Sports: There are 8 intercollegiate sports for men and 7 for women, and 10 intramural sports for men and 10 for women. Facilities include an activity center housing a 1200-seat gym, basketball and racquetball courts, wrestling and weight rooms, and a swimming pool. The field house includes an indoor track, 3 basketball/volleyball/tennis courts, and a climbing wall. There are also track/football, intramural, and softball fields, tennis courts, a fitness center, and a 1200-seat stadium.

Disabled Students: All of the campus is accessible. Wheelchair ramps, elevators, special parking, specially equipped rest rooms, special class scheduling, lowered telephones, and special housing are available.

Services: Counseling and information services are available, as is tutoring in every subject. There is a reader service for the blind, and remedial math, reading, and writing.

Campus Safety and Security: Measures include security escort services, shuttle buses, informal discussions, and pamphlets/posters/films. There are emergency telephones and lighted pathways/sidewalks.

Programs of Study: Mary confers B.A., B.S., and B.Univ.Studies degrees. Master's degrees are also awarded. Bachelor's degrees are awarded in BIOLOGICAL SCIENCE (biology/biological science), BUSINESS (accounting, business administration and management, business communications, and management information systems), COMMUNICA-

TIONS AND THE ARTS (communications, English, and music), COMPUTER AND PHYSICAL SCIENCE (information sciences and systems, mathematics, and radiological technology), EDUCATION (athletic training, early childhood, elementary, English, mathematics, music, physical, science, social science, social studies, and special), ENGINEERING AND ENVIRONMENTAL DESIGN (engineering and applied science), HEALTH PROFESSIONS (exercise science, medical laboratory science, nursing, occupational therapy, physical therapy, premedicine, and respiratory therapy), SOCIAL SCIENCE (addiction studies, behavioral science, criminal justice, liberal arts/general studies, ministries, pastoral studies, prelaw, psychology, social science, social work, and theological studies). Business administration, education, and nursing are the strongest academically. Business, nursing, and elementary education are the largest.

Required: To graduate, students must complete 128 semester hours, with 32 to 56 in the major and 44 at the 300-400 level, and have a minimum GPA of 2.0. At least 56 semester hours must be in liberal arts courses. In addition, a B.A. degree requires 16 semester hours of a foreign language or 20 semester hours of philosophy/theology, with 12 such hours at the 300-400 level. All students must take 3 courses each in humanities, math/science, philosophy/theology, and social sciences.

Special: A co-op program in engineering is available as is cross-registration with the University of Minnesota. Special academic programs include internships in all fields and all programs, study abroad in France, Germany, and Spain, on-campus work-study, and a general studies degree. Dual majors include elementary education/early childhood, elementary education/special education, athletic training/biology, athletic training/phys ed, business/accounting, and business/computer information systems. There are accelerated degree programs in several majors, and a 3-2 engineering program with the University of Minnesota. There are 3 national honor societies, a freshman honors program, and 2 departmental honors programs.

Faculty/Classroom: 50% of faculty are male; 50%, female. 95% teach undergraduates and 15% both teach and do research. No introductory courses are taught by graduate students. The average class size in an introductory lecture is 15; in a laboratory, 20; and in a regular course, 20.

Admissions: 86% of the 2005-2006 applicants were accepted. The ACT scores for the 2005-2006 freshman class were: 45% below 21, 20% between 21 and 23, 23% between 24 and 26, 8% between 27 and 28, and 4% above 28. 34% of the current freshmen were in the top fifth of their class; 69% were in the top two fifths. 30 freshmen graduated first in their class.

Requirements: The SAT or ACT is recommended. The ACT Optional Writing test is also recommended. In addition, applicants should be graduates of an accredited secondary school; the GED is accepted. For automatic acceptance, 3 requirements must be met: a minimum 2.5 GPA; an 18 or higher score on the ACT; and rank in the upper half of the graduating class. The school's own testing can also be used to determine acceptance. A recommendation from a school counselor, teacher, or employer is requested. An interview is advised. AP and CLEP credits are accepted. Important factors in the admissions decision are evidence of special talent, leadership record, and advanced placement or honor courses.

Procedure: Freshmen are admitted fall and spring. Entrance exams should be taken in the fall of the senior year. There are early admissions and deferred admissions plans. Applications should be filed by August 15 for fall entry and December 15 for spring entry, along with a $15 fee. Notification is sent on a rolling basis. Applications are accepted on-line.

Transfer: 243 transfer students enrolled in 2004-2005. Transfer students should have a 2.0 minimum GPA and should present a recommendation from a school counselor, instructor, or employer. 32 of 128 credits required for the bachelor's degree must be completed at Mary.

Visiting: There are regularly scheduled orientations for prospective students, including a campus tour and meetings with individual professors, coaches, students, and music instructors. There are guides for informal visits and visitors may sit in on classes and stay overnight. To schedule a visit, contact the Admissions Office at *marauder@umary.edu*.

Financial Aid: In 2005-2006, 95% of all full-time freshmen and 85% of continuing full-time students received some form of financial aid. 85% of full-time freshmen and 75% of continuing full-time students received need-based aid. Need-based scholarships or need-based grants averaged $1840 ($4050 maximum); need-based self-help aid (loans and jobs) averaged $1800 ($2625 maximum); non-need-based athletic scholarships averaged $5500 ($9000 maximum); and other non-need-based awards and non-need-based scholarships averaged $3850 ($10,600 maximum). 70% of undergraduates work part time. Average annual earnings from campus work are $1000. The average financial indebtedness of the 2005 graduate was $15,500. The FAFSA is required. The priority date for freshman financial aid applications for fall entry is March 15. The deadline for filing freshman financial aid applications for fall entry is August 1.

International Students: There are 25 international students enrolled. The school actively recruits these students. They must take the TOEFL.

Computers: 235 computer stations are available for student use, all with connection to the college's network and the Internet. These are located in several labs as well as in all residence facilities. All students may access the system 24 hours a day. There are no time limits. The fee is $4 per credit enrolled. It is recommended that students in computer information systems have personal computers.

Graduates: From July 1, 2004 to June 30, 2005, 506 bachelor's degrees were awarded. The most popular majors were education (23%), management (19%), and nursing (13%). In an average class, 5% graduate in 3 years or less, 42% graduate in 4 years or less, 55% graduate in 5 years or less, and 57% graduate in 6 years or less. 30 companies recruited on campus in 2004-2005. Of the 2004 graduating class, 17% were enrolled in graduate school within 6 months of graduation and 80% were employed.

Admissions Contact: Dave Heringer, Vice President For Enrollment. A video is available. E-mail: *heringer@umary.edu* Web: *www.umary.edu*

UNIVERSITY OF NORTH DAKOTA E-2

Grand Forks, ND 58202
(701) 777-4463
(800) 225-5863; Fax: (701) 777-2696

Full-time: 5052 men, 4312 women	**Faculty:** 723; I, --$
Part-time: 638 men, 496 women	**Ph.D.s:** 93%
Graduate: 1029 men, 1427 women	**Student/Faculty:** 13 to 1
Year: semesters, summer session	**Tuition:** $5327 ($12,659)
Application Deadline: July 1	**Room & Board:** $4787
Freshman Class: 3749 applied, 2725 accepted, 1884 enrolled	
ACT: 23	**VERY COMPETITIVE**

The University of North Dakota, established in 1883, is a state-supported comprehensive institution. Its undergraduate and graduate programs emphasize the liberal arts, fine arts, engineering, medicine, aerospace sciences, nursing, professional training, business and public administration, health science, teacher preparation, law, and computer science. There are 8 undergraduate and 3 graduate schools. In addition to regional accreditation, UND has baccalaureate program accreditation with AACSB, ABET, ACEJMC, ADA, APTA, CSAB, CSWE, NASAD, NASM, NCATE, and NLN. The 3 libraries contain 1,444,396 volumes, 1,676,498 microform items, and 31,010 audio/video tapes/CDs/DVDs, and subscribe to 16,494 periodicals including electronic. Computerized library services include the card catalog, interlibrary loans, database searching, Internet access, and laptop Internet portals. Special learning facilities include a learning resource center, art gallery, natural history museum, radio station, TV station, an entrepreneur center, an atmospherium, and an art museum and gallery. The 550-acre campus is in an urban area 4 hours from Minneapolis/St. Paul and 2 hours from Winnipeg, Manitoba. Including any residence halls, there are 235 buildings.

Student Life: 53% of undergraduates are from North Dakota. Students are from 49 states, 64 foreign countries, and Canada. 95% are from public schools. 91% are white. The average age of freshmen is 18; all undergraduates, 22. 25% do not continue beyond their first year; 75% remain to graduate.

Housing: 4271 students can be accommodated in college housing, which includes single-sex and coed dorms, on-campus apartments, married-student housing, and sorority houses. In addition, there are special-interest houses. On-campus housing is guaranteed for all 4 years. 71% of students commute. Alcohol is not permitted. All students may keep cars.

Activities: 10% of men belong to 13 national fraternities; 8% of women belong to 7 national sororities. There are 200 groups on campus, including art, band, cheerleading, chess, choir, chorale, chorus, computers, dance, debate, departmental, drama, drill team, ethnic, film, gay, honors, international, jazz band, literary magazine, marching band, musical theater, newspaper, orchestra, pep band, photography, political, professional, radio and TV, religious, social, social service, special interest, student government, and symphony. Popular campus events include Honors Day, Potato Bowl, and Spring Concert.

Sports: There are 8 intercollegiate sports for men and 10 for women, and 21 intramural sports for men and 21 for women. Facilities include an ice arena, a golf course, a 15,000-seat stadium, a 11,499-seat hockey arena, a 6,100-seat basketball center, a sports/field house with racquetball and basketball courts, weight rooms, a dance studio, and a wellness center.

Disabled Students: 99% of the campus is accessible. Wheelchair ramps, elevators, special parking, specially equipped rest rooms, special class scheduling, lowered drinking fountains, lowered telephones, special housing, accessible transportation, academic and personal support services are available.

Services: Counseling and information services are available, as is tutoring in every subject. There is a reader service for the blind.

Campus Safety and Security: Measures include 24-hour foot and vehicle patrol, self-defense education, security escort services, and shuttle buses. There are informal discussions, pamphlets/posters/films, emergency telephones, lighted pathways/sidewalks, and emergency phones throughout the campus.

Programs of Study: UND confers B.A., B.S., B.Acc., B.B.A., B.F.A., B.G.S., B.Mus., B.S.A., B.S.A.T., B.S.At.Sc., B.S.C.E., B.S.Ch.E., B.S. Chem., B.S.C.J.S., B.S.C.L.S., B.S.C.N., B.S.C.S.C.I., B.S.Cyto., B.S.D., B.S.Ed., B.S.E.E., B.S.E.G., B.S.F.W.B., B.S.G.E., B.S.Geol., B.S.I.T., B.S.M.E., B.S.N., B.S.O.S.E.H., B.S.P.A., B.S.P.E., B.S.P.T., B.S.R.H.S., B.S.R.L.S., and B.S.S.W. degrees. Master's and doctoral degrees are also awarded. Bachelor's degrees are awarded in AGRICULTURE (fish and game management), BIOLOGICAL SCIENCE (biology/biological science), BUSINESS (accounting, banking and finance, business economics, entrepreneurial studies, management information systems, management science, marketing/retailing/merchandising, and recreation and leisure services), COMMUNICATIONS AND THE ARTS (communications, dramatic arts, English, French, German, music, music performance, Norwegian, Spanish, and visual and performing arts), COMPUTER AND PHYSICAL SCIENCE (atmospheric sciences and meteorology, chemistry, computer science, geoenvironmental studies, geology, information sciences and systems, mathematics, and physics), EDUCATION (athletic training, business, early childhood, elementary, marketing and distribution, mathematics, middle school, music, physical, science, and social studies), ENGINEERING AND ENVIRONMENTAL DESIGN (aerospace studies, air traffic control, airline piloting and navigation, aviation administration/management, aviation maintenance management, chemical engineering, civil engineering, electrical/electronics engineering, geological engineering, industrial engineering technology, mechanical engineering, and occupational safety and health), HEALTH PROFESSIONS (clinical science, community health work, cytotechnology, exercise science, music therapy, nursing, physical therapy, preallied health, and rehabilitation therapy), SOCIAL SCIENCE (American Indian studies, anthropology, classical/ancient civilization, criminal justice, dietetics, economics, forensic studies, geography, history, interdisciplinary studies, international studies, liberal arts/general studies, philosophy, political science/government, psychology, public administration, religion, social science, social work, and sociology). Physical therapy is the strongest academically. Health, liberal arts, and business are the largest.

Required: To graduate, students must complete at least 125 credit hours, 30 in the major, with a minimum GPA of 2.0. At least 36 credits must be numbered 300 or above, and at least 60 credits must be from a 4-year institution. Distribution requirements include 12 credits of math, science, and technology, 9 each of social sciences and arts, and humanities, and 6 of English composition. One course in social science or arts and humanities must meet the world cultures designation.

Special: Special academic programs include cooperative programs, accelerated degree programs in most majors, internships in many majors, study abroad in at least 20 countries, work-study, and dual majors in all areas. Also offered are a general studies degree, honors programs, student-designed majors, B.A.-B.S. degees, nondegree study, and pass/fail options. Alternative academic programs include the Division of Continuing Education's correspondence study, the Integrated Studies Program, which offers a means of fulfilling general education requirements by a semester of related course work, and study via telecommunications. Cross-registration with all North Dakota 2- and 4-year public institutions is possible. There are 28 national honor societies, including Phi Beta Kappa, a freshman honors program, and 1 departmental honors program.

Faculty/Classroom: 61% of faculty are male; 39%, female. 90% teach undergraduates. The average class size in an introductory lecture is 34; in a laboratory, 21; and in a regular course, 36.

Admissions: 73% of the 2005-2006 applicants were accepted. The ACT scores for the 2005-2006 freshman class were: 22% below 21, 34% between 21 and 23, 25% between 24 and 26, 10% between 27 and 28, and 9% above 28. There were 9 National Merit finalists. 90 freshmen graduated first in their class.

Requirements: The SAT or ACT is required; the ACT is preferred, but the SAT will be accepted. Applicants must be graduates of an accredited secondary school or have passed to GED with an average of 50. A GPA of 2.5 is required. AP and CLEP credits are accepted.

Procedure: Freshmen are admitted to all sessions. Entrance exams should be taken in spring of the junior year or fall of the senior year. There are early decision and rolling admissions plans. Applications should be filed by July 1 for fall entry. Deadlines are rolling for spring and summer entry. Notification is sent on a rolling basis. The fall 2005 application fee was $35.

Transfer: 781 transfer students enrolled in 2004-2005. Transfer students must have a minimum GPA of 2.0 and be in good academic standing. A higher GPA may be required in specific programs. 30 of 125 credits required for the bachelor's degree must be completed at UND.

Visiting: There are regularly scheduled orientations for prospective students, including a visit with an admissions counselor, a campus tour, an academic appointment, and an athletic appointment (if applicable). There are guides for informal visits and visitors may sit in on classes and stay overnight. To schedule a visit, contact Enrollment Services.

Financial Aid: In a recent year, 81% of all full-time freshmen and 78% of continuing full-time students received some form of financial aid. 47% of full-time freshmen and 50% of continuing full-time students received need-based aid. The average freshman award was $7722. Need-based

scholarships or need-based grants averaged $2999 ($4050 maximum); need-based self-help aid (loans and jobs) averaged $4241 ($8820 maximum); non-need-based athletic scholarships averaged $4822 ($14,136 maximum); and other non-need-based awards and non-need-based scholarships averaged $2889 ($3593 maximum). The average financial indebtedness of a recent graduate was $22,733. UND is a member of CSS. The FAFSA is required. Check with the school for current application deadlines.

International Students: There are 189 international students enrolled. They must achieve a satisfactory score on the TOEFL and also take the SAT or the ACT.

Computers: All students may access the system 24 hours a day. It is recommended that students in aviation and medical programs have PCs.

Graduates: From July 1, 2004 to June 30, 2005, 1757 bachelor's degrees were awarded. The most popular majors were commercial aviation (11%), nursing (5%), and communications (5%). In an average class, 22% graduate in 4 years or less, 49% graduate in 5 years or less, and 54% graduate in 6 years or less. 253 companies recruited on campus in 2004-2005. Of the 2004 graduating class, 20% were enrolled in graduate school within 6 months of graduation and 85% were employed.

Admissions Contact: Kenton Pauls, Director, Enrollment Services. A video is available. E-mail: *kenton_pauls@mail.und.nodak.edu* Web: *http://www.go.und.edu*

VALLEY CITY STATE UNIVERSITY — E-3
Valley City, ND 58072

(701) 845-7101
(800) 532-8641; Fax: (701) 845-7299

Full-time: 403 men, 380 women	**Faculty:** 55
Part-time: 78 men, 152 women	**Ph.D.s:** 36%
Graduate: 10 men, 12 women	**Student/Faculty:** 14 to 1
Year: semesters, summer session	**Tuition:** $5160 ($11,265)
Application Deadline: open	**Room & Board:** $4694
Freshman Class: 256 applied, 240 accepted, 176 enrolled	
SAT Verbal/Math: 515/505*	**ACT:** 20　　**LESS COMPETITIVE**

Valley City State University, founded in 1890, is a state-supported institution offering degree programs in the arts and sciences, business, and teacher education. In addition to regional accreditation, VCSU has baccalaureate program accreditation with NASM and NCATE. The library contains 97,500 volumes, 30,000 microform items, and 7900 audio/video tapes/CDs/DVDs, and subscribes to 13,000 periodicals including electronic. Computerized library services include the card catalog, interlibrary loans, database searching, Internet access, and laptop Internet portals. Special learning facilities include a learning resource center, art gallery, and planetarium. The 64-acre campus is in a small town 58 miles west of Fargo. Including any residence halls, there are 29 buildings.

Student Life: 72% of undergraduates are from North Dakota. Others are from 21 states, 8 foreign countries, and Canada. 90% are from public schools. 89% are white. The average age of freshmen is 18; all undergraduates, 23. 35% do not continue beyond their first year.

Housing: 514 students can be accommodated in college housing, which includes single-sex and coed dorms and married-student housing. On-campus housing is guaranteed for all 4 years. 70% of students commute. Alcohol is not permitted. All students may keep cars.

Activities: 1% of men belong to 1 local fraternity; 1% of women belong to 1 local sorority. There are 22 groups on campus, including art, band, cheerleading, choir, chorus, computers, drama, honors, international, jazz band, musical theater, newspaper, pep band, photography, political, professional, religious, social, and student government. Popular campus events include Sno-Daze and Medicine Wheel Seasonal Celebrations.

Sports: There are 3 intercollegiate sports for men and 3 for women, and 9 intramural sports for men and 9 for women. Facilities include a 2500-seat football stadium with an all-weather track, a 2500-seat arena, an indoor pool, a field house, tennis and racquetball courts, a cross-country course, softball and baseball fields, a golf course, weight rooms, and a fitness room.

Disabled Students: 97% of the campus is accessible. Wheelchair ramps, elevators, special parking, specially equipped rest rooms, special class scheduling, lowered drinking fountains, and lowered telephones are available.

Services: Counseling and information services are available, as is tutoring in most subjects. There is remedial writing.

Campus Safety and Security: Measures include 24-hour foot and vehicle patrol, self-defense education, informal discussions, and pamphlets/posters/films. There are lighted pathways/sidewalks and a night patrol.

Programs of Study: VCSU confers B.A., B.S., B.S.Ed., and B.University Studies degrees. Master's degrees are also awarded. Bachelor's degrees are awarded in BIOLOGICAL SCIENCE (biology/biological science), BUSINESS (business administration and management, human resources, and office supervision and management), COMMUNICATIONS AND THE ARTS (art, English, music, and Spanish), COMPUTER AND PHYSICAL SCIENCE (chemistry, information sciences and systems, mathematics, and science), EDUCATION (business, elementary, health, physical, technical, and vocational), SOCIAL SCIENCE (history and social science). Education, business, and computer information systems are the strongest academically. Elementary education and business are the largest.

Required: To graduate, students must complete at least 128 semester hours with a minimum GPA of 2.0, or 2.5 for a B.S.Ed. degree. Except for those pursuing the Bachelor of University Studies degree, all students must complete the foundation studies curriculum, which includes 15 to 16 hours in foreign language, 12 in problem solving, 9 in communication, 6 each in aesthetic engagement and wellness, 5 in global perspective, and 3 in technology. Students must complete 48 hours in their major if they do not have a minor, or 36 hours in their major if they have a minor. All students must complete a digital portfolio specific to their major.

Special: VCSU offers internships, dual majors, on-campus work-study, study abroad in 2 countries, pass/fail options for some courses, and credit for life, military, and work experience. There are 6 national honor societies and 4 departmental honors programs.

Faculty/Classroom: 53% of faculty are male; 47%, female. All teach undergraduates, and 25% both teach and do research. The average class size in an introductory lecture is 40; in a laboratory, 20; and in a regular course, 25.

Admissions: 94% of the 2005-2006 applicants were accepted. The SAT scores for the 2005-2006 freshman class were: Verbal--45% below 500, 40% between 500 and 599, and 15% between 600 and 700; Math--45% below 500, 40% between 500 and 599, and 15% between 600 and 700. The ACT scores were 54% below 21, 24% between 21 and 23, 14% between 24 and 26, 5% between 27 and 28, and 2% above 28. 22% of the current freshmen were in the top fifth of their class. 6 freshmen graduated first in their class.

Requirements: The ACT is required. In addition, applicants must be graduates of an accredited secondary school or have a GED certificate. Core curriculum requirements include 4 units of English and 3 units each of math, lab science, and social science. AP and CLEP credits are accepted.

Procedure: Freshmen are admitted to all sessions. There is a deferred admissions plan. There is a rolling admission plan. Application deadlines are open. Application fee is $35. Notification is sent on a rolling basis. Applications are accepted on-line.

Transfer: 73 transfer students enrolled in 2004-2005. Applicants must be in good academic standing, have a minimum GPA of 2.0, and be eligible to return to their previous institution. Official transcripts from all colleges attended are required. Some students may be required to submit high school transcripts and standardized test scores. 24 of 120 credits required for the bachelor's degree must be completed at VCSU.

Visiting: There are regularly scheduled orientations for prospective students. There are guides for informal visits and visitors may sit in on classes and stay overnight. To schedule a visit, contact the Office of Enrollment Services.

Financial Aid: In 2005-2006, 90% of all full-time freshmen and 72% of continuing full-time students received some form of financial aid. 54% of full-time freshmen and 46% of continuing full-time students received need-based aid. The average freshman award was $8024. Need-based scholarships or need-based grants averaged $4691 ($12,450 maximum); need-based self-help aid (loans and jobs) averaged $3273 ($6171 maximum); non-need-based athletic scholarships averaged $843 ($3000 maximum); and other non-need-based awards and non-need-based scholarships averaged $2869 ($12,030 maximum). 22% of undergraduates work part time. Average annual earnings from campus work were $989. The average financial indebtedness of the 2005 graduate was $18,394. VCSU is a member of CSS. The FAFSA is required. The deadline for filing freshman financial aid applications for fall entry is April 15.

International Students: There are 54 international students enrolled. A satisfactory score on the TOEFL is required.

Computers: Wireless access is available. Each student is provided with a PC. Students can connect to any of 2500 Internet connections on campus. All students may access the system 24 hours a day. There are no time limits and no fees.

Graduates: From July 1, 2004 to June 30, 2005, 191 bachelor's degrees were awarded. The most popular majors were elementary education (45%), business administration (29%), and human resources (6%). In an average class, 24% graduate in 4 years or less, 44% graduate in 5 years or less, and 48% graduate in 6 years or less.

Admissions Contact: Dan Klein, Director of Enrollment Management. E-mail: *enrollment_services@vcsu.edu* Web: *www.vcsu.edu*

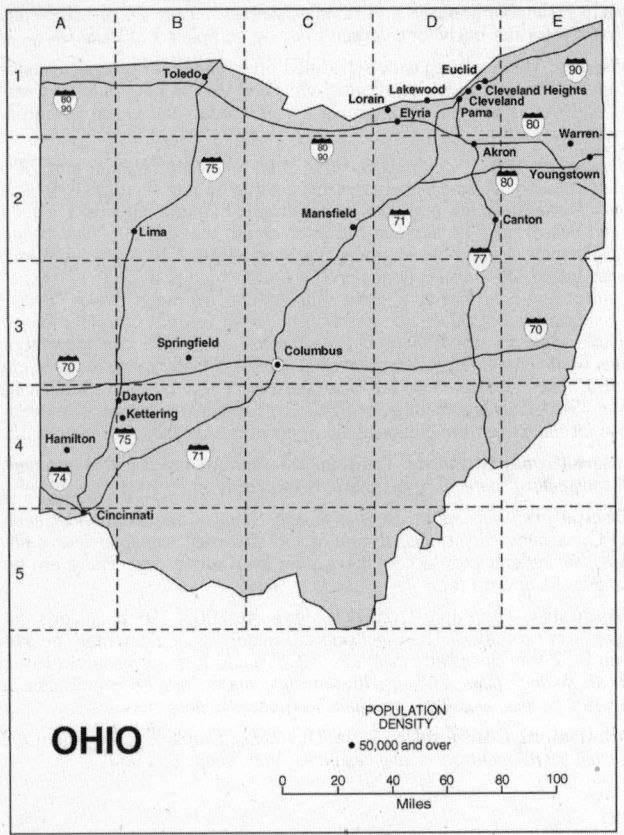

OHIO

POPULATION
DENSITY
● 50,000 and over

0   20   40   60   80   100
Miles

ANTIOCH COLLEGE
Yellow Springs, OH 45387

B-4

(937) 769-1100
(800) 543-9436; Fax: (937) 769-1111

Full-time: 161 men, 218 women
Part-time: none
Graduate: none
Year: trimesters, summer session
Application Deadline: February 1
Freshman Class: 368 applied, 187 accepted, 53 enrolled
SAT or ACT: recommended

Faculty: IIB, --$
Ph.Ds: 65%
Student/Faculty: n/av
Tuition: $26,700
Room & Board: $7000

COMPETITIVE

Antioch College, established in 1852, is private liberal arts institution where students alternate full-time study on campus with full-time related work experience off campus. The library contains 300,024 volumes, 48,320 microform items, and 6340 audio/video tapes/CDs/DVDs, and subscribes to 10,920 periodicals including electronic. Computerized library services include the card catalog, interlibrary loans, database searching, and Internet access. Special learning facilities include a learning resource center, art gallery, radio station, and archives. The 100-acre campus is in a small town 18 miles east of Dayton. Including any residence halls, there are 34 buildings.

Student Life: 68% of undergraduates are from out of state, mostly the Northeast. Students are from 43 states and 6 foreign countries. 49% are white. The average age of freshmen is 18; all undergraduates, 21. 50% of freshmen remain to graduate.

Housing: 592 students can be accommodated in college housing, which includes coed dorms and on-campus apartments. In addition, there are language houses, special-interest houses, single-sex floors, and food cooperative in the dorms. On-campus housing is guaranteed for all 4 years. 95% of students live on campus; of those, 95% remain on campus on weekends. Alcohol is not permitted. All students may keep cars.

Activities: There are no fraternities or sororities. There are 27 groups on campus, including art, choir, dance, drama, ethnic, film, gay, international, literary magazine, newspaper, photography, political, radio and TV, social, social service, and student government.

Sports: There are 16 intramural sports for men and 16 for women.

Disabled Students: 10% of the campus is accessible. Wheelchair ramps, elevators, special parking, specially equipped rest rooms, and special housing are available.

Services: Counseling and information services are available, as is tutoring in most subjects. There is a reader service for the blind and remedial math and writing.

Campus Safety and Security: Measures include 24-hour foot and vehicle patrol, security escort services, informal discussions, and pamphlets/posters/films. There are lighted pathways/sidewalks.

Programs of Study: Antioch confers B.A. and B.S. degrees. Bachelor's degrees are awarded in BUSINESS (entrepreneurial studies), COMMUNICATIONS AND THE ARTS (communications, languages, and visual and performing arts), COMPUTER AND PHYSICAL SCIENCE (physical sciences), ENGINEERING AND ENVIRONMENTAL DESIGN (environmental science), SOCIAL SCIENCE (crosscultural studies, humanities and social science, and interdisciplinary studies). Social sciences and environmental studies are the largest.

Required: To graduate, students must complete at least 107 academic credits, with 40 to 56 in the major, and 5 co-op experiences. The general education program consists of 8 4-credit courses. The core curriculum includes writing, math, and foreign language. Distribution requirements include 32 credits in arts, humanities, social sciences, natural sciences, and physical sciences. In addition, students must demonstrate proficiency in a foreign language and must successfully complete a work-study experience of at least 1 term in an international or cross-cultural setting.

Special: An alternating work-study program is required of all students; co-op jobs, normally 16 weeks long and resulting in 1 block of co-op credit, are individually arranged according to the needs, interests, and qualifications of each student. There is cross-registration with 17 higher education institutions in southwestern Ohio, and Antioch's membership in the Great Lakes Colleges Association allows for opportunities for special off-campus programs. An extensive study abroad program in 15 countries is based on student-designed majors and accelerated degree programs in all majors. Within the 8 interdisciplinary majors offered at Antioch, there are dual majors and 25 concentrations available. Nondegree study is possible. All courses are graded on a credit/no credit basis with faculty giving narrative evaluations of each student's work.

Faculty/Classroom: 49% of faculty are male; 51%, female. All teach undergraduates. The average class size in a regular course is 12.

Admissions: 51% of the 2005-2006 applicants were accepted.

Requirements: The SAT or ACT is recommended. A GPA of 2.5 is required. AP and CLEP credits are accepted. Important factors in the admissions decision are personality/intangible qualities, recommendations by school officials, and evidence of special talent.

Procedure: Freshmen are admitted fall, spring, and summer. There are early action, early admissions, deferred admissions, and rolling admissions plans. Early action applications should be filed by January 1; regular decision priority date for applications, is February 1 for fall entry. Notification of early action is sent February 1; regular decision, on a rolling basis beginning April 1. Applications are accepted on-line.

Transfer: 10 transfer students enrolled in fall 2005. Official college transcripts from previous institutions and a dean's recommendation form are required. 54 of 107 credits required for the bachelor's degree must be completed at Antioch.

Visiting: There are regularly scheduled orientations for prospective students, including admissions interviews, co-op presentations, tours, and special events. There are guides for informal visits and visitors may sit in on classes and stay overnight. To schedule a visit, contact the Admissions Office.

Financial Aid: In 2005-2006, 100% of all full-time freshmen and 95% of continuing full-time students received some form of financial aid. At least 72% of full-time freshmen and 73% of continuing full-time students received need-based aid. The average freshman award was $17,521. Need-based scholarships or need-based grants averaged $11,898; need-based self-help aid (loans and jobs) averaged $4689; and other institutional non-need-based awards and non-need-based scholarships averaged $15,929. The average financial indebtedness of the 2005 graduate was $17,125. The FAFSA and the college's own financial statement are required. The priority date for freshman financial aid applications for fall entry is February 1.

International Students: There were 10 international students enrolled in a recent year. A satisfactory score is required on the written TOEFL.

Computers: All students may access the system. There are no time limits. The fee is $156.

Graduates: From July 1, 2004 to June 30, 2005, 60 bachelor's degrees were awarded. The most popular majors were area and ethnic studies (33%), interdisciplinary studies (28%), and liberal arts/general studies (13%). In an average class, 32% graduate in 4 years or less, 42% graduate in 5 years or less, and 48% graduate in 6 years or less.

Admissions Contact: Dean of Admission and Financial Aid. A video is available. E-mail: *admissions@antioch-college.edu*
Web: *antioch-college.edu*

ART ACADEMY OF CINCINNATI
A-5
Cincinnati, OH 45202-7106

(513) 562-8744
(800) 323-5692; Fax: (513) 562-8778

Full-time: 72 men, 83 women	**Faculty:** 16
Part-time: 1 man, 7 women	**Ph.D.s:** 99%
Graduate: 1 woman	**Student/Faculty:** 10 to 1
Year: semesters, summer session	**Tuition:** $18,100
Application Deadline: June 30	**Room & Board:** n/app
Freshman Class: 144 applied, 143 accepted, 52 enrolled	
SAT Verbal/Math: 514/500*	**ACT:** 21 SPECIAL

The Art Academy of Cincinnati, founded in 1887, is a private professional college offering B.F.A. degrees in fine art, communication arts, and art history, an associate degree in graphic design, and a master's degree in art education. In addition to regional accreditation, The Art Academy has baccalaureate program accreditation with NASAD. Collaboration with the Cincinnati Public Library is offered. Special learning facilities include a learning resource center and art gallery. The 120,000-square foot campus is in an urban area 2 miles northeast of downtown Cincinnati. There are 2 buildings.

Student Life: 65% of undergraduates are from Ohio. Others are from 6 states and 6 foreign countries. 89% are white. The average age of freshmen is 19; all undergraduates, 23. 20% do not continue beyond their first year; 60% remain to graduate.

Housing: There are no residence halls. All of students commute. All students may keep cars.

Activities: There are no fraternities or sororities. There are some groups and organizations on campus, including art and literary magazine. Popular campus events include field trips, Career Week, and Performance Day.

Disabled Students: All of the campus is accessible. Wheelchair ramps, elevators, special parking, specially equiped rest rooms, and lowered drinking fountains are available.

Services: Counseling and information services are available, as is tutoring in some subjects, including drawing and most academics.

Campus Safety and Security: Measures include 24-hour foot and vehicle patrol, security escort services, informal discussions, and pamphlets/posters/films.

Programs of Study: The Art Academy confers the B.F.A. degree. Associate and master's degrees are also awarded. Bachelor's degrees are awarded in COMMUNICATIONS AND THE ARTS (art history and appreciation, fine arts, graphic design, and illustration). Art history is the strongest academically. Graphic design and fine arts are the largest.

Required: To graduate, students must complete 132 semester hours, including 30 to 45 in the major, with a GPA of 2.0. The 21-credit foundation curriculum is required of all students, as are a senior thesis and a senior exhibition. Distribution requirements include 15 credits in art history and 6 each in English, social science, natural science, and humanities, as well as 3 each in a cross-disciplinary, aesthetics, and electives.

Special: Students may cross-register with member institutions of the Greater Cincinnati Consortium. Co-op programs are available in graphic design, illustration, and art history. Work-study programs are available with various local graphic design firms. Art history majors may intern at the Cincinnati Art Museum.

Faculty/Classroom: 50% of faculty are male; 50%, female. All teach undergraduates. The average class size in an introductory lecture is 25 and in a regular course, 12.

Admissions: 99% of the 2005-2006 applicants were accepted. The SAT scores for the 2005-2006 freshman class were: Verbal--25% below 500, 25% between 500 and 599, 44% between 600 and 700, and 1% above 700; Math--44% below 500, 37% between 500 and 599, and 19% between 600 and 700. The ACT scores were 57% below 21, 19% between 21 and 23, 19% between 24 and 26, and 5% between 27 and 28.

Requirements: The SAT or ACT is required. In addition, applicants should be graduates of an accredited secondary school. The GED is accepted. A portfolio review and an interview are necessary. A GPA of 2.0 is required. AP and CLEP credits are accepted. Important factors in the admissions decision are evidence of special talent, personality/intangible qualities, and recommendations by school officials.

Procedure: Freshmen are admitted in the fall. There is a deferred admissions plan and a rolling admissions plan. Early decision applications should be filed by March 1; regular applications, by June 30 for fall entry, along with a $25 fee. Notification is sent on a rolling basis. Applications are accepted on-line.

Transfer: 13 transfer students enrolled in 2004-2005. Applicants must present academic transcripts and a portfolio. 66 of 132 credits required for the bachelor's degree must be completed at the Art Academy.

Visiting: There are guides for informal visits and visitors may sit in on classes. To schedule a visit, contact Admissions at (513) 562-8740.

Financial Aid: In 2005-2006, 80% of all full-time freshmen and 81% of continuing full-time students received some form of financial aid. 60% of full-time freshmen and 66% of continuing full-time students received

need-based aid. The average freshman award was $10,505. Need-based scholarships or need-based grants averaged $6830; need-based self-help aid (loans and jobs) averaged $4634; and other non-need-based awards and non-need-based scholarships averaged $11,558. All undergraduates work part time. Average annual earnings from campus work are $1750. The average financial indebtedness of the 2005 graduate was $25,233. The FAFSA is required. The priority date for freshman financial aid applications for fall entry is March 1. There is a rolling deadline for filing freshman financial aid applications for fall entry.

International Students: There are 6 international students enrolled. They must take the TOEFL.

Computers: There are 80 PCs available in 4 different labs, open 24 hours a day, all with Internet access. All students may access the system. There are no time limits and no fees.

Graduates: From July 1, 2004 to June 30, 2005, 43 bachelor's degrees were awarded. The most popular majors were fine art (49%), communications design (49%), and art history (2%). In an average class, 73% graduate in 4 years, 22% graduate in 5 years, and 5% graduate in 6 years. 20 companies recruited on campus in 2004-2005. Of the 2004 graduating class, 10% were enrolled in graduate school within 6 months of graduation and 90% were employed.

Admissions Contact: Mary Jane Zumwalde, Director of Admissions. E-mail: *admissions@artacademy.edu* Web: *artacademy.edu*

ASHLAND UNIVERSITY
C-2
Ashland, OH 44805

(419) 289-5052
(800) 882-1548; Fax: (419) 289-5333

Full-time: 995 men, 1425 women	**Faculty:** 215; IIB, av$
Part-time: 95 men, 270 women	**Ph.D.s:** 79%
Graduate: 1470 men, 2475 women	**Student/Faculty:** 11 to 1
Year: semesters, summer session	**Tuition:** $18,000
Application Deadline: open	**Room & Board:** $7000
Freshman Class: n/av	
SAT or ACT: required	COMPETITIVE

Ashland University, founded in 1878, is a private liberal arts institution affiliated with the Brethren Church, offering undergraduate and graduate programs in the arts and sciences, business, education, and health services. There are 3 undergraduate and 3 graduate schools. Figures above capsule and profile are approximate. In addition to regional accreditation, AU has baccalaureate program accreditation with AACSB, AHEA, CSWE, NASM, NCATE, and NLN. The 2 libraries contain 270,000 volumes, 250,000 microform items, and 8800 audio/video tapes/CDs/DVDs, and subscribe to 700 periodicals including electronic. Computerized library services include the card catalog, interlibrary loans, and database searching. Special learning facilities include a learning resource center, art gallery, radio station, TV station, writing center, media center, and theater.. The 150-acre campus is in a small town midway between Cleveland and Columbus. Including any residence halls, there are 38 buildings.

Student Life: 94% of undergraduates are from Ohio. Others are from 29 states, 13 foreign countries, and Canada. 86% are white. 46% claim no religious affiliation; 34% Protestant; 14% Catholic. The average age of freshmen is 18; all undergraduates, 23. 42% do not continue beyond their first year; 58% remain to graduate.

Housing: 1620 students can be accommodated in college housing, which includes single-sex and coed dormitories, on-campus apartments, and fraternity houses. In addition, there are honors houses, honor floors, sorority suites, and a resource management residence. On-campus housing is guaranteed for all 4 years. 72% of students live on campus. Alcohol is not permitted. All students may keep cars.

Activities: 14% of men belong to 4 national fraternities; 22% of women belong to 5 national sororities. There are 100 groups on campus, including art, band, cheerleading, choir, chorus, dance, drama, drill team, environmental, ethnic, health, honors, international, jazz band, literary magazine, marching band, musical theater, newspaper, orchestra, pep band, photography, political, professional, radio and TV, religious, social service, student government, symphony, and yearbook. Popular campus events include Spectrum Series, plays, and Little Sibs Weekend.

Sports: There are 10 intercollegiate sports for men and 9 for women, and 20 intramural sports for men and 20 for women. Facilities include a 5800-seat stadium, a 3000-seat gym, an all-weather track, a field house, a weight-training center, an 8-lane swimming pool with diving board, saunas, exercise rooms, 3 basketball courts, 2 handball/racquetball courts, playing fields, a fitness center, and a soccer complex with 2 full-size fields.

Disabled Students: 5% of the campus is accessible. Wheelchair ramps, elevators, special parking, specially equipped rest rooms, special class scheduling, lowered drinking fountains, lowered telephones, and special housing are available.

Services: Counseling and information services are available, as is tutoring in every subject. There is a reader service for the blind.

Campus Safety and Security: Measures include 24-hour foot and vehicle patrol, self-defense education, security escort services, and informal discussions. There are pamphlets/posters/films, emergency telephones, lighted pathways/sidewalks, encoded student identification cards, and an electronic-access system in residence halls.

Programs of Study: AU confers B.A., B.S., B.M., B.S.B.A., B.S.Ed., B.S.N., and B.S.W. degrees. Associate, master's, and doctoral degrees are also awarded. Bachelor's degrees are awarded in BIOLOGICAL SCIENCE (biology/biological science and toxicology), BUSINESS (accounting, banking and finance, business administration and management, business economics, fashion merchandising, hotel/motel and restaurant management, management information systems, marketing/retailing/merchandising, and recreational facilities management), COMMUNICATIONS AND THE ARTS (art, broadcasting, communications, creative writing, dramatic arts, English, fine arts, French, journalism, media arts, music, musical theater, Spanish, and speech/debate/rhetoric), COMPUTER AND PHYSICAL SCIENCE (chemistry, computer science, geology, mathematics, and physics), EDUCATION (art, athletic training, early childhood, education administration, education of the exceptional child, elementary, English, foreign languages, health, home economics, music, physical, science, and secondary), ENGINEERING AND ENVIRONMENTAL DESIGN (commercial art and environmental science), HEALTH PROFESSIONS (predentistry, premedicine, preoptometry, preveterinary science, and recreation therapy), SOCIAL SCIENCE (American studies, child care/child and family studies, criminal justice, economics, food science, history, international studies, philosophy, physical fitness/movement, political science/government, prelaw, psychology, religion, social science, social work, and sociology). Preprofessional science is the strongest academically. Business and teacher education are the largest.

Required: To graduate, students must complete at least 128 semester hours with a minimum GPA of 2.0 overall and 2.25 in the major. All students must complete 3 semester hours of freshman studies and 44 semester hours of interdisciplinary studies, including courses in English, phys ed, religion, speech, business or economics, fine arts, humanities, science, and social science.

Special: Opportunities are provided for internships, co-op programs in all business majors, work-study programs, dual majors, credit by exam, study abroad in 27 countries, a Washington semester, and pass/fail options. There are 17 national honor societies, a freshman honors program, and 10 departmental honors programs.

Faculty/Classroom: 61% of faculty are male; 39%, female. 81% teach undergraduates. No introductory courses are taught by graduate students. The average class size in an introductory lecture is 20; in a laboratory, 11; and in a regular course, 18.

Requirements: The SAT or ACT is required. In addition, applicants must be graduates of an accredited secondary school. The GED is accepted. The recommended preparatory program includes 4 units of English, 3 each of science, social studies, and math, and 2 of foreign language. An interview is recommended. A GPA of 2.5 is required. AP and CLEP credits are accepted. Important factors in the admissions decision are advanced placement or honor courses, evidence of special talent, and leadership record.

Procedure: Freshmen are admitted to all sessions. Entrance exams should be taken in the spring of the junior year. There are deferred admissions and rolling admissions plans. Application deadlines are open. Applications are accepted on-line. The fall 2005 application fee was $25.

Transfer: Official transcripts from all previous colleges, showing course credits and a minimum GPA of 2.25, must be submitted when applying for transfer. Generally, if the student has successfully completed a minimum of 1 year of college, the SAT or ACT will not be required. 32 of 128 credits required for the bachelor's degree must be completed at AU.

Visiting: There are regularly scheduled orientations for prospective students. There are guides for informal visits and visitors may sit in on classes and stay overnight. To schedule a visit, contact the Office of Admissions at (800) 882-1548, ext. 5052.

Financial Aid: In a recent year, 99% of all full-time freshmen and 98% of continuing full-time students received some form of financial aid. 82% of full-time freshmen and 78% of continuing full-time students received need-based aid. The average freshman award was $17,408. Need-based scholarships or need-based grants averaged $10,382 ($18,687 maximum); need-based self-help aid (loans and jobs) averaged $4785 ($6625 maximum); non-need-based athletic scholarships averaged $434 ($24,464 maximum); other non-need-based awards and non-need-based scholarships averaged $843 ($17,974 maximum); and outside scholarships averaged $964. 30% of undergraduates worked part time. Average annual earnings from campus work were $954. The average financial indebtedness of a recent graduate was $18,250. The FAFSA, the college's own financial statement, and federal tax returns are required. Check with the school for current application deadlines.

International Students: The school actively recruits these students. They must score satisfactorily on the written TOEFL.

Computers: All students may access the system. There are no time limits. The fee is $1.50 per credit hour.

Admissions Contact: Office of Admissions.
E-mail: *auadmsn@ashland.edu* Web: *http://www.ashland.edu*

BALDWIN-WALLACE COLLEGE   D-1

Berea, OH 44017-2088   (440) 826-2222; Fax: (440) 826-3830

Full-time: 1242 men, 1746 women	**Faculty:** 160; IIB, av$
Part-time: 217 men, 470 women	**Ph.D.s:** 73%
Graduate: 390 men, 398 women	**Student/Faculty:** 19 to 1
Year: semesters, summer session	**Tuition:** $20,518
Application Deadline: May 1	**Room & Board:** $6738
Freshman Class: 2366 applied, 1870 accepted, 599 enrolled	
SAT Verbal/Math: 547/557	**ACT:** 23 **VERY COMPETITIVE**

Baldwin-Wallace College, established in 1845, is a private liberal arts institution affiliated with the United Methodist Church. In addition to regional accreditation, B-W has baccalaureate program accreditation with NASM and NCATE. The 3 libraries contain 200,000 volumes and 103,000 microform items, and subscribe to 20,000 periodicals including electronic. Computerized library services include the card catalog, interlibrary loans, database searching, and Internet access. Special learning facilities include a learning resource center, art gallery, radio station, neuroscience lab, and observatory. The 100-acre campus is in a suburban area 14 miles southwest of Cleveland. Including any residence halls, there are 60 buildings.

Student Life: 89% of undergraduates are from Ohio. Others are from 32 states, 13 foreign countries, and Canada. 85% are from public schools. 86% are white. 46% are Catholic; 30% Protestant; 14% Buddhist, Hindu, Muslim, Orthodox, Unitarian, nondenominational. The average age of freshmen is 18; all undergraduates, 20. 21% do not continue beyond their first year; 67% remain to graduate.

Housing: 1955 students can be accommodated in college housing, which includes single-sex and coed dorms and on-campus apartments. In addition, there are honors houses, special-interest house, freshman only houses, wellness halls, Sprout Houses for single mothers and children, and Carmel Living and Learning Center. On-campus housing is guaranteed for all 4 years. 55% of students live on campus; of those, 40% remain on campus on weekends. Upperclassmen may keep cars.

Activities: 20% of men belong to 3 national fraternities; 22% of women belong to 6 national sororities. There are 135 groups on campus, including art, band, cheerleading, chess, choir, chorale, chorus, computers, dance, drama, drill team, ethnic, gay, honors, international, jazz band, literary magazine, musical theater, newspaper, opera, orchestra, pep band, political, professional, radio and TV, religious, social, social service, student government, symphony, and yearbook. Popular campus events include April Reign Games and Dance Marathon.

Sports: There are 11 intercollegiate sports for men and 10 for women, and 18 intramural sports for men and 18 for women. Facilities include an 8000-seat stadium with polyturf and an all-weather track, a 3000-seat gym, baseball fields, and a 6-court tennis complex. The recreation center houses a 200-meter track, a swimming pool, a dance studio, wrestling, gymnastics, and weight rooms, and facilities for basketball, racquetball, volleyball, bowling, and billiards.

Disabled Students: 75% of the campus is accessible. Wheelchair ramps, elevators, special parking, specially equipped rest rooms, special class scheduling, and lowered telephones are available.

Services: Counseling and information services are available, as is tutoring in every subject. There is a reader service for the blind, and remedial math, reading, and writing.

Campus Safety and Security: Measures include 24-hour foot and vehicle patrol, security escort services, shuttle buses, and informal discussions. There are pamphlets/posters/films, emergency telephones, and lighted pathways/sidewalks.

Programs of Study: B-W confers B.A., B.S., B.M., B.M.E, and B.S.Ed. degrees. Master's degrees are also awarded. Bachelor's degrees are awarded in BIOLOGICAL SCIENCE (biology/biological science and neurosciences), BUSINESS (accounting, banking and finance, business administration and management, human resources, management science, marketing management, organizational behavior, and sports management), COMMUNICATIONS AND THE ARTS (art history and appreciation, broadcasting, communications, English, film arts, French, German, music, music history and appreciation, music performance, music theory and composition, musical theater, public relations, Spanish, and studio art), COMPUTER AND PHYSICAL SCIENCE (chemistry, computer science, information sciences and systems, mathematics, and physics), EDUCATION (art, athletic training, early childhood, health, middle school, music, physical, science, and specific learning disabilities), ENGINEERING AND ENVIRONMENTAL DESIGN (preengineering), HEALTH PROFESSIONS (exercise science, music therapy, physical therapy, predentistry, and premedicine), SOCIAL SCIENCE (criminal justice, economics, history, international studies, philosophy, political science/government, prelaw, psychology, religion, and sociology). Business, education, and sports and fitness administration are the largest.

Required: All students must complete 124 semester hours and have at least a 2.0 GPA. A total of 45 semester hours must be taken in the liberal arts core, including 20 in humanities, 10 each in natural science and social science, 3 in math/computer science/statistics, and 2 in health and phys ed. Comprehensive exams are required in some majors.

Special: Special academic programs include internships that can qualify for credit, work-study programs, student teaching in England, and study abroad in Europe, India, Japan, Central America, and the Middle East. There is cross-registration within the Cleveland Commission on Higher Education, as well as 3-2 programs in social work and biology with Case Western Reserve University, and in engineering with Columbia, Washington, and Case Western Reserve Universities; a 2-2 co-op allied health program is offered with local community colleges and a 3-2 masters program in accounting and human resources. B-W also offers the Consortium for Music Therapy, accelerated degree programs, a general studies degree, a B.A.-B.S. degree, dual and student-designed majors, credit for life, military, and work experience, and pass/fail options. The Continuing Education Program offers degrees through evening and weekend colleges. Concentrations in business include accounting, banking and finance, and marketing. There are 5 national honor societies, a freshman honors program, and 8 departmental honors programs.

Faculty/Classroom: 56% of faculty are male; 44%, female. 99% teach undergraduates. No introductory courses are taught by graduate students. The average class size in an introductory lecture is 21; in a laboratory, 10; and in a regular course, 19.

Admissions: 79% of the 2005-2006 applicants were accepted. The SAT scores for the 2005-2006 freshman class were: Verbal--25% below 500, 45% between 500 and 599, 26% between 600 and 700, and 4% above 700; Math--25% below 500, 43% between 500 and 599, 28% between 600 and 700, and 4% above 700. The ACT scores were 23% below 21, 27% between 21 and 23, 29% between 24 and 26, 14% between 27 and 28, and 7% above 28. 49% of the current freshmen were in the top fifth of their class; 80% were in the top two fifths. There were 2 National Merit finalists. 15 freshmen graduated first in their class.

Requirements: Satisfactory score is required on the SAT or ACT. The scores are used to support data from the high school record; alternative scores are considered. Applicants must be graduates of an accredited secondary school or have earned a GED. 16 academic credits are required, including 4 in English, 3 each in math, natural science, and social science, and 2 in a foreign language; alternative distributions are considered. A teacher's recommendation is required. B-W requires applicants to be in the upper 50% of their class. A GPA of 2.75 is required. AP and CLEP credits are accepted. Important factors in the admissions decision are leadership record, advanced placement or honor courses, and extracurricular activities record.

Procedure: Freshmen are admitted to all sessions. Entrance exams should be taken late in the junior year or early in the senior year. There is a deferred admissions plan and a rolling admissions plan. Applications should be filed by May 1 for fall entry, March 15 for spring entry, and June 15 for summer entry, along with a $25 fee. Notification is sent on a rolling basis. Applications are accepted on-line.

Transfer: 363 transfer students enrolled in 2004-2005. Students must be in good academic standing at prior institution(s). 32 of 124 credits required for the bachelor's degree must be completed at B-W.

Visiting: There are regularly scheduled orientations for prospective students, including an interview, a tour, and classroom visits. There are guides for informal visits and visitors may sit in on classes and stay overnight. To schedule a visit, contact the Admission Office at admission@bw.edu.

Financial Aid: In 2005-2006, 97% of all full-time students received some form of financial aid. 81% of full-time freshmen and 77% of continuing full-time students received need-based aid. The average freshman award was $16,321. Need-based scholarships or need-based grants averaged $11,837 ($19,079 maximum); need-based self-help aid (loans and jobs) averaged $4393 ($5325 maximum); and other non-need-based awards and non-need-based scholarships averaged $7975 ($14,900 maximum). 80% of undergraduates work part time. Average annual earnings from campus work are $1000. The average financial indebtedness of the 2005 graduate was $16,250. The FAFSA is required. The priority date for freshman financial aid applications for fall entry is April 1. The deadline for filing freshman financial aid applications for fall entry is September 1.

International Students: There are 32 international students enrolled. The school actively recruits these students. They must score satisfactorily on the written TOEFL and also take the SAT or the ACT.

Computers: Wireless access is available. All students may access the system 24 hours a day. There are no time limits and no fees.

Graduates: From July 1, 2004 to June 30, 2005, 748 bachelor's degrees were awarded. The most popular majors were business (28%), education (16%), and psychology (10%). In an average class, 2% graduate in 3 years or less, 50% graduate in 4 years or less, 65% graduate in 5 years or less, and 67% graduate in 6 years or less. 29 companies recruited on campus in 2004-2005. Of the 2004 graduating class, 19% were enrolled in graduate school within 6 months of graduation and 70% were employed.

Admissions Contact: Susan Dileno, Dean of Admission and Financial Aid. E-mail: sdileno@bw.edu

BLUFFTON COLLEGE B-2
Bluffton, OH 45817

(419) 358-3257
(800) 488-3257; Fax: (419) 358-3232

Full-time: 427 men, 578 women	**Faculty:** 64; IIB, --$
Part-time: 30 men, 44 women	**Ph.D.s:** 70%
Graduate: 56 men, 76 women	**Student/Faculty:** 16 to 1
Year: semesters, summer session	**Tuition:** $19,428
Application Deadline: May 31	**Room & Board:** $6682
Freshman Class: 1065 applied, 805 accepted, 266 enrolled	
SAT Verbal/Math: 536/529	**ACT:** 23 COMPETITIVE

Bluffton College, founded in 1899, is a private, Christian, liberal arts institution affiliated with Mennonite Church, U.S.A. In addition to regional accreditation, Bluffton College has baccalaureate program accreditation with ADA, CSWE, and NASM. The library contains 165,679 volumes, 135,354 microform items, and 1295 audio/video tapes/CDs/DVDs, and subscribes to 5525 periodicals including electronic. Computerized library services include the card catalog, interlibrary loans, database searching, Internet access, and laptop Internet portals. Special learning facilities include a learning resource center, art gallery, radio station, and the Lion and the Lamb Peace Arts Center. The 65-acre campus is in a small town 60 miles south of Toledo and 75 miles north of Dayton. Including any residence halls, there are 25 buildings.

Student Life: 86% of undergraduates are from Ohio. Others are from 21 states, 15 foreign countries, and Canada. 95% are from public schools. 92% are white. 63% are Protestant; 21% Muslim, Hindu, and Buddhist; 16% Catholic. The average age of freshmen is 18; all undergraduates, 22. 25% do not continue beyond their first year; 58% remain to graduate.

Housing: 828 students can be accommodated in college housing, which includes single-sex and coed dorms. On-campus housing is guaranteed for all 4 years. All full-time students must live in residence halls unless commuting from home. 75% of students live on campus; of those, 50% remain on campus on weekends. Alcohol is not permitted. All students may keep cars.

Activities: There are no fraternities or sororities. There are 40 groups on campus, including art, band, cheerleading, choir, chorale, chorus, dance, drama, ethnic, honors, international, jazz band, literary magazine, musical theater, newspaper, political, professional, radio and TV, religious, social, social service, student government, and yearbook. Popular campus events include International Week, Spiritual Emphasis Weeks, and Artist Series.

Sports: There are 8 intercollegiate sports for men and 8 for women, and 7 intramural sports for men and 7 for women. Facilities include 2 gyms, an athletic complex, baseball/softball and football fields, an all-weather track, and a 2600-seat stadium.

Disabled Students: 33% of the campus is accessible. Wheelchair ramps, elevators, special parking, specially equipped rest rooms, special class scheduling, lowered drinking fountains, lowered telephones, and special computers for visually impaired students are available.

Services: Counseling and information services are available, as is tutoring in every subject. There is a reader service for the blind, and remedial math, reading, and writing. Tutoring is available for most students, as are classes at the student's request and/or faculty designation.

Campus Safety and Security: Measures include informal discussions, pamphlets/posters/films, emergency telephones, and lighted pathways/sidewalks. In a town of only 3500, village police cruisers regularly patrol the campus during night hours. There are also 2 night security officers who communicate directly with village police and routinely patrol campus at night.

Programs of Study: Bluffton College confers the B.A. degree. Master's degrees are also awarded. Bachelor's degrees are awarded in BIOLOGICAL SCIENCE (biology/biological science), BUSINESS (accounting, apparel and accessories marketing, business administration and management, organizational behavior, recreational facilities management, and sports management), COMMUNICATIONS AND THE ARTS (art, communications, creative writing, English, music, and Spanish), COMPUTER AND PHYSICAL SCIENCE (chemistry, computer science, information sciences and systems, mathematics, and physical sciences), EDUCATION (early childhood, home economics, middle school, music, and physical), HEALTH PROFESSIONS (premedicine), SOCIAL SCIENCE (child psychology/development, criminal justice, economics, family/consumer studies, food science, history, psychology, religion, social science, social work, and sociology). Business, early childhood education, and organizational management are the largest.

Required: To graduate, students must complete 124 semester hours with 40 to 60 in the major, and have a minimum GPA of 2.0. The general education requirements must be met, and satisfactory achievement in departmental senior comprehensives demonstrated. Distribution requirements are approximately one third for general education requirements, including 6 hours of religion, and one third to one half for the major.

Special: Special arrangements include internships in business, recreation, social work, and education, a Washington semester through the Council for Christian Colleges and Universities, and study abroad. Student-designed majors and independent study are possible, as is credit for prior learning and for learning in voluntary service. There is an accelerated degree program in organizational management. Nondegree study and pass/fail options are offered. There are 2 national honor societies and a freshman honors program.

Faculty/Classroom: 60% of faculty are male; 40%, female. All teach undergraduates. No introductory courses are taught by graduate students. The average class size in an introductory lecture is 23; in a laboratory, 12; and in a regular course, 17.

Admissions: 76% of the 2005-2006 applicants were accepted. The SAT scores for the 2005-2006 freshman class were: Verbal--37% below 500, 46% between 500 and 599, 14% between 600 and 700, and 3% above 700; Math--41% below 500, 32% between 500 and 599, 24% between 600 and 700, and 3% above 700. The ACT scores were 24% below 21, 30% between 21 and 23, 33% between 24 and 26, 10% between 27 and 28, and 3% above 28. 39% of the current freshmen were in the top fifth of their class; 75% were in the top two fifths. 11 freshmen graduated first in their class in a recent year.

Requirements: A satisfactory score is required on the SAT or ACT; the ACT is preferred. Other admissions requirements include graduation from an accredited secondary school, with a 2.3 GPA or class rank above 50%. Recommended courses include 4 units of English and 3 units each of math, science, social studies, and a foreign language. The GED is accepted. A personal campus visit and an interview are strongly recommended. Music students must audition. AP and CLEP credits are accepted. Important factors in the admissions decision are recommendations by school officials and extracurricular activities record.

Procedure: Freshmen are admitted to all sessions. Entrance exams should be taken in the spring of the junior year or fall of the senior year. There is a deferred admissions plan. There is a rolling admissions plan. The priority deadline for applications for fall entry is May 31.The fee is $20. Notification is sent on a rolling basis. Applications are accepted online.

Transfer: 88 transfer students enrolled in 2004-2005. Transfer students must have a minimum college GPA of 2.0, meet eligibility criteria from previous institutions, and have met their financial obligations at the former institution. A signed transfer recommendation must be submitted from each college attended. 30 of 124 credits required for the bachelor's degree must be completed at Bluffton College.

Visiting: There are regularly scheduled orientations for prospective students, including high school preview days on Saturdays and overnight visit programs; personal visits are arranged on a daily basis and are strongly encouraged. There are guides for informal visits and visitors may sit in on classes and stay overnight. To schedule a visit, contact the Office of Admission.

Financial Aid: In 2005-2006, all full-time students received some form of financial aid. 88% of full-time freshmen and 71% of continuing full-time students received need-based aid. The average freshman award was $17,726. Need-based scholarships or need-based grants averaged $12,869 ($21,565 maximum); need-based self-help aid (loans and jobs) averaged $4945 ($5475 maximum); and other non-need-based awards and non-need-based scholarships averaged $8061 ($12,388 maximum). 66% of undergraduates work part time. Average annual earnings from campus work are $1052. The average financial indebtedness of the 2005 graduate was $20,039. The FAFSA is required. The priority date for freshman financial aid applications for fall entry is May 1. The deadline for filing freshman financial aid applications for fall entry is October 1.

International Students: There are 18 international students enrolled. A satisfactory score on the TOEFL and/or SAT is required.

Computers: Wireless access is available. Networked PCs are available to all students in a central lab and other locations, inlcuding many academic departments. Wireless networks are available in major buildings. All students may access the system any time. There are no time limits and no fees.

Graduates: From July 1, 2004 to June 30, 2005, 242 bachelor's degrees were awarded. The most popular majors were organizational management (25%), early childhood education (11%), and business administration (7%). In an average class, 1% graduate in 3 years or less, 49% graduate in 4 years or less, 57% graduate in 5 years or less, and 57% graduate in 6 years or less. 200 companies recruited on campus in 2004-2005. Of the 2004 graduating class, 9% were enrolled in graduate school within 6 months of graduation and 74% were employed.

Admissions Contact: Chris Jebsen, Director of Admissions. A video is available. E-mail: *admissions@bluffton.edu* Web: *www.bluffton.edu*

BOWLING GREEN STATE UNIVERSITY   B-1
Bowling Green, OH 43403

(419) 372-7799
(866) 246-6732; Fax: (419) 372-6955

Full-time: 6693 men, 8321 women	Faculty: 739; I, --$
Part-time: 531 men, 534 women	Ph.D.s: 77%
Graduate: 1112 men, 1825 women	Student/Faculty: 20 to 1
Year: semesters, summer session	Tuition: $8560 ($15,868)
Application Deadline: July 15	Room & Board: $6434
Freshman Class: 11,168 applied, 10,058 accepted, 3585 enrolled	
SAT Verbal/Math: 516/516	ACT: 22 COMPETITIVE

Bowling Green State University, founded in 1910, is a public Doctoral I/Research II institution offering more than 200 undergraduate majors and programs and more than 80 graduate programs. There are 6 undergraduate schools and 1 graduate school. In addition to regional accreditation, BGSU has baccalaureate program accreditation with AACSB, ACCE, ACEJMC, ACS, APA, APTA, CAAHEP, CADE, CAHEA, CCNE, CSWE, NAIT, NASAD, NASM, NASPE, NAST, NCATE, NEHSPAC, and NRPA. The 2 libraries contain 2,468,812 volumes and 2,364,679 microform items, and subscribe to 9502 periodicals including electronic. Computerized library services include the card catalog, interlibrary loans, and database searching. Special learning facilities include a learning resource center, art gallery, planetarium, radio station, and TV station. The 1230-acre campus is in a small town 25 miles south of Toledo. Including any residence halls, there are 127 buildings.

Student Life: 90% of undergraduates are from Ohio. Others are from 50 states, 36 foreign countries, and Canada. 84% are white. The average age of freshmen is 19; all undergraduates, 21. 21% do not continue beyond their first year; 60% remain to graduate.

Housing: 7330 students can be accommodated in college housing, which includes single-sex and coed dorms, on-campus apartments, fraternity houses, and sorority houses. In addition, there are honors houses, language houses, special-interest houses, and a living-learning center. 55% of students commute. All students may keep cars.

Activities: 11% of men belong to 19 national fraternities; 11% of women belong to 19 national sororities. There are more than 280 groups on campus, including art, band, cheerleading, chess, choir, chorale, chorus, computers, dance, debate, drama, drill team, ethnic, film, gay, honors, international, jazz band, marching band, musical theater, newspaper, orchestra, photography, political, professional, radio and TV, religious, social, social service, student government, symphony, and yearbook. Popular campus events include Greek Week, International Festival, and all-campus picnic.

Sports: There are 11 intercollegiate sports for men and 11 for women, and 13 intramural sports for men and 13 for women. Facilities include 4 buildings, including a student recreation center and an intramural field house facility, a 30,000-seat football stadium, a 5000-seat gym, tennis courts, a golf course, basketball and ice arenas, and softball and intramural fields.

Disabled Students: 80% of the campus is accessible. Wheelchair ramps, elevators, special parking, specially equipped rest rooms, special class scheduling, lowered drinking fountains, lowered telephones, and a shuttle van with lift capabilities are available.

Services: Counseling and information services are available, as is tutoring in some subjects, including writing, math, and 100-level content area classes such as biology, chemistry, and sociology. There is a reader service for the blind, and remedial math, reading, and writing.

Campus Safety and Security: Measures include 24-hour foot and vehicle patrol, self-defense education, security escort services, and shuttle buses. There are informal discussions, pamphlets/posters/films, emergency telephones, lighted pathways/sidewalks, and a campus 911 number.

Programs of Study: BGSU confers B.A., B.S., B.A.H.S., B.F.A., B.L.S., and B.Mus. degrees. Master's and doctoral degrees are also awarded. Bachelor's degrees are awarded in BIOLOGICAL SCIENCE (biology/biological science, life science, and neurosciences), BUSINESS (accounting, apparel and accessories marketing, banking and finance, business administration and management, business economics, business law, hospitality management services, institutional management, international business management, management information systems, marketing/retailing/merchandising, personnel management, recreation and leisure services, and sports management), COMMUNICATIONS AND THE ARTS (art, art history and appreciation, broadcasting, communications, creative writing, dance, design, dramatic arts, English, film arts, fine arts, French, German, journalism, Latin, music, Russian, Spanish, and telecommunications), COMPUTER AND PHYSICAL SCIENCE (chemistry, computer science, geology, information sciences and systems, mathematics, physical sciences, physics, and statistics), EDUCATION (art, business, early childhood, health, marketing and distribution, middle school, physical, and special), ENGINEERING AND ENVIRONMENTAL DESIGN (environmental science), HEALTH PROFESSIONS (exercise science, health care administration, health science, physical therapy, and speech pathology/audiology), SOCIAL SCIENCE (African studies, American studies, Asian/Oriental studies, child care/child and family studies, classical/ancient civilization, criminal justice, early childhood studies, economics, ethnic studies, family/consumer resource management, geography, history, international studies, liberal arts/general studies, philosophy, physical fitness/movement, political science/government, psychology, public administration, social science, sociology, Western civilization/culture, and women's studies). Biology, psychology, and marketing are the largest.

Required: To graduate, students must complete a minimum of 122 semester hours, including at least 30 in the major, depending on the major, and maintain a minimum 2.0 GPA. The 8-course mandatory general education core includes 2 courses each from natural sciences, social sciences, and humanities and the arts, 1 course from cultural diversity in the United States, and 1 additional course from among natural sciences, social sciences, humanities and the arts, and foreign languages and cultures. At least 1 of the courses in the social sciences or humanities and arts must be designated as foreign cultures or foreign language at the 200 level or above.

Special: Special academic programs include co-op programs in all majors with the National Student Exchange, internships, a Washington semester, work-study, and study abroad. Dual majors are available in all programs, and a B.A.-B.S. degree is offered in computer science, geology, math, psychology, statistics, scientific and technical communication, and individualized planned program. Student-designed majors, independent study, credit for experience, nondegree study, and pass/fail options are possible. There are 20 national honor societies, including Phi Beta Kappa, and a freshman honors program.

Faculty/Classroom: 55% of faculty are male; 45%, female. 88% teach undergraduates. Graduate students teach 23% of introductory courses. The average class size in an introductory lecture is 27; in a laboratory, 18; and in a regular course, 23.

Admissions: 90% of the 2005-2006 applicants were accepted. The SAT scores for the 2005-2006 freshman class were: Verbal--44% below 500, 38% between 500 and 599, 14% between 600 and 700, and 4% above 700; Math--43% below 500, 37% between 500 and 599, 17% between 600 and 700, and 3% above 700. The ACT scores were 40% below 21, 31% between 21 and 23, 16% between 24 and 26, 6% between 27 and 28, and 7% above 28. 28% of the current freshmen were in the top fifth of their class; 58% were in the top two fifths. There were 20 National Merit finalists.

Requirements: The ACT is required and the SAT is recommended. In addition, for all freshmen except those out of high school for 3 or more years, SAT score must be satisfactory and the minimum ACT score is 20. Performance and test scores must be at minimum and above to be considered. There is no automatic admission. Special circumstances are reviewed as applicable. Other admissions requirements include graduation from an accredited secondary school with a recommended 4 years of English, 3 years each of math, science, and social studies/history, 2 years of a foreign language, and 1 year of art or music. The GED is accepted. Music students must audition. A GPA of 2.5 is required. AP and CLEP credits are accepted. Important factors in the admissions decision are advanced placement or honor courses, recommendations by school officials, and evidence of special talent.

Procedure: Freshmen are admitted to all sessions. There is a rolling admissions plan. Entrance exams should be taken in the junior year. There is a deferred admissions plan. Applications should be filed by July 15 for fall entry, December 15 for spring entry, and May 15 for summer entry. The fall 2005 application fee was $35. Notification is sent on a rolling basis. Applications are accepted on-line.

Transfer: 983 transfer students enrolled in 2004-2005. Transfer students must either have an associate's degree or have a 2.5 GPA (60 hours or more), or a 2.0 GPA (fewer than 60 hours). 30 of 122 credits required for the bachelor's degree must be completed at BGSU.

Visiting: There are regularly scheduled orientations for prospective students. There are guides for informal visits and visitors may sit in on classes and stay overnight. To schedule a visit, contact the Office of Admissions at (419) 372-BGSU or *admissions@bgnet.bgsu.edu*.

Financial Aid: The FAFSA is required.

International Students: There were 153 international students enrolled in a recent year. The school actively recruits these students. They must take the written TOEFL or the MELAB.

Computers: All students may access the system during operating hours. There are no time limits and no fees.

Graduates: From July 1, 2004 to June 30, 2005, 2960 bachelor's degrees were awarded. The most popular majors were kindergarten/preschool education (7%), speech and rhetorical studies (5%), and middle school education (4%). In an average class, 33% graduate in 4 years or less, 56% graduate in 5 years or less, and 60% graduate in 6 years or less.

Admissions Contact: Gary Swegan, Director of Admissions. A video is available. E-mail: *admissions@bgnet.bgsu.edu*
Web: *http://go2.bgsu.edu/choose/welcome/*

CAPITAL UNIVERSITY   C-3
Columbus, OH 43209-2394
(614) 236-6101
(800) 289-6289; Fax: (614) 236-6926

Full-time: 868 men, 1374 women	**Faculty:** 178; IIA, av$
Part-time: 161 men, 459 women	**Ph.D.s:** 33%
Graduate: 514 men, 515 women	**Student/Faculty:** 13 to 1
Year: semesters, summer session	**Tuition:** $24,100
Application Deadline: April 15	**Room & Board:** $6340
Freshman Class: n/av	
SAT or ACT: required	**COMPETITIVE**

Capital University, established in 1830, is a private institution affiliated with the Evangelical Lutheran Church in America. Its undergraduate and graduate programs emphasize the liberal arts and sciences, music, and nursing. There are 5 undergraduate and 3 graduate schools. In addition to regional accreditation, Capital has baccalaureate program accreditation with ABA, ACBSP, ACS, CCNE, CSWE, NASM, NCATE. The 2 libraries contain 190,987 volumes, 148,561 microform items, and 15,299 audio/video tapes/CDs/DVDs, and subscribe to 5765 periodicals including electronic. Computerized library services include the card catalog, interlibrary loans, and database searching. Special learning facilities include an art gallery, radio station, and a TV studio. The 48-acre campus is in a suburban area 3 miles east of downtown Columbus. Including any residence halls, there are 24 buildings.

Student Life: 96% of undergraduates are from Ohio. 78% are white; 12% African American. The average age of freshmen is 19; all undergraduates, 23.

Housing: University housing includes coed dorms, on-campus apartments, and off-campus apartments. In addition, there are special-interest floors, substance-free floors, Greek organization floors, and a self-governing unit. On-campus housing is guaranteed for all 4 years. 64% of students commute. Upperclassmen may keep cars.

Activities: 7% of men belong to 2 local and 4 national fraternities; 8% of women belong to 3 local and 1 national sorority. There are many groups and organizations on campus, including art, band, cheerleading, choir, chorale, chorus, dance, debate, drama, drill team, ethnic, gay, honors, international, jazz band, literary magazine, musical theater, newspaper, opera, orchestra, pep band, political, professional, radio and TV, religious, social, social service, student government, symphony, and yearbook. Popular campus events include Greek Week, Martin Luther King Jr. Day of Learning; and Kids and Sibs Weekend.

Sports: There are 8 intercollegiate sports for men and 6 for women, and 9 intramural sports for men and 9 for women. Facilities include a 2500-seat football stadium, a 2400-seat gym, tennis courts, and weight and game rooms. The recreation center offers bowling, billiards, and other game facilities.

Disabled Students: Wheelchair ramps, elevators, special parking, specially equipped rest rooms, special class scheduling, and special housing are available.

Services: Counseling and information services are available, as is tutoring in most subjects. There is remedial math and writing.

Campus Safety and Security: Measures include 24-hour foot and vehicle patrol, self-defense education, security escort services, and shuttle buses. There are pamphlets/posters/films and lighted pathways/sidewalks.

Programs of Study: Capital confers B.A., B.F.A., B.G.S., B.M., B.S.N., and B.S.W. degrees. Master's degrees are also awarded. Bachelor's degrees are awarded in BIOLOGICAL SCIENCE (biochemistry and biology/biological science), BUSINESS (accounting and business administration and management), COMMUNICATIONS AND THE ARTS (communications, dramatic arts, English, fine arts, French, music, public relations, Spanish, and speech/debate/rhetoric), COMPUTER AND PHYSICAL SCIENCE (chemistry, computer science, and mathematics), EDUCATION (elementary, middle school, physical, and secondary), ENGINEERING AND ENVIRONMENTAL DESIGN (environmental science), HEALTH PROFESSIONS (art therapy, nursing, predentistry, premedicine, and sports medicine), SOCIAL SCIENCE (behavioral science, criminal justice, economics, history, international relations, philosophy, physical fitness/movement, political science/government, prelaw, psychology, religion, social work, and sociology). Business, education, and history are the largest.

Required: To graduate, all students must complete at least 124 semester hours, with a varying number of hours in the major, and maintain a minimum 2.0 GPA. The university core, 36 semester hours, must be followed in an ordered sequence throughout the 4 years; considered an assessment program, it includes specific courses in reading and writing, communication, health, art, science, social science, the humanities, ethics, and religion.

Special: Special academic programs include cross-registration with the Higher Education Council of Columbus, semester internships in most majors, and a Washington semester. Study abroad in 21 countries on 5 continents includes opportunities in Jamaica and at the Kodaly Institute of Music in Hungary. Also possible are a general studies degree and student-designed majors. A dual degree in engineering is offered with Case

Western Reserve University and Washington University in St. Louis. Credit for life, military, and work experience may be granted, and non-degree study and pass/fail options are offered. There is a freshman honors program.

Faculty/Classroom: 55% of faculty are male; 45%, female. 80% teach undergraduates. No introductory courses are taught by graduate students. The average class size in an introductory lecture is 30; in a laboratory, 12; and in a regular course, 17.

Admissions: The SAT scores for the 2005-2006 freshman class were: Verbal--30% below 500, 42% between 500 and 599, 24% between 600 and 700, and 4% above 700; Math--28% below 500, 45% between 500 and 599, 22% between 600 and 700, and 5% above 700. The ACT scores were 26% below 21, 31% between 21 and 23, 24% between 24 and 26, 10% between 27 and 28, and 9% above 28. 42% of the current freshmen were in the top fifth of their class; 74% were in the top two fifths.

Requirements: The SAT or ACT is required. Other admissions requirements include graduation from an accredited secondary school with 16 academic credits, including 4 units of English, 3 each of math, science, and social science, 2 units of a foreign language, and 1 of electives; nursing applicants need chemistry. The GED is accepted. High school students must submit recommendations from their guidance counselor. An interview is recommended. Students must audition for entry to the Conservatory of Music. A GPA of 2.6 is required. AP and CLEP credits are accepted. Important factors in the admissions decision are advanced placement or honor courses, recommendations by school officials, and evidence of special talent.

Procedure: Freshmen are admitted fall, spring, and summer. Entrance exams should be taken by December of the senior year. There is a deferred admissions plan and a rolling admissions plan. Applications should be filed by April 15 for fall entry, December 1 for winter entry, and April 1 for summer entry, along with a $25 fee. Notification is sent on a rolling basis. 846 early decision candidates were accepted for the 2005-2006 class. Applications are accepted on-line.

Transfer: 72 transfer students enrolled in 2004-2005. Transfer students must have a minimum college GPA of 2.25. The SAT or ACT is recommended, as is an interview. 30 of 124 credits required for the bachelor's degree must be completed at Capital.

Visiting: There are regularly scheduled orientations for prospective students, including an interview with a counselor and a campus tour. There are guides for informal visits and visitors may sit in on classes and stay overnight. To schedule a visit, contact the Admissions Office at *admissions@capital.edu.*

Financial Aid: In 2005-2006, 88% of all full-time freshmen and 82% of continuing full-time students received some form of financial aid. The average freshman award was $19,487. Need-based scholarships or need-based grants averaged $15,032; and need-based self-help aid (loans and jobs) averaged $5025. The average financial indebtedness of the 2005 graduate was $25,171. The FAFSA is required. The deadline for filing freshman financial aid applications for fall entry is April 1.

International Students: There are 16 international students enrolled. The school actively recruits these students. They must score satisfactorily on the written TOEFL.

Computers: Wireless access is available. All students may access the system 24 hours per day. There are no time limits and no fees.

Graduates: From July 1, 2004 to June 30, 2005, 590 bachelor's degrees were awarded. In an average class, 48% graduate in 4 years or less, 57% graduate in 5 years or less, and 59% graduate in 6 years or less. 27 companies recruited on campus in 2004-2005.

Admissions Contact: Kimberly V. Ebbrecht, Director of Admission. A video is available. E-mail: *admissions@capital.edu* Web: *www.capital.edu*

CASE WESTERN RESERVE UNIVERSITY · D-1

Cleveland, OH 44106 · **(216) 368-4450; Fax: (216) 368-5111**

Full-time: 2214 men, 1500 women	Faculty: 464; I, av$
Part-time: 132 men, 103 women	Ph.D.s: 95%
Graduate: 2865 men, 2801 women	Student/Faculty: 8 to 1
Year: semesters, summer session	Tuition: $28,678
Application Deadline: January 15	Room & Board: $8636
Freshman Class: 7181 applied, 4916 accepted, 1162 enrolled	
SAT Verbal/Math: 660/690*	ACT: 29 MOST COMPETITVE

Case Western Reserve University, founded in 1826, is a private institution offering undergraduate, graduate, and professional programs in arts and sciences, dentistry, engineering, law, management, medicine, nursing, and social work. There are 4 undergraduate and 8 graduate schools. In addition to regional accreditation, Case has baccalaureate program accreditation with AACSB, ABET, CAHEA, CSAB, NASM, and NLN. The 7 libraries contain 2,452,731 volumes, 2,524,889 microform items, and 54,343 audio/video tapes/CDs/DVDs, and subscribe to 20,678 periodicals including electronic. Computerized library services include the card catalog, interlibrary loans, database searching, Internet access, and laptop Internet portals. Special learning facilities include a learning re-

source center, art gallery, natural history museum, planetarium, radio station, and a biology field station. The 155-acre campus is in an urban area 4 miles east of downtown Cleveland. Including any residence halls, there are 94 buildings.

Student Life: 55% of undergraduates are from Ohio. Students are from 47 states, 31 foreign countries, and Canada. 70% are from public schools. 65% are white; 15% Asian American. The average age of freshmen is 18; all undergraduates, 20. 8% do not continue beyond their first year; 79% remain to graduate.

Housing: 3095 students can be accommodated in college housing, which includes single-sex and coed dorms, on-campus apartments, fraternity houses, sorority houses, and special housing for students in the College Scholars Program. On-campus housing is guaranteed for all 4 years. 85% of students live on campus; of those, 85% remain on campus on weekends. All students may keep cars.

Activities: 34% of men belong to 17 national fraternities; 23% of women belong to 1 local and 4 national sororities. There are 100 groups on campus, including art, cheerleading, chess, choir, chorale, chorus, computers, dance, debate, drama, ethnic, film, gay, honors, international, jazz band, literary magazine, marching band, musical theater, newspaper, orchestra, percussion ensemble, photography, political, professional, radio, religious, social, social service, student government, symphonic wind ensemble, symphony, and yearbook. Popular campus events include Hudson Relays, Greek Week, and Springfest.

Sports: There are 10 intercollegiate sports for men and 9 for women, and 30 intramural sports for men and 30 for women. Facilities include a gym with multipurpose courts, football, baseball, and soccer fields, indoor and all-weather tracks, softball diamonds, 2 swimming pools, weight and wrestling rooms, basketball, badminton, volleyball, squash, tennis, and racquetball courts, a multipurpose aerobics room, cardio exercise room, rock climbing wall, and an archery range.

Disabled Students: Wheelchair ramps, elevators, special parking, specially equipped rest rooms, special class scheduling, lowered drinking fountains, lowered telephones, TDD, special testing arrangements, note-taking assistance, individualized academic counseling and planning, adaptive equipment, interpreters, and access to audiotaped text materials are available.

Services: Counseling and information services are available, as is tutoring in every subject. There is a reader service for the blind, seminars to improve computing skills and study strategies and supplemental instruction in designated courses in biology, chemistry, math, and physics.

Campus Safety and Security: Measures include 24-hour foot and vehicle patrol, self-defense education, security escort services, and shuttle buses. There are informal discussions, pamphlets/posters/films, emergency telephones, lighted pathways/sidewalks, and property crime prevention programs, including bicycle lock rental, vehicle ID etching, and equipment bolting.

Programs of Study: Case confers B.A., B.S., B.S.E., and B.S.N. degrees. Master's and doctoral degrees are also awarded. Bachelor's degrees are awarded in BIOLOGICAL SCIENCE (biochemistry, biology/biological science, evolutionary biology, and nutrition), BUSINESS (accounting and business administration and management), COMMUNICATIONS AND THE ARTS (art history and appreciation, classics, comparative literature, dramatic arts, English, French, German, music, and Spanish), COMPUTER AND PHYSICAL SCIENCE (applied mathematics, astronomy, chemistry, computer science, fluid and thermal science, geology, mathematics, natural sciences, physics, polymer science, and statistics), EDUCATION (art, education, and music), ENGINEERING AND ENVIRONMENTAL DESIGN (aeronautical engineering, architecture, biomedical engineering, chemical engineering, civil engineering, computer engineering, electrical/electronics engineering, engineering, engineering physics, environmental science, materials science, mechanical engineering, and systems engineering), HEALTH PROFESSIONS (nursing, public health, and speech pathology/audiology), SOCIAL SCIENCE (American studies, anthropology, Asian/Oriental studies, cognitive science, economics, food science, French studies, German area studies, gerontology, history, history of science, international studies, Japanese studies, philosophy, political science/government, psychology, religion, sociology, and women's studies). Engineering, accounting, and biology are the strongest academically. Engineering, biology, and management are the largest.

Required: To graduate, students must complete a minimum of 120 semester hours, with at least 30 hours in the major, and maintain a minimum GPA of 2.0. Students must complete the SAGES (Seminar Approach to General Education and Scholarship) core curriculum and two semesters of physical education.

Special: Case offers co-op programs with more than 160 employers; students may alternate classroom study with full-time employment. Cross-registration with 13 institutions in the Cleveland area is available, as well as internships in government, corporations, and nonprofit agencies. Students may participate in study abroad, a Washington semester, work-study programs, and accelerated-degree programs. B.A.-B.S. degrees, dual and student-designed majors, 3-2 engineering degrees, non-degree study, independent study, and pass/fail options are possible. There are extensive opportunities for undergraduates to work with faculty on research projects. Preprofessional Scholars Programs in medicine, dental medicine, social work, and law are availble. Interdisciplinary majors, such as environmental geology and a double major in pre-architecture, and intradisciplinary majors, such as nutritional biochemistry and metabolism, are available. There are 3 national honor societies, including Phi Beta Kappa.

Faculty/Classroom: 68% of faculty are male; 32%, female. 77% teach undergraduates, 95% do research, and 77% do both. Graduate students teach 5% of introductory courses. The average class size in an introductory lecture is 18 and in a regular course, 27.

Admissions: 68% of the 2005-2006 applicants were accepted. The SAT scores for the 2005-2006 freshman class were: Verbal--3% below 500, 18% between 500 and 599, 48% between 600 and 700, and 31% above 700; Math--1% below 500, 11% between 500 and 599, 42% between 600 and 700, and 46% above 700. The ACT scores were 2% below 21, 6% between 21 and 23, 15% between 24 and 26, 17% between 27 and 28, and 60% above 28. 86% of the current freshmen were in the top fifth of their class; 98% were in the top two fifths. There were 58 National Merit finalists. 100 freshmen graduated first in their class.

Requirements: The SAT or ACT is required. The ACT Optional Writing test is also required. In addition, SAT: Subject tests in writing plus 2 others of the student's choice are strongly recommended for students who take the SAT. Applicants must be graduates of an accredited secondary school. The GED is accepted. 16 high school academic credits are required, including 4 years of English, 3 of math (4 for science, math, and engineering majors), and 1 of lab science (2 for science and math majors and premedical students). 2 to 4 years of foreign language are strongly recommended. Engineering, math, and science students should take the SAT: Subject tests in math I/IC of IIC and physics and/or chemistry. A writing sample of the student's choice is required, and an interview is recommended. AP credits are accepted. Important factors in the admissions decision are advanced placement or honor courses, leadership record, and recommendations by school officials.

Procedure: Freshmen are admitted fall, spring, and summer. Entrance exams should be taken by the fall of the senior year; Case recommends also taking the test during the spring of the junior year. There are early admissions and deferred admissions plans. Applications should be filed by January 15 for fall entry. The fall 2005 application fee was $35. Notification is sent March 1. 705 applicants were on the 2005 waiting list; 45 were admitted. Applications are accepted on-line.

Transfer: 75 transfer students enrolled in 2004-2005. Transfer students should have a minimum GPA of 3.0 and meet all high school requirements. Grades of C or better transfer for credit. 60 of 120 credits required for the bachelor's degree must be completed at Case.

Visiting: There are regularly scheduled orientations for prospective students. There are guides for informal visits and visitors may sit in on classes and stay overnight. To schedule a visit, contact the Office of Undergraduate Admission.

Financial Aid: In 2005-2006, 95% of all full-time freshmen and 89% of continuing full-time students received some form of financial aid. 71% of full-time freshmen and 60% of continuing full-time students received need-based aid. The average freshman award was $27,107. 70% of undergraduates work part time. Average annual earnings from campus work are $2900. The FAFSA, the college's own financial statement and the Parent and student income tax returns and W-2 forms are required. The priority date for freshman financial aid applications for fall entry is February 1.

International Students: There are 154 international students enrolled. The school actively recruits these students. A satisfactory score is required on the written TOEFL or complete 30 hours of instruction at Case's English Language Center.

Computers: Wireless access is available. All residence halls, classrooms, libraries, and lounges feature a switched gig-to-the desktop network, providing short download times, wireless access, and high-performance networking at speeds about 1,000 times faster than the typical home broadband network. All students may access the system 24 hours a day. There are no time limits and no fees. It is strongly recommended that all students have a PC. Case recommends Windows and Mac models configured to use Case's network.

Graduates: From July 1, 2004 to June 30, 2005, 705 bachelor's degrees were awarded. The most popular majors were psychology (11%), biology (10%), and management (7%). In an average class, 1% graduate in 3 years or less, 55% graduate in 4 years or less, 75% graduate in 5 years or less, and 79% graduate in 6 years or less. 93 companies recruited on campus in 2004-2005. Of the 2004 graduating class, 47% were enrolled in graduate school within 6 months of graduation and 40% were employed.

Admissions Contact: Director of Undergraduate Admission. A video is available. E-mail: *admission@case.edu* Web: *http://www.case.edu*

CEDARVILLE UNIVERSITY B-4
Cedarville, OH 45314-0601

(937) 766-7700
(800) CEDARVILLE; Fax: (937) 766-2760

Full-time: 1289 men, 1641 women	**Faculty:** 211; IIB, -$
Part-time: 73 men, 87 women	**Ph.D.s:** 63%
Graduate: 6 men, 30 women	**Student/Faculty:** 14 to 1
Year: semesters, summer session	**Tuition:** $17,120
Application Deadline: open	**Room & Board:** $4784

Freshman Class: 2017 applied, 1679 accepted, 763 enrolled
SAT Verbal/Math: 600/580*   **ACT:** 25   **VERY COMPETITIVE**

Cedarville University, founded in 1887, is a private Baptist college of arts and sciences offering programs in engineering, nursing, accounting, computer information systems, and education. The school is known for its religious commitment, conservative values, and community outreach programs. In addition to regional accreditation, Cedarville has baccalaureate program accreditation with ABET and NLN. The library contains 187,880 volumes, 21,396 microform items, and 9130 audio/video tapes/CDs/DVDs, and subscribes to 6931 periodicals including electronic. Computerized library services include the card catalog, interlibrary loans, database searching, Internet access, and laptop Internet portals. Special learning facilities include a learning resource center, radio station, and media resource center, and observatory. The 400-acre campus is in a small town 12 miles south of Springfield. Including any residence halls, there are 45 buildings.

Student Life: 63% of undergraduates are from out of state, mostly the Midwest. Students are from 48 states, 11 foreign countries, and Canada. 51% are from public schools. 95% are white. Most are Protestant. The average age of freshmen is 18; all undergraduates, 20. 19% do not continue beyond their first year; 54% remain to graduate.

Housing: 2524 students can be accommodated in college housing, which includes single-sex dorms and married-student housing. On-campus housing is guaranteed for all 4 years. 88% of students live on campus; of those, 80% remain on campus on weekends. Alcohol is not permitted. All students may keep cars.

Activities: There are no fraternities or sororities. There are 59 groups on campus, including band, cheerleading, chess, choir, chorale, chorus, debate, drama, ethnic, forensics, honors, international, jazz band, newspaper, orchestra, pep band, photography, political, professional, radio and TV, religious, social, social service, student government, and yearbook. Popular campus events include Lil' Sibs Weekend.

Sports: There are 7 intercollegiate sports for men and 7 for women, and 28 intramural sports for men and 28 for women. Facilities include a 3500-seat gym, 5 volleyball and badminton courts, a fitness center with 3 racquetball courts, a climbing wall, an exercise studio, a free weight room, Nautilus strength training areas, and cardiovascular areas, a field house with a 200-meter track, basketball, volleyball, tennis, and indoor soccer courts, indoor batting cages, and a training room, and outdoor facilities including tennis and sand volleyball courts, a track, soccer, baseball, and softball fields, a golf driving range, and intramural sports playing fields.

Disabled Students: 60% of the campus is accessible. Wheelchair ramps, elevators, special parking, specially equipped rest rooms, special class scheduling, lowered drinking fountains, and lowered telephones are available.

Services: Counseling and information services are available, as is tutoring in some subjects, including specific social science, calculus, and science courses. There is a reader service for the blind, and remedial math, reading, and writing.

Campus Safety and Security: Measures include 24-hour foot and vehicle patrol, security escort services, informal discussions, and pamphlets/posters/films. There are emergency telephones and lighted pathways/sidewalks.

Programs of Study: Cedarville confers B.A., B.S., B.M., B.M.E., B.S.E.E., B.S.M.E., and B.S.N. degrees. Associate and master's degrees are also awarded. Bachelor's degrees are awarded in BIOLOGICAL SCIENCE (biology/biological science), BUSINESS (accounting, banking and finance, business administration and management, management information systems, marketing/retailing/merchandising, and sports management), COMMUNICATIONS AND THE ARTS (communications, dramatic arts, English, graphic design, multimedia, music, Spanish, and technical and business writing), COMPUTER AND PHYSICAL SCIENCE (chemistry, computer science, information sciences and systems, mathematics, and physics), EDUCATION (athletic training, Christian, early childhood, English, foreign languages, mathematics, middle school, music, physical, science, social studies, and special), ENGINEERING AND ENVIRONMENTAL DESIGN (computer engineering, electrical/electronics engineering, and mechanical engineering), HEALTH PROFESSIONS (exercise science and nursing), SOCIAL SCIENCE (American studies, biblical studies, criminal justice, history, international studies, missions, pastoral studies, philosophy, political science/government, prelaw, psychology, public administration, religious music, social work, and sociology). Business, education, and science are the largest.

Required: To graduate, all students must maintain a minimum GPA of 2.0 while taking 128 semester hours, with a minimum of 32 in specific disciplines. General education requirements include 16 semester hours of biblical education, 10 of science and math, 9 each of humanities, social sciences, and history, 6 of communication, and 2 of phys ed. Students must demonstrate proficiency in English and math and must fulfill the global awareness requirement through foreign language study or intercultural experience. Specific courses required include English composition, fundamentals of speech, and politics and American culture.

Special: Internships, study abroad in 25 countries, a Washington semester, dual majors, student-designed majors, B.A.-B.S. degrees in biology, physics, chemistry, and math, work-study programs with the college, and pass/fail options are available. Cross-registration with the Southwest Ohio Consortium for Higher Education and the Ohio Learning Network is possible. There are 3 national honor societies, a freshman honors program, and 1 departmental honors program.

Faculty/Classroom: 70% of faculty are male; 30%, female. All teach undergraduates. The average class size in an introductory lecture is 38; in a laboratory, 15; and in a regular course, 20.

Admissions: 83% of the 2005-2006 applicants were accepted. The SAT scores for the 2005-2006 freshman class were: Verbal--9% below 500, 39% between 500 and 599, 41% between 600 and 700, and 11% above 700; Math--15% below 500, 41% between 500 and 599, 37% between 600 and 700, and 7% above 700. The ACT scores were 8% below 21, 27% between 21 and 23, 30% between 24 and 26, 17% between 27 and 28, and 18% above 28. 55% of the current freshmen were in the top fifth of their class; 81% were in the top two fifths. There were 9 National Merit finalists and 40 semifinalists. 63 freshmen graduated first in their class.

Requirements: The SAT or ACT is required, with scores above the national average preferred. The ACT Optional Writing test is also recommended. The college recommends that applicants have 4 years of English, 3 to 4 of math, and 3 each of social studies, math, science, and a foreign language. The GED is accepted. Recommendations from a local pastor and a high school counselor are required. An interview is recommended. Cedarville requires applicants to be in the upper 50% of their class. A GPA of 3.0 is required. AP and CLEP credits are accepted. Important factors in the admissions decision are personality/intangible qualities, recommendations by school officials, and advanced placement or honor courses.

Procedure: Freshmen are admitted to all sessions. Entrance exams should be taken by late junior year or early senior year. There are early admissions and deferred admissions plans. Application deadlines are open. Application fee is $30. Notification is sent on a rolling basis. A waiting list is an active part of the admissions procedure. Applications are accepted on-line.

Transfer: 123 transfer students enrolled in 2004-2005. Applicants must have a minimum college GPA of 3.0. The SAT or ACT (preferred) is strongly recommended. 32 of 128 credits required for the bachelor's degree must be completed at Cedarville.

Visiting: There are regularly scheduled orientations for prospective students, including campus tours, chapel services, class visits, and meetings with faculty, coaches, and admissions counselors. There are guides for informal visits and visitors may sit in on classes and stay overnight. To schedule a visit, contact the Admissions Office at *admissions@cedarville.edu.*

Financial Aid: In 2005-2006, 95% of all full-time freshmen and 86% of continuing full-time students received some form of financial aid. 76% of full-time freshmen and 66% of continuing full-time students received need-based aid. The average freshman award was $15,956. Need-based scholarships or need-based grants averaged $4454 ($17,141 maximum); need-based self-help aid (loans and jobs) averaged $3196 ($12,000 maximum); non-need-based athletic scholarships averaged $3715 ($21,403 maximum); and other non-need-based awards and non-need-based scholarships averaged $12,482 ($33,803 maximum). 49% of undergraduates work part time. Average annual earnings from campus work are $758. The average financial indebtedness of the 2005 graduate was $31,840. The FAFSA and the college's own financial statement are required. The deadline for filing freshman financial aid applications for fall entry is March 1.

International Students: There are 14 international students enrolled. They must score satisfactorily on the written TOEFL or on the electronic version and also take the SAT or the ACT.

Computers: Wireless access is available. 5 public computer labs contain 180 PCs and about 1250 residence hall rooms are equipped with PCs and printers, for a total of 1800 computers available to students. The network provides access to more than 150 software packages, library resources, e-mail, and the Internet. Cedarville is a participant in Internet 2. All students may access the system 24 hours a day for dorm rooms or up to 93 hours a week in the labs. There are no time limits and no fees.

Graduates: From July 1, 2004 to June 30, 2005, 603 bachelor's degrees were awarded. The most popular majors were nursing (9%), early childhood education (6%), and communication arts (5%). In an average class, 42% graduate in 3 years or less, 54% graduate in 4 years or less, 67% graduate in 5 years or less, and 71% graduate in 6 years or less.

246 companies recruited on campus in 2004-2005. Of the 2004 graduating class, 17% were enrolled in graduate school within 6 months of graduation and 87% were employed.

Admissions Contact: Roscoe Smith, Director of Admissions. A video is available. E-mail: *admissions@cedarville.edu*
Web: *http://www.cedarville.edu*

CENTRAL STATE UNIVERSITY   B-4
Wilberforce, OH 45384   (937) 376-6348
                                        (800) 388-CSU1; Fax: (937) 376-6648

Full-time: 560 men, 650 women	**Faculty:** 77; IIB, -$
Part-time: 55 men, 70 women	**Ph.D.s:** 62%
Graduate: 30 men, 55 women	**Student/Faculty:** 16 to 1
Year: quarters, summer session	**Tuition:** $3800 ($8200)
Application Deadline: see profile	**Room & Board:** $5210
Freshman Class: n/av	
ACT: required	**COMPETITIVE+**

Central State University, founded in 1887, is a public institution offering programs in liberal arts, business, engineering, teacher preparation, and professional training. There are 3 undergraduate schools and 1 graduate school. Figures in the above capsule and profile are approximate. In addition to regional accreditation, Central State has baccalaureate program accreditation with ABET and NASM. The library contains 179,241 volumes, 622,727 microform items, and 500 audio/video tapes/CDs/DVDs, and subscribes to 26,316 periodicals including electronic. Computerized library services include the card catalog, interlibrary loans, and database searching. Special learning facilities include a learning resource center, art gallery, radio station, and the National Afro-American Museum and Cultural Center. The 60-acre campus is in a rural area 18 miles east of Dayton. Including any residence halls, there are 34 buildings.

Student Life: 77% of undergraduates are from Ohio. Others are from 24 states and 2 foreign countries. 96% are African American. The average age of freshmen is 18; all undergraduates, 22. 42% do not continue beyond their first year; 23% remain to graduate.

Housing: 745 students can be accommodated in college housing, which includes single-sex dormitories. On-campus housing is guaranteed for the freshman year only and is available on a first-come, first-served basis. 57% of students live on campus. Alcohol is not permitted. All students may keep cars.

Activities: 1% of men belong to 2 national fraternities; 1% of women belong to 2 national sororities. There are 30 groups on campus, including art, band, cheerleading, choir, chorale, chorus, drama, drill team, ethnic, honors, jazz band, marching band, pep band, political, professional, radio and TV, religious, social, and student government. Popular campus events include Career Day and May Week.

Sports: There are 3 intercollegiate sports for men and 4 for women, and 8 intramural sports for men and 7 for women. Facilities include 2 gyms, a stadium, a swimming pool, a pool room, a baseball diamond, tennis courts, and a weight room.

Disabled Students: All of the campus is accessible. Wheelchair ramps, elevators, special parking, specially equipped rest rooms, lowered drinking fountains, and lowered telephones are available.

Services: Counseling and information services are available, as is tutoring in most subjects.

Campus Safety and Security: Measures include 24-hour foot and vehicle patrol and lighted pathways/sidewalks.

Programs of Study: Central State confers B.A., B.S., B.M., B.S.Ed., and B.S.M.E. degrees. Master's degrees are also awarded. Bachelor's degrees are awarded in BIOLOGICAL SCIENCE (biology/biological science), BUSINESS (accounting, banking and finance, business administration and management, and marketing/retailing/merchandising), COMMUNICATIONS AND THE ARTS (advertising, broadcasting, English, journalism, and music), COMPUTER AND PHYSICAL SCIENCE (chemistry, computer science, and mathematics), EDUCATION (art, elementary, health, music, physical, secondary, and special), ENGINEERING AND ENVIRONMENTAL DESIGN (graphic arts technology and manufacturing engineering), SOCIAL SCIENCE (economics, history, political science/government, psychology, public administration, social work, sociology, and water resources). Communication, music, and education are the strongest academically. Business administration is the largest.

Required: To graduate, students must complete 186 quarter credits, with a minimum GPA of 2.0 (2.5 in education). Required university core courses include 64 credits in English composition, math, computer skills, humanities, natural sciences, social sciences, health and phys ed, and African American history.

Special: Central State offers co-op programs in all majors, cross-registration with 15 area colleges, study abroad in 3 countries, internships, on-campus work-study programs, and B.A.-B.S. degrees. There is a freshman honors program.

Faculty/Classroom: 77% of faculty are male; 23%, female. All teach undergraduates and 75% both teach and do research. No introductory

courses are taught by graduate students. The average class size in an introductory lecture is 25; in a laboratory, 20; and in a regular course, 15.

Requirements: The ACT is required; the SAT is accepted. Applicants must be graduates of an accredited secondary school. The GED is accepted. Students should have completed 4 years of high school English, 3 years each of math, science, and social studies, and 2 years of the same foreign language. Ohio applicants should have a GPA of 2.0 and a minimum ACT composite score of 15 or a satisfactory SAT score. Criteria are higher for out-of-state applicants. A GPA of 2.0 is required. AP and CLEP credits are accepted.

Procedure: Freshmen are admitted to all sessions. There are early admissions, deferred admissions, and rolling admissions plan. Check with the school for application deadlines. The application fee is $15. Notification is sent on a rolling basis. Applications are accepted on-line.

Transfer: Applicants should have a minimum college GPA of 2.0. Grades of C or better transfer for credit. Transfer students with fewer than 47 quarter hours must submit high school transcripts and test scores. Transfers are admitted every term. 45 of 186 credits required for the bachelor's degree must be completed at Central State.

Visiting: There are regularly scheduled orientations for prospective students. There are guides for informal visits and visitors may sit in on classes. To schedule a visit, contact the Admissions Office.

Financial Aid: The FAFSA and the college's own financial statement are required. Check with the school for current deadlines.

International Students: They must score satisfactorily on the written TOEFL and also take the SAT or the ACT.

Computers: All students may access the system.

Admissions Contact: Thandabantu Maceo, Director of Admissions. A video is available. E-mail: *admissions@csu.ces.edu* Web: *www.centralstate.edu*

CINCINNATI COLLEGE OF MORTUARY SCIENCE   A-4
Cincinnati, OH 45224-1462

(513) 761-2020
(888) 377-8433; Fax: (513) 761-3333

Full-time: 80 men, 55 women	**Faculty:** 7
Part-time: 1 man, 1 woman	**Ph.D.s:** 33%
Graduate: none	**Student/Faculty:** 18 to 1
Year: quarters, summer session	**Tuition:** $12,000
Application Deadline: see profile	**Room & Board:** n/app
Freshman Class: n/av	
SAT or ACT: required	SPECIAL

The Cincinnati College of Mortuary Science, founded in 1882, is the only private mortuary college in the country that is regionally accredited at the bachelor's level. Figures above capsule and profile are approximate. The curriculum encompasses the embalming sciences, funeral directing, and the liberal arts. In addition to regional accreditation, CCMS has baccalaureate program accreditation with ABFSE. The 2 libraries contain 6000 volumes. Computerized library services include the card catalog. Special learning facilities include a clinical embalming lab. The 16-acre campus is in an urban area 8 miles from downtown Cincinnati. There is 1 building.

Student Life: 50% of undergraduates are from out of state, mostly the Midwest. Students are from 15 states. 93% are white. The average age of all undergraduates is 24. 15% do not continue beyond their first year; 85% remain to graduate.

Housing: There are no residence halls. Alcohol is not permitted.

Activities: There are no fraternities or sororities. There are some groups and organizations on campus, including student government and yearbook. Popular campus events include field trips, guest lectures, and welcoming and farewell parties.

Sports: There is no sports program at CCMS.

Disabled Students: All of the campus is accessible. Wheelchair ramps, elevators, special parking, and specially equipped rest rooms are available.

Campus Safety and Security: Measures include informal discussions, pamphlets/posters/films, emergency telephones, and lighted pathways/sidewalks.

Programs of Study: CCMS confers the Bachelor of Mortuary Science degree. Associate degrees are also awarded. Bachelor's degrees are awarded in BUSINESS (funeral home services).

Required: To graduate, students must complete 180 quarter credit hours, including 90 in the major, with a minimum GPA of 2.0. General education requirements consist of 18 quarter hours each in natural science/math, social science, and humanities/arts, and 12 each in English composition and literature, business management, and free electives.

Special: Limited credit may be given for life, military, and work experience.

Faculty/Classroom: 87% of faculty are male; 13%, female. All teach undergraduates. The average class size in an introductory lecture is 50 and in a laboratory, 20.

Requirements: The SAT or ACT is required. Applicants must be graduates of an accredited secondary school. The GED is accepted. Students

must complete 16 high school units, including 8 of electives, 3 of English, 2 each of science and history, and 1 of math. An interview is recommended. A GPA of 2.0 is required. AP and CLEP credits are accepted. Important factors in the admissions decision are leadership record, recommendations by alumni, and parents or siblings attending the school.

Procedure: Freshmen are admitted fall and spring. There is a rolling admissions plan. Check with the school for current application deadlines. Notification is sent on a rolling basis. Applications are accepted on-line. The fall 2005 application fee was $25.

Transfer: Applicants must submit transcripts from all colleges attended. Grades of D+ or better transfer for credit if students have a GPA of 2.0. Transfers are admitted for the fall and spring terms. 90 of 180 credits required for the bachelor's degree must be completed at CCMS.

Visiting: There are regularly scheduled orientations for prospective students, including open house programs in August and February. There are guides for informal visits. To schedule a visit, contact Patsy Leon.

Financial Aid: In a recent year, 87% of all full-time freshmen and 89% of continuing full-time students received some form of financial aid. 90% of full-time freshmen and 89% of continuing full-time students received need-based aid. The average freshman award was $6625. Need-based self-help aid (loans and jobs) averaged $6625 ($6625 maximum). 80% of undergraduates worked part time. The average financial indebtedness of a recent graduate was $10,500. CCMS is a member of CSS. The CSS/Profile is required. Check with the school for current application deadlines.

Computers: All students may access the system during supervised lab hours. There are no fees.

Graduates: In a recent year, 40 bachelor's degrees were awarded. The most popular major was mortuary science (100%). In an average class, all graduate in 4 years or less. 4 companies recruited on campus in a recent year.

Admissions Contact: Patsy Leon, Admissions/Financial Aid. E-mail: *ccms@eos.net* Web: *www.ccms.edu*

CLEVELAND INSTITUTE OF ART   D-1
Cleveland, OH 44106

(216) 421-7418
(800) 223-4700; Fax: (216) 754-3634

Full-time: 254 men, 258 women	**Faculty:** 48
Part-time: 7 men, 21 women	**Ph.D.s:** 90%
Graduate: 3 men, 5 women	**Student/Faculty:** 11 to 1
Year: semesters	**Tuition:** $26,567
Application Deadline: July 1	**Room & Board:** $7542
Freshman Class: 329 applied, 310 accepted, 123 enrolled	
SAT Verbal/Math: 580/494*	**ACT:** 21 SPECIAL

Cleveland Institute of Art, founded in 1882, is an independent professional school of art offering a 5-year B.F.A. degree. In addition to regional accreditation, CIA has baccalaureate program accreditation with NASAD. The 3 libraries contain 42,000 volumes and 2800 audio/video tapes/CDs/DVDs, and subscribe to 260 periodicals including electronic. Computerized library services include the card catalog, interlibrary loans, and database searching. Special learning facilities include an art gallery, natural history museum, planetarium, radio station, auto aviation museum, symphony orchestra, art museum, botanical gardens, and historical society. The 500-acre campus is in an urban area 4 miles east of downtown Cleveland, sharing a campus with Case Western Reserve University. Including any residence halls, there are 3 buildings.

Student Life: 67% of undergraduates are from Ohio. Others are from 27 states and 10 foreign countries. 97% are from public schools. 88% are white. The average age of freshmen is 20; all undergraduates, 22. 10% do not continue beyond their first year; 50% remain to graduate.

Housing: 100 students can be accommodated in college housing, which includes single-sex and coed dormitories and on-campus apartments. On-campus housing is guaranteed for the freshman year only, is available on a first-come, first-served basis, and is available on a lottery system for upperclassmen. Priority is given to out-of-town students. 84% of students commute. Upperclassmen may keep cars.

Activities: There are 6 national fraternities and 6 national sororities. There are 9 groups on campus, including art, artists for Christ, ethnic, gay, ghost hunting club, international, photography, professional, student activities program board, student artist association, student government, student leadership council, and survey student gallery. The institute also shares many, social cultural, and extracurricular activies with Case Western Reserve University. Popular campus events include museum trips, an-end-of-school-year cookout, and student art exhibits.

Sports: For a fee, students may use the recreation facilities of Case Western Reserve.

Disabled Students: 90% of the campus is accessible. Wheelchair ramps, elevators, special parking, and specially equipped rest rooms are available.

Services: Counseling and information services are available, as is tutoring in most subjects. There is remedial writing.

Campus Safety and Security: Measures include 24-hour foot and vehicle patrol, security escort services, shuttle buses, and informal discussions. There are pamphlets/posters/films, emergency telephones, and lighted pathways/sidewalks.

Programs of Study: CIA confers the B.F.A. degree. Master's degrees are also awarded. Bachelor's degrees are awarded in COMMUNICATIONS AND THE ARTS (advertising, applied art, design, drawing, fiber/textiles/weaving, glass, graphic design, illustration, industrial design, metal/jewelry, painting, photography, printmaking, sculpture, and studio art), ENGINEERING AND ENVIRONMENTAL DESIGN (engineering chemistry and interior design). Industrial design, painting, jewelry and metals are the strongest academically. Industrial design, painting, and technology and integrated media environment (digital arts) are the largest.

Required: To graduate, students must complete 150 to 153 credit hours, with 42 to 51 in the major, and must maintain a minimum GPA of 2.0. Distribution requirements call for 105 studio credits and 48 academic credits. A thesis is required, which is encompassed in the B.F.A. show that each student mounts in the spring of the fifth year.

Special: Cross-registration through the Northeast Ohio Council on Higher Education, internships for third-, fourth-, and fifth-year students with business and industry, and study abroad in 6 countries are available. There are joint programs with Case Western Reserve University in art education and medical illustration.

Faculty/Classroom: 70% of faculty are male; 30%, female. All teach undergraduates. The average class size in an introductory lecture is 40 and in a regular course, 20.

Admissions: 94% of the 2005-2006 applicants were accepted. The SAT scores for the 2005-2006 freshman class were: Verbal--23% below 500, 41% between 500 and 599, 27% between 600 and 700, and 9% above 700; Math--55% below 500, 27% between 500 and 599, and 18% between 600 and 700. The ACT scores were 37% below 21, 28% between 21 and 23, 21% between 24 and 26, 9% between 27 and 28, and 5% above 28. 28% of the current freshmen were in the top fifth of their class; 54% were in the top two fifths. 2 freshmen graduated first in their class.

Requirements: The SAT or ACT is required. Applicants must be graduates of an accredited secondary school. The GED is accepted. An essay and a portfolio are required. An interview is strongly recommended. A GPA of 2.0 is required. AP and CLEP credits are accepted. Important factors in the admissions decision are evidence of special talent, personality/intangible qualities, and leadership record.

Procedure: Freshmen are admitted in the fall. Entrance exams should be taken during the junior year. There are deferred admissions and rolling admissions plans. Applications should be filed by July 1 for fall entry, along with a $30 fee. Notification is sent on a rolling basis. A waiting list is an active part of the admissions procedure.Applications are accepted on-line.

Transfer: 27 transfer students enrolled in 2004-2005. Applicants must have a 2.0 GPA and must submit a portfolio. Those who have 30 to 36 credits in comparable studio courses or a strong portfolio will be reviewed by department faculty. Grades of C or better transfer for credit. 30 of 153 credits required for the bachelor's degree must be completed at CIA.

Visiting: There are guides for informal visits. To schedule a visit, contact Corey Thrush, Director of Admissions.

Financial Aid: In 2005-2006, 85% of all full-time students received some form of financial aid. 68% of full-time freshmen and 63% of continuing full-time students received need-based aid. The average freshman award was $20,072. Need-based scholarships or need-based grants averaged $3000 ($7000 maximum); need-based self-help aid (loans and jobs) averaged $4125 ($5625 maximum); and other non-need-based awards and non-need-based scholarships averaged $7200 ($24,917 maximum). 33% of undergraduates work part time. Average annual earnings from campus work are $1200. The average financial indebtedness of the 2005 graduate was $24,979. The FAFSA and the college's own financial statement are required. The deadline for filing freshman financial aid applications for fall entry is March 15.

International Students: There are 17 international students enrolled. The school actively recruits these students. They must score satisfactorily on the written TOEFL or complete Level 109 at an ELS center.

Computers: Students may access the system 2 hours. There are no fees.

Graduates: From July 1, 2004 to June 30, 2005, 109 bachelor's degrees were awarded. The most popular majors were industrial design (14%), technology and integrated media environm (14%), and painting (9%). In an average class, 55% graduate in 5 years or less, and 65% graduate in 6 years or less.

Admissions Contact: Corey Thrush, Director of Admissions.
E-mail: *admissions@cia.edu* Web: *www.cia.edu*

Cleveland, OH 44106   (216) 795-3107; Fax: (216) 791-1530

Full-time: 105 men, 120 women	**Faculty:** 31
Part-time: none	**Ph.D.s:** 9%
Graduate: 60 men, 90 women	**Student/Faculty:** 7 to 1
Year: semesters, summer session	**Tuition:** $20,500
Application Deadline: see profile	**Room & Board:** $6000
Freshman Class: n/av	
SAT or ACT: required	**SPECIAL**

Cleveland Institute of Music, founded in 1920, is a private music conservatory offering education and training in the arts of performance, composition, and related musical disciplines. Figures in above capsule and in this profile are approximate. In addition to regional accreditation, CIM has baccalaureate program accreditation with NASM. The library contains 47,878 volumes and 20,500 audio/video tapes/CDs/DVDs, and subscribes to 115 periodicals including electronic. Computerized library services include the card catalog, interlibrary loans, and database searching. Special learning facilities include concert and recital halls, teaching studios, practice rooms, a technology learning center, a specially designed eurhythmics studio, an orchestra library, an opera theater workshop and studio, and music store. The 480-acre campus is in an urban area.

Student Life: 68% of undergraduates are from out of state, mostly the Midwest. Students are from 40 states, 21 foreign countries, and Canada. 95% are from public schools. 71% are white; 20% foreign nationals. The average age of freshmen is 18; all undergraduates, 21. 2% do not continue beyond their first year; 85% remain to graduate.

Housing: College-sponsored housing is coed. On-campus housing is guaranteed for the freshman year only. Alcohol is not permitted. All students may keep cars.

Activities: There are no fraternities or sororities. There are 8 groups on campus, including chorale, chorus, jazz band, opera, orchestra, religious, student government, and symphony. Popular campus events include weekly concerts by the Cleveland Orchestra.

Sports: Athletic facilities and a fitness center are available.

Disabled Students: Wheelchair ramps, elevators, special parking, specially equipped rest rooms, and lowered drinking fountains are available.

Services: Counseling and information services are available, as is tutoring in some subjects.

Campus Safety and Security: Measures include 24-hour foot and vehicle patrol, security escort services, shuttle buses, and informal discussions. There are pamphlets/posters/films, emergency telephones, and lighted pathways/sidewalks.

Programs of Study: CIM confers B.M.; B.A.Mus.Ed. and B.S.Mus.Ed. degrees. Master's and doctoral degrees are also awarded. Bachelor's degrees are awarded in COMMUNICATIONS AND THE ARTS (music), EDUCATION (music).

Required: CIM requires a minimum of 126 credits with a GPA of 2.0 or higher for graduation. A core curriculum of general education courses, music history, theory, and literature is required. Performance evaluation is based on jury exams and recitals.

Special: Students may take a 5-year double major in performance and audio recording. Cross-registration with schools in the Cleveland Commission on Higher Education Consortium is possible. Music education degrees are offered in conjunction with Case Western Reserve University. There are 2 national honor societies.

Faculty/Classroom: 68% of faculty are male; 32%, female. All teach undergraduates.

Requirements: The SAT or ACT is required. In addition, an audition and interview are required, at which time freshman applicants must also complete a questionnaire pertaining to general knowledge of music, and diagnostic evaluations of rhythmic comprehension as well as sight singing and ear training. Applicants majoring in composition must submit scores and tapes. Other factors in the admissions decision are GPA, class rank, test scores, and recommendations. Applicants should complete a 16 unit college preparatory program. The GED is accepted. AP credits are accepted.

Procedure: Freshmen are admitted fall and spring. Entrance exams should be taken at the time of the entrance audition. A waiting list is an active part of the admissions procedure. Applications are accepted online. Check with the school for current application deadlines. The fall 2005 application fee was $70.

Transfer: Applicants must meet the same criteria as entering freshmen and submit transcripts and letters of recommendation. 48 of 126 credits required for the bachelor's degree must be completed at CIM.

Visiting: Visitors may sit in on classes. To schedule a visit, contact the Admissions Office.

Financial Aid: CIM is a member of CSS. The CSS/Profile or FAFSA is required. Check with school for current application deadlines.

International Students: They must score satisfactorily on the written TOEFL or take the MELAB.

Computers: All students may access the system. There are no time limits and no fees. It is strongly recommended that all students have a personal computer.

Admissions Contact: Admission Office.
E-mail: *cimadmission@po.cwru.edu* Web: *www.cim.edu*

CLEVELAND STATE UNIVERSITY   D-1
Cleveland, OH 44115-2403   (216) 687-2100
(800) CSU-OHIO; Fax: (216) 687-9210

Full-time: 3071 men, 3566 women	Faculty: 575; I, --$
Part-time: 1080 men, 1438 women	Ph.D.s: 86%
Graduate: 1586 men, 2425 women	Student/Faculty: 12 to 1
Year: semesters, summer session	Tuition: $7394 ($9926)
Application Deadline: August	Room & Board: $3404
Freshman Class: 3153 applied, 2520 accepted, 1079 enrolled	
SAT Verbal/Math: 490/480*	ACT: 19 NONCOMPETITIVE

Cleveland State University, founded in 1964, is a primarily commuter public institution offering undergraduate and graduate programs through the colleges of arts and sciences, business administration, education, engineering, and urban affairs. There are 7 undergraduate and 7 graduate schools. In addition to regional accreditation, CSU has baccalaureate program accreditation with AACSB, ABET, CSWE, NCATE, and NLN. The 2 libraries contain 484,914 volumes and 690,023 microform items, and subscribe to 6186 periodicals including electronic. Computerized library services include the card catalog, interlibrary loans, and database searching. Special learning facilities include a learning resource center, art gallery, and radio station. The 70-acre campus is in an urban area in downtown Cleveland. Including any residence halls, there are 38 buildings.

Student Life: 96% of undergraduates are from Ohio. Others are from 20 states, 79 foreign countries, and Canada. 59% are white; 30% African American. The average age of freshmen is 19; all undergraduates, 26. 39% do not continue beyond their first year; 30% remain to graduate.

Housing: 475 students can be accommodated in university housing, which includes coed dorms and off-campus apartments, law, quiet study, and first-year experience floors. 95% of students commute. All students may keep cars.

Activities: 5% of men belong to 2 local and 6 national fraternities; 5% of women belong to 8 national sororities. There are 150 groups on campus, including art, cheerleading, chess, choir, chorale, chorus, computers, dance, drama, ethnic, film, gay, honors, international, jazz band, literary magazine, musical theater, newspaper, opera, orchestra, pep band, photography, political, professional, radio and TV, religious, social, social service, student government, and symphony. Popular campus events include Black Aspiration Week and Springfest.

Sports: There are 8 intercollegiate sports for men and 7 for women, and 5 intramural sports for men and 5 for women. Facilities include a gym, gymnastics and weight rooms, a dance studio, a swimming pool, a fitness trail, an indoor track, handball and squash courts, a 2500-seat soccer stadium, and a convocation center.

Disabled Students: 99% of the campus is accessible. Wheelchair ramps, elevators, special parking, specially equipped rest rooms, and lowered drinking fountains are available.

Services: There is a reader service for the blind, and remedial math, reading, and writing.

Campus Safety and Security: Measures include 24-hour foot and vehicle patrol, security escort services, informal discussions, and pamphlets/posters/films. There are emergency telephones, lighted pathways/sidewalks, and a campus watch organization for faculty and staff.

Programs of Study: CSU confers B.A., B.S., B.B.A., B.C.E., B.Ch.E., B.E.E., B.M., B.M.E., B.S.C.I.S., B.S.Ed., B.S.I.E., B.S.N., and B.S.T. degrees. Master's and doctoral degrees are also awarded. Bachelor's degrees are awarded in BIOLOGICAL SCIENCE (biology/biological science), BUSINESS (accounting, banking and finance, business economics, labor studies, management information systems, management science, and marketing/retailing/merchandising), COMMUNICATIONS AND THE ARTS (art, communications, dramatic arts, English, French, German, linguistics, music, and Spanish), COMPUTER AND PHYSICAL SCIENCE (chemistry, computer science, geology, information sciences and systems, mathematics, and physics), EDUCATION (early childhood, elementary, physical, secondary, and special), ENGINEERING AND ENVIRONMENTAL DESIGN (chemical engineering, civil engineering, electrical/electronics engineering, electromechanical technology, environmental science, industrial engineering, mechanical engineering, and mechanical engineering technology), HEALTH PROFESSIONS (medical technology, nursing, occupational therapy, physical therapy, premedicine, and speech therapy), SOCIAL SCIENCE (anthropology, classical/ancient civilization, economics, history, international relations, liberal arts/general studies, philosophy, political science/government, psychology, religion, social science, social studies, social work, sociology, and urban studies). Communications, psychology, and social work are the largest.

Required: Students must complete at least 120 semester hours with a minimum 2.0 GPA for graduation. Requirements include a core curriculum containing courses in English composition, arts and humanities, social science, natural sciences, math and logic, nonwestern culture and civilization, Western culture and civilization, and human diversity and the African American experience.

Special: CSU offers a developmental program for Ohio students not qualified for regular freshman admission. There are also cooperative education programs, nondegree study, work-study programs, accelerated degree programs, internships, pass/fail options, and cross-registration at other Cleveland area colleges. Student-designed and dual majors, study abroad in 10 countries, and volunteer opportunities are available, as well as a combined liberal arts and engineering degree and a 3-2 engineering degree. There are 6 national honor societies and 5 departmental honors programs.

Faculty/Classroom: 59% of faculty are male; 41%, female.

Admissions: 80% of the 2005-2006 applicants were accepted. The SAT scores for the 2005-2006 freshman class were: Verbal--53% below 500, 35% between 500 and 599, 12% between 600 and 700, and 1% above 700; Math--54% below 500, 30% between 500 and 599, 14% between 600 and 700, and 2% above 700. The ACT scores were 65% below 21, 19% between 21 and 23, 10% between 24 and 26, 4% between 27 and 28, and 2% above 28. 21% of the current freshmen were in the top fifth of their class; 44% were in the top two fifths.

Requirements: The SAT or ACT is required. The ACT Optional Writing test is also recommended. In addition, a high school diploma is required or the GED is accepted. Students should have completed the following academic credits: 4 years of English, 3 of math, social studies, and science (1 of which must be a lab), and 2 of a foreign language. A general college-preparatory program is recommended. AP and CLEP credits are accepted.

Procedure: Freshmen are admitted to all sessions. Entrance exams should be taken prior to application. There is a deferred admissions plan. Applications should be filed by August for fall entry, December 1 for spring entry, and April 1 for summer entry. The university accepts all applicants. Notification is sent on a rolling basis beginning September 1. Applications are accepted on-line.

Transfer: 1040 transfer students enrolled in 2004-2005. Applicants must have a minimum GPA of 2.0 and submit previous college transcripts. Transfer students entering with fewer than 24 semester hours must submit official high school transcripts and test scores if they have been out of high school less than 5 years. 30 of 120 credits required for the bachelor's degree must be completed at CSU.

Visiting: There are regularly scheduled orientations for prospective students, including general visitation days for the university (in the fall) and each of the colleges (in the spring). There are guides for informal visits and visitors may sit in on classes and stay overnight. To schedule a visit, contact the Office of Undergraduate Admissions at (216) 687-3755.

Financial Aid: In 2005-2006, 70% of all full-time students received some form of financial aid. 56% of full-time freshmen and 51% of continuing full-time students received need-based aid. The average freshman award was $6510. Need-based scholarships or need-based grants averaged $5200; need-based self-help aid (loans and jobs) averaged $2776; non-need-based athletic scholarships averaged $9523; and other non-need-based awards and non-need-based scholarships averaged $8887. The FAFSA is required. The priority date for freshman financial aid applications for fall entry is February 15.

International Students: There are 220 international students enrolled. They must score satisfactorily on the TOEFL.

Computers: All students may access the system. Hours vary by input center. Modem access is available 24 hours per day.

Graduates: From July 1, 2004 to June 30, 2005, 1690 bachelor's degrees were awarded. The most popular majors were business/marketing (21%), education (12%), and social sciences (12%). In an average class, 11% graduate in 4 years or less, 23% graduate in 5 years or less, and 30% graduate in 6 years or less.

Admissions Contact: Gerald Kiel, Vice Provost of Enrollment Management Services. A video is available. Web: *http://www.csuohio.edu*

COLLEGE OF MOUNT ST. JOSEPH   A-5
Cincinnati, OH 45233-1672   (513) 244-4531
(800) 654-9314; Fax: (513) 244-4851

Full-time: 458 men, 847 women	Faculty: 117; IIA, --$
Part-time: 109 men, 487 women	Ph.D.s: 59%
Graduate: 64 men, 235 women	Student/Faculty: 11 to 1
Year: semesters, summer session	Tuition: $18,790
Application Deadline: August 15	Room & Board: $6070
Freshman Class: 1087 applied, 793 accepted, 307 enrolled	
SAT Verbal/Math: 500/490*	ACT: 21 COMPETITIVE

The College of Mount St. Joseph is a Catholic college focused on preparing its students to succeed academically and personally. Degree programs are based on an interdisciplinary liberal arts core curriculum that integrates life learning with an emphasis on values, integrity, and social responsibility. Students study in 34 undergraduate or five graduate degree programs, including the Doctor of Physical Therapy. In addition to regional accreditation, the Mount has baccalaureate program accreditation with ACS, CAPTE, CSWE, NASM, and NLN. The library contains 97,576 volumes, 380,391 microform items, and 3414 audio/video tapes/CDs/DVDs, and subscribes to 10,434 periodicals including electronic. Computerized library services include the card catalog, interlibrary loans, database searching, and laptop Internet portals. Special learning facilities include a learning resource center and art gallery. The 92-acre campus is in a suburban area 7 miles west of downtown Cincinnati. Including any residence halls, there are 9 buildings.

Student Life: 88% of undergraduates are from Ohio. Others are from 27 states and 7 foreign countries. 70% are from public schools. 84% are white; 10% African American. 41% are Catholic; 39% claim no religious affiliation; 19% Protestant. The average age of freshmen is 18; all undergraduates, 26. 22% do not continue beyond their first year; 68% remain to graduate.

Housing: 460 students can be accommodated in college housing, which includes coed dorms. On-campus housing is guaranteed for all 4 years. 79% of students commute. All students may keep cars.

Activities: There are no fraternities or sororities. There are 43 groups on campus, including art, band, cheerleading, choir, chorale, chorus, computers, dance, drama, ethnic, honors, international, jazz band, literary magazine, marching band, musical theater, newspaper, orchestra, pep band, photography, professional, religious, social, social service, specific academic program clubs, and student government. Popular campus events include Laughter on the Hill, Spring Formal, and Studio Guiseppe Art Gallery Exhibits.

Sports: There are 11 intercollegiate sports for men and 10 for women, and 6 intramural sports for men and 6 for women. Facilities include a sports complex and field for football, soccer, lacrosse, and track and field with an 8-lane running track and athletic training facilities. The student center also includes courts used for basketball and wrestling, a running track, handball/racquetball courts, a fitness center, athletic training center, and a wellness center. Facilities also include tennis courts and a practice facility for soccer, lacrosse, and baseball.

Disabled Students: 95% of the campus is accessible. Wheelchair ramps, elevators, special parking, specially equipped rest rooms, special class scheduling, lowered drinking fountains, lowered telephones, special door openings for wheelchair access, and a chairlift between levels where the science building and classroom building meet are available.

Services: Counseling and information services are available, as is tutoring in every subject. There is remedial math and writing. Peer tutoring, services to students with learning disabilities, and math and writing centers are also available.

Campus Safety and Security: Measures include 24-hour foot and vehicle patrol, security escort services, informal discussions, and pamphlets/posters/films. There are emergency telephones and lighted pathways/sidewalks.

Programs of Study: The Mount confers B.A., B.S., B.F.A., and B.S.N. degrees. Associate and master's degrees are also awarded. Bachelor's degrees are awarded in BIOLOGICAL SCIENCE (biochemistry and biology/biological science), BUSINESS (accounting, business administration and management, and management information systems), COMMUNICATIONS AND THE ARTS (art, communications, English, fine arts, graphic design, and music), COMPUTER AND PHYSICAL SCIENCE (chemistry, mathematics, and natural sciences), EDUCATION (art, athletic training, early childhood, elementary, middle school, and special), ENGINEERING AND ENVIRONMENTAL DESIGN (interior design), HEALTH PROFESSIONS (nursing), SOCIAL SCIENCE (criminology, history, liberal arts/general studies, paralegal studies, pastoral studies, psychology, religion, religious education, social work, and sociology). Athletic training, biology, and criminology/sociology are the strongest academically. Athletic training, biology, and business administration are the largest.

Required: To graduate, students must complete a minimum of 128 credits with an overall minimum GPA of 2.0 and 2.0 in the major. 52 semester hours of interdisciplinary liberal arts and sciences and hours in the majors as required. All students must take 12 hours of humanities, 9 hours of social science/history, 7 hours of natural sciences/mathematics, 6 hours of religious studies/philosophy and interdisciplinary studies, 3 hours of ethics, 9 hours of electives from the liberal arts and sciences or interdisciplinary studies, and a capstone synthesis reflection.

Special: The college offers co-op programs in all majors, cross-registration with the Greater Cincinnati Consortium of Colleges and Universities, internships, and study abroad in 8 countries, work-study programs, accelerated degree programs, dual majors, credit for experiential learning, cultural immersion courses in U.S. and abroad, dual enrollment program (transition for transfer students), evening programs, off-campus study for RNs in area hospitals, service learning, and program for students with learning disabilities (Project EXCEL). There are 5 national honor societies and a freshman honors program.

Faculty/Classroom: 65% of faculty are male; 35%, female. All teach undergraduates and 54% both teach and do research. No introductory courses are taught by graduate students. The average class size in an introductory lecture is 17; in a laboratory, 14; and in a regular course, 13.

Admissions: 73% of the 2005-2006 applicants were accepted. The SAT scores for the 2005-2006 freshman class were: Verbal--50% below 500, 37% between 500 and 599, and 13% between 600 and 700; Math--55% below 500, 34% between 500 and 599, 9% between 600 and 700, and 2% above 700. The ACT scores were 43% below 21, 32% between 21 and 23, 17% between 24 and 26, 5% between 27 and 28, and 2% above 28. 29% of the current freshmen were in the top fifth of their class; 59% were in the top two fifths. There was 1 National Merit finalist. 2 freshmen graduated first in their class.

Requirements: The SAT or ACT is required. The Mount reviews every candidate's credentials for admission, including: a college prep high school curriculum, strong grade point average, standardized test scores, evidence of leadership, and extracurricular involvement. An ACT score at or above the national average is recommended. In addition, students' personal background, attributes, and individual life circumstances are taken into consideration. A GPA of 2.5 is required. AP and CLEP credits are accepted.

Procedure: Freshmen are admitted to all sessions. There is a rolling admissions plan. Applications should be filed by August 15 for fall entry, along with a $25 fee. Notification is sent on a rolling basis. Applications are accepted on-line.

Transfer: 122 transfer students enrolled in a recent year. Transfer students must have a college GPA of 2.0 or better in a minimum of 12 semester or 18 quarter hours. All college hours must be presented. 27 of 128 credits required for the bachelor's degree must be completed at the Mount.

Visiting: There are regularly scheduled orientations for prospective students, including a meeting with an admissions counselor, a student-guided tour, a visit to financial aid, and a meeting with a faculty member, if requested. There are guides for informal visits and visitors may sit in on classes and stay overnight. To schedule a visit, contact the Office of Admission at (513) 244-4531 or admission@mail.edu.

Financial Aid: In 2005-2006, 99% of all full-time freshmen and 90% of continuing full-time students received some form of financial aid. 90% of all full-time students received need-based aid. The average freshman award was $14,773. Need-based scholarships or need-based grants averaged $5827 ($20,620 maximum); need-based self-help aid (loans and jobs) averaged $3941 ($6125 maximum); and other non-need-based awards and non-need-based scholarships averaged $4098 ($16,000 maximum). 19% of undergraduates work part time. Average annual earnings from campus work are $1329. The average financial indebtedness of the 2005 graduate was $9100. the Mount is a member of CSS. The FAFSA is required. The priority date for freshman financial aid applications for fall entry is March 1.

International Students: There are 7 international students enrolled. They must score satisfactorily on the written TOEFL, scholarship applicants must also take the SAT or the ACT and receive a satisfactory score.

Computers: Wireless access is available. Students may use the network, including access to e-mail and the Internet, throughout the campus via their own wireless laptop computer, one of 40 available wireless laptop computers, or from one of 201 desktop computers located in 13 computer labs. All students may access the system 24 hours a day. There are no time limits. The fee is $250/year for full-time students; $80/year for part-time students. All students are required to have personal computers; IBM ThinkPad is recommended.

Graduates: From July 1, 2004 to June 30, 2005, 330 bachelor's degrees were awarded. The most popular majors were business administration (9%), nursing (9%), and rehabilitation science (7%). In an average class, 1% graduate in 3 years or less, 68% graduate in 4 years or less, and 70% graduate in 6 years or less. 72 companies recruited on campus in 2004-2005. Of the 2004 graduating class, 18% were enrolled in graduate school within 6 months of graduation and 80% were employed.

Admissions Contact: Peggy Minnich, Director of Admission.
E-mail: admission@mail.msj.edu Web: www.msj.edu

COLLEGE OF WOOSTER   D-2
Wooster, OH 44691   **(330) 263-2322**
                                        (800) 877-9905; Fax: (330) 263-2621

Full-time: 857 men, 945 women	Faculty: 133; IIB, av$
Part-time: 2 men, 6 women	Ph.D.s: 91%
Graduate: none	Student/Faculty: 14 to 1
Year: semesters, summer session	Tuition: $25,050
Application Deadline: February 15	Room & Board: $6260
Freshman Class: 2542 applied, 1900 accepted, 559 enrolled	
SAT Verbal/Math: 620/610*	ACT: 26 VERY COMPETITIVE+

The College of Wooster, founded in 1866, is a private liberal arts college. The tuition and enrollment figures in the above capsule and in this profile are approximate. In addition to regional accreditation, Wooster has baccalaureate program accreditation with NASM. The 3 libraries contain 622,672 volumes, 210,094 microform items, and 24,149 audio/video tapes/CDs/DVDs, and subscribe to 6696 periodicals including electronic.

Computerized library services include the card catalog, interlibrary loans, and database searching. Special learning facilities include a learning resource center, art gallery, and radio station. The 240-acre campus is in a suburban area 55 miles southwest of Cleveland. Including any residence halls, there are 37 buildings.

Student Life: 52% of undergraduates are from Ohio. Others are from 44 states, 35 foreign countries, and Canada. 74% are from public schools. 76% are white. The average age of freshmen is 19; all undergraduates, 20. 12% do not continue beyond their first year; 68% remain to graduate.

Housing: 1859 students can be accommodated in college housing, which includes single-sex and coed dormitories, fraternity houses, and sorority houses. In addition, there are language houses special-interest houses, and almost 3 dozen small house residential options most of wich are associated with Community service/volunteer programs. On-campus housing is guaranteed for all 4 years. 99% of students live on campus; of those, 80% remain on campus on weekends. All students may keep cars.

Activities: 10% of men belong to 3 local fraternities; 17% of women belong to 6 local sororities. There are 11 groups on campus, including art, bagpipe band, band, cheerleading, chess, choir, chorale, chorus, dance, debate, drama, ethnic, film, forensics, gay, honors, international, jazz band, literary magazine, marching band, musical theater, newspaper, orchestra, pep band, photography, political, religious, social service, student government, symphony, and yearbook. Popular campus events include Party on the Green, Winter Gala, and Scot Spirit Day.

Sports: There are 11 intercollegiate sports for men and 11 for women, and 11 intramural sports for men and 11 for women. Facilities include a phys ed center, a stadium, a golf course, tennis courts, a track, baseball and softball fields, a soccer field, a hockey and lacrosse field, a natatorium, and a fitness center.

Disabled Students: 95% of the campus is accessible. Wheelchair ramps, elevators, special parking, specially equipped rest rooms, special class scheduling, and lowered drinking fountains are available.

Services: Counseling and information services are available, as is tutoring in every subject. There is a reader service for the blind, and remedial math, reading, and writing.

Campus Safety and Security: Measures include 24-hour foot and vehicle patrol, security escort services, informal discussions, and pamphlets/posters/films. There are emergency telephones and lighted pathways/sidewalks.

Programs of Study: Wooster confers B.A., B.Mus., and B.Mus.Ed. degrees. Bachelor's degrees are awarded in BIOLOGICAL SCIENCE (biochemistry and biology/biological science), BUSINESS (business economics), COMMUNICATIONS AND THE ARTS (communications, comparative literature, dramatic arts, English, fine arts, French, German, Greek (classical), Latin, music, and Spanish), COMPUTER AND PHYSICAL SCIENCE (chemistry, computer science, geology, mathematics, and physics), SOCIAL SCIENCE (African American studies, anthropology, archeology, area studies, economics, history, interdisciplinary studies, international relations, philosophy, political science/government, psychology, religion, Russian and Slavic studies, sociology, urban studies, and women's studies). Chemistry, history, and English are the strongest academically. History, English, and sociology are the largest.

Required: To graduate students must complete 32 course credits, with 9 to 13 in the major and a minimum GPA of 2.0. All students must take 1 course each in critical inquiry, studies in cultural differences, religious perspectives, and quantitative reasoning, and demonstrate basic writing and foreign language proficiency. Two courses each in English, foreign languages, social science/history, natural science/math, and arts/humanities are required.

Special: A 3-2 engineering degree is offered in conjunction with Case Western Reserve and Washington universities. A B.A.-B.S. degree is offered in music/music education. Cross-registration is possible with off-campus programs of the Great Lakes Colleges Association. Internships are available in American politics in Washington, D.C., the Ohio State Legislature, and the U.S. State Department, as well as in professional theater and economics. Student-designed majors, dual majors, study abroad in 50 countries, a Washington semester, accelerated degree programs, nondegree study, and pass/fail options for a limited number of courses are available. All seniors participate in a 2-term independent-study project in the major. The student chooses the topic and works on a one-to-one basis with a faculty mentor. A sophomore research program is available by application. There are 12 national honor societies, including Phi Beta Kappa.

Faculty/Classroom: 55% of faculty are male; 45%, female. All both teach and do research. The average class size in an introductory lecture is 15 and in a regular course, 20.

Admissions: 75% of the 2005-2006 applicants were accepted. The SAT scores for the 2005-2006 freshman class were: Verbal--7% below 500, 31% between 500 and 599, 44% between 600 and 700, and 18% above 700; Math--5% below 500, 38% between 500 and 599, 45% between 600 and 700, and 12% above 700. The ACT scores were 7% below 21, 22% between 21 and 23, 31% between 24 and 26, 16% be-

tween 27 and 28, and 24% above 28. 55% of the current freshmen were in the top fifth of their class; 86% were in the top two fifths.

Requirements: The SAT or ACT is required with a satisfactory score. In addition, applicants should be graduates of an accredited secondary school. The GED is accepted. Students should have completed a minimum of 17 high school academic credits. The school also requires an essay and recommends an interview. AP credits are accepted. Important factors in the admissions decision are advanced placement or honor courses, recommendations by school officials, and leadership record.

Procedure: Freshmen are admitted fall and winter. Entrance exams should be taken in the fall of the senior year. There are early decision, early admissions, and deferred admissions plans. Early decision applications should be filed by December 1; regular applications, by February 15 for fall entry, along with a $40 fee. Notification of early decision is sent December 15; regular decision, April 1. 70 early decision candidates were accepted for the 2005-2006 class. 147 applicants were on the 2005 waiting list; 6 were admitted. Applications are accepted on-line.

Transfer: 22 transfer students enrolled in 2004-2005. Applicants for transfer must have a minimum GPA of 2.5 and must submit either the SAT or ACT scores as well as a dean's reference, a high school transcript, and an essay or personal statement. An interview is recommended. Grades of C or better transfer for credit. Transfers are admitted every semester. 17 of 32 credits required for the bachelor's degree must be completed at Wooster.

Visiting: There are regularly scheduled orientations for prospective students, including an interview, tour, class visits, and meetings with faculty and coaches. There are guides for informal visits and visitors may sit in on classes and stay overnight. To schedule a visit, contact the Admissions Office.

Financial Aid: In 2005-2006, 59% of all full-time freshmen and 57% of continuing full-time students received some form of financial aid. At least 44% of full-time freshmen and at least 48% of continuing full-time students received need-based aid. The average freshman award was $23,486. Need-based scholarships or need-based grants averaged $17,281; need-based self-help aid (loans and jobs) averaged $5407; and institutional non-need-based awards and non-need-based scholarships averaged $12,591. 50% of undergraduates work part time. The average financial indebtedness of the 2005 graduate was $19,989. Wooster is a member of CSS. The CSS/Profile or FAFSA and the college's own financial statement are required. The priority date for freshman financial aid applications for fall entry is February 15. The deadline for filing freshman financial aid applications for fall entry is September 1.

International Students: The school actively recruits these students. They must score satisfactorily on the written TOEFL or take the MELAB or the American Language Institute test and also take the SAT or the ACT.

Computers: All students may access the system any time.

Graduates: From July 1, 2004 to June 30, 2005, 435 bachelor's degrees were awarded. The most popular majors were social sciences (22%), history (11%), and English (9%). In an average class, 68% graduate in 4 years or less, 74% graduate in 5 years or less, and 75% graduate in 6 years or less. Of the 2004 graduating class, 28% were enrolled in graduate school within 6 months of graduation and 70% were employed.

Admissions Contact: Carol Wheatley, Director of Admissions. A video is available. E-mail: *admissions@wooster.edu* Web: *http://www.wooster.edu*

COLUMBUS COLLEGE OF ART AND DESIGN   C-3
Columbus, OH 43215 (614) 222-3261
(877) 997-CCAD; Fax: (614) 232-8344

Full-time: 655 men, 690 women	Faculty: 75
Part-time: 200 men, 205 women	Ph.D.s: 47%
Graduate: none	Student/Faculty: 18 to 1
Year: semesters, summer session	Tuition: $18,000
Application Deadline: open	Room & Board: $6500
Freshman Class: n/av	
SAT or ACT: required	SPECIAL

Columbus College of Art and Design, founded in 1879, is a private institution offering undergraduate programs in art and fine arts. Figures above capsule and profile are approximate. In addition to regional accreditation, CCAD has baccalaureate program accreditation with NASAD. The library contains 41,396 volumes and 13,475 microform items, and subscribes to 254 periodicals including electronic. Computerized library services include the card catalog and database searching. Special learning facilities include a learning resource center, art gallery, and an art museum. The 17-acre campus is in an urban area in Columbus. Including any residence halls, there are 15 buildings.

Student Life: 63% of undergraduates are from Ohio. Others are from 47 states, 27 foreign countries, and Canada. 89% are white. The average age of freshmen is 19; all undergraduates, 21. 22% do not continue beyond their first year; 36% remain to graduate.

Housing: 300 students can be accommodated in college housing, which includes single-sex and coed dormitories and off-campus apartments. On-campus housing is guaranteed for the freshman year only and is available on a first-come, first-served basis. Priority is given to out-of-town students. 82% of students commute. Alcohol is not permitted. Upperclassmen may keep cars.

Activities: There are no fraternities or sororities. There are 7 groups on campus, including ethnic, international, literary magazine, newspaper, professional, religious, and student government. Popular campus events include biannual student art sales, International Reception, and International Students Holiday Brunch.

Sports: There are 4 intramural sports for men and 2 for women. Facilities include a game room in the student center.

Disabled Students: 50% of the campus is accessible. Wheelchair ramps, elevators, special parking, specially equipped rest rooms, special class scheduling, and lowered telephones are available.

Services: There is remedial reading and writing.

Campus Safety and Security: Measures include 24-hour foot and vehicle patrol, security escort services, informal discussions, and pamphlets/posters/films. There are emergency telephones and lighted pathways/sidewalks.

Programs of Study: CCAD confers the B.F.A. degree. Bachelor's degrees are awarded in COMMUNICATIONS AND THE ARTS (advertising, fine arts, graphic design, illustration, industrial design, and media arts), ENGINEERING AND ENVIRONMENTAL DESIGN (interior design), SOCIAL SCIENCE (fashion design and technology). Media arts and fine arts are the largest.

Required: All students must complete foundation studies, including 4 years of drawing and 3 years of design/color, and courses in English, sociology, psychology, business, art history, science, literature, and painting. A total of 129 credit hours, with 75 to 90 in the major depending on the major, and a minimum GPA of 2.0 are required to graduate. A sophomore English exam must be passed. Students must complete a portfolio of professional caliber, and students in fine arts must have an individual showing of recent works.

Special: Cross-registration is offered with Franklin, Ohio State, and Capital Universities, Ohio Dominican, Otterbein, and Pontifical Colleges, Columbus State Community College, Mount Carmel College of Nursing, and DeVry Institute of Technology. Internships are available, as are on-campus work-study, dual majors, and nondegree study.

Faculty/Classroom: 71% of faculty are male; 29%, female. All teach undergraduates. The average class size in an introductory lecture is 23; in a laboratory, 18; and in a regular course, 20.

Requirements: The SAT or ACT is required. In addition, applicants should be graduates of an accredited secondary school or have the GED. A portfolio of artwork indicative of abilities must be submitted. An interview is advised. A GPA of 2.0 is required. AP credits are accepted. Important factors in the admissions decision are evidence of special talent, recommendations by school officials, and recommendations by alumni.

Procedure: Freshmen are admitted fall and spring. There is a rolling admissions plan. Application deadlines are open. Application fee is $25. Applications are accepted on-line.

Transfer: 75 transfer students enrolled in a recent year. Applicants must submit an acceptable portfolio of artwork as well as all high school and college transcripts. A minimum GPA of 2.0 is required. An interview is recommended. 60 of 129 credits required for the bachelor's degree must be completed at CCAD.

Visiting: There are regularly scheduled orientations for prospective students, including a personal interview, a portfolio review, and a tour. There are guides for informal visits. To schedule a visit, contact the Admissions Office.

Financial Aid: In a recent year, 72% of all full-time freshmen and 85% of continuing full-time students received some form of financial aid. 60% of full-time freshmen and 80% of continuing full-time students received need-based aid. The average freshman award was $6500. Need-based scholarships or need-based grants averaged $8839. 53% of undergraduates work part time. Average annual earnings from campus work were $3126. The average financial indebtedness of a recent graduate was $21,730. CCAD is a member of CSS. The FAFSA and the college's own financial statement are required. Check with the school for application deadlines.

International Students: In a recent year there were 73 international students enrolled. The school actively recruits these students. They must score satisfactorily on the written TOEFL or take the MELAB and also take the SAT or the ACT.

Computers: All students may access the system during scheduled lab hours and class time. There are no time limits and no fees.

Admissions Contact: Thomas Green, Director of Admissions.
E-mail: admissions@ccad.edu Web: www.ccad.edu

DAVID N. MYERS COLLEGE   D-1
Cleveland, OH 44115

	(216) 523-3800
	(877) DNMYERS; Fax: (216) 696-6430

Full-time: 130 men, 445 women	**Faculty:** 17
Part-time: 195 men, 335 women	**Ph.D.s:** 23%
Graduate: 50 men, 35 women	**Student/Faculty:** 12 to 1
Year: semesters, summer session	**Tuition:** $9500
Application Deadline: open	**Room & Board:** n/app
Freshman Class: n/av	
SAT or ACT: required	**COMPETITIVE**

David H. Myers College, founded in 1848, is a private institution offering undergraduate programs in business to commuting students. Figures above capsule and profile are approximate. The library contains 13,250 volumes, 616 microform items, and 471 audio/video tapes/CDs/DVDs, and subscribes to 140 periodicals including electronic. Computerized library services include the card catalog, interlibrary loans, and database searching. Special learning facilities include a learning resource center. The 2-acre campus is in an urban area in Cleveland. There is 1 building.

Student Life: 45% are African American; 42% white. The average age of all undergraduates is 26.

Housing: There are no residence halls. All of students commute. Alcohol is not permitted.

Activities: There are no fraternities. There are some groups and organizations on campus, including chorale, student government, and yearbook.

Disabled Students: All of the campus is accessible. Wheelchair ramps, elevators, specially equipped rest rooms, special class scheduling, lowered drinking fountains, and lowered telephones are available.

Services: Counseling and information services are available, as is tutoring in most subjects. There is a reader service for the blind, and remedial math, reading, and writing.

Programs of Study: Myers College confers the B.S. degree. Associate and master's degrees are also awarded. Bachelor's degrees are awarded in BUSINESS (accounting, business administration and management, marketing/retailing/merchandising, office supervision and management, real estate, retailing, and secretarial studies/office management), COMPUTER AND PHYSICAL SCIENCE (information sciences and systems), ENGINEERING AND ENVIRONMENTAL DESIGN (industrial administration/management), HEALTH PROFESSIONS (health care administration), SOCIAL SCIENCE (economics, paralegal studies, public administration, and social science).

Required: All students must complete 51 hours of general education requirements, and 27 hours in the business core, plus major requirements and electives. A minimum of 120 semester hours with a minimum GPA of 2.0 is required in order to graduate.

Special: The external degree program enables working adults to earn a bachelor's degree in a nontraditional manner, including credit by exam and credit for life/work experience. Work-study programs, co-op programs in 7 majors, internships, dual majors, pass/fail options, and cross-registration with other area colleges are offered. Evening and Saturday classes are also available.

Faculty/Classroom: 72% of faculty are male; 28%, female. All teach undergraduates. The average class size in an introductory lecture is 11; in a laboratory,16; and in a regular course,11.

Requirements: The SAT or ACT is required for recent high school graduates. Applicants should have completed 19 Carnegie units, including 4 years of high school English, 3 each of math and science, and 2 each of social studies and history. The GED is accepted. An interview is recommended. AP and CLEP credits are accepted. Important factors in the admissions decision are ability to finance college education, advanced placement or honor courses, and recommendations by school officials.

Procedure: Freshmen are admitted to all sessions. Entrance exams should be taken by March of the senior year. There are deferred admissions and rolling admissions plans. Application deadlines are open. Application fee is $25.

Transfer: Applicants should have a minimum GPA of 2.0 in at least 24 semester hours. An associate's degree and an interview are recommended. 30 of 126 credits required for the bachelor's degree must be completed at Myers College.

Visiting: There are guides for informal visits and visitors may sit in on classes. To schedule a visit, contact the Admissions Services.

Financial Aid: Myers College is a member of CSS. The FAFSA is required. Check with the school for current application deadlines

International Students: They must score satisfactorily on the written TOEFL.

Computers: All students may access the system on or off campus. There are no time limits and no fees.

Admissions Contact: Tiffiney Payton, Interim Director of Admissions.
E-mail: tpayton@dnmyers.edu Web: www.dnmyers.edu

DEFIANCE COLLEGE   A-2
Defiance, OH 43512

(419) 783-2361
(800) 520-GODC (4632); Fax: (419) 783-2468

Full-time: 315 men, 359 women	**Faculty:** 40
Part-time: 52 men, 102 women	**Ph.Ds:** 70%
Graduate: 103 men and women	**Student/Faculty:** 17 to 1
Year: semesters, summer session	**Tuition:** $18,930
Application Deadline: open	**Room & Board:** $5860
Freshman Class: n/av	
SAT Verbal/Math: 484/480*	**ACT:** 21 **COMPETITIVE**

Defiance College is an independent, coeducational institution affiliated with the United Church of Christ and home to the McMaster School for Advancing Humanity. Our vision calls for an educational esperience of engagement - civic, cultural, and learning - for all students. In addition to regional accreditation, Defiance has baccalaureate program accreditation with CSWE and NCATE. The library contains 124,500 volumes, 7400 microform items, and 4577 audio/video tapes/CDs/DVDs, and subscribes to 330 periodicals including electronic. Computerized library services include the card catalog, interlibrary loans, database searching, Internet access, and laptop Internet portals. Special learning facilities include a learning resource center, art gallery, and Thoreau Wildlife Sanctuary, and a greenhouse. The 150-acre campus is in a small town 55 miles southwest of Toledo, and 50 miles east of Fort Wayne. Including any residence halls, there are 24 buildings.

Student Life: 89% of undergraduates are from Ohio. Students are from 8 states and 2 foreign countries. 96% are from public schools. 90% are white. The average age of freshmen is 18. 31% do not continue beyond their first year; 58% remain to graduate.

Housing: 505 students can be accommodated in college housing, which includes single-sex and coed dorms and on-campus apartments. In addition, there are academic floors in the residence halls with additional academic programming and resources. On-campus housing is guaranteed for all 4 years and is available on a lottery system for upperclassmen. 66% of students live on campus; of those, 50% remain on campus on weekends. Alcohol is not permitted. All students may keep cars.

Activities: 6% of men belong to 1 national fraternity; 6% of women belong to 2 national sororities. There are 33 groups on campus, including art, band, choir, dance, drama, ethnic, honors, international, literary magazine, musical theater, newspaper, pep band, political, professional, religious, social, social service, student government, and yearbook. Popular campus events include Freshman Service Day, Arts on the Quad, and Thanksgiving Dinner.

Sports: There are 9 intercollegiate sports for men and 9 for women, and 10 intramural sports for men and 10 for women. Facilities include a 4,000-seat stadium, baseball, softball, and soccer field, a cross-country course, gymnasium, racquetball courts, indoor track, weight-lifting, basketball courts, tennis courts, 8-lane all-weather outdoor track, and a fitness center.

Disabled Students: 80% of the campus is accessible. Wheelchair ramps, elevators, special parking, specially equipped rest rooms, special class scheduling, lowered drinking fountains, and lowered telephones are available.

Services: Counseling and information services are available, as is tutoring in every subject. There is a reader service for the blind.

Campus Safety and Security: Measures include security escort services, informal discussions, pamphlets/posters/films, and lighted pathways/sidewalks. There are nighttime security guards in residence halls, security cameras in residence hall entrances, and a security guard on the grounds from dusk to dawn.

Programs of Study: Defiance confers B.A. and B.S. degrees. Associate and master's degrees are also awarded. Bachelor's degrees are awarded in BIOLOGICAL SCIENCE (biology/biological science, and ecology), BUSINESS (accounting, banking and finance, business administration and management, human resources, management science, marketing/retailing/merchandising, organizational leadership and management, and sports management), COMMUNICATIONS AND THE ARTS (art, communications, and graphic design), COMPUTER AND PHYSICAL SCIENCE (information sciences and systems, and mathematics), EDUCATION (art, athletic training, Christian, early childhood, elementary, health, mathematics, physical, reading, science, secondary, and social studies), ENGINEERING AND ENVIRONMENTAL DESIGN (environmental science), HEALTH PROFESSIONS (medical laboratory technology), SOCIAL SCIENCE (criminal justice, forensic studies, history, humanities, international studies, physical fitness/movement, psychology, religion, and social work). Education and sciences are the strongest academically. Business, forensic sciences, and education are the largest.

Required: All students must fulfill general education requirements, including communication skills, arts and humanities, natural science, and social science. Freshman Seminar, Fitness for Life as well as senior assessment in the major, are also required. A total of 120 semester credits, with at least 30 in the major, and a minimum GPA of 2.0 are required to graduate. Service is required in all majors; computer proficency must be demonstrated.

Special: Co-op programs and internships are available in all majors, as are B.A.-B.S. degrees and dual majors. Work study and student-designed majors are also available. The McMaster School for Advancing Humanity allows students and faculty to more closely examine global issues and how they effect the human condition. There are 8 national honor societies, a freshman honors program, and 1 departmental honors program.

Faculty/Classroom: 58% of faculty are male; 42%, female. All teach undergraduates and 30% both teach and do research. The average class size in an introductory lecture is 22; in a laboratory, 18; and in a regular course, 16.

Admissions: The SAT scores for the 2005-2006 freshman class were: Verbal--51% below 500, 45% between 500 and 599, and 4% between 600 and 700; Math--55% below 500, 33% between 500 and 599, and 12% between 600 and 700. The ACT scores were 47% below 21, 25% between 21 and 23, 17% between 24 and 26, and 10% between 27 and 28. 28% of the current freshmen were in the top fifth of their class; 51% were in the top two fifths. 2 freshmen graduated first in their class.

Requirements: The ACT is required and the SAT is recommended. In addition, applicants should be graduates of an accredited secondary school or have a GED, with 15 Carnegie units completed, including 4 in English, 3 each in math, science, and social studies, and 2 in foreign language. An essay and an interview are recommended. A GPA of 2.25 is required. AP and CLEP credits are accepted. Important factors in the admissions decision are advanced placement or honor courses, personality/intangible qualities, and leadership record.

Procedure: Freshmen are admitted to all sessions. Entrance exams should be taken in the spring of the junior year or the fall of the senior year. There are early admissions, deferred admissions, and rolling admissions plans. Application deadlines are open. Application fee is $25. Applications are accepted on-line.

Transfer: 53 transfer students enrolled in 2004-2005. A high school diploma, GED certificate or equivalent; official transcript from each college or university attended; minimum college GPA of 2.0 from the last college attended; record indicating good standing socially from each college or university attended is required. An interview is recommended. 35 of 120 credits required for the bachelor's degree must be completed at Defiance.

Visiting: There are regularly scheduled orientations for prospective students, including admissions, financial aid, and special interest sessions, campus tour, complimentary lunch, meetings with faculty, observing a class in session. Interested applicants can meet with a coach. There are guides for informal visits and visitors may sit in on classes and stay overnight. To schedule a visit, contact the Office of Admission at (419) 783-2359 or admissions@defiance.edu.

Financial Aid: In a recent year, all full-time freshmen and 99% of continuing full-time students received some form of financial aid. 70% of full-time freshmen and 66% of continuing full-time students received need-based aid. The average freshman award was $18,699. Need-based scholarships or need-based grants averaged $1707; need-based self-help aid (loans and jobs) averaged $1590; and other non-need-based awards and non-need-based scholarships averaged $15,402. 30% of undergraduates work part time. Average annual earnings from campus work are $645. The average financial indebtedness of the 2005 graduate was $14,061. The FAFSA and the college's own financial statement are required. The deadline for filing freshman financial aid applications for fall entry is March 1.

International Students: There is 1 international student enrolled. The school actively recruits these students. A satisfactory score is required on the written TOEFL and the SAT or the ACT.

Computers: Wireless access is available. All students may access the system 24 hours a day, every day. There are no time limits. The fee is $260 per semester.

Graduates: From July 1, 2004 to June 30, 2005, 197 bachelor's degrees were awarded. In a recent year, the most popular majors were management (23%), elementary education (13%), and communications (10%). In an average class, 46% graduate in 4 years or less, 56% graduate in 5 years or less, and 58% graduate in 6 years or less. 390 companies recruited on campus in a recent year. Of the 2004 graduating class, 10% were enrolled in graduate school within 6 months of graduation and 92% were employed.

Admissions Contact: William Nunn, Dean of Enrollment Management. E-mail: admissions@defiance.edu Web: www.defiance.edu

DENISON UNIVERSITY C-3
Granville, OH 43023

(740) 587-6276
(800) DENISON; Fax: (740) 587-6306

Full-time: 1003 men, 1289 women	**Faculty:** 183; IIB, +$
Part-time: 15 men, 22 women	**Ph.D.s:** 97%
Graduate: none	**Student/Faculty:** 13 to 1
Year: semesters	**Tuition:** $28,920
Application Deadline: February 15	**Room & Board:** $8120
Freshman Class: 5122 applied, 1997 accepted, 622 enrolled	
SAT Verbal/Math: 615/620*	**ACT:** 27 **HIGHLY COMPETITIVE**

Denison University, founded in 1831, is a private independent institution of liberal arts and sciences. The library contains 411,395 volumes, 122,351 microform items, and 6465 audio/video tapes/CDs/DVDs, and subscribes to 7465 periodicals including electronic. Computerized library services include the card catalog, interlibrary loans, and database searching. Special learning facilities include a learning resource center, art gallery, planetarium, radio station, TV station, an observatory, a field research station in a 350-acre biological reserve, high resolution spectometer, economics computer labs, and modern languages laboratory. The 1200-acre campus is in a suburban area 30 miles east of Columbus. Including any residence halls, there are 62 buildings.

Student Life: 60% of undergraduates are from out of state, mostly the Midwest. Students are from 49 states, 34 foreign countries, and Canada. 69% are from public schools. 84% are white. 33% are Catholic; 33% Protestant; 28% Muslim, Hindu, Buddhist, nondenominational Christian; 6% claim no religious affiliation. The average age of freshmen is 18; all undergraduates, 20. 10% do not continue beyond their first year; 79% remain to graduate.

Housing: 2253 students can be accommodated in college housing, which includes single-sex and coed dorms and on-campus apartments. In addition, there are honors houses, special-interest houses, first-year center, substance-free dorms, quiet dorms, all-womaen dorms, suite-style dorms, and apartments for juniors and seniors with high grade point average/leadership. On-campus housing is guaranteed for all 4 years. 98% of students live on campus; of those, 92% remain on campus on weekends. All students may keep cars.

Activities: 28% of men belong to 12 national fraternities; 30% of women belong to 9 national sororities. There are 130 groups on campus, including art, cheerleading, choir, chorale, chorus, computers, dance, drama, ethnic, film, gay, honors, international, jazz band, literary magazine, musical theater, newspaper, orchestra, pep band, photography, political, professional, radio and TV, religious, social, social service, student government, symphony, and yearbook. Popular campus events include an all-campus community picnic and fair, All-Campus Gala, and Academic Awards Convocation.

Sports: There are 11 intercollegiate sports for men and 11 for women, and 12 intramural sports for men and 12 for women. Facilities include a 6000-seat stadium, a 1500-seat gym, 12 outdoor tennis courts, squash courts, an 8-lane quarter-mile track, a field house with a 200-meter track and 4 tennis courts, baseball/softball fields, a recreation gym with 3 volleyball/basketball courts, weight, aerobic, fitness rooms, soccer and men's lacrosse stadium, women's field hockey and lacrosse field, and multiple practice fields.

Disabled Students: 66% of the campus is accessible. Wheelchair ramps, elevators, special parking, specially equipped rest rooms, special class scheduling, lowered drinking fountains, and lowered telephones are available.

Services: Counseling and information services are available, as is tutoring in most subjects. There is a reader service for the blind. A reading and writing center is available, as are study sessions for math, chemistry, and some languages, reduced courseloads, special counselor services, note taking services, oral tests, extended time for tests, untimed tests, talking books, tape recorders, and readers.

Campus Safety and Security: Measures include 24-hour foot and vehicle patrol, self-defense education, security escort services, and informal discussions. There are pamphlets/posters/films, emergency telephones and lighted pathways/sidewalks. Residence halls are locked 24 hours a day with entry through a card access system.

Programs of Study: Denison confers B.A., B.S., and B.F.A. degrees. Bachelor's degrees are awarded in AGRICULTURE (environmental studies), BIOLOGICAL SCIENCE (biochemistry and molecular/biological science), COMMUNICATIONS AND THE ARTS (art history and appreciation, communications, dance, dramatic arts, English, film arts, fine arts, French, German, languages, Latin, media arts, music, Spanish, speech/debate/rhetoric, and studio art), COMPUTER AND PHYSICAL SCIENCE (chemistry, computer science, geology, mathematics, and physics), EDUCATION (education and physical), SOCIAL SCIENCE (African American studies, anthropology, classical/ancient civilization, East Asian studies, economics, history, international studies, Latin American studies, philosophy, political science/government, psychology, religion, sociology, Western European studies, and women's studies). Psychology, philosophy, and physics are the strongest academically. Communication, biology, and economics are the largest.

Required: All students must fulfill aproximately 13 courses of the general education program, including freshman studies in textual, critical, social, scientific, and artistic inquiries, along with oral communication, minority/women's studies, and 2 choices from Western Studies, non-Western studies and American social institutions. A total of 127 semester hours, with 36 in the major and a minimum GPA of 2.0, is required in order to graduate.

Special: Work-study programs, a Washington semester, study-abroad programs in more than 35 countries, student-designed majors, a math/economics dual major, a dual major in education and various other majors, a philosophy, political science, and economics interdisciplinary major, and pass/fail options are available. A 3-2 engineering program is offered with Rensselaer Polytechnic Institute, Case Western Reserve, and Washington Universities. A May-term internship is available at more than 200 U.S. locations. A B.A.-B.S. degree, accelerated degree programs, a media technology and arts interdisciplinary major, and nondegree study are possible. There are 15 national honor societies, including Phi Beta Kappa, a freshman honors program, and 100 departmental honors programs.

Faculty/Classroom: 63% of faculty are male; 37%, female. All both teach and do research. The average class size in an introductory lecture is 19; in a laboratory, 21; and in a regular course, 20.

Admissions: 39% of the 2005-2006 applicants were accepted. The SAT scores for the 2005-2006 freshman class were: Verbal--5% below 500, 36% between 500 and 599, 51% between 600 and 700, and 8% above 700; Math--6% below 500, 29% between 500 and 599, 57% between 600 and 700, and 8% above 700. The ACT scores were 6% below 21, 13% between 21 and 23, 25% between 24 and 26, 25% between 27 and 28, and 31% above 28. 75% of the current freshmen were in the top fifth of their class; 93% were in the top two fifths. There were 9 National Merit finalists and 12 semifinalists. In a recent year, 40 freshmen graduated first in their class.

Requirements: The SAT or ACT is required. The ACT Optional Writing test is also required. In addition, applicants should have completed 19 Carnegie units, including 4 each in English, math and science, 3 in foreign language, 2 in social studies, and 1 each in history and academic electives. An essay is part of the application process. An interview is advised, and a portfolio or an audition is recommended for art or music majors, respectively. AP credits are accepted. Important factors in the admissions decision are personality/intangible qualities, evidence of special talent, and advanced placement or honor courses.

Procedure: Freshmen are admitted in the fall. Entrance exams should be taken by December of the senior year. There are early decision, early admissions, and deferred admissions plans. Early decision applications should be filed by November 1; regular applications, by January 15 for fall entry, along with a $40 fee. Notification is sent April 1. 164 early decision candidates were accepted for the 2005-2006 class. 134 applicants were on the 2005 waiting list. Applications are accepted on-line.

Transfer: 18 transfer students enrolled in 2004-2005. A minimum GPA of 2.75 is required. The SAT or ACT scores should be submitted, as well as high school and college transcripts, an essay, and a statement of good standing from previous institutions. An interview is recommended. 64 of 127 credits required for the bachelor's degree must be completed at Denison.

Visiting: There are regularly scheduled orientations for prospective students, including orientation programs, class visits, tours, and interviews. There are guides for informal visits and visitors may sit in on classes and stay overnight. To schedule a visit, contact the Admissions Office at *www.denison.edu/admissions/visit.*

Financial Aid: In 2005-2006, 97% of all full-time freshmen and 66% of continuing full-time students received some form of financial aid. The average freshman award was $24,545. Need-based scholarships or need-based grants averaged $24,545; need-based self-help aid (loans and jobs) averaged $5142; and other institutional non-need-based awards and non-need-based scholarships averaged $12,213. 50% of undergraduates work part time. Average annual earnings from campus work are $1776. The average financial indebtedness of the 2005 graduate was $14,657. The FAFSA and the college's own financial statement are required. The deadline for filing freshman financial aid applications for fall entry is February 15.

International Students: There are 105 international students enrolled. The school actively recruits these students. A satisfactory score is required on the written TOEFL, the SATor the ACT.

Computers: All students may access the system 24 hours a day. There are no time limits and no fees.

Graduates: From July 1, 2004 to June 30, 2005, 515 bachelor's degrees were awarded. The most popular majors were biology (10%), economics (10%), and communications (9%). In an average class, 75% graduate in 4 years or less, 78% graduate in 5 years or less, and 79% graduate in 6 years or less. 85 companies recruited on campus in 2004-2005. Of the 2004 graduating class, 22% were enrolled in graduate school within 6 months of graduation and 65% were employed.

Admissions Contact: Perry Robinson, Vice President and Director of Admissions. E-mail: *admissions@denison.edu* Web: *http://denison.edu/admissions/*

DEVRY UNIVERSITY/COLUMBUS

C-3

Columbus, OH 43209-2705
(614) 253-1525
(800) 426-2206; Fax: (614) 253-0843

Full-time: 1706 men, 465 women
Part-time: 655 men, 335 women
Graduate: none
Year: semesters, summer session
Application Deadline: open
Freshman Class: n/av
SAT or ACT: n/av

Faculty: n/av
Ph.D.s: n/av
Student/Faculty: n/av
Tuition: $11,000
Room & Board: n/app

LESS COMPETITIVE

DeVry University/Columbus, 1 of 67 DeVry University locations in the United States and Canada, opened in 1952. The institute offers undergraduate degrees in business administration, electronics, computer information systems, technical management, information technology, and computer engineering technology. Figures above capsule and profile are approximate. In addition to regional accreditation, DeVry has baccalaureate program accreditation with ABET. The library contains 28,000 volumes, and subscribes to 60 periodicals including electronic. Computerized library services include the card catalog, interlibrary loans, and database searching. Special learning facilities include a learning resource center and electronics and other labs. The 13-acre campus is in an urban area. There is 1 building.

Student Life: 73% are white; 20% African American. The average age of all undergraduates is 24.

Housing: There are no residence halls. Housing referrals may be obtained through the Student Housing Office. Threre are private apartments, student-plan housing, and private rooms. All students commute. Alcohol is not permitted. All students may keep cars.

Activities: There are no fraternities or sororities. There are 9 groups on campus, including ethnic, honors, newspaper, professional, religious, and student government. Popular campus events include Parents Weekend, Student Appreciation Week, and New Student Days.

Sports: There are 3 intramural sports for men and 1 for women.

Disabled Students: 90% of the campus is accessible. Wheelchair ramps, elevators, special parking, specially equipped rest rooms, and special class scheduling are available.

Services: Counseling and information services are available, as is tutoring in every subject.

Campus Safety and Security: Measures include informal discussions, pamphlets/posters/films, emergency telephones, and lighted pathways/sidewalks. Daytime and evening security is provided until the building is closed. Security systems and motion detectors are utilized after business hours.

Programs of Study: DeVry confers the B.S. degree. Associate and master's degrees are also awarded. Bachelor's degrees are awarded in BUSINESS (business administration and management), COMMUNICATIONS AND THE ARTS (telecommunications), COMPUTER AND PHYSICAL SCIENCE (information sciences and systems), ENGINEERING AND ENVIRONMENTAL DESIGN (computer engineering, electrical/electronics engineering technology, and technological management). Computer information systems and computer engineering technology are the largest.

Required: To graduate, students must achieve a GPA of at least 2.0 and satisfactorily complete all curriculum requirements. Course requirements vary according to program. All first-semester students take courses in business organization, computer applications, algebra, psychology, and student success strategies.

Special: Accelerated degrees, co-op programs, nondegree study, distance learning, and evening classes are possible. There is 1 national honor society.

Faculty/Classroom: All teach undergraduates.

Requirements: Admissions requirements include graduation from a secondary school; the GED is also accepted. Applicants must pass the DeVry entrance exam or present satisfactory ACT or SAT scores. An interview is required. CLEP credit is accepted.

Procedure: Freshmen are admitted fall, spring, and summer. There are early admissions, and deferred admissions and rolling admissions plans. Application deadlines are open. Application fee is $50. Applications are accepted on-line.

Transfer: Applicants must present passing grades in all completed college course work, demonstrate language skills proficiency with at least 24 completed semester hours, and evidence math proficiency by appropriate college-level credits. 25 of 48 credits required for the bachelor's degree must be completed at DeVry.

Visiting: There are regularly scheduled orientations for prospective students. There are guides for informal visits and visitors may sit in on classes. To schedule a visit, contact the New Student Coordinator at (800) 426-3916.

Financial Aid: In a recent year, 52% of all full-time freshmen and 73% of continuing full-time students received some form of financial aid. 50% of full-time freshmen and 72% of continuing full-time students received need-based aid. The average freshman award was $7530. Need-based

scholarships or need-based grants averaged $3713; need-based self-help aid (loans and jobs) averaged $4443; and other non-need-based awards and non-need-based scholarships averaged $5783. DeVry is a member of CSS. The FAFSA is required. Check with school for current application deadlines.

International Students: They must score satisfactorily on the written TOEFL or on the electronic version and also take the college's own entrance exam.

Computers: Students in the computer information systems program may access the system during lab hours. There are no fees. It is recommended that students in the information technology program must have DeVry-issued laptops.

Graduates: In a recent year, 474 bachelor's degrees were awarded. The most popular majors were computer information systems (52%), business (32%), and electronics engineering technology (16%). 175 companies recruited on campus in a recent year.

Admissions Contact: Bill Holtry, Dean of Admissions.
E-mail: *admissions@devry.edu* Web: *www.devry.cols.edu*

FRANCISCAN UNIVERSITY OF STEUBENVILLE

E-3

Steubenville, OH 43952-1763
(740) 283-6226, ext.1220
(800) 783-6220; Fax: (740) 284-5456

Full-time: 675 men, 1020 women
Part-time: 60 men, 100 women
Graduate: 190 men, 250 women
Year: semesters, summer session
Application Deadline: see profile
Freshman Class: n/av
SAT or ACT: required

Faculty: 96; IIA, --$
Ph.D.s: 73%
Student/Faculty: 18 to 1
Tuition: $16,000
Room & Board: $5500

VERY COMPETITIVE

Franciscan University of Steubenville, founded in 1946 by the Franciscan Friars, is a private, liberal arts, professional and preprofessional institution committed to the Catholic Church and its renewal. Figures above capsule and profile are approximate. In addition to regional accreditation, Franciscan University has baccalaureate program accreditation with NLN. The library contains 232,013 volumes, 250,968 microform items, and 892 audio/video tapes/CDs/DVDs, and subscribes to 5874 periodicals including electronic. Computerized library services include the card catalog, interlibrary loans, and database searching. Special learning facilities include a radio station. The 124-acre campus is in a small town 40 miles west of Pittsburgh. Including any residence halls, there are 21 buildings.

Student Life: 76% of undergraduates are from out of state, mostly the Midwest. Students are from 49 states, 23 foreign countries, and Canada. 59% are from public schools. 83% are white. Most are Catholic. The average age of freshmen is 18; all undergraduates, 21. 16% do not continue beyond their first year; 71% remain to graduate.

Housing: 1155 students can be accommodated in college housing, which includes single-sex dormitories and Christian faith households in residence halls. On-campus housing is available on a first-come, first-served basis. 61% of students live on campus; of those, 70% remain on campus on weekends. Upperclassmen may keep cars.

Activities: There is 1 local and 1 national fraternity; 1% of women belong to 1 national sorority. There are 25 groups on campus, including choir, chorale, chorus, computers, drama, ethnic, honors, international, literary magazine, newspaper, orchestra, political, professional, profile, radio and TV, religious, social, social service, student government, and yearbook. Popular campus events include the Feast of St. Francis, Pro-Life Rally, and all school evangelism events.

Sports: There are 4 intramural sports for men and 4 for women. Facilities include a campus athletic center, which houses 2 full-size basketball courts, racquetball courts, saunas, whirlpools, and locker rooms, and provides indoor seating for 2000. Outdoor athletic facilities include a basketball court, 4 tennis courts, and baseball, softball, flag football, and soccer fields.

Disabled Students: 75% of the campus is accessible. Wheelchair ramps, elevators, special parking, specially equipped rest rooms, special class scheduling, lowered drinking fountains, lowered telephones, fire alarm devices, wider doorways, and curb cuts are available.

Services: Counseling and information services are available, as is tutoring in most subjects. There is a reader service for the blind and remedial reading. Tutoring and counseling are available for learning-disabled students. Tutoring is also available for students on academic probation.

Campus Safety and Security: Measures include 24-hour foot and vehicle patrol, self-defense education, security escort services, and shuttle buses. There are informal discussions, pamphlets/posters/films, emergency telephones, and lighted pathways/sidewalks.

Programs of Study: Franciscan University confers B.A., B.S., and B.S.N. degrees. Associate and master's degrees are also awarded. Bachelor's degrees are awarded in BIOLOGICAL SCIENCE (biology/biological science), BUSINESS (accounting and business administration and management), COMMUNICATIONS AND THE ARTS (classics, communications, English, French, German, and Spanish), COMPUTER AND PHYSICAL SCIENCE (chemistry, computer science, information sciences and systems, and mathematics), EDUCATION (elementary), ENGINEERING AND ENVIRONMENTAL DESIGN (engineering and applied science), HEALTH PROFESSIONS (mental health/human services and nursing), SOCIAL SCIENCE (anthropology, economics, history, humanities and social science, paralegal studies, philosophy, political science/government, psychology, religion, religious education, social work, sociology, and theological studies). Theology, psychology, and education are the strongest academically. Theology, education, and business are the largest.

Required: All students must complete core liberal arts courses, including 15 credits each in humanities and communications and 6 credits each in theology, social science, and natural science. A 1-credit thesis seminar is required in all majors. A total of 124 credit hours, with at least 24 in the major, and a minimum GPA of 2.0 are required to graduate.

Special: Dual majors and internships for up to 6 credit hours are available in most majors. A humanities and Catholic culture major in Western tradition and minors in human life issues and music are offered. Study abroad is offered through the university's course location in Gaming, Austria, where students spend a semester studying humanities as well as traveling through Europe. There are 5 national honor societies, a freshman honors program, and 25 departmental honors programs.

Faculty/Classroom: 65% of faculty are male; 35%, female. 93% teach undergraduates. No introductory courses are taught by graduate students. The average class size in an introductory lecture is 28; in a laboratory, 15; and in a regular course, 21.

Requirements: The SAT or ACT is required. In addition, applicants should have completed 15 academic high school units, including 10 in 4 of the 5 following areas: English, foreign language, social science, math, and natural sciences. The GED is accepted. An essay and an interview are recommended. A GPA of 2.4 is required. AP and CLEP credits are accepted. Important factors in the admissions decision are advanced placement or honor courses, evidence of special talent, and leadership record.

Procedure: Freshmen are admitted fall and spring. Entrance exams should be taken in the spring of the junior year or the fall of the senior year. There is a rolling admissions plan. Check with the school for current application deadlines. Application fee is $20. Notification is sent on a rolling basis. Applications are accepted on-line.

Transfer: 221 transfer students enrolled in a recent year. A minimum 2.0 college GPA is required. High school and college transcripts must be submitted. An interview is recommended. 30 of 124 credits required for the bachelor's degree must be completed at Franciscan University.

Visiting: There are regularly scheduled orientations for prospective students, including tours, interviews with professors, admissions, and financial aid officers, and class visits. There are guides for informal visits and visitors may sit in on classes and stay overnight. To schedule a visit, contact the Admissions Office at (800) 783-6220.

Financial Aid: In a recent year, 92% of all full-time freshmen and 87% of continuing full-time students received some form of financial aid. 61% of full-time freshmen and 67% of continuing full-time students received need-based aid. The average freshman award was $10,126. Need-based scholarships or need-based grants averaged $7190 ($21,000 maximum); and need-based self-help aid (loans and jobs) averaged $3866 ($9625 maximum). 50% of undergraduates worked part time. Average annual earnings from campus work were $1000. The average financial indebtedness of a recent graduate was $21,616. The FAFSA is required. Check with schools for current application deadlines.

International Students: In a recent year there were 61 international students enrolled. The school actively recruits these students. They must score satisfactorily on the written TOEFL or on the electronic version.

Computers: All students may access the system from 9 A.M. to 11 P.M. Monday through Friday, 10 A.M. to 6 P.M. Saturday, and 1 P.M. to 11 P.M. Sunday. There are no time limits and no fees.

Graduates: In a recent year, 400 bachelor's degrees were awarded. The most popular majors were theology (21%), business (11%), and education (10%). In an average class, 3% graduate in 3 years or less, 63% graduate in 4 years or less, 70% graduate in 5 years or less, and 71% graduate in 6 years or less. 35 companies recruited on campus in a recent year.

Admissions Contact: Margaret Weber, Director of Admissions. A video is available. E-mail: admissions@franciscan.edu Web: www.franciscan.edu

---

FRANKLIN UNIVERSITY
Columbus, OH 43215-5399

C-3

(614) 797-4700
(877) 341-6300; Fax: (614) 224-8027

Full-time: 810 men, 1045 women	**Faculty:** 13
Part-time: 1610 men, 1855 women	**Ph.D.s:** 57%
Graduate: 450 men, 520 women	**Student/Faculty:** n/av
Year: trimesters, summer session	**Tuition:** $7000
Application Deadline: open	**Room & Board:** n/app
Freshman Class: n/av	
SAT or ACT: not required	SPECIAL

Franklin University is a student-centered, independent, regional institution of lifelong higher education (undergraduate and graduate) working in partnership with Central Ohio's business and professional community in a global context. Figures above capsule and profile are approximate. The library contains 15,000 volumes, 7920 microform items, and 132 audio/video tapes/CDs/DVDs, and subscribes to 200 periodicals including electronic. Computerized library services include the card catalog, interlibrary loans, and database searching. Special learning facilities include a learning resource center and art gallery. The 14-acre campus is in an urban area located in downtown Columbus. There are 7 buildings.

Student Life: 82% of undergraduates are from Ohio. Students are from 42 states, 77 foreign countries, and Canada. 66% are white; 18% African American. The average age of freshmen is 28; all undergraduates, 32.

Housing: There are no residence halls. All students commute. Alcohol is not permitted. All students may keep cars.

Activities: There are no fraternities or sororities. There are 6 groups on campus, including computers, international, and professional. Popular campus events include New student orientation, awards/scholarship reception, and opening week activities.

Sports: There is no sports program at Franklin.

Disabled Students: All of the campus is accessible. Wheelchair ramps, elevators, special parking, specially equipped rest rooms, special class scheduling, lowered drinking fountains, and lowered telephones are available.

Services: Counseling and information services are available, as is tutoring in most subjects. There is a reader service for the blind, and remedial math, reading, and writing.

Campus Safety and Security: Measures include security escort services. There is a parking guard on duty in each lot and a city police officer on duty during class hours. All such personnel are connected by an emergency radio system.

Programs of Study: Franklin confers the B.S. degree. Associate and master's degrees are also awarded. Bachelor's degrees are awarded in BUSINESS (accounting, banking and finance, business administration and management, human resources, management science, marketing and distribution, and organizational behavior), COMPUTER AND PHYSICAL SCIENCE (computer science), ENGINEERING AND ENVIRONMENTAL DESIGN (technological management), HEALTH PROFESSIONS (health care administration), SOCIAL SCIENCE (safety management). Business administration and computer science are the largest.

Required: Students must complete general education core requirements in communication, math, humanities, socal and behavioral sciences, and science. A total of 122 to 132 semester hours with a minimum GPA of 2.0 (2.25 for some majors) is required to graduate.

Special: Cross-registration is possible with other area colleges and universities through the Higher Education Council of Columbus. Internships are available for accounting, finance, marketing, business administration, computer science, human resources management, and management information sciences. Student-designed majors, ESL, and some pass/fail courses are offered. Bachelor of Science degree completion programs are available through alliances with community colleges in the United States and Canada. Accelerated delivery of specific courses is possible, as are integrated B.S./B.A. degrees in accounting, organizational leaderhip, financial management, and business administration.

Faculty/Classroom: 60% of faculty are male; 40%, female. 84% teach undergraduates. No introductory courses are taught by graduate students. The average class size in a regular course is 18.

Requirements: Applicants should be graduates of an accredited secondary school or have a GED. AP and CLEP credits are accepted.

Procedure: Freshmen are admitted fall, winter, and summer. There are early admissions, and deferred admissions, and rolling admissions plans. Application deadlines are open.

Transfer: 2528 transfer students enrolled in a recent year. The open admission policy applies to transfer students as well as freshmen. 40 of 122 credits required for the bachelor's degree must be completed at Franklin.

Visiting: There are guides for informal visits and visitors may sit in on classes. To schedule a visit, contact the Admission Office.

Financial Aid: The FAFSA and the college's own financial statement are required. Check with the school for current application deadlines.

International Students: In a recent year, there were 295 international students enrolled. The school actively recruits these students. They must score satisfactorily on the written TOEFL or on the electronic version or take the MELAB.

Computers: All students may access the system. There are no time limits and no fees.

Graduates: In a recent year, 814 bachelor's degrees were awarded. The most popular majors were business administration (39%), accounting (11%), and computer science (9%).

Admissions Contact: Student Services Office.
E-mail: *info@franklin.edu* Web: *www.franklin.edu*

HEIDELBERG COLLEGE   C-2

Tiffin, OH 44883-2434   **(419) 448-2330**
                            (800) HEIDELBERG; Fax: (419) 448-2334

Full-time: 565 men, 525 women	**Faculty:** IIB, -$
Part-time: 12 men, 19 women	**Ph.Ds:** 77%
Graduate: 60 men, 145 women	**Student/Faculty:** n/av
Year: semesters, summer session	**Tuition:** $16,134
Application Deadline: May 1	**Room & Board:** $7108
Freshman Class: 1529 applied, 1370 accepted, 330 enrolled	
SAT Verbal/Math: 510/520*	**COMPETITIVE**

Heidelberg College, founded in 1850, is a private liberal arts institution affiliated with the United Church of Christ/Congregational. In addition to regional accreditation, Heidelberg has baccalaureate program accreditation with CAAHEP and NASM. The library contains 260,055 volumes, 108,640 microform items, and 8300 audio/video tapes/CDs/DVDs, and subscribes to 829 periodicals including electronic. Computerized library services include the card catalog, interlibrary loans, database searching, Internet access, and laptop Internet portals. Special learning facilities include a learning resource center, radio station, TV station, a media center, an anthropology museum, a human cadaver lab, a water quality lab, an archeology lab, a physiology lab, and a computer-assisted writing classroom. The 120-acre campus is in a small town 50 miles south of Toledo. Including any residence halls, there are 27 buildings.

Student Life: 94% of undergraduates are from Ohio. Others are from 18 states and 14 foreign countries. 61% are from public schools. 89% are white. 61% are Protestant; 33% Catholic. The average age of freshmen is 18; all undergraduates, 23. 20% do not continue beyond their first year; 56% remain to graduate.

Housing: 900 students can be accommodated in college housing, which includes single-sex and coed dorms. In addition, there are special-interest houses. On-campus housing is guaranteed for all 4 years. 86% of students live on campus; of those, 86% remain on campus on weekends. Upperclassmen may keep cars.

Activities: 30% of men belong to 4 local fraternities; 36% of women belong to 4 local sororities. There are 65 groups on campus, including art, band, cheerleading, choir, chorale, chorus, computers, dance, drama, drill team, ethnic, forensics, gay, honors, international, jazz band, literary magazine, musical theater, newspaper, opera, orchestra, pep band, political, professional, radio and TV, religious, social, social service, student government, symphony, and yearbook. Popular campus events include Greek Sing, Tuba Christmas, and Soul Food Dinner.

Sports: There are 9 intercollegiate sports for men and 8 for women, and 9 intramural sports for men and 8 for women. Facilities include a wrestling arena, an all-weather track, indoor courts for volleyball, basketball, racquetball, and tennis, a weight room and fitness area, a sports medicine clinic, and outdoor tennis, soccer, lacrosse, and football facilities. A YMCA adjacent to the college provides additional recreation options.

Disabled Students: 20% of the campus is accessible. Wheelchair ramps, elevators, special parking, specially equipped rest rooms, special class scheduling, and lowered drinking fountains are available.

Services: Counseling and information services are available, as is tutoring in every subject. There is remedial math.

Campus Safety and Security: Measures include 24-hour foot and vehicle patrol, self-defense education, security escort services, and informal discussions. There are pamphlets/posters/films, emergency telephones, and lighted pathways/sidewalks.

Programs of Study: Heidelberg confers B.A., B.S., and B.Mus. degrees. Master's degrees are also awarded. Bachelor's degrees are awarded in BIOLOGICAL SCIENCE (biology/biological science and environmental biology), BUSINESS (accounting, business administration and management, business economics, management science, and sports management), COMMUNICATIONS AND THE ARTS (communications, dramatic arts, English, German, music, public relations, and Spanish), COMPUTER AND PHYSICAL SCIENCE (chemistry, computer science, information sciences and systems, mathematics, and physics), EDUCATION (athletic training, elementary, foreign languages, middle school, music, physical, science, and secondary), ENGINEERING AND ENVIRONMENTAL DESIGN (preengineering), HEALTH PROFESSIONS (predentistry and premedicine), SOCIAL SCIENCE (anthropology, economics, history, international studies, philosophy, political science/government, prelaw, psychology, public administration, religion, social science, and water resources). Business administration, education,

and sciences are the strongest academically. Business administration, physical sciences, and education are the largest.

Required: Students must fulfill 40 semester hours of general education requirements, including English composition and public speaking, arts, languages and literature, civilization, religion and philosophy, social sciences, natural sciences, and math, and 40 semester hours each in the major and electives. Four units of health and phys ed are needed. A total of 120 semester hours with a minimum GPA of 2.0 overall and 2.5 in the major is required to graduate.

Special: There are co-op programs in preengineering, prenursing, environmental management, and medical technology. A 3-2 engineering degree and a 3-3 nursing degree are offered in cooperation with Case Western Reserve University. Study abroad is possible at the University of Heidelberg, Germany, Seville, Spain, and in Mexico, UK, Cuba, and others. A Washington semester is available at American University. Dual majors in any combination, an honors program, credit for life experience, internships, and pass/fail options are possible. There are 10 national honor societies, a freshman honors program, and 15 departmental honors programs.

Faculty/Classroom: 67% of faculty are male; 33%, female. 95% teach undergraduates. No introductory courses are taught by graduate students. The average class size in an introductory lecture is 20; in a laboratory, 15; and in a regular course, 15.

Admissions: 90% of the 2005-2006 applicants were accepted. The SAT scores for the 2005-2006 freshman class were: Verbal--50% below 500, 36% between 500 and 599, and 14% between 600 and 700; Math--50% below 500, 34% between 500 and 599, and 16% between 600 and 700. The ACT scores were 51% below 21, 23% between 21 and 23, 16% between 24 and 26, 5% between 27 and 28, and 5% above 28. 28% of the current freshmen were in the top fifth of their class; 58% were in the top two fifths. There were 2 National Merit semifinalists. 1 freshman graduated first in their class.

Requirements: The SAT or ACT is required. The ACT Optional Writing test is also recommended. In addition, applicants should have completed 22 high school academic credits, including 4 years each of English and social studies, 3 each of math and science, and 2 of a foreign language. An audition is required for music majors. Recommendations and an interview are recommended. A GPA of 2.7 is required. AP and CLEP credits are accepted. Important factors in the admissions decision are leadership record, advanced placement or honor courses, and extracurricular activities record.

Procedure: Freshmen are admitted to all sessions. Entrance exams should be taken by the end of the junior year or the beginning of the senior year. There is a deferred admissions plan. Applications should be filed by May 1 for fall entry, December 1 for spring entry, and June 1 for summer entry, along with a $25 fee. Notification is sent on a rolling basis. Applications are accepted on-line.

Transfer: 51 transfer students enrolled in 2004-2005. A minimum GPA of 2.0 and a character reference from the institution most recently attended are required. 30 of 120 credits required for the bachelor's degree must be completed at Heidelberg.

Visiting: There are regularly scheduled orientations for prospective students, including coach and faculty sessions, academic overview, student panel, admissions and financial aid presentations, a tour of the college, and lunch. There are guides for informal visits and visitors may sit in on classes and stay overnight. To schedule a visit, contact the Office of Admission at 1-800-434-3352 or *imapus@heidelberg.edu*.

Financial Aid: In 2005-2006, 98% of all full-time freshmen and 99% of continuing full-time students received some form of financial aid. 84% of full-time freshmen received need-based aid. The average freshman award was $13,000. Need-based scholarships or need-based grants averaged $10,705 ($16,510 maximum); need-based self-help aid (loans and jobs) averaged $4268 ($5125 maximum); and Ohio Choice Award, outside scholarships, awards of circumstances averaged $6771 ($14,840 maximum). 65% of undergraduates work part time. Average annual earnings from campus work are $450. The average financial indebtedness of the 2005 graduate was $20,886. The FAFSA is required. The priority date for freshman financial aid applications for fall entry is March 1.

International Students: There are 30 international students enrolled. The school actively recruits these students. They must receive a satisfactory score on the TOEFL and the college's own test and also take the college's own entrance exam.

Computers: Wireless access is available. Main buildings are wireless; also some housing facilities, Many PCs are available. Students may check out labtops in the library, and server space is given to all students. All students may access the system. There are no time limits and no fees.

Graduates: In a recent year, 261 bachelor's degrees were awarded. The most popular majors were education (22%), business (18%), and psychology (15%). In an average class, 50% graduate in 4 years or less, 52% graduate in 5 years or less, and 54% graduate in 6 years or less. 50 companies recruited on campus in. Of a recent graduating class, 17% were enrolled in graduate school within 6 months of graduation and 94% were employed.

Admissions Contact: Lindsay Sooy, Director of Admission.
E-mail: *adminfo@mail.heidelberg.edu* Web: *http://www.heidelberg.edu*

HIRAM COLLEGE   E-1

Hiram, OH 44234

(330) 569-5169
(800) 362-5280; Fax: (330) 569-5944

Full-time: 390 men, 435 women	**Faculty:** 72; IIB, av$
Part-time: 115 men, 180 women	**Ph.D.s:** 92%
Graduate: none	**Student/Faculty:** 11 to 1
Year: summer session	**Tuition:** $21,500
Application Deadline: see profile	**Room & Board:** $7200
Freshman Class: n/av	
SAT or ACT: required	**VERY COMPETITIVE**

Hiram College, founded in 1850, is a private, residential liberal arts and sciences institution. In addition to regional accreditation, Hiram has baccalaureate program accreditation with NASM. Figures in the above capsule and profile are aproximate. The library contains 483,564 volumes, 123,474 microform items, and 8054 audio/video tapes/CDs/DVDs, and subscribes to 891 periodicals including electronic. Computerized library services include the card catalog, interlibrary loans, and database searching. Special learning facilities include a learning resource center, art gallery, planetarium, radio station, a 260-acre biological field station, and a field station in the Upper Peninsula of Michigan. The 110-acre campus is in a rural area 35 miles southeast of Cleveland. Including any residence halls, there are 28 buildings.

Student Life: 79% of undergraduates are from Ohio. Others are from 23 states and 13 foreign countries. 86% are from public schools. 83% are white; 10% African American. 52% claim no religious affiliation; 21% Catholic; 21% Protestant. The average age of freshmen is 18; all undergraduates, 20. 14% do not continue beyond their first year; 68% remain to graduate.

Housing: 1000 students can be accommodated in college housing, which includes single-sex and coed dormitories. In addition, there is an international theme house. On-campus housing is guaranteed for all 4 years. 93% of students live on campus; of those, 75% remain on campus on weekends. All students may keep cars.

Activities: There are no fraternities or sororities. There are 90 groups on campus, including art, band, cheerleading, choir, chorale, chorus, computers, dance, drama, ethnic, gay, honors, international, jazz band, literary magazine, musical theater, newspaper, opera, orchestra, photography, political, professional, radio and TV, religious, social, social service, student government, and yearbook. Popular campus events include Campus Days, Springfest, and Madrigal Revels.

Sports: There are 9 intercollegiate sports for men and 8 for women, and 10 intramural sports for men and 10 for women. Facilities include a 4000-seat stadium, a gym, sports fields, an all-weather track, a fitness room, a sauna, racquetball and tennis courts, an indoor swimming pool with diving area, an outdoor exercise and fitness trail, a cross-country ski trail, and a fully equipped athletic training facility.

Disabled Students: 40% of the campus is accessible. Wheelchair ramps, elevators, special parking, and specially equipped rest rooms are available.

Services: Counseling and information services are available, as is tutoring in every subject. There is a reader service for the blind. Note takers are available for most classes.

Campus Safety and Security: Measures include 24-hour foot and vehicle patrol, self-defense education, security escort services, and informal discussions. There are pamphlets/posters/films, emergency telephones, and lighted pathways/sidewalks.

Programs of Study: Hiram confers the B.A. degree. Bachelor's degrees are awarded in BIOLOGICAL SCIENCE (biology/biological science), BUSINESS (international economics and management science), COMMUNICATIONS AND THE ARTS (art, art history and appreciation, classics, communications, dramatic arts, English, French, German, language arts, music, and Spanish), COMPUTER AND PHYSICAL SCIENCE (applied physics, chemistry, computer science, and mathematics), EDUCATION (elementary), ENGINEERING AND ENVIRONMENTAL DESIGN (environmental science), SOCIAL SCIENCE (economics, history, philosophy, political science/government, psychobiology, psychology, religion, social studies, and sociology). Biology, computer science, and education are the strongest academically. Biology, education, and management are the largest.

Required: All students must complete distribution requirement courses in the fine arts, humanities, natural sciences, and social sciences; the Freshman Institute and Colloquium; a first-year seminar in writing and speaking skills; and 1 upper-division interdisciplinary requirement. A total of 120 academic semester hours and a minimum GPA of 2.0 are required to graduate.

Special: There is cross-registration through the Cleveland Commission on Higher Education and a 3-2 engineering program with Case Western Reserve and Washington Universities. There is a Washington semester and study abroad in many countries with courses taught by Hiram faculty. Double majors and individually arranged internships in all fields, stu-

dent-designed majors, and pass/no credit options are possible. There are 8 national honor societies, including Phi Beta Kappa.

Faculty/Classroom: 54% of faculty are male; 46%, female. All teach undergraduates. The average class size in an introductory lecture is 19; in a laboratory, 11; and in a regular course, 13.

Requirements: The SAT or ACT is required. In addition, applicants should have completed 16 academic units or the GED equivalent. An essay is required. A portfolio, audition, and interview are recommended. AP and CLEP credits are accepted. Important factors in the admissions decision are advanced placement or honor courses, leadership record, and extracurricular activities record.

Procedure: Freshmen are admitted fall and spring. Entrance exams should be taken no later than the fall of the senior year. There are early decision, early admissions, deferred admissions, and rolling admissions plans. Check with the school for current application deadlines. Application fee is $35. Notification is sent on a rolling basis. Applications are accepted on-line.

Transfer: 27 transfer students enrolled in a recent year. Applicants should have at least a 2.5 GPA and be in good academic and social standing with the previous institution. An interview is recommended. 60 of 120 credits required for the bachelor's degree must be completed at Hiram.

Visiting: There are regularly scheduled orientations for prospective students, 1 week before the semester begins, and campus visits are encouraged while school is in session. There are guides for informal visits and visitors may sit in on classes and stay overnight. To schedule a visit, contact the Admissions Office.

Financial Aid: In a recent year, 94% of all full-time freshmen and 93% of continuing full-time students received some form of financial aid. 82% of all full-time students received need-based aid. The average freshman award was $17,172. Need-based scholarships or need-based grants averaged $11,565; and need-based self-help aid (loans and jobs) averaged $5607. 71% of undergraduates worked part time. Average annual earnings from campus work were $1251. The average financial indebtedness of a recent graduate was $17,125. Hiram is a member of CSS. The FAFSA is required. Check with school for current application deadlines.

International Students: In a recent year, there were 39 international students enrolled. The school actively recruits these students. They must score satisfactorily on the written TOEFL and also take the SAT or the ACT.

Computers: All students may access the system 24 hours a day, 7 days per week. There are no time limits and no fees.

Graduates: In a recent year, 261 bachelor's degrees were awarded. The most popular majors were biology (13%), communication (9%), and history (9%). In an average class, 1% graduate in 3 years or less, 60% graduate in 4 years or less, 66% graduate in 5 years or less, and 68% graduate in 6 years or less. Of a recent year graduating class, 23% were enrolled in graduate school within 6 months of graduation and 71% were employed.

Admissions Contact: Brenda Swihart-Meyer, Director of Admission. A video is available. E-mail: *admission@hiram.edu* Web: *www.hiram.edu*

JOHN CARROLL UNIVERSITY   D-1

University Heights, OH 44118

(216) 397-4294
Fax: (216) 397-4981

Full-time: 1510 men, 1775 women	**Faculty:** 236; IIA, +$
Part-time: 90 men, 85 women	**Ph.D.s:** 89%
Graduate: 283 men, 510 women	**Student/Faculty:** 14 to 1
Year: semesters, summer session	**Tuition:** $25,072
Application Deadline: see profile	**Room & Board:** $7790
Freshman Class: n/av	
SAT or ACT: required	**COMPETITIVE+**

John Carroll University, founded in 1886, is a private Catholic institution operated by the Jesuits. It offers undergraduate degree programs in the arts, sciences, and business. There are 2 undergraduate schools and 1 graduate school. Figures in the above capsule and profile are aproximate. In addition to regional accreditation, John Carroll has baccalaureate program accreditation with AACSB and NCATE. The library contains 710,403 microform items and 4880 audio/video tapes/CDs/DVDs, and subscribes to 1975 periodicals including electronic. Computerized library services include the card catalog, interlibrary loans, and database searching. Special learning facilities include a learning resource center, radio station, and TV station. The 62-acre campus is in a suburban area 10 miles east of Cleveland. Including any residence halls, there are 26 buildings.

Student Life: 75% of undergraduates are from Ohio. Others are from 35 states, 21 foreign countries, and Canada. 53% are from public schools. 87% are white. 71% are Catholic; 15% Protestant; 7% claim no religious affiliation. The average age of freshmen is 18; all undergraduates, 21. 14% do not continue beyond their first year; 81% remain to graduate.

Housing: 2016 students can be accommodated in college housing, which includes single-sex and coed dormitories. 58% of students live on campus. Upperclassmen may keep cars.

Activities: 13% of men belong to 4 national fraternities; 18% of women belong to 5 national sororities. There are 87 groups on campus, including band, cheerleading, chess, choir, chorale, chorus, computers, dance, debate, drama, drill team, ethnic, honors, international, jazz band, literary magazine, musical theater, newspaper, pep band, photography, political, professional, radio and TV, religious, social, social service, student government, symphony, and yearbook. Popular campus events include Welcome Back Week, Little Siblings Weekend, and Dance Marathon.

Sports: There are 11 intercollegiate sports for men and 10 for women, and 8 intramural sports for men and 8 for women. Facilities include a swimming pool and diving well, a 3800-seat football stadium and track, a baseball stadium, soccer and softball fields, an indoor track, tennis, volleyball, racquetball, and basketball courts, a weight room, a fitness center, and a 33-acre off-campus student villa. Club sports include hockey, rugby, lacrosse, skiing, and sailing.

Disabled Students: 96% of the campus is accessible. Wheelchair ramps, elevators, special parking, specially equipped rest rooms, special class scheduling, lowered drinking fountains, and lowered telephones are available.

Services: Counseling and information services are available, as is tutoring in every subject. There is a reader service for the blind.

Campus Safety and Security: Measures include 24-hour foot and vehicle patrol, self-defense education, security escort services, and shuttle buses. There are informal discussions, pamphlets/posters/films, emergency telephones, and lighted pathways/sidewalks.

Programs of Study: John Carroll confers B.A., B.S., B.A.Classics, B.S.B.A., and B.S.Econ. degrees. Master's degrees are also awarded. Bachelor's degrees are awarded in BIOLOGICAL SCIENCE (biology/biological science), BUSINESS (accounting, banking and finance, business administration and management, and marketing/retailing/merchandising), COMMUNICATIONS AND THE ARTS (art history and appreciation, communications, English, French, German, Greek, Latin, literature, and Spanish), COMPUTER AND PHYSICAL SCIENCE (chemistry, computer science, mathematics, and physics), EDUCATION (early childhood, elementary, mathematics, physical, and secondary), ENGINEERING AND ENVIRONMENTAL DESIGN (engineering physics), SOCIAL SCIENCE (economics, history, humanities, philosophy, political science/government, psychology, public administration, religion, and sociology). Accounting, biology, and English are the strongest academically. Communications, biology, and marketing are the largest.

Required: All students must complete a liberal arts core curriculum, which includes 6 credits each in English composition and foreign language, 3 in first-year seminar, and 2 in speech communication. Also, students must take 4 courses each in science/math and the humanities, 3 each in social sciences and philosophy, and 2 in religious studies. Additional requirements include 1 writing-intensive course beyond English composition, 2 international courses, and 1 course in issues of diversity. A total of 128 credit hours with a minimum GPA of 2.0 is required for graduation.

Special: Co-op programs are available, and cross-registration is offered with 16 area colleges through the Northeast Ohio Commission on Higher Education. Study abroad is possible in many countries. Joint engineering degrees are offered with Case Western Reserve University, the University of Detroit Mercy, and Washington University. Work-study programs with local corporations, internships, a Washington semester, student-designed majors, dual majors, and some pass/fail options are available. There are 13 national honor societies and a freshman honors program.

Faculty/Classroom: 59% of faculty are male; 41%, female. All teach undergraduates, 95% do research, and 95% do both. Graduate students teach 4% of introductory courses. The average class size in an introductory lecture is 21; in a laboratory, 20; and in a regular course, 21.

Requirements: The SAT or ACT is required. In addition, applicants should be graduates of an accredited secondary school with 16 academic credits, including 4 in English, 3 in math, 2 each in foreign language, lab science, and social studies, and 3 in electives. An essay is part of the application process, and an interview is recommended. AP credits are accepted. Important factors in the admissions decision are advanced placement or honor courses, extracurricular activities record, and recommendations by school officials.

Procedure: Freshmen are admitted fall and spring. Entrance exams should be taken in the spring of the junior year or the fall of the senior year. There are deferred admissions and rolling admissions plans. Check with the school for current application deadlines. Notification is sent on a rolling basis. Applications are accepted on-line.

Transfer: Students must be in good standing at the time of application. The most recent term average and the cumulative average at the home school must be 2.0 or better to be considered for admission, and the cumulative average for all schools attended must be 2.0 or better. A GPA of at least 2.5 is recommended. 30 of 128 credits required for the bachelor's degree must be completed at John Carroll.

Visiting: There are regularly scheduled orientations for prospective students, consisting of open houses, admission and financial aid presentations, campus and Cleveland tours, opportunities to meet faculty and students and to stay overnight on campus. There are guides for informal visits and visitors may sit in on classes and stay overnight. To schedule a visit, contact the Office of Admissions.

Financial Aid: In a recent year, 97% of all full-time freshmen and 94% of continuing full-time students received some form of financial aid. 76% of full-time freshmen and 79% of continuing full-time students received need-based aid. The average freshman award was $15,577. Need-based scholarships or need-based grants averaged $4226 ($8000 maximum); need-based self-help aid (loans and jobs) averaged $4155 ($6425 maximum); and other non-need-based awards and non-need-based scholarships averaged $3737 ($13,000 maximum). 34% of undergraduates worked part time. The FAFSA is required. Check with the school for current application deadlines.

International Students: The school actively recruits these students. They must score satisfactorily on the written TOEFL or on the electronic version and also take the SAT or the ACT.

Computers: All students may access the system 24 hours a day in some locations. There are no time limits. The fee $300.

Admissions Contact: Thomas P. Fanning, Director of Admission. A video is available. E-mail: *admission@jcu.edu*
Web: *http://explore.jcu.edu*

KENT STATE UNIVERSITY   D-2
Kent, OH 44242-0001   (330) 672-2444
(800) 988-KENT; Fax: (330) 672-2499

Full-time: 6263 men, 9565 women	**Faculty:** 731; I, --$
Part-time: 1205 men, 1712 women	**Ph.D.s:** 70%
Graduate: 1588 men, 3289 women	**Student/Faculty:** 19 to 1
Year: semesters, summer session	**Tuition:** $7954 ($15,386)
Application Deadline: May 1	**Room & Board:** $6640
Freshman Class: 11,407 applied, 9852 accepted, 3628 enrolled	
SAT Verbal/Math: 517/517*	**ACT:** 22 **COMPETITIVE**

Kent State University, founded in 1910, is a public university offering degree programs in liberal and fine arts, business, health science, teacher and professional training, and aviation. There are 10 undergraduate and 8 graduate schools. In addition to regional accreditation, KSU has baccalaureate program accreditation with AACSB, ABET, ACEJMC, ADA, CAAHEP, FIDER, NAAB, NASAD, NASM, NASPE, NCATE, and NLN. The 6 libraries contain 2,614,797 volumes, 1,318,427 microform items, and 19,002 audio/video tapes/CDs/DVDs, and subscribe to 12,348 periodicals including electronic. Computerized library services include the card catalog, interlibrary loans, database searching, Internet access, and laptop Internet portals. Special learning facilities include an art gallery, planetarium, radio station, TV station, fashion museum, and Liquid Crystal Institute. The 1398-acre campus is in a suburban area 45 miles southeast of Cleveland. Including any residence halls, there are 127 buildings.

Student Life: 92% of undergraduates are from Ohio. Others are from 46 states, 9 foreign countries, and Canada. 86% are white. The average age of freshmen is 19; all undergraduates, 22. 28% do not continue beyond their first year; 46% remain to graduate.

Housing: 6800 students can be accommodated in college housing, which includes single-sex and coed dorms, on-campus apartments, and married-student housing. In addition, there are honors houses and special-interest houses. On-campus housing is guaranteed for all 4 years. 64% of students commute. Alcohol is not permitted. Upperclassmen may keep cars.

Activities: 8% of men belong to 20 national fraternities; 5% of women belong to 1 local and 9 national sororities. There are 197 groups on campus, including academic, art, band, cheerleading, chess, choir, chorale, chorus, computers, dance, drama, ethnic, gay, honors, international, jazz band, marching band, musical theater, newspaper, opera, orchestra, photography, political, professional, radio and TV, religious, social, social service, and student government. Popular campus events include Black Squirrel Festival, Folk Festival, and Experience Kent State-Community/Parents Day.

Sports: There are 8 intercollegiate sports for men and 10 for women, and 22 intramural sports for men and 22 for women. Facilities include a gym, a recreation and wellness center, a football stadium, a field house, 2 fitness circuits, a golf course, a bowling alley, tennis courts, lighted basketball courts, an ice arena, a pool, a weight room, and soccer, lacrosse, rugby, baseball, softball, and field hockey fields, indoor track, outdoor track, and wrestling room.

Disabled Students: 90% of the campus is accessible. Wheelchair ramps, elevators, special parking, specially equipped rest rooms, special class scheduling, lowered drinking fountains, lowered telephones, special housing, and transportation services are available.

Services: Counseling and information services are available, as is tutoring in some subjects. There is a reader service for the blind, remedial math, reading, and writing, and a writing clinic.

Campus Safety and Security: Measures include 24-hour foot and vehicle patrol, security escort services, shuttle buses, and informal discussions. There are pamphlets/posters/films, emergency telephones, lighted pathways/sidewalks, a 24-hour campus police department, overnight security guards, and a 2-key system for residence halls.

Programs of Study: KSU confers B.A., B.S., B.A.R.C., B.B.A., B.F.A., B.G.S., B.M., B.R.I.T., B.S.E., and B.S.N. degrees. Associate, master's, and doctoral degrees are also awarded. Bachelor's degrees are awarded in AGRICULTURE (animal science, conservation and regulation, horticulture, and natural resource management), BIOLOGICAL SCIENCE (anatomy, biology/biological science, biotechnology, botany, cell biology, ecology, neurosciences, nutrition, and zoology), BUSINESS (accounting, business administration and management, business economics, business systems analysis, fashion merchandising, international economics, marketing and distribution, marketing management, recreation and leisure services, and secretarial studies/office management), COMMUNICATIONS AND THE ARTS (advertising, art history and appreciation, audio technology, communications, crafts, creative writing, dance, dramatic arts, English, English literature, French, Germanic languages and literature, journalism, language arts, Latin, music, music history and appreciation, music performance, music theory and composition, public relations, radio/television technology, Russian languages and literature, Spanish, speech/debate/rhetoric, telecommunications, and visual and performing arts), COMPUTER AND PHYSICAL SCIENCE (actuarial science, applied mathematics, chemistry, computer programming, computer science, information sciences and systems, mathematics, physics, and radiological technology), EDUCATION (agricultural, art, athletic training, bilingual/bicultural, business, early childhood, education, education of the deaf and hearing impaired, elementary, health, library science, marketing and distribution, mathematics, music, physical, reading, school psychology, science, secondary, social studies, special, teaching English as a second/foreign language (TESOL/TEFOL), and trade and industrial), ENGINEERING AND ENVIRONMENTAL DESIGN (aeronautical engineering, aeronautical science, aeronautical technology, aerospace studies, aircraft mechanics, architecture, city/community/regional planning, commercial art, computer technology, electrical/electronics engineering technology, engineering, engineering technology, industrial engineering, industrial engineering technology, interior design, mechanical engineering, mechanical engineering technology, plastics engineering, and plastics technology), HEALTH PROFESSIONS (allied health, biomedical science, clinical science, emergency medical technologies, health, health care administration, nuclear medical technology, nursing, pharmacology, physical therapy, predentistry, premedicine, prepharmacy, public health, radiation therapy, and speech pathology/audiology), SOCIAL SCIENCE (addiction studies, African American studies, American studies, anthropology, child care/child and family studies, clinical psychology, community psychology, counseling/psychology, criminal justice, economics, ethnic studies, experimental psychology, family/consumer studies, fashion design and technology, food science, gender studies, history, human development, humanities, international relations, Latin American studies, liberal arts/general studies, paralegal studies, parks and recreation management, peace studies, philosophy, political science/government, psychology, public administration, Russian and Slavic studies, safety science, sociology, and systems science). Architecture, education, and fashion design and merchandising are the strongest academically. Business, psychology, and nursing are the largest.

Required: Students are required to complete 121 credit hours, of which 39 must be upper division. Distribution requirements include 9 hours in humanities and fine arts, 9 hours in social sciences and 6 hours each in basic sciences, composition, math, logic, and foreign languages. Students must maintain an overall GPA of 2.0.

Special: A co-op program is available with the School of Technology, and cross-registration is available with the University of Akron, Cleveland State University, and Northeastern Ohio University's College of Medicine (NEOUCOM). Work-study programs and internships are offered. Study abroad in 18 countries, a Washington semester, an accelerated medical degree program, B.A.-B.S. degrees, dual majors, a general studies degree, student-designed majors, credit for military education, nondegree study, and pass/fail options are also possible. The Honors College provides honors course work in all majors. Dual admission with Cuyahoga Community, Lakeland Community, NEOUCOM, and Lorain County Commmunity Colleges is available. Kent is a member of the national student exchange program. There are 14 national honor societies, including Phi Beta Kappa, and a freshman honors program.

Faculty/Classroom: 51% of faculty are male; 49%, female. Graduate students teach 29% of introductory courses. The average class size in an introductory lecture is 34; in a laboratory, 17; and in a regular course, 29.

Admissions: 86% of the 2005-2006 applicants were accepted. The SAT scores for the 2005-2006 freshman class were: Verbal--39% below 500, 43% between 500 and 599, 16% between 600 and 700, and 1% above 700; Math--43% below 500, 39% between 500 and 599, 16% between 600 and 700, and 2% above 700. The ACT scores were 42% below 21, 30% between 21 and 23, 17% between 24 and 26, 6% between

27 and 28, and 5% above 28. 28% of the current freshmen were in the top fifth of their class; 58% were in the top two fifths. 43 freshmen graduated first in their class.

Requirements: The SAT or ACT is required. Applicants most likely to be admitted will have at least a 2.5 cumulative GPA (on a 4.0 scale) in a solid college-preparatory program and a satisfactory ACT or SAT score. A GPA of 2.5 is required. AP and CLEP credits are accepted.

Procedure: Freshmen are admitted fall, spring, and summer. Entrance exams should be taken in the spring of the junior year or the fall of the senior year. There is a rolling admissions plan. Applications should be filed by May 1 for fall entry, along with a $30 fee. Notification is sent on a rolling basis. 1116 applicants were on the 2005 waiting list; 704 were admitted. Applications are accepted on-line.

Transfer: 1352 transfer students enrolled in 2004-2005. Applicants must present a minimum GPA of 2.0 on completed college course work. For students with fewer than 24 semester hours or 36 quarter hours, a high school transcript and ACT or SAT scores are also required. 30 of 121 credits required for the bachelor's degree must be completed at KSU.

Visiting: There are regularly scheduled orientations for prospective students, including information sessions (financial aid, residence halls, student panel), a campus tour, and meetings with academic representatives. There are guides for informal visits. To schedule a visit, contact the Admissions Office.

Financial Aid: In 2005-2006, 80% of all full-time freshmen and 70% of continuing full-time students received some form of financial aid. 63% of full-time freshmen and 58% of continuing full-time students received need-based aid. The average freshman award was $13,228. The average financial indebtedness of the 2005 graduate was $21,066. The FAFSA and the college's own financial statement are required. The priority date for freshman financial aid applications for fall entry is March 1.

International Students: There are 182 international students enrolled. The school actively recruits these students. They must score satisfactorily on the TOEFL and also take the MELAB.

Computers: Wireless access is available. Available in several labs and buildings at the Kent campus, the wireless network allows students, faculty, and staff to work anywhere in a coverage area and still have access to all university computing resources. Students with departmental authorization may access the system 24 hours a day, 7 days a week. There are no time limits and no fees.

Graduates: From July 1, 2004 to June 30, 2005, 3755 bachelor's degrees were awarded. The most popular majors were business management (20%), psychology (6%), and nursing (5%). In an average class, 19% graduate in 4 years or less, 40% graduate in 5 years or less, and 46% graduate in 6 years or less. 111 companies recruited on campus in 2004-2005.

Admissions Contact: Nancy Dellavecchia, Director of Admissions. A video is available. E-mail: admissions@kent.edu
Web: www.admissions.kent.edu

KENYON COLLEGE C-3
Gambier, OH 43022-9623

(740) 427-5776
(800) 848-2468; Fax: (740) 427-5770

Full-time: 770 men, 870 women	Faculty: 151; IIB,
Part-time: 8 men, 13 women	Ph.D.s: 99%
Graduate: none	Student/Faculty: 11 to 1
Year: semesters	Tuition: $33,930
Application Deadline: February 2	Room & Board: $5570
Freshman Class: 3929 applied, 1420 accepted, 441 enrolled	
SAT Verbal/Math: 670/660*	ACT: 29 MOST COMPETITIVE

Kenyon College is a private liberal arts and sciences undergraduate college founded in 1824 by Philander Chase, the first Episcopal Bishop of Ohio. The library contains 808,005 volumes, 141,663 microform items, and 1738 audio/video tapes/CDs/DVDs, and subscribes to 1796 periodicals including electronic. Computerized library services include the card catalog, interlibrary loans, database searching, Internet access, and laptop Internet portals. Special learning facilities include a learning resource center, art gallery, radio station, an observatory, and an environmental center. The 1000-acre campus is in a rural area 50 miles northeast of Columbus. Including any residence halls, there are 65 buildings.

Student Life: 79% of undergraduates are from out of state, mostly the Midwest. Students are from 46 states, 27 foreign countries, and Canada. 53% are from public schools. 87% are white. 31% claim no religious affiliation; 19% Protestant; 18% Catholic; 18% a variety of religious practices from Quaker to Zen Buddhists; 14% Jewish. The average age of freshmen is 18; all undergraduates, 20. 4% do not continue beyond their first year; 84% remain to graduate.

Housing: 1589 students can be accommodated in college housing, which includes single-sex and coed dorms and on-campus apartments. In addition, there are special-interest floors, including community service or social group halls, a substance-free hall, a wellness hall, an international wing, kosher living, and Township Fire Department. On-campus housing is guaranteed for all 4 years. All students live on campus; of those, 99% remain on campus on weekends. All students may keep cars.

Activities: 27% of men belong to 1 local fraternity and 7 national fraternities; 9% of women belong to 4 local sororities. There are 120 groups on campus, including art, band, chess, choir, chorale, chorus, dance, debate, drama, enviromental/conservation, ethnic, film, gay, international, jazz band, literary magazine, martial arts, musical theater, newspaper, opera, orchestra, pep band, photography, political, professional, radio and TV, religious, social, social service, student government, students lectureships, symphony, and yearbook. Popular campus events include Philander's Phling, Summer Send-Off, and dance, drama, music, and athletic events.

Sports: There are 9 intercollegiate sports for men and 9 for women, and 9 intramural sports for men and 9 for women. Facilities include 70 acres of playing, football, softball, and soccer fields, a 50-yard pool, a field house, a Nautilus center and weight rooms, and basketball, tennis, squash, and racquetball courts.

Disabled Students: 13% of the campus is accessible. Wheelchair ramps, elevators, special parking, specially equipped rest rooms, special class scheduling, lowered drinking fountains, lowered telephones, and audio and visual equipment are available.

Services: Counseling and information services are available, as is tutoring in some subjects upon request. There is a reader service for the blind, remedial writing, note-taking services, oral tests, and extended time on tests.

Campus Safety and Security: Measures include 24-hour foot and vehicle patrol, self-defense education, security escort services, and informal discussions. There are pamphlets/posters/films, emergency telephones, lighted pathways/sidewalks, and formal safety awareness events.

Programs of Study: Kenyon confers the B.A. degree. Bachelor's degrees are awarded in BIOLOGICAL SCIENCE (biochemistry, biology/ biological science, molecular biology, and neurosciences), COMMUNICATIONS AND THE ARTS (art history and appreciation, classics, dance, dramatic arts, English, French, German, Greek (classical), Latin, modern language, music, Spanish, and studio art), COMPUTER AND PHYSICAL SCIENCE (chemistry, mathematics, and physics), SOCIAL SCIENCE (anthropology, economics, history, international studies, philosophy, political science/government, psychology, religion, and sociology). English, history, and political science are the largest.

Required: Students are required to complete a total of 16 units, including 4 to 7 units in the major, 1 unit in each of 4 divisions representing the arts, humanities, natural sciences, and social sciences, a unit of foreign language, and 1/2 unit of quantitative reasoning. Students must maintain a minimum GPA of 2.0 and complete the senior exercise in their major. A thesis is required for honor students.

Special: Students may study abroad in many countries. The college also offers dual and student-designed majors, pass/fail options, internships, winter and/or spring break externship programs, a Washington semester consisting of apprenticeships in any of several U.S. programs, and a 3-2 engineering degree with Case Western Reserve University, Washington University in St. Louis, and Rensselaer Polytechnic Institute, as well as a 3-2 nursing degree with Case Western Reserve and a 3-2 environmental studies program with Duke University. 3-2 or 4-1 master's (certification) programs with The Bank Street College of Education are also possible. Kenyon's Interdisciplinary Program in Humane Studies offers a tutorial-based concentration on the human predicament. There are 3 national honor societies, including Phi Beta Kappa, and 30 departmental honors programs.

Faculty/Classroom: 59% of faculty are male; 41%, female. All both teach and do research.

Admissions: 36% of the 2005-2006 applicants were accepted. The SAT scores for the 2005-2006 freshman class were: Verbal--1% below 500, 8% between 500 and 599, 50% between 600 and 700, and 41% above 700; Math--1% below 500, 14% between 500 and 599, 60% between 600 and 700, and 25% above 700. The ACT scores were 4% between 21 and 23, 9% between 24 and 26, 23% between 27 and 28, and 64% above 28. 85% of the current freshmen were in the top fifth of their class; 98% were in the top two fifths. There were 90 National Merit finalists. 29 freshmen graduated first in their class.

Requirements: The SAT or ACT is required. In addition, applicants should be graduates of an accredited secondary school. Kenyon recommends 4 units each of English, foreign language, and math and 3 units each of science and social studies. Candidates are encouraged to exceed the minimum requirements, especially in math and science, and to take advanced placement or honors work in at least 2 subjects. An essay and an interview are important criteria in the admissions decision. Talent in music, theater, art, writing, and athletics is given extra consideration. AP credits are accepted. Important factors in the admissions decision are advanced placement or honor courses, evidence of special talent, and leadership record.

Procedure: Freshmen are admitted in the fall. Entrance exams should be taken in the fall of the senior year. There are early decision and deferred admissions plans. Early decision applications should be filed by December 1; regular applications, by February 2 for fall entry, along with a $45 fee. Notification of early decision is sent December 15; regular decision, April 1. 135 early decision candidates were accepted for the 2005-2006 class. 932 applicants were on the 2005 waiting list; 8 were admitted. Applications are accepted on-line.

Transfer: 15 transfer students enrolled in 2004-2005. Transfer applicants must have a minimum college GPA of 3.0 and a high school record suggesting ability and potential. 8 of 16 units required for the bachelor's degree must be completed at Kenyon.

Visiting: There are regularly scheduled orientations for prospective students, Including interviews with staff, a campus tour, and a class visit. Students may also request to meet with faculty and coaches, Kenyon students are also available to host a prospective student overnight in the dorm weekly Sunday through Thursday. There are guides for informal visits and visitors may sit in on classes and stay overnight. To schedule a visit, contact the Admissions Office.

Financial Aid: In 2005-2006, 67% of all full-time freshmen and 70% of continuing full-time students received some form of financial aid. 40% of full-time freshmen and 46% of continuing full-time students received need-based aid. The average freshman award was $23,097. Need-based scholarships or need-based grants averaged $19,729; need-based self-help aid (loans and jobs) averaged $4917; and Stafford loans and state and federal loans averaged $1750. 35% of undergraduates work part time. Average annual earnings from campus work are $635. Kenyon is a member of CSS. The CSS/Profile or FAFSA is required. The deadline for filing freshman financial aid applications for fall entry is February 15.

International Students: There are 45 international students enrolled. The school actively recruits these students. They must achieve a satisfactory score on the TOEFL or take the SAT or ACT or the GRE.

Computers: Wireless access is available. There are 530 public computers, ports to all beds, and wireless to all dorms and most classrooms. All students may access the system 24 hours a day. There are no time limits and no fees. It is strongly recommended that all students have a personal computer. A Windows NT, Windows 2000, or any Apple running OS X or higher is recommended.

Graduates: From July 1, 2004 to June 30, 2005, 395 bachelor's degrees were awarded. The most popular majors were English (20%), political science (11%), and history (11%). In an average class, 2% graduate in 3 years or less, 80% graduate in 4 years or less, 82% graduate in 5 years or less, and 84% graduate in 6 years or less. 40 companies recruited on campus in 2004-2005. Of the 2004 graduating class, 17% were enrolled in graduate school within 6 months of graduation and 95% were employed.

Admissions Contact: Jennifer Britz, Dean of Admissions and Financial Aid. A video is available. E-mail: *admissions@kenyon.edu* Web: *www.kenyon.edu*

LAKE ERIE COLLEGE   E-1

Painesville, OH 44077

(440) 375-7050
(800) 916-0904; Fax: (440) 375-7005

Full-time: 157 men, 417 women	**Faculty:** 34; II B, -$
Part-time: 28 men, 80 women	**Ph.D.s:** 76%
Graduate: 72 men, 255 women	**Student/Faculty:** 17 to 1
Year: semesters, summer session	**Tuition:** $21,390
Application Deadline: open	**Room & Board:** $6335
Freshman Class: n/av	
SAT or ACT: required	**COMPETITIVE**

Lake Erie College, founded in 1856, is a private liberal arts institution offering 22 undergraduate majors and master's degrees in business administration and education. The college is nationally recognized for its equine studies programs and international learning opportunities. The library contains 87,500 volumes, 11,000 microform items, and 724 audio/video tapes/CDs/DVDs, and subscribes to 7500 periodicals including electronic. Computerized library services include the card catalog, interlibrary loans, database searching, Internet access, and laptop Internet portals. Special learning facilities include a learning resource center, art gallery, radio station, a theater and an equestrian center. The 133-acre campus is in a small town 30 miles east of Cleveland. Including any residence halls, there are 15 buildings.

Student Life: 85% of undergraduates are from Ohio. Others are from 31 states, 6 foreign countries, and Canada. 90% are from public schools. 90% are white. The average age of freshmen is 18; all undergraduates, 23. 37% do not continue beyond their first year; 50% remain to graduate.

Housing: 291 students can be accommodated in college housing, which includes single-sex and coed dorms. On-campus housing is guaranteed for all 4 years. 52% of students commute. All students may keep cars.

Activities: 33% of women belong to 1 local sorority. There are no fraternities. There are 21 groups on campus, including art, cheerleading, choir, chorus, dance, drama, equestrian, ethnic, gay, honors, international, musical theater, newspaper, pep band, photography, political, professional, religious, social, social service, and student government. Popular campus events include Prix de Ville of North America, international dinners, and mountain day.

Sports: There are 5 intercollegiate sports for men and 5 for women, and 5 intramural sports for men and 5 for women. Facilities include on-campus soccer and softball fields, a nearby off-campus baseball field and an 85-acre equestrian center, including a competition arena. The college also has an athletic and wellness center with an indoor basketball/volleyball arena, a multi-purpose practice/intramural and recreational gym with a suspended indoor jogging track, and a 4000-square foot fitness center and weight room.

Disabled Students: 20% of the campus is accessible. Wheelchair ramps, elevators, special parking, specially equipped rest rooms, special class scheduling, lowered drinking fountains, and lowered telephones are available.

Services: Counseling and information services are available, as is tutoring in most subjects. There is remedial math, reading, and writing.

Campus Safety and Security: Measures include 24-hour foot and vehicle patrol, self-defense education, security escort services, and informal discussions. There are pamphlets/posters/films, emergency telephones, and lighted pathways/sidewalks.

Programs of Study: Lake Erie confers B.A., B.S., and B.F.A. degrees. Master's degrees are also awarded. Bachelor's degrees are awarded in AGRICULTURE (equine science and range/farm management), BIOLOGICAL SCIENCE (biology/biological science), BUSINESS (accounting, business administration and management, and international business management), COMMUNICATIONS AND THE ARTS (arts administration/management, communications, English, fine arts, and language arts), COMPUTER AND PHYSICAL SCIENCE (chemistry and mathematics), EDUCATION (early childhood and middle school), ENGINEERING AND ENVIRONMENTAL DESIGN (environmental science), SOCIAL SCIENCE (interdisciplinary studies, law enforcement and corrections, paralegal studies, psychology, and social science). Biology, equestrian, and business are the strongest academically. Equestrian science, elementary education, and business are the largest.

Required: General education requirements include 4 hours each of math and English, 8 hours of a foreign language, and 2 hours of public speaking. A computer literacy course is required. There are specific core requirements for 25 additional semester hours. Students must complete 128 credits, including an average of 64 in the major, with a minimum GPA of 2.0.

Special: Students may choose either national or international internships or study abroad in the Netherlands, France, Germany, Spain, England, Italy, or another country, as arranged by the student, B.A.-B.S. degrees, including a B.F.A. in fine arts, music, dance, or an individual major, student-designed majors, and potential credit for life, military, or work experience are offered. Cross-registration is available with the Northeast Ohio Commission on Higher Education. There is 1 national honor society and a freshman honors program.

Faculty/Classroom: 51% of faculty are male; 49%, female. All teach undergraduates. The average class size in an introductory lecture is 15; in a laboratory, 16; and in a regular course, 11.

Admissions: The SAT scores for the 2005-2006 freshman class were: Verbal--49% below 500, 35% between 500 and 599, 12% between 600 and 700, and 4% above 700; Math--63% below 500, 27% between 500 and 599, and 10% between 600 and 700. The ACT scores were 58% below 21, 26% between 21 and 23, 10% between 24 and 26, 4% between 27 and 28, and 2% above 28. 17% of the current freshmen were in the top fifth of their class; 30% were in the top two fifths. 2 freshmen graduated first in their class.

Requirements: The SAT or ACT is required. In addition, applicants should be graduates of an accredited secondary school with a minimum GPA of 2.0. The high school program should include 4 years each of English, math, and science (including 2 years of lab science), and 2 years each of history and social studies, with 2 years of a foreign language recommended. A GPA of 2.0 is required. AP and CLEP credits are accepted. Important factors in the admissions decision are advanced placement or honor courses, recommendations by school officials, and extracurricular activities record.

Procedure: Freshmen are admitted fall, spring, and summer. Entrance exams should be taken by November of the senior year. There is a deferred admissions plan. Application deadlines are open. The application fee is $25. Applications are accepted on-line.

Transfer: 75 transfer students enrolled in 2004-2005. Applicants should submit transcripts from all schools attended and show a GPA of 2.0 in all college work. 32 of 128 credits required for the bachelor's degree must be completed at Lake Erie.

Visiting: There are regularly scheduled orientations for prospective students, including a campus tour, a financial aid information session, classroom observation, and faculty or department head interviews. There are guides for informal visits and visitors may sit in on classes and stay overnight. To schedule a visit, contact the Admissions Office at admissions@lec.edu.

Financial Aid: In 2005-2006, all full-time students received some form of financial aid. 95% of all full-time students received need-based aid. The average freshman award was $18,100. 25% of undergraduates work part time. Average annual earnings from campus work are $2000.

The average financial indebtedness of the 2005 graduate was $17,125. Lake Erie is a member of CSS. The FAFSA and the college's own financial statement are required. The priority date for freshman financial aid applications for fall entry is March 1. The deadline for filing freshman financial aid applications for fall entry is rolling.

International Students: There are 7 international students enrolled. They must score satisfactorily on the TOEFL and also take the SAT or the ACT.

Computers: All students may access the system. There are no time limits and no fees.

Graduates: From July 1, 2004 to June 30, 2005, 153 bachelor's degrees were awarded. The most popular majors were early childhood education (18%), equine science (10%), and individualized (8%). In an average class, 47% graduate in 4 years, 50% graduate in 5 years, and 3% graduate in 6 years.

Admissions Contact: Jennifer Calhoun, Director of Admissions. E-mail: admissions@lec.edu Web: www.lec.edu

LOURDES COLLEGE | B-1

Sylvania, OH 43560 | **(419) 885-5291, ext. 299**
(800) 878-3210, ext. 1299; Fax: (419) 882-3987

Full-time: 90 men, 405 women	**Faculty:** 60; IIB, --$
Part-time: 110 men, 605 women	**Ph.D.s:** 32%
Graduate: 15 men, 40 women	**Student/Faculty:** 8 to 1
Year: semesters, summer session	**Tuition:** $15,500
Application Deadline: open	**Room & Board:** n/app
Freshman Class: n/av	
SAT or ACT: required	**LESS COMPETITIVE**

Lourdes College, founded in 1958, is a private liberal arts college affiliated with the Roman Catholic Church and sponsored by the Sisters of St. Francis. Figures in the above capsule and profile are approximate. In addition to regional accreditation, Lourdes has baccalaureate program accreditation with CSWE and NLN. The library contains 59,236 volumes, 10,807 microform items, and 1451 audio/video tapes/CDs/DVDs, and subscribes to 388 periodicals including electronic. Computerized library services include the card catalog, interlibrary loans, and database searching. Special learning facilities include a learning resource center, art gallery, planetarium, and an environmental science lab. The 89-acre campus is in a suburban area 10 miles west of Toledo. There are 8 buildings.

Student Life: 93% of undergraduates are from Ohio. Others are from 2 states and 2 foreign countries. 12% are African American. The average age of freshmen is 21; all undergraduates, 30.

Housing: There are no residence halls. All of students commute. Alcohol is not permitted. All students may keep cars.

Activities: There are no fraternities or sororities. There are 15 groups on campus, including art, choir, chorus, honors, international, literary magazine, newspaper, political, professional, religious, social service, and student government. Popular campus events include End-of-the-Year Picnic, Convocation, and Christmas dinner.

Sports: There are 4 intramural sports for men and 4 for women. Facilities include a gym and exercise room.

Disabled Students: 95% of the campus is accessible. Wheelchair ramps, elevators, special parking, specially equipped rest rooms, special class scheduling, lowered drinking fountains, lowered telephones, and accessible computer stations are available.

Services: Counseling and information services are available, as is tutoring in most subjects. There is remedial math, reading, and writing. Windows for Intellectual Networking Center offers computer-assisted instruction for self-paced learning/tutoring in remedial math, reading, writing, study skills, APA style documentation, Spanish tutorials, advanced math programs, as well as offering professional tutoring services in writing. The center also works with instructors to offer in-class tutorial workshops on specific topics as requested.

Campus Safety and Security: Measures include security escort services, pamphlets/posters/films, and lighted pathways/sidewalks.

Programs of Study: Lourdes confers B.A., B.S., B.I.S., B.S.N. degrees. Associate and master's degrees are also awarded. Bachelor's degrees are awarded in BIOLOGICAL SCIENCE (biology/biological science), BUSINESS (accounting, business administration and management, human resources, and marketing management), COMMUNICATIONS AND THE ARTS (art, art history and appreciation, English, and fine arts), EDUCATION (education), ENGINEERING AND ENVIRONMENTAL DESIGN (environmental science), HEALTH PROFESSIONS (health care administration and nursing), SOCIAL SCIENCE (criminal justice, history, psychology, religion, social work, and sociology). Nursing, chemistry, and education are the strongest academically. Business, nursing, and criminal justice are the largest.

Required: Students are required to maintain at least a 2.0 overall GPA, although most disciplines require 2.5. The total number of hours in the major varies from 36 to 59 semester hours depending on the major. Students must complete 120 credit hours, the requirements varying according to the degree sought. Most students will need courses in art/music, religious studies, composition, literature, phys ed, social science, and philosophy.

Special: The college offers internships in social work, criminal justice, occupational therapy, and business, co-op programs in business, work-study programs, B.A.-B.S. degrees in biology, chemistry, and education, and an accelerated degree program in business and criminal justice. Students may pursue dual majors, nondegree study, student-designed majors, or select pass/fail options. The college gives credit for life, military, or work experience.

Faculty/Classroom: 30% of faculty are male; 70%, female. 99% teach undergraduates. No introductory courses are taught by graduate students. The average class size in an introductory lecture is 16; in a laboratory, 8; and in a regular course, 12.

Requirements: The SAT or ACT is required. Candidates for admission should have completed 4 units of English and 3 each of math, science, and social studies. If a GED recipient, a passing score on the GED and satisfactory placement test scores are required. A GPA of 2.0 is required. AP and CLEP credits are accepted.

Procedure: Freshmen are admitted to all sessions. Entrance exams should be taken at least 30 days prior to the beginning of the freshman year of college. There are early admissions, deferred admissions, and rolling admissions plans. Application deadlines are open. Applications are accepted on-line. The fall application fee was $25.

Transfer: 200 transfer students enrolled in a recent year. Transfer students need to submit official transcripts from previously attended colleges/universities, a completed application and fee, and placement tests when necessary. Regular admission is granted to transfer students with a GPA of 2.0 or better and satisfactory placement test scores, if required. 30 of 120 credits required for the bachelor's degree must be completed at Lourdes.

Visiting: There are guides for informal visits and visitors may sit in on classes. To schedule a visit, contact the Office of Admissions at (419) 885-3211.

Financial Aid: Ina recent year, 91% of all full-time freshmen and 96% of continuing full-time students received some form of financial aid. 93% of full-time freshmen and 94% of continuing full-time students received need-based aid. The average freshman award was $13,732. Need-based scholarships or need-based grants averaged $4475 ($5466 maximum); need-based self-help aid (loans and jobs) averaged $6620 ($7876 maximum); and other non-need-based awards and non-need-based scholarships averaged $4439 ($5000 maximum). 6% of undergraduates worked part time. Lourdes is a member of CSS. The FAFSA is required. Check with the school for current application deadlines.

International Students: In a recent year, there were 2 international students enrolled. They must score satisfactorily on the written TOEFL or on the electronic version.

Computers: All students may access the system. PCs may be used any time during open lab hours. There are no time limits and no fees.

Graduates: In a recent year, 195 bachelor's degrees were awarded. The most popular majors were business (25%), nursing (20%), and education (15%). In an average class, 28% graduate in 6 years or less. 7 companies recruited on campus in a recent year.

Admissions Contact: Amy L. Megen, Director of Admissions. E-mail: *lcadmits@lourdes.edu* Web: *www.lourdes.edu*

MALONE COLLEGE   D-2
Canton, OH 44709
(330) 471-8139
(800) 521-1146; Fax: (330) 471-8149

Full-time: 676 men, 1000 women	**Faculty:** 101; IIA, --$
Part-time: 75 men, 169 women	**Ph.D.s:** 70%
Graduate: 101 men, 256 women	**Student/Faculty:** 17 to 1
Year: semesters, summer session	**Tuition:** $16,790
Application Deadline: July 1	**Room & Board:** $6250
Freshman Class: 1036 applied, 839 accepted, 361 enrolled	
SAT Verbal/Math: 530/520	**COMPETITIVE**

Malone College, founded in 1892, is a private (not for profit) Christian college for the arts, sciences, and professions in the liberal arts tradition. There are 6 undergraduate schools and 1 graduate school. In addition to regional accreditation, Malone has baccalaureate program accreditation with CCNE, CSWE, and IACBE. The library contains 169,655 volumes, 674,090 microform items, and 8557 audio/video tapes/CDs/DVDs, and subscribes to 21,804 periodicals including electronic. Computerized library services include the card catalog, interlibrary loans, database searching, and Internet access. Special learning facilities include a learning resource center, radio station, writing lab, and subject area tutoring. The 78-acre campus is in a suburban area 56 miles southeast of Cleveland. Including any residence halls, there are 21 buildings.

Student Life: 90% of undergraduates are from Ohio. Others are from 25 states and 15 foreign countries. 84% are from public schools. 92% are white. 89% are Protestant; 6% Catholic. The average age of freshmen is 18; all undergraduates, 24. 25% do not continue beyond their first year; 54% remain to graduate.

Housing: 974 students can be accommodated in college housing, which includes single-sex dorms. In addition, there are special topic/discipleship floors for upperclassmen. On-campus housing is guaranteed for the freshman year only, is available on a first-come, first-served basis, and is available on a lottery system for upperclassmen. 56% of students live on campus; of those, 40% remain on campus on weekends. Alcohol is not permitted. All students may keep cars.

Activities: There are no fraternities or sororities. There are 56 groups on campus, including art, band, cheerleading, choir, chorale, chorus, computers, dance, debate, drama, drill team, ethnic, forensics, honors, international, jazz band, literary magazine, marching band, musical theater, newspaper, photography, political, professional, radio and TV, religious, social, social service, student government, and yearbook. Popular campus events include Little Sibs Weekend, Christman Celebration, and Culture Fest.

Sports: There are 9 intercollegiate sports for men and 9 for women, and 14 intramural sports for men and 13 for women. Facilities include a gym, a wellness center with strength and cardio rooms, an outdoor track, baseball, softball, and soccer fields, practice soccer and football fields, intramural fields, a cross-country course, and outdoor volleyball and basketball courts.

Disabled Students: Wheelchair ramps, elevators, special parking, specially equipped rest rooms, special class scheduling, lowered drinking fountains, and lowered telephones are available.

Services: Counseling and information services are available, as is tutoring in most subjects. There is a reader service for the blind and remedial math and writing. There are also disability support services such as a distraction reduced testing room.

Campus Safety and Security: Measures include 24-hour foot and vehicle patrol, self-defense education, security escort services, and shuttle buses. There are informal discussions, emergency telephones, and lighted pathways/sidewalks.

Programs of Study: Malone confers B.A., B.S.Ed., and B.S.N. degrees. Master's degrees are also awarded. Bachelor's degrees are awarded in BIOLOGICAL SCIENCE (biology/biological science, life science, and zoology), BUSINESS (accounting, business administration and management, recreational facilities management, and sports management), COMMUNICATIONS AND THE ARTS (art, communications, English, language arts, music, music technology, and Spanish), COMPUTER AND PHYSICAL SCIENCE (chemistry, computer science, mathematics, physical sciences, and science), EDUCATION (art, Christian, early childhood, foreign languages, health, middle school, music, physical, science, secondary, social studies, and special), HEALTH PROFESSIONS (community health work, exercise science, medical laboratory technology, and nursing), SOCIAL SCIENCE (biblical studies, history, liberal arts/general studies, ministries, physical fitness/movement, political science/government, psychology, religious music, social work, theological studies, and youth ministry). Biology, chemistry, and math are the strongest academically. Business administration, early childhood education, and nursing are the largest.

Required: Students must maintain a GPA of 2.0 overall and 2.25 to 2.75 in the major, depending upon the major. At least 30 hours in the major and 39 hours at the 300 or 400 level are required. To graduate, all students must complete at least 124 credit hours, including a general education curriculum requiring 63 to 64 semester hours focusing on stewardship: Stewardship Under God (14 hours), Stewardship and Skills (15 to 16 hours), Stewardship and the Sciences (12 to 13 hours), and Stewardship and Society (15 to 18 hours). Courses in phys ed and data analysis are also required.

Special: Students may participate in co-op programs and internships in many majors and may cross-register within the Christian College Consortium. Malone offers study abroad in Guatemala, Costa Rica, England, Russia, China, Egypt, Australia, Uganda, and Kenya; and Hollywood (film studies), Martha's Vineyard (contemporary music), or Washington semesters through the Council for Christian Colleges and Universities. A liberal arts degree, dual and student-designed majors, and credit for life, military, or work experience are also available. The Malone College Management Program offers accelerated degree completion for students age 25 or older who have the equivalent of 2 years of college. The BS-NDC program offers degree completion for RNs. There are 10 national honor societies and a freshman honors program.

Faculty/Classroom: 59% of faculty are male; 41%, female. 93% teach undergraduates and 40% both teach and do research. No introductory courses are taught by graduate students. The average class size in an introductory lecture is 29; in a laboratory, 13; and in a regular course, 20.

Admissions: 81% of the 2005-2006 applicants were accepted. The SAT scores for the 2005-2006 freshman class were: Verbal--28% below 500, 49% between 500 and 599, and 23% between 600 and 700; Math--38% below 500, 40% between 500 and 599, 21% between 600 and 700, and 1% above 700. The ACT scores were 27% below 21, 30% between 21 and 23, 25% between 24 and 26, 11% between 27 and 28, and 7% above 28. 45% of the current freshmen were in the top fifth of their class; 74% were in the top two fifths. 11 freshmen graduated first in their class.

Requirements: The ACT or SAT is required for traditional students. The ACT is preferred. In addition, applicants should be graduates of an accredited secondary school with a minimum GPA of 2.5. The GED is accepted. AP and CLEP credits are accepted. Important factors in the admissions decision are advanced placement or honor courses, leadership record, and extracurricular activities record.

Procedure: Freshmen are admitted fall, spring, and summer. Entrance exams should be taken in the junior year. There is a rolling admissions and a deferred admissions plan. Applications should be filed by July 1 for fall entry. The fall 2005 fee was $20. Notification is sent on a rolling basis. Applications are accepted on-line.

Transfer: 117 transfer students enrolled in 2004-2005. Applicants must submit an official transcript and a financial aid transcript from each college attended and a transfer reference form from the most recent school. 30 of 124 credits required for the bachelor's degree must be completed at Malone.

Visiting: There are regularly scheduled orientations for prospective students. There are guides for informal visits and visitors may sit in on classes and stay overnight. To schedule a visit, contact Jody Dimit, Campus Visit Coordinator at (330) 471-8147 or jdimit@malone.edu.

Financial Aid: In 2005-2006, 99% of all full-time freshmen and 95% of continuing full-time students received some form of financial aid. 74% of full-time freshmen and 66% of continuing full-time students received need-based aid. The average freshman award was $16,091. Need-based scholarships or need-based grants averaged $5903 ($16,600 maximum); need-based self-help aid (loans and jobs) averaged $3897 ($8825 maximum); non-need-based athletic scholarships averaged $6286 ($15,000 maximum); other non-need-based awards and non-need-based scholarships averaged $6999 ($25,225 maximum); and parent loans averaged $10,296 ($20,000 maximum). 25% of undergraduates work part time. Average annual earnings from campus work are $968. The average financial indebtedness of the 2005 graduate was $18,482. The FAFSA and for returning students, and the college's own form are required. The priority date for freshman financial aid applications for fall entry is March 1. The deadline for filing freshman financial aid applications for fall entry is July 31.

International Students: There are 21 international students enrolled. They must score satisfactorily on the TOEFL.

Computers: Wireless access is available. PC labs are available in the library, in classroom buildings, and all residence halls. Students have 24/7 access in the residence halls. The library and classrooms are available most all day during classes. Wireless is available 24/7 in Meyer's Lounge (Women's Residence Hall), during the day and evenings in the Student Center, and in Mitchell Hall classrooms and the library. All students may access the system 24/7. There are no time limits and no fees.

Graduates: From July 1, 2004 to June 30, 2005, 461 bachelor's degrees were awarded. The most popular majors were nursing (9%), business administration (6%), and early childhood education (5%). In an average class, 1% graduate in 3 years or less, 40% graduate in 4 years or less, 53% graduate in 5 years or less, and 54% graduate in 6 years or less. 300 companies recruited on campus in 2004-2005. Of the 2004 graduating class, 14% were enrolled in graduate school within 6 months of graduation and 82% were employed.

Admissions Contact: John Russell, Director of Admissions. A video is available. E-mail: admissions@malone.edu
Web: http://www.malone.edu

MARIETTA COLLEGE
Marietta, OH 45750-4005

E-5

(740) 376-4600
(800) 331-7896; Fax: (740) 376-8888

Full-time: 671 men, 679 women	**Faculty:** 140; IIB, -$
Part-time: 20 men, 51 women	**Ph.D.s:** 92%
Graduate: 10 men, 36 women	**Student/Faculty:** 10 to 1
Year: semesters, summer session	**Tuition:** $22,879
Application Deadline: April 15	**Room & Board:** $6448
Freshman Class: 1852 applied, 1748 accepted, 391 enrolled	
SAT Verbal/Math: 534/530*	**ACT:** 23 COMPETITIVE

Marietta College, founded in 1835, is a private liberal arts college. In addition to regional accreditation, Marietta has baccalaureate program accreditation with ABET and CAAHEP. The library contains 249,122 volumes and 133,116 microform items, and subscribes to 550 periodicals including electronic. Computerized library services include the card catalog, interlibrary loans, database searching, and Internet access. Special learning facilities include a learning resource center, an art gallery, a radio station, a TV station, an observatory, a greenhouse, and a geology annex. The 120-acre campus is in a small town 115 miles southeast of Columbus. Including any residence halls, there are 40 buildings.

Student Life: 50% of undergraduates are from out of state, mostly the Middle Atlantic. Students are from 43 states, 13 foreign countries, and Canada. 89% are from public schools. 88% are white. 60% are Protestant; 30% Catholic; 10% Jewish. The average age of freshmen is 18; all undergraduates, 20. 20% do not continue beyond their first year; 65% remain to graduate.

Housing: 1250 students can be accommodated in college housing, which includes single-sex and coed dorms, on-campus apartments, fraternity houses, and sorority houses. In addition, there are honors houses and special-interest houses. On-campus housing is guaranteed for all 4 years. 90% of students live on campus; of those, 80% remain on campus on weekends. All students may keep cars.

Activities: 22% of men belong to 4 national fraternities; 22% of women belong to 3 national sororities. There are 65 groups on campus, including art, band, cheerleading, choir, chorale, chorus, Circle K, computers, dance, debate, drama, drill team, ethnic, film, forensics, gay, honors, human rights, international, jazz band, literary magazine, musical theater, newspaper, orchestra, outdoor, pep band, philanthropy, photography, political, professional, radio and TV, religious, rowing, skiing, social, social service, student government, swing dancing, and yearbook. Popular campus events include DooDah Day, Winter Weekend, and Welcome Back Bash.

Sports: There are 9 intercollegiate sports for men and 9 for women, and 7 intramural sports for men and 7 for women. Facilities include a 7000-seat stadium, a 1500-seat performance gym, a 3500-seat field house, baseball, softball, and soccer fields, a boat house, a cross-country course, tennis courts, and a recreational center housing a 200-meter track, multipurpose and racquetball courts, an ergometer training room, cardio equipment, and a climbing wall.

Disabled Students: 70% of the campus is accessible. Wheelchair ramps, elevators, special parking, specially equipped rest rooms, special class scheduling, lowered drinking fountains, and individual accommodations for students with disabilities are available.

Services: Counseling and information services are available, as is peer tutoring in most subjects. There is a reader service for the blind, remedial math and writing.

Campus Safety and Security: Measures include 24-hour foot and vehicle patrol, self-defense education, security escort services, and informal discussions. There are pamphlets/posters/films, emergency telephones, lighted pathways/sidewalks, and airport shuttles available upon request.

Programs of Study: Marietta confers B.A., B.S., B.F.A., and B.S. degrees. Associate and master's degrees are also awarded. Bachelor's degrees are awarded in AGRICULTURE (environmental studies), BIOLOGICAL SCIENCE (biochemistry and biology/biological science), BUSINESS (accounting, banking and finance, business administration and management, human resources, international business management, management information systems, and marketing/retailing/merchandising), COMMUNICATIONS AND THE ARTS (advertising, broadcasting, communications, dramatic arts, English, graphic design, journalism, music, musical theater, public relations, radio/television technology, Spanish, speech/debate/rhetoric, and studio art), COMPUTER AND PHYSICAL SCIENCE (applied physics, chemistry, computer science, geology, information sciences and systems, mathematics, and physics), EDUCATION (athletic training and early childhood), ENGINEERING AND ENVIRONMENTAL DESIGN (environmental science and petroleum/natural gas engineering), HEALTH PROFESSIONS (health science and physician's assistant), SOCIAL SCIENCE (economics, history, interdisciplinary studies, political science/government, and psychology). Petroleum engineering is the strongest academically. Economics, management and accounting, and elementary education are the largest.

Required: To graduate, students must complete at least 120 total credit hours, with general education requirements.The minimum number of hours required for a major is 36. A minimum GPA of 2.0 must be maintained. Seniors must complete a capstone project.

Special: There are 3-2 binary engineering programs with Case Western Reserve, Columbia, and the University of Pennsylvania. Internships are available in many majors, and students may study abroad in numerous countries and participate in a Washington semester through American University. Preprofessional programs, work-study programs, B.A.-B.S. degrees in all majors, student-designed majors, pass/fail options, and credit for life, military, and work experience are also available. There are 23 national honor societies, including Phi Beta Kappa, a freshman honors program, and 17 departmental honors programs.

Faculty/Classroom: 57% of faculty are male; 43%, female. All teach undergraduates and 30% do research. No introductory courses are taught by graduate students. The average class size in an introductory lecture is 22; in a laboratory, 12; and in a regular course, 22.

Admissions: 94% of the 2005-2006 applicants were accepted. The SAT scores for the 2005-2006 freshman class were: Verbal--31% below 500, 44% between 500 and 599, 21% between 600 and 700, and 5% above 700; Math--33% below 500, 41% between 500 and 599, 22% between 600 and 700, and 4% above 700. The ACT scores were 30% below 21, 27% between 21 and 23, 22% between 24 and 26, 15% between 27 and 28, and 6% above 28. 41% of the current freshmen were in the top fifth of their class; 67% were in the top two fifths. There were 10 National Merit semifinalists. 67 freshmen graduated first in their class.

Requirements: The SAT or ACT is required. In addition, students seeking admission should have completed 4 years of English and 3 of history, math, and science; 2 years of a foreign language is also recommended. An interview is strongly recommended. A GPA of 2.0 is required. AP and CLEP credits are accepted. Important factors in the admissions decision are advanced placement or honor courses, evidence of special talent, and leadership record.

Procedure: Freshmen are admitted fall and spring. Entrance exams should be taken no later than February of the senior year. Applications should be filed by April 15 for fall entry. The fall 2005 application fee was $25. Notification is sent on a rolling basis. Applications are accepted on-line.

Transfer: 55 transfer students enrolled in 2004-2005. A minimum GPA of 2.5, a recommendation, and an essay are required. 36 of 120 credits required for the bachelor's degree must be completed at Marietta.

Visiting: There are regularly scheduled orientations for prospective students, including fall and spring open houses, tours, and meetings with faculty, coaches, and financial aid representatives. There are guides for informal visits and visitors may sit in on classes and stay overnight. To schedule a visit, contact the Office of Admissions at (740) 376-4600 or (800) 331-7896 or admit@marietta.edu.

Financial Aid: In 2005-2006, 96% of all full-time freshmen and 95% of continuing full-time students received some form of financial aid. 77% of all full-time students received need-based aid. The average freshman award was $19,000. Need-based scholarships or need-based grants averaged $6815 ($16,000 maximum); need-based self-help aid (loans and jobs) averaged $5138 ($5625 maximum); and other non-need-based awards and non-need-based scholarships averaged $6893 ($20,500 maximum). 77% of undergraduates work part time. Average annual earnings from campus work are $2000. The average financial indebtedness of the 2005 graduate was $17,000. The FAFSA is required. The deadline for filing freshman financial aid applications for fall entry is March 1.

International Students: There are 62 international students enrolled. The school actively recruits these students. They must score satisfactorily on the written TOEFL or on the electronic version or take the college's own test and also take the SAT or the ACT.

Computers: All students may access the system. It is strongly recommended that all students have a personal computer.

Graduates: From July 1, 2004 to June 30, 2005, 222 bachelor's degrees were awarded. The most popular majors were management (11%), elementary education (9%), and psychology (8%). 45 companies recruited on campus in 2004-2005. Of the 2004 graduating class, 25% were enrolled in graduate school within 6 months of graduation and 70% were employed.

Admissions Contact: Marke M. Vickers, Director of Admission. A video is available. E-mail: admit@mcnet.marietta.edu
Web: http://www.marietta.edu

MIAMI UNIVERSITY — A-4

Oxford, OH 45056 (513) 529-2531; Fax: (513) 529-1550

Full-time: 6669 men, 7643 women	Faculty: 842; I, --$
Part-time: 164 men, 167 women	Ph.D.s: 90%
Graduate: 609 men, 1086 women	Student/Faculty: 17 to 1
Year: semesters, summer session	Tuition: $21,487
Application Deadline: January 31	Room & Board: $7610
Freshman Class: 15,579 applied, 10,823 accepted, 3162 enrolled	
SAT Verbal/Math: 590/610*	ACT: 27 HIGHLY COMPETITIVE

Miami University, founded in 1809, is a public institution offering a variety of programs in the liberal arts and pre-professional-vocational training. There are 6 undergraduate schools and 1 graduate school. In addition to regional accreditation, Miami University has baccalaureate program accreditation with AACSB, ABET, ADA, AHEA, ASLA, FIDER, NAAB, NASAD, NASM, NCATE, and NLN. The 4 libraries contain 2,373,050 volumes, 3,031,242 microform items, and 26,468 audio/video tapes/CDs/DVDs, and subscribe to 13,710 periodicals including electronic. Computerized library services include the card catalog, interlibrary loans, and database searching. Special learning facilities include a learning resource center, art gallery, natural history museum, radio station, and TV station. The 1921-acre campus is in a small town 35 miles northwest of Cincinnati. Including any residence halls, there are 162 buildings.

Student Life: 72% of undergraduates are from Ohio. Others are from 50 states, 48 foreign countries, and Canada. 75% are from public schools. 86% are white. The average age of freshmen is 18; all undergraduates, 20. 10% do not continue beyond their first year; 80% remain to graduate.

Housing: 7080 students can be accommodated in college housing, which includes single-sex and coed dorms, married-student housing, and sorority houses. In addition, there are honors houses, language houses, special-interest houses, international houses, and freshman-only houses. On-campus housing is guaranteed for the freshman year only and is available on a lottery system for upperclassmen. 56% of students commute. Alcohol is not permitted. All students may keep cars.

Activities: 22% of men belong to 28 national fraternities; 25% of women belong to 22 national sororities. There are 350 groups on campus, including art, band, cheerleading, choir, chorale, chorus, dance, debate, drama, drill team, ethnic, forensics, gay, honors, international, jazz band, literary magazine, marching band, musical theater, newspaper, opera, orchestra, pep band, political, professional, radio and TV, religious, social, social service, student government, and symphony. Popular campus events include Parents Weekend, Kidsfest Weekend, and Unity Fest.

Sports: There are 8 intercollegiate sports for men and 11 for women, and 25 intramural sports for men and 25 for women. Facilities include a 25,000-seat football stadium, 70 acres of playing fields, 30 outdoor tennis courts, a recreational sports center, 10 indoor basketball/volleyball courts, racquetball, handball, and squash courts, a floor hockey/indoor soccer court, a climbing wall, equestrian stables and dressage course, an aquatic center containing 3 indoor swimming pools, jogging paths, a par course, sand volleyball courts, aerobics and weight rooms, a Frisbee golf course, and an outdoor in-line skating court.

Disabled Students: All of the campus is accessible. Wheelchair ramps, elevators, special parking, specially equipped rest rooms, special class scheduling, lowered drinking fountains, and lowered telephones are available.

Services: Counseling and information services are available, as is tutoring in most subjects. There is a reader service for the blind. Assistance in study skills is available.

Campus Safety and Security: Measures include 24-hour foot and vehicle patrol, self-defense education, security escort services, and shuttle buses. There are informal discussions, pamphlets/posters/films, emergency telephones, lighted pathways/sidewalks, formal crime prevention programs, a community relations officer, a bicycle patrol, and card access into dorms.

Programs of Study: Miami University confers B.A., B.S., B.E.D., B.F.A., B.Mus., and B.Phil. degrees. Master's and doctoral degrees are also awarded. Bachelor's degrees are awarded in BIOLOGICAL SCIENCE (biochemistry, biology/biological science, botany, microbiology, and zoology), BUSINESS (accounting, banking and finance, business administration and management, business economics, human resources, management information systems, management science, marketing/retailing/merchandising, operations research, organizational behavior, personnel management, purchasing/inventory management, and sports management), COMMUNICATIONS AND THE ARTS (art, art history and appreciation, broadcasting, communications, dramatic arts, English, fine arts, French, German, graphic design, Greek, Latin, linguistics, music, music performance, Russian, Spanish, speech/debate/rhetoric, and telecommunications), COMPUTER AND PHYSICAL SCIENCE (chemistry, computer science, geology, mathematics, physics, and statistics), EDUCATION (art, athletic training, early childhood, elementary, foreign languages, health, middle school, music, physical, science, secondary, and special), ENGINEERING AND ENVIRONMENTAL DESIGN (architecture, electrical/electronics engineering, engineering, engineering management, engineering physics, engineering technology, environmental design, environmental science, interior design, manufacturing engineering, mechanical engineering, and paper and pulp science), HEALTH PROFESSIONS (exercise science, health, medical technology, nursing, premedicine, and speech pathology/audiology), SOCIAL SCIENCE (African American studies, American studies, anthropology, classical/ancient civilization, dietetics, economics, family/consumer studies, geography, history, interdisciplinary studies, international relations, international studies, philosophy, physical fitness/movement, political science/government, prelaw, psychology, public administration, religion, social science, social work, sociology, urban studies, and women's studies). Zoology, chemistry, and accountancy are the strongest academically. Accountancy, elementary education, and marketing are the largest.

Required: To graduate students must complete 128 semester hours, with a minimum 2.0 GPA. Distribution requirements include a total of 36 hours in English composition, fine arts, humanities, social science, world cultures, natural science, math, formal reasoning, and technology. A minimum of 9 hours in a Thematic Sequence outside the major department, and a 3-hour Senior Capstone Experience, which integrates liberal learning and specialized knowledge, are also required.

Special: The university offers cross-registration with Cincinnati area colleges, study abroad in 15 countries, co-op programs in the School of Applied Science, internships in health and sport studies and applied science, a 3-2 engineering degree with Case Western Reserve and Columbia Universities, and a 3-2 forestry degree with Duke University. Students may pursue student-designed majors through the School of Interdisciplinary Studies or interdisciplinary majors, including decision sciences and history of art and architecture. There are 30 national honor societies, including Phi Beta Kappa, and a freshman honors program.

Faculty/Classroom: 60% of faculty are male; 40%, female. All teach undergraduates. Graduate students teach 20% of introductory courses. The average class size in a laboratory is 15 and in a regular course, 29.

Admissions: 69% of the 2005-2006 applicants were accepted. The SAT scores for the 2005-2006 freshman class were: Verbal--5% below 500, 41% between 500 and 599, 45% between 600 and 700, and 9% above 700; Math--3% below 500, 27% between 500 and 599, 56% between 600 and 700, and 14% above 700. The ACT scores were 2% below 21, 14% between 21 and 23, 38% between 24 and 26, 23% between 27 and 28, and 23% above 28. 69% of the current freshmen were in the top fifth of their class; 96% were in the top two fifths. There were 13 National Merit finalists and 7 semifinalists.

Requirements: The SAT or ACT is required. In addition, candidates for admission must ordinarily be graduates of accredited secondary schools or hold the GED and should have completed 4 units of English, 3 each of math, science, and social studies/history, 2 of a foreign language, and 1 of fine arts. An audition, a portfolio, or an interview is required for direct admission to majors in the School of Fine Arts. AP and CLEP credits are accepted. Important factors in the admissions decision are advanced placement or honor courses, evidence of special talent, and extracurricular activities record.

Procedure: Freshmen are admitted to all sessions. Entrance exams should be taken no later than December of the senior year. There is an early decision plan. Early decision applications should be filed by November 1; regular applications, by January 31 for fall entry and November 15 for spring entry, along with a $45 fee. Notification of early decision is sent December 15; regular decision, March 15. A waiting list is an active part of the admissions procedure. Applications are accepted on-line.

Transfer: 237 transfer students enrolled in 2004-2005. A limited number of transfer students can be accepted. A GPA of 2.00 or higher is necessary. 32 of 128 credits required for the bachelor's degree must be completed at Miami University.

Visiting: There are regularly scheduled orientations for prospective students, consisting of open houses in February and April. There are guides for informal visits and visitors may sit in on classes and stay overnight. To schedule a visit, contact the Office of Admissions, Visit Coordinator at (513) 529-4632 or *visitcoor@muohio.edu*.

Financial Aid: In 2005-2006, 82% of all full-time freshmen and 80% of continuing full-time students received some form of financial aid. 46% of full-time freshmen and 40% of continuing full-time students received need-based aid. The average freshman award was $13,903. 30% of undergraduates work part time. Average annual earnings from campus work are $1084. The average financial indebtedness of the 2005 graduate was $21,522. The FAFSA is required. The deadline for filing freshman financial aid applications for fall entry is February 15.

International Students: There are 113 international students enrolled. They must take the TOEFL or the MELAB. The SAT or ACT is required only for Canadian applicants, athletes, and those students who have followed a U.S. high school curriculum at a secondary school in the United States or abroad.

Computers: Wireless access is available. All students may access the system. There are no time limits. It is strongly recommended that all students have a personal computer.

Graduates: From July 1, 2004 to June 30, 2005, 4100 bachelor's degrees were awarded. The most popular majors were marketing (8%), finance (7%), and psychology (6%). In an average class, 3% graduate in 3 years or less, 66% graduate in 4 years or less, 78% graduate in 5 years or less, and 80% graduate in 6 years or less. 336 companies recruited on campus in a recent year.

Admissions Contact: Ann Larson, Interim Director of Admissions. A video is available. E-mail: *admissions@muohio.edu*
Web: *www.muohio.edu*

MOUNT UNION COLLEGE   E-2
Alliance, OH 44601

	(330) 821-5320
	(800) 992-6682; Fax: (330) 823-3457
Full-time: 993 men, 1028 women	**Faculty:** 123; IIB, av$
Part-time: 44 men, 140 women	**Ph.D.s:** 77%
Graduate: none	**Student/Faculty:** 16 to 1
Year: semesters, summer session	**Tuition:** $19,850
Application Deadline: open	**Room & Board:** $5990
Freshman Class: 1925 applied, 1494 accepted, 560 enrolled	
SAT Verbal/Math: 500/520*	**ACT:** 22 **COMPETITIVE**

Mount Union College, founded in 1846, is a private, liberal arts college affiliated with the United Methodist Church. In addition to regional accreditation, Mount Union has baccalaureate program accreditation with CAAHEP, JRC-AT, NASM, NASPE, and NCATE. The 3 libraries contain 230,000 volumes and 43,000 microform items, and subscribe to 950 periodicals including electronic. Computerized library services include interlibrary loans, database searching, Internet access, and laptop Internet portals. Special learning facilities include a learning resource center, art gallery, radio station, two astronomical observatories, a university theater, a playhouse, and a nature center. The 115-acre campus is in a suburban area 20 miles east of Canton. Including any residence halls, there are 35 buildings.

Student Life: 89% of undergraduates are from Ohio. Others are from 28 states and 7 foreign countries. 89% are from public schools. 90% are white. 40% are Protestant; 32% Catholic; 30% claim no religious affiliation. The average age of freshmen is 18; all undergraduates, 21. 21% do not continue beyond their first year; 61% remain to graduate.

Housing: 1350 students can be accommodated in college housing, which includes single-sex and coed dormitories and fraternity houses. In

addition, there are honors houses, special-interest houses and substance-free (tobacco/alachol) houses. On-campus housing is guaranteed for the freshman year only, is available on a first-come, first-served basis, and is available on a lottery system for upperclassmen. 64% of students live on campus; of those, 60% remain on campus on weekends. All students may keep cars.

Activities: 12% of men belong to 4 national fraternities; 20% of women belong to 1 local and 3 national sororities. There are 76 groups on campus, including art, band, cheerleading, chess, choir, chorale, chorus, computers, dance, debate, drama, drill team, ethnic, forensics, gay, honors, international, jazz band, literary magazine, marching band, musical theater, newspaper, orchestra, pep band, political, professional, radio and TV, religious, social, social service, student government, symphony, and yearbook. Popular campus events include Spring Fest, Greek Week, and Schooler Lecture series.

Sports: There are 11 intercollegiate sports for men and 10 for women, and 16 intramural sports for men and 16 for women. Facilities include a gym, field house, stadium, tennis courts, wellness center, exercise and aerobics rooms, and the Hoover-Price Campus Center.

Disabled Students: 90% of the campus is accessible. Wheelchair ramps, elevators, special parking, specially equipped rest rooms, special class scheduling, lowered drinking fountains, and special housing are available.

Services: Counseling and information services are available, as is tutoring in most subjects, including general education courses and most introductory courses. There is a reader service for the blind and remedial writing, and facilitated study groups for most general education courses that meet once a week.

Campus Safety and Security: Measures include 24-hour foot and vehicle patrol, self-defense education, security escort services, and informal discussions. There are pamphlets/posters/films, emergency telephones, and lighted pathways/sidewalks.

Programs of Study: Mount Union confers B.A., B.S., B.Mus., and B.Mus.Ed. degrees. Bachelor's degrees are awarded in BIOLOGICAL SCIENCE (biochemistry, biology/biological science, and environmental biology), BUSINESS (accounting, business administration and management, international business management, and sports management), COMMUNICATIONS AND THE ARTS (art, communications, creative writing, dramatic arts, English, French, German, Japanese, media arts, music, music performance, and Spanish), COMPUTER AND PHYSICAL SCIENCE (astronomy, chemistry, computer science, geology, information sciences and systems, mathematics, and physics), EDUCATION (athletic training, early childhood, elementary, middle school, music, and physical), HEALTH PROFESSIONS (health), SOCIAL SCIENCE (American studies, cognitive science, economics, history, international studies, Near Eastern studies, philosophy, physical fitness/movement, political science/government, psychology, religion, social science, and sociology). Business, education, and psychology are the largest.

Required: To graduate, students must complete a minimum of 120 semester hours, including 30 in upper division courses and up to 48 in the major, with a minimum GPA of 2.0. General requirements include 49 hours in a core curriculum encompassing communication skills, analytical skills, religion/philosophy, international studies, Western history, literature, fine arts, phys ed, and the freshman liberal arts experience. Students must also complete a minor requirement and the senior year culminating experience.

Special: Mount Union offers internships for credit in many majors, study abroad in 12 countries, co-op programs in business, work-study programs with various employers, student-designed majors, and pass/fail options. Adults in the nontraditional study program may receive credit for life, military, or work experience. There are 18 national honor societies, a freshman honors program, and 19 departmental honors programs.

Faculty/Classroom: 67% of faculty are male; 33%, female. All teach undergraduates. The average class size in an introductory lecture is 19; in a laboratory, 12; and in a regular course, 18.

Admissions: 78% of the 2005-2006 applicants were accepted. The SAT scores for the 2005-2006 freshman class were: Verbal--47% below 500, 38% between 500 and 599, 14% between 600 and 700, and 2% above 700; Math--41% below 500, 41% between 500 and 599, 17% between 600 and 700, and 1% above 700. The ACT scores were 34% below 21, 31% between 21 and 23, 22% between 24 and 26, 8% between 27 and 28, and 5% above 28. 35% of the current freshmen were in the top fifth of their class; 64% were in the top two fifths. There were 2 National Merit finalists. 8 freshmen graduated first in their class.

Requirements: The SAT or ACT is required. Preference is given to high school graduates who have completed a minimum of 15 academic units, including 4 in English, 3 each in math, social science, and lab science, and 2 in foreign language. A GPA of 2.0 is required. AP and CLEP credits are accepted. Important factors in the admissions decision are advanced placement or honor courses, recommendations by school officials, and personality/intangible qualities.

Procedure: Freshmen are admitted fall and spring. Entrance exams should be taken for the first time in the spring of the junior year. There is a deferred admission and rolling admissions plan. Application deadlines are open. Applications are accepted on-line. The fall 2005 application fee was $20.

Transfer: 76 transfer students enrolled in 2004-2005. Applicants must have a college GPA of 2.0 for consideration and must submit a statement of honorable dismissal and an official transcript from the last college attended. A personal statement must accompany the transfer application. 45 of 120 credits required for the bachelor's degree must be completed at Mount Union.

Visiting: There are regularly scheduled orientations for prospective students, including interviews, a campus tour, meetings with faculty, and classroom visits. There are guides for informal visits and visitors may sit in on classes and stay overnight. To schedule a visit, contact the Admissions Office at (330) 823-2590.

Financial Aid: In 2005-2006, 99% of all full-time freshmen and 95% of continuing full-time students received some form of financial aid. 79% of full-time freshmen and 74% of continuing full-time students received need-based aid. The average freshman award was $15,835. Need-based scholarships or need-based grants averaged $12,109 ($19,600 maximum); need-based self-help aid (loans and jobs) averaged $5456 ($5825 maximum); and other non-need-based awards and non-need-based scholarships averaged $9905 ($19,600 maximum). 29% of undergraduates work part time. Average annual earnings from campus work are $1155. The average financial indebtedness of the 2005 graduate was $17,852. Mount Union is a member of CSS. The FAFSA is required. The priority date for freshman financial aid applications for fall entry is March 1. The deadline for filing freshman financial aid applications for fall entry is September 1.

International Students: There are 45 international students enrolled. The school actively recruits these students. They must take the TOEFL and also take the International English Language Testing System (IELTS) or certification of completion of ELS.

Computers: Wireless access is available. The campus is fully wired with high speed Internet access and wireless access that accommodates 2000 users in all academic buildings and residence halls. Over 200 PCs are available to students in lab setting for use, many 24 hours a day. All students are provided with an e-mail account and network space. A help desk provides technology support for students, faculty, and staff. All students may access the system. There are no time limits. The fee is $250 annually. It is strongly recommended that all students have a personal computer.

Graduates: From July 1, 2004 to June 30, 2005, 434 bachelor's degrees were awarded. The most popular majors were education (25%), business (17%), and psychology (6%). In an average class, 1% graduate in 3 years or less, 51% graduate in 4 years or less, 61% graduate in 5 years or less, and 61% graduate in 6 years or less. 20 companies recruited on campus in 2004-2005. Of the 2004 graduating class, 29% were enrolled in graduate school within 6 months of graduation and 71% were employed.

Admissions Contact: Amy Tomko, Vice President, Enrollment Services. A video is available. E-mail: *admission@muc.edu*
Web: *www.muc.edu*

MOUNT VERNON NAZARENE UNIVERSITY C-3

Mt. Vernon, OH 43050 (740) 392-6868, ext. 4510
(866) 462-MVNU; Fax: (740) 393-0511

Full-time: 779 men, 1121 women	**Faculty:** 78; IIA, --$
Part-time: 157 men, 155 women	**Ph.D.s:** 63%
Graduate: 118 men, 219 women	**Student/Faculty:** 24 to 1
Year: 4-1-4, summer session	**Tuition:** $15,886
Application Deadline: May 1	**Room & Board:** $4924
Freshman Class: 741 applied, 603 accepted, 380 enrolled	
SAT Verbal/Math: 537/517*	**ACT:** 22 COMPETITIVE

Mount Vernon Nazarene University, founded in 1968, is a private liberal arts college affiliated with the Church of the Nazarene. The library contains 104,066 volumes, 3382 microform items, and 6104 audio/video tapes/CDs/DVDs, and subscribes to 6324 periodicals including electronic. Computerized library services include the card catalog, interlibrary loans, database searching, and Internet access. Special learning facilities include a learning resource center, art gallery, radio station, and a nature center. The 401-acre campus is in a small town 45 miles northeast of Columbus. Including any residence halls, there are 49 buildings.

Student Life: 90% of undergraduates are from Ohio. Students are from 29 states, 9 foreign countries, and Canada. 77% are from public schools. 93% are white. Most are Protestant. The average age of freshmen is 18; all undergraduates, 20. 22% do not continue beyond their first year; 52% remain to graduate.

Housing: 1138 students can be accommodated in college housing, which includes single-sex dorms and on-campus apartments. On-campus housing is available on a first-come, first-served basis. 75% of students live on campus; of those, 55% remain on campus on weekends. Alcohol is not permitted. All students may keep cars.

Activities: There are no fraternities or sororities. There are 37 groups on campus, including art, band, cheerleading, choir, chorale, chorus,

computers, drama, ethnic, honors, international, jazz band, musical theater, newspaper, orchestra, pep band, photography, political, professional, radio and TV, religious, social, social service, student government, symphony, and yearbook. Popular campus events include Sonfest, community service week, and Spring Luau.

Sports: There are 4 intercollegiate sports for men and 4 for women, and 9 intramural sports for men and 9 for women. Facilities include a main gym, an intramural/practice gym, a weight room, a game room, a fitness/exercise facility, tennis courts, intramural, baseball, softball, and soccer fields, and a baseball/softball batting facility.

Disabled Students: 95% of the campus is accessible. Wheelchair ramps, elevators, special parking, specially equipped rest rooms, special class scheduling, lowered drinking fountains, and lowered telephones are available.

Services: Counseling and information services are available, as is tutoring in most subjects. There is a reader service for the blind, and remedial math, reading, and writing. Students in the at-risk program are required to take University Success Strategies.

Campus Safety and Security: Measures include 24-hour foot and vehicle patrol, self-defense education, informal discussions, and pamphlets/posters/films. There are emergency telephones, lighted pathways/sidewalks, and fire safety training with student leadership, and blood-borne pathogen seminars. Campus-wide sexual harassment training is required of all faculty, staff and students, and there is a campus safety and security review committee.

Programs of Study: MVNU confers B.A., B.S., and B.B.A. degrees. Associate and master's degrees are also awarded. Bachelor's degrees are awarded in BIOLOGICAL SCIENCE (biology/biological science), BUSINESS (accounting, business administration and management, business communications, business economics, international business management, office supervision and management, and sports management), COMMUNICATIONS AND THE ARTS (art, communications, English, graphic design, journalism, music, music performance, and Spanish), COMPUTER AND PHYSICAL SCIENCE (chemistry, computer science, and mathematics), EDUCATION (art, business, Christian, early childhood, elementary, English, foreign languages, home economics, mathematics, middle school, music, physical, science, secondary, social studies, and special), HEALTH PROFESSIONS (exercise science and medical technology), SOCIAL SCIENCE (child care/child and family studies, criminal justice, family/consumer studies, history, philosophy, psychology, religion, religious education, social work, sociology, and youth ministry). Education, premedicine, and biology are the strongest academically. Business, teacher education, and biology are the largest.

Required: Students must complete 124 semester hours, at least 40 to 60 hours in the major and 40 in upper-division courses, and maintain a minimum GPA of 2.0. The 43- to 50-hour B.A. general education core includes 12 to 15 hours of general requirements, 18 to 21 in the humanities, 7 to 8 in natural sciences, 6 in social sciences, and 2 hours in physical education for life. Students must also complete 1 semester of a foreign language (or 2 years of 1 language in high school), intermediate algebra (or complete 2 years of algebra and/or geometry in high school), and the junior-senior testing program.

Special: MVNU offers internships with local businesses/organizations, on-campus work-study programs, study abroad in 13 countries, dual majors, a general studies degree, and non-degree study. A 2-2 nursing degree in cooperation with Capital University is also available, as is a 2-2 engineering degree with Olivet Nazarene University. Cross-registration is available with Nazarene Colleges and Universities, and the Council for Christian College and Universities program, and a Washington semester is offered through the American Studies Program. There are 3 national honor societies, a freshman honors program, and 19 departmental honors programs.

Faculty/Classroom: 72% of faculty are male; 28%, female. 95% teach undergraduates and 20% both teach and do research. No introductory courses are taught by graduate students. The average class size in an introductory lecture is 24; in a laboratory, 17; and in a regular course, 15.

Admissions: 81% of the 2005-2006 applicants were accepted. The SAT scores for the 2005-2006 freshman class were: Verbal--31% below 500, 50% between 500 and 599, 16% between 600 and 700, and 3% above 700; Math--40% below 500, 40% between 500 and 599, 18% between 600 and 700, and 1% above 700. The ACT scores were 34% below 21, 28% between 21 and 23, 23% between 24 and 26, 8% between 27 and 28, and 7% above 28. 38% of the current freshmen were in the top fifth of their class; 64% were in the top two fifths. 10 freshmen graduated first in their class.

Requirements: A satisfactory score on the ACT is required. Applicants should be graduates of an accredited high school and be in the upper two-thirds of their class. Required preparatory courses include 4 units in English, 3 units each in math (algebra I and II, and geometry) and social studies, and 3 units in science. In addition, 3 units of 1 foreign language and 3 laboratory science courses are recommended. A GPA of 2.3 is required. AP and CLEP credits are accepted. Important factors in the admissions decision are recommendations by school officials, personality/intangible qualities, and leadership record.

Procedure: Freshmen are admitted fall, winter, and spring. Entrance exams should be taken in early fall. There is a rolling admissions plan. Applications should be filed by May 1 for fall entry, December 1 for winter entry, January 1 for spring entry, and May 15 for summer entry, along with a $25 fee. Notification is sent on a rolling basis. Applications are accepted on-line.

Transfer: 69 transfer students enrolled in 2004-2005. Transfer students must be in good standing academically and financially. Official transcripts from all colleges attended must be submitted. 30 of 124 credits required for the bachelor's degree must be completed at MVNU.

Visiting: There are regularly scheduled orientations for prospective students. There are guides for informal visits and visitors may sit in on classes and stay overnight. To schedule a visit, contact the Admissions Office at (800) 782-2435 or admissions@mvnu.edu.

Financial Aid: In 2005-2006, 100% of all full-time freshmen and 99% of continuing full-time students received some form of financial aid. 89% of full-time freshmen and 81% of continuing full-time students received need-based aid. The average freshman award was $15,690. Need-based scholarships or need-based grants averaged $6829 ($15,384 maximum); need-based self-help aid (loans and jobs) averaged $3726 ($16,500 maximum); non-need-based athletic scholarships averaged $363 ($12,000 maximum); and other non-need-based awards and non-need-based scholarships averaged $1045 ($15,384 maximum). 48% of undergraduates work part time. Average annual earnings from campus work are $1631. The average financial indebtedness of the 2005 graduate was $22,710. The FAFSA and the college's own financial statement are required. The priority date for freshman financial aid applications for fall entry is April 15.

International Students: There are 12 international students enrolled. Satisfactory scores are required on the written TOEFL and the SAT or the ACT.

Computers: Wireless access is available. All residence halls and apartments are wired for Internet and there are open computer labs in each dorm. There are several computer labs on campus, including a general usage lab with 30 PCs and 7 Macs, general classroom classroom lab with 33 PCs, a MAC lab with 25 Imac G5 systems, 2 business labs with 25 PCs each, and several other departmental or general labs. There are 9 walk-up kiosks for Internet use and wireless access in the student union and the library. All students may access the system 24 hours, 7 days a week. There are no time limits and no fees.

Graduates: From July 1, 2004 to June 30, 2005, 459 bachelor's degrees were awarded. The most popular majors were business (18%), education (15%), and religion (13%). In an average class, 1% graduate in 3 years or less, 54% graduate in 4 years or less, 67% graduate in 5 years or less, and 70% graduate in 6 years or less. 63 companies recruited on campus in 2004-2005. Of the 2004 graduating class, 16% were enrolled in graduate school within 6 months of graduation and 98% were employed.

Admissions Contact: Tim Eades, Director of Admissions and Recruitment. A video is available. E-mail: admissions@mvnu.edu
Web: wwwgotomvnu.com

MUSKINGUM COLLEGE D-3

New Concord, OH 43762

(740) 826-8137
(800) 752-6082; Fax: (740) 826-8100

Full-time: 803 men, 782 women	**Faculty:** 94; IIB, -$
Part-time: 30 men, 69 women	**Ph.D.s:** 91%
Graduate: 128 men, 382 women	**Student/Faculty:** 17 to 1
Year: semesters, summer session	**Tuition:** $16,450
Application Deadline: August 15	**Room & Board:** $6520
Freshman Class: 1756 applied, 1401 accepted, 434 enrolled	
SAT Verbal/Math: 529/522*	**ACT:** 22 COMPETITIVE

Muskingum College, founded in 1837, is a private liberal arts and sciences institution affiliated with the Presbyterian Church (U.S.A.). In addition to regional accreditation, Muskingum has baccalaureate program accreditation with NASM and NCATE. The library contains 202,866 volumes, 17,000 microform items, and 2675 audio/video tapes/CDs/DVDs, and subscribes to 5655 periodicals including electronic. Computerized library services include the card catalog, interlibrary loans, database searching, and Internet access. Special learning facilities include a learning resource center, art gallery, radio station, TV station, and greenhouse. The 215-acre campus is in a small town 9 miles west of Cambridge and 50 miles east of Columbus. Including any residence halls, there are 34 buildings.

Student Life: 87% of undergraduates are from Ohio. Others are from 28 states and 15 foreign countries. 85% are from public schools. 91% are white. 44% are Protestant; 36% claim no religious affiliation; 19% Catholic. The average age of freshmen is 18; all undergraduates, 21. 24% do not continue beyond their first year; 62% remain to graduate.

Housing: 1300 students can be accommodated in college housing, which includes single-sex and coed dormitories, on-campus apartments, fraternity houses, and sorority houses. In addition, there are language houses, special-interest houses, and upper classman apartments and

townhouses. On-campus housing is guaranteed for all 4 years. 80% of students live on campus; of those, 65% remain on campus on weekends. All students may keep cars.

Activities: 25% of men belong to 3 local and 2 national fraternities; 30% of women belong to 4 local and 2 national sororities. There are 90 groups on campus, including art, band, cheerleading, choir, chorus, computers, dance, debate, drama, forensics, gay, honors, international, jazz band, literary magazine, musical theater, newspaper, orchestra, pep band, political, professional, radio and TV, religious, social, social service, student government, symphony, and yearbook. Popular campus events include Parents Weekend, Li'l Sibs Weekend, and Muskie-palooza.

Sports: There are 9 intercollegiate sports for men and 8 for women, and 8 intramural sports for men and 8 for women. Facilities include gyms, weightlifting/training rooms, an aerobics room, a baseball batting cage, a swimming pool, a walking/jogging trail, an all-weather track, football, baseball, and soccer fields, and tennis, basketball, and racquetball courts.

Disabled Students: 40% of the campus is accessible. Wheelchair ramps, elevators, special parking, and lowered drinking fountains are available.

Services: Counseling and information services are available, as is tutoring in every subject. There is a reader service for the blind. The PLUS program is available for learning-disabled and disabled students.

Campus Safety and Security: Measures include 24-hour foot and vehicle patrol, security escort services, informal discussions, and pamphlets/posters/films. There are emergency telephones and lighted pathways/sidewalks.

Programs of Study: Muskingum confers B.A. and B.S. degrees. Master's degrees are also awarded. Bachelor's degrees are awarded in AGRICULTURE (conservation and regulation), BIOLOGICAL SCIENCE (biology/biological science, molecular biology, and neurosciences), BUSINESS (accounting, business administration and management, and international business management), COMMUNICATIONS AND THE ARTS (art, communications, dramatic arts, English, French, German, journalism, music, Spanish, and speech/debate/rhetoric), COMPUTER AND PHYSICAL SCIENCE (chemistry, computer science, earth science, geology, mathematics, and physics), EDUCATION (Christian, early childhood, elementary, foreign languages, music, physical, reading, science, secondary, and special), ENGINEERING AND ENVIRONMENTAL DESIGN (environmental science), SOCIAL SCIENCE (American studies, criminal justice, economics, history, international relations, philosophy, political science/government, psychology, public affairs, religion, religious education, social science, and sociology). Sciences, education, and industry are the strongest academically. Education, business, and psychology are the largest.

Required: To graduate, students must complete a minimum of 124 credit hours, including at least 30 in a major and 40 in upper-level courses. Students must maintain a GPA of at least 2.0, and must also complete the 50 to 55 credit hours of Liberal Arts Essentials, with courses in writing, speech, math, arts and humanities, religion and ethics, science, social science, American studies, and phys ed. Senior capstone experience is required in all areas.

Special: Internships, both national and regional, work-study programs, study abroad in 12 countries, and a Washington semester are possible. Students may earn a 3-2 engineering degree with Case Western Reserve University, a B.A.-B.S. degree, or a general studies degree; nearly a third of students pursue dual and student-designed majors. Nondegree study, pass/fail options, and credit for life, military, or work experience are also available. There are 13 national honor societies.

Faculty/Classroom: 57% of faculty are male; 43%, female. 87% teach undergraduates, 85% do research, and 85% do both. No introductory courses are taught by graduate students. The average class size in an introductory lecture is 25; in a laboratory, 16; and in a regular course, 22.

Admissions: 80% of the 2005-2006 applicants were accepted. The SAT scores for the 2005-2006 freshman class were: Verbal--36% below 500, 39% between 500 and 599, 22% between 600 and 700, and 3% above 700; Math--37% below 500, 41% between 500 and 599, 18% between 600 and 700, and 4% above 700. The ACT scores were 40% below 21, 32% between 21 and 23, 18% between 24 and 26, 5% between 27 and 28, and 5% above 28. 43% of the current freshmen were in the top fifth of their class; 65% were in the top two fifths. 6 freshmen graduated first in their class.

Requirements: The SAT or ACT is required. In addition, candidates for admission must have a high school diploma or its equivalent, and should have 4 years of English, 3 years of college preparatory math, and 2 years each of science, social science, and foreign language. A GPA of 2.0 is required. AP and CLEP credits are accepted. Important factors in the admissions decision are advanced placement or honor courses, extracurricular activities record, and leadership record.

Procedure: Freshmen are admitted fall and spring. Entrance exams should be taken in the junior year or the fall of the senior year. There are early admissions, deferred admissions, and rolling admissions plans. Applications should be filed by August 15 for fall entry. Notification is sent on a rolling basis. Applications are accepted on-line.

Transfer: 67 transfer students enrolled in 2004-2005. Applicants must submit an official college transcript and be in good academic standing from their previous institution. 48 of 124 credits required for the bachelor's degree must be completed at Muskingum.

Visiting: There are regularly scheduled orientations for prospective students, consisting of an admission presentation, faculty panel, student panel, and class attendance. There are guides for informal visits and visitors may sit in on classes and stay overnight. To schedule a visit, contact the Admission Office.

Financial Aid: In 2005-2006, 98% of all full-time students received some form of financial aid. 78% of full-time freshmen and 77% of continuing full-time students received need-based aid. The average freshman award was $15,527. Need-based scholarships or need-based grants averaged $11,276 ($23,962 maximum); and need-based self-help aid (loans and jobs) averaged $4225 ($5825 maximum). 45% of undergraduates work part time. Average annual earnings from campus work are $1000. The average financial indebtedness of the 2005 graduate was $17,300 (excluding alternative loans). Muskingum is a member of CSS. The FAFSA and student and parents' tax returns are required. The priority date for freshman financial aid applications for fall entry is March 15.

International Students: In a recent year there were 33 international students enrolled. The school actively recruits these students. They must score satisfactorily on the written TOEFL or on the electronic version.

Computers: Students may access the network from residence hall rooms or from various labs on campus, including the library, academic buildings, and residence halls. Limited wireless capability is also available. All students may access the system 24 hours a day. There are no time limits and no fees.

Graduates: From July 1, 2004 to June 30, 2005, 264 bachelor's degrees were awarded. The most popular majors were business (18%), early childhood education (13%), and biology (10%). In an average class, 1% graduate in 3 years or less, 48% graduate in 4 years or less, 61% graduate in 5 years or less, and 62% graduate in 6 years or less. 25 companies recruited on campus in 2004-2005. Of the 2004 graduating class, 18% were enrolled in graduate school within 6 months of graduation and 95% were employed.

Admissions Contact: Beth DaLonzo, Senior Director of Admission and Student Financial Services. E-mail: *adminfo@muskingum.edu* Web: *www.muskingum.edu*

NOTRE DAME COLLEGE   D-1
South Euclid, OH 44121   (216) 373-5383
(800) NDC-1680, ext. 355; Fax: (216) 381-3802

Full-time: 60 men, 250 women	Faculty: 26; IIB, --$
Part-time: 500 men and women	Ph.D.s: 65%
Graduate: 125 men and women	Student/Faculty: 12 to 1
Year: semesters, summer session	Tuition: $15,000
Application Deadline: open	Room & Board: $5700
Freshman Class: n/av	
SAT or ACT: required	**COMPETITIVE**

Notre Dame College, founded in 1922, is a private liberal arts and sciences college affiliated with the Roman Catholic Church. Figures in the above capsule and profile are aproximate. In addition to regional accreditation, NDC has baccalaureate program accreditation with ADA. The library contains 89,292 volumes, 14,200 microform items, and 1768 audio/video tapes/CDs/DVDs, and subscribes to 300 periodicals including electronic. Computerized library services include the card catalog, interlibrary loans, and database searching. Special learning facilities include a learning resource center and tolerance resource center. The 53-acre campus is in a suburban area 13 miles east of Cleveland. Including any residence halls, there are 6 buildings.

Student Life: 95% of undergraduates are from Ohio. Students are from 8 states, 7 foreign countries, and Canada. 65% are from public schools. 65% are white; 23% African American. 55% are Catholic; 20% Baptist, Muslim, and other Christian; 15% Protestant; 8% claim no religious affiliation. The average age of freshmen is 18; all undergraduates, 26. 34% do not continue beyond their first year; 52% remain to graduate.

Housing: 222 students can be accommodated in college housing, which includes dorms. There are non-smoking floors and quiet floors. Housing ia available for weekend college students on WECO weekends. On-campus housing is guaranteed for all 4 years and is available on a lottery system for upperclassmen. 78% of students commute. Alcohol is not permitted. All students may keep cars.

Activities: There are no fraternities or sororities. There are 32 groups on campus, including art, choir, computers, dance, drama, ethnic, honors, international, literary magazine, newspaper, political, professional, religious, social, social service, and student government. Popular campus events include Parents Day, Founders Weekend, and Christmas Happening.

Sports: There are 5 intercollegiate sports for men and 7 for women, and 4 intramural sports for men and 4 for women. Facilities include a 500-seat gym, a pool, and a fitness center.

Disabled Students: 75% of the campus is accessible. Wheelchair ramps, elevators, special parking, specially equipped rest rooms, lowered drinking fountains, and lowered telephones are available.

Services: Counseling and information services are available, as is tutoring in most subjects. There is remedial math, reading, and writing.

Campus Safety and Security: Measures include 24-hour foot and vehicle patrol, security escort services, informal discussions, and pamphlets/posters/films. There are emergency telephones and lighted pathways/sidewalks.

Programs of Study: NDC confers B.A. and B.S. degrees. Associate and master's degrees are also awarded. Bachelor's degrees are awarded in BIOLOGICAL SCIENCE (biology/biological science), BUSINESS (accounting, business economics, human resources, management science, and marketing/retailing/merchandising), COMMUNICATIONS AND THE ARTS (art, communications, English, graphic design, studio art, and visual and performing arts), COMPUTER AND PHYSICAL SCIENCE (chemistry, information sciences and systems, and mathematics), EDUCATION (early childhood, elementary, middle school, and secondary), ENGINEERING AND ENVIRONMENTAL DESIGN (environmental science), SOCIAL SCIENCE (economics, history, ministries, political science/government, psychology, and theological studies). Business, education, and science are the strongest academically. Business administration, education, and sciences are the largest.

Required: To graduate, students must complete 128 semester hours with a minimum GPA of 2.0. Core requirements include English, speech, literature, fine arts, foreign language, health and phys ed, math, science, social or behavioral science, philosophy/theology, world civilization, and senior seminar.

Special: Students may cross-register with the Cleveland Institutes of Music and Art and through the Northeast Ohio Council on Higher Education. The college offers co-op programs in most majors, internships with local businesses, special degrees, including a B.A. with a diploma in theology, and interdisciplinary majors, including visual arts management, credit by exam, nondegree study, and pass/fail options. NDC also offers Weekend College. There are 5 national honor societies.

Faculty/Classroom: 30% of faculty are male; 70%, female. All teach undergraduates. No introductory courses are taught by graduate students. The average class size in an introductory lecture is 20; in a laboratory, 11; and in a regular course, 11.

Requirements: The SAT or ACT is required. Applicants should be graduates of an accredited secondary school with 15 academic credits, including 4 of English, 2 of foreign language, 1 each of math, social studies, and science, plus 5 electives. The GED is accepted. An interview is recommended. A GPA of 2.5 is required. AP and CLEP credits are accepted. Important factors in the admissions decision are advanced placement or honor courses, evidence of special talent, and extracurricular activities record.

Procedure: Freshmen are admitted fall and spring. Entrance exams should be taken in the spring of the junior year or the fall of the senior year. There are deferred admissions, and rolling admissions plans. Application deadlines are open. The fall 2005 application fee was $30.

Transfer: Applicants must have a college GPA of at least 2.5. An interview is required. 32 of 128 credits required for the bachelor's degree must be completed at NDC.

Visiting: There are regularly scheduled orientations for prospective students, including placement testing, academic advising, scheduling, an overview of student services, and a tour of Cleveland. There are guides for informal visits and visitors may sit in on classes and stay overnight. To schedule a visit, contact the Admissions Office.

Financial Aid: The FAFSA is required. Checkwith the school for current application deadlines.

International Students: The school actively recruits these students. They must score satisfactorily on the written TOEFL or take the ELS Proficiency Test 109.

Computers: All students may access the system. There are no time limits. The fee $200.

Admissions Contact: Meredith Young, Director of Admissions. E-mail: *myoung@ndc.edu* Web: *http://www.ndc.edu*

OBERLIN COLLEGE   D-2
Oberlin, OH 44074   (440) 775-8411
(800) 622-6243; Fax: (440) 775-6905

Full-time: 1218 men, 1537 women	Faculty: 288; IIB, +$
Part-time: 46 men, 44 women	Ph.D.s: 96%
Graduate: 9 men, 10 women	Student/Faculty: 10 to 1
Year: 4-1-4	Tuition: $32,724
Application Deadline: January 15	Room & Board: $8180
Freshman Class: 4553 applied, 2016 accepted, 792 enrolled	
SAT Verbal/Math: 698/663*	ACT: 30 **MOST COMPETITIVE**

Oberlin College, founded in 1833, is an independent institution offering degree programs in the liberal arts and sciences and music. There are 2 undergraduate schools. In addition to regional accreditation, Oberlin has baccalaureate program accreditation with NASM. The 4 libraries contain

1,352,932 volumes, 345,918 microform items, and 87,066 audio/video tapes/CDs/DVDs, and subscribe to 20,936 periodicals including electronic. Computerized library services include the card catalog, interlibrary loans, database searching, and Internet access. Special learning facilities include a learning resource center, art gallery, radio station, observatory, art museum, art library, arboretum, conservatory of music, and music library. The 440-acre campus is in a small town 35 miles southwest of Cleveland. Including any residence halls, there are 65 buildings.

Student Life: 90% of undergraduates are from out of state, mostly the Middle Atlantic. Students are from 48 states, 49 foreign countries, and Canada. 67% are from public schools. 76% are white. 48% are claim no religious affiliation; 19% Protestant; 13% Jewish; 12% Islamic, Buddhist; 8% Catholic. The average age of freshmen is 18; all undergraduates, 20. 9% do not continue beyond their first year; 81% remain to graduate.

Housing: 2336 students can be accommodated in college housing, which includes single-sex and coed dorms and on-campus apartments. In addition, there are language houses, special-interest houses and co-ops. On-campus housing is guaranteed for all 4 years. 75% of students live on campus; of those, 99% remain on campus on weekends. All students may keep cars.

Activities: There are no fraternities or sororities. There are 120 groups on campus, including art, band, cheerleading, chess, choir, chorale, chorus, computers, dance, drama, ethnic, film, gay, honors, international, jazz band, literary magazine, marching band, musical theater, newspaper, opera, orchestra, photography, political, professional, radio and TV, religious, social, social service, student government, symphony, and yearbook. Popular campus events include the Big Parade and Drag Ball.

Sports: There are 11 intercollegiate sports for men and 11 for women, and 10 intramural sports for men and 10 for women. Facilities include a gym, an enclosed and a semienclosed field house, a stadium, an indoor 6-lane, 200-meter track, an 8-lane outdoor track, 12 outdoor and 4 indoor tennis courts, a cross-country course, a fitness trail, a swimming pool, a Nautilus center, a free-weight room, 22 practice/play fields, and indoor space for football, soccer, and lacrosse practice.

Disabled Students: 90% of the campus is accessible. Wheelchair ramps, elevators, special parking, specially equipped rest rooms, special class scheduling, lowered drinking fountains, lowered telephones, special housing, and an indoor/outdoor lift are available.

Services: Counseling and information services are available, as is tutoring in every subject. There is a reader service for the blind, and remedial math, reading, and writing. Computer-assisted services for hearing and visually impaired students and special tutoring and peer-counseling services for learning-disabled students are available.

Campus Safety and Security: Measures include 24-hour foot and vehicle patrol, self-defense education, security escort services, and informal discussions. There are pamphlets/posters/films, emergency telephones, lighted pathways/sidewalks, a full-time crime prevention officer, a 24-hour headquarters facility staffed by professional dispatchers, and an electronic card-access system in all dorms. All security officers are state-certified academy graduates.

Programs of Study: Oberlin confers B.A. and B.Mus. degrees. Master's degrees are also awarded. Bachelor's degrees are awarded in BIOLOGICAL SCIENCE (biochemistry, biology/biological science, and neurosciences), COMMUNICATIONS AND THE ARTS (art, classics, comparative literature, creative writing, dance, dramatic arts, English, film arts, fine arts, French, German, music, music history and appreciation, music performance, music theory and composition, romance languages and literature, Russian, and Spanish), COMPUTER AND PHYSICAL SCIENCE (astronomy, chemistry, computer science, geology, mathematics, and physics), EDUCATION (music), ENGINEERING AND ENVIRONMENTAL DESIGN (environmental science), SOCIAL SCIENCE (African American studies, American studies, anthropology, archeology, East Asian studies, economics, history, humanities, Judaic studies, Latin American studies, law, Near Eastern studies, philosophy, political science/government, psychology, religion, sociology, and women's studies). Sciences, art and humanities, and music are the strongest academically. English, biology, and history are the largest.

Required: Students are required to complete 112 to 124 total credit hours, including 9 hours each in arts/humanities, social/behavioral sciences, natural science/math, and courses dealing with cultural diversity, and 3 winter term projects. In addition, they must earn writing and quantitative proficiency certification. A minimum of 24 credits is required for the major.

Special: Internships are available through the Business Initiatives Program. Students may study abroad in more than 25 countries. The college offers independent and dual majors, 3-2 engineering programs with other institutions, nondegree study for special and visiting students, and a 5-year B.A.-B.Mus. double degree. Pass/no credit options are available to all students. There are 4 national honor societies, including Phi Beta Kappa, and 25 departmental honors programs.

Faculty/Classroom: 59% of faculty are male; 41%, female. All both teach and do research. No introductory courses are taught by graduate students. The average class size in a laboratory is 14 and in a regular course, 18.

Admissions: 44% of the 2005-2006 applicants were accepted. The SAT scores for the 2005-2006 freshman class were: Verbal--1% below 500, 8% between 500 and 599, 42% between 600 and 700, and 49% above 700; Math--2% below 500, 13% between 500 and 599, 54% between 600 and 700, and 31% above 700. 90% of the current freshmen were in the top fifth of their class; 99% were in the top two fifths. There were 45 National Merit finalists. 22 freshmen graduated first in their class.

Requirements: The SAT or ACT is required. In addition, candidates for admission should have completed 4 years each of English and math and 3 each of science, social studies, and a foreign language. AP credits are accepted. Important factors in the admissions decision are advanced placement or honor courses, personality/intangible qualities, and leadership record.

Procedure: Freshmen are admitted in the fall. Entrance exams should be taken in the junior year or early in the senior year. There are early decision and deferred admissions plans. Early decision applications should be filed by November 15; regular applications, by January 15 for fall entry and November 15 for spring entry, along with a $35 fee. Notification of early decision is sent December 15; regular decision, April 1. 236 early decision candidates were accepted for the 2005-2006 class. 640 applicants were on the 2005 waiting list; 33 were admitted. Applications are accepted on-line.

Transfer: 37 transfer students enrolled in 2004-2005. Applicants should submit official transcripts of all college work completed, plus a list of current courses and midterm grades. An average of B or better should be presented. A high school transcript, recommendations, and standardized test scores are also required. 56 of 112 credits required for the bachelor's degree must be completed at Oberlin.

Visiting: There are regularly scheduled orientations for prospective students, including campus tours, class visits, an interview with an admissions staffmember, and an overnight stay in the dorm. There are guides for informal visits and visitors may sit in on classes and stay overnight. To schedule a visit, contact the Admissions Office.

Financial Aid: In 2005-2006, 55% of all full-time freshmen and 59% of continuing full-time students received some form of financial aid. 43% of full-time freshmen and 50% of continuing full-time students received need-based aid. The average freshman award was $22,145. Need-based scholarships or need-based grants averaged $14,590 ($32,971 maximum); need-based self-help aid (loans and jobs) averaged $3058 ($8275 maximum); and other non-need-based awards and non-need-based scholarships averaged $2459 ($36,938 maximum). 57% of undergraduates work part time. Average annual earnings from campus work are $1450. The average financial indebtedness of the 2005 graduate was $13,926. Oberlin is a member of CSS. The CSS/Profile or FAFSA and the college's own financial statement are required. The deadline for filing freshman financial aid applications for fall entry is February 15.

International Students: There are 199 international students enrolled. The school actively recruits these students. They must score satisfactorily on the written TOEFL.

Computers: All students may access the system. There are no time limits and no fees.

Graduates: From July 1, 2004 to June 30, 2005, 564 bachelor's degrees were awarded. The most popular majors were English (12%), politics (9%), and biology (8%). In an average class, 1% graduate in 3 years or less, 67% graduate in 4 years or less, 79% graduate in 5 years or less, and 81% graduate in 6 years or less. 18 companies recruited on campus in 2004-2005. Of the 2004 graduating class, 20% were enrolled in graduate school within 6 months of graduation and 77% were employed.

Admissions Contact: Debra Chermonte, Dean of Admissions and Financial Aid. E-mail: *college.admissions@oberlin.edu*
Web: *www.oberlin.edu*

OHIO DOMINICAN UNIVERSITY　　C-3
Columbus, OH 43219　　　　　(614) 251-4500
(800) 955-OHIO; Fax: (614) 252-0776

Full-time: 687 men, 1015 women	**Faculty:** 66; IIB, --$
Part-time: 263 men, 594 women	**Ph.D.s:** 86%
Graduate: 184 men, 199 women	**Student/Faculty:** 26 to 1
Year: semesters, summer session	**Tuition:** $19,454
Application Deadline: open	**Room & Board:** $6500
Freshman Class: 1902 applied, 1374 accepted, 381 enrolled	
SAT or ACT: required	**COMPETITIVE**

Ohio Dominican University, founded in 1911 by the Dominican Sisters of St. Mary of the Springs, is a private liberal arts university affiliated with the Roman Catholic Church. There are 2 undergraduate schools and 1 graduate school. The library contains 105,500 volumes, 9882 microform items, and 4284 audio/video tapes/CDs/DVDs, and subscribes to 588 periodicals including electronic. Computerized library services include the card catalog, interlibrary loans, database searching, and Internet access. Special learning facilities include a learning resource center, art gallery, and radio station. The 68-acre campus is in an urban area 5 miles from downtown Columbus. Including any residence halls, there are 9 buildings.

Student Life: 97% of undergraduates are from Ohio. Students are from 16 states, 9 foreign countries, and Canada. 77% are from public schools. 76% are white; 21% African American. 41% are Protestant; 28% Catholic. The average age of freshmen is 18; all undergraduates, 26. 38% do not continue beyond their first year; 48% remain to graduate.

Housing: 780 students can be accommodated in college housing, which includes single-sex and coed dorms and off-campus apartments. In addition, there are honors houses. On-campus housing is available on a first-come, first-served basis. 74% of students commute. Alcohol is not permitted. All students may keep cars.

Activities: There are no fraternities or sororities. There are 32 groups on campus, including academic Association of Commuters, art, association of resident students, board games, cheerleading, choir, dance, drama, drill team, English circle, ethnic, honors, international, literary magazine, newspaper, Palette Club, pep band, political, professional, radio and TV, religious, social, social service, and student government. Popular campus events include Black History Week, International Student Week, and ODU Day in the Spring.

Sports: There are 7 intercollegiate sports for men and 7 for women, and 6 intramural sports for men and 6 for women. Facilities include an athletic center, a gym, a baseball and softball field, a soccer field, and tennis courts.

Disabled Students: 90% of the campus is accessible. Wheelchair ramps, elevators, special parking, specially equipped rest rooms, and special class scheduling are available.

Services: Counseling and information services are available, as is tutoring in most subjects. There is remedial math, reading, and writing. The Academic Center is a support unit designed to help all students meet their academic commitment and improve their learning skills. The staff offers workshops in study-related topics, provides professional and peer tutoring in a variety of subjects, and counsels students and faculty on learning and study problems.

Campus Safety and Security: Measures include 24-hour foot and vehicle patrol, self-defense education, security escort services, and shuttle buses. There are informal discussions, pamphlets/posters/films, emergency telephones, and lighted pathways/sidewalks.

Programs of Study: ODU confers B.A., B.S., and B.S.Ed. degrees. Associate and master's degrees are also awarded. Bachelor's degrees are awarded in BIOLOGICAL SCIENCE (biology/biological science), BUSINESS (accounting, banking and finance, business administration and management, international business management, management information systems, and sports management), COMMUNICATIONS AND THE ARTS (art, communications, English, graphic design, public relations, and technical and business writing), COMPUTER AND PHYSICAL SCIENCE (chemistry, computer science, information sciences and systems, and mathematics), EDUCATION (early childhood, middle school, and special), SOCIAL SCIENCE (criminal justice, economics, history, interdisciplinary studies, liberal arts/general studies, philosophy, political science/government, psychology, social work, and sociology). Business, education, and psychology are the largest.

Required: Core curriculum requirements include 4 semester credits each in philosophy and theology, plus 4 additional credits in either, 8 each in humanities, English, and behavioral science, 4 each in literature, math, and science, 4 or 8 in language, and 1 in phys ed. All students beyond the freshman year must maintain a GPA of 2.0. Students must complete 124 semester credits. The total hours in the major is set by individual departments.

Special: Students may cross-register with members of the Higher Education Council of Columbus Consortium, study abroad in various countries, and participate in a Washington semester. Internships are required in some majors. ODU offers dual majors and pass/fail options in some courses. Nondegree study and credit for life, military, and work experience are available. The Weekend College Program allows students to attend classes scheduled every other weekend. There are 4 national honor societies and a freshman honors program.

Faculty/Classroom: 49% of faculty are male; 51%, female. All teach undergraduates. The average class size in an introductory lecture is 20 and in a regular course, 20.

Admissions: 72% of the 2005-2006 applicants were accepted. The ACT scores for the 2005-2006 freshman class were: 49% below 21, 35% between 21 and 23, 11% between 24 and 26, 4% between 27 and 28, and 1% above 28.

Requirements: The SAT or ACT is required. In addition, candidates for admission should have completed 4 units of English and 3 units each of a foreign language, math, science, and social studies. The freshman applicant is required to submit a completed application, transcripts of secondary courses and grades, and official scores from standardized testing (ACT or SAT). An essay and an interview (in-state applicants) are required. A GPA of 2.0 is required. AP and CLEP credits are accepted.

Procedure: Freshmen are admitted to all sessions. There are deferred admissions and enrolling admissions plans. Application deadlines are open. Application fee is $25.

Transfer: 140 transfer students enrolled in 2004-2005. A completed application, an interview, and transcripts of all college work are required of transfer applicants. 32 of 124 credits required for the bachelor's degree must be completed at ODU.

Visiting: There are regularly scheduled orientations for prospective students, including an August orientation for fall entry and a January orientation for the second semester. Individual appointments can be arranged. There are guides for informal visits and visitors may sit in on classes and stay overnight. To schedule a visit, contact Nicole Evans, Acting Director of Admissions.

Financial Aid: In a recent year, 97% of all full-time freshmen and 67% of continuing full-time students received some form of financial aid. 80% of full-time freshmen and 78% of continuing full-time students received need-based aid. The average freshman award was $18,242. 93% of undergraduates worked part time. Average annual earnings from campus work were $2000. The FAFSA is required. The priority date for freshman financial aid applications for fall entry is April 1.

International Students: There are 9 international students enrolled. The school actively recruits these students. They must score satisfactorily on the written TOEFL or on the electronic version.

Computers: All students may access the system. There are no time limits and no fees. It is strongly recommended that all students have a personal computer.

Graduates: From July 1, 2004 to June 30, 2005, 377 bachelor's degrees were awarded. The most popular majors were business (39%), early childhood education (14%), and criminal justice (4%). In an average class, 1% graduate in 3 years or less, 36% graduate in 4 years or less, 47% graduate in 5 years or less, and 48% graduate in 6 years or less. 15 companies recruited on campus in 2004-2005.

Admissions Contact: Nicole Evans, Acting Director of Admissions. E-mail: *admissions@ohiodominican.edu* Web: *www.ohiodominican.edu*

OHIO NORTHERN UNIVERSITY — B-2
Ada, OH 45810

(419) 772-2260
(800) 408-4668; Fax: (419) 772-2313

Full-time: 1185 men, 1050 women	**Faculty:** 169; IIB, +$
Part-time: 35 men, 35 women	**Ph.D.s:** 82%
Graduate: 410 men, 570 women	**Student/Faculty:** 13 to 1
Year: quarters, summer session	**Tuition:** $22,500
Application Deadline: see profile	**Room & Board:** $6000
Freshman Class: n/av	
SAT or ACT: required	**VERY COMPETITVE**

Ohio Northern University, founded in 1871, is a private institution affiliated with the United Methodist Church. Undergraduate programs are offered in arts and sciences, business administration, engineering, and pharmacy. There are 4 undergraduate schools and 1 graduate school. Figures in the above capsule and profile are aproximate. In addition to regional accreditation, ONU has baccalaureate program accreditation with ABET, ACPE, ACS, CAAHEP, NASM, and NCATE. The 2 libraries contain 250,518 volumes, 72,067 microform items, and 10,815 audio/video tapes/CDs/DVDs, and subscribe to 1038 periodicals including electronic. Computerized library services include the card catalog, interlibrary loans, and database searching. Special learning facilities include a learning resource center, art gallery, radio station, TV station, and pharmacy museum. The 285-acre campus is in a small town about 75 miles south of Toledo. Including any residence halls, there are 39 buildings.

Student Life: 86% of undergraduates are from Ohio. Students are from 42 states, 17 foreign countries, and Canada. 82% are from public schools. 95% are white. 43% are Baptist, Muslim, Lutheran, Presbyterian, United Church of Christ; 26% Catholic; 12% claim no religious affiliation. The average age of freshmen is 18; all undergraduates, 20. 18% do not continue beyond their first year; 66% remain to graduate.

Housing: 1915 students can be accommodated in college housing, which includes single-sex and coed dorms, on-campus apartments, off-campus apartments, fraternity houses, and sorority houses. In addition, there are honors houses and special-interest houses. On-campus housing is guaranteed for all 4 years. 64% of students live on campus; of those, 70% remain on campus on weekends. All students may keep cars.

Activities: 25% of men belong to 8 national fraternities; 22% of women belong to 4 national sororities. There are 170 groups on campus, including art, band, cheerleading, chess, choir, chorale, chorus, computers, dance, debate, drama, drill team, ethnic, honors, international, jazz band, literary magazine, marching band, musical theater, newspaper, orchestra, pep band, political, professional, radio and TV, religious, social, social service, student government, symphony, and yearbook. Popular campus events include Tunes on the Tundra, International Week, and Little Sibs Weekend.

Sports: There are 11 intercollegiate sports for men and 10 for women, and 12 intramural sports for men and 11 for women. Facilities include a 6-lane pool, a wrestling room, weight rooms, indoor/outdoor tennis courts, 3 basketball courts, a football stadium, a training room, bowling lanes, a billiards room, a dance room, a fitness lab, a 200-meter indoor track, an 8-lane, 400-meter outdoor track, 3 racquetball courts, a Nautilus room, and a 2.5-mile jogging/walking path.

Disabled Students: 95% of the campus is accessible. Wheelchair ramps, elevators, special parking, specially equipped rest rooms, special class scheduling, lowered drinking fountains, and lowered telephones are available.

Services: Counseling and information services are available, as is tutoring in most subjects. There is a reader service for the blind and remedial math and writing.

Campus Safety and Security: Measures include 24-hour foot and vehicle patrol, self-defense education, security escort services, and informal discussions. There are pamphlets/posters/films, emergency telephones, and lighted pathways/sidewalks.

Programs of Study: ONU confers B.A., B.S., B.F.A., B.M., B.S.B.A., B.S.C.E., B.S.C.P.E., B.S.E.E., B.S.M.E., B.S.M.T., and B.S.Ph. degrees. Doctoral degrees are also awarded. Bachelor's degrees are awarded in AGRICULTURE (environmental studies), BIOLOGICAL SCIENCE (biochemistry, biology/biological science, and molecular biology), BUSINESS (accounting, business administration and management, business economics, international business management, management science, and sports management), COMMUNICATIONS AND THE ARTS (broadcasting, ceramic art and design, communications, creative writing, dramatic arts, English, fine arts, French, graphic design, journalism, language arts, literature, music, music business management, music performance, music theory and composition, public relations, and Spanish), COMPUTER AND PHYSICAL SCIENCE (chemistry, computer science, mathematics, physics, and statistics), EDUCATION (athletic training, early childhood, health, middle school, music, and physical), ENGINEERING AND ENVIRONMENTAL DESIGN (civil engineering, computer engineering, electrical/electronics engineering, mechanical engineering, and technological management), HEALTH PROFESSIONS (health, medical technology, and pharmacy), SOCIAL SCIENCE (criminal justice, history, international studies, philosophy, political science/government, psychology, religion, social studies, sociology, and youth ministry). Chemistry, engineering, and pharmacy are the strongest academically. Pharmacy, engineering, and biology are the largest.

Required: To graduate, students must complete a minimum of 182 quarter hours, maintain a cumulative GPA of 2.0, and fulfill all departmental/college core requirements. Also, students must submit a formal application for graduation.

Special: Co-op programs are available in civil, electrical, computer, and mechanical engineering and technology, computer science, and math. Students may take internships in pharmacy, engineering, and business and may study abroad in 15 countries. B.A.-B.S. degrees and dual majors are available in arts/engineering, arts/pharmacy, and arts/business. The university also offers pass/fail options and work-study programs. There are 38 national honor societies, a freshman honors program, and 21 departmental honors programs.

Faculty/Classroom: 67% of faculty are male; 33%, female. 90% teach undergraduates. No introductory courses are taught by graduate students. The average class size in an introductory lecture is 29; in a laboratory, 14; and in a regular course, 25.

Requirements: The SAT or ACT is required. In addition, the preparatory program should include 4 years of English, 3 of math, and 2 each of science, social studies, art, history, and music; 2 years of foreign language are recommended. ONU requires applicants to be in the upper 50% of their class. A GPA of 2.5 is required. AP and CLEP credits are accepted. Important factors in the admissions decision are advanced placement or honor courses, leadership record, and extracurricular activities record.

Procedure: Freshmen are admitted to all sessions. Entrance exams should be taken in the spring of the junior year or the fall of the senior year. There are deferred admissions and rolling admissions plans. Check with the school for current application deadlines. Application fee is $30. Notification is sent on a rolling basis. Applications are accepted on-line.

Transfer: Applicants should have a minimum college GPA of 2.0 and submit official transcripts from all the schools they have attended. 45 of 182 credits required for the bachelor's degree must be completed at ONU.

Visiting: There are regularly scheduled orientations for prospective students, including a tour, lunch, and appointments with academics, admissions, and financial aid departments. A meeting with a coach can also be arranged. There are guides for informal visits and visitors may sit in on classes and stay overnight. To schedule a visit, contact the Admissions Office.

Financial Aid: ONU is a member of CSS. The FAFSA and the college's own financial statement are required. Check with the school for current application deadlines.

International Students: The school actively recruits these students. They must score satisfactorily on the written TOEFL or on the electronic version or take the MELAB.

Computers: All students may access the system during building hours and 24 hours a day via modem. There are no time limits and no fees.

Admissions Contact: Karen P. Condeni, VP, Admissions. A video is available. E-mail: *admissions-ug@onu.edu* Web: *www.onu.edu*

OHIO STATE UNIVERSITY SYSTEM

The Ohio State University System, established in 1870, is a land-grant university. It is governed by a board of trustees and publicly funded through the Ohio Board of Regents. The chief administrator is the president. As a comprehensive flagship institution, its mission includes teaching, research, and public service. The main campus is in Columbus, and regional campuses are located in Lima, Mansfield, Marion, and Newark, while the 2-year Agricultural Technical Institute is in Wooster. The undergraduate enrollment of the five 4-year campuses is about 57,000, with some 4,500 faculty members. There are more than 170 baccalaureate, 127 master's, and 96 doctoral degree programs. Profiles of the 4-year campuses are included in this section. For more information, visit *http://www.osu.edu.*

OHIO STATE UNIVERSITY   C-3

Columbus, OH 43210-1200   (614) 292-3980; Fax: (614) 292-4818

Full-time: 17,773 men, 16,044 women	**Faculty:** 2782; I, av$
Part-time: 1871 men, 1723 women	**Ph.D.s:** 99%
Graduate: 4440 men, 5384 women	**Student/Faculty:** 12 to 1
Year: trimesters, summer session	**Tuition:** $8082 ($19,305)
Application Deadline: February 1	**Room & Board:** $7275
Freshman Class: 17,542 applied, 12,863 accepted, 5860 enrolled	
SAT Verbal/Math: 590/610*	**ACT:** 26 **HIGHLY COMPETITIVE**

The Ohio State University, founded in 1870, is a public land-grant institution offering programs in agriculture and natural resources, arts and sciences, business, education, architecture and engineering, nursing, pharmacy, social work, dental hygiene, and human ecology. There are 5 other campuses. There are 14 undergraduate schools and 1 graduate school. In addition to regional accreditation, Ohio State has baccalaureate program accreditation with AACSB, ABET, ACPE, ADA, APTA, ASLA, CAAHEP, CSAB, FIDER, NASAD, NASM, NCATE, NLN, and SAF. The 18 libraries contain 5,809,505 volumes, 5,749,143 microform items, and 54,823 audio/video tapes/CDs/DVDs, and subscribe to 35,561 periodicals including electronic. Computerized library services include the card catalog, interlibrary loans, and database searching. Special learning facilities include a learning resource center, art gallery, planetarium, radio station, TV station, the Museum of Biological Diversity, the John Glenn Institute for Public Service and Public Policy, and the Cartoon Research Library. The 1755-acre campus is in an urban area 2 miles north of downtown Columbus. Including any residence halls, there are 460 buildings.

Student Life: 87% of undergraduates are from Ohio. Students are from 50 states, 81 foreign countries, and Canada. 87% are from public schools. 79% are white. 44% are Protestant; 31% Catholic; 17% claim no religious affiliation. The average age of freshmen is 18; all undergraduates, 21. 10% do not continue beyond their first year; 68% remain to graduate.

Housing: 10,104 students can be accommodated in college housing, which includes coed dorms, on-campus apartments, off-campus apartments, and married-student housing. In addition, there are honors houses, special-interest houses, international houses, language floors, and an alumnae scholarship house. On-campus housing is guaranteed for the freshman year only and is available on a first-come, first-served basis. 76% of students commute. All students may keep cars.

Activities: 6% of men belong to 2 local and 35 national fraternities; 6% of women belong to 2 local and 17 national sororities. There are 750 groups on campus, including art, band, cheerleading, chess, choir, chorale, chorus, computers, dance, debate, drama, drill team, ethnic, film, forensics, gay, honors, international, jazz band, literary magazine, marching band, musical theater, newspaper, opera, orchestra, pep band, photography, political, professional, radio and TV, religious, social, social service, student government, symphony, and yearbook. Popular campus events include United Black World Month, Medieval and Renaissance Festival, and Greek Week.

Sports: There are 18 intercollegiate sports for men and 19 for women, and 48 intramural sports for men and 47 for women. Facilities include a 100,000-seat football stadium, a 17,500-to-21,000-seat multipurpose event center, a 13,000-seat arena, an archery range, a running track, sand volleyball courts, a cricket field, an in-line hockey rink, weight rooms, swimming pools, basketball, volleyball, and racquetball courts, field houses for tennis, volleyball, basketball, and soccer, and baseball and softball fields.

Disabled Students: 85% of the campus is accessible. Wheelchair ramps, elevators, special parking, specially equipped rest rooms, special class scheduling, lowered drinking fountains, lowered telephones, special housing, adaptive transportations, and adaptive technology are available.

Services: Counseling and information services are available, as is tutoring in most subjects. There is a reader service for the blind, and remedial math, reading, and writing.

Campus Safety and Security: Measures include 24-hour foot and vehicle patrol, self-defense education, security escort services, and shuttle buses. There are informal discussions, pamphlets/posters/films, emergency telephones, lighted pathways/sidewalks, crisis action teams, and off-campus patrols in cooperation with the city police.

Programs of Study: Ohio State confers B.A., B.S., B.A.E., B.F.A., B.Mus., and B.Mus.Ed. degrees. Master's and doctoral degrees are also awarded. Bachelor's degrees are awarded in AGRICULTURE (agricultural economics, animal science, fishing and fisheries, forestry and related sciences, natural resource management, and plant science), BIOLOGICAL SCIENCE (biochemistry, biology/biological science, entomology, evolutionary biology, microbiology, nutrition, plant physiology, and zoology), BUSINESS (accounting, banking and finance, business economics, hospitality management services, human resources, insurance and risk management, international business management, management information systems, marketing and distribution, real estate, and transportation management), COMMUNICATIONS AND THE ARTS (Arabic, art, Chinese, classics, communications, dance, English, French, German, Greek, Hebrew, industrial design, Italian, Japanese, jazz, journalism, linguistics, music, music history and appreciation, music performance, music theory and composition, Portuguese, Russian, and Spanish), COMPUTER AND PHYSICAL SCIENCE (actuarial science, astronomy, chemistry, computer science, geology, information sciences and systems, mathematics, and physics), EDUCATION (agricultural, art, dance, environmental, music, and technical), ENGINEERING AND ENVIRONMENTAL DESIGN (aeronautical engineering, architecture, ceramic engineering, chemical engineering, civil engineering, computer engineering, electrical/electronics engineering, engineering physics, environmental science, industrial engineering, interior design, landscape architecture/design, materials engineering, materials science, mechanical engineering, metallurgical engineering, and welding engineering), HEALTH PROFESSIONS (dental hygiene, medical technology, nursing, occupational therapy, physical therapy, radiograph medical technology, respiratory therapy, and speech pathology/audiology), SOCIAL SCIENCE (African American studies, anthropology, clothing and textiles management/production/services, criminology, economics, geography, history, human development, human ecology, industrial and organizational psychology, international studies, Islamic studies, Judaic studies, medieval studies, philosophy, political science/government, psychology, social work, sociology, and women's studies). Engineering, business, and social and behavioral sciences are the largest.

Required: To graduate, students must complete 181 to 220 quarter hours, including 40 to 60 in the major, with a minimum GPA of 2.0. The core curriculum consists of courses in writing skills, quantitative and logical skills, foreign language, the sciences, math, and the arts. Distribution requirements include 5 courses in arts and humanities, 4 to 5 courses in natural science, and 3 in social science.

Special: Students may cross-register with all central Ohio colleges. OSU offers internships, co-op programs, extensive study abroad in about 40 countries, work-study programs, dual and student-designed majors, a general degree, an accelerated degree, credit by exam, nondegree study, and pass/fail options. There are 39 national honor societies, including Phi Beta Kappa, a freshman honors program, and 14 departmental honors programs.

Faculty/Classroom: 66% of faculty are male; 34%, female. 75% teach undergraduates, 98% do research, and 74% do both. Graduate students teach 39% of introductory courses. The average class size in an introductory lecture is 68; in a laboratory, 18; and in a regular course, 23.

Admissions: 73% of the 2005-2006 applicants were accepted. The SAT scores for the 2005-2006 freshman class were: Verbal--11% below 500, 43% between 500 and 599, 39% between 600 and 700, and 8% above 700; Math--7% below 500, 35% between 500 and 599, 46% between 600 and 700, and 12% above 700. The ACT scores were 5% below 21, 19% between 21 and 23, 35% between 24 and 26, 18% between 27 and 28, and 23% above 28. 66% of the current freshmen were in the top fifth of their class; 93% were in the top two fifths. There were 95 National Merit finalists. 240 freshmen graduated first in their class.

Requirements: The SAT or ACT is required. In addition, applicants must complete high school with at least 18 academic credits, including 4 in English, 3 in math, 2 each in foreign language, science, and history or social studies, and 1 in art or music. The GED is accepted. AP and CLEP credits are accepted. Important factors in the admissions decision are advanced placement or honor courses, evidence of special talent, and extracurricular activities record.

Procedure: Freshmen are admitted to all sessions. Entrance exams should be taken by October of the senior year. There is a rolling admissions plan. Applications should be filed by February 1 for fall entry, November 1 for winter entry, February 1 for spring entry, and February 1 for summer entry, along with a $40 fee. Notification is sent on a rolling basis. 134 applicants were on the 2005 waiting list. Applications are accepted on-line.

Transfer: 2916 transfer students enrolled in 2004-2005. High school graduates with 45 hours of college credit and a minimum GPA of 2.0 are admitted for transfer. Those with fewer than 45 hours apply on a competitive basis. 45 of 181 to 220 credits required for the bachelor's degree must be completed at Ohio State.

Visiting: There are regularly scheduled orientations for prospective students, including campus tours, placement tests, course scheduling, and special sessions designed for parents. There are guides for informal visits and visitors may sit in on classes and stay overnight. To schedule a visit, contact the Student Visitor Center.

Financial Aid: In 2005-2006, 88% of all full-time freshmen and 78% of continuing full-time students received some form of financial aid. 51% of full-time freshmen and 50% of continuing full-time students received need-based aid. The average freshman award was $11,698. Need-based scholarships or need-based grants averaged $3764 ($23,194 maximum); need-based self-help aid (loans and jobs) averaged $3571 ($10,525 maximum); non-need-based athletic scholarships averaged $15,352 ($37,049 maximum); and other non-need-based awards and non-need-based scholarships averaged $8542 ($39,000 maximum). The average financial indebtedness of the 2005 graduate was $17,821. Ohio State is a member of CSS. The FAFSA is required. The deadline for filing freshman financial aid applications for fall entry is March 1.

International Students: There were 1289 international students enrolled in a recent year. The school actively recruits these students. They must achieve a satisfactory score on the TOEFL and also take the SAT or the ACT.

Computers: Students may connect to the wireless system at student gathering places all over campus. 4000 Internet-connected computers are available in public student computing centers, libraries, and college computing labs throughout campus. Most centers, libraries, and labs also provide laptop hookup Internet access stations. All residence hall students have Internet access in their rooms. All students may access the system 24 hours a day. There are no time limits and no fees. It is strongly recommended that all students have a personal computer. Students in the Fisher College of Business Executive MBA program and students in the Department of Industrial, Interior, and Visual Communication Design within the College of Arts must have a personal computer.

Graduates: From July 1, 2004 to June 30, 2005, 8508 bachelor's degrees were awarded. The most popular majors were psychology (6%), communication (4%), and English (4%). In an average class, 1% graduate in 3 years or less, 35% graduate in 4 years or less, 63% graduate in 5 years or less, and 68% graduate in 6 years or less.

Admissions Contact: Undergraduate Admissions and First Year Experience. A video is available. E-mail: *askabuckeye@osu.edu* Web: *www.osu.edu*

OHIO STATE UNIVERSITY AT LIMA   B-2

Lima, OH 45804   (419) 995-8396

Full-time: 550 men, 790 women	**Faculty:** 56; IIB, av$
Part-time: 435 men, 570 women	**Ph.D.s:** 84%
Graduate: 15 men, 75 women	**Student/Faculty:** 15 to 1
Year: quarters, summer session	**Tuition:** $4500 ($14,500)
Application Deadline: see profile	**Room & Board:** n/app
Freshman Class: n/av	
ACT: required	**NONCOMPETITIVE**

Ohio State University at Lima, founded in 1960, is a regional commuter campus in the Ohio State University system. At Lima, students may earn a bachelor's degree in education, English, and psychology as well as 1 to 3 years of credit toward any degree conferred by OSU. The student may finish the degree at the Columbus campus or transfer to another institution. There are 19 undergraduate and 2 graduate schools. Figures in the above capsule and profile are approximate. In addition to regional accreditation, Ohio State Lima has baccalaureate program accreditation with NCATE. The library contains 77,984 volumes, 9040 microform items, and 7715 audio/video tapes/CDs/DVDs, and subscribes to 517 periodicals including electronic. Computerized library services include the card catalog, interlibrary loans, and database searching. Special learning facilities include a learning resource center, a greenhouse, and a geology museum. The 565-acre campus is in a suburban area 3 miles east of Lima. There are 7 buildings.

Student Life: 95% are from public schools. 94% are white. 27% are Protestant; 25% Catholic; 10% claim no religious affiliation. The average age of freshmen is 19; all undergraduates, 24. 35% do not continue beyond their first year; 50% remain to graduate.

Housing: There are no residence halls. Alcohol is not permitted. All students may keep cars.

Activities: There are no fraternities or sororities. There are 24 groups on campus, including cheerleading, chess, chorus, computers, drama, ethnic, honors, musical theater, political, religious, social, and student government. Popular campus events include May Week, Back to School Weiner Roast, and movies.

Sports: There are 3 intramural sports for men and 3 for women. Facilities include a gym and a weight room.

Disabled Students: All of the campus is accessible. Wheelchair ramps, elevators, special parking, specially equipped rest rooms, special class scheduling, and lowered drinking fountains are available.

Services: Counseling and information services are available, as is tutoring in most subjects. There is a reader service for the blind, and remedial math, reading, and writing. Developmental education, taped textbooks, oral testing, test readers and scribes, tape recorders, note takers, and a learning disabilities coordinator/counselor are also available.

Campus Safety and Security: Measures include 24-hour foot and vehicle patrol, self-defense education, security escort services, and informal discussions. There are pamphlets/posters/films, emergency telephones, and lighted pathways/sidewalks.

Programs of Study: Ohio State Lima confers B.A., B.S., and B.S.Ed. degrees. Associate and master's degrees are also awarded. Bachelor's degrees are awarded in BUSINESS (business administration and management and hospitality management services), COMMUNICATIONS AND THE ARTS (English), EDUCATION (education), SOCIAL SCIENCE (family/consumer resource management, history, and psychology). Education is the strongest academically.

Required: To graduate, all students must complete 181 to 220 quarter hours, with a minimum GPA of 2.0, and fulfill the general education curriculum requirements.

Special: Students may cross-register with Rhodes State College. Work-study programs, nondegree study, pass/fail options, and credit for life, military, or work experience are available. There is 1 national honor society, a freshman honors program, and 4 departmental honors programs.

Faculty/Classroom: 60% of faculty are male; 40%, female. All teach undergraduates and 50% do research. No introductory courses are taught by graduate students. The average class size in an introductory lecture is 35; in a laboratory, 25; and in a regular course, 20.

Requirements: The ACT is required. In addition, candidates should be high school graduates with 4 years of English, 3 of math, 2 each of foreign language, science, and social studies, 1 of visual or performing arts, and 2 additional years of any of the above subjects. AP and CLEP credits are accepted.

Procedure: Freshmen are admitted to all sessions. Entrance exams should be taken in the spring of the junior year or early fall of the senior year. There is a rolling admissions plan. Check with the school for current deadlines. Application fee is 40. The college accepts all in-state residents. Notification is sent on a rolling basis.

Transfer: An overall GPA of 2.0 on all previous college work is required of applicants. 45 of 181 credits required for the bachelor's degree must be completed at Ohio State Lima.

Visiting: There are regularly scheduled orientations for prospective students. There are guides for informal visits and visitors may sit in on classes. To schedule a visit, contact the Admissions Office.

Financial Aid: In a recent year, 56% of all full-time freshmen and 58% of continuing full-time students received some form of financial aid. 45% of full-time freshmen and 50% of continuing full-time students received need-based aid. The average freshman award was $3160. Need-based scholarships or need-based grants averaged $450 ($4050 maximum); need-based self-help aid (loans and jobs) averaged $2625 ($10,000 maximum); and other non-need-based awards and non-need-based scholarships averaged $450 ($1500 maximum). 95% of undergraduates worked part time. Average annual earnings from campus work were $2000. The average financial indebtedness of a recent graduate was $12,000. The FAFSA is required. Check with the school for current application deadlines.

International Students: They must score satisfactorily on the written TOEFL and also take the ACT.

Computers: All students may access the system. There are no time limits and no fees.

Admissions Contact: Admissions Office.
Web: *www.lima.ohio-state.edu*

OHIO STATE UNIVERSITY AT MANSFIELD   C-2
Mansfield, OH 44906   (419) 755-4226

Full-time: 330 men, 450 women	Faculty: 42; IIB, av$
Part-time: 150 men, 300 women	Ph.D.s: 95%
Graduate: 20 men, 95 women	Student/Faculty: 19 to 1
Year: quarters, summer session	Tuition: $3700 ($12,500)
Application Deadline: open	Room & Board: n/app
Freshman Class: n/av	
SAT or ACT: required	NONCOMPETITIVE

Ohio State University at Mansfield, founded in 1958, is a regional commuter campus of the Ohio State University system. At Mansfield, students may earn an undergraduate degree in elementary education. Figures given in the above capsule and in this profile are approximate. There are 19 undergraduate schools and 1 graduate school. In addition to regional accreditation, OSU Mansfield has baccalaureate program accreditation with NCATE. The library contains 38,874 volumes, 17,559 microform items, and 2155 audio/video tapes/CDs/DVDs, and subscribes to 410 periodicals including electronic. Special learning facilities include a learning resource center, art gallery, radio station, and TV station. The 600-acre campus is in a suburban area 2 miles from Mansfield. There are 7 buildings.

Student Life: 91% are white. The average age of freshmen is 19; all undergraduates, 24.

Housing: There are no residence halls. All of students commute. Alcohol is not permitted.

Activities: There are no fraternities or sororities. There are 50 groups on campus, including chorale, drama, ethnic, film, musical theater, newspaper, radio and TV, religious, social, social service, student ambassadors, and student government. Popular campus events include May Day and Buckeye Week.

Sports: There are 12 intramural sports for men and 12 for women. Facilities include a gym and a weight room.

Disabled Students: All of the campus is accessible. Wheelchair ramps, elevators, special parking, specially equipped rest rooms, special class scheduling, lowered drinking fountains, and lowered telephones are available.

Services: Counseling and information services are available, as is tutoring in most subjects. There is a reader service for the blind, and remedial math, reading, and writing. Writing and math labs are provided. Books on tape, test readers and scribes, and priority scheduling are available.

Campus Safety and Security: Measures include 24-hour foot and vehicle patrol, self-defense education, security escort services, and informal discussions. There are pamphlets/posters/films, emergency telephones, and lighted pathways/sidewalks.

Programs of Study: OSU Mansfield confers the B.S. in Elem.Ed. degree. Associate degrees are also awarded. Bachelor's degrees are awarded in EDUCATION (elementary).

Required: To graduate, all students must complete 181 to 220 quarter hours, with a minimum GPA of 2.0. General education curriculum requirements must be met.

Special: OSU Mansfield offers co-op programs, study abroad, internships, a general studies degree (no major), nondegree study, pass/fail options, and work-study programs. There are 3 national honor societies and a freshman honors program.

Faculty/Classroom: 92% teach undergraduates.

Requirements: The SAT or ACT is required. The GED is accepted. OSU Mansfield follows an open admissions policy. AP and CLEP credits are accepted.

Procedure: Freshmen are admitted to all sessions. There are early admissions and deferred admissions plans. Application deadlines are open.

Transfer: Applicants must present a minimum 2.0 GPA on previous university course work. 45 of 181 credits required for the bachelor's degree must be completed at OSU Mansfield.

Visiting: There are regularly scheduled orientations for prospective students. There are guides for informal visits and visitors may sit in on classes. To schedule a visit, contact Henry Thomas, Coordinator of Admissions.

Financial Aid: OSU Mansfield is a member of CSS. The FAFSA is required. Check with the school for current application deadlines.

International Students: They must score satisfactorily on the written TOEFL.

Computers: All students may access the system. There are no time limits and no fees.

Admissions Contact: Henry Thomas, Coordinator of Admissions.

OHIO STATE UNIVERSITY AT MARION   C-3
Marion, OH 43302   (614) 389-6786, ext. 6337; Fax: (614) 292-5817

Full-time and part time: 1365 men and women	Faculty: 26; IIB, +$
	Ph.D.s: 94%
Graduate: n/av	Student/Faculty: 18 to 1
Year: quarters, summer session	Tuition: $4850 ($12,300)
Application Deadline: open	Room & Board: n/app
Freshman Class: n/av	
SAT or ACT: recommended	NONCOMPETITIVE

Ohio State University at Marion, founded in 1957, is a commuter campus of the Ohio State University system. At Marion, students may earn a bachelor's degree in elementary education, English, accounting, business management, and psychology as well as 1 to 3 years of credit applicable to any other degree, including more than 170 academic programs, conferred by OSU, provided the program is completed at the main campus in Columbus. Figures in the above capsule and in this profile are approximate. In addition to regional accreditation, OSU Marion has baccalaureate program accreditation with NCATE. The library contains 44,000 volumes, 2906 microform items, and 8000 audio/video tapes/CDs/DVDs, and subscribes to 322 periodicals including electronic. Computerized library services include the card catalog, interlibrary loans, and database searching. Special learning facilities include a learning resource center, art gallery, natural reconstructed prairie site, greenhouse, psychology lab, and early childhood education center. The 180-acre campus is in a rural area 45 miles north of Columbus. There are 6 buildings.

Student Life: 99% of undergraduates are from Ohio. Students are from 3 states. 98% are from public schools. 86% are white. The average age of freshmen is 20; all undergraduates, 24.

Housing: There are no residence halls. All of students commute. Alcohol is not permitted. All students may keep cars.

Activities: There are no fraternities or sororities. There are 8 groups on campus, including art, choir, chorale, chorus, dance, drama, ethnic, honors, international, jazz band, literary magazine, musical theater, newspaper, political, professional, religious, social, social service, and student government. Popular campus events include Buckeye Week, May Day, and cultural arts events.

Sports: There are 4 intercollegiate sports for men and 3 for women, and 5 intramural sports for men and 5 for women. Facilities include a 740-seat gym, an outdoor fitness court, a weight room, a game room, a rock climbing wall, volleyball courts, and an exercise room.

Disabled Students: All of the campus is accessible. Wheelchair ramps, elevators, special parking, specially equipped rest rooms, lowered drinking fountains, and lowered telephones are available.

Services: Counseling and information services are available, as is tutoring in most subjects. There is remedial math, reading, and writing.

Campus Safety and Security: Measures include self-defense education, informal discussions, pamphlets/posters/films, and emergency telephones. There are lighted pathways/sidewalks.

Programs of Study: OSU Marion confers B.A., B.S., and B.S.Ed. degrees. Associate and master's degrees are also awarded. Bachelor's degrees are awarded in BUSINESS (accounting), COMMUNICATIONS AND THE ARTS (English), EDUCATION (elementary), SOCIAL SCIENCE (psychology). Elementary education and psychology are the strongest academically. Elementary education, psychology, and English are the largest.

Required: Between 181 and 220 credit hours are needed for graduation. Students must complete general education curriculum requirements and maintain a 2.0 GPA.

Special: OSU Marion offers cross-registration with Ohio State University Columbus, various co-op and work-study programs, nondegree study in continuing education, and pass/fail options. There is a freshman honors program.

Faculty/Classroom: 70% of faculty are male; 30%, female. All both teach and do research. The average class size in an introductory lecture is 18; in a laboratory, 24; and in a regular course, 25.

Requirements: The SAT or ACT is recommended. OSU Marion follows an open admissions policy for in-state students. Applicants should be high school graduates with 4 units of English, 3 of math, 2 each of foreign language, history or social studies, and science, and 1 of art or music. AP and CLEP credits are accepted.

Procedure: Freshmen are admitted to all sessions. Entrance exams should be taken before fall of the senior year in high school. There is a rolling admissions plan. Application deadlines are open. Applications are accepted on-line.

Transfer: A GPA of 2.0 is required. 45 of 181 credits required for the bachelor's degree must be completed at OSU Marion.

Visiting: There are regularly scheduled orientations for prospective students. There are guides for informal visits and visitors may sit in on classes. To schedule a visit, contact the Admissions Office.

Financial Aid: The FAFSA is required. Check with the school for current application deadlines.

International Students: They must score satisfactorily on the written TOEFL.

Computers: All students may access the system. There are no time limits and no fees. It is strongly recommended that all students have a personal computer.

Admissions Contact: Mathieu Moreau, Director of Admissions.
E-mail: *moreau.1@osu.edu* Web: *www.marion.ohio-state.edu*

OHIO STATE UNIVERSITY AT NEWARK   C-3

Newark, OH 43055 (740) 366-9333
(800) 9NEWARK; Fax: (740) 366-9460

Full-time:Undergraduate 2088 men and women	Faculty: IIB, av$
	Ph.Ds: 88%
Graduate: 95 men and women	Student/Faculty: n/av
Year: quarters, summer session	Tuition: $5310 ($11,223)
Application Deadline: July 1	Room & Board: $6037
Freshman Class: 1512 applied, 1501 accepted, 759 enrolled	
SAT Verbal/Math: 490/500*	ACT: 20 NONCOMPETITIVE

The Ohio State University at Newark, founded in 1957, is a regional public commuter campus of the Ohio State University system. At Newark, students may earn a bachelor's degree in elementary education, psychology, history, or English as well as 1 to 3 years of credit applicable to any other degree, including 219 academic programs, conferred by OSU, provided the program is completed at the main campus in Columbus. The library contains 50,008 volumes, 17,465 microform items, and 3649 audio/video tapes/CDs/DVDs, and subscribes to 427 periodicals including electronic. Computerized library services include the card catalog, interlibrary loans, database searching, and Internet access. Special learning facilities include a learning resource center and art gallery. The

150-acre campus is in a suburban area 40 miles east of Columbus. Including any residence halls, there are 5 buildings.

Student Life: 99% of undergraduates are from Ohio. Students are from 3 states and 1 foreign country. 98% are from public schools. 92% are white. The average age of freshmen is 19; all undergraduates, 24. 65% do not continue beyond their first year.

Housing: 140 students can be accommodated in college housing, which includes coed on-campus apartments. On-campus housing is available on a first-come, first-served basis. 95% of students commute. Alcohol is not permitted. All students may keep cars.

Activities: There are no fraternities or sororities. There are 25 groups on campus, including cheerleading, choir, chorale, chorus, circle K, drama, ethnic, ebonye horizons, gay, honors, professional, religious, social, social service, student government and young democrats. Popular campus events include Welcome Week, Spring Fling, and Community Service Programs.

Sports: There are 3 intercollegiate sports for men and 3 for women, and 7 intramural sports for men and 7 for women. Facilities include 2 weight rooms, a double gym, and a vita course.

Disabled Students: All of the campus is accessible. Wheelchair ramps, elevators, special parking, specially equipped rest rooms, special class scheduling, lowered drinking fountains, and lowered telephones are available.

Services: Counseling and information services are available, as is tutoring in every subject. There is a reader service for the blind and remedial math and writing. Books on tape, extended test time, readers, scribes, word processing assistance, and loans of specialized equipment are available.

Campus Safety and Security: Measures include 24-hour foot and vehicle patrol, self-defense education, security escort services, and informal discussions. There are pamphlets/posters/films and emergency telephones.

Programs of Study: OSU Newark confers B.A. and B.S.Ed. degrees. Associate and master's degrees are also awarded. Bachelor's degrees are awarded in BUSINESS (business administration and management), COMMUNICATIONS AND THE ARTS (English), EDUCATION (elementary), SOCIAL SCIENCE (history and psychology). Elementary education, English, and psychology are the strongest academically. Elementary education is the largest.

Required: Between 181 and 220 credit hours are necessary for graduation, as is a GPA of 2.0. General education requirements include courses in English, math, natural sciences, social sciences, humanities, and foreign language.

Special: Co-op programs and internships are available in some majors, and study abroad is available in some departments. Cross-registration is possible with Central Ohio Technical College and HECC member schools, and there is work-study with Ohio State. B.A.-B.S. degrees are offered in elementary education, general business, English, history, and psychology. Dual and student-designed majors and nondegree study are possible, and pass/fail options are available. There is a freshman honors program.

Faculty/Classroom: 60% of faculty are male; 40%, female. All teach undergraduates. Graduate students teach 10% of introductory courses. The average class size in an introductory lecture is 35; in a laboratory, 24; and in a regular course, 24.

Admissions: 99% of the 2005-2006 applicants were accepted. The SAT scores for the 2005-2006 freshman class were: Verbal--54% below 500, 35% between 500 and 599, and 11% between 600 and 700; Math--46% below 500, 41% between 500 and 599, and 12% between 600 and 700. The ACT scores were 54% below 21, 29% between 21 and 23, 13% between 24 and 26, 3% between 27 and 28, and 1% above 28. 14% of the current freshmen were in the top fifth of their class; 39% were in the top two fifths. 4 freshmen graduated first in their class.

Requirements: The SAT or ACT is recommended. For applicants who graduated from high school within the previous 3 years. Candidates should be high school graduates with 4 units of English, 3 of math, 2 each of science, foreign language, and history or social studies, and 1 of visual or performing arts. OSU Newark follows an open admissions policy for Ohio resident applicants. AP and CLEP credits are accepted.

Procedure: Freshmen are admitted to all sessions. Entrance exams should be taken in the junior year of high school. There is a rolling admissions plan. Applications should be filed by July 1 for fall entry, December 1 for winter entry, March 1 for spring entry, and June 1 for summer entry, along with a $40 fee. The college accepts all in-state residents. Notification is sent on a rolling basis. Applications are accepted on-line.

Transfer: 140 transfer students enrolled in 2004-2005. A GPA of 2.0 is required. 45 of 181 to 220 credits required for the bachelor's degree must be completed at OSU Newark.

Visiting: There are regularly scheduled orientations for prospective students, including a campus tour, meeting with faculty, financial aid, and student services, a placement test, and class scheduling. There are guides for informal visits and visitors may sit in on classes and stay overnight. To schedule a visit, contact Admissions at (740) 366-9333 or *bruner.4@osu.edu*.

Financial Aid: In a recent year, 75% of all full-time freshmen and 62% of continuing full-time students received some form of financial aid. 67% of full-time freshmen and 60% of continuing full-time students received need-based aid. The average freshman award was $11,000, with need-based scholarships or need-based grants $3000 ($9000 maximum) from need-based self-help aid (loans and jobs) $7000 ($23,000 maximum) from and $1000 ($4000) from other non-need-based awards and non-need-based scholarships. 7% of undergraduates work part time. Average annual earnings from campus work are $1250. The average financial indebtedness of a recent year's graduate was $12,250. The FAFSA is required. The priority date for freshman financial aid applications for fall entry is December 15. The deadline for filing freshman financial aid applications for fall entry is April 1.

International Students: They must achieve a satisfactory score on the TOEFL or take the MELAB.

Computers: All students may access the system. There are no time limits and no fees.

Graduates: In a recent year, 125 bachelor's degrees were awarded. The most popular majors were elementary education (50%), arts and sciences (40%), and business (10%). Of a recent year graduating class, 24% were enrolled in graduate school within 6 months of graduation and 97% were employed.

Admissions Contact: Ann Donahue, Director of Enrollment. A video is available. E-mail: *donahue.5@osu.edu* Web: *http://newark.osu.edu*

OHIO UNIVERSITY   D-4

Athens, OH 45701-2979   **(740) 593-4100; Fax: (740) 593-0560**

Full-time: 7682 men, 8408 women	**Faculty:** 920; I, av$
Part-time: 459 men, 642 women	**Ph.D.s:** 88%
Graduate: 1398 men, 1378 women	**Student/Faculty:** 17 to 1
Year: quarters, summer session	**Tuition:** $8235 ($17,199)
Application Deadline: February 1	**Room & Board:** $7686
Freshman Class: 12,367 applied, 11,027 accepted, 4165 enrolled	
SAT Verbal/Math: 540/540*	**ACT:** 23 **COMPETITIVE**

Ohio University, founded in 1804, is a public university offering programs in liberal and fine arts, aviation, business, communication, engineering, health science, osteopathic medicine, professional training, sciences, and teacher preparation. There are 9 undergraduate and 8 graduate schools. In addition to regional accreditation, Ohio has baccalaureate program accreditation with AACSB, ABET, ACEJMC, ADA, AHEA, CSWE, FIDER, NASAD, NASM, NCATE, and NLN. The 9 libraries contain 2,550,511 volumes, 3,197,485 microform items, and 86,574 audio/video tapes/CDs/DVDs, and subscribe to 25,557 periodicals including electronic. Computerized library services include the card catalog, interlibrary loans, database searching, Internet access, and laptop Internet portals. Special learning facilities include a learning resource center, art gallery, radio station, TV station, quarterly magazine, accelerator lab, and hearing and speech clinic. The 1700-acre campus is in a small town 75 miles southeast of Columbus. Including any residence halls, there are 201 buildings.

Student Life: 92% of undergraduates are from Ohio. Others are from 50 states, 104 foreign countries, and Canada. 86% are from public schools. 92% are white. 50% are Protestant; 30% Catholic; 9% claim no religious affiliation. The average age of freshmen is 19; all undergraduates, 21. 19% do not continue beyond their first year; 70% remain to graduate.

Housing: 7825 students can be accommodated in college housing, which includes single-sex and coed dorms, on-campus apartments, married-student housing, fraternity houses, and sorority houses. In addition, there are honors houses, language houses, special-interest houses, international houses, quiet halls, and engineering, business, and communication halls. On-campus housing is guaranteed for all 4 years. 55% of students commute. Alcohol is not permitted. Upperclassmen may keep cars.

Activities: 12% of men belong to 18 local and 20 national fraternities; 13% of women belong to 13 local and 12 national sororities. There are 333 groups on campus, including art, band, cheerleading, chess, choir, chorale, chorus, computers, dance, drama, ethnic, film, forensics, gay, honors, international, jazz band, literary magazine, marching band, musical theater, newspaper, opera, orchestra, pep band, photography, political, professional, radio and TV, religious, social, social service, student government, and symphony. Popular campus events include International Street Fair and Communication Week.

Sports: There are 9 intercollegiate sports for men and 12 for women, and 48 intramural sports for men and 48 for women. Facilities include a recreation center, a football stadium, a basketball and convocation center, an aquatic center, an ice rink, tennis courts, a golf course, an intramural gym, a running track, a fitness and aerobics center, baseball, softball, and soccer fields, and an artificial turf field with track.

Disabled Students: 82% of the campus is accessible. Wheelchair ramps, elevators, special parking, specially equipped rest rooms, special class scheduling, lowered drinking fountains, and lowered telephones are available.

Services: Counseling and information services are available, as is tutoring in most subjects. There is a reader service for the blind, and remedial math, reading, and writing.

Campus Safety and Security: Measures include 24-hour foot and vehicle patrol, self-defense education, security escort services, and pamphlets/posters/films. There are emergency telephones and lighted pathways/sidewalks.

Programs of Study: Ohio confers B.A., B.S., B.B.A., B.C.J., B.F.A., B.Mus., B.S.A., B.S.A.S., B.S.A.T., B.S.C., B.S.C.E., B.S.C.S., B.S.Ch.E., B.S.Ed., B.S.E.E., B.S.E.H., B.S.H., B.S.H.C.S., B.S.H.L.S., B.S.I.H., B.S.I.S.E., B.S.I.T., B.S.J., B.S.M.E., B.S.N., B.S.P.E., B.S.R.S., B.S.S., B.S.S.P.S., and B.S.V.C. degrees. Associate, master's, and doctoral degrees are also awarded. Bachelor's degrees are awarded in AGRICULTURE (plant science), BIOLOGICAL SCIENCE (biochemistry, biology/biological science, cell biology, environmental biology, microbiology, molecular biology, nutrition, and wildlife biology), BUSINESS (accounting, banking and finance, business economics, business law, international business management, management science, marketing management, personnel management, recreation and leisure services, and sports management), COMMUNICATIONS AND THE ARTS (art, art history and appreciation, broadcasting, ceramic art and design, classical languages, communications, creative writing, dance, dramatic arts, English, fiber/textiles/weaving, fine arts, French, German, Greek (classical), journalism, Latin, linguistics, music, music history and appreciation, music theory and composition, painting, printmaking, Russian, Spanish, speech/debate/rhetoric, telecommunications, visual and performing arts, and voice), COMPUTER AND PHYSICAL SCIENCE (actuarial science, applied mathematics, applied physics, astrophysics, atmospheric sciences and meteorology, chemistry, computer science, earth science, geology, geoscience, mathematics, and physics), EDUCATION (art, athletic training, business, early childhood, education of the multiply handicapped, education of the physically handicapped, elementary, middle school, music, science, and secondary), ENGINEERING AND ENVIRONMENTAL DESIGN (airline piloting and navigation, aviation administration/management, cartography, chemical engineering, civil engineering, computer engineering, electrical/electronics engineering, environmental science, industrial engineering, and mechanical engineering), HEALTH PROFESSIONS (community health work, health care administration, nursing, physical therapy, predentistry, premedicine, prepharmacy, recreation therapy, speech pathology/audiology, and sports medicine), SOCIAL SCIENCE (African American studies, African studies, anthropology, classical/ancient civilization, community services, criminal justice, criminology, dietetics, economics, family/consumer resource management, food production/management/services, forensic studies, geography, history, international public service, international relations, international studies, Latin American studies, parks and recreation management, philosophy, political science/government, prelaw, psychology, public administration, social studies, social work, sociology, theological studies, and urban studies). Recreation, journalism, and psychology are the strongest academically and are the largest.

Required: To graduate, students must complete 192 quarter hours, including 45 to 55 in the major, with a minimum GPA of 2.0 in most departments. General education requirements include 2 courses in English composition plus 30 quarter hours in social sciences, natural sciences, humanities, and third world cultures, a minimum of 1 course in math or quantitative skills, and a senior year interdisciplinary course.

Special: The university offers co-op programs in engineering and computer science, internships, study abroad, work-study programs, and an accelerated degree program for students in the Honors Tutorial College. Students may earn a B.A.-B.S. degree in most arts and sciences majors, or a general studies degree. Dual and student-designed majors, nondegree study, limited pass/fail options, and credit for life, military, or work experience are also available. There are 36 national honor societies, including Phi Beta Kappa, and a freshman honors program.

Faculty/Classroom: 63% of faculty are male; 37%, female. All both teach and do research. Graduate students teach 17% of introductory courses. The average class size in an introductory lecture is 37; in a laboratory, 17; and in a regular course, 25.

Admissions: 89% of the 2005-2006 applicants were accepted. The SAT scores for the 2005-2006 freshman class were: Verbal--28% below 500, 46% between 500 and 599, 22% between 600 and 700, and 4% above 700; Math--26% below 500, 45% between 500 and 599, 25% between 600 and 700, and 4% above 700. The ACT scores were 23% below 21, 36% between 21 and 23, 25% between 24 and 26, 9% between 27 and 28, and 8% above 28. 33% of the current freshmen were in the top fifth of their class; 67% were in the top two fifths. There were 8 National Merit finalists. 101 freshmen graduated first in their class.

Requirements: The SAT or ACT is required. In addition, applicants should graduate with 4 units of English, 3 each of math, science, and social studies, 2 of foreign language, and 1 each of history and visual or performing arts. Ohio requires applicants to be in the upper 50% of their class. A GPA of 2.0 is required. AP and CLEP credits are accepted. Important factors in the admissions decision are advanced placement or honor courses, recommendations by school officials, and evidence of special talent.

Procedure: Freshmen are admitted to all sessions. Entrance exams should be taken in spring of the junior year or fall of the senior year. There is a rolling admissions plan. Applications should be filed by February 1 for fall entry, December 1 for winter entry, March 1 for spring entry, and May 1 for summer entry. Notification is sent on a rolling basis.

Transfer: 469 transfer students enrolled in 2004-2005. Transfer students are evaluated individually but must have a GPA of at least 2.5 and 30 quarter hours of transferable college credit. Business and journalism majors usually require a GPA of 3.0 or higher. 48 of 192 credits required for the bachelor's degree must be completed at Ohio.

Visiting: There are regularly scheduled orientations for prospective students, including information sessions and campus tours conducted daily Monday to Saturday. There are guides for informal visits and visitors may sit in on classes. To schedule a visit, contact the Admissions Office.

Financial Aid: In 2005-2006, 83% of all full-time freshmen and 72% of continuing full-time students received some form of financial aid. 46% of full-time freshmen and 44% of continuing full-time students received need-based aid. The average freshman award was $9400. Need-based scholarships or need-based grants averaged $4046 ($8835 maximum); need-based self-help aid (loans and jobs) averaged $2835 ($5500 maximum); non-need-based athletic scholarships averaged $13,074 ($25,453 maximum); and other non-need-based awards and non-need-based scholarships averaged $8809 ($26,577 maximum). 40% of undergraduates work part time. Average annual earnings from campus work are $1464. The FAFSA is required.

International Students: There are 144 international students enrolled. They must take the TOEFL and also take the SAT.

Computers: All students may access the system. There are no time limits and no fees.

Graduates: From July 1, 2004 to June 30, 2005, 4222 bachelor's degrees were awarded. The most popular majors were recreation (6%), journalism (5%), and psychology (4%). In an average class, 44% graduate in 4 years or less, 67% graduate in 5 years or less, and 70% graduate in 6 years or less. 525 companies recruited on campus in 2004-2005. Of the 2004 graduating class, 26% were enrolled in graduate school within 6 months of graduation and 74% were employed.

Admissions Contact: Director of Admissions.
E-mail: *admissions.freshmen@ohiou.edu*

OHIO WESLEYAN UNIVERSITY   C-3
Delaware, OH 43015

(740) 368-3020
(800) 922-8953; Fax: (740) 368-3314

Full-time: 925 men, 1016 women	Faculty: 130; IIB, av$
Part-time: 13 men, 22 women	Ph.Ds: 100%
Graduate: none	Student/Faculty: 15 to 1
Year: semesters, summer session	Tuition: $28,280
Application Deadline: March 1	Room & Board: $7550
Freshman Class: 2929 applied, 2187 accepted, 595 enrolled	
SAT Verbal/Math: 605/610*	ACT: 26 VERY COMPETITIVE+

Ohio Wesleyan University, founded in 1842, is an independent liberal arts institution affiliated with the United Methodist Church. In addition to regional accreditation, Ohio Wesleyan has baccalaureate program accreditation with NASM. The 3 libraries contain 461,758 volumes, 115,768 microform items, and 3407 audio/video tapes/CDs/DVDs, and subscribe to 8125 periodicals including electronic. Computerized library services include the card catalog, interlibrary loans, database searching, Internet access, and laptop Internet portals. Special learning facilities include a learning resource center, art gallery, radio station, TV station, and an astronomical observatory. The 200-acre campus is in a small town 20 miles north of Columbus. Including any residence halls, there are 55 buildings.

Student Life: 59% of undergraduates are from Ohio. Students are from 43 states and 41 foreign countries. 77% are from public schools. 83% are white. 59% are claim no religious affiliation; 24% Protestant; 14% Catholic. The average age of freshmen is 18; all undergraduates, 20. 19% do not continue beyond their first year; 68% remain to graduate.

Housing: 1720 students can be accommodated in college housing, which includes single-sex and coed dorms, on-campus apartments, and fraternity houses. In addition, there are honors houses, language houses, and special-interest houses. Students are invited to submit theme proposals to run a residential house for 10 to 15 studentes. On-campus housing is guaranteed for all 4 years. 85% of students live on campus; of those, 85% remain on campus on weekends. All students may keep cars.

Activities: 39% of men belong to 10 national fraternities; 26% of women belong to 6 national sororities. There are 75 groups on campus, including art, cheerleading, chess, choir, chorale, chorus, computers, dance, drama, ethnic, gay, honors, international, jazz band, literary magazine, newspaper, opera, orchestra, pep band, political, professional, radio and TV, religious, social, social service, student government, symphony, and yearbook. Popular campus events include National Colloquium, Fallfest, and Monett Weekend.

Sports: There are 11 intercollegiate sports for men and 11 for women, and 17 intramural sports for men and 17 for women. Facilities include a gym, a football and lacrosse stadium, field hockey and soccer fields, practice fields, a weight room, indoor and outdoor tracks, handball and squash courts, an indoor pool, an exercise facility, and weight resistance equipment.

Disabled Students: 60% of the campus is accessible. Wheelchair ramps, elevators, special parking, specially equipped rest rooms, special class scheduling, lowered drinking fountains, lowered telephones, and special housing are available.

Services: Counseling and information services are available, as is tutoring in most subjects. Students with learning disabilities may receive special help in writing and organization and in quantitative areas.

Campus Safety and Security: Measures include 24-hour foot and vehicle patrol, self-defense education, security escort services, and informal discussions. There are pamphlets/posters/films, emergency telephones, and lighted pathways/sidewalks.

Programs of Study: Ohio Wesleyan confers B.A., B.F.A., and B.M. degrees. Bachelor's degrees are awarded in BIOLOGICAL SCIENCE (biochemistry, biology/biological science, botany, genetics, microbiology, and zoology), BUSINESS (accounting, business economics, and international business management), COMMUNICATIONS AND THE ARTS (dramatic arts, English, fine arts, French, German, journalism, music, and Spanish), COMPUTER AND PHYSICAL SCIENCE (chemistry, computer science, earth science, geology, mathematics, and physics), EDUCATION (art, early childhood, elementary, foreign languages, middle school, music, physical, and science), ENGINEERING AND ENVIRONMENTAL DESIGN (environmental science), HEALTH PROFESSIONS (predentistry, premedicine, and preveterinary science), SOCIAL SCIENCE (African American studies, anthropology, economics, geography, history, international relations, philosophy, political science/government, prelaw, psychology, religion, social science, sociology, and women's studies). Psychology, political science and prelaw, and biological sciences are the strongest academically. Economics and business, biological sciences, and psychology are the largest.

Required: Most students are required to complete at least 34 units, including 3 units each of humanities/English, social sciences, and science, 2 units of foreign languages, and 1 unit of fine or performing arts. Each unit equals a full course and 3.75 semester hours. All students must also take 8 to 12 units in the major, maintain a minimum GPA of 2.0, and satisfy the university writing skills requirements.

Special: Cross-registration is available with members of the Great Lakes Colleges Association. Students may study abroad in 20 countries or participate in a Washington semester or a departmental internship. Students may also take dual majors in any combination, design their own majors, or pursue a 3-2 engineering degree in conjunction with 4 major universities. Nondegree study and pass/fail options are available. There are 27 national honor societies, including Phi Beta Kappa, a freshman honors program, and 22 departmental honors programs.

Faculty/Classroom: 63% of faculty are male; 37%, female. All both teach and do research. The average class size in an introductory lecture is 32; in a laboratory, 19; and in a regular course, 16.

Admissions: 75% of the 2005-2006 applicants were accepted. The SAT scores for the 2005-2006 freshman class were: Verbal--8% below 500, 35% between 500 and 599, 41% between 600 and 700, and 16% above 700; Math--7% below 500, 34% between 500 and 599, 44% between 600 and 700, and 16% above 700. The ACT scores were 21% between 21 and 23, 32% between 24 and 26, 21% between 27 and 28, and 26% above 28. 47% of the current freshmen were in the top fifth of their class; 70% were in the top two fifths. There were 2 National Merit semifinalists. 17 freshmen graduated first in their class.

Requirements: The SAT or ACT is required. In addition, candidates for admission should complete a recommended 4 units of English and 3 each of math, foreign language, social studies, and science. AP credits are accepted. Important factors in the admissions decision are recommendations by school officials, extracurricular activities record, and advanced placement or honor courses.

Procedure: Freshmen are admitted fall and spring. Entrance exams should be taken in the spring of the junior year or fall of the senior year. There is an early decision plan. There is a rolling admissions plan. Early decision applications should be filed by December 1; regular applications, by March 1 for fall entry, along with a $35 fee. Notification of early decision is sent December 30; regular decision, on a rolling basis. 26 early decision candidates were accepted for the 2005-2006 class. 20 applicants were on the 2005 waiting list; 1 was admitted. Applications are accepted on-line.

Transfer: 35 transfer students enrolled in 2004-2005. Applicants should have better than a 2.5 college GPA and at least 8 course units of credit. High school and college transcripts and an essay are required, along with a statement of good standing from the previous institution. An interview is recommended. 16 of 34 units of credit (127.5 semester credit hour) required for the bachelor's degree must be completed at Ohio Wesleyan.

Visiting: There are regularly scheduled orientations for prospective students. There are guides for informal visits and visitors may sit in on classes and stay overnight. To schedule a visit, contact the Office of Admission.

Financial Aid: In 2005-2006, 99% of all full-time freshmen and 98% of continuing full-time students received some form of financial aid. 59% of full-time freshmen and 65% of continuing full-time students received need-based aid. The average freshman award was $21,893. Need-based scholarships or need-based grants averaged $15,595; need-based self-help aid (loans and jobs) averaged $4170; and other non-need-based awards and non-need-based scholarships averaged $3286. 25% of undergraduates work part time. Average annual earnings from campus work are $774. The average financial indebtedness of the 2005 graduate was $22,619. The FAFSA and the college's own financial statement are required. The priority date for freshman financial aid applications for fall entry is March 15. The deadline for filing freshman financial aid applications for fall entry is May 15.

International Students: There are 153 international students enrolled. The school actively recruits these students. They must take the TOEFL, achieving a satisfactory score, or take the IELTS. They must also take the SAT or the ACT.

Computers: Wireless access is available. There are 260 PCs and laptops located in 6 academic labs, 4 dorm labs, and 1 information commons. All students may access the system 24 hours a day. There are no time limits and no fees. It is strongly recommended that all students have a personal computer.

Graduates: From July 1, 2004 to June 30, 2005, 400 bachelor's degrees were awarded. The most popular majors were biological science (13%), psychology (11%), and economics management (9%). In an average class, 1% graduate in 3 years or less, 58% graduate in 4 years or less, 62% graduate in 5 years or less, and 68% graduate in 6 years or less. 23 companies recruited on campus in 2004-2005. Of the 2004 graduating class, 33% were enrolled in graduate school within 6 months of graduation and 95% were employed.

Admissions Contact: Margaret Drugovich, Vice President of Admission and Financial Aid. E-mail: *owuadmit@owu.edu*
Web: *www.owu.edu*

OTTERBEIN COLLEGE   C-3
Westerville, OH 43081
(614) 823-1500
(800) 488-8144; Fax: (614) 823-1200

Full-time: 815 men, 1446 women	Faculty: 143
Part-time: 131 men, 332 women	Ph.D.s: 91%
Graduate: 116 men, 254 women	Student/Faculty: 16 to 1
Year: quarters, summer session	Tuition: $22,518
Application Deadline: March 1	Room & Board: $6468
Freshman Class: 2708 applied, 2093 accepted, 630 enrolled	
SAT or ACT: required	COMPETITIVE

Otterbein College, founded in 1847, is an independent institution affiliated with the United Methodist Church. The college provides a solid liberal arts education combined with professional/career preparation. In addition to regional accreditation, Otterbein College has baccalaureate program accreditation with CAAHEP, NASM, NCATE, and NLN. The library contains 300,000 volumes. Computerized library services include the card catalog, interlibrary loans, and database searching. Special learning facilities include a learning resource center, art gallery, planetarium, radio station, TV station, an equine facility, 2 theaters, and a recital hall. The 142-acre campus is in a suburban area 12 miles northeast of Columbus. Including any residence halls, there are 28 buildings.

Student Life: 89% of undergraduates are from Ohio. Students are from 29 states, 28 foreign countries, and Canada. 88% are white. 76% are Protestant; 22% Catholic; 12% claim no religious affiliation. The average age of freshmen is 18; all undergraduates, 22. 7% do not continue beyond their first year; 74% remain to graduate.

Housing: 1029 students can be accommodated in college housing, which includes single-sex and coed dorms, on-campus apartments, fraternity houses, and sorority houses. In addition, there are honors houses and special-interest houses. On-campus housing is guaranteed for the freshman year only, is available on a first-come, first-served basis, and is available on a lottery system for upperclassmen. Priority is given to out-of-town students. 60% of students live on campus; of those, 55% remain on campus on weekends. Alcohol is not permitted. All students may keep cars.

Activities: 28% of men belong to 5 local and 1 national fraternity; 28% of women belong to 6 local sororities. There are 90 groups on campus, including art, band, cheerleading, choir, chorale, chorus, dance, debate, drama, drill team, equestrian, ethnic, forensics, gay, honors, international, intramurals, jazz band, literary magazine, marching band, musical theater, newspaper, opera, orchestra, pep band, photography, political, professional, radio and TV, religious, social, social service, student government, symphony, and yearbook. Popular campus events include athletics and music and theater events.

Sports: There are 8 intercollegiate sports for men and 8 for women, and 11 intramural sports for men and 11 for women. Facilities include a basketball and volleyball center, a football stadium, a soccer field, a weight room, tennis courts, a cross-country course, and a student recreation center.

Disabled Students: 81% of the campus is accessible. Wheelchair ramps, elevators, special parking, specially equipped rest rooms, special class scheduling, lowered drinking fountains, and lowered telephones are available.

Services: Counseling and information services are available, as is tutoring in every subject. There is a reader service for the blind, and remedial math, reading, and writing.

Campus Safety and Security: Measures include 24-hour foot and vehicle patrol, self-defense education, security escort services, and informal discussions. There are pamphlets/posters/films, emergency telephones, lighted pathways/sidewalks, and 24-hour locked dorm facilities.

Programs of Study: Otterbein College confers B.A., B.S., B.F.A., B.M., B.Mus.Ed., B.S.E., and B.S.N. degrees. Master's degrees are also awarded. Bachelor's degrees are awarded in AGRICULTURE (equine science), BIOLOGICAL SCIENCE (biochemistry, life science, and molecular biology), BUSINESS (accounting and business administration and management), COMMUNICATIONS AND THE ARTS (art, broadcasting, communications, dramatic arts, English, French, journalism, music, music performance, musical theater, public relations, Spanish, speech/debate/rhetoric, and visual and performing arts), COMPUTER AND PHYSICAL SCIENCE (chemistry, computer science, mathematics, and physics), EDUCATION (athletic training, elementary, health, music, and physical), HEALTH PROFESSIONS (nursing), SOCIAL SCIENCE (economics, history, international studies, liberal arts/general studies, philosophy, political science/government, psychology, religion, and sociology). Life science, chemistry, and athletic training are the strongest academically. Business, education, and communications are the largest.

Required: All students must complete 180 quarter hours, including 50 to 100 in the major, with a minimum GPA of 2.0. The liberal arts core includes 15 hours in English composition and literature, 10 hours each in natural and social sciences, 5 hours each in religion/philosophy, fine arts, and non-Western cultures, and 3 in phys ed.

Special: Students may cross-register with members of the Higher Education Council of Columbus, study abroad in 9 countries, have an internship in most majors, or participate in a Washington semester. B.A.-B.S. degrees, 3-2 engineering degrees with Case Western Reserve and Washington Universities, credit for military experience, student-designed majors, nondegree study, and limited pass/fail options are also available. There are 9 national honor societies and a freshman honors program.

Faculty/Classroom: 52% of faculty are male; 48%, female. All teach undergraduates. No introductory courses are taught by graduate students. The average class size in an introductory lecture is 20; in a laboratory, 10; and in a regular course, 20.

Admissions: 77% of the 2005-2006 applicants were accepted.

Requirements: The SAT or ACT is required. In addition, applicants should be graduates of an accredited secondary school. The recommended preparatory program includes 4 units of English, 3 to 4 units each of math, science, and social studies, 2 to 3 units of foreign language, and 1 to 2 units of performing arts. A high school GPA of 2.5 or better is recommended. Otterbein College requires applicants to be in the upper 50% of their class. A GPA of 2.5 is required. AP and CLEP credits are accepted. Important factors in the admissions decision are advanced placement or honor courses, evidence of special talent, and recommendations by school officials.

Procedure: Freshmen are admitted to all sessions. Entrance exams should be taken in the spring of the junior year. There are deferred admissions and rolling admissions plans. Applications should be filed by March 1 for fall entry, along with a $25 fee. Notification is sent on a rolling basis. Applications are accepted on-line.

Transfer: 92 transfer students enrolled in 2004-2005. Applicants should present a college GPA of 2.5. 60 of 180 credits required for the bachelor's degree must be completed at Otterbein College.

Visiting: There are regularly scheduled orientations for prospective students, including conference with an admissions counselor, and a campus tour. There are guides for informal visits and visitors may sit in on classes and stay overnight. To schedule a visit, contact Debbie Jamieson at *uotter@otterbein.edu*.

Financial Aid: 28% of undergraduates work part time. Average annual earnings from campus work are $1500. The FAFSA is required. The deadline for filing freshman financial aid applications for fall entry is April 1.

International Students: The school actively recruits these students. A satisfactory score is required on the written TOEFL. Students must also take the SAT or the ACT.

Computers: All students may access the system. There are no time limits and no fees.

Graduates: In an average class, 4% graduate in 3 years or less, 80% graduate in 4 years or less, and 88% graduate in 5 years or less. Of a recent year's graduating class, 95% were employed within 6 months of graduation.

Admissions Contact: Dr. Cass Johnson, Director of Admissions.
E-mail: *uotterb@otterbein.edu* Web: *www.otterbein.edu*

SHAWNEE STATE UNIVERSITY C-5
Portsmouth, OH 45662

(740) 351-4778
(800) 959-2778; Fax: (740) 351-3111

Full-time: 1291 men, 1906 women	Faculty: 138; IIB, -$
Part-time: 205 men, 418 women	Ph.D.s: 54%
Graduate: none	Student/Faculty: 23 to 1
Year: quarters, summer session	Tuition: $5508 ($9396)
Application Deadline: open	Room & Board: $6729
Freshman Class: 2917 applied, 2917 accepted, 898 enrolled	
SAT or ACT: not required	NONCOMPETITIVE

Shawnee State University, founded in 1975, is a public institution offering programs in arts and sciences, business, engineering, health sciences, and education. There are 2 undergraduate schools. In addition to regional accreditation, Shawnee State has baccalaureate program accreditation with ACBSP and ADA. The library contains 131,540 volumes, 68,394 microform items, and 4804 audio/video tapes/CDs/DVDs, and subscribes to 15,759 periodicals including electronic. Computerized library services include interlibrary loans, database searching, Internet access, and laptop Internet portals. Special learning facilities include a learning resource center, art gallery, and planetarium. The 50-acre campus is in a small town 90 miles south of Columbus. Including any residence halls, there are 29 buildings.

Student Life: 91% of undergraduates are from Ohio. Others are from 14 states and 11 foreign countries. 86% are white. The average age of freshmen is 20; all undergraduates, 24. 39% do not continue beyond their first year; 61% remain to graduate.

Housing: 519 students can be accommodated in university housing, which includes single-sex on-campus apartments. On-campus housing is available on a first-come, first-served basis. 90% of students commute. Alcohol is not permitted. All students may keep cars.

Activities: 5% of men belong to 3 national fraternities; 3% of women belong to 2 local sororities. There are 5 groups on campus, including art, cheerleading, choir, chorus, computers, ethnic, honors, international, literary magazine, newspaper, pep band, photography, professional, social, and student government. Popular campus events include Fall Fest, Spring Fest, and Scare Week.

Sports: There are 5 intercollegiate sports for men and 6 for women, and 9 intramural sports for men and 9 for women. Facilities include an activities center with basketball and volleyball courts; a sports center with racquetball courts, Nautilus and weight rooms, a pool, a sauna, and a whirlpool; and a soccer field.

Disabled Students: All of the campus is accessible. Wheelchair ramps, elevators, special parking, specially equipped rest rooms, lowered drinking fountains, and lowered telephones are available.

Services: Counseling and information services are available, as is tutoring in most subjects. There is a reader service for the blind, and remedial math, reading, and writing.

Campus Safety and Security: Measures include 24-hour foot and vehicle patrol, pamphlets/posters/films, emergency telephones, and lighted pathways/sidewalks.

Programs of Study: Shawnee State confers B.A., B.S., B.F.A., B.I.S., and B.S.N. degrees. Associate degrees are also awarded. Bachelor's degrees are awarded in BIOLOGICAL SCIENCE (biology/biological science), BUSINESS (business administration and management and sports management), COMMUNICATIONS AND THE ARTS (English and fine arts), COMPUTER AND PHYSICAL SCIENCE (chemistry, mathematics, natural sciences, and physical sciences), EDUCATION (early childhood, education, elementary, and special), ENGINEERING AND ENVIRONMENTAL DESIGN (computer technology, engineering technology, environmental engineering technology, and plastics technology), HEALTH PROFESSIONS (medical laboratory science, nursing, occupational therapy, and premedicine), SOCIAL SCIENCE (history, humanities, interdisciplinary studies, international relations, prelaw, psychology, social science, and sociology). Early childhood education is the strongest academically and has the largest enrollments.

Required: To graduate, students must complete a general education program and a senior seminar. A total of 180 to 190 quarter credit hours, with a 2.0 GPA in all course work and in the major, is required.

Special: Study abroad in China, Germany, Morocco, and Spain, internships, and student-designed programs are available. Cross-registration with Miami University, 2+2 programs, and a Washington semester are also possible. There is 1 national honor society and a freshman honors program.

Faculty/Classroom: 59% of faculty are male; 41%, female. All teach undergraduates. The average class size in an introductory lecture is 19; in a laboratory, 16; and in a regular course, 14.

Admissions: 100% of the 2005-2006 applicants were accepted. The ACT scores for the 2005-2006 freshman class were: 68% below 21, 21% between 21 and 23, 7% between 24 and 26, 3% between 27 and 28, and 1% above 28. 25% of the current freshmen were in the top fifth of their class; 51% were in the top two fifths. 15 freshmen graduated first in their class.

Requirements: Applicants must graduate from an accredited high school or have a GED. AP and CLEP credits are accepted.

Procedure: Freshmen are admitted to all sessions. Entrance exams should be taken in late spring or early summer. Application deadlines are open. Applications are accepted on-line.

Transfer: 223 transfer students enrolled in 2004-2005. A completed application and college and high school transcripts sent directly to SSU from previous institutions are required. 45 of 180 credits required for the bachelor's degree must be completed at Shawnee State.

Visiting: There are regularly scheduled orientations for prospective students, including fall and spring visitation days, which consist of small sessions with deans and faculty, orientation by student affairs offices, and tours with current college students. There are guides for informal visits and visitors may sit in on classes. To schedule a visit, contact the Office of Admissions at To SSU@shawnee.edu.

Financial Aid: Shawnee State is a member of CSS. The FAFSA is required. The deadline for filing freshman financial aid applications for fall entry is March 1.

International Students: There are 31 international students enrolled. The school actively recruits these students. They must take the written TOEFL.

Computers: Wireless access is available. Computer labs are located in nearly every building on campus, and all 39 labs are networked to the campus or ATC network. There are 9 open labs offering students walk-in availability, while others may be open during non-class hours. In all, there are 620 workstations for student usage. All students may access the system. There are no time limits and no fees.

Graduates: From July 1, 2004 to June 30, 2005, 377 bachelor's degrees were awarded. The most popular majors were business administration (26%), social sciences (13%), and early childhood education (8%). In an average class, 17% graduate in 4 years or less, 27% graduate in 5 years or less, and 31% graduate in 6 years or less. 130 companies recruited on campus in 2004-2005.

Admissions Contact: Bob Trusz, Director of Admissions and Retention. A video is available. E-mail: To_SSU@shawnee.edu
Web: www.shawnee.edu

TIFFIN UNIVERSITY C-2
Tiffin, OH 44883

(419) 447-6443
(800) 968-6446; Fax: (419) 443-5006

Full-time: 420 men, 450 women	Faculty: 49; IIB, av$
Part-time: 55 men, 105 women	Ph.D.s: 69%
Graduate: 175 men, 210 women	Student/Faculty: 18 to 1
Year: semesters, summer session	Tuition: $13,600
Application Deadline: open	Room & Board: $6000
Freshman Class: n/av	
SAT or ACT: required	LESS COMPETITIVE

Tiffin University, established in 1888, is a private institution emphasizing degree programs in business, liberal studies, and criminal justice. There are 3 undergraduate and 2 graduate schools. Figures in the above capsule and profile are approximate. In addition to regional accreditation, TU has baccalaureate program accreditation with ACBSP. The library contains 30,000 volumes, 32,500 microform items, and 830 audio/video tapes/CDs/DVDs, and subscribes to 255 periodicals including electronic. Computerized library services include the card catalog, interlibrary loans, database searching, and Internet access. Special learning facilities include a learning resource center, art gallery, and the Ohio Council on Holocaust Education Information Center. The 110-acre campus is in a small town 90 miles north of Columbus and 60 miles southeast of Toledo. Including any residence halls, there are 25 buildings.

Student Life: 85% of undergraduates are from Ohio. Others are from 19 states, 13 foreign countries, and Canada. 78% are from public schools. 85% are white; 10% African American. The average age of freshmen is 18; all undergraduates, 24. 39% do not continue beyond their first year; 25% remain to graduate.

Housing: 450 students can be accommodated in college housing, which includes single-sex and coed dormitories, on-campus apartments, off-campus apartments, fraternity houses, and sorority houses. In addition, there are honors houses and student development housing, bringing together students who are involved in a number of activities and maintaine a 3.2 CPA. On-campus housing is guaranteed for all 4 years. 50% of students live on campus; of those, 60% remain on campus on weekends. All students may keep cars.

Activities: 1% of men belong to 1 local and 1 national fraternity; 1% of women belong to 2 local and 1 national sorority. There are 16 groups on campus, including band, cheerleading, choir, chorale, chorus, computers, drama, drill team, ethnic, gay, honors, international, jazz band, marching band, pep band, political, professional, religious, social, social service, student government and vocal jazz. Popular campus events include Spring Fest and the faculty vs. student basketball game.

Sports: There are 9 intercollegiate sports for men and 9 for women, and 10 intramural sports for men and 8 for women. Facilities include a

student center gym, indoor batting cages, a weight room, tennis courts, and soccer, baseball, and softball fields.

Disabled Students: 90% of the campus is accessible. Wheelchair ramps, elevators, special parking, specially equipped rest rooms, special class scheduling, lowered drinking fountains, and lowered telephones are available.

Services: Counseling and information services are available, as is tutoring in most subjects. There is a reader service for the blind, and remedial math, reading, and writing.

Campus Safety and Security: Measures include self-defense education, security escort services, informal discussions, and pamphlets/posters/films. There are lighted pathways/sidewalks.

Programs of Study: TU confers B.A., B.B.A., and B.C.J. degrees. Associate and master's degrees are also awarded. Bachelor's degrees are awarded in BUSINESS (accounting, banking and finance, business administration and management, hotel/motel and restaurant management, marketing/retailing/merchandising, and personnel management), COMPUTER AND PHYSICAL SCIENCE (information sciences and systems), SOCIAL SCIENCE (corrections, criminology, international studies, law enforcement and corrections, and liberal arts/general studies). Accounting and forensic psychology are the strongest academically. Accounting and management are the largest.

Required: To graduate, all students must complete 130 to 133 semester hours, including 51 to 54 in the major, with a GPA of 2.0 cumulatively and 2.5 in the major. The 61-semester-hour integrated core curriculum includes courses in computer systems, speech and writing, math and statistics, economics, psychology, and sociology, history, literature, philosophy, and cultural heritage.

Special: Internships are recommended for all students. An accelerated degree program in finance, work-study programs, a junior semester in England, nondegree study, and pass/fail options are also available. There is 1 national honor society.

Faculty/Classroom: 70% of faculty are male; 30%, female. All teach undergraduates. No introductory courses are taught by graduate students. The average class size in an introductory lecture is 24 and in a regular course, 23.

Requirements: The SAT or ACT is required. In addition, candidates should be graduates of an accredited secondary school, with 4 units of English, 3 of math, 2 each of science and social studies, and 5 of electives. The GED is accepted. An interview is recommended. A GPA of 3.0 is required. AP and CLEP credits are accepted. Important factors in the admissions decision are leadership record, recommendations by school officials, and extracurricular activities record.

Procedure: Freshmen are admitted to all sessions. There is a rolling admissions plan. Entrance exams should be taken as early as possible. Application deadlines are open. Applications are accepted on-line. The fall 2005 application fee was $20.

Transfer: 21 transfer students enrolled in a recent year. Applicants with 12 or more hours of credit must have a minimum college GPA of 2.0; applicants with fewer hours of credit need a minimum GPA of 1.8 to enter in good standing. The SAT or ACT and an interview are recommended. 30 of 130 credits required for the bachelor's degree must be completed at TU.

Visiting: There are regularly scheduled orientations for prospective students, consisting of placement testing, tours of the campus, lunch with advisers, and an appointment with an individual adviser to schedule fall classes. There are guides for informal visits and visitors may sit in on classes and stay overnight. To schedule a visit, contact the Admissions Office at (419) 448-3423 or (800) 968-6446.

Financial Aid: In a recent year, 90% of all full-time freshmen and 87% of continuing full-time students received some form of financial aid. 88% of full-time freshmen and 86% of continuing full-time students received need-based aid. The average freshman award was $12,458. Need-based scholarships or need-based grants averaged $5180 ($11,016 maximum); need-based self-help aid (loans and jobs) averaged $3294 ($6500 maximum); non-need-based athletic scholarships averaged $4243 ($13,590 maximum); and other non-need-based awards and non-need-based scholarships averaged $6192 ($19,492 maximum). 13% of undergraduates worked part time. Average annual earnings from campus work were $874. The average financial indebtedness of a recent graduate was $17,125. The FAFSA is required. Check with the school for current application deadlines.

International Students: In a recent year, there were 26 international students enrolled. The school actively recruits these students. They must score satisfactorily on the written TOEFL.

Computers: All students may access the system. There are no time limits. The fee is $35.

Graduates: In a recent year, 268 bachelor's degrees were awarded. The most popular majors were management (59%), forensic psychology (8%), and accounting (5%). 8 companies recruited on campus in a recent year. Of a recent graduating class, 18% were enrolled in graduate school within 6 months of graduation and 97% were employed.

Admissions Contact: Cam Cruickshank, Director of Admissions. A video is available. E-mail: *cacruick@tiffin.edu* Web: *www.tiffin.edu*

UNION INSTITUTE & UNIVERSITY   A-5
Cincinnati, OH 45206-1925

(513) 861-6400
(800) 486-3116; Fax: (513) 861-0779

Full-time: 177 men, 496 women	**Faculty:** 42
Part-time: 184 men, 265 women	**Ph.D.s:** 86%
Graduate: 375 men, 882 women	**Student/Faculty:** 20 to 1
Year: semesters, summer session	**Tuition:** $8912
Application Deadline: October 1	**Room & Board:** n/app
Freshman Class: n/av	
SAT or ACT: not required	**SPECIAL**

The Union Institute and University, established in 1964, serves the academic needs of mature working adults seeking to earn the B.A. or B.S. degree. In addition to the main Cincinnati campus, there are learning centers in Miami, Los Angeles, San Diego, and Sacramento. The Institute's Center for Distance Learning enables individuals to earn their degrees through a computer-based educational delivery system. There are 2 undergraduate and 2 graduate schools. The library contains 45,000 volumes and 450 audio/video tapes/CDs/DVDs, and subscribes to 150 periodicals including electronic. Computerized library services include database searching. Special learning facilities include a learning resource center and an art gallery. The campus is in an urban area 2 miles from downtown Cincinnati. There are 3 buildings.

Student Life: 77% of undergraduates are from Ohio. Students are from 45 states, 6 foreign countries, and Canada. 52% are white; 26% African American. The average age of freshmen is 38; all undergraduates, 38.

Housing: There are no residence halls. 90% of students commute. Alcohol is not permitted. All students may keep cars.

Activities: There are no fraternities or sororities. Popular campus events include Commencement.

Sports: There is no sports program at Union.

Disabled Students: All of the campus is accessible. Wheelchair ramps, elevators, special parking, specially equipped rest rooms, lowered drinking fountains, lowered telephones, and audio/visual fire alarms are available.

Services: Counseling and information services are available. Scholar skills development is available.

Campus Safety and Security: Measures include lighted pathways/sidewalks and a security guard during operating hours.

Programs of Study: Union confers B.A. and B.S. degrees. Master's and doctoral degrees are also awarded. Bachelor's degrees are awarded in BUSINESS (business administration and management), COMMUNICATIONS AND THE ARTS (communications), COMPUTER AND PHYSICAL SCIENCE (computer science), EDUCATION (education), HEALTH PROFESSIONS (health), SOCIAL SCIENCE (criminal justice, liberal arts/general studies, psychology, public administration, social science, and social work). Criminal justice studies, business, and education are the largest.

Required: To graduate, students must complete a total of 128 semester credit hours. Distribution requirements include a minimum of 16 semester credits each in humanities and arts, social sciences, language and communications, and natural sciences and math, plus 64 credits in electives and the area of concentration. A senior project, including an oral presentation and thesis, is required.

Special: Programs are designed to meet individual learning needs, with tutorial-based courses, often one-on-one. Scheduling is flexible, and there are part-time enrollment options. Dual majors and student-designed majors are offered.

Faculty/Classroom: 46% of faculty are male; 54%, female. 35% teach undergraduates. No introductory courses are taught by graduate students. The average class size in an introductory lecture is 8 and in a regular course, 1.

Requirements: Applicants must show evidence of ability to do college-level work, to be highly motivated, and to have the capacity for self-directed learning. All applicants should present 2 letters of recommendation, a structured personal essay, and transcripts of any previous college work. An interview is required. AP and CLEP credits are accepted. Important factors in the admissions decision are evidence of special talent, personality/intangible qualities, and leadership record.

Procedure: Freshmen are admitted to all sessions. There are deferred admissions and rolling admissions plans. Applications should be filed by October 1 for fall entry, February 1 for spring entry, and June 1 for summer entry. The fall 2005 application fee was $35. Notification is sent on a rolling basis. Applications are accepted on-line.

Transfer: Grades of C or better from a regionally accredited institution may be transferable. 30 of 120 credits required for the bachelor's degree must be completed at Union.

Visiting: There are guides for informal visits and visitors may sit in on classes. To schedule a visit, contact local campuses.

Financial Aid: In 2005-2006, 70% of continuing full-time students received some form of financial aid. 94% of undergraduates work part time. The FAFSA and the college's own financial statement are required. Check with the school for current deadlines.

International Students: There are 8 international students enrolled.

Computers: All students may access the system. There are no time limits and no fees. It is strongly recommended that all students have a PC.
Graduates: From July 1, 2004 to June 30, 2005, 260 bachelor's degrees were awarded. The most popular majors were criminal justice studies (22%), education (19%), and liberal studies (17%).
Admissions Contact: Admissions Office. E-mail: *admissions@tui.edu* Web: *www.tui.edu*

UNIVERSITY OF AKRON   D-2
Akron, OH 44325

	(330) 972-7077
	(800) 655-4884; Fax: (330) 972-7022
Full-time: 6533 men, 6988 women	Faculty: 715; I, --$
Part-time: 2154 men, 3048 women	Ph.D.s: 87%
Graduate: 1727 men, 2186 women	Student/Faculty: 19 to 1
Year: semesters, summer session	Tuition: $7958 ($16,682)
Application Deadline: open	Room & Board: $7208
Freshman Class: 9214 applied, 7656 accepted, 3395 enrolled	
SAT Verbal/Math: 505/515*	ACT: 21 NONCOMPETITIVE

University of Akron, founded in 1870, is the public research university for northern Ohio. Primarily a commuter institution, the university offers more than 350 associate, bachelor's, master's, doctoral, and law degree programs and approximately 100 certificate programs at its main campus in Akron, its Wayne College branch campus in Orrville, and in sites throughout Medina and Summit counties. There are 9 undergraduate and 8 graduate schools. In addition to regional accreditation, UA has baccalaureate program accreditation with AACSB, AAFCS, ABET, ADA, CAHEA, CCNE, CSWE, FIDER, NASAD, NASD, NASM, and NCATE. The 4 libraries contain 1,233,833 volumes, 1,675,948 microform items, and 45,631 audio/video tapes/CDs/DVDs, and subscribe to 12,438 periodicals including electronic. Computerized library services include the card catalog, interlibrary loans, database searching, Internet access, and laptop Internet portals. Special learning facilities include a learning resource center, art gallery, radio station, TV station, nursing center, speech and hearing center, dance institute, educational media lab, and synchro hours learning classrooms. The 218-acre campus is in an urban area in downtown Akron, 35 miles south of Cleveland. Including any residence halls, there are 82 buildings.
Student Life: 98% of undergraduates are from Ohio. Others are from 42 states, 68 foreign countries, and Canada. 77% are white; 12% African American. The average age of freshmen is 20; all undergraduates, 25. 36% do not continue beyond their first year; 34% remain to graduate.
Housing: 2366 students can be accommodated in college housing, which includes single-sex and coed dorms, on-campus apartments, fraternity houses, and sorority houses. In addition, there are honors houses, special-interest houses, private apartment-type halls, and private residence halls. On-campus housing is available on a first-come, first-served basis. Priority is given to out-of-town students. 90% of students commute. Alcohol is not permitted. All students may keep cars.
Activities: 2% of men belong to 1 local and 13 national fraternities; 2% of women belong to 8 national sororities. There are 200 groups on campus, including art, band, cheerleading, chess, choir, chorale, chorus, computers, dance, drama, ethnic, gay, honors, international, jazz band, marching band, musical theater, newspaper, opera, orchestra, pep band, photography, political, professional, radio and TV, religious, social, social service, student government, symphony, and yearbook. Popular campus events include Celebrating Akron Traditions and Zips Fest.
Sports: There are 8 intercollegiate sports for men and 9 for women, and 12 intramural sports for men and 12 for women. Facilities include a recreation and wellness center, a natatorium, an athletic field house and indoor varsity golf practice facility with 120-yard football field and a 6-lane, 300 meter track, a 5500-seat basketball/volleyball arena, a 35,000-seat football stadium, weight and athletic training rooms, and an outdoor 100-yard artificial turf practice field.
Disabled Students: 90% of the campus is accessible. Wheelchair ramps, elevators, special parking, specially equipped rest rooms, special class scheduling, lowered drinking fountains, lowered telephones, special housing, city/campus bus service, residence hall accommodations, and priority registration for disabled students are available.
Services: Counseling and information services are available, as is tutoring in most subjects. There is a reader service for the blind, and remedial math, reading, and writing. TDDs are available.
Campus Safety and Security: Measures include 24-hour foot and vehicle patrol, self-defense education, security escort services, and shuttle buses. There are informal discussions, pamphlets/posters/films, emergency telephones, and lighted pathways/sidewalks.
Programs of Study: UA confers B.A., B.S., and B.F.A. degrees. Associate, master's, and doctoral degrees are also awarded. Bachelor's degrees are awarded in BIOLOGICAL SCIENCE (biology/biological science, botany, microbiology, and zoology), BUSINESS (accounting, banking and finance, business administration and management, business economics, hospitality management services, international business management, marketing/retailing/merchandising, and personnel man-

agement), COMMUNICATIONS AND THE ARTS (advertising, art, broadcasting, classics, communications, dance, design, dramatic arts, English, fine arts, French, German, Latin, music, photography, Russian, Spanish, and speech/debate/rhetoric), COMPUTER AND PHYSICAL SCIENCE (chemistry, computer science, earth science, geology, mathematics, natural sciences, physics, and statistics), EDUCATION (art, athletic training, business, early childhood, elementary, foreign languages, guidance, health, home economics, music, physical, science, secondary, special, and technical), ENGINEERING AND ENVIRONMENTAL DESIGN (biomedical engineering, chemical engineering, civil engineering, computer engineering, construction technology, electrical/electronics engineering, emergency/disaster science, manufacturing technology, mechanical engineering, mechanical engineering technology, and survey and mapping technology), HEALTH PROFESSIONS (emergency medical technologies, medical laboratory technology, nursing, predentistry, premedicine, prepharmacy, preveterinary science, and speech pathology/audiology), SOCIAL SCIENCE (anthropology, criminal justice, dietetics, economics, family/consumer studies, geography, history, home economics, humanities, philosophy, political science/government, prelaw, psychology, public administration, social science, social work, and sociology). Engineering, nursing, and business are the strongest academically. Business, education, and engineering are the largest.
Required: To graduate, all students must complete at least 128 credits, with a varying number of hours in the major, and maintain a GPA of 2.0. Specific course requirements include English, Western cultural traditions, math, natural science, social science, humanities, speech, cultural diversity, and phys ed.
Special: UA offers co-op programs with local and out-of-state employers, study abroad in 22 countries, internships and work-study opportunities with community employers, a 6-year accelerated B.S.-M.D. program, B.A.-B.S. degrees in 10 majors, credit for military experience, nondegree study, and pass/fail options. There are 25 national honor societies, a freshman honors program, and 100 departmental honors programs.
Faculty/Classroom: 53% of faculty are male; 47%, female. Graduate students teach 8% of introductory courses. The average class size in a regular course is 25.
Admissions: 83% of the 2005-2006 applicants were accepted. The SAT scores for the 2005-2006 freshman class were: Verbal--46% below 500, 37% between 500 and 599, 15% between 600 and 700, and 2% above 700; Math--42% below 500, 36% between 500 and 599, 20% between 600 and 700, and 2% above 700. The ACT scores were 54% below 21, 23% between 21 and 23, 14% between 24 and 26, 6% between 27 and 28, and 4% above 28. 23% of the current freshmen were in the top fifth of their class; 46% were in the top two fifths. There were 3 National Merit finalists and 3 semifinalists. 40 freshmen graduated first in their class.
Requirements: The SAT or ACT is required. Students who demonstrate outstanding college preparation through completion of a college prep curriculum may be admitted directly to a specific academic program. Criteria considered include high school GPA, test scores, class rank, and in some majors/programs additional information is reviewed, such as activities, leadership, recommendations, essays, portfolios, and auditions. AP and CLEP credits are accepted. Important factors in the admissions decision are advanced placement or honor courses, leadership record, and evidence of special talent.
Procedure: Freshmen are admitted to all sessions. Entrance exams should be taken by November 1 for scholarship consideration. Contact the school for additional deadlines. There are early admissions and deferred admissions plans. Application deadlines are open. The application fee is $30. The college accepts all in-state residents. Notification is sent on a rolling basis. Applications are accepted on-line.
Transfer: 883 transfer students enrolled in 2004-2005. Applicants should present a minimum college GPA of 2.0. There are other requirements for direct admission to specific academic programs. 32 of 128 credits required for the bachelor's degree must be completed at UA.
Visiting: There are regularly scheduled orientations for prospective students, including small groups for information on financial aid, student organizations, campus tours, and meetings with college faculty. There are guides for informal visits and visitors may sit in on classes and stay overnight. To schedule a visit, contact the Office of Undergraduate Admissions at *admissions@uakron.edu*.
Financial Aid: In 2005-2006, 63% of all full-time freshmen and 61% of continuing full-time students received some form of financial aid. 57% of full-time freshmen and 56% of continuing full-time students received need-based aid. The average freshman award was $3453. Need-based scholarships or need-based grants averaged $4513 ($7240 maximum); need-based self-help aid (loans and jobs) averaged $2503 ($4046 maximum); non-need-based athletic scholarships averaged $9783 ($18,976 maximum); and other non-need-based awards and non-need-based scholarships averaged $3200 ($13,000 maximum). 65% of undergraduates work part time. Average annual earnings from campus work are $1500. The average financial indebtedness of the 2005 graduate was $15,036. The FAFSA is required. The priority date for freshman finan-

cial aid applications for fall entry is March 1. The deadline for filing freshman financial aid applications for fall entry is June 30.

International Students: There are 114 international students enrolled. The school actively recruits these students. They must score satisfactorily on the written TOEFL or on the electronic version or the MELAB, or the International Engish Language Testing System (IELTS). Students under age 21 or transfers with fewer than 12 credits must also take the SAT or ACT.

Computers: Wireless access is available. Students can check out laptops that provide access to the Internet. There are also approximately 150 computer labs with approximately 2,900 PCs for student use. Students can also access the network utilizing their own laptops. There are 20 Apple laptops available for checkout on the main campus. All access requires a valid ID and password. All students may access the system from 7 A.M. to 1 A.M. The network and access to the Internet are generally available 24/7, except for scheduled maintenance outages. There are no time limits and no fees.

Graduates: From July 1, 2004 to June 30, 2005, 2271 bachelor's degrees were awarded. The most popular majors were early childhood education (8%), accounting (4%), and nursing (4%). In an average class, 13% graduate in 4 years or less, 28% graduate in 5 years or less, and 34% graduate in 6 years or less. 275 companies recruited on campus in 2004-2005.

Admissions Contact: Diane Raybuck, Director of Admissions. A video is available. E-mail: *admissions@uakron.edu*
Web: *www.uakron.edu/admissions*

UNIVERSITY OF CINCINNATI   A-5

Cincinnati, OH 45221-0127	(513) 556-1100; Fax: (513) 556-1105
Full-time: 8453 men, 7645 women	Faculty: 1151; I, -$
Part-time: 1236 men, 2178 women	Ph.D.s: 70%
Graduate: 3946 men, 4474 women	Student/Faculty: 14 to 1
Year: quarters, summer session	Tuition: $8877 ($22,629)
Application Deadline: July 31	Room & Board: $8805
Freshman Class: 10,840 applied, 8788 accepted, 3138 enrolled	
SAT Verbal/Math: 540/550*	COMPETITIVE

The University of Cincinnati, founded in 1819, is a state-supported institution offering undergraduate programs in art and architecture, business, engineering, health science, liberal arts and sciences, music, and technical training. There are 11 undergraduate and 12 graduate schools. In addition to regional accreditation, UC has baccalaureate program accreditation with AACSB and NCATE. The 18 libraries contain 2,977,475 volumes, 3,287,318 microform items, and 544,245 audio/video tapes/CDs/DVDs, and subscribe to 33,568 periodicals including electronic. Computerized library services include the card catalog, interlibrary loans, database searching, and Internet access. Special learning facilities include a learning resource center, art gallery, and radio station. The 270-acre campus is in an urban area downtown Cincinnati. Including any residence halls, there are 90 buildings.

Student Life: 89% of undergraduates are from Ohio. Others are from 50 states, 92 foreign countries, and Canada. 70% are white; 12% African American. The average age of freshmen is 19; all undergraduates, 25. 21% do not continue beyond their first year.

Housing: 3200 students can be accommodated in college housing, which includes coed dormitories and on-campus apartments. In addition, there are honors houses and language houses. On-campus housing is guaranteed for the freshman year only. Priority is given to out-of-town students. 80% of students commute. Alcohol is not permitted. All students may keep cars.

Activities: 11% of men belong to 24 local fraternities; 10% of women belong to 11 local sororities. There are 31 groups on campus, including art, band, cheerleading, chess, choir, chorale, chorus, computers, dance, drama, ethnic, gay, honors, international, jazz band, literary magazine, marching band, musical theater, newspaper, opera, orchestra, pep band, photography, political, professional, radio and TV, religious, social, social service, student government, symphony, and yearbook. Popular campus events include College Conservatory of Music productions.

Sports: There are 8 intercollegiate sports for men and 10 for women, and 32 intramural sports for men and 32 for women. Facilities include a 30,000-seat stadium, a field house, a 13,000-seat gym, indoor and outdoor tracks, a swimming pool, tennis courts, and athletic fields.

Disabled Students: 95% of the campus is accessible. Wheelchair ramps, elevators, special parking, specially equipped rest rooms, special class scheduling, lowered drinking fountains, and lowered telephones are available.

Services: Counseling and information services are available, as is tutoring in most subjects. There is remedial math, reading, and writing. Other services offered include note taking and reading services for the blind, and interpreting services for the hearing-impaired.

Campus Safety and Security: Measures include security escort services, shuttle buses, emergency telephones, and lighted pathways/sidewalks.

Programs of Study: UC confers B.A., B.S., B.Arch., B.B.A., B.F.A., B.G.S., B.M., B.S.Des., B.S.E., B.S.I.M., B.S.N., B.S.Pharm., B.S.W,

and B.U.P. degrees. Associate, master's, and doctoral degrees are also awarded. Bachelor's degrees are awarded in BIOLOGICAL SCIENCE (biochemistry and biology/biological science), BUSINESS (accounting, banking and finance, business administration and management, management science, marketing/retailing/merchandising, and real estate), COMMUNICATIONS AND THE ARTS (broadcasting, communications, comparative literature, dance, design, dramatic arts, English, fine arts, French, German, jazz, linguistics, music, music history and appreciation, music theory and composition, piano/organ, Spanish, theater design, and voice), COMPUTER AND PHYSICAL SCIENCE (chemical technology, chemistry, computer science, geology, information sciences and systems, mathematics, physics, and quantitative methods), EDUCATION (art, business, early childhood, elementary, foreign languages, guidance, health, industrial arts, middle school, music, nutrition, science, secondary, and special), ENGINEERING AND ENVIRONMENTAL DESIGN (aeronautical engineering, architectural engineering, architectural technology, chemical engineering, city/community/regional planning, civil engineering, computer engineering, construction management, electrical/electronics engineering, electrical/electronics engineering technology, engineering, engineering mechanics, engineering technology, industrial administration/management, industrial engineering technology, materials engineering, mechanical engineering, mechanical engineering technology, metallurgical engineering, and nuclear engineering), HEALTH PROFESSIONS (medical laboratory technology, nuclear medical technology, nursing, pharmacy, predentistry, premedicine, and speech pathology/audiology), SOCIAL SCIENCE (African American studies, anthropology, Asian/Oriental studies, classical/ancient civilization, criminal justice, economics, geography, history, international studies, Judaic studies, Latin American studies, philosophy, political science/government, prelaw, psychology, social science, social work, sociology, and urban studies). Engineering is the strongest academically. Arts and sciences is the largest.

Required: All students must complete English and humanities requirements. A minimum of 185 quarter credits is required for the baccalaureate degree.

Special: The Professional Practice Program, a 5-year cooperative plan offering alternate work in academic subjects and industry, is available for students in engineering, business, arts and sciences, and design, architecture, and art. Study abroad opportunities include a winter quarter in Spain, an academic program in Paris, and a language/area studies work program in Germany. A general studies degree and nondegree study are available. There is a chapter of Phi Beta Kappa and a freshman honors program.

Faculty/Classroom: 63% of faculty are male; 37%, female.

Admissions: 81% of the 2005-2006 applicants were accepted. The SAT scores for the 2005-2006 freshman class were: Verbal--32% below 500, 39% between 500 and 599, 25% between 600 and 700, and 4% above 700; Math--30% below 500, 36% between 500 and 599, 28% between 600 and 700, and 6% above 700. The ACT scores were 36% below 21, 20% between 24 and 26, 11% between 27 and 28, and 10% above 28. 31% of the current freshmen were in the top fifth of their class; 58% were in the top two fifths. There were 19 National Merit finalists. 58 freshmen graduated first in their class.

Requirements: The SAT or ACT is required. In addition, applicants should be graduates of an accredited secondary school with 4 units of high school English, 3 of math, 2 each of science, social science, foreign language, and electives, and 1 of fine arts. A GPA of 2.0 is required. AP and CLEP credits are accepted.

Procedure: Freshmen are admitted to all sessions. Entrance exams should be taken in May of the junior year or January or March of the senior year. There is a rolling admissions plan. Applications should be filed by July 31 for fall entry, along with a $35 fee. Notification of early decision is sent rolling ; regular decision, on a rolling basis.

Transfer: 1256 transfer students enrolled in 2004-2005. A GPA of 2.0 is required to apply from a 4-year college; a GPA of 2.5 or an associate degree if applying from a 2-year college.

Visiting: There are regularly scheduled orientations for prospective students. There are guides for informal visits and visitors may sit in on classes and stay overnight. To schedule a visit, contact the Admissions Office.

Financial Aid: In a recent year, 57% of all full-time freshmen and 52% of continuing full-time students received some form of financial aid. 41% of full-time freshmen and 35% of continuing full-time students received need-based aid. The average freshman award was $6840. Need-based scholarships or need-based grants averaged $3888; need-based self-help aid (loans and jobs) averaged $1835; and non-need-based athletic scholarships averaged $5171. The CSS/Profile or FAFSA is required.

International Students: There are 234 international students enrolled. The school actively recruits these students. They must score satisfactorily on the written TOEFL and also take IELTS (International English Language Testing System).

Computers: Wireless access is available. All students may access the system. There are no time limits and no fees.

Graduates: From July 1, 2004 to June 30, 2005, 2938 bachelor's degrees were awarded. The most popular majors were marketing (7%), communication (6%), and criminal justice (5%). In an average class, 1%

graduate in 3 years or less, 17% graduate in 4 years or less, 43% graduate in 5 years or less, and 50% graduate in 6 years or less.

Admissions Contact: Director of Admissions.
E-mail: *admissions@uc.edu* Web: *www.uc.edu*

UNIVERSITY OF DAYTON   B-4
Dayton, OH 45469   (937) 229-4411
(800) 837-7433; Fax: (937) 229-4729

Full-time: 3476 men, 3437 women	Faculty: 353; IIA, av$
Part-time: 280 men, 233 women	Ph.D.s: 94%
Graduate: 1316 men, 1827 women	Student/Faculty: 20 to 1
Year: semesters, summer session	Tuition: $22,046
Application Deadline: open	Room & Board: $6780
Freshman Class: 8679 applied, 6899 accepted, 1981 enrolled	
SAT Verbal/Math: 560/580*	ACT: 25 VERY COMPETITIVE

The University of Dayton, founded in 1850, is a nonprofit, private, comprehensive institution affiliated with the Roman Catholic Church. Part of the Southwestern Ohio Council for Higher Education, it has undergraduate and graduate programs emphasizing the arts and sciences, business administration, engineering, education, allied professions and law. There are 4 undergraduate schools and 1 graduate school. In addition to regional accreditation, UD has baccalaureate program accreditation with AACSB, ABET, ADA, NASM, and NCATE. The 3 libraries contain 1million volumes, 800,000 microform items, and 3030 audio/video tapes/CDs/DVDs, and subscribe to 8000 periodicals including electronic. Computerized library services include the card catalog, interlibrary loans, and database searching. Special learning facilities include a learning resource center, art gallery, radio station, TV station, UD Research Institute, Bombeck Family Learning Center, a learning teaching center, and Davis Center for Portfolio Management. The 123-acre campus is in a suburban area 2 miles south of downtown Dayton. Including any residence halls, there are 46 buildings.

Student Life: 66% of undergraduates are from Ohio. Others are from 46 states, 32 foreign countries, and Canada. 52% are from public schools. 87% are white. 67% are Catholic; 12% Protestant. The average age of freshmen is 18; all undergraduates, 19. 14% do not continue beyond their first year; 73% remain to graduate.

Housing: 5760 students can be accommodated in college housing, which includes single-sex and coed dormitories, on-campus apartments, fraternity houses, and sorority houses. In addition, there are honors houses and special-interest houses. On-campus housing is available on a first-come, first-served basis and is available on a lottery system for upperclassmen. 95% of students live on campus; of those, 85% remain on campus on weekends. Upperclassmen may keep cars.

Activities: 15% of men belong to 2 local and 11 national fraternities; 18% of women belong to 1 local and 9 national sororities. There are 190 groups on campus, including art, band, cheerleading, chess, choir, chorale, chorus, computers, dance, debate, drama, drill team, ethnic, gay, honors, international, jazz band, literary magazine, marching band, musical theater, newspaper, orchestra, pep band, photography, political, professional, radio and TV, religious, social, social service, student government, symphony, and yearbook. Popular campus events include Christmas on Campus, Distinguished Speakers Series, and The Weekend Scene.

Sports: There are 7 intercollegiate sports for men and 10 for women, and 13 intramural sports for men and 13 for women. Facilities include a physical activities center, a field house, a 13,455-seat arena, a 11,000-seat football stadium, soccer and baseball fields, an outdoor track, indoor and outdoor tennis courts, racquetball and squash courts, a swimming pool, a basketball court, weight rooms, a fully equipped aerobic conditioning center, a strength and conditioning facility, a weight room, and a sports medicine complex.

Disabled Students: Wheelchair ramps, elevators, special parking, specially equipped rest rooms, special class scheduling, lowered drinking fountains, lowered telephones, a note-taking service, Braille services, interpreters for hearing impaired, talking books, electronic text, adaptive computer lab, oral tests, and untimed tests are available.

Services: Counseling and information services are available, as is tutoring in every subject. There is a reader service for the blind and remedial math. Developmental math, reading and writing, and nonremedial tutoring are available.

Campus Safety and Security: Measures include 24-hour foot and vehicle patrol, security escort services, informal discussions, and pamphlets/posters/films. There are emergency telephones, lighted pathways/sidewalks, bike patrol, controlled dorm access, video cameras, and on-campus EMTs.

Programs of Study: UD confers B.A., B.S., B.C.E., B.Ch.E., B.E.E., B.F.A., B.G.S., B.M.E., and B.Mus. degrees. Master's and doctoral degrees are also awarded. Bachelor's degrees are awarded in BIOLOGICAL SCIENCE (biochemistry, biology/biological science, environmental biology, and nutrition), BUSINESS (accounting, banking and finance, business economics, international business management, management information systems, management science, marketing/retailing/ merchandising, operations research, and sports management), COMMUNICATIONS AND THE ARTS (art history and appreciation, broadcasting, communications, design, dramatic arts, English, fine arts, French, German, journalism, music, music performance, music theory and composition, photography, public relations, and Spanish), COMPUTER AND PHYSICAL SCIENCE (chemistry, computer science, geology, information sciences and systems, mathematics, physical sciences, and physics), EDUCATION (art, early childhood, elementary, music, physical, secondary, and special), ENGINEERING AND ENVIRONMENTAL DESIGN (chemical engineering, civil engineering, computer engineering, computer technology, electrical/electronics engineering, electrical/ electronics engineering technology, engineering technology, industrial engineering technology, manufacturing technology, mechanical engineering, and mechanical engineering technology), HEALTH PROFESSIONS (exercise science, music therapy, predentistry, and premedicine), SOCIAL SCIENCE (American studies, criminal justice, dietetics, economics, history, international studies, philosophy, political science/ government, prelaw, psychology, religion, and sociology). Engineering, business, and education are the strongest academically. Business/ marketing and engineering/engineering technologies are the largest.

Required: To graduate, all students must complete a minimum of 120 semester hours with at least 30 hours of residence, and maintain a minimum GPA of 2.0. The curricula must include general education requirements, including 4 classes in religious studies and philosophy as well as basic skills requirements. Departmental requirements vary.

Special: Co-op programs are available in 24 majors; students in other majors may participate in the co-op program with the approval of their department. Internships are available in all majors. More than 100 companies participate in the work-study programs. Cross-registration is available with the Southwestern Ohio Council for Higher Education. Study abroad, a Washigton semester, accelerated degree programs in business and engineering, and B.A.-B.S. degrees in chemistry, math, economics, and psychology are available. For students who wish to have a dual major, almost all programs may be combined. Student designed majors include general studies and interdisciplinary studies. An engineering curriculum agreement exist's with Sinclair Community College. There are 14 national honor societies, a freshman honors program, and all departments have honors programs.

Faculty/Classroom: 73% of faculty are male; 27%, female. 88% teach undergraduates. The average class size in an introductory lecture is 32; in a laboratory, 15; and in a regular course, 27.

Admissions: 79% of the 2005-2006 applicants were accepted. The SAT scores for the 2005-2006 freshman class were: Verbal--16% below 500, 47% between 500 and 599, 33% between 600 and 700, and 4% above 700; Math--10% below 500, 40% between 500 and 599, 40% between 600 and 700, and 10% above 700. The ACT scores were 8% below 21, 24% between 21 and 23, 30% between 24 and 26, 16% between 27 and 28, and 22% above 28. 42% of the current freshmen were in the top fifth of their class; 71% were in the top two fifths. There were 3 National Merit finalists and 13 semifinalists. 36 freshmen graduated first in their class.

Requirements: The SAT or ACT is required. In addition, applicants should be graduates of an accredited secondary school with 16 units in English, math, science, social studies, and academic electives. In addition, 2 units of foreign language are required for admission to the College of Arts and Sciences. The GED is accepted. High school transcripts and official scores from the ACT or SAT must be submitted. An essay or personal statement, recommendation from the high school guidance counselor, and an interview are recommended. Music students must audition. AP and CLEP credits are accepted.

Procedure: Freshmen are admitted fall, winter, and summer. Entrance exams should be taken by December of the senior year. There are deferred admissions and rolling admissions plans. Application deadlines are open. 69 applicants were on the 2005 waiting list; 4 were admitted. Applications are accepted on-line.

Transfer: 112 transfer students enrolled in a recent year. Attention is directed to college and high school GPA and course selection. The minimum grade point average is 2.0. The School of Education and Allied Professions requires a minimum 2.5 GPA in previous college work. Achievement of the minimum GPA does not guarantee admission. For students under 21 years of age, results of the SAT or ACT are required. All students applying to the School of Education and Allied Professions, must submit SAT or ACT and Praxis I scores. 30 of 120 credits required for the bachelor's degree must be completed at UD.

Visiting: There are regularly scheduled orientations for prospective students, including an admission interview, financial aid consultation, campus tour, residence hall tour, and faculty or class visit. High school seniors who have been accepted to the university may participate in an overnight visit during the winter semester. There are guides for informal visits and visitors may sit in on classes and stay overnight. To schedule a visit, contact campus visit coordinator, Office of Admission.

Financial Aid: In 2005-2006, 93% of all full-time freshmen and 90% of continuing full-time students received some form of financial aid. 57% of full-time freshmen and 58% of continuing full-time students received need-based aid. The average freshman award was $13,473. Need-based

scholarships or need-based grants averaged $9185; need-based self-help aid (loans and jobs) averaged $3332; non-need-based athletic scholarships averaged $15,512; and other non-need-based awards and non-need-based scholarships averaged $5320. The FAFSA is required. The priority date for freshman financial aid applications for fall entry is March 31.

International Students: In a recent year, there were 39 international students enrolled. The school actively recruits these students. A satisfactory score is required on the written TOEFL or take the English Language Proficiency Test, or the Advanced Placement International English Language Examination.

Computers: All students may access the system 24 hours a day, 7 day a week. There are no time limits and no fees. All students are required to have personal computers.

Graduates: In a recent year, 1654 bachelor's degrees were awarded. The most popular majors were business/marketing (26%), engineering/engineering technologies (15%), and education (12%). In an average class, 57% graduate in 4 years or less, 75% graduate in 5 years or less, and 76% graduate in 6 years or less. 210 companies recruited on campus in a recent year.

Admissions Contact: Robert F. Durkle, Director of Admission. E-mail: *admission@udayton.edu* Web: *http://admission.udayton.edu*

UNIVERSITY OF FINDLAY   B-2
Findlay, OH 45840

(419) 424-4732
(800) 548-0932; Fax: (419) 424-4822

Total Enrollment: 4600 men and women	Faculty: 160; IIA, --$
	Ph.D.s: 51%
Part-time: n/av	Student/Faculty: 16 to 1
Graduate: n/av	Tuition: $21,746
Year: semesters, summer session	Room & Board: $7492
Application Deadline: June 1	
Freshman Class: 3220 applied, 2110 accepted, 776 enrolled	
SAT Verbal/Math: 520/530*	ACT: 22 COMPETITIVE

The University of Findlay, founded in 1882, is a private, independent institution affiliated with the Churches of God, General Conference, offering liberal arts and sciences and career preparation programs. There are 4 undergraduate and 7 graduate schools. Enrollment figures in the above capsule are approximate. In addition to regional accreditation, Findlay has baccalaureate program accreditation with NCATE. The library contains 135,000 volumes, 90,000 microform items, and 1200 audio/video tapes/CDs/DVDs, and subscribes to 2500 periodicals including electronic. Computerized library services include interlibrary loans and database searching. Special learning facilities include a learning resource center, art gallery, planetarium, radio station, university-owned farm, equine facility, and emergency response training center. The 135-acre campus is in a small town 45 miles south of Toledo and 100 miles north of Columbus. Including any residence halls, there are 55 buildings.

Student Life: 80% of undergraduates are from Ohio. Students are from 45 states, 41 foreign countries, and Canada. 80% are from public schools. 85% are white. 60% are Protestant; 35% Catholic. The average age of freshmen is 18; all undergraduates, 22. 25% do not continue beyond their first year; 55% remain to graduate.

Housing: 1000 students can be accommodated in college housing, which includes single-sex dorms, on-campus apartments, fraternity houses, and sorority houses. In addition, there are honors houses, language houses, and special-interest houses. On-campus housing is guaranteed for all 4 years. 65% of students commute. Alcohol is not permitted. All students may keep cars.

Activities: 4% of men belong to 3 national fraternities; 1% of women belong to 2 national sororities. There are 40 groups on campus, including art, band, cheerleading, choir, chorale, chorus, computers, drama, drum and bugle corps, ethnic, honors, international, jazz band, literary magazine, marching band, musical theater, newspaper, pep band, political, professional, radio and TV, religious, social, social service, student government, and yearbook. Popular campus events include Family Weekend, International Night, and Spring Bash.

Sports: There are 14 intercollegiate sports for men and 12 for women, and 15 intramural sports for men and 15 for women. Facilities include a fitness center, a 7200-seat stadium, a 25-meter pool, racquetball courts, a phys ed center with a 3200-seat gym, an ice arena, indoor track, and 4-court athletic building.

Disabled Students: 90% of the campus is accessible. Wheelchair ramps, elevators, special parking, specially equipped rest rooms, special class scheduling, lowered drinking fountains, and specially equipped residence hall rooms are available.

Services: Counseling and information services are available, as is tutoring in most subjects. There is a reader service for the blind, and remedial math, reading, and writing. Other services include assistance with note taking, test taking, research papers, and study skills, and support for the hearing impaired, including interpreters.

Campus Safety and Security: Measures include 24-hour foot and vehicle patrol, self-defense education, security escort services, and informal discussions. There are pamphlets/posters/films, emergency telephones, and lighted pathways/sidewalks.

Programs of Study: Findlay confers B.A. and B.S. degrees. Associate and master's degrees are also awarded. Bachelor's degrees are awarded in AGRICULTURE (equine science), BIOLOGICAL SCIENCE (biology/biological science), BUSINESS (accounting, banking and finance, business administration and management, business economics, business systems analysis, hospitality management services, human resources, international business management, and marketing/retailing/merchandising), COMMUNICATIONS AND THE ARTS (arts administration/management, broadcasting, communications, dramatic arts, English, English as a second/foreign language, illustration, Japanese, Spanish, studio art, and technical and business writing), COMPUTER AND PHYSICAL SCIENCE (chemistry, computer science, mathematics, and science), EDUCATION (art, athletic training, bilingual/bicultural, business, elementary, foreign languages, middle school, physical, and secondary), ENGINEERING AND ENVIRONMENTAL DESIGN (environmental science, occupational safety and health, and technological management), HEALTH PROFESSIONS (health science, nuclear medical technology, nursing, occupational therapy, physician's assistant, premedicine, and preveterinary science), SOCIAL SCIENCE (criminal justice, economics, forensic studies, history, international studies, philosophy, political science/government, prelaw, psychology, religion, social work, and sociology). Business administration, preveterinary medicine, and education are the strongest academically. Business administration, equestrian studies, and education are the largest.

Required: All students must complete 36 semester hours of general education requirements, including fine arts, humanities, natural science, math, social science, and religion or philosophy, and most take courses in wellness, computer science, and statistics. There are competency requirements in library use, English and reading, and a wellness course. A total of 124 semester hours with a minimum GPA of 2.0 is required in order to graduate.

Special: Co-op programs are available in accounting and occupational health and safety. There is cross-registration with Mount Carmel College of Nursing. The field experience program provides up to 20 semester hours in field placement. Internships are available for business, business education, communication, hazardous materials management, and theater majors. Through the College Consortium for International Studies, study abroad is possible in 16 countries. Work-study, a Washington semester, dual and student-designed majors, a general studies degree, pass/fail options, and credit for life experience are offered. Nondegree study is possible. There is a freshman honors program.

Faculty/Classroom: 60% of faculty are male; 40%, female. All teach undergraduates. The average class size in an introductory lecture is 23; in a laboratory, 15; and in a regular course, 22.

Admissions: 66% of the 2005-2006 applicants were accepted. The SAT scores for the 2005-2006 freshman class were: Verbal--38% below 500, 43% between 500 and 599, 16% between 600 and 700, and 3% above 700; Math--34% below 500, 46% between 500 and 599, 19% between 600 and 700, and 1% above 700. The ACT scores were 41% below 21, 26% between 21 and 23, 18% between 24 and 26, 10% between 27 and 28, and 5% above 28. 49% of the current freshmen were in the top fifth of their class; 80% were in the top two fifths. 137 freshmen graduated first in their class.

Requirements: The SAT or ACT is required. In addition, applicants should have completed 16 high school credits or GED equivalents, including 4 years of English, 2 years of social studies/history, 3 to 4 math courses, and 2 to 3 science courses. A letter of recommendation and an essay are required for all applicants. A GPA of 2.3 is required. AP and CLEP credits are accepted. Important factors in the admissions decision are advanced placement or honor courses, evidence of special talent, and extracurricular activities record.

Procedure: Freshmen are admitted to all sessions. Entrance exams should be taken during fall of the senior year or the spring of the junior year. There are deferred admissions and rolling admissions plans. Applications should be filed by June 1 for fall entry and December 1 for winter entry. Notification is sent on a rolling basis. Applications are accepted on-line.

Transfer: A minimum 2.0 GPA and eligibility to return to the current institution are required. An interview is recommended. 30 of 124 credits required for the bachelor's degree must be completed at Findlay.

Visiting: There are regularly scheduled orientations for prospective students, including a tour, interview, coach/faculty visits, and lunch. There are guides for informal visits and visitors may sit in on classes and stay overnight. To schedule a visit, contact the Admissions Office at (800) 548-0932, ext. 4732.

Financial Aid: The FAFSA is required. Check with the school for application deadlines.

International Students: The school actively recruits these students. A satisfactory score is required on the written TOEFL.

Computers: All students may access the system. There are no time limits and no fees.

Admissions Contact: Randall Langston, Director of Undergraduate Admissions. A video is available. E-mail: *admissions@findlay.edu* Web: *www.findlay.edu*

UNIVERSITY OF RIO GRANDE D-5

Rio Grande, OH 45674 **(740) 245-5353**

(800) 282-7201; Fax: (740) 245-7260

Full-time: 620 men, 900 women	**Faculty:** 84; IIB, -$
Part-time: 115 men, 220 women	**Ph.D.s:** 52%
Graduate: 25 men, 75 women	**Student/Faculty:** 20 to 1
Year: quarters, summer session	**Tuition:** $4500 ($5000)
Application Deadline: n/av	**Room & Board:** $4250
Freshman Class: n/av	**ACT:** required
	NONCOMPETITIVE

The University of Rio Grande, founded in 1876, is a private institution offering degree programs in the liberal arts and sciences, business, and education. Check with the school for specific tuition rates that vary by program. Figures in above capsule and in this profile are approximate. There are 9 undergraduate schools and 1 graduate school. In addition to regional accreditation, Rio has baccalaureate program accreditation with CSWE, NASDTEC, and NLN. The library contains 96,731 volumes, 274,400 microform items, and 1835 audio/video tapes/CDs/DVDs, and subscribes to 850 periodicals including electronic. Computerized library services include the card catalog, interlibrary loans, and database searching. Special learning facilities include a learning resource center, art gallery, radio station, and TV station. The 194-acre campus is in a rural area 100 miles southeast of Columbus. Including any residence halls, there are 27 buildings.

Student Life: 94% of undergraduates are from Ohio. Students are from 12 states, 15 foreign countries, and Canada. 98% are from public schools. 97% are white. The average age of freshmen is 23; all undergraduates, 24.

Housing: 640 students can be accommodated in college housing, which includes single-sex and coed dorms. In addition, there are special-interest houses. On-campus housing is guaranteed for all 4 years. 76% of students commute. All students may keep cars.

Activities: 6% of men belong to 2 local and 2 national fraternities; 4% of women belong to 5 local sororities. There are 39 groups on campus, including band, cheerleading, choir, chorale, chorus, drama, ecology, ethnic, gay, honors, international, jazz band, musical theater, newspaper, orchestra, pep band, photography, political, professional, radio and TV, religious, social, social service, and student government. Popular campus events include Ethnofest, Bob Evans Farm Festival, and Community Service Day.

Sports: There are 5 intercollegiate sports for men and 5 for women, and 10 intramural sports for men and 10 for women. Facilities include 2 gyms, tennis courts, an indoor Olympic-size pool, an outdoor track, handball, racquetball, and sand volleyball courts, a fitness center, a cross-country track, and soccer, baseball, and softball fields.

Disabled Students: 70% of the campus is accessible. Wheelchair ramps, elevators, special parking, specially equipped rest rooms, special class scheduling, lowered drinking fountains, lowered telephones, note takers, tape recorders, and closed-caption TV are available.

Services: Counseling and information services are available, as is tutoring in every subject. There is a reader service for the blind, and remedial math, reading, and writing. There is also an Accessibility Office.

Campus Safety and Security: Measures include 24-hour foot and vehicle patrol, security escort services, informal discussions, and pamphlets/posters/films. There are emergency telephones and lighted pathways/sidewalks.

Programs of Study: Rio confers B.A., B.S., B.S.I.T., B.S.N., and B.S.W. degrees. Associate and master's degrees are also awarded. Bachelor's degrees are awarded in BIOLOGICAL SCIENCE (biology/biological science), BUSINESS (accounting, business administration and management, business economics, international business management, and marketing management), COMMUNICATIONS AND THE ARTS (art, communications, English, fine arts, music, and public relations), COMPUTER AND PHYSICAL SCIENCE (chemistry, computer science, mathematics, and physical sciences), EDUCATION (art, business, early childhood, education of the mentally handicapped, elementary, English, health, mathematics, music, physical, psychology, reading, science, secondary, social science, and social studies), ENGINEERING AND ENVIRONMENTAL DESIGN (computer technology, drafting and design technology, electrical/electronics engineering technology, environmental science, industrial engineering technology, manufacturing technology, preengineering, and woodworking), HEALTH PROFESSIONS (medical technology, nursing, predentistry, premedicine, and preveterinary science), SOCIAL SCIENCE (American studies, behavioral science, economics, history, humanities, physical fitness/movement, political science/government, prelaw, psychology, social work, and sociology). Education, business, and nursing are the strongest academically. Education, general studies, and business are the largest.

Required: Students must complete 190 to 198 quarter hours, including 47 to 53 in the major, with a minimum GPA of 2.0. The required general studies program, for all but teacher certification and industrial technology majors, includes 13 credit hours in communication skills, 12 hours each in the humanities, math, natural sciences, and social sciences, 3 hours in health and phys ed, and 1 hour in liberal arts.

Special: Rio offers internships in social work, communications, and business, a Washington semester, student-designed majors, limited pass/fail options, and credit for life, military, or work experience. Nondegree study for 1-year certificates in secretarial science and personal computer applications is also available. A community college on the same campus offers technical degree programs that are built into 4-year degrees. There are 3 national honor societies, a freshman honors program, and 1 departmental honors program.

Faculty/Classroom: 67% of faculty are male; 33%, female. All teach undergraduates. The average class size in an introductory lecture is 30; in a laboratory, 20; and in a regular course, 20.

Requirements: The ACT is required for applicants who are less than 5 years out of high school. Rio follows an open admissions policy for all applicants. A high school diploma or GED is required. For on-line applications, consult the Rio web site. A GPA of 2.0 is required. AP and CLEP credits are accepted.

Procedure: Freshmen are admitted to all sessions. Entrance exams should be taken no later than December of the senior year for those entering college the following fall. There are early admissions and rolling admissions plans. The college accepts all applicants. Notification is sent on a rolling basis. Check with the school for application deadlines. The application fee is $15.

Transfer: Candidates must submit a final transcript and a dean's evaluation form from the last school attended. 45 of 190 credits required for the bachelor's degree must be completed at Rio.

Visiting: There are regularly scheduled orientations for prospective students, with parents and students participating in 1- or 2-day sessions. The program includes half-day placement testing and presentations from various offices, campus e-mail, advising, and registration. Residential students stay in the dorms and have dinner with the president. There are guides for informal visits and visitors may sit in on classes and stay overnight. To schedule a visit, contact the Admissions Office.

Financial Aid: Rio is a member of CSS. The FAFSA and the college's own financial statement are required. Check with the school for current application deadlines.

International Students: The school actively recruits these students. They must score satisfactorily on the written TOEFL.

Computers: All students may access the system. The fee is $7 per quarter. It is strongly recommended that all students have a personal computer.

Admissions Contact: Mark F. Abell, Executive Director, Admissions. E-mail: *mabell@rio.edu* Web: *www.rio.edu*

UNIVERSITY OF TOLEDO B-1

Toledo, OH 43606-3398 **(419) 530-5720**

(800) 5TOLEDO; Fax: (419) 530-5745

Full-time: 6575 men, 6503 women	**Faculty:** 776; I, --$
Part-time: 1441 men, 1539 women	**Ph.D.s:** 75%
Graduate: 1448 men, 1195 women	**Student/Faculty:** 17 to 1
Year: semesters, summer session	**Tuition:** $7494 ($16,305)
Application Deadline: open	**Room & Board:** $8312
Freshman Class: 10,357 applied, 9737 accepted, 4494 enrolled	
SAT Verbal/Math: 510/530*	**ACT:** 22 **NONCOMPETITIVE**

The University of Toledo, founded in 1872, is a public comprehensive institution emphasizing undergraduate degree programs in the liberal arts and sciences, business, engineering, teacher preparation, and health professions. There are 8 undergraduate and 7 graduate schools. In addition to regional accreditation, UT has baccalaureate program accreditation with AACSB, ABET, ACPE, APTA, NASM, and NCATE. The 3 libraries contain 1,610,000 volumes, 1,614,490 microform items, and 7800 audio/video tapes/CDs/DVDs, and subscribe to 8000 periodicals including electronic. Computerized library services include the card catalog, interlibrary loans, and database searching. Special learning facilities include a learning resource center, art gallery, planetarium, and radio station. The 450-acre campus is in a suburban area 6 miles northwest of downtown Toledo. Including any residence halls, there are 98 buildings.

Student Life: 90% of undergraduates are from Ohio. Others are from 45 states, 105 foreign countries, and Canada. 75% are white; 13% African American. The average age of freshmen is 19; all undergraduates, 22. 28% do not continue beyond their first year; 45% remain to graduate.

Housing: 4098 students can be accommodated in college housing, which includes single-sex and coed dorms, fraternity houses, and sorority houses. In addition, there are honors houses, special-interest houses, and international house. On-campus housing is available on a first-come, first-served basis. 86% of students commute. All students may keep cars.

Activities: 6% of men belong to 16 national fraternities; 7% of women belong to 1 local and 12 national sororities. There are 200 groups on campus, including art, band, cheerleading, chess, choir, chorale, chorus, computers, dance, drama, drill team, ethnic, film, gay, honors, international, jazz band, literary magazine, marching band, musical theater, newspaper, orchestra, pep band, photography, political, professional, radio and TV, religious, social, social service, student government, and symphony. Popular campus events include Songfest and Greek Week.

Sports: There are 9 intercollegiate sports for men and 10 for women, and 48 intramural sports for men and 48 for women. Facilities include a recreation center, a 27,000-seat stadium, a 9000-seat arena, a field house, 3 pools, 12 tennis courts, an indoor/outdoor track, a 4-field recreational softball complex, and recreational/sport club fields.

Disabled Students: 96% of the campus is accessible. Wheelchair ramps, elevators, special parking, specially equipped rest rooms, special class scheduling, lowered drinking fountains, and lowered telephones are available.

Services: Counseling and information services are available, as is tutoring in every subject. There is a reader service for the blind, and remedial math, reading, and writing.

Campus Safety and Security: Measures include 24-hour foot and vehicle patrol, self-defense education, security escort services, and shuttle buses. There are informal discussions, pamphlets/posters/films, emergency telephones, lighted pathways/sidewalks, and student patrols. All security officers are state-certified with full arrest authority.

Programs of Study: UT confers B.A., B.A.T., B.A.Env.Studies, B.A. in Africana Studies, B.B.A., B.Ed., B.E.T., B.F.A., B.M., B.S.Admin. Svcs, B.S.C.E., B.S.Chem.Eng., B.S.Comp.Sci. and Eng., B.S.Const.Eng., B.S.Crim.Just., B.S.C.S.E., B.S.E., B.S.E.E., B.S.El.Eng.Tech., B.S.Eng.Phys., B.S. Env. Sci., B.S. Exer. Sci., B.S.HealthCareSpvsn., B.S.I.E., B.S. in Bioeng., B.S. in Comp.Sci. and Eng. Tech., B.S.M.E., B.S. Med.Tech., B.S.N., B.S.Pharm., B.S.P.T., B.S.Rad.Sci., B.S. Resp.Care, B.S.W., and B.Voc.Ed. degrees. Associate, master's, and doctoral degrees are also awarded. Bachelor's degrees are awarded in BIOLOGICAL SCIENCE (biology/biological science), BUSINESS (accounting, banking and finance, business administration and management, marketing/retailing/merchandising, and recreation and leisure services), COMMUNICATIONS AND THE ARTS (art history and appreciation, communications, dramatic arts, English, film arts, fine arts, French, German, linguistics, music, and Spanish), COMPUTER AND PHYSICAL SCIENCE (chemistry, computer science, geology, information sciences and systems, mathematics, and physics), EDUCATION (art, business, early childhood, elementary, foreign languages, health, music, physical, science, secondary, special, and vocational), ENGINEERING AND ENVIRONMENTAL DESIGN (bioengineering, chemical engineering, civil engineering, computer engineering, electrical/electronics engineering, electromechanical technology, engineering, engineering technology, environmental science, industrial engineering, and mechanical engineering), HEALTH PROFESSIONS (nursing, pharmacy, physical therapy, and speech pathology/audiology), SOCIAL SCIENCE (anthropology, community services, criminal justice, economics, geography, history, humanities, international relations, philosophy, physical fitness/movement, political science/government, psychology, social work, sociology, and women's studies). Engineering, pharmacy, and business are the strongest academically.

Required: To graduate, all students must complete 124 to 169 hours of credit, with a minimum of 60 in the major, and maintain a minimum GPA of 2.0. A core curriculum is required of all students. A thesis is required in the honors program. The number of hours required in the major varies.

Special: Special academic programs include internships in most majors, study abroad in 14 countries, and on-campus employment through the Financial Aid Office. There is a co-op program with the College of Engineering and cross-registration with Bowling Green State University. The B.A.-B.S. degree and dual majors are available in many areas of study. A general studies degree, student-designed majors, accelerated degrees, credit for life, military, and work experience, nondegree study, and pass/fail options are also offered. There are 56 national honor societies, a freshman honors program, and 21 departmental honors programs.

Faculty/Classroom: 60% of faculty are male; 40%, female. The average class size in an introductory lecture is 33; in a laboratory, 19; and in a regular course, 28.

Admissions: 94% of the 2005-2006 applicants were accepted. The SAT scores for the 2005-2006 freshman class were: Verbal--42% below 500, 39% between 500 and 599, 17% between 600 and 700, and 1% above 700; Math--34% below 500, 39% between 500 and 599, 24% between 600 and 700, and 2% above 700. The ACT scores were 38% below 21, 27% between 21 and 23, 21% between 24 and 26, 7% between 27 and 28, and 7% above 28. 29% of the current freshmen were in the top fifth of their class; 54% were in the top two fifths.

Requirements: The SAT or ACT is required. The ACT Optional Writing test is also required. In addition, the university follows an open admissions policy for Ohio applicants. Students should be graduates of an accredited secondary school or hold the GED. The preparatory program should include 4 years of English, 3 each of math, natural science, and social studies, and 2 of a foreign language. A GPA of 2.0 is required for out-of-state applicants. AP and CLEP credits are accepted.

Procedure: Freshmen are admitted to all sessions. Entrance exams should be taken late in the junior year or early in the senior year. There is a deferred admissions plan. Application deadlines are open. Application fee is $40. Applications are accepted on-line.

Transfer: 855 transfer students enrolled in 2004-2005. Applicants must have a minimum of 12 quarter or 8 semester college credits and a GPA of 2.0. An interview is recommended.

Visiting: There are regularly scheduled orientations for prospective students, including an interview with an admissions representative and a student-guided campus tour. Academic appointments are availabel by request. There are guides for informal visits and visitors may sit in on classes and stay overnight. To schedule a visit, contact the Office of Undergraduate Admissions at (419) 530-8700 or *enroll@utoledo.edu*.

Financial Aid: In 2005-2006, 85% of all full-time freshmen and 79% of continuing full-time students received some form of financial aid. 57% of full-time freshmen and 51% of continuing full-time students received need-based aid. The average freshman award was $10,445. Need-based scholarships or need-based grants averaged $3866 ($12,692 maximum); need-based self-help aid (loans and jobs) averaged $2942 ($8945 maximum); non-need-based athletic scholarships averaged $15,211 ($25,232 maximum); and other non-need-based awards and non-need-based scholarships averaged $8202 ($29,105 maximum). Average annual earnings from campus work are $2304. The average financial indebtedness of the 2005 graduate was $18,629. UT is a member of CSS. The FAFSA is required. The priority date for freshman financial aid applications for fall entry is April 1.

International Students: The school actively recruits these students. A satisfactory score is required on the written TOEFL.

Computers: All students may access the system 24 hours per day, except from Saturday at 5 P.M. to Sunday at noon. There are no time limits and no fees.

Graduates: From July 1, 2004 to June 30, 2005, 2775 bachelor's degrees were awarded. The most popular majors were business (21%), education (15%), and health and human services (11%).

Admissions Contact: Jennifer Kwiatkowski, Interim Director of Freshman Admissions. A video is available. E-mail: *enroll@.utoledo.edu* Web: *www.utoledo.edu*

URBANA UNIVERSITY

Urbana, OH 43078-2091

B-3

(937) 484-1356
(800) 7-URBANA; Fax: (937) 484-1322

Full-time: 495 men, 415 women	**Faculty:** 55
Part-time: 191 men, 346 women	**Ph.Ds:** 74%
Graduate: 32 men, 58 women	**Student/Faculty:** 17 to 1
Year: semesters, summer session	**Tuition:** $15,180
Application Deadline: open	**Room & Board:** $6010
Freshman Class: n/av	
SAT or ACT: required	**COMPETITIVE**

Urbana University, founded in 1850 and affiliated with the Swedenborgian Church, is a independent institution emphasizing programs in liberal arts, business, professional training, and teacher preparation. Some of the figures in the above capsule and in this profile are approximate. There are 2 undergraduate and 2 graduate schools. The library contains 70,000 volumes, 8176 microform items, and 2099 audio/video tapes/CDs/DVDs, and subscribes to 328 periodicals including electronic. Computerized library services include interlibrary loans, database searching, and Internet access. Special learning facilities include a learning resource center, TV station, a rare book room, and a history museum. The 128-acre campus is in a small town 40 miles west of Columbus and 50 miles north of Dayton. Including any residence halls, there are 30 buildings.

Student Life: 90% of undergraduates are from Ohio. Students are from 5 states and 5 foreign countries. 95% are from public schools. 79% are white; 17% African American. The average age of freshmen is 20; all undergraduates, 24. 23% do not continue beyond their first year; 35% remain to graduate.

Housing: 450 students can be accommodated in college housing, which includes single-sex and coed dorms. In addition, there are honors houses. On-campus housing is available on a lottery system for upperclassmen. 58% of students commute. All students may keep cars.

Activities: There are no fraternities or sororities. There are 20 groups on campus, including art, band, cheerleading, choir, chorus, drama, ethnic, honors, international, literary magazine, marching band, musical theater, newspaper, pep band, political, professional, religious, social service, and student government. Popular campus events include Spring Week, Founders Day, and Activities Fair.

Sports: There are 5 intercollegiate sports for men and 4 for women, and 6 intramural sports for men and 6 for women. Facilities include a community center with a 3500-seat gym, a pool, handball and racquetball courts, a weight room, and outdoor tennis courts.

Disabled Students: 30% of the campus is accessible. Wheelchair ramps, elevators, special parking, and special class scheduling are available.

Services: Counseling and information services are available, as is tutoring in most subjects. There is remedial math, reading, and writing. Taped textbooks, reading and writing labs, and study skills seminars are also available.

Campus Safety and Security: Measures include 24-hour foot and vehicle patrol, self-defense education, security escort services, and informal discussions. There are pamphlets/posters/films, emergency telephones, and lighted pathways/sidewalks.

Programs of Study: Urbana confers B.A., B.S., and B.S.Ed. degrees. Associate and master's degrees are also awarded. Bachelor's degrees are awarded in BUSINESS (business administration and management and sports management), COMMUNICATIONS AND THE ARTS (communications and English), COMPUTER AND PHYSICAL SCIENCE (science), EDUCATION (elementary, middle school, and secondary), HEALTH PROFESSIONS (premedicine and sports medicine), SOCIAL SCIENCE (criminal justice, liberal arts/general studies, philosophy, physical fitness/movement, prelaw, psychology, and sociology). Business and education are the strongest programs academically and the largest.

Required: To graduate, all students must complete 126 semester hours, with a minimum overall GPA of 2.0 and 2.5 in the major. Distribution requirements in a 47-49-hour core curriculum include 12 to 13 credit hours in math and science, 12 each in humanities and social sciences, 9 in communications, and 2 to 3 in health, phys ed, and recreation. The number of hours in the major varies. The business program requires business seminars; education graduates must take the NTE.

Special: Special academic programs include internships, cross-registration with the Southwestern Ohio Council for Higher Education, study abroad, and accelerated degree programs in teacher certification. B.A.-B.S. degrees, dual and student-designed majors, credit for life, military, and work experience, and nondegree study are also available. There is 1 national honor society, a freshman honors program, and 4 departmental honors program.

Faculty/Classroom: 60% of faculty are male; 40%, female. All teach undergraduates. No introductory courses are taught by graduate students. The average class size in an introductory lecture is 18; in a laboratory, 7; and in a regular course, 19.

Requirements: A satisfactory score on the SAT or ACT is required for applicants under 23 years of age; the ACT is preferred. Applicants must be graduates of an accredited secondary school with a GPA of 2.0. The GED is accepted. An essay is required of all applicants, and in interview is recommended. A GPA of 2.0 is required. CLEP credit is accepted. Important factors in the admissions decision are advanced placement or honor courses, evidence of special talent, and extracurricular activities record.

Procedure: Freshmen are admitted to all sessions. Entrance exams should be taken during the junior or senior year. There is a deferred admissions plan. Application deadlines are open. Applications are accepted on-line.

Transfer: 50 transfer students enrolled in 2004-2005. Applicants must have at least 30 college credits with a GPA of 2.25 and must be in good standing at their previous institution. 30 of 126 credits required for the bachelor's degree must be completed at Urbana.

Visiting: There are regularly scheduled orientations for prospective students, consisting of a campus tour and sessions on academics, athletics, performing arts, financial aid, and student life. There are guides for informal visits and visitors may sit in on classes and stay overnight. To schedule a visit, contact the Admissions Office.

Financial Aid: In a reent year need-based scholarships or need-based grants averaged $10,343; need-based self-help aid (loans and jobs) averaged $7532; other non-need-based awards and non-need-based scholarships averaged $3445; and need-based loans averaged $3157. The FAFSA, the state aid form, and the college's own financial statement are required.

International Students: There were 4 international students enrolled in a recent year. The school actively recruits these students. A satisfactory score is required on the written TOEFL.

Computers: All students may access the system. There are no time limits and no fees.

Admissions Contact: Melissa Tolle, Director of Admissions.
E-mail: *mtolle@urbana.edu* Web: *www.urbana.edu*

URSULINE COLLEGE — D-1
Pepper Pike, OH 44124

(440) 442-4203
(888) URSULINE; Fax: (440) 684-6138

Full-time: 39 men, 716 women	**Faculty:** 58; IIB, --$
Part-time: 48 men, 349 women	**Ph.D.s:** 63%
Graduate: 56 men, 286 women	**Student/Faculty:** 13 to 1
Year: semesters, summer session	**Tuition:** $19,090
Application Deadline: open	**Room & Board:** $6366
Freshman Class: 439 applied, 286 accepted, 138 enrolled	
SAT Verbal/Math: 480/480*	**ACT:** 21	**COMPETITIVE**

Ursuline College, established in 1871, is a private, liberal arts, primarily women's college affiliated with the Roman Catholic Church. There are 3 undergraduate and 2 graduate schools. In addition to regional accreditation, Ursuline has baccalaureate program accreditation with CSWE and NLN. The library contains 142,906 volumes, 4675 microform items, and 8394 audio/video tapes/CDs/DVDs, and subscribes to 13,317 periodicals including electronic. Computerized library services include the card catalog, interlibrary loans, database searching, and Internet access. Special learning facilities include a learning resource center, art gallery, a media center, and curriculum library. The 114-acre campus is in a suburban area 13 miles east of Cleveland. Including any residence halls, there are 16 buildings.

Student Life: 99% of undergraduates are from Ohio. Students are from 6 states and 5 foreign countries. 80% are from public schools. 69% are white; 26% African American. 42% are claim no religious affiliation; 30% Catholic; 11% Protestant. The average age of freshmen is 18; all undergraduates, 29. 35% do not continue beyond their first year; 50% remain to graduate.

Housing: 184 students can be accommodated in college housing, which includes single-sex and coed dorms. On-campus housing is guaranteed for all 4 years. 86% of students commute. Alcohol is not permitted. All students may keep cars.

Activities: There are no fraternities or sororities. There are 19 groups on campus, including choir, drama, ethnic, international, literary magazine, professional, religious, social, social service, and student government. Popular campus events include All College Day, a formal dance, and charity benefits.

Sports: There are 7 intercollegiate sports for women and 5 intramural sports for women. Facilities include a fitness center, a swimming pool, a gym, and a campus center.

Disabled Students: 90% of the campus is accessible. Wheelchair ramps, elevators, special parking, and specially equipped rest rooms are available.

Services: Counseling and information services are available, as is tutoring in most subjects. There is a reader service for the blind, and remedial math, reading, and writing.

Campus Safety and Security: Measures include 24-hour foot and vehicle patrol, security escort services, informal discussions, and pamphlets/posters/films. There are emergency telephones and lighted pathways/sidewalks.

Programs of Study: Ursuline confers B.A. and B.S.N. degrees. Master's degrees are also awarded. Bachelor's degrees are awarded in BIOLOGICAL SCIENCE (biology/biological science and biotechnology), BUSINESS (accounting, business administration and management, fashion merchandising, human resources, management information systems, and marketing management), COMMUNICATIONS AND THE ARTS (art, English, graphic design, historic preservation, and public relations), COMPUTER AND PHYSICAL SCIENCE (mathematics), EDUCATION (early childhood, elementary, middle school, secondary, and special), HEALTH PROFESSIONS (allied health, health care administration, nursing, and premedicine), SOCIAL SCIENCE (American studies, child care/child and family studies, fashion design and technology, history, humanities, law, philosophy, prelaw, psychology, religion, social work, and sociology). Nursing is the strongest academically. Nursing and business are the largest.

Required: To graduate, students must complete 128 semester hours for the B.A. and 129 for the B.S.N., with a minimum GPA of 2.0 (2.5 in education courses). All students must take 49 credits of general education courses, structured to develop progressive stages of learning.

Special: Co-op programs are generally available to business, public relations, and fashion merchandising majors. Ursuline offers cross-registration with colleges in the NE Ohio Commission of Higher Education. Internships, a general studies degree, dual and student-designed majors, nondegree study, and accelerated degree programs in business management, health care administration, legal studies, and management information systems are available. Students may receive credit for life, military, or work experience. There are pass/fail options and a continuing studies program for nontraditional students. There are 2 national honor societies and 3 departmental honors programs.

Faculty/Classroom: 27% of faculty are male; 73%, female. 80% teach undergraduates. No introductory courses are taught by graduate students. The average class size in an introductory lecture is 14; in a laboratory, 10; and in a regular course, 13.

Admissions: 65% of the 2005-2006 applicants were accepted. The SAT scores for the 2005-2006 freshman class were: Verbal--62% below 500, 33% between 500 and 599, and 5% between 600 and 700; Math--59% below 500, 34% between 500 and 599, and 7% between 600 and 700. The ACT scores were 51% below 21, 28% between 21 and 23, 15% between 24 and 26, 5% between 27 and 28, and 1% above 28. 51% of the current freshmen were in the top fifth of their class; 78% were in the top two fifths. 3 freshmen graduated first in their class.

Requirements: The SAT or ACT is required. In addition, students should be graduates of an accredited secondary school and have a GPA of 2.5. Recommended college preparatory courses include 4 units of English, 3 each of social studies, math, and science, 2 of a foreign language, and 1 each of fine/performing arts and phys ed/health. A recommendation from a teacher or counselor is required and an interview is encouraged. A GPA of 2.5 is required. AP and CLEP credits are accepted. Important factors in the admissions decision are advanced placement or honor courses, recommendations by school officials, and leadership record.

Procedure: Freshmen are admitted fall, spring, and summer. Entrance exams should be taken in the junior year. There are deferred admissions and rolling admissions plans. Application deadlines are open. Notification is sent on a rolling basis. Application fee is $25. Applications are accepted on-line.

Transfer: 161 transfer students enrolled in 2004-2005. Offical copies of all transcripts and a 2.5 GPA are required. Students with less than 24 semester hours must provide high school transcripts. 43 of 128 credits required for the bachelor's degree must be completed at Ursuline.

Visiting: There are regularly scheduled orientations for prospective students, including an open house and overnight visit. There are guides for informal visits and visitors may sit in on classes and stay overnight. To schedule a visit, contact the Admissions Office.

Financial Aid: In 2005-2006, all full-time freshmen and 93% of continuing full-time students received some form of financial aid. 94% of full-time freshmen received need-based aid. The average freshman award was $17,703. Need-based scholarships or need-based grants averaged $8179 ($17,516 maximum); need-based self-help aid (loans and jobs) averaged $4392 ($9625 maximum); non-need-based athletic scholarships averaged $4293 ($9000 maximum); and other non-need-based awards and non-need-based scholarships averaged $4966 ($12,900 maximum). All of undergraduates work part time. Average annual earnings from campus work are $620. The average financial indebtedness of the 2005 graduate was $23,000. The FAFSA and the college's own financial statement are required. The deadline for filing freshman financial aid applications for fall entry is March 1.

International Students: There are 6 international students enrolled. The school actively recruits these students. Satisfactory scores are required on the written TOEFL and the SAT or the ACT.

Computers: Wireless access is available. Access to the college's network is available on 72 PCs in labs in 3 buildings and the library. Wired drops are available in the Pilla Center and library, and wireless APs are available in the Pilla Center, Science Building, and library. All students may access the system daily at designated hours. There are no time limits. The fee is $95 per semester.

Graduates: From July 1, 2004 to June 30, 2005, 240 bachelor's degrees were awarded. The most popular majors were nursing (29%), business (27%), and education (15%). In an average class, 31% graduate in 4 years or less, 43% graduate in 5 years or less, and 47% graduate in 6 years or less.

Admissions Contact: Sarah Carr, Director of Admission.
E-mail: *admission@ursuline.edu* Web: *ursuline.edu*

WALSH UNIVERSITY　　　　　　　　　　　　　D-2

North Canton, OH 44720-3396　　　　　　　(330) 490-7172
　　　　　　　　　　　　(800) 362-9846; Fax: (330) 490-7165

Full-time: 557 men, 865 women	**Faculty:** 79; IIB, --$
Part-time: 127 men, 320 women	**Ph.D.s:** 79%
Graduate: 96 men, 230 women	**Student/Faculty:** 18 to 1
Year: semesters, summer session	**Tuition:** $16,540
Application Deadline: see profile	**Room & Board:** $6900
Freshman Class: 1061 applied, 946 accepted, 447 enrolled	
ACT: 22	**COMPETITIVE**

Walsh University was established in 1958 by the Brothers of Christian Instruction, a religious order of the Roman Catholic Church. The private institution offers undergraduate programs in liberal arts, business, communication, education, professional training, and nursing. There are 5 graduate programs. In addition to regional accreditation, Walsh has baccalaureate program accreditation with NLN. The library contains 138,985 volumes, 8634 microform items, and 1468 audio/video tapes/CDs/DVDs, and subscribes to 24,867 periodicals including electronic. Computerized library services include the card catalog, interlibrary loans, database searching, and Internet access. Special learning facilities include a learning resource center, radio station, a child development center, and a museum for vacuum sweepers. The 143-acre campus is in a small town 20 miles south of Akron. Including any residence halls, there are 15 buildings.

Student Life: 97% of undergraduates are from Ohio. Others are from 15 states, 20 foreign countries, and Canada. 73% are from public schools. 78% are white. Most are Catholic. The average age of freshmen is 20; all undergraduates, 22. 22% do not continue beyond their first year; 54% remain to graduate.

Housing: 731 students can be accommodated in college housing, which includes single-sex and coed dormitories and on-campus apartments. In addition, there are special-interest houses, study floors, and substance-free floors. On-campus housing is guaranteed for all 4 years. 65% of students commute. All students may keep cars.

Activities: There are no fraternities or sororities. There are 25 groups on campus, including cheerleading, chess, choir, chorale, computers, dance, drama, ethnic, forensics, honors, international, leadership honor societies, literary magazine, newspaper, pep band, political, professional, radio and TV, religious, social, social service, student government, and yearbook. Popular campus events include Fall Fest, Apollo Night, and Late Night Finals Breakfast.

Sports: There are 9 intercollegiate sports for men and 10 for women, and 9 intramural sports for men and 9 for women. Facilities include a 1200-seat gym, outdoor basketball and tennis courts, a track, softball and baseball fields, practice and intramural fields, a soccer field, a game room, and a student exercise and weight room.

Disabled Students: All of the campus is accessible. Wheelchair ramps, elevators, special parking, specially equipped rest rooms, special class scheduling, lowered drinking fountains, lowered telephones, and special housing are available.

Services: Counseling and information services are available, as is tutoring in every subject. There is remedial math, reading, and writing.

Campus Safety and Security: Measures include 24-hour foot and vehicle patrol, self-defense education, security escort services, and informal discussions. There are pamphlets/posters/films, emergency telephones, and lighted pathways/sidewalks.

Programs of Study: Walsh confers B.A., B.S., B.S.Ed., and B.S.N. degrees. Associate and master's degrees are also awarded. Bachelor's degrees are awarded in BIOLOGICAL SCIENCE (biology/biological science), BUSINESS (accounting, banking and finance, business administration and management, management information systems, and marketing/retailing/merchandising), COMMUNICATIONS AND THE ARTS (communications, English, French, and Spanish), COMPUTER AND PHYSICAL SCIENCE (chemistry, computer science, mathematics, and science), EDUCATION (early childhood, elementary, middle school, physical, secondary, and special), HEALTH PROFESSIONS (clinical science, nursing, physical therapy, predentistry, premedicine, prephysical therapy, and preveterinary science), SOCIAL SCIENCE (history, international studies, pastoral studies, philosophy, political science/government, prelaw, psychology, sociology, and theological studies). Business, psychology, and nursing are the strongest academically. Education, business, and biology are the largest.

Required: To graduate, students must complete 130 semester hours with a minimum 2.0 GPA. The number of hours required in the major varies. A core curriculum of 37 hours is required, including courses in English, art or music appreciation, science, social science, math, humanities, theology, philosophy, and possibly a foreign language.

Special: Work-study programs are available to students having substantial financial need. A 3-2 program in natural resources, including forestry, conservation teaching, fisheries, and wildlife management, is offered with the University of Michigan. Walsh offers co-op programs in business, internships in several majors, study abroad in 6 countries, accelerated degree programs in business, management, and nursing, evening and continuing education programs, and credit for life experience. There is a freshman honors program.

Faculty/Classroom: 49% of faculty are male; 51%, female. 90% teach undergraduates, 45% do research, and 40% do both. No introductory courses are taught by graduate students. The average class size in an introductory lecture is 28; in a laboratory, 15; and in a regular course, 15.

Admissions: 89% of the 2005-2006 applicants were accepted. The SAT scores for the 2005-2006 freshman class were: Verbal--49% below 500, 31% between 500 and 599, 18% between 600 and 700, and 2% above 700; Math--46% below 500, 35% between 500 and 599, 17% between 600 and 700, and 2% above 700. The ACT scores were 42% below 21, 31% between 21 and 23, 18% between 24 and 26, 6% between 27 and 28, and 3% above 28. 33% of the current freshmen were in the top fifth of their class; 62% were in the top two fifths. 10 freshmen graduated first in their class.

Requirements: The SAT or ACT is required. In addition, the applicant must be a graduate of an accredited secondary school; the GED is accepted. Walsh recommends completion of 4 units of English, 3 each of math, science, and social studies, 2 of foreign language, and 1 of fine or performing arts. An essay and an interview are recommended. A GPA of 2.1 is required. AP and CLEP credits are accepted. Important factors in the admissions decision are recommendations by school officials and leadership record.

Procedure: Freshmen are admitted to all sessions. Entrance exams should be taken during the junior year. There is a deferred admissions plan and a rolling admissions plan. Notification is sent on a rolling basis. Applications are accepted on-line. Check with the school for current application deadlines. The application fee is $25.

Transfer: 277 transfer students enrolled in 2004-2005. Applicants must have a minimum GPA of 2.0 from previous colleges attended. 32 of 130 credits required for the bachelor's degree must be completed at Walsh.

Visiting: There are regularly scheduled orientations for prospective students, consisting of a campus tour, a session with financial aid and admissions staff, and an opportunity to meet with faculty, coaches, and other personnel. There are guides for informal visits and visitors may sit in on classes and stay overnight. To schedule a visit, contact the Admissions Office at *bfreshour@walsh.edu*.

Financial Aid: In 2005-2006, 94% of all full-time freshmen and 91% of continuing full-time students received some form of financial aid. 82% of full-time freshmen and 74% of continuing full-time students received need-based aid. The average freshman award was $14,765, with $3,250 ($11,416 maximum) from need-based scholarships or grants, $4,237 ($5,125 maximum) from need-based self-help aid (loans and jobs), $2,402 ($12,000 maximum) from non-need-based athletic scholarships, and $4,876 ($25,440 maximum) from other non-need-based awards and non-need-based scholarships. 24% of undergraduates work part time. Average annual earnings from campus work are $1095. The average financial indebtedness of the 2005 graduate was $17,334. Walsh is a member of CSS. The FAFSA and the college's own financial statement are required. The priority date for freshman financial aid applications for fall entry is March 1. There is a rolling deadline for filing freshman financial aid applications for fall entry.

International Students: There are 43 international students enrolled. The school actively recruits these students. They must take the TOEFL.

Computers: There are more than 260 computers available in 16 different sites on 4 campuses. All have access to the Internet. All students may access the system. There are no time limits and no fees.

Graduates: From July 1, 2004 to June 30, 2005, 281 bachelor's degrees were awarded. The most popular majors were management (22%), early childhood education (13%), and nursing (11%). In an average class, 42% graduate in 4 years or less, 53% graduate in 5 years or less, and 54% graduate in 6 years or less. 21 companies recruited on campus in 2004-2005. Of the 2004 graduating class, 12% were enrolled in graduate school within 6 months of graduation and 86% were employed.

Admissions Contact: Brett Freshhour, Dean of Enrollment Management. E-mail: *admissions@walsh.edu* Web: *www.walsh.edu*

WILBERFORCE UNIVERSITY   B-4

Wilberforce, OH 45384-1091   (937) 376-2911, ext. 721
                                       (800) 367-8568; Fax: (937) 376-4751

Full-time: 300 men, 480 women	**Faculty:** 46
Part-time: 10 men, 10 women	**Ph.D.s:** 53%
Graduate: none	**Student/Faculty:** 17 to 1
Year: semesters	**Tuition:** $10,700
Application Deadline: open	**Room & Board:** $4400
Freshman Class: n/av	
SAT or ACT: recommended	**LESS COMPETITIVE**

Wilberforce University, founded in 1856, is a nonprofit, private institution operated under the auspices of the African Methodist Episcopal Church; it was the first black college in America. Its programs emphasize the liberal arts, business, art and fine arts, engineering, and music. Figures given in the above capsule and in this profile are approximate. The library contains 60,000 volumes, 12,000 microform items, and 200 audio/video tapes/CDs/DVDs, and subscribes to 350 periodicals including electronic. Special learning facilities include a learning resource center, radio station, and the nearby National Afro-American Museum. The 125-acre campus is in a rural area 20 miles east of Dayton. Including any residence halls, there are 21 buildings.

Student Life: 64% of undergraduates are from out of state, mostly the Midwest. Students are from 32 states and 2 foreign countries. All are African American. The average age of freshmen is 18; all undergraduates, 20.

Housing: 775 students can be accommodated in college housing, which includes dorms and married-student housing. In addition, there are honors houses. On-campus housing is guaranteed for all 4 years. 85% of students live on campus; of those, 70% remain on campus on weekends. Alcohol is not permitted. All students may keep cars.

Activities: 10% of men belong to 3 national fraternities; 10% of women belong to 3 national sororities. There are 30 groups on campus, including choir, computers, dance, ethnic, honors, international, literary magazine, newspaper, political, religious, social, student government, and yearbook. Popular campus events include Fall Festival and Dawn Dance.

Sports: There are 5 intercollegiate sports for men and 4 for women, and 4 intramural sports for men and 4 for women. Facilities include a

1500-seat gym, outdoor and cross-country track, a softball field, and basketball, volleyball, and tennis courts.

Disabled Students: 50% of the campus is accessible. Wheelchair ramps, special parking, specially equipped rest rooms, and limited elevator service in classroom buildings only are available.

Services: Counseling and information services are available, as is tutoring in most subjects. There is a reader service for the blind, and remedial math, reading, and writing.

Programs of Study: Wilberforce confers B.A. and B.S. degrees. Bachelor's degrees are awarded in BIOLOGICAL SCIENCE (biology/biological science), BUSINESS (accounting, banking and finance, business administration and management, business economics, management science, and marketing/retailing/merchandising), COMMUNICATIONS AND THE ARTS (communications, fine arts, literature, and music), COMPUTER AND PHYSICAL SCIENCE (chemistry, computer science, information sciences and systems, mathematics, and science), ENGINEERING AND ENVIRONMENTAL DESIGN (preengineering), HEALTH PROFESSIONS (health care administration and rehabilitation therapy), SOCIAL SCIENCE (economics, liberal arts/general studies, political science/government, prelaw, psychology, social science, social work, and sociology). Business administration, accounting, and banking and finance are the strongest academically.

Required: To graduate, students must complete 126 credit hours with a minimum GPA of 2.0 and no grade in the major below a C. To fulfill the general studies requirements, all students must complete a first-year program, which includes composition and computer literacy courses, and they must also take at least 1 course from each of the following areas: humanistic traditions, music, art, religion, communication arts, literature and language, non-Western studies, behavioral sciences, economics and political science, physical sciences, and life science. 2 credits in health and phys ed and completion of 2 cooperative education experiences are also required.

Special: Wilberforce offers a co-op arrangement with St. John's University School of Law and cross-registration through the Southwestern Ohio Council for Higher Education. B.A.-B.S. degrees are available in all majors, and there are dual majors in engineering along with a 3-2 engineering degree with the University of Dayton. Credit is given for the mandatory co-op education program, in which students participate in paid work experience in their chosen field. Nondegree study is possible in military science. There is 1 national honor society, including Phi Beta Kappa, a freshman honors program, and 4 departmental honors programs.

Faculty/Classroom: 50% of faculty are male; 50%, female. The average class size in an introductory lecture is 12 and in a regular course, 18.

Requirements: The SAT or ACT is recommended. Students should be graduates of an accredited secondary school and have 15 Carnegie units, including 4 units of English, 2 to 3 of math, including algebra, 2 to 3 of science, including a lab course, and 2 of social studies, including U.S. history. The GED is accepted with a score of 45 or better. SAT: Subject tests are recommended. A GPA of 2.0 is required. AP and CLEP credits are accepted. Important factors in the admissions decision are recommendations by school officials, advanced placement or honor courses, and evidence of special talent.

Procedure: Freshmen are admitted fall and spring. Entrance exams should be taken by the fall of the senior year. There are early decision, early admissions and rolling admissions plans. Application deadlines are open. A waiting list is an active part of the admissions procedure.

Transfer: A minimum college GPA of 2.0 is required. 30 of 126 credits required for the bachelor's degree must be completed at Wilberforce.

Visiting: There are regularly scheduled orientations for prospective students. There are guides for informal visits. To schedule a visit, contact the Office of Admissions.

Financial Aid: Wilberforce is a member of CSS. The FAFSA, the college's own financial statement, and the parent and student federal income tax returns are required. Check with the school for current application deadlines.

International Students: They must score satisfactorily on the written TOEFL and also take the SAT or the ACT.

Computers: Students enrolled in computer and engineering programs may access the system. There are no time limits and no fees.

Admissions Contact: Kenneth C. Christmon, Director of Admissions. E-mail: *admissions@payne.wilberforce.edu* Web: *www.wilberforce.edu*

WILMINGTON COLLEGE   B-4
Wilmington, OH 45177

(937) 382-6661, ext. 260
(800) 341-9318; Fax: (937) 383-8542

Full-time: 646 men, 737 women	**Faculty:** IIB, --$
Part-time: 145 men, 195 women	**Ph.D.s:** 69%
Graduate: none	**Student/Faculty:** n/av
Year: semesters, summer session	**Tuition:** $20,656
Application Deadline: open	**Room & Board:** $7406
Freshman Class: 1409 applied, 1381 accepted, 366 enrolled	
SAT or ACT: required	**NONCOMPETITIVE**

Wilmington College, established in 1870, is a private institution sponsored by the Society of Friends. The college offers programs in the liberal arts, business, health science, teacher preparation, agricultural studies, religious studies, and athletic training. In addition to regional accreditation, Wilmington has baccalaureate program accreditation with CAAHEP and NCATE. The library contains 110,000 volumes, 42,000 microform items, and 1400 audio/video tapes/CDs/DVDs, and subscribes to 400 periodicals including electronic. Computerized library services include the card catalog, interlibrary loans, and database searching. Special learning facilities include a learning resource center, art gallery, Peace Resource Center, Quaker museum, observatory, greenhouse, and academic farm. The 65-acre campus is in a small town 50 miles from Cincinnati and from Columbus. Including any residence halls, there are 20 buildings.

Student Life: 96% of undergraduates are from Ohio. Students are from 13 states and 4 foreign countries. 74% are white. 40% are claim no religious affiliation; 17% Catholic. The average age of freshmen is 19; all undergraduates, 21. 27% do not continue beyond their first year.

Housing: 833 students can be accommodated in college housing, which includes single-sex and coed dorms, on-campus apartments, fraternity houses, and sorority houses. On-campus housing is guaranteed for all 4 years. 67% of students live on campus. All students may keep cars.

Activities: 7% of men belong to 4 local and 1 national fraternity; 11% of women belong to 4 local sororities. There are 63 groups on campus, including cheerleading, choir, chorale, drama, ethnic, gay, honors, international, jazz band, literary magazine, musical theater, newspaper, orchestra, photography, political, professional, religious, social, social service, student government, and yearbook. Popular campus events include Community Day, Westheimer Peace Symposium, and Fall Fest.

Sports: There are 11 intercollegiate sports for men and 10 for women, and 8 intramural sports for men and 8 for women. Facilities include an Olympic-size pool, a Nautilus weight-training room, an exercise room, racquetball courts, a 4500-seat gym, and a 3000-seat stadium.

Disabled Students: 20% of the campus is accessible. Wheelchair ramps, elevators, special parking, specially equipped rest rooms, and special class scheduling are available.

Services: Counseling and information services are available, as is tutoring in every subject. There is remedial math, reading, and writing.

Campus Safety and Security: Measures include 24-hour foot and vehicle patrol, security escort services, informal discussions, and pamphlets/posters/films. There are emergency telephones and lighted pathways/sidewalks.

Programs of Study: Wilmington confers B.A. and B.S. degrees. Master's degrees are also awarded. Bachelor's degrees are awarded in AGRICULTURE (agriculture), BIOLOGICAL SCIENCE (biology/biological science), BUSINESS (accounting, business administration and management, organizational behavior, and sports management), COMMUNICATIONS AND THE ARTS (art, communications, dramatic arts, English, and Spanish), COMPUTER AND PHYSICAL SCIENCE (chemistry, computer science, and mathematics), EDUCATION (athletic training, early childhood, elementary, physical, and secondary), HEALTH PROFESSIONS (predentistry, premedicine, and preveterinary science), SOCIAL SCIENCE (criminal justice, history, liberal arts/general studies, prelaw, psychology, religion, social science, social work, and sociology). Chemistry, biology, and athletic training are the strongest academically. Business, agriculture, and athletic training are the largest.

Required: To graduate, students must complete 124 semester hours, with no more than 60 hours in the major, with a minimum GPA of 2.0. At least 40 hours must be in upper-division work. General education requirements include courses in English and math competence, international knowledge, basic areas of thought and expression, and personal fitness.

Special: Special academic programs include work-study, internships, a Washington semester, and cross-registration with the Southwest Ohio Consortium. Study abroad may be arranged in Mexico, Austria, France, and other countries. Dual majors in any subject and student-designed majors are offered. Credit for experience, nondegree study, and pass/fail options are possible. There are 5 national honor societies, a freshman honors program, and 3 departmental honors programs.

Faculty/Classroom: 42% of faculty are male; 58%, female. All teach undergraduates. The average class size in an introductory lecture is 25 and in a regular course, 19.

Admissions: 98% of the 2005-2006 applicants were accepted. 8 freshmen graduated first in their class in a recent year.

Requirements: The SAT or ACT is required. In addition, applicants must be graduates of an accredited secondary school, with 4 units of English, 2 units each of math, science, and social studies, and a recommended 2 units of a foreign language. An additional 6 units is required in other areas. The GED is accepted. An interview is recommended. An essay may be required. AP and CLEP credits are accepted. Important factors in the admissions decision are recommendations by school officials, parents or siblings attending the school, and recommendations by alumni.

Procedure: Freshmen are admitted fall and spring. Entrance exams should be taken as early as possible. There is a deferred admissions plan and a rolling addmissions plan. Application deadlines are open. Application fee is $25. Notification is sent on a rolling basis.

Transfer: 64 transfer students enrolled in fall 2005. Applicants' college and high school transcripts are evaluated on an individual basis. They must have a 2.0 GPA and a completed transfer recommendation form. 30 of 124 credits required for the bachelor's degree must be completed at Wilmington.

Visiting: There are regularly scheduled orientations for prospective students, including meetings with faculty and a tour of the campus. There are guides for informal visits and visitors may sit in on classes and stay overnight. To schedule a visit, contact the Admissions Office.

Financial Aid: In a recent year, 99% of all full-time students received some form of financial aid. 84% of full-time freshmen and 83% of continuing full-time students received need-based aid. The average freshman award was $17,520. Need-based scholarships or need-based grants averaged $5816 ($15,300 maximum); need-based self-help aid (loans and jobs) averaged $4096 ($8175 maximum); other non-need-based awards and non-need-based scholarships averaged $6678 ($15,002 maximum); and from unsubsidized Stafford Loans. Total award does not include Parent Plus loans or alternative educational loans. averaged $930 ($6625 maximum). 35% of undergraduates work part time. Average annual earnings from campus work are $1400. The average financial indebtedness of a recent year's graduate was $19,306. The FAFSA is required. Check with the school for current application deadlines.

International Students: There were 5 international students enrolled in a recent year. The school actively recruits these students. A satisfactory score is required on the written TOEFL. The TOEFL is not required if the SAT is taken. Students who have been previously enrolled in a U.S. high school must also take the SAT or ACT.

Computers: All students may access the system at any time. There are no time limits and no fees.

Admissions Contact: Tina Garland, Director of Admissions.
E-mail: *admissions@wilmington.edu* Web: *www.wilmington.edu*

WITTENBERG UNIVERSITY   B-3
Springfield, OH 45501

(937) 327-6314
(877) 206-0332; Fax: (937) 327-6379

Full-time: 842 men, 1120 women	**Faculty:** 148; IIB, av$
Part-time: 54 men, 9 women	**Ph.D.s:** 89%
Graduate: 1 man, 14 women	**Student/Faculty:** 13 to 1
Year: semesters, summer session	**Tuition:** $27,542
Application Deadline: March 15	**Room & Board:** $7054
Freshman Class: 2607 applied, 2176 accepted, 496 enrolled	
SAT Verbal/Math: 571/564*	**ACT:** 24 **VERY COMPETITIVE**

Wittenberg University, founded in 1845, is a private liberal arts and sciences institution affiliated with the Evangelical Lutheran Church in America. In addition to regional accreditation, Wittenberg has baccalaureate program accreditation with ACS, NASM, and NCATE. The 2 libraries contain 424,502 volumes, 82,109 microform items, and 23,171 audio/video tapes/CDs/DVDs, and subscribe to 6613 periodicals including electronic. Computerized library services include the card catalog, interlibrary loans, database searching, Internet access, and laptop Internet portals. Special learning facilities include a learning resource center, art gallery, radio station, geology museum, observatory, GIS lab with supercomputer, and a parallel processing lab. The 100-acre campus is in a suburban area 25 miles east of Dayton, 40 miles west of Columbus, and 75 miles from Cincinatti. Including any residence halls, there are 35 buildings.

Student Life: 75% of undergraduates are from Ohio. Student are from 40 states and 17 foreign countries. 80% are from public schools. 90% are white. 39% are Protestant; 38% claim no religious affiliation; 20% Catholic. The average age of freshmen is 18; all undergraduates, 20. 21% do not continue beyond their first year; 69% remain to graduate.

Housing: 1711 students can be accommodated in college housing, which includes single-sex and coed dorms, on-campus apartments, off-campus apartments, married-student housing, fraternity houses, and sorority houses. In addition, there are honors houses, language houses, special-interest houses, a substance-free residence hall, and an international awareness house. On-campus housing is guaranteed for the freshman year only and is available on a lottery system for upperclassmen.

63% of students live on campus; of those, 85% remain on campus on weekends. All students may keep cars.

Activities: 20% of men belong to 7 national fraternities; 35% of women belong to 7 national sororities. There are 129 groups on campus, including art, band, caving, cheerleading, choir, chorale, chorus, computers, conservation, dance, drama, ethnic, gay, Habitat for Humanity, honors, international, literary magazine, musical theater, newspaper, opera, pep band, photography, political, professional, radio and TV, religious, social, social service, and student government. Popular campus events include Wittenberg Series, International Festival, and Professional Alumni Days.

Sports: There are 11 intercollegiate sports for men and 11 for women, and 12 intramural sports for men and 12 for women. Facilities include a multipurpose field house, a swimming pool, 6 racquetball/handball courts, a fitness center, and sports medicine rooms. There is also a 3200-seat gym, a 3200-seat arena, 12 acres of playing fields, and a 500-seat stadium with playing field, track, and 12 tennis courts. Fitness equipment includes treadmills, rowing machines, and lifting equipment.

Disabled Students: 75% of the campus is accessible. Wheelchair ramps, elevators, special parking, specially equipped rest rooms, special class scheduling, lowered drinking fountains, and lowered telephones are available.

Services: Counseling and information services are available, as is tutoring in most subjects. There is also a math workshop and writing and oral communication centers.

Campus Safety and Security: Measures include 24-hour foot and vehicle patrol, self-defense education, security escort services, and informal discussions. There are pamphlets/posters/films, emergency telephones, lighted pathways/sidewalks, a bicycle patrol, and various prevention programs. City police support campus police during the evening. There is also a student Eyes and Ears Program and a campus security committee made up of students and faculty.

Programs of Study: Wittenberg confers B.A., B.S., B.F.A., B.M., and B.M.E. degrees. Master's degrees are also awarded. Bachelor's degrees are awarded in BIOLOGICAL SCIENCE (biology/biological science), BUSINESS (business administration and management), COMMUNICATIONS AND THE ARTS (communications, dramatic arts, English, fine arts, French, German, music, Russian, and Spanish), COMPUTER AND PHYSICAL SCIENCE (chemistry, computer science, geology, mathematics, and physics), EDUCATION (elementary, foreign languages, middle school, music, science, secondary, and special), HEALTH PROFESSIONS (predentistry and premedicine), SOCIAL SCIENCE (American studies, East Asian studies, economics, geography, history, international relations, philosophy, political science/government, prelaw, psychology, religion, and sociology). Biology, communication, and East Asian studies are the strongest academically. Biology, communication, and education are the largest.

Required: To graduate, students must complete at least 130 credits and have a minimum GPA of 2.0. The required minimum GPA and number of hours in the major vary by department. All Wittenberg students complete a program of general education built on 16 learning goals. These include acquisition of foundations skills in writing, math, foreign language, speaking, research, and computing, the understanding of the different arts and sciences disciplines and their distinct methodological approaches to knowledge, and an introduction to non-Western culture, the diversity of human experience, and inter- and transdisciplinary knowledge. Students achieve each general education learning goal by completing 1 to 2 courses. As part of general education, students also complete 2 physical activity classes and perform 30 hours of community service.

Special: Special academic programs include internships, cross-registration through the Southwest Ohio Consortium, a Washington semester, work-study programs, study-abroad opportunities in many countries, accelerated degree programs, dual and student-designed majors, nondegree study, and pass/fail options. A 3-2 engineering degree is offered through Washington, Columbia, and Case Western Reserve Universities and Georgia Institute of Technology. There is also a 3-2 nursing program with Johns Hopkins University and an occupational therapy program with Washington University. There are 7 national honor societies, including Phi Beta Kappa, a freshman honors program, and 18 departmental honors programs.

Faculty/Classroom: 57% of faculty are male; 43%, female. All teach undergraduates. No introductory courses are taught by graduate students. The average class size in an introductory lecture is 25; in a laboratory, 20; and in a regular course, 18.

Admissions: 83% of the 2005-2006 applicants were accepted. The SAT scores for the 2005-2006 freshman class were: Verbal--20% below 500, 41% between 500 and 599, 32% between 600 and 700, and 7% above 700; Math--22% below 500, 41% between 500 and 599, 31% between 600 and 700, and 6% above 700. The ACT scores were 19% below 21, 29% between 21 and 23, 23% between 24 and 26, 14% between 27 and 28, and 15% above 28. 49% of the current freshmen were in the top fifth of their class; 74% were in the top two fifths. There were 2 National Merit finalists. 8 freshmen graduated first in their class.

Requirements: The SAT or ACT is required. In addition, students should have graduated from an accredited secondary school with 16 academic credits, including 4 units of English and 3 each of a foreign language, math, science, and social studies, which includes history. An essay is required and an interview advised. Art students must present a portfolio, and music students must audition. AP credits are accepted. Important factors in the admissions decision are advanced placement or honor courses, evidence of special talent, and extracurricular activities record.

Procedure: Freshmen are admitted to all sessions. Entrance exams should be taken by the fall of the senior year, but as early as possible. There are early decision, early admissions, and deferred admissions plans. There is a rolling admissions plan. Early decision applications should be filed by November 15; regular applications, by March 15 for fall entry, December 1 for winter entry, and May 1 for summer entry, along with a $40 fee. Notification of early decision is sent December 15; regular decision, on a rolling basis. 22 early decision candidates were accepted for the 2005-2006 class. A waiting list is an active part of the admissions procedure. Applications are accepted on-line.

Transfer: 30 transfer students enrolled in 2004-2005. Applicants should have a minimum GPA of 2.0 at an accredited college and be in good academic and social standing. High school transcripts are required in some cases. An interview is recommended. 65 of 130 credits required for the bachelor's degree must be completed at Wittenberg.

Visiting: There are regularly scheduled orientations for prospective students, including a tour and interview. Year-round "Tiger Days" are information sessions that include a tour, academic and services fair, financial aid presentation, current student panel, and classroom experience/faculty engagement. Accepted students may stay overnight and the "fly-in" program can subsidize the cost of the trip. There are guides for informal visits and visitors may sit in on classes and stay overnight. To schedule a visit, contact the Admissions Office.

Financial Aid: In 2005-2006, 99% of all full-time students received some form of financial aid. 70% of full-time freshmen and 71% of continuing full-time students received need-based aid. The average freshman award was $22,180. Need-based scholarships or need-based grants averaged $18,258; need-based self-help aid (loans and jobs) averaged $4461; and other non-need-based awards and non-need-based scholarships averaged $12,186. 53% of undergraduates work part time. Average annual earnings from campus work are $1500. The average financial indebtedness of the 2005 graduate was $21,665. The FAFSA is required. The deadline for filing freshman financial aid applications for fall entry is March 15.

International Students: There are 40 international students enrolled. The school actively recruits these students. They must stake the SAT, ACT, or TOEFL.

Computers: Wireless access is available. Students have access to computer labs 24 hours a day. Specialized academic software is available in labs near those departments. There are no time limits and no fees. It is strongly recommended that all students have a personal computer.

Graduates: From July 1, 2004 to June 30, 2005, 407 bachelor's degrees were awarded. The most popular majors were management (17%), education (14%), and psychology (10%). In an average class, 1% graduate in 3 years or less, 63% graduate in 4 years or less, 68% graduate in 5 years or less, and 69% graduate in 6 years or less. 64 companies recruited on campus in 2004-2005.

Admissions Contact: Kurt V. Schmidt, Director of Admissions. A video is available. E-mail: admission@wittenberg.edu
Web: www.wittenberg.edu

WRIGHT STATE UNIVERSITY B-4

Dayton, OH 45435　　　　　　　　　　　　**(937) 775-5700**
(800) 247-1770; Fax: (937) 775-5795

Full-time: 4509 men, 5941 women	Faculty: I, --$
Part-time: 856 men, 962 women	Ph.Ds: n/av
Graduate: 1641 men, 2298 women	Student/Faculty: 19 to 1
Year: quarters, summer session	Tuition: $6864 ($13,239)
Application Deadline: open	Room & Board: $6752
Freshman Class: 5497 applied, 4763 accepted, 2336 enrolled	
SAT Verbal/Math: 500/500*	ACT: 21　　LESS COMPETITIVE

Wright State University, founded in 1964, is a state-supported institution offering undergraduate programs in business and administration, education and human services, engineering and computer science, liberal arts, math and science, and nursing and health. There are 6 undergraduate and 8 graduate schools. In addition to regional accreditation, Wright State has baccalaureate program accreditation with AACSB, ABET, CSWE, NASM, NCATE, and NLN. The 2 libraries contain 703,000 volumes, 1,278,767 microform items, and 29,800 audio/video tapes/CDs/DVDs, and subscribe to 5700 periodicals including electronic. Computerized library services include the card catalog, interlibrary loans, database searching, and Internet access. Special learning facilities include a learning resource center, art gallery, radio station, TV station, and a TV production studio. The Department of Archives and Special Collections houses one of the most complete depositories of information on the Wright Brothers in the world. The 557-acre campus is in a suburban area 8 miles northeast of Dayton. Including any residence halls, there are 50 buildings.

Student Life: 96% of undergraduates are from Ohio. Others are from 49 states, 67 foreign countries, and Canada. 76% are white; 11% African American. The average age of freshmen is 19; all undergraduates, 23. 29% do not continue beyond their first year; 42% remain to graduate.

Housing: 3000 students can be accommodated in college housing, which includes coed dorms, on-campus apartments, and married-student housing. In addition, there are honors houses and special-interest houses. On-campus housing is available on a first-come, first-served basis and is available on a lottery system for upperclassmen. 77% of students commute. All students may keep cars.

Activities: 5% of men belong to 2 local and 8 national fraternities; 3% of women belong to 5 national sororities. There are 140 groups on campus, including band, cheerleading, chess, choir, chorale, chorus, computers, drill team, ethnic, film, gay, honors, international, jazz band, literary magazine, newspaper, orchestra, pep band, political, professional, radio and TV, religious, social, social service, and student government. Popular campus events include Fall Fest, May Daze, and Madrigal Dinner.

Sports: There are 7 intercollegiate sports for men and 7 for women, and 12 intramural sports for men and 12 for women. Facilities include an athletic and entertainment center with an arena seating 13,000 spectators, break-off rooms, auxiliary gym, and baseball and practice fields. The student union houses a natatorium, weight rooms, game rooms, and playing courts.

Disabled Students: All of the campus is accessible. Wheelchair ramps, elevators, special parking, specially equipped rest rooms, lowered drinking fountains, lowered telephones, special housing, and adaptive technology are available. An underground tunnel system connects all academic buildings.

Services: Counseling and information services are available, as is tutoring in most subjects. There is a reader service for the blind, and remedial math, reading, and writing.

Campus Safety and Security: Measures include 24-hour foot and vehicle patrol, self-defense education, security escort services, and shuttle buses. There are informal discussions, pamphlets/posters/films, emergency telephones, and lighted pathways/sidewalks.

Programs of Study: Wright State confers B.A., B.S., B.F.A., B.Mus., B.S.B., B.S.Comp.Eng., B.S.E., B.S.Ed., B.S.M.T., and B.S.N. degrees. Master's and doctoral degrees are also awarded. Bachelor's degrees are awarded in BIOLOGICAL SCIENCE (biology/biological science), BUSINESS (accounting, banking and finance, business economics, management information systems, management science, and marketing/retailing/merchandising), COMMUNICATIONS AND THE ARTS (art history and appreciation, arts administration/management, classical languages, communications, dance, dramatic arts, English, film arts, fine arts, French, German, modern language, music, music history and appreciation, music theory and composition, Spanish, and theater design), COMPUTER AND PHYSICAL SCIENCE (chemistry, computer science, geology, geophysics and seismology, mathematics, and physics), EDUCATION (art, business, elementary, foreign languages, music, physical, science, secondary, and special), ENGINEERING AND ENVIRONMENTAL DESIGN (biomedical engineering, computer engineering, electrical/electronics engineering, engineering physics, materials engineering, mechanical engineering, systems engineering, and water and wastewater technology), HEALTH PROFESSIONS (environmental health science, medical laboratory technology, nursing, predentistry, premedicine, and rehabilitation therapy), SOCIAL SCIENCE (anthropology, economics, geography, history, humanities, international relations, philosophy, political science/government, prelaw, psychology, religion, social work, sociology, and urban studies). Business education, theater arts, and engineering are the strongest academically. Elementary education, accounting, and nursing are the largest.

Required: To graduate, students must complete 183 quarter hours, with a minimum GPA of 2.0. All students are required to take 56 credit hours of general education courses in 4 areas: communication and math skills, the Western experience, the non-Western world, and understanding the contemporary world.

Special: B.A.-B.S. degrees are offered in computer science, geography, urban affairs, biological sciences, chemistry, geological sciences, math, and psychology. Cross-registration with other area colleges is available through the Southwestern Ohio Council for Higher Education. Dual majors, co-op programs, internships, study abroad, work-study programs, student-designed majors, nondegree study, and credit for military experience are available. There are 13 national honor societies, a freshman honors program, and 62 departmental honors programs.

Faculty/Classroom: 58% of faculty are male; 42%, female. The average class size in an introductory lecture is 41; in a laboratory, 27; and in a regular course, 32.

Admissions: 87% of the 2005-2006 applicants were accepted. The SAT scores for the 2005-2006 freshman class were: Verbal--50% below 500, 33% between 500 and 599, 15% between 600 and 700, and 2% above 700; Math--49% below 500, 34% between 500 and 599, 15% between 600 and 700, and 2% above 700. The ACT scores were 50% below 21, 25% between 21 and 23, 15% between 24 and 26, 6% between 27 and 28, and 4% above 28. 29% of the current freshmen were in the top fifth of their class; 55% were in the top two fifths.

Requirements: The SAT or ACT is required. In addition, applicants should be graduates of an accredited secondary school and have 4 units in English, 3 units each in math, science, and social studies, 2 units in a foreign language, and 1 unit in the arts. A portfolio is required for art majors, an audition for theater and music majors. The GED is accepted. A GPA of 2.0 is required. AP and CLEP credits are accepted.

Procedure: Freshmen are admitted to all sessions. Entrance exams should be taken in the spring of the junior year. There are deferred admissions and rolling admissions plans. Application deadlines are open. Applications are accepted on-line.

Transfer: 967 transfer students enrolled in 2004-2005. Applicants must have a 2.0 GPA. 45 of 183 quarter hours required for the bachelor's degree must be completed at Wright State.

Visiting: There are regularly scheduled orientations for prospective students, including a campus tour and information on academic and student services. There are guides for informal visits and visitors may sit in on classes. To schedule a visit, contact the Office of Admissions.

Financial Aid: 60% of full-time freshmen and 63% of continuing full-time students received need-based aid. The average freshman award was $9267. Need-based scholarships or need-based grants averaged $3982; need-based self-help aid (loans and jobs) averaged $2814; non-need-based athletic scholarships averaged $10,907; and other non-need-based awards and non-need-based scholarships averaged $3055. Wright State is a member of CSS. The CSS/Profile, FAFSA, FFS or SFS, and the college's own financial statement are required.

International Students: There are 517 international students enrolled. They must score satisfactorily on the written TOEFL.

Computers: Wireless access is available. All students may access the system. There are no time limits and no fees.

Graduates: From July 1, 2004 to June 30, 2005, 2035 bachelor's degrees were awarded. The most popular majors were liberal arts (27%), education (22%), and business (20%). In an average class, 17% graduate in 4 years or less, 18% graduate in 5 years or less, and 40% graduate in 6 years or less.

Admissions Contact: Cathy Davis, Director of Undergraduate Admissions. E-mail: *admissions@wright.edu* Web: *www.wright.edu*

XAVIER UNIVERSITY

A-5

Cincinnati, OH 45207

(513) 745-3301
(877) 982-3648; Fax: (513) 745-4319

Full-time: 1489 men, 1844 women	**Faculty:** 286; IIA, -$
Part-time: 207 men, 339 women	**Ph.D.s:** 80%
Graduate: 1097 men, 689 women	**Student/Faculty:** 11 to 1
Year: semesters, summer session	**Tuition:** $22,430
Application Deadline: February 1	**Room & Board:** $8060
Freshman Class: 5468 applied, 3612 accepted, 765 enrolled	
SAT Verbal/Math: 593/591*	**ACT:** 26 **HIGHLY COMPETITIVE**

Xavier University, founded in 1831, is a comprehensive Jesuit institution affiliated with the Roman Catholic Church. There are 3 undergraduate schools. In addition to regional accreditation, Xavier has baccalaureate program accreditation with AACSB, AOTA, CAAHEP, CCNE, CSWE and MACTE. The library contains 366,282 volumes, 749,259 microform items, and 9382 audio/video tapes/CDs/DVDs, and subscribes to 3793 periodicals including electronic. Computerized library services include the card catalog, interlibrary loans, database searching, Internet access, and laptop Internet portals. Special learning facilities include a learning resource center, art gallery, radio station, TV station, and an observatory. The 146-acre campus is in a suburban area 5 miles northeast of the center of Cincinnati in a residential area. Including any residence halls, there are 36 buildings.

Student Life: 61% of undergraduates are from Ohio. Others are from 46 states, 34 foreign countries, and Canada. 47% are from public schools. 81% are white; 11% African American. 66% are Catholic; 21% Buddhist, Hindu, Muslim, other, Christian; 12% claim no religious affiliation. The average age of freshmen is 18; all undergraduates, 21. 11% do not continue beyond their first year; 78% remain to graduate.

Housing: 1815 students can be accommodated in college housing, which includes coed dorms, on-campus apartments, and off-campus apartments. In addition, there are honors houses and special-interest houses. On-campus housing is available on a first-come, first-served basis and is available on a lottery system for upperclassmen. 54% of students commute. All students may keep cars.

Activities: There are no fraternities or sororities. There are 102 groups on campus, including art, band, cheerleading, choir, chorale, chorus, computers, dance, drama, ethnic, film, gay, honors, international, jazz band, literary magazine, musical theater, newspaper, pep band, photography, political, professional, radio and TV, religious, social, social service, student government, and yearbook. Popular campus events include Family Weekend, Academic Day, and Spirit Celebration.

Sports: There are 8 intercollegiate sports for men and 8 for women, and 13 intramural sports for men and 11 for women. Facilities include a fieldhouse, sports center, basketball and volleyball courts, baseball, soccer, and softball fields, rifle range, and tennis courts.

Disabled Students: 98% of the campus is accessible. Wheelchair ramps, elevators, special parking, specially equipped rest rooms, lowered drinking fountains, and lowered telephones are available.

Services: Counseling and information services are available, as is tutoring in most subjects. There are math and writing labs, an efficient reading and study skills class, and drop-in sessions for many disciplines. Individual group study skills workshops are also offered. There is a reader service for the blind and remedial math.

Campus Safety and Security: Measures include 24-hour foot and vehicle patrol, self-defense education, security escort services, and shuttle buses. There are informal discussions, pamphlets/posters/films, emergency telephones, lighted pathways/sidewalks, and alcohol awareness, drug awareness, and sexual assault programs.

Programs of Study: Xavier confers B.A., B.S., Honors A.B., B.F.A., B.L.A., B.S.B.A., B.S.N. and B.S.W. degrees. Associate, master's, and doctoral degrees are also awarded. Bachelor's degrees are awarded in BIOLOGICAL SCIENCE (biology/biological science), BUSINESS (accounting, banking and finance, business administration and management, business economics, entrepreneurial studies, human resources, international business management, management science, marketing/retailing/merchandising, and sports management), COMMUNICATIONS AND THE ARTS (advertising, art, classics, communications, English, fine arts, French, German, music, public relations, and Spanish), COMPUTER AND PHYSICAL SCIENCE (applied physics, chemistry, computer science, information sciences and systems, mathematics, natural sciences, and physics), EDUCATION (athletic training, early childhood, education, middle school, music, science, and special), ENGINEERING AND ENVIRONMENTAL DESIGN (chemical engineering), HEALTH PROFESSIONS (medical laboratory technology, nursing, and prepharmacy), SOCIAL SCIENCE (criminal justice, economics, history, international relations, liberal arts/general studies, philosophy, political science/government, psychology, social work, sociology, and theological studies). Philosophy, politics and the public honors program are the strongest academically. Business, communications, and education are the largest.

Required: To graduate, students must complete a minimum of 120 credit hours with a minimum GPA of 2.0. The total number of hours required in the major varies. All students must take core curriculum courses in English composition, cultural diversity, math, science, social science, history, theology, philosophy, a foreign language, literature, fine arts, and an ethics/religion and society focus.

Special: Xavier offers internships related to some majors, cross-registration through the Greater Cincinnati Consortium, and co-op programs in business and computer science. Students may study abroad in 10 countries. A Washington semester and nondegree study are available. A 3-2 applied biology degree is offered with Duke University. A Professional Accountancy B.S.B.A and M.B.A Program are also offered. There are 8 national honor societies, a freshman honors program, and 1 departmental honors program.

Faculty/Classroom: 52% of faculty are male; 48%, female. 97% teach undergraduates. No introductory courses are taught by graduate students. The average class size in an introductory lecture is 24; in a laboratory, 17; and in a regular course, 19.

Admissions: 66% of the 2005-2006 applicants were accepted. The SAT scores for the 2005-2006 freshman class were: Verbal--10% below 500, 43% between 500 and 599, 38% between 600 and 700, and 9% above 700; Math--11% below 500, 42% between 500 and 599, 37% between 600 and 700, and 11% above 700. The ACT scores were 9% below 21, 21% between 21 and 23, 25% between 24 and 26, 21% between 27 and 28, and 24% above 28. 56% of the current freshmen were in the top fifth of their class; 82% were in the top two fifths. There were 6 National Merit finalists. 24 freshmen graduated first in their class.

Requirements: The SAT or ACT is required. In addition, graduation from an accredited secondary school or satisfactory scores on the GED is required for admission. The school requires 21 academic credits, including 4 years of English, 3 each of math, social studies, and science, 2 of foreign language, 1 of health/phys ed, plus 5 electives. Xavier recommends an interview. AP and CLEP credits are accepted. Important factors in the admissions decision are advanced placement or honor courses, leadership record, and extracurricular activities record.

Procedure: Freshmen are admitted fall and spring. Entrance exams should be taken by fall of senior year. There are early action and deferred admissions plans. Early action applications should be filed by December 1; regular applications, by February 1 for fall entry, along with a $35 fee. Notification of early action is sent January 15; regular decision, March 15. 599 applicants were on the 2005 waiting list; 109 were admitted. Applications are accepted on-line.

Transfer: 115 transfer students enrolled in 2004-2005. Transfer students must have a minimum GPA of 2.0 in all college-level work. An in-

terview is also recommended. Students who transfer to Xavier with 30 or more semester hours are not required to submit results of the ACT or SAT tests, an essay, or counselor recommendation. 30 of 120 credits required for the bachelor's degree must be completed at Xavier.

Visiting: There are regularly scheduled orientations for prospective students, including an interview and a tour of the campus. There are guides for informal visits and visitors may sit in on classes and stay overnight. To schedule a visit, contact the Admissions Office at (877) XU ADMIT or *xuadmit@xavier.edu*.

Financial Aid: In 2005-2006, 96% of all full-time freshmen and 92% of continuing full-time students received some form of financial aid. 57% of full-time freshmen and 54% of continuing full-time students received need-based aid. The average freshman award was $14,057. Need-based scholarships or need-based grants averaged $10,778; need-based self-help aid (loans and jobs) averaged $5640; and non-need-based athletic scholarships averaged $9737. 20% of undergraduates work part time. Average annual earnings from campus work are $2100. The average financial indebtedness of the 2005 graduate was $19,300. Xavier is a member of CSS. The FAFSA is required. The deadline for filing freshman financial aid applications for fall entry is February 15.

International Students: There are 49 international students enrolled. The school actively recruits these students. A satisfactory score is required on the written TOEFL. Applicants must also take the SAT, ACT, or TOEFL.

Computers: Wireless access is available. There are more than 200 PCs for public use in labs. Wireless laptops may be checked out at the student center or library. Network connections for PCs are provided for all resident students as well as for students bringing wireless laptops to campus. Internet access is available at all locations. All students may access the system 24 hours a day, 7 days a week. There are no time limits and no fees.

Graduates: From July 1, 2004 to June 30, 2005, 861 bachelor's degrees were awarded. The most popular majors were business/marketing (26%), liberal arts (14%), and communications (9%). In an average class, 3% graduate in 3 years or less, 70% graduate in 4 years or less, 75% graduate in 5 years or less, and 79% graduate in 6 years or less. 130 companies recruited on campus in 2004-2005. Of the 2004 graduating class, 26% were enrolled in graduate school within 6 months of graduation and 66% were employed.

Admissions Contact: Marc Camille, Dean of Admission. A video is available. E-mail: *xuadmit@xu.edu* Web: *www.xavier.edu*

YOUNGSTOWN STATE UNIVERSITY   C-2

Youngstown, OH 44555-0001

(330) 941-2000
(877) 468-6978; Fax: (330) 941-3674

Full-time: 4236 men, 5005 women	**Faculty:** 427; IIA, av$
Part-time: 957 men, 1504 women	**Ph.D.s:** 82%
Graduate: 404 men, 706 women	**Student/Faculty:** 22 to 1
Year: semesters, summer session	**Tuition:** $6333 ($11,541)
Application Deadline: August 15	**Room & Board:** $6280
Freshman Class: 3904 applied, 3879 accepted, 2142 enrolled	
SAT Verbal/Math: 490/490*	**ACT:** 20 NONCOMPETITIVE

Youngstown State University, founded in 1908, is a publicly funded, primarily commuter institution offering undergraduate and graduate programs in the arts and sciences, education, business, engineering, fine and performing arts, and health and human services. There are 6 undergraduate schools and 1 graduate school. In addition to regional accreditation, YSU has baccalaureate program accreditation with AACSB, ABET, ADA, CAAHEP, CAHEA, CAPTE, CSWE, NAACLS, NASAD, NAST, NASM, NCATE, and NLN. The library contains 923,356 volumes, 942,061 microform items, and 20,456 audio/video tapes/CDs/DVDs, and subscribes to 9722 periodicals including electronic. Computerized library services include the card catalog, interlibrary loans, database searching, and Internet access. Special learning facilities include a learning resource center, art gallery, planetarium, radio station, and center for historic preservation. The 200-acre campus is in an urban area 65 miles southeast of Cleveland. Including any residence halls, there are 47 buildings.

Student Life: 91% of undergraduates are from Ohio. Students are from 35 states, 54 foreign countries, and Canada. 76% are white; 12% African American. The average age of freshmen is 20; all undergraduates, 24. 29% do not continue beyond their first year; 37% remain to graduate.

Housing: 1300 students can be accommodated in college housing, which includes single-sex and coed dorms and on-campus apartments. In addition, there are honors houses, off-campus fraternity and sorority houses, and a leadership community. On-campus housing is guaranteed for all 4 years. 93% of students live on campus. Alcohol is not permitted. All students may keep cars.

Activities: 3% of men belong to 8 national fraternities; 3% of women belong to 1 local sorority and 5 national sororities. There are 150 groups on campus, including art, band, cheerleading, chess, choir, chorale, chorus, computers, dance, drama, ethnic, film, gay, honors, international, jazz band, literary magazine, marching band, musical theater, newspaper, opera, orchestra, photography, political, professional, radio and TV, religious, social, social service, student government, symphony, and yearbook. Popular campus events include Organizational Fair, Greek Sing, and Career Night.

Sports: There are 8 intercollegiate sports for men and 10 for women, and 26 intramural sports for men and 26 for women. Facilities include a sports complex with a 20630-seat stadium, an artificial turf field for football and soccer, racquetball courts, gyms, weight rooms, an all-weather 400-meter track, outdoor basketball, handball, and volleyball courts, and 10 lighted tennis courts. There is also a phys ed center with a 7000-spectator gym, an Olympic-size swimming pool, a dance studio, a rifle range, a fitness center, racquetball and squash courts, and separate gyms for wrestling, weight lifting, gymnastics, and the disabled. A 70,000-square-foot recreation and wellness center includes a cardio fitness and free-weight area and a sports forum.

Disabled Students: 98% of the campus is accessible. Wheelchair ramps, elevators, special parking, specially equipped rest rooms, special class scheduling, lowered drinking fountains, lowered telephones, an escort service, adaptive computers, a lounge, books on tape, institutional memberships, interpreters, a test proctoring program, TDD, a campus shuttle, a note-taker program, C-Print and E-Text, and other adaptive equipment are available.

Services: Counseling and information services are available, as is tutoring in most subjects. There is remedial math, reading, and writing. A foreign language lab is also available.

Campus Safety and Security: Measures include 24-hour foot and vehicle patrol, self-defense education, security escort services, and shuttle buses. There are informal discussions, pamphlets/posters/films, emergency telephones, lighted pathways/sidewalks, night security posts in dorms, and concentrated security in parking and other critical areas.

Programs of Study: YSU confers A.B., B.S., B.Eng., B.F.A., B.G.S., B.M., B.S.Appl.Sci., B.S.B.A., B.S.Ed., B.S.N., B.S.R.C., and B.S.W. degrees. Associate, master's, and doctoral degrees are also awarded. Bachelor's degrees are awarded in BIOLOGICAL SCIENCE (biology/biological science, and nutrition), BUSINESS (accounting, apparel and accessories marketing, banking and finance, business administration and management, business economics, fashion merchandising, hospitality management services, hotel/motel and restaurant management, human resources, international economics, management information systems, marketing and distribution, marketing management, marketing/retailing/merchandising, office supervision and management, personnel management, retailing, and secretarial studies/office management), COMMUNICATIONS AND THE ARTS (advertising, art, art history and appreciation, broadcasting, communications, dramatic arts, drawing, English, French, German, graphic design, Italian, journalism, languages, music, music history and appreciation, music performance, music theory and composition, musical theater, painting, percussion, performing arts, photography, piano/organ, printmaking, public relations, Spanish, speech/debate/rhetoric, studio art, technical and business writing, telecommunications, voice, and winds), COMPUTER AND PHYSICAL SCIENCE (astronomy, chemistry, computer programming, computer science, earth science, geology, information sciences and systems, mathematics, physics, and science), EDUCATION (art, business, computer, drama, early childhood, education, education of the emotionally handicapped, education of the mentally handicapped, education of the multiply handicapped, elementary, English, foreign languages, health, home economics, mathematics, middle school, music, physical, science, secondary, social science, social studies, special, specific learning disabilities, and vocational), ENGINEERING AND ENVIRONMENTAL DESIGN (chemical engineering, civil engineering, civil engineering technology, computer technology, electrical/electronics engineering, electrical/electronics engineering technology, engineering, engineering technology, environmental science, industrial administration/management, industrial engineering, materials engineering, mechanical engineering, mechanical engineering technology, preengineering, and systems engineering), HEALTH PROFESSIONS (allied health, clinical science, community health work, health, health science, medical laboratory technology, medical technology, nursing, nursing home administration, predentistry, premedicine, preoptometry, preosteopathy, prepharmacy, preveterinary science, and respiratory therapy), SOCIAL SCIENCE (African studies, American studies, anthropology, child care/child and family studies, corrections, criminal justice, dietetics, early childhood studies, economics, family and community services, family/consumer studies, fashion design and technology, forensic studies, geography, history, home economics, human ecology, law enforcement and corrections, philosophy, physical fitness/movement, political science/government, prelaw, psychology, public administration, religion, safety and security technology, social science, social studies, social work, and sociology). Early childhood education, management, and nursing are the largest.

Required: To graduate, students must complete 124 to 132 semester hours, depending on the major, with a minimum GPA of 2.0. At least 30 to 48 semester hours in the major are required. All students must fulfill core requirements, including 2 to 3 courses each in natural science, artistic and literary perspectives, and societies and institutions and 2 courses in personal and social responsibility. Requirements must also be met in English, speech, and math.

Special: YSU offers co-op programs in business and engineering, internships, dual majors, credit for military experience, nondegree study, honors degree programs, distance learning, a joint engineering program, accelerated degrees in medicine and chemistry, and pass/fail options. Student-designed majors are available through the Individualized Curriculum Program. There are 25 national honor societies, a freshman honors program, and 6 departmental honors programs.

Faculty/Classroom: 63% of faculty are male; 37%, female. All teach undergraduates. Graduate students teach 10% of introductory courses. The average class size in an introductory lecture is 30; in a laboratory, 10; and in a regular course, 22.

Admissions: 99% of the 2005-2006 applicants were accepted. The SAT scores for the 2005-2006 freshman class were: Verbal--55% below 500, 29% between 500 and 599, 14% between 600 and 700, and 2% above 700; Math--52% below 500, 31% between 500 and 599, 14% between 600 and 700, and 3% above 700. The ACT scores were 59% below 21, 19% between 21 and 23, 12% between 24 and 26, 5% between 27 and 28, and 5% above 28. 22% of the current freshmen were in the top fifth of their class; 43% were in the top two fifths.

Requirements: The SAT or ACT is required. Those who have been out of school for 2 or more years, and who are not pursuing a restricted program of study, are exempt from test requirements. By special agreement, residents of Mercer and Lawrence Counties in Pennsylvania are afforded the same admission requirements as Ohio residents. Out-of-state applicants must rank in the upper two-thirds of their class or have a satisfactory SAT or ACT score. Graduation from an accredited secondary school or satisfactory scores on the GED are required for all applicants. High school courses recommended are 4 units of English, 3 each of math, science, and social studies, 2 of foreign language, and 1 of fine or performing arts. AP and CLEP credits are accepted.

Procedure: Freshmen are admitted fall, spring, and summer. Entrance exams should be taken in spring of the junior year or fall of the senior year. There are early admissions and deferred admissions plans. There is a rolling admissions plan. Early decision applications should be filed by February 15; regular applications, by August 15 for fall entry, December 15 for spring entry, and April 15 for summer entry. The fall 2005 application fee was $30. The college accepts all in-state residents. Notification is sent on a rolling basis.

Transfer: 1063 transfer students enrolled in 2004-2005. Transfer applicants in good standing at the last institution attended and who have an aggregate cumulative point average of 2.0 or higher for all courses taken at other colleges or universities are admitted in good standing. Those with an aggregate cumulative point average of less than 2.0 or on probation may be considered for probationary transfer if their overall academic record, including high school grades and test scores, indicates potential success. Applicants suspended or dismissed from other institutions are not eligible for consideration (without appeal to the Office of Undergraduate Admission) until at least 1 semester has passed following the term in which the suspension occurred. 30 of 124 to 132 credits required for the bachelor's degree must be completed at YSU.

Visiting: There are regularly scheduled orientations for prospective students. There are guides for informal visits and visitors may sit in on classes. To schedule a visit, contact the Office of Undergraduate Admissions.

Financial Aid: In 2005-2006, 82% of all full-time freshmen and 83% of continuing full-time students received some form of financial aid. 42% of all full-time students received need-based aid. Average annual earnings from campus work are $6000. YSU is a member of CSS. The FAFSA and the college's own financial statement are required. The deadline for filing freshman financial aid applications for fall entry is February 15.

International Students: There are 112 international students enrolled. They must achieve a satisfactory score on the TOEFL or take the MELAB.

Computers: Wireless access is available. All students may access the system. There are no time limits and no fees.

Graduates: From July 1, 2004 to June 30, 2005, 1537 bachelor's degrees were awarded. The most popular majors were early childhood education (10%), criminal justice (5%), and marketing management (5%). In an average class, 14% graduate in 4 years or less, 30% graduate in 5 years or less, and 37% graduate in 6 years or less.

Admissions Contact: Sue Davis, Director, Undergraduate Admissions. E-mail: *enroll@ysu.edu* Web: *www.ysu.edu*

OKLAHOMA

POPULATION
DENSITY

• 25,000 and over

0   20   40   60   80   100
Miles

CAMERON UNIVERSITY   D-4
Lawton, OK 73505-6377

(580) 581-2230 or 2289
(888) 454-7600; Fax: (580) 581-5514

Full-time: 1423 men, 2076 women
Part-time: 699 men, 1205 women
Graduate: 118 men, 292 women
Year: semesters, summer session
Application Deadline: open
Freshman Class: 1727 applied, 1727 accepted, 1150 enrolled
ACT: 19

Faculty: 185
Ph.D.s: 70%
Student/Faculty: 19 to 1
Tuition: $3300 ($7890)
Room & Board: $3014

NONCOMPETITIVE

Cameron University, founded in 1908, is a publicly funded institution offering undergraduate programs in business, education and psychology, fine arts, liberal arts, science, math, and technology. There are 4 undergraduate schools and 1 graduate school. In addition to regional accreditation, Cameron has baccalaureate program accreditation with ACBSP, ADDA, NASM, NCATE, and NLN . The library contains 262,215 volumes, 46,567 microform items, and 2868 audio/video tapes/CDs/DVDs, and subscribes to 17,425 periodicals including electronic. Computerized library services include the card catalog, interlibrary loans, database searching, Internet access, and laptop Internet portals. Special learning facilities include a learning resource center, art gallery, radio station, and TV station. The 160-acre campus is in a suburban area 90 miles southwest of Oklahoma City. Including any residence halls, there are 34 buildings.

Student Life: 84% of undergraduates are from Oklahoma. Others are from 49 states, 50 foreign countries, and Canada. 97% are from public schools. 61% are white; 20% African American. The average age of freshmen is 24; all undergraduates, 26.

Housing: 752 students can be accommodated in college housing, which includes single-sex dorms. On-campus housing is guaranteed for all 4 years. 99% of students commute. Alcohol is not permitted. All students may keep cars.

Activities: 4% of men belong to 2 national fraternities; 6% of women belong to 2 national sororities. There are 65 groups on campus, including art, band, cheerleading, computers, debate, drama, drill team, ethnic, forensics, gay, honors, international, jazz band, literary magazine, newspaper, orchestra, pep band, political, professional, radio and TV, religious, social, social service, student government, and yearbook. Popular campus events include Spring Fling, Diversity Week, and Organizational Day.

Sports: There are 5 intercollegiate sports for men and 5 for women, and 6 intramural sports for men and 6 for women. Facilities include a 10,000-seat football stadium, an 1800-seat gym, an 800-seat baseball park, a running track, Nautilus and free-weight rooms, an indoor swimming pool, and basketball, volleyball, and racquetball courts.

Disabled Students: 88% of the campus is accessible. Wheelchair ramps, elevators, special parking, specially equipped rest rooms, special class scheduling, lowered drinking fountains, and lowered telephones are available.

Services: Counseling and information services are available, as is tutoring in some subjects, including writing, reading, accounting, math, fine arts, technology, and computer science. There is remedial math, reading, and writing.

Campus Safety and Security: Measures include 24-hour foot and vehicle patrol, security escort services, pamphlets/posters/films, and emergency telephones. There are lighted pathways/sidewalks.

Programs of Study: Cameron confers B.A., B.S., B.Acctg., B.B.A., B.F.A., and B.Mus. degrees. Associate and master's degrees are also awarded. Bachelor's degrees are awarded in AGRICULTURE (agriculture), BIOLOGICAL SCIENCE (biology/biological science), BUSINESS (accounting and business administration and management), COMMUNICATIONS AND THE ARTS (art, communications, English, multimedia, music, and romance languages and literature), COMPUTER AND PHYSICAL SCIENCE (chemistry, computer science, mathematics, natural sciences, and physics), EDUCATION (elementary and physical), ENGINEERING AND ENVIRONMENTAL DESIGN (technology and public affairs), HEALTH PROFESSIONS (health), SOCIAL SCIENCE (criminal justice, history, human ecology, interdisciplinary studies, liberal arts/general studies, political science/government, psychology, and sociology). Elementary education and criminal justice are the largest.

Required: To graduate, students must complete a total of 128 credit hours with a minimum GPA of 2.0. All students must take courses in English, math, science, U.S. history and government, humanities, behavioral science, economics, and phys ed.

Special: Cameron offers dual majors in several fields, an interdisciplinary studies degree, nondegree study, and credit for military experience. There are 20 national honor societies, and a freshman honors program.

Faculty/Classroom: 64% of faculty are male; 36%, female. All both teach and do research. The average class size in an introductory lecture is 28; in a laboratory, 17; and in a regular course, 15.

Admissions: All of the 2005-2006 applicants were accepted. The ACT scores for the 2005-2006 freshman class were: 64% below 21, 19% between 21 and 23, 11% between 24 and 26, 4% between 27 and 28, and 4% above 28. 19% of the current freshmen were in the top fifth of their class; 48% were in the top two fifths. 19 freshmen graduated first in their class.

Requirements: The SAT or ACT is required, with a minimum score or applicants must rank in the top 50% of their graduating class and have a GPA of at least 2.7. High school courses must include 4 years of English, 3 of math (including algebra I and above), 2 each of history and lab science, 1 each of economics, geography, government, or non-Western culture, and an additional 3 years of any of the previous subjects or of computer science or foreign language. AP and CLEP credits are accepted.

Procedure: Freshmen are admitted to all sessions. Entrance exams should be taken late in the junior year or early in the senior year. Application deadlines are open. Application fee is $15. Notification is sent on a rolling basis. Applications are accepted on-line.

Transfer: Transfer students must have a minimum GPA of 2.0 and be in good standing at the institution last attended. 30 of 128 credits required for the bachelor's degree must be completed at Cameron.

Visiting: There are regularly scheduled orientations for prospective students, including introductory sessions on college life and student services, and with department chairs and enrollment, and campus tours. There are guides for informal visits and visitors may sit in on classes and stay overnight. To schedule a visit, contact Vanessa Arterberry, Admissions Counselor at (580) 581-5760 or *varterbe@cameron.edu*.

Financial Aid: In a recent year, 90% of all full-time freshmen and 85% of continuing full-time students received some form of financial aid. 85% of full-time freshmen and 83% of continuing full-time students received need-based aid. The average freshman award was $3000. Need-based scholarships or need-based grants averaged $2000 ($9376 maximum); need-based self-help aid (loans and jobs) averaged $1500 ($4625 maximum); and other non-need-based awards and non-need-based scholarships averaged $800. 70% of undergraduates work part time. Average annual earnings from campus work are $800. The average financial indebtedness of a recent graduate was $6300. The FAFSA is required. Check with the school for current application deadlines.

International Students: There are 133 international students enrolled. They must score satisfactorily on the written TOEFL or on the electronic version and also take the SAT if under 21 years of age.

Computers: All students have user accounts for any location on campus as well as e-mail accounts, central file storage, and unlimited black-and-white and color printing. Wireless connectivity is available in common areas of both residential housing locations, the student union, classroom buildings, and a central courtyard. All students may access the system at any time. There are no time limits. There is a $10 per credit hour student technology fee.

Graduates: From July 1, 2004 to June 30, 2005, 469 bachelor's degrees were awarded. The most popular majors were business (20%), education (14%), and technology (12%). In an average class, 31% graduate in 6 years or less. 50 companies recruited on campus in 2004-2005.

Admissions Contact: Zoe Du Rant, Director of Admissions.
E-mail: *zoed@cameron.edu* Web: *www.cameron.edu*

EAST CENTRAL UNIVERSITY　　　　E-4

Ada, OK 74820　　　　(580) 332-8000; Fax: (580) 310-5432

Full-time: 1286 men, 1886 women	**Faculty:** 156; IIA, --$
Part-time: 208 men, 423 women	**Ph.D.s:** 72%
Graduate: 189 men, 579 women	**Student/Faculty:** 20 to 1
Year: semesters, summer session	**Tuition:** $3207 ($7841)
Application Deadline: open	**Room & Board:** $3000
Freshman Class: 572 enrolled	
ACT: 20	**COMPETITIVE**

East Central University, founded in 1909, is a publicly funded institution offering undergraduate programs in liberal arts and sciences, education, business, and health-related fields, and graduate programs in education, human resources, and psychology. There are 4 undergraduate schools and 1 graduate school. In addition to regional accreditation, ECU has baccalaureate program accreditation with ACBSP, CSWE, NASM, NCATE, and NLN. The library contains 174,905 volumes, 700,000 microform items, and 13,509 audio/video tapes/CDs/DVDs, and subscribes to 17,098 periodicals including electronic. Computerized library services include the card catalog, interlibrary loans, database searching, and Internet access. Special learning facilities include a learning resource center, art gallery, and an observatory. The 140-acre campus is in a small town 90 miles south of Oklahoma City. Including any residence halls, there are 28 buildings.

Student Life: 94% of undergraduates are from Oklahoma. Others are from 25 states, 23 foreign countries, and Canada. 99% are from public schools. 69% are white; 21% Native American/Eskimo. The average age of freshmen is 19; all undergraduates, 25. 38% do not continue beyond their first year; 34% remain to graduate.

Housing: 1064 students can be accommodated in college housing, which includes single-sex and coed dorms, on-campus apartments, mar-

ried-student housing, fraternity houses, and sorority houses. On-campus housing is available on a first-come, first-served basis. 50% of students live on campus; of those, 5% remain on campus on weekends. Alcohol is not permitted. All students may keep cars.

Activities: 2% of men belong to 1 local and 3 national fraternities; 2% of women belong to 3 national sororities. There are 88 groups on campus, including art, band, cheerleading, choir, chorale, chorus, computers, dance, debate, drama, drill team, ethnic, film, forensics, gay, honors, international, jazz band, literary magazine, marching band, musical theater, newspaper, nontrational students, opera, pep band, photography, political, professional, radio and TV, religious, social, social service, student government, and yearbook. Popular campus events include Welcome Week, Don't Go Home This Weekend Weekend, and Christmas in the Eyes of a Child.

Sports: There are 6 intercollegiate sports for men and 5 for women, and 8 intramural sports for men and 8 for women. Facilities include an indoor swimming pool, a fitness/aerobics center, tennis, basketball, and racquetball courts, a weight room, football, soccer, baseball, and softball fields, and indoor and outdoor tracks.

Disabled Students: All of the campus is accessible. Wheelchair ramps, elevators, special parking, specially equipped rest rooms, special class scheduling, lowered drinking fountains, lowered telephones, special housing, adaptive swimming, and weight training are available.

Services: Counseling and information services are available, as is tutoring in every subject. There is a reader service for the blind, and remedial math, reading, and writing. Interpreters for the deaf, note taking/typing, and tape transcription are available.

Campus Safety and Security: Measures include 24-hour foot and vehicle patrol, lighted pathways/sidewalks, and training in the freshman seminar class.

Programs of Study: ECU confers B.A., B.S., B.G.S., B.S.Ed., and B.S.W. degrees. Master's degrees are also awarded. Bachelor's degrees are awarded in BIOLOGICAL SCIENCE (biology/biological science), BUSINESS (accounting, banking and finance, business administration and management, management information systems, marketing/retailing/merchandising, recreation and leisure services, and retailing), COMMUNICATIONS AND THE ARTS (advertising, art, communications, dramatic arts, English, journalism, music, piano/organ, public relations, speech/debate/rhetoric, and voice), COMPUTER AND PHYSICAL SCIENCE (applied mathematics, chemistry, computer science, mathematics, and physics), EDUCATION (art, athletic training, business, drama, early childhood, elementary, English, health, home economics, mathematics, music, physical, science, and special), ENGINEERING AND ENVIRONMENTAL DESIGN (cartography), HEALTH PROFESSIONS (environmental health science, exercise science, medical laboratory technology, medical records administration/services, nursing, and rehabilitation therapy), SOCIAL SCIENCE (criminal justice, family/consumer resource management, gerontology, history, human services, liberal arts/general studies, paralegal studies, political science/government, prelaw, psychology, social work, and sociology). Nursing, human resources, and elementary education are the largest.

Required: To graduate, students must complete a minimum of 124 credit hours with a minimum GPA of 2.0. 60 hours must be from a 4-year college/university. Between 45 to 55 hours must be completed in the major and 18 to 21 hours in the minor. All students must take 40 hours of upper-level courses, as well as 45 hours in general studies, and must meet computer proficiency requirements.

Special: The school offers co-op programs with the Ardmore Higher Education Center and is a member of the National Student Exchange Program. Internships are available in human resources, environmental health, political science, office technology, mass communications, and cartography. Students may participate in a work-study program with the Veterans Administration. Nondegree study, student designed majors, and credit for military experience are available. The school offers special rates for nonresidents from approved states who wish to major in specialized fields. There is 1 university-wide honors program and a freshman honors program.

Faculty/Classroom: 55% of faculty are male; 45%, female. 96% teach undergraduates, 50% do research, and 50% do both. Graduate students teach 1% of introductory courses. The average class size in an introductory lecture is 30 and in a laboratory, 30.

Admissions: The ACT scores for the 2005-2006 freshman class were: 52% below 21, 26% between 21 and 23, 16% between 24 and 26, 4% between 27 and 28, and 2% above 28. 31% of the current freshmen were in the top fifth of their class; 59% were in the top two fifths.

Requirements: The ACT is required, with a minimum composite score of 20. The SAT will be accepted in place of the ACT. Applicants must be graduates of an accredited secondary school or have the GED. High school courses must include 4 years of English, 3 years of math, and 2 years each of history and science. ECU requires applicants to be in the upper 50% of their class. A GPA of 2.7 is required. AP and CLEP credits are accepted.

Procedure: Freshmen are admitted to all sessions. Entrance exams should be taken during the junior or senior year of high school. Application deadlines are open. Applications are accepted on-line.

Transfer: Applicants having fewer than 24 credit hours must meet the criteria for entering freshmen. The required minimum GPA for transfer students is 2.0. 30 of 124 credits required for the bachelor's degree must be completed at ECU.

Visiting: There are regularly scheduled orientations for prospective students. There are guides for informal visits. To schedule a visit, contact the Student Services Office at (877) 310-5628.

Financial Aid: In 2005-2006, 53% of all full-time freshmen and 54% of continuing full-time students received some form of financial aid. 39% of all full-time students received need-based aid. The average freshman award was $7292. Need-based scholarships or need-based grants averaged $4910 ($14,330 maximum); need-based self-help aid (loans and jobs) averaged $5921 ($9921 maximum); non-need-based athletic scholarships averaged $4546 ($18,964 maximum); and other non-need-based awards and non-need-based scholarships averaged $1856. 22% of undergraduates work part time. Average annual earnings from campus work are $1732. The FAFSA, the college's own financial statement, and federal tax returns are required. The priority date for freshman financial aid applications for fall entry is July 1.

International Students: There are 49 international students enrolled. The school actively recruits these students. They must score satisfactorily on the written TOEFL or on the electronic version.

Computers: Wireless access is available. Students have access to 500 Pcs in 25 computer labs across campus. They are each issued a network ID and password. All students may access the system when labs are open. There are no time limits and no fees.

Admissions Contact: Pamla Armstrong, Registrar and Director of Admissions. E-mail: *parmstro@mailclerk.ecok.edu* Web: *www.ecok.edu*

LANGSTON UNIVERSITY — D-3

Langston, OK 73050 — (405) 466-3224; Fax: (405) 466-3381

Full-time: 1290 men, 1920 women	Faculty: 105
Part-time: 290 men, 520 women	Ph.D.s: 50%
Graduate: 20 men, 40 women	Student/Faculty: 31 to 1
Year: semesters, summer session	Tuition: $2500 ($5100)
Application Deadline: open	Room & Board: n/app
Freshman Class: n/av	
SAT or ACT: required	LESS COMPETITIVE

Langston University, founded in 1897 as the Colored Agricultural and Normal University, is today a multiracial, public institution offering programs in liberal arts, business, allied health, and teacher preparation. Figures in above capsule and in this profile are approximate. In addition to regional accreditation, Langston has baccalaureate program accreditation with ADA, APTA, NCATE, and NLN. The 6 libraries contain 110,248 volumes and 465,319 microform items, and subscribe to 80 periodicals including electronic. Computerized library services include the card catalog and interlibrary loans. Special learning facilities include a learning resource center, satellite teaching, a black heritage center, an institute for goat research, and a state research group in catfish production. The 40-acre campus is in a rural area 45 miles from Oklahoma City. Including any residence halls, there are 20 buildings.

Student Life: 98% are from public schools. 50% are African American; 50% white. 65% of freshmen remain to graduate.

Housing: 676 students can be accommodated in college housing, which includes dorms and married-student housing. Alcohol is not permitted. All students may keep cars.

Activities: 25% of men belong to 4 national fraternities; 30% of women belong to 4 national sororities. There are 30 groups on campus, including band, cheerleading, choir, drama, ethnic, international, jazz band, marching band, newspaper, professional, religious, social service, student government, and yearbook. Popular campus events include student theater productions and a performing arts series.

Sports: There are 4 intercollegiate sports for men and 2 for women, and 6 intramural sports for men and 5 for women. Facilities include a gym, tennis courts, a baseball field, and a track.

Disabled Students: 70% of the campus is accessible. Wheelchair ramps, elevators, special parking, specially equipped rest rooms, and special class scheduling are available.

Services: Counseling and information services are available, as is tutoring in some subjects. There is remedial math, reading, and writing.

Programs of Study: Langston confers B.A., B.B.A., B.S., B.S.Ed., and B.S.N. degrees. Associate and master's degrees are also awarded. Bachelor's degrees are awarded in AGRICULTURE (agricultural economics and animal science), BIOLOGICAL SCIENCE (biology/biological science and nutrition), BUSINESS (accounting, business administration and management, and management science), COMMUNICATIONS AND THE ARTS (dramatic arts, English, music, and speech/debate/rhetoric), COMPUTER AND PHYSICAL SCIENCE (chemistry, computer science, and mathematics), EDUCATION (business, elementary, home economics, industrial arts, mathematics, physical, and science), ENGINEERING AND ENVIRONMENTAL DESIGN (industrial engineering technology), HEALTH PROFESSIONS (health care administration, medical laboratory technology, nursing, and physical therapy), SOCIAL

SCIENCE (criminal justice, early childhood studies, economics, gerontology, history, home economics, psychology, social science, sociology, and urban studies).

Required: To graduate, students must complete a total of 124 semester hours, with a GPA of 2.0. The required general education core consists of 50 credits in English, math, computer science, biological and physical sciences, social science, and health and phys ed. 6 credits are required in American history and government, and all students must complete an internship or field experience.

Special: Work-study programs, internships, and nondegree and noncredit study are available. There are 6 national honor societies and a freshman honors program.

Faculty/Classroom: All teach undergraduates.

Requirements: The SAT or ACT is required. In general, test scores should place students in the upper 60 percent of Oklahoma high school seniors. Applicants should be graduates of accredited high schools with at least a C average (2.7 on a 4.0 scale) and rank in the upper 60 percent of their graduating classes. Required secondary preparation includes 4 years of English, 3 years of math, and 2 years each of lab science and history, including 1 year of American history. 4 additional academic units, including a foreign language, are strongly recommended. There are alternative admission programs for students with varying backgrounds. Langston requires applicants to be in the upper 50% of their class. A GPA of 2.7 is required. AP and CLEP credits are accepted.

Procedure: Freshmen are admitted to all sessions. There is a rolling admissions plan. Application deadlines are open. The fall 2005 application fee was $15.

Transfer: Applicants should be in good standing and have earned at least a C average in previous college work. 30 of 124 credits required for the bachelor's degree must be completed at Langston.

Visiting: There are regularly scheduled orientations for prospective students. There are guides for informal visits and visitors may sit in on classes and stay overnight. To schedule a visit, contact the High School/College Relations Office.

Financial Aid: The CSS/Profile, FAFSA, FFS or SFS is required. Check with the school for current application deadlines.

International Students: They must score satisfactorily on the written TOEFL.

Computers: There are no time limits and no fees.

Admissions Contact: Ms. Gayle T. Robertson, Driector of Admissions and Enrollment Management. E-mail: *gtrobertson@lunet.edu*

NORTHEASTERN STATE UNIVERSITY — F-3

Tahlequah, OK 74464 — (918) 456-5511, ext. 2200 (800) 722-9614; Fax: (918) 458-2342

Full-time: 2664 men, 3852 women	Faculty: 314; II A, --$
Part-time: 716 men, 1393 women	Ph.D.s: 72%
Graduate: 334 men, 743 women	Student/Faculty: 21 to 1
Year: semesters, summer session	Tuition: $2616 ($6432)
Application Deadline: open	Room & Board: $3280
Freshman Class: 1651 accepted, 1102 enrolled	
ACT: 24	LESS COMPETITIVE

Northeastern State University, founded in 1846, is a public institution offering programs in arts and sciences, professional training, teacher preparation, and business. There are 4 undergraduate and 5 graduate schools. In addition to regional accreditation, NSU has baccalaureate program accreditation with ACBSP, ADA, ASLA, CSWE, NASM, NCATE, and NLN. The library contains 400,000 volumes, 766,300 microform items, and 8659 audio/video tapes/CDs/DVDs, and subscribes to 15,000 periodicals including electronic. Computerized library services include the card catalog, interlibrary loans, database searching, Internet access, and laptop Internet portals. Special learning facilities include a learning resource center. The 200-acre campus is in a small town 70 miles from Tulsa. Including any residence halls, there are 51 buildings.

Student Life: 94% of undergraduates are from Oklahoma. Others are from 34 states, 47 foreign countries, and Canada. 61% are white; 28% Native American/Eskimo. The average age of freshmen is 19; all undergraduates, 26. 30% do not continue beyond their first year.

Housing: 1653 students can be accommodated in college housing, which includes single-sex and coed dorms, on-campus apartments, married-student housing and rooming arrangements for special-interest groups. On-campus housing is available on a first-come, first-served basis. 80% of students commute. Alcohol is not permitted. All students may keep cars.

Activities: 5% of men belong to 7 national fraternities; 2% of women belong to 5 national sororities. There are 80 groups on campus, including art, band, cheerleading, choir, chorus, dance, drama, drill team, ethnic, film, gay, honors, international, jazz band, literary magazine, marching band, musical theater, newspaper, orchestra, pep band, photography, political, professional, radio and TV, religious, social service, student government, and symphony. Popular campus events include Cherokee Seminaries, Symposium on the American Indian, and Sequoyah Institute shows.

Sports: There are 5 intercollegiate sports for men and 5 for women, and 16 intramural sports for men and 16 for women. Facilities include a 12,500-seat football stadium, an indoor practice facility, an exercise/fitness track, baseball, softball and soccer fields, tennis courts, baseball and soccer/softball field houses, and a 1,200-seat basketball gym and basketball court used for academics.

Disabled Students: 70% of the campus is accessible. Wheelchair ramps, elevators, special parking, specially equipped rest rooms, special class scheduling, lowered drinking fountains, lowered telephones, and special housing are available.

Services: Counseling and information services are available, as is tutoring in most subjects. There is remedial math, reading, and writing.

Campus Safety and Security: Measures include 24-hour foot and vehicle patrol, self-defense education, security escort services, and shuttle buses. There are informal discussions, pamphlets/posters/films, emergency telephones, and lighted pathways/sidewalks. There is a campus security police department.

Programs of Study: NSU confers B.A., B.S., B.A.Ed., B.B.A., B.S.Ed., B.S.N., B.S.Sci.Ed., and B.S.W. degrees. Master's and doctoral degrees are also awarded. Bachelor's degrees are awarded in BIOLOGICAL SCIENCE (biology/biological science), BUSINESS (accounting, banking and finance, business administration and management, and marketing/retailing/merchandising), COMMUNICATIONS AND THE ARTS (advertising, communications, English, fine arts, journalism, music, Spanish, and speech/debate/rhetoric), COMPUTER AND PHYSICAL SCIENCE (chemistry, computer science, information sciences and systems, and mathematics), EDUCATION (art, early childhood, elementary, health, industrial arts, music, science, secondary, and special), HEALTH PROFESSIONS (medical laboratory technology and nursing), SOCIAL SCIENCE (criminal justice, geography, history, political science/government, social science, social work, and sociology). Elementary education, early childhood education, business administration, psychology, and criminal justice are the largest.

Required: To graduate, students must complete at least 124 credit hours, with 24 to 50 in the major. General education requirements include 40 hours in language arts, social science, natural science, humanities, and phys ed. Freshman orientation and English proficiency are required.

Special: Internships are offered in business, mass communications, and education. There are 10 national honor societies, a freshman honors program, and 5 departmental honors programs.

Faculty/Classroom: 56% of faculty are male; 44%, female. 90% teach undergraduates. Graduate students teach 5% of introductory courses. The average class size in an introductory lecture is 60; in a laboratory, 24; and in a regular course, 20 to 30.

Requirements: The ACT is required, with satisfactory scores. Applicants should be high school graduates or have a GED. Students should have completed 4 years of English, 3 of math, and 2 each of history and science. NSU requires applicants to be in the upper 50% of their class. A GPA of 2.7 is required. AP and CLEP credits are accepted.

Procedure: Freshmen are admitted to all sessions. There is a rolling admissions plan. Application deadlines are open.

Transfer: 1404 transfer students enrolled in 2004-2005. Transfer applicants must have a minimum GPA of 2.0, with 24 transfer hours completed, and be in good standing at the last institution attended. 30 of 124 credits required for the bachelor's degree must be completed at NSU.

Visiting: There are regularly scheduled orientations for prospective students, including a general campus visit with highlights presented by trained tour guides. Visitors may sit in on classes and stay overnight. To schedule a visit, contact High School and College Relations at (918) 458-2130 or sneed@nsuok.edu.

Financial Aid: In 2005-2006, 86% of all full-time freshmen and 85% of continuing full-time students received some form of financial aid. 67% of full-time freshmen and 63% of continuing full-time students received need-based aid. Need-based scholarships or need-based grants averaged $3370; need-based self-help aid (loans and jobs) averaged $2425 ($13,100 maximum); and non-need-based athletic scholarships averaged $5426. 7% of undergraduates work part time. Average annual earnings from campus work are $2850. The average financial indebtedness of the 2005 graduate was $17,824. The FAFSA and the college's own financial statement are required. The priority date for freshman financial aid applications for fall entry is March 1.

International Students: There are 252 international students enrolled. They must take the TOEFL.

Computers: Wireless access is available. All students may access the system.

Graduates: From July 1, 2004 to June 30, 2005, 1404 bachelor's degrees were awarded. 254 companies recruited on campus in 2004-2005.

Admissions Contact: Dawn Cain, Director of Admissions.
E-mail: *nsuinfo@nsuok.edu* Web: *www.nsuok.edu*

NORTHWESTERN OKLAHOMA STATE UNIVERSITY   C-1

Alva, OK 73717   (580) 327-8546; Fax: (580) 327-8413

Full-time: 550 men, 755 women | **Faculty:** n/av
Part-time: 224 men, 332 women | **Ph.Ds:** n/av
Graduate: 62 men, 178 women | **Student/Faculty:** n/av
Year: semesters, summer session | **Tuition:** $3270 ($8100)
Application Deadline: open | **Room & Board:** $2980
Freshman Class: 438 applied, 434 accepted, 275 enrolled
ACT: 20   **NONCOMPETITIVE**

Northwestern Oklahoma State University, founded in 1897, is a public institution offering programs in liberal and fine arts, agriculture, business, professional training, and teacher preparation. There are 2 undergraduate schools and 1 graduate school. In addition to regional accreditation, Northwestern has baccalaureate program accreditation with NCATE and NLN. The library contains 135,000 volumes, 366,000 microform items, and 1100 audio/video tapes/CDs/DVDs, and subscribes to 1480 periodicals including electronic. Computerized library services include interlibrary loans, database searching, and Internet access. Special learning facilities include a learning resource center, natural history museum, radio station, TV station, and a cable channel. The 70-acre campus is in a small town 150 miles northwest of Oklahoma City. Including any residence halls, there are 35 buildings.

Student Life: 80% of undergraduates are from Oklahoma. Others are from 29 states, 28 foreign countries, and Canada. 86% are white. The average age of freshmen is 21; all undergraduates, 24. 34% do not continue beyond their first year; 35% remain to graduate.

Housing: 872 students can be accommodated in college housing, which includes single-sex dorms. In addition, there is a dorm with all private rooms for junior and senior women. On-campus housing is guaranteed for all 4 years. 75% of students commute. Alcohol is not permitted. All students may keep cars.

Activities: 1% of men belong to 1 national fraternity and 1 local and 1 national sorority. There are 39 groups on campus, including art, band, cheerleading, choir, chorale, computers, dance, drama, ethnic, forensics, honors, international, jazz band, marching band, musical theater, newspaper, pep band, photography, political, professional, radio and TV, religious, social, student government, and yearbook. Popular campus events include Foundation Scholarship Banquet, Alumni Banquet, and Science Fair.

Sports: There are 4 intercollegiate sports for men and 2 for women, and 4 intramural sports for men and 4 for women. Facilities include a field house, playing fields, a basketball court, a pool, and racquetball and tennis courts.

Disabled Students: Wheelchair ramps, elevators, special parking, specially equipped rest rooms, special class scheduling, and lowered drinking fountains are available. In addition, Northwestern works with disabled students to accommodate their special needs.

Services: Counseling and information services are available, as is tutoring in most subjects. There is remedial math, reading, and writing.

Campus Safety and Security: Measures include 24-hour foot and vehicle patrol and lighted pathways/sidewalks.

Programs of Study: Northwestern confers B.A., B.S., B.A.Ed., B.S.Ed., and B.S.N. degrees. Master's degrees are also awarded. Bachelor's degrees are awarded in AGRICULTURE (agricultural business management, agriculture, and conservation and regulation), BIOLOGICAL SCIENCE (biology/biological science), BUSINESS (accounting, business administration and management, and office supervision and management), COMMUNICATIONS AND THE ARTS (broadcasting, communications, dramatic arts, English, music, public relations, and speech/debate/rhetoric), COMPUTER AND PHYSICAL SCIENCE (chemistry, computer science, mathematics, and physics), EDUCATION (business, early childhood, elementary, English, library science, mathematics, music, physical, science, secondary, and special), HEALTH PROFESSIONS (medical laboratory technology and nursing), SOCIAL SCIENCE (criminal justice, economics, history, political science/government, psychology, social science, social work, and sociology). Education and business are the strongest academically.

Required: A total of 124 credit hours is required, including at least 40 in the major, with a minimum GPA of 2.0. General education courses total 54 semester hours, including 19 hours in communication and humanities, 15 in social and behavioral science, 11 in math and natural science, and 9 in phys ed and other practical arts. This general sequence totals 50 hours for education majors.

Special: Northwestern offers credit by exam and for military experience. There are 4 national honor societies and a freshman honors program.

Faculty/Classroom: 49% of faculty are male; 51%, female. All teach undergraduates. No introductory courses are taught by graduate students. The average class size in an introductory lecture is 38; in a laboratory, 24; and in a regular course, 19.

Admissions: 99% of the 2005-2006 applicants were accepted. The ACT scores for the 2005-2006 freshman class were: 59% below 21, 26%

between 21 and 23, 9% between 24 and 26, 5% between 27 and 28, and 2% above 28.

Requirements: The ACT is required. Applicants must be graduates of an accredited secondary school or have earned a GED. Northwestern requires 20 academic credits, including 4 in English, 3 in math, and 2 each in history and lab science. Northwestern requires applicants to be in the upper 50% of their class. A GPA of 2.7 is required. CLEP credit is accepted.

Procedure: Freshmen are admitted to all sessions. Entrance exams should be taken in the junior or senior year. There is a rolling admissions plan. The fall 2005 application fee was $15. Application deadlines are open.

Transfer: 258 transfer students enrolled in 2004-2005. Applicants must have a GPA of at least 2.0. 40 of 124 credits required for the bachelor's degree must be completed at Northwestern.

Visiting: There are regularly scheduled orientations for prospective students, in April, usually during 2 sessions. Entering freshmen receive information, tour the campus, and enroll. There are guides for informal visits and visitors may sit in on classes and stay overnight. To schedule a visit, contact the Recruitment Office.

Financial Aid: 57% of undergraduates work part time. Average annual earnings from campus work are $2040. The FAFSA is required. The deadline for filing freshman financial aid applications for fall entry is June 1.

International Students: There were 27 international students enrolled in a recent year. The school actively recruits these students. They must score satisfactorily on the TOEFL.

Computers: All students may access the system 8 A.M. to 8 P.M. There are no time limits and no fees.

Graduates: From July 1, 2004 to June 30, 2005, 368 bachelor's degrees were awarded. The most popular majors were business administration (15%), elementary education (9%), and psychology (9%). In an average class, 25% graduate in 4 years or less, 32% graduate in 5 years or less, and 35% graduate in 6 years or less. 25 companies recruited on campus in 2004-2005.

Admissions Contact: Jennifer Goucher, Director of Recruitment. A video is available. E-mail: *dpsmith@nwosu.edu* Web: *www.nwosu.edu*

OKLAHOMA BAPTIST UNIVERSITY   E-3
Shawnee, OK 74804   (405) 878-2033
    (800) 654-3285; Fax: (405) 878-2046

Full-time: 564 men, 841 women	Faculty: n/av
Part-time: 170 men, 74 women	Ph.D.s: n/av
Graduate: none	Student/Faculty: n/av
Year: 4-1-4, summer session	Tuition: $13,846
Application Deadline: August 1	Room & Board: $4140
Freshman Class: 1026 applied, 854 accepted, 371 enrolled	
SAT Verbal/Math: 590/560*	ACT: 24 VERY COMPETITIVE

Oklahoma Baptist University, founded in 1910, is a liberal arts institution affiliated with the Southern Baptist Convention. OBU offers degrees in Christian service, business, nursing, fine arts, telecommunications, teacher education, and the traditional liberal arts areas. There are 5 undergraduate schools and 1 graduate school. In addition to regional accreditation, OBU has baccalaureate program accreditation with ACBSP, NASM, NCATE, and NLN. The library contains 290,000 volumes, 230,000 microform items, and 1500 audio/video tapes/CDs/DVDs, and subscribes to 600 periodicals including electronic. Computerized library services include the card catalog, interlibrary loans, database searching, Internet access, and laptop Internet portals. Special learning facilities include a learning resource center, art gallery, planetarium, TV station, a language lab, and a biblical research library. The 189-acre campus is in a small town 30 miles east of Oklahoma City and 90 miles southwest of Tulsa. Including any residence halls, there are 53 buildings.

Student Life: 57% of undergraduates are from Oklahoma. Students are from 42 states, 20 foreign countries, and Canada. 84% are from public schools. 82% are white. 78% are Protestant; 17% claim no religious affiliation. The average age of freshmen is 18; all undergraduates, 22. 24% do not continue beyond their first year; 58% remain to graduate.

Housing: 1400 students can be accommodated in college housing, which includes single-sex dorms, on-campus apartments, and married-student housing. On-campus housing is guaranteed for all 4 years. 70% of students live on campus; of those, 75% remain on campus on weekends. Alcohol is not permitted. All students may keep cars.

Activities: 16% of men belong to 5 local fraternities; 15% of women belong to 5 local sororities. There are 95 groups on campus, including art, band, cheerleading, choir, chorale, chorus, computers, drama, ethnic, film, honors, international, jazz band, literary magazine, musical theater, newspaper, opera, orchestra, pep band, photography, political, professional, radio and TV, religious, social, social service, student government, and yearbook. Popular campus events include Stampede of Stars, International Awareness Day, and Hanging of the Green.

Sports: There are 8 intercollegiate sports for men and 8 for women, and 10 intramural sports for men and 8 for women. Facilities include a sports complex, which houses a 2500-seat arena, a swimming pool, tennis and racquetball courts, weight rooms, an all-weather track, and baseball, softball, and sand volleyball facilities.

Disabled Students: 95% of the campus is accessible. Wheelchair ramps, elevators, special parking, specially equipped rest rooms, lowered drinking fountains, lowered telephones, and special housing are available.

Services: Counseling and information services are available, as is tutoring in most subjects. There is a reader service for the blind, and remedial math, reading, and writing.

Campus Safety and Security: Measures include 24-hour foot and vehicle patrol, self-defense education, security escort services, and pamphlets/posters/films. There are emergency telephones and lighted pathways/sidewalks.

Programs of Study: OBU confers B.A., B.S., B.B.A., B.F.A., B.Hum., B.M., B.M.A., B.Mus.Ed., and B.S.E. degrees. Associate and master's degrees are also awarded. Bachelor's degrees are awarded in BIOLOGICAL SCIENCE (biology/biological science), BUSINESS (accounting, banking and finance, business administration and management, and marketing/retailing/merchandising), COMMUNICATIONS AND THE ARTS (broadcasting, communications, dramatic arts, English, fine arts, French, German, journalism, music, Spanish, speech/debate/rhetoric, and telecommunications), COMPUTER AND PHYSICAL SCIENCE (chemistry, computer science, information sciences and systems, mathematics, and physics), EDUCATION (art, early childhood, elementary, foreign languages, music, physical, science, and secondary), HEALTH PROFESSIONS (nursing, physical therapy, predentistry, and premedicine), SOCIAL SCIENCE (history, political science/government, prelaw, psychology, religion, social science, social work, and sociology). Teacher education, biology, and religion are the strongest academically. Biology, elementary education, and nursing are the largest.

Required: To graduate, students must complete a total of 128 credit hours, including 30 to 48 hours in the major, with a 2.0 GPA. Students are also required to complete 6 credits each of English, literature, history, science, Bible, social sciences, and language; 3 each in math, fine arts, and comparative civilization; 2 each in speech, philosophy, and phys ed; and 1 in computer literacy.

Special: OBU offers co-op programs in business, and a 3-2 engineering degree with Oklahoma State University. Students may study abroad in Europe, Central America, Uganda, China, Japan, Australia, Mexico, Haiti, and Russia. Internships in several fields, student-designed majors, including an interdisciplinary program in humanities, and pass/fail options are available. There are 4 national honor societies and a freshman honors program.

Faculty/Classroom: 58% of faculty are male; 42%, female. All teach undergraduates. The average class size in an introductory lecture is 25; in a laboratory, 19; and in a regular course, 18.

Admissions: 83% of the 2005-2006 applicants were accepted. The SAT scores for the 2005-2006 freshman class were: Verbal--16% below 500, 36% between 500 and 599, 36% between 600 and 700, and 12% above 700; Math--19% below 500, 43% between 500 and 599, 29% between 600 and 700, and 9% above 700. The ACT scores were 10% below 21, 30% between 21 and 23, 25% between 24 and 26, 16% between 27 and 28, and 19% above 28. 60% of the current freshmen were in the top fifth of their class; 83% were in the top two fifths. There were 5 National Merit finalists and 5 semifinalists. 40 freshmen graduated first in their class.

Requirements: The SAT or ACT is required. Admission is granted to students with minimum composite scores on the SAT or ACT and with a 3.0 GPA. Graduation from an accredited secondary school or satisfactory scores on the GED are required for admission. The recommended high school courses should include 4 units of English, 3 units of math, and 2 units each of social studies, lab science, and a foreign language. OBU requires applicants to be in the upper 50% of their class. A GPA of 3.0 is required. AP and CLEP credits are accepted. Important factors in the admissions decision are advanced placement or honor courses, recommendations by school officials, and leadership record.

Procedure: Freshmen are admitted to all sessions. Entrance exams should be taken during the spring of the junior year. There is a deferred admissions plan. There is a rolling admissions plan. Applications should be filed by August 1 for fall entry, December 15 for winter entry, January 15 for spring entry, and May 15 for summer entry, along with a $25 fee. Notification is sent on a rolling basis. Applications are accepted on-line.

Transfer: 110 transfer students enrolled in 2004-2005. Transfer students must have a GPA of 2.5 for all college work attempted. 33 of 128 credits required for the bachelor's degree must be completed at OBU.

Visiting: There are regularly scheduled orientations for prospective students, including tours, faculty visits, and general information sessions. There are guides for informal visits and visitors may sit in on classes with advance notice and stay overnight with prior approval. To schedule a visit, contact the Admissions Office.

Financial Aid: In a recent year, 94% of all full-time freshmen and 92% of continuing full-time students received some form of financial aid. 62%

of full-time freshmen and 65% of continuing full-time students received need-based aid. The average freshman award was $11,312. Need-based scholarships or need-based grants averaged $3523; need-based self-help aid (loans and jobs) averaged $3151; and non-need-based athletic scholarships averaged $5139. 95% of undergraduates work part time. Average annual earnings from campus work are $1648. The average financial indebtedness of a receny year's graduate was $14,000. The FAFSA is required. The priority date for freshman financial aid applications for fall entry is April 1.

International Students: There are 52 international students enrolled. The school actively recruits these students. They must achieve a satisfactory score on the TOEFL and also take the SAT or the ACT, scoring 20 on the ACT.

Computers: Wireless access is available. All students may access the system 75 hours per week. There are no time limits and no fees. It is strongly recommended that all students have a personal computer.

Admissions Contact: Trent Argo, Enrollment Management. A video is available. E-mail: *admissions@okbu.edu* Web: *www.okbu.edu*

OKLAHOMA CHRISTIAN UNIVERSITY D-3

Oklahoma City, OK 73136-1100 (405) 425-5050
(800) 877-5010; Fax: (405) 425-5069

Full-time: 886 men, 869 women	**Faculty:** 89
Part-time: 38 men, 42 women	**Ph.D.s:** 71%
Graduate: 136 men, 81 women	**Student/Faculty:** 20 to 1
Year: semesters, summer session	**Tuition:** $13,932
Application Deadline: open	**Room & Board:** $5060
Freshman Class: 1676 applied, 1676 accepted, 709 enrolled	
SAT Verbal/Math: 551/618*	**ACT:** 23 **NONCOMPETITIVE**

Oklahoma Christian University, founded in 1950, is a private liberal arts institution affiliated with the Church of Christ. There are 3 undergraduate and 2 graduate schools. In addition to regional accreditation, OC has baccalaureate program accreditation with ABET, ACBSP, NASM, and NCATE. The library contains 115,299 volumes, 741,211 microform items, and 5714 audio/video tapes/CDs/DVDs, and subscribes to 7255 periodicals including electronic. Computerized library services include the card catalog, interlibrary loans, database searching, Internet access, and laptop Internet portals. Special learning facilities include a learning resource center, art gallery, radio station, and , free enterprise museum, and journalism lab. The 200-acre campus is in a suburban area on the north side of Oklahoma City. Including any residence halls, there are 33 buildings.

Student Life: 58% of undergraduates are from out of state, mostly the Midwest. Students are from 45 states, 33 foreign countries, and Canada. 85% are white. Most are Protestant. The average age of freshmen is 18. 34% do not continue beyond their first year; 41% remain to graduate.

Housing: 1480 students can be accommodated in college housing, which includes single-sex dorms, on-campus apartments, and married-student housing. In addition, there are honors houses. On-campus housing is guaranteed for all 4 years. 80% of students live on campus. Alcohol is not permitted. All students may keep cars.

Activities: There are no fraternities or sororities. There are 19 groups on campus, including band, cheerleading, choir, chorale, computers, drama, ethnic, honors, international, jazz band, literary magazine, musical theater, newspaper, opera, pep band, photography, political, professional, radio and TV, religious, social service, student government, and symphony. Popular campus events include High School Day, Spring Sing, and Special Olympics Banquet.

Sports: There are 6 intercollegiate sports for men and 6 for women, and 20 intramural sports for men and 20 for women. Facilities include a swimming pool, softball, football, and soccer fields, and a fitness center with weight training, stair, and bicycle machines.

Disabled Students: 98% of the campus is accessible. Wheelchair ramps, elevators, special parking, specially equipped rest rooms, special class scheduling, lowered drinking fountains, lowered telephones, and special housing are available.

Services: Counseling and information services are available, as is tutoring in some subjects, including English, math speech, chemistry, physics, business, education, and computer science. There is remedial math, reading, and writing.

Campus Safety and Security: Measures include 24-hour foot and vehicle patrol, security escort services, informal discussions, and pamphlets/posters/films. There are lighted pathways/sidewalks and security officers.

Programs of Study: OC confers B.A., B.S., B.B.A., B.F.A., B.M.E., B.Mus.Ed., B.S.C.E., B.S.Ed., B.S.E., B.S.E.E., and B.S.M.E. degrees. Master's degrees are also awarded. Bachelor's degrees are awarded in BIOLOGICAL SCIENCE (biochemistry and biology/biological science), BUSINESS (accounting, business administration and management, and marketing/retailing/merchandising), COMMUNICATIONS AND THE ARTS (advertising, art, broadcasting, communications, creative writing, design, English, journalism, music, and Spanish), COMPUTER AND PHYSICAL SCIENCE (chemistry, computer science, information sci-

ences and systems, and mathematics), EDUCATION (art, early childhood, elementary, English, mathematics, middle school, music, physical, science, social studies, special, and teaching English as a second/foreign language (TESOL/TEFOL)), ENGINEERING AND ENVIRONMENTAL DESIGN (computer engineering, electrical/electronics engineering, engineering physics, interior design, and mechanical engineering), HEALTH PROFESSIONS (medical laboratory technology and premedicine), SOCIAL SCIENCE (biblical studies, child care/child and family studies, history, liberal arts/general studies, ministries, missions, prelaw, psychology, religious education, and youth ministry). Science and engineering business and communication are the largest.

Required: To graduate, students must have a minimum of 126 credit hours, including 30 to 104 in the major, with a GPA of 2.0. All students must complete 60 to 61 hours in the general education program, which includes courses in Bible, English, speech, American studies, math, literature, fine arts, economics, biology, physical science, philosophy, Western civilization, phys ed, personal development, and social science.

Special: OC offers cross-registration with the University of Central Oklahoma, a liberal studies degree, internships in various majors, on-campus work-study, and credit for military experience. Students may study abroad in Austria, Japan, and the Pacific Rim. Major-minor combinations are offered in mass communication, family life, engineering, prelaw, advertising design, speech communication, English, music, education, and math. There are 3 national honor societies, a freshman honors program, and 1 departmental honors program.

Faculty/Classroom: 64% of faculty are male; 36%, female. All teach undergraduates and 25% do research. No introductory courses are taught by graduate students. The average class size in an introductory lecture is 50; in a laboratory, 19; and in a regular course, 30.

Admissions: All of the 2005-2006 applicants were accepted. The SAT scores for the 2005-2006 freshman class were: Verbal--27% below 500, 35% between 500 and 599, 27% between 600 and 700, and 10% above 700; Math--27% below 500, 33% between 500 and 599, 22% between 600 and 700, and 10% above 700. The ACT scores were 27% below 21, 26% between 21 and 23, 19% between 24 and 26, 13% between 27 and 28, and 15% above 28.

Requirements: The SAT or ACT is required. In addition, graduation from an accredited secondary school or satisfactory scores on the GED are required for admission. AP and CLEP credits are accepted.

Procedure: Freshmen are admitted to all sessions. There is a deferred admissions plan. Application deadlines are open. The fall 2005 application $25.

Transfer: 101 transfer students enrolled in 2004-2005. Applicants must be eligible to return to the school from which they are transferring. 30 of 126 credits required for the bachelor's degree must be completed at OC.

Visiting: There are regularly scheduled orientations for prospective students, including fall and spring visits in September and February. There are guides for informal visits and visitors may sit in on classes and stay overnight. To schedule a visit, contact the Admissions Office at *info@oc.edu.*

Financial Aid: In 2005-2006, 76% of all full-time freshmen and 66% of continuing full-time students received some form of financial aid. 57% of full-time freshmen and 54% of continuing full-time students received need-based aid. The average freshman award was $13,881. Need-based scholarships or need-based grants averaged $1503 ($12,486 maximum); need-based self-help aid (loans and jobs) averaged $3453 ($18,955 maximum); and non-need-based athletic scholarships averaged $5670 ($15,756 maximum). 32% of undergraduates work part time. Average annual earnings from campus work are $1219. The average financial indebtedness of the 2005 graduate was $18,065. The FAFSA is required. The priority date for freshman financial aid applications for fall entry is March 15. The deadline for filing freshman financial aid applications for fall entry is April 15.

International Students: There are 55 international students enrolled. The school actively recruits these students. They must score satisfactorily on the written TOEFL or on the electronic version and also take the SAT or the ACT.

Computers: Wireless access is available. All students may access the system 24 hours, 7 days a week. There are no time limits and no fees. It is strongly recommended that all students have a personal computer.

Graduates: From July 1, 2004 to June 30, 2005, 266 bachelor's degrees were awarded. The most popular majors were liberal studies (11%), engineering (10%), and biology (6%). In an average class, 23% graduate in 4 years or less, 39% graduate in 5 years or less, and 41% graduate in 6 years or less. 50 companies recruited on campus in 2004-2005.

Admissions Contact: Risa Forrester, Director of Enrollment Development. A video is available. E-mail: *info@oc.edu* Web: *oc.edu*

OKLAHOMA CITY UNIVERSITY | D-3

Oklahoma City, OK 73106-1493   **(405) 208-5050**
(800) 633-7242; Fax: (405) 208-5916

Full-time: 569 men, 897 women	**Faculty:** 139; IIA, --$
Part-time: 146 men, 299 women	**Ph.D.s:** 78%
Graduate: 1001 men, 776 women	**Student/Faculty:** 11 to 1
Year: semesters, summer session	**Tuition:** $17,715
Application Deadline: August 20	**Room & Board:** $6250
Freshman Class: 1144 applied, 846 accepted, 370 enrolled	
SAT Verbal/Math: 580/555*	**ACT:** 24 **VERY COMPETITIVE**

Oklahoma City University, founded in 1904, is a private, comprehensive university affiliated with the United Methodist Church, offering undergraduate and graduate programs in arts and sciences, business, music and performing arts, religion and church vocations, nursing, and law. There are 6 undergraduate and 6 graduate schools. In addition to regional accreditation, OCU has baccalaureate program accreditation with ACBSP, NASM, and NLN. The 2 libraries contain 451,966 volumes, 958,998 microform items, and 10,396 audio/video tapes/CDs/DVDs, and subscribe to 4975 periodicals including electronic. Computerized library services include the card catalog, interlibrary loans, and database searching. Special learning facilities include a learning resource center, art gallery, and TV station. The 75-acre campus is in an urban area within Oklahoma City. Including any residence halls, there are 34 buildings.

Student Life: 63% of undergraduates are from Oklahoma. Others are from 48 states, 58 foreign countries, and Canada. 57% are white; 26% foreign nationals. 54% are Protestant; 17% claim no religious affiliation; 10% Catholic. The average age of freshmen is 19; all undergraduates, 23. 28% do not continue beyond their first year; 56% remain to graduate.

Housing: 1021 students can be accommodated in college housing, which includes single-sex dorms, on-campus apartments, and fraternity houses. In addition, there are special-interest houses and learning communities. On-campus housing is guaranteed for all 4 years. 54% of students live on campus. Alcohol is not permitted. All students may keep cars.

Activities: 9% of men belong to 3 national fraternities; 11% of women belong to 3 national sororities. There are 70 groups on campus, including art, band, cheerleading, choir, chorus, computers, dance, drama, drill team, ethnic, film, gay, honors, international, jazz band, literary magazine, musical theater, newspaper, opera, orchestra, pep band, photography, political, professional, radio and TV, religious, social, social service, student government, symphony, and yearbook. Popular campus events include theater, dance, and music programs, international fair, and oozeball.

Sports: There are 4 intercollegiate sports for men and 4 for women, and 9 intramural sports for men and 8 for women. Facilities include a field house, tennis courts, baseball and soccer fields, and a wellness and activity center.

Disabled Students: 96% of the campus is accessible. Wheelchair ramps, elevators, special parking, specially equipped rest rooms, lowered drinking fountains, and lowered telephones are available.

Services: Counseling and information services are available, as is tutoring in most subjects. There is a reader service for the blind, and remedial math, reading, and writing. There are writing and learning enhancement centers and a math lab.

Campus Safety and Security: Measures include 24-hour foot and vehicle patrol, security escort services, informal discussions, and pamphlets/posters/films. There are emergency telephones, lighted pathways/sidewalks, an inner-campus bicycle patrol.

Programs of Study: OCU confers B.A., B.S., B.F.A., B.M., B.Perf.Arts, B.S.B., and B.S.N. degrees. Master's degrees are also awarded. Bachelor's degrees are awarded in BIOLOGICAL SCIENCE (biochemistry, biology/biological science, and biophysics), BUSINESS (accounting, banking and finance, and business administration and management), COMMUNICATIONS AND THE ARTS (advertising, art, broadcasting, communications, dance, dramatic arts, English, French, German, graphic design, journalism, music, piano/organ, Spanish, and speech/debate/rhetoric), COMPUTER AND PHYSICAL SCIENCE (chemistry, computer management, computer science, mathematics, physics, and science), EDUCATION (early childhood, elementary, foreign languages, music, physical, and science), HEALTH PROFESSIONS (nursing, and premedicine), SOCIAL SCIENCE (criminal justice, economics, history, humanities, philosophy, political science/government, prelaw, psychology, religion, and sociology). Business, performing arts, and sciences are the strongest academically. Sciences, performing arts, and mass communications are the largest.

Required: To graduate, students must complete a total of 124 credit hours, including 30 to 80 in the major, with a minimum GPA of 2.0. Students must complete their last 15 hours, including the last 6 in the major, at OCU with a minimum GPA of 2.0. All students must take 43 hours in the core curriculum as specified by their college or department.

Special: OCU offers internships, a Washington semester, work-study programs, a general studies degree, dual and student-designed majors,

credit for life experience, and study-abroad programs in 5 countries. B.A.-B.S. degrees and an accelerated degree program in nursing are also available. There are 9 national honor societies, a freshman honors program, and 10 departmental honors programs.

Faculty/Classroom: 57% of faculty are male; 43%, female. 80% teach undergraduates. No introductory courses are taught by graduate students. The average class size in an introductory lecture is 22; in a laboratory, 9; and in a regular course, 13.

Admissions: 74% of the 2005-2006 applicants were accepted. The SAT scores for the 2005-2006 freshman class were: Verbal--16% below 500, 42% between 500 and 599, 35% between 600 and 700, and 7% above 700; Math--22% below 500, 45% between 500 and 599, 29% between 600 and 700, and 4% above 700. The ACT scores were 17% below 21, 24% between 21 and 23, 26% between 24 and 26, 15% between 27 and 28, and 18% above 28. 52% of the current freshmen were in the top fifth of their class; 87% were in the top two fifths. 21 freshmen graduated first in their class.

Requirements: The SAT or ACT is required. Graduation from an accredited secondary school or satisfactory scores on the GED are also required for admission. High school courses must include 4 units of English, 3 units each of science, social studies, and math, and 2 units of a foreign language. Music and dance students are required to audition. OCU requires applicants to be in the upper 50% of their class. A GPA of 3.0 is required. AP and CLEP credits are accepted. Important factors in the admissions decision are evidence of special talent, advanced placement or honor courses, and leadership record.

Procedure: Freshmen are admitted to all sessions. Entrance exams should be taken by February of the senior year. There is a deferred admissions plan. Applications should be filed by August 20 for fall entry. The fall 2005 application fee was $35. Notification is sent on a rolling basis. Applications are accepted on-line.

Transfer: 155 transfer students enrolled in a recent year. Applicants must submit a transcript from each college attended and must have a minimum GPA of 2.0 from an accredited institution. Applicants having fewer than 29 credit hours must submit a high school transcript and ACT or SAT scores. 30 of 124 credits required for the bachelor's degree must be completed at OCU.

Visiting: There are regularly scheduled orientations for prospective students. There are guides for informal visits and visitors may sit in on classes and stay overnight. To schedule a visit, contact Visitor Services or Undergraduate Admissions at *visitocu@okcu.edu*.

Financial Aid: In 2005-2006, 99% of all full-time freshmen and 84% of continuing full-time students received some form of financial aid. 71% of full-time freshmen and 69% of continuing full-time students received need-based aid. The average freshman award was $16,895. Need-based scholarships or need-based grants averaged $12,416 ($29,355 maximum); need-based self-help aid (loans and jobs) averaged $9246 ($27,945 maximum); non-need-based athletic scholarships averaged $3449 ($12,508 maximum); and other non-need-based awards and non-need-based scholarships averaged $8493 ($24,715 maximum). 14% of undergraduates work part time. Average annual earnings from campus work are $2318. The average financial indebtedness of the 2005 graduate was $20,584. OCU is a member of CSS. The FAFSA, the college's own financial statement and the and tax returns, if selected for verification are required. The priority date for freshman financial aid applications for fall entry is March 1. The deadline for filing freshman financial aid applications for fall entry is June 30.

International Students: There are 377 international students enrolled. The school actively recruits these students. A satisfactory score is required on the written TOEFL.

Computers: All students may access the system 24 hours a day. There are no time limits. The fee is $230.

Graduates: From July 1, 2004 to June 30, 2005, 415 bachelor's degrees were awarded. In a recent year, most popular majors were business (15%), nursing (6%), and dance (5%). In an average class, 38% graduate in 4 years or less, 48% graduate in 5 years or less, and 50% graduate in 6 years or less. 65 companies recruited on campus in 2004-2005.

Admissions Contact: Dr. Lloyd Musselman, Interim Dean, Enrollment Services. A video is available. E-mail: *uadmissions@okcu.edu* Web: *www.okcu.edu* or *www.tgimatocu.com*

OKLAHOMA PANHANDLE STATE UNIVERSITY   B-2
Goodwell, OK 73939

(580) 349-1376
(800) 664-6778; Fax: (580) 349-1371

Full-time: 454 men, 466 women	Faculty: 56
Part-time: 65 men, 159 women	Ph.D.s: 22%
Graduate: none	Student/Faculty: 16 to 1
Year: semesters, summer session	Tuition: $3365 ($5618)
Application Deadline: open	Room & Board: $4270
Freshman Class: 257 applied, 257 accepted, 206 enrolled	
ACT: 21	NONCOMPETITIVE

Oklahoma Panhandle State University, founded in 1909, is a publicly funded institution offering undergraduate programs in the liberal arts, business and technology, education, agriculture, mathematics, sciences, and nursing. There are 5 undergraduate schools. In addition to regional accreditation, OPSU has baccalaureate program accreditation with NCATE and NLN. The library contains 130,133 volumes, 12,690 microform items, and 6217 audio/video tapes/CDs/DVDs, and subscribes to 318 periodicals including electronic. Computerized library services include the card catalog, interlibrary loans, database searching, and Internet access. Special learning facilities include a learning resource center, natural history museum, radio station, a writing lab, academic support lab, farm lab, children's collection library, and 2 instructional TV facilities. The 120-acre campus is in a rural area 100 miles north of Amarillo, Texas. Including any residence halls, there are 27 buildings.

Student Life: 57% of undergraduates are from Oklahoma. Others are from 34 states, 15 foreign countries, and Canada. 98% are from public schools. 73% are white; 12% Hispanic. The average age of freshmen is 19; all undergraduates, 25. 50% do not continue beyond their first year; 25% remain to graduate.

Housing: 613 students can be accommodated in college housing, which includes single-sex and coed dorms, on-campus apartments, and married-student housing. On-campus housing is guaranteed for all 4 years. 66% of students commute. Alcohol is not permitted. All students may keep cars.

Activities: There are no fraternities or sororities. There are 45 groups on campus, including art, band, cheerleading, choir, chorale, chorus, computers, dance, debate, drama, drill team, ethnic, forensics, honors, international, jazz band, marching band, musical theater, newspaper, pep band, photography, professional, radio and TV, religious, Rodeo Club, social, social service, and student government.

Sports: There are 10 intercollegiate sports for men and 8 for women. Facilities include a field house, an athletic field, a golf course, tennis courts, and an activity center. Waterskiing and fishing spots are nearby.

Disabled Students: 90% of the campus is accessible. Wheelchair ramps, elevators, special parking, and special class scheduling are available.

Services: Counseling and information services are available, as is tutoring in every subject. There is remedial math, reading, and writing. Free tutoring is provided through the peer counseling center.

Campus Safety and Security: Measures include 24-hour foot and vehicle patrol, self-defense education, pamphlets/posters/films, and emergency telephones. There are lighted pathways/sidewalks.

Programs of Study: OPSU confers B.A., B.S., B.B.A., B.F.A., B.I.T., B.M., B.S.N., B.T. degrees. Associate degrees are also awarded. Bachelor's degrees are awarded in AGRICULTURE (agricultural business management, agronomy, and animal science), BIOLOGICAL SCIENCE (biology/biological science), BUSINESS (accounting and business administration and management), COMMUNICATIONS AND THE ARTS (English and music), COMPUTER AND PHYSICAL SCIENCE (chemistry, information sciences and systems, mathematics, and physical sciences), EDUCATION (agricultural, business, elementary, English, health, mathematics, music, physical, science, and social studies), ENGINEERING AND ENVIRONMENTAL DESIGN (industrial engineering technology), HEALTH PROFESSIONS (medical technology and nursing), SOCIAL SCIENCE (fire protection, history, humanities, psychology, and social studies).

Required: To graduate, students must complete a total of 124 semester hours with a minimum GPA of 2.0. The number of hours required in the major varies. All students must complete 45 hours of general education courses, with at least 1 course at the upper-division level. Students must complete 40 upper-level hours and must have completed 60 hours at a 4-year institution.

Special: There is 1 national honor society and 1 departmental honors program.

Faculty/Classroom: 49% of faculty are male; 51%, female. All teach undergraduates. The average class size in an introductory lecture is 30; in a laboratory, 20; and in a regular course, 20.

Admissions: All 2005-2006 applicants were accepted. The ACT scores for the 2005-2006 freshman class were: 72% below 21, 18% between 21 and 23, 8% between 24 and 26, 1% between 27 and 28, and 1% above 28.

Requirements: The SAT or ACT is required. Graduation from an accredited secondary school or satisfactory scores on the GED are required. High school courses must include 4 units of English, 3 units of math (beginning with algebra I), 3 units of other courses such as foreign language or computer application courses, 2 units each of history (including 1 unit of American history) and lab science, and 1 unit of citizenship (for example, government, civics). AP and CLEP credits are accepted.

Procedure: Freshmen are admitted to all sessions. There is a rolling admissions plan. Application deadlines are open.

Transfer: 164 transfer students enrolled in 2004-2005. An application for admission, a medical history form, college transcripts, high school transcripts, and ACT scores are required. If students are transferring in with a GPA below 2.0, they come in on academic probation. 30 of 124 credits required for the bachelor's degree must be completed at OPSU.

Visiting: There are regularly scheduled orientations for prospective students. There are guides for informal visits and visitors may sit in on classes and stay overnight. To schedule a visit, contact High School and Community Relations.

Financial Aid: The FAFSA and the college's own financial statement are required. Check with the school for current application deadlines.

International Students: The school actively recruits these students. They must take the TOEFL, achieving a satisfactory score, and also take the SAT or ACTor or any other country's equivalent.

Computers: Wireless access is available. All students may access the system. There are no time limits and no fees.

Graduates: From July 1, 2004 to June 30, 2005, 197 bachelor's degrees were awarded. The most popular majors were agriculture (21%), education (17%), and business (11%).

Admissions Contact: Bobby Jenkins, Registrar and Director of Admissions. E-mail: *jolie@opsu.edu* Web: *www.opsu.edu*

OKLAHOMA STATE SYSTEM OF HIGHER EDUCATION

The Oklahoma State System of Higher Education, established in 1941, is a public system in Oklahoma. It is governed by the Oklahoma State Regents for Higher Education, whose chief administrator is the chancellor. The primary goals of the system are teaching, research, and public service. The main priorities are student success, excellence, and system efficiency. The total enrollment of all 25 campuses is usually about 235,000; there were about 6780 faculty members. Altogether there are 596 baccalaureate, 266 master's, and 106 doctoral programs offered in Oklahoma State System of Higher Education. 4-year campuses are located in Stillwater, Norman, Edmond, Ada, Tahlequah, Alva, Durant, Weatherford, Lawton, Langston, Goodwell, and Chickasha. Profiles of the 4-year campuses are included in this section.

OKLAHOMA STATE UNIVERSITY   E-2
Stillwater, OK 74078

(405) 744-5358
(800) 852-1255; Fax: (405) 744-7092

Full-time: 8654 men, 8077 women	Faculty: 765
Part-time: 1145 men, 1033 women	Ph.D.s: 91%
Graduate: 2348 men, 2204 women	Student/Faculty: 22 to 1
Year: semesters, summer session	Tuition: $4365 ($12,389)
Application Deadline: open	Room & Board: $5848
Freshman Class: 6533 applied, 5719 accepted, 3315 enrolled	
SAT Verbal/Math: 550/570*	ACT: 24 VERY COMPETITIVE

Oklahoma State University, founded in 1890, is a publicly funded land-grant institution, offering undergraduate programs in agricultural sciences and natural resources, arts and sciences, business, education, engineering, architecture, technology, and human environmental resources. There are 6 undergraduate schools and 1 graduate school. In addition to regional accreditation, OSU has baccalaureate program accreditation with AACSB, ABET, ACEJMC, ACS, ADA, AHEA, APA, ASLHA, ASLA, FIDER, NAAB, NAACLS, NASM, NRPA, and SAF. The 5 libraries contain 2,491,438 volumes, 4,410,122 microform items, and 391,710 audio/video tapes/CDs/DVDs, and subscribe to 35,751 periodicals including electronic. Computerized library services include interlibrary loans, database searching, Internet access, and laptop Internet portals. Special learning facilities include a learning resource center, art gallery, natural history museum, and radio station. The 840-acre campus is in a small town 65 miles north of Oklahoma City. Including any residence halls, there are 200 buildings.

Student Life: 82% of undergraduates are from Oklahoma. Others are from 49 states, 119 foreign countries, and Canada. 76% are white. The average age of freshmen is 19; all undergraduates, 22. 21% do not continue beyond their first year; 79% remain to graduate.

Housing: 5813 students can be accommodated in college housing, which includes single-sex and coed dorms, on-campus apartments, off-campus apartments, married-student housing, fraternity houses, and sorority houses. In addition, there are honors houses, language houses, special-interest houses, floors for fine arts, engineering, and fire protection majors. On-campus housing is guaranteed for all 4 years. 63% of students commute. Alcohol is not permitted. All students may keep cars.

Activities: 13% of men belong to 23 national fraternities; 17% of women belong to 16 national sororities. There are 350 groups on campus, including art, band, cheerleading, choir, chorale, chorus, computers, dance, drama, ethnic, gay, honors, international, jazz band, literary magazine, marching band, musical theater, newspaper, opera, orchestra, pep band, political, professional, radio and TV, religious, social, social service, student government, and symphony. Popular campus events include Freshmen Follies, Special Olympics, and Diwali Night.

Sports: There are 8 intercollegiate sports for men and 8 for women, and 48 intramural sports for men and 46 for women. Facilities include the recreation center, with more than 240,00 square feet of activity space, includes: 10 basketball-volleyball courts, a large multi-purpose court, 30,00 square feet of weight and fitness equipment, cardio-theater, indoor climbing wall, golf practice area including 2 golf simulators, a 4-lane jogging track, indoor and outdoor swimming pools, 12 racquetball-handball courts, and 5 large multi-purpose activity rooms.

Disabled Students: 99% of the campus is accessible. Wheelchair ramps, elevators, special parking, specially equipped rest rooms, special class scheduling, lowered drinking fountains, lowered telephones, special housing, and adaptive technology are available.

Services: Counseling and information services are available, as is tutoring in most subjects, including math. Tutoring is not disability-specific. There is a reader service for the blind, and remedial math, reading, and writing. Academic assessment and minority programs are also available.

Campus Safety and Security: Measures include 24-hour foot and vehicle patrol, self-defense education, security escort services, and shuttle buses. There are informal discussions, pamphlets/posters/films, emergency telephones, and lighted pathways/sidewalks.

Programs of Study: OSU confers B.A., B.S., B.Arch., B.Arch.Eng., B.F.A., B.Land.Arch., B.M., and B.U.S. degrees. Master's and doctoral degrees are also awarded. Bachelor's degrees are awarded in AGRICULTURE (agricultural business management, agricultural economics, animal science, fish and game management, forestry and related sciences, horticulture, and plant science), BIOLOGICAL SCIENCE (biochemistry, biology/biological science, botany, cell biology, entomology, microbiology, molecular biology, nutrition, physiology, and zoology), BUSINESS (accounting, banking and finance, business administration and management, business economics, hotel/motel and restaurant management, international business management, management information systems, management science, marketing/retailing/merchandising, and recreation and leisure services), COMMUNICATIONS AND THE ARTS (art, communications, design, dramatic arts, English, French, German, journalism, music, Russian, and Spanish), COMPUTER AND PHYSICAL SCIENCE (chemistry, computer science, geology, mathematics, physics, and statistics), EDUCATION (agricultural, elementary, health, music, physical, secondary, and technical), ENGINEERING AND ENVIRONMENTAL DESIGN (aeronautical engineering, architectural engineering, architecture, aviation computer technology, bioengineering, chemical engineering, civil engineering, construction management, electrical/electronics engineering, electrical/electronics engineering technology, engineering, environmental science, industrial engineering, landscape architecture/design, mechanical engineering, and mechanical engineering technology), HEALTH PROFESSIONS (biomedical science, medical technology, premedicine, preveterinary science, and speech pathology/audiology), SOCIAL SCIENCE (American studies, child care/child and family studies, economics, fire control and safety technology, geography, history, liberal arts/general studies, philosophy, political science/government, prelaw, psychology, and sociology). Animal sciences, marketing, and elementary education are the strongest academically.

Required: To graduate, students must have a minimum GPA of 2.0 and at least 120 hours, including a minimum of 30 hours in the major, for most programs. A higher GPA may be required in some majors. All students must take a minimum of 40 credit hours of core courses, including 6 each of English, humanities, analytical and quantitative thought, natural sciences, and social and behavioral sciences, 3 each of American history and government, and 1 each of scientific investigation and international studies.

Special: OSU offers cross-registration with Northern Oklahoma College and Tulsa Community College, a Washington semester, and an internship program. A B.A.-B.S. degree, dual majors, an individualized university studies degree, multidisciplinary majors in biosystems engineering and in cell and molecular biology, credit for life experience, nondegree study, and pass/fail options are available. Students may study abroad in several countries. The school also sponsors Semester at Sea, a 1-semester program of study on a ship traveling to ports throughout the world. There is a freshman honors program.

Faculty/Classroom: 68% of faculty are male; 32%, female. Graduate students teach 26% of introductory courses. The average class size in an introductory lecture is 31 and in a laboratory, 19.

Admissions: 88% of the 2005-2006 applicants were accepted. The SAT scores for the 2005-2006 freshman class were: Verbal--22% below 500, 48% between 500 and 599, 25% between 600 and 700, and 5% above 700; Math--19% below 500, 44% between 500 and 599, 30% between 600 and 700, and 7% above 700. The ACT scores were 14% below 21, 29% between 21 and 23, 29% between 24 and 26, 11% be-

tween 27 and 28, and 17% above 28. 46% of the current freshmen were in the top fifth of their class; 76% were in the top two fifths. There were 16 National Merit finalists and 4 semifinalists. 426 freshmen graduated first in their class.

Requirements: The SAT or ACT is required. In addition, for admission in good standing, freshman applicants must have a cumulative high school GPA of 3.0 and rank in the upper third of their graduating class, or achieve a satisfactory score on the ACT or on the SAT, or have a 3.0 GPA in the required 15 curricular units, which include 4 years of English, 3 of math (algebra I and above), 2 each of history and lab science, 1 of citizenship skills, and 3 more from any of the above or computer science or foreign language. OSU requires applicants to be in the upper 33% of their class. A GPA of 3.0 is required. AP and CLEP credits are accepted. Important factors in the admissions decision are advanced placement or honor courses, evidence of special talent, and recommendations by school officials.

Procedure: Freshmen are admitted fall, spring, and summer. Entrance exams should be taken during the junior or senior year. There is a rolling admissions plan. Application deadlines are open. Notification is sent on a rolling basis beginning on October 1. Application fee is $40. Applications are accepted on-line.

Transfer: 1755 transfer students enrolled in 2004-2005. Applicants must submit official transcripts from all colleges attended. Students having fewer than 24 credit hours must also meet the requirements for entering freshmen and have a 2.25 GPA. 30 of 120 credits required for the bachelor's degree must be completed at OSU.

Visiting: There are regularly scheduled orientations for prospective students, including personal meetings and tours. Appointments are scheduled with other campus departments, as needed, to assist prospective students. There are guides for informal visits and visitors may sit in on classes and stay overnight. To schedule a visit, contact the Undergraduate Admissions Office at (800) 223-5019 (in Oklahoma) or (800) 852-1255.

Financial Aid: The FAFSA is required. The deadline for filing freshman financial aid applications for fall entry is March 1.

International Students: There are 586 international students enrolled. The school actively recruits these students. They must score satisfactorily on the written TOEFL or on the electronic version.

Computers: Wireless access is available. Students receive computer access, network data storage space, and e-mail upon enrollment. Students may use any of the 5 general campus labs (3 are open24/7), and 24 departmental labs. Student technology resources are provided via an Ethernet-based network. All campus residences provide each resident and common living space with a 10/100 megabit per second dedicated connection to the Internet. Some areas provide wireless access for central campus. All students may access the system. There are no time limits. The fee is $5 per credit hour.

Graduates: From July 1, 2004 to June 30, 2005, 3549 bachelor's degrees were awarded. The most popular majors were business/marketing (8%), teaching and curriculum leadership (6%), and finance (5%). In an average class, 2% graduate in 3 years or less, 26% graduate in 4 years or less, 53% graduate in 5 years or less, and 59% graduate in 6 years or less. 158 companies recruited on campus in 2004-2005.

Admissions Contact: Dr. Paul Carney, Director Undergraduate Admissions. E-mail: *admit@okstate.edu* Web: *www.okstate.edu*

OKLAHOMA WESLEYAN UNIVERSITY E-1
Bartlesville, OK 74006

(918) 335-6219
(866) 222-8226; Fax: (918) 335-6229

Full-time: 196 men, 325 women	**Faculty:** IIB, --$
Part-time: 250 men, 245 women	**Ph.D.s:** 51%
Graduate: none	**Student/Faculty:** n/av
Year: semesters, summer session	**Tuition:** $13,750
Application Deadline: open	**Room & Board:** $5200
Freshman Class: n/av	
SAT or ACT: recommended	**NONCOMPETITIVE**

Oklahoma Wesleyan University, founded in 1909, is a private liberal arts institution affiliated with the Wesleyan Church. In addition to regional accreditation, OWU has baccalaureate program accreditation with CCNE, IACBE, and NCATE. The library contains 120,000 volumes, 20,000 microform items, and 500 audio/video tapes/CDs/DVDs, and subscribes to 18,000 periodicals including electronic. Computerized library services include the card catalog, interlibrary loans, and database searching. Special learning facilities include a learning resource center. The 101-acre campus is in a suburban area 40 miles north of Tulsa. Including any residence halls, there are 15 buildings.

Student Life: 64% of undergraduates are from Oklahoma. Students are from 30 states, 12 foreign countries, and Canada. 80% are from public schools. 83% are white. 55% are Protestant; 15% claim no religious affiliation. The average age of freshmen is 18; all undergraduates, 26. 20% do not continue beyond their first year; 60% remain to graduate.

Housing: 300 students can be accommodated in college housing, which includes single-sex dorms. On-campus housing is guaranteed for all 4 years. 69% of students commute. Alcohol is not permitted. All students may keep cars.

Activities: There are no fraternities or sororities. There are more than 10 groups on campus, including band, cheerleading, choir, chorale, chorus, computers, drama, ethnic, honors, international, musical theater, photography, political, professional, religious, social service, and student government. Popular campus events include Spiritual Emphasis Week and Youth Conference.

Sports: There are 7 intercollegiate sports for men and 7 for women, and 10 intramural sports for men and 10 for women. Facilities include a 2000-seat indoor gym and an 8-acre athletic field.

Disabled Students: 73% of the campus is accessible. Wheelchair ramps, elevators, special parking, and specially equipped rest rooms are available.

Services: Counseling and information services are available, as is tutoring in most subjects. There is remedial math, reading, and writing.

Campus Safety and Security: Measures include informal discussions, lighted pathways/sidewalks, and an evening patrol by a security guard.

Programs of Study: OWU confers B.A. and B.S. degrees. Associate and master's degrees are also awarded. Bachelor's degrees are awarded in BIOLOGICAL SCIENCE (biology/biological science), BUSINESS (accounting, business administration and management, and human resources), COMMUNICATIONS AND THE ARTS (communications, English, and music), COMPUTER AND PHYSICAL SCIENCE (chemistry, mathematics, and science), EDUCATION (business, elementary, English, mathematics, middle school, music, physical, science, secondary, and social studies), HEALTH PROFESSIONS (predentistry and premedicine), SOCIAL SCIENCE (behavioral science, history, liberal arts/general studies, pastoral studies, political science/government, prelaw, religion, religious music, social studies, sociology, and youth ministry). Business and education are the largest and the strongest academically.

Required: To graduate, students must complete a total of 126 credit hours with a minimum GPA of 2.0. About 40 hours are required in the major. All students must take 9 hours of religion and a writing proficiency exam.

Special: OWU offers cross-registration with Tri-County Tech, a Washington semester, a co-op program, internships, a general studies degree, credit for life experience, and an accelerated degree program in business and the B.S.N.

Faculty/Classroom: 60% of faculty are male; 40%, female. The average class size in an introductory lecture is 20; in a laboratory, 20; and in a regular course, 20.

Requirements: The SAT or ACT is recommended. In addition, graduation from an accredited secondary school or satisfactory scores on the GED are required for admission. 18 academic credits must be completed, including 4 credits of English and 2 credits each of history, math, science, and social studies. OWU requires applicants to be in the upper 50% of their class. A GPA of 2.0 is required. AP and CLEP credits are accepted.

Procedure: Freshmen are admitted to all sessions. Entrance exams should be taken during the senior year. There is a rolling admissions plan. Application deadlines are open. Application fee is $25. Applications are accepted on-line.

Transfer: 56 transfer students enrolled in 2004-2005. Applicants must have a minimum GPA of 2.0. 24 of 126 credit hours required for the bachelor's degree must be completed at OWU.

Visiting: There are regularly scheduled orientations for prospective students. There are guides for informal visits and visitors may sit in on classes and stay overnight. To schedule a visit, contact the Enrollment Services Office.

Financial Aid: In 2005-2006, 98% of all full-time students received some form of financial aid. 90% of all full-time students received need-based aid. 60% of undergraduates work part time. The average financial indebtedness of the 2005 graduate was $20,000. The FAFSA and the college's own financial statement are required. The deadline for filing freshman financial aid applications for fall entry is open.

International Students: There are 15 international students enrolled. A satisfactory score is required on the written TOEFL or the MELAB.

Computers: All students may access the system. There are no time limits and no fees.

Admissions Contact: Jim Eeidman, Vice President for Enrollment. E-mail: *admissions@okwu.edu* Web: *www.bwc.edu*

ORAL ROBERTS UNIVERSITY
Tulsa, OK 74171

E-2

(918) 495-6529
(800) 678-8876; Fax: (918) 495-6222

Full-time: 2451 men and women	**Faculty:** 164; IIA, --$
Part-time: 814 men and women	**Ph.D.s:** 57%
Graduate: 821 men and women	**Student/Faculty:** 15 to 1
Year: semesters, summer session	**Tuition:** $15,880
Application Deadline: open	**Room & Board:** $6770
Freshman Class: 594 applied, 577 accepted, 463 enrolled	
SAT Verbal/Math: 520/510*	**ACT:** 21 **COMPETITIVE**

Oral Roberts University, founded in 1963, is a private liberal arts university committed to the Christian faith. There are 5 undergraduate and 3 graduate schools. In addition to regional accreditation, ORU has baccalaureate program accreditation with ABET, CSWE, NASM, and NLN. The library contains 750,000 volumes, 200,000 microform items, and 500,000 audio/video tapes/CDs/DVDs, and subscribes to 2100 periodicals including electronic. Computerized library services include the card catalog, database searching, Internet access, and laptop Internet portals. Special learning facilities include a learning resource center, natural history museum, radio station, TV station, and and a TV production studio. The 400-acre campus is in an urban area. Including any residence halls, there are 27 buildings.

Student Life: 86% of undergraduates are from out of state, mostly the Midwest. Others are from 50 states, 59 foreign countries, and Canada. 50% are from public schools. 63% are white; 23% African American. Most are Protestant. The average age of freshmen is 19. 15% do not continue beyond their first year; 54% remain to graduate.

Housing: 2700 students can be accommodated in college housing, which includes single-sex dorms and honors wings in several dorms. On-campus housing is available on a first-come, first-served basis. 57% of students live on campus; of those, 99% remain on campus on weekends. Alcohol is not permitted. All students may keep cars.

Activities: There are no fraternities or sororities. There are 60 groups on campus, including art, band, cheerleading, choir, chorale, chorus, community outreach and summer mission, computers, drama, ethnic, film, honors, international, jazz band leadership academy, newspaper, opera, pep band, photography, political, professional, radio and TV, religious, social, social service, student government, symphony, and yearbook. Popular campus events include Fall Break and College Weekend.

Sports: There are 8 intercollegiate sports for men and 8 for women, and 20 intramural sports for men and 20 for women. Facilities include a physical fitness center, a track, tennis, racquetball, squash, volleyball, and basketball courts, and baseball and soccer fields.

Disabled Students: 90% of the campus is accessible. Wheelchair ramps, elevators, special parking, specially equipped rest rooms, special class scheduling, lowered drinking fountains, and lowered telephones are available.

Services: Counseling and information services are available, as is tutoring in most subjects. There is a reader service for the blind, and remedial math, reading, and writing.

Campus Safety and Security: Measures include 24-hour foot and vehicle patrol, self-defense education, security escort services, and shuttle buses. There are lighted pathways/sidewalks.

Programs of Study: ORU confers B.A., B.S., B.M., B.Mus.Ed., B.S.E., B.S.N., and B.S.W. degrees. Master's and doctoral degrees are also awarded. Bachelor's degrees are awarded in BIOLOGICAL SCIENCE (biology/biological science), BUSINESS (accounting, banking and finance, business administration and management, international business management, management information systems, management science, marketing/retailing/merchandising, organizational behavior, and recreation and leisure services), COMMUNICATIONS AND THE ARTS (applied art, broadcasting, communications, dramatic arts, English, English literature, film arts, French, German, literature, music, music performance, music theory and composition, Spanish, speech/debate/rhetoric, and studio art), COMPUTER AND PHYSICAL SCIENCE (chemistry, computer science, mathematics, and physics), EDUCATION (art, business, drama, early childhood, elementary, English, foreign languages, health, mathematics, music, physical, recreation, science, social studies, and special), ENGINEERING AND ENVIRONMENTAL DESIGN (bioengineering, commercial art, computer engineering, electrical/electronics engineering, engineering, engineering management, mechanical engineering, and preengineering), HEALTH PROFESSIONS (biomedical science, health science, medical laboratory technology, nursing, optometry, predentistry, and premedicine), SOCIAL SCIENCE (biblical studies, history, international relations, international studies, liberal arts/general studies, ministries, philosophy, political science/government, prelaw, psychology, religion, religious education, religious music, and social work). All science programs, music, and theology are the strongest academically. Business is the largest.

Required: A minimum of 128 credit hours, with a minimum of 30 hours in the major, and a 2.0 GPA are required to graduate. All students must complete specific courses in the Bible, theology, and English, plus 12 hours in social sciences, 11 in biological, physical, and mathematical sciences, 6 to 7 in a modern foreign language, 3 in communication arts, and 2 in fine arts. 1 physical activity course is required per semester, along with regular, semiweekly chapel attendance. A senior paper must be completed in most majors.

Special: ORU offers combined B.A.-B.S. degrees, internships, 3-2 programs, a Washington semester, work-study programs, dual and student-designed majors, study abroad in 5 countries, independent study, non-degree study, an accelerated degree in business and education, and a liberal arts degree. An honors program/leadership academy is also offered. There are 4 national honor societies, a freshman honors program, and 12 departmental honors programs.

Faculty/Classroom: 61% of faculty are male; 39%, female. 78% both teach and do research. No introductory courses are taught by graduate students. The average class size in an introductory lecture is 30; in a laboratory, 20; and in a regular course, 20.

Admissions: 97% of the 2005-2006 applicants were accepted. The SAT scores for the 2005-2006 freshman class were: Verbal--35% below 500, 39% between 500 and 599, 19% between 600 and 700, and 7% above 700; Math--33% below 500, 41% between 500 and 599, 23% between 600 and 700, and 3% above 700. The ACT scores were 30% below 21, 24% between 21 and 23, 27% between 24 and 26, 8% between 27 and 28, and 11% above 28. 40% of the current freshmen were in the top fifth of their class; 69% were in the top two fifths. There were 6 National Merit finalists. 44 freshmen graduated first in their class.

Requirements: The SAT or ACT is required. In addition, students should be graduates of an accredited secondary school or hold a GED. High school preparation should include 4 years of English, 2 of math, including algebra and geometry or 2 years of algebra, and 2 each of foreign language, social studies, and science, including lab science. A recommendation from the student's minister is required. An academic recommendation and an interview are recommended. ORU requires applicants to be in the upper 40% of their class. A GPA of 2.6 is required. AP and CLEP credits are accepted. Important factors in the admissions decision are advanced placement or honor courses, evidence of special talent, and leadership record.

Procedure: Freshmen are admitted to all sessions. Entrance exams should be taken during the last semester of the junior year or during the senior year. There are early decision, early admissions, rolling admissions, and deferred admissions plans. Application deadlines are open. 80 early decision candidates were accepted for the 2005-2006 class.

Transfer: 890 transfer students enrolled in 2004-2005. An official transcript showing honorable dismissal from each previous institution is required. 30 of 128 credits required for the bachelor's degree must be completed at ORU.

Visiting: There are regularly scheduled orientations for prospective students, including College Weekend, which consists of visiting classes, meeting with faculty and staff, attending chapel services, and attending student life events. Visitors may sit in on classes and stay overnight. To schedule a visit, contact Chris Belcher, the Admissions Office at (918) 495-6530 or admissions@oru.edu.

Financial Aid: 73% of full-time freshmen and 70% of continuing full-time students received need-based aid. Need-based scholarships or need-based grants averaged $8029 ($29,650 maximum); need-based self-help aid (loans and jobs) averaged $8864 ($22,625 maximum); and non-need-based athletic scholarships averaged $18,678 ($24,035 maximum). 100% of undergraduates work part time. Average annual earnings from campus work are $571. The average financial indebtedness of the 2005 graduate was $30,409. The FAFSA and the federal income tax return are required. The priority date for freshman financial aid applications for fall entry is March 15. The deadline for filing freshman financial aid applications for fall entry is July 30.

International Students: There are 167 international students enrolled. Satisfactory scores are required on the TOEFL and either the ACT or the SAT.

Computers: Wireless access is available. Wireless and the Internet are available across the entire campus, including dorms. There are also multiple computer labs, the largest with more than 100 computers and scanners. Business students may access the system. There are no time limits. The fee is $10 per semster. It is strongly recommended that all students have a personal computer.

Graduates: From July 1, 2004 to June 30, 2005, 547 bachelor's degrees were awarded. The most popular majors were mass communication/media studies (10%), psychology (7%), and business administration/management (7%). In an average class, 36% graduate in 4 years or less, 40% graduate in 5 years or less, and 54% graduate in 6 years or less. 286 companies recruited on campus in 2004-2005.

Admissions Contact: Chris Belcher, Admissions.
E-mail: admission@oru.edu Web: www.oru.edu

SAINT GREGORY'S UNIVERSITY E-3
Shawnee, OK 74804
(405) 878-5444
(888) 784-7347; Fax: (405) 878-5198

Full-time: 280 men, 335 women	**Faculty:** 30
Part-time: 65 men, 90 women	**Ph.Ds:** 57%
Graduate: none	**Student/Faculty:** 20 to 1
Year: semesters, summer session	**Tuition:** $12,363
Application Deadline: open	**Room & Board:** $5320
Freshman Class: n/av	
ACT: required	**NONCOMPETITIVE**

Saint Gregory's University, founded in 1875, is a private instituition affiliated with the Roman Catholic Church. Students design personalized degree programs within the integrative areas of humanities, natural science, social science, business, and theology. The enrollment figures in the above capsule are approximate. There are 5 undergraduate schools and 1 graduate school. The library contains 80,000 volumes, 3526 microform items, and 450 audio/video tapes/CDs/DVDs, and subscribes to 150 periodicals including electronic. Computerized library services include the card catalog, interlibrary loans, database searching, Internet access, and laptop Internet portals. Special learning facilities include an art gallery. The 300-acre campus is in a suburban area about 30 miles east of Oklahoma City. Including any residence halls, there are 12 buildings.

Student Life: 70% of undergraduates are from Oklahoma. Others are from 13 states, 15 foreign countries, and Canada. 80% are from public schools. 65% are white; 15% foreign nationals. 40% are Catholic; 24% claim no religious affiliation. The average age of freshmen is 18. 35% do not continue beyond their first year.

Housing: 415 students can be accommodated in college housing, which includes single-sex and coed dorms. In addition, there are language houses and a dorm floor dedicated to honors students. On-campus housing is guaranteed for the freshman year only and is available on a first-come, first-served basis. Priority is given to out-of-town students. 70% of students live on campus; of those, 60% remain on campus on weekends. Alcohol is not permitted. All students may keep cars.

Activities: 10% of men belong to 3 local fraternities; 10% of women belong to 3 local sororities. There are 24 groups on campus, including art, cheerleading, choir, chorale, computers, dance, drama, ethnic, history, honors, international, musical theater, newspaper, photography, professional, radio and TV, religious, social, social service, student government, and yearbook. Popular campus events include sporting events, movie nights, and dances.

Sports: There are 5 intercollegiate sports for men and 7 for women, and 4 intramural sports for men and 4 for women. Facilities include soccer, baseball, and softball facilities, a wellness center with 2 gyms, Cybex equipment, and a free-weight facility.

Disabled Students: 90% of the campus is accessible. Wheelchair ramps, elevators, special parking, specially equipped rest rooms, special class scheduling, and lowered drinking fountains are available.

Services: Counseling and information services are available, as is tutoring in every subject. Partners in Learning is a program designed to aid those students with learning disabilities. There is a reader service for the blind. learning disabilities.

Campus Safety and Security: Measures include 24-hour foot and vehicle patrol, security escort services, informal discussions, and lighted pathways/sidewalks, and card access to residence halls.

Programs of Study: Saint Gregory's University confers B.A. in Humanities, B.A. in Theology, B.S. in Business, B.S. in Natural Science, and B.S. in Social Science degrees. Students follows personalized degree programs under these five integrative degrees. Associate and master's degrees are also awarded. Life sciences, premedicine, and conservation biology are the strongest academically. Natural sciences, business, and social sciences are the largest.

Required: To graduate, students must complete 128 credits, including approximately 40 in the major, with a minimum 2.0 GPA. The core curriculum focuses on professional communication, creative thinking, self leadership, and informational technology, including specific courses in English, speech, math, life science, physical science, philosophy, and theology. Students must pass a comprehensive exam at the end of sophomore year and complete a senior research project.

Special: There are 4 national honor societies, a freshman honors program, and all departments have honors programs.

Faculty/Classroom: 45% of faculty are male; 55%, female. All teach undergraduates. The average class size in an introductory lecture is 16; in a laboratory, 14; and in a regular course, 9.

Requirements: The ACT is required. Saint Gregory's University requires applicants to be in the upper 50% of their class. A GPA of 2.75 is required. AP and CLEP credits are accepted. Important factors in the admissions decision are leadership record, parents or siblings attending the school, and recommendations by alumni.

Procedure: Freshmen are admitted to all sessions. Entrance exams should be taken in October. There are deferred admissions and rolling admissions plans. Application deadlines are open. Application fee is $25. Applications are accepted on-line with a $15 fee.

Transfer: Applicants must have either an associate degree or a cumulative 2.0 GPA in all completed college courses. 30 of 128 credits required for the bachelor's degree must be completed at Saint Gregory's University.

Visiting: There are regularly scheduled orientations for prospective students, consisting of a private tour by an admissions counselor. There are guides for informal visits and visitors may sit in on classes and stay overnight. To schedule a visit, contact the Office of Admissions at (405) 878-5444.

Financial Aid: 38% of undergraduates work part time. Average annual earnings from campus work are $1000. The average financial indebtedness of the 2005 graduate was $17,959. The FAFSA is required. The deadline for filing freshman financial aid applications for fall entry is July 15.

International Students: The school actively recruits these students. They must score satisfactorily on the written TOEFL or on the electronic version or complete an on-campus intensive English program.

Computers: Wireless access is available. All students may access the system. There are no time limits and no fees. All students are required to have personal computers. Any model that meets minimum 650 MHz, 10 GB hard disk, and 128 M is recommended.

Admissions Contact: Judy Chance, Office Manager. A video is available. E-mail: *jmchance@stgregorys.edu* Web: *www.stgregorys.edu*

SOUTHEASTERN OKLAHOMA STATE UNIVERSITY D-3
Durant, OK 74701

(580) 745-2060
(800) 435-1327; Fax: (580) 745-7502

Full-time: 1400 men, 1500 women	Faculty: 153; IIA, --$
Part-time: 280 men, 490 women	Ph.D.s: 65%
Graduate: 180 men, 290 women	Student/Faculty: 19 to 1
Year: semesters, summer session	Tuition: $2684 ($5708)
Application Deadline: open	Room & Board: $3250
Freshman Class: 1067 applied, 856 accepted, 649 enrolled	
ACT: required	COMPETITIVE

Southeastern Oklahoma State University, founded in 1909, is a public institution offering programs in the arts and sciences, business, education, music, and technology to a primarily commuter student body. There are 3 undergraduate schools and 1 graduate school. Some figures in the above capsule and in this profile are approximate. In addition to regional accreditation, Southeastern has baccalaureate program accreditation with AACSB, ACBSP, NASM, and NCATE. The library contains 288,030 volumes, 563,955 microform items, and 7084 audio/video tapes/CDs/DVDs, and subscribes to 1017 periodicals including electronic. Computerized library services include the card catalog, interlibrary loans, database searching, and Internet access. Special learning facilities include a learning resource center, radio station, and an herbarium. The 177-acre campus is in a rural area 90 miles north of Dallas. Including any residence halls, there are 46 buildings.

Student Life: 77% of undergraduates are from Oklahoma. Students are from 34 states, 32 foreign countries, and Canada. 99% are from public schools. 64% are white; 28% Native American/Eskimo. The average age of freshmen is 22; all undergraduates, 25. 42% do not continue beyond their first year; 40% remain to graduate.

Housing: 648 students can be accommodated in college housing, which includes single-sex and coed dorms on-campus apartments, and married-student housing. In addition, there are special-interest houses. On-campus housing is guaranteed for all 4 years. 80% of students commute. Alcohol is not permitted. All students may keep cars.

Activities: 1% of men belong to 3 national fraternities; 5% of women belong to 2 national sororities. There are 70 groups on campus, including art, band, cheerleading, chess, choir, chorale, chorus, computers, dance, debate, drama, ethnic, forensics, honors, international, jazz band, literary magazine, marching band, musical theater, newspaper, opera, pep band, photography, political, professional, radio and TV, religious, social, social service, student government, and yearbook. Popular campus events include Parents Day, Candlelighting, and Springfest.

Sports: There are 4 intercollegiate sports for men and 5 for women, and 2 intramural sports for men and 1 for women. Facilities include a 4000-seat football stadium, a 2000-seat gym, baseball and softball fields, a track, tennis courts, playing fields, and a swimming pool.

Disabled Students: 70% of the campus is accessible. Wheelchair ramps, elevators, special parking, specially equipped rest rooms, special class scheduling, lowered drinking fountains, lowered telephones, and special housing are available.

Services: Counseling and information services are available, as is tutoring in every subject. There is a reader service for the blind, remedial math, reading, and writing, and tutoring in study skills.

Campus Safety and Security: Measures include 24-hour foot and vehicle patrol, self-defense education, security escort services, and informal discussions. There are pamphlets/posters/films, lighted pathways/sidewalks, and safety training.

Programs of Study: Southeastern confers B.A., B.S., B.A.A.S., B.B.A., B.G.S., B.M., and B.M.Ed. degrees. Master's degrees are also awarded. Bachelor's degrees are awarded in AGRICULTURE (conservation and regulation and environmental studies), BIOLOGICAL SCIENCE (biology/biological science and biotechnology), BUSINESS (accounting, business administration and management, recreation and leisure services, and secretarial studies/office management), COMMUNICATIONS AND THE ARTS (art, communications, dramatic arts, English, fine arts, music, and speech/debate/rhetoric), COMPUTER AND PHYSICAL SCIENCE (chemistry, computer science, information sciences and systems, mathematics, and physics), EDUCATION (art, business, early childhood, education of the mentally handicapped, elementary, mathematics, music, physical, science, secondary, and social studies), ENGINEERING AND ENVIRONMENTAL DESIGN (aviation administration/management and occupational safety and health), HEALTH PROFESSIONS (medical laboratory technology), SOCIAL SCIENCE (criminal justice, economics, gerontology, history, political science/government, psychology, social science, and sociology). Chemistry, history, and music are the strongest academically. Occupational safety and health, elementary education, and criminal justice are the largest.

Required: A total of 124 credit hours with a minimum GPA of 2.0 (2.5 for teacher education majors) is required for graduation. All students must complete 41 semester hours of general education requirements, including English, American history, government, humanities, arts, social and lab sciences, math, communications, and health education, and 3 hours of computer science.

Special: Internships, study abroad, credit for military experience, pass/fail options in some courses, and nondegree study are available. There are 15 national honor societies and 9 departmental honors programs.

Faculty/Classroom: 64% of faculty are male; 36%, female. All teach undergraduates and 10% do research. No introductory courses are taught by graduate students. The average class size in an introductory lecture is 28; in a laboratory, 18; and in a regular course, 23.

Admissions: 16 freshmen graduated first in their class in a recent year.

Requirements: The ACT is required. In addition, applicants should be graduates of an accredited secondary school or have earned a GED. High school courses must include 4 years of English, 3 of math, 2 each of lab science and history, 1 of citizenship skills (from the subjects of economics, geography, government, or non-Western culture), and 3 additional units of subjects previously listed or of computer science or foreign language. Southeastern requires applicants to be in the upper 50% of their class. A GPA of 2.7 is required. AP and CLEP credits are accepted.

Procedure: Freshmen are admitted to all sessions. Entrance exams should be taken by the fall of the senior year. Application deadlines are open. Application fee is $20. Applications are accepted on-line.

Transfer: 445 transfer students enrolled in a recent year. Out-of-state applicants must have a 2.0 GPA. In-state applicants must have a 1.7 GPA with 24 to 36 credit hours earned, 1.8 with 37 to 72 hours, and 2.0 with 73 or more hours. 30 of 124 credits required for the bachelor's degree must be completed at Southeastern.

Visiting: There are guides for informal visits and visitors may sit in on classes. To schedule a visit, contact Admissions and Recruitment Services.

Financial Aid: In a recent year, 76% of all full-time freshmen and 70% of continuing full-time students received some form of financial aid. 51% of full-time freshmen and 55% of continuing full-time students received need-based aid. The average freshman award was $2585. Need-based scholarships or need-based grants averaged $1171 ($6050 maximum); need-based self-help aid (loans and jobs) averaged $1226 ($7560 maximum); non-need-based athletic scholarships averaged $1678 ($6764 maximum); and other non-need-based awards and non-need-based scholarships averaged $1350 ($3000 maximum). 45% of undergraduates work part time. Average annual earnings from campus work are $1200. The average financial indebtedness of arecent year's graduate was $8000. Southeastern is a member of CSS. The FAFSA is required. Check with the school for current deadlines.

International Students: There were 46 international students enrolled in a recent year. They must achieve a satisfactory score on the TOEFL and also take the SATor the ACT.

Computers: All students may access the system. There are no time limits. The fee is $11 per credit hour.

Graduates: In a recent year, 618 bachelor's degrees were awarded. The most popular majors were elementary education (27%), business and marketing (17%), and engineering (9%). In an average class, 2% graduate in 3 years or less, 18% graduate in 4 years or less, 35% graduate in 5 years or less, and 40% graduate in 6 years or less. 130 companies recruited on campus in a recent year..

Admissions Contact: Kyle Stafford, Director, Admissions and Recruitment Services. E-mail: *admissions@sosu.edu* Web: *www.sosu.edu*

SOUTHERN NAZARENE UNIVERSITY — D-3

Bethany, OK 73008

(405) 491-6324
(800) 648-9899; Fax: (405) 491-6320

Full-time: 770 men, 860 women	**Faculty:** 53
Part-time: 30 men, 50 women	**Ph.D.s:** 58%
Graduate: 135 men, 170 women	**Student/Faculty:** 31 to 1
Year: semesters, summer session	**Tuition:** $10,500
Application Deadline: see profile	**Room & Board:** $4500
Freshman Class: n/av	
SAT or ACT: required	**NONCOMPETITIVE**

Southern Nazarene University, founded in 1899, is a private, coeducational institution affiliated with the Church of the Nazarene. It offers programs in liberal arts and sciences, health fields, business, and education. Figures in above capsule and in this profile are approximate. There are 3 undergraduate schools and 1 graduate school. In addition to regional accreditation, SNU has baccalaureate program accreditation with NASM, NCATE, and NLN. The library contains 112,673 volumes, 219,576 microform items, and 3543 audio/video tapes/CDs/DVDs, and subscribes to 667 periodicals including electronic. Computerized library services include the card catalog, interlibrary loans, and database searching. Special learning facilities include a learning resource center and TV station. The 40-acre campus is in a suburban area 10 miles northwest of Oklahoma City. Including any residence halls, there are 20 buildings.

Student Life: 55% of undergraduates are from out of state, mostly the South. Students are from 31 states, 22 foreign countries, and Canada. 90% are white. 90% are Protestant; 7% claim no religious affiliation. The average age of freshmen is 18; all undergraduates, 23. 10% do not continue beyond their first year; 45% remain to graduate.

Housing: 938 students can be accommodated in college housing, which includes single-sex dorms, on-campus apartments, and married-student housing. On-campus housing is guaranteed for all 4 years. 55% of students live on campus; of those, 80% remain on campus on weekends. Alcohol is not permitted. All students may keep cars.

Activities: There are no fraternities or sororities. There are 40 groups on campus, including band, cheerleading, choir, chorale, chorus, computers, drama, drum and bugle corps, honors, international, jazz band, literary magazine, musical theater, newspaper, orchestra, pep band, photography, political, professional, radio and TV, religious, social, social service, student government, symphony, and yearbook. Popular campus events include Valentine Banquet, Fall Fest, and Yule Feast.

Sports: There are 7 intercollegiate sports for men and 7 for women, and 3 intramural sports for men and 3 for women. Facilities include a 1824-seat phys ed center, gyms, a soccer complex, and tennis courts, and a new athletic convocation center that seats 4000.

Disabled Students: 95% of the campus is accessible. Wheelchair ramps, elevators, special parking, specially equipped rest rooms, special class scheduling, lowered drinking fountains and lowered telephones are available. Dormitory rooms may be adapted for handicapped students.

Services: Counseling and information services are available, as is tutoring in most subjects. There is remedial math, reading, and writing. Services may be arranged for deaf or learning-disabled students.

Campus Safety and Security: Measures include 24-hour foot and vehicle patrol, self-defense education, security escort services, and informal discussions. There are lighted pathways/sidewalks and 24-hour controlled access into dormitories.

Programs of Study: SNU confers A.B., B.S., and B.Mus.Ed. degrees. Associate and master's degrees are also awarded. Bachelor's degrees are awarded in AGRICULTURE (agriculture), BIOLOGICAL SCIENCE (biology/biological science), BUSINESS (accounting, banking and finance, business administration and management, business economics, management information systems, marketing/retailing/merchandising, office supervision and management, personnel management, and sports management), COMMUNICATIONS AND THE ARTS (communications, creative writing, English, fine arts, journalism, music, music business management, music performance, piano/organ, Spanish, speech/debate/rhetoric, and voice), COMPUTER AND PHYSICAL SCIENCE (chemistry, computer science, mathematics, and physics), EDUCATION (athletic training, business, early childhood, elementary, foreign languages, music, physical, and secondary), ENGINEERING AND ENVIRONMENTAL DESIGN (aviation administration/management and preengineering), HEALTH PROFESSIONS (exercise science, nursing, physical therapy, predentistry, premedicine, and prepharmacy), SOCIAL SCIENCE (biblical languages, criminal justice, history, international studies, missions, philosophy, political science/government, prelaw, psychology, religion, religious education, social science, and sociology). Premedicine, physics, and theology are the strongest academically. Business, and education are the largest.

Required: A total of 124 semester hours, including at least 32 hours in the major, with a minimum GPA of 2.0 is required to graduate. All students must complete 53 hours of general education requirements covering core areas of self and identity, faith and tradition, and service and society. Skills courses must be taken in computer science, composition, speech communication, math, natural science, citizenship, foreign language, and phy ed.

Special: Cross-registration and co-op programs are available through the Southwestern Colleges of Christian Ministry. Internships may be arranged in the major. A Washington semester, study abroad in Latin America, England, Russia, and the Middle East, work-study programs in sociology, and dual and student-designed majors are available. There is an accelerated degree program in management of human resources and family studies and gerontology. SNU offers nondegree study for life/military/work experience. A Hollywood semester may be arranged through the Christian College Coalition. There are 6 national honor societies, including Phi Beta Kappa, and a freshman honors program.

Faculty/Classroom: 57% of faculty are male; 43%, female. All teach undergraduates and 15% do research. Graduate students teach 1% of introductory courses. The average class size in an introductory lecture is 20 and in a laboratory, 15.

Requirements: The SAT or ACT is required. In addition, applicants must be graduates of an accredited secondary school or have a GED. SNU requires applicants to be in the upper 40% of their class. A GPA of 2.5 is required. AP and CLEP credits are accepted. Important factors in the admissions decision are advanced placement or honor courses, extracurricular activities record, and leadership record.

Procedure: Freshmen are admitted fall and spring. Entrance exams should be taken by April of the senior year or at orientation prior to the beginning of classes. There are early admissions, deferred admissions, and rolling admissions plans. The college accepts all applicants. Notification is sent on a rolling basis. The fall 2005 application fee was $25.

Transfer: Transfer applicants must have a 2.0 GPA and be in good standing at their previous college. 30 of 124 credits required for the bachelor's degree must be completed at SNU.

Visiting: There are regularly scheduled orientations for prospective students, including visits with faculty and students and seminars on financial aid and admissions. There are campus tours, group social activities, and small group mentoring throughout the fall semester. There are guides for informal visits and visitors may sit in on classes and stay overnight. To schedule a visit, contact the Office of Admissions.

Financial Aid: The FAFSA is required. Check with the school for current application deadlines.

International Students: They must take the TOEFL.

Computers: All students may access the system Monday through Saturday. There are no time limits. The fee is $140 per year.

Admissions Contact: Brad Townley, Director of Admissions. A video is available. E-mail: *admiss@snu.edu* Web: *www.snu.edu*

SOUTHWESTERN OKLAHOMA STATE UNIVERSITY — D-3

Weatherford, OK 73096

(580) 774-3009; Fax: (580) 774-3795

Full-time: 1525 men, 1900 women	**Faculty:** 190; IIA, --$
Part-time: 170 men, 275 women	**Ph.D.s:** 65%
Graduate: 245 men, 365 women	**Student/Faculty:** 18 to 1
Year: semesters, summer session	**Tuition:** $2200 ($5000)
Application Deadline: see profile	**Room & Board:** $2700
Freshman Class: n/av	
ACT: required	**COMPETITIVE**

Southwestern Oklahoma State University, founded in 1901, is a public institution offering programs in education, arts and sciences, business, health sciences, and pharmacy. There are 4 undergraduate and 3 graduate schools. Figures in the above capsule and profile are approximate. In addition to regional accreditation, SWOSU has baccalaureate program accreditation with ABET, ABHES, ACBSP, ACOTE, ACPE, ACS, APTA, CAAHEP, CAHEA, CSWE, JRCERT, NAMT, NASM, NCATE, and NLN. The library contains 287,572 volumes, 1,168,558 microform items, and 872 audio/video tapes/CDs/DVDs, and subscribes to 1551 periodicals including electronic. Computerized library services include the card catalog, interlibrary loans, and database searching. The 73-acre campus is in a small town 70 miles west of Oklahoma City. Including any residence halls, there are 30 buildings.

Student Life: 90% of undergraduates are from Oklahoma. Students are from 37 states, 36 foreign countries, and Canada. 98% are from public schools. 86% are white. The average age of freshmen is 19; all undergraduates, 23. 35% do not continue beyond their first year; 32% remain to graduate.

Housing: 1255 students can be accommodated in college housing, which includes single-sex dorms and married-student housing. On-campus housing is guaranteed for all 4 years. 73% of students commute. Alcohol is not permitted. All students may keep cars.

Activities: 2% of men belong to 2 local and 1 national fraternity; 2% of women belong to 3 local sororities. There are 66 groups on campus, including art, band, cheerleading, choir, chorale, chorus, computers, debate, drama, drill team, ethnic, forensics, honors, international, jazz band, marching band, musical theater, newspaper, opera, orchestra, pep band, political, professional, religious, social, social service, student government, symphony, and yearbook. Popular campus events include Howdy Week, Miss Southwestern Pageant, and Panorama Series.

Sports: There are 6 intercollegiate sports for men and 6 for women, and 8 intramural sports for men and 8 for women. Facilities include 2 gyms, a weight room, an indoor pool, an outdoor track, tennis courts, an outdoor football field and baseball diamond, 2 football practice fields, a rodeo arena, an exercise equipment room, a ropes course, and a lake. A soccer practice field, sand volleyball courts, and outdoor basketball courts are also available.

Disabled Students: 98% of the campus is accessible. Wheelchair ramps, elevators, special parking, specially equipped rest rooms, special class scheduling, lowered drinking fountains, and lowered telephones are available.

Services: Counseling and information services are available, as is tutoring in some subjects, including math, science, business, English, and social sciences. There is remedial math, reading, and writing. A student development center offers counseling and tutoring on an individual basis.

Campus Safety and Security: Measures include 24-hour foot and vehicle patrol, self-defense education, informal discussions, and pamphlets/posters/films. There are emergency telephones and lighted pathways/sidewalks.

Programs of Study: SWOSU confers B.A., B.S., B.A.Ed., B.Art, B.B.A., B.Comm.Art, B.Gen.Tech., B.M., B.M.Ed., B.Rec., B.S.Ed., B.S.Eng.Tech., B.S.H.I.M., B.S.M.T., B.S.N., and B.S.P. degrees. Associate, master's, and doctoral degrees are also awarded. Bachelor's degrees are awarded in BIOLOGICAL SCIENCE (biology/biological science and biophysics), BUSINESS (accounting, banking and finance, business administration and management, management information systems, management science, marketing/retailing/merchandising, and recreational facilities management), COMMUNICATIONS AND THE ARTS (communications, English, and graphic design), COMPUTER AND PHYSICAL SCIENCE (chemistry, computer programming, computer science, information sciences and systems, mathematics, natural sciences, and physics), EDUCATION (art, athletic training, education administration, elementary, English, health, industrial arts, mathematics, music, physical, school psychology, science, secondary, social science, special, and technical), ENGINEERING AND ENVIRONMENTAL DESIGN (computer engineering, electrical/electronics engineering technology, engineering physics, engineering technology, environmental engineering technology, industrial administration/management, industrial engineering technology, manufacturing engineering, and manufacturing technology), HEALTH PROFESSIONS (health care administration, health science, medical records administration/services, medical technology, music therapy, and nursing), SOCIAL SCIENCE (community psychology, criminal justice, history, political science/government, psychology, and social work). Chemistry is the strongest academically. Business and education are the largest.

Required: To graduate, students must complete 124 semester hours with a minimum GPA of 2.0. Distribution requirements include 8 hours in communication and natural sciences, 6 each in history and government, fine arts and humanities, and international and cultural studies, 3 each in economics, health and phys ed, behavioral/social science, and math, and 2 in computer applications.

Special: SWOSU offers work-study programs and a program allowing high school seniors to earn college credits. Preprofessional curricula are offered in numerous areas including medicine, law, engineering, and allied health professions. There are 4 national honor societies.

Faculty/Classroom: 63% of faculty are male; 37%, female. All teach undergraduates, 10% do research, and 10% do both. Graduate students teach 1% of introductory courses. The average class size in a laboratory is 15 and in a regular course, 27.

Requirements: The ACT is required. Applicants should be graduates of an accredited secondary school. The GED is accepted. Students should present at least 15 academic credits, including 4 in English, 3 in math, 2 each in history and lab science, 1 in citizenship, and 3 additional units in computer science or foreign language. SWOSU requires applicants to be in the upper 50% of their class. A GPA of 2.7 is required. AP and CLEP credits are accepted.

Procedure: Freshmen are admitted to all sessions. There is a rolling admissions plan. Entrance exams should be taken during the senior year. Check with the school for current application deadlines. Notification is sent on a rolling basis. The fall 2005 applicatin fee was $15.

Transfer: Applicants must have a minimum college GPA of 2.0 and submit official transcripts from all institutions attended. 30 of 124 credits required for the bachelor's degree must be completed at SWOSU.

Visiting: There are regularly scheduled orientations for prospective students, including counseling sessions on careers, financial aid, social activities, and enrollment procedures. There are guides for informal visits and visitors may sit in on classes and stay overnight. To schedule a visit, contact the Director of High School and College Relations at (580) 774-3782.

Financial Aid: The FAFSA and the college's own financial statement are required. Check with the school for current application deadlines.

International Students: They must score satisfactorily on the written TOEFL and also take the ACT.

Computers: All students may access the system from 8 A.M. to midnight Monday through Thursday, 8 A.M. to 5 P.M. Friday, 10 A.M. to 2 P.M. Saturday, and 2 P.M. to midnight Sunday. There are no time limits and no fees.

Admissions Contact: Connie Phillips, Admissions Coordinator. A video is available. E-mail: *phillic@swosu.edu* Web: *www.swosu.edu*

UNIVERSITY OF CENTRAL OKLAHOMA
E-5

Edmond, OK 73034

(405) 974-2338

(800) 254-4215; Fax: (405) 341-4964

Full-time: 4414 men, 6098 women	**Faculty:** 413; IIA, -$
Part-time: 1653 men, 2463 women	**Ph.D.s:** 70%
Graduate: 382 men, 943 women	**Student/Faculty:** 25 to 1
Year: semesters, summer session	**Tuition:** $3618 ($8628)
Application Deadline: August 15	**Room & Board:** $4476
Freshman Class: n/av	
ACT: required	**COMPETITIVE**

The University of Central Oklahoma, founded in 1890, is a state-supported institution offering undergraduate and graduate programs in the liberal arts and sciences, education, business, and music. There are 5 undergraduate schools and 1 graduate school. In addition to regional accreditation, UCO has baccalaureate program accreditation with ABFSE, ACBSP, ADA, NASM, NCATE, and NLN. The library contains 438,975 volumes, 989,936 microform items, and 30,202 audio/video tapes/CDs/DVDs, and subscribes to 5244 periodicals including electronic. Computerized library services include the card catalog, interlibrary loans, database searching, and Internet access. Special learning facilities include a learning resource center, art gallery, radio station, and TV station. The 200-acre campus is in a suburban area north of Oklahoma City. Including any residence halls, there are 43 buildings.

Student Life: 82% of undergraduates are from Oklahoma. Others are from 44 states, 81 foreign countries, and Canada. 83% are from public schools. 68% are white. The average age of freshmen is 20; all undergraduates, 24. 33% do not continue beyond their first year; 27% remain to graduate.

Housing: 1900 students can be accommodated in college housing, which includes single-sex and coed dorms, on-campus apartments, off-campus apartments, and married-student housing. On-campus housing is available on a first-come, first-served basis and is available on a lottery system for upperclassmen. 90% of students commute. Alcohol is not permitted. All students may keep cars.

Activities: 5% of men belong to 11 national fraternities; 7% of women belong to 7 national sororities. There are 170 groups on campus, including art, band, cheerleading, choir, computers, dance, debate, ethnic, gay, honors, international, jazz band, literary magazine, marching band, musical theater, newspaper, opera, orchestra, political, professional, radio and TV, religious, social, and student government. Popular campus events include International Week, Black Heritage Week, and Indian Heritage Week.

Sports: There are 8 intercollegiate sports for men and 7 for women, and 21 intramural sports for men and 21 for women. Facilities include a field house with a gym, a swimming pool, a track, a weight room, a stadium with a track and a softball field, and a wellness center with basketball courts, aerobic classes, cardiovascular equipment, weights, and various classes.

Disabled Students: All of the campus is accessible. Wheelchair ramps, elevators, special parking, specially equipped rest rooms, special class scheduling, and lowered drinking fountains, are available.

Services: Counseling and information services are available, as is tutoring in some subjects, including English, math, reading, and writing. There is remedial math.

Campus Safety and Security: Measures include 24-hour foot and vehicle patrol, security escort services, emergency telephones, and lighted pathways/sidewalks. There is a crime and terrorism tip line.

Programs of Study: UCO confers B.A., B.S., B.A.Ed., B.B.A., B.F.A., B.F.A.Ed., B.M.Ed., B.Mus., and B.S.Ed. degrees. Master's degrees are also awarded. Bachelor's degrees are awarded in BIOLOGICAL SCIENCE (biology/biological science and nutrition), BUSINESS (accounting, banking and finance, business administration and management, business economics, fashion merchandising, funeral home services, hotel/motel and restaurant management, human resources, insurance, management information systems, marketing/retailing/merchandising, and recreational facilities management), COMMUNICATIONS AND THE ARTS (advertising, broadcasting, communications, creative writing, dramatic arts, English, fine arts, French, German, graphic design, journalism, music, photography, public relations, Spanish, and speech/debate/rhetoric), COMPUTER AND PHYSICAL SCIENCE (actuarial science, chemistry, computer science, and mathematics), EDUCATION (art, business, dance, early childhood, elementary, English, foreign languages, industrial arts, marketing and distribution, mathematics, museum studies, music, physical, science, social studies, and special), ENGINEERING AND ENVIRONMENTAL DESIGN (engineering physics and interior design), HEALTH PROFESSIONS (community health work, industrial hygiene, medical laboratory technology, nursing, and speech pathology/audiology), SOCIAL SCIENCE (addiction studies, criminal justice, economics, family/consumer studies, forensic studies, geography, history, liberal arts/general studies, philosophy, physical fitness/movement, political science/government, psychology, public administration, and sociology). Nursing, business administration, and elementary education are the largest.

Required: Students must complete 124 semester hours with a 2.25 GPA. At least 15 hours in upper-division courses in the major are required. Students must also complete a maximum of 12 semester hours in general education requirements, including phys ed.

Special: There is cross-registration with the Downtown Consortium. Opportunities are provided for internships, B.A.-B.S. degrees, dual majors, a general studies degree, credit by exam, nondegree study, and credit for military experience. Work-study programs may be arranged through the Federal College Work-Study Program. There are 6 national honor societies.

Faculty/Classroom: 54% of faculty are male; 46%, female. No introductory courses are taught by graduate students.

Requirements: The ACT is required. Graduation from an accredited secondary school is required. A GED will be accepted for adult students. The applicant's academic record should include 4 years of English, 3 years of math, first-year algebra and beyond, and 2 years each of lab science and history, of which 1 year must be in American history. UCO requires applicants to be in the upper 50% of their class. A GPA of 2.7 is required. AP and CLEP credits are accepted. Important factors in the admissions decision are evidence of special talent, extracurricular activities record, and leadership record.

Procedure: Freshmen are admitted to all sessions. Entrance exams should be taken within 30 days of submitting the application. There are early admissions and rolling admissions plans. Applications should be filed by August 15 for fall entry, January 2 for spring entry, and May 25 for summer entry, along with a $25 fee. Notification is sent on a rolling basis.

Transfer: 1545 transfer students enrolled in a recent year. Applicants must submit official transcripts from previous colleges attended and have a minimum GPA of 2.0. Students who have completed fewer than 24 hours of transferable credit must meet the requirements for entering freshmen. 30 of 124 credits required for the bachelor's degree must be completed at UCO.

Visiting: There are regularly scheduled orientations for prospective students, including a brief tour, a question-and-answer period, and access to an information booth. There are guides for informal visits and visitors may sit in on classes. To schedule a visit, contact Prospective Student Services at (405) 974-2727.

Financial Aid: The CSS/Profile or FFS and the college's own financial statement are required. Check with the school for current application deadlines.

International Students: There are 1193 international students enrolled. The school actively recruits these students. They must score satisfactorily on the written TOEFL and on the ACT.

Computers: Wireless access is available. All students may access the system. There are no time limits and no fees.

Graduates: From July 1, 2004 to June 30, 2005, 2114 bachelor's degrees were awarded. The most popular majors were general studies (11%), information and operations management (7%), and accounting (5%). In an average class, 9% graduate in 4 years or less, 24% graduate in 5 years or less, and 27% graduate in 6 years or less. 68 companies recruited on campus in 2004-2005.

Admissions Contact: Linda Lofton, Director, Admissions.
E-mail: *admissions@ucok.edu* Web: *www.ucok.edu*

UNIVERSITY OF OKLAHOMA D-3

Norman, OK 73019

(405) 325-2252
(800) 234-6868; Fax: (405) 325-7124

Full-time: 8967 men, 8749 women	Faculty: 980; I, --$
Part-time: 1404 men, 1304 women	Ph.D.s: 85%
Graduate: 3186 men, 3384 women	Student/Faculty: 18 to 1
Year: semesters, summer session	Tuition: $4408 ($12,301)
Application Deadline: April 1	Room & Board: $6361
Freshman Class: 7388 applied, 6331 accepted, 3245 enrolled	
SAT Verbal/Math: 591/600*	ACT: 26 VERY COMPETITIVE+

The University of Oklahoma, founded in 1890, is a comprehensive research university offering 160 areas for undergraduate study. There are 13 undergraduate and 13 graduate schools. In addition to regional accreditation, OU has baccalaureate program accreditation with AACSB, ABET, ACCE, ACEJMC, APA, CAA, CSWE, FIDER, NAAB, NASM, and NCATE. The 9 libraries contain 4,736,213 volumes, 4,147,765 microform items, and 12,338 audio/video tapes/CDs/DVDs, and subscribe to 31,235 periodicals including electronic. Computerized library services include the card catalog, interlibrary loans, database searching, Internet access, and laptop Internet portals. Special learning facilities include an art gallery, natural history museum, radio station, TV station, and observatory. The 3757-acre campus is in a suburban area 18 miles south of Oklahoma City. Including any residence halls, there are 227 buildings.

Student Life: 74% of undergraduates are from Oklahoma. Others are from 50 states, 82 foreign countries, and Canada. 75% are white. The average age of freshmen is 19; all undergraduates, 22. 15% do not continue beyond their first year; 56% remain to graduate.

Housing: 4526 students can be accommodated in college housing, which includes single-sex and coed dorms, on-campus apartments, and married-student housing. In addition, there are honors houses, special-interest houses and international, scholastic, and quiet floors. On-campus housing is guaranteed for all 4 years. 74% of students commute. All students may keep cars.

Activities: 17% of men belong to 24 national fraternities; 25% of women belong to 17 national sororities. There are 456 groups on campus, including art, band, cheerleading, chess, choir, chorale, chorus, computers, dance, debate, drama, drill team, ethnic, film, forensics, gay, honors, international, jazz band, literary magazine, marching band, musical theater, newspaper, opera, orchestra, pep band, photography, political, professional, radio and TV, religious, social, social service, student government, symphony, and yearbook. Popular campus events include Moms and Dads Days, Theater and Dance season, and Big Event Community Service.

Sports: There are 10 intercollegiate sports for men and 10 for women, and 42 intramural sports for men and 42 for women. Facilities include a golf course, a field house, an arena, a gymnastics center, tennis courts, a swimming pool complex, a fitness center, a football stadium, track and field facilities, and baseball, soccer, and softball fields.

Disabled Students: 90% of the campus is accessible. Wheelchair ramps, elevators, special parking, specially equipped rest rooms, special class scheduling, lowered drinking fountains, lowered telephones, special housing, 25 TDDs, automatic door openers, adaptive computer labs, and an office of disability services are available.

Services: Counseling and information services are available, as is tutoring in most subjects. There is a reader service for the blind, and remedial math, reading, and writing. There are also volunteer note takers, interpreter and real-time reporting services for the deaf or hearing impaired, and alternative testing services.

Campus Safety and Security: Measures include 24-hour foot and vehicle patrol, self-defense education, security escort services, and shuttle buses. There are informal discussions, pamphlets/posters/films, emergency telephones, lighted pathways/sidewalks, a modified 911 system, a bicycle patrol, and formal presentations.

Programs of Study: OU confers B.A., B.Arch., B.S., B.B.A., B.F.A., B.Int.Des., B.Lib.Studies, B.Mus, B.Mus.Arts, B.Mus.Ed. degrees. Master's and doctoral degrees are also awarded. Bachelor's degrees are awarded in BIOLOGICAL SCIENCE (biochemistry, botany, microbiology, and zoology), BUSINESS (accounting, banking and finance, business administration and management, business economics, human resources, international business management, management information systems, marketing/retailing/merchandising, and real estate), COMMUNICATIONS AND THE ARTS (advertising, art, art history and appreciation, broadcasting, classics, communications, dance, dramatic arts, English, film arts, French, German, journalism, languages, linguistics, music, photography, public relations, Russian, Spanish, and video), COMPUTER AND PHYSICAL SCIENCE (astronomy, astrophysics, atmospheric sciences and meteorology, chemistry, computer science, environmental geology, geology, geophysics and seismology, geoscience, information sciences and systems, mathematics, paleontology, and physics), EDUCATION (early childhood, elementary, foreign languages, mathematics, music, science, social studies, and special), ENGINEERING AND ENVIRONMENTAL DESIGN (aeronautical engineering, architectural engineering, architecture, aviation administration/management, chemical engineering, civil engineering, computer engineering, construction management, electrical/electronics engineering, engineering, engineering physics, environmental design, environmental engineering, environmental science, industrial engineering, interior design, land use management and reclamation, mechanical engineering, and petroleum/natural gas engineering), HEALTH PROFESSIONS (health science and medical laboratory technology), SOCIAL SCIENCE (African American studies, anthropology, area studies, Asian/Oriental studies, Eastern European studies, economics, European studies, geography, history, international studies, Latin American studies, liberal arts/general studies, Native American studies, philosophy, political science/government, psychology, public affairs, religion, Russian and Slavic studies, social work, sociology, and women's studies). Meteorology, finance and accounting, and chemistry are the strongest academically. Journalism and mass communication, psychology, and zoology are the largest.

Required: To graduate, students must have a minimum 2.0 GPA, depending on the major, and complete a minimum of 124 semester hours, the last 30 hours of which must be in residence. The number of hours required in the major varies. A 40-hour general education core includes courses in arts and humanities, oral and symbolic communication, natural science, and social science. All students must take 6 hours each of English composition, American history and government, and general education requirements. Seniors must take a 3-credit-hour capstone experience course integrating their undergraduate studies, and it must include writing.

Special: Co-op programs are available in arts and sciences, business, and engineering. A variety of voluntary and required internships are available in more than 50 fields of study. OU offers study abroad in 66 countries, work-study programs, a Washington semester, a general studies degree, dual and student-designed majors, nondegree study, pass/fail options, and credit for life experience. B.A.-B.S. degrees are offered in many subjects and an accelerated degree is offered in 13 majors. The interdisciplinary major in letters combines the classics, history, philosophy, and languages. A professional studies major is offered through the continuing education program. There are 37 national honor societies, including Phi Beta Kappa, a freshman honors program and all departments have an honors program.

Faculty/Classroom: 66% of faculty are male; 34%, female. Graduate students teach 37% of introductory courses. The average class size in an introductory lecture is 46; in a laboratory, 23; and in a regular course, 24.

Admissions: 86% of the 2005-2006 applicants were accepted. The ACT scores for the 2005-2006 freshman class were: 9% below 21, 16% between 21 and 23, 34% between 24 and 26, 17% between 27 and 28, and 24% above 28. 62% of the current freshmen were in the top fifth of their class; 88% were in the top two fifths. There were 147 National Merit finalists. 275 freshmen graduated first in their class.

Requirements: The SAT or ACT is required. Performance requirements can be met by residents of Oklahoma with a high school GPA of 3.0 and a class ranking in the upper 25% or a minimum composite score of 24 on the ACT or a comparable SAT score. Nonresidents must have a high school GPA of 3.5 and rank in the top 25% or have a composite score of 26 on the ACT or a comparable combined verbal and math score on the SAT. Graduation from an accredited secondary school or a satisfactory score on the GED is required. Students must have a total of 15 curricular units, including 4 years of English, 3 of math, 2 each of history and lab science, 1 unit of citizenship skills, and 3 elective units from areas previously mentioned or computer science or foreign language. Some alternative admission opportunities are available but are limited. AP and CLEP credits are accepted.

Procedure: Freshmen are admitted to all sessions. Entrance exams should be taken during the junior year or the first part of the senior year. Applications should be filed by April 1 for fall entry, November 1 for spring entry, and April 1 for summer entry, along with a $40 fee. Notification is sent on a rolling basis. 950 applicants were on the 2005 waiting list; 544 were admitted.

Transfer: 1259 transfer students enrolled in 2004-2005. Applicants who have attempted 7 to 59 semester hours of college work must have a minimum GPA of 2.5. Applicants with 60 or more semester hours attempted must have a minimum GPA of 2.0; education and journalism and mass communication majors must have a minimum GPA of 2.75; nonresident applicants with engineering majors must have a minimum 3.0 GPA. Applicants with fewer than 24 semester hours of college level work must also meet freshman admission requirements. Nonresidents must be in good standing at the last institution attended. 30 of 124 credits required for the bachelor's degree must be completed at OU.

Visiting: There are regularly scheduled orientations for prospective students, consisting of sessions tailored to individual needs and interests. There are guides for informal visits and visitors may sit in on classes and stay overnight. To schedule a visit, contact Prospective Student Services at (405) 325-2151 or ou-pss@ou.edu.

Financial Aid: In 2005-2006, 72% of all full-time freshmen and 86% of continuing full-time students received some form of financial aid. 47% of full-time freshmen and 66% of continuing full-time students received need-based aid. The average freshman award was $7346. Need-based scholarships or need-based grants averaged $3660 ($8512 maximum); need-based self-help aid (loans and jobs) averaged $6065 ($9825 maximum); non-need-based athletic scholarships averaged $3674 ($22,736 maximum); and other non-need-based awards and non-need-based scholarships averaged $3282. 4% of undergraduates work part time. Average annual earnings from campus work are $2481. The average financial indebtedness of the 2005 graduate was $18,494. OU is a member of CSS. The FAFSA is required. The priority date for freshman financial aid applications for fall entry is March 1. The deadline for filing freshman financial aid applications for fall entry is June 1.

International Students: There are 505 international students enrolled. They must score satisfactorily on the written TOEFL or on the electronic version.

Computers: Wireless access is available. All students may access the system 24 hours per day. There are no time limits. The fee is $12 per credit hour. It is strongly recommended that all students have a personal computer and students in engineering programs are required to have personal computers. A special OU student PC package is available through Dell.

Graduates: From July 1, 2004 to June 30, 2005, 3624 bachelor's degrees were awarded. The most popular majors were sociology (7%), liberal studies (6%), and psychology (5%). In an average class, 1% graduate in 3 years or less, 20% graduate in 4 years or less, 47% graduate in 5 years or less, and 56% graduate in 6 years or less. 1450 companies recruited on campus in 2004-2005.

Admissions Contact: Pat Lynch, Director of Admissions. A video is available. E-mail: admrec@ou.edu Web: www.ou.edu

UNIVERSITY OF SCIENCE AND ARTS OF OKLAHOMA D-4
Chickasha, OK 73018-5322

(405) 574-1357
(800) 933-8726; Fax: (405) 574-1220

Full-time: 426 men, 638 women	**Faculty:** 48; IIB, --$
Part-time: 94 men, 272 women	**Ph.D.s:** 92%
Graduate: none	**Student/Faculty:** 22 to 1
Year: trimesters, summer session	**Tuition:** $3480 ($8220)
Application Deadline: September 8	**Room & Board:** $4170
Freshman Class: 448 applied, 397 accepted, 282 enrolled	
ACT: 21	COMPETITIVE

The University of Science and Arts of Oklahoma, founded in 1908, is a publicly funded liberal arts college, providing interdisciplinary learning opportunities. In addition to regional accreditation, USAO has baccalaureate program accreditation with CED, NASM, and NCATE. The library contains 68,897 volumes, 153,980 microform items, and 4689 audio/video tapes/CDs/DVDs, and subscribes to 137 periodicals including electronic. Computerized library services include the card catalog, interlibrary loans, database searching, and Internet access. Special learning facilities include a learning resource center, an art gallery, a commercial art computer lab, a TV studio, a child development center, and a speech pathology clinic. The 75-acre campus is in a small town 40 miles southwest of Oklahoma City. Including any residence halls, there are 14 buildings.

Student Life: 93% of undergraduates are from Oklahoma. Others are from 20 states, 14 foreign countries, and Canada. 90% are from public schools. 76% are white; 13% Native American/Eskimo. The average age of freshmen is 19; all undergraduates, 23. 40% do not continue beyond their first year; 32% remain to graduate.

Housing: 504 students can be accommodated in college housing, which includes single-sex and coed dorms and on-campus apartments. On-campus housing is guaranteed for the freshman year only and is available on a first-come, first-served basis. Priority is given to out-of-town students. 63% of students commute. All students may keep cars.

Activities: 3% of men belong to 1 national fraternity; 2% of women belong to 1 national sorority. There are 24 groups on campus, including art, band, cheerleading, choir, chorale, chorus, computers, drama, drill team, ethnic, gay, honors, international, jazz band, literary magazine, musical theater, newspaper, opera, orchestra, pep band, photography, political, professional, radio and TV, religious, social, social service, and student government. Popular campus events include Montmartre Art Festival, Droverstock, and Tinsel Ball.

Sports: There are 3 intercollegiate sports for men and 3 for women, and 4 intramural sports for men and 4 for women. Facilities include a field house, a 2000-seat gym, a 1000-seat auditorium, a ballpark with baseball and softball fields, each seating 200, a soccer field with seating for 250, tennis courts, a weight room, a fitness center, an indoor pool, an outdoor pool with hot tub, and volleyball courts.

Disabled Students: All of the campus is accessible. Wheelchair ramps, elevators, special parking, specially equipped rest rooms, special class scheduling, lowered drinking fountains, and lowered telephones are available.

Services: Counseling and information services are available, as is tutoring in some subjects, including math, writing, and reading. There is remedial math, reading, and writing. Tutors and interpreters are available for hearing-impaired students.

Campus Safety and Security: Measures include 24-hour foot and vehicle patrol, informal discussions, pamphlets/posters/films, and lighted pathways/sidewalks.

Programs of Study: USAO confers B.A., B.S., and B.F.A. degrees. Bachelor's degrees are awarded in BIOLOGICAL SCIENCE (biology/biological science), BUSINESS (business administration and management), COMMUNICATIONS AND THE ARTS (art, communications, dramatic arts, English, fine arts, and music), COMPUTER AND PHYSICAL SCIENCE (chemistry, computer science, mathematics, natural sciences, and physics), EDUCATION (early childhood, education of the deaf and hearing impaired, elementary, and physical), HEALTH PROFESSIONS (speech pathology/audiology), SOCIAL SCIENCE (American Indian studies, economics, history, political science/government, psychology, and sociology). Humanities and physical science are the strongest academically. Business administration, elementary education, and psychology are the largest.

Required: To graduate, students must complete a total of 124 credit hours with a minimum GPA of 2.0. Required core courses include 29 hours of team-taught interdisciplinary ideas in math, science, and social science, 15 of interdisciplinary skills in logic and critical thinking, writing, and computer science, 2 each of artistic and physical expression, and 3 of freshman seminar. Other requirements include a 2-hour senior seminar, an English proficiency exam, and entry-, junior-, and senior-level academic assessments.

Special: USAO offers dual majors, accelerated degree programs in all majors through year-round study, work-study programs, internship placement in community institutions, a Tutorial Scholars Program for student-designed majors, an interdisciplinary studies program, and a limited number of pass/fail options. There are 5 national honor societies, a freshman honors program, and 1 departmental honors program.

Faculty/Classroom: 61% of faculty are male; 39%, female. All teach undergraduates, and 56% do research. The average class size in an introductory lecture is 25; in a laboratory, 10; and in a regular course, 21.

Admissions: 89% of the 2005-2006 applicants were accepted. The ACT scores for the 2005-2006 freshman class were: 48% below 21, 21% between 21 and 23, 18% between 24 and 26, 7% between 27 and 28, and 6% above 28. 29% of the current freshmen were in the top fifth of their class; 66% were in the top two fifths. 10 freshmen graduated first in their class.

Requirements: A satisfactory score on the ACT is required. In addition, applicants must be graduates of an accredited secondary school or have a GED. They must complete 20 high school academic credits, including 4 years of English, 3 of math, and 2 each of lab science and history, 1 of which is American history. USAO requires applicants to be in the upper 50% of their class. A GPA of 2.85 is required. AP and CLEP credits are accepted.

Procedure: Freshmen are admitted to all sessions. Entrance exams should be taken by May of the preceding spring. There is a rolling admissions plan. Applications should be filed by September 8 for fall entry, along with a $15 fee. Notification is sent on a rolling basis. Applications are accepted on-line.

Transfer: 124 transfer students enrolled in 2004-2005. Applicants must have a minimum GPA of 2.0. Those students with fewer than 30 college-level credit hours must submit a high school transcript or GED and ACT scores. 30 of 124 credits required for the bachelor's degree must be completed at USAO.

Visiting: There are guides for informal visits and visitors may sit in on classes. To schedule a visit, contact the Admissions Office at *usao-admissions@usao.edu.*

Financial Aid: In 2005-2006, 64% of all full-time freshmen and 66% of continuing full-time students received some form of financial aid. 61% of all full-time students received need-based aid. The average freshman award was $6034. Need-based scholarships or need-based grants averaged $4948 (13,104 maximum); need-based self-help aid (loans and jobs) averaged $2,491 (5625 maximum); non-need-based athletic scholarships averaged $6969 ($12,480 maximum); and other non-need-based awards and non-need-based scholarships averaged $3,957. 18% of undergraduates work part time. Average annual earnings from campus work are $1688. The average financial indebtedness of the 2005 graduate was $11,378. The FAFSA and Institution Information Sheet are required. The priority date for freshman financial aid applications for fall entry is March 15. The deadline for filing freshman financial aid applications for fall entry is open.

International Students: There are 25 international students enrolled. The school actively recruits these students. They must score satisfactorily on the written TOEFL or on the electronic version.

Computers: The entire campus has wireless coverage. Every academic building has at least one computer lab accessible by all students. All students may access the system at any time. There are no time limits and no fees.

Graduates: From July 1, 2004 to June 30, 2005, 182 bachelor's degrees were awarded. The most popular majors were business administration (17%), elementary education (9%), and physical education (9%). In an average class, 14% graduate in 4 years or less, 25% graduate in 5 years or less, and 33% graduate in 6 years or less. 30 companies recruited on campus in 2004-2005. Of the 2004 graduating class, 10% were enrolled in graduate school within 6 months of graduation and 90% were employed.

Admissions Contact: Chris Crumley, Recruiting Coordinator.
E-mail: *ccrumley@usao.edu or usao-admissions@usao.edu*
Web: *http://www.usao.edu*

UNIVERSITY OF TULSA   E-2

Tulsa, OK, USA 74104-3189

(918) 631-2307
(800) 331-3050; Fax: (918) 631-5003

Full-time: 1338 men, 1297 women	**Faculty:** 271; IIA, +$
Part-time: 75 men, 86 women	**Ph.D.s:** 96%
Graduate: 768 men, 520 women	**Student/Faculty:** 10 to 1
Year: semesters, summer session	**Tuition:** $18,860
Application Deadline: open	**Room & Board:** $6488
Freshman Class: 2687 applied, 2017 accepted, 631 enrolled	
SAT Verbal/Math: 620/620*	**ACT:** 26 **HIGHLY COMPETITIVE**

The University of Tulsa, founded in 1894, is a private comprehensive institution offering 60 undergraduate major areas of study through its programs in liberal arts and sciences, engineering and natural sciences, and business administration. There are 3 undergraduate and 2 graduate schools. In addition to regional accreditation, TU has baccalaureate program accreditation with AACSB, ABET, CSAB, NASM, NCATE, and NLN. The 2 libraries contain 1,033,604 volumes, 3,338,713 microform

items, and 16,385 audio/video tapes/CDs/DVDs, and subscribe to 27,604 periodicals including electronic. Computerized library services include the card catalog, interlibrary loans, database searching, and Internet access. Special learning facilities include an art gallery, radio station, and TV station. The 209-acre campus is in an urban area in the city of Tulsa. Including any residence halls, there are 78 buildings.

Student Life: 59% of undergraduates are from Oklahoma. Others are from 43 states, 49 foreign countries, and Canada. 72% are from public schools. 66% are white. 42% claim no religious affiliation; 42% Protestant; 14% Catholic. The average age of freshmen is 18; all undergraduates, 21. 16% do not continue beyond their first year.

Housing: 2197 students can be accommodated in college housing, which includes single-sex and coed dorms, on-campus apartments, off-campus apartments, married-student housing, and sorority houses. In addition, there are honors houses and language houses. On-campus housing is guaranteed for the freshman and sophomore year only and is available on a lottery system for upperclassmen. 64% of students live on campus; of those, 93% remain on campus on weekends. All students may keep cars.

Activities: 21% of men belong to 7 national fraternities; 23% of women belong to 9 national sororities. There are 245 groups on campus, including art, band, cheerleading, chess, choir, chorale, chorus, computers, dance, drama, drill team, ethnic, film, gay, honors, international, jazz band, literary magazine, marching band, musical theater, newspaper, opera, orchestra, pep band, photography, political, professional, radio and TV, religious, social, social service, student government, and symphony. Popular campus events include Springfest and Black Heritage Month.

Sports: There are 8 intercollegiate sports for men and 10 for women, and 25 intramural sports for men and 25 for women. Facilities include a 40,000-seat stadium, an 8300-seat basketball arena, a gym, an athletic field, indoor racquetball courts, basketball and tennis courts, an indoor swimming pool, a handball court, a weight room, a dance studio, student fitness center, soccer fields, softball field, track, multi-purpose recreational field, and outdoor tennis courts.

Disabled Students: 80% of the campus is accessible. Wheelchair ramps, elevators, special parking, specially equipped rest rooms, special class scheduling, lowered drinking fountains, lowered telephones, and sidewalks and curb cuts are available.

Services: Counseling and information services are available, as is tutoring in most subjects. There is a reader service for the blind. Special labs are available to students in need of assistance in math and writing.

Campus Safety and Security: Measures include 24-hour foot and vehicle patrol, self-defense education, security escort services, and informal discussions. There are pamphlets/posters/films, emergency telephones, lighted pathways/sidewalks, and electronic door locks on residence halls open only with student identification.

Programs of Study: TU confers B.A., B.S., B.F.A., B.Mus.Ed., B.S.A.M., B.S.A.T., B.S.B., B.S.B.A., B.S.C., B.S.C.E., B.S.C.S., B.S.D.E., B.S.E., B.S.E.E., B.S.E.P., B.S.E.S.S., B.S.G.S., B.S.I.B.L., B.S.M.E., B.S.N., B.S.P.E., B.S.S.P. degrees. Master's and doctoral degrees are also awarded. Bachelor's degrees are awarded in AGRICULTURE (environmental studies), BIOLOGICAL SCIENCE (biochemistry and biology/biological science), BUSINESS (accounting, banking and finance, international business management, management information systems, management science, marketing/retailing/merchandising, and sports management), COMMUNICATIONS AND THE ARTS (art, arts administration/management, communications, English, film arts, French, German, music, music performance, musical theater, piano/organ, Spanish, and voice), COMPUTER AND PHYSICAL SCIENCE (chemistry, computer science, geology, geoscience, information sciences and systems, mathematics, and physics), EDUCATION (athletic training, education, education of the deaf and hearing impaired, elementary, and music), ENGINEERING AND ENVIRONMENTAL DESIGN (chemical engineering, electrical/electronics engineering, engineering physics, mechanical engineering, and petroleum/natural gas engineering), HEALTH PROFESSIONS (exercise science, nursing, premedicine, and speech pathology/audiology), SOCIAL SCIENCE (anthropology, economics, history, philosophy, political science/government, prelaw, psychology, religion, Russian and Slavic studies, and sociology). Petroleum engineering, psychology, and English are the strongest academically. Management, mechanical engineering, and biology are the largest.

Required: To graduate, students must complete 124 to 136 credit hours, including 24 to 51 in the major, with a minimum GPA determined by the major. Freshmen in liberal arts and business administration must complete the First Seminar. All students must complete the core curriculum, which includes 3 writing courses and at least 1 course in math. All students must also complete the general curriculum, which requires 8 courses in 4 categories (artistic imagination, social inquiry, cultural interpretation, and scientific investigation). A foreign language requirement of 2 years for liberal arts and sciences students and 1 year for business majors must be completed.

Special: Internships are available in the Tulsa area during the school year and in cities throughout the United States during the summer. Students may participate in more than 40 study-abroad programs, most of them arranged through the Institute of European Studies. TU offers a Washington semester, B.A.-B.S. degrees, cross-registration with the 3 undergraduate schools, dual and student-designed majors, accelerated degree programs, nondegree study, work-study programs, and pass/fail options. There are 40 national honor societies, including Phi Beta Kappa, and a freshman honors program.

Faculty/Classroom: 66% of faculty are male; 34%, female. All both teach and do research. Graduate students teach 4% of introductory courses. The average class size in an introductory lecture is 24; in a laboratory, 17; and in a regular course, 20.

Admissions: 75% of the 2005-2006 applicants were accepted. The SAT scores for the 2005-2006 freshman class were: Verbal--12% below 500, 30% between 500 and 599, 32% between 600 and 700, and 28% above 700; Math--10% below 500, 30% between 500 and 599, 34% between 600 and 700, and 26% above 700. The ACT scores were 6% below 21, 20% between 21 and 23, 24% between 24 and 26, 14% between 27 and 28, and 36% above 28. 75% of the current freshmen were in the top fifth of their class; 90% were in the top two fifths. There were 83 National Merit finalists. 35 freshmen graduated first in their class.

Requirements: The SAT or ACT is required. In addition, graduation from an accredited secondary school or satisfactory scores on the GED are also required for admission. The school recommends a minimum of 15 academic credits, including 4 years of English, 3 to 4 years each of math, science, and social studies (including history), and 2 years of a single foreign language. An essay and an interview are highly recommended. An audition or a portfolio is required for students applying for music, theater, or art scholarships. TU requires applicants to be in the upper 33% of their class. A GPA of 3.0 is required. AP and CLEP credits are accepted. Important factors in the admissions decision are advanced placement or honor courses, leadership record, and extracurricular activities record.

Procedure: Freshmen are admitted fall, spring, and summer. Entrance exams should be taken during spring of the junior year or fall of the senior year. There are deferred admissions and rolling admissions plans. Application deadlines are open. Application fee is $35. 272 applicants were on the 2005 waiting list; 95 were admitted. Applications are accepted on-line.

Transfer: 173 transfer students enrolled in 2004-2005. Transfer students must submit official transcripts from all colleges attended and should have a minimum GPA of 2.5 for all college and high school work. Applicants with fewer than 30 credit hours must submit ACT or SAT scores. Those with fewer than 60 credit hours must submit an official high school transcript. Applicants 25 years of age or older are exempt from submitting ACT or SAT scores unless requested to do so by the Admission Office. 45 of 126 credits required for the bachelor's degree must be completed at TU.

Visiting: There are regularly scheduled orientations for prospective students, including overnight programs in the fall and spring. Students stay on campus and attend special information sessions. There are guides for informal visits and visitors may sit in on classes and stay overnight. To schedule a visit, contact the Office of Admission.

Financial Aid: In 2005-2006, 94% of all full-time freshmen and 79% of continuing full-time students received some form of financial aid. 36% of full-time freshmen and 41% of continuing full-time students received need-based aid. The average freshman award was $15,840. Need-based scholarships or need-based grants averaged $4123 ($9050 maximum); need-based self-help aid (loans and jobs) averaged $5922 ($13,715 maximum); non-need-based athletic scholarships averaged $16,224 ($26,759 maximum); and other non-need-based awards and non-need-based scholarships averaged $11,292 ($27,123 maximum). 23% of undergraduates work part time. Average annual earnings from campus work are $3500. The average financial indebtedness of the 2005 graduate was $23,824. The FAFSA and the college's own financial statement are required. The deadline for filing freshman financial aid applications for fall entry is April 1.

International Students: There are 235 international students enrolled. The school actively recruits these students. A satisfactory score is required on the written TOEFL or on the electronic version.

Computers: Wireless access is available. All students may access the system 24 hours per day. There are no time limits and no fees.

Graduates: From July 1, 2004 to June 30, 2005, 536 bachelor's degrees were awarded. The most popular majors were management (7%), petroleum engineering (7%), and mechanical engineering (5%). In an average class, 43% graduate in 4 years or less, 59% graduate in 5 years or less, and 60% graduate in 6 years or less. 137 companies recruited on campus in 2004-2005. Of the 2004 graduating class, 31% were enrolled in graduate school within 6 months of graduation and 80% were employed.

Admissions Contact: John C. Corso, Associate Vice President for Enrollment and Student Services,. A video is available.
E-mail: *admission@utulsa.edu* Web: *www.utulsa.edu*

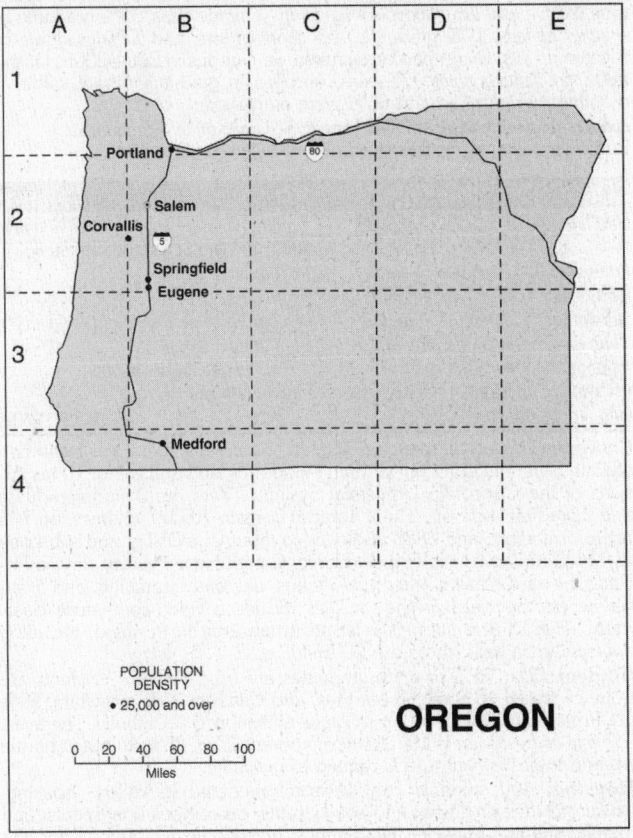

A B C D E

Portland

Salem
Corvallis
Springfield
Eugene

Medford

POPULATION
DENSITY
• 25,000 and over

0 20 40 60 80 100
Miles

OREGON

ART INSTITUTE OF PORTLAND
B-1
Portland, OR 97209-2911
(503) 228-6528
(888) 228-6528; Fax: (503) 227-1945

Full-time: 470 men, 550 women	Faculty: 27
Part-time: 150 men, 180 women	Ph.D.s: 52%
Graduate: none	Student/Faculty: 37 to 1
Year: quarters, summer session	Tuition: $15,500
Application Deadline: open	Room & Board: $8000
Freshman Class: n/av	
SAT or ACT: recommended	SPECIAL

The Art Institute of Portland, is a private institution offering undergraduate programs in interior, graphic, and apparel design; media arts and animation; and multimedia and web design, game art and design, digital media production, and advertising. Figures in the above capsule and profile are approximate. The library contains 22,289 volumes and 1000 audio/video tapes/CDs/DVDs, and subscribes to 200 periodicals including electronic. Computerized library services include the card catalog, interlibrary loans, database searching, and Internet access. Special learning facilities include a learning resource center. The 1-acre campus is in an urban area in downtown Portland. Including any residence halls, there are 2 buildings.

Student Life: 69% of undergraduates are from Oregon. 81% are white. The average age of freshmen is 23; all undergraduates, 25.

Housing: 110 students can be accommodated in college housing, which includes coed off-campus apartments. On-campus housing is available on a first-come, first-served basis. 92% of students commute. Alcohol is not permitted. No one may keep cars.

Activities: There are no fraternities or sororities. There are 3 groups on campus, including art, computers, film, international, professional, and student government. Popular campus events include portfolio review, animation shows, and Halloween and Valentine's Day activities.

Sports: There is no sports program at AIPD.

Disabled Students: All of the campus is accessible. Wheelchair ramps, elevators, special parking, specially equipped rest rooms, special class scheduling, lowered drinking fountains, and lowered telephones are available.

Services: Counseling and information services are available, as is tutoring in most subjects. There is remedial math, reading, and writing.

Campus Safety and Security: Measures include informal discussions, pamphlets/posters/films, emergency telephones, lighted pathways/sidewalks, and a night security guard.

Programs of Study: AIPD confers the B.S. degree. Associate degrees are also awarded. Bachelor's degrees are awarded in COMMUNICATIONS AND THE ARTS (advertising, animation, apparel design, graphic design, media arts, and multimedia), ENGINEERING AND ENVIRONMENTAL DESIGN (interior design). Interior design is the strongest academically. Graphic design is the largest.

Required: To graduate, students must complete 180 quarter hours, including 111 in the major, with a minimum GPA of 2.0. Distribution requirements include 9 credits each in English composition and history of material culture, 6 credits in basic design, and 3 credits each in drawing, computer fundamentals, physics, math, art history, and critical thinking.

Special: Accelerated degree programs and field trips to San Francisco and annually to Europe are available. Internships are required for most programs.

Faculty/Classroom: 44% of faculty are male; 56%, female. All teach undergraduates. The average class size in an introductory lecture is 25; in a laboratory, 25; and in a regular course, 20.

Requirements: The SAT or ACT is recommended. In addition, a high school diploma or GED is required. An interview with an admissions officer and an essay are required. A GPA of 2.5 is required. AP and CLEP credits are accepted. Important factors in the admissions decision are evidence of special talent, personality/intangible qualities, and recommendations by school officials.

Procedure: Freshmen are admitted to all sessions. There are deferred admissions and rolling admissions plans. Application deadlines are open. Application fee is $50. Applications are accepted on-line.

Transfer: 185 transfer students enrolled in a recent year. Requirements are the same as for new students. 45 of 180 credits required for the bachelor's degree must be completed at AIPD.

Visiting: There are regularly scheduled orientations for prospective students, including college tours, mini class sessions, financial aid and financial planning meetings, and career assessment. There are guides for informal visits and visitors may sit in on classes. To schedule a visit, contact the Admissions Office.

Financial Aid: In a recent year, 84% of all full-time freshmen and 80% of continuing full-time students received some form of financial aid. 82% of full-time freshmen and 75% of continuing full-time students received need-based aid. The average freshman award was $11,093. Need-based scholarships or need-based grants averaged $3784 ($4050 maximum); need-based self-help aid (loans and jobs) averaged $3051 ($5500 maximum); and other non-need-based awards and non-need-based scholarships averaged $3495 ($6252 maximum). 4% of undergraduates worked part time. Average annual earnings from campus work were $2431. The average financial indebtedness of a recent graduate was $19,400. AIPD is a member of CSS. The FAFSA is required. Check with the school for current application deadlines.

International Students: In a recent year, there were 37 international students enrolled. The school actively recruits these students. They must score satisfactorily on the written TOEFL or on the electronic version.

Computers: All students may access the system weekdays and weekends, daytime and evening. There are no time limits and no fees. It is strongly recommended that all students have a personal computer.

Admissions Contact: Kelly Alston, Director of Admissions.
E-mail: *aipdadm@aii.edu* Web: *www.aipd.artinstitutes.edu*

CASCADE COLLEGE
B-2
Portland, OR 97216-1515
(503) 255-7060
(800) 550-7678; Fax: (503) 257-1222

Full-time: 125 men, 149 women	Faculty: n/av
Part-time: 8 men, 4 women	Ph.D.s: 47%
Graduate: none	Student/Faculty: 22 to 1
Year: semesters, summer session	Tuition: $11,930
Application Deadline: open	Room & Board: $6050
Freshman Class: 199 applied, 108 accepted, 76 enrolled	
SAT Verbal/Math: 490/500*	ACT: 20 NONCOMPETITIVE

Cascade College is a Christian liberal arts college offering bachelor's degrees in interdisciplinary studies, business, biblical studies, English, psychology, communication, science, and early childhood education. The library contains 25,000 volumes, 62,045 microform items, and 1200 audio/video tapes/CDs/DVDs, and subscribes to 110 periodicals including electronic. Computerized library services include the card catalog, interlibrary loans, database searching, and Internet access. Special learning facilities include a learning resource center. The 12-acre campus is in a suburban area 8 miles east of downtown Portland. Including any residence halls, there are 16 buildings.

Student Life: 64% of undergraduates are from out of state, mostly the Northwest. Students are from 16 states, 6 foreign countries, and Canada.

76% are from public schools; 7% are home-schooled. 80% are white. 81% are Protestant; 8% claim no religious affiliation. The average age of freshmen is 19; all undergraduates, 21. 40% do not continue beyond their first year; 25% remain to graduate.

Housing: 240 students can be accommodated in college housing, which includes single-sex dorms. On-campus housing is guaranteed for all 4 years. 75% of students live on campus; of those, 65% remain on campus on weekends. Alcohol is not permitted. All students may keep cars.

Activities: There are no fraternities or sororities. There are 20 groups on campus, including art, band, choir, chorale, chorus, drama, honors, literary magazine, professional, religious, social service, student government, and yearbook. Popular campus events include a campus variety show, formal banquets, and Youth Venture.

Sports: There are 4 intercollegiate sports for men and 5 for women, and 5 intramural sports for men and 5 for women. Facilities include a gym, a weight room, a team room, a soccer field, and basketball, volleyball, badminton, and tennis courts.

Disabled Students: 70% of the campus is accessible. Wheelchair ramps, elevators, special parking, specially equipped rest rooms, special class scheduling, and special housing are available.

Services: Counseling and information services are available, as is tutoring in most subjects. There is remedial math, reading, and writing. Other services may be available as needed.

Campus Safety and Security: Measures include 24-hour foot and vehicle patrol, security escort services, informal discussions, and pamphlets/posters/films. There are lighted pathways/sidewalks and a nighttime security patrol.

Programs of Study: Cascade confers B.A., B.S., and B.S.E. degrees. Bachelor's degrees are awarded in BUSINESS (business administration and management and marketing management), COMMUNICATIONS AND THE ARTS (communications and English), COMPUTER AND PHYSICAL SCIENCE (science), SOCIAL SCIENCE (biblical studies, interdisciplinary studies, and psychology). Business, psychology, and elementary education are the largest.

Required: To graduate, students must complete a minimum of 126 semester hours, including a minimum of 40 in upper-division courses, with a GPA of 2.0. At least 30 hours must be taken in the major, 20 of them being upper division. In addition to biblical and religious curriculum requirements, 1 hour of phys ed is required.

Special: Cascade College offers internships and practica in some areas of study, including psychology, business, communication, science, and ministry. Study abroad in Austria and the Pacific Rim is possible, as are student-designed majors. Christian service is available as a second major and, with approval, other majors may be combined for a double major. There is 1 national honor society.

Faculty/Classroom: 74% of faculty are male; 26%, female. All teach undergraduates. The average class size in an introductory lecture is 25; in a laboratory, 20; and in a regular course, 19.

Admissions: 54% of the 2005-2006 applicants were accepted. The SAT scores for the 2005-2006 freshman class were: Verbal--47% below 500, 42% between 500 and 599, and 11% between 600 and 700; Math--45% below 500, 41% between 500 and 599, and 14% between 600 and 700. The ACT scores were 49% below 21, 22% between 21 and 23, 22% between 24 and 26, 6% between 27 and 28, and 1% above 28.

Requirements: The SAT or ACT is required; the ACT is preferred. The ACT Optional Writing test is also recommended. Scores are used for placement in classes only. Applicants must provide a high school transcript that shows evidence of graduation, or evidence of having passed the GED. Home-schooled students may provide a transcript and graduation records from a recognized home-school program. AP and CLEP credits are accepted.

Procedure: Freshmen are admitted to all sessions. Entrance exams should be taken at any national test date prior to fall enrollment. There is a deferred admissions and a rolling admissioins plan. Application deadlines are open. Applications are accepted on-line. The fall 2005 application fee was $25.

Transfer: 37 transfer students enrolled in 2004-2005. Official transcripts from all institutions attended are required. 30 of 126 credits required for the bachelor's degree must be completed at Cascade.

Visiting: There are regularly scheduled orientations for prospective students, including a meeting with faculty members, a financial aid workshop, and a survey of college programs. There are guides for informal visits and visitors may sit in on classes and stay overnight. To schedule a visit, contact the Admissions Office at (503) 257-1202.

Financial Aid: In 2005-2006, 100% of all full-time freshmen and 98% of continuing full-time students received some form of financial aid. 76% of full-time freshmen and 69% of continuing full-time students received need-based aid. The average freshman award was $8100. 26% of undergraduates work part time. Average annual earnings from campus work are $1400. The FAFSA is required.

International Students: There are 12 international students enrolled. The school actively recruits these students. They must score satisfactorily on the written TOEFL and also take the SAT, ACTor , with the ACT preferred.

Computers: Wireless access is available. All students may access the system 8 A.M. to 10:30 P.M. There are no time limits and no fees.

Graduates: From July 1, 2004 to June 30, 2005, 50 bachelor's degrees were awarded. The most popular majors were liberal arts (29%), business (22%), and education (18%). In an average class, 13% graduate in 4 years or less, 17% graduate in 5 years or less, and 17% graduate in 6 years or less. 3 companies recruited on campus in 2004-2005. Of the 2004 graduating class, 6% were enrolled in graduate school within 6 months of graduation and 85% were employed.

Admissions Contact: Pearl Howarth, Director of Admissions.
E-mail: *admissions@cascade.edu* Web: *www.cascade.edu*

CONCORDIA UNIVERSITY   B-1
Portland, OR 97211-6099

(503) 280-8501
(800) 321-9371; Fax: (503) 280-8531

Full-time: 304 men, 504 women	**Faculty:** 40; IIB, --$
Part-time: 73 men, 125 women	**Ph.D.s:** 57%
Graduate: 179 men, 321 women	**Student/Faculty:** 20 to 1
Year: semesters, summer session	**Tuition:** $18,900
Application Deadline: open	**Room & Board:** $5500
Freshman Class: 804 applied, 532 accepted, 171 enrolled	
SAT Verbal/Math: 500/520*	**ACT:** 21 COMPETITIVE

Concordia University, founded in 1905, is a private liberal arts institution affiliated with the Lutheran Church Missouri Synod and is 1 of 10 institutions of the Concordia University System. There are 3 undergraduate and 2 graduate schools. The 2 libraries contain 70,000 volumes, 56,706 microform items, and 2888 audio/video tapes/CDs/DVDs, and subscribe to 424 periodicals including electronic. Computerized library services include the card catalog, interlibrary loans, database searching, and Internet access. Special learning facilities include a video-conference classroom. The 13-acre campus is in an urban area in Portland. Including any residence halls, there are 20 buildings.

Student Life: 75% of undergraduates are from Oregon. Students are from 14 states, 18 foreign countries, and Canada. 75% are white. 59% are Protestant; 30% claim no religious affiliation; 8% Catholic. The average age of freshmen is 19; all undergraduates, 25. 25% do not continue beyond their first year; 45% remain to graduate.

Housing: 400 students can be accommodated in college housing, which includes single-sex and coed dorms, on-campus apartments, and married-student housing. On-campus housing is guaranteed for the freshman year only, is available on a first-come, first-served basis, and is available on a lottery system for upperclassmen. 59% of students live on campus; of those, 95% remain on campus on weekends. Alcohol is not permitted. All students may keep cars.

Activities: There are no fraternities or sororities. There are 14 groups on campus, including brass ensemble, choir, chorus, drama, handbell choir, honors, international, literary magazine, newspaper, professional, religious, social, social service, and student government.

Sports: There are 4 intercollegiate sports for men and 5 for women, and 10 intramural sports for men and 10 for women. Facilities include a weight room, a 1200-seat gym, and a baseball/soccer field.

Disabled Students: 80% of the campus is accessible. Wheelchair ramps, elevators, special parking, specially equipped rest rooms, special class scheduling, and lowered telephones are available.

Services: Counseling and information services are available, as is tutoring in most subjects. There is remedial math, reading, and writing. There is also student-supported individual help and media resources.

Campus Safety and Security: Measures include 24-hour foot and vehicle patrol, self-defense education, security escort services, and informal discussions. There are pamphlets/posters/films, emergency telephones, lighted pathways/sidewalks, and emergency cell phone available 24 hours.

Programs of Study: Concordia confers B.A. and B.S. degrees. Associate and master's degrees are also awarded. Bachelor's degrees are awarded in BIOLOGICAL SCIENCE (biology/biological science), BUSINESS (business administration and management), COMMUNICATIONS AND THE ARTS (English), COMPUTER AND PHYSICAL SCIENCE (chemistry), EDUCATION (early childhood, elementary, and secondary), ENGINEERING AND ENVIRONMENTAL DESIGN (environmental science), HEALTH PROFESSIONS (health care administration, nursing, and premedicine), SOCIAL SCIENCE (humanities, psychology, social work, theological studies, and youth ministry). Business administration, education, and psychology are the strongest academically. Education and business are the largest.

Required: To graduate, students must complete a total of 124 semester hours, with a minimum GPA of 2.0. General education requirements total 48 semester hours. All students must take freshman composition and courses in math, phys ed, humanities, religion, science, writing, fine arts, and social sciences. In the major, 45 hours of 300-400 level courses must be taken.

Special: Cross-registration may be arranged through the Concordia University System and with Oregon Independent. There is a dual enrollment program with Portland Community College. There are also internships, study abroad in more than 20 countries, and an accelerated degree program in business, health care administration, and social work. There is 1 national honor society, a freshman honors program, and 1 departmental honors program.

Faculty/Classroom: 67% of faculty are male; 33%, female. All teach undergraduates and 5% do research. No introductory courses are taught by graduate students. The average class size in an introductory lecture is 19; in a laboratory, 19; and in a regular course, 17.

Admissions: 66% of the 2005-2006 applicants were accepted. The SAT scores for the 2005-2006 freshman class were: Verbal--50% below 500, 34% between 500 and 599, 15% between 600 and 700, and 1% above 700; Math--44% below 500, 39% between 500 and 599, and 17% between 600 and 700. The ACT scores were 40% below 21, 35% between 21 and 23, 16% between 24 and 26, 9% between 27 and 28, and 2% above 28. 42% of the current freshmen were in the top fifth of their class; 69% were in the top two fifths.

Requirements: The SAT or ACT is required, with satisfactory SAT verbal scores recommended. Graduation from an accredited secondary school or satisfactory scores on the GED are required. The school recommends that high school courses include 4 units of English, 3 units each of social studies, math, and science, 2 units of a foreign language, and 1 unit of art and music. An interview is recommended. A GPA of 2.5 is required. AP and CLEP credits are accepted. Important factors in the admissions decision are recommendations by school officials, leadership record, and personality/intangible qualities.

Procedure: Freshmen are admitted fall, spring, and summer. Entrance exams should be taken during the junior year or early in the senior year. There is a rolling admissions plan. Early decision applications should be filed by March 1; regular application deadlines are open for fall entry. The fall 2005 application fee was $20. Notification is sent on a rolling basis. A waiting list is an active part of the admissions procedure. Applications are accepted on-line.

Transfer: 141 transfer students enrolled in a recent year. Transfer students must have a minimum GPA of 2.0. 45 of 124 credits required for the bachelor's degree must be completed at Concordia.

Visiting: There are regularly scheduled orientations for prospective students, including class visitations and meetings with program deans and faculty. There are guides for informal visits and visitors may sit in on classes and stay overnight. To schedule a visit, contact the Admissions Office.

Financial Aid: The average freshman award was $10,000. The FAFSA is required.

International Students: There are 15 international students enrolled. The school actively recruits these students. They must achieve a satisfactory score on the TOEFL and also take the SAT or the ACT.

Computers: Wireless access is available. All students may access the system. There are no time limits and no fees. It is strongly recommended that all students have a personal computer, specifically a Windows 2000 or greater compatible.

Graduates: In a recent year, 219 bachelor's degrees were awarded. The most popular majors were business administration (36%), education (34%), and health care administration (7%). In an average class, 30% graduate in 4 years or less, 39% graduate in 5 years or less, and 43% graduate in 6 years or less. 35 companies recruited on campus in a recent year.

Admissions Contact: Admissions Office.
E-mail: *admissions@cu-portland.edu* Web: *www.cu-portland.edu*

EASTERN OREGON UNIVERSITY — D-2
La Grande, OR 97850-2807
(541) 962-3393
(800) 452-8639; Fax: (541) 962-3418

Full-time: 860 men, 1090 women	Faculty: 93; IIB, --$
Part-time: 420 men, 680 women	Ph.D.s: 88%
Graduate: 60 men, 190 women	Student/Faculty: 21 to 1
Year: terms, summer session	Tuition: $4400
Application Deadline: open	Room & Board: $6000
Freshman Class: n/av	
SAT or ACT: required	NONCOMPETITIVE

Eastern Oregon University, founded in 1929, is a public institution that is part of the Oregon University System. It offers programs in liberal and fine arts, agriculture, business, health science, and teacher preparation. There are 3 undergraduate schools and 1 graduate school. Figures in the above capsule and profile are approximate. In addition to regional accreditation, Eastern has baccalaureate program accreditation with NCATE. The library contains 335,455 volumes, 250,834 microform items, and 34,176 audio/video tapes/CDs/DVDs, and subscribes to 893 periodicals including electronic. Computerized library services include the card catalog, interlibrary loans, database searching, and Internet access. Special learning facilities include a learning resource center, art gallery, natural history museum, and radio station. The 121-acre campus is in a rural area 260 miles east of Portland. Including any residence halls, there are 13 buildings.

Student Life: 70% of undergraduates are from Oregon. Students are from 42 states, 25 foreign countries, and Canada. 96% are from public schools. 82% are white. The average age of freshmen is 19; all undergraduates, 27. 32% do not continue beyond their first year; 37% remain to graduate.

Housing: 436 students can be accommodated in college housing, which includes single-sex and coed dorms and married-student housing. In addition, there is a wellness floor and on academic focus floor. On-campus housing is available on a first-come, first-served basis. 85% of students commute. All students may keep cars.

Activities: There are no fraternities or sororities. There are 44 groups on campus, including art, band, cheerleading, choir, chorale, chorus, computers, dance, drama, ethnic, international, jazz band, literary magazine, musical theater, newspaper, orchestra, pep band, photography, professional, radio and TV, religious, social, student government, symphony, and yearbook. Popular campus events include Casino Night, Spring Fling, and Spring Symposium.

Sports: There are 6 intercollegiate sports for men and 6 for women, and 6 intramural sports for men and 6 for women. Facilities include racquetball courts, a weight room, 3 gyms, a swimming pool, aerobics facilities, a track, and indoor and outdoor tennis courts.

Disabled Students: 80% of the campus is accessible. Wheelchair ramps, elevators, special parking, and specially equipped rest rooms are available.

Services: Counseling and information services are available, as is tutoring in most subjects. There is a reader service for the blind, and remedial math, reading, and writing.

Campus Safety and Security: Measures include 24-hour foot and vehicle patrol, security escort services, informal discussions, and pamphlets/posters/films. There are emergency telephones and lighted pathways/sidewalks.

Programs of Study: Eastern confers B.A. and B.S degrees. Master's degrees are also awarded. Bachelor's degrees are awarded in AGRICULTURE (agricultural business management, agricultural economics, forestry and related sciences, range/farm management, and soil science), BIOLOGICAL SCIENCE (biology/biological science), BUSINESS (accounting and business administration and management), COMMUNICATIONS AND THE ARTS (art, dramatic arts, English, and music), COMPUTER AND PHYSICAL SCIENCE (chemistry, computer science, mathematics, and physics), EDUCATION (education and physical), HEALTH PROFESSIONS (health and nursing), SOCIAL SCIENCE (anthropology, history, liberal arts/general studies, psychology, and sociology). Sciences is the strongest academically. Business and education are the largest.

Required: Students must complete 180 credit hours, including 60 hours of general education courses that include 15 hours each of social science, natural science, humanities, art-language, and logic, with a GPA of at least 2.0. They must demonstrate computer competency and pass a writing proficiency exam. A senior capstone experience is required.

Special: There are cooperative and 3-2 engineering degree programs with Oregon State University. The university offers internships, work-study with federal agencies, accelerated degree program, student-designed and dual majors, study abroad in 8 countries, a general studies degree, B.A.-B.S. degrees, a multidisciplinary degree, numerous pre-professional programs, credit by exam, external degrees, and pass/fail options. The university also serves students with course work via telecommunications and video and with a weekend University. There are 6 national honor societies, including Phi Beta Kappa, and 6 departmental honors programs.

Faculty/Classroom: 57% of faculty are male; 43%, female. All both teach and do research. No introductory courses are taught by graduate students. The average class size in an introductory lecture is 60; in a laboratory, 20; and in a regular course, 35.

Requirements: The SAT or ACT is required. A GED is accepted. Applicants must complete 14 academic credits, including 4 years of English, 3 each of math and social studies, and 2 of science. A GPA of 3.0 is required. AP and CLEP credits are accepted. Important factors in the admissions decision are extracurricular activities record and geographic diversity.

Procedure: Freshmen are admitted to all sessions. Entrance exams should be taken in the senior year. There are deferred admissions and rolling admissions plans. Application deadlines are open. Application fee is $50.

Transfer: 463 transfer students enrolled in a recent year. Applicants must have 30 credits of transferable academic work with a GPA of 2.25. 45 of 180 credits required for the bachelor's degree must be completed at Eastern.

Visiting: There are regularly scheduled orientations for prospective students, including a campus tour, academic advising, and information sessions on financial aid and residence life. There are guides for informal visits and visitors may sit in on classes and stay overnight. To schedule a visit, contact Admissions/New Student Programs.

Financial Aid: In a recent year, 60% of all full-time freshmen and 66% of continuing full-time students received some form of financial aid. 37%

of full-time freshmen and 44% of continuing full-time students received need-based aid. The average freshman award was $7558. 35% of undergraduates worked part time. Average annual earnings from campus work were $1003. The average financial indebtedness of a recent graduate was $14,185. Eastern is a member of CSS. The FAFSA is required. Check with the school for current application deadlines.

International Students: In a recent year, there were 92 international students enrolled. They must score satisfactorily on the written TOEFL or on the electronic version or take the MELAB and also take the University of Michigan Language Test for placement.

Computers: All students may access the system at various posted hours. There are no time limits and no fees.

Graduates: In a recent year, 494 bachelor's degrees were awarded. The most popular majors were liberal studies (25%), interdisciplinary studies (20%), and business marketing (19%). In an average class, 20% graduate in 4 years or less, 45% graduate in 5 years or less, and 37% graduate in 6 years or less. 30 companies recruited on campus in a recent year.

Admissions Contact: Sherri Edvalson, Director of Admissions. E-mail: *admissions@eou.edu* Web: *http://www.eou.edu*

GEORGE FOX UNIVERSITY B-2
Newberg, OR 97132

(503) 554-2240
(800) 765-4369; Fax: (503) 554-3110

Full-time: 593 men, 948 women	**Faculty:** 99; I, --$
Part-time: 136 men, 183 women	**Ph.Ds:** 59%
Graduate: 541 men, 798 women	**Student/Faculty:** 16 to 1
Year: semesters	**Tuition:** $21,710
Application Deadline: February 1	**Room & Board:** $6780
Freshman Class: 1186 applied, 1031 accepted, 451 enrolled	
SAT Verbal/Math: 560/560*	**ACT:** 23 **COMPETITIVE**

George Fox University is a Christian university of the arts and sciences and professional studies, founded by the Northwest Yearly Meeting of Friends in 1891. In addition to regional accreditation, George Fox has baccalaureate program accreditation with ABET and NASM. The 2 libraries contain 202,852 volumes, 211,669 microform items, and 5942 audio/video tapes/CDs/DVDs, and subscribe to 1345 periodicals including electronic. Computerized library services include the card catalog, interlibrary loans, database searching, Internet access, and laptop Internet portals. Special learning facilities include a learning resource center, art gallery, radio station, and a television production studio. The 77-acre campus is in a small town 23 miles southwest of Portland. Including any residence halls, there are 73 buildings.

Student Life: 67% of undergraduates are from Oregon. Students are from 28 states and 7 foreign countries. 75% are from public schools. 83% are white. Most are Protestant. The average age of freshmen is 18; all undergraduates, 24. 18% do not continue beyond their first year; 60% remain to graduate.

Housing: 1055 students can be accommodated in college housing, which includes single-sex dorms, on-campus apartments, and married-student housing. In addition, there are special-interest houses. On-campus housing is available on a first-come, first-served basis. 66% of students live on campus; of those, 50% remain on campus on weekends. Alcohol is not permitted. All students may keep cars.

Activities: There are no fraternities or sororities. There are 31 groups on campus, including art, band, cheerleading, choir, chorale, chorus, computers, debate, drama, drill team, ethnic, film, forensics, honors, international, jazz band, literary magazine, newspaper, orchestra, outdoor club, pep band, political, professional, radio and TV, religious, social, social service, student government, symphony, and yearbook. Popular campus events include Quaker Heritage Week, Christian Emphasis Week, and Mr. Bruin.

Sports: There are 6 intercollegiate sports for men and 7 for women, and 4 intramural sports for men and 4 for women. Facilities include an all-weather track, a fitness center, tennis and handball/racquetball courts, a climbing wall, a 2500-seat gym, and baseball, softball, and soccer fields.

Disabled Students: 80% of the campus is accessible. Wheelchair ramps, elevators, special parking, specially equipped rest rooms, special class scheduling, lowered drinking fountains, lowered telephones, and special housing are available.

Services: Counseling and information services are available, as is tutoring in most subjects. There is a reader service for the blind, and remedial math, reading, and writing.

Campus Safety and Security: Measures include 24-hour foot and vehicle patrol, self-defense education, security escort services, and informal discussions. There are pamphlets/posters/films, emergency telephones, lighted pathways/sidewalks, parking lot cameras, and video surveillance of key buildings.

Programs of Study: George Fox confers B.A. and B.S. degrees. Master's and doctoral degrees are also awarded. Bachelor's degrees are awarded in BIOLOGICAL SCIENCE (biology/biological science), BUSINESS (business economics, human resources, and management science), COMMUNICATIONS AND THE ARTS (art, communications, literature, music, Spanish, and telecommunications), COMPUTER AND PHYSICAL SCIENCE (chemistry, computer science, information sciences and systems, and mathematics), EDUCATION (elementary, health, home economics, mathematics, middle school, music, physical, science, secondary, and social studies), ENGINEERING AND ENVIRONMENTAL DESIGN (engineering), HEALTH PROFESSIONS (nursing, predentistry, premedicine, and preveterinary science), SOCIAL SCIENCE (biblical studies, cognitive science, economics, history, home economics, international studies, ministries, political science/government, prelaw, psychology, religion, social work, and sociology). Business is the largest.

Required: To graduate, students must have a minimum 2.0 GPA and complete 126 semester hours, including 48 in the major. 20 of the last 30 hours must be completed at George Fox. The required core curriculum of 57 semester hours includes 18 hours total in math/language, natural science, and social science, 14 to 15 hours of humanities, 10 hours of Bible/religious studies, 6 hours each in communication, language, and global studies, and 3 hours of health/phys ed. A thesis is required in some majors.

Special: There is a 3-2 engineering degree with the University of Portland, Oregon State University, and Washington University in St. Louis, and cross-registration through the Oregon Independent College Association. George Fox also offers internships with area companies, study abroad, and a Washington semester through the Christian College Coalition. Work-study programs, accelerated degrees, B.A.-B.S. degrees in all majors, dual and student-designed interdisciplinary majors, and pass/fail options in upper-division courses outside of the major also are offered. There are 3 national honor societies, and a freshman honors program.

Faculty/Classroom: 55% of faculty are male; 45%, female. 66% teach undergraduates. The average class size in an introductory lecture is 50; in a laboratory, 20; and in a regular course, 25.

Admissions: 87% of the 2005-2006 applicants were accepted. The SAT scores for the 2005-2006 freshman class were: Verbal--27% below 500, 40% between 500 and 599, 29% between 600 and 700, and 4% above 700; Math--24% below 500, 43% between 500 and 599, 30% between 600 and 700, and 3% above 700. The ACT scores were 29% below 21, 23% between 21 and 23, 33% between 24 and 26, 9% between 27 and 28, and 6% above 28. 57% of the current freshmen were in the top fifth of their class; 80% were in the top two fifths. 38 freshmen graduated first in their class.

Requirements: The SAT or ACT is required. The ACT Optional Writing test is also recommended. In addition, applicants need 16 academic credits or 14 Carnegie units, including a suggested 4 units of English and 2 units each of a foreign language, math, science, and social studies. An essay and 2 personal recommendations are required; a portfolio, audition, and interview are recommended in certain majors. A GPA of 2.6 is required. AP and CLEP credits are accepted. Important factors in the admissions decision are advanced placement or honor courses, extracurricular activities record, and leadership record.

Procedure: Freshmen are admitted fall and spring. Entrance exams should be taken in fall or winter. There are early admissions and deferred admissions plans. There is a rolling admissions plan. Applications should be filed by February 1 for fall entry and December 1 for spring entry. Notification is sent on a rolling basis. The fall 2005 application fee was $40. Applications are accepted on-line.

Transfer: 109 transfer students enrolled in 2004-2005. Transfers must have a minimum 2.3 GPA and 14 earned credits from their previous college. A personal recommendation is required. 30 of 126 credits required for the bachelor's degree must be completed at George Fox.

Visiting: There are regularly scheduled orientations for prospective students, including observation of classes and talking with professors. There are guides for informal visits and visitors may sit in on classes and stay overnight. To schedule a visit, contact the Office of Admissions at (800) 765-4369, ext. 2240 or *admissions@georgefox.edu*.

Financial Aid: In 2005-2006, 93% of all full-time freshmen and 80% of continuing full-time students received some form of financial aid. 74% of all full-time students received need-based aid. The average freshman award was $20,820. Need-based scholarships or need-based grants averaged $11,800; need-based self-help aid (loans and jobs) averaged $4350; and other non-need-based awards and non-need-based scholarships averaged $4670. 34% of undergraduates work part time. Average annual earnings from campus work are $1445. George Fox is a member of CSS. The FAFSA is required. The priority date for freshman financial aid applications for fall entry is February 1.

International Students: There are 40 international students enrolled. The school actively recruits these students. They must score satisfactorily on the TOEFL and also take the college's own test.

Computers: Wireless access is available. All freshmen are provided with a computer as part of their tuition. The wireless network is accessible in all academic classrooms, the library, meeting areas, the student union, and dorm lobbies. All students may access the system. There are no time limits and no fees. It is strongly recommended that all students have a personal computer. It is required that students in in some of our seminary programs have personal computers.

Graduates: From July 1, 2004 to June 30, 2005, 538 bachelor's degrees were awarded. The most popular majors were business (24%), social and behavioral sciences (6%), and elementary education (5%). In an average class, 11% graduate in 3 years or less, 52% graduate in 4 years or less, 58% graduate in 5 years or less, and 60% graduate in 6 years or less. 285 companies recruited on campus in 2004-2005. Of the 2004 graduating class, 18% were enrolled in graduate school within 6 months of graduation and 47% were employed.

Admissions Contact: Ryan Dougherty, Director of Undergraduate Admission. E-mail: *admissions@georgefox.edu* Web: *www.georgefox.edu*

LEWIS AND CLARK COLLEGE   B-1
Portland, OR 97219-7899

	(503) 768-7040
	(800) 444-4111; Fax: (503) 768-7055
Full-time: 745 men, 1153 women	Faculty: 129; IIB, +$
Part-time: 5 men, 6 women	Ph.D.s: 94%
Graduate: 169 men, 553 women	Student/Faculty: 15 to 1
Year: semesters, summer session	Tuition: $27,710
Application Deadline: February 1	Room & Board: $7648
Freshman Class: 4196 applied, 2495 accepted, 490 enrolled	
SAT Verbal/Math: 600/570*	ACT: 26 VERY COMPETITIVE+

Lewis & Clark College, founded in 1867, is a private, independent liberal arts and sciences institution, with a global reach. In addition to regional accreditation, LC has baccalaureate program accreditation with NASM. The 2 libraries contain 501,169 volumes, 711,175 microform items, and 14,990 audio/video tapes/CDs/DVDs, and subscribe to 6942 periodicals including electronic. Computerized library services include the card catalog, interlibrary loans, database searching, Internet access, and laptop Internet portals. Special learning facilities include a learning resource center, art gallery, radio station, TV station, telescope, research astronomical observatory, language lab, and greenhouse. The 137-acre campus is in a suburban area 6 miles south of downtown Portland. Including any residence halls, there are 54 buildings.

Student Life: 80% of undergraduates are from out of state, mostly the West. Students are from 46 states, 41 foreign countries, and Canada. 74% are from public schools. 67% are white. 78% claim no religious affiliation; 12% Protestant. The average age of freshmen is 18; all undergraduates, 20. 14% do not continue beyond their first year; 67% remain to graduate.

Housing: 1165 students can be accommodated in college housing, which includes single-sex and coed dorms and on-campus apartments. In addition, there are language houses and international awareness, outdoor pursuits, visual and performance arts, and substance-free floors. On-campus housing is guaranteed for the freshman year only and is available on a lottery system for upperclassmen. 64% of students live on campus; of those, 98% remain on campus on weekends. Upperclassmen may keep cars.

Activities: There are no fraternities or sororities. There are 75 groups on campus, including art, band, choir, chorale, chorus, computers, cross-cultural journal, dance, debate, drama, ethnic, film, forensics, gay, honors, international, jazz band, literary magazine, newspaper, orchestra, outdoors, pep band, photography, political, professional, radio and TV, religious, social, social service, student government, and symphony. Popular campus events include Gender Studies Symposium, International Affairs Symposium, and Environmental Studies Symposium.

Sports: There are 9 intercollegiate sports for men and 10 for women, and 10 intramural sports for men and 10 for women. Facilities include indoor and outdoor swimming pools, 6 tennis courts (3 covered), Astroturf football field, basketball and volleyball courts, softball and baseball fields, a track, and weight and aerobics rooms. There is also a 3700-seat stadium and a 2200-seat auditorium/arena.

Disabled Students: 80% of the campus is accessible. Wheelchair ramps, elevators, special parking, specially equipped rest rooms, special class scheduling, lowered drinking fountains, lowered telephones, and special housing are available.

Services: Counseling and information services are available, as is tutoring in every subject. There are mentors, note takers, books on tape, and math and writing skills centers. There is a reader service for the blind.

Campus Safety and Security: Measures include 24-hour foot and vehicle patrol, self-defense education, security escort services, and shuttle buses. There are informal discussions, pamphlets/posters/films, emergency telephones, lighted pathways/sidewalks, and card key locks in all residence halls.

Programs of Study: LC confers the B.A. degree. Master's degrees are also awarded. Bachelor's degrees are awarded in AGRICULTURE (environmental studies), BIOLOGICAL SCIENCE (biochemistry and biology/biological science), COMMUNICATIONS AND THE ARTS (art history and appreciation, communications, dramatic arts, English, fine arts, languages, music, and studio art), COMPUTER AND PHYSICAL SCIENCE (chemistry, computer science, mathematics, and physics), SOCIAL SCIENCE (anthropology, East Asian studies, economics, French studies, German area studies, Hispanic American studies, history, interdisciplinary studies, international relations, philosophy, political science/

government, psychology, religion, and sociology). Biology, psychology, and history are the largest.

Required: To graduate, students must complete a total of 128 semester hours with a 2.0 GPA. A third of this total generally falls in the major program, a third in electives, and a third in general requirements, which includes a required first-year course, 12 hours in scientific and quantitative reasoning, 8 hours in international studies, 3 semesters of a foreign language, 2 semesters of phys ed, and 1 course in creative arts. Certain majors require a thesis or a senior project/recital.

Special: LC offers cross-registration with the Oregon Independent College Association, which includes Reed College and the University of Portland; internships; study-abroad programs encompassing 60 countries; semesters in Washington and New York City; and dual and student-designed majors. A 3-2 engineering program is available with Columbia and Washington Universities, the University of Southern California, and the Oregon Graduate Institute. There are 5 national honor societies, including Phi Beta Kappa.

Faculty/Classroom: 52% of faculty are male; 48%, female. 100% both teach and do research. No introductory courses are taught by graduate students. The average class size in an introductory lecture is 25; in a laboratory, 21; and in a regular course, 20.

Admissions: 59% of the 2005-2006 applicants were accepted. The SAT scores for the 2005-2006 freshman class were: Verbal--1% below 500, 21% between 500 and 599, 48% between 600 and 700, and 30% above 700; Math--1% below 500, 31% between 500 and 599, 51% between 600 and 700, and 17% above 700. The ACT scores were 3% below 21, 12% between 21 and 23, 18% between 24 and 26, 23% between 27 and 28, and 44% above 28. 70% of the current freshmen were in the top fifth of their class; 93% were in the top two fifths.

Requirements: The SAT or ACT is required. In addition, a GED may be accepted. It is recommended that applicants have 4 years each of English and math, 3 to 4 years of science, 3 years each of history/social studies and foreign language, and 1 year of fine arts. An essay is required and an interview recommended. The college also admits exceptional students through the Portfolio Path option. Portfolios should include 4 samples of graded work from junior or senior year: 2 writing, 1 quantitative, and 1 of the student's choice. A GPA of 2.0 is required. AP credits are accepted. Important factors in the admissions decision are advanced placement or honor courses, recommendations by school officials, and extracurricular activities record.

Procedure: Freshmen are admitted fall and spring. Entrance exams should be taken during the spring of the junior year and the fall of the senior year. There is a deferred admissions plan. Early decision applications should be filed by December 1; regular applications, by February 1 for fall entry, December 1 for spring entry, and May 1 for summer entry, along with a $50 fee. Notification of early decision is sent January 15; regular decision, April 1. 170 applicants were on the 2005 waiting list; 43 were admitted. Applications are accepted on-line.

Transfer: 56 transfer students enrolled in 2004-2005. Applicants must submit high school and college transcripts, 2 essays, and SAT or ACT scores, if they have less than 2 years of transferable credit. 60 of 128 credits required for the bachelor's degree must be completed at LC.

Visiting: There are regularly scheduled orientations for prospective students, including campus tours, class visits, interviews, special-interest appointments, overnight stays in residence halls, and 4 open house events. There are guides for informal visits and visitors may sit in on classes and stay overnight. To schedule a visit, contact the Visit Coordinator, Office of Admissions.

Financial Aid: In 2005-2006, 60% of all full-time freshmen and 61% of continuing full-time students received some form of financial aid. 60% of full-time freshmen and 61% of continuing full-time students received need-based aid. The average freshman award was $23,873. Need-based scholarships or need-based grants averaged $20,519 ($34,440 maximum); need-based self-help aid (loans and jobs) averaged $5330 ($7125 maximum); and other non-need-based awards and non-need-based scholarships averaged $6753. The average financial indebtedness of the 2005 graduate was $19,156. The FAFSA is required. The deadline for filing freshman financial aid applications for fall entry is March 1.

International Students: There were 96 international students enrolled in a recent year. The school actively recruits these students. They must take the TOEFL and also take ECPE, FCE, CAE, CPE, or IELTS.

Computers: Wireless access is available. Approximately 160 PCs are available to undergraduate students in open labs. In addition, wireless network access is available in the Boley Law Library, other student areas on the law campus, Watzek Library, the Dovecote Coffee house, and Maggie's Café. It is possible to access online reserves, read e-mail, and browse the Web from anywhere in the libraries. All students may access the system 24 hours a day. There are no time limits and no fees.

Graduates: In a recent year, 377 bachelor's degrees were awarded. The most popular majors were social sciences (19%), biology/life sciences (11%), and psychology (11%). In an average class, 1% graduate in 3 years or less, 59% graduate in 4 years or less, 66% graduate in 5 years or less, and 66% graduate in 6 years or less. 37 companies recruited on campus in a recent year. Of a recent graduating class, 13% were enrolled in graduate school within 6 months of graduation and 70% were employed.

Admissions Contact: Michael B. Sexton, Dean of Admissions.
E-mail: *admissions@lclark.edu* Web: *www.lclark.edu*

LINFIELD COLLEGE   B-2
McMinnville, OR 97128-6894

	(503) 883-2213
	(800) 640-2287; Fax: (503) 883-2472
Full-time: 773 men, 935 women	Faculty: 107; IIB, -$
Part-time: 28 men, 14 women	Ph.D.s: 92%
Graduate: none	Student/Faculty: 16 to 1
Year: 4-1-4, summer session	Tuition: $23,022
Application Deadline: February 15	Room & Board: $6610
Freshman Class: 2131 applied, 1560 accepted, 488 enrolled	
SAT Verbal/Math: 560/580*	ACT: 24* VERY COMPETITIVE

Linfield College, chartered in 1858 by the Oregon Territorial Legislature, is an independent, comprehensive undergraduate institution with a broad liberal arts core. There are 3 undergraduate schools. In addition to regional accreditation, Linfield has baccalaureate program accreditation with CAAHEP, CCNE, and NASM. The library contains 173,960 volumes, 17,649 microform items, and 32,537 audio/video tapes/CDs/DVDs, and subscribes to 1275 periodicals including electronic. Computerized library services include the card catalog, interlibrary loans, database searching, Internet access, and laptop Internet portals. Special learning facilities include a learning resource center, art gallery, radio station, a writing center, psychology lab, computer lab, anthropology museum, multimedia studio, speaking center, and the Linfield Research Institute. The 193-acre campus is in a small town 40 miles southwest of Portland. Including any residence halls, there are 66 buildings.

Student Life: 57% of undergraduates are from Oregon. Students are from 26 states, 19 foreign countries, and Canada. 85% are from public schools. 79% are white. 38% are Protestant; 11% Catholic. The average age of freshmen is 18; all undergraduates, 20. 18% do not continue beyond their first year; 68% remain to graduate.

Housing: 1287 students can be accommodated in college housing, which includes single-sex and coed dorms, on-campus apartments, off-campus apartments, and fraternity houses. On-campus housing is guaranteed for all 4 years. 74% of students live on campus; of those, 80% remain on campus on weekends. All students may keep cars.

Activities: 26% of men belong to 1 local and 3 national fraternities; 30% of women belong to 1 local and 3 national sororities. There are 60 groups on campus, including art, band, bowling, cheerleading, choir, chorale, chorus, computers, dance, debate, drama, ethnic, fishing, forensics, gay, honors, international, Isis (women's issues), jazz band, literary magazine, musical theater, newspaper, opera, orchestra, pep band, photography, political, professional, radio and TV, religious, social, social service, student government, symphony, tennis, ultimate frisbee, vegan and yearbook. Popular campus events include Multicultural Club Talent Show and Oregon Nobel Laureate Symposium.

Sports: There are 9 intercollegiate sports for men and 10 for women, and 7 intramural sports for men and 7 for women. Facilities include a football field and all-weather track, a complex with a 2200-seat gym, 3 basketball courts, a 25-yard swimming pool, 4 racquetball courts, a 3200-square-foot weight room, a field house with 3 tennis courts, 4 hitting cages, an indoor track, and a baseball facility. There also are soccer fields, and additional basketball, tennis, and racquetball courts.

Disabled Students: 80% of the campus is accessible. Wheelchair ramps, elevators, special parking, specially equipped rest rooms, special class scheduling, lowered drinking fountains, lowered telephones, and special housing are available.

Services: Counseling and information services are available, as is tutoring in every subject. There is a reader service for the blind and remedial math. There is also the Linfield Speaking Center and Linfield Writing Lab.

Campus Safety and Security: Measures include 24-hour foot and vehicle patrol, self-defense education, security escort services, and informal discussions. There are pamphlets/posters/films, emergency telephones, and lighted pathways/sidewalks.

Programs of Study: Linfield confers B.A., B.S., and B.S.N. degrees. Bachelor's degrees are awarded in BIOLOGICAL SCIENCE (biology/biological science), BUSINESS (accounting, banking and finance, business administration and management, and international business management), COMMUNICATIONS AND THE ARTS (art, communications, creative writing, dramatic arts, English, French, German, Japanese, music, and Spanish), COMPUTER AND PHYSICAL SCIENCE (applied physics, chemistry, computer science, mathematics, physics, and science), EDUCATION (athletic training, elementary, health, and physical), ENGINEERING AND ENVIRONMENTAL DESIGN (environmental science), HEALTH PROFESSIONS (exercise science), SOCIAL SCIENCE (anthropology, economics, history, philosophy, political science/government, psychology, religion, and sociology). Business, elementary education, and biology are the strongest academically.

Required: To graduate, students must have a 2.0 GPA and complete 125 credit hours, including 35 to 45 in the major. Core requirements include courses from the sciences, literature, fine arts, religion or philosophy, the social sciences, and history. Math proficiency and an inquiry seminar in writing are required. Students must also take courses in American pluralism and global diversity, and also 3 credits of activity courses (phys ed, music, or community service).

Special: During the January term, academic classes are conducted in such areas as New York City, Hawaii, China, Japan, Ireland, Mexico, and Ghana. Linfield also has a Division Continuing Education with majors offered throughout Oregon and online. Cross-registration with the Oregon Independent Colles Association, internships, study-abroad for a semester in 11 countries, a Washington semester, work-study programs, B.A.-B.S. degrees, an accelerated degree, student-designed majors and a 3-2 engineering degree with Oregon State and Washington State Universities, and the University of Southern California are available. There are 16 national honor societies and 12 departmental honors programs.

Faculty/Classroom: 59% of faculty are male; 41%, female. All both teach and do research. The average class size in a laboratory is 11 and in a regular course, 17.

Admissions: 73% of the 2005-2006 applicants were accepted. The SAT scores for the 2005-2006 freshman class were: Verbal--19% below 500, 46% between 500 and 599, 31% between 600 and 700, and 5% above 700; Math--17% below 500, 40% between 500 and 599, 37% between 600 and 700, and 7% above 700. The ACT scores were 11% below 21, 38% between 21 and 23, 23% between 24 and 26, 13% between 27 and 28, and 15% above 28. 59% of the current freshmen were in the top fifth of their class; 86% were in the top two fifths. There were 3 National Merit finalists and 1 semifinalist. 29 freshmen graduated first in their class.

Requirements: The SAT or ACT is required. In addition, applicants should have 4 years each of English and math, 3 years of science, and 2 years each of foreign language, history, and social studies. An essay is required, and an interview is recommended. The GED is accepted. AP and CLEP credits are accepted. Important factors in the admissions decision are advanced placement or honor courses, evidence of special talent, and recommendations by school officials.

Procedure: Freshmen are admitted fall and spring. Entrance exams should be taken during the fall of the senior year. There are early admissions and deferred admissions plans. Early decision applications should be filed by November 15; regular applications, by February 15 for fall entry and December 1 for spring entry, along with a $40 fee. Notification of early decision is sent January 15; regular decision, April 1. 15 applicants were on the 2005 waiting list. Applications are accepted on-line.

Transfer: Applicants must have a minimum 2.0 GPA from an accredited institution to be considered. An interview is also recommended. 30 of 125 credits required for the bachelor's degree must be completed at Linfield.

Visiting: There are regularly scheduled orientations for prospective students, including tours and interviews. There are guides for informal visits and visitors may sit in on classes and stay overnight. To schedule a visit, contact the Admissions Office.

Financial Aid: In 2005-2006, 90% of all full-time freshmen and 89% of continuing full-time students received some form of financial aid. 65% of full-time freshmen and 67% of continuing full-time students received need-based aid. The average freshman award was $18,671. Need-based scholarships or need-based grants averaged $7730; and need-based self-help aid (loans and jobs) averaged $5944. All of undergraduates work part time. Average annual earnings from campus work are $1010. The average financial indebtedness of the 2005 graduate was $24,594. Linfield is a member of CSS. The FAFSA and CSS profile for early action applicants only are required. The priority date for freshman financial aid applications for fall entry is February 1.

International Students: There are 70 international students enrolled. The school actively recruits these students. They must score satisfactorily on the written TOEFL or on the electronic version and also take the MELAB.

Computers: Wireless access is available. The main campus has 228 PCs in 8 public labs and 10 departmental labs for student use. Some labs are open 24 hours a day, 7 days per week. Approximately 45% of the computers are Macs, while the other 55% are PCs. All residences have high-speed Internet access and wireless network access is available in many public and classroom areas. All students may access the system. There are no time limits and no fees.

Graduates: From July 1, 2004 to June 30, 2005, 311 bachelor's degrees were awarded. The most popular majors were elementary education (11%), business (6%), and psychology (6%). In an average class, 2% graduate in 3 years or less, 59% graduate in 4 years or less, 67% graduate in 5 years or less, and 68% graduate in 6 years or less. 10 companies recruited on campus in 2004-2005. Of the 2004 graduating class, 22% were enrolled in graduate school within 6 months of graduation and 84% were employed.

Admissions Contact: Lisa Knodle-Bragiel, Director of Admissions.
E-mail: *admission@linfield.edu* Web: *www.linfield.edu*

MARYLHURST UNIVERSITY · B-1

Marylhurst, OR 97036
(503) 699-6268
(800) 634-9982; Fax: (503) 635-6585

Full-time: 66 men, 178 women	Faculty: 38
Part-time: 146 men, 427 women	Ph.D.s: 56%
Graduate: 132 men, 251 women	Student/Faculty: 6 to 1
Year: quarters, summer session	Tuition: $14,220
Application Deadline: open	Room & Board: n/app
Freshman Class: n/av	
SAT or ACT: not required	NONCOMPETITIVE

Marylhurst University, founded in 1893, is a private, commuter, liberal arts institution affiliated with the Roman Catholic Church. The primary emphasis is on innovative programs and flexible options for adults. There are 17 undergraduate and 4 graduate schools. In addition to regional accreditation, Marylhurst has baccalaureate program accreditation with NASM. The library contains 89,391 volumes, 16 microform items, and 3790 audio/video tapes/CDs/DVDs, and subscribes to 403 periodicals including electronic. Computerized library services include the card catalog, interlibrary loans, database searching, Internet access, and laptop Internet portals. Special learning facilities include an art gallery. The 68-acre campus is in a suburban area 10 miles south of Portland. Including any residence halls, there are 14 buildings.

Student Life: 89% of undergraduates are from Oregon. Students are from 28 states, 16 foreign countries, and Canada. 78% are white. The average age of freshmen is 34; all undergraduates, 36.

Housing: All students commute. Alcohol is not permitted. All students may keep cars.

Activities: There are no fraternities or sororities. There are 6 groups on campus, including art, chorale, honors, international, jazz band, orchestra, professional, and symphony. Popular campus events include Alumni Days and Commencement Weekend.

Sports: There is no sports program at Marylhurst.

Disabled Students: 75% of the campus is accessible. Wheelchair ramps, elevators, special parking, specially equipped rest rooms, lowered drinking fountains, and lowered telephones are available.

Services: Counseling and information services are available, as is tutoring in some subjects, including math and writing. There is a reader service for the blind.

Campus Safety and Security: Measures include 24-hour foot and vehicle patrol, security escort services, emergency telephones, and lighted pathways/sidewalks.

Programs of Study: Marylhurst confers B.A., B.S., B.F.A., and B.Music Therapy degrees. Master's degrees are also awarded. Bachelor's degrees are awarded in BUSINESS (business administration and management, management science, and real estate), COMMUNICATIONS AND THE ARTS (art, communications, English as a second/foreign language, fine arts, and music), COMPUTER AND PHYSICAL SCIENCE (science), HEALTH PROFESSIONS (art therapy and music therapy), SOCIAL SCIENCE (anthropology, human development, interdisciplinary studies, ministries, psychology, religion, social science, and sociology). Business and leadership, human sciences, and communication are the largest.

Required: To graduate, students must have a minimum 2.0 GPA and complete 180 quarter credits, including 60 to 145 in the major. 60 credits must be upper division. Distribution requirements vary according to major but include: Life and Learning Skills--9 outcomes; Arts and Ideas--5 outcomes; The Human Community--6 outcomes; and Natural World--3 outcomes. Some majors also require internship.

Special: Cross-registration may be arranged through the Oregon Independent College Association. Marylhurst offers work-study programs, B.A.-B.S. degrees, internships, an interdisciplinary studies degree, dual and student-designed majors, accelerated degree programs in all majors, credit for college-level learning, non-degree study, and pass/fail options. There is 1 national honor society.

Faculty/Classroom: 51% of faculty are male; 49%, female. 84% teach undergraduates. No introductory courses are taught by graduate students. The average class size in an introductory lecture is 10 and in a regular course, 10.

Requirements: Applicants who have graduated within two years of application must supply SAT or ACT scores; one letter of recommendation; high school GPA of 2.5 or GED score of 50. AP and CLEP credits are accepted.

Procedure: Freshmen are admitted to all sessions. Application deadlines are open. Applications are accepted on-line.

Transfer: 400 transfer students enrolled in 2004-2005. Almost all students are returning adults who have transferred prior college credit. Grades of C- or better transfer for credit. 45 of 180 quarter credits required for the bachelor's degree must be completed at Marylhurst.

Visiting: There are regularly scheduled orientations for prospective students, including addressing registration and financial aid issues, academic advising, and use of the library, cafeteria, and bookstore. There are guides for informal visits and visitors may sit in on classes and stay overnight. To schedule a visit, contact the Admissions Department at *admissions@marylhurst.edu*.

Financial Aid: In 2005-2006, 70% of all full-time students received some form of financial aid. 60% of full-time freshmen and 66% of continuing full-time students received need-based aid. The average freshman award was $10,000. The FAFSA and an institutional application are required.

International Students: International students must take the TOEFL.

Computers: All students may access the system. There are no time limits and no fees.

Graduates: From July 1, 2004 to June 30, 2005, 138 bachelor's degrees were awarded. The most popular majors were business and leadership (24%), communications (12%), and interdisciplinary studies (10%).

Admissions Contact: Katie Abbott, Assistant Director of Admissions. E-mail: *admissions@marylhurst.edu* Web: *www.marylhurst.edu*

NORTHWEST CHRISTIAN COLLEGE · B-2

Eugene, OR 97401-3727
(541) 684-7201
(877) 463-6622; Fax: (541) 684-7317

Full-time: 151 men, 226 women	Faculty: 19
Part-time: 10 men, 15 women	Ph.D.s: 47%
Graduate: 42 men, 47 women	Student/Faculty: 20 to 1
Year: quarters, summer session	Tuition: $18,380
Application Deadline: n/av	Room & Board: $591
Freshman Class: 179 applied, 114 accepted, 50 enrolled	
SAT Verbal/Math: 500/460*	ACT: 20 COMPETITIVE

Northwest Christian College, founded in 1895, is a private institution affiliated with the Christian Church, offering programs in the arts and sciences, business, education, and ministries. In addition to regional accreditation, NCC has baccalaureate program accreditation with IACBE. The library contains 60,250 volumes, 766 microform items, and 10,367 audio/video tapes/CDs/DVDs, and subscribes to 261 periodicals including electronic. Computerized library services include the card catalog, interlibrary loans, database searching, and Internet access. Special learning facilities include a learning resource center. The 8-acre campus is in an urban area 125 miles south of Portland. Including any residence halls, there are 14 buildings.

Student Life: 92% of undergraduates are from Oregon. Students are from 8 states. 94% are from public schools. 70% are white. 64% are claim no religious affiliation; 35% Protestant. The average age of freshmen is 18; all undergraduates, 30. 38% do not continue beyond their first year; 38% remain to graduate.

Housing: 213 students can be accommodated in college housing, which includes single-sex and coed dorms and off-campus apartments. On-campus housing is guaranteed for the freshman year only. 73% of students commute. Alcohol is not permitted. All students may keep cars.

Activities: There are no fraternities or sororities. There are 15 groups on campus, including cheerleading, choir, chorale, debate, drama, forensics, literary magazine, musical theater, newspaper, religious, social service, student government, and yearbook. Popular campus events include Annual Musical, Spirit Week, and Wellness Week.

Sports: There is 1 intercollegiate sport for men and 2 for women, and 4 intramural sports for men and 4 for women. Facilities include an event center with a basketball court, fitness rooms, locker rooms, and softball practice area.

Disabled Students: 60% of the campus is accessible. Wheelchair ramps, elevators, special parking, specially equipped rest rooms, special class scheduling, lowered drinking fountains, and lowered telephones are available.

Services: Counseling and information services are available, as is tutoring in most subjects. There is remedial math, reading, and writing.

Campus Safety and Security: Measures include 24-hour foot and vehicle patrol, security escort services, emergency telephones, and lighted pathways/sidewalks.

Programs of Study: NCC confers B.A. and B.S. degrees. Associate and master's degrees are also awarded. Bachelor's degrees are awarded in BUSINESS (accounting, business administration and management, and management information systems), COMMUNICATIONS AND THE ARTS (communications and music), COMPUTER AND PHYSICAL SCIENCE (computer science), EDUCATION (education and elementary), HEALTH PROFESSIONS (exercise science and health care administration), SOCIAL SCIENCE (human services, humanities, interdisciplinary studies, international studies, ministries, psychology, and social science). Business administration, and elementary education are the strongest academically. Elementary education and psychology are the largest.

Required: To graduate, students must complete 124-186 quarter credits with at least 40 in the major and a minimum GPA of 2.00. The core curriculum consists of 55-86 credit hours in humanities, social sciences, math and science, and Bible; a 1-credit-hour chapel for every term enrolled is also required as are 3 service credits.

Special: NCC offers internships, study abroad in 4 countries, a Washington semester, work study, accelerated degree programs, and student-designed majors.

Faculty/Classroom: 58% of faculty are male; 42%, female. All teach undergraduates. No introductory courses are taught by graduate students. The average class size in an introductory lecture is 40 and in a regular course, 25.

Admissions: 64% of the 2005-2006 applicants were accepted. The SAT scores for the 2005-2006 freshman class were: Verbal--50% below 500, 27% between 500 and 599, and 23% between 600 and 700; Math--61% below 500, 30% between 500 and 599, and 9% between 600 and 700. The ACT scores were 57% below 21, 21% between 21 and 23, 7% between 24 and 26, and 14% between 27 and 28. 36% of the current freshmen were in the top fifth of their class; 67% were in the top two fifths. 1 freshman graduated first in the class.

Requirements: The SAT or ACT is required. In addition, students are required to submit a completed admission application, high school transcripts, and 2 references. An interview is recommended. A GPA of 2.5 is required. AP and CLEP credits are accepted. Important factors in the admissions decision are advanced placement or honor courses, recommendations by school officials, and extracurricular activities record.

Procedure: Freshmen are admitted fall and spring. There are early admissions, deferred admissions, and rolling admissions plans. Notification is sent on a rolling basis. Applications are accepted on-line. Check with the school for current deadlines and fee.

Transfer: 55 transfer students enrolled in a recent year. Students are required to submit a completed application, official transcripts from each college or university attended, an academic reference, and official high school transcripts if they have fewer than 36 transferable credits. 30 of 124 credits required for the bachelor's degree must be completed at NCC.

Visiting: There are regularly scheduled orientations for prospective students. There are guides for informal visits and visitors may sit in on classes and stay overnight. To schedule a visit, contact Admissions at (541) 684-7209.

Financial Aid: In 2005-2006, all full-time students received some form of financial aid. Need-based scholarships or need-based grants averaged $15,076; and need-based self-help aid (loans and jobs) averaged $3694. The average financial indebtedness of the 2005 graduate was $17,585. NCC is a member of CSS. The FAFSA and the college's own financial statement are required.

International Students: No international students are currently enrolled. A satisfactory score is required on the written TOEFL.

Computers: Wireless access is available in the library and bookstore/café. All students may access the system. There are no time limits and no fees. It is strongly recommended that all students have a PC.

Graduates: From July 1, 2004 to June 30, 2005, 103 bachelor's degrees were awarded. The most popular majors were management (51%), teacher education (27%), and psychology (6%). In an average class, 30% graduate in 4 years or less, 38% graduate in 5 years or less, and 38% graduate in 6 years or less. Of the 2004 graduating class, 13% were enrolled in graduate school within 6 months of graduation and 72% were employed.

Admissions Contact: Randy Jones, Dean of Admissions.
E-mail: *admissions@nwcc.edu* Web: *www.nwcc.edu*

OREGON INSTITUTE OF TECHNOLOGY

Klamath Falls, OR 97601-8801

B-4

(541) 885-1150
Fax: (541) 885-1115

Full-time: 1115 men, 840 women	**Faculty:** 107; IIB, -$
Part-time: 590 men, 555 women	**Ph.D.s:** 31%
Graduate: 15 men	**Student/Faculty:** 18 to 1
Year: quarters, summer session	**Tuition:** $3750 ($12,530)
Application Deadline: see profile	**Room & Board:** $5160
Freshman Class: n/av	
SAT or ACT: required	**COMPETITIVE**

Oregon Institute of Technology, the only public institute of technology in the Pacific Northwest, provides degree programs in engineering and health technologies, management, communications and applied sciences that prepare students to be effective participants in their professional, public and international communities. There are 3 undergraduate schools and 1 graduate school. Figures in the above capsule and in this profile are approximate. In addition to regional accreditation, OIT has baccalaureate program accreditation with ABET and NLN. The library contains 145,988 volumes, 158,278 microform items, and 2069 audio/video tapes/CDs/DVDs, and subscribes to 1815 periodicals including electronic. Computerized library services include the card catalog, interlibrary loans, and database searching. Special learning facilities include a learning resource center, art gallery, and radio station. The 173-acre campus is in a small town 60 miles east of Medford in south central Oregon. Including any residence halls, there are 12 buildings.

Student Life: 85% of undergraduates are from Oregon. Students are from 35 states and 17 foreign countries. 95% are from public schools. 80% are white. The average age of freshmen is 23; all undergraduates, 26. 26% do not continue beyond their first year; 29% remain to graduate.

Housing: 500 students can be accommodated in college housing, which includes single-sex and coed dorms. On-campus housing is guaranteed for all 4 years. 82% of students commute. All students may keep cars.

Activities: 3% of men belong to 1 local and 1 national fraternity; 3% of women belong to 1 local and 1 national sorority. There are 37 groups on campus, including cheerleading, computers, ethnic, honors, international, newspaper, pep band, professional, radio and TV, religious, social, and student government. Popular campus events include Tech Challenge, Family Weekend Tech Fest, and a skills contest for business and math students.

Sports: There are 4 intercollegiate sports for men and 6 for women. Facilities include a 3000-seat stadium, a 2066-seat gym, football, baseball, and softball fields, free weights and aerobics areas, an indoor swimming pool, a track, and tennis, volleyball, basketball, and badminton courts.

Disabled Students: 90% of the campus is accessible. Wheelchair ramps, elevators, special parking, specially equipped rest rooms, and special class scheduling are available.

Services: Counseling and information services are available, as is tutoring in some subjects, including math, sciences, and computers. There is a reader service for the blind, and remedial math, reading, and writing.

Campus Safety and Security: Measures include 24-hour foot and vehicle patrol, security escort services, and lighted pathways/sidewalks.

Programs of Study: OIT confers the B.S. degree. Associate and master's degrees are also awarded. Bachelor's degrees are awarded in BUSINESS (management information systems), ENGINEERING AND ENVIRONMENTAL DESIGN (civil engineering, computer technology, electrical/electronics engineering technology, engineering technology, environmental science, industrial administration/management, laser electro-optics technology, manufacturing technology, mechanical engineering technology, and surveying engineering), HEALTH PROFESSIONS (dental hygiene, health science, radiograph medical technology, and ultrasound technology), SOCIAL SCIENCE (industrial and organizational psychology). Engineering technology programs are the largest.

Required: General education requirements include 12 hours in social science and 9 hours each in communication, business, and humanities. Students also must take 9 hours in English composition and technical report writing. Completion of about 200 quarter hours, with a minimum GPA of 2.0, is required to graduate.

Special: Cross-registration with Klamath Community College, internships in all majors, and co-op programs in all engineering technologies are available. OIT also offers advanced degree programs in software engineering technology and vascular imaging. There are 2 national honor societies.

Faculty/Classroom: 77% of faculty are male; 23%, female. All teach undergraduates. The average class size in an introductory lecture is 30; in a laboratory, 18; and in a regular course, 30.

Requirements: The SAT or ACT is required, for placement purposes; however, a satisfactory score on the SAT or on the ACT is required for applicants who do not meet the minimum GPA requirement. Applicants must have 14 academic units, including 4 years of English, 3 each of math and social sciences, and 2 each of science and a foreign language. The GED is accepted. A GPA of 2.5 is required. AP and CLEP credits are accepted.

Procedure: Freshmen are admitted to all sessions. Entrance exams should be taken The SAT or ACT should be taken during the senior year, and placement tests just prior to registration. There are early admissions and rolling admissions plan. Check with the school for current deadlines. Notification is sent on a rolling basis. The fall 2005 application fee was $50.

Transfer: Applicants must have a minimum GPA of 2.0 and at least 24 quarter credit hours; students with fewer credit hours must submit high school transcripts or GED scores. An associate degree is recommended. 45 of 190 credits required for the bachelor's degree must be completed at OIT.

Visiting: There are regularly scheduled orientations for prospective students, including tours and meetings with admissions counselors, faculty, and students. There are guides for informal visits and visitors may sit in on classes and stay overnight. To schedule a visit, contact the Admissions Office.

Financial Aid: The FAFSA is required. Check with the school for current application deadlines.

International Students: The school actively recruits these students. They must score satisfactorily on the written TOEFL.

Computers: All students may access the system 24 hours daily during the last 2 weeks of the quarter and 18 hours daily otherwise. There are no time limits and no fees.

Admissions Contact: Palmer Muntz, Director of Admissions. A video is available. E-mail: *muntzp@oit.edu* Web: *www.oit.edu*

OREGON STATE UNIVERSITY
Corvallis, OR 97331-2106

B-2

(541) 737-4411
(800) 291-4192; Fax: (541) 737-2482

Full-time: 7510 men, 6480 women
Part-time: 810 men, 805 women
Graduate: 1710 men, 1650 women
Year: quarters, summer session
Application Deadline: see profile
Freshman Class: n/av
SAT or ACT: required

Faculty: 1352; I, --$
Ph.D.s: 85%
Student/Faculty: 10 to 1
Tuition: $4710 ($17,500)
Room & Board: $6400

COMPETITIVE

Oregon State University, founded in 1868, is the oldest institution in the Oregon state system, offering liberal arts and preprofessional programs. There are 10 undergraduate and 12 graduate schools. Figures in the above capsule and profile are approximate. In addition to regional accreditation, OSU has baccalaureate program accreditation with AACSB, ABET, ACCE, ACEJMC, ACPE, AHEA, NASM, NCATE, and SAF. The 4 libraries contain 1,403,451 volumes, 1,912,023 microform items, and 6225 audio/video tapes/CDs/DVDs, and subscribe to 14,777 periodicals including electronic. Computerized library services include the card catalog and database searching. Special learning facilities include a learning resource center, art gallery, natural history museum, radio station, TV station, arboretum, wave research lab, research farm, research vessel, and the Linus Pauling Collection. The 400-acre campus is in a small town 80 miles south of Portland. Including any residence halls, there are 203 buildings.

Student Life: 85% of undergraduates are from Oregon. Students are from 49 states, 90 foreign countries, and Canada. 75% are white. The average age of freshmen is 19; all undergraduates, 23. 20% do not continue beyond their first year; 60% remain to graduate.

Housing: 5593 students can be accommodated in college housing, which includes coed dorms, married-student housing, fraternity houses, and sorority houses. In addition, there are honors houses, special-interest houses, and cooperative houses. All residences are smoke free. On-campus housing is available on a first-come, first-served basis. 71% of students commute. Alcohol is not permitted. All students may keep cars.

Activities: 15% of men belong to 25 national fraternities; 11% of women belong to 13 national sororities. There are 350 groups on campus, including art, band, cheerleading, chess, choir, chorale, chorus, computers, dance, drama, drill team, drum and bugle corps, ethnic, film, gay, honors, international, jazz band, literary magazine, marching band, musical theater, newspaper, orchestra, pep band, photography, political, professional, radio and TV, religious, social, social service, student government, symphony, and yearbook. Popular campus events include Renaissance Fair and Native American Pow Wow.

Sports: There are 7 intercollegiate sports for men and 8 for women, and 19 intramural sports for men and 17 for women. Facilities include 2 fitness centers, a 10,400-seat gym, a 40,000-seat stadium, indoor and outdoor recreation centers, weight and exercise rooms, bowling alleys, and numerous courts and playing fields.

Disabled Students: 92% of the campus is accessible. Wheelchair ramps, elevators, special parking, specially equipped rest rooms, special class scheduling, lowered drinking fountains, lowered telephones, note takers, interpreters for the deaf, and visual-aid equipment for the blind are available.

Services: Counseling and information services are available, as is tutoring in most subjects, including chemistry, computer science, math, psychology and counseling, and physics. There is a reader service for the blind, and remedial math, reading, and writing. Facilities include a communication skills center and a math sciences learning center.

Campus Safety and Security: Measures include emergency telephones and lighted pathways/sidewalks.

Programs of Study: OSU confers B.A., B.S., and B.F.A. degrees. Master's and doctoral degrees are also awarded. Bachelor's degrees are awarded in AGRICULTURE (agricultural business management, agricultural economics, agriculture, animal science, fishing and fisheries, forest engineering, forestry and related sciences, forestry production and processing, horticulture, poultry science, range/farm management, and soil science), BIOLOGICAL SCIENCE (biochemistry, biology/biological science, biophysics, botany, entomology, microbiology, nutrition, plant pathology, wildlife biology, and zoology), BUSINESS (accounting, business administration and management, hotel/motel and restaurant management, marketing management, and marketing/retailing/merchandising), COMMUNICATIONS AND THE ARTS (apparel design, art, dramatic arts, English, French, German, music, Spanish, speech/debate/rhetoric, and visual and performing arts), COMPUTER AND PHYSICAL SCIENCE (chemistry, computer science, geology, mathematics, physics, and science), EDUCATION (health), ENGINEERING AND ENVIRONMENTAL DESIGN (chemical engineering, civil engineering, computer engineering, construction management, environmental science, industrial engineering technology, landscape architecture/design, mechanical engineering, nuclear engineering, and urban design), HEALTH PROFESSIONS (environmental health science, health, health care adminis-

tration, medical technology, and nursing), SOCIAL SCIENCE (American studies, anthropology, economics, family/consumer studies, fashion design and technology, food science, geography, history, home economics, human development, liberal arts/general studies, philosophy, political science/government, psychology, sociology, and textiles and clothing). Engineering, biochemistry, and forestry are the strongest academically. Business, liberal arts, and mechanical engineering are the largest.

Required: To graduate, students must complete at least 192 quarter credits with a GPA of 2.0. The required core curriculum includes a total of 37 credits in writing and communications, math, humanities and social studies, natural sciences, and fitness. Students must take a writing-intensive course in their major field and meet additional distribution requirements.

Special: OSU offers cooperative veterinary medicine programs with Washington State University and the University of Idaho; geological, metallurgical, and mining engineering programs with the University of Idaho; and an education program with the University of Oregon. Students may cross-register at any college in the Oregon state system, at member colleges of the Western Interstate Commission, and with any member of the National Student Exchange. Study abroad is possible in any of 13 countries, including New Zealand and the former Soviet Union. There is a 5-year B.A.-B.S. program in civil engineering and forest engineering, and a 3-2 engineering program with the University of Oregon. Internships, a liberal studies degree, nondegree study, and pass/fail options are also available. There are 7 national honor societies, a freshman honors program, and 20 departmental honors programs.

Faculty/Classroom: 58% of faculty are male; 42%, female. 67% teach undergraduates, 24% do research, and 67% do both.

Requirements: The SAT or ACT is required. In addition, applicants should be high school graduates or hold the GED. Required high school preparation includes 4 years of English; 3 years of math, including algebra I; 2 years of natural science; and 1 year each of U.S history, world history, and social science. Among electives, government and foreign language are strongly recommended. Some subject requirements may be fulfilled by test scores. A GPA of 3.0 is required. AP and CLEP credits are accepted. Advanced placement or honor courses is an important factor in the admission decision.

Procedure: Freshmen are admitted to all sessions. Entrance exams should be taken during the junior or senior year. There are early admissions and rolling admissions plans. Notification is sent on a rolling basis. The fall 2005 application fee was $50. Check with the school for current appication deadlines.

Transfer: Applicants who are Oregon residents must present a GPA of at least 2.25 in previous college work; for nonresidents, a GPA of 2.5. Students should have completed at least 36 hours of college credit. Either SAT or ACT scores must be submitted. 36 of 192 credits required for the bachelor's degree must be completed at OSU.

Visiting: There are regularly scheduled orientations for prospective students. There are guides for informal visits and visitors may sit in on classes and stay overnight. To schedule a visit, contact the Office of New Student Programs.

Financial Aid: OSU is a member of CSS. The FAFSA is required. Check with the school for current application deadlines.

International Students: The school actively recruits these students. They must score satisfactorily on the written TOEFL.

Computers: All students may access the system at any time. There are no time limits and no fees.

Admissions Contact: Michelle Sandlin, Director of Admissions.
E-mail: osuadmit@orst.edu
Web: http://www.oregonstate.edu/admissions

OREGON UNIVERSITY SYSTEM

The Oregon University System (OUS), is comprised of 7 distinguished public universities, reaching more than 1 million persons each year through on-campus classes, statewide public services, and lifelong learning. OUS provides the central administration for the Oregon State Board of Higher Education, an 11-member volunteer board appointed by the governor and confirmed by the Oregon legislature. The chancellor serves as the system's chief administrative officer. OUS has a three-part mission: to provide affordable access to high-quality post-secondary education for all qualified Oregonians; to improve and enrich learning in the sciences, the social sciences, the humanities, the arts, and the professions; and to help Oregon respond effectively to social, economic, and environmental challenges and opportunities. Total campus enrollment exceeds 80,000 with nearly 3,400 faculty. Campuses of the system include Eastern Oregon University, Oregon Institute of Technology, Oregon State University, Portland State University, Southern Oregon University, the University of Oregon, and Western Oregon University.

PACIFIC NORTHWEST COLLEGE OF ART B-1

Portland, OR 97209 (503) 821-8972; Fax: (503) 821-8978

Full-time: 103 men, 150 women	Faculty: n/av
Part-time: 16 men, 22 women	Ph.D.s: 79%
Graduate: none	Student/Faculty: n/av
Year: semesters	Tuition: $17,296
Application Deadline: August 15	Room & Board: n/app
Freshman Class: 120 applied, 87 accepted, 30 enrolled	
SAT or ACT: not required	SPECIAL

Pacific Northwest College of Art, founded in 1909, offers professional training in the fine and visual arts. In addition to regional accreditation, PNCA has baccalaureate program accreditation with NASAD. The library contains 12,742 volumes and 459 audio/video tapes/CDs/DVDs, and subscribes to 65 periodicals including electronic. Computerized library services include interlibrary loans. Special learning facilities include an art gallery. The 1-acre campus is in an urban area in downtown Portland. There are 3 buildings.

Student Life: 74% of undergraduates are from Oregon. Others are from 20 states, 5 foreign countries, and Canada. 87% are white. The average age of freshmen is 20; all undergraduates, 25. 37% do not continue beyond their first year; 35% remain to graduate.

Housing: There are no residence halls. All students commute.

Activities: There are no fraternities or sororities. There are some groups and organizations on campus, including art, photography, professional, and student government.

Sports: There is no sports program at PNCA.

Disabled Students: 90% of the campus is accessible. Wheelchair ramps, elevators, specially equipped rest rooms, and lowered drinking fountains are available.

Services: There is remedial writing.

Campus Safety and Security: Measures include pamphlets/posters/films, emergency telephones, and guards at building entrances.

Programs of Study: PNCA confers the B.F.A. degree. Bachelor's degrees are awarded in COMMUNICATIONS AND THE ARTS (fine arts, graphic design, illustration, painting, photography, printmaking, and sculpture). Painting is the largest.

Required: To graduate, all students must complete 120 credits, including 45 in liberal arts and science courses and 57 in a studio major. All seniors must earn a 2.0 GPA for both semesters and must complete a thesis, which is critiqued by the faculty and later exhibited.

Special: A joint B.A./B.F.A. degree is offered with Reed College. Students may cross-register with members of the Oregon Independent Colleges Association. There is a Mobility Program for 1 semester or 1 year with member schools of the Association of Schools of Art and Design. Fourth-year graphic design majors may undertake a 1-semester professional internship; internships also are strongly encouraged for juniors in all majors. Students may study abroad in 3 countries through PNCA's program or in any other country through the programs of other accredited institutions. Nondegree study and student-designed majors are possible.

Faculty/Classroom: 62% of faculty are male; 38%, female. All teach undergraduates. The average class size in a regular course is 17.

Admissions: 72% of the 2005-2006 applicants were accepted. The SAT scores for the 2005-2006 freshman class were: Verbal--37% below 500, 25% between 500 and 599, and 38% between 600 and 700; Math--50% below 500, 25% between 500 and 599, and 25% between 600 and 700. The ACT scores were 25% below 21, 25% between 21 and 23, and 50% between 24 and 26.

Requirements: Applicants should be high school graduates or have earned the GED. The application consists of high school transcripts, 2 essays, and a portfolio of at least 12 pieces of artwork. A GPA of 2.0 is required. AP credits are accepted. Evidence of special talent is an important factor in the admission decision.

Procedure: Freshmen are admitted fall and spring. There is a deferred admissions and a rolling admissions plan. Recommend application deadlines are August 15 for fall entry and December 15 for spring entry. The fall 2005 application fee was $35. Notification is sent on a rolling basis.

Transfer: 70 transfer students enrolled in 2004-2005. Applicants must submit official copies of transcripts from high school and all colleges attended. Also required are 2 essays, a resume, a portfolio of 12 to 20 images, and a portfolio index. A minimum 2.0 GPA is required. 48 of 120 credits required for the bachelor's degree must be completed at PNCA.

Visiting: There are guides for informal visits and visitors may sit in on classes. To schedule a visit, contact the Admissions Office.

Financial Aid: The FAFSA is required. The priority date for freshman financial aid applications for fall entry is March 1.

International Students: A satisfactory score is required on the written TOEFL.

Computers: All students may access the system. There are no time limits and no fees.

Graduates: In a recent year, 57 bachelor's degrees were awarded. The most popular majors were painting (32%), graphic design (18%), and photography (15%). In an average class, 26% graduate in 4 years or less, and 26% graduate in 6 years or less.

Admissions Contact: Rebecca Haas, Director of Admissions.
E-mail: *admissions@pnca.edu* Web: *www.pnca.edu*

PACIFIC UNIVERSITY B-1

Forest Grove, OR 97116 (503) 359-2218
(800) PAC-UNIV; Fax: (503) 359-2975

Full-time: 390 men, 625 women	Faculty: 87; IIA, --$
Part-time: 40 men, 40 women	Ph.D.s: 78%
Graduate: 375 men, 625 women	Student/Faculty: 12 to 1
Year: 4-1-4, summer session	Tuition: $18,570
Application Deadline: see profile	Room & Board: $5750
Freshman Class: n/av	
SAT or ACT: required	COMPETITIVE

Pacific University, founded in 1849, is an independent institution affiliated with the Congregational Church (United Church of Christ), offering degree programs in liberal arts, science, business, education, and health professions. Figures in above capsule and in this profile are approximate. In addition to regional accreditation, Pacific has baccalaureate program accreditation with NASM. The library contains 152,060 volumes, 76,609 microform items, and 3708 audio/video tapes/CDs/DVDs, and subscribes to 945 periodicals including electronic. Computerized library services include the card catalog, interlibrary loans, and database searching. Special learning facilities include a learning resource center, art gallery, radio station, TV station, and museum of the history of the university. The 55-acre campus is in a small town 25 miles west of Portland. Including any residence halls, there are 18 buildings.

Student Life: 50% of undergraduates are from out of state, mostly the West. Students are from 31 states, 7 foreign countries, and Canada. 91% are from public schools. 64% are white; 17% Asian American. The average age of freshmen is 18; all undergraduates, 20. 22% do not continue beyond their first year; 54% remain to graduate.

Housing: 680 students can be accommodated in college housing, which includes single-sex and coed dorms, off-campus apartments, and married-student housing. In addition, there are special-interest houses. On-campus housing is guaranteed for the freshman year only, is available on a first-come, first-served basis, and is available on a lottery system for upperclassmen. 50% of students live on campus; of those, 90% remain on campus on weekends. All students may keep cars.

Activities: 2% of men belong to 3 local fraternities; 6% of women belong to 3 local sororities. There are 35 groups on campus, including art, band, cheerleading, choir, chorale, chorus, computers, dance, debate, drama, ethnic, forensics, gay, honors, international, jazz band, literary magazine, musical theater, newspaper, opera, outdoor and urban recreation, orchestra, pep band, photography, political, professional, radio and TV, religious, social, social service, student government, and yearbook. Popular campus events include Hawaiian Club Luau, International Club Banquet, and Japan Day.

Sports: There are 8 intercollegiate sports for men and 8 for women, and 10 intramural sports for men and 10 for women. Facilities include a gym, various courts, a sauna, weight and wrestling rooms, a dance studio, outdoor playing fields, a field house, and racquetball courts.

Disabled Students: 80% of the campus is accessible. Wheelchair ramps, elevators, special parking, specially equipped rest rooms, and lowered drinking fountains are available.

Services: Counseling and information services are available, as is tutoring in most subjects. There is a reader service for the blind.

Campus Safety and Security: Measures include 24-hour foot and vehicle patrol, security escort services, informal discussions, and pamphlets/posters/films. There are emergency telephones and lighted pathways/sidewalks.

Programs of Study: Pacific confers B.A., B.S., and B.M. degrees. Master's and doctoral degrees are also awarded. Bachelor's degrees are awarded in BIOLOGICAL SCIENCE (biology/biological science), BUSINESS (business administration and management), COMMUNICATIONS AND THE ARTS (creative writing, dramatic arts, Japanese, literature, music, and Spanish), COMPUTER AND PHYSICAL SCIENCE (chemistry, computer science, mathematics, and physics), SOCIAL SCIENCE (economics, history, humanities, philosophy, political science/government, psychology, social work, and sociology). Natural sciences, literature, and creative writing are the strongest academically. Business administration, English and psychology are the largest.

Required: All students take a core curriculum that includes a first-year seminar and courses in writing, foreign language, social and natural sciences, art, and cross-cultural studies. A cumulative GPA of 2.0 in 124 semester hours is required for graduation. 34 to 64 hours are required in the major, depending on the discipline.

Special: Cross-registration is available with Oregon Independent Colleges and Oregon Graduate Institute of Science and Technology (OGIST). The university also offers cooperative programs with Washington University in St. Louis, OGIST, and Oregon School of Arts and Crafts, as well as study abroad in 13 countries. Full-time, semester-long internships, including one in Washington D.C., are possible. Dual majors, a general studies degree in humanities, nondegree study, 3-2 engineering programs with Washington University in St. Louis and OGIST, and an interdisciplinary program in peace and conflict studies are available. There are 2 national honor societies, a freshman honors program, and 1 departmental honors program.

Faculty/Classroom: 52% of faculty are male; 48%, female. All both teach and do research. No introductory courses are taught by graduate students. The average class size in an introductory lecture is 35; in a laboratory, 20; and in a regular course, 19.

Requirements: The SAT or ACT is required. In addition, applicants are expected to be high school graduates or to hold the GED. A personal essay is required, and an interview is recommended. A GPA of 3.0 is required. AP and CLEP credits are accepted. Important factors in the admissions decision are advanced placement or honor courses, recommendations by school officials, and extracurricular activities record.

Procedure: Freshmen are admitted fall and spring. There are deferred admissions and rolling admissions plans. Application fee is $30. Check with school for application deadliness. Notification of early decision is sent rolling ; regular decision, on a rolling basis. Applications are accepted on-line.

Transfer: 67 transfer students enrolled in a recent year. Transfer applicants must present at least a 2.75 GPA in previous college work; those with fewer than 30 semester hours or 45 quarter hours must also submit SAT or ACT test scores and high school transcripts. A personal interview is strongly recommended. 30 of 124 credits required for the bachelor's degree must be completed at Pacific.

Visiting: There are regularly scheduled orientations for prospective students, including overnight housing with current students, a campus tour, classroom visitations, and meetings with faculty and coaches. There are guides for informal visits and visitors may sit in on classes and stay overnight. To schedule a visit, contact the Admissions Office.

Financial Aid: In a recent year, 92% of all full-time freshmen and 97% of continuing full-time students received some form of financial aid. 82% of full-time freshmen and 70% of continuing full-time students received need-based aid. The average freshman award was $15,957. 54% of undergraduates worked part time. Average annual earnings from campus work were $823. The average financial indebtedness of a recent graduate was $18,500. Pacific is a member of CSS. The FAFSA is required. Check with the school for current application deadlines.

International Students: In a recent year, there were 48 international students enrolled. The school actively recruits these students. They must score satisfactorily on the written TOEFL.

Computers: All students may access the system. There are no time limits and no fees.

Graduates: In a recent year, 285 bachelor's degrees were awarded. The most popular majors were foreign language and English (11%), business and biology (11%), and physical education (9%). In an average class, 44% graduate in 4 years or less, 57% graduate in 5 years or less, and 63% graduate in 6 years or less. 10 companies recruited on campus in a recent year. Of a recent graduating class, 34% were enrolled in graduate school within 6 months of graduation and 60% were employed.

Admissions Contact: Beth Woodward, Director of Admissions.
E-mail: *admissions@pacificu.edu* Web: *www.pacificu.edu*

PORTLAND STATE UNIVERSITY   B-1
Portland, OR 97207-0751

	(503) 725-3511
	(800) 547-8887; Fax: (503) 725-5525
Full-time: 4673 men, 5415 women	**Faculty:** 635; I, --$
Part-time: 2655 men, 3174 women	**Ph.Ds:** 78%
Graduate: 2118 men, 2995 women	**Student/Faculty:** 16 to 1
Year: quarters, summer session	**Tuition:** $4278 ($13,674)
Application Deadline: open	**Room & Board:** $8175
Freshman Class: n/av	
SAT or ACT: required	**COMPETITIVE**

Portland State University, founded in 1946, is a comprehensive public institution serving a primarily commuter student body. Graduate and undergraduate degree programs are offered in liberal arts and sciences, business, education, engineering and applied science, fine and performing arts, social work, and urban and public affairs. There are 5 undergraduate and 7 graduate schools. In addition to regional accreditation, PSU has baccalaureate program accreditation with AACSB, ABET, ASLA, NASAD, and NASM. The library contains 1,300,919 volumes, 2,362,836 microform items, and 87,092 audio/video tapes/CDs/DVDs, and subscribes to 9730 periodicals including electronic. Computerized library services include the card catalog, interlibrary loans, database searching, and Internet access. Special learning facilities include a learning resource center, art gallery, radio station, a multicultural center, and a Native American center. The 49-acre campus is in an urban area in the center of Portland. Including any residence halls, there are 43 buildings.

Student Life: 87% of undergraduates are from Oregon. Students are from 47 states, 67 foreign countries, and Canada. 66% are white; 10% Asian American. The average age of freshmen is 19; all undergraduates, 26. 34% do not continue beyond their first year; 32% remain to graduate.

Housing: 1600 students can be accommodated in college housing, which includes coed dorms, on-campus apartments, off-campus apartments, fraternity houses, and freshman experience. On-campus housing is available on a first-come, first-served basis. Priority is given to out-of-town students. 89% of students commute. All students may keep cars.

Activities: 1% of men belong to 3 national fraternities; 1% of women belong to 1 local and 2 national sororities. There are 148 groups on campus, including art, band, cheerleading, chess, choir, chorale, chorus, computers, dance, debate, drama, drill team, ethnic, film, forensics, gay, honors, international, jazz band, literary magazine, musical theater, newspaper, opera, orchestra, outdoor, pep band, photography, political, professional, radio and TV, religious, social, social service, student government, students with disabilities, and symphony. Popular campus events include International Student Cultural Night, Friends of Chamber Music, and LunchBox Theater.

Sports: There are 8 intercollegiate sports for men and 9 for women, and 7 intramural sports for men and 6 for women. Facilities include a practice field, a swimming pool, an all-weather tennis facility, gyms, circuit training and weight rooms, a golf putting green, running track, and racquetball, handball, and squash courts. Nearby Civic Stadium and Duniway Park provide football, baseball, and track and field facilities.

Disabled Students: 95% of the campus is accessible. Wheelchair ramps, elevators, special parking, specially equipped rest rooms, special class scheduling, lowered drinking fountains, lowered telephones, and special housing are available.

Services: Counseling and information services are available, as is tutoring in most subjects. There is a reader service for the blind and remedial math and writing. Student Support Services, provides assistance to students who are low-income, who have a physical disability, or whose parents did not graduate from college.

Campus Safety and Security: Measures include 24-hour foot and vehicle patrol, self-defense education, security escort services, and informal discussions. There are pamphlets/posters/films, emergency telephones, lighted pathways/sidewalks, a campus watch newsletter, information lectures, and community liaison.

Programs of Study: PSU confers B.A., B.S., and B.M. degrees. Master's and doctoral degrees are also awarded. Bachelor's degrees are awarded in BIOLOGICAL SCIENCE (biochemistry and biology/biological science), BUSINESS (accounting, business administration and management, management science, marketing/retailing/merchandising, and personnel management), COMMUNICATIONS AND THE ARTS (advertising, art history and appreciation, Chinese, dramatic arts, English, fine arts, French, German, Japanese, languages, music, Russian, Spanish, and speech/debate/rhetoric), COMPUTER AND PHYSICAL SCIENCE (chemistry, computer science, geology, information sciences and systems, mathematics, and physics), EDUCATION (health), ENGINEERING AND ENVIRONMENTAL DESIGN (architecture, civil engineering, computer engineering, electrical/electronics engineering, and environmental science), SOCIAL SCIENCE (anthropology, child care/child and family studies, community services, economics, geography, history, international studies, law enforcement and corrections, liberal arts/general studies, philosophy, political science/government, psychology, sociology, and women's studies). Electrical engineering, environmental science, and physics are the strongest academically. Psychology, business administration, and art are the largest.

Required: All students must complete at least 180 quarter credits with a 2.0 GPA in all courses in the major, and in all residence work. Other requirements and the number of hours that must be completed in the major vary by degree program. Freshmen must complete 3 5-credit freshman inquiry courses; sophomores, 3 4-credit courses from different interdisciplinary programs or general education clusters; juniors and seniors, 1 interdisciplinary program or general education cluster (4 3-credit courses); and seniors must complete a Senior Capstone. A thesis is required in the honors program only.

Special: Students may study abroad in 34 countries. Numerous internships, co-op programs, a Washington semester, and work-study programs are available. Most undergraduate programs may be taken on an accelerated basis, and students in all programs may undertake dual majors or design their own majors. A general studies program is available in arts and letters, science, or social science. Nondegree study and pass/fail grading options are possible. Students may enroll for 7 or fewer credits per term without formal admission. There are 18 national honor societies, a freshman honors program, and 10 departmental honors programs.

Faculty/Classroom: 55% of faculty are male; 45%, female. All both teach and do research. The average class size in an introductory lecture is 23; in a laboratory, 19; and in a regular course, 28.

Admissions: 18 freshmen graduated first in their class.

Requirements: Satisfactory scores are required on the SAT or ACT. Addition, applicants should be high school graduates or have earned the

GED. Secondary preparation should include 4 years of English, 3 years each of social studies and math, and 2 years each of science and foreign language. A GPA of 3.0 is required. AP and CLEP credits are accepted.

Procedure: Freshmen are admitted to all sessions. Entrance exams should be taken as early as possible. There is a deferred admissions and a rolling admissions plan. Application deadlines are open. Application fee is $50. Notification is sent on a rolling basis. Applications are accepted on-line.

Transfer: 2516 transfer students enrolled in a recent year. Applicants who are Oregon residents must have earned at least a 2.0 GPA in 30 college credits; those with 12 to 30 credits must meet freshman admission requirements and have a 2.0 GPA in all college work attempted. Nonresident applicants must have at least a 2.25 GPA in 30 hours of college work; those with 12 to 30 hours must meet freshman requirements and have a 2.5 GPA in all college work attempted. 45 of 180 credits required for the bachelor's degree must be completed at PSU.

Visiting: There are regularly scheduled orientations for prospective students, including twice-daily campus tours led by student guides and opportunities for prospective students to meet with faculty, staff, and advisers. There are guides for informal visits and visitors may sit in on classes and stay overnight. To schedule a visit, contact Campus Tour Coordinator, Office of Admissions and Records at (503) 725-5555 or psutours@pdx.edu.

Financial Aid: In a recent year, 63% of all full-time freshmen and 58% of continuing full-time students received some form of financial aid. 46% of full-time freshmen and 51% of continuing full-time students received need-based aid. The average freshman award was $6203. Need-based scholarships or need-based grants averaged $7343 ($21,681 maximum). 80% of undergraduates work part time. Average annual earnings from campus work are $1716. The FAFSA and the college's own financial statement are required. The deadline for filing freshman financial aid applications for fall entry is June 15.

International Students: In a recent year, there were 363 international students enrolled. The school actively recruits these students. Satisfactory scores are required on the written TOEFL and the college's own test. Only the international TOEFL exam or the PSU institutional TOEFL exam will be accepted.

Computers: All students may access the system 24 hours a day, except during the scheduled weekly maintenance period. Lab time is not limited, but dial-in is 90 limited to minutes per session. There are no fees.

Graduates: In a recent year, 2596 bachelor's degrees were awarded. The most popular majors were general studies/social science (11%), management (8%), and psychology (7%). In an average class, 8% graduate in 4 years or less, 24% graduate in 5 years or less, and 32% graduate in 6 years or less. 130 companies recruited on campus in a recent year.

Admissions Contact: Samuel Collie, Executive Director of Admissions, Records and Financial Aid. E-mail: askadm@ess.pdx.edu Web: http://www.ess.pdx.edu/adm/

REED COLLEGE
B-1

Portland, OR 97202-8199

(503) 777-7511
(800) 547-4750; Fax: (503) 777-7553

Full-time: 575 men, 697 women	**Faculty:** 116; IIB, +$
Part-time: 15 men, 22 women	**Ph.D.s:** 89%
Graduate: 13 men, 18 women	**Student/Faculty:** 11 to 1
Year: semesters	**Tuition:** $32,590
Application Deadline: January 15	**Room & Board:** $8516
Freshman Class: 2646 applied, 1200 accepted, 353 enrolled	
SAT Verbal/Math: 710/670*	**ACT:** 30 **MOST COMPETITIVE**

Reed College, founded in 1908, is a private, nonsectarian institution offering programs in liberal arts and sciences and emphasizing instruction through small conference-style classes. In addition to regional accreditation, Reed has baccalaureate program accreditation with ACS. The library contains 544,616 volumes, 242,537 microform items, and 20,470 audio/video tapes/CDs/DVDs, and subscribes to 16,447 periodicals including electronic. Computerized library services include the card catalog, interlibrary loans, database searching, Internet access, and laptop Internet portals. Special learning facilities include a learning resource center, art gallery, radio station, a reactor, and centers for bio science, math, quantitative skills, science, and writing. The 110-acre campus is in an urban area in Portland. Including any residence halls, there are 40 buildings.

Student Life: 86% of undergraduates are from out of state, mostly the West. Students are from 42 states, 33 foreign countries, and Canada. 61% are from public schools. 63% are white. The average age of freshmen is 18; all undergraduates, 20. 15% do not continue beyond their first year; 73% remain to graduate.

Housing: 803 students can be accommodated in college housing, which includes coed dorms, on-campus apartments, and off-campus apartments. In addition, there are language houses and special-interest houses. On-campus housing is guaranteed for the freshman year only, is available on a first-come, first-served basis, and is available on a lot-

tery system for upperclassmen. 65% of students live on campus; of those, 95% remain on campus on weekends. Alcohol is not permitted. All students may keep cars.

Activities: There are no fraternities or sororities. There are 65 groups on campus, including art, chess, choir, chorale, chorus, computers, dance, debate, drama, ethnic, gay, international, literary magazine, newspaper, orchestra, photography, radio and TV, religious, social service, and student government. Popular campus events include Performing Arts Festival, Campus Clean Up Day (Canyon Day), and Renaissance Fair.

Sports: There are 6 intercollegiate sports for men and 4 for women, and 4 intramural sports for men and 4 for women. Facilities include a sports center that houses 2 gyms (1 seating 1200), an indoor pool, squash and racquetball courts, saunas, a weight room, an exercise room, and a dance studio. Outdoor facilities include tennis courts, a track, and areas for soccer, rugby, volleyball, and baseball.

Disabled Students: 68% of the campus is accessible. Wheelchair ramps, elevators, special parking, specially equipped rest rooms, special class scheduling, lowered drinking fountains, and lowered telephones are available.

Services: Counseling and information services are available, as is tutoring in every subject. There is a reader service for the blind, and remedial math, reading, and writing.

Campus Safety and Security: Measures include 24-hour foot and vehicle patrol, self-defense education, security escort services, and shuttle buses. There are informal discussions, pamphlets/posters/films, emergency telephones, and lighted pathways/sidewalks.

Programs of Study: Reed confers the B.A. degree. Master's degrees are also awarded. Bachelor's degrees are awarded in BIOLOGICAL SCIENCE (biology/biological science), COMMUNICATIONS AND THE ARTS (art, Chinese, classics, dramatic arts, English literature, Germanic languages and literature, linguistics, music, and Russian languages and literature), COMPUTER AND PHYSICAL SCIENCE (chemistry, mathematics, and physics), SOCIAL SCIENCE (anthropology, economics, French studies, history, philosophy, political science/government, psychology, religion, sociology, and Spanish studies). Biology, English, and psychology are the largest.

Required: All students are required to maintain a C average while taking 120 semester hours. The liberal arts program also requires 1 year of humanities and 1 year for a senior research project, in addition to 1 year each from literature and the arts, history, social science, psychology, natural science, math, logic, foreign languages, and linguistics. Students also must take 6 quarters of phys ed.

Special: Cross-registration is available through the Oregon Independent Colleges organization and Pacific Northwest College of Art. Also available are 3-2 engineering degrees with California Institute of Technology, Columbia University, and Rensselaer Polytechnic Institute, combined 3-2 programs in science, and programs with the Pacific Northwest College of Art. Study abroad in 15 countries, a domestic exchange program with Howard University in Washington, D.C., Sarah Lawrence College, and Sea Education Association (SEA), accelerated degree programs, dual majors, student-designed majors, numerous interdisciplinary majors, nondegree study, and pass/fail options are also offered. There is a chapter of Phi Beta Kappa.

Faculty/Classroom: 66% of faculty are male; 34%, female. All both teach and do research. No introductory courses are taught by graduate students. The average class size in a laboratory is 17 and in a regular course, 14.

Admissions: 45% of the 2005-2006 applicants were accepted. The SAT scores for the 2005-2006 freshman class were: Verbal--6% between 500 and 599, 37% between 600 and 700, and 57% above 700; Math--1% below 500, 13% between 500 and 599, 53% between 600 and 700, and 33% above 700. The ACT scores were 1% below 21, 2% between 21 and 23, 6% between 24 and 26, 14% between 27 and 28, and 77% above 28. 81% of the current freshmen were in the top fifth of their class; 97% were in the top two fifths. There were 6 National Merit finalists. 16 freshmen graduated first in their class.

Requirements: The SAT is required. In addition, Reed strongly recommends that applicants have 4 years of English, 3 each of math and science, and 2 each of foreign language, history, and social studies. An essay is required, and an interview is recommended. The GED is accepted. AP credits are accepted. Important factors in the admissions decision are advanced placement or honor courses, personality/intangible qualities, and evidence of special talent.

Procedure: Freshmen are admitted fall and spring. There are early decision, early admissions, and deferred admissions plans. Early decision applications should be filed by November 15; regular applications, by January 15 for fall entry and November 15 for winter entry. Notification of early decision is sent December 15; regular decision, April 1. The fall 2005 application fee was $40. 124 early decision candidates were accepted for the 2005-2006 class. 775 applicants were on the 2005 waiting list; 15 were admitted. Applications are accepted on-line.

Transfer: 46 transfer students enrolled in 2004-2005. Transfer students must have a GPA of 3.0. 60 of 120 credits required for the bachelor's degree must be completed at Reed.

Visiting: There are regularly scheduled orientations for prospective students, including an information session, campus tour, and an admission interview. Visitors may sit in on classes and stay overnight. To schedule a visit, contact the Office of Admission at *admission@reed.edu.*

Financial Aid: In 2005-2006, 47% of all full-time freshmen and 52% of continuing full-time students received some form of financial aid. 43% of full-time freshmen and 49% of continuing full-time students received need-based aid. The average freshman award was $28,205. Need-based scholarships or need-based grants averaged $27,387 and need-based self-help aid (loans and jobs) averaged $3154. 49% of undergraduates work part time. Average annual earnings from campus work are $1760. The average financial indebtedness of the 2005 graduate was $17,175. Reed is a member of CSS. The CSS/Profile or FAFSA, the college's own financial statement, and the parent and student federal tax forms are required. The deadline for filing freshman financial aid applications for fall entry is March 1.

International Students: There are 51 international students enrolled. The school actively recruits these students. They must score satisfactorily on the TOEFL and also take the SAT or the ACT.

Computers: Wireless access is available. High-speed networking is available in all residence hall rooms, classrooms, labs, and offices. All students may access the system 24 hours daily. There are no time limits and no fees.

Graduates: From July 1, 2004 to June 30, 2005, 299 bachelor's degrees were awarded. The most popular majors were biology (14%), English (12%), and anthropology (10%). In an average class, 58% graduate in 4 years or less, 72% graduate in 5 years or less, and 73% graduate in 6 years or less. 45 companies recruited on campus in 2004-2005.

Admissions Contact: Paul Marthers, Dean.
E-mail: *admission@reed.edu* Web: *http://www.reed.edu*

SOUTHERN OREGON UNIVERSITY   B-4

Ashland, OR 97520-5005   **(541) 552-6411**
                            (800) 482-7672; Fax: (541) 552-6614

Full-time: 3475 men and women	**Faculty:** 197; IIA, --$
Part-time: 963 men and women	**Ph.Ds:** 93%
Graduate: 539 men and women	**Student/Faculty:** 18 to 1
Year: quarters, summer session	**Tuition:** $4932 ($10,137)
Application Deadline: open	**Room & Board:** $7254
Freshman Class: 1847 applied, 1530 accepted, 793 enrolled	
SAT Verbal/Math: 520/510*	**ACT:** 21 **COMPETITIVE**

Southern Oregon University, founded in 1882, is a public comprehensive university providing undergraduate and graduate programs in humanities, science, business, fine and performing arts, social sciences, and teacher education. There are 4 undergraduate schools and 1 graduate school. In addition to regional accreditation, Southern has baccalaureate program accreditation with NASM and NLN. The library contains 300,000 volumes, 750,000 microform items, and 6000 audio/video tapes/CDs/DVDs, and subscribes to 2000 periodicals including electronic. Computerized library services include interlibrary loans, database searching, and Internet access. Special learning facilities include a learning resource center, art gallery, radio station, TV station, art museum, 8 art galleries, a wildlife forensics lab, a music recital hall, 2 theaters, a greenhouse, and an ecology center. The 175-acre campus is in a small town 10 miles southeast of Medford. Including any residence halls, there are 38 buildings.

Student Life: 79% of undergraduates are from Oregon. Students are from 43 states, 35 foreign countries, and Canada. 85% are from public schools. 86% are white. The average age of all undergraduates is 24. 30% do not continue beyond their first year; 37% remain to graduate.

Housing: 1300 students can be accommodated in college housing, which includes coed dorms, off-campus apartments, and married-student housing. In addition, there are special-interest house; 24-hour and 12-hour quiet halls, a wellness hall, a freshman hall, a smoke-and-incense-free hall, and an age 21+ hall.. On-campus housing is guaranteed for the freshman year only and is available on a first-come, first-served basis. 75% of students commute. Alcohol is not permitted. All students may keep cars.

Activities: There are no fraternities or sororities. There are 84 groups on campus, including art, band, cheerleading, choir, chorale, chorus, computers, dance, drama, ethnic, gay, honors, international, jazz band, literary magazine, musical theater, newspaper, pep band, photography, political, professional, radio and TV, religious, social, student government, and symphony. Popular campus events include Commencement weekend, International Week, and One World Series.

Sports: There are 6 intercollegiate sports for men and 7 for women, and 11 intramural sports for men and 7 for women. Facilities include an indoor swimming pool, 6 racquetball courts, 12 tennis courts, 4 gyms, a climbing-wall gym, a dance studio, wrestling and weight rooms, a sauna, a football stadium, and an all-weather track.

Disabled Students: 95% of the campus is accessible. Wheelchair ramps, elevators, special parking, specially equipped rest rooms, lowered drinking fountains, and individualized programming are available.

Services: Counseling and information services are available, as is tutoring in some subjects, including math and writing. There is a reader service for the blind and remedial math and writing. Program design is offered for students with learning disabilities.

Campus Safety and Security: Measures include 24-hour foot and vehicle patrol, self-defense education, informal discussions, and pamphlets/posters/films. There are emergency telephones and lighted pathways/sidewalks.

Programs of Study: Southern confers B.A., B.S., and B.F.A. degrees. Master's degrees are also awarded. Bachelor's degrees are awarded in BIOLOGICAL SCIENCE (biology/biological science), BUSINESS (accounting, business administration and management, and marketing/retailing/merchandising), COMMUNICATIONS AND THE ARTS (art, communications, dramatic arts, English, languages, music, music business management, Spanish, and visual and performing arts), COMPUTER AND PHYSICAL SCIENCE (chemistry, computer science, geology, mathematics, physics, and science), EDUCATION (physical), HEALTH PROFESSIONS (health, nursing, and premedicine), SOCIAL SCIENCE (anthropology, criminology, economics, geography, history, international studies, liberal arts/general studies, political science/government, pre-law, psychology, social science, and sociology). Fine and performing arts, sciences, and social sciences are the strongest academically. Business and social sciences are the largest.

Required: Students need a minimum GPA of 2.0 earned over 180 quarter hours, with 50 to 100 in the major and at least 60 in upper-division course work. Competency must be demonstrated through course work in writing and research. General education requirements include a year long course in speaking, writing, and critical thinking, and both lower- and upper-division courses in arts and letters, natural sciences, social sciences, and quantitative reasoning. There is a required senior capstone experience.

Special: Cross-registration through the National Student and Western Student Exchanges, study abroad in 23 countries, internships, and federal work-study are all available. Accelerated degrees in business, communication, computer science, economics, geography, math, political science, foreign languages and literature, and sociology; dual majors in business and chemistry, physics, math, or music, and in math and computer science; and interdisciplinary majors in environmental or international studies are all offered. There are 13 national honor societies, a freshman honors program, and 3 departmental honors programs.

Faculty/Classroom: 54% of faculty are male; 46%, female. Almost all teach undergraduates and 1% both teach and do research. No introductory courses are taught by graduate students. The average class size in a regular course is 25.

Admissions: 83% of the 2005-2006 applicants were accepted. The SAT scores for the 2005-2006 freshman class were: Verbal--32% below 500, 45% between 500 and 599, 19% between 600 and 700, and 4% above 700; Math--39% below 500, 45% between 500 and 599, 15% between 600 and 700, and 1% above 700. The ACT scores were 24% below 21, 34% between 21 and 23, 32% between 24 and 26, 5% between 27 and 28, and 5% above 28.

Requirements: The SAT or ACT is required. In addition, a satisfactorily score on the SAT is needed if the high school GPA is less than 2.75. Applicants need 14 academic credits, including 4 years of English, 3 each of math and social studies, 2 of science, and 2 years of 1 foreign language. The GED is accepted. A GPA of 2.75 is required. AP and CLEP credits are accepted.

Procedure: Freshmen are admitted to all sessions. Entrance exams should be taken in the senior year. There are early admissions rolling admissions, and deferred admissions plans. Application deadlines are open. The application fee is $50. Applications are accepted on-line.

Transfer: 444 transfer students enrolled in 2004-2005. Transfer students need a minimum GPA of 2.25 and at least 36 quarter credits. 45 of 180 credits required for the bachelor's degree must be completed at Southern.

Visiting: There are regularly scheduled orientations for prospective students, including tours of the campus and residence halls and a meeting with an admissions representative. Appointments with faculty and class visits can be arranged. There are guides for informal visits and visitors may sit in on classes. To schedule a visit, contact the Admissions Office.

Financial Aid: 46% of undergraduates work part time. Average annual earnings from campus work are $809. Southern is a member of CSS. The FAFSA is required. The priority date for freshman financial aid applications for fall entry is February 22. The deadline for filing freshman financial aid applications for fall entry is March 1.

International Students: There are 135 international students enrolled. The school actively recruits these students. They must score satisfactorily on the TOEFL.

Computers: Wireless access is available. There are 27 labs, more than 600 terminals, and 5 hot spots. All students may access the system 7:30 A.M. to 10 P.M. Monday through Thursday, 7:30 A.M. to 5 P.M. Friday through Sunday.

Admissions Contact: Mara Affre, Director of Admissions.
E-mail: *admissions@sou.edu* Web: *www.sou.edu*

UNIVERSITY OF OREGON
B-2

Eugene, OR 97403-1227

(541) 346-3201
(800) 232-3825; Fax: (541) 346-5815

Full-time: 7086 men, 7910 women
Part-time: 711 men, 766 women
Graduate: 1812 men, 2062 women
Year: quarters, summer session
Application Deadline: January 15
Freshman Class: 10,012 applied, 9048 accepted, 3062 enrolled
SAT Verbal/Math: 560/580*

Faculty: 785; I, --$
Ph.D.s: 98%
Student/Faculty: 19 to 1
Tuition: $5613 ($17,445)
Room & Board: $7496

VERY COMPETITIVE

The University of Oregon, founded in 1876, is a public liberal arts institution within the Oregon University System. There are 7 undergraduate and 7 graduate schools. In addition to regional accreditation, UO has baccalaureate program accreditation with AACSB, ACEJMC, ASLA, FIDER, NAAB, NASM, and NRPA. The 6 libraries contain 2,665,518 volumes, 2,909,868 microform items, and 106,111 audio/video tapes/CDs/DVDs, and subscribe to 18,165 periodicals including electronic. Computerized library services include the card catalog, interlibrary loans, database searching, Internet access, and laptop Internet portals. Special learning facilities include a learning resource center, art gallery, natural history museum, radio station, TV station, more than 50 interdisciplinary institutes, centers, and research related facilities across campus, a computer music center, the Jordan Schnitzer Museum of Art, Museum of Natural and Cultural History, and University of Oregon Many Nations Longhouse. The 295-acre campus is in a suburban area near downtown Eugene. Including any residence halls, there are 118 buildings.

Student Life: 76% of undergraduates are from Oregon. Students are from 49 states, 81 foreign countries, and Canada. 91% are from public schools. 78% are white. The average age of freshmen is 18; all undergraduates, 21. 16% do not continue beyond their first year; 65% remain to graduate.

Housing: 3200 students can be accommodated in college housing, which includes single-sex and coed dorms and married-student housing. In addition, there are honors houses, language houses, special-interest houses, an international house, and a graduate student residence hall. On-campus housing is available on a first-come, first-served basis. 79% of students commute. Alcohol is not permitted. All students may keep cars.

Activities: 8% of men belong to 13 national fraternities; 8% of women belong to 8 national sororities. There are approximately 300 groups on campus, including art, band, cheerleading, choir, chorale, chorus, computers, dance, drama, drill team, ethnic, film, forensics, gay, honors, international, jazz band, literary magazine, marching band, musical theater, newspaper, opera, orchestra, pep band, photography, political, professional, radio and TV, religious, social, social service, student government, symphony, and yearbook. Popular campus events include University Day, Family Weekends, and Convocation.

Sports: There are 8 intercollegiate sports for men and 10 for women, and 16 intramural sports for men and 15 for women. Facilities include a 58,000-seat stadium with 40 private suites, a 9,000-seat arena, an 8-lane 400-meter track and field complex with seating for 9,500 spectators, a softball complex, 12 tennis courts, a practice putting green, and grass fields for soccer and lacrosse and football practices. The student recreation center includes several gyms and training facilities with exercise and weight training equipment, a swimming pool, an indoor track, a climbing wall, and an indoor practice facility for athletic teams.

Disabled Students: 90% of the campus is accessible. Wheelchair ramps, elevators, special parking, specially equipped rest rooms, special class scheduling, lowered drinking fountains, lowered telephones, special housing, and a counselor for students with disabilities are available. Other accomodations are made upon request.

Services: Counseling and information services are available, as is tutoring in every subject. There is a reader service for the blind and remedial math and writing. Peer tutors in entry-level undergraduate courses are available through the Academic Learning Services Center. Students can drop in to receive free assistance with math and writing at the center's lab.

Campus Safety and Security: Measures include 24-hour foot and vehicle patrol, self-defense education, security escort services, and shuttle buses. There are informal discussions, pamphlets/posters/films, emergency telephones, and lighted pathways/sidewalks.

Programs of Study: UO confers B.A., B.S., B.Arch., B.Ed., B.F.A., B.I.Arch., B.L.A., and B.Mus. degrees. Master's and doctoral degrees are also awarded. Bachelor's degrees are awarded in BIOLOGICAL SCIENCE (biochemistry, biology/biological science, and physiology), BUSINESS (accounting and business administration and management), COMMUNICATIONS AND THE ARTS (art history and appreciation, ceramic art and design, Chinese, classics, comparative literature, dance, design, dramatic arts, English, fiber/textiles/weaving, fine arts, French, German, graphic design, Greek, Italian, Japanese, jazz, journalism, Latin, linguistics, metal/jewelry, multimedia, music, music performance, music theory and composition, painting, photography, printmaking, romance languages and literature, Russian, sculpture, and Spanish),

COMPUTER AND PHYSICAL SCIENCE (chemistry, computer science, digital arts/technology, geology, mathematics, physics, and science), EDUCATION (education and music), ENGINEERING AND ENVIRONMENTAL DESIGN (architecture, environmental science, interior design, and landscape architecture/design), HEALTH PROFESSIONS (speech pathology/audiology), SOCIAL SCIENCE (anthropology, Asian/Oriental studies, classical/ancient civilization, economics, ethnic studies, family and community services, geography, history, humanities, international studies, Judaic studies, philosophy, political science/government, psychology, public administration, religion, sociology, and women's studies). Architecture, journalism, and biology are the strongest academically. Business, psychology, and journalism are the largest.

Required: For graduation, at least 180 quarter credits are required of all students, with a minimum GPA of 2.0. A minimum of 36 credits must be in the major, including 24 in upper-division work. Basic courses vary by major, but all students must complete 12 to 16 credits each in the areas of arts and letters, social science, and science, as well as 2 courses in written English and 2 courses each in multicultural studies.

Special: UO offers cross-registration with other schools in the Oregon University System, matriculation agreements with over 25 Oregon and Washington community colleges, dual enrollment with Lane Community College, study abroad in at least 70 countries, pre-engineering in conjunction with Lane Community College, an engineering/physics program with Oregon State University, and numerous internship opportunities, B.A.-B.S. degrees, dual majors, a 3-2 engineering degree, and pass/fail options are available. There are 14 national honor societies, including Phi Beta Kappa, a freshman honors program, and 54 departmental honors programs.

Faculty/Classroom: 58% of faculty are male; 42%, female. All teach undergraduates. Graduate students teach 14% of introductory courses. The average class size in a regular course is 26.

Admissions: 90% of the 2005-2006 applicants were accepted. The SAT scores for the 2005-2006 freshman class were: Verbal--24% below 500, 43% between 500 and 599, 27% between 600 and 700, and 6% above 700; Math--22% below 500, 44% between 500 and 599, 28% between 600 and 700, and 5% above 700. There were 10 National Merit finalists. 86 freshmen graduated first in their class.

Requirements: The SAT or ACT is required. Students from accredited high schools with minimum 3.25 high school GPA and 16 college preparatory units are guaranteed admission. For all others, secondary school record and test scores are most important. A minimum 3.25 high school GPA in all academic subjects or predicated first-term GPA of 2.0 or better based on a combination of high school GPA and SAT/ACT scores are required. Admissions essay is required for all students with fewer than 16 college preparatory units or a cumulative high school GPA below 3.25. AP and CLEP credits are accepted.

Procedure: Freshmen are admitted to all sessions. Entrance exams should be taken after October 15 of the junior year and before March of the senior year. There is a rolling admissions plan. Applications should be filed by January 15 for fall entry, October 16 for winter entry, February 1 for spring entry, and March 1 for summer entry, along with a $50 fee. Notification is sent on a rolling basis. Applications are accepted online.

Transfer: 1436 transfer students enrolled in 2004-2005. Students who have completed 36 or more credits with a minimum 2.25 GPA for residents and 2.5 for nonresidents, and whose college record includes passing 1 college-level course each in writing and math with a C- or better, may be admitted as transfer students. An official transcript from each college and university attended must be submitted. Students who have completed 12 to 35 credits must also meet freshman requirements. 45 of 180 credits required for the bachelor's degree must be completed at UO.

Visiting: There are regularly scheduled orientations for prospective students, including 2-day programs scheduled for late July that include both advising and web-based registration. There are guides for informal visits and visitors may sit in on classes. To schedule a visit, contact the Ambassador Program at (541) 346-1274.

Financial Aid: In 2005-2006, 74% of all full-time freshmen and 60% of continuing full-time students received some form of financial aid. 44% of full-time freshmen and 53% of continuing full-time students received need-based aid. The average freshman award was $7138. The average financial indebtedness of the 2005 graduate was $18,029. The FAFSA is required. The deadline for filing freshman financial aid applications for fall entry is March 1.

International Students: There are 667 international students enrolled. The school actively recruits these students. They must score satisfactorily on the written TOEFL and also take the SAT or the ACT.

Computers: Wireless access is available. Access to the campus network and the Internet is provided via 40 computer labs with approximately 950 workstations for student use; approximately 5000 ethernet connections in student residences; and the campus wireless network that covers the majority of the public space on campus. All students may access the system 24 hours a day. There are no time limits. The fee is $75 per term. It is strongly recommended that all students have a personal computer. Students in architecture and law must have personal computers.

Graduates: From July 1, 2004 to June 30, 2005, 3984 bachelor's degrees were awarded. The most popular majors were business administration (10%), architecture and arts (7%), and journalism/communications (7%). In an average class, 1% graduate in 3 years or less, 37% graduate in 4 years or less, 56% graduate in 5 years or less, and 61% graduate in 6 years or less. 175 companies recruited on campus in 2004-2005. Of the 2004 graduating class, 20% were enrolled in graduate school within 6 months of graduation and 81% were employed.

Admissions Contact: Martha Pitts, Assistant Vice President for Enrollment Services. A video is available.
E-mail: *uoadmit@oregon.uoregon.edu* Web: *www.uoregon.edu*

UNIVERSITY OF PORTLAND	B-1
Portland, OR 97203	**(503) 943-7147**
	(888) 627-5601; Fax: (503) 943-7315
Full-time: 1076 men, 1756 women	**Faculty:** 188; IIA, -$
Part-time: 7 men, 21 women	**Ph.D.s:** 86%
Graduate: 177 men, 260 women	**Student/Faculty:** 15 to 1
Year: semesters, summer session	**Tuition:** $24,900
Application Deadline: February 1	**Room & Board:** $7400
Freshman Class: 3026 applied, 2445 accepted, 724 enrolled	
SAT Verbal/Math: 591/591*	**VERY COMPETITIVE**

The University of Portland, founded in 1901, is an independent institution affiliated with the Roman Catholic Church. It offers degree programs in the arts and sciences, business administration, education, engineering, and nursing. There are 5 undergraduate schools and 1 graduate school. In addition to regional accreditation, UP has baccalaureate program accreditation with AACSB, ABET, NASM, NCATE, and NLN. The library contains 380,000 volumes, 524,861 microform items, and 7827 audio/video tapes/CDs/DVDs, and subscribes to 1446 periodicals including electronic. Computerized library services include interlibrary loans, database searching, Internet access, and laptop Internet portals. Special learning facilities include a learning resource center, art gallery, radio station, and an observatory. The 155-acre campus is in an urban area 4 miles north of downtown Portland. Including any residence halls, there are 30 buildings.

Student Life: 54% of undergraduates are from out of state, mostly the West. Others are from 44 states, 37 foreign countries, and Canada. 62% are from public schools. 79% are white. Most are Catholic. The average age of freshmen is 19; all undergraduates, 21. 14% do not continue beyond their first year; 68% remain to graduate.

Housing: 1425 students can be accommodated in college housing, which includes single-sex and coed dorms and off-campus apartments. In addition, there are special-interest houses. On-campus housing is guaranteed for the freshman year only. 49% of students live on campus; of those, % remain on campus on weekends. Upperclassmen may keep cars.

Activities: There are no fraternities or sororities. There are 62 groups on campus, including art, band, cheerleading, choir, chorale, chorus, computers, dance, debate, drama, ethnic, honors, international, jazz band, literary magazine, musical theater, newspaper, orchestra, pep band, photography, political, professional, radio and TV, religious, social, social service, student government, symphony, and yearbook. Popular campus events include Christmas in April, Casino Night, and Luau.

Sports: There are 7 intercollegiate sports for men and 7 for women, and 20 intramural sports for men and 20 for women. Facilities include weight rooms, an indoor track, a gym, a swimming pool, and a 5000-seat athletic and convocation center. Rental equipment is available for biking and camping activities.

Disabled Students: 95% of the campus is accessible. Wheelchair ramps, elevators, special parking, specially equipped rest rooms, special class scheduling, lowered drinking fountains, and lowered telephones are available.

Services: Counseling and information services are available, as is tutoring in most subjects, including including English and math. The faculty is available for individual assistance.

Campus Safety and Security: Measures include 24-hour foot and vehicle patrol, self-defense education, security escort services, and informal discussions. There are pamphlets/posters/films, emergency telephones, and lighted pathways/sidewalks.

Programs of Study: UP confers B.A., B.S., B.A.Ed., B.B.A., B.M.Ed., B.S.C.E., B.S.E.E., B.S.E.M., B.S.E.S., B.S.M.E., and B.S.N. degrees. Master's degrees are also awarded. Bachelor's degrees are awarded in BIOLOGICAL SCIENCE (biology/biological science), BUSINESS (accounting, banking and finance, international business management, and marketing/retailing/merchandising), COMMUNICATIONS AND THE ARTS (communications, dramatic arts, English, music, Spanish, and theater management), COMPUTER AND PHYSICAL SCIENCE (chemistry, computer science, mathematics, and physics), EDUCATION (elementary, music, and secondary), ENGINEERING AND ENVIRONMENTAL DESIGN (civil engineering, electrical/electronics engineering, engineering, engineering management, environmental science, and mechanical engineering), HEALTH PROFESSIONS (nursing), SOCIAL SCIENCE

(criminal justice, history, interdisciplinary studies, philosophy, political science/government, psychology, social work, sociology, and theological studies). Engineering, business, and nursing are the strongest academically. Business administration, engineering, and nursing are the largest.

Required: To graduate, students must complete 120 credit hours, including at least 24 upper-division classes in the major, with a minimum GPA of 2.0. Required courses include 9 hours each of philosophy and theology, 6 each of science, social sciences, and electives, and 3 each of fine arts, history, math, and literature. Some majors may require a comprehensive exam and/or thesis.

Special: UP offers internships through individual departments, cross-registration with members of the Oregon Independent College Association, dual and interdisciplinary majors, including engineering chemistry and organizational communications, work-study programs, and pass/fail options. Study abroad may be arranged in Japan, Mexico, Australia, Chile, and several European countries. There are 9 national honor societies and a freshman honors program.

Faculty/Classroom: 58% of faculty are male; 42%, female. All teach undergraduates. No introductory courses are taught by graduate students. The average class size in an introductory lecture is 25; in a laboratory, 20; and in a regular course, 20.

Admissions: 81% of the 2005-2006 applicants were accepted. The SAT scores for the 2005-2006 freshman class were: Verbal--10% below 500, 44% between 500 and 599, 36% between 600 and 700, and 10% above 700; Math--8% below 500, 43% between 500 and 599, 41% between 600 and 700, and 8% above 700. 74% of the current freshmen were in the top fifth of their class; 95% were in the top two fifths. 39 freshmen graduated first in their class.

Requirements: A satisfactory score is required on the SAT or ACT. Graduation from an accredited secondary school or satisfactory scores on the GED are required. The high school curriculum should include courses in English composition, math, social studies, science, and a foreign language. 2 essays are required, as is a letter of recommendation from the high school counselor or principal. UP requires applicants to be in the upper 50% of their class. A GPA of 3.0 is required. AP and CLEP credits are accepted.

Procedure: Freshmen are admitted to all sessions. Entrance exams should be taken preferably before February 1 but no later than June 1 of the senior year. There is a deferred admissions plan. Applications should be filed by February 1 for fall entry, along with a $50 fee. Notification is sent on a rolling basis. 145 applicants were on the 2005 waiting list; 102 were admitted. Applications are accepted on-line.

Transfer: 88 transfer students enrolled in 2004-2005. Applicants with 26 or more credits must have a minimum GPA of 2.5 and be in good standing at their previous school. Students with fewer credits may need to meet freshman requirements. 30 of 120 credits required for the bachelor's degree must be completed at UP.

Visiting: There are regularly scheduled orientations for prospective students, including a campus tour, class attendance, and a meeting with an admissions counselor. There are guides for informal visits and visitors may sit in on classes and stay overnight. To schedule a visit, contact the Office of Admissions at *admissio@up.edu*.

Financial Aid: In 2005-2006, 93% of all full-time freshmen and 89% of continuing full-time students received some form of financial aid. 65% of full-time freshmen and 57% of continuing full-time students received need-based aid. The average freshman award was $19,726. Need-based scholarships or need-based grants averaged $13,807; and need-based self-help aid (loans and jobs) averaged $3900. 55% of undergraduates work part time. Average annual earnings from campus work are $2100. The average financial indebtedness of the 2005 graduate was $18,900. The FAFSA and the college's own financial statement are required. The deadline for filing freshman financial aid applications for fall entry is March 1.

International Students: There are 61 international students enrolled. The school actively recruits these students. They must receive a satisfactory score on the TOEFL.

Computers: Wireless access is available. All students may access the system. There are no time limits and no fees. It is strongly recommended that all students have a personal computer.

Graduates: From July 1, 2004 to June 30, 2005, 606 bachelor's degrees were awarded. The most popular majors were nursing (18%), business (17%), and engineering (9%). In an average class, 59% graduate in 4 years or less and 68% graduate in 5 years or less. 85 companies recruited on campus in 2004-2005.

Admissions Contact: James Lyons, Dean of Admissions. A video is available. E-mail: *admissio@up.edu* Web: *www.up.edu*

WARNER PACIFIC COLLEGE — B-1
Portland, OR 97215

(503) 517-1024
(800) 582-7885; Fax: (503) 517-1352

Full-time: 195 men, 365 women	Faculty: 39
Part-time: 35 men, 70 women	Ph.D.s: 50%
Graduate: 10 men and women	Student/Faculty: 14 to 1
Year: semesters, summer session	Tuition: $16,930
Application Deadline: open	Room & Board: $5000
Freshman Class: n/av	
SAT or ACT: required	COMPETITIVE

Warner Pacific College, founded in 1937, is a private Christian liberal arts college affiliated with the Church of God. Enrollment figures in above capsule and in this profile are approximate. The library contains 53,000 volumes, 1155 microform items, and 1110 audio/video tapes/CDs/DVDs, and subscribes to 400 periodicals including electronic. Computerized library services include the card catalog, interlibrary loans, and database searching. Special learning facilities include a learning resource center, 2 electron microscopes, and an early childhood learning center. The 14-acre campus is in an urban area 5 miles east of downtown Portland. Including any residence halls, there are 30 buildings.

Student Life: 80% of undergraduates are from Oregon. Students are from 18 states, 7 foreign countries, and Canada. 78% are from public schools. 83% are white. 51% claim no religious affiliation; 42% Protestant. The average age of freshmen is 21; all undergraduates, 28. 25% do not continue beyond their first year; 45% remain to graduate.

Housing: 250 students can be accommodated in college housing, which includes single-sex dorms, on-campus apartments, and married-student housing. On-campus housing is guaranteed for the freshman year only, is available on a first-come, first-served basis, and is available on a lottery system for upperclassmen. Priority is given to out-of-town students. 70% of students commute. Alcohol is not permitted. All students may keep cars.

Activities: There are no fraternities or sororities. There are 6 groups on campus, including art, band, bible study, choir, chorale, chorus, dance, drama, ethnic, international, jazz band, musical theater, orchestra, photography, professional, religious, social, social service, spiritual growth groups, student government, and yearbook. Popular campus events include Winter Banquet, Spring Banquet, and Western Fling.

Sports: There are 4 intercollegiate sports for men and 5 for women, and 10 intramural sports for men and 10 for women. Facilities include a gym, a weight-training room, and hiking trails.

Disabled Students: 75% of the campus is accessible. Wheelchair ramps, special parking, specially equipped rest rooms, special class scheduling, lowered drinking fountains, and personalized care and services are available.

Services: Counseling and information services are available, as is tutoring in most subjects. There is remedial math, reading, and writing and testing and study skills workshops.

Campus Safety and Security: Measures include 24-hour foot and vehicle patrol, self-defense education, security escort services, and informal discussions. There are pamphlets/posters/films and lighted pathways/sidewalks.

Programs of Study: Warner Pacific confers B.A. and B.S degrees. Associate and master's degrees are also awarded. Bachelor's degrees are awarded in BIOLOGICAL SCIENCE (biology/biological science), BUSINESS (business administration and management), COMMUNICATIONS AND THE ARTS (English and music), EDUCATION (music and physical), SOCIAL SCIENCE (American studies, history, human development, liberal arts/general studies, ministries, religious music, social science, and sociology). Biological science and business administration are the strongest academically. Business administration, human development, and music education are the largest.

Required: To graduate, students must complete 124 credits with a minimum GPA of 2.0. All students must take a core curriculum of 42 credits, consisting of 15 hours in humanities, 9 in communication, 7 to 9 in religion, 6 in social science, 4 in fine arts, and 3 each in science and health and phys ed.

Special: Warner Pacific offers cross-registration through OICA, a Washington semester, a co-op nursing program, accelerated degree programs in human development and business administration, and study abroad in Latin America, the Middle East, and Russia. Internships, work-study programs, double majors, individualized majors, independent study credit for life and military experience, and pass/fail options are available.

Faculty/Classroom: 62% of faculty are male; 38%, female. All teach undergraduates and 40% do research. No introductory courses are taught by graduate students. The average class size in an introductory lecture is 15; in a laboratory, 10; and in a regular course, 15.

Requirements: The SAT or ACT is required. In addition, applicants must be graduates of an accredited secondary school. The GED is accepted. High school preparation should include 4 years of English, 3 of social studies, and 2 each of math and lab science. A GPA of 2.25 is required. AP and CLEP credits are accepted. Important factors in the admissions decision are evidence of special talent, leadership record, and advanced placement or honor courses.

Procedure: Freshmen are admitted to all sessions. There is a rolling admissions plan. Entrance exams should be taken no later than the early fall of the senior year. Application deadlines are open. Application fee is $25. Applications are accepted on-line.

Transfer: 54 transfer students enrolled in a recent year. Applicants must provide transcripts from their previous college. A minimum GPA of 2.0 is required. 30 of 124 credits required for the bachelor's degree must be completed at Warner Pacific.

Visiting: There are regularly scheduled orientations for prospective students, including 6 visitation weekends, academic fairs, scholarship days, and a retreat. There are guides for informal visits and visitors may sit in on classes and stay overnight. To schedule a visit, contact the Office of Admissions and Financial Aid.

Financial Aid: In a recent year, 98% of all full-time students received some form of financial aid. 98% of all full-time students received need-based aid. The average freshman award was $18,282. Average annual earnings from campus work were $2000. Warner Pacific is a member of CSS. The FAFSA is required. Check with the school for current application deadlines.

International Students: In a recent year, there are 12 international students enrolled. The school actively recruits these students. They must score satisfactorily on the written TOEFL or on the electronic version and also take the college's own test.

Computers: All students may access the system 24 hours a day. There are no time limits and no fees. It is strongly recommended that all students have a personal computer.

Graduates: In a recent year, 149 bachelor's degrees were awarded. The most popular majors were psychology (48%), business (34%), and religion (5%). In an average class, 2% graduate in 3 years or less, 29% graduate in 4 years or less, 8% graduate in 5 years or less, and 2% graduate in 6 years or less.

Admissions Contact: Dr. Jack P. Powell, Dean of Enrollment Management. E-mail: *admiss@warnerpacific.edu*
Web: *www.warnerpacific.edu*

WESTERN BAPTIST COLLEGE — B-2
Salem, OR 97301-9392

(503) 375-7005
(800) 845-3005; Fax: (503) 585-4316

Full-time: 245 men, 380 women	Faculty: 33
Part-time: 60 men, 60 women	Ph.D.s: 39%
Graduate: none	Student/Faculty: 19 to 1
Year: semesters, summer session	Tuition: $16,115
Application Deadline: see profile	Room & Board: $5725
Freshman Class: n/av	
SAT or ACT: required	COMPETITIVE

Western Baptist College is a Christian, liberal arts institution offering degrees in biblical-theological studies, business administration, education, humanities, math, phys ed, social sciences, psychology, intercultural studies, and youth work. Figures in the above capsule and in this profile are approximate. The library contains 82,000 volumes, 4100 microform items, and 4532 audio/video tapes/CDs/DVDs, and subscribes to 552 periodicals including electronic. Computerized library services include the card catalog, interlibrary loans, database searching, and Internet access. Special learning facilities include a learning resource center and an archaeological museum. The 107-acre campus is in a suburban area in Salem. Including any residence halls, there are 20 buildings.

Student Life: 70% of undergraduates are from Oregon. Students are from 30 states and 5 foreign countries. 72% are from public schools. 93% are white. Most are Protestant. The average age of freshmen is 19; all undergraduates, 23. 30% do not continue beyond their first year; 50% remain to graduate.

Housing: 390 students can be accommodated in college housing, which includes single-sex dorms, on-campus apartments, and married-student housing. On-campus housing is guaranteed for the freshman year only and is available on a first-come, first-served basis. Priority is given to out-of-town students. 53% of students live on campus; of those, 90% remain on campus on weekends. Alcohol is not permitted. All students may keep cars.

Activities: There are no fraternities or sororities. There are 16 groups on campus, including band, cheerleading, choir, chorale, chorus, drama, honors, jazz band, literary magazine, newspaper, orchestra, pep band, religious, social, social service, student government, and yearbook. Popular campus events include Western Weekends, Sports Weekends, and chapel services.

Sports: There are 4 intercollegiate sports for men and 5 for women, and 3 intramural sports for men and 3 for women. Facilities include a sports center with a gym and soccer and baseball fields.

Disabled Students: 95% of the campus is accessible. Elevators, special parking, specially equipped rest rooms, and lowered telephones are available.

Services: Counseling and information services are available, as is tutoring in most subjects.

Campus Safety and Security: Measures include security escort services, informal discussions, emergency telephones, and lighted pathways/sidewalks. There is a campus security patrol, and a vehicle patrol.

Programs of Study: Western confers B.A., B.S., and Th.B. degrees. Associate degrees are also awarded. Bachelor's degrees are awarded in BUSINESS (accounting and business administration and management), COMMUNICATIONS AND THE ARTS (communications, English, and music), COMPUTER AND PHYSICAL SCIENCE (computer science and mathematics), EDUCATION (education and physical), HEALTH PROFESSIONS (health science), SOCIAL SCIENCE (biblical studies, crosscultural studies, history, humanities, ministries, psychology, and social science). Education, psychology, and business are the largest.

Required: To graduate, students must complete 128 credits, with 40 to 64 in the major. The minimum required GPA is 2.0 for most programs; the education major requires a 3.0 GPA. The general education core consists of 68 credits. Courses must be taken in the Bible, humanities, social sciences, math, science, and phys ed.

Special: Western offers a preseminary co-op program, cross-registration with Oregon Independent Colleges, study abroad in 4 countries, a Washington semester, internships with the approval of a program adviser, accelerated programs in management and communication and in family studies, and student-designed majors with adviser approval. There is a freshman honors program.

Faculty/Classroom: 79% of faculty are male; 21%, female. All teach undergraduates. The average class size in an introductory lecture is 38; in a laboratory, 15; and in a regular course, 25.

Requirements: The SAT or ACT is required, as is an essay. A GPA of 2.5 is required. AP and CLEP credits are accepted. Important factors in the admissions decision are extracurricular activities record, leadership record, and evidence of special talent.

Procedure: Freshmen are admitted fall and spring. There are rolling admissions plans. The application fee is $35. Notification is sent on a rolling basis. Applications are accepted on-line. Check with the school for application deadlines.

Transfer: 117 transfer students enrolled in a recent year. Transfer applicants are required to have a minimum 2.0 cumulative college GPA and submit the college transcript and 3 references. 30 of 128 credits required for the bachelor's degree must be completed at Western.

Visiting: There are regularly scheduled orientations for prospective students, including scheduled weekend visits and Western Daze. There are guides for informal visits and visitors may sit in on classes and stay overnight. To schedule a visit, contact the Admissions Office at (503) 581-8600.

Financial Aid: The FAFSA is required. Check with the school for current application deadlines.

International Students: In a recent year, there were 5 international students enrolled. They must score satisfactorily on the written TOEFL and also take the SAT or the ACT.

Computers: All students may access the system 7 days per week/24 hours per day. There are no time limits and no fees. It is strongly recommended that all students have a personal computer. It is strongly recommended that students in business information systems and computer science have personal computers.

Graduates: In a recent year, 173 bachelor's degrees were awarded. The most popular majors were business (26%), pyschology (24%), and education (14%). In an average class, 2% graduate in 3 years or less, 49% graduate in 4 years or less, 54% graduate in 5 years or less, and 54% graduate in 6 years or less.

Admissions Contact: Marty Ziesemer, Dean of Enrollment Management. E-mail: admissions@wbc.edu Web: www.wbc.edu

WESTERN OREGON UNIVERSITY

B-2

Monmouth, OR 97361

(503) 838-8211
(877) 877-1593; Fax: (503) 838-8067

Full-time: 1600 men, 2425 women	Faculty: 182; IIA, --$
Part-time: 245 men, 210 women	Ph.D.s: 81%
Graduate: 175 men, 395 women	Student/Faculty: 22 to 1
Year: quarters, summer session	Tuition: $4315 ($12,580)
Application Deadline: open	Room & Board: $5980
Freshman Class: n/av	
SAT or ACT: required	COMPETITIVE

Western Oregon University, founded in 1856, is a publicly funded institution and a member of the Oregon University System. WOU offers undergraduate programs through the Colleges of Education and Liberal Arts and Sciences. There are 2 undergraduate schools and 1 graduate school. Figures in the above capsule and in this profile are approximate. In addition to regional accreditation, WOU has baccalaureate program accreditation with NASM and NCATE. Computerized library services include the card catalog, interlibrary loans, and database searching. Special learning facilities include a learning resource center, art gallery, TV station, and the Paul Jensen Arctic Museum. The 157-acre campus is in a rural area 15 miles west of Salem. Including any residence halls, there are 36 buildings.

Student Life: 91% of undergraduates are from Oregon. Students are from 23 states, 19 foreign countries, and Canada. 99% are from public schools. 81% are white. The average age of freshmen is 19; all undergraduates, 22. 29% do not continue beyond their first year; 50% remain to graduate.

Housing: 1275 students can be accommodated in college housing, which includes coed dorms and married-student housing. In addition,there wellness, honors, multicultural,and quiet communities. On-campus housing is guaranteed for the freshman year only and is available on a first-come, first-served basis. 76% of students commute. Alcohol is not permitted. All students may keep cars.

Activities: There are no fraternities or sororities. There are 50 groups on campus, including art, band, cheerleading, chess, choir, chorale, chorus, computers, dance, debate, drama, drill team, ethnic, gay, honors, international, jazz band, literary magazine, marching band, model U.N., musical theater, newspaper, orchestra, pep band, political, radio and TV, religious, social, social service, and student government. Popular campus events include Annual Christmas Tree Lighting, Alcohol Awareness Week, and Family Day.

Sports: There are 5 intercollegiate sports for men and 6 for women, and 25 intramural sports for men and 25 for women. Facilities include a sports field, a phys ed building, a swimming pool, a weight room, indoor/outdoor tennis courts, handball and racquetball courts, a dance studio, archery facilities, and baseball, softball, and soccer fields.

Disabled Students: 90% of the campus is accessible. Wheelchair ramps, elevators, special parking, specially equipped rest rooms, special class scheduling, lowered drinking fountains, lowered telephones, and the Regional Resource Center of Deafness are available.

Services: Counseling and information services are available, as is tutoring in most subjects. There is a reader service for the blind, and remedial math, reading, and writing. There is also a student support and services program for first-generation, low-income, and physically disabled students.

Campus Safety and Security: Measures include 24-hour foot and vehicle patrol, self-defense education, security escort services, and informal discussions. There are pamphlets/posters/films, emergency telephones, and lighted pathways/sidewalks.

Programs of Study: WOU confers B.A., B.S., and B.Mus. degrees. Associate and master's degrees are also awarded. Bachelor's degrees are awarded in BIOLOGICAL SCIENCE (biology/biological science), BUSINESS (business administration and management), COMMUNICATIONS AND THE ARTS (American Sign Language, art, dance, dramatic arts, English, music, Spanish, and speech/debate/rhetoric), COMPUTER AND PHYSICAL SCIENCE (chemistry, computer science, earth science, information sciences and systems, mathematics, and natural sciences), EDUCATION (education and health), SOCIAL SCIENCE (anthropology, corrections, economics, fire protection, geography, history, humanities, interdisciplinary studies, international studies, interpreter for the deaf, law enforcement and corrections, philosophy, political science/government, psychology, public administration, social science, and sociology). Education, business, and psychology are the strongest academically. Education, criminal justice, and psychology are the largest.

Required: To graduate, students must complete a total of 180 quarter hours with a minimum GPA of 2.0. Between 45 and 120 quarter hours are required in the major. All students must fulfill the requirements of the 55-quarter hour liberal arts core curriculum, which includes 12 credits each of lab science and social sciences, 9 each of literature and fine arts, 4 of phys ed, and 3 each of philosophy, speech, and writing. Students must also satisfy graduation requirements in math, comuter science or technology, writing-intensive, and cultural diversity.

Special: Most academic majors in liberal arts and sciences offer a B.A.-B.S degree option. Dual majors, internships, study abroad through international exchange programs and the Oregon University System, and student-designed majors in interdisciplinary studies are available. Nondegree study and pass/fail options are possible. There are 7 national honor societies, and a freshman honors program.

Faculty/Classroom: 51% of faculty are male; 49%, female. All teach undergraduates. Graduate students teach 1% of introductory courses. The average class size in an introductory lecture is 40; in a laboratory, 25; and in a regular course, 30.

Requirements: The SAT or ACT is required. In addition, graduation from an accredited secondary school or satisfactory scores on the GED are required. Students must have 14 academic credits or Carnegie units. High school courses must include 4 years of English, 3 each of math and social studies, and 2 each of science and a foreign language. A GPA of 2.75 is required. AP and CLEP credits are accepted. Important factors in the admissions decision are evidence of special talent, recommendations by alumni, and parents or siblings attending the school.

Procedure: Freshmen are admitted to all sessions. There is a rolling admissions plan. Entrance exams should be taken during the junior or senior year. Application deadlines are open. Application fee is $50. Applications are accepted on-line.

Transfer: Applicants must have a minimum GPA of 2.0. Applicants with fewer than 24 quarter hours must also meet freshman admission requirements. 45 of 180 credits required for the bachelor's degree must be completed at WOU.

Visiting: There are regularly scheduled orientations for prospective students, consisting of a 1-day program for students and a parent program; all newly admitted students must make arrangements to register during orientation in July to reserve their enrollment slot. There are guides for informal visits and visitors may sit in on classes. To schedule a visit, contact the Admissions Office.

Financial Aid: The FAFSA is required. Check with the school for current application deadlines.

International Students: In a recent year, there were 75 international students enrolled. The school actively recruits these students. They must score satisfactorily on the written TOEFL or on the electronic version or take the MELAB.

Computers: All students may access the system. There are no time limits. The fee is $70.

Admissions Contact: Rob Kvidt, Director of Admissions.
E-mail: *wolfgram@wou.edu* Web: *www.wou.edu*

WILLAMETTE UNIVERSITY   B-2

Salem, OR 97301

(503) 370-6303
(877) 542-2787; Fax: (503) 375-5363

Full-time: 827 men, 996 women	**Faculty:** 137; IIA, +$
Part-time: 80 men, 51 women	**Ph.D.s:** 91%
Graduate: 360 men, 328 women	**Student/Faculty:** 13 to 1
Year: semesters	**Tuition:** $28,416
Application Deadline: February 1	**Room & Board:** $7000
Freshman Class: 2498 applied, 2072 accepted, 444 enrolled	
SAT Verbal/Math: 620/620*	**ACT:** 27 **VERY COMPETITIVE+**

Willamette University, founded in 1842, is an independent liberal arts institution affiliated with the Methodist Church. In addition to regional accreditation, Willamette has baccalaureate program accreditation with NASM. The 2 libraries contain 372,571 volumes, 333,664 microform items, and 10,440 audio/video tapes/CDs/DVDs, and subscribe to 1623 periodicals including electronic. Computerized library services include the card catalog, interlibrary loans, database searching, and Internet access. Special learning facilities include a learning resource center, art gallery, natural history museum, radio station, botanical and Japanese gardens, multimedia center, and "smart" classrooms. The 72-acre campus is in an urban area 50 minutes south of Portland. Including any residence halls, there are 44 buildings.

Student Life: 60% of undergraduates are from out of state, mostly the West. Students are from 41 states, 17 foreign countries, and Canada. 81% are from public schools. 56% are white. 66% are claim no religious affiliation; 24% Protestant; 8% Catholic. The average age of freshmen is 18; all undergraduates, 20. 12% do not continue beyond their first year; 74% remain to graduate.

Housing: 1420 students can be accommodated in college housing, which includes coed dorms, on-campus apartments, fraternity houses, and sorority houses. In addition, there are language houses special-interest houses, a 24-hour quiet dorm (intensive study), and substance-free options. On-campus housing is guaranteed for the freshman year only and is available on a lottery system for upperclassmen. 67% of students live on campus; of those, 67% remain on campus on weekends. All students may keep cars.

Activities: 35% of men belong to 5 national fraternities; 29% of women belong to 3 national sororities. There are 109 groups on campus, including art, band, cheerleading, chess, choir, chorale, chorus, computers, dance, debate, drama, ethnic, film, forensics, gay, honors, international, jazz band, literary magazine, musical theater, newspaper, orchestra, pep band, photography, political, professional, radio and TV, religious, social, social service, student government, symphony, and yearbook. Popular campus events include International Extravaganza, Wulapalooza, and Hawaiian Luau.

Sports: There are 10 intercollegiate sports for men and 10 for women, and 10 intramural sports for men and 10 for women. Facilities include a phys ed and recreation center, a 4000-seat football stadium, a 3000-seat indoor gym, a 1200-seat auditorium, a baseball stadium, a soccer field, an all-weather track, a track building, 2 other gyms, a mini-Olympic-size indoor swimming pool, an outdoor swimming pool, 3 indoor and 10 outdoor tennis courts, handball/racquetball courts, weight training facilities, and other practice fields.

Disabled Students: 90% of the campus is accessible. Wheelchair ramps, elevators, special parking, specially equipped rest rooms, special class scheduling, lowered drinking fountains, lowered telephones, and special equipment, readers, and braille services are available.

Services: Counseling and information services are available, as is tutoring in most subjects. There is a reader service for the blind. Therapists are available for students on an individual need basis.

Campus Safety and Security: Measures include 24-hour foot and vehicle patrol, self-defense education, security escort services, and informal discussions. There are pamphlets/posters/films, emergency telephones, lighted pathways/sidewalks, formal programs and education, and a weekly published campus safety report.

Programs of Study: Willamette confers B.A. and B.M. degrees. Master's and doctoral degrees are also awarded. Bachelor's degrees are awarded in BIOLOGICAL SCIENCE (biology/biological science), COMMUNICATIONS AND THE ARTS (art history and appreciation, comparative literature, dramatic arts, English, French, German, music, music performance, music theory and composition, Spanish, speech/debate/rhetoric, and studio art), COMPUTER AND PHYSICAL SCIENCE (chemistry, computer science, mathematics, physics, and science), EDUCATION (music), ENGINEERING AND ENVIRONMENTAL DESIGN (environmental science), HEALTH PROFESSIONS (exercise science), SOCIAL SCIENCE (American studies, anthropology, Asian/Oriental studies, classical/ancient civilization, economics, history, humanities, international studies, Japanese studies, Latin American studies, philosophy, political science/government, psychology, religion, sociology, and women's studies). Social sciences, natural science, and humanities are the strongest academically. Psychology, politics, and biology are the largest.

Required: To graduate, students must complete a total of 124 semester hours, including a minimum of 32 in the major, with a minimum GPA of 2.0. All students must complete general education requirements in fine arts, humanities, literature, foreign language, interdisciplinary courses, natural sciences, and social sciences, and meet math and English proficiency levels. Freshmen are required to take a World Views seminar. Seniors are required to complete a senior thesis or other project in their major.

Special: Willamette offers internships with the state and city governments, a Chicago semester, a Washington semester, and a 3-2 engineering degree with Washington University, University of Southern California, and Columbia University. Nondegree study, B.A.-B.S. degrees, dual majors, work-study programs with numerous employers in the Salem area and at the university, and credit/no-credit options are also available. Study abroad programs are available in 14 countries. There are 3-2 degrees in management, forestry, and computer science. There are 7 national honor societies, including Phi Beta Kappa.

Faculty/Classroom: 58% of faculty are male; 42%, female. All both teach and do research. No introductory courses are taught by graduate students. The average class size in an introductory lecture is 19; in a laboratory, 14; and in a regular course, 16.

Admissions: 83% of the 2005-2006 applicants were accepted. The SAT scores for the 2005-2006 freshman class were: Verbal--7% below 500, 30% between 500 and 599, 46% between 600 and 700, and 17% above 700; Math--6% below 500, 33% between 500 and 599, 48% between 600 and 700, and 13% above 700. The ACT scores were 5% below 21, 11% between 21 and 23, 28% between 24 and 26, 27% between 27 and 28, and 29% above 28. 64% of the current freshmen were in the top fifth of their class; 91% were in the top two fifths. 30 freshmen graduated first in their class.

Requirements: The SAT or ACT is required. The ACT Optional Writing test is also required. In addition, graduation from an accredited secondary school or satisfactory scores on the GED are required. Institutional preferences include 4 years each of English and math, and 3 years each of foreign language, lab science, and social studies or history. 2 essays are required, and an interview is recommended. Portfolios or auditions are recommended for art and music students. A GPA of 2.0 is required. AP credits are accepted. Important factors in the admissions decision are advanced placement or honor courses and recommendations by school officials.

Procedure: Freshmen are admitted fall and spring. Entrance exams should be taken by the end of December. There is a deferred admissions plan. Applications should be filed by February 1 for fall entry and November 1 for spring entry, along with a $50 fee. Notification is sent April 1. 509 early decision candidates were accepted for the 2005-2006 class. A waiting list is an active part of the admissions procedure. Applications are accepted on-line.

Transfer: 65 transfer students enrolled in 2004-2005. Transfer students must submit transcripts for all college and high school courses. A minimum GPA of 2.0 is required, as is a Transfer Reference Form (recommendation form). 60 of 124 credits required for the bachelor's degree must be completed at Willamette.

Visiting: There are regularly scheduled orientations for prospective students, consisting of fall and spring campus preview days, tours, and faculty and student presentations. There are guides for informal visits and visitors may sit in on classes and stay overnight. To schedule a visit, contact Martha Cripe at *liberts@willamette.edu.*

Financial Aid: In 2005-2006, 95% of all full-time freshmen and 94% of continuing full-time students received some form of financial aid. In a recent year, all full-time freshmen and 94% of continuing full-time students received need-based aid. The average freshman award in 2005-2006 was $23,382. Need-based scholarships or need-based grants averaged $18,666; need-based self-help aid (loans and jobs) averaged $5130 ($7313 maximum); and other non-need-based awards and non-need-based scholarships averaged $8340. 55% of undergraduates work part time. Average annual earnings from campus work are $1855. The average financial indebtedness of the 2005 graduate was $18,756. Willamette is a member of CSS. The FAFSA is required. Students applying for admission under the early action program must also file the CSS. The deadline for filing freshman financial aid applications for fall entry is February 1.

International Students: There are 36 international students enrolled. The school actively recruits these students. A satisfactory score is required on the written TOEFL. Students must also take the ELPT (English Language Placement Test) as well as the SAT or the ACT.

Computers: Wireless access is available. Computers connected to the college's network are available at several different locations. There are 2 24-hour PC labs. Wireless internet connection is available in all administrative buildings, the library, and student dorm lounges. All students may access the system 24 hours per day. There are no time limits and no fees.

Graduates: From July 1, 2004 to June 30, 2005, 442 bachelor's degrees were awarded. The most popular majors were politics (12%), biology (10%), and economics (10%). In an average class, 67% graduate in 4 years or less, 74% graduate in 5 years or less, and 74% graduate in 6 years or less. 109 companies recruited on campus in 2004-2005.

Admissions Contact: Robin Brown, Vice President, Enrollment. E-mail: *libarts@willamette.edu* Web: *http://www.willamette.edu*

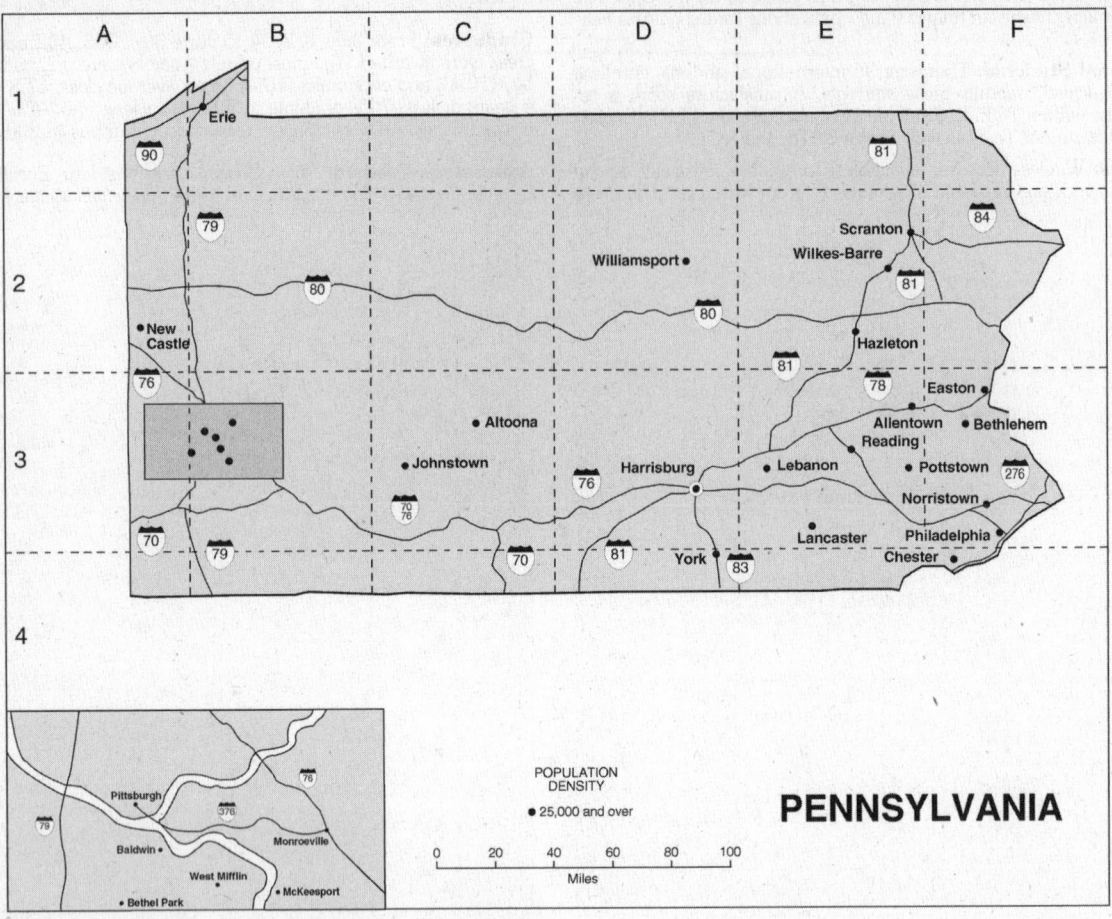

POPULATION
DENSITY

● 25,000 and over

PENNSYLVANIA

0 20 40 60 80 100
Miles

ALBRIGHT COLLEGE   E-3
Reading, PA 19612-5234   (610) 921-7512
                        (800) 252-1856; Fax: (610) 921-7294

Full-time: 662 men, 961 women	**Faculty:** 105; IIB, -$
Part-time: 235 men, 307 women	**Ph.D.s:** 2%
Graduate: 23 men, 55 women	**Student/Faculty:** 15 to 1
Year: 4-1-4, summer session	**Tuition:** $26,032
Application Deadline: open	**Room & Board:** $7888

Freshman Class: 3058 applied, 2125 accepted, 451 enrolled
SAT Verbal/Math: 520/510*   **COMPETITIVE**

Albright College, founded in 1856, is a private liberal arts institution affiliated with the United Methodist Church. There is 1 undergraduate and 1 graduate school. The 2 libraries contain 218,465 volumes, 83,934 microform items, and 23,435 audio/video tapes/CDs/DVDs, and subscribe to 725 periodicals including electronic. Computerized library services include the card catalog, interlibrary loans, database searching, and Internet access. Special learning facilities include a learning resource center, art gallery, radio station, a multicultural center, and centers for women and child development. The 118-acre campus is in a suburban area 55 miles west of Philadelphia. Including any residence halls, there are 36 buildings.

Student Life: 63% of undergraduates are from Pennsylvania. Others are from 26 states and 28 foreign countries. 73% are from public schools. 79% are white. 51% are claim no religious affiliation; 24% Catholic; 23% Protestant. The average age of freshmen is 18; all undergraduates, 22. 21% do not continue beyond their first year; 59% remain to graduate.

Housing: 1104 students can be accommodated in college housing, which includes single-sex and coed dormitories and on-campus apartments. In addition, there are honors houses and special-interest houses. On-campus housing is guaranteed for all 4 years. 69% of students live on campus; of those, 95% remain on campus on weekends. Upperclassmen may keep cars.

Activities: 28% of men belong to 3 national fraternities; 32% of women belong to 3 national sororities. There are 70 groups on campus, including band, cheerleading, chess, choir, chorus, computers, dance, drama, ethnic, film, honors, international, jazz band, literary magazine, musical theater, newspaper, pep band, photography, political, professional, radio and TV, religious, social, social service, student government, and yearbook. Popular campus events include Dance Marathon, Greek Weekend, and Spring Fever Weekend.

Sports: There are 11 intercollegiate sports for men and 11 for women, and 3 intramural sports for men and 4 for women. Facilities include a 5000-seat stadium, baseball, softball, and soccer fields, fitness center, weight room, indoor and outdoor tracks, bowling alley, a swimming pool, and racquetball courts.

Disabled Students: 75% of the campus is accessible. Wheelchair ramps, elevators, special parking, specially equipped rest rooms, and special class scheduling are available.

Services: Counseling and information services are available, as is tutoring in most subjects. There is a reader service for the blind. An academic learning center, a writing center, and an ESL program are available.

Campus Safety and Security: Measures include 24-hour foot and vehicle patrol, self-defense education, security escort services, and shuttle buses. There are informal discussions, pamphlets/posters/films, emergency telephones, lighted pathways/sidewalks, a Comprehensive Crisis Action Plan, and a bicycle patrol. All officers are CPR, AED, and first aid certified.

Programs of Study: Albright confers B.A. and B.S. degrees. Master's degrees are also awarded. Bachelor's degrees are awarded in BIOLOGICAL SCIENCE (biochemistry and biology/biological science), BUSINESS (accounting, business administration and management, and fashion merchandising), COMMUNICATIONS AND THE ARTS (art, communications, digital communications, dramatic arts, English, French, music business management, and Spanish), COMPUTER AND PHYSICAL SCIENCE (chemistry, computer science, information sciences and systems, mathematics, and physics), EDUCATION (elementary, secondary, and special), ENGINEERING AND ENVIRONMENTAL DESIGN (environmental science), SOCIAL SCIENCE (American studies, child care/child and family studies, criminal justice, economics, history, Latin American studies, philosophy, political science/government, psychobiology, psychology, religion, sociology, textiles and clothing, and women's studies). Biology, psychology, and business are the largest.

Required: To graduate, students must complete 32 courses, including 13 to 14 in the major, with a minimum GPA of 2.0. All students take 1 interdisciplinary course, and they must fulfill the cultural experience requirement. General studies requirements include 11 to 15 courses in English composition, a foreign language, natural science, quantitative reasoning, social science, the arts, and humanities (literature, history, philosophy and religion).

Special: Co-op programs are available in forestry, environmental studies, and natural resources with Duke University and the University of Michigan. The school offers credit and noncredit internships, a Washington semester, an accelerated degree program, cross-registration, dual majors, student-designed majors, nondegree study, and pass/fail options. Study abroad may be arranged in any country. There are 11 national honor societies, and a freshman honors program.

Faculty/Classroom: 52% of faculty are male; 48%, female. All teach undergraduates. The average class size in an introductory lecture is 25; in a laboratory, 15; and in a regular course, 18.

Admissions: 69% of the 2005-2006 applicants were accepted. The SAT scores for the 2005-2006 freshman class were: Verbal--41% below 500, 42% between 500 and 599, 16% between 600 and 700, and 1% above 700; Math--38% below 500, 44% between 500 and 599, 17% between 600 and 700, and 1% above 700. 79% were in the top two fifths. 6 freshmen graduated first in their class.

Requirements: The SAT is required. In addition, graduation from an accredited secondary school or satisfactory scores on the GED are required for admission. Students must have a total of 16 Carnegie units, including 4 years of English, 3 in science, including 1 lab, 2 years each of a foreign language, math, and social studies, and 3 electives in college preparatory subjects. An essay is required, and an interview recommended. AP and CLEP credits are accepted. Important factors in the admissions decision are advanced placement or honor courses, leadership record, and recommendations by school officials.

Procedure: Freshmen are admitted fall, spring, and summer. Entrance exams should be taken during the spring of the junior year or the fall of the senior year. There are early admissions, deferred and rolliong admissions plans. Application deadlines are open. Applications are accepted on-line. The fall 2005 application fee was $25.

Transfer: 51 transfer students enrolled in 2004-2005. Transfer students must have a minimum GPA of 2.5 and be in good standing. 64 of 128 credits required for the bachelor's degree must be completed at Albright.

Visiting: There are regularly scheduled orientations for prospective students, including an interview with a counselor and a tour of the campus with a currently enrolled student. There are guides for informal visits and visitors may sit in on classes and stay overnight. To schedule a visit, contact the Admissions Office.

Financial Aid: In 2005-2006, 95% of all full-time freshmen and 87% of continuing full-time students received some form of financial aid. 87% of full-time freshmen and 86% of continuing full-time students received need-based aid. The average freshman award was $26,120. Need-based scholarships or need-based grants averaged $5533 ($25,232 maximum); need-based self-help aid (loans and jobs) averaged $5142 ($9125 maximum); and other non-need-based awards and non-need-based scholarships averaged $10,046 ($15,000 maximum). 44% of undergraduates work part time. Average annual earnings from campus work are $840. The average financial indebtedness of the 2005 graduate was $23,000. The FAFSA is required. The priority date for freshman financial aid applications for fall entry is March 1.

International Students: There are 83 international students enrolled. The school actively recruits these students. They must take the TOEFL or the MELAB, the Comprehensive English Language Test, or the college's own test and also take the SAT or ACT. They can take the TOEFL in lieu of the SAT.

Computers: Wireless access is available. There is a separate logical network, wired throughout the dorms, allowing students to attach a registered PC or MAC computing device to the Internet. Students may also register a wireless connection to the wireless LAN, which is available in all classrooms and in many public areas. There are more than 10 computer labs providing access to popular shrink-wrap software such as MS-Office and the Internet. All students may access the system 24 hours/day, 7 days/week. There are no time limits and no fees. It is strongly recommended that all students have a personal computer.

Graduates: From July 1, 2004 to June 30, 2005, 349 bachelor's degrees were awarded. The most popular majors were business administration (13%), psychology/psychobiology (11%), and biology/biochemistry (7%). In an average class, 1% graduate in 3 years or less, 52% graduate in 4 years or less, 56% graduate in 5 years or less, and 59% graduate in 6 years or less. 68 companies recruited on campus in 2004-2005. Of the 2004 graduating class, 23% were enrolled in graduate school within 6 months of graduation and 98% were employed.

Admissions Contact: Gregory E. Eichhorn, Vice President for Enrollment Management and Dean of Admissions. E-mail: *albright@alb.edu* Web: *www.albright.edu*

ALLEGHENY COLLEGE   B-1
Meadville, PA 16335

(814) 332-4351
(800) 521-5293; Fax: (814) 337-0431

Full-time: 945 men, 1065 women	**Faculty:** 135; IIB, av$
Part-time: 17 men, 26 women	**Ph.D.s:** 95%
Graduate: none	**Student/Faculty:** 15 to 1
Year: semesters	**Tuition:** $26,950
Application Deadline: February 15	**Room & Board:** $6550
Freshman Class: 3540 applied, 2206 accepted, 561 enrolled	
SAT Verbal/Math: 610/610*	**ACT:** 25 **HIGHLY COMPETITIVE**

Allegheny College, founded in 1815, is a private liberal arts institution affiliated with the United Methodist Church. The library contains 957,724 volumes, 488,286 microform items, and 6754 audio/video tapes/CDs/DVDs, and subscribes to 4542 periodicals including electronic. Computerized library services include the card catalog, interlibrary loans, database searching, Internet access, and laptop Internet portals. Special learning facilities include a learning resource center, art gallery, planetarium, radio station, TV station, and TV studio, observatory, 283-acre experimental research reserve, art studio, 80-acre protected forest, dance studio, Geographic Information Systems Learning Laboratory, language learning center, and a nationally acclaimed science complex. The 542-acre campus is in a small town 90 miles north of Pittsburgh and east of Cleveland. Including any residence halls, there are 33 buildings.

Student Life: 64% of undergraduates are from Pennsylvania. Students are from 33 states, 27 foreign countries, and Canada. 82% are from public schools. 93% are white. 37% are Catholic; 31% Protestant; 24% claim no religious affiliation; 6% Buddhist, Hindu, Moslem, Orthodox, Jesus Christ Latter-Day Saint, Christian Disciples, Christian Scientist, Jehovah Witness, Quaker, Unitarian. The average age of freshmen is 19; all undergraduates, 20. 10% do not continue beyond their first year; 69% remain to graduate.

Housing: 1450 students can be accommodated in college housing, which includes single-sex and coed dorms, on-campus apartments, off-campus apartments, and fraternity houses. In addition, there are language houses special-interest houses, and wellness floors. On-campus housing is guaranteed for all 4 years. 97% of students live on campus; of those, 75% remain on campus on weekends. All students may keep cars.

Activities: 24% of men belong to 5 national fraternities; 26% of women belong to 4 national sororities. There are 100 groups on campus, including academic, art, band, cheerleading, choir, chorale, chorus, computers, dance, debate, drama, ethnic, environmental, gay, honors, international, jazz band, literary magazine, music ensembles, musical theater, newspaper, orchestra, outdoor, pep band, photography, political, professional, radio and TV, religious, social, social service, student government, symphony, and yearbook. Popular campus events include Black History Month, Latino Heritage Month, Celebrate Asia.

Sports: There are 10 intercollegiate sports for men and 11 for women, and 13 intramural sports for men and 14 for women. Facilities include a sports and fitness center that includes a training track, weight rooms, a variety of cardio machines, 4 multipurpose courts (volleyball, basketball, tennis, badminton, putting green, batting cage), a natatorium, a dance studio, 3 racquetball courts, and a performance floor, an outdoor complex with a stadium, cross-country course, 8 fields, 12 lighted tennis courts, a challenge course, and picnic shelter. In addition, there are 80 wooded acres for mountain biking, hiking, and cross-country skiing.

Disabled Students: 35% of the campus is accessible. Wheelchair ramps, elevators, special parking, specially equipped rest rooms, special class scheduling, lowered drinking fountains and special housing. Reasonable accommodations are made for all special needs.

Services: Counseling and information services are available, as is tutoring in some subjects, including biology, chemistry, economics, computer science, environmental science, geology, math, physics, psychology, foreign languages, writing, technology and speech. There is a reader service for the blind, and remedial math, reading, and writing. There is also help with study skills, a speech center, a learning center, a note-taking scribe services, tape recorders, and books on tape.

Campus Safety and Security: Measures include 24-hour foot and vehicle patrol, self-defense education, security escort services, and informal discussions. There are pamphlets/posters/films, emergency telephones, lighted pathways/sidewalks, and TTY phones, emergency medical dispatching, AED certified officers, van driving training, parking issues, access to dorms with key only, motorist assistance, smoke detectors in all residence halls, and student patrols.

Programs of Study: Allegheny confers B.A. and B.S. degrees. Bachelor's degrees are awarded in AGRICULTURE (environmental studies), BIOLOGICAL SCIENCE (biochemistry, biology/biological science, and neurosciences), COMMUNICATIONS AND THE ARTS (art, art history and appreciation, communications, dramatic arts, English, French, German, music, Spanish, and studio art), COMPUTER AND PHYSICAL SCIENCE (chemistry, computer science, environmental geology, geology, mathematics, physics, and software engineering), ENGINEERING AND ENVIRONMENTAL DESIGN (environmental science), SOCIAL

SCIENCE (economics, history, international studies, philosophy, political science/government, psychology, religion, and women's studies). Physical and biological sciences, political science, and English are the strongest academically. Psychology, English, and political science are the largest.

Required: To graduate, students must complete 131 credit hours with a minimum GPA of 2.0 in both the major and minor. Between 32 and 64 hours are required in the major, including the junior seminar and senior research project. All students must fulfill liberal studies requirements of 8 credits each in arts and humanities, natural sciences, and social sciences. The liberal studies program extends through all 4 years and promotes breadth at both introductory and advanced levels of study. Additional required courses include freshman first seminar, freshman second seminar, a sophomore writing and speaking seminar, and academic planning seminars. All graduating seniors complete independent research project. Most departments require an oral defense of the project.

Special: Allegheny offers a Washington semester, internships, dual majors, student-designed majors, study abroad in 14 countries, work study, and co-op programs. A 3-2 engineering degree is available with Case Western Reserve, Columbia, Duke, Pittsburgh, and Washington Universities. An accelerated masters program through Carnegie Mellon University for public policy and management programs, reprofessional programs, independent study, a marine biology study program, and an experiential learning term are also available. There are 13 national honor societies, including Phi Beta Kappa, and 18 departmental honors programs.

Faculty/Classroom: 61% of faculty are male; 39%, female. 100% both teach and do research. The average class size in an introductory lecture is 22; in a laboratory, 22; and in a regular course, 22.

Admissions: 62% of the 2005-2006 applicants were accepted. The SAT scores for the 2005-2006 freshman class were: Verbal--6% below 500, 31% between 500 and 599, 49% between 600 and 700, and 14% above 700; Math--4% below 500, 36% between 500 and 599, 51% between 600 and 700, and 9% above 700. The ACT scores were 9% below 21, 21% between 21 and 23, 30% between 24 and 26, 21% between 27 and 28, and 19% above 28. 70% of the current freshmen were in the top fifth of their class; 91% were in the top two fifths. There were 3 National Merit semifinalists.

Requirements: The SAT or ACT is required. In addition, SAT subject tests are recommended in writing and in the student's expected major. Graduation from an accredited secondary school is required for admission. Students must have 16 Carnegie units, including 4 years of English, 3 years each of math, science, and social studies, and 2 years of a foreign language. An essay is required, and an interview is recommended. The GED is accepted. A college prep program is required, along with 2 letters of recommendation (1 from guidance counselor, 1 from teacher). AP and CLEP credits are accepted.

Procedure: Freshmen are admitted fall and spring. Entrance exams should be taken by January of the senior year. There are early decision, early admissions, and deferred admissions plans. Early decision applications should be filed by November 15; regular applications, by February 15 for fall entry and November 1 for spring entry, along with a $35 fee. Notification of early decision is sent December 15; regular decision, April 1. 68 early decision candidates were accepted for the 2005-2006 class. 352 applicants were on the 2005 waiting list; 32 were admitted. Applications are accepted on-line.

Transfer: 16 transfer students enrolled in 2004-2005. Transfer applicants must submit a transcript of all college courses, a high school transcript, standardized test scores, a statement of good standing, a letter describing reasons for transfer, and have a minimum GPA of 2.5, with 3.0 recommended. 67 of 131 credits required for the bachelor's degree must be completed at Allegheny.

Visiting: There are regularly scheduled orientations for prospective students, consisting of tours, panels, and presentations on academic programs, student life, admissions, and financial aid. There are guides for informal visits and visitors may sit in on classes and stay overnight. To schedule a visit, contact the Office of Admissions at admissions@allegheny.edu.

Financial Aid: In 2005-2006, 99% of all full-time freshmen and 97% of continuing full-time students received some form of financial aid. 70% of full-time freshmen and 67% of continuing full-time students received need-based aid. The average freshman award was $19,600. Need-based scholarships or need-based grants averaged $15,625 ($33,500 maximum); need-based self-help aid (loans and jobs) averaged $5560 ($10,625 maximum); other non-need-based awards and non-need-based scholarships averaged $10,835 ($17,000 maximum); and tuition remission to students without regard to financial need. averaged $24,900 ($26,650 maximum). 66% of undergraduates work part time. Average annual earnings from campus work are $810. The average financial indebtedness of the 2005 graduate was $24,825. The FAFSA is required. The priority date for freshman financial aid applications for fall entry is February 15.

International Students: There are 38 international students enrolled. The school actively recruits these students. A satisfactory score is required. written TOEFL also take the SAT or the ACT.

Computers: Wireless access is available. 311 PCs are networked and available for students to use in the library, residence halls, the campus center, academic buildings, and computer services. The wireless system can accommodate approximately 500 simultaneous us. Wireless access is available in residence hall lounges and patios, the library, campus center, and food court area. All students may access the system 24 hours per day. There are no time limits and no fees. It is strongly recommended that all students have a personal computer. A computer with Intel/Windows is recommended.

Graduates: From July 1, 2004 to June 30, 2005, 381 bachelor's degrees were awarded. The most popular majors were psychology (16%), biology (13%), and political science (12%). In an average class, 67% graduate in 4 years, 71% graduate in 5 ears, and 69% graduate in 6 years or less. 9 companies recruited on campus in 2004-2005. Of the 2004 graduating class, 52% were enrolled in graduate school within 6 months of graduation and 92% were employed.

Admissions Contact: Jennifer Winge, Director of Admissions.
E-mail: admissions@allegheny.edu Web: www.allegheny.edu

ALVERNIA COLLEGE   E-3

Reading, PA 19607

(610) 796-8220
(888) Alvernia; Fax: (610) 796-8336

Full-time: 506 men, 1009 women	**Faculty:** IIB, --$
Part-time: 120 men, 361 women	**Ph.D.s:** n/av
Graduate: 241 men, 498 women	**Student/Faculty:** 17 to 1
Year: semesters, summer session	**Tuition:** $19,089
Application Deadline: open	**Room & Board:** $7299
Freshman Class: 922 applied, 699 accepted, 274 enrolled	
SAT or ACT: n/av	**COMPETITIVE**

Alvernia College, established in 1958, is a Roman Catholic liberal arts institution. Some figures in the above capsule and in this profile are approximate. In addition to regional accreditation, Alvernia has baccalaureate program accreditation with ACOTE, APTA, CCNE, CSWE, NCATE, and NLN. The library contains 86,647 volumes and 1967 audio/video tapes/CDs/DVDs, and subscribes to 390 periodicals including electronic. Computerized library services include the card catalog, interlibrary loans, and database searching. The 85-acre campus is in a suburban area 3 miles southwest of Reading. Including any residence halls, there are 14 buildings.

Student Life: 88% of undergraduates are from Pennsylvania. Others are from 12 states and 9 foreign countries. 76% are from public schools. 84% are white. 29% are Catholic; 19% claim no religious affiliation. The average age of freshmen is 19; all undergraduates, 24.

Housing: 500 students can be accommodated in college housing, which includes single-sex and coed dormitories and on-campus apartments. In addition, there are honors houses. On-campus housing is guaranteed for the freshman year only and is available on a first-come, first-served basis. Priority is given to out-of-town students. 60% of students commute. Alcohol is not permitted. All students may keep cars.

Activities: There are no fraternities or sororities. There are 31 groups on campus, including cheerleading, chorus, computers, drama, ethnic, honors, international, literary magazine, newspaper, political, professional, religious, student government, and yearbook. Popular campus events include Christmas on Campus, Spring Fling, and Club Fair.

Sports: There are 6 intercollegiate sports for men and 8 for women, and 4 intramural sports for men and 2 for women. Facilities include a gym, a physical fitness and recreation center, playing fields, and outdoor tennis, basketball, and volleyball courts.

Disabled Students: 75% of the campus is accessible. Wheelchair ramps, elevators, special parking, specially equipped rest rooms, special class scheduling, lowered drinking fountains, lowered telephones, and special housing are available.

Services: Counseling and information services are available, as is tutoring in every subject. There is remedial math, reading, and writing. Facilities include a writing center and a math/science tutorial lab.

Campus Safety and Security: Measures include 24-hour foot and vehicle patrol, security escort services, informal discussions, and pamphlets/posters/films. There are emergency telephones and lighted pathways/sidewalks. Photo ID cards must be carried by students.

Programs of Study: Alvernia confers B.A., B.S., B.S.N., and B.S.W. degrees. Associate and master's degrees are also awarded. Bachelor's degrees are awarded in BIOLOGICAL SCIENCE (biochemistry and biology/biological science), BUSINESS (accounting, business administration and management, marketing and distribution, and sports management), COMMUNICATIONS AND THE ARTS (communications and English), COMPUTER AND PHYSICAL SCIENCE (chemistry, information sciences and systems, mathematics, and science), EDUCATION (athletic training, elementary, and secondary), HEALTH PROFESSIONS (nursing), SOCIAL SCIENCE (addiction studies, criminal justice, forensic studies, history, liberal arts/general studies, philosophy, political science/government, psychology, social studies, social work, and theological studies). Biology, chemistry, and occupational therapy are the strongest academically. Criminal justice, education, and forensic science are the largest.

Required: To graduate, all students must complete at least 123 credit hours with a minimum GPA of 2.0 overall and in the major (2.5 for elementary education and nursing majors). Requirements include 54 to 55 credits in a liberal arts core, consisting of theology and philosophy, social science, communications, literature, fine arts, math, and science. All students also must perform 40 clock hours of service to others before graduation, complete course work in college success skills and in human diversity, and demonstrate computer proficiency.

Special: The college offers co-op programs in business and sports management, internships, cross-registration with Kutztown University, Pennsylvania State University, Albright College, and Reading area community colleges, a Washington semester, dual and student-designed majors, and practicums in psychology, criminal justice, education, addiction studies, social work, athletic training, and occupational therapy. There is a freshman honors program.

Faculty/Classroom: 43% of faculty are male; 57%, female. All teach undergraduates. No introductory courses are taught by graduate students. The average class size in an introductory lecture is 21; in a laboratory, 15; and in a regular course, 18.

Admissions: 76% of the 2005-2006 applicants were accepted. The SAT scores for the 2005-2006 freshman class were: Verbal--58% below 500, 31% between 500 and 599, and 11% between 600 and 700; Math--61% below 500, 33% between 500 and 599, and 6% between 600 and 700. 35% of the current freshmen were in the top fifth of their class; 53% were in the top two fifths.

Requirements: All applicants must be graduates of an accredited secondary school or have a GED certificate. They should have completed at least 16 academic units, including 4 in English and electives and 2 each in math, foreign language, science, and social studies. An interview is required for nursing applicants and strongly recommended for all others. A GPA of 2.0 is required. AP and CLEP credits are accepted. Important factors in the admissions decision are advanced placement or honor courses, recommendations by school officials, and extracurricular activities record.

Procedure: Freshmen are admitted fall and spring. Entrance exams should be taken in the spring of the junior year or fall of the senior year. There are deferred admissions and rolling admissions plans. Application deadlines are open. Applications are accepted on-line. The fall 2005 application fee was $25.

Transfer: 107 transfer students enrolled in 2004-2005. Applicants must have a college GPA of 2.0 or better. 45 of 123 credits required for the bachelor's degree must be completed at Alvernia.

Visiting: There are regularly scheduled orientations for prospective students, including faculty displays, lunch, tours of the campus, and the opportunity to interact with current students. There are guides for informal visits and visitors may sit in on classes and stay overnight. To schedule a visit, contact the Admissions Office.

Financial Aid: In 2005-2006, 91% of all full-time students received some form of financial aid. 84% of full-time freshmen and 79% of continuing full-time students received need-based aid. The average freshman award was $13,986. Need-based scholarships or need-based grants averaged $6784; and need-based self-help aid (loans and jobs) averaged $4825. In a recent year, 80% of undergraduates worked part time. Average annual earnings from campus work were $1000. The average financial indebtedness of a recent graduate was $6749. Alvernia is a member of CSS. The FAFSA, the state aid form, and the noncustodial parent's statement, if applicable are required.

International Students: They must score satisfactorily on the written TOEFL.

Computers: All students may access the system. Labs are open 17 hours per day, and the network is available 24 hours per day. There are no time limits and no fees. It is strongly recommended that all students have a personal computer.

Admissions Contact: Catherine Emery, Dean of Enrollment.
E-mail: *admissions@alvernia.edu* Web: *www.alvernia.edu*

ARCADIA UNIVERSITY

Glenside, PA 19038

F-3

(215) 572-2910
(877) ARCADIA; Fax: (215) 572-4049

Full-time: 482 men, 1266 women	**Faculty:** 103; IIA, av$
Part-time: 71 men, 136 women	**Ph.D.s:** 89%
Graduate: 353 men, 1095 women	**Student/Faculty:** 17 to 1
Year: semesters, summer session	**Tuition:** $24,270
Application Deadline: open	**Room & Board:** $9300
Freshman Class: 2432 applied, 2056 accepted, 440 enrolled	
SAT Verbal/Math: 569/553*	**ACT:** 25 **VERY COMPETITIVE**

Arcadia University, founded in 1853, is a private institution offering undergraduate and graduate programs in the fine arts, the sciences, business, education, and preprofessional fields. In addition to regional accreditation, Arcadia University has baccalaureate program accreditation with ACBSP, APTA, CAHEA, and NASAD. The library contains 148,271 volumes, 50,301 microform items, and 3236 audio/video tapes/CDs/DVDs, and subscribes to 7832 periodicals including electronic. Computerized library services include the card catalog, interlibrary loans, database searching, Internet access, and laptop Internet portals. Special learning facilities include a learning resource center, art gallery, radio station, observatory, theater, computer graphics and communication labs, and multimedia classrooms. The 76-acre campus is in a suburban area 10 miles north of Philadelphia. Including any residence halls, there are 21 buildings.

Student Life: 68% of undergraduates are from Pennsylvania. Students are from 24 states and 12 foreign countries. 70% are from public schools. 70% are white. 77% are claim no religious affiliation; 13% Catholic; 8% Protestant. The average age of freshmen is 18; all undergraduates, 22. 19% do not continue beyond their first year; 64% remain to graduate.

Housing: 1284 students can be accommodated in college housing, which includes single-sex and coed dorms, on-campus apartments, and off-campus apartments. On-campus housing is guaranteed for all 4 years. 68% of students live on campus. Upperclassmen may keep cars.

Activities: There are no fraternities or sororities. There are 40 groups on campus, including art, cheerleading, choir, chorale, chorus, computers, dance, drama, ethnic, gay, honors, international, literary magazine, musical theater, newspaper, photography, political, professional, radio and TV, religious, social, social service, student government, and yearbook. Popular campus events include Mr. Beaver contest, Woodstock Weekend, and International Festival.

Sports: There are 6 intercollegiate sports for men and 9 for women, and 5 intramural sports for men and 5 for women. Facilities include a softball field, outdoor tennis and basketball courts, field hockey and soccer/lacrosse fields, and an athletic and recreation center with a 1500-seat gym for basketball and volleyball, an indoor track, an indoor NCAA regulation swimming pool, an aerobics and dance studio, and fitness and training rooms.

Disabled Students: 70% of the campus is accessible. Wheelchair ramps, elevators, special parking, specially equipped rest rooms, special class scheduling, lowered drinking fountains, and lowered telephones are available.

Services: Counseling and information services are available, as is tutoring in every subject. There is a reader service for the blind, and remedial math, reading, and writing.

Campus Safety and Security: Measures include 24-hour foot and vehicle patrol, self-defense education, security escort services, and shuttle buses. There are informal discussions, pamphlets/posters/films, emergency telephones, lighted pathways/sidewalks, alarmed doors, night receptionists, and card access to residence halls.

Programs of Study: Arcadia University confers B.A., B.S., and B.F.A. degrees. Master's and doctoral degrees are also awarded. Bachelor's degrees are awarded in BIOLOGICAL SCIENCE (biology/biological science), BUSINESS (accounting, banking and finance, business administration and management, international business management, marketing/retailing/merchandising, and personnel management), COMMUNICATIONS AND THE ARTS (art history and appreciation, communications, dramatic arts, English, fine arts, graphic design, illustration, photography, and theater design), COMPUTER AND PHYSICAL SCIENCE (chemistry, computer science, mathematics, and science), EDUCATION (art, early childhood, elementary, music, secondary, and special), ENGINEERING AND ENVIRONMENTAL DESIGN (engineering, environmental science, and interior design), HEALTH PROFESSIONS (art therapy, health care administration, predentistry, premedicine, preoptometry, and preveterinary science), SOCIAL SCIENCE (criminal justice, history, international studies, liberal arts/general studies, philosophy, political science/government, prelaw, psychobiology, psychology, and sociology). Biology, psychology, and math are the strongest academically. Fine arts, business, and education are the largest.

Required: Students must take English composition, math, 2 semesters of a lab science, and a foreign language. They must also fulfill 24 credits of distribution requirements in the arts, humanities, and social sciences; core courses in American pluralism and non-Western cultures; and a final project or thesis. 128 credit hours are required to graduate, including 40 to 52 in the major, with a minimum GPA of 2.0.

Special: Internships are encouraged in all majors. There are study-abroad programs in 13 countries and co-op programs in business, computer science, chemistry, actuarial science, and accounting. There is a 3-2 engineering program with Columbia University, a 3-4 optometry program with Jefferson University, and a 3-4 optometry program with the Pennsylvania College of Optometry. Arcadia also offers a Washington semester, work-study, student-designed majors, a dual major in chemistry and business, interdisciplinary majors in scientific illustration, and credit by exam. There are 13 national honor societies and a freshman honors program.

Faculty/Classroom: 44% of faculty are male; 56%, female. All do research. No introductory courses are taught by graduate students. The average class size in an introductory lecture is 28; in a laboratory, 20; and in a regular course, 16.

Admissions: 85% of the 2005-2006 applicants were accepted. The SAT scores for the 2005-2006 freshman class were: Verbal--18% below

500, 47% between 500 and 599, 30% between 600 and 700, and 5% above 700; Math--22% below 500, 47% between 500 and 599, 28% between 600 and 700, and 3% above 700. 51% of the current freshmen were in the top fifth of their class; 86% were in the top two fifths. 4 freshmen graduated first in their class.

Requirements: The SAT is required and the ACT is recommended. The ACT Optional Writing test is also recommended. In addition, applicants must be graduates of an accredited secondary school or have a GED. A total of 16 academic credits is required, including 4 years of English, 3 each of math and social studies, and 2 each of a foreign language and science. An essay is required. All art and illustration majors (except art education) must submit a portfolio. AP and CLEP credits are accepted. Important factors in the admissions decision are advanced placement or honor courses, recommendations by school officials, and extracurricular activities record.

Procedure: Freshmen are admitted fall and spring. Entrance exams should be taken during orientation. There are early decision, early admissions, and deferred admissions plans. There is a rolling admissions plan. Application deadlines are open. Application fee is $30. 12 early decision candidates were accepted for a recent class. Applications are accepted on-line.

Transfer: 167 transfer students enrolled in 2004-2005. Applicants must have a GPA of 2.5. Art majors must submit a portfolio. The SAT or the ACT is required if the student has earned less than 1 year of college credit. An interview is encouraged. 32 of 128 credits required for the bachelor's degree must be completed at Arcadia University.

Visiting: There are regularly scheduled orientations for prospective students, including personal interviews Monday through Saturday, open houses, and opportunities to dine on campus and to meet with faculty, financial aid officers, and current students. There are guides for informal visits and visitors may sit in on classes and stay overnight. To schedule a visit, contact the Office of Enrollment Management.

Financial Aid: In 2005-2006, 99% of all full-time freshmen and 94% of continuing full-time students received some form of financial aid. 77% of full-time freshmen received need-based aid. Need-based scholarships or need-based grants averaged $7992 ($17,735 maximum); need-based self-help aid (loans and jobs) averaged $5594 ($7825 maximum); and other non-need-based awards and non-need-based scholarships averaged $8865 ($23,990 maximum). 30% of undergraduates work part time. Average annual earnings from campus work are $709. The average financial indebtedness of the 2005 graduate was $31,923. The FAFSA, the college's own financial statement, the PHEAA, and parent and student tax returns are required. The priority date for freshman financial aid applications for fall entry is March 1.

International Students: There are 41 international students enrolled. The school actively recruits these students. They must take the TOEFL, achieving a satisfactory score, or take the ILET.

Computers: Wireless access is available. All students may access the system. There are no time limits and no fees.

Graduates: From July 1, 2004 to June 30, 2005, 381 bachelor's degrees were awarded. The most popular majors were business (15%), education (15%), and psychology (11%).

Admissions Contact: Office of Enrollment Management. A video is available. E-mail: *admiss@arcadia.edu* Web: *www.arcadia.edu*

BLOOMSBURG UNIVERSITY OF PENNSYLVANIA   E-2

Bloomsburg, PA 17815   (570) 389-4316; Fax: (570) 389-4741

Full-time: 2889 men, 4368 women | Faculty: 339; IIA, +$
Part-time: 189 men, 337 women | Ph.Ds: 85%
Graduate: 249 men, 538 women | Student/Faculty: 21 to 1
Year: semesters, summer session | Tuition: $6226 ($13,586)
Application Deadline: open | Room & Board: $5376
Freshman Class: 8237 applied, 5570 accepted, 1697 enrolled
SAT Verbal/Math: 500/510*   **COMPETITIVE**

Bloomsburg University of Pennsylvania, founded in 1839, is a public institution offering undergraduate programs in the liberal arts, sciences, business, teacher education, technology, and health professions. There are 4 undergraduate schools and 1 graduate school. In addition to regional accreditation, BU has baccalaureate program accreditation with AACSB, CCNE, CSWE, and NCATE. The library contains 450,700 volumes, 2,111,791 microform items, and 10,195 audio/video tapes/CDs/DVDs, and subscribes to 2826 periodicals including electronic. Computerized library services include the card catalog, interlibrary loans, database searching, Internet access, and laptop Internet portals. Special learning facilities include a learning resource center, art gallery, radio station, and TV station. The 282-acre campus is in a small town 80 miles northeast of Harrisburg. Including any residence halls, there are 54 buildings.

Student Life: 89% of undergraduates are from Pennsylvania. Others are from 25 states, 34 foreign countries, and Canada. 91% are from public schools. 86% are white. The average age of freshmen is 18; all undergraduates, 21. 18% do not continue beyond their first year; 63% remain to graduate.

Housing: 2980 students can be accommodated in college housing, which includes coed dorms, on-campus apartments, and off-campus apartments. In addition, there are honors houses and special-interest houses. On-campus housing is guaranteed for the freshman year only and is available on a first-come, first-served basis. Alcohol is not permitted. All students may keep cars.

Activities: 4% of men belong to 3 local and 12 national fraternities; 6% of women belong to 5 local and 7 national sororities. There are 188 groups on campus, including art, band, cheerleading, chess, choir, chorale, chorus, computers, dance, drama, drill team, ethnic, film, forensics, gay, honors, international, jazz band, literary magazine, marching band, musical theater, newspaper, orchestra, pep band, political, professional, radio and TV, religious, social, social service, student government, and yearbook. Popular campus events include Parents Weekend, Renaissance Jamboree, and Siblings and Children Weekend.

Sports: There are 9 intercollegiate sports for men and 9 for women. Facilities include a 5000-seat stadium, a gym, an athletic field, an indoor track, a 6-lane swimming pool, 9 practice fields, 18 Grasstex tennis courts, racquetball/handball courts, and a 57,000-square-foot recreation facility.

Disabled Students: Wheelchair ramps, elevators, special parking, specially equipped rest rooms, special class scheduling, lowered drinking fountains, and lowered telephones are available.

Services: Counseling and information services are available, as is tutoring in some subjects. There is a reader service for the blind, and remedial math, reading, and writing.

Campus Safety and Security: Measures include 24-hour foot and vehicle patrol, self-defense education, security escort services, and shuttle buses. There are emergency telephones, lighted pathways/sidewalks, monitored surveillance cameras, and strict residence hall security.

Programs of Study: BU confers B.A., B.S., B.S.Ed., and B.S.N. degrees. Associate, master's, and doctoral degrees are also awarded. Bachelor's degrees are awarded in BIOLOGICAL SCIENCE (biology/biological science), BUSINESS (accounting, business administration and management, and business economics), COMMUNICATIONS AND THE ARTS (art history and appreciation, communications, dramatic arts, English, French, German, music, Spanish, speech/debate/rhetoric, and studio art), COMPUTER AND PHYSICAL SCIENCE (chemistry, computer science, earth science, geology, mathematics, physics, and radiological technology), EDUCATION (business, early childhood, elementary, science, secondary, social studies, and special), ENGINEERING AND ENVIRONMENTAL DESIGN (electrical/electronics engineering), HEALTH PROFESSIONS (medical laboratory technology, nursing, and speech pathology/audiology), SOCIAL SCIENCE (anthropology, criminal justice, economics, geography, history, philosophy, physical fitness/movement, political science/government, psychology, social work, and sociology). Elementary education, business adminstration, and special education are the largest.

Required: To graduate, students must complete 120 credit hours with a minimum GPA of 2.0. BU requires 12 semester hours each in humanities, social sciences, natural sciences, and math. There are specific course requirements in communication, quantitative/analytical reasoning, values, ethics, responsible decision making, and survival, fitness, and recreational skills.

Special: Internships for upperclassmen, study abroad in more than 11 countries, work-study programs, and dual majors are available. BU offers a 3-2 engineering degree with Pennsylvania State and Wilkes Universities. There is nondegree study, pass/fail, and credit for life, military, and work experience. The school uses telecourses and interactive video. There are 8 national honor societies, a freshman honors program, and 15 departmental honors programs.

Faculty/Classroom: 59% of faculty are male; 41%, female. No introductory courses are taught by graduate students. The average class size in a laboratory is 14 and in a regular course, 29.

Admissions: 68% of the 2005-2006 applicants were accepted. The SAT scores for the 2005-2006 freshman class were: Verbal--48% below 500, 43% between 500 and 599, and 9% between 600 and 700; Math--41% below 500, 47% between 500 and 599, and 12% between 600 and 700. 25% of the current freshmen were in the top fifth of their class; 60% were in the top two fifths. 9 freshmen graduated first in their class.

Requirements: A satisfactory score on the SAT or ACT is required. In addition, applicants must be graduates of an accredited secondary school. To be competitive, a student should also rank in the top 30% of the high school class with a B average. The GED is accepted. Applicants should complete 4 years each of English and social studies, 3 each of math and science, and 2 of a foreign language. An interview is recommended. AP and CLEP credits are accepted.

Procedure: Freshmen are admitted to all sessions. Entrance exams should be taken during the junior year. There are early decision, early admissions, and deferred admissions plans. Early decision applications should be filed by November 15; deadline are open for regular applications. The fall 2005 application fee was $30. Notification is sent on a rolling basis. 303 early decision candidates were accepted for the 2005-2006 class. 71 applicants were on the 2005 waiting list. Applications are accepted on-line.

Transfer: 413 transfer students enrolled in 2004-2005. Either the SAT or ACT is required from applicants who have completed fewer than 24 semester hours of college credits. An official secondary school transcript or a GED and official transcripts from any post-secondary schools attended are also required. Applicants must have a minimum GPA of 2.0 (2.5 or 2.8 for some majors) and be in good standing at the college last attended. Those who have completed 30 semester hours must select a major upon entering BU. 30 of 120 credits required for the bachelor's degree must be completed at BU.

Visiting: There are regularly scheduled orientations for prospective students, consisting of a general meeting with admissions staff, a question-and-answer session, a campus tour, lunch, and meetings with academic faculty. There are guides for informal visits and visitors may sit in on classes. To schedule a visit, contact the Admissions Office.

Financial Aid: In 2005-2006, 81% of all full-time freshmen and 78% of continuing full-time students received some form of financial aid. 65% of all full-time students received need-based aid. The average freshman award was $9362. Need-based scholarships or need-based grants averaged $4491; need-based self-help aid (loans and jobs) averaged $3449; and non-need-based athletic scholarships averaged $2111. The average financial indebtedness of the 2005 graduate was $16,442. The FAFSA and PHEAA Aid Information Request (PAIR) are required. The priority date for freshman financial aid applications for fall entry is March 15.

International Students: There are 50 international students enrolled. They must score satisfactorily on the written TOEFL.

Computers: Wireless access is available on a selected-service basis. There are no time limits and no fees.

Graduates: From July 1, 2004 to June 30, 2005, 1403 bachelor's degrees were awarded. The most popular majors were business administration (16%), elementary education (13%), and communications (6%). In an average class, 37% graduate in 4 years or less, 60% graduate in 5 years or less, and 63% graduate in 6 years or less. 28 companies recruited on campus in 2003-2004. Of the 2004 graduating class, 15% were enrolled in graduate school within 6 months of graduation and 87% were employed.

Admissions Contact: Christopher Keller, Director of Admissions. E-mail: *buadmiss@bloomu.edu* Web: *www.bloomu.edu/admissions/*

BRYN ATHYN COLLEGE OF THE NEW CHURCH F-3

Bryn Athyn, PA 19009   (267) 502-2511; Fax: (267) 502-2658

Full-time: 53 men, 80 women	**Faculty:** 20
Part-time: 4 men, 5 women	**Ph.D.s:** 75%
Graduate: 2 men, 3 women	**Student/Faculty:** 7 to 1
Year: trimesters	**Tuition:** $9639
Application Deadline: February 1	**Room & Board:** $5360
Freshman Class: 52 applied, 50 accepted, 45 enrolled	
SAT Verbal/Math: 550/530*	**NONCOMPETITIVE**

Bryn Athyn College of the New Church, founded in 1877, is a private, independent, liberal arts institution affiliated with the General Church of the New Jerusalem. The 2 libraries contain 104,358 volumes, 3404 microform items, and 1250 audio/video tapes/CDs/DVDs, and subscribe to 319 periodicals including electronic. Computerized library services include the card catalog, interlibrary loans, database searching, and Internet access. Special learning facilities include a museum, performing arts center, and archives. The 130-acre campus is in a suburban area 15 miles northeast of Philadelphia. Including any residence halls, there are 13 buildings.

Student Life: 61% of undergraduates are from Pennsylvania. Others are from 12 states, 10 foreign countries, and Canada. 18% are from public schools. 71% are white; 19% foreign nationals. Most are General Church of the New Jerusalem. The average age of freshmen is 18; all undergraduates, 20. 34% do not continue beyond their first year; 20% remain to graduate.

Housing: 98 students can be accommodated in college housing, which includes single-sex dorms and off-campus apartments. On-campus housing is guaranteed for all 4 years. 63% of students live on campus; and all remain on campus on weekends. Alcohol is not permitted. All students may keep cars.

Activities: 115% of women belong to 1 local sorority. There are no fraternities. There are 13 groups on campus, including business, chorale, drama, international, newspaper, outing, psychology, social, social service, and student government. Popular campus events include charter day, service day, and alumni weekend.

Sports: There are 5 intercollegiate sports for men and 4 for women. Facilities include a 500-seat gym, an outdoor skating rink, tennis courts, 2 athletic fields, a fitness center, and a dance studio.

Disabled Students: 35% of the campus is accessible. Wheelchair ramps, special parking, and specially equipped rest rooms are available.

Services: Counseling and information services are available, as is tutoring in most subjects.

Campus Safety and Security: Measures include informal discussions, emergency telephones, lighted pathways/sidewalks, and an 18-hour foot and vehicle patrol.

Programs of Study: Bryn Athyn College confers B.A. and B.S. degrees. Associate and master's degrees are also awarded. Bachelor's degrees are awarded in BIOLOGICAL SCIENCE (biology/biological science), COMMUNICATIONS AND THE ARTS (English), EDUCATION (education), SOCIAL SCIENCE (history, interdisciplinary studies, and religion). Interdisciplinary studies, history, and education are the largest.

Required: To graduate, students must complete a total of 136 credit hours with a minimum GPA of 1.9. All students must take required courses in religion, writing, philosophy, and phys ed. Some majors require a comprehensive exam or thesis.

Special: Cross-registration is available with Holy Family University. Also available are co-op programs, internships, B.A.-B.S. degrees, student-designed majors, nondegree study, and study-abroad opportunites.

Faculty/Classroom: 59% of faculty are male; 41%, female. All teach undergraduates and 45% both teach and do research. No introductory courses are taught by graduate students. The average class size in a regular course is 10.

Admissions: 96% of the 2005-2006 applicants were accepted. The SAT scores for the 2005-2006 freshman class were: Verbal--35% below 500, 20% between 500 and 599, 33% between 600 and 700, and 5% above 700; Math--35% below 500, 31% between 500 and 599, and 4% above 700. The ACT scores were 50% above 28. There were 2 National Merit finalists.

Requirements: The SAT or ACT is required. Applicants must be graduates of an accredited secondary school or achieve satisfactory scores on the GED. An interview is recommended. A GPA of 2.2 is required. AP and CLEP credits are accepted. Important factors in the admissions decision are recommendations by school officials, personality/intangible qualities, and advanced placement or honor courses.

Procedure: Freshmen are admitted to all sessions. Entrance exams should be taken by fall of senior year. Applications should be filed by February 1 for fall entry, October 1 for winter entry, and January 1 for spring entry, along with a $30 fee. Notification is sent on a rolling basis. Applications are accepted on-line.

Transfer: 6 transfer students enrolled in 2004-2005. Transfer students must supply SAT or ACT scores, transcripts, course descriptions, and teacher, adviser, and employer recommendations. An interview is recommended. 60 of 136 credits required for the bachelor's degree must be completed at Bryn Athyn College.

Visiting: There are regularly scheduled orientations for prospective students, consisting of campus tours, chapel attendance, and visiting classes. There are guides for informal visits and visitors may sit in on classes and stay overnight. To schedule a visit, contact Brittany Barnett at *Brittany.barnett@brynathyn.edu.*

Financial Aid: In 2005-2006, 70% of all full-time freshmen and 66% of continuing full-time students received some form of financial aid. 50% of full-time freshmen and 46% of continuing full-time students received need-based aid. The average freshman award was $6689. Need-based scholarships or need-based grants averaged $4274 ($11,143 maximum); need-based self-help aid (loans and jobs) averaged $1063 ($4625 maximum); and other non-need-based awards and non-need-based scholarships averaged $1352 ($6000 maximum). 22% of undergraduates work part time. The average financial indebtedness of the 2005 graduate was $1431. The FAFSA and the college's own financial statement are required. The deadline for filing freshman financial aid applications for fall entry is June 1.

International Students: There are 27 international students enrolled. They must score satisfactorily on the TOEFL.

Computers: All students may access the system 8 A.M. to 1 A.M. There are no time limits and no fees.

Graduates: From July 1, 2004, to June 30, 2005, 20 bachelor's degrees were awarded. The most popular majors were interdisciplinary studies (43%), history (13%), and education (13%). In an average class, 13% graduate in 4 years or less, 16% graduate in 5 years or less, and 20% graduate in 6 years or less.

Admissions Contact: Brittany Barnett, Counselor. A video is available. E-mail: *Brittany.barnett@brynathyn.edu*
Web: *www.brynathyn.edu*

BRYN MAWR COLLEGE F-3

Bryn Mawr, PA 19010-2899   (610) 526-5152
(800) 262-1885; Fax: (610) 526-7471

Full-time: 25 men, 1260 women	**Faculty:** 146; IIA, ++$
Part-time: 50 women	**Ph.D.s:** 97%
Graduate: 85 men, 370 women	**Student/Faculty:** 9 to 1
Year: semesters, summer session	**Tuition:** $32,230
Application Deadline: see profile	**Room & Board:** $10,550
Freshman Class: n/av	
SAT: required	**HIGHLY COMPETITIVE+**

Bryn Mawr College, founded in 1885, is an independent liberal arts institution, primarily for women. The undergraduate college is for women only. The two graduate schools and postbaccalaureate program are coeducational. Figures in the above capsule and in this profile are approximate. The 4 libraries contain 1,125,116 volumes, 157,521 microform items, and 4008 audio/video tapes/CDs/DVDs, and subscribe to 1859 periodicals including electronic. Computerized library services include the card catalog, interlibrary loans, database searching, and Internet access. Special learning facilities include a learning resource center, art gallery, radio station, an archeological museum, and a language learning center with audio, video, and computer technology. The 135-acre campus is in a suburban area 11 miles west of Philadelphia. Including any residence halls, there are 57 buildings.

Student Life: 80% of undergraduates are from out of state, mostly the Middle Atlantic. Students are from 47 states, 44 foreign countries, and Canada. 62% are from public schools. 50% are white; 12% Asian American. The average age of freshmen is 18; all undergraduates, 20. 3% do not continue beyond their first year; 85% remain to graduate.

Housing: 1218 students can be accommodated in college housing, which includes single-sex and coed dorms and off-campus apartments. In addition, there are language houses, special-interest houses, an African American culture center that houses several students, and a co-op house. On-campus housing is guaranteed for all 4 years. 95% of students live on campus; of those, 85% remain on campus on weekends. Alcohol is not permitted. Upperclassmen may keep cars.

Activities: There are no fraternities. There are 100 groups on campus, including art, chess, choir, chorale, chorus, computers, dance, drama, environmental, ethnic, film, gay, honors, international, literary magazine, musical theater, newspaper, orchestra, photography, political, professional, radio and TV, religious, science fiction, social, social service, student government, and yearbook. Popular campus events include May Day, Lantern Night, and Fall Frolic.

Sports: Facilities include 3 playing fields with access to an indoor track, a gym with an 8-lane pool and diving well, basketball, badminton, and volleyball courts, a gymnastics room and dance studio, a weight-training and fitness room, a 1000-seat auditorium, and a student center.

Disabled Students: Wheelchair ramps, elevators, special parking, specially equipped rest rooms, special class scheduling, lowered drinking fountains, lowered telephones, and special housing are available.

Services: Counseling and information services are available, as is tutoring in every subject. There is a reader service for the blind.

Campus Safety and Security: Measures include 24-hour foot and vehicle patrol, self-defense education, security escort services, and shuttle buses. There are informal discussions, pamphlets/posters/films, emergency telephones, lighted pathways/sidewalks, a web page, and bicycle registration.

Programs of Study: Bryn Mawr confers the A.B. degree. Master's and doctoral degrees are also awarded. Bachelor's degrees are awarded in BIOLOGICAL SCIENCE (biology/biological science), COMMUNICATIONS AND THE ARTS (art history and appreciation, classical languages, classics, comparative literature, English, fine arts, French, German, Greek, Italian, Latin, music, romance languages and literature, Russian, and Spanish), COMPUTER AND PHYSICAL SCIENCE (astronomy, chemistry, geology, mathematics, and physics), SOCIAL SCIENCE (anthropology, archeology, East Asian studies, economics, history, philosophy, political science/government, psychology, religion, sociology, and urban studies). Growth and structure of cities, classical and Near Eastern archeology, and physics are the strongest academically. English, math, and biology are the largest.

Required: To graduate, students must complete 128 semester hours, with 40 to 60 in the major and a minimum GPA of 2.0. All students must complete 2 courses each in the social sciences, the humanities, and natural sciences or math, including 1 lab science. Additional required courses include 2 college seminars and 1 quantitative skills course. Students must be able to demonstrate proficiency in 1 foreign language.

Special: Students may cross-register with Haverford and Swarthmore colleges and the University of Pennsylvania. Internships are available in the cities, sociology, education, and science programs through the Career Development Office. Bryn Mawr sponsors and cosponsors study abroad in 27 countries. Student-designed and dual majors are possible. Pass/fail options, work-study programs, and 3-2 degrees in engineering and city and regional planning with the University of Pennsylvania are offered.

Faculty/Classroom: 50% of faculty are male; 50%, female. All both teach and do research. No introductory courses are taught by graduate students. The average class size in an introductory lecture is 25; in a laboratory, 15; and in a regular course, 16.

Requirements: The SAT is required, the ACT may be substituted. SAT: Subject Tests in writing and 2 other areas are required. Applicants must be graduates of an accredited secondary school. The GED is accepted. Applicants should complete 4 years of English, at least 3 years of foreign language, 3 years of math, and 1 year each of science and history. An essay is required. An interview is strongly recommended. AP credits are accepted. Important factors in the admissions decision are advanced placement or honor courses, evidence of special talent, and extracurricular activities record.

Procedure: Freshmen are admitted in the fall. Entrance exams should be taken in the spring of the junior year or the fall of the senior year.

There are early decision and deferred admissions plans. The application fee is $50. 78 early decision candidates were accepted for a recent class. 176 applicants were on a recent waiting list; 1 were admitted. Applications are accepted on-line. Check with the school for application deadlines.

Transfer: Applicants for transfer must have a minimum college GPA of 3.0. The SAT and recommendations from both college and high school are required. 96 of 128 credits required for the bachelor's degree must be completed at Bryn Mawr.

Visiting: There are regularly scheduled orientations for prospective students, including student-guided campus tours and interviews can be arranged. There are guides for informal visits and visitors may sit in on classes and stay overnight. To schedule a visit, contact the Office of Admissions.

Financial Aid: In a recent year, 59% of all full-time freshmen and 62% of continuing full-time students received some form of financial aid. 58% of full-time freshmen and 56% of continuing full-time students received need-based aid. The average freshman award was $24,500. Need-based scholarships or need-based grants averaged $21,413; and need-based self-help aid (loans and jobs) averaged $5721. 75% of undergraduates worked part time. Average annual earnings from campus work are $1500. The average financial indebtedness of a recent graduate was $17,827. Bryn Mawr is a member of CSS. The CSS/Profile or FAFSA and the prior year's tax returns, the noncustodial parent statement, and the business/farm supplement are required. Check with the school for application deadlines.

International Students: In a recent year, there were 100 international students enrolled. The school actively recruits these students. They must score satisfactorily on the written TOEFL or on the electronic version and also take the SAT or the ACT.

Computers: All students may access the system every day. There are no time limits and no fees.

Graduates: In a recent year, 304 bachelor's degrees were awarded. The most popular majors were political science (12%), English (11%), and biology (9%). In an average class, 2% graduate in 3 years or less, 78% graduate in 4 years or less, 84% graduate in 5 years or less, and 85% graduate in 6 years or less. 175 companies recruited on campus in a recent year. Of a recent graduating class, 20% were enrolled in graduate school within 6 months of graduation and 64% were employed.

Admissions Contact: Jennifer Rickard, Dean of Admissions and Financial Aid. A video is available. E-mail: *admissions@brynmawr.edu* Web: *http://www.brynmawr.edu*

BUCKNELL UNIVERSITY D-2

Lewisburg, PA 17837	**(570) 577-1101; Fax: (570) 577-3538**
Full-time: 1702 men, 1767 women	Faculty: 299; IIA, +$
Part-time: 11 men, 25 women	Ph.D.s: 97%
Graduate: 53 men, 90 women	Student/Faculty: 12 to 1
Year: semesters, summer session	Tuition: $32,788
Application Deadline: January 1	Room & Board: $6872
Freshman Class: 8306 applied, 2820 accepted, 924 enrolled	
SAT Verbal/Math: 640/670*	ACT: 29 MOST COMPETITIVE

Bucknell University, established in 1846, is a private independent institution offering undergraduate and graduate programs in arts, music, education, humanities, management, engineering, sciences, and social sciences. There are 2 undergraduate schools and 1 graduate school. In addition to regional accreditation, Bucknell has baccalaureate program accreditation with ABET, CSAB, NASM, and ACS. The library contains 793,936 volumes, 63 microform items, and 12,468 audio/video tapes/CDs/DVDs, and subscribes to 6059 periodicals including electronic. Computerized library services include the card catalog, interlibrary loans, database searching, Internet access, and laptop Internet portals. Special learning facilities include an art gallery, radio station, outdoor natural area, greenhouse, primate facility, observatory, photography lab, race and gender resource center, library resources training lab, electronic classroom, multimedia lab, conference center, performing arts center, multicultural, writing, craft, and poetry centers, herbarium, and engineering structural test lab. The 450-acre campus is in a small town 75 miles north of Harrisburg. Including any residence halls, there are 123 buildings.

Student Life: 72% of undergraduates are from out of state, mostly the Middle Atlantic. Others are from 46 states, 37 foreign countries, and Canada. 83% are white. 32% are claim no religious affiliation; 29% Catholic; 27% Protestant; 7% Jewish. The average age of freshmen is 18; all undergraduates, 20. 5% do not continue beyond their first year; 90% remain to graduate.

Housing: 2695 students can be accommodated in college housing, which includes single-sex and coed dorms, on-campus apartments, and fraternity houses. In addition, there are special-interest houses and substance-free houses. There are 6 residential colleges for the first year (arts, environmental, humanities, global science and technology, and social justice). On-campus housing is guaranteed for all 4 years. 89% of students live on campus; of those, 85% remain on campus on weekends. Upperclassmen may keep cars.

Activities: 37% of men belong to 11 national fraternities; 39% of women belong to 7 national sororities. There are 135 groups on campus, including art, band, cheerleading, chess, choir, chorale, chorus, dance, drama, ethnic, film, forensics, gay, honors, international, jazz band, literary magazine, newspaper, opera, orchestra, pep band, photography, political, professional, radio, religious, social, social service, student government, symphony, and yearbook. Popular campus events include Celebration for the Arts, and Spring Greek Weekend.

Sports: There are 13 intercollegiate sports for men and 14 for women, and 18 intramural sports for men and 21 for women. Facilities include an athletic and recreation center with an Olympic-size pool a 16,000-sq. foot fitness center, a 4,000-seat basketball arena, a 13,000-seat stadium with 8-lane track, hockey and lacrosse fields, baseball fields, and recreational fields for soccer, softball, and other activities, a field house with a 4-lane track, tennis, squash, and racquetball courts, climbing wall, and dance studio, an 18-hole golf course, and tennnis courts.

Disabled Students: 70% of the campus is accessible. Wheelchair ramps, elevators, special parking, specially equipped rest rooms, special class scheduling, lowered drinking fountains, lowered telephones, and special housing are available. Individual arrangements may be made with faculty for students with disabilities.

Services: Counseling and information services are available, as is tutoring in some subjects, including biology, chemistry, physics, math, and writing across the curriculum.

Campus Safety and Security: Measures include 24-hour foot and vehicle patrol, self-defense education, security escort services, and informal discussions. There are pamphlets/posters/films, emergency telephones, lighted pathways/sidewalks, campus safety alerts, and intrusion alarms in residence halls.

Programs of Study: Bucknell confers B.A., B.S., B.S.B.A., B.S.B.E., B.S.C.E., B.S.Ch.E., B.S.C.S.E., B.S.Ed., B.S.E.E., B.S.M.E and B.Mus. degrees. Master's degrees are also awarded. Bachelor's degrees are awarded in BIOLOGICAL SCIENCE (biochemistry, biology/biological science, and cell biology), BUSINESS (accounting, and business administration and management), COMMUNICATIONS AND THE ARTS (art, art history and appreciation, classics, dramatic arts, English, fine arts, French, German, music, music history and appreciation, music performance, music theory and composition, Russian, and Spanish), COMPUTER AND PHYSICAL SCIENCE (chemistry, computer science, geology, mathematics, and physics), EDUCATION (early childhood, education, educational statistics and research, elementary, music, and secondary), ENGINEERING AND ENVIRONMENTAL DESIGN (biomedical engineering, chemical engineering, civil engineering, computer engineering, electrical/electronics engineering, engineering, environmental science, and mechanical engineering), SOCIAL SCIENCE (anthropology, East Asian studies, economics, geography, history, humanities, interdisciplinary studies, international relations, Latin American studies, philosophy, political science/government, psychology, religion, sociology, and women's studies). Humanities, biology, engineering, and English are the strongest academically. Biology, management, and mechanical engineering are the largest.

Required: All students enrolled in the College of Arts and Sciences must complete a foundation seminar during the first semester; distribution selections include 4 courses in humanities, 3 in natural science and math, 2 in social science, 2 in broadened perspectives for the 21st century addressing issues of the natural and fabricated worlds and issues in human diversity, and a capstone seminar or experience during the senior year. In addition, Bucknell requires a minimum writing competency for graduation. All students enrolled in the College of Engineering have a common first semester and must complete Exploring Engineering (EG 100). A total of 32 courses (34 courses for engineering) and a minimum GPA of 2.0 are required to graduate.

Special: Bucknell offers internships, study abroad in more than 60 countries, a Washington semester, a 5-year B.A.-B.S. degree in arts and engineering, a 3-2 engineering degree, and dual and student-designed majors. An interdisciplinary major in animal behavior is offered through the biology and psychology departments. Nondegree study is possible, and a pass/fail grading option is offered in some courses. The Residential College program offers opportunities for an academic-residential mix and faculty-student collaborative learning. Undergraduate research opportunities are available in the humanities/social sciences and the sciences and engineering. There are 23 national honor societies, including Phi Beta Kappa, and 55 departmental honors programs.

Faculty/Classroom: 65% of faculty are male; 35%, female. All teach undergraduates, and do research. No introductory courses are taught by graduate students. The average class size in an introductory lecture is 24; in a laboratory, 17; and in a regular course, 21.

Admissions: 34% of the 2005-2006 applicants were accepted. The SAT scores for the 2005-2006 freshman class were: Verbal--2% below 500, 22% between 500 and 599, 56% between 600 and 700, and 20% above 700; Math--1% below 500, 11% between 500 and 599, 55% between 600 and 700, and 34% above 700. The ACT scores were 1% below 21, 5% between 21 and 23, 15% between 24 and 26, 21% between 27 and 28, and 59% above 28. 89% of the current freshmen were in the top fifth of their class; 98% were in the top two fifths.

Requirements: The SAT is required. The ACT Optional Writing test is also required. In addition, applicants must graduate from an accredited secondary school or have a GED. 16 units must be earned, including 4 in English, 3 in math, and 2 each in history, science, social studies, and a foreign language. An essay is required, and, an interview is recommended. Music applicants are required to audition. A portfolio is recommended for art applicants. AP and CLEP credits are accepted. Important factors in the admissions decision are advanced placement or honor courses, evidence of special talent, and extracurricular activities record.

Procedure: Freshmen are admitted in the fall. Entrance exams should be taken before January 1. There are early decision and deferred admissions plans. Early decision applications should be filed by November 15; regular applications, by January 1 for fall entry. Notification of early decision is sent December 15; second early decision February 1; regular decision, April 1. 387 early decision candidates were accepted for the 2005-2006 class. 860 applicants were on the 2005 waiting list; 101 were admitted. Applications are accepted on-line.

Transfer: 28 transfer students enrolled in 2004-2005. Transfer students must have a minimum GPA of 2.5 in courses comparable to those offered at Bucknell. The SAT or ACT is required. A minimum of 16 credit hours must have been earned; 32 are recommended. Students are accepted on a space-available basis. An interview is recommended. 48 of 128 credits required for the bachelor's degree must be completed at Bucknell.

Visiting: There are regularly scheduled orientations for prospective students, including an open house for admitted students on the middle Saturday in April and fall visitation program for minority students, and open houses for prospective students in September and November. There are guides for informal visits and visitors may sit in on classes and stay overnight. To schedule a visit, contact the Admissions Office at (570) 577-1101 or *admissions@bucknell.edu.*

Financial Aid: In 2005-2006, 55% of all full-time freshmen and 50% of continuing full-time students received some form of financial aid. 45% of full-time freshmen and 48% of continuing full-time students received need-based aid. The average freshman award was $23,100. Need-based scholarships or need-based grants averaged $18,400; need-based self-help aid (loans and jobs) averaged $5700; non-need-based athletic scholarships averaged $10,000; and other non-need-based awards and non-need-based scholarships averaged $1040. 45% of undergraduates work part time. Average annual earnings from campus work are $1500 to $1800. The average financial indebtedness of the 2005 graduate was $17,400. Bucknell is a member of CSS. The CSS/Profile or FAFSA and noncustodial parent's statement are required. The deadline for filing freshman financial aid applications for fall entry is January 1.

International Students: There are 94 international students enrolled. The school actively recruits these students. They must have satisfactory scores on the TOEFL.

Computers: Wireless access is available. All spaces in academic, administrative, and co-curricular locations (such as lounges) in residence halls are wireless, and several outdoor spaces. There are 620 student accessible PCs throughout campus, some of which are located in 34 labs and classrooms. All students may access the system 24 hours per day, 7 days per week. There are no time limits and no fees. It is strongly recommended that all students have a personal computer.

Graduates: From July 1, 2004, to June 30, 2005, 860 bachelor's degrees were awarded. The most popular majors were management (14%), economics (14%), and biology (7%). In an average class, 85% graduate in 4 years or less, 90% graduate in 5 years or less, and 90% graduate in 6 years or less. 639 companies recruited on campus in 2004-2005. Of the 2004 graduating class, 24% were enrolled in graduate school within 6 months of graduation and 64% were employed.

Admissions Contact: Mark D. Davies, Director of Admissions. A video is available. E-mail: *admissions@bucknell.edu* Web: *http://www.bucknell.edu*

CABRINI COLLEGE   F-4
Radnor, PA 19087-3698

(610) 902-8552
(800) 848-1003; Fax: (610) 902-8508

Full-time: 488 men, 1062 women	**Faculty:** 64; IIB, -$
Part-time: 74 men, 115 women	**Ph.D.s:** 77%
Graduate: 164 men, 415 women	**Student/Faculty:** 24 to 1
Year: semesters, summer session	**Tuition:** $24,000
Application Deadline: open	**Room & Board:** $9340
Freshman Class: 2535 applied, 1648 accepted, 539 enrolled	
SAT Verbal/Math: 490/480*	**ACT:** not required **COMPETITIVE**

Cabrini College, founded in 1957, is a private liberal arts and professional institution founded by the Missionary Sisters of the Sacred Heart of Jesus, a Roman Catholic order. The college is known for its service learning emphasis. In addition to regional accreditation, Cabrini has baccalaureate program accreditation with CSWE. The library contains 243,073 volumes, 118,585 microform items, and 1848 audio/video tapes/CDs/DVDs, and subscribes to 465 periodicals including electronic. Computerized library services include the card catalog, interlibrary loans, database searching, Internet access, and laptop Internet portals. Special learning facilities include a learning resource center, art gallery, radio station, a communications lab with a TV studio, a graphic design lab, a newsroom for the student newspaper, and a science education and technology building with biology, chemistry, biotechnology, and physics labs. There are also information science labs. The 112-acre campus is in a suburban area 20 miles west of Philadelphia. Including any residence halls, there are 23 buildings.

Student Life: 59% of undergraduates are from Pennsylvania. Others are from 21 states, 8 foreign countries, and Canada. 84% are white. 72% are Catholic; 18% Protestant; 7% claim no religious affiliation. The average age of freshmen is 18; all undergraduates, 20. 28% do not continue beyond their first year; 60% remain to graduate.

Housing: 999 students can be accommodated in college housing, which includes single-sex and coed dorms, on-campus apartments, and off-campus apartments. In addition, there are honors houses, language houses, and special-interest houses. On-campus housing is available on a first-come, first-served basis and is available on a lottery system for upperclassmen. Priority is given to out-of-town students. 63% of students live on campus; of those, 63% remain on campus on weekends. Upperclassmen may keep cars.

Activities: There are no fraternities or sororities. There are 41 groups on campus, including cheerleading, choir, chorus, computers, dance, drama, ethnic, honors, international, literary magazine, musical theater, newspaper, photography, political, professional, radio and TV, religious, social, social service, student government, and yearbook. Popular campus events include Cabrini Day, Yule Log, and Spring Fling.

Sports: There are 7 intercollegiate sports for men and 10 for women, and 12 intramural sports for men and 12 for women. Facilities include a weight room, athletic fields, a 1500-seat gym, tennis courts, an Olympic-size pool, an indoor jogging track, squash courts, and an aerobic dance studio.

Disabled Students: 90% of the campus is accessible. Wheelchair ramps, elevators, special parking, specially equipped rest rooms, special class scheduling, lowered drinking fountains, lowered telephones, and special housing are available. Accommodations are made on an individual basis, with appropriate documentation.

Services: Counseling and information services are available, as is tutoring in most subjects. There is a reader service for the blind. Students may enroll in a study skills course or utilize individual tutoring to acquire learning skills.

Campus Safety and Security: Measures include 24-hour foot and vehicle patrol, self-defense education, security escort services, and shuttle buses until 1 A.M.. There are informal discussions, pamphlets/posters/films, emergency telephones, and lighted pathways/sidewalks.

Programs of Study: Cabrini confers B.A., B.S., B.S.Ed., and B.S.W. degrees. Master's degrees are also awarded. Bachelor's degrees are awarded in BIOLOGICAL SCIENCE (biology/biological science and biotechnology), BUSINESS (accounting, banking and finance, business administration and management, human resources, and marketing/retailing/merchandising), COMMUNICATIONS AND THE ARTS (communications, English, French, graphic design, Spanish, and visual and performing arts), COMPUTER AND PHYSICAL SCIENCE (chemistry, information sciences and systems, mathematics, and web technology), EDUCATION (early childhood, education, elementary, and special), HEALTH PROFESSIONS (medical laboratory technology and sports medicine), SOCIAL SCIENCE (American studies, criminal justice, history, liberal arts/general studies, philosophy, political science/government, psychology, religion, social work, and sociology). Education, English/communication, and biology/biotechnology are the strongest academically. Business, education, and English/communication are the largest.

Required: To graduate, students must complete a minimum of 123 credits with a minimum GPA of 2.0. All students must complete a core curriculum, which includes English, math, foreign language, information technology, an interdisciplinary seminar in self-understanding, and a junior seminar exploring the common good, which includes a community service project. Distribution requirements cover science, heritage, cultural diversity, values, the individual and society, contemporary issues, creativity, and religious studies. Most majors require a capstone experience, which can include an internship, student teaching, or a comprehensive project or paper. The average number of hours in the major is 45. A thesis is required in some majors.

Special: Cabrini offers cooperative programs, internships, study abroad, work-study programs, and cross-registration with Eastern University, Rosemont and Valley Forge Colleges, and other SEPCHE colleges and universities. B.A.-B.S. degrees, dual majors and minors, a liberal arts degree, and student-designed majors are available, as are 3 accelerated interdisciplinary degree programs in organizational management, history or liberal arts. Credit by exam, credit for life/military/work experience, nondegree study, and pass/fail options are also offered. A Washington semester with the Washington Center for Internships and Academic Seminars is available. There are 15 national honor societies, a freshman honors program, and 11 departmental honors programs.

Faculty/Classroom: 46% of faculty are male; 54%, female. 86% teach undergraduates and 60% both teach and do research. No introductory courses are taught by graduate students. The average class size in an introductory lecture is 19; in a laboratory, 15; and in a regular course, 18.

Admissions: 65% of the 2005-2006 applicants were accepted. The SAT scores for the 2005-2006 freshman class were: Verbal--52% below 500, 38% between 500 and 599, 10% between 600 and 700, and 1% above 700; Math--58% below 500, 34% between 500 and 599, 9% between 600 and 700, and 1% above 700. 21% of the current freshmen were in the top fifth of their class; 48% were in the top two fifths.

Requirements: The SAT is required. All students must be graduates of an accredited secondary school or have a GED. A minimum of 17 Carnegie units are required, consisting of 4 in English, 3 each in math, science, and social studies, 2 in a foreign language, and the rest in electives. An interview is recommended. A GPA of 2.0 is required. AP and CLEP credits are accepted. Important factors in the admissions decision are advanced placement or honor courses, extracurricular activities record, and leadership record.

Procedure: Freshmen are admitted to all sessions. Entrance exams should be taken before December of the senior year. There is a deferred admissions plan and a rolling admissions plan. Application deadlines are open. Applications are accepted on-line. The fall 2005 application fee was $35.

Transfer: 75 transfer students enrolled in 2004-2005. A minimum of 15 credit hours with at least a GPA of 2.2 overall is required; a 2.5 GPA is preferred. Some programs may have higher requirements. 45 of 123 credits required for the bachelor's degree must be completed at Cabrini.

Visiting: There are regularly scheduled orientations for prospective students, including fall orientations held 3 to 5 days before classes begin, with students completing an electronic gateway prior to arriving. There are guides for informal visits and visitors may sit in on classes and stay overnight. To schedule a visit, contact the Admissions Office.

Financial Aid: In 2005-2006, all full-time freshmen and 82% of continuing full-time students received some form of financial aid. 88% of full-time freshmen and 73% of continuing full-time students received need-based aid. The average freshman award was $16,345. Need-based scholarships or need-based grants averaged $4969 ($16,900 maximum); need-based self-help aid (loans and jobs) averaged $3218 ($6500 maximum); and other non-need-based awards and non-need-based scholarships averaged $10,401 ($26,000 maximum). 15% of undergraduates work part time. Average annual earnings from campus work are $765. The average financial indebtedness of the 2005 graduate was $17,400. The FAFSA is required. The deadline for filing freshman financial aid applications for fall entry is April 1.

International Students: There are 10 international students enrolled. The school actively recruits these students. They must take the TOEFL or the MELAB, and successfully complete ESL if they are not fron am English-speaking country.

Computers: Wireless access is available. Every student receives a domain account and a campus e-mail address. With those accounts, students can log in to any PC on campus and access the College's network. Students can access the Internet anywhere on campus, which is 90% wireless. All students may access the system 24 hours a day, 7 days a week. There are no time limits and no fees. It is strongly recommended that all students have a personal computer. A Celeron at 600 MHZ or a 1-GHz or faster PowerMac G4, or a Dell is recommended.

Graduates: From July 1, 2004 to June 30, 2005, 339 bachelor's degrees were awarded. The most popular majors were English/communication (14%), business (7%), and educational studies (6%). In an average class, 1% graduate in 3 years or less, 53% graduate in 4 years or less, 58% graduate in 5 years or less, and 61% graduate in 6 years or less. 85 companies recruited on campus in 2004-2005. Of the 2004 graduating class, 13% were enrolled in graduate school within 6 months of graduation and 92% were employed.

Admissions Contact: Mark Osborn, Vice President for Enrollment Management. E-mail: admit@cabrini.edu Web: http://www.cabrini.edu

CALIFORNIA UNIVERSITY OF PENNSYLVANIA   B-3

California, PA 15419-1394	(724) 938-4404; Fax: (724) 938-4564
Full-time: 2587 men, 2686 women	**Faculty:** 266; IIA, +$
Part-time: 249 men, 421 women	**Ph.D.s:** 55%
Graduate: 485 men, 756 women	**Student/Faculty:** 20 to 1
Year: semesters, summer session	**Tuition:** $6429 ($8946)
Application Deadline: open	**Room & Board:** $7788
Freshman Class: 3385 applied, 2633 accepted, 1285 enrolled	
SAT Verbal/Math: 493/493*	**ACT:** not required **COMPETITIVE**

California University of Pennsylvania, founded in 1852, is a state-supported institution offering degree programs in the arts and sciences, engineering, and education. There are 3 undergraduate schools and 1 graduate school. In addition to regional accreditation, the university has baccalaureate program accreditation with CSWE, NCATE, NLN, ASHA, CAAHEP, CAPTE, CCNE, NASPE, NAST, and and NATA. The library contains 451,382 volumes, 830,298 microform items, and 60,416 audio/video tapes/CDs/DVDs, and subscribes to 822 periodicals including electronic. Computerized library services include the card catalog, interlibrary loans, and database searching. Special learning facilities include a learning resource center, art gallery, natural history museum, radio station, and TV station. The 148-acre campus is in a small town 35 miles south of Pittsburgh. Including any residence halls, there are 38 buildings.

Student Life: 95% of undergraduates are from Pennsylvania. Others are from 35 states, 21 foreign countries, and Canada. 95% are from public schools. 93% are white. The average age of freshmen is 19; all undergraduates, 23. 25% do not continue beyond their first year; 50% remain to graduate.

Housing: 1467 students can be accommodated in college housing, which includes single-sex and coed dorms and off-campus apartments. In addition, there are honors houses, wellness, and quiet floors. On-campus housing is available on a first-come, first-served basis and is available on a lottery system for upperclassmen. 80% of students commute. Alcohol is not permitted. All students may keep cars.

Activities: 10% of men belong to 7 national fraternities; 6% of women belong to 7 national sororities. There are 78 groups on campus, including art, band, cheerleading, chess, choir, chorale, chorus, computers, dance, debate, drama, drill team, ethnic, forensics, honors, international, jazz band, literary magazine, marching band, musical theater, newspaper, pep band, professional, radio and TV, religious, student government, and yearbook.

Sports: There are 12 intercollegiate sports for men and 10 for women, and 13 intramural sports for men and 14 for women. Facilities include tennis and basketball courts, an all-weather track, a swimming pool, and a 4500-seat stadium.

Disabled Students: 95% of the campus is accessible. Wheelchair ramps, elevators, special parking, specially equipped rest rooms, special class scheduling, lowered drinking fountains, and lowered telephones are available.

Services: Counseling and information services are available, as is tutoring in most subjects. There is a reader service for the blind, and remedial math, reading, and writing.

Campus Safety and Security: Measures include 24-hour foot and vehicle patrol, self-defense education, security escort services, and shuttle buses. There are informal discussions, pamphlets/posters/films, and lighted pathways/sidewalks.

Programs of Study: the university confers B.A., B.S., B.S.Ed., and B.S.N. degrees. Associate and master's degrees are also awarded. Bachelor's degrees are awarded in BIOLOGICAL SCIENCE (biology/ biological science), BUSINESS (accounting, business administration and management, management science, and sports management), COMMUNICATIONS AND THE ARTS (art, dramatic arts, English, French, graphic design, Spanish, and speech/debate/rhetoric), COMPUTER AND PHYSICAL SCIENCE (chemistry, geology, information sciences and systems, mathematics, physical sciences, and physics), EDUCATION (athletic training, early childhood, education, elementary, guidance, reading, school psychology, secondary, and special), ENGINEERING AND ENVIRONMENTAL DESIGN (commercial art, computer technology, electrical/electronics engineering technology, engineering technology, environmental science, and industrial engineering technology), HEALTH PROFESSIONS (medical laboratory technology, mental health/human services, nursing, and physical therapy assistant), SOCIAL SCIENCE (criminal justice, geography, gerontology, history, liberal arts/general studies, parks and recreation management, philosophy, political science/ government, psychology, social science, and social work).

Required: Students must complete a minimum of 120 semester credits and must maintain a minimum GPA of 2.5 in teacher education curricula, 2.3 in the student's area of concentration, and 2.0 overall.

Special: Cooperative programs are available in all academic areas when eligibility requirements have been met. Opportunities are provided for internships, and an accelerated degree program in justice studies is also available. There are 25 national honor societies, a freshman honors program.

Faculty/Classroom: 58% of faculty are male; 42%, female. All teach undergraduates. No introductory courses are taught by graduate students. The average class size in an introductory lecture is 30; in a laboratory, 24; and in a regular course, 30.

Admissions: 78% of the 2005-2006 applicants were accepted. The SAT scores for the 2005-2006 freshman class were: Verbal--57% below 500, 36% between 500 and 599, 6% between 600 and 700, and 1% above 700; Math--55% below 500, 36% between 500 and 599, 8% between 600 and 700, and 1% above 700. The ACT scores were 68% below 21, 21% between 21 and 23, 7% between 24 and 26, 3% between 27 and 28, and 1% above 28. 17% of the current freshmen were in the top fifth of their class; 44% were in the top two fifths. 3 freshmen graduated first in their class.

Requirements: A satisfactory score on the SAT is required. In addition, the ACT may be substituted. Graduation from an accredited secondary school is required; a GED will be accepted. Applicants should submit an academic record that includes 4 credits each in English and history, 3 each in math and academic electives, 2 in science, and 1 each in social

studies and a foreign language. An essay and an interview are recommended. A GPA of 2.5 is required. AP and CLEP credits are accepted.

Procedure: Freshmen are admitted to all sessions. Entrance exams should be taken during the senior year. There is a rolling admissions plan. Application deadlines are open. Application fee is $25. Applications are accepted on-line.

Transfer: 619 transfer students enrolled in 2004-2005. Applicants must submit official transcripts from all previous colleges attended. If fewer than 30 transferable credits are submitted, applicants must also include a high school transcript and standardized test score. Grades of D are not transferable. 30 of 120 credits required for the bachelor's degree must be completed at the university.

Visiting: There are regularly scheduled orientations for prospective students. There are guides for informal visits and visitors may sit in on classes and stay overnight. To schedule a visit, contact the Admissions Office.

Financial Aid: The FAFSA and Pennsylvania State Grant and Federal Financial Aid Application are required. The priority date for freshman financial aid applications for fall entry is April 1. The deadline for filing freshman financial aid applications for fall entry is April 1.

International Students: There are 48 international students enrolled. Satisfactory scores are required on the written TOEFL and the SAT, The SAT is recommended.

Computers: Wireless access is available. All students may access the system. There are no time limits and no fees.

Graduates: From July 1, 2004 to June 30, 2005, 983 bachelor's degrees were awarded. The most popular majors were education (21%), business (12%), and justice studies (8%). In an average class, 21% graduate in 4 years or less, 43% graduate in 5 years or less, and 49% graduate in 6 years or less. 62 companies recruited on campus in 2004-2005. Of the 2004 graduating class, 18% were enrolled in graduate school within 6 months of graduation and 95% were employed.

Admissions Contact: William Edmonds, Director of Admissions. A video is available. E-mail: *inquiry@cup.edu* Web: *www.cup.edu*

CARLOW UNIVERSITY (Formerly Carlow College)
B-3

Pittsburgh, PA 15213

(412) 578-6059
(800) 333-CARLOW; Fax: (412) 578-6668

Full-time: 62 men, 1105 women	**Faculty:** 72; IIA, --$
Part-time: 29 men, 427 women	**Ph.Ds:** 62%
Graduate: 54 men, 446 women	**Student/Faculty:** 16 to 1
Year: semesters, summer session	**Tuition:** $17,443
Application Deadline: July 1	**Room & Board:** $6870
Freshman Class: 1076 applied, 684 accepted, 274 enrolled	
SAT Verbal/Math: 520/500	**ACT:** 21 **COMPETITIVE**

Carlow University, formerly Carlow College and founded in 1929, is a private, primarily women's college affiliated with the Roman Catholic Church, offering programs in liberal and fine arts, business, health science, professional training, and teacher preparation. There are 4 undergraduate and 4 graduate schools. In addition to regional accreditation, Carlow has baccalaureate program accreditation with AACN, CCNE and CSWE. The library contains 127,367 volumes, 11,674 microform items, and 4830 audio/video tapes/CDs/DVDs, and subscribes to 10,362 periodicals including electronic. Computerized library services include the card catalog, interlibrary loans, database searching, and Internet access. Special learning facilities include a learning resource center, art gallery, and a TV studio. The 14-acre campus is in an urban area, the Oakland section of Pittsburgh. Including any residence halls, there are 14 buildings.

Student Life: 95% of undergraduates are from Pennsylvania. Others are from 10 states and 9 foreign countries. 90% are from public schools. 73% are white; 18% African American. 42% are Catholic; 13% claim no religious affiliation; 12% Protestant. The average age of freshmen is 18; all undergraduates, 31. 35% do not continue beyond their first year; 52% remain to graduate.

Housing: 393 students can be accommodated in college housing, which includes single-sex dorms. There are quiet floors. On-campus housing is available on a first-come, first-served basis and is available on a lottery system for upperclassmen. 79% of students commute. Alcohol is not permitted. All students may keep cars.

Activities: There are no fraternities or sororities. There are 25 groups on campus, including art, choir, community service, computers, drama, ethnic, honors, instrumental ensembles, international, literary magazine, newspaper, philosophy, photography, political, professional, religious, social, social service, student government, and yearbook. Popular campus events include International Fair, Fall Festival, and Spring Carnival.

Sports: There are 5 intercollegiate sports for women. Facilities include a gym, a pool, a fitness center, and an aerobics room.

Disabled Students: 15% of the campus is accessible. Wheelchair ramps, elevators, special parking, specially equipped rest rooms, special class scheduling, lowered drinking fountains, lowered telephones, 3 power doors, and 1 doorbell are available.

Services: Counseling and information services are available, as is tutoring in most subjects. There is remedial math, reading, and writing. Professional tutoring is available for reading, writing, study skills, math, and sciences. Peer tutoring is available in other subject areas.

Campus Safety and Security: Measures include 24-hour foot and vehicle patrol, self-defense education, security escort services, and shuttle buses. There are informal discussions, pamphlets/posters/films, emergency telephones, lighted pathways/sidewalks, and an electronically secured dorm entrance.

Programs of Study: Carlow confers B.A., B.S., B.S.N., and B.S.W. degrees. Master's degrees are also awarded. Bachelor's degrees are awarded in BIOLOGICAL SCIENCE (biology/biological science), BUSINESS (accounting, business administration and management, human resources, international business management, and marketing and distribution), COMMUNICATIONS AND THE ARTS (art, art history and appreciation, communications, creative writing, English, Spanish, and technical and business writing), COMPUTER AND PHYSICAL SCIENCE (chemistry, computer science, information sciences and systems, and mathematics), EDUCATION (art, early childhood, elementary, secondary, and special), ENGINEERING AND ENVIRONMENTAL DESIGN (computer graphics), HEALTH PROFESSIONS (health science, nursing, and scientific/medical marketing), SOCIAL SCIENCE (criminal justice, forensic studies, history, liberal arts/general studies, philosophy, political science/government, psychology, public administration, social studies, social work, sociology, and theological studies). Nursing, creative writing, and education are the strongest academically. Nursing, business management, and elementary education are the largest.

Required: A total of 120 credit hours (125 for nursing students), including 27 to 44 in the major, is required to graduate. Credits must be earned in history, literature, art or music, math or logic, theology, philosophy, psychology or sociology, biology or chemistry, women's studies, and cross-cultural understanding. An interdisciplinary course, a course with a peace and justice overlay, English, and communication studies are also required. A minimum GPA of 2.0 is required. All students must demonstrate competence in writing, reading comprehension, and math and must take basic skills courses in public speaking and research paper writing. All students undergo a comprehensive evaluation in their senior year.

Special: Carlow offers cross-registration through the Pittsburgh Council for Higher Education, internships in all areas, and work-study. There are accelerated degree programs, and dual majors are possible in most majors, as are student-designed majors. There are 3-2 engineering programs with Carnegie Mellon University, as well as 2-2 and 3-3 programs in athletic training, physician assistant, physical therapy, and occupational therapy with Dusquesne University. There are 4 national honor societies, and a freshman honors program. All departments have honors programs.

Faculty/Classroom: 32% of faculty are male; 68%, female. 82% teach undergraduates. No introductory courses are taught by graduate students. The average class size in an introductory lecture is 14; in a laboratory, 12; and in a regular course, 13.

Admissions: 64% of the 2005-2006 applicants were accepted. The SAT scores for the 2005-2006 freshman class were: Verbal--37% below 500, 49% between 500 and 599, 12% between 600 and 700, and 2% above 700; Math--44% below 500, 42% between 500 and 599, 13% between 600 and 700, and 1% above 700. The ACT scores were 45% below 21, 23% between 21 and 23, 18% between 24 and 26, 9% between 27 and 28, and 5% above 28. 33% of the current freshmen were in the top fifth of their class; 69% were in the top two fifths. 4 freshmen graduated first in their class.

Requirements: The SAT or ACT is required; the minimum scores depend on the major selected. Candidates must be graduates of an accredited secondary school. 18 Carnegie units are required, including 4 each in English and arts/humanities, 3 each in math and science, and 4 in electives. Applicants for nursing must have completed a minimum 4 units in English, 3 in social studies, and 2 each in math (including algebra) and lab science (including chemistry), as required by the State Board of Nursing. The GED is accepted. An essay and/or interview may be required. Art majors may submit a portfolio. In some cases where preferred admission requirements are not met, provisional admission is possible. Carlow requires applicants to be in the upper 40% of their class. A GPA of 2.0 is required. AP and CLEP credits are accepted. Important factors in the admissions decision are advanced placement or honor courses, leadership record, and extracurricular activities record.

Procedure: Freshmen are admitted fall and spring. Entrance exams should be taken late in the junior year or early in the senior year. There are early action and deferred admissions plans. There is a rolling admission plan. Early action applications should be filed by September 30; regular applications, by July 1 for fall entry (preferred date) and December 1 for spring entry, along with a $20 fee. Notification of early action is sent October 30; regular decision, on a rolling basis. Applications are accepted on-line.

Transfer: 121 transfer students enrolled in 2004-2005. Transfer students must have a minimum GPA of 2.0 and submit high school and college transcripts. A 3.0 GPA is required for education and nursing; a

2.5 for science, math, and social work; a 2.8 for perfusion technology. An interview is also recommended. 32 of 120 credits required for the bachelor's degree must be completed at Carlow.

Visiting: There are regularly scheduled orientations for prospective students, including a campus tour, information sessions on admission and financial aid, and interaction with faculty and students regarding academic and student life. There are guides for informal visits and visitors may sit in on classes and stay overnight. To schedule a visit, contact the Admissions Office.

Financial Aid: In 2005-2006, 89% of all full-time freshmen and 68% of continuing full-time students received some form of financial aid. 86% of full-time freshmen and 58% of continuing full-time students received need-based aid. The average freshman award was $14,093. Need-based scholarships or need-based grants averaged $3013 ($9000 maximum); need-based self-help aid (loans and jobs) averaged $1706 ($2625 maximum); non-need-based athletic scholarships averaged $3976 ($8000 maximum); and other non-need-based awards and non-need-based scholarships averaged $5192 ($16,754 maximum). 18% of undergraduates work part time. Average annual earnings from campus work are $800. Carlow is a member of CSS. The FAFSA, verification worksheets, and tax returns when applicable are required. The deadline for filing freshman financial aid applications for fall entry is April 1.

International Students: There are 10 international students enrolled. A satisfactory score on the TOEFL is required. In some cases the SAT can replace the TOEFL; otherwise, the SAT is recommended only.

Computers: Wireless access is available. They are approximately 182 PCs in computing labs. All students may access the system anytime. There are no time limits and no fees. It is strongly recommended that all students have a personal computer, specifically an IBM ThinkPad.

Graduates: From July 1, 2004 to June 30, 2005, 326 bachelor's degrees were awarded. The most popular majors were nursing (20%), education (18%), and business management (11%). In an average class, 1% graduate in 3 years or less, 35% graduate in 4 years or less, 48% graduate in 5 years or less, and 52% graduate in 6 years or less. 4 companies recruited on campus in 2004-2005. Of the 2004 graduating class, 22% were enrolled in graduate school within 6 months of graduation and 73% were employed.

Admissions Contact: Christine Bell, Director of Admissions. A video is available. E-mail: *admissions@carlow.edu* Web: *www.carlow.edu*

CARNEGIE MELLON UNIVERSITY B-3

Pittsburgh, PA 15213   (412) 268-2082; Fax: (412) 268-7838

Full-time: 3245 men, 1810 women	**Faculty:** 1042; I, +$
Part-time: 65 men, 35 women	**Ph.D.s:** 96%
Graduate: 2240 men, 945 women	**Student/Faculty:** 5 to 1
Year: semesters, summer session	**Tuition:** $25,880
Application Deadline: see profile	**Room & Board:** $6820
Freshman Class: n/av	
SAT or ACT: required	**MOST COMPETITIVE**

Carnegie Mellon University, established in 1900, is a private nonsectarian institution offering undergraduate programs in liberal arts and science and professional technology. Figures in above capsule and in this profile are approximate. There are 6 undergraduate and 7 graduate schools. In addition to regional accreditation, Carnegie Mellon has baccalaureate program accreditation with AACSB, ABET, NAAB, NASAD, and NASM. The 3 libraries contain 935,888 volumes, 885,422 microform items, and 50,465 audio/video tapes/CDs/DVDs, and subscribe to 3209 periodicals including electronic. Computerized library services include the card catalog, interlibrary loans, and database searching. Special learning facilities include a learning resource center, art gallery, and radio station. The 103-acre campus is in a suburban area 4 miles from downtown Pittsburgh. Including any residence halls, there are 80 buildings.

Student Life: 78% of undergraduates are from out of state, mostly the Middle Atlantic. Students are from 50 states, 102 foreign countries, and Canada. 70% are from public schools. 53% are white; 21% foreign nationals; 17% Asian American. The average age of freshmen is 18; all undergraduates, 20. 8% do not continue beyond their first year; 76% remain to graduate.

Housing: 3538 students can be accommodated in college housing, which includes single-sex and coed dorms, on-campus apartments, off-campus apartments, fraternity houses, and sorority houses. In addition, there are honors houses, language houses, and special-interest houses. On-campus housing is guaranteed for all 4 years. 59% of students live on campus; of those, 90% remain on campus on weekends. Alcohol is not permitted. Upperclassmen may keep cars.

Activities: 13% of men belong to 13 national fraternities; 9% of women belong to 1 local and 4 national sororities. There are 120 groups on campus, including art, bagpipe band, band, cheerleading, chess, choir, chorale, chorus, computers, debate, drama, ethnic, film, gay, honors, international, jazz band, literary magazine, marching band, musical theater, newspaper, opera, orchestra, pep band, photography, political, professional, radio and TV, religious, social, social service, student government, symphony, and yearbook. Popular campus events include Spring Carnival, International Festival, and Watson Arts Festival.

Sports: There are 9 intercollegiate sports for men and 8 for women, and 22 intramural sports for men and 16 for women. Facilities include a gym, a stadium, athletic fields, tennis and racquetball courts, and a pool.

Disabled Students: 98% of the campus is accessible. Wheelchair ramps, elevators, special parking, specially equipped rest rooms, special class scheduling, lowered drinking fountains, and lowered telephones are available.

Services: Counseling and information services are available, as is tutoring in most subjects. There is a reader service for the blind.

Campus Safety and Security: Measures include 24-hour foot and vehicle patrol, self-defense education, security escort services, and shuttle buses. There are informal discussions, pamphlets/posters/films, emergency telephones, lighted pathways/sidewalks, and and a SafeWalk Program.

Programs of Study: Carnegie Mellon confers B.A., B.S., B.A.H., B.Arch., B.F.A., and B.S.A. degrees. Master's and doctoral degrees are also awarded. Bachelor's degrees are awarded in BIOLOGICAL SCIENCE (biology/biological science), BUSINESS (business administration and management, business economics, and marketing/retailing/merchandising), COMMUNICATIONS AND THE ARTS (communications, design, dramatic arts, English, fine arts, French, German, journalism, languages, music, and Spanish), COMPUTER AND PHYSICAL SCIENCE (chemistry, computer programming, computer science, information sciences and systems, mathematics, physics, and statistics), EDUCATION (music), ENGINEERING AND ENVIRONMENTAL DESIGN (chemical engineering, civil engineering, computer engineering, electrical/electronics engineering, engineering, and mechanical engineering), SOCIAL SCIENCE (economics, history, philosophy, political science/government, psychology, public administration, social science, and urban studies). Computer Science, engineering, and business administration are the strongest academically. Engineering is the largest.

Required: To graduate, students must complete requirements in English, history, and computing skills, and they must have a GPA of 2.0. Distribution requirements, the number of credits needed to graduate, and the number of credits required in the major vary by college.

Special: Students may cross-register with other Pittsburgh Council of Higher Education institutions. Also available are internships, work-study programs, study abroad in Germany, Switzerland, and Japan, a Washington semester, accelerated degrees, B.A.-B.S. degrees, co-op programs, dual majors, and limited student-designed majors. There are 10 national honor societies, including Phi Beta Kappa and a freshman honors program.

Faculty/Classroom: 72% of faculty are male; 28%, female. All both teach and do research.

Requirements: The SAT or ACT is required. In addition, SAT: Subject tests in writing and math are required for all applicants. Engineering applicants must take the chemistry or physics test. Science applicants may take either of these or the biology test. Business and liberal arts applicants must take a third test of their choice. Applicants must graduate from an accredited secondary school or have a GED. They must earn 16 Carnegie units. All applicants must have completed 4 years of English. Applicants to the Carnegie Institute of Technology and the Mellon College of Science must take 4 years of math and 1 year each of biology, chemistry, and physics. Essays are required, and interviews are recommended. Art and design applicants must submit a portfolio. Drama and music applicants must audition. AP credits are accepted. Important factors in the admissions decision are advanced placement or honor courses, leadership record, and evidence of special talent.

Procedure: Freshmen are admitted in the fall. Entrance exams should be taken be received by February 15. There are early decision, early admissions, and deferred admissions plans. 95 early decision candidates were accepted for a recent class. Check with the school for current application deadlines. The fall 2005 application fee was $50. A waiting list is an active part of the admissions procedure. Applications are accepted on-line.

Transfer: 37 transfer students enrolled in a recent year. Applicants must have a minimum GPA of 3.3 in all previous college-level work. 1 academic year must be completed at Carnegie Mellon.

Visiting: There are regularly scheduled orientations for prospective students, including Saturday group sessions in September, October, November, and April. There are guides for informal visits and visitors may sit in on classes and stay overnight. To schedule a visit, contact the Admissions Office.

Financial Aid: Carnegie Mellon is a member of CSS. The FAFSA, the college's own financial statement and the parent and student federal tax returns and W-2 forms are required. Check with the school for current application deadlines.

International Students: The school actively recruits these students. They must score satisfactorily on the written TOEFL or take the MELAB and also take the SAT or the ACT. Students must take SAT: Subject tests in writing and math level I or II.

Computers: All students may access the system 24 hours per day. There are no time limits and no fees.

Admissions Contact: Michael Steidel, Director of Admissions.
E-mail: *undergraduate-admissions+@andrew.cmu.edu*
Web: *www.cmu.edu/enrollment/admission*

CEDAR CREST COLLEGE E-3
Allentown, PA 18104-6196
(610) 740-3780
(800) 360-1222; Fax: (610) 606-4647

Full-time: 15 men, 932 women	**Faculty:** IIB, -$
Part-time: 71 men, 803 women	**Ph.Ds:** n/av
Graduate: 15 men, 70 women	**Student/Faculty:** 11 to 1
Year: semesters, summer session	**Tuition:** $22,712
Application Deadline: open	**Room & Board:** $7903
Freshman Class: 1444 applied, 955 accepted, 204 enrolled	
SAT Verbal/Math: 480/460*	**ACT:** 23 COMPETITIVE

Cedar Crest College, founded in 1867 by the United Church of Christ, is a private, women's liberal arts college. Some information in this profile is approximate. In addition to regional accreditation, Cedar Crest has baccalaureate program accreditation with CAHEA, CSWE, and NLN. The library contains 135,088 volumes, 12,941 microform items, and 16,126 audio/video tapes/CDs/DVDs, and subscribes to 6650 periodicals including electronic. Computerized library services include the card catalog, interlibrary loans, and database searching. Special learning facilities include a learning resource center, art gallery, radio station, arboretum, theaters, and sculpture garden. The 84-acre campus is in a suburban area 55 miles north of Philadelphia and 90 miles west of New York City. Including any residence halls, there are 18 buildings.

Student Life: 82% of undergraduates are from Pennsylvania. Students are from 31 states, 35 foreign countries, and Canada. 95% are from public schools. 83% are white. 45% are claim no religious affiliation; 26% Protestant; 25% Catholic. The average age of freshmen is 18; all undergraduates, 29. 20% do not continue beyond their first year; 83% remain to graduate.

Housing: 550 students can be accommodated in college housing, which includes single-sex dorms and smoke-free floors. On-campus housing is guaranteed for all 4 years. 80% of students live on campus; of those, 70% remain on campus on weekends. All students may keep cars.

Activities: There are no fraternities. There are 46 groups on campus, including art, choir, chorus, computers, dance, drama, ethnic, gay, honors, international, literary magazine, musical theater, newspaper, political, professional, radio and TV, religious, social, social service, student government, and yearbook. Popular campus events include Student Faculty Frolic, Midnight Breakfast, and Ring Ceremony.

Sports: Facilities include 5 tennis courts, softball, field hockey, soccer, and lacrosse fields, a cross-country course, a gym with basketball, volleyball, and badminton courts, dance and aerobics studios, weight training, and a fitness center.

Disabled Students: 35% of the campus is accessible. Wheelchair ramps, elevators, special parking, specially equipped rest rooms, special class scheduling, lowered drinking fountains, and lowered telephones are available.

Services: Counseling and information services are available, as is tutoring in most subjects. There is remedial math and writing and a computer software skills program for underprepared students.

Campus Safety and Security: Measures include 24-hour foot and vehicle patrol, self-defense education, security escort services, and informal discussions. There are pamphlets/posters/films, emergency telephones, and lighted pathways/sidewalks. Residence halls are equipped with fire/intrusion alarms, which are monitored 24 hours a day. A keyless access system is in place; exterior doors are locked 24 hours a day.

Programs of Study: Cedar Crest confers B.A. and B.S degrees. Associate degrees are also awarded. Bachelor's degrees are awarded in BIOLOGICAL SCIENCE (biochemistry, biology/biological science, genetics, and neurosciences), BUSINESS (accounting and business administration and management), COMMUNICATIONS AND THE ARTS (art, communications, comparative literature, dance, dramatic arts, English, fine arts, French, music, and Spanish), COMPUTER AND PHYSICAL SCIENCE (chemistry, computer science, information sciences and systems, and mathematics), EDUCATION (elementary, science, and secondary), ENGINEERING AND ENVIRONMENTAL DESIGN (environmental science), HEALTH PROFESSIONS (medical laboratory technology, nuclear medical technology, and nursing), SOCIAL SCIENCE (history, liberal arts/general studies, philosophy, political science/government, prelaw, psychology, social work, and sociology). Genetic engineering, nursing, and sciences are the strongest academically. Sciences, nursing, and psychology are the largest.

Required: To graduate, students must complete 120 credit hours (122 for nursing) with a minimum GPA of 2.0 (some majors have higher requirements). Distribution requirements include 8 credits in science; 6 each in humanistic studies, primary texts, creativity and the arts, and global issues and world cultures; and 3 each in writing, research, math, and ethics. A major capstone experience is required.

Special: Cross-registration is available through the Lehigh Valley Association of Independent Colleges. Also available are internships, a Washington semester with American University, work-study programs, an accelerated degree program in business, and B.A.-B.S. degrees in math, biology, and psychology. Dual majors, student-designed majors, 3-2 engineering degrees with Georgia Institute of Technology and Washington University, pass/fail options, and credit for life, military, and work experience are offered. There are 13 national honor societies, a freshman honors program, and 1 departmental honors program.

Faculty/Classroom: All teach undergraduates. The average class size in an introductory lecture is 20; in a laboratory, 13; and in a regular course, 14.

Admissions: 66% of the 2005-2006 applicants were accepted. The SAT scores for the 2005-2006 freshman class were: Verbal--35% below 500, 39% between 500 and 599, 24% between 600 and 700, and 2% above 700; Math--40% below 500, 40% between 500 and 599, 18% between 600 and 700, and 2% above 700. The ACT scores were 15% below 21, 35% between 21 and 23, 25% between 24 and 26, 15% between 27 and 28, and 10% above 28. 41% of the current freshmen were in the top fifth of their class; 76% were in the top two fifths. 2 freshmen graduated first in their class.

Requirements: The SAT is required. In addition, applicants must be graduates of an accredited secondary school. The GED is accepted. Students should have completed 16 high school academic credits, including 4 years of English, 3 of math, 2 each of science, history, and foreign language, and 1 each of art, music, and social studies. An essay is required. Cedar Crest requires applicants to be in the upper 50% of their class. A GPA of 2.0 is required. AP and CLEP credits are accepted. Important factors in the admissions decision are advanced placement or honor courses, leadership record, and evidence of special talent.

Procedure: Freshmen are admitted fall and spring. Entrance exams should be taken in the junior year or early in the senior year. There are early admissions, deferred admissions, and rolling admissions plans. Application deadlines are open. Application fee is $30. Applications are accepted on-line.

Transfer: 64 transfer students enrolled in 2004-2005. Applicants should have a minimum college GPA of 2.0. An interview is recommended. 30 of 120 credits required for the bachelor's degree must be completed at Cedar Crest.

Visiting: There are regularly scheduled orientations for prospective students. There are guides for informal visits and visitors may sit in on classes and stay overnight. To schedule a visit, contact the Admissions Office at cccadmis@cedarcrest.edu.

Financial Aid: In 2005-2006, 98% of all full-time freshmen and 95% of continuing full-time students received some form of financial aid. 87% of full-time freshmen and 91% of continuing full-time students received need-based aid. The average freshman award was $17,103. Need-based scholarships or need-based grants averaged $13,349; need-based self-help aid (loans and jobs) averaged $4366; and other non-need-based awards and non-need-based scholarships averaged $3391. 50% of undergraduates work part time. Cedar Crest is a member of CSS. The FAFSA and the college's own financial statement are required. Check with the school for current deadlines.

International Students: The school actively recruits these students. Satisfactory scores are required on the written TOEFL and the SAT or the ACT.

Computers: All students may access the system. There are no time limits and no fees. It is strongly recommended that all students have a personal computer.

Graduates: In an average class, 1% graduate in 3 years or less, 63% graduate in 4 years or less, and 68% graduate in 5 years or less.

Admissions Contact: Judith Neyhart, Vice President for Enrollment and Advancement. A video is available.
E-mail: judyn.@cedarcrest.edu Web: www.cedarcrest.edu

CHATHAM COLLEGE   B-3
Pittsburgh, PA 15232   **(412) 365-1290**
                            (800) 837-1290; Fax: (412) 365-1609

Full-time: 410 women	**Faculty:** 71; IIA, --$
Part-time: 265 women	**Ph.D.s:** 89%
Graduate: 95 men, 465 women	**Student/Faculty:** 6 to 1
Year: 4-1-4, summer session	**Tuition:** $20,570
Application Deadline: open	**Room & Board:** $6720
Freshman Class: n/av	
SAT or ACT: required	**COMPETITIVE+**

Chatham College, founded in 1869, is a private college offering undergraduate degree programs only to women in more than 30 liberal arts and preprofessional majors. Graduate degree programs in health sciences, education, management, writing, biology, counseling psychology, and landscape architecture are coeducational. Figures in the above capsule and in this profile are approximate. In addition to regional accreditation, Chatham has baccalaureate program accreditation with ACS. The library contains 93,100 volumes, 8500 microform items, and 385 audio/

video tapes/CDs/DVDs, and subscribes to 8500 periodicals including electronic. Computerized library services include the card catalog, interlibrary loans, database searching, and Internet access. Special learning facilities include a learning resource center, art gallery, theaters, a media center, and an arboretum. The 32-acre campus is in an urban area 8 miles east of downtown Pittsburgh. Including any residence halls, there are 33 buildings.

Student Life: 75% of undergraduates are from Pennsylvania. Students are from 25 states, 18 foreign countries, and Canada. 96% are from public schools. 77% are white; 10% African American. The average age of freshmen is 18; all undergraduates, 21. 35% do not continue beyond their first year; 54% remain to graduate.

Housing: 380 students can be accommodated in college housing, which includes single-sex dorms, on-campus apartments, and off-campus apartments. In addition, there are special-interest houses and an intercultural residence hall. On-campus housing is available on a lottery system for upperclassmen. 66% of students live on campus; of those, 75% remain on campus on weekends. Upperclassmen may keep cars.

Activities: There are 28 groups on campus, including choir, dance, drama, environmental, ethnic, feminist, film, gay, honors, international, literary magazine, newspaper, photography, political, professional, religious, social service, student government, and yearbook. Popular campus events include Fall Festival, Spring Fling, and Air Band Contest.

Sports: Facilities include a swimming pool, a gym, an athletic and fitness center, a dance studio, an athletic field, free weights, a cardiovascular room, and a Cybex system.

Disabled Students: 75% of the campus is accessible. Wheelchair ramps, elevators, special parking, specially equipped rest rooms, and special class scheduling are available.

Services: Counseling and information services are available, as is tutoring in every subject. There is a reader service for the blind, and remedial math, reading, and writing. One-on-one and group tutoring are available by both students and professional specialists, and there is also computer-aided tutoring and an organized study group.

Campus Safety and Security: Measures include 24-hour foot and vehicle patrol, self-defense education, security escort services, and shuttle buses. There are informal discussions, pamphlets/posters/films, emergency telephones, and lighted pathways/sidewalks.

Programs of Study: Chatham confers B.A., B.S., and B.S.W. degrees. Master's and doctoral degrees are also awarded. Bachelor's degrees are awarded in AGRICULTURE (environmental studies), BIOLOGICAL SCIENCE (biochemistry, bioinformatics, and biology/biological science), BUSINESS (accounting, business administration and management, international business management, management information systems, and marketing management), COMMUNICATIONS AND THE ARTS (art history and appreciation, arts administration/management, communications, dramatic arts, English, English literature, French, media arts, music, Spanish, and visual and performing arts), COMPUTER AND PHYSICAL SCIENCE (chemistry, computer science, mathematics, and physics), EDUCATION (education), ENGINEERING AND ENVIRONMENTAL DESIGN (environmental science), HEALTH PROFESSIONS (exercise science), SOCIAL SCIENCE (crosscultural studies, economics, forensic studies, history, interdisciplinary studies, international relations, political science/government, psychology, public affairs, social work, and women's studies). Biology, psychology, and English are the strongest academically and have the largest enrollments.

Required: To graduate, students must complete 120 credit hours, including a general education curriculum of 7 courses and a senior tutorial, with a minimum GPA of 2.0. Students must also demonstrate proficiencies in writing, math, and computer literacy.

Special: Chatham offers a study-abroad program in 7 countries, cross-registration with other Pittsburgh Council on Higher Education institutions, co-op programs in all majors, several multidisciplinary majors, internships in the public and private sectors, and a Washington semester in conjunction with American University and the Public Leadership Education Network. Accelerated degree programs, work-study, combined B.A.-B.S. degrees, multidisciplinary majors, and dual and student-designed majors are available. There are 3-2 engineering degrees with Carnegie Mellon and Penn State Universities and the University of Pittsburgh, dual degree programs, and an accelerated Master's program with Carnegie Mellon's Heinz School also available. There are 7 national honor societies, including Phi Beta Kappa, and 100 departmental honors programs.

Faculty/Classroom: 37% of faculty are male; 63%, female. All both teach and do research. No introductory courses are taught by graduate students. The average class size in an introductory lecture is 16; in a laboratory, 12; and in a regular course, 12.

Requirements: The SAT or ACT is required. In addition, applicants must be graduates of an accredited secondary school or have earned the GED. Students are encouraged to have completed 4 years of high school English and 2 years each of math, science, and social studies. A foreign language and an interview are recommended. An essay is required. Chatham requires applicants to be in the upper 50% of their class. A GPA of 2.8 is required. AP and CLEP credits are accepted. Important factors in the admissions decision are recommendations by school officials, leadership record, and extracurricular activities record.

Procedure: Freshmen are admitted fall, winter, and spring. Entrance exams should be taken by fall of the senior year. There are deferred admissions and rolling admissions plans. Application deadlines are open. Application fee is $35. Applications are accepted on-line.

Transfer: 28 transfer students enrolled in a recent year. Applicants must present high school and college transcripts. The SAT or ACT and an interview are required. 45 of 120 credits required for the bachelor's degree must be completed at Chatham.

Visiting: There are regularly scheduled orientations for prospective students, including campus tours, student and faculty panels, financial aid presentations, and athletic coach meetings. There are guides for informal visits and visitors may sit in on classes and stay overnight. To schedule a visit, contact the Admissions Office.

Financial Aid: In a recent year, 99% of all full-time freshmen and 95% of continuing full-time students received some form of financial aid. 86% of full-time freshmen and 80% of continuing full-time students received need-based aid. The average freshman award was $18,231. Need-based scholarships or need-based grants averaged $9427 ($16,330 maximum); need-based self-help aid (loans and jobs) averaged $4746 ($7779 maximum); other non-need-based awards and non-need-based scholarships averaged $2397 ($7000 maximum); and parent Plus averaged $9794 ($18,642 maximum). 90% of undergraduates worked part time. Average annual earnings from campus work were $2200. The average financial indebtedness of a recent graduate was $20,125. The FAFSA is required. Check with the school for current application deadlines.

International Students: In a recent year, there were 29 international students enrolled. The school actively recruits these students. They must score satisfactorily on the written TOEFL or on the electronic version or take the MELAB. The SAT is required unless TOEFL score is available.

Computers: All students may access the system 24 hours per day from their own or residence hall cluster computers. There are no time limits and no fees.

Graduates: In a recent year, 118 bachelor's degrees were awarded. The most popular majors were biology (15%), psychology (15%), and English (10%). In an average class, 54% graduate in 4 years or less, 59% graduate in 5 years or less, and 60% graduate in 6 years or less. 62 companies recruited on campus in a recent year. Of a recent graduating class, 36% were enrolled in graduate school within 6 months of graduation and 53% were employed.

Admissions Contact: Alan G. McIvor, Vice President of Enrollment Management. E-mail: *admissions@chatham.edu*
Web: *www.chatham.edu*

CHESTNUT HILL COLLEGE   F-3
Philadelphia, PA 19118-2693   **(215) 248-7001**
(800) 248-0052; Fax: (215) 248-7082

Full-time: 120 men, 530 women	**Faculty:** 56
Part-time: 55 men, 210 women	**Ph.Ds:** 82%
Graduate: 125 men, 535 women	**Student/Faculty:** 12 to 1
Year: semesters, summer session	**Tuition:** $19,100
Application Deadline: open	**Room & Board:** $7500
Freshman Class: n/av	
SAT or ACT: required	**LESS COMPETITIVE**

Chestnut Hill College, founded in 1924, is a private, liberal arts, institution, affiliated with the Roman Catholic Church. In addition to the traditional program, CHC also offers an accelerated evening and weekend program for working adults. Courses in the accelerated program are offered in 6 8-week sessions per year, with 11 career-oriented majors. There are 2 undergraduate schools and 1 graduate school. Figures in the above capsule and in this profile are approximate. The library contains 128,489 volumes, 203,958 microform items, and 2089 audio/video tapes/CDs/DVDs, and subscribes to 484 periodicals including electronic. Computerized library services include the card catalog, interlibrary loans, database searching, and Internet access. Special learning facilities include a learning resource center, art gallery, planetarium, rotating observatory, and technology center. The 45-acre campus is in a suburban area 25 miles northwest of downtown Philadelphia. Including any residence halls, there are 11 buildings.

Student Life: 85% of undergraduates are from Pennsylvania. Students are from 13 states, 12 foreign countries, and Canada. 47% are from public schools. 64% are white; 28% African American. 59% are Catholic; 26% claim no religious affiliation; 11% Protestant. The average age of freshmen is 18; all undergraduates, 21. 25% do not continue beyond their first year; 66% remain to graduate.

Housing: 350 students can be accommodated in college housing, which includes coed dorms. On-campus housing is guaranteed for all 4 years. 66% of students live on campus; of those, 60% remain on campus on weekends. Alcohol is not permitted. All students may keep cars.

Activities: There are no fraternities or sororities. There are 25 groups on campus, including chorale, chorus, drama, environmental, ethnic, honors, instrumental ensembles, international, literary magazine, musical

theater, newspaper, opera, orchestra, political, professional, religious, social, social service, student government, and yearbook. Popular campus events include International Gourmet Day, Intramural One-Act Play Night, and concerts.

Sports: There are 5 intercollegiate sports for men and 7 for women. Facilities include a gym and an auxiliary gym, an athletic training room, locker facilities, fitness room, indoor swimming pool, 8 tennis courts, playing fields for hockey, lacrosse, softball, and soccer, as well as neighboring stables and a golf course.

Disabled Students: 90% of the campus is accessible. Wheelchair ramps, elevators, special parking, specially equipped rest rooms, and a shower area in residence halls are available.

Services: Counseling and information services are available, as is tutoring in most subjects, including . There is a reader service for the blind and remedial math and writing. .

Campus Safety and Security: Measures include 24-hour foot and vehicle patrol, security escort services, informal discussions, and pamphlets/posters/films. There are lighted pathways/sidewalks. Doors are locked after 6 P.M. and on weekends and are monitored by cameras. Escorted shuttle cars to parking lots are available in the evenings.

Programs of Study: CHC confers B.A. and B.S. degrees. Associate, master's, and doctoral degrees are also awarded. Bachelor's degrees are awarded in BIOLOGICAL SCIENCE (biochemistry, biology/biological science, and molecular biology), BUSINESS (accounting, banking and finance, business administration and management, business communications, human resources, management science, and marketing/retailing/merchandising), COMMUNICATIONS AND THE ARTS (art history and appreciation, communications technology, English, French, and Spanish), COMPUTER AND PHYSICAL SCIENCE (chemistry, computer science, and mathematics), EDUCATION (early childhood and elementary), ENGINEERING AND ENVIRONMENTAL DESIGN (environmental science), HEALTH PROFESSIONS (health care administration), SOCIAL SCIENCE (child care/child and family studies, criminal justice, gerontology, history, human services, political science/government, psychology, and sociology). Biological/computer/physical sciences, humanities, and social sciences are the strongest academically. Education, biological sciences, and psychology are the largest.

Required: To graduate, students must complete at least 120 credit hours with a general average of 2.0 overall and in the major. Course work must include 12 to 15 courses in the major; Introduction to the Liberal Arts; Interdisciplinary Global Studies Seminar; a writing course; 2 courses in religious studies; the College Experience; Career Connections; 2 1-credit courses in phys ed; courses in various ways of knowing, including historical (2 courses), literary (1), aesthetic (1), scientific (2 or 3), analytic (1) and interpreting human behavior (2); and a senior seminar and senior thesis. Proficiency must be demonstrated in math, computers, oral communication, and swimming. Students may choose from a wide variety of minors.

Special: Cross-registration is available with LaSalle University and at the 10 colleges in the Sisters of St. Joseph College Consortium Student Exchange Program. The college offers internships, study abroad in England, Spain, Italy, Austria, and France, work-study programs, interdisciplinary majors, and dual and student-designed majors. Up to 6 credits may be given for life experience. Nondegree study and pass/fail options are available. The school offers unique career preparation programs in communications, international studies, environmental science, and international business. There are 4 national honor societies, a freshman honors program, and 11 departmental honors programs.

Faculty/Classroom: 39% of faculty are male; 61%, female. 92% teach undergraduates and 40% both teach and do research. No introductory courses are taught by graduate students. The average class size in an introductory lecture is 25; in a laboratory, 15; and in a regular course, 15.

Requirements: The SAT or ACT is required. Applicants must be graduates of an accredited secondary school. 16 Carnegie units are required, with a recommended 4 units each of English, math, science, and social studies and 3 of foreign language. An interview is recommended for all students. An essay is required. A GPA of 2.0 is required. AP and CLEP credits are accepted. Important factors in the admissions decision are leadership record, recommendations by alumni, and evidence of special talent.

Procedure: Freshmen are admitted fall and spring. Entrance exams should be taken early in the senior year. There are early admissions, deferred admissions and rolling admissions plans. Application deadlines are open. Application fee is $35. Applications are accepted on-line.

Transfer: 39 transfer students enrolled in a recent year. Applicants must have a minimum GPA of 2.0; a 2.5 is recommended. 45 of 120 credits required for the bachelor's degree must be completed at CHC.

Visiting: There are regularly scheduled orientations for prospective students, including faculty presentations and workshops on specific issues. There are guides for informal visits and visitors may sit in on classes and stay overnight. To schedule a visit, contact the Admissions Office.

Financial Aid: In a recent year, 83% of all full-time freshmen and 93% of continuing full-time students received some form of financial aid. 77% of full-time freshmen and 90% of continuing full-time students received

need-based aid. The average freshman award was $14,050. Need-based scholarships or need-based grants averaged $8125; need-based self-help aid (loans and jobs) averaged $4625; and other non-need-based awards and non-need-based scholarships averaged $6050. 50% of undergraduates worked part time. Average annual earnings from campus work were $1500. The average financial indebtedness of the 2005 graduate was $17,125. CHC is a member of CSS. The FAFSA is required. Check with the school for current application deadlines.

International Students: In a recent year, there were 12 international students enrolled. The school actively recruits these students. They must score satisfactorily on the written TOEFL.

Computers: All students may access the system. There are no time limits and no fees. All students are required to have personal computers.

Graduates: In a recent year, 205 bachelor's degrees were awarded. The most popular majors were business (26%), sociology (25%), and education (11%). In an average class, 58% graduate in 4 years or less, 60% graduate in 5 years or less, and 62% graduate in 6 years or less. 25 companies recruited on campus in a recent year.

Admissions Contact: Jodie King, Director of Admissions. A video is available. E-mail: *chcapply@chc.edu* Web: *www.chc.edu*

CHEYNEY UNIVERSITY OF PENNSYLVANIA   F-4

Cheyney, PA 19319

(610) 399-2275
(800) 223-3608; Fax: (610) 399-2099

Full-time: 605 men, 690 women	**Faculty:** n/av
Part-time: 39 men, 67 women	**Ph.D.s:** 33%
Graduate: 51 men, 108 women	**Student/Faculty:** n/av
Year: semesters, summer session	**Tuition:** $5818 ($13,178)
Application Deadline: May 30	**Room & Board:** $5679
Freshman Class: n/av	
SAT or ACT: required	**LESS COMPETITIVE**

Cheyney University of Pennsylvania, founded in 1837, is a public, liberal arts institution offering programs in art, business, music, and teacher preparation. Cheyney University of Pennsylvania cherishes its legacy as the oldest historically black institution of higher education. There are 2 undergraduate schools and 1 graduate school. In addition to regional accreditation, Cheyney has baccalaureate program accreditation with NCATE and IACBE. The library contains 290,000 volumes, 795,000 microform items, and 1451 audio/video tapes/CDs/DVDs, and subscribes to 485 periodicals including electronic. Computerized library services include the card catalog and Internet access. Special learning facilities include a planetarium, radio station, TV station, weather station, world cultures center, and theater arts center. The 275-acre campus is in a suburban area 24 miles west of Philadelphia. Including any residence halls, there are 33 buildings.

Student Life: 82% of undergraduates are from Pennsylvania. Others are from 21 states and 6 foreign countries. 93% are African American. The average age of freshmen is 20; all undergraduates, 21. 43% do not continue beyond their first year; 33% remain to graduate.

Housing: 1273 students can be accommodated in college housing, which includes single-sex and coed dorms. In addition, there are honors houses. On-campus housing is available on a first-come, first-served basis. 76% of students live on campus. Alcohol is not permitted. All students may keep cars.

Activities: There are 5 national fraternities and 5 national sororities. There are 30 groups on campus, including art, cheerleading, chess, choir, computers, drama, ethnic, honors, international, jazz band, newspaper, political, professional, radio and TV, religious, social, social service, and student government. Popular campus events include Founders Day Ball and Wade Wilson Football Classic.

Sports: There are 5 intercollegiate sports for men and 5 for women, and 3 intramural sports for men and 2 for women. Facilities include a track, tennis courts, outdoor and indoor basketball courts, a pool, a gym, and a weight room.

Disabled Students: 90% of the campus is accessible. Wheelchair ramps, elevators, special parking, specially equipped rest rooms, lowered drinking fountains, and lowered telephones are available.

Services: Counseling and information services are available, as is tutoring in most subjects. There is remedial math, reading, and writing. Both peers and professionals serve as tutors.

Campus Safety and Security: Measures include 24-hour foot and vehicle patrol, emergency telephones, and lighted pathways/sidewalks.

Programs of Study: Cheyney confers B.A., B.S., and B.S. Ed. degrees. Associate and master's degrees are also awarded. Bachelor's degrees are awarded in BIOLOGICAL SCIENCE (biology/biological science), BUSINESS (business administration and management and hotel/motel and restaurant management), COMMUNICATIONS AND THE ARTS (communications, dramatic arts, English, and music), COMPUTER AND PHYSICAL SCIENCE (chemistry, computer science, mathematics, and science), EDUCATION (early childhood, elementary, home economics, secondary, and special), HEALTH PROFESSIONS (medical laboratory technology), SOCIAL SCIENCE (clothing and textiles management/production/services, economics, geography, parks and recreation man-

agement, political science/government, psychology, and social science). Psychology, political science, and social relations are the strongest academically. Business administration and social relations are the largest.

Required: To graduate, students must complete at least 124 credit hours, with 30 in the major and a minimum GPA of 2.0. Distribution requirements include 6 credits each in communications, humanities, science, and social science, 4 in health and phys ed, and 3 in math.

Special: Students may participate in a co-op program and cross-register with West Chester University of Pennsylvania. Internships, study abroad, work-study programs, a chemistry-biology dual degree, nondegree study, pass/fail options, and credit for life, military, and work experience are available. There are 10 national honor societies, a freshman honors program, and 6 departmental honors programs.

Faculty/Classroom: 50% of faculty are male; 50%, female. 76% teach undergraduates. No introductory courses are taught by graduate students.

Requirements: The SAT or ACT is required. In addition, applicants must be graduates of an accredited secondary school or hold a GED. An interview is recommended. CLEP credit is accepted. Important factors in the admissions decision are ability to finance college education, extracurricular activities record, and geographic diversity.

Procedure: Freshmen are admitted fall and spring. Entrance exams should be taken during the junior or senior year. There are early decision and early admissions plans. There is a rolling admissions plan. Early decision applications should be filed by November 30; regular applications, by May 30 for fall entry and November 15 for spring entry. Notification is sent on a rolling basis.

Transfer: 79 transfer students enrolled in 2004-2005. Applicants must have a C average from an accredited postsecondary institution; others may be admitted on probation. Students with fewer than 30 credits must submit a high school transcript. 30 of 124 credits required for the bachelor's degree must be completed at Cheyney.

Visiting: There are regularly scheduled orientations for prospective students. There are guides for informal visits and visitors may sit in on classes. To schedule a visit, contact the Office of Admissions at (800) CHEYNEY.

Financial Aid: In 2005-2006, 87% of all full-time freshmen and 90% of continuing full-time students received some form of financial aid. 85% of full-time freshmen and 83% of continuing full-time students received need-based aid. Cheyney is a member of CSS. The FAFSA is required. Check with the school for current deadlines.

International Students: The school actively recruits these students. They must score satisfactorily on the written TOEFL.

Computers: Only authorized terminal operators may access the system 24 hours a day. There are no time limits and no fees.

Graduates: From July 1, 2004 to June 30, 2005, 138 bachelor's degrees were awarded. The most popular majors were social relations (42%), business administration (30%), and elementary education (26%).

Admissions Contact: Gemma Stemley, Director of Admission. A video is available. E-mail: *gstemley@cheyney.edu* Web: *www.cheyney.edu*

CLARION UNIVERSITY OF PENNSYLVANIA   B-2

Clarion, PA 16214

(814) 393-2306
(800) 672-7171; Fax: (814) 393-2030

Full-time: 2040 men, 3029 women	**Faculty:** IIA, +$
Part-time: 194 men, 481 women	**Ph.D.s:** 87%
Graduate: 140 men, 454 women	**Student/Faculty:** 17 to 1
Year: semesters, summer session	**Tuition:** $6598 ($11,568)
Application Deadline: open	**Room & Board:** $5246
Freshman Class: n/av	
SAT Verbal/Math: 505/502*	**COMPETITIVE**

Clarion University of Pennsylvania, founded in 1867, is a public institution and part of the Pennsylvania State System of Higher Education. There are 4 undergraduate and 4 graduate schools. In addition to regional accreditation, Clarion University has baccalaureate program accreditation with AACSB, ACS, ASHLA, NASM, NASPE, and NCATE. The 2 libraries contain 439,810 volumes, 1,603,663 microform items, and 7044 audio/video tapes/CDs/DVDs, and subscribe to 20,684 periodicals including electronic. Computerized library services include the card catalog, interlibrary loans, database searching, Internet access, and laptop Internet portals. Special learning facilities include a learning resource center, art gallery, planetarium, radio station, and TV station. The 201-acre campus is in a small town 85 miles northeast of Pittsburgh. Including any residence halls, there are 48 buildings.

Student Life: 94% of undergraduates are from Pennsylvania. Others are from 36 states, 34 foreign countries, and Canada. 89% are from public schools. 91% are white. The average age of freshmen is 18; all undergraduates, 22. 25% do not continue beyond their first year; 50% remain to graduate.

Housing: 2205 students can be accommodated in college housing, which includes single-sex and coed dorms and off-campus apartments.

75% of students commute. Alcohol is not permitted. All students may keep cars.

Activities: 4% of men belong to 6 national fraternities; 7% of women belong to 8 national sororities. There are 150 groups on campus, including art, band, cheerleading, choir, chorus, computers, dance, debate, drama, ethnic, forensics, gay, honors, international, jazz band, literary magazine, marching band, musical theater, newspaper, orchestra, pep band, photography, political, professional, radio and TV, religious, social, social service, student government, and symphony. Popular campus events include Autumn Leaf Festival, Activities Day, and Martin Luther King Cultural Series.

Sports: There are 8 intercollegiate sports for men and 8 for women, and 50 intramural sports for men and 50 for women. Facilities include a 5000-seat stadium; a gym with physical fitness center and recreational swimming; a natatorium; baseball, softball, and soccer fields; a 48,000-square-foot recreation building with 3 full-size multipurpose courts, a 4-lane elevated track, and a 4,800-square-foot weight room; tennis and basketball courts; sand volleyball pits; and an in-line hockey rink.

Disabled Students: 98% of the campus is accessible. Wheelchair ramps, elevators, special parking, specially equipped rest rooms, special class scheduling, lowered drinking fountains, lowered telephones, and priority registration are available.

Services: Counseling and information services are available, as is tutoring in some subjects, including math, economics, accounting, biology, chemistry, physics, earth science, history, sociology, political science, psychology, and computer information sciences. There is a reader service for the blind, remedial math, reading, and writing, computer-assisted instruction, and a learning skills lab.

Campus Safety and Security: Measures include 24-hour foot and vehicle patrol, self-defense education, security escort services, and informal discussions. There are pamphlets/posters/films, emergency telephones, lighted pathways/sidewalks, video surveillance cameras on campus, a bicycle patrol program, and a rape/aggressive defense program.

Programs of Study: Clarion University confers B.A., B.S., B.F.A., B.Mus., B.S.B.A., B.S.Ed., and B.S.N. degrees. Associate and master's degrees are also awarded. Bachelor's degrees are awarded in BIOLOGICAL SCIENCE (biology/biological science and molecular biology), BUSINESS (accounting, banking and finance, business administration and management, business economics, international business management, marketing/retailing/merchandising, and real estate), COMMUNICATIONS AND THE ARTS (art, communications, dramatic arts, English, French, music, Spanish, and speech/debate/rhetoric), COMPUTER AND PHYSICAL SCIENCE (chemistry, computer science, earth science, geology, information sciences and systems, mathematics, natural sciences, physics, quantitative methods, and radiological technology), EDUCATION (athletic training, early childhood, elementary, foreign languages, library science, music, secondary, and special), ENGINEERING AND ENVIRONMENTAL DESIGN (environmental science, and industrial administration/management), HEALTH PROFESSIONS (medical technology, nursing, rehabilitation therapy, and speech pathology/audiology), SOCIAL SCIENCE (anthropology, economics, geography, history, humanities, liberal arts/general studies, philosophy, political science/government, psychology, social psychology, social science, and sociology). Education, mass media and journalism, and biology are the strongest academically. Elementary education, secondary education, and communication are the largest.

Required: To graduate, student must complete at least 120 credits, with a minimum GPA of 2.0 (2.8 for the College of Education and Human Services). Degree requirements include Writing II, completion of general education courses, including a mandated 12 credits in liberal education skills, 27 credits in liberal knowledge (9 credits each in physical and social sciences, social and behavioral sciences, and arts and humanities), and 3 credits in health and personal performance. Specific degree and class requirements vary by major.

Special: Clarion University has co-op programs in engineering with the University of Pittsburgh and Case Western Reserve University and in speech pathology and audiology with Gallaudet University and a cooperative M.S.L.S./J.D. with Widener University. Internships, study abroad, work-study programs, and dual and student-designed majors are also available. There are 15 national honor societies and a freshman honors program.

Faculty/Classroom: 51% of faculty are male; 49%, female. All teach undergraduates. No introductory courses are taught by graduate students.

Admissions: The SAT scores for the 2005-2006 freshman class were: Verbal--56% below 500, 35% between 500 and 599, 8% between 600 and 700, and 1% above 700; Math--57% below 500, 35% between 500 and 599, 7% between 600 and 700, and 1% above 700. 58% of the current freshmen were in the top two fifths of their class.

Requirements: The ACT is recommended. In addition, applicants must be graduates of an accredited secondary school. The GED is accepted. Clarion University requires 4 years each of English and social studies and 3 years each of math and science and recommends 2 years of a foreign language. An essay and interview are recommended. A GPA of 2.0 is required. AP and CLEP credits are accepted. Important factors in the

admissions decision are advanced placement or honor courses, evidence of special talent, and leadership record.

Procedure: Freshmen are admitted fall and spring. Entrance exams should be taken in the spring of the junior year or early fall of the senior year. There is a deferred admissions plan and a rolling admissions plan. Application deadlines are open. Application fee is $30. Notification is sent 2 weeks after receipt of the completed application. Applications are accepted on-line.

Transfer: 358 transfer students enrolled in 2004-2005. Applicants for transfer shoulder have completed at least 6 college credit hours with a GPA of 2.8 for education and communication sciences and disorders majors, 2.5 for business majors, and 2.0 for other programs. An audition is required for music majors, and an interview and national test are required for nursing students. 45 of 120 credits required for the bachelor's degree must be completed at Clarion University.

Visiting: There are regularly scheduled orientations for prospective students, including 4 1-day orientation sessions in the spring for students who commit to Clarion early, as well as numerous 1-day orientation sessions during the summer for all other new students. There are guides for informal visits and visitors may sit in on classes. To schedule a visit, contact the Admissions Office.

Financial Aid: In 2005-2006, 64% of all full-time freshmen and 74% of continuing full-time students received some form of financial aid. 56% of full-time freshmen and 67% of continuing full-time students received need-based aid. Need-based scholarships or need-based grants averaged $5520 ($9800 maximum); need-based self-help aid (loans and jobs) averaged $2475 ($8175 maximum); and other non-need-based awards and non-need-based scholarships averaged $1367 ($11,694 maximum). Average annual earnings from campus work are $1275. The average financial indebtedness of the 2005 graduate was $16,500. The FAFSA is required. The priority date for freshman financial aid applications for fall entry is April 1. The deadline for filing freshman financial aid applications for fall entry is May 1.

International Students: There are 41 international students enrolled. The school actively recruits these students. A satisfactory score is required on the TOEFL.

Computers: Wireless access is available. Clarion University has 12 computer labs located in convenient locations across the campus, including in specially-designated rooms in classroom buildings and the campus library. All students may access the system 24 hours a day. There are no time limits and no fees.

Graduates: From July 1, 2004 to June 30, 2005, 1019 bachelor's degrees were awarded. The most popular majors were education (27%), business/marketing (19%), and communication/journalism (10%). In an average class, 26% graduate in 4 years or less, 48% graduate in 5 years or less, and 50% graduate in 6 years or less. 98 companies recruited on campus in 2004-2005.

Admissions Contact: Admissions Officer. A video is available. E-mail: *admissions@clarion.edu* Web: *www.clarion.edu*

COLLEGE MISERICORDIA   B-2
Dallas, PA 18612   (570) 674-6400
(866) 262-6363; Fax: (570) 675-2441

Full-time: 397 men, 1031 women	**Faculty:** 87; IIB, -$
Part-time: 143 men, 501 women	**Ph.Ds:** 80%
Graduate: 62 men, 209 women	**Student/Faculty:** 16 to 1
Year: semesters, summer session	**Tuition:** $19,700
Application Deadline: open	**Room & Board:** $8250
Freshman Class: 1071 applied, 865 accepted, 324 enrolled	
SAT Verbal/Math: 500/510*	**COMPETITIVE**

College Misericordia, established in 1924 and sponsored by the Religious Sisters of Mercy, is a private liberal arts institution affiliated with the Roman Catholic Church and offering professional programs in health-related fields. In addition to regional accreditation, College Misericordia has baccalaureate program accreditation with ACOTE, CAHEA, CCNE, CSWE, JRCERT, and NLN. The library contains 82,955 volumes, 7697 microform items, and 2240 audio/video tapes/CDs/DVDs, and subscribes to 575 periodicals including electronic. Computerized library services include the card catalog, interlibrary loans, database searching, and Internet access. Special learning facilities include a learning resource center, art gallery, radio station, and TV station. The 120-acre campus is in a suburban area 9 miles north of Wilkes-Barre. Including any residence halls, there are 16 buildings.

Student Life: 84% of undergraduates are from Pennsylvania. Others are from 20 states and 2 foreign countries. 79% are from public schools. 96% are white. 59% are Catholic; 26% Protestant; 6% claim no religious affiliation. The average age of freshmen is 18; all undergraduates, 21. 21% do not continue beyond their first year; 73% remain to graduate.

Housing: 750 students can be accommodated in college housing, which includes coed dorms and on-campus apartments. In addition, there are special-interest houses. On-campus housing is guaranteed for all 4 years. 53% of students live on campus; of those, 25% remain on campus on weekends. Upperclassmen may keep cars.

Activities: There are no fraternities or sororities. There are 26 groups on campus, including cheerleading, choir, chorale, chorus, drama, ethnic, honors, international, literary magazine, musical theater, newspaper, political, professional, radio and TV, religious, social service, student government, and yearbook. Popular campus events include Winter Snowball dance.

Sports: There are 8 intercollegiate sports for men and 11 for women, and 13 intramural sports for men and 13 for women. Facilities include the sports and health center, a 78,000 square-foot multipurpose facility with a competitive wood floor, 3 cross courts, a synthetic surfaced indoor running track, a six-lane NCAA competitive pool with observation deck, and an athletic complex and field, a 23-acre facility for field hockey, soccer, lacrosse, and track. A six-lane synthetic track encircles the field.

Disabled Students: 95% of the campus is accessible. Wheelchair ramps, elevators, special parking, specially equipped rest rooms, special class scheduling, and lowered drinking fountains are available.

Services: Counseling and information services are available, as is tutoring in every subject. There is remedial math and reading. Services for students with disabilities are provided through the Alternative Learners Program.

Campus Safety and Security: Measures include 24-hour foot and vehicle patrol, security escort services, informal discussions, and pamphlets/posters/films. There are emergency telephones and lighted pathways/sidewalks.

Programs of Study: College Misericordia confers B.A., B.S., B.S.N., and B.S.W. degrees. Master's and doctoral degrees are also awarded. Bachelor's degrees are awarded in BIOLOGICAL SCIENCE (biochemistry and biology/biological science), BUSINESS (accounting, business administration and management, marketing/retailing/merchandising, and sports management), COMMUNICATIONS AND THE ARTS (communications and English), COMPUTER AND PHYSICAL SCIENCE (chemistry, computer science, information sciences and systems, and mathematics), EDUCATION (early childhood, elementary, secondary, and special), HEALTH PROFESSIONS (medical laboratory technology, nursing, occupational therapy, physical therapy, radiograph medical technology, and speech therapy), SOCIAL SCIENCE (history, interdisciplinary studies, liberal arts/general studies, philosophy, psychology, and social work). Occupational therapy, physical therapy, and nursing are the strongest academically. Nursing, physical therapy, and business are the largest.

Required: To graduate, students must earn a minimum of 120 credits, with at least 60 credits in the major. The required 48-credit core curriculum includes courses in anthropology, English composition and literature, fine arts, history, math, philosophy, political science, psychology, religious studies, and science. A minimum GPA of 2.0 is required.

Special: Students may cross-register with King's College and Wilkes University. The college offers co-op programs, internships for all majors, work-study programs, study abroad in Guyana, Haiti, and Ireland, an accelerated degree program in business and nursing for adult students, student-designed majors, and dual majors in elementary and early childhood education, elementary and special education, and math and computer science. Credit may be granted for life, military, and work experience. Nondegree study is also available. The college offers an alternative learner's project, which accepts a limited number of learning disabled students each year. There are 5 national honor societies, a freshman honors program, and 1 departmental honors program.

Faculty/Classroom: 49% of faculty are male; 51%, female. 90% teach undergraduates, 10% do research, and 10% do both. No introductory courses are taught by graduate students. The average class size in an introductory lecture is 21; in a laboratory, 14; and in a regular course, 17.

Admissions: 81% of the 2005-2006 applicants were accepted. The SAT scores for the 2005-2006 freshman class were: Verbal--48% below 500, 43% between 500 and 599, 8% between 600 and 700, and 1% above 700; Math--44% below 500, 44% between 500 and 599, and 12% between 600 and 700. The ACT scores were 60% below 21, 30% between 21 and 23, and 10% between 27 and 28. 29% of the current freshmen were in the top fifth of their class; 60% were in the top two fifths. 1 freshman graduated first in class.

Requirements: The SAT is required. In addition, applicants must graduate from an accredited secondary school or have a GED. 16 Carnegie units must be earned, and students must complete 3 years each in English, math, history, and science, and 2 to 3 years in social studies. College Misericordia requires applicants to be in the upper 50% of their class. A GPA of 2.0 is required. AP and CLEP credits are accepted. Important factors in the admissions decision are advanced placement or honor courses, personality/intangible qualities, and extracurricular activities record.

Procedure: Freshmen are admitted fall and spring. Entrance exams should be taken during the junior year. There are early admissions and deferred admissions plans. Application deadlines are open. Application fee is $25. A waiting list is an active part of the admissions procedure. Applications are accepted on-line.

Transfer: 166 transfer students enrolled in 2004-2005. Applicants must have a minimum GPA of 2.0. Requirements may be higher for selected majors. 30 of 120 credits required for the bachelor's degree must be completed at College Misericordia.

Visiting: There are regularly scheduled orientations for prospective students, including meetings with admissions and financial aid counselors, a tour of the campus, and optional meetings with faculty and coaches. There are guides for informal visits and visitors may sit in on classes and stay overnight. To schedule a visit, contact the Admissions Office.

Financial Aid: In 2005-2006, 99% of all full-time freshmen and 98% of continuing full-time students received some form of financial aid. 73% of full-time freshmen and 75% of continuing full-time students received need-based aid. The average freshman award was $13,619. Need-based scholarships or need-based grants averaged $5377 ($12,600 maximum); need-based self-help aid (loans and jobs) averaged $4326 ($6025 maximum); and other non-need-based awards and non-need-based scholarships averaged $7074 ($24,576 maximum). 23% of undergraduates work part time. Average annual earnings from campus work are $801. The average financial indebtedness of the 2005 graduate was $12,066. College Misericordia is a member of CSS. The FAFSA and the college's own financial statement are required. The priority date for freshman financial aid applications for fall entry is March 1. The deadline for filing freshman financial aid applications for fall entry is May 1.

International Students: There are 3 international students enrolled. The school actively recruits these students. They must take the TOEFL.

Computers: Wireless access is available. The College has 4 open computer labs with 50 computers and 3 teaching labs, in addition to 20 PCs in the residence halls. Wireless laptops are loaned to students through the library. The student center is wireless. All students may access the system. There are no time limits and no fees.

Graduates: From July 1, 2004 to June 30, 2005, 397 bachelor's degrees were awarded. The most popular majors were nursing (20%), business (16%), and elementary education (10%). In an average class, 67% graduate in 4 years or less, 72% graduate in 5 years or less, and 73% graduate in 6 years or less. Of the 2004 graduating class, 43% were enrolled in graduate school within 6 months of graduation and 96% were employed.

Admissions Contact: Jane F. Dessoye, Executive Director of Admissions and Financial Aid. E-mail: *admiss@misericordia.edu* Web: *www.misericordia.edu*

CURTIS INSTITUTE OF MUSIC   F-3
Philadelphia, PA 19103-6187   (215) 893-5262
Fax: (215) 893-9065

Full-time: 45 men, 85 women	Faculty: n/av
Part-time: none	Ph.D.s: n/av
Graduate: 10 men, 10 women	Student/Faculty: n/av
Year: n/app	Tuition: see profile
Application Deadline: open	Room & Board: n/app
Freshman Class: n/av	
SAT: required	SPECIAL

Curtis Institute of Music, founded in 1924, is a private conservatory offering undergraduate, graduate, and professional programs in music. The institution serves an entirely commuter student body. All applicants are accepted on full-tuition scholarships. However, they must pay about $700 in fees and provide all their living expenses. Figures given in the above capsule and in this profile are approximate. In addition to regional accreditation, Curtis has baccalaureate program accreditation with NASM. The library contains 60,000 volumes, 100 microform items, and 10,000 audio/video tapes/CDs/DVDs, and subscribes to 40 periodicals including electronic. Special learning facilities include the Leonard Stolowski Collection. The campus is in an urban area. There are 3 buildings.

Student Life: 92% of undergraduates are from out of state, mostly the Northeast. Students are from 30 states, 21 foreign countries, and Canada. 90% are from public schools. 62% are white. The average age of freshmen is 18. 2% do not continue beyond their first year; 98% remain to graduate.

Housing: There are no residence halls. Alcohol is not permitted.

Activities: There are no fraternities or sororities. There are some groups and organizations on campus, including student government.

Sports: There is no sports program at Curtis.

Disabled Students: 1% of the campus is accessible. Elevators and specially equipped rest rooms are available.

Services: Counseling and information services are available. Tutoring is provided on an individual basis in every subject.

Campus Safety and Security: Measures include informal discussions, 24-hour security guards in the main building, and buzzer entry to other buildings.

Programs of Study: Bachelor's degrees are awarded in COMMUNICATIONS AND THE ARTS (music).

Requirements: The SAT is required. In addition, applicants must be graduates of an accredited secondary school or have earned a GED. Confidential letters of recommendation from 2 qualified musicians are required. Admission is based primarily on evidence of the applicant's special talent. An audition is required. AP and CLEP credits are accepted.

Procedure: Freshmen are admitted in the fall. Entrance exams should be taken by March of the senior year. Application deadlines are open.

Transfer: 97 of 131 credits required for the bachelor's degree must be completed at Curtis.

Financial Aid: Curtis is a member of CSS. The CSS/Profile and the college's own financial statement are required. Check with the school for current application deadlines.

International Students: They must score satisfactory on the written TOEFL and also take the SAT.

Computers: All students may access the system. There are no time limits and no fees.

Admissions Contact: Judi L. Gattone, Director of Admissions.

DE SALES UNIVERSITY E-3
Center Valley, PA 18034-9568

(610) 282-1100, ext. 1475
(877) 433-7253; Fax: (610) 282-0131

Full-time: 777 men, 989 women	Faculty: 83; IIA, --$
Part-time: 518 men and women	Ph.D.s: 72%
Graduate: 793 men and women	Student/Faculty: 21 to 1
Year: semesters, summer session	Tuition: $20,700
Application Deadline: open	Room & Board: $7880
Freshman Class: 1728 applied, 1365 accepted, 434 enrolled	
SAT Verbal/Math: 548/541*	ACT: 22 VERY COMPETITIVE

De Sales University, founded in 1964, is a private liberal arts institution affiliated with the Roman Catholic Church. In addition to regional accreditation, DSU has baccalaureate program accreditation with ACBSP, ARC-PA, and NLN. The library contains 148,743 volumes, 460,812 microform items, and 4551 audio/video tapes/CDs/DVDs, and subscribes to 8541 periodicals including electronic. Computerized library services include the card catalog, interlibrary loans, database searching, and Internet access. Special learning facilities include a learning resource center, radio station, TV station, 2 theaters, 2 dance studios, a distant learning center, and a science center. The 400-acre campus is in a suburban area 50 miles north of Philadelphia. Including any residence halls, there are 27 buildings.

Student Life: 70% of undergraduates are from Pennsylvania. Others are from 15 states. 46% are from public schools. 78% are white; 14% Asian American. 71% are Catholic; 15% Protestant; 8% claim no religious affiliation. The average age of freshmen is 18. 18% do not continue beyond their first year; 70% remain to graduate.

Housing: 952 students can be accommodated in college housing, which includes single-sex and coed dorms. In addition, there are special-interest houses. On-campus housing is guaranteed for all 4 years. 80% of students live on campus; of those, 60% remain on campus on weekends. All students may keep cars.

Activities: There is 1 local sorority. There are no fraternities. There are 21 groups on campus, including cheerleading, chorale, chorus, computers, dance, debate, drama, ethnic, honors, international, literary magazine, musical theater, newspaper, political, professional, radio and TV, religious, social, social service, student government, and yearbook. Popular campus events include Act One Plays, Annual Lecture Series, and Fall Fest.

Sports: There are 8 intercollegiate sports for men and 8 for women, and 8 intramural sports for men and 8 for women. Facilities include facilities for soccer, baseball, softball, tennis, basketball, lacrosse, track and cross country, volleyball, and a state-of-the-art sports and recreation facility featuring a fitness center, a student lounge, and multi-purpose athletic courts.

Disabled Students: 95% of the campus is accessible. Wheelchair ramps, elevators, special parking, specially equipped rest rooms, special class scheduling, lowered drinking fountains, and lowered telephones are available.

Services: Counseling and information services are available, as is tutoring in most subjects. There is a reader service for the blind and remedial reading and writing. The Academic Resource Center provides services (including tutoring) to all students.

Campus Safety and Security: Measures include 24-hour foot and vehicle patrol, self-defense education, security escort services, and informal discussions. There are pamphlets/posters/films, emergency telephones, lighted pathways/sidewalks, and 24-hour desk security in residence halls.

Programs of Study: DSU confers B.A., B.S., and B.S.N. degrees. Master's degrees are also awarded. Bachelor's degrees are awarded in BIOLOGICAL SCIENCE (biology/biological science), BUSINESS (accounting, banking and finance, business administration and management, electronic business, human resources, management information systems, marketing/retailing/merchandising, and sports management), COMMUNICATIONS AND THE ARTS (communications, dance, dramatic arts, English, film arts, performing arts, radio/television technology, and Spanish), COMPUTER AND PHYSICAL SCIENCE (chemistry, computer science, and mathematics), EDUCATION (elementary), ENGINEERING AND ENVIRONMENTAL DESIGN (environmental science), HEALTH

PROFESSIONS (nursing, physician's assistant, and sports medicine), SOCIAL SCIENCE (criminal justice, family/consumer studies, history, liberal arts/general studies, philosophy, political science/government, psychology, social work, and theological studies). Performing arts, nursing, and natural sciences are the strongest academically. Elementary education, theater/tv/film, and criminal justice are the largest.

Required: For graduation, students must complete a minimum of 120 credit hours, including a maximum of 48 in the major, with a minimum GPA of 2.0. Liberal arts distribution requirements consist of 12 to 16 courses including cultural literacy, modes of thinking, and Christian values and theology, as well as 3 units in phys ed. Internships are strongly encouraged for all majors.

Special: Students may cross-register with schools in the Lehigh Valley Association of Independent Colleges. Internships are strongly encouraged in all majors and study abroad in 10 countries is possible. Dual majors, a Washington semester, pass/fail options, accelerated degree programs, and credit for life, military, and work experience are offered. There are 11 national honor societies and a freshman honors program.

Faculty/Classroom: 63% of faculty are male; 37%, female. All teach undergraduates and do research. No introductory courses are taught by graduate students. The average class size in an introductory lecture is 20; in a laboratory, 20; and in a regular course, 20.

Admissions: 79% of the 2005-2006 applicants were accepted. The SAT scores for the 2005-2006 freshman class were: Verbal--26% below 500, 52% between 500 and 599, 19% between 600 and 700, and 3% above 700; Math--30% below 500, 48% between 500 and 599, 21% between 600 and 700, and 1% above 700. 48% of the current freshmen were in the top quarter of their class; 79% were in the top half.

Requirements: The SAT is required. In addition, applicants must be graduates of an accredited secondary school. The GED is accepted. Applicants should have completed 17 college preparatory courses, including 4 years each of English, history, and math, 3 years of science, and 2 years of foreign language. The school will accept an essay, but strongly recommends an interview. For theater students, a performance appraisal is required. For dance students, an audition is required. A GPA of 3.0 is required. AP and CLEP credits are accepted. Important factors in the admissions decision are advanced placement or honor courses, leadership record, and evidence of special talent.

Procedure: Freshmen are admitted fall and spring. Entrance exams should be taken during the junior or senior year. There are deferred admissions and rolling admissions plans. Application deadlines are open. Application fee is $30. Notification is sent on a rolling basis. Applications are accepted on-line.

Transfer: 51 transfer students enrolled in 2004-2005. Applicants for transfer should have completed a minimum of 24 college credit hours with a GPA of 2.5. An interview is recommended. 45 of 120 credits required for the bachelor's degree must be completed at DSU.

Visiting: There are regularly scheduled orientations for prospective students, including meetings with faculty advisers and social activities. There are guides for informal visits and visitors may sit in on classes and stay overnight. To schedule a visit, contact the Enrollment Management Office at (610) 282-4443 or admiss@desales.edu.

Financial Aid: In 2005-2006, 72% of all full-time freshmen and 71% of continuing full-time students received some form of financial aid. 72% of full-time freshmen and 69% of continuing full-time students received need-based aid. The average freshman award was $14,325. Need-based scholarships or need-based grants averaged $10,044; need-based self-help aid (loans and jobs) averaged $5240; and other non-need-based awards and non-need-based scholarships averaged $5097. 51% of undergraduates work part time. Average annual earnings from campus work are $833. The average financial indebtedness of the 2005 graduate was $13,997. DSU is a member of CSS. The FAFSA and the college's own financial statement are required. The deadline for filing freshman financial aid applications for fall entry is February 1.

International Students: There are 10 international students enrolled. A satisfactory score is required on the written TOEFL.

Computers: Wireless access is available. There is wireless access to the Internet in all residence hall rooms and all public places. There are special PC labs and approximately 150 PCs in the Dooling Hall, the academic building, and the Trexler Library. All students may access the system 24/hours a day from residence hall rooms, and 7 A.M. to 11 P.M. in public computing rooms. There are no time limits and no fees. It is strongly recommended that all students have a personal computer.

Graduates: From July 1, 2004 to June 30, 2005, 443 bachelor's degrees were awarded. The most popular majors were elementary education (12%), accounting (9%), and criminal justice (7%). In an average class, 62% graduate in 4 years or less, 69% graduate in 5 years or less, and 70% graduate in 6 years or less. 29 companies recruited on campus in 2004-2005. Of the 2004 graduating class, 9% were enrolled in graduate school within 6 months of graduation and 85% were employed.

Admissions Contact: Peter Rautzhan, Dean of Enrollment Management. E-mail: admiss@desales.edu Web: www.desales.edu

DELAWARE VALLEY COLLEGE   F-3
Doylestown, PA 18901-2697   (215) 489-2372
(800) 2-DEL-VAL; Fax: (215) 230-2968

Full-time: 702 men, 898 women	Faculty: 79; IIB, --$
Part-time: 209 men, 191 women	Ph.D.s: 62%
Graduate: 27 men, 43 women	Student/Faculty: 20 to 1
Year: semesters, summer session	Tuition: $21,814
Application Deadline: open	Room & Board: $8130
Freshman Class: 1476 applied, 1164 accepted, 451 enrolled	
SAT Verbal/Math: 510/510*	ACT: 22 COMPETITIVE

Delaware Valley College, founded in 1896, is a private institution offering undergraduate programs in specialized fields of agriculture, business administration, English, the sciences, math, criminal justice administration, and secondary education. The college also offers graduate programs in educational leadership and in food and agribusiness. The library contains 70,000 volumes and 162,914 microform items, and subscribes to 728 periodicals including electronic. Computerized library services include interlibrary loans, database searching, Internet access, and laptop Internet portals. Special learning facilities include a learning resource center, radio station, TV station, a dairy science center, a livestock farm, horse facilities, an apiary, a small animal lab, a tissue culture lab, an arboretum, and greenhouses. The 550-acre campus is in a suburban area 20 miles north of Philadelphia. Including any residence halls, there are 36 buildings.

Student Life: 67% of undergraduates are from Pennsylvania. Others are from 22 states, 1 foreign countries, and Canada. 85% are from public schools. 80% are white. 35% are Catholic; 32% Protestant; 16% claim no religious affiliation; 14% Buddhist, Seventh-day Adventist, and others. The average age of freshmen is 18; all undergraduates, 21. 26% do not continue beyond their first year; 75% remain to graduate.

Housing: 960 students can be accommodated in college housing, which includes single-sex and coed dorms. In addition, there are honors houses. On-campus housing is available on a first-come, first-served basis and is available on a lottery system for upperclassmen. 63% of students live on campus; of those, 65% remain on campus on weekends. Upperclassmen may keep cars.

Activities: 4% of men belong to 5 national fraternities; 5% of women belong to 3 national sororities. There are 40 groups on campus, including art, band, cheerleading, chess, choir, chorale, chorus, computers, dance, drama, ethnic, honors, international, literary magazine, newspaper, pep band, photography, professional, radio and TV, religious, social, social service, student government, and yearbook. Popular campus events include A-Day, Parents Day, and Family Weekend.

Sports: There are 8 intercollegiate sports for men and 7 for women, and 9 intramural sports for men and 9 for women. Facilities include 2 gyms, tennis courts, outdoor playing courts and fields, a football stadium, a running track, a small lake, a video game room, picnic areas, nature walks, riding trails, and indoor and outdoor equine facilities.

Disabled Students: 85% of the campus is accessible. Wheelchair ramps, elevators, special parking, specially equipped rest rooms, special class scheduling, and lowered drinking fountains are available.

Services: Counseling and information services are available, as is tutoring in most subjects. There is a reader service for the blind, and remedial math, reading, and writing.

Campus Safety and Security: Measures include 24-hour foot and vehicle patrol, self-defense education, security escort services, and shuttle buses. There are informal discussions, pamphlets/posters/films, emergency telephones, and lighted pathways/sidewalks.

Programs of Study: DVC confers B.A. and B.S. degrees. Associate and master's degrees are also awarded. Bachelor's degrees are awarded in AGRICULTURE (agronomy, animal science, dairy science, equine science, horticulture, and wildlife management), BIOLOGICAL SCIENCE (biology/biological science and zoology), BUSINESS (accounting, business administration and management, marketing/retailing/merchandising, and sports management), COMMUNICATIONS AND THE ARTS (English), COMPUTER AND PHYSICAL SCIENCE (chemistr, and computer science), EDUCATION (secondary), ENGINEERING AND ENVIRONMENTAL DESIGN (environmental science and food services technology), SOCIAL SCIENCE (criminal justice, food production/management/services, and food science). Physical and biological science and animal science are the strongest academically. Business administration and animal science are the largest.

Required: The bachelor's degree requires completion of at least 128 credits, including 48 in the major, with a minimum GPA of 2.0. The core curriculum consists of 48 credits of liberal arts courses, including cultural enrichment, phys ed, and an introduction to computers. Students must also fulfill employment program requirements.

Special: DVC offers a specialized methods and techniques program that enables students to learn lab techniques and gain experience in the practical aspects of their majors. There is a zoo science major that prepares students for careers in zoo management and animal conservation. There are co-op programs in all majors, dual majors, study abroad in England, internships, and work-study programs in a wide variety of employment

and research settings. Cross-registration is available with Rutgers University and Middle Bucks Technical Institute. Nondegree study and pass/fail options are also available. There are 3 national honor societies, a freshman honors program, and 2 departmental honors programs.

Faculty/Classroom: 66% of faculty are male; 34%, female. All teach undergraduates. The average class size in an introductory lecture is 24; in a laboratory, 21; and in a regular course, 20.

Admissions: 79% of the 2005-2006 applicants were accepted. The SAT scores for the 2005-2006 freshman class were: Verbal--43% below 500, 43% between 500 and 599, 13% between 600 and 700, and 1% above 700; Math--41% below 500, 46% between 500 and 599, 12% between 600 and 700, and 1% above 700. The ACT scores were 38% below 21, 25% between 21 and 23, 25% between 24 and 26, and 13% between 27 and 28. 25% of the current freshmen were in the top fifth of their class; 49% were in the top two fifths. 1 freshman graduated first in the class.

Requirements: The SAT or ACT is required. In addition, applicants must be graduates of accredited secondary schools or have earned a GED. The college requires 15 academic units, including 6 in electives, 3 in English, and 2 each in math, science, and social studies. An interview is recommended. DVC requires applicants to be in the upper 50% of their class. A GPA of 2.75 is required. AP and CLEP credits are accepted. Important factors in the admissions decision are leadership record, personality/intangible qualities, and extracurricular activities record.

Procedure: Freshmen are admitted fall and spring. Entrance exams should be taken in the junior or senior year. There are deferred admissions and rolling admissions plans. Application deadlines are open. Application fee is $35. Applications are accepted on-line.

Transfer: 109 transfer students enrolled in 2004-2005. Applicants must have a minimum GPA of 2.0 and must submit SAT scores. An interview is recommended. 60 of 130 credits required for the bachelor's degree must be completed at DVC.

Visiting: There are regularly scheduled orientations for prospective students, consisting of a student panel, meetings with department chairs, and general information sessions. There are guides for informal visits and visitors may sit in on classes and stay overnight. To schedule a visit, contact the Admissions Department.

Financial Aid: In 2005-2006, 98% of all full-time freshmen and 94% of continuing full-time students received some form of financial aid. 78% of all full-time students received need-based aid. The average freshman award was $16,050. 20% of undergraduates work part time. Average annual earnings from campus work are $1600. The average financial indebtedness of the 2005 graduate was $17,760. The FAFSA is required. The deadline for filing freshman financial aid applications for fall entry is April 1.

International Students: There is 1 international student enrolled. A satisfactory score is required on the written TOEFL and the SAT or the ACT.

Computers: Wireless access is available. Wireless access is available in the library. All students may access the system at designated times in the labs and 24 hours per day in most other areas. There are no time limits and no fees.

Graduates: From July 1, 2004 to June 30, 2005, 281 bachelor's degrees were awarded. The most popular majors were business administration (30%), animal science (22%), and ornamental horticulture (10%). In an average class, 44% graduate in 4 years or less, 54% graduate in 5 years or less, and 57% graduate in 6 years or less. 310 companies recruited on campus in 2004-2005. Of the 2004 graduating class, 24% were enrolled in graduate school within 6 months of graduation and 80% were employed.

Admissions Contact: Stephen W. Zenko, Director of Admissions. A video is available. E-mail: *admitme@devalcol.edu*
Web: *www.devalcol.edu*

DEVRY UNIVERSITY/FORT WASHINGTON
Fort Washington, PA 19034-3204   (215) 591-5700
(866) 303-3879; Fax: (251) 591-5745

Full-time: 350 men, 100 women	Faculty: n/av
Part-time: 150 men, 75 women	Ph.D.s: n/av
Graduate: none	Student/Faculty: n/av
Year: semesters, summer session	Tuition: $12,000
Application Deadline: open	Room & Board: n/app
Freshman Class: n/av	
SAT or ACT: n/av	LESS COMPETITIVE

DeVry University/Fort Washington. 1 of 67 DeVry University locations in the United States and Canada, opened in 2002. It offers programs in business administration, computer engineering technology, computer information systems, electronics engineering technology, network and communications management, and technical management. Figures in the above capsule and in this profile are approximate. The library contains 4200 volumes and 620 audio/video tapes/CDs/DVDs, and subscribes to 70 periodicals including electronic. The campus is located 25 miles from downtown Philadelphia.

Student Life: 46% are white; 39% African American.

Housing: There are no residence halls. All students commute.

Activities: There are no fraternities or sororities.

Programs of Study: DeVry confers B.A. degrees. Associate and master's degrees are also awarded. Bachelor's degrees are awarded in BUSINESS (business administration and management), COMMUNICATIONS AND THE ARTS (telecommunications), COMPUTER AND PHYSICAL SCIENCE (information sciences and systems), ENGINEERING AND ENVIRONMENTAL DESIGN (computer engineering, electrical/electronics engineering technology, and technological management).

Required: To graduate, students must achieve a GPA of at least 2.0, complete 48 to 154 credit hours, and satisfactorily complete all curriculum requirements. Course requirements vary according to program. All first-semester students take course in business organization, computer applications, algebra, psychology, and student success strategies.

Special: Accelerated degree programs in computer information systems and technical management, co-op programs, and distance learning are available.

Requirements: Admissions requirements include graduation from a secondary school; the GED is accepted. Applicants must pass the DeVry entrance exam or present satisfactory SAT or ACT scores. An interview is required.

Procedure: Freshmen are admitted fall, spring, and summer. There are early admissions and deferred admissions plans. Application deadlines are open. Check with the school for application fee. Applications are accepted on-line.

Transfer: 25 of 48 credits required for the bachelor's degree must be completed at DeVry University/Fort Washington.

Financial Aid: In a recent year, 74% of all full-time freshmen and 75% of continuing full-time students received some form of financial aid. 73% of all full-time students received need-based aid. The average freshman award was $6884. Need-based scholarships or need-based grants averaged $4120; need-based self-help aid (loans and jobs) averaged $4201; and other non-need-based awards and non-need-based scholarships averaged $8122. The FAFSA is required. The deadline for filing freshman financial aid applications is rolling.

International Students: International students must take the TOEFL and also take the college's own entrance exam.

Admissions Contact: Director of Admissions.
E-mail: *admissions@phi.devry.edu*
Web: *www.devry.edu/fortwashington*

DICKINSON COLLEGE D-3

Carlisle, PA 17013

(717) 245-1231
(800) 644-1773; Fax: (717) 245-1442

Full-time: 1010 men, 1301 women	**Faculty:** 175; IIB, +$
Part-time: 14 men, 27 women	**Ph.D.s:** 94%
Graduate: none	**Student/Faculty:** 13 to 1
Year: semesters, summer session	**Tuition:** $32,120
Application Deadline: February 1	**Room & Board:** $8050
Freshman Class: 4784 applied, 2359 accepted, 648 enrolled	
SAT Verbal/Math: 640/650*	**ACT:** 28

HIGHLY COMPETITIVE+

Dickinson College, founded in 1783, is a private institution offering a liberal arts curriculum including international education and science. The library contains 520,449 volumes, 167,434 microform items, and 12,510 audio/video tapes/CDs/DVDs, and subscribes to 1303 periodicals including electronic. Computerized library services include the card catalog, interlibrary loans, database searching, and Internet access. Special learning facilities include an art gallery, planetarium, radio station, fiber optic and satellite telecommunications networks, telescope observatory, and an archival collection. The 120-acre campus is in a suburban area about 20 miles west of Harrisburg and 2 hours from Washington, DC. Including any residence halls, there are 118 buildings.

Student Life: 72% of undergraduates are from out of state, mostly the Middle Atlantic. Students are from 40 states, 30 foreign countries, and Canada. 64% are from public schools. 82% are white. 31% are Protestant; 29% Catholic; 24% claim no religious affiliation; 10% Jewish. The average age of freshmen is 18; all undergraduates, 20. 11% do not continue beyond their first year; 81% remain to graduate.

Housing: 1933 students can be accommodated in college housing, which includes coed dorms, on-campus apartments, fraternity houses, and sorority houses. In addition, there are language houses and special-interest houses. On-campus housing is guaranteed for all 4 years. 92% of students live on campus; of those, 85% remain on campus on weekends. Upperclassmen may keep cars.

Activities: 19% of men belong to 6 national fraternities; 24% of women belong to 1 local and 3 national sororities. There are 120 groups on campus, including art, band, cheerleading, chess, choir, chorale, chorus, computers, dance, debate, drama, ethnic, film, gay, honors, international, jazz band, literary magazine, musical theater, newspaper, orchestra, photography, political, professional, radio and TV, religious, social, social service, student government, symphony, and yearbook. Popular

campus events include Black Arts Festival, Multicultural Fair, and Public Affairs Symposium.

Sports: There are 11 intercollegiate sports for men and 12 for women, and 13 intramural sports for men and 10 for women. Facilities include an 8000 square-foot fitness center with weight training and 40 cardiorespiratory conditioning machines. The 38,600 square-foot Kline Center includes basketball, squash, racquetball, and handball courts. The gym area features a multipurpose synthetic floor covering that includes an indoor 200-meter 4-lane track with a jump pit. There is a 20-yard competition swimming pool with separate diving well and seating for 350 spectators, and there are tennis courts, a varsity football field, lacrosse, baseball, and soccer fields, all comprising nearly 30 acres. There is also an outdoor track, jogging trails, and an indoor rock-climbing wall.

Disabled Students: 58% of the campus is accessible. Wheelchair ramps, elevators, special parking, specially equipped rest rooms, special class scheduling, lowered drinking fountains, lowered telephones, and special housing are available.

Services: Counseling and information services are available, as is tutoring in every subject. Services are provided as necessary on a case-by-case basis. There is a reader service for the blind and a writing center.

Campus Safety and Security: Measures include 24-hour foot and vehicle patrol, self-defense education, security escort services, and informal discussions. There are pamphlets/posters/films, emergency telephones, lighted pathways/sidewalks, and electronic access to residence halls.

Programs of Study: Dickinson confers B.A. and B.S. degrees. Bachelor's degrees are awarded in BIOLOGICAL SCIENCE (biochemistry, biology/biological science, and neurosciences), BUSINESS (international business management), COMMUNICATIONS AND THE ARTS (classical languages, dance, dramatic arts, English, fine arts, French, German, Greek, Latin, music, Russian, and Spanish), COMPUTER AND PHYSICAL SCIENCE (chemistry, computer science, geology, mathematics, and physics), ENGINEERING AND ENVIRONMENTAL DESIGN (environmental science), HEALTH PROFESSIONS (environmental health science), SOCIAL SCIENCE (American studies, anthropology, archeology, classical/ancient civilization, East Asian studies, economics, history, international studies, Italian studies, Judaic studies, law, medieval studies, philosophy, political science/government, psychology, public affairs, religion, Russian and Slavic studies, sociology, and women's studies). International education/foreign languages, natural sciences, and preprofessional programs are the strongest academically. Psychology, political science, international business and managament/international studies are the largest.

Required: To graduate, students must complete 32 courses with a minimum GPA of 2.0. The school requires 2 courses each in humanities, social sciences, and lab sciences. Also required are 3 courses of crosscultural studies (including foreign language, comparative civilizations, and U.S. diversity), a first-year seminar, phys ed, and the completion of a major averaging 9 to 15 courses. Writing intensive and quantitative reasoning courses are also required.

Special: Students may cross-register with Central Pennsylvania Consortium Colleges. 32 academic year or summer study abroad programs are offered in 24 countries. A Washington semester, work-study, and accelerated degree programs are available, as are dual majors, student-designed majors, nondegree study, pass/fail options, and a 3-3 law degree with the Dickinson School of Law of Pennsylvania State University. There are 3-2 engineering degrees offered with Case Western Reserve University, Rensselaer Polytechnic Institute, and the University of Pennsylvania. Instruction in 12 languages is available. There is a certification program in Latin American studies. Linkage programs are available with 7 graduate programs in business, accounting, and public administration at various institutions. There are 15 national honor societies, including Phi Beta Kappa, and 41 departmental honors programs.

Faculty/Classroom: 55% of faculty are male; 45%, female. All both teach and do research. The average class size in an introductory lecture is 35; in a laboratory, 18; and in a regular course, 18.

Admissions: 49% of the 2005-2006 applicants were accepted. The SAT scores for the 2005-2006 freshman class were: Verbal--2% below 500, 21% between 500 and 599, 52% between 600 and 700, and 25% above 700; Math--1% below 500, 21% between 500 and 599, 59% between 600 and 700, and 19% above 700. The ACT scores were 1% below 21, 4% between 21 and 23, 23% between 24 and 26, 29% between 27 and 28, and 43% above 28. 76% of the current freshmen were in the top fifth of their class; 93% were in the top two fifths. 17 freshmen graduated first in their class.

Requirements: The SAT or ACT is recommended. The ACT Optional Writing test is also recommended. In addition, the SAT and SAT Subject Tests are optional submissions. The GED is accepted. Applicants should have completed 16 academic credits, including 4 years of English, 3 each of math and science, 2 (preferably 3) of foreign language, 2 of social studies, and 2 additional courses drawn from the above areas. An essay is required and an interview is recommended. AP credits are accepted. Important factors in the admissions decision are advanced placement or honor courses, extracurricular activities record, and recommendations by school officials.

Procedure: Freshmen are admitted in the fall. Entrance exams should be taken in the spring of the junior year or the fall of the senior year. There are early decision, early admissions, and deferred admissions plans. Early decision applications should be filed by January 15; regular applications, by February 1 for fall entry. The fall application fee was $50. Notification of early decision is sent February 15; regular decision, March 31. 312 early decision candidates were accepted for the 2005-2006 class. 278 applicants were on the 2005 waiting list; 20 were admitted. Applications are accepted on-line.

Transfer: 10 transfer students enrolled in 2004-2005. Applicants for transfer must have at least a 2.0 cumulative GPA and must submit secondary school and college transcripts and one professor recommendation in addition to the standard application for admission. 16 of 32 credits required for the bachelor's degree must be completed at Dickinson.

Visiting: There are regularly scheduled orientations for prospective students, including campus tours, individual interviews, group information sessions, class visits, overnight stays in residence halls, and open houses. There are guides for informal visits and visitors may sit in on classes and stay overnight. To schedule a visit, contact the Admissions Office at *admit@dickinson.edu*.

Financial Aid: In 2005-2006, 59% of all full-time freshmen and 62% of continuing full-time students received some form of financial aid. 50% of full-time freshmen and 49% of continuing full-time students received need-based aid. The average freshman award was $23,563. Need-based scholarships or need-based grants averaged $16,471 ($42,061 maximum); need-based self-help aid (loans and jobs) averaged $3492 ($14,615 maximum); and federal, state, outside grants/scholarships averaged $1896 ($37,303 maximum). 50% of undergraduates work part time. Average annual earnings from campus work are $1332. The average financial indebtedness of the 2005 graduate was $20,982. Dickinson is a member of CSS. The CSS/Profile or FAFSA, the state aid form noncustodial parent statement, and business farm supplement are required. The deadline for filing freshman financial aid applications for fall entry is February 1.

International Students: There are 107 international students enrolled. The school actively recruits these students. They must score satisfactorily on the TOEFL.

Computers: Wireless access is available. The library hosts over 100 computers equipped with the Microsoft Office suite and other applications, as well as laptop computers that may be borrowed by students. The campus has a range of computer labs with 284 PCs and 276 Mac computers for student use. Laser printers are available. The campus is completely networked and every student room has at least 1 Ethernet network connection. Students may access the Internet from any location on campus through wired Ethernet connections or through the wireless network in the Waider-Spahr Library, the Quarry, and the Holland Union Building. All students may access the system. There are no time limits and no fees.

Graduates: From July 1, 2004 to June 30, 2005, 536 bachelor's degrees were awarded. The most popular majors were psychology (9%), political science (8%), and English (7%). In an average class, 81% graduate in 4 years or less, 84% graduate in 5 years or less, and 84% graduate in 6 years or less. 37 companies recruited on campus in 2004-2005. Of the 2004 graduating class, 36% were enrolled in graduate school within 6 months of graduation and 69% were employed.

Admissions Contact: Christopher Seth Allen, Dean of Admissions. A video is available. E-mail: *admit@dickinson.edu*
Web: *http://www.dickinson.edu*

DREXEL UNIVERSITY		**F-3**
Philadelphia, PA 19104		**(215) 895-2400**
	(800) 2-DREXEL; Fax: (215) 895-5939	
Full-time: 5700 men, 3650 women	**Faculty:** 653; I, -$	
Part-time: 945 men, 735 women	**Ph.D.s:** 90%	
Graduate: 2045 men, 2265 women	**Student/Faculty:** 14 to 1	
Year: quarters, summer session	**Tuition:** $19,000	
Application Deadline: see profile	**Room & Board:** $8700	
Freshman Class: n/av		
SAT or ACT: required		**VERY COMPETITIVE**

Drexel University, established in 1891, is a private institution with undergraduate programs in business and administration, engineering, information studies, design arts, and arts and sciences. Figures in the above capsule and this profile are approximate. There are 9 undergraduate and 8 graduate schools. In addition to regional accreditation, Drexel has baccalaureate program accreditation with AACSB, ABET, ADA, APA., CSAB, FIDER, and NAAB. The library contains 290,000 volumes, 651,500 microform items, and 32,935 audio/video tapes/CDs/DVDs, and subscribes to 9662 periodicals including electronic. Computerized library services include the card catalog, interlibrary loans, and database searching. Special learning facilities include a learning resource center, art gallery, radio station, and TV station. The 49-acre campus is in an urban area near the center of Philadelphia. Including any residence halls, there are 34 buildings.

Student Life: 40% of undergraduates are from out of state, mostly the Middle Atlantic. Students are from 40 states, 121 foreign countries, and Canada. 61% are white; 13% Asian American; 10% African American. The average age of freshmen is 18; all undergraduates, 21. 14% do not continue beyond their first year; 54% remain to graduate.

Housing: 2600 students can be accommodated in college housing, which includes coed dorms, on-campus apartments, and fraternity houses. In addition, there are honors floors in residence halls and internation student housing. On-campus housing is available on a first-come, first-served basis and is available on a lottery system for upperclassmen. 63% of students commute. All students may keep cars.

Activities: 12% of men belong to 14 national fraternities; 8% of women belong to 4 national sororities. There are 103 groups on campus, including art, band, cheerleading, chess, choir, chorus, computers, dance, drama, ethnic, film, gay, honors, international, jazz band, literary magazine, musical theater, newspaper, orchestra, pep band, photography, political, professional, radio and TV, religious, social, social service, student government, and yearbook. Popular campus events include Spring Jam, Winter Weekend, and an ongoing program of musical, cultural, and art events.

Sports: There are 10 intercollegiate sports for men and 10 for women, and 15 intramural sports for men and 12 for women. Facilities include a phys ed and activity center with 3 gyms, 6 squash courts, a swimming pool, a diving well, a wrestling room, a dance studio, a fencing room, Nautilus weight training rooms, and special exercise rooms; a field house; a bowling alley and game room with billiard, table tennis, and arcade games; and an outdoor volleyball court.

Disabled Students: 75% of the campus is accessible. Wheelchair ramps, elevators, special parking, specially equipped rest rooms, special class scheduling, lowered drinking fountains, lowered telephones, and special housing are available.

Services: Counseling and information services are available, as is tutoring in most subjects. There is remedial math, reading, and writing and a resident tutor program.

Campus Safety and Security: Measures include 24-hour foot and vehicle patrol, self-defense education, security escort services, and shuttle buses. There are pamphlets/posters/films, emergency telephones, lighted pathways/sidewalks, and residential and commuter safety and security programs.

Programs of Study: Drexel confers B.A., B.S., and B.Arch. degrees. Master's and doctoral degrees are also awarded. Bachelor's degrees are awarded in BIOLOGICAL SCIENCE (biology/biological science and nutrition), BUSINESS (business administration and management, fashion merchandising, hotel/motel and restaurant management, and marketing/retailing/merchandising), COMMUNICATIONS AND THE ARTS (communications, creative writing, design, film arts, graphic design, literature, music, photography, and video), COMPUTER AND PHYSICAL SCIENCE (chemistry, computer science, digital arts/technology, information sciences and systems, mathematics, physics, and science), EDUCATION (education), ENGINEERING AND ENVIRONMENTAL DESIGN (architectural engineering, architecture, biomedical engineering, chemical engineering, civil engineering, computer engineering, construction management, electrical/electronics engineering, environmental engineering, environmental science, interior design, materials engineering, and mechanical engineering), HEALTH PROFESSIONS (predentistry and premedicine), SOCIAL SCIENCE (fashion design and technology, food production/management/services, history, international studies, political science/government, prelaw, psychology, and sociology). Engineering, business, and design arts are the strongest academically. Electrical and computer engineering, business, and architecture are the largest.

Required: To graduate, students must complete 180 to 192 term credits with a minimum GPA of 2.0 and must earn the number of Drexel Co-op Units determined by the major. There are requirements in math, computer literacy, English, lab science, humanities, and history.

Special: The Drexel Plan of Cooperative Education enables students to alternate periods of full-time classroom studies and full-time employment with university-approved employers. Participation in cooperative education is mandatory, for most students. Cross-registration is available with Eastern Mennonite College, Indiana University of Pennsylvania, and Lincoln University. Drexel also offers study abroad, internships, accelerated degrees, 3-3 engineering degrees, dual majors, nondegree study, credit/no credit options, and a Sea Education Association semester. There is a freshman honors program.

Faculty/Classroom: 63% of faculty are male; 37%, female. The average class size in an introductory lecture is 35; in a laboratory, 24; and in a regular course, 24.

Requirements: The SAT or ACT is required. In addition, ; the SAT I is preferred. Applicants must be graduates of an accredited secondary school. The GED is accepted. An interview is recommended. A GPA of 2.0 is required. AP and CLEP credits are accepted. Important factors in the admissions decision are advanced placement or honor courses, evidence of special talent, and recommendations by school officials.

Procedure: Freshmen are admitted to all sessions. Entrance exams should be taken by January 1 of the senior year. There are early admissions and deferred admissions plans. Applications should be filed by March 1 for fall entry, along with a $50 fee. Notification is sent on a rolling basis. A waiting list is an active part of the admissions procedure.Applications are accepted on-line.

Transfer: 850 transfer students enrolled in 2004-2005. Applicants must have a minimum GPA of 2.5. Other requirements vary among the individual colleges within the university. 45 of 192 credits required for the bachelor's degree must be completed at Drexel.

Visiting: There are regularly scheduled orientations for prospective students, consisting of a 2-day program for new freshmen and their parents in late July. There are guides for informal visits and visitors may sit in on classes and stay overnight. To schedule a visit, contact the Admissions Office at enroll@drexel.edu.

Financial Aid: In 2005-2006, 70% of all full-time freshmen and 89% of continuing full-time students received some form of financial aid. The average freshman award was $10,728. Need-based scholarships or need-based grants averaged $4603; need-based self-help aid (loans and jobs) averaged $4989; non-need-based athletic scholarships averaged $24,014; and other non-need-based awards and non-need-based scholarships averaged $7045. 16% of undergraduates work part time. Average annual earnings from campus work are $800. The average financial indebtedness of the 2005 graduate was $22,234. The FAFSA is required. The deadline for filing freshman financial aid applications for fall entry is February 15.

International Students: There are 594 international students enrolled. The school actively recruits these students. They must score satisfactorily on the written TOEFL.

Computers: All students may access the system 24 hours a day. There are no time limits and no fees. All students are required to have personal computers.

Graduates: In a recent year, 1942 bachelor's degrees were awarded. The most popular majors were business/marketing (27%), engineering/engineering technologies (23%), and computer and information sciences (15%). In an average class, 57% graduate in 6 years or less. 300 companies recruited on campus in a recent year. Of a recent graduating class, 14% were enrolled in graduate school within 6 months of graduation and 81% were employed.

Admissions Contact: David Eddy, Director of Admissions. A video is available. Email: enroll@drexel.edu Web:www.drexel.edu

DUQUESNE UNIVERSITY B-3
Pittsburgh, PA 15282-0201

(412) 396-5002
(800) 456-0590; Fax: (412) 396-6223

Full-time: 2163 men, 3160 women	**Faculty:** 427; IIA, av$
Part-time: 142 men, 185 women	**Ph.D.s:** 89%
Graduate: 1771 men, 2495 women	**Student/Faculty:** 12 to 1
Year: semesters, summer session	**Tuition:** $21,480
Application Deadline: July 1	**Room & Board:** $8054
Freshman Class: n/av	
SAT or ACT: required	**VERY COMPETITIVE**

Duquesne University, founded in 1878 by the Spiritan Congregation, is a private Roman Catholic institution offering programs in liberal arts, natural and environmental sciences, nursing, health sciences, pharmacy, business, music, teacher preparation, preprofessional training, law, and leadership and professional development. There are 9 undergraduate and 10 graduate schools. In addition to regional accreditation, Duquesne has baccalaureate program accreditation with AACSB, ACOTE, ACPE, APTA, CAAHEP, CAPTE, and NASM. The 2 libraries contain 690,904 volumes and 331,806 microform items, and subscribe to 17,437 periodicals including electronic. Computerized library services include the card catalog, interlibrary loans, database searching, and Internet access. Special learning facilities include a learning resource center, art gallery, radio station, TV station, and 144 multimedia enhanced teaching facilities. The 50-acre campus is in an urban area on a private, self-contained campus in the center of Pittsburgh. Including any residence halls, there are 29 buildings.

Student Life: 80% of undergraduates are from Pennsylvania. Others are from 43 states, 55 foreign countries, and Canada. 79% are from public schools. 82% are white. 49% are Catholic; 34% claim no religious affiliation. The average age of freshmen is 18; all undergraduates, 21. 11% do not continue beyond their first year; 71% remain to graduate.

Housing: 3574 students can be accommodated in college housing, which includes single-sex and coed dorms and on-campus apartments. In addition, there are honors houses, special-interest houses, fraternity and sorority wings, no-smoking wings, international wings, and club wings. On-campus housing is guaranteed for the freshman and sophomore year's only, is available on a first-come, first-served basis, and is available on a lottery system for upperclassmen. 56% of students live on campus; of those, 70% remain on campus on weekends. All students may keep cars.

Activities: 14% of men belong to 1 local and 8 national fraternities; 18% of women belong to 8 national sororities. There are 145 groups on campus, including art, band, cheerleading, chess, choir, chorale, chorus,

computers, dance, debate, drama, ethnic, film, honors, international, jazz band, literary magazine, marching band, musical theater, newspaper, opera, orchestra, pep band, photography, political, professional, radio and TV, religious, social, social programming, social service, student government, symphony, and yearbook. Popular campus events include Carnival, Bluffstock Music Festival, and Valentine, Halloween, and Christmas balls.

Sports: There are 10 intercollegiate sports for men and 10 for women, and 9 intramural sports for men and 9 for women. Facilities include an athletic center, a swimming pool, a football and soccer field, a baseball field, an intramural field with an all-weather track, a weight room and exercise facilities, and volleyball, tennis, basketball, and street hockey courts.

Disabled Students: 95% of the campus is accessible. Wheelchair ramps, elevators, special parking, specially equipped rest rooms, special class scheduling, lowered drinking fountains, lowered telephones, special housing, and special assistive technology in the Gumberg Library for certain disabilities, including the visually impaired, are available.

Services: Counseling and information services are available, as is tutoring in every subject, in anything requested. There is a reader service for the blind, and remedial math, reading, and writing.

Campus Safety and Security: Measures include 24-hour foot and vehicle patrol, self-defense education, security escort services, and informal discussions. There are pamphlets/posters/films, emergency telephones, lighted pathways/sidewalks, and security cameras throughout campus that monitor exterior areas. All academic buildings have card access. Security measures for residence halls include card access, security cameras, and entrances that are monitored by residence life staff 24 hours a day.

Programs of Study: Duquesne confers B.A., B.S., B.M., B.S.A.T., B.S.B.A., B.S.Ed., B.S.H.M.S., B.S.H.S., B.S.N., and B.S.P.S. degrees. Master's and doctoral degrees are also awarded. Bachelor's degrees are awarded in BIOLOGICAL SCIENCE (biochemistry and biology/biological science), BUSINESS (accounting, banking and finance, business administration and management, entrepreneurial studies, international business management, investments and securities, management information systems, management science, marketing and distribution, marketing/retailing/merchandising, and purchasing/inventory management), COMMUNICATIONS AND THE ARTS (art history and appreciation, classical languages, classics, communications, dramatic arts, English, Greek (classical), journalism, Latin, literature, modern language, multimedia, music, music performance, music technology, Spanish, and studio art), COMPUTER AND PHYSICAL SCIENCE (chemistry, computer science, mathematics, physics, and web technology), EDUCATION (athletic training, early childhood, education, educational media, elementary, English, music, and secondary), ENGINEERING AND ENVIRONMENTAL DESIGN (environmental science), HEALTH PROFESSIONS (health care administration, health science, music therapy, and nursing), SOCIAL SCIENCE (classical/ancient civilization, economics, history, international relations, liberal arts/general studies, philosophy, political science/government, psychology, sociology, and theological studies). Liberal arts, business, and health sciences are the largest.

Required: To graduate, students are required to complete at least 120 credit hours, including a specified number in the major (varies by program), with a minimum 2.0 GPA. General requirements vary by department, but there is a 27-credit liberal arts core curriculum.

Special: The university offers cross-registration through the Pittsburgh Council on Higher Education, internships, study abroad in 21 countries, and a Washington semester. Also available are B.A.-B.S. degrees, Saturday College, a general studies degree, an accelerated degree program, dual and student-designed majors, a 3-2 engineering program with Case Western Reserve University and University of Pittsburgh, a 3-3 law degree and a 3-2 business degree, pass/fail options, and credit for life, military, and work experience. There are 26 national honor societies and a freshman honors program. Most departments have honors programs.

Faculty/Classroom: 58% of faculty are male; 42%, female. The average class size in an introductory lecture is 27; in a laboratory, 23; and in a regular course, 26.

Admissions: 80% of the 2005-2006 applicants were accepted. 77% were in the top two fifths. 45 freshmen graduated first in their class.

Requirements: The SAT or ACT is required. In addition, students should have either a high school diploma or the GED. Applicants are required to have 16 academic credits, including 4 each in English and academic electives, and 8 combined in social studies, language, math, and science. An audition is required for music majors. An essay is required and an interview is recommended. A GPA of 3.0 is required. AP and CLEP credits are accepted.

Procedure: Freshmen are admitted to all sessions. Entrance exams should be taken during the spring of the junior year or the fall of the senior year. There are early decision, early admissions, and deferred admissions plans. Early decision applications should be filed by November 1; regular applications, by July 1 for fall entry, December 1 for spring entry, and April 1 for summer entry, along with a $50 fee. There is a rolling admissions plan. Notification of early decision is sent December 15; regular decision, on a rolling basis. 63 early decision candidates were accepted for the 2005-2006 class. Applications are accepted on-line.

Transfer: 166 transfer students enrolled in 2004-2005. Applicants must submit complete high school and college transcripts. Students should have a minimum GPA of 2.5 for the university, but some schools require a higher average. A minimum of 12 credits earned is required and an interview is recommended. 30 of 120 credits required for the bachelor's degree must be completed at Duquesne.

Visiting: There are regularly scheduled orientations for prospective students, consisting of a campus tour and individual interviews with counselors and professors. There are guides for informal visits and visitors may sit in on classes. To schedule a visit, contact the Office of Admissions at (412) 396-6222 or *admissions@duq.edu*.

Financial Aid: In 2005-2006, 98% of all full-time freshmen and 88% of continuing full-time students received some form of financial aid. 74% of full-time freshmen and 64% of continuing full-time students received need-based aid. The average freshman award was $19,486 with $8,361 ($20,000 maximum) from need-based scholarships or need-based grants, $8,023 ($28,778 maximum) from need-based self-help aid (loans and jobs), $466 ($32,259 maximum) from non-need-based athletic scholarships, and $2,636 ($25,486 maximum) from other non-need-based awards and non-need-based scholarships averaged $2636 ($25,486 maximum). The average financial indebtedness of the 2005 graduate was $23,205. The FAFSA and the college's own financial statement are required. The deadline for filing freshman financial aid applications for fall entry is May 1.

International Students: There are 117 international students enrolled. The school actively recruits these students. They must take the TOEFL or the MELAB.

Computers: Wireless access is available. The campus is covered by a 7000-node Ethernet network, a wireless network, and more than 850 computers in computer labs. All students may access the system. There are no time limits and no fees. It is strongly recommended that all students have a personal computer. Dell, IBM, or Mac is recommended.

Graduates: From July 1, 2004 to June 30, 2005, 1115 bachelor's degrees were awarded. The most popular majors were liberal arts (31%), business (26%), and education (10%). In an average class, 55% graduate in 4 years or less, 67% graduate in 5 years or less, and 69% graduate in 6 years or less. 60 companies recruited on campus in 2004-2005. Of the 2004 graduating class, 20% were enrolled in graduate school within 6 months of graduation and 70% to 75% were employed.

Admissions Contact: Paul-James Cukanna, Executive Director of Admissions. A video is available. E-mail: *admissions@duq.edu* Web: *www.admissions.duq.edu*

EAST STROUDSBURG UNIVERSITY OF PENNSYLVANIA   F-2

East Stroudsburg, PA 18301   **(570) 422-3542**
(877) 230-5547; Fax: (570) 422-3933

Full-time: 1940 men, 2720 women	**Faculty:** n/av
Part-time: 210 men, 265 women	**Ph.D.s:** n/av
Graduate: 320 men, 730 women	**Student/Faculty:** n/av
Year: semesters, summer session	**Tuition:** $5950 ($12,900)
Application Deadline: see profile	**Room & Board:** $4400
Freshman Class: n/av	
SAT Verbal/Math: 490/490	**COMPETITIVE**

East Stroudsburg University of Pennsylvania, founded in 1893, is a part of the Pennsylvania State System of Higher Education and offers programs in arts and science, health sciences and human performance, and professional studies. There are 3 undergraduate schools and 1 graduate school. Figures in the above capsule and in this profile are approximate. In addition to regional accreditation, East Stroudsburg has baccalaureate program accreditation with NLN. The library contains 428,000 volumes, 1,238,040 microform items, and 7650 audio/video tapes/CDs/DVDs, and subscribes to 2200 periodicals including electronic. Computerized library services include the card catalog, interlibrary loans, and database searching. Special learning facilities include a learning resource center, art gallery, radio station, and wildlife museum. The 183-acre campus is in a small town 75 miles west of New York City. Including any residence halls, there are 39 buildings.

Student Life: 81% of undergraduates are from Pennsylvania.Students are from 22 states, 21 foreign countries, and Canada. 92% are white. The average age of freshmen is 18; all undergraduates, 23. 17% do not continue beyond their first year; 60% remain to graduate.

Housing: 2140 students can be accommodated in college housing, which includes single-sex and coed dorms, on-campus apartments, and honors floors. 53% of students commute. Alcohol is not permitted. Upperclassmen may keep cars.

Activities: 12% of men belong to 8 national fraternities; 15% of women belong to 2 local and 6 national sororities. There are 76 groups on campus, including art, band, cheerleading, chess, choir, chorus, computers, dance, drama, ethnic, gay, honors, international, jazz band, literary magazine, musical theater, newspaper, pep band, political, professional, radio and TV, religious, social, social service, student government, and yearbook. Popular campus events include concerts, Spring Music Festival, and International Celebrations.

Sports: There are 9 intercollegiate sports for men and 9 for women, and 11 intramural sports for men and 11 for women. Facilities include a 5000-seat stadium, a 2600-seat gym, another gym, 8 athletic fields, 12 outdoor tennis courts, 1 indoor tennis court, a swimming pool, indoor and outdoor tracks, and weight rooms.

Disabled Students: 98% of the campus is accessible. Wheelchair ramps, elevators, special parking, specially equipped rest rooms, special class scheduling, lowered drinking fountains, lowered telephones, and visual fire alarms for hearing impaired persons are available.

Services: Counseling and information services are available, as is tutoring in every subject. There is remedial math, reading, and writing.

Campus Safety and Security: Measures include 24-hour foot and vehicle patrol, self-defense education, security escort services, and informal discussions. There are pamphlets/posters/films, emergency telephones, lighted pathways/sidewalks, and a police bicycle patrol.

Programs of Study: East Stroudsburg confers B.A. and B.S. degrees. Master's degrees are also awarded. Bachelor's degrees are awarded in BIOLOGICAL SCIENCE (biochemistry, biology/biological science, and marine science), BUSINESS (business administration and management and hotel/motel and restaurant management), COMMUNICATIONS AND THE ARTS (art, communications, dramatic arts, English, fine arts, French, media arts, music, and Spanish), COMPUTER AND PHYSICAL SCIENCE (chemistry, computer science, earth science, mathematics, physical sciences, and science), EDUCATION (early childhood, elementary, foreign languages, health, secondary, and special), ENGINEERING AND ENVIRONMENTAL DESIGN (environmental science), HEALTH PROFESSIONS (allied health, medical laboratory technology, nursing, premedicine, and speech pathology/audiology), SOCIAL SCIENCE (economics, geography, history, parks and recreation management, philosophy, physical fitness/movement, political science/government, psychology, social studies, and sociology). Computer science, nursing, and math are the strongest academically. Education, hospitality management, and phys ed are the largest.

Required: All students must maintain a GPA of at least 2.0 while taking 128 semester hours, including 27 to 83 hours in the major. General education courses total 50 credits, with English composition and phys ed required courses. Distribution requirements include 15 hours in arts and letters, science, and social science.

Special: Internships are offered in most programs, as are dual majors. Also offered are B.A.-B.S. degrees, 3-2 engineering degrees with Pennsylvania State University or the University of Pittsburgh, and a transfer program in podiatry. Nondegree study, study abroad, and cross-registration through the National Student Exchange are possible. There are 16 national honor societies and a freshman honors program.

Faculty/Classroom: All teach undergraduates. No introductory courses are taught by graduate students. The average class size in an introductory lecture is 40; in a laboratory, 25; and in a regular course, 25.

Requirements: The SAT is required. In addition, applicants must be graduates of an accredited secondary school. The GED is accepted. AP and CLEP credits are accepted. Important factors in the admissions decision are advanced placement or honor courses, evidence of special talent, and leadership record.

Procedure: Freshmen are admitted in the fall. Entrance exams should be taken during the fall of the senior year. Check witrh school for current appication deadlines. Notification is sent March 1. The fall 2005 application fee was $35.

Transfer: Transfer students must have a 2.0 GPA earned over at least 24 credit hours. 32 of 128 credits required for the bachelor's degree must be completed at East Stroudsburg.

Visiting: There are regularly scheduled orientations for prospective students. There are guides for informal visits and visitors may sit in on classes. To schedule a visit, contact the Admissions Office.

Financial Aid: In a recent year, 67% of all full-time freshmen and 72% of continuing full-time students received some form of financial aid. East Stroudsburg is a member of CSS. The FAFSA is required. Check with the school for current application deadlines.

International Students: They must score satisfactory on the written TOEFL.

Computers: All students may access the system. Most computers are available 7 A.M. to 10 P.M., with some available on a 24-hour basis. There are no time limits and no fees.

Admissions Contact: Alan T. Chesterton, Director of Admission. E-mail: *undergrads@esu.edu* Web: *www.esu.edu*

EASTERN UNIVERSITY   F-3
St. Davids, PA 19087-3696   **(610) 341-5967**
(800) 452-0996; Fax: (610) 341-1723

Full-time: 525 men, 1035 women	Faculty: 64; IIA, --$
Part-time: 125 men, 235 women	Ph.D.s: 75%
Graduate: 340 men, 540 women	Student/Faculty: 24 to 1
Year: semesters, summer session	Tuition: $16,850
Application Deadline: see profile	Room & Board: $7225
Freshman Class: n/av	
SAT or ACT: required	COMPETITIVE

Eastern University, founded in 1932, is a private liberal arts institution affiliated with the American Baptist Church. Figures in the above capsule and in this profile are approximate. In addition to regional accreditation, Eastern has baccalaureate program accreditation with CSWE and NLN. The 2 libraries contain 131,000 volumes, 716,396 microform items, and 13,242 audio/video tapes/CDs/DVDs, and subscribe to 1079 periodicals including electronic. Computerized library services include the card catalog, interlibrary loans, and database searching. Special learning facilities include a planetarium and radio station. The 106-acre campus is in a small town 20 miles northwest of Philadelphia. Including any residence halls, there are 23 buildings.

Student Life: 60% of undergraduates are from Pennsylvania. Students are from 38 states, 26 foreign countries, and Canada. 72% are from public schools. 81% are white; 14% African American. 68% are Assembly of God, Christian, Evangelical, Mennonite, Pentecostal; 13% claim no religious affiliation; 11% Catholic. The average age of freshmen is 19; all undergraduates, 27. 28% do not continue beyond their first year; 55% remain to graduate.

Housing: 840 students can be accommodated in college housing, which includes single-sex and coed dorms and on-campus apartments, and apartment living by application. On-campus housing is guaranteed for all 4 years. 53% of students commute. Alcohol is not permitted. All students may keep cars.

Activities: There are no fraternities or sororities. There are 70 groups on campus, including band, cheerleading, choir, chorale, chorus, computers, dance, drama, drill team, ethnic, honors, international, jazz band, literary magazine, musical theater, newspaper, orchestra, pep band, political, professional, radio and TV, religious, social, social service, student government, and yearbook. Popular campus events include President's Christmas Party, Spring Banquet, and World Culture Day.

Sports: There are 5 intercollegiate sports for men and 7 for women, and 3 intramural sports for men and 3 for women. Facilities include a gym, a soccer pitch, a baseball/field hockey/softball field, a weight room, an outdoor track, 4 tennis courts, a health fitness trail, an outdoor pool, and basketball/volleyball courts.

Disabled Students: 75% of the campus is accessible. Wheelchair ramps, elevators, special parking, specially equipped rest rooms, special class scheduling, lowered drinking fountains, lowered telephones, and special housing are available.

Services: Counseling and information services are available, as is tutoring in every subject. There is a reader service for the blind, and remedial math, reading, and writing and a summer skills workshop.

Campus Safety and Security: Measures include 24-hour foot and vehicle patrol, self-defense education, security escort services, and shuttle buses. There are informal discussions, pamphlets/posters/films, emergency telephones, and lighted pathways/sidewalks.

Programs of Study: Eastern confers B.A., B.S., B.S.N., and B.S.W. degrees. Associate and master's degrees are also awarded. Bachelor's degrees are awarded in AGRICULTURE (environmental studies), BIOLOGICAL SCIENCE (biochemistry and biology/biological science), BUSINESS (accounting, business administration and management, management information systems, and marketing/retailing/merchandising), COMMUNICATIONS AND THE ARTS (art history and appreciation, communications, dance, English literature, French, music, Spanish, and studio art), COMPUTER AND PHYSICAL SCIENCE (astronomy, chemistry, and mathematics), EDUCATION (elementary, English, secondary, and special), ENGINEERING AND ENVIRONMENTAL DESIGN (city/community/regional planning), HEALTH PROFESSIONS (health care administration and health science), SOCIAL SCIENCE (biblical studies, history, missions, political science/government, psychology, social work, sociology, theological studies, urban studies, and youth ministry). Biblical/theological studies and English literature are the strongest academically. Youth ministries and elementary education are the largest.

Required: To graduate, all students must complete at least 127 credit hours with a minimum 2.0 GPA. The required hours in the major vary. Students must take courses in the Old and New Testament, humanities, social sciences, non-Western heritage, natural sciences, college writing, Living and Learning in Community, Heritage of Western Thought and Civilization, Science Technology and Values, and Justice in a Pluralistic Society and complete a capstone.

Special: The college offers cross-registration with Cabrini and Rosemont Colleges, Valley Forge Military Academy, and Villanova University, internships, a Washington semester in the American studies program, and student-designed majors. Also available are accelerated degree programs in organizational management and management of information systems, credit for experience, nondegree study, and pass/fail options. There is a different calendar for the organizational management program. There are 10 national honor societies, a freshman honors program, and 1 departmental honors program.

Faculty/Classroom: 54% of faculty are male; 46%, female. 83% teach undergraduates. No introductory courses are taught by graduate students. The average class size in an introductory lecture is 45; in a laboratory, 14; and in a regular course, 14.

Requirements: The SAT or ACT is required. A GPA of 2.0 is required. AP and CLEP credits are accepted.

Procedure: Freshmen are admitted to all sessions. Entrance exams should be taken as early as possible. There are early admissions and deferred admissions and rolling admissions plans.Check with the school for current application deadlines. Notification is sent on a rolling basis. Applications are accepted on-line. The fall 2005 application fee was $25.

Transfer: Applicants should have a 2.0 GPA with more than 24 credits, and a 2.5 GPA with fewer than 24 credits. Candidates must be in good standing at their previous institution. 32 of 127 credits required for the bachelor's degree must be completed at Eastern.

Visiting: There are regularly scheduled orientations for prospective students, including a preview of academics, student life, and athletics. There are guides for informal visits and visitors may sit in on classes and stay overnight. To schedule a visit, contact the Admissions Office.

Financial Aid: In a recent year, 95% of all full-time freshmen received some form of financial aid. 95% of full-time freshmen received need-based aid. Eastern is a member of CSS. The FAFSA, the college's own financial statement and the income tax forms are required. Check with the school for current application deadlines.

International Students: The school actively recruits these students. They must score satisfactorily on the written TOEFL.

Computers: All students may access the system. There are no time limits and no fees. It is strongly recommended that all students have a personal computer.

Admissions Contact: David Urban/Jim Henderson, Executive Director of Enrollment Management. E-mail: ugadm@eastern.edu
Web: www.eastern.edu

EDINBORO UNIVERSITY OF PENNSYLVANIA   B-1
Edinboro, PA 16444   **(814) 732-2761**
(888) 8GO-BORO; Fax: (814) 732-2420

Full-time: 2422 men, 3227 women	Faculty: IIA, av$
Part-time: 314 men, 487 women	Ph.D.s: 69%
Graduate: 246 men, 656 women	Student/Faculty: n/av
Year: semesters, summer session	Tuition: $6291 ($11,198)
Application Deadline: open	Room & Board: $5518
Freshman Class: 3541 applied, 2903 accepted, 1268 enrolled	
SAT or ACT: required	LESS COMPETITIVE

Edinboro University of Pennsylvania, founded in 1857, is a public institution and a member of the Pennsylvania State System of Higher Education. The university offers programs in fine and liberal arts, business, engineering, health science, and teacher preparation. There are 3 undergraduate schools and 1 graduate school. In addition to regional accreditation, EUP has baccalaureate program accreditation with ACBSP, ADA, CSWE, NASM, NCATE, and NLN. The 2 libraries contain 468,887 volumes, 1,354,837 microform items, and 32,413 audio/video tapes/CDs/DVDs, and subscribe to 1669 periodicals including electronic. Computerized library services include the card catalog, interlibrary loans, and database searching. Special learning facilities include an art gallery, planetarium, radio station, TV station, and a newspaper. The 585-acre campus is in a small town 18 miles south of Erie. Including any residence halls, there are 43 buildings.

Student Life: 89% of undergraduates are from Pennsylvania. Students are from 34 states, 49 foreign countries, and Canada. 88% are white. The average age of freshmen is 19; all undergraduates, 22. 34% do not continue beyond their first year; 49% remain to graduate.

Housing: 2500 students can be accommodated in college housing, which includes single-sex and coed dorms. In addition, there are honors houses and special-interest houses. On-campus housing is guaranteed for the freshman year only and is available on a first-come, first-served basis. 73% of students commute. Alcohol is not permitted. All students may keep cars.

Activities: There are 8 national fraternities and 8 national sororities. There are 129 groups on campus, including art, bagpipe band, band, cheerleading, chess, choir, chorale, chorus, computers, dance, debate, drama, drill team, ethnic, film, forensics, gay, honors, international, literary magazine, marching band, musical theater, opera, orchestra, pep band, photography, political, professional, radio and TV, religious, social, social service, student government, symphony, and yearbook. Popular campus events include Academic Festival, Snowfest, and Greek Week.

Sports: There are 6 intercollegiate sports for men and 7 for women, and 12 intramural sports for men and 12 for women. Facilities include a field house, a stadium, a gym, a swimming pool, racquetball courts, an aerobics room, an indoor track, a fitness center, saunas, steamrooms, 2 weight rooms, and a climbing wall.

Disabled Students: 97% of the campus is accessible. Wheelchair ramps, elevators, special parking, specially equipped rest rooms, special class scheduling, lowered drinking fountains, lowered telephones, special housing, computer facilities, and transportation services are available.

Services: Counseling and information services are available, as is tutoring in most subjects. There is a reader service for the blind, and remedial math, reading, and writing. Academic aides are available as are services in the academic support library.

Campus Safety and Security: Measures include 24-hour foot and vehicle patrol, self-defense education, informal discussions, and pamphlets/posters/films. There are emergency telephones, lighted pathways/sidewalks, 14 commissioned police officers, and optional engraving of personal property.

Programs of Study: EUP confers B.A., B.S., B.F.A., B.S.A.E., B.S.Ed., B.S.H.P.E., and B.S.N. degrees. Associate and master's degrees are also awarded. Bachelor's degrees are awarded in BIOLOGICAL SCIENCE (biochemistry, biology/biological science, and nutrition), BUSINESS (accounting, banking and finance, business administration and management, marketing management, and sports management), COMMUNICATIONS AND THE ARTS (advertising, applied art, art, art history and appreciation, broadcasting, ceramic art and design, creative writing, dramatic arts, drawing, English, English literature, fiber/textiles/weaving, film arts, fine arts, German, graphic design, media arts, metal/jewelry, music, painting, photography, printmaking, sculpture, Spanish, and speech/debate/rhetoric), COMPUTER AND PHYSICAL SCIENCE (chemistry, computer science, earth science, geology, mathematics, natural sciences, and physics), EDUCATION (art, early childhood, elementary, English, foreign languages, health, mathematics, music, physical, science, secondary, social studies, and special), ENGINEERING AND ENVIRONMENTAL DESIGN (engineering physics, environmental science, and woodworking), HEALTH PROFESSIONS (medical laboratory technology, nuclear medical technology, nursing, predentistry, premedicine, preveterinary science, public health, and speech pathology/audiology), SOCIAL SCIENCE (anthropology, criminal justice, economics, forensic studies, geography, history, humanities, liberal arts/general studies, philosophy, political science/government, prelaw, psychology, social science, social work, and sociology). Applied media arts, business administration, and criminal justice are the largest.

Required: To graduate, students must complete a minimum of 120 semester hours with a minimum GPA of 2.0. General education requirements include 48 hours of courses, consisting of a 21-semester-hour core with 3 hours each in artistic expression, world civilizations, American civilizations, human behavior, cultural diversity and social pluralism, ethics, and science and technology, and a 12-hour distribution with 9 hours in English and math skills and 3 hours of health and phys ed.

Special: The university offers cooperative programs in engineering, prelaw, and osteopathic medicine, and cross-registration through the Pennsylvania State System of Higher Education and the Marine Science Consortium at Wallops Island, Virginia, and with Mercyhurst College and Gannon University. A Harrisburg semester, internships in most majors, a general studies program, student-designed majors, dual majors in education, a 3-2 engineering degree, study abroad in more than 10 countries, and nondegree study are also offered. Students may select pass/fail options and receive credit for life, military, and work experience. There are 10 national honor societies, a freshman honors program, and 9 departmental honors programs.

Faculty/Classroom: 56% of faculty are male; 44%, female. 92% teach undergraduates. No introductory courses are taught by graduate students. The average class size in an introductory lecture is 30.

Admissions: 82% of the 2005-2006 applicants were accepted. 5 freshmen graduated first in their class.

Requirements: The SAT or ACT is required. In addition, candidates for admission should be graduates of an accredited secondary school or the equivalent. The GED is accepted. A GPA of 2.0 is recommended. A portfolio is recommended for art students and an audition is required for music students. An interview is recommended for all. Admissions decisions are based upon the academic major requested, high school curriculum, grades, GPA, class rank, SAT or ACT scores, and leadership and extracurricular activities record. AP and CLEP credits are accepted. Important factors in the admissions decision are advanced placement or honor courses, extracurricular activities record, and personality/intangible qualities.

Procedure: Freshmen are admitted to all sessions. Entrance exams should be taken in the junior year or early in the senior year. There are early admissions, deferred admissions, and rolling admissions plans. Application deadlines are open. Application fee is $30. Applications are accepted on-line.

Transfer: 480 transfer students enrolled in 2004-2005. Applicants should have a 2.0 GPA and must submit transcripts from previous insti-

tutions. An interview is recommended. 32 of 120 credits required for the bachelor's degree must be completed at EUP.

Visiting: There are regularly scheduled orientations for prospective students, including admissions, financial aid, and academic affairs presentations followed by campus tours. There are guides for informal visits and visitors may sit in on classes and stay overnight. To schedule a visit, contact the Admissions Office.

Financial Aid: In 2005-2006, 80% of all full-time freshmen and 76% of continuing full-time students received some form of financial aid. 80% of full-time freshmen and 76% of continuing full-time students received need-based aid. The average freshman award was $5639. Need-based scholarships or need-based grants averaged $2832; need-based self-help aid (loans and jobs) averaged $2802; institutional non-need-based athletic scholarships averaged $1808; and other institutional non-need-based awards and non-need-based scholarships averaged $2444. 10% of undergraduates work part time. Average annual earnings from campus work are $1800. The average financial indebtedness of the 2005 graduate was $17,034. The FAFSA is required. The priority date for freshman financial aid applications for fall entry is March 15. The deadline for filing freshman financial aid applications for fall entry is May 1.

International Students: There were 215 international students enrolled in a recent year. The school actively recruits these students. A satisfactory score is required on the written TOEFL.

Computers: All students may access the system; lab hours vary. There are no time limits and no fees.

Graduates: From July 1, 2004 to June 30, 2005, 1174 bachelor's degrees were awarded. The most popular majors were visual and performing arts (15%), education (14%), health professions and related sciences (8%), and security and protective services (8%). In an average class, 18% graduate in 4 years or less, 41% graduate in 5 years or less, and 49% graduate in 6 years or less.

Admissions Contact: Admissions Office.
E-mail: *eup_admissions@edinboro.edu* Web: *www.edinboro.edu*

ELIZABETHTOWN COLLEGE — D-3

Elizabethtown, PA 17022 — (717) 361-1400; Fax: (717) 361-1365

Full-time: 644 men, 1251 women	Faculty: 125
Part-time: 110 men, 201 women	Ph.D.s: 82%
Graduate: 9 men, 29 women	Student/Faculty: 15 to 1
Year: semesters, summer session	Tuition: $25,200
Application Deadline: open	Room & Board: $6900
Freshman Class: 2688 applied, 1674 accepted, 521 enrolled	
SAT Verbal/Math: 560/550*	VERY COMPETITIVE

Elizabethtown College, founded in 1899, is a private college founded by members of the Church of the Brethren and offers 45 majors and more than 60 minors and concentrations in the arts, sciences, humanities, and professional programs and a master's program in occupational therapy. In addition to regional accreditation, E-town has baccalaureate program accreditation with ACBSP, ACOTE, CSWE, and NASM. The library contains 197,468 volumes, 20,646 microform items, and 32,389 audio/video tapes/CDs/DVDs, and subscribes to 912 periodicals including electronic. Computerized library services include the card catalog, interlibrary loans, database searching, Internet access, and laptop Internet portals. Special learning facilities include a learning resource center, art gallery, radio station, TV station, and the Young Center for Anabaptist and Pietist Studies a nationally unique academic research facility. The 215-acre campus is in a small town 10 minutes from Hershey and 25 minutes from Lancaster and Harrisburg. Including any residence halls, there are 25 buildings.

Student Life: 38% of undergraduates are from Pennsylvania. Others are from 35 states and 40 foreign countries. 81% are from public schools. 92% are white. 31% are Protestant; 23% Catholic. The average age of freshmen is 18; all undergraduates, 20. 16% do not continue beyond their first year; 72% remain to graduate.

Housing: 1490 students can be accommodated in college housing, which includes single-sex and coed dorms and on-campus apartments. In addition, there are honors houses, special-interest houses, chemical-free, health, living, and quiet areas. On-campus housing is guaranteed for all 4 years. 85% of students live on campus; of those, 70% remain on campus on weekends. All students may keep cars.

Activities: There are no fraternities or sororities. There are 70 groups on campus, including academic, art, band, cheerleading, choir, chorale, chorus, computers, dance, drama, ethnic, forensics, gay, honors, international, jazz band, learning communities, literary magazine, musical theater, newspaper, orchestra, photography, political, professional, radio and TV, religious, residential, social, social service, student government, and yearbook. Popular campus events include lecture series, Thank God It's Spring, and International Fest.

Sports: There are 11 intercollegiate sports for men and 11 for women, and 5 intramural sports for men and 5 for women. Facilities include a swimming pool, weight training rooms, a 2200-seat soccer complex, a 2400-seat gym, a track and field complex, racquetball and tennis courts, basketball and sand volleyball courts, a fitness center, and baseball, softball, lacrosse, and hockey fields.

Disabled Students: 75% of the campus is accessible. Wheelchair ramps, elevators, special parking, specially equipped rest rooms, special class scheduling, lowered drinking fountains, and lowered telephones are available.

Services: Counseling and information services are available, as is tutoring in most subjects. There is a reader service for the blind, and remedial math, reading, and writing. Workshops and individual help with study skills, as well as some technological assistance are also available.

Campus Safety and Security: Measures include 24-hour foot and vehicle patrol, self-defense education, security escort services, and informal discussions. There are pamphlets/posters/films, emergency telephones, lighted pathways/sidewalks, and a crime prevention program.

Programs of Study: E-town confers B.A., B.S., and B.M. degrees. Associate and master's degrees are also awarded. Bachelor's degrees are awarded in AGRICULTURE (forestry and related sciences), BIOLOGICAL SCIENCE (biochemistry, biology/biological science, and biotechnology), BUSINESS (accounting, business administration and management, and international business management), COMMUNICATIONS AND THE ARTS (art, communications, dramatic arts, English, French, German, music, and Spanish), COMPUTER AND PHYSICAL SCIENCE (actuarial science, chemistry, computer science, information sciences and systems, mathematics, physics, and science), EDUCATION (early childhood, elementary, music, and secondary), ENGINEERING AND ENVIRONMENTAL DESIGN (computer engineering, engineering, engineering physics, environmental science, and industrial engineering), HEALTH PROFESSIONS (allied health, clinical science, music therapy, occupational therapy, and premedicine), SOCIAL SCIENCE (criminal justice, economics, history, law, philosophy, political science/government, psychology, religion, social studies, social work, and sociology). Business administration, communications, and elementary education are the largest.

Required: The core curriculum includes a first-year seminar and a colloquium, and courses in math, language, creative expression, Western cultural heritage, non-Western cultural heritage, the natural and social sciences, and humanities. Distribution requirements include 40 hours in 8 areas of understanding. Students must complete 125 credit hours and maintain a GPA of 2.0 overall and in their major.

Special: Students can participate in semester-long study-abroad experiences in 16 countries through partnerships with Brethren Colleges Abroad; Nihon University in Japan; Queen's University, in England; and the University of Newcastle in Australia. Additionally, the college's faculty offers several short-term study-abroad opportunities to countries like Japan, the Czech Republic, Costa Rica, Ecuador, Ireland, England, and China. Also available are work-study programs, internships, a Washington semester, accelerated degrees, and dual majors, including sociology and anthropology. There is a 3-2 engineering degree with Pennsylvania State University; a 2-2 allied health degree and a 4-2 physical therapy degree with Thomas Jefferson University, Widener University, and the University of Maryland/Baltimore County; and a 3-2 forestry or environmental management degree with Duke University. There are 19 national honor societies and a freshman honors program.

Faculty/Classroom: 60% of faculty are male; 40%, female. All teach and do research. The average class size in an introductory lecture is 23; in a laboratory, 18; and in a regular course, 20.

Admissions: 62% of the 2005-2006 applicants were accepted. The SAT scores for the 2005-2006 freshman class were: Verbal--25% below 500, 46% between 500 and 599, 26% between 600 and 700, and 3% above 700; Math--21% below 500, 46% between 500 and 599, 27% between 600 and 700, and 6% above 700. 53% of the current freshmen were in the top fifth of their class; 82% were in the top two fifths. There was 1 National Merit semifinalist. 11 freshmen graduated first in their class.

Requirements: Satisfactory scores are required on the SAT or ACT. Applicants must be graduates of an accredited secondary school or have earned a GED. The college encourages completion of 18 academic credits, based on 4 years of English, 3 of math, 2 each of lab science, social studies, and consecutive foreign language, and 5 additional college preparatory units. An audition is required for music majors and an interview is required for occupational therapy majors. AP and CLEP credits are accepted. Important factors in the admissions decision are advanced placement or honor courses, recommendations by school officials, and extracurricular activities record.

Procedure: Freshmen are admitted to all sessions. Entrance exams should be taken in spring of the junior year or fall of the senior year. There are early admissions, deferred admissions, and rolling admissions plans. Application deadlines are open. Application fee is $30. Applications are accepted on-line.

Transfer: 42 transfer students enrolled in 2004-2005. Applicants should present a minimum GPA of 3.0 in at least 15 credit hours earned from a community college, or 2.5 from a 4-year institution. 30 of 125 credits required for the bachelor's degree must be completed at E-town.

Visiting: There are regularly scheduled orientations for prospective students, including 5 open houses and weekday appointments throughout

the year. Special academic department days are also hosted. There are guides for informal visits and visitors may sit in on classes and stay overnight. To schedule a visit, contact the Admissions Office.

Financial Aid: In 2005-2006, 98% of all full-time freshmen and 95% of continuing full-time students received some form of financial aid. 71% of all full-time students received need-based aid. The average freshman award was $17,517. Need-based scholarships or need-based grants averaged $12,559 ($29,250 maximum); and need-based self-help aid (loans and jobs) averaged $4018 ($5125 maximum). 56% of undergraduates work part time. Average annual earnings from campus work are $843. The average financial indebtedness of the 2005 graduate was $20,944. E-town is a member of CSS. The FAFSA, the college's own financial statement and the family federal tax returns are required. The deadline for filing freshman financial aid applications for fall entry is March 15.

International Students: There are 70 international students enrolled. The school actively recruits these students. A satisfactory score is required on the written TOEFL.

Computers: Wireless access is available. All students are provided with Internet access and e-mail service. PCs are avilable in computer centers and labs, residence halls, the library and the student center. There are open, wied network connections in the library, computer labs, and elsewhere on campus. All of the college-owned and college-operated housing units are wired for high-speed Internet access. All students may access the system any time. There are no time limits and no fees. It is strongly recommended that all students have a personal computer.

Graduates: From July 1, 2004 to June 30, 2005, 454 bachelor's degrees were awarded. The most popular majors were business (25%), education (19%), and health professional and related science (11%). In an average class, 65% graduate in 4 years or less, 66% graduate in 5 years or less, and 67% graduate in 6 years or less. 32 companies recruited on campus in 2004-2005. Of the 2004 graduating class, 28% were enrolled in graduate school within 6 months of graduation and 70% were employed.

Admissions Contact: Paul Cramer, Vice President for Enrollment. E-mail: *admissions@etown.edu* Web: *www.etown.edu*

FRANKLIN AND MARSHALL COLLEGE E-3

Lancaster, PA 17604-3003 (717) 291-3953; Fax: (717) 291-4389

Full-time: 1041 men, 941 women	**Faculty:** 175; IIB, +$
Part-time: 30 men, 13 women	**Ph.D.s:** 97%
Graduate: none	**Student/Faculty:** 11 to 1
Year: semesters, summer session	**Tuition:** $32,530
Application Deadline: February 1	**Room & Board:** $8060
Freshman Class: 4227 applied, 1921 accepted, 582 enrolled	
SAT Verbal/Math: 630/640*	**HIGHLY COMPETITIVE**

Franklin and Marshall College, founded in 1787, is a private liberal arts institution. The 2 libraries contain 473,036 volumes, 335,882 microform items, and 13,703 audio/video tapes/CDs/DVDs, and subscribe to 2025 periodicals including electronic. Computerized library services include the card catalog, interlibrary loans, database searching, and Internet access. Special learning facilities include an art gallery, natural history museum, planetarium, radio station, TV station, academic technology services, an advanced language lab, a writing center, and a student newspaper. The 125-acre campus is in a suburban area 60 miles west of Philadelphia. Including any residence halls, there are 45 buildings.

Student Life: 65% of undergraduates are from out of state, mostly the Middle Atlantic. Students are from 43 states, 47 foreign countries, and Canada. 53% are from public schools. 77% are white. 43% claim no religious affiliation; 21% Catholic; 18% Protestant; 9% Jewish; 9% Orthodox Christian, Moslem, Hindu, Buddhist, Unitarian. The average age of freshmen is 18; all undergraduates, 20. 8% do not continue beyond their first year; 82% remain to graduate.

Housing: 1320 students can be accommodated in college housing, which includes single-sex and coed dorms and off-campus apartments. In addition, there are language houses and special-interest houses, including a French house, an arts house, an international living center, and a community outreach house. On-campus housing is guaranteed for the freshman year only and is available on a lottery system for upperclassmen. 64% of students live on campus. Upperclassmen may keep cars.

Activities: 25% of men belong to 7 national fraternities; 10% of women belong to 2 national sororities. There are 110 groups on campus, including art, band, Ben's Underground (a student-run club/restaurant), cheerleading, chess, choir, chorale, chorus, computers, dance, debate, drama, ethnic, film, forensics, gay, honors, international, jazz band, literary magazine, musical theater, newspaper, opera, orchestra, photography, political, professional, radio and TV, religious, social, social service, student government, and symphony. Popular campus events include Spring Arts Weekend, Freshman Feast, and Senior Surprise.

Sports: There are 13 intercollegiate sports for men and 13 for women, and 12 intramural sports for men and 12 for women. Facilities include a 3000-seat gym, 4 squash courts, a wrestling room, 54 acres of playing fields, a 400-meter all-weather track, a wellness/aerobic center, a strength training center, and tennis courts. A sport center features a fitness center, 5 multipurpose courts, 2 jogging tracks, and an Olympic-size pool.

Disabled Students: 71% of the campus is accessible. Wheelchair ramps, elevators, special parking, specially equipped rest rooms, special class scheduling, lowered drinking fountains, lowered telephones, and special housing are available.

Services: Counseling and information services are available, as is tutoring in every subject.

Campus Safety and Security: Measures include 24-hour foot and vehicle patrol, self-defense education, security escort services, and informal discussions. There are pamphlets/posters/films, emergency telephones, and lighted pathways/sidewalks. Regular fire safety drills are held in residence halls and academic buildings, and residence hall access requires a fob.

Programs of Study: F & M confers the B.A. degree. Bachelor's degrees are awarded in AGRICULTURE (environmental studies), BIOLOGICAL SCIENCE (biochemistry, biology/biological science, and neurosciences), BUSINESS (business administration and management), COMMUNICATIONS AND THE ARTS (art history and appreciation, classics, dramatic arts, English, fine arts, French, German, Greek, Latin, music, Spanish, and studio art), COMPUTER AND PHYSICAL SCIENCE (astronomy, astrophysics, chemistry, geology, mathematics, and physics), ENGINEERING AND ENVIRONMENTAL DESIGN (environmental science), SOCIAL SCIENCE (African studies, American studies, anthropology, economics, history, interdisciplinary studies, philosophy, political science/government, psychology, religion, and sociology). Chemistry, geosciences, and psychology are the strongest academically. Government, business administration, and biology are the largest.

Required: General eduation requirements proceed from 3 foundations courses and a distribution requirement to an upper-level coherent exploration and a major. Students must take at least 1 course in arts, humanities, social science, and natural sciences (including a lab). There are also language studies and non-Western culture studies requirements. Students must also satisfy the writing proficiency requirement. The bachelor's degree requires completion of 32 courses, including a minimum of 8 in the major, with a minimum GPA of 2.0.

Special: There is a 3-2 degree program in forestry and environmental studies with Duke University as well as 3-2 degree programs in engineering with the Pennsylvania State University College of Engineering, Columbia University, Rensselaer Polytechnic Institute, Case Western Reserve, and Washington University in St. Louis. Cross-registration is possible with the Lancaster Theological Seminary, the Central Pennsylvania Consortium, and Millersville University, allowing students to study at nearby Dickinson or Gettysburg Colleges. Students may also study architecture and urban planning at Columbia University, studio art at the School of Visual Arts in New York City, theater in Connecticut, oceanography in Massachusetts, and American studies at American University. There are study-abroad programs in England, France, Germany, Greece, Italy, Denmark, India, Japan, and other countries. There are internships for credit, joint majors, many minors, dual and student-designed majors, independent study, interdisciplinary studies, optional first-year seminars, collaborative projects, pass/fail options, and nondegree study. There are 12 national honor societies, including Phi Beta Kappa.

Faculty/Classroom: 61% of faculty are male; 39%, female. All both teach undergraduates and do research. The average class size in an introductory lecture is 23; in a laboratory, 19; and in a regular course, 19.

Admissions: 45% of the 2005-2006 applicants were accepted. The SAT scores for the 2005-2006 freshman class were: Verbal--3% below 500, 26% between 500 and 599, 50% between 600 and 700, and 20% above 700; Math--3% below 500, 20% between 500 and 599, 59% between 600 and 700, and 18% above 700. 76% of the current freshmen were in the top fifth of their class; 93% were in the top two fifths. There were 3 National Merit finalists.

Requirements: The SAT is required. Standardized tests are optional for students in the top 10% of their class; if this option is selected, 2 graded writing samples are required. Applicants must be graduates of accredited secondary schools. Recommended college preparatory study includes 4 years each of English and math, 3 or 4 of foreign language, 3 each of lab science and history/social studies, and 1 or 2 courses in art or music. All students must also submit high school transcripts, recommendations from a teacher and a counselor, and a personal essay. An interview is recommended. AP and CLEP credits are accepted. Important factors in the admissions decision are advanced placement or honor courses, recommendations by school officials, and extracurricular activities record.

Procedure: Freshmen are admitted fall and spring. Entrance exams should be taken by December of the senior year. There are early decision, early admissions, and deferred admissions plans. Early decision applications should be filed by November 15; regular applications, by February 1 for fall entry, along with a $50 fee. Notification of early decision is sent December 15; regular decision, April 1. 277 early decision candidates were accepted for the 2005-2006 class. 1028 applicants were on the 2005 waiting list; 25 were admitted. Applications are accepted online.

Transfer: 15 transfer students enrolled in 2004-2005. Applicants must present a minimum of 4 course credits (16 semester hours) completed at an accredited college. An interview, SAT or ACT scores, college and secondary school transcripts, a dean's form, recommendations from 2 professors, and a letter explaining the reason for transfer are also required. 16 of 32 credits required for the bachelor's degree must be completed at F & M.

Visiting: There are regularly scheduled orientations for prospective students, including a campus tour, an interview, and a class visit. There are guides for informal visits and visitors may sit in on classes. To schedule a visit, contact the Admission Office at admission@fandm.edu.

Financial Aid: In 2005-2006, 68% of all full-time freshmen and 71% of continuing full-time students received some form of financial aid. 63% of full-time freshmen and 48% of continuing full-time students received need-based aid. The average freshman award was $20,472. Need-based scholarships or need-based grants averaged $20,967; need-based self-help aid (loans and jobs) averaged $4598; and other non-need-based awards and non-need-based scholarships averaged $8209. 44% of undergraduates work part time. Average annual earnings from campus work are $1390. The average financial indebtedness of the 2005 graduate was $19,391. F & M is a member of CSS. The CSS/Profile, FAFSA, the college's own financial statement, and, if applicable, the business/farm supplement and noncustodial parents statement are required. The deadline for filing freshman financial aid applications for fall entry is February 1.

International Students: There are 142 international students enrolled. The school actively recruits these students. They must take the TOEFL and also take the SAT or the ACT.

Computers: Wireless access is available. All students may access the system 24 hours a day, 7 days a week. There are no time limits and no fees. It is strongly recommended that all students have a personal computer. A MAC iBook or PowerBook is recommended.

Graduates: From July 1, 2004 to June 30, 2005, 449 bachelor's degrees were awarded. The most popular majors were government (21%), business management (9%), and biology (6%). In an average class, 75% graduate in 4 years or less, 81% graduate in 5 years or less, and 82% graduate in 6 years or less. 26 companies recruited on campus in 2004-2005. Of the 2004 graduating class, 25% were enrolled in graduate school within 6 months of graduation and 75% were employed.

Admissions Contact: Dennis Trotter, Vice President for Enrollment Management and Dean of Admissions. A video is available.
E-mail: admission@fandm.edu Web: admission@fandm.edu

GANNON UNIVERSITY   B-1
Erie, PA 16541

(814) 871-5696
(800) GANNON U; Fax: (814) 871-5803

Full-time: 888 men, 1296 women	**Faculty:** 172; IIA, --$
Part-time: 147 men, 243 women	**Ph.D.s:** 68%
Graduate: 346 men, 670 women	**Student/Faculty:** 13 to 1
Year: semesters, summer session	**Tuition:** $18,690
Application Deadline: open	**Room & Board:** $7410
Freshman Class: 2443 applied, 2111 accepted, 622 enrolled	
SAT Verbal/Math: 520/530*	**ACT:** 21 COMPETITIVE

Gannon University, founded in 1925, is a private liberal arts and teaching-oriented university affiliated with the Roman Catholic Church. There are 2 undergraduate schools and 1 graduate school. In addition to regional accreditation, Gannon has baccalaureate program accreditation with ABET, ACOTE, ADA, ARC-PA, CAAHEP, CAHEA, CoARCH, CSWE, JRCET, MSCHE, and NLN. The library contains 270,349 volumes, 190,433 microform items, and 3666 audio/video tapes/CDs/DVDs, and subscribes to 14,000 periodicals including electronic. Computerized library services include the card catalog, interlibrary loans, database searching, Internet access, and laptop Internet portals. Special learning facilities include a learning resource center, art gallery, and radio station. The 13-acre campus is in an urban area 128 miles north of Pittsburgh, and 99 miles east of Cleveland. Including any residence halls, there are 27 buildings.

Student Life: 79% of undergraduates are from Pennsylvania. Others are from 27 states, 12 foreign countries, and Canada. 80% are from public schools. 89% are white. 56% are Catholic; 24% Protestant; 10% Buddhist, Hindu, Muslim, and Orthodox. The average age of freshmen is 18; all undergraduates, 21. 17% do not continue beyond their first year; 64% remain to graduate.

Housing: 1065 students can be accommodated in college housing, which includes coed dorm, on-campus apartments, and off-campus apartments. On-campus housing is guaranteed for the freshman year only and is available on a lottery system for upperclassmen. Priority is given to out-of-town students. 51% of students live on campus; of those, 85% remain on campus on weekends. Alcohol is not permitted. Upperclassmen may keep cars.

Activities: 9% of men belong to 6 national fraternities; 13% of women belong to 6 national sororities. There are 69 groups on campus, including art, activies programming board, cheerleading, chess, chorus, computers, debate, drama, ethnic, honors, international, literary magazine, musical theater, newspaper, orchestra, pep band, political, professional, radio, religious, residence union, social, social service, and student government. Popular campus events include Family Weekend, Distinguished Speaker Series, and Springtopia.

Sports: There are 9 intercollegiate sports for men and 9 for women, and 20 intramural sports for men and 20 for women. Facilities include a pool, 3 indoor gyms, a track, 6 racquetball courts, an outdoor recreation field, outdoor sand volleyball and tennis courts, a 3000-seat basketball and volleyball venue, exercise equipment, and a dance room.

Disabled Students: 80% of the campus is accessible. Wheelchair ramps, elevators, special parking, specially equipped rest rooms, special class scheduling, lowered drinking fountains, lowered telephones, and special drop-off points are available.

Services: Counseling and information services are available, as is tutoring in most subjects. There is a reader service for the blind and remedial math and writing. There are math, writing, and advising centers.

Campus Safety and Security: Measures include 24-hour foot and vehicle patrol, security escort services, informal discussions, and pamphlets/posters/films. There are emergency telephones, lighted pathways/sidewalks, and security cameras in buildings.

Programs of Study: Gannon confers B.A., B.S., B.S.E.E., B.S.M.E., and B.S.N. degrees. Associate, master's, and doctoral degrees are also awarded. Bachelor's degrees are awarded in BIOLOGICAL SCIENCE (bioinformatics, biology/biological science, and biotechnology), BUSINESS (accounting, banking and finance, business administration and management, funeral home services, insurance and risk management, international business management, management information systems, and marketing/retailing/merchandising), COMMUNICATIONS AND THE ARTS (advertising, communications, dramatic arts, English, and languages), COMPUTER AND PHYSICAL SCIENCE (chemistry, computer science, mathematics, and science), EDUCATION (early childhood, elementary, foreign languages, secondary, and special), ENGINEERING AND ENVIRONMENTAL DESIGN (electrical/electronics engineering, environmental engineering, environmental science, and mechanical engineering), HEALTH PROFESSIONS (medical technology, nursing, occupational therapy, optometry, physical therapy, physician's assistant, predentistry, premedicine, preoptometry, preosteopathy, prepharmacy, prepodiatry, preveterinary science, respiratory therapy, and sports medicine), SOCIAL SCIENCE (criminal justice, dietetics, history, international studies, liberal arts/general studies, paralegal studies, philosophy, political science/government, prelaw, psychology, social science, social work, and theological studies). Engineering, preprofessional, and nursing are the strongest academically. Nursing, physician's assistant, and criminal justice are the largest.

Required: Students must complete at least 128 hours of academic work. Each academic program has specific course requirements. Students must have a cumulative GPA of at least 2.0 overall and in the area of concentration. 3 writing-intensive courses must be completed after the freshman year; 1 must be taken in the senior year. There is a liberal studies core curriculum.

Special: The university offers study abroad in more than 5 countries, co-op programs, dual majors, B.A.-B.S. degrees, summer internships, a Washington semester, pass/fail options, work-study programs, a general studies program, accelerated degree programs in law, optometry, podiatry, and pharmacy, a 3-2 chemical engineering degree with the Universities of Akron, Pittsburgh, and Detroit Mercy, a 4-4 medical program and 3-4 accelerated osteopathic preprofessional program, with Lake Erie College of Osteopathic Medicine, a 3-3 pre-law early admission, and 2-4 prepharmacy program with Duquesne University, and nondegree study. The B.S. in mortuary science program consists of 2 or 3 years of study at Gannon with degree completion at a school of mortuary science. There are 12 national honor societies, a freshman honors program, and 11 departmental honors programs.

Faculty/Classroom: 57% of faculty are male; 43%, female. 97% teach undergraduates and 3% do research. Graduate students teach 3% of introductory courses. The average class size in an introductory lecture is 23; in a laboratory, 17; and in a regular course, 17.

Admissions: 86% of the 2005-2006 applicants were accepted. The SAT scores for the 2005-2006 freshman class were: Verbal--38% below 500, 49% between 500 and 599, 12% between 600 and 700, and 2% above 700; Math--34% below 500, 45% between 500 and 599, 19% between 600 and 700, and 2% above 700. The ACT scores were 41% below 21, 30% between 21 and 23, 18% between 24 and 26, 7% between 27 and 28, and 4% above 28. 40% of the current freshmen were in the top fifth of their class; 67% were in the top two fifths. 28 freshmen graduated first in their class.

Requirements: The SAT or ACT is required. In addition, candidates should have completed 16 academic units including 4 in English and 12 in social sciences, foreign languages, math, and science, depending on the degree sought. Specific courses in math and science are required for some majors in health sciences and engineering. Gannon requires applicants to be in the upper 60% of their class. A GPA of 2.0 is required. AP and CLEP credits are accepted. Important factors in the admissions deci-

sion are advanced placement or honor courses, leadership record, and recommendations by school officials.

Procedure: Freshmen are admitted to all sessions. Entrance exams should be taken at the end of the junior year or the beginning of the senior year. There are early admissions and deferred admissions plans. There is a rolling admissions plan. Application deadlines are open. Application fee is $25. Notification is sent on a rolling basis. A waiting list is an active part of the admissions procedure. Applications are accepted on-line.

Transfer: 59 transfer students enrolled in 2004-2005. Transfer students should be in good standing at their previous institution with at least a 2.0 GPA. They must submit a college clearance from the college most recently attended and all transcripts. A high school transcript is required from transfer students with fewer than 60 credits. Several health science programs are not designed to accommodate transfers. At least 30 of 128 credits required for the bachelor's degree must be completed at Gannon.

Visiting: There are regularly scheduled orientations for prospective students, consisting of open houses for prospective students in the fall and spring. Students may meet with faculty, tour the campus, and sit in on a variety of presentations. There are guides for informal visits and visitors may sit in on classes and stay overnight. To schedule a visit, contact Linda Kish, Campus Visit Coordinator.

Financial Aid: In 2005-2006, 97% of all full-time freshmen and 95% of continuing full-time students received some form of financial aid. 86% of full-time freshmen and 85% of continuing full-time students received need-based aid. The average freshman award was $11,441. Need-based scholarships or need-based grants averaged $10,314; need-based self-help aid (loans and jobs) averaged $2606; non-need-based athletic scholarships averaged $11,000; and other non-need-based awards and non-need-based scholarships averaged $6527. 24% of undergraduates work part time. Average annual earnings from campus work are $1700. Gannon is a member of CSS. The FAFSA and the college's own financial statement are required. The priority date for freshman financial aid applications for fall entry is March 15.

International Students: There are 26 international students enrolled. The school actively recruits these students. They must take the TOEFL.

Computers: Wireless access is available. All students may access the system 24 hours a day. There are no time limits and no fees.

Graduates: From July 1, 2004 to June 30, 2005, 423 bachelor's degrees were awarded. The most popular majors were criminal justice (9%), biology (6%), and nursing (6%). In an average class, 49% graduate in 4 years or less, 63% graduate in 5 years or less, and 64% graduate in 6 years or less. 6 companies recruited on campus in 2004-2005. Of the 2004 graduating class, 35% were enrolled in graduate school within 6 months of graduation and 62% were employed.

Admissions Contact: Bill Eilola, Dean of Enrollment.
E-mail: *admissions@gannon.edu* Web: *www.gannon.edu*

GENEVA COLLEGE   A-3
Beaver Falls, PA 15010   (724) 847-6500
                                   (800) 847-8255; Fax: (724) 847-6776

Full-time: 600 men, 725 women	**Faculty:** 75; IIB, -$
Part-time: 30 men, 30 women	**Ph.D.s:** 76%
Graduate: 130 men, 190 women	**Student/Faculty:** 18 to 1
Year: semesters, summer session	**Tuition:** $15,525
Application Deadline: open	**Room & Board:** $6380
Freshman Class: n/av	
SAT or ACT: required	**COMPETITIVE**

Geneva College, founded in 1848, is a private institution affiliated with the Reformed Presbyterian Church of North America. The college offers undergraduate programs in the arts and sciences, business, education, health science, biblical and religious studies, engineering, and preprofessional training. In addition to the above figures, there are 440 nontraditional undergraduates. Figures in the above capsule and in this profile are approximate. In addition to regional accreditation, Geneva has baccalaureate program accreditation with ABET and ACBSP. The library contains 167,206 volumes, 198,624 microform items, and 12,901 audio/video tapes/CDs/DVDs, and subscribes to 879 periodicals including electronic. Computerized library services include the card catalog, interlibrary loans, database searching, and Internet access. Special learning facilities include a radio station, TV station, and an observatory. The 50-acre campus is in a small town 35 miles northwest of Pittsburgh. Including any residence halls, there are 30 buildings.

Student Life: 73% of undergraduates are from Pennsylvania. Students are from 37 states, 19 foreign countries, and Canada. 87% are from public schools. 91% are white. 89% are Protestant; 7% Catholic. The average age of freshmen is 19; all undergraduates, 26. 23% do not continue beyond their first year; 55% remain to graduate.

Housing: 994 students can be accommodated in college housing, which includes single-sex dorms, on-campus apartments, and off-campus apartments. In addition, there is a Discipleship House for those interested in structural growth opporrtunities. On-campus housing is guaranteed for all 4 years. 73% of students live on campus; of those,

70% remain on campus on weekends. Alcohol is not permitted. Upperclassmen may keep cars.

Activities: There are no fraternities or sororities. There are 50 groups on campus, including band, cheerleading, chess, choir, chorale, chorus, computers, drama, ethnic, forensics, honors, international, literary magazine, marching band, newspaper, photography, political, professional, radio, religious, social, social service, student government, and yearbook. Popular campus events include International Day, Fall Fest, and The Big Event.

Sports: There are 6 intercollegiate sports for men and 5 for women, and 6 intramural sports for men and 5 for women. Facilities include a 5600-seat stadium, a field house, a 3200-seat gym, a practice gym, a track, athletic fields, racquetball and tennis courts, weight training rooms, and the Merriman Athletic Soccer/ Track Complex.

Disabled Students: 90% of the campus is accessible. Wheelchair ramps, elevators, special parking, specially equipped rest rooms, special class scheduling, lowered drinking fountains, and lowered telephones are available.

Services: Counseling and information services are available, as is tutoring in most subjects. There is remedial math, reading, and writing.

Campus Safety and Security: Measures include security escort services, informal discussions, pamphlets/posters/films, and emergency telephones. There are lighted pathways/sidewalks, off-duty city policemen on campus from 4:30 P.M. to 7 A.M. daily, and a full-time Director of Campus Security.

Programs of Study: Geneva confers B.A., B.S., B.S.B.A., B.S.E., and B.S.Ed. degrees. Associate and master's degrees are also awarded. Bachelor's degrees are awarded in BIOLOGICAL SCIENCE (biology/ biological science), BUSINESS (accounting and business administration and management), COMMUNICATIONS AND THE ARTS (applied music, broadcasting, communications, creative writing, English, music, music business management, Spanish, and speech/debate/rhetoric), COMPUTER AND PHYSICAL SCIENCE (applied mathematics, chemistry, computer science, and physics), EDUCATION (elementary, mathematics, and music), ENGINEERING AND ENVIRONMENTAL DESIGN (aviation administration/management, chemical engineering, and engineering), HEALTH PROFESSIONS (speech pathology/audiology), SOCIAL SCIENCE (biblical studies, counseling/psychology, history, human services, interdisciplinary studies, ministries, philosophy, political science/ government, psychology, and sociology). Engineering, business administration, and education are the strongest academically. Elementary education, business administration, and psychology are the largest.

Required: The core curriculum includes 12 hours of humanities, 9 each of biblical studies and social science, 8 to 10 of natural science, 6 of communications, 2 of phys ed, and the 1-hour Freshman Experience course. Students must also fulfill a chapel requirement per semester. To graduate, students must complete 126 to 138 semester hours, including those required for a major, with a minimum GPA of 2.0 in the major.

Special: Cross-registration is offered in conjunction with Pennsylvania State University/Beaver Campus and Community College of Beaver County. There is a 3-1 degree program in cardiovascular technology, and an accelerated degree program in human resources and community ministry. Off-campus study includes programs at the Philadelphia Center for Urban Theological Studies, a Washington semester, a summer program at AuSable, Institute of Environmental Studies in Michigan, art studies in Pittsburgh, CCCU music program in Martha's Vineyard, film studies in Los Angeles, and study abroad in Costa Rica, Egypt, China, England, Russia, and Israel. Geneva also offers internships, independent study, and credit by proficiency exam. Nondegree study is available through adult education programs. There are 2 national honor societies, a freshman honors program, and 1 departmental honors program.

Faculty/Classroom: 76% of faculty are male; 24%, female. 95% teach undergraduates. No introductory courses are taught by graduate students. The average class size in an introductory lecture is 135; in a laboratory, 22; and in a regular course, 20.

Requirements: The SAT or ACT is required. In addition, applicants must be graduates of an accredited secondary school or have earned a GED. Geneva requires 16 academic units, based on 4 each of English and electives, 3 of social studies, 2 each of math and foreign language, and 1 of science. An essay is required and an interview is recommended. Geneva requires applicants to be in the upper 50% of their class. A GPA of 2.5 is required. AP and CLEP credits are accepted. Important factors in the admissions decision are recommendations by school officials, advanced placement or honor courses, and leadership record.

Procedure: Freshmen are admitted to all sessions. Entrance exams should be taken during the junior or senior year. There are deferred admissions and rolling admissions plans. Application deadlines are open. Application fee is $25. Applications are accepted on-line.

Transfer: 96 transfer students enrolled in a recent year. Applicants must have a GPA of 2.0 from College, must complete 48 semester hours at Geneva, including 15 in a chosen major, have a high school diploma or GED, and take the SAT/ ACT if less than 3 years out of high school. Letters of recommendation are required. 48 of 126 credits required for the bachelor's degree must be completed at Geneva.

Visiting: There are regularly scheduled orientations for prospective students, including class visits, a campus tour, meetings with faculty, admissions, and financial aid counselors, and meetings with coaches. There are guides for informal visits and visitors may sit in on classes and stay overnight. To schedule a visit, contact Victoria Chapoloko, Campus Visit Coordinator.

Financial Aid: In a recent year, 90% of all full-time students received some form of financial aid. 70% of all full-time students received need-based aid. The average freshman award was $13,785. Need-based scholarships or need-based grants averaged $10,241 ($22,000 maximum); need-based self-help aid (loans and jobs) averaged $4212 ($5625 maximum); and non-need-based athletic scholarships averaged $2542 ($14,980 maximum). 75% of undergraduates worked part time. Average annual earnings from campus work were $1000. The average financial indebtedness of a recent graduate was $20,000. Geneva is a member of CSS. The FAFSA is required. Check with the school for current application deadlines.

International Students: In a recent year, there were 18 international students enrolled. The school actively recruits these students. They must score satisfactorily on the written TOEFL and also take the college's own test.

Computers: All students may access the system. There are no time limits. The fee is $100 per semester.

Graduates: In a recent year, 454 bachelor's degrees were awarded. The most popular majors were business and marketing (40%), philosophy/religion/theology (14%), and education (12%). In an average class, 1% graduate in 3 years or less, 42% graduate in 4 years or less, 55% graduate in 5 years or less, and 56% graduate in 6 years or less.

Admissions Contact: Director of Admissions. A video is available. E-mail: *admissions@geneva.edu* Web: *www.geneva.edu*

GETTYSBURG COLLEGE   D-4

Gettysburg, PA 17325-1484

(717) 337-6100
(800) 431-0803; Fax: (717) 337-6145

Full-time: 1223 men, 1384 women	**Faculty:** IIB, +$
Part-time: 4 men, 5 women	**Ph.D.s:** 95%
Graduate: none	**Student/Faculty:** n/av
Year: semesters	**Tuition:** $32,070
Application Deadline: February 15	**Room & Board:** $7794
Freshman Class: 5097 applied, 2183 accepted, 697 enrolled	
SAT Verbal/Math: 640/640*	**HIGHLY COMPETITIVE**

Gettysburg College, founded in 1832, is a nationally ranked college offering programs in the liberal arts and sciences. The library contains 484,357 volumes, 75,067 microform items, and 21,128 audio/video tapes/CDs/DVDs, and subscribes to 23,208 periodicals including electronic. Computerized library services include the card catalog, interlibrary loans, database searching, Internet access, and laptop Internet portals. Special learning facilities include an art gallery, planetarium, radio station, TV station, electron microscopes, spectrometers, optics lab, plasma physics lab, greenhouse, observatory, child study lab, fine and performing arts facilities, and challenge course. The 200-acre campus is in a suburban area 30 miles south of Harrisburg, 55 miles from Baltimore, and 80 miles from Washington, D.C. Including any residence halls, there are 63 buildings.

Student Life: 75% of undergraduates are from out of state, mostly the Middle Atlantic. Sudents are from 40 states, 35 foreign countries, and Canada. 70% are from public schools. 89% are white. 34% are Protestant; 30% Catholic; 6% claim no religious affiliation. The average age of freshmen is 18; all undergraduates, 20. 10% do not continue beyond their first year; 80% remain to graduate.

Housing: 2220 students can be accommodated in college housing, which includes single-sex and coed dorms, on-campus apartments, off-campus apartments, and fraternity houses. In addition, there are honors houses, language houses, and special-interest houses. On-campus housing is guaranteed for all 4 years. 93% of students live on campus; of those, 95% remain on campus on weekends. All students may keep cars.

Activities: 40% of men belong to 10 national fraternities; 26% of women belong to 6 national sororities. There are 120 groups on campus, including art, band, cheerleading, choir, chorale, chorus, computers, dance, drama, ethnic, film, gay, honors, international, jazz band, literary magazine, marching band, musical theater, newspaper, opera, orchestra, outdoor, pep band, photography, political, professional, radio and TV, religious, social, social service, student activities, student government, symphony, and yearbook. Popular campus events include Holiday Concert, all-campus picnics, and Family Weekend.

Sports: There are 12 intercollegiate sports for men and 12 for women. Facilities include basketball courts, indoor and outdoor tennis courts, a pool, several tracks and fields, 2 outdoor turf fields, a field house, fitness and weight rooms, and an athletic complex.

Disabled Students: 90% of the campus is accessible. Wheelchair ramps, elevators, special parking, specially equipped rest rooms, special class scheduling, lowered drinking fountains, and special housing are available.

Services: Counseling and information services are available, as is tutoring in most subjects.

Campus Safety and Security: Measures include 24-hour foot and vehicle patrol, self-defense education, security escort services, and informal discussions. There are pamphlets/posters/films, emergency telephones, and lighted pathways/sidewalks.

Programs of Study: Gettysburg confers B.A., B.S., B.M. (Performance), and B.S. (Music Education) degrees. Bachelor's degrees are awarded in BIOLOGICAL SCIENCE (biochemistry and biology/biological science), BUSINESS (business administration and management), COMMUNICATIONS AND THE ARTS (art history and appreciation, classics, dramatic arts, English, French, German, Greek, Latin, music, Spanish, and studio art), COMPUTER AND PHYSICAL SCIENCE (chemistry, computer science, mathematics, and physics), EDUCATION (elementary, foreign languages, music, science, and secondary), ENGINEERING AND ENVIRONMENTAL DESIGN (environmental science), HEALTH PROFESSIONS (health science, predentistry, and premedicine), SOCIAL SCIENCE (anthropology, economics, history, international relations, Japanese studies, philosophy, political science/government, prelaw, psychology, religion, sociology, and women's studies). The sciences, psychology, and history are the strongest academically. Management, political science, and psychology are the largest.

Required: All students must complete 32 courses including a concentration in a major field of study culminating with a capstone experience; 1 course each in humanities, social studies, reasoning, composition, non-Western culture; diversity, science, technology, and society; 2 courses in natural sciences; and 4 courses in a foreign language. The minimum GPA is 2.0.

Special: The college offers cross-registration with the Central Pennsylvania Consortium, an extensive study-abroad program and has special centers worldwide. There are summer internships and a Washington semester with American University. There is a United Nations semester at Drew University, and a 3-2 engineering program with Columbia University, Rensselaer Polytechnic, and Washington University in St. Louis. There are also joint programs in optometry with the Pennsylvania College of Optometry, and forestry and environmental studies with Duke University. The college also offers double majors, student-designed majors, and B.A.-B.S. degrees in biology, chemistry, physics, biochemistry, molecular biology, environmental studies, and health and exercise sciences. Education certification is also available. There are 16 national honor societies, including Phi Beta Kappa.

Faculty/Classroom: 55% of faculty are male; 45%, female. All both teach and do research. The average class size in an introductory lecture is 19; in a laboratory, 15; and in a regular course, 18.

Admissions: 43% of the 2005-2006 applicants were accepted. The SAT scores for the 2005-2006 freshman class were: Verbal--22% between 500 and 599, 63% between 600 and 700, and 15% above 700; Math--19% between 500 and 599, 70% between 600 and 700, and 11% above 700. 81% of the current freshmen were in the top fifth of their class; 99% were in the top two fifths.

Requirements: The SAT or ACT is required. In addition, an essay is required. Art students can submit a portfolio, and music students must audition. An interview and SAT; Subject tests are recommended. A GPA of 3.0 is required. AP credits are accepted. Important factors in the admissions decision are evidence of special talent, recommendations by school officials, and advanced placement or honor courses.

Procedure: Freshmen are admitted fall and spring. Entrance exams should be taken by the January testing date of the senior year. There are early decision, early admissions, and deferred admissions plans. Early decision applications should be filed by November 15 or January 15; regular applications, by February 15 for fall entry and December 1 for spring entry, along with a $45 fee. Notification is sent April 1. 249 early decision candidates were accepted for the 2005-2006 class. A waiting list is an active part of the admissions procedure. Applications are accepted on-line.

Transfer: 25 transfer students enrolled in a recent year. Transfer applicants must have a GPA of at least 2.5. An interview is recommended. The high school record, test scores, and a dean's transfer recommendation form are also considered. 16 of 32 courses required for the bachelor's degree must be completed at Gettysburg.

Visiting: There are regularly scheduled orientations for prospective students, including interviews, tours, open houses, and group sesions. There are guides for informal visits and visitors may sit in on classes and stay overnight. To schedule a visit, contact the Admissions Office at 800-431-0803 or admiss@gettysburg.edu.

Financial Aid: In 2005-2006, 75% of all full-time freshmen and 70% of continuing full-time students received some form of financial aid. 55% of full-time freshmen and 60% of continuing full-time students received need-based aid. The average freshman award was $24,487. 46% of undergraduates work part time. Average annual earnings from campus work are $1500. The average financial indebtedness of the 2005 graduate was $21,810. Gettysburg is a member of CSS. The CSS/Profile or FAFSA is required. The deadline for filing freshman financial aid applications for fall entry is February 15.

International Students: There are 62 international students enrolled. The school actively recruits these students. They must score satisfactorily on the written TOEFL or on the electronic version and also take the SAT or the ACT.

Computers: Wireless access is available. All students may access the system 24 hours a day. There are no time limits and no fees. It is strongly recommended that all students have a personal computer.

Graduates: From July 1, 2004 to June 30, 2005, 681 bachelor's degrees were awarded. The most popular majors were management (22%), political science (9%), and history (8%). In an average class, 75% graduate in 4 years or less, 76% graduate in 5 years or less, and 77% graduate in 6 years or less. 160 companies recruited on campus in 2004-2005. Of the 2004 graduating class, 18% were enrolled in graduate school within 6 months of graduation and 78% were employed.

Admissions Contact: Gail Sweezey, Director of Admissions.
E-mail: admiss@gettysburg.edu Web: www.gettysburg.edu

GROVE CITY COLLEGE   B-2

Grove City, PA 16127-2104   (724) 458-2100; Fax: (724) 458-3395

Full-time: 1162 men, 1137 women	**Faculty:** 125
Part-time: 5 men, 6 women	**Ph.D.s:** 88%
Graduate: none	**Student/Faculty:** 18 to 1
Year: semesters	**Tuition:** $10,440
Application Deadline: February 1	**Room & Board:** $5344
Freshman Class: 2077 applied, 925 accepted, 582 enrolled	
SAT Verbal/Math: 640/640*	**ACT:** 28

HIGHLY COMPETITIVE+

Grove City College, founded in 1876, is a private, liberal arts and science Christian college affiliated with the Presbyterian Church (U.S.A.). There are 2 undergraduate schools. In addition to regional accreditation, Grove City has baccalaureate program accreditation with ABET. The library contains 140,000 volumes, 10,000 microform items, and 70 audio/video tapes/CDs/DVDs, and subscribes to 1200 periodicals including electronic. Computerized library services include the card catalog, interlibrary loans, database searching, and Internet access. Special learning facilities include an art gallery and radio station. The 150-acre campus is in a small town 60 miles north of Pittsburgh. Including any residence halls, there are 27 buildings.

Student Life: 50% of undergraduates are from out of state, mostly the Middle Atlantic. Others are from 43 states, 8 foreign countries, and Canada. 85% are from public schools. 95% are white. 54% are Protestant; 20% claim no religious affiliation; 7% Catholic. The average age of freshmen is 18; all undergraduates, 20. 9% do not continue beyond their first year; 77% remain to graduate.

Housing: 2048 students can be accommodated in college housing, which includes single-sex dorms and on-campus apartments. On-campus housing is guaranteed for all 4 years. 93% of students live on campus; of those, 90% remain on campus on weekends. Alcohol is not permitted. Upperclassmen may keep cars.

Activities: 15% of men belong to 7 local fraternities; 17% of women belong to 8 local sororities. There are 120 groups on campus, including art, band, cheerleading, choir, chorale, chorus, computers, dance, debate, drama, drill team, ethnic, film, forensics, honors, international, jazz band, literary magazine, marching band, musical theater, newspaper, opera, orchestra, pep band, photography, political, professional, radio and TV, religious, social, social service, student government, symphony, and yearbook. Popular campus events include Parents Weekend, Christmas Candlelight Service, and President's Gala.

Sports: There are 9 intercollegiate sports for men and 10 for women, and 10 intramural sports for men and 11 for women. Facilities include a field house, a recreation building that includes 2 indoor pools, an indoor running track, 4 basketball, volleyball, or tennis courts, 3 racquetball courts, bowling lanes, and a weight room, 10 outdoor tennis courts, a football stadium with an all-weather track, baseball, soccer, and softball fields, and a basketball arena.

Disabled Students: All of the campus is accessible. Wheelchair ramps, elevators, special parking, specially equipped rest rooms, special class scheduling, lowered drinking fountains, and lowered telephones. The college's hillside location presents some difficulty for the seriously disabled.

Services: Counseling and information services are available, as is tutoring in most subjects. A student tutoring program is available for a small fee.

Campus Safety and Security: Measures include 24-hour foot and vehicle patrol, self-defense education, security escort services, and pamphlets/posters/films. There are emergency telephones and lighted pathways/sidewalks.

Programs of Study: Grove City confers B.A., B.S., B.Mus., B.S.E.E., and B.S.M.E. degrees. Bachelor's degrees are awarded in BIOLOGICAL SCIENCE (biochemistry and biology/biological science), BUSINESS (accounting, banking and finance, business administration and management, international business management, management information systems, and marketing/retailing/merchandising), COMMUNICATIONS AND THE ARTS (communications, English, French, music, music business management, music performance, and Spanish), COMPUTER AND PHYSICAL SCIENCE (chemistry, computer science, mathematics, and physics), EDUCATION (elementary, music, science, and secondary), ENGINEERING AND ENVIRONMENTAL DESIGN (electrical/electronics engineering, industrial administration/management, and mechanical engineering), HEALTH PROFESSIONS (predentistry and premedicine), SOCIAL SCIENCE (economics, history, philosophy, political science/government, prelaw, psychology, religion, and religious music). Engineering, education, and premedicine are the strongest academically. Business, education, and engineering are the largest.

Required: Students are required to complete a minimum of 128 credit hours (136 for engineering students). All students must complete the 38-semester-hour general education curriculum, which includes 18 hours of humanities, 8 of natural science, and 6 each of social science and quantitative and logical reasoning. Specific courses required include 4 chapel credits, 2 hours of phys ed, and 2 years demonstrated proficiency in a foreign language. A minimum GPA of 2.0 is required.

Special: The college offers study abroad, accelerated and dual degrees, summer internships, student-designed interdisciplinary majors, and a Washington semester. There are 9 national honor societies, and 14 departmental honors programs.

Faculty/Classroom: 78% of faculty are male; 22%, female. All teach undergraduates and 40% both teach and do research. The average class size in an introductory lecture is 33; in a laboratory, 20; and in a regular course, 28.

Admissions: 45% of the 2005-2006 applicants were accepted. The SAT scores for the 2005-2006 freshman class were: Verbal--5% below 500, 25% between 500 and 599, 47% between 600 and 700, and 23% above 700; Math--3% below 500, 24% between 500 and 599, 50% between 600 and 700, and 23% above 700. The ACT scores were 2% below 21, 7% between 21 and 23, 29% between 24 and 26, 20% between 27 and 28, and 42% above 28. 77% of the current freshmen were in the top fifth of their class; 91% were in the top two fifths. There were 24 National Merit finalists and 2 semifinalists. 75 freshmen graduated first in their class.

Requirements: The SAT or ACT is required. In addition, the academic or college preparatory course is highly recommended, including 4 units each of English, history, math, science, and a foreign language. An essay is required of all applicants, and an audition is required of music students. An interview is highly recommended. AP and CLEP credits are accepted. Important factors in the admissions decision are extracurricular activities record, personality/intangible qualities, and ability to finance college education.

Procedure: Freshmen are admitted fall and spring. Entrance exams should be taken in the spring of the junior year or the fall of the senior year. There are early decision, early admissions, and deferred admissions plans. Early decision applications should be filed by November 15; regular applications, by February 1 for fall entry and December 15 for spring entry, along with a $50 fee. Notification of early decision is sent December 15; regular decision, March 15. 320 early decision candidates were accepted for the 2005-2006 class. 246 applicants were on the 2005 waiting list; 32 were admitted. Applications are accepted on-line.

Transfer: 26 transfer students enrolled in 2004-2005. Applicants should have a minimum 2.0 GPA. Either the SAT or the ACT is recommended, as is an interview. 64 of 128 credits required for the bachelor's degree must be completed at Grove City.

Visiting: There are regularly scheduled orientations for prospective students, consisting of daily interviews and tours, 2 high school visitation days in the fall, and a career day in the spring. There are science, engineering, math, and computer open houses. There are guides for informal visits and visitors may sit in on classes and stay overnight. To schedule a visit, contact the Admissions Office at 724-458-2100 or *admissions@gcc.edu.*

Financial Aid: In 2005-2006, 47% of all full-time freshmen and 38% of continuing full-time students received some form of financial aid. 41% of full-time freshmen and 33% of continuing full-time students received need-based aid. The average freshman award was $5393. Need-based scholarships or need-based grants averaged $5104; and other non-need-based awards and non-need-based scholarships averaged $4919. 52% of undergraduates work part time. Average annual earnings from campus work are $450. The average financial indebtedness of the 2005 graduate was $23,409. The college's own financial statement is required. The deadline for filing freshman financial aid applications for fall entry is April 15.

International Students: There are 13 international students enrolled. Satisfactory scores are required on the written TOEFL and the SAT. If the TOEFL is not available, either the SAT or the ACT is required.

Computers: Wireless access is available. All students are provided a tablet PC and have access to the network via their residence hall rooms and wireless areas on campus. All students may access the system at any time. There are no time limits and no fees. All students are required to have personal computers. All freshmen receive an HP Tablet PC.

Graduates: From July 1, 2004 to June 30, 2005, 530 bachelor's degrees were awarded. The most popular majors were elementary educa-

tion (9%), English (7%), and mechanical engineering (6%). In an average class, 3% graduate in 3 years or less, 77% graduate in 4 years or less, 80% graduate in 5 years or less, and 80% graduate in 6 years or less. 183 companies recruited on campus in 2004-2005. Of the 2004 graduating class, 20% were enrolled in graduate school within 6 months of graduation and 80% were employed.

Admissions Contact: Jeffrey C. Mincey, Director of Admissions.
E-mail: *admissions@gcc.edu* Web: *www.gcc.edu*

GWYNEDD-MERCY COLLEGE   F-4
Gwynedd Valley, PA 19437   **(215) 641-5510**
(800) DIAL-GMC; Fax: (215) 641-5556

Full-time: 324 men, 949 women	**Faculty:** 75
Part-time: 227 men, 680 women	**Ph.D.s:** 54%
Graduate: 105 men, 438 women	**Student/Faculty:** 17 to 1
Year: semesters, summer session	**Tuition:** $18,080
Application Deadline: August 1	**Room & Board:** $8000
Freshman Class: 2797 applied, 1929 accepted, 442 enrolled	
SAT Verbal/Math: 490/490*	**COMPETITIVE**

Gwynedd-Mercy College, founded in 1948, is a private institution affiliated with the Roman Catholic Church and offering degree programs in the arts and sciences, business, education, and health fields. There are 5 undergraduate and 2 graduate schools. In addition to regional accreditation, Gwynedd-Mercy has baccalaureate program accreditation with NLN. The library contains 99,493 volumes, 15,140 microform items, and 49,664 audio/video tapes/CDs/DVDs, and subscribes to 685 periodicals including electronic. Computerized library services include the card catalog, interlibrary loans, database searching, and Internet access. Special learning facilities include a learning resource center and a lab school for education majors. The 170-acre campus is in a suburban area 20 miles northwest of Philadelphia. Including any residence halls, there are 21 buildings.

Student Life: 94% of undergraduates are from Pennsylvania. Others are from 11 states, 36 foreign countries, and Canada. 51% are from public schools. 79% are white; 13% African American. 51% are Catholic; 20% Protestant; 7% claim no religious affiliation. The average age of freshmen is 23; all undergraduates, 28. 13% do not continue beyond their first year; 76% remain to graduate.

Housing: 550 students can be accommodated in college housing, which includes coed dorms. On-campus housing is available on a first-come, first-served basis. 76% of students commute. Alcohol is not permitted. All students may keep cars.

Activities: There are no fraternities or sororities. There are 21 groups on campus, including choir, chorus, drama, ethnic, honors, international, literary magazine, newspaper, professional, religious, social, social service, student government, and yearbook. Popular campus events include Fall Fest, Carol Night, and International Night.

Sports: There are 8 intercollegiate sports for men and 10 for women. Facilities include a recreation center housing men's and women's basketball, women's volleyball, a walking track, indoor racquetball courts, a weight room, team locker rooms, and a sauna. Outdoor facilities include soccer, baseball, softball, and field hockey fields.

Disabled Students: 75% of the campus is accessible. Wheelchair ramps, elevators, special parking, specially equipped rest rooms, and special class scheduling are available.

Services: Counseling and information services are available, as is tutoring in most subjects. There is remedial math, reading, and writing. Tutoring is made available in conjunction with student needs.

Campus Safety and Security: Measures include 24-hour foot and vehicle patrol, security escort services, shuttle buses, and informal discussions. There are emergency telephones and lighted pathways/sidewalks.

Programs of Study: Gwynedd-Mercy confers B.A., B.S., and B.H.S. degrees. Associate and master's degrees are also awarded. Bachelor's degrees are awarded in BIOLOGICAL SCIENCE (biology/biological science), BUSINESS (accounting, banking and finance, business administration and management, human resources, international business management, management science, marketing and distribution, office supervision and management, and sports management), COMMUNICATIONS AND THE ARTS (communications, English, and public relations), COMPUTER AND PHYSICAL SCIENCE (computer science, information sciences and systems, mathematics, and natural sciences), EDUCATION (business, elementary, mathematics, science, secondary, social studies, and special), HEALTH PROFESSIONS (clinical science, health care administration, medical laboratory technology, nursing, radiation therapy, and respiratory therapy), SOCIAL SCIENCE (criminal justice, history, psychology, social work, and sociology). Nursing, biology, and medical technology are the strongest academically. Nursing, business, and education are the largest.

Required: All students must complete at least 125 credit hours, including 60 in the major, with a minimum GPA of 2.0. (Some programs require a higher GPA.) General education courses cover language, literature and fine arts, behavioral and social sciences, humanities, and natural science. Specific courses in English composition, literature, philosophy, and religious studies are required.

Special: The college offers co-op programs in computer science, business administration, and accounting, as well as internships, dual majors, accelerated degree programs, B.A.-B.S. degrees, and pass/fail options.Cross-registration is offered with South Eastern Pennsylvania Consortium for Higher Education. All programs require or have the option for hands-on experience. There is a 3-1 program in medical technology available wherein the last year is a hospital rotation. There are 4 national honor societies, a freshman honors program, and 1 departmental honors program.

Faculty/Classroom: 35% of faculty are male; 65%, female. 96% teach undergraduates. No introductory courses are taught by graduate students. The average class size in an introductory lecture is 20; in a laboratory, 10; and in a regular course, 18.

Admissions: 69% of the 2005-2006 applicants were accepted. The SAT scores for the 2005-2006 freshman class were: Verbal--51% below 500, 38% between 500 and 599, 10% between 600 and 700, and 1% above 700; Math--51% below 500, 41% between 500 and 599, and 8% between 600 and 700. 21% of the current freshmen were in the top fifth of their class; 49% were in the top two fifths.

Requirements: The SAT is required. In addition, candidates for admission must be graduates of accredited secondary schools and have completed 16 academic credits/Carnegie units, including 4 credits in English, 3 each in math, science, and college preparatory electives, 2 in a foreign language, and 1 in history. The GED is accepted. An interview is recommended for all candidates and is required for some programs. Gwynedd-Mercy requires applicants to be in the upper 71% of their class. A GPA of 2.0 is required. AP and CLEP credits are accepted. Important factors in the admissions decision are advanced placement or honor courses, parents or siblings attending the school, and recommendations by alumni.

Procedure: Freshmen are admitted fall and spring. Entrance exams should be taken in the spring of the junior year or the fall of the senior year. There are deferred admissions and rolling admissions plans. Applications should be filed by August 1 for fall entry and December 15 for spring entry, along with a $25 fee. Notification is sent on a rolling basis. Applications are accepted on-line.

Transfer: 134 transfer students enrolled in 2004-2005. Neither the SAT nor the ACT is required for transfer students out of high school for 2 or more years. A minimum GPA of 2.0 is necessary; some programs require a higher GPA. An interview is recommended. 45 of 125 credits required for the bachelor's degree must be completed at Gwynedd-Mercy.

Visiting: There are regularly scheduled orientations for prospective students, consisting of open houses with formal presentations and campus tours, and class days with class visitations and campus tours. There are guides for informal visits and visitors may sit in on classes and stay overnight. To schedule a visit, contact the Admissions Office.

Financial Aid: In 2005-2006, 76% of all full-time freshmen and 71% of continuing full-time students received some form of financial aid. 76% of full-time freshmen and 62% of continuing full-time students received need-based aid. The average freshman award was $14,446. Need-based scholarships or need-based grants averaged $10,686; and need-based self-help aid (loans and jobs) averaged $3660. The average financial indebtedness of the 2005 graduate was $18,708. The FAFSA, the college's own financial statement and federal income tax returns are required. The deadline for filing freshman financial aid applications for fall entry is March 15.

International Students: There were 38 international students enrolled in a recent year. Satisfactory scores are required on the written TOEFL and the MELAB or the MTELP.

Computers: Wireless access is available. All students may access the system 65 hours a week.

Graduates: From July 1, 2004 to June 30, 2005, 362 bachelor's degrees were awarded. The most popular majors were business administration (27%), nursing (23%), and education (12%). In an average class, 57% graduate in 4 years or less, 75% graduate in 5 years or less, and 76% graduate in 6 years or less.

Admissions Contact: James Abbuhl, Vice President of Enrollment Management. E-mail: *admissions@gmc.edu* Web: *www.gmc.edu*

HAVERFORD COLLEGE — E-4

Haverford, PA 19041-1392 (610) 896-1350; Fax: (610) 896-1338

Full-time: 546 men, 622 women	Faculty: 111; IIB, +$
Part-time: none	Ph.D.s: 98%
Graduate: none	Student/Faculty: 11 to 1
Year: semesters	Tuition: $31,760
Application Deadline: January 15	Room & Board: $9840
Freshman Class: 3112 applied, 816 accepted, 316 enrolled	
SAT Verbal/Math: 690/690*	ACT: required

MOST COMPETITIVE

Haverford College, founded in 1833, is a private liberal arts college. The 5 libraries contain 757,759 volumes, 4809 microform items, and 11,921

audio/video tapes/CDs/DVDs, and subscribe to 4506 periodicals including electronic. Computerized library services include the card catalog, interlibrary loans, database searching, Internet access, and laptop Internet portals. Special learning facilities include an art gallery, radio station, an observatory, and an arboretum. The 200-acre campus is in a suburban area 10 miles west of Philadelphia. Including any residence halls, there are 72 buildings.

Student Life: 85% of undergraduates are from out of state, mostly the Middle Atlantic. Students are from 48 states, 38 foreign countries, and Canada. 61% are from public schools. 68% are white; 13% Asian American. The average age of freshmen is 18; all undergraduates, 20. 1% do not continue beyond their first year; 99% remain to graduate.

Housing: 1150 students can be accommodated in college housing, which includes single-sex and coed dormitories and on-campus apartments. In addition, there are language houses, and special-interest houses and Haverford students may live at Bryn Mawr College through a dorm exchange program. On-campus housing is guaranteed for all 4 years. 98% of students live on campus; of those, 90% remain on campus on weekends. Upperclassmen may keep cars.

Activities: There are no fraternities or sororities. There are 75 groups on campus, including chorale, dance, drama, ethnic, gay, international, jazz band, literary magazine, musical theater, newspaper, orchestra, political, radio and TV, religious, social service, student government, and yearbook. Popular campus events include Haverfest, Snowball, and Swarthmore athletic competitions.

Sports: There are 10 intercollegiate sports for men and 12 for women, and 3 intramural sports for men and 3 for women. Facilities include a 100,00-square-foot gym with a 1,200-seat arena, basketball/volleyball/badminton courts, aerobics, dance, and martial arts room, a fencing salle, 5 international squash courts, a conference room, and a 7,200-square foot fitness center. The alumni field house provides additional extensive facilities including a track, a batting field, and playing fields.

Disabled Students: 60% of the campus is accessible. Wheelchair ramps, elevators, special parking, specially equipped rest rooms, special class scheduling, lowered drinking fountains, lowered telephones, and reasonable accommodations are available.

Services: Counseling and information services are available, as is tutoring in every subject. There is a reader service for the blind.

Campus Safety and Security: Measures include 24-hour foot and vehicle patrol, self-defense education, security escort services, and shuttle buses. There are informal discussions, pamphlets/posters/films, emergency telephones, lighted pathways/sidewalks, and a fire safety program.

Programs of Study: Haverford confers B.A. and B.S. degrees. Bachelor's degrees are awarded in BIOLOGICAL SCIENCE (biology/biological science), COMMUNICATIONS AND THE ARTS (art history and appreciation, classics, comparative literature, English, fine arts, French, German, Greek, Italian, Latin, linguistics, music, romance languages and literature, Russian, Spanish, and visual and performing arts), COMPUTER AND PHYSICAL SCIENCE (astronomy, chemistry, computer science, geology, information sciences and systems, mathematics, and physics), SOCIAL SCIENCE (anthropology, archeology, East Asian studies, economics, history, interdisciplinary studies, liberal arts/general studies, philosophy, political science/government, psychology, religion, sociology, and urban studies). Natural and physical sciences, English, and history are the strongest academically. Biology, history, and English are the largest.

Required: All students must take a minimum of 32 course credits, including freshman writing and 3 courses each in social science, natural science, and the humanities. One of the distribution courses must be quantitative and 1 must meet the social justice requirement. Students must also take 3 semesters of phys ed and demonstrate proficiency in a foreign language. Students must take a minimum of 6 courses in the major and 6 in related fields. Each major includes a capstone experience (a comprehensive exam, thesis, or advanced project, a specially designed course, or some combination), which varies by department.

Special: Haverford offers internship programs, cross-registration with Bryn Mawr College and Swarthmore College, study abroad in 35 countries, dual majors, student-designed majors. Pass/fail options are limited to 4 in 4 years. There is 1 national honor society, including Phi Beta Kappa, and 28 departmental honors programs.

Faculty/Classroom: 53% of faculty are male; 47%, female. All teach undergraduates. The average class size in an introductory lecture is 30.

Admissions: 26% of the 2005-2006 applicants were accepted. The SAT scores for the 2005-2006 freshman class were: Verbal--8% between 500 and 599, 44% between 600 and 700, and 48% above 700; Math--10% between 500 and 599, 43% between 600 and 700, and 47% above 700. 97% of the current freshmen were in the top fifth of their class; All were in the top two fifths.

Requirements: The SAT or ACT is required. In addition, first-year applicants must take the SAT Writing test and 2 others or the ACT and 2 SAT subject tests before the deadline for the decision plan chosen. Candidates for admission must be graduates of an accredited secondary school and have taken 4 courses in English, 3 each in a foreign language and math, and 1 each in science and history. The GED is accepted. An essay is required and an interview is recommended. AP credits are accepted. Important factors in the admissions decision are advanced placement or honor courses, leadership record, and recommendations by school officials.

Procedure: Freshmen are admitted in the fall. Entrance exams should be taken by January 15. There are early decision, early admissions, and deferred admissions plans. Early decision applications should be filed by November 15; regular applications, by January 15 for fall entry, along with a $60 fee. Notification of early decision is sent December 15; regular decision, April 15. 104 early decision candidates were accepted for the 2005-2006 class. 169 applicants were on the 2005 waiting list; 28 were admitted. Applications are accepted on-line.

Transfer: 2 transfer students enrolled in 2004-2005. Transfer students must be able to enter the sophomore or junior class. Admission depends mainly on the strength of college grades. A minimum GPA of 3.0 is necessary and the SAT is recommended. The equivalent of 1 year of courses must have been earned. A liberal arts curriculum is also recommended. 64 of 128 credits required for the bachelor's degree must be completed at Haverford.

Visiting: There are guides for informal visits and visitors may sit in on classes and stay overnight. To schedule a visit, contact the Admissions Office.

Financial Aid: In 2005-2006, 54% of all full-time freshmen and 53% of continuing full-time students received some form of financial aid. 42% of full-time freshmen and 43% of continuing full-time students received need-based aid. The average freshman award was $29,172. The average financial indebtedness of the 2005 graduate was $16,330. Haverford is a member of CSS. The CSS/Profile or FAFSA is required. The deadline for filing freshman financial aid applications for fall entry is January 31.

International Students: There are 57 international students enrolled. The school actively recruits these students. They must score satisfactorily on the written TOEFL or on the electronic version and also take the SAT. Haverfod requires the SAT writing test and 2 others or the ACT plus 2 SAT subject tests.

Computers: Wireless access is available. All students may access the system. There are no time limits and no fees.

Graduates: From July 1, 2004 to June 30, 2005, 278 bachelor's degrees were awarded. The most popular majors were biology (12%), history (9%), and English (9%). In an average class, 81% graduate in 4 years or less, 85% graduate in 5 years or less, and 88% graduate in 6 years or less. 172 companies recruited on campus in 2004-2005. Of the 2004 graduating class, 16% were enrolled in graduate school within 6 months of graduation and 51% were employed.

Admissions Contact: Jess Lord, Director of Admission. A video is available. E-mail: *admitme@haverford.edu*
Web: *http://www.haverford.edu*

HOLY FAMILY UNIVERSITY F-3
(Formerly Holy Family College)

Philadelphia, PA 19114

(215) 637-3050
(800) 637-1191; Fax: (215) 281-1022

Full-time: 322 men, 1057 women	**Faculty:** 75; IIB, -$
Part-time: 153 men, 533 women	**Ph.D.s:** 69%
Graduate: 215 men, 908 women	**Student/Faculty:** 18 to 1
Year: semesters, summer session	**Tuition:** $17,740
Application Deadline: open	**Room & Board:** $8000
Freshman Class: n/av	
SAT Verbal/Math: 505/495	**COMPETITIVE**

Holy Family University (Formerly Holy Family College), established in 1954 and affiliated with the Roman Catholic Church, is a private, non-residential institution with a liberal arts core. In addition to regional accreditation, Holy Family has baccalaureate program accreditation with AACSB and NLN. The library contains 101,392 volumes, 8588 microform items, and 2975 audio/video tapes/CDs/DVDs, and subscribes to 709 periodicals including electronic. Computerized library services include the card catalog, interlibrary loans, and database searching. Special learning facilities include a learning resource center and writing resource center. The 46-acre campus is in a suburban area within city limits. There are 8 buildings.

Student Life: 90% of undergraduates are from Pennsylvania. Others are from 7 states and 17 foreign countries. 24% are from public schools. 92% are white. 78% are Catholic; 9% Protestant. The average age of freshmen is 18; all undergraduates, 21. 18% do not continue beyond their first year; 65% remain to graduate.

Housing: Holy Family provides 2 residential-living experiences: a residence hall and independent apartments. First-year students selected to participate in the Residence-Life Program are guaranteed housing for 2 years.. Alcohol is not permitted. All students may keep cars.

Activities: There are no fraternities or sororities. There are 62 groups on campus, including cheerleading, drama, honors, international, literary magazine, newspaper, professional, religious, social service, student gov-

ernment, and yearbook. Popular campus events include Buddy Day, Christmas Rose, and Spring Fling.

Sports: There are 3 intercollegiate sports for men and 4 for women, and 5 intramural sports for men and 5 for women. Facilities include a gym, a weight room, racquetball courts, and soccer and softball fields.

Disabled Students: All of the campus is accessible. Wheelchair ramps, elevators, special parking, specially equipped rest rooms, lowered drinking fountains, and lowered telephones are available.

Services: Counseling and information services are available, as is tutoring in some subjects, including writing, reading, and math.

Campus Safety and Security: Measures include 24-hour foot and vehicle patrol, security escort services, pamphlets/posters/films, and emergency telephones. There are lighted pathways/sidewalks.

Programs of Study: Holy Family confers B.A., B.S., and B.S.N. degrees. Associate and master's degrees are also awarded. Bachelor's degrees are awarded in BIOLOGICAL SCIENCE (biochemistry and biology/biological science), BUSINESS (accounting, business administration and management, and marketing/retailing/merchandising), COMMUNICATIONS AND THE ARTS (art, English, French, and Spanish), COMPUTER AND PHYSICAL SCIENCE (chemistry, information sciences and systems, and mathematics), EDUCATION (early childhood, elementary, foreign languages, science, secondary, and special), HEALTH PROFESSIONS (medical laboratory technology, nursing, and premedicine), SOCIAL SCIENCE (criminal justice, economics, history, humanities, prelaw, psychology, religion, social work, and sociology). Nursing, elementary education, and accounting are the strongest academically. Nursing, education, and business are the largest.

Required: Students must complete 120 to 130 semester hours, including at least 30 in the major, with a minimum GPA of 2.0. Nursing, medical technology, and education majors must maintain a GPA of 2.5. Specific discipline requirements include English, science, math, philosophy, religious studies, social studies, humanities, and foreign language. A core curriculum of communication, quantification, philosophy, humanities, social science, natural sciences, senior ethics, and religious studies must be fulfilled. All majors require satisfactory performance on a comprehensive exam.

Special: Opportunities are provided for study abroad, co-op programs in 23 majors with more than 200 companies, a B.A.-B.S. degree, an accelerated degree program, independent study, credit by exam, nondegree study, and pass/fail options. Students may pursue dual majors in business and French or Spanish, international business and French or Spanish, and elementary and special education. There are 10 national honor societies, a freshman honors program, and 2 departmental honors programs.

Faculty/Classroom: 44% of faculty are male; 56%, female. No introductory courses are taught by graduate students. The average class size in an introductory lecture is 20; in a laboratory, 17; and in a regular course, 21.

Requirements: The SAT or ACT is required. In addition, graduation from an accredited secondary school is required; a GED is accepted. Applicants must submit 16 academic credits, including 4 courses in English, 3 each in history and math, 2 each in foreign language and science, 1 in social studies, and the remainder in academic electives. Holy Family requires applicants to be in the upper 40% of their class. A GPA of 2.5 is required. AP and CLEP credits are accepted.

Procedure: Freshmen are admitted to all sessions. Entrance exams should be taken by October or November of the senior year. There are early decision and deferred admissions plans. There is a rolling admissions plan. Application deadlines are open. Application fee is $25. Notification is sent on a rolling basis. Applications are accepted on-line.

Transfer: 172 transfer students enrolled in 2004-2005. Applicants must submit official transcripts from all previous colleges. Grades of D are not transferable. A maximum of 75 credits will be accepted for transfer. 45 of 120 credits required for the bachelor's degree must be completed at Holy Family.

Visiting: There are regularly scheduled orientations for prospective students. There are guides for informal visits and visitors may sit in on classes and stay overnight. To schedule a visit, contact the Office of Admissions.

Financial Aid: In 2005-2006, 85% of all full-time students received some form of financial aid, including need-based aid. The average financial indebtedness of a recent graduate was $17,125. Holy Family is a member of CSS. The FAFSA is required. The deadline for filing freshman financial aid applications for fall entry is May 1.

International Students: A satisfactory score on the TOEFL is required.

Computers: All students may access the system 6 days a week (7-day remote Internet access for subscribers). There are no time limits and no fees.

Admissions Contact: Lauren Campbell, Director of Undergraduate Admissions. E-mail: *admissions@holyfamily.edu*
Web: *www.holyfamily.edu*

IMMACULATA UNIVERSITY   E-4

Immaculata, PA 19345   **(610) 647-4400, ext. 3015**
    (877) IC-TODAY; Fax: (610) 640-0836

Full-time: 390 women	**Faculty:** 76; IIA, --$
Part-time: none	**Ph.D.s:** 64%
Graduate: none	**Student/Faculty:** 5 to 1
Year: semesters, summer session	**Tuition:** $17,300
Application Deadline: see profile	**Room & Board:** $8050
Freshman Class: n/av	
SAT: required	**COMPETITIVE**

Immaculata University, founded in 1920, is a private Catholic, women's liberal arts and career preparation college. Figures in the above capsule and profile are approximate. In addition to regional accreditation, Immaculata has baccalaureate program accreditation with ADA, AHEA, NASM, and NLN. The library contains 130,000 volumes, 1373 microform items, and 1500 audio/video tapes/CDs/DVDs, and subscribes to 760 periodicals including electronic. Computerized library services include the card catalog, interlibrary loans, database searching, and Internet access. Special learning facilities include a learning resource center and computer and language labs. The 400-acre campus is in a suburban area 20 miles west of Philadelphia. Including any residence halls, there are 13 buildings.

Student Life: 71% of undergraduates are from Pennsylvania. Others are from 10 states and 1 foreign country. 38% are from public schools. 85% are white. 76% are Catholic; 16% Protestant; 7% Muslim, Hindu, and Shinto. The average age of freshmen is 18; all undergraduates, 20. 31% do not continue beyond their first year; 55% remain to graduate.

Housing: 380 students can be accommodated in college housing, which includes single-sex dormitories. On-campus housing is guaranteed for all 4 years. 74% of students live on campus; of those, 55% remain on campus on weekends. Alcohol is not permitted. All students may keep cars.

Activities: There are no fraternities. There are 32 groups on campus, including art, choir, chorale, chorus, computers, dance, debate, drama, ethnic, honors, international, literary magazine, musical theater, newspaper, orchestra, photography, political, professional, religious, social, social service, student government, and yearbook. Popular campus events include Rose Arbor Dinner, class proms, and Friday's Pub.

Sports: Facilities include tennis courts, a full gym, a handball gym, an Olympic-size swimming pool, hockey and softball fields, and a weight room.

Disabled Students: All of the campus is accessible. Wheelchair ramps, elevators, special parking, specially equipped rest rooms, special class scheduling, lowered drinking fountains, lowered telephones, and special housing are available.

Services: Counseling and information services are available, as is tutoring in most subjects. There is a reader service for the blind, and remedial math, reading, and writing.

Campus Safety and Security: Measures include 24-hour foot and vehicle patrol, self-defense education, security escort services, and informal discussions. There are pamphlets/posters/films, emergency telephones, and lighted pathways/sidewalks.

Programs of Study: Immaculata confers B.A., B.S., B.Mus., and B.S.N. degrees. Associate, master's, and doctoral degrees are also awarded. Bachelor's degrees are awarded in BIOLOGICAL SCIENCE (biochemistry, and biology/biological science), BUSINESS (accounting, banking and finance, business administration and management, and fashion merchandising), COMMUNICATIONS AND THE ARTS (English, French, music, and Spanish), COMPUTER AND PHYSICAL SCIENCE (information sciences and systems and mathematics), EDUCATION (early childhood, elementary, foreign languages, home economics, middle school, music, science, and secondary), HEALTH PROFESSIONS (music therapy, nursing, and premedicine), SOCIAL SCIENCE (dietetics, economics, experimental psychology, food science, history, international relations, prelaw, psychology, social science, sociology, and theological studies). Premedicine, education, and dietetics are the strongest academically. Education, business, and music therapy are the largest.

Required: To graduate, all students must complete 54 credits in liberal arts, including distribution requirements in humanities, social sciences, and sciences. Students must take a minimum of 126 credits, including 36 to 52 in the major. 2 credits of phys ed are also required. The college requires a minimum GPA of 2.0. A thesis, which is the outcome of a required senior seminar, is also required. Internships are required for dietetics, music therapy, and education.

Special: All majors offer opportunities for internships, and most require them. Students may study abroad in 6 countries. The college offers dual-majors, 3 accelerated degree programs in organization dynamics, human resource management, and nursing, and nondegree study and pass/fail options. There are 16 national honor societies, including Phi Beta Kappa, a freshman honors program, and 13 departmental honors programs.

Faculty/Classroom: 28% of faculty are male; 72%, female. 92% teach undergraduates and 4% both teach and do research. The average class size in an introductory lecture is 15; in a laboratory, 12; and in a regular course, 15.

Requirements: The SAT is required. Candidates for admission should be graduates of an accredited secondary school with a minimum of 16 academic credits including 4 in English, 2 each in a foreign language, math, science, and social studies, 1 in history, and 3 more in college preparatory courses. The GED is accepted. An audition is required for music students and an essay and an interview are recommended for all. Immaculata requires applicants to be in the upper 60% of their class. A GPA of 2.0 is required. AP and CLEP credits are accepted. Important factors in the admissions decision are advanced placement or honor courses, recommendations by school officials, and extracurricular activities record.

Procedure: Freshmen are admitted fall and spring. Entrance exams should be taken in the spring of the junior year. There are early decision, deferred admissions, and rolling admissions plans. Check with the school for application deadlines. The application fee is $25. Notification of early decision is sent December 1; regular decision, on a rolling basis.

Transfer: 23 transfer students enrolled in a recent year. In addition to high school credentials, transfer applicants must present college transcripts. Courses in which the student has achieved a C or better are accepted if they are comparable to Immaculata's courses. A satisfactory score on the SAT is required, as is an interview. Students must have a minimum GPA of 2.0. 36 of 126 credits required for the bachelor's degree must be completed at Immaculata.

Visiting: There are regularly scheduled orientations for prospective students, including an open house and class visit. There are guides for informal visits and visitors may sit in on classes and stay overnight. To schedule a visit, contact the Office of Admissions.

Financial Aid: In a recent year, 91% of all full-time freshmen and 86% of continuing full-time students received some form of financial aid. 91% of full-time freshmen and 75% of continuing full-time students received need-based aid. The average freshman award was $13,500. Need-based scholarships or need-based grants averaged $2318 ($4050 maximum); need-based self-help aid (loans and jobs) averaged $1578 ($2625 maximum); and other non-need-based awards and non-need-based scholarships averaged $15,488 ($17,200 maximum). 120% of undergraduates worked part time. Average annual earnings from campus work were $700. The average financial indebtedness of a recent graduate was $17,125. Immaculata is a member of CSS. The FAFSA and are required. Check with the school for application deadlines.

International Students: The school actively recruits these students. They must score satisfactorily on the written TOEFL.

Computers: All students may access the system. There are no time limits and no fees.

Graduates: In a recent yaer; 94 bachelor's degrees were awarded. In an average class, 1% graduate in 3 years or less, 71% graduate in 4 years or less, 3% graduate in 5 years or less, and 4% graduate in 6 years or less. 18 companies recruited on campus in a recent year. Of a recent graduating class, 7% were enrolled in graduate school within 6 months of graduation and 85% were employed.

Admissions Contact: Sarah Fox, Assistant Director of Admissions. A video is available. E-mail: *admiss@immaculata.edu* Web: *http://www.immaculata.edu*

INDIANA UNIVERSITY OF PENNSYLVANIA   B-3

Indiana, PA 15705   **(724) 357-2230; (800) 442-6830**

Full-time: 5011 men, 6212 women	**Faculty:** n/av
Part-time: 381 men, 443 women	**Ph.D.s:** 86%
Graduate: 693 men, 1341 women	**Student/Faculty:** n/av
Year: semesters, summer session	**Tuition:** $6221 ($13,581)
Application Deadline: open	**Room & Board:** $4988
Freshman Class: 8618 applied, 4887 accepted, 2654 enrolled	
SAT Verbal/Math: 536/532*	**COMPETITIVE**

Indiana University of Pennsylvania, founded in 1875, is a public member of the Pennsylvania State System of Higher Education offering programs in liberal and fine arts, business, preengineering, health science, military science, teacher preparation, basic and applied science, social science and humanities, criminology, and safety science. There are 7 undergraduate schools and 1 graduate school. In addition to regional accreditation, IUP has baccalaureate program accreditation with AACSB, ABET, ACS, ADA, APA, ASLHA, CAHEA, CCNE, JRCERT, NASM, NCATE, and NAST. The library contains 840,000 volumes, 2,376,446 microform items, and 3000 audio/video tapes/CDs/DVDs, and subscribes to 14,700 periodicals including electronic. Computerized library services include the card catalog, interlibrary loans, database searching, Internet access, and laptop Internet portals. Special learning facilities include a learning resource center, art gallery, planetarium, radio station, and TV station. The 342-acre campus is in a small town 50 miles northeast of Pittsburgh. Including any residence halls, there are 79 buildings.

Student Life: 95% of undergraduates are from Pennsylvania. Others are from 37 states, 52 foreign countries, and Canada. 95% are from public schools. 79% are white. The average age of freshmen is 20; all undergraduates, 21. 23% do not continue beyond their first year; 50% remain to graduate.

Housing: 3993 students can be accommodated in college housing, which includes single-sex and coed dorms and on-campus apartments. In addition, there are honors houses, 24-hour intensified study floors, substance-free housing, academic specialty housing, and an international house. On-campus housing is guaranteed for the freshman year only and is available on a lottery system for upperclassmen. 69% of students commute. Alcohol is not permitted. All students may keep cars.

Activities: 10% of men belong to 19 national fraternities; 11% of women belong to 14 national sororities. There are 251 groups on campus, including art, band, cheerleading, choir, chorale, chorus, computers, dance, drama, ethnic, film, gay, honors, international, jazz band, marching band, musical theater, newspaper, opera, orchestra, pep band, political, professional, radio and TV, religious, social, social service, student government, symphony, and yearbook. Popular campus events include International Day, Pantiellenic Recruitment, and Student Organizational Fair.

Sports: There are 7 intercollegiate sports for men and 10 for women, and 24 intramural sports for men and 21 for women. Facilities include a 7600-seat stadium, swimming pools, a fitness trail, softball fields, and courts for tennis, badminton, handball/racquetball, basketball, and volleyball, and a fitness center.

Disabled Students: 98% of the campus is accessible. Wheelchair ramps, elevators, special parking, specially equipped rest rooms, special class scheduling, lowered drinking fountains, and lowered telephones are available.

Services: There is a reader service for the blind, and remedial math, reading, and writing.

Campus Safety and Security: Measures include 24-hour foot and vehicle patrol, self-defense education, security escort services, and shuttle buses. There are informal discussions, pamphlets/posters/films, emergency telephones, lighted pathways/sidewalks, and bicycle registration, operation ID, and crime tip hotline.

Programs of Study: IUP confers B.A., B.S., B.F.A., and B.S.Ed. degrees. Associate, master's, and doctoral degrees are also awarded. Bachelor's degrees are awarded in BIOLOGICAL SCIENCE (biochemistry and biology/biological science), BUSINESS (accounting, banking and finance, business administration and management, fashion merchandising, hotel/motel and restaurant management, human resources, international business management, management information systems, and marketing/retailing/merchandising), COMMUNICATIONS AND THE ARTS (art, communications, dramatic arts, English, fine arts, French, German, journalism, media arts, music, music performance, Russian, Spanish, and studio art), COMPUTER AND PHYSICAL SCIENCE (applied mathematics, applied physics, chemistry, computer science, geology, geoscience, mathematics, natural sciences, and physics), EDUCATION (art, business, early childhood, education of the deaf and hearing impaired, education of the mentally handicapped, education of the physically handicapped, elementary, English, foreign languages, mathematics, music, nutrition, physical, science, social science, special, and vocational), ENGINEERING AND ENVIRONMENTAL DESIGN (city/community/regional planning and interior design), HEALTH PROFESSIONS (environmental health science, medical technology, nuclear medical technology, nursing, premedicine, rehabilitation therapy, respiratory therapy, and speech pathology/audiology), SOCIAL SCIENCE (anthropology, child care/child and family studies, consumer services, criminology, dietetics, economics, family/consumer studies, food production/management/services, food science, geography, history, international studies, philosophy, political science/government, prelaw, psychology, religion, safety and security technology, social science, and sociology). Elementary education, criminology, and communications media are the largest.

Required: All candidates for graduation must complete approximately 120 credits, including 48 credits in the liberal studies core. The total number of hours and the minimum GPA vary with the major.

Special: IUP offers co-op programs, cross-registration through the National Student Exchange Consortium, a 3-2 engineering degree with the University of Pittsburgh and Drexel University, and a B.A.-B.S. degree. Internships and dual and student-designed majors are available. Students may study abroad in 28 countries. Also available are work-study programs, a Washington semester, an accelerated degree program, and credit for military experience. There are 21 national honor societies, and a freshman honors program.

Faculty/Classroom: 56% of faculty are male; 44%, female. 91% teach undergraduates. No introductory courses are taught by graduate students. The average class size in an introductory lecture is 43; in a laboratory, 16; and in a regular course, 25.

Admissions: 57% of the 2005-2006 applicants were accepted. The SAT scores for the 2005-2006 freshman class were: Verbal--35% below 500, 48% between 500 and 599, 15% between 600 and 700, and 2% above 700; Math--38% below 500, 48% between 500 and 599, 13% between 600 and 700, and 1% above 700. 35% of the current freshmen were in the top fifth of their class; 74% were in the top two fifths.

Requirements: The SAT is required. In addition, candidates for admission should be graduates of an accredited secondary school. There are no specific course requirements. Art majors must have a portfolio and music majors must audition. AP and CLEP credits are accepted. Important factors in the admissions decision are advanced placement or honor courses, extracurricular activities record, and evidence of special talent.

Procedure: Freshmen are admitted fall and spring. Entrance exams should be taken by December of the preceding year. There are deferred admissions and rolling admissions plans. Notification is sent on a rolling basis. The fall 2005 application fee was $30. Application deadlines are open. Applications are accepted on-line.

Transfer: 601 transfer students enrolled in 2004-2005. Transfer students must have a minimum GPA of 2.0 for all subjects (2.5 for education students). 45 of 120 credits required for the bachelor's degree must be completed at IUP.

Visiting: There are regularly scheduled orientations for prospective students. There are guides for informal visits and visitors may sit in on classes. To schedule a visit, contact the Admissions Office at *admission_inquiry@iup.edu.*

Financial Aid: In 2005-2006, 66% of all full-time freshmen and 69% of continuing full-time students received some form of financial aid. 47% of full-time freshmen and 48% of continuing full-time students received need-based aid. The average freshman award was $7772. Need-based scholarships or need-based grants averaged $4052; need-based self-help aid (loans and jobs) averaged $4272; and non-need-based athletic scholarships averaged $3478. 18% of undergraduates work part time. Average annual earnings from campus work are $1500. The FAFSA and Pennsylvania State Grant form are required. The priority date for freshman financial aid applications for fall entry is April 15.

International Students: There are 122 international students enrolled. A satisfactory score is required on the written TOEFL.

Computers: Wireless access is available. Students have access to the network in nearly all areas of campus, with half of classrooms wireless accessible. The most used areas are library, student union, and residence halls. There is virtual access to many services on campus such as dining service menu, advising, financial aid, applying for admission, and registering for classes. While PCs are not required, Dell computers are recommended for students who have PCs. All students may access the system 24 hours a day, 7 days a week.

Graduates: From July 1, 2004 to June 30, 2005, 1976 bachelor's degrees were awarded. The most popular majors were elementary education (10%), criminology (9%), and communication media (6%). In an average class, 55% graduate in 6 years or less. 129 companies recruited on campus in a recent year.

Admissions Contact: Rhonda Luckey, Interim Vice President for Student Affairs. A video is available. Web: *www.iup.edu/admissions*

JUNIATA COLLEGE   C-3
Huntingdon, PA 16652   (814) 641-3420
                                (877) JUNIATA; Fax: (814) 641-3100

Full-time: 649 men, 740 women	**Faculty:** 94; IIB, av$
Part-time: 34 men, 26 women	**Ph.Ds:** 91%
Graduate: none	**Student/Faculty:** 15 to 1
Year: semesters, summer session	**Tuition:** $25,890
Application Deadline: March 15	**Room & Board:** $7240
Freshman Class: 1745 applied, 1219 accepted, 388 enrolled	
SAT Verbal/Math: 570/600*	**VERY COMPETITIVE**

Juniata College, founded in 1876, is an independent liberal arts college affiliated with the Church of the Brethren. In addition to regional accreditation, Juniata has baccalaureate program accreditation with ACS and CSWE. The library contains 280,000 volumes, 400 microform items, and 1800 audio/video tapes/CDs/DVDs, and subscribes to 1000 periodicals including electronic. Computerized library services include the card catalog, interlibrary loans, database searching, Internet access, and laptop Internet portals. Special learning facilities include a learning resource center, art gallery, radio station, an observatory, an environmental studies field station, a nature preserve, an early childhood education center, and a ceramics studio with an Anagama kiln. The 110-acre campus is in a small town 31 miles south of State College, in the heart of rural Pennsylvania. Including any residence halls, there are 43 buildings.

Student Life: 75% of undergraduates are from Pennsylvania. Others are from 31 states and 31 foreign countries. 87% are from public schools. 90% are white. 63% are Protestant; 32% Catholic. The average age of freshmen is 18; all undergraduates, 20. 15% do not continue beyond their first year; 75% remain to graduate.

Housing: 1142 students can be accommodated in college housing, which includes single-sex and coed dorms, on-campus apartments, and off-campus apartments. In addition, there are special-interest houses. On-campus housing is guaranteed for all 4 years. 82% of students live on campus; of those, 75% remain on campus on weekends. All students may keep cars.

Activities: There are no fraternities or sororities. There are 83 groups on campus, including art, band, cheerleading, chess, choir, chorale, chorus, computers, dance, debate, drama, ethnic, forensics, gay, honors, international, literary magazine, model UN, musical theater, newspaper, orchestra, outing, pep band, photography, political, professional, radio and TV, religious, social, social service, student government, symphony, and yearbook. Popular campus events include Mountain Day, Christmas Madrigal Dinner, and Mr. Juniata.

Sports: There are 9 intercollegiate sports for men and 10 for women, and 4 intramural sports for men and 4 for women. Facilities include 2 gyms, a swimming pool, a fitness center, 4 racquetball courts, a multipurpose room, a sauna, a whirlpool, a varsity football field and stadium, baseball, soccer, softball, and hockey fields, an outdoor running track, 7 tennis courts, and 1 outdoor basketball court.

Disabled Students: 75% of the campus is accessible. Wheelchair ramps, elevators, special parking, specially equipped rest rooms, lowered drinking fountains, wide doors, and stairlifts are available.

Services: Counseling and information services are available, as is tutoring in most subjects. There is a reader service for the blind. Juniata also offers courses and workshops in study, reading, and writing skills.

Campus Safety and Security: Measures include 24-hour foot and vehicle patrol, self-defense education, security escort services, and informal discussions. There are pamphlets/posters/films, emergency telephones, awareness programs, fire safety training, weather alerts, terror alerts, an emergency operation plan, a firearms storage vault, a vehicle lockout service, identification processing, and evacuation mapping.

Programs of Study: Juniata confers B.A. and B.S. degrees. Bachelor's degrees are awarded in AGRICULTURE (environmental studies), BIOLOGICAL SCIENCE (biochemistry, biology/biological science, botany, ecology, marine science, microbiology, molecular biology, and zoology), BUSINESS (accounting, banking and finance, business administration and management, human resources, international business management, management information systems, and marketing/retailing/merchandising), COMMUNICATIONS AND THE ARTS (art history and appreciation, communications, English, French, German, Russian, Spanish, and studio art), COMPUTER AND PHYSICAL SCIENCE (chemistry, computer science, earth science, geology, information sciences and systems, mathematics, natural sciences, physics, and planetary and space science), EDUCATION (early childhood, elementary, English, foreign languages, mathematics, museum studies, science, secondary, social studies, and special), ENGINEERING AND ENVIRONMENTAL DESIGN (engineering physics, environmental science, and preengineering), HEALTH PROFESSIONS (chiropractic, physician's assistant, preallied health, predentistry, premedicine, preoptometry, prepharmacy, prepodiatry, and preveterinary science), SOCIAL SCIENCE (anthropology, criminal justice, economics, history, humanities, international relations, international studies, peace studies, philosophy, political science/government, prelaw, psychology, public administration, social science, social work, sociology, and theological studies). Biology, chemistry, and psychology are the strongest academically. Biology, business, and education are the largest.

Required: Students are required to complete a minimum of 120 credit hours, including courses in fine arts, international studies, social sciences, humanities, and natural sciences, as well as 4 communications-based courses, 2 cultural analysis courses, a math and statistics course, and the college writing seminar. The total number of hours required for the program of emphasis varies from 45 to 60; majors do not exist as such, and students must develop a program of emphasis and complete it to obtain their degree. Students must have a minimum GPA of 2.0.

Special: Juniata offers cooperative programs in marine science, cytogenetics, cytotechnology, marine biology, biotechnology, nursing, medical technology, diagnostic imaging, occupational and physical therapy, dentistry, medicine, optometry, and podiatry. Internships, study abroad in 19 countries, Washington and Philadelphia semesters, and nondegree study are also offered. There are 3-2 engineering degrees with Columbia, Clarkson, Washington, and Pennsylvania State Universities, a 3-3 law program with Duquesne University, and various preprofessional programs, including optometry, chiropractic, medicine, dentistry, pharmacy, physician assistant, and podiatry. With the assistance of faculty advisers, most students design their own majors to meet their individual goals. There are 12 national honor societies, a freshman honors program, and 12 departmental honors programs.

Faculty/Classroom: 59% of faculty are male; 41%, female. All teach undergraduates. The average class size in an introductory lecture is 19; in a laboratory, 15; and in a regular course, 14.

Admissions: 70% of the 2005-2006 applicants were accepted. The SAT scores for the 2005-2006 freshman class were: Verbal--9% below 500, 51% between 500 and 599, 31% between 600 and 700, and 8% above 700; Math--7% below 500, 40% between 500 and 599, 46% between 600 and 700, and 7% above 700. 68% of the current freshmen were in the top fifth of their class; 92% were in the top two fifths. There was 1 National Merit semifinalist. 9 freshmen graduated first in their class.

Requirements: The SAT or ACT is required. In addition, candidates for admission should be graduates of an accredited secondary school and have completed 16 academic credits, including 4 in English, 2 in a foreign language, and a combination of 10 in math, social studies, and lab

science. The GED is accepted, and homeschoolers are encouraged to apply. An essay is required, and an interview is recommended. A GPA of 3.0 is required. AP credits are accepted. Important factors in the admissions decision are advanced placement or honor courses, leadership record, and recommendations by school officials.

Procedure: Freshmen are admitted fall and spring. Entrance exams should be taken in the junior or senior years of high school. There are early decision, early admissions, and deferred admissions plans. There is a rolling admissions plan. Early decision applications should be filed by November 15; regular applications, by March 15 for fall entry and December 1 for spring entry, along with a $30 fee. Notification of early decision is sent December 31; regular decision, on a rolling basis. 74 early decision candidates were accepted for the 2005-2006 class. Applications are accepted on-line.

Transfer: 23 transfer students enrolled in 2004-2005. A GPA of 2.5 is required. Applicants must submit a high school transcript, a college transcript, and an essay. SAT scores are required of some students. 30 of 120 credits required for the bachelor's degree must be completed at Juniata.

Visiting: There are regularly scheduled orientations for prospective students, including a campus tour, interviews, and a department fair. There are guides for informal visits and visitors may sit in on classes and stay overnight. To schedule a visit, contact Norma Jennings, Enrollment Assistant at (814) 641-3428 or jenninn@juniata.edu.

Financial Aid: In 2005-2006, all full-time freshmen and 97% of continuing full-time students received some form of financial aid. 79% of full-time freshmen and 77% of continuing full-time students received need-based aid. The average freshman award was $18,763. Need-based scholarships or need-based grants averaged $15,668 ($22,900 maximum); and need-based self-help aid (loans and jobs) averaged $4551 ($5325 maximum). 54% of undergraduates work part time. Average annual earnings from campus work are $626. The average financial indebtedness of the 2005 graduate was $22,131. The FAFSA is required. The priority date for freshman financial aid applications for fall entry is March 1. The deadline for filing freshman financial aid applications for fall entry is May 1.

International Students: There are 77 international students enrolled. The school actively recruits these students. A satisfactory score on the TOEFL is required.

Computers: Wireless access is available. All students may access the system. There are no time limits and no fees. It is strongly recommended that all students have a personal computer.

Graduates: From July 1, 2004 to June 30, 2005, 296 bachelor's degrees were awarded. The most popular majors were biology/pre-health (15%), business/accounting (15%), and education (14%). In an average class, 68% graduate in 4 years or less, 74% graduate in 5 years or less, and 75% graduate in 6 years or less. 20 companies recruited on campus in 2004-2005. Of the 2004 graduating class, 35% were enrolled in graduate school within 6 months of graduation and 60% were employed.

Admissions Contact: Office of Enrollment.
E-mail: admissions@juniata.edu Web: www.juniata.edu

KEYSTONE COLLEGE E-4
La Plume, PA 18440
(570) 945-8112
(877) 4COLLEGE; Fax: (570) 945-7916

Full-time: 526 men, 788 women	Faculty: n/av
Part-time: 104 men, 300 women	Ph.D.s: n/av
Graduate: none	Student/Faculty: n/av
Year: semesters, summer session	Tuition: $15,020
Application Deadline: open	Room & Board: $7790
Freshman Class: 908 applied, 832 accepted, 374 enrolled	
SAT Verbal/Math: 450/440*	ACT: 17 LESS COMPETITIVE

Keystone College, founded in 1868, is a small private college offering 13 bachelor's degrees and 17 associate degrees. The library contains 39,977 volumes, 41,449 microform items, and 1516 audio/video tapes/CDs/DVDs, and subscribes to 179 periodicals including electronic. Computerized library services include the card catalog, interlibrary loans, database searching, and Internet access. Special learning facilities include a learning resource center, art gallery, radio station, and observatory. The 270-acre campus is in a rural area 15 miles north of Scranton and 40 miles south of Binghamton, New York. Including any residence halls, there are 29 buildings.

Student Life: 90% of undergraduates are from Pennsylvania. Others are from 18 states, 9 foreign countries, and Canada. 94% are white. The average age of freshmen is 21; all undergraduates, 24. 41% do not continue beyond their first year; 41% remain to graduate.

Housing: 404 students can be accommodated in college housing, which includes single-sex and coed dormitories and single rooms for upper classmen. On-campus housing is guaranteed for all 4 years. 71% of students commute. Alcohol is not permitted. All students may keep cars.

Activities: There are no fraternities or sororities. There are 19 groups on campus, including art, cheerleading, drama, equestrian, ethnic, forensics, gay, honors, international, literary magazine, newspaper co-op, photography, radio and TV, religious, social, social service, ski, student government, and yearbook. Popular campus events include United Nations Day, Winterfest, and Spring Fling.

Sports: There are 7 intercollegiate sports for men and 7 for women, and 6 intramural sports for men and 6 for women. Facilities include an athletic center, tennis courts, playing fields, and a trail system.

Disabled Students: 90% of the campus is accessible. Wheelchair ramps, elevators, special parking, specially equipped rest rooms, special class scheduling, lowered drinking fountains, lowered telephones, and special housing are available.

Services: Counseling and information services are available, as is tutoring in every subject. There is remedial math, reading, and writing. A writing center is available and there are some services with documented learning disabilities (extended test time, preferential seating, notetakers).

Campus Safety and Security: Measures include 24-hour foot and vehicle patrol, security escort services, informal discussions, and pamphlets/posters/films. There are emergency telephones and lighted pathways/sidewalks.

Programs of Study: Keystone College confers B.S. and B.A. degrees. Associate degrees are also awarded. Bachelor's degrees are awarded in AGRICULTURE (natural resource management), BUSINESS (accounting, business administration and management, and recreational facilities management), COMMUNICATIONS AND THE ARTS (communications and visual and performing arts), COMPUTER AND PHYSICAL SCIENCE (information sciences and systems and natural sciences), EDUCATION (art, early childhood, and elementary), ENGINEERING AND ENVIRONMENTAL DESIGN (environmental science), SOCIAL SCIENCE (criminal justice). Visual art, environmental resource management, and natural sciences are the strongest academically. Criminal justice is the largest.

Required: To graduate, students must complete 123 to 130 credit hours and maintain a GPA of 2.0. The required core curriculum includes courses in interdisciplinary studies, math, English, speech, computer, and fitness. Distribution requirements and total credit hours vary with the major.

Special: Keystone offers co-op programs in all majors, as well as paid and unpaid internships. Study abroad is available and dependent on major interest or program. The Weekender program accommodates the needs of busy adult students and operates on a trimester basis. There are 3 national honor societies and a freshman honors program.

Faculty/Classroom: 43% of faculty are male; 58%, female. All teach undergraduates. The average class size in an introductory lecture is 18; in a laboratory, 9; and in a regular course, 15.

Admissions: 92% of the 2005-2006 applicants were accepted. The SAT scores for the 2005-2006 freshman class were: Verbal--74% below 500, 23% between 500 and 599, and 3% between 600 and 700; Math--74% below 500, 23% between 500 and 599, and 3% between 600 and 700. The ACT scores were 75% below 21, 17% between 21 and 23, and 8% between 24 and 26. 11% of the current freshmen were in the top fifth of their class; 34% were in the top two fifths.

Requirements: The SAT or ACT is required, the SAT is preferred. An interview is recommended for all. An art portfolio is required for all students whose intended major is art or art education. A GPA of 2.0 is required. AP and CLEP credits are accepted. Important factors in the admissions decision are extracurricular activities record, leadership record, and parents or siblings attending the school.

Procedure: Freshmen are admitted to all sessions. Entrance exams should be taken in the spring of the junior year or early fall of the senior year. There are deferred admissions and rolling admissions plans. Application deadlines are open. Applications are accepted on-line. The fall 2005 application fee was $25.

Transfer: 101 transfer students enrolled in 2004-2005. Applicants with more than 12 academic college credits must have a minimum GPA of 2.0. A letter of recommendation is required. 32 of 123 to 130 credits required for the bachelor's degree must be completed at Keystone College.

Visiting: There are regularly scheduled orientations for prospective students, consisting of 7 open houses and 3 visitation days. There are guides for informal visits and visitors may sit in on classes and stay overnight. To schedule a visit, contact the Admissions Office at 570-945-8111.

Financial Aid: In 2005-2006, 98% of all full-time freshmen and 96% of continuing full-time students received some form of financial aid. 86% of full-time freshmen and 87% of continuing full-time students received need-based aid. The average freshman award was $18,002. Need-based scholarships or need-based grants averaged $5093 ($16,756 maximum); need-based self-help aid (loans and jobs) averaged $3853 ($8075 maximum); and other non-need-based awards and non-need-based scholarships averaged $11,109 ($26,135 maximum). 55% of undergraduates work part time. Average annual earnings from campus work are $1393. The average financial indebtedness of the 2005 graduate was $20,628. Keystone College is a member of CSS. The FAFSA and the state aid form for Pennsylvania residents are required. The priority date for freshman financial aid applications for fall entry is April 1. The deadline for filing freshman financial aid applications for fall entry is August 1.

International Students: There are 15 international students enrolled. They must score satisfactorily on the written TOEFL or on the electronic version or the college's own test.

Computers: Wireless access is available. All students are provided with a network sign-on as well as an e-mail address. Most of the campus, including the residence halls, is wireless. Computer labs are located throughout the campus for student use. All students may access the system. There are no time limits. The fee is $300.

Graduates: From July 1, 2004 to June 30, 2005, 157 bachelor's degrees were awarded. The most popular majors were information technology (13%), sports and recreation management (12%), and elementary education (12%).

Admissions Contact: Sarah S. Keating, Director of Admissions. E-mail: *admissions@keystone.edu* Web: *www.keystone.edu*

KING'S COLLEGE
E-2
Wilkes Barre, PA 18711
(570) 208-5858
(888) 546-4772; Fax: (570) 208-5971

Full-time: 1009 men, 840 women	**Faculty:** 110; IIB, av$
Part-time: 95 men, 161 women	**Ph.D.s:** 83%
Graduate: 38 men, 161 women	**Student/Faculty:** 17 to 1
Year: semesters, summer session	**Tuition:** $21,220
Application Deadline: open	**Room & Board:** $8590
Freshman Class: n/av	
SAT or ACT: required	**COMPETITIVE**

King's College, founded in 1946, is a private institution affiliated with the Roman Catholic Church. The college offers undergraduate programs in humanities and natural and social sciences, specialized programs in business and other professions, and graduate programs in reading, health care administration, and physician assistant. In addition to regional accreditation, King's has baccalaureate program accreditation with AACSB, AMA, ACS, and CAAHEP. The library contains 171,558 volumes, 562,996 microform items, and 2719 audio/video tapes/CDs/DVDs, and subscribes to 15,750 periodicals including electronic. Computerized library services include the card catalog, interlibrary loans, database searching, Internet access, and laptop Internet portals. Special learning facilities include a learning resource center, art gallery, radio station, and a TV studio. The 48-acre campus is in an urban area in northeastern Pennsylvania 19 miles south of Scranton. Including any residence halls, there are 19 buildings.

Student Life: 77% of undergraduates are from Pennsylvania. Others are from 17 states, 7 foreign countries, and Canada. 67% are from public schools. 85% are white. 59% are Catholic; 27%; 13% Protestant. The average age of freshmen is 18; all undergraduates, 20. 19% do not continue beyond their first year; 70% remain to graduate.

Housing: 866 students can be accommodated in college housing, which includes single-sex dorms and on-campus apartments. On-campus housing is guaranteed for all 4 years. 57% of students commute. Alcohol is not permitted. All students may keep cars.

Activities: There are no fraternities or sororities. There are 50 groups on campus, including art, cheerleading, choir, chorale, chorus, computers, dance, debate, drama, ethnic, film, honors, international, jazz band, literary magazine, musical theater, newspaper, pep band, photography, political, professional, radio and TV, religious, social, social service, student government, and yearbook. Popular campus events include All College Ball, Student Activities Fair, and Friends and Family Weekend.

Sports: There are 11 intercollegiate sports for men and 10 for women, and 7 intramural sports for men and 6 for women. Facilities include a phys ed center, outdoor basketball courts, a fitness center, a wrestling room, racquetball courts, a swimming pool, a multipurpose area, a 3200-seat gym, a free weight area, an outdoor athletic complex with a field house, a field hockey field, a football stadium, and baseball, softball, and soccer fields.

Disabled Students: 99% of the campus is accessible. Wheelchair ramps, elevators, special parking, specially equipped rest rooms, special class scheduling, lowered drinking fountains, and lowered telephones are available.

Services: Counseling and information services are available, as is tutoring in every subject. The academic skills center provides a writing center, learning skills workshops, a tutoring program, and learning disability services.

Campus Safety and Security: Measures include 24-hour foot and vehicle patrol, self-defense education, security escort services, and informal discussions. There are pamphlets/posters/films, emergency telephones, and lighted pathways/sidewalks.

Programs of Study: King's confers B.A. and B.S. degrees. Associate and master's degrees are also awarded. Bachelor's degrees are awarded in AGRICULTURE (environmental studies), BIOLOGICAL SCIENCE (biology/biological science and neurosciences), BUSINESS (accounting, banking and finance, business administration and management, international business management, marketing/retailing/merchandising, and personnel management), COMMUNICATIONS AND THE ARTS (communications, dramatic arts, English, French, and Spanish), COMPUTER

AND PHYSICAL SCIENCE (chemistry, computer science, information sciences and systems, mathematics, and science), EDUCATION (early childhood, elementary, foreign languages, middle school, science, secondary, and special), HEALTH PROFESSIONS (medical laboratory technology, predentistry, premedicine, and sports medicine), SOCIAL SCIENCE (criminal justice, economics, history, philosophy, political science/government, prelaw, psychology, sociology, and theological studies). Accounting, English, and biology are the strongest academically. Business administration, elementary education, and criminal justice are the largest.

Required: All students must earn a minimum of 120 credits and maintain a GPA of 2.0. The core requirements represent 54 credits. The major comprises a maximum of 60 credits, of which up to 40 can be specified in the major department, with the balance designated for related fields.

Special: A co-op program in special education and cross-registration with Wilkes University and College Misericordia are offered. The Experiential Learning Program provides internship opportunities in all majors with a variety of employers. King's also offers study abroad through an agreement with Webster University and John Cabot University, a Washington semester, work-study programs in 6 countries, an accelerated degree program in business administration, B.A.-B.S. degrees in psychology, dual majors, credit for life experience, and pass/fail options on a few courses. Student-designed majors are available through the King's honors program. There are 11 national honor societies and a freshman honors program.

Faculty/Classroom: 65% of faculty are male; 35%, female. All teach undergraduates. No introductory courses are taught by graduate students. The average class size in an introductory lecture is 21; in a laboratory, 11; and in a regular course, 18.

Admissions: The SAT scores for the 2005-2006 freshman class were: Verbal--38% below 500, 46% between 500 and 599, 14% between 600 and 700, and 2% above 700; Math--35% below 500, 46% between 500 and 599, 17% between 600 and 700, and 2% above 700. 33% of the current freshmen were in the top fifth of their class; 60% were in the top two fifths. 2 freshmen graduated first in their class.

Requirements: The SAT or ACT is required. In addition, King's requires 16 academic credits, although 22 are recommended, including 4 in English, 3 each in science, math, and social studies, 2 in foreign language, and 1 in history. AP and CLEP credits are accepted. Important factors in the admissions decision are advanced placement or honor courses, extracurricular activities record, and leadership record.

Procedure: Freshmen are admitted fall and spring. Entrance exams should be taken so that scores are received by April 1. There is a deferred admissions plan. There is a rolling admissions plan. The fall 2005 application fee was $30. Application deadlines are open. Applications are accepted on-line.

Transfer: 90 transfer students enrolled in 2004-2005. Applicants must present a minimum GPA of 2.5. Students must have earned at least 12 credit hours at another college. An interview is recommended. 60 of 120 credits required for the bachelor's degree must be completed at King's.

Visiting: There are regularly scheduled orientations for prospective students, consisting of admissions interviews, financial aid presentations, faculty one-on-one meetings, and campus tours. There are guides for informal visits and visitors may sit in on classes and stay overnight. To schedule a visit, contact the Admissions Office at admissions@kings.edu.

Financial Aid: In 2005-2006, 98% of all full-time freshmen and 96% of continuing full-time students received some form of financial aid. 71% of full-time freshmen and 70% of continuing full-time students received need-based aid. The average freshman award was $16,135. Need-based scholarships or need-based grants averaged $5700 ($17,800 maximum); need-based self-help aid (loans and jobs) averaged $4400 ($6875 maximum); and other non-need-based awards and non-need-based scholarships averaged $7964 ($20,320 maximum). 26% of undergraduates work part time. Average annual earnings from campus work are $1200. The average financial indebtedness of the 2005 graduate was $17,263. King's is a member of CSS. The FAFSA and the college's own financial statement are required. The priority date for freshman financial aid applications for fall entry is February 15.

International Students: There are 7 international students enrolled. The school actively recruits these students. They must take the written TOEFL and also take the SAT or the ACT, scoring satisfactorily.

Computers: Wireless access is available. All students may access the system. 1 24-hour networked public lab exists, and 15 other networked labs. There are no time limits and no fees.

Graduates: From July 1, 2004 to June 30, 2005, 439 bachelor's degrees were awarded. The most popular majors were elementary education (12%), business administration (10%), and accounting (8%). In an average class, 62% graduate in 4 years or less, 69% graduate in 5 years or less, and 70% graduate in 6 years or less. 40 companies recruited on campus in 2004-2005. Of the 2004 graduating class, 18% were enrolled in graduate school within 6 months of graduation and 80% were employed.

Admissions Contact: Michelle Lawrence-Schmude, Director of Admissions. A video is available. E-mail: admissions@kings.edu Web: http://www.kings.edu

KUTZTOWN UNIVERSITY OF PENNSYLVANIA — E-3

Kutztown, PA 19530
(610) 683-4060
(877) 628-1915; Fax: (610) 683-1375

Full-time: 2985 men, 4260 women	Faculty: 343; IIA, +$
Part-time: 205 men, 615 women	Ph.D.s: 75%
Graduate: 280 men, 680 women	Student/Faculty: 21 to 1
Year: semesters, summer session	Tuition: $6000 ($12,950)
Application Deadline: open	Room & Board: $4820
Freshman Class: n/av	
SAT or ACT: required	COMPETITIVE

Kutztown University of Pennsylvania, founded in 1866, is a public institution within the Pennsylvania State System of Higher Education. The university offers undergraduate programs in the arts and sciences, business, education, and visual and performing arts. There are 4 undergraduate schools and 1 graduate school. Figures in the above capsule and profile are approximate. In addition to regional accreditation, KU has baccalaureate program accreditation with CSWE, NASAD, NASM, NCATE, and NLN. The library contains 497,752 volumes, 1,307,315 microform items, and 14,858 audio/video tapes/CDs/DVDs, and subscribes to 4265 periodicals including electronic. Computerized library services include the card catalog, interlibrary loans, and database searching. Special learning facilities include a learning resource center, art gallery, planetarium, radio station, TV station, a women's center, cartography lab, German Cultural Heritage Center, computer labs, and tutorial labs. The 326-acre campus is in a small town 90 miles north of Philadelphia, midway between Reading and Allentown. Including any residence halls, there are 61 buildings.

Student Life: 91% of undergraduates are from Pennsylvania. Others are from 21 states, 44 foreign countries, and Canada. 89% are white. The average age of freshmen is 19; all undergraduates, 22.

Housing: 3442 students can be accommodated in college housing, which includes single-sex and coed dormitories and on-campus apartments. In addition, there are honors houses and special-interest houses. On-campus housing is guaranteed for the freshman year only and is available on a first-come, first-served basis. 59% of students commute. Alcohol is not permitted. Upperclassmen may keep cars.

Activities: 1% of men belong to 4 national fraternities; 1% of women belong to 1 local and 4 national sororities. There are 140 groups on campus, including art, band, cheerleading, chess, choir, chorus, computers, dance, drama, ethnic, gay, honors, international, jazz band, literary magazine, marching band, musical theater, newspaper, orchestra, political, professional, prgramming board, radio and TV, recreational sports, religious, social, social service, student government, and yearbook. Popular campus events include Bearfest, Preforming Diversity, Welcome Week, and Five Days of Justice.

Sports: There are 10 intercollegiate sports for men and 12 for women, and 22 intramural sports for men and 19 for women. Facilities include a 7500-seat stadium and outdoor track, a 55,000-square-foot field house and 200-meter indoor track, a swimming pool, 9 outdoor tennis courts, a 4000-seat arena, athletic fields, a street hockey rink, basketball courts, a rifle range, a fitness center, and a free-weight room.

Disabled Students: 90% of the campus is accessible. Wheelchair ramps, elevators, special parking, specially equipped rest rooms, special class scheduling, and lowered drinking fountains are available. All programs are accessible to students with disabilities.

Services: Counseling and information services are available, as is tutoring in most subjects. There is a reader service for the blind, and remedial math, reading, and writing.

Campus Safety and Security: Measures include 24-hour foot and vehicle patrol, self-defense education, security escort services, and shuttle buses. There are informal discussions, pamphlets/posters/films, emergency telephones, lighted pathways/sidewalks, a bike patrol, crime prevention programs, automatic fire protection systems, door alarms, safety screens, and student monitors in the dorms.

Programs of Study: KU confers B.A., B.S., B.F.A., B.S.B.A., B.S.Ed., and B.S.N. degrees. Master's degrees are also awarded. Bachelor's degrees are awarded in BIOLOGICAL SCIENCE (biology/biological science and marine science), BUSINESS (accounting, banking and finance, business administration and management, business economics, international business management, and marketing/retailing/merchandising), COMMUNICATIONS AND THE ARTS (crafts, dramatic arts, English, fine arts, French, graphic design, music, Spanish, speech/debate/rhetoric, telecommunications, and visual and performing arts), COMPUTER AND PHYSICAL SCIENCE (chemistry, computer science, geology, mathematics, and physics), EDUCATION (art, early childhood, elementary, library science, secondary, and special), ENGINEERING AND ENVIRONMENTAL DESIGN (environmental science), HEALTH PROFESSIONS (medical laboratory technology, nursing, and speech pathology/audiology), SOCIAL SCIENCE (anthropology, criminal justice, geography, history, liberal arts/general studies, philosophy, political science/government, psychology, public administration, social work, and sociology). Physical science and math are the strongest academically. Business, psychology, and elementary education are the largest.

Required: General education requirements vary by program, but all students must take phys ed, speech, English composition, or introduction to dance. Distribution requirements also include courses in humanities, social sciences, natural sciences, and math. To graduate, students must complete at least 120 semester hours, including 33 to 80 in a major field, with a minimum GPA of 2.0. Students in the College of Liberal Arts and Sciences must take a comprehensive exam.

Special: Students may study abroad in 11 countries. There is a 3-2 engineering degree program with Pennsylvania State University and cross-registration with area colleges. KU also offers internships, student-designed majors, dual majors, and a general studies degree. Nondegree study is possible. There are 15 national honor societies, a freshman honors program, and 30 departmental honors programs.

Faculty/Classroom: 55% of faculty are male; 45%, female. 97% teach undergraduates. No introductory courses are taught by graduate students. The average class size in an introductory lecture is 35; in a laboratory, 20; and in a regular course, 22.

Requirements: The SAT or ACT is required. In addition, applicants must be graduates of accredited secondary schools or have earned a GED. Recommended Carnegie units include 4 each of English and social studies, 3 each of science and math, and 2 of foreign language. SAT: Subject tests in biology/chemistry are required for medical technology. Portfolios or auditions are required for art or music majors. KU requires applicants to be in the upper 50% of their class. A GPA of 2.0 is required. AP and CLEP credits are accepted.

Procedure: Freshmen are admitted fall and spring. Entrance exams should be taken no later than fall of the senior year. There are early admissions, deferred admissions, and rolling admissions plans. Application deadlines are open. Applications are accepted on-line. The fall 2005 application fee was $30.

Transfer: 555 transfer students enrolled in 2004-2005. Applicants must present a GPA of 2.0 (2.8 for education) and official transcripts from all colleges and secondary schools previously attended. Students transferring fewer than 30 credit hours must also submit the SAT I or ACT scores. 33 of 120 credits required for the bachelor's degree must be completed at KU.

Visiting: There are regularly scheduled orientations for prospective students, consisting of daily visits, including group tours. There is a comprehensive summer orientation program for enrolling students. There are guides for informal visits and visitors may sit in on classes. To schedule a visit, contact the Admissions Office.

Financial Aid: In a recent year, 67% of all full-time freshmen and 61% of continuing full-time students received some form of financial aid. 62% of full-time freshmen and 56% of continuing full-time students received need-based aid. The average freshman award was $5483. Need-based scholarships or need-based grants averaged $3792 ($7950 maximum); need-based self-help aid (loans and jobs) averaged $2545 ($5125 maximum); non-need-based athletic scholarships averaged $1027 ($8000 maximum); and other non-need-based awards and non-need-based scholarships averaged $1342 ($4600 maximum). 55% of undergraduates worked part time. Average annual earnings from campus work were $1002. The average financial indebtedness of ta recent graduate was $14,594. The FAFSA is required. Check with school for application deadlines.

International Students: They must score satisfactorily on the written TOEFL or on the electronic version.

Computers: All students may access the system. There are no time limits and no fees.

Graduates: In a recent year, 1575 bachelor's degrees were awarded. The most popular majors were elementary education (12%), psychology (7%), and English (5%). 50 companies recruited on campus in a recent year. Of a recent graduating class, 6% were enrolled in graduate school within 6 months of graduation and 96% were employed.

Admissions Contact: William Stahler, Director of Admissions.
E-mail: *admissions@kutztown.edu*
Web: *http://www.kutztown.edu/admissions*

LA ROCHE COLLEGE   B-3
Pittsburgh, PA 15237

	(412) 536-1275
	(800) 838-4LRC; Fax: (412) 847-1820
Full-time: 414 men, 788 women	Faculty: 64; IIA, --$
Part-time: 72 men, 26 women	Ph.D.s: 86%
Graduate: 72 men, 83 women	Student/Faculty: 19 to 1
Year: semesters, summer session	Tuition: $17,380
Application Deadline: open	Room & Board: $7344
Freshman Class: n/av	
SAT Verbal/Math: 490/480*	LESS COMPETITIVE

La Roche College, founded in 1963, is a private Catholic institution offering undergraduate programs in arts and sciences, business, graphic and interior design, health science, nursing, professional training, and religious studies. There are 2 undergraduate and 3 graduate schools. In addition to regional accreditation, La Roche has baccalaureate program accreditation with ACBSP, FIDER, NASAD, and NLN. The library contains 110,762 volumes, 33,760 microform items, and 825 audio/video tapes/CDs/DVDs, and subscribes to 7900 periodicals including electronic. Computerized library services include the card catalog, interlibrary loans, database searching, and Internet access. Special learning facilities include a learning resource center, art gallery, radio station, and interior and graphic design studios. The 100-acre campus is in a suburban area 10 miles north of Pittsburgh. Including any residence halls, there are 15 buildings.

Student Life: 85% of undergraduates are from Pennsylvania. Others are from 15 states, 32 foreign countries, and Canada. 82% are white; 11% foreign nationals. 49% claim no religious affiliation; 31% are Catholic; 12% Protestant; 7% Orthodox, Muslim, and Hindu. The average age of freshmen is 18; all undergraduates, 24. 27% do not continue beyond their first year; 62% remain to graduate.

Housing: 627 students can be accommodated in college housing, which includes coed dorms. On-campus housing is guaranteed for all 4 years. 65% of students commute. All students may keep cars.

Activities: There are no fraternities or sororities. There are 39 groups on campus, including art, cheerleading, chorus, computers, dance, ethnic, honors, international, literary magazine, newspaper, photography, political, professional, radio and TV, religious, social, social service, and student government. Popular campus events include Battle of the Bands, the Gateway Clipper Cruise, and the Spring Fling.

Sports: There are 5 intercollegiate sports for men and 5 for women, and 10 intramural sports for men and 9 for women. Facilities include soccer, softball, and baseball fields, a gym, tennis courts, hiking trails, a fitness/sports center that houses a gym, racquetball courts, an indoor track, an aerobics room, and a weight room, and a nearby county park with tennis courts and a swimming pool.

Disabled Students: 80% of the campus is accessible. Wheelchair ramps, elevators, special parking, specially equipped rest rooms, special class scheduling, lowered drinking fountains, and lowered telephones are available.

Services: Counseling and information services are available, as is tutoring in every subject. There is a reader service for the blind and remedial math and writing.

Campus Safety and Security: Measures include 24-hour foot and vehicle patrol, security escort service, shuttle buses, and informal discussions. There are pamphlets/posters/films, emergency telephones, lighted pathways/sidewalks, an intercom security system, and residence halls that are locked 24 hours a day.

Programs of Study: La Roche confers B.A., B.S., B.S.I.D., and B.S.N. degrees. Associate and master's degrees are also awarded. Bachelor's degrees are awarded in BIOLOGICAL SCIENCE (biology/biological science), BUSINESS (accounting, banking and finance, business administration and management, institutional management, international business management, marketing management, and real estate), COMMUNICATIONS AND THE ARTS (communications, creative writing, dance, English, and graphic design), COMPUTER AND PHYSICAL SCIENCE (chemistry, computer science, information sciences and systems, and mathematics), EDUCATION (elementary, English, foreign languages, and science), ENGINEERING AND ENVIRONMENTAL DESIGN (interior design), HEALTH PROFESSIONS (nursing, radiograph medical technology, and respiratory therapy), SOCIAL SCIENCE (criminal justice, history, human services, international studies, liberal arts/general studies, psychology, religion, religious education, and sociology). Graphic design, interior design, and professional writing are the strongest academically. Design areas, elementary education, and criminal justice are the largest.

Required: 12 credits in basic skills areas, including math and computer applications, and 12 credits in liberal arts areas, including history, science, religion or philosophy, aesthetics, literature, and social and cultural systems, are required. Also, a 9-credit sequence of 3 interdisciplinary courses that emphasizes the concepts of community, the individual, and global perspectives is required. A minimum of 120 credit hours and a GPA of 2.0 are requirements for graduation, as is a senior seminar in most majors. Some majors require a higher GPA and slightly more credit hours.

Special: There is cross-registration with members of the Pittsburgh Council of Higher Education. Internships, for which students may receive up to 6 credits, are available for juniors and seniors with numerous employers in the Pittsburgh area. La Roche also offers study abroad in 13 countries, a Washington semester, dual majors, credit for life experience, directed research, honors programs, independent study, and pass/fail options. Accelerated degrees may be earned in management, criminal justice, and nursing. A 3-2 engineering degree with the University of Pittsburgh is possible, as are cooperative programs in athletic training, physician's assistant, physical therapy, speech/language pathology, and occupational therapy with Duquesne University.

Faculty/Classroom: 53% of faculty are male; 47%, female. 95% teach undergraduates. No introductory courses are taught by graduate stu-

dents. The average class size in an introductory lecture is 28; in a laboratory, 12; and in a regular course, 14.

Admissions: The SAT scores for the 2005-2006 freshman class were: Verbal--53% below 500, 40% between 500 and 599, 6% between 600 and 700, and 1% above 700; Math--57% below 500, 36% between 500 and 599, 6% between 600 and 700, and 1% above 700. The ACT scores were 52% below 21, 24% between 21 and 23, 12% between 24 and 26, and 12% between 27 and 28. 25% of the current freshmen were in the top fifth of their class; 48% were in the top two fifths.

Requirements: The SAT or ACT is required. In addition, applicants must be graduates of accredited secondary schools or have earned a GED. An interview is recommended for all applicants. At least 2 letters of recommendation are required. A GPA of 2.0 is required. AP and CLEP credits are accepted. Important factors in the admissions decision are advanced placement or honor courses, personality/intangible qualities, and recommendations by school officials.

Procedure: Freshmen are admitted to all sessions. Entrance exams should be taken by the fall of the senior year. There is a rolling admissions plan. Application deadlines are open. The fall 2005 application fee was $50. Applications are accepted on-line.

Transfer: 167 transfer students enrolled in 2004-2005. Transfer design students may be required to submit a portfolio and must have a 2.0 GPA. 30 of 120 credits required for the bachelor's degree must be completed at La Roche.

Visiting: There are regularly scheduled orientations for prospective students, including an overnight stay, information and interactive sessions, class attendance, and meeting with faculty. There are also 1-day visits on Saturday. There are guides for informal visits and visitors may sit in on classes and stay overnight. To schedule a visit, contact the Admissions Office at *admissions@laroche.edu*.

Financial Aid: In 2005-2006, 98% of all full-time freshmen and 90% of continuing full-time students received some form of financial aid. 62% of full-time freshmen and 76% of continuing full-time students received need-based aid. The average freshman award was $16,855. Need-based scholarships or need-based grants averaged $3030; need-based self-help aid (loans and jobs) averaged $4379; and other non-need-based awards and non-need-based scholarships averaged $7732 ($10,000 maximum). 15% of undergraduates work part time. Average annual earnings from campus work are $900. The average financial indebtedness of the 2005 graduate was $18,000. La Roche is a member of CSS. The FAFSA and the college's own financial statement are required. The priority date for freshman financial aid applications for fall entry is February 15. The deadline for filing freshman financial aid applications for fall entry is April 15.

International Students: There are 153 international students enrolled. The school actively recruits these students. They must score satisfactorily on the electronic TOEFL or if their native language is English, they must take the SAT or ACT.

Computers: All students may access the system. There are no time limits and no fees. It is recommended that students in facility management, graphic design, interior design, and communication have personal computers. IBM ThinkPads and Apple PowerBooks are recommended.

Graduates: From July 1, 2004 to June 30, 2005, 323 bachelor's degrees were awarded. The most popular majors were elementary education (10%), graphic design (8%), and psychology, management, and information technology (7%).

Admissions Contact: Thomas Hassett, Director of Admissions. A video is available. E-mail: *admissions@laroche.edu*
Web: *www.laroche.edu*

LA SALLE UNIVERSITY F-3
Philadelphia, PA 19141-1199

(215) 951-1500
(800) 328-1910; Fax: (215) 951-1656

Full-time: 1488 men, 1847 women	**Faculty:** 188; IIA, av$
Part-time: 247 men, 757 women	**Ph.D.s:** 88%
Graduate: 651 men, 1148 women	**Student/Faculty:** 18 to 1
Year: semesters, summer session	**Tuition:** $26,080
Application Deadline: April 1	**Room & Board:** $8870
Freshman Class: 4565 applied, 3248 accepted, 756 enrolled	
SAT Verbal/Math: 550/550*	**ACT:** required **COMPETITIVE**

La Salle University, founded in 1863, is a private institution conducted under the auspices of the Christian Brothers of the Roman Catholic Church. The university offers undergraduate and graduate programs in the arts and sciences, business, education, fine arts, religious studies, and nursing. There are 3 undergraduate and 3 graduate schools. In addition to regional accreditation, La Salle has baccalaureate program accreditation with AACSB, AACTE, ACS, CAA=ASHA, CADE=ADA, CCNE, CSWE, and NLN. The library contains 370,000 volumes, 265,000 microform items, and 10,000 audio/video tapes/CDs/DVDs, and subscribes to 7450 periodicals including electronic. Computerized library services include the card catalog, interlibrary loans, database searching, Internet access, and laptop Internet portals. Special learning facilities include a learning resource center, art gallery, radio station, and TV station. The 100-acre campus is in an urban area 8 miles northwest of the center of Philadelphia. Including any residence halls, there are 49 buildings.

Student Life: 59% of undergraduates are from Pennsylvania. Others are from 33 states, 25 foreign countries, and Canada. 50% are from public schools. 81% are white; 10% African American. 81% are Catholic; 15% Protestant. The average age of freshmen is 19; all undergraduates, 21. 16% do not continue beyond their first year; 70% remain to graduate.

Housing: 2204 students can be accommodated in college housing, which includes single-sex and coed dorms and on-campus apartments. In addition, there are honors houses, for which student groups may submit proposals for use. Townhouses and apartments are available to juniors and seniors. On-campus housing is guaranteed for all 4 years. 64% of students live on campus; of those, 70% remain on campus on weekends. All students may keep cars.

Activities: 14% of men belong to 1 local and 6 national fraternities; 14% of women belong to 1 local and 4 national sororities. There are 111 groups on campus, including band, cheerleading, choir, computers, dance, drama, drill team, ethnic, film, honors, international, jazz band, literary magazine, newspaper, orchestra, pep band, political, professional, radio and TV, religious, social, social service, student government, and yearbook. Popular campus events include Oktoberfest, Family Weekend, and Diplomat in Residence Program.

Sports: There are 11 intercollegiate sports for men and 12 for women, and 14 intramural sports for men and 14 for women. Facilities include a 7000-seat stadium, a 4000-seat gym, a 500-seat auditorium, 4 playing fields, 6 tennis courts, a fully equipped athletic and exercise facility, wrestling rooms, a sauna, racquetball and squash courts, outdoor tracks, basketball and volleyball courts, and an indoor swimming pool.

Disabled Students: 95% of the campus is accessible. Wheelchair ramps, elevators, special parking, specially equipped rest rooms, special class scheduling, and lowered drinking fountains are available.

Services: Counseling and information services are available, as is tutoring in some subjects, including English, math, and accounting. A writing center is also available.

Campus Safety and Security: Measures include 24-hour foot and vehicle patrol, security escort services, shuttle buses, and emergency telephones. There are lighted pathways/sidewalks and magnetic card access to residence facilities.

Programs of Study: La Salle confers B.A., B.S., B.S.N., and B.S.W. degrees. Associate, master's, and doctoral degrees are also awarded. Bachelor's degrees are awarded in BIOLOGICAL SCIENCE (biochemistry, biology/biological science, and nutrition), BUSINESS (accounting, banking and finance, business administration and management, international economics, management information systems, marketing/retailing/merchandising, and organizational behavior), COMMUNICATIONS AND THE ARTS (classical languages, communications, English, fine arts, French, German, Italian, multimedia, music, Russian, and Spanish), COMPUTER AND PHYSICAL SCIENCE (chemistry, computer science, geology, information sciences and systems, mathematics, and science), EDUCATION (elementary, foreign languages, science, secondary, social studies, and special), ENGINEERING AND ENVIRONMENTAL DESIGN (computer graphics and environmental science), HEALTH PROFESSIONS (nursing, preallied health, predentistry, premedicine, and speech pathology/audiology), SOCIAL SCIENCE (criminal justice, economics, history, philosophy, political science/government, prelaw, psychology, public administration, religion, social work, and sociology). English, accounting, and education are the strongest academically. Communication, education, and nursing are the largest.

Required: Students take courses in writing, computer science, religion, philosophy, history, literature, math, the natural sciences, the social sciences, and information technology. The core curriculum is distinguished by 2 requirements: the "double," a thematically linked pair of courses taught by 2 facility partners from different disciplines, and the "metro," a year-long program of cocurricular activities conducted by a faculty member and designed to help students take advantage of the resources of the City of Philadelphia.

Special: Cross-registration is offered in conjunction with Chestnut Hill College, and there is a 2-2 program in allied health with Thomas Jefferson University. La Salle also offers study abroad, co-op programs in business and computer science, work-study programs, internships in most majors, dual majors, an honors program for gifted students, and pass/fail options. An E-Commerce Institute has been created to educate all students about this business tool. An integrated science, business, and technology program is offered. There are 14 national honor societies and a freshman honors program.

Faculty/Classroom: 52% of faculty are male; 48%, female. 88% teach undergraduates and 60% do research. No introductory courses are taught by graduate students. The average class size in an introductory lecture is 23; in a laboratory, 14; and in a regular course, 19.

Admissions: 71% of the 2005-2006 applicants were accepted. The SAT scores for the 2005-2006 freshman class were: Verbal--25% below 500, 45% between 500 and 599, 29% between 600 and 700, and 2% above 700; Math--23% below 500, 50% between 500 and 599, 24% be-

tween 600 and 700, and 3% above 700. 36% of the current freshmen were in the top fifth of their class; 63% were in the top two fifths. 11 freshmen graduated first in their class in a recent year.

Requirements: The SAT or ACT is required. In addition, the SAT: Subject test in math is recommended. Applicants must be graduates of accredited secondary schools or have earned a GED. La Salle requires 16 academic units, based on 4 years of English, 3 of math, 2 of foreign language, and 1 of history, with the remaining 5 units in academic electives; science and math majors must have an additional one-half unit of math. An essay is required, and an interview is recommended. La Salle requires applicants to be in the upper 50% of their class. AP and CLEP credits are accepted. Important factors in the admissions decision are advanced placement or honor courses, leadership record, and recommendations by school officials.

Procedure: Freshmen are admitted fall and spring. Entrance exams should be taken before January of the senior year. There is a rolling admissions and a deferred admissions plan. Applications should be filed by April 1 for fall entry and December 15 for spring entry, along with a $35 fee. Notification is sent on a rolling basis. Applications are accepted online.

Transfer: 196 transfer students enrolled in 2004-2005. Transfer applicants should have a minimum cumulative GPA of 2.5. Nursing applicants should have at least a 3.0. 50 of 120 credits required for the bachelor's degree must be completed at La Salle.

Visiting: There are regularly scheduled orientations for prospective students, including campus tours 7 Saturdays throughout the fall, 1 Saturday during the winter, and 3 Saturdays during the spring. There are guides for informal visits and visitors may sit in on classes and stay overnight. To schedule a visit, contact the Admissions Office at *admissions@lasalle.edu*.

Financial Aid: In 2005-2006, 93% of all full-time freshmen and 86% of continuing full-time students received some form of financial aid. 79% of full-time freshmen and 68% of continuing full-time students received need-based aid. The average freshman award was $17,858. Need-based scholarships or need-based grants averaged $15,838 ($36,190 maximum); need-based self-help aid (loans and jobs) averaged $11,297 ($30,629 maximum); and non-need-based athletic scholarships averaged $11,553 ($15,688 maximum). 15% of undergraduates work part time. Average annual earnings from campus work are $1800. The average financial indebtedness of the 2005 graduate was $26,405. The FAFSA is required. The deadline for filing freshman financial aid applications for fall entry is February 15.

International Students: There are 75 international students enrolled. The school actively recruits these students. They must score satisfactorily on the written TOEFL or on the electronic version.

Computers: A wireless network extends through every academic building and most nonresidence campus areas. Internet bandwidth is based on Gigabit Ethernet technology, at T3 capacity. There are student PC labs and classrooms, and SunRay Smart terminals in kiosks in common areas and lounges. Student help desk support is available from 8 A.M. until 11P.M. as well as on-line support. The university's web portal includes innovative applications, as well as the customary on-line registration, financial aid information, grades, and so on. Student subscriptions to RealNetworks Rhapsody are also offered at a greatly reduced rate. All students may access the system 8 A.M. to 11 P.M. weekdays, 9 A.M. to 7 P.M. Saturday, and noon to 11 P.M. Sunday. There are no time limits and no fees.

Graduates: From July 1, 2004 to June 30, 2005, 893 bachelor's degrees were awarded. The most popular majors were communications (13%), education (11%), and nursing (9%). In an average class, 56% graduate in 4 years or less, 70% graduate in 5 years or less, and 72% graduate in 6 years or less. 198 companies recruited on campus in 2004-2005. Of the 2004 graduating class, 18% were enrolled in graduate school within 6 months of graduation and 91% were employed.

Admissions Contact: Robert Voss, Dean of Admissions and Financial Aid. E-mail: *admiss@lasalle.edu* Web: *lasalle.edu*

LAFAYETTE COLLEGE	F-3
Easton, PA 18042	(610) 330-5100; Fax: (610) 330-5355
Full-time: 1198 men, 1083 women	Faculty: 195; IIB, ++$
Part-time: 32 men, 33 women	Ph.D.s: 100%
Graduate: none	Student/Faculty: 12 to 1
Year: semesters, summer session	Tuition: $29,982
Application Deadline: January 1	Room & Board: $9285
Freshman Class: n/av	
SAT or ACT: required	MOST COMPETITIVE

Lafayette College, founded in 1826 is a highly selective, private institution emphasizing the liberal arts, sciences, and engineering. In addition to regional accreditation, Lafayette has baccalaureate program accreditation with ABET and ACS. The 2 libraries contain 510,000 volumes and 120,000 microform items, and subscribe to 2600 periodicals including electronic. Computerized library services include the card catalog, interlibrary loans, and database searching. Special learning facilities in-

clude a learning resource center, art gallery, radio station, geological museum, foreign languages lab, and calculus lab. The 342-acre campus is in a suburban area 70 miles west of New York City. Including any residence halls, there are 65 buildings.

Student Life: 72% of undergraduates are from out of state, mostly the Middle Atlantic. Students are from 30 states, 40 foreign countries, and Canada. 70% are from public schools. 82% are white. 37% are Catholic; 30% Protestant; 15% claim no religious affiliation; 11% Jewish; 7% Hindu, Muslim, and others. The average age of freshmen is 18; all undergraduates, 20. 5% do not continue beyond their first year; 92% remain to graduate.

Housing: 2100 students can be accommodated in college housing, which includes single-sex and coed dorms, on-campus apartments, off-campus apartments, fraternity houses, and sorority houses. In addition, there are honors houses and special-interest houses. On-campus housing is guaranteed for all 4 years. 98% of students live on campus; of those, 95% remain on campus on weekends. Upperclassmen may keep cars.

Activities: 26% of men belong to 8 national fraternities; 45% of women belong to 6 national sororities. There are 250 groups on campus, including AIDS awareness,art, band, cheerleading, chess, choir, chorale, chorus, computers, dance, debate, drama, ethnic, film, forensics, gay, honors, international, jazz band, literary magazine, musical theater, newspaper, orchestra, pep band, photography, political, professional, radio and TV, religious, social, social service, student government, and yearbook. Popular campus events include All College Day, Earth Day, and International Extravaganza.

Sports: There are 11 intercollegiate sports for men and 11 for women, and 22 intramural sports for men and 22 for women. Facilities include a 14,000-seat stadium; a sports center containing a 3500-seat gym, a field house, a varsity house, a natatorium, a fitness center, 2 exercise rooms, a weight training room, an outdoor track, an indoor track, a climbing wall, 6 racquet courts, and 3 multipurpose courts; and a 230-acre athletic complex for lacrosse, field hockey, soccer, and baseball.

Disabled Students: 95% of the campus is accessible. Wheelchair ramps, elevators, special parking, specially equipped rest rooms, special class scheduling, lowered drinking fountains, and lowered telephones are available.

Services: Counseling and information services are available, as is tutoring in most subjects, including most 100-level and many 200-level classes.

Campus Safety and Security: Measures include 24-hour foot and vehicle patrol, self-defense education, security escort services, and shuttle buses. There are informal discussions, pamphlets/posters/films, emergency telephones, lighted pathways/sidewalks, and advisers in all residence halls. Residence halls are locked from 8 P.M. to 7 A.M. and are accessible by room keys and outside telephones.

Programs of Study: Lafayette confers A.B., B.S., and B.S.Eng. degrees. Bachelor's degrees are awarded in BIOLOGICAL SCIENCE (biochemistry, biology/biological science, and neurosciences), BUSINESS (business economics and international economics), COMMUNICATIONS AND THE ARTS (art, English, French, German, music, and Spanish), COMPUTER AND PHYSICAL SCIENCE (chemistry, computer science, geology, mathematics, and physics), ENGINEERING AND ENVIRONMENTAL DESIGN (chemical engineering, civil engineering, electrical/electronics engineering, engineering, and mechanical engineering), SOCIAL SCIENCE (African studies, American studies, anthropology, economics, history, interdisciplinary studies, international relations, philosophy, political science/government, prelaw, psychology, religion, Russian and Slavic studies, and sociology). Engineering, psychology, and English are the strongest academically. Economics, business, and engineering are the largest.

Required: To graduate, students must maintain a GPA of 2.0 over a minimum of 32 to 38 courses. The common course of study, designed to build a background in the liberal arts and sciences in the first 2 years, includes interdisciplinary seminars, 3 courses in humanities/social science, 2 in natural science, and 1 each in college writing and math/computer science/philosophy. Students must fulfill a foreign culture requirement, and A.B. and B.S. majors must take 2 upper-level writing courses.

Special: Cross-registration through the Lehigh Valley Association of Independent Colleges, internships in all academic departments, study abroad in 3 countries as well as through other individually arranged plans, a Washington semester at American University, and work-study programs with area employers are possible. An accelerated degree plan in all majors, dual and student-designed majors, 5-year dual-degree programs, and pass/fail options in any nonmajor subject also are available. There are 12 national honor societies, including Phi Beta Kappa, and 24 departmental honors programs.

Faculty/Classroom: 74% of faculty are male; 26%, female. All both teach and do research. The average class size in a laboratory is 12 and in a regular course, 17.

Requirements: The SAT or ACT is required. The ACT Optional Writing test is also required. In addition, applicants need 4 years of English, 3 of math (4 for science or engineering majors), 2 each of a foreign language and lab science (with physics and chemistry for science or engineering students), and at least an additional 5 units in academic subjects. An essay is required and an interview recommended. Evaluations from the secondary school counselor and a teacher are required. The GED is accepted. AP credits are accepted. Important factors in the admissions decision are advanced placement or honor courses, evidence of special talent, and personality/intangible qualities.

Procedure: Freshmen are admitted in the fall. Entrance exams should be taken by January of the senior year. There are early decision and deferred admissions plans. Early decision applications should be filed by January 1; regular applications, by January 1 for fall entry, along with a $60 fee. Notification of early decision is sent within 30 days of receipt of the application; regular decision, mid-March. 249 early decision candidates were accepted for the 2005-2006 class. 650 applicants were on the 2005 waiting list; 67 were admitted. Applications are accepted online.

Transfer: 4 transfer students enrolled in 2004-2005. Acceptance usually depends on college-level performance and achievements. An interview is required if the student lives within 200 miles of the college. No minimum GPA is required, and neither the SAT nor the ACT is needed. The number of credit hours required varies with the program, but usually enough for freshman status with advanced standing is needed. 16 of 32 credits required for the bachelor's degree must be completed at Lafayette.

Visiting: There are regularly scheduled orientations for prospective students, including student/faculty panel discussions, tours, and departmental open houses. There are guides for informal visits and visitors may sit in on classes and stay overnight. To schedule a visit, contact the Admissions Office at *admissions@lafayette.edu*.

Financial Aid: In 2005-2006, 44% of all full-time freshmen and 55% of continuing full-time students received some form of financial aid. 45% of full-time freshmen and 48% of continuing full-time students received need-based aid. The average freshman award was $26,435. Need-based scholarships or need-based grants averaged $26,435 ($29,822 maximum). 54% of undergraduates work part time. Average annual earnings from campus work are $900. The average financial indebtedness of the 2005 graduate was $19,373. The CSS Profile or FAFSA, the college's own financial statement, and the Business/Farm supplement and Divorce/Separation parent statement (if applicable) are required. The deadline for filing freshman financial aid applications for fall entry is February 15.

International Students: There are 128 international students enrolled. The school actively recruits these students. A satisfactory score is required on the written TOEFL. Students must also take the SAT, or the ACT.

Computers: Wireless access is available. All students may access the system 24 hours per day. There are no time limits and no fees.

Graduates: From July 1, 2004 to June 30, 2005, 558 bachelor's degrees were awarded. The most popular majors were engineering (16%), economics and business (14%), and government and law (10%). In an average class, 1% graduate in 3 years or less, 89% graduate in 4 years or less, and 93% graduate in 5 years or less. 250 companies recruited on campus in 2004-2005. Of the 2004 graduating class, 24% were enrolled in graduate school within 6 months of graduation and 76% were employed.

Admissions Contact: Carol Rowlands, Director of Admissions. A video is available. E-mail: *rowlandc@lafayette.edu*
Web: *www.lafayette.edu*

LEBANON VALLEY COLLEGE E-3
Annville, PA 17003-1400

	(717) 867-6181
	(866) LVC-4ADM; Fax: (717) 867-6026
Full-time: 747 men, 867 women	Faculty: 100; IIB, av$
Part-time: 39 men, 121 women	Ph.D.s: 84%
Graduate: 56 men, 85 women	Student/Faculty: 16 to 1
Year: semesters, summer session	Tuition: $24,860
Application Deadline: open	Room & Board: $6840
Freshman Class: 2005 applied, 1537 accepted, 454 enrolled	
SAT Verbal/Math: 554/569*	**VERY COMPETITIVE**

Founded in 1866, Lebanon Valley College offers 33 major fields of study, students can developed their own individualized major. LVC offers graduate programs in physical therapy, business, education, and science. In addition to regional accreditation, LVC has baccalaureate program accreditation with NASM. The library contains 184,189 volumes, 14,290 microform items, and 11,143 audio/video tapes/CDs/DVDs, and subscribes to 820 periodicals including electronic. Computerized library services include the card catalog, interlibrary loans, database searching, Internet access, and laptop Internet portals. Special learning facilities include a learning resource center, art gallery, and radio station. The 340-acre campus is in a small town 6 miles east of Hershey. Including any residence halls, there are 46 buildings.

Student Life: 79% of undergraduates are from Pennsylvania. Students are from 20 states, 4 foreign countries, and Canada. 94% are from pub-

lic schools. 89% are white. Most claim no religious affiliation. The average age of freshmen is 18; all undergraduates, 21. 15% do not continue beyond their first year; 74% remain to graduate.

Housing: 1173 students can be accommodated in college housing, which includes single-sex and coed dorms and on-campus apartments. In addition, there are special-interest houses, suite-style living, substance-free and clean air halls. On-campus housing is guaranteed for all 4 years. 76% of students live on campus; of those, 60% remain on campus on weekends. All students may keep cars.

Activities: 14% of men and about 1% of women belong to 2 local and 2 national fraternities; 12% of women belong to 1 local and 3 national sororities. There are 77 groups on campus, including band, cheerleading, choir, chorus, computers, concert band, drama, drill team, ethnic, gay, honors, international, jazz band, literary magazine, marching band, music ensembles, musical theater, newspaper, orchestra, photography, political, professional, radio and TV, religious, social, social service, student government, symphony, and yearbook. Popular campus events include Christmas at the Valley and Valley Festival.

Sports: There are 11 intercollegiate sports for men and 10 for women, and 9 intramural sports for men and 9 for women. Facilities include a 3000-seat stadium, a sports center, more than 60 acres of athletic fields, indoor and outdoor tracks, a 1660 seat gym, playing courts for basketball, handball, squash, and tennis, a 500-seat baseball grandstand, and a football field.

Disabled Students: 80% of the campus is accessible. Wheelchair ramps, elevators, special parking, specially equipped rest rooms, special class scheduling, lowered drinking fountains, lowered telephones, and special housing are available.

Services: Counseling and information services are available, as is tutoring in every subject. There is a reader service for the blind.

Campus Safety and Security: Measures include 24-hour foot and vehicle patrol, self-defense education, security escort services, and informal discussions. There are pamphlets/posters/films, emergency telephones, and lighted pathways/sidewalks.

Programs of Study: LVC confers B.A., B.S., B.M., B.S.Ch., and B.S.Med.Tech. degrees. Associate, master's, and doctoral degrees are also awarded. Bachelor's degrees are awarded in BIOLOGICAL SCIENCE (biochemistry and biology/biological science), BUSINESS (accounting and business administration and management), COMMUNICATIONS AND THE ARTS (art, audio technology, communications technology, English, French, German, music, and Spanish), COMPUTER AND PHYSICAL SCIENCE (actuarial science, chemistry, computer science, mathematics, and physics), EDUCATION (elementary and music), HEALTH PROFESSIONS (health, medical laboratory technology, and physical therapy), SOCIAL SCIENCE (American studies, economics, history, philosophy, political science/government, psychobiology, psychology, religion, and sociology). Actuarial science, natural sciences, and education are the strongest academically. Education, business, and natural sciences are the largest.

Required: The general education program consists of course work in these areas: communications, liberal studies, foreign studies, cultural diversity studies, and disciplinary perspectives. Students are required to complete 3 writing-intensive courses and be proficient in computer applications and modes of information access and retrieval. To graduate, students must complete at least 120 credit hours, 2 units of phys ed, and the requirements for the major with a minimum GPA of 2.0.

Special: Study abroad opportunities are available in Argentina, Australia, England, France, Germany, Greece, Sweden, Spain, the Netherlands, and New Zealand. There are also 2 off-campus domestic programs in Philadelphia and Washingtgon, D.C. There are 3-2 degree programs in engineering with Penn State University, Case Western Reserve, and Widener Universities, and in forestry with Duke University. There is also a 2-2 degree program in allied health sciences with Thomas Jefferson University. LVC offers internships in a number of areas. There are 6 national honor societies, and 11 departmental honors programs.

Faculty/Classroom: 59% of faculty are male; 41%, female. 92% teach undergraduates. No introductory courses are taught by graduate students. The average class size in an introductory lecture is 22; in a laboratory, 14; and in a regular course, 16.

Admissions: 77% of the 2005-2006 applicants were accepted. The SAT scores for the 2005-2006 freshman class were: Verbal--22% below 500, 50% between 500 and 599, 26% between 600 and 700, and 2% above 700; Math--18% below 500, 44% between 500 and 599, 34% between 600 and 700, and 4% above 700. 56% of the current freshmen were in the top fifth of their class; 79% were in the top two fifths. 7 freshmen graduated first in their class.

Requirements: The SAT or ACT is required. In addition, applicants must be graduates of accredited secondary schools or have earned a GED. LVC requires 16 academic units or 16 Carnegie units, including 4 in English, 2 each in math and foreign language, and 1 each in science and social studies. An interview is recommended. Students applying as music majors must audition. AP and CLEP credits are accepted. Important factors in the admissions decision are advanced placement or honor courses, leadership record, and personality/intangible qualities.

Procedure: Freshmen are admitted fall and spring. Entrance exams should be taken in the spring of the junior year. Application deadlines are open. There is a rolling admissions plan. Application fee is $30. 15 applicants were on the 2005 waiting list; 10 were admitted. Applications are accepted on-line.

Transfer: 52 transfer students enrolled in 2004-2005. Requirements for transfer applicants include a minimum GPA of 2.0, SAT scores, and an interview. 30 of 120 credits required for the bachelor's degree must be completed at LVC.

Visiting: There are regularly scheduled orientations for prospective students, including tours, interviews, and meetings with professors. There are guides for informal visits and visitors may sit in on classes. To schedule a visit, contact Susan Sarisky, Director of Admission.

Financial Aid: In 2005-2006, 99% of all full-time freshmen and 97% of continuing full-time students received some form of financial aid. 80% of full-time freshmen and 76% of continuing full-time students received need-based aid. The average freshman award was $20,556. Need-based scholarships or need-based grants averaged $15,235 ($21,260 maximum); need-based self-help aid (loans and jobs) averaged $4558 ($6125 maximum); and other non-need-based awards and non-need-based scholarships averaged $10,125 ($24,210 maximum). 50% of undergraduates work part time. Average annual earnings from campus work are $853. The average financial indebtedness of the 2005 graduate was $24,236. LVC is a member of CSS. The FAFSA and the college's own financial statement are required. The priority date for freshman financial aid applications for fall entry is March 1.

International Students: There are 8 international students enrolled. They must score satisfactorily on the written TOEFL or on the electronic version and also take the SAT or the ACT.

Computers: Wireless access is available. Students use the network and other computer facilities for academic or other pruposes. There are more than 200 PC's for student use in the library, academic buildings, and student center. Internet access is available throughout campus including the residence halls. All students may access the system. This fee is $100/semester for full-time residents and $50/semester for full-time commuters.

Graduates: From July 1, 2004 to June 30, 2005, 374 bachelor's degrees were awarded. The most popular majors were business administration (22%), education (18%), and psychology (11%). In an average class, 69% graduate in 4 years or less, 73% graduate in 5 years or less, and 74% graduate in 6 years or less. 39 companies recruited on campus in 2004-2005. Of the 2004 graduating class, 13% were enrolled in graduate school within 6 months of graduation and 87% were employed.

Admissions Contact: Susan Sarisky, Director of Admission.
E-mail: *admission@lvc.edu* Web: *www.lvc.edu*

LEHIGH UNIVERSITY
F-3

Bethlehem, PA 18015

	(610) 758-3100; Fax: (610) 758-4361
Full-time: 2724 men, 1897 women	Faculty: 434; I, av$
Part-time: 40 men, 18 women	Ph.Ds: 99%
Graduate: 1114 men, 955 women	Student/Faculty: 11 to 1
Year: semesters, summer session	Tuition: $33,770
Application Deadline: January 1	Room & Board: $8920
Freshman Class: 10,501 applied, 4340 accepted, 1223 enrolled	
SAT Verbal/Math: 625/670*	ACT: required
	HIGHLY COMPETITIVE+

Lehigh University, founded in 1865, is a private university offering both undergraduate and graduate programs in liberal arts, science, engineering, and business, and graduate programs in education. There are 3 undergraduate and 4 graduate schools. In addition to regional accreditation, Lehigh has baccalaureate program accreditation with AACSB, ABET, and NCATE. The 2 libraries contain 1,354,100 volumes, 2,113,130 microform items, and 3915 audio/video tapes/CDs/DVDs, and subscribe to 10,797 periodicals including electronic. Computerized library services include the card catalog, interlibrary loans, and database searching. Special learning facilities include a learning resource center, art gallery, radio station, TV station, Special Collections/Rare Book Reading Room, and International Multimedia Resource Center. The 1600-acre campus is in a suburban area 60 miles north of Philadelphia and 80 miles southwest of New York City. Including any residence halls, there are 153 buildings.

Student Life: 72% of undergraduates are from out of state, mostly the Middle Atlantic. Students are from 49 states, 45 foreign countries, and Canada. 70% are from public schools. 76% are white. The average age of freshmen is 18; all undergraduates, 20. 7% do not continue beyond their first year; 85% remain to graduate.

Housing: 3240 students can be accommodated in college housing, which includes coed dormitories, on-campus apartments, married-student housing, fraternity houses, and sorority houses. In addition, there are special-interest houses. A students -of -color house, a creative arts house, an ROTC house, substance-free housing, and special housing for international students. On-campus housing is guaranteed for the freshman year only, is available on a first-come, first-served basis, and

is available on a lottery system for upperclassmen. 69% of students live on campus; of those, 75% remain on campus on weekends. Upperclassmen may keep cars.

Activities: 33% of men belong to 27 national fraternities; 39% of women belong to 8 national sororities. There are 200 groups on campus, including art, band, cheerleading, chess, choir, chorale, chorus, computers, dance, drama, ethnic, gay, honors, international, jazz band, literary magazine, marching band, musical theater, newspaper, orchestra, photography, political, professional, radio and TV, religious, social, social service, student government, and yearbook. Popular campus events include Greek Week, Spring Fest, and South Side Alive (carnival with the community).

Sports: There are 12 intercollegiate sports for men and 11 for women, and 23 intramural sports for men and 22 for women. Facilities include a 16,000-seat stadium, a 6500-seat arena, a gym, a champion cross-country course, a field house with basketball and tennis courts, swimming pools, a track, indoor squash and racquetball courts, playing fields including astro-turf for field hockey, football, lacrosse, and soccer, weight rooms, a fitness center, and an indoor tennis center.

Disabled Students: 35% of the campus is accessible. Wheelchair ramps, elevators, special parking, specially equipped rest rooms, special class scheduling, lowered drinking fountains, and lowered telephones are available.

Services: Counseling and information services are available, as is tutoring in most subjects, including calculus, physics, English, accounting, finance, and economics. Tutoring in other subjects is available on request. There is a reader service for the blind. There are special programs for students with learning disabilities.

Campus Safety and Security: Measures include 24-hour foot and vehicle patrol, self-defense education, security escort services, and shuttle buses. There are informal discussions, pamphlets/posters/films, emergency telephones, and lighted pathways/sidewalks.

Programs of Study: Lehigh confers B.A., B.S., B.S.B.A., and B.S.E. degrees. Master's and doctoral degrees are also awarded. Bachelor's degrees are awarded in AGRICULTURE (environmental studies), BIOLOGICAL SCIENCE (biochemistry, biology/biological science, ecology, life science, and molecular biology), BUSINESS (accounting, banking and finance, business administration and management, business economics, business systems analysis, marketing/retailing/merchandising, and supply chain management), COMMUNICATIONS AND THE ARTS (art, art history and appreciation, classics, design, dramatic arts, English, French, German, journalism, music, music theory and composition, and Spanish), COMPUTER AND PHYSICAL SCIENCE (applied science, astronomy, astrophysics, chemistry, computer science, geology, information sciences and systems, mathematics, physics, science technology, and statistics), ENGINEERING AND ENVIRONMENTAL DESIGN (architectural history, architecture, bioengineering, chemical engineering, civil engineering, computer engineering, construction engineering, electrical/electronics engineering, engineering, engineering mechanics, engineering physics, environmental engineering, environmental science, industrial engineering, materials engineering, and mechanical engineering), HEALTH PROFESSIONS (predentistry, premedicine, and preoptometry), SOCIAL SCIENCE (African studies, American studies, anthropology, Asian/Oriental studies, behavioral science, classical/ancient civilization, cognitive science, economics, history, international relations, philosophy, political science/government, psychology, religion, Russian and Slavic studies, sociology, and urban studies). Architecture, accounting, and mechanical engineering are the largest.

Required: Graduation requirements vary by degree sought, but all students must complete 2 semesters of English, at least 30 credits in the chosen major, and a minimum of 121 credit hours. Students must also maintain a minimum GPA of 2.0.

Special: The university offers co-op programs through the Colleges of Engineering and Applied Science and Business and Economics, cross-registration with the Lehigh Valley Association of Independent Colleges, study abroad in 40 countries, internships, a Washington semester, several work-study programs, accelerated degree programs in medicine, dentistry and optometry, student-designed majors, many combinations of dual majors, a B.A.-B.S. degree, a 3-2 engineering degree, and pass/fail options. A 6-year B.A.-M.D. degree with the Medical College of Pennsylvania and a 7-year B.A.-D.D.S. degree with Pennsylvania State University are possible. There are 18 national honor societies, including Phi Beta Kappa, and a freshman honors program.

Faculty/Classroom: 69% of faculty are male; 31%, female. All both teach and do research. No introductory courses are taught by graduate students. The average class size in an introductory lecture is 150 and in a regular course, 29.

Admissions: 41% of the 2005-2006 applicants were accepted. The SAT scores for the 2005-2006 freshman class were: Verbal--1% below 500, 23% between 500 and 599, 57% between 600 and 700, and 18% above 700; Math--9% between 500 and 599, 51% between 600 and 700, and 40% above 700.

Requirements: The SAT or ACT is required. The ACT Optional Writing test is also required. In addition, candidates for admission should have completed 4 years of English, 3 years of math and electives, and

2 years each of a foreign language, science, and social science. Most students present 4 years each of science, math, and English. An on-campus interview is recommended. AP credits are accepted. Important factors in the admissions decision are advanced placement or honor courses, evidence of special talent, and leadership record.

Procedure: Freshmen are admitted fall and spring. Entrance exams should be taken by the January test date. There is an early decision plan. Early decision applications should be filed by November 15; regular applications, by January 1 for fall entry and November 15 for spring entry, along with a $60 fee. Notification of early decision is sent December 15; regular decision, by April 1. 752 applicants were on the 2005 waiting list.

Transfer: 46 transfer students enrolled in 2004-2005. Transfer candidates should have a minimum GPA of 3.25 and submit high school and college transcripts, an essay, and a statement of good standing from previous institutions. 30 of 121 credits required for the bachelor's degree must be completed at Lehigh.

Visiting: There are regularly scheduled orientations for prospective students, consisting of interviews scheduled Monday through Friday, 9 A.M. to 3:30 P.M.; tours scheduled Monday through Friday, 10:15 A.M., 11:15 A.M., 1 P.M., and 3 P.M., and interviews and tours also available on some Saturdays. General information sessions are offered Monday through Friday at 9:30 A.M., 10:30 A.M., and 2:15 P.M. There are guides for informal visits and visitors may sit in on classes and stay overnight. To schedule a visit, contact the Office of Admissions.

Financial Aid: In 2005-2006, 46% of all full-time students received some form of financial aid. 42% of all full-time students received need-based aid. The average freshman award was $24,245. Need-based scholarships or need-based grants averaged $19,990 ($35,275 maximum); need-based self-help aid (loans and jobs) averaged $4205 ($7425 maximum); non-need-based athletic scholarships averaged $38,068 ($34,670 maximum); and institutional non-need-based awards and non-need-based scholarships averaged $10,759 ($37,320 maximum). 27% of undergraduates work part time. Average annual earnings from campus work are $980. The average financial indebtedness of the 2005 graduate was $23,418. Lehigh is a member of CSS. The CSS/Profile or FAFSA, the college's own financial statement, the Noncustodial Profile, and the Business/Farm supplement are required. The deadline for filing freshman financial aid applications for fall entry is February 15.

International Students: There are 131 international students enrolled. The school actively recruits these students. They must score satisfactorily on the TOEFL and also take the SAT or the ACT. Students must take SAT: Subject tests in English, math, and 1 other.

Computers: All students may access the system 24 hours per day, 7 days per week. There are no time limits and no fees.

Graduates: From July 1, 2004 to June 30, 2005, 1113 bachelor's degrees were awarded. The most popular majors were health professions and related science (27%), engineering (26%), and social sciences (9%). In an average class, 71% graduate in 4 years or less, 83% graduate in 5 years or less, and 84% graduate in 6 years or less.

Admissions Contact: J. Bruce Gardiner, Director (Interim). E-mail: *inado@lehigh.edu; www.lehigh.edu* Web: *www.lehigh.edu*

LINCOLN UNIVERSITY — E-4

Lincoln University, PA 19352	(610) 932-8300, ext. 3206
	(800) 790-0191; Fax: (610) 932-1209
Full-time: 639 men, 1013 women	Faculty: 96; IIA, --$
Part-time: 26 men, 36 women	Ph.D.s: 77%
Graduate: 177 men, 387 women	Student/Faculty: 17 to 1
Year: semesters, summer session	Tuition: $6866 ($11,406)
Application Deadline: open	Room & Board: $6792
Freshman Class: 5525 applied, 1914 accepted, 665 enrolled	
SAT Verbal/Math: 410/400*	COMPETITIVE+

Lincoln University, founded in 1854, is a public institution offering programs in liberal arts and teacher preparation. There are 3 undergraduate schools and 1 graduate school. The library contains 189,350 volumes, 212,000 microform items, and 2700 audio/video tapes/CDs/DVDs. Computerized library services include the card catalog, interlibrary loans, and database searching. Special learning facilities include an art gallery, radio station, and TV station. The 422-acre campus is in a rural area 45 miles southwest of Philadelphia. Including any residence halls, there are 38 buildings.

Student Life: 51% of undergraduates are from Pennsylvania. Others are from 25 states, 34 foreign countries, and Canada. 92% are African American. The average age of freshmen is 18; all undergraduates, 19. 32% do not continue beyond their first year; 44% remain to graduate.

Housing: 1590 students can be accommodated in college housing, which includes single-sex and coed dorms and on-campus apartments. On-campus housing is guaranteed for the freshman year only and is available on a first-come, first-served basis. 96% of students live on campus; of those, 80% remain on campus on weekends. Upperclassmen may keep cars.

Activities: 5% of men belong to 4 national fraternities; 5% of women belong to 4 national sororities. There are 90 groups on campus, including art, band, cheerleading, choir, chorale, computers, dance, drama, drill team, honors, international, jazz band, newspaper, pep band, political, radio and TV, religious, social, social service, student government, and yearbook. Popular campus events include lectures and recitals, Black History Month, and convocations.

Sports: There are 7 intercollegiate sports for men and 8 for women, and 2 intramural sports for men and 2 for women. Facilities include a 2000-seat gym, softball and track fields, a fitness trail, a swimming pool, big screen TV, games, table tennis, a pool table, and a bowling alley.

Disabled Students: Wheelchair ramps, elevators, special parking, and specially equipped rest rooms are available.

Services: Counseling and information services are available, as is tutoring in every subject. There is remedial math, reading, and writing.

Campus Safety and Security: Measures include 24-hour foot and vehicle patrol, self-defense education, security escort services, and shuttle buses. There are informal discussions, pamphlets/posters/films, emergency telephones, and lighted pathways/sidewalks.

Programs of Study: Lincoln confers B.A. and B.S. degrees. Master's degrees are also awarded. Bachelor's degrees are awarded in BIOLOGICAL SCIENCE (biology/biological science), BUSINESS (accounting, banking and finance, and business administration and management), COMMUNICATIONS AND THE ARTS (communications, English, French, journalism, music, Spanish, and studio art), COMPUTER AND PHYSICAL SCIENCE (actuarial science, chemistry, computer science, mathematics, physics, and science), EDUCATION (early childhood, elementary, English, mathematics, music, physical, secondary, and special), ENGINEERING AND ENVIRONMENTAL DESIGN (environmental science and preengineering), HEALTH PROFESSIONS (health science and recreation therapy), SOCIAL SCIENCE (anthropology, criminal justice, economics, history, human services, industrial and organizational psychology, international relations, liberal arts/general studies, philosophy, political science/government, psychobiology, psychology, religion, and sociology). Physics, chemistry, and biology are the strongest academically. Business administration, elementary education, and criminal justice are the largest.

Required: Required courses include 8 in the humanities, 3 each in the social and natural sciences, 2 to 4 in foreign language, 2 each in phys ed, writing emphasis, speaking emphasis, critical thinking, and university seminar, and 1 in computer applications. Students must take Integrative Themes in the Liberal Arts, pass a writing proficiency exam, and participate in the Major Field Achievement Assessment. For graduation, a total of 120 semester hours is required, including 60 in the major, with a GPA of 2.0.

Special: Lincoln offers co-op programs, internships, study abroad in 18 countries, work-study, and pass/fail options. 3-2 engineering degrees are offered with 7 other universities and institutes. Accelerated degree programs, B.A.-B.S. degrees, and dual majors are possible. There are 7 national honor societies, a freshman honors program, and 3 departmental honors programs.

Faculty/Classroom: 65% of faculty are male; 35%, female. 81% teach undergraduates. No introductory courses are taught by graduate students.

Admissions: 35% of the 2005-2006 applicants were accepted. The SAT scores for the 2005-2006 freshman class were: Verbal--84% below 500, 14% between 500 and 599, and 2% between 600 and 700; Math--86% below 500, 12% between 500 and 599, and 2% between 600 and 700.

Requirements: The SAT or ACT is required. In addition, applicants should complete 21 credit hours, including 4 credits in English, 3 each in math, science, and social studies, 2 in art, and 1 in phys ed. The GED is accepted. An essay and an interview are required. Lincoln requires applicants to be in the upper 50% of their class. A GPA of 2.0 is required. AP and CLEP credits are accepted. Important factors in the admissions decision are advanced placement or honor courses, evidence of special talent, and leadership record.

Procedure: Freshmen are admitted fall and spring. Entrance exams should be taken prior to admission. There is a rolling admissions plan. Application deadlines are open. The fall 2005 application fee was $20. Applications are accepted on-line.

Transfer: 43 transfer students enrolled in a recent year. Applicants must have completed at least 12 semester hours, be in good standing at all previously attended institutions, and submit official transcripts. 60 of 120 credits required for the bachelor's degree must be completed at Lincoln.

Visiting: There are regularly scheduled orientations for prospective students. There are guides for informal visits and visitors may sit in on classes and stay overnight. To schedule a visit, contact Michael Taylor, Director of Admissions at (800) 790-0191 or *admiss@lincoln.edu.*

Financial Aid: In 2005-2006, 94% of all full-time freshmen and 90% of continuing full-time students received some form of financial aid. 90% of full-time freshmen received need-based aid. The average freshman award was $14,000. Need-based scholarships or need-based grants averaged $5142 ($9350 maximum); need-based self-help aid (loans and jobs) averaged $3000 ($9625 maximum); and other non-need-based awards and non-need-based scholarships averaged $8000 ($21,000 maximum). 24% of undergraduates work part time. Average annual earnings from campus work are $3900. The average financial indebtedness of the 2005 graduate was $21,000. The FAFSA and PHEAA are required. The deadline for filing freshman financial aid applications for fall entry is April 1.

International Students: There are 100 international students enrolled. The school actively recruits these students. They must take the written TOEFL and also take the SAT or the ACT, scoring satisfactorily.

Computers: Wireless access is available. There are computer labs, and free email accounts available. All students may access the system. There are no time limits and no fees.

Graduates: From July 1, 2004 to June 30, 2005, 240 bachelor's degrees were awarded. The most popular majors were criminal justice (10%), communication (9%), and elementary education (9%). In an average class, 1% graduate in 3 years or less, 28% graduate in 4 years or less, 41% graduate in 5 years or less, and 44% graduate in 6 years or less. 48 companies recruited on campus in 2004-2005.

Admissions Contact: Mr. Micheal Taylor, Director of Admissions. E-mail: *admiss@lincoln.edu* Web: *www.lincoln.edu*

LOCK HAVEN UNIVERSITY OF PENNSYLVANIA — D-2

Lock Haven, PA 17745　　　　　　　　　**(570) 893-2027**
(800) 233-8978; Fax: (570) 893-2201

Full-time: 1948 men, 2608 women	Faculty: 270
Part-time: 133 men, 288 women	Ph.D.s: 69%
Graduate: 87 men, 219 women	Student/Faculty: 17 to 1
Year: semesters, summer session	Tuition: $6258 ($11,618)
Application Deadline: open	Room & Board: $5840
Freshman Class: n/av	
SAT or ACT: n/av	LESS COMPETITIVE

Lock Haven University, established in 1870, is a public institution offering undergraduate degrees in arts and sciences, education, and human services. The university maintains a branch campus in Clearfield. There are 2 undergraduate and 3 graduate schools. In addition to regional accreditation, LHUP has baccalaureate program accreditation with CSWE, NCATE, and NLN. Computerized library services include the card catalog, interlibrary loans, database searching, and Internet access. Special learning facilities include a learning resource center, art gallery, planetarium, radio station, TV station, primate and human performance labs, and a cadaver dissection lab. The 135-acre campus is in a rural area 30 miles west of Williamsport.

Student Life: 91% of undergraduates are from Pennsylvania. Others are from Canada. 88% are white. The average age of freshmen is 19; all undergraduates, 22. 27% do not continue beyond their first year; 52% remain to graduate.

Housing: More than 1700 students can be accommodated in college housing, which includes single-sex and coed dormitories and off-campus apartments. On-campus housing is guaranteed for the freshman year only and is available on a lottery system for upperclassmen. 83% of students commute. Alcohol is not permitted. All students may keep cars.

Activities: 8% of men belong to 6 national fraternities; 5% of women belong to 4 national sororities. There are more than 100 groups on campus, including art, band, cheerleading, chess, choir, chorale, chorus, computers, dance, drama, ethnic, forensics, gay, honors, international, jazz band, literary magazine, marching band, newspaper, orchestra, pep band, photography, political, professional, radio and TV, religious, social, social service, student government, and symphony. Popular campus events include Family Day, Alcohol Awareness Week, and Spring Carnival.

Sports: There are 7 intercollegiate sports for men and 9 for women. Facilities include a 5000-seat stadium containing a football field and an all-weather track, a 2500-seat field house with a wrestling room, a recreation facility, a gym used for intramurals and weight training, and a gym that houses a swimming pool.

Disabled Students: 95% of the campus is accessible. Wheelchair ramps, elevators, special parking, specially equipped rest rooms, special class scheduling, lowered drinking fountains, and lowered telephones are available.

Services: Counseling and information services are available, as is tutoring in most subjects. There is remedial math. Reader services for the blind can be arranged. There are also writing and math centers.

Campus Safety and Security: Measures include 24-hour foot and vehicle patrol, security escort services, informal discussions, and pamphlets/posters/films. There are emergency telephones and lighted pathways/sidewalks.

Programs of Study: LHUP confers B.A., B.S., B.F.A., and B.S.Ed. degrees. Associate and master's degrees are also awarded. Bachelor's degrees are awarded in BIOLOGICAL SCIENCE (biology/biological science and environmental science), BUSINESS (business administration and management), COMMUNICATIONS AND THE ARTS (communications, English, fine arts, French, German, journalism, music, Spanish, and speech/debate/rhetoric), COMPUTER AND PHYSICAL SCIENCE (chemistry, computer science, earth science, geology, information sci-

ences and systems, mathematics, and physics), EDUCATION (early childhood, elementary, foreign languages, physical, science, secondary, and special), HEALTH PROFESSIONS (health science and medical laboratory technology), SOCIAL SCIENCE (criminal justice, economics, geography, history, humanities and social science, international studies, Latin American studies, liberal arts/general studies, paralegal studies, philosophy, political science/government, psychology, social science, social work, and sociology). Health science and biological sciences are the strongest academically. Education, health science, and recreation are the largest.

Required: To graduate, students must complete 60 hours of general education, including 12 in humanities and in social and behavioral sciences, 9 in skills core, 6 in science, 3 in wellness core, and the rest in electives. A total of 120 credit hours is required, including 61 to 68 in the major, with a minimum GPA of 2.0.

Special: There are cooperative programs in music education and engineering, including a 3-2 engineering degree with Pennsylvania State University. Lock Haven also offers study-abroad programs in more than 20 countries, a dual major in education, work-study options, an accelerated degree program for honor students, a student-designed general studies major, and internships, which are required in some majors. Pass/fail grading options are limited to 1 course outside the major per semester, not to exceed 12 credit hours. There are 11 national honor societies, a freshman honors program, and 6 departmental honors programs.

Faculty/Classroom: 54% of faculty are male; 46%, female. No introductory courses are taught by graduate students.

Admissions: 3 freshmen graduated first in their class.

Requirements: The SAT is required. In addition, applicants must graduate from an accredited secondary school or have a GED. 16 academic credits are required, and a college preparatory course is recommended. AP and CLEP credits are accepted. Important factors in the admissions decision are advanced placement or honor courses, evidence of special talent, and personality/intangible qualities.

Procedure: Freshmen are admitted to all sessions. Entrance exams should be taken during the spring of the junior year and the fall of the senior year. There is a deferred admissions and a rolling admissions plan. Application deadlines are open. Application fee is $25. Applications are accepted on-line.

Transfer: 197 transfer students enrolled in 2004-2005. Priority is given to applicants who have completed 24 or more transferable credits. A minimum GPA of 2.0 is required. 30 of 120 credits required for the bachelor's degree must be completed at LHUP.

Visiting: There are regularly scheduled orientations for prospective students, consisting of an introduction to the administration, sessions with faculty, and an information arena/departmental showcase; small group visits are also scheduled. There are guides for informal visits and visitors may sit in on classes. To schedule a visit, contact the Admissions Office.

Financial Aid: The FAFSA and PHEAA are required.

International Students: There are 111 international students enrolled. The school actively recruits these students. They must score satisfactorily on the written TOEFL.

Computers: Wireless access is available. All students may access the system. There are no time limits and no fees.

Graduates: From July 1, 2004 to June 30, 2005, 671 bachelor's degrees were awarded. The most popular majors were education (21%), parks and recreation (19%), and health professional (11%). In an average class, 25% graduate in 4 years or less, 49% graduate in 5 years or less, and 52% graduate in 6 years or less. Of the 2004 graduating class, 13% were enrolled in graduate school within 6 months of graduation and 82% were employed.

Admissions Contact: Stephen Lee, Director of Admissions. A video is available. E-mail: *admissions@lhup.edu* Web: *www.lhup.edu*

LYCOMING COLLEGE — D-2

Williamsport, PA 17701-5192　　　　　　**(570) 321-4026**
(800) 345-3920; Fax: (570) 321-4317

Full-time: 633 men, 822 women	Faculty: 88; IIB, -$
Part-time: 10 men, 20 women	Ph.D.s: 92%
Graduate: none	Student/Faculty: 17 to 1
Year: semesters, summer session	Tuition: $24,255
Application Deadline: April 1	Room & Board: $6542
Freshman Class: 1511 applied, 1157 accepted, 359 enrolled	
SAT Verbal/Math: 530/530*	ACT: 24　COMPETITIVE+

Lycoming College, established in 1812, is a private, residential, liberal arts institution affiliated with the Methodist Church. In addition to regional accreditation, Lycoming has baccalaureate program accreditation with AACSB. The library contains 170,000 volumes and 2400 audio/video tapes/CDs/DVDs, and subscribes to 1100 periodicals including electronic. Computerized library services include the card catalog, interlibrary loans, database searching, and Internet access. Special learning facilities include a learning resource center, art gallery, planetarium, radio station, and TV station. The 35-acre campus is in a small town in north central Pennsylvania. Including any residence halls, there are 24 buildings.

Student Life: 70% of undergraduates are from Pennsylvania. Others are from 22 states, 11 foreign countries, and Canada. 81% are from public schools. 94% are white. 64% are Protestant; 30% Catholic. The average age of freshmen is 18; all undergraduates, 19. 17% do not continue beyond their first year; 65% remain to graduate.

Housing: 1240 students can be accommodated in college housing, which includes single-sex and coed dorms, on-campus apartments, and off-campus apartments. In addition, there are language houses special-interest houses, and nonsmoking, intensive study, and Greek floors. On-campus housing is guaranteed for all 4 years. 83% of students live on campus; of those, 67% remain on campus on weekends. All students may keep cars.

Activities: 16% of men belong to 5 national fraternities; 24% of women belong to 3 local and 2 national sororities. There are 70 groups on campus, including art, band, cheerleading, choir, chorus, computers, dance, drama, ethnic, film, gay, honors, international, jazz band, literary magazine, musical theater, newspaper, photography, political, professional, radio and TV, religious, social, social service, student government, and yearbook. Popular campus events include Campus Carnival, Annual Christmas Candlelight Service, and Choir Concert.

Sports: There are 9 intercollegiate sports for men and 9 for women, and 6 intramural sports for men and 6 for women. Facilities include an outdoor softball, football, soccer, and lacrosse complex, indoor basketball courts, weight and exercise rooms, indoor pool, and intramural fields.

Disabled Students: 85% of the campus is accessible. Wheelchair ramps, elevators, special parking, specially equipped rest rooms, special class scheduling, lowered drinking fountains, lowered telephones, and special housing are available.

Services: Counseling and information services are available, as is tutoring in every subject. There is remedial math, reading, and writing.

Campus Safety and Security: Measures include 24-hour foot and vehicle patrol, self-defense education, security escort services, and informal discussions. There are pamphlets/posters/films, emergency telephones and lighted pathways/sidewalk.

Programs of Study: Lycoming confers B.A. and B.S. degrees. Bachelor's degrees are awarded in BIOLOGICAL SCIENCE (biology/biological science), BUSINESS (accounting and business administration and management), COMMUNICATIONS AND THE ARTS (art history and appreciation, communications, dramatic arts, English, French, German, music, Spanish, and studio art), COMPUTER AND PHYSICAL SCIENCE (astronomy, chemistry, computer science, mathematics, and physics), SOCIAL SCIENCE (anthropology, criminal justice, economics, history, international studies, philosophy, political science/government, psychology, religion, and sociology). Business, psychology, and biology are the largest.

Required: To graduate, students must complete 128 credits with a minimum GPA of 2.0. Distribution requirements include 4 courses in humanities and 2 each in English, foreign language, math, fine arts, natural science, social science, and cultural diversity. Students must also complete 2 semesters of phys ed, wellness, or community service.

Special: Cooperative programs are available with the Ohio and Pennsylvania Colleges of Podiatric Medicine, Pennsylvania College of Optometry, and Penn State and Duke Universities. Cross-registration is available with the Pennsylvania College of Technology. More than 200 internships, including teacher programs, study abroad in 5 countries, and a Washington semester at American University are available. Lycoming offers work-study programs, dual and student-designed majors, and an accelerated degree program in conjunction with the college's Scholar Program in optometry, podiatric medicine, and dentistry. Nondegree study and pass/fail grading options are available. There are 12 national honor societies, a freshman honors program, and 11 departmental honors programs.

Faculty/Classroom: 63% of faculty are male; 37%, female. All teach undergraduates. The average class size in an introductory lecture is 25; in a laboratory, 15; and in a regular course, 18.

Admissions: 77% of the 2005-2006 applicants were accepted. The SAT scores for the 2005-2006 freshman class were: Verbal--30% below 500, 49% between 500 and 599, 19% between 600 and 700, and 2% above 700; Math--28% below 500, 53% between 500 and 599, 18% between 600 and 700, and 1% above 700. The ACT scores were 14% below 21, 29% between 21 and 23, 43% between 24 and 26, and 14% between 27 and 28. 36% of the current freshmen were in the top fifth of their class; 68% were in the top two fifths. 10 freshmen graduated first in their class.

Requirements: A satisfactory score is required on the SAT or ACT. Applicants must graduate from an accredited secondary school or have a GED. They must have earned 16 academic or Carnegie units, completing 4 years of English, 3 each of math and social studies, and 2 each of science, a foreign language, and academic electives. 2 personal letters of recommendation are required. An essay is required and an interview is recommended. Portfolios and auditions may be required for students seeking scholarships. AP and CLEP credits are accepted. Important factors in the admissions decision are advanced placement or honor courses, leadership record, and evidence of special talent.

Procedure: Freshmen are admitted fall and spring. Entrance exams should be taken during the junior year or by January of the senior year. There are early admissions and deferred admissions plans. There is a rolling admissions plan. Applications should be filed by April 1 for fall entry and December 1 for spring entry, along with a $35 fee. Notification is sent on a rolling basis. Applications are accepted on-line.

Transfer: 29 transfer students enrolled in 2004-2005. Applicants must submit appropriate transcripts and have a minimum GPA of 2.0 in transferable courses. Students who have completed 24 transferable semester hours are not required to submit the SAT or ACT results. 32 of 128 credits required for the bachelor's degree must be completed at Lycoming.

Visiting: There are regularly scheduled orientations for prospective students, consisting of a student-guided tour of campus and an interview with an admissions counselor. Meetings with professors and coaches and attending a class are possible upon request. There are guides for informal visits and visitors may sit in on classes and stay overnight. To schedule a visit, contact the Admissions House at (800) 345-3920, ext. 4026 or *admissions@lycoming.edu*.

Financial Aid: In 2005-2006, 82% of all full-time freshmen and 83% of continuing full-time students received some form of financial aid. 82% of full-time freshmen and 83% of continuing full-time students received need-based aid. The average freshman award was $18,277. Need-based scholarships or need-based grants averaged $14,694 ($19,000 maximum); need-based self-help aid (loans and jobs) averaged $4095 ($12,500 maximum); and other non-need-based awards and non-need-based scholarships averaged $9504 ($16,000 maximum). 55% of undergraduates work part time. Average annual earnings from campus work are $1110. The average financial indebtedness of the 2005 graduate was $23,343. Lycoming is a member of CSS. The FAFSA and the college's own financial statement are required. The priority date for freshman financial aid applications for fall entry is March 1. The deadline for filing freshman financial aid applications for fall entry is April 15.

International Students: There are 10 international students enrolled. They must score satisfactorily on the TOEFL and also take the SAT or ACT. This requirement may be waived, however.

Computers: All students may access the system 8 A.M. to midnight. There are no time limits and no fees. It is strongly recommended that all students have a personal computer. A Pentium 4 or IBM Think Pad is recommended.

Graduates: From July 1, 2004 to June 30, 2005, 293 bachelor's degrees were awarded. The most popular majors were business (17%), psychology (15%), and biology (12%). In an average class, 2% graduate in 3 years or less, 61% graduate in 4 years or less, and 69% graduate in 5 years or less. 25 companies recruited on campus in 2004-2005. Of the 2004 graduating class, 24% were enrolled in graduate school within 6 months of graduation and 97% were employed.

Admissions Contact: James Spencer, Dean of Admissions and Financial Aid. E-mail: *admissions@lycoming.edu* Web: *www.lycoming.edu*

MANSFIELD UNIVERSITY　　　　　　　　　　　　D-1
Mansfield, PA 16933　　　　　　　　　　　　　　(570) 662-4243
　　　　　　　　　　　　(800) 577-6826; Fax: (570) 662-4121

Full-time: 1038 men, 1649 women	**Faculty:** 155
Part-time: 49 men, 150 women	**Ph.D.s:** 93%
Graduate: 49 men, 308 women	**Student/Faculty:** 17 to 1
Year: semesters, summer session	**Tuition:** $6433 ($13,793)
Application Deadline: open	**Room & Board:** $5868
Freshman Class: 2348 applied, 1689 accepted, 680 enrolled	
SAT Verbal/Math: 500/490*	**COMPETITIVE**

Mansfield University, founded in 1857, is a public university that is part of the Pennsylvania State System of Higher Education. It offers programs in professional studies and the arts and sciences. In addition to regional accreditation, Mansfield has baccalaureate program accreditation with CAHEA, CSWE, NASM, and NCATE. The library contains 246,141 volumes, 818,288 microform items, and 26,742 audio/video tapes/CDs/DVDs, and subscribes to 2948 periodicals including electronic. Computerized library services include the card catalog, interlibrary loans, database searching, and Internet access. Special learning facilities include a learning resource center, art gallery, natural history museum, planetarium, radio station, TV station, and a high-tech lecture lab. The 175-acre campus is in a rural area 28 miles south of Corning/Elmira, New York, and 58 miles north of Williamsport. Including any residence halls, there are 41 buildings.

Student Life: 80% of undergraduates are from Pennsylvania. Others are from 25 states, 21 foreign countries, and Canada. 87% are white. The average age of freshmen is 19; all undergraduates, 22. 36% do not continue beyond their first year; 52% remain to graduate.

Housing: 1800 students can be accommodated in college housing, which includes coed dorms, fraternity houses, and sorority houses. In addition, there are special-interest houses, wellness floors, nonsmoking floors, 24-hour quiet floors, and honors floors in residence halls. On-campus housing is guaranteed for all 4 years. 52% of students commute. Alcohol is not permitted. All students may keep cars.

Activities: 5% of men belong to 4 national fraternities; 4% of women belong to 4 national sororities. There are 108 groups on campus, including art, band, cheerleading, choir, chorus, computers, dance, debate, drama, ethnic, forensics, honors, international, jazz band, literary magazine, marching band, musical theater, newspaper, orchestra, pep band, photography, political, professional, radio and TV, religious, social, social service, student government, and symphony. Popular campus events include Fabulous 1890s Weekend.

Sports: There are 6 intercollegiate sports for men and 8 for women, and 8 intramural sports for men and 8 for women. Facilities include a track, a recreation center, a 4000-seat stadium, a 1500-seat indoor gym, a 1200-seat auditorium, and football, baseball, and hockey fields.

Disabled Students: 80% of the campus is accessible. Wheelchair ramps, elevators, special parking, specially equipped rest rooms, special class scheduling, lowered drinking fountains, lowered telephones, and a wheelchair lift are available.

Services: Counseling and information services are available, as is tutoring in most subjects. There is a reader service for the blind, and remedial math, reading, and writing.

Campus Safety and Security: Measures include 24-hour foot and vehicle patrol, self-defense education, security escort services, and shuttle buses. There are informal discussions, pamphlets/posters/films, emergency telephones, and lighted pathways/sidewalks.

Programs of Study: Mansfield confers B.A., B.S., B.M., B.M.E., B.S.Ed., B.S.N., and B.S.W. degrees. Associate and master's degrees are also awarded. Bachelor's degrees are awarded in AGRICULTURE (fishing and fisheries), BIOLOGICAL SCIENCE (biochemistry, biology/biological science, cell biology, and molecular biology), BUSINESS (accounting, business administration and management, business economics, international business management, marketing/retailing/merchandising, personnel management, and tourism), COMMUNICATIONS AND THE ARTS (art history and appreciation, broadcasting, dramatic arts, English, French, German, journalism, music, music business management, music performance, public relations, Spanish, speech/debate/rhetoric, and studio art), COMPUTER AND PHYSICAL SCIENCE (chemistry, computer science, information sciences and systems, mathematics, and physics), EDUCATION (art, early childhood, education of the exceptional child, elementary, English, foreign languages, mathematics, music, science, secondary, social studies, and special), ENGINEERING AND ENVIRONMENTAL DESIGN (city/community/regional planning, environmental science, and preengineering), HEALTH PROFESSIONS (medical technology, music therapy, nursing, and premedicine), SOCIAL SCIENCE (anthropology, criminal justice, dietetics, economics, geography, history, international studies, liberal arts/general studies, philosophy, political science/government, prelaw, psychology, social science, social work, and sociology). Music, physical sciences, and social sciences are the strongest academically. Education, music, and social sciences are the largest.

Required: To graduate, students must complete 120 credit hours with a 2.0 GPA in core courses, distribution requirements, general education electives, and major requirements. Some degrees require a higher GPA.

Special: There are co-op programs in preengineering, predentistry, premedicine, and medical technology and study abroad in England, Spain, and Germany. There is a 3-2 engineering program with several major universities. The university also offers work-study, dual majors, a liberal studies degree, credit by exam, credit for military experience, nondegree study, and pass/fail options. There are 6 national honor societies, including Phi Beta Kappa, and a freshman honors program.

Faculty/Classroom: 50% of faculty are male; 50%, female. All teach undergraduates. No introductory courses are taught by graduate students. The average class size in an introductory lecture is 32; in a laboratory, 19; and in a regular course, 30.

Admissions: 72% of the applicants for a recent class were accepted. The SAT scores for the a recent freshman class were: Verbal--38% below 500, 48% between 500 and 599, 13% between 600 and 700, and 1% above 700; Math--39% below 500, 46% between 500 and 599, 13% between 600 and 700, and 2% above 700. The ACT scores were 50% below 21, 30% between 21 and 23, 14% between 24 and 26, 3% between 27 and 28, and 3% above 28. 26% of the current freshmen were in the top fifth of their class; 53% were in the top two fifths. 6 freshmen graduated first in their class.

Requirements: The SAT or ACT is required. A GED is accepted. Applicants should prepare with 4 credits of English and history, 3 each of math, science, and social studies, 2 of foreign language, and 6 of additional academic electives. Art students must submit a portfolio; music students must audition. Mansfield requires applicants to be in the upper 60% of their class. A GPA of 2.5 is required. AP and CLEP credits are accepted. Important factors in the admissions decision are advanced placement or honor courses, evidence of special talent, and leadership record.

Procedure: Freshmen are admitted fall and spring. Entrance exams should be taken by the junior or senior year of high school. There are early admissions and deferred admissions plans. There is a rolling admissions plan. Application deadlines are open. Application fee is $25.Notifi-

cation is sent on a rolling basis beginning July 1. Applications are accepted on-line.

Transfer: 248 transfer students enrolled in 2004-2005. Applicants must have a GPA of at least 2.0 and must submit all college transcripts. 32 of 120 credits required for the bachelor's degree must be completed at Mansfield.

Visiting: There are regularly scheduled orientations for prospective students. There are guides for informal visits and visitors may sit in on classes. To schedule a visit, contact the Admissions Office.

Financial Aid: In 2005-2006, 75% of all full-time freshmen and 74% of continuing full-time students received some form of financial aid. At least 55% of all full-time students received need-based aid. The average freshman award was $10,082. Need-based scholarships or need-based grants averaged $4051; need-based self-help aid (loans and jobs) averaged $2805; institutional non-need-based athletic scholarships averaged $1630; and other institutional non-need-based awards and non-need-based scholarships averaged $1534. 28% of undergraduates work part time. Average annual earnings from campus work are $1200. The average financial indebtedness of the 2005 graduate was $22,821. Mansfield is a member of CSS. The FAFSA and the college's own financial statement are required. The priority date for freshman financial aid applications for fall entry is March 15.

International Students: There were 29 international students enrolled in a recent year. The school actively recruits these students. A satisfactory score on the TOEFL is required.

Computers: All students may access the system. There are no time limits and no fees.

Graduates: From July 1, 2004 to June 30, 2005, 577 bachelor's degrees were awarded. The most popular majors were education (14%), business/marketing (12%), and communications/journalism (10%). In an average class, 2% graduate in 3 years, 30% graduate in 4 years, 65% graduate in 5 years, and 51% graduate in 6 years. 20 companies recruited on campus in 2004-2005. Of the 2004 graduating class, 8% were enrolled in graduate school within 6 months of graduation and 89% were employed.

Admissions Contact: Brian D. Barden, Director, Enrollment Management. E-mail: *admissns@mansfield.edu* Web: *www.mansfield.edu*

MARYWOOD UNIVERSITY   E-2
Scranton, PA 18509-1598
(570) 348-6234
(800) 346-5014; Fax: (570) 961-4763

Full-time: 444 men, 1218 women	**Faculty:** IIA, -$
Part-time: 62 men, 143 women	**Ph.D.s:** 88%
Graduate: 250 men, 997 women	**Student/Faculty:** n/av
Year: semesters, summer session	**Tuition:** $21,580
Application Deadline: open	**Room & Board:** $9100
Freshman Class: 1441 applied, 1104 accepted, 372 enrolled	
SAT Verbal/Math: 527/521*	**ACT:** 22 COMPETITIVE

Marywood University, founded in 1915, is an independent comprehensive Catholic institution committed to the integration of liberal arts and professional studies in the context of ethical and religious values. There are 4 undergraduate and 4 graduate schools. In addition to regional accreditation, Marywood has baccalaureate program accreditation with AATA, ABA, ACBSP, ADA, AMTA, ARC-PA, ASLHA, CAAHEP, CACREP, CSWE, NASAD, NASM, NCATE, and NLN. The library contains 219,770 volumes, 364,690 microform items, and 23,183 audio/video tapes/CDs/DVDs, and subscribes to 8918 periodicals including electronic. Computerized library services include the card catalog, interlibrary loans, database searching, and Internet access. Special learning facilities include a learning resource center, art gallery, radio station, TV station, communication disorders clinic, on-campus preschool and day care center, psychology/education research lab, science multimedia lab, distance education, human performance lab, videoconferencing classroom, and studio arts center, including 2 art museums. The 115-acre campus is in a suburban area 120 miles west of New York City and 115 miles north of Philadelphia. Including any residence halls, there are 30 buildings.

Student Life: 78% of undergraduates are from Pennsylvania. Others are from 21 states and 16 foreign countries. 76% are from public schools. 91% are white. 61% are Catholic; 25% Protestant; 8% claim no religious affiliation. The average age of freshmen is 19; all undergraduates, 22. 15% do not continue beyond their first year; 70% remain to graduate.

Housing: 677 students can be accommodated in college housing, which includes single-sex and coed dormitories and on-campus apartments. In addition, there are honors houses, a community service residence, and an American-International student wing. On-campus housing is guaranteed for all 4 years. 63% of students commute. Alcohol is not permitted. All students may keep cars.

Activities: 44% of women belong to 1 local sorority. There are no fraternities. There are 78 groups on campus, including art, band, cheerleading, choir, chorus, commuter, computers, dance, drama, ethnic, film, gay, honors, international, jazz band, literary magazine, musical theater, newspaper, orchestra, photography, political, professional, radio and TV, religious, social, social service, student government, symphony, and volunteer yearbook. Popular campus events include Family Weekend, Halloween Haunted House, and Spring Fling.

Sports: There are 5 intercollegiate sports for men and 7 for women, and 40 intramural sports for men and 40 for women. Facilities include an Olympic-size pool, a human performance lab, a gym, an athletic training room, outdoor tennis courts, racquetball courts, an aerobic room, a game room, saunas, a fitness center and weight room, 3 athletic fields for baseball, softball, field hockey, and soccer, and volleyball and horseshoe courts.

Disabled Students: 98% of the campus is accessible. Wheelchair ramps, elevators, special parking, specially equipped rest rooms, special class scheduling, lowered drinking fountains, lowered telephones, special housing, electronic doors, and full assistive technology labs are available.

Services: Counseling and information services are available, as is tutoring in every subject. There is a reader service for the blind, and remedial math, reading, and writing. Remedial study skills and nonremedial tutoring, oral tests, note taking, tutors, tape recorders for physically challenged students, and interpreters for students with hearing impairments are available.

Campus Safety and Security: Measures include 24-hour foot and vehicle patrol, self-defense education, security escort services, and informal discussions. There are pamphlets/posters/films, emergency telephones, lighted pathways/sidewalks, night security in dorms, card access to dorm floors, and transportation on request.

Programs of Study: Marywood confers B.A., B.S., B.B.A., B.F.A., B.M., B.S.N., and B.S.W. degrees. Associate, master's, and doctoral degrees are also awarded. Bachelor's degrees are awarded in BIOLOGICAL SCIENCE (biology/biological science and biotechnology), BUSINESS (accounting, banking and finance, business administration and management, hospitality management services, international business management, and marketing/retailing/merchandising), COMMUNICATIONS AND THE ARTS (advertising, arts administration/management, communications, design, digital communications, dramatic arts, English, French, music, music performance, musical theater, performing arts, Spanish, studio art, and telecommunications), COMPUTER AND PHYSICAL SCIENCE (information sciences and systems and mathematics), EDUCATION (art, athletic training, early childhood, elementary, home economics, music, physical, science, secondary, and special), ENGINEERING AND ENVIRONMENTAL DESIGN (aviation administration/management and environmental science), HEALTH PROFESSIONS (art therapy, health care administration, health science, medical laboratory technology, medical technology, music therapy, nursing, and speech pathology/audiology), SOCIAL SCIENCE (clinical psychology, criminal justice, dietetics, family/consumer studies, history, industrial and organizational psychology, paralegal studies, psychology, religion, religious music, social science, social work, and sociology). Nutrition and dietetics, education, and biotechnology are the strongest academically. Education, business, and visual and performing arts are the largest.

Required: To graduate, students must complete a liberal arts requirement consisting of religious studies, philosophy, math, science, psychology, history, social science, world literature, foreign language, and fine arts. Additional course requirements include speech, writing, and phys ed. Students must have a GPA of 2.0, with 2.5 in the major. A minimum of 126 credits must be earned, with the number of credits required in the major varying.

Special: Marywood offers cross-registration with the University of Scranton, internships, study abroad, accelerated degree programs in dietetics and social work, dual majors, and student-designed majors. A semester at a fashion institute, student teaching abroad, credit for life, military, and work experience, off-campus degree programs, and nondegree study are also offered. There are 23 national honor societies, a freshman honors program, and 18 departmental honors programs.

Faculty/Classroom: 44% of faculty are male; 56%, female. 72% teach undergraduates and All do research. No introductory courses are taught by graduate students. The average class size in an introductory lecture is 17; in a laboratory, 14; and in a regular course, 16.

Admissions: 77% of the 2005-2006 applicants were accepted. The SAT scores for the 2005-2006 freshman class were: Verbal--37% below 500, 46% between 500 and 599, 14% between 600 and 700, and 3% above 700; Math--41% below 500, 42% between 500 and 599, 15% between 600 and 700, and 2% above 700. The ACT scores were 59% below 21, 18% between 21 and 23, 14% between 24 and 26, and 9% above 28. 41% of the current freshmen were in the top fifth of their class; 78% were in the top half.

Requirements: The SAT is required and the ACT is recommended. In addition, applicants are expected to be graduates of an accredited secondary school or have the GED. A minimum of 16 academic credits is required, including 4 in English, 3 each in social studies and science (1 as lab), and 2 in math. A letter of support is required in selected majors, as is a portfolio or an audition where appropriate. A personal interview is strongly recommended. A GPA of 2.5 is required. AP and CLEP credits are accepted. Important factors in the admissions decision are ad-

vanced placement or honor courses, extracurricular activities record, and leadership record.

Procedure: Freshmen are admitted to all sessions. Entrance exams should be taken in the junior year or the senior year before February 1. There are early decision, early admissions, deferred admissions and rolling admissions plans. Application deadlines are open. Applications are accepted on-line. The fall 2005 application fee was $35.

Transfer: 157 transfer students enrolled in 2004-2005. SAT or ACT scores are required of transfer applicants who have earned fewer than 12 college credits; both secondary school and college transcripts are required. Transfer students are required to have earned a minimum GPA of 2.5 at the college most recently attended. A grade of C is the minimum requirement for transfer of academic credit. 60 of 126 credits required for the bachelor's degree must be completed at Marywood.

Visiting: There are regularly scheduled orientations for prospective students, including a campus tour, individual visits with admissions counselors, an appointment with an academic adviser, and a financial aid appointment. A full summer orientation program for first-year students is available. There are guides for informal visits and visitors may sit in on classes and stay overnight. To schedule a visit, contact the Office of Undergraduate Admissions.

Financial Aid: In 2005-2006, all full-time freshmen and 94% of continuing full-time students received some form of financial aid. 94% of full-time freshmen received need-based aid. The average freshman award was $14,150. 20% of undergraduates work part time. Average annual earnings from campus work are $1800. The FAFSA and the college's own financial statement are required. The deadline for filing freshman financial aid applications for fall entry is February 15.

International Students: In a recent year, there were 33 international students enrolled. The school actively recruits these students. They must score satisfactorily on the written TOEFL or on the electronic version and also take the SAT or the ACT for applicants whose native language is English.

Computers: All students may access the system 24 hours per day. There are no time limits and no fees. It is strongly recommended that all students have a personal computer.

Graduates: From July 1, 2004 to June 30, 2005, 349 bachelor's degrees were awarded. The most popular majors were business (28%), health sciences (23%), and education (21%). In an average class, 40% graduate in 4 years or less, 58% graduate in 5 years or less, and 64% graduate in 6 years or less. 84 companies recruited on campus in 2004-2005. Of the 2004 graduating class, 31% were enrolled in graduate school within 6 months of graduation and 94% were employed.

Admissions Contact: Robert W. Reese, Director of Undergraduate Admissions. A video is available. E-mail: ugadm@ac.marywood.edu Web: www.marywood.edu

MERCYHURST COLLEGE B-1

Erie, PA 16546

(814) 824-2202
(800) 825-1926; Fax: (814) 824-2071

Full-time: 1390 men, 1988 women	**Faculty:** IIB, --$
Part-time: 129 men, 333 women	**Ph.D.s:** 60%
Graduate: 140 men, 140 women	**Student/Faculty:** 21 to 1
Year: semesters, summer session	**Tuition:** $21,175
Application Deadline: open	**Room & Board:** $7458
Freshman Class: 2154 accepted, 705 enrolled	
SAT or ACT: required	**VERY COMPETITIVE**

Mercyhurst College, established in 1926, is a private, nonprofit institution affiliated with the Roman Catholic Church. The college offers undergraduate degrees in the arts, business, health science, liberal arts, religious studies, and teacher preparation as well as a degree-directed program for the learning disabled. Some information in this profile is approximate. In addition to regional accreditation, Mercyhurst has baccalaureate program accreditation with ADA and CSWE. The library contains 165,644 volumes, 50,631 microform items, and 9309 audio/video tapes/CDs/DVDs, and subscribes to 848 periodicals including electronic. Computerized library services include the card catalog, interlibrary loans, and database searching. Special learning facilities include a learning resource center, art gallery, planetarium, radio station, TV station, northwestern Pennsylvania historical archives, and archeological institute. The 88-acre campus is in a suburban area within Erie. Including any residence halls, there are 44 buildings.

Student Life: 63% of undergraduates are from Pennsylvania. Others are from 37 states, 14 foreign countries, and Canada. 76% are from public schools. 91% are white. 53% are Catholic; 21% Protestant; 18% claim no religious affiliation. The average age of freshmen is 18; all undergraduates, 26. 20% do not continue beyond their first year; 62% remain to graduate.

Housing: 1718 students can be accommodated in college housing, which includes single-sex and coed dorms, on-campus apartments, and married-student housing. On-campus housing is guaranteed for all 4 years. 61% of students live on campus; of those, 91% remain on campus on weekends. Upperclassmen may keep cars.

Activities: There are no fraternities or sororities. There are 49 groups on campus, including art, band, cheerleading, choir, chorus, computers, dance, debate, drama, ethnic, film, gay, honors, international, jazz band, literary magazine, musical theater, newspaper, opera, orchestra, pep band, photography, political, professional, radio and TV, religious, social, social service, student government, and yearbook. Popular campus events include Activities Day, Parents Weekend, and winter and spring formals.

Sports: There are 13 intercollegiate sports for men and 12 for women, and 9 intramural sports for men and 9 for women. Facilities include a pool, indoor crew tanks, football, field hockey,·lacrosse, and soccer fields, an ice hockey rink/arena, Nautilus facilities, a free-weight room, a baseball/softball complex, a training room, and a basketball arena.

Disabled Students: 90% of the campus is accessible. Wheelchair ramps, elevators, special parking, specially equipped rest rooms, and lowered drinking fountains are available.

Services: Counseling and information services are available, as is tutoring in every subject. There is remedial math, reading, and writing.

Campus Safety and Security: Measures include 24-hour foot and vehicle patrol, self-defense education, shuttle buses, and informal discussions. There are pamphlets/posters/films, emergency telephones, lighted pathways/sidewalks, and a 24-hour security camera surveillance system.

Programs of Study: Mercyhurst confers B.A., B.S., and B.M. degrees. Associate and master's degrees are also awarded. Bachelor's degrees are awarded in BIOLOGICAL SCIENCE (biochemistry and biology/ biological science), BUSINESS (accounting, banking and finance, business administration and management, fashion merchandising, hotel/ motel and restaurant management, insurance and risk management, management information systems, and marketing/retailing/ merchandising), COMMUNICATIONS AND THE ARTS (advertising, broadcasting, communications, dance, English, graphic design, journalism, languages, music, musical theater, public relations, and studio art), COMPUTER AND PHYSICAL SCIENCE (chemistry, earth science, geology, mathematics, web services, and web technology), EDUCATION (art, athletic training, business, early childhood, elementary, home economics, mathematics, music, science, secondary, social science, and special), ENGINEERING AND ENVIRONMENTAL DESIGN (environmental science and interior design), HEALTH PROFESSIONS (art therapy, medical laboratory technology, predentistry, premedicine, preosteopathy, prepharmacy, preveterinary science, and sports medicine), SOCIAL SCIENCE (anthropology, archeology, criminal justice, dietetics, family/consumer studies, forensic studies, history, philosophy, political science/government, prelaw, psychology, religion, religious education, social work, and sociology). Archeology/anthropology, research intelligence, and sports medicine are the strongest academically. Business, education, and sports medicine are the largest.

Required: To graduate, students must complete the core curriculum, which includes English, math, science, religion, philosophy, history, and a computer course. Distribution requirements include American history, cultural appreciation, human behavior, and ethics. A minimum GPA of 2.0 is required, with a 2.5 in the major, and a minimum total of 123 credit hours. The number of credit hours in the major varies, with a minimum of 30. A thesis is necessary for history and English majors.

Special: Mercyhurst offers cross-registration with Gannon University, internships in all majors through the co-op office, and study abroad in London and Dublin. Dual and student-designed majors, credit for life, military, or work experience, nondegree study, work-study, and a pass/ fail grading option are also available. There are 7 national honor societies, a freshman honors program, and 4 departmental honors programs.

Faculty/Classroom: 57% of faculty are male; 43%, female. All teach undergraduates and 30% do research. No introductory courses are taught by graduate students. The average class size in an introductory lecture is 35; in a laboratory, 12; and in a regular course, 25.

Admissions: The SAT scores for the 2005-2006 freshman class were: Verbal--31% below 500, 46% between 500 and 599, 20% between 600 and 700, and 3% above 700; Math--29% below 500, 47% between 500 and 599, 22% between 600 and 700, and 2% above 700. The ACT scores were 21% below 21, 46% between 21 and 23, and 33% between 24 and 26. 79% of the current freshmen were in the top two fifths of their class. There were 2 National Merit semifinalists. 20 freshmen graduated first in their class.

Requirements: The SAT or ACT is required. In addition, applicants must graduate from an accredited secondary school or have a GED. 16 academic credits are required, including 4 years of English, 3 each of math and social studies, and 2 each of history, science, and a foreign language. Interviews are recommended. Art applicants must submit portfolios; auditions are required of music and dance applicants. Mercyhurst requires applicants to be in the upper 50% of their class. A GPA of 2.75 is required. AP and CLEP credits are accepted. Important factors in the admissions decision are recommendations by alumni, evidence of special talent, and personality/intangible qualities.

Procedure: Freshmen are admitted to all sessions. Entrance exams should be taken during the spring of the junior year. There are early admissions and deferred admissions plans.There is a rolling admissions plan. Application deadlines are open. Application fee is $30 (free on-

line). Notification is sent on a rolling basis beginning in November. Applications are accepted on-line.

Transfer: 68 transfer students enrolled in 2004-2005. A minimum GPA of 2.0 on previous college work is required. 45 of 123 credits required for the bachelor's degree must be completed at Mercyhurst.

Visiting: There are regularly scheduled orientations for prospective students, including tours, class visits, faculty meetings, and interviews with financial aid and admissions counselors. There are guides for informal visits and visitors may sit in on classes and stay overnight. To schedule a visit, contact the Admissions Office at admissions@mercyhurst.edu.

Financial Aid: In 2005-2006, 93% of all full-time freshmen received some form of financial aid. 76% of full-time freshmen received need-based aid. The average freshman award was $12,094. Mercyhurst is a member of CSS. The FAFSA is required. Check with the school for current deadlines.

International Students: The school actively recruits these students. They must achieve a satisfactory score on the TOEFL and also take the SAT or the ACT.

Computers: All students may access the system 24 hours a day, 7 days a week. There are no time limits.

Admissions Contact: J.P. Cooney, Director of Admissions. A video is available. E-mail: jcooney@mercyhusrt.edu Web: www.mercyhurst.edu

MESSIAH COLLEGE   D-3
Grantham, PA 17027
(717) 691-6000
(800) 233-4220; Fax: (717) 796-5374

Full-time: 1070 men, 1794 women	Faculty: 170; IIB, -$
Part-time: 22 men, 30 women	Ph.D.s: 71%
Graduate: none	Student/Faculty: 17 to 1
Year: semesters, summer session	Tuition: $22,110
Application Deadline: open	Room & Board: $6800
Freshman Class: 2730 applied, 2036 accepted, 707 enrolled	
SAT Verbal/Math: 600/590*	ACT: 26 VERY COMPETITIVE+

Messiah College, founded in 1909, is a private Christian college of the liberal and applied arts and sciences. The college is committed to the evangelical spirit rooted in the Anabaptist, Pietist, and Wesleyan traditions of Christian churches. There are 5 undergraduate schools. In addition to regional accreditation, Messiah has baccalaureate program accreditation with ABET, ADA, CAAHEP, CCNE, CSWE, NASAD, and NASM. The library contains 295,518 volumes, 118,682 microform items, and 18,528 audio/video tapes/CDs/DVDs, and subscribes to 11,036 periodicals including electronic. Computerized library services include the card catalog, interlibrary loans, database searching, and Internet access. Special learning facilities include a learning resource center, art gallery, natural history museum, and radio station. The 485-acre campus is in a small town 12 miles southwest of Harrisburg. Including any residence halls, there are 50 buildings.

Student Life: 52% of undergraduates are from Pennsylvania. Others are from 39 states and 28 foreign countries. 75% are from public schools. 89% are white. Most are Protestant. The average age of freshmen is 18; all undergraduates, 20. 15% do not continue beyond their first year; 75% remain to graduate.

Housing: 2369 students can be accommodated in college housing, which includes single-sex and coed dorms, on-campus apartments, and off-campus apartments. In addition, there are special-interest houses. On-campus housing is guaranteed for all 4 years. 84% of students live on campus; of those, 65% remain on campus on weekends. Alcohol is not permitted. All students may keep cars.

Activities: There are no fraternities or sororities. There are 54 groups on campus, including art, band, cheerleading, choir, chorale, chorus, dance, drama, ethnic, film, honors, international, jazz band, literary magazine, musical theater, newspaper, orchestra, pep band, political, professional, radio and TV, religious, social, social service, student government, symphony, and yearbook. Popular campus events include cultural series, traveling music ensembles, and Theatre Messiah.

Sports: There are 10 intercollegiate sports for men and 10 for women, and 8 intramural sports for men and 9 for women. Facilities include indoor and outdoor tracks, a pool with separate diving well, wrestling and gymnastics areas, a weight room, numerous playing fields, and courts for racquetball, basketball, and tennis. The campus center provides additional recreational facilities.

Disabled Students: 85% of the campus is accessible. Wheelchair ramps, elevators, special parking, specially equipped rest rooms, special class scheduling, and lowered drinking fountains are available.

Services: Counseling and information services are available, as is tutoring in some subjects. There is a reader service for the blind and remedial reading and writing.

Campus Safety and Security: Measures include 24-hour foot and vehicle patrol, self-defense education, security escort services, and informal discussions. There are pamphlets/posters/films, emergency telephones, and lighted pathways/sidewalks.

Programs of Study: Messiah confers B.A., B.S., B.S.E., B.S.N., and B.S.W. degrees. Bachelor's degrees are awarded in AGRICULTURE (environmental studies), BIOLOGICAL SCIENCE (biochemistry and biology/biological science), BUSINESS (accounting, business administration and management, business economics, business systems analysis, electronic business, entrepreneurial studies, international business management, marketing/retailing/merchandising, and personnel management), COMMUNICATIONS AND THE ARTS (art history and appreciation, broadcasting, communications, dramatic arts, English, French, German, journalism, music, Spanish, and studio art), COMPUTER AND PHYSICAL SCIENCE (chemistry, computer science, mathematics, and physics), EDUCATION (art, athletic training, early childhood, elementary, English, environmental, foreign languages, mathematics, music, physical, science, and social studies), ENGINEERING AND ENVIRONMENTAL DESIGN (engineering and environmental science), HEALTH PROFESSIONS (exercise science, nursing, and recreation therapy), SOCIAL SCIENCE (biblical studies, biopsychology, criminal justice, dietetics, economics, history, human development, humanities, ministries, philosophy, political science/government, psychology, religion, social work, and sociology). Elementary education, nursing, and biology are the largest.

Required: All students must complete at least 126 credits with a minimum GPA of 2.0. The last 30 credits must be taken at Messiah College and a minimum of 12 credits must be in the major. For general education requirements, students must take 9 credits each in Christian faith, math, natural sciences, humanities and arts, and languages and cultures; 6 credits each in social sciences and history and in interdisciplinary studies; 3 credits in first-year seminar, oral communications, a writing enrichment course, ethics, world views/pluralism, and health/phys ed; and 2 to 3 credits in non-Western studies.

Special: Students may cross-register at Temple University in Philadelphia. Off-campus study is available at Daystar University in Kenya, through Brethren Colleges Abroad, at Jerusalem University College at Oxford University, in Thailand, and through Latin American, Central American, Middle East, and Russian studies programs, among others. Off-campus options within the United States include the American Studies program, the Au Sable Institute of Environmental Studies, Los Angeles Film Studies, Oregon Extension, and others. Students may also spend a semester or year at any of 12 other Christian Consortium colleges in a student exchange program. Numerous internships, practicums, and ministry opportunities are available. There are 2 national honor societies, a freshman honors program, and 16 departmental honors programs.

Faculty/Classroom: 65% of faculty are male; 35%, female. All teach undergraduates. The average class size in an introductory lecture is 27; in a laboratory, 18; and in a regular course, 24.

Admissions: 75% of the 2005-2006 applicants were accepted. The SAT scores for the 2005-2006 freshman class were: Verbal--8% below 500, 39% between 500 and 599, 40% between 600 and 700, and 12% above 700; Math--12% below 500, 41% between 500 and 599, 39% between 600 and 700, and 9% above 700. The ACT scores were 11% below 21, 17% between 21 and 23, 28% between 24 and 26, 20% between 27 and 28, and 24% above 28. 63% of the current freshmen were in the top fifth of their class; 88% were in the top two fifths. There were 7 National Merit finalists. 33 freshmen graduated first in their class.

Requirements: Messiah requires the SAT or ACT exam for most students. Applicants graduating in the top 20% of their class have a score-less option that requires an interview. Applicants must have graduated from an accredited high school or the equivalent. Secondary preparation of students who enroll usually includes 4 units in English, 3 or 4 in math, 3 each in natural science, social studies, and foreign languages, and 4 in academic electives. Students who enroll are usually in the top one third of their class and have a B average or better. A campus visit with an interview/information session is recommended. Potential music majors must audition. AP and CLEP credits are accepted. Important factors in the admissions decision are leadership record, recommendations by school officials, and advanced placement or honor courses.

Procedure: Freshmen are admitted fall and spring. Entrance exams should be taken in the spring of the junior year. There is an early admissions plan. Application deadlines are open. The application fee is $30. Notification is sent on a rolling basis. A waiting list is an active part of the admissions procedure. Applications are accepted on-line.

Transfer: 85 transfer students enrolled in 2004-2005. Transfer applicants should have earned a 2.5 GPA in at least 30 college credits. The college prefers that applicants also have composite SAT or ACT scores and that they seek a campus visit. Students with fewer than 30 credits in college should submit a high school transcript as well. 30 of 126 credits required for the bachelor's degree must be completed at Messiah.

Visiting: There are regularly scheduled orientations for prospective students, including a campus tour, academic and career advising, and a financial aid information session. There are guides for informal visits and visitors may sit in on classes and stay overnight. To schedule a visit, contact Ellen Ferris at *Eferris@messiah.edu.*

Financial Aid: In 2005-2006, 99% of all full-time freshmen and 96% of continuing full-time students received some form of financial aid. 77% of full-time freshmen and 78% of continuing full-time students received need-based aid. The average freshman award was $14,789. Need-based scholarships or need-based grants averaged $4879; need-based self-help

aid (loans and jobs) averaged $5885; and other non-need-based awards and non-need-based scholarships averaged $5906. 55% of undergraduates work part time. Average annual earnings from campus work are $1783. The average financial indebtedness of the 2005 graduate was $23,249. The FAFSA is required. The priority date for freshman financial aid applications for fall entry is April 1.

International Students: There are 74 international students enrolled. The school actively recruits these students. They must score satisfactorily on the written TOEFL or on the electronic version and also take the SAT or the ACT.

Computers: Limited wireless access is available in certain buildings. All students may access the system 24 hours a day. There are no time limits and no fees.

Graduates: From July 1, 2004 to June 30, 2005, 633 bachelor's degrees were awarded. The most popular majors were elementary education (8%), psychology (7%), and nursing (7%). Of the 2004 graduating class, 14% were enrolled in graduate school within 6 months of graduation and 86% were employed.

Admissions Contact: William G. Strausbaugh, Dean for Enrollment Management. A video is available. E-mail: *admiss@messiah.edu* Web: *www.messiah.edu*

MILLERSVILLE UNIVERSITY OF PENNSYLVANIA E-4
Millersville, PA 17551-0302
(717) 872-3371
(800) MU-ADMIT; Fax: (717) 871-2147

Full-time: 2714 men, 3599 women	**Faculty:** 334
Part-time: 284 men, 338 women	**Ph.D.s:** 95%
Graduate: 283 men, 701 women	**Student/Faculty:** 19 to 1
Year: 4-1-4, summer session	**Tuition:** $6235 ($13,658)
Application Deadline: open	**Room & Board:** $5875
Freshman Class: 6411 applied, 3553 accepted, 1318 enrolled	
SAT Verbal/Math: 520/540*	**COMPETITIVE**

Millersville University, founded as Lancaster County Normal School in 1855, is a public institution offering undergraduate and graduate programs in liberal arts and sciences and education. There are 3 undergraduate schools and 1 graduate school. In addition to regional accreditation, Millersville has baccalaureate program accreditation with AACTE, ABET, ACBSP, ACS, CAHEA, CSAB, CSWE, NASM, NCATE, NLN, NAIT, and NASPE. The library contains 505,601 volumes, 560,716 microform items, and 32,034 audio/video tapes/CDs/DVDs, and subscribes to 10,776 periodicals including electronic. Computerized library services include the card catalog, interlibrary loans, database searching, Internet access, and laptop Internet portals. Special learning facilities include a learning resource center, art gallery, radio station, TV station, an early childhood center, and a foreign language lab. The 220-acre campus is in a small town 5 miles west of Lancaster. Including any residence halls, there are 102 buildings.

Student Life: 97% of undergraduates are from Pennsylvania. Others are from 22 states, 67 foreign countries, and Canada. 79% are white. The average age of freshmen is 19; all undergraduates, 21. 17% do not continue beyond their first year; 67% remain to graduate.

Housing: 2384 students can be accommodated in college housing, which includes coed dormitories, on-campus apartments, and off-campus apartments. In addition, there are honors houses and special-interest houses, including service learning/leadership and an internation student house. On-campus housing is available on a first-come, first-served basis. 67% of students commute. Alcohol is not permitted. Upperclassmen may keep cars.

Activities: 3% of men belong to 1 local and 8 national fraternities; 4% of women belong to 2 local and 6 national sororities. There are 113 groups on campus, including art, band, cheerleading, choir, chorale, chorus, dance, drama, ethnic, film, forensics, gay, honors, international, jazz band, literary magazine, marching band, musical theater, newspaper, orchestra, pep band, political, professional, radio and TV, religious, social, social service, student government, symphony, and yearbook. Popular campus events include Parents Day, Wellness Week, and International Week.

Sports: There are 9 intercollegiate sports for men and 11 for women, and 13 intramural sports for men and 13 for women. Facilities include a football stadium, 2 pools, 2 gyms, 2 fitness centers, a dance studio, a ropes course, wrestling and weight rooms, basketball, volleyball, tennis, and badminton courts, and various playing fields.

Disabled Students: 85% of the campus is accessible. Wheelchair ramps, elevators, special parking, specially equipped rest rooms, special class scheduling, lowered drinking fountains, lowered telephones, special housing, and transportation assistance within campus are available.

Services: Counseling and information services are available, as is tutoring in most subjects. There is a reader service for the blind, and remedial math, reading, and writing. Every effort is made to tailor a tutoring program to individual needs. Note takers, interpreters, and some physical aids and other specialized equipment are provided, as available.

Campus Safety and Security: Measures include 24-hour foot and vehicle patrol, self-defense education, security escort services, and shuttle

buses. There are informal discussions, pamphlets/posters/films, emergency telephones, lighted pathways/sidewalks, and regularly scheduled crime awareness programs.

Programs of Study: Millersville confers B.A., B.S., B.F.A., B.S.Ed., and B.S.N. degrees. Associate and master's degrees are also awarded. Bachelor's degrees are awarded in BIOLOGICAL SCIENCE (biology/biological science), BUSINESS (business administration and management), COMMUNICATIONS AND THE ARTS (art, communications, English, French, German, music, and Spanish), COMPUTER AND PHYSICAL SCIENCE (atmospheric sciences and meteorology, chemistry, computer science, earth science, geology, mathematics, oceanography, and physics), EDUCATION (art, elementary, music, social studies, special, and technical), ENGINEERING AND ENVIRONMENTAL DESIGN (industrial engineering technology and occupational safety and health), HEALTH PROFESSIONS (nursing), SOCIAL SCIENCE (anthropology, economics, geography, history, international studies, philosophy, political science/government, psychology, social work, and sociology). Physical sciences and teacher education are the strongest academically. Elementary education, business administration, and biology are the largest.

Required: All students must complete at least 120 hours, including 30 in the major, with a minimum 2.0 GPA. Courses are required in humanities, science and math, social sciences, and perspectives as part of a core curriculum. Specific courses are required in writing, speech, wellness, and phys ed.

Special: Numerous co-op and internship programs, including student teaching opportunities, are available. Millersville has exchange agreements with Franklin and Marshall College, Lancaster Theological Seminary, and Wallops Island Consortium, and 3-2 engineering programs with Pennsylvania State University and the University of Pennsylvania for chemistry and physics majors. Study abroad is offered in Germany, England, Japan, Scotland, Chile, and Spain. Dual majors are possible in most disciplines, and accelerated degrees and B.A.-B.S. degrees are available in many. Nondegree study is offered, and there are limited pass/fail options. There are 6 national honor societies, a freshman honors program, and 11 departmental honors programs.

Faculty/Classroom: 52% of faculty are male; 48%, female. All teach undergraduates. No introductory courses are taught by graduate students. The average class size in an introductory lecture is 35; in a laboratory, 24; and in a regular course, 25.

Admissions: 55% of the 2005-2006 applicants were accepted. The SAT scores for the 2005-2006 freshman class were: Verbal--33% below 500, 50% between 500 and 599, 16% between 600 and 700, and 1% above 700; Math--28% below 500, 52% between 500 and 599, 19% between 600 and 700, and 1% above 700. 31% of the current freshmen were in the top fifth of their class; 66% were in the top two fifths. 7 freshmen graduated first in their class.

Requirements: The SAT is required, and the ACT is accepted. Applicants must be graduates of approved secondary schools or hold a GED. Secondary preparation should include 4 credits in English, 3 credits each in math and social studies, and 2 credits each in science and history. Music program applicants must audition. An interview is optional for all applicants. Millersville requires applicants to be in the upper 40% of their class. A GPA of 2.0 is required. AP and CLEP credits are accepted. Important factors in the admissions decision are advanced placement or honor courses, evidence of special talent, and recommendations by school officials.

Procedure: Freshmen are admitted to all sessions. Entrance exams should be taken in the spring of the junior year. There are early admissions, deferred admissions and rolling admissions plans. Application deadlines are open. Applications are accepted on-line. The fall 2005 application fee was $35.

Transfer: 439 transfer students enrolled in 2004-2005. All applicants must submit high school as well as college transcripts. Graduates of state community colleges are given preference over applicants with fewer than 2 and more than 5 semesters of study at other colleges. Applicants must have at least a 2.0 GPA. A personal interview is recommended. 30 of 120 credits required for the bachelor's degree must be completed at Millersville.

Visiting: There are regularly scheduled orientations for prospective students, including a president's welcome and admissions, financial aid, student organization, and department conferences. There are guides for informal visits and visitors may sit in on classes. To schedule a visit, contact the Campus Visit Coordinator at the Admissions Office at (717) 872-3371.

Financial Aid: In 2005-2006, 83% of all full-time freshmen and 73% of continuing full-time students received some form of financial aid. 55% of full-time freshmen and 50% of continuing full-time students received need-based aid. The average freshman award was $7744. Need-based scholarships or need-based grants averaged $2812 ($15,252 maximum); need-based self-help aid (loans and jobs) averaged $3667 ($21,761 maximum); non-need-based athletic scholarships averaged $31 ($4000 maximum); and other non-need-based awards and non-need-based scholarships averaged $1264 ($20,370 maximum). 31% of undergraduates work part time. Average annual earnings from campus work are

$1129. The average financial indebtedness of the 2005 graduate was $16,103. The FAFSA is required. The deadline for filing freshman financial aid applications for fall entry is March 15.

International Students: There are 138 international students enrolled. The school actively recruits these students. They must score satisfactorily on the written TOEFL or on the electronic version and also take the SAT.

Computers: Wireless access is available. Approved students are entitled to computer accounts to access the mainframes for e-mail, the Internet and coursework. There are 20 general-purpose PC labs on campus, housing IBM and Mac PCs and Sun work stations. Most Pcs are local area networked. All students may access the system 24 hours, 7 days a week. There are no time limits and no fees. It is strongly recommended that all students have a personal computer.

Graduates: From July 1, 2004 to June 30, 2005, 1402 bachelor's degrees were awarded. The most popular majors were elementary education (16%), business administration (11%), and communications and theatre (8%). In an average class, 1% graduate in 3 years or less, 36% graduate in 4 years or less, 57% graduate in 5 years or less, and 59% graduate in 6 years or less. 75 companies recruited on campus in 2004-2005.

Admissions Contact: Douglas Zander, Director of Admissions.
E-mail: *admissions@millersville.edu* Web: *www.millersville.edu/~admit*

MOORE COLLEGE OF ART AND DESIGN   F-3

Philadelphia, PA 19103   (215) 568-4515, ext. 1105
                    (800) 523-2025, ext. 1105; Fax: (215) 568-8017

Full-time: 480 women	**Faculty:** 34
Part-time: 150 women	**Ph.D.s:** 83%
Graduate: none	**Student/Faculty:** 14 to 1
Year: semesters, summer session	**Tuition:** $19,750
Application Deadline: open	**Room & Board:** $7450
Freshman Class: n/av	
SAT: recommended	**SPECIAL**

Moore College of Art and Design, founded in 1844, is a private professional and fine arts college for women in the country. Figures in the above capsule and profile are approximate. In addition to regional accreditation, Moore has baccalaureate program accreditation with FIDER and NASAD. The library contains 34,000 volumes, and subscribes to 250 periodicals including electronic. Computerized library services include the card catalog, interlibrary loans, database searching, and Internet access. Special learning facilities include 2 art galleries. The 4-acre campus is in an urban area in Philadelphia. Including any residence halls, there are 4 buildings.

Student Life: 61% of undergraduates are from Pennsylvania. Others are from 29 states and 7 foreign countries. 60% are from public schools. 77% are white. The average age of freshmen is 19; all undergraduates, 23. 15% do not continue beyond their first year; 55% remain to graduate.

Housing: 194 students can be accommodated in college housing, which includes single-sex dormitories and off-campus apartments. On-campus housing is guaranteed for all 4 years. 70% of students commute. Alcohol is not permitted. All students may keep cars.

Activities: There are no fraternities. There are 10 groups on campus, including computers, enviromental action, ethnic, film, gay, international, newspaper, professional, social service, student government, and yearbook. Popular campus events include Family Day, Spring Fling, and Convocation.

Sports: There is no sports program at Moore. Facilities include a fitness center with a weight room.

Disabled Students: All of the campus is accessible. Wheelchair ramps, elevators, special parking, specially equipped rest rooms, lowered drinking fountains, and lowered telephones are available.

Services: Counseling and information services are available, as is tutoring in most subjects. English as a second language is offered.

Campus Safety and Security: Measures include 24-hour foot and vehicle patrol, self-defense education, security escort services, and shuttle buses. There are informal discussions, pamphlets/posters/films, emergency telephones, and lighted pathways/sidewalks.

Programs of Study: Moore confers the B.F.A. degree. Bachelor's degrees are awarded in COMMUNICATIONS AND THE ARTS (fine arts, graphic design, illustration, painting, and sculpture), EDUCATION (art), ENGINEERING AND ENVIRONMENTAL DESIGN (interior design), SOCIAL SCIENCE (fashion design and technology and textiles and clothing). Interior design is the strongest academically. Graphic design is the largest.

Required: All students take 36 credits in basic arts, including design, drawing, color, and art history, and a liberal arts core in history, humanities, and social science. A total of 125.5 to 137 credits, with a 2.0 minimum GPA, is required for graduation. A thesis is required in some programs.

Special: Moore has long-established cooperative relationships with various employers who provide training to supplement academic studies in all majors. Dual majors, nondegree study, study abroad, and continuing education programs are offered.

Faculty/Classroom: 38% of faculty are male; 62%, female. All teach undergraduates. The average class size in an introductory lecture is 20 and in a regular course, 10.

Requirements: The SAT is recommended. Applicants should be graduates of accredited high schools or the equivalent, having taken 4 years of English and 2 years each of social studies, science, and math. At least 2 years of art study are also recommended. The most important part of the application is the portfolio of 8 to 12 original pieces, 6 of which should be drawings from observation. In addition, Moore strongly recommends a personal interview. A GPA of 2.5 is required. AP and CLEP credits are accepted. Important factors in the admissions decision are evidence of special talent, personality/intangible qualities, and extracurricular activities record.

Procedure: Freshmen are admitted fall and spring. There are early admissions, deferred admissions, and rolling admissions plans. Application deadlines are open. The fall 2005 application fee was $40.

Transfer: Transfer applicants from non-art programs must meet freshman admission requirements. Others must submit a portfolio for review. Applicants should have at least a 2.0 GPA in previous college work, and submit satisfactory SAT scores. A personal interview is required. 50 of 126 credits required for the bachelor's degree must be completed at Moore.

Visiting: There are regularly scheduled orientations for prospective students, including an open house in November. There are guides for informal visits and visitors may sit in on classes and stay overnight. To schedule a visit, contact the Admissions Office.

Financial Aid: In a recent year, all full-time students received some form of financial aid. 85% of full-time freshmen and 83% of continuing full-time students received need-based aid. The average freshman award was $16,250. Need-based scholarships or need-based grants averaged $4400 ($9000 maximum); need-based self-help aid (loans and jobs) averaged $2500 ($5125 maximum); other non-need-based awards and non-need-based scholarships averaged $4100 ($8500 maximum); and non-need based self-help loans and work-study averaged $5250. 30% of undergraduates worked part time. Average annual earnings from campus work were $2000. The average financial indebtedness of a recent graduate was $25,000. Moore is a member of CSS. The CSS/Profile and the college's own financial statement are required. Check with school for application deadlines.

International Students: In a recent year, there were 8 international students enrolled. The school actively recruits these students. They must score satisfactorily on the written TOEFL.

Computers: There are no time limits and no fees.

Graduates: In a recent year, 104 bachelor's degrees were awarded. The most popular majors were graphic design (28%), fashion design (22%), and fine arts (20%). In an average class, 55% graduate in 4 years or less. Of a recent graduating class, 5% were enrolled in graduate school within 6 months of graduation and 80% were employed.

Admissions Contact: Wendy Pyle Elliott, Director of Admissions. E-mail: *admiss@moore.edu* Web: *www.moore.edu*

MORAVIAN COLLEGE F-3
Bethlehem, PA 18018

	(610) 861-1320
	(800) 441-3191; Fax: (610) 625-7930
Full-time: 565 men, 965 women	**Faculty:** 114; IIB, +$
Part-time: 110 men, 210 women	**Ph.D.s:** 78%
Graduate: 50 men, 125 women	**Student/Faculty:** 13 to 1
Year: semesters, summer session	**Tuition:** $22,100
Application Deadline: see profile	**Room & Board:** $6850
Freshman Class: n/av	
SAT or ACT: required	**VERY COMPETITIVE**

Moravian College, established in 1742, is a private, liberal arts institution affiliated with the Moravian Church. There are 2 undergraduate schools and 1 graduate school. The figures in the above capsule and in this profile are approximate. In addition to regional accreditation, Moravian has baccalaureate program accreditation with ACS, CCNE, CAHEA, and NASM. The library contains 257,650 volumes, 11,680 microform items, and 4800 audio/video tapes/CDs/DVDs, and subscribes to 1185 periodicals including electronic. Computerized library services include the card catalog, interlibrary loans, database searching, and Internet access. Special learning facilities include a learning resource center, art gallery, and radio station. The 80-acre campus is in a suburban area 60 miles north of Philadelphia and 90 miles west of New York City. Including any residence halls, there are 127 buildings.

Student Life: 61% of undergraduates are from Pennsylvania. Others are from 22 states, 16 foreign countries, and Canada. 80% are from public schools. 92% are white. 41% are Catholic; 29% Protestant; 9% claim no religious affiliation. The average age of freshmen is 18; all undergraduates, 20. 14% do not continue beyond their first year; 74% remain to graduate.

Housing: 1047 students can be accommodated in college housing, which includes single-sex and coed dormitories, on-campus apartments, fraternity houses, and sorority houses. In addition, there are special-interest houses. On-campus housing is guaranteed for all 4 years. 71% of students live on campus; of those, 65% remain on campus on weekends. Upperclassmen may keep cars.

Activities: 14% of men belong to 1 local and 2 national fraternities; 22% of women belong to 4 national sororities. There are 77 groups on campus, including alumni, art, band, cheerleading, choir, chorale, chorus, computers, dance, debate, drama, ethnic, gay, honors, international, jazz band, literary magazine, marching band, newspaper, orchestra, outdoor recreation, pep band, photography, political, professional, radio, religious, social, social service, student government, and yearbook. Popular campus events include arts and lecture series, Christmas vesper services, and Mardi Gras dance.

Sports: There are 10 intercollegiate sports for men and 10 for women, and 11 intramural sports for men and 11 for women. Facilities include a 1200-seat gym, football, soccer, field hockey, and lacrosse fields, baseball and softball diamonds, indoor and all-weather tracks, indoor and outdoor tennis courts, a field house, a fitness room, an aerobics and dance studio, and 4 multipurpose courts.

Disabled Students: Wheelchair ramps, elevators, special parking, specially equipped rest rooms, special class scheduling, lowered drinking fountains, lowered telephones, and special housing are available.

Services: Counseling and information services are available, as is tutoring in most subjects. There is a reader service for the blind, peer assistance, and a writing center.

Campus Safety and Security: Measures include 24-hour foot and vehicle patrol, self-defense education, security escort services, and shuttle buses. There are informal discussions, pamphlets/posters/films, emergency telephones, lighted pathways/sidewalks, and an and ongoing crime prevention program supervised by a crime prevention officer.

Programs of Study: Moravian confers B.A., B.S., and B.Mus. degrees. Master's degrees are also awarded. Bachelor's degrees are awarded in BIOLOGICAL SCIENCE (biology/biological science), BUSINESS (accounting, business administration and management, business economics, and international business management), COMMUNICATIONS AND THE ARTS (art history and appreciation, classics, dramatic arts, English, French, German, graphic design, music, Spanish, and studio art), COMPUTER AND PHYSICAL SCIENCE (chemistry, computer science, mathematics, and physics), EDUCATION (art, elementary, music, and secondary), HEALTH PROFESSIONS (nursing), SOCIAL SCIENCE (counseling/psychology, criminal justice, developmental psychology, economics, experimental psychology, history, industrial and organizational psychology, philosophy, political science/government, psychology, religion, social science, and sociology). Physics, chemistry, and math are the strongest academically. Psychology, management, and sociology are the largest.

Required: To graduate, students must complete a Learning in Common curriculum, which includes courses in writing, quantitative reasoning, historical studies, ultimate questions, cultural values and global issues, natural sciences, a foreign language, social sciences, aesthetic expression, literature, moral life, and phys ed. They must maintain a minimum GPA of 2.0 and complete 32 courses equivalent to 128 credits. The number of hours required in the major varies.

Special: The college offers 3-2 engineering degrees in conjunction with Washington University and a 4-1 engineering program with Lehigh University. Moravian also offers cooperative programs in allied health, natural resource management, and geology with Lehigh, Duke, and Thomas Jefferson Universities. Cross-registration is available with Lehigh and DeSales Universities and Lafayette, Muhlenberg, and Cedar Crest. Internships, study abroad in many countries, a Washington semester, and student-designed majors may be pursued. There are 17 national honor societies and all departments have honors programs.

Faculty/Classroom: 57% of faculty are male; 43%, female. All both teach and do research. No introductory courses are taught by graduate students. The average class size in an introductory lecture is 20; in a laboratory, 14; and in a regular course, 18.

Requirements: The SAT or ACT is required. In addition, applicants must graduate from an accredited secondary school or have a GED. Moravian requires 16 Carnegie units, based on 4 years each of English and social science, 3 to 4 of math, and 2 each of lab science, a foreign language, and electives. Essays are required and interviews are recommended. For music students, auditions are required; for art students, portfolios are recommended. AP and CLEP credits are accepted. Important factors in the admissions decision are advanced placement or honor courses, recommendations by school officials, and leadership record.

Procedure: Freshmen are admitted fall and spring. Entrance exams should be taken with enough time to submit scores by the application deadline. There are early decision and deferred admissions plans. Check with the school for application deadlines. Notification of early decision is sent December 15; regular decision, March 15. Applications are accepted on-line.

Transfer: 106 transfer students enrolled in a recent year. Applicants must have a minimum GPA of 2.5 and are required to submit recommendations, secondary and postsecondary transcripts, and standardized test scores. 32 of 128 credits required for the bachelor's degree must be completed at Moravian.

Visiting: There are regularly scheduled orientations for prospective students, including tours and interviews with admissions staff. There are guides for informal visits and visitors may sit in on classes and stay overnight. To schedule a visit, contact the Office of Admission.

Financial Aid: In a recent year, 94% of all full-time freshmen and 93% of continuing full-time students received some form of financial aid. 77% of full-time freshmen and 75% of continuing full-time students received need-based aid. The average freshman award was $15,227. Need-based scholarships or need-based grants averaged $11,851; and need-based self-help aid (loans and jobs) averaged $5044. 51% of undergraduates worked part time. Average annual earnings from campus work were $804. Moravian is a member of CSS. The CSS/Profile or FAFSA is required. Check with the school for application deadlines.

International Students: In a recent year, there were 25 international students enrolled. The school actively recruits these students. They must score satisfactorily on the written TOEFL or on the electronic version. The SAT or ACT is preferred for all students and required if the student's first language is English.

Computers: All students may access the system 24 hours per day. There are no time limits and no fees.

Graduates: In a recent year, 339 bachelor's degrees were awarded. The most popular majors were psychology (14%), sociology (12%), and management (11%). In an average class, 56% graduate in 4 years or less, and 74% graduate in 5 years or less. 22 companies recruited on campus in a recent year. Of a recent graduating class, 23% were enrolled in graduate school within 6 months of graduation and 69% were employed.

Admissions Contact: James P. Mackin, Director of Admission. E-mail: *admissions@moravian.edu* Web: *www.moravian.edu*

MOUNT ALOYSIUS COLLEGE   C-3
Cresson, PA 16630

	(814) 886-6383
	(888) 823-2220; Fax: (814) 886-6441
Full-time: 330 men, 817 women	**Faculty:** 62; IIB, --$
Part-time: 83 men, 252 women	**Ph.D.s:** 35%
Graduate: 14 men, 43 women	**Student/Faculty:** 19 to 1
Year: semesters, summer session	**Tuition:** $14,710
Application Deadline: see profile	**Room & Board:** $6190
Freshman Class: 949 applied, 728 accepted, 293 enrolled	
SAT Verbal/Math: 460/460*	**ACT:** 18 **Less Competitive**

Mount Aloysius, established 1853 by the Sisters of Mercy, is a private, liberal arts college affiliated with the Roman Catholic Church. In addition to regional accreditation, Mount Aloysius College has baccalaureate program accreditation with APTA and NLN. The library contains 77,186 volumes, 4680 microform items, and 2431 audio/video tapes/CDs/DVDs, and subscribes to 275 periodicals including electronic. Computerized library services include the card catalog, interlibrary loans, and database searching. Special learning facilities include a learning resource center and art gallery. The 165-acre campus is in a small town located in the southern Allegheny Mountains between Altoona and Johnstown. Including any residence halls, there are 8 buildings.

Student Life: 96% of undergraduates are from Pennsylvania. Others are from 20 states, 15 foreign countries, and Canada. 94% are white. 43% are Catholic; 13% Protestant. The average age of freshmen is 21; all undergraduates, 27. 28% do not continue beyond their first year; 67% remain to graduate.

Housing: 237 students can be accommodated in college housing, which includes single-sex and coed dorms. In adition, there are rooms for hearing-impaired students. On-campus housing is guaranteed for all 4 years. 85% of students commute. Alcohol is not permitted. All students may keep cars.

Activities: There are no fraternities or sororities. There are 30 groups on campus, including art, campus ministry, cheerleading, chorale, chorus, computers, drama, ethnic, honors, musical theater, newspaper, photography, professional, religious, social, social service, student government, and yearbook. Popular campus events include Madrigal Dinner, Heritage days, and Christmas at the Mount.

Sports: There are 5 intercollegiate sports for men and 5 for women, and 13 intramural sports for men and 12 for women. Facilities include an 1800-seat health and physical fitness center with 3 basketball courts, 2 tennis courts, a volleyball court, a weight-and-exercise room equipped with a sauna, and 2 locker rooms.

Disabled Students: 95% of the campus is accessible. Wheelchair ramps, elevators, special parking, specially equipped rest rooms, lowered drinking fountains, lowered telephones, and special housing are available.

Services: Counseling and information services are available, as is tutoring in every subject. There is remedial math, reading, and writing.

Campus Safety and Security: Measures include 24-hour foot and vehicle patrol, security escort services, informal discussions, and pamphlets/posters/films. There are emergency telephones and lighted pathways/sidewalks.

Programs of Study: Mount Aloysius College confers B.A., and B.S. degrees. Associate and master's degrees are also awarded. Bachelor's degrees are awarded in BUSINESS (accounting and business administration and management), COMMUNICATIONS AND THE ARTS (English), COMPUTER AND PHYSICAL SCIENCE (information sciences and systems and science), EDUCATION (elementary), HEALTH PROFESSIONS (medical laboratory technology, nursing, and occupational therapy), SOCIAL SCIENCE (criminology, history, interpreter for the deaf, prelaw, and psychology). Nursing, prelaw, and criminology are the strongest academically. Nursing, criminology, and elementary education are the largest.

Required: Baccalaureate-level students are required during their final semester of study to complete 2 3-credit courses designed to integrate and synthesize scientific, behavioral, and moral concepts. Students in allied health programs must complete an approved clinical experience. Courses in research writing and speech are required. A total of 120 credits is required with an overall 2.0 GPA, including a C average in all core courses.

Special: The Professional Studies curriculum provides a student-designed course of study, with an emphasis in behavior and social science, humanities, math/science/computer science, or prelaw. B.A.-B.S. degrees are offered, as are internships in nursing, business, criminology, and student teaching. Dual majors are possible in elementary education/early childhood education. There are 3 national honor societies, a freshman honors program, and 1 departmental honors program.

Faculty/Classroom: 37% of faculty are male; 63%, female. All both teach and do research. The average class size in an introductory lecture is 17; in a laboratory, 12; and in a regular course, 17.

Admissions: 77% of the 2005-2006 applicants were accepted. The SAT scores for the 2005-2006 freshman class were: Verbal--67% below 500, 30% between 500 and 599, and 3% between 600 and 700; Math--67% below 500, 28% between 500 and 599, and 5% between 600 and 700. The ACT scores were 84% below 21, 15% between 21 and 23, and 1% between 24 and 26. 5 freshmen graduated first in their class.

Requirements: The SAT or ACT is required. In addition, applicants must graduate from an accredited high school or have the GED. A placement test and any necessary developmental studies classes may need to be taken. Science classes and an interview are required of some allied health programs. A GPA of 2.5 is required. AP and CLEP credits are accepted. Important factors in the admissions decision are recommendations by school officials, advanced placement or honor courses, and leadership record.

Procedure: Freshmen are admitted fall and spring. Entrance exams should be taken as early as possible. For the nursing and health studies programs, applications should be filed by June 1. Application deadlines are open for other programs. Application fee is $30. Notification is sent on a rolling basis. Applications are accepted on-line.

Transfer: 200 transfer students enrolled in 2004-2005. Transfer students must have a 2.0 GPA. Only courses with a C or better will be considered for transfer; all other requirements are the same as for freshmen. 30 of 120 credits required for the bachelor's degree must be completed at Mount Aloysius College.

Visiting: There are regularly scheduled orientations for prospective students, including 3 daily sessions. There are guides for informal visits and visitors may sit in on classes and stay overnight. To schedule a visit, contact the Admissions Office at *admissions@mtaloy.edu*.

Financial Aid: In a recent year, 90% of all full-time freshmen and 95% of continuing full-time students received some form of financial aid. 94% of full-time freshmen and 86% of continuing full-time students received need-based aid. The average freshman award was $9000. Need-based scholarships or need-based grants averaged $3000 ($5000 maximum); need-based self-help aid (loans and jobs) averaged $3000 ($5000 maximum); and other non-need-based awards and non-need-based scholarships averaged $3000 ($7000 maximum). All undergraduates work part time. Average annual earnings from campus work are $750. The average financial indebtedness of the 2005 graduate was $17,125. Mount Aloysius College is a member of CSS. The FAFSA is required. The priority date for freshman financial aid applications for fall entry is February 15. The deadline for filing freshman financial aid applications for fall entry is May 1.

International Students: There are 23 international students enrolled. The school actively recruits these students. They must score 500 on the written TOEFL or 173 on the electronic version and also take the SAT, ACT, or New Jersey Basic Skills Test.

Computers: Wireless access is available. All students may access the system from 8 A.M. to 10 P.M. There are no time limits and no fees.

Graduates: From July 1, 2004 to June 30, 2005, 123 bachelor's degrees were awarded. 30 companies recruited on campus in 2004-2005. Of the 2004 graduating class, 22% were enrolled in graduate school within 6 months of graduation and 97% were employed.

Admissions Contact: Francis Crouse, Jr., Dean of Enrollment Management. E-mail: *admissions@mtaloy.edu* Web: *www.mtaloy.edu*

MUHLENBERG COLLEGE
Allentown, PA 18104 E-3
(484) 664-3200; Fax: (484) 664-3234

Full-time: 961 men, 1306 women	Faculty: 156; IIB, -$
Part-time: 78 men, 112 women	Ph.Ds: 86%
Graduate: none	Student/Faculty: 15 to 1
Year: semesters, summer session	Tuition: $28,760
Application Deadline: February 15	Room & Board: $7270
Freshman Class: 4217 applied, 1809 accepted, 576 enrolled	
SAT Verbal/Math: 610/620*	ACT: 28

HIGHLY COMPETITIVE+

Muhlenberg College, established in 1848, is a private liberal arts institution affiliated with the Lutheran Church. The library contains 226,746 volumes, 136,124 microform items, and 14,222 audio/video tapes/CDs/DVDs, and subscribes to 14,760 periodicals including electronic. Computerized library services include the card catalog, interlibrary loans, database searching, Internet access, and laptop Internet portals. Special learning facilities include a learning resource center, art gallery, natural history museum, radio station, TV station, and 2 more than 50-acre environmental field stations. The 80-acre campus is in a suburban area 50 miles north of Philadelphia and 90 miles west of New York City. Including any residence halls, there are 70 buildings.

Student Life: 74% of undergraduates are from out of state, mostly the Middle Atlantic. Students are from 34 states, 6 foreign countries, and Canada. 70% are from public schools. 92% are white. 31% are Catholic; 26% Jewish; 13% Protestant. The average age of freshmen is 18; all undergraduates, 19. 7% do not continue beyond their first year; 81% remain to graduate.

Housing: 1968 students can be accommodated in college housing, which includes single-sex and coed dorms, on-campus apartments, off-campus apartments, fraternity houses, and sorority houses. In addition, there are language houses special-interest houses, and college-owned houses in the surrounding community. On-campus housing is guaranteed for all 4 years. 90% of students live on campus; of those, 80% remain on campus on weekends. Upperclassmen may keep cars.

Activities: 14% of men belong to 4 national fraternities; 18% of women belong to 4 national sororities. There are 100 groups on campus, including art, band, cheerleading, chess, choir, chorale, chorus, computers, dance, drama, ethnic, film, gay, honors, human rights, international, jazz band, literary magazine, musical theater, newspaper, opera, orchestra, pep band, photography, political, professional, radio and TV, religious, social, social service, step team, student government, and yearbook. Popular campus events include Spring Fling Weekend, Candlelight Carols, and Jefferson Field Day.

Sports: There are 11 intercollegiate sports for men and 11 for women, and 13 intramural sports for men and 13 for women. Facilities include a sports center, which contains a 6-lane swimming pool, racquetball and squash courts, wrestling and weight training rooms; a multipurpose field house with indoor tennis courts, a running track, and a fitness loft; and outdoor volleyball courts, athletic fields, tennis courts, a soccer stadium, an all-weather track, and a football stadium.

Disabled Students: 95% of the campus is accessible. Wheelchair ramps, elevators, special parking, specially equipped rest rooms, special class scheduling, lowered drinking fountains, lowered telephones, extra time on tests, tutors, and books on tape are available.

Services: Counseling and information services are available, as is tutoring in every subject. There is a reader service for the blind and a writing center.

Campus Safety and Security: Measures include 24-hour foot and vehicle patrol, self-defense education, security escort services, and shuttle buses. There are informal discussions, pamphlets/posters/films, emergency telephones, and lighted pathways/sidewalks.

Programs of Study: Berg confers B.A. and B.S. degrees. Bachelor's degrees are awarded in BIOLOGICAL SCIENCE (biochemistry, biology/biological science, and neurosciences), BUSINESS (accounting and business administration and management), COMMUNICATIONS AND THE ARTS (art, communications, dance, English, German, music, and Spanish), COMPUTER AND PHYSICAL SCIENCE (chemistry, computer science, mathematics, natural sciences, physical sciences, and physics), ENGINEERING AND ENVIRONMENTAL DESIGN (environmental science), SOCIAL SCIENCE (American studies, anthropology, economics, German area studies, history, international studies, philosophy, political science/government, psychology, religion, Russian and Slavic studies, and sociology). Biology, theater, and English are the strongest academically. Biology, business administration, and communication are the largest.

Required: To graduate, students must complete requirements in literature and the arts, religion or philosophy, human behavior and social institutions, historical studies, physical and life sciences, and other cultures. They must have a minimum GPA of 2.0 in a total of 34 course units, with 9 to 14 units in the major. All students must take 1 quarter of phys ed, including a wellness course, as well as freshman and senior seminars.

Special: Students may cross-register with Lehigh, Lafayette, Cedar Crest, Moravian, and Allentown Colleges. Internships, work-study pro-

grams, B.A.-B.S. degrees, study abroad in Asia, Australia, Latin America, Russia, and Europe, and a Washington semester are available. Dual majors and student-designed majors may be pursued. A 3-2 engineering degree is available in cooperation with Columbia and Washington Universities, a 4-4 assured admission medical program is offered with Drexel University College of Medicine, a 3-4 dental program is offered with University of Pennsylvania, and a 3-2 forestry degree is offered in cooperation with Duke University. Nondegree study and a pass/fail grading option are also offered. There are 12 national honor societies, including Phi Beta Kappa, a freshman honors program, and 9 departmental honors programs.

Faculty/Classroom: 54% of faculty are male; 46%, female. All teach undergraduates, 84% do research, and 84% do both. The average class size in an introductory lecture is 30; in a laboratory, 18; and in a regular course, 19.

Admissions: 43% of the 2005-2006 applicants were accepted. The SAT scores for the 2005-2006 freshman class were: Verbal--3% below 500, 40% between 500 and 599, 45% between 600 and 700, and 12% above 700; Math--4% below 500, 28% between 500 and 599, 58% between 600 and 700, and 10% above 700. The ACT scores were 7% between 21 and 23, 30% between 24 and 26, 26% between 27 and 28, and 37% above 28. 75% of the current freshmen were in the top fifth of their class; 96% were in the top two fifths. There were 2 National Merit semifinalists. 4 freshmen graduated first in their class.

Requirements: The SAT or ACT is required for some programs. The ACT Optional Writing Test is also required for some programs. In addition, applicants must graduate from an accredited secondary school or have a GED. 16 Carnegie units are required, and students must complete 4 courses in English, 3 in math, and 2 each in history, science, and a foreign language. All students must submit essays. Interviews are recommended and are required for those who do not submit SAT scores. AP and CLEP credits are accepted. Important factors in the admissions decision are advanced placement or honor courses, leadership record, and evidence of special talent.

Procedure: Freshmen are admitted fall and spring. Entrance exams should be taken during the spring of the junior year or the fall of the senior year. There are early decision, early admissions, and deferred admissions plans. Early decision applications should be filed by February 1; regular applications, by February 15 for fall entry, along with a $45 fee. Notification of early decision is sent on a rolling basis; regular decision, March 15. 309 early decision candidates were accepted for the 2005-2006 class. 465 applicants were on the 2005 waiting list; 41 were admitted. Applications are accepted on-line.

Transfer: 6 transfer students enrolled in 2004-2005. A minimum college GPA of 2.5 and an interview are required. 17 of 34 credits required for the bachelor's degree must be completed at Berg.

Visiting: There are regularly scheduled orientations for prospective students, consisting of a tour of the campus and a personal interview. There are 2 open houses in the fall and 1 in the spring. There are guides for informal visits and visitors may sit in on classes and stay overnight. To schedule a visit, contact Bonnie Reabold or Alyssa Rabenold at (484) 664-3202 or reabold@muhlenberg.edu.

Financial Aid: In 2005-2006, 75% of all full-time freshmen and 73% of continuing full-time students received some form of financial aid. 46% of full-time freshmen and 42% of continuing full-time students received need-based aid. The average freshman award was $15,517. Need-based scholarships or need-based grants averaged $16,155 ($33,405 maximum); need-based self-help aid (loans and jobs) averaged $4054 ($7425 maximum); and other non-need-based awards and non-need-based scholarships averaged $11,331 ($19,000 maximum). 41% of undergraduates work part time. Average annual earnings from campus work are $1086. The average financial indebtedness of the 2005 graduate was $15,292. Berg is a member of CSS. The CSS/Profile, FAFSA, the college's own financial statement, and parent and student tax returns and W-2 forms are required. The deadline for filing freshman financial aid applications for fall entry is February 15.

International Students: There are 11 international students enrolled. The school actively recruits these students. They must take the written TOEFL.

Computers: Wireless access is available. There are student computers throughout campus and in residence halls. All students may access the system 24 hours a day. There are no time limits and no fees. It is strongly recommended that all students have a personal computer.

Graduates: From July 1, 2004 to June 30, 2005, 589 bachelor's degrees were awarded. The most popular majors were business (17%), psychology (9%), and communication (9%). In an average class, 1% graduate in 3 years or less, 81% graduate in 4 years or less, and 85% graduate in 5 or 6 years or less. 68 companies recruited on campus in 2004-2005. Of the 2004 graduating class, 29% were enrolled in graduate school within 6 months of graduation and 68% were employed.

Admissions Contact: Christopher Hooker-Haring, Dean, Admissions. E-mail: admissions@muhlenberg.edu Web: www.muhlenberg.edu

NEUMANN COLLEGE
E-4
Aston, PA 19014-1298
(610) 558-5616
(800) 9NEUMAN; Fax: (610) 558-5652

Full-time: 652 men, 1180 women	Faculty: 80; IIB, --$
Part-time: 118 men, 363 women	Ph.D.s: 62%
Graduate: 170 men, 327 women	Student/Faculty: 23 to 1
Year: semesters, summer session	Tuition: $17,920
Application Deadline: open	Room & Board: $8076
Freshman Class: 2080 applied, 1996 accepted, 522 enrolled	
SAT Verbal/Math: 450/430*	LESS COMPETITIVE

Neumann College, founded in 1965 by the Sisters of St. Francis, is a private liberal arts institution affiliated with the Roman Catholic Church. In addition to regional accreditation, Neumann has baccalaureate program accreditation with ACBSP, CAHEA, CAPTE and NLN. The library contains 90,000 volumes, 99,758 microform items, and 36,562 audio/video tapes/CDs/DVDs, and subscribes to 700 periodicals including electronic. Computerized library services include the card catalog, interlibrary loans, database searching, and Internet access. Special learning facilities include a learning resource center and a learning assistance center. The 50-acre campus is in a suburban area 15 miles southwest of Philadelphia. Including any residence halls, there are 6 buildings.

Student Life: 70% of undergraduates are from Pennsylvania. Others are from 24 states, 7 foreign countries, and Canada. 35% are from public schools. 68% are white; 13% African American. 67% are Catholic; 23% Protestant; 7% claim no religious affiliation. The average age of freshmen is 18; all undergraduates, 20. 23% do not continue beyond their first year; 55% remain to graduate.

Housing: 800 students can be accommodated in college housing, which includes coed dormitories and off-campus apartments. On-campus housing is available on a first-come, first-served basis. Priority is given to out-of-town students. 54% of students commute. Alcohol is not permitted. All students may keep cars.

Activities: There are no fraternities or sororities. There are 17 groups on campus, including choir, chorus, dance, drama, ethnic, honors, literary magazine, newspaper, photography, political, professional, religious, social, social service, and student government. Popular campus events include dinner dances, Spring Fling, and charity fund-raising.

Sports: There are 7 intercollegiate sports for men and 8 for women, and 5 intramural sports for men and 5 for women. Facilities include a 350-seat gym, weight and fitness rooms, tennis courts, baseball and softball fields, an ice hockey rink, video games, and a theater.

Disabled Students: All of the campus is accessible. Wheelchair ramps, elevators, special parking, specially equipped rest rooms, and special class scheduling are available.

Services: Counseling and information services are available, as is tutoring in most subjects. There is a reader service for the blind, and remedial math, reading, and writing.

Campus Safety and Security: Measures include 24-hour foot and vehicle patrol, self-defense education, security escort services, and shuttle buses. There are informal discussions, pamphlets/posters/films, emergency telephones, and lighted pathways/sidewalks.

Programs of Study: Neumann confers B.A. and B.S. degrees. Associate and master's degrees are also awarded. Bachelor's degrees are awarded in AGRICULTURE (environmental studies), BIOLOGICAL SCIENCE (biology/biological science), BUSINESS (accounting, business administration and management, international business management, marketing and distribution, and sports management), COMMUNICATIONS AND THE ARTS (communications, English, and performing arts), COMPUTER AND PHYSICAL SCIENCE (computer science), EDUCATION (athletic training, early childhood, and elementary), HEALTH PROFESSIONS (nursing), SOCIAL SCIENCE (criminal justice, liberal arts/general studies, political science/government, and psychology). Biology, nursing, and elementary education are the strongest academically. Nursing, elementary education, and liberal studies are the largest.

Required: To graduate, all students must complete 120 to 130 credits, including 44 credits of core requirements, with 30 to 50 in the major. A minimum 2.0 GPA is required.

Special: The college offers co-op programs in all majors, study abroad in England, internships, work-study programs, dual majors, and a general studies degree. Credit for life, work, and military experience, nondegree study, an accelerated degree liberal studies program, and pass/fail options are available. There are 4 national honor societies, a freshman honors program, and 1 departmental honors program.

Faculty/Classroom: 35% of faculty are male; 65%, female. 94% teach undergraduates and 15% both teach and do research. No introductory courses are taught by graduate students. The average class size in an introductory lecture is 24; in a laboratory, 17; and in a regular course, 20.

Admissions: 96% of the 2005-2006 applicants were accepted. The SAT scores for the 2005-2006 freshman class were: Verbal--81% below 500, 16% between 500 and 599, 2% between 600 and 700, and 1% above 700; Math--81% below 500, 17% between 500 and 599, and 2% between 600 and 700. 25% of the current freshmen were in the top fifth of their class; 80% were in the top two fifths.

Requirements: The SAT is required. In addition, applicants must be graduates of an accredited secondary school or have a GED. High school courses must include 4 years of English and 2 years each of a foreign language, history, and science. An interview is recommended. A GPA of 2.0 is required. AP and CLEP credits are accepted. Recommendations by school officials is an important factor in the admission decision.

Procedure: Freshmen are admitted fall and spring. Entrance exams should be taken by December of the senior year. There are deferred admissions and rolling admissions plans. Application deadlines are open. Application fee is $35. Applications are accepted on-line.

Transfer: 79 transfer students enrolled in a recent year. Applicants should submit transcripts from all institutions attended. 30 of 120 to 130 credits required for the bachelor's degree must be completed at Neumann.

Visiting: There are regularly scheduled orientations for prospective students, including class visits and informal meetings with faculty. There are guides for informal visits and visitors may sit in on classes. To schedule a visit, contact the Admissions Office.

Financial Aid: In a recent year, 95% of all full-time freshmen and 90% of continuing full-time students received some form of financial aid. 90% of all full-time students received need-based aid. The average freshman award was $15,000. Need-based scholarships or need-based grants averaged $10,000 ($15,000 maximum); and need-based self-help aid (loans and jobs) averaged $5000 ($7000 maximum). 89% of undergraduates worked part time. Average annual earnings from campus work were $1200. The average financial indebtedness of a recent year graduate was $15,000. The FAFSA is required. The deadline for filing freshman financial aid applications for fall entry is March 15.

International Students: There are 14 international students enrolled. They must score satisfactorily on the written TOEFL or on the electronic version and also take the SAT.

Computers: Wireless access is available. Every student has access to the college's network and the campus is wireless. Dormitories have Internet cable connection. All students may access the system any time. There are no time limits and no fees. It is strongly recommended that all students have a personal computer.

Graduates: From July 1, 2004 to June 30, 2005, 395 bachelor's degrees were awarded. The most popular majors were liberal studies (29%), elementary education (15%), and nursing (15%). In an average class, 40% graduate in 4 years or less, 50% graduate in 5 years or less, and 55% graduate in 6 years or less. 55 companies recruited on campus in 2004-2005. Of the 2004 graduating class, 15% were enrolled in graduate school within 6 months of graduation and 95% were employed.

Admissions Contact: Dennis Murphy, Vice President for enrollment management. E-mail: *neumann@neumann.edu*
Web: *www.neumann.edu*

PEIRCE COLLEGE
F-3
Philadelphia, PA 19102
(215) 670-9214
(888) 467-3472; Fax: (888)467-3472

Full-time: 200 men, 600 women	Faculty: 30; III, --$
Part-time: 319 men, 843 women	Ph.D.s: 43%
Graduate: none	Student/Faculty: 27 to 1
Year: sessions, summer session	Tuition: $12,760
Application Deadline: open	Room & Board: n/app
Freshman Class: 593 applied, 593 accepted, 218 enrolled	
SAT or ACT: not required	NONCOMPETITIVE

Peirce College, founded in 1865, is a private specialized institution providing practical curricula to primarily working adults. Peirce offers accelerated bachelor's and associate degree programs in business administration, information technology, and paralegal studies, utilizing 3 interchangeable delivery formats: on campus, in Center City Philadelphia; on site at corporate and community locations throughout the region; and on line through web-based distance learning. There is 1 undergraduate school. In addition to regional accreditation, Peirce has baccalaureate program accreditation with ACBSP and ABA. The library contains 30,000 volumes, and subscribes to 25,000 periodicals including electronic. Computerized library services include the card catalog, interlibrary loans, database searching, and Internet access. Special learning facilities include a learning resource center and the Walker Center for Academic Excellence. The 1-acre campus is in an urban area in the Center City Business District. There are 2 buildings.

Student Life: 80% of undergraduates are from Pennsylvania. Others are from 40 states, 30 foreign countries, and Canada. 50% are African American; 31% white. The average age of freshmen is 31; all undergraduates, 33. 7% do not continue beyond their first year; 53% remain to graduate.

Housing: There are no residence halls. 100% of students commute. Alcohol is not permitted. No one may keep cars.

Activities: There are no fraternities or sororities. There are 3 groups on campus, including honors and professional. Popular campus events include Student Leadership Retreat, Welcome Back Day, and Annual Awards Induction Ceremony.

Sports: There is no sports program at Peirce.

Disabled Students: All of the campus is accessible. Wheelchair ramps, elevators, specially equipped rest rooms, special class scheduling, lowered drinking fountains, and lowered telephones are available.

Services: Counseling and information services are available, as is tutoring in most subjects. There is a reader service for the blind, and remedial math, reading, and writing.

Campus Safety and Security: Measures include 24-hour foot and vehicle patrol, security escort services, informal discussions, and pamphlets/posters/films. There are emergency telephones, lighted pathways/sidewalks, and security cameras throughout the campus.

Programs of Study: Peirce confers the B.S. degree. Associate degrees are also awarded. Bachelor's degrees are awarded in BUSINESS (accounting, business administration and management, business law, entrepreneurial studies, human resources, management information systems, marketing management, and real estate), COMPUTER AND PHYSICAL SCIENCE (computer management, computer programming, and information sciences and systems), ENGINEERING AND ENVIRONMENTAL DESIGN (computer technology), SOCIAL SCIENCE (paralegal studies). Paralegal studies is the strongest academically. Business administration is the largest.

Required: To graduate, all students must complete 121 credit hours, including a core curriculum, and maintain a minimum cumulative GPA of 2.0.

Special: The college offers accelerated degrees and co-op programs in most major programs of study. There are 2 national honor societies.

Faculty/Classroom: 62% of faculty are male; 38%, female. All teach undergraduates. The average class size in an introductory lecture is 19 and in a regular course, 18.

Admissions: 100% of the 2005-2006 applicants were accepted.

Requirements: Applicants for a degree program must submit a completed application for admission and application fee and an official transcript documenting high school graduation or a copy of the GED or state equivalency diploma and scores. AP and CLEP credits are accepted.

Procedure: Freshmen are admitted to all sessions. Entrance exams are offered continuously. There is a deferred admissions plan. Application deadlines are open. Application fee is $50. Applications are accepted on-line.

Transfer: 1224 transfer students enrolled in 2004-2005. Transcripts from other colleges attended must be submitted. 31 of 121 credits required for the bachelor's degree must be completed at Peirce.

Visiting: There are regularly scheduled orientations for prospective students, including a campus tour and a meeting with an adviser. There are guides for informal visits and visitors may sit in on classes. To schedule a visit, contact Enrollment Services at info@peirce.edu.

Financial Aid: In 2005-2006, 72% of all full-time students received some form of financial aid. 72% of all full-time students received need-based aid. The average freshman award was $4000. Need-based scholarships or need-based grants averaged $2000 (maximum); need-based self-help aid (loans and jobs) averaged $3500 ($7500 maximum); and other non-need-based awards and non-need-based scholarships averaged $4500 (maximum). 15% of undergraduates work part time. Average annual earnings from campus work are $2000. The average financial indebtedness of the 2005 graduate was $15,000. The FAFSA and the college's own financial statement are required. The priority date for freshman financial aid applications for fall entry is April 15. The deadline for filing freshman financial aid applications for fall entry is June 1.

International Students: There are 22 international students enrolled. The school actively recruits these students.

Computers: Over 230 computers are available for student use on campus in classrooms, labs, and the library. Students may access electronic courseware, e-mail, the Internet, and library databases. Students can register for courses and pay bills online. Through electronic courseware, they can participate in lectures, student organizations, and discussions. They can also view grades, and communicate with classmates and instructors. Wireless connectivity is available in the library and labs. All students may access the system. There are no time limits and no fees. All students are required to have personal computers.

Graduates: From July 1, 2004 to June 30, 2005, 253 bachelor's degrees were awarded. The most popular majors were business administration (65%), information technology (23%), and paralegal studies (12%). In an average class, 2% graduate in 3 years or less, 20% graduate in 4 years or less, 56% graduate in 5 years or less, and 69% graduate in 6 years or less. 15 companies recruited on campus in 2004-2005. Of the 2004 graduating class, 32% were enrolled in graduate school within 6 months of graduation and 86% were employed.

Admissions Contact: Admissions, Enrollment Representative. E-mail: info@peirce.edu Web: www.peirce.edu

PENN STATE ERIE/THE BEHREND COLLEGE   B-1

Erie, PA 16563

(814) 898-6100
(866) 374-3378; Fax: (814) 898-6044

Full-time: 2154 men, 1067 women	**Faculty:** 204; IIB, av$
Part-time: 150 men, 69 women	**Ph.D.s:** 61%
Graduate: 98 men, 55 women	**Student/Faculty:** 16 to 1
Year: semesters, summer session	**Tuition:** $10,026 ($15,910)
Application Deadline: open	**Room & Board:** $6230

Freshman Class: 2590 applied, 2092 accepted, 854 enrolled

SAT or ACT: required   **COMPETITIVE**

Penn State Erie The Behrend College, founded in 1948, offers 26 baccalaureate programs as well as the first 2 years of most Penn State University Park baccalaureate programs. It offers courses in business, humanities, social sciences, science, engineering technology, and engineering. There are 4 undergraduate and 2 graduate schools. In addition to regional accreditation, Penn State Behrend or Penn State Erie has baccalaureate program accreditation with AACSB and ABET. The library contains 100,000 volumes, 75,190 microform items, and 351 audio/video tapes/CDs/DVDs, and subscribes to 700 periodicals including electronic. Computerized library services include the card catalog, interlibrary loans, database searching, Internet access, and laptop Internet portals. Special learning facilities include a learning resource center, radio station, and engineering workstation labs, media labs, and an observatory. The 725-acre campus is in a suburban area 5 miles east of Erie. Including any residence halls, there are 42 buildings.

Student Life: 92% of undergraduates are from Pennsylvania. Others are from 28 states, 23 foreign countries, and Canada. 79% are white; 14% foreign nationals. The average age of freshmen is 18; all undergraduates, 22. 9% do not continue beyond their first year; 61% remain to graduate.

Housing: 1650 students can be accommodated in college housing, which includes single-sex and coed dorms and on-campus apartments. In addition, there are honors houses, special-interest houses, and freshman interest groups housing. On-campus housing is guaranteed for the freshman year only, is available on a first-come, first-served basis, and is available on a lottery system for upperclassmen. 53% of students commute. Alcohol is not permitted. All students may keep cars.

Activities: 5% of men belong to 3 national fraternities; 16% of women belong to 3 national sororities. There are 80 groups on campus, including band, cheerleading, chess, choir, computers, dance, drama, ethnic, gay, honors, international, jazz band, literary magazine, newspaper, pep band, political, professional, radio and TV, religious, social, social service, student government, and yearbook. Popular campus events include a speaker series, parents events, and Black Cultural Awareness Month.

Sports: There are 10 intercollegiate sports for men and 11 for women, and 18 intramural sports for men and 18 for women. Facilities include a new athletic center with an indoor track and an 8-lane pool, tennis courts, a weight room, a fitness trail, basketball courts, and baseball, softball, and soccer fields.

Disabled Students: 90% of the campus is accessible. Wheelchair ramps, elevators, special parking, specially equipped rest rooms, special class scheduling, lowered drinking fountains, and lowered telephones are available.

Services: Counseling and information services are available, as is tutoring in every subject. There is a reader service for the blind, and remedial math, reading, and writing.

Campus Safety and Security: Measures include 24-hour foot and vehicle patrol, self-defense education, security escort services, and informal discussions. There are pamphlets/posters/films, emergency telephones, and lighted pathways/sidewalks.

Programs of Study: Penn State Behrend or Penn State Erie confers B.A., B.S., and B.F.A. degrees. Associate and master's degrees are also awarded. Bachelor's degrees are awarded in BIOLOGICAL SCIENCE (biology/biological science), BUSINESS (accounting, banking and finance, business administration and management, business economics, management information systems, and marketing management), COMMUNICATIONS AND THE ARTS (communications and English), COMPUTER AND PHYSICAL SCIENCE (chemistry, computer science, mathematics, physics, and science), ENGINEERING AND ENVIRONMENTAL DESIGN (computer engineering, engineering, engineering technology, mechanical engineering technology, and plastics technology), SOCIAL SCIENCE (economics, history, political science/government, and psychology). Management information systems, psychology, and math are the strongest academically. Engineering, business, and psychology are the largest.

Required: All baccalaureate degree candidates must take 46 general education credits, including 27 in arts, humanities, natural science, and social and behavioral sciences including a cultural diversity course, 15 in quantification and communication skills including a writing intensive course, and 3 in health, phys ed, and a freshman seminar. All students must complete a minimum of 120 credit hours with a minimum GPA of 2.0. Further requirements vary by degree program.

Special: Internships, study abroad in 14 countries, work-study programs, and accelerated degree programs are available. In addition, a B.A.-B.S. degree in psychology, a 3-2 engineering degree with Edinboro University, dual majors, a general studies degree, and student-designed majors in business and general arts and sciences are offered. Nondegree study and up to 12 credits of pass/fail options are possible. There are 4 national honor societies and a freshman honors program.

Faculty/Classroom: 70% of faculty are male; 30%, female. 100% both teach and do research. No introductory courses are taught by graduate students. The average class size in an introductory lecture is 35; in a laboratory, 18; and in a regular course, 29.

Admissions: 81% of the 2005-2006 applicants were accepted. The SAT is required. 12 freshmen graduated first in their class.

Requirements: The SAT or ACT is required. The ACT Optional Writing test is also recommended. In addition, candidates for admission must have 15 academic credits or 15 Carnegie units, including 5 in social studies, 4 in English, 3 each in math and science, and 2 in foreign language. The GED is accepted. AP and CLEP credits are accepted.

Procedure: Freshmen are admitted to all sessions. Entrance exams should be taken during the junior year. There is a deferred admissions and a rolling admissions plans. Application deadlines are open. Application fee is $50. Notification is sent on a rolling basis. Applications are accepted on-line.

Transfer: Transfer candidates need a minimum GPA of 2.4, good academic standing, and 18 or more credits from a regionally accredited institution at the college level. 36 of 120 credits required for the bachelor's degree must be completed at Penn State Behrend or Penn State Erie.

Visiting: There are regularly scheduled orientations for prospective students, including meetings with a counselor and faculty, a campus tour, and a class visit. There are guides for informal visits and visitors may sit in on classes and stay overnight. To schedule a visit, contact the Admissions Office.

Financial Aid: The FAFSA is required. The priority date for freshman financial aid applications for fall entry is February 15.

International Students: There are 32 international students enrolled. The school actively recruits these students. A satisfactory score is required on the written TOEFL.

Computers: Wireless access is available. All students may access the system any time by modem or network. There are no time limits and no fees. It is strongly recommended that all students have a personal computer.

Admissions Contact: Mary-Ellen Madigan, Director of Admissions. E-mail: *behrend.admissions@psu.edu* Web: *www.pserie.psu.edu*

PENN STATE UNIVERSITY/ALTOONA

Altoona, PA 16601	(814) 949-5466; (800) 848-9843
Full-time: 1795 men, 1670 women	Faculty: 122
Part-time: 130 men, 230 women	Ph.D.s: 71%
Graduate: 2 men, 10 women	Student/Faculty: 28 to 1
Year: semesters, summer session	Tuition: $7285 ($11,120)
Application Deadline: open	Room & Board: $5350
Freshman Class: n/av	
SAT or ACT: required	COMPETITIVE

Penn State Altoona, founded in 1939, offers more than 10 baccalaureate degree programs, as well as a number of associate degrees. Figures in the above capsule and this profile are approximate. In addition to regional accreditation, Penn State University/Altoona has baccalaureate program accreditation with ABET. The library contains 58,596 microform items and 5680 audio/video tapes/CDs/DVDs, and subscribes to 291 periodicals including electronic. Computerized library services include the card catalog, interlibrary loans, and database searching. Special learning facilities include a learning resource center, art gallery, Pic-Tel teleconferencing, 5 state-of-the-art engineering labs, and CAD/CAM computer lab facilities. The 123-acre campus is in a suburban area. Including any residence halls, there are 25 buildings.

Student Life: 88% of undergraduates are from Pennsylvania. Others are from 29 states and 11 foreign countries. 85% are white. 54% claim no religious affiliation; 25% various Christian and non-Christian denominations; 18% Catholic. The average age of freshmen is 19; all undergraduates, 22.

Housing: 900 students can be accommodated in college housing, which includes single-sex and coed dormitories. In addition, there are honors houses, special-interest houses, and alcohol-free and substance-free housing. On-campus housing is available on a first-come, first-served basis and is available on a lottery system for upperclassmen. 76% of students commute. Alcohol is not permitted. All students may keep cars.

Activities: 4% of men belong to 4 national fraternities; 3% of women belong to 3 local sororities. There are 50 groups on campus, including cheerleading, choir, dance, drama, ethnic, gay, honors, horticulture, international, jazz band, literary magazine, newspaper, pep band, political, professional, religious, social, social service, step team, student government, and yearbook. Popular campus events include Distinguished

Speaker Series, Hoops Hysteria, and Black History and Women's History Month events.

Sports: There are 6 intercollegiate sports for men and 6 for women. Facilities include a large gym, an indoor pool, racquetball courts, a weight room, a fitness loft, tennis courts, an outdoor track, sand volleyball courts, and baseball, softball, and soccer fields.

Disabled Students: 95% of the campus is accessible. Wheelchair ramps, elevators, special parking, specially equipped rest rooms, special class scheduling, lowered drinking fountains, and lowered telephones are available.

Services: Counseling and information services are available, as is tutoring in most subjects. There is remedial math, reading, and writing.

Campus Safety and Security: Measures include 24-hour foot and vehicle patrol, self-defense education, security escort services, and shuttle buses. There are informal discussions, pamphlets/posters/films, emergency telephones, and lighted pathways/sidewalks.

Programs of Study: Penn State University/Altoona confers B.A. and B.S. degrees. Associate degrees are also awarded. Bachelor's degrees are awarded in AGRICULTURE (environmental studies), BUSINESS (business administration and management), COMMUNICATIONS AND THE ARTS (English), COMPUTER AND PHYSICAL SCIENCE (science), ENGINEERING AND ENVIRONMENTAL DESIGN (electromechanical technology), HEALTH PROFESSIONS (nursing), SOCIAL SCIENCE (criminal justice, human development, and liberal arts/general studies). Engineering is the strongest academically. Business, engineering, and criminal justice are the largest.

Required: To graduate, students must complete a minimum of 120 credit hours with a minimum GPA of 2.0. They must complete 46 general education credits, including 27 in arts, humanities, natural science, and social and behavioral sciences and 15 in quantification and communication skills.

Special: Internships, study abroad in 2 countries, work-study programs, accelerated degree programs, and dual and student-designed majors are available. There is an integrative arts major, which allows students to pursue interest across artistic boundaries. There are 2 national honor societies, including Phi Beta Kappa, and a freshman honors program.

Faculty/Classroom: 59% of faculty are male; 41%, female. No introductory courses are taught by graduate students. The average class size in an introductory lecture is 35; in a laboratory, 20; and in a regular course, 24.

Requirements: The SAT or ACT is required. In addition, applicants should have 15 academic or Carnegie units, including 4 in English, 3 each in math, science, and social studies, and 2 in foreign language (required for some majors). The GED is accepted. AP and CLEP credits are accepted. Advanced placement or honor courses is an important factor in the admission decision.

Procedure: Freshmen are admitted to all sessions. Entrance exams should be taken during the junior year. There are early admissions, deferred admissions, and rolling admissions plans. Application deadlines are open. Applications are accepted on-line. The fall 2005 application fee was $50.

Transfer: High school and college transcripts are required, as is good academic standing. The minimum GPA varies by major. 36 of 120 credits required for the bachelor's degree must be completed at Penn State University/Altoona.

Visiting: There are regularly scheduled orientations for prospective students, including campus tours and meetings with academic counselors and faculty. There are guides for informal visits and visitors may sit in on classes and stay overnight. To schedule a visit, contact the Admissions Office.

Financial Aid: The FAFSA and some academic scholarships require a specific application, which varies according to the college/major. are required. Check with the school for application deadlines.

International Students: The school actively recruits these students. They must score satisfactorily on the written TOEFL and also take the SAT or the ACT.

Computers: All students may access the system. There are no time limits and no fees. It is strongly recommended that all students have a personal computer.

Admissions Contact: Richard Shaffer, Director of Admissions. A video is available. E-mail: *rks8@psu.edu* Web: *www.aa.psu.edu*

PENN STATE UNIVERSITY/UNIVERSITY PARK CAMPUS C-3

University Park, PA 16802	**(814) 865-5471; Fax: (814) 863-7590**
Full-time: 18,013 men, 15,195 women	**Faculty:** I, -$
Part-time: 868 men, 561 women	**Ph.D.s:** 77%
Graduate: 3301 men, 2771 women	**Student/Faculty:** n/av
Year: semesters, summer session	**Tuition:** $11,508 ($21,744)
Application Deadline: open	**Room & Board:** $6530
Freshman Class: 29,904 applied, 18,423 accepted, 6496 enrolled	
SAT Verbal/Math: 580/620*	**HIGHLY COMPETITIVE**

Penn State University/University Park Campus, founded in 1855, is the oldest and largest of 24 campuses in the Penn State system, offering undergraduate and graduate degrees in agricultural science, arts and architecture, business administration, earth and mineral sciences, education, engineering, health and human development, liberal arts, science, and communications. There are 12 undergraduate schools and 1 graduate school. In addition to regional accreditation, Penn State has baccalaureate program accreditation with AACSB, ABET, ACEJMC, ACOTE, ACS, APTA, ASLA, CAAHEP, CCNE, CSAB, NAAB, NASAD, NASM, NAST, NASPE, NCATE, NLN, and SAF. The 14 libraries contain 4,975,339 volumes, 5,202,694 microform items, and 163,643 audio/video tapes/CDs/DVDs, and subscribe to 58,459 periodicals including electronic. Computerized library services include the card catalog, interlibrary loans, database searching, Internet access, and laptop Internet portals. Special learning facilities include a learning resource center, art gallery, planetarium, radio station, TV station, and five major museums at University Park house significant research and educational collections in the fields of agriculture, anthropology, entomology, earth and mineral sciences, and the fine arts. The 15,984-acre campus is in a suburban area 90 miles west of Harrisburg. Including any residence halls, there are 758 buildings.

Student Life: 75% of undergraduates are from Pennsylvania. Others are from 50 states and Canada. 80% are white. The average age of freshmen is 18; all undergraduates, 20. 7% do not continue beyond their first year; 93% remain to graduate.

Housing: More than 13,000 students can be accommodated in college housing, which includes single-sex and coed dorms, on-campus apartments, married-student housing, fraternity houses, and sorority houses. In addition, there are honors houses, language houses, and special-interest houses. On-campus housing is guaranteed for all 4 years and is available on a lottery system for upperclassmen. 62% of students commute. Alcohol is not permitted. Upperclassmen may keep cars.

Activities: 13% of men belong to 59 national fraternities; 10% of women belong to 31 national sororities. There are more than 600 groups on campus, including art, band, cheerleading, chess, choir, chorale, chorus, computers, dance, debate, drama, drill team, ethnic, film, forensics, gay, honors, international, jazz band, literary magazine, marching band, musical theater, newspaper, opera, orchestra, pep band, photography, political, professional, radio and TV, religious, social, social service, student government, symphony, and yearbook. Popular campus events include Late Night Penn State, Dance Marathon, and Distinguished Speaker Series.

Sports: There are 15 intercollegiate sports for men and 14 for women, and 15 intramural sports for men and 14 for women. Facilities include 6 gyms, 5 swimming pools, indoor and outdoor tracks, 2 golf courses, a jogging course, a rink, 2 rifle ranges, 32 acres of practice fields, and numerous courts for tennis, handball, squash, and paddleball.

Disabled Students: All of the campus is accessible. Wheelchair ramps, elevators, special parking, specially equipped rest rooms, special class scheduling, lowered drinking fountains, lowered telephones, and special housing are available.

Services: Counseling and information services are available, as is tutoring in most subjects. There is a reader service for the blind, and remedial math, reading, and writing.

Campus Safety and Security: Measures include 24-hour foot and vehicle patrol, self-defense education, security escort services, and shuttle buses. There are informal discussions, pamphlets/posters/films, emergency telephones, and lighted pathways/sidewalks.

Programs of Study: Penn State confers B.A., B.S., B.Arch., B.Arch.Eng., B.F.A., B.M., B.Mus.Arts, and B.Ph. degrees. Associate, master's, and doctoral degrees are also awarded. Bachelor's degrees are awarded in AGRICULTURE (agricultural business management, agriculture, agronomy, animal science, dairy science, fishing and fisheries, forestry and related sciences, forestry production and processing, horticulture, natural resource management, plant science, poultry science, and soil science), BIOLOGICAL SCIENCE (biochemistry, biology/biological science, ecology, microbiology, molecular biology, nutrition, and wildlife biology), BUSINESS (accounting, banking and finance, business administration and management, hotel/motel and restaurant management, insurance, international business management, labor studies, management information systems, management science, marketing/retailing/merchandising, real estate, and transportation management), COMMUNICATIONS AND THE ARTS (advertising, art, art history and apprecia-

tion, broadcasting, classics, communications, comparative literature, dramatic arts, English, film arts, fine arts, French, German, Italian, journalism, music, Russian, Spanish, and speech/debate/rhetoric), COMPUTER AND PHYSICAL SCIENCE (actuarial science, astronomy, atmospheric sciences and meteorology, chemistry, computer science, earth science, geoscience, mathematics, physics, science, and statistics), EDUCATION (agricultural, art, elementary, health, industrial arts, music, secondary, and special), ENGINEERING AND ENVIRONMENTAL DESIGN (aeronautical engineering, agricultural engineering, architectural engineering, architecture, chemical engineering, civil engineering, computer engineering, electrical/electronics engineering, energy management technology, engineering, environmental engineering, industrial administration/management, industrial engineering, landscape architecture/design, materials science, mechanical engineering, mining and mineral engineering, nuclear engineering, and petroleum/natural gas engineering), HEALTH PROFESSIONS (health care administration, nursing, premedicine, public health, rehabilitation therapy, and speech pathology/audiology), SOCIAL SCIENCE (African American studies, American studies, anthropology, criminal justice, East Asian studies, economics, food science, geography, history, human development, international relations, Latin American studies, liberal arts/general studies, medieval studies, parks and recreation management, philosophy, physical fitness/movement, political science/government, prelaw, psychology, public administration, religion, sociology, and women's studies). Agriculture, architecture, and meteorology are the strongest academically. Engineering, liberal arts, and business are the largest.

Required: The typical baccalaureate Penn State academic program requires the completion of between 120 and 130 credits. The General Education requirements are common to all degree programs and compose about one-third of the course work (45 credits). All students must also complete a Writing-Across-The-Curriculum course (3 credits), a first-year seminar (1 credit), United States Culture (3 credits), and International Cultures (3 credits) as part of their degree program.

Special: Co-op programs, internships, study-abroad in 46 countries, and work-study programs are available. Dual majors and student-designed majors are possible. Accelerated degree programs and a 3-2 engineering degree are also offered. There are 5 national honor societies, including Phi Beta Kappa, and a freshman honors program.

Faculty/Classroom: 68% of faculty are male; 33%, female.

Admissions: 62% of the 2005-2006 applicants were accepted. The SAT scores for the 2005-2006 freshman class were: Verbal--12% below 500, 44% between 500 and 599, 36% between 600 and 700, and 8% above 700; Math--6% below 500, 32% between 500 and 599, 47% between 600 and 700, and 15% above 700. 68% of the current freshmen were in the top fifth of their class; 94% were in the top two fifths.

Requirements: The SAT or ACT is required. The SAT is preferred. Applicants should be graduates of accredited high schools or have earned the GED. Required secondary preparation varies by the college or other academic unit applied to. Generally, all applicants should have 5 years in arts, humanities, and social studies, 4 of English, and 3 each of science and math. 2 years of the same foreign language are required for the College of Liberal Arts and School of Communications, and recommended for all other programs. AP and CLEP credits are accepted. Important factors in the admissions decision are advanced placement or honor courses and evidence of special talent.

Procedure: Freshmen are admitted fall, spring, and summer. Entrance exams should be taken in the junior year. There are early admissions, deferred admissions, and rolling admissions plans. Application deadlines are open. Application fee is $50. Applications are accepted on-line.

Transfer: 362 transfer students enrolled in 2004-2005. Transfer applicants need a minimum GPA of 2.0, good academic standing, and 18 or more credits from any regionally accredited college or institution at the college level. 36 of 120 to 130 credits required for the bachelor's degree must be completed at Penn State.

Visiting: There are regularly scheduled orientations for prospective students. There are guides for informal visits and visitors may sit in on classes and stay overnight. To schedule a visit, contact the Undergraduate Admissions Office.

Financial Aid: In a recent year, 45% of all full-time freshmen and 50% of continuing full-time students received some form of financial aid. 26% of full-time freshmen and 33% of continuing full-time students received need-based aid. The average freshman award was $10,915. Need-based scholarships or need-based grants averaged $4459; need-based self-help aid (loans and jobs) averaged $2830; non-need-based athletic scholarships averaged $3849; and other non-need-based awards and non-need-based scholarships averaged $13,941. The average financial indebtedness of the 2005 graduate was $22,420. The FAFSA is required. The deadline for filing freshman financial aid applications for fall entry is February 15.

International Students: There are 824 international students enrolled. A satisfactory score is required on the written TOEFL. Students whose native language is English or if US citizen or permanent resident must submit SAT or ACT scores; others submit TOEFL.

Computers: There are 52 labs and 247 tech classrooms. All students may access the system 24 hours a day, every day. There are no time limits. The fee is $190 per semester. It is strongly recommended that all students have a personal computer.

Graduates: From July 1, 2004 to June 30, 2005, 9840 bachelor's degrees were awarded. The most popular majors were business (21%), engineering (13%), and communications (9%). In an average class, 56% graduate in 4 years or less, 81% graduate in 5 years or less, and 84% graduate in 6 years or less. 997 companies recruited on campus in 2004-2005. Of the 2004 graduating class, 24% were enrolled in graduate school within 6 months of graduation and 74% were employed.

Admissions Contact: Dr. Randall C. Deike, Assistant Vice President for Undergraduate Education and Executive Vice President for admissions E-mail: *admissions@psu.edu*
Web: *http://www.psu.edu/dept/admissions/*

PENNSYLVANIA COLLEGE OF TECHNOLOGY   D-2

Williamsport, PA 17701

(570) 327-4761
(800) 367-9222; Fax: (570) 321-5536

Full-time: 3858 men, 1657 women	**Faculty:** 283
Part-time: 402 men, 620 women	**Ph.D.s:** 20%
Graduate: none	**Student/Faculty:** 19 to 1
Year: semesters, summer session	**Tuition:** $10,080 ($12,660)
Application Deadline: July 1	**Room & Board:** $6900
Freshman Class: 2830 applied, 2156 enrolled	
SAT Verbal/Math: 460/460*	**LESS COMPETITIVE**

Pennsylvania College of Technology, founded in 1989, is a public technical college affiliated with Pennsylvania State University. There are 9 undergraduate schools. The library contains 113,343 volumes, 12,806 microform items, and 13,494 audio/video tapes/CDs/DVDs, and subscribes to 827 periodicals including electronic. Computerized library services include the card catalog, interlibrary loans, database searching, Internet access, and laptop Internet portals. Special learning facilities include a learning resource center, radio station, a restaurant and a dental hygiene clinic that are open to the public, and the Penn College Child Care Center. The 114-acre campus is in an urban area 80 miles west of Wilkes Barre. Including any residence halls, there are 26 buildings.

Student Life: 91% of undergraduates are from Pennsylvania. Others are from 32 states, 18 foreign countries, and Canada. 94% are white. 57% are Protestant; 23% Catholic; 19% claim no religious affiliation. The average age of freshmen is 19; all undergraduates, 23.

Housing: 1500 students can be accommodated in college housing, which includes single-sex and coed on-campus apartments, first-year experience housing, and academic themed housing. On-campus housing is available on a first-come, first-served basis. 77% of students commute. Alcohol is not permitted. All students may keep cars.

Activities: There are no fraternities or sororities. There are 50 groups on campus, including computers, dance, ethnic, gay, honors, international, professional, radio, religious, social, social service, student government, and yearbook. Popular campus events include a cultural series, Spring Fling Week, and Penn Environment Week.

Sports: There are 9 intercollegiate sports for men and 9 for women, and 35 intramural sports for men and 35 for women. Facilities include a fitness center, a field house, a gym, a soccer field, 5 tennis courts, a sand volleyball court, outdoor basketball court, and an intramural field.

Disabled Students: All of the campus is accessible. Wheelchair ramps, elevators, special parking, specially equipped rest rooms, lowered drinking fountains, and lowered telephones are available.

Services: Counseling and information services are available, as is tutoring in every subject, provided on request, if tutors are available. There is a reader service for the blind, and remedial math, reading, and writing. Services for hearing-impaired students, adaptive equipment, and note takers are available.

Campus Safety and Security: Measures include 24-hour foot and vehicle patrol, self-defense education, security escort services, and shuttle buses. There are informal discussions, pamphlets/posters/films, and lighted pathways/sidewalks.

Programs of Study: Penn College confers B.S. and B.S.N. degrees. Associate degrees are also awarded. Bachelor's degrees are awarded in AGRICULTURE (environmental studies), BUSINESS (accounting, banking and finance, business administration and management, management information systems, marketing and distribution, and marketing management), COMMUNICATIONS AND THE ARTS (graphic design and technical and business writing), COMPUTER AND PHYSICAL SCIENCE (computer programming and polymer science), EDUCATION (vocational), ENGINEERING AND ENVIRONMENTAL DESIGN (aircraft mechanics, automotive technology, civil engineering, civil engineering technology, computer engineering, computer graphics, computer technology, construction management, construction technology, drafting and design, electrical/electronics engineering technology, engineering, food services technology, graphic arts technology, manufacturing engineering, mechanical design technology, mechanical engineering technology, plastics engineering, plastics technology, printing technology, survey and mapping technology, surveying engineering, technological management, transportation technology, and welding engineering), HEALTH PRO-

FESSIONS (dental hygiene,, health care administration, health science, mental health/human services, nursing, occupational therapy, physician's assistant, radiograph medical technology, and radiological science), SOCIAL SCIENCE (culinary arts, human services, and paralegal studies). Information technology, electronics technology, nursing, and business management are the largest.

Required: To graduate, students must complete at least 120 credits with a minimum GPA of 2.0 overall and in the major. The core curriculum consists of 18 to 21 credits in humanities, social science, art, and foreign language, 9 in communications, 7 in science, 6 in math, 2 in health and fitness, and a course in computer information.

Special: Penn College offers cooperative and internship programs, cross-registration with Lycoming College and Penn State, dual and student-designed majors, and credit by exam and for work and/or life experience. There is a chapter of Phi Beta Kappa.

Faculty/Classroom: 62% of faculty are male; 37%, female. All teach undergraduates. The average class size in a regular course is 18.

Admissions: 15% of the current freshmen were in the top fifth of their class; 32% were in the top two fifths.

Requirements: The SAT or ACT is required. In addition, applicants must have a high school diploma or GED and must take the college's placement exams. Other admissions criteria vary by program. AP and CLEP credits are accepted.

Procedure: Freshmen are admitted to all sessions. Entrance exams should be taken prior to scheduling classes. There are early decision, early admissions, and deferred admissions plans. Applications should be filed by July 1 for fall entry. Notification of early decision and regular decision is sent on a rolling basis. 1030 applicants were on the 2005 waiting list; 377 were admitted. Applications are accepted on-line.

Transfer: In a recent year. Transfer procedures vary with each degree program. Courses are evaluated for transfer equivalency. 60 of 120 credits required for the bachelor's degree must be completed at Penn College.

Visiting: There are regularly scheduled orientations for prospective students, including registration, a multimedia presentation, admission and financial aid sessions, a question-and-answer period, a tour of campus facilities, and a reception. There are guides for informal visits and visitors may sit in on classes. To schedule a visit, contact the Office of Admissions at *admissions@pct.edu*.

Financial Aid: In 2005-2006, 76% of all full-time students received some form of financial aid. 76% of all full-time students received need-based aid. The average freshman award was $7277. 6% of undergraduates work part time. Average annual earnings from campus work are $2400. The average financial indebtedness of the 2005 graduate was $12,005. The FAFSA and the college's own financial statement are required. The priority date for freshman financial aid applications for fall entry is April 1.

International Students: There are 30 international students enrolled. The school actively recruits these students. They must receive a satisfactory score on the TOEFL.

Computers: Wireless access is available. There are 50 computer labs with more than 1500 PCs all networked with a 100 MBPS Internet connection. 80% of campus inside spaces have wireless coverage. All students may access the system. There are no time limits and no fees. It is recommended that students in Information Technology have personal computers.

Graduates: From July 1, 2004 to June 30, 2005, 393 bachelor's degrees were awarded. The most popular majors were computer information technology (5%), building construction technology (5%), and nursing (5%). In an average class, 13% graduate in 3 years, 23% graduate in 4 years, 49% graduate in 5 years, and 5% graduate in 6 years. Of the 2004 graduating class, 65% were employed within 6 months of graduation.

Admissions Contact: Chester D. Schuman, Director of Admissions. E-mail: *cschuman@pct.edu* Web: *www.pct.edu*

PENNSYLVANIA STATE SYSTEM OF HIGHER EDUCATION

The Pennsylvania State System of Higher Education, established in 1983, is a public system in Pennsylvania. It is governed by a board of governors, whose chief administrator is the chancellor. The primary goal of the system is to provide high-quality liberal arts education at an affordable cost with a central mission of teaching and service. The main priorities are capital facilities matters of maintenance and funding, social equity, and tuition stabilization through appropriate funding. The total enrollment is usually about 99,000; with 5200 faculty members. Altogether there are some 200 baccalaureate, 100 master's, and 6 doctoral programs offered in Pennsylvania State System of Higher Education. 4-year campuses are located in Bloomsburg, California, Cheyney, Clarion, East Stroudsberg, Edinboro,, Indiana, Kutztown, Lock Haven, Mansfield, Millersville, Shippensburg, Slippery Rock, and West Chester. Profiles of the 4-year campuses are included in this section.

PHILADELPHIA BIBLICAL UNIVERSITY   F-3
Langhorne, PA 19047-2990   (215) 752-5800
(800) 366-0049; Fax: (215) 702-4248

Full-time: 425 men, 553 women	Faculty: 64; IIB, --$
Part-time: 50 men, 35 women	Ph.Ds: 41%
Graduate: 109 men, 147 women	Student/Faculty: 15 to 1
Year: semesters, summer session	Tuition: $15,875
Application Deadline: open	Room & Board: $6550
Freshman Class: 520 applied, 487 accepted, 238 enrolled	
SAT Verbal/Math: 540/520*	ACT: 23 COMPETITIVE

Philadelphia Biblical University, founded in 1913, is a private institution offering instruction in the Scriptures and liberal arts and professional theory. There are 7 undergraduate and 4 graduate schools. In addition to regional accreditation, PBU has baccalaureate program accreditation with CSWE, IACBE, NASM, and NCATE. The library contains 162,850 volumes, 63,827 microform items, and 8312 audio/video tapes/CDs/DVDs, and subscribes to 8064 periodicals including electronic. Computerized library services include the card catalog, interlibrary loans, database searching, Internet access, and laptop Internet portals. Special learning facilities include a learning resource center. The 114-acre campus is in a suburban area 30 miles north of Philadelphia. Including any residence halls, there are 25 buildings.

Student Life: 56% of undergraduates are from Pennsylvania. Others are from 41 states, 18 foreign countries, and Canada. 60% are from public schools. 89% are white; 11% African American. Most are Protestant. The average age of freshmen is 18; all undergraduates, 23. 25% do not continue beyond their first year; 60% remain to graduate.

Housing: 666 students can be accommodated in university housing, which includes single-sex dorms, on-campus apartments, and married-student housing. On-campus housing is guaranteed for all 4 years. 55% of students live on campus. Alcohol is not permitted. All students may keep cars.

Activities: There are no fraternities or sororities. There are 21 groups on campus, including art, band, cheerleading, choir, chorale, chorus, computers, drama, ethnic, honors, international, musical theater, newspaper, opera, orchestra, professional, religious, social, student government, symphony, and yearbook. Popular campus events include Late Skates, Christmas and Valentine socials, and Spring Formal.

Sports: There are 6 intercollegiate sports for men and 6 for women, and 7 intramural sports for men and 7 for women. Facilities include a gym, a baseball diamond, soccer, hockey, and softball fields, a sand volleyball court, 4 tennis courts, a fitness circuit, and a weight room.

Disabled Students: All of the campus is accessible. Wheelchair ramps, elevators, special parking, specially equipped rest rooms, lowered drinking fountains, and special housing are available.

Services: Counseling and information services are available, as is tutoring in most subjects. The AIMS Program provides academic support for freshmen who need it.

Campus Safety and Security: Measures include 24-hour foot and vehicle patrol, security escort services, shuttle buses, and informal discussions. There are pamphlets/posters/films, emergency telephones, and lighted pathways/sidewalks.

Programs of Study: PBU confers B.S., B.Mus., B.S.B.A., B.S.Ed., and B.S.W. degrees. Master's degrees are also awarded. Bachelor's degrees are awarded in BUSINESS (business administration and management), COMMUNICATIONS AND THE ARTS (music), EDUCATION (education), SOCIAL SCIENCE (biblical studies and social work). Bible is the strongest academically. Teacher education and Bible are the largest.

Required: Students must complete 51 credits in Bible, 48 in general education, and 27 in professional studies. A total of 126 credits, with a minimum GPA of 2.0, is required. 3 credits in phys ed must be taken. The number of hours in the major varies: 57 in Bible, 80 in music, 43 in social work, and 47 in education. All matriculating baccalaureate students major in Bible and receive a B.S. in Bible degree. About 48% of those students are enrolled in dual degree programs and receive the B.S. in Bible degree plus a degree in their professional area.

Special: PBU offers co-op programs in accounting, computer and microcomputer applications, and office administration; cross-registration with Bucks County Community College; various church ministries, education, social work, and music internships; and study abroad in Israel. An accelerated degree program in Biblical Leadership is offered. There are dual majors in social work, music, education, and business administration. Student-designed interdisciplinary majors are possible. There is 1 national honor society and a freshman honors program.

Faculty/Classroom: 68% of faculty are male; 32%, female. All teach undergraduates. No introductory courses are taught by graduate students. The average class size in an introductory lecture is 25; in a laboratory, 9; and in a regular course, 20.

Admissions: 94% of the 2005-2006 applicants were accepted. The SAT scores for the 2005-2006 freshman class were: Verbal--29% below 500, 50% between 500 and 599, 19% between 600 and 700, and 2% above 700; Math--42% below 500, 41% between 500 and 599, 15% be-

tween 600 and 700, and 2% above 700. The ACT scores were 25% below 21, 29% between 21 and 23, 17% between 24 and 26, 21% between 27 and 28, and 8% above 28. 34% of the current freshmen were in the top fifth of their class; 60% were in the top two fifths. 3 freshmen graduated first in their class.

Requirements: The SAT or ACT is required. A high school diploma or the GED is needed. An essay and a pastor's reference are required. A GPA of 2.0 is required. AP and CLEP credits are accepted. Important factors in the admissions decision are advanced placement or honor courses, personality/intangible qualities, and leadership record.

Procedure: Freshmen are admitted fall and spring. Entrance exams should be taken in the junior or senior year of high school. There is a deferred admissions plan. Application deadlines are open. Application fee is $25. Applications are accepted on-line.

Transfer: 144 transfer students enrolled in 2004-2005. Tranfers must submit an application, a pastor's reference, college transcripts, and a health form. SAT and high school transcripts are required if the student has fewer than 60 college credit hours. 60 of 126 credits required for the bachelor's degree must be completed at PBU.

Visiting: There are regularly scheduled orientations for prospective students,. including chapel, class visits, a meal in the dining room, and an interview with a counselor. There are guides for informal visits and visitors may sit in on classes and stay overnight. To schedule a visit, contact the Admissions Department at (215) 702-4235.

Financial Aid: In 2005-2006, 97% of all full-time freshmen and 85% of continuing full-time students received some form of financial aid. 80% of full-time freshmen and 65% of continuing full-time students received need-based aid. The average freshman award was $12,597. Need-based scholarships or need-based grants averaged $10,075; need-based self-help aid (loans and jobs) averaged $3229; and other non-need-based awards and non-need-based scholarships averaged $7670. 55% of undergraduates work part time. Average annual earnings from campus work are $1750. The average financial indebtedness of the 2005 graduate was $15,000. The FAFSA is required. The deadline for filing freshman financial aid applications for fall entry is May 1.

International Students: There are 19 international students enrolled. They must score satisfactorily on the written TOEFL or on the electronic version.

Computers: Wireless access is available. All students may access the system. There are no time limits and no fees. It is strongly recommended that all students have a personal computer.

Graduates: From July 1, 2004 to June 30, 2005, 295 bachelor's degrees were awarded. The most popular majors were Bible (72%), education (12%), and social work (9%). In an average class, 18% graduate in 4 years or less, 52% graduate in 5 years or less, and 53% graduate in 6 years or less. 75 companies recruited on campus in 2004-2005. Of the 2004 graduating class, 38% were enrolled in graduate school within 6 months of graduation and 87% were employed.

Admissions Contact: Lisa Yoder, Director of Admissions. A video is available. E-mail: admissions@pbu.edu Web: pbu.edu

PHILADELPHIA UNIVERSITY   F-3
Philadelphia, PA 19144-5497   (215) 951-2800
(800) 951-7287; Fax: (215) 951-2907

Full-time: 730 men, 1647 women	Faculty: 104; IIA, -$
Part-time: 92 men, 234 women	Ph.Ds: 76%
Graduate: 203 men, 303 women	Student/Faculty: 23 to 1
Year: semesters, summer session	Tuition: $22,070
Application Deadline: open	Room & Board: $7936
Freshman Class: 4180 applied, 2682 accepted, 692 enrolled	
SAT Verbal/Math: 535/542*	COMPETITIVE

Philadelphia University, founded in 1884, is a private institution offering preprofessional programs in architecture, design, business, sciences, textiles, fashion, and health. There are 6 undergraduate schools and 1 graduate school. In addition to regional accreditation, Phila. U. has baccalaureate program accreditation with ABET, ACS, FIDER, NAAB, and NASAD. The library contains 109,235 volumes, 125,000 microform items, and 50,630 audio/video tapes/CDs/DVDs, and subscribes to 1011 periodicals including electronic. Computerized library services include the card catalog, interlibrary loans, and database searching. Special learning facilities include a learning resource center, art gallery, and design center. The 100-acre campus is in a suburban area 10 minutes west of metropolitan Philadelphia. Including any residence halls, there are 56 buildings.

Student Life: 50% of undergraduates are from out of state, mostly the Middle Atlantic. Students are from 37 states, 24 foreign countries, and Canada. 65% are from public schools. 80% are white; 10% African American. The average age of freshmen is 18; all undergraduates, 20. 26% do not continue beyond their first year; 54% remain to graduate.

Housing: 1265 students can be accommodated in college housing, which includes single-sex and coed dorms, on-campus apartments, and off-campus apartments. On-campus housing is guaranteed for the freshman year only, is available on a first-come, first-served basis, and is available on a lottery system for upperclassmen. Priority is given to out-of-town students. 50% of students live on campus; of those, 60% remain on campus on weekends. Upperclassmen may keep cars.

Activities: 1% of men belong to 1 national fraternity; 1% of women belong to 1 national sorority. There are 30 groups on campus, including cheerleading, choir, dance, drama, ethnic, gay, honors, international, newspaper, professional, religious, social, social service, and student government. Popular campus events include annual fashion show and design competition, Welcome Week, and Spring Weekend.

Sports: There are 6 intercollegiate sports for men and 8 for women, and 13 intramural sports for men and 13 for women. Facilities include 2 gyms, a fitness center, 6 tennis courts, 3 athletic fields, and a student center recreation room.

Disabled Students: 85% of the campus is accessible. Wheelchair ramps, elevators, special parking, specially equipped rest rooms, special class scheduling, lowered drinking fountains, and lowered telephones are available.

Services: Counseling and information services are available, as is tutoring in every subject. There is a reader service for the blind, and remedial math, reading, and writing. There also are study skills workshops, course-related workshops, math review sessions, writing review sessions, and time management and stress reduction workshops.

Campus Safety and Security: Measures include 24-hour foot and vehicle patrol, self-defense education, security escort services, and shuttle buses. There are informal discussions, pamphlets/posters/films, emergency telephones, and lighted pathways/sidewalks.

Programs of Study: Phila. U. confers B.S. and B.Arch. degrees. Master's and doctoral degrees are also awarded. Bachelor's degrees are awarded in BIOLOGICAL SCIENCE (biochemistry and biology/biological science), BUSINESS (accounting, banking and finance, fashion merchandising, international business management, management information systems, management science, and marketing/retailing/merchandising), COMMUNICATIONS AND THE ARTS (graphic design and industrial design), COMPUTER AND PHYSICAL SCIENCE (chemistry, digital arts/technology, and science and management), ENGINEERING AND ENVIRONMENTAL DESIGN (architecture, engineering, environmental science, industrial engineering, interior design, landscape architecture/design, textile engineering, and textile technology), HEALTH PROFESSIONS (physician's assistant and premedicine), SOCIAL SCIENCE (biopsychology, fashion design and technology, and psychology). Physician's assistant, architecture, and engineering are the strongest academically. Architecture, fashion merchandising, and fashion design are the largest.

Required: All students are required to complete a 60-credit residency with courses in math, science, social science, and the humanities, 2 semesters of phys ed. and a professional studies core curriculum, which differs by major program. A number of requirements may be satisfied and elective credits earned by proficiency exam. A total of 121 to 146 credits is required with an overall GPA of 2.0.

Special: Internships in all academic majors, study abroad, a dual major in international business, an accelerated business administration degree program, and an intergrated major in business and science are available. There is a freshman honors program.

Faculty/Classroom: 59% of faculty are male; 41%, female. All teach undergraduates and 50% do research. No introductory courses are taught by graduate students. The average class size in an introductory lecture is 25; in a laboratory, 14; and in a regular course, 17.

Admissions: 64% of the 2005-2006 applicants were accepted. The SAT scores for the 2005-2006 freshman class were: Verbal--27% below 500, 56% between 500 and 599, 16% between 600 and 700, and 1% above 700; Math--26% below 500, 51% between 500 and 599, 20% between 600 and 700, and 3% above 700. 31% of the current freshmen were in the top fifth of their class; 65% were in the top two fifths.

Requirements: The SAT or ACT is required. In addition, applicants should be high school graduates or have earned the GED. Recommended secondary preparation includes 4 years each of English and history, 3 years of math, which must include algebra II and geometry, and 2 years of science. Potential science majors are strongly urged to take 4 years of math and 4 years of science. A GPA of 2.5 is required. AP and CLEP credits are accepted. Important factors in the admissions decision are evidence of special talent, extracurricular activities record, and leadership record.

Procedure: Freshmen are admitted fall and spring. There is a deferred admissions plan. Application deadlines are open. Application fee is $35. Notification is sent on a rolling basis. 140 applicants were on the 2005 waiting list; 20 were admitted. Applications are accepted on-line.

Transfer: A 2.5 GPA is usually required. 60 of 121 to 146 credits required for the bachelor's degree must be completed at Phila. U.

Visiting: There are regularly scheduled orientations for prospective students, including an interview and a campus tour. There are guides for informal visits and visitors may sit in on classes and stay overnight. To schedule a visit, contact the Admissions Office or Patricia Coleman at colemanp@philau.edu.

Financial Aid: In 2005-2006, 99% of all full-time freshmen and 97% of continuing full-time students received some form of financial aid. 75%

of full-time freshmen and 69% of continuing full-time students received need-based aid. The average freshman award was $16,642. Need-based scholarships or need-based grants averaged $11,323 ($20,450 maximum); need-based self-help aid (loans and jobs) averaged $4635 ($5425 maximum); non-need-based athletic scholarships averaged $9260 ($30,006 maximum); and other awards averaged $4660 ($8000 maximum). 28% of undergraduates work part time. Average annual earnings from campus work are $1067. The average financial indebtedness of the 2005 graduate was $14,820. The FAFSA is required. The deadline for filing freshman financial aid applications for fall entry is April 15.

International Students: There are 49 international students enrolled. The school actively recruits these students. They must score satisfactorily on the written TOEFL and also take an English placement test.

Computers: Wireless access is available. There are more than 250 PCs available in general purpose labs, specific labs, all facilities on campus, and in the library. All students may access the system 7 days a week. There are no time limits and no fees. It is strongly recommended that all students have a personal computer.

Graduates: From July 1, 2004 to June 30, 2005, 508 bachelor's degrees were awarded. The most popular majors were fashion merchandising (15%), architecture (11%), and graphic design (8%). In an average class, 35% graduate in 4 years or less, 51% graduate in 5 years or less, and 54% graduate in 6 years or less. 70 companies recruited on campus in 2004-2005. Of the 2004 graduating class, 19% were enrolled in graduate school within 6 months of graduation and 71% were employed.

Admissions Contact: Christine Greb, Director of Admissions.
E-mail: *admissions@philau.edu* Web: *www.philau.edu*

POINT PARK UNIVERSITY   B-3
Pittsburgh, PA 15222   (412) 392-3430
                                    (800) 321-0129; Fax: (412) 392-3902

Full-time: 904 men, 1359 women	**Faculty:** n/av
Part-time: 322 men, 377 women	**Ph.D.s:** 36%
Graduate: 189 men, 256 women	**Student/Faculty:** n/av
Year: semesters, summer session	**Tuition:** $16,740
Application Deadline: open	**Room & Board:** $7420
Freshman Class: 2453 applied, 1866 accepted, 472 enrolled	
SAT Verbal/Math: 524/501*	**ACT:** 22 **COMPETITIVE**

Point Park University, founded in 1960, is an independent institution offering programs in liberal arts, fine arts, business, engineering, health science, professional training, and teacher preparation. There are 4 undergraduate and 6 graduate schools. In addition to regional accreditation, Point Park has baccalaureate program accreditation with ABET, IACBE, and NASD. The library contains 95,000 volumes, 9589 microform items, and 1439 audio/video tapes/CDs/DVDs, and subscribes to 15,714 periodicals including electronic. Computerized library services include the card catalog, interlibrary loans, database searching, and Internet access. Special learning facilities include a learning resource center, radio station, TV station, theaters, dance studios, and digital film-editing suites. The campus is in an urban area in downtown Pittsburgh. Including any residence halls, there are 5 buildings.

Student Life: 84% of undergraduates are from Pennsylvania. Others are from 47 states, 35 foreign countries, and Canada. 76% are white; 18% African American. The average age of freshmen is 18; all undergraduates, 25.

Housing: 760 students can be accommodated in college housing, which includes single-sex and coed dormitories. On-campus housing is guaranteed for all 4 years. 77% of students commute. No one may keep cars.

Activities: There are no fraternities or sororities. There are 18 groups on campus, including choir, chorale, computers, dance, drama, ethnic, film, honors, international, literary magazine, musical theater, newspaper, photography, political, professional, radio and TV, religious, social, social service, student government, and yearbook. Popular campus events include Snowball (Christmas) Dance, Spring Fling (spring dance), and dance and theater productions.

Sports: There are 4 intercollegiate sports for men and 4 for women, and 7 intramural sports for men and 7 for women. Facilities include a recreation center and a 130-seat auditorium.

Disabled Students: 99% of the campus is accessible. Wheelchair ramps, elevators, specially equipped rest rooms, special class scheduling, lowered drinking fountains, and lowered telephones are available.

Services: Counseling and information services are available, as is tutoring in most subjects. Learning-disabled services are available on a case-by-case basis. There is a reader service for the blind, and remedial math, reading, and writing.

Campus Safety and Security: Measures include 24-hour foot and vehicle patrol, security escort services, shuttle buses, and informal discussions. There are pamphlets/posters/films, emergency telephones, and lighted pathways/sidewalks.

Programs of Study: Point Park confers B.A., B.S., and B.F.A. degrees. Associate and master's degrees are also awarded. Bachelor's degrees are awarded in BIOLOGICAL SCIENCE (biology/biological science and biotechnology), BUSINESS (accounting, business administration and management, funeral home services, human resources, management science, and sports management), COMMUNICATIONS AND THE ARTS (advertising, applied art, arts administration/management, broadcasting, communications, dance, dramatic arts, English, film arts, journalism, media arts, photography, and video), COMPUTER AND PHYSICAL SCIENCE (computer science, digital arts/technology, and information sciences and systems), EDUCATION (dance, drama, early childhood, elementary, and secondary), ENGINEERING AND ENVIRONMENTAL DESIGN (civil engineering technology, electrical/electronics engineering technology, engineering management, environmental science, mechanical engineering technology, and systems engineering), HEALTH PROFESSIONS (health care administration and respiratory therapy), SOCIAL SCIENCE (behavioral science, criminal justice, history, international studies, law enforcement and corrections, liberal arts/general studies, paralegal studies, political science/government, psychology, and public administration). Accelerated business, dance, and theater are the largest.

Required: All majors leading to a baccalaureate degree require a minimum of 120 credits. Most programs require 42 core curriculum credits, with at least 30 completed in residence. A 2.0 GPA is required.

Special: Cross-registration is available through the Pittsburgh Council on Higher Education. The university offers internships, study abroad, a Washington semester, work-study, dual and student-designed majors, credit by exam and for life/military/work experience, nondegree study, and pass/fail options. Capstone programs are available for students with associate degrees. The film and video major is offered in conjunction with Pittsburgh Filmmakers. Accelerated degree programs are available. There are 2 national honor societies, and a freshman honors program.

Faculty/Classroom: 61% of faculty are male; 39%, female. No introductory courses are taught by graduate students.

Admissions: 76% of the 2005-2006 applicants were accepted. The SAT scores for the 2005-2006 freshman class were: Verbal--37% below 500, 44% between 500 and 599, 17% between 600 and 700, and 2% above 700; Math--46% below 500, 41% between 500 and 599, 12% between 600 and 700, and 1% above 700. The ACT scores were 32% below 21, 37% between 21 and 23, 21% between 24 and 26, 7% between 27 and 28, and 3% above 28. 29% of the current freshmen were in the top fifth of their class; 62% were in the top two fifths. 1 freshman graduated first in the class.

Requirements: The SAT or ACT is required. In addition, students should have completed 12 academic credits or 16 Carnegie units consisting of 4 in English, 3 in history, science, and math, and 2 years of foreign language. The GED is accepted. Theater and dance students must audition, and an interview is requested for all candidates. A GPA of 2.5 is required. AP and CLEP credits are accepted. Important factors in the admissions decision are advanced placement or honor courses, evidence of special talent, and personality/intangible qualities.

Procedure: Freshmen are admitted to all sessions. Entrance exams should be taken in the junior or senior year. There are early admissions and deferred admissions plans. Application deadlines are open. Application fee is $40. Notification is sent on a rolling basis. Applications are accepted on-line.

Transfer: 202 transfer students enrolled in a recent year. Applicants must have completed 12 credit hours with at least a 2.0 GPA. The SAT or ACT and an interview are recommended. 30 of 120 credits required for the bachelor's degree must be completed at Point Park.

Visiting: There are regularly scheduled orientations for prospective students. There are guides for informal visits and visitors may sit in on classes. To schedule a visit, contact the Office of Admissions.

Financial Aid: In 2005-2006, 95% of all full-time students received some form of financial aid. 65% of full-time freshmen and 77% of continuing full-time students received need-based aid. The average freshman award was $13,266. The average financial indebtedness of the 2005 graduate was $25,288. The FAFSA is required. Point Park is a member of CSS. The priority date for freshman financial aid applications for fall entry is May 1. The deadline for filing freshman financial aid applications for fall entry is December 1.

International Students: There were 40 international students enrolled in a recent year. The school actively recruits these students. They must score 500 on the written TOEFL or take the MELAB or the college's own test. Students who do not take the TOEFL, score a satisfactorily on either of the other tests, or a 6 on the Test of Written English (TWE) must be tested upon arrival at the college.

Computers: Wireless access is available. All students may access the system 7 days a week; lab hours vary by facility. There are no time limits and no fees.

Graduates: From July 1, 2004 to June 30, 2005, 610 bachelor's degrees were awarded. The most popular majors were business (accelerated) (15%), criminal justice (9%), and theater arts (7%). In an average class, 43% graduate in 6 years or less.

Admissions Contact: Joell Minford, Full-Time Admissions. A video is available. E-mail: *enroll@pointpark.edu* Web: *www.pointpark.edu*

ROBERT MORRIS UNIVERSITY
Moon Township, PA 15108-1189

B-3

(412) 262-8402
(800) 762-0097; Fax: (412) 299-2425

Full-time: 1759 men, 1344 women	**Faculty:** 155
Part-time: 396 men, 472 women	**Ph.D.s:** 82%
Graduate: 609 men, 515 women	**Student/Faculty:** 20 to 1
Year: semesters, summer session	**Tuition:** $15,152
Application Deadline: July 1	**Room & Board:** $7670
Freshman Class: 2584 applied, 2024 accepted, 685 enrolled	
SAT Verbal/Math: 500/520*	**ACT:** 21 **COMPETITIVE**

Robert Morris University, founded in 1921, is a private institution offering 34 undergraduate degree programs and 18 master's and doctoral degree programs. There are 6 undergraduate and 6 graduate schools. In addition to regional accreditation, RMU has baccalaureate program accreditation with ABET. The 2 libraries contain 138,676 volumes, 325,563 microform items, and 2863 audio/video tapes/CDs/DVDs, and subscribe to 685 periodicals including electronic. Computerized library services include the card catalog, interlibrary loans, database searching, and Internet access. Special learning facilities include a learning resource center, art gallery, TV station, and a manufacturing lab for engineering and other students. The 230-acre campus is in a suburban area 17 miles southwest of Pittsburgh. Including any residence halls, there are 25 buildings.

Student Life: 90% of undergraduates are from Pennsylvania. Others are from 33 states, 26 foreign countries, and Canada. 90% are from public schools. 86% are white. 41% are Catholic; 35% Protestant. The average age of freshmen is 18; all undergraduates, 24. 22% do not continue beyond their first year; 55% remain to graduate.

Housing: 1096 students can be accommodated in college housing, which includes single-sex and coed dorms and on-campus apartments. On-campus housing is guaranteed for all 4 years. 72% of students commute. Alcohol is not permitted. All students may keep cars.

Activities: 4% of men belong to 5 national fraternities; 3% of women belong to 3 national sororities. There are 50 groups on campus, including cheerleading, computers, drama, ethnic, film, honors, international, marching band, musical theater, newspaper, pep band, photography, professional, radio and TV, religious, social, social service, student government, and yearbook. Popular campus events include Snow Ball and Spring Fest.

Sports: There are 10 intercollegiate sports for men and 13 for women, and 15 intramural sports for men and 15 for women. RMU's Moon Campus offers a field house, gym, health club, and 11 athletic fields. The RMU Island Sports Center (4 miles away) has 2 hockey rinks, golf dome, batting cages, health club, and an 8-lane track.

Disabled Students: 75% of the campus is accessible. Wheelchair ramps, elevators, special parking, specially equipped rest rooms, special class scheduling, lowered drinking fountains, and lowered telephones are available.

Services: Counseling and information services are available, as is tutoring in most subjects. There is a reader service for the blind, and remedial math, reading, and writing.

Campus Safety and Security: Measures include 24-hour foot and vehicle patrol, security escort services, shuttle buses, and informal discussions. There are pamphlets/posters/films, emergency telephones, and lighted pathways/sidewalks.

Programs of Study: RMU confers B.A., B.S., B.F.A., and B.S.B.A. degrees. Master's and doctoral degrees are also awarded. Bachelor's degrees are awarded in BUSINESS (accounting, banking and finance, business administration and management, entrepreneurial studies, hospitality management services, human resources, management science, marketing/retailing/merchandising, organizational behavior, sports management, supply chain management, and transportation management), COMMUNICATIONS AND THE ARTS (communications, English, and media arts), COMPUTER AND PHYSICAL SCIENCE (actuarial science, information sciences and systems, and mathematics), EDUCATION (business and elementary), ENGINEERING AND ENVIRONMENTAL DESIGN (aviation administration/management, engineering, environmental science, and manufacturing engineering), HEALTH PROFESSIONS (health care administration and nursing), SOCIAL SCIENCE (applied psychology, economics, and social science). Engineering and mathematics are the strongest academically. Management, marketing, and information sciences are the largest.

Required: All candidates must complete 126 to 135 credit hours, including 24 to 31 in the major, with a 2.0 GPA overall and a 2.5 in the major. A core curriculum varies with each major, and consists of humanities, communication skills, social sciences, computing, and math. All students must demonstrate competency in computer software applications.

Special: The university offers cooperative programs in all majors, cross-registration with the 9 schools of the Pittsburgh Council of Higher Education, internships, work-study programs, study abroad in 4 countries, and nondegree study. Credit by exam and pass/fail options are available. There are 2 national honor societies, a freshman honors program, and 1 departmental honors program.

Faculty/Classroom: 66% of faculty are male; 34%, female. 99% teach undergraduates, 80% do research, and 80% do both. No introductory courses are taught by graduate students. The average class size in an introductory lecture is 23; in a laboratory, 12; and in a regular course, 23.

Admissions: 78% of the 2005-2006 applicants were accepted. The SAT scores for the 2005-2006 freshman class were: Verbal--48% below 500, 42% between 500 and 599, and 10% between 600 and 700; Math--38% below 500, 46% between 500 and 599, 14% between 600 and 700, and 2% above 700. 6 freshmen graduated first in their class.

Requirements: The SAT is required. In addition, candidates should be graduates of an accredited secondary school or hold a GED diploma. They must have completed 16 Carnegie units, including 4 in English, 3 each in math and social studies, 2 in science, and 1 in history. An interview is required for some and recommended for all others. A GPA of 2.0 is required. AP and CLEP credits are accepted. Important factors in the admissions decision are advanced placement or honor courses, leadership record, and personality/intangible qualities.

Procedure: Freshmen are admitted fall and spring. Entrance exams should be taken by fall or late winter of the senior year. There is a deferred admissions plan and a rolling admissions plan. Applications should be filed by July 1 for fall entry and December 1 for spring entry. Notification is sent on a rolling basis. The fall 2005 application fee was $30. Applications are accepted on-line.

Transfer: 387 transfer students enrolled in 2004-2005. Students must have a minimum 2.0 GPA in nondevelopmental academic courses. Those with fewer than 30 earned credits must also submit an official high school transcript and test results of the SAT or ACT. An interview is recommended. 30 of 126 credits required for the bachelor's degree must be completed at RMU.

Visiting: There are regularly scheduled orientations for prospective students, consisting of placement testing, orientation, and academic advising. There are guides for informal visits and visitors may sit in on classes and stay overnight. To schedule a visit, contact the Enrollment Office at (412) 262-8206 or enrollmentoffice@rmu.edu.

Financial Aid: In 2005-2006, 78% of all full-time freshmen and 75% of continuing full-time students received some form of financial aid. 77% of full-time freshmen and 68% of continuing full-time students received need-based aid. The average freshman award was $13,207. Need-based scholarships or need-based grants averaged $7960; need-based self-help aid (loans and jobs) averaged $5914; and non-need-based athletic scholarships averaged $7151. RMU is a member of CSS. The FAFSA and PHEAA are required. The deadline for filing freshman financial aid applications for fall entry is May 1.

International Students: There are 61 international students enrolled. The school actively recruits these students. Satisfactory scores are required on the written TOEFL and the SAT.

Computers: Wireless access is available. Computer labs with a total of 300 PCs are provided in several classroom buildings as well as in the library and residence halls. Dorm rooms are wired for high speed Internet access and wireless nodes are provided in several campus locations. All students may access the system. There are no time limits and no fees.

Graduates: From July 1, 2004 to June 30, 2005, 773 bachelor's degrees were awarded. The most popular majors were management (16%), marketing (12%), and communication (10%). In an average class, 27% graduate in 4 years or less, 50% graduate in 5 years or less, and 55% graduate in 6 years or less. 140 companies recruited on campus in 2004-2005. Of the 2004 graduating class, 3% were enrolled in graduate school within 6 months of graduation and 95% were employed.

Admissions Contact: Marianne L. Budziszewski, Associate VP, Academic and Enrollment Services. A video is available.
E-mail: enrollmentoffice@rmu.edu Web: http://www.rmu.edu

ROSEMONT COLLEGE
F-4

Rosemont, PA 19010-1699

(610) 526-2952
(800) 331-0708; Fax: (610) 520-4399

Full-time: 425 women	Faculty: 31
Part-time: 82 men, 137 women	Ph.D.s: 91%
Graduate: 74 men, 330 women	Student/Faculty: 14 to 1
Year: semesters, summer session	Tuition: $20,550
Application Deadline: open	Room & Board: $8800
Freshman Class: 434 applied, 285 accepted, 120 enrolled	
SAT Verbal/Math: 509/493*	ACT: 21 COMPETITIVE

Rosemont College, founded in 1921, is an independent primarily women's liberal arts and sciences college, affiliated with the Roman Catholic Church. Accelerated degree and graduate programs are open to men and women. The library contains 159,731 volumes, 24,981 microform items, and 2784 audio/video tapes/CDs/DVDs, and subscribes to 563 periodicals including electronic. Computerized library services include the card catalog, interlibrary loans, and database searching. Special learning facilities include a learning resource center and art gallery. The 56-acre campus is in a suburban area 11 miles west of Philadelphia. Including any residence halls, there are 15 buildings.

Student Life: 72% of undergraduates are from Pennsylvania. Others are from 18 states and 12 foreign countries. 57% are white; 19% African American; 11% Asian American. 60% are Catholic; 17% Protestant; 15% Muslim, Quaker, and not indicated. The average age of freshmen is 18; all undergraduates, 23. 8% do not continue beyond their first year; 72% remain to graduate.

Housing: 410 students can be accommodated in college housing, which includes single-sex dorms. In addition, there are special-interest houses. On-campus housing is guaranteed for all 4 years. 68% of students live on campus; of those, 60% remain on campus on weekends. All students may keep cars.

Activities: There are no fraternities or sororities. There are 23 groups on campus, including art, band, choir, chorus, dance, drama, ethnic, honors, international, jazz band, literary magazine, marching band, musical theater, newspaper, orchestra, photography, political, professional, religious, social service, student government, symphony, and yearbook. Popular campus events include Oktoberfest, Founders Day, and International/Multi-Cultural Festival.

Sports: There are 6 intercollegiate sports for women. Facilities include hockey and softball fields, tennis courts, treadmills, weight equipment, a 500-seat auditorium, and indoor basketball, badminton, and volleyball courts.

Disabled Students: 20% of the campus is accessible. Wheelchair ramps, elevators, special parking, specially equipped rest rooms, special class scheduling, lowered drinking fountains, and lowered telephones are available.

Services: Counseling and information services are available, as is tutoring in every subject. There is a writing and learning resource center.

Campus Safety and Security: Measures include 24-hour foot and vehicle patrol, self-defense education, security escort services, and shuttle buses. There are informal discussions, pamphlets/posters/films, emergency telephones, lighted pathways/sidewalks, and electronically operated residence hall entrances activated by security cards.

Programs of Study: Rosemont confers B.A., B.S., and B.F.A. degrees. Master's degrees are also awarded. Bachelor's degrees are awarded in BIOLOGICAL SCIENCE (biochemistry and biology/biological science), BUSINESS (accounting and business administration and management), COMMUNICATIONS AND THE ARTS (communications, English, fine arts, French, German, and Spanish), COMPUTER AND PHYSICAL SCIENCE (chemistry and mathematics), EDUCATION (art, foreign languages, and secondary), ENGINEERING AND ENVIRONMENTAL DESIGN (environmental science), HEALTH PROFESSIONS (predentistry and premedicine), SOCIAL SCIENCE (economics, history, humanities, Italian studies, liberal arts/general studies, philosophy, political science/government, prelaw, psychology, religion, social science, sociology, and women's studies). Psychology, English, and chemistry are the largest.

Required: All students take classes in writing, literature, religious studies, foreign language, philosophy, history, math or natural science, social science, and art. A total of 128 credits is required for graduation, with 40 to 48 in the major, and a minimum GPA of 2.0. A comprehensive exam must be taken in the major.

Special: Cross-registration with Villanova and Arcadia Universities and Eastern, Cabrini, Gwynedd-Mercy, Holy Family, Chestnut Hill, Immaculata, and Neumann Colleges, the Art Institute Exchange Program, internships, study abroad, a Washington semester, dual and student-designed majors, and accelerated degree programs are available. Also offered are a joint admission program with MCP/Hahnemann School of Medicine, 5-year accelerated programs in English and publishing, and in counseling psychology, and elementary and secondary teacher certification. A transfer nursing program with Villanova University is also available. There are 6 national honor societies and a freshman honors program.

Faculty/Classroom: 41% of faculty are male; 59%, female. All teach undergraduates and 70% both teach and do research. No introductory courses are taught by graduate students. The average class size in an introductory lecture is 20; in a laboratory, 10; and in a regular course, 12.

Admissions: 66% of the 2005-2006 applicants were accepted. The SAT scores for the 2005-2006 freshman class were: Verbal--24% below 500, 44% between 500 and 599, 25% between 600 and 700, and 4% above 700; Math--38% below 500, 42% between 500 and 599, 15% between 600 and 700, and 3% above 700. The ACT scores were 100% between 21 and 23. 35% of the current freshmen were in the top fifth of their class; 55% were in the top two fifths. 2 freshmen graduated first in their class.

Requirements: The SAT is required. In addition, a GED is accepted. Applicants must complete 16 academic credits, including 4 in English and 2 each in foreign language, history, math, and science. An interview is recommended. A GPA of 2.0 is required. AP and CLEP credits are accepted. Important factors in the admissions decision are advanced placement or honor courses, leadership record, and recommendations by school officials.

Procedure: Freshmen are admitted fall and spring. Entrance exams should be taken before January of the senior year. There is a deferred admissions plan and a rolling admissions plan. Application deadlines are open. Application fee is $35. Notification is sent on a rolling basis. Applications are accepted on-line.

Transfer: 27 transfer students enrolled in 2005-2006. Transfer applicants should submit transcripts from each college attended, a letter of good standing from the dean at the last college attended, and catalogs from the colleges from which the student wishes to transfer credits. Students with fewer than 30 credits are required to submit high school transcripts and SAT scores. The minimum GPA is 2.0. An associate degree and interview are recommended. 48 of 128 credits required for the bachelor's degree must be completed at Rosemont.

Visiting: There are regularly scheduled orientations for prospective students, including campus visit days, overnight visits, and class visitations. There are guides for informal visits and visitors may sit in on classes and stay overnight. To schedule a visit, contact the Admissions Office.

Financial Aid: In a recent year, 97% of all full-time freshmen and 95% of continuing full-time students received some form of financial aid. 78% of full-time freshmen and 76% of continuing full-time students received need-based aid. The average freshman award was $17,409, with $10,784 ($20,150 maximum) from need-based scholarships or need-based grants, $4625 (6625 maximum) from need-based self-help aid (loans and jobs), and $2000 (maximum) from federal and state grants. $2000 (maximum). 39% of undergraduates work part time. Average annual earnings from campus work are $750. The average financial indebtedness of a recent year's graduate was $16,000. The FAFSA is required. The priority date for freshman financial aid applications for fall entry is February 15. The deadline for filing freshman financial aid applications for fall entry is March 15.

International Students: There are 15 international students enrolled. The school actively recruits these students. A satisfactory score on the TOEFL is required.

Computers: All students may access the system. There are no time limits and no fees.

Graduates: From July 1, 2004 to June 30, 2005, 135 bachelor's degrees were awarded. The most popular majors were psychology (23%), English literature (15%), and accounting/business (13%). In an average class, 74% graduate in 4 years or less, and 77% graduate in 5 years or less. 25 companies recruited on campus in 2004-2005. Of the 2004 graduating class, 40% were enrolled in graduate school within 6 months of graduation and 60% were employed.

Admissions Contact: Rennie H. Andrews, Dean of Admissions. A video is available. E-mail: *admissions@rosemont.edu* Web: *www.rosemont.edu*

SAINT FRANCIS UNIVERSITY C-3
Loretto, PA 15940
(814) 472-3100
(866) 342-5738; Fax: (814) 472-3335

Full-time: 485 men, 675 women	Faculty: 90
Part-time: 50 men, 130 women	Ph.D.s: 74%
Graduate: 190 men, 310 women	Student/Faculty: 13 to 1
Year: semesters, summer session	Tuition: $18,295
Application Deadline: see profile	Room & Board: $7585
Freshman Class: n/av	
SAT or ACT: required	LESS COMPETITIVE

Saint Francis University, founded in 1847, is a private Franciscan institution affiliated with the Roman Catholic Church. Figures in the above capsule and this profile are approximate. It offers programs in business, education, humanities, sciences, social science, and preprofessional programs. In addition to regional accreditation, Saint Francis has baccalaureate program accreditation with APTA, CAHEA, and CSWE. The library contains 117,870 volumes, 7648 microform items, and 2701 audio/video tapes/CDs/DVDs, and subscribes to 7293 periodicals including electronic. Computerized library services include the card catalog, interlibrary loans, database searching, and Internet access. Special learning facilities include a learning resource center, art gallery, radio station, TV station, classroom satellite hookup, art studio, wireless technology lab, and computer assurance lab. The 600-acre campus is in a rural area 85 miles east of Pittsburgh. Including any residence halls, there are 23 buildings.

Student Life: 77% of undergraduates are from Pennsylvania. Others are from 27 states, 6 foreign countries, and Canada. 66% are from public schools. 85% are white; 11% African American. 55% are Catholic; 40% Protestant. The average age of freshmen is 19; all undergraduates, 21. 21% do not continue beyond their first year; 62% remain to graduate.

Housing: 983 students can be accommodated in college housing, which includes single-sex dormitories, on-campus apartments, off-campus apartments, married-student housing, and intensive study floors. On-campus housing is guaranteed for all 4 years. 56% of students live on campus; of those, 20% remain on campus on weekends. Alcohol is not permitted. Upperclassmen may keep cars.

Activities: 1% of men belong to 1 national fraternity; 2% of women belong to 1 local and 2 national sororities. There are 54 groups on campus, including academis department clubs, art, cheerleading, choir, comput-

ers, drama, ethnic, honors, international, literary magazine, newspaper, pep band, photography, political, professional, radio and TV, religious, social, social service, student government, theater production, and yearbook. Popular campus events include Days of Reflection, Winter Weekend, and Christmas Mass.

Sports: There are 9 intercollegiate sports for men and 12 for women, and 8 intramural sports for men and 8 for women. Facilities include an athletic center with a 6-lane swimming pool, 3 racquetball courts, a suspended running track, a weight room, a 3500-seat basketball arena, and a multipurpose gym. Outdoor facilities include recreational areas and game fields, jogging/walking trails, 9-hole golf course, a lake, and beach volleyball pits.

Disabled Students: Wheelchair ramps, elevators, special parking, specially equipped rest rooms, lowered drinking fountains, lowered telephones, and special housing are available.

Services: Counseling and information services are available, as is tutoring in most subjects. There is remedial math, reading, and writing.

Campus Safety and Security: Measures include 24-hour foot and vehicle patrol, self-defense education, security escort services, and informal discussions. There are pamphlets/posters/films, emergency telephones, lighted pathways/sidewalks, and a certified police force.

Programs of Study: Saint Francis confers B.A., B.S., B.S.N., and B.S.W. degrees. Master's degrees are also awarded. Bachelor's degrees are awarded in BIOLOGICAL SCIENCE (biology/biological science), BUSINESS (accounting, management information systems, and management science), COMMUNICATIONS AND THE ARTS (communications, English, French, modern language, and Spanish), COMPUTER AND PHYSICAL SCIENCE (chemistry, computer science, and mathematics), EDUCATION (elementary and secondary), HEALTH PROFESSIONS (medical laboratory technology, nursing, occupational therapy, physical therapy, and physician's assistant), SOCIAL SCIENCE (criminal justice, economics, history, international studies, philosophy, political science/government, psychology, public administration, religion, social work, and sociology). Business, occupational therapy, and chemistry are the strongest academically. Business, physician's assistant, and education are the largest.

Required: Students must complete 128 credits, with at least 36 in the major, while maintaining a 2.0 GPA. The core curriculum, totaling 58 credits, includes writing, public speaking, fine arts, foreign language, history, philosophy, religious studies (with required service component), psychology, sociology, political science, and economics. A word processing and research workshop is required in the freshman year. In addition to a comprehensive exam in the major, an English proficiency exam must be taken in the junior year.

Special: The university offers internships, co-op programs, study abroad in 10 countries, a Washington semester, work-study programs, and nondegree study. Student-designed majors and 3-2 engineering degrees with Pennsylvania State and Clarkson Universities and the University of Pittsburgh are available. There is a dual major available in international business/modern languages. Credit by exam and pass/fail options are also offered. There are 11 national honor societies, a freshman honors program, and 10 departmental honors programs.

Faculty/Classroom: 56% of faculty are male; 44%, female. 99% teach undergraduates, 50% do research, and 50% do both. No introductory courses are taught by graduate students. The average class size in an introductory lecture is 23; in a laboratory, 16; and in a regular course, 19.

Requirements: The SAT or ACT is required. In addition, applicants must be graduates of an accredited secondary school or have earned a GED certificate. All applicants must have completed 16 Carnegie units, consisting of 4 years of English, 2 each of math and social science, 1 lab science, and 7 academic electives. Applicants to biology and allied health majors need an additional unit of science. Chemistry, computer science, engineering, and math applicants need 4 math units and 2 science units. Physical therapy applicants must have 4 units of math and 4 of science. AP and CLEP credits are accepted. Important factors in the admissions decision are advanced placement or honor courses, extracurricular activities record, and recommendations by school officials.

Procedure: Freshmen are admitted to all sessions. Entrance exams should be taken in spring of the junior year and fall of the senior year. There are deferred admissions and rolling admissions plans. Check with the school for application deadlines. Notification is sent on a rolling basis. Applications are accepted on-line. The fall 2005 application fee was $30.

Transfer: 32 transfer students enrolled in a recent year. Applicants must have a minimum GPA of 2.0 for consideration, 2.5 for nursing majors, and 2.75 for physician's assistant majors. 64 of 128 credits required for the bachelor's degree must be completed at Saint Francis.

Visiting: There are regularly scheduled orientations for prospective students, including an interview by financial aid and admission staff, tour, meeting with faculty, and attending class. There are guides for informal visits and visitors may sit in on classes and stay overnight. To schedule a visit, contact the Admissions Office.

Financial Aid: In a recent year, 96% of all full-time freshmen and 91% of continuing full-time students received some form of financial aid. 86%

of full-time freshmen and 83% of continuing full-time students received need-based aid. The average freshman award was $16,962. Need-based scholarships or need-based grants averaged $6866 ($14,350 maximum); need-based self-help aid (loans and jobs) averaged $2976 ($4625 maximum); non-need-based athletic scholarships averaged $1812 ($26,688 maximum); other non-need-based awards and non-need-based scholarships averaged $3531 ($18,292 maximum); and non need-based self-help and other miscellaneous funds averaged $1777 ($15,000 maximum). 32% of undergraduates worked part time. Average annual earnings from campus work were $794. The average financial indebtedness of a recent graduate was $17,000. The FAFSA and the college's own financial statement are required. Check with the school for application deadlines.

International Students: In a recent year, there were 48 international students enrolled. The school actively recruits these students. They must score satisfactorily on the written TOEFL or on the electronic version and also take the SAT or the ACT.

Computers: All students may access the system. There are no time limits and no fees. All students are required to have personal computers.

Graduates: In a recent year, 261 bachelor's degrees were awarded. The most popular majors were elementary education (12%), occupational therapy (11%), and accounting (10%). In an average class, 1% graduate in 3 years or less, 47% graduate in 4 years or less, 60% graduate in 5 years or less, and 65% graduate in 6 years or less. 60 companies recruited on campus in a recent year. Of a recent graduating class, 23% were enrolled in graduate school within 6 months of graduation and 75% were employed.

Admissions Contact: Evan Lipp, Dean for Enrollment Management. E-mail: *admissions@francis.edu* Web: *www.francis.edu*

SAINT JOSEPH'S UNIVERSITY	**F-3**
Philadelphia, PA 19131	**(610) 660-1300**
	(888) BE-A-HAWK; Fax: (610) 660-1314

Full-time: 2054 men, 2193 women	**Faculty:** 262; IIA, +$
Part-time: 383 men, 513 women	**Ph.D.s:** 98%
Graduate: 1047 men, 1524 women	**Student/Faculty:** 16 to 1
Year: semesters, summer session	**Tuition:** $27,455
Application Deadline: February 1	**Room & Board:** $9973
Freshman Class: 9021 applied, 4280 accepted, 1129 enrolled	
SAT Verbal/Math: 570/570*	**ACT:** 25 **VERY COMPETITIVE**

Saint Joseph's University, founded in 1851, is a Catholic, private college affiliated with the Jesuit order. It offers undergraduate programs in arts and sciences and business administration. It is a comprehensive school in the Carnegie classification system. There are 3 undergraduate and 2 graduate schools. In addition to regional accreditation, Saint Joseph's has baccalaureate program accreditation with AACSB. The 2 libraries contain 352,500 volumes, 848,000 microform items, and 4700 audio/video tapes/CDs/DVDs, and subscribe to 8900 periodicals including electronic. Computerized library services include the card catalog, interlibrary loans, database searching, and Internet access. Special learning facilities include a learning resource center, art gallery, radio station, instructional media center, foreign language labs, Mandeville Hall, wall street trading room, and Clover Honors House. The 65-acre campus is in a suburban area on the western edge of Philadelphia and eastern Montgomery county. Including any residence halls, there are 53 buildings.

Student Life: 53% of undergraduates are from Pennsylvania. Others are from 39 states, 34 foreign countries, and Canada. 81% are white. 64% are Catholic; 18% claim no religious affiliation; 11% Protestant; 6% other on non-Christian & non Jewish. The average age of freshmen is 18; all undergraduates, 20. 10% do not continue beyond their first year; 78% remain to graduate.

Housing: 2450 students can be accommodated in college housing, which includes single-sex and coed dorms, on-campus apartments, and off-campus apartments. In addition, there are honors houses, special-interest houses, and special interest floors. On-campus housing is guaranteed for freshman and sophomore years and is available on a lottery system for upperclassmen. 60% of students live on campus. Upperclassmen may keep cars.

Activities: 8% of men belong to 3 national fraternities; 13% of women belong to 4 national sororities. There are 94 groups on campus, including art, cheerleading, choir, chorale, dance, debate, drama, ethnic, forensics, gay, honors, international, jazz band, literary magazine, musical theater, newspaper, pep band, political, professional, radio, religious, social, social service, student government, and yearbook. Popular campus events include Hand in Hand, Up 'Til Dawn, and Mass of the Holy Spirit.

Sports: There are 9 intercollegiate sports for men and 9 for women, and 30 intramural sports for men and 30 for women. The Sports/Recreation Complex consist of the Alumni Memorial Fieldhouse, a 240' by 120' four-court area, convertible for basketball, tennis, and volleyball, an indoor, four-lane, 200-yard practice running track, a 25 meter, 8-lane indoor pool with a 300-seat observation area, 4 racquetball/handball

courts, spacious locker rooms and saunas, a fitness center featuring state-of-the-art cardiovascular, and resistance and free weight equipment. There is a 400-meter, 6-lane Balsam track, an all pro field, and 4 tennis courts.

Disabled Students: 85% of the campus is accessible. Wheelchair ramps, elevators, special parking, specially equipped rest rooms, special class scheduling, lowered drinking fountains, lowered telephones, special housing, automatic eye doors, curb cuts, a specially equipped van for wheelchairs, a pool lift, and a bell system at major road crossings are available.

Services: Counseling and information services are available, as is tutoring in most subjects. There is a reader service for the blind. In addition to tutoring, there are study and life skills workshops, supplemental instruction, a writing center, and other educational support services to help students.

Campus Safety and Security: Measures include 24-hour foot and vehicle patrol, self-defense education, security escort services, and shuttle buses. There are informal discussions, pamphlets/posters/films, emergency telephones, lighted pathways/sidewalks, and a bicycle patrol.

Programs of Study: Saint Joseph's confers B.A., B.S., and B.B.A. degrees. Associate, master's, and doctoral degrees are also awarded. Bachelor's degrees are awarded in BIOLOGICAL SCIENCE (biology/biological science), BUSINESS (accounting, banking and finance, business administration and management, international business management, management information systems, marketing/retailing/merchandising, and purchasing/inventory management), COMMUNICATIONS AND THE ARTS (communications, English, fine arts, French, German, Latin, and Spanish), COMPUTER AND PHYSICAL SCIENCE (actuarial science, chemistry, computer science, information sciences and systems, mathematics, and physics), EDUCATION (elementary, secondary, and special), ENGINEERING AND ENVIRONMENTAL DESIGN (environmental science), HEALTH PROFESSIONS (health care administration), SOCIAL SCIENCE (criminal justice, economics, European studies, French studies, history, humanities, industrial and organizational psychology, international relations, law, philosophy, political science/government, psychology, public administration, religion, social science, and sociology). Social sciences, natural sciences, and English are the strongest academically. Marketing, food marketing, and finance are the largest.

Required: All students must take general education common courses in English, theology, philosophy, and history. Distribution requirements include courses in social/behavioral sciences, theology, foreign language at the intermediate level, math, natural sciences, and philosophy. A minimum of 120 credit hours is required for graduation.

Special: There is an exchange program with a Japanese university and study abroad in 7 countries. The university offers internships, a Washington semester, advanced 5-year degrees in international marketing and in psychology, dual majors, minor concentrations, and special programs in American, Latin American, European, gender, and medieval studies. There is a co-op program for food marketing, accounting, finance, marketing, pharmaceutical marketing, decision/system science, management majors, and an interdisciplinary major in health services. There are 17 national honor societies, including Phi Beta Kappa, and a freshman honors program.

Faculty/Classroom: 60% of faculty are male; 40%, female. 80% teach undergraduates. No introductory courses are taught by graduate students. The average class size in an introductory lecture is 25 and in a laboratory, 13.

Admissions: 47% of the 2005-2006 applicants were accepted. 45% of the current freshmen were in the top fifth of their class; 76% were in the top two fifths.

Requirements: The SAT or ACT is required. In addition, careful consideration is given to the applicant's high school curriculum, extracurricular activities, recalculated academic grade point average, and standardized test scores. Preference is given to those applicants who have taken a more demanding curriculum, maintained a B grade point average, and rank in the upper 40% of their high school class. A GPA of 3.0 is required. AP credits are accepted. Important factors in the admissions decision are advanced placement or honor courses, extracurricular activities record, and leadership record.

Procedure: Freshmen are admitted fall and spring. Entrance exams should be taken in the spring of the junior year and/or the fall of the senior year. There are early decision and deferred admissions plans. Early decision applications should be filed by November 15; regular applications, by February 1 for fall entry, along with a $55 fee. Notification of early decision is sent December 15; regular decision, March 15. 2932 applicants were on the 2005 waiting list. Applications are accepted online.

Transfer: 40 transfer students enrolled in 2005-2006. Transfer applicants must have a GPA of at least 2.5 and must submit former test scores and high school and college transcripts. Applicants must apply by November 1 for the spring term and by March 1 for the fall term. 60 of the minimum 120 credits required for the bachelor's degree must be completed at Saint Joseph's.

Visiting: There are regularly scheduled orientations for prospective students, consisting of open houses, tours, and information sessions. There are guides for informal visits and visitors may sit in on classes and stay overnight. To schedule a visit, contact the Admissions Office at *admit@sju.edu*.

Financial Aid: In 2005-2006, 85% of all full-time freshmen and 80% of continuing full-time students received some form of financial aid. 80% of all full-time students received need-based aid. The average freshman award was $12,450. Need-based scholarships or need-based grants averaged $8400; need-based self-help aid (loans and jobs) averaged $3800; and non-need-based athletic scholarships averaged $12,000. The average financial indebtedness of the 2005 graduate was $15,734. Saint Joseph's is a member of CSS. The FAFSA is required. The priority date for freshman financial aid applications for fall entry is February 15. The deadline for filing freshman financial aid applications for fall entry is May 1.

International Students: There are 58 international students enrolled. The school actively recruits these students. Satisfactory scores are required on the written TOEFL and the SAT or the ACT. Students who matriculate through ELS must achieve Level 112.

Computers: Wireless access is available. All students may access the system. There are no time limits and no fees. It is strongly recommended that all students have a personal computer. Laptops are required for psychology majors and students in the business school. St. Josephis recommends IBM for the business school and Mac for psychology majors.

Graduates: From July 1, 2004 to June 30, 2005, 918 bachelor's degrees were awarded. The most popular majors were marketing (12%), finance (8%), and food marketing (7%). In an average class, 68% graduate in 4 years or less, 75% graduate in 5 years or less, and 78% graduate in 6 years or less. Over 400 companies recruited on campus in 2004-2005. Of the 2004 graduating class, 25% were enrolled in graduate school within 6 months of graduation and 66% were employed.

Admissions Contact: Susan P. Kassab, Director of Admissions. A video is available. E-mail: *admit@sju.edu* Web: *http://www.sju.edu*

SAINT VINCENT COLLEGE   B-2

Latrobe, PA 15650   (724) 537-4540
                                    (800) SVC-5549; Fax: (724) 532-5069

Full-time: 630 men, 635 women	**Faculty:** 90; IIB, av$
Part-time: 85 men, 95 women	**Ph.D.s:** 81%
Graduate: 30 men, 45 women	**Student/Faculty:** 14 to 1
Year: semesters, summer session	**Tuition:** $20,000
Application Deadline: see profile	**Room & Board:** $6160
Freshman Class: n/av	
SAT or ACT: required	**VERY COMPETITIVE**

Saint Vincent College, founded in 1846, is a private Catholic college of liberal arts and sciences sponsored by the Benedictine monks. There are 4 undergraduate schools and 1 graduate school. Figures in the above capsule and profile are approximate. In addition to regional accreditation, Saint Vincent has baccalaureate program accreditation with ACB-SP. The library contains 368,688 volumes, 98,951 microform items, and 4195 audio/video tapes/CDs/DVDs, and subscribes to 738 periodicals including electronic. Computerized library services include the card catalog, interlibrary loans, database searching, and Internet access. Special learning facilities include a learning resource center, art gallery, planetarium, radio station, TV station, an observatory, a radio telescope, and a small business development center. The 200-acre campus is in a suburban area 35 miles east of Pittsburgh. Including any residence halls, there are 22 buildings.

Student Life: 84% of undergraduates are from Pennsylvania. Others are from 26 states, 18 foreign countries, and Canada. 76% are from public schools. 93% are white. 68% are Catholic; 24% Protestant; 8% claim no religious affiliation; 8% unknown, no preference. The average age of freshmen is 18; all undergraduates, 21. 13% do not continue beyond their first year; 74% remain to graduate.

Housing: 1063 students can be accommodated in college housing, which includes coed dormitories and a 24-hour quiet, private study dorm. On-campus housing is guaranteed for all 4 years. 69% of students live on campus; of those, 80% remain on campus on weekends. All students may keep cars.

Activities: There are no fraternities or sororities. There are 57 groups on campus, including art, band, campus ministry/service, cheerleading, choir, chorale, chorus, dance, drama, ethnic, honors, international, literary magazine, musical theater, newspaper, pep band, political, professional, radio and TV, religious, social, social service, student government, and yearbook. Popular campus events include Founder's Day, the Threshold Lecture Series, and Pittsburgh Steeler training camp.

Sports: There are 6 intercollegiate sports for men and 7 for women, and 6 intramural sports for men and 6 for women. Facilities include a 2400-seat gym, basketball and volleyball facilities, a weight and exercise room, an indoor pool, tennis courts, baseball, soccer, and football fields, a mini movie theater, a 999-seat auditorium/arena, and a student union and game room area.

Disabled Students: 95% of the campus is accessible. Wheelchair ramps, elevators, special parking, specially equipped rest rooms, special class scheduling, lowered drinking fountains, lowered telephones, and lowered computer desks are available.

Services: Counseling and information services are available, as is tutoring in every subject. There is remedial math, reading, and writing. The Opportunity Office provides individual counseling and a freshman study skills class.

Campus Safety and Security: Measures include 24-hour foot and vehicle patrol, security escort services, informal discussions, and pamphlets/posters/films. There are emergency telephones and lighted pathways/sidewalks.

Programs of Study: Saint Vincent confers B.A., and B.S. degrees. Master's degrees are also awarded. Bachelor's degrees are awarded in BIOLOGICAL SCIENCE (biochemistry and biology/biological science), BUSINESS (accounting, banking and finance, business administration and management, international business management, and marketing/retailing/merchandising), COMMUNICATIONS AND THE ARTS (art, art history and appreciation, communications, English, fine arts, French, music, music performance, Spanish, studio art, and visual and performing arts), COMPUTER AND PHYSICAL SCIENCE (chemistry, computer science, information sciences and systems, mathematics, and physics), EDUCATION (art, business, music, psychology, and science), ENGINEERING AND ENVIRONMENTAL DESIGN (environmental science), HEALTH PROFESSIONS (occupational therapy, physical therapy, physician's assistant, predentistry, premedicine, prepharmacy, and preveterinary science), SOCIAL SCIENCE (anthropology, economics, history, liberal arts/general studies, philosophy, political science/government, prelaw, psychology, public affairs, religious education, sociology, and theological studies). Biology, accounting, and chemistry are the strongest academically. Biology, psychology, and history are the largest.

Required: To graduate, students must complete 124 credit hours with a minimum GPA of 2.0. All students are required to take Language and Rhetoric, Exploring Religious Meaning, and Philosophy I. The core curriculum includes 9 hours each of social science, religious studies, and English. 8 of natural sciences, 6 hours each of history, philosophy, and foreign language, and 3 of math. Total number of hours in major varies depending on the program. All majors require a culminating activity, such as a thesis, research project, or capstone course/seminar.

Special: There is cross-registration with Seton Hill College, co-op programs, internships, study abroad in Europe and Asia, a Washington semester, a work-study program, dual majors, a general studies degree, credit by exam and for life/military/work experience, nondegree study, and pass/fail options. There is an accelerated degree engineering program and a 3-2 engineering option with Boston University, Pennsylvania state universities, the University of Pittsburgh, and the Catholic University of America. The college offers teacher certificate programs in early childhood, elementary, and secondary education. There are 9 national honor societies, a freshman honors program, and a campus-wide honors program.

Faculty/Classroom: 73% of faculty are male; 27%, female. All both teach and do research. No introductory courses are taught by graduate students. The average class size in an introductory lecture is 34; in a laboratory, 21; and in a regular course, 19.

Requirements: The SAT or ACT is required. In addition, applicants must complete 15 academic credits, including 4 of English, 3 each of social studies and math, 2 of foreign language, and 1 of a lab science. Art students must submit a portfolio, and music and theater students must audition. An essay is required. A GED is accepted. A GPA of 3.2 is required. AP and CLEP credits are accepted. Important factors in the admissions decision are advanced placement or honor courses, evidence of special talent, and recommendations by school officials.

Procedure: Freshmen are admitted fall and spring. Entrance exams should be taken at the end of the junior year or the beginning of the senior year. There are early admissions, deferred admissions and rolling admissions plans. Check with the school for application deadlines. Notification is sent on a rolling basis. Applications are accepted on-line. The fall 2005 application fee was $25.

Transfer: 99 transfer students enrolled in a recent year. Transfer applicants must submit transcripts from postsecondary schools attended and a catalog describing courses taken, plus secondary school transcript(s). 34 of 124 credits required for the bachelor's degree must be completed at Saint Vincent.

Visiting: There are regularly scheduled orientations for prospective students, consisting of a general information session, an informal meeting with faculty, and campus tours. There are guides for informal visits and visitors may sit in on classes and stay overnight. To schedule a visit, contact the Admission and Financial Aid Office.

Financial Aid: In a recent year, 95% of all full-time freshmen and 93% of continuing full-time students received some form of financial aid. 80% of all full-time students received need-based aid. The average freshman award was $18,544. Need-based scholarships or need-based grants averaged $3883 ($15,000 maximum); need-based self-help aid (loans and jobs) averaged $3087 ($6175 maximum); non-need-based athletic scholarships averaged $1132 ($20,440 maximum); and other non-need-based awards and non-need-based scholarships averaged $7784 ($25,677 maximum). 54% of undergraduates worked part time. Average annual earnings from campus work were $1600. The average financial indebtedness of a recent graduate was $17,000. The FAFSA is required. Check with the school for application deadlines.

International Students: In a recent year there were 18 international students enrolled. They must score satisfactorily on the written TOEFL.

Computers: All students may access the system during computer lab hours and 24 hours from dorm rooms. Computer labs are open an average of 18 hours per day. There are no fees.

Graduates: In a recent year, 235 bachelor's degrees were awarded. The most popular majors were psychology (12%), communication (12%), and computing (8%). In an average class, 1% graduate in 3 years or less, 59% graduate in 4 years or less, 65% graduate in 5 years or less, and 74% graduate in 6 years or less. 140 companies recruited on campus in a recent year. Of a recent graduating class, 23% were enrolled in graduate school within 6 months of graduation and 53% were employed.

Admissions Contact: Admission and Financial Aid Office. A video is available. E-mail: *admission@stvincent.edu*
Web: *http://www.stuincent.edu/admin-faid/admin-faid.html*

SETON HILL UNIVERSITY   B-4
Greensburg, PA 15601-1599

	(724) 838-4255
	(800) 826-6234; Fax: (724) 830-1294
Full-time: 482 men, 744 women	**Faculty:** 60; IIB, -$
Part-time: 69 men, 231 women	**Ph.D.s:** 85%
Graduate: 71 men, 266 women	**Student/Faculty:** 20 to 1
Year: varies by program, summer session	**Tuition:** $21,990
	Room & Board: $6820

Application Deadline: open
Freshman Class: 2133 applied, 1500 accepted, 336 enrolled
SAT or ACT: recommended   **COMPETITIVE**

Seton Hill University, founded in 1883, is a private university affiliated with the Roman Catholic Church and offers programs in liberal arts and career preparation. In addition to regional accreditation, Seton Hill has baccalaureate program accreditation with ADA, ARC-PA,CSWE, and NASM. The library contains 96,872 volumes, 5819 microform items, and 6631 audio/video tapes/CDs/DVDs, and subscribes to 360 periodicals including electronic. Computerized library services include the card catalog, interlibrary loans, database searching, and Internet access. Special learning facilities include an art gallery, TV station, a nursery school and kindergarten that function as laboratory schools for education students, a performance hall, and 2 theaters. The 200-acre campus is in a small town 35 miles east of Pittsburgh. Including any residence halls, there are 19 buildings.

Student Life: 82% of undergraduates are from Pennsylvania. Others are from 33 states, 14 foreign countries, and Canada. 83% are white; 10% African American. The average age of freshmen is 18; all undergraduates, 22. 22% do not continue beyond their first year; 60% remain to graduate.

Housing: 685 students can be accommodated in college housing, which includes single-sex and coed dorms. On-campus housing is guaranteed for all 4 years. 61% of students live on campus. Alcohol is not permitted. All students may keep cars.

Activities: There are no fraternities or sororities. There are 35 groups on campus, including art, cheerleading, choir, chorale, chorus, dance, drama, environmental, entrpreneurial, ethnic, gay, honors, international, jazz band, literary magazine, musical theater, newspaper, orchestra, pep band, political, professional, religious, social, social service, student government, symphony, and yearbook. Popular campus events include Christmas on the Hill, Family Weekend, and President's Reception.

Sports: There are 9 intercollegiate sports for men and 10 for women. Facilities include 2 gyms, one with a seating capacity of 1200, a fitness center, an aerobics room, a swimming pool, a field house with weight and training rooms, 3 natural grass playing fields, and a football stadium.

Disabled Students: 95% of the campus is accessible. Wheelchair ramps, elevators, special parking, specially equipped rest rooms, special class scheduling, lowered drinking fountains, and lowered telephones are available.

Services: Counseling and information services are available, as is tutoring in most subjects. There is a reader service for the blind and remedial math and writing.

Campus Safety and Security: Measures include 24-hour foot and vehicle patrol, self-defense education, security escort services, and shuttle buses. There are informal discussions, pamphlets/posters/films, emergency telephones, and lighted pathways/sidewalks.

Programs of Study: Seton Hill confers B.A., B.S., B.F.A., B.Mus., B.S.Med.Tech., and B.S.W. degrees. Master's degrees are also awarded. Bachelor's degrees are awarded in BIOLOGICAL SCIENCE (biochemistry and biology/biological science), BUSINESS (accounting, business administration and management, business economics, entrepreneurial studies, human resources, international business management, manage-

ment information systems, marketing/retailing/merchandising, personnel management, and tourism), COMMUNICATIONS AND THE ARTS (art history and appreciation, arts administration/management, communications, creative writing, dramatic arts, English, fine arts, graphic design, journalism, music, musical theater, performing arts, Spanish, studio art, theater design, and theater management), COMPUTER AND PHYSICAL SCIENCE (actuarial science, chemistry, computer science, mathematics, and physics), EDUCATION (art, early childhood, elementary, English, foreign languages, home economics, mathematics, music, science, secondary, social science, and special), ENGINEERING AND ENVIRONMENTAL DESIGN (engineering), HEALTH PROFESSIONS (art therapy, medical laboratory technology, music therapy, nursing, physician's assistant, predentistry, premedicine, and preveterinary science), SOCIAL SCIENCE (child care/child and family studies, criminal justice, dietetics, economics, family/consumer resource management, family/consumer studies, food production/management/services, forensic studies, history, human services, international studies, liberal arts/general studies, political science/government, prelaw, psychology, religion, religious music, social work, and sociology). Sciences, education, and fine arts are the strongest academically. Psychology, art, and business are the largest.

Required: The core corriculum requires 6 credits in Western cultures, 6 credits in writing, and 3 each in theology, philosophy/senior seminar, math, computer science, science, college-level foreign language, U.S. cultures, non-western cultures, and artistic expression. A portfolio is required. A total of 120 credit hours with a minimum GPA of 2.0 is required for graduation.

Special: There are cooperative programs in all majors and cross-registration with St. Vincent College, the University of Pittsburgh at Greensburg, and Westmoreland County Community College. Internships are encouraged. Seton Hill offers study abroad, a Washington semester, work-study, dual and student-designed majors, accelerated degree programs, a 3-2 engineering program with Pennsylvania State University and Georgia Institute of Technology, a 2-2 nursing program with Catholic University of America, a 3-2 or 3-1 medical technology program with area hospitals, credit by exam and for life/military/work experience, non-degree study, and pass/fail options. There are 5 national honor societies, and a freshman honors program.

Faculty/Classroom: 42% of faculty are male; 58%, female. 85% teach undergraduates and 60% do research. No introductory courses are taught by graduate students. The average class size in an introductory lecture is 25; in a laboratory, 16; and in a regular course, 18.

Admissions: 70% of the 2005-2006 applicants were accepted. 31% of the current freshmen were in the top fifth of their class; 60% were in the top two fifths. 6 freshmen graduated first in their class.

Requirements: The SAT or ACT is recommended. Two graded writing samples are accepted in place of SAT or ACT scores. A total of 15 Carnegie units is required, including 4 each of English and electives, 2 each of math, social studies, and foreign language, and 1 of a lab science. Art students must submit a portfolio; music and theater students must audition. An interview is recommended. The GED is accepted with supporting recommendations. A GPA of 2.5 is required. AP and CLEP credits are accepted. Important factors in the admissions decision are advanced placement or honor courses, evidence of special talent, and leadership record.

Procedure: Freshmen are admitted fall and spring. Entrance exams should be taken in spring of the junior year or fall of the senior year. There is a deferred admissions plan and a rolling admissions plans. Application deadlines are open. Application fee is $35. Applications are accepted on-line.

Transfer: 64 transfer students enrolled in 2004-2005. Applicants must submit college transcripts and have a GPA of at least 2.0. An interview is recommended, as are supporting letters. 48 of 120 credits required for the bachelor's degree must be completed at Seton Hill.

Visiting: There are regularly scheduled orientations for prospective students, consisting of an introduction, an address by the president or dean, an open reception with faculty, a financial aid session, a student panel, and a campus tour. There are guides for informal visits and visitors may sit in on classes and stay overnight. To schedule a visit, contact the Director of Admissions.

Financial Aid: In 2005-2006, 99% of all full-time freshmen and 79% of continuing full-time students received some form of financial aid. 96% of full-time freshmen and 70% of continuing full-time students received need-based aid. The average freshman award was $21,896. Need-based scholarships or need-based grants averaged $8616 ($20,500 maximum); need-based self-help aid (loans and jobs) averaged $3857 ($9861 maximum); non-need-based athletic scholarships averaged $5000 ($28,900 maximum); and other non-need-based awards and non-need-based scholarships averaged $4423 ($28,900 maximum). 53% of undergraduates work part time. Average annual earnings from campus work are $1300. The average financial indebtedness of the 2005 graduate was $22,085. The FAFSA and the college's own financial statement are required. The priority date for freshman financial aid applications for fall entry is April 30. The deadline for filing freshman financial aid applications for fall entry is August 1.

International Students: There are 22 international students enrolled. The school actively recruits these students. They must score satisfactorily on the TOEFL.

Computers: Wireless access is available. All classrooms, labs, offices, and dorm rooms have Internet access. There are approximately 600 university-owned computers used daily on campus. The Management/Student Information System and the course Management System as well as all e-mail accounts are accessible from off campus via web portals. All students may access the system 24 hours per day. There are no time limits and no fees.

Graduates: From July 1, 2004 to June 30, 2005, 199 bachelor's degrees were awarded. The most popular majors were business (33%), art (11%), and social sciences (10%). In an average class, 45% graduate in 4 years or less, 55% graduate in 5 years or less, and 60% graduate in 6 years or less. 51 companies recruited on campus in 2004-2005. Of the 2004 graduating class, 31% were enrolled in graduate school within 6 months of graduation and 92% were employed.

Admissions Contact: Kim McCarty, Director of Admissions and Graduate Student Services. E-mail: *admit@setonhill.edu* Web: *setonhill.edu*

SHIPPENSBURG UNIVERSITY OF PENNSYLVANIA   C-4

Shippensburg, PA 17257-2299

(717) 477-1231
(800) 822-8028; Fax: (717) 477-4016

Full-time: 2956 men, 3219 women	**Faculty:** 292; IIA, +$
Part-time: 120 men, 164 women	**Ph.D.s:** 87%
Graduate: 306 men, 720 women	**Student/Faculty:** 21 to 1
Year: semesters, summer session	**Tuition:** $6175 ($13,598)
Application Deadline: open	**Room & Board:** $5446
Freshman Class: 6282 applied, 4131 accepted, 1504 enrolled	
SAT Verbal/Math: 520/520*	**COMPETITIVE**

Shippensburg University, founded in 1871, is a public university that is part of the Pennsylvania State System of Higher Education offering undergraduate and graduate degree programs in the College of Arts and Sciences, College of Business, and College of Education and Human Services. There are 4 undergraduate schools and 1 graduate school. In addition to regional accreditation, Ship has baccalaureate program accreditation with AACSB, ACS, CACREP, CEC, CSWE, IACS, NCACE, and NCATE. The library contains 449,125 volumes, 1,285,048 microform items, and 77,847 audio/video tapes/CDs/DVDs, and subscribes to 1243 periodicals including electronic. Computerized library services include the card catalog, interlibrary loans, database searching, Internet access, and laptop Internet portals. Special learning facilities include a learning resource center, art gallery, planetarium, radio station, TV station, a closed-circuit television, fashion archives center, vertebrate museum, women's center, on-campus elementary school, electron microscope, greenhouse, and herbarium. The 204-acre campus is in a rural area 40 miles southwest of Harrisburg. Including any residence halls, there are 49 buildings.

Student Life: 94% of undergraduates are from Pennsylvania. Others are from 23 states, 12 foreign countries, and Canada. 88% are from public schools. 87% are white. The average age of freshmen is 18; all undergraduates, 21. 24% do not continue beyond their first year; 63% remain to graduate.

Housing: 2646 students can be accommodated in college housing, which includes single-sex and coed dormitories, on-campus apartments, and off-campus apartments. In addition, there is a designated "quiet" hall and a scholars hall. On-campus housing is guaranteed for the freshman year only. 60% of students commute. Alcohol is not permitted. All students may keep cars.

Activities: 6% of men belong to 10 national fraternities; 8% of women belong to 1 local and 10 national sororities. There are 247 groups on campus, including art, band, cheerleading, choir, chorale, chorus, computers, dance, debate, drama, ethnic, gay, honors, international, jazz band, literary magazine, marching band, musical theater, newspaper, orchestra, pep band, photography, political, professional, radio and TV, religious, social, social service, student government, and yearbook. Popular campus events include planetarium shows, Senior Olympics, and Summer Music Festival.

Sports: There are 8 intercollegiate sports for men and 10 for women, and 12 intramural sports for men and 12 for women. Facilities include a 7700-seat stadium for football and track and field events and complexes for varsity baseball, softball, and tennis. There is a 450-seat stadium with an artficial turf surface for soccer, field hockey, and lacrosse. Basketball, volleyball, and wrestling competitions are conducted within a 2700-seat facility, with swimming facilities. Outdoor recreational facilities include a 12-acre sports complex.

Disabled Students: 90% of the campus is accessible. Wheelchair ramps, elevators, special parking, specially equipped rest rooms, special class scheduling, lowered drinking fountains, lowered telephones, enlarged printing, extended time for tests, classroom accessibility, note taking, reader services, alternative testing sites, prior scheduling, and a Kurzweil reader are available.

Services: Counseling and information services are available, as is tutoring in most subjects, including writing and study skills assessment and resources. Workshops, supplemental instruction, and learning specialists are available.

Campus Safety and Security: Measures include 24-hour foot and vehicle patrol, self-defense education, security escort services, and shuttle buses. There are informal discussions, pamphlets/posters/films, emergency telephones and lighted pathways/sidewalks. Residence halls are equipped with an automatic heat/smoke detection sprinkler system monitored 24 hours a day by police. A strobe light unit notifies students who are hearing impaired. Residence hall doors are locked 24 hours a day. There are digital cameras at the main entrance to residence halls, computer labs, and other buildings, as well as many exterior cameras covering parking lots and other campus areas. There is also a bicycle patrol.

Programs of Study: Ship confers B.A., B.S., B.S.B.A., B.S.Ed., and B.S.W. degrees. Master's degrees are also awarded. Bachelor's degrees are awarded in BIOLOGICAL SCIENCE (biology/biological science), BUSINESS (accounting, banking and finance, business administration and management, business systems analysis, management information systems, and marketing/retailing/merchandising), COMMUNICATIONS AND THE ARTS (art, communications, English, French, journalism, Spanish, and speech/debate/rhetoric), COMPUTER AND PHYSICAL SCIENCE (applied physics, chemistry, computer science, earth science, geoenvironmental studies, information sciences and systems, mathematics, and physics), EDUCATION (art, business, elementary, English, foreign languages, mathematics, science, secondary, and social studies), ENGINEERING AND ENVIRONMENTAL DESIGN (environmental science), HEALTH PROFESSIONS (exercise science and health care administration), SOCIAL SCIENCE (criminal justice, economics, geography, history, interdisciplinary studies, political science/government, psychology, public administration, social work, and sociology). Elementary education, criminal justice, and communication/journalism are the largest.

Required: General education courses include English composition, oral communications, math, and history, as well as courses in logic and numbers for rational thinking; linguistic, literary, artistic, and cultural traditions; lab science; biological and physical science; political, economic, and geographic sciences; and social and behavioral sciences. The core curriculum varies for degree programs. Most degree programs require 120 credit hours, with 22 to 30 hours in the major, and a 2.0 minimum GPA for graduation.

Special: The university offers internships, study abroad in the Netherlands, South Korea,, Denmark, and other countries and a 3-2 engineering degree with Pennsylvania State University and the University of Maryland. There is a cooperative art program with the Art Institutes International (Art Institutes of Pittsburgh and Art Institutes of Philadelphia) in Pennsylvania and 6 other states, as well as a cooperative program in the health sciences. Students have the option of taking courses for a semester at one of the 13 other schools in the Pennsylvania State System of Higher Education. There is also a Visiting Student Program with Wilson College and with the Fashion Institute of Technology of New York City. As a member of the Marine Science Consortium, the university also offers opportunities for field and laboratory studies in marine science at Wallops Island, Virginia. There are 17 national honor societies, a freshman honors program, and 1 departmental honors program.

Faculty/Classroom: 56% of faculty are male; 44%, female. 95% teach undergraduates, 31% do research, and 31% do both. No introductory courses are taught by graduate students. The average class size in an introductory lecture is 35; in a laboratory, 16; and in a regular course, 28.

Admissions: 66% of the 2005-2006 applicants were accepted. The SAT scores for the 2005-2006 freshman class were: Verbal--38% below 500, 47% between 500 and 599, 14% between 600 and 700, and 1% above 700; Math--34% below 500, 50% between 500 and 599, 16% between 600 and 700, and 1% above 700. 23% of the current freshmen were in the top fifth of their class; 56% were in the top two fifths. 2 freshmen graduated first in their class.

Requirements: The SAT is required. In addition, applicants are urged to pursue a typical college preparatory program, which should include 4 years of English, 3 each of social sciences, sequential math, and lab science, and 2 of 1 foreign language. A GED is accepted. AP and CLEP credits are accepted. Important factors in the admissions decision are advanced placement or honor courses, recommendations by school officials, and evidence of special talent.

Procedure: Freshmen are admitted fall and spring. Entrance exams should be taken in the junior year and senior year. There is a deferred admissions and a rolling admissions plan. Application deadlines are open. Applications are accepted on-line. The fall 2005 application fee was $30.

Transfer: 469 transfer students enrolled in 2004-2005. Applicants must provide high school and college transcripts and SAT or ACT scores if they have less than 30 college credits. 45 of 120 credits required for the bachelor's degree must be completed at Ship.

Visiting: There are regularly scheduled orientations for prospective students, including daily academic group meetings, campus tours, and 5 weekend open house programs per year. There are guides for informal visits and visitors may sit in on classes. To schedule a visit, contact the Admissions Office.

Financial Aid: In 2005-2006, 76% of all full-time freshmen and 71% of continuing full-time students received some form of financial aid. 51% of full-time freshmen and 45% of continuing full-time students received need-based aid. The average freshman award was $6422. Need-based scholarships or need-based grants averaged $3923 ($14,717 maximum); need-based self-help aid (loans and jobs) averaged $4531 ($18,025 maximum); non-need-based athletic scholarships averaged $2057 ($11,732 maximum); and other non-need-based awards and non-need-based scholarships averaged $5980 ($26,388 maximum). 9% of undergraduates work part time. Average annual earnings from campus work are $2040. The average financial indebtedness of the 2005 graduate was $17,984. Ship is a member of CSS. The FAFSA and PHEAA are required. The deadline for filing freshman financial aid applications for fall entry is May 1.

International Students: There are 15 international students enrolled. They must score satisfactorily on the written TOEFL or on the electronic version and also take the SAT or the ACT. Students whose native language is English must submit SAT scores instead of TOEFL.

Computers: Wireless access is available. Students may use their PCs to access the campus network from residence halls using both wired and wireless connectivity. Additionally, wireless is available in common areas and academic classrooms throughout the campus. Public and department-specific computer classrooms and labs allow students access to the campus network. All students may access the system 24 hours a day. There are no time limits and no fees.

Graduates: From July 1, 2004 to June 30, 2005, 1388 bachelor's degrees were awarded. The most popular majors were elementary education (17%), criminal justice (7%), and marketing (6%). In an average class, 42% graduate in 4 years or less, 61% graduate in 5 years or less, and 63% graduate in 6 years or less. 70 companies recruited on campus in 2004-2005.

Admissions Contact: Dr. Thomas Speakman, Enrollment Services. A video is available. E-mail: *admiss@ship.edu*
Web: *www.ship.edu/admiss*

SLIPPERY ROCK UNIVERSITY OF PENNSYLVANIA   B-2
Slippery Rock, PA 16057

	(724) 738-2015
	(800) 929-4778; Fax: (724) 738-2913
Full-time: 2860 men, 3565 women	Faculty: 366; IIA, +$
Part-time: 225 men, 415 women	Ph.D.s: 78%
Graduate: 235 men, 510 women	Student/Faculty: 18 to 1
Year: semesters, summer session	Tuition: $5810 ($12,710)
Application Deadline: see profile	Room & Board: $4550
Freshman Class: n/a	
SAT or ACT: required	**LESS COMPETITIVE**

Slippery Rock University of Pennsylvania, founded in 1889, is a public institution that is part of the Pennsylvania State System of Higher Education. It offers programs in business, information, social sciences, education, health, environment, science, humanities, and fine and performing arts. There are 4 undergraduate schools and 1 graduate school. Figures in the above capsule and profile are approximate. In addition to regional accreditation, The Rock has baccalaureate program accreditation with ACBSP, APTA, CAAHEP, CSWE, NASAD, NASM, NCATE, NLN, and NRPA. The library contains 502,974 volumes, 1,497,469 microform items, and 22,707 audio/video tapes/CDs/DVDs, and subscribes to 1300 periodicals including electronic. Computerized library services include the card catalog, interlibrary loans, database searching, and Internet access. Special learning facilities include a learning resource center, art gallery, natural history museum, planetarium, radio station, TV station, and a wellness center. The 600-acre campus is in a small town 50 miles north of Pittsburgh. Including any residence halls, there are 60 buildings.

Student Life: 96% of undergraduates are from Pennsylvania. Others are from 35 states, 47 foreign countries, and Canada. 70% are from public schools. 87% are white. The average age of freshmen is 18; all undergraduates, 22. 22% do not continue beyond their first year; 49% remain to graduate.

Housing: 2810 students can be accommodated in college housing, which includes single-sex and coed dormitories, on-campus apartments, off-campus apartments, married-student housing, fraternity houses, and sorority houses. In addition, there are honors houses, language houses, and special-interest houses. On-campus housing is guaranteed for the freshman year only and is available on a first-come, first-served basis. 62% of students commute. Alcohol is not permitted. All students may keep cars.

Activities: 7% of men belong to 11 national fraternities; 6% of women belong to 9 national sororities. There are 100 groups on campus, including art, band, cheerleading, chess, choir, chorale, chorus, computers, dance, drama, ethnic, film, gay, honors, international, jazz band, literary magazine, marching band, musical theater, newspaper, orchestra, pep band, photography, political, professional, radio and TV, religious, so-

cial, social service, student government, symphony, and yearbook. Popular campus events include Spring Weekend.

Sports: There are 12 intercollegiate sports for men and 12 for women, and 7 intramural sports for men and 7 for women. Facilities include a field house, a gym, and a fitness center. The campus stadium seats 10,000, the indoor gym seats 3000, and the largest auditorium/arena seats 1000.

Disabled Students: 80% of the campus is accessible. Wheelchair ramps, elevators, special parking, specially equipped rest rooms, special class scheduling, lowered drinking fountains, lowered telephones, and special housing are available.

Services: Counseling and information services are available, as is tutoring in some subjects, including about 60 introductory-level general liberal studies courses. There is a reader service for the blind and remedial math and writing.

Campus Safety and Security: Measures include 24-hour foot and vehicle patrol, self-defense education, security escort services, and shuttle buses. There are informal discussions, pamphlets/posters/films, emergency telephones, lighted pathways/sidewalks, and the university maintains its own police department, with officers having the same powers as municipal police.

Programs of Study: The Rock confers B.A., B.S., B.F.A., B.Mus., B.Mus.Ed., B.S.B.A., B.S.Ed., and B.S.N. degrees. Master's and doctoral degrees are also awarded. Bachelor's degrees are awarded in BIOLOGICAL SCIENCE (biology/biological science), BUSINESS (accounting, business administration and management, international business management, and marketing/retailing/merchandising), COMMUNICATIONS AND THE ARTS (communications, dance, English, fine arts, French, German, music, and Spanish), COMPUTER AND PHYSICAL SCIENCE (chemistry, computer science, earth science, geology, information sciences and systems, mathematics, and physics), EDUCATION (early childhood, elementary, foreign languages, health, music, science, secondary, and special), HEALTH PROFESSIONS (community health work, medical laboratory technology, and nursing), SOCIAL SCIENCE (anthropology, economics, geography, history, parks and recreation management, philosophy, political science/government, psychology, public administration, social science, social work, and sociology). Business, education, and health science areas are the largest.

Required: B.A. students must demonstrate proficiency in a foreign language, and all must complete 42 to 53 credits in a 7-part liberal studies program, including basic competencies, arts, cultural diversity/global perspective, human institutions, science and math, natural experience, and modern age. Specific requirements include public speaking, college writing, algebra, and phys ed. A minimum of 120 credit hours, with at least 30 in the major, is required for graduation.

Special: Study abroad is available in 16 countries. Internships are offered in most majors, and international internships are available in Scotland and England. There is a 3-2 engineering program with Pennsylvania State University. The dual major is an option and credit is given for military experience. Pass/fail options also are available. There are 26 national honor societies, a freshman honors program, and 33 departmental honors programs.

Faculty/Classroom: 53% of faculty are male; 47%, female. All teach undergraduates. No introductory courses are taught by graduate students. The average class size in an introductory lecture is 33; in a laboratory, 20; and in a regular course, 25.

Requirements: The SAT is required and the ACT is recommended. Students should graduate from an accredited secondary school or have a GED. A total of 16 academic credits is required. The recommended college preparatory program includes 4 years of English and social studies, 3 each of science and math, and 2 of a foreign language. An interview is recommended. AP and CLEP credits are accepted. Important factors in the admissions decision are advanced placement or honor courses, extracurricular activities record, and evidence of special talent.

Procedure: Freshmen are admitted fall, spring, and summer. Entrance exams should be taken in the junior year or fall of the senior year. There are deferred admissions, and rolling admissions plans. Check with the school for application deadlines. Notification is sent on a rolling basis. A waiting list is an active part of the admissions procedure. Applications are accepted on-line. The fall 2005 application fee was $25.

Transfer: 559 transfer students enrolled in a recent year. Applicants should have completed at least 24 credit hours with a GPA of 2.5. The SAT or ACT, as well as an interview, are recommended. 36 of 120 credits required for the bachelor's degree must be completed at The Rock.

Visiting: There are regularly scheduled orientations for prospective students, including a meeting with faculty, an information fair, and a campus tour. There are guides for informal visits and visitors may sit in on classes and stay overnight. To schedule a visit, contact the Admissions Office.

Financial Aid: In a recent year, 64% of all full-time freshmen and 58% of continuing full-time students received some form of financial aid. 51% of full-time freshmen and 43% of continuing full-time students received need-based aid. The average freshman award was $6074. Need-based scholarships or need-based grants averaged $2907; need-based self-help aid (loans and jobs) averaged $2437; non-need-based athletic scholarships averaged $2507; and other non-need-based awards and non-need-based scholarships averaged $3590. 30% of undergraduates worked part time. Average annual earnings from campus work were $1000. The average financial indebtedness of a recent graduate was $19,195. The Rock is a member of CSS. The FAFSA is required. Check with the school for application deadlines.

International Students: In a recent year, there were 130 international students enrolled. The school actively recruits these students. They must score satisfactorily on the written TOEFL.

Computers: All students may access the system The mainframe system is accessible 24 hours a day. Campus terminal and PC labs are generally open more than 100 hours per week. There are no time limits and no fees.

Graduates: In a recent year, 1190 bachelor's degrees were awarded. The most popular majors were education (23%), marketing (15%), and parks and recreation (13%). In an average class, 24% graduate in 4 years or less, 46% graduate in 5 years or less, and 49% graduate in 6 years or less. 260 companies recruited on campus in a recent year. Of a recent graduating class, 12% were enrolled in graduate school within 6 months of graduation and 81% were employed.

Admissions Contact: Jim Barrett, Director of Admissions. A video is available. E-mail: *asktherock@sru.edu* Web: *http://www.sru.edu*

SUSQUEHANNA UNIVERSITY D-3

Selinsgrove, PA 17870-1001

(570) 372-4260
(800) 326-9672; Fax: (570) 372-2722

Full-time: 844 men, 1050 women	**Faculty:** 122; IIB, av$
Part-time: 32 men, 63 women	**Ph.D.s:** 93%
Graduate: none	**Student/Faculty:** 16 to 1
Year: semesters, summer session	**Tuition:** $26,265
Application Deadline: March 1	**Room & Board:** $7200
Freshman Class: n/av	
SAT or ACT: not required	**VERY COMPETITIVE**

Susquehanna University, founded in 1858, is an independent, selective, residential institution affiliated with the Lutheran Church. It offers programs through schools of arts, humanities and communications, natural and social sciences, and business. There are 3 undergraduate schools. In addition to regional accreditation, S.U. has baccalaureate program accreditation with AACSB, ACS, and NASM. The library contains 292,235 volumes, 125,121 microform items, and 7368 audio/video tapes/CDs/DVDs, and subscribes to 15,935 periodicals including electronic. Computerized library services include the card catalog, interlibrary loans, database searching, and Internet access. Special learning facilities include a learning resource center, art gallery, radio station, multimedia classrooms, video studios, a campuswide telecommunications network, satellite dishes and distribution system for foreign-language broadcasts, a video conferencing facility, an ecological field station, observatory, a child development center, and an electronic music lab. The 307-acre campus is in a small town 50 miles north of Harrisburg. Including any residence halls, there are 52 buildings.

Student Life: 60% of undergraduates are from Pennsylvania. Others are from 26 states, 10 foreign countries, and Canada. 84% are from public schools. 93% are white. 52% are Protestant; 38% Catholic. The average age of freshmen is 18; all undergraduates, 20. 12% do not continue beyond their first year; 78% remain to graduate.

Housing: 1410 students can be accommodated in college housing, which includes coed dorms, on-campus apartments, off-campus apartments, fraternity houses, and sorority houses. In addition, there are honors houses and special-interest houses. On-campus housing is guaranteed for all 4 years. 80% of students live on campus; of those, 86% remain on campus on weekends. All students may keep cars.

Activities: 20% of men belong to 4 national fraternities; 25% of women belong to 4 national sororities. There are 100 groups on campus, including art, band, cheerleading, chess, choir, chorale, chorus, computers, dance, drama, ethnic, film, gay, honors, international, jazz band, literary magazine, musical theater, newspaper, National Organization for women, opera, orchestra, outdoors, pep band, photography, political, professional, radio and TV, religious, social, social service, student government, and yearbook. Popular campus events include Spring Weekend, Candlelight Christmas Service, and Family Weekend.

Sports: There are 11 intercollegiate sports for men and 12 for women, and 22 intramural sports for men and 22 for women. Facilities include a field house with indoor track, tennis and basketball courts, football stadium and track, soccer, baseball, lacrosse, rugby, and hockey fields, basketball and tennis courts, a swimming pool, racquetball courts, a weight-training room, a fitness center, and a sauna.

Disabled Students: 90% of the campus is accessible. Wheelchair ramps, elevators, special parking, specially equipped rest rooms, special class scheduling, lowered drinking fountains, and lowered telephones are available.

Services: Counseling and information services are available, as is tutoring in some subjects, including writing, math, foreign languages, and study skills. Academic departments also provide tutoring.

Campus Safety and Security: Measures include 24-hour foot and vehicle patrol, self-defense education, security escort services, and informal discussions. There are pamphlets/posters/films, emergency telephones, and lighted pathways/sidewalks.

Programs of Study: S.U. confers B.A., B.S., and B.M. degrees. Associate degrees are also awarded. Bachelor's degrees are awarded in BIOLOGICAL SCIENCE (biochemistry, biology/biological science, and ecology), BUSINESS (accounting and business administration and management), COMMUNICATIONS AND THE ARTS (art, art history and appreciation, communications, creative writing, dramatic arts, English, French, German, graphic design, music, music performance, and Spanish), COMPUTER AND PHYSICAL SCIENCE (chemistry, computer science, earth science, information sciences and systems, mathematics, and physics), EDUCATION (early childhood, education, elementary, and music), ENGINEERING AND ENVIRONMENTAL DESIGN (environmental science), SOCIAL SCIENCE (economics, history, international studies, philosophy, political science/government, psychology, religion, religious music, and sociology). Natural sciences, business administration, and psychology are the strongest academically. Business administration, communications, and psychology are the largest.

Required: All students must complete a 3-part core curriculum of about 40 semester hours, including academic requirements in history, fine arts, literature, science, and social science, as well as philosophy or religion; skills in computers, math/logic, and foreign language; and courses in academic skills, wellness/fitness, and career development. An additional 36 to 44 hours are required in the major, and the remainder of a 130-hour minimum required total in electives or a minor. A minimum GPA of 2.0 is also required to graduate.

Special: There is cross-registration with Bucknell University. Internships are offered in almost all majors, and study abroad is available on 6 continents. The School of Business offers a semester in London for junior business majors. 2-week study seminars in Australia are available, as are a Boston semester, a Washington semester, a United Nations semester, and a work and study semester through the Philadelphia Center. The university offers dual and student-designed majors, work-study programs, credit by exam, nondegree study, and pass/fail options. The B.A.-B.S. degree is available in several majors, and there is a 3-2 program in forestry with Duke University, a 2-2 program in allied health with Thomas Jefferson University, and a 3-2 program in dentistry with Temple University. Highly motivated students have the option of earning their baccalureate degree in 3 years. There are 21 national honor societies, a freshman honors program, and 16 departmental honors programs.

Faculty/Classroom: 60% of faculty are male; 40%, female. All both teach and do research. The average class size in an introductory lecture is 23; in a laboratory, 13; and in a regular course, 19.

Requirements: All students have the option of submitting either the SAT, ACT, or 2 graded writing samples. Students should be graduates of an accredited high school. Preparation should include 4 years of English and math, 3 to 4 years of science, and 2 to 3 years each of social studies and foreign language. In addition, 1 unit of art or music is recommended. An essay is required, as are, for relevant fields, a music audition or writing portfolio. An interview is strongly recommended. S.U. requires applicants to be in the upper 40% of their class. A GPA of 3.0 is required. AP and CLEP credits are accepted. Important factors in the admissions decision are advanced placement or honor courses, evidence of special talent, and recommendations by school officials.

Procedure: Freshmen are admitted fall and spring. Entrance exams should be taken by January of the senior year. There are early decision and deferred admissions plans. There is a rolling admission plan. Early decision I applications should be filed by November 15 and early decision II by January I; regular applications, by March 1 for fall entry and December 1 for spring entry, along with a $35 fee. Notification of early decision I is sent December 1 and early decision II January 15; regular decision, on a rolling basis. 136 early decision candidates were accepted for the 2005-2006 class. 89 applicants were on the 2005 waiting list; 7 were admitted. Applications are accepted on-line.

Transfer: 36 transfer students enrolled in 2005-2006. Applicants must submit high school and college transcripts, test scores, and a recommendation from a dean. An interview is strongly recommended. A music audition or writing portfolio is required for relevant fields. 65 of 130 credits required for the bachelor's degree must be completed at S.U.

Visiting: There are regularly scheduled orientations for prospective students, including special visiting days for prospective students and their parents held in the spring and fall, which consist of sessions with faculty, admissions, financial aid, and placement staff and tours of the campus. There are guides for informal visits and visitors may sit in on classes and stay overnight. To schedule a visit, contact the Office of Admissions.

Financial Aid: In 2005-2006, 93% of all full-time freshmen and 94% of continuing full-time students received some form of financial aid. 66% of full-time freshmen and 64% of continuing full-time students received need-based aid. The average freshman award was $18,460. Need-based scholarships or need-based grants averaged $14,710 ($25,950 maximum); need-based self-help aid (loans and jobs) averaged $3525 ($6425 maximum); and other non-need-based awards and non-need-based scholarships averaged $8435 ($25,950 maximum). 54% of undergraduates work part time. Average annual earnings from campus work are $770. The average financial indebtedness of the 2005 graduate was $12,500. S.U. is a member of CSS. The CSS/Profile or FAFSA and federal tax return are required. The priority date for freshman financial aid applications for fall entry is March 1. The deadline for filing freshman financial aid applications for fall entry is May 1.

International Students: There are 17 international students enrolled. The school actively recruits these students. A satisfactory score on the TOEFL is required.

Computers: More than 300 PCs are located in classrooms, the library, residence hall rooms, and the campus center. There are wireless areas in the major campus buildings. All students may access the system 24 hours a day. There are no time limits and no fees. It is strongly recommended that all students have a personal computer, specifically a 3.0 GHz Pentium 4 with 1 GB of RAM.

Graduates: From July 1, 2004 to June 30, 2005, 515 bachelor's degrees were awarded. The most popular majors were business administration (23%), communications and theater arts (15%), and psychology (7%). In an average class, 1% graduate in 3 years or less, 79% graduate in 4 years or less, 82% graduate in 5 years or less, and 82% graduate in 6 years or less. 51 companies recruited on campus in 2004-2005. Of the 2004 graduating class, 21% were enrolled in graduate school within 6 months of graduation and 75% were employed.

Admissions Contact: Chris Markle, Director of Admissions. E-mail: *suadmiss@susqu.edu* Web: *www.susqu.edu/admissions/*

SWARTHMORE COLLEGE   F-4
Swarthmore, PA 19081-1397

	(610) 328-8300
	(800) 667-3110; Fax: (610) 328-8580
Full-time: 708 men, 764 women	**Faculty:** 171; IIB, ++$
Part-time: 3 men, 4 women	**Ph.D.s:** 98%
Graduate: none	**Student/Faculty:** 9 to 1
Year: semesters	**Tuition:** $31,516
Application Deadline: January 1	**Room & Board:** $9764
Freshman Class: 4085 applied, 917 accepted, 389 enrolled	
SAT Verbal/Math: 730/710*	**MOST COMPETITIVE**

Swarthmore College, established in 1864, is a private, nonprofit institution offering undergraduate courses in engineering and liberal arts. In addition to regional accreditation, Swarthmore has baccalaureate program accreditation with ABET. The 7 libraries contain 762,747 volumes, 70,288 microform items, and 21,748 audio/video tapes/CDs/DVDs, and subscribe to 6457 periodicals including electronic. Computerized library services include the card catalog, interlibrary loans, database searching, Internet access, and laptop Internet portals. Special learning facilities include an art gallery, a radio station, an observatory, a performing arts center, Center for the Study of Classical Jewish Texts, a solar energy lab, an arboretum, and a library of documents and memorabilia of the peace movement. The 357-acre campus is in a suburban area 10 miles southwest of Philadelphia. Including any residence halls, there are 49 buildings.

Student Life: 84% of undergraduates are from out of state, mostly the Middle Atlantic. Students are from 48 states, 38 foreign countries, and Canada. 62% are from public schools. 47% are white; 15% Asian American; 10% Hispanic. The average age of freshmen is 18; all undergraduates, 20. 4% do not continue beyond their first year; 92% remain to graduate.

Housing: 1352 students can be accommodated in college housing, which includes single-sex and coed dorms. On-campus housing is guaranteed for all 4 years and is available on a lottery system for upperclassmen. 96% of students live on campus. Upperclassmen may keep cars.

Activities: 6% of men belong to 1 local and 1 national fraternity. There are no sororities. There are more than 100 groups on campus, including a acppella, art, band, chess, choir, chorus, club sports, computers, dance, debate, drama, ethnic, film, gay, honors, international, jazz band, literary magazine, musical theater, newspaper, orchestra, photography, political, radio and TV, religious, social, social service, student government, and yearbook. Popular campus events include Crain Regatta, McCabe Mile, and Screw Your Roommate.

Sports: There are 10 intercollegiate sports for men and 12 for women, and 9 intramural sports for men and 9 for women. Facilities include 12 outdoor and 6 indoor tennis courts; 6 full-length indoor basketball courts; 10 outdoor playing fields; a lighted stadium with synthetic grass surface, an athletic events center with seating for 1,800; a field house large enough to accommodate team practices during inclement weather; an outdoor 8-lane, 400-meter Versaturf track; an indoor 215-meter banked Tartan track; an indoor swimming pool with electronic timing system; 5 squash courts; a fitness center with aerobic and Medx equipment; and a professionally staffed sports medicine facility with three full-time trainers.

Disabled Students: 80% of the campus is accessible. Wheelchair ramps, elevators, special parking, specially equipped rest rooms, special class scheduling, lowered drinking fountains, lowered telephones, and special housing are available.

Services: Counseling and information services are available, as is tutoring in most subjects. There is a reader service for the blind. Writing and computing support are also available.

Campus Safety and Security: Measures include 24-hour foot and vehicle patrol, self-defense education, security escort services, and shuttle buses. There are informal discussions, pamphlets/posters/films, emergency telephones, and lighted pathways/sidewalks.

Programs of Study: Swarthmore confers B.A. and B.S. degrees. Bachelor's degrees are awarded in BIOLOGICAL SCIENCE (biochemistry and biology/biological science), COMMUNICATIONS AND THE ARTS (art, art history and appreciation, Chinese, classics, comparative literature, dance, dramatic arts, English literature, French, German, Greek, Latin, linguistics, literature, music, Russian, and Spanish), COMPUTER AND PHYSICAL SCIENCE (astronomy, astrophysics, chemistry, computer science, mathematics, and physics), EDUCATION (education), ENGINEERING AND ENVIRONMENTAL DESIGN (engineering), SOCIAL SCIENCE (anthropology, Asian/Oriental studies, classical/ancient civilization, economics, German area studies, history, medieval studies, philosophy, political science/government, psychobiology, psychology, religion, and sociology). Biology, economics, and political science are the largest.

Required: To graduate, students must complete 3 courses in each of 3 divisions consisting of humanities, natural sciences and engineering, and social sciences. Concurrent with distribution and/or major requirements, there is a requirement of 3 writing courses and a science laboratory.They must have completed 32 courses or the equivalent, with a minimum of 20 courses outside the major and 8 to 12 courses in the major. They must have a GPA of 2.0. Students must demonstrate foreign language competency and fulfill a phys ed requirement including a swimming test. Each major has a culminating experience, which may be a thesis, project, or comprehensive exam.

Special: Students may cross-register with Haverford and Bryn Mawr Colleges and the University of Pennsylvania. They may study abroad in their country of choice. Dual majors in physics and astronomy and in sociology and anthropology, student-designed majors, and a 4-year program leading to a B.A.-B.S. degree in engineering and liberal arts are available. Swarthmore offers a unique honors program whose features are student independence and responsibility and collegial relationship with faculty; students are evaluated by external examiners. There are 3 national honor societies, including Phi Beta Kappa, and 100 departmental honors programs.

Faculty/Classroom: 61% of faculty are male; 39%, female. All both teach and do research. The average class size in an introductory lecture is 22; in a laboratory, 10; and in a regular course, 15.

Admissions: 22% of the 2005-2006 applicants were accepted. The SAT scores for the 2005-2006 freshman class were: Verbal--1% below 500, 4% between 500 and 599, 26% between 600 and 700, and 69% above 700; Math--5% between 500 and 599, 33% between 600 and 700, and 62% above 700. 95% of the current freshmen were in the top fifth of their class; 99% were in the top two fifths. 37 freshmen graduated first in their class.

Requirements: The SAT or ACT is required. In addition, SAT Subject tests in 2 areas of choice are required. Swarthmore does not require a specific high school curriculum. It does, however, recommend the inclusion of English, math, 1 or 2 foreign languages, history and social studies, literature, art and music, and the sciences. Interviews are strongly recommended. AP credits are accepted. Important factors in the admissions decision are advanced placement or honor courses, personality/intangible qualities, and recommendations by school officials.

Procedure: Freshmen are admitted in the fall. Entrance exams should be taken in spring of the junior year or fall of the senior year. There are early decision and deferred admissions plans. Early decision applications should be filed by November 15; regular applications, by January 1 for fall entry. Notification of early decision is sent December 15; regular decision, April 1. 160 early decision candidates were accepted for the 2005-2006 class. A waiting list is an active part of the admissions procedure. Applications are accepted on-line.

Transfer: 8 transfer students enrolled in 2004-2005. The SAT is required if not taken previously. An essay is required. 16 of 32 credits required for the bachelor's degree must be completed at Swarthmore.

Visiting: There are regularly scheduled orientations for prospective students, including group information sessions and campus tours, offered at regular times throughout the year. There are guides for informal visits and visitors may sit in on classes and stay overnight. To schedule a visit, contact the admissions receptionist at (610) 328-8300 or *admissions@swarthmore.edu*.

Financial Aid: In 2005-2006, 51% of all full-time freshmen and 50% of continuing full-time students received some form of financial aid. 51% of full-time freshmen and 50% of continuing full-time students received need-based aid. The average freshman award was $29,945. Need-based

scholarships or need-based grants averaged $26,838; need-based self-help aid (loans and jobs) averaged $3106; and other non-need-based awards and non-need-based scholarships averaged $31,196. 81% of undergraduates work part time. Average annual earnings from campus work are $1501. The average financial indebtedness of the 2005 graduate was $14,100. Swarthmore is a member of CSS. The CSS/Profile or FAFSA, the college's own financial statement, and tax returns, W-2 statements, and year-end paycheck stubs are required. The deadline for filing freshman financial aid applications for fall entry is February 15.

International Students: There are 93 international students enrolled. The school actively recruits these students. They must take the SAT or the ACT and 2 SAT subject tests in subjects that will reflect their academic strengths. Math Level is strongly encouraged for potential engineering students.

Computers: Wireless access is available. Students may use any residence hall room, libraries, public spaces, some classrooms, and some outdoor spaces. All students may access the system. There are no time limits and no fees.

Graduates: From July 1, 2004 to June 30, 2005, 395 bachelor's degrees were awarded. The most popular majors were biology (14%), economics (13%), and political science (12%). In an average class, 1% graduate in 3 years or less, 86% graduate in 4 years or less, 91% graduate in 5 years or less, and 92% graduate in 6 years or less. 65 companies recruited on campus in 2004-2005. Of the 2004 graduating class, 26% were enrolled in graduate school within 6 months of graduation, and 61% were employed upon graduation.

Admissions Contact: James L. Bock, Dean of Admissions and Financial Aid. E-mail: *admissions@swarthmore.edu*
Web: *http://www.swarthmore.edu/admissions/*

TEMPLE UNIVERSITY
F-3

Philadelphia, PA 19122-1803

(215) 204-7200
(888) 340-2222; Fax: (215) 204-5694

Full-time: 9123 men, 11,813 women	**Faculty:** 1232; I, av$
Part-time: 1375 men, 1883 women	**Ph.D.s:** 82%
Graduate: 4173 men, 5328 women	**Student/Faculty:** 17 to 1
Year: semesters, summer session	**Tuition:** $9640 ($17,236)
Application Deadline: April 1	**Room & Board:** $7798
Freshman Class: 17,352 applied, 10,989 accepted, 3871 enrolled	
SAT Verbal/Math: 540/540*	**COMPETITIVE**

Temple University, founded in 1888, is part of the Commonwealth System of Higher Education in Pennsylvania. It offers programs in the liberal arts and science and technology; health professions; education; engineering; art; business and management; communications and theater; architecture, landscape architecture and horticulture; music and dance; and social administration. Temple has 6 other campuses, including one in Rome and one in Tokyo. There are 13 undergraduate and 16 graduate schools. In addition to regional accreditation, Temple has baccalaureate program accreditation with AACSB, ABET, ACEJMC, ACPE, ADA, APTA, CAHEA, CSWE, NAAB, NASAD, NASM, NCATE, NLN, and NRPA. The 11 libraries contain 3 million volumes, 3.1 million microform items, and 27,000 audio/video tapes/CDs/DVDs, and subscribe to 24,000 periodicals including electronic. Computerized library services include the card catalog, interlibrary loans, database searching, Internet access, and laptop Internet portals. Special learning facilities include a learning resource center, art gallery, planetarium, radio station, dance lab theater, media learning center for the study of critical languages, and multimedia lab for teacher education in music. The 430-acre campus is in an urban area 1 mile north of Center City, Philadelphia. Including any residence halls, there are 236 buildings.

Student Life: 75% of undergraduates are from Pennsylvania. Others are from 42 states, 101 foreign countries, and Canada. 82% are from public schools. 63% are white; 20% African American; 10% Asian American. The average age of freshmen is 18; all undergraduates, 21. 15% do not continue beyond their first year; 54% remain to graduate.

Housing: 5131 students can be accommodated in college housing, which includes coed dormitories, on-campus apartments, off-campus apartments, and married-student housing. In addition, there are honors houses, language houses, special-interest houses, and living-learning communities. On-campus housing is available on a lottery system for upperclassmen. 80% of students commute. Alcohol is not permitted. All students may keep cars.

Activities: 1% of men belong to 12 local fraternities; 1% of women belong to 11 local sororities. There are 125 groups on campus, including art, band, cheerleading, chess, choir, chorus, computers, dance, drama, drill team, ethnic, film, honors, international, jazz band, literary magazine, marching band, musical theater, newspaper, orchestra, pep band, photography, political, professional, radio and TV, religious, social, social service, student government, and yearbook. Popular campus events include Spring Fling, Fall Fest, and Freshmen Summer reading project contest.

Sports: There are 13 intercollegiate sports for men and 13 for women, and 12 intramural sports for men and 12 for women. Facilities include

fitness areas with free weight and cardiovascular equipment, circuit training area, stretch abs/back area, tread wall, 4 racquetball courts, a group fitness room, martial arts/aerobic room, indoor walking/jogging track, and 4 indoor multi-purpose courts. There are also 2 large playing fields, a 6-lane, 1/4 mile track with synthetic surface, sand volleyball court, outdoor basketball, volleyball, and tennis courts, outdoor in-line skating, and 2 Olympic size swimming pools.

Disabled Students: All of the campus is accessible. Wheelchair ramps, elevators, special parking, specially equipped rest rooms, special class scheduling, lowered drinking fountains, and lowered telephones are available. Additional services may be arranged through the Disabled Student Services Office.

Services: Counseling and information services are available, as is tutoring in most subjects. There is a reader service for the blind, and remedial math, reading, and writing.

Campus Safety and Security: Measures include 24-hour foot and vehicle patrol, self-defense education, security escort services, and shuttle buses. There are informal discussions, pamphlets/posters/films, emergency telephones, lighted pathways/sidewalks, and 24-hour security in residence halls. Residence halls have fire safety features including smoke detectors, alarmed fire-exit doors, fire extinguishers and automated exit doors.

Programs of Study: Temple confers B.A., B.S., B.Ar., B.B.A., B.F.A., B.M., B.S.Ar., B.S.E., B.S.Ed., B.S.E.E., B.S.N., and B.S.W. degrees. Associate, master's, and doctoral degrees are also awarded. Bachelor's degrees are awarded in AGRICULTURE (environmental studies and horticulture), BIOLOGICAL SCIENCE (biochemistry, biology/biological science, and biophysics), BUSINESS (accounting, banking and finance, business administration and management, business economics, business law, electronic business, entrepreneurial studies, human resources, international business management, management information systems, marketing/retailing/merchandising, personnel management, real estate, sports management, and tourism), COMMUNICATIONS AND THE ARTS (art, art history and appreciation, broadcasting, classics, communications, dance, dramatic arts, English, film arts, fine arts, French, German, Germanic languages and literature, Greek, guitar, Hebrew, Italian, jazz, journalism, linguistics, music, music history and appreciation, music performance, music theory and composition, percussion, performing arts, photography, piano/organ, Russian, Spanish, speech/debate/rhetoric, strings, telecommunications, voice, and winds), COMPUTER AND PHYSICAL SCIENCE (actuarial science, chemistry, computer science, earth science, geology, information sciences and systems, mathematics, physics, and statistics), EDUCATION (art, business, early childhood, education, elementary, English, foreign languages, industrial arts, marketing and distribution, mathematics, middle school, music, physical, science, secondary, social studies, and teaching English as a second/foreign language (TESOL/TEFOL), ENGINEERING AND ENVIRONMENTAL DESIGN (architecture, civil engineering, electrical/electronics engineering, electrical/electronics engineering technology, engineering, engineering technology, environmental engineering technology, environmental science, landscape architecture/design, materials science, mechanical engineering, and mechanical engineering technology), HEALTH PROFESSIONS (health science, music therapy, nursing, occupational therapy, pharmacy, predentistry, and premedicine), SOCIAL SCIENCE (African American studies, American studies, anthropology, Asian/Oriental studies, criminal justice, economics, geography, history, interdisciplinary studies, Latin American studies, parks and recreation management, philosophy, physical fitness/movement, political science/government, prelaw, psychology, religion, social science, social work, sociology, urban studies, and women's studies). Business administration, psychology, and elementary education are the largest.

Required: The required core curriculum includes English composition, intellectual heritage, American culture, the arts, the individual and society, foreign language/international studies, math/statistics/logic, and science and technology. A minimum 2.0 GPA and a total of 128 credit hours are required for graduation, including 24 credits in the major.

Special: The university offers study abroad, work-study programs, and up to 30 credits for life/military/work experience. There is a chapter of Phi Beta Kappa and a freshman honors program.

Faculty/Classroom: 60% of faculty are male; 40%, female. The average class size in a regular course is 24.

Admissions: 63% of the 2005-2006 applicants were accepted. The SAT scores for the 2005-2006 freshman class were: Verbal--24% below 500, 51% between 500 and 599, 23% between 600 and 700, and 2% above 700; Math--21% below 500, 52% between 500 and 599, 24% between 600 and 700, and 3% above 700. The ACT scores were 32% below 21, 37% between 21 and 23, 19% between 24 and 26, 8% between 27 and 28, and 4% above 28. 40% of the current freshmen were in the top fifth of their class; 77% were in the top two fifths. 19 freshmen graduated first in their class.

Requirements: The SAT or ACT is required. In addition, applicants should complete 16 academic credits/Carnegie units, including 4 years of English, 2 each of math and a foreign language, and 1 each of history and a lab science. A GED is accepted. A portfolio and audition are required in relevant fields. AP and CLEP credits are accepted. Important factors in the admissions decision are advanced placement or honor courses, recommendations by school officials, and parents or siblings attending the school.

Procedure: Freshmen are admitted fall and spring. Entrance exams should be taken by March of the junior year or April of the senior year. There is a rolling admissions plan. Applications should be filed by April 1 for fall entry and November 15 for spring entry. Notification is sent on a rolling basis. Applications are accepted on-line. The fall 2005 application fee was $35.

Transfer: 2596 transfer students enrolled in a recent year. Applicants must have earned at least 15 college credit hours with at least a 2.3 GPA and must submit official high school and college transcripts. 30 of 128 credits required for the bachelor's degree must be completed at Temple.

Visiting: There are regularly scheduled orientations for prospective students. There are guides for informal visits and visitors may sit in on classes. To schedule a visit, contact the Office of Undergraduate Admissions.

Financial Aid: In 2005-2006, 70% of all full-time freshmen and 67% of continuing full-time students received some form of financial aid. 70% of full-time freshmen and 67% of continuing full-time students received need-based aid. The average freshman award was $12,488. Need-based scholarships or need-based grants averaged $5010; need-based self-help aid (loans and jobs) averaged $2778; and non-need-based athletic scholarships averaged $12,828. The average financial indebtedness of the 2005 graduate was $23,772. The FAFSA, the college's own financial statement and the and the PHEAA (Pennsylvania residents) are required. The deadline for filing freshman financial aid applications for fall entry is March 31.

International Students: There are 683 international students enrolled. The school actively recruits these students. They must score satisfactorily on the written TOEFL or on the electronic version and also take the SAT or the ACT.

Computers: Wireless access is available. From the outside, students may sign on to university systems using their assigned user ID and a secure password. They may also plug into the network in labs, dorms, and smart classrooms. Students have access to 2200 Windows based PCs, 400 MACs and 100 Unix machines. Wireless access is available in approximately 95% of classrooms and common areas. Students need only register their computer to gain access. All students may access the system 24 hours per day. There are no time limits and no fees.

Graduates: From July 1, 2004 to June 30, 2005, 4263 bachelor's degrees were awarded. The most popular majors were elementary education (8%), psychology (7%), and criminal justice (5%). In an average class, 1% graduate in 3 years or less, 20% graduate in 4 years or less, 38% graduate in 5 years or less, and 44% graduate in 6 years or less. 269 companies recruited on campus in 2004-2005.

Admissions Contact: Dr. Timm Rinehart, Director, Undergraduate Admissions. E-mail: *tuadm@temple.edu* Web: *http://www.temple.edu*

THIEL COLLEGE A-2

Greenville, PA 16125

(724) 589-2226
(800) 24-THIEL; Fax: (724) 589-2013

Full-time: 688 men, 565 women	**Faculty:** 61; IIB, --$
Part-time: 35 men, 32 women	**Ph.D.s:** 64%
Graduate: none	**Student/Faculty:** 21 to 1
Year: semesters, summer session	**Tuition:** $17,590
Application Deadline: June 30	**Room & Board:** $6990
Freshman Class: 2397 applied, 1803 accepted, 427 enrolled	
SAT Verbal/Math: 480/480*	**ACT:** 19 **COMPETITIVE**

Thiel College, founded in 1866, is a private independent college affiliated with the Lutheran Church. It offers programs in liberal arts, business, engineering, religion, teacher preparation, and professional programs. The library contains 180,708 volumes, 148,520 microform items, and 6522 audio/video tapes/CDs/DVDs, and subscribes to 415 periodicals including electronic. Computerized library services include the card catalog, interlibrary loans, database searching, Internet access, and laptop Internet portals. Special learning facilities include a learning resource center, art gallery, radio station, and a wildlife sanctuary. The 135-acre campus is in a rural area 75 miles north of Pittsburgh and 75 miles southeast of Cleveland. Including any residence halls, there are 51 buildings.

Student Life: 72% of undergraduates are from Pennsylvania. Others are from 21 states and 14 foreign countries. 90% are from public schools. 60% are white. 36% claim no religious affiliation; 19% Catholic; 18% Protestant. The average age of freshmen is 18; all undergraduates, 20. 35% do not continue beyond their first year; 41% remain to graduate.

Housing: 1129 students can be accommodated in college housing, which includes single-sex and coed dorms and on-campus apartments. In addition, there are special-interest houses, an honors residence hall, and living-learning centers. On-campus housing is guaranteed for all 4 years. 82% of students live on campus; of those, 60% remain on campus on weekends. Alcohol is not permitted. All students may keep cars.

Activities: 10% of men belong to 4 national fraternities; 19% of women belong to 4 national sororities. There are 36 groups on campus, including art, band, cheerleading, choir, chorus, computers, dance, drama, drill team, ethnic, forensics, gay, honors, international, literary magazine, musical theater, newspaper, pep band, political, professional, radio and TV, religious, social, social service, student government, symphony, and yearbook. Popular campus events include Spring Weekend, Greek Week, and theatrical productions.

Sports: There are 10 intercollegiate sports for men and 9 for women, and 4 intramural sports for men and 3 for women. Facilities include a 1200-seat gym, basketball and handball courts, playing fields, a fitness center, tennis courts, and a football stadium.

Disabled Students: 75% of the campus is accessible. Wheelchair ramps, elevators, special parking, specially equipped rest rooms, and special class scheduling are available.

Services: Counseling and information services are available, as is tutoring in most subjects. There is remedial math, reading, and writing.

Campus Safety and Security: Measures include 24-hour foot and vehicle patrol, security escort services, shuttle buses, and pamphlets/posters/films. There are emergency telephones and lighted pathways/sidewalks.

Programs of Study: Thiel confers the B.A. degree. Associate degrees are also awarded. Bachelor's degrees are awarded in BIOLOGICAL SCIENCE (biology/biological science), BUSINESS (accounting, business administration and management, electronic business, international business management, and management information systems), COMMUNICATIONS AND THE ARTS (art, communications, English, and Spanish), COMPUTER AND PHYSICAL SCIENCE (actuarial science, chemistry, computer science, mathematics, physics, and web services), EDUCATION (elementary and secondary), ENGINEERING AND ENVIRONMENTAL DESIGN (environmental science and preengineering), HEALTH PROFESSIONS (cytotechnology, medical laboratory technology, physical therapy, predentistry, premedicine, prepharmacy, preveterinary science, and speech pathology/audiology), SOCIAL SCIENCE (family/juvenile justice, history, philosophy, political science/government, prelaw, psychology, religion, religious education, and sociology). Binary engineering, biology, and chemistry are the strongest academically. Business administration, social sciences, and psychology are the largest.

Required: To graduate, students must complete a total of 124 credit hours, with 35 to 55 in the major and a minimum GPA of 2.0. Integrative distribution requirements include 8 hours of Western humanities, 4 hours each of global heritage, health and phys ed, and lab science, and 3 each of religion, humanities, social science, and math/sciences. Math must be college algebra or higher. Some majors require a comprehensive exam or thesis.

Special: Students may spend a semester at Argonne National Laboratories, the Art Institute of Pittsburgh, or Drew University. Special programs include a UN semester, a Washington semester, an Appalachian semester, study at Pittsburgh Institute of Mortuary Science, and a forestry and environmental management semester at Duke University. There is a 3-2 engineering program with Case Western Reserve University and the University of Pittsburgh. Internships, study abroad, work-study, dual majors, nondegree study, cooperative programs in all majors, credit by exam, and credit for life, military, and work experience are also available. There are 11 national honor societies, a freshman honors program, and 10 departmental honors programs.

Faculty/Classroom: 62% of faculty are male; 38%, female. All teach undergraduates. The average class size in an introductory lecture is 25; in a laboratory, 15; and in a regular course, 15.

Admissions: 75% of the 2005-2006 applicants were accepted. The SAT scores for the 2005-2006 freshman class were: Verbal--58% below 500, 34% between 500 and 599, 7% between 600 and 700, and 1% above 700; Math--56% below 500, 35% between 500 and 599, 8% between 600 and 700, and 1% above 700. The ACT scores were 66% below 21, 21% between 21 and 23, 9% between 24 and 26, 2% between 27 and 28, and 2% above 28. 21% of the current freshmen were in the top fifth of their class; 36% were in the top two fifths.

Requirements: The SAT or ACT is required. The ACT Optional Writing test is also required. In addition, applicants should be high school graduates who have completed 16 academic units, including 4 years of English, 3 of social science, and 2 each of foreign language, math, and science. The GED is accepted. An essay and an interview are recommended. Thiel requires applicants to be in the upper 60% of their class. A GPA of 2.0 is required. AP and CLEP credits are accepted. Important factors in the admissions decision are advanced placement or honor courses, evidence of special talent, and leadership record.

Procedure: Freshmen are admitted to all sessions. Entrance exams should be taken by May 1 of each year. Regular applications for fall entry should be filed no later than June 30, along with a $25 fee. There is a deferred admissions plan and a rolling admissions plan. Notification is sent on a rolling basis. Applications are accepted on-line.

Transfer: 55 transfer students enrolled in 2004-2005. Applicants should meet the same criteria as entering freshmen and should submit official transcripts, statements of good standing, financial aid transcripts, and transfer forms from all colleges previously attended. Students must have a 2.0 GPA to transfer. 30 of 124 credits required for the bachelor's degree must be completed at Thiel.

Visiting: There are regularly scheduled orientations for prospective students, including orientation sessions for students enrolling in the fall and monthly sessions beginning in February. There are guides for informal visits and visitors may sit in on classes and stay overnight. To schedule a visit, contact the Admissions Office at *mknapp@thiel.edu*.

Financial Aid: In 2005-2006, 99% of all full-time students received some form of financial aid. 83% of full-time freshmen and 87% of continuing full-time students received need-based aid. The average freshman award was $14,960. Need-based scholarships or need-based grants averaged $11,135 ($16,200 maximum); need-based self-help aid (loans and jobs) averaged $4264 ($16,200 maximum); and other non-need-based awards and non-need-based scholarships averaged $6250 ($16,200 maximum). 39% of undergraduates work part time. Average annual earnings from campus work are $1300. The average financial indebtedness of the 2005 graduate was $20,000. The CSS/Profile, FAFSA, FFS, or SFS are required; the FAFSA is preferred. The deadline for filing freshman financial aid applications for fall entry is May 1.

International Students: There are 61 international students enrolled. The school actively recruits these students. They must take the TOEFL.

Computers: Wireless access is available. All students may access the system. There are no time limits and no fees. All students are required to have personal computers. The college providees an IBM ThinkPad to each of its students.

Graduates: From July 1, 2004 to June 30, 2005, 214 bachelor's degrees were awarded. The most popular majors were business (34%), accounting (11%), and psychology (11%). In an average class, 32% graduate in 4 years or less, 41% graduate in 5 years or less, and 42% graduate in 6 years or less. 40 companies recruited on campus in 2004-2005. Of the 2004 graduating class, 13% were enrolled in graduate school within 6 months of graduation and 87% were employed.

Admissions Contact: Gary Kelsey, Dean of Admissions.
Web: *http://www.thiel.edu*

UNIVERSITY OF PENNSYLVANIA   F-3

Philadelphia, PA 19104   (215) 898-7507

Full-time: 4735 men, 4810 women	**Faculty:** 3258; I, ++$
Part-time: 170 men, 126 women	**Ph.D.s:** 99%
Graduate: 4461 men, 4512 women	**Student/Faculty:** 3 to 1
Year: semesters, summer session	**Tuition:** $32,364
Application Deadline: January 1	**Room & Board:** $9402
Freshman Class: 18,824 applied, 3913 accepted, 2552 enrolled	
SAT Verbal/Math: 700/720*	**ACT:** 31 **MOST COMPETITIVE**

University of Pennsylvania, founded in 1740, is a private institution offering undergraduate and graduate degrees in arts and sciences, business, engineering and applied science, and nursing. There are 4 undergraduate and 21 graduate schools. In addition to regional accreditation, Penn has baccalaureate program accreditation with AACSB, ABA, ABET, ADA, APA, ASLA, AVMA, CSWE, LCM, NAAB, NCATE, and NLN. The 15 libraries contain 5,760,065 volumes, 4,048,727 microform items, and 73,489 audio/video tapes/CDs/DVDs, and subscribe to 43,931 periodicals including electronic. Computerized library services include the card catalog, interlibrary loans, database searching, Internet access, and laptop Internet portals. Special learning facilities include a learning resource center, an art gallery, a planetarium, a radio station, a TV station, an arboretum, an animal research center, a primate research center, a language lab, a center for performing arts, an institute for contemporary art, a wind tunnel, an electron microscope, and a museum of anthropology and archeology. The 269-acre campus is in an urban area in Philadelphia. Including any residence halls, there are 151 buildings.

Student Life: 82% of undergraduates are from out of state, mostly the Middle Atlantic. Students are from 50 states, 109 foreign countries, and Canada. 54% are from public schools. 48% are white; 18% Asian American. 23% claim no religious affiliation; 22% are Jewish; 20% Catholic; 19% Protestant; 16% Buddhist, Islamic, and Mormon. The average age of freshmen is 18; all undergraduates, 20. 4% do not continue beyond their first year; 94% remain to graduate.

Housing: 6625 students can be accommodated in college housing, which includes coed dorms, on-campus apartments, off-campus apartments, married-student housing, fraternity houses, and sorority houses. In addition, there are language houses, special-interest houses, and 35 academic residence programs, including the areas of art, biophysics, entrepeneuship, international studies, media, visual arts, and women in science. On-campus housing is available on a first-come, first-served basis and is available on a lottery system for upperclassmen. 63% of students live on campus; of those, 97% remain on campus on weekends. All students may keep cars.

Activities: 21% of men belong to 32 national fraternities; 17% of women belong to 14 national sororities. There are 450 groups on campus, including art, band, cheerleading, chess, choir, chorale, chorus, computers, dance, debate, drama, ethnic, film, forensics, gay, honors, international, jazz band, literary magazine, marching band, musical theater, newspaper, orchestra, pep band, photography, political, professional, radio and TV, religious, social, social service, student government, symphony, and yearbook.

Sports: There are 17 intercollegiate sports for men and 16 for women, and 11 intramural sports for men and 11 for women. Facilities include 4 gyms, 2 swimming pools, squash courts, indoor and outdoor tennis courts, 7 playing fields, an indoor ice rink, rowing tanks, saunas, weight rooms, exercise facilities, a boathouse, and a stadium.

Disabled Students: 90% of the campus is accessible. Wheelchair ramps, elevators, special parking, specially equipped rest rooms, special class scheduling, lowered drinking fountains, lowered telephones, special housing, TDD, accessible housing, and an accessible van shuttle are available.

Services: Counseling and information services are available, as is tutoring in most subjects. There is a reader service for the blind. The WHEEL academic support program is available in all residences.

Campus Safety and Security: Measures include 24-hour foot and vehicle patrol, self-defense education, security escort services, and shuttle buses. There are informal discussions, pamphlets/posters/films, emergency telephones, lighted pathways/sidewalks, a bicycle patrol, 100 commissioned police officers, victim support and special services, Students Together Against Acquaintance Rape, Penn Watch, Student Walking Escort, and 200 security guard personnel, many on public patrol.

Programs of Study: Penn confers B.A., B.S., B.Applied Sc., B.B.A., B.F.A., B.S.E., and B.S.N. degrees. Associate, master's, and doctoral degrees are also awarded. Bachelor's degrees are awarded in AGRICULTURE (environmental studies), BIOLOGICAL SCIENCE (biochemistry, biology/biological science, biometrics and biostatistics, biophysics, and neurosciences), BUSINESS (accounting, banking and finance, business administration and management, business law, electronic business, entrepreneurial studies, insurance and risk management, international business management, management information systems, marketing/retailing/merchandising, operations research, real estate, and transportation management), COMMUNICATIONS AND THE ARTS (art history and appreciation, classics, communications, comparative literature, dramatic arts, East Asian languages and literature, English, fine arts, folklore and mythology, French, German, Italian, linguistics, music, romance languages and literature, Russian, Slavic languages, Spanish, video, and visual and performing arts), COMPUTER AND PHYSICAL SCIENCE (actuarial science, chemistry, computer science, digital arts/technology, geology, mathematics, physics, and statistics), EDUCATION (education, and elementary), ENGINEERING AND ENVIRONMENTAL DESIGN (architecture, bioengineering, chemical engineering, civil engineering, computer engineering, electrical/electronics engineering, engineering, environmental design, environmental science, materials engineering, mechanical engineering, and systems engineering), HEALTH PROFESSIONS (biomedical science, health, health care administration, and nursing), SOCIAL SCIENCE (African American studies, African studies, anthropology, Asian/Oriental studies, cognitive science, East Asian studies, economics, history, history of science, humanities, international relations, international studies, Italian studies, Judaic studies, Latin American studies, liberal arts/general studies, philosophy, political science/government, psychobiology, psychology, public administration, religion, sociology, South Asian studies, urban studies, and women's studies). Liberal arts, engineering and management are the strongest academically. Finance, economics, and history are the largest.

Required: The bachelor's degree requires completion of 32 to 40 course units, depending on the student's major, with 12 to 18 of these units in the major and a GPA of 2.0.

Special: Cross-registration is permitted with Haverford, Swarthmore, and Bryn Mawr Colleges and through the Quaker Consortium. Opportunities are provided for internships, a Washington semester, accelerated degree programs, joint degree programs, preprofessional programs, B.A.-B.S. degrees, dual and student-designed majors, credit by exam, limited pass/fail options, and study abroad in 39 countries. Through the "one university" concept, students in one undergraduate school may study in any of the other three. There are 10 national honor societies, including Phi Beta Kappa, a freshman honors program, and 27 departmental honors programs.

Faculty/Classroom: 65% of faculty are male; 35%, female. All both teach and do research. No introductory courses are taught by graduate students. The average class size in an introductory lecture is 44; in a laboratory, 15; and in a regular course, 23.

Admissions: 21% of the 2005-2006 applicants were accepted. The SAT scores for the 2005-2006 freshman class were: Verbal--6% between 500 and 599, 46% between 600 and 700, and 48% above 700; Math--3% between 500 and 599, 34% between 600 and 700, and 63% above 700. The ACT scores were 3% between 21 and 23, 8% between 24 and 26, 13% between 27 and 28, and 76% above 28. 98% of the current freshmen were in the top fifth of their class; All were in the top two fifths. There were 68 National Merit finalists. 365 freshmen graduated first in their class.

Requirements: The SAT or ACT is required. Graduation from an accredited secondary school is not required. Recommended preparation includes 4 years of high school English, 3 or 4 each of a foreign language and math, and 3 each of history and science. An essay is required. A portfolio and an audition are recommended for prospective art and music majors, respectively. AP credits are accepted. Important factors in the admissions decision are advanced placement or honor courses, recommendations by school officials, and parents or siblings attending the school.

Procedure: Freshmen are admitted in the fall. Entrance exams should be taken by December of the senior year. There are early decision, early admissions, and deferred admissions plans. Early decision applications should be filed by November 1; regular applications, by January 1 for fall entry, along with a $70 fee. Notification of early decision is sent December 15; regular decision, April 1. 1169 early decision candidates were accepted for the 2005-2006 class. 1269 applicants were on the 2005 waiting list; 35 were admitted. Applications are accepted on-line.

Transfer: 175 transfer students enrolled in 2004-2005. Applicants must provide college and high school transcripts, essays, and 2 recommendations. SAT or ACT scores are required for transfer students. 16 of 32 credits to 40 courses units required for the bachelor's degree must be completed at Penn.

Visiting: There are regularly scheduled orientations for prospective students, including an information session by the Admissions Office and a tour of the campus led by current students. There are guides for informal visits and visitors may sit in on classes and stay overnight with prior notice. To schedule a visit, contact the Admissions Office at *www.admissions.upenn.edu.*

Financial Aid: In 2005-2006, 58% of all full-time freshmen and 57% of continuing full-time students received some form of financial aid. 41% of full-time freshmen and 42% of continuing full-time students received need-based aid. The average freshman award was $27,110. Need-based scholarships or need-based grants averaged $23,855 ($39,000 maximum); and need-based self-help aid (loans and jobs) averaged $5512 ($12,850 maximum). The average financial indebtedness of the 2005 graduate was $21,217. Penn is a member of CSS. The CSS/Profile or FAFSA, the college's own financial statement, parent and student federal income tax returns, and the CSS Noncustodial Parent Profile are required. The priority date for freshman financial aid applications for fall entry is February 15.

International Students: There are 921 international students enrolled. The school actively recruits these students. They must score satisfactorily on the written TOEFL on the electronic version and also take the SAT and 2 SAT: Subject tests or the ACT with writing.

Computers: All campus buildings are wired for Ethernet, and students residing in campus residences and in Greek houses have Ethernet connections in their rooms. Students may also use the more than 1000 networked PCs in computer labs, libraries, and other locations on campus. Wireless services are available in a large number of academic buildings, libraries, and public spaces. All students may access the system. There are no time limits and no fees. It is strongly recommended that all students have a personal computer.

Graduates: From July 1, 2004 to June 30, 2005, 2854 bachelor's degrees were awarded. The most popular majors were finance (12%), economics (8%), and history (6%). In an average class, 3% graduate in 3 years or less, 87% graduate in 4 years or less, 93% graduate in 5 years or less, and 94% graduate in 6 years or less. 566 companies recruited on campus in 2004-2005. Of the 2004 graduating class, 22% were enrolled in graduate school within 6 months of graduation and 66% were employed.

Admissions Contact: Willis Stetson, Jr., Dean of Admissions. A video is available. Web: *www.upenn.edu/admissions/*

UNIVERSITY OF PITTSBURGH SYSTEM

The University of Pittsburgh, established in 1787, is a state-related public research University in Pennsylvania. It is governed by the board of trustees of the University of Pittsburgh, whose chief administrator is the chancellor. The primary goal of the system is enhancing educational opportunities for the citizens of Pennsylvania and contributing to the state's social, intellectual, and economic development. The main priorities are to engage in research, artistic, and scholarly activities; to provide high-quality undergraduate, graduate, and professional programs; and to offer expertise and educational services to meet the needs of the region and state. The total enrollment for the University of Pittsburgh (all five campuses) in Fall Term, 2005 is 33,393. There are 4,696 faculty members. There are 206 baccalaureate, 116 master's, 83 doctoral, and 4 first professional degree programs offered at the University of Pittsburgh. 4-year campuses are located in Pittsburgh, Johnstown, Greensburg, and Bradford. A two-year campus is located in Titusville. The University of Pittsburgh web site is *www.pitt.edu.* Profiles of the 4-year campuses are included in this section.

UNIVERSITY OF PITTSBURGH AT BRADFORD | C-2

Bradford, PA 16701-2898

(814) 362-7555
(800) 872-1787; Fax: (814) 362-7578

Full-time: 436 men, 555 women	**Faculty:** 65; IIB, -$
Part-time: 88 men, 222 women	**Ph.D.s:** 62%
Graduate: none	**Student/Faculty:** 15 to 1
Year: semesters, summer session	**Tuition:** $10,538 ($20,426)
Application Deadline: open	**Room & Board:** $6470
Freshman Class: 592 applied, 449 accepted, 239 enrolled	
SAT Verbal/Math: 510/520*	**ACT:** 21	**COMPETITIVE**

The University of Pittsburgh at Bradford, established in 1963, is a public, state-related liberal arts institution. Figures in the above capsule and profile are approximate. In addition to regional accreditation, Pitt-Bradford has baccalaureate program accreditation with NLN. The library contains 92,740 volumes, 14,481 microform items, and 5551 audio/video tapes/CDs/DVDs, and subscribes to 343 periodicals including electronic. Computerized library services include the card catalog, interlibrary loans, database searching, and Internet access. Special learning facilities include a learning resource center, radio station, and a sports medicine and rehabilitative therapy clinic. The 317-acre campus is in a small town 160 miles northeast of Pittsburgh and 80 miles south of Buffalo. Including any residence halls, there are 28 buildings.

Student Life: 90% of undergraduates are from Pennsylvania. Others are from 13 states, 3 foreign countries, and Canada. 82% are white. The average age of freshmen is 18; all undergraduates, 24. 35% do not continue beyond their first year; 41% remain to graduate.

Housing: 641 students can be accommodated in college housing, which includes single-sex and coed on-campus apartments. On-campus housing is available on a first-come, first-served basis. 51% of students live on campus; of those, 43% remain on campus on weekends. All students may keep cars.

Activities: 3% of men belong to 3 local fraternities; 3% of women belong to 3 local sororities. There are 50 groups on campus, including art, choir, computers, dance, drama, ethnic, honors, international, literary magazine, newspaper, political, professional, radio and TV, religious, social, social service, and student government. Popular campus events include Winter Weekend, Spring Fling, and Alumni Weekend.

Sports: There are 5 intercollegiate sports for men and 6 for women, and 11 intramural sports for men and 11 for women. Facilities include a sport and fitness center that includes a 1200-seat performance arena for basketball, volleyball, and general recreation; a fitness center with physical conditioning equipment; and an exercise arts studio for dance, martial arts, and aerobics. There is also an auxiliary gym for recreation and intramurals, phys ed classes, and other events and a 6-lane swimming pool. Outdoor facilities include a lighted softball field, a baseball field, tennis courts, 2 handball courts, several basketball courts, football/softball fields, and a sand volleyball court.

Disabled Students: 99% of the campus is accessible. Elevators, special parking, specially equipped rest rooms, lowered drinking fountains, lowered telephones, and special housing are available.

Services: Counseling and information services are available, as is tutoring in most subjects. There is remedial math, reading, and writing. There is a writing lab.

Campus Safety and Security: Measures include 24-hour foot and vehicle patrol, security escort services, informal discussions, and pamphlets/posters/films. There are emergency telephones and lighted pathways/sidewalks.

Programs of Study: Pitt-Bradford confers B.A., B.S., and B.S.N. degrees. Associate degrees are also awarded. Bachelor's degrees are awarded in AGRICULTURE (environmental studies), BIOLOGICAL SCIENCE (biology/biological science), BUSINESS (business administration and management, and sports management), COMMUNICATIONS AND THE ARTS (communications, creative writing, English, and public relations), COMPUTER AND PHYSICAL SCIENCE (chemistry, computer science, mathematics, and physical sciences), EDUCATION (athletic training and elementary), ENGINEERING AND ENVIRONMENTAL DESIGN (engineering), HEALTH PROFESSIONS (nursing, radiological science, and sports medicine), SOCIAL SCIENCE (criminal justice, economics, history, human development, liberal arts/general studies, political science/government, psychology, social science, and sociology). Business administration, nursing, and administration of justice are the largest.

Required: To graduate, students must complete a minimum of 120 credits with 30 to 76 in the major, and maintan a minimum GPA of 2.0. At least 30 should be un upper-level courses. The core curriculum varies from 12 to 30 credits and distribution requirements from 56 to 59. English, math competency, and phys ed courses are required.

Special: Students may cross-register with colleges in the University of Pittsburgh system. Internships are required or strongly recommended for all majors. The school offers study abroad, dual majors, nondegree study, and a 3-2 engineering degree with the University of Pittsburgh (Oakland campus). Interdisciplinary majors are offered in human relations combining anthropology, psychology, and sociology; social sciences, combining anthropology, economics, history, political science, and sociology; and interdisciplinary arts, combining art, music, and theater. Professional preparation is available in many areas, including premedicine, prelaw, preveterinary science, prepharmacy, and predentistry. Teacher certification is also offered. There are 8 national honor societies and 5 departmental honors programs.

Faculty/Classroom: 55% of faculty are male; 45%, female. All teach undergraduates. The average class size in an introductory lecture is 22; in a laboratory, 14; and in a regular course, 17.

Admissions: 76% of the 2005-2006 applicants were accepted. The SAT scores for the 2005-2006 freshman class were: Verbal--47% below 500, 42% between 500 and 599, 11% between 600 and 700, and 1% above 700; Math--43% below 500, 49% between 500 and 599, and 7% between 600 and 700. The ACT scores were 41% below 21, 45% between 21 and 23, 7% between 24 and 26, 7% between 27 and 28, and 2% above 28. 24% of the current freshman were in the top fifth of their class; 57% were in the top two fifths.

Requirements: The SAT is required. The ACT Optional Writing test is also required. In addition, students must be graduates of an accredited secondary school with 16 Carnegie units, including 4 in English, 3 in history or social studies, and 3 each in science and math. The GED is accepted. Also used in the admissions decision are standardized test scores, rank in class, extracurricular activities, and recommendations. An essay is strongly recommended, as is an interview. A GPA of 2.0 is required. AP and CLEP credits are accepted. Important factors in the admissions decision are advanced placement or honor courses, extracurricular activities record, and leadership record.

Procedure: Freshmen are admitted fall, spring, and summer. Entrance exams should be taken during the junior year or the fall of the senior year. There are early admissions, deferred admissions, and rolling admissions plans. There is a rolling admissions plan. Application deadlines are open. Application fee is $35. Applications are accepted on-line.

Transfer: 95 transfer students enrolled in a recent year. A GPA of 2.0 or higher is required. 30 of 120 credits required for the bachelor's degree must be completed at Pitt-Bradford.

Visiting: There are regularly scheduled orientations for prospective students, consisting of 1-day open house programs throughout the year, offering a workshop with admissions representatives on academics, admissions, guidance, standardized tests, the application process, and financial aid. Tours led by students, a financial aid presentation, and a special campus event are also offered. There are guides for informal visits and visitors may sit in on classes. To schedule a visit, contact the Admissions Office.

Financial Aid: 13% of undergraduates worked part time. Average annual earnings from campus work are $1120. The average financial indebtedness of the 2005 graduate was $19,313. The FAFSA is required. The priority date for frshman financial aid applications dor fall entry is March 1.

International Students: There were 3 international students enrolled in a recent year. A satisfactory score on the TOEFL is required.

Computers: Internet access is available to each student on campus (1 port per pillow) and in 5 computer labs with an average of 20 computers each. 91% of classrooms allow student laptops; all classrooms allow wireless connectivity. Wireless connectivity is available campuswide. Student web pages are permitted. All students may access the system. There are no time limits. The fee is $130 per term for full-time students.

Graduates: In a recent year, 151 bachelor's degrees were awarded. The most popular majors were business (19%), administration of justice (15%), and human relations (9%). In an average class, 1% graduate in 3 years or less, 17% graduate in 4 years or less, 35% graduate in 5 years or less, and 41% graduate in 6 years or less. 49 companies recruited on campus in a recent year. Of a recent graduating class, 20% were enrolled in graduate school within 6 months of graduation and 93% were employed.

Admissions Contact: Alexander P. Nazemetz, Director of Admissions. A video is available. E-mail: *admissions@upb.pitt.edu*
Web: *www.upb.pitt.edu*

UNIVERSITY OF PITTSBURGH AT GREENSBURG   B-3
Greensburg, PA 15601-5898

	(724) 836-9880
	Fax: (724) 836-7160
Full-time: 798 men, 840 women	**Faculty:** 89; IIB, --$
Part-time: 79 men, 78 women	**Ph.D.s:** 84%
Graduate: none	**Student/Faculty:** 18 to 1
Year: semesters, summer session	**Tuition:** $10,350 ($20,244)
Application Deadline: open	**Room & Board:** $7290
Freshman Class: 1568 applied, 1405 accepted, 424 enrolled	
SAT Verbal/Math: 519/520*	**COMPETITIVE**

The University of Pittsburgh at Greensburg, established in 1963, is a public state-related institution, offering undergraduate majors that can be completed at Pitt-Greensburg, as well as relocation programs that are begun at Greensburg and completed at another Pitt campus. The library contains 75,000 volumes, 9458 microform items, and 1280 audio/video

tapes/CDs/DVDs. Computerized library services include the card catalog, interlibrary loans, database searching, Internet access, and laptop Internet portals. Special learning facilities include a learning resource center. The 219-acre campus is in a suburban area 33 miles southeast of Pittsburgh. Including any residence halls, there are 25 buildings.

Student Life: 99% of undergraduates are from Pennsylvania. Others are from 5 states, 1 foreign countries, and Canada. 94% are white. The average age of freshmen is 18; all undergraduates, 21. 25% do not continue beyond their first year; 55% remain to graduate.

Housing: 585 students can be accommodated in college housing, which includes coed dorms and on-campus apartments. In addition, there are special-interest houses. On-campus housing is available on a first-come, first-served basis. 68% of students commute. Alcohol is not permitted. All students may keep cars.

Activities: There are no fraternities or sororities. There are 44 groups on campus, including academic, band, cheerleading, chess, choir, chorale, chorus, computers, dance, debate, drama, ethnic, honors, literary magazine, newspaper, pep band, political, religious, social, social service, and student government. Popular campus events include a La Cultura study of a different historically significant era each year, the St. Clair history lecture, and Westmoreland Forum on a topic of countywide significance.

Sports: There are 6 intercollegiate sports for men and 6 for women, and 8 intramural sports for men and 8 for women. Facilities include a gym, a weight room, playing fields, and tennis and racquetball courts.

Disabled Students: 95% of the campus is accessible. Wheelchair ramps, elevators, special parking, specially equipped rest rooms, special class scheduling, lowered drinking fountains, lowered telephones, and special housing are available.

Services: Counseling and information services are available, as is tutoring in most subjects, including math, computer science, and English. There is remedial math, reading, and writing.

Campus Safety and Security: Measures include 24-hour foot and vehicle patrol, security escort services, informal discussions, and pamphlets/posters/films. There are emergency telephones and lighted pathways/sidewalks.

Programs of Study: Pitt-Greensburg confers B.A. and B.S. degrees. Bachelor's degrees are awarded in BIOLOGICAL SCIENCE (biology/ biological science), BUSINESS (accounting and management science), COMMUNICATIONS AND THE ARTS (communications, creative writing, and English literature), COMPUTER AND PHYSICAL SCIENCE (applied mathematics and natural sciences), SOCIAL SCIENCE (American studies, anthropology, humanities, political science/government, psychology, and social science). Management and psychology are the strongest academically. Management and administration of justice are the largest.

Required: To graduate, students must complete 120 to 126 hours, with 24 to 36 in the major, and maintain a minimum GPA of 2.0. General education requirements include 15 credits each in humanities, social sciences, and natural sciences, 6 to 15 in writing courses, 3 each in speech and critical reasoning, and 2 to 3 in math.

Special: Pitt-Greensburg offers cross-registration with the Pittsburgh and Johnstown campuses of the university system and with Seton Hill College and Westmoreland County Community College. Internships are available in all majors and required for English writing and criminology. Double majors, student-designed majors, a Washington semester, nondegree study, and pass/fail options are available. There are 2 national honor societies, including Phi Beta Kappa.

Faculty/Classroom: 52% of faculty are male; 48%, female. All teach undergraduates and 50% do research. The average class size in an introductory lecture is 30; in a laboratory, 15; and in a regular course, 25.

Admissions: 90% of the 2005-2006 applicants were accepted. The SAT scores for the 2005-2006 freshman class were: Verbal--34% below 500, 52% between 500 and 599, 13% between 600 and 700, and 1% above 700; Math--26% below 500, 58% between 500 and 599, 15% between 600 and 700, and 1% above 700. 22% of the current freshmen were in the top fifth of their class; 60% were in the top two fifths.

Requirements: The SAT is required. In addition, students must be graduates of an accredited secondary school. The GED is also accepted. Students must complete 15 college-preparatory high school units, including 4 each of English and academic electives, 3 of a single foreign language (recommended), 2 of math, and 1 each of history and a lab science; additional units in all but English are recommended. An essay is optional; an interview is recommended. Students must also submit scores from the SAT or ACT (including the Writing test). GPA and class rank are also considered heavily. Pitt-Greensburg requires applicants to be in the upper 60% of their class. A GPA of 2.0 is required. AP and CLEP credits are accepted. Important factors in the admissions decision are advanced placement or honor courses, recommendations by school officials, and leadership record.

Procedure: Freshmen are admitted fall and spring. Entrance exams should be taken by November. There are deferred admissions and rolling admissions plans. Application deadlines are open. The application fee is $35. Notification is sent within 15 days after receiving application. Applications are accepted on-line.

Transfer: 139 transfer students enrolled in 2005-2006. Applicants must have a minimum GPA of 2.0 and at least 12 college credits. 30 of 120 credits required for the bachelor's degree must be completed at Pitt-Greensburg.

Visiting: There are regularly scheduled orientations for prospective students, including Open House, Preview Day, and Junior Jump Start, and weekday visits that include campus tours and information sessions. There are guides for informal visits and visitors may sit in on classes. To schedule a visit, contact the Admissions Office at (724) 836-9881 or *upgadmit@pitt.edu.*

Financial Aid: In 2005-2006, 85% of all full-time students received some form of financial aid. 67% of all full-time students received need-based aid. The average freshman award was $7200. Need-based scholarships or need-based grants averaged $4000 ($9050 maximum); need-based self-help aid (loans and jobs) averaged $5700 ($5700 maximum); and other non-need-based awards and non-need-based scholarships averaged $3000 ($5000 maximum). 10% of undergraduates work part time. Average annual earnings from campus work are $2250. The average financial indebtedness of the 2005 graduate was $17,000. The FAFSA and the college's own financial statement are required. The priority date for freshman financial aid applications for fall entry is March 1. The deadline for filing freshman financial aid applications for fall entry is April 1.

International Students: A satisfactory score is required on the written TOEFL.

Computers: Wireless access is available. There are wireless sites at the student union, library, and coffeehouse. All students may access the system. There are no time limits and no fees.

Graduates: From July 1, 2004 to June 30, 2005, 212 bachelor's degrees were awarded. The most popular majors were management (23%), psychology (21%), and accounting (15%). In an average class, 27% graduate in 4 years, 52% graduate in 5 years, and 2% graduate in 6 years. 5 companies recruited on campus in 2004-2005. Of the 2004 graduating class, 23% were enrolled in graduate school within 6 months of graduation and 56% were employed.

Admissions Contact: Brandi S. Darr, Director of Admissions and Financial Aid. E-mail: *upgadmit@pitt.edu*

UNIVERSITY OF PITTSBURGH AT JOHNSTOWN   C-3

Johnstown, PA 15904

(814) 269-7050
(800) 765-4875; Fax: (814) 269-7044

Full-time: 1402 men, 1420 women	**Faculty:** IIB, -$
Part-time: 121 men, 203 women	**Ph.D.s:** n/av
Graduate: none	**Student/Faculty:** n/av
Year: trimesters, summer session	**Tuition:** $10,500 ($20,388)
Application Deadline: open	**Room & Board:** $6240
Freshman Class: 2589 applied, 2189 accepted, 781 enrolled	
SAT Verbal/Math: 506/517*	**ACT:** 21 **LESS COMPETITIVE**

The University of Pittsburgh at Johnstown is a 4-year institution offering programs in arts and sciences, education, and engineering technology. In addition to regional accreditation, Pitt-Johnstown has baccalaureate program accreditation with ABET. Computerized library services include the card catalog, interlibrary loans, database searching, and Internet access. Special learning facilities include a learning resource center, art gallery, radio station, and TV station. The 650-acre campus is in a suburban area 70 miles east of Pittsburgh. Including any residence halls, there are 35 buildings.

Student Life: 99% of undergraduates are from Pennsylvania. Others are from 9 states. 89% are from public schools. 96% are white. The average age of freshmen is 18; all undergraduates, 21. 24% do not continue beyond their first year; 63% remain to graduate.

Housing: 1700 students can be accommodated in college housing, which includes single-sex and coed dorms, on-campus apartments, off-campus apartments, fraternity houses, and sorority houses. In addition, there are special-interest houses and clubs and organizations that provide housing. On-campus housing is guaranteed for all 4 years. 67% of students live on campus; of those, 65% remain on campus on weekends. All students may keep cars.

Activities: 3% of men belong to 1 local and 3 national fraternities; 3% of women belong to sororities. There are 70 groups on campus, including band, cheerleading, choir, chorus, computers, dance, drama, ethnic, gay, honors, literary magazine, musical theater, newspaper, political, professional, radio and TV, religious, social, social service, student government, symphony, and yearbook. Popular campus events include Spring Concert, Pitt Fest, and Sephia Fashion Show.

Sports: There are 5 intercollegiate sports for men and 6 for women, and 11 intramural sports for men and 11 for women. Facilities include a 2300-seat gym, a pool, a dance studio, a weight room, a sauna, a cross-country track, basketball courts, and a nature area.

Disabled Students: 80% of the campus is accessible. Elevators, special parking, specially equipped rest rooms, special class scheduling, lowered drinking fountains, lowered telephones, and special housing are available.

Services: Counseling and information services are available, as is tutoring in most subjects. There is a reader service for the blind and remedial math.

Campus Safety and Security: Measures include 24-hour foot and vehicle patrol, self-defense education, security escort services, and shuttle buses. There are informal discussions, pamphlets/posters/films, emergency telephones, and lighted pathways/sidewalks.

Programs of Study: Pitt-Johnstown confers B.A. and B.S. degrees. Associate degrees are also awarded. Bachelor's degrees are awarded in AGRICULTURE (environmental studies), BIOLOGICAL SCIENCE (biology/biological science), BUSINESS (accounting, banking and finance, business administration and management, and business economics), COMMUNICATIONS AND THE ARTS (communications, creative writing, dramatic arts, English, and journalism), COMPUTER AND PHYSICAL SCIENCE (chemistry, computer science, geology, and mathematics), EDUCATION (elementary, English, mathematics, science, secondary, and social science), ENGINEERING AND ENVIRONMENTAL DESIGN (civil engineering technology, electrical/electronics engineering technology, and mechanical engineering technology), HEALTH PROFESSIONS (medical laboratory technology), SOCIAL SCIENCE (American studies, economics, geography, history, humanities, political science/government, psychology, social science, and sociology). Business, biology, and engineering technology are the largest.

Required: To graduate, students must complete 120 to 139 credits, with 30 to 36 credits in the major and a minimum GPA of 2.0. The school requires a core set of general education to include 12 credits each in humanities, natural sciences, and social sciences.

Special: Students may cross-register with schools in the Pittsburgh Council for Higher Education. Internships are available both on and off campus for credit, pay, or both. The school offers study abroad, work-study programs, accelerated degree programs, dual majors, student-designed majors, nondegree study, and pass/fail options. There are 10 national honor societies.

Faculty/Classroom: The average class size in an introductory lecture is 30; in a laboratory, 18; and in a regular course, 25.

Admissions: 85% of the 2005-2006 applicants were accepted. The SAT scores for the 2005-2006 freshman class were: Verbal--42% below 500, 47% between 500 and 599, 10% between 600 and 700, and 1% above 700; Math--36% below 500, 47% between 500 and 599, 16% between 600 and 700, and 1% above 700. The ACT scores were 52% below 21, 36% between 21 and 23, 10% between 24 and 26, 1% between 27 and 28, and 1% above 28. 23% of the current freshmen were in the top fifth of their class; 58% were in the top two fifths.

Requirements: The SAT or ACT is required. In addition, applicants must be graduates of an accredited secondary school. The GED is accepted. For admission to freshman standing, 15 academic credits are required, including 4 each of English and history, 3 each of social studies and math (2 of algebra, 1 of geometry preferred), 2 of foreign language, and 1 to 2 of lab science. Engineering students must have completed chemistry, physics, and trigonometry. An interview is recommended, and an essay is required. AP credits are accepted. Important factors in the admissions decision are advanced placement or honor courses, leadership record, and recommendations by school officials.

Procedure: Freshmen are admitted to all sessions. Entrance exams should be taken between April and June of the junior year or by November of the senior year. There are early admissions and deferred admissions plans. There is a rolling admissions plan. Application deadlines are open. Application fee is $45.

Transfer: 128 transfer students enrolled in 2004-2005. Students wishing to transfer must have a minimum GPA of 2.5 and at least 15 credit hours earned. The SAT or ACT is required. Grades of C or better transfer for credit. 30 of 120 to 139 credits required for the bachelor's degree must be completed at Pitt-Johnstown.

Visiting: There are regularly scheduled orientations for prospective students, including 5 programs held on Saturdays in the fall, 2 Saturdays in the spring, 1 Friday in the spring, and 3 Fridays in the summer. There are guides for informal visits and visitors may sit in on classes and stay overnight. To schedule a visit, contact the Admissions Office at *upjadmit@pitt.edu.*

Financial Aid: In 2005-2006, 72% of all full-time freshmen and 69% of continuing full-time students received some form of financial aid. 68% of full-time freshmen and 67% of continuing full-time students received need-based aid. The average freshman award was $8013. Need-based scholarships or need-based grants averaged $4061; need-based self-help aid (loans and jobs) averaged $2577; non-need-based athletic scholarships averaged $4573; and other non-need-based awards and non-need-based scholarships averaged $2438. The average financial indebtedness of the 2005 graduate was $18,962. The FAFSA, PHEAA Application, and State Grant are required.

International Students: They must score satisfactorily on the written TOEFL.

Computers: All students may access the system. There are no time limits. The fee is $130/semester.

Graduates: The most popular majors were business marketing (24%), education (19%), and engineering technologies (12%). In an average class, 41% graduate in 4 years or less, 60% graduate in 5 years or less, and 63% graduate in 6 years or less.

Admissions Contact: James F. Gyure, Director of Admissions.
E-mail: *gyure@.pitt.edu* Web: *www.upj.pitt.edu*

UNIVERSITY OF PITTSBURGH AT PITTSBURGH   B-3

Pittsburgh, PA 15260	**(412) 624-PITT; Fax: (412) 648-8815**
Full-time: 7368 men, 7732 women	Faculty: I, av$
Part-time: 833 men, 1091 women	Ph.D.s: 88%
Graduate: 4119 men, 5416 women	Student/Faculty: n/av
Year: semesters, summer session	Tuition: $11,436 ($20,784)
Application Deadline: open	Room & Board: $7430
Freshman Class: 18,153 applied, 9654 accepted, 3249 enrolled	
SAT Verbal/Math: 610/620*	**HIGHLY COMPETITIVE**

The University of Pittsburgh, founded in 1787, is a state-related, public research university with programs in arts and sciences, education, engineering, law, social work, business, health science, information sciences, and public and international affairs. There are 11 undergraduate and 14 graduate schools. In addition to regional accreditation, Pitt has baccalaureate program accreditation with AACSB, ABET, ACPE, ACS, ADA, APA, ASLHA, CAAHEP, CADE, CCNE, CED, LCME, and NASPAA. The 21 libraries contain 4,182,324 volumes and 4,360,230 microform items, and subscribe to 23,377 periodicals including electronic. Computerized library services include the card catalog, interlibrary loans, database searching, Internet access, and laptop Internet portals. Special learning facilities include a learning resource center, art gallery, radio station, and international classrooms, located in the 42-story Cathedral of Learning, an observatory, and a music hall. A natural history museum is also located near the campus. The 132-acre campus is in an urban area 3 miles east of downtown Pittsburgh. Including any residence halls, there are 122 buildings.

Student Life: 85% of undergraduates are from Pennsylvania. Others are from Canada. 81% are white. The average age of freshmen is 18; all undergraduates, 22.

Housing: 6300 students can be accommodated in college housing, which includes single-sex and coed dorms, off-campus apartments, fraternity houses, and sorority houses. In addition, there are honors houses, special-interest houses, engineering, nursing, health-related business, international living, alcohol-free, and quiet living communities. On-campus housing is guaranteed for the freshman year only, is available on a first-come, first-served basis, and is available on a lottery system for upperclassmen. 56% of students commute. All students may keep cars.

Activities: There are 16 national fraternities and 11 national sororities. There are 450 groups on campus, including art, band, cheerleading, chess, choir, chorus, computers, dance, debate, drama, ethnic, film, gay, honors, international, jazz band, literary magazine, marching band, newspaper, orchestra, pep band, political, professional, radio and TV, religious, social, social service, student government, and symphony. Popular campus events include Jazz Seminar, Black Week, and Greek Week.

Sports: There are 9 intercollegiate sports for men and 9 for women, and 13 intramural sports for men and 11 for women. Facilities include a 12,000-seat field house for hosting basketball games and concert; the complex also has a fitness center for student use as well as a food court and shops; a field house with volleyball, gymnastics, wrestling and an indoor track and field; a pool; a gymnastics training center; and a baseball field. There are billiard tables, table tennis, video games, and televisions in the student union.

Disabled Students: 90% of the campus is accessible. Wheelchair ramps, elevators, special parking, specially equipped rest rooms, special class scheduling, lowered drinking fountains, lowered telephones, special housing, disability shuttle, and wheelchair-accessible computer facilities in the computing labs are available.

Services: Counseling and information services are available, as is tutoring in some subjects, including many lower-level undergraduate science and humanities courses. There is a reader service for the blind and remedial writing.

Campus Safety and Security: Measures include 24-hour foot and vehicle patrol, self-defense education, security escort services, and shuttle buses. There are informal discussions, pamphlets/posters/films, emergency telephones, lighted pathways/sidewalks, taxi service, and crime alerts and notices distributed when an immediate danger to faculty, students, or staff is presented.

Programs of Study: Pitt confers B.A., B.S., B.A.S.W., B.Phil., B.S.B.A., B.S.E., and B.S.N. degrees. Master's and doctoral degrees are also awarded. Bachelor's degrees are awarded in BIOLOGICAL SCIENCE (biology/biological science, ecology, evolutionary biology, microbiology, molecular biology, and neurosciences), BUSINESS (accounting, banking and finance, business administration and management, management science, and marketing/retailing/merchandising), COMMUNICATIONS AND THE ARTS (art, Chinese, classics, communications, dramatic arts, English literature, film arts, French, Italian, Japanese, linguistics, music, Polish, Russian, Spanish, and studio art), COMPUTER AND PHYSICAL SCIENCE (applied mathematics, astronomy, chemistry, computer science, environmental geology, geology, mathematics, natural sciences, physics, and statistics), EDUCATION (education), ENGINEERING AND ENVIRONMENTAL DESIGN (architecture, bioengineering, chemical engineering, civil engineering, computer engineering, electrical/electronics engineering, engineering physics, environmental science, industrial engineering, materials engineering, materials science, and mechanical engineering), HEALTH PROFESSIONS (clinical science, dental hygiene, emergency medical technologies, health, nursing, occupational therapy, and rehabilitation therapy), SOCIAL SCIENCE (African American studies, African studies, anthropology, economics, history of philosophy, humanities, interdisciplinary studies, law, liberal arts/general studies, philosophy, political science/government, psychology, public administration, religion, social science, social work, sociology, and urban studies). Philosophy, history and philosophy of science, and chemistry are the strongest academically.

Required: All students in the School of Arts and Sciences must take a minimum of 120 credits. Skills and general education requirements vary by high school achievement but include course work in the humanities, social and natural sciences, and foreign culture. A minimum of 24 credits in the major and a 2.0 GPA are required. Requirements for other schools may vary.

Special: Students may cross-register with 9 neighboring colleges and universities. Internships, unlimited study abroad, a Washington semester, work-study programs, a dual major in business and any other subject in arts and sciences, and student-designed majors are available. There are freshman seminars and a 5-year joint degree in arts and sciences/engineering. There are co-op programs in engineering, computer science, and chemistry. There are 22 national honor societies, including Phi Beta Kappa and a freshman honors program.

Admissions: 53% of the 2005-2006 applicants were accepted. The SAT scores for the 2005-2006 freshman class were: Verbal--5% below 500, 39% between 500 and 599, 42% between 600 and 700, and 14% above 700; Math--4% below 500, 32% between 500 and 599, 49% between 600 and 700, and 15% above 700. 73% of the current freshmen were in the top fifth of their class; 96% were in the top two fifths. 101 freshmen graduated first in their class.

Requirements: The SAT or ACT is required. In addition, applicants for admission to the School of Arts and Sciences must be graduates of an accredited secondary school. Students must have 15 high school academic credits, including 4 units of English, 3 each of math and lab science, and 1 of social studies, plus 4 units in academic electives. Pitt recommends that the student have 3 or more years of a single foreign language. An essay is recommended if the student is seeking scholarship consideration, and music students must audition. AP and CLEP credits are accepted.

Procedure: Freshmen are admitted to all sessions. Entrance exams should be taken preferably by January for September admission. There is a deferred admissions and a rolling admissions plan. Application deadlines are open. Application fee is $35. Notifcation is sent on a rolling basis. 226 applicants were on the 2005 waiting list; 24 were admitted. Applications are accepted on-line.

Transfer: 536 transfer students enrolled in 2004-2005. Applicants for transfer to the School of Arts and Sciences must supply transcripts of all secondary school and college course work and have a minimum GPA of 2.75. An interview is recommended. Grades of C or better transfer for credit. Application deadlines vary by school. 30 of 120 credits required for the bachelor's degree must be completed at Pitt.

Visiting: There are regularly scheduled orientations for prospective students, including information sessions, student-guided tours, and class attendance. There are guides for informal visits and visitors may sit in on classes. To schedule a visit, contact the Office of Admissions and Financial Aid at 1-877-see-pitt or *http://www.admissions.pitt.edu/reservations.aspx.*

Financial Aid: In a recent year, 87% of all full-time freshmen and 77% of continuing full-time students received some form of financial aid. The average freshman award was $10,118. Need-based scholarships or need-based grants averaged $7518; need-based self-help aid (loans and jobs) averaged $4380; and non-need-based athletic scholarships averaged $13,247. 19% of undergraduates work part time. Average annual earnings from campus work are $1722. The average financial indebtedness of the recent year's graduate was $20,154. The FAFSA and the college's own financial statement are required. The deadline for filing freshman financial aid applications for fall entry is January 15.

International Students: There are 118 international students enrolled. Satisfactory scores are required on the written TOEFL and the SAT. SAT scores are required only from applicants currently attending a high school in the United States.

Computers: Students have access to the University's wired network from seven campus computing labs, all university residence halls, and wireless access from six common areas with high student traffic. Students may also access the wireless network from selected departmental areas and classrooms. The university provides 650 PCs in the central campus computing labs. Students also have access to the Internet from approximately 500 additional PCs in departmental computing labs. Students bring their own computers to the residence halls and wireless network areas. All students may access the system 24 hours a day. The dialup modem pool is the only service with time limits in place. Access by students, faculty, or staff is limited to 2 hours during peak times and 4 hours during non-peak times. Students may be required to provide PCs by certain departments or programs, the largest of which is the Katz Graduate School of Business.

Graduates: From July 1, 2004 to June 30, 2005, 3989 bachelor's degrees were awarded. The most popular majors were business (14%), social sciences and history (13%), and English language and literature (12%). 386 companies recruited on campus in 2004-2005. Of the 2004 graduating class, 40% were enrolled in graduate school within 6 months of graduation.

Admissions Contact: Dr. Betsy A. Porter, Director, Admissions and Financial Aid. A video is available. E-mail: *oafa@pitt.edu* Web: *www.pitt.edu/admissions.html*

UNIVERSITY OF SCRANTON   E-2

Scranton, PA 18510-4699   (570) 941-7540
                                 (888) SCRANTON; Fax: (570) 941-5928

Full-time: 1630 men, 2150 women	**Faculty:** 247; IIA, +$
Part-time: 120 men, 190 women	**Ph.D.s:** 86%
Graduate: 235 men, 380 women	**Student/Faculty:** 15 to 1
Year: semesters, summer session	**Tuition:** $21,600
Application Deadline: see profile	**Room & Board:** $9500
Freshman Class: n/av	
SAT or ACT: required	**VERY COMPETITIVE**

The University of Scranton, founded in 1888, is a private institution operated by the Jesuit order of the Roman Catholic Church. It offers programs in business, behavioral sciences, education, health science, humanities, math, science, and social science. There are 4 undergraduate schools and 1 graduate school. Figures in the above capsule and profile are approximate. In addition to regional accreditation, the university has baccalaureate program accreditation with AACSB, APTA, CSAB, NCATE, and NLN. The library contains 454,098 volumes, 104,639 microform items, and 13,367 audio/video tapes/CDs/DVDs, and subscribes to 16,745 periodicals including electronic. Computerized library services include the card catalog, interlibrary loans, database searching, and Internet access. Special learning facilities include a learning resource center, art gallery, radio station, TV station, and satellite dish for telecommunication reception, music center, language lab, and a greenhouse. The 50-acre campus is in an urban area 125 miles north of Philadelphia. Including any residence halls, there are 60 buildings.

Student Life: 51% of undergraduates are from Pennsylvania. Others are from 29 states, 12 foreign countries, and Canada. 51% are from public schools. 85% are white. 84% are Catholic; 10% Protestant. The average age of freshmen is 18; all undergraduates, 20. 10% do not continue beyond their first year; 80% remain to graduate.

Housing: 2112 students can be accommodated in college housing, which includes single-sex and coed dormitories and on-campus apartments. In addition, there are language houses, special-interest houses, an international house, a residential college, a Spanish house, a performing arts house, an education house, a volunteer/service house, 2 wellness dorms, a theter house, and 2 wellness floors. On-campus housing is guaranteed for all 4 years. 80% of students live on campus; of those, 65% remain on campus on weekends. Upperclassmen may keep cars.

Activities: There are no fraternities or sororities. There are 80 groups on campus, including art, band, cheerleading, chess, choir, chorale, chorus, computers, dance, debate, drama, drill team, ethnic, film, honors, international, jazz band, literary magazine, musical theater, newspaper, orchestra, pep band, photography, political, professional, radio and TV, religious, social, social service, student government, and yearbook. Popular campus events include Spring Fling, Senior Formal, and President's Ball.

Sports: There are 10 intercollegiate sports for men and 8 for women, and 17 intramural sports for men and 14 for women. Facilities include a 3000-seat gym, basketball courts, wrestling and weight rooms, handball/racquetball and tennis courts, a sand volleyball court, a soccer/lacrosse field, a softball field, a swimming pool, a physical therapy room, a 3-court multipurpose gym, a fitness center, a sauna and steamroom, a dance aerobics room, and a turfed recreation/utility field.

Disabled Students: All of the campus is accessible. Wheelchair ramps, elevators, special parking, specially equipped rest rooms, special class scheduling, lowered drinking fountains, and lowered telephones are available.

Services: Counseling and information services are available, as is tutoring in most subjects. There is a reader service for the blind and computing and study skills seminars.

Campus Safety and Security: Measures include 24-hour foot and vehicle patrol, self-defense education, security escort services, and informal discussions. There are pamphlets/posters/films, emergency telephones, and lighted pathways/sidewalks.

Programs of Study: the university confers B.A. and B.S. degrees. Associate, master's, and doctoral degrees are also awarded. Bachelor's degrees are awarded in BIOLOGICAL SCIENCE (biochemistry, biology/biological science, biophysics, and neurosciences), BUSINESS (accounting, banking and finance, business administration and management, business economics, electronic business, human resources, international business management, marketing/retailing/merchandising, and operations research), COMMUNICATIONS AND THE ARTS (communications, dramatic arts, English, French, German, Greek, Latin, and Spanish), COMPUTER AND PHYSICAL SCIENCE (chemistry, computer management, computer science, information sciences and systems, mathematics, and physics), EDUCATION (early childhood, elementary, science, secondary, and special), ENGINEERING AND ENVIRONMENTAL DESIGN (electrical/electronics engineering and environmental science), HEALTH PROFESSIONS (exercise science, health care administration, medical laboratory technology, nursing, occupational therapy, and physical therapy), SOCIAL SCIENCE (criminal justice, economics, gerontology, history, human services, international relations, philosophy, political science/government, psychology, sociology, and theological studies). Chemistry, biology, and physical therapy are the strongest academically. Biology, communication, and elementary education are the largest.

Required: Students take distribution requirements according to their general area of study. All are required to take philosophy/theology, phys ed, English composition, speech, and computer literacy. A total of 130 credit hours is required for graduation, with 36 in the major. The minimum GPA is 2.0, although some majors require a higher GPA.

Special: There are cooperative programs with the University of Detroit Mercy and cross-registration with 27 other Jesuit colleges. Internships are available in all career-oriented majors, and foreign study is offered in many countries. There is a Washington semester for history and political science majors. Students may earn a B.A.-B.S. degree in economics and accelerated degrees in history, chemistry, and biochemistry. The university also offers dual, student-designed, and interdisciplinary majors, including chemistry-business, chemistry-computers, electronics-business, and international language-business, credit by exam and for life/military/work experience, work-study, nondegree study, and pass/fail options. There is also a special Jesuit-oriented general education program. There are 26 national honor societies, including Phi Beta Kappa, a freshman honors program, and 2 departmental honors programs.

Faculty/Classroom: 69% of faculty are male; 31%, female. 97% teach undergraduates, 80% do research, and 77% do both. No introductory courses are taught by graduate students. The average class size in an introductory lecture is 22; in a laboratory, 12; and in a regular course, 21.

Requirements: The SAT or ACT is required. In addition, applicants should be graduates of an accredited secondary school, though in some cases a GED may be accepted. They should complete 18 academic or Carnegie units, including 4 years of high school English, 3 each of math, science, history, and social studies, and 2 of foreign language. 2 letters of reference/recommendation are required. Essays are not required, but for some students the additional information can be of assistance. Interviews are recommended. AP and CLEP credits are accepted. Important factors in the admissions decision are leadership record, advanced placement or honor courses, and extracurricular activities record.

Procedure: Freshmen are admitted fall and spring. Entrance exams should be taken by fall of the senior year. There are early admissions, deferred admissions and rolling admissions plans. Check with the school for application deadlines. The application fee is $40. Notification is sent on a rolling basis. Applications are accepted on-line.

Transfer: 128 transfer students enrolled in a recent year. Applicants should have earned a GPA of at least 2.5. 63 of 130 credits required for the bachelor's degree must be completed at the university.

Visiting: There are regularly scheduled orientations for prospective students, including private interviews conducted Monday through Friday throughout the school year. Group information sessions are offered on Saturdays and holidays in the fall and spring and during the week in the summer. There are guides for informal visits and visitors may sit in on classes and stay overnight. To schedule a visit, contact the Office of Admissions.

Financial Aid: In a recent year, 71% of all full-time freshmen and 66% of continuing full-time students received some form of financial aid. 70% of full-time freshmen and 64% of continuing full-time students received need-based aid. The average freshman award was $14,317. Need-based scholarships or need-based grants averaged $10,771; need-based self-help aid (loans and jobs) averaged $4070; and other non-need-based awards and non-need-based scholarships averaged $7635. 17% of undergraduates worked part time. Average annual earnings from campus work were $900. The average financial indebtedness of a recent graduate was $15,800. The university is a member of CSS. The FAFSA is required. Check with the school for application deadlines.

International Students: In a recent year, there were 15 international students enrolled. The school actively recruits these students. They must score satisfactorily on the written TOEFL.

Computers: All students may access the system 24 hours a day. There are no time limits and no fees.

Graduates: In a recent year, 915 bachelor's degrees were awarded. The most popular majors were communications (10%), biology (8%), and elementary education (7%). In an average class, 67% graduate in 4 years or less, 76% graduate in 5 years or less, and 82% graduate in 6 years or less. Of a recent graduating class, 33% were enrolled in graduate school within 6 months of graduation and 65% were employed.

Admissions Contact: Joseph M. Roback, Director of Admissions. A video is available. E-mail: *admissions@scranton.edu* Web: *www.scranton.edu*

UNIVERSITY OF THE ARTS   F-3

Philadelphia, PA 19102   **(215) 717-6039**
                                         (800) 616-2787; Fax: (215) 717-6045

Full-time: 925 men, 1110 women	**Faculty:** 110
Part-time: 13 men, 31 women	**Ph.D.s:** 47%
Graduate: 61 men, 137 women	**Student/Faculty:** 19 to 1
Year: semesters	**Tuition:** $24,330
Application Deadline: open	**Room & Board:** $8000
Freshman Class: 2286 applied, 1118 accepted, 510 enrolled	
SAT Verbal/Math: 550/520*	**ACT:** 22 **SPECIAL**

University of the Arts, founded in 1870, is a private institution offering education and professional training in visual, media, and performing arts, with an emphasis on the humanities and interdisciplinary exploration. There are 3 undergraduate and 2 graduate schools. In addition to regional accreditation, UArts has baccalaureate program accreditation with NASAD and NASM. The 3 libraries contain 144,700 volumes, 461 microform items, and 21,200 audio/video tapes/CDs/DVDs, and subscribe to 541 periodicals including electronic. Computerized library services include the card catalog, interlibrary loans, database searching, and Internet access. Special learning facilities include an art gallery and several theaters, and music, animation, and recording studios. The 18-acre campus is in an urban area in Philadelphia. Including any residence halls, there are 8 buildings.

Student Life: 61% of undergraduates are from out of state, mostly the Middle Atlantic. Students are from 43 states, 42 foreign countries, and Canada. 73% are from public schools. 67% are white; 10% African American. The average age of freshmen is 18; all undergraduates, 20. 18% do not continue beyond their first year; 55% remain to graduate.

Housing: 690 students can be accommodated in college housing, which includes coed dorms, on-campus apartments, and off-campus apartments. On-campus housing is guaranteed for the freshman year only and is available on a first-come, first-served basis. Priority is given to out-of-town students. 65% of students commute. Alcohol is not permitted. No one may keep cars.

Activities: There are no fraternities or sororities. There are 20 groups on campus, including art, band, choir, chorale, chorus, dance, drama, ethnic, film, gay, international, jazz band, musical theater, photography, professional, religious, and student government. Popular campus events include exhibitions and performances.

Sports: There is no sports program at UArts. Athletic facilities are available at area gyms, for which the university provides discount membership.

Disabled Students: 65% of the campus is accessible. Wheelchair ramps, elevators, specially equipped rest rooms, lowered drinking fountains, lowered telephones, and sign language interpreters are available.

Services: Counseling and information services are available, as is tutoring in every subject. There is remedial math, reading, and writing. There also is assistance with study skills.

Campus Safety and Security: Measures include 24-hour foot and vehicle patrol, self-defense education, security escort services, and informal discussions. There are pamphlets/posters/films and lighted pathways/ sidewalks.

Programs of Study: UArts confers B.S., B.F.A., and B.M. degrees. Master's degrees are also awarded. Bachelor's degrees are awarded in COMMUNICATIONS AND THE ARTS (communications, dance, film arts, graphic design, illustration, industrial design, multimedia, music performance, music theory and composition, musical theater, painting, photography, printmaking, and sculpture), EDUCATION (dance). Dance, music, and illustration are the largest.

Required: All students must complete a core program consisting of liberal arts courses in languages and literature, arts history, philosophy and religion, science and math, and social sciences. A GPA of 2.0 overall for 123-143 credits, with 21 to 45 in the major, depending on the curriculum, must be achieved for graduation.

Special: UArts offers cross-registration with the 10-member Consortium East Coast Art Schools. Internships may be arranged, and there are extensive summer programs and opportunities to study abroad.

Faculty/Classroom: 60% of faculty are male; 40%, female. 95% teach undergraduates. No introductory courses are taught by graduate students. The average class size in an introductory lecture is 18 and in a regular course, 14.

Admissions: 49% of the 2005-2006 applicants were accepted. The SAT scores for the 2005-2006 freshman class were: Verbal--31% below 500, 42% between 500 and 599, 24% between 600 and 700, and 3% above 700; Math--44% below 500, 40% between 500 and 599, 15% between 600 and 700, and 1% above 700. The ACT scores were 48% below 21, 11% between 21 and 23, 27% between 24 and 26, 7% between 27 and 28, and 7% above 28. 27% of the current freshmen were in the top fifth of their class; 55% were in the top two fifths. 3 freshmen graduated first in their class.

Requirements: The SAT or ACT is required. In addition, students must have graduated from an accredited secondary school or hold a GED certificate. A minimum of 16 academic credits consisting of 4 each in English and math and 2 each in music or art and history is recommended. An essay and either a portfolio or an audition are required of all applicants. An interview is recommended. A GPA of 2.0 is required. AP and CLEP credits are accepted. Important factors in the admissions decision are evidence of special talent, advanced placement or honor courses, and personality/intangible qualities.

Procedure: Freshmen are admitted fall and spring. Entrance exams should be taken late in the junior year or early in the senior year. There is a deferred admissions and a rolling admissions plan. Application deadlines are open. Application fee is $60. Notification is sent on a rolling basis. 44 applicants were on the 2005 waiting list; 10 were admitted. Applications are accepted on-line.

Transfer: 138 transfer students enrolled in 2004-2005. Candidates must have a minimum 2.0 GPA overall. An interview is recommended, as well as test scores for either the SAT or ACT if English composition has not been completed. 48 of 123 credits required for the bachelor's degree must be completed at UArts.

Visiting: There are regularly scheduled orientations for prospective students, including a spring and fall open house. There are guides for informal visits. To schedule a visit, contact the Office of Admissions.

Financial Aid: The FAFSA is required. The deadline for filing freshman financial aid applications for fall entry is March 1.

International Students: There are 52 international students enrolled. The school actively recruits these students. A satisfactory score is required on the written TOEFL.

Computers: Wireless access is available. All students may access the system. There are no time limits and no fees. It is strongly recommended that all students have a personal computer.

Graduates: From July 1, 2004 to June 30, 2005, 406 bachelor's degrees were awarded. The most popular majors were dance (11%), crafts (9%), and graphic design (8%). In an average class, 49% graduate in 4 years or less, 55% graduate in 5 years or less, and 56% graduate in 6 years or less. 30 companies recruited on campus in 2004-2005.

Admissions Contact: Susan Gandy, Director of Admissions. A video is available. E-mail: *admissions@uarts.edu* Web: *http://www.uarts.edu*

UNIVERSITY OF THE SCIENCES IN PHILADELPHIA   F-3

Philadelphia, PA 19104-4495   **(215) 596-8810**
                                         (888) 996-8747; Fax: (215) 596-8821

Full-time: 898 men, 1505 women	**Faculty:** 147
Part-time: 16 men, 49 women	**Ph.D.s:** 5%
Graduate: 138 men, 202 women	**Student/Faculty:** 16 to 1
Year: semesters, summer session	**Tuition:** $24,000
Application Deadline: open	**Room & Board:** $9380
Freshman Class: 3057 applied, 1876 accepted, 536 enrolled	
SAT Verbal/Math: 560/600*	**ACT:** 25 **VERY COMPETITIVE**

University of the Sciences in Philadelphia, founded in 1821, is a private institution offering degree programs in the health sciences, pharmaceutical sciences, and arts and sciences. There are 3 undergraduate and 4 graduate schools. In addition to regional accreditation, USP has baccalaureate program accreditation with ACPE, ACS, APTA, CAAHEP, and NAACLS. The library contains 85,939 volumes, 27,637 microform items, and 4376 audio/video tapes/CDs/DVDs, and subscribes to 6700 periodicals including electronic. Computerized library services include the card catalog, interlibrary loans, and database searching. Special learning facilities include a learning resource center, a pharmaceutical history museum, and the Center for Advanced Pharmacy Studies (CAPS). The 35-acre campus is in an urban area in the University City section of Philadelphia. Including any residence halls, there are 19 buildings.

Student Life: 53% of undergraduates are from Pennsylvania. Others are from 33 states, 17 foreign countries, and Canada. 47% are white; 34% Asian American. The average age of freshmen is 18; all undergraduates, 21. 17% do not continue beyond their first year; 60% remain to graduate.

Housing: 694 students can be accommodated in college housing, which includes coed dorms. In addition, there are honors houses, honor halls in certain dorms, and an upper-level floor for upper-level students. On-campus housing is guaranteed for the freshman year only, is available on a first-come, first-served basis, and is available on a lottery system for upperclassmen. Priority is given to out-of-town students. 72% of students commute. Alcohol is not permitted. Upperclassmen may keep cars.

Activities: There are 2 local and 10 national fraternities and 2 national sororities. There are 66 groups on campus, including band, cheerleading, chess, chorale, chorus, computers, dance, drama, ethnic, gay, honors, international, literary magazine, martial arts, musical theater, newspaper, orchestra, political, professional, religious, social, social service, student government, and yearbook. Popular campus events include Greek Week, Student Appreciation Day, and Misher Week (highlighting the richness of world music).

Sports: There are 6 intercollegiate sports for men and 7 for women, and 17 intramural sports for men and 17 for women. Facilities include an athletic and recreation center with swimming pool and indoor track, a gym, a rifle range, tennis courts, a softball field, a jogging path, and recreational areas in the residence halls.

Disabled Students: 90% of the campus is accessible. Wheelchair ramps, elevators, special parking, specially equipped rest rooms, and special class scheduling are available. Each student is accommodated on an individual basis.

Services: Counseling and information services are available, as is tutoring in every subject. There is remedial math and writing.

Campus Safety and Security: Measures include 24-hour foot and vehicle patrol, self-defense education, security escort services, and shuttle buses. There are informal discussions, pamphlets/posters/films, emergency telephones, lighted pathways/sidewalks, and required key and student identification for dorm entry.

Programs of Study: USP confers B.S. and B.S.Ed. degrees. Master's and doctoral degrees are also awarded. Bachelor's degrees are awarded in BIOLOGICAL SCIENCE (biochemistry, bioinformatics, biology/biological science, microbiology, and toxicology), BUSINESS (marketing management), COMPUTER AND PHYSICAL SCIENCE (chemistry and computer science), ENGINEERING AND ENVIRONMENTAL DESIGN (environmental science), HEALTH PROFESSIONS (health psychology, health science, medical technology, mental health/human services, occupational therapy, pharmaceutical chemistry, pharmaceutical science, pharmacology, pharmacy, physical therapy, and physician's assistant), SOCIAL SCIENCE (psychology). Pharmacy and physical therapy are the strongest academically. Pharmacy, physical therapy, and biology are the largest.

Required: Total credits required for graduation range from 120 to 149 depending on the major, with a 2.0 GPA, or 2.5 for pharmacy, physical therapy, and physician's assistant majors, and a 2.3 for occupational therapy majors. The core curriculum includes 16 credits of natural science, 6 each of math, social sciences, communication, and an intellectual heritage sequence, 3 of literature, world culture, history, and advanced social sciences, and 1 of phys ed, along with 3 of electives. Students must pass a writing proficiency exam and demonstrate proficiency in computer applications.

Special: USP offers 5- and 6-year integrated professional programs in occupational therapy, physical therapy, and physician's assistant studies. Internships are required in all health science disciplines. A 1-year undeclared major program is offered, as is a program of curriculum and advisement to prepare students to enter medical school. Students may elect dual majors or a minor in communications, economics, psychology, sociology, math, physics, computer science, biochemistry, biology, chemistry, forensic science, humanities, math, microbiology, social sciences, and writing. Study abroad can be arranged. There are 5 national honor societies.

Faculty/Classroom: 51% of faculty are male; 49%, female. 99% teach undergraduates. No introductory courses are taught by graduate students. The average class size in an introductory lecture is 100; in a laboratory, 28; and in a regular course, 25.

Admissions: 61% of the 2005-2006 applicants were accepted. The SAT scores for the 2005-2006 freshman class were: Verbal--10% below 500, 58% between 500 and 599, 30% between 600 and 700, and 2% above 700; Math--5% below 500, 42% between 500 and 599, 48% between 600 and 700, and 5% above 700. The ACT scores were 14% below 21, 24% between 21 and 23, 30% between 24 and 26, 26% between 27 and 28, and 6% above 28. 62% of the current freshmen were in the top fifth of their class; 95% were in the top two fifths. 4 freshmen graduated first in their class.

Requirements: The SAT or ACT is required. In addition, applicants must be high school graduates or hold the GED. Minimum academic requirements include 4 credits in English, 1 credit each in American history and social science, and 4 credits in academic electives. Math requirements include 2 years of algebra and 1 year of plane geometry; the university strongly recommends an additional year of higher-level math, such as precalculus or calculus. 3 science credits are required; strongly recommended are 1 credit each in biology, chemistry, and physics. A strong background in English, science, and math is recommended. USP requires applicants to be in the upper 50% of their class. AP and CLEP credits are accepted. Important factors in the admissions decision are extracurricular activities record, leadership record, and advanced placement or honor courses.

Procedure: Freshmen are admitted in the fall. Entrance exams should be taken at the end of the junior year and in the fall of the senior year. There is a deferred admissions plan and a rolling admissions plan. Appli-

cation deadlines are open. Application fee is $45. Notification is sent on a rolling basis. 250 applicants were on the 2005 waiting list. Applications are accepted on-line.

Transfer: 49 transfer students enrolled in 2004-2005. To be considered, pharmacy and physical therapy applicants must present a minimum GPA of 3.0. All other majors must have at least a 2.7 GPA. All applicants must meet high school requirements as well. 51 credits required for the bachelor's degree must be completed at USP.

Visiting: There are regularly scheduled orientations for prospective students, consisting of summer open houses for rising seniors, campus day visits, campus tours, and meetings with faculty members. There are guides for informal visits and visitors may sit in on classes. To schedule a visit, contact the Admission Office.

Financial Aid: In 2005-2006, 95% of all full-time students received some form of financial aid. 28% of undergraduates work part time. The FAFSA is required. The priority date for freshman financial aid applications for fall entry is March 15.

International Students: There are 31 international students enrolled. They must submit scores from the SAT or ACT as well as scores from the TOEFL of ELPT if their native language is not English.

Computers: Wireless access is available. All students may use the network and wireless system on their own computers. There are 120 college-owned workstations in the dorms, library, computer center, and student center. All dorm rooms are wired for high-speed Internet connections and have access to the campus-wide network. All students may access the system. There are no time limits and no fees. It is strongly recommended that all students have a personal computer, specifically a computer with a Windows operating system.

Graduates: From July 1, 2004 to June 30, 2005, 149 bachelor's degrees were awarded. The most popular majors were pharmacy (64%), physical therapy (8%), and biology (5%). In an average class, 17% graduate in 4 years or less, 31% graduate in 5 years or less, and 60% graduate in 6 years or less. 150 companies recruited on campus in 2004-2005.

Admissions Contact: Louis L. Hegyes, Director of Admission. E-mail: *admit@usip.edu* Web: *www.usip.edu*

URSINUS COLLEGE
E-3

Collegeville, PA 19426   (610) 409-3200; Fax: (610) 409-3662

Full-time: 740 men, 812 women	**Faculty:** 115; IIB, +$
Part-time: 4 men, 15 women	**Ph.D.s:** 92%
Graduate: none	**Student/Faculty:** 13 to 1
Year: semesters	**Tuition:** $33.200
Application Deadline: February 15	**Room & Board:** $7,600
Freshman Class: 1776 applied, 1326 accepted, 426 enrolled	
SAT Verbal/Math: 596/600*	**ACT:** 23 VERY COMPETITIVE

Ursinus College, founded in 1869, is a private residential college offering programs in the liberal arts. In addition to regional accreditation, Ursinus has baccalaureate program accreditation with ACS. The library contains 400,000 volumes, 200,000 microform items, and 30,000 audio/video tapes/CDs/DVDs, and subscribes to 5815 periodicals including electronic. Computerized library services include the card catalog, interlibrary loans, database searching, Internet access, and laptop Internet portals. Special learning facilities include an art gallery, planetarium, radio station, TV station, and observatory. The 170-acre campus is in a suburban area 28 miles west of Philadelphia. Including any residence halls, there are 65 buildings.

Student Life: 62% of undergraduates are from Pennsylvania. Others are from 29 states and 15 foreign countries. 75% are from public schools. 76% are white. The average age of freshmen is 18; all undergraduates, 20. 8% do not continue beyond their first year; 78% remain to graduate.

Housing: 1380 students can be accommodated in college housing, which includes single-sex and coed dorms and on-campus apartments. In addition, there are honors houses, language houses, special-interest houses, and multicultural, wellness, art, biology, and quiet houses. On-campus housing is guaranteed for all 4 years. 95% of students live on campus; of those, 85% remain on campus on weekends. Upperclassmen may keep cars.

Activities: 17% of men belong to 6 local and 3 national fraternities; 28% of women belong to 6 local and 2 national sororities. There are 85 groups on campus, including art, band, cheerleading, chess, choir, chorale, chorus, computers, dance, debate, drama, ethnic, fencing, film, folksong, forensics, gay, gospel, honors, international, jazz band, literary magazine, men's chorus, museum friends, musical theater, newspaper, orchestra, pep band, political, professional, radio and TV, religious, social, social service, student government, and yearbook. Popular campus events include Family Day, Homecoming, and Air Band Competition.

Sports: There are 12 intercollegiate sports for men and 13 for women, and 14 intramural sports for men and 12 for women. Facilities include racquetball and squash courts, a dance studio, tennis courts, a field house, a fitness center, and all types of playing fields.

Disabled Students: 95% of the campus is accessible. Wheelchair ramps, elevators, special parking, specially equipped rest rooms, special class scheduling, lowered drinking fountains, and lowered telephones are available.

Services: Counseling and information services are available, as is tutoring in every subject. The college provides appropriate services on an as-needed basis.

Campus Safety and Security: Measures include 24-hour foot and vehicle patrol, self-defense education, security escort services, and informal discussions. There are pamphlets/posters/films, emergency telephones, and lighted pathways/sidewalks.

Programs of Study: Ursinus confers B.A. and B.S. degrees. Bachelor's degrees are awarded in BIOLOGICAL SCIENCE (biochemistry, biology/biological science, and neurosciences), BUSINESS (business economics), COMMUNICATIONS AND THE ARTS (art, classics, communications, dance, dramatic arts, English, French, German, and Spanish), COMPUTER AND PHYSICAL SCIENCE (chemistry, computer science, mathematics, and physics), EDUCATION (secondary), ENGINEERING AND ENVIRONMENTAL DESIGN (environmental science), HEALTH PROFESSIONS (exercise science), SOCIAL SCIENCE (American studies, anthropology, East Asian studies, history, international relations, philosophy, philosophy and religion, political science/government, psychology, religion, and sociology). Biology, chemistry, and English are the strongest academically. Economics, biology, and psychology are the largest.

Required: All students must fulfill requirements in the common intellectual experience, math or logic, foreign language, humanities, and natural and social science, and complete an independent learning experience. A total of 128 semester hours, with 32 to 40 in the major, is required, as is a GPA of 2.0.

Special: The college offers study abroad, student-designed majors, internships, a Washington semester, dual majors, and a 3-2 engineering degree with Columbia University and Washington University of St. Louis. There are 14 national honor societies, including Phi Beta Kappa, and 14 departmental honors programs.

Faculty/Classroom: 50% of faculty are male; 50%, female. All both teach and do research. The average class size in a laboratory is 22 and in a regular course, 18.

Admissions: 75% of the 2005-2006 applicants were accepted. The SAT scores for the 2005-2006 freshman class were: Verbal--9% below 500, 40% between 500 and 599, 38% between 600 and 700, and 13% above 700; Math--12% below 500, 29% between 500 and 599, 47% between 600 and 700, and 12% above 700. 62% of the current freshmen were in the top fifth of their class; 91% were in the top two fifths. There were 3 National Merit finalists. 6 freshmen graduated first in their class.

Requirements: The SAT or ACT is required. In addition, SAT: Subject tests are recommended. Applicants should prepare with 16 academic credits, including 4 years of English, 3 of math, 2 of foreign language, and 1 each of science and social studies. An interview is recommended. Any student in the top 10% of his or her high school class may elect to waive the SAT/ACT requirement. AP and CLEP credits are accepted. Important factors in the admissions decision are advanced placement or honor courses, recommendations by school officials, and leadership record.

Procedure: Freshmen are admitted fall and spring. Entrance exams should be taken in the junior or senior year. There are early decision, early admissions, and deferred admissions plans. Early decision applications should be filed by January 15; regular applications, by February 15 for fall entry and December 1 for spring entry, along with a $50 fee. Notification of early decision is sent January 15; regular decision, on April 1. 114 early decision candidates were accepted for the 2005-2006 class. 19 applicants were on the 2005 waiting list; none were admitted. Applications are accepted on-line.

Transfer: 13 transfer students enrolled in 2004-2005. Transfer applicants must submit transcripts from all institutions attended. 64 of 128 credits required for the bachelor's degree must be completed at Ursinus.

Visiting: There are regularly scheduled orientations for prospective students, including a campus interview and a tour. There are guides for informal visits and visitors may sit in on classes and stay overnight. To schedule a visit, contact the Admissions Office at *admissions@ursinus.edu*.

Financial Aid: In 2005-2006, 95% of all full-time freshmen and 93% of continuing full-time students received some form of financial aid. 85% of full-time freshmen and 80% of continuing full-time students received need-based aid. The average freshman award was $24,219. Need-based scholarships or need-based grants averaged $16,301 ($25,000 maximum); need-based self-help aid (loans and jobs) averaged $5519 ($8000 maximum); and other non-need-based awards and non-need-based scholarships averaged $10,000 ($25,000 maximum). 50% of undergraduates work part time. Average annual earnings from campus work are $1900. The average financial indebtedness of the 2005 graduate was $20,000. Ursinus is a member of CSS. The CSS/Profile or FAFSA is required. The deadline for filing freshman financial aid applications for fall entry is February 15.

International Students: There are 20 international students enrolled. The school actively recruits these students. They must score satisfactorily on the written TOEFL or on the electronic version and also take the SAT or the ACT.

Computers: Every classroom and dorm room is wired for network and Internet access, and some areas of the campus (the library, the student, selected classrooms, and athletic fields) have wireless access. In addition, there are 4 public computer labs with about 130 PCs throughout the campus.There are no time limits and no fees. All students are provided with a laptop computer.

Graduates: From July 1, 2004 to June 30, 2005, 295 bachelor's degrees were awarded. The most popular majors were biology (13%), psychology (12%), and business and economics (11%). In an average class, 75% graduate in 4 years or less, and 78% graduate in 5 years or less. 34 companies recruited on campus in 2004-2005. Of the 2004 graduating class, 34% were enrolled in graduate school within 6 months of graduation and 57% were employed.

Admissions Contact: Director of Admissions.
E-mail: *admissions@ursinus.edu* Web: *http://www.ursinus.edu/*

VILLANOVA UNIVERSITY — F-4

Villanova, PA 19085-1672   (610) 519-4000; Fax: (610) 519-6450

Full-time: 3139 men, 3254 women	**Faculty:** 545; IIA, +$
Part-time: 353 men, 341 women	**Ph.D.s:** 88%
Graduate: 1228 men, 1061 women	**Student/Faculty:** 12 to 1
Year: semesters, summer session	**Tuition:** $29,310
Application Deadline: January 7	**Room & Board:** $9362
Freshman Class: 10,394 applied, 5338 accepted, 1625 enrolled	
SAT Verbal/Math: 620/650*	**ACT:** 28

HIGHLY COMPETITIVE+

Villanova University, founded in 1842 and affiliated with the Roman Catholic Church, offers undergraduate programs in liberal arts and sciences, commerce and finance, engineering, and nursing. Tuition figure in above capsule is an average; exact costs vary by college. There are 4 undergraduate and 5 graduate schools. In addition to regional accreditation, Villanova has baccalaureate program accreditation with AACSB, ABA, ABET, and NLN. The 2 libraries contain 800,000 volumes, 1,800,000 microform items, and 6500 audio/video tapes/CDs/DVDs, and subscribe to 12,000 periodicals including electronic. Computerized library services include the card catalog, interlibrary loans, database searching, Internet access, and laptop Internet portals. Special learning facilities include a learning resource center, art gallery, radio station, TV station, and 2 observatories. The 254-acre campus is in a suburban area 12 miles west of Philadelphia. Including any residence halls, there are 60 buildings.

Student Life: 67% of undergraduates are from out of state, mostly the Middle Atlantic. Students are from 45 states, 33 foreign countries, and Canada. 52% are from public schools. 80% are white. 77% are Catholic; 14% Protestant. The average age of freshmen is 18; all undergraduates, 20. 5% do not continue beyond their first year; 85% remain to graduate.

Housing: 4365 students can be accommodated in college housing, which includes single-sex and coed dorms and on-campus apartments. In addition, there are learning communities for freshmen, 2 special sophomore residence halls, a Service Learning Community, and a 24-hour quiet study hall. On-campus housing is guaranteed for all 4 years and is available on a lottery system for upperclassmen. 74% of students live on campus; of those, 90% remain on campus on weekends. All students may keep cars.

Activities: 11% of men belong to 14 national fraternities; 31% of women belong to 11 national sororities. There are 272 groups on campus, including band, blue key, cheerleading, chess, choir, chorale, chorus, computers, dance, debate, drama, ethnic, forensics, gay, honors, international, jazz band, literary magazine, marching band, multicultural musical theater, newspaper, pep band, photography, political, professional, radio and TV, religious, social, social service, student government, and yearbook. Popular campus events include Balloon Day, Nova Fest, and Hoops Mania.

Sports: There are 10 intercollegiate sports for men and 12 for women, and 15 intramural sports for men and 15 for women. Facilities include a 200-meter indoor track, 2 swimming pools, weight rooms, a field house, and basketball, volleyball, and tennis courts. The football stadium seats 11,800; the pavilion, 6400.

Disabled Students: All of the campus is accessible. Wheelchair ramps, elevators, special parking, specially equipped rest rooms, special class scheduling, lowered drinking fountains, lowered telephones, a specially equipped van for campus transportation, and proximity card readers for several buildings with automatic doors are available.

Services: Counseling and information services are available, as is tutoring in most subjects. There is a reader service for the blind. Tutoring services are administered through each department on an individual basis. There is a writing center and a math resource center.

Campus Safety and Security: Measures include 24-hour foot and vehicle patrol, self-defense education, security escort services, and shuttle buses. There are informal discussions, pamphlets/posters/films, emergency telephones, and lighted pathways/sidewalks. Public Safety officers are on duty all night in women's residence halls, and there is a card access system to all residence halls.

Programs of Study: Villanova confers B.A., B.S., and B.S.N. degrees. Associate, master's, and doctoral degrees are also awarded. Bachelor's degrees are awarded in BIOLOGICAL SCIENCE (biology/biological science), BUSINESS (accounting, banking and finance, business administration and management, business economics, international business management, management information systems, and marketing/retailing/merchandising), COMMUNICATIONS AND THE ARTS (art history and appreciation, classics, communications, English, French, German, Italian, and Spanish), COMPUTER AND PHYSICAL SCIENCE (astronomy, astrophysics, chemistry, computer science, information sciences and systems, mathematics, physics, and science), EDUCATION (elementary and secondary), ENGINEERING AND ENVIRONMENTAL DESIGN (chemical engineering, civil engineering, computer engineering, electrical/electronics engineering, and mechanical engineering), HEALTH PROFESSIONS (nursing), SOCIAL SCIENCE (criminal justice, economics, geography, history, human services, humanities, liberal arts/general studies, philosophy, political science/government, psychology, religion, sociology, and theological studies). Sciences, business, and liberal arts are the strongest academically. Liberal arts and commerce and finance are the largest.

Required: All students are required to take core courses in core humanities, English, social science, religious studies, natural sciences, philosophy, and math. Students must complete a total of 122 credit hours with a 2.0 overall GPA and a 2.2 GPA in the major.

Special: Cross-registration is possible with Rosemont College. Internships are available for each college in the Philadelphia area as well as in New York City and Washington D.C. Students may study abroad worldwide. Villanova offers a Washington semester, an accelerated degree program in biology for allied health program, dual majors, a general studies degree, and credit by exam. There are 35 national honor societies, including Phi Beta Kappa, a freshman honors program, and a honors department that serves all colleges.

Faculty/Classroom: 69% of faculty are male; 31%, female. All teach undergraduates and 78% do research. No introductory courses are taught by graduate students. The average class size in an introductory lecture is 24; in a laboratory, 17; and in a regular course, 23.

Admissions: 51% of the 2005-2006 applicants were accepted. The SAT scores for the 2005-2006 freshman class were: Verbal--5% below 500, 29% between 500 and 599, 54% between 600 and 700, and 13% above 700; Math--3% below 500, 18% between 500 and 599, 58% between 600 and 700, and 22% above 700. The ACT scores were 4% between 21 and 23, 14% between 24 and 26, 41% between 27 and 28, and 41% above 28. 73% of the current freshmen were in the top fifth of their class; 92% were in the top two fifths. 31 freshmen graduated first in their class.

Requirements: The SAT or ACT is required. The ACT Optional Writing test is also required. In addition, applicants must be graduates of an accredited secondary school and should have completed 16 academic units. The specific courses required vary according to college. A GED is accepted. An essay is required. AP and CLEP credits are accepted. Important factors in the admissions decision are evidence of special talent, leadership record, and advanced placement or honor courses.

Procedure: Freshmen are admitted in the fall. Entrance exams should be taken by December of the senior year. There is a deferred admissions plan. Early action applications should be filed by November 1; regular applications, by January 7 for fall entry. The fall 2005 application fee was $70. Notification of early action is sent December 20; regular decision, April 1. 1525 applicants were on the 2005 waiting list; 116 were admitted. Applications are accepted on-line.

Transfer: 133 transfer students enrolled in 2004-2005. A cumulative GPA of 3.0 is recommended for students interested in transferring into the College of Liberal Arts and Sciences. Students interested in transferring into the College of Nursing must have maintained at least a 2.5 cumulative GPA. Required GPAs for the College of Commerce and Finance and the College of Engineering vary. 60 of 122 credits required for the bachelor's degree must be completed at Villanova.

Visiting: There are regularly scheduled orientations for prospective students, including campus tours and information sessions conducted several times daily and on selected Saturdays throughout the academic year. There are guides for informal visits and visitors may sit in on classes. To schedule a visit, contact the Office of University Admission at *gotovu@villanova.edu*.

Financial Aid: In 2005-2006, 70% of all full-time freshmen and 66% of continuing full-time students received some form of financial aid. 42% of full-time freshmen and 40% of continuing full-time students received need-based aid. The average freshman award was $20,752. Need-based scholarships or need-based grants averaged $16,355 ($32,480 maximum); need-based self-help aid (loans and jobs) averaged $4655 ($6625 maximum); non-need-based athletic scholarships averaged $27,033 ($43,705 maximum); and other non-need-based awards and non-need-based scholarships averaged $15,905 ($42,775 maximum). 35% of undergraduates work part time. Average annual earnings from campus work are $1275. The average financial indebtedness of the

2005 graduate was $28,367. The FAFSA, the college's own financial statement, and the parent and student federal income tax return and W2s are required. The deadline for filing freshman financial aid applications for fall entry is February 13.

International Students: The school actively recruits these students. They must score satisfactorily on the written TOEFL and also take the SAT, or the ACT.

Computers: Wireless access is available. The University provides Dell laptops to students in Colleges of Commerce and Finance and Engineering as part of tuition. In all other colleges, a personal PC is recommended, although many computer labs are also available to all students. Students connect in their residence halls via Internet T1 lines. Most academic buildings and the student center are wireless. Students must purchase a network/wireless card (s). All students may access the system. There are no time limits and no fees.

Graduates: From July 1, 2004 to June 30, 2005, 1852 bachelor's degrees were awarded. The most popular majors were finance (11%), communications (9%), and accountancy (9%). In an average class, 80% graduate in 4 years or less, 85% graduate in 5 years or less, and 86% graduate in 6 years or less. 330 companies recruited on campus in 2004-2005. Of the 2004 graduating class, 16% were enrolled in graduate school within 6 months of graduation and 74% were employed.

Admissions Contact: Michael Gaynor, Director of Admission. E-mail: *gotovu@villanova.edu* Web: *www.admission.villanova.edu*

WASHINGTON AND JEFFERSON COLLEGE A-3
Washington, PA 15301
(724) 223-6025
(888) 926-3529; Fax: (724) 223-6534

Full-time: 726 men, 674 women	**Faculty:** 97; IIB, av$
Part-time: 7 men, 11 women	**Ph.D.s:** 86%
Graduate: none	**Student/Faculty:** 15 to 1
Year: 4-1-4, summer session	**Tuition:** $26,330
Application Deadline: March 1	**Room & Board:** $7160
Freshman Class: 4477 applied, 1737 accepted, 388 enrolled	
SAT Verbal/Math: 560/570*	**ACT:** 25 **VERY COMPETITIVE**

Washington & Jefferson College, founded in 1781, is a private institution offering instruction in liberal arts. The library contains 192,787 volumes, 14,882 microform items, and 5006 audio/video tapes/CDs/DVDs, and subscribes to 503 periodicals including electronic. Computerized library services include the card catalog, interlibrary loans, database searching, Internet access, and laptop Internet portals. Special learning facilities include a learning resource center, art gallery, radio station, and a biological field station. The 60-acre campus is in a small town 27 miles southwest of Pittsburgh. Including any residence halls, there are 52 buildings.

Student Life: 75% of undergraduates are from Pennsylvania. Others are from 33 states and 42 foreign countries. 86% are from public schools. 95% are white. The average age of freshmen is 18; all undergraduates, 20. 14% do not continue beyond their first year; 68% remain to graduate.

Housing: 1216 students can be accommodated in college housing, which includes single-sex and coed dorms, on-campus apartments, fraternity houses, and sorority houses. In addition, there are special-interest houses. On-campus housing is guaranteed for all 4 years. 81% of students live on campus; of those, 75% remain on campus on weekends. All students may keep cars.

Activities: 43% of men belong to 7 national fraternities; 37% of women belong to 4 national sororities. There are 79 groups on campus, including art, band, cheerleading, choir, chorale, chorus, computers, dance, debate, drama, ethnic, honors, international, jazz band, literary magazine, musical theater, newspaper, orchestra, pep band, photography, political, professional, radio and TV, religious, social, social service, student government, and yearbook. Popular campus events include International Week, Greek Week, and Spring Concert.

Sports: There are 12 intercollegiate sports for men and 11 for women, and 20 intramural sports for men and 19 for women. Facilities include swimming and diving pools, a track, a weight room, football, baseball, and soccer fields, and basketball, volleyball, squash, and racquetball courts. The stadium seats 4000, the largest auditorium/arena, 3500.

Disabled Students: 48% of the campus is accessible. Wheelchair ramps, elevators, special parking, specially equipped rest rooms, special class scheduling, and special housing are available.

Services: Counseling and information services are available, as is tutoring in most subjects. There is a reader service for the blind, and remedial math, reading, and writing.

Campus Safety and Security: Measures include 24-hour foot and vehicle patrol, security escort services, informal discussions, and pamphlets/posters/films. There are emergency telephones and lighted pathways/sidewalks.

Programs of Study: W & J confers the B.A. degree. Associate degrees are also awarded. Bachelor's degrees are awarded in BIOLOGICAL SCIENCE (biochemistry, biology/biological science, and biophysics), BUSINESS (accounting, business administration and management, and international business management), COMMUNICATIONS AND THE ARTS (art, English, French, German, music, and Spanish), COMPUTER AND PHYSICAL SCIENCE (chemistry, information sciences and systems, mathematics, and physics), EDUCATION (art), ENGINEERING AND ENVIRONMENTAL DESIGN (industrial administration/management), SOCIAL SCIENCE (economics, history, philosophy, political science/government, psychology, and sociology). Psychology, business administration, and English are the largest.

Required: Students must complete the general education requirement of at least 8 courses in 4 divisions. Other requirements include phys ed, freshman forum, foreign language, cultural diversity, and academic skills. A total of 34 courses, with 8 to 10 courses in the major, is required for graduation, as is a 2.0 GPA.

Special: The college offers study abroad in Russsia, Germany, Colombia, and Mexico, internships in all majors, a Washington semester with American University, dual and student-designed majors, credit by exam, and pass/fail options. There is a 3-2 engineering program with Case Western Reserve University in Cleveland and Washington University in St. Louis. The college offers special human resources management, entrepreneurial studies programs, pre-health programs, pre-physical therapy programs, pre-occupational therapy programs, and physician assistant programs. There is also a 3-4 podiatry program with the Pennsylvania and Ohio Colleges of Podiatry and a 3-4 optometry program with Pennsylvania College of Optometry. There is a 3-3 law program with Duquesne University School of Law and University of Pittsburgh School of Law. There are 19 national honor societies, including Phi Beta Kappa, and 16 departmental honors programs.

Faculty/Classroom: 60% of faculty are male; 40%, female. All teach undergraduates. The average class size in an introductory lecture is 21; in a laboratory, 13; and in a regular course, 16.

Admissions: 39% of the 2005-2006 applicants were accepted. The SAT scores for the 2005-2006 freshman class were: Verbal--12% below 500, 57% between 500 and 599, 26% between 600 and 700, and 5% above 700; Math--11% below 500, 51% between 500 and 599, 32% between 600 and 700, and 6% above 700. The ACT scores were 8% below 21, 25% between 21 and 23, 41% between 24 and 26, 14% between 27 and 28, and 11% above 28. 51% of the current freshmen were in the top fifth of their class; 85% were in the top two fifths. 14 freshmen graduated first in their class.

Requirements: The SAT or ACT is required. In addition, a GED is accepted. Applicants must complete 15 academic credits or Carnegie units, including 3 credits of English and math, 2 of foreign language, and 1 of science. An essay is required and interviews are recommended. AP and CLEP credits are accepted. Important factors in the admissions decision are advanced placement or honor courses, evidence of special talent, and personality/intangible qualities.

Procedure: Freshmen are admitted to all sessions. Entrance exams should be taken in the junior or senior year. There are early decision, early admissions, and deferred admissions plans. Early decision applications should be filed by December 1; regular applications, by March 1 for fall entry, January 1 for winter entry, February 1 for spring entry, and June 1 for summer entry, along with a $25 fee. Notification of early decision is sent December 15; regular decision, April 1. 14 early decision candidates were accepted for the 2005-2006 class. 285 applicants were on the 2005 waiting list; 35 were admitted. Applications are accepted on-line.

Transfer: 17 transfer students enrolled in 2004-2005. Applicants must have a college GPA of at least 2.5 and must take the SAT or ACT. 68 of 140 credits required for the bachelor's degree must be completed at W & J.

Visiting: There are regularly scheduled orientations for prospective students, including a general session, departmental meetings, preprofessional meetings, a financial aid meeting, and class scheduling. There are guides for informal visits and visitors may sit in on classes and stay overnight. To schedule a visit, contact the Admission Office at *visitorservices@washjeff.edu.*

Financial Aid: In 2005-2006, 98% of all full-time freshmen and 96% of continuing full-time students received some form of financial aid. 70% of full-time freshmen and 64% of continuing full-time students received need-based aid. The average freshman award was $17,999. Need-based scholarships or need-based grants averaged $5410; need-based self-help aid (loans and jobs) averaged $2865; and other non-need-based awards and non-need-based scholarships averaged $9724. 45% of undergraduates work part time. Average annual earnings from campus work are $830. The average financial indebtedness of the 2005 graduate was $17,500. The FAFSA is required. The priority date for freshman financial aid applications for fall entry is February 15.

International Students: There are 3 international students enrolled. Satisfactory scores are required on the written TOEFL and the SAT or the ACT.

Computers: Wireless access is available. W & J supports wireless computing in and around many buildings and dorms, including the library, the student center and dining halls, as well as most outdoor locations. Wired connections are available in public access areas such as study lounges, the library, dining areas, and meeting rooms. Open computing labs are available in several classroom buildings and the library. Some labs are open 24 hours a day for student use during the academic year. Through any point of connection on the college's network, students can access all services including Internet and the Web, email, home drives, Blackboard, and on-line financial and academic services via W & J Advisor. All students may access the system any time. There are no time limits and no fees. It is strongly recommended that all students have a personal computer. It is recommended that students in Notebook computer section of Freshman Forum have personal computers.

Graduates: From July 1, 2004 to June 30, 2005, 258 bachelor's degrees were awarded. The most popular majors were business administration (17%), accounting (14%), and psychology (13%). In an average class, 1% graduate in 3 years or less, 66% graduate in 4 years or less, 68% graduate in 5 years or less, and 68% graduate in 6 years or less. 32 companies recruited on campus in 2004-2005. Of the 2004 graduating class, 32% were enrolled in graduate school within 6 months of graduation and 73% were employed.

Admissions Contact: Alton E. Newell, Vice President of Enrollment Management. E-mail: *admission@washjeff.edu*
Web: *http://www.washjeff.edu*

WAYNESBURG COLLEGE   B-4
Waynesburg, PA 15370-9930

(724) 852-3248
(800) 225-7393; Fax: (724) 627-8124

Full-time: 563 men, 780 women	**Faculty:** 62; IIB, --$
Part-time: 53 men, 218 women	**Ph.D.s:** 56%
Graduate: 195 men, 325 women	**Student/Faculty:** 22 to 1
Year: semesters, summer session	**Tuition:** $15,150
Application Deadline: open	**Room & Board:** $6080
Freshman Class: n/av	
SAT or ACT: required	**COMPETITIVE**

Waynesburg College, founded in 1849, is a private liberal arts institution affiliated with the Presbyterian Church (U.S.A.). In addition to regional accreditation, Waynesburg has baccalaureate program accreditation with ACS, CAAHEP, and NLN.The library contains 100,000 volumes, 82,911 microform items, and 2788 audio/video tapes/CDs/DVDs, and subscribes to 395 periodicals including electronic. Computerized library services include the card catalog, interlibrary loans, database searching, and Internet access. Special learning facilities include a learning resource center, art gallery, natural history museum, radio station, and TV station. The 30-acre campus is in a small town 50 miles south of Pittsburgh. Including any residence halls, there are 15 buildings.

Student Life: 88% of undergraduates are from Pennsylvania. Others are from 20 states, 4 foreign countries, and Canada. 91% are from public schools. 91% are white. 30% are Protestant; 19% Catholic; 12% unknown 35. The average age of freshmen is 18; all undergraduates, 24. 28% do not continue beyond their first year; 55% remain to graduate.

Housing: 887 students can be accommodated in college housing, which includes single-sex and coed dormitories. On-campus housing is guaranteed for all 4 years. 52% of students live on campus; of those, 60% remain on campus on weekends. Alcohol is not permitted. Upperclassmen may keep cars.

Activities: There are no fraternities or sororities. There are 36 groups on campus, including band, cheerleading, chorale, drama, ethnic, film, honors, international, jazz band, literary magazine, marching band, musical theater, newspaper, orchestra, pep band, photography, professional, radio and TV, religious, social, social service, and student government. Popular campus events include Spring Weekend Formal, VIP Forum, and Fine Arts Series.

Sports: There are 9 intercollegiate sports for men and 8 for women, and 7 intramural sports for men and 7 for women. Facilities include a 1500-seat stadium, a 1500-seat gym, a 250-seat arena, a fitness center, basketball and racquetball courts, wrestling and weight rooms, a golf driving net, 3 all-weather tennis courts, and table tennis and billiards tables.

Disabled Students: 90% of the campus is accessible. Wheelchair ramps, elevators, special parking, specially equipped rest rooms, special class scheduling, and lowered drinking fountains are available.

Services: Counseling and information services are available, as is tutoring in every subject. There is remedial math and writing.

Campus Safety and Security: Measures include 24-hour foot and vehicle patrol, self-defense education, security escort services, and informal discussions. There are pamphlets/posters/films, lighted pathways/sidewalks, and 24-hour security access.

Programs of Study: Waynesburg confers B.A., B.S., B.S.B.A., B.S.M.B., and B.S.N. degrees. Associate and master's degrees are also awarded. Bachelor's degrees are awarded in BIOLOGICAL SCIENCE (biology/biological science and marine biology), BUSINESS (accounting, banking and finance, international business management, management science, marketing/retailing/merchandising, and small business management), COMMUNICATIONS AND THE ARTS (advertising, art, arts administration/management, broadcasting, communications, creative writing, English, graphic design, literature, and multimedia), COMPUTER AND PHYSICAL SCIENCE (chemistry, computer science, information sciences and systems, and mathematics), EDUCATION (athletic training, elementary, and special), ENGINEERING AND ENVIRONMENTAL DESIGN (engineering and environmental science), HEALTH PROFESSIONS (exercise science, medical laboratory technology, nursing, predentistry, premedicine, prephysical therapy, and preveterinary science), SOCIAL SCIENCE (criminal justice, crosscultural studies, forensic studies, history, human services, ministries, political science/government, prelaw, psychology, social science, and sociology). Nursing, business, and education are the strongest academically. Business administration, education, and nursing are the largest.

Required: To graduate, students must complete a minimum of 124 semester hours, including at least 30 in the major, with a minimum 2.0 GPA. Requirements include 15 credits of humanities and social and behavioral sciences, 8 of natural and physical sciences, 6 each of English and literature/arts, 3 credits each in math and computer science and I each of life skills, service learning, and Fiat Lux. Students must also pass an English usage and written competency test as well as a math test.

Special: The college offers internships, an accelerated degree program in marketing, dual majors, a student-designed interdisciplinary major, credit for experience, nondegree study, and pass/fail options. There is a 3-2 engineering degree program with Case Western Reserve, Washington, and Penn State Universities and a 3-1 in marine biology with Florida Institute of Technology. A Washington semester is offered, as is study abroad in South Korea and Northern Ireland through the Council for Christian Colleges and the Universities Study Abroad program. There are 15 national honor societies and a freshman honors program.

Faculty/Classroom: 50% of faculty are male; 50%, female. All teach undergraduates. No introductory courses are taught by graduate students. The average class size in an introductory lecture is 30; in a laboratory, 20; and in a regular course, 22.

Admissions: 28% of the current freshmen were in the top fifth of their class; 57% were in the top two fifths. 19 freshmen graduated first in their class.

Requirements: The SAT or ACT is required. In addition, applicants must be graduates of an accredited secondary school or have a GED certificate and have completed 16 academic credits, including 4 in English, 3 in math, and 2 in sciences, history, or social studies. Waynesburg requires applicants to be in the upper 40% of their class. A GPA of 2.75 is required. AP and CLEP credits are accepted. Important factors in the admissions decision are advanced placement or honor courses, recommendations by school officials, and extracurricular activities record.

Procedure: Freshmen are admitted to all sessions. Entrance exams should be taken in April of the junior year or December of the senior year. There are early admissions and rolling admissions plan. Application deadlines are open. Application fee is $20. Applications are accepted on-line.

Transfer: 57 transfer students enrolled in 2004-2005. Students must submit a high school transcript and complete transcripts from all colleges previously attended. 45 of 124 credits required for the bachelor's degree must be completed at Waynesburg.

Visiting: There are regularly scheduled orientations for prospective students, including visits with faculty, students, administrators, and financial aid officers, and a tour of the campus. There are guides for informal visits and visitors may sit in on classes and stay overnight. To schedule a visit, contact Robin L. King, Admissions Office at (724) 852-3333.

Financial Aid: In 2005-2006, 92% of all full-time freshmen and 90% of continuing full-time students received some form of financial aid. 84% of all full-time students received need-based aid. The average freshman award was $12,375. Need-based scholarships or need-based grants averaged $3934 ($11,000 maximum); need-based self-help aid (loans and jobs) averaged $3082 ($5625 maximum); and other non-need-based awards and non-need-based scholarships averaged $4500 ($19,370 maximum). 26% of undergraduates work part time. Average annual earnings from campus work are $900. The average financial indebtedness of the 2005 graduate was $17,125. Waynesburg is a member of CSS. The FAFSA, the state aid form, and the college's own financial statement are required. The priority date for freshman financial aid applications for fall entry is March 15. The deadline for filing freshman financial aid applications for fall entry is rolling.

International Students: There are 5 international students enrolled. The school actively recruits these students. They must score satisfactorily on the written TOEFL.

Computers: Wireless access is available. The students use the college's network through a web portal, which gives them access to their class schedules, grades, e-mail, electronic portfolio, and file storage, from anywhere the Internet is available and at any time day or night. The students can access the Internet on campus via a free wired connection in their dorm room and also via a wireless connection in any academic building on campus. Students have access to 145 PCs across 7 computing labs on campus, 2 PCs in each residence hall lobby, and 4 Internet kiosks in the Stover Campus Center. All students may access the system. There are no time limits and no fees.

Graduates: From July 1, 2004 to June 30, 2005, 320 bachelor's degrees were awarded. The most popular majors were business administra-

tion (23%), nursing (22%), and criminal justice (12%). In an average class, 44% graduate in 4 years or less, 50% graduate in 5 years or less, and 53% graduate in 6 years or less. Of the 2004 graduating class, 55% were enrolled in graduate school within 6 months of graduation and 90% were employed.

Admissions Contact: Robin L. King, Dean of Admissions. E-mail: *admissions@waynesburg.edu* Web: *www.waynesburg.edu*

WEST CHESTER UNIVERSITY OF PENNSYLVANIA   F-4
West Chester, PA 19383

(610) 436-3411
(877) 315-2165; Fax: (610) 436-2907

Full-time: 3761 men, 6027 women	**Faculty:** n/av
Part-time: 443 men, 607 women	**Ph.D.s:** 74%
Graduate: 545 men, 1605 women	**Student/Faculty:** 18 to 1
Year: semesters, summer session	**Tuition:** $6147 ($13,507)
Application Deadline: open	**Room & Board:** $6208
Freshman Class: 11,013 applied, 5438 accepted, 1901 enrolled	
SAT Verbal/Math: 530/530*	**COMPETITIVE+**

West Chester University, founded in 1871, is a public institution that is part of the Pennsylvania State System of Higher Education. It offers programs through the College of Arts and Sciences, and Schools of Business and Public Affairs, Education, Health Sciences, and Music. There are 5 undergraduate and 7 graduate schools. In addition to regional accreditation, West Chester University has baccalaureate program accreditation with CSWE, NASM, NCATE, and NLN. The 2 libraries contain 606,000 volumes, 900,000 microform items, and 71,000 audio/video tapes/CDs/DVDs, and subscribe to 4200 periodicals including electronic. Computerized library services include the card catalog, interlibrary loans, database searching, and Internet access. Special learning facilities include a learning resource center, art gallery, planetarium, radio station, TV station, an herbarium, a speech and hearing clinic, a center for government and community affairs, and a 100-acre natural area for environmental studies. The 388-acre campus is in a suburban area 25 miles west of Philadelphia. Including any residence halls, there are 62 buildings.

Student Life: 89% of undergraduates are from Pennsylvania. Students are from 31 states, 61 foreign countries, and Canada. 84% are white; 11% African American. The average age of freshmen is 18; all undergraduates, 22. 16% do not continue beyond their first year; 51% remain to graduate.

Housing: 3600 students can be accommodated in college housing, which includes single-sex and coed dormitories and on-campus apartments. In addition, there are honors houses, and international students sections. On-campus housing is guaranteed for all 4 years. 64% of students commute. Alcohol is not permitted. Upperclassmen may keep cars.

Activities: 8% of men belong to 14 national fraternities; 9% of women belong to 12 national sororities. There are 200 groups on campus, including art, band, cheerleading, chess, choir, chorale, chorus, computers, dance, drama, drill team, drum and bugle corps, ethnic, film, forensics, gay, honors, international, jazz band, literary magazine, marching band, musical theater, newspaper, orchestra, photography, political, professional, radio and TV, religious, social, social service, student government, symphony, and yearbook. Popular campus events include Martin Luther King Day and University Festival.

Sports: There are 10 intercollegiate sports for men and 12 for women, and 11 intramural sports for men and 7 for women. Facilities include a 2500-seat field house, a gymnastics room, 4 gyms, swimming pools, 2 game fields, 3 practice fields, a softball complex, tennis courts, a 500-seat baseball stadium, and a 7500-seat stadium.

Disabled Students: 80% of the campus is accessible. Wheelchair ramps, elevators, special parking, specially equipped rest rooms, special class scheduling, lowered drinking fountains, and lowered telephones are available.

Services: Counseling and information services are available, as is tutoring in every subject. There is a reader service for the blind, and remedial math, reading, and writing.

Campus Safety and Security: Measures include 24-hour foot and vehicle patrol, self-defense education, security escort services, and shuttle buses. There are informal discussions, pamphlets/posters/films, emergency telephones, lighted pathways/sidewalks, bike patrol, card access/security alarms, and resident hall security.

Programs of Study: West Chester University confers B.A., B.S., B.F.A., B.Mus., B.S.Ed., and B.S.N. degrees. Associate and master's degrees are also awarded. Bachelor's degrees are awarded in BIOLOGICAL SCIENCE (biochemistry and biology/biological science), BUSINESS (accounting, business administration and management, business economics, and marketing/retailing/merchandising), COMMUNICATIONS AND THE ARTS (art, communications, comparative literature, dramatic arts, English, French, German, Latin, literature, music, music performance, music theory and composition, Russian, Spanish, speech/debate/rhetoric, and studio art), COMPUTER AND PHYSICAL SCIENCE (chemistry, computer science, earth science, geoscience, mathematics, and physics), EDUCATION (athletic training, early childhood, elementary, foreign languages, health, music, physical, secondary, social studies, and special), HEALTH PROFESSIONS (health, health science, nursing, predentistry, premedicine, public health, and speech pathology/audiology), SOCIAL SCIENCE (American studies, anthropology, criminal justice, economics, geography, history, liberal arts/general studies, philosophy, political science/government, prelaw, psychology, public administration, religion, social work, sociology, and women's studies). Premedical is the strongest academically. Physical education, elementary/early childhood education, and business management are the largest.

Required: All students must satisfy requirements in English composition, math, interdisciplinary study, and phys ed. Distribution requirements include 9 hours each of science, behavioral and social science, and humanities, and 3 hours in the arts. A total of 120 (126 for some degrees) credit hours and a 2.0 GPA are required.

Special: There is cross-registration with Cheyney University and a 3-2 engineering program with Pennsylvania State University. The university offers internships in most majors, an accelerated degree program in business, study abroad in France, Austria, Scotland, England, and Wales, a Washington semester, work-study, some student-designed majors, credit by examination and for life, military, and work experience, and pass/fail options. There are 23 national honor societies, a freshman honors program, and 10 departmental honors programs.

Faculty/Classroom: 54% of faculty are male; 46%, female. No introductory courses are taught by graduate students. The average class size in an introductory lecture is 35; in a laboratory, 24; and in a regular course, 30.

Admissions: 49% of the 2005-2006 applicants were accepted. The SAT scores for the 2005-2006 freshman class were: Verbal--28% below 500, 56% between 500 and 599, 16% between 600 and 700, and 1% above 700; Math--26% below 500, 57% between 500 and 599, 16% between 600 and 700, and 1% above 700. 23% of the current freshmen were in the top fifth of their class; 53% were in the top two fifths.

Requirements: The SAT is required. In addition, a college preparatory curriculum in high school, standardized test scores from either the SAT or ACT, and a personal statement is required. An interview is required for athletic tranning, premedical, and pharmaceutical product development programs, and an audition is required for music. Specific course prerequisites depend on major selection. Additional documentation is required of candidates for the summer academic development program. The GED is acceptable. West Chester University requires applicants to be in the upper 50% of their class. A GPA of 3.0 is required. AP and CLEP credits are accepted. Important factors in the admissions decision are advanced placement or honor courses, recommendations by school officials, and evidence of special talent.

Procedure: Freshmen are admitted fall and spring. Entrance exams should be taken in spring of the junior year or fall of the senior year. There is an early admissions plan and a rolling admissions plan. Application deadlines are open. Application fee is $35. 307 applicants were on the 2005 waiting list; 30 were admitted. Applications are accepted online.

Transfer: 961 transfer students enrolled in 2004-2005. Applicants should have earned at least 30 credits and must have a recommended GPA of at least 2.0 Some departments require a higher GPA and specific course requirements. Transfers who have earned fewer than 30 credits must submit a high school transcript and standardized test scores. 30 of 120 credits required for the bachelor's degree must be completed at West Chester University.

Visiting: There are regularly scheduled orientations for prospective students including campus tours, available 20 times each week during the academic year. During the fall, there are 2 preview Saturdays. The agenda includes academic presentations, a faculty and student services, and a tour. There are guides for informal visits and visitors may sit in on classes. To schedule a visit, contact the Office of Admissions at (877) 315-2165.

Financial Aid: In 2004-2005, 85% of all full-time freshmen and 84% of continuing full-time students received some form of financial aid. 73% of full-time freshmen and 66% of continuing full-time students received need-based aid. The average freshman award was $6190. Need-based scholarships or need-based grants averaged $3453 ($8225 maximum); need-based self-help aid (loans and jobs) averaged $2337 ($3500 maximum); non-need-based athletic scholarships averaged $2197 ($8000 maximum); and other non-need-based awards and non-need-based scholarships averaged $3765 ($13,931 maximum). 17% of undergraduates work part time. Average annual earnings from campus work are $1553. The average financial indebtedness of a recent graduate was $17,500. West Chester University is a member of CSS. The FAFSA is required. Check with the school for current application deadlines.

International Students: There are 53 international students enrolled. They must score satisfactorily on the written TOEFL or on the electronic version.

Computers: All students may access the system.

Admissions Contact: Marsha Haug, Interim Ass't VP for Admissions and Enrollment Services. E-mail: ugadmiss@wcupa.edu Web: www.wcupa.edu

WESTMINSTER COLLEGE A-2

New Wilmington, PA 16172 (724) 946-7100
(800) 942-8033; Fax: (724) 946-6171

Full-time: 508 men, 902 women	**Faculty:** 100; IIB, -$
Part-time: 20 men, 34 women	**Ph.D.s:** 83%
Graduate: 43 men, 86 women	**Student/Faculty:** 14 to 1
Year: semesters, summer session	**Tuition:** $24,220
Application Deadline: open	**Room & Board:** $7070
Freshman Class: 1302 applied, 1006 accepted, 359 enrolled	
SAT Verbal/Math: 544/543*	**ACT:** 24 COMPETITIVE+

Westminster College, founded in 1852, is a private liberal arts institution related to the Presbyterian Church (U.S.A.). In addition to regional accreditation, Westminster has baccalaureate program accreditation with NASM. The 2 libraries contain 283,070 volumes, 9737 microform items, and 14,251 audio/video tapes/CDs/DVDs, and subscribe to 848 periodicals including electronic. Computerized library services include interlibrary loans, database searching, Internet access, and laptop Internet portals. Special learning facilities include a learning resource center, art gallery, planetarium, radio station, TV station, electron microscope labs in the science center, and a graphics computer center. The 350-acre campus is in a rural area 60 miles north of Pittsburgh. Including any residence halls, there are 25 buildings.

Student Life: 79% of undergraduates are from Pennsylvania. Students are from 23 states and 1 foreign country. 90% are from public schools. 97% are white. 56% are Protestant; 34% Catholic; 10% claim no religious affiliation. The average age of freshmen is 18; all undergraduates, 20. 11% do not continue beyond their first year; 76% remain to graduate.

Housing: 1098 students can be accommodated in college housing, which includes single-sex dorms, on-campus apartments, and fraternity houses. Some residence hall floors have 24 hour weekend visitation. On-campus housing is guaranteed for all 4 years. 90% of students live on campus; of those, 70% remain on campus on weekends. Alcohol is not permitted. All students may keep cars.

Activities: 33% of men belong to 5 national fraternities; 34% of women belong to 5 national sororities. There are 60 groups on campus, including band, cheerleading, choir, chorale, chorus, dance, debate, drama, drill team, ethnic, forensics, gay, honors, jazz band, literary magazine, marching band, musical theater, newspaper, orchestra, pep band, political, radio and TV, religious, social, social service, student government, and symphony. Popular campus events include Mock Conventions, Mardi Gras, and Volleyrock.

Sports: There are 9 intercollegiate sports for men and 9 for women, and 7 intramural sports for men and 6 for women. Facilities include a natatorium, racquetball, tennis, and basketball courts, an all-weather track, and weight and aerobics rooms. Canoeing on the lake is available.

Disabled Students: 50% of the campus is accessible. Wheelchair ramps, elevators, special parking, specially equipped rest rooms, and special class scheduling are available.

Services: Counseling and information services are available, as is tutoring in most subjects through the learning center. There is a reader service for the blind, and remedial math, reading, and writing.

Campus Safety and Security: Measures include 24-hour foot and vehicle patrol, self-defense education, security escort services, and shuttle buses. There are informal discussions, pamphlets/posters/films, emergency telephones, and lighted pathways/sidewalks.

Programs of Study: Westminster confers B.A., B.S., and B.M. degrees. Master's degrees are also awarded. Bachelor's degrees are awarded in BIOLOGICAL SCIENCE (biology/biological science and molecular biology), BUSINESS (accounting, banking and finance, business administration and management, international business management, and marketing/retailing/merchandising), COMMUNICATIONS AND THE ARTS (art, broadcasting, communications, dramatic arts, English, fine arts, French, German, Latin, music, music performance, music theory and composition, public relations, and Spanish), COMPUTER AND PHYSICAL SCIENCE (chemistry, computer science, mathematics, and physics), EDUCATION (Christian, elementary, guidance, music, and secondary), HEALTH PROFESSIONS (predentistry and premedicine), SOCIAL SCIENCE (criminal justice, economics, history, international relations, philosophy, political science/government, prelaw, psychology, religion, religious music, social science, and sociology). Sciences, business, and education are the strongest academically and have the largest enrollments.

Required: First-year students are required to take Inquiry I and II, as well as writing and a speech course. Students must fullfill a distribution requirement by taking a course in one of each of the Intellectual Perspectives: Visual and Performing Arts, Quantitative Reasoning, Social Thought and Tradition, Humanity and Culture, Scientific Discovery, Foreign Language, and Religious and Philosophical Thought. A capstone experience in their major and community service are also required. Students must complete 132 semester hours with a minimum of 84 outside their majors, and have a minimum of 2.0 GPA in all courses. Majors require between 32 and 60 hours of coursework.

Special: The college offers internships, study abroad in many countries, a Washington semester, various dual and student-designed majors, a 3-2 engineering degree with Case Western Reserve, Pennsylvania State, and Washington Universities, London study at Regent's College, a 3-3 J.D. program with Duquesne, and nondegree study. There are 12 national honor societies and a freshman honors program.

Faculty/Classroom: 53% of faculty are male; 47%, female. All teach undergraduates. No introductory courses are taught by graduate students. The average class size in an introductory lecture is 20; in a laboratory, 20; and in a regular course, 22.

Admissions: 77% of the 2005-2006 applicants were accepted. The SAT scores for the 2005-2006 freshman class were: Verbal--32% below 500, 44% between 500 and 599, 21% between 600 and 700, and 3% above 700; Math--31% below 500, 44% between 500 and 599, 23% between 600 and 700, and 2% above 700. The ACT scores were 73% below 21, 13% between 21 and 23, 8% between 24 and 26, 2% between 27 and 28, and 3% above 28. 48% of the current freshmen were in the top fifth of their class; 80% were in the top two fifths. 8 freshmen graduated first in their class.

Requirements: The SAT or ACT is required. Applicants must be graduates of an accredited secondary school and have a minimum of 16 academic credits, including 4 units in English, 3 in math, and 2 each in foreign language, science, and social studies. The GED will be considered with a minimum composite score of 270. A portfolio, audition, and interview are recommended. An essay is required. Westminster requires applicants to be in the upper 50% of their class. A GPA of 2.5 is required. AP and CLEP credits are accepted. Important factors in the admissions decision are advanced placement or honor courses, leadership record, and recommendations by school officials.

Procedure: Freshmen are admitted fall, winter, and spring. Entrance exams should be taken during the junior year. There are deferred admissions and rolling admissions plans. Early decision applications should be filed by November 15; regular applications, by open for fall entry, along with a $35 fee. Notification of early decision is sent December 1; regular decision, on a rolling basis. Applications are accepted on-line.

Transfer: 11 transfer students enrolled in 2004-2005. Applicants must have a college GPA of 2.0 or better. 60 of 132 credits required for the bachelor's degree must be completed at Westminster.

Visiting: There are regularly scheduled orientations for prospective students, consisting of an introduction, a student panel, a financial aid workshop, a campus tour, a faculty fair, and a lunch. Optional activities include a tour of residence halls and radio and TV stations and a football game. There are 2 visitation days in the fall and 2 in the spring. There are guides for informal visits and visitors may sit in on classes and stay overnight. To schedule a visit, contact the Office of Admissions.

Financial Aid: In 2005-2006, 98% of all full-time freshmen and 97% of continuing full-time students received some form of financial aid. 81% of full-time freshmen and 78% of continuing full-time students received need-based aid. The average freshman award was $16,427. 40% of undergraduates work part time. Average annual earnings from campus work are $1650. The average financial indebtedness of the 2005 graduate was $20,386. Westminster is a member of CSS. The FAFSA and the college's own financial statement are required. The deadline for filing freshman financial aid applications for fall entry is May 1.

International Students: There are 2 international students enrolled. They must score satisfactorily on the written TOEFL take the MELAB, or the SAT for students who come from a country where English is the spoken language.

Computers: Wireless access is available. Every residence room has ports. The college has several labs that are available to all students. All students may access the system. There are no time limits and no fees.

Graduates: From July 1, 2004 to June 30, 2005, 222 bachelor's degrees were awarded. The most popular majors were elementary education (21%), business administration (16%), and social sciences and history (13%). In an average class, 74% graduate in 4 years or less, 75% graduate in 5 years or less, and 76% graduate in 6 years or less. Of the 2004 graduating class, 90% were employed within 6 months of graduation.

Admissions Contact: Dean of Admissions.
E-mail: *admis@westminster.edu* Web: *www.westminster.edu*

WIDENER UNIVERSITY	F-4
Chester, PA 19013	**(610) 499-4126**
	(888)-Widener; Fax: (610) 499-4676
Full-time: 1115 men, 1075 women	Faculty: 171; IIA, +$
Part-time: 100 men, 50 women	Ph.D.s: 92%
Graduate: 510 men, 1015 women	Student/Faculty: 13 to 1
Year: semesters, summer session	Tuition: $19,650
Application Deadline: see profile	Room & Board: $7625
Freshman Class: n/av	
SAT: required	**COMPETITIVE**

Widener University, founded in 1821, is a private liberal arts institution offering undergraduate programs in the arts and sciences, business ad-

ministration, engineering, nursing, and hospitality management. Other campuses are in Harrisburg and Wilmington, Delaware. There are 6 undergraduate and 5 graduate schools. Figures in the above capsule and profile are approximate. In addition to regional accreditation, Widener has baccalaureate program accreditation with AACSB, ABET, APTA, CSWE, and NLN. The library contains 241,491 volumes, 174,632 microform items, and 6463 audio/video tapes/CDs/DVDs, and subscribes to 1959 periodicals including electronic. Computerized library services include the card catalog, interlibrary loans, database searching, and Internet access. Special learning facilities include a learning resource center, art gallery, radio station, TV station, a child development center, and a wireless accessible library. The 105-acre campus is in a suburban area 12 miles south of Philadelphia. Including any residence halls, there are 87 buildings.

Student Life: 64% of undergraduates are from Pennsylvania. Others are from 21 states and 15 foreign countries. 51% are from public schools. 78% are white; 10% African American. 45% are Catholic; 44% Protestant. The average age of freshmen is 18; all undergraduates, 20. 18% do not continue beyond their first year; 62% remain to graduate.

Housing: 1375 students can be accommodated in college housing, which includes single-sex and coed dormitories, on-campus apartments, fraternity houses, and sorority houses. In addition, there are honors houses, special-interest houses, substance-free housing, affinity housing, wellness housing, and quiet/study wings. On-campus housing is guaranteed for all 4 years. 65% of students live on campus; of those, 75% remain on campus on weekends. All students may keep cars.

Activities: 25% of men belong to 7 national fraternities; 14% of women belong to 3 national sororities. There are 106 groups on campus, including art, band, cheerleading, chess, choir, chorale, chorus, computers, dance, drama, ethnic, film, gay, honors, ice hockey, international, jazz band, literary magazine, men's hockey clubs, model UN, musical theater, newspaper, outdoor, pep band, photography, political, professional, radio and TV, religious, rigby, ski and snowboard, social, social service, student government, video and yearbook. Popular campus events include Greek Week, Hundredth Night, and Honors Week.

Sports: There are 11 intercollegiate sports for men and 11 for women, and 7 intramural sports for men and 7 for women. Facilities include a 4000-seat stadium, an 1800-seat basketball gym, a field house, a championship pool, a weight training room, an exercise room, tennis courts, outdoor game and practice fields, and an 8-lane, all-weather championship track.

Disabled Students: All of the campus is accessible. Wheelchair ramps, elevators, special parking, specially equipped rest rooms, special class scheduling, lowered drinking fountains, and lowered telephones are available.

Services: Counseling and information services are available, as is tutoring in every subject. There is a reader service for the blind. Academic support is offered as needed for all students.

Campus Safety and Security: Measures include 24-hour foot and vehicle patrol, self-defense education, security escort services, and shuttle buses. There are informal discussions, pamphlets/posters/films, emergency telephones, lighted pathways/sidewalks, residence hall briefings on personal safety, housing security, and enforcement procedures. There are bike patrols.

Programs of Study: Widener confers B.A., B.S., B.S.B., B.S.C.E., B.S.Ch.E., B.S.E.E., B.S. in H.M., B.S.M.E., B.S.N., and B.S.W. degrees. Associate, master's, and doctoral degrees are also awarded. Bachelor's degrees are awarded in BIOLOGICAL SCIENCE (biochemistry and biology/biological science), BUSINESS (accounting, business administration and management, business economics, hospitality management services, and international business management), COMMUNICATIONS AND THE ARTS (communications, English, and modern language), COMPUTER AND PHYSICAL SCIENCE (chemistry, computer science, information sciences and systems, mathematics, and physics), EDUCATION (early childhood, elementary, and science), ENGINEERING AND ENVIRONMENTAL DESIGN (chemical engineering, civil engineering, electrical/electronics engineering, environmental science, and mechanical engineering), HEALTH PROFESSIONS (nursing, predentistry, and premedicine), SOCIAL SCIENCE (anthropology, behavioral science, criminal justice, economics, history, humanities, international relations, political science/government, prelaw, psychology, social work, and sociology). Computer science, biology, and psychology are the strongest academically. Arts and sciences, business administration, and engineering are the largest.

Required: All students must complete 12 credits each in humanities, social sciences, and science/math, and 1 credit in phys ed. For graduation, students must have 121 credit hours and a GPA of 2.0. Hours in the major vary by program. There is a university-wide writing requirement for all students.

Special: Widener offers internships, study abroad in 12 countries, a Washington semester, accelerated degree programs, dual, student-designed, and interdisciplinary majors, including chemistry management, nondegree study, and pass/fail options. Co-op programs are available in business administration, computer science, and engineering and are required in hospitality management. There is also cross-registration with Boston, Syracuse, Swarthmore College, and American Universities, work-study programs, and B.A.-B.S. degrees. There are 26 national honor societies, a freshman honors program, and 8 departmental honors programs.

Faculty/Classroom: 54% of faculty are male; 46%, female. 82% teach undergraduates, 70% do research, and 70% do both. No introductory courses are taught by graduate students. The average class size in an introductory lecture is 30; in a laboratory, 14; and in a regular course, 24.

Requirements: The SAT is required. In addition, applicants must be graduates of an accredited secondary school and have completed 4 units each of English and social studies, 3 units each of math and science, and 1 unit each of art, history, and music. The GED is accepted under limited circumstances. An interview is recommended. Widener requires applicants to be in the upper 50% of their class. A GPA of 3.0 is required. AP credits are accepted. Important factors in the admissions decision are advanced placement or honor courses, recommendations by school officials, and extracurricular activities record.

Procedure: Freshmen are admitted fall and spring. Entrance exams should be taken in the junior year and November or December of the senior year. There are early admissions, deferred admissions, and rolling admissions plans. Check with the school for application deadlines. The application fee is $35. Notification of early decision is sent December 15; regular decision, on a rolling basis. Applications are accepted on-line.

Transfer: Applicants must have at least 12 college credits with a minimum GPA of 2.0 (2.5 for nursing students). An associate's degree and an interview are recommended. 45 of 121 credits required for the bachelor's degree must be completed at Widener.

Visiting: There are regularly scheduled orientations for prospective students. There are guides for informal visits and visitors may sit in on classes and stay overnight. To schedule a visit, contact Office of Admissions.

Financial Aid: Widener is a member of CSS. The FAFSA and the college's own financial statement are required. Check with the school for application deaadlines.

International Students: In a recent year, there were 45 international students enrolled. The school actively recruits these students. They must score satisfactorily on the written TOEFL or on the electronic version.

Computers: All students may access the system. Resources are generally available 24 hours a day, 7 days a week. Student computer labs are open from 8 A.M. to 11 P.M. There are no time limits. The fee is $75. It is strongly recommended that all students have a personal computer.

Graduates: In a recent year, 493 bachelor's degrees were awarded. The most popular majors were arts and sciences (38%), business administration (26%), and engineering (13%). In an average class, 46% graduate in 4 years or less, 66% graduate in 5 years or less, and 70% graduate in 6 years or less. 102 companies recruited on campus in a recent year. Of a recent graduating class, 14% were enrolled in graduate school within 6 months of graduation and 86% were employed.

Admissions Contact: M. Hendricks, Jr., Dean of Admissions.
E-mail: *admissions.office@widener.edu* Web: *http://www.widener.edu*

WILKES UNIVERSITY — E-2

Wilkes Barre, PA 18766

(570) 408-4400
(800) WILKESU; Fax: (570) 408-4904

Full-time: 969 men, 1131 women	Faculty: 133; IIA, -$
Part-time: 107 men, 113 women	Ph.Ds: 87%
Graduate: 711 men, 1449 women	Student/Faculty: 16 to 1
Year: semesters, summer session	Tuition: $21,646
Application Deadline: open	Room & Board: $9240
Freshman Class: 2702 applied, 2084 accepted, 572 enrolled	
SAT Verbal/Math: 520/540*	COMPETITIVE

Wilkes University, founded in 1933, is an independent comprehensive university offering undergraduate programs in 40 fields, including the arts and sciences, business, and engineering. There are 5 undergraduate schools and 1 graduate school. In addition to regional accreditation, Wilkes has baccalaureate program accreditation with ABET, ACBSP, ACPE, CCNE, and NLN. The library contains 220,000 volumes, 800,000 microform items, and 10,358 audio/video tapes/CDs/DVDs, and subscribes to 650 periodicals including electronic. Computerized library services include the card catalog, interlibrary loans, database searching, Internet access, and laptop Internet portals. Special learning facilities include a learning resource center, art gallery, radio station, and TV station. The 27-acre campus is in an urban area 120 miles west of New York City. Including any residence halls, there are 48 buildings.

Student Life: 83% of undergraduates are from Pennsylvania. Others are from 23 states and 7 foreign countries. 80% are from public schools. 93% are white. The average age of freshmen is 18; all undergraduates, 21. 20% do not continue beyond their first year; 59% remain to graduate.

Housing: 974 students can be accommodated in college housing, which includes single-sex and coed dorms. On-campus housing is guaranteed for all 4 years. 55% of students commute. Alcohol is not permitted. All students may keep cars.

Activities: There are no fraternities or sororities. There are 60 groups on campus, including art, band, cheerleading, choir, chorus, computers, debate, drama, ethnic, gay, honors, international, jazz band, literary magazine, musical theater, newspaper, orchestra, pep band, political, professional, radio and TV, religious, social, social service, student government, and yearbook. Popular campus events include Casino Night, Junior-Senior Dinner Dance, and Winter Weekend.

Sports: There are 7 intercollegiate sports for men and 7 for women, and 7 intramural sports for men and 3 for women. Facilities include tennis courts, a 5000-seat stadium, a 3500-seat gym, a game room, and weight and exercise rooms.

Disabled Students: All of the campus is accessible. Wheelchair ramps, elevators, special parking, specially equipped rest rooms, special class scheduling, lowered drinking fountains, and lowered telephones are available.

Services: Counseling and information services are available, as is tutoring in every subject. There is remedial math, reading, and writing. The Learning Center also provides individual tutoring, group study sessions, and small-group supplemental instruction seminars.

Campus Safety and Security: Measures include 24-hour foot and vehicle patrol, security escort services, shuttle buses, and informal discussions. There are pamphlets/posters/films, emergency telephones, lighted pathways/sidewalks, personal alarm devices for students who wish to carry one, and engraving of personal belongings. Students and others may contact security anonymously.

Programs of Study: Wilkes confers B.A., B.S., B.B.A., and B.M. degrees. Master's degrees are also awarded. Bachelor's degrees are awarded in BIOLOGICAL SCIENCE (biochemistry and biology/biological science), BUSINESS (accounting, business administration and management, and entrepreneurial studies), COMMUNICATIONS AND THE ARTS (communications, dramatic arts, English, French, media arts, music, musical theater, and Spanish), COMPUTER AND PHYSICAL SCIENCE (chemistry, computer science, earth science, information sciences and systems, and mathematics), EDUCATION (elementary and music), ENGINEERING AND ENVIRONMENTAL DESIGN (electrical/electronics engineering, engineering and applied science, engineering management, environmental engineering, and mechanical engineering), HEALTH PROFESSIONS (medical technology, nursing, pharmacology, predentistry, premedicine, prepharmacy, prepodiatry, and preveterinary science), SOCIAL SCIENCE (criminology, history, international studies, liberal arts/general studies, philosophy, political science/government, prelaw, psychology, and sociology). Prepharmacy, biology, and engineering are the strongest academically. Nursing, prepharmacy, and business administration are the largest.

Required: To graduate, all students must complete at least 120 credit hours, with a minimum of 30 in the major, and a cumulative GPA of at least 2.0 overall and in the major. Students must demonstrate competency in written expression, computer literacy, oral expression, and math. General education requirements consist of 12 to 15 credits in humanities, 9 to 12 in sciences, 6 to 9 in social sciences, and 3 in fine arts.

Special: Wilkes offers cooperative education, cross-registration with King's College and Misericordia, internships, and study abroad in more than 50 countries. Dual majors in all disciplines, credit for military experience, and nondegree study are also offered. Preprofessional programs include medicine, dentistry, podiatry, optometry, veterinary medicine, and pharmacy. There are 16 national honor societies, a freshman honors program, and 6 departmental honors programs.

Faculty/Classroom: 61% of faculty are male; 39%, female. No introductory courses are taught by graduate students. The average class size in an introductory lecture is 26; in a laboratory, 14; and in a regular course, 22.

Admissions: 77% of the 2005-2006 applicants were accepted. The SAT scores for the 2005-2006 freshman class were: Verbal--33% below 500, 47% between 500 and 599, 19% between 600 and 700, and 1% above 700; Math--30% below 500, 42% between 500 and 599, 26% between 600 and 700, and 2% above 700. 40% of the current freshmen were in the top fifth of their class; 62% were in the top two fifths. 11 freshmen graduated first in their class.

Requirements: The SAT or ACT is required. In addition, applicants must be graduates of an accredited secondary school or have the GED. Secondary-school preparation should include 4 years of English, 3 years each of math and social studies, and 2 years of science. Music majors and theater arts majors must audition. Wilkes requires applicants to be in the upper 50% of their class. A GPA of 2.5 is required. AP and CLEP credits are accepted. Important factors in the admissions decision are recommendations by school officials, advanced placement or honor courses, and leadership record.

Procedure: Freshmen are admitted to all sessions. Entrance exams should be taken before the second semester of the senior year in high school. There is a deferred admissions plan and a rolling admissions plan. Application deadlines are open. The fall 2005 application fee was $35. Applications are accepted on-line.

Transfer: 133 transfer students enrolled in 2004-2005. Applicants must have a minimum college GPA of 2.0 and at least 30 earned credits. A

GPA of 2.5 is required for engineering majors. Students with fewer than 30 credits must submit official high school transcripts and SAT or ACT scores. An interview is recommended. 60 of 120 credits required for the bachelor's degree must be completed at Wilkes.

Visiting: There are regularly scheduled orientations for prospective students, including a general orientation session, a tour of the campus, and a meeting with faculty from the department of the student's intended major. There are guides for informal visits and visitors may sit in on classes and stay overnight. To schedule a visit, contact the Admissions Office at *admissions@wilkes.edu.*

Financial Aid: In 2005-2006, 99% of all full-time freshmen and 92% of continuing full-time students received some form of financial aid. 86% of full-time freshmen and 81% of continuing full-time students received need-based aid. The average freshman award was $16,751. 36% of undergraduates work part time. Average annual earnings from campus work are $700. The average financial indebtedness of the 2005 graduate was $25,164. The FAFSA and PHEAA are required. The deadline for filing freshman financial aid applications for fall entry is March 1.

International Students: There are 6 international students enrolled. The school actively recruits these students. They must score satisfactorily on the TOEFL and also take the SAT or the ACT.

Computers: Wireless access is available. All students may access the system 24 hours daily. There are no time limits. The fee is $80 per semester. It is strongly recommended that all students have a personal computer.

Graduates: From July 1, 2004 to June 30, 2005, 405 bachelor's degrees were awarded. The most popular majors were business (16%), education (10%), and engineering (9%). In an average class, 44% graduate in 4 years or less, 55% graduate in 5 years or less, and 59% graduate in 6 years or less. 75 companies recruited on campus in 2004-2005. Of the 2004 graduating class, 26% were enrolled in graduate school within 6 months of graduation and 73% were employed.

Admissions Contact: Michael J. Frantz, Vice President for Enrollment Services. E-mail: *frantz@wilkes.edu* Web: *www.wilkes.edu*

WILSON COLLEGE
D-4

Chambersburg, PA 17201-1285

(717) 262-2025
(800) 421-8402; Fax: (717) 264-1578

Full-time: 14 men, 334 women	Faculty: 40
Part-time: 70 men, 314 women	Ph.D.s: 78%
Graduate: none	Student/Faculty: 9 to 1
Year: 4-1-4, summer session	Tuition: $20,050
Application Deadline: open	Room & Board: $7610
Freshman Class: 441 applied, 250 accepted, 76 enrolled	
SAT Verbal/Math: 530/500*	ACT: 22 COMPETITIVE

Wilson College, founded in 1869, is a private liberal arts institution for women that is affiliated with the Presbyterian Church (U.S.A.). In addition to regional accreditation, Wilson has baccalaureate program accreditation with AVMA. The library contains 175,000 volumes, 10,933 microform items, and 2007 audio/video tapes/CDs/DVDs, and subscribes to 293 periodicals including electronic. Computerized library services include the card catalog, interlibrary loans, database searching, and Internet access. Special learning facilities include a learning resource center, art gallery, natural history museum, radio station, a veterinary technology center, a transmission electron microscope, a classics collection, stables, a center for sustainable living, and an on-campus equestrian center. The 300-acre campus is in a small town 55 miles south of Harrisburg, 76 miles west of Baltimore, 90 miles west of Washington, D.C. Including any residence halls, there are 34 buildings.

Student Life: 83% of undergraduates are from Pennsylvania. Others are from 19 states and 10 foreign countries. 91% are from public schools. 85% are white. 51% are claim no religious affiliation; 31% Protestant; 11% Catholic. The average age of freshmen is 18; all undergraduates, 30. 33% do not continue beyond their first year; 48% remain to graduate.

Housing: 473 students can be accommodated in college housing, which includes single-sex dorms, on-campus apartments, and single-mother housing for women with children. On-campus housing is guaranteed for all 4 years. 59% of students commute. All students may keep cars.

Activities: There are no fraternities. There are 23 groups on campus, including art, cheerleading, choir, chorale, dance, drama, ethnic, gay, honors, international, literary magazine, newspaper, photography, political, professional, radio and TV, religious, social, social service, and student government. Popular campus events include May Weekend and Thanksgiving, Christmas, and Muhibbah International Dinners.

Sports: Facilities include a 400-seat gym, a field house, a pool, a gymnastics gym, an archery range, a hockey field, a softball field, tennis courts, a 2-lane bowling alley, an equestrian center (indoor and outdoor arena), a soccer field, and a fitness center.

Disabled Students: 55% of the campus is accessible. Wheelchair ramps, elevators, special parking, specially equipped rest rooms, and special class scheduling are available.

Services: Counseling and information services are available, as is tutoring in every subject. There is remedial math, reading, and writing, and study skills workshops.

Campus Safety and Security: Measures include 24-hour foot and vehicle patrol, shuttle buses, informal discussions, and pamphlets/posters/films. There are emergency telephones and lighted pathways/sidewalks.

Programs of Study: Wilson confers B.A. and B.S. degrees. Associate degrees are also awarded. Bachelor's degrees are awarded in AGRICULTURE (equine science), BIOLOGICAL SCIENCE (biology/biological science), BUSINESS (accounting and business economics), COMMUNICATIONS AND THE ARTS (communications, English, fine arts, French, languages, and Spanish), COMPUTER AND PHYSICAL SCIENCE (chemistry and mathematics), EDUCATION (elementary), ENGINEERING AND ENVIRONMENTAL DESIGN (environmental science), HEALTH PROFESSIONS (exercise science and veterinary science), SOCIAL SCIENCE (history, international studies, law, philosophy, political science/government, psychobiology, psychology, religion, and sociology). Business and economics, education, and veterinary medical technology, have the largest enrollments and are the strongest academically.

Required: To graduate, students must complete a minimum of 36 courses, with a minimum GPA of 2.0. At least 18 of the 36 courses must be outside any single discipline.

Special: Cross-registration is available with Shippensburg University and Gettysburg College. Wilson offers internships, a Washington semester, student-designed majors, B.A.-B.S. degree in psychology and sociology, credit by exam, pass/fail options, and credit for noncollegiate learning. Students may participate in study-abroad programs sponsored by other colleges. There is a chapter of Phi Beta Kappa and a freshman honors program.

Faculty/Classroom: 47% of faculty are male; 53%, female. All teach undergraduates. The average class size in an introductory lecture is 20; in a laboratory, 14; and in a regular course, 14.

Admissions: 57% of the 2005-2006 applicants were accepted. The SAT scores for the 2005-2006 freshman class were: Verbal--36% below 500, 42% between 500 and 599, 15% between 600 and 700, and 7% above 700; Math--45% below 500, 40% between 500 and 599, and 15% between 600 and 700. The ACT scores were 50% below 21, 10% between 21 and 23, 30% between 24 and 26, and 10% above 28. 21% of the current freshmen were in the top fifth of their class; 43% were in the top two fifths. 1 freshman graduated first in the class.

Requirements: The SAT is required, the ACT is recommended. In addition, applicants should prepare with 4 years each of English and social studies/history, 3 of math, and 2 of science with a lab, and a foreign language. An essay and at least one academic reference are required, and an interview is recommended. Wilson requires applicants to be in the upper 50% of their class. A GPA of 2.5 is required. AP and CLEP credits are accepted. Important factors in the admissions decision are personality/intangible qualities, advanced placement or honor courses, and leadership record.

Procedure: Freshmen are admitted fall and spring. Entrance exams should be taken in the spring of the junior year. There is a deferred admissions and a rolling admissions plan. Application deadlines are open. Application fee is $35. Notification is sent on a rolling basis. Applications are accepted on-line.

Transfer: 22 transfer students enrolled in 2004-2005. Applicants must have a college GPA of at least 2.0. The SAT or ACT may be waived after discussion with the Admissions Office. 14 of 36 credits required for the bachelor's degree must be completed at Wilson.

Visiting: There are regularly scheduled orientations for prospective students, consisting of a campus tour, meetings with faculty, students, or administration, and an interview with an admissions counselor. There are guides for informal visits and visitors may sit in on classes and stay overnight. To schedule a visit, contact the Office of Admissions at (800) 421-8402 or (717) 262-2002 or *admissions@wilson.edu.*

Financial Aid: In 2005-2006, 99% of all full-time students received some form of financial aid. 77% of full-time freshmen and 71% of continuing full-time students received need-based aid. The average freshman award was $15,469. Need-based scholarships or need-based grants averaged $12,411; need-based self-help aid (loans and jobs) averaged $3855; and other non-need-based awards and non-need-based scholarships averaged $11,381. 40% of undergraduates work part time. Average annual earnings from campus work are $1340. The average financial indebtedness of the 2005 graduate was $25,534. The FAFSA and the college's own financial statement are required. The priority date for freshman financial aid applications for fall entry is April 30.

International Students: In a recent year, there were 31 international students enrolled. The school actively recruits these students. Satisfactory scores are required on the TOEFL and the SAT or the ACT. The SAT is recommended.

Computers: Wireless access is available. All residence halls and lounges wire to the network. All students may access the system. There are no time limits and no fees.

Graduates: From July 1, 2004 to June 30, 2005, 95 bachelor's degrees were awarded. The most popular majors were veterinary medical (21%), elementary education (13%), and business economics (10%). In an average class, 58% graduate in 4 years or less, 59% graduate in 5 years or less, and 62% graduate in 6 years or less.

Admissions Contact: Mary Ann Naso, Director of Admissions.
E-mail: *admissions @wilson.edu* Web: *www.wilson.edu*

YORK COLLEGE OF PENNSYLVANIA   D-4

York, PA 17405-7199   **(717) 849-1600**
                                        (800) 455-8018; Fax: (717) 849-1607

Full-time: 1909 men, 2560 women	**Faculty:** 134; IIB, +$
Part-time: 304 men, 632 women	**Ph.D.s:** n/av
Graduate: 125 men, 163 women	**Student/Faculty:** 33 to 1
Year: semesters, summer session	**Tuition:** $10,050
Application Deadline: open	**Room & Board:** $6500
Freshman Class: 4152 applied, 3101 accepted, 1079 enrolled	
SAT Verbal/Math: 544/551*	**ACT:** 23 **VERY COMPETITIVE**

York College of Pennsylvania, founded in 1787, is a private institution offering undergraduate programs in the liberal arts and sciences, as well as professional programs. There is 1 graduate school. In addition to regional accreditation, YCP has baccalaureate program accreditation with ABET, ACBSP, CAAHEP, NLN, and NRPA. The library contains 300,000 volumes, 500,000 microform items, and 11,000 audio/video tapes/CDs/DVDs, and subscribes to 1500 periodicals including electronic. Computerized library services include interlibrary loans and database searching. Special learning facilities include a learning resource center, art gallery, radio station, TV station, telecommunications center, Abraham Lincoln artifacts collection, rare books collection, oral history room, and a nursing education center. The 118-acre campus is in a suburban area 45 miles north of Baltimore. Including any residence halls, there are 30 buildings.

Student Life: 58% of undergraduates are from Pennsylvania. Others are from 30 states, 36 foreign countries, and Canada. 86% are from public schools. 94% are white. 44% are Catholic; 42% Protestant. The average age of freshmen is 19; all undergraduates, 24. 17% do not continue beyond their first year; 62% remain to graduate.

Housing: 2009 students can be accommodated in college housing, which includes single-sex and coed dorms, on-campus apartments, and fraternity houses. On-campus housing is guaranteed for the freshman year only and is available on a first-come, first-served basis. Alcohol is not permitted. All students may keep cars.

Activities: 10% of men belong to 8 national fraternities; 10% of women belong to 6 national sororities. There are 80 groups on campus, including band, cheerleading, chess, choir, chorale, chorus, computers, debate, drama, ethnic, film, forensics, gay, honors, international, jazz band, literary magazine, musical theater, newspaper, orchestra, photography, political, professional, radio and TV, religious, social, social service, student government, and symphony. Popular campus events include Family Weekend, Spring Weekend Festival, and live Sparts Den performers.

Sports: There are 10 intercollegiate sports for men and 10 for women, and 10 intramural sports for men and 10 for women. Facilities include 2 gyms, a track, a swimming pool, a game room, a fitness center, weight training rooms, tennis courts, and soccer, hockey, baseball, softball, and athletic/intramural fields.

Disabled Students: 60% of the campus is accessible. Wheelchair ramps, elevators, special parking, specially equipped rest rooms, special class scheduling, lowered drinking fountains, and lowered telephones are available.

Services: Counseling and information services are available, as is tutoring in most subjects. There is remedial math and writing. There is also an education learning resource center.

Campus Safety and Security: Measures include 24-hour foot and vehicle patrol, self-defense education, security escort services, and shuttle buses. There are informal discussions, pamphlets/posters/films, emergency telephones, lighted pathways/sidewalks, a 24-hour foot patrol, safety seminars, crime prevention speakers, a desk monitor in residence halls, and a personal property engraving program.

Programs of Study: YCP confers B.A. and B.S. degrees. Associate and master's degrees are also awarded. Bachelor's degrees are awarded in BIOLOGICAL SCIENCE (biology/biological science), BUSINESS (accounting, banking and finance, business administration and management, international business management, management science, marketing/retailing/merchandising, and sports management), COMMUNICATIONS AND THE ARTS (broadcasting, communications, English, fine arts, graphic design, music, music technology, Spanish, and speech/debate/rhetoric), COMPUTER AND PHYSICAL SCIENCE (chemistry, computer programming, information sciences and systems, and mathematics), EDUCATION (business, education, elementary, science, secondary, social studies, and special), ENGINEERING AND ENVIRONMENTAL DESIGN (engineering, engineering management, and mechanical engineering), HEALTH PROFESSIONS (medical laboratory technology, nuclear medical technology, nursing, premedicine, and respiratory therapy), SOCIAL SCIENCE (behavioral science, criminal jus-

tice, economics, history, humanities, parks and recreation management, political science/government, prelaw, psychology, and sociology). Electrical and computer engineering, mechanical engineering, and nursing are the strongest academically. Nursing, business administration, and criminal justice are the largest.

Required: To graduate, all students must complete at least 124 credit hours, with 60 to 80 in the major. The required core curriculum consists of English Composition, Writing about Literature, Human Communications, Critical Thinking and Problem Solving in Mathematics, Information Literacy, and physical education. Distribution requirements include 6 credits in fine arts and humanities, 6 in social and behavioral sciences, 6 to 8 in laboratory sciences, 6 in American civilization/government and Western civilization, and 6 in international studies/foreign language. A minimum GPA of 2.0 is required.

Special: YCP offers internships for upper-division students and a co-op program in mechanical engineering. Exchange programs are offered with York St. John College in York, England; Huron University in London, England; Honam University in Kwanju, South Korea; Pontificia Universidad Catolica del Equador in Quito, Equador; and Cemanahuac Educational Community in Cuernavaca, Mexico. Dual majors in any combination, nondegree study, and pass/fail options are available. There are 2 national honor societies and, a freshman honors program.

Faculty/Classroom: 55% of faculty are male; 45%, female. All teach undergraduates. No introductory courses are taught by graduate students. The average class size in an introductory lecture is 30; in a laboratory, 20; and in a regular course, 30.

Admissions: 75% of the 2005-2006 applicants were accepted. 4 freshmen graduated first in their class.

Requirements: The SAT or ACT is required. In addition, applicants must be graduates of an accredited secondary school or have a GED certificate. 15 academic credits are required, including 4 units in English, 3 or 4 in math, 2 or 3 in science, 2 in history, and 1 in social studies. Music students must audition. YCP requires applicants to be in the upper 60% of their class. A GPA of 2.5 is required. AP and CLEP credits are accepted. Important factors in the admissions decision are advanced placement or honor courses, leadership record, and extracurricular activities record.

Procedure: Freshmen are admitted fall and spring. Entrance exams should be taken in the spring of the junior year or the fall of the senior year. There is a deferred admissions and a rolling admissions plan. Application deadlines are open. The application fee is $30. Applications are accepted on-line.

Transfer: 210 transfer students enrolled in 2004-2005. Applicants must have a minimum GPA of 2.0 from a regionally accredited institution. Students with fewer than 30 credit hours must submit a high school transcript. An interview is recommended. 30 of 124 credits required for the bachelor's degree must be completed at YCP.

Visiting: There are regularly scheduled orientations for prospective students, including 2 open houses in October/November; 1 junior open house in April; and 2 spring orientation programs in April/May, featuring a general orientation, academic and support services sessions, and campus tours. There are guides for informal visits and visitors may sit in on classes. To schedule a visit, contact the Admissions Office.

Financial Aid: In 2005-2006, 84% of all full-time freshmen and 76% of continuing full-time students received some form of financial aid. 48% of full-time freshmen and 49% of continuing full-time students received need-based aid. The average freshman award was $7597. Need-based scholarships or need-based grants averaged $3247 ($14,350 maximum); need-based self-help aid (loans and jobs) averaged $2352 ($7225 maximum); and other non-need-based awards and non-need-based scholarships averaged $6270 ($18,890 maximum). 20% of undergraduates work part time. Average annual earnings from campus work are $1500. The average financial indebtedness of the 2005 graduate was $15,621. YCP is a member of CSS. The FAFSA and the college's own financial statement are required. The deadline for filing freshman financial aid applications for fall entry is April 15.

International Students: They must score satisfactorily on the written TOEFL and also take the SAT or the ACT.

Computers: Wireless access is available. There are more than 450 computers available in 6 public labs and 13 special-purpose labs for various disciplines, all using wireless technology. There are 70 wireless access points in the library, public lobbies, and student union for mobile users. All students may access the system. There are no time limits and no fees.

Graduates: In a recent year, 892 bachelor's degrees were awarded. The most popular majors were elementary education (10%), criminal justice (7%), and mass communications (7%). In an average class, 15% graduate in 3 years or less, 42% graduate in 4 years or less, 61% graduate in 5 years or less, and 62% graduate in 6 years or less. 173 companies recruited on campus in 2004-2005. Of the 2004 graduating class, 15% were enrolled in graduate school within 6 months of graduation and 90% were employed.

Admissions Contact: Director of Admissions. A video is available.
E-mail: *admissions@ycp.edu* Web: *http://www.ycp.edu*

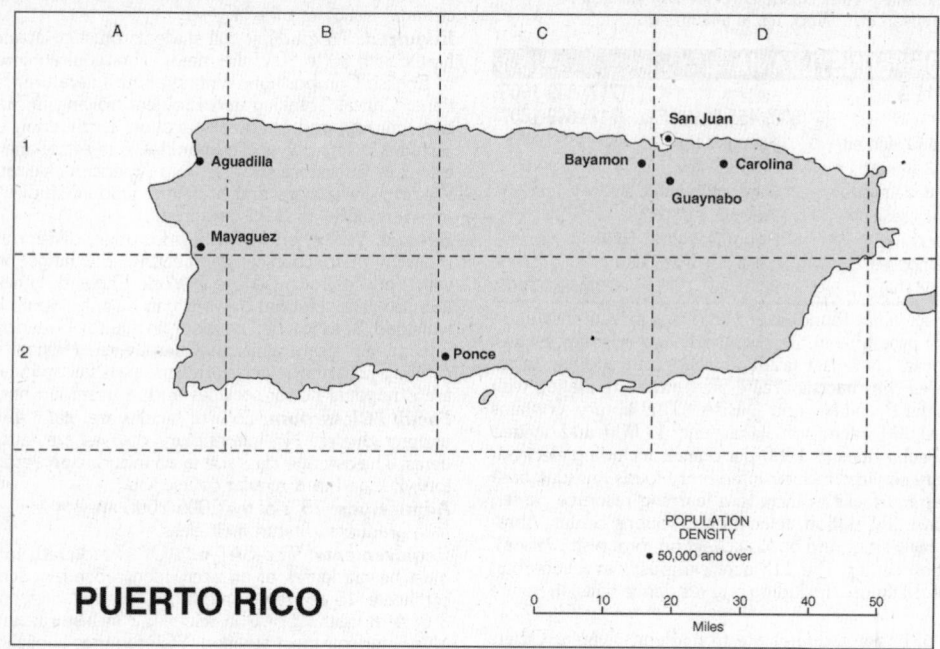

PUERTO RICO

POPULATION
DENSITY
● 50,000 and over

0   10   20   30   40   50
Miles

AMERICAN UNIVERSITY OF PUERTO RICO   C-1
Bayamon, PR 00960-2037   (787) 740-6410; Fax: (787) 785-7377

Full-time: 1190 men, 1860 women	**Faculty:** n/av
Part-time: none	**Ph.D.s:** n/av
Graduate: none	**Student/Faculty:** n/av
Year: semesters, summer session	**Tuition:** $4000
Application Deadline: open	**Room & Board:** n/app
Freshman Class: n/av	
SAT or ACT: required	

American University in Puerto Rico, founded in 1963, is a private non-sectarian institution offering undergraduate programs in business administration, secretarial training, and computer science. There are 4 undergraduate schools. Figures in the above capsule and profile are approximate. The 2 libraries contain 10,000 volumes, 1000 microform items, and 1000 audio/video tapes/CDs/DVDs, and subscribe to 50 periodicals including electronic. Computerized library services include the card catalog, interlibrary loans, and database searching. Special learning facilities include a learning resource center. The 21-acre campus is in an urban area south of San Juan. There are 9 buildings.

Student Life: 99% of undergraduates are from Puerto Rico. 80% are from public schools. All are Hispanic. The average age of freshmen is 18; all undergraduates, 21. 3% do not continue beyond their first year; 97% remain to graduate.

Housing: There are no residence halls. Alcohol is not permitted.

Activities: There are no fraternities or sororities. There are some groups and organizations on campus, including art and photography.

Sports: There are 3 intercollegiate sports for men and 3 for women, and 3 intramural sports for men and 3 for women. Facilities include an indoor basketball and volleyball court, a soccer field, and a pool.

Disabled Students: All of the campus is accessible. Wheelchair ramps, elevators, special parking, specially equipped rest rooms, lowered drinking fountains, and lowered telephones are available.

Services: Counseling and information services are available, as is tutoring in every subject.

Campus Safety and Security: Measures include 24-hour foot and vehicle patrol, self-defense education, security escort services, and shuttle buses. There are informal discussions, pamphlets/posters/films, and lighted pathways/sidewalks.

Programs of Study: American confers B.A. and B.B.A. degrees. Associate degrees are also awarded. Business and communications are the largest.

Required: A GPA of 2.0 is required to graduate.

Special: Work-study programs are available.

Requirements: The SAT or ACT is required. A GPA of 2.0 is required.

Procedure: Freshmen are admitted in the fall. Application deadlines are open.

Visiting: There are guides for informal visits and visitors may sit in on classes. To schedule a visit, contact the school at (787) 798-2040.

Computers: All students may access the system. There are no time limits and no fees.

Admissions Contact: Admissions Office. Web: *www.aupr.edu*

CARIBBEAN UNIVERSITY   C-1
Bayamon, PR 00960-0493   (787) 780-0070, ext. 224

Full-time: 550 men, 1000 women	**Faculty:** n/av
Part-time: 550 men, 1000 women	**Ph.D.s:** n/av
Graduate: none	**Student/Faculty:** n/av
Year: n/av	**Tuition:** $3050
Application Deadline: open	**Room & Board:** n/app
Freshman Class: n/av	
SAT or ACT: not required	

Caribbean University, founded in 1969, is an independent, commuter institution offering undergraduate programs in business, engineering, health science and liberal arts. There are extension centers in Vega Baja, Carolina, and Ponce. Figures given in above capsule and in this profile are approximate. There are 6 undergraduate schools. The library contains 32,620 volumes, 1200 microform items, and 200 audio/video tapes/CDs/DVDs, and subscribes to 210 periodicals including electronic. Computerized library services include interlibrary loans and database searching. Special learning facilities include a learning resource center. The 21-acre campus is in an urban area. There are 8 buildings.

Housing: There are no residence halls. All students commute. Alcohol is not permitted.

Activities: There are 10 groups on campus, including chess, professional, social, and student government.

Sports: Facilities include a gym, basketball and tennis courts, and a track and field arena.

Disabled Students: All of the campus is accessible. Wheelchair ramps, elevators, special parking, and specially equipped rest rooms are available. Special counseling is provided.

Services: Counseling and information services are available, as is tutoring in every subject. There is remedial math, reading, and writing.

Campus Safety and Security: Measures include campus security guards, student ID cards, and regular fire drills.

Programs of Study: Bachelor's degrees are awarded in BIOLOGICAL SCIENCE (biology/biological science), BUSINESS (accounting, banking and finance, business administration and management, marketing/retailing/merchandising, and secretarial studies/office management), COMPUTER AND PHYSICAL SCIENCE (computer programming, computer science, mathematics, and science), EDUCATION (business, elementary, middle school, science, secondary, special, and teaching English as a second/foreign language (TESOL/TEFOL)), ENGINEERING AND ENVIRONMENTAL DESIGN (civil engineering and industrial engineering technology), HEALTH PROFESSIONS (nursing), SOCIAL SCIENCE (criminal justice, social science, and social work).

Requirements: Applicants must be graduates of an accredited secondary school with a GPA of 2.0 or a CEEB score of 4.0. The GED is accepted. High school preparation should include 3 years each of art, English, Spanish, and social studies, 2 years each of history and math, and 1 year of science. A GPA of 2.0 is required.

Procedure: Freshmen are admitted to all sessions. There is a rolling admissions plan. Entrance exams should be taken in the junior or senior year. Application deadlines are open.

Transfer: A minimum college GPA of 2.0 is recommended. Applicants should submit two official transcripts and a catalog from each previous college attended, along with a written recommendation from the dean at the last institution. 30 of 135 credits required for the bachelor's degree must be completed at CU.

Visiting: There are regularly scheduled orientations for prospective students. To schedule a visit, contact the Director of Admissions.

Financial Aid: CU is a member of CSS. The CSS/Profile and income tax returns are required. Check with the school for application deadlines.

Computers: There are no time limits and no fees.

Admissions Contact: Director of Admissions.

CENTRAL UNIVERSITY OF BAYAMON C-1

Bayamon, PR 00960-1725   **(787) 786-3030, ext. 2100**

Full-time: 850 men, 1605 women	Faculty: 61
Part-time: 160 men, 295 women	Ph.D.s: 28%
Graduate: 100 men, 180 women	Student/Faculty: 40 to 1
Year: semesters, summer session	Tuition: $3350
Application Deadline: see profile	Room & Board: n/app
Freshman Class: n/av	
SAT or ACT: not required	

Central University of Bayamon, founded in 1970, is a private Catholic institution offering degree programs primarily to commuter students in the arts and sciences, business, education, nursing, and religious studies. Figures in the above capsule and in this profile are approximate. There are 4 undergraduate and 3 graduate schools. The 2 libraries contain 51,500 volumes and 40 microform items, and subscribe to 370 periodicals including electronic. Computerized library services include the card catalog. The 55-acre campus is in an urban area 4 miles west of Bayamon. There are 13 buildings.

Student Life: 90% are from public schools. All are Hispanic. The average age of freshmen is 17; all undergraduates, 20.

Housing: There are no residence halls. All of students commute. Alcohol is not permitted. All students may keep cars.

Activities: There are no fraternities or sororities. There are 13 groups on campus, including computers, film, literary magazine, photography, professional, radio and TV, religious, social service, and student government.

Sports: There are 10 intercollegiate sports for men and 10 for women. Facilities include a 400-seat gym, basketball and volleyball courts, a swimming pool, and a weight-training room.

Disabled Students: All of the campus is accessible. Wheelchair ramps, elevators, special parking, specially equipped rest rooms, special class scheduling, lowered drinking fountains, and lowered telephones are available.

Services: Counseling and information services are available, as is tutoring in some subjects, including English, Spanish, philosophy, accounting, math, biology, and computer science. There is a reader service for the blind, and remedial math, reading, and writing.

Campus Safety and Security: Measures include 24-hour foot and vehicle patrol.

Programs of Study: UCB confers B.A., B.S., B.B.A., B.S.N., and B.S.S. degrees. Associate and master's degrees are also awarded. Bachelor's degrees are awarded in BIOLOGICAL SCIENCE (biology/biological science), BUSINESS (accounting, business administration and management, and marketing/retailing/merchandising), COMMUNICATIONS AND THE ARTS (journalism and Spanish), COMPUTER AND PHYSICAL SCIENCE (chemistry and computer science), EDUCATION (elementary, English, science, and secondary), HEALTH PROFESSIONS (nursing and premedicine), SOCIAL SCIENCE (philosophy, psychology, religion, social work, and sociology). Business administration is the strongest academically.

Required: Students must complete 48 credits distributed among specific courses in theology, philosophy, Spanish, English, humanities, social science, math, science, and phys ed. The bachelor's degree requires completion of 124 to 141 credits, including 33 to 43 in the major, with a minimum GPA of 2.0.

Special: The university offers limited pass/fail options, work-study programs, and nondegree study.

Faculty/Classroom: All teach undergraduates. The average class size in an introductory lecture is 35; in a laboratory, 20; and in a regular course, 35.

Requirements: The CEEB Spanish test is required. Applicants must be graduates of accredited secondary schools or have earned a GED. They must speak Spanish and have a good knowledge of English. The university requires 15.5 academic credits, including 3 credits each in English, Spanish, math, and science, 1.5 in history, and 1 each in social studies and electives. An interview is recommended. A GPA of 2.0 is required. CLEP credit is accepted. Important factors in the admissions decision are personality/intangible qualities, recommendations by school officials, and ability to finance college education.

Procedure: Freshmen are admitted to all sessions. Entrance exams should be taken by October of the senior year. Check with the school for current application deadlines.

Transfer: A minimum college GPA of 2.0 is required. 30 of 124 credits required for the bachelor's degree must be completed at UCB.

Visiting: There are regularly scheduled orientations for prospective students. There are guides for informal visits and visitors may sit in on classes. To schedule a visit, contact the Admissions Office.

Financial Aid: In a recent year, 94% of all full-time freshmen received some form of financial aid. The college's own financial statement is required. Check with the school for current application deadlines.

Computers: Those students registered with the computer lab may access the mainframe from 9 A.M. to 7 P.M. Monday through Thursday and from 9 A.M. to noon on Friday. Students may access the system 2 hours per week. The fee is $30.

Admissions Contact: Christine M. Hernandez, Dir, Admissions. Web: www.ucb.edu.pr

CONSERVATORY OF MUSIC OF PUERTO RICO D-1

San Juan, PR 00918   **(787) 751-0160; Fax: (787) 758-8258**

Full-time: 110 men, 30 women	Faculty: 30
Part-time: 85 men, 30 women	Ph.D.s: 2%
Graduate: none	Student/Faculty: 5 to 1
Year: semesters	Tuition: $1430
Application Deadline: see profile	Room & Board: n/app
Freshman Class: n/av	
SAT: required	

The Conservatory of Music of Puerto Rico, founded in 1959, is a specialized commuter school supported by the Commonwealth of Puerto Rico, offering 4- and 5-year degree programs. Figures given in above capsule and in this profile are approximate. The library contains 23,608 volumes, 11 microform items, and 5000 audio/video tapes/CDs/DVDs, and subscribes to 2 periodicals including electronic. Special learning facilities include a learning resource center and and a computer-based ear-training lab. The 3-acre campus is in an urban area in the Hato Rey section of San Juan. There are 3 buildings.

Programs of Study: The conservatory confers B.F.A., B.M., and B.Perf.Arts degrees.

Required: To graduate, students must complete 142 credit hours (158 for music education) with a minimum GPA of 2.0. Requirements include 4 years of courses in the principal instrument and specific courses in music theory, including solfege, harmony, and counterpoint. All students must present a graduation recital.

Special: A dual major is available in the principal instrument and music education.

Faculty/Classroom: 70% of faculty are male; 30%, female. All teach undergraduates.

Requirements: The SAT is required, or the CEEB's Spanish version. Applicants must be graduates of an accredited secondary school. An interview and audition are required. A GPA of 2.0 is required. AP credits are accepted. Important factors in the admissions decision are leadership record, parents or siblings attending the school, and ability to finance college education.

Procedure: Freshmen are admitted to all sessions. Entrance exams should be taken in May of the junior year or December of the senior year. There is an early admissions plan. A waiting list is an active part of the admissions procedure. Check with the school for current application deadlines.

Transfer: 100 of 142 credits required for the bachelor's degree must be completed at the conservatory.

Visiting: There are regularly scheduled orientations for prospective students. To schedule a visit, contact Pilar Ruibal, Counselor, or Zulma Palos, Admissions Director.

Financial Aid: The conservatory is a member of CSS. The CSS/Profile is required. Check with the school for current application deadlines.

Computers: There are no time limits and no fees.

Admissions Contact: Zulma Palos-Santini, Admissions Director.

ESCUELA DE ARTES PLASTICAS DE PUERTO RICO D-1

San Juan, PR 00902-1112   (787) 725-8120, ext. 233
                                     Fax: (787) 725-8111

Full-time: 197 men, 171 women   **Faculty:** 12
Part-time: 49 men, 34 women   **Ph.D.s:** 20%
Graduate: none   **Student/Faculty:** 26 to 1
Year: semesters   **Tuition:** $2372
Application Deadline: May 16   **Room & Board:** n/app
Freshman Class: 157 applied, 86 accepted, 86 enrolled
SAT: required

Escuela de Artes Plasticas de Puerto Rico, founded in 1966, is a public institution considered to be the national art school of Puerto Rico. The library contains 12,429 volumes, 10,000 microform items, and 300 audio/video tapes/CDs/DVDs, and subscribes to 40 periodicals including electronic. Computerized library services include the card catalog and Internet access. Special learning facilities include a learning resource center and art gallery. The 1-acre campus is in an urban area in Old San Juan. There are 3 buildings.
Student Life: 61% are from public schools. 100% are Hispanic. The average age of freshmen is 18; all undergraduates, 25. 5% do not continue beyond their first year; 35% remain to graduate.
Housing: There are no residence halls. All students commute. Alcohol is not permitted. No one may keep cars.
Activities: There are no fraternities or sororities. There are 2 groups on campus, art and student government. Popular campus events include Student Day, Health Fair, and Halloween Costume Party.
Sports: There is no sports program at Escuela de Artes Plasticas de Puerto Rico.
Disabled Students: All of the campus is accessible. Wheelchair ramps, elevators, special parking, and special class scheduling are available.
Services: Counseling and information services are available, as is tutoring in some subjects, including all the general studies courses. There is remedial writing.
Campus Safety and Security: Measures include 24-hour foot and vehicle patrol, pamphlets/posters/films, and safety training.
Programs of Study: Escuela de Artes Plasticas de Puerto Rico confers the B.A. degree. Bachelor's degrees are awarded in COMMUNICATIONS AND THE ARTS (graphic design, industrial design, painting, and sculpture), EDUCATION (art), ENGINEERING AND ENVIRONMENTAL DESIGN (computer graphics). Computer graphics is the largest.
Required: To graduate, students must maintain a minimum GPA of 2.0 in 132 credits, including 36 in art fundamentals and 48 in general education courses.
Special: Accelerated degree programs are offered.
Faculty/Classroom: 56% of faculty are male; 44%, female. All teach undergraduates. The average class size in an introductory lecture is 25 and in a laboratory, 18.
Admissions: 55% of the 2005-2006 applicants were accepted.
Requirements: The SAT, or the CEEB Spanish equivalent of the SAT is required. Applicants must be graduates of an accredited secondary school or have earned a GED. A portfolio and interview are required, with an essay recommended. A GPA of 2.0 is required. Important factors in the admissions decision are evidence of special talent, recommendations by school officials, and personality/intangible qualities.
Procedure: Freshmen are admitted in the fall. There is a rolling admission plan. Applications should be filed by May 16 for fall entry, along with a $20 fee. Notification is sent on a rolling basis.
Transfer: 22 transfer students enrolled in a recent year. Admission requirements are the same as for first-year applicants.
Visiting: There are regularly scheduled orientations for prospective students. There are guides for informal visits. To schedule a visit, contact the Student Affairs Office.
Financial Aid: In a recent year, 56% of all full-time freshmen and 73% of continuing full-time students received some form of financial aid. 33% of full-time freshmen and 52% of continuing full-time students received need-based aid. The average freshman award was $3250. 12% of undergraduates work part time. Average annual earnings from campus work are $1300. Escuela de Artes Plasticas de Puerto Rico is a member of CSS. The FAFSA is required.
International Students: The school actively recruits these students. A satisfactory score is required on the SAT or or the CEEB Spanish equivalent of the SAT.
Computers: All students may access the system Monday through Saturday from 8:00 A.M. to 5:30 P.M. Students may access the system 1 hour. There are no fees.
Graduates: In a recent year, 47 bachelor's degrees were awarded. The most popular majors were graphic design (47%), painting (27%), and art education (10%). In an average class, 6% graduate in 3 years or less, 17% graduate in 4 years or less, 38% graduate in 5 years or less, and 39% graduate in 6 years or less. 4 companies recruited on campus in 2004-2005. Of the 2004 graduating class, 14% were enrolled in graduate school within 6 months of graduation and 57% were employed.

Admissions Contact: Juan Negroni, Recruiting Officer. A video is available. E-mail: *planificacioneap@yahoo.com* Web: *www.eap.edu.pr*

INTER AMERICAN UNIVERSITY OF PUERTO RICO/AGUADILLA CAMPUS A-1

Aguadilla, PR 00605   (787) 891-0925; Fax: (787) 882-3020
Full-time: 1453 men, 2026 women   **Faculty:** 75
Part-time: 244 men, 363 women   **Ph.D.s:** 24%
Graduate: 26 men, 44 women   **Student/Faculty:** 46 to 1
Year: semesters, summer session   **Tuition:** $3784
Application Deadline: May 1   **Room & Board:** n/app
Freshman Class: 1568 applied, 1065 accepted, 978 enrolled
SAT: required

Inter American University of Puerto Rico/Aguadilla Campus, a private, nonsectarian institution, was founded in 1957 and is a part of the Inter American University of Puerto Rico. Programs offered include business, fine and liberal arts, health sciences, and teacher and professional preparation. The library contains 58,702 volumes, 2628 microform items, and 24,870 audio/video tapes/CDs/DVDs, and subscribes to 270 periodicals including electronic. Computerized library services include the card catalog, interlibrary loans, database searching, and Internet access. Special learning facilities include a learning resource center, a radio station, a multimedia center, an instructional development center, and an electronic classroom. The 54-acre campus is in a suburban area in northwestern Puerto Rico, near the Atlantic Ocean. There are 6 buildings.
Student Life: 99% of undergraduates are from Puerto Rico. 96% are from public schools. 100% are Hispanic. 70% are Catholic; 30% Protestant. The average age of freshmen is 20; all undergraduates, 24. 20% do not continue beyond their first year.
Housing: There are no residence halls. Alcohol is not permitted. All students may keep cars.
Activities: There are no fraternities or sororities. There are 22 groups on campus, including academics, chess, choir, computers, cultural, debate, drama, film, honors, newspaper, professional, religious, social, social service, and student government. Popular campus events include Flora and Fauna Festival and Achievement Night.
Sports: There are 11 intercollegiate sports for men and 9 for women, and 8 intramural sports for men and 8 for women. Facilities include a 2000-person-capacity multiuse coliseum with basketball and volleyball courts and a small indoor track. There is also a gym with exercise equipment and an area with 3 platforms for weight-lifting. The recreation facility has table tennis and table and video arcade games.
Disabled Students: Wheelchair ramps, elevators, special parking, lowered drinking fountains, and lowered telephones are available.
Services: Counseling and information services are available, as is tutoring in some subjects, including Spanish, math, English, and accounting. There is a reader service for the blind. There is a computerized center for skills development, and there are language and math labs.
Campus Safety and Security: Measures include 24-hour foot and vehicle patrol, pamphlets/posters/films, and lighted pathways/sidewalks.
Programs of Study: Inter confers B.A., B.S., B.B.A., and B.S.N. degrees. Associate and master's degrees are also awarded. Bachelor's degrees are awarded in BIOLOGICAL SCIENCE (biology/biological science and microbiology), BUSINESS (accounting, business administration and management, management information systems, marketing/retailing/merchandising, recreational facilities management, and secretarial studies/office management), COMPUTER AND PHYSICAL SCIENCE (computer science), EDUCATION (early childhood, elementary, and secondary), ENGINEERING AND ENVIRONMENTAL DESIGN (electrical/electronics engineering technology), HEALTH PROFESSIONS (mental health/human services and nursing), SOCIAL SCIENCE (criminal justice). Human psychosocial services, criminal justice, and education are the strongest academically. Human psychosocial services, criminal justice, and elementary education are the largest.
Required: To graduate, students must fulfill 44 to 47 general education credits depending on the major and including 23 credits in basic skills, 9 in historical and social context, 6 in philosophical and esthetic thought, and 3 each in Christian thought and science and technological context. A total of 120 credit hours is required; the number required in the major varies. A 2.0 GPA overall and in the major is required.
Special: The university offers internships in and out of Puerto Rico, work-study, and adult and continuing education programs,. There is a freshman honors program.
Faculty/Classroom: 48% of faculty are male; 52%, female. 86% teach undergraduates. The average class size in an introductory lecture is 30; in a laboratory, 25; and in a regular course, 28.
Admissions: 68% of the 2005-2006 applicants were accepted.
Requirements: The SAT is required. In addition, native Spanish speakers may take the Spanish version of the SAT. Applicants must be graduates of an accredited secondary school. An interview may be required. A GPA of 2.0 is required. AP and CLEP credits are accepted.
Procedure: Freshmen are admitted to all sessions. There are early admissions and rolling admissions plans. Applications should be filed by

May 1 for fall entry, November 15 for winter entry, and April 15 for summer entry. Notification is sent on a rolling basis. Applications are accepted on-line.

Transfer: 81 transfer students enrolled in 2004-2005. Transfer applicants must submit all college transcripts and must be in good standing at their previous institution. A minimum of 15 transferable credits with a grade of at least C must have been completed.

Visiting: There are regularly scheduled orientations for prospective students.

Financial Aid: In 2005-2006, 92% of all full-time freshmen and 94% of continuing full-time students received some form of financial aid. 90% of full-time freshmen and 94% of continuing full-time students received need-based aid. The average freshman award was $7625. Need-based scholarships or need-based grants averaged $400 ($600 maximum); need-based self-help aid (loans and jobs) averaged $1000 ($3625 maximum); and other non-need-based awards and non-need-based scholarships averaged $780 ($2000 maximum). 32% of undergraduates work part time. Average annual earnings from campus work are $800. Inter is a member of CSS. The FAFSA and the college's own financial statement are required. The deadline for filing freshman financial aid applications for fall entry is April 28.

International Students: A personal interview is required, as are satisfactory scores on an appropriate comprehensive exam.

Computers: Wireless access is available. Open-wireless, network use, and access to the Internet are available to all students. All students may access the system for distance learning, Web browsing, e-mail, and library searches. There are no time limits and no fees.

Graduates: From July 1, 2004 to June 30, 2005, 350 bachelor's degrees were awarded. The most popular majors were elementary teacher education (20%), criminal justice (12%), and human psychosocial services (10%).

Admissions Contact: Doris Perez, Director of Admissions.
Web: www.interaguadilla.edu

INTER AMERICAN UNIVERSITY OF PUERTO RICO/ARECIBO CAMPUS
B-1

Arecibo, PR 00614-4050   (787) 878-5195; Fax: (787) 880-1624

Full-time: 1105 men, 2205 women	**Faculty:** 82
Part-time: 275 men, 550 women	**Ph.D.s:** 21%
Graduate: 5 men, 10 women	**Student/Faculty:** 40 to 1
Year: semesters, summer session	**Tuition:** $3350
Application Deadline: see profile	**Room & Board:** n/app
Freshman Class: n/av	
SAT or ACT: n/av	

Inter-American Arecibo, founded in 1957, is a private, nonsectarian unit of the Inter-American University of Puerto Rico system. It offers programs in business, health sciences, liberal arts, and teacher preparation. Figures given in above capsule and in this profile are approximate. The library contains 74,991 volumes, 82 microform items, and 28,665 audio/video tapes/CDs/DVDs, and subscribes to 739 periodicals including electronic. Computerized library services include interlibrary loans and database searching. Special learning facilities include a learning resource center and a library exhibition area. The 20-acre campus is in a suburban area 50 miles west of San Juan. There are 9 buildings.

Student Life: 99% of undergraduates are from Puerto Rico. Students are from 1 state. 93% are from public schools. All are Hispanic. The average age of freshmen is 18; all undergraduates, 24. 11% do not continue beyond their first year.

Housing: There are no residence halls. All of students commute. Alcohol is not permitted. All students may keep cars.

Activities: There are 2 local fraternities and 1 local sorority. There are 12 groups on campus, including drama, film, honors, newspaper, professional, religious, social, and student government. Popular campus events include Open House, Talent Festival, and sports events.

Sports: There are 7 intercollegiate sports for men and 7 for women, and 10 intramural sports for men and 10 for women. Facilities include a tennis court, a basketball court, and a student center with Ping-Pong tables and weight-lifting equipment.

Disabled Students: Wheelchair ramps, elevators, special parking, specially equipped rest rooms, lowered drinking fountains, and lowered telephones are available.

Services: Counseling and information services are available, as is tutoring in some subjects, including accounting, secretarial sciences, math, Spanish, English, and computer sciences. There is a reader service for the blind and remedial math.

Campus Safety and Security: Measures include 24-hour foot and vehicle patrol, pamphlets/posters/films, and lighted pathways/sidewalks.

Programs of Study: Inter-American Arecibo confers B.A. and B.S. degrees. Associate and master's degrees are also awarded. Bachelor's degrees are awarded in BIOLOGICAL SCIENCE (biology/biological science and microbiology), BUSINESS (accounting, business administration and management, and marketing and distribution),

COMPUTER AND PHYSICAL SCIENCE (chemical technology, chemistry, and computer science), EDUCATION (elementary, secondary, special, and teaching English as a second/foreign language (TESOL/TEFOL)), HEALTH PROFESSIONS (nursing), SOCIAL SCIENCE (criminal justice and social work). Biology, criminal justice, and business administration are the strongest academically. Business administration is the largest.

Required: To graduate, all students must complete at least 130 credits with a GPA of 2.0. General education requirements include 55 credits in Spanish, English, math, logic, computers, Puerto Rican history, humanities, health, social studies, environment, and religion. Noncredit courses are required in phys ed and orientation.

Special: The university offers 3-2 programs with Pennsylvania State University in engineering and earth and mineral sciences, and with Universidad Catolica Madre y Maestra of the Dominican Republic in medicine. Independent research, work-study, and independent study programs are available. Professional certificate programs are offered in nurse anesthetist and intensive nursing care. There is a freshman honors program.

Faculty/Classroom: 45% of faculty are male; 55%, female. All teach undergraduates. The average class size in an introductory lecture is 27 and in a laboratory, 25.

Requirements: Applicants must present satisfactory scores on the aptitude and English tests of the CEEB. Students whose first language is English may take the SAT. In addition, applicants should be graduates of an accredited high school. The GED is accepted. Secondary school preparation should include 15 to 30 academic credits. Some applicants may be required to schedule an interview. A GPA of 2.0 is required. Important factors in the admissions decision are advanced placement or honor courses, evidence of special talent, and leadership record.

Procedure: Freshmen are admitted to all sessions. Entrance exams should be taken in October or February of the senior year. There are early decision and rolling admissions plans. Notification is sent on a rolling basis. Check with the school for current application deadlines.

Transfer: Applicants should present a C average in at least 15 college credits. Those with fewer transferable credits must meet freshman entrance requirements.

Visiting: There are regularly scheduled orientations for prospective students. There are guides for informal visits. To schedule a visit, contact the Admissions Office.

Financial Aid: Inter-American Arecibo is a member of CSS. The CSS/Profile and the college's own financial statement are required. Check with the school for current application deadlines.

International Students: They must take the TOEFL and also take the SAT.

Computers: All students may access the system. There are no time limits and no fees. It is strongly recommended that all students have a personal computer.

Admissions Contact: Provi Montalvo, Director of Admissions.
Web: www.arecibo.inter.edu

INTER AMERICAN UNIVERSITY OF PUERTO RICO/BARRANQUITAS REGIONAL COLLEGE
C-2

Barranquitas, PR 00794   (787) 857-3600

Full-time: 305 men, 835 women	**Faculty:** 40
Part-time: 155 men, 425 women	**Ph.D.s:** 1%
Graduate: none	**Student/Faculty:** 28 to 1
Year: semesters, summer session	**Tuition:** $3350
Application Deadline: see profile	**Room & Board:** n/app
Freshman Class: n/av	
SAT or ACT: required	

Inter-American University of Puerto Rico/Barranquitas Regional College, founded in 1957 and part of the Inter-American University system, is a private college whose primary focus is teacher education. Figures given in the above capsule and in this profile are approximate. There are 6 undergraduate schools. The library contains 32,275 volumes, 23,657 microform items, and 926 audio/video tapes/CDs/DVDs, and subscribes to 223 periodicals including electronic. Computerized library services include the card catalog and interlibrary loans. Special learning facilities include a learning resource center. The 36-acre campus is in a small town. There are 5 buildings.

Student Life: Students are from 1 state and 1 foreign country. 99% of undergraduates are from Puerto Rico. All are Hispanic. The average age of freshmen is 18; all undergraduates, 22. 4% do not continue beyond their first year; 96% remain to graduate.

Housing: There are no residence halls. All of students commute. Alcohol is not permitted. All students may keep cars.

Activities: There are no fraternities or sororities. There are 9 groups on campus, including chorus, dance, honors, religious, social, and student government. Popular campus events include Competencias LAI y LIDE, Health Fair, and Open House.

Sports: There are 8 intercollegiate sports for men and 7 for women, and 7 intramural sports for men and 6 for women. Facilities include a

student center, a gym, volleyball and basketball courts, and a softball park.

Disabled Students: 1% of the campus is accessible. Wheelchair ramps and special parking are available.

Services: Counseling and information services are available, as is tutoring in some subjects, including Spanish, English, and math. There is a reader service for the blind, and remedial math, reading, and writing.

Campus Safety and Security: Measures include 24-hour foot and vehicle patrol, pamphlets/posters/films, emergency telephones, and lighted pathways/sidewalks.

Programs of Study: Inter-American at Barranquitas confers B.A. and B.B.A. degrees. Associate degrees are also awarded. Bachelor's degrees are awarded in BUSINESS (accounting, business administration and management and secretarial studies/office management), EDUCATION (early childhood, elementary and secondary), SOCIAL SCIENCE (criminal justice). Education, business administration and secretarial studies are the strongest academically.

Required: In order to graduate, students must complete 120 to 132 credit hours with a minimum GPA of 2.0.

Special: Internships are available in education, secretarial studies, and criminal justice. There is 1 national honor society.

Requirements: The SAT or ACT is required. SAT: Subject tests are also required. A GPA of 2.0 is required. AP credits are accepted. Important factors in the admissions decision are evidence of special talent, advanced placement or honor courses, and leadership record.

Procedure: Freshmen are admitted fall, winter, and summer. Entrance exams should be taken in October, February, or June. There are early admissions and rolling admissions plans. Notification is sent on a rolling basis. Check with the school for current application deadlines.

Transfer: Transfer applicants must submit a university transcript, dean's recommendation, and financial aid transcript. 36 of 120 credits required for the bachelor's degree must be completed at Inter-American at Barranquitas.

Visiting: There are regularly scheduled orientations for prospective students. There are guides for informal visits. To schedule a visit, contact the Admissions Director.

Financial Aid: Inter-American at Barranquitas is a member of CSS.

International Students: They must take the college's own test and also take SAT: Subject tests.

Computers: There are no time limits and no fees.

Admissions Contact: Maribel Diaz Pena, Director of Admissions.

INTER AMERICAN UNIVERSITY OF PUERTO RICO/BAYAMON UNIVERSITY COLLEGE C-1

Bayamon, PR 00957	**(787) 279-1912, ext. 2017**
	Fax: (787) 279-2205
Full-time: 2300 men, 1900 women	**Faculty:** 95
Part-time: 500 men, 390 women	**Ph.Ds:** 27%
Graduate: none	**Student/Faculty:** 44 to 1
Year: trimesters, summer session	**Tuition:** $3522
Application Deadline: May 1	**Room & Board:** n/app
Freshman Class: 3944 applied, 1347 accepted, 1239 enrolled	
SAT or ACT: required	

Inter American University of Puerto Rico/Bayamon University College, a private, nonsectarian institution founded in 1912, is part of the Inter American University of Puerto Rico. Students may pursue undergraduate and graduate study in business, health sciences, liberal and fine arts, and teacher preparation. There are 3 undergraduate schools. Figures in the above capsule and in this profile are approximate. In addition to regional accreditation, Inter American at Bayamon has baccalaureate program accreditation with CSWE. Computerized library services include the card catalog. Special learning facilities include an audiovisual center, an instructional development center, and a publication center. The campus is in an urban area in a medium-size city.

Student Life: 67% are from public schools. The average age of freshmen is 19; all undergraduates, 21.

Activities: There are many groups and organizations on campus, including band, cheerleading, chess, choir, computers, dance, debate, drama, ethnic, film, honors, international, newspaper, photography, professional, radio and TV, religious, social service, and student government.

Sports: There are 10 intercollegiate sports for men and 10 for women, and 10 intramural sports for men and 10 for women.

Disabled Students: Wheelchair ramps, elevators, special parking, lowered drinking fountains, and lowered telephones are available.

Campus Safety and Security: Measures include 24-hour foot and vehicle patrol, security escort services, informal discussions, and pamphlets/posters/films. There are lighted pathways/sidewalks.

Programs of Study: Inter American at Bayamon confers B.A., B.S., and B.B.A. degrees. Associate degrees are also awarded. Bachelor's degrees are awarded in BIOLOGICAL SCIENCE (bioinformatics, biology/biological science, and biotechnology), BUSINESS (accounting, banking and finance, business administration and management, business eco-

nomics, human resources, logistics, management information systems, marketing/retailing/merchandising, office supervision and management, and secretarial studies/office management), COMMUNICATIONS AND THE ARTS (communications technology, and visual and performing arts), COMPUTER AND PHYSICAL SCIENCE (chemical technology, chemistry, computer science, and mathematics), ENGINEERING AND ENVIRONMENTAL DESIGN (aeronautical science, aeronautical technology, aviation administration/management, aviation computer technology, computer technology, electrical/electronics engineering, electrical/electronics engineering technology, environmental engineering technology, food services technology, industrial administration/management, industrial engineering, and mechanical engineering), SOCIAL SCIENCE (forensic studies). Business administration is the largest.

Required: To graduate, students must earn a minimum of 110 academic credits, with a minimum GPA of 2.0 overall and in the major.

Faculty/Classroom: 60% of faculty are male; 40%, female. All teach undergraduates. The average class size in an introductory lecture is 19 and in a regular course, 23.

Admissions: 34% of the 2005-2006 applicants were accepted.

Requirements: The SAT is required. In addition, or its Spanish equivalent is required, along with the SAT II: Writing test. Applicants must be graduates of an accredited secondary school or its equivalent. A GPA of 2.0 is required.

Procedure: There is an early admissions plan. Applications should be filed by May 1 for fall entry, November 15 for winter entry, February 15 for spring entry, and April 15 for summer entry. Applications are accepted on-line.

Transfer: 132 transfer students enrolled in 2004-2005.

Financial Aid: The FAFSA and the college's own financial statement are required.

International Students: There are 5 international students enrolled. A personal interview is required, as is satisfactory completion of an appropriate comprehensive exam.

Computers: There are no time limits and no fees.

Graduates: From July 1, 2004 to June 30, 2005, 529 bachelor's degrees were awarded. The most popular majors were accounting (10%), management (10%), and human resources management (10%).

Admissions Contact: Carlos Alicea, Director of Admissions.
E-mail: *calicea@bc.inter.edu* Web: *www.bc.inter.edu*

INTER AMERICAN UNIVERSITY OF PUERTO RICO/FAJARDO CAMPUS D-1

Fajardo, PR 00738-7003	**(787) 860-3100, ext. 2210**
	Fax: (787) 860-3470
Full-time: 570 men, 1170 women	**Faculty:** 37
Part-time: 170 men, 350 women	**Ph.Ds:** 9%
Graduate: none	**Student/Faculty:** 47 to 1
Year: 4-1-4, summer session	**Tuition:** $4000
Application Deadline: August 15	**Room & Board:** n/app
Freshman Class: 1381 applied, 727 accepted, 507 enrolled	
SAT or ACT: required	

Inter American University of Puerto Rico/Fajardo Campus, founded in 1912 and a unit of the Inter American University of Puerto Rico, is a private, nonsectarian college offering undergraduate and graduate degrees in business, fine and liberal arts, health sciences, and teacher preparation. Figures in the above capsule and in this profile are approximate. In addition to regional accreditation, Inter at Fajardo has baccalaureate program accreditation with CSWE. The library contains 39,968 volumes and 1822 audio/video tapes/CDs/DVDs. Computerized library services include the card catalog. Special learning facilities include an audiovisual center, a publication center, and an instructional development center. The 11-acre campus is in an urban area in a small city. There are 10 buildings.

Student Life: 90% are from public schools. The average age of freshmen is 18.

Housing: There are no residence halls. Alcohol is not permitted.

Activities: There are no fraternities or sororities. There are some groups and organizations on campus, including chorale, professional, religious, and social.

Sports: There are 3 intercollegiate sports for men and 2 for women, and 4 intramural sports for men and 3 for women. Facilities include a multipurpose building.

Disabled Students: Wheelchair ramps, elevators, special parking, and specially equipped rest rooms are available.

Services: There is remedial math and reading.

Campus Safety and Security: Measures include pamphlets/posters/films.

Programs of Study: Inter at Fajardo confers B.A., B.S., and B.B.A. degrees. Associate, master's, and doctoral degrees are also awarded. Bachelor's degrees are awarded in BIOLOGICAL SCIENCE (biology/biological science), BUSINESS (accounting, banking and finance, business administration and management, insurance, management information systems, marketing/retailing/merchandising, and secretarial studies/office management), COMMUNICATIONS AND THE ARTS (applied music, Spanish, and visual and performing arts), COMPUTER AND PHYSICAL SCIENCE (chemical technology, chemistry, computer science, and mathematics), EDUCATION (early childhood, elementary, music, secondary, and special), ENGINEERING AND ENVIRONMENTAL DESIGN (electrical/electronics engineering technology), HEALTH PROFESSIONS (medical technology and nursing), SOCIAL SCIENCE (criminal justice, history, political science/government, psychology, public administration, social work, and sociology).

Required: To graduate, all students must complete 120 credit hours with a minimum GPA of 2.0 overall and in the major. General education requirements total 59 credits, including 18 credits in communication skills, 12 in historical-cultural heritage, 11 in ability to integrate, apply, and create, 8 in reasoning skills, 6 in methods of interpreting reality, and 2 nonacademic credits each in Introduction to University Life and health, phys ed, or recreation.

Special: Co-op programs in engineering and earth and mineral sciences with Pennsylvania State University, cross-registration, internships, work-study, and adult and continuing education programs are available. There is a freshman honors program.

Faculty/Classroom: 42% of faculty are male; 58%, female. The average class size in an introductory lecture is 25; in a laboratory, 20; and in a regular course, 25.

Requirements: Satisfacory scores are required on the SAT or the ACT and the SAT: Writing test. Native Spanish-speaking students may take the CEEB Spanish version of the SAT. Students must have graduated from an accredited secondary school. An interview may be required. A GPA of 2.0 is required. AP credits are accepted.

Procedure: Freshmen are admitted to all sessions. There is an early admissions plan. Check with the school for current deadlines and fee.

Transfer: Applicants must have completed at least 15 transferable semester credits with a minimum grade of C and must be in good standing at their previous institution. All college transcripts must be submitted.

Financial Aid: In a recent year, 98% of all full-time freshmen received some form of financial aid. Need-based scholarships or need-based grants averaged $3600. Average annual earnings from campus work are $400. The FAFSA and the college's own financial statement are required. Check with the school for current deadlines.

International Students: A personal interview and satisfactory scores on an appropriate comprehensive exam are required.

Computers: All students may access the system. There are no time limits and no fees.

Graduates: From July 1, 2004 to June 30, 2005, 204 bachelor's degrees were awarded. The most popular majors were business administration (77%), education (19%), and science and technology (4%).

Admissions Contact: Ada Caraballo, Admissions Director.
E-mail: *adcaraba@inter.edu* Web: *www.inter.edu*

INTER AMERICAN UNIVERSITY OF PUERTO RICO/METROPOLITAN CAMPUS
D-1

San Juan, PR 00919-1293   (787) 765-1270; Fax: (787) 764-6963

Full-time: 2110 men, 2730 women	**Faculty:** 159
Part-time: 965 men, 2790 women	**Ph.D.s:** 52%
Graduate: 1120 men, 2320 women	**Student/Faculty:** 30 to 1
Year: trimesters, summer session	**Tuition:** $4320
Application Deadline: see profile	**Room & Board:** n/app
Freshman Class: n/av	
SAT: recommended	

Inter American University of Puerto Rico/Metropolitan Campus, a private, nonsectarian institution founded in 1912, is a unit of the Inter American University of Puerto Rico. Students may pursue undergraduate and graduate study in business, fine and liberal arts, health sciences, and teacher preparation. There are 6 undergraduate and 2 graduate schools. Figures in the above capsule and in this profile are approximate. In addition to regional accreditation, Inter American Metro has baccalaureate program accreditation with ACS, CSWE, NAACLS, and NLN. The library contains 112,018 volumes, 638,026 microform items, and 1350 audio/video tapes/CDs/DVDs, and subscribes to 2798 periodicals including electronic. Computerized library services include the card catalog, interlibrary loans, database searching, and Internet access. Special learning facilities include a learning resource center, art gallery, an audiovisual center, an instructional development center, and a publication center. The 20-acre campus is in an urban area 9 miles from San Juan. There are 13 buildings.

Student Life: 99% of undergraduates are from Puerto Rico. 59% are from public schools. 98% are Hispanic. The average age of freshmen is 18; all undergraduates, 18.

Housing: 100% of students commute. Alcohol is not permitted. All students may keep cars.

Activities: There are no fraternities or sororities. There are 23 groups on campus, including art, cheerleading, chorus, debate, drama, interna-

tional, jazz band, orchestra, professional, religious, student government, symphony, and yearbook.

Sports: There are 7 intercollegiate sports for men and 7 for women, and 7 intramural sports for men and 7 for women.

Disabled Students: 90% of the campus is accessible. Wheelchair ramps, elevators, special parking, lowered drinking fountains, and lowered telephones are available.

Services: Counseling and information services are available, as is tutoring in some subjects, including Spanish, English, and math. There is a reader service for the blind. There also are interpreters for the hearing impaired.

Campus Safety and Security: Measures include 24-hour foot and vehicle patrol and pamphlets/posters/films.

Programs of Study: Inter American Metro confers B.A., B.S., and B.B.A. degrees. Associate, master's, and doctoral degrees are also awarded. Bachelor's degrees are awarded in BIOLOGICAL SCIENCE (biology/biological science), BUSINESS (accounting, banking and finance, business administration and management, management information systems, marketing/retailing/merchandising, and secretarial studies/office management), COMMUNICATIONS AND THE ARTS (music performance and Spanish), COMPUTER AND PHYSICAL SCIENCE (chemistry, computer science, and mathematics), EDUCATION (early childhood, elementary, secondary, and special), HEALTH PROFESSIONS (medical technology and nursing), SOCIAL SCIENCE (criminal justice, history, political science/government, psychology, social work, and sociology). Chemistry is the strongest academically.

Required: To graduate, students must complete 47 general education credits: 23 credits in basic skills, 9 credits in philosophical and esthetic thought, 9 in the historical process of Puerto Rico, 3 in scientific and technological context, and 3 in well-being and quality of life. A total of 120 credit hours must be completed; the number in the major varies. A minimum 2.0 GPA overall and in the major is required.

Special: Cross-registration, internship and work-study programs, and adult education programs are available. There is 1 national honor society and a freshman honors program.

Faculty/Classroom: 49% of faculty are male; 51%, female. 65% teach undergraduates and 5% both teach and do research. The average class size in an introductory lecture is 20 and in a laboratory, 22.

Requirements: The SAT is recommended. In addition, students whose first language is Spanish may take the CEEB Spanish version of the SAT. A GPA of 2.0 is required.

Procedure: Freshmen are admitted to all sessions. Entrance exams should be taken by October. Check with the school for current deadlines and fee. Applications are accepted on-line.

Transfer: Applicants must have completed at least 12 transferable semester credits with a minimum grade of C and be in good standing at the previous institution. 40 of 120 credits required for the bachelor's degree must be completed at Inter American Metro.

Visiting: There are regularly scheduled orientations for prospective students, including an open house twice a year. To schedule a visit, contact Edwin Mendez, Recruiter at (787) 250-1912, ext. 2102, 2463 or *edmendez@inter.edu*.

Financial Aid: In a recent year, 80% of all full-time freshmen and 82% of continuing full-time students received some form of financial aid. 79% of full-time freshmen and 81% of continuing full-time students received need-based aid. The FAFSA and the college's own financial statement are required. Check with the school for current deadlines.

International Students: A personal interview is required, as are satisfactory scores on an appropriate comprehensive exam.

Computers: All students may access the system Monday through Saturday. It is recommended that students in It is recommended that students in Economics and Administrative Sciences, Science and Technology, and distance education have personal computers.

Admissions Contact: Lisette Rivera-Ortiz, Director of Admissions. A video is available. E-mail: *lisriver@inter.edu* Web: *metro.inter.edu*

INTER AMERICAN UNIVERSITY OF PUERTO RICO/PONCE REGIONAL COLLEGE
C-2

Ponce, PR 00715-2201   (787) 840-9090; Fax: (787) 841-0103

Full-time: none	**Faculty:** n/av
Part-time: none	**Ph.D.s:** n/av
Graduate: none	**Student/Faculty:** n/av
Year: n/app	**Tuition:** $3700
Application Deadline: see profile	**Room & Board:** n/app
Freshman Class: n/av	
SAT or ACT: n/av	

Inter-American University of Puerto Rico/Ponce Regional College, founded in 1912 and a unit of the Inter-American University of Puerto Rico, is a private, nonsectarian institution offering undergraduate and graduate programs in business, liberal and fine arts, health sciences, and teacher preparation. Figures given in the above capsule and in this profile are approximate. In addition to regional accreditation, Inter-

American at Ponce has baccalaureate program accreditation with CSWE. Computerized library services include the card catalog. Special learning facilities include an audiovisual center, an instructional development center, and a publication center. The campus is in an urban area in a medium-size city.

Programs of Study: Bachelor's degrees are awarded in BIOLOGICAL SCIENCE (biology/biological science), BUSINESS (accounting, banking and finance, business administration and management, insurance, management information systems, marketing/retailing/merchandising, and secretarial studies/office management), COMMUNICATIONS AND THE ARTS (applied music, Spanish, and visual and performing arts), COMPUTER AND PHYSICAL SCIENCE (chemical technology, chemistry, computer science, and mathematics), EDUCATION (early childhood, elementary, music, secondary, and special), ENGINEERING AND ENVIRONMENTAL DESIGN (electrical/electronics engineering technology), HEALTH PROFESSIONS (medical technology and nursing), SOCIAL SCIENCE (criminal justice, history, political science/government, psychology, public administration, social work, and sociology).

Financial Aid: The FAFSA and the college's own financial statement are required. Check with the school for current deadlines.

International Students: A personal interview is required, as are satisfactory scores on an appropriate comprehensive exam.

Computers: There are no time limits and no fees.

Admissions Contact: Director of Admissions.

INTER AMERICAN UNIVERSITY OF PUERTO RICO/SAN GERMAN

B-2

San German, PR 00683-9801

(787) 892-3090
(800) 981-8075; Fax: (787) 892-6350

Full-time: 3880 men and women	**Faculty:** 116
Part-time: 1210 men and women	**Ph.D.s:** 43%
Graduate: 950 men and women	**Student/Faculty:** 33 to 1
Year: semesters, summer session	**Tuition:** $4316
Application Deadline: see profile	**Room & Board:** $2400
Freshman Class: n/av	
SAT: required	

Inter-American University of Puerto Rico/San German, founded in 1912, is a private institution that is part of the Inter-American University of Puerto Rico system. It offers programs in fine and liberal arts, business, health science, and teacher preparation. Figures in the above capsule and in this profile are approximate. In addition to regional accreditation, the university has baccalaureate program accreditation with CAHEA. The library contains 153,431 volumes, 571,116 microform items, and 30,777 audio/video tapes/CDs/DVDs, and subscribes to 3818 periodicals including electronic. Computerized library services include interlibrary loans. Special learning facilities include a learning resource center, art gallery, and natural history museum. The 260-acre campus is in a rural area 14 miles from Mayaguez. Including any residence halls, there are 64 buildings.

Student Life: 99% of undergraduates are from Puerto Rico. Others are from 9 foreign countries and Canada. 83% are from public schools. 99% are Hispanic. The average age of freshmen is 18; all undergraduates, 22. 28% do not continue beyond their first year; 41% remain to graduate.

Housing: 512 students can be accommodated in college housing, which includes single-sex dormitories, on-campus apartments, and married-student housing. On-campus housing is guaranteed for all 4 years. 89% of students commute. Alcohol is not permitted. All students may keep cars.

Activities: There are no fraternities or sororities. There are 34 groups on campus, including art, band, choir, chorale, computers, dance, drama, ethnic, honors, international, jazz band, marching band, musical theater, newspaper, orchestra, political, professional, religious, social, social service, and student government. Popular campus events include Feria Tipica, Founders Celebration Dances, and intercollegiate sport events.

Sports: There are 11 intercollegiate sports for men and 6 for women, and 11 intramural sports for men and 6 for women. Facilities include a gym, dirt and tartan tracks, tennis courts, a jogging course, table tennis, a billiards room, table games, aerobics areas, a small gym in residence halls, and a gym with a basketball court.

Disabled Students: 80% of the campus is accessible. Wheelchair ramps, special parking, specially equipped rest rooms, special class scheduling, lowered drinking fountains, lowered telephones, and elevators in some buildings are available.

Services: Counseling and information services are available, as is tutoring in some subjects, including Spanish, English, math, and computer science.

Campus Safety and Security: Measures include 24-hour foot and vehicle patrol, shuttle buses, pamphlets/posters/films, and emergency telephones. There is an electronic security system.

Programs of Study: The university confers B.A., B.S., and B.B.A. degrees. Associate, master's, and doctoral degrees are also awarded. Bachelor's degrees are awarded in BIOLOGICAL SCIENCE (biology/biological science), BUSINESS (accounting, banking and finance, business administration and management, marketing/retailing/merchandising, and secretarial studies/office management), COMMUNICATIONS AND THE ARTS (English, fine arts, music, and Spanish), COMPUTER AND PHYSICAL SCIENCE (chemistry, computer science, and mathematics), EDUCATION (art, early childhood, elementary, health, music, science, secondary, special, and teaching English as a second/foreign language (TESOL/TEFOL)), HEALTH PROFESSIONS (medical laboratory technology, nursing, and premedicine), SOCIAL SCIENCE (economics, history, political science/government, psychology, public administration, and sociology). Business administration and medical technology are the strongest academically. Computer science, business administration, and biology are the largest.

Required: To graduate, students must complete at least 124 credits, with a minimum GPA of 2.5. General education requirements include courses in Spanish, English, mathematical reasoning, logical and critical reasoning, computer programming, and Puerto Rican history. In addition, students must take 6 credits in methods of interpreting reality, 2 in phys ed, computer science, and community service, and 1 each in art, music, ethics, and Puerto Rican culture.

Special: The university offers internships, credit by exam, and nondegree study. A 3-2 engineering degree is available with Penn State University. There are 2 national honor societies and a freshman honors program.

Faculty/Classroom: 48% of faculty are male; 52%, female. 89% teach undergraduates. The average class size in an introductory lecture is 25; in a laboratory, 10; and in a regular course, 25.

Requirements: The SAT is required or the CEEB Spanish equivalent. Applicants must be high school graduates and have completed 15 credits, including 3 each in Spanish, English, and electives, and 2 each in math and science. A GPA of 2.5 is required. AP and CLEP credits are accepted. Important factors in the admissions decision are advanced placement or honor courses, evidence of special talent, and recommendations by school officials.

Procedure: Freshmen are admitted to all sessions. Entrance exams should be taken in the first or second semester of the senior year. There is an early admissions plan. Check with the school for current deadlines and fee. Applications are accepted on-line.

Transfer: Applicants should have at least 15 college credits with a minimum GPA of 2.5. The SAT, or the CEEB Spanish version, is required, as is a letter of recommendation from the dean of students at the student's previous college. 30 of 124 credits required for the bachelor's degree must be completed at the university.

Visiting: There are regularly scheduled orientations for prospective students, during the summer. There are guides for informal visits and visitors may sit in on classes and stay overnight. To schedule a visit, contact Professor Celia Gonzalez in Communications at (787) 264-1912 or cgonzalez@sg.inter.edu.

Financial Aid: The university is a member of CSS. The FAFSA, the college's own financial statement and the application for Federal Student Aid (Pell Grant) are required. Check with the school for current deadlines.

International Students: In a recent year, there were 50 international students enrolled. and also take English or Spanish SAT.

Computers: All students may access the system designated hours. There are no time limits. Check with the school for the current fee.

Admissions Contact: Mildred Camacho, Director of Admissions. A video is available. E-mail: milcama@sg.inter.edu
Web: www.sg.inter.edu

INTER-AMERICAN UNIVERSITY OF PUERTO RICO SYSTEM

The Inter-American University of Puerto Rico System, established in 1912, is a private system in Puerto Rico. It is governed by a board of trustees, whose chief administrator is the president. The primary goal of the system is teaching. The main priorities are to provide quality education and public service, and devote attention to students' needs. The total enrollment is usually about 43,000; with 900 faculty members. Altogether there are some 35 baccalaureate, 28 master's, and 1 doctoral programs offered in Inter-American University of Puerto Rico System. 4-year campuses are located in San Juan and, and San German. Profiles of the 4-year campuses are included in this section.

PONTIFICAL CATHOLIC UNIVERSITY OF PUERTO RICO/PONCE
C-2

Ponce, PR 00717-0777

(787) 841-2000, ext. 1000
(800) 981-5040; Fax: (787) 651-2044

Full-time: 2280 men, 4470 women	**Faculty:** 307
Part-time: 480 men, 790 women	**Ph.D.s:** n/av
Graduate: 670 men, 1200 women	**Student/Faculty:** 22 to 1
Year: semesters, summer session	**Tuition:** $4460
Application Deadline: see profile	**Room & Board:** $2850
Freshman Class: n/av	
SAT: required	

Pontifical Catholic University of Puerto Rico, founded in 1948, is a private institution affiliated with the Roman Catholic Church of Puerto Rico. The school offers undergraduate and graduate programs in liberal arts, the sciences, education, and business. There are 4 undergraduate and 6 graduate schools. Figures in the above capsule and in this profile are approximate. In addition to regional accreditation, La Catolica has baccalaureate program accreditation with CSWE and NLN. The 2 libraries contain 238,033 volumes, 514,440 microform items, and 13,456 audio/video tapes/CDs/DVDs, and subscribe to 58,183 periodicals including electronic. Computerized library services include the card catalog, interlibrary loans, and database searching. Special learning facilities include a learning resource center, radio station, TV station, and an electronic information center. The 55-acre campus is in an urban area 35 miles south of San Juan. Including any residence halls, there are 40 buildings.

Student Life: The majority of students are fom Puerto Rico. Others are from 4 foreign countries. 80% are from public schools. 100% are Hispanic. The average age of freshmen is 19; all undergraduates, 22.

Housing: 180 students can be accommodated in college housing, which includes single-sex dormitories. Priority for on-campus housing is given to out-of-town students. 97% of students commute. Alcohol is not permitted. All students may keep cars.

Activities: 1% of men belong to 11 local fraternities; 1% of women belong to 7 local sororities. There are 50 groups on campus, including art, band, choir, chorale, computers, dance, drama, honors, literary magazine, newspaper, photography, professional, radio and TV, religious, social service, student government, and yearbook. Popular campus events include freshman activities at the beginning of the academic year; religious and social activities celebrated on Thanksgiving, Christmas, and Holy Week; and Puerto Rican Culture Week.

Sports: There are 7 intercollegiate sports for men and 5 for women, and 6 intramural sports for men and 4 for women. Facilities include a gym, a 6000-seat arena, an Olympic-size pool, 5 tennis courts, 1 baseball field, 3 basketball courts, 3 volleyball courts, and a synthetic track and field.

Disabled Students: 95% of the campus is accessible. Wheelchair ramps, elevators, special parking, specially equipped rest rooms, special class scheduling, lowered drinking fountains, lowered telephones, a braille typewriter, an English and Spanish book reader, and a text enlarger are available.

Services: Counseling and information services are available, as is tutoring in some subjects, including math, chemistry, physics, English, Spanish, philosophy, statistics, accounting, and political science. There is a reader service for the blind, and remedial math, reading, and writing. .

Campus Safety and Security: Measures include 24-hour foot and vehicle patrol, informal discussions, pamphlets/posters/films, and emergency telephones. There are lighted pathways/sidewalks.

Programs of Study: La Catolica confers B.A., B.S., B.B.A., and B.S.Ed. degrees. Associate, master's, and doctoral degrees are also awarded. Bachelor's degrees are awarded in BIOLOGICAL SCIENCE (biology/biological science), BUSINESS (accounting, banking and finance, business administration and management, business economics, international economics, and marketing/retailing/merchandising), COMMUNICATIONS AND THE ARTS (communications, English, fine arts, public relations, and Spanish), COMPUTER AND PHYSICAL SCIENCE (chemistry, computer programming, mathematics, and physics), EDUCATION (art, business, elementary, home economics, mathematics, music, physical, science, secondary, social studies, special, and teaching English as a second/foreign language (TESOL/TEFOL)), HEALTH PROFESSIONS (medical laboratory technology and nursing), SOCIAL SCIENCE (criminology, gerontology, history, liberal arts/general studies, philosophy, political science/government, psychology, public administration, religion, social science, social work, sociology, and theological studies). Physical sciences is the strongest academically. General studies is the largest.

Required: Bachelor's candidates must complete a 136-credit program in not more than twice the usual number of years and maintain a GPA of 2.0. Required courses include theology, philosophy, humanities, English, Spanish, math, science, phys ed, social or political science, music or art, and basic computer. A thesis is required of Institute of Graduate Studies candidates.

Special: The university offers co-op programs in medicine, engineering, veterinary, and pharmacy, as well as cross-registration with the University of Valladolid and a 3-2 engineering degree with Case Western Reserve University. A Washington semester, work-study programs within the university, nondegree study, pass/fail options in elective courses, and a student-designed major in liberal arts are also available. There are 8 national honor societies, a freshman honors program, and 3 departmental honors programs.

Faculty/Classroom: 85% teach undergraduates and 1% do research. The average class size in an introductory lecture is 35; in a laboratory, 32; and in a regular course, 35.

Requirements: The SAT is required, along with SAT: Subject tests in math, Spanish, and English as a second language. In addition, applicants must be high school graduates or hold a GED. Students from 3-year senior high schools should have earned 10 units consisting of 3 each of English and Spanish, 2 of math, and 1 each of science and history. Students from 4-year high schools should have earned 15 units consisting of 4 each of English and Spanish, 3 of math, and 2 each of science and history. Students from outside Puerto Rico may substitute 2 years of another foreign language for the Spanish requirement. An interview is required for special programs. A GPA of 2.0 is required. AP and CLEP credits are accepted. Important factors in the admissions decision are advanced placement or honor courses, evidence of special talent, and leadership record.

Procedure: Freshmen are admitted to all sessions. Entrance exams should be taken during the fall of the senior year. Check with the school for current deadlines and fee.

Transfer: Applicants must supply a college transcript. A GPA of 2.0 and 30 credit hours are required. An associate degree is recommended. 30 of 136 credits required for the bachelor's degree must be completed at La Catolica.

Visiting: There are guides for informal visits and visitors may sit in on classes. To schedule a visit, contact Irem Poventud at (787) 841-2000, ext. 1245 or ipoventud@pucpr.edu.

Financial Aid: The FAFSA, the college's own financial statement and income certification documents are required. Check with the school for current deadlines.

International Students: The school actively recruits these students. They must take the SAT or the ACT.

Computers: All students may access the system 8 A.M. to 10 P.M. Monday through Thursday, and 8 A.M. to 5 P.M. Friday and Saturday. There are no time limits. The fee is included in the university fee.

Admissions Contact: Admissions Office. A video is available.
E-mail: *admisiones@pucpr.edu* Web: *www.pucpr.edu*

TURABO UNIVERSITY
D-1

Gurabo, PR 00658

(787) 746-3009

Full-time: none	**Faculty:** 100
Part-time: none	**Ph.D.s:** 33%
Graduate: none	**Student/Faculty:** 30 to 1
Year: semesters, summer session	**Tuition:** $4110
Application Deadline: see profile	**Room & Board:** n/app
Freshman Class: n/av	
SAT or ACT: n/av	

Turabo University, founded in 1972, is a private nonsectarian institution offering undergraduate programs in business administration, education, Spanish, social sciences, natural sciences and technology, English and communications, and graduate programs in business administration and education. Figures given in above capsule and in this profile are approximate. There are 2 graduate schools. The library contains 126,000 volumes. Computerized library services include the card catalog and database searching. Special learning facilities include a learning resource center, an archeological-folkloric museum, and language lab. The 116-acre campus is in a suburban area 15 miles south of San Juan. There are 15 buildings.

Programs of Study: the university confers B.A., B.S., and B.B.A. degrees. Associate and master's degrees are also awarded. Bachelor's degrees are awarded in BIOLOGICAL SCIENCE (biology/biological science), BUSINESS (accounting, business administration and management, management science, marketing/retailing/merchandising, and secretarial studies/office management), COMMUNICATIONS AND THE ARTS (English and Spanish), COMPUTER AND PHYSICAL SCIENCE (chemistry, computer programming, mathematics, and natural sciences), EDUCATION (elementary, English, foreign languages, mathematics, physical, science, secondary, social science, and special), SOCIAL SCIENCE (criminology, economics, history, humanities, psychology, public administration, social science, and sociology).

Required: To graduate, students must complete course requirements with a minimum 2.0 GPA overall and 2.0 to 2.3 in the major.

Special: The university offers a general studies degree, graduate-level night courses in business and education, work-study, and nondegree study.

Faculty/Classroom: 50% of faculty are male; 50%, female.

Procedure: Check with the school for current deadlines and fee.

Financial Aid: The FAFSA is required. Check with the school for current deadlines.
Computers: There are no time limits and no fees.
Admissions Contact: Admissions Office Director.

UNIVERSIDAD ADVENTISTA DE LAS ANTILLAS — A-1

Mayaguez, PR 00681-0118

(787) 834-9595, ext. 2261
Fax: (787) 834-9597

Full-time: 288 men, 416 women	**Faculty:** 42
Part-time: 19 men, 37 women	**Ph.D.s:** 26%
Graduate: 18 men, 53 women	**Student/Faculty:** 17 to 1
Year: semesters, summer session	**Tuition:** $4760
Application Deadline: open	**Room & Board:** $2600
Freshman Class: n/av	
SAT or ACT: required	

Universidad Adventista de las Antillas, established in 1961 and affiliated with the Seventh-day Adventist Church, offers undergraduate programs in business administration, sciences and computers, education and psychology, nursing and allied health, music and fine arts, religion, and humanities. There are 7 undergraduate schools. In addition to regional accreditation, UAA has baccalaureate program accreditation with NLN and AHIMA. The library contains 88,432 volumes, 2603 microform items, and 1717 audio/video tapes/CDs/DVDs, and subscribes to 392 periodicals including electronic. Computerized library services include the card catalog, interlibrary loans, database searching, and Internet access. Special learning facilities include a learning resource center. The 284-acre campus is in a small town on the west coast of Puerto Rico. Including any residence halls, there are 6 buildings.
Student Life: 72% of undergraduates are from Puerto Rico. Others are from 15 states, 22 foreign countries, and Canada. 50% are from public schools. 96% are Hispanic. 66% are Seventh-day Adventist; 14% claim no religious affiliation; 13% Catholic; 6% Protestant. The average age of freshmen is 19; all undergraduates, 22. 30% do not continue beyond their first year; 70% remain to graduate.
Housing: 252 students can be accommodated in college housing, which includes single-sex dorms, on-campus apartments, and married-student housing. On-campus housing is guaranteed for all 4 years. 70% of students commute. Alcohol is not permitted. All students may keep cars.
Activities: 75% of men belong to 1 local fraternity; 80% of women belong to 1 local sorority. There are 20 groups on campus, including band, choir, chorale, chorus, drama, film, international, literary magazine, newspaper, orchestra, photography, professional, religious, social, social service, and student government. Popular campus events include International Fair, Columbus Day, and Discovering Puerto Rico.
Sports: There are 4 intercollegiate sports for men and 3 for women, and 4 intramural sports for men and 3 for women. Facilities include a gym, a swimming pool, and a tennis court.
Disabled Students: 90% of the campus is accessible. Wheelchair ramps, special parking, specially equipped rest rooms, lowered drinking fountains, and lowered telephones are available.
Services: Counseling and information services are available, as is tutoring in some subjects, including math, English, and Spanish. There is remedial math, reading, and writing.
Campus Safety and Security: Measures include 24-hour foot and vehicle patrol.
Programs of Study: UAA confers B.A. and B.S. degrees. Associate and master's degrees are also awarded. Bachelor's degrees are awarded in BIOLOGICAL SCIENCE (biology/biological science), BUSINESS (business administration and management and office supervision and management), COMMUNICATIONS AND THE ARTS (music and Spanish), COMPUTER AND PHYSICAL SCIENCE (computer science), EDUCATION (elementary, music, and secondary), HEALTH PROFESSIONS (health science and nursing), SOCIAL SCIENCE (history, pastoral studies, religion, and theological studies). Business administration, nursing, and computer science are the strongest academically. Nursing is is the largest.
Required: Students must complete 128 credits, with 44 to 66 in the major and a minimum GPA of 2.0. General education requirements include courses in religion, music or art, math, phys ed, computer science, Spanish, English, philosophy of education, and biological and physical sciences.
Special: Work-study programs, B.A.-B.S. degrees, credit by exam, and pass/fail options are available. There is a 3-2 engineering degree with Walla Walla University in Washington State.
Faculty/Classroom: 51% of faculty are male; 47%, female. All teach undergraduates. The average class size in an introductory lecture is 30; in a laboratory, 35; and in a regular course, 30.
Requirements: The SAT or ACT is required. In addition, graduation from an accredited secondary school is required; the GED is accepted. Applicants must submit 12 to 15 academic credits, including 3 each in English and a foreign language, 2 each in history, math, science, and social studies, and 1 to 2 in other electives. An interview is recommended.

A GPA of 2.0 is required. AP and CLEP credits are accepted. Important factors in the admissions decision are advanced placement or honor courses, ability to finance college education, and parents or siblings attending the school.
Procedure: Freshmen are admitted to all sessions. Application deadlines are open. Application fee is $20.
Transfer: 62 transfer students enrolled in 2004-2005. Applicants must be in good standing at the previous institution, with a GPA of at least 2.0, and must submit official transcripts of high school and college credit. An official report of the CEEB Spanish equivalent of the SAT must be provided if the applicant has completed fewer than 24 semester credits. 30 of 128 credits required for the bachelor's degree must be completed at UAA.
Visiting: There are regularly scheduled orientations for prospective students. There are guides for informal visits and visitors may sit in on classes and stay overnight. To schedule a visit, contact Dr. Myrna Costa at (787) 834-9595, ext. 2210 or *mcosta@uaa.edu*.
Financial Aid: 35% of undergraduates work part time. Average annual earnings from campus work are $1400. UAA is a member of CSS. The CSS/Profile or FAFSA and the college's own financial statement are required.
International Students: There are 39 international students enrolled. They must take the college's own test aor the CEEB Spanish equivalent of the SAT.
Computers: Wireless access is available. All students may access the system 7:30 A.M. to 10 P.M. The fee is $50. It is strongly recommended that all students have a personal computer.
Graduates: From July 1, 2004 to June 30, 2005, 108 bachelor's degrees were awarded. The most popular majors were nursing (33%), business administration (19%), and education (16%). In an average class, 30% graduate in 4 years or less, and 60% graduate in 5 years or less. Of the 2004 graduating class, 40% were enrolled in graduate school within 6 months of graduation and 50% were employed.
Admissions Contact: Evelyn del Valle, Director, Admissions and Continuing Education. A video is available. E-mail: *edelvalle@uaa.edu* or *admissions@uaa.edu* Web: *www.uaa.edu*

UNIVERSIDAD METROPOLITANA — D-1

Rio Piedras, PR 00928

(787) 765-6262

Full-time: none	**Faculty:** n/av
Part-time: none	**Ph.D.s:** n/av
Graduate: none	**Student/Faculty:** 45 to 1
Year: semesters, summer session	**Tuition:** $3330
Application Deadline: open	**Room & Board:** n/app
Freshman Class: n/av	
SAT: required	

Universidad Metropolitana, founded in 1980, is a private, commuter institution offering undergraduate programs in the liberal arts and sciences, business, nursing, and education. Figures given in above capsule and in this profile are approximate. There are 6 undergraduate schools. In addition to regional accreditation, UMET has baccalaureate program accreditation with NLN. The library contains 34,445 volumes and 5000 microform items. Special learning facilities include a learning resource center and TV station. The campus is in an urban area. There are 11 buildings.
Programs of Study: UMET confers B.A., B.S., B.B.A., and B.S.N. degrees. Associate and master's degrees are also awarded. Bachelor's degrees are awarded in BUSINESS (accounting, business administration and management, and management science), COMPUTER AND PHYSICAL SCIENCE (natural sciences), EDUCATION (elementary and secondary), ENGINEERING AND ENVIRONMENTAL DESIGN (surveying engineering), HEALTH PROFESSIONS (nursing), SOCIAL SCIENCE (humanities, psychology, social science, and sociology). Business is the strongest academically. Education and natural sciences are the largest.
Required: To graduate, students must complete an average of 135 credits, including at least 30 in the major field. Specific GPA requirements vary by department. All students must take a computer course and complete a general education core.
Special: UMET offers work-study programs, B.A.-B.S. degrees, and an honors program in the natural sciences. The Televised Education Center (CET) offers students an opportunity for independent study.
Faculty/Classroom: 40% of faculty are male; 60%, female.
Requirements: The SAT is required. In addition, applicants must be graduates of an accredited secondary school with a GPA of 2.0. Some programs have higher GPA requirements.
Procedure: Freshmen are admitted to all sessions. Check with the school for current deadlines and fee.
Transfer: All applicants must meet the GPA requirements of the program they wish to enter. Students should submit transcripts from all previous colleges attended as well as a letter of recommendation from the dean of the most recent institution. Grades of C or better transfer for credit.
Financial Aid: The college's own financial statement is required. Check with the school for current deadlines.
Admissions Contact: Office of Admissions.

UNIVERSIDAD POLITECNICA DE PUERTO RICO D-1

Hato Rey, PR 00918 (787) 754-8000, ext. 240

Full-time: 1980 men, 670 women	**Faculty:** 147
Part-time: 2000 men, 530 women	**Ph.D.s:** 20%
Graduate: 290 men 205 women	**Student/Faculty:** 18 to 1
Year: trimesters, summer session	**Tuition:** $5400
Application Deadline: see profile	**Room & Board:** n/app
Freshman Class: n/av	
SAT: required	

Universidad Politecnica de Puerto Rico is a private institution offering undergraduate programs in engineering, business administration, and architecture, and graduate programs in engineering management, civil engineering, manufacturing business administration, and environmental protection. There are 3 undergraduate schools and 1 graduate school. Figures in the above capsule and in this profile are approximate. In addition to regional accreditation, La Poli has baccalaureate program accreditation with ABET. The library contains 90,346 volumes, 100 microform items, and 1971 audio/video tapes/CDs/DVDs, and subscribes to 8376 periodicals including electronic. Computerized library services include the card catalog, interlibrary loans, database searching, and Internet access. Special learning facilities include a learning resource center, art gallery, TV studio, satellite dish, museum and historical archive of the university, and projection room. The 8-acre campus is in an urban area in the Hato Rey section of San Juan. There are 8 buildings.

Student Life: The majority of students are from Puerto Rico. Others are from 4 foreign countries. 50% are from public schools. 100% are Hispanic. Most are Catholic. The average age of freshmen is 18; all undergraduates, 25. 30% do not continue beyond their first year; 20% remain to graduate.

Housing: There are no residence halls. Alcohol is not permitted. All students may keep cars.

Activities: There are no fraternities or sororities. There are 8 groups on campus, including choir, honors, newspaper, political, professional, religious, and student government. Popular campus events include Student Night, Library Week, and Education Weeks.

Sports: There are 8 intercollegiate sports for men and 8 for women, and 10 intramural sports for men and 10 for women. Facilities include basketball and volleyball courts, a game room, and a gym.

Disabled Students: 90% of the campus is accessible. Wheelchair ramps, elevators, special parking, specially equipped rest rooms, and special class scheduling are available.

Services: Counseling and information services are available, as is tutoring in some subjects, including Spanish, English, math, and engineering. There is remedial math.

Campus Safety and Security: Measures include 24-hour foot and vehicle patrol, informal discussions, pamphlets/posters/films, and lighted pathways/sidewalks.

Programs of Study: La Poli confers B.S., B.B.A., and B.S.E. degrees. Master's degrees are also awarded. Bachelor's degrees are awarded in BUSINESS (business administration and management), ENGINEERING AND ENVIRONMENTAL DESIGN (chemical engineering, civil engineering, electrical/electronics engineering, environmental engineering, industrial administration/management, industrial engineering, mechanical engineering, and surveying engineering). Electrical and civil engineering are the strongest programs academically and have the largest enrollments.

Required: All graduating students must complete 128 to 176 quarter credits, with a minimum GPA of 2.0. There are distribution requirements in Spanish, English, humanities, social sciences, and math, and within the chosen field. All students must take 6 credits in Computer Science. All majors require a practicum course before graduation.

Special: Co-op programs are available in all majors. There is a freshman honors program.

Faculty/Classroom: 64% of faculty are male; 36%, female. All teach undergraduates. The average class size in an introductory lecture is 30; in a laboratory, 20; and in a regular course, 22.

Requirements: The SAT is required. In addition, the CEEB Spanish equivalents of the SAT: Subject tests are required. Applicants must be graduates of an accredited secondary school, with 15 high school academic units. An interview is recommended. A GPA of 2.5 is required.

Procedure: Freshmen are admitted to all sessions. There are early decision and early admissions plans. Check with the school for current deadlines and fee.

Transfer: Applicants must present an official transcript and letters of recommendation. They must also have a GPA of 2.0 or higher and approved credits.

Visiting: There are regularly scheduled orientations for prospective students. To schedule a visit, contact Teresa Cardona, Director of Admissions.

Financial Aid: La Poli is a member of CSS. The FAFSA and the college's own financial statement are required. Check with the school for current deadlines.

International Students: These students must take the Spanish equivalent of the SAT.

Computers: All students may access the system. There are no time limits. Check with the school for current fee.

Admissions Contact: Teresa Cardona, Director of Admissions.
E-mail: *tcardona@pupr.edu* Web: *www.pupr.edu*

UNIVERSITY OF PUERTO RICO SYSTEM

The University of Puerto Rico System, established in 1903, is a public system in Puerto Rico. It is governed by the Puerto Rico Council on Higher Education, whose chief administrator is the president. The primary goal of the system is to serve as a center for scholarly research, to develop academic excellence, and to capitalize on its location as a focal point of the Caribbean region and the international community by developing programs germane to the residents of the region. The main priorities are to improve academic programs in key areas, to strengthen research and research training, and to upgrade physical facilities. The total enrollment is usually about 55,000, with 4500 faculty members. Altogether there are 194 baccalaureate, 97 master's, and 15 doctoral programs offered in University of Puerto Rico System. 4-year campuses are located in Cayey,, Humacao,, Mayaguez,, Rio Piedras,, Arecibo,, Bayamon,, and Ponce, and San Juan. Profiles of the 4-year campuses are included in this section.

UNIVERSITY OF PUERTO RICO AT HUMACAO D-2

Humacao, PR 00791-4300 (787) 850-0000, ext. 9301
Fax: (787) 850-9428

Full-time: 1033 men, 2486 women	**Faculty:** 249; IIB, -$
Part-time: 216 men, 547 women	**Ph.D.s:** 34%
Graduate: none	**Student/Faculty:** 14 to 1
Year: semesters, summer session	**Tuition:** $1707
Application Deadline: November 14	**Room & Board:** n/app
Freshman Class: 2178 applied, 1015 accepted, 857 enrolled	
SAT Verbal/Math: 525/539*	

The University of Puerto Rico at Humacao, founded in 1962, is a public institution offering undergraduate programs in the arts and sciences, business, education, and nursing to an entirely commuter student body. Annual tuition and fees for nonresident U.S. citizens are an amount equal to the nonresident rate at a state university in their home state. In addition to regional accreditation, University of Puerto Rico at Humacao has baccalaureate program accreditation with ACOTE, APTA, CSWE, and NLN. The library contains 117,629 volumes, 10,248 microform items, and 1613 audio/video tapes/CDs/DVDs, and subscribes to 18,697 periodicals including electronic. Computerized library services include the card catalog, interlibrary loans, database searching, and Internet access. Special learning facilities include a learning resource center and a museum, an observatory, a census data center, and web radio. The 62-acre campus is in a suburban area 30 miles southeast of San Juan. There are 29 buildings.

Student Life: 99% of undergraduates are from Puerto Rico. Others are from 5 states and 4 foreign countries. 75% are from public schools. 100% are Hispanic. The average age of freshmen is 18; all undergraduates, 21. 13% do not continue beyond their first year; 87% remain to graduate.

Housing: There are no residence halls. All students commute. Alcohol is not permitted. All students may keep cars.

Activities: There are 2 local fraternities and 1 local sorority. There are no fraternities. There are 30 groups on campus, including cheerleading, chorus, computers, dance, honors, literary magazine, pep band, photography, professional, religious, social, social service, student government, and web radio. Popular campus events include Shakespeare Festival, Women's Week, and Puerto Rican Culture Week.

Sports: There are 8 intercollegiate sports for men and 8 for women, and 3 intramural sports for men and 4 for women. Facilities include a 1000-seat gym, a track, 2 tennis courts, a softball field, a swimming pool, wrestling mats, and a student center.

Disabled Students: 60% of the campus is accessible. Wheelchair ramps, elevators, special parking, specially equipped rest rooms, special class scheduling, lowered drinking fountains, and lowered telephones are available.

Services: Counseling and information services are available, as is tutoring in some subjects, including English, Spanish, and math. There is a reader service for the blind, and remedial math, reading, and writing.

Campus Safety and Security: Measures include 24-hour foot and vehicle patrol, pamphlets/posters/films, emergency telephones, and lighted pathways/sidewalks.

Programs of Study: University of Puerto Rico at Humacao confers B.A., B.S., and B.B.A. degrees. Associate degrees are also awarded. Bachelor's degrees are awarded in AGRICULTURE (wildlife management), BIOLOGICAL SCIENCE (biology/biological science, marine biology, and microbiology), BUSINESS (accounting, business administration and management, human resources, international business management, and secretarial studies/office management), COMMUNICATIONS AND THE ARTS (English), COMPUTER AND PHYSICAL SCIENCE (chemistry, mathematics, and physics), EDUCATION (elementary), HEALTH PROFESSIONS (nursing and occupational therapy), SOCIAL SCIENCE (social work). Natural sciences is the strongest academically. Business administration is the largest.

Required: To graduate, students must complete 127 to 136 credit hours, including 18 to 56 in a major field, with a minimum GPA of 2.0. General education requirements include 33 to 73 liberal arts credits, with 6 credits in Spanish and 6 in English, humanities, and social sciences. Other distribution requirements vary by program.

Special: Students may study abroad through the National Student Exchange program. There are also co-op programs, internships in accounting, management, human resources, and physics work-study programs, credit for work experience, and a pass/fail option in remedial courses. Nondegree study is available through the Division of Continuing Education. The college offers programs in coastal marine biology, industrial microbiology, and industrial chemistry, and sponsors a Puerto Rican plain pigeon conservation project. There is 1 national honor society, and a freshman honors program.

Faculty/Classroom: 44% of faculty are male; 56%, female. 85% teach undergraduates and 1% do research. The average class size in a laboratory is 17 and in a regular course, 21.

Admissions: 47% of the 2005-2006 applicants were accepted. The SAT scores for the 2005-2006 freshman class were: Verbal--39% below 500, 46% between 500 and 599, 14% between 600 and 700, and 1% above 700; Math--34% below 500, 43% between 500 and 599, 21% between 600 and 700, and 2% above 700.

Requirements: The SAT is required for U.S. applicants, or the CEEB's Spanish equivalent, as well as SAT: Subject tests in Spanish and math level I. Applicants must be graduates of an accredited secondary school or have earned the GED. College preparatory study should include 3 credits each in English, Spanish, and math, 2 in history, and 1 in social studies. All courses are conducted in Spanish only. Nonnative speakers of Spanish are required to demonstrate fluency through institutional exam interviews. A GPA of 2.0 is required. AP credits are accepted.

Procedure: Freshmen are admitted in the fall. Entrance exams should be taken by October or February of the senior year. There are early decision and deferred admissions plans. Early decision applications should be filed by November 30; regular decisions, by November 14 for fall entry, along with a $20 fee. Notification of early decision is sent in February; regular decision, in April. 250 early decision candidates were accepted for the 2005-2006 class. Applications are accepted on-line.

Transfer: 26 transfer students enrolled in 2004-2005. Applicants to the bachelor's programs must have at least 30 college credits with a minimum GPA of 3.0 and must be in good standing at their previous institution. 30 of 136 credits required for the bachelor's degree must be completed at University of Puerto Rico at Humacao.

Visiting: There are regularly scheduled orientations for prospective students. To schedule a visit, contact Milagros Alvarez at (809) 850-0000, ext. 9238 or mi_alvarez@webmail.uprh.edu.

Financial Aid: In 2005-2006, 76% of all full-time freshmen and 77% of continuing full-time students received some form of financial aid. 76% of all full-time students received need-based aid. The average freshman award was $4087. Need-based scholarships or need-based grants averaged $4077; and need-based self-help aid (loans and jobs) averaged $2158. The FAFSA is required. The deadline for filing freshman financial aid applications for fall entry is June 30.

International Students: There are 7 international students enrolled. Applicants must take the CEEB's Spanish version of the SAT. This consists of an aptitude test (verbal and math) and an achievement test battery (Spanish, English, and math).

Computers: Wireless access is available. All students may access the system daily until 10 P.M. There are no time limits and no fees.

Graduates: From July 1, 2004 to June 30, 2005, 564 bachelor's degrees were awarded. The most popular majors were elementary education (15%), accounting (12%), and office systems administration (9%). In an average class, 7% graduate in 3 years or less, 19% graduate in 4 years or less, 40% graduate in 5 years or less, and 47% graduate in 6 years or less.

Admissions Contact: Inara Ferrer, Director of Admissions.
E-mail: i_ferrer@webmail.uprh.edu

UNIVERSITY OF PUERTO RICO/ARECIBO   B-1

Arecibo, PR 00613   (787) 815-0000, ext. 4110; Fax: (787) 880-4972

Full-time: 1150 men, 2338 women	Faculty: 199
Part-time: 194 men, 464 women	Ph.D.s: 22%
Graduate: none	Student/Faculty: 18 to 1
Year: semesters, summer session	Tuition: $1707 ($3539)
Application Deadline: November 30	Room & Board: $5520 ($6620)
Freshman Class: 3715 applied, 1152 accepted, 941 enrolled	
SAT: required	

University of Puerto Rico/Arecib, founded in 1967, offers undergraduate programs in business administration, health sciences, natural sciences, education, computer sciences, telecommunications, and others. Tuition and fees for Puerto Rican residents total $1,707 per year; nonresidents pay an amount equal to the nonresident rate at a state university in their home state. In addition to regional accreditation, UPRA has baccalaureate program accreditation with NLN. The library contains 82,316 volumes, 7266 microform items, and 2510 audio/video tapes/CDs/DVDs, and subscribes to 1500 periodicals including electronic. Computerized library services include interlibrary loans, database searching, and Internet access. Special learning facilities include a learning resource center and art gallery. The 49-acre campus is in an urban area 40 miles west of San Juan. There are 14 buildings.

Student Life: Students are from Puerto Rico and 2 foreign countries. 84% are from public schools. All are Hispanic. The average age of freshmen is 18; all undergraduates, 21. 18% do not continue beyond their first year.

Housing: There are no residence halls. All students commute. Alcohol is not permitted. All students may keep cars.

Activities: There are no fraternities or sororities. There are 29 groups on campus, including art, band, cheerleading, chorus, computers, dance, drama, film, honors, newspaper, photography, political, professional, radio and TV, religious, social, social service, and student government. Popular campus events include fairs, plays, and concerts.

Sports: There are 8 intercollegiate sports for men and 6 for women, and 4 intramural sports for men and 3 for women. Facilities include basketball and tennis courts, baseball/softball and soccer fields, a gym, track and field facilities, and an activity room.

Disabled Students: 90% of the campus is accessible. Wheelchair ramps, elevators, special parking, specially equipped rest rooms, lowered drinking fountains, and lowered telephones are available.

Services: Counseling and information services are available, as is tutoring in most subjects. There is a reader service for the blind, and remedial math, reading, and writing.

Campus Safety and Security: Measures include 24-hour foot and vehicle patrol, informal discussions, pamphlets/posters/films, and lighted pathways/sidewalks.

Programs of Study: UPRA confers B.A. and B.S. B.S.N., B.B.A degrees. Associate degrees are also awarded. Bachelor's degrees are awarded in BIOLOGICAL SCIENCE (microbiology), BUSINESS (accounting, banking and finance, business administration and management, marketing/retailing/merchandising, and secretarial studies/office management), COMMUNICATIONS AND THE ARTS (telecommunications), COMPUTER AND PHYSICAL SCIENCE (computer science), EDUCATION (elementary and physical), ENGINEERING AND ENVIRONMENTAL DESIGN (chemical engineering technology), HEALTH PROFESSIONS (nursing), SOCIAL SCIENCE (Iberian studies and industrial and organizational psychology). Microbiology is the strongest academically. Accounting is the largest.

Required: To graduate, students must have a 2.0 GPA. The total number of credit hours required varies according to major. The core curriculum includes 2 semesters each of English, Spanish, math, and social sciences or humanities.

Special: There are internships, an exchange program with Spain, and a 3-2 engineering degree with the University of Puero Rico/Mayaguez. There is a freshman honors program.

Faculty/Classroom: 44% of faculty are male; 56%, female. 89% teach undergraduates and 35% do research. The average class size in an introductory lecture is 25; in a laboratory, 20; and in a regular course, 23.

Admissions: 31% of the 2005-2006 applicants were accepted.

Requirements: A Spanish version of the SAT or the College Entrance Examination Board test (CEEB) is required. A GPA of 2.0 is required. AP credits are accepted.

Procedure: Freshmen are admitted in the fall. Entrance exams should be taken by October of the senior year. There are early admissions and rolling admissions plans. Applications should be filed by November 30 for fall entry. Notification of early decision is sent February 30; regular decision, April 30. The fall 2005 application fee was $20.

Transfer: 40 transfer students enrolled in 2004-2005. Applicants should have a minimum of 24 credits with a 2.5 GPA.

Visiting: There are regularly scheduled orientations for prospective students. To schedule a visit, contact Prof. Celia Medina.

Financial Aid: 79% of full-time freshmen and 69% of continuing full-time students received need-based aid. The average freshman award was $4050. 9% of undergraduates work part time. Average annual earnings from campus work are $1500. UPRA is a member of CSS. The FAFSA and the college's own financial statement are required. The deadline for filing freshman financial aid applications for fall entry is April 13.

International Students: There are 2 international students enrolled. They must take the College Entrance Examination Board test.

Computers: Wireless access is available. Several computer labs are available to students. Wireless access is available in main buildings. All students may access the system. There are no time limits and no fees.

Graduates: From July 1, 2004 to June 30, 2005, 581 bachelor's degrees were awarded. The most popular majors were elementary education (12%), nursing (11%), and secretarial studies (9%). In an average class, 3% graduate in 3 years or less, 11% graduate in 4 years or less, 31% graduate in 5 years or less, and 38% graduate in 6 years or less. 37 companies recruited on campus in 2004-2005.

Admissions Contact: Delma Barrios, Admissions Director. E-mail: *dbarrios@upra.edu* Web: *www.upra.edu*

UNIVERSITY OF PUERTO RICO/BAYAMON UNIVERSITY COLLEGE CAMPUS   A-1

Bayamon, PR 00959-1919	(787) 786-2885, ext. 2426
Full-time: 1785 men, 2320 women	Faculty: 230
Part-time: 550 men, 680 women	Ph.D.s: 21%
Graduate: none	Student/Faculty: 18 to 1
Year: semesters, summer session	Tuition: $1600
Application Deadline: see profile	Room & Board: n/app
Freshman Class: n/av	
SAT or ACT: required	

Bayamon University College, a commuter institution founded in 1971, is part of the University of Puerto Rico system. It offers undergraduate business, education, and technical programs. Figures in the above capsule and in this profile are approximate. Approximate tuition and fees for Puerto Rican residents total $1600 per year; nonresident U.S. citizens pay an amount equal to the nonresident rate at a state university in their home state. The library contains 67,020 volumes, 247,302 microform items, and 5103 audio/video tapes/CDs/DVDs, and subscribes to 273 periodicals including electronic. Computerized library services include the card catalog and database searching. Special learning facilities include a learning resource center. The 78-acre campus is in a suburban area 9 miles west of San Juan. There are 20 buildings.

Student Life: 53% are from public schools. 100% are Hispanic. The average age of freshmen is 18; all undergraduates, 21. 24% do not continue beyond their first year; 75% remain to graduate.

Housing: There are no residence halls. 100% of students commute. Alcohol is not permitted. All students may keep cars.

Activities: There are no fraternities or sororities. There are 15 groups on campus, including art, band, cheerleading, chess, choir, chorus, computers, drama, drill team, honors, professional, religious, social, social service, and student government. Popular campus events include an annual sports tournament, recognition of distinguished athletes, and the college anniversary.

Sports: There are 13 intercollegiate sports for men and 10 for women. Facilities include a basketball/volleyball court, a tennis court, a track and field site, an exercise gym, and a recreation room with table tennis, electronic games, and pool tables.

Disabled Students: 90% of the campus is accessible. Wheelchair ramps, special parking, specially equipped rest rooms, lowered drinking fountains, and lowered telephones are available.

Services: Counseling and information services are available, as is tutoring in some subjects, including English, math, Spanish, and physics for engineering and electronics students. There is a reader service for the blind and remedial math.

Campus Safety and Security: Measures include 24-hour foot and vehicle patrol and pamphlets/posters/films.

Programs of Study: UPR-Bayamon confers the B.A. degree. Associate degrees are also awarded. Bachelor's degrees are awarded in BUSINESS (accounting, banking and finance, business administration and management, management engineering, and marketing/retailing/merchandising), COMPUTER AND PHYSICAL SCIENCE (computer science, and information sciences and systems), EDUCATION (early childhood and elementary), ENGINEERING AND ENVIRONMENTAL DESIGN (electrical/electronics engineering technology). Electronics, computer science, and office systems are the strongest academically. Business administration is the largest.

Required: General education requirements include courses in Spanish, English, math, social sciences or humanities, and biological or physical sciences. To graduate, students must complete 130 to 135 credits, including 29 to 34 in the major, with a minimum GPA of 2.0.

Special: Students may cross-register with any campus in the University of Puerto Rico system. Work-study programs, dual majors, pass/fail options, and a 3-2 engineering degree with the Mayaguez campus are also available. There is a freshman honors program.

Faculty/Classroom: 44% of faculty are male; 56%, female. All teach undergraduates. The average class size in an introductory lecture is 23 and in a laboratory, 20.

Requirements: The SAT or ACT is required, or the CEEB's Spanish version of the SAT, along with SAT: Subject tests in Spanish, writing, and math. Applicants must be graduates of accredited secondary schools. The GED is accepted. A GPA of 2.0 is required.

Procedure: Freshmen are admitted in the fall. Entrance exams should be taken by October of the senior year. There is an early decision plan. Check with the school for current deadlines and fee.

Transfer: Applicants must present an associate degree or at least 30 college credits and a minimum GPA of 2.5. 28 of 130 credits required for the bachelor's degree must be completed at UPR-Bayamon.

Visiting: There are regularly scheduled orientations for prospective students. To schedule a visit, contact the Director of Admissions.

Financial Aid: In a recent year, 29% of all full-time freshmen and 71% of continuing full-time students received some form of financial aid. 29% of full-time freshmen and 71% of continuing full-time students received need-based aid. The average freshman award was $3726. UPR-Bayamon is a member of CSS. The CSS/Profile, the college's own financial statement and the income tax forms, medical receipts, and social security information, are required. Check with the school for current deadlines.

International Students: Applicants must take the SAT or or the Spanish equivalent version of the SAT, along with SAT: Subject tests in Spanish, writing, and math.

Computers: All students may access the system daily from 8 A.M. to 10 P.M. and Saturday from 8 A.M. to 4:30 P.M. There are no time limits and no fees.

Graduates: In a recent year, 551 bachelor's degrees were awarded. The most popular majors were accounting (11%), office systems (10%), and management (7%). In an average class, 16% graduate in 4 years or less, 31% graduate in 5 years or less, and 13% graduate in 6 years or less.

Admissions Contact: Vivian Rivera, Director of Admissions.

UNIVERSITY OF PUERTO RICO/CAYEY UNIVERSITY COLLEGE   C-2

Cayey, PR 00736	(809) 738-2161, ext. 2208
Full-time: 1030 men, 2570 women	Faculty: 181
Part-time: 105 men, 290 women	Ph.D.s: 48%
Graduate: none	Student/Faculty: 20 to 1
Year: semesters, summer session	Tuition: $1250 ($2400)
Application Deadline: see profile	Room & Board: n/app
Freshman Class: n/av	
SAT: required	ACT: not required

Cayey University College, founded in 1967, is a public liberal arts institution and part of the University of Puerto Rico. Figures in the above capsule and in this profile are approximate. The library contains 107,365 volumes, 49 microform items, and 3965 audio/video tapes/CDs/DVDs, and subscribes to 424 periodicals including electronic. Computerized library services include the card catalog, interlibrary loans, and database searching. Special learning facilities include a learning resource center and an art museum. The 167-acre campus is in an urban area 30 miles south of San Juan. There are 54 buildings.

Student Life: 85% are from public schools. 100% are Hispanic. The average age of freshmen is 18; all undergraduates, 22. 15% do not continue beyond their first year; 85% remain to graduate.

Housing: There are no residence halls. 100% of students commute. Alcohol is not permitted. All students may keep cars.

Activities: There is 1 local fraternity. There are no sororities. There are 17 groups on campus, including band, cheerleading, chorus, drama, honors, marching band, orchestra, political, professional, religious, and student government. Popular campus events include Student Day.

Sports: There are 10 intercollegiate sports for men and 6 for women, and 9 intramural sports for men and 8 for women. Facilities include a gym, a pool, and tennis, basketball, and volleyball courts.

Disabled Students: All of the campus is accessible. Wheelchair ramps, elevators, special parking, specially equipped rest rooms, lowered drinking fountains, and lowered telephones are available.

Services: Counseling and information services are available, as is tutoring in most subjects. There is a reader service for the blind, and remedial math, reading, and writing.

Campus Safety and Security: Measures include 24-hour foot and vehicle patrol, shuttle buses, and lighted pathways/sidewalks.

Programs of Study: Cayey University College confers B.A., B.S., B.B.A., B.Ed., and B.S.Ed. degrees. Associate degrees are also awarded. Bachelor's degrees are awarded in BIOLOGICAL SCIENCE (biology/biological science), BUSINESS (accounting, business administration and management, management science, and secretarial studies/office management), COMMUNICATIONS AND THE ARTS (English), COMPUTER AND PHYSICAL SCIENCE (chemistry, mathematics, and natural sciences), EDUCATION (elementary, secondary, and special), SOCIAL SCIENCE (economics, Hispanic American studies, history, humanities, and psychology). Natural science is the strongest academically. Natural science, secondary education, and biology are the largest.

Required: To graduate, students must complete 129 to 135 credits, including 28 in the major, with a minimum GPA of 2.0. There are requirements in humanities, social science, Spanish, English, and natural science. All students must take 2 courses in phys ed.

Special: The university offers cross-registration through the National Student Exchange, study abroad in Toledo, Spain, and a Washington semester. There is 1 national honor society, including Phi Beta Kappa, and a freshman honors program.

Faculty/Classroom: 55% of faculty are male; 45%, female. 99% teach undergraduates and 1% do research. The average class size in an introductory lecture is 30; in a laboratory, 20; and in a regular course, 30.

Requirements: The SAT is required or its CEEB Spanish equivalent. Applicants must be graduates of an accredited secondary school. The GED is accepted. Students should complete 3 high school courses each in English, Spanish, math, science, and social studies. A GPA of 2.0 is required. CLEP credit is accepted. Advanced placement or honor courses is an important factor in the admission decision.

Procedure: Freshmen are admitted in the fall. Entrance exams should be taken in October of the senior year. There is a deferred admissions plan. Check with the school for current deadlines and fee. Applications are accepted on-line.

Transfer: Applicants should have 48 approved credit hours toward the program they are entering. 40 of 129 credits required for the bachelor's degree must be completed at Cayey University College.

Visiting: Visitors may sit in on classes. To schedule a visit, contact Maria Montalvo at (809) 738-2161, ext. 2053.

Financial Aid: In a recent year, 86% of all full-time freshmen and 78% of continuing full-time students received some form of financial aid. 71% of full-time freshmen and 78% of continuing full-time students received need-based aid. The average freshman award was $5485. 6% of undergraduates work part time. The CSS/Profile or FAFSA is required. Check with the school for current deadlines.

International Students: Applicants must take the SAT, the ACT or the CEEB Spanish equivalent of the SAT.

Computers: All students may access the system from 7 P.M. to 9 P.M. Monday through Thursday, and Friday from 7 A.M. to 4:30 P.M. There are no time limits and no fees.

Admissions Contact: Wilfredo Lopez, Admissions Office.
Web: www@cayey.upr.edu

UNIVERSITY OF PUERTO RICO/MAYAGUEZ A-1

Mayaguez, PR 00680 (787) 265-3811; Fax: (787) 834-5265

Full-time: 5100 men, 4950 women	Faculty: 666
Part-time: 475 men, 570 women	Ph.D.s: 64%
Graduate: 545 men, 530 women	Student/Faculty: 15 to 1
Year: semesters, summer session	Tuition: $1250 ($2820)
Application Deadline: see profile	Room & Board: n/app
Freshman Class: n/av	
SAT: required	

The University of Puerto Rico/Mayaguez, founded in 1911, is a bilingual land-grant institution offering undergraduate programs in arts and sciences, business administration, agricultural sciences, and engineering. There are 4 undergraduate and 4 graduate schools. Figures in the above capsule and in this profile are approximate. In addition to regional accreditation, the university has baccalaureate program accreditation with ABET and NLN. The library contains 783,905 volumes, 345,052 microform items, and 43,610 audio/video tapes/CDs/DVDs, and subscribes to 2171 periodicals including electronic. Computerized library services include interlibrary loans, database searching, and Internet access. Special learning facilities include a learning resource center, art gallery, natural history museum, planetarium, and sea grant program, and resource center for science and engineering. The 520-acre campus is in an urban area 70 miles west of San Juan. There are 63 buildings.

Student Life: 99% of students are from Puerto Rico. Others are from 9 foreign countries and Canada. 59% are from public schools. 99% are Hispanic. The average age of freshmen is 18; all undergraduates, 21. 10% do not continue beyond their first year; 52% remain to graduate.

Housing: There are no residence halls. Alcohol is not permitted. All students may keep cars.

Activities: 5% of men belong to 6 local and 1 national fraternity; 2% of women belong to 3 local sororities. There are 90 groups on campus, including band, cheerleading, chess, choir, chorale, chorus, computers, dance, debate, drama, drill team, drum and bugle corps, ethnic, honors, international, jazz band, literary magazine, marching band, newspaper, orchestra, photography, political, professional, religious, social, social service, student government, and yearbook. Popular campus events include fairs, concerts, and dances.

Sports: There are 12 intercollegiate sports for men and 9 for women, and 15 intramural sports for men and 11 for women. Facilities include a gym, a coliseum, a swimming pool, and 2 playing fields.

Disabled Students: 90% of the campus is accessible. Wheelchair ramps, elevators, special parking, specially equipped rest rooms, special class scheduling, lowered drinking fountains, and lowered telephones are available.

Services: Counseling and information services are available, as is tutoring in most subjects. There is a reader service for the blind and remedial math and reading.

Campus Safety and Security: Measures include 24-hour foot and vehicle patrol, shuttle buses, informal discussions, and pamphlets/posters/films. There are emergency telephones and lighted pathways/sidewalks.

Programs of Study: The university confers B.A., B.S., B.B.A., and B.S.A. degrees. Associate, master's, and doctoral degrees are also awarded. Bachelor's degrees are awarded in AGRICULTURE (animal science and horticulture), BIOLOGICAL SCIENCE (biochemistry, biology/biological science, biotechnology, and microbiology), BUSINESS (accounting, banking and finance, business administration and management, business economics, and marketing/retailing/merchandising), COMMUNICATIONS AND THE ARTS (English, fine arts, and French), COMPUTER AND PHYSICAL SCIENCE (chemistry, computer science, geology, information sciences and systems, mathematics, and physics), EDUCATION (foreign languages, and teaching English as a second/foreign language (TESOL/TEFOL)), ENGINEERING AND ENVIRONMENTAL DESIGN (chemical engineering, civil engineering, computer engineering, electrical/electronics engineering, engineering, industrial engineering, mechanical engineering, and surveying engineering), HEALTH PROFESSIONS (nursing, and premedicine), SOCIAL SCIENCE (economics, history, philosophy, political science/government, psychology, social science, and sociology). Engineering, business administration, and agricultural science are the strongest academically. Electrical, chemical, and civil engineering are the largest.

Required: To graduate, students must complete 172 credit hours with a GPA of 2.0. Required disciplines include humanities, English, Spanish, physical science, biology, social science, math, and phys ed.

Special: The university offers co-op programs in engineering, business, and nursing, as well as some study abroad. There is 1 national honor society and a freshman honors program.

Faculty/Classroom: 65% of faculty are male; 35%, female. 23% do research. The average class size in an introductory lecture is 30; in a laboratory, 20; and in a regular course, 30.

Requirements: The SAT is required, or the CEEB's Spanish equivalent, along with SAT: Subject tests in writing, Spanish and Spanish reading, and math. Applicants must be high school graduates or hold the GED. CLEP credit is accepted.

Procedure: Freshmen are admitted in the fall. Entrance exams should be taken during the first semester of the senior year. There is an early admissions plan. Check with the school for current deadlines and fee.

Transfer: Applicants must have 48 college credits with a GPA of 2.0.

Financial Aid: The university is a member of CSS. The college's own financial statement is required. Check with school for current deadlines.

International Students: The school actively recruits these students. Students must take the SAT and SAT: Subject tests in math, Spanish (reading), and English (literature or writing).

Computers: All students may access the system 24 hours a day. There are no fees.

Admissions Contact: Norma Torres, Director.
E-mail: norma@rectoria.uprm.edu Web: www.uprm.edu

UNIVERSITY OF PUERTO RICO/RIO PIEDRAS D-1

San Juan, PR 00931-3344 (787) 764-0000, ext. 5666
Fax: (787) 764-3680, ext. 1375

Full-time: 4900 men, 9770 women	Faculty: n/av
Part-time: 1060 men, 2130 women	Ph.D.s: 41%
Graduate: 1280 men, 2760 women	Student/Faculty: n/av
Year: semesters, summer session	Tuition: $800 ($2480)
Application Deadline: see profile	Room & Board: $4950
Freshman Class: n/av	
SAT: required	

The University of Puerto Rico/Rio Piedras, founded in 1903, is a public institution offering undergraduate programs in arts and sciences, business, and education. Figures in the above capsule and in this profile are approximate. Nonresident U.S. citizens pay annual tuition and fees equal to what Puerto Rican students would pay at a public university in the home states. There are 8 undergraduate and 10 graduate schools. In addition to regional accreditation, UPR/Rio Piedras has baccalaureate program accreditation with ADA, CSWE, NAAB, and NCATE. The 10 libraries contain 1,804,010 volumes and 1,678,239 microform items, and subscribe to 5600 periodicals including electronic. Computerized library services include the card catalog. Special learning facilities include a learning resource center, art gallery, natural history museum, radio station, audiovisual services, and television production facilities. The 271-

acre campus is in an urban area in the Rio Piedras section of San Juan. Including any residence halls, there are 134 buildings.

Student Life: 99% of undergraduates are from Puerto Rico. Others are from 28 foreign countries and Canada. 49% are from public schools. 100% are Hispanic. The average age of freshmen is 18; all undergraduates, 20. 9% do not continue beyond their first year; 46% remain to graduate.

Housing: 789 students can be accommodated in college housing, which includes coed dormitories. On-campus housing is available on a first-come, first-served basis and is available on a lottery system for upperclassmen. Priority is given to out-of-town students. Alcohol is not permitted. All students may keep cars.

Activities: There is 1 local fraternity. There are 63 groups on campus, including art, band, chorus, drama, honors, international, literary magazine, newspaper, pep band, political, professional, radio and TV, religious, social, social service, and student government. Popular campus events include sports events and spring and Christmas concerts.

Sports: There are 12 intercollegiate sports for men and 8 for women, and 15 intramural sports for men and 10 for women. Facilities include a sports complex with a swimming pool, a gym, track and field areas, and tennis, basketball, and volleyball courts.

Disabled Students: 80% of the campus is accessible. Wheelchair ramps, elevators, special parking, specially equipped rest rooms, special class scheduling, lowered drinking fountains, and lowered telephones are available.

Services: There is a reader service for the blind, and remedial math, reading, and writing.

Campus Safety and Security: Measures include 24-hour foot and vehicle patrol, shuttle buses, pamphlets/posters/films, and emergency telephones. There are lighted pathways/sidewalks.

Programs of Study: UPR/Rio Piedras confers B.A., B.S., B.B.A., B.E.D., and B. in Secretarial Science degrees. Master's and doctoral degrees are also awarded. Bachelor's degrees are awarded in AGRICULTURE (natural resource management), BIOLOGICAL SCIENCE (biology/biological science and nutrition), BUSINESS (accounting, banking and finance, business administration and management, business economics, business statistics, labor studies, management science, marketing management, personnel management, and secretarial studies/office management), COMMUNICATIONS AND THE ARTS (comparative literature, dramatic arts, English, fine arts, journalism, languages, music, and romance languages and literature), COMPUTER AND PHYSICAL SCIENCE (applied mathematics, chemistry, computer science, and information sciences and systems), EDUCATION (education, elementary, secondary, and special), ENGINEERING AND ENVIRONMENTAL DESIGN (environmental design), SOCIAL SCIENCE (anthropology, economics, family/consumer studies, geography, history, home economics, interdisciplinary studies, liberal arts/general studies, philosophy, political science/government, psychology, social science, social work, and sociology). Natural sciences is the strongest academically. Secondary education is the largest.

Required: To graduate, students must complete 117 to 147 credits, with a minimum GPA of 2.0. All students must take basic courses in biological sciences, physical sciences, social sciences, Spanish, humanities, and English. Spanish is the language of instruction in most courses, but students are required to have a working knowledge of English.

Special: The university offers a co-op program in accounting, internships at local government and private agencies, study abroad in 11 countries, a Washington semester, a general studies degree, and nondegree study. There is 1 national honor society.

Faculty/Classroom: 48% of faculty are male; 52%, female. No introductory courses are taught by graduate students. The average class size in an introductory lecture is 23; in a laboratory, 20; and in a regular course, 23.

Requirements: The SAT is required or the CEEB's Spanish equivalent. Applicants must be graduates of an accredited secondary school. The GED is accepted. Students should have completed 3 courses each of English and Spanish, 2 courses each of math and science, and 3 electives. A GPA of 2.0 is required. AP credits are accepted. Important factors in the admissions decision are advanced placement or honor courses, evidence of special talent, and extracurricular activities record.

Procedure: Freshmen are admitted in the fall. Entrance exams should be taken in November or February of the senior year. Check with the school for current deadlines and fee.

Transfer: 592 transfer students enrolled in a recent year. Applicants from within Puerto Rico should have a minimum of 48 credits with a 2.5 GPA; out-of-state applicants, 30 credits with a 2.5 GPA.

Visiting: To schedule a visit, contact the Dean of Students at (787) 764-0000, ext. 5540 or 5541.

Financial Aid: The CSS/Profile and the Puerto Rico Income Tax Revenue Report are required. Check with the school for current deadlines.

International Students: In a recent year, there were 19 international students enrolled. The school actively recruits therse students. They must take the Spanish or English SAT.

Computers: All students may access the system according to schedules provided during the semester. There are no time limits and no fees.

Admissions Contact: Cruz B. Valentin, Admissions Director. Web: *www.uprrp.edu*

UNIVERSITY OF THE SACRED HEART   D-1

Santurce, PR 00914   (787) 728-1199; Fax: (787) 727-7880

Full-time: 1150 men, 2100 women	**Faculty:** 134; IIB, --$
Part-time: 440 men, 875 women	**Ph.Ds:** 30%
Graduate: 170 men, 485 women	**Student/Faculty:** 24 to 1
Year: semesters, summer session	**Tuition:** $4640
Application Deadline: see profile	**Room & Board:** $950
Freshman Class: n/av	
SAT: required	

University of the Sacred Heart, founded in 1935, is a private, comprehensive Roman Catholic institution. There are 6 undergraduate and 4 graduate schools. Figures in the above capsule and in the profile are approximate. In addition to regional accreditation, the university has baccalaureate program accreditation with CAHEA, CSWE, and NLN. The library contains 124,936 volumes, 49,086 microform items, and 10,366 audio/video tapes/CDs/DVDs, and subscribes to 1525 periodicals including electronic. Computerized library services include the card catalog and database searching. Special learning facilities include a learning resource center, art gallery, natural history museum, TV station, and a communication center, and secretarial, human performance, and art labs. The 33-acre campus is in an urban area in San Juan. Including any residence halls, there are 14 buildings.

Student Life: 44% are from public schools. 100% are Hispanic. The average age of freshmen is 19; all undergraduates, 22.

Housing: 422 students can be accommodated in college housing, which includes single-sex dormitories. On-campus housing is available on a first-come, first-served basis. Alcohol is not permitted. All students may keep cars.

Activities: There are no fraternities or sororities.

Sports: There are 12 intercollegiate sports for men and 10 for women, and 8 intramural sports for men and 8 for women. Facilities include 1 volleyball and basketball court with 1500 seating capacity, Nautilus and free-weight gym, 4 tennis courts, a softball field, 3 beach volley courts, an Olympic swimming pool, a game room, locker area, judo area, and weight-lifting area.

Disabled Students: Wheelchair ramps, elevators, special parking, specially equipped rest rooms, lowered drinking fountains, and lowered telephones are available.

Campus Safety and Security: Measures include 24-hour foot and vehicle patrol.

Programs of Study: The university confers B.A., B.S., B.A.C., B.B.A., B.Ed., B.O.S.A., and B.S.N. degrees. Associate and master's degrees are also awarded. Bachelor's degrees are awarded in BIOLOGICAL SCIENCE (biology/biological science), BUSINESS (accounting, business administration and management, management information systems, marketing/retailing/merchandising, personnel management, secretarial studies/office management, and tourism), COMMUNICATIONS AND THE ARTS (advertising, communications, telecommunications, and visual and performing arts), COMPUTER AND PHYSICAL SCIENCE (chemistry, computer science, and mathematics), EDUCATION (elementary, and physical), HEALTH PROFESSIONS (medical technology and nursing), SOCIAL SCIENCE (criminal justice, psychology, social work, and urban studies). Business administration and communications are the largest.

Required: To graduate, students must complete between 133 and 145 credits, including 22 to 45 in the major, with a minimum GPA of 2.1 in the major and 2.0 overall. All students must take 12 credits of English, 9 credits of Spanish, 6 credits each of theology, humanities, social sciences, and biology, and 3 credits each of logic and philosophy, arts, computer science, and physical fitness. Some programs require a fieldwork practicum.

Special: The university offers a Washington semester, work-study, and nondegree programs in continuing education and basic skills. Study in the mainland United States is possible through the National Student Exchange and through independent agreements with various private and public colleges and universities. There are also opportunities for study in Spain and Mexico. A 3-2 engineering degree is offered with Manhattan College in New York. There is 1 national honor society.

Faculty/Classroom: 47% of faculty are male; 53%, female.

Requirements: The SAT is required, or the CEEB's Spanish equivalent, along with SAT: Subject tests in Spanish, English, and math. Applicants must be graduates of an accredited secondary school. The GED is accepted. The admissions formula is based on GPA (x 600) + CEEB (verbal + math + English). Applicants whose index is 3300 will be admitted to the university. Those who comply with only 1 (GPA or CEEB) will be considered individually by the evaluation committee. A GPA of 2.5 is required. AP credits are accepted.

Procedure: Entrance exams should be taken in October of the senior year. There are early decision and early admissions plans. Check with the school for current deadlines and fee.

Transfer: Applicants with at least 30 college credits and a high school and college GPA of 2.5 are eligible for transfer. Students must submit CEEB scores and a letter of recommendation. Three quarters of the credits needed in the major must be taken at the university.

Visiting: There are regularly scheduled orientations for prospective students. Visitors may sit in on classes. To schedule a visit, contact the Admission, Promotion, and Recruitment Office at (787) 728-1602 or (787) 728-1515, ext. 3237.

Financial Aid: The university is a member of CSS. The CSS/Profile, the college's own financial statement, and the AFSA are required. Check with the school for current deadlines.

International Students: In a recent year, there were 75 international students enrolled. They must take the SAT or or the CEEB's Spanish equivalent.

Computers: All students may access the system. There are no time limits. The fee is $25 to $75. It is strongly recommended that all students have a personal computer.

Admissions Contact: Luis A. Henriquez, Director of Admission and Promotion. A video is available. E-mail: *nuevoingreso@sagrado.edu* Web: *www.sagrado.edu*

RHODE ISLAND

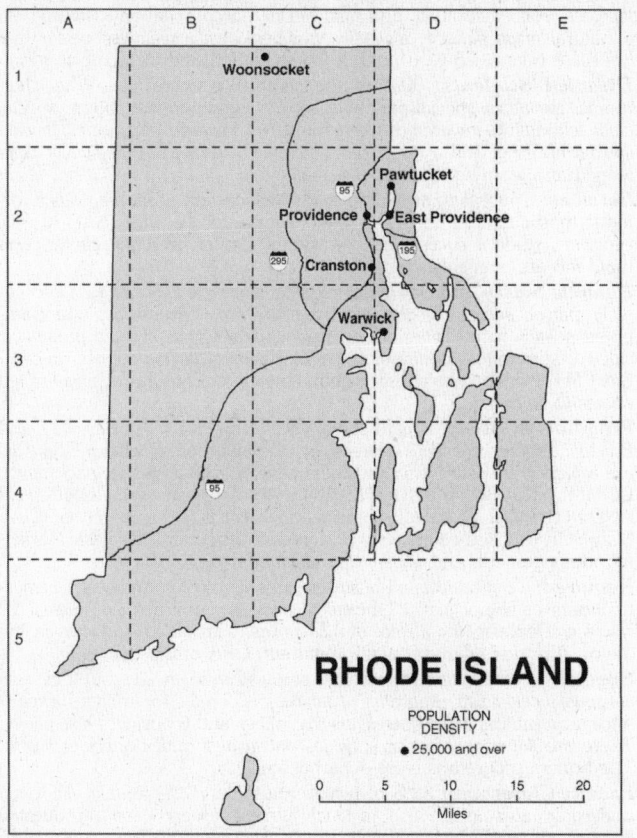

RHODE ISLAND

POPULATION DENSITY

● 25,000 and over

0   5   10   15   20
Miles

BROWN UNIVERSITY   C-2
Providence, RI 02912   (401) 863-2378; Fax: (401) 863-9300
Full-time: 2771 men, 3160 women   **Faculty:** 630; I, +$
Part-time: 88 men, 157 women   **Ph.D.s:** 98%
Graduate: 1065 men, 1020 women   **Student/Faculty:** 9 to 1
Year: semesters, summer session   **Tuition:** $33,219
Application Deadline: January 1   **Room & Board:** $8796
Freshman Class: 16,911 applied, 2587 accepted, 1475 enrolled
SAT Verbal/Math: 720/720*   **ACT:** 30   **MOST COMPETITIVE**

Brown University, founded in 1764, is a co-educational liberal arts institution and a member of the Ivy League. In addition to regional accreditation, Brown has baccalaureate program accreditation with ABET. The 6 libraries contain 3,000,000 volumes, 1,000,000 microform items, and 28,000 audio/video tapes/CDs/DVDs, and subscribe to 16,000 periodicals including electronic. Computerized library services include the card catalog, interlibrary loans, database searching, and Internet access. Special learning facilities include a learning resource center, art gallery, planetarium, radio station, TV station, and an anthropology museum. The 140-acre campus is in an urban area 45 miles south of Boston. Including any residence halls, there are 243 buildings.

Student Life: 96% of undergraduates are from out of state, mostly the Middle Atlantic. Students are from 50 states, 72 foreign countries, and Canada. 56% are from public schools. 52% are white; 14% Asian American. The average age of freshmen is 18; all undergraduates, 20. 4% do not continue beyond their first year; 96% remain to graduate.

Housing: 4350 students can be accommodated in college housing, which includes single-sex and coed dormitories, on-campus apartments, off-campus apartments, fraternity houses, and sorority houses. In addition, there are language houses, special-interest houses, international house, technology house, environmental studies house, and cooperatives. On-campus housing is guaranteed for all 4 years. 85% of students live on campus; of those, 90% remain on campus on weekends. Upperclassmen may keep cars.

Activities: 12% of men belong to 10 national fraternities; 2% of women belong to 3 national sororities. There are 240 groups on campus, including art, band, cheerleading, chess, choir, chorale, chorus, computers, dance, debate, drama, ethnic, film, gay, honors, international, jazz band, literary magazine, marching band, musical theater, newspaper, orchestra, photography, political, professional, radio and TV, religious, social,

social service, student government, and yearbook. Popular campus events include Commencement, Spring Weekend, and Parents Weekend.

Sports: There are 17 intercollegiate sports for men and 20 for women, and 15 intramural sports for men and 15 for women. Facilities include a 25,000-seat stadium, an Olympic-size pool, a 200-meter, 6-lane track, a hockey rink, playing fields, weight-training rooms, facilities for wrestling, and courts for squash, handball, racquetball, tennis, basketball, and volleyball.

Disabled Students: Wheelchair ramps, elevators, special parking, and specially equipped rest rooms are available.

Services: Counseling and information services are available, as is tutoring in most subjects. There is a reader service for the blind. Other services include class note taking, books on tape, diagnostic testing services, oral tests, tutors, and untimed tests.

Campus Safety and Security: Measures include 24-hour foot and vehicle patrol, self-defense education, security escort services, and shuttle buses. There are informal discussions, pamphlets/posters/films, emergency telephones, lighted pathways/sidewalks, and the Safe Walk program.

Programs of Study: Brown confers A.B. and Sc.B. degrees. Master's and doctoral degrees are also awarded. Bachelor's degrees are awarded in BIOLOGICAL SCIENCE (biochemistry, biology/biological science, biophysics, marine biology, and neurosciences), COMMUNICATIONS AND THE ARTS (American literature, art, art history and appreciation, classics, comparative literature, English, linguistics, media arts, music, performing arts, Portuguese, and visual and performing arts), COMPUTER AND PHYSICAL SCIENCE (applied mathematics, chemical physics, chemistry, computer science, geology, mathematics, physics, and statistics), EDUCATION (education), ENGINEERING AND ENVIRONMENTAL DESIGN (architectural technology, architecture, computational sciences, engineering, and environmental science), HEALTH PROFESSIONS (biomedical science and community health work), SOCIAL SCIENCE (African American studies, African studies, American studies, anthropology, archeology, classical/ancient civilization, cognitive science, East Asian studies, economics, ethnic studies, French studies, gender studies, German area studies, Hispanic American studies, history, international relations, Italian studies, Judaic studies, Latin American studies, medieval studies, Middle Eastern studies, philosophy, political science/government, psychology, public administration, religious education, Russian and Slavic studies, sociology, South Asian studies, urban studies, and women's studies). Biological sciences, international relations, and history and economics are the largest.

Required: To graduate, students must pass 30 of 32 courses taken (4 each semester), including 8 to 21 courses in the major. There are no distribution requirements or specific required courses.(except for the required courses in a major). Honors thesis are available in each concentration program.

Special: Students may cross-register with Rhode Island School of Design, or study abroad in any of 50 programs in 15 countries. A combined A.B.-S.C.B. degree is possible in any major field with 5 years of study. Dual and student-designed majors, community internships, and pass/fail options are available. Students may pursue 5-year programs in the arts or sciences, or the 8-year program in the liberal medical education continuum. There is a chapter of Phi Beta Kappa.

Faculty/Classroom: 68% of faculty are male; 32%, female. All both teach and do research. Graduate students teach 13% of introductory courses. The average class size in an introductory lecture is 200; in a laboratory, 20; and in a regular course, 40.

Admissions: 15% of the 2005-2006 applicants were accepted. The SAT scores for the 2005-2006 freshman class were: Verbal--8% between 500 and 599, 28% between 600 and 700, and 64% above 700; Math--5% between 500 and 599, 29% between 600 and 700, and 66% above 700. The ACT scores were 7% between 21 and 23, 16% between 24 and 26, 15% between 27 and 28, and 62% above 28. 97% of the current freshmen were in the top fifth of their class; 100% were in the top two fifths. 171 freshmen graduated first in their class.

Requirements: The SAT or ACT is required. The ACT Optional Writing test is also required, along with any 2 SAT Subject tests. The ACT may be substituted for both the SAT Reasoning and Subject tests. Applicants must be graduates of accredited high schools. Secondary preparation is expected to include courses in English, foreign language, math, laboratory science, the arts (music or art), and history. A personal essay is required. The high school transcript is a most important criterion for admission. AP credits are accepted. Important factors in the admissions decision are advanced placement or honor courses, evidence of special talent, and recommendations by school officials.

Procedure: Freshmen are admitted in the fall. Entrance exams should be taken in the junior or senior year. There are early decision and deferred admissions plans. Early decision applications should be filed by November 1; regular applications, by January 1 for fall entry, along with a $70 fee. Notification of early decision is sent December 15; regular decision, April 1. 571 early decision candidates were accepted for the 2005-2006 class. 450 applicants were on the 2005 waiting list; 97 were admitted. Applications are accepted on-line.

Transfer: 142 transfer students enrolled in 2005. Transfer applicants must submit high school and college transcripts, 2 recommendations from college professors, scores on the ACT or on the SAT and any 2 SAT Subject tests, a letter of good standing, and a personal essay. 15 of 30 credits required for the bachelor's degree must be completed at Brown.

Visiting: There are regularly scheduled orientations for prospective students, Group Information Sessions are usually conducted Monday through Friday at 2 P.M. and at 10 A.M. from mid-February through November and on Saturday mornings from mid-September to mid-November. Check the web site for schedule variations. There are guides for informal visits and visitors may sit in on classes and stay overnight. To schedule a visit, contact the Admission Office Receptionist at *admission-undergraduate@brown.edu*.

Financial Aid: Brown is a member of CSS. The CSS/Profile or FAFSA, the college's own financial statement and the some state forms are required. The deadline for filing freshman financial aid applications for fall entry is January 1.

International Students: There are 365 international students enrolled. The school actively recruits these students. Satisfactory scores are required on the written TOEFL and the SAT or the ACT. Students must also take 2 SAT: Subject tests and the SAT Reasoning test.

Computers: Wireless access is available. There are 400 workstations on campus for student use. Students all have access to the main frame. All students may access the system at any time. There are no time limits and no fees.

Graduates: From July 1, 2004 to June 30, 2005, 1449 bachelor's degrees were awarded. The most popular majors were biological sciences (9%), international relations (9%), and history (9%). In an average class, 84% graduate in 4 years or less, 93% graduate in 5 years or less, and 95% graduate in 6 years or less. 400 companies recruited on campus in 2004-2005. Of the 2004 graduating class, 35% were enrolled in graduate school within 6 months of graduation and 65% were employed.

Admissions Contact: James Miller, Dean of Admission.
E-mail: *admission_undergraduate@brown.edu* Web: *www.brown.edu*

BRYANT COLLEGE		C-2
Smithfield, RI 02917-1284		**(401) 232-6100**
		(800) 622-7001; Fax: (401) 232-6741
Full-time: 1802 men, 1210 women	**Faculty:** 133; IIB, ++$	
Part-time: 96 men, 95 women	**Ph.D.s:** 86%	
Graduate: 260 men, 179 women	**Student/Faculty:** 23 to 1	
Year: semesters, summer session	**Tuition:** $24,762	
Application Deadline: February 15	**Room & Board:** $9568	
Freshman Class: 4214 applied, 2430 accepted, 822 enrolled		
SAT Verbal/Math: 540/570*	**ACT:** 23	**VERY COMPETITIVE**

Bryant College, founded in 1863, is a private, primarily residential institution that offers degrees in business, liberal arts, and technology. There are 2 undergraduate schools and 1 graduate school. In addition to regional accreditation, Bryant has baccalaureate program accreditation with AACSB. The library contains 154,353 volumes, 14,500 microform items, and 1148 audio/video tapes/CDs/DVDs, subscribes to 200 periodicals including electronic and has access to 20,518 e-journals. Computerized library services include the card catalog, interlibrary loans, database searching, Internet access, and laptop Internet portals. Special learning facilities include a learning resource center, a communication complex housing an all-digital television studio and radio station, a learning/language lab, a writing center, academic center, a center for international business, and a center for information and technology. The 420-acre campus is in a suburban area 12 miles northwest of Providence. Including any residence halls, there are 46 buildings.

Student Life: 84% of undergraduates are from out of state, mostly the Northeast. Students are from 31 states, 30 foreign countries, and Canada. 85% are white. The average age of freshmen is 18; all undergraduates, 20. 12% do not continue beyond their first year; 69% remain to graduate.

Housing: Approximately 2500 students can be accommodated in college housing, which includes single-sex and coed dormitories and on-campus apartments. In addition, there are honor houses, special-interest houses, housing for international business students, and 24 hour quiet housing. On-campus housing is guaranteed for all 4 years. 83% of students live on campus; of those, 75% remain on campus on weekends. All students may keep cars.

Activities: 6% of men belong to 5 national fraternities; 4% of women belong to 3 national sororities. There are 60 groups on campus, including art, cheerleading, chorus, computers, dance, drama, ethnic, film, gay, international, jazz band, literary magazine, newspaper, pep band, political, professional, radio and TV, religious, social, social service, student government, and yearbook. Popular campus events include Parents and Family Weekend, Spring Weekend, and Festival of Lights.

Sports: There are 11 intercollegiate sports for men and 11 for women, and 8 intramural sports for men and 7 for women. Facilities include a 2700-seat gym, tennis, squash, racquetball, and multipurpose courts, a 400-meter track, cross-country trails, playing fields for baseball, softball, lacrosse, soccer, football, and field hockey, a competition stadium with a natural grass surface, a varsity weight room, a wellness center that houses a 6-lane, 25-yard pool, a fitness center, and an aerobics room.

Disabled Students: 90% of the campus is accessible. Wheelchair ramps, elevators, special parking, specially equipped rest rooms, special class scheduling, lowered drinking fountains, lowered telephones, limited special housing, and a range of support services for the physically challenged and learning disabled are available.

Services: Counseling and information services are available, as is tutoring in most subjects. There is a reader service for the blind. A study skills program, student success course, writing center, learning center, and math lab are available.

Campus Safety and Security: Measures include 24-hour foot and vehicle patrol, security escort services, informal discussions, and pamphlets/posters/films. There are emergency telephones, lighted pathways/sidewalks, monitored one point of access/egress, bicycle patrols, on-campus EMTs, video cameras, prevention/awareness programs, and limited access to dorms.

Programs of Study: Bryant confers B.A, B.S., B.S.B.A., B.Sc.I.T., and B.S.I.B. degrees. Master's degrees are also awarded. Bachelor's degrees are awarded in BUSINESS (business administration and management), COMMUNICATIONS AND THE ARTS (communications), COMPUTER AND PHYSICAL SCIENCE (information sciences and systems), SOCIAL SCIENCE (applied psychology and liberal arts/general studies). Marketing, management, and accounting are the largest.

Required: To graduate, all business students must complete 61 semester hours of liberal arts, 31 hours of business, and a maximum of 12 hours of electives, for a total of 123 hours, with 18 to 33 hours in the major. All students must have a minimum GPA of 2.0 overall.

Special: Bryant offers internships, study abroad in 21 countries, on-campus work-study programs, dual majors, credit for military experience, and minors in 16 liberal arts disciplines and 6 business disciplines. There are 4 national honor societies and a freshman honors program. The honors program is cross-departmental.

Faculty/Classroom: 68% of faculty are male; 32%, female. All teach undergraduates and 79% both teach and do research. No introductory courses are taught by graduate students. The average class size in an introductory lecture is 28; in a laboratory, 25; and in a regular course, 27.

Admissions: 58% of the 2005-2006 applicants were accepted. The SAT scores for the 2005-2006 freshman class were: Verbal--21% below 500, 60% between 500 and 599, 18% between 600 and 700, and 1% above 700; Math--9% below 500, 53% between 500 and 599, 35% between 600 and 700, and 3% above 700. The ACT scores were 15% below 21, 37% between 21 and 23, 33% between 24 and 26, 4% between 27 and 28, and 11% above 28. 43% of the current freshmen were in the top fifth of their class; 80% were in the top two fifths. 2 freshmen graduated first in their class.

Requirements: The SAT or ACT is required. In addition, applicants must be graduates of an accredited secondary school or have a GED certificate. A total of 16 Carnegie units is required, including 4 years of English, 4 of math (minimum of 1 year beyond algebra II), and 2 years each of social studies, lab science, and foreign language. An essay is required. A GPA of 3.3 is recommended. AP and CLEP credits are accepted.

Procedure: Freshmen are admitted fall and spring. Entrance exams should be taken before January of the senior year. There are early decision, early admissions, and deferred admissions plans. Early decision applications should be filed by November 15; regular applications, by February 15 for fall entry. Notification of early decision is sent December 15; regular decision, mid-March. 96 early decision candidates were accepted for the 2005-2006 class. 310 applicants were on the 2005 waiting list; 78 were admitted. Application fee is $50. Applications are accepted on-line.

Transfer: 193 transfer students enrolled in 2004-2005. Applicants must have a minimum college GPA of 2.5, although a 3.0 is recommended. Applicants must be high school graduates or have a GED, with a minimum of a year of math beyond algebra ll in high school or college level math. 30 of 123 credits required for the bachelor's degree must be completed at Bryant.

Visiting: There are regularly scheduled orientations for prospective students, includes a campus tour and an admission/financial aid presentation. There are guides for informal visits and visitors may sit in on classes. Only admitted students can stay overnight and on a limited basis. To schedule a visit, contact the Office of Admission.

Financial Aid: In 2005-2006, 85% of all full-time freshmen and 84% of continuing full-time students received some form of financial aid. 63% of full-time freshmen and 59% of continuing full-time students received need-based aid. The average freshman award was $15,176. Need-based scholarships or need-based grants averaged $9485 ($16,000 maximum); need-based self-help aid (loans and jobs) averaged $5485 ($4000 maximum); non-need-based athletic scholarships averaged $16,355 ($34,830 maximum); and other non-need-based awards and non-need-based scholarships averaged $8303 ($24,762 maximum). 19% of undergraduates work part time. Average annual earnings from campus work are $1530. The average financial indebtedness of the 2005 graduate was $22,340. Bryant is a member of CSS. The FAFSA is required. The deadline for filing freshman financial aid applications for fall entry is February 15.

International Students: There are 48 international students enrolled. The school actively recruits these students. They must score satisfactorily on the written TOEFL or on the electronic version and also take the SAT or the ACT.

Computers: Wireless access is available. All freshmen are provided with a wireless labtop and can access the Internet, e-mail, Blackboard (course management), Banner (financial), and web services at anytime. These services can also be accessed on any of the 539 accessible PCs on campus or a student-owned computer. All students may access the system. There are no time limits and no fees. All students are required to have personal computers.

Graduates: From July 1, 2004 to June 30, 2005, 644 bachelor's degrees were awarded. The most popular majors were marketing (26%), management (23%), and accounting (17%). In an average class, 63% graduate in 4 years or less, 68% graduate in 5 years or less, and 69% graduate in 6 years or less. 197 companies recruited on campus in 2004-2005. Of the 2004 graduating class, 4% were enrolled in graduate school within 6 months of graduation and 90% were employed.

Admissions Contact: Cynthia Bonn, Director of Admission. A video is available. E-mail: *admission@bryant.edu* Web: *www.bryant.edu*

JOHNSON AND WALES UNIVERSITY/PROVIDENCE CAMPUS

Providence, RI 02903	(401) 598-1000; (800) 342-5598
Full-time: 4024 men, 4375 women	Faculty: n/av
Part-time: 411 men, 527 women	Ph.D.s: 25%
Graduate: 408 men, 426 women	Student/Faculty: n/av
Year: quarters, summer session	Tuition: $20,826
Application Deadline: open	Room & Board: $7300
Freshman Class: 15,258 applied, 12,235 accepted, 2792 enrolled	
SAT or ACT required for some programs	LESS COMPETITIVE

Johnson & Wales University/Providence Campus, founded in 1914, is the largest of the J&W campuses and offers more than 50 majors in business, hospitality, culinary arts, technology, and graduate programs. There are 4 undergraduate schools. The 2 libraries contain 94,969 volumes, 439,822 microform items, and 3405 audio/video tapes/CDs/DVDs, and subscribe to 2242 periodicals including electronic. Computerized library services include interlibrary loans, database searching, Internet access, and laptop Internet portals. Special learning facilities include a learning resource center and J&W practicum facilities, the Radisson Airport Hotel and the J&W Inn, are owned and operated by the university and provide students with practical traning serving the public. The Culinary Archives Museum is a resource for culinary research. The 166-acre campus is in an urban area in Providence, 45 minutes from Boston, Cape Cod, and Newport and 3 hours from New York. Including any residence halls, there are 38 buildings.

Student Life: 83% of undergraduates are from out of state, mostly the Northeast. Students are from 50 states, 98 foreign countries, and Canada. 50% are white. The average age of freshmen is 19; all undergraduates, 20.

Housing: 3337 students can be accommodated in college housing, which includes coed dorms and on-campus apartments. In addition, there are honors floors, quiet floors, international housing, national student organization housing, and access student housing. Housing is available to freshmen on a first-deposited, first-contract-received basis. On-campus housing is available on a lottery system for upperclassmen. 70% of students commute. Alcohol is not permitted. All students may keep cars.

Activities: 3% of men belong to 6 national fraternities; 4% of women belong to 7 national sororities. There are 54 groups on campus, including cheerleading, chorale, dance, debate, drama, ethnic, gay, honors, international, newspaper, pep band, political, professional, religious, social, social service, student government, and yearbook.

Sports: There are 8 intercollegiate sports for men, 6 for women, and 2 coed. There are 7 intramural sports for men, 4 for women, and 4 coed. Facilities include state-of-the-art exercise machines and numerous programs, including weight management, personal exercise, wellness programs, body composition analysis, strength training, physical fitness testing, nutritional analysis, physical fitness assessments, life saving, and stress relief days.

Disabled Students: All of the campus is accessible. Wheelchair ramps, elevators, special parking, specially equipped rest rooms, special class scheduling, lowered drinking fountains, and lowered telephones are available.

Services: Counseling and information services are available, as is tutoring in every subject. Workshops in stress and time management and wellness and learning centers are available.

Campus Safety and Security: Measures include 24-hour foot and vehicle patrol, security escort services, shuttle buses, and informal discussions. There are pamphlets/posters/films, emergency telephones, lighted pathways/sidewalks, 24-hour dorm coverage, a phone hot line for campus emergencies, and crime alerts in the student weekly newspaper.

Programs of Study: J&W confers the B.S. degree. Associate, master's, and doctoral degrees are also awarded. Bachelor's degrees are awarded in AGRICULTURE (equine science), BUSINESS (accounting, business administration and management, entrepreneurial studies, fashion merchandising, hospitality management services, hotel/motel and restaurant management, international business management, management information systems, marketing and distribution, marketing management, marketing/retailing/merchandising, office supervision and management, recreation and leisure services, recreational facilities management, retailing, secretarial studies/office management, small business management, sports management, tourism, and transportation and travel marketing), COMMUNICATIONS AND THE ARTS (advertising), COMPUTER AND PHYSICAL SCIENCE (computer management, computer science, information sciences and systems, systems analysis, and web services), EDUCATION (marketing and distribution), ENGINEERING AND ENVIRONMENTAL DESIGN (electrical/electronics engineering, food services technology, and technological management), SOCIAL SCIENCE (clothing and textiles management/production/services, criminal justice, food production/management/services, paralegal studies, parks and recreation management, and systems science). Culinary arts, hotel/restaurant management, and marketing are the strongest academically. Culinary arts, hotel/restaurant management, and sports entertainment event management are the largest.

Required: To graduate, students must complete 180 quarter credit hours, including at least 36 in the major, with a minimum GPA of 2.0. Required classes include English, math, history, economics, science, psychology, sociology, and professional development.

Special: The university offers co-op programs, accelerated degree programs, dual majors, study abroad, and worldwide work-study opportunities in business, hospitality, technology, and culinary arts. Most majors require 11-week internships. There is 1 national honor society, a freshman honors program, and 5 departmental honors program.

Faculty/Classroom: 50% of faculty are male; 41%, female.

Admissions: 80% of the 2005-2006 applicants were accepted.

Requirements: The SAT or ACT is required for some programs. In addition, although SAT and ACT scores are required only for students applying for honors admissions, students who have taken these tests are encouraged to submit their scores. A GPA of 2.0 is required. AP and CLEP credits are accepted. Important factors in the admissions decision are advanced placement or honor courses, extracurricular activities record, and recommendations by school officials.

Procedure: Freshmen are admitted to all sessions. There is a deferred admissions and a rolling admissions plan. Application deadlines are open.

Transfer: 358 transfer students enrolled in 2004-2005. Applicants are required to submit official high school and college transcripts and must have earned a minimum college GPA of 2.0. 45 of 180 quarter credit hours required for the bachelor's degree must be completed at J&W.

Visiting: There are regularly scheduled orientations for prospective students, including an introduction to the academic and social aspects of the campus experience through interactive sessions. There are guides for informal visits and visitors may sit in on classes and stay overnight. To schedule a visit, contact Admissions.

Financial Aid: In 2005-2006, 73% of all full-time freshmen and 67% of continuing full-time students received some form of financial aid. 71% of full-time freshmen and 57% of continuing full-time students received need-based aid. Need-based scholarships or need-based grants averaged $5175; need-based self-help aid (loans and jobs) averaged $7295; and other non-need-based awards and non-need-based scholarships averaged $4090. The average financial indebtedness of the 2005 graduate was $17,704. J&W is a member of CSS. The FAFSA is required. Check with the school for current deadlines.

International Students: There are 777 international students enrolled. The school actively recruits these students. A satisfactory score is required on the written TOEFL.

Computers: Wireless access is available. There are 3 computer centers. The Academic Center labs house more than 300 workstations. There is software for drafting, programming, and electronic engineering. The Harborside labs have 128 networked and Internet-ready computers. Software includes a powerful statistical package, as well as nutrition and menu planning templates.The Xavier labs have 110 networked and 68 nonnetworked computers, all Internet ready, for general use and specialized use, such as for hotel property management and business administration. All students may access the system. There are no fees.

Graduates: From July 1, 2004 to June 30, 2005, 1328 bachelor's degrees were awarded. The most popular majors were culinary (23%), food service (9%), and business marketing (7%). 93 companies recruited on campus in 2004-2005. Of the 2004 graduating class, 35% were enrolled in graduate school within 6 months of graduation.

Admissions Contact: Maureen Dumas, Dean of Admissions. A video is available. E-mail: *admissions.pvd@jwu.edu* Web: *www.jwu.edu*

PROVIDENCE COLLEGE   C-2
Providence, RI 02918

	(401) 865-2535
	(800) 721-6444; Fax: (401) 865-2826
Full-time: 1733 men, 2233 women	**Faculty:** 287; IIA, +$
Part-time: 240 men, 381 women	**Ph.D s:** 92%
Graduate: 320 men, 600 women	**Student/Faculty:** 14 to 1
Year: semesters, summer session	**Tuition:** $25,310
Application Deadline: January 15	**Room & Board:** $9270
Freshman Class: 8237 applied, 4484 accepted, 1069 enrolled	
SAT Verbal/Math: 597/606*	**ACT:** 25 **HIGHLY COMPETITIVE**

Providence College, founded in 1917, is a liberal arts and sciences institution operated by the Dominican order of the Catholic Church. There is 1 undergraduate and 1 graduate school. In addition to regional accreditation, Providence has baccalaureate program accreditation with CSWE and NCATE. The library contains 331,093 volumes and 211,406 microform items, and subscribes to 1600 periodicals including electronic. Computerized library services include interlibrary loans, database searching, Internet access, and laptop Internet portals. Special learning facilities include a learning resource center, art gallery, radio station, Blackfriars Theater, and the Smith Center for the Arts. The 105-acre campus is in a suburban area 50 miles south of Boston. Including any residence halls, there are 41 buildings.

Student Life: 88% of undergraduates are from out of state, mostly the Northeast. Students are from 41 states, 17 foreign countries, and Canada. 63% are from public schools. 83% are white. 67% are Catholic; 21% claim no religious affiliation; 8% Greek Orthodox, Islamic. The average age of freshmen is 18; all undergraduates, 20. 7% do not continue beyond their first year; 83% remain to graduate.

Housing: 3113 students can be accommodated in college housing, which includes single-sex and coed dormitories and on-campus apartments. On-campus housing is available on a first-come, first-served basis and is available on a lottery system for upperclassmen. 83% of students live on campus; of those, 80% remain on campus on weekends. Upperclassmen may keep cars.

Activities: There are no fraternities or sororities. There are 95 groups on campus, including art, band, cheerleading, choir, chorale, chorus, computers, dance, debate, drama, ethnic, honors, international, jazz band, literary magazine, musical theater, newspaper, pep band, photography, political, professional, radio and TV, religious, social, social service, student government, and yearbook. Popular campus events include Multicultural Awareness Week, Midnight Madness, and Junior Ring Weekend.

Sports: There are 7 intercollegiate sports for men and 10 for women, and 2 intramural sports for men and 3 for women. Facilities include an ice arena, indoor track, courts for tennis, racquetball, handball, squash, basketball and volleyball, a pool, a Nautilus program, facilities for weight lifting, aerobics, and ballet studio, a soccer field, softball field, and a turf field.

Disabled Students: 90% of the campus is accessible. Wheelchair ramps, elevators, special parking, specially equipped rest rooms, special class scheduling, lowered drinking fountains, lowered telephones, and special housing are available.

Services: Counseling and information services are available, as is tutoring in most subjects. There is a reader service for the blind and academic support services, including evaluation of learning-disabled students.

Campus Safety and Security: Measures include 24-hour foot and vehicle patrol, self-defense education, security escort services, and shuttle buses. There are informal discussions, pamphlets/posters/films, emergency telephones, lighted pathways/sidewalks, and and a campuswide computerized card access system for entry into all dorms and apartment buildings.

Programs of Study: Providence confers B.A. and B.S. degrees. Associate and master's degrees are also awarded. Bachelor's degrees are awarded in BIOLOGICAL SCIENCE (biochemistry and biology/ biological science), BUSINESS (accounting, banking and finance, business administration and management, and marketing/retailing/ merchandising), COMMUNICATIONS AND THE ARTS (art history and appreciation, dramatic arts, English, French, Italian, music, Spanish, and studio art), COMPUTER AND PHYSICAL SCIENCE (applied physics, chemistry, computer science, and mathematics), EDUCATION (elementary, English, foreign languages, mathematics, music, secondary, social studies, and special), ENGINEERING AND ENVIRONMENTAL DESIGN (preengineering), HEALTH PROFESSIONS (health care administration), SOCIAL SCIENCE (American studies, community services, economics, history, humanities, international studies, philosophy, political science/government, psychology, social science, social work, sociology, and theological studies). Biology, chemistry, and business are the strong-

est academically. Marketing, business administration, and management, and English are the largest.

Required: To graduate, all students must complete at least 116 credit hours, with 24 upper-division hours in the major, and maintain a GPA of 2.0. Students must also meet an English proficiency requirement, complete 20 credits in Western civilization, and fulfill the 30-credit core curriculum, including 6 credits each in natural science, social science, philosophy, and theology, and 3 each in math and fine arts.

Special: Providence offers internships in politics, broadcasting, journalism, and business, and study abroad in 6 countries. Other opportunities for study-abroad are available through AIFS. Also available are dual and student-designed majors, a 3-2 engineering degree with Columbia University or Washington University in St. Louis, nondegree study, and pass/fail options. There are 17 national honor societies and a freshman honors program.

Faculty/Classroom: 63% of faculty are male; 37%, female. All teach undergraduates. No introductory courses are taught by graduate students. The average class size in an introductory lecture is 24; in a laboratory, 15; and in a regular course, 16.

Admissions: 54% of the 2005-2006 applicants were accepted. The SAT scores for the 2005-2006 freshman class were: Verbal--7% below 500, 42% between 500 and 599, 43% between 600 and 700, and 8% above 700; Math--7% below 500, 35% between 500 and 599, 48% between 600 and 700, and 10% above 700. The ACT scores were 9% below 21, 22% between 21 and 23, 32% between 24 and 26, 23% between 27 and 28, and 14% above 28. 71% of the current freshmen were in the top fifth of their class; 94% were in the top two fifths. There were 19 National Merit finalists. 15 freshmen graduated first in their class.

Requirements: The SAT or ACT is required. In addition, applicants must be graduates of an accredited secondary school. A GPA of 3.25 is recommended. High school preparation should include 4 years of English, 3 years of math, 3 years of 1 foreign language, 2 years of lab science, 2 years of history/social studies, and 2 other academic subjects. Either the SAT or ACT with writing is required. An essay and 2 academic letters of recommendation are required. SAT subject tests in 2 areas of the applicants choice are recommended. AP credits are accepted. Important factors in the admissions decision are advanced placement or honor courses, leadership record, and evidence of special talent.

Procedure: Freshmen are admitted fall and spring. Entrance exams should be taken in the junior or senior year. There are early admissions and deferred admissions plans. Early decision applications should be filed by November 1; regular applications, by January 15 for fall entry and December 1 for spring entry. Notification of early decision is sent January 1; regular decision, April 1. 1647 applicants were on the 2005 waiting list; 355 were admitted. Applications are accepted on-line. The fall 2005 application fee was $55.

Transfer: 67 transfer students enrolled in 2004-2005. The application, college transcripts, and courses in progress, high school records, standardized testing scores (SAT and/or ACT), a required essay, an intended major (if one has been selected), and college disciplinary records are reviewed to ensure that the "match" to PC is a good one. 60 of 116 credits required for the bachelor's degree must be completed at Providence.

Visiting: There are regularly scheduled orientations for prospective students, including campus tours and information sessions. There are guides for informal visits and visitors may sit in on classes. To schedule a visit, contact the Admissions Office.

Financial Aid: In 2005-2006, 81% of all full-time freshmen and 78% of continuing full-time students received some form of financial aid. 65% of full-time freshmen and 63% of continuing full-time students received need-based aid. The average freshman award was $18,221. Need-based scholarships or need-based grants averaged $8060 ($24,800 maximum); need-based self-help aid (loans and jobs) averaged $3625 ($5425 maximum); non-need-based athletic scholarships averaged $13,766 ($34,500 maximum); and other non-need-based awards and non-need-based scholarships averaged $12,965 ($24,800 maximum). 20% of undergraduates work part time. Average annual earnings from campus work are $1200. The average financial indebtedness of the 2005 graduate was $23,125. Providence is a member of CSS. The CSS/Profile or FAFSA is required. The deadline for filing freshman financial aid applications for fall entry is February 1.

International Students: There are 41 international students enrolled. The school actively recruits these students. They must score satisfactorily on the written TOEFL or on the electronic version and also take the SAT or the ACT.

Computers: Wireless access is available. Students use the college's network to access on-campus resources and the Internet. The Internet itself can be used by students for research, e-mail, and instant messaging. Every resident student has a network connection for a PC. There are a few wireless areas that students with labtops are able to access by the college network or Internet. All students may access the system. There are no time limits. The fee is $270.

Graduates: From July 1, 2004 to June 30, 2005, 974 bachelor's degrees were awarded. The most popular majors were marketing (10%), business administration and management (9%), and English (7%). In an average class, 82% graduate in 4 years or less, 83% graduate in 5 years or less, and 83% graduate in 6 years or less.

Admissions Contact: Christopher P. Lydon, Associate Vice President for Admission and Enrollment Planning.
E-mail: *pcadmiss@providence.edu* Web: *www.providence.edu*

RHODE ISLAND COLLEGE   C-2

Providence, RI 02908   **(401) 456-8234**
   (800) 669-5760; Fax: (401) 456-8817

Full-time: 1655 men, 3320 women	**Faculty:** 300; IIA, av$
Part-time: 760 men, 1585 women	**Ph.D.s:** 76%
Graduate: 320 men, 1300 women	**Student/Faculty:** 17 to 1
Year: semesters, summer session	**Tuition:** $4000 ($10,200)
Application Deadline: see profile	**Room & Board:** $7570
Freshman Class: n/av	
SAT: required	**COMPETITIVE**

Rhode Island College, founded in 1854, is a state-supported liberal arts institution offering undergraduate and graduate programs in the liberal arts and sciences, social work, education, and human development. There are 4 undergraduate schools and 1 graduate school. Figures in the above capsule and in this profile are approximate. In addition to regional accreditation, RIC has baccalaureate program accreditation with NASAD, NASM, NCATE, and NLN. The library contains 634,000 volumes, 1,338,000 microform items, and 3300 audio/video tapes/CDs/DVDs, and subscribes to 1500 periodicals including electronic. Computerized library services include the card catalog, interlibrary loans, database searching, and Internet access. Special learning facilities include an art gallery and radio station. The 180-acre campus is in a suburban area 50 miles southwest of Boston. Including any residence halls, there are 42 buildings.

Student Life: 90% of undergraduates are from Rhode Island. Others are from 29 states and 4 foreign countries. 90% are white. 60% are Catholic; 14% Protestant. The average age of freshmen is 18; all undergraduates, 24. 28% do not continue beyond their first year; 45% remain to graduate.

Housing: 830 students can be accommodated in college housing, which includes single-sex and coed dormitories. In addition, there are honors houses. On-campus housing is available on a first-come, first-served basis. Priority is given to out-of-town students. 75% of students commute. Alcohol is not permitted. All students may keep cars.

Activities: There are no fraternities or sororities. There are 64 groups on campus, including art, band, cheerleading, chess, chorale, chorus, dance, debate, drama, ethnic, gay, honors, international, literary magazine, musical theater, newspaper, orchestra, political, professional, radio and TV, religious, social, social service, student government, symphony, and yearbook. Popular campus events include a fine and performing arts calendar, chess tournaments, and campus center activities.

Sports: There are 9 intercollegiate sports for men and 10 for women, and 5 intramural sports for men and 5 for women. Facilities include an intercollegiate facility with a 2500-seat arena and student athlete support areas; a recreation center that includes a field house with indoor track, multiuse courts, swimming pool, cardiovascular center, dance studio, and wrestling facility; and outdoor facilities that include varsity baseball and tennis complexes, a track, and a softball facility.

Disabled Students: All of the campus is accessible. Wheelchair ramps, elevators, special parking, specially equipped rest rooms, special class scheduling are available. A peer adviser is available to assist disabled students.

Services: Counseling and information services are available, as is tutoring in most subjects. There is a reader service for the blind, and remedial math, reading, and writing, and services for learning-disabled students and any student needing academic assistance.

Campus Safety and Security: Measures include 24-hour foot and vehicle patrol, self-defense education, security escort services, and informal discussions. There are pamphlets/posters/films, emergency telephones, and lighted pathways/sidewalks.

Programs of Study: RIC confers B.A., B.S., B.F.A., B.G.A., B.M., and B.S.W. degrees. Master's and doctoral degrees are also awarded. Bachelor's degrees are awarded in BIOLOGICAL SCIENCE (biology/biological science), BUSINESS (accounting, business administration and management, business economics, labor studies, marketing/retailing/merchandising, and personnel management), COMMUNICATIONS AND THE ARTS (communications, dramatic arts, English, film arts, fine arts, French, music, photography, and Spanish), COMPUTER AND PHYSICAL SCIENCE (chemistry, computer programming, computer science, information sciences and systems, mathematics, physics, and radiological technology), EDUCATION (art, early childhood, elementary, foreign languages, health, industrial arts, middle school, music, physical, science, secondary, and special), HEALTH PROFESSIONS (medical laboratory technology, and nursing), SOCIAL SCIENCE (African American studies, anthropology, economics, geography, history, philosophy, political science/government, prelaw, psychology, public administration,

social science, social work, sociology, and women's studies). Education, management, and psychology are the largest.

Required: To graduate, students must complete 120 credits and maintain a minimum GPA of 2.0. All students must complete the college's general education program, which consists of 4 core requirements in cultural legacies and critical thinking, and 6 distribution requirements. In addition, all students must complete the college writing and math competeny requirements.

Special: Cross-registration is available with other Rhode Island schools and the National Student Exchange. The college offers internships, study abroad, work-study programs, a general studies degree, dual and student-designed majors, credit by exam, credit for prior learning, and pass/fail options. There are 6 national honor societies, a freshman honors program, and 21 departmental honors programs.

Faculty/Classroom: 56% of faculty are male; 44%, female. 98% both teach and do research. No introductory courses are taught by graduate students. The average class size in an introductory lecture is 30; in a laboratory, 14; and in a regular course, 30.

Requirements: The SAT is required, ACT scores will be accepted. Applicants should be graduates of an accredited secondary school with 18 academic credits, including 4 in English, 3 in math, 2 each in foreign languages (2 years of same language), science (biology plus chemistry or physics), and social studies, 1/2 credit each in the arts, and computer literacy, and the remainder in academic electives. The GED is accepted. An essay is required along with a portfolio for art students and an audition for music students. AP and CLEP credits are accepted. Important factors in the admissions decision are advanced placement or honor courses, evidence of special talent, and leadership record.

Procedure: Freshmen are admitted fall and spring. Entrance exams should be taken by December of the senior year. There are early admissions and deferred admissions plans. Check with the school for current deadlines and fee.

Transfer: Applicants must submit 24 transferable credits with a minimum GPA of 2.25 or 30 college credits and a minimum GPA of 2.0. 45 of 120 credits required for the bachelor's degree must be completed at RIC.

Visiting: There are regularly scheduled orientations for prospective students, including information sessions and a campus tour. There are guides for informal visits and visitors may sit in on classes. To schedule a visit, contact the Admissions Office.

Financial Aid: In a recent year, 76% of all full-time freshmen and 60% of continuing full-time students received some form of financial aid. 65% of full-time freshmen and 60% of continuing full-time students received need-based aid. The average freshman award was $5695. RIC is a member of CSS. The FAFSA and the college's own financial statement are required. Check with the school for current deadlines.

International Students: Satisfactory scores are required on the written TOEFL or the SAT.

Computers: All students may access the system. There are no time limits. The fall 2003 fee was $40.

Admissions Contact: Holly L. Shadoian, Director of Admissions.
E-mail: *hshadoian@ric.edu* or *admissions@ric.edu*
Web: *http://www.ric.edu*

RHODE ISLAND SCHOOL OF DESIGN   C-2

Providence, RI 02903   **(401) 454-6300**
   (800) 364-7473; Fax: (401) 454-6309

Full-time: 640 men, 1238 women	**Faculty:** IIB, ++$
Part-time: 155 men, 225 women	**Ph.D.s:** n/av
Graduate: none	**Student/Faculty:** n/av
Year: 4-1-4	**Tuition:** $26,775
Application Deadline: February 15	**Room & Board:** $8355
Freshman Class: 2512 applied, 870 accepted, 420 enrolled	
SAT Verbal/Math: 600/620*	**SPECIAL**

Rhode Island School of Design, founded in 1877, is a private institution offering degree programs in fine arts, design, and architecture. In addition to regional accreditation, RISD has baccalaureate program accreditation with NAAB and NASAD. The library contains 120,000 volumes, 1855 microform items, and 2100 audio/video tapes/CDs/DVDs, and subscribes to 400 periodicals including electronic. Computerized library services include the card catalog, interlibrary loans, database searching, and Internet access. Special learning facilities include an art gallery, an art museum, nature lab, and writing center. The 13-acre campus is in an urban area 50 miles south of Boston. Including any residence halls, there are 42 buildings.

Student Life: 94% of undergraduates are from out of state, mostly the Northeast. Students are from 50 states, 44 foreign countries, and Canada. 60% are from public schools. 54% are white; 13% Asian American; 12% foreign nationals. The average age of freshmen is 18; all undergraduates, 23. 8% do not continue beyond their first year; 90% remain to graduate.

Housing: Approximate 1200 students can be accommodated in college housing, which includes coed dorms and on-campus apartments. On-campus housing is guaranteed for the freshman year only and is available on a lottery system for upperclassmen. 52% of students live on campus; of those, 90% remain on campus on weekends. Alcohol is not permitted. No one may keep cars.

Activities: There are no fraternities or sororities. There are 60 groups on campus, including art, computers, dance, drama, ethnic, film, gay, international, literary magazine, newspaper, photography, political, professional, religious, social, social service, and student government. Popular campus events include Talent Show, Artists Ball, and Beaux Arts.

Sports: There are 7 intramural sports for men and 7 for women. Facilities include a student center with areas and equipment for dance, aerobics, and weight and fitness training, and Tillinghast Farm, a retreat on Narragansett Bay, 15 minutes from campus. Students may also enroll in activity classes at Brown University and use its athletic complex, which includes a swimming pool, an ice skating rink, a track, weight training equipment, and courts for basketball, tennis, and squash.

Disabled Students: Wheelchair ramps, elevators, special parking, specially equipped rest rooms, and special class scheduling are available.

Services: A writing program is available to all students. Taped lectures, note takers, and alternative test-taking procedures are also available, particularly for students with learning disabilities.

Campus Safety and Security: Measures include 24-hour foot and vehicle patrol, security escort services, shuttle buses, and informal discussions. There are pamphlets/posters/films, emergency telephones, lighted pathways/sidewalks, and building access cards.

Programs of Study: RISD confers B.Arch., B.F.A., B.G.D., B.I.A., and B.I.D. degrees. Master's degrees are also awarded. Bachelor's degrees are awarded in COMMUNICATIONS AND THE ARTS (apparel design, ceramic art and design, film arts, glass, graphic design, illustration, industrial design, metal/jewelry, painting, photography, printmaking, and sculpture), ENGINEERING AND ENVIRONMENTAL DESIGN (architecture, furniture design, and interior design), SOCIAL SCIENCE (textiles and clothing). Illustration, graphic design, and architecture are the largest.

Required: To graduate, all students must complete at least 126 credit hours, including 54 in the major, 42 in liberal arts, 18 in the freshman foundation program, and 12 in nonmajor, art department electives. Liberal arts credits must include 12 each in art/architectural history and electives, and 9 each in English and history/philosophy/social science. Core courses include 2 semesters each of foundation drawing, 2-dimensional design, and 3-dimensional design. A minimum GPA of 2.0 and completion of the final-year project are required.

Special: RISD offers cross-registration with Brown University and through the AICAD mobility program, credit or noncredit summer programs, 6-week internships during the midyear winter session, and study abroad in 21 countries and through the senior-year European Honors Program in Rome. Students may also elect a liberal arts concentration in art/architectural history, literary studies, creative writing, or social sciences.

Faculty/Classroom: 55% of faculty are male; 45%, female. All teach undergraduates. The average class size in an introductory lecture is 20 and in a laboratory, 17.

Admissions: 35% of the 2005-2006 applicants were accepted. The SAT scores for the 2005-2006 freshman class were: Verbal--12% below 500, 35% between 500 and 599, 37% between 600 and 700, and 15% above 700; Math--10% below 500, 35% between 500 and 599, 43% between 600 and 700, and 12% above 700. 62% of the current freshmen were in the top fifth of their class; 90% were in the top two fifths.

Requirements: The SAT is required, the ACT may be substituted. The ACT Optional Writing test is also required. Applicants must be graduates of an accredited secondary school or have a GED. An essay, assigned drawings, a portfolio, and a statement of purpose are also required. Up to 3 letters of recommendation are recommended. AP credits are accepted. Important factors in the admissions decision are evidence of special talent, advanced placement or honor courses, and personality/intangible qualities.

Procedure: Freshmen are admitted fall and spring. Entrance exams should be taken at least 6 weeks before the application deadline. There are early admissions and deferred admissions plans. Applications should be filed by February 15 for fall entry and November 25 for spring entry, along with a $50 fee. Notification is sent April 1. A waiting list is an active part of the admissions procedure. Applications are accepted on-line.

Transfer: 110 transfer students enrolled in 2004-2005. Applicants must have at least 27 college credits and should submit an essay along with academic transcripts from the previous 3 years. All students must submit a portfolio and complete a drawing assignment. Letters of recommendation are encouraged. The SAT or ACT is required for architecture and industrial design applicants. 66 of 126 credits required for the bachelor's degree must be completed at RISD.

Visiting: There are regularly scheduled orientations for prospective students, including a presentation by the admissions staff and a campus tour by a student. Visitors may sit in on classes. To schedule a visit, contact the Admissions Office at *admissions@risd.edu*.

Financial Aid: In a recent year, 62% of all full-time freshmen and 66% of continuing full-time students received some form of financial aid. 54% of full-time freshmen and 58% of continuing full-time students received need-based aid. The average freshman award was $16,000. Need-based scholarships or need-based grants averaged $12,340 ($31,575 maximum); need-based self-help aid (loans and jobs) averaged $3700 ($9100 maximum); other non-need-based awards and non-need-based scholarships averaged $5000 (maximum); and the SEOG Pell State Grant averaged $2250 ($6500 maximum). 59% of undergraduates work part time. Average annual earnings from campus work are $1100. The average financial indebtedness of the 2005 graduate was $24,300. RISD is a member of CSS. The CSS Profile, FAFSA, and parents' income tax returns are required. The deadline for filing freshman financial aid applications for fall entry is February 15.

International Students: There are 294 international students enrolled. They must take the TOEFL and also take the SAT or the ACT.

Computers: Wireless access is available. All students may access the system. There are no time limits. The fee is $150. It is recommended that students in industrial design, interior architecture, furniture design, graphic design, and architecture have personal computers. The preferred model varies by department.

Graduates: From July 1, 2004 to June 30, 2005, 518 bachelor's degrees were awarded. In an average class, 87% graduate in 5 years or less.

Admissions Contact: Edward Newhall, Director of Admissions. E-mail: *admissions@risd.edu* Web: *www.risd.edu*

ROGER WILLIAMS UNIVERSITY   D-3
Bristol, RI 02809-2921

(401) 254-3500
(800) 458-7144; Fax: (401) 254-3557

Full-time: 1650 men, 1730 women	**Faculty:** 173
Part-time: 40 men, 20 women	**Ph.D.s:** 70%
Graduate: 75 men, 140 women	**Student/Faculty:** 19 to 1
Year: semesters, summer session	**Tuition:** $21,000
Application Deadline: rolling	**Room & Board:** $9,500
Freshman Class: n/av	
SAT Verbal/Math: required	**COMPETITIVE**

Roger Williams University, founded in 1956, is a private, liberal arts institution that offers programs in the arts and sciences, professional studies, architecture, and law. There are 6 undergraduate and 3 graduate schools. Figures in the above capsule and in this profile are approximate. In addition to regional accreditation, RWU has baccalaureate program accreditation with AACSB, ABA, ABET, ACCE, NAAB, NASDTEC, and NCATE. The 3 libraries contain 187,930 volumes, 17,055 microform items, and 5012 audio/video tapes/CDs/DVDs, and subscribe to 2779 periodicals including electronic. Computerized library services include the card catalog, interlibrary loans, database searching, and Internet access. Special learning facilities include a learning resource center, art gallery, radio station, a greenhouse, and a wet lab. The 140-acre campus is in a small town 18 miles southeast of Providence. Including any residence halls, there are 42 buildings.

Student Life: 87% of undergraduates are from out of state, mostly the Northeast. Others are from 25 states, 38 foreign countries, and Canada. 75% are from public schools. 93% are white. The average age of freshmen is 18; all undergraduates, 20. 25% do not continue beyond their first year; 50% remain to graduate.

Housing: 2729 students can be accommodated in college housing, which includes single-sex and coed dormitories, on-campus apartments, off-campus apartments, and married-student housing. In addition, there are special-interest houses. On-campus housing is guaranteed for the freshman year only and is available on a lottery system for upperclassmen. 77% of students live on campus; of those, 70% remain on campus on weekends. Upperclassmen may keep cars.

Activities: There are no fraternities or sororities. There are 56 groups on campus, including art, band, cheerleading, chess, choir, chorus, computers, dance, drama, ethnic, film, gay, honors, international, jazz band, literary magazine, musical theater, newspaper, orchestra, photography, political, professional, radio and TV, religious, social service, student government, and yearbook. Popular campus events include Spring Weekend, International Dinner, and Campus Entertainment Network (concerts and comedians).

Sports: There are 11 intercollegiate sports for men and 9 for women, and 17 intramural sports for men and 16 for women. Facilities include a 2500-seat gym, exercise and weight rooms, jogging facilities, and tennis, volleyball, and basketball courts.

Disabled Students: 80% of the campus is accessible. Wheelchair ramps, elevators, special parking, specially equipped rest rooms, special class scheduling, lowered drinking fountains, and lowered telephones are available.

Services: Counseling and information services are available, as is tutoring in every subject. There is a reader service for the blind, and remedial math, reading, and writing.

Campus Safety and Security: Measures include 24-hour foot and vehicle patrol, security escort services, shuttle buses, and pamphlets/

posters/films. There are emergency telephones and lighted pathways/sidewalks.

Programs of Study: RWU confers B.A., B.S., B.Arch., and B.F.A. degrees. Master's degrees are also awarded. Bachelor's degrees are awarded in BIOLOGICAL SCIENCE (biology/biological science and marine biology), BUSINESS (accounting, banking and finance, business administration and management, international business management, and marketing/retailing/merchandising), COMMUNICATIONS AND THE ARTS (art history and appreciation, communications, creative writing, dance, dramatic arts, English, historic preservation, languages, and visual and performing arts), COMPUTER AND PHYSICAL SCIENCE (chemistry, computer science, information sciences and systems, and mathematics), EDUCATION (elementary and secondary), ENGINEERING AND ENVIRONMENTAL DESIGN (architecture, computer engineering, construction management, engineering, environmental engineering, and environmental science), HEALTH PROFESSIONS (premedicine and preveterinary science), SOCIAL SCIENCE (American studies, criminal justice, history, paralegal studies, philosophy, political science/government, prelaw, psychology, and social science). Architecture, construction management, and engineering are the strongest academically. Architecture, criminal justice, and psychology are the largest.

Required: To graduate, all students must complete 3 skills courses, 5 courses in interdisciplinary studies, 5 courses within a specific concentration, and an integrative senior seminar. A minimum of 120 credit hours, with 30 to 66 hours in the major and a GPA of 2.0, is required.

Special: RWU offers co-op programs, internships, accelerated degree programs, study abroad in 3 countries, a Washington semester, work-study, individualized majors, and dual majors. There are 7 national honor societies, a freshman honors program, and 6 departmental honors programs.

Faculty/Classroom: 59% of faculty are male; 41%, female. All teach undergraduates. No introductory courses are taught by graduate students. The average class size in an introductory lecture is 23; in a laboratory, 22; and in a regular course, 23.

Requirements: The SAT is required. In addition, applicants should be graduates of an accredited secondary school with a minimum GPA of 2.0. The GED is accepted. Students should have 4 years of English, 3 years of math, 2 years each of social and natural sciences, and 4 to 6 electives, for a total of 16 Carnegie units. Art and architecture students must submit portfolios. An essay is required, and an interview is recommended. Dance students must audition. A GPA of 2.0 is required. AP and CLEP credits are accepted. Important factors in the admissions decision are recommendations by school officials, leadership record, and advanced placement or honor courses.

Procedure: Freshmen are admitted fall and spring. Entrance exams should be taken in September or October of the senior year. There are early decision and deferred admissions plans. Check with the school for current application deadlines and fee.125 applicants were on the waiting list in a recent year, 14 were admitted. Applications are accepted on-line.

Transfer: 134 transfer students enrolled in a recent year. Applicants need a minimum college GPA of 2.0. The SAT I is required if the transfer student has less than 24 transfer credits. 45 of 120 credits required for the bachelor's degree must be completed at RWU.

Visiting: There are regularly scheduled orientations for prospective students. There are guides for informal visits and visitors may sit in on classes. To schedule a visit, contact the Office of Admissions at *admit@rwu.edu*.

Financial Aid: In a recent year, 80% of all full-time freshmen and 77% of continuing full-time students received some form of financial aid. 65% of full-time freshmen and 69% of continuing full-time students received need-based aid. The average freshman award was $15,300. Need-based scholarships or need-based grants averaged $8905 ($19,920 maximum); need-based self-help aid (loans and jobs) averaged $4780 ($7800 maximum); and other non-need-based awards and non-need-based scholarships averaged $6700 ($19,920 maximum). 36% of undergraduates work part time. Average annual earnings from campus work are $1600. The average financial indebtedness of the recent year's graduate was $17,125. RWU is a member of CSS. The CSS/Profile or FAFSA is required. Check with the school for current deadlines.

International Students: In a recent year, there were 87 international students enrolled. The school actively recruits these students. A satisfactory score is required on the MELAB or the college's own test.

Computers: All students may access the system. There are no time limits and no fees. It is strongly recommended that all students have a personal computer.

Graduates: In a recent year, 664 bachelor's degrees were awarded. The most popular majors were law/legal studies (24%), business/marketing (15%), and engineering/engineering technology (9%). In an average class, 39% graduate in 4 years or less, 9% graduate in 5 years or less, and 5% graduate in 6 years or less. 80 companies recruited on campus in a recent year. In a recent graduating class, 25% were enrolled in graduate school within 6 months of graduation and 98% were employed.

Admissions Contact: Michelle Beauregard, Associate Director of Admissions. E-mail: *admit@rwu.edu* Web: *www.rwu.edu*

SALVE REGINA UNIVERSITY   D-4
Newport, RI 02840-4192

(401) 341-2908
(888) GO-SALVE; Fax: (401) 848-2823

Full-time: 571 men, 1416 women	**Faculty:** 118; IIA, -$
Part-time: 25 men, 79 women	**Ph.D.s:** 77%
Graduate: 179 men, 229 women	**Student/Faculty:** 17 to 1
Year: semesters, summer session	**Tuition:** $23,950
Application Deadline: March 1	**Room & Board:** $9500
Freshman Class: 4555 applied, 2727 accepted, 569 enrolled	
SAT or ACT: required	**COMPETITIVE**

Salve Regina University, founded in 1934 and sponsored by the Sisters of Mercy, is an independent institution affiliated with the Roman Catholic Church. The university offers programs in liberal arts, business, health science, and professional training. In addition to regional accreditation, Salve has baccalaureate program accreditation with CSWE, IACBE, NASAD, and NLN. The library contains 139,161 volumes, 43,146 microform items, and 19,420 audio/video tapes/CDs/DVDs, and subscribes to 1041 periodicals including electronic. Computerized library services include the card catalog, interlibrary loans, database searching, Internet access, and laptop Internet portals. Special learning facilities include a learning resource center, art gallery, radio station, and information systems and computer science labs. The 75-acre campus is in a suburban area on Newport's waterfront, 60 miles south of Boston. Including any residence halls, there are 45 buildings.

Student Life: 83% of undergraduates are from out of state, mostly the Northeast. Students are from 38 states, 16 foreign countries, and Canada. 68% are from public schools. 92% are white. The average age of freshmen is 18; all undergraduates, 21. 20% do not continue beyond their first year; 62% remain to graduate.

Housing: 1170 students can be accommodated in college housing, which includes single-sex and coed dorms, on-campus apartments, and off-campus apartments. On-campus housing is guaranteed for the freshman and sophomore year only and is available on a lottery system for upperclassmen. 56% of students live on campus; of those, 75% remain on campus on weekends. Alcohol is not permitted. Upperclassmen may keep cars.

Activities: There are no fraternities or sororities. There are 30 groups on campus, including art, band, cheerleading, choir, chorus, computers, dance, drama, ethnic, gay, honors, international, jazz band, literary magazine, musical theater, newspaper, outdoor, pep band, photography, political, professional, radio and TV, religious, social, social service, student government, and yearbook. Popular campus events include September Welcome-Back Weekend, Octoberfest Weekend, and New Year's Eve Ball.

Sports: There are 9 intercollegiate sports for men and 11 for women, and 8 intramural sports for men and 9 for women. Facilities include a recreation center, tennis courts, outdoor basketball courts, a weight room, a fitness center, and soccer, baseball, and softball fields.

Disabled Students: 75% of the campus is accessible. Wheelchair ramps, elevators, special parking, specially equipped rest rooms, special class scheduling, lowered drinking fountains, and lowered telephones are available.

Services: Counseling and information services are available, as is tutoring in most subjects. There is remedial math, reading, and writing. There also is a writing center and a computer-based tutorial program.

Campus Safety and Security: Measures include 24-hour foot and vehicle patrol, self-defense education, security escort services, and shuttle buses. There are informal discussions, pamphlets/posters/films, emergency telephones, and lighted pathways/sidewalks.

Programs of Study: Salve confers B.A., B.S., and B.A.S. degrees. Associate, master's, and doctoral degrees are also awarded. Bachelor's degrees are awarded in BIOLOGICAL SCIENCE (biology/biological science), BUSINESS (accounting, business administration and management, and management science), COMMUNICATIONS AND THE ARTS (art history and appreciation, communications, communications technology, dramatic arts, English, French, historic preservation, media arts, music, Spanish, and studio art), COMPUTER AND PHYSICAL SCIENCE (chemistry, information sciences and systems, and mathematics), EDUCATION (early childhood, elementary, secondary, and special), HEALTH PROFESSIONS (cytotechnology and nursing), SOCIAL SCIENCE (American studies, criminal justice, economics, history, philosophy, political science/government, psychology, religion, social work, and sociology). Psychology, social work, and accounting are the strongest academically. Business, administration of justice, and elementary education are the largest.

Required: To graduate, students must have 128 credit hours, with about 36 in the major, and must maintain a minimum GPA of 2.0. Distribution requirements include 9 credit hours in social science, 6 each in religious studies, science, English, and a foreign language, and 3 each in visual and performing arts, philosophy, and math.

Special: Salve offers internships in most academic disciplines as well as work-study programs on campus. Study abroad in more than 6 countries, a Washington semester, B.A.-B.S. degrees in biology, business, and economics, dual majors in many programs, and accelerated degree programs in administration of justice, health services administration, business, and international relations are available. A liberal studies degree, credit for life, military, and work experience, nondegree study, and pass/fail options are also offered. There are 15 national honor societies, a freshman honors program, and 10 departmental honors programs.

Faculty/Classroom: 44% of faculty are male; 56%, female. 97% teach undergraduates and 50% both teach and do research. No introductory courses are taught by graduate students. The average class size in an introductory lecture is 22; in a laboratory, 17; and in a regular course, 18.

Admissions: 60% of the 2005-2006 applicants were accepted. The SAT scores for the 2005-2006 freshman class were: Verbal--23% below 500, 56% between 500 and 599, 20% between 600 and 700, and 2% above 700; Math--22% below 500, 59% between 500 and 599, 18% between 600 and 700, and 1% above 700. The ACT scores were 24% below 21, 37% between 21 and 23, 27% between 24 and 26, and 11% between 27 and 28. 44% of the current freshmen were in the top fifth of their class; 77% were in the top two fifths. There was 1 National Merit semifinalist.

Requirements: The SAT or ACT is required. In addition, applicants must be high school graduates or hold a GED. Students should have 16 Carnegie units, consisting of 4 each in English, 3 each in math including algebra and geometry, 2 each in science and foreign language, and 1 in history, and electives. An essay is required. A GPA of 2.7 is required. AP and CLEP credits are accepted. Important factors in the admissions decision are advanced placement or honor courses, recommendations by school officials, and leadership record.

Procedure: Freshmen are admitted fall and spring. Entrance exams should be taken as early as possible. There are early admissions and deferred admissions plans. Applications should be filed by March 1 for fall entry and December 15 for spring entry, along with a $40 fee. Notification is sent rolling. 498 applicants were on the 2005 waiting list; 24 were admitted. Applications are accepted on-line.

Transfer: 45 transfer students enrolled in 2004-2005. Applicants must have a college GPA of 2.7. 36 of 128 credits required for the bachelor's degree must be completed at Salve.

Visiting: There are regularly scheduled orientations for prospective students, including information sessions led by an admissions professional with question / answer sessions and a student-led campus tour. There are guides for informal visits and visitors may sit in on classes. Accepted applicants may stay overnight. To schedule a visit, contact the Admissions Office at sruadmis@salve.edu.

Financial Aid: In 2005-2006, 66% of all full-time students received some form of financial aid. 63% of full-time freshmen and 60% of continuing full-time students received need-based aid. The average freshman award was $16,244. Need-based scholarships or need-based grants averaged $13,425; need-based self-help aid (loans and jobs) averaged $3565; and other non-need-based awards and non-need-based scholarships averaged $3915. 33% of undergraduates work part time. Average annual earnings from campus work are $1000. The average financial indebtedness of the 2005 graduate was $21,925. Salve is a member of CSS. The CSS/Profile or FAFSA, the college's own financial statement, and tax forms are required. The deadline for filing freshman financial aid applications for fall entry is March 1.

International Students: There are 21 international students enrolled. The school actively recruits these students. A satisfactory score on the TOEFL is required.

Computers: There are more than 1200 data connection points throughout the residence hall system; each resident student is provided a data connectiom point for Internet access. More than 130 general use computers are available in the University Computer Lab area and more than 45 general use computers are in the library for access to the Internet. Wireless access capabilities are present in various locations. All students may access the system 16 hours per day in labs and 24 hours per day by dial-in access to the Internet. There are no time limits. The fee is $125 per semester. All students are required to have personal computers.

Graduates: From July 1, 2004 to June 30, 2005, 427 bachelor's degrees were awarded. The most popular majors were education (18%), business (18%), and administration of justice (10%). In an average class, 58% graduate in 4 years or less, 59% graduate in 5 years or less, and 60% graduate in 6 years or less. 105 companies recruited on campus in 2004-2005. Of a recent year's graduating class, 20% were enrolled in graduate school within 6 months of graduation and 85% were employed.

Admissions Contact: Laura E. McPhie-Oliveira, Vice President for Enrollment and Dean of Admissions. A video is available.
E-mail: sruadmis@salve.edu Web: www.salve.edu

UNIVERSITY OF RHODE ISLAND   C-4

Kingston, RI 02881	(401) 874-7100; Fax: (401) 874-5523
Full-time: 4293 men, 5473 women	Faculty: I, -$
Part-time: 676 men, 1104 women	Ph.D.s: 90%
Graduate: 1052 men, 1944 women	Student/Faculty: 15 to 1
Year: semesters, summer session	Tuition: $7284 ($19,926)
Application Deadline: February 1	Room & Board: $8114
Freshman Class: 13,388 applied, 10,327 accepted, 2461 enrolled	
SAT or ACT: required	COMPETITIVE

The University of Rhode Island, founded in 1892, is a land-grant, sea-grant, and urban-grant institution offering programs in liberal arts, business, engineering, human services, nursing, and pharmacy. Located near the ocean and the bay, the university has strong marine and environmental programs. There are satellite campuses in Providence, West Greenwich, and Narragansett. There are 8 undergraduate and 3 graduate schools. In addition to regional accreditation, URI has baccalaureate program accreditation with AACSB, ABET, ACPE, ADA, ASLA, NASM, NCATE, and NLN. The 3 libraries contain 1,205,138 volumes, 1,655,084 microform items, and 11,671 audio/video tapes/CDs/DVDs, and subscribe to 7926 periodicals including electronic. Computerized library services include the card catalog, interlibrary loans, and database searching. Special learning facilities include a learning resource center, art gallery, planetarium, radio station, TV station, historic textile collection, and early childhood education center. The 1248-acre campus is in a small town 30 miles south of Providence. Including any residence halls, there are 314 buildings.

Student Life: 61% of undergraduates are from Rhode Island. Others are from 50 states, 53 foreign countries, and Canada. 85% are from public schools. 76% are white. The average age of freshmen is 19; all undergraduates, 22. 20% do not continue beyond their first year; 56% remain to graduate.

Housing: 4100 students can be accommodated in college housing, which includes single-sex and coed dorms, on-campus apartments, married-student housing, fraternity houses, and sorority houses. In addition, there are language houses, special-interest houses, a freshman dorm, and a wellness dorm. 63% of students commute. All students may keep cars.

Activities: 10% of men belong to 11 national fraternities; 10% of women belong to 9 national sororities. There are 90 groups on campus, including band, cheerleading, chess, choir, chorale, chorus, computers, dance, drama, ethnic, gay, honors, international, jazz band, literary magazine, marching band, musical theater, newspaper, opera, orchestra, pep band, photography, political, professional, radio and TV, religious, social, social service, student government, and yearbook. Popular campus events include Winterfest, Martin Luther King Week, and International Week.

Sports: There are 10 intercollegiate sports for men and 11 for women, and 18 intramural sports for men and 18 for women. Facilities include a 4000-seat area, a 10,000-seat stadium, 3 pools, a multipurpose field house with an indoor track, a gymnastics center, 3 fitness rooms, and courts for basketball, tennis, and volleyball. There are also outdoor tennis courts, an all-weather track, 2 beach volleyball courts, and varsity and practice fields.

Disabled Students: Wheelchair ramps, elevators, special parking, specially equipped rest rooms, special class scheduling, lowered drinking fountains, lowered telephones, special housing, and special transportation around campus are available.

Services: Counseling and information services are available, as is tutoring in some subjects, including ESL and popular freshman courses. There is a reader service for the blind, and remedial math, reading, and writing.

Campus Safety and Security: Measures include 24-hour foot and vehicle patrol, self-defense education, security escort services, and shuttle buses. There are informal discussions, pamphlets/posters/films, emergency telephones, and lighted pathways/sidewalks.

Programs of Study: URI confers B.A., B.S., B.F.A., B.G.S., B.L.A., and B.M. degrees. Master's and doctoral degrees are also awarded. Bachelor's degrees are awarded in AGRICULTURE (animal science, fishing and fisheries, horticulture, natural resource management, and wildlife management), BIOLOGICAL SCIENCE (biology/biological science, marine science, microbiology, nutrition, and zoology), BUSINESS (accounting, banking and finance, business administration and management, fashion merchandising, management information systems, and marketing/retailing/merchandising), COMMUNICATIONS AND THE ARTS (art, classics, communications, comparative literature, dramatic arts, English, fine arts, French, German, Italian, journalism, literature, music, Spanish, and speech/debate/rhetoric), COMPUTER AND PHYSICAL SCIENCE (chemistry, computer science, geology, mathematics, physics, and statistics), EDUCATION (elementary, music, physical, and secondary), ENGINEERING AND ENVIRONMENTAL DESIGN (biomedical engineering, chemical engineering, civil engineering, computer engineering, electrical/electronics engineering, environmental science, industrial engineering, landscape architecture/design, mechanical engineering, and ocean engineering), HEALTH PROFESSIONS (clinical science, dental hygiene, health care administration, medical laboratory technology, nursing, pharmacy, and speech pathology/audiology), SOCIAL SCIENCE (anthropology, dietetics, economics, family/consumer studies, food science, geography, history, human development, human services, Latin American studies, philosophy, political science/government, psychology, sociology, textiles and clothing, water resources, and women's studies). Pharmacy, engineering, and biology are the strongest academically. Psychology, communication studies, and pharmacy are the largest.

Required: To graduate, the student must earn 120 to 150 credit hours, at least 30 in the major, with a GPA of 2.0. Distribution requirements include 6 credits each in English communication, fine arts and literature, foreign language or culture, letters, natural science, and social sciences, as well as 3 credits in math.

Special: Cross-registration is available with Rhode Island College and Community College of Rhode Island. URI also offers a Washington semester as well as semester-long internships with businesses and state agencies, study abroad in 6 countries, a B.A.-B.S. degree in German and engineering and in languages and business, a general studies degree, dual majors, pass/fail options, and credit for life, military, and work experience. The College of Engineering offers co-op programs and an international internship. There are 30 national honor societies, including Phi Beta Kappa, and a freshman honors program.

Faculty/Classroom: 62% of faculty are male; 38%, female. All both teach and do research. Graduate students teach 7% of introductory courses. The average class size in an introductory lecture is 30 and in a laboratory, 14.

Admissions: 77% of the 2005-2006 applicants were accepted.

Requirements: The SAT or ACT is required. In addition, applicants should be high school graduates, having completed 18 courses, including 4 of English, 3 to 4 of math, and 2 each of science (chemistry and physics for engineering majors), foreign language, and history or social studies. Remaining units should be college preparatory. Music majors must audition. AP and CLEP credits are accepted. Important factors in the admissions decision are advanced placement or honor courses, evidence of special talent, and recommendations by school officials.

Procedure: Freshmen are admitted fall and spring. Entrance exams should be taken during the spring of the junior year or fall of the senior year. There is an early admissions plan. Early decision applications should be filed by December 15; regular applications, by February 1 for fall entry and November 1 for spring entry, along with a $50 fee. Notification is sent on a rolling basis. Applications are accepted on-line.

Transfer: 512 transfer students enrolled in 2004-2005. Applicants must submit transcripts from high school and all colleges or universities attended. A minimum GPA of 2.5 is required; many programs require higher. 24 of 120 credits required for the bachelor's degree must be completed at URI.

Visiting: There are regularly scheduled orientations for prospective students, including open house programs in October and campus tours. There are guides for informal visits and visitors may sit in on classes. To schedule a visit, contact the Admissions Office at (401) 874-9800.

Financial Aid: In 2005-2006, 57% of all full-time freshmen and 51% of continuing full-time students received some form of financial aid. The average freshman award was $12,009. Need-based scholarships or need-based grants averaged $6353; need-based self-help aid (loans and jobs) averaged $5966; non-need-based athletic scholarships averaged $1179; and other non-need-based awards and non-need-based scholarships averaged $4711. The average financial indebtedness of the 2005 graduate was $16,200. URI is a member of CSS. The FAFSA is required. The priority date for freshman financial aid applications for fall entry is March 1. The deadline for filing freshman financial aid applications for fall entry is rolling.

International Students: The school actively recruits these students. They must take the TOEFL or the English proficiency test administered by the American Consulate and also take the SAT or the ACT.

Computers: All students may access the system 24 hours per day. There are no time limits and no fees.

Graduates: From July 1, 2004 to June 30, 2005, 1889 bachelor's degrees were awarded. The most popular majors were business/marketing (16%), communications/journalism (12%), and engineering (10%). In an average class, 34% graduate in 4 years or less, 52% graduate in 5 years or less, and 55% graduate in 6 years or less.

Admissions Contact: David Taggart, Dean of Admissions.
E-mail: *uriadmit@etal.uri.edu* Web: *www.uri.edu/admissions*

POPULATION
DENSITY
• 25,000 and over

0 20 40 60 80 100
Miles

SOUTH CAROLINA

sociology). Sociology/social work and business administration are the largest.

Required: To graduate, all students must complete 120 credit hours with a minimum 2.0 GPA. Students must demonstrate competence in reading, composition, speech, and fundamental math skills.

Special: Allen offers internships with businesses and federal, state, and local agencies, and work-study with the Columbia Housing Authority. A certificate in gerontology is possible. There is 1 national honor society, and 20 departmental honors programs.

Faculty/Classroom: All teach undergraduates.

Requirements: Applicants should be graduates of accredited high schools or have earned the GED. Secondary preparation should total 20 academic credits. A personal interview is recommended. Important factors in the admissions decision are leadership record, advanced placement or honor courses, and evidence of special talent.

Procedure: Freshmen are admitted to all sessions. Entrance exams should be taken in the spring. There is an early decision plan. Check with the school for current application deadlines and fee.

Transfer: An official transcript from each school attended is required at least 1 month prior to the beginning of the semester in which admission is desired. 30 of 120 credits required for the bachelor's degree must be completed at Allen.

Visiting: There are regularly scheduled orientations for prospective students. There are guides for informal visits and visitors may sit in on classes. To schedule a visit, contact Dr. John Waddell, Dean of Student Development Services at (803) 376-5741.

Financial Aid: Allen is a member of CSS. The CSS/Profile and the college's own financial statement are required. Check with the school for current deadlines.

International Students: The school actively recruits these students.

Computers: All students may access the system. There are no time limits and no fees.

Graduates: In an average class, 40% graduate in 4 years or less, and 20% graduate in 5 years or less.

Admissions Contact: Admissions Office.

E-mail: *auniv@minspring.com*

ALLEN UNIVERSITY
C-3
Columbia, SC 29204

(803) 376-5735
(888) 425-5360; Fax: (803) 376-5715

Full-time: 130 men, 200 women	**Faculty:** 14
Part-time: 10 men, 10 women	**Ph.Ds:** 54%
Graduate: none	**Student/Faculty:** 23 to 1
Year: semesters, summer session	**Tuition:** $5400
Application Deadline: open	**Room & Board:** $5100
Freshman Class: n/av	
SAT or ACT: not required	**NONCOMPETITIVE**

Allen University, founded in 1870, is a small private institution affiliated with the African Methodist Episcopal (A.M.E.) Church. It offers undergraduate programs in liberal arts and sciences, business, and social work. Figures in the above capsule and in this profile are approximate. The library contains 40,558 volumes, 2883 microform items, and 2527 audio/video tapes/CDs/DVDs, and subscribes to 106 periodicals including electronic. Special learning facilities include a learning resource center. The 4-acre campus is in a small town. Including any residence halls, there are 84 buildings.

Student Life: Students are from 20 states and 9 foreign countries. 95% are from public schools. 99% are African American. Most are Protestant. The average age of freshmen is 18; all undergraduates, 24. 20% do not continue beyond their first year.

Housing: 405 students can be accommodated in college housing, which includes single-sex dormitories and off-campus apartments. On-campus housing is guaranteed for all 4 years. 95% of students live on campus. Alcohol is not permitted. All students may keep cars.

Activities: 8% of men belong to 4 national fraternities; 6% of women belong to 4 national sororities. There are 20 groups on campus, including art, band, cheerleading, choir, chorus, drama, honors, international, newspaper, religious, social service, student government, and yearbook. Popular campus events include Cultural, Academic, and Religious Series (CARS), International Day, and Founders Day.

Sports: There are 2 intercollegiate sports for men, and 1 intramural sport for men and 1 for women.

Disabled Students: Special parking is available.

Services: Counseling and information services are available, as is tutoring in most subjects. There is remedial math, reading, and writing. There are math, science, reading, and writing labs.

Campus Safety and Security: Measures include 24-hour foot and vehicle patrol, self-defense education, security escort services, and pamphlets/posters/films. There are emergency telephones and lighted pathways/sidewalks.

Programs of Study: Allen confers B.A. and B.S. degrees. Associate degrees are also awarded. Bachelor's degrees are awarded in BIOLOGICAL SCIENCE (biology/biological science), BUSINESS (business administration and management), COMMUNICATIONS AND THE ARTS (English and music), COMPUTER AND PHYSICAL SCIENCE (mathematics), SOCIAL SCIENCE (history, political science/government, and

BENEDICT COLLEGE
C-3
Columbia, SC 29204

(803) 253-5143
(800) 868-6598; Fax: (803) 253-5167

Full-time: 1228 men, 1262 women	**Faculty:** 118
Part-time: 32 men, 30 women	**Ph.Ds:** 59%
Graduate: none	**Student/Faculty:** 21 to 1
Year: semesters, summer session	**Tuition:** $13,156
Application Deadline: open	**Room & Board:** $5958
Freshman Class: n/av	
SAT: required	**LESS COMPETITIVE**

Benedict College, founded in 1870, is a private liberal arts institution affiliated with the Baptist Church. There are 4 undergraduate schools. In addition to regional accreditation, Benedict College has baccalaureate program accreditation with CSWE and NCATE. The library contains 119,594 volumes, 164,317 microform items, and 6648 audio/video tapes/CDs/DVDs, and subscribes to 314 periodicals including electronic. Computerized library services include interlibrary loans, database searching, Internet access, and laptop Internet portals. Special learning facilities include a learning resource center and art gallery. The 110-acre campus is in an urban area 90 miles south of Charlotte, North Carolina. Including any residence halls, there are 37 buildings.

Student Life: 71% of undergraduates are from South Carolina. Others are from 32 states and 17 foreign countries. 99% are from public schools. 99% are African American. The average age of freshmen is 19; all undergraduates, 21. 35% do not continue beyond their first year; 30% remain to graduate.

Housing: 2072 students can be accommodated in college housing, which includes single-sex dorms and off-campus apartments. In addition, there are honors dorms. On-campus housing is available on a first-come, first-served basis. Priority is given to out-of-town students. 68% of students live on campus. Alcohol is not permitted. Upperclassmen may keep cars.

Activities: 3% of men belong to 4 local and 4 national fraternities; 6% of women belong to 4 local and 4 national sororities. There are 42 groups on campus, including art, cheerleading, choir, chorale, chorus, dance, drama, drill team, honors, international, marching band, newspaper, pep band, photography, religious, social, social service, and student government. Popular campus events include Fall Convocation, Crowning of Miss Benedict, and Religion Emphasis Week.

Sports: There are 7 intercollegiate sports for men and 7 for women, and 2 intramural sports for men. Facilities include a gym and a student center.

Disabled Students: 85% of the campus is accessible. Wheelchair ramps, elevators, and special parking are available.

Services: Counseling and information services are available, as is tutoring in every subject. There is remedial math, reading, and writing.

Campus Safety and Security: Measures include 24-hour foot and vehicle patrol, shuttle buses, informal discussions, and pamphlets/posters/films. There are lighted pathways/sidewalks.

Programs of Study: Benedict College confers B.A., B.S., and B.S.W. degrees. Bachelor's degrees are awarded in BIOLOGICAL SCIENCE (biology/biological science), BUSINESS (accounting and business administration and management), COMMUNICATIONS AND THE ARTS (English, journalism, music, and studio art), COMPUTER AND PHYSICAL SCIENCE (chemistry, computer science, mathematics, and physics), EDUCATION (early childhood, elementary, and recreation), ENGINEERING AND ENVIRONMENTAL DESIGN (computer engineering and electrical/electronics engineering), HEALTH PROFESSIONS (environmental health science and public health), SOCIAL SCIENCE (criminal justice, economics, history, philosophy, political science/government, religion, social science, social work, and sociology). Physics, engineering, and chemistry are the strongest academically. Business administration is the largest.

Required: Students must complete 125 credit hours, including 24 to 32 in the major, with a minimum GPA of 2.0; some degrees require a higher GPA. The 57-hour general education requirements include 15 hours of English, 9 of social science, 8 of natural science, 6 each of math and a foreign language, 4 of humanities, and 2 each of health education, freshman seminar, phys ed, and religion.

Special: Benedict offers work-study programs, a physics/engineering dual major, internships, a B.A./B.S. degree, and preprofessional programs in dentistry, engineering, law, and medicine. There are 6 national honor societies.

Faculty/Classroom: 55% of faculty are male; 45%, female. All teach undergraduates and 1% both teach and do research. The average class size in an introductory lecture is 30; in a laboratory, 27; and in a regular course, 24.

Requirements: The SAT is required. In addition, students should have taken 4 secondary school units of English, 3 each of math and social science, 2 of natural science, 7 of electives, and 1 of phys or ROTC. The GED is accepted. Benedict requires applicants to be in the upper 75% of their class. A GPA of 2.0 is required. AP and CLEP credits are accepted.

Procedure: Freshmen are admitted fall and spring. Entrance exams should be taken prior to registration. There is a deferred admissions plan. There is a rolling admissions plan. Application deadlines are open. The fall 2005 application fee was $25.

Transfer: 106 transfer students enrolled in 2004-2005. Applicants must submit transcripts from previous institutions attended plus evidence of honorable withdrawal. The SAT is required. Only courses in which a C or better was earned will be considered for credit. 30 of 125 credits required for the bachelor's degree must be completed at Benedict College.

Visiting: There are regularly scheduled orientations for prospective students. There are guides for informal visits and visitors may sit in on classes. To schedule a visit, contact the Admissions Office.

Financial Aid: The average freshman award was $12,000. 50% of undergraduates work part time. Average annual earnings from campus work are $1800. The average financial indebtedness of the 2005 graduate was $25,000. The CSS/Profile or FAFSA, the college's own financial statement, and the South Carolina Tuition Grant applications are required.

International Students: There are 99 international students enrolled. A satisfactory score on the TOEFL is required. Some students may be required to complete an ESL program. The SAT or the ACT is recommended.

Computers: Wireless access is available. All students may access the system. There are no time limits and no fees.

Graduates: From July 1, 2004 to June 30, 2005, 312 bachelor's degrees were awarded. The most popular majors were business administration (18%), criminal justice (12%), and biology, and computer science (11%). In an average class, 9% graduate in 4 years or less, 21% graduate in 5 years or less, and 26% graduate in 6 years or less. Of the 2004 graduating class, 8% were enrolled in graduate school within 6 months of graduation.

Admissions Contact: Phyllis Thompson, Director of Enrollment Management. A video is available. E-mail: *admissions@benedict.edu* Web: *www.benedict.edu*

CHARLESTON SOUTHERN UNIVERSITY   D-4
Charleston, SC 29423-8087

(843) 863-7050
(800) 947-7474; Fax: (843) 863-7070

Full-time: 800 men, 1200 women	**Faculty:** 93; IIB, --$
Part-time: 160 men, 320 women	**Ph.D.s:** 71%
Graduate: 100 men, 140 women	**Student/Faculty:** 21 to 1
Year: semesters, summer session	**Tuition:** $13,000
Application Deadline: open	**Room & Board:** $4,800
Freshman Class: n/av	
SAT or ACT: recommended	**COMPETITIVE**

Charleston Southern University, founded in 1964, is a private liberal arts institution affiliated with the South Carolina Baptist Convention. There are 4 undergraduate and 3 graduate schools. Figures in the above capsule and in this profile are approximate. In addition to regional accreditation, CSU has baccalaureate program accreditation with NASDTEC, NASM, and NLN. The library contains 212,666 volumes, 212,539 microform items, and 7527 audio/video tapes/CDs/DVDs, and subscribes to 9788 periodicals including electronic. Computerized library services include the card catalog and database searching. Special learning facilities include a learning resource center an earthquake education center, and a field physics laboratory. The 500-acre campus is in a suburban area 20 miles west of Charleston. Including any residence halls, there are 16 buildings.

Student Life: 81% of undergraduates are from South Carolina. Others are from 45 states, 35 foreign countries, and Canada. 85% are from public schools. 47% are white; 27% African American. 50% are claim no religious affiliation; 42% Protestant; 7% Catholic. The average age of freshmen is 18; all undergraduates, 25. 28% do not continue beyond their first year; 31% remain to graduate.

Housing: 1250 students can be accommodated in college housing, which includes single-sex dormitories and married-student housing. On-campus housing is guaranteed for the freshman year only and is available on a first-come, first-served basis. 56% of students commute. Alcohol is not permitted. All students may keep cars.

Activities: There are no fraternities or sororities. There are 20 groups on campus, including art, band, cheerleading, choir, chorus, drama, honors, jazz band, literary magazine, marching band, newspaper, religious, social service, student government, and yearbook.

Sports: There are 9 intercollegiate sports for men and 9 for women, and 4 intramural sports for men and 4 for women. Facilities include a gym, tennis courts, a track center, football and soccer fields, a baseball diamond, training and weight rooms, a 3-hole golf course with driving range, and a Wellness Center.

Disabled Students: All of the campus is accessible. Wheelchair ramps, elevators, special parking, specially equipped rest rooms, and lowered drinking fountains are available.

Services: Counseling and information services are available, as is tutoring in most subjects. There is remedial math, reading, and writing.

Campus Safety and Security: Measures include 24-hour foot and vehicle patrol, security escort services, emergency telephones, and lighted pathways/sidewalks.

Programs of Study: CSU confers B.A., B.S., and B.Tech. degrees. Associate and master's degrees are also awarded. Bachelor's degrees are awarded in BIOLOGICAL SCIENCE (biochemistry and biology/biological science), BUSINESS (business administration and management), COMMUNICATIONS AND THE ARTS (dramatic arts, English, fine arts, music, Spanish, and speech/debate/rhetoric), COMPUTER AND PHYSICAL SCIENCE (chemistry, computer science, geology, mathematics, and natural sciences), EDUCATION (early childhood, elementary, music, physical, and science), ENGINEERING AND ENVIRONMENTAL DESIGN (environmental science), HEALTH PROFESSIONS (music therapy and nursing), SOCIAL SCIENCE (criminal justice, economics, geography, history, humanities, political science/government, psychology, religion, religious music, social science, sociology, and youth ministry).

Required: To graduate, students must complete 125 credit hours, including all core curriculum, major, and minor requirements, with a GPA of 2.0. At least 45 hours must be in the major. Core courses include 24 hours of communications and fine arts, 11 of natural science/math, and 9 of social studies.

Special: CSU offers internships, cross-registration through the Trident Area Consortium, work-study programs, dual majors, and nondegree study. Nonmajor preprofessional programs are available in dentistry, engineering, law, medicine, and ministry. There are 5 national honor societies, a freshman honors program, and 100 departmental honors programs.

Faculty/Classroom: 55% of faculty are male; 45%, female. All teach undergraduates. No introductory courses are taught by graduate students. The average class size in an introductory lecture is 40; in a laboratory, 15; and in a regular course, 25.

Requirements: The SAT or ACT is recommended. In addition, applicants must be graduates of an accredited secondary school. The GED is accepted. Character references are preferred. An English proficiency exam is required for all entering students. CSU requires applicants to be in the upper 60% of their class. A GPA of 2.0 is required. AP and CLEP credits are accepted. Important factors in the admissions decision are evidence of special talent, leadership record, and advanced placement or honor courses.

Procedure: Freshmen are admitted to all sessions. Entrance exams should be taken any time before filing for admission. Check with the school for current application deadlines and fee. Applications are accepted on-line.

Transfer: 278 transfer students enrolled in a recent year. Applicants must submit official transcripts from all previous colleges attended. Accepted transfers must take an English proficiency exam. 30 of 125 credits required for the bachelor's degree must be completed at CSU.

Visiting: There are regularly scheduled orientations for prospective students, consisting of orientation for students, orientation for parents, placement testing for students, a tour, and lunch. There are guides for informal visits and visitors may sit in on classes. To schedule a visit, contact the Office of Enrollment Services.

Financial Aid: In a recent year, the average freshman award was $8000. 26% of undergraduates work part time. Average annual earnings from campus work are $2000. The average financial indebtedness of the recent year's graduate was $20,000. CSU is a member of CSS. The CSS/Profile or FAFSA is required. Check with the school for current deadlines.

International Students: In a recent year, there were 69 international students enrolled. Satisfactory scores are required on the written TOEFL and the SAT or the ACT.

Computers: All students may access the system. There are no time limits and no fees. It is strongly recommended that all students have a personal computer.

Graduates: In a recent year, 275 bachelor's degrees were awarded. The most popular majors were business administration (21%), education (14%), and psychology/social science (9%). In an average class, 31% graduate in 4 years or less. 30 companies recruited on campus in 2004-2005. Of the 2004 graduating class, 27% were enrolled in graduate school within 6 months of graduation and 63% were employed.

Admissions Contact: Cheryl Burton, Director of Enrollment Services. A video is available. E-mail: *enroll@csuniv.edu* Web: *www.csuniv.edu*

CITADEL, THE   D-4
Charleston, SC 29409   (843) 953-5230
(800) 868-1842; Fax: (843) 953-7036

Full-time: 1979 men, 132 women	**Faculty:** 193; IIA, av$
Part-time: 58 men, 7 women	**Ph.D.s:** 94%
Graduate: 319 men, 487 women	**Student/Faculty:** 11 to 1
Year: semesters, summer session	**Tuition:** n/av
Application Deadline: open	**Room & Board:** n/app
Freshman Class: 1913 applied, 1496 accepted, 585 enrolled	
SAT or ACT: required	**COMPETITIVE+**

The Citadel, established in 1842 by the South Carolina legislature, is a liberal arts military college supported by the state. Tuition figures in the above capsule are for students in the Corps of Cadets and include charges for lab fees, athletic fees, most books, school supplies, uniforms, alterations, and laundry and dry cleaning. Freshmen pay an additional $3,360. In addition to regional accreditation, The Citadel has baccalaureate program accreditation with AACSB, ABET, and NCATE. The library contains 236,418 volumes, 1,193,192 microform items, and 2656 audio/video tapes/CDs/DVDs, and subscribes to 504 periodicals including electronic. Computerized library services include the card catalog, interlibrary loans, database searching, Internet access, and laptop Internet portals. Special learning facilities include a military museum and archives and a writing center. The 100-acre campus is in a suburban area in Charleston. Including any residence halls, there are 69 buildings.

Student Life: 51% of undergraduates are from out of state, mostly the South. Students are from 46 states, 29 foreign countries, and Canada. 70% are from public schools. 84% are white. 68% are Protestant; 23% Catholic. The average age of freshmen is 18; all undergraduates, 20. 18% do not continue beyond their first year; 66% remain to graduate.

Housing: 1928 students can be accommodated in college housing, which includes coed barracks. On-campus housing is guaranteed for all 4 years. All of students live on campus; of those, All remain on campus on weekends. Alcohol is not permitted. Upperclassmen may keep cars.

Activities: There are no fraternities or sororities. There are 37 groups on campus, including bagpipe band, band, choir, chorale, drama, literary magazine, marching band, newspaper, pep band, student government, and yearbook. Popular campus events include Parents Weekend and Corps Day.

Sports: There are 9 intercollegiate sports for men and 5 for women, and 20 intramural sports for men and 20 for women. Facilities include a 22,000-seat stadium, a 6000-seat field house, fitness centers, weight and wrestling rooms, tennis courts, an all-weather track, and playing fields. The boating center and beach club are within a half-hour drive of the college.

Disabled Students: 80% of the campus is accessible. Wheelchair ramps, elevators, special parking, and specially equipped rest rooms are available.

Services: Counseling and information services are available, as is tutoring in every subject.

Campus Safety and Security: Measures include 24-hour foot and vehicle patrol, security escort services, lighted pathways/sidewalks, lock out, and jump start services.

Programs of Study: The Citadel confers B.A., B.S., B.S.B.A., B.S.C.E., and B.S.E.E. degrees. Master's degrees are also awarded. Bachelor's degrees are awarded in BIOLOGICAL SCIENCE (biology/biological science), BUSINESS (business administration and management), COMMUNICATIONS AND THE ARTS (English, French, German, and Spanish), COMPUTER AND PHYSICAL SCIENCE (chemistry, computer science, mathematics, and physics), EDUCATION (health, physical, and secondary), ENGINEERING AND ENVIRONMENTAL DESIGN (civil engineering and electrical/electronics engineering), HEALTH PROFESSIONS (predentistry and premedicine), SOCIAL SCIENCE (criminal justice, history, political science/government, and psychology). English is the strongest academically. Business administration is the largest.

Required: To graduate, students must complete 121 to 139 credit hours, depending on the major, with an overall GPA of 2.0 (2.5 for education majors). The required core curriculum for all majors includes study in the following areas: English, history, math, science, social sciences, computer literacy, and foreign languages. Specific course requirements include 8 semesters of ROTC, 4 of English, and 4 of phys ed. In addition, cadets must satisfy disciplinary requirements and observe the honor system.

Special: Students may earn a combined B.A.-B.S. degree, design their own majors, and take a 3-2 program in engineering. Work-study programs, internships, dual majors, independent study, study abroad, and pass/fail options are also available. Qualified students may enroll in a separate honors program. There is a teacher certification program. There are 7 national honor societies, including Phi Beta Kappa, a freshman honors program, and 1 departmental honors program.

Faculty/Classroom: 69% of faculty are male; 31%, female. 95% teach undergraduates. The average class size in an introductory lecture is 25 and in a regular course, 20.

Admissions: 78% of the 2005-2006 applicants were accepted. The SAT scores for the 2005-2006 freshman class were: Verbal--33% below 500, 41% between 500 and 599, 22% between 600 and 700, and 4% above 700; Math--21% below 500, 54% between 500 and 599, 23% between 600 and 700, and 3% above 700. 31% of the current freshmen were in the top fifth of their class; 67% were in the top two fifths.

Requirements: The SAT or ACT is required. In addition, the SAT: Subject test in math level II is strongly recommended for engineering, science, and math applicants. Also required are recommendations from high school principals or guidance counselors. A high school diploma is required and the GED is accepted. Applicants must be between 16 and 22, and unmarried, and must meet certain physical requirements. High school preparation should include 4 units in English; 3 in math, including algebra I and II; biology, chemistry, or physics; 2 each in foreign language and social science; 1 in phys ed or ROTC; and 1 in history. AP and CLEP credits are accepted. Important factors in the admissions decision are advanced placement or honor courses, extracurricular activities record, and leadership record.

Procedure: Freshmen are admitted in the fall. Entrance exams should be taken by February of the senior year. Early decision applications should be filed by October 26. Application deadlines are open for regular applications. The fee is $40. Notification of early decision is sent on a rolling basis; regular decision, on a rolling basis beginning July 16. 119 early decision candidates were accepted for the 2005-2006 class. Applications are accepted on-line.

Transfer: 41 transfer students enrolled in 2004-2005. Applicants must meet freshmen entrance requirements and submit official transcripts from high school and all previous colleges attended. Transfer students must have completed a minimum of 2 semesters as full-time students (minimum 12 hours each semester) and maintained a GPA of 2.0. A full year of course work, including half the required hours in the major, must be completed at The Citadel. A statement of good standing from prior institutions and an interview are required.

Visiting: There are regularly scheduled orientations for prospective students, including an interview with an admissions counselor and a campus tour guided by a cadet. There are guides for informal visits and visitors may sit in on classes and stay overnight. To schedule a visit, contact the Admissions Office.

Financial Aid: In 2005-2006, 52% of all full-time freshmen and 47% of continuing full-time students received some form of financial aid. At least 39% of full-time freshmen and at least 32% of continuing full-time students received need-based aid. The average freshman award was $9217. Need-based scholarships or need-based grants averaged $9231; need-based self-help aid (loans and jobs) averaged $3154; and other non-need-based awards and non-need-based scholarships averaged $8756. 3% of undergraduates work part time. Average annual earnings from campus work are $675. The average financial indebtedness of the 2005 graduate was $9300. The Citadel is a member of CSS. The FAFSA is required. The priority date for freshman financial aid applications for fall entry is March 1.

International Students: There are 61 international students enrolled. They must score satisfactorily on the written TOEFL.

Computers: All students may access the system. It is strongly recommended that all students have a personal computer. A 486-OX- or Pentium-based PC is recommended.

Graduates: From July 1, 2004 to June 30, 2005, 471 bachelor's degrees were awarded. The most popular majors were business/marketing (36%), security and protection services (12%), and social sciences (10%). In an average class, 57% graduate in 4 years or less, 64% graduate in 5 years or less, and 66% graduate in 6 years or less. 89 companies recruited on campus in 2004-2005. Of the 2004 graduating class, 15% were enrolled in graduate school within 6 months of graduation and 96% were employed.

Admissions Contact: Lt. Col. John Powell, Acting Dean of Enrollment Management. A video is available. E-mail: *admissions@citadel.edu* Web: *www.citadel.edu*

CLAFLIN UNIVERSITY   C-3

Orangeburg, SC 29115   (803) 535-5340
                                   (800) 922-1246; Fax: (803) 535-5387

Full-time: 528 men, 1070 women	**Faculty:** 90; IIB, --$
Part-time: 33 men, 47 women	**Ph.D.s:** 70%
Graduate: 17 men, 33 women	**Student/Faculty:** 18 to 1
Year: semesters, summer session	**Tuition:** $10,890
Application Deadline: open	**Room & Board:** $5908
Freshman Class: 2744 applied, 1103 accepted, 385 enrolled	
SAT Verbal/Math: 463/460*	**ACT:** 18 COMPETITIVE+

Claflin University, established in 1869 and affiliated with the United Methodist Church, is a small, private liberal arts institution offering undergraduate programs in education, humanities, social sciences, business, natural sciences, and math, and graduate programs in business administration and biotechnology. There are 4 undergraduate schools. In addition to regional accreditation, Claflin University has baccalaureate program accreditation with ACBSP, NASM, and NCATE. The library contains 158,310 volumes, 63,085 microform items, and 1041 audio/video tapes/CDs/DVDs, and subscribes to 447 periodicals including electronic. Computerized library services include the card catalog, interlibrary loans, database searching, Internet access, and laptop Internet portals. Special learning facilities include a learning resource center, art gallery, radio station, and TV station. The 43-acre campus is in a suburban area between Columbia and Charleston. Including any residence halls, there are 27 buildings.

Student Life: 86% of undergraduates are from South Carolina. Others are from 24 states and 14 foreign countries. 99% are from public schools. 94% are African American. Most are Protestant. The average age of all undergraduates is 19. 17% do not continue beyond their first year; 83% remain to graduate.

Housing: 1003 students can be accommodated in college housing, which includes single-sex dorms and off-campus apartments. On-campus housing is available on a first-come, first-served basis. 60% of students live on campus; of those, 70% remain on campus on weekends. Alcohol is not permitted. Upperclassmen may keep cars.

Activities: 15% of men belong to 4 national fraternities; 15% of women belong to 4 national sororities. There are 49 groups on campus, including band, cheerleading, choir, drama, ethnic, film, honors, international, jazz band, literary magazine, marching band, newspaper, radio and TV, religious, social, social service, student government, and yearbook. Popular campus events include Founders Day, Pantherfest, and Claflin Pride Day.

Sports: There are 5 intercollegiate sports for men and 7 for women, and 4 intramural sports for men and 4 for women. Facilities include a gym, tennis courts, a game room, and basketball courts.

Disabled Students: 95% of the campus is accessible. Wheelchair ramps, elevators, special parking, and specially equipped rest rooms are available.

Services: Counseling and information services are available, as is tutoring in most subjects. There is remedial math, reading, and writing.

Campus Safety and Security: Measures include 24-hour foot and vehicle patrol, security escort services, informal discussions, and lighted pathways/sidewalks.

Programs of Study: Claflin University confers B.A., B.S., and B.S.B.A. degrees. Master's degrees are also awarded. Bachelor's degrees are awarded in BIOLOGICAL SCIENCE (biochemistry, bioinformatics, biology/biological science, and biotechnology), BUSINESS (business administration and management, management information systems, marketing management, organizational behavior, and sports management), COMMUNICATIONS AND THE ARTS (art, English, and music), COMPUTER

AND PHYSICAL SCIENCE (chemistry, computer science, and mathematics), EDUCATION (art, early childhood, elementary, English, mathematics, middle school, music, and physical), ENGINEERING AND ENVIRONMENTAL DESIGN (computer engineering and environmental science), SOCIAL SCIENCE (African American studies, American studies, criminal justice, history, philosophy and religion, and sociology). Biology, business administration, and sociology are the strongest academically and the largest.

Required: To graduate, all students must complete 120 to 130 semester hours with a minimum GPA of 2.0. General education requirements include courses in education, English, humanities, math, phys ed, natural science, computer science, and analytical reasoning. An exit exam is required, and honors college students must complete a capstone project.

Special: Claflin offers co-op and accelerated degree programs in all majors, cross-registration with South Carolina State University and Orangeburg-Calhoun Technical College, study abroad, B.A.-B.S. degrees, and a 3-2 engineering degree with Clemson University and South Carolina State University. There are 7 national honor societies and a freshman honors program.

Faculty/Classroom: 60% of faculty are male; 40%, female. All both teach and do research. The average class size in an introductory lecture is 25; in a laboratory, 25; and in a regular course, 25.

Admissions: 40% of the 2005-2006 applicants were accepted. The SAT scores for the 2005-2006 freshman class were: Verbal--51% below 500, 41% between 500 and 599, 7% between 600 and 700, and 1% above 700; Math--69% below 500, 22% between 500 and 599, 8% between 600 and 700, and 1% above 700. 46% of the current freshmen were in the top fifth of their class; 75% were in the top two fifths. 5 freshmen graduated first in their class in a recent year.

Requirements: The SAT or ACT is required. In addition, applicants should be high school graduates who have completed 16 to 18 units, including 4 units in English, 2 in math, and 1 each in social studies and natural science. Admissions decisions are based on the secondary school record, test scores, recommendations from the secondary school, personal qualities, and health record. A GPA of 2.0 is required. AP and CLEP credits are accepted. Important factors in the admissions decision are recommendations by school officials, evidence of special talent, and leadership record.

Procedure: Freshmen are admitted fall and spring. There is a rolling admission plan. Application deadlines are open. Notification is sent on a rolling basis. Application fee is $20. Applications are accepted on-line.

Transfer: 42 transfer students enrolled in 2004-2005. Applicants with fewer than 60 semester hours of college credit must submit test scores and meet the other criteria for entering freshmen. Official transcripts of all colleges attended are required. 25 of 126 credits required for the bachelor's degree must be completed at Claflin University.

Visiting: There are regularly scheduled orientations for prospective students. There are guides for informal visits and visitors may sit in on classes and stay overnight. To schedule a visit, contact the Admissions Office at *mzeigler@claflin.edu*.

Financial Aid: In 2005-2006, 98% of all full-time students received some form of financial aid. 92% of all full-time students received need-based aid. The average freshman award was $10,699. Need-based scholarships or need-based grants averaged $1980 ($2190 maximum); need-based self-help aid (loans and jobs) averaged $4500 ($5500 maximum); non-need-based athletic scholarships averaged $2000 ($14,000 maximum); and other non-need-based awards and non-need-based scholarships averaged $1000 ($15,000 maximum). 35% of undergraduates work part time. The average financial indebtedness of the 2005 graduate was $14,412. The FAFSA is required. The priority date for freshman financial aid applications for fall entry is April 15. The deadline for filing freshman financial aid applications for fall entry is June 1.

International Students: There are 90 international students enrolled. The school actively recruits these students. They must take the TOEFL and also take the SAT or the ACT.

Computers: Wireless access is available. All students may access the system. There are no time limits. The fee is $162.

Graduates: From July 1, 2004 to June 30, 2005, 284 bachelor's degrees were awarded. The most popular majors were criminal justice/law (14%), sociology (12%), and child development (8%). In an average class, 61% graduate in 6 years or less. Of the 2004 graduating class, 17% were enrolled in graduate school within 6 months of graduation and 55% were employed.

Admissions Contact: Michael Zeigler. A video is available. E-mail: *mzeigler@claflin.edu* Web: *htttp://www.claflin.edu*

CLEMSON UNIVERSITY · A-2

Clemson, SC 29634-5124   (864) 656-2287; Fax: (864) 656-0622

Full-time: 7133 men, 5933 women	**Faculty:** 952; I, -$
Part-time: 515 men, 355 women	**Ph.D.s:** 83%
Graduate: 1736 men, 1438 women	**Student/Faculty:** 14 to 1
Year: semesters, summer session	**Tuition:** $8074 ($16,638)
Application Deadline: May 1	**Room & Board:** $5292
Freshman Class: 12,463 applied, 7154 accepted, 2904 enrolled	
SAT Verbal/Math: 600/625	**ACT:** 26 **HIGHLY COMPETITIVE**

Clemson University, founded in 1889, is a public institution with programs in agriculture, architecture, commerce and industry, education, engineering, forest and recreation resources, liberal arts, nursing, and sciences. There are 5 undergraduate schools and 1 graduate school. In addition to regional accreditation, Clemson has baccalaureate program accreditation with AACSB, ABET, CSAB, NAAB, NCATE, NLN, and NRPA. The 3 libraries contain 1,228,473 volumes, 1,168,491 microform items, and 139,666 audio/video tapes/CDs/DVDs, and subscribe to 11,374 periodicals including electronic. Computerized library services include the card catalog, interlibrary loans, database searching, Internet access, and laptop Internet portals. Special learning facilities include a learning resource center, art gallery, natural history museum, planetarium, radio station, TV station, geology museum, experimental forest, research park, and state botanical gardens. The 1400-acre campus is in a small town 32 miles west of Greenville. Including any residence halls, there are 584 buildings.

Student Life: 68% of undergraduates are from South Carolina. Others are from 49 states, 84 foreign countries, and Canada. 81% are from public schools. 79% are white. The average age of freshmen is 18; all undergraduates, 21. 11% do not continue beyond their first year; 72% remain to graduate.

Housing: 6346 students can be accommodated in college housing, which includes single-sex and coed dorms, on-campus apartments, off-campus apartments, married-student housing, fraternity houses, and sorority houses. In addition, there are honors houses. On-campus housing is guaranteed for the freshman year only. 54% of students commute. All students may keep cars.

Activities: 17% of men belong to 19 national fraternities; 31% of women belong to 17 national sororities. There are 300 groups on campus, including band, cheerleading, choir, chorus, computers, dance, debate, drama, drill team, ethnic, gay, honors, international, jazz band, literary magazine, marching band, musical theater, newspaper, orchestra, pep band, photography, political, professional, radio and TV, religious, social, social service, student government, and yearbook. Popular campus events include Tigerama, Welcome Back Festival, and Annual Shakespeare.

Sports: There are 10 intercollegiate sports for men and 9 for women, and 45 intramural sports for men and 45 for women. Facilities include a newly renovated recreation center, an 89,000-seat stadium, and a 10,251-seat coliseum.

Disabled Students: 75% of the campus is accessible. Wheelchair ramps, elevators, special parking, specially equipped rest rooms, special class scheduling, lowered drinking fountains, lowered telephones, and special housing are available.

Services: Counseling and information services are available, as is tutoring in some subjects. There is a reader service for the blind. Other services include textbooks on tape, testing modifications, library assistance, interpreters, note takers, and letters to faculty members.

Campus Safety and Security: Measures include 24-hour foot and vehicle patrol, self-defense education, security escort services, and shuttle buses. There are informal discussions, pamphlets/posters/films, emergency telephones, lighted pathways/sidewalks, electronic card access to residence halls, and limited outdoor surveillance cameras.

Programs of Study: Clemson confers B.A., B.S., B.F.A., and B.L.A. degrees. Master's and doctoral degrees are also awarded. Bachelor's degrees are awarded in AGRICULTURE (agriculture, animal science, forestry and related sciences, forestry production and processing, horticulture, and soil science), BIOLOGICAL SCIENCE (biochemistry, biology/biological science, and microbiology), BUSINESS (accounting, banking and finance, business administration and management, management science, and marketing/retailing/merchandising), COMMUNICATIONS AND THE ARTS (communications, design, English, fine arts, French, German, modern language, and Spanish), COMPUTER AND PHYSICAL SCIENCE (chemistry, computer science, geology, information sciences and systems, mathematics, and physics), EDUCATION (agricultural, early childhood, elementary, industrial arts, secondary, and special), ENGINEERING AND ENVIRONMENTAL DESIGN (agricultural engineering, ceramic engineering, chemical engineering, civil engineering, computer engineering, construction management, electrical/electronics engineering, graphic arts technology, industrial administration/management, industrial engineering, landscape architecture/design, mechanical engineering, and textile technology), HEALTH PROFESSIONS (medical laboratory technology, nursing, predentistry, premedicine, prepharmacy, preveterinary science, and speech pathology/audiology), SO-CIAL SCIENCE (economics, food science, history, parks and recreation management, philosophy, political science/government, prelaw, psychology, and sociology). Engineering, architecture, and biological sciences are the strongest academically. Marketing and engineering are the largest.

Required: To graduate, students must complete 120 to 157 credit hours, including 89 to 108 hours in the major, with a GPA of 2.0. Courses are required in English, humanities, math, science, and social science.

Special: Co-op programs are available in all majors except nursing. Work-study programs and study abroad in 38 countries are offered. There are 22 national honor societies, a freshman honors program, and 40 departmental honors programs.

Faculty/Classroom: 67% of faculty are male; 33%, female. 99% teach undergraduates, 73% do research, and 72% do both. Graduate students teach 18% of introductory courses. The average class size in an introductory lecture is 45; in a laboratory, 19; and in a regular course, 29.

Admissions: 57% of the 2005-2006 applicants were accepted. The SAT scores for the 2005-2006 freshman class were: Verbal--8% below 500, 45% between 500 and 599, 40% between 600 and 700, and 7% above 700; Math--5% below 500, 32% between 500 and 599, 50% between 600 and 700, and 13% above 700. The ACT scores were 8% below 21, 15% between 21 and 23, 31% between 24 and 26, 15% between 27 and 28, and 31% above 28. 61% of the current freshmen were in the top fifth of their class; 96% were in the top two fifths. There were 24 National Merit finalists in a recent year. 100 freshmen graduated first in their class in a recent year.

Requirements: The SAT or ACT is required. The ACT Optional Writing test is also required. In addition, applicants should be graduates of an accredited secondary school. The GED is accepted. AP and CLEP credits are accepted. Important factors in the admissions decision are advanced placement or honor courses, parents or siblings attending the school, and recommendations by school officials.

Procedure: Freshmen are admitted fall, spring, and summer. Entrance exams should be taken during spring of the junior year or fall of the senior year. Applications should be filed by May 1 for fall entry and December 15 for spring entry. The fall 2005 application fee was $50. Notification is sent February 17. 109 applicants were on the 2005 waiting list; 14 were admitted. Applications are accepted on-line.

Transfer: 689 transfer students enrolled in 2004-2005. Transfer applicants must have completed at least 30 semester hours with approximately a 2.5 GPA. 37 of 120 to 157 credits required for the bachelor's degree must be completed at Clemson.

Visiting: There are regularly scheduled orientations for prospective students, including a series of 2-day summer programs of advisement, student services presentations, and registration for the fall semester. There are guides for informal visits and visitors may sit in on classes (see http://dcit.clemson.edu). To schedule a visit, contact the Class of 1944 Visitor's Center at (864) 656-4789 or http://www.clemson.edu/welcome/vcenter/center/reserve.htm.

Financial Aid: In 2005-2006, 87% of all full-time freshmen and 71% of continuing full-time students received some form of financial aid. 28% of full-time freshmen and 31% of continuing full-time students received need-based aid. The average freshman award was $9147. Need-based scholarships or need-based grants averaged $3264 ($7500 maximum); need-based self-help aid (loans and jobs) averaged $3394 ($7125 maximum); non-need-based athletic scholarships averaged $11,925 ($25,409 maximum); and other non-need-based awards and non-need-based scholarships averaged $7075 ($24,426 maximum). 57% of undergraduates work part time. Average annual earnings from campus work are $2302. The average financial indebtedness of the 2005 graduate was $14,307. The FAFSA is required. The priority date for freshman financial aid applications for fall entry is April 1.

International Students: There are 995 international students enrolled. The school actively recruits these students. A satisfactory score is required on the TOEFL as well as on the SAT or ACT.

Computers: Wireless access is available almost everywhere on campus, including at several outdoor locations. All students may access the system. There are no time limits and no fees. All students are required to have personal computers. An IBM ThinkPad T43 was required for 2005-2006.

Graduates: From July 1, 2004 to June 30, 2005, 2941 bachelor's degrees were awarded. The most popular majors were management (6%), marketing (6%), and mechanical engineering (5%). In an average class, 1% graduate in 3 years or less, 40% graduate in 4 years or less, 68% graduate in 5 years or less, and 72% graduate in 6 years or less. 340 companies recruited on campus in 2004-2005.

Admissions Contact: Robert S. Barkley, Director of Admissions. A video is available. E-mail: cuadmissions@clemson.edu Web: http://www.clemson.edu

COASTAL CAROLINA UNIVERSITY   E-3
Conway, SC 29528   **(843) 349-2026**
(800) 277-7000; Fax: (843) 349-2127

Full-time: 2780 men, 2973 women	Faculty: 233; IIB, -$
Part-time: 253 men, 391 women	Ph.D.s: 78%
Graduate: 143 men, 1073 women	Student/Faculty: 25 to 1
Year: semesters, summer session	Tuition: $6860 ($15,100)
Application Deadline: August 15	Room & Board: $6280
Freshman Class: 5427 applied, 4015 accepted, 1498 enrolled	
SAT Verbal/Math: 510/520*	ACT: 22 COMPETITIVE

Coastal Carolina University, established in 1954, is a public liberal arts institution offering undergraduate programs through the colleges of business administration, natural and applied sciences, education, and humanities and fine arts. Graduate programs are offered through the College of Education, College of Natural and Applied Science and the College of Business. There are 4 undergraduate schools and 1 graduate school. In addition to regional accreditation, Coastal Carolina has baccalaureate program accreditation with AACSB, ABET, NASAD, and NCATE. The library contains 146,509 volumes, 18,059 microform items, and 4233 audio/video tapes/CDs/DVDs, and subscribes to 24,010 periodicals including electronic. Computerized library services include the card catalog, interlibrary loans, and database searching. Special learning facilities include a learning resource center, art gallery, and a marine science research center. The 302-acre campus is in a suburban area 9 miles west of Myrtle Beach. Including any residence halls, there are 52 buildings.

Student Life: 54% of undergraduates are from South Carolina. Others are from 48 states, 49 foreign countries, and Canada. 95% are from public schools. 82% are white; 13% African American. The average age of freshmen is 18; all undergraduates, 22. 36% do not continue beyond their first year; 43% remain to graduate.

Housing: 2168 students can be accommodated in college housing, which includes coed dormitories. On-campus housing is available on a first-come, first-served basis. 68% of students commute. Alcohol is not permitted. All students may keep cars.

Activities: 7% of men belong to 9 national fraternities; 6% of women belong to 6 national sororities. There are 95 groups on campus, including art, band, cheerleading, chess, choir, chorale, chorus, computers, dance, drama, ethnic, gay, honors, international, jazz band, literary magazine, marching band, musical theater, newspaper, pep band, political, professional, religious, social, social service, and student government. Popular campus events include CINO Day, Christmas formal, and Welcome Back Dance.

Sports: There are 8 intercollegiate sports for men and 9 for women, and 17 intramural sports for men and 16 for women. Facilities include a gym; a football stadium; baseball, soccer, and softball fields; tennis, basketball, volleyball, and racquetball courts; indoor Olympic-size swimming pool; aerobic dance room; weight rooms; and track.

Disabled Students: 95% of the campus is accessible. Wheelchair ramps, elevators, special parking, specially equipped rest rooms, special class scheduling, lowered drinking fountains, and special housing are available.

Services: Counseling and information services are available, as is tutoring in some subjects, including English, foreign languages, math, and statistics. There is a reader service for the blind.

Campus Safety and Security: Measures include 24-hour foot and vehicle patrol, self-defense education, security escort services, and informal discussions. There are pamphlets/posters/films, emergency telephones, and lighted pathways/sidewalks.

Programs of Study: Coastal Carolina confers B.A., B.S., B.A.Ed., B.A.I.S., B.S.B.A., B.S.Ed., B.S.I.S., and B.S.P.E. degrees. Master's degrees are also awarded. Bachelor's degrees are awarded in BIOLOGICAL SCIENCE (biology/biological science and marine science), BUSINESS (accounting, banking and finance, business administration and management, marketing/retailing/merchandising, sports management, and tourism), COMMUNICATIONS AND THE ARTS (communications, dramatic arts, English, fine arts, music, musical theater, Spanish, and studio art), COMPUTER AND PHYSICAL SCIENCE (chemistry, computer science, mathematics, and physics), EDUCATION (early childhood, elementary, middle school, physical, and special), HEALTH PROFESSIONS (health, predentistry, and premedicine), SOCIAL SCIENCE (economics, history, interdisciplinary studies, philosophy, political science/government, prelaw, psychology, and sociology). Accounting, finance, and management are the strongest academically. Marine science, management, and marketing are the largest.

Required: Students must successfully complete a minimum of 120 credits, varying with major department requirements, and must maintain a minimum GPA of 2.0. A 4-year core curriculum of 44 to 52 hours is required for proficiency in the broad areas of writing, library research, a foreign language, and computer usage.

Special: Internships are offered in most majors, as well as study abroad in 19 countries. Interdisciplinary studies and a 3-2 engineering degree

with Clemson University are available. There are 20 national honor societies and a freshman honors program.

Faculty/Classroom: 57% of faculty are male; 43%, female. 95% teach undergraduates and 33% both teach and do research. No introductory courses are taught by graduate students. The average class size in an introductory lecture is 30; in a laboratory, 19; and in a regular course, 25.

Admissions: 74% of the 2005-2006 applicants were accepted. The SAT scores for the 2005-2006 freshman class were: Verbal--41% below 500, 49% between 500 and 599, 9% between 600 and 700, and 1% above 700; Math--31% below 500, 53% between 500 and 599, 15% between 600 and 700, and 1% above 700. The ACT scores were 42% below 21, 33% between 21 and 23, 17% between 24 and 26, 5% between 27 and 28, and 3% above 28. 26% of the current freshmen were in the top fifth of their class; 57% were in the top two fifths. 6 freshmen graduated first in their class.

Requirements: The SAT or ACT is required. In addition, graduation from an accredited secondary or home school program is required; a GED will be accepted with appropriate scores. Applicants are required to submit complete specific high school credits, including 4 years of college prep, English, 3 units of mathematics (Algebra ll required) , 3 units of laboratory science, 3 units of social sciences (U.S. History required), 2 units of the same foreign language, 4 advance electives (from computer science, math, additional science, foreign language, social science, humanities, and arts), and 1 unit of physical education or ROTC. An interview is recommended. A GPA of 2.25 is required. AP and CLEP credits are accepted. Important factors in the admissions decision are advanced placement or honor courses, recommendations by school officials, and evidence of special talent.

Procedure: Freshmen are admitted to all sessions. Entrance exams should be taken in spring of the junior year or fall of the senior year. There are deferred admissions and rolling admissions plans. Applications should be filed by August 15 for fall entry and December 15 for spring entry. Notification is sent on a rolling basis. Applications are accepted on-line. The fall 2005 application fee was $45.

Transfer: 587 transfer students enrolled in 2004-2005. A minimum GPA of 2.0 is required. Transfers with fewer than 30 hours earned must also meet freshman admission requirements. Students must submit college transcripts and must be eligible to return to the last institution attended. 30 of 120 credits required for the bachelor's degree must be completed at Coastal Carolina.

Visiting: There are regularly scheduled orientations for prospective students, including sessions for academic requirements, housing, financial aid, student life, parents' orientation, tours, cookouts, and entertainment. There are guides for informal visits and visitors may sit in on classes. To schedule a visit, contact the Admissions Office.

Financial Aid: In 2005-2006, 63% of all full-time freshmen and 66% of continuing full-time students received some form of financial aid. 64% of full-time freshmen and 72% of continuing full-time students received need-based aid. The average freshman award was $6868. Need-based scholarships or need-based grants averaged $3347; need-based self-help aid (loans and jobs) averaged $6213; and non-need-based athletic scholarships averaged $5645. 81% of undergraduates work part time. Average annual earnings from campus work are $2000. The average financial indebtedness of the 2005 graduate was $20,923. The FAFSA and the college's own financial statement are required. The deadline for filing freshman financial aid applications for fall entry is April 1.

International Students: In a recent year there were 135 international students enrolled. They must score satisfactorily on the written TOEFL or on the electronic version. The SAT or ACT is also required for first-time fresman.

Computers: All students may access the system 24 hours via dial-in. There are no time limits and no fees. It is strongly recommended that all students have a personal computer. It is recommended that students in Computer Science: Introduction to Algorithmic Design have personal computers.

Graduates: From July 1, 2004 to June 30, 2005, 887 bachelor's degrees were awarded. The most popular majors were marketing (12%), marine science (9%), and management (9%). In an average class, 23% graduate in 4 years or less, 38% graduate in 5 years or less, and 43% graduate in 6 years or less. 71 companies recruited on campus in a recent year.

Admissions Contact: Judy W. Vogt, Associate Vice President, Enrollment Service. E-mail: *admissions@coastal.edu*
Web: *www.coastal.edu/admissions*

COKER COLLEGE
D-2
Hartsville, SC 29550

(843) 383-8050
(800) 950-1908; Fax: (843) 383-8056

Full-time: 200 men, 280 women	**Faculty:** 53
Part-time: 4 men, 5 women	**Ph.D.s:** 72%
Graduate: none	**Student/Faculty:** 9 to 1
Year: semesters, summer session	**Tuition:** $16,200
Application Deadline: open	**Room & Board:** $5,400
Freshman Class: n/av	
SAT or ACT: required	**COMPETITIVE**

Coker College, founded in 1908, is a private institution offering undergraduate programs in business, education, and the arts and sciences. Figures in the above capsule and in this profile are approximate. In addition to regional accreditation, Coker has baccalaureate program accreditation with NASDTEC and NASM. The library contains 67,956 volumes, 43,182 microform items, and 4412 audio/video tapes/CDs/DVDs, and subscribes to 531 periodicals including electronic. Computerized library services include the card catalog, interlibrary loans, and database searching. Special learning facilities include an art gallery a botanical garden, and a nature preserve. The 15-acre campus is in a small town 25 miles west of Florence, 70 miles northeast of Columbia, and 85 miles southeast of Charlotte, North Carolina. Including any residence halls, there are 17 buildings.

Student Life: 79% of undergraduates are from South Carolina. Others are from 25 states, 6 foreign countries, and Canada. 69% are white; 26% African American. The average age of freshmen is 19; all undergraduates, 21. 23% do not continue beyond their first year; 50% remain to graduate.

Housing: 358 students can be accommodated in college housing, which includes single-sex and coed dormitories. On-campus housing is available on a first-come, first-served basis and is available on a lottery system for upperclassmen. 70% of students live on campus; of those, 75% remain on campus on weekends. All students may keep cars.

Activities: There are no fraternities or sororities. There are 27 groups on campus, including art, band, cheerleading, choir, chorus, dance, drama, ethnic, honors, musical theater, newspaper, photography, political, religious, social service, student government, and yearbook. Popular campus events include Black History Month, Apollo Night, and Bandfest.

Sports: There are 6 intercollegiate sports for men and 6 for women, and 17 intramural sports for men and 18 for women. Facilities include a gym, a weight room, an aerobic/dance room, soccer, baseball, and softball fields, tennis courts, a boat house with canoes, and access to a golf course. The gym seats approximately 500.

Disabled Students: 63% of the campus is accessible. Wheelchair ramps, elevators, special parking, specially equipped rest rooms, special class scheduling, and lowered drinking fountains are available.

Services: Counseling and information services are available, as is tutoring in English and math. There is a writing lab.

Campus Safety and Security: Measures include 24-hour foot and vehicle patrol, informal discussions, pamphlets/posters/films, and lighted pathways/sidewalks.

Programs of Study: Coker confers B.A., B.S., B.M.Ed., and B.S.W. degrees. Bachelor's degrees are awarded in BIOLOGICAL SCIENCE (biology/biological science), BUSINESS (business administration and management), COMMUNICATIONS AND THE ARTS (art, communications, dance, dramatic arts, English, French, graphic design, music, musical theater, photography, and Spanish), COMPUTER AND PHYSICAL SCIENCE (chemistry, computer science, and mathematics), EDUCATION (art, early childhood, education, elementary, English, mathematics, music, physical, science, and social science), HEALTH PROFESSIONS (medical laboratory technology), SOCIAL SCIENCE (criminology, history, political science/government, psychology, social work, and sociology). Biology, math, and education are the strongest academically. Business, education, and visual and performing arts are the largest.

Required: Distribution requirements include 9 hours each in humanities and oral and written rhetoric, 7 in science, 6 each in the arts and behavioral sciences, and 3 each in nonnative language, math, and phys ed. A total of 120 credit hours, with 30 to 45 in the major, and a minimum 2.0 GPA are required to graduate.

Special: Internships, study abroad in many countries, on-campus and community service work-study programs, cross-registration with Central College, and dual and student-designed majors are offered. A 3-1 in medical technology with McCleod Regional Medical Center is possible. Also available are credit for military experience, nondegree study, and pass/fail options. The college's round-table approach to teaching allows students and professors to discuss topics and research in small, round-table settings. There are 3 national honor societies, and 3 departmental honors programs.

Faculty/Classroom: 56% of faculty are male; 44%, female. All teach undergraduates and 60% both teach and do research. The average class size in an introductory lecture is 18; in a laboratory, 10; and in a regular course, 9.

Requirements: The SAT or ACT is required. In addition, applicants must be graduates of an accredited secondary school or have a GED. A recommendation from a high school guidance counselor or teacher may be required. An audition or portfolio review is required for music, dance, art, and drama. AP and CLEP credits are accepted. Important factors in the admissions decision are advanced placement or honor courses, extracurricular activities record, and leadership record.

Procedure: Freshmen are admitted fall, spring, and summer. Entrance exams should be taken during the junior year or the first part of the senior year. There are early decision and deferred admissions plans. Check with the school for current application deadlines and fees. Applications are accepted on-line.

Transfer: 42 transfer students enrolled in a recent year. Applicants with fewer than 30 semester hours must submit high school transcripts and SAT scores. A minimum 2.0 GPA is required. 30 of 120 credits required for the bachelor's degree must be completed at Coker.

Visiting: There are regularly scheduled orientations for prospective students, consisting of orientation, a meal, campus tours, and discussions with faculty and a student panel. There are guides for informal visits and visitors may sit in on classes and stay overnight. To schedule a visit, contact the Admissions Office at *admissions@coker.edu*.

Financial Aid: In a recent year, 100% of all full-time freshmen and 98% of continuing full-time students received some form of financial aid. 89% of full-time freshmen and 90% of continuing full-time students received need-based aid. The average freshman award was $17,206. Need-based scholarships or need-based grants averaged $4808 ($14,550 maximum); need-based self-help aid (loans and jobs) averaged $3851 ($9625 maximum); non-need-based athletic scholarships averaged $3685 ($12,750 maximum); and other non-need-based awards and non-need-based scholarships averaged $8565 ($17,250 maximum). 37% of undergraduates work part time. Average annual earnings from campus work are $1211. The average financial indebtedness of the recent year's graduate was $17,323. Coker is a member of CSS. The FAFSA is required. Check with the school for current deadlines.

International Students: In a recent year, there were 8 international students enrolled. A satisfactory score is required on the written TOEFL.

Computers: All students may access the system regular hours in labs and at all times in dorm rooms. There are no time limits and no fees.

Graduates: In a recent year, 84 bachelor's degrees were awarded. The most popular majors were education (11%), business/marketing (11%), and visual and performing arts (8%). In an average class, 51% graduate in 4 years or less.

Admissions Contact: Perry Kirven, Director of Admissions. A video is available. E-mail: *admission@coker.edu* Web: *www.coker.edu*

COLLEGE OF CHARLESTON
C-3
Charleston, SC 29424

(843) 953-5670; Fax: (843) 953-6322

Full-time: 3230 men, 5825 women	**Faculty:** 509; IIA, --$
Part-time: 350 men, 473 women	**Ph.D.s:** 85%
Graduate: 260 men, 1194 women	**Student/Faculty:** 18 to 1
Year: semesters, summer session	**Tuition:** $6668 ($15,342)
Application Deadline: April 1	**Room & Board:** $6948
Freshman Class: 8217 applied, 5436 accepted, 1993 enrolled	
SAT Verbal/Math: 609/604*	**ACT:** 24 **VERY COMPETITIVE**

The College of Charleston, founded in 1770, is a state-assisted institution offering liberal arts programs, including business and education. There are 5 undergraduate schools and 1 graduate school. In addition to regional accreditation, C of C has baccalaureate program accreditation with AACSB, CSAB, NASM, NCATE, and NAST. The 2 libraries contain 679,661 volumes, 866,116 microform items, and 6729 audio/video tapes/CDs/DVDs, and subscribe to 3818 periodicals including electronic. Computerized library services include the card catalog, interlibrary loans, database searching, and Internet access. Special learning facilities include a learning resource center, art gallery, radio station, TV station, an observatory, a communications museum, a marine lab, an Afro-American research center, and a bronze sculpture foundry. The 52-acre campus is in an urban area in the heart of historic Charleston, by the Atlantic Ocean. Including any residence halls, there are 111 buildings.

Student Life: 65% of undergraduates are from South Carolina. Others are from 49 states, 75 foreign countries, and Canada. 82% are from public schools. 82% are white. The average age of freshmen is 18; all undergraduates, 21. 17% do not continue beyond their first year; 83% remain to graduate.

Housing: 2770 students can be accommodated in college housing, which includes single-sex and coed dormitories, on-campus apartments, fraternity houses, and sorority houses. In addition, there are honors houses, language houses, and special-interest houses. On-campus housing is available on a first-come, first-served basis. 74% of students commute. Upperclassmen may keep cars.

Activities: 13% of men belong to 13 national fraternities; 16% of women belong to 11 national sororities. There are 143 groups on campus, including art, band, cheerleading, chess, choir, chorale, chorus, computers, dance, drama, ethnic, film, forensics, gay, honors, international, jazz band, literary magazine, musical theater, newspaper, opera, orchestra, pep band, political, professional, radio and TV, religious, social, social service, student government, and symphony. Popular campus events include Sports Rally, Thursday Entertainment and Food Specials, and Black History Month.

Sports: There are 8 intercollegiate sports for men and 11 for women, and 16 intramural sports for men and 16 for women. Facilities include a phys ed center with racquetball courts and a weight and workout room, pool, outdoor recreation center with baseball and soccer fields, tennis courts, sailing marina, and student center with a movie theater, game room, weight room, meeting facilities, ballroom, and garden.

Disabled Students: 80% of the campus is accessible. Wheelchair ramps, elevators, special parking, specially equipped rest rooms, special class scheduling, lowered drinking fountains, lowered telephones, and special housing are available.

Services: Counseling and information services are available, as is tutoring in every subject. There is a reader service for the blind, and remedial math, reading, and writing.

Campus Safety and Security: Measures include 24-hour foot and vehicle patrol, self-defense education, security escort services, and informal discussions. There are pamphlets/posters/films, emergency telephones, and lighted pathways/sidewalks.

Programs of Study: C of C confers B.A., B.S., A.B., B.S.D., and B.S.M. degrees. Master's degrees are also awarded. Bachelor's degrees are awarded in BIOLOGICAL SCIENCE (biochemistry, biology/biological science, and marine biology), BUSINESS (accounting, business administration and management, and international business management), COMMUNICATIONS AND THE ARTS (art history and appreciation, arts administration/management, classics, communications, dramatic arts, English, French, German, historic preservation, music, Spanish, and studio art), COMPUTER AND PHYSICAL SCIENCE (chemistry, computer science, geology, information sciences and systems, mathematics, and physics), EDUCATION (athletic training, early childhood, elementary, middle school, physical, and special), HEALTH PROFESSIONS (predentistry and premedicine), SOCIAL SCIENCE (anthropology, economics, history, Latin American studies, philosophy, political science/government, psychology, religion, sociology, and urban studies). Sciences and business are the strongest academically. Business and communication are the largest.

Required: All students must complete a core curriculum, including English and history courses, 12 hours each of language and humanities, 8 hours of lab science and 6 hours each of English, history, math or logic, and social science. A total of 122 credit hours, including 24 to 43 in the major, with a minimum overall GPA of 2.0 (2.5 in some majors) is required to graduate. The average number of hours in the major is 40.

Special: Cross-registration is possible with the Medical University of South Carolina, Trident Technical College, The Citadel, and Charleston Southern University. Co-op programs and internships in all majors, a Washington semester, study abroad in about 39 countries, work-study programs, B.A.-B.S. degrees, and dual majors are offered. The B.S.D. and B.S.M. degrees provide 3 years in predentistry or premedicine, with the fourth year of completion at a medical school. 3-2 engineering degrees are available with Case Western Reserve University, Clemson University, Georgia Institute of Technology, University of South Carolina, and Washington University of St. Louis. A 2-2 program in allied health, biometry, or nursing is offered with the Medical University of South Carolina. The college's 3-week Maymester session offers unconventional courses and programs using alternative methods of instruction. There is an interdisciplinary honors program available to talented students. There are 10 national honor societies, a freshman honors program, and 10 departmental honors programs.

Faculty/Classroom: 52% of faculty are male; 48%, female. 91% teach undergraduates. No introductory courses are taught by graduate students. The average class size in an introductory lecture is 28; in a laboratory, 20; and in a regular course, 21.

Admissions: 66% of the 2005-2006 applicants were accepted. The SAT scores for the 2005-2006 freshman class were: Verbal--1% below 500, 41% between 500 and 599, 50% between 600 and 700, and 8% above 700; Math--2% below 500, 40% between 500 and 599, 52% between 600 and 700, and 6% above 700. The ACT scores were 7% below 21, 43% between 21 and 23, 41% between 24 and 26, 7% between 27 and 28, and 2% above 28. 55% of the current freshmen were in the top fifth of their class; 86% were in the top two fifths. There were 5 National Merit finalists. 18 freshmen graduated first in their class.

Requirements: The SAT or ACT is required. In addition, applicants should have completed 4 units of high school English, 3 each of math, lab science, and social science (including 1 unit of U.S. history and 1/2 unit each of economics and government), 2 of foreign language, and 1 of phys ed. In addition, students should have 1 unit of advanced math or computer science or a combination of these, or 1 unit of world history, world geography, or Western civilization. The GED is accepted. An essay is required. A GPA of 2.0 in-state, 2.3 out-of-state is required. AP and CLEP credits are accepted. Important factors in the admissions deci-

sion are ability to finance college education, leadership record, and evidence of special talent.

Procedure: Freshmen are admitted fall and spring. Entrance exams should be taken by March 1 or earlier. There are early decision, early admissions, deferred admissions, and rolling admissions plans. Early decision applications should be filed by November 1; regular applications, by April 1 for fall entry and November 1 for spring entry, along with a $45 fee. Notification of early decision is sent December 15; regular decision, on a rolling basis. Applications are accepted on-line.

Transfer: 689 transfer students enrolled in 2004-2005. Applicants must have 30 hours and must have a 2.6 GPA for in-state residence and 3.0 for out-ot-state students. 36 of 122 credits required for the bachelor's degree must be completed at C of C.

Visiting: There are regularly scheduled orientations for prospective students, consisting of 1-day open houses throughout the year and 6 2-day orientation sessions throughout the summer, including a family session. Academic requirements and expectations, services offered, placement testing, individual academic advising, registration, and introduction to residence life and cultural offerings are included. There are guides for informal visits and visitors may sit in on classes. To schedule a visit, contact the Admissions Office.

Financial Aid: The FAFSA is required. The priority date for freshman financial aid applications for fall entry is March 1.

International Students: There are 270 international students enrolled. They must score satisfactorily on the written TOEFL or on the electronic version.

Computers: All students may access the system 24 hours a day. There are no time limits. The fee is $35.

Graduates: From July 1, 2004 to June 30, 2005, 2098 bachelor's degrees were awarded. The most popular majors were communications (15%), business administration (14%), and elementary education (3%). In an average class, 2% graduate in 3 years or less, 46% graduate in 4 years or less, 59% graduate in 5 years or less, and 59% graduate in 6 years or less. Of the 2004 graduating class, 26% were enrolled in graduate school within 6 months of graduation and 84% were employed.

Admissions Contact: Suzette Stille, Dean of Undergraduate Admissions. A video is available. E-mail: *admissions@cofc.edu*
Web: *www.cofc.edu/admissions*

COLUMBIA COLLEGE   C-3
Columbia, SC 29203   **(803) 786-3871**
                            (800) 277-1301; Fax: (803) 786-3674

Full-time: 9 men, 858 women	**Faculty:** n/av
Part-time: 14 men, 227 women	**Ph.Ds:** 80%
Graduate: 26 men, 359 women	**Student/Faculty:** n/av
Year: semesters, summer session	**Tuition:** $19,164
Application Deadline: February 15	**Room & Board:** $5818
Freshman Class: n/av	
SAT or ACT: required	**LESS COMPETITIVE**

Columbia College, founded in 1854, is a private primarily women's liberal arts college affiliated with the United Methodist Church. In addition to regional accreditation, Columbia College has baccalaureate program accreditation with CSWE, NASAD, NASDTEC, and NASM. The library contains 170,000 volumes, 8353 microform items, and 29,834 audio/video tapes/CDs/DVDs, and subscribes to 633 periodicals including electronic. Computerized library services include interlibrary loans and database searching. Special learning facilities include a learning resource center, art gallery, women's leadership center, and a science and technology center. The 53-acre campus is in an urban area in the northern section of Columbia. Including any residence halls, there are 26 buildings.

Student Life: 93% of undergraduates are from South Carolina. Students are from 16 states, 12 foreign countries, and Canada. 52% are white; 43% African American. 84% are Protestant; 17% claim no religious affiliation; 6% Catholic. The average age of freshmen is 18; all undergraduates, 23. 28% do not continue beyond their first year; 72% remain to graduate.

Housing: 650 students can be accommodated in college housing, which includes single-sex dorms. In addition, there are honors houses. On-campus housing is guaranteed for all 4 years. 58% of students live on campus. Alcohol is not permitted. All students may keep cars.

Activities: There are no fraternities or sororities. There are 57 groups on campus, including art, band, choir, chorus, computers, dance, drama, ethnic, honors, international, literary magazine, musical theater, newspaper, opera, photography, political, professional, radio and TV, religious, social, social service, student government, and yearbook. Popular campus events include Fine Arts Series, Follies, and Ludy Bowl.

Sports: There are 4 intercollegiate sports for women and 4 intramural sports for women. Facilities include an athletic field, tennis courts, a gym, an Olympic-size pool, a fitness lab, and a dance studio.

Disabled Students: 90% of the campus is accessible. Wheelchair ramps, elevators, special parking, specially equipped rest rooms, and special class scheduling are available.

Services: Counseling and information services are available. Peer tutoring and remedial instruction are offered in some subjects.

Campus Safety and Security: Measures include 24-hour foot and vehicle patrol, self-defense education, security escort services, and informal discussions. There are pamphlets/posters/films, emergency telephones, and lighted pathways/sidewalks.

Programs of Study: Columbia College confers B.A., B.F.A., and B.Mus. degrees. Master's degrees are also awarded. Bachelor's degrees are awarded in BIOLOGICAL SCIENCE (biology/biological science), BUSINESS (accounting and business administration and management), COMMUNICATIONS AND THE ARTS (communications, dance, English, French, languages, music, music performance, performing arts, piano/organ, Spanish, and studio art), COMPUTER AND PHYSICAL SCIENCE (chemistry, information sciences and systems, and mathematics), EDUCATION (Christian, dance, early childhood, elementary, music, special, and speech correction), HEALTH PROFESSIONS (medical laboratory technology), SOCIAL SCIENCE (history, political science/government, psychology, public affairs, religion, religious music, social work, and sociology). Education, sciences, and performing arts are the largest.

Required: To graduate, students must complete 127 semester hours, with a minimum GPA of 2.5 in the major and 2.0 overall. General education requirements for the B.A. degree include 15 hours of communication skills, 12 of social science, 9 of aesthetics, 8 of natural science, 6 of religion, and 3 each of math and phys ed. Students also must satisfy proficiency requirements in English and math.

Special: The Center for Contractual Studies allows qualified students to pursue individualized programs through independent study, practicums, and a senior project. The college also offers internships, study abroad, a Washington semester, dual majors, and credit for life, military, and work experience. Nondegree study and pass/fail options are available. There is a freshman honors program.

Faculty/Classroom: 36% of faculty are male; 64%, female. 95% teach undergraduates. No introductory courses are taught by graduate students. The average class size in an introductory lecture is 20 and in a laboratory, 20.

Admissions: 42% of the current freshmen were in the top fifth of their class; 71% were in the top two fifths.

Requirements: The SAT or ACT is required. In addition, applicants must be graduates of an accredited secondary school or have earned a GED. They should complete 16 Carnegie units, including 4 years of English, 3 of math, and 2 each of foreign language and lab science, as well as courses in history and social studies. An essay and an interview are recommended, as is a portfolio or an audition for fine or performing arts students. AP and CLEP credits are accepted. Important factors in the admissions decision are recommendations by school officials, advanced placement or honor courses, and leadership record.

Procedure: Freshmen are admitted to all sessions. Entrance exams should be taken near the end of the junior year or by December of the senior year. There is a rolling admission plan. Priority applications should be filed by February 15 for fall entry. The fall 2005 application fee was $25. Notification is sent on a rolling basis. Applications are accepted on-line.

Transfer: 111 transfer students enrolled in 2004-2005. An interview is recommended for transfer students. Applicants with fewer than 24 semester hours must present ACT or SAT scores and high school transcripts. Grades of C or better transfer for credit. 30 of 127 credits required for the bachelor's degree must be completed at Columbia College.

Visiting: There are regularly scheduled orientations for prospective students, consisting of meetings with faculty advisers, classroom visits, campus tours, lunch, and student life and financial aid presentations. There are guides for informal visits and visitors may sit in on classes. To schedule a visit, contact the Admissions Office.

Financial Aid: The average freshman award in a recent year was $17,000. 34% of undergraduates work part time. Average annual earnings from campus work are $700. The FAFSA is required. Check with the school for current application deadlines.

International Students: There are 18 international students enrolled in a recent year. The school actively recruits these students. They must score satisfactorily on TOEFL and also take the SAT or the ACT.

Computers: All students may access the system. There are no time limits. The fee is $15 per semester. It is strongly recommended that all students have a personal computer.

Graduates: 218 bachelor's degrees were awarded in a recent year. The most popular majors were business administration (14%), speech correction (13%), and early childhood education (10%). In an average class, 52% graduate in 4 years or less, 55% graduate in 5 years or less, and 57% graduate in 6 years or less.

Admissions Contact: Julie A. King, Director of Admissions.
E-mail: *admissions@colacoll.edu*
Web: *http://www.columbiacollegesc.edu*

CONVERSE COLLEGE B-1

Spartanburg, SC 29302 (864) 596-9040
(800) 766-1125; Fax: (864) 596-9225

Full-time: 600 women	**Faculty:** 68; IIB, -$
Part-time: 120 women	**Ph.D.s:** 89%
Graduate: 65 men, 380 women	**Student/Faculty:** 9 to 1
Year: 4-1-4, summer session	**Tuition:** $19,000
Application Deadline: see profile	**Room & Board:** $5800
Freshman Class: n/av	
SAT or ACT: recommended	**VERY COMPETITIVE**

Converse College, founded in 1889, is a private women's liberal arts college. Men are admitted to the graduate programs. There are 2 undergraduate and 2 graduate schools. Figures in the above capsule and in this profile are approximate. In addition to regional accreditation, Converse College has baccalaureate program accreditation with NASM. The library contains 150,000 volumes, 310 microform items, and 12,000 audio/video tapes/CDs/DVDs, and subscribes to 700 periodicals including electronic. Computerized library services include the card catalog, interlibrary loans, and database searching. Special learning facilities include a learning resource center, art gallery, and natural history museum. The 72-acre campus is in an urban area 80 miles southwest of Charlotte. Including any residence halls, there are 27 buildings.

Student Life: 65% of undergraduates are from South Carolina. Others are from 25 states and 10 foreign countries. 70% are from public schools. 85% are white; 12% African American. The average age of freshmen is 18; all undergraduates, 20. 26% do not continue beyond their first year; 56% remain to graduate.

Housing: 700 students can be accommodated in college housing, which includes single-sex dormitories. On-campus housing is guaranteed for all 4 years. 90% of students live on campus; of those, 40% remain on campus on weekends. Alcohol is not permitted. All students may keep cars.

Activities: There are 50 groups on campus, including art, cheerleading, choir, chorale, chorus, computers, dance, debate, drama, ethnic, gay, honors, international, literary magazine, musical theater, newspaper, opera, orchestra, photography, political, professional, religious, social service, student government, symphony, and yearbook. Popular campus events include Founders Day, May Day, and Family Weekend.

Sports: Facilities include a gym, a pool, a dance studio, a weight room, tennis courts, and bowling lanes.

Disabled Students: 50% of the campus is accessible. Wheelchair ramps, elevators, special parking, and specially equipped rest rooms are available.

Services: Counseling and information services are available, as is tutoring in most subjects. There is a reader service for the blind.

Campus Safety and Security: Measures include 24-hour foot and vehicle patrol, self-defense education, security escort services, and informal discussions. There are pamphlets/posters/films, emergency telephones, and lighted pathways/sidewalks.

Programs of Study: Converse College confers B.A., B.S., B.F.A., and B.Mus. degrees. Master's degrees are also awarded. Bachelor's degrees are awarded in BIOLOGICAL SCIENCE (biology/biological science), BUSINESS (accounting and business administration and management), COMMUNICATIONS AND THE ARTS (English, fine arts, French, languages, modern language, music, and Spanish), COMPUTER AND PHYSICAL SCIENCE (chemistry, computer science, and mathematics), EDUCATION (art, early childhood, elementary, foreign languages, music, science, and secondary), ENGINEERING AND ENVIRONMENTAL DESIGN (interior design), HEALTH PROFESSIONS (art therapy, predentistry, and premedicine), SOCIAL SCIENCE (economics, history, political science/government, prelaw, psychology, and religion). English, politics, and biology are the strongest academically. Music, education, and business are the largest.

Required: To graduate, students must complete 120 semester hours, including 52 hours across the liberal arts discipline, with a minimum GPA of 2.0. Courses in ideas and culture, computer literacy, public speaking, and phys ed are required.

Special: There are co-op programs and cross-registration with Wofford College. Internships, study abroad, a work-study program, accelerated degree programs, B.A.-B.S. degrees in business, economics, sociology, biology, and chemistry, and dual and student-designed majors are offered. There are 10 national honor societies, a freshman honors program, and 100 departmental honors programs.

Faculty/Classroom: 46% of faculty are male; 54%, female. 95% teach undergraduates and 50% both teach and do research. No introductory courses are taught by graduate students. The average class size in an introductory lecture is 20; in a laboratory, 15; and in a regular course, 11.

Requirements: The SAT or ACT is recommended. In addition, applicants should be graduates of an accredited secondary school, having completed 20 Carnegie units, including 4 years of English, 3 of math, 2 each of foreign language, science, and social studies, and 1 of history. The GED is accepted. An interview is recommended for all students and an audition is recommended for music students. A GPA of 2.0 is required. AP and CLEP credits are accepted. Important factors in the admissions decision are advanced placement or honor courses, recommendations by school officials, and leadership record.

Procedure: Freshmen are admitted to all sessions. Entrance exams should be taken by the senior year of high school. There is an early decision plan. Check with school for current application deadlines and fee. 4 early decision candidates were accepted in a recent year. Applications are accepted on-line.

Transfer: 20 transfer students enrolled in 2004-2005. Transfer applicants should have a minimum GPA of 2.0. 42 of 120 credits required for the bachelor's degree must be completed at Converse College.

Visiting: There are regularly scheduled orientations for prospective students, consisting of faculty meetings, panel discussions, campus tours, tours of Spartanburg, and private interview sessions. There are guides for informal visits and visitors may sit in on classes and stay overnight. To schedule a visit, contact the Admissions Office at (864) 596-9090 or *admissions@converse.edu*.

Financial Aid: In a recent year, 80% of all full-time freshmen and 75% of continuing full-time students received some form of financial aid. 72% of full-time freshmen and 69% of continuing full-time students received need-based aid. The average freshman award was $18,039. Need-based scholarships or need-based grants averaged $15,866; need-based self-help aid (loans and jobs) averaged $3593; non-need-based athletic scholarships averaged $9488; and other non-need-based awards and non-need-based scholarships averaged $17,061. 33% of undergraduates work part time. Average annual earnings from campus work are $915. The average financial indebtedness of the recent year's graduate was $18,036. The FAFSA is required. Check with the school for current deadlines.

International Students: In a recent year, there were 10 international students enrolled. The school actively recruits these students. A satisfactory score is required on the written TOEFL.

Computers: All students may access the system. There are no time limits and no fees. It is strongly recommended that all students have a personal computer.

Admissions Contact: Director of Admissions. A video is available. Web: *www.converse.edu*

ERSKINE COLLEGE   B-2
Due West, SC 29639

(864) 379-8830
(800) 241-8721; Fax: (864) 379-2167

Full-time: 266 men, 319 women	**Faculty:** 37
Part-time: 4 men, 5 women	**Ph.D.s:** 92%
Graduate: none	**Student/Faculty:** 16 to 1
Year: 4-1-4, summer session	**Tuition:** $19,042
Application Deadline: open	**Room & Board:** $6426
Freshman Class: 854 applied, 596 accepted, 181 enrolled	
SAT Verbal/Math: 550/570*	**VERY COMPETITIVE**

Erskine College, founded in 1839, is a private liberal arts college affiliated with the Associate Reformed Presbyterian Church. The library contains 198,099 volumes, 62,897 microform items, and 1826 audio/video tapes/CDs/DVDs, and subscribes to 1040 periodicals including electronic. Computerized library services include the card catalog, interlibrary loans, and database searching. Special learning facilities include an art gallery and radio station. The 85-acre campus is in a rural area 90 miles west of Columbia. Including any residence halls, there are 30 buildings.

Student Life: 66% of undergraduates are from South Carolina. Others are from 20 states, 7 foreign countries, and Canada. 85% are from public schools. 85% are white. Most are Protestant. The average age of freshmen is 18; all undergraduates, 20. 23% do not continue beyond their first year; 69% remain to graduate.

Housing: 654 students can be accommodated in college housing, which includes single-sex dorms. On-campus housing is guaranteed for all 4 years. 90% of students live on campus; of those, 50% remain on campus on weekends. Alcohol is not permitted. All students may keep cars.

Activities: There are no fraternities or sororities. There are 49 groups on campus, including cheerleading, choir, chorale, chorus, computers, dance, drama, ethnic, honors, jazz band, literary magazine, newspaper, pep band, political, professional, radio and TV, religious, social, social service, student government, and yearbook. Popular campus events include Spring Fling, Back to School Bash, and Freshman Follies.

Sports: There are 5 intercollegiate sports for men and 5 for women. Facilities include a physical activities center, 2 gyms, racquetball courts, soccer and baseball fields, tennis and basketball courts, an outdoor pavilion, an outdoor pool, 2 sand volleyball courts, a weight room, a dance/aerobics studio, and a climbing wall.

Disabled Students: 75% of the campus is accessible. Wheelchair ramps, elevators, special parking, specially equipped rest rooms, and special class scheduling are available.

Services: Counseling and information services are available, as is tutoring in every subject. There is a reader service for the blind.

Campus Safety and Security: Measures include security escort services, informal discussions, pamphlets/posters/films, and lighted pathways/sidewalks.

Programs of Study: Erskine confers A.B. and B.S. degrees. Master's and doctoral degrees are also awarded. Bachelor's degrees are awarded in BIOLOGICAL SCIENCE (biology/biological science), BUSINESS (business administration and management and sports management), COMMUNICATIONS AND THE ARTS (art, English, music, and visual and performing arts), COMPUTER AND PHYSICAL SCIENCE (chemistry, mathematics, natural sciences, and physics), EDUCATION (athletic training, Christian, early childhood, elementary, foreign languages, music, physical, and special), HEALTH PROFESSIONS (medical laboratory technology), SOCIAL SCIENCE (American studies, behavioral science, history, philosophy, psychology, religion, and social studies). Philosophy, music, and Spanish are the strongest academically. Business administration and biology are the largest.

Required: Students must complete 124 semester hours with an average of 27 credits in a major and a minimum GPA of 2.0. A basic curriculum of arts and letters, humanities, natural science and math, social sciences, and phys ed is required. Attendance at 17 convocations per semester is also required.

Special: Externships are available during the January term. Study abroad in 5 countries, 3-2 engineering degrees with Clemson University, the University of Tennessee at Knoxville, and Medical University of South Carolina, and pass/fail options are offered. There are 6 national honor societies and 6 departmental honors programs.

Faculty/Classroom: 57% of faculty are male; 43%, female. All teach undergraduates and 25% both teach and do research. The average class size in an introductory lecture is 22; in a laboratory, 25; and in a regular course, 14.

Admissions: 70% of the 2005-2006 applicants were accepted. The SAT scores for the 2005-2006 freshman class were: Verbal--28% below 500, 35% between 500 and 599, 29% between 600 and 700, and 8% above 700; Math--19% below 500, 48% between 500 and 599, 29% between 600 and 700, and 3% above 700. The ACT scores were 26% below 21, 22% between 21 and 23, 26% between 24 and 26, 13% between 27 and 28, and 13% above 28. 50% of the current freshmen were in the top fifth of their class; 78% were in the top two fifths. 5 freshmen graduated first in their class.

Requirements: The SAT or ACT is required, but grades from college preparatory courses are weighed twice as heavily as the SAT or ACT scores. Applicants must be graduates of an accredited secondary school. The GED is accepted. Applicants should have a minimum of 14 high school academic credits, including 4 credits of English and 2 credits each of math, science, and history. AP and CLEP credits are accepted. Important factors in the admissions decision are advanced placement or honor courses, recommendations by school officials, and extracurricular activities record.

Procedure: Freshmen are admitted to all sessions. Entrance exams should be taken in the spring of the junior year or the fall of the senior year. There is a rolling admissions plan. Application deadlines are open. The fall 2005 application fee was $25. Notification is sent on a rolling basis. Applications are accepted on-line.

Transfer: 12 transfer students enrolled in 2004-2005. Transfer applicants should have a minimum GPA of 2.0. An interview is recommended. 30 of 124 credits required for the bachelor's degree must be completed at Erskine.

Visiting: There are guides for informal visits and visitors may sit in on classes and stay overnight. To schedule a visit, contact Kimberly Yates at (864) 379-6682 or *admissions@erskine.edu*.

Financial Aid: In 2005-2006, 95% of all full-time freshmen and 91% of continuing full-time students received some form of financial aid. 77% of full-time freshmen and 81% of continuing full-time students received need-based aid. The average freshman award was $19,264. Need-based scholarships or need-based grants averaged $6935; and need-based self-help aid (loans and jobs) averaged $2356. The average financial indebtedness of the 2005 graduate was $10,250. The FAFSA and the college's own financial statement are required. The deadline for filing freshman financial aid applications for fall entry is April 1.

International Students: There are 9 international students enrolled. They must achieve a satisfactory score on the TOEFL and also take the SAT.

Computers: All students may access the system from 7 A.M. to 1 A.M. Monday to Saturday, and from 1 P.M. to 1 A.M. Sunday. There are no time limits. The fee is $175. It is strongly recommended that all students have a personal computer.

Graduates: From July 1, 2004 to June 30, 2005, 145 bachelor's degrees were awarded. The most popular majors were business (23%), education (14%), and biology (10%). In an average class, 60% graduate in 4 years or less, and 67% graduate in 5 years or less. 38 companies recruited on campus in 2004-2005. Of the 2004 graduating class, 38% were enrolled in graduate school within 6 months of graduation and 76% were employed.

Admissions Contact: Bart Walker, Director of Admissions. E-mail: *admissions@erskine.edu* Web: *www.erskine.edu*

FRANCIS MARION UNIVERSITY   D-2

Florence, SC 29501-0547   (843) 661-1231
                                        (800) 368-7551; Fax: (843) 661-4635

Full-time: 1099 men, 1959 women	**Faculty:** 179; IIA, --$
Part-time: 119 men, 323 women	**Ph.D.s:** 80%
Graduate: 82 men, 423 women	**Student/Faculty:** 17 to 1
Year: semesters, summer session	**Tuition:** $5984 ($11,833)
Application Deadline: open	**Room & Board:** $5130
Freshman Class: 2524 applied, 1804 accepted, 803 enrolled	
SAT Verbal/Math: 491/490*	**COMPETITIVE**

Francis Marion University, founded in 1970, is a state-supported liberal arts, business, and teachers college. There are 3 undergraduate and 3 graduate schools. In addition to regional accreditation, FMU has baccalaureate program accreditation with AACSB, NASAD, NASDTEC, and NCATE. The library contains 391,457 volumes, 524,242 microform items, and 8894 audio/video tapes/CDs/DVDs, and subscribes to 1538 periodicals including electronic. Computerized library services include the card catalog, interlibrary loans, and database searching. Special learning facilities include a learning resource center and planetarium. The 300-acre campus is in a rural area 8 miles east of Florence. Including any residence halls, there are 34 buildings.

Student Life: 95% of undergraduates are from South Carolina. Others are from 27 states, 20 foreign countries, and Canada. 90% are from public schools. 54% are white; 40% African American. The average age of freshmen is 18; all undergraduates, 21. 40% do not continue beyond their first year; 37% remain to graduate.

Housing: 1381 students can be accommodated in college housing, which includes single-sex dormitories and on-campus apartments. On-campus housing is available on a first-come, first-served basis. 60% of students commute. All students may keep cars.

Activities: 7% of men belong to 7 national fraternities; 7% of women belong to 7 national sororities. There are 60 groups on campus, including art, cheerleading, choir, chorus, drama, ethnic, gay, honors, international, jazz band, literary magazine, newspaper, pep band, photography, political, professional, religious, social, social service, and student government. Popular campus events include Holiday Ball, Spring Fling, and Fall Fling.

Sports: There are 7 intercollegiate sports for men and 7 for women, and 26 intramural sports for men and 26 for women. Facilities include a 3200-seat gym, Olympic-size and outdoor leisure pools, baseball, softball, soccer, and intramural fields, tennis, racquetball, and sand volleyball courts, a track, and weight, fitness, and game rooms.

Disabled Students: All of the campus is accessible. Wheelchair ramps, elevators, special parking, specially equipped rest rooms, special class scheduling, and lowered drinking fountains are available.

Services: There is a reader service for the blind and remedial reading and writing.

Campus Safety and Security: Measures include 24-hour foot and vehicle patrol, security escort services, pamphlets/posters/films, and emergency telephones. There are lighted pathways/sidewalks.

Programs of Study: FMU confers B.A., B.S., B.B.A., B.G.S., and B.S.N degrees. Master's degrees are also awarded. Bachelor's degrees are awarded in BIOLOGICAL SCIENCE (biology/biological science), BUSINESS (accounting, banking and finance, business administration and management, business economics, and marketing/retailing/merchandising), COMMUNICATIONS AND THE ARTS (communications, dramatic arts, English, modern language, and Spanish), COMPUTER AND PHYSICAL SCIENCE (chemistry, computer science, information sciences and systems, mathematics, and physics), EDUCATION (art, early childhood, and elementary), HEALTH PROFESSIONS (nursing), SOCIAL SCIENCE (economics, history, international studies, liberal arts/general studies, political science/government, psychology, and sociology). Premedicine and predentistry are the strongest academically. Business, education, and biology are the largest.

Required: Students must complete 120 to 132 credit hours, including 30 to 60 in the major, with a GPA of 2.0. Distribution requirements include 15 hours of humanities, 12 each of sciences and basic communications (6 of English composition and 6 of math or logic), up to 12 hours of a foreign language, and 9 of social sciences.

Special: There are co-op programs in civil engineering technology and electronic engineering technology with Florence Darlington Technical College, in engineering and forest management with Clemson University, and in medical technology with the McLeod Regional Medical Center. Internships are required in the communications and health physics programs. Accelerated degree programs, preprofessional programs, and dual majors are possible. Nondegree study is permitted. Self-paced courses are offered in math and French. Study abroad is possible in Mexico, Switzerland, Germany, New Zealand, Australia, and England. There are 13 national honor societies and a freshman honors program.

Faculty/Classroom: 58% of faculty are male; 42%, female. No introductory courses are taught by graduate students. The average class size in a regular course is 22.

Admissions: 71% of the 2005-2006 applicants were accepted. The SAT scores for the 2005-2006 freshman class were: Verbal--57% below 500, 32% between 500 and 599, 10% between 600 and 700, and 1% above 700; Math--53% below 500, 38% between 500 and 599, 8% between 600 and 700, and 1% above 700. The ACT scores were 73% below 21, 13% between 21 and 23, 10% between 24 and 26, 3% between 27 and 28, and 1% above 28. 16% of the current freshmen were in the top fifth of their class; 54% were in the top two fifths. 1 freshman graduated first in their class.

Requirements: The SAT is required. In addition, students should have earned 20 credits, consisting of 4 each in academic electives and English, 3 each in math (including algebra I and II), social science, and lab science, 2 in a foreign language, and 1 of phys ed or ROTC. A GPA of 2.0 is required. AP and CLEP credits are accepted.

Procedure: Freshmen are admitted to all sessions. Entrance exams should be taken in the fall of the senior year or spring of the junior year. There is a deferred admissions and a rolling admissions plan. Application deadlines are open. Application fee is $30. Applications are accepted on-line.

Transfer: 840 transfer students enrolled in 2004-2005. Transfer students should have earned 24 hours of college credit, with a GPA of at least 2.0. 36 of 120 to 132 credits required for the bachelor's degree must be completed at FMU.

Visiting: There are regularly scheduled orientations for prospective students, including campus tours and registering for classes. There are guides for informal visits and visitors may sit in on classes. To schedule a visit, contact the Admissions Office.

Financial Aid: In 2005-2006, 83% of all full-time freshmen and 82% of continuing full-time students received some form of financial aid. 44% of full-time freshmen and 55% of continuing full-time students received need-based aid. The average freshman award was $5250. 18% of undergraduates work part time. Average annual earnings from campus work are $5720. The average financial indebtedness of the 2005 graduate was $19,968. FMU is a member of CSS. The FAFSA and the college's own financial statement are required. The priority date for freshman financial aid applications for fall entry is March 1. The deadline for filing freshman financial aid applications for fall entry is February 15.

International Students: In a recent year there were 52 international students enrolled. The school actively recruits these students. They must score satisfactorily on the written TOEFL or on the electronic version. The TOEFL may be submitted in place of the SAT.

Computers: All students may access the system at various hours.

Graduates: From July 1, 2004 to June 30, 2005, 493 bachelor's degrees were awarded. The most popular majors were business administration (35%), biology (11%), and education (10%). In an average class, 16% graduate in 4 years or less, 32% graduate in 5 years or less, and 37% graduate in 6 years or less. 106 companies recruited on campus in 2004-2005.

Admissions Contact: Cynthia Lawson, Director of Admissions. A video is available. E-mail: *admission@fmarion.edu*
Web: *www.fmarion.edu*

FURMAN UNIVERSITY   B-1

Greenville, SC 29613   (864) 294-2034; Fax: (864) 294-3127

Full-time: 1175 men, 1511 women	**Faculty:** 219; IIB, +$
Part-time: 58 men, 59 women	**Ph.D.s:** 96%
Graduate: 57 men, 253 women	**Student/Faculty:** 12 to 1
Year: summer session	**Tuition:** $26,352
Application Deadline: January 15	**Room & Board:** $6912
Freshman Class: 4012 applied, 2127 accepted, 691 enrolled	
SAT Verbal/Math: 650/650*	**ACT:** 28
	HIGHLY COMPETITIVE+

Founded in 1826, Furman University is an independent liberal arts institution offering undergraduate and graduate programs. In addition to regional accreditation, Furman has baccalaureate program accreditation with ACS, NASM, and NCATE. The 3 libraries contain 436,000 volumes, 857,000 microform items, and 8269 audio/video tapes/CDs/DVDs, and subscribe to 4230 periodicals including electronic. Computerized library services include the card catalog, interlibrary loans, database searching, Internet access, and laptop Internet portals. Special learning facilities include a learning resource center, art gallery, radio station, observatory, and cable TV with on-campus broadcasting. The 750-acre campus is in a suburban area 5 miles north of Greenville. Including any residence halls, there are 69 buildings.

Student Life: 71% of undergraduates are from out of state, mostly the South. Students are from 46 states, 27 foreign countries, and Canada. 65% are from public schools. 86% are white. 77% are Protestant; 13% Catholic; 6% claim no religious affiliation. The average age of freshmen is 18; all undergraduates, 20. 7% do not continue beyond their first year; 84% remain to graduate.

Housing: 2452 students can be accommodated in college housing, which includes single-sex and coed dorms and on-campus apartments. In addition, there are language houses, special-interest houses, small houses, lakeside cabins,an eco-cottage, and a healthy living dorm. On-campus housing is guaranteed for all 4 years, is available on a first-come, first-served basis, and is available on a lottery system for upper-classmen. 91% of students live on campus; of those, 75% remain on campus on weekends. Alcohol is not permitted. All students may keep cars.

Activities: 35% of men belong to 8 national fraternities; 40% of women belong to 7 national sororities. There are 130 groups on campus, including art, band, cheerleading, chess, choir, chorale, chorus, computers, dance, debate, drama, drill team, ethnic, forensics, gay, international, jazz band, literary magazine, marching band, musical theater, newspaper, opera, orchestra, pep band, photography, political, professional, radio and TV, religious, social, social service, student government, symphony, and yearbook. Popular campus events include Parents Weekend, Beach Weekend, and Mountain Weekend.

Sports: There are 8 intercollegiate sports for men and 9 for women, and 20 intramural sports for men and 20 for women. Facilities include a 16,500-seat football stadium, a 5800-seat arena, a gym, a pool, an 18-hole golf course, a tennis center with indoor and outdoor courts, a 3000-seat soccer stadium, 12 playing fields, a varsity softball field, and a baseball stadium. The gym includes 6 racquetball courts and a fitness center.

Disabled Students: All of the campus is accessible. Wheelchair ramps, elevators, special parking, specially equipped rest rooms, special class scheduling, lowered drinking fountains, lowered telephones, and special housing are available.

Services: Counseling and information services are available, as is tutoring in every subject. There is a reader service for the blind.

Campus Safety and Security: Measures include 24-hour foot and vehicle patrol, self-defense education, security escort services, and shuttle buses. There are informal discussions, pamphlets/posters/films, emergency telephones, and lighted pathways/sidewalks.

Programs of Study: Furman confers B.A., B.S., B.L.A., and B.M. degrees. Master's degrees are also awarded. Bachelor's degrees are awarded in BIOLOGICAL SCIENCE (biology/biological science and neurosciences), BUSINESS (accounting and business administration and management), COMMUNICATIONS AND THE ARTS (art, communications, dramatic arts, English, French, German, Greek, Latin, music, music performance, music theory and composition, piano/organ, and Spanish), COMPUTER AND PHYSICAL SCIENCE (chemistry, computer science, geology, mathematics, and physics), EDUCATION (education, elementary, and music), ENGINEERING AND ENVIRONMENTAL DESIGN (environmental science and preengineering), HEALTH PROFESSIONS (health science), SOCIAL SCIENCE (Asian/Oriental studies, economics, history, philosophy, political science/government, psychology, religion, religious music, sociology, and urban studies). Chemistry, biology, and music are the strongest academically. Political science, history, and business administration are the largest.

Required: To graduate, students must complete 128 credit hours, including 24 to 44 in the major, with a GPA of 2.0. Distribution requirements include 64 hours of general education courses in English composition, foreign language, health and exercise science, natural sciences, social sciences, fine Asian-African program, arts, math, and humanities. Students must attend 36 cultural events before graduation.

Special: A 3-2 engineering degree is offered with Georgia Institute of Technology, Clemson, North Carolina State, Auburn, and Washington University at St. Louis. Internships, study abroad in at least 17 countries, a Washington semester with an internship in a government agency or political organization, and work-study programs are offered. B.A.-B.S. degrees, dual majors, interdisciplinary majors such as computer science-math, math-economics, and computing-business, and student-designed majors are available. A bachelor of general studies degree is granted in the evening division. Nondegree study and pass/fail options are possible. Furman features student/faculty research programs. There are 20 national honor societies, including Phi Beta Kappa.

Faculty/Classroom: 68% of faculty are male; 32%, female. All teach undergraduates. No introductory courses are taught by graduate students. The average class size in an introductory lecture is 23; in a laboratory, 10; and in a regular course, 17.

Admissions: 53% of the 2005-2006 applicants were accepted. The SAT scores for the 2005-2006 freshman class were: Verbal--2% below 500, 20% between 500 and 599, 56% between 600 and 700, and 22% above 700; Math--2% below 500, 19% between 500 and 599, 61% between 600 and 700, and 18% above 700. The ACT scores were 4% below 21, 10% between 21 and 23, 23% between 24 and 26, 22% between 27 and 28, and 41% above 28. 84% of the current freshmen were in the top fifth of their class; 96% were in the top two fifths. There were 26 National Merit finalists. 47 freshmen graduated first in their class.

Requirements: The SAT or ACT is required. In addition, applicants must be high school graduates or hold a GED. Students should have earned at least 20 units in high school, including 4 of English, 3 each of history, math, and science, and 2 each of social studies and foreign language. 2 essays are required. A portfolio or an audition, where appropriate, is recommended. AP credits are accepted. Important factors in the admissions decision are advanced placement or honor courses, extracurricular activities record, and leadership record.

Procedure: Freshmen are admitted to all sessions. Entrance exams should be taken by late junior or early senior year. There are early decision and early admissions plans. Early decision applications should be filed by November 15; regular applications, by January 15 for fall entry, December 1 for winter entry, February 1 for spring entry, and February 1 for summer entry, along with a $40 fee. Notification of early decision is sent December 15; regular decision, March 15. 497 early decision candidates were accepted for the 2005-2006 class. 597 applicants were on the 2005 waiting list; 7 were admitted. Applications are accepted on-line.

Transfer: 17 transfer students enrolled in 2004-2005. Applicants should complete at least 1 year elsewhere before seeking admission. Admission is competitive. 60 of 128 credits required for the bachelor's degree must be completed at Furman.

Visiting: There are regularly scheduled orientations for prospective students, consisting of an individual or group session with an admissions officer and a campus tour. There are guides for informal visits and visitors may sit in on classes and stay overnight. To schedule a visit, contact the Admissions Office at (864) 294-2034 or *admissions@furman.edu*.

Financial Aid: In 2005-2006, 85% of all full-time freshmen and 82% of continuing full-time students received some form of financial aid. 43% of all full-time students received need-based aid. The average freshman award was $17,800. 44% of undergraduates work part time. Average annual earnings from campus work are $1071. The average financial indebtedness of the 2005 graduate was $21,194. Furman is a member of CSS. The FAFSA and the state aid form are required. The deadline for filing freshman financial aid applications for fall entry is February 1.

International Students: The school actively recruits these students. Satisfactory scores are required on the TOEFL or and the SAT or the ACT.

Computers: Wireless access is available. 98% of students have PCs (the majority--laptops); all have wired connections to network; 95% of classrooms and public spaces have wireless access. All students may access the system 24 hours a day. There are no time limits and no fees.

Graduates: From July 1, 2004 to June 30, 2005, 661 bachelor's degrees were awarded. The most popular majors were political science (13%), history (9%), and business administration (8%). In an average class, 1% graduate in 3 years or less, 79% graduate in 4 years or less, 83% graduate in 5 years or less, and 84% graduate in 6 years or less. 86 companies recruited on campus in 2004-2005. Of the 2004 graduating class, 37% were enrolled in graduate school within 6 months of graduation and 61% were employed.

Admissions Contact: Woody O'Cain, Director of Admissions. A video is available. E-mail: *admissions@furman.edu*
Web: *www.engage.furman.edu*

LANDER UNIVERSITY B-2

Greenwood, SC 29649
(864) 388-8307
(888) 4LANDER; Fax: (864) 388-8125

Full-time: 810 men, 1480 women	**Faculty:** 114; IIB, av$
Part-time: 120 men, 240 women	**Ph.D.s:** 80%
Graduate: 30 men, 290 women	**Student/Faculty:** 20 to 1
Year: semesters, summer session	**Tuition:** $5600 ($11,300)
Application Deadline: open	**Room & Board:** $5000 ($10,600)
Freshman Class: n/av	
SAT or ACT: required	**COMPETITIVE**

Lander University, founded in 1872, is a state-supported institution offering undergraduate programs in liberal arts, science and math, business, education, nursing, and phys ed and exercise studies. There are 10 undergraduate schools and 1 graduate school. Figures in the above capsule and in this profile are approximate. In addition to regional accreditation, Lander has baccalaureate program accreditation with AACSB, NASAD, NASM, and NCATE. The library contains 170,091 volumes, 141,945 microform items, and 2170 audio/video tapes/CDs/DVDs, and subscribes to 692 periodicals including electronic. Computerized library services include the card catalog, interlibrary loans, database searching, and Internet access. Special learning facilities include a learning resource center, art gallery, and a media center. The 100-acre campus is in a small town 75 miles west of Columbia. Including any residence halls, there are 33 buildings.

Student Life: 96% of undergraduates are from South Carolina. Others are from 30 states, 19 foreign countries, and Canada. 77% are white; 19% African American. The average age of freshmen is 19; all undergraduates, 22. 32% do not continue beyond their first year; 68% remain to graduate.

Housing: 1082 students can be accommodated in college housing, which includes single-sex and coed dormitories, on-campus apartments, and off-campus apartments. On-campus housing is available on a first-come, first-served basis. 68% of students commute. Alcohol is not permitted. All students may keep cars.

Activities: 11% of men belong to 5 national fraternities; 12% of women belong to 5 national sororities. There are 65 groups on campus, including art, band, cheerleading, choir, chorale, chorus, computers, dance, drama, ethnic, honors, international, jazz band, literary magazine, musical theater, newspaper, orchestra, pep band, political, professional, religious, social, social service, and student government. Popular campus events include The Greenwood Performing Arts Series.

Sports: There are 4 intercollegiate sports for men and 5 for women, and 11 intramural sports for men and 11 for women. Facilities include a gym, basketball courts, a weight room, a softball field, tennis courts, an indoor pool, and an indoor suspended track.

Disabled Students: 90% of the campus is accessible. Wheelchair ramps, elevators, special parking, specially equipped rest rooms, special class scheduling, lowered drinking fountains, and lowered telephones are available.

Services: Counseling and information services are available, as is tutoring in most subjects. There is a reader service for the blind, and remedial math, reading, and writing.

Campus Safety and Security: Measures include 24-hour foot and vehicle patrol, self-defense education, security escort services, and emergency telephones. There are lighted pathways/sidewalks.

Programs of Study: Lander confers B.A., B.S., and B.M.Ed. degrees. Master's degrees are also awarded. Bachelor's degrees are awarded in BIOLOGICAL SCIENCE (biology/biological science), BUSINESS (business administration and management), COMMUNICATIONS AND THE ARTS (communications, dramatic arts, English, music, Spanish, speech/debate/rhetoric, and visual and performing arts), COMPUTER AND PHYSICAL SCIENCE (chemistry, computer science, and mathematics), EDUCATION (early childhood, elementary, music, physical, and special), ENGINEERING AND ENVIRONMENTAL DESIGN (environmental science), HEALTH PROFESSIONS (exercise science, nursing, and sports medicine), SOCIAL SCIENCE (history, interdisciplinary studies, political science/government, psychology, and sociology). Premedical and dual engineering are the strongest academically. Business administration, education, and behavorial science are the largest.

Required: To graduate, students must complete 125 semester hours, including 36 in the major, with a GPA of 2.0.

Special: Lander offers internships, co-op and work-study programs, accelerated degrees, B.A.-B.S. degrees, dual engineering degrees with Clemson University, student-designed majors in interdisciplinary studies, credit for military experience, and nondegree study. Students in the Honors International Program study abroad in England for 1 semester during their sophomore year. There are 7 national honor societies and a freshman honors program.

Faculty/Classroom: 50% of faculty are male; 50%, female. All teach undergraduates. No introductory courses are taught by graduate students. The average class size in a regular course is 29.

Requirements: The SAT or ACT is required. In addition, applicants must be high school graduates with 20 credits, including 4 each of English and academic electives, and 3 each of math and lab science, 2 each of foreign language and social studies, and 1 each of American history and phys ed or ROTC. An interview and a portfolio or an audition, if appropriate, are recommended. Lander requires applicants to be in the upper 50% of their class. A GPA of 2.0 is required. AP and CLEP credits are accepted.

Procedure: Freshmen are admitted to all sessions. Entrance exams should be taken in the junior year. There are early admissions and deferred admissions plans. Application deadlines are open. Check with the school for current application deadlines and fee. Applications are accepted on-line.

Transfer: 242 transfer students enrolled in a recent year. Applicants must have a minimum college GPA of 2.0, otherwise they may be considered on the strength of military or work experience. Transcripts from every school attended should be submitted. Students under 21 with fewer than 30 semester credits must submit high school transcripts and SAT or ACT results. An interview is recommended. 30 of 125 credits required for the bachelor's degree must be completed at Lander.

Visiting: There are regularly scheduled orientations for prospective students, consisting of open houses. There are guides for informal visits and visitors may sit in on classes. To schedule a visit, contact the Admissions Office.

Financial Aid: In a recent year, 48% of all full-time freshmen and 54% of continuing full-time students received some form of financial aid. 29% of full-time freshmen and 38% of continuing full-time students received need-based aid. The average freshman award was $1392. 20% of undergraduates work part time. The average financial indebtedness of the recent year's graduate was $12,500. The FAFSA is required. Check with the school for current deadlines.

International Students: In a recent year there were 42 international students enrolled. The school actively recruits these students. Satisfactory scores are required on the written TOEFL and the SAT or the ACT.

Computers: All students may access the system. There are no time limits. Check with the school for current fee. It is strongly recommended that all students have a personal computer.

Graduates: In a recent year, 393 bachelor's degrees were awarded. The most popular majors were business (25%), nursing (8%), and elementary education (8%). In an average class, 2% graduate in 3 years or less, 34% graduate in 4 years or less, 44% graduate in 5 years or less,

and 49% graduate in 6 years or less. 20 companies recruited on campus in a recent year.

Admissions Contact: Jonathan T. Reece, Director of Admissions. E-mail: *admissions@lander.edu* Web: *www.lander.edu*

LIMESTONE COLLEGE   B-1

Gaffney, SC 29340-3799

(864) 489-7151 ext. 4554
(800) 795-7151; Fax: (864) 487-8706

Full-time: 356 men, 303 women	**Faculty:** 55; IIB, --$
Part-time: 11 men, 7 women	**Ph.Ds:** 74%
Graduate: none	**Student/Faculty:** 12 to 1
Year: semesters, summer session	**Tuition:** $14,040
Application Deadline: open	**Room & Board:** $5800

Freshman Class: 884 applied, 512 accepted, 172 enrolled
SAT Verbal/Math: 480/490*   **ACT:** 19   **COMPETITIVE**

Limestone College, founded in 1845, is a private, nondenominational Christian institution offering programs in liberal arts, the sciences, business, and teacher preparation. In addition to regional accreditation, Limestone has baccalaureate program accreditation with CAAHEP, CSWE, and NASM. The library contains 109,900 volumes, 2915 microform items, and 3441 audio/video tapes/CDs/DVDs, and subscribes to 281 periodicals including electronic. Computerized library services include the card catalog, interlibrary loans, database searching, Internet access, and laptop Internet portals. Special learning facilities include a learning resource center, a writing and math lab with computer workstations, a center for tutorial services, and a computer graphics art lab. The 115-acre campus is in a suburban area 50 miles southwest of Charlotte, North Carolina, and 25 miles north of Spartanburg. Including any residence halls, there are 20 buildings.

Student Life: 57% of undergraduates are from South Carolina. Others are from 28 states, 11 foreign countries, and Canada. 77% are white; 18% African American. 53% are Protestant; 36% claim no religious affiliation; 11% Catholic. The average age of freshmen is 19; all undergraduates, 21. 35% do not continue beyond their first year; 43% remain to graduate.

Housing: 345 students can be accommodated in college housing, which includes single-sex dorms. On-campus housing is guaranteed for the freshman year only and is available on a first-come, first-served basis. 50% of students live on campus; of those, 65% remain on campus on weekends. Alcohol is not permitted. All students may keep cars.

Activities: 22% of women belong to 1 local sorority. There are no fraternities. There are 17 groups on campus, including art, cheerleading, choir, chorus, computers, drama, honors, jazz band, literary magazine, musical theater, orchestra, professional, religious, social, social service, student government, and yearbook. Popular campus events include Christmas Luminaries, Midterm Madness, and Earth Day.

Sports: There are 9 intercollegiate sports for men and 9 for women, and 9 intramural sports for men and 9 for women. Facilities include a 1500-seat gym, an indoor pool, 8 lighted tennis courts, baseball, softball, soccer, and lacrosse fields, 4 practice fields, a student center with a game room, and a phys ed center.

Disabled Students: 75% of the campus is accessible. Wheelchair ramps, elevators, special parking, specially equipped rest rooms, special class scheduling, and lowered drinking fountains are available. Accommodations are made on an as-needed basis.

Services: Counseling and information services are available, as is tutoring in every subject. There is remedial math, reading, and writing. Special assistance is also available to students with documented learning disabilities through the PALS Program.

Campus Safety and Security: Measures include 24-hour foot and vehicle patrol, security escort services, informal discussions, and lighted pathways/sidewalks.

Programs of Study: Limestone confers B.A., B.S., B.A.S., and B.S.W. degrees. Associate degrees are also awarded. Bachelor's degrees are awarded in BIOLOGICAL SCIENCE (biology/biological science), BUSINESS (accounting, business administration and management, business economics, human resources, marketing management, and sports management), COMMUNICATIONS AND THE ARTS (dramatic arts, English, graphic design, jazz, music, and studio art), COMPUTER AND PHYSICAL SCIENCE (chemistry, computer programming, computer science, information sciences and systems, mathematics, software engineering, and web services), EDUCATION (art, athletic training, elementary, English, mathematics, music, physical, science, and social studies), ENGINEERING AND ENVIRONMENTAL DESIGN (industrial administration/management), SOCIAL SCIENCE (corrections, counseling/psychology, criminal justice, criminology, history, human services, liberal arts/general studies, prelaw, psychology, and social work). Business administration, elementary education, and sports management are the largest.

Required: To graduate, students must complete a minimum of 120 semester hours with 30 to 56 hours in the major and a minimum GPA of 2.0. General education requirements are as follows: 18 hours of fine arts and humanities, 13 to 14 of science and math, and 12 of social science, for a total of 43 hours minimum. A senior exit exam in the major is required.

Special: The college offers senior internships in public and private organizations for 3 credits, as well as a work-study program and off-campus evening courses. Students may have divisional and multidisciplinary dual majors. The college confers a liberal studies degree and may grant credit for military experience. Double majors are possible; however, granting of 2 B.A. degrees requires an additional 30 semester hours. There are 4 national honor societies, a freshman honors program, and 15 departmental honors programs.

Faculty/Classroom: 65% of faculty are male; 35%, female. All teach undergraduates. The average class size in an introductory lecture is 17; in a laboratory, 17; and in a regular course, 11.

Admissions: 58% of the 2005-2006 applicants were accepted. The SAT scores for the 2005-2006 freshman class were: Verbal--63% below 500, 32% between 500 and 599, and 5% between 600 and 700; Math--53% below 500, 34% between 500 and 599, and 13% between 600 and 700. The ACT scores were 71% below 21, 21% between 21 and 23, 6% between 24 and 26, and 2% between 27 and 28. 17% of the current freshmen were in the top fifth of their class; 39% were in the top two fifths.

Requirements: A satisfactory score on the SAT or ACT. The college recommends that students present 4 units of English, 3 of math, and 2 each of lab science and social science. The GED is accepted. An interview is recommended. A GPA of 2.0 is required. AP and CLEP credits are accepted. Important factors in the admissions decision are advanced placement or honor courses, leadership record, and evidence of special talent.

Procedure: Freshmen are admitted fall and spring. Entrance exams should be taken during the fall of the senior year of high school. There is a deferred admissions plan. There is a rolling admissions plan. Application deadlines are open. Application fee is $25. Notification is sent March 1. Applications are accepted on-line.

Transfer: 72 transfer students enrolled in 2004-2005. Applicants must have a minimum GPA of 2.0 and be in good standing at their previous school. 30 of 120 credits required for the bachelor's degree must be completed at Limestone.

Visiting: There are regularly scheduled orientations for prospective students. There are guides for informal visits and visitors may sit in on classes and stay overnight. To schedule a visit, contact Sharon Chery at the Admissions Office.

Financial Aid: In 2005-2006, all full-time freshmen and 85% of continuing full-time students received some form of financial aid. 86% of full-time freshmen and 79% of continuing full-time students received need-based aid. The average freshman award was $13,829. Need-based scholarships or need-based grants averaged $4019 ($4050 maximum); need-based self-help aid (loans and jobs) averaged $2990 ($5500 maximum); non-need-based athletic scholarships averaged $5565 ($13,440 maximum); other non-need-based awards and non-need-based scholarships averaged $5646 ($19,990 maximum); and private scholarships averaged $1511 ($9000 maximum). 13% of undergraduates work part time. Average annual earnings from campus work are $1545. The average financial indebtedness of the 2005 graduate was $8031. Limestone is a member of CSS. The FAFSA is required. The priority date for freshman financial aid applications for fall entry is February 1. The deadline for filing freshman financial aid applications for fall entry is July 1.

International Students: There are 33 international students enrolled. The school actively recruits these students. They must achieve a satisfactory score on the TOEFL as well as on the SAT or ACT.

Computers: Wireless access is available. The Internet is accessible through 70 PCs in the library, the student success center, and the graphics art and computer labs, as well as in residence hall rooms and via wireless access at the phys ed center. All students may access the system 7 days a week, 7 A.M. to 11 P.M. There are no time limits and no fees.

Graduates: From July 1, 2004 to June 30, 2005, 98 bachelor's degrees were awarded. The most popular majors were elementary education (27%), business administration (21%), and social work (10%). In an average class, 1% graduate in 3 years or less, 26% graduate in 4 years or less, 37% graduate in 5 years or less, and 43% graduate in 6 years or less.

Admissions Contact: Chris Phenicie, Vice President, Enrollment Services. E-mail: cphenicie@limestone.edu Web: www.limestone.edu

MORRIS COLLEGE D-3

Sumter, SC 29150-3599
(803) 934-3225
(888) 775-1345; Fax: (803) 773-3687

Full-time: 307 men, 537 women	Faculty: 47
Part-time: 6 men, 13 women	Ph.D.s: 64%
Graduate: none	Student/Faculty: 18 to 1
Year: semesters, summer session	Tuition: $8163
Application Deadline: April 30	Room & Board: $3836
Freshman Class: 931 applied, 749 accepted, 209 enrolled	
SAT or ACT: not required	LESS COMPETITIVE

Morris College, founded in 1908, is a private liberal arts institution affiliated with the Baptist Church. The library contains 102,206 volumes, 202,608 microform items, and 1337 audio/video tapes/CDs/DVDs, and subscribes to 414 periodicals including electronic. Computerized library services include the card catalog, interlibrary loans, database searching, and Internet access. Special learning facilities include a learning resource center, radio station, a TV production studio, and a photography workroom. The 34-acre campus is in an urban area 40 miles east of Columbia. Including any residence halls, there are 20 buildings.

Student Life: 84% of undergraduates are from South Carolina. Others are from 19 states. 99% are from public schools. Almost all are African American. The average age of freshmen is 19; all undergraduates, 22. 45% do not continue beyond their first year; 40% remain to graduate.

Housing: 689 students can be accommodated in college housing, which includes single-sex dorms. On-campus housing is guaranteed for the freshman year only and is available on a first-come, first-served basis. 71% of students live on campus; of those, 25% remain on campus on weekends. Alcohol is not permitted. Upperclassmen may keep cars.

Activities: 12% of men belong to 4 national fraternities; 11% of women belong to 4 national sororities. There are 56 groups on campus, including cheerleading, chess, choir, chorale, dance, drama, honors, literary magazine, newspaper, pep band, photography, political, professional, radio and TV, religious, social, social service, student government, and yearbook. Popular campus events include Coronation of Miss Morris College, Christmas and gospel choir concerts, and Martin Luther King Celebration.

Sports: There are 6 intercollegiate sports for men and 6 for women, and 5 intramural sports for men and 5 for women. Facilities include a weight room, an athletic field complex, a 1700-seat gym, and a 600-seat auditorium.

Disabled Students: 30% of the campus is accessible. Wheelchair ramps, elevators, special parking, specially equipped rest rooms, and lowered drinking fountains are available.

Services: Counseling and information services are available, as is tutoring in every subject. There is remedial math, reading, and writing. Skill-building materials are available on computer.

Campus Safety and Security: Measures include 24-hour foot and vehicle patrol, security escort services, informal discussions, and lighted pathways/sidewalks.

Programs of Study: Morris confers B.A., B.S., B.F.A., and B.S.Ed. degrees. Bachelor's degrees are awarded in BIOLOGICAL SCIENCE (biology/biological science), BUSINESS (business administration and management and recreation and leisure services), COMMUNICATIONS AND THE ARTS (broadcasting, English, and journalism), COMPUTER AND PHYSICAL SCIENCE (mathematics), EDUCATION (early childhood, elementary, English, mathematics, science, and social studies), HEALTH PROFESSIONS (community health work), SOCIAL SCIENCE (criminal justice, history, liberal arts/general studies, pastoral studies, political science/government, religious education, and sociology). Christian education, pastoral ministry, and English are the strongest academically. Business administration, biology, and criminal justice are the largest.

Required: All students must complete 124 to 143 credit hours with a 2.0 GPA overall. General education requirements, with a core curriculum of 60 to 62 credits, include 12 credits each in English and social sciences, 8 to 16 in natural sciences, 6 in religion, 4 in fine arts, 3 to 9 in math, 3 in health education, 2 to 3 each in computers and speech, and a freshman seminar. A comprehensive exam in the major is required prior to graduation.

Special: Internships, co-op programs, and work-study programs on and off campus are offered. A B.A.-B.S. degree in organizational management is available. A B.S. degree in nursing is offered in conjunction with the University of South Carolina. A cooperative 3-2 engineering degree program with Clemson University and a dual degree program with North Carolina A&T University are available. Credit by exam and credit for military experience are possible. There is 1 national honor society, a freshman honors program, and 1 departmental honors program.

Faculty/Classroom: 51% of faculty are male; 49%, female. All teach undergraduates. The average class size in an introductory lecture is 30; in a laboratory, 20; and in a regular course, 25.

Admissions: 80% of the 2005-2006 applicants were accepted. 4% of the current freshmen were in the top fifth of their class; 22% were in the top two fifths.

Requirements: In addition, candidates should be graduates of an accredited secondary school or have the GED. They must have completed 24 Carnegie units, consisting of 4 each in high school English and math, 3 in natural science, 2 in social sciences, and 1 each in U.S. history, phys ed, computer science, and foreign language, and 7 in electives. A GPA of 2.0 is required. AP and CLEP credits are accepted.

Procedure: Freshmen are admitted to all sessions. There is a deferred admissions and a rolling admissions plan. Applications should be filed by April 30 for fall entry, October 30 for spring entry, and March 30 for summer entry, along with a $20 fee. Notification is sent on a rolling basis.

Transfer: 25 transfer students enrolled in 2004-2005. Applicants must submit transcripts and evidence of honorable release. A minimum GPA of 2.0 is required. 30 of 124 credits required for the bachelor's degree must be completed at Morris.

Visiting: There are regularly scheduled orientations for prospective students, consisting of a campus tour, visits with division chairs and faculty members to discuss majors, scheduled activities, and lunch. There are guides for informal visits. To schedule a visit, contact Deborah Calhoun at dcalhoun@morris.edu.

Financial Aid: In 2005-2006, 98% of all full-time freshmen and 97% of continuing full-time students received some form of financial aid. 96% of all full-time students received need-based aid. The average freshman award was $12,000. Need-based scholarships or need-based grants averaged $3900 ($4050 maximum); need-based self-help aid (loans and jobs) averaged $4000 ($5000 maximum); non-need-based athletic scholarships averaged $750 ($10,500 maximum); and other non-need-based awards and non-need-based scholarships averaged $3500 ($5000 maximum). 49% of undergraduates work part time. Average annual earnings from campus work are $1500. The average financial indebtedness of the 2005 graduate was $17,000. Morris is a member of CSS. The FAFSA and the college's own financial statement are required. The deadline for filing freshman financial aid applications for fall entry is April 30.

International Students: Satisfactory scores are required on the TOEFL and the SAT or the ACT.

Computers: There are 5 computer labs and computers in all dorms and the library, with Internet access in all of these locations. All students may access the system 78 hours per week. The fee is $90 per year.

Graduates: From July 1, 2004 to June 30, 2005, 163 bachelor's degrees were awarded. The most popular majors were business administration (19%), health science (18%), and criminal justice (10%). In an average class, 18% graduate in 4 years or less, 38% graduate in 5 years or less, and 40% graduate in 6 years or less. 80 companies recruited on campus in 2004-2005. Of the 2004 graduating class, 15% were enrolled in graduate school within 6 months of graduation and 75% were employed.

Admissions Contact: Deborah Calhoun, Director of Admissions and Records. A video is available. Web: www.morris.edu

NEWBERRY COLLEGE

B-2

Newberry, SC 29108

(803) 321-5127
(800) 845-4955; Fax: (803) 321-5138

Full-time: 430 men, 320 women	Faculty: 46; IIB, --$
Part-time: 10 men, 25 women	Ph.D.s: 70%
Graduate: none	Student/Faculty: 16 to 1
Year: semesters, summer session	Tuition: $17,300
Application Deadline: open	Room & Board: $5,700
Freshman Class: 942 applied, 744 accepted, 234 enrolled	
SAT or ACT required	LESS COMPETITIVE

Newberry College, founded in 1856, is a private liberal arts institution affiliated with the Evangelical Lutheran Church in America. Figures in the above capsule and in this profile are approximate. In addition to regional accreditation, Newberry has baccalaureate program accreditation with NASM, NCATE, and AVMA. The 2 libraries contain 79,464 volumes, 7153 microform items, and 1217 audio/video tapes/CDs/DVDs, and subscribe to 258 periodicals including electronic. Computerized library services include the card catalog, interlibrary loans, database searching, and Internet access. Special learning facilities include a learning resource center, radio station, TV station, and an herbarium. The 60-acre campus is in a small town 40 miles northwest of Columbia. Including any residence halls, there are 22 buildings.

Student Life: 84% of undergraduates are from South Carolina. Others are from 13 states, 8 foreign countries, and Canada. 90% are from public schools. 71% are white; 26% African American. 80% are Protestant; 12% claim no religious affiliation; 6% Catholic. The average age of freshmen is 18; all undergraduates, 20. 49% do not continue beyond their first year; 47% remain to graduate.

Housing: 622 students can be accommodated in college housing, which includes single-sex and coed dormitories. In addition, there are honors houses. On-campus housing is guaranteed for all 4 years. 77% of students live on campus; of those, 66% remain on campus on weekends. All students may keep cars.

Activities: 11% of men belong to 6 national fraternities; 13% of women belong to 3 national sororities. There are 50 groups on campus, including band, cheerleading, choir, chorale, chorus, computers, dance, drama, ethnic, honors, international, jazz band, literary magazine, marching band, musical theater, newspaper, orchestra, pep band, political, professional, radio and TV, religious, social, social service, student government, and yearbook. Popular campus events include Fall Fling and Spring Fling.

Sports: There are 7 intercollegiate sports for men and 7 for women, and 6 intramural sports for men and 5 for women. Facilities include a 4000-seat stadium, a phys ed complex with a 1600-seat basketball arena and racquetball courts, an outdoor pool, tennis courts, and baseball, softball, and soccer fields.

Disabled Students: 90% of the campus is accessible. Wheelchair ramps, elevators, special parking, specially equipped rest rooms, and special class scheduling are available.

Services: Counseling and information services are available, as is tutoring in most subjects. There is remedial math, reading, and writing.

Campus Safety and Security: Measures include 24-hour foot and vehicle patrol, security escort services, informal discussions, and pamphlets/posters/films. There are emergency telephones and lighted pathways/sidewalks.

Programs of Study: Newberry confers B.A., B.S., B.M., and B.M.E. degrees. Bachelor's degrees are awarded in BIOLOGICAL SCIENCE (biology/biological science), BUSINESS (business administration and management), COMMUNICATIONS AND THE ARTS (applied music, art, communications, dramatic arts, English, French, German, languages, music, music performance, music theory and composition, and Spanish), COMPUTER AND PHYSICAL SCIENCE (chemistry, computer science, and mathematics), EDUCATION (early childhood, elementary, music, and physical), HEALTH PROFESSIONS (veterinary science), SOCIAL SCIENCE (history, philosophy, political science/government, psychology, religion, and sociology). Education and natural sciences are the strongest academically. Business administration, education, and physical education are the largest.

Required: To graduate, students must complete 126 semester hours, with a minimum GPA of 2.0. Core curriculum requirements include 10 to 11 hours of math and natural science, 9 each of communication skills, humanities or fine arts, and history or social sciences, up to 6 of foreign language, 3 of religion, and 2 of phys ed. There is also a 24-event fine arts and lectures requirement. All students must fulfill Communications Across the Curriculum writing projects.

Special: Internships, dual and student-designed majors, study abroad, a Washington semester, work-study programs, independent study, and cooperative education are offered. A 3-2 engineering degree program with Clemson University, a 3-2 forestry program with Duke University, a 3-3 cytotechnology program, and a 3-1 medical technology program are available. Nondegree study is possible. There are 3 national honor societies, a freshman honors program, and 3 departmental honors programs.

Faculty/Classroom: 58% of faculty are male; 41%, female. All teach undergraduates. The average class size in an introductory lecture is 30; in a laboratory, 30; and in a regular course, 25.

Requirements: The SAT or ACT is required. In addition, applicants should have completed 18 high school academic units, including 4 of English, 3 each of math and social science (1 of U.S. history), 2 each of lab science and a foreign language, and 1 elective. The GED is accepted. An essay is recommended. A GPA of 2.0 is required. AP and CLEP credits are accepted. Important factors in the admissions decision are leadership record, evidence of special talent, and recommendations by school officials.

Procedure: Freshmen are admitted to all sessions. Entrance exams should be taken in the spring of the junior year or the fall of the senior year. There is a deferred admissions plan. Application deadlines are open. Check with the school for current deadlines and fee.

Transfer: 57 transfer students enrolled in a recent year. Applicants must be eligible to return to their previous school. A 2.0 minimum GPA is recommended. 32 of 126 credits required for the bachelor's degree must be completed at Newberry.

Visiting: There are regularly scheduled orientations for prospective students, including a campus tour, informational sessions, and meetings with faculty, staff, and students. There are guides for informal visits and visitors may sit in on classes and stay overnight. To schedule a visit, contact the Admissions Office.

Financial Aid: In a recent year, 91% of all full-time freshmen and 96% of continuing full-time students received some form of financial aid. 63% of full-time freshmen and 65% of continuing full-time students received need-based aid. The average freshman award was $12,450. 12% of undergraduates work part time. Average annual earnings from campus work are $625. The average financial indebtedness of the recent year's graduate was $3135. Newberry is a member of CSS. The FAFSA is required. Check with the school for current deadlines.

International Students: In a recent year, there were 8 international students enrolled. The school actively recruits these students. Satisfactory scores are required on the written TOEFL, the college's own test, and the SAT or the ACT.

Computers: All students may access the system. There are no time limits and no fees.

Admissions Contact: Director of Admissions. A video is available. E-mail: *admissions@newberry.edu* Web: *www.newberry.edu*

PRESBYTERIAN COLLEGE   B-2
Clinton, SC 29325

	(864) 833-8230
	(800) 476-7272; Fax: (864) 833-8481
Full-time: 554 men, 584 women	Faculty: 83; IIB, -$
Part-time: 21 men, 37 women	Ph.D.s: 94%
Graduate: none	Student/Faculty: 14 to 1
Year: semesters, summer session	Tuition: $23,244
Application Deadline: open	Room & Board: $6800
Freshman Class: 1110 applied, 846 accepted, 313 enrolled	
SAT Verbal/Math: 567/570*	ACT: 23 VERY COMPETITIVE

Presbyterian College, founded in 1880, is a private liberal arts institution affiliated with the Presbyterian Church (U.S.A.). In addition to regional accreditation, PC has baccalaureate program accreditation with AACSB, NCATE, and SACS. The library contains 154,730 volumes, 9454 microform items, and 7962 audio/video tapes/CDs/DVDs, and subscribes to 684 periodicals including electronic. Computerized library services include the card catalog, interlibrary loans, database searching, Internet access, and laptop Internet portals. Special learning facilities include a learning resource center, art gallery, and radio station. The 240-acre campus is in a small town 40 miles south of Greenville. Including any residence halls, there are 39 buildings.

Student Life: 64% of undergraduates are from South Carolina. Others are from 26 states, 12 foreign countries, and Canada. 71% are from public schools. 91% are white. 87% are Protestant; 6% Catholic; 6% claim no religious affiliation. The average age of freshmen is 18; all undergraduates, 20. 17% do not continue beyond their first year; 73% remain to graduate.

Housing: 1138 students can be accommodated in college housing, which includes single-sex and coed dormitories, on-campus apartments, and fraternity houses. In addition, there are special-interest houses. Carol Internation House serves as housing for international students and students with an interest in studing abroad or experiencing international cultures. On-campus housing is guaranteed for all 4 years. 92% of students live on campus; of those, 75% remain on campus on weekends. All students may keep cars.

Activities: 44% of men belong to 7 national fraternities; 36% of women belong to 3 national sororities. There are 48 groups on campus, including art, band, cheerleading, choir, chorale, chorus, computers, drama, ethnic, gay, honors, international, jazz band, literary magazine, newspaper, pep band, photography, political, professional, radio and TV, religious, social, social service, student government, and yearbook. Popular campus events include Fall Fling, Spring Swing, and Greek Week.

Sports: There are 7 intercollegiate sports for men and 6 for women, and 10 intramural sports for ment and 10 for women. Facilities include a phys ed center, tennis courts, a soccer stadium, a baseball complex, a softball complex, and 2 additional stadiums. Springs Campus Center contains a canteen, table tennis and pool tables, a fitness center, an aerobics room, and a gym.

Disabled Students: 90% of the campus is accessible. Wheelchair ramps, elevators, special parking, specially equipped rest rooms, special class scheduling, lowered drinking fountains, and special housing are available.

Services: Counseling and information services are available, as is tutoring in every subject. There is a reader service for the blind.

Campus Safety and Security: Measures include 24-hour foot and vehicle patrol, security escort services, informal discussions, and pamphlets/posters/films. There are emergency telephones, lighted pathways/sidewalks, and 24-hour key card dorm locks.

Programs of Study: PC confers B.A. and B.S degrees. Bachelor's degrees are awarded in BIOLOGICAL SCIENCE (biology/biological science), BUSINESS (accounting and business administration and management), COMMUNICATIONS AND THE ARTS (art, English, fine arts, French, German, modern language, music, music performance, Spanish, and visual and performing arts), COMPUTER AND PHYSICAL SCIENCE (chemistry, computer science, mathematics, and physics), EDUCATION (early childhood, elementary, middle school, music, secondary, social studies, and special), SOCIAL SCIENCE (economics, history, political science/government, psychology, religion, religious education, religious music, and sociology). Business administration, biology, and English are the largest.

Required: To graduate, students must complete a minimum of 122 semester hours, including 30 to 48 in the major, with a minimum GPA of 2.0. General education requirements of 46 to 55 credits include 16 hours of foreign language, 8 of lab science, 6 each of religion, English, world history, and social science, 3 to 4 of math, 3 of fine arts, and 2 of phys ed.

Special: Educational internships, study abroad in 43 countries, and a Washington semester are available. Dual majors, work-study programs, accelerated degree programs, B.A.-B.S. degrees, and a 3-2 engineering degree with Auburn, Clemson, Vanderbilt, and Mercer Universities are offered. There is a forestry environmental studies program with Duke University and a Christian education program with Presbyterian School of Christian Education. Credit for military experience, auditing courses, and pass/fail options are possible. There are 9 national honor societies, a freshman honors program, and 26 departmental honors programs.

Faculty/Classroom: 68% of faculty are male; 32%, female. All teach undergraduates. The average class size in an introductory lecture is 15; in a laboratory, 17; and in a regular course, 13.

Admissions: 76% of the 2005-2006 applicants were accepted. The SAT scores for the 2005-2006 freshman class were: Verbal--22% below 500, 43% between 500 and 599, 30% between 600 and 700, and 5% above 700; Math--17% below 500, 44% between 500 and 599, 35% between 600 and 700, and 3% above 700. The ACT scores were 20% below 21, 31% between 21 and 23, 31% between 24 and 26, 8% between 27 and 28, and 10% above 28. 52% of the current freshmen were in the top fifth of their class; 74% were in the top two fifths.

Requirements: The SAT or ACT is required. In addition, applicants must be graduates of an accredited secondary school with 18 academic credits, including 4 years of English, 3 years of math, and 2 or more years each of foreign language, history, science, and social studies. The GED is accepted. An essay is required. For music scholarships, an audition is necessary. A GPA of 2.25 is required. AP and CLEP credits are accepted. Important factors in the admissions decision are advanced placement or honor courses, recommendations by school officials, and leadership record.

Procedure: Freshmen are admitted to all sessions. Entrance exams should be taken during the spring of the junior year. There are early decision, early admissions, deferred admissions, and rolling admissions plans. Application deadlines are open. Application fee is $30. 84 early decision candidates were accepted for the 2005-2006 class. Applications are accepted on-line.

Transfer: 14 transfer students enrolled in 2004-2005. Transfer applicants must have a minimum GPA of 2.0. 48 of 122 credits required for the bachelor's degree must be completed at PC.

Visiting: There are regularly scheduled orientations for prospective students, including academic, activity, and financial aid information sessions, tours, and lunch. There are guides for informal visits and visitors may sit in on classes and stay overnight. To schedule a visit, contact the Office of Admissions at (800) 960-7587.

Financial Aid: In 2005-2006, 61% of all full-time freshmen and 60% of continuing full-time students received some form of financial aid. 92% of full-time freshmen and 91% of continuing full-time students received need-based aid. The average freshman award was $23,791. The average financial indebtedness of the 2005 graduate was $21,517. The FAFSA and the college's own financial statement are required. The deadline for filing freshman financial aid applications for fall entry is March 1.

International Students: In a recent year, there were 20 international students enrolled. They must score satisfactorily on the written TOEFL and also take the SAT or the ACT.

Computers: Wireless access is available. There are ports in every residence hall room that allow students to connect to the college network and the Internet, and there is wireless coverage from more than 90% of the open spaces on campus. There is also wireless coverage in the library and several academic buildings. There are approximately 125 student-accessible PCs located in 3 labs, the library, and other smaller installations. All students may access the system any time. There are no time limits and no fees.

Graduates: From July 1, 2004 to June 30, 2005, 229 bachelor's degrees were awarded. The most popular majors were economics/business (22%), biology (14%), and psychology (12%). In an average class, 62% graduate in 4 years or less, 72% graduate in 5 years or less, and 73% graduate in 6 years or less. 48 companies recruited on campus in 2004-2005. Of the 2004 graduating class, 25% were enrolled in graduate school within 6 months of graduation and 66% were employed.

Admissions Contact: Leni Patterson, Interim Vice President of Enrollment and Dean of Admissions. A video is available. E-mail: *lpatters@presby.edu* Web: *www.presby.edu*

SOUTH CAROLINA STATE UNIVERSITY   C-3

Orangeburg, SC 29117   (803) 536-7185
                                      (800) 260-5956; Fax: (803) 536-8990

Full-time: 1600 men, 2000 women	**Faculty:** 211
Part-time: 120 men, 300 women	**Ph.D.s:** 62%
Graduate: 120 men, 530 women	**Student/Faculty:** 16 to 1
Year: semesters, summer session	**Tuition:** $3500 ($6800)
Application Deadline: see profile	**Room & Board:** $3200
Freshman Class: n/av	
SAT or ACT: required	**LESS COMPETITIVE**

South Carolina State University, a historically black, land-grant institution founded in 1896, offers undergraduate programs in liberal arts and sciences, business, education, engineering technology, and human sciences. There are 5 undergraduate schools and 1 graduate school. Figures in the above capsule and in this profile are approximate. In addition to regional accreditation, State or SCSU has baccalaureate program accreditation with ABET, ADA, AHEA, CSWE, NASDTEC, and NCATE. The library contains 277,438 volumes and 686,225 microform items, and subscribes to 1394 periodicals including electronic. Computerized library services include the card catalog, interlibrary loans, and database searching. Special learning facilities include a learning resource center, art gallery, planetarium, radio station, and an instructional media center. The 160-acre campus is in a small town 40 miles east of Columbia. Including any residence halls, there are 60 buildings.

Student Life: 83% of undergraduates are from South Carolina. 95% are African American. The average age of freshmen is 18; all undergraduates, 19. 22% do not continue beyond their first year; 32% remain to graduate.

Housing: 2242 students can be accommodated in college housing, which includes single-sex dormitories and married-student housing. On-campus housing is available on a first-come, first-served basis and is available on a lottery system for upperclassmen. 80% of students live on campus. Alcohol is not permitted. Upperclassmen may keep cars.

Activities: 25% of men belong to 4 national fraternities; 32% of women belong to 4 national sororities. There are 85 groups on campus, including band, cheerleading, choir, chorus, dance, drama, drill team, honors, international, jazz band, marching band, newspaper, orchestra, pep band, political, religious, social, social service, student government, and yearbook. Popular campus events include Colloquium Series, game nights, Leadership Training, and Bulldog Fest.

Sports: There are 7 intercollegiate sports for men and 8 for women, and 8 intramural sports for men and 7 for women. Facilities include a student center with a game room and bowling alley, a gym, tennis courts, a 22,000-seat stadium, an 8-lane asphalt track, and swimming pools.

Disabled Students: 60% of the campus is accessible. Wheelchair ramps, elevators, special parking, specially equipped rest rooms, lowered drinking fountains, and lowered telephones are available.

Services: Counseling and information services are available, as is tutoring in most subjects. There is a reader service for the blind, and remedial math, reading, and writing. Free counseling is also available.

Campus Safety and Security: Measures include 24-hour foot and vehicle patrol, shuttle buses, pamphlets/posters/films, and lighted pathways/sidewalks. There is a campus police department with 25 safety and security officers.

Programs of Study: State or SCSU confers B.A. and B.S. degrees. Master's and doctoral degrees are also awarded. Bachelor's degrees are awarded in AGRICULTURE (agricultural business management), BIOLOGICAL SCIENCE (biology/biological science and nutrition), BUSINESS (accounting, business administration and management, business economics, marketing/retailing/merchandising, and office supervision and management), COMMUNICATIONS AND THE ARTS (dramatic arts, English, fine arts, French, music business management, and Spanish), COMPUTER AND PHYSICAL SCIENCE (chemistry, computer science, mathematics, and physics), EDUCATION (art, business, early childhood, elementary, guidance, health, home economics, industrial arts, music, physical, reading, and special), ENGINEERING AND ENVIRONMENTAL DESIGN (civil engineering technology, electrical/electronics engineering technology, engineering technology, and mechanical engineering technology), HEALTH PROFESSIONS (nursing and speech pathology/audiology), SOCIAL SCIENCE (criminal justice, food science, history, human services, political science/government, psychology, social studies, social work, and sociology). Science, engineering technology, and business education are the strongest academically.

Required: To graduate, all students must complete at least 128 credit hours with a minimum GPA of 2.0. Students must attend the freshman orientation program, take a general education examination in their sophomore year, satisfy the general education program requirements, and pass an English proficiency test.

Special: The college offers co-op education and work-study programs, cross-registration with Claflin College, internships, study abroad in 2 countries, combined B.A.-B.S. degrees, credit for educational and work experience, nondegree study, and pass/fail options for juniors and se-

niors. Also available are an electrical engineering technology program at Midlands, Greenville, and Trident Technical colleges, an evening school program, and a program for educationally disadvantaged students who do not meet traditional entrance requirements. There are 12 national honor societies and a freshman honors program.

Faculty/Classroom: No introductory courses are taught by graduate students.

Requirements: The SAT or ACT is required. In addition, applicants must rank in the upper half of their graduating class at an accredited secondary school. The GED is accepted. High school preparation should include 4 units of English, 3 of math, 2 each of foreign language and lab science, and 1 each of history, social studies, and phys ed or ROTC, plus 1/2 unit each in economics and government. A GPA of 2.0 is required. AP and CLEP credits are accepted. Important factors in the admissions decision are advanced placement or honor courses, leadership record, and personality/intangible qualities.

Procedure: Freshmen are admitted fall and spring. Entrance exams should be taken before filing an application. Check with school for current deadlines and fee.

Transfer: 120 transfer students enrolled in a recent year. Transfer applicants should have a college GPA of 2.0. Students with fewer than 30 credit hours must submit high school and college transcripts and SAT or ACT scores. 30 of 128 credits required for the bachelor's degree must be completed at State or SCSU.

Visiting: There are guides for informal visits and visitors may sit in on classes. To schedule a visit, contact the Office of Admissions and Recruitment.

Financial Aid: In a recent year, 85% of all full-time freshmen and 94% of continuing full-time students received some form of financial aid. 88% of full-time freshmen and 64% of continuing full-time students received need-based aid. The average freshman award was $4000. State or SCSU is a member of CSS. The CSS/Profile is required. Check with school for current deadlines.

International Students: In a recent year, there were 8 international students enrolled. Satisfactory scores are required on the TOEFL and the SAT or the ACT. Check with school for current deadlines.

Computers: All students may access the system. There are no time limits and no fees.

Admissions Contact: Dorothy L. Brown, Director of Admissions.
E-mail: *admissions@scsu.edu*

SOUTHERN WESLEYAN UNIVERSITY   A-2

Central, SC 29630-1020   (864) 644-5550
                                      (800) 282-8798; Fax: (864) 644-5972

Full-time: 650 men, 1259 women	**Faculty:** 63
Part-time: 26 men, 60 women	**Ph.D.s:** 77%
Graduate: 183 men, 454 women	**Student/Faculty:** 29 to 1
Year: semesters, summer session	**Tuition:** $15,450
Application Deadline: see profile	**Room & Board:** $6225
Freshman Class: 264 accepted, 138 enrolled	
SAT Verbal/Math: 520/510*	**ACT:** 21 **COMPETITIVE**

Southern Wesleyan University, founded in 1906, and part of the Council for Christian Colleges and Universities, is a private liberal arts institution affiliated with the Wesleyan Church. In addition to regional accreditation, SWU has baccalaureate program accreditation with NASDTEC. The library contains 90,000 volumes, 160 microform items, and 3500 audio/video tapes/CDs/DVDs, and subscribes to 525 periodicals including electronic. Computerized library services include the card catalog, interlibrary loans, and database searching. Special learning facilities include a learning resource center and an electron microscope lab. The 200-acre campus is in a small town 30 miles southwest of Greenville. Including any residence halls, there are 21 buildings.

Student Life: 84% of undergraduates are from South Carolina. Students are from 24 states, 7 foreign countries, and Canada. 98% are from public schools. 63% are white; 32% African American. 86% are Protestant; 9% claim no religious affiliation. The average age of freshmen is 19; all undergraduates, 25. 25% do not continue beyond their first year; 34% remain to graduate.

Housing: 362 students can be accommodated in college housing, which includes single-sex and coed dorms and on-campus apartments. On-campus housing is guaranteed for all 4 years. 84% of students commute. Alcohol is not permitted. All students may keep cars.

Activities: There are no fraternities or sororities. There are 20 groups on campus, including cheerleading, choir, computers, drama, ethnic, honors, jazz band, literary magazine, musical theater, newspaper, orchestra, professional, religious, social, social service, and student government. Popular campus events include Christmas Banquet and Junior/Senior Banquet, Coffee House, and Late Night Breakfast.

Sports: There are 5 intercollegiate sports for men and 5 for women, and 5 intramural sports for men and 4 for women. Facilities include a gym, soccer, softball and baseball fields, tennis courts, a fitness center, and a cross-country trail.

Disabled Students: 90% of the campus is accessible. Wheelchair ramps, elevators, special parking, and specially equipped rest rooms are available.

Services: Counseling and information services are available, as is tutoring in some subjects. There is remedial math, reading, and writing.

Campus Safety and Security: Measures include informal discussions, pamphlets/posters/films, emergency telephones, lighted pathways/ sidewalks, and night security.

Programs of Study: SWU confers B.A., B.S., and B.Acct. degrees. Associate and master's degrees are also awarded. Bachelor's degrees are awarded in BIOLOGICAL SCIENCE (biology/biological science), BUSINESS (accounting, business administration and management, personnel management, and recreation and leisure services), COMMUNICATIONS AND THE ARTS (English and music), COMPUTER AND PHYSICAL SCIENCE (chemistry, information sciences and systems, mathematics, and web services), EDUCATION (elementary, music, physical, and special), HEALTH PROFESSIONS (medical laboratory technology), SOCIAL SCIENCE (history, psychology, religion, and social science). Education, business, and religion are the largest.

Required: To graduate, students must complete 128 credit hours with 54 hours in general education courses and a minimum GPA of 2.0. All students must take 12 hours each of English and religion, 6 of history, 3 of social sciences, and 3 of math or statistics, plus 2 science lab courses. Specific required courses include aesthetics, introduction to computer science, phys ed, and interdisciplinary seminars.

Special: There is a co-op program with Clemson University and in medical technology and criminal justice with other institutions. Study abroad in 6 countries and internships in psychology, English, and business are available. A Washington semester with the Council for Christian Colleges and Universities, a semester at the Los Angeles Film Studies center, a session at the Summer Institute of Journalism in Washington D.C., and dual majors are available. The Leadership Education for the Adult Professional Program offers degrees for working professionals. There is 1 national honor society, a freshman honors program, and 7 departmental honors program.

Faculty/Classroom: 78% of faculty are male; 22%, female. All both teach and do research. No introductory courses are taught by graduate students. The average class size in an introductory lecture is 25; in a laboratory, 15; and in a regular course, 20.

Admissions: The SAT scores for the 2005-2006 freshman class were: Verbal--37% below 500, 47% between 500 and 599, 15% between 600 and 700, and 2% above 700; Math--38% below 500, 45% between 500 and 599, 15% between 600 and 700, and 1% above 700. The ACT scores were 29% below 21, 47% between 21 and 23, and 24% between 24 and 26. 23% of the current freshmen were in the top fifth of their class; 74% were in the top two fifths.

Requirements: A Satisfactory score is required on the SAT or ACT. Applicants must be graduates of an accredited secondary school. The GED is accepted. Students should complete 16 Carnegie units, including 4 credits of English and 2 each of math, science, and social studies, as well as 6 electives. SWU requires applicants to be in the upper 50% of their class. A GPA of 2.0 is required. AP and CLEP credits are accepted. Important factors in the admissions decision are leadership record, advanced placement or honor courses, and personality/intangible qualities.

Procedure: Freshmen are admitted fall and spring. Entrance exams should be taken prior to application. There are early admissions, deferred admissions and rolling admissions plans. The application fee is $25. Notification is sent on a rolling basis. Check with the school for application deadlines.

Transfer: 64 transfer students enrolled in 2004-2005. SWU recommends that transfer applicants have a minimum GPA of 2.0 in at least 29 credit hours. 32 of 128 credits required for the bachelor's degree must be completed at SWU.

Visiting: There are regularly scheduled orientations for prospective students. There are guides for informal visits and visitors may sit in on classes and stay overnight. To schedule a visit, contact the Admissions Office.

Financial Aid: 65% of all full-time students received need-based aid. Need-based scholarships or need-based grants averaged $9171; need-based self-help aid (loans and jobs) averaged $2754; and non-need-based athletic scholarships averaged $6471. The FAFSA and the college's own financial statement are required. Check with the school for current deadlines.

International Students: There are 11 international students enrolled. A satisfactory score is required on the written TOEFL and the SAT or the ACT.

Computers: All students may access the system. There are no time limits. The fee $50.

Graduates: In a recent year, 357 bachelor's degrees were awarded. The most popular majors in a recent year were business (48%), education (12%), and religion (3%). In an average class, 16% graduate in 4 years or less, 41% graduate in 5 years or less, and 42% graduate in 6 years or less.

Admissions Contact: Chad Peters, Director of Admissions. A video is available. E-mail: admissions@swu.edu Web: www.swu.edu

UNIVERSITY OF SOUTH CAROLINA SYSTEM

The University of South Carolina System, established in 1801, is a public system in South Carolina. It is governed by a board of trustees, whose chief administrator is president. The primary goal of the system is to prepare informed and productive citizens to adapt to an increasingly complex environment. The main priorities are to foster excellence in undergraduate and graduate education, research, and service programs. The total enrollment of all 8 campuses is usually about 40,000; there were more than 1700 faculty members. Altogether there are 85 baccalaureate, 135 master's, and 62 doctoral, and 3 professional programs offered in University of South Carolina System. Profiles of the 4-year campuses are included in this section.

UNIVERSITY OF SOUTH CAROLINA AT AIKEN   C-3

Aiken, SC 29801 (803) 641-3366
(888) WOW-USCA; Fax: (803) 641-3727

Full-time: 760 men, 1510 women	Faculty: 142; IIB, -$
Part-time: 285 men, 596 women	Ph.D.s: 80%
Graduate: 25 men, 191 women	Student/Faculty: 16 to 1
Year: semesters, summer session	Tuition: $6158 ($12,300)
Application Deadline: open	Room & Board: $5560
Freshman Class: 976 accepted, 603 enrolled	
SAT Verbal/Math: 490/505*	ACT: 20 LESS COMPETITIVE

The University of South Carolina Aiken (USCA), founded in 1961 is a comprehensive liberal arts institution committed to active learning through teaching, faculty and student scholarship, research, creative activities and service. The university offers degrees in the arts and sciences and in the professional disciplines of business, education, and nursing. There are 5 undergraduate and 3 graduate schools. In addition to regional accreditation, USCA has baccalaureate program accreditation with AACSB, NCATE, and NLN. The library contains 133,452 volumes, 72,700 microform items, and 810 audio/video tapes/CDs/DVDs, and subscribes to 853 periodicals including electronic. Computerized library services include the card catalog, interlibrary loans, database searching, Internet access, and laptop Internet portals. Special learning facilities include a learning resource center, art gallery, planetarium, a science education center, and a language lab. The 354-acre campus is in a suburban area 14 miles east of Augusta, Georgia. Including any residence halls, there are 17 buildings.

Student Life: 87% of undergraduates are from South Carolina. Others are from 32 states, 19 foreign countries, and Canada. 98% are from public schools. 67% are white; 25% African American. The average age of freshmen is 18; all undergraduates, 24.

Housing: 680 students can be accommodated in college housing, which includes coed on-campus apartments. On-campus housing is available on a first-come, first-served basis and is available on a lottery system for upperclassmen. 80% of students commute. Alcohol is not permitted. All students may keep cars.

Activities: 1% of men belong to 3 national fraternities; 1% of women belong to 3 national sororities. There are 53 groups on campus, including cheerleading, choir, chorus, computers, drama, ethnic, gay, honors, international, literary magazine, musical theater, newspaper, nontraditional students, pep band, photography, political, professional, religious, social, social service, and student government. Popular campus events include International Week and Alcohol/Health Awareness Week.

Sports: There are 6 intercollegiate sports for men and 6 for women, and 20 intramural sports for men and 20 for women. Facilities include an activities center, the Roberto Hernandez baseball stadium, a soccer/intramural/softball field, tennis courts, and a wellness/exercise center.

Disabled Students: All of the campus is accessible. Wheelchair ramps, elevators, special parking, specially equipped rest rooms, lowered drinking fountains, lowered telephones, and special housing are available. Special administration of tests, note taking, and free copying of notes if needed are also available.

Services: Counseling and information services are available, as is tutoring in most subjects, including math and writing. There is a reader service for the blind.

Campus Safety and Security: Measures include 24-hour foot and vehicle patrol, self-defense education, security escort services, and informal discussions. There are pamphlets/posters/films, emergency telephones, and lighted pathways/sidewalks.

Programs of Study: USCA confers B.A., B.S., and B.I.S. degrees. Master's degrees are also awarded. Bachelor's degrees are awarded in BIOLOGICAL SCIENCE (biology/biological science), BUSINESS (business administration and management), COMMUNICATIONS AND THE ARTS (communications, English, and fine arts), COMPUTER AND PHYSICAL SCIENCE (applied mathematics, chemistry, and computer mathematics), EDUCATION (early childhood, elementary, music, secondary, and special), HEALTH PROFESSIONS (nursing), SOCIAL SCIENCE (history, interdisciplinary studies, physical fitness/movement, political science/government, psychology, and sociology). Nursing, history, and biology are the strongest academically. Business, education, and nursing are the largest.

Required: Students must complete a minimum of 120 credit hours, with at least a 2.0 GPA. General education requirements include courses in English, math, applied speech, natural science, social and behavioral sciences, humanities, non-western studies course, and history.

Special: Cross-registration is permitted with other schools in the University of South Carolina system. Co-op programs in engineering, business, math/cs, communications and chemistry, business internships, study abroad in 19 countries, student-designed majors, and work-study programs are offered. B.A.-B.S. degrees in psychology and education, non-degree study, and pass/fail options are possible. There are 7 national honor societies, a freshman honors program, and 4 departmental honors programs.

Faculty/Classroom: 54% of faculty are male; 46%, female. 97% teach undergraduates. No introductory courses are taught by graduate students. The average class size in an introductory lecture is 24; in a laboratory, 18; and in a regular course, 16.

Admissions: The SAT scores for the 2005-2006 freshman class were: Verbal--57% below 500, 35% between 500 and 599, 7% between 600 and 700, and 1% above 700; Math--47% below 500, 43% between 500 and 599, and 10% between 600 and 700. The ACT scores were 63% below 21, 25% between 21 and 23, 11% between 24 and 26, and 1% above 28. 9 freshmen graduated first in their class.

Requirements: The SAT is required. In addition, admission is based on a combination of an applicant's scores on college entrance exams and high school GPA. Applicants are required to submit 21 academic credits, including 4 years of high school English, 3 units of math, 3 units of social studies, 2 units of foreign language, 3 units of a lab science, 1 of US history, and 1 year of phys ed or ROTC, and 4 electives from 3 different areas such as computer science, English, fine arts, foreign language, humanities, certain lab sciences, math above algebra II, and social science. It is strongly suggested that 1 be in computer science programming. AP and CLEP credits are accepted. Important factors in the admissions decision are advanced placement or honor courses, recommendations by school officials, and leadership record.

Procedure: Freshmen are admitted to all sessions. Entrance exams should be taken by the fall of the senior year. There are early admissions, deferred admissions, and rolling admissions plans. Application deadlines are open. Applications are accepted on-line. The fal 2005 application fee was $35.

Transfer: The college GPA is considered. A high school transcript is required of applicants with fewer than 30 semester hours. 30 of 120 credits required for the bachelor's degree must be completed at USCA.

Visiting: There are regularly scheduled orientations for prospective students, including regularly scheduled 3-day orientations for prospective students. There are guides for informal visits and visitors may sit in on classes. To schedule a visit, contact the Admissions Office.

Financial Aid: In 2005-2006, 70% of all full-time freshmen and 75% of continuing full-time students received some form of financial aid. 51% of full-time freshmen and 50% of continuing full-time students received need-based aid. The average freshman award was $2950. 9% of undergraduates work part time. Average annual earnings from campus work are $1700. The average financial indebtedness of the 2005 graduate was $13,200. The FAFSA is required. The priority date for freshman financial aid applications for fall entry is February 15. The deadline for filing freshman financial aid applications for fall entry is March 15.

International Students: There are 45 international students enrolled. They must score satisfactorily on the written TOEFL and also take the SAT or the ACT.

Computers: Wireless access is available. All students may access the system 24 hours a day, 7 days a week. There are no time limits. The fee is $100 which is charged at registration.

Graduates: From July 1, 2004 to June 30, 2005, 517 bachelor's degrees were awarded. The most popular majors were business (28%), education (16%), and sociology (8%). In an average class, 13% graduate in 4 years or less, 36% graduate in 5 years or less, and 42% graduate in 6 years or less. 30 companies recruited on campus in 2004-2005.

Admissions Contact: Andrew Hendrix, Director of Admissions. E-mail: *admit@sc.edu* Web: *www.usca.edu*

UNIVERSITY OF SOUTH CAROLINA AT COLUMBIA   C-3
Columbia, SC 29208

(803) 777-7700
(800) 868-5872; Fax: (803) 777-0101

Full-time: 7425 men, 8974 women	**Faculty:** 849; I, -$
Part-time: 983 men, 980 women	**Ph.D.s:** 84%
Graduate: 3020 men, 5683 women	**Student/Faculty:** 19 to 1
Year: semesters, summer session	**Tuition:** $7314 ($18,956)
Application Deadline: December 1	**Room & Board:** $6083
Freshman Class: 13,023 applied, 8812 accepted, 3734 enrolled	
SAT Verbal/Math: 570/590*	**ACT:** 25 **VERY COMPETITIVE**

The University of South Carolina at Columbia, founded in 1801, is a publicly assisted institution serving the entire state of South Carolina. In addition to the main campus at Columbia, there are 3 senior campuses at Aiken, Beaufort and Upstate, and 4 regional campuses at Lancaster, Salkehatchie, Sumter and Union. There are 10 undergraduate and 14 graduate schools. In addition to regional accreditation, Carolina has baccalaureate program accreditation with AACSB, ABET, ACEJMC, ACPE, CSAB, NASM, NCATE, and NLN. The 7 libraries contain 3,498,445 volumes, 5,116,024 microform items, and 47,815 audio/video tapes/CDs/DVDs, and subscribe to 23,740 periodicals including electronic. Computerized library services include the card catalog, interlibrary loans, and database searching. Special learning facilities include a learning resource center, art gallery, natural history museum, planetarium, and radio station. The 372-acre campus is in an urban area in the downtown area of Columbia. Including any residence halls, there are 169 buildings.

Student Life: 78% of undergraduates are from South Carolina. Others are from 50 states, 67 foreign countries, and Canada. 71% are white; 14% African American. The average age of freshmen is 18; all undergraduates, 21. 17% do not continue beyond their first year; 65% remain to graduate.

Housing: 7387 students can be accommodated in college housing, which includes single-sex and coed dorms, on-campus apartments, married-student housing, fraternity houses, and sorority houses. In addition, there are honors houses, special-interest houses, wellness, residential college, U.S. international community, teaching fellows residence, athletic, Greek houses, and a French house. On-campus housing is guaranteed for the freshman year only and is available on a lottery system for upperclassmen. 60% of students commute. All students may keep cars.

Activities: 14% of men belong to 18 national fraternities; 15% of women belong to 14 national sororities. There are 300 groups on campus, including art, band, cheerleading, chess, choir, chorale, chorus, computers, dance, debate, drama, drill team, ethnic, forensics, gay, honors, international, jazz band, literary magazine, marching band, musical theater, newspaper, opera, orchestra, pep band, photography, political, professional, radio and TV, religious, social, social service, student government, symphony, and yearbook. Popular campus events include Parents Weekend, Black History Month, and Carolina Spirit Week.

Sports: There are 9 intercollegiate sports for men and 11 for women, and 29 intramural sports for men and 29 for women. Facilities include football and soccer stadiums, a basketball coliseum, a field house, a volleyball and basketball practice facility, baseball, softball, and practice fields, and an all-weather track. There is also a recreation center with badminton, basketball, handball/racquetball, an aquatics center, a weight room, areobics, and tennis court space.

Disabled Students: 95% of the campus is accessible. Wheelchair ramps, elevators, special parking, specially equipped rest rooms, special class scheduling, lowered drinking fountains, lowered telephones, special housing, listening devices, sign language interpreting, and adapted transportation and computers are available.

Services: Counseling and information services are available, as is tutoring in every subject, including reader services for LD students. There is a reader service for the blind.

Campus Safety and Security: Measures include 24-hour foot and vehicle patrol, self-defense education, security escort services, and shuttle buses. There are informal discussions, pamphlets/posters/films, emergency telephones, and lighted pathways/sidewalks. The USC police department is a nationally accredited campus law enforcement agency. All police officers have state wide police authority.

Programs of Study: Carolina confers B.A., B.S., B.A.I.S., B.A.J., B.A.P.E./B.S.P.E., B.A.R.S.C., B.F.A., B.M., B.M.A., B.S.B.A., B.S.Chem., B.S.C.S., B.S.E., B.S.I.S., and B.S.N. degrees. Associate, master's, and doctoral degrees are also awarded. Bachelor's degrees are awarded in BIOLOGICAL SCIENCE (biology/biological science and marine science), BUSINESS (accounting, banking and finance, business administration and management, business economics, hotel/motel and restaurant management, insurance, management science, marketing/retailing/merchandising, office supervision and management, real estate, retailing, and sports management), COMMUNICATIONS AND THE ARTS (advertising, art history and appreciation, broadcasting, classics, communications, comparative literature, dance, dramatic arts, English, film arts, fine arts, French, German, Italian, journalism, media arts, music, music performance, public relations, Russian, Spanish, speech/debate/rhetoric, and studio art), COMPUTER AND PHYSICAL SCIENCE (chemistry, computer science, geology, geophysics and seismology, mathematics, physics, and statistics), EDUCATION (art, early childhood, elementary, music, physical, and secondary), ENGINEERING AND ENVIRONMENTAL DESIGN (chemical engineering, civil engineering, computer engineering, electrical/electronics engineering, and mechanical engineering), HEALTH PROFESSIONS (exercise science, medical laboratory technology, and nursing), SOCIAL SCIENCE (African American studies, anthropology, criminal justice, economics, European studies, geography, history, interdisciplinary studies, international relations, Latin American studies, philosophy, political science/government, psychology, religion, sociology, and women's studies). Biology, experimental psychology, and engineering are the largest.

Required: All students must maintain a GPA of 2.0 in 120 semester hours, including 24 in their major. Distribution requirements include 7 in natural science, 6 hours each in English and numerical and analytical reasoning, and a demonstrated ability in foreign languages.

Special: USC transmits live interactive televised instruction to more than 20 locations in the state. Cross-registration is offered with the National Technological University in Engineering and through the National Student Exchange. Internships in many fields, study abroad in many countries through the Byrnes International Center, co-op programs, and work-study programs are available. Double majors through the colleges of humanities and social sciences and science and math, student-designed majors, an interdisciplinary studies degree, and a 3-2 engineering degree with the College of Charleston are offered. Credit for military experience, nondegree study, and pass/fail options are also possible. There are 34 national honor societies, including Phi Beta Kappa, and a freshman honors program.

Faculty/Classroom: 63% of faculty are male; 37%, female. 61% teach undergraduates and 100% do research. Graduate students teach 23% of introductory courses. The average class size in an introductory lecture is 31; in a laboratory, 22; and in a regular course, 32.

Admissions: 68% of the 2005-2006 applicants were accepted. The SAT scores for the 2005-2006 freshman class were: Verbal--14% below 500, 47% between 500 and 599, 31% between 600 and 700, and 8% above 700; Math--10% below 500, 44% between 500 and 599, 37% between 600 and 700, and 9% above 700. The ACT scores were 12% below 21, 26% between 21 and 23, 30% between 24 and 26, 15% between 27 and 28, and 17% above 28. 49% of the current freshmen were in the top fifth of their class; 82% were in the top two fifths. There were 50 National Merit finalists. 73 freshmen graduated first in their class.

Requirements: The SAT or ACT is required. In addition, students are evaluated primarily on high school curriculum, grades on the required high school courses, and on SAT or ACT scores. A GPA of 2.0 is required. AP and CLEP credits are accepted. Important factors in the admissions decision are evidence of special talent and recommendations by school officials.

Procedure: Freshmen are admitted to all sessions. Entrance exams should be taken during spring of the junior year and fall of the senior year, if necessary. There is a rolling admissions plan. Applications should be filed by December 1 for fall entry, December 1 for spring entry, and May 15 for summer entry, along with a $50 fee. Notification is sent on a rolling basis. Applications are accepted on-line.

Transfer: 1997 transfer students enrolled in 2004-2005. Transfer students must have a cumulative 2.25 GPA from regionally accredited institutions. The SAT or ACT is required for transfers who have attempted fewer than 30 semester hours of college credit. These students must meet both freshman and transfer requirements. Requirements are higher for some majors. 30 of 120 credits required for the bachelor's degree must be completed at Carolina.

Visiting: There are regularly scheduled orientations for prospective students. There are guides for informal visits and visitors may sit in on classes. To schedule a visit, contact the USC Visitor's Center at (803) 777-2125.

Financial Aid: In 2005-2006, 95% of all full-time freshmen and 83% of continuing full-time students received some form of financial aid. 36% of full-time freshmen and 42% of continuing full-time students received need-based aid. The average freshman award was $2442. Need-based scholarships or need-based grants averaged $6834 ($23,642 maximum). 14% of undergraduates work part time. Average annual earnings from campus work are $2858. The average financial indebtedness of the 2005 graduate was $18,699. Carolina is a member of CSS. The FAFSA is required. The deadline for filing freshman financial aid applications for fall entry is April 15.

International Students: There are 205 international students enrolled. The school actively recruits these students. A satisfactory score is required on the written TOEFL.

Computers: Wireless access is available. Students can register, check grades, pay fees, search the Internet, and access the library and e-mail on the system. All students may access the system. There are no time limits and no fees. It is strongly recommended that all students have a PC.

Graduates: From July 1, 2004 to June 30, 2005, 3286 bachelor's degrees were awarded. The most popular majors were business administration (8%), public relations (7%), and experimental psychology (7%). In an average class, 40% graduate in 4 years or less, 59% graduate in 5 years or less, and 65% graduate in 6 years or less. 16,351 companies recruited on campus in 2004-2005.

Admissions Contact: R. Scott Verzyl, Director of Undergraduate Admissions. A video is available. E-mail: *admissions-ugrad@sc.edu* Web: *www.sc.edu/admissions*

UNIVERSITY OF SOUTH CAROLINA AT SPARTANBURG
(See University of South Carolina Upstate)

UNIVERSITY OF SOUTH CAROLINA UPSTATE   B-1
(Formerly University of South Carolina at Spartanburg)

Spartanburg, SC 29303
(864) 503-5280
(800) 277-8727; Fax: (864) 503-5727

Full-time: 1253 men, 2403 women	**Faculty:** 162; IIB, --$
Part-time: 217 men, 459 women	**Ph.D.s:** 68%
Graduate: 5 men, 48 women	**Student/Faculty:** 23 to 1
Year: semesters, summer session	**Tuition:** $6762 ($13,502)
Application Deadline: open	**Room & Board:** $5195
Freshman Class: 2273 applied, 1464 accepted, 736 enrolled	
SAT Verbal/Math: 490/500*	**ACT:** not required **COMPETITIVE**

The University of South Carolina Upstate, established in 1967, is a public institution offering undergraduate programs in the liberal arts and sciences, business administration, education, and nursing. There are 4 undergraduate schools and 1 graduate school. In addition to regional accreditation, USC Upstate has baccalaureate program accreditation with AACSB, NCATE, and NLN. The library contains 235,576 volumes, 55,051 microform items, and 7985 audio/video tapes/CDs/DVDs, and subscribes to 14,953 periodicals including electronic. Computerized library services include the card catalog, interlibrary loans, database searching, Internet access, and laptop Internet portals. Special learning facilities include an art gallery and a greenhouse. The 298-acre campus is in an urban area 100 miles north of Columbia. Including any residence halls, there are 18 buildings.

Student Life: 96% of undergraduates are from South Carolina. Others are from 32 states and 30 foreign countries. 62% are white; 26% African American. The average age of freshmen is 18; all undergraduates, 24. 34% do not continue beyond their first year; 41% remain to graduate.

Housing: 699 students can be accommodated in college housing, which includes coed on-campus apartments and off-campus apartments. In addition, there is an honors floor. On-campus housing is available on a first-come, first-served basis. 85% of students commute. Alcohol is not permitted. All students may keep cars.

Activities: 4% of men belong to 5 national fraternities; 5% of women belong to 6 national sororities. There are 50 groups on campus, including band, cheerleading, choir, chorus, computers, dance, debate, drama, ethnic, forensics, gay, honors, international, literary magazine, newspaper, pep band, photography, political, professional, religious, social, social service, and student government. Popular campus events include RIOTS, Wet and Wild Day, and intramural tournaments.

Sports: There are 5 intercollegiate sports for men and 6 for women, and 13 intramural sports for men and 12 for women. Facilities include a soccer field, baseball fields, a basketball gym, racquetball courts, and an auxiliary gym.

Disabled Students: Wheelchair ramps, elevators, special parking, specially equipped rest rooms, special class scheduling, lowered drinking fountains, and lowered telephones are available.

Services: Counseling and information services are available, as is tutoring in most subjects. There is remedial math, reading, and writing.

Campus Safety and Security: Measures include 24-hour foot and vehicle patrol, self-defense education, security escort services, and pamphlets/posters/films. There are emergency telephones and lighted pathways/sidewalks.

Programs of Study: USC Upstate confers B.A., B.S., and B.S.N. degrees. Associate and master's degrees are also awarded. Bachelor's degrees are awarded in BIOLOGICAL SCIENCE (biology/biological science), BUSINESS (accounting, business administration and management, marketing management, and nonprofit/public organization management), COMMUNICATIONS AND THE ARTS (communications, English, French, graphic design, Spanish, and studio art), COMPUTER AND PHYSICAL SCIENCE (chemistry, computer science, information sciences and systems, and mathematics), EDUCATION (early childhood, elementary, English, mathematics, middle school, physical, secondary, social studies, and special), ENGINEERING AND ENVIRONMENTAL DESIGN (commercial art), HEALTH PROFESSIONS (nursing), SOCIAL SCIENCE (criminal justice, economics, history, interdisciplinary studies, liberal arts/general studies, political science/government, psychology, and sociology). Business administration is the largest.

Required: Students must complete 120 to 136 credits, including 69 to 82 in the major, with a minimum GPA of 2.0. General education requirements include courses in communications, math, arts and humanities, social and behavioral sciences, natural science, foreign culture, computer studies, and a senior seminar.

Special: Cross-registration is permitted within the University of South Carolina system and with Wofford College and Greenville Technical College. Opportunities are provided for B.A.-B.S. degrees, student-designed majors, a 3-2 engineering degree, nondegree study, credit for military service, and study abroad in Mexico, France, Germany, England, Spain, and Italy. There are 6 national honor societies, including Phi Beta Kappa.

Faculty/Classroom: 47% of faculty are male; 53%, female. All teach undergraduates. No introductory courses are taught by graduate stu-

dents. The average class size in an introductory lecture is 22; in a laboratory, 20; and in a regular course, 15.

Admissions: 64% of the 2005-2006 applicants were accepted. The SAT scores for the 2005-2006 freshman class were: Verbal--55% below 500, 35% between 500 and 599, 9% between 600 and 700, and 1% above 700; Math--50% below 500, 38% between 500 and 599, and 12% between 600 and 700. The ACT scores were 66% below 21, 23% between 21 and 23, 7% between 24 and 26, 2% between 27 and 28, and 2% above 28. 29% of the current freshmen were in the top fifth of their class; 60% were in the top two fifths. 6 freshmen graduated first in their class.

Requirements: A satisfactory score is required on the SAT is required. In addition, graduation from an accredited secondary school with a GPA of 2.0 is required. The GED is accepted. Applicants must submit 20 academic credits, distributed as follows: 4 years of English, 3 of math, 2 each of lab science, foreign language, and social studies, 1 each of history and phys ed or ROTC, and the remainder in electives. A GPA of 2.0 is required. AP and CLEP credits are accepted.

Procedure: Entrance exams should be taken at the beginning of the senior year. There is a rolling admissions plan. Application deadlines are open. Application fee is $40.

Transfer: 524 transfer students enrolled in 2004-2005. Applicants must have a minimum college GPA of 2.0 and submit final transcripts from all schools attended. Students transferring with fewer than 30 semester credits must submit a satisfactory SAT score or ACT score of 18 and meet other freshman requirements. 30 of 120 credits required for the bachelor's degree must be completed at USC Upstate.

Visiting: There are regularly scheduled orientations for prospective students. There are guides for informal visits and visitors may sit in on classes. To schedule a visit, contact the Admissions Office.

Financial Aid: The CSS/Profile, FAFSA, FFS, or SFS is required.

International Students: International students must score satisfactorily on the written TOEFL and also take the SAT or the ACT.

Computers: All students may access the system during school hours. There are no time limits and no fees.

Graduates: From July 1, 2004 to June 30, 2005, 839 bachelor's degrees were awarded. The most popular majors were education (19%), nursing (15%), and business administration (15%). In an average class, 15% graduate in 4 years or less, and 42% graduate in 6 years or less. 120 companies recruited on campus in 2004-2005.

Admissions Contact: Donette Stewart, Assistant Vice Chancellor for Enrollment Services. E-mail: *dstewart@uscupstate.edu*
Web: *www.uscupstate.edu*

VOORHEES COLLEGE C-3

Denmark, SC 29042 **(803) 793-3351**
(800) 446-6250; Fax: (803) 793-1112

Full-time: 300 men, 550 women	Faculty: n/av
Part-time: 10 men, 30 women	Ph.Ds: n/av
Graduate: none	Student/Faculty: n/av
Year: semesters, summer session	Tuition: $7200
Application Deadline: see profile	Room & Board: $4600
Freshman Class: n/av	
SAT or ACT: required	LESS COMPETITIVE

Voorhees College, founded in 1897, is a historically black liberal arts college affiliated with the Protestant Episcopal Church. Undergraduate programs are offered in accounting, biology, business administration, English, health and recreation, political science, sociology, criminal justice, computer science, teacher education, and math. Figures in the above capsule and in this profile are approximate. The library contains 111,057 volumes, 23,387 microform items, and 238 audio/video tapes/CDs/DVDs, and subscribes to 417 periodicals including electronic. Computerized library services include the card catalog and interlibrary loans. Special learning facilities include a learning resource center. The 350-acre campus is in a rural area 50 miles south of Columbia. Including any residence halls, there are 23 buildings.

Student Life: 78% of undergraduates are from South Carolina. Others are from 20 states and 2 foreign countries. 100% are from public schools. 99% are African American. Most are Protestant. The average age of freshmen is 17; all undergraduates, 23. 38% do not continue beyond their first year; 55% remain to graduate.

Housing: 521 students can be accommodated in college housing, which includes single-sex dormitories. On-campus housing is guaranteed for all 4 years. 75% of students live on campus; of those, 50% remain on campus on weekends. Alcohol is not permitted. All students may keep cars.

Activities: 20% of men belong to 4 national fraternities; 14% of women belong to 4 national sororities. There are 20 groups on campus, including cheerleading, choir, computers, dance, drama, honors, newspaper, pep band, political, professional, religious, social, student government, and yearbook. Popular campus events include Career Awareness Week, Black History Month, and Religious Emphasis Week.

Sports: There are 3 intercollegiate sports for men and 4 for women, and 4 intramural sports for men and 4 for women. Facilities include a gym, tennis courts, baseball and softball fields, a weight room, a dance studio, and a student center.

Disabled Students: 80% of the campus is accessible. Wheelchair ramps, elevators, special parking, specially equipped rest rooms, lowered drinking fountains, and mobile carts are available.

Services: Counseling and information services are available, as is tutoring in most subjects. There is remedial math, reading, and writing.

Campus Safety and Security: Measures include 24-hour foot and vehicle patrol, informal discussions, and lighted pathways/sidewalks.

Programs of Study: Voorhees confers B.A. and B.S. degrees. Bachelor's degrees are awarded in BIOLOGICAL SCIENCE (biology/biological science), BUSINESS (accounting, business administration and management, and recreation and leisure services), COMMUNICATIONS AND THE ARTS (English), COMPUTER AND PHYSICAL SCIENCE (computer science and mathematics), HEALTH PROFESSIONS (health), SOCIAL SCIENCE (criminal justice and sociology). Biology and business administration are the strongest academically. Business and organizational management are the largest.

Required: To graduate, students must earn at least 122 credit hours, with at least 30 in the major, and have a minimum GPA of 2.0. The 55-hour general education requirement includes 13 hours of humanities, 9 of English, 6 each of social science, natural science, math, and foreign language, 3 of computer science, 2 of phys ed, and 1 of freshman orientation. A number of free electives and a senior seminar are also required. An English proficiency exam and an exit exam must be passed.

Special: Voorhees offers cooperative education, study abroad in England, internships in some programs, work-study, an evening/Saturday program, off-campus summer study, dual majors, credit by exam, and a degree completion program. Cross-registration with Denmark Technical College and interdisciplinary majors, such as health and recreation, are possible. There are 3 national honor societies and 1 departmental honors program.

Faculty/Classroom: All teach undergraduates. The average class size in an introductory lecture is 30; in a laboratory, 20; and in a regular course, 25.

Requirements: The SAT or ACT is required. Applicants must be high school graduates or hold a GED. Students should have earned 20 academic credits in high school, including 4 of English, 3 of math, 2 each of science and foreign language (optional), and 1 each of history, social studies, economics/government, and phys ed. Letters of recommendation and a campus visit are advised. Voorhees requires applicants to be in the upper 75% of their class. A GPA of 2.0 is required. AP and CLEP credits are accepted. Important factors in the admissions decision are advanced placement or honor courses, recommendations by school officials, and recommendations by alumni.

Procedure: Freshmen are admitted to all sessions. Entrance exams should be taken in the senior year. There is a deferred admissions plan. Check with the school for current deadlines and fees.

Transfer: 31 transfer students enrolled in 2004-2005. Transfer students must submit complete records, including a confidential report from each college attended. The confidential report form is provided by the Office of Admission and Recruitment. Students with fewer than 30 semester hours must submit their high school record with rank in class and GPA. The SAT I is recommended; a minimum composite score of 600 is expected. An interview is advised. 30 of 122 credits required for the bachelor's degree must be completed at Voorhees.

Visiting: There are regularly scheduled orientations for prospective students, consisting of senior visitation days held January through April. There are guides for informal visits and visitors may sit in on classes and stay overnight. To schedule a visit, contact Willie Jefferson, Vice President for Student Affairs at (803) 703-7173 or *williej@voorhees.edu*.

Financial Aid: In a reent year, 98% of all full-time freshmen and 80% of continuing full-time students received some form of financial aid. 94% of full-time freshmen and 74% of continuing full-time students received need-based aid. The average freshman award was $10,150. 42% of undergraduates work part time. Average annual earnings from campus work are $1720. Voorhees is a member of CSS. The FAFSA, the college's own financial statement, or the SAR is required. The FAFSA is preferred. Check with the school for current deadlines.

International Students: In a recent year, there are 3 international students enrolled. Satisfactory scores are required on the written TOEFL and the SAT or the ACT.

Computers: All students may access the system. There are no time limits and no fees.

Admissions Contact: Benjamin Watson, Director of Admissions and Recruitment. A video is available. E-mail: *bwatson@voorhees.edu*
Web: *www.voorhees.edu*

WINTHROP UNIVERSITY
C-1

Rock Hill, SC 29733

(803) 323-2191
(800) 763-0230; Fax: (803) 323-2137

Full-time: 1400 men, 3220 women	**Faculty:** 264; IIA, --$
Part-time: 180 men, 400 women	**Ph.D.s:** 53%
Graduate: 370 men, 1050 women	**Student/Faculty:** 17 to 1
Year: semesters, summer session	**Tuition:** $6700 ($12,300)
Application Deadline: see profile	**Room & Board:** $4650
Freshman Class: n/av	
SAT or ACT: required	**COMPETITIVE**

Winthrop University, founded in 1886, is a state-supported institution offering undergraduate and graduate programs in liberal arts and sciences, business administration, education, and visual and performing arts. There are 4 undergraduate and 4 graduate schools. Figures in the above capsule and in this profile are approximate. In addition to regional accreditation, Winthrop has baccalaureate program accreditation with AACSB, CSAB, CSWE, FIDER, NASAD, NASM, and NCATE. The library contains 414,879 volumes, 1,236,619 microform items, and 2884 audio/video tapes/CDs/DVDs, and subscribes to 1446 periodicals including electronic. Computerized library services include the card catalog, interlibrary loans, and database searching. Special learning facilities include an art gallery, radio station, TV station, an audio recording studio, an early childhood lab school, the MIDI lab, the Instructional Technology Center, and the Conservatory of Music. The 418-acre campus is in a small town 23 miles south of Charlotte, North Carolina. Including any residence halls, there are 43 buildings.

Student Life: 88% of undergraduates are from South Carolina. Others are from 41 states, 33 foreign countries, and Canada. 69% are white; 26% African American. The average age of freshmen is 18; all undergraduates, 21. 25% do not continue beyond their first year; 75% remain to graduate.

Housing: 2336 students can be accommodated in college housing, which includes single-sex and coed dormitories, on-campus apartments, and married-student housing. On-campus housing is guaranteed for the freshman year only and is available on a first-come, first-served basis. 52% of students commute. All students may keep cars.

Activities: 11% of men belong to 8 national fraternities; 14% of women belong to 8 national sororities. There are 115 groups on campus, including art, band, cheerleading, chess, choir, chorale, chorus, computers, dance, drama, ethnic, gay, honors, international, jazz band, literary magazine, musical theater, newspaper, opera, orchestra, pep band, political, professional, radio and TV, religious, social, social service, student government, and yearbook. Popular campus events include convocation, Fall Fest, and Fine Arts Series.

Sports: There are 7 intercollegiate sports for men and 7 for women, and 30 intramural sports for men and 30 for women. Facilities include a golf course, a 6000-seat coliseum, a swimming pool, a cross-country course, tennis courts, racquetball courts, a weight room, a training room, baseball, softball, and soccer fields, a ropes course, and an 18-hole disc golf course.

Disabled Students: 90% of the campus is accessible. Wheelchair ramps, elevators, special parking, specially equipped rest rooms, special class scheduling, lowered drinking fountains, lowered telephones, and special housing are available.

Services: There is a reader service for the blind. All tutoring is the responsibility of the students to arrange with their professors or specific departments.

Campus Safety and Security: Measures include 24-hour foot and vehicle patrol, self-defense education, security escort services, and informal discussions. There are pamphlets/posters/films, emergency telephones, and lighted pathways/sidewalks.

Programs of Study: Winthrop confers B.A., B.S., B.F.A., B.M., B.M.E., and B.S.W. degrees. Master's degrees are also awarded. Bachelor's degrees are awarded in BIOLOGICAL SCIENCE (biology/biological science), BUSINESS (business administration and management and sports management), COMMUNICATIONS AND THE ARTS (art, art history and appreciation, communications, dance, dramatic arts, English, fine arts, French, music, public relations, Spanish, and speech/debate/rhetoric), COMPUTER AND PHYSICAL SCIENCE (chemistry, computer science, and mathematics), EDUCATION (early childhood, elementary, home economics, music, physical, secondary, and special), HEALTH PROFESSIONS (medical laboratory technology and speech pathology/audiology), SOCIAL SCIENCE (food science, history, home economics, philosophy, political science/government, psychology, religion, social work, and sociology). Business administration, elementary education, and fine arts are the largest.

Required: Students must complete a minimum of 124 semester hours, including a 59-hour general education distribution requirement, and maintain a minimum GPA of 2.0. Specific courses in writing, oral communication, computer information systems, critical issues, and the American Constitution are required.

Special: Cross-registration is permitted with the Charlotte Area Educational Consortium. Co-op programs and internships in most professional

areas, study abroad in 14 countries, and on-campus work-study programs are offered. Interdisciplinary majors such as science communication, nondegree study, and pass/fail options are possible. There are 3 national honor societies, a freshman honors program, and 18 departmental honors programs.

Faculty/Classroom: 47% of faculty are male; 56%, female. 98% teach undergraduates, 90% do research, and 90% do both. No introductory courses are taught by graduate students. The average class size in an introductory lecture is 26; in a laboratory, 16; and in a regular course, 22.

Requirements: The SAT or ACT is required. In addition, graduation from an accredited secondary school is required; a GED will be accepted. Applicants must have successfully completed 4 credits in high school English, 3 in math, 2 each in lab science, social studies, and a foreign language, 1 in United States history, and 1 in phys ed or ROTC. A GPA of 3.5 is required. AP and CLEP credits are accepted. Important factors in the admissions decision are recommendations by school officials and evidence of special talent.

Procedure: Freshmen are admitted to all sessions. There is a deferred admissions plan. Check with the school for current deadlines and fees. Applications are accepted on-line.

Transfer: 173 transfer students enrolled in 2004-2005. Applicants must be eligible to return to the previous institution and submit college transcripts. 30 of 124 credits required for the bachelor's degree must be completed at Winthrop.

Visiting: There are regularly scheduled orientations for prospective students, consisting of the Winthrop Festival, with all academic areas and student life areas represented, a general session, minisessions, and a campus tour. There are guides for informal visits and visitors may sit in on classes. To schedule a visit, contact the Admissions Office.

Financial Aid: In a recent year, 53% of all full-time freshmen and 50% of continuing full-time students received some form of financial aid. 42% of full-time freshmen and 50% of continuing full-time students received need-based aid. The average freshman award was $6750. Need-based scholarships or need-based grants averaged $5513; need-based self-help aid (loans and jobs) averaged $2376; non-need-based athletic scholarships averaged $3673; and other non-need-based awards and non-need-based scholarships averaged $5086. 20% of undergraduates work part time. Average annual earnings from campus work are $800. The average financial indebtedness of a recent year's graduate was $17,482. Winthrop is a member of CSS. The FAFSA and the college's own financial statement are required. Check with the school for current deadlines.

International Students: In a recent year, there were 99 international students enrolled. The school actively recruits these students. A satisfactory score is required on the written TOEFL.

Computers: All students may access the system 95 hours a week, weekdays until 1 A.M. There are no time limits and no fees.

Graduates: In a recent year, 834 bachelor's degrees were awarded. The most popular majors were business/marketing (26%), education (24%), and visual and performing arts (11%). In an average class, 1% graduate in 3 years or less, 33% graduate in 4 years or less, 51% graduate in 5 years or less, and 53% graduate in 6 years or less. 45 companies recruited on campus in 2004-2005.

Admissions Contact: Deborah Barber, Director of Admissions. A video is available. E-mail: *admissions@winthrop.edu*
Web: *www.winthrop.edu/admissions/admissions.html*

WOFFORD COLLEGE
B-1

Spartanburg, SC 29303-3663

(864) 597-4130
Fax: (864) 597-4147

Full-time: 603 men, 555 women	**Faculty:** 89; IIB, av$
Part-time: 10 men, 6 women	**Ph.D.s:** 92%
Graduate: none	**Student/Faculty:** 13 to 1
Year: 4-1-4, summer session	**Tuition:** $24,130
Application Deadline: February 1	**Room & Board:** $6805
Freshman Class: 1871 applied, 1237 accepted, 321 enrolled	
SAT Verbal/Math: 616/628*	**ACT:** 25 **HIGHLY COMPETITIVE**

Wofford College, founded in 1854, is a private institution affiliated with the United Methodist Church, offering programs in liberal arts and pre-professional studies. There is 1 undergraduate school. In addition to regional accreditation, Wofford has baccalaureate program accreditation with NASDTEC. The library contains 197,077 volumes, 38,259 microform items, and 3133 audio/video tapes/CDs/DVDs, and subscribes to 4489 periodicals including electronic. Computerized library services include the card catalog, interlibrary loans, database searching, Internet access, and laptop Internet portals. Special learning facilities include a learning resource center, art gallery, foreign language center, satellite earth station, and international studies center with simultaneous translation capabilities. The 150-acre campus is in an urban area 65 miles southeast of Charlotte. Including any residence halls, there are 35 buildings.

Student Life: 64% of undergraduates are from South Carolina. Others are from 29 states and 8 foreign countries. 77% are from public schools. 89% are white. 70% are Protestant; 11% Catholic. The average age of freshmen is 18; all undergraduates, 20. 11% do not continue beyond their first year; 78% remain to graduate.

Housing: 1065 students can be accommodated in college housing, which includes single-sex and coed dorms and fraternity houses. In addition, there is experimental residential grouping of science majors and some freshman humanities sections. On-campus housing is guaranteed for all 4 years. 90% of students live on campus; of those, 75% remain on campus on weekends. All students may keep cars.

Activities: 51% of men belong to 8 national fraternities; 59% of women belong to 4 national sororities. There are 82 groups on campus, including band, cheerleading, choir, chorale, chorus, College bowl team, computers, drama, enviromental, ethnic, international, literary magazine, newspaper, pep band, photography, political, professional, religious, social, social service, student government, and yearbook. Popular campus events include Phi Beta Kappa Day, Christmas concert, and Spring weekend/Greek games.

Sports: There are 10 intercollegiate sports for men and 9 for women, and 7 intramural sports for men and 7 for women. Facilities include an 8500-seat campus stadium, a 3500-seat arena, a tennis complex, a soccer field, and a wellness and athletic center built to the specifications of the Carolina Panthers.

Disabled Students: 90% of the campus is accessible. Wheelchair ramps, elevators, special parking, specially equipped rest rooms, special class scheduling, lowered drinking fountains, and lowered telephones are available.

Services: Counseling and information services are available, as is tutoring in every subject. There is a reader service for the blind.

Campus Safety and Security: Measures include 24-hour foot and vehicle patrol, self-defense education, security escort services, and informal discussions. There are pamphlets/posters/films, emergency telephones, and lighted pathways/sidewalks.

Programs of Study: Wofford confers B.A. and B.S. degrees. Bachelor's degrees are awarded in BIOLOGICAL SCIENCE (biology/biological science), BUSINESS (accounting, banking and finance, and business economics), COMMUNICATIONS AND THE ARTS (art history and appreciation, dramatic arts, English, French, German, and Spanish), COMPUTER AND PHYSICAL SCIENCE (chemistry, computer science, mathematics, and physics), SOCIAL SCIENCE (crosscultural studies, economics, history, humanities, philosophy, political science/government, psychology, religion, and sociology). Biology, foreign languages, and finance/accounting are the strongest academically. Biology, business economics, and government are the largest.

Required: To graduate, students must complete 124 credits, with 21 to 38 credits in the major and a minimum GPA of 2.0. General education requirements include 12 credits of history/philosophy/religion, 8 of natural sciences, 6 of English, 3 each of fine arts and math, and 2 of phys ed. Students must complete 4 interim projects, a career workshop, and a freshman humanities seminar.

Special: Special academic programs include limited cross-registration with Converse College and USC/Spartanburg, study abroad in more than 30 countries, a Washington semester, and a concentration in Latin American and Caribbean studies. In addition, students can major in 2 fields or complete interdisciplinary, humanities, or intercultural studies majors. Wofford participates in 3-2 programs in engineering with Clemson and Columbia Universities. The January interim allows students to concentrate on a single study project, internship, or travel experience. There are 9 national honor societies, including Phi Beta Kappa.

Faculty/Classroom: 65% of faculty are male; 35%, female. All teach undergraduates and 30% both teach and do research. The average class size in an introductory lecture is 20; in a laboratory, 15; and in a regular course, 10.

Admissions: 66% of the 2005-2006 applicants were accepted. The SAT scores for the 2005-2006 freshman class were: Verbal--5% below 500, 43% between 500 and 599, 43% between 600 and 700, and 9% above 700; Math--5% below 500, 35% between 500 and 599, 49% between 600 and 700, and 11% above 700. The ACT scores were 15% below 21, 23% between 21 and 23, 33% between 24 and 26, 12% between 27 and 28, and 17% above 28. 78% of the current freshmen were in the top fifth of their class; 95% were in the top two fifths. There were 5 National Merit finalists. 10 freshmen graduated first in their class.

Requirements: The SAT or ACT is required. In addition, SAT Subject tests are recommended. Applicants must be graduates of an accredited secondary school. The GED is accepted. Students should have completed 4 years each of high school English and math, 3 of lab science, and 2 each of a foreign language and social studies. An essay is required and an interview is strongly recommended. AP and CLEP credits are accepted. Important factors in the admissions decision are advanced placement or honor courses, leadership record, and personality/intangible qualities.

Procedure: Freshmen are admitted to all sessions. Entrance exams should be taken in the spring of the junior year or fall of the senior year. There are early decision and deferred admissions plans. Early decision applications should be filed by November 15; regular applications, by February 1 for fall entry. The fall 2005 application fee was $40. Notification of early decision is sent January 15; regular decision, March 15. 370 early decision candidates were accepted for the 2005-2006 class. A waiting list is an active part of the admissions procedure. Applications are accepted on-line.

Transfer: 10 transfer students enrolled in 2004-2005. Transfers should have a minimum GPA of 2.5 from a 4-year college or 3.0 from a 2-year college, or they may submit ACT or SAT scores. An interview is recommended. 30 of 124 credits required for the bachelor's degree must be completed at Wofford.

Visiting: There are regularly scheduled orientations for prospective students. There are guides for informal visits and visitors may sit in on classes and stay overnight. To schedule a visit, contact the Director of Admissions at (864) 597-4130 or *admissions@wofford.edu*.

Financial Aid: In 2005-2006, 92% of all full-time freshmen and 85% of continuing full-time students received some form of financial aid. 48% of full-time freshmen and 51% of continuing full-time students received need-based aid. The average freshman award was $16,689. Need-based scholarships or need-based grants averaged $6957 ($30,935 maximum); need-based self-help aid (loans and jobs) averaged $1882 ($5500 maximum); non-need-based athletic scholarships averaged $17,311 ($30,935 maximum); and other non-need-based awards and non-need-based scholarships averaged $13,782 ($30,935 maximum). 28% of undergraduates work part time. Average annual earnings from campus work are $1230. The average financial indebtedness of the 2005 graduate was $14,444. The FAFSA is required. The deadline for filing freshman financial aid applications for fall entry is March 15.

International Students: There are 8 international students enrolled. A satisfactory score is required on the written TOEFL.

Computers: Wireless access is available. All students may access the system 24 hours per day. There are no time limits and no fees. It is strongly recommended that all students have a personal computer.

Graduates: From July 1, 2004 to June 30, 2005, 257 bachelor's degrees were awarded. The most popular majors were biology (18%), business economics (16%), and government (11%). In an average class, 74% graduate in 4 years or less, 77% graduate in 5 years or less, and 78% graduate in 6 years or less. Of the 2004 graduating class, 35% were enrolled in graduate school within 6 months of graduation and 62% were employed.

Admissions Contact: Brand R. Stille, Director of Admissions. A video is available. E-mail: *admissions@wofford.edu* Web: *www.wofford.edu*

SOUTH DAKOTA

POPULATION
DENSITY
• 10,000 and over

0 20 40 60 80 100
Miles

AUGUSTANA COLLEGE   F-3
Sioux Falls, SD 57197   (605) 274-5516
(800) 727-2844; Fax: (605) 274-5518

Full-time: 617 men, 1004 women	**Faculty:** IIB, --$
Part-time: 32 men, 61 women	**Ph.D.s:** 90%
Graduate: 6 men, 25 women	**Student/Faculty:** n/av
Year: 4-1-4, summer session	**Tuition:** $18,860
Application Deadline: open	**Room & Board:** $5520
Freshman Class: 1544 applied, 1229 accepted, 393 enrolled	
SAT Verbal/Math: 595/595*	**VERY COMPETITIVE**

Augustana College, founded in 1860, is a private liberal arts institution affiliated with the Evangelical Lutheran Church in America. In addition to regional accreditation, Augie has baccalaureate program accreditation with CSWE, NASM, NCATE, and NLN. The library contains 234,515 volumes, 85,938 microform items, and 6147 audio/video tapes/CDs/DVDs, and subscribes to 1085 periodicals including electronic. Computerized library services include the card catalog, interlibrary loans, and database searching. Special learning facilities include an art gallery, natural history museum, radio station, and a Center for Western Studies. The 100-acre campus is in a suburban area 150 miles north of Omaha, Nebraska. Including any residence halls, there are 30 buildings.

Student Life: 55% of undergraduates are from out of state, mostly the Midwest. Students are from 30 states, 12 foreign countries, and Canada. 95% are from public schools. 96% are white. Most are Catholic. The average age of freshmen is 18; all undergraduates, 20. 21% do not continue beyond their first year; 64% remain to graduate.

Housing: 1100 students can be accommodated in college housing, which includes coed dorms and married-student housing. In addition, there are special-interest houses, independent student housing for those with children, and a theme house. On-campus housing is guaranteed for all 4 years. 65% of students live on campus; of those, 70% remain on campus on weekends. Alcohol is not permitted. All students may keep cars.

Activities: There are no fraternities or sororities. There are 55 groups on campus, including art, band, cheerleading, choir, chorale, chorus, computers, dance, debate, drama, ethnic, gay, honors, international, jazz band, literary magazine, musical theater, newspaper, opera, orchestra, pep band, photography, political, professional, radio and TV, religious, social, social service, student government, symphony, and yearbook.

Popular campus events include Christmas Vespers, Viking Days, and Boe Forum on Public Affairs.

Sports: There are 9 intercollegiate sports for men and 9 for women, and 26 intramural sports for men and 26 for women. Facilities include a 3600-seat gym and a health, phys ed, and recreation center.

Disabled Students: 75% of the campus is accessible. Wheelchair ramps, elevators, special parking, specially equipped rest rooms, special class scheduling, lowered drinking fountains, lowered telephones, special housing, Arkenstone reader, Dragon Dictate, TTYs, and doorbell lights are available.

Services: Counseling and information services are available, as is tutoring in every subject. There is a reader service for the blind and remedial math and writing. A special writing lab is available 3 nights per week.

Campus Safety and Security: Measures include 24-hour foot and vehicle patrol, self-defense education, security escort services, and informal discussions. There are pamphlets/posters/films, emergency telephones, lighted pathways/sidewalks, and key card access to residence halls.

Programs of Study: Augie confers the B.A. degree. Master's degrees are also awarded. Bachelor's degrees are awarded in BIOLOGICAL SCIENCE (biology/biological science), BUSINESS (accounting, business administration and management, and management information systems), COMMUNICATIONS AND THE ARTS (art, communications, dramatic arts, English, French, German, journalism, modern language, music, and Spanish), COMPUTER AND PHYSICAL SCIENCE (chemistry, computer science, mathematics, and physics), EDUCATION (athletic training, drama, education of the deaf and hearing impaired, elementary, music, physical, secondary, social studies, and special), ENGINEERING AND ENVIRONMENTAL DESIGN (engineering physics), HEALTH PROFESSIONS (exercise science, medical technology, nursing, and speech pathology/audiology), SOCIAL SCIENCE (economics, history, international relations, international studies, philosophy, physical fitness/movement, political science/government, psychology, religion, social work, and sociology). Education, biology, and business are the largest.

Required: Students must complete 130 semester hours, with a minimum GPA of 2.0. General education requirements total 59 semester hours, including component courses in writing for graduation. 2 phys ed. activity courses are required; there is a computer component and a capstone course.

Special: Cross-registration with Upper Midwest Association for Intercultural Education and Higher Education Consortium for Urban Affairs is available. Internships (both national and local), study abroad in 40 countries, and a 3-2 engineering degree with Columbia University, Washington University in St. Louis, or University of Minnesota are offered. A Washington semester with Lutheran College Washington Consortium or American University is offered. Credit for life experience is possible. There are 12 national honor societies and 3 departmental honors programs.

Faculty/Classroom: 60% of faculty are male; 40%, female. All both teach and do research. No introductory courses are taught by graduate students. The average class size in an introductory lecture is 25; in a laboratory, 18; and in a regular course, 20.

Admissions: 80% of the 2005-2006 applicants were accepted. The SAT scores for the 2005-2006 freshman class were: Verbal--12% below 500, 38% between 500 and 599, 38% between 600 and 700, and 12% above 700; Math--25% below 500, 25% between 500 and 599, 38% between 600 and 700, and 12% above 700. The ACT scores were 15% below 21, 28% between 21 and 23, 29% between 24 and 26, 16% between 27 and 28, and 12% above 28. 45% of the current freshmen were in the top fifth of their class; 78% were in the top two fifths. There was 1 National Merit finalist. 27 freshmen graduated first in their class.

Requirements: The SAT or ACT is required. The ACT Optional Writing test is also recommended. In addition, graduation from an accredited secondary school is preferred; however, a GED will be accepted. Applicants should have completed 4 years of high school English, 3 each of math and science, and 2 each of a foreign language and history. An interview is recommended. Augie requires applicants to be in the upper 50% of their class. A GPA of 2.5 is required. AP and CLEP credits are accepted. Important factors in the admissions decision are advanced placement or honor courses, leadership record, and parents or siblings attending the school.

Procedure: Freshmen are admitted to all sessions. Entrance exams should be taken in the spring of the junior year or early fall of the senior year. There are early admissions and deferred admissions plans. There is a rolling admissions plan. Application deadlines are open. Notification is sent on a rolling basis. Applications are accepted on-line.

Transfer: 119 transfer students enrolled in 2004-2005. Applicants must have a 2.0 GPA in previous college work. If only 1 semester or 1 quarter has been completed, and the applicant has just graduated from high school, then Augustana requires a high school transcript. 30 of 130 credits required for the bachelor's degree must be completed at Augie.

Visiting: There are regularly scheduled orientations for prospective students, including Explore Augustana days, which offer tours, and visits with faculty, current students, and coaches. Admitted Student Days (fall) and Decision Days (spring) offer the chance to shadow a current student for a day. The school also hosts Junior Visit Day and Summer Visit Days for juniors. There are guides for informal visits and visitors may sit in on classes and stay overnight. To schedule a visit, contact Pam Wentzlaff, Visit Coordinator, the Office of Admissions at (800) 727-2844 or *pam.wentzlaff@augie.edu.*

Financial Aid: In 2005-2006, 99% of all full-time students received some form of financial aid. 87% of full-time freshmen and 85% of continuing full-time students received need-based aid. The average freshman award was $15,017. 32% of undergraduates work part time. Average annual earnings from campus work are $1350. The average financial indebtedness of the 2005 graduate was $18,956. The FAFSA is required. The priority date for freshman financial aid applications for fall entry is March 1.

International Students: There are 33 international students enrolled. The school actively recruits these students. They must achieve satisfactory scores on both the TOEFL and the SAT or ACT.

Computers: Wireless access is available. Each dorm and academic building has 1 computer lab for student use. All dorm rooms are wired with free Internet and access to the Augustana system. Students are able to check out laptops for wireless use in the library. All students may access the system.

Graduates: From July 1, 2004 to June 30, 2005, 360 bachelor's degrees were awarded. The most popular majors were business (16%), education (15%), and nursing (12%). In an average class, 1% graduate in 3 years or less, 49% graduate in 4 years or less, 62% graduate in 5 years or less, and 62% graduate in 6 years or less. 50 companies recruited on campus in 2004-2005. Of the 2004 graduating class, 25% were enrolled in graduate school within 6 months of graduation and 98% were employed.

Admissions Contact: Nancy L. Davidson, Dean of Admission.
E-mail: *info@augie.edu* Web: *www.augie.edu*

BLACK HILLS STATE UNIVERSITY	A-2
Spearfish, SD 57799-9500	(605) 642-6343
	(800) ALL-BHSU; Fax: (605) 642-6022

Full-time: 1020 men, 1700 women	**Faculty:** 110; IIB, -$
Part-time: 310 men, 690 women	**Ph.D.s:** 78%
Graduate: 30 men, 180 women	**Student/Faculty:** 24 to 1
Year: semesters, summer session	**Tuition:** $4600 ($9600)
Application Deadline: see profile	**Room & Board:** $3200
Freshman Class: n/av	
ACT: required	**LESS COMPETITIVE**

Black Hills State University, founded in 1883, is a public institution offering undergraduate programs in applied science and technology, arts and humanities, business and public affairs, and education and human resources development. There are 3 undergraduate schools and 1 graduate school. Figures in the above capsule and in this profile are approximate. In addition to regional accreditation, BHSU has baccalaureate program accreditation with NCATE. The library contains 235,000 volumes, 118,572 microform items, and 1300 audio/video tapes/CDs/DVDs, and subscribes to 1800 periodicals including electronic. Computerized library services include the card catalog, interlibrary loans, and database searching. Special learning facilities include a learning resource center, art gallery, radio station, and TV station. The 123-acre campus is in a small town 45 miles northwest of Rapid City. Including any residence halls, there are 13 buildings.

Student Life: 81% of undergraduates are from South Dakota. Others are from 32 states, 7 foreign countries, and Canada. 89% are white. The average age of freshmen is 22; all undergraduates, 25. 53% do not continue beyond their first year.

Housing: 788 students can be accommodated in college housing, which includes single-sex and coed dormitories, on-campus apartments, and married-student housing. On-campus housing is available on a first-come, first-served basis. 79% of students commute. Alcohol is not permitted. All students may keep cars.

Activities: 2% of men belong to 1 local and 1 national fraternity; 2% of women belong to 1 local and 1 national sorority. There are 77 groups on campus, including art, band, cheerleading, choir, chorale, chorus, computers, dance, debate, drama, drill team, ethnic, honors, international, jazz band, musical theater, newspaper, pep band, photography, political, professional, radio and TV, religious, social, social service, student government, and yearbook. Popular campus events include Swarm Week and Big 100 Week.

Sports: There are 4 intercollegiate sports for men and 4 for women, and 20 intramural sports for men and 20 for women. Facilities include a stadium, a sport and fitness center, tennis courts, swimming pools, a track, a gym, a golf course, and a baseball and softball complex.

Disabled Students: Wheelchair ramps, elevators, special parking, specially equipped rest rooms, lowered drinking fountains, and special housing are available.

Services: Counseling and information services are available, as is tutoring in most subjects. There is remedial math.

Campus Safety and Security: Measures include 24-hour foot and vehicle patrol, security escort services, and lighted pathways/sidewalks.

Programs of Study: BHSU confers B.A., B.S., and B.S.Ed. degrees. Associate and master's degrees are also awarded. Bachelor's degrees are awarded in BIOLOGICAL SCIENCE (biology/biological science), BUSINESS (accounting, business administration and management, hotel/motel and restaurant management, human resources, and marketing/retailing/merchandising), COMMUNICATIONS AND THE ARTS (art, broadcasting, communications, English, fine arts, music, Spanish, and speech/debate/rhetoric), COMPUTER AND PHYSICAL SCIENCE (chemistry, mathematics, and physical sciences), EDUCATION (art, business, elementary, health, music, physical, science, secondary, and special), HEALTH PROFESSIONS (health care administration), SOCIAL SCIENCE (American Indian studies, history, human services, political science/government, prelaw, psychology, social science, and sociology).

Required: Students must successfully complete 128 credits, with at least 36 in the major, and must maintain a minimum GPA of 2.0. Core curriculum requirements include courses in English, speech, psychology, math, science, non-Western cultures, and phys ed. All students must pass an English proficiency exam.

Special: The university offers a co-op program in social work, cross-registration with the University of South Dakota, internships, work-study programs, a B.A.-B.S. degree, dual majors, a general studies degree, credit by exam, credit for military service, nondegree study, and pass/fail options. Composite majors offered include marketing, environmental physical science, outdoor education, tourism, and wellness management. A library media major is possible in conjunction with a second major. There are 5 national honor societies and a freshman honors program.

Faculty/Classroom: 66% of faculty are male; 24%, female. All teach undergraduates. No introductory courses are taught by graduate students. The average class size in an introductory lecture is 120; in a laboratory, 20; and in a regular course, 30.

Requirements: The ACT is required; the ACT is preferred. Graduation from an accredited secondary school is required; a GED will be accepted. Applicants must have completed the following academic credits with a minimum GPA of 2.0: 4 years of English, 3 each of social studies, math, and science, and 1/2 year of fine arts. BHSU requires applicants to be in the upper 60% of their class. A GPA of 2.0 is required. AP and CLEP credits are accepted.

Procedure: Freshmen are admitted to all sessions. Entrance exams should be taken during the senior year of high school. Application deadlines are open. Check with the school for current deadlines and fee.

Transfer: 523 transfer students enrolled in a recent year. Applicants must supply transcripts from all previous schools attended, high school and college, and must have maintained a minimum college GPA of 2.0. 32 of 128 credits required for the bachelor's degree must be completed at BHSU.

Visiting: There are regularly scheduled orientations for prospective students. There are guides for informal visits and visitors may sit in on classes and stay overnight. To schedule a visit, contact the Admissions Office at *admissions@bhsu.edu*.

Financial Aid: The FAFSA and state aid form are required. Check with the school for current deadlines.

International Students: In a recent year there were 7 international students enrolled. Satisfactory scores, are required on the written TOEFL take the ACT.

Computers: All students may access the system during lab and library hours. There are no time limits and no fees. It is strongly recommended that all students have a personal computer.

Graduates: In a recent year, 478 bachelor's degrees were awarded. The most popular majors were elementary education (17%), curriculum and instruction (13%), and business administration (9%). In an average class, 15% graduate in 3 years or less, 25% graduate in 4 years or less, 27% graduate in 5 years or less, and 29% graduate in 6 years or less. 127 companies recruited on campus in a recent year.

Admissions Contact: Admissions Officer, Enrollment Services Center. E-mail: *admissions@bhsu.edu* Web: *www.bhsu.edu*

DAKOTA STATE UNIVERSITY
Madison, SD 57042

E-3

(605) 256-5139
(888) DSU-9988; Fax: (605) 256-5020

Full-time: 700 men, 560 women	**Faculty:** 73; IIB, -$
Part-time: 850 men and women	**Ph.D.s:** 58%
Graduate: 85 men, 75 women	**Student/Faculty:** 17 to 1
Year: semesters, summer session	**Tuition:** $4400 ($9100)
Application Deadline: open	**Room & Board:** $3100
Freshman Class: n/av	
SAT or ACT: required	**COMPETITIVE**

Dakota State University, founded in 1881, is a public institution offering undergraduate programs through the Colleges of Business and Information Systems, Education, and Arts and Sciences. There are 3 undergraduate schools and 1 graduate school. Figures in the above capsule and in this profile are approximate. In addition to regional accreditation, DSU has baccalaureate program accreditation with AHEA and NCATE. The library contains 125,461 volumes, 3728 microform items, and 3728 audio/video tapes/CDs/DVDs, and subscribes to 350 periodicals including electronic. Computerized library services include the card catalog, interlibrary loans, and database searching. Special learning facilities include a learning resource center, art gallery, and natural history museum. The 20-acre campus is in a small town 45 miles northwest of Sioux Falls. Including any residence halls, there are 17 buildings.

Student Life: 85% of undergraduates are from South Dakota. Others are from 22 states, 10 foreign countries, and Canada. The average age of all undergraduates is 22.

Housing: 702 students can be accommodated in college housing, which includes single-sex and coed dormitories and on-campus apartments. On-campus housing is guaranteed for the freshman year only, is available on a first-come, first-served basis, and is available on a lottery system for upperclassmen. 63% of students commute. Alcohol is not permitted. All students may keep cars.

Activities: There are no fraternities or sororities. There are 30 groups on campus, including art, band, cheerleading, choir, chorale, chorus, computers, dance, drama, ethnic, honors, international, jazz band, literary magazine, marching band, musical theater, newspaper, pep band, political, religious, student government, and yearbook. Popular campus events include Discover DSU Days, Zimmfest, and Diversity Week.

Sports: There are 6 intercollegiate sports for men and 6 for women, and 20 intramural sports for men and 20 for women. Facilities include courts for basketball and racquetball, a football field, a weight room, and a swimming pool.

Disabled Students: 80% of the campus is accessible. Wheelchair ramps, elevators, special parking, specially equipped rest rooms, special class scheduling, and lowered drinking fountains are available.

Services: Counseling and information services are available, as is tutoring in every subject. There is a reader service for the blind, and remedial math, reading, and writing.

Campus Safety and Security: Measures include self-defense education, security escort services, informal discussions, and pamphlets/posters/films. There are emergency telephones, lighted pathways/sidewalks, and a foot patrol.

Programs of Study: DSU confers B.S., B.B.A., and B.S.Ed. degrees. Associate and master's degrees are also awarded. Bachelor's degrees are awarded in BIOLOGICAL SCIENCE (biology/biological science), BUSINESS (business administration and management and electronic business), COMMUNICATIONS AND THE ARTS (English, fine arts, and music), COMPUTER AND PHYSICAL SCIENCE (chemistry, computer programming, computer science, information sciences and systems, mathematics, and physics), EDUCATION (art, business, elementary, English, health, marketing and distribution, music, and secondary), ENGINEERING AND ENVIRONMENTAL DESIGN (computer graphics), HEALTH PROFESSIONS (medical laboratory technology, medical records administration/services, premedicine, and respiratory therapy). Computer science, information systems, and education are the largest.

Required: To graduate, students must complete 128 semester hours, 85 of which must be in the major and 16 at the 300-400 course level. A 2.0 GPA and 43 hours of general education are also required. Students must take the Computer Concepts and Health courses. All candidates for graduation must apply formally to the Registration and Academic Records Office.

Special: The university offers co-op programs with South Dakota State University, internships, study abroad in London, and on-campus work-study programs. Also available are the general studies degree, a 3-2 engineering degree with the University of Minnesota/Twin Cities, credit for life, military, and work experience, nondegree study, and pass/fail options. There are 2 national honor societies and a freshman honors program.

Faculty/Classroom: 66% of faculty are male; 34%, female. All teach undergraduates. Graduate students teach 1% of introductory courses. The average class size in an introductory lecture is 40; in a laboratory, 25; and in a regular course, 20.

Requirements: The SAT or ACT is required. In addition, applicants must be graduates of an accredited secondary school or have a GED certificate, and have completed 4 years of English, 3 years each of math, science, and social studies, and 1/2 year of computer science and the fine arts. DSU requires applicants to be in the upper 60% of their class. A GPA of 2.6 is required. AP and CLEP credits are accepted.

Procedure: Freshmen are admitted to all sessions. Entrance exams should be taken before students register for classes. Application deadlines are open. Check with the school for current deadlines and fees. Applications are accepted on-line.

Transfer: 67 transfer students enrolled in a recent year. Transfer applicants must have a minimum 2.0 GPA. 32 of 128 credits required for the bachelor's degree must be completed at DSU.

Visiting: There are regularly scheduled orientations for prospective students, including general information and academic sessions, a campus tour, and financial aid information. There are guides for informal visits and visitors may sit in on classes and stay overnight. To schedule a visit, contact the Admissions Office.

Financial Aid: In a recent year, 88% of continuing full-time students received some form of financial aid. The average freshman award was $5836. Need-based scholarships or need-based grants averaged $641. 50% of undergraduates work part time. Average annual earnings from campus work are $1405. The average financial indebtedness of the recent year's graduate was $16,588. The FAFSA is required. Check with the school for current deadlines.

International Students: In a recent year, there are 120 international students enrolled. The school actively recruits these students. A satisfactory score is required on the written TOEFL.

Computers: All students may access the system. There are no time limits and no fees.

Graduates: In a recent year, 145 bachelor's degrees were awarded. In an average class, 24% graduate in 4 years or less, 42% graduate in 5 years or less, and 15% graduate in 6 years or less. 25 companies recruited on campus in a recent year. Of the recent year's graduating class, 1% were enrolled in graduate school within 6 months of graduation and 96% were employed.

Admissions Contact: Amy Crissinger, Director of Admission. E-mail: *yourfuture@dsu.edu* Web: *www.dsu.edu*

DAKOTA WESLEYAN UNIVERSITY

E-3

Mitchell, SD 57301

(605) 995-2650
(800) 333-8506; Fax: (605) 995-2699

Full-time: 300 men, 380 women
Part-time: 25 men, 55 women
Graduate: 5 men, 10 women
Year: semesters, summer session
Application Deadline: see profile
Freshman Class: n/av
SAT or ACT: required

Faculty: 42; IIB, --$
Ph.D.s: 52%
Student/Faculty: 16 to 1
Tuition: $13,600
Room & Board: $4300

COMPETITIVE

Dakota Wesleyan University, founded in 1885, is a private liberal arts institution affiliated with the United Methodist Church. Figures in the above capsule and in this profile are approximate. In addition to regional accreditation, DWU has baccalaureate program accreditation with CAAHEP and NLN. The library contains 62,500 volumes, 72,500 microform items, and 3700 audio/video tapes/CDs/DVDs, and subscribes to 620 periodicals including electronic. Computerized library services include the card catalog, interlibrary loans, database searching, and Internet access. Special learning facilities include a learning resource center and an observatory, as well as a history museum with art gallery adjacent to the campus. The 50-acre campus is in a small town 70 miles west of Sioux Falls. Including any residence halls, there are 18 buildings.
Student Life: 72% of undergraduates are from South Dakota. Others are from 31 states, 5 foreign countries, and Canada. 99% are from public schools. 89% are white. 50% are Protestant; 24% Catholic. The average age of freshmen is 19; all undergraduates, 23. 37% do not continue beyond their first year.
Housing: 385 students can be accommodated in college housing, which includes single-sex and coed dormitories and on-campus apartments. In addition, there are honors houses. On-campus housing is guaranteed for the freshman year only and is available on a first-come, first-served basis. 60% of students commute. Alcohol is not permitted. All students may keep cars.
Activities: There are no fraternities or sororities. There are 30 groups on campus, including art, band, cheerleading, choir, chorale, chorus, dance, drama, drill team, ethnic, forensics, honors, international, literary magazine, musical theater, newspaper, political, professional, religious, social, social service, student government, and yearbook. Popular campus events include Prom, Spring Week, and Family Life Conference.
Sports: There are 7 intercollegiate sports for men and 6 for women, and 3 intramural sports for men and 3 for women. Facilities include a 500-seat stadium, a 3200-seat auditorium/arena, and a wellness center with a double gym and cardio, weight training, and cybex rooms. City facilities include a 1500-seat baseball stadium, a 500-seat softball field, and a 1000-seat outdoor track.
Disabled Students: 20% of the campus is accessible. Wheelchair ramps, elevators, special parking, specially equipped rest rooms, special class scheduling, lowered telephones, and class relocation are available.
Services: Counseling and information services are available, as is tutoring in every subject. There is a reader service for the blind, and remedial math, reading, and writing.
Campus Safety and Security: Measures include self-defense education, security escort services, informal discussions, and emergency telephones. There are lighted pathways/sidewalks, safety and security personnel trained in first aid and self-defense, 20-hour foot and vehicle patrol, and pamphlets and posters.
Programs of Study: DWU confers the B.A. degree. Associate and master's degrees are also awarded. Bachelor's degrees are awarded in BIOLOGICAL SCIENCE (biology/biological science), BUSINESS (accounting, business administration and management, and sports management), COMMUNICATIONS AND THE ARTS (art, communications, dramatic arts, English, and multimedia), COMPUTER AND PHYSICAL SCIENCE (computer science and mathematics), EDUCATION (athletic training, elementary, physical, and secondary), HEALTH PROFESSIONS (predentistry and premedicine), SOCIAL SCIENCE (behavioral science, criminal justice, history, human services, ministries, philosophy, psychology, religion, sociology, and youth ministry). Business and education are the largest.
Required: To graduate, students must complete a total of 125 credit hours, including 30 or more in the major, and at least 42 in upper-level courses, with a minimum 2.0 GPA. General education requirements include 6 hours of communication, literature and the arts, and social, psychological, and political thought, 3 to 5 of physical science, 3 to 4 each of math and cultural awareness, 3 each of history and philosophy/theology, and 2 of physical activities; students must demonstrate basic skills in reading, writing, and math. All new freshmen must take Forum and Advising courses.
Special: DWU offers internships, study abroad on a limited basis, work-study programs, a general studies degree, dual majors, student-designed minors, credit for experience, and credit/no credit options. There are 4 national honor societies and a freshman honors program.
Faculty/Classroom: 52% of faculty are male; 48%, female. All teach undergraduates. No introductory courses are taught by graduate students. The average class size in an introductory lecture is 32; in a laboratory, 17; and in a regular course, 20.
Requirements: The SAT or ACT is required. In addition, applicants must be graduates of an accredited secondary school or have a GED certificate. An interview is recommended. DWU requires applicants to be in the upper 50% of their class. A GPA of 2.0 is required. AP and CLEP credits are accepted. Important factors in the admissions decision are advanced placement or honor courses, extracurricular activities record, and parents or siblings attending the school.
Procedure: Freshmen are admitted fall, spring, and summer. Entrance exams should be taken during the senior year. Check with the school for current deadlines and fees. Applications are accepted on-line.
Transfer: 98 transfer students enrolled in a recent year. Students must submit official transcripts from all previous colleges attended. DWU will accept credits from regionally accredited institutions, but half the credits for the student's major must be completed at DWU. 30 of 125 credits required for the bachelor's degree must be completed at DWU.
Visiting: There are regularly scheduled orientations for prospective students, including a campus tour and meetings with faculty and students. There are guides for informal visits and visitors may sit in on classes and stay overnight. To schedule a visit, contact Enrollment Services.
Financial Aid: In a recent year, 100% of all full-time students received some form of financial aid. 87% of all full-time students received need-based aid. The average freshman award was $14,634. Need-based scholarships or need-based grants averaged $3829 ($4000 maximum); need-based self-help aid (loans and jobs) averaged $3262 ($4825 maximum); non-need-based athletic scholarships averaged $2807 ($10,070 maximum); and other non-need-based awards and non-need-based scholarships averaged $3654 ($13,170 maximum). 52% of undergraduates work part time. Average annual earnings from campus work are $860. The average financial indebtedness of the recent year's graduate was $17,125. DWU is a member of CSS. The FAFSA is required. Check with the school for current deadlines.
International Students: In a recent year, there were 8 international students enrolled. The school actively recruits these students. Satisfactory scores are required on the written TOEFL, the MELAB, and the SAT or the ACT.
Computers: All students may access the system 24 hours a day. There are no time limits and no fees. It is strongly recommended that all students have a personal computer. It is recommended that students in music, education, and computers and technology have personal computers.
Graduates: In a recent year, 96 bachelor's degrees were awarded. The most popular majors were business administration (28%), elementary education (15%), and criminal justice (10%). 3 companies recruited on campus in a recent year. Of the recent year's graduating class, 8% were enrolled in graduate school within 6 months of graduation.
Admissions Contact: Laura Miller, Director of Admissions Operations and Outreach Programming. A video is available.
E-mail: *admissions@dwu.edu* Web: *www.dwu.edu*

HURON UNIVERSITY

E-2

Huron, SD 57350-2798

(605) 352-8721
(800) 710-7159; Fax: (605) 352-7421

Full-time: 240 men, 205 women
Part-time: 40 men, 70 women
Graduate: 20 men, 10 women
Year: semesters, summer session
Application Deadline: see profile
Freshman Class: n/av
SAT or ACT: recommended

Faculty: 36
Ph.D.s: 25%
Student/Faculty: 9 to 1
Tuition: $7700
Room & Board: $3000

COMPETITIVE

Huron University, established as Huron College in 1883, is a private institution offering career-oriented programs in the arts and sciences, nursing, and professional studies. There are 4 undergraduate schools and 1 graduate school. Figures in the above capsule and in this profile are approximate. The library contains 62,000 volumes, and subscribes to 300 periodicals including electronic. Special learning facilities include a learning resource center. The 15-acre campus is in a small town 120 miles northwest of Sioux Falls. Including any residence halls, there are 7 buildings.
Student Life: Others are from 26 states, 14 foreign countries, and Canada. 68% are white. The average age of all undergraduates is 23.
Housing: 300 students can be accommodated in college housing, which includes coed dormitories and on-campus apartments. On-campus housing is guaranteed for all 4 years. 50% of students live on campus; of those, 85% remain on campus on weekends. Alcohol is not permitted. All students may keep cars.
Activities: There are no fraternities or sororities. There are 15 groups on campus, including cheerleading, choir, computers, ethnic, honors, international, newspaper, pep band, photography, professional, religious, social, social service, and student government. Popular campus events include Pow Wow Days, Paddle Days, and International Student Day.
Sports: There are 4 intercollegiate sports for men and 4 for women, and 15 intramural sports for men and 14 for women. Facilities include

saunas, an exercise room, a 2800-seat recreation center, and a 5000-seat arena.

Disabled Students: 75% of the campus is accessible. Wheelchair ramps, special parking, specially equipped rest rooms, special class scheduling, lowered drinking fountains, and a portable chair lift are available.

Services: Counseling and information services are available, as is tutoring in every subject. There is remedial math, reading, and writing.

Campus Safety and Security: Measures include informal discussions, pamphlets/posters/films, lighted pathways/sidewalks, and a night watchman.

Programs of Study: H.U. confers B.S. and B.S.N. degrees. Associate and master's degrees are also awarded. Bachelor's degrees are awarded in BUSINESS (banking and finance, business administration and management, human resources, management information systems, management science, marketing/retailing/merchandising, organizational behavior, and sports management), COMPUTER AND PHYSICAL SCIENCE (computer science), EDUCATION (elementary, physical, science, and secondary), ENGINEERING AND ENVIRONMENTAL DESIGN (systems engineering), HEALTH PROFESSIONS (health care administration and nursing), SOCIAL SCIENCE (criminal justice). Nursing is the strongest academically. Business administration is the largest.

Required: To graduate, students must complete at least 120 to 128 credit hours with a minimum GPA of 2.0. Required courses include an introduction to higher education, computers, career planning, and other general education classes.

Special: The university offers cooperative programs, cross-registration, internships, study abroad in England or Japan, work-study programs, general studies and B.A.-B.S. degrees, dual majors, credit for life experience, nondegree study, and pass/fail options. There are 5 national honor societies and 5 departmental honors programs.

Faculty/Classroom: 50% of faculty are male; 50%, female. The average class size in an introductory lecture is 30; in a laboratory, 15; and in a regular course, 20.

Requirements: The SAT or ACT is recommended. Applicants must be graduates of an accredited secondary school or have a GED certificate. An interview is recommended. A GPA of 2.0 is required. CLEP credit is accepted. Important factors in the admissions decision are advanced placement or honor courses, leadership record, and recommendations by school officials.

Procedure: Freshmen are admitted to all sessions. Entrance exams should be taken during the senior year. Check with the school for current deadlines and fee.

Transfer: 32 of 120 credits required for the bachelor's degree must be completed at H.U.

Visiting: There are regularly scheduled orientations for prospective students. There are guides for informal visits and visitors may sit in on classes and stay overnight. To schedule a visit, contact Director of Admissions.

Financial Aid: The CSS/Profile or FFS and PHEAA are required. Check with the school for current deadlines.

International Students: The school actively recruits these students. A satisfactory score is required on the written TOEFL.

Computers: There are no time limits and no fees.

Admissions Contact: Brad Smith, Director of Admissions. E-mail: *admissions@huron.edu* Web: *www.huron.edu*

MOUNT MARTY COLLEGE
C-4

Yankton, SD 57078-3724

(605) 668-1545
(800) 658-4552; Fax: (605) 668-1607

Full-time: 214 men, 498 women	**Faculty:** 35; IIB, --$
Part-time: 76 men, 301 women	**Ph.D.s:** 64%
Graduate: 50 men, 50 women	**Student/Faculty:** 20 to 1
Year: semesters, summer session	**Tuition:** $15,730
Application Deadline: open	**Room & Board:** $4860
Freshman Class: 397 accepted, 190 enrolled	
ACT: required	**COMPETITIVE**

Mount Marty College is a private, Catholic Benedictine liberal arts college, open to students of all faiths and backgrounds. Mount Marty prepares students for a contemporary world of work, service to the human community, and personal growth. There are 2 undergraduate and 3 graduate schools. In addition to regional accreditation, Mount Marty has baccalaureate program accreditation with ADA and NLN. The library contains 79,228 volumes, 11,624 microform items, and 8465 audio/video tapes/CDs/DVDs, and subscribes to 439 periodicals including electronic. Computerized library services include the card catalog, interlibrary loans, database searching, Internet access, and laptop Internet portals. Special learning facilities include a learning resource center and art gallery. The 80-acre campus is in a small town 60 miles northwest of Sioux City, Iowa, and 80 miles southwest of Sioux Falls. Including any residence halls, there are 11 buildings.

Student Life: 60% of undergraduates are from South Dakota. Students are from 25 states and 5 foreign countries. 79% are from public schools.

94% are white. 42% are Catholic; 36% claim no religious affiliation. The average age of freshmen is 19; all undergraduates, 26. 22% do not continue beyond their first year; 61% remain to graduate.

Housing: 352 students can be accommodated in college housing, which includes single-sex dorms. On-campus housing is guaranteed for all 4 years. 75% of students live on campus; of those, 60% remain on campus on weekends. Alcohol is not permitted. All students may keep cars.

Activities: There are no fraternities or sororities. There are 50 groups on campus, including band, cheerleading, choir, chorus, computers, dance, debate, drama, drill team, forensics, honors, jazz band, literary magazine, musical theater, newspaper, pep band, photography, political, professional, religious, social, social service, and student government. Popular campus events include Blue & Gold Days, formal dances, and Benedictine lecture series.

Sports: There are 6 intercollegiate sports for men and 6 for women, and 4 intramural sports for men and 4 for women. Facilities include volleyball and basketball courts, a jogging track, 2 racquetball courts, weight and training rooms, a 2220-seat stadium, a 1500-seat indoor gym, and a 700-seat auditorium.

Disabled Students: All of the campus is accessible. Wheelchair ramps, elevators, special parking, specially equipped rest rooms, special class scheduling, lowered drinking fountains, and lowered telephones are available.

Services: Counseling and information services are available, as is tutoring in most subjects. There is remedial math, reading, and writing.

Campus Safety and Security: Measures include 24-hour foot and vehicle patrol, security escort services, informal discussions, and emergency telephones. There are lighted pathways/sidewalks.

Programs of Study: Mount Marty confers B.A., B.S., and B.S.N. degrees. Associate and master's degrees are also awarded. Bachelor's degrees are awarded in BIOLOGICAL SCIENCE (biology/biological science), BUSINESS (accounting and business administration and management), COMMUNICATIONS AND THE ARTS (English, journalism, and music), COMPUTER AND PHYSICAL SCIENCE (chemistry, computer science, mathematics, and radiological technology), EDUCATION (athletic training, elementary, physical, secondary, and special), ENGINEERING AND ENVIRONMENTAL DESIGN (environmental science), HEALTH PROFESSIONS (health care administration, medical technology, and nursing), SOCIAL SCIENCE (behavioral science, criminal justice, food production/management/services, history, religion, and social science). Nursing, business, and teacher education are the strongest academically.

Required: To graduate, all students must complete at least 128 credit hours, with a minimum GPA of 2.0. General education requirements include 10 credit hours in religious studies/philosophy, 9 in humanities, 6 in English, 4 each in math, natural science, and lab science, and 3 in speech.

Special: Mount Marty offers co-op programs, internships, student-designed majors in selected studies, an accelerated degree program in business administration, credit for work, life, and military experience, and pass/fail options. There are 8 national honor societies, a freshman honors program, and 7 departmental honors programs.

Faculty/Classroom: 54% of faculty are male; 46%, female. All teach undergraduates. No introductory courses are taught by graduate students. The average class size in an introductory lecture is 30; in a laboratory, 15; and in a regular course, 20.

Admissions: The ACT scores for the 2005-2006 freshman class were: 10% below 21, 50% between 21 and 23, 30% between 24 and 26, 5% between 27 and 28, and 5% above 28. 10% of the current freshmen were in the top fifth of their class; 56% were in the top two fifths. 5 freshmen graduated first in their class.

Requirements: The ACT is required. In addition, applicants must be graduates of an accredited secondary school or have a GED certificate. An audition and an interview are recommended. A GPA of 2.0 is required. AP and CLEP credits are accepted.

Procedure: Freshmen are admitted fall, spring, and summer. Entrance exams should be taken by October of the senior year. There is a deferred admissions plan. Application deadlines are open. Applications are accepted on-line.

Transfer: 60 transfer students enrolled in 2004-2005. Transfer students with fewer than 28 semester hours must submit high school and college transcripts. A minimum GPA of 2.0 and at least 64 credit hours are required. An interview is recommended. 32 of 128 credits required for the bachelor's degree must be completed at Mount Marty.

Visiting: There are regularly scheduled orientations for prospective students, including campus tours, faculty appointments, and admission and financial aid information. There are guides for informal visits and visitors may sit in on classes and stay overnight. To schedule a visit, contact Director of Admissions.

Financial Aid: In 2005-2006, 99% of all full-time students received some form of financial aid. 84% of all full-time students received need-based aid. The average freshman award was $12,343. 60% of undergraduates work part time. Average annual earnings from campus work are $1500. The average financial indebtedness of the 2005 graduate was $17,407. The FAFSA is required. The deadline for filing freshman financial aid applications for fall entry is March 1.

International Students: There are 5 international students enrolled. The school actively recruits these students. They must receive a satisfactory score on the TOEFL.

Computers: Wireless access is available. All full-time students receive laptop computers to utilize the wireless Internet connections. All students may access the system 24 hours, 7 days per week. There are no time limits and no fees.

Graduates: The most popular majors were health professions (28%), business (23%), and education (15%). In an average class, 30% graduate in 4 years or less, 41% graduate in 5 years or less, and 44% graduate in 6 years or less. Of the 2004 graduating class, 5% were enrolled in graduate school within 6 months of graduation and 94% were employed.

Admissions Contact: Brandi Tschumper, Director of Admissions.
E-mail: *mmcadmit@mtmc.edu* Web: *http://www.mtmc.edu*

NATIONAL AMERICAN UNIVERSITY   B-3

Rapid City, SD 57701   (605) 394-4827
                                   (800) 843-8892; Fax: (605) 394-4871

Full-time: 158 men, 153 women	**Faculty:** 15
Part-time: 77 men, 75 women	**Ph.D.s:** 5%
Graduate: 37 men, 31 women	**Student/Faculty:** 21 to 1
Year: quarters, summer session	**Tuition:** $11,090
Application Deadline: open	**Room & Board:** $3730
Freshman Class: n/av	
SAT or ACT: not required	**NONCOMPETITIVE**

National American University, founded in 1941, is a private institution that offers undergraduate programs in all aspects of business. The college has branch campuses in Sioux Falls and at Ellsworth Air Force Base, South Dakota; Albuquerque, New Mexico; Minneapolis/St. Paul, Minnesota; Kansas City, Missouri; Colorado Springs and Denver, Colorado; Rio Rancho, New Mexico, Mall of America, Bloomington, Minnesota, and Brooklyn Center, Minnesota. In addition to regional accreditation, NAU has baccalaureate program accreditation with CAHEA. The library contains 31,018 volumes and 71 audio/video tapes/CDs/DVDs, and subscribes to 268 periodicals including electronic. Computerized library services include interlibrary loans, database searching, and Internet access. Special learning facilities include a learning resource center. The Animal Health Care Center and Medical Assisting Room are instructional facilities set up as doctors' offices. The 8-acre campus is in a small town 360 miles from Sioux Falls and 420 miles from Denver, Colorado. Including any residence halls, there are 7 buildings.

Student Life: 60% of undergraduates are from South Dakota. Students are from 23 states, 6 foreign countries, and Canada. 75% are white; 13% foreign nationals. The average age of freshmen is 35; all undergraduates, 30. 43% do not continue beyond their first year.

Housing: 260 students can be accommodated in college housing, which includes single-sex and coed dorms. On-campus housing is guaranteed for all 4 years. 79% of students commute. Alcohol is not permitted. All students may keep cars.

Activities: There are no fraternities or sororities. There are 10 groups on campus, including arts and music, computers, ethnic, international, political, professional, social, social service, and student government. Popular campus events include Maverick Day, spring and fall picnics, and dances.

Sports: There is 1 intercollegiate sport for men and 2 for women, and 2 intramural sports for men and 2 for women. Facilities include a 500-seat gym, a weight room,and rodeo facilities.

Disabled Students: 99% of the campus is accessible. Wheelchair ramps, elevators, special parking, and lowered drinking fountains are available.

Services: Counseling and information services are available, as is tutoring in most subjects. There is remedial math, reading, and writing. Some technical classes are tutored by instructors.

Campus Safety and Security: Measures include informal discussions, pamphlets/posters/films, emergency telephones, and lighted pathways/sidewalks. There are and security guards on duty all evenings until morning.

Programs of Study: NAU confers the B.S. degree. Associate and master's degrees are also awarded. Bachelor's degrees are awarded in AGRICULTURE (equine science), BUSINESS (accounting, business administration and management, and tourism), COMPUTER AND PHYSICAL SCIENCE (information sciences and systems), EDUCATION (athletic training), HEALTH PROFESSIONS (allied health, and veterinary science), SOCIAL SCIENCE (paralegal studies). Accounting, veterinary technology, and business administration are the strongest academically. Business administration, accounting, and equine studies are the largest.

Required: To graduate, students must complete 192 quarter credit hours with a 2.0 GPA in major courses. Students are required to take 76 hours of general education courses, including 12 hours each of communications, math, social science, and humanities, 8 hours of science, 4 hours of speech, and 16 hours of electives.

Special: National offers internships in veterinary technology equine studies, and paralegal studies, study abroad, work-study programs on campus and with nonprofit organizations, accelerated degree programs in all majors, B.A.-B.S. degrees in accounting, computer information systems, management information systems, business administration, paralegal studies, and applied management. A general studies degree, credit for life experience, nondegree study, and pass/fail options are also available. Operation Bootstrap allows qualified U.S. Air Force personnel to complete their college degrees on an accelerated basis. There is 1 national honor society.

Faculty/Classroom: 38% of faculty are male; 62%, female. The average class size in an introductory lecture is 30; in a laboratory, 10; and in a regular course, 25.

Requirements: Applicants must be graduates of an accredited secondary school or have the GED. An interview is recommended. CLEP credit is accepted.

Procedure: Freshmen are admitted to all sessions. Entrance exams should be taken before classes begin. There are early admissions deferred admissions and rolling admissions plans. Application deadlines are open. Application fee is $25. Applications are accepted on-line.

Transfer: Applicants must submit transcripts of all high school and college work. Grades of C or better transfer for credit. An interview is recommended. 48 of 192 quarter credit hours required for the bachelor's degree must be completed at NAU.

Visiting: There are regularly scheduled orientations for prospective students. Visits or tours are available anytime with 1 day's notice. Orientations are scheduled at the beginning of each quarter. There are guides for informal visits and visitors may sit in on classes and stay overnight. To schedule a visit, contact the Admissions Office.

Financial Aid: In 2005-2006, 91% of all full-time freshmen and 89% of continuing full-time students received some form of financial aid. The average freshman award was $2500. The FAFSA, and the college's own financial statement are required.

International Students: There are 19 international students enrolled. The school actively recruits these students. They must score satisfactorily on the written TOEFL.

Computers: Wireless access is available. The library has computer labs available for student use. All students may access the system from 7 A.M. to 8 P.M. Students may access the system 90 minutes if another student is waiting. There are no fees.

Graduates: From July 1, 2004 to June 30, 2005, 56 bachelor's degrees were awarded. The most popular majors were business administration (50%), health care management (16%), and accounting (5%).

Admissions Contact: Angela Beck, Director of Admissions.
E-mail: *abeck@rc.national.edu* Web: *www.national.edu*

NORTHERN STATE UNIVERSITY   D-1

Aberdeen, SD 57401   (605) 626-2544
                                   (800) 678-5330; Fax: (605) 626-2587

Full-time: 683 men, 912 women	**Faculty:** 94; IIA, --$
Part-time: 306 men, 524 women	**Ph.D.s:** 80%
Graduate: 62 men, 144 women	**Student/Faculty:** 17 to 1
Year: semesters, summer session	**Tuition:** $4699 ($9687)
Application Deadline: August 15	**Room & Board:** $3558
Freshman Class: 783 applied, 737 accepted, 383 enrolled	
SAT Verbal/Math: 550/525*	**ACT:** 21 **COMPETITIVE**

Northern State University, established in 1901, is a state-supported institution offering undergraduate and graduate programs in the liberal arts and sciences, business, and education. Distance delivery technology is a core mission in all programs, especially all levels of teacher preparation. There are 4 undergraduate schools and 1 graduate school. In addition to regional accreditation, Northern State has baccalaureate program accreditation with NASM and NCATE. The library contains 199,064 volumes and 397,614 microform items, and subscribes to 150 periodicals including electronic. Computerized library services include the card catalog, interlibrary loans, database searching, Internet access, and laptop Internet portals. Special learning facilities include a learning resource center, art gallery, radio station, TV station, and fine arts center. The 72-acre campus is in an urban area one-half mile south of Aberdeen's city center. Including any residence halls, there are 21 buildings.

Student Life: 80% of undergraduates are from South Dakota. Others are from 33 states, 15 foreign countries, and Canada. 79% are white. The average age of freshmen is 18; all undergraduates, 23. 30% do not continue beyond their first year; 45% remain to graduate.

Housing: 930 students can be accommodated in college housing, which includes single-sex and coed dorms. On-campus housing is guaranteed for all 4 years. 64% of students commute. Alcohol is not permitted. All students may keep cars.

Activities: There are no fraternities or sororities. There are 100 groups on campus, including art, band, cheerleading, chess, choir, chorale, chorus, computers, dance, debate, drama, drill team, honors, international, jazz band, marching band, musical theater, newspaper, orchestra, pep band, photography, political, professional, radio and TV, religious, social, social service, student government, and symphony. Popular campus events include Gypsy Day, Gypsy Week, and I Hate Winter Weekend.

Sports: There are 7 intercollegiate sports for men and 5 for women, and 14 intramural sports for men and 12 for women. Facilities include a sports complex that houses a football stadium and an all-weather track, and a phys ed building that houses a 160-meter track, an Olympic-size pool, a weight room, 3 racquetball courts, a human performance lab, 2 basketball courts, and an 8300-seat arena.

Disabled Students: 90% of the campus is accessible. Wheelchair ramps, elevators, special parking, specially equipped rest rooms, lowered drinking fountains, lowered telephones, and curb cuts are available.

Services: Counseling and information services are available, as is tutoring in most subjects. There is remedial math, reading, and writing. There is an educational media center, a math lab, reading and writing centers, an ASL interpreter for the deaf, and a speech, language, and hearing clinic.

Campus Safety and Security: Measures include 24-hour foot and vehicle patrol, self-defense education, security escort services, and informal discussions. There are pamphlets/posters/films, emergency telephones, and lighted pathways/sidewalks.

Programs of Study: Northern State confers B.A., B.S., B.M.E., and B.S.Ed. degrees. Associate and master's degrees are also awarded. Bachelor's degrees are awarded in BIOLOGICAL SCIENCE (biology/biological science), BUSINESS (accounting, banking and finance, business administration and management, business economics, international business management, marketing/retailing/merchandising, and personnel management), COMMUNICATIONS AND THE ARTS (English, fine arts, French, German, music, and Spanish), COMPUTER AND PHYSICAL SCIENCE (chemistry, and mathematics), EDUCATION (art, business, early childhood, elementary, foreign languages, health, middle school, music, physical, science, secondary, and special), ENGINEERING AND ENVIRONMENTAL DESIGN (environmental science), HEALTH PROFESSIONS (medical laboratory technology, predentistry, premedicine, and speech pathology/audiology), SOCIAL SCIENCE (community services, criminal justice, economics, history, human services, physical fitness/movement, political science/government, prelaw, psychology, social science, and sociology). Business and education are the strongest academically.

Required: Students must complete a minimum of 128 semester hours, with 27 to 36 in the major, and must maintain a 2.0 minimum GPA. The core curriculum consists of courses in English, history, fine arts, science, math, and psychology. In addition, there are specific course requirements. All students must pass a comprehensive exam.

Special: Opportunities are provided for internships, a Washington semester, work-study programs, a B.A.-B.S. degree, dual majors, a general studies degree, credit by exam, and nondegree study. Study abroad and a co-op program in international business are available. Technology proficiency certification is available with a diverse selection of certifications. There are 4 national honor societies, a freshman honors program, and 4 departmental honors programs.

Faculty/Classroom: 70% of faculty are male; 30%, female. 100% both teach and do research. No introductory courses are taught by graduate students. The average class size in an introductory lecture is 15 and in a laboratory, 18.

Admissions: 94% of the 2005-2006 applicants were accepted. 19% of the current freshmen were in the top fifth of their class; 43% were in the top two fifths.

Requirements: The ACT is required with a minimum composite score of 18, or students must earn a high school GPA of at least 2.6 on a 4.0 scale, or rank in the top 60% of their graduating class. Graduation from an accredited secondary school is required; a GED will be accepted. Applicants should submit a minimum academic record distributed as follows: 4 years of English, 3 each of math, science, and social studies, and one-half year of fine arts. A GPA of 2.0 is required. AP and CLEP credits are accepted. Important factors in the admissions decision are evidence of special talent, advanced placement or honor courses, and extracurricular activities record.

Procedure: Freshmen are admitted fall, spring, and summer. Entrance exams should be taken during the summer before the senior year. There are early admissions, deferred admissions, and rolling admissions plans. Applications should be filed by August 15 for fall entry. Notification is sent on a rolling basis. The fall 2005 application fee was $20.

Transfer: 253 transfer students enrolled in 2004-2005. Applicants must submit official transcripts from all previous colleges attended. D grades do not transfer. If the applicant has not maintained a C average, an ACT score that places the applicant in the upper 50% of college-bound freshmen may be submitted for consideration.

Visiting: There are regularly scheduled orientations for prospective students, consisting of a welcome presentation, registration, refreshments, an academic visit, a campus tour, lunch, a financial aid presentation, student panel, and a cost and scholarship presentation. There are guides for informal visits and visitors may sit in on classes and stay overnight. To schedule a visit, contact the Admissions Office.

Financial Aid: In a recent year, 80% of continuing full-time students received some form of financial aid. Northern State is a member of CSS. The CSS/Profile, FAFSA, FFS or SFS is required. The priority date for freshman financial aid applications for fall entry is March 1.

International Students: Satisfactory scores are required on the written TOEFL and the SAT or the ACT.

Computers: All students may access the system. There are no time limits and no fees.

Graduates: From July 1, 2004 to June 30, 2005, 339 bachelor's degrees were awarded. The most popular majors were business (35%), education (24%), and social sciences (16%). 5 companies recruited on campus in 2004-2005. Of the 2004 graduating class, 16% were enrolled in graduate school within 6 months of graduation and 84% were employed.

Admissions Contact: Allan Vogel, Director of Admissions.
E-mail: *admissions@wolf.northern.edu* Web: *www.northern.edu*

OGLALA LAKOTA COLLEGE   B-3

Kyle, SD 57752	(605) 455-2321; Fax: (605) 455-2787
Full-time: none	Faculty: n/av
Part-time: none	Ph.D.s: n/av
Graduate: none	Student/Faculty: n/av
Year: n/app	Tuition: $2000
Application Deadline: open	Room & Board: n/app
Freshman Class: n/av	
SAT or ACT: n/av	NONCOMPETITIVE

Oglala Lakota College was founded in 1971 by the Oglala Sioux Tribal Council to provide academic, tribal, and cultural resources for the Pine Ridge Reservation community, offering programs in business, teaching, and human services. There are 10 regional centers in addition to the central campus. Figures in the above capsule and in this profile are approximate. Special learning facilities include a learning resource center and archives, an American Indians collection, and an audio video studio. The campus is in a rural area spread over the 5,000 square miles of the Pine Ridge Indian Reservation in the state's Southwest corner. There are 5 buildings.

Programs of Study: Bachelor's degrees are awarded in BUSINESS (business administration and management), EDUCATION (business and elementary), SOCIAL SCIENCE (history, human services, and sociology).

Requirements: The SAT or ACT is not required. Applicants should be high school graduates or have the GED. Certification of degree of Indian blood from the tribal census office is required.

Procedure: Application deadlines are open.

Transfer: 30 of 128 credits required for the bachelor's degree must be completed at OLC.

Visiting: Visitors may sit in on classes.

Financial Aid: The FFS is required. Check with the school for current deadlines.

Computers: There are no time limits and no fees.

Admissions Contact: Billi K. Hornbeck, Registrar.

PRESENTATION COLLEGE   D-1

Aberdeen, SD 57401	(605) 229-8492
	(800) 437-6060; Fax: (605) 229-8518
Full-time: 60 men, 380 women	Faculty: 28; II B, --$
Part-time: 20 men, 170 women	Ph.D.s: 25%
Graduate: none	Student/Faculty: 16 to 1
Year: semesters, summer session	Tuition: $10,600
Application Deadline: open	Room & Board: $4200
Freshman Class: n/av	
ACT: required	LESS COMPETITIVE

Presentation College, founded in 1922 as Notre Dame Junior College, is an independent Catholic institution offering undergraduate degrees in nursing and allied health service management. Figures in the above capsule and in this profile are approximate. In addition to regional accreditation, Presentation has baccalaureate program accreditation with AHEA. The library contains 33,725 volumes, and subscribes to 221 periodicals including electronic. Computerized library services include the card catalog and interlibrary loans. Special learning facilities include a learning resource center. The 100-acre campus is in a small town. Including any residence halls, there are 8 buildings.

Student Life: 76% of undergraduates are from South Dakota. Others are from 6 states and Canada. 78% are white. 30% are Catholic; 29% Protestant.

Housing: 137 students can be accommodated in college housing, which includes single-sex dormitories. On-campus housing is guaranteed for all 4 years and is available on a first-come, first-served basis. 81% of students commute. Alcohol is not permitted. All students may keep cars.

Activities: There are no fraternities or sororities. There are some groups and organizations on campus, including chorus.

Sports: There are 5 intercollegiate sports for men and 5 for women, and 3 intramural sports for men and 3 for women.

Disabled Students: All of the campus is accessible. Wheelchair ramps, elevators, special parking, and specially equipped rest rooms are available.

Services: Counseling and information services are available, as is tutoring in every subject. There is remedial math, reading, and writing.

Campus Safety and Security: Measures include 24-hour foot and vehicle patrol, informal discussions, pamphlets/posters/films, and emergency telephones. There are lighted pathways/sidewalks.

Programs of Study: Presentation confers B.S., B.S.N., and B.S.W. degrees. Associate degrees are also awarded. Bachelor's degrees are awarded in BIOLOGICAL SCIENCE (biology/biological science), BUSINESS (business administration and management), COMMUNICATIONS AND THE ARTS (communications), COMPUTER AND PHYSICAL SCIENCE (radiological technology), HEALTH PROFESSIONS (health care administration and nursing), SOCIAL SCIENCE (social work). Nursing is the largest.

Required: Students must complete 128 semester hours, including 48 in upper-division courses and 36 in the major, with a minimum GPA of 2.0. The core curriculum consists of 18 hours of humanities and fine arts, 12 of social and behavioral sciences, 11 of natural sciences and math, and 10 of religious studies and philosophy.

Special: Certificate programs are available in phlebotomy, surgical technology, administrative assistance, business/accounting, and computer operating. An external degree program offers an accelerated schedule for working adults. Limited credit for experiential learning is possible. There is 1 national honor society and 2 departmental honors program.

Faculty/Classroom: 32% of faculty are male; 68%, female. All teach undergraduates.

Requirements: The ACT is required. In addition, prospective students must graduate from high school or hold a GED, and a GPA of 2.0 is recommended. A GPA of 2.0 is required. AP and CLEP credits are accepted. Important factors in the admissions decision are ability to finance college education, extracurricular activities record, and leadership record.

Procedure: Freshmen are admitted to all sessions. Check with the school for current application deadlines and fee. The college accepts all applicants. Applications are accepted on-line.

Transfer: 115 transfer students enrolled in a recent year. A 2.0 GPA on previous college work is recommended. 30 of 127 credits required for the bachelor's degree must be completed at Presentation.

Visiting: To schedule a visit, contact the Admissions Office at (605) 229-8492 or (800) 437-6060 ext.492 or admit@presentation.edu.

Financial Aid: In a recent year, 94% of all full-time freshmen and 97% of continuing full-time students received some form of financial aid. 88% of full-time freshmen and 89% of continuing full-time students received need-based aid. The average freshman award was $11,339. Need-based scholarships or need-based grants averaged $3933 ($7050 maximum); need-based self-help aid (loans and jobs) averaged $6694 ($7125 maximum); and other non-need-based awards and non-need-based scholarships averaged $9109 ($11,650 maximum). 100% of undergraduates work part time. Average annual earnings from campus work are $1500. The average financial indebtedness of the recent year's graduate was $26,737. Presentation is a member of CSS. The FAFSA is required. Check with the school for current deadlines.

International Students: There are 4 international students enrolled. A satisfactory score is required on the written TOEFL.

Computers: Computer students may access the system.

Graduates: 116 bachelor's degrees were awarded. The most popular majors were nursing (54%), radiologic technician (7%), and surgical technician (6%).

Admissions Contact: Joddy Meidinger, Director of Admissions and Financial Aid. E-mail: meidinger@presentation.edu

SINTE GLESKA UNIVERSITY   C-3

Rosebud, SD 57570   (605) 747-2263; Fax: (605) 747-2098

Full-time: 100 men, 240 women	**Faculty:** 23
Part-time: 1 woman	**Ph.Ds:** n/av
Graduate: 120 men, 320 women	**Student/Faculty:** 14 to 1
Year: semesters, summer session	**Tuition:** $2300
Application Deadline: open	**Room & Board:** n/app
Freshman Class: n/av	
SAT or ACT: not required	**NONCOMPETITIVE**

Sinte Gleska University, founded in 1970, is an independent institution offering undergraduate programs in business, fine arts, professional training, and technical studies. Figures in the above capsule and in this profile are approximate. There is 1 graduate school. The library contains 85,000 volumes. The 52-acre campus is in a rural area east of Mission. There are 7 buildings.

Student Life: 92% of undergraduates are from South Dakota. Others are from 1 state. All are from public schools. 85% are Native American/Eskimo; 15% white. The average age of all undergraduates is 31. 10% do not continue beyond their first year; 90% remain to graduate.

Housing: There are no residence halls. 100% of students commute. Alcohol is not permitted.

Activities: There are no fraternities or sororities. There are some groups and organizations on campus, including newspaper and photography. Popular campus events include Founders Day.

Sports: There are 4 intramural sports for men and 3 for women.

Disabled Students: All of the campus is accessible. Wheelchair ramps, special parking, specially equipped rest rooms, and lowered drinking fountains are available.

Services: Counseling and information services are available, as is tutoring in every subject.

Campus Safety and Security: Measures include shuttle buses, informal discussions, and an evening security guard.

Programs of Study: Sinte Gleska confers B.A. and B.S. degrees. Associate and master's degrees are also awarded. Bachelor's degrees are awarded in COMMUNICATIONS AND THE ARTS (art), EDUCATION (early childhood and elementary), HEALTH PROFESSIONS (mental health/human services), SOCIAL SCIENCE (human services). Education and human services are the strongest academically.

Required: To graduate, students must complete at least 128 credits with a GPA of 2.0; education majors must have a 2.5. All students must fulfill the core curriculum requirements.

Special: The college offers work-study programs, accelerated degree programs, a general studies degree, and pass/fail options.

Requirements: In addition, applicants must be graduates of accredited secondary schools or have earned a GED.

Procedure: Freshmen are admitted to all sessions. Entrance exams should be taken before admission. Application deadlines are open. Check with the school for current fee.

Transfer: Applicants must submit an official transcript from their previous college. 68 of 128 credits required for the bachelor's degree must be completed at Sinte Gleska.

Visiting: There are regularly scheduled orientations for prospective students. There are guides for informal visits and visitors may stay overnight. To schedule a visit, contact Cheryl Crazy Bull, Vice President at (605) 747-2263, ext. 52.

Financial Aid: The SFS is required. Check with the school for current deadlines.

Computers: Students may access the system 3 lab hours. Check with the school for current fee.

Admissions Contact: Michelle Zephier, Registrar.
E-mail: mzephr@rosebud.sinte.edu

SOUTH DAKOTA BOARD OF REGENTS

The South Dakota Board of Regents governs the 6 public universities: Black Hills State University, Dakota State University, Northern State University, South Dakota School of Mines and Technology, South Dakota State University, and the University of South Dakota. In addition, the regents operate off-campus attendance centers in several locations statewide. In 2000, the Regents created the Electronic University Consortium, offering courses and degrees on-line from the six universities. In the past decade, the thrust of Regental policies has been to foster a unified system of public higher education while maintaining quality and accountability through wise resource management. To that end, at least one center of excellence has been established at each university. Additional initiatives include a proficiency exam of all rising juniors, information technology proficiency requirements, interuniversity faculty discipline councils, common course numbering among the six universities, student technology fellows, and faculty salary increases based on performance and market. The Regents have integrated technology throughout the system by wiring all campus buildings, and establishing a statewide e-learning center to enhance teacher education and delivery of distance education courses for high school students. Total 2005 fall enrollment is 30,720. For more info, visit www.sdbor.edu. Profiles of the universities appear in this section.

SOUTH DAKOTA SCHOOL OF MINES AND TECHNOLOGY   B-3

Rapid City, SD 57701-3995   (605) 394-2414
(800) 544-8162, ext. 2400; Fax: (605) 394-1268

Full-time: 1202 men, 390 women	**Faculty:** 107; IIA, av$
Part-time: 206 men, 259 women	**Ph.Ds:** 85%
Graduate: 195 men, 61 women	**Student/Faculty:** 15 to 1
Year: semesters, summer session	**Tuition:** $4757 ($9744)
Application Deadline: August 15	**Room & Board:** $2867
Freshman Class: 727 applied, 682 accepted, 365 enrolled	
SAT Verbal/Math: 555/555*	**ACT:** 25 **COMPETITIVE+**

South Dakota School of Mines and Technology, founded in 1885, is a public university offering undergraduate and graduate programs in engineering, science, and mathematics. There are 4 undergraduate schools and 1 graduate school. In addition to regional accreditation, SDSM&T has baccalaureate program accreditation with ABET, ACS, and CSAB. The library contains 365,367 volumes, 71,285 microform items, and 1455 audio/video tapes/CDs/DVDs, and subscribes to 516 periodicals including electronic. Computerized library services include the card catalog, interlibrary loans, database searching, and Internet access. Special learning facilities include a learning resource center, art gallery, natural history museum, planetarium, radio station, and a geology museum. The 120-acre campus is in a suburban area 350 miles northeast of Denver. Including any residence halls, there are 18 buildings.

Student Life: 69% of undergraduates are from South Dakota. Others are from 34 states, 12 foreign countries, and Canada. 86% are white. The average age of freshmen is 19; all undergraduates, 22. 27% do not continue beyond their first year; 40% remain to graduate.

Housing: 560 students can be accommodated in college housing, which includes single-sex and coed dormitories, fraternity houses, and sorority houses. On-campus housing is available on a first-come, first-served basis. 68% of students commute. Alcohol is not permitted. All students may keep cars.

Activities: 22% of men belong to 4 national fraternities; 23% of women belong to 2 national sororities. There are 74 groups on campus, including art, band, biking, choir, chorale, chorus, computers, drama, drill team, ethnic, film, honors, international, jazz band, newspaper, orchestra, pep band, political, professional, radio and TV, religious, SAAD, ski club, social, social service, student government, and yearbook. Popular campus events include M-Week, Christmas chorale concert, and International Cultural Exposition.

Sports: There are 5 intercollegiate sports for men and 5 for women, and 15 intramural sports for men and 15 for women. Facilities include a football field, track, a 2350-seat gym, sand volleyball court, swimming pool, squash/racquetball courts, and a weight room.

Disabled Students: 90% of the campus is accessible. Wheelchair ramps, elevators, special parking, specially equipped rest rooms, special class scheduling, lowered drinking fountains, and an ADA lab with specialized workstations, software, and hardware to aid students with visual, auditory, and mobility impairments and dyslexia are available.

Services: Counseling and information services are available, as is tutoring in most subjects. There is a reader service for the blind and remedial math.

Campus Safety and Security: Measures include 24-hour foot and vehicle patrol, security escort services, informal discussions, and pamphlets/posters/films. There are emergency telephones and lighted pathways/sidewalks.

Programs of Study: SDSM&T confers the B.S. degree. Associate, master's, and doctoral degrees are also awarded. Bachelor's degrees are awarded in COMPUTER AND PHYSICAL SCIENCE (chemistry, computer science, geology, mathematics, and physics), ENGINEERING AND ENVIRONMENTAL DESIGN (chemical engineering, civil engineering, computer engineering, electrical/electronics engineering, geological engineering, industrial engineering, mechanical engineering, metallurgical engineering, and mining and mineral engineering), SOCIAL SCIENCE (interdisciplinary studies). Engineering is the strongest academically. Mechanical engineering, electrical engineering, and civil engineering are the largest.

Required: Students must complete 128 credits for the science major or 136 credits for the engineering major, and maintain a minimum GPA of 2.0. Included in these requirements are 16 credit hours each of math at a level of calculus and above, basic science, and humanities/social science (for engineering, 3 credits must be at the 300 or above level). State regents mandated distribution requirements include 6 credits each of written communications, social sciences, arts/humanities, science, and cultural diversity; 3 credits each of speech communications and math; and 2 credits of information technology literacy, plus completion of an exam.

Special: Opportunities are provided for study abroad, co-op programs, internships, work-study programs, dual majors, an interdisciplinary science major, credit by exam, student-designed majors in interdisciplinary studies, and nondegree study. There are 5 national honor societies, including Phi Beta Kappa.

Faculty/Classroom: 80% of faculty are male; 20%, female. 95% teach undergraduates, 20% do research, and 90% do both. Graduate students teach 4% of introductory courses. The average class size in an introductory lecture is 50; in a laboratory, 24; and in a regular course, 25.

Admissions: 94% of the 2005-2006 applicants were accepted. The ACT scores for the 2005-2006 freshman class were: 20% below 21, 29% between 21 and 23, 26% between 24 and 26, 13% between 27 and 28, and 11% above 28. 35% of the current freshmen were in the top fifth of their class; 62% were in the top two fifths. In a recent year, there were 2 National Merit finalists and 7 semifinalists. 18 freshmen graduated first in their class.

Requirements: The SAT is accepted, but the ACT is preferred, with a minimum composite score. Graduation from an accredited secondary school is required. A GED is accepted. Applicants must submit high school credits, distributed as follows: 4 years of English, 3 each of math,

lab science, social studies, and 1/2 year each of fine arts and computer science. SDSM&T requires applicants to be in the upper 60% of their class. A GPA of 2.6 is required. AP and CLEP credits are accepted.

Procedure: Freshmen are admitted fall and spring. Entrance exams should be taken preferably in October and December. There is a rolling admissions plan. Applications should be filed by August 15 for fall entry and January 15 for spring entry. Notification is sent on a rolling basis. The fall 2005 application fee was $20. Applications are accepted on-line.

Transfer: 110 transfer students enrolled in 2004-2005. Transfer students must submit an official transcript from the previous college and must have maintained a minimum GPA of 2.0, with 2.5 recommended. 32 of 128 credits required for the bachelor's degree must be completed at SDSM&T.

Visiting: There are regularly scheduled orientations for prospective students, including a campus tour, discussions, training, and a meal. There are guides for informal visits and visitors may sit in on classes. To schedule a visit, contact the Admissions Office at *admissions@sdsmt.edu.*

Financial Aid: In 2004-2005, 56% of all full-time freshmen received some form of financial aid. 33% of full-time freshmen and 29% of continuing full-time students received need-based aid. The average freshman award was $6631. Need-based scholarships or need-based grants averaged $520; need-based self-help aid (loans and jobs) averaged $3383; non-need-based athletic scholarships averaged $2515; and other non-need-based awards and non-need-based scholarships averaged $2465. 23% of undergraduates work part time. Average annual earnings from campus work are $1500. The average financial indebtedness of the 2005 graduate was $1623. The FAFSA is required. The deadline for filing freshman financial aid applications for fall entry is March 15.

International Students: In a recent year 22 international students were enrolled. The school actively recruits these students. Satisfactory scores are required on the written TOEFL, the IELTS, and the ACT.

Computers: Wireless access is available. All students may access the system 24 hours per day. There are no time limits and no fees.

Graduates: From July 1, 2004 to June 30, 2005, 249 bachelor's degrees were awarded. The most popular majors were mechanical engineering (22%), civil engineering (3%), and interdisciplinary sciences (1%). In an average class, 12% graduate in 4 years or less, 28% graduate in 5 years or less, and 40% graduate in 6 years or less. 116 companies recruited on campus in 2004-2005. Of the 2004 graduating class, 21% were enrolled in graduate school within 6 months of graduation and 83% were employed.

Admissions Contact: Office of Admissions.
E-mail: *admissions@.sdsmt.edu* Web: *http://www.sdsmt.edu/admissions*

SOUTH DAKOTA STATE UNIVERSITY

F-3

Brookings, SD 57007

(605) 688-4121
(800) 952-3541; Fax: (605) 688-6891

Full-time: 4022 men, 3727 women	**Faculty:** IIA, --$
Part-time: 575 men, 1270 women	**Ph.D.s:** 78%
Graduate: 555 men, 789 women	**Student/Faculty:** n/av
Year: semesters, summer session	**Tuition:** $5046 ($9969)
Application Deadline: open	**Room & Board:** $4769
Freshman Class: 3641 applied, 3376 accepted, 1869 enrolled	
ACT: 23	**SAT:** not required **COMPETITIVE**

South Dakota State University, founded in 1881, is a public land-grant institution offering undergraduate programs in agriculture and biological sciences, arts and science, engineering, family and consumer sciences, nursing, pharmacy, education and counseling, and general registration. There are 8 undergraduate schools and 1 graduate school. In addition to regional accreditation, SDSU has baccalaureate program accreditation with AAFCS, ABET, ACEJMC, ACPE, ACS, ADA, AHEA, CCNE, NASM, NCATE, and NLN. The library contains 890,319 volumes, 923,269 microform items, and 3217 audio/video tapes/CDs/DVDs, and subscribes to 27,754 periodicals including electronic. Computerized library services include the card catalog, interlibrary loans, database searching, and Internet access. Special learning facilities include an art gallery, radio station, TV station, arboretum, Agricultural Heritage Museum, Northern Plains Biostress Lab, and animal disease research and diagnostic lab, and South Dakota Art Museum. The 272-acre campus is in a small town 50 miles north of Sioux Falls, 200 miles west of Minneapolis. Including any residence halls, there are 152 buildings.

Student Life: 71% of undergraduates are from South Dakota. Others are from 39 states, 19 foreign countries, and Canada. 89% are white. The average age of freshmen is 19; all undergraduates, 22. 25% do not continue beyond their first year; 53% remain to graduate.

Housing: 3652 students can be accommodated in college housing, which includes coed dorms, on-campus apartments, married-student housing, fraternity houses, and sorority houses. In addition, there are honors houses special-interest houses, a health professions learning community (first-year students), an engineering learning community, and substance-free house. On-campus housing is available on a first-come, first-served basis. 67% of students commute. Alcohol is not permitted. All students may keep cars.

Activities: 5% of men belong to 7 national fraternities; 2% of women belong to 3 national sororities. There are 200 groups on campus, including art, band, cheerleading, chess, choir, chorale, chorus, computers, dance, debate, drama, drill team, ethnic, film, forensics, gay, honors, international, jazz band, literary magazine, marching band, musical theater, newspaper, opera, orchestra, pep band, photography, political, professional, radio and TV, religious, social, social service, student government, and symphony. Popular campus events include Little International, Engineering Exploration Days, and Hobo Days.

Sports: There are 10 intercollegiate sports for men and 11 for women, and 12 intramural sports for men and 12 for women. Facilities include a phys ed complex, an intramural building, an outdoor track, lighted tennis courts, a wellness center, intramural football and softball fields, and soccer and rugby fields.

Disabled Students: Wheelchair ramps, elevators, special parking, specially equipped rest rooms, special class scheduling, lowered drinking fountains, lowered telephones, and special housing are available. All academic programs can be made accessible.

Services: Counseling and information services are available, as is tutoring in most subjects, including accounting, biology, chemistry, economics, physics, Spanish and speech. There is a reader service for the blind, and remedial math, reading, and writing.

Campus Safety and Security: Measures include 24-hour foot and vehicle patrol, self-defense education, security escort services, and informal discussions. There are pamphlets/posters/films, emergency telephones, and lighted pathways/sidewalks.

Programs of Study: SDSU confers B.A., B.S., B.A.T.S., B.M.E., and B.S.E.D. degrees. Associate, master's, and doctoral degrees are also awarded. Bachelor's degrees are awarded in AGRICULTURE (agricultural business management, agricultural economics, agriculture, agronomy, animal science, dairy science, fish and game management, horticulture, and range/farm management), BIOLOGICAL SCIENCE (biochemistry, biology/biological science, microbiology, and nutrition), BUSINESS (apparel and accessories marketing and hotel/motel and restaurant management), COMMUNICATIONS AND THE ARTS (art, communications, dramatic arts, English, German, graphic design, journalism, music, music business management, and Spanish), COMPUTER AND PHYSICAL SCIENCE (chemistry, computer science, mathematics, physics, and software engineering), EDUCATION (agricultural, art, athletic training, early childhood, health, home economics, music, physical, secondary, and vocational), ENGINEERING AND ENVIRONMENTAL DESIGN (agricultural engineering, agricultural engineering technology, civil engineering, construction management, electrical/electronics engineering, electrical/electronics engineering technology, engineering physics, engineering technology, environmental engineering, industrial administration/management, interior design, landscape architecture/design, manufacturing technology, and mechanical engineering), HEALTH PROFESSIONS (clinical science, nursing, and pharmacy), SOCIAL SCIENCE (consumer services, economics, family/consumer studies, food production/management/services, food science, French studies, geography, history, human development, liberal arts/general studies, parks and recreation management, political science/government, psychology, rural sociology, safety management, and sociology). Pharmacy, engineering, and nursing are the strongest academically. Nursing, sociology, and economics are the largest.

Required: Students must complete 128 credits (136 for engineering and nursing), with at least 32 in the major, and must maintain a 2.0 minimum GPA. Additional requirements for graduation are 6 credits each in natural sciences, written communication, social sciences/diversity, and humanities and arts/diversity, 3 credits each in social responsibility/cultural and aesthetic awareness, math, oral communications, and land and natural resources, and 2 credits in personal wellness. There are also expectations in globalization, advance writing requirements, and computer and information literacy.

Special: Co-op programs in elementary education and social work, internships, work-study programs, B.A.-B.S. degrees, and interdisciplinary majors including agricultural journalism, environmental management, and wildlife and fisheries science are available. SDSU offers cross-registration with Dakota State University, Black Hills State University, the University of South Dakota, Northern State University, and South Dakota School of Mines and Technology. Opportunities are provided for dual majors, study abroad in more than 40 countries, credit by exam, student-designed majors, credit for military experience, nondegree study, a general studies degree, and pass/fail options. There are 32 national honor societies and a freshman honors program.

Faculty/Classroom: 63% of faculty are male; 37%, female. 78% teach undergraduates, 14% do research, and 87% do both. Graduate students teach 30% of introductory courses. The average class size in an introductory lecture is 50; in a laboratory, 30; and in a regular course, 30.

Admissions: 93% of the 2005-2006 applicants were accepted. The ACT scores for the 2005-2006 freshman class were: 33% below 21, 23% between 21 and 23, 28% between 24 and 26, 10% between 27 and 28, and 6% above 28. 30% of the current freshmen were in the top fifth of their class; 59% were in the top two fifths. There was 1 National Merit finalist and 3 semifinalists. 106 freshmen graduated first in their class.

Requirements: The ACT is required. Students must be in the top 60% of their class, or have a 2.6 GPA in required classes. Graduation from an accredited secondary school is required. A GED will be accepted. Applicants must submit 4 years of English, 3 years each of social studies, math, and science, and 1 year of fine arts and have a GPA of 2.0 in the required courses. SDSU requires applicants to be in the upper 60% of their class. A GPA of 2.6 is required. AP and CLEP credits are accepted. Important factors in the admissions decision are advanced placement or honor courses, evidence of special talent, and extracurricular activities record.

Procedure: Freshmen are admitted to all sessions. Entrance exams should be taken by spring of the junior year. There is a rolling admissions plan. Application deadlines are open. Application fee is $20. Notification is sent on a rolling basis. Applications are accepted on-line.

Transfer: 729 transfer students enrolled in 2004-2005. To be eligible for transfer, students must have been in good standing at the previous college and must have maintained a minimum GPA of 2.0 to 2.5, depending on the student's major. 32 of 128 credits required for most majors for the bachelor's degree must be completed at SDSU.

Visiting: There are regularly scheduled orientations for prospective students, including several new student orientation sessions which are offered each June. Students become acquainted with the university and student resources. They also meet with an academic adviser and register for fall semester classes. Information is sent to all admitted students. There are guides for informal visits and visitors may sit in on classes and stay overnight. To schedule a visit, contact the Admissions Office at *SDSU_Admissions@sdstate.edu.*

Financial Aid: In 2005-2006, 88% of all full-time freshmen and 84% of continuing full-time students received some form of financial aid. 74% of full-time freshmen and 71% of continuing full-time students received need-based aid. The average freshman award was $6140. Need-based scholarships or need-based grants averaged $3126 ($5410 maximum); need-based self-help aid (loans and jobs) averaged $2976 ($8425 maximum); non-need-based athletic scholarships averaged $5420 ($12,037 maximum); and other non-need-based awards and non-need-based scholarships averaged $1041 ($8500 maximum). 91% of undergraduates work part time. Average annual earnings from campus work are $1440. The average financial indebtedness of the 2005 graduate was $19,520. SDSU is a member of CSS. The FAFSA is required. The priority date for freshman financial aid applications for fall entry is March 10.

International Students: There are 26 international students enrolled. They must take the TOEFL.

Computers: Wireless access is available. All students have an e-mail address through the university, which can be accessed by their personal computer or on 1 of the 1022 computers in 8 labs that are located all across campus. Any student that lives in the residence halls can hook up to the Internet through the college network and has access to the wireless system on campus. Students off campus can request authorization for wireless access but laptops must have the required anti-virus software loaded before access is given. All students may access the system. There are no time limits and no fees. Nursing students are required to have laptops once in the accelerated program and graduate program. All students in the College of Engineering are required to have a personal computer.

Graduates: From July 1, 2004 to June 30, 2005, 1321 bachelor's degrees were awarded. The most popular majors were nursing (17%), economics (5%), and biology/biological sciences, general (4%). In an average class, 26% graduate in 4 years, 24% graduate in 5 years, and 5% graduate in 6 years.

Admissions Contact: Megan Dombek, Admissions Counselor.
E-mail: *Megan_Dombek@sdstate.edu* Web: *http://www.sdstate.edu*

UNIVERSITY OF SIOUX FALLS   F-3

Sioux Falls, SD 57105   (605) 331-6600
(800) 888-1047; Fax: (605) 331-6615

Full-time: 472 men, 554 women	**Faculty:** IIB, --$
Part-time: 94 men, 142 women	**Ph.D.s:** 68%
Graduate: 146 men, 198 women	**Student/Faculty:** n/av
Year: 4-1-4, summer session	**Tuition:** $15,900
Application Deadline: open	**Room & Board:** $4900
Freshman Class: 891 applied, 816 accepted, 254 enrolled	
SAT or ACT: required	**COMPETITIVE**

University of Sioux Falls, founded in 1883, is a private liberal arts institution affiliated with the American Baptist Churches. In addition to regional accreditation, USF has baccalaureate program accreditation with CSWE and NCATE. The library contains 78,000 volumes and 4600 audio/video tapes/CDs/DVDs, and subscribes to 450 periodicals including electronic. Computerized library services include the card catalog, interlibrary loans, and database searching. Special learning facilities include a learning resource center, radio station, and TV station. The 22-acre campus is in a suburban area 250 miles from Minneapolis/St. Paul, Minnesota and 180 miles from Omaha, Nebraska. Including any residence halls, there are 13 buildings.

Student Life: 65% of undergraduates are from South Dakota. Others are from 21 states, 10 foreign countries, and Canada. 95% are from public schools. 94% are white. 73% are Protestant; 14% Catholic; 13% claim no religious affiliation. The average age of freshmen is 18; all undergraduates, 21. 37% do not continue beyond their first year; 48% remain to graduate.

Housing: 350 students can be accommodated in college housing, which includes single-sex and coed dorms, on-campus apartments, and married-student housing. On-campus housing is guaranteed for the freshman year only, is available on a first-come, first-served basis, and is available on a lottery system for upperclassmen. Priority is given to out-of-town students. 62% of students commute. Alcohol is not permitted. All students may keep cars.

Activities: There are no fraternities or sororities. There are 35 groups on campus, including art, band, cheerleading, choir, chorale, chorus, computers, drama, ethnic, honors, international, jazz band, musical theater, newspaper, opera, orchestra, pep band, photography, political, professional, radio and TV, religious, social, social service, and student government. Popular campus events include Spring Formal, Staley Lectures, and Madrigals.

Sports: There are 8 intercollegiate sports for men and 8 for women, and 8 intramural sports for men and 8 for women. Facilities include a student lounge, a 160-meter running track, volleyball, tennis, badminton, racquetball, and basketball courts, aerobics facilities, exercise machines, a whirlpool, and a 700-seat gym.

Disabled Students: 54% of the campus is accessible. Wheelchair ramps, elevators, special parking, specially equipped rest rooms, special class scheduling, lowered drinking fountains, and lowered telephones are available.

Services: There is remedial math and reading.

Campus Safety and Security: Measures include self-defense education, security escort services, informal discussions, and pamphlets/posters/films. There are emergency telephones and lighted pathways/sidewalks.

Programs of Study: USF confers B.A. and B.S. degrees. Associate and master's degrees are also awarded. Bachelor's degrees are awarded in BIOLOGICAL SCIENCE (biology/biological science), BUSINESS (accounting, business administration and management, business economics, and marketing/retailing/merchandising), COMMUNICATIONS AND THE ARTS (communications, English, music, and speech/debate/rhetoric), COMPUTER AND PHYSICAL SCIENCE (chemistry, computer science, and mathematics), EDUCATION (art, early childhood, elementary, middle school, music, science, and secondary), HEALTH PROFESSIONS (medical laboratory technology and premedicine), SOCIAL SCIENCE (history, philosophy, political science/government, prelaw, psychology, religion, social work, and sociology). Business and elementary education are the strongest academically and are the largest.

Required: To graduate, all students must complete a minimum of 128 credit hours, with 64 hours in the major. Required courses include phys ed, computer science, religion, history, English, science, economics, political science, psychology, math, social science, cross-cultural experience, speech, and fine arts. A writing proficiency test and a minimum 2.0 GPA are also required.

Special: There are co-op programs with Augustana College, the Center for Public Higher Education, Dakota State University, and the North American Baptist Seminary. USF offers internships, study abroad in Japan, Central America, and China, an American Studies Program in Washington, D.C., and a January interim. Also available are on-campus work-study programs, B.A.-B.S. degrees, dual and student-designed interdisciplinary majors, a general studies degree, a 3-2 engineering degree, credit for life and work experience, and pass/fail options. There are 3 national honor societies, a freshman honors program, and 2 departmental honors programs.

Faculty/Classroom: 69% of faculty are male; 31%, female. All teach undergraduates and 60% do research. No introductory courses are taught by graduate students. The average class size in an introductory lecture is 40; in a laboratory, 15; and in a regular course, 20.

Admissions: 92% of the 2005-2006 applicants were accepted.

Requirements: The SAT or ACT is required. Applicants must be graduates of an accredited secondary school or have a GED certificate. Students should have completed 4 years each of English and math and 2 years each of foreign language, science, and social studies. USF requires applicants to be in the upper 50% of their class. A GPA of 2.5 is required. AP and CLEP credits are accepted. Important factors in the admissions decision are advanced placement or honor courses, evidence of special talent, and leadership record.

Procedure: Freshmen are admitted to all sessions. Entrance exams should be taken during the junior or senior year of high school. There is an early admissions and rolling admissions plan. Application deadlines are open. Application fee is $25.

Transfer: Transfer students must meet freshman admission requirements and have completed at least 24 hours of college courses with a minimum 2.0 GPA. The SAT or the ACT and an interview are recommended. 30 of 128 credits required for the bachelor's degree must be completed at USF.

Visiting: There are regularly scheduled orientations for prospective students, including meetings with faculty and staff, attendance at class, a campus tour, and a financial aid session. There are guides for informal visits and visitors may sit in on classes and stay overnight. To schedule a visit, contact the Admissions Office.

Financial Aid: In 2004-2005, 96% of all students received some form of financial aid. The average aid per student was $10,200. USF is a member of CSS. The CSS/Profile, FAFSA, FFS or SFS is required. The deadline for filing freshman financial aid applications for fall entry is April 1.

International Students: The school actively recruits these students. They must score satisfactorily on the written TOEFL or on the electronic version and also take the ACT if the examination is available to the student.

Computers: All students may access the system 8 A.M. to 11 P.M. There are no time limits and no fees.

Admissions Contact: Greg Fritz, Vice President for Enrollment Management. E-mail: *greg.fritz@usiouxfalls.edu* Web: *www.usiouxfalls.edu*

UNIVERSITY OF SOUTH DAKOTA   F-4
Vermillion, SD 57069

	(605) 677-5434
	(877) COYOTES; Fax: (605) 677-6323
Full-time: 1852 men, 2422 women	**Faculty:** 323; I, --$
Part-time: 578 men, 1556 women	**Ph.D.s:** 76%
Graduate: 909 men, 1324 women	**Student/Faculty:** 13 to 1
Year: semesters, summer session	**Tuition:** $4828 ($9816)
Application Deadline: open	**Room & Board:** $4240
Freshman Class: 2795 applied, 2405 accepted, 1165 enrolled	
SAT Verbal/Math: 535/535*	**COMPETITIVE**

The University of South Dakota, founded in 1862, is a public institution with undergraduate programs in arts and sciences, education, fine arts, and business, and professional schools of law and medicine. There are 4 undergraduate and 6 graduate schools. In addition to regional accreditation, USD has baccalaureate program accreditation with AACSB, ACS, APTA, CSWE, NASAD, NASM, NCATE, and NLN. The 4 libraries contain 892,356 volumes, 759,475 microform items, and 21,626 audio/video tapes/CDs/DVDs, and subscribe to 3480 periodicals including electronic. Computerized library services include the card catalog, interlibrary loans, database searching, and Internet access. Special learning facilities include a learning resource center, art gallery, natural history museum, planetarium, radio station, TV station, music museum and historical study center, institutes of American Indian studies, social science research, and child welfare training, business and governmental research bureaus, centers for speech and hearing, international studies, fine arts, telecommunications, natural sciences field station, and archeology and human factors labs. The 274-acre campus is in a rural area 31 miles from Sioux City, Iowa, and 64 miles from Sioux Falls. Including any residence halls, there are 61 buildings.

Student Life: 77% of undergraduates are from South Dakota. Others are from 42 states, 14 foreign countries, and Canada. 94% are white. 52% are claim no religious affiliation; 25% Protestant; 21% Catholic. The average age of freshmen is 21; all undergraduates, 23. 31% do not continue beyond their first year; 48% remain to graduate.

Housing: 2076 students can be accommodated in college housing, which includes single-sex and coed dormitories, on-campus apartments, married-student housing, and fraternity houses. On-campus housing is available on a first-come, first-served basis. 77% of students commute. Alcohol is not permitted. All students may keep cars.

Activities: 20% of men belong to 8 national fraternities; 13% of women belong to 4 national sororities. There are 120 groups on campus, including art, band, cheerleading, chess, choir, chorale, chorus, computers, dance, debate, drama, drill team, ethnic, forensics, gay, honors, international, jazz band, literary magazine, marching band, musical theater, newspaper, opera, orchestra, pep band, photography, political, professional, radio and TV, religious, social, social service, student government, and symphony. Popular campus events include Dakota Days, Strollers (a variety production), and Rockfest.

Sports: There are 7 intercollegiate sports for men and 7 for women, and 37 intramural sports for men and 37 for women. Facilities include an indoor football field, 5 basketball courts, a 25-meter swimming pool, an 8-lane, 200-meter track, a fitness center, a fitness room, batting cages, and racquetball, volleyball, and tennis courts. Outdoor areas include a softball complex, soccer fields, flag football fields, and tennis courts.

Disabled Students: 95% of the campus is accessible. Wheelchair ramps, elevators, special parking, specially equipped rest rooms, special class scheduling, lowered drinking fountains and lowered telephones.

Services: Counseling and information services are available, as is tutoring in most subjects. There is a reader service for the blind, and remedial math, reading, and writing. There is an academic advising and testing center.

Campus Safety and Security: Measures include 24-hour foot and vehicle patrol, self-defense education, security escort services, and shuttle buses. There are informal discussions, pamphlets/posters/films, emergency telephones, and lighted pathways/sidewalks.

Programs of Study: USD confers B.A., B.S., B.F.A., B.L.S., B.M., B.S.A.H., B.S.B.A, B.S.D.H., B.S.Ed., B.S.H.A., B.S.Med., B.S.Med.Tech., and B.S.Rec. degrees. Associate, master's, and doctoral degrees are also awarded. Bachelor's degrees are awarded in BIOLOGICAL SCIENCE (biology/biological science), BUSINESS (accounting, management science, and recreation and leisure services), COMMUNICATIONS AND THE ARTS (art, communications technology, dramatic arts, English, German, journalism, music, music performance, and Spanish), COMPUTER AND PHYSICAL SCIENCE (chemistry, computer science, earth science, mathematics, and physics), EDUCATION (art, elementary, music, physical, secondary, and special), HEALTH PROFESSIONS (dental hygiene, health care administration, medical technology, and speech pathology/audiology), SOCIAL SCIENCE (addiction studies, American Indian studies, anthropology, criminal justice, economics, French studies, history, international studies, liberal arts/general studies, philosophy, political science/government, psychology, social work, and sociology). Business, biology, and chemistry are the strongest academically. Business, biology, and elementary education are the largest.

Required: Students must complete 132 hours with a minimum GPA of 2.0. At least 32 hours must be at the 300/400 level. All students should complete 9 hours of interdisciplinary course work, 6 hours each in composition, humanities, social science, natural science, and multicultural diversity, 1 hour in fine arts, and a computer literacy course.

Special: USD offers internships, study abroad in 8 countries, and work-study programs. B.A.-B.S. degrees in 33 majors, a student-designed liberal studies major, dual majors, nondegree study, and pass/fail options are available. The Arts Outreach program provides arts activities and noncredit classes. There are 16 national honor societies, including Phi Beta Kappa, a freshman honors program, and 43 departmental honors programs.

Faculty/Classroom: 52% of faculty are male; 48%, female. 97% both teach and do research. Graduate students teach 3% of introductory courses. The average class size in an introductory lecture is 39; in a laboratory, 20; and in a regular course, 22.

Admissions: 86% of the 2005-2006 applicants were accepted. The SAT scores for the 2005-2006 freshman class were: Verbal--42% below 500, 25% between 500 and 599, 28% between 600 and 700, and 3% above 700; Math--33% below 500, 38% between 500 and 599, 18% between 600 and 700, and 8% above 700. The ACT scores were 33% below 21, 28% between 21 and 23, 26% between 24 and 26, 6% between 27 and 28, and 6% above 28. 17% of the current freshmen were in the top fifth of their class; 25% were in the top two fifths. In a recent year there were 4 National Merit finalists. 76 freshmen graduated first in their class.

Requirements: The ACT is required. In addition, applicants must have earned a 2.0 GPA in 4 years of English, 3 years each of lab science, math, and social studies, and 2 semesters of fine arts. They must also rank in the top 60% of their graduation class, have a satisfactory ACT score, or have a high school GPA of 2.6. AP and CLEP credits are accepted.

Procedure: Freshmen are admitted fall, spring, and summer. Entrance exams should be taken prior to enrollment. There is a deferred admissions and a rolling admissions plan. Application deadlines are open. Application fee is $20. Applications are accepted on-line.

Transfer: 686 transfer students enrolled in a recent year. Applicants should have a minimum college GPA of 2.0 and be in good standing at their previous school. 30 of 132 credits required for the bachelor's degree must be completed at USD.

Visiting: There are regularly scheduled orientations for prospective students, including an introductory session with an admission counselor, academic department visits, a campus tour with a student guide and any other requested units. There are guides for informal visits and visitors may sit in on classes and stay overnight. To schedule a visit, contact the Admissions Office.

Financial Aid: In 2005-2006, 93% of all full-time freshmen and 89% of continuing full-time students received some form of financial aid. 80% of all full-time students received need-based aid. The average freshman award was $5483. Need-based scholarships or need-based grants averaged $2973; need-based self-help aid (loans and jobs) averaged $3533; non-need-based athletic scholarships averaged $2714; and other non-need-based awards and non-need-based scholarships averaged $2991. The average financial indebtedness of the 2005 graduate was $19,535. The FAFSA is required. The priority date for freshman financial aid applications for fall entry is March 15.

International Students: There are 68 international students enrolled. They must score satisfactorily on the written TOEFL or on the electronic version.

Computers: Wireless access is available. All dorm rooms have a network connection available for student use. There are 862 PCs in 61 labs and clusters that students can use to access the Internet. 20% of the campus is covered by wireless. All students may access the system 24 hours a day. There are no time limits and no fees. It is recommended that students in nursing have personal computers. Gateway is recommended.

Graduates: From July 1, 2004 to June 30, 2005, 757 bachelor's degrees were awarded. The most popular majors were business management (11%), psychology (11%), and contemporary media and journalism (9%). In an average class, 2% graduate in 3 years or less, 21% graduate in 4 years or less, 42% graduate in 5 years or less, and 46% graduate in 6 years or less. 112 companies recruited on campus in a recent year. Of recent graduating class, 25% were enrolled in graduate school within 6 months of graduation and 78% were employed.

Admissions Contact: Cecil Foster, Assistant Vice President for Enrollment. E-mail: *admiss@usd.edu* Web: *http://www.usd.edu*

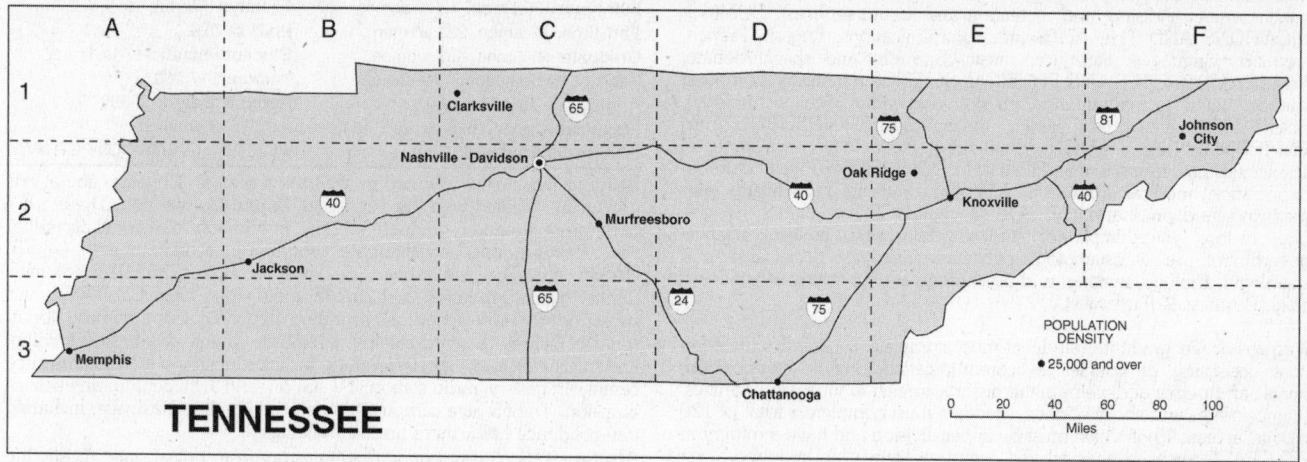

TENNESSEE

AQUINAS COLLEGE C-2

Nashville, TN 37205 (615) 297-7545 ext. 428; Fax: (615) 279-3893

Full-time: 520 men and women	**Faculty:** 29
Part-time: none	**Ph.Ds:** 20%
Graduate: none	**Student/Faculty:** 18 to 1
Year: semesters, summer session	**Tuition:** $10,700
Application Deadline: open	**Room & Board:** n/app
Freshman Class: n/av	
ACT: required	**LESS COMPETITIVE**

Aquinas College is a private Catholic institution offering an academically challenging liberal arts and sciences curriculum. The figures in the above capsule and in this profile are approximate. In addition to regional accreditation, the college has baccalaureate program accreditation with NLN. The library contains 45,762 volumes, 140,602 microform items, and 1820 audio/video tapes/CDs/DVDs, and subscribes to 301 periodicals including electronic. Computerized library services include the card catalog, interlibrary loans, and database searching. Special learning facilities include a learning resource center. The 92-acre campus is in an urban area in the western section of metropolitan Nashville. There are 4 buildings.

Programs of Study: The college confers B.A., B.B.A.,and B.S.N. degrees. Associate degrees are also awarded. Bachelor's degrees are awarded in BUSINESS (business administration and management), EDUCATION (elementary), HEALTH PROFESSIONS (nursing), SOCIAL SCIENCE (liberal arts/general studies). Nursing is the largest.

Required: All students must complete 124 to 134 credit hours, including the liberal arts core, and must maintain a minimum GPA of 2.0 in the B.S.N., A.S.N., and A.A. programs, 2.2 in the B.B.A. program, and 2.6 in the B.A. programs.

Special: There is a Weekend College for working adult students and evening courses are also offered. There is 1 national honor society.

Faculty/Classroom: 25% of faculty are male; 75%, female. All teach undergraduates. The average class size in an introductory lecture is 25; in a laboratory, 20; and in a regular course, 25.

Requirements: The ACT is required. In addition, the GED is accepted. An essay and an interview are required for some majors. A GPA of 2.0 is required. AP and CLEP credits are accepted.

Procedure: Freshmen are admitted to all sessions. Application deadlines are open. Applications are accepted on-line.

Transfer: Transfer applicants must have a 2.0 GPA in previous college work. 32 of 124 credits required for the bachelor's degree must be completed at the college.

Visiting: There are regularly scheduled orientations for prospective students, including campus tours and information on admissions, financial aid, student life, and degree programs. There are guides for informal visits and visitors may sit in on classes. To schedule a visit, contact Sarah Curtis at (615) 297-7545, ext. 436.

Financial Aid: The college is a member of CSS. The FAFSA and the college's own financial statement are required. Check with the school for current deadlines.

International Students: A satisfactory score is required on the written TOEFL.

Computers: All students may access the system all hours of college operation. There are no time limits. Check with the school for current fee.

Admissions Contact: Diane C. LeJeune, Director of Admissions. E-mail: *lejeuned@aquinas-tn.edu* Web: *www.aquinas-tn.edu.*

AUSTIN PEAY STATE UNIVERSITY C-2

Clarksville, TN 37040 (931) 221-7661
(800) 844-2778; Fax: (931) 221-6168

Full-time: 2339 men, 4009 women	**Faculty:** 274; IIA, --$
Part-time: 691 men, 1177 women	**Ph.Ds:** 91%
Graduate: 164 men, 433 women	**Student/Faculty:** 23 to 1
Year: semesters, summer session	**Tuition:** $4635 ($13,947)
Application Deadline: July 29	**Room & Board:** $2900
Freshman Class: 2608 applied, 2367 accepted, 1408 enrolled	
SAT Verbal/Math: 500/485*	**ACT:** 21 **COMPETITIVE**

Austin Peay State University, established in 1927, is a public institution offering undergraduate degrees in the liberal arts and sciences and professional preparation. There are 5 undergraduate schools and 1 graduate school. In addition to regional accreditation, APSU has baccalaureate program accreditation with CSWE, NASAD, NASM, NCATE, and NLN. The library contains 196,826 volumes, 520,732 microform items, and 6844 audio/video tapes/CDs/DVDs, and subscribes to 1736 periodicals including electronic. Computerized library services include the card catalog, interlibrary loans, and database searching. Special learning facilities include a learning resource center, art gallery, and radio station. The 150-acre campus is in an urban area 47 miles from Nashville. Including any residence halls, there are 42 buildings.

Student Life: 85% of undergraduates are from Tennessee. Students are from 29 states, 14 foreign countries, and Canada. 90% are from public schools. 68% are white; 18% African American. The average age of freshmen is 20; all undergraduates, 26. 36% do not continue beyond their first year; 32% remain to graduate.

Housing: 1100 students can be accommodated in college housing, which includes single-sex and coed dorms, on-campus apartments, and married-student housing. In addition, there are honors houses. On-campus housing is available on a first-come, first-served basis. 81% of students commute. Alcohol is not permitted. All students may keep cars.

Activities: 10% of men belong to 7 national fraternities; 3% of women belong to 7 national sororities. There are 80 groups on campus, including art, band, cheerleading, choir, chorus, debate, drama, ethnic, gay, honors, international, jazz band, literary magazine, marching band, newspaper, orchestra, pep band, political, professional, radio and TV, religious, social, social service, and student government. Popular campus events include Graduation, Parents Day, and Jazz Festival.

Sports: There are 6 intercollegiate sports for men and 8 for women, and 11 intramural sports for men and 11 for women. Facilities include a gym, an exercise room, a jogging fitness trail, and a weight room.

Disabled Students: 95% of the campus is accessible. Wheelchair ramps, elevators, special parking, specially equipped rest rooms, special class scheduling, lowered drinking fountains, and lowered telephones are available.

Services: There is a reader service for the blind, and remedial math, reading, and writing. The university provides help with academic, learning, and test-taking problems.

Campus Safety and Security: Measures include 24-hour foot and vehicle patrol, security escort services, shuttle buses, and informal discussions. There are pamphlets/posters/films, emergency telephones, and lighted pathways/sidewalks.

Programs of Study: APSU confers B.A., B.S., B.B.A., B.F.A., B.S.Ed., and B.S.N. degrees. Associate and master's degrees are also awarded.

Bachelor's degrees are awarded in AGRICULTURE (agriculture and conservation and regulation), BIOLOGICAL SCIENCE (biology/biological science), BUSINESS (accounting, banking and finance, business administration and management, management science, marketing/retailing/merchandising, and recreation and leisure services), COMMUNICATIONS AND THE ARTS (art, communications, English, French, German, languages, literature, music, Spanish, and speech/debate/rhetoric), COMPUTER AND PHYSICAL SCIENCE (chemistry, computer science, geology, mathematics, physics, and radiological technology), EDUCATION (elementary, health, and special), ENGINEERING AND ENVIRONMENTAL DESIGN (engineering technology, environmental science, and military science), HEALTH PROFESSIONS (health care administration, medical laboratory technology, nursing, predentistry, premedicine, and prepharmacy), SOCIAL SCIENCE (economics, geography, history, interdisciplinary studies, philosophy, political science/government, prelaw, psychology, public administration, social work, and sociology). Biology, nursing, and psychology are the strongest academically. Business is the largest.

Required: To graduate, students must complete a general education core consisting of courses in communications/English composition, health and personal development, history, foreign language/humanities, science/math, and social science. Students must complete a total of 120 credits, at least 45 of which must be upper division and have a minimum 2.0 GPA. Courses in phys ed and computer literacy are required.

Special: APSU offers cooperative programs in nuclear medicine and radiological technology with Vanderbilt University. Work-study programs and dual majors are available. Credit may be granted for military experience. Pass/fail grading options are available. There are 21 national honor societies and a freshman honors program.

Faculty/Classroom: 59% of faculty are male; 41%, female. All teach undergraduates. No introductory courses are taught by graduate students. The average class size in an introductory lecture is 24; in a laboratory, 16; and in a regular course, 25.

Admissions: 91% of the 2005-2006 applicants were accepted. The SAT scores for the 2005-2006 freshman class were: Verbal--42% below 500, 34% between 500 and 599, 21% between 600 and 700, and 3% above 700; Math--53% below 500, 29% between 500 and 599, 15% between 600 and 700, and 2% above 700. The ACT scores were 29% below 21, 46% between 21 and 23, 16% between 24 and 26, 5% between 27 and 28, and 4% above 28. 29% of the current freshmen were in the top fifth of their class; 57% were in the top two fifths.

Requirements: The ACT is required for some programs. In addition, applicants must be graduates of an accredited secondary school or have a GED. 14 academic units are required, including 4 units of English, 2 units each of algebra, natural/physical science, and a foreign language, and 1 unit each of visual and/or performing arts, geometry, social studies, and U.S. history. Applicants who do not meet these requirements may be considered for admission. A GPA of 2.75 is required. AP and CLEP credits are accepted.

Procedure: Freshmen are admitted to all sessions. There is a rolling admissions plan. Applications should be filed by July 29 for fall entry, December 16 for spring entry, and May 20 for summer entry. The fall 2005 application fee was $15. Notification is sent on a rolling basis. Applications are accepted on-line.

Transfer: 942 transfer students enrolled in 2004-2005. Applicants must have a 2.0 GPA. Grades of D or better will be considered for credit. Application deadlines are the same as those for freshmen. 24 of 120 credits required for the bachelor's degree must be completed at APSU.

Visiting: There are regularly scheduled orientations for prospective students. There are guides for informal visits. To schedule a visit, contact the Admissions Office.

Financial Aid: In 2005-2006, 87% of all full-time freshmen and 78% of continuing full-time students received some form of financial aid. 78% of full-time freshmen and 72% of continuing full-time students received need-based aid. 25% of undergraduates work part time. The FFS is required. Tennessee residents should submit the Tennessee edition of the FFS.

International Students: A satisfactory score on the TOEFL is required.

Computers: All students may access the system. There are no time limits and no fees.

Admissions Contact: Scott Mc Donald, Director of Admissions. A video is available. E-mail: *admission@apsu.edu* Web: *www.apsu.edu/admissions/index.htm*

BELMONT UNIVERSITY   C-2

Nashville, TN 37212-3757

(615) 460-6785
(800) 56E-NROL; Fax: (615) 460-5434

Full-time: 1292 men, 1996 women	**Faculty:** 198; IIA, -$
Part-time: 125 men, 232 women	**Ph.D.s:** 75%
Graduate: 237 men, 437 women	**Student/Faculty:** 17 to 1
Year: semesters, summer session	**Tuition:** $17,260
Application Deadline: August 1	**Room & Board:** $6850
Freshman Class: 1626 applied, 1212 accepted, 603 enrolled	
SAT Verbal/Math: 580/580*	**ACT:** 25 **VERY COMPETITIVE**

Belmont University, founded in 1890, is a private, Christian liberal arts university affiliated with the Tennessee Baptist Convention. There are 7 undergraduate and 6 graduate schools. In addition to regional accreditation, Belmont has baccalaureate program accreditation with CSWE, NASM, NCATE, and NLN. The library contains 252,923 volumes, 22,981 microform items, and 25,248 audio/video tapes/CDs/DVDs, and subscribes to 1430 periodicals including electronic. Computerized library services include the card catalog, interlibrary loans, database searching, and Internet access. Special learning facilities include a learning resource center, art gallery, radio station, TV station, and 19th century antebellum mansion. The 65-acre campus is in an urban area in Nashville. Including any residence halls, there are 30 buildings.

Student Life: 56% of undergraduates are from out of state, mostly the South. Students are from 48 states, 27 foreign countries, and Canada. 77% are from public schools. 89% are white. 44% are Protestant; 40% claim no religious affiliation; 8% Catholic. The average age of freshmen is 18; all undergraduates, 22. 21% do not continue beyond their first year; 60% remain to graduate.

Housing: 1755 students can be accommodated in college housing, which includes single-sex dormitories, on-campus apartments, off-campus apartments, and married-student housing. In addition, there are honors houses, language houses, and special-interest houses. On-campus housing is guaranteed for the freshman year only and is available on a first-come, first-served basis. 52% of students commute. Alcohol is not permitted. All students may keep cars.

Activities: 1% of men belong to 2 national fraternities; 3% of women belong to 3 national sororities. There are 67 groups on campus, including art, band, cheerleading, choir, chorale, chorus, computers, dance, debate, drama, ethnic, film, honors, international, jazz band, literary magazine, marching band, musical theater, newspaper, orchestra, pep band, photography, political, professional, radio and TV, religious, social, social service, student government, and symphony. Popular campus events include formal dance events.

Sports: Facilities include an event center and a student center.

Disabled Students: 98% of the campus is accessible. Wheelchair ramps, elevators, special parking, specially equipped rest rooms, special class scheduling, and lowered drinking fountains are available.

Services: Counseling and information services are available, as is tutoring in some subjects. There is remedial math, reading, and writing. Writing and computer labs are available.

Campus Safety and Security: Measures include 24-hour foot and vehicle patrol, self-defense education, security escort services, and shuttle buses. There are informal discussions, pamphlets/posters/films, emergency telephones, and lighted pathways/sidewalks.

Programs of Study: Belmont confers B.A., B.S., B.B.A., B.F.A., B.M., and B.S.N. degrees. Master's degrees are also awarded. Bachelor's degrees are awarded in BIOLOGICAL SCIENCE (biology/biological science and environmental biology), BUSINESS (accounting, business administration and management, hotel/motel and restaurant management, management science, and marketing/retailing/merchandising), COMMUNICATIONS AND THE ARTS (communications, English, French, music, music business management, music performance, and public relations), COMPUTER AND PHYSICAL SCIENCE (chemistry, computer science, mathematics, and physics), EDUCATION (elementary, physical, and science), HEALTH PROFESSIONS (nursing), SOCIAL SCIENCE (economics, history, liberal arts/general studies, philosophy, political science/government, psychology, religion, and social work). Music, business, and humanities are the strongest academically. Business, music, nursing, and music business management are the largest.

Required: All students must complete at least 128 hours with a C average, including 22 to 24 hours in the major field. B.A. candidates are required to pursue a minor field. All programs except the B.B.A. require a core curriculum, which includes courses in language and literature, humanities (including religion), social sciences, science, math, and phys ed.

Special: Belmont offers study abroad, student-designed majors, and dual majors in math, physics, and chemistry. Dual degree programs are available with Auburn University and the University of Tennessee at Knoxville. Programs require 3 years of study at Belmont followed by 2 years at the other institution. There are 11 national honor societies, a freshman honors program, and 3 departmental honors programs.

Faculty/Classroom: 50% of faculty are male; 50%, female. 92% teach undergraduates, 2% do research, and 3% do both. No introductory

courses are taught by graduate students. The average class size in an introductory lecture is 25; in a laboratory, 24; and in a regular course, 25.

Admissions: 75% of the 2005-2006 applicants were accepted. The SAT scores for the 2005-2006 freshman class were: Verbal--9% below 500, 47% between 500 and 599, 36% between 600 and 700, and 8% above 700; Math--11% below 500, 47% between 500 and 599, 32% between 600 and 700, and 9% above 700. The ACT scores were 7% below 21, 26% between 21 and 23, 32% between 24 and 26, 16% between 27 and 28, and 19% above 28. 60% of the current freshmen were in the top fifth of their class; 80% were in the top two fifths. 22 freshmen graduated first in their class.

Requirements: The ACT is required and the SAT is recommended. Applicants should be high school graduates or hold the GED. Secondary preparation should include 4 units of English, 3 of math, and 2 each of a foreign language, history, science, and social studies. Potential music majors must audition. Belmont requires applicants to be in the upper 50% of their class. A GPA of 3.0 is required. AP and CLEP credits are accepted. Important factors in the admissions decision are advanced placement or honor courses, recommendations by school officials, and evidence of special talent.

Procedure: Freshmen are admitted fall, spring, and summer. Entrance exams should be taken during the junior or senior year. There is a rolling admissions plan. Applications should be filed by August 1 for fall entry and December 1 for spring entry. Notification is sent on a rolling basis. Application fee is $35. Applications are accepted on-line.

Transfer: 376 transfer students enrolled in 2004-2005. Applicants should present an above average GPA in previous college work and be able to meet freshman entrance requirements. Those with fewer than 64 credit hours must also submit SAT or ACT scores. 32 of 128 credits required for the bachelor's degree must be completed at Belmont.

Visiting: There are regularly scheduled orientations for prospective students, consisting of a 2-day program in summer and a 4-day program right before classes begin. There are guides for informal visits and visitors may sit in on classes and stay overnight. To schedule a visit, contact the Admissions Office.

Financial Aid: In 2005-2006, 81% of all full-time freshmen and 74% of continuing full-time students received some form of financial aid. 46% of full-time freshmen and 52% of continuing full-time students received need-based aid. The average freshman award was $5237. Need-based scholarships or need-based grants averaged $4797; need-based self-help aid (loans and jobs) averaged $2956; non-need-based athletic scholarships averaged $9556; and other non-need-based awards and non-need-based scholarships averaged $4344. 17% of undergraduates work part time. Average annual earnings from campus work are $2500. The average financial indebtedness of the 2005 graduate was $18,007. The FAFSA is required. The deadline for filing freshman financial aid applications for fall entry is March 1.

International Students: There are 44 international students enrolled. They must score satisfactorily on the written TOEFL.

Computers: Wireless access is available. There are 500 PCs in student labs; and 98% wireless acessibility. All students may access the system. There are no time limits and no fees.

Graduates: From July 1, 2004 to June 30, 2005, 649 bachelor's degrees were awarded. The most popular majors were music business (24%), business administration (17%), and liberal arts (6%). In an average class, 2% graduate in 3 years or less, 37% graduate in 4 years or less, 53% graduate in 5 years or less, and 54% graduate in 6 years or less. 83 companies recruited on campus in a recent year. Of a recent graduating class, 31% were enrolled in graduate school within 6 months of graduation and 35% were employed.

Admissions Contact: Kathryn H. Baugher, Dean of Enrollment Services. A video is available. E-mail: buadmission@belmont.edu
Web: www.belmont@edu

BETHEL COLLEGE
B-3

McKenzie, TN 38201   (731) 352-4030; Fax: (731) 352-4069

Full-time: 432 men, 541 women	**Faculty:** n/av
Part-time: 77 men, 176 women	**Ph.Ds:** n/av
Graduate: 64 men, 91 women	**Student/Faculty:** n/av
Year: varies by program, summer session	**Tuition:** $10,306
	Room & Board: $5760

Application Deadline: August 30

Freshman Class: 755 applied, 449 accepted, 258 enrolled

SAT or ACT: required   **NONCOMPETITIVE**

Bethel College, established in 1842, is a private institution affiliated with the Cumberland Presbyterian Church offering undergraduate degrees through its divisions of humanities, natural sciences, social sciences, education, and health science. The library contains 79,164 volumes, 185 microform items, and 2166 audio/video tapes/CDs/DVDs, and subscribes to 1208 periodicals including electronic. Computerized library services include the card catalog, interlibrary loans, database searching, and laptop Internet portals. Special learning facilities include a learning resource center and Jack's Place Pizza Business operated by Students in Free Enterprise (SIFE). The 100-acre campus is in a small town 120 miles northeast of Memphis. Including any residence halls, there are 18 buildings.

Student Life: 87% of undergraduates are from Tennessee. Others are from 28 states, 18 foreign countries, and Canada. 99% are from public schools. 57% are white; 22% African American. Most are Protestant. The average age of freshmen is 18; all undergraduates, 28.

Housing: 486 students can be accommodated in college housing, which includes single-sex and coed dorms. On-campus housing is guaranteed for the freshman year only and is available on a first-come, first-served basis. 68% of students commute. Alcohol is not permitted. All students may keep cars.

Activities: 25% of men belong to 5 local fraternities; 25% of women belong to 5 local sororities. There are 25 groups on campus, including art, band, cheerleading, choir, chorus, drama, honors, international, marching band, musical theater, newspaper, opera, pep band, political, professional, religious, social, and student government.

Sports: There are 8 intercollegiate sports for men and 7 for women, and 9 intramural sports for men and 8 for women. Facilities include a gym with a heated indoor pool and weight room, a field house, pool tables, and Ping-Pong tables. There are tennis courts, a track, and fields for football, soccer, and a baseball field.

Disabled Students: 75% of the campus is accessible. Wheelchair ramps, special parking, specially equipped rest rooms, special class scheduling, lowered drinking fountains, and lowered telephones are available.

Services: Counseling and information services are available, as is tutoring in every subject. There is remedial math, reading, and writing. Tutoring is available free of charge to students.

Campus Safety and Security: Measures include 24-hour foot and vehicle patrol, self-defense education, security escort services, and informal discussions. There are pamphlets/posters/films, emergency telephones, lighted pathways/sidewalks, and a security guard at night.

Programs of Study: Bethel confers B.A. and B.S. degrees. Master's degrees are also awarded. Bachelor's degrees are awarded in BIOLOGICAL SCIENCE (biology/biological science and zoology), BUSINESS (business administration and management and management science), COMMUNICATIONS AND THE ARTS (English), COMPUTER AND PHYSICAL SCIENCE (chemistry and mathematics), EDUCATION (early childhood, education of the exceptional child, health, and physical), ENGINEERING AND ENVIRONMENTAL DESIGN (preengineering), SOCIAL SCIENCE (child psychology/development, history, human services, liberal arts/general studies, physical fitness/movement, psychology, and sociology). Education, organizational management, and biology are the strongest academically. Education and organizational management are the largest.

Required: Requirements for graduation include courses in English, Western literature and arts, history, lab science, math, phys ed, and religion. Students must complete 128 to 132 hours with a minimum GPA of 2.0. A thesis is required in some majors.

Special: Bethel offers evening classes for adults, in-service training for teachers, off-site classes, an accelerated degree program in organizational management, student-designed majors, a 3-2 engineering program with Tennessee Technical University, internships, work-study, nondegree study, a pass/fail option, and portfolio credit for prior learning and work experience. There is 1 national honor society and a freshman honors program.

Faculty/Classroom: 5% of faculty both teach and do research. No introductory courses are taught by graduate students.

Admissions: 59% of the 2005-2006 applicants were accepted.

Requirements: The SAT or ACT is required. In addition, applicants must graduate from an accredited secondary school. Those ranking in the upper half of their class or achieving a certain minumum score on the SAT or ACT are granted regular acceptance. Other applicants may be admitted conditionally. Other factors in the admission procedure are standardized test scores, an interview, evidence of special talent, and personality. A GPA of 2.25 is required. AP and CLEP credits are accepted. Important factors in the admissions decision are advanced placement or honor courses, leadership record, and parents or siblings attending the school.

Procedure: Freshmen are admitted to all sessions. Entrance exams should be taken prior to enrollment, preferably by fall of the senior year. There is a rolling admissions plan. Applications should be filed by August 30 for fall entry, January 10 for spring entry, and June 5 for summer entry, along with a $30 fee. Notification is sent on a rolling basis.

Transfer: 52 transfer students enrolled in 2004-2005. Applicants must meet the GPA requirements for the number of hours they previously earned. Up to 68 hours may be transferred from community or junior colleges. Students with fewer than 12 semester hours must submit high school transcripts and ACT or SAT scores and take Bethel's placement test. 32 of 128 to 132 credits required for the bachelor's degree must be completed at Bethel.

Visiting: There are regularly scheduled orientations for prospective students. Students receive information about the college, dorms, and the laptop program, meet advisers, register for classes, and meet with the financial aid and business office. There are guides for informal visits and visitors may sit in on classes and stay overnight. To schedule a visit, contact the Admissions Office at *hodgest@bethel-college.edu*.

Financial Aid: 14% of undergraduates work part time. Average annual earnings from campus work are $1187. The FAFSA and the college's own financial statement are required. The deadline for filing freshman financial aid applications for fall entry is March 15.

International Students: There are 37 international students enrolled. The school actively recruits these students. It is suggested that they take the TOEFL, achieving a satisfactory score. A satisfactory score on the SAT or ACT is required.

Computers: Wireless access is available. Each full-time student receives a laptop. Several buildings are wireless, and there are hubs to hook up laptops all over campus. Connections to the campus LAN and the Internet are available throughout the campus and in each dorm room. There are no time limits and no fees. All students are required to have personal computers.

Graduates: From July 1, 2004 to June 30, 2005, 380 bachelor's degrees were awarded. The most popular majors were management and organizational development (60%), education (4%), and biology (2%).

Admissions Contact: Tina Hodges, Director of Admissions.
E-mail: *admissions@bethel-college.edu* Web: *www.bethel-college.edu*

BRYAN COLLEGE   D-3
Dayton, TN 37321-7000
(423) 775-7204
(800) 277-9522; Fax: (423) 775-7199

Full-time: 757 men and women	**Faculty:** IIB, --$
Part-time: 18 men and women	**Ph.Ds:** 90%
Graduate: none	**Student/Faculty:** n/av
Year: semesters, summer session	**Tuition:** $14,800
Application Deadline: open	**Room & Board:** $4470
Freshman Class: n/av	
SAT or ACT: required	**COMPETITIVE**

Bryan College, founded in 1930, is a private, Christian institution that is evangelical and interdenominational. Its emphases are on the liberal arts, business, health science, fine arts, Bible and religious studies, music, and teacher preparation. The library contains 150,000 volumes, 13,489 microform items, and 3015 audio/video tapes/CDs/DVDs, and subscribes to 10,000 periodicals including electronic. Computerized library services include the card catalog, interlibrary loans, database searching, Internet access, and laptop Internet portals. Special learning facilities include a museum of natural science. The 130-acre campus is in a small town 40 miles north of Chattanooga. Including any residence halls, there are 28 buildings.

Student Life: 61% of undergraduates are from out of state, mostly the South. Others are from 39 states, 6 foreign countries, and Canada. 94% are white. Most are Protestant. The average age of freshmen is 18; all undergraduates, 20. 24% do not continue beyond their first year; 55% remain to graduate.

Housing: 497 students can be accommodated in college housing, which includes single-sex dorms and married-student housing. On-campus housing is guaranteed for all 4 years. 80% of students live on campus; of those, 75% remain on campus on weekends. Alcohol is not permitted. All students may keep cars.

Activities: There are no fraternities or sororities. There are 17 groups on campus, including art, cheerleading, choir, chorale, computers, drama, honors, international, literary magazine, mock trial, musical theater, newspaper, orchestra, pep band, photography, religious, social, social service, student government, and yearbook. Popular campus events include a fine arts series.

Sports: There are 3 intercollegiate sports for men and 4 for women, and 6 intramural sports for men and 6 for women. Facilities include a 1200-seat gym, soccer fields, a baseball field, an outdoor swimming pool, and 4 tennis courts.

Disabled Students: All of the campus is accessible. Wheelchair ramps, elevators, special parking, specially equipped rest rooms, and lowered drinking fountains are available.

Services: Counseling and information services are available, as is tutoring in some subjects, including math and English. There is remedial math, reading, and writing.

Campus Safety and Security: Measures include self-defense education, security escort services, informal discussions, and pamphlets/posters/films. There are lighted pathways/sidewalks and a night security patrol.

Programs of Study: Bryan confers B.A. and B.S. degrees. Associate degrees are also awarded. Bachelor's degrees are awarded in BIOLOGICAL SCIENCE (biology/biological science), BUSINESS (business administration and management), COMMUNICATIONS AND THE ARTS (communications, English, music, and Spanish), COMPUTER AND PHYSICAL SCIENCE (computer science and mathematics), EDUCATION (athletic training, elementary, physical, and science), HEALTH PROFESSIONS (exercise science), SOCIAL SCIENCE (Christian studies,

history, liberal arts/general studies, psychology, and religion). Communication,studies and business administration are the largest.

Required: To graduate, students must complete 124 semester hours, with a minimum of 30 in the major, and maintain a GPA of at least 2.0. Distributions requirements include 16 semester hours in Bible, 9 in communications, 7 each in personal development and natural science, and 6 each in the humanities and social science. Specific courses that must be taken include 7 semester hours in science, 6 hours each in freshman English, a foreign language, and history of Western civilization, and 3 each in speech, general psychology, introduction to literature, fine arts, and phys ed. In addition, matn and English proficiency must be met; a comprehensive exam in the major is also required.

Special: Special academic programs include practicums in business and psychology, and psychology internships. An American Studies Program in Washington and a study-abroad Latin American Studies Program are offered through the Christian College Coalition. A dual major in Christian education and church music is available. There is a freshman honors program.

Faculty/Classroom: 64% of faculty are male; 36%, female. All teach undergraduates. The average class size in an introductory lecture is 27; in a laboratory, 13; and in a regular course, 16.

Requirements: The SAT or ACT is required. In addition, clear admission is granted to applicants who have graduated from an approved high school and who have a minimum GPA of 2.5 with a satisfactory minimun composite score on the ACT or on the SAT; clear admission is also granted to applicants with a minimum GPA of 2.0 and a satisfactory composite score on the ACT or on the SAT. The high school record should include a minimum of 18 academic credits with a recommended distribution of 4 units of English, 3 each of math, science, and social science/humanities, and 2 of a foreign language. The GED is also accepted. References are required, and an interview is recommended. A GPA of 2.0 is required. AP and CLEP credits are accepted. Important factors in the admissions decision are parents or siblings attending the school, recommendations by alumni, and recommendations by school officials.

Procedure: Freshmen are admitted fall and spring. Entrance exams should be taken before the fall of the senior year in high school. There are deferred admissions and rolling admissions plans. Application deadlines are open. Application fee is $30. Applications are accepted on-line.

Transfer: 40 transfer students enrolled in 2004-2005. Applicants need a minimum GPA of 2.0. 31 of 124 credits required for the bachelor's degree must be completed at Bryan.

Visiting: There are regularly scheduled orientations for prospective students, consisting of college visitation weekends, which include a tour of the campus, sitting in on classes and chapel, meeting with professors in the area of academic interest, staying with current students in residence halls, and eating meals in the dining room. There are guides for informal visits and visitors may sit in on classes and stay overnight. To schedule a visit, contact Kim Tuttle at (423) 775-7211 or *admissions@bryan.edu*.

Financial Aid: In 2005-2006, 98% of all full-time freshmen and 94% of continuing full-time students received some form of financial aid. 65% of full-time freshmen and 56% of continuing full-time students received need-based aid. The average freshman award was $9373. 55% of undergraduates work part time. Average annual earnings from campus work are $1500. The average financial indebtedness of the 2005 graduate was $14,500. The FAFSA and the college's own financial statement are required. The deadline for filing freshman financial aid applications for fall entry is May 1.

International Students: There are 9 international students enrolled. Satisfactory scores are required on the written TOEFL and the SAT or the ACT.

Computers: All students may access the system at all times. There are no time limits and no fees.

Graduates: From July 1, 2004 to June 30, 2005, 136 bachelor's degrees were awarded. In an average class, 50% graduate in 4 years, 58% graduate in 5 years, and 60% graduate in 6 years.

Admissions Contact: Michael Sapienza, Director of Admissions. A video is available. E-mail: *admiss@bryan.edu* Web: *www.bryan.edu*

CARSON-NEWMAN COLLEGE   E-2
Jefferson City, TN 37760
(865) 471-2000
(800) 678-9061; Fax: (865) 471-3502

Full-time: 820 men, 980 women	**Faculty:** 122; IIB, --$
Part-time: 55 men, 105 women	**Ph.Ds:** 65%
Graduate: 45 men, 130 women	**Student/Faculty:** 15 to 1
Year: semesters, summer session	**Tuition:** $13,300
Application Deadline: see profile	**Room & Board:** $3500
Freshman Class: 1153 applied, 1014 accepted, 366 enrolled	
SAT or ACT: required	**COMPETITIVE**

Carson-Newman College, founded in 1851, is a private liberal arts college affiliated with the Tennessee Baptist Convention. Figures in the above capsule and in this profile are approximate. In addition to regional accreditation, Carson-Newman has baccalaureate program accreditation with ADA, AHEA, NASAD, NASM, NCATE, and NLN. The library contains 300,000 volumes, 221,960 microform items, and 15,000 audio/video tapes/CDs/DVDs, and subscribes to 2000 periodicals including electronic. Computerized library services include the card catalog, interlibrary loans, and database searching. Special learning facilities include a learning resource center, art gallery, natural history museum, radio station, and TV station. The 100-acre campus is in a small town 27 miles northeast of Knoxville. Including any residence halls, there are 27 buildings.

Student Life: 67% of undergraduates are from Tennessee. Others are from 36 states and 13 foreign countries. 92% are from public schools. 87% are white. 84% are Protestant; 8% claim no religious affiliation. The average age of freshmen is 18; all undergraduates, 22. 25% do not continue beyond their first year; 57% remain to graduate.

Housing: 1430 students can be accommodated in college housing, which includes single-sex dormitories, on-campus apartments, and married-student housing. In addition, there are honors houses. On-campus housing is guaranteed for all 4 years. 50% of students live on campus; of those, 50% remain on campus on weekends. Alcohol is not permitted. All students may keep cars.

Activities: 20% of men belong to 2 local and 1 national fraternity; 20% of women belong to 2 local and 1 national sorority.There are 55 groups on campus, including art, band, cheerleading, chess, choir, chorale, chorus, computers, dance, debate, drama, drill team, ethnic, film, forensics, honors, international, jazz band, literary magazine, marching band, musical theater, newspaper, orchestra, pep band, photography, political, professional, radio and TV, religious, social, social service, student government, and yearbook. Popular campus events include Spring Fest, Fall Formal, and Honors Convocation.

Sports: There are 10 intercollegiate sports for men and 6 for women, and 40 intramural sports for men and 40 for women. Facilities include a gym, a football stadium, soccer, baseball, softball, and intramural fields, a pool, and a student center with 3 racquetball courts, 3 gyms, a weight room, an Olympic-size pool, a Jacuzzi, and an outdoor café.

Disabled Students: 10% of the campus is accessible. Wheelchair ramps, elevators, special parking, and special class scheduling are available.

Services: Counseling and information services are available, as is tutoring in most subjects, including English, math, and science. There is remedial math, reading, and writing.

Campus Safety and Security: Measures include 24-hour foot and vehicle patrol, self-defense education, security escort services, and informal discussions. There are pamphlets/posters/films and lighted pathways/sidewalks.

Programs of Study: Carson-Newman confers B.A., B.S., B.M., B.S.M., and B.S.N. degrees. Associate and master's degrees are also awarded. Bachelor's degrees are awarded in BIOLOGICAL SCIENCE (biology/biological science), BUSINESS (accounting, business administration and management, and business economics), COMMUNICATIONS AND THE ARTS (communications, English, fine arts, French, languages, music, and Spanish), EDUCATION (art, early childhood, elementary, foreign languages, health, home economics, middle school, music, science, and secondary), HEALTH PROFESSIONS (nursing and physical therapy), SOCIAL SCIENCE (economics, history, philosophy, psychology, religion, social science, and sociology). Nursing, music, and biology are the strongest academically. Communication arts, and biology are the largest.

Required: All students must complete 128 credit hours, including Composition I and II, Survey of Old Testament, Survey of New Testament, 15 hours in English and communications, 9 in social sciences, 6 each in religion, humanities, and science, and 3 each in history, literature, and math. The major requires 40 to 48 hours. Students must achieve a minimum GPA of 2.0.

Special: The college offers internships, study in England, France, Japan, Hong Kong, and Spain, a Washington semester, on-campus work-study programs, B.A.-B.S. degrees, dual majors, a general studies degree, student-designed majors, and pass/fail options. Students may receive credit for life, military, or work experience. There is 1 national honor society, a freshman honors program, and 16 departmental honors program.

Faculty/Classroom: 57% of faculty are male; 43%, female. All teach undergraduates and 40% do research. No introductory courses are taught by graduate students. The average class size in an introductory lecture is 20; in a laboratory, 16; and in a regular course, 17.

Requirements: A satisfactory score is required on the SAT or the ACT is required. Applicants should be graduates of an accredited secondary school. The GED is accepted. 20 academic credits are required, including 4 units of English and 2 units each of history, math, science, and social studies. An essay, a portfolio, an audition, and an interview are recommended. Carson-Newman requires applicants to be in the upper 50% of their class. A GPA of 2.25 is required. AP and CLEP credits are accepted. Important factors in the admissions decision are advanced placement or honor courses, leadership record, and parents or siblings attending the school.

Procedure: Freshmen are admitted to all sessions. Entrance exams should be taken in the fall of the senior year or the spring of the junior year. There is a deferred admissions plan. Check with the school for current deadlines and fee. Applications are accepted on-line.

Transfer: 189 transfer students enrolled in a recent year. Transfer students should have a minimum GPA of 2.0. Either the SAT I or the ACT is required if the student has fewer than 32 hours of college credit. An interview is recommended. 32 of 128 credits required for the bachelor's degree must be completed at Carson-Newman.

Visiting: There are regularly scheduled orientations for prospective students, including information sessions, meetings with advisers, and pre-registration. There are guides for informal visits and visitors may sit in on classes and stay overnight. To schedule a visit, contact the Admissions Office.

Financial Aid: In a recent year, 92% of all full-time freshmen and 90% of continuing full-time students received some form of financial aid. 75% of full-time freshmen and 70% of continuing full-time students received need-based aid. The average freshman award was $12,500. Need-based scholarships or need-based grants averaged $4300 ($5000 maximum); need-based self-help aid (loans and jobs) averaged $3835 ($6125 maximum); non-need-based athletic scholarships averaged $2000 ($12,500 maximum); and other non-need-based awards and non-need-based scholarships averaged $7500 ($12,500 maximum). 31% of undergraduates work part time. Average annual earnings from campus work are $1500. The average financial indebtedness of the recent year's graduate was $14,800. Carson-Newman is a member of CSS. The FAFSA and the college's own financial statement are required. Check with the school for current dealines. The deadline for filing freshman financial aid applications for fall entry is March 1.

International Students: The school actively recruits these students. Satisfactory scores are required on the written TOEFL, the APIEL, and English proficiency and math placement exams.

Computers: All students may access the system until the lab closes at 11 P.M. There are no time limits. Check with the school for current fee. It is strongly recommended that all students have a personal computer.

Graduates: In a recent year, 420 bachelor's degrees were awarded. The most popular majors were education (22%), business administration (7%), and biology (7%). In an average class, 47% graduate in 4 years or less, 57% graduate in 5 years or less, and 58% graduate in 6 years or less. 35 companies recruited on campus in a recent year.

Admissions Contact: Sheryl M. Gray, Director of Admissions. A video is available. E-mail: *sgray@cn.edu* Web: *www.cn.edu*

CHRISTIAN BROTHERS UNIVERSITY   A-4
Memphis, TN 38104-5581   (901) 321-4213
(800) 288-7576; Fax: (901) 321-3202

Full-time: 552 men, 599 women	Faculty: 94; IIB, av$
Part-time: 120 men, 222 women	Ph.Ds: 88%
Graduate: 119 men, 166 women	Student/Faculty: 12 to 1
Year: semesters, summer session	Tuition: $19,150
Application Deadline: August 1	Room & Board: $5500
Freshman Class: 1144 applied, 783 accepted, 312 enrolled	
SAT Verbal/Math: 539/544*	ACT: 24 VERY COMPETITIVE

Christian Brothers University, founded in 1871, is a private, nonprofit institution affiliated with the Roman Catholic Church. Its undergraduate and graduate programs emphasize the liberal arts and sciences, business, engineering, and teacher preparation. There are 4 undergraduate and 3 graduate schools. In addition to regional accreditation, CBU has baccalaureate program accreditation with ABET and IACBE. The library contains 154,000 volumes, 60,342 microform items, and 900 audio/video tapes/CDs/DVDs, and subscribes to 550 periodicals including electronic. Computerized library services include the card catalog, interlibrary loans, database searching, Internet access, and laptop Internet portals. Special learning facilities include a learning resource center and art gallery. The 75-acre campus is in an urban area in Memphis. Including any residence halls, there are 23 buildings.

Student Life: 83% of undergraduates are from Tennessee. Others are from 27 states, 22 foreign countries, and Canada. 68% are from public schools. 51% are white. 35% African American. 42% are Protestant; 34% claim no religious affiliation; 20% Catholic. The average age of freshmen is 18; all undergraduates, 25. 21% do not continue beyond their first year; 63% remain to graduate.

Housing: 576 students can be accommodated in college housing, which includes single-sex and coed dorms and on-campus apartments. In addition, there are quiet floors in residence halls. On-campus housing is guaranteed for the freshman year only, is available on a first-come, first-served basis, and is available on a lottery system for upperclassmen. Priority is given to out-of-town students. 70% of students commute. All students may keep cars.

Activities: 30% of men belong to 5 national fraternities; 24% of women belong to 1 local and 4 national sororities. There are 34 groups on campus, including art, cheerleading, chess, chorale, chorus, computers, drama, ethnic, honors, international, literary magazine, musical theater, political, professional, religious, social, social service, student government, and yearbook. Popular campus events include Bacchus, Sofapalooza, and SGA.

Sports: There are 5 intercollegiate sports for men and 6 for women, and 10 intramural sports for men and 10 for women. Facilities include a swimming pool, gym, theater, multimedia auditorium, batting cage, jogging track, basketball/volleyball and handball/racquetball courts, baseball and soccer fields, tennis courts, and weight-training facilities.

Disabled Students: 90% of the campus is accessible. Wheelchair ramps, elevators, special parking, specially equipped rest rooms, and lowered drinking fountains are available.

Services: Counseling and information services are available, as is tutoring in most subjects. CBU also has centers for math, language, and writing.

Campus Safety and Security: Measures include 24-hour foot and vehicle patrol, self-defense education, security escort services, and pamphlets/posters/films. There are emergency telephones and lighted pathways/sidewalks.

Programs of Study: CBU confers B.A. and B.S. degrees. Master's degrees are also awarded. Bachelor's degrees are awarded in BIOLOGICAL SCIENCE (biology/biological science), BUSINESS (business administration and management, management science, and marketing/retailing/merchandising), COMMUNICATIONS AND THE ARTS (English and language arts), COMPUTER AND PHYSICAL SCIENCE (chemistry, computer science, information sciences and systems, mathematics, natural sciences, and physics), ENGINEERING AND ENVIRONMENTAL DESIGN (chemical engineering, civil engineering, electrical/electronics engineering, engineering physics, and mechanical engineering), SOCIAL SCIENCE (applied psychology, history, liberal arts/general studies, psychology, and religion). Engineering, business, and psychology are the strongest academically. Psychology, business, and biology are the largest.

Required: To graduate, students must complete at least 122 semester hours, with a varying number of hours in the major, and maintain a minimum GPA of 2.0. General education requirements, totaling 37 semester hours, consist of 9 hours each of English, religion, and social science, 4 of science, and 3 each of math and technology. Individual schools vary in their core requirements.

Special: Special academic programs include on-campus work-study, study abroad in 4 countries, and internships for all juniors and seniors. There is cross-registration with Memphis College of Art, Memphis Theological Seminary, and LeMoyne-Owen College. An accelerated degree program is available to all business and psychology majors through the evening program, and a general studies degree is offered. Up to 36 hours of nondegree study is possible, as are dual majors and pass/fail options. Numerous teacher licensure programs are also offered. There are 9 national honor societies and a freshman honors program.

Faculty/Classroom: 64% of faculty are male; 36%, female. 92% teach undergraduates. No introductory courses are taught by graduate students. The average class size in an introductory lecture is 22; in a laboratory, 15; and in a regular course, 16.

Admissions: 68% of the 2005-2006 applicants were accepted. The SAT scores for the 2005-2006 freshman class were: Verbal--30% below 500, 46% between 500 and 599, 20% between 600 and 700, and 4% above 700; Math--29% below 500, 41% between 500 and 599, and 30% between 600 and 700. The ACT scores were 17% below 21, 32% between 21 and 23, 21% between 24 and 26, 16% between 27 and 28, and 14% above 28. 44% of the current freshmen were in the top fifth of their class; 74% were in the top two fifths. 5 freshmen graduated first in their class.

Requirements: The SAT or ACT is required with a satisfactory score. Other admissions requirements include graduation from an accredited secondary school, with a college-preparatory curriculum recommended. The GED is also accepted. An interview is advised. A GPA of 2.5 is required. AP and CLEP credits are accepted. Important factors in the admissions decision are advanced placement or honor courses, leadership record, and recommendations by school officials.

Procedure: Freshmen are admitted to all sessions. Entrance exams should be taken by the end of the junior year. There is a deferred admissions plan and a rolling admissions plan. Applications should be filed by August 1 for fall entry, December 1 for spring entry, and May 1 for summer entry. Notification is sent on a rolling basis. Applications are accepted on-line.

Transfer: 51 transfer students enrolled in 2004-2005. Transfer students should have a minimum GPA of 2.5 and be in good academic and disciplinary standing. A satisfactory score is required on the SAT or ACT. An interview is advised. 35 of 122 credits required for the bachelor's degree must be completed at CBU.

Visiting: There are regularly scheduled orientations for prospective students, including attendance at classes, meetings with professors and students, a campus tour, and meetings with admissions and financial aid representatives. There are guides for informal visits and visitors may sit in on classes and stay overnight. To schedule a visit, contact Jim Shannon, Dean of Admissions at *jshannon@cbu.edu.*

Financial Aid: All undergraduates work part time. Average annual earnings from campus work are $1250. The average financial indebtedness of the 2005 graduate was $17,600. The FAFSA is required.

International Students: There are 28 international students enrolled. The school actively recruits these students. They must score satisfactorily on the written TOEFL.

Computers: Wireless access is available. All students may access the system during the 93.5 hours per week of computer center operation; 24-hour dial-in phone access is available. There are no time limits and no fees.

Graduates: From July 1, 2004 to June 30, 2005, 313 bachelor's degrees were awarded. The most popular majors were business (39%), psychology (22%), and engineering (15%). In an average class, 45% graduate in 4 years or less, 60% graduate in 5 years or less, and 63% graduate in 6 years or less.

Admissions Contact: Tracy Dysart-Ford, Dean of Admissions. E-mail: *admissions@cbu.edu* Web: *http://www.cbu.edu*

CRICHTON COLLEGE   A-3
Memphis, TN 38111-1375   (901) 320-9797, ext. 1041
                                        (800) 960-9777; Fax: (901) 320-9709

Full-time: 250 men, 470 women	**Faculty:** 30; IIB, --$
Part-time: 80 men, 85 women	**Ph.D.s:** 60%
Graduate: none	**Student/Faculty:** 24 to 1
Year: semesters, summer session	**Tuition:** $11,700
Application Deadline: open	**Room & Board:** $3600
Freshman Class: n/av	**ACT:** required COMPETITIVE

Crichton College, founded in 1941, is an independent Christian liberal arts college offering programs in liberal arts, Bible, business, health science, religion, and teacher preparation. There are 5 undergraduate schools. Figures in the above capsule and in this profile are approximate. The 2 libraries contain 46,777 volumes, 54,308 microform items, and 1580 audio/video tapes/CDs/DVDs, and subscribe to 303 periodicals including electronic. Computerized library services include the card catalog, interlibrary loans, database searching, and Internet access. Special learning facilities include a learning resource center, 21st Century Classroom, and a tutoring center. The 7-acre campus is in an urban area in midtown Memphis. Including any residence halls, there is 1 building.

Student Life: 86% of undergraduates are from Tennessee. Others are from 11 states and 4 foreign countries. 95% are from public schools. 45% are African American; 41% white. The average age of freshmen is 18; all undergraduates, 32. 50% do not continue beyond their first year; 50% remain to graduate.

Housing: 100 students can be accommodated in college housing, which includes single-sex off-campus apartments. On-campus housing is guaranteed for all 4 years. 96% of students commute. Alcohol is not permitted. All students may keep cars.

Activities: There are no fraternities or sororities. There are 12 groups on campus, including chorale, chorus, debate, drama, ethnic, forensics, honors, musical theater, professional, religious, social, social service, student government, and yearbook. Popular campus events include film, drama, and lecture series; concerts; and Marriage and Family Conference.

Sports: There are 2 intercollegiate sports for men, and 4 intramural sports for men and 4 for women.

Disabled Students: All of the campus is accessible. Wheelchair ramps, elevators, special parking, specially equipped rest rooms, lowered drinking fountains, and lowered telephones are available.

Services: Counseling and information services are available, as is tutoring in most subjects. There is remedial math, reading, and writing.

Campus Safety and Security: Measures include 24-hour foot and vehicle patrol, security escort services, informal discussions, and pamphlets/posters/films. There are lighted pathways/sidewalks, security gates at entrances, monitored security systems, and alarm buttons in each apartment unit.

Programs of Study: Crichton confers B.A. and B.S. degrees. Bachelor's degrees are awarded in BIOLOGICAL SCIENCE (biology/biological science), BUSINESS (business administration and management, human resources, and management information systems), COMMUNICATIONS AND THE ARTS (English), COMPUTER AND PHYSICAL SCIENCE (chemistry), EDUCATION (elementary, school psychology, science, and secondary), HEALTH PROFESSIONS (nursing), SOCIAL SCIENCE (biblical studies, clinical psychology, counseling/psychology, history, interdisciplinary studies, liberal arts/general studies, ministries, psychology, and youth ministry). Organizational management, elementary education, and liberal arts are the largest.

Required: Students must complete a minimum of 128 credit hours, and some disciplines require more. The number of hours for the major varies, but all students must take 15 hours of humanities, 3 to 12 of biblical studies, 8 of natural science, 4 of health/phys ed, and 3 each of math and computer science. The minimum GPA required is 2.0; for teacher education students, 2.5.

Special: B.A.-B.S. degrees, dual majors, and limited nondegree study are available. The college also offers internships with area businesses and institutions, a study-abroad program in London, accelerated degrees in organizational management and teacher education, student-designed majors, and work-study programs. There are 2 national honor societies, a freshman honors program, and 100 departmental honors programs.

Faculty/Classroom: 19% of faculty are male; 9%, female. All teach undergraduates, 4% do research, and 8% do both. The average class size in an introductory lecture is 33; in a laboratory, 15; and in a regular course, 17.

Admissions: In a recent year, 79% of the 2005-2006 applicants were accepted.

Requirements: A satisfactory score on the ACT is required. In addition, students must have a high school diploma or hold the GED. An essay is required. A GPA of 2.0 is required. AP and CLEP credits are accepted. Important factors in the admissions decision are advanced placement or honor courses, evidence of special talent, and leadership record.

Procedure: Freshmen are admitted to all sessions. Entrance exams should be taken during orientation. There is a deferred admissions plan. Application deadlines are open. Check with the school for current fee. Applications are accepted on-line.

Transfer: 570 transfer students enrolled in a recent year. Transfer students must have a minimum GPA of 2.0. An interview is required. 30 of 128 credits required for the bachelor's degree must be completed at Crichton.

Visiting: There are regularly scheduled orientations for prospective students, including a preview of all college departments. There are guides for informal visits and visitors may sit in on classes and stay overnight. To schedule a visit, contact the Admissions Office at *info@crichton.edu*.

Financial Aid: In a recent year, 75% of all full-time freshmen and 69% of continuing full-time students received some form of financial aid. 59% of full-time freshmen and 53% of continuing full-time students received need-based aid. The average freshman award was $11,522. Need-based scholarships or need-based grants averaged $5478 ($11,530 maximum); need-based self-help aid (loans and jobs) averaged $3595 ($10,575 maximum); non-need-based athletic scholarships averaged $6702 ($11,785 maximum); and other non-need-based awards and non-need-based scholarships averaged $6631 ($21,393 maximum). 5% of undergraduates work part time. Average annual earnings from campus work are $3671. The average financial indebtedness of the recent year's graduate was $22,514. The FAFSA, and the college's own financial statement are required. Contact the school for current deadlines.

International Students: In a recent year, there were 4 international students enrolled. Satisfactory scores are required on the TOEFL and the SAT or the ACT.

Computers: All students may access the system 24 hours a day, 7 days a week. There are no time limits. Check with the school for current fee. It is recommended that students in business administration with information management concentration. have personal computers. Dell Inspiron 1100/2650 is recommended.

Graduates: In a recent year, 110 bachelor's degrees were awarded.

Admissions Contact: David Wilson, Director of Admissions.
E-mail: *info@crichton.edu* Web: *http://www.crichton.edu*

CUMBERLAND UNIVERSITY — C-2

Lebanon, TN 37087

(615) 444-2562, ext 1225
(800) 467-0562; Fax: (615) 444-2569

Full-time: 409 men, 528 women	Faculty: 60
Part-time: 57 men, 89 women	Ph.D.s: 49%
Graduate: 96 men, 329 women	Student/Faculty: 16 to 1
Year: semesters, summer session	Tuition: $13,744
Application Deadline: open	Room & Board: $5150
Freshman Class: 1038 applied, 717 accepted, 262 enrolled	
SAT Verbal/Math: 490/485*	ACT: 21 COMPETITIVE

Cumberland University, founded in 1842, is a private institution offering undergraduate and graduate degrees in business, education, and social sciences. In addition to regional accreditation, Cumberland has baccalaureate program accreditation with AACSB and NLN. The library contains 37,056 volumes, 590 microform items, and 1260 audio/video tapes/CDs/DVDs, and subscribes to 357 periodicals including electronic. Computerized library services include the card catalog, interlibrary loans, database searching, and Internet access. Special learning facilities include a learning resource center, art gallery, natural history museum, and radio station. The 44-acre campus is in a small town 28 miles east of Nashville. Including any residence halls, there are 17 buildings.

Student Life: 88% of undergraduates are from Tennessee. Others are from 26 states, 32 foreign countries, and Canada. 89% are from public schools. 79% are white; 15% African American. The average age of freshmen is 18; all undergraduates, 24. 30% do not continue beyond their first year; 39% remain to graduate.

Housing: 400 students can be accommodated in college housing, which includes single-sex dormitories. On-campus housing is available on a first-come, first-served basis. 67% of students commute. Alcohol is not permitted. All students may keep cars.

Activities: 17% of men belong to 3 national fraternities; 7% of women belong to 2 national sororities. There are 15 groups on campus, including art, band, cheerleading, chorale, chorus, computers, dance, drama, honors, international, jazz band, marching band, musical theater, newspaper, pep band, political, professional, religious, social, social service, and student government. Popular campus events include Fall Frolic, Halloween at CU, and Fall and Spring Preview Days.

Sports: There are 9 intercollegiate sports for men and 8 for women, and 4 intramural sports for men and 5 for women. Facilities include a gym, field house, weight room, baseball and soccer fields, tennis courts, outdoor volleyball courts, football field, and softball field.

Disabled Students: All of the campus is accessible. Wheelchair ramps, special parking, and lowered telephones are available.

Services: Counseling and information services are available, as is tutoring in most subjects. There is remedial math, reading, and writing.

Campus Safety and Security: Measures include 24-hour foot and vehicle patrol, informal discussions, and lighted pathways/sidewalks. The outside entrances of the dorms are always secured; only residents have keys.

Programs of Study: Cumberland confers B.A., B.S., B.B.A., and B.S.N. degrees. Associate and master's degrees are also awarded. Bachelor's degrees are awarded in BIOLOGICAL SCIENCE (biology/biological science), BUSINESS (accounting, business administration and management, management science, marketing management, and recreation and leisure services), COMMUNICATIONS AND THE ARTS (English, fine arts, and music), COMPUTER AND PHYSICAL SCIENCE (mathematics), EDUCATION (elementary, middle school, music, physical, secondary, and special), HEALTH PROFESSIONS (nursing), SOCIAL SCIENCE (American studies, criminal justice, history, political science/government, psychology, social science, and sociology). Business, education, and nursing are the largest.

Required: To graduate, students must complete 120 to 132 (depending on major) semester hours, including a 41-hour core curriculum, and maintain a GPA of 2.0.

Special: Internships with local businesses and with the state legislature are available. Nondegree study, pass/fail options, and an accelerated degree program in general business are offered. There are 13 national honor societies, a freshman honors program, and 5 departmental honors programs.

Faculty/Classroom: 52% of faculty are male; 48%, female. 82% teach undergraduates. No introductory courses are taught by graduate students. The average class size in an introductory lecture is 20; in a laboratory, 20; and in a regular course, 20.

Admissions: 69% of the 2005-2006 applicants were accepted. The SAT scores for the 2005-2006 freshman class were: Verbal--60% below 500, 30% between 500 and 599, and 10% between 600 and 700; Math--65% below 500, 25% between 500 and 599, and 10% between 600 and 700. The ACT scores were 62% below 21, 22% between 21 and 23, 12% between 24 and 26, 3% between 27 and 28, and 1% above 28. 24% of the current freshmen were in the top fifth of their class; 53% were in the top two fifths.

Requirements: The ACT is required and the SAT is recommended. The ACT Optional Writing test is also recommended. In addition, a minimum GPA of 2.5 is expected. Applicants must be high school graduates or have earned the GED with a composite 50 score. A GPA of 2.5 is required (or the student goes before the Admissions committee). AP and CLEP credits are accepted.

Procedure: Freshmen are admitted fall, spring, and summer. Entrance exams should be taken during spring of the junior year ro fall of the senior year. There is a rolling admissions plan. Application deadlines are open. Application fee is $25. Applications are accepted on-line.

Transfer: 140 transfer students enrolled in 2004-2005. Transfer applicants should have a GPA of at least 2.0. 33 of 120 to 132 credits required for the bachelor's degree must be completed at Cumberland.

Visiting: There are regularly scheduled orientations for prospective students, consisting of campus tours, testing, information sessions pertaining to college life, and academic advising. A parent orientation is provided in conjunction with student orientation programs. There are guides for informal visits and visitors may sit in on classes. To schedule a visit, contact the Admissions Office.

Financial Aid: In 2005-2006, 88% of all full-time students received some form of financial aid. 35% of all full-time students received need-based aid. The average freshman award was $5986. Need-based scholarships or need-based grants averaged $5191 ($9588 maximum); need-based self-help aid (loans and jobs) averaged $4484 ($10,500 maximum); non-need-based athletic scholarships averaged $5388 ($16,510 maximum); and other non-need-based awards and non-need-based scholarships averaged $3990 ($12,750 maximum). Average annual earnings from campus work are $1000. The FAFSA and the college's own financial statement are required. The priority date for freshman financial aid applications for fall entry is February 1. The deadline for filing freshman financial aid applications for fall entry is July 15.

International Students: There are 40 international students enrolled. The school actively recruits these students. A satisfactory score is required on the written TOEFL or the MELAB and the SAT or the ACT.

Computers: Wireless access is available. All students may access the system. There are no time limits and no fees.

Graduates: From July 1, 2004 to June 30, 2005, 175 bachelor's degrees were awarded. The most popular majors were business administration (26%), education (18%), and nursing (18%). In an average class, 12% graduate in 4 years, 20% graduate in 5 years, and 8% graduate in 6 years.

Admissions Contact: Eddie Pawlawski, VP of Enrollment Management. E-mail: *epawlawski@cumberland.edu* Web: *cumberland.edu*

DAVID LIPSCOMB UNIVERSITY
(See Lipscomb University)

EAST TENNESSEE STATE UNIVERSITY   F-2
Johnson City, TN 37614

(423) 439-4213
(800) 462-3878; Fax: (423) 439-7156

Full-time: 3400 men, 4546 women	Faculty: 350; IIA, --$
Part-time: 650 men, 980 women	Ph.D.s: 75%
Graduate: 620 men, 1230 women	Student/Faculty: 23 to 1
Year: semesters, summer session	Tuition: $3840 ($11,800)
Application Deadline: open	Room & Board: $4700
Freshman Class: n/av	
SAT or ACT: required	**COMPETITIVE**

East Tennessee State University, founded in 1911, is a public institution that is part of the State University and Community College System of Tennessee. ETSU's undergraduate and graduate programs stress the liberal arts, business, art, fine arts, professional training, music, teacher preparation, technical studies, and health science. There are 6 undergraduate and 2 graduate schools. Figures in the above capsule and in this profile are approximate. In addition to regional accreditation, ETSU has baccalaureate program accreditation with AACSB, ABET, ACEJMC, ACS, ADA, CAAHEP, CSAB, CSWE, NASAD, NASM, NCATE, NEHSPAC, and NLN. The library contains 1,073,382 volumes, 1,692,830 microform items, and 23,658 audio/video tapes/CDs/DVDs, and subscribes to 3714 periodicals including electronic. Computerized library services include the card catalog, interlibrary loans, database searching, and Internet access. Special learning facilities include a learning resource center, art gallery, planetarium, radio station, TV station, and a regional art and history museum. The 366-acre campus is in a small town 90 miles northeast of Knoxville; 130 miles southwest of Roanoke, VA.; 60 miles northwest of Asheville, NC. Including any residence halls, there are 68 buildings.

Student Life: 89% of undergraduates are from Tennessee. Others are from 38 states, 46 foreign countries, and Canada. 97% are from public schools. 91% are white. The average age of freshmen is 19; all undergraduates, 23. 33% do not continue beyond their first year; 38% remain to graduate.

Housing: 2478 students can be accommodated in college housing, which includes single-sex and coed dormitories, on-campus apartments, and married-student housing. On-campus housing is available on a first-come, first-served basis. 79% of students commute. Alcohol is not permitted. All students may keep cars.

Activities: 4% of men belong to 8 national fraternities; 4% of women belong to 1 local and 6 national sororities. There are 200 groups on campus, including art, band, cheerleading, choir, chorale, chorus, computers, dance, drama, drill team, ethnic, forensics, gay, honors, international, jazz band, literary magazine, newspaper, pep band, photography, political, professional, radio and TV, religious, social, social service, and student government. Popular campus events include Leadership Retreat, National Clean Up for Hunger, and Winter Cruise.

Sports: There are 6 intercollegiate sports for men and 8 for women, and 8 intramural sports for men and 8 for women. Facilities include a 4000-seat gym and a domed stadium seating 12,000, which includes a basketball arena, tennis and handball/racquetball courts, a track, and weight and training rooms.

Disabled Students: 75% of the campus is accessible. Wheelchair ramps, elevators, special parking, specially equipped rest rooms, special class scheduling, lowered drinking fountains, lowered telephones, special housing, and adaptive computer equipment are available.

Services: Counseling and information services are available, as is tutoring in most subjects. There is a reader service for the blind, and remedial math, reading, and writing. The Office for Students with Disabilities, Student Support Services, and the Undergraduate Academic Advisement administer these sciences.

Campus Safety and Security: Measures include 24-hour foot and vehicle patrol, self-defense education, security escort services, and shuttle buses. There are informal discussions, pamphlets/posters/films, emergency telephones, lighted pathways/sidewalks, and engravers available to identify personal property.

Programs of Study: ETSU confers B.A., B.S., B.A.S., B.B.A., B.F.A. B.G.S., B.M., B.S.D.H., B.S.Ed., B.S.E.H., B.S.M.T., B.S.N., and B.S.W. degrees. Associate, master's, and doctoral degrees are also awarded. Bachelor's degrees are awarded in BIOLOGICAL SCIENCE (biology/biological science), BUSINESS (accounting, management science, and marketing/retailing/merchandising), COMMUNICATIONS AND THE ARTS (art, communications, English, fine arts, music, and speech/debate/rhetoric), COMPUTER AND PHYSICAL SCIENCE (chemistry, computer science, information sciences and systems, mathematics, and physics), EDUCATION (foreign languages, physical, and special), ENGINEERING AND ENVIRONMENTAL DESIGN (engineering technology, and survey and mapping technology), HEALTH PROFESSIONS (allied health, dental hygiene, environmental health science, health science, nursing, and public health), SOCIAL SCIENCE (child psychology/development, criminal justice, economics, geography, history, human development, interdisciplinary studies, liberal arts/general studies, philosophy, political science/government, psychology, social work, and sociology). Engineering technology, computer science, and nursing are the largest.

Required: All students must complete 120 semester hours, with 30 to 60 in the major, and maintain a minimum GPA of 2.0. Distribution requirements, which total 46 semester hours, include English, American history, phys ed, natural science, social and behavioral science, the humanities, analysis, and a 3-hour computer literacy course. An exit exam is also required.

Special: Special academic programs include cooperative education programs, cross-registration with Milligan College, internships in political science, applied human sciences, and management,and dual majors study abroad in Scotland, England, France, and Spain, and B.A.-B.S. degrees and dual majors in most arts and sciences undergraduate majors. A general studies degree is offered. Credit for military experience may be granted, and nondegree study and pass/fail options are possible. There are 19 national honor societies, a freshman honors program, and 12 departmental honors programs.

Faculty/Classroom: 55% of faculty are male; 45%, female. 85% teach undergraduates. The average class size in an introductory lecture is 30; in a laboratory, 15; and in a regular course, 25.

Requirements: A satisfactory score is required on the SAT or ACT. Other admissions requirements include graduation from an accredited secondary school, with 20 Carnegie units and 14 academic credits, including 4 of English, 3 of math, 2 each of a foreign language and science, and 1 each of history, social studies, and art. In-state students who pass the Tennessee State Proficiency Test are eligible to apply for admission. Applicants whose ACT/SAT is below a certain score must complete the Academic Assessment Placement Program (AAPP) test battery before registration for classes. The GED is also accepted. A GPA of 2.3 is required. AP and CLEP credits are accepted.

Procedure: Freshmen are admitted to all sessions. Entrance exams should be taken during the junior and/or senior year. Application deadlines are open. Applications are accepted on-line. Check with the school for current deadlines and fee.

Transfer: 857 transfer students enrolled in a recent year. Transfer students must have a minimum GPA of 2.0 in 12 or more semester credit hours of course work from a regionally accredited institution. Transfer students must also satisfy high school unit requirements if deficiencies exist. 34 of 120 credits required for the bachelor's degree must be completed at ETSU.

Visiting: There are regularly scheduled orientations for prospective students, including 5 2-day orientation programs held during spring and summer for new students admitted to fall term. There are guides for informal visits and visitors may sit in on classes and stay overnight. To schedule a visit, contact the Admissions Office at *go2etsu@etsu.edu*.

Financial Aid: In a recent year, 74% of all full-time freshmen and 75% of continuing full-time students received some form of financial aid. 55% of all full-time students received need-based aid. The average freshman award was $7407. Need-based scholarships or need-based grants averaged $5002; need-based self-help aid (loans and jobs) averaged $2992; and other non-need-based awards and non-need-based scholarships averaged $1760. 28% of undergraduates work part time. Average annual earnings from campus work are $2119. The average financial indebtedness of the recent year's graduate was $17,668. The FAFSA is required. Check with the school for current deadlines.

International Students: In a recent year, there were 99 international students enrolled. Satisfactory scores are required on the written TOEFL and the SAT or the ACT.

Computers: All students may access the system Students may access the system 24 hours per day. There are no time limits and no fees.

Graduates: In a recent year, 1499 bachelor's degrees were awarded. The most popular majors were nursing (8%), psychology (6%), and finance and elementary education (5%). In an average class, 12% graduate in 4 years or less, 29% graduate in 5 years or less, and 38% graduate in 6 years or less. 200 companies recruited on campus in a recent year.

Admissions Contact: Mike Pitts, Director of Admissions. A video is available. E-mail: *go2etsu@etsu.edu* Web: *www.etsu.edu*

FISK UNIVERSITY
Nashville, TN 37208-3051
C-2

(615) 329-8665
(888) 702-0022; Fax: (615) 329-8774

Full-time: 243 men, 575 women	**Faculty:** 66
Part-time: 21 men, 27 women	**Ph.D.s:** 76%
Graduate: 16 men, 39 women	**Student/Faculty:** 12 to 1
Year: semesters	**Tuition:** $13,100
Application Deadline: open	**Room & Board:** $6730
Freshman Class: 1643 applied, 1310 accepted, 214 enrolled	
SAT Verbal/Math: 480/470*	**ACT:** 20	**COMPETITIVE**

Fisk University, founded in 1866, is a private, nonsectarian, liberal arts institution . Estabished as a college for African Americans, Fisk has always accepted students regardless of race. In addition to regional accreditation, Fisk University has baccalaureate program accreditation with NASM. The library contains 210,000 volumes, 114,998 microform items, and 3880 audio/video tapes/CDs/DVDs, and subscribes to 844 periodicals including electronic. Computerized library services include the card catalog, database searching, Internet access, and laptop Internet portals. Special learning facilities include an art gallery and radio station. The 40-acre campus is in an urban area. Including any residence halls, there are 21 buildings.

Student Life: 69% of undergraduates are from out of state, mostly the South. Others are from 39 states and 6 foreign countries. 87% are from public schools. 92% are African American. The average age of freshmen is 18; all undergraduates, 20. 16% do not continue beyond their first year; 68% remain to graduate.

Housing: 852 students can be accommodated in college housing, which includes single-sex dorms and married-student housing. On-campus housing is guaranteed for all 4 years. 67% of students live on campus; of those, 80% remain on campus on weekends. Alcohol is not permitted. All students may keep cars.

Activities: 25% of men belong to 4 national fraternities; 20% of women belong to 4 national sororities. There are 102 groups on campus, including cheerleading, choir, dance, drama, honors, international, literary magazine, newspaper, political, professional, radio and TV, religious, social, student government, and yearbook. Popular campus events include Jubilee Day.

Sports: There are 7 intercollegiate sports for men and 8 for women. Facilities include a gym and a student center.

Disabled Students: 80% of the campus is accessible. Wheelchair ramps and elevators are available.

Services: Counseling and information services are available, as is tutoring in every subject. There is remedial math, reading, and writing.

Campus Safety and Security: Measures include 24-hour foot and vehicle patrol, security escort services, and lighted pathways/sidewalks.

Programs of Study: Fisk University confers B.A., B.S., and B.M. degrees. Master's degrees are also awarded. Bachelor's degrees are awarded in BIOLOGICAL SCIENCE (biology/biological science), BUSINESS (business administration and management), COMMUNICATIONS AND THE ARTS (dramatic arts, English, fine arts, French, music, Spanish, and speech/debate/rhetoric), COMPUTER AND PHYSICAL SCIENCE (chemistry, computer science, mathematics, and physics), EDUCATION (art and music), SOCIAL SCIENCE (economics, history, philosophy, political science/government, psychology, religion, and sociology). Biology, chemistry, and physics are the strongest academically. Biology is the largest.

Required: To graduate, students must complete 120 credits, including a 32-credit core curriculum in communications, creative arts, humanistic experience and thought, natural sciences or math, social sciences, and world civilization. In addition, students must complete 8 hours of written and computational skills and 24 hours of interdisciplinary courses, plus a foreign language. A minimum 2.0 GPA must be maintained.

Special: Fisk offers cross-registration with Vanderbilt University, study abroad, dual majors in engineering and pharmacy, student-designed majors, and campus work-study. Students may take a 5-year B.S.-B.E. program or a combined B.S.-M.B.A. program with Vanderbilt University. There are 8 national honor societies, including Phi Beta Kappa, and 6 departmental honors programs.

Faculty/Classroom: 61% of faculty are male; 39%, female. All teach undergraduates, 22% do research, and 24% do both. No introductory courses are taught by graduate students. The average class size in an introductory lecture is 30; in a laboratory, 15; and in a regular course, 19.

Admissions: 80% of the 2005-2006 applicants were accepted. The SAT scores for the 2005-2006 freshman class were: Verbal--53% below 500, 33% between 500 and 599, 13% between 600 and 700, and 1% above 700; Math--57% below 500, 33% between 500 and 599, 10% between 600 and 700, and 1% above 700. The ACT scores were 60% below 21, 21% between 21 and 23, 14% between 24 and 26, 3% between 27 and 28, and 1% above 28. 32% of the current freshmen were in the top fifth of their class; 67% were in the top two fifths. 3 freshmen graduated first in their class.

Requirements: The SAT or ACT is required. In addition, applicants should be high school graduates with 14 academic credits. A GPA of 2.5

is required. AP credits are accepted. Important factors in the admissions decision are advanced placement or honor courses, leadership record, and evidence of special talent.

Procedure: Freshmen are admitted fall and spring. There are early admissions, deferred admissions, and rolling admissions plans. Application deadlines are open. Application fee is $50. Applications are accepted on-line.

Transfer: 42 transfer students enrolled in 2004-2005. Applicants for transfer should have a minimum college GPA of 2.0.

Visiting: There are guides for informal visits and visitors may sit in on classes and stay overnight. To schedule a visit, contact the Admissions Office at (615) 329-8666.

Financial Aid: In 2005-2006, 92% of all full-time students received some form of financial aid. 86% of full-time freshmen and 74% of continuing full-time students received need-based aid. The average freshman award was $16,831. Need-based scholarships or need-based grants averaged $6044; need-based self-help aid (loans and jobs) averaged $10,502; and other non-need-based awards and non-need-based scholarships averaged $285. The FAFSA and the college's own financial statement are required. The priority date for freshman financial aid applications for fall entry is February 15.

International Students: A satisfactory score is required on the written TOEFL.

Computers: All students may access the system. There are no time limits and no fees.

Graduates: From July 1, 2004 to June 30, 2005, 140 bachelor's degrees were awarded. The most popular majors were psychology (22%), business administration (20%), and biology (12%). In an average class, 41% graduate in 4 years or less, 55% graduate in 5 years or less, and 68% graduate in 6 years or less.

Admissions Contact: Keith Chandler, Director of Admissions.
E-mail: *admit@fisk.edu* Web: *www.fisk.edu*

FREED-HARDEMAN UNIVERSITY
Henderson, TN 38340
B-3

(731) 989-6651
(800) 630-3480; Fax: (731) 989-6047

Full-time: 640 men, 740 women	**Faculty:** 90; IIA, --$
Part-time: 40 men, 35 women	**Ph.D.s:** 78%
Graduate: 195 men, 330 women	**Student/Faculty:** 15 to 1
Year: semesters, summer session	**Tuition:** $11,050
Application Deadline: open	**Room & Board:** $5320
Freshman Class: n/av	
ACT: required	**NONCOMPETITIVE**

Freed-Hardeman University, founded in 1869, is a private, liberal arts institution associated with Churches of Christ. There are 6 undergraduate and 3 graduate schools. Figures in the above capsule and in this profile are approximate. In addition to regional accreditation, FHU has baccalaureate program accreditation with ACBSP, CSWE, and NCATE. The library contains 158,565 volumes, 240,000 microform items, and 43,000 audio/video tapes/CDs/DVDs, and subscribes to 1650 periodicals including electronic. Computerized library services include the card catalog, interlibrary loans, database searching, and Internet access. Special learning facilities include a learning resource center, art gallery, radio station, TV station, and a Cancer Research Institute. The 120-acre campus is in a small town 85 miles east of Memphis and 13 miles south of Jackson. Including any residence halls, there are 34 buildings.

Student Life: 52% of undergraduates are from out of state, mostly the South. Others are from 36 states, 17 foreign countries, and Canada. 75% are from public schools. 87% are white. Most are Protestant. The average age of freshmen is 19; all undergraduates, 21. 26% do not continue beyond their first year; 57% remain to graduate.

Housing: 1303 students can be accommodated in college housing, which includes single-sex dormitories and on-campus apartments. On-campus housing is guaranteed for all 4 years. 78% of students live on campus; of those, 55% remain on campus on weekends. Alcohol is not permitted. All students may keep cars.

Activities: There are no fraternities or sororities. There are 52 groups on campus, including art, band, cheerleading, choir, chorus, computers, drama, drum and bugle corps, ethnic, honors, international, jazz band, musical theater, newspaper, orchestra, pep band, photography, political, professional, radio and TV, religious, social, social service, student government, and yearbook. Popular campus events include Makin' Music and Annual Bible Lectureship.

Sports: There are 6 intercollegiate sports for men and 7 for women, and 7 intramural sports for men and 7 for women. Facilities include 3 gyms, lighted playing fields, lighted tennis courts, a swimming pool, a walking track, a weight room, racquetball courts, and a game room.

Disabled Students: 70% of the campus is accessible. Wheelchair ramps, elevators, special parking, specially equipped rest rooms, special class scheduling, lowered drinking fountains, and lowered telephones are available.

Services: Counseling and information services are available, as is tutoring in most subjects. There is remedial math, reading, and writing.

Campus Safety and Security: Measures include 24-hour foot and vehicle patrol, security escort services, informal discussions, and lighted pathways/sidewalks.

Programs of Study: FHU confers B.A., B.S., B.B.A., and B.S.W. degrees. Master's degrees are also awarded. Bachelor's degrees are awarded in AGRICULTURE (agricultural business management), BIOLOGICAL SCIENCE (biology/biological science), BUSINESS (accounting, banking and finance, business administration and management, and marketing/retailing/merchandising), COMMUNICATIONS AND THE ARTS (art, broadcasting, communications, dramatic arts, English, fine arts, public relations, and speech/debate/rhetoric), COMPUTER AND PHYSICAL SCIENCE (chemistry, computer programming, computer science, information sciences and systems, mathematics, and physical sciences), EDUCATION (art, early childhood, elementary, health, middle school, music, physical, science, secondary, and special), ENGINEERING AND ENVIRONMENTAL DESIGN (preengineering), HEALTH PROFESSIONS (predentistry, premedicine, preoptometry, prepharmacy, and preveterinary science), SOCIAL SCIENCE (biblical studies, child care/child and family studies, family/consumer studies, history, ministries, psychology, and social work). Premedicine, preengineering, and business are the strongest academically. Business, Bible, and elementary education are the largest.

Required: To graduate, students must complete 132 semester hours, including 44 in upper-division courses in Bible, skills, humanities, and science, plus 3 hours of speech communication and 2 hours of phys ed. The major requires a minimum of 30 semester hours, including 15 upper-division hours. Students must maintain a GPA of 2.0. All students must demonstrate, by approved tests or criteria, basic competence in reading, writing, oral communication, math, and computers.

Special: FHU offers cross-registration with Lambuth University and Union University, study abroad in Belgium, a B.A.-B.S. degree in Bible, biology, communication, and arts and humanities, co-op programs, a dual major, field practium opportunities in several majors, student-designed majors, 3-2 engineering degrees with 6 universities, and non-degree study. There are 4 national honor societies, a freshman honors program, and 13 departmental honors programs.

Faculty/Classroom: 66% of faculty are male; 34%, female. 91% teach undergraduates. No introductory courses are taught by graduate students. The average class size in a laboratory is 22 and in a regular course, 20.

Requirements: A satisfactory score is required on the ACT is required. In addition, candidates for admission should be graduates of an accredited secondary school. An interview is recommended. A GPA of 2.25 is required. AP and CLEP credits are accepted. Important factors in the admissions decision are personality/intangible qualities, recommendations by school officials, and leadership record.

Procedure: Freshmen are admitted fall, spring, and summer. Entrance exams should be taken in early fall or summer before senior year. There is an early admissions plan. Application deadlines are open. Applications are accepted on-line. Check with the school for current deadlines and fee.

Transfer: Applicants should have a minimum college GPA of 2.0. Those with fewer than 30 college credits must also submit a high school transcript and ACT or SAT scores. 33 of 132 credits required for the bachelor's degree must be completed at FHU.

Visiting: There are regularly scheduled orientations for prospective students, including an orientation during the 5 days prior to classes beginning in the fall. There are guides for informal visits and visitors may sit in on classes and stay overnight. To schedule a visit, contact Jim Brown.

Financial Aid: In a recent year, 87% of all full-time freshmen and 88% of continuing full-time students received some form of financial aid. 51% of full-time freshmen and 74% of continuing full-time students received need-based aid. 31% of undergraduates work part time. Average annual earnings from campus work are $1080. The FAFSA is required. Check with the school for current deadlines.

International Students: In a recent year, there were 27 international students enrolled. Satisfactory scores are required on the written TOEFL and the ACT.

Computers: All students may access the system.

Graduates: In a recent year, 296 bachelor's degrees were awarded. The most popular majors were Bible (14%), elementary education (14%), and biology (6%). In an average class, 2% graduate in 3 years or less, 39% graduate in 4 years or less, 55% graduate in 5 years or less, and 57% graduate in 6 years or less. 84 companies recruited on campus in a recent year.

Admissions Contact: Jim Brown, Director of Admissions. A video is available. E-mail: jbrown@fhu.edu Web: http://www.fhu.edu

KING COLLEGE   F-2

Bristol, TN 37620-2699

(423) 652-4861
(800) 362-0014; Fax: (423) 652-4727

Full-time: 314 men, 489 women	**Faculty:** 50; IIB, --$
Part-time: 30 men, 34 women	**Ph.D.s:** 76%
Graduate: 52 men, 45 women	**Student/Faculty:** 16 to 1
Year: semesters, summer session	**Tuition:** $17,680
Application Deadline: open	**Room & Board:** $5720
Freshman Class: 1331 applied, 524 accepted, 209 enrolled	
SAT Verbal/Math: 515/524*	**COMPETITIVE**

King College, founded in 1867, is a private liberal arts college affiliated with the Presbyterian Church (U.S.A.). There are 5 undergraduate schools and 1 graduate school. In addition to regional accreditation, King has baccalaureate program accreditation with CCNE and IACBE. The library contains 110,000 volumes, 40,408 microform items, and 5832 audio/video tapes/CDs/DVDs, and subscribes to 389 periodicals including electronic. Computerized library services include the card catalog, interlibrary loans, database searching, Internet access, and laptop Internet portals. Special learning facilities include a learning resource center and an observatory. The 135-acre campus is in a small town 2 miles east of Bristol. Including any residence halls, there are 17 buildings.

Student Life: 54% of undergraduates are from Tennessee. Others are from 30 states, 17 foreign countries, and Canada. 83% are from public schools. 89% are white. Most are Protestant. The average age of freshmen is 18; all undergraduates, 24. 67% do not continue beyond their first year; 59% remain to graduate.

Housing: 485 students can be accommodated in college housing, which includes single-sex dorms and married-student housing. In addition, there are honors houses. On-campus housing is guaranteed for all 4 years. Alcohol is not permitted. All students may keep cars.

Activities: There are no fraternities or sororities. There are 35 groups on campus, including art, band, cheerleading, choir, chorale, chorus, dance, debate, drama, honors, international, literary magazine, musical theater, newspaper, pep band, photography, political, professional, religious, social service, student government, and yearbook. Popular campus events include International Fair, Fall Ball, and Dogwood Ball and Weekend.

Sports: There are 10 intercollegiate sports for men and 11 for women, and 7 intramural sports for men and 6 for women. Facilities include a gym, soccer and baseball fields, 6 tennis courts, and a fitness trail. A student center complex provides a facility for sporting events, convocations, student activities, and fitness. The 68,000-square-foot building has a basketball court, running track, racquetball courts, offices, a boardroom, a weight room, cardio equipment, and a medical suite.

Disabled Students: 80% of the campus is accessible. Wheelchair ramps, elevators, special parking, and specially equipped rest rooms are available.

Services: Counseling and information services are available, as is tutoring in most subjects.

Campus Safety and Security: Measures include security escort services, informal discussions, lighted pathways/sidewalks, and 24-hour foot and vehicle patrol on weekends and 12-hour patrol Monday through Friday.

Programs of Study: King confers B.A., B.S., B.B.A., B.S. Med.Tech., and B.S.N. degrees. Master's degrees are also awarded. Bachelor's degrees are awarded in BIOLOGICAL SCIENCE (biochemistry, biology/biological science, and neurosciences), BUSINESS (business administration and management, business economics, electronic business, international business management, marketing management, and sports management), COMMUNICATIONS AND THE ARTS (English, French, modern language, Spanish, technical and business writing, and visual and performing arts), COMPUTER AND PHYSICAL SCIENCE (applied mathematics, chemistry, computer science, mathematics, and physics), EDUCATION (elementary, physical, and secondary), HEALTH PROFESSIONS (health science, medical technology, nursing, and physical therapy), SOCIAL SCIENCE (American studies, behavioral science, biblical studies, forensic studies, history, interdisciplinary studies, missions, philosophy, political science/government, psychology, and youth ministry). Business and economics, English, and natural sciences are the strongest academically. Business and economics, nursing, and social sciences are the largest.

Required: Students must complete a minimum of 124 semester hours with 27 to 53 in the major. The minimum 49 semester hours of core curriculum include courses in English, history, math, Bible, humanities, science, social science, and phys ed. Students must have a minimum GPA of 2.0 in most majors (may vary according to field of study). A comprehensive exam in the student's major area of concentration is required.

Special: King offers co-op programs, cross-registration with Virginia Intermont College, internships, study abroad in approximately 50 countries, a Washington semester, and work-study programs. There are 3-2 engineering degrees available with Vanderbilt University and University of Tennessee. Dual degrees in pharmacy, engineering, and physical therapy are offered. Nondegree study and pass/fail options for special students are available. There is 1 national honor society, a freshman honors program, and 1 departmental honors program.

Faculty/Classroom: 52% of faculty are male; 48%, female. All teach undergraduates and 45% both teach and do research. The average class size in an introductory lecture is 30; in a laboratory, 30; and in a regular course, 15.

Admissions: 39% of the 2005-2006 applicants were accepted. The SAT scores for the 2005-2006 freshman class were: Verbal--40% below 500, 43% between 500 and 599, 16% between 600 and 700, and 1% above 700; Math--26% below 500, 63% between 500 and 599, and 11% between 600 and 700. The ACT scores were 28% below 21, 39% between 21 and 23, 20% between 24 and 26, 7% between 27 and 28, and 6% above 28. 35% of the current freshmen were in the top fifth of their class; 66% were in the top two fifths. 1 freshman graduated first in the class.

Requirements: The SAT or ACT is required. In addition, graduation from an accredited or recognized secondary institution is required with a minimum of 16 academic units, distributed as follows: 4 of English; 2 of algebra (algebra I and II); 1 of geometry; 2 of foreign language; 2 from history and social studies; 1 of natural science; and 4 of other academic electives. A GPA of 2.4 is required. AP and CLEP credits are accepted. Important factors in the admissions decision are advanced placement or honor courses, extracurricular activities record, and leadership record.

Procedure: Freshmen are admitted to all sessions. Entrance exams should be taken by May 1. There are early admissions and deferred admissions plans. There is a rolling admissions plan. Application deadlines are open. The fall 2005 application fee was $20. Applications are accepted on-line.

Transfer: 81 transfer students enrolled in 2004-2005. Transfer applicants should have a minimum 2.0 GPA and 30 semester hours. If fewer hours have been completed, a 2.4 high school GPA and a minimum ACT or SAT score are required. 50 of 124 credits required for the bachelor's degree must be completed at King.

Visiting: There are regularly scheduled orientations for prospective students, including a campus tour, a financial aid seminar, faculty sessions, an overnight visit in a dorm, and admissions counseling. There are guides for informal visits and visitors may sit in on classes and stay overnight. To schedule a visit, contact the Admissions Office.

Financial Aid: In 2005-2006, 99% of all full-time students received some form of financial aid. 52% of full-time freshmen and 70% of continuing full-time students received need-based aid. The average freshman award was $14,907. Need-based scholarships or need-based grants averaged $13,391; need-based self-help aid (loans and jobs) averaged $2664; non-need-based athletic scholarships averaged $5894; and other non-need-based awards and non-need-based scholarships averaged $7459. 22% of undergraduates work part time. Average annual earnings from campus work are $877. The average financial indebtedness of the 2005 graduate was $16,635. King is a member of CSS. The FAFSA and the college's own financial statement are required. The priority date for freshman financial aid applications for fall entry is March 15. The deadline for filing freshman financial aid applications for fall entry is rolling.

International Students: There are 37 international students enrolled. The school actively recruits these students. They must achieve a satisfactory score on the TOEFL and also take the college's own test. Students outside the United States where English is the primary language are required to take the SAT in place of the TOEFL.

Computers: Wireless access is available. All students may access the system. There are no time limits and no fees. All students are required to have personal computers and are provided with IBM ThinkPads at campus check-in day.

Graduates: From July 1, 2004 to June 30, 2005, 151 bachelor's degrees were awarded. The most popular majors were nursing (24%), business (18%), and English (6%). In an average class, 5% graduate in 3 years or less, 48% graduate in 4 years or less, and 59% graduate in 5 years or less. Of the 2004 graduating class, 24% were enrolled in graduate school within 6 months of graduation and 63% were employed.

Admissions Contact: Melinda Clark, Associate Vice President of Enrollment Management. E-mail: *admissions@king.edu*
Web: *www.king.edu*

KNOXVILLE COLLEGE
Knoxville, TN 37921

E-3

(865) 524-6500
(800) 743-5669; Fax: (865) 524-6686

Full-time: none	Faculty: 47
Part-time: none	Ph.D.s: 55%
Graduate: none	Student/Faculty: n/av
Year: semesters	Tuition: $6200
Application Deadline: open	Room & Board: n/app
Freshman Class: n/av	
SAT or ACT: recommended	LESS COMPETITIVE

Knoxville College, founded in 1875, is a small, private liberal arts institution affiliated with the United Presbyterian Church. Figures in the above

capsule and in this profile are approximate. The library contains 79,000 volumes and 11,000 microform items, and subscribes to 450 periodicals including electronic. The 39-acre campus is in an urban area. There are 22 buildings.

Programs of Study: KC confers B.A., B.S., B.S.Ed., B.S.M.T., and B.S. in Tourism, Food, and Lodging Administration. degrees. Associate degrees are also awarded. Bachelor's degrees are awarded in BIOLOGICAL SCIENCE (biology/biological science), BUSINESS (accounting and business administration and management), COMMUNICATIONS AND THE ARTS (English and music), COMPUTER AND PHYSICAL SCIENCE (chemistry), EDUCATION (business, early childhood, elementary, health, mathematics, music, physical, recreation, and science), HEALTH PROFESSIONS (health care administration and medical laboratory technology), SOCIAL SCIENCE (political science/government, psychology, and sociology).

Required: To graduate, all students must complete 124 semester hours with at least a 2.0 GPA. 66 hours in a core curriculum are required, including courses in English, speech, history, math, natural and social sciences, religion, philosophy, humanities and the arts, computer science, health, and phys ed. Between 26 and 40 hours are required in the major.

Special: A 3-2 engineering degree is offered with the University of Tennessee. Students seeking degrees in tourism, food and lodging administration, or recreation leadership may take some courses at the University of Tennessee. Cooperative programs, nondegree study, internships, and dual majors are possible. There is a freshman honors program.

Requirements: The SAT or ACT is recommended. In addition, SAT or ACT scores should be submitted for placement purposes. Applicants should be graduates of an accredited high school or have earned the GED. Secondary preparation should include a total of 15 Carnegie units. Music program applicants must audition. Culturally disadvantaged students may be admitted under a special program. A GPA of 2.0 is required.

Procedure: Application deadlines are open. Check with the school for current fee.

Transfer: Applicants with fewer than 15 college credits must submit a high school transcript. 30 of 124 credits required for the bachelor's degree must be completed at KC.

Visiting: There are guides for informal visits. To schedule a visit, contact Director of Admissions.

Financial Aid: In a recent year, 100% of all full-time freshmen received some form of financial aid. The FAFSA and the college's own financial statement are required. Check with the school for current deadlines.

International Students: A satisfactory score is required on the written TOEFL.

Computers: All students may access the system. There are no time limits and no fees.

Admissions Contact: Director of Admissions. A video is available.

LAMBUTH UNIVERSITY
Jackson, TN 38301

B-3

(731) 425-3322
(800) 526-2884; Fax: (731) 425-3496

Full-time: 351 men, 415 women	Faculty: 52
Part-time: 21 men, 18 women	Ph.D.s: 80%
Graduate: none	Student/Faculty: 15 to 1
Year: semesters, summer session	Tuition: $15,400
Application Deadline: open	Room & Board: $6300
Freshman Class: 1333 applied, 861 accepted, 234 enrolled	
SAT : not required	ACT: 24 COMPETITIVE+

Lambuth University, founded in 1843, is a private liberal arts and sciences institution affiliated with the United Methodist Church. There are 6 undergraduate schools. In addition to regional accreditation, Lambuth has baccalaureate program accreditation with ACBSP. The library contains 137,914 volumes, 203,130 microform items, and 2296 audio/video tapes/CDs/DVDs, and subscribes to 13,999 periodicals including electronic. Computerized library services include the card catalog, interlibrary loans, database searching, Internet access, and laptop Internet portals. Special learning facilities include a learning resource center, art gallery, planetarium, radio station, and video studio. The 50-acre campus is in an urban area 75 miles northeast of Memphis. Including any residence halls, there are 16 buildings.

Student Life: 75% of undergraduates are from Tennessee. Students are from 30 states, 12 foreign countries, and Canada. 81% are from public schools. 76% are white; 16% African American. 70% are Protestant; 28% claim no religious affiliation; 8% Catholic. The average age of freshmen is 18; all undergraduates, 22. 42% do not continue beyond their first year; 38% remain to graduate.

Housing: 628 students can be accommodated in college housing, which includes single-sex and coed dormitories, on-campus apartments, fraternity houses, and sorority houses. In addition, there are honors houses. 62% of students live on campus; of those, 60% remain on campus on weekends. Alcohol is not permitted. All students may keep cars.

Activities: 11% of men belong to 3 national fraternities; 15% of women belong to 3 national sororities. There are 26 groups on campus, including art, band, cheerleading, chess, choir, computers, dance, drama, ethnic, film, honors, international, jazz band, literary magazine, musical theater, newspaper, pep band, photography, political, professional, radio and TV, religious, social, social service, student government, and yearbook. Popular campus events include Hawaiian Bash, FOCUS, Christmas Candlelight Service, and All-Sing.

Sports: There are 7 intercollegiate sports for men and 7 for women, and 10 intramural sports for men and 10 for women. Facilities include an indoor swimming pool, racquetball and tennis courts, a weight room, a gym, and football, baseball, and soccer fields.

Disabled Students: 75% of the campus is accessible. Wheelchair ramps, elevators, special parking, specially equipped rest rooms, special class scheduling, and special housing are available.

Services: Counseling and information services are available, as is tutoring in most subjects. There is remedial math, reading, and writing.

Campus Safety and Security: Measures include 24-hour foot and vehicle patrol, self-defense education, security escort services, and informal discussions. There are pamphlets/posters/films, emergency telephones, and lighted pathways/sidewalks.

Programs of Study: Lambuth confers B.A., B.S., B.B.A., and B.M. degrees. Bachelor's degrees are awarded in BIOLOGICAL SCIENCE (biology/biological science), BUSINESS (business administration and management), COMMUNICATIONS AND THE ARTS (communications, dramatic arts, English, fine arts, French, German, music, Spanish, and visual and performing arts), COMPUTER AND PHYSICAL SCIENCE (chemistry and mathematics), EDUCATION (elementary, music, physical, secondary, and special), ENGINEERING AND ENVIRONMENTAL DESIGN (interior design), SOCIAL SCIENCE (family/consumer studies, history, interdisciplinary studies, international relations, political science/government, psychology, religion, and sociology). Biological science, art, and business are the strongest academically. Business, education, and health and human performance are the largest.

Required: All students must complete a minimum of 128 semester hours, including Freshman Seminar, 9 hours in English, 8 in biological/physical sciences, 6 each in religion, writing courses, and interdisciplinary courses, and 3 each in speech, computer science, social science, and math. Students must have a minimum GPA of 2.0. Students must have 18 hours in a minor field of study. A comprehensive exam in major field is required. Juniors must take a test of core curriculum skills. Portfolios and research projects may also be required.

Special: Lambuth offers cross-registration with Union University and Freed-Hardeman University, internships in several disciplines, study abroad in England, Mexico, and France, a Washington semester, work-study programs, dual majors in all areas, student-designed majors in most areas, a 3-2 engineering degree, nondegree study, and pass/fail options. Pre-professional programs have a three-year residence program. There are 6 national honor societies, a freshman honors program, and 10 departmental honors programs.

Faculty/Classroom: 58% of faculty are male; 42%, female. All teach undergraduates. The average class size in an introductory lecture is 23; in a laboratory, 23; and in a regular course, 20.

Admissions: 65% of the 2005-2006 applicants were accepted. The SAT scores for the 2005-2006 freshman class were: Verbal--31% below 500, 43% between 500 and 599, 24% between 600 and 700, and 2% above 700; Math--24% below 500, 52% between 500 and 599, 21% between 600 and 700, and 3% above 700. The ACT scores were 19% below 21, 32% between 21 and 23, 27% between 24 and 26, 12% between 27 and 28, and 10% above 28. 42% of the current freshmen were in the top fifth of their class; 66% were in the top two fifths. 8 freshmen graduated first in their class.

Requirements: The ACT is required. Other students are admitted at the discretion of the admissions committee. Candidates for admission should be graduates of accredited secondary schools. The GED is accepted. It is preferred that students have completed 4 courses each in English, history, math, science, and social studies, and 2 courses in foreign language, art, and music. An essay and interview are recommended. A GPA of 2.0 is required. AP and CLEP credits are accepted. Important factors in the admissions decision are advanced placement or honor courses, leadership record, and recommendations by school officials.

Procedure: Freshmen are admitted to all sessions. Entrance exams should be taken by February of the senior year. There is a deferred admissions and rolling admissions plan. Application deadlines are open. Applications are accepted on-line. The fall 2003 application fee was $25.

Transfer: 74 transfer students enrolled in 2004-2005. A minimum 2.0 GPA in college-level courses taken, transcripts from all colleges attended, and a statement of honorable dismissal are required. An associate degree usually guarantees admission. A minimum of 12 successfully completed credit hours is recommended. 32 of 128 credits required for the bachelor's degree must be completed at Lambuth.

Visiting: There are regularly scheduled orientations for prospective students, consisting of students and parents touring the campus, participating in the students panel discussion, and attending a luncheon. Students

visit a class. Parents participate in seminars. There are guides for informal visits and visitors may sit in on classes and stay overnight. To schedule a visit, contact the Office of Admissions.

Financial Aid: In 2005-2006, 97% of all full-time freshmen and 86% of continuing full-time students received some form of financial aid. 58% of full-time freshmen and 75% of continuing full-time students received need-based aid. The average freshman award was $10,116. Need-based scholarships or need-based grants averaged $12,871; need-based self-help aid (loans and jobs) averaged $3960; non-need-based athletic scholarships averaged $6713; and other non-need-based awards and non-need-based scholarships averaged $10,459. 32% of undergraduates work part time. Average annual earnings from campus work are $112. The average financial indebtedness of the 2005 graduate was $17,000. Lambuth is a member of CSS. The FAFSA is required. The priority date for freshman financial aid applications for fall entry is January 15. The deadline for filing freshman financial aid applications for fall entry is May 1.

International Students: There are 27 international students enrolled. The school actively recruits these students. They must score satisfactorily on the written TOEFL or on the electronic version and also take the SAT or the ACT, with a score of 20 on the ACT. Others are admitted at the discretion of the admissions committee.

Computers: Wireless access is available. All PCs (including labtops) have access to the Internet. There is a teaching lab with 24 PCs that students may use for specific classes. The Student Union has 22 PCs, the computer lab has 12 PCs, and the library has 14 PCs plus 5 portals. All students may access the system 8 A.M. to 10 P.M. when classes are not in session (computer lab). There are no time limits and no fees. It is strongly recommended that all students have a personal computer.

Graduates: From July 1, 2004 to June 30, 2005, 154 bachelor's degrees were awarded. The most popular majors were business (30%), education (10%), and health and human performance (9%). In an average class, 1% graduate in 3 years or less, 25% graduate in 4 years or less, 37% graduate in 5 years or less, and 38% graduate in 6 years or less. 4 companies recruited on campus in 2004-2005. Of the 2004 graduating class, 30% were enrolled in graduate school within 6 months of graduation and 46% were employed.

Admissions Contact: Sandy Maxwell, Associate Director of Admissions. E-mail: *admit@lambuth.edu* Web: *www.lambuth.edu*

LANE COLLEGE   B-3
Jackson, TN 38301-4598

	(731) 426-7532
	(800) 960-7533; Fax: (731) 426-7559
Full-time: 455 men, 490 women	**Faculty:** 50; IIB, --$
Part-time: 10 men, 10 women	**Ph.D.s:** 60%
Graduate: none	**Student/Faculty:** 19 to 1
Year: semesters, summer session	**Tuition:** $6820
Application Deadline: see profile	**Room & Board:** $4400
Freshman Class: n/av	
ACT: required	**COMPETITIVE+**

Lane College, founded in 1882, is a private liberal arts institution affiliated with the Christian Methodist Episcopal Church. Figures in the above capsule and in this profile are approximate. The library contains 98,619 volumes, 53,125 microform items, and 820 audio/video tapes/CDs/DVDs, and subscribes to 226 periodicals including electronic. Computerized library services include the card catalog, interlibrary loans, database searching, and Internet access. Special learning facilities include a learning resource center, a media center, several computer labs for students majoring in education and other areas, a curriculum lab, a video teleconferencing center, a math lab, a writing center, and a mass communications lab. The 25-acre campus is in a small town 79 miles from Memphis, 122 miles from Nashville. Including any residence halls, there are 23 buildings.

Student Life: 57% of undergraduates are from Tennessee. Others are from 30 states and 1 foreign country. 85% are from public schools. 99% are African American. Most are Protestant. The average age of freshmen is 19; all undergraduates, 21. 20% do not continue beyond their first year; 65% remain to graduate.

Housing: 638 students can be accommodated in college housing, which includes single-sex dormitories and on-campus apartments. On-campus housing is guaranteed for all 4 years. 63% of students live on campus; of those, 40% remain on campus on weekends. Alcohol is not permitted. All students may keep cars.

Activities: 3% of men belong to 2 local and 2 national fraternities; 9% of women belong to 4 local and 4 national sororities. There are 21 groups on campus, including band, cheerleading, chess, choir, chorus, computers, debate, drama, honors, marching band, newspaper, pep band, religious, social, social service, student government, and yearbook. Popular campus events include Founders Day, Fine Arts Week, and Religious Emphasis Week.

Sports: There are 6 intercollegiate sports for men and 6 for women, and 4 intramural sports for men and 4 for women. Facilities include an Olympic-size swimming pool, a multipurpose/weight room, a gym, off-campus football and baseball fields, and a campus recreation center with a theater area, dance floor, billiards, Ping-Pong, table games, and a lounge area.

Disabled Students: 70% of the campus is accessible. Wheelchair ramps, elevators, special parking, specially equipped rest rooms, and wheelchair lifts in some buildings are available.

Services: Counseling and information services are available, as is tutoring in most subjects. The writing center provides tutoring in writing and the mathematics lab offers tutoring in math. Student Support Services provides tutoring in English, math, reading, computer science, computer literacy, test-taking, and study skills.

Campus Safety and Security: Measures include 24-hour foot and vehicle patrol, security escort services, informal discussions, and pamphlets/posters/films. There are emergency telephones, lighted pathways/sidewalks, a security guard at the entrance to the campus, and camera surveillance in parking lots and dorms.

Programs of Study: Lane confers B.A. and B.S. degrees. Bachelor's degrees are awarded in BIOLOGICAL SCIENCE (biology/biological science), BUSINESS (business administration and management), COMMUNICATIONS AND THE ARTS (communications, English, French, and music), COMPUTER AND PHYSICAL SCIENCE (chemistry, computer science, mathematics, and physics), EDUCATION (physical), SOCIAL SCIENCE (criminal justice, history, interdisciplinary studies, religion, and sociology). Business, education, and criminal justice are the strongest academically. Education, business, and sociology are the largest.

Required: Students must complete a minimum of 124 semester hours with a 2.0 GPA. 50 to 69 hours are required in the general studies curriculum, which includes courses in art, music, personal finance, foreign language, speech, composition, literature, history, sociology, math, physical science, biology, computer literacy, foundations of education, religion, and phys ed. The ETS Academic Profile is also required. ETS Major Field Tests are given as exit exams by major.

Special: Cooperative programs are available in engineering with Tennessee State University School of Engineering and Technology. The College also offers work-study programs, dual majors, student-designed majors, and nondegree study. Internships are available in many fields in various corporations, universities, and federal agencies. The college also has a cooperative agreement with Milwaukee Area Technical College. There are 2 national honor societies.

Faculty/Classroom: 72% of faculty are male; 28%, female. All teach undergraduates. The average class size in an introductory lecture is 25; in a laboratory, 16; and in a regular course, 16.

Requirements: A satisfactory score is required on the ACT. In addition, graduation from an accredited secondary school is required; a GED will be accepted. Applicants' academic record must include 16 credits, including 4 credits in English, and 2 credits each in math, science, and social studies. An additional 2 credits in a foreign language is recommended. An interview is recommended. A GPA of 2.0 is required. AP and CLEP credits are accepted. Important factors in the admissions decision are evidence of special talent, recommendations by school officials, and ability to finance college education.

Procedure: Freshmen are admitted to all sessions. Entrance exams should be taken by October of the senior year. There are early decision and early admissions plans. Check with the school for current deadlines and fee. Notification is sent on a rolling basis. Applications are accepted on-line.

Transfer: 103 transfer students enrolled in a recent year. Applicants must submit transcripts from previous colleges attended and be in good standing at the time of application. Students having an associate degree will be given credit for a maximum of 68 semester hours in general education courses with a grade of C or higher. 31 of 124 credits required for the bachelor's degree must be completed at Lane.

Visiting: There are regularly scheduled orientations for prospective students, including meetings on financial aid, residential life, rules and regulations of the college, course requirements, and registration. There are guides for informal visits and visitors may sit in on classes and stay overnight. To schedule a visit, contact the Office of Recruitment/Admissions at ebrown@lanecollege.edu.

Financial Aid: In a recent year, the average freshman award was $9318. 39% of undergraduates work part time. Average annual earnings from campus work are $971. The average financial indebtedness of the recent year's graduate was $19,275. The CSS/Profile, FAFSA, FFS or SFS is required. Check with the school for current deadlines.

International Students: In a recent year, there were 1 international students enrolled. The school actively recruits these students. Satisfactory scores are required on the written TOEFL and the ACT.

Computers: All students may access the system. There are no time limits and no fees.

Graduates: In a recent year, 88 bachelor's degrees were awarded. The most popular majors were interdisciplinary studies (23%), computer science (14%), and criminal justice (12%). In an average class, 39% graduate in 4 years or less, 54% graduate in 5 years or less, and 61% graduate in 6 years or less. 31 companies recruited on campus in a recent year.

Of the recent year's graduating class, 32% were enrolled in graduate school within 6 months of graduation and 63% were employed.

Admissions Contact: Evelyn L. Brown, Director of Admissions. A video is available. E-mail: *ebrown@lanecollege.edu*
Web: *www.lanecollege.edu*

LEE UNIVERSITY   D-4
Cleveland, TN 37311
(423) 614-8500
(800) 533-9930; Fax: (423) 614-8533

Full-time: 1392 men, 1924 women	Faculty: 148; IIB, --$
Part-time: 150 men, 182 women	Ph.D.s: 76%
Graduate: 117 men, 165 women	Student/Faculty: 22 to 1
Year: semesters, summer session	Tuition: $9610
Application Deadline: September 1	Room & Board: $5170
Freshman Class: 1465 applied, 895 accepted, 761 enrolled	
SAT Verbal/Math: 538/524*	ACT: 23 NONCOMPETITIVE

Lee University, founded in 1918, is a private liberal arts institution affiliated with the Church of God. There are 4 undergraduate and 4 graduate schools. In addition to regional accreditation, Lee has baccalaureate program accreditation with NASM. The 2 libraries contain 127,714 volumes, 50,946 microform items, and 8453 audio/video tapes/CDs/DVDs, and subscribe to 516 periodicals including electronic. Computerized library services include the card catalog, interlibrary loans, database searching, and Internet access. Special learning facilities include a learning resource center and an audiovisual center. The 115-acre campus is in a suburban area 25 miles north of Chattanooga. Including any residence halls, there are 50 buildings.

Student Life: 62% of undergraduates are from out of state, mostly the South. Students are from 49 states, 54 foreign countries, and Canada. 82% are white. The average age of freshmen is 18; all undergraduates, 21. 28% do not continue beyond their first year; 72% remain to graduate.

Housing: 1840 students can be accommodated in college housing, which includes single-sex dormitories, on-campus apartments, off-campus apartments, and married-student housing. On-campus housing is guaranteed for the freshman year only and is available on a first-come, first-served basis. 56% of students commute. Alcohol is not permitted. All students may keep cars.

Activities: There are no fraternities or sororities. There are 63 groups on campus, including art, band, cheerleading, choir, chorale, chorus, computers, debate, drama, ethnic, film, honors, international, jazz band, literary magazine, musical theater, newspaper, opera, orchestra, pep band, photography, political, professional, radio and TV, religious, social, social service, student government, symphony, and yearbook. Popular campus events include College Day, Parade of Favorites, and Dorm Wars.

Sports: There are 6 intercollegiate sports for men and 6 for women, and 23 intramural sports for men and 23 for women. Facilities include an arena, a recreation complex, a softball field, a tennis center, a soccer field, a baseball field, and a playing field.

Disabled Students: 69% of the campus is accessible. Wheelchair ramps, elevators, special parking, specially equipped rest rooms, special class scheduling, lowered drinking fountains, and lowered telephones are available.

Services: Counseling and information services are available, as is tutoring in every subject. There is a reader service for the blind, and remedial math, reading, and writing.

Campus Safety and Security: Measures include 24-hour foot and vehicle patrol, security escort services, shuttle buses, and informal discussions. There are pamphlets/posters/films, emergency telephones, and lighted pathways/sidewalks.

Programs of Study: Lee confers B.A., B.S., B.C.M., B.M., and B.M.E. degrees. Master's degrees are also awarded. Bachelor's degrees are awarded in BIOLOGICAL SCIENCE (biology/biological science), BUSINESS (accounting and business administration and management), COMMUNICATIONS AND THE ARTS (communications, English, French, German, music, and Spanish), COMPUTER AND PHYSICAL SCIENCE (chemistry, computer programming, mathematics, and science), EDUCATION (elementary, music, and physical), HEALTH PROFESSIONS (medical laboratory technology), SOCIAL SCIENCE (crosscultural studies, history, human development, psychology, religious education, social science, and sociology). Business administration, communication, and human development are the strongest academically. Business, human development, and psychology are the largest.

Required: All students must complete a minimum of 130 credit hours, including a core curriculum and 36 hours in the major, with a 2.0 GPA (2.5 for education majors). A Global Perpectives seminar and cross-cultural experience are required, in addition to a major field test the last semester before graduation in all fields except preprofessional science and teacher licensure.

Special: Lee offers internships, cross-registration with the Coalition for Christian Colleges and Universities, study abroad, a Washington semester, numerous work-study programs, an accelerated degree program, dual and student-designed majors, nondegree study, and limited pass/ fail options. Every student completes a minor in religion. There are 13 national honor societies, a freshman honors program, and 6 departmental honors programs.

Faculty/Classroom: 64% of faculty are male; 36%, female. All teach undergraduates and 20% both teach and do research. No introductory courses are taught by graduate students. The average class size in an introductory lecture is 25; in a laboratory, 15; and in a regular course, 28.

Admissions: 61% of the 2005-2006 applicants were accepted. The SAT scores for the 2005-2006 freshman class were: Verbal--32% below 500, 39% between 500 and 599, 24% between 600 and 700, and 5% above 700; Math--40% below 500, 33% between 500 and 599, 21% between 600 and 700, and 6% above 700. The ACT scores were 35% below 21, 21% between 21 and 23, 20% between 24 and 26, 16% between 27 and 28, and 8% above 28. 16% of the current freshmen were in the top fifth of their class; 65% were in the top two fifths. 18 freshmen graduated first in their class.

Requirements: The SAT or ACT is required for admission. Students must be graduates of accredited secondary schools. The GED is accepted. A portfolio is recommended. A GPA of 2.0 is required. AP and CLEP credits are accepted. Important factors in the admissions decision are advanced placement or honor courses, leadership record, and recommendations by school officials.

Procedure: Freshmen are admitted fall and spring. Entrance exams should be taken prior to registration. There are early admissions, deferred admissions, and rolling admissions plans. Early decision applications should be filed by January 1; regular applications, by September 1 for fall entry, along with a $25 fee. The college accepts all applicants. Notification is sent on a rolling basis. Applications are accepted on-line.

Transfer: 294 transfer students enrolled in 2004-2005. Transfer students must take the SAT, scoring satisfactorily, or the ACT, scoring 17, unless they have 16 credit hours with a GPA of 2.0 or better. Must have official transcripts from all prior colleges. 30 of 130 credits required for the bachelor's degree must be completed at Lee.

Visiting: There are regularly scheduled orientations for prospective students. The Admissions Office will arrange a complete campus tour upon request. There are guides for informal visits and visitors may sit in on classes. To schedule a visit, contact the Admissions Center at (423) 614-8500.

Financial Aid: In 2005-2006, 86% of all full-time freshmen received some form of financial aid. 61% of full-time freshmen received need-based aid. The average freshman award was $11,460. Need-based scholarships or need-based grants averaged $7000; need-based self-help aid (loans and jobs) averaged $2937; and average need-based loan (excluding PLUS, unsubsidized, and private loans) averaged $2819. Average annual earnings from campus work are $2000. The FAFSA and the college's own financial statement are required. The deadline for filing freshman financial aid applications for fall entry is April 15.

International Students: There are 180 international students enrolled. The school actively recruits these students. They must score satisfactorily on the written TOEFL or on the electronic version.

Computers: Wireless access is available. All students may access the system. There are no time limits. The fee is $25 per semester.

Graduates: From July 1, 2004 to June 30, 2005, 738 bachelor's degrees were awarded. The most popular majors were education (24%), philosophy, religion, and theology (18%), and business marketing (12%). In an average class, 1% graduate in 3 years or less, 43% graduate in 4 years or less, 44% graduate in 5 years or less, and 42% graduate in 6 years or less.

Admissions Contact: Phil Cook, Assistant Vice President for Enrollment. E-mail: *admissions@leeuniversity.edu*
Web: *http://www.leeuniversity.edu*

LEMOYNE-OWEN COLLEGE   A-4

Memphis, TN 38126

(901) 942-7302
(800) 737-7778; Fax: (901) 942-6233

Full-time: 640 men and women	**Faculty:** 45
Part-time: 145 men and women	**Ph.D.s:** 80%
Graduate: none	**Student/Faculty:** 14 to 1
Year: semesters, summer session	**Tuition:** $8500
Application Deadline: see profile	**Room & Board:** $4650
Freshman Class: n/av	
SAT or ACT: required	**LESS COMPETITIVE**

LeMoyne-Owen College, established in 1872, is a private, liberal arts college affiliated with the United Church of Christ and the Tennessee Baptist, Missionary and Educational Convention, offering degrees in the liberal arts and sciences and business administration. Figures in the above capsule and in this profile are approximate. In addition to regional accreditation, LOC has baccalaureate program accreditation with NCATE. The library contains 90,000 volumes and 1000 audio/video tapes/CDs/DVDs, and subscribes to 300 periodicals including electronic. Computerized library services include the card catalog, interlibrary loans, database searching, and Internet access. Special learning facilities include a learning resource center and an art gallery. The 15-acre campus is in an urban area. Including any residence halls, there are 18 buildings.

Student Life: 86% of undergraduates are from Tennessee. Others are from 20 states and 3 foreign countries. 95% are from public schools. 94% are African American. 90% are Protestant; 8% claim no religious affiliation. The average age of all undergraduates is 23. 30% do not continue beyond their first year; 20% remain to graduate.

Housing: 140 students can be accommodated in college housing, which includes single-sex and coed dormitories. On-campus housing is available on a first-come, first-served basis. Priority is given to out-of-town students. 80% of students commute. Alcohol is not permitted. All students may keep cars.

Activities: 20% of men belong to 4 local and 4 national fraternities; 20% of women belong to 4 local and 4 national sororities. There are 15 groups on campus, including cheerleading, choir, chorus, computers, drama, ethnic, newspaper, photography, professional, religious, social service, student government, and yearbook.

Sports: There are 4 intercollegiate sports for men and 5 for women, and 1 intramural sport for men and 5 for women. Facilities include a gym, a pool, and other phys ed installations.

Disabled Students: 80% of the campus is accessible. Wheelchair ramps and elevators are available.

Services: Counseling and information services are available, as is tutoring in every subject. There is remedial math, reading, and writing.

Campus Safety and Security: Measures include 24-hour foot and vehicle patrol, security escort services, emergency telephones, and lighted pathways/sidewalks.

Programs of Study: LOC confers B.A., B.S., and B.B.A. degrees. Bachelor's degrees are awarded in BIOLOGICAL SCIENCE (biology/ biological science), BUSINESS (accounting and business administration and management), COMMUNICATIONS AND THE ARTS (art, English, language arts, and music), COMPUTER AND PHYSICAL SCIENCE (chemistry, computer science, mathematics, natural sciences, and science), EDUCATION (early childhood and special), SOCIAL SCIENCE (criminal justice, history, humanities, political science/government, social science, social work, and sociology). Business, biology, and education are the strongest academically. Business and biology are the largest.

Required: To graduate, students must satisfy 42 hours of core requirements in communication, math, natural and computer sciences, literature and the humanities, African and African American history, social and behavioral sciences, and physical fitness. They must have a minimum GPA of 2.0 and grades of C or better in all major courses. The college requires 120 credits for graduation, including at least 45 in upper-division courses. All recent high school graduates must participate in the Freshman Year Experience Program.

Special: Students may cross-register with other institutions of the Greater Memphis Consortium. The college offers a work-study program, dual and student-designed majors, internships, nondegree study, and a pass/ fail grading option. There are dual-degree programs in pharmacy with Xavier School of Pharmacy, in optometry with Southern College of Optometry, and in engineering with Christian Brothers University. There is 1 national honor society, a freshman honors program, and 100 departmental honors program.

Faculty/Classroom: All teach undergraduates and 40% do research. The average class size in an introductory lecture is 15; in a laboratory, 15; and in a regular course, 12.

Requirements: The SAT or ACT is required. In addition, applicants must graduate from an accredited secondary school, having completed 20 high school units. The college recommends 4 years of English, 2 each of math, science, and social studies, and 1 of a foreign language. Applicants must submit 2 letters of recommendation. Students 23 or older may be admitted to the division of lifelong learning, which accepts the GED. A GPA of 2.0 is required. AP and CLEP credits are accepted. Important factors in the admissions decision are advanced placement or honor courses, evidence of special talent, and parents or siblings attending the school.

Procedure: Freshmen are admitted to all sessions. Entrance exams should be taken in the spring of the junior year. There are early admissions and deferred admissions plans. Check with the school for current deadlines and fee.

Transfer: 122 transfer students enrolled in a recent year. Applicants should have a GPA of 2.0 and must submit 2 copies of official transcripts plus a statement of good standing from the previous college attended. Students with fewer than 28 college credit hours must also submit a high school transcript and, if below age 21, ACT or SAT scores. 30 of 120 credits required for the bachelor's degree must be completed at LOC.

Visiting: There are regularly scheduled orientations for prospective students. There are guides for informal visits and visitors may sit in on classes. To schedule a visit, contact Lonnie Morris.

Financial Aid: In a recent year, 90% of all full-time students received some form of financial aid. 80% of full-time freshmen and 90% of continuing full-time students received need-based aid. 90% of undergraduates work part time. Average annual earnings from campus work are $2880. LOC is a member of CSS. The FAFSA and the college's own financial statement are required. Check with the school for current deadlines.

International Students: Satisfactory scores are required on the written TOEFL and the ACT.

Computers: All students may access the system. There are no time limits and no fees.

Admissions Contact: Lonnie Morris, Director of Admissions.
E-mail: *lonnie_morris@nile.lemoyne-owen.edu*
Web: *www.lemoyne-owen.edu*

LINCOLN MEMORIAL UNIVERSITY   E-2
Harrogate, TN 37752-0901

(423) 869-6280
(800) 325-0900; Fax: (423) 869-6370

Full-time: 281 men, 731 women	**Faculty:** n/av
Part-time: 84 men, 220 women	**Ph.Ds:** n/av
Graduate: 408 men, 1078 women	**Student/Faculty:** 12 to 1
Year: semesters, summer session	**Tuition:** $13,104
Application Deadline: open	**Room & Board:** $5040
Freshman Class: n/av	
SAT or ACT: required	**COMPETITIVE**

Lincoln Memorial University, founded in 1897, is an independent institution offering degree programs in the arts and sciences, business, education, and preprofessional training. Some figures in the above capsule and in this profile are approximate. There are 4 undergraduate and 2 graduate schools. In addition to regional accreditation, LMU has baccalaureate program accreditation with CAHEA and NLN. The library contains 200,000 volumes, 160,506 microform items, and 254 audio/video tapes/CDs/DVDs, and subscribes to 893 periodicals including electronic. Computerized library services include the card catalog, interlibrary loans, database searching, and Internet access. Special learning facilities include a learning resource center, radio station, TV station, and the Lincoln Museum. The 1000-acre campus is in a rural area 55 miles north of Knoxville. Including any residence halls, there are 32 buildings.

Student Life: 67% of undergraduates are from Tennessee. Others are from 25 states, 22 foreign countries, and Canada. 89% are from public schools. 94% are white. The average age of freshmen is 19; all undergraduates, 23. 20% do not continue beyond their first year; 50% remain to graduate.

Housing: 500 students can be accommodated in college housing, which includes single-sex and coed dormitories, on-campus apartments, and married-student housing. On-campus housing is guaranteed for the freshman year only and is available on a first-come, first-served basis. Priority is given to out-of-town students. 70% of students commute. Alcohol is not permitted. All students may keep cars.

Activities: There are 3 local fraternities and 3 local sororities. There are 26 groups on campus, including art, cheerleading, choir, chorus, computers, drama, drill team, honors, international, literary magazine, newspaper, photography, radio and TV, religious, social service, student government, and yearbook. Popular campus events include Lincoln Day.

Sports: There are 6 intercollegiate sports for men and 6 for women, and 4 intramural sports for men and 4 for women. Facilities include a 5000-seat arena, a baseball field, a playing field, and a natatorium.

Disabled Students: 60% of the campus is accessible. Wheelchair ramps, elevators, special parking, and special class scheduling are available.

Services: Counseling and information services are available, as is tutoring in most subjects. There is remedial math, reading, and writing.

Campus Safety and Security: Measures include 24-hour foot and vehicle patrol, informal discussions, pamphlets/posters/films, and lighted pathways/sidewalks.

Programs of Study: LMU confers B.A., B.S., B.B.A., B.S.N., and B.S.W. degrees. Associate and master's degrees are also awarded. Bachelor's degrees are awarded in AGRICULTURE (wildlife management), BIOLOGICAL SCIENCE (biology/biological science), BUSINESS (accounting and business administration and management), COMMUNICATIONS AND THE ARTS (broadcasting, communications, English, and fine arts), COMPUTER AND PHYSICAL SCIENCE (chemistry, information sciences and systems, and mathematics), EDUCATION (athletic training, business, early childhood, elementary, health, middle school, science, and secondary), ENGINEERING AND ENVIRONMENTAL DESIGN (environmental science), HEALTH PROFESSIONS (medical laboratory technology, nursing, predentistry, premedicine, and veterinary science), SOCIAL SCIENCE (history, prelaw, psychology, social science, and social work). Nursing, business, and education are the largest.

Required: To graduate, all students must complete at least 128 semester credit hours, including the general studies requirements of the declared major and a minimum of 30 hours of in the major. Students must achieve a minimum GPA of 2.0.

Special: LMU offers pass/fail options and credit for life, military, and work experience. Some internships are available.

Faculty/Classroom: 49% of faculty are male; 51%, female. 80% teach undergraduates. No introductory courses are taught by graduate students. The average class size in an introductory lecture is 20; in a laboratory, 25; and in a regular course, 20.

Admissions: 37% of the 2005-2006 applicants were accepted.

Requirements: The SAT or ACT is required. In addition, applicants must graduate with a GPA of at least 2.3. Candidates for admission should be graduates of accredited secondary schools or have the GED. Students should have completed 4 years of English, 2 each of math and science, and 1 each of history and social studies. LMU requires applicants to be in the upper 50% of their class. A GPA of 2.3 is required. AP and CLEP credits are accepted. Important factors in the admissions decision are recommendations by school officials, personality/intangible qualities, and leadership record.

Procedure: Freshmen are admitted fall, spring, and summer. Entrance exams should be taken in the spring of the junior year. There are early admissions, deferred admissions and rolling admissions plans. Application deadlines are open. The fall 2005 application fee was $25.

Transfer: Trasfer students who have completed 12 or more semester credit hours of potentially transferable course work at a regionally accredited college or uinversity will be considered for transfer admissions. Students with fewe that 12 semester credit hours are subject to freshman admission procedures. Official transcripts from all colleges and universities must be summbitted. 32 of 128 credits required for the bachelor's degree must be completed at LMU.

Visiting: There are regularly scheduled orientations for prospective students, including introductory sessions for both students and their parents and opportunities for advising, and registration sessions. There are guides for informal visits and visitors may sit in on classes and stay overnight. To schedule a visit, contact the Office of Admissions and Recruitment.

Financial Aid: LMU is a member of CSS. The CSS/Profile, FAFSA, FFS or SFS is required. Check with the school for current application deadlines.

International Students: In a recent year there are 48 international students enrolled. They must score satisfactorily on the written TOEFL.

Computers: All students may access the system. There are no time limits and no fees. It is strongly recommended that all students have a personal computer.

Graduates: In a recent year, 145 bachelor's degrees were awarded. The most popular majors were nursing (30%), elementary education (27%), and business (26%). In an average class, 42% graduate in 4 years or less.

Admissions Contact: Conrad Daniels, Dean of Admissions.
E-mail: *cdaniels@inetlmu.lmunet.edu* Web: *www.lmunet.edu*

LIPSCOMB UNIVERSITY   C-3
(Formerly David Lipscomb University)
Nashville, TN 37204-3951

(615) 269-1776
(800) 333-4358; Fax: (615) 269-1804

Full-time: 897 men, 1173 women	**Faculty:** 115; IIA, --$
Part-time: 98 men, 129 women	**Ph.D.s:** 77%
Graduate: 124 men, 97 women	**Student/Faculty:** 18 to 1
Year: semesters, summer session	**Tuition:** $14,557
Application Deadline: open	**Room & Board:** $6410
Freshman Class: 1599 applied, 1210 accepted, 535 enrolled	
SAT Verbal/Math: 570/550*	**VERY COMPETITIVE**

Lipscomb University, founded in 1891, is a private liberal arts university affiliated with the Church of Christ. There are 5 undergraduate and 3 graduate schools. In addition to regional accreditation, Lipscomb has baccalaureate program accreditation with ABET, ACBSP, ADA, CAAHEP, CSWE, NASM, and NCATE. The library contains 202,378 volumes (includes periodicals), 39,539 microform items, and 726 audio/video tapes/CDs/DVDs. Computerized library services include the card catalog, interlibrary loans, database searching, Internet access, and laptop Internet portals. Special learning facilities include a learning resource center and radio station. The 65-acre campus is in a suburban area 2 miles south of downtown Nashville. Including any residence halls, there are 19 buildings.

Student Life: 64% of undergraduates are from Tennessee. Others are from 43 states, 20 foreign countries, and Canada. 81% are white. Most are Protestant. The average age of freshmen is 18; all undergraduates, 21. 29% do not continue beyond their first year; 58% remain to graduate.

Housing: 1496 students can be accommodated in college housing, which includes single-sex dorms. 54% of students live on campus. Alcohol is not permitted. All students may keep cars.

Activities: There are no fraternities or sororities. There are many groups and organizations on campus, including art, band, cheerleading, chorale, chorus, computers, drama, ethnic, honors, international, jazz band, literary magazine, musical theater, newspaper, orchestra, photography, political, professional, radio and TV, religious, social, social service, student government, and yearbook. Popular campus events include Sing-a-rama (spring talent show) and multicultural events.

Sports: There are 7 intercollegiate sports for men and 8 for women, and 8 intramural sports for men and 8 for women. Facilities include an arena with a basketball court and a student activity center with 2 full-size basketball courts, 4 racquetball courts, a jogging course, and weight, aerobics, and recreation rooms for both men and women.

Disabled Students: 95% of the campus is accessible. Wheelchair ramps, elevators, special parking, specially equipped rest rooms, special class scheduling, and lowered drinking fountains are available.

Services: Counseling and information services are available, as is tutoring in some subjects. There is a reader service for the blind, and remedial math, reading, and writing.

Campus Safety and Security: Measures include 24-hour foot and vehicle patrol, security escort services, pamphlets/posters/films, and emergency telephones. There are lighted pathways/sidewalks and residence hall security systems.

Programs of Study: Lipscomb confers B.A. and B.S. degrees. Master's degrees are also awarded. Bachelor's degrees are awarded in BIOLOGICAL SCIENCE (biochemistry and biology/biological science), BUSINESS (accounting, banking and finance, business administration and management, fashion merchandising, and marketing management), COMMUNICATIONS AND THE ARTS (art, communications, English, French, German, journalism, music, music performance, Spanish, and visual and performing arts), COMPUTER AND PHYSICAL SCIENCE (chemistry, computer science, mathematics, and physics), EDUCATION (art, athletic training, education, elementary, English, health, mathematics, music, physical, and special), ENGINEERING AND ENVIRONMENTAL DESIGN (computer engineering, engineering, engineering mechanics, environmental science, and preengineering), HEALTH PROFESSIONS (exercise science, nursing, predentistry, premedicine, preoptometry, and prepharmacy), SOCIAL SCIENCE (American studies, biblical studies, dietetics, economics, family/consumer studies, food production/management/services, political science/government, prelaw, psychology, textiles and clothing, and urban studies). Biologym and engineering are the strongest academically. Business, biology, and education are the largest.

Required: All full-time students must take and pass a Bible class meeting each day the student has classes. Other general education requirements include 9 semester hours in communication, 6 each in humanities, science, history, and social science, 3 in math, and 2 in phys ed. Students must complete a total of 132 semester hours and have a minimum GPA of 2.0. At least 25% of credit hours must be earned at Lipscomb.

Special: Some majors require an internship. There is study abroad in England, Germany, Greece, and Mexico. There is 1 national honor society and a freshman honors program.

Faculty/Classroom: 76% of faculty are male; 24%, female. All teach undergraduates. No introductory courses are taught by graduate students. The average class size in an introductory lecture is 20; in a laboratory, 20; and in a regular course, 15.

Admissions: 76% of the 2005-2006 applicants were accepted. The SAT scores for the 2005-2006 freshman class were: Verbal--23% below 500, 36% between 500 and 599, 34% between 600 and 700, and 7% above 700; Math--27% below 500, 37% between 500 and 599, 30% between 600 and 700, and 6% above 700. The ACT scores were 22% below 21, 27% between 21 and 23, 25% between 24 and 26, 10% between 27 and 28, and 15% above 28.

Requirements: The SAT or ACT is required. In addition, candidates for admission should be graduates of accredited secondary schools. The GED is accepted. 14 academic units are required. Students should have completed 4 units of English and 2 units each of history, math, and science. 2 units of a foreign language are highly recommended. 2 additional units from the areas of English, foreign language, history, math, science, and social studies are also required. A GPA of 2.25 is required. AP and CLEP credits are accepted.

Procedure: Freshmen are admitted to all sessions. There is an early decision plan. There is a rolling admissions plan. Application deadlines are open. The fall 2005 application fee was $50. Applications are accepted on-line.

Transfer: Students must be in good standing at their previous institution. 33 of 132 credits required for the bachelor's degree must be completed at Lipscomb.

Visiting: There are regularly scheduled orientations for prospective students. There are guides for informal visits and visitors may sit in on classes and stay overnight. To schedule a visit, contact the Office of Undergraduate Admissions.

Financial Aid: The FAFSA is required. Check with the school for current application deadlines.

International Students: There are 36 international students enrolled. The school actively recruits these students. They must take the TOEFL, achieving a satisfactory score, or take the MELAB, they must also take the SAT or the ACT.

Computers: Wireless access is available. There are several computer labs on campus, as well as in the dorms. All students may access the system 24 hours per day, 7 days per week. There are no time limits and no fees. It is strongly recommended that all students have a personal computer.

Graduates: From July 1, 2004 to June 30, 2005, 488 bachelor's degrees were awarded.

Admissions Contact: Ricky Holaway, Director of Admissions. A video is available. E-mail: *ricky.holaway@lipscomb.edu* Web: *www.lipscomb.edu*

MARYVILLE COLLEGE   E-3
Maryville, TN 37804   **(865) 981-8206**
(800) 597-2687; Fax: (865) 981-8005

Full-time: 515 men, 605 women	**Faculty:** 73; IIB, -$
Part-time: 16 men, 10 women	**Ph.D.s:** 93%
Graduate: none	**Student/Faculty:** 15 to 1
Year: 4-1-4, summer session	**Tuition:** $22,224
Application Deadline: March 1	**Room & Board:** $7000
Freshman Class: 1496 applied, 1183 accepted, 333 enrolled	
SAT Verbal/Math: 560/530*	**ACT:** 24 **VERY COMPETITIVE**

Maryville College, founded in 1819, is a private liberal arts college affiliated with the Presbyterian Church (U.S.A.). In addition to regional accreditation, Maryville has baccalaureate program accreditation with NASM. The 2 libraries contain 130,168 volumes and 7749 microform items, and subscribe to 10,884 periodicals including electronic. Computerized library services include the card catalog, interlibrary loans, database searching, and Internet access. Special learning facilities include a learning resource center, art gallery, radio station, a greenhouse, and college woods. The 350-acre campus is in a suburban area 15 miles south of Knoxville. Including any residence halls, there are 24 buildings.

Student Life: 75% of undergraduates are from Tennessee. Others are from 31 states and 24 foreign countries. 87% are from public schools. 86% are white. 64% are Protestant; 10% Catholic. The average age of freshmen is 18; all undergraduates, 21. 29% do not continue beyond their first year; 55% remain to graduate.

Housing: 788 students can be accommodated in college housing, which includes single-sex and coed dorms, on-campus apartments, and off-campus apartments. In addition, there are language houses and special-interest houses. On-campus housing is guaranteed for all 4 years. 67% of students live on campus; of those, 68% remain on campus on weekends. All students may keep cars.

Activities: There are no fraternities or sororities. There are 55 groups on campus, including art, band, cheerleading, choir, chorus, computers, dance, drama, equestrian, ethnic, gay, gospel music, honors, international, jazz band, literary magazine, musical theater, newspaper, orchestra, pep band, photography, political, professional, radio and TV, religious, social service, student government, and symphony. Popular campus events include Dogwood Arts Festival, Blister-in-the-Sun, and Spring Fling.

Sports: There are 7 intercollegiate sports for men and 7 for women, and 12 intramural sports for men and 11 for women. Facilities include a phys ed building with an indoor pool, tennis and racquetball courts, and a weight room; football, soccer, baseball, and softball fields; and an off-campus equestrian arena.

Disabled Students: 75% of the campus is accessible. Wheelchair ramps, elevators, special parking, specially equipped rest rooms, special class scheduling, lowered drinking fountains, lowered telephones, and special housing are available.

Services: Counseling and information services are available, as is tutoring in every subject. There is a reader service for the blind, remedial math, and sign language interpreters for deaf students.

Campus Safety and Security: Measures include 24-hour foot and vehicle patrol, security escort services, informal discussions, and lighted pathways/sidewalks.

Programs of Study: Maryville confers B.A. and B.Mus. degrees. Bachelor's degrees are awarded in AGRICULTURE (environmental studies), BIOLOGICAL SCIENCE (biochemistry and biology/biological science), BUSINESS (business administration and management and recreation and leisure services), COMMUNICATIONS AND THE ARTS (American Sign Language, art, art history and appreciation, creative writing, dramatic arts, English, English as a second/foreign language, music, music performance, and Spanish), COMPUTER AND PHYSICAL SCIENCE (chemical physics, chemistry, computer science, and mathematics), EDUCATION (elementary, music, physical, science, and secondary), ENGINEERING AND ENVIRONMENTAL DESIGN (engineering and preengineering), HEALTH PROFESSIONS (nursing, predentistry, and premedicine), SOCIAL SCIENCE (economics, history, international relations, interpreter for the deaf, political science/government, prelaw, psychology, religion, social science, and sociology). Biology, chemistry, and English are the strongest academically. Business, biology, and psychology are the largest.

Required: Each degree has its own general education requirements, which include humanities and a foreign language. Students must complete at least 128 total credit hours, including 48 in the major, and must maintain a minimum 2.0 GPA. A year-long freshman seminar and orientation are required in addition to a senior thesis in all majors and senior comprehensive exams.

Special: Maryville offers cross-registration with the University of Tennessee and Vanderbilt University, internships, study abroad in 9 countries, a Washington semester, accelerated degree programs, a B.A.-B.S. degree in engineering, and dual and student-designed majors. There are 3-2 engineering degrees offered with regional universities. Nondegree study and pass/fail options are possible. There are 6 national honor societies, a freshman honors program, honors programs in all departments.

Faculty/Classroom: 48% of faculty are male; 52%, female. All both teach and do research. The average class size in an introductory lecture is 28; in a laboratory, 15; and in a regular course, 16.

Admissions: 79% of the 2005-2006 applicants were accepted. The SAT scores for the 2005-2006 freshman class were: Verbal--28% below 500, 37% between 500 and 599, 27% between 600 and 700, and 8% above 700; Math--38% below 500, 35% between 500 and 599, 24% between 600 and 700, and 3% above 700. The ACT scores were 20% below 21, 28% between 21 and 23, 18% between 24 and 26, 17% between 27 and 28, and 17% above 28. 44% of the current freshmen were in the top fifth of their class; 74% were in the top two fifths. 6 freshmen graduated first in their class.

Requirements: A satisfactory score is required on the SAT and the ACT. Candidates should be graduates of accredited secondary schools or have the GED. They should also have 15 academic credits with 4 years of English, 3 each of math and science, 2 years of foreign language, and 2 of history or social studies. An essay, portfolio, audition, and interview are all recommended. A GPA of 2.5 is required. AP and CLEP credits are accepted. Important factors in the admissions decision are advanced placement or honor courses, extracurricular activities record, and leadership record.

Procedure: Freshmen are admitted fall, spring, and summer. Entrance exams should be taken by October of the senior year. There are early decision, early admissions, and deferred admissions plans. Early decision applications should be filed by November 15; regular applications, by March 1 for fall entry, November 1 for spring entry, and May 1 for summer entry. Notification of early decision is sent November 15; regular decision, April 1. Applications are accepted on-line.

Transfer: In a recent year 63 transfer students enrolled. Transfer applicants must have a minimum GPA of 2.0 and a recommended 15 credit hours earned. An interview is also recommended. 45 of 128 credits required for the bachelor's degree must be completed at Maryville.

Visiting: There are regularly scheduled orientations for prospective students, including an overnight in a residence hall, class attendance, meeting with students and faculty, a campus tour, and an interview. There are guides for informal visits and visitors may sit in on classes and stay overnight. To schedule a visit, contact the Admissions Office at 1-800-597-2687 or admissions@maryvillecollege.edu.

Financial Aid: In 2005-2006, 100% of all full-time freshmen and 97% of continuing full-time students received some form of financial aid. 81% of full-time freshmen and 73% of continuing full-time students received need-based aid. The average freshman award was $22,060. Need-based scholarships or need-based grants averaged $17,351 ($35,702 maximum); need-based self-help aid (loans and jobs) averaged $1244 ($3300 maximum); and other non-need-based awards and non-need-based scholarships averaged $19,233 ($41,753 maximum). 49% of undergraduates work part time. Average annual earnings from campus work are $1559. The FAFSA is required. The priority date for freshman financial aid applications for fall entry is March 1.

International Students: There are 49 international students enrolled. The school actively recruits these students. They must receive a satisfactory score on TOEFL.

Computers: All students may access the system 7 days a week, 16 hours a day. There are no time limits and no fees. It is strongly recommended that all students have a personal computer.

Graduates: From July 1, 2004 to June 30, 2005, 172 bacherlor's degrees were awarded. The most popular majors were business/commerce (16%), education (10%), and psychology (9%). In an average class, 40% graduate in 4 years or less, 52% graduate in 5 years or less, and 55% graduate in 6 years or less. 80 companies recruited on campus in 2004-2005. Of the 2004 graduating class, 29% were enrolled in graduate school within 6 months of graduation and 67% were employed.

Admissions Contact: Ned Willard, Assistant Vice President for Admissions. E-mail: ned.willard@maryvillecollege.edu
Web: maryvillecollege.edu

MEMPHIS COLLEGE OF ART   A-4
Memphis, TN 38104   (901) 272-5151
                                     (800) 727-1088; Fax: (901) 272-5158

Full-time: 130 men, 140 women	**Faculty:** n/av
Part-time: 28 men, 16 women	**Ph.Ds:** n/av
Graduate: 6 men, 6 women	**Student/Faculty:** n/av
Year: semesters, summer session	**Tuition:** $17,460
Application Deadline: open	**Room & Board:** $7500
Freshman Class: 322 applied, 311 accepted, 109 enrolled	
SATor ACT: required	**SPECIAL**

Memphis College of Art, established in 1936, is a private, independent institution offering degree programs in fine arts and design arts, including studio art, fiber/surface design, computer arts, and photography. In addition to regional accreditation, MCA has baccalaureate program accreditation with NASAD. The library contains 18,000 volumes, and subscribes to 120 periodicals including electronic. Computerized library services include interlibrary loans. Special learning facilities include a learning resource center and art gallery. The 200-acre campus is in an urban area in Memphis. Including any residence halls, there are 4 buildings.

Student Life: 60% of undergraduates are from Tennessee. Others are from 20 states and 4 foreign countries. 69% are from public schools. 78% are white; 15% African American. The average age of freshmen is 20; all undergraduates, 23. 30% do not continue beyond their first year; 45% remain to graduate.

Housing: 108 students can be accommodated in college housing, which includes coed on-campus apartments and off-campus apartments. On-campus housing is available on a first-come, first-served basis. Priority is given to out-of-town students. Alcohol is not permitted. All students may keep cars.

Activities: There are no fraternities or sororities. There are 3 groups on campus, including art, ethnic, and student government. Popular campus events include Holiday Bazaar, gallery openings, and community dinners.

Sports: There is no sports program at MCA. Facilities include those provided by the 200-acre city park on which MCA is located. There is an adjacent public golf course, playing fields, and a volleyball court. Regular Saturday football, soccer, and bicycling are popular activities.

Disabled Students: All of the campus is accessible. Wheelchair ramps, elevators, special parking, specially equipped rest rooms, lowered drinking fountains, and lowered telephones are available.

Services: Counseling and information services are available, as is tutoring in some subjects, including liberal studies classes. There is remedial writing.

Campus Safety and Security: Measures include 24-hour foot and vehicle patrol, security escort services, shuttle buses, and informal discussions. There are pamphlets/posters/films, lighted pathways/sidewalks, and a security guard in the buildings in the evening, at night, and on weekends.

Programs of Study: MCA confers the B.F.A. degree. Master's degrees are also awarded. Bachelor's degrees are awarded in COMMUNICATIONS AND THE ARTS (design and fine arts).

Required: Students must complete 120 credit hours, including 33 in the major, with a minimum GPA of 2.0. Distribution requirements comprise 45 credits in liberal studies, including 12 in art history, 6 in English, and 3 each in literature, social sciences, and natural sciences; 30 credits in elective studio art; and 18 credits in foundation classes, including drawing, design, and first-year studio.

Special: Special academic programs include off-campus internships for juniors in advertising agencies, design firms, or other educational situations; on-campus work-study, including an in-house student advertising agency where students can get paid work experience dealing with clients; and study abroad in Europe, Canada, Japan, Italy, or Ireland. There are co-op programs with Rhodes, Lemoyne-Owen, and Christian Brothers Colleges as well as with Memphis Theological Seminary, and there is cross-registration with the Association of Independent Colleges of Art and Design, and the Memphis area consortium. There is a variety of art internships and credit for life and work experience are available.

Faculty/Classroom: 75% of faculty are male; 25%, female. 93% teach undergraduates. Graduate students teach 2% of introductory courses. The average class size in an introductory lecture is 20 and in a regular course, 15.

Admissions: 97% of the 2005-2006 applicants were accepted. The ACT scores for the 2005-2006 freshman class were: 46% below 21, 26% between 21 and 23, 24% between 24 and 26, 2% between 27 and 28, and 2% above 28.

Requirements: The SAT or ACT is required. Test scores are used for admissions and placement purposes. Other admissions requirements include a completed application form, high school transcripts (the GED is accepted), and a portfolio. An interview is recommended. A GPA of 2.0 is required. AP and CLEP credits are accepted. Important factors in the admissions decision are evidence of special talent, advanced placement or honor courses, and extracurricular activities record.

Procedure: Freshmen are admitted fall and spring. Application deadlines are open. There is a rolling admissions plan. Application fee is $25. Applications are accepted on-line.

Transfer: 45 transfer students enrolled in 2005-2006. Applicants must submit official college transcripts and a portfolio. 48 of 120 credits required for the bachelor's degree must be completed at MCA.

Visiting: There are regularly scheduled orientations for prospective students. There are guides for informal visits and visitors may sit in on classes. To schedule a visit, contact the Admissions Office at *info@mca.edu*.

Financial Aid: In 2005-2006, 97% of all full-time freshmen received some form of financial aid. Need-based scholarships or need-based grants averaged $1000 ($2000 maximum); and other non-need-based awards and non-need-based scholarships averaged $4000 ($17,460 maximum). 75% of undergraduates work part time. MCA is a member of CSS. The FAFSA is required.

International Students: There are 5 international students enrolled. The school actively recruits these students. They must take the TOEFL and also take the SAT or the ACT.

Computers: All students may access the system. There are no time limits and no fees. It is strongly recommended that all students have a personal computer especially students in computer arts and design. A Mac is recommended.

Graduates: 25 companies recruited on campus in 2004-2005.

Admissions Contact: Annette Moore, Director of Admissions.
E-mail: *info@mca.edu* Web: *www.mca.edu*

MIDDLE TENNESSEE STATE UNIVERSITY   C-3

Murfreesboro, TN 37132   (615) 898-2111
(800) 433-MTSU; Fax: (615) 898-5478

Full-time: 8201 men, 9056 women	Faculty: IIA, -$
Part-time: 1369 men, 1653 women	Ph.D.s: 68%
Graduate: 745 men, 1208 women	Student/Faculty: n/av
Year: semesters, summer session	Tuition: $3915 ($11,845)
Application Deadline: July 1	Room & Board: $4625
Freshman Class: 6395 applied, 5430 accepted, 3208 enrolled	
SAT Verbal/Math: 540/530*	ACT: 22 COMPETITIVE

Middle Tennessee State University, founded in 1911, is a comprehensive public university that offers undergraduate and graduate programs reflecting an emphasis on research, creative arts, and public and professional service activities. The tuition figures in the above capsule are approximate There are 6 undergraduate schools and 1 graduate school. In addition to regional accreditation, MTSU has baccalaureate program accreditation with AACSB, AAFCS, ABET, ACEJMC, ACS, ADA, CAA, CACREP, CSAB, CSWE, FIDER, NAIT, NASAD, NASM, NASP, NCATE, NLN, and NRPA. The library contains 702,764 volumes and 1,281,160 microform items, and subscribes to 3798 periodicals including electronic. Computerized library services include the card catalog, interlibrary loans, database searching, and Internet access. Special learning facilities include a learning resource center, art gallery, planetarium, radio station, TV station, and numerous research centers. The 500-acre campus is in an urban area 32 miles southeast of Nashville. Including any residence halls, there are 159 buildings.

Student Life: 93% of undergraduates are from Tennessee. Others are from 47 states, 70 foreign countries, and Canada. 75% are white; 11% African American. 45% are Protestant; 43% claim no religious affiliation; 6% Catholic. The average age of freshmen is 18; all undergraduates, 19.

Housing: 3294 students can be accommodated in college housing, which includes single-sex and coed dormitories, on-campus apartments, married-student housing, fraternity houses, and sorority houses. In addition, there are honors houses, a First Year Experience program, and various Learning Community programs. On-campus housing is available on a first-come, first-served basis. 85% of students commute. Alcohol is not permitted. All students may keep cars.

Activities: 3% of men belong to 16 national fraternities; 4% of women belong to 1 local and 11 national sororities. There are 153 groups on campus, including art, band, cheerleading, chess, choir, chorale, chorus, computers, dance, debate, drama, drill team, ethnic, gay, honors, international, jazz band, literary magazine, marching band, musical theater, newspaper, pep band, photography, political, professional, radio and TV, religious, social, social service, student government, and symphony. Popular campus events include Founders Day, Family Day, and African American History Month.

Sports: There are 8 intercollegiate sports for men and 9 for women, and 13 intramural sports for men and 13 for women. Facilities include an athletic center with a 30,000-seat stadium, a 12,000-seat gym, a soccer/track complex, tennis courts, and baseball and softball fields, and a recreation center with 12 courts, an indoor track, indoor and outdoor pools, a rock-climbing wall, and a sand volleyball court.

Disabled Students: All of the campus is accessible. Wheelchair ramps, elevators, special parking, specially equipped rest rooms, special class scheduling, lowered drinking fountains, and lowered telephones are available.

Services: Counseling and information services are available, as is tutoring in most subjects. There is a reader service for the blind, and remedial math, reading, and writing.

Campus Safety and Security: Measures include 24-hour foot and vehicle patrol, self-defense education, security escort services, and shuttle buses. There are pamphlets/posters/films, emergency telephones, and lighted pathways/sidewalks.

Programs of Study: MTSU confers B.A., B.S., B.B.A., B.F.A., B.Mus., B.S.N., B.S.W., and B.U.S. degrees. Master's and doctoral degrees are also awarded. Bachelor's degrees are awarded in AGRICULTURE (agricultural business management, animal science, and plant science), BIOLOGICAL SCIENCE (biology/biological science and nutrition), BUSINESS (accounting, banking and finance, business administration and management, entrepreneurial studies, marketing/retailing/merchandising, office supervision and management, and recreation and leisure services), COMMUNICATIONS AND THE ARTS (communications, English, French, German, graphic design, music, music business management, public relations, Spanish, and studio art), COMPUTER AND PHYSICAL SCIENCE (chemistry, computer science, information sciences and systems, mathematics, physics, and science), EDUCATION (art, athletic training, business, early childhood, health, physical, and special), ENGINEERING AND ENVIRONMENTAL DESIGN (engineering technology, environmental science, industrial engineering technology, and interior design), HEALTH PROFESSIONS (health science and nursing), SOCIAL SCIENCE (anthropology, criminal justice, economics, family/consumer studies, geography, history, interdisciplinary studies, international relations, philosophy, political science/government, prelaw, psychology, public administration, social work, sociology, and textiles and clothing). Nursing and science are the strongest academically. Recording industry is the largest.

Required: To graduate, a total of at least 132 hours, including at least 48 of upper-level courses, is needed with a minimum overall GPA of 2.0. All students must complete the general studies requirements, including 9 hours each of natural science/math and humanities, 6 each of English composition and history, 2 each of phys ed, arts/fine arts, and social science, and demonstrate computer literacy. A major field test and general studies exam are required.

Special: MTSU offers co-op programs in aerospace, computer science, math, engineering technology, and industrial studies, cross-registration with Tennessee State University, internships, study abroad, work-study, double majors, a general studies degree, student-designed majors, non-degree study, and pass/fail options. Credit for life, military, and work experience may be granted. There are 2 national honor societies, a freshman honors program, and 25 departmental honors programs.

Faculty/Classroom: 56% of faculty are male; 44%, female. The average class size in an introductory lecture is 24; in a laboratory, 18; and in a regular course, 23.

Admissions: 85% of the 2005-2006 applicants were accepted. The SAT scores for the 2005-2006 freshman class were: Verbal--30% below 500, 46% between 500 and 599, 21% between 600 and 700, and 3% above 700; Math--36% below 500, 47% between 500 and 599, and 17% between 600 and 700. The ACT scores were 31% below 21, 36% between 21 and 23, 21% between 24 and 26, 7% between 27 and 28, and 5% above 28. 27% of the current freshmen were in the top fifth of their class; 50% were in the top two fifths. There were 2 National Merit finalists. 31 freshmen graduated first in their class.

Requirements: The SAT or ACT is required, with a minimum composite score of 22 on the ACT if the GPA is less than 3.0. A high school diploma is required; the GED is accepted. The number of academic credits required is 14, including 4 years of English, 3 of math, 2 each of a foreign language and science, and 1 each of social studies, U.S. history, and visual and/or performance arts, with an additional unit of math, language, or art recommended. A GPA of 3.0 is required. AP and CLEP credits are accepted.

Procedure: Freshmen are admitted to all sessions. Entrance exams should be taken in the first half of the senior year. There are early admissions and deferred admissions plans. There is a rolling admissions plan. Applications should be filed by July 1 for fall entry, along with a $25 fee. Notification is sent on a rolling basis. Applications are accepted on-line.

Transfer: 1996 transfer students enrolled in 2004-2005. Applicants must have a minimum 2.0 GPA and submit official transcripts from all previous colleges attended. If transferring fewer than 9 semester hours, they must also meet freshman admission requirements. 30 of 132 credits required for the bachelor's degree must be completed at MTSU.

Visiting: There are regularly scheduled orientations for prospective students, including campus tours and meeting with a departmental adviser. There are guides for informal visits and visitors may sit in on classes. To schedule a visit, contact the Office of Admissions at (615) 898-5670 or (800) 331-MTSU (in-state) or *admissions@mtsu.edu*.

Financial Aid: In 2005-2006, 35% of all full-time freshmen and 52% of continuing full-time students received some form of financial aid. At least 19% of full-time freshmen and 29% of continuing full-time students received need-based aid. The average freshman award was $6265. Need-based scholarships or need-based grants averaged $2295 ($6150 maximum); need-based self-help aid (loans and jobs) averaged $1589

($10,500 maximum); institutional non-need-based athletic scholarships and other institutional non-need-based awards and non-need-based scholarships averaged $4057 ($5000 maximum). 84% of undergraduates work part time. Average annual earnings from campus work are $3200. The average financial indebtedness of the 2005 graduate was $19,800. The FAFSA is required. The priority date for freshman financial aid applications for fall entry is May 1.

International Students: There were 124 international students enrolled in a recent year.They must take the TOEFL or the MELAB and also take the SAT or the ACT, scoring 20 on the ACT.

Computers: All students may access the system 24 hours a day. There are no time limits and no fees.

Graduates: From July 1, 2004 to June 30, 2005, 3475 bachelor's degrees were awarded. The most popular majors were business/marketing (21%), visual and performing arts (13%), and communication/journalism (11%). 297 companies recruited on campus in a recent year. Of a recent graduating class, 20% were enrolled in graduate school within 6 months of graduation and 7% were employed.

Admissions Contact: Sherian Huddleston, Interim Assistant Vice President, Enrollment Management. E-mail: *admissions@mtsu.edu* Web: *www.mtsu.edu*

MILLIGAN COLLEGE F-2

Milligan College, TN 37682 (423) 461-8730
(800) 262-8337; Fax: (423) 461-8982

Full-time: 286 men, 444 women	**Faculty:** 66; IIB, --$
Part-time: 6 men, 17 women	**Ph.D.s:** 68%
Graduate: 71 men, 130 women	**Student/Faculty:** 11 to 1
Year: semesters, summer session	**Tuition:** $17,240
Application Deadline: August 15	**Room & Board:** $4750
Freshman Class: 686 applied, 536 accepted, 168 enrolled	
SAT Verbal/Math: 560/550*	**ACT:** 24 **VERY COMPETITIVE**

Milligan College, founded in 1866, is a private institution affiliated with the Christian Church and Churches of Christ. Its degree programs stress the liberal arts and biblical studies. In addition to regional accreditation, Milligan has baccalaureate program accreditation with ACOTE, CCNE and NCATE. The library contains 212,861 volumes, 493,520 microform items, and 3394 audio/video tapes/CDs/DVDs, and subscribes to 7313 periodicals including electronic. Computerized library services include the card catalog, interlibrary loans, database searching, and Internet access. Special learning facilities include a learning resource center, art gallery, radio station, TV station, editing rooms, and darkroom. The 181-acre campus is in a suburban area 4 miles south of Johnson City. Including any residence halls, there are 23 buildings.

Student Life: 55% of undergraduates are from out of state, mostly the Midwest. Students are from 35 states, 11 foreign countries, and Canada. 80% are from public schools. 94% are white. Most are Protestant. The average age of freshmen is 18; all undergraduates, 22. 24% do not continue beyond their first year; 54% remain to graduate.

Housing: 572 students can be accommodated in college housing, which includes single-sex dorms, on-campus apartments, and married-student housing. On-campus housing is guaranteed for all 4 years. 76% of students live on campus; of those, 85% remain on campus on weekends. Alcohol is not permitted. All students may keep cars.

Activities: There are no fraternities or sororities. There are 40 groups on campus, including art, band, cheerleading, choir, chorus, drama, drill team, film, honors, jazz band, literary magazine, musical theater, newspaper, orchestra, pep band, photography, political, professional, radio and TV, religious, social, social service, student government, symphony, and yearbook. Popular campus events include Wonderful Wednesday, campus theater productions, and a faculty auction.

Sports: There are 6 intercollegiate sports for men and 6 for women, and 7 intramural sports for men and 7 for women. Facilities include a 25-meter swimming pool, a basketball court, a 500-seat stadium, a 1500-seat gym, tennis courts, and baseball, softball, and soccer fields.

Disabled Students: 80% of the campus is accessible. Wheelchair ramps, elevators, special parking, specially equipped rest rooms, and lowered drinking fountains are available.

Services: Counseling and information services are available, as is tutoring in most subjects. There is remedial math, reading, and writing.

Campus Safety and Security: Measures include informal discussions, pamphlets/posters/films, lighted pathways/sidewalks, and an evening vehicle patrol.

Programs of Study: Milligan confers B.A., B.S., and B.S.N. degrees. Master's degrees are also awarded. Bachelor's degrees are awarded in BIOLOGICAL SCIENCE (biology/biological science), BUSINESS (accounting and business administration and management), COMMUNICATIONS AND THE ARTS (communications, English, fine arts, and music), COMPUTER AND PHYSICAL SCIENCE (chemistry, information sciences and systems, and mathematics), EDUCATION (early childhood and music), HEALTH PROFESSIONS (exercise science, nursing, and premedicine), SOCIAL SCIENCE (biblical studies, history, humani-

ties, psychology, religious music, and sociology). Business, nursing, and Bible are the largest.

Required: Students must complete at least 128 semester hours, including 24 to 62 in the major, and 59 to 71 in the general education core, with a minimum GPA of 2.0. Required disciplines include 24 credit hours of humanities, 9 of Bible studies, 8 of lab science, 6 of social science, 3 each of math, speech, and ethnic studies, 2 of phys ed, and 1 of introduction to college; B.A. candidates must also complete 6 to 12 in foreign language. All students must demonstrate computer literacy and attend all required chapel/convocation sessions.

Special: Milligan offers a Washington semester, study abroad in England, Australia, China, Costa Rica, Egypt, Russia, and Uganda, co-op programs and internships in several majors, cross-registration with East Tennessee State University, work-study, nondegree study, and dual majors. 3 credits are offered for students participating in the annual summer tour of Europe. There are 5 national honor societies.

Faculty/Classroom: 49% of faculty are male; 51%, female. 96% teach undergraduates. No introductory courses are taught by graduate students. The average class size in an introductory lecture is 50; in a laboratory, 15; and in a regular course, 15.

Admissions: 78% of the 2005-2006 applicants were accepted. The SAT scores for the 2005-2006 freshman class were: Verbal--20% below 500, 51% between 500 and 599, 23% between 600 and 700, and 6% above 700; Math--27% below 500, 49% between 500 and 599, 22% between 600 and 700, and 2% above 700. The ACT scores were 12% below 21, 37% between 21 and 23, 27% between 24 and 26, 14% between 27 and 28, and 10% above 28.

Requirements: The SAT or ACT is required. In addition, students must be graduates of an accredited secondary school, with 18 Carnegie units and 18 academic credits, including courses in English, math, science, history and social studies, and speech, music, or art, along with 2 years of a foreign language. Music students must audition. The GED is accepted. Other factors in the admission decision include character, recommendations by school officials, advanced placement or honor courses, ability, preparation, and Christian commitment. AP and CLEP credits are accepted. Important factors in the admissions decision are leadership record, recommendations by school officials, and personality/intangible qualities.

Procedure: Freshmen are admitted to all sessions. Entrance exams should be taken beginning in the spring of the junior year. There is a deferred admissions plan and a rolling admissions plan. Applications should be filed by August 15 for fall entry and December 15 for spring entry, along with a $30 fee. Notification is sent on a rolling basis. Applications are accepted on-line.

Transfer: 62 transfer students enrolled in 2004-2005. A minimum GPA of 2.5 is preferred. Applicants must submit transcripts of all previous college work. 45 of 128 credits required for the bachelor's degree must be completed at Milligan.

Visiting: There are regularly scheduled orientations for prospective students, consisting of 1-day open houses in November and March that include a campus tour, a financial aid workshop, a meal in the cafeteria, and the opportunity to meet faculty and to learn about student life. There are new student orientation weekends in April, June, and August. There are guides for informal visits and visitors may sit in on classes and stay overnight. To schedule a visit, contact the Campus Visits Coordinator at *visits@milligan.edu*.

Financial Aid: In 2005-2006, 95% of all full-time freshmen and 98% of continuing full-time students received some form of financial aid. 42% of full-time freshmen and 50% of continuing full-time students received need-based aid. The average freshman award was $16,462. Need-based scholarships or need-based grants averaged $3425 ($9694 maximum); need-based self-help aid (loans and jobs) averaged $7377 ($21,625 maximum); non-need-based athletic scholarships averaged $6846 ($17,990 maximum); other non-need-based awards and non-need-based scholarships averaged $8045 ($20,000 maximum); and personnel grants and tuition exchange averaged $16,730 (maximum). 40% of undergraduates work part time. Average annual earnings from campus work are $1184. The average financial indebtedness of the 2005 graduate was $20,506. The FAFSA and the college's own financial statement are required. The priority date for freshman financial aid applications for fall entry is March 1.

International Students: There are 18 international students enrolled. They must take the TOEFL. If no TOEFL is available, they must take the SAT or ACT.

Computers: Wireless access is available. 2 network ports are provided in each residence hall room. Dial-up network service is provided for local commuting students. Wireless access is available in 2 classroom buildings, the student center, the library, and the faculty office building. 102 lab and public access computers are available throughout the campus. All students may access the system. There are no time limits. The fee is $175 per semester. It is strongly recommended that all students have a personal computer.

Graduates: From July 1, 2004 to June 30, 2005, 177 bachelor's degrees were awarded. The most popular majors were business administration (20%), communications (13%), and psychology (8%). In an average class, 2% graduate in 3 years or less, 49% graduate in 4 years or less, 59% graduate in 5 years or less, and 59% graduate in 6 years or less.

Admissions Contact: Tracy Brinn, Director of Enrollment Management. E-mail: *admissions@milligan.edu* Web: *www.milligan.edu*

RHODES COLLEGE   A-3
Memphis, TN 38112

	(901) 843-3700
	(800) 844-5969; Fax: (901) 843-3631
Full-time: 705 men, 965 women	**Faculty:** 141; IIB, av$
Part-time: 25 men, 14 women	**Ph.D.s:** 95%
Graduate: 9 men, 7 women	**Student/Faculty:** 12 to 1
Year: semesters	**Tuition:** $25,956
Application Deadline: February 1	**Room & Board:** $6904
Freshman Class: 3597 applied, 1785 accepted, 442 enrolled	
SAT Verbal/Math: 630/630*	**ACT:** 27 **HIGHLY COMPETITIVE**

Rhodes College, founded in 1848, is a private liberal arts institution affiliated with the Presbyterian Church (U.S.A.). The 2 libraries contain 278,392 volumes, 95,034 microform items, and 10,600 audio/video tapes/CDs/DVDs, and subscribe to 1683 periodicals including electronic. Computerized library services include the card catalog, interlibrary loans, database searching, Internet access, and laptop Internet portals. Special learning facilities include an art gallery, 2 electron microscopes, a 0.8-meter infrared optimized telescope, a cell culture lab, and the Human Relations Area Files, containing 2 million pages of human behavior resources materials on microfiche. The 100-acre campus is in an urban area in Memphis. Including any residence halls, there are 44 buildings.

Student Life: 73% of undergraduates are from out of state, mostly the South. Students are from 41 states, 8 foreign countries, and Canada. 60% are from public schools. 85% are white. 62% are Protestant; 14% Catholic. The average age of freshmen is 18; all undergraduates, 19. 12% do not continue beyond their first year; 79% remain to graduate.

Housing: 1212 students can be accommodated in college housing, which includes single-sex and coed dorms and on-campus apartments. In addition, there are special-interest houses, theme, substance-free,quiet-study, and non-smoking housing. On-campus housing is guaranteed for the freshman year only and is available on a lottery system for upperclassmen. 77% of students live on campus; of those, 90% remain on campus on weekends. All students may keep cars.

Activities: 48% of men belong to 7 national fraternities; 53% of women belong to 6 national sororities. There are 131 groups on campus, including art, black student association, cheerleading, chess, choir, chorale, chorus, club sport, computers, contents under pressure (comedy improv troupe), dance, debate, drama, ethnic, film, gay, honor council, honors, international, literary magazine, mock trial team, model, musical theater, newspaper, orchestra, pep band, photography, political, professional, religious, social, social service, student government, symphony, and yearbook. Popular campus events include Rites of Spring, All-Sing, and Hunger for Homelessness.

Sports: There are 9 intercollegiate sports for men and 10 for women, and 16 intramural sports for men and 16 for women. Facilities include a campus life center, which includes a performance gym, a 3-court multi-use gym, racquetball, and squash courts, a fitness center, and an indoor jogging track. Outdoor facilities include a pool, 10 lighted tennis courts, 2 soccer fields, a football field, a track, and baseball, softball and intramural fields.

Disabled Students: 90% of the campus is accessible. Wheelchair ramps, elevators, special parking, specially equipped rest rooms, special class scheduling, lowered drinking fountains, lowered telephones, and an infrared hearing system in 1 of the auditoriums are available.

Services: Counseling and information services are available, as is tutoring in some subjects, including math, writing, modern languages, biology, chemistry, economics, business, computer science, and physics. There is a reader service for the blind.

Campus Safety and Security: Measures include 24-hour foot and vehicle patrol, self-defense education, security escort services, and informal discussions. There are pamphlets/posters/films, emergency telephones, lighted pathways/sidewalks, a 24/7 staffed guard house, electronic readers on all gate entrances and residential dorms, security cameras monitored 24 hours a day, a fenced campus, and city cab service billed to student accounts.

Programs of Study: Rhodes confers B.A. and B.S. degrees. Master's degrees are also awarded. Bachelor's degrees are awarded in BIOLOGICAL SCIENCE (biology/biological science), BUSINESS (business administration and management), COMMUNICATIONS AND THE ARTS (art, dramatic arts, English, French, German, music, and Spanish), COMPUTER AND PHYSICAL SCIENCE (chemistry, computer science, mathematics, and physics), SOCIAL SCIENCE (anthropology, classical/ancient civilization, economics, history, interdisciplinary studies, international studies, Latin American studies, philosophy, political science/government, psychology, religion, Russian and Slavic studies, sociology, and urban studies). Biology, English, and business administration are the strongest academically and have the largest enrollments.

Required: To graduate, students must complete 124 credit hours with a variable number of hours in the major, and maintain a minimum GPA of 2.0. There is a basic degree requirement in 12 foundation areas. Students must complete 3 courses examining questions of meaning and value; 2 courses in writing; 1 course in each of literature, art, marth, natural science, human interaction and contemporary institutions, and cultural perspective. Students must further demonstrate intermediate proficiency with a second language, engage in 1 for-credit activity broadening connections between the classroom and the world, participate in three half-semesters of physical education, and complete a senior seminar in the major.

Special: More than half of Rhodes students have an internship experience, in which off-campus work and significant academic work are combined for credit. Study abroad in 11 countries, a Washington semester, cross-registration with Memphis College of Art and Christian Brothers University, and a science semester at Oak Ridge National Laboratory are offered. A 3-2 engineering degree with Washington University is available. The B.A.-B.S. degree and dual majors are offered in any combination, and student-designed majors can be arranged. Nondegree study and pass/fail options are possible. There are 19 national honor societies, including Phi Beta Kappa. All departments have honors programs.

Faculty/Classroom: 59% of faculty are male; 41%, female. All both teach and do research. No introductory courses are taught by graduate students. The average class size in an introductory lecture is 17; in a laboratory, 17; and in a regular course, 17.

Admissions: 50% of the 2005-2006 applicants were accepted. The SAT scores for the 2005-2006 freshman class were: Verbal--3% below 500, 28% between 500 and 599, 50% between 600 and 700, and 19% above 700; Math--4% below 500, 27% between 500 and 599, 49% between 600 and 700, and 19% above 700. The ACT scores were 9% between 21 and 23, 31% between 24 and 26, 23% between 27 and 28, and 37% above 28. 73% of the current freshmen were in the top fifth of their class; 92% were in the top two fifths. 13 freshmen graduated first in their class.

Requirements: The SAT or ACT is required. In addition, graduation from an accredited secondary school is required, with 16 or more academic credits, including 4 years of English, 3 of math, and 2 each of a foreign language, science, and social studies/history. The GED is accepted. An essay is required; an interview is recommended. Applications may be submitted on-line at the school's web site or via Common App. AP credits are accepted. Important factors in the admissions decision are advanced placement or honor courses, recommendations by school officials, and extracurricular activities record.

Procedure: Freshmen are admitted fall and spring. Entrance exams should be taken prior to December of the senior year. There are early decision and deferred admissions plans. Early decision applications should be filed by November 1; regular applications, by February 1 for fall entry and December 1 for spring entry. Notification of early decision is sent December 1; regular decision, April 1. 80 early decision candidates were accepted for the 2005-2006 class. 184 applicants were on the 2005 waiting list; 73 were admitted. Applications are accepted on-line.

Transfer: 23 transfer students enrolled in 2004-2005. Applicants must submit all high school and college transcripts, as well as SAT or ACT scores, and must be in good standing at the last institution they attended. 56 of 124 credits required for the bachelor's degree must be completed at Rhodes.

Visiting: There are regularly scheduled orientations for prospective students, including class visits, meetings with students and faculty, tours, and an overnight stay with students if desired. Interviews also are available. There are guides for informal visits and visitors may sit in on classes and stay overnight. To schedule a visit, contact the Admissions Office.

Financial Aid: In 2005-2006, 36% of all full-time freshmen and 34% of continuing full-time students received some form of financial aid. 36% of full-time freshmen and 34% of continuing full-time students received need-based aid. The average freshman award was $25,834. Need-based scholarships or need-based grants averaged $15,873; need-based self-help aid (loans and jobs) averaged $5432; and other non-need-based awards and non-need-based scholarships averaged $10,367. 31% of undergraduates work part time. Average annual earnings from campus work are $1537. The average financial indebtedness of the 2005 graduate was $45,151. The CSS/Profile or FAFSA is required. The deadline for filing freshman financial aid applications for fall entry is January 15.

International Students: There are 11 international students enrolled. The school actively recruits these students. A satisfactory score is required on the written TOEFL. Students also take the SAT or the ACT.

Computers: Wireless access is available. More than 220 PCs are available for use by students. Wired Ethernet ports are available in each room for all students living in the residence halls. Wireless computing is available in selected locations in the residence halls and in many public locations on campus. The Barret Library provides wireless throughout. Access to the Internet is provided by a 48Mb link shared by the entire campus. All students may access the system 24 hours per day. There are no time limits and no fees. It is strongly recommended that all students have a PC.

Graduates: From July 1, 2004 to June 30, 2005, 317 bachelor's degrees were awarded. The most popular majors were English (14%), biology (12%), and business administration (12%). In an average class, 76% graduate in 4 years or less, 79% graduate in 5 years or less, and 79% graduate in 6 years or less. 121 companies recruited on campus in 2004-2005. Of the 2004 graduating class, 34% were enrolled in graduate school within 6 months of graduation and 55% were employed.

Admissions Contact: David J. Wottle, Dean of Admissions and Financial Aid. A video is available. E-mail: *adminfo@rhodes.edu* Web: *http://www.rhodes.edu/Admissions*

SOUTHERN ADVENTIST UNIVERSITY   D-4
Collegedale, TN 37315

(423) 238-2844
(800) 768-8437; Fax: (423) 238-1845

2522 men and women none	**Faculty:** 131
Year: semesters, summer session	**Ph.D.s:** 66%
Application Deadline: open	**Student/Faculty:** n/av
	Tuition: $14,020
	Room & Board: $4480

Freshman Class: 1471 applied, 1022 accepted, 605 enrolled
ACT: 21   **COMPETITIVE**

Southern Adventist University, founded in 1892, is a private liberal arts institution affiliated with the Seventh-day Adventist Church. There are 9 undergraduate schools. In addition to regional accreditation, Southern has baccalaureate program accreditation with CSWE, NASM, NCATE, and NLN. The library contains 153,283 volumes, 476,838 microform items, and 6382 audio/video tapes/CDs/DVDs, and subscribes to 18,429 periodicals including electronic. Computerized library services include the card catalog, interlibrary loans, database searching, Internet access, and laptop Internet portals. Special learning facilities include a learning resource center, art gallery, and radio station. The 1000-acre campus is in a small town 18 miles southeast of Chattanooga. Including any residence halls, there are 17 buildings.

Student Life: 78% of undergraduates are from out of state, mostly the South. Students are from 46 states, 55 foreign countries, and Canada. 16% are from public schools. 74% are white; 10% Hispanic. Most are Protestant. The average age of freshmen is 19; all undergraduates, 21. 27% do not continue beyond their first year; 55% remain to graduate.

Housing: 1749 students can be accommodated in college housing, which includes single-sex dorms, on-campus apartments, and married-student housing. On-campus housing is guaranteed for all 4 years. 71% of students live on campus; of those, 70% remain on campus on weekends. Alcohol is not permitted. All students may keep cars.

Activities: There are no fraternities or sororities. There are 30 groups on campus, including band, choir, chorus, drama, ethnic, honors, international, newspaper, orchestra, professional, radio and TV, religious, social, student government, symphony, and yearbook. Popular campus events include Alumni Weekend, Strawberry Festival, and Week of Spiritual Emphasis.

Sports: There are 10 intramural sports for men and 10 for women. Facilities include 8 tennis courts, 3 athletic fields, a field house, a pool, 4 racquetball courts, a track, soccer fields, a 23,000-square-foot gym that can seat 3000 when used as an auditorium, 3 weight rooms, and a 3-hole golf course.

Disabled Students: 70% of the campus is accessible. Wheelchair ramps, elevators, special parking, specially equipped rest rooms, and special class scheduling are available.

Services: Counseling and information services are available, as is tutoring in most subjects. There is remedial math, reading, and writing.

Campus Safety and Security: Measures include 24-hour foot and vehicle patrol, security escort services, informal discussions, and pamphlets/posters/films. There are emergency telephones and lighted pathways/sidewalks.

Programs of Study: Southern confers B.A., B.S., B.B.A., B.F.A., B.Mus., and B.S.W. degrees. Associate and master's degrees are also awarded. Bachelor's degrees are awarded in BIOLOGICAL SCIENCE (biology/biological science), BUSINESS (accounting, banking and finance, business administration and management, entrepreneurial studies, international business management, marketing/retailing/merchandising, and nonprofit/public organization management), COMMUNICATIONS AND THE ARTS (animation, art, broadcasting, communications, English, film arts, fine arts, graphic design, journalism, music, and public relations), COMPUTER AND PHYSICAL SCIENCE (actuarial science, chemistry, computer management, computer science, information sciences and systems, mathematics, physics, and web services), EDUCATION (elementary, music, physical, and recreation), HEALTH PROFESSIONS (health care administration, health science, medical technology, and nursing), SOCIAL SCIENCE (behavioral science, history, international studies, psychology, public administration, religious education, social work, and theological studies). Business, nursing, and education are the strongest academically. Nursing and business are the largest.

Required: Students must complete 124 semester hours with at least 30 in the major, and maintain a minimum GPA of 2.0. General education requirements include 12 semester hours of religion; 6 of language, literature, and fine arts; 6 to 9 of English and natural science; 6 of history; 5 of behavioral, family, and health science; 3 each of activity skills, computer competencies, oral communication, and political and economic systems; and up to 3 of math, depending on the ACT scores.

Special: Internships in long-term life care, nursing, and journalism, a social work practicum, an accelerated degree program in nursing, and study abroad in Austria, Spain, Argentina, Italy, Germany, Mexico, and France are offered. The B.A.-B.S. degree and dual majors in any combination including business administration and automotive service and business administration and public relations, and interdisciplinary student-designed majors are available. Credit may be granted for 4 years of military experience. Pass/fail options are possible only for phys ed activity classes. There are paraprofessional and preprofessional programs in dentistry and medicine and various other health-related fields, as well as in law. There are 9 national honor societies.

Faculty/Classroom: 65% of faculty are male; 35%, female. All teach undergraduates. The average class size in an introductory lecture is 40; in a laboratory, 20; and in a regular course, 13.

Admissions: 69% of the 2005-2006 applicants were accepted. The ACT scores for the 2005-2006 freshman class were: 43% below 21, 26% between 21 and 23, 19% between 24 and 26, 7% between 27 and 28, and 5% above 28. There were 2 National Merit finalists.

Requirements: The SAT or ACT is required; the ACT is preferred. Students must graduate from an accredited secondary school with 14 academic credits, including 4 units of English and 2 each of a foreign language, math, science, social studies, and history. The GED is accepted. An essay must be submitted, if homeschooled. A GPA of 2.0 is required. AP and CLEP credits are accepted. Important factors in the admissions decision are advanced placement or honor courses, recommendations by school officials, and leadership record.

Procedure: Freshmen are admitted to all sessions. Entrance exams should be taken prior to admission. There is a rolling admissions plan. Application deadlines are open. Application fee is $25. Applications are accepted on-line.

Transfer: 152 transfer students enrolled in 2004-2005. Transfer applicants must have a cumulative GPA of at least 2.0 and a satisfactory ACT score. 2 letters of recommendation are also required. 30 of 124 credits required for the bachelor's degree must be completed at Southern.

Visiting: There are regularly scheduled orientations for prospective students, including a tour of the campus and dorms, appointments with academic departments, and an interview with an admissions officer. There are guides for informal visits and visitors may sit in on classes and stay overnight. To schedule a visit, contact the Admissions Office at (423) 236-2807 or *admissions@southern.edu*.

Financial Aid: In 2005-2006, 93% of all full-time freshmen and 90% of continuing full-time students received some form of financial aid. 77% of full-time freshmen and 76% of continuing full-time students received need-based aid. The average freshman award was $10,727. Need-based scholarships or need-based grants averaged $4697 ($10,000 maximum); need-based self-help aid (loans and jobs) averaged $3740 ($5800 maximum); and other non-need-based awards and non-need-based scholarships averaged $2290 ($16,205 maximum). 43% of undergraduates work part time. Average annual earnings from campus work are $2300. The average financial indebtedness of the 2005 graduate was $15,540. The FAFSA is required. The priority date for freshman financial aid applications for fall entry is March 1.

International Students: There are 110 international students enrolled. The school actively recruits these students. They must score satisfactorily on the TOEFL and also take the MELAB and the ACT, scoring satisfactorily.

Computers: Wireless access is available. All students may access the system 24 hours per day. There are no time limits and no fees. It is strongly recommended that all students have a personal computer.

Graduates: From July 1, 2004 to June 30, 2005, 381 bachelor's degrees were awarded. The most popular majors were business (16%), nursing (15%), and religion (9%). In an average class, 24% graduate in 4 years or less, 41% graduate in 5 years or less, and 55% graduate in 6 years or less.

Admissions Contact: Marc Grundy, Director, Enrollment Services. A video is available. E-mail: *admissions@southern.edu* Web: *www.southern.edu*

STATE UNIVERSITY AND COMMUNITY COLLEGE SYSTEM OF TENNESSEE

The State University and Community College System of Tennessee, established in 1972, is a private system in Tennessee. It is governed by the Tennessee Board of Regents, whose chief administrator is chancellor. The primary goal of the system is teaching, research, and public service. The main priorities are to provide quality programs accessible to state residents with equal opportunity in education and employment. The total enrollment is usually about 135,000; with 4100 faculty members. Altogether there are some 300 baccalaureate, 195 master's, and 29 doctoral programs offered in State University and Community College System of Tennessee. Profiles of the 4-year campuses are included in this section.

TENNESSEE STATE UNIVERSITY   C-3
Nashville, TN 37209-1561   (615) 963-5101
                                (888) 463-6878; Fax: (615) 963-5108

Full-time: 2208 men, 3741 women	**Faculty:** 434
Part-time: 411 men, 758 women	**Ph.Ds:** 80%
Graduate: 626 men, 1280 women	**Student/Faculty:** 15 to 1
Year: semesters, summer session	**Tuition:** $3818 ($11,750)
Application Deadline: August 1	**Room & Board:** $5230
Freshman Class: 6069 applied, 3799 accepted, 1509 enrolled	
SAT or ACT: required	**Less Competitive**

Tennessee State University, founded in 1912, is a state-supported land-grant institution offering undergraduate and graduate programs in arts and sciences, agriculture, health professions, business, education, engineering and technology, and nursing. Some of the figures in the above capsule and in this profile are approximate. There are 7 undergraduate schools and 1 graduate school. In addition to regional accreditation, TSU has baccalaureate program accreditation with AACSB, AAFCS, ABET, AHEA, APA, ASLHA, AUPHA, CSWE, NAACLS, NASAD, NASM, NCATE, and NLN. The 2 libraries contain 463,621 volumes, 754,955 microform items, and 5125 audio/video tapes/CDs/DVDs, and subscribe to 1272 periodicals including electronic. Computerized library services include the card catalog, interlibrary loans, and database searching. Special learning facilities include a learning resource center, art gallery, and radio station. The 450-acre campus is in an urban area in Nashville. Including any residence halls, there are 66 buildings.

Student Life: 67% of undergraduates are from Tennessee. Students are from 44 states, 42 foreign countries, and Canada. 90% are from public schools. 74% are African American; 21% white. The average age of freshmen is 18; all undergraduates, 25.

Housing: 3225 students can be accommodated in college housing, which includes single-sex and coed dorms and off-campus apartments. In addition, there are honors houses. On-campus housing is guaranteed for all 4 years. 58% of students commute. Alcohol is not permitted. All students may keep cars.

Activities: 1% of men belong to 4 national fraternities; 2% of women belong to 4 national sororities. There are 63 groups on campus, including band, cheerleading, choir, chorale, computers, dance, drama, forensics, honors, jazz band, literary magazine, marching band, newspaper, pep band, professional, radio and TV, religious, social, social service, and student government. Popular campus events include Miss TSU Pageant and Inauguration, Greek Show, and Christmas Tree Lighting Ceremony.

Sports: There are 8 intercollegiate sports for men and 7 for women. Facilities include a major convocation and athletic center that accommodates intramural sports, swimming, handball, and intercollegiate basketball, and a campus center that provides extensive recreational facilities.

Disabled Students: 90% of the campus is accessible. Wheelchair ramps, elevators, special parking, specially equipped rest rooms, and lowered drinking fountains are available. A campus improvement program makes all new and renovated buildings accessible.

Services: Counseling and information services are available, as is tutoring in some subjects, including all general education courses and many major-field courses. There is a reader service for the blind, and remedial math, reading, and writing. A writing clinic, math lab, and reading center provide individualized assistance.

Campus Safety and Security: Measures include 24-hour foot and vehicle patrol, shuttle buses, informal discussions, and pamphlets/posters/films. There are emergency telephones and lighted pathways/sidewalks.

Programs of Study: TSU confers B.A., B.S., B.B.A., and B.S.N. degrees. Associate, master's, and doctoral degrees are also awarded. Bachelor's degrees are awarded in AGRICULTURE (agriculture), BIOLOGICAL SCIENCE (biology/biological science), BUSINESS (accounting, business administration and management, business economics, and hotel/motel and restaurant management), COMMUNICATIONS AND THE ARTS (art, dramatic arts, English, languages, music, and speech/debate/rhetoric), COMPUTER AND PHYSICAL SCIENCE (chemistry, computer science, mathematics, and physics), EDUCATION (early childhood, health, and special), ENGINEERING AND ENVIRONMENTAL DESIGN (aeronautical technology, architectural engineering, civil engineering, electrical/electronics engineering, and mechanical engineering), HEALTH PROFESSIONS (dental hygiene, health care administration, medical records administration/services, medical technology, nursing, occupational therapy, physical therapy, respiratory therapy, and speech pathology/audiology), SOCIAL SCIENCE (African studies, criminal justice, family/consumer studies, history, interdisciplinary studies, political science/government, psychology, social work, and sociology). Engineer-

ing, allied health professions, and nursing are the strongest academically. Allied health, nursing, and engineering are the largest.

Required: To graduate, students must complete at least 120 semester hours, with 25% in the major, and maintain a minimum GPA of 2.0. Additional requirements include demonstration of proficiency in English composition, completion of a senior project, and courses in English, math, social sciences, American history, humanities, and natural sciences.

Special: Opportunities are provided for co-op programs in business and engineering, cross-registration with Middle Tennessee State University and Meharry Medical College, a B.A.-B.S. degree in interdisciplinary studies, credit by exam, and nondegree study. There are 19 national honor societies, a freshman honors program, and 5 departmental honors programs.

Faculty/Classroom: 55% of faculty are male; 45%, female. 90% teach undergraduates, 20% do research, and 85% do both. No introductory courses are taught by graduate students. The average class size in an introductory lecture is 30; in a laboratory, 35; and in a regular course, 30.

Admissions: 63% of the 2005-2006 applicants were accepted. The SAT scores for the 2005-2006 freshman class were: Verbal--76% below 500, 21% between 500 and 599, and 4% between 600 and 700; Math--74% below 500, 23% between 500 and 599, and 3% between 600 and 700. The ACT scores were 77% below 21, 17% between 21 and 23, 5% between 24 and 26, 1% between 27 and 28, and 1% above 28.

Requirements: A satisfactory score on the SAT or ACT is required. In addition, graduation from an accredited secondary school is required; the GED is accepted. Applicants should have 4 credits in English, 3 in math, 2 each in science and a foreign language, and 1 each in history, social studies, and art. A GPA of 2.25 is required. AP and CLEP credits are accepted.

Procedure: Freshmen are admitted to all sessions. Entrance exams should be taken in the junior year. There is an early admissions plan. Applications should be filed by August 1 for fall entry, December 1 for spring entry, and May 1 for summer entry. The fall 2005 application fee was $15.

Transfer: 631 transfer students enrolled in 2004-2005. Applicants must submit official transcripts from all previous colleges attended. Students from other than Tennessee colleges must have maintained a minimum GPA of 2.0. The GPA requirements for students transferring from Tennessee colleges vary according to the number of semester hours being submitted for transfer credit. 30 of 120 credits required for the bachelor's degree must be completed at TSU.

Visiting: There are guides for informal visits and visitors may sit in on classes and stay overnight. To schedule a visit, contact the recruiting staff.

Financial Aid: In 2005-2006, 74% of all full-time freshmen and 79% of continuing full-time students received some form of financial aid. 71% of full-time freshmen and 69% of continuing full-time students received need-based aid. In a recent year, the average freshman award was $5316. Need-based scholarships or need-based grants averaged $6288 ($6581 maximum); need-based self-help aid (loans and jobs) averaged $4680 ($6375 maximum); non-need-based athletic scholarships averaged $5894 ($19,075 maximum); and other non-need-based awards and non-need-based scholarships averaged $146 ($1000 maximum). The FAFSA is required. The deadline for filing freshman financial aid applications for fall entry is April 1.

International Students: There are 63 international students enrolled. A satisfactory score is required on the written TOEFL. Students must also take the SAT or the ACT.

Computers: All students may access the system. There are no time limits and no fees.

Graduates: In a recent year, 988 bachelor's degrees were awarded. The most popular majors in a recent year were arts and sciences (14%), business administration (12%), and biology (7%). In an average class, 9% graduate in 3 years or less, 13% graduate in 4 years or less, and 5% graduate in 5 years or less. 250 companies recruited on campus in a recent year. Of the 2004 graduating class, 7% were enrolled in graduate school within 6 months of graduation.

Admissions Contact: John Cade, Dean of Admissions and Records. A video is available. E-mail: *jcade@picard.tnstate.edu* Web: *www.tnstate.edu*

TENNESSEE TECHNOLOGICAL UNIVERSITY

D-3

Cookeville, TN 38505

(931) 372-3888
(800) 255-8881; Fax: (931) 372-6250

Full-time: 3449 men, 2954 women	**Faculty:** 381; IIA, -$
Part-time: 411 men, 391 women	**Ph.Ds:** 83%
Graduate: 619 men, 1439 women	**Student/Faculty:** 17 to 1
Year: semesters, summer session	**Tuition:** $4424 ($13,736)
Application Deadline: August 1	**Room & Board:** $5620
Freshman Class: 3292 applied, 2475 accepted, 1409 enrolled	
ACT: 23	**COMPETITIVE**

Tennessee Technological University, founded in 1915 and a member of the state university and community college system of Tennessee, is a public institution offering undergraduate and graduate programs in the liberal arts, business, engineering, agriculture studies, art and fine arts, music, professional training, teacher preparation, nursing, home economics, and crafts. There are 8 undergraduate and 4 graduate schools. In addition to regional accreditation, Tennessee Tech has baccalaureate program accreditation with AACSB, AAFCS, ABET, NASAD, NASM, NCATE, and NLN. The library contains 336,000 volumes, 1 million microform items, and 18,000 audio/video tapes/CDs/DVDs, and subscribes to 3800 periodicals including electronic. Computerized library services include the card catalog, interlibrary loans, database searching, and Internet access. Special learning facilities include a learning resource center, art gallery, radio station, and TV station. The 235-acre campus is in a small town 78 miles east of Nashville. Including any residence halls, there are 97 buildings.

Student Life: 93% of undergraduates are from Tennessee. Others are from 41 states, 55 foreign countries, and Canada. 88% are white. Most claim no religious affiliation. The average age of freshmen is 19; all undergraduates, 22. 27% do not continue beyond their first year; 44% remain to graduate.

Housing: 3100 students can be accommodated in college housing, which includes single-sex and coed dorms, on-campus apartments, and married-student housing. In addition, there are honors houses, special-interest houses, and private room dorms for upperclassmen. On-campus housing is guaranteed for all 4 years. 70% of students commute. Alcohol is not permitted. All students may keep cars.

Activities: 18% of men belong to 11 national fraternities; 7% of women belong to 5 national sororities. There are 178 groups on campus, including art, band, cheerleading, chess, choir, chorale, chorus, computers, dance, debate, drama, drill team, ethnic, forensics, gay, honors, international, jazz band, literary magazine, marching band, musical theater, newspaper, opera, orchestra, pep band, photography, political, professional, radio and TV, religious, social, social service, student government, symphony, and yearbook. Popular campus events include intramural events, Greek Week, and Parents Day.

Sports: There are 7 intercollegiate sports for men and 9 for women, and 10 intramural sports for men and 8 for women. Facilities include 2 gyms seating 10,500 and 4000; a 16,500-seat stadium with track facilities, an indoor pool, indoor and outdoor tennis courts, handball and basketball courts, baseball, softball, and football fields, a track, a rifle range, apparatus rooms, and a health and wellness center with an indoor track, 8 racquetball courts, a weight room, an aerobics classroom, a pool, and basketball/volleyball courts.

Disabled Students: 95% of the campus is accessible. Wheelchair ramps, elevators, special parking, specially equipped rest rooms, special class scheduling, lowered drinking fountains, lowered telephones, and special housing are available.

Services: Counseling and information services are available, as is tutoring in some subjects, including English and lower levels of mathematics. There is a reader service for the blind, and remedial math, reading, and writing.

Campus Safety and Security: Measures include 24-hour foot and vehicle patrol, self-defense education, security escort services, and informal discussions. There are pamphlets/posters/films, emergency telephones, lighted pathways/sidewalks, and a student safety organization.

Programs of Study: Tennessee Tech confers B.A., B.S., B.F.A., B.M., B.S.Agr., B.S.B.A., B.S.C.E., B.S.Ch.E., B.S.Ed., B.S.E.E., B.S.H.E., B.S.I.E., B.S.Ind.Tech., B.S.M.E., and B.S.N. degrees. Master's and doctoral degrees are also awarded. Bachelor's degrees are awarded in AGRICULTURE (agricultural economics, agriculture, animal science, fish and game management, plant science, soil science, and wildlife management), BIOLOGICAL SCIENCE (biochemistry and biology/biological science), BUSINESS (accounting, banking and finance, business administration and management, management science, and marketing/retailing/merchandising), COMMUNICATIONS AND THE ARTS (English, fine arts, French, German, journalism, Spanish, and technical and business writing), COMPUTER AND PHYSICAL SCIENCE (chemistry, computer science, geology, mathematics, physics, and web technology), EDUCATION (agricultural, art, home economics, music, physical, secondary, and special), ENGINEERING AND ENVIRONMENTAL DESIGN (chemical engineering, civil engineering, electrical/electronics engineering, engineering, environmental engineering, industrial engineering, industrial

engineering technology, manufacturing engineering, and mechanical engineering), HEALTH PROFESSIONS (nursing), SOCIAL SCIENCE (child care/child and family studies, economics, history, human ecology, political science/government, psychology, and sociology). Engineering, business, and education are the strongest academically. Engineering is the largest.

Required: Students must complete 120 semester hours, with a variable number of hours in the major, and maintain a minimum GPA of 2.0. 9 semester hours of English, 8 of a lab science, 6 each of American history, social sciences, and humanities, and 3 hours each of math and speech and required.

Special: Co-op programs in most academic areas, internships in community-based programs, study abroad, a Washington semester, multidisciplinary majors, and work-study programs are available. Accelerated degree programs are offered in all specified majors with 3 calendar years of continuous studies. A B.A.-B.S. degree is available, as are dual majors in all areas. Credit may be granted for military experience, and nondegree study and pass/fail options are offered. There are 29 national honor societies and a freshman honors program.

Faculty/Classroom: 66% of faculty are male; 34%, female. 99% teach undergraduates, 73% do research, and 70% do both. Graduate students teach 5% of introductory courses. The average class size in an introductory lecture is 27; in a laboratory, 30; and in a regular course, 26.

Admissions: 75% of the 2005-2006 applicants were accepted. The SAT scores for the 2005-2006 freshman class were: Verbal--26% below 500, 46% between 500 and 599, 23% between 600 and 700, and 5% above 700; Math--23% below 500, 40% between 500 and 599, 29% between 600 and 700, and 8% above 700. The ACT scores were 30% below 21, 25% between 21 and 23, 23% between 24 and 26, 12% between 27 and 28, and 10% above 28. 48% of the current freshmen were in the top fifth of their class; 80% were in the top two fifths. There was 1 National Merit finalist. 36 freshmen graduated first in their class.

Requirements: A satisfactory score is required on the ACT is required. Other admissions requirements include graduation from an accredited secondary school with 14 academic credits, including 4 of English, 3 of math, 2 each in science and a single foreign language, 1 in American history, 1 in world history, ancient history, modern history, world geography, or European history, and 1 in music/art. The GED is also accepted. A GPA of 2.5 is required. AP and CLEP credits are accepted.

Procedure: Freshmen are admitted to all sessions. Entrance exams should be taken during the senior year. There is a deferred admissions plan. There is a rolling admissions plan. Applications should be filed by August 1 for fall entry, December 1 for spring entry, and May 1 for summer entry, along with a $15 fee. Notification is sent on a rolling basis. Applications are accepted on-line.

Transfer: 641 transfer students enrolled in 2004-2005. Transfer students should have a minimum of 12 credit hours earned; the minimum GPA depends on the number of credit hours accumulated. Official transcripts must be submitted, and the ACT is required, depending on age (for applicants 21 or older it is not required). If an applicant has fewer than 12 credit hours, admissions requirements are the same as for freshmen. 30 of 120 credits required for the bachelor's degree must be completed at Tennessee Tech.

Visiting: There are regularly scheduled orientations for prospective students, including visits either morning or afternoon each weekday and meetings with an admission officer, faculty member in the student's major, and a campus tour. There are guides for informal visits and visitors may sit in on classes. To schedule a visit, contact the Admissions Office at (866) SEE-TECH or visit@tntech.edu.

Financial Aid: In 2005-2006, 91% of all full-time freshmen and 89% of continuing full-time students received some form of financial aid. 58% of full-time freshmen and 62% of continuing full-time students received need-based aid. The average freshman award was $7324. Need-based scholarships or need-based grants averaged $3476; need-based self-help aid (loans and jobs) averaged $1780; non-need-based athletic scholarships averaged $9814; and other non-need-based awards and non-need-based scholarships averaged $5092. 97% of undergraduates work part time. Average annual earnings from campus work are $1403. The average financial indebtedness of the 2005 graduate was $18,286. The FAFSA is required. The priority date for freshman financial aid applications for fall entry is March 15. The deadline for filing freshman financial aid applications for fall entry is May 1.

International Students: There are 300 international students enrolled. The school actively recruits these students. A satisfactory score on the TOEFL is required. SAT or ACT scores should be submitted if available.

Computers: All students may access the system 24 hours a day. There are no time limits and no fees.

Graduates: From July 1, 2004 to June 30, 2005, 1270 bachelor's degrees were awarded. The most popular majors were elementary education (14%), business management (10%), and mechanical engineering (6%). In an average class, 14% graduate in 4 years or less, 35% graduate in 5 years or less, and 44% graduate in 6 years or less. 309 companies recruited on campus in 2004-2005. Of the 2004 graduating class, 10% were enrolled in graduate school within 6 months of graduation and 80% were employed.

Admissions Contact: Robert L. Hodum, Assistant Director of Admissions. E-mail: *admissions@tntech.edu* Web: *www.tntech.edu*

TENNESSEE WESLEYAN COLLEGE D-3
Athens, TN 37371-0040
(423) 746-5286
(800) PICK-TWC; Fax: (423) 744-9968

Full-time: 240 men, 493 women	**Faculty:** 46; --$
Part-time: 38 men, 94 women	**Ph.D.s:** 53%
Graduate: none	**Student/Faculty:** 16 to 1
Year: semesters, summer session	**Tuition:** $13,550
Application Deadline: open	**Room & Board:** $5100
Freshman Class: n/av	
ACT: 21	**COMPETITIVE**

Tennessee Wesleyan College, founded in 1857, is a private institution affiliated with the United Methodist Church. Its undergraduate programs stress the liberal arts, teacher preparation, and nursing. There are 2 undergraduate schools. In addition to regional accreditation, TWC has baccalaureate program accreditation with CCNE. The library contains 153,505 volumes, 9668 microform items, and 3558 audio/video tapes/CDs/DVDs, and subscribes to 9663 periodicals including electronic. Computerized library services include the card catalog, interlibrary loans, database searching, and Internet access. Special learning facilities include a learning resource center, art gallery, and an education technology lab. The 40-acre campus is in a small town 55 miles south of Knoxville. Including any residence halls, there are 19 buildings.

Student Life: 94% of undergraduates are from Tennessee. Students are from 18 states, 13 foreign countries, and Canada. 98% are from public schools. 75% are white. Most are Protestant. The average age of freshmen is 19; all undergraduates, 24. 35% do not continue beyond their first year; 35% remain to graduate.

Housing: 327 students can be accommodated in college housing, which includes single-sex and coed dorms, on-campus apartments, and fraternity houses. On-campus housing is guaranteed for all 4 years. 73% of students commute. Alcohol is not permitted. All students may keep cars.

Activities: 11% of women belong to 1 local and 1 national sorority. There are no fraternities. There are 24 groups on campus, including art, cheerleading, choir, chorale, computers, dance, drama, ethnic, honors, international, literary magazine, musical theater, newspaper, professional, religious, social, social service, and student government. Popular campus events include skiing trips and annual spring Dodge Ball Tournament.

Sports: There are 7 intercollegiate sports for men and 6 for women, and 4 intramural sports for men and 4 for women. Facilities include a 2000-seat stadium, an 800-seat gym, a fitness center, and a YMCA adjacent to campus with an indoor/outdoor swimming pool available to all full-time students.

Disabled Students: 56% of the campus is accessible. Wheelchair ramps, elevators, special parking, specially equipped rest rooms, and special class scheduling are available.

Services: Counseling and information services are available, as is tutoring in every subject, including English, math, computers, and sciences. There is a reader service for the blind and remedial math and writing.

Campus Safety and Security: Measures include self-defense education, security escort services, informal discussions, and pamphlets/posters/films. There are lighted pathways/sidewalks and an evening security patrol 7 days per week.

Programs of Study: TWC confers B.A., B.S., B.Applied Sc., B.Mus.Ed., and B.S.N. degrees. Bachelor's degrees are awarded in BIOLOGICAL SCIENCE (biology/biological science), BUSINESS (accounting and business administration and management), COMMUNICATIONS AND THE ARTS (English and music), COMPUTER AND PHYSICAL SCIENCE (chemistry and mathematics), EDUCATION (music and physical), HEALTH PROFESSIONS (nursing), SOCIAL SCIENCE (behavioral science, history, human development, human services, interdisciplinary studies, international studies, ministries, pastoral studies, psychology, religious education, and religious music). History, English, and preseminary are the strongest academically. Business administration, education, and nursing are the largest.

Required: Students must complete 128 semester hours, fulfilling the requirements of the major and taking 30 semester hours at the upper-division level, and maintain a minimum GPA of 2.0. Distribution requirements include 12 semester hours of the humanities, 9 of social and behavioral sciences, 8 of science, 6 each of math and English composition, and 3 each of speech and fine arts. B.A. candidates must also take 12 hours of a single foreign language. 2 semester hours of phys ed are also needed. Internships are required for human services students, and all students must take an exit exam. The number of hours required for the major varies.

Special: The college offers cross-registration, for credit internships in business and behavioral science, study abroad, an accelerated degree program, B.A.-B.S. degrees, and dual and student-designed majors. Students in natural science programs may take summer courses offered by the Gulf Coast Research Laboratory of the University of Southern Mississippi Institute of Marine Sciences. There are 3 national honor societies and a freshman honors program.

Faculty/Classroom: 52% of faculty are male; 48%, female. All teach undergraduates and 40% both teach and do research. The average class size in an introductory lecture is 15; in a laboratory, 15; and in a regular course, 15.

Admissions: 122% of the 2005-2006 applicants were accepted. The ACT scores for the 2005-2006 freshman class were: 49% below 21, 28% between 21 and 23, 13% between 24 and 26, 9% between 27 and 28, and 2% above 28.

Requirements: The ACT is required. In addition, other admission requirements include graduation from an accredited secondary school with 16 academic credits, including 4 units in English, 2 each in math and science, and 1 each in social studies and history. Foreign language is recommended. The GED is also accepted. A GPA of 2.0 is required. AP and CLEP credits are accepted. Important factors in the admissions decision are recommendations by school officials and personality/intangible qualities.

Procedure: Freshmen are admitted to all sessions. Entrance exams should be taken during high school. There is a rolling admissions plan. Application deadlines are open. Application fee is $25. Notification is sent on a rolling basis. Applications are accepted on-line.

Transfer: 144 transfer students enrolled in 2004-2005. Transfer students must have a minimum GPA of 2.0; an associate degree is recommended. 32 of 128 credits required for the bachelor's degree must be completed at TWC.

Visiting: There are regularly scheduled orientations for prospective students. There are guides for informal visits and visitors may sit in on classes and stay overnight. To schedule a visit, contact the Office of Admissions at (423) 746-5287 or *cawoodr@twcnet.edu*.

Financial Aid: In 2005-2006, all full-time freshmen and 96% of continuing full-time students received some form of financial aid. 34% of full-time freshmen and 32% of continuing full-time students received need-based aid. The average freshman award was $10,668. Need-based scholarships or need-based grants averaged $2462 ($10,194 maximum); need-based self-help aid (loans and jobs) averaged $3091 ($3125 maximum); non-need-based athletic scholarships averaged $2796 ($13,000 maximum); and other non-need-based awards and non-need-based scholarships averaged $5004 ($14,550 maximum). 13% of undergraduates work part time. Average annual earnings from campus work are $859. The average financial indebtedness of the 2005 graduate was $15,154. The FAFSA and the college's own financial statement are required. The priority date for freshman financial aid applications for fall entry is March 1.

International Students: There are 23 international students enrolled. The school actively recruits these students. A satisfactory score is required on the written TOEFL.

Computers: All students may access the system during lab hours. There are no time limits and no fees. It is strongly recommended that all students have a PC.

Graduates: From July 1, 2004 to June 30, 2005, 195 bachelor's degrees were awarded. The most popular majors were business administration (36%), nursing (15%), and education (12%). In an average class, 35% graduate in 4 years or less, 44% graduate in 5 years or less, and 46% graduate in 6 years or less. Of the 2004 graduating class, 28% were enrolled in graduate school within 6 months of graduation.

Admissions Contact: Michelle Boyd, Office Coordinator. A video is available. E-mail: *shellyb@twcnet.edu* Web: *www.twcnet.edu*

TREVECCA NAZARENE UNIVERSITY C-3
Nashville, TN 37210-2877
(615) 248-1320
(888) 210-4TNU; Fax: (615) 248-7406

Full-time: 455 men, 532 women	**Faculty:** 63; IIA, --$
Part-time: 105 men, 153 women	**Ph.D.s:** 76%
Graduate: 296 men, 655 women	**Student/Faculty:** 16 to 1
Year: semesters, summer session	**Tuition:** $13,432
Application Deadline: open	**Room & Board:** $6162
Freshman Class: 762 applied, 522 accepted, 250 enrolled	
SAT Verbal/Math: 510/510*	**ACT:** 22 **COMPETITIVE**

Trevecca Nazarene University, founded in 1901, is a private institution affiliated with the Church of the Nazarene. Trevecca offers programs in liberal arts and sciences and a number of professional content areas. The university also provides a variety of nontraditional continuing education professional programs at the undergraduate and graduate levels. There are 4 undergraduate and 4 graduate schools. In addition to regional accreditation, TNU has baccalaureate program accreditation with CAHEA and NASM. The library contains 108,570 volumes, 309,315 microform items, and 4161 audio/video tapes/CDs/DVDs, and subscribes to 703 periodicals including electronic. Computerized library services include the card catalog, interlibrary loans, database searching, Internet access, and laptop Internet portals. Special learning facilities include a learning resource center, radio station, and curriculum library. The 80-acre campus is in an urban area. Including any residence halls, there are 25 buildings.

Student Life: 57% of undergraduates are from Tennessee. Others are from 39 states, 14 foreign countries, and Canada. 85% are white. 84% are Protestant; 12% claim no religious affiliation. The average age of freshmen is 19; all undergraduates, 28. 32% do not continue beyond their first year; 40% remain to graduate.

Housing: 733 students can be accommodated in college housing, which includes single-sex dorms, on-campus apartments, off-campus apartments, and married-student housing. On-campus housing is guaranteed for all 4 years. 56% of students live on campus. Alcohol is not permitted. All students may keep cars.

Activities: There are no fraternities or sororities. There are 18 groups on campus, including band, cheerleading, choir, chorale, chorus, drama, forensics, honors, jazz band, literary magazine, marching band, newspaper, orchestra, pep band, professional, radio, religious, social service, student government, symphony, and yearbook. Popular campus events include Valentine's Banquet, Junior-Senior Banquets, and Fall Retreat.

Sports: There are 4 intercollegiate sports for men and 5 for women, and 9 intramural sports for men and 8 for women. Facilities include a gym, a pool, a jogging track, handball, racquetball, and tennis courts, exercise and weight rooms, and playing fields.

Disabled Students: Wheelchair ramps, elevators, special parking, specially equipped rest rooms, and special class scheduling are available.

Services: Counseling and information services are available, as is tutoring in every subject. There is a reader service for the blind, and remedial math, reading, and writing. An academic enrichment program for students scoring below 19 on the ACT provides tutoring in math, reading, writing, and study skills.

Campus Safety and Security: Measures include 24-hour foot and vehicle patrol, informal discussions, and lighted pathways/sidewalks.

Programs of Study: TNU confers B.A., B.S., B.B.A., and B.S.S.W. degrees. Associate, master's, and doctoral degrees are also awarded. Bachelor's degrees are awarded in BIOLOGICAL SCIENCE (biology/biological science), BUSINESS (accounting, business administration and management, and marketing/retailing/merchandising), COMMUNICATIONS AND THE ARTS (broadcasting, communications, communications technology, dramatic arts, English, music, and music business management), COMPUTER AND PHYSICAL SCIENCE (chemistry, information sciences and systems, mathematics, physics, and science), EDUCATION (early childhood, education, English, mathematics, music, physical, and science), HEALTH PROFESSIONS (medical laboratory technology), SOCIAL SCIENCE (behavioral science, history, political science/government, psychology, religion, religious music, social science, and social work). Teacher education, business, and music are the strongest academically. Management and human relations, religion, and education are the largest.

Required: To graduate, students must complete at least 120 semester hours with a minimum 2.0 GPA. The required 57-hour general education curriculum includes courses in English, communications, religion and philosophy, fine arts, history and social science (including foreign language), science and math, phys ed, and computer literacy.

Special: There is cross-registration with other Nazarene colleges and universities in the United States, and work-study programs, internships, a Washington semester, and nondegree study are offered. Study abroad is possible. An evening program leads to the B.A. in management and human relations for adult learners over 23 with 62 semester hours of college work. A 3-2 nursing program is offered with Belmont University. There are preprofessional studies in nursing, physical therapy, medicine, dentistry, pharmacy, veterinary science, law, and engineering. There is 1 national honor society.

Faculty/Classroom: 64% of faculty are male; 36%, female. 76% teach undergraduates. No introductory courses are taught by graduate students.

Admissions: 69% of the 2005-2006 applicants were accepted. The ACT scores for the 2005-2006 freshman class were: 36% below 21, 29% between 21 and 23, 15% between 24 and 26, 11% between 27 and 28, and 8% above 28.

Requirements: The SAT or ACT is required; the ACT is preferred, with a composite score of at least 18. In addition, candidates should have completed at least 15 academic secondary credits, including 4 units in English, 2 each in math, foreign language, and social science, and 1 in natural science. A GED of at least 45 is also accepted. The medical technology and teacher education programs have special admission requirements. A GPA of 2.5 is required. AP and CLEP credits are accepted.

Procedure: Freshmen are admitted fall, spring, and summer. Entrance exams should be taken in the junior or senior year. There is a deferred admissions plan. Application deadlines are open. Application fee is $25. Notification is sent on a rolling basis.

Transfer: 50 transfer students enrolled in 2004-2005. Transfer applicants must present official transcripts and recommendations. 30 of 120 credits required for the bachelor's degree must be completed at TNU.

Visiting: There are regularly scheduled orientations for prospective students, including a tour and meetings with admissions and financial aid

personnel and faculty. There are guides for informal visits and visitors may sit in on classes and stay overnight. To schedule a visit, contact the Admissions Office at admissions_und@trevecca.edu.

Financial Aid: In 2005-2006, 43% of all full-time freshmen received some form of financial aid. 41% of full-time freshmen received need-based aid. The average freshman award was $10,502. Need-based scholarships or need-based grants averaged $8176; and need-based self-help aid (loans and jobs) averaged $3955. The average financial indebtedness of the 2005 graduate was $24,000. The FAFSA is required. The deadline for filing freshman financial aid applications for fall entry is March 1.

International Students: There are 21 international students enrolled. They must score satisfactorily on the written TOEFL on the electronic version and also take the SAT or the ACT.

Computers: Wireless access is available. All students may access the system from 8 A.M. to 11 P.M. every day, with residence hall labs open 24 hours per day. There are no time limits and no fees.

Graduates: From July 1, 2004 to June 30, 2005, 459 bachelor's degrees were awarded. The most popular majors were management and human resources (62%), religion (4%), and education (4%). In an average class, 1% graduate in 3 years or less, 24% graduate in 4 years or less, 35% graduate in 5 years or less, and 41% graduate in 6 years or less. 25 companies recruited on campus in 2004-2005.

Admissions Contact: Patty Cook, Director of Admissions.
E-mail: admissions_und@trevecca.edu Web: www.trevecca.edu

TUSCULUM COLLEGE   F-3

Greeneville, TN 37743   (423) 636-7300
(800) 729-0256; Fax: (423) 638-7166

Full-time: 983 men, 1257 women	**Faculty:** 60
Part-time: 23 men, 26 women	**Ph.D.s:** 65%
Graduate: 114 men, 253 women	**Student/Faculty:** 37 to 1
Year: semesters, summer session	**Tuition:** $15,110
Application Deadline: open	**Room & Board:** $6230
Freshman Class: 1969 applied, 1320 accepted, 259 enrolled	
SAT Verbal/Math: 470/470*	**ACT:** 20 **LESS COMPETITIVE**

Tusculum College, a civic arts institution chartered in 1794, is the oldest college in Tennessee and the oldest coeducational college affiliated with the Presbyterian Church (U.S.A.). The 2 libraries contain 67,202 volumes, 210,798 microform items, and 966 audio/video tapes/CDs/DVDs, and subscribe to 300 periodicals including electronic. Computerized library services include the card catalog, interlibrary loans, database searching, and Internet access. Special learning facilities include an art gallery, radio station, TV station, and President Andrew Johnson Museum. The 142-acre campus is in a small town 30 miles south of Johnson City, in the foothills of the Great Smoky Mountains. Including any residence halls, there are 21 buildings.

Student Life: 80% of undergraduates are from Tennessee. Students are from 36 states, 18 foreign countries, and Canada. 97% are from public schools. 87% are white. The average age of freshmen is 19; all undergraduates, 28. 32% do not continue beyond their first year; 68% remain to graduate.

Housing: 607 students can be accommodated in college housing, which includes single-sex dorms. On-campus housing is guaranteed for all 4 years. 72% of students commute. Alcohol is not permitted. All students may keep cars.

Activities: There are no fraternities or sororities. There are 21 groups on campus, including art, cheerleading, chorale, dance, drama, ethnic, honors, international, newspaper, pep band, photography, professional, radio and TV, religious, social service, student government, and yearbook. Popular campus events include McCormick Day, Opening Convocation, and Honors Convocation.

Sports: There are 7 intercollegiate sports for men and 7 for women, and 12 intramural sports for men and 13 for women. Facilities include a 2000-seat gym, a gym/pool complex, tennis courts, and football, soccer, softball, and baseball fields.

Disabled Students: 50% of the campus is accessible. Wheelchair ramps, elevators, special parking, specially equipped rest rooms, special class scheduling, lowered drinking fountains, lowered telephones and special housing are available. Classes and activities are scheduled in accessible areas.

Services: Counseling and information services are available, as is tutoring in most subjects. There is a reader service for the blind, and remedial math, reading, and writing. Math and English tutoring are available on a limited basis through the College Learning Center.

Campus Safety and Security: Measures include 24-hour foot and vehicle patrol, informal discussions, emergency telephones, and lighted pathways/sidewalks.

Programs of Study: Tusculum confers B.A. and B.S. degrees. Master's degrees are also awarded. Bachelor's degrees are awarded in BIOLOGICAL SCIENCE (biology/biological science), BUSINESS (management information systems, management science, small business management, and sports management), COMMUNICATIONS AND THE ARTS (English and fine arts), COMPUTER AND PHYSICAL SCIENCE (computer science and information sciences and systems), EDUCATION (early childhood, education, elementary, middle school, museum studies, physical, and special), ENGINEERING AND ENVIRONMENTAL DESIGN (environmental science), HEALTH PROFESSIONS (medical technology, premedicine, and sports medicine), SOCIAL SCIENCE (history and psychology). Management, education, and biology are the strongest academically. Management and education are the largest.

Required: All students must complete at least 128 hours, a minimum GPA of 2.0 overall and 2.25 in the major. Specific degree programs have varying requirements. B.S. candidates must take a core curriculum consisting of courses in English, art, music, sociology, economics, and psychology. B.A. candidates must complete a set of interdisciplinary courses, validate 15 competencies, complete a civic arts project, and fulfill the requirements of a major.

Special: Each semester is divided into four 3 1/2-week blocks, with 1 course taken per block. Internships, practicums, and student-teaching opportunities are offered in business administration, professional and special education, social services, psychology, biology, chemistry, and medical technology. The B.S. in applied organizational management is designed for adult students with previous training and work experience. The medical technology program is offered in cooperation with a medical center in Kingsport. Study abroad, independent majors, nondegree study, an accelerated degree program in applied organizational management, work-study programs, student-designed majors, and pass/fail options are available. There is an accelerated evening program for working adults. There is 1 national honor society.

Faculty/Classroom: 67% of faculty are male; 33%, female. 89% teach undergraduates. No introductory courses are taught by graduate students. The average class size in an introductory lecture is 25; in a laboratory, 20; and in a regular course, 15.

Admissions: 67% of the 2005-2006 applicants were accepted. The SAT scores for the 2005-2006 freshman class were: Math--60% below 500, 30% between 500 and 599, and 9% between 600 and 700. The ACT scores for the 2005-2006 freshman class were: 56% below 21, 26% between 21 and 23, 12% between 24 and 26, 4% between 27 and 28, and 2% above 28. 3 freshmen graduated first in their class.

Requirements: The SAT or ACT is required. Applicants should be high school graduates or have the GED. Secondary school preparation should include 4 units of English, 2 units each of foreign language, math, and science, and 1 unit of history. A personal essay is also required and an interview may be necessary. Tusculum requires applicants to be in the upper 50% of their class. A GPA of 2.0 is required. AP and CLEP credits are accepted. Important factors in the admissions decision are advanced placement or honor courses, leadership record, and evidence of special talent.

Procedure: Freshmen are admitted to all sessions. Entrance exams should be taken in the spring of the junior year. There are deferred admissions and rolling admissions plans. Application deadlines are open. Applications are accepted on-line.

Transfer: 99 transfer students enrolled in 2004-2005. Transfer applicants should present at least a 2.0 GPA in previous college work. Tusculum recommends that applicants also submit SAT or ACT scores. 32 of 128 credits required for the bachelor's degree must be completed at Tusculum.

Visiting: There are regularly scheduled orientations for prospective students, including a fall and spring open house during which students are given campus tours, financial aid information, and application materials. There are guides for informal visits and visitors may sit in on classes and stay overnight. To schedule a visit, contact the Admissions Office.

Financial Aid: In a recent year, 80% of all full-time freshmen and 61% of continuing full-time students received some form of financial aid. 62% of full-time freshmen and 49% of continuing full-time students received need-based aid. The average freshman award in a recent year was $11,975. Need-based scholarships or need-based grants averaged $1467; need-based self-help aid (loans and jobs) averaged $2855; and other non-need-based awards and non-need-based scholarships averaged $6438. 20% of undergraduates work part time. Average annual earnings from campus work are $1045. The average financial indebtedness of the 2005 graduate was $14,633. The FAFSA is required. The priority date for freshman financial aid applications for fall entry is February 5.

International Students: There are 30 international students enrolled. Satisfactory scores are required on the written TOEFL and the SAT or the ACT.

Computers: All students may access the system 24 hours a day, 7 days a week. There are no time limits and no fees.

Admissions Contact: Nancy Kilday, Admission Coordinator. E-mail: admissions@tusculum.edu Web: www.tusculum.edu

UNION UNIVERSITY
B-3
Jackson, TN 38305-3697

(731) 661-5102
(800) 33-UNION; Fax: (731) 338-6466

Full-time: 637 men, 974 women	**Faculty:** 146; IIA, -$
Part-time: 183 men, 292 women	**Ph.Ds:** 80%
Graduate: 240 men, 540 women	**Student/Faculty:** 11 to 1
Year: 4-1-4, summer session	**Tuition:** $16,400
Application Deadline: open	**Room & Board:** $4350
Freshman Class: 1090 applied, 936 accepted, 408 enrolled	
SAT Verbal/Math: 560/550*	**ACT:** 24 **VERY COMPETITIVE**

Union University, founded in 1823, is a private, nonprofit institution affiliated with the Southern Baptist Convention. The university offers programs in arts and sciences, education, business, and nursing. There are 4 undergraduate and 3 graduate schools. In addition to regional accreditation, Union has baccalaureate program accreditation with AACSB, ABET, ACS, CAAHEP, CCNE, CSWE, NASAD, NASM, NCATE, and NLN. The 2 libraries contain 146,055 volumes, 479,357 microform items, and 11,088 audio/video tapes/CDs/DVDs, and subscribe to 705 periodicals including electronic. Computerized library services include the card catalog, interlibrary loans, database searching, and Internet access. Special learning facilities include a learning resource center, art gallery, and radio and TV lab facilities. The 290-acre campus is in a suburban area 80 miles east of Memphis. Including any residence halls, there are 34 buildings.

Student Life: 68% of undergraduates are from Tennessee. Students are from 44 states, 36 foreign countries, and Canada. 75% are from public schools. 90% are white. Most are Protestant. The average age of freshmen is 18; all undergraduates, 20. 7% do not continue beyond their first year; 59% remain to graduate.

Housing: 1114 students can be accommodated in college housing, which includes single-sex dorms, on-campus apartments, and married-student housing. On-campus housing is guaranteed for all 4 years. 68% of students live on campus; of those, 35% remain on campus on weekends. Alcohol is not permitted. All students may keep cars.

Activities: 12% of men belong to 3 national fraternities; 15% of women belong to 3 national sororities. There are 73 groups on campus, including art, band, cheerleading, choir, chorus, computers, concert band, drama, ethnic, film, honors, international, jazz band, literary magazine, music ensembles, musical theater, newspaper, opera, orchestra, photography, political, professional, radio and TV, religious, social, social service, student government, and symphony. Popular campus events include Campus Day, Parents Weekend, and Variety Show.

Sports: There are 5 intercollegiate sports for men and 5 for women, and 12 intramural sports for men and 12 for women. Facilities include racquetball courts, a student recreation center, an indoor swimming pool, a wellness center, 2 gyms, 2 soccer fields, and baseball and softball complexes.

Disabled Students: 98% of the campus is accessible. Wheelchair ramps, elevators, special parking, specially equipped rest rooms, special class scheduling, lowered drinking fountains, lowered telephones, and special housing are available.

Services: Counseling and information services are available, as is tutoring in most subjects. There is also assistance with study skills, time management, note taking, reading comprehension, and writing.

Campus Safety and Security: Measures include 24-hour foot and vehicle patrol, self-defense education, security escort services, and informal discussions. There are pamphlets/posters/films, emergency telephones, and lighted pathways/sidewalks.

Programs of Study: Union confers B.A., B.S., B.M., B.S.B.A., B.S.M.T., and B.S.N. degrees. Associate, master's, and doctoral degrees are also awarded. Bachelor's degrees are awarded in BIOLOGICAL SCIENCE (biology/biological science), BUSINESS (accounting, banking and finance, business administration and management, management science, marketing management, marketing/retailing/merchandising, and sports management), COMMUNICATIONS AND THE ARTS (advertising, art, broadcasting, communications, dramatic arts, English, English as a second/foreign language, English literature, French, graphic design, Greek, journalism, music, music performance, music theory and composition, piano/organ, public relations, Spanish, and voice), COMPUTER AND PHYSICAL SCIENCE (chemistry, computer science, mathematics, physical chemistry, physical sciences, and physics), EDUCATION (education, elementary, middle school, music, physical, secondary, special, and teaching English as a second/foreign language (TESOL/TEFOL)), ENGINEERING AND ENVIRONMENTAL DESIGN (preengineering), HEALTH PROFESSIONS (medical laboratory technology, nursing, predentistry, premedicine, prepharmacy, and sports medicine), SOCIAL SCIENCE (biblical languages, biblical studies, Christian studies, economics, family and community services, history, ministries, missions, pastoral studies, philosophy, political science/government, prelaw, psychology, religion, religious music, social work, sociology, and youth ministry). Business, nursing, and education are the largest.

Required: All students must complete 128 credit hours, with at least 30 in the major, and maintain a minimum overall GPA of 2.0. The general core requirements are 8 credit hours of lab sciences, 6 each of history, composition, literature, and religion, 3 each of math, oral communication, social sciences/humanities, and fine arts, and 2 of phys ed. Students must pass comprehensive exams in each course and at completion of the major.

Special: Cooperative and accelerated degree programs are available in business department majors. Cross-registration with Lambuth and Freed-Hardeman Universities, internships, study abroad in 7 countries, a Washington semester, work-study programs, composite majors in religion and church ministry, religion and Greek, and religion and philosophy, dual and student-designed majors, 3-2 engineering degrees, and nondegree study are also offered. There are 15 national honor societies, a freshman honors program, and 14 departmental honors programs.

Faculty/Classroom: 54% of faculty are male; 46%, female. All teach undergraduates and 25% do research. No introductory courses are taught by graduate students. The average class size in an introductory lecture is 25; in a laboratory, 18; and in a regular course, 15.

Admissions: 86% of the 2005-2006 applicants were accepted. The SAT scores for the 2005-2006 freshman class were: Verbal--15% below 500, 41% between 500 and 599, 32% between 600 and 700, and 11% above 700; Math--22% below 500, 41% between 500 and 599, 30% between 600 and 700, and 7% above 700. The ACT scores were 20% below 21, 25% between 21 and 23, 26% between 24 and 26, 12% between 27 and 28, and 17% above 28. 66% of the current freshmen were in the top fifth of their class; 89% were in the top two fifths. In a recent year, there were 6 National Merit finalists and 2 semifinalists. 44 freshmen graduated first in their class in a recent year.

Requirements: The SAT or ACT is required; the ACT is preferred. Candidates must be graduates of an accredited secondary school or have the GED. A minimum of 20 academic credits is required, including at least 14 in English, math, foreign language, and social and natural sciences. An interview is also recommended. Union requires applicants to be in the upper 50% of their class. A GPA of 2.5 is required. AP and CLEP credits are accepted. Important factors in the admissions decision are leadership record, advanced placement or honor courses, and recommendations by school officials.

Procedure: Freshmen are admitted to all sessions. Entrance exams should be taken in the spring of the junior year. There are early decision, early admissions, deferred admissions and rolling admissions plans. Application deadlines are open. Application fee is $25. 14 early decision candidates were accepted in a recent year. Applications are accepted online.

Transfer: 183 transfer students enrolled in a recent year. Candidates must have a minimum GPA of 2.0 in more than 12 semester hours and submit a student transfer form from the last institution attended. 32 of 128 credits required for the bachelor's degree must be completed at Union.

Visiting: There are regularly scheduled orientations for prospective students, including campus tours, class visits, and appointments with counselors. There are guides for informal visits and visitors may sit in on classes and stay overnight. To schedule a visit, contact Robbie Graves, Director of Enrollment at (731) 661-5590 or rgraves@uu.edu.

Financial Aid: In a recent year, 81% of all full-time freshmen and 80% of continuing full-time students received some form of financial aid. 70% of full-time freshmen and 71% of continuing full-time students received need-based aid. Need-based scholarships or need-based grants averaged $2585; need-based self-help aid (loans and jobs) averaged $2851; and other non-need-based awards and non-need-based scholarships averaged $2655. 35% of undergraduates work part time. Average annual earnings from campus work are $1000. The average financial indebtedness of a recent year's graduate was $7800. The FAFSA and the college's own financial statement are required. Check with the school for current application deadlines.

International Students: There were 40 international students enrolled in a recent year. The school actively recruits these students. A satisfactory score is required on the written TOEFL. If the TOEFL has not been taken, a satisfactory score is required on the ACT or the SAT.

Computers: All students may access the system during lab hours. There are no time limits and no fees.

Graduates: From July 1, 2004 to June 30, 2005, 428 bachelor's degrees were awarded. The most popular majors were business/marketing (26%), health professions and related sciences (20%), and education (15%). In an average class, 4% graduate in 3 years or less, 47% graduate in 4 years or less, 59% graduate in 5 years or less, and 60% graduate in 6 years or less. 47 companies recruited on campus in 2004-2005.

Admissions Contact: Rich Grimm, Vice President for Enrollment Service. E-mail: info@uu.edu Web: www.uu.edu

UNIVERSITY OF MEMPHIS   A-4
Memphis, TN 38152   (901) 678-2111
                                   (800) 669-2678; Fax: (901) 678-3053

Full-time: 4634 men, 6934 women	**Faculty:** 600; I, --$
Part-time: 1568 men, 2629 women	**Ph.D.s:** 70%
Graduate: 1803 men, 2897 women	**Student/Faculty:** 19 to 1
Year: semesters, summer session	**Tuition:** $5084 ($14,898)
Application Deadline: July 1	**Room & Board:** $6069
Freshman Class: 5131 applied, 3665 accepted, 2073 enrolled	
SAT Verbal/Math: 525/530*	**ACT:** 21 COMPETITIVE

The University of Memphis, founded in 1912, is a public liberal arts and sciences institution and is part of the Tennessee Board of Regents system. There are 9 undergraduate and 2 graduate schools. In addition to regional accreditation, U of M has baccalaureate program accreditation with AACSB, AAFCS, ABET, ACEJMC, ACS, ADA, AHEA, APA, ASHA, ASLA, CACREP, CCNE, CSWE, FIDER, NASAD, NASM, NASPAA, NAST, NCATE, and NLN. The 6 libraries contain 1,854,768 volumes, 3,497,860 microform items, and 33,363 audio/video tapes/CDs/DVDs, and subscribe to 11,541 periodicals including electronic. Computerized library services include the card catalog, interlibrary loans, database searching, Internet access, and laptop Internet portals. Special learning facilities include a learning resource center, art gallery, radio station, TV station, an earthquake research center, a center for electron microscopy, Chucalissa Indian Village and Museum, and a speech and hearing center. The 1160-acre campus is in an urban area. Including any residence halls, there are 202 buildings.

Student Life: 93% of undergraduates are from Tennessee. Others are from 48 states, 97 foreign countries, and Canada. 57% are white; 35% African American. The average age of freshmen is 19; all undergraduates, 24. 29% do not continue beyond their first year; 35% remain to graduate.

Housing: 2448 students can be accommodated in college housing, which includes single-sex and coed dormitories, on-campus apartments, married-student housing, fraternity houses, and sorority houses. In addition, there are special-interest houses and family housing. On-campus housing is guaranteed for all 4 years. 87% of students commute. Alcohol is not permitted. All students may keep cars.

Activities: 7% of men belong to 10 national fraternities; 5% of women belong to 2 local and 12 national sororities. There are 151 groups on campus, including art, band, cheerleading, chess, choir, chorale, chorus, computers, dance, drama, ethnic, film, gay, honors, international, jazz band, literary magazine, marching band, musical theater, newspaper, opera, orchestra, pep band, photography, political, professional, radio and TV, religious, social, social service, student government, symphony, and yearbook. Popular campus events include Black History Month, step shows by Greek organizations, and Internationmal Night.

Sports: There are 9 intercollegiate sports for men and 9 for women, and 11 intramural sports for men and 11 for women. Facilities include a gym, a football stadium, a baseball field, swimming pools, a track, a weight room, and tennis, handball, and racquetball courts.

Disabled Students: 95% of the campus is accessible. Wheelchair ramps, elevators, special parking, specially equipped rest rooms, special class scheduling, lowered drinking fountains, lowered telephones, special housing, and a transportation service are available.

Services: Counseling and information services are available, as is tutoring in most subjects. There is a reader service for the blind, and remedial math, reading, and writing.

Campus Safety and Security: Measures include 24-hour foot and vehicle patrol, security escort services, informal discussions, and pamphlets/posters/films. There are emergency telephones, lighted pathways/sidewalks, digital video cameras, a computerized entry system, a gated parking lot, parking lot fences, parking lot security towers, campus safety forums, and a personal safety program.

Programs of Study: U of M confers B.A., B.S., B.B.A., B.F.A., B.L.S., B.M., B.P.S., B.S.C.E., B.S.Ch., B.S.CpE., B.S.C.P., B.S.Ed., B.S.E.E., B.S.E.T., B.S.I.S., B.S.M.E., and B.S.N. degrees. Master's and doctoral degrees are also awarded. Bachelor's degrees are awarded in BIOLOGICAL SCIENCE (biology/biological science and microbiology), BUSINESS (accounting, banking and finance, business administration and management, business economics, hospitality management services, insurance and risk management, international business management, logistics, management information systems, management science, marketing and distribution, marketing management, marketing/retailing/merchandising, operations management, organizational behavior, real estate, recreation and leisure services, and retailing), COMMUNICATIONS AND THE ARTS (applied music, art, art history and appreciation, communications, dramatic arts, English, journalism, languages, music, and music business management), COMPUTER AND PHYSICAL SCIENCE (chemistry, computer science, geology, information sciences and systems, mathematics, and physics), EDUCATION (education, elementary, physical, and special), ENGINEERING AND ENVIRONMENTAL DESIGN (architectural technology, architecture, biomedical engineering, civil engineering, computer engineering, computer technology, electrical/electronics engineering, electrical/electronics engineering technology, industrial engineering, manufacturing technology, and mechanical engineering), HEALTH PROFESSIONS (exercise science and nursing), SOCIAL SCIENCE (African American studies, anthropology, consumer services, criminal justice, criminology, economics, geography, history, human development, interdisciplinary studies, international relations, international studies, liberal arts/general studies, paralegal studies, parks and recreation management, philosophy, political science/government, psychology, social work, and sociology). Nursing, integrative studies, and individual studies are the largest.

Required: To graduate, students must complete a minimum of 120 credit hours with a GPA of 2.0 and demonstrate proficiency in computer skills. Distribution requirements include 9 hours of humanitites and fine arts with at least 1 literature course, 8 of natural science, 6 each of English composition, social and behavioral science, and U.S. history, and 3 each of math, oral communication, and writing intensive, computation intensive, and integrative courses.

Special: The university offers co-op programs, dual enrollment, internships, study abroad and domestic student exchange, accelerated degree programs, double and student-designed majors, independent study, distance learning, an external degree program, preprofessional and professional studies program, teacher certification, ESL, nondegree study, and pass/fail options. Students may receive credit for life, military, and work experience. There are 12 national honor societies, a freshman honors program, and 13 departmental honors programs.

Faculty/Classroom: 54% of faculty are male; 46%, female. 66% teach undergraduates. Graduate students teach 22% of introductory courses.

Admissions: 71% of the 2005-2006 applicants were accepted. The SAT scores for the 2005-2006 freshman class were: Verbal--37% below 500, 36% between 500 and 599, 23% between 600 and 700, and 3% above 700; Math--34% below 500, 41% between 500 and 599, 22% between 600 and 700, and 3% above 700. The ACT scores were 44% below 21, 28% between 21 and 23, 16% between 24 and 26, 7% between 27 and 28, and 5% above 28.

Requirements: The SAT or ACT is required. Candidates for admission should be graduates of an accredited secondary school and have 15 academic credits or 20 Carnegie units. The GED is accepted. Academic preparation should include 4 units in English, 3 in math, 2 each in science, social studies, and foreign language, 1 in history, and 1 in visual and performing arts. An interview is required for University College applicants, a portfolio is required for art program applicants, and an audition is required for music applicants. A GPA of 2.0 is required. AP and CLEP credits are accepted. Important factors in the admissions decision are advanced placement or honor courses, evidence of special talent, and recommendations by school officials.

Procedure: Freshmen are admitted fall, spring, and summer. There are early admissions and rolling admissions plans. Entrance exams should be taken in the spring of the junior year or October of the senior year. Applications should be filed by July 1 for fall entry, December 1 for spring entry, and May 1 for summer entry. Notification is sent on a rolling basis. Applications are accepted on-line. The fall 2005 application fee was $25.

Transfer: 2248 transfer students enrolled in 2004-2005. They must meet cumulative GPA requirements established by the state board and have an honorable dismissal from the previous institution. 33 of 120 credits required for the bachelor's degree must be completed at U of M.

Visiting: There are regularly scheduled orientations for prospective students, including Fall Campus Day for high school seniors. There are guides for informal visits and visitors may sit in on classes and stay overnight. To schedule a visit, contact Brian Meredith, Recruitment and Orientation Services at (800) 669-2678.

Financial Aid: In 2004-2005, 75% of all full-time freshmen and 85% of continuing full-time students received some form of financial aid. 82% of full-time freshmen and 78% of continuing full-time students received need-based aid. The average freshman award was $4310. Need-based scholarships or need-based grants averaged $3449; need-based self-help aid (loans and jobs) averaged $1720; non-need-based athletic scholarships averaged $4915; and other non-need-based awards and non-need-based scholarships averaged $3786. 12% of undergraduates work part time. Average annual earnings from campus work are $1808. The average financial indebtedness of the 2005 graduate was $21,487. The FAFSA is required. The priority date for freshman financial aid applications for fall entry is March 1. The deadline for filing freshman financial aid applications for fall entry is June 30.

International Students: There are 269 international students enrolled. The school actively recruits these students. They must score satisfactorily on the written TOEFL or on the electronic version and also take the SAT or ACT. The minimum score is tied to the applicant's GPA.

Computers: Wireless access is available. A total of 2000 PCs are available to all students. 3025 open, wired network connections are available to students in the library, classrooms, computer labs, and elsewhere. The wireless network is available in the libraries, classrooms, computer labs, administrative and faculty offices, and work areas, and in college-owned, -operated, or -affiliated housing. All students may access the system. There are no time limits and no fees.

Graduates: From July 1, 2004 to June 30, 2005, 2282 bachelor's degrees were awarded. The most popular majors were individual studies (9%), intergrative studies (7%), and psychology (6%). In an average class, 11% graduate in 4 years or less, 26% graduate in 5 years or less, and 35% graduate in 6 years or less.

Admissions Contact: David Wallace, Director, Admissions. A video is available. E-mail: *recruitment@memphis.edu* Web: *http://www.memphis.edu*

UNIVERSITY OF TENNESSEE SYSTEM

The University of Tennessee System, established in 1794, is a land-grand system in Tennessee. It is governed by a board of trustees, whose chief administrator is president. The primary goal of the system is to provide a full range of teaching, research, and service programs at all levels. The main priorities are to provide quality learning and research opportunities for students from Tennessee and throughout the country. The total enrollment is usually about 38,000, with 3100 faculty members. Altogether there are some 180 baccalaureate, 125 master's, and 60 doctoral programs offered in University of Tennessee System. Profiles of the 4-year campuses are included in this section.

UNIVERSITY OF TENNESSEE AT CHATTANOOGA   D-4
Chattanooga, TN 37403   (423) 755-4662
(800) UTC-6627; Fax: (423) 755-4157

Full-time: 2400 men, 3360 women	Faculty: 307; IIA, --$
Part-time: 615 men, 750 women	Ph.D s: 80%
Graduate: 550 men, 840 women	Student/Faculty: 19 to 1
Year: semesters, summer session	Tuition: $3240 ($9800)
Application Deadline: see profile	Room & Board: $4550
Freshman Class: n/av	
SAT or ACT: required	COMPETITIVE

The University of Tennessee at Chattanooga, founded in 1886, is a public institution. Part of the state's university system, it offers programs in liberal and fine arts, business, engineering, health science, and teacher preparation. There are 5 undergraduate and 5 graduate schools. Figures in the above capsule and in this profile are approximate. In addition to regional accreditation, UTC has baccalaureate program accreditation with AACSB, ABET, ACEJMC, AHEA, APTA, CSWE, NASAD, NASM, NCATE, and NLN. The library contains 486,978 volumes, 1,338,193 microform items, and 16,451 audio/video tapes/CDs/DVDs, and subscribes to 2768 periodicals including electronic. Computerized library services include the card catalog, interlibrary loans, and database searching. Special learning facilities include a learning resource center, art gallery, radio station, and an observatory. The 116-acre campus is in an urban area 105 miles north of Atlanta. Including any residence halls, there are 76 buildings.

Student Life: 92% of undergraduates are from Tennessee. Others are from 41 states, 49 foreign countries, and Canada. 79% are white; 16% African American. The average age of freshmen is 20; all undergraduates, 24. 26% do not continue beyond their first year; 44% remain to graduate.

Housing: 1830 students can be accommodated in college housing, which includes single-sex and coed dormitories, on-campus apartments, off-campus apartments, married-student housing, and fraternity houses. On-campus housing is available on a first-come, first-served basis. 74% of students commute. Alcohol is not permitted. All students may keep cars.

Activities: 8% of men belong to 8 national fraternities; 7% of women belong to 7 national sororities. There are 130 groups on campus, including band, cheerleading, chess, choir, chorale, chorus, computers, dance, drama, drill team, ethnic, gay, honors, international, jazz band, literary magazine, marching band, musical theater, newspaper, orchestra, pep band, photography, political, professional, radio and TV, religious, social, social service, student government, symphony, and yearbook. Popular campus events include Homecoming.

Sports: There are 6 intercollegiate sports for men and 6 for women, and 12 intramural sports for men and 7 for women. Facilities include a gym, an arena, a tennis and racquet center, a swimming pool, and 2 fields, including a soccer field.

Disabled Students: 98% of the campus is accessible. Wheelchair ramps, elevators, special parking, specially equipped rest rooms, special class scheduling, lowered drinking fountains, and lowered telephones are available.

Services: Counseling and information services are available, as is tutoring in most subjects. There is a reader service for the blind, and remedial math, reading, and writing.

Campus Safety and Security: Measures include 24-hour foot and vehicle patrol, security escort services, shuttle buses, and informal discussions. There are pamphlets/posters/films, emergency telephones, and lighted pathways/sidewalks.

Programs of Study: UTC confers B.A., B.S., B.F.A., B.M., B.S.E., B.S.N., B.S.O.T., and B.S.W. degrees. Master's degrees are also awarded. Bachelor's degrees are awarded in BIOLOGICAL SCIENCE (biology/biological science), BUSINESS (business administration and management and recreation and leisure services), COMMUNICATIONS AND THE ARTS (communications, dramatic arts, English, fine arts, French, Greek, Latin, music, and Spanish), COMPUTER AND PHYSICAL SCIENCE (applied mathematics, chemistry, computer science, geology, mathematics, and physics), EDUCATION (art, education, music, secondary, and special), ENGINEERING AND ENVIRONMENTAL DESIGN (engineering, engineering management, and environmental science), HEALTH PROFESSIONS (medical laboratory technology, nursing, occupational therapy, and rehabilitation therapy), SOCIAL SCIENCE (criminal justice, economics, history, home economics, human services, humanities, paralegal studies, philosophy, political science/government, psychology, social work, sociology, and women's studies). Business and nursing are the strongest academically. Business is the largest.

Required: All students must complete at least 128 semester hours and maintain a minimum GPA of 2.0. General education requirements include 9 hours in humanities and fine arts, 6 hours each in written communication in English and behavioral and social sciences, 4 hours in physical and natural sciences, and 3 hours each in math, and perspectives. A health and phys ed course is required in the first year, and another phys ed activity course must be taken before graduation. Requirements vary by major.

Special: Cooperative programs are offered in accounting, business systems, chemistry, communications, engineering, environmental studies, nursing, and psychology. UTC offers internships, study abroad in England, work-study and accelerated degree programs, B.A.-B.S. degrees, dual majors,interdisciplinary majors, including theater and speech, 3-2 engineering degrees, and nondegree study. Credit is given for life, military, or work experience. There are 30 national honor societies, a freshman honors program, and 25 departmental honors programs.

Faculty/Classroom: 65% of faculty are male; 35%, female. No introductory courses are taught by graduate students. The average class size in an introductory lecture is 25.

Requirements: The SAT or ACT is required. In addition, secondary school credits should include 4 in English, 3 in math, and 2 each in science, social studies, and a foreign language. The GED is accepted. Applicatioons are accepted on-line at the school's web site. A GPA of 2.0 is required. AP and CLEP credits are accepted. Important factors in the admissions decision are recommendations by school officials, advanced placement or honor courses, and evidence of special talent.

Procedure: Freshmen are admitted to all sessions. Entrance exams should be taken in spring of the junior year. There is a deferred admissions plan. Check with the school for current deadlines and fee. Applications are accepted on-line.

Transfer: 631 transfer students enrolled in a recent year. A minimum GPA of 2.0 is required. 30 of 128 credits required for the bachelor's degree must be completed at UTC.

Visiting: There are regularly scheduled orientations for prospective students. There are guides for informal visits and visitors may sit in on classes and stay overnight. To schedule a visit, contact the Admissions Office.

Financial Aid: In a recent year, 70% of all full-time freshmen and 65% of continuing full-time students received some form of financial aid. 48% of full-time freshmen and 56% of continuing full-time students received need-based aid. The average freshman award was $3305. 78% of undergraduates work part time. Average annual earnings from campus work are $1900. The FAFSA is required. Check with the school for current dedlines

International Students: The school actively recruits these students. A satisfactory score is required on the written TOEFL.

Computers: There are no time limits and no fees.

Graduates: In a recent year, 1377 bachelor's degrees were awarded. The most popular majors were business administration (23%), education (15%), and psychology (9%). In an average class, 18% graduate in 4 years or less, 37% graduate in 5 years or less, and 44% graduate in 6 years or less. 100 companies recruited on campus in a recent year.

Admissions Contact: Yancy Freeman, Director of Admissions & Recruitment. E-mail: *yancy-freeman@utc.edu* Web: *www.utc.edu*

UNIVERSITY OF TENNESSEE AT KNOXVILLE	E-2
Knoxville, TN 37996-0230	(865) 974-2184
	(800) 221-VOLS; Fax: (865) 974-6341

Full-time: 9173 men, 9385 women	Faculty: 1253
Part-time: 693 men, 801 women	Ph.D.s: 82%
Graduate: 2607 men, 3379 women	Student/Faculty: n/av
Year: semesters, summer session	Tuition: $5290 ($16,360)
Application Deadline: February 1	Room & Board: $6430
Freshman Class: n/av	
SAT or ACT: required	COMPETITIVE

The University of Tennessee, Knoxville, founded in 1794 and the original campus of the state university system, is now a large public institution offering more than 300 graduate and undergraduate programs. There are 11 undergraduate and 14 graduate schools. In addition to regional accreditation, UT Knoxville has baccalaureate program accreditation with AACSB, ABET, ACEJMC, ADA, AHEA, ASLA, CSWE, FIDER, NAAB, NASAD, NASM, NCATE, NLN, NRPA, and SAF. The 4 libraries contain 2,492,953 volumes, 3,502,541 microform items, and 173,506 audio/video tapes/CDs/DVDs, and subscribe to 16,656 periodicals including electronic. Computerized library services include the card catalog, interlibrary loans, and database searching. Special learning facilities include a learning resource center, art gallery, natural history museum, radio station, and science and engineering research facility. The 533-acre campus is in an urban area adjacent to downtown Knoxville. Including any residence halls, there are 220 buildings.

Student Life: 85% of undergraduates are from Tennessee. Others are from 50 states, 94 foreign countries, and Canada. 83% are white. The average age of freshmen is 18; all undergraduates, 22. 21% do not continue beyond their first year; 57% remain to graduate.

Housing: 7000 students can be accommodated in college housing, which includes single-sex and coed dorms, on-campus apartments, off-campus apartments, married-student housing, and fraternity houses. In addition, there are language houses, special-interest houses, sority housing within a residence hall, and EXCEL, a specialized housing program for freshmen. On-campus housing is available on a first-come, first-served basis. 62% of students commute. Alcohol is not permitted. All students may keep cars.

Activities: 8% of men belong to 26 national fraternities; 8% of women belong to 17 national sororities. There are 300 groups on campus, including art, band, cheerleading, chess, choir, chorale, chorus, computers, dance, drama, ethnic, film, gay, honors, international, jazz band, literary magazine, marching band, musical theater, newspaper, opera, orchestra, pep band, photography, political, professional, radio and TV, religious, social, social service, student government, symphony, and yearbook. Popular campus events include All-Sing, Torch Night, and International Festival.

Sports: There are 8 intercollegiate sports for men and 10 for women, and 22 intramural sports for men and 22 for women. Facilities include a 25,000-seat basketball arena, the second largest collegiate football stadium in the United States, an Olympic track, Olympic indoor and outdoor pools, various outdoor facilities, a baseball stadium, and softball and soccer fields.

Disabled Students: 95% of the campus is accessible. Wheelchair ramps, elevators, special parking, specially equipped rest rooms, special class scheduling, lowered drinking fountains, lowered telephones, and an escort service are available.

Services: There is a reader service for the blind. Tutoring in math, English, and most lower-division courses can be arranged.

Campus Safety and Security: Measures include 24-hour foot and vehicle patrol, self-defense education, security escort services, and shuttle buses. There are informal discussions, pamphlets/posters/films, emergency telephones, lighted pathways/sidewalks, and campus safety educational programs.

Programs of Study: UT Knoxville confers B.A., B.S.,,B.Arch., B.F.A., B.M., and specialized B.S. degrees in 25 fields, including business administration, nursing, and social work. Master's and doctoral degrees are also awarded. Bachelor's degrees are awarded in AGRICULTURE (agricultural economics, agriculture, animal science, fishing and fisheries, forestry and related sciences, plant science, and soil science), BIOLOGICAL SCIENCE (biochemistry, biology/biological science, botany, microbiology, and nutrition), BUSINESS (accounting, banking and finance, business administration and management, business economics, hotel/motel and restaurant management, management science, marketing/retailing/merchandising, retailing, sports management, tourism, and transportation management), COMMUNICATIONS AND THE ARTS (advertising, art history and appreciation, broadcasting, classics, comparative literature, dramatic arts, English, film arts, fine arts, French, German, graphic design, Italian, journalism, languages, linguistics, music, Russian, Spanish, speech/debate/rhetoric, and studio art), COMPUTER AND PHYSICAL SCIENCE (chemistry, computer science, geology, mathematics, physics, and statistics), EDUCATION (agricultural, art, elementary, health, marketing and distribution, music, physical, recreation, and special), ENGINEERING AND ENVIRONMENTAL DESIGN (aerospace studies, agricultural engineering, architecture, chemical engineering, civil engineering, electrical/electronics engineering, engineering, engineering and applied science, engineering physics, environmental science, food services technology, industrial engineering, interior design, landscape architecture/design, materials engineering, materials science, mechanical engineering, and nuclear engineering), HEALTH PROFESSIONS (community health work, health science, nursing, predentistry, premedicine, preveterinary science, and speech pathology/audiology), SOCIAL SCIENCE (African American studies, anthropology, Asian/Oriental studies, child care/child and family studies, classical/ancient civilization, economics, food science, geography, history, human services, Latin American studies, medieval studies, philosophy, political science/government, psychology, public administration, religion, Russian and Slavic studies, social work, sociology, textiles and clothing, urban studies, and women's studies). Engineering, physical sciences, and English are the strongest academically. Business administration is the largest.

Required: All students must complete at least 120 credits with a minimum 2.0 GPA. Many degree programs require higher credit totals and GPAs. All students take 2 English composition courses and a core curriculum including 2 courses each in math sciences, humanities and the arts, history, social sciences, natural sciences, and foreign language or integrative studies.

Special: Cooperative programs are offered in engineering, communications, liberal arts, and business. Cross-registration is possible through the Academic Common Market, a Southern 14-state consortium, in any of 11 programs. Internships are available in social work, education, and architecture, and there are a number of work-study programs. Study abroad in more than 25 countries is possible. Dual and student-designed majors, accelerated study, nondegree study, and pass/fail options are offered. There are 51 national honor societies, including Phi Beta Kappa, a freshman honors program, and 13 departmental honors programs.

Faculty/Classroom: 65% of faculty are male; 35%, female. 6% do research and 94% both teach and do research. The average class size in an introductory lecture is 26; in a laboratory, 14; and in a regular course, 29.

Requirements: The SAT or ACT is required; the ACT is preferred. Applicants should be high school graduates or have the GED. Required secondary school courses include 4 credits in English, 3 in math, 2 each in science and a single foreign language, 1 each in history and world history or world geography, and 1 unit of visual/performing arts. A GPA of 2.0 is required. AP and CLEP credits are accepted. Important factors in the admissions decision are advanced placement or honor courses, leadership record, and parents or siblings attending the school.

Procedure: Freshmen are admitted to all sessions. Entrance exams should be taken in spring of the junior year or fall of the senior year. There are early admissions and deferred admissions plans. There is a rolling admissions plan. Applications should be filed by February 1 for fall entry, November 1 for spring entry, and April 1 for summer entry, along with a $30 fee. Notification is sent on a rolling basis.

Transfer: 1398 transfer students enrolled in 2004-2005. Transfer applicants should present a minimum 2.0 GPA in previous college work, although many specific programs have higher requirements. 30 of 120 credits required for the bachelor's degree must be completed at UT Knoxville.

Visiting: There are regularly scheduled orientations for prospective students, including 2 open houses yearly where prospective students can meet with faculty, administrators, and students to discuss admissions, housing, financial aid, student activities, academic colleges and departments, and organizations. There are guides for informal visits and visitors may sit in on classes. To schedule a visit, contact Undergraduate Admissions at (865) 974-2184.

Financial Aid: The average financial indebtedness of the 2005 graduate was $19,624. The CSS/Profile or FFS and the Academic College Scholarship Application are required. Check with the school for current deadlines.

International Students: They must score satisfactorily on the written TOEFL.

Computers: All students may access the system. There are no time limits and no fees.

Admissions Contact: Marshall Rose, Director of Admissions.
E-mail: *admissions@utk.edu* Web: *www.utk.edu*

UNIVERSITY OF TENNESSEE AT MARTIN
B-2

Martin, TN 38238

(731) 587-7020
(800) 829-8861; Fax: (731) 587-7029

Full-time: 2203 men, 2813 women	Faculty: 245; IIA, --$
Part-time: 368 men, 558 women	Ph.D.s: 69%
Graduate: 172 men, 370 women	Student/Faculty: 20 to 1
Year: semesters, summer session	Tuition: $4493 ($13,547)
Application Deadline: open	Room & Board: $4200
Freshman Class: 2803 applied, 2184 accepted, 1250 enrolled	
ACT: 21	COMPETITIVE

The University of Tennessee at Martin, founded in 1900, is a public university offering undergraduate programs in natural and social sciences, humanities, fine and performing arts, computer science, nursing, agriculture, teacher education, business administration, engineering, and the online Bachelor of University Studies. Graduate degrees are offered in accounting and business administration, counseling and teacher education, family and consumer sciences, and agricultural operations management. Master's degrees in education and agricultural operations management are available online. There are 5 undergraduate and 4 graduate schools. In addition to regional accreditation, UT Martin has baccalaureate program accreditation with AACSB, ABET, ACEJMC, ACS, ADA, AHEA, CSWE, NASM, NCATE and NLN. The library contains 493,492 volumes, 701,177 microform items, and 12,688 audio/video tapes/CDs/DVDs, and subscribes to 1198 periodicals including electronic. Computerized library services include the card catalog, interlibrary loans, database searching, Internet access, and laptop Internet portals. Special learning facilities include a learning resource center, natural history museum, radio station, TV station, a teacher resource center, a 680-acre Agricultural Experiment Station, a teaching/research facility at Reelfoot Lake State Resort, and a Center for Environmental and Conservation Education. The 250-acre campus is in a rural area 125 miles northeast of Memphis and 150 miles northwest of Nashville. Including any residence halls, there are 46 buildings.

Student Life: 94% of undergraduates are from Tennessee. Others are from 40 states, 28 foreign countries, and Canada. 90% are from public schools. 81% are white; 15% African American. Most are Protestant. The average age of freshmen is 19; all undergraduates, 22. 29% do not continue beyond their first year; 40% remain to graduate.

Housing: 1949 students can be accommodated in college housing, which includes single-sex and coed dorms, on-campus apartments, and married-student housing. In addition, there are special-interest houses. On-campus housing is available on a first-come, first-served basis. 60% of students commute. Alcohol is not permitted. All students may keep cars.

Activities: 7% of men belong to 11 national fraternities; 5% of women belong to 1 local and 7 national sororities. There are 125 groups on campus, including art, band, cheerleading, choir, chorale, chorus, computers, dance, drama, ethnic, film, gay, honors, international, jazz band, literary magazine, marching band, musical theater, newspaper, opera, pep band, photography, political, professional, radio and TV, religious, social, social service, student government, and yearbook. Popular campus events include Greekfest, UTM Rodeo-N-Roundup Days, and All-Niter.

Sports: There are 9 intercollegiate sports for men and 9 for women, and 18 intramural sports for men and 18 for women. Facilities include indoor: an Olympic-size swimming pool, 7 racquetball courts, a running/walking track, a weight room, 6 basketball, volleyball, badminton and tennis court combinations, and outdoor: a 1.5 mile fitness track, 16 tennis courts, a soccer field, and lighted intramural playing fields.

Disabled Students: All of the campus is accessible. Wheelchair ramps, elevators, special parking, specially equipped rest rooms, special class scheduling, lowered drinking fountains, lowered telephones, and special housing are available.

Services: Counseling and information services are available, as is tutoring in every subject, including biology, chemistry, computer science, English, finance, geology, German, history, math, nursing, political science, psychology, sociology, Spanish, and zoology. There is a reader service for the blind and remedial math and reading.

Campus Safety and Security: Measures include 24-hour foot and vehicle patrol, self-defense education, informal discussions, and pamphlets/posters/films. There are emergency telephones, lighted pathways/sidewalks, a bicycle patrol, and security cameras in the 4 largest residence halls.

Programs of Study: UT Martin confers B.A., B.S., B.A.Mus., B.F.A., B.Mus., B.S.Agri., B.S.Bus.Admn., B.S.Chem., B.S.Crim.Just., B.S.Ed., B.S.Eng., B.S., B.S. Fam.C.S., B.S.Health/HP, B.S.N.R.M., B.S.N., B.S.S.W., and B.U.S. degrees. Master's degrees are also awarded. Bachelor's degrees are awarded in AGRICULTURE (agricultural business management, agriculture, animal science, natural resource management, and plant science), BIOLOGICAL SCIENCE (biology/biological science and nutrition), BUSINESS (accounting, business administration and management, business economics, management science, and marketing/retailing/merchandising), COMMUNICATIONS AND THE ARTS (communications, English, fine arts, French, music, performing arts, and Spanish), COMPUTER AND PHYSICAL SCIENCE (chemistry, computer science, geology, and mathematics), EDUCATION (early childhood, education administration, elementary, secondary, and special), ENGINEERING AND ENVIRONMENTAL DESIGN (engineering), HEALTH PROFESSIONS (nursing, predentistry, premedicine, preoptometry, and prepharmacy), SOCIAL SCIENCE (child care/child and family studies, criminal justice, economics, geography, history, international studies, philosophy, political science/government, prelaw, psychology, public administration, social work, and sociology). Preprofessional health programs, biology, and engineering are the strongest academically. Nursing, human learning, and biology are the largest.

Required: The number of credit hours required for graduation ranges from 120 to 134 (based on degree). All students must have at least a 2.0 GPA. Specific courses and major requirements vary by the program selected. There is a 1 year or 30 hour UTM residency requirement. The general education core curriculum is 38 hours; English and communications courses are required. Major field and general education tests are required.

Special: UTM offers co-op programs in engineering, agriculture, computer science, business, and chemistry, for-credit internships, cross-registration through the Gulf Coast consortium, study abroad, B.A.-B.S. degrees, dual and student-designed majors, and pass/fail options. There are 30 national honor societies, a freshman honors program, and 5 departmental honors programs.

Faculty/Classroom: 55% of faculty are male; 45%, female. All teach undergraduates, 83% do research, and 83% do both. No introductory courses are taught by graduate students. The average class size in an introductory lecture is 27; in a laboratory, 16; and in a regular course, 18.

Admissions: 78% of the 2005-2006 applicants were accepted. The ACT scores for the 2005-2006 freshman class were: 37% below 21, 32% between 21 and 23, 20% between 24 and 26, 7% between 27 and 28, and 5% above 28. 41% of the current freshmen were in the top fifth of their class; 72% were in the top two fifths. 20 freshmen graduated first in their class.

Requirements: The ACT is required. In addition, students should have a minimum composite score of 19 on the ACT with a 2.25 minimum GPA, or 16 on the ACT with a minimum 2.6 GPA. Candidates for admission should be graduates of an accredited secondary school with 14 academic credits. The GED is accepted with a score of 50. Secondary school units should include 4 of English, 3 of math, 2 of a foreign language, and 1 each of science, history, social studies, and fine and performing arts. A GPA of 2.4 is required. AP and CLEP credits are accepted.

Procedure: Freshmen are admitted to all sessions. Entrance exams should be taken in the fall of the senior year. There is a deferred admissions plan. Application deadlines are open. Applications are accepted on-line.

Transfer: 421 transfer students enrolled in 2004-2005. Transfer students should have a minimum GPA of 2.0. 30 of 120 credits required for the bachelor's degree must be completed at UT Martin.

Visiting: There are regularly scheduled orientations for prospective students, including Summer Orientation and Registration (SOAR); 4 sessions conducted for students and parents that include information sessions and class registration. There are guides for informal visits and visitors may sit in on classes and stay overnight. To schedule a visit, contact the Admissions Office at *admitme@utm.edu*.

Financial Aid: In 2005-2006, 75% of all full-time freshmen and 77% of continuing full-time students received some form of financial aid. 62% of full-time freshmen and 57% of continuing full-time students received need-based aid. The average freshman award was $8275. Need-based scholarships or need-based grants averaged $4493; need-based self-help aid (loans and jobs) averaged $5462; and non-need-based athletic scholarships averaged $11,206. 22% of undergraduates work part time. Average annual earnings from campus work are $1738. The average financial indebtedness of the 2005 graduate was $16,749. The FAFSA is required. The deadline for filing freshman financial aid applications for fall entry is March 1.

International Students: There are 116 international students enrolled. The school actively recruits these students. They must score satisfactorily on the written TOEFL or on the electronic version and also take and also take the college's own entrance exam or a writing proficiency exam.

Computers: Wireless access is available. There is both wired and wireless access in all buildings and classrooms, for research, homework, the Internet, e-mail, projects, and labs. All students may access the system 24 hours. There are no time limits. The fee is $100. It is strongly recommended that all students have a personal computer.

Graduates: From July 1, 2004 to June 30, 2005, 835 bachelor's degrees were awarded. The most popular majors were Individual area of interest (12%), human learning (7%), and agriculture (6%). In an average class, 2% graduate in 3 years or less, 18% graduate in 4 years or less, 27% graduate in 5 years or less, and 40% graduate in 6 years or less. 88 companies recruited on campus in 2004-2005. Of the 2004 graduating class, 20% were enrolled in graduate school within 6 months of graduation and 71% were employed.

Admissions Contact: Judy Rayburn, Director of Admissions. A video is available. E-mail: *jrayburn@utm.edu* Web: *www.utm.edu*

UNIVERSITY OF THE SOUTH — D-4

Sewanee, TN 37383-1000

(931) 598-1238
(800) 522-2234; Fax: (931) 538-3248

Full-time: 632 men, 751 women	**Faculty:** 137; IIB, +$
Part-time: 10 men, 12 women	**Ph.D.s:** 97%
Graduate: 62 men, 34 women	**Student/Faculty:** 10 to 1
Year: semesters, summer session	**Tuition:** $27,095
Application Deadline: February 1	**Room & Board:** $7550
Freshman Class: 2070 applied, 1328 accepted, 398 enrolled	
SAT or ACT: required	**HIGHLY COMPETITIVE**

The University of the South, founded in 1857, is an independent liberal arts institution affiliated with the Episcopal Church. There is 1 undergraduate and 1 graduate school. The library contains 648,459 volumes, 328,090 microform items, and 72,964 audio/video tapes/CDs/DVDs, and subscribes to 3444 periodicals including electronic. Computerized library services include the card catalog, interlibrary loans, database searching, and Internet access. Special learning facilities include a learning resource center, art gallery, radio station, an observatory, a materials analysis lab with an electron scanning microscope, and a rare books collection. The 10,000-acre campus is in a small town 45 miles west of Chattanooga. Including any residence halls, there are 43 buildings.

Student Life: 80% of undergraduates are from out of state, mostly the South. Others are from 44 states, 23 foreign countries, and Canada. 55% are from public schools. 92% are white. 60% are Protestant; 21%

claim no religious affiliation; 9% Catholic. The average age of freshmen is 18; all undergraduates, 20. 12% do not continue beyond their first year; 79% remain to graduate.

Housing: 1275 students can be accommodated in college housing, which includes single-sex and coed dorms, on-campus apartments, and married-student housing. In addition, there are language houses. On-campus housing is guaranteed for all 4 years. 92% of students live on campus; of those, 90% remain on campus on weekends. All students may keep cars.

Activities: 46% of men belong to 11 national fraternities; 39% of women belong to 6 local sororities. There are 110 groups on campus, including art, cheerleading, choir, chorale, chorus, computers, dance, drama, ethnic, film, gay, honors, international, jazz band, literary magazine, musical theater, newspaper, orchestra, photography, political, professional, radio and TV, religious, social, social service, student government, and symphony. Popular campus events include Spring Festival Weekend.

Sports: There are 10 intercollegiate sports for men and 11 for women, and 15 intramural sports for men and 16 for women. Facilities include a sport and fitness center with multipurpose volleyball and basketball courts, an indoor pool with diving well, an indoor track, a batting cage, racquetball and squash courts, indoor tennis courts, and dance and fitness studios; a golf course; outdoor tennis courts; a multiweather track; an equestrian center and stables; 15 playing fields, a lake; and areas for rappelling, caving, hiking, and rock climbing.

Disabled Students: 75% of the campus is accessible. Wheelchair ramps, elevators, special parking, specially equipped rest rooms, special class scheduling, lowered drinking fountains, special administrative services, and a telecommunications device for the deaf are available.

Services: Counseling and information services are available, as is tutoring in most subjects. Study skills training is also offered.

Campus Safety and Security: Measures include 24-hour foot and vehicle patrol, self-defense education, security escort services, and shuttle buses. There are informal discussions, pamphlets/posters/films, emergency telephones, and lighted pathways/sidewalks.

Programs of Study: Sewanee confers B.A. and B.S. degrees. Master's and doctoral degrees are also awarded. Bachelor's degrees are awarded in AGRICULTURE (environmental studies, forestry and related sciences, and natural resource management), BIOLOGICAL SCIENCE (biology/biological science), COMMUNICATIONS AND THE ARTS (art, art history and appreciation, dramatic arts, English, French, German, Greek, Latin, music, Russian, and Spanish), COMPUTER AND PHYSICAL SCIENCE (chemistry, computer science, geology, mathematics, and physics), SOCIAL SCIENCE (American studies, anthropology, Asian/Oriental studies, economics, French studies, German area studies, history, medieval studies, philosophy, political science/government, psychology, religion, Russian and Slavic studies, social science, and Third World studies). English and environmental studies are the strongest academically. English, economics, and history are the largest.

Required: To graduate, students must complete at least 32 full courses (130 semester hours), 21 of which must be outside the major, with a minimum GPA of 2.0. The core curriculum includes 4 courses in language and literature, 3 in math and natural science, 2 each in social science and phys ed, and 1 each in the arts and in religion or philosophy. Comprehensive exams in the major field of study are required.

Special: Sewanee offers internships in economics and public affairs, study abroad in 13 countries, a Washington semester, and student-designed majors. Teacher certification and Peace Corps, medical, law, and veterinary preparation are available. A 3-2 engineering degree is offered with Columbia, Washington, and Vanderbilt Universities, Georgia Institute of Technology, and Rensselaer Polytechnic Institute. Pass/fail options are possible. There are 10 national honor societies, including Phi Beta Kappa, a freshman honors program, and 28 departmental honors programs.

Faculty/Classroom: 65% of faculty are male; 35%, female. All teach undergraduates. No introductory courses are taught by graduate students. The average class size in an introductory lecture is 20; in a laboratory, 16; and in a regular course, 12.

Admissions: 64% of the 2005-2006 applicants were accepted. The SAT scores for the 2005-2006 freshman class were: Verbal--4% below 500, 31% between 500 and 599, 52% between 600 and 700, and 13% above 700; Math--3% below 500, 37% between 500 and 599, 50% between 600 and 700, and 10% above 700. The ACT scores were 1% below 21, 22% between 21 and 23, 20% between 24 and 26, 43% between 27 and 28, and 14% above 28. 70% of the current freshmen were in the top fifth of their class; 95% were in the top two fifths.

Requirements: The SAT or ACT is required. In addition, candidates for admission should have 15 secondary school academic credits, including 4 years of English, 3 of math, and 2 each of lab science, a foreign language, and history or social science. An essay and recommendation are required and an interview is recommended. AP credits are accepted. Important factors in the admissions decision are advanced placement or honor courses, leadership record, and evidence of special talent.

Procedure: Freshmen are admitted in the fall. Entrance exams should be taken by December of the senior year. There are early decision, early admissions, and deferred admissions plans. Early decision applications should be filed by November 15; regular applications, by February 1 for fall entry. Notification of early decision is sent December 15; regular decision, April 1. A waiting list is an active part of the admissions procedure. Applications are accepted on-line.

Transfer: 15 transfer students enrolled in 2004-2005. Applicants should have a minimum GPA of 3.0 and take the SAT or ACT. They must submit official transcripts from all previous colleges attended and 2 letters of recommendation from college instructors, and they must be eligible to continue in their present school. An interview is recommended. 64 of 130 credits required for the bachelor's degree must be completed at Sewanee.

Visiting: There are regularly scheduled orientations for prospective students, including a tour, an interview, class visits, and a meeting with a counselor. There are guides for informal visits and visitors may sit in on classes and stay overnight. To schedule a visit, contact the Office of Admission at *admiss@sewanee.edu*.

Financial Aid: 35% of full-time freshmen and 37% of continuing full-time students received need-based aid. The average freshman award was $21,185. Need-based scholarships or need-based grants averaged $18,342; need-based self-help aid (loans and jobs) averaged $4720; and other non-need-based awards and non-need-based scholarships averaged $10,638. 33% of undergraduates work part time. Average annual earnings from campus work are $1000. The average financial indebtedness of the 2005 graduate was $13,244. The FAFSA and the college's own financial statement are required. The deadline for filing freshman financial aid applications for fall entry is March 1.

International Students: The school actively recruits these students. Satisfactory scores are required on the written TOEFL and the SAT or the ACT.

Computers: Wireless access is available. Students may access the network through a wired connection, which all rooms have, or through wireless hotspots across campus. All students may access the system 24 hours a day. There are no time limits and no fees.

Graduates: In a recent year, 309 bachelor's degrees were awarded. The most popular majors were social sciences and history (29%), English (13%), and foreign languages and literature (10%). In an average class, 1% graduate in 3 years or less, 78% graduate in 4 years or less, 79% graduate in 5 years or less, and 80% graduate in 6 years or less. 30 companies recruited on campus in a recent year. In a recent graduating class, 35% were enrolled in graduate school within 6 months of graduation and 95% were employed.

Admissions Contact: David Lessene, Dean of Admission. A video is available. E-mail: *collegeadmission@sewanee.edu*
Web: *www.sewanee.edu*

VANDERBILT UNIVERSITY C-2

Nashville, TN 37203-1700 (615) 322-2561
(800) 288-0432; Fax: (615) 343-7765

Full-time: 3018 men, 3228 women	**Faculty:** 785; I, +$
Part-time: 25 men, 15 women	**Ph.D.s:** n/av
Graduate: 1681 men, 2022 women	**Student/Faculty:** 8 to 1
Year: semesters, summer session	**Tuition:** $31,700
Application Deadline: January 3	**Room & Board:** $10,286
Freshman Class: 11,663 applied, 4115 accepted, 1622 enrolled	
SAT or ACT: required	**MOST COMPETITIVE**

Vanderbilt University, founded in 1873, is a private university offering programs in liberal and fine arts, business, engineering, health science, military science, religion, law, music, and teacher preparation. There are 4 undergraduate and 6 graduate schools. In addition to regional accreditation, Vanderbilt has baccalaureate program accreditation with AACSB, ABET, CAHEA, and NCATE. The 9 libraries contain 2,882,057 volumes, 2,968,668 microform items, and 63,403 audio/video tapes/CDs/DVDs, and subscribe to 29,173 periodicals including electronic. Computerized library services include the card catalog, interlibrary loans, and database searching. Special learning facilities include a learning resource center, art gallery, radio station, TV station, 2 observatories, and TV news archive. The 330-acre campus is in an urban area less than a mile and a half from downtown Nashville. Including any residence halls, there are 209 buildings.

Student Life: 83% of undergraduates are from out of state, mostly the South. Students are from 50 states, 52 foreign countries, and Canada. 55% are from public schools. 70% are white. The average age of freshmen is 18; all undergraduates, 20. 5% do not continue beyond their first year.

Housing: 4942 students can be accommodated in college housing, which includes single-sex and coed dorms, on-campus apartments, and married-student housing. In addition, there are language houses and special-interest houses. On-campus housing is guaranteed for the freshman year only, is available on a first-come, first-served basis, and is available on a lottery system for upperclassmen. Priority is given to out-of-town students. 83% of students live on campus. Alcohol is not permitted. Upperclassmen may keep cars.

Activities: 34% of men belong to 18 national fraternities; 50% of women belong to 12 national sororities. There are 375 groups on campus, including art, band, cheerleading, chess, choir, chorale, chorus, computers, dance, drama, drill team, ethnic, film, gay, honors, international, jazz band, literary magazine, marching band, musical theater, newspaper, opera, orchestra, pep band, photography, political, professional, radio and TV, religious, social, social service, student government, symphony, video production, and yearbook. Popular campus events include Rites of Spring, Blue Fest, IMPACT Speakers Series, and Homecoming.

Sports: There are 7 intercollegiate sports for men and 8 for women, and 45 intramural sports for men and 44 for women. Facilities include a gym, a pool, football and intramural fields, student recreation and tennis centers, basketball and racquetball courts, a suspended indoor track, and a climbing wall.

Disabled Students: 90% of the campus is accessible. Wheelchair ramps, elevators, special parking, specially equipped rest rooms, special class scheduling, lowered drinking fountains, and lowered telephones are available.

Services: Counseling and information services are available, as is tutoring in most subjects. There is a reader service for the blind.

Campus Safety and Security: Measures include 24-hour foot and vehicle patrol, self-defense education, security escort services, and shuttle buses. There are informal discussions, pamphlets/posters/films, emergency telephones, lighted pathways/sidewalks, a bicycle patrol, and student dorm monitors.

Programs of Study: Master's and doctoral degrees are also awarded. Bachelor's degrees are awarded in BIOLOGICAL SCIENCE (biology/biological science and molecular biology), COMMUNICATIONS AND THE ARTS (classical languages, classics, communications, English, fine arts, French, German, music history and appreciation, music performance, music theory and composition, Russian, Spanish, and theater design), COMPUTER AND PHYSICAL SCIENCE (chemistry, geology, mathematics, and physics), EDUCATION (early childhood, education, elementary, secondary, and special), ENGINEERING AND ENVIRONMENTAL DESIGN (bioengineering, chemical engineering, civil engineering, computer engineering, electrical/electronics engineering, engineering and applied science, and mechanical engineering), SOCIAL SCIENCE (African American studies, American studies, anthropology, child psychology/development, cognitive science, East Asian studies, economics, European studies, history, human development, interdisciplinary studies, Latin American studies, philosophy, political science/government, psychology, public affairs, religion, sociology, and urban studies). Social science, engineering, and education are the largest.

Required: All students must take at least 120 total credit hours. General requirements vary, as do specific major requirements, depending on the chosen program. A minimum GPA of 2.0 is usually needed. There is a mandatory writing requirement. Students majoring in human development must complete an internship in the fall semester of the senior year.

Special: Vanderbilt offers cross-registration with Fisk and Howard Universities and Meharry Medical College, study abroad in 18 countries, a Washington semester, a work-study program, B.A.-B.S. degrees, dual and student-designed majors, an accelerated degree in engineering, non-degree study, and pass/fail options. Internships, required for human development majors, are available in human service agencies, city and state government, and businesses. A 3-2 engineering degree is offered with Fisk University. The school belongs to NASA's Tennessee Space Grant Consortium and the Intercollegiate Center for Classical Studies in Rome. There are 19 national honor societies, including Phi Beta Kappa, a freshman honors program, and 21 departmental honors programs.

Faculty/Classroom: 90% teach undergraduates and 90% do research. Graduate students teach 10% of introductory courses. The average class size in an introductory lecture is 20; in a laboratory, 31; and in a regular course, 19.

Admissions: 35% of the 2005-2006 applicants were accepted. There were 132 National Merit finalists. 177 freshmen graduated first in their class.

Requirements: The SAT or ACT is required. In addition, SAT Subject tests are recommended in math level I, II, or IIc, writing, and foreign language. Admission requirements vary by school. Candidates should be graduates of an accredited secondary school with a minimum of 15 academic credits. Most programs require 4 years of English, 3 of math, and 2 of a foreign language and recommend 2 of history and of social studies. An essay is required. An audition is required for Blair School of Music. AP credits are accepted. Important factors in the admissions decision are advanced placement or honor courses and evidence of special talent.

Procedure: Freshmen are admitted in the fall. Entrance exams should be taken in the spring of the junior year or the fall of the senior year. There are early decision and deferred admissions plans. Early decision applications should be filed by November 1; regular applications, due January 3 for fall entry, along with a $50 fee. Notification of early decision is sent December 15; regular decision, April 1. 446 early decision candidates were accepted for the 2005-2006 class. 1360 applicants were on the 2005 waiting list; 50 were admitted. Applications are accepted on-line.

Transfer: 58 transfer students enrolled in 2004-2005. Transfers must take the SAT or the ACT. A minimum of 12 hours of college credit must have been earned. Students must meet all freshman requirements and be in good standing at the previous institution attended. Applicants must submit high school and college transcripts and an essay or personal statement. 60 of 120 credits required for the bachelor's degree must be completed at Vanderbilt.

Visiting: There are regularly scheduled orientations for prospective students, including group information sessions and campus tours available Monday through Saturday during the academic year and Monday through Friday during the summer. Schedules vary, so visitors must call in advance. There are guides for informal visits and visitors may sit in on classes and stay overnight. To schedule a visit, contact the Office of Undergraduate Admissions.

Financial Aid: In 2005-2006, 46% of all full-time freshmen and 38% of continuing full-time students received some form of financial aid. At least 26% of full-time freshmen and at least 25% of continuing full-time students received need-based aid. The average freshman award was $32,265. Need-based scholarships or need-based grants averaged $25,749; need-based self-help aid (loans and jobs) averaged $4169; non-need-based athletic scholarships averaged $26,741; and other institutional non-need-based awards and non-need-based scholarships averaged $13,216. 24% of undergraduates work part time. Average annual earnings from campus work are $3700. The average financial indebtedness of the 2005 graduate was $19,585. The CSS/Profile or FAFSA and tax return information are required. The priority date for freshman financial aid applications for fall entry is February 1.

International Students: The school actively recruits these students. They must score satisfactorily on the written TOEFL and also take SAT Subject tests in writing, math, and 1 other test.

Computers: All students may access the system any time.

Graduates: From July 1, 2004 to June 30, 2005, 1519 bachelor's degrees were awarded. The most popular majors were social sciences (27%), engineering (14%), and psychology (7%). In an average class, 83% graduate in 4 years or less, 87% graduate in 5 years or less, and 88% graduate in 6 years or less. 250 companies recruited on campus in 2004-2005. Of the 2004 graduating class, 32% were enrolled in graduate school within 6 months of graduation and 63% were employed.

Admissions Contact: Admissions Officer. A video is available. E-mail: *admissions@vanderbilt.edu* Web: *vanderbilt.edu*

POPULATION DENSITY
●50,000 and over

0 40 80 120 160
Miles

TEXAS

ABILENE CHRISTIAN UNIVERSITY   C-2

Abilene, TX 79699-9000

(325) 674-2650
(800) 460-6228; Fax: (325) 674-2130

Full-time: 1792 men, 2137 women	**Faculty:** 210; IIA, --$
Part-time: 67 men, 124 women	**Ph.D.s:** 78%
Graduate: 307 men, 258 women	**Student/Faculty:** 19 to 1
Year: semesters, summer session	**Tuition:** $15,160
Application Deadline: open	**Room & Board:** $5670

Freshman Class: 4011 applied, 2097 accepted, 1031 enrolled

SAT: recommended   **COMPETITIVE**

Abilene Christian University, founded in 1906, is a private institution affiliated with the Churches of Christ. The university offers a wide range of programs through the colleges of Biblical Studies, Business Administration, Arts and Sciences, and Education and Human Services. There are 6 undergraduate schools and 1 graduate school. In addition to regional accreditation, ACU has baccalaureate program accreditation with AACSB, ACEJMC, ADA, CCNE, CSWE, and NASM. The library contains 497,000 volumes, 1,200,000 microform items, and 60,000 audio/video tapes/CDs/DVDs, and subscribes to 2425 periodicals including electronic. Computerized library services include the card catalog, interlibrary loans, database searching, Internet access, and laptop Internet portals. Special learning facilities include an art gallery, planetarium, radio station, TV station, and a volunteer and service learning center. The 208-acre campus is in an urban area 150 miles west of the Dallas-Fort Worth metroplex. Including any residence halls, there are 41 buildings.

Student Life: 74% of undergraduates are from Texas. Others are from 49 states, 52 foreign countries, and Canada. 88% are from public schools. 79% are white. Most are Protestant. The average age of freshmen is 18; all undergraduates, 21. 28% do not continue beyond their first year; 54% remain to graduate.

Housing: 2050 students can be accommodated in college housing, which includes single-sex dorms, on-campus apartments, and married-student housing. On-campus housing is available on a first-come, first-served basis and is available on a lottery system for upperclassmen. 56% of students commute. Alcohol is not permitted. All students may keep cars.

Activities: 18% of men belong to 8 local fraternities; 22% of women belong to 7 local sororities. There are 108 groups on campus, including art, band, cheerleading, chess, choir, chorale, chorus, computers, de-

bate, drama, ethnic, film, forensics, honors, integrated marketing, international, jazz band, literary magazine, marching band, musical theater, newspaper, opera, orchestra, photography, political, professional, public relations, radio and TV, religious, social, social service, steel drum band, student government, symphony, volunteer and service-learning center, and yearbook. Popular campus events include Sing Song Festival, Bible lectures, and Freshman Follies.

Sports: There are 7 intercollegiate sports for men and 6 for women, and 27 intramural sports for men and 27 for women. Facilities include a coliseum, track, baseball and softball stadiums, soccer fields, an indoor swimming pool, gyms, a weight training facility, aerobic fitness exercise equipment, and tennis, racquetball, and basketball courts.

Disabled Students: 95% of the campus is accessible. Wheelchair ramps, elevators, special parking, specially equipped rest rooms, special class scheduling, lowered drinking fountains, and lowered telephones are available.

Services: There is a reader service for the blind, remedial math and writing, and a sign language interpreter.

Campus Safety and Security: Measures include 24-hour foot and vehicle patrol, self-defense education, security escort services, and shuttle buses. There are informal discussions, pamphlets/posters/films, emergency telephones, lighted pathways/sidewalks, and and Fire Safety discussions.

Programs of Study: ACU confers B.A., B.S., B.B.A., B.F.A., B.M., and B.S.N. degrees. Associate, master's, and doctoral degrees are also awarded. Bachelor's degrees are awarded in AGRICULTURE (animal science), BIOLOGICAL SCIENCE (biochemistry, biology/biological science, and nutrition), BUSINESS (accounting, banking and finance, management science, and marketing/retailing/merchandising), COMMUNICATIONS AND THE ARTS (advertising, art, broadcasting, communications, design, dramatic arts, English, fine arts, journalism, music, Spanish, and speech/debate/rhetoric), COMPUTER AND PHYSICAL SCIENCE (chemistry, computer science, information sciences and systems, mathematics, and physics), EDUCATION (art, business, early childhood, elementary, foreign languages, middle school, music, physical, science, secondary, and teaching English as a second/foreign language (TESOL/TEFOL)), ENGINEERING AND ENVIRONMENTAL DESIGN (engineering and applied science, engineering physics, and environmental science), HEALTH PROFESSIONS (nursing, predentistry, premedicine, and speech pathology/audiology), SOCIAL SCIENCE (biblical languages, biblical studies, criminal justice, history, international relations, ministries, missions, political science/government, prelaw, psychology, religion, social science, social work, and sociology). Biology, chemistry, and education are the strongest academically. Elementary education, management, and psychology are the largest.

Required: To graduate, students must complete courses in Bible (15 hours), science, English, history, behavioral science, communication, phys ed (4 hours), fine arts, and math. 33 semester hours of advanced work must be taken and a minimum 2.0 GPA maintained. A minimum of 128 credit hours is needed, more in some programs, plus 30 to 64 hours in the major, 18 of which must be upper division.

Special: ACU offers cross-registration with Hardin-Simmons and McMurry, Universities and study abroad in 4 countries. Double majors and credit for military training are available. Internships are possible in most majors, as are B.A.-B.S. degrees in biology, bio-chemistry, communication, communication sciences and disorders, and math. A 3-2 engineering degree is offered with the University of Texas at Arlington and an admissions agreement with Texas Tech for applied physics MS program. Student designed majors (interdisciplinary studies) are available. The applied studies program enables degree completion for adult students. There are 14 national honor societies, a freshman honors program, and 15 departmental honors programs.

Faculty/Classroom: 67% of faculty are male; 33%, female. 93% teach undergraduates and 19% both teach and do research. Graduate students teach 1% of introductory courses. The average class size in an introductory lecture is 30; in a laboratory, 16; and in a regular course, 20.

Admissions: 52% of the 2005-2006 applicants were accepted. The SAT scores for the 2005-2006 freshman class were: Verbal--27% below 500, 40% between 500 and 599, 26% between 600 and 700, and 7% above 700; Math--26% below 500, 38% between 500 and 599, 31% between 600 and 700, and 5% above 700. The ACT scores were 30% below 21, 27% between 21 and 23, 25% between 24 and 26, 8% between 27 and 28, and 11% above 28. 24% of the current freshmen were in the top fifth of their class; 41% were in the top two fifths. There were 11 National Merit finalists. 13 freshmen graduated first in their class.

Requirements: The SAT is recommended. In addition, SAT: Subject tests in English composition and essay, math level II, and foreign language (French, German, Spanish, or Latin) are required. Applicants must be graduates of an accredited secondary school or have the GED and have completed 22 academic credits, including 4 in English, 2 each in math and science, and 1 each in history and social studies. Two years of the same foreign language are required. Art majors need to submit a portfolio, and music and theater majors must audition. ACU requires applicants to be in the upper 50% of their class. AP and CLEP credits are accepted. Important factors in the admissions decision are leadership record, recommendations by alumni, and advanced placement or honor courses.

Procedure: Freshmen are admitted to all sessions. Entrance exams should be taken by October of the senior year. There is a rolling admissions plan. Application deadlines are open. Application fee is $25. Notification is sent on a rolling basis. Applications are accepted on-line.

Transfer: 240 transfer students enrolled in 2004-2005. Transfer students must be in good standing at previously attended universities/colleges and have a minimum 2.0 GPA. Satisfactory scores are required on the SAT or the ACT for students with fewer than 64 semester hours. A maximum of 66 semester hours from community or junior colleges will be accepted. An interview is required. 32 of 128 credits required for the bachelor's degree must be completed at ACU.

Visiting: There are regularly scheduled orientations for prospective students, including tours and interviews with faculty, administrators, admissions/financial aid counselors, and current students. There are guides for informal visits and visitors may sit in on classes and stay overnight. To schedule a visit, contact Gretchen Etheredge, Campus Visit Coordinator at (915) 674-2664.

Financial Aid: In 2005-2006, 93% of all full-time freshmen and 89% of continuing full-time students received some form of financial aid. 63% of full-time freshmen and 59% of continuing full-time students received need-based aid. The average freshman award was $12,029. 21% of undergraduates work part time. Average annual earnings from campus work are $1850. The average financial indebtedness of the 2005 graduate was $26,413. The FAFSA is required. The deadline for filing freshman financial aid applications for fall entry is March 1.

International Students: There are 159 international students enrolled. The school actively recruits these students. A satisfactory score is required on the written TOEFL.

Computers: Wireless access is available. All residence halls and most departments have a PC lab with approximately 700 available PCs. The library and several other buildings on-campus are equipped with wireless Internet access. All students may access the system 24 hours a day. There are no time limits and no fees.

Graduates: From July 1, 2004 to June 30, 2005, 815 bachelor's degrees were awarded. The most popular majors were management (9%), elementary education (8%), and psychology (5%). In an average class, 3% graduate in 3 years or less, 37% graduate in 4 years or less, 51% graduate in 5 years or less, and 56% graduate in 6 years or less. 208 companies recruited on campus in 2004-2005. Of the 2004 graduating class, 21% were enrolled in graduate school within 6 months of graduation and 72% were employed.

Admissions Contact: Robert Heil, Director of Admissions and Enrollment Management. E-mail: *info@admissions.acu.edu*
Web: *http://www.acu.edu/admissions*

ANGELO STATE UNIVERSITY

C-3

San Angelo, TX 76909

(325) 942-2041
(800) 946-8627; Fax: (325) 942-2078

Full-time: 2257 men, 2583 women	**Faculty:** 240; IIA, --$
Part-time: 363 men, 506 women	**Ph.D.s:** 75%
Graduate: 170 men, 277 women	**Student/Faculty:** 20 to 1
Year: semesters, summer session	**Tuition:** $3521 ($10,145)
Application Deadline: August 9	**Room & Board:** $4819
Freshman Class: 2222 applied, 2214 accepted, 1304 enrolled	
SAT Verbal/Math: 480/490*	**ACT:** 20 NONCOMPETITIVE

Angelo State University, founded in 1928 and part of the Texas State University System, offers degrees through the Colleges of Liberal and Fine Arts, Business, Sciences, and Education. There are 4 undergraduate schools and 1 graduate school. In addition to regional accreditation, ASU has baccalaureate program accreditation with ACBSP, NASM, and NLN. The library contains 482,000 volumes, 975,000 microform items, and 11,000 audio/video tapes/CDs/DVDs, and subscribes to 1628 periodicals including electronic. Computerized library services include the card catalog, interlibrary loans, database searching, Internet access, and laptop Internet portals. Special learning facilities include a learning resource center, art gallery, planetarium and Internet radio station, and cable TV station. The 268-acre campus is in an urban area 200 miles west of Austin. Including any residence halls, there are 43 buildings.

Student Life: 97% of undergraduates are from Texas. Students are from 40 states, 22 foreign countries, and Canada. 98% are from public schools. 69% are white; 22% Hispanic. The average age of freshmen is 19; all undergraduates, 23. 36% do not continue beyond their first year; 34% remain to graduate.

Housing: 1544 students can be accommodated in college housing, which includes single-sex and coed dorms and on-campus apartments. There are designated honors room in 1 dorm. On-campus housing is available on a first-come, first-served basis. Priority is given to out-of-

town students. 75% of students commute. Alcohol is not permitted. All students may keep cars.

Activities: 3% of men belong to 4 national fraternities; 4% of women belong to 2 national sororities. There are 76 groups on campus, including art, band, cheerleading, chess, choir, chorale, chorus, computers, dance, debate, drama, drill team, ethnic, film, gay, honors, international, jazz band, marching band, musical theater, newspaper, opera, pep band, political, professional, radio and TV, religious, rodeo, social, social service, student government and wool judging. Popular campus events include Fish Splash, Madrigal Dinner, and musical theater.

Sports: There are 4 intercollegiate sports for men and 5 for women, and 15 intramural sports for men and 15 for women. Facilities include a gym, racquetball, basketball, volleyball, badminton, and tennis courts, an all-weather Tartan track, 2 regulation softball fields, and a 25-meter Olympic-size pool. The campus track stadium seats 3500, and the indoor gym, 4000. There is a multipurpose arena seating up to 6300 people that has an auxiliary practice gym, two weight rooms, and a sports medicine area. There is also a multipurpose complex.

Disabled Students: 98% of the campus is accessible. Wheelchair ramps, elevators, special parking, specially equipped rest rooms, special class scheduling, lowered drinking fountains, and lowered telephones are available.

Services: Counseling and information services are available, as is tutoring in most subjects. There is remedial math, reading, and writing.

Campus Safety and Security: Measures include 24-hour foot and vehicle patrol, self-defense education, security escort services, and informal discussions. There are pamphlets/posters/films, emergency telephones, and lighted pathways/sidewalks.

Programs of Study: ASU confers B.A., B.S., B.B.A., B.F.A., B.G.S., B.M., and B.S.N. degrees. Associate and master's degrees are also awarded. Bachelor's degrees are awarded in AGRICULTURE (agricultural business management, animal science, and natural resource management), BIOLOGICAL SCIENCE (biochemistry and biology/biological science), BUSINESS (accounting, banking and finance, business administration and management, international business management, marketing/retailing/merchandising, and real estate), COMMUNICATIONS AND THE ARTS (art, communications, dramatic arts, English, French, German, journalism, music, Spanish, and studio art), COMPUTER AND PHYSICAL SCIENCE (applied physics, chemistry, computer science, mathematics, and physics), EDUCATION (athletic training), HEALTH PROFESSIONS (exercise science, medical laboratory technology, and nursing), SOCIAL SCIENCE (child psychology/development, criminal justice, history, liberal arts/general studies, political science/government, psychology, and sociology). Math, biology, and physics are the strongest academically. Business-related programs and kinesiology are the largest.

Required: To graduate, students must complete a total of 130 semester hours with a minimum GPA of 2.0 (2.5 for all programs leading to teacher certification). Between 30 and 36 hours are required in the major. General education core courses must be taken in English, government, history, modern language, and phys ed. Students must also fulfill distributional requirements of 6 to 8 credits each in art, communication, drama, journalism, music, and philosophy; economics, geography, linguistics, psychology and sociology; and lab science.

Special: ASU offers co-op programs with the University of Texas at El Paso; study abroad in 4 countries; internships in psychology, public administration, sociology, and journalism; work-study programs; dual majors, a 3-2 engineering degree with the University of Texas at El Paso, and a 5-year integrated accounting program. There are 10 national honor societies, a freshman honors program.

Faculty/Classroom: 55% of faculty are male; 45%, female. 97% teach undergraduates and 75% both teach and do research. Graduate students teach 3% of introductory courses. The average class size in an introductory lecture is 34; in a laboratory, 23; and in a regular course, 28.

Admissions: 100% of the 2005-2006 applicants were accepted. The SAT scores for the 2005-2006 freshman class were: Verbal--56% below 500, 32% between 500 and 599, 11% between 600 and 700, and 1% above 700; Math--51% below 500, 35% between 500 and 599, 13% between 600 and 700, and 1% above 700. The ACT scores were 53% below 21, 27% between 21 and 23, 13% between 24 and 26, 4% between 27 and 28, and 3% above 28. 31% of the current freshmen were in the top fifth of their class; 62% were in the top two fifths. 23 freshmen graduated first in their class.

Requirements: The SAT or ACT is required. In addition, applicants must be graduates of an accredited secondary school or have the GED. ASU requires applicants to be in the upper 50% of their class. AP and CLEP credits are accepted.

Procedure: Freshmen are admitted to all sessions. Entrance exams should be taken during spring of the junior year or fall of the senior year. There is a rolling admissions and deferred admissions plan. Applications should be filed by August 9 for fall entry, December 13 for spring entry, and May 9 for summer entry, along with a $20 fee. The university accepts all applicants. Notification is sent on a rolling basis. Applications are accepted on-line.

Transfer: 610 transfer students enrolled in a recent year. Transfer students must have a minimum 2.0 GPA; those with fewer than 18 hours must meet high school admission requirements. 33 of 130 credits required for the bachelor's degree must be completed at ASU.

Visiting: There are regularly scheduled orientations for prospective students, including orientation, a tour, advising, and lunch. There are guides for informal visits and visitors may sit in on classes and stay overnight. To schedule a visit, contact the Recruiting Office/Office of Admissions at (325) 942-2185 or *admissions@angelo.edu*.

Financial Aid: In a recent year, 49% of all full-time freshmen and 70% of continuing full-time students received some form of financial aid. 27% of full-time freshmen and 46% of continuing full-time students received need-based aid. 9% of undergraduates work part time. Average annual earnings from campus work are $4000. The average financial indebtedness of the 2005 graduate was $15,000. The FAFSA is required. The deadline for filing freshman financial aid applications for fall entry is June 1.

International Students: There are 83 international students enrolled. The school actively recruits these students. They must score satisfactorily on the TOEFL or on the electronic version or take the SAT or ACT if English is the native language

Computers: All students may access the system 24 hours a day on weekdays, and modified hours on weekends. There are no time limits. The fee is $6 per semester.

Graduates: From July 1, 2004 to June 30, 2005, 883 bachelor's degrees were awarded. The most popular majors were business (20%), education (13%), and kinesiology (11%). In an average class, 16% graduate in 4 years or less, 30% graduate in 5 years or less, and 34% graduate in 6 years or less. 141 companies recruited on campus ina recent year.

Admissions Contact: Office of Admissions. A video is available. E-mail: *admissions@angelo.edu* Web: *www.angelo.edu*

AUSTIN COLLEGE

D-2

Sherman, TX 75090-4400

(903) 813-3000
(800) 442-5363; Fax: (903) 813-3198

Full-time: 581 men, 705 women	**Faculty:** 91; IIB, av$
Part-time: 6 men, 6 women	**Ph.D.s:** 98%
Graduate: 5 men, 24 women	**Student/Faculty:** 14 to 1
Year: 4-1-4, summer session	**Tuition:** $20,495
Application Deadline: March 1	**Room & Board:** $7376
Freshman Class: 1530 applied, 1029 accepted, 348 enrolled	
SAT Verbal/Math: 628/623*	**ACT:** 26 **HIGHLY COMPETITIVE**

Austin College, founded in 1849, is a private liberal arts institution affiliated with the Presbyterian Church (U.S.A.) and offering programs in business, liberal arts, and health field. The library contains 239,986 volumes, 113,834 microform items, and 8374 audio/video tapes/CDs/DVDs, and subscribes to 2835 periodicals including electronic. Computerized library services include the card catalog, interlibrary loans, database searching, Internet access, and laptop Internet portals. Special learning facilities include a learning resource center and a social science lab, television studios for media instruction, environmental research areas near Lake Texoma, and a facility for advanced computing and 3-D graphics. The 70-acre campus is in a suburban area 60 miles north of Dallas. Including any residence halls, there are 33 buildings.

Student Life: 93% of undergraduates are from Texas. Students are from 32 states, 12 foreign countries, and Canada. 86% are from public schools. 74% are white; 12% Asian American. 50% are Protestant; 18% Catholic. The average age of freshmen is 18; all undergraduates, 20. 12% do not continue beyond their first year; 75% remain to graduate.

Housing: 951 students can be accommodated in college housing, which includes single-sex and coed dorms and on-campus apartments. In addition, there are language houses and a suite-style residence hall. On-campus housing is available on a lottery system for upperclassmen. 69% of students live on campus; of those, 60% remain on campus on weekends. All students may keep cars.

Activities: 20% of men belong to 9 local fraternities; 23% of women belong to 7 local sororities. There are 50 groups on campus, including art, cheerleading, choir, chorale, chorus, drama, ethnic, film, gay, honors, international, jazz band, literary magazine, musical theater, newspaper, orchestra, pep band, photography, political, professional, radio and TV, religious, social, social service, student government, symphony, and yearbook. Popular campus events include Christmas Pops, Film Series, and Diwali Dinner.

Sports: There are 6 intercollegiate sports for men and 5 for women, and 9 intramural sports for men and 9 for women. Facilities include an athletic/recreation complex that includes 2 gyms, a natatorium, and a fitness pavilion; a tennis stadium; a 2500-seat stadium; and soccer and baseball fields.

Disabled Students: 99% of the campus is accessible. Wheelchair ramps, elevators, special parking, specially equipped rest rooms, special class scheduling, and lowered drinking fountains are available.

Services: Counseling and information services are available, as is tutoring in some subjects, including introductory-level courses. Individual and group assistance to strengthen reading, writing, and study skills is available.

Campus Safety and Security: Measures include 24-hour foot and vehicle patrol, self-defense education, security escort services, and informal discussions. There are pamphlets/posters/films, emergency telephones, and lighted pathways/sidewalks.

Programs of Study: AC confers the B.A. degree. Master's degrees are also awarded. Bachelor's degrees are awarded in BIOLOGICAL SCIENCE (biochemistry and biology/biological science), BUSINESS (business administration and management and international economics), COMMUNICATIONS AND THE ARTS (art, classics, communications, English, French, German, Latin, music, and Spanish), COMPUTER AND PHYSICAL SCIENCE (chemistry, computer science, mathematics, and physics), SOCIAL SCIENCE (American studies, economics, history, interdisciplinary studies, international studies, Latin American studies, philosophy, political science/government, psychology, religion, and sociology). Biology, English, and political science are the strongest academically. Business Administration and psychology are the largest.

Required: Core requirements for graduation include Freshman Communication Inquiry, a physical profile and activity course, 3 Heritage of Western Culture courses, and 3 courses in humanities, 2 courses in social science, and 1 course in natural science.To graduate, students must have a minimum 2.0 GPA and a total of 34 course credits (136 semester hours), with 7 to 11 course credits in the major. Students must demonstrate an ability in a modern or classical language other than their own, quantitative competency with an approved course or test, and the required skills in written communication with approved course work. A minor or a 2nd major is required.

Special: AC offers cooperative programs with Butler University, Arcadia University, Central College, and the Institute for International Education of Students, internships during the January and summer terms, study abroad in 58 countries, and fall, spring, and summer internships in Washington, D.C. Work-study, accelerated degree programs in all majors, and dual and student-designed majors are available. There is a 3-2 engineering degree program in conjunction with the University of Texas at Dallas and Washington University in St. Louis, as well as cooperative agreements with Columbia University at Texas A&M University. There are 14 national honor societies, including Phi Beta Kappa.

Faculty/Classroom: 66% of faculty are male; 34%, female. All both teach and do research. No introductory courses are taught by graduate students. The average class size in an introductory lecture is 19; in a laboratory, 16; and in a regular course, 20.

Admissions: 67% of the 2005-2006 applicants were accepted. The SAT scores for the 2005-2006 freshman class were: Verbal--3% below 500, 30% between 500 and 599, 47% between 600 and 700, and 19% above 700; Math--3% below 500, 31% between 500 and 599, 50% between 600 and 700, and 16% above 700. The ACT scores were 6% below 21, 21% between 21 and 23, 33% between 24 and 26, 17% between 27 and 28, and 22% above 28. 64% of the current freshmen were in the top fifth of their class; 92% were in the top two fifths. There were 4 National Merit finalists and 4 semifinalists. 11 freshmen graduated first in their class.

Requirements: The SAT or ACT is required. In addition, applicants must be graduates of an accredited secondary school, home school, or have a GED. The minimum recommended academic requirements are 4 credits in English, 3 each in math and science, 2 each in social studies and foreign language, and 1 in art/music/theater. An essay is required, and an interview is recommended. AP and CLEP credits are accepted. Important factors in the admissions decision are advanced placement or honor courses, leadership record, and extracurricular activities record.

Procedure: Freshmen are admitted fall and summer. Entrance exams should be taken in the junior year or the fall of the senior year. There are early decision, early admissions, deferred admissions, and rolling admissions plans. Early decision applications should be filed by December 1; regular applications, by March 1 for fall entry, along with a $35 fee. Notification of early decision is sent January 10; regular decision, April 1. 21 early decision candidates were accepted for the 2005-2006 class. 56 applicants were on the 2005 waiting list; 9 were admitted. Applications are accepted on-line.

Transfer: 44 transfer students enrolled in 2004-2005. Applicants must have a minimum 3.0 GPA, submit official college transcripts and 2 recommendations, and be in good standing at most recently attended schools. Students with fewer than 30 credit hours must submit SAT or ACT scores and their high school transcript or GED. 17 of 34 course credit units required for the bachelor's degree must be completed at AC.

Visiting: There are regularly scheduled orientations for prospective students, 1-day and 2-day preview programs held for high school juniors, seniors and parents. Individual appointments may be made as well. There are guides for informal visits and visitors may sit in on classes and stay overnight. To schedule a visit, contact the Admission Office.

Financial Aid: In 2005-2006, 97% of all full-time freshmen and 96% of continuing full-time students received some form of financial aid. 59% of full-time freshmen and 55% of continuing full-time students received need-based aid. The average freshman award was $22,232. Need-based scholarships or need-based grants averaged $8352 ($23,540 maximum); need-based self-help aid (loans and jobs) averaged $4518 ($8198 maximum); and other non-need-based awards and non-need-based scholarships averaged $15,094 ($30,225 maximum). 30% of undergraduates work part time. Average annual earnings from campus work are $1230. The average financial indebtedness of the 2005 graduate was $26,164. AC is a member of CSS. The FAFSA is required. The deadline for filing freshman financial aid applications for fall entry is April 1.

International Students: There are 18 international students enrolled. A satisfactory score is required on the written TOEFL. Students must also take the SAT or the ACT.

Computers: Wireless access is available. All students may access the system 24 hours a day in some locations. There are no time limits and no fees.

Graduates: From July 1, 2004 to June 30, 2005, 290 bachelor's degrees were awarded. The most popular majors were psychology (15%), business administration (15%), and English (9%). In an average class, 3% graduate in 3 years or less, 73% graduate in 4 years or less, 74% graduate in 5 years or less, and 75% graduate in 6 years or less. 43 companies recruited on campus in 2004-2005. Of the 2004 graduating class, 36% were enrolled in graduate school within 6 months of graduation and 39% were employed.

Admissions Contact: h, VP for Institutional Enrollment. A video is available. E-mail: *admission@austincollege.edu*
Web: *www.austincollege.edu*

BAYLOR UNIVERSITY   D-3

Waco, TX 76798   (254) 710-3435; (800) BAYLOR-U

Full-time: 4750 men, 6715 women	Faculty: I, --$
Part-time: 159 men, 201 women	Ph.D.s: 77%
Graduate: 1180 men, 970 women	Student/Faculty: n/av
Year: semesters, summer session	Tuition: $21,070
Application Deadline: open	Room & Board: $6485
Freshman Class: 15,485 applied, 10,170 accepted, 3168 enrolled	
SAT Verbal/Math: 600/610*	ACT: 25 HIGHLY COMPETITIVE

Baylor University, founded in 1845, is an independent institution affiliated with the Baptist Church and offering undergraduate programs in liberal arts and sciences, business, computer science, education, engineering, music, nursing, social work, and an honors college. There are 8 undergraduate and 10 graduate schools. In addition to regional accreditation, Baylor has baccalaureate program accreditation with AACSB, AALE, ABET, ACEJMC, ADA, AHEA, APTA, CAHEA, CSWE, NASM, NCATE, and NLN. The 9 libraries contain 2,140,168 volumes, 2,059,235 microform items, and 83,165 audio/video tapes/CDs/DVDs, and subscribe to 18,940 periodicals including electronic. Computerized library services include the card catalog, interlibrary loans, database searching, and Internet access. Special learning facilities include a learning resource center, art gallery, natural history museum, radio station, TV station, and speech/hearing clinic. The 508-acre campus is in an urban area 100 miles south of Dallas/Fort Worth. Including any residence halls, there are 88 buildings.

Student Life: 82% of undergraduates are from Texas. Others are from 50 states, 74 foreign countries, and Canada. 72% are white; 10% Hispanic. 77% are Protestant; 13% Catholic. The average age of freshmen is 19; all undergraduates, 21. 16% do not continue beyond their first year; 71% remain to graduate.

Housing: 4172 students can be accommodated in college housing, which includes single-sex dorms, on-campus apartments, off-campus apartments, and married-student housing. There are also academic wings. On-campus housing is guaranteed for the freshman year only and is available on a first-come, first-served basis. 66% of students commute. Alcohol is not permitted. All students may keep cars.

Activities: 18% of men belong to 2 local and 14 national fraternities; 17% of women belong to 1 local and 9 national sororities. There are 309 groups on campus, including art, band, cheerleading, chess, choir, chorale, chorus, computers, dance, debate, drama, ethnic, film, forensics, honors, international, jazz band, literary magazine, marching band, musical theater, newspaper, opera, orchestra, pep band, photography, political, professional, radio and TV, religious, social, social service, student government, symphony, and yearbook. Popular campus events include Dia del Oso (Day of the Bear), Campus Sing, and Pigskin Review.

Sports: There are 8 intercollegiate sports for men and 9 for women, and 17 intramural sports for men and 17 for women. Facilities include a 50,000-seat football stadium, gyms, intramural fields, tennis courts, a swimming pool, a marina, and a 10,000-seat special events center that seats. A 158,000-square-foot student life center has a 52-foot climbing rock, fitness center, aerobics room, racquetball/squash courts, basketball courts, pool, indoor walking/jogging track, and outdoor sand volleyball courts.

Disabled Students: 95% of the campus is accessible. Wheelchair ramps, elevators, special parking, specially equipped rest rooms, and lowered drinking fountains are available.

Services: There is a reader service for the blind and remedial reading and writing. Taped textbooks are available through the Commission for the Blind. The Office of Student Access and Learning provides study skills and time management sessions for students with disabilities.

Campus Safety and Security: Measures include 24-hour foot and vehicle patrol, security escort services, shuttle buses, and informal discussions. There are pamphlets/posters/films, emergency telephones, and lighted pathways/sidewalks.

Programs of Study: Baylor confers B.A., B.S., B.B.A., B.F.A., B.M., B.M.E., B.S.Av.Sc., B.S.C.S., B.S.E., B.S.E.C.E., B.S.Ed., B.S.F.C.S., B.S.I., B.S.M.E., B.S.N., and B.S.W. degrees. Master's and doctoral degrees are also awarded. Bachelor's degrees are awarded in AGRICULTURE (forestry and related sciences and soil science), BIOLOGICAL SCIENCE (biochemistry, bioinformatics, biology/biological science, life science, neurosciences, and nutrition), BUSINESS (accounting, banking and finance, business administration and management, business economics, business statistics, business systems analysis, entrepreneurial studies, fashion merchandising, human resources, insurance, international business management, management information systems, marketing/retailing/merchandising, personnel management, real estate, and sports marketing), COMMUNICATIONS AND THE ARTS (applied music, art, art history and appreciation, broadcasting, choral music, classics, communications, creative writing, dramatic arts, English, French, German, Greek (classical), journalism, languages, Latin, literature, music, music history and appreciation, music performance, music theory and composition, performing arts, Russian, Spanish, speech/debate/rhetoric, studio art, telecommunications, and theater design), COMPUTER AND PHYSICAL SCIENCE (applied mathematics, chemistry, computer science, earth science, geology, geophysics and seismology, information sciences and systems, mathematics, and physics), EDUCATION (art, athletic training, business, computer, drama, elementary, English, foreign languages, health, home economics, journalism, mathematics, museum studies, music, physical, reading, recreation, science, secondary, social science, social studies, and special), ENGINEERING AND ENVIRONMENTAL DESIGN (airline piloting and navigation, architecture, computer engineering, electrical/electronics engineering, engineering, environmental science, interior design, and mechanical engineering), HEALTH PROFESSIONS (community health work, health science, medical laboratory technology, nursing, optometry, predentistry, premedicine, speech pathology/audiology, and speech therapy), SOCIAL SCIENCE (American studies, anthropology, archeology, Asian/Oriental studies, biblical languages, child care/child and family studies, dietetics, economics, family/consumer studies, fashion design and technology, forensic studies, geography, history, interdisciplinary studies, international public service, Latin American studies, philosophy, physical fitness/movement, political science/government, psychology, public administration, religion, religious education, religious music, Russian and Slavic studies, social work, sociology, and urban studies). Business, biology, and psychology are the largest.

Required: All degree programs require a minimum of 124 hours and a 2.0 GPA to graduate. Basic requirements for the B.A. degree include 18 semester hours of social science, 12 each of English and science, 6 to 9 of fine arts, 6 of religion, 4 of phys ed, 3 to 16 of foreign language, 3 of math, and 2 semesters of chapel forum. Requirements for other degrees vary.

Special: Baylor offers cooperative programs in architecture, business, dentistry, medicine, and optometry, internships in each school, study abroad and student exchange in more than 30 countries, and pass/fail options. There are also honors and university scholars programs and faculty exchange with 4 schools in China, and 1 each in Japan, Thailand, and Russia. There are 35 national honor societies, including Phi Beta Kappa, and a freshman honors program.

Faculty/Classroom: 63% of faculty are male; 37%, female. The average class size in a regular course is 31.

Admissions: 66% of the 2005-2006 applicants were accepted. The SAT scores for the 2005-2006 freshman class were: Verbal--7% below 500, 43% between 500 and 599, 39% between 600 and 700, and 11% above 700; Math--4% below 500, 37% between 500 and 599, 49% between 600 and 700, and 10% above 700. The ACT scores were 1% below 21, 30% between 21 and 23, 32% between 24 and 26, 20% between 27 and 28, and 17% above 28. 61% of the current freshmen were in the top fifth of their class; 84% were in the top two fifths. There were 37 National Merit finalists.

Requirements: The SAT or ACT is required. The ACT Optional Writing test is also required. In addition, minimum composite scores are required on the SAT or the ACT. Applicants must be graduates of an accredited secondary school. An interview is recommended. Baylor requires applicants to be in the upper 50% of their class. AP and CLEP credits are accepted.

Procedure: Freshmen are admitted fall, spring, and summer. Entrance exams should be taken in spring of the junior year or fall of the senior year. There is a rolling admission plan. Application deadlines are open. Application fee is $50. A waiting list is an active part of the admissions procedure. Applications are accepted on-line, and the application fee is waived for on-line applications.

Transfer: 422 transfer students enrolled in 2004-2005. Transfer students should begin studies no later than the end of the sophomore year because of the 60-semester-hour residence requirement for a bachelor's degree. A minimum 2.5 GPA is required. Students with fewer than 30

credit hours earned must meet the entrance requirements for freshmen. 60 of 124 credits required for the bachelor's degree must be completed at Baylor.

Visiting: There are regularly scheduled orientations for prospective students, including day-and-a-half sessions in June and a Welcome Week in August. There are guides for informal visits and visitors may sit in on classes and stay overnight. To schedule a visit, contact the Campus Visitation Program at (254) 710-2407.

Financial Aid: In 2005-2006, 91% of all full-time freshmen and 84% of continuing full-time students received some form of financial aid. 51% of full-time freshmen and 48% of continuing full-time students received need-based aid. The average freshman award was $16,817. Need-based scholarships or need-based grants averaged $7682 ($33,050 maximum); need-based self-help aid (loans and jobs) averaged $4691 ($11,455 maximum); non-need-based athletic scholarships averaged $19,812 ($29,711 maximum); and other non-need-based awards and non-need-based scholarships averaged $11,273 ($33,496 maximum). 13% of undergraduates work part time. Average annual earnings from campus work are $1288. The FAFSA is required. The deadline for filing freshman financial aid applications for fall entry is May 1.

International Students: There are 255 international students enrolled. The school actively recruits these students. A satisfactory score is required on the written TOEFL. Applicants must also take the SAT, the ACT or the ACT Optional Writing.

Computers: Wireless access is available. All students may access the system. Most systems are accessible 24 hours a day, 7 days per week. It is strongly recommended that all students have a personal computer. It is recommended that students in Baylor Interdisciplinary Core (BIC) and MBA programs have personal computers.

Graduates: From July 1, 2004 to June 30, 2005, 2533 bachelor's degrees were awarded. The most popular majors were business marketing (6%), biology (6%), and psychology (6%). In an average class, 1% graduate in 3 years or less, 45% graduate in 4 years or less, 68% graduate in 5 years or less, and 71% graduate in 6 years or less. 153 companies recruited on campus in 2004-2005.

Admissions Contact: Diana M. Ramey, Director, Undergraduate Admissions. A video is available. E-mail: *addmissions@baylor.edu* Web: *http://www.baylor.edu*

CONCORDIA UNIVERSITY AT AUSTIN   D-3

Austin, TX 78705-2799   (512) 486-2000
(800) 865-4282; Fax: (512) 486-1350

Full-time: 345 men, 406 women	**Faculty:** n/av
Part-time: 85 men, 185 women	**Ph.D.s:** 74%
Graduate: 20 men, 70 women	**Student/Faculty:** n/av
Year: semesters, summer session	**Tuition:** $16,740
Application Deadline: August 15	**Room & Board:** $6900
Freshman Class: 728 applied, 532 accepted, 194 enrolled	
SAT or ACT: required	**LESS COMPETITIVE**

Concordia University at Austin, founded in 1926, is a private college affiliated with the Lutheran Church-Missouri Synod. It offers undergraduate programs in liberal arts, behavioral science, business, communication, education, environmental science, and church music. There are 4 undergraduate schools. The library contains 56,146 volumes, 8504 microform items, and 3213 audio/video tapes/CDs/DVDs, and subscribes to 514 periodicals including electronic. Computerized library services include the card catalog, interlibrary loans, and database searching. Special learning facilities include a TV station. The 20-acre campus is in an urban area in the heart of Austin. Including any residence halls, there are 20 buildings.

Student Life: 93% of undergraduates are from Texas. Students are from 21 states and 13 foreign countries. 89% are from public schools. 63% are white; 16% Hispanic. 78% are Protestant; 16% Catholic; 6% claim no religious affiliation. The average age of freshmen is 19; all undergraduates, 25. 40% do not continue beyond their first year; 35% remain to graduate.

Housing: 245 students can be accommodated in college housing, which includes single-sex and coed dorms. On-campus housing is guaranteed for the freshman year only and is available on a first-come, first-served basis. 68% of students commute. All students may keep cars.

Activities: There are no fraternities or sororities. There are 9 groups on campus, including band, choir, chorus, dance, drama, ethnic, religious, social, and student government. Popular campus events include Fall Festival Weekend, Parents Day, and Founders Day.

Sports: There are 6 intercollegiate sports for men and 5 for women, and 10 intramural sports for men and 9 for women. Facilities include an activities center, a 1600-seat gym, a 250-seat auditorium, a baseball field, a beach volleyball court, and tennis courts.

Disabled Students: 75% of the campus is accessible. Wheelchair ramps, elevators, special parking, specially equipped rest rooms, and lowered drinking fountains are available.

Services: Counseling and information services are available, as is tutoring in most subjects.

Campus Safety and Security: Measures include 24-hour foot and vehicle patrol, security escort services, informal discussions, and pamphlets/posters/films. There are lighted pathways/sidewalks.

Programs of Study: Concordia confers the B.A. degree. Associate and master's degrees are also awarded. Bachelor's degrees are awarded in BUSINESS (accounting and business administration and management), COMMUNICATIONS AND THE ARTS (communications, English, music, and Spanish), COMPUTER AND PHYSICAL SCIENCE (computer science), EDUCATION (elementary and secondary), ENGINEERING AND ENVIRONMENTAL DESIGN (environmental science), SOCIAL SCIENCE (behavioral science, history, liberal arts/general studies, Mexican-American/Chicano studies, and religious music). Education is the strongest academically. Business management, education, and communication are the largest.

Required: To graduate, all students must complete 12 hours each of English, social/behavioral science, and religion, 6 to 8 hours of natural science, and 3 hours each of fine arts, math, phys ed, and speech. Students must earn 128 semester hours, including 39 upper-level hours and 33 to 48 hours in the major. A minimum 2.0 GPA is required, plus a 2.25 GPA in the major.

Special: Concordia offers internships in communications, behavioral science, business, environmental science, and Mexican-American studies, study abroad in Mexico, an accelerated degree program in business management, dual majors, credit for prior experiential learning, nondegree study, pass/fail options, and a preseminary program. There is 1 national honor society.

Faculty/Classroom: 69% of faculty are male; 31%, female. All teach undergraduates. The average class size in a laboratory is 16 and in a regular course, 21.

Admissions: 73% of the 2005-2006 applicants were accepted.

Requirements: The SAT or ACT is required. Applicants must be graduates of an accredited secondary school or have the GED. A GPA of 2.5 is required. AP and CLEP credits are accepted.

Procedure: Freshmen are admitted fall, spring, and summer. There are early admissions, deferred admissions, and rolling admissions plans. Applications should be filed by August 15 for fall entry. The fall 2005 application fee was $25. Notification is sent on a rolling basis.

Transfer: 71 transfer students enrolled in fall 2005. Transfer students with fewer than 18 hours earned must meet freshman admissions requirements and submit high school and college transcripts; those with 18 or more hours earned must be in good standing at the previously attended college with a minimum 2.5 GPA. 45 of 128 credits required for the bachelor's degree must be completed at Concordia.

Visiting: There are regularly scheduled orientations for prospective students, consisting of placement exams, scheduling and registration of classes, and information sessions for parents with faculty and administrators. There are guides for informal visits and visitors may sit in on classes and stay overnight. To schedule a visit, contact the Admissions Office.

Financial Aid: In 2005-2006, 65% of all full-time freshmen and 66% of continuing full-time students received some form of financial aid. At least 63% of full-time freshmen and 58% of continuing full-time students received need-based aid. The average freshman award was $16,678. Need-based scholarships or need-based grants averaged $10,250; need-based self-help aid (loans and jobs) averaged $3034; and other institutional non-need-based awards and non-need-based scholarships averaged $6896. The average financial indebtedness of the 2005 graduate was $15,084. The FAFSA and the college's own financial statement are required. The priority date for freshman financial aid applications for fall entry is May 1. The deadline for filing freshman financial aid applications for fall entry is rolling.

International Students: The school actively recruits these students. A satisfactory score is required on the written TOEFL.

Computers: All students may access the system. There are no time limits and no fees.

Graduates: From July 1, 2004 to June 30, 2005, 151 bachelor's degrees were awarded. The most popular majors were business/marketing (44%), education (12%), and social sciences (9%). In an average class, 20% graduate in 4 years or less, and 30% graduate in 5 years or less.

Admissions Contact: Dr. Michael Mogavero, Vice President, Enrollment Services. E-mail: *admissions@concordia.edu* Web: *www.concordia.edu*

DALLAS BAPTIST UNIVERSITY   D-2
Dallas, TX 75211-9299   (214) 333-5360
(800) 460-1328; Fax: (214) 333-5447

Full-time: 877 men, 1223 women	**Faculty:** 85
Part-time: 562 men, 905 women	**Ph.D.s:** 80%
Graduate: 499 men, 922 women	**Student/Faculty:** 25 to 1
Year: 4-1-4, summer session	**Tuition:** $12,270
Application Deadline: open	**Room & Board:** $4770
Freshman Class: 937 applied, 599 accepted, 362 enrolled	
SAT Verbal/Math: 550/540*	**ACT:** 23 **VERY COMPETITIVE**

Dallas Baptist University, established in 1898, is a private institution affil-iated with the Baptist General Convention of Texas. The university offers degrees in the arts, sciences, music, and business while integrating faith and learning. There are 7 undergraduate and 11 graduate schools. In addition to regional accreditation, DBU has baccalaureate program ac-creditation with ACBSP and NASM. The library contains 276,945 vol-umes, 517,334 microform items, and 6171 audio/video tapes/CDs/DVDs, and subscribes to 637 periodicals including electronic. Computer-ized library services include the card catalog, interlibrary loans, database searching, and laptop Internet portals. Special learning facilities include a Corrie Ten Boom collection. The 292-acre campus is in a suburban area 13 miles from downtown Dallas and 19 miles from Fort Worth. In-cluding any residence halls, there are 20 buildings.

Student Life: 96% of undergraduates are from Texas. Others are from 43 states, 41 foreign countries, and Canada. 57% are white; 21% Afri-can American. 73% are Protestant; 17% claim no religious affiliation; 9% Catholic. The average age of freshmen is 18; all undergraduates, 29. 32% do not continue beyond their first year; 68% remain to graduate.

Housing: 1270 students can be accommodated in college housing, which includes coed dorms, on-campus apartments, and married-student housing. On-campus housing is available on a first-come, first-served basis. 66% of students commute. Alcohol is not permitted. All stu-dents may keep cars.

Activities: There are no fraternities or sororities. There are 36 groups on campus, including art, band, choir, chorale, civil service, community outreach, drama, ethnic, honors, international, leadership/mission work, musical theater, political, professional, religious, social, social service, student government, and yearbook. Popular campus events include Family Weekend, Spiritual Rush, and Habitat for Humanity.

Sports: There are 6 intercollegiate sports for men and 6 for women, and 18 intramural sports for men and 18 for women. Facilities include a gym, tennis courts, a baseball diamond, a soccer field, 2 pools, a sand volleyball court, a basketball court, table tennis and foosball tables, and an intramural field.

Disabled Students: 74% of the campus is accessible. Wheelchair ramps, elevators, special parking, specially equipped rest rooms, special class scheduling, lowered drinking fountains, lowered telephones, and special housing are available.

Services: Counseling and information services are available, as is tutor-ing in most subjects, including math, writing, English, computer, study skills, and adult education. There is a reader service for the blind and re-medial math. Student counseling is also available.

Campus Safety and Security: Measures include 24-hour foot and ve-hicle patrol, security escort services, shuttle buses, and informal discus-sions. There are pamphlets/posters/films, emergency telephones, and lighted pathways/sidewalks.

Programs of Study: DBU confers B.A., B.S., B.A.S., B.B.A., B.B.S., and B.M. degrees. Associate, master's, and doctoral degrees are also awarded. Bachelor's degrees are awarded in BIOLOGICAL SCIENCE (biology/biological science), BUSINESS (accounting, banking and fi-nance, business administration and management, management informa-tion systems, and marketing/retailing/merchandising), COMMUNICA-TIONS AND THE ARTS (applied music, communications, English, fine arts, music, and music performance), COMPUTER AND PHYSICAL SCIENCE (computer science and mathematics), EDUCATION (elemen-tary and physical), SOCIAL SCIENCE (biblical studies, counseling/psychology, criminal justice, history, interdisciplinary studies, liberal arts/general studies, pastoral studies, philosophy, physical fitness/movement, psychology, religious education, and sociology). Business administration and multi/interdisciplinary studies are the largest.

Required: To graduate, students must have a minimum GPA of 2.0 and complete 126 credit hours, including 24 hours in the major and 42 upper-division hours. Students must also take additional credit hours of general studies courses, including computer science, English, fine arts, foreign language, history, math, natural science, phys ed, religion, speech, and social science, to total 126. Chapel attendance is required. All freshmen must take 2 semesters of an orientation course.

Special: Work-study programs, study abroad, and a Washington se-mester are available. There are 4 national honor societies, a freshman honors program, and 8 departmental honors programs.

Faculty/Classroom: 59% of faculty are male; 41%, female. All teach undergraduates. No introductory courses are taught by graduate stu-dents. The average class size in an introductory lecture is 26; in a labora-tory, 20; and in a regular course, 15.

Admissions: 64% of the 2005-2006 applicants were accepted. The SAT scores for the 2005-2006 freshman class were: Verbal--19% below 500, 55% between 500 and 599, 21% between 600 and 700, and 5% above 700; Math--20% below 500, 51% between 500 and 599, 22% be-tween 600 and 700, and 7% above 700. The ACT scores were 27% be-low 21, 37% between 21 and 23, 25% between 24 and 26, 6% between 27 and 28, and 7% above 28. 39% of the current freshmen were in the top fifth of their class; 62% were in the top two fifths. 7 freshmen gradu-ated first in their class.

Requirements: The SAT or ACT is required. In addition, applicants must be graduates of an accredited secondary school or home school or have a GED and meet one of the following criteria: a satisfactory SAT score; a composite ACT score of at least 21; or a high school average of 2.5. High school courses should include 4 years of English, 3 years each of math and social studies, 2 to 3 years of a foreign language, and 2 years each of history and science. An essay is required. DBU requires applicants to be in the upper 50% of their class. A GPA of 2.5 is re-quired. AP and CLEP credits are accepted. Important factors in the ad-missions decision are personality/intangible qualities, leadership record, and extracurricular activities record.

Procedure: Freshmen are admitted to all sessions. Entrance exams should be taken during the spring of the junior year and/or the fall of the senior year. There is a rolling admissions plan. Application deadlines are open. Application fee is $25. Applications are accepted on-line.

Transfer: 308 transfer students enrolled in 2004-2005. Applicants must submit an essay and transcripts of all previous college work and should have a cumulative GPA of 2.2 or higher. Students with fewer than 30 credit hours must furnish high school transcripts and ACT or SAT scores. 32 of 126 credits required for the bachelor's degree must be completed at DBU.

Visiting: There are regularly scheduled orientations for prospective stu-dents, including a Patriot Weekend and Patriot Day conducted each fall and spring semester to provide information on financial aid and admis-sions. There are guides for informal visits and visitors may sit in on class-es and stay overnight. To schedule a visit, contact the Undergraduate Admissions Office.

Financial Aid: In 2005-2006, 85% of all full-time freshmen and 86% of continuing full-time students received some form of financial aid. 50% of all full-time students received need-based aid. The average freshman award was $11,572. Need-based scholarships or need-based grants av-eraged $4454 ($4050 maximum); need-based self-help aid (loans and jobs) averaged $3463 ($4180 maximum); non-need-based athletic scholarships averaged $6896 ($14,000 maximum); other non-need-based awards and non-need-based scholarships averaged $5448 ($11,000 maximum); and outside benefits and scholarships and non-need-based loans averaged $3598 ($15,000 maximum). 20% of under-graduates work part time. Average annual earnings from campus work are $2880. The average financial indebtedness of the 2005 graduate was $22,921. The FAFSA and the college's own financial statement are re-quired. The priority date for freshman financial aid applications for fall entry is March 15. The deadline for filing freshman financial aid applica-tions for fall entry is May 15.

International Students: There are 190 international students enrolled. The school actively recruits these students. Satisfactory scores are re-quired on the written TOEFL and the SAT or the ACT.

Computers: Wireless access is available. There are 220 PCs available for students, use in various locations on campus. All students may access the system. There are no time limits and no fees.

Graduates: From July 1, 2004 to June 30, 2005, 803 bachelor's de-grees were awarded. The most popular majors were business administra-tion (24%), general studies (19%), and psychology (9%). In an average class, 33% graduate in 4 years or less, 43% graduate in 5 years or less, and 48% graduate in 6 years or less. 201 companies recruited on cam-pus in 2004-2005.

Admissions Contact: Erin Spivay, Director of Undergraduate Admis-sions. A video is available. E-mail: *admiss@dbu.edu* Web: *www.dbu.edu*

DEVRY UNIVERSITY/DALLAS   D-2
Irving, TX 75063-2439   (972) 929-5777
(800) 633-3879; Fax: (972) 929-2860

Full-time: 960 men, 350 women	**Faculty:** n/av
Part-time: 825 men, 375 women	**Ph.D.s:** n/av
Graduate: none	**Student/Faculty:** n/av
Year: semesters, summer session	**Tuition:** $10,700
Application Deadline: open	**Room & Board:** n/app
Freshman Class: n/av	
SAT or ACT: n/av	**LESS COMPETITIVE**

DeVry University/Dallas, founded in 1969, is 1 of 67 DeVry University locations in the United States and Canada. The private institution offers career-oriented degree programs with hands-on training in various fields of business and technology. Figures in the above capsule and in this profile are approximate. In addition to regional accreditation, DeVry has baccalaureate program accreditation with ABET. The library contains 16,500 volumes and 1800 audio/video tapes/CDs/DVDs. Computerized library services include the card catalog, interlibrary loans, and database searching. Special learning facilities include a learning resource center and electronics and other labs. The 14-acre campus is in a suburban area 12 miles northwest of Dallas. There is one building.

Student Life: 42% are white; 32% African American; 19% Hispanic. The average age of all undergraduates is 26.

Housing: There are no residence halls. 100% of students commute. All students may keep cars.

Activities: There are no fraternities or sororities. There are 15 groups on campus, including computers, ethnic, international, newspaper, professional, religious, and social. Popular campus events include Thanksgiving Dinner, Club Fair Day, and Block Party.

Sports: There are 5 intramural sports for men and 5 for women.

Disabled Students: 90% of the campus is accessible. Wheelchair ramps, elevators, special parking, specially equipped rest rooms, lowered drinking fountains, and lowered telephones are available.

Services: Counseling and information services are available, as is tutoring in every subject.

Campus Safety and Security: Measures include security escort services, informal discussions, pamphlets/posters/films, and emergency telephones. There are lighted pathways/sidewalks. Daytime and evening security is provided until the building is closed. Security systems and motion detectors are utilized after business hours.

Programs of Study: DeVry confers the B.S. degree. Associate and master's degrees are also awarded. Bachelor's degrees are awarded in BIOLOGICAL SCIENCE (bioinformatics), BUSINESS (business administration and management), COMMUNICATIONS AND THE ARTS (telecommunications), COMPUTER AND PHYSICAL SCIENCE (information sciences and systems), ENGINEERING AND ENVIRONMENTAL DESIGN (biomedical engineering, computer engineering, electrical/electronics engineering technology, and technological management). Telecommunications and computer information systems are the largest.

Required: To graduate, students must achieve a GPA of at least 2.0 and satisfactorily complete all curriculum requirements. Course requirements vary according to program. All first-semester students take courses in business organization, computer applications, algebra, psychology, and student success strategies.

Special: Accelerated degree programs are offered in business administration, computer information systems, and telecommunications. Co-op programs, nondegree study, and evening and weekend classes are possible.

Faculty/Classroom: All teach undergraduates.

Requirements: Admissions requirements include graduation from a secondary school; the GED is also accepted. Applicants must pass the DeVry entrance exam or present satisfactory ACT or SAT scores. An interview is required. CLEP credit is accepted.

Procedure: Freshmen are admitted to all sessions. There are early admissions and deferred admissions plans. Application deadlines are open. Check with the school for current application fee. Applications are accepted on-line.

Transfer: 268 transfer students enrolled in a recent year. Applicants must submit official transcripts from all previous colleges attended indicating passing grades in all completed course work, demonstrate language skills proficiency with at least 24 completed semester hours, and evidence math proficiency by appropriate college-level credits. 25 of 48 credits required for the bachelor's degree must be completed at DeVry.

Visiting: There are regularly scheduled orientations for prospective students. There are guides for informal visits and visitors may sit in on classes. To schedule a visit, contact Vicki Carroll, New Student Coordinator at (972) 929-6777.

Financial Aid: In a recent year, 51% of all full-time freshmen and 73% of continuing full-time students received some form of financial aid. 50% of full-time freshmen and 72% of continuing full-time students received need-based aid. The average freshman award was $7433. Need-based scholarships or need-based grants averaged $4174; need-based self-help aid (loans and jobs) averaged $4868; and other non-need-based awards and non-need-based scholarships averaged $10,487. The FAFSA is required. Check with the school for current deadlines.

International Students: Satisfactory scores are required on the written TOEFL and the college's own entrance exam.

Computers: Students in the computer information systems program may access the system during lab hours. Check with the school for current fee. It is recommended that students in the information technology program have DeVry-issued laptop computers.

Graduates: In a recent year, 444 bachelor's degrees were awarded. The most popular majors were computer information systems (68%), business (20%), and electronics engineering technology (11%). 67 companies recruited on campus in a recent year.

Admissions Contact: Chad Williams, Director of Admissions. E-mail: *cwilliams@mail.dal.devry.edu* Web: *www.dal.devry.edu*

EAST TEXAS BAPTIST UNIVERSITY   E-2
Marshall, TX 75670-1498   (903) 923-2000
                             (800) 804-ETBU; Fax: (903) 923-2001

Full-time: 522 men, 654 women	Faculty: 66; IIB, --$
Part-time: 81 men, 69 women	Ph.D.s: 85%
Graduate: none	Student/Faculty: 18 to 1
Year: semesters, summer session	Tuition: $12,840
Application Deadline: open	Room & Board: $3873
Freshman Class: 852 applied, 670 accepted, 303 enrolled	
SAT Verbal/Math: 480/490*	ACT: 21 COMPETITIVE

East Texas Baptist University, founded in 1912, is affiliated with the Baptist General Convention of Texas. The private liberal arts university offers undergraduate programs in the arts and sciences and professional areas, such as business, teacher education, nursing, and Christian ministry. There are 7 undergraduate schools. In addition to regional accreditation, ETBU has baccalaureate program accreditation with NASM and CCNE. The library contains 216,000 volumes, 9250 microform items, and 1216 audio/video tapes/CDs/DVDs, and subscribes to 15,000 periodicals including electronic. Computerized library services include the card catalog, interlibrary loans, and database searching. Special learning facilities include a learning resource center, a math learning center, and a writing lab. The 200-acre campus is in a small town 35 miles west of Shreveport, Louisana, and 140 miles east of Dallas. Including any residence halls, there are 26 buildings.

Student Life: 87% of undergraduates are from Texas. Others are from 29 states and 7 foreign countries. 79% are white; 15% African American. 79% are Protestant; 16% claim no religious affiliation. The average age of freshmen is 18; all undergraduates, 22. 35% do not continue beyond their first year; 45% remain to graduate.

Housing: 1090 students can be accommodated in college housing, which includes single-sex dorms, on-campus apartments, and married-student housing. On-campus housing is available on a first-come, first-served basis. 71% of students live on campus; of those, 40% remain on campus on weekends. Alcohol is not permitted. All students may keep cars.

Activities: 2% of men belong to 2 local fraternities; 3% of women belong to 2 local sororities. There are 35 groups on campus, including band, cheerleading, choir, chorale, chorus, debate, drama, drill team, ethnic, honors, international, jazz band, marching band, newspaper, opera, pep band, political, professional, religious, social, social service, student government, and yearbook. Popular campus events include Week-0-Fun, Tiger Awards, and the Great Pumpkin Schmumpkin.

Sports: There are 5 intercollegiate sports for men and 5 for women, and 7 intramural sports for men and 6 for women. Facilities include a baseball field, tennis courts, a weight room, a 1500-seat gym, a soccer field, a softball field, an intramural field, a practice gym, football practice fields, a football field, and a stadium.

Disabled Students: 95% of the campus is accessible. Wheelchair ramps, elevators, special parking, specially equipped rest rooms, special class scheduling, and lowered drinking fountains are available.

Services: Counseling and information services are available, as is tutoring in some subjects, including math and English. There is remedial math and writing.

Campus Safety and Security: Measures include 24-hour foot and vehicle patrol, self-defense education, informal discussions, and pamphlets/posters/films. There are emergency telephones and lighted pathways/sidewalks.

Programs of Study: ETBU confers B.A., B.S., B.A.S., B.B.A., B.M., B.S.E., and B.S.N. degrees. Associate degrees are also awarded. Bachelor's degrees are awarded in BIOLOGICAL SCIENCE (biology/biological science), BUSINESS (accounting, banking and finance, business administration and management, human resources, and marketing management), COMMUNICATIONS AND THE ARTS (dramatic arts, English, music, music performance, piano/organ, Spanish, speech/debate/rhetoric, and voice), COMPUTER AND PHYSICAL SCIENCE (chemistry, information sciences and systems, and mathematics), EDUCATION (athletic training, drama, education, elementary, English, foreign languages, mathematics, music, physical, science, secondary, social studies, and speech correction), HEALTH PROFESSIONS (medical technology and nursing), SOCIAL SCIENCE (community psychology, history, ministries, physical fitness/movement, psychology, religion, religious music, and sociology). Religion and teacher education are the largest.

Required: To graduate, students must complete general education requirements, ranging from 34 hours for B.M. degrees to 48 hours for B.A. and 47 hours for B.S. degrees, and have a minimum GPA of 2.0. A total of 120 to 131 semester hours, with at least 30 in the major, is required, including 9 to 12 of English, 6 to 9 of religion, 3 to 6 of history, 3 to 6 of math, at least 3 of lab science, and 3 of physical activity.

Special: Internships are offered in social work, management, and computer information systems, as is study abroad in 5 countries and a Washington semester through the American Studies Program. There are 6 national honor societies.

Faculty/Classroom: 67% of faculty are male; 33%, female. All teach undergraduates and 20% do research. The average class size in an introductory lecture is 30; in a laboratory, 15; and in a regular course, 21.

Admissions: 79% of the 2005-2006 applicants were accepted. The SAT scores for the 2005-2006 freshman class were: Verbal--61% below 500, 30% between 500 and 599, 7% between 600 and 700, and 2% above 700; Math--55% below 500, 31% between 500 and 599, and 14% between 600 and 700. The ACT scores were 48% below 21, 25% between 21 and 23, 17% between 24 and 26, 4% between 27 and 28, and 6% above 28.

Requirements: The SAT or ACT is required. In addition, applicants must be graduates of an accredited secondary school or have the GED, and must have satisfactory composite scores on the ACT or on the SAT, or rank in the top 60% of their graduating class. Students not meeting these requirements may be admitted conditionally for 1 term or semester. An essay is required for all students. ETBU requires applicants to be in the upper 60% of their class. A GPA of 2.0 is required. AP and CLEP credits are accepted.

Procedure: Freshmen are admitted to all sessions. Entrance exams should be taken in the first semester of the senior year. There are a deferred admissions and rolling admissions plans. Application deadlines are open. The fall 2005 application fee was $25. Applications are accepted on-line.

Transfer: 127 transfer students enrolled in 2004-2005. Transfer students must have a minimum GPA of 2.0 and be eligible to return to the last college attended. 36 of 120 to 131 credits required for the bachelor's degree must be completed at ETBU.

Visiting: There are regularly scheduled orientations for prospective students, including campus tours, meals, scholarship interviews/testing, faculty visits, class visits, sports/entertainment, and financial aid seminars. There are guides for informal visits and visitors may sit in on classes and stay overnight. To schedule a visit, contact the Campus Visit Coordinator.

Financial Aid: In 2005-2006, 93% of all full-time freshmen and 95% of continuing full-time students received some form of financial aid. 89% of full-time freshmen and 85% of continuing full-time students received need-based aid. The average freshman award was $11,930. The average financial indebtedness of the 2005 graduate was $16,777. The FAFSA and the college's own financial statement are required. The deadline for filing freshman financial aid applications for fall entry is June 1.

International Students: There are 10 international students enrolled. The school actively recruits these students. A satisfactory score is required on the written TOEFL. Applicants must also take the MELAB and the SAT or the ACT, scoring 18.

Computers: All students may access the system. There are no time limits and no fees.

Graduates: From July 1, 2004 to June 30, 2005, 265 bachelor's degrees were awarded. The most popular majors were elementary education (22%), business (16%), and religion (14%). In an average class, 26% graduate in 4 years or less, 45% graduate in 5 years or less, and 48% graduate in 6 years or less. 60 companies recruited on campus in a recent year.

Admissions Contact: Vince Blankenship, Dean of Admissions and Marketing. A video is available. E-mail: *admissions@etbu.edu* Web: *www.etbu.edu*

HARDIN-SIMMONS UNIVERSITY   C-2

Abilene, TX 79698

(325) 670-1206
(877) 464-7889; Fax: (325) 670-1527

Full-time: 816 men, 963 women	**Faculty:** 121; IIA, --$
Part-time: 6 men, 126 women	**Ph.D.s:** 74%
Graduate: 193 men, 251 women	**Student/Faculty:** 15 to 1
Year: semesters, summer session	**Tuition:** $14,426
Application Deadline: open	**Room & Board:** $4215
Freshman Class: 1179 applied, 782 accepted, 436 enrolled	
SAT Verbal/Math: 517/520*	**COMPETITIVE**

Hardin-Simmons University, founded in 1891, is a private liberal arts institution affiliated with the Baptist General Convention of Texas. There are 7 undergraduate schools and 1 graduate school. In addition to regional accreditation, HSU has baccalaureate program accreditation with ACBSP, CAPT, CCNE, CSWE, and NASM. The 2 libraries contain 245,006 volumes, 21,914 microform items, and 9256 audio/video tapes/CDs/DVDs, and subscribe to 36,225 periodicals including electronic. Computerized library services include the card catalog, interlibrary loans, database searching, Internet access, and laptop Internet portals. Special learning facilities include an art gallery and an observatory. The 120-acre campus is in an urban area 150 miles west of Fort Worth. Including any residence halls, there are 42 buildings.

Student Life: 95% of undergraduates are from Texas. Others are from 31 states, 11 foreign countries, and Canada. 93% are from public schools. 79% are white; 10% Hispanic. 16% are claim no religious affiliation; 13% Protestant; 10% unknown; 6% Catholic. The average age of

freshmen is 18; all undergraduates, 21. 31% do not continue beyond their first year; 48% remain to graduate.

Housing: 1114 students can be accommodated in college housing, which includes single-sex dormitories, off-campus apartments, and married-student housing. On-campus housing is available on a first-come, first-served basis. 57% of students commute. Alcohol is not permitted. All students may keep cars.

Activities: 8% of men belong to 4 local fraternities; 11% of women belong to 4 local sororities. There are 55 groups on campus, including art, band, cheerleading, choir, chorale, computers, debate, drama, drill team, ethnic, honors, international, literary magazine, marching band, musical theater, newspaper, opera, orchestra, pep band, photography, political, professional, radio and TV, religious, social, social service, student government, symphony, and yearbook. Popular campus events include Western Heritage Day and May Day.

Sports: There are 6 intercollegiate sports for men and 6 for women, and 17 intramural sports for men and 17 for women. Facilities include a rodeo arena, 2 running ovals, a practice field, a football stadium, a soccer field, softball and baseball fields, outdoor and indoor swimming pools, 6 bowling alleys, a fitness course, 4 basketball, 4 racquetball, 8 tennis, and 8 badminton/paddleball courts, and a Nautilus weight-lifting room.

Disabled Students: All of the campus is accessible. Wheelchair ramps, elevators, special parking, specially equipped rest rooms, special class scheduling, lowered drinking fountains, lowered telephones, special housing, and an office to coordinate disability services are available.

Services: Counseling and information services are available, as is tutoring in most subjects. There is remedial math, reading, and writing. and free counseling services.

Campus Safety and Security: Measures include 24-hour foot and vehicle patrol, informal discussions, pamphlets/posters/films, and emergency telephones. There are lighted pathways/sidewalks.

Programs of Study: HSU confers B.A., B.S., B.B.A., B.B.S., B.Mus., and B.S.N. degrees. Master's degrees are also awarded. Bachelor's degrees are awarded in AGRICULTURE (agricultural business management, agriculture, and animal science), BIOLOGICAL SCIENCE (biochemistry, biology/biological science, and molecular biology), BUSINESS (accounting, banking and finance, business administration and management, management science, and marketing management), COMMUNICATIONS AND THE ARTS (art, broadcasting, communications, dramatic arts, English, graphic design, music, music business management, music history and appreciation, music performance, music theory and composition, piano/organ, public relations, radio/television technology, Spanish, speech/debate/rhetoric, strings, and voice), COMPUTER AND PHYSICAL SCIENCE (chemistry, computer science, geology, mathematics, and physics), EDUCATION (art, athletic training, business, computer, drama, early childhood, education, elementary, English, foreign languages, mathematics, middle school, music, physical, reading, science, secondary, and social studies), ENGINEERING AND ENVIRONMENTAL DESIGN (environmental science), HEALTH PROFESSIONS (exercise science, health science, nursing, predentistry, premedicine, and speech pathology/audiology), SOCIAL SCIENCE (biblical studies, corrections, criminal justice, economics, history, ministries, missions, philosophy, political science/government, prelaw, psychology, religious music, social work, sociology, theological studies, and youth ministry). English, speech pathology, and edcuation are the strongest academically. Education, biology, and nursing are the largest.

Required: To graduate, students must complete a minimum of 124 semester hours with a minimum 2.0 GPA. At minimum of 18 to 30 hours are required in the major (18 must be advanced and 12 of the advanced must be from HSU). 42 hours in upper-division courses. Core courses that must be taken include 12 to 18 hours of social science, 9 of English, 7 of natural science (from 2 separate fields and 1 requiring a lab), 6 each of Bible and humanities (3 of fine arts and 3 of non-fine arts) , 3 to 6 each of math, 3 to 4 of phys ed, 3 of oral communication, and computer science. All students must satisfy chapel attendance requirements and must demonstrate proficiency in written English.

Special: Cross-registration may be arranged with Abilene Christian and McMurry Universities. HSU offers cooperative programs, internships, dual majors, credit by exam, nondegree study, and pass/fail options. Students may study abroad in England, Austria, China, Spain, Italy and Israel, where HSU is involved in an ongoing archeological excavation of early Christian sites. There are 9 national honor societies and a freshman honors program.

Faculty/Classroom: 64% of faculty are male; 36%, female. 90% teach undergraduates. No introductory courses are taught by graduate students. The average class size in an introductory lecture is 23; in a laboratory, 13; and in a regular course, 18.

Admissions: 66% of the 2005-2006 applicants were accepted. The SAT scores for the 2005-2006 freshman class were: Verbal--41% below 500, 42% between 500 and 599, and 17% between 600 and 700; Math--38% below 500, 45% between 500 and 599, 14% between 600 and 700, and 3% above 700. The ACT scores were 40% below 21, 28% between 21 and 23, 18% between 24 and 26, 8% between 27 and 28, and 6% above 28. 44% of the current freshmen were in the top fifth of their class; 76% were in the top two fifths. 5 freshmen graduated first in their class.

Requirements: The SAT or ACT is required. The ACT Optional Writing test is also required. Graduation from an accredited secondary school is required; a GED will be accepted. Applicants should submit an academic record of at least 16 units, distributed as follows: 3 units of English, 2 units each of math, science, and social studies, and 7 units of electives. 3 letters of recommendation are also required. HSU requires applicants to be in the upper 75% of their class. A GPA of 2.0 is required. AP and CLEP credits are accepted.

Procedure: Freshmen are admitted to all sessions. There are early admissions, deferred admissions, and rolling admissions plans. Application deadlines are open. Application fee is $50. Applications are accepted on-line.

Transfer: 168 transfer students enrolled in 2005-2006. Applicants must submit official transcripts from all previous colleges. Students may petition to transfer up to 2 D grades if the overall GPA is 2.0 or higher. Students transferring from a 2-year college may receive credit for up to 66 semester hours of transferable courses. Applicants with fewer than 24 semester hours must submit a high school transcript and official report of ACT or SAT scores. Students ineligible to continue at another institution are not eligible for regular admission to HSU. 31 of 124 credits required for the bachelor's degree must be completed at HSU.

Visiting: There are regularly scheduled orientations for prospective students, including Cowboy Fridays, plus spring and fall preview for prospective students. There are guides for informal visits and visitors may sit in on classes. To schedule a visit, contact Jenni Williams, Visitor Coordinator at (325) 670-5890 or (877) GO-HSUTX.

Financial Aid: In 2005-2006, 99% of all full-time freshmen and 89% of continuing full-time students received some form of financial aid. 65% of full-time freshmen and 62% of continuing full-time students received need-based aid. The average freshman award was $13,492. Need-based scholarships or need-based grants averaged $4431 ($8494 maximum); need-based self-help aid (loans and jobs) averaged $4044 ($9025 maximum); and other non-need-based awards and non-need-based scholarships averaged $4548 ($26,030 maximum). 17% of undergraduates work part time. Average annual earnings from campus work are $2400. The average financial indebtedness of the 2005 graduate was $26,144. The FAFSA is required. The priority date for freshman financial aid applications for fall entry is March 15. The deadline for filing freshman financial aid applications for fall entry is open.

International Students: There are 79 international students enrolled. The school actively recruits these students. They must score satisfactorily on the written TOEFL or on the electronic version and also take the SAT or the ACT.

Computers: Wireless access is available. There are approximately 192 PCs in about 15 labs across campus. Most of the PCs are used for classroom instruction and are open to the HSU community. All are equipped with the entire Microsoft Office Suite, and many are equipped with discipline-specific software such as SPSS and Manifold. All students may access the system. There are no time limits and no fees.

Graduates: From July 1, 2004 to June 30, 2005, 308 bachelor's degrees were awarded. The most popular majors were education (18%), biology (8%), and psychology (7%). In an average class, 2% graduate in 3 years or less, 27% graduate in 4 years or less, 45% graduate in 5 years or less, and 48% graduate in 6 years or less. 12 companies recruited on campus in 2004-2005.

Admissions Contact: Shane Davidson, Associate, Vice President for Enrollment Services. A video is available. E-mail: *jdsd@hsutx.edu* Web: *hsutx.edu*

HOUSTON BAPTIST UNIVERSITY E-3
Houston, TX 77074-3298

	(281) 649-3211
	(800) 969-3210; Fax: (281) 649-3217
Full-time: 556 men, 1097 women	**Faculty:** 110; IIA, --$
Part-time: 80 men, 201 women	**Ph.D.s:** 78%
Graduate: 101 men, 261 women	**Student/Faculty:** 15 to 1
Year: quarters, summer session	**Tuition:** $13,950
Application Deadline: open	**Room & Board:** $4710
Freshman Class: 867 applied, 567 accepted, 313 enrolled	
SAT Verbal/Math: 540/560*	**ACT:** 22 **COMPETITIVE**

Houston Baptist University, founded in 1960, is a private institution affiliated with the Baptist General Convention of Texas and offering undergraduate programs in nursing, arts and science, music, and business administration. There are 7 undergraduate and 4 graduate schools. In addition to regional accreditation, HBU has baccalaureate program accreditation with NLN. The library contains 218,505 volumes, 105,991 microform items, and 10,100 audio/video tapes/CDs/DVDs, and subscribes to 1010 periodicals including electronic. Computerized library services include the card catalog, interlibrary loans, and database searching. Special learning facilities include a learning resource center, a TV station, a museum of decorative arts, and the Bible in America Museum.

The 100-acre campus is in an urban area in southwest Houston. Including any residence halls, there are 25 buildings.

Student Life: 92% of undergraduates are from Texas. Others are from 26 states, 35 foreign countries, and Canada. 84% are from public schools. 46% are white; 20% African American; 14% Hispanic; 13% Asian American. 51% are Protestant; 15% Catholic. The average age of freshmen is 18; all undergraduates, 23. 26% do not continue beyond their first year; 74% remain to graduate.

Housing: 718 students can be accommodated in college housing, which includes single-sex dorms and on-campus apartments. On-campus housing is available on a first-come, first-served basis and is available on a lottery system for upperclassmen. Priority is given to out-of-town students. 69% of students commute. Alcohol is not permitted. All students may keep cars.

Activities: 5% of men belong to 1 local and 1 national fraternity; 5% of women belong to 3 national sororities. Women may be belong to professional/and service fraternities. 5% to 10% belong. There are 45 groups on campus, including art, band, cheerleading, choir, chorale, chorus, computers, debate, drama, ethnic, forensics, honors, international, jazz band, newspaper, opera, pep band, photography, political, professional, radio and TV, religious, social service, student government, symphony, and yearbook. Popular campus events include Welcome Days for new students, Husky Fest Fall Festival, and Winter Formal.

Sports: There are 2 intercollegiate sports for men and 3 for women, and 12 intramural sports for men and 12 for women. Facilities include volleyball, basketball, and tennis courts, an indoor track, softball, baseball, and soccer fields, and areas for track.

Disabled Students: 90% of the campus is accessible. Wheelchair ramps, elevators, special parking, specially equipped rest rooms, lowered drinking fountains, lowered telephones, and special housing are available.

Services: There is remedial math and writing.

Campus Safety and Security: Measures include 24-hour foot and vehicle patrol, security escort services, emergency telephones, and lighted pathways/sidewalks.

Programs of Study: HBU confers B.A., B.S., B.B.A., B.M., and B.S.N. degrees. Associate and master's degrees are also awarded. Bachelor's degrees are awarded in BIOLOGICAL SCIENCE (biology/biological science and molecular biology), BUSINESS (accounting, banking and finance, business administration and management, and entrepreneurial studies), COMMUNICATIONS AND THE ARTS (art, communications, English, French, music, music performance, music theory and composition, and Spanish), COMPUTER AND PHYSICAL SCIENCE (chemistry, information sciences and systems, mathematics, and physics), EDUCATION (art, early childhood, elementary, mathematics, music, physical, reading, secondary, special, and teaching English as a second/foreign language (TESOL/TEFOL)), HEALTH PROFESSIONS (nursing), SOCIAL SCIENCE (biblical languages, Christian studies, economics, history, liberal arts/general studies, physical fitness/movement, political science/government, psychology, religious music, and sociology). Premedical studies, health professions, and education are the strongest academically. Biology, nursing, and business administration are the largest.

Required: To graduate, students must complete a minimum of 130 semester hours, including at least 48 semester hours of upper-level courses and 24 to 36 hours in the major. They must complete courses in Christianity, written and oral communications, math, lab science, computer, kinetics, social and behavioral sciences, humanities, and fine arts. No grade below "C" within majors and program requirements and a cumulative GPA of 2.0 are required. Proficiency is required in reading, computer, communication, and math. Spiritual Life Program participation is also a graduation requirement.

Special: HBU offers internships through its academic colleges, B.A.-B.S. degrees, dual majors in most areas, work-study programs, credit for military experience, and pass/fail options. There is a freshman honors program.

Faculty/Classroom: 52% of faculty are male; 48%, female. 94% teach undergraduates. No introductory courses are taught by graduate students. The average class size in an introductory lecture is 20; in a laboratory, 20; and in a regular course, 15.

Admissions: 65% of the 2005-2006 applicants were accepted. The SAT scores for the 2005-2006 freshman class were: Verbal--24% below 500, 47% between 500 and 599, 23% between 600 and 700, and 6% above 700; Math--23% below 500, 42% between 500 and 599, 30% between 600 and 700, and 5% above 700. The ACT scores were 39% below 21, 24% between 21 and 23, 23% between 24 and 26, 8% between 27 and 28, and 6% above 28. 39% of the current freshmen were in the top fifth of their class; 65% were in the top two fifths. 6 freshmen graduated first in their class.

Requirements: The SAT or ACT is required. In addition one recommendation, and an official high school transcript or GED scores are also required. AP and CLEP credits are accepted. Important factors in the admissions decision are recommendations by school officials, personality/intangible qualities, and advanced placement or honor courses.

Procedure: Freshmen are admitted to all sessions. Entrance exams should be taken in the fall of the senior year. There are early decision and early admissions plans. Application deadlines are open. Application fee is $25. Notification is sent on a rolling basis. Applications are accepted on-line.

Transfer: 420 transfer students enrolled in 2004-2005. Applicants with fewer than 30 semester hours earned must submit a high school transcript and SAT or ACT scores. All students must have a minimum 2.0 GPA and submit all previous college transcripts. 32 of 130 credits required for the bachelor's degree must be completed at HBU.

Visiting: There are guides for informal visits and visitors may sit in on classes and stay overnight. To schedule a visit, contact the Office of Admissions at *unadm@hbu.edu.*

Financial Aid: In 2005-2006, 81% of all full-time freshmen and 87% of continuing full-time students received some form of financial aid. 60% of full-time freshmen and 75% of continuing full-time students received need-based aid. The average freshman award was $14,239. Need-based scholarships or need-based grants averaged $2846 ($4050 maximum); need-based self-help aid (loans and jobs) averaged $2797 ($8125 maximum); non-need-based athletic scholarships averaged $8988 ($15,345 maximum); and other non-need-based awards and non-need-based scholarships averaged $3255 ($6000 maximum). 8% of undergraduates work part time. Average annual earnings from campus work are $985. The average financial indebtedness of the 2005 graduate was $17,642. The FAFSA and the college's own financial statement are required. The priority date for freshman financial aid applications for fall entry is March 1. The deadline for filing freshman financial aid applications for fall entry is April 15.

International Students: There are 109 international students enrolled. The school actively recruits these students. They must score satisfactorily on the written TOEFL or on the electronic version.

Computers: All students may access the system. There are no time limits and no fees.

Graduates: From July 1, 2004 to June 30, 2005, 349 bachelor's degrees were awarded. The most popular majors were business administration (12%), psychology (11%), and biology (10%). In an average class, 1% graduate in 3 years or less, 32% graduate in 4 years or less, 52% graduate in 5 years or less, and 59% graduate in 6 years or less.

Admissions Contact: David Melton, Associate Vice President for Admission / Marketing. E-mail: *unadm@hbu.edu* Web: *www.hbu.edu*

HOWARD PAYNE UNIVERSITY C-3
Brownwood, TX 76801-2794

(325) 649-8027
(800) 880-4478; Fax: (325) 649-8901

Full-time: 509 men, 534 women	Faculty: 75; II B, --$
Part-time: 159 men, 162 women	Ph.D.s: 49%
Graduate: none	Student/Faculty: 14 to 1
Year: semesters, summer session	Tuition: $12,500
Application Deadline: August 1	Room & Board: $4615
Freshman Class: 1076 applied, 763 accepted, 478 enrolled	
SAT Verbal/Math: 495/500*	ACT: 21	COMPETITIVE

Howard Payne University, founded in 1889 and affiliated with the Baptist General Convention of Texas, offers undergraduate programs in the arts and sciences, business administration, education, Christianity, music, and social sciences. There are 6 undergraduate schools. In addition to regional accreditation, HPU has baccalaureate program accreditation with CSWE, IACBE, and NASM. The library contains 118,825 volumes and 271,542 microform items, and subscribes to 30,598 periodicals including electronic. Computerized library services include the card catalog, interlibrary loans, database searching, Internet access, and laptop Internet portals. Special learning facilities include a radio station children's literature center, audio production facility, TV production studio, and video editing facility. The 29-acre campus is in a small town 120 miles southwest of Dallas/Fort Worth. Including any residence halls, there are 31 buildings.

Student Life: 96% of undergraduates are from Texas. Others are from 18 states and 2 foreign countries. 93% are from public schools. 74% are white; 14% Hispanic. 85% are Protestant; 9% claim no religious affiliation. The average age of freshmen is 18; all undergraduates, 22. 40% do not continue beyond their first year; 33% remain to graduate.

Housing: 764 students can be accommodated in college housing, which includes single-sex dorms, on-campus apartments, and married-student housing. On-campus housing is available on a lottery system for upperclassmen. 54% of students commute. Alcohol is not permitted. All students may keep cars.

Activities: 14% of men belong to 5 local fraternities; 16% of women belong to 6 local sororities. There are 33 groups on campus, including art, band, cheerleading, choir, chorus, drama, drill team, ethnic, honors, jazz band, literary magazine, marching band, musical theater, newspaper, photography, professional, radio and TV, religious, social, social service, student government, and yearbook. Popular campus events include Christian Concerts and College Preview Weekends.

Sports: There are 5 intercollegiate sports for men and 5 for women, and 5 intramural sports for men and 5 for women. Facilities include an 8000-seat stadium and an 800-seat auditorium; a remodeled wellness center with basketball and volleyball courts, an indoor walking track, and free weights and exercise equipment; tennis and sand volleyball courts; a practice field; a student union; and nearby baseball and softball parks.

Disabled Students: 90% of the campus is accessible. Wheelchair ramps, elevators, special parking, specially equipped rest rooms, special class scheduling, and lowered drinking fountains are available.

Services: Counseling and information services are available, as is tutoring in some subjects, including math and English. There is remedial math, reading, and writing. A writing lab and computer lab are available for English, math, and computer science.

Campus Safety and Security: Measures include informal discussions, pamphlets/posters/films, emergency telephones, and lighted pathways/sidewalks. In addition, there are 12-hour foot patrols, monthly dorm meetings, 2 security seminars for the entire campus, and 24-hour telephone availability with on-duty officers carrying cell phones.

Programs of Study: HPU confers B.A., B.S., B.A.A.S., B.B.A., and B.M. degrees. Associate degrees are also awarded. Bachelor's degrees are awarded in BIOLOGICAL SCIENCE (biology/biological science), BUSINESS (accounting and business administration and management), COMMUNICATIONS AND THE ARTS (art, communications, dramatic arts, English, multimedia, music, and Spanish), COMPUTER AND PHYSICAL SCIENCE (chemistry, computer science, and mathematics), EDUCATION (athletic training, elementary, secondary, and teaching English as a second/foreign language (TESOL/TEFOL)), ENGINEERING AND ENVIRONMENTAL DESIGN (occupational safety and health), HEALTH PROFESSIONS (exercise science), SOCIAL SCIENCE (Christian studies, history, liberal arts/general studies, political science/government, psychology, social work, and sociology). Biology, chemistry, and political science are the strongest academically. Business management, elementary education, and exercise and sports science are the largest.

Required: To graduate, students must complete a minimum of 128 credit hours, 49 in general education courses, 30 to 36 in the major, and 18 to 24 in a minor, plus electives. A minimum 2.0 GPA is required. The general education core includes Bible, English, social science, computer science, fine arts, phys ed, lab science, speech, and math courses. Requirements for students not obtaining the B.A. or B.S. vary. All students must complete 6 semester credits of chapel/convocation attendance.

Special: Cross-registration is offered with several hospitals, and internships are available in many fields. HPU offers credit for experience for B.A.A.S. candidates only, study abroad in Israel and England, pass/fail options, and work-study programs. Special programs include the Douglas MacArthur Academy of Freedom, an interdisciplinary honors program in the social sciences; a chemistry honors program; and a provisional program for underprepared students. There are 4 national honor societies, a freshman honors program, and 1 departmental honors program.

Faculty/Classroom: 64% of faculty are male; 36%, female. All teach undergraduates. The average class size in an introductory lecture is 22; in a laboratory, 20; and in a regular course, 18.

Admissions: 71% of the 2005-2006 applicants were accepted. The SAT scores for the 2005-2006 freshman class were: Verbal--52% below 500, 32% between 500 and 599, 11% between 600 and 700, and 5% above 700; Math--56% below 500, 29% between 500 and 599, 13% between 600 and 700, and 2% above 700. The ACT scores were 47% below 21, 29% between 21 and 23, 14% between 24 and 26, 7% between 27 and 28, and 3% above 28. 32% of the current freshmen were in the top fifth of their class; 60% were in the top two fifths. 4 freshmen graduated first in their class.

Requirements: The SAT or ACT is required. In addition, applicants must be graduates of an accredited secondary school or have a GED. It is recommended that they have completed 4 credits of English, 3 of math including algebra I, 2.5 of social studies, 2 of science, 1.5 of phys ed, and 1 each of technology applications and a science/social studies elective, along with courses in economics, health, and speech; the remaining credits should be earned in courses approved by the Texas Board of Education. Graduates of high schools or home study programs that are not accredited by a regional or state accrediting agency will have their work reviewed by the admissions committee on an individual basis. A GPA of 3.0 is required. AP and CLEP credits are accepted. Important factors in the admissions decision are recommendations by school officials, leadership record, and personality/intangible qualities.

Procedure: Freshmen are admitted to all sessions. Entrance exams should be taken during the senior year. There is an early admissions plan and a rolling admissions plan. Applications should be filed by August 1 for fall entry and January 1 for spring entry, along with a $25 fee. Notification is sent on a rolling basis.

Transfer: 67 transfer students enrolled in 2004-2005. Transfer students must be able to return to the university they are leaving and submit official transcripts from all previously attended colleges/universities. Students younger than 21 with fewer than 12 semester hours must submit the SAT or ACT scores. The same GPA per number of hours attempted is required of transfers as for continuing HPU students. 32 of 128 credits required for the bachelor's degree must be completed at HPU.

Visiting: There are regularly scheduled orientations for prospective students, including college preview weekends in the fall and spring. There are guides for informal visits and visitors may sit in on classes and stay overnight. To schedule a visit, contact the Enrollment Services Office at (915) 649-8020 or enroll@hputx.edu.

Financial Aid: 65% of undergraduates work part time. Average annual earnings from campus work are $2000. The FAFSA is required. The deadline for filing freshman financial aid applications for fall entry is March 1.

International Students: In a recent year, there were 11 international students enrolled. The school actively recruits these students. A satisfactory score is required on the written TOEFL. Applicants must also achieve minimum scores on the SAT or the ACT for unconditional admission; otherwise, a provisional program may be available. A TOEFL score is not required for International students entering the English as a Second Language (ESL) program.

Computers: All students may access the system 24 hours a day in 3 labs in the dorms and 8 A.M. to 10 P.M., Monday through Friday in the Instructional Building labs. There are no time limits and no fees.

Graduates: From July 1, 2004 to June 30, 2005, 240 bachelor's degrees were awarded. The most popular majors were Christian studies (20%), business management (16%), and education (16%). In an average class, 2% graduate in 3 years or less, 23% graduate in 4 years or less, 34% graduate in 5 years or less, and 37% graduate in 6 years or less. Of the 2004 graduating class, 20% were enrolled in graduate school within 6 months of graduation.

Admissions Contact: Cheryl Mangrum, Coordinator of Admissions Services. E-mail: enroll@hputx.edu Web: www.hputx.edu

HUSTON-TILLOTSON UNIVERSITY D-3
(Formerly Huston-Tillotson College)

Austin, TX 78702 (512) 505-3027
(877) 505-3026; Fax: (512) 505-3192

Full-time: 293 men, 332 women	**Faculty:** 39
Part-time: 21 men, 28 women	**Ph.Ds:** 64%
Graduate: 11 men, 21 women	**Student/Faculty:** 16 to 1
Year: semesters, summer session	**Tuition:** $8190
Application Deadline: March 1	**Room & Board:** $6042
Freshman Class: 332 applied, 227 accepted, 168 enrolled	
SAT Verbal/Math: 406/403*	**ACT:** 14 LESS COMPETITIVE

Huston-Tillotson University, formerly Huston-Tillotson College and formed in 1952 by the merger of Tillotson College and Samuel Huston College (both founded in the mid-1870s), is a private liberal arts institution affiliated with the United Church of Christ and the United Methodist Church. The library contains 88,455 volumes, 69,216 microform items, and 8753 audio/video tapes/CDs/DVDs, and subscribes to 2353 periodicals including electronic. Computerized library services include the card catalog, interlibrary loans, database searching, and Internet access. Special learning facilities include a learning resource center. The 23-acre campus is in an urban area, downtown Austin. Including any residence halls, there are 12 buildings.

Student Life: 93% of undergraduates are from Texas. Others are from 16 states and 6 foreign countries. 85% are from public schools. 74% are African American; 13% Hispanic. 74% are Protestant; 13% Catholic; 9% claim no religious affiliation. The average age of freshmen is 19; all undergraduates, 22. 50% do not continue beyond their first year; 20% remain to graduate.

Housing: 457 students can be accommodated in college housing, which includes single-sex dorms. On-campus housing is guaranteed for all 4 years. 63% of students commute. Alcohol is not permitted. All students may keep pets.

Activities: 3% of men belong to 4 national fraternities; 8% of women belong to 4 local and 4 national sororities. There are 17 groups on campus, including band, cheerleading, choir, chorus, drama, drill team, honors, international, jazz band, newspaper, professional, radio and TV, religious, social, social service, student government, and yearbook. Popular campus events include Charter Day, Alumni Weekend, and Miss UNCF Contest.

Sports: There are 3 intercollegiate sports for men and 3 for women, and 2 intramural sports for men and 2 for women. Facilities include an 800-seat gym and soccer and baseball fields.

Disabled Students: 82% of the campus is accessible. Wheelchair ramps, elevators, special parking, and specially equipped rest rooms are available.

Services: Counseling and information services are available, as is tutoring in every subject. There is remedial math, reading, and writing.

Campus Safety and Security: Measures include 24-hour foot and vehicle patrol, security escort services, and lighted pathways/sidewalks.

Programs of Study: HT confers B.A. and B.S. degrees. Bachelor's degrees are awarded in BIOLOGICAL SCIENCE (biology/biological science), BUSINESS (business administration and management and marketing/retailing/merchandising), COMMUNICATIONS AND THE ARTS (communications, English, and music), COMPUTER AND PHYSICAL SCIENCE (chemistry, computer science, and mathematics), EDUCATION (education, elementary, and physical), SOCIAL SCIENCE (interdisciplinary studies, political science/government, psychology, and sociology). Biology, computer science, and education are the strongest academically. Business studies, computer science, and education are the largest.

Required: All students must complete 120 credit hours, including 54 in the general education required curriculum and 30 in the major, with a minimum GPA of 2.0. Core requirements include 18 hours of English and foreign languages, 9 each of math/computer science and social sciences, 8 of natural science, 6 of phys ed and health, 3 of philosophy, and 1 of psychology.

Special: The university offers co-op programs, internships, work-study programs, and dual majors. A 3-2 engineering degree with Prairie View A&M University is also available. There are 4 national honor societies, a freshman honors program, and 1 departmental honors program.

Faculty/Classroom: 48% of faculty are male; 52%, female. All teach undergraduates and 4% do research. The average class size in an introductory lecture is 16; in a laboratory, 16; and in a regular course, 20.

Admissions: 68% of the 2005-2006 applicants were accepted. The SAT scores for the 2005-2006 freshman class were: Verbal--83% below 500, 16% between 500 and 599, and 1% between 600 and 700; Math--85% below 500, 12% between 500 and 599, and 3% between 600 and 700. The ACT scores were 92% below 21, 4% between 21 and 23, and 4% between 24 and 26. 12% of the current freshmen were in the top fifth of their class; 34% were in the top two fifths.

Requirements: The SAT or ACT is required. The ACT Optional Writing test is also required. Applicants should be high school graduates with 18 academic credits, including 4 in English, 3 in math, 2 each in science and social studies, and 1 in phys ed. AP and CLEP credits are accepted. Important factors in the admissions decision are advanced placement or honor courses, extracurricular activities record, and parents or siblings attending the school.

Procedure: Freshmen are admitted to all sessions. There is an early admissions plan. Applications should be filed by March 1 for fall entry, October 1 for spring entry, and March 1 for summer entry, along with a $25 fee. Notification is sent on a rolling basis. Applications are accepted online.

Transfer: 121 transfer students enrolled in a recent year. Applicants must submit transcripts from all colleges or universities attended and must have an overall GPA of 2.0. Students with fewer than 15 credit hours must meet freshman entrance requirements. 30 of 120 credits required for the bachelor's degree must be completed at HT.

Visiting: There are regularly scheduled orientations for prospective students. There are guides for informal visits and visitors may sit in on classes and stay overnight. To schedule a visit, contact the Dean of Enrollment Services.

Financial Aid: The FAFSA and the college's own financial statement are required. The deadline for filing freshman financial aid applications for fall entry is March 15.

International Students: There are 14 international students enrolled. They must score satisfactorily on the written TOEFL and also take the SAT.

Computers: Wireless access is available. Students with a network card can log into the wireless network automatically. All students may access the system during lab hours. There are no time limits. The fee is $15.

Graduates: From July 1, 2004 to June 30, 2005, 69 bachelor's degrees were awarded. The most popular majors were business administration (23%), computer science (16%), and political science (11%).

Admissions Contact: Doris Price, Ph.D., Dean of Enrollment Management. E-mail: dfprice@htu.edu Web: www.htu.edu

JARVIS CHRISTIAN COLLEGE E-2

Hawkins, TX 75765 (903) 769-5730
(800) 292-9517; Fax: (903) 769-1282

Full-time: 256 men, 303 women	**Faculty:** 36
Part-time: 7 men, 6 women	**Ph.Ds:** 54%
Graduate: none	**Student/Faculty:** 16 to 1
Year: semesters, summer session	**Tuition:** $6980
Application Deadline: August 1	**Room & Board:** $4156
Freshman Class: n/av	
SAT: recommended	**ACT:** required
	NONCOMPETITIVE

Jarvis Christian College, founded in 1912, is a private liberal arts institution affiliated with the Disciples of Christ. The library contains 54,170 volumes, 4339 microform items, and 2431 audio/video tapes/CDs/DVDs, and subscribes to 152 periodicals including electronic. Computerized library services include the card catalog, interlibrary loans, database searching, Internet access, and laptop Internet portals. Special learning facilities include a learning resource center, planetarium, and archives of the Black Disciples in Texas. The 243-acre campus is in a rural area 100 miles southeast of Dallas. Including any residence halls, there are 18 buildings.

Student Life: 86% of undergraduates are from Texas. Others are from 24 states and 1 foreign country. 99% are from public schools. 97% are African American. 79% are Protestant; 20% claim no religious affiliation. The average age of freshmen is 19; all undergraduates, 21. 40% do not continue beyond their first year; 15% remain to graduate.

Housing: 750 students can be accommodated in college housing, which includes single-sex dorms, on-campus apartments, and married-student housing. In addition, there are honors houses. On-campus housing is guaranteed for all 4 years. 86% of students live on campus; of those, 50% remain on campus on weekends. Alcohol is not permitted. All students may keep cars.

Activities: 5% of men belong to 4 national fraternities; 10% of women belong to 4 national sororities. There are 47 groups on campus, including band, cheerleading, chess, choir, chorale, chorus, drama, drill team, honors, newspaper, political, professional, religious, social, social service, and student government. Popular campus events include Miss/Mr. Jarvis Coronation, Hall of Fame Weekend, and Christmas Concert.

Sports: There are 2 intercollegiate sports for men and 2 for women, and 11 intramural sports for men and 11 for women. Facilities include 2 basketball gyms, a pool, tennis and volleyball courts, a soccer field, billiards, a flag football field, and a softball/baseball diamond.

Disabled Students: 83% of the campus is accessible. Wheelchair ramps, special parking, specially equipped rest rooms, special class scheduling, lowered drinking fountains, and special housing are available.

Services: Counseling and information services are available, as is tutoring in every subject. There is remedial math, reading, and writing.

Campus Safety and Security: Measures include 24-hour foot and vehicle patrol, self-defense education, security escort services, and informal discussions. There are pamphlets/posters/films and lighted pathways/sidewalks.

Programs of Study: Jarvis confers B.A., B.S., and B.B.A. degrees. Bachelor's degrees are awarded in BIOLOGICAL SCIENCE (biology/biological science), COMMUNICATIONS AND THE ARTS (English), COMPUTER AND PHYSICAL SCIENCE (chemistry, computer science, and mathematics), EDUCATION (elementary, music, reading, secondary, and special), HEALTH PROFESSIONS (premedicine), SOCIAL SCIENCE (criminal justice, history, religion, and sociology). Sociology, business, and computer science are the strongest academically. Business administration is the largest.

Required: A 54-credit general education requirement includes at least 36 hours in the major, plus courses in English, literature, math, religion, science, speech, social science, health, and phys ed. Other graduation requirements include a minimum 2.0 GPA, at least 124 credit hours, math and writing proficiencies, and satisfactory scores on the sophomore comprehensive exam and on the GRE.

Special: Jarvis offers co-op and work-study programs, an accelerated degree in education, internships, dual and student-designed majors, a Washington semester, and a general studies degree. Cross-registration is offered with members of the TADC consortium. Also available are the Brookhaven National Laboratory Semester Program, the UNCF Premedical Summer Program with Fisk University, and the Biomedical Sciences Program with Meharry Medical College. A 3-2 engineering degree is available with Texas at Arlington and a 3-2 nursing degree with University of Texas at Tyler. A mass communication degree with University of North Texas is also possible. There are 4 national honor societies, a freshman honors program, and 2 departmental honors programs.

Faculty/Classroom: 61% of faculty are male; 39%, female. 99% teach undergraduates, 1% do research, and 10% do both. The average class size in an introductory lecture is 30; in a laboratory, 16; and in a regular course, 16.

Admissions: The SAT scores for the 2005-2006 freshman class were: Verbal--99% below 500, and 1% between 500 and 599; Math--99% below 500, and 2% between 500 and 599. The ACT scores were 98% below 21, and 2% between 21 and 23. 10% of the current freshmen were in the top fifth of their class; 26% were in the top two fifths.

Requirements: The ACT is required and the SAT is accepted. In addition, applicants should graduate from an accredited secondary school with 16 academic credits, including 3 each in English and social science, 2 in math, and 1 in science. The GED is accepted. Graduates of nonaccredited high schools are given conditional admission. A GPA of 2.0 is required. AP and CLEP credits are accepted. Important factors in the admissions decision are parents or siblings attending the school, recommendations by alumni, and advanced placement or honor courses.

Procedure: Freshmen are admitted fall, spring, and summer. Entrance exams should be taken before entrance or during orientation week. Early decision applications should be filed by April 1; regular applications, by August 1 for fall entry, December 1 for spring entry, and May 1 for summer entry, along with a $25 fee. There is a rolling admissions plan. The college accepts all applicants. Notification is sent on a rolling basis.

Transfer: Applicants must submit official transcripts from all schools of higher education attended and provide proof of honorable dismissal

from the most recent one. 30 of 124 credits required for the bachelor's degree must be completed at Jarvis.

Visiting: There are regularly scheduled orientations for prospective students, including classroom visits, a tour of the campus, and review of the orientation guidebook. There are guides for informal visits and visitors may sit in on classes and stay overnight. To schedule a visit, contact the Office of Admissions.

Financial Aid: 97% of full-time freshmen received need-based aid. The average freshman award was $9815. Need-based scholarships or need-based grants averaged $7877 ($10,615 maximum); need-based self-help aid (loans and jobs) averaged $2625 ($4185 maximum); non-need-based athletic scholarships averaged $5800 ($10,615 maximum); and other non-need-based awards and non-need-based scholarships averaged $800 ($8000 maximum). External funds are available for students. 6% of undergraduates work part time. Average annual earnings from campus work are $1560. The average financial indebtedness of the 2005 graduate was $4067. The FAFSA, FFS, and the college's own financial statement are required.

International Students: There is 1 international student enrolled. Students must take the TOEFL and also take the ACT or SAT.

Computers: Wireless access is available. All students may access the system 8 A.M. to 10 P.M. There are no time limits. The fee is $500.

Graduates: From July 1, 2004 to June 30, 2005, 57 bachelor's degrees were awarded. The most popular majors were business (21%), criminal justice (7%), and biology (7%). In an average class, 8% graduate in 4 years or less, 23% graduate in 5 years or less, and 24% graduate in 6 years or less. 85 companies recruited on campus in 2004-2005. Of the 2004 graduating class, 10% were enrolled in graduate school within 6 months of graduation and 10% were employed.

Admissions Contact: Felecia Tyiska, Director. A video is available. E-mail: *mary_mckinney@jarvis.edu* Web: *www.jarvis.edu*

LAMAR UNIVERSITY — E-3

Beaumont, TX 77710 — (409) 880-8888; Fax: (409) 880-8463

Full-time: 2330 men, 2830 women	**Faculty:** 303; IIA, --$
Part-time: 1310 men, 1960 women	**Ph.D's:** 48%
Graduate: 260 men, 305 women	**Student/Faculty:** 15 to 1
Year: semesters, summer session	**Tuition:** $2620 ($9010)
Application Deadline: see profile	**Room & Board:** $4200
Freshman Class: n/av	
SAT or ACT: required	**LESS COMPETITIVE**

Lamar University-Beaumont, founded in 1923, is part of the Lamar University system. The university offers undergraduate degrees in arts and sciences, business, education, engineering, fine arts, communications, health and behavioral science, and technical arts. There are 7 undergraduate and 5 graduate schools. Figures in the above capsule and in this profile are approximate. In addition to regional accreditation, LU has baccalaureate program accreditation with AACSB, ABET, CSWE, NASM, and NCATE. The library contains 900,000 volumes, and subscribes to 2800 periodicals including electronic. Computerized library services include the card catalog, interlibrary loans, and database searching. Special learning facilities include a learning resource center, art gallery, and radio station. The 200-acre campus is in an urban area 90 miles east of Houston. Including any residence halls, there are 90 buildings.

Student Life: Students are from 39 states, 61 foreign countries, and Canada. 95% are from public schools. 79% are white; 16% African American. The average age of freshmen is 19; all undergraduates, 25. 40% do not continue beyond their first year; 19% remain to graduate.

Housing: 1700 students can be accommodated in college housing, which includes dormitories, on-campus apartments, fraternity houses, and sorority houses. In addition, there are special-interest houses. On-campus housing is guaranteed for all 4 years. 91% of students commute. Alcohol is not permitted. All students may keep cars.

Activities: 5% of men belong to 11 national fraternities; 5% of women belong to 7 national sororities. There are 120 groups on campus, including art, band, cheerleading, choir, chorale, chorus, computers, dance, drama, ethnic, film, honors, international, jazz band, literary magazine, marching band, musical theater, newspaper, opera, orchestra, pep band, photography, political, professional, radio and TV, religious, social, social service, student government, and symphony. Popular campus events include Springfest, Birdfeed, and Love Lamar Week.

Sports: There are 7 intercollegiate sports for men and 6 for women, and 15 intramural sports for men and 15 for women. Facilities include a 10,000-seat multipurpose facility for basketball and other sports; a student center with games areas and a video lounge; a gym; an indoor/outdoor pool; a track; and a 17,000-seat stadium.

Disabled Students: All of the campus is accessible. Wheelchair ramps, elevators, special parking, specially equipped rest rooms, special class scheduling, lowered drinking fountains, and lowered telephones are available.

Services: Counseling and information services are available, as is tutoring in some subjects, including math and English. There is a reader service for the blind, and remedial math, reading, and writing.

Campus Safety and Security: Measures include 24-hour foot and vehicle patrol, self-defense education, informal discussions, and pamphlets/posters/films. There are lighted pathways/sidewalks.

Programs of Study: LU confers B.A., B.S., B.A.A.S., B.B.A., B.F.A., B.G.S., B.Mus., and B.S.W. degrees. Associate, master's, and doctoral degrees are also awarded. Bachelor's degrees are awarded in BIOLOGICAL SCIENCE (biology/biological science), BUSINESS (accounting, business administration and management, business economics, business law, marketing/retailing/merchandising, and personnel management), COMMUNICATIONS AND THE ARTS (advertising, communications, design, dramatic arts, English, fine arts, French, music, Spanish, and speech/debate/rhetoric), COMPUTER AND PHYSICAL SCIENCE (chemistry, computer programming, computer science, geology, information sciences and systems, mathematics, and physics), EDUCATION (art, early childhood, elementary, foreign languages, health, music, science, secondary, and special), ENGINEERING AND ENVIRONMENTAL DESIGN (chemical engineering, civil engineering, electrical/electronics engineering, industrial engineering, industrial engineering technology, and mechanical engineering), HEALTH PROFESSIONS (medical laboratory technology, nursing, occupational therapy, pharmacy, physical therapy, predentistry, premedicine, and speech pathology/audiology), SOCIAL SCIENCE (criminal justice, economics, family/consumer studies, history, political science/government, prelaw, psychology, public administration, social science, social work, and sociology). Engineering is the strongest academically. Arts and sciences are the largest.

Required: To graduate, all students must complete 124 to 132 total credit hours, with 30 hours in the major. Required courses include 12 hours of English, 6 hours each of electives, political science, and American history, and 4 hours each of lab science or math and physical activity and/or marching band and/or ROTC. Students must have a minimum 2.0 GPA.

Special: The university offers internships in social work, work-study programs, B.A.-B.S. degrees, a dual major in biochemistry, the general studies degree, credit for experience, nondegree study, and pass/fail options. There are 2 national honor societies, including Phi Beta Kappa, and a freshman honors program.

Faculty/Classroom: 58% of faculty are male; 42%, female. All teach undergraduates. The average class size in an introductory lecture is 50; in a laboratory, 25; and in a regular course, 24.

Requirements: A satisfactory score is required on the SAT or the ACT. In addition, SAT: Subject tests in math are required for engineering and physical science majors. Applicants must be graduates of an accredited secondary school or have a GED certificate and must have completed 4 credits of English, 3 of math, 2 of science, and 2 1/2 of history. LU requires applicants to be in the upper 50% of their class. A GPA of 2.0 is required. AP and CLEP credits are accepted. Important factors in the admissions decision are advanced placement or honor courses, evidence of special talent, and leadership record.

Procedure: Freshmen are admitted to all sessions. Entrance exams should be taken in the fall of the senior year. Check with the school for current deadlines and fee.

Transfer: 483 transfer students enrolled in a recent year. Applicants must have a minimum 2.0 GPA and at least 18 credit hours earned. 30 of 132 credits required for the bachelor's degree must be completed at LU.

Visiting: There are regularly scheduled orientations for prospective students. There are guides for informal visits. To schedule a visit, contact the Admissions Office.

Financial Aid: LU is a member of CSS. The CSS/Profile and the college's own financial statement are required. Check with the school for current deadlines.

International Students: A satisfactory score is required on the written TOEFL and the SAT or the ACT.

Computers: All students may access the system. There are no time limits. Check with the school for the current fee. It is strongly recommended that all students have a personal computer.

Admissions Contact: James Rush, Director of Academic Services. A video is available. E-mail: *admissions@hal.lamar.edu* Web: *lamar.edu*

LETOURNEAU UNIVERSITY   E-2
Longview, TX 75607   (903) 233-3400
                                          (800) 759-8811; Fax: (903) 233-3411

Full-time: 880 men, 410 women	**Faculty:** IIA, --$
Part-time: 620 men, 1280 women	**Ph.D.s:** 67%
Graduate: 220 men, 220 women	**Student/Faculty:** n/av
Year: semesters, summer session	**Tuition:** $15,100
Application Deadline: see profile	**Room & Board:** $6100
Freshman Class: n/av	
SAT or ACT: required	**COMPETITIVE**

Le Tourneau University, founded in 1946, is a private, nondenominational Christian institution offering programs in aeronautical science, business administration, engineering, education, liberal arts, technology, computer science, natural and mathematical sciences, kinesiology, and others. There are 6 undergraduate schools and 1 graduate school. Figures in the above capsule and in this profile are approximate. In addition to regional accreditation, LeTourneau has baccalaureate program accreditation with ABET and IACBE. The library contains 84,779 volumes, 50,481 microform items, and 3144 audio/video tapes/CDs/DVDs, and subscribes to 383 periodicals including electronic. Computerized library services include the card catalog, interlibrary loans, and database searching. Special learning facilities include a learning resource center and a museum. The 162-acre campus is in an urban area 60 miles west of Shreveport, Louisiana, and 120 miles east of the Dallas/Fort Worth metroplex. Including any residence halls, there are 55 buildings.

Student Life: 50% of undergraduates are from out of state, mostly the West. Others are from 49 states and 19 foreign countries. 57% are from public schools. 69% are white; 19% African American. The average age of freshmen is 18; all undergraduates, 20.

Housing: 863 students can be accommodated in college housing, which includes single-sex dormitories, on-campus apartments, and married-student housing. On-campus housing is guaranteed for all 4 years. 74% of students live on campus; of those, 70% remain on campus on weekends. Alcohol is not permitted. All students may keep cars.

Activities: There are no fraternities or sororities. There are 22 groups on campus, including choir, chorale, chorus, computers, drama, honors, international, jazz band, newspaper, pep band, photography, political, professional, religious, social, social service, student government, and yearbook. Popular campus events include Spiritual Emphasis Week, Longview Blitz, and Longview Symphony.

Sports: There are 6 intercollegiate sports for men and 7 for women, and 16 intramural sports for men and 16 for women. Facilities include soccer, softball, baseball, and intramural fields, a 1000-seat gym, a 1000-seat arena/auditorium, 8 tennis courts, 3 racquetball courts, a weight room, a Nautilus room, a swimming pool, and an indoor running track.

Disabled Students: 90% of the campus is accessible. Wheelchair ramps, elevators, special parking, specially equipped rest rooms, special class scheduling, lowered drinking fountains, lowered telephones, special housing, and automated doors are available.

Services: Counseling and information services are available, as is tutoring in most subjects. There is remedial math and writing.

Campus Safety and Security: Measures include 24-hour foot and vehicle patrol, self-defense education, security escort services, and informal discussions. There are pamphlets/posters/films and lighted pathways/sidewalks.

Programs of Study: LeTourneau confers B.A., B.S., and B.B.A. degrees. Associate and master's degrees are also awarded. Bachelor's degrees are awarded in BIOLOGICAL SCIENCE (biology/biological science), BUSINESS (accounting, business administration and management, management information systems, marketing management, and marketing/retailing/merchandising), COMMUNICATIONS AND THE ARTS (English), COMPUTER AND PHYSICAL SCIENCE (chemistry, computer mathematics, computer science, and mathematics), EDUCATION (business, elementary, physical, science, and secondary), ENGINEERING AND ENVIRONMENTAL DESIGN (aeronautical science, aeronautical technology, computer engineering, computer technology, electrical/electronics engineering, engineering, engineering technology, industrial administration/management, mechanical engineering, and welding engineering), HEALTH PROFESSIONS (health, premedicine, and preveterinary science), SOCIAL SCIENCE (biblical studies, history, interdisciplinary studies, prelaw, psychology, and public administration). Engineering, computer science, and math are the strongest academically. Engineering, aeronautical science, and business are the largest.

Required: All students must fulfill general curricula requirements, including 12 hours of biblical studies, 9 of English, 3 each of lab science, math, history, and humanities and social science, as well as 2 of phys ed and 1 of introduction to the university. A minimum of 126 semester credit hours, including at least 24 in the major, with a minimum GPA of 2.0 is required to graduate.

Special: Le Tourneau offers co-op programs in engineering, business, accounting, computer science, biology, design technology, and others, internships through business and liberal arts programs, an American studies program with the Council for Christian Colleges and Universities, credit for experience, and study abroad in 7 countries. There is a freshman honors program.

Faculty/Classroom: 82% of faculty are male; 18%, female. 96% teach undergraduates and 20% both teach and do research. No introductory courses are taught by graduate students. The average class size in an introductory lecture is 24; in a laboratory, 16; and in a regular course, 18.

Admissions: I

Requirements: The SAT or ACT is required. Applicants must be graduates of an accredited secondary school or have the GED. They should have completed 16 academic credits, including 4 in English, 3 each in math, social studies, and natural science, and 1 in computer science. An essay is required. LeTourneau requires applicants to be in the upper 50% of their class. A GPA of 2.5 is required. AP and CLEP credits are accepted. Important factors in the admissions decision are advanced placement or honor courses, personality/intangible qualities, and extracurricular activities record.

Procedure: Freshmen are admitted to all sessions. Entrance exams should be taken by the fall of the senior year. There is a deferred admissions plan. Check with school for current application deadlines and fee. Notification is sent on a rolling basis. Applications are accepted on-line.

Transfer: 99 transfer students enrolled in a recent year. Applicants with at least 26 semester hours must have a minimum 2.0 GPA. Other students must satisfy freshman entrance requirements. 36 of 126 credits required for the bachelor's degree must be completed at LeTourneau.

Visiting: There are regularly scheduled orientations for prospective students. Visits are individualized and may include touring the school, attending classes, special events, or chapel, meeting with faculty and financial aid personnel, and staying in a dorm. There are guides for informal visits and visitors may sit in on classes and stay overnight. To schedule a visit, contact the Visitor Coordinator at (903) 233-3454.

Financial Aid: In a recent year, 80% of all full-time freshmen and 78% of continuing full-time students received some form of financial aid. 73% of full-time freshmen and 72% of continuing full-time students received need-based aid. The average freshman award was $12,728. Need-based scholarships or need-based grants averaged $5724; need-based self-help aid (loans and jobs) averaged $4454; and other non-need-based awards and non-need-based scholarships averaged $3964. The average financial indebtedness of the recent year's graduate was $20,055. LeTourneau is a member of CSS. The FAFSA is required. Check with the school for current deadlines.

International Students: In a recent year,35 international students enrolled. The school actively recruits these students. Satisfactory scores are required on the written TOEFL and the SAT or the ACT.

Computers: All students may access the system. There are no time limits and no fees.

Graduates: In a recent year , 719 bachelor's degrees were awarded. The most popular majors were engineering/engineering technologies (54%), business/marketing (14%), and education (7%). In an average class, 32% graduate in 4 years or less, 50% graduate in 5 years or less, and 52% graduate in 6 years or less. Of a recent graduating class, 5% were enrolled in graduate school within 6 months of graduation and 94% were employed.

Admissions Contact: James Townsend, Director of Admissions. A video is available. E-mail: *admissions@letu.edu* Web: *www.letu.edu*

LUBBOCK CHRISTIAN UNIVERSITY B-2
Lubbock, TX 79407

(806) 720-7151
(800) 933-7601; Fax: (806) 720-7255

Full-time: 601 men, 783 women	Faculty: 81; IIB, --$
Part-time: 196 men, 255 women	Ph.D.s: 59%
Graduate: 117 men, 127 women	Student/Faculty: 17 to 1
Year: semesters, summer session	Tuition: $12,710
Application Deadline: open	Room & Board: $4250

Freshman Class: 912 applied, 671 accepted, 320 enrolled
SAT Verbal/Math: 490/490*   ACT: 20   COMPETITIVE

Lubbock Christian University, founded in 1957 in affiliation with the Churches of Christ, offers undergraduate degrees in liberal arts and professional studies, and graduate degrees in biblical studies and education, behavioral sciences, and nursing. There are 3 undergraduate and 2 graduate schools. In addition to regional accreditation, LCU has baccalaureate program accreditation with CSWE and NLN. The library contains 117,508 volumes, 103,812 microform items, and 566 audio/video tapes/CDs/DVDs, and subscribes to 543 periodicals including electronic. Computerized library services include the card catalog, interlibrary loans, database searching, and Internet access. Special learning facilities include a learning resource center and art gallery. The 65-acre campus is in a suburban area 350 miles from Dallas and 325 miles from Albuquerque. Including any residence halls, there are 22 buildings.

Student Life: 90% of undergraduates are from Texas. Others are from 27 states, 17 foreign countries, and Canada. 78% are white; 14% Hispanic. 87% are Protestant; 7% Catholic. The average age of freshmen

is 18; all undergraduates, 25. 41% do not continue beyond their first year; 31% remain to graduate.

Housing: 612 students can be accommodated in college housing, which includes single-sex dorms, on-campus apartments, and married-student housing. On-campus housing is guaranteed for the freshman year only and is available on a first-come, first-served basis. 69% of students commute. Alcohol is not permitted. All students may keep cars.

Activities: There are 32 groups on campus, including cheerleading, chorus, drama, ethnic, honors, jazz band, newspaper, professional, religious, social, social service, student government, and yearbook. Popular campus events include Master Follies, Family Weekend, and Spiritual Renewal Week.

Sports: There are 3 intercollegiate sports for men and 3 for women, and 7 intramural sports for men and 8 for women. Facilities include the Rip Griffin Center, which serves as the home for the university's intercollegiate teams. The field house is the center for intramural and phys ed activities with an indoor track, badminton, volleyball, and basketball courts, and a fitness center.

Disabled Students: Wheelchair ramps, elevators, special parking, and specially equipped rest rooms are available.

Services: Counseling and information services are available, as is tutoring in every subject. There is a reader service for the blind, and remedial math, reading, and writing.

Campus Safety and Security: Measures include 24-hour foot and vehicle patrol and lighted pathways/sidewalks.

Programs of Study: LCU confers B.A., B.S., B.B.A., B.S.I.S., B.S.N., and B.S.W. degrees. Associate and master's degrees are also awarded. Bachelor's degrees are awarded in AGRICULTURE (agricultural business management, and animal science), BIOLOGICAL SCIENCE (biology/biological science), BUSINESS (accounting, banking and finance, business administration and management, organizational leadership and management, and sports management), COMMUNICATIONS AND THE ARTS (communications and music), COMPUTER AND PHYSICAL SCIENCE (chemistry, information sciences and systems, and mathematics), EDUCATION (art, business, early childhood, elementary, middle school, music, physical, science, and secondary), ENGINEERING AND ENVIRONMENTAL DESIGN (engineering), HEALTH PROFESSIONS (exercise science, medical technology, and nursing), SOCIAL SCIENCE (biblical studies, criminal justice, family/consumer studies, humanities, ministries, missions, physical fitness/movement, psychology, social work, and youth ministry). Education, business administration, and social work are the strongest academically. Organizational management, early childhood/elementary education, and humanities are the largest.

Required: To graduate, students must complete 126 credit hours, including at least 42 in upper-division courses, 30 to 42 in the major, and 32 in residence after achieving senior status, with a minimum GPA of 2.25 overall and 2.5 in the major. All students must fulfill general education and biblical studies course requirements, including courses in English, math, history, science, communication, computer science, and kinesiology. The core curriculum totals 33 hours.

Special: LCU offers co-op programs in engineering, medical technology, and criminal justice, internships in several fields, and cross-registration with Texas Tech University and other regional schools. A general studies degree, nondegree study, and pass/fail options are also available. A 3-2 engineering degree with Texas Tech University is offered. There are 3 national honor societies, a freshman honors program, and 1 departmental honors program.

Faculty/Classroom: 59% of faculty are male; 41%, female. All teach undergraduates. No introductory courses are taught by graduate students. The average class size in an introductory lecture is 20; in a laboratory, 15; and in a regular course, 16.

Admissions: 74% of the 2005-2006 applicants were accepted. The SAT scores for the 2005-2006 freshman class were: Verbal--52% below 500, 31% between 500 and 599, 14% between 600 and 700, and 3% above 700; Math--50% below 500, 34% between 500 and 599, 15% between 600 and 700, and 1% above 700. The ACT scores were 52% below 21, 18% between 21 and 23, 19% between 24 and 26, 7% between 27 and 28, and 4% above 28. 34% of the current freshmen were in the top fifth of their class; 61% were in the top two fifths. 1 freshman graduated first in their class.

Requirements: The SAT or ACT is required. In addition, applicants must be graduates of an accredited secondary school or have a GED certificate. Unconditional admission is granted to freshmen who score 18 or higher on the ACT or who achieve a comparable score on the SAT, and who meet all other admission requirements. AP and CLEP credits are accepted. Important factors in the admissions decision are personality/intangible qualities, parents or siblings attending the school, and geographic diversity.

Procedure: Freshmen are admitted fall, spring, and summer. Entrance exams should be taken before registration. There is a deferred admissions plan. Application deadlines are open. Notification is sent on a rolling basis. The application fee is $25. Applications are accepted on-line.

Transfer: 436 transfer students enrolled in 2004-2005. Transfer students with fewer than 16 hours of college credit must meet freshman admission requirements. All transfers must submit an official transcript from previously attended colleges or universities and be in good academic standing. Only courses with a grade of C or above are transferred from another institution. 32 of 126 credits required for the bachelor's degree must be completed at LCU.

Visiting: There are regularly scheduled orientations for prospective students. There are guides for informal visits and visitors may sit in on classes and stay overnight. To schedule a visit, contact Admissions at (806) 720-7151 or *admissions@lcu.edu*.

Financial Aid: In 2005-2006, 96% of all full-time freshmen and 92% of continuing full-time students received some form of financial aid. 78% of full-time freshmen and 73% of continuing full-time students received need-based aid. The average freshman award was $10,417. Need-based scholarships or need-based grants averaged $6796; need-based self-help aid (loans and jobs) averaged $4319; non-need-based athletic scholarships averaged $5705; and other non-need-based awards and non-need-based scholarships averaged $10,685. 15% of undergraduates work part time. Average annual earnings from campus work are $905. The average financial indebtedness of the 2005 graduate was $22,192. The FAFSA and the college's own financial statement are required. The priority date for freshman financial aid applications for fall entry is June 1.

International Students: There are 15 international students enrolled. They must score a satisfactory score on the written TOEFL on the electronic version or the MELAB, and must also take the SAT or the ACT, scoring 18 on the ACT.

Computers: Students may access the network from dorm rooms through Ethernet connection although there is no wireless access available in dorms. If a student has wireless, they may access the network throughout campus. Labs are available in the library as well as every educational building on campus. All students may access the system. There are no time limits. The fee is $315.

Graduates: From July 1, 2004 to June 30, 2005, 387 bachelor's degrees were awarded. The most popular majors were business (27%), education (19%), and behavioral sciences (12%). In an average class, 2% graduate in 3 years or less, 21% graduate in 4 years or less, 35% graduate in 5 years or less, and 41% graduate in 6 years or less.

Admissions Contact: Brad Rogers, Director of Admissions. A video is available. E-mail: *brad.rogers@lcu.edu* Web: *www.lcu.edu*

MCMURRY UNIVERSITY | C-2

Abilene, TX 79697

(325) 793-4700
(800) 460-2392; Fax: (325) 793-4718

Full-time: 600 men, 600 women	**Faculty:** 78
Part-time: 120 men, 100 women	**Ph.D.s:** 80%
Graduate: none	**Student/Faculty:** 15 to 1
Year: semesters, summer session	**Tuition:** $13,00
Application Deadline: see profile	**Room & Board:** $5100
Freshman Class: n/av	
SAT or ACT: required	**LESS COMPETITIVE**

McMurry University, chartered in 1923, is a private liberal arts institution affiliated with the United Methodist Church. There are 4 undergraduate schools. Figures in the above capsule and in this profile are approximate. The library contains 153,118 volumes, 4437 microform items, and 1692 audio/video tapes/CDs/DVDs, and subscribes to 503 periodicals including electronic. Computerized library services include the card catalog, interlibrary loans, and database searching. Special learning facilities include a learning resource center, art gallery, and several special book collections, including the McWhiney collection of Civil War-era books. The 41-acre campus is in an urban area 180 miles west of Dallas. Including any residence halls, there are 25 buildings.

Student Life: 95% of undergraduates are from Texas. Others are from 17 states and 7 foreign countries. 74% are white; 12% Hispanic. 67% are Protestant; 21% claim no religious affiliation; 12% Catholic. The average age of freshmen is 18; all undergraduates, 23. 38% do not continue beyond their first year; 40% remain to graduate.

Housing: 667 students can be accommodated in college housing, which includes single-sex dormitories and on-campus apartments. On-campus housing is guaranteed for all 4 years and is available on a first-come, first-served basis. 60% of students commute. Alcohol is not permitted. All students may keep cars.

Activities: 10% of men belong to 6 local fraternities; 10% of women belong to 6 local sororities. There are 46 groups on campus, including art, band, cheerleading, choir, chorale, computers, drama, ethnic, honors, jazz band, literary magazine, marching band, musical theater, newspaper, political, professional, religious, social, social service, student government, and yearbook. Popular campus events include Parents Weekend, Sing Song, and Big Event.

Sports: There are 9 intercollegiate sports for men and 8 for women, and 15 intramural sports for men and 15 for women. Facilities include a 4500-seat track and football stadium, a 2200-seat gym, a 1500-seat auditorium, an intramural gym, a swimming pool and diving area, 2 racquetball courts, basketball, volleyball, and badminton courts, a soccer field, and a 875-seat baseball stadium.

Disabled Students: 70% of the campus is accessible. Wheelchair ramps, elevators, special parking, specially equipped rest rooms, special class scheduling, and special housing are available.

Services: Counseling and information services are available, as is tutoring in most subjects. There is remedial math, reading, and writing.

Campus Safety and Security: Measures include 24-hour foot and vehicle patrol and lighted pathways/sidewalks.

Programs of Study: McMurry confers B.A., B.S., B.B.A., B.F.A., B.Mus., B.Mus.Ed., B.S. Multidisciplinary Studies, and B.S.N. degrees. Bachelor's degrees are awarded in BIOLOGICAL SCIENCE (biochemistry and biology/biological science), BUSINESS (accounting, banking and finance, business administration and management, business economics, management information systems, management science, and marketing/retailing/merchandising), COMMUNICATIONS AND THE ARTS (art, ceramic art and design, communications, dramatic arts, English, French, German, graphic design, multimedia, music, music performance, painting, piano/organ, Spanish, and voice), COMPUTER AND PHYSICAL SCIENCE (chemistry, computer science, information sciences and systems, mathematics, natural sciences, and physics), EDUCATION (art, athletic training, bilingual/bicultural, elementary, middle school, music, physical, and secondary), ENGINEERING AND ENVIRONMENTAL DESIGN (environmental science), HEALTH PROFESSIONS (nursing), SOCIAL SCIENCE (economics, history, interdisciplinary studies, philosophy, political science/government, psychology, religion, and sociology). Education, biology, and chemistry are the strongest academically. Education, business, and biology are the largest.

Required: Students must complete 126 semester hours, including 27 in the major, with a GPA of at least 2.0. Distribution requirements vary with the degree but include courses in English, ethics, humanities, fine arts, science, math, social science, religion, political science, sociology, history, foreign language, and health fitness. A 9-hour freshman core curriculum focuses on ethics; sophmore and junior year the focus is humanities.

Special: McMurry offers internships, co-op programs, and cross-registration with Abilene Christian and Hardin-Simmons Universities. There are work-study programs with the university and area businesses for seniors. B.A.-B.S. degrees in business administration, accounting, banking and finance, biology, chemistry, multidisciplinary studies, nursing, and computer science are available. A 3-2 engineering degree with Texas Tech University is offered, as is a Servant Leadership program, designed to instill principles of leadership in the betterment of community and society. There are 16 national honor societies, a freshman honors program, and 22 departmental honors programs.

Faculty/Classroom: 74% of faculty are male; 26%, female. All teach undergraduates and 64% do research. The average class size in an introductory lecture is 27; in a laboratory, 14; and in a regular course, 17.

Requirements: A satisfactory score on the SAT or ACT is required. Those meeting the minimum score must rank in the top 40% of their high school class. Applicants need 16 academic credits, including 4 units of English, 3 each in math and social studies, and 2 each in foreign language and science. An interview is recommended. The GED is accepted with an average score of 55. A GPA of 2.0 is required. AP and CLEP credits are accepted.

Procedure: Freshmen are admitted to all sessions. Entrance exams should be taken in the junior year. There is a deferred admissions plan. Check with the school for current application deadllines and fee. Notification is sent on a rolling basis. Applications are accepted on-line.

Transfer: 155 transfer students enrolled in a recent year. All transfer students must have a GPA of at least 2.0. Those with fewer than 15 credit hours must submit high school transcripts and SAT or ACT scores; those with 15 to 23 hours need only school transcripts. 30 of 126 credits required for the bachelor's degree must be completed at McMurry.

Visiting: There are regularly scheduled orientations for prospective students. There are guides for informal visits and visitors may sit in on classes and stay overnight. To schedule a visit, contact the Admissions Office at *admissions@mcm.edu*.

Financial Aid: In a recent year, 98% of all full-time freshmen and 99% of continuing full-time students received some form of financial aid. 82% of full-time freshmen and 81% of continuing full-time students received need-based aid. The average freshman award was $15,853. Need-based scholarships or need-based grants averaged $7390 ($14,480 maximum); need-based self-help aid (loans and jobs) averaged $2892 ($5595 maximum); and other non-need-based awards and non-need-based scholarships averaged $8487 ($21,925 maximum). 57% of undergraduates work part time. Average annual earnings from campus work are $987. The average financial indebtedness of the recent year's graduate was $15,125. The FAFSA and the college's own financial statement are required. Check with the school for current deadlines.

International Students: In a recent year, there were 7 international students enrolled. The school actively recruits these students. Satisfactory scores are required on the written TOEFL and the SAT or the ACT.

Computers: All students may access the system at any time. There are no time limits and no fees.

Graduates: In a recent year, 228 bachelor's degrees were awarded. The most popular majors were education (29%), business (24%), and biology (6%). In an average class, 1% graduate in 3 years or less, 25% graduate in 4 years or less, 37% graduate in 5 years or less, and 40% graduate in 6 years or less. 10 companies recruited on campus in a recent year. In a recent graduating class, 10% were enrolled in graduate school within 6 months of graduation and 80% were employed.

Admissions Contact: Amy Weyant, Director of Admissions.
E-mail: *weyanta@mcmurryadjm.mcm.edu* Web: *http://www.mcm.edu*

MIDWESTERN STATE UNIVERSITY   D-2
Wichita Falls, TX 76308-2099   (940) 397-4334
                                   (800) 842-1922; Fax: (940) 397-4672

Full-time: 1732 men, 2277 women	Faculty: IIA, --$
Part-time: 626 men, 902 women	Ph.D.s: 70%
Graduate: 210 men, 369 women	Student/Faculty: n/av
Year: semesters, summer session	Tuition: $4461 ($12,741)
Application Deadline: August 7	Room & Board: $4920
Freshman Class: 1561 applied, 1291 accepted, 706 enrolled	
SAT Verbal/Math: 480/480*	LESS COMPETITIVE

Midwestern State University, founded in 1922, is a public liberal arts institution offering courses in business administration, education, fine arts, health sciences, humanities, math and science, political science and public administration, and social and behavioral sciences. There are 6 undergraduate and 5 graduate schools. In addition to regional accreditation, MSU has baccalaureate program accreditation with ABET, ACBSP, ADA, NASM, NCATE, and NLN. The library contains 241,000 volumes, 158,000 microform items, and 6757 audio/video tapes/CDs/DVDs, and subscribes to 1100 periodicals including electronic. Computerized library services include the card catalog, interlibrary loans, and database searching. Special learning facilities include an art gallery, planetarium, TV station, greenhouse, and TTVN studio. The 172-acre campus is in an urban area 135 miles northwest of Dallas. Including any residence halls, there are 31 buildings.

Student Life: 95% of undergraduates are from Texas. Others are from 49 states, 40 foreign countries, and Canada. 67% are white; 13% African American; 11% foreign nationals. The average age of freshmen is 19; all undergraduates, 24. 40% do not continue beyond their first year; 31% remain to graduate.

Housing: 733 students can be accommodated in college housing, which includes single-sex and coed dormitories, on-campus apartments, off-campus apartments, and married-student housing. In addition, there are honors houses and a Biology House. On-campus housing is guaranteed for the freshman year only and is available on a first-come, first-served basis. Priority is given to out-of-town students. 80% of students commute. Alcohol is not permitted. All students may keep cars.

Activities: 13% of men belong to 6 national fraternities; 11% of women belong to 6 national sororities. There are 102 groups on campus, including art, band, cheerleading, choir, chorale, chorus, computers, dance, drama, environmental, ethnic, honors, international, jazz band, literary magazine, marching band, newspaper, pep band, political, professional, religious, social, social service, student government, symphony, TV, and yearbook. Popular campus events include Family Day, Spirit Days, and College Day Preview.

Sports: There are 4 intercollegiate sports for men and 4 for women, and 18 intramural sports for men and 21 for women. Facilities include a 5000-seat gym, a soccer stadium, tennis courts, an indoor swimming pool, a sand volleyball court, and a walking track.

Disabled Students: 99% of the campus is accessible. Wheelchair ramps, elevators, special parking, specially equipped rest rooms, special class scheduling, lowered drinking fountains, lowered telephones, and special housing are available.

Services: Counseling and information services are available, as is tutoring in some subjects, including algebra, sciences, and history. There is a reader service for the blind, and remedial math, reading, and writing.

Campus Safety and Security: Measures include 24-hour foot and vehicle patrol, self-defense education, informal discussions, and pamphlets/posters/films. There are lighted pathways/sidewalks and seminars on safety and living on campus.

Programs of Study: MSU confers B.A., B.S., B.A.A.S., B.B.A., B.F.A., B.M., B.S.C.J., B.S.D.H., B.S.I.S., B.S.M.T., B.S.N., B.S.R.C., B.S.R.S., and B.S.W. degrees. Associate and master's degrees are also awarded. Bachelor's degrees are awarded in BIOLOGICAL SCIENCE (biology/biological science), BUSINESS (accounting, banking and finance, business administration and management, business economics, international economics, management science, and marketing/retailing/merchandising), COMMUNICATIONS AND THE ARTS (communications, dramatic arts, English, fine arts, music, and Spanish), COMPUTER AND PHYSICAL SCIENCE (chemical technology, chemistry, computer science, geology, information sciences and systems, and mathematics), EDUCATION (music and physical), ENGINEERING AND ENVIRONMENTAL DESIGN (engineering technology, environmental science, manufacturing engineering, and preengineering), HEALTH PROFESSIONS (dental hygiene, health care administration, health science, medical laboratory technology, nursing, predentistry, premedicine, prephar-

macy, preveterinary science, radiological science, and respiratory therapy), SOCIAL SCIENCE (criminal justice, economics, history, humanities, interdisciplinary studies, political science/government, prelaw, psychology, social work, and sociology). Business and nursing are the largest.

Required: All students must earn a minimum GPA of 2.0 while taking 120 semester hours, 24 in the major. Distribution requirements include 6 hours from a list of humanities classes, 6 from social science, 7 to 10 hours from natural science, and additional phys ed requirements.

Special: An exchange program with the Monterrey Institute of Technology, internships with local firms and agencies, and study abroad in London are available. Dual majors, co-op programs in all majors, a general studies degree, credit for military experience, and nondegree study up to 12 hours are also offered. There are 23 national honor societies and a freshman honors program.

Faculty/Classroom: 53% of faculty are male; 47%, female. All teach undergraduates. Graduate students teach 10% of introductory courses. The average class size in an introductory lecture is 25; in a laboratory, 20; and in a regular course, 25.

Admissions: 83% of the 2005-2006 applicants were accepted. The SAT scores for the 2005-2006 freshman class were: Verbal--57% below 500, 35% between 500 and 599, 7% between 600 and 700, and 1% above 700; Math--56% below 500, 35% between 500 and 599, and 9% between 600 and 700. The ACT scores were 60% below 21, 26% between 21 and 23, 10% between 24 and 26, 3% between 27 and 28, and 2% above 28. 29% of the current freshmen were in the top fifth of their class; 60% were in the top two fifths.

Requirements: The SAT or ACT is required. In addition, the minimum required composite score on the SAT or ACT is dependent on class rank. For students in the top quarter of the class, there is no minimum requirement. High school credits should include 4 years of English, 3 years of math, 2 years of science, and 6 units of electives. The GED is accepted. AP and CLEP credits are accepted.

Procedure: Freshmen are admitted to all sessions. Entrance exams should be taken before applying for admission. There is an early action and a rolling admissioins plan. Applications should be filed by August 7 for fall entry, December 15 for spring entry, and May 15 for summer entry. Notification is sent on a rolling basis beginning September 1. Applications are accepted on-line. The fall 2005 application fee was $25.

Transfer: 586 transfer students enrolled in the Fall 2005. Transfer students with fewer than 18 semester hours must meet beginning freshman criteria. A minimum GPA of a 2.0, college transcripts, and a statement of good standing from prior institutions are required. 31 of 120 credits required for the bachelor's degree must be completed at MSU.

Visiting: There are regularly scheduled orientations for prospective students, consisting of a college day preview each February, which introduces high school juniors, seniors, and their parents to the campus and faculty. There are also daily tours. There are guides for informal visits and visitors may sit in on classes and stay overnight. To schedule a visit, contact MSU Admissions.

Financial Aid: In 2005-2006, 47% of all full-time freshmen and 46% of continuing full-time students received some form of financial aid. At least 42% of full-time freshmen and at least 40% of continuing full-time students received need-based aid. The average freshman award was $6147. Need-based scholarships or need-based grants averaged $4387; need-based self-help aid (loans and jobs) averaged $2581; non-need-based athletic scholarships averaged $1909; and other non-need-based awards and non-need-based scholarships averaged $1460. 8% of undergraduates work part time. Average annual earnings from campus work are $3710. MSU is a member of CSS. The FAFSA and the college's own financial statement are required. The priority date for freshman financial aid applications for fall entry is May 1.

International Students: The school actively recruits these students. They must score satisfactorily on the written TOEFL and also take the SAT or the ACT.

Computers: All students may access the system. There are no time limits and no fees.

Graduates: From July 1, 2004 to June 30, 2005, 934 bachelor's degrees were awarded. The most popular majors were business/marketing (22%) and health professions and related sciences (13%). In an average class, 9% graduate in 4 years or less, 24% graduate in 5 years or less, and 31% graduate in 6 years or less.

Admissions Contact: Barbara Ramos Merkle, Director of Admissions.
E-mail: *admissions@mwsu.edu* Web: *www.mwsu.edu*

NORTHWOOD UNIVERSITY

D-2

Cedar Hill, TX 75104

(972) 293-5400
(800) 927-9663; Fax: (972) 291-3824

Full-time: 320 men, 330 women	**Faculty:** 23
Part-time: 10 men, 1 woman	**Ph.D.s:** 13%
Graduate: none	**Student/Faculty:** 28 to 1
Year: quarters, summer session	**Tuition:** $14,000
Application Deadline: see profile	**Room & Board:** $6200
Freshman Class: n/av	
SATor ACT required	LESS COMPETITIVE

Northwood University, founded in 1959 and whose Texas campus opened in 1966, is a private institution offering undergraduate degrees in business administration. Campuses are located in Florida, Michigan, and Texas. Figures in the above capsule and in this profile are approximate. The library contains 11,000 volumes and 350 audio/video tapes/CDs/DVDs, and subscribes to 160 periodicals including electronic. Computerized library services include the card catalog, interlibrary loans, database searching, and Internet access. Special learning facilities include a learning resource center and art gallery. The 360-acre campus is in a suburban area 18 miles southwest of Dallas. Including any residence halls, there are 18 buildings.

Student Life: 92% of undergraduates are from Texas. Others are from 17 states, 8 foreign countries, and Canada. 90% are from public schools. 43% are white; 28% Hispanic; 20% African American. The average age of freshmen is 19; all undergraduates, 21. 39% do not continue beyond their first year; 55% remain to graduate.

Housing: 260 students can be accommodated in college housing, which includes single-sex dormitories and on-campus apartments. On-campus housing is guaranteed for the freshman year only and is available on a first-come, first-served basis. 73% of students commute. All students may keep cars.

Activities: There are no fraternities or sororities. There are 17 groups on campus, including computers, dance, debate, ethnic, forensics, honors, international, literary magazine, professional, religious, social, social service, and student government. Popular campus events include Sanity Inn (talent show) and Spring Formal.

Sports: There are 5 intercollegiate sports for men and 5 for women, and 6 intramural sports for men and 5 for women. Facilities include an outdoor swimming pool, tennis court, baseball/softball fields, and jogging trails, along with a state recreational area adjacent to the campus.

Disabled Students: 75% of the campus is accessible. Wheelchair ramps, special parking, specially equipped rest rooms, special class scheduling, lowered drinking fountains, and lowered telephones are available.

Services: Counseling and information services are available, as is tutoring in most subjects. There is a reader service for the blind, and remedial math, reading, and writing. tutoring for any subject at student's request.

Campus Safety and Security: Measures include 24-hour foot and vehicle patrol, informal discussions, pamphlets/posters/films, and lighted pathways/sidewalks.

Programs of Study: Northwood confers the B.B.A. degree. Associate degrees are also awarded. Bachelor's degrees are awarded in BUSINESS (accounting, apparel and accessories marketing, banking and finance, business administration and management, court reporting, entrepreneurial studies, hotel/motel and restaurant management, international business management, management information systems, marketing management, sports management, and transportation and travel marketing), COMMUNICATIONS AND THE ARTS (advertising), COMPUTER AND PHYSICAL SCIENCE (computer management). Management, international business, and entertainment, sport, and promotion management are the largest.

Required: To graduate, all students must complete at least 180 term credit hours, including 36 in the major, with a minimum GPA of 2.0. Students must complete the general studies core curriculum, 6 credits of computer science management, and 2 credits of executive fitness. Internships for 1 to 6 credits are required in some majors.

Special: Study abroad in 20 countries, accelerated degree programs, and dual majors and externships in most majors are offered. There is a freshman honors program.

Faculty/Classroom: 61% of faculty are male; 39%, female. All teach undergraduates. The average class size in an introductory lecture is 22; in a laboratory, 15; and in a regular course, 19.

Requirements: The SAT or ACT is required. In addition, applicants must be graduates of an accredited secondary school with a 2.0 GPA or have a GED certificate. An interview and essay are recommended. A GPA of 2.0 is required. AP and CLEP credits are accepted. Important factors in the admissions decision are advanced placement or honor courses, evidence of special talent, and leadership record.

Procedure: Freshmen are admitted to all sessions. There are early admissions and deferred admissions plans. Check with the school for current application deadlines and fee. Notification is sent on a rolling basis. Applications are accepted on-line.

Transfer: 76 transfer students enrolled in a recent year. Applicants must have earned a minimum of 12 credit hours and a 2.0 GPA. They must submit official transcripts from all previous colleges attended and the final high school transcript. 45 of 180 credits required for the bachelor's degree must be completed at Northwood.

Visiting: There are regularly scheduled orientations for prospective students. There are guides for informal visits and visitors may sit in on classes and stay overnight. To schedule a visit, contact the Admissions Office at txadmit@northwood.edu.

Financial Aid: In a recent year, 99% of all full-time students received some form of financial aid. 76% of full-time freshmen and 70% of continuing full-time students received need-based aid. The average freshman award was $13,756. Need-based scholarships or need-based grants averaged $9211 ($13,485 maximum); need-based self-help aid (loans and jobs) averaged $4230 ($10,625 maximum); non-need-based athletic scholarships averaged $5715 ($15,702 maximum); and other non-need-based awards and non-need-based scholarships averaged $6830 ($23,711 maximum). 11% of undergraduates work part time. Average annual earnings from campus work are $1911. The average financial indebtedness of the recent year's graduate was $13,101. The FAFSA and are required. Check with the school for current deadlines.

International Students: In a recent year, there were 33 international students enrolled. The school actively recruits these students. A satisfactory score is required on the written TOEFL.

Computers: All students may access the system any time. There are no time limits and no fees.

Graduates: In a recent year, 115 bachelor's degrees were awarded. The most popular majors were marketing/management (23%), international business (16%), and banking/finance (12%). In an average class, 41% graduate in 4 years or less, and 55% graduate in 6 years or less.

Admissions Contact: James R. Hickerson, Admissions Director. A video is available. E-mail: txadmit@northwood.edu
Web: www.northwood.edu

OUR LADY OF THE LAKE UNIVERSITY OF SAN ANTONIO

D-4

San Antonio, TX 78207-4689

(210) 434-6711, ext. 314
(800) 436-6558; Fax: (210) 431-4036

Full-time: 300 men, 942 women	**Faculty:** IIA, --$
Part-time: 131 men, 419 women	**Ph.D.s:** n/av
Graduate: 296 men, 784 women	**Student/Faculty:** n/av
Year: semesters, summer session	**Tuition:** $17,048
Application Deadline: open	**Room & Board:** $5382
Freshman Class: n/av	
SAT Verbal/Math: 460/450*	**ACT:** 19 LESS COMPETITIVE

Our Lady of the Lake, founded as a private Catholic institution in 1895 by the Sisters of Divine Providence, offers programs in the arts and sciences, business, education, and social service. There are 4 undergraduate and 4 graduate schools. In addition to regional accreditation, The Lake has baccalaureate program accreditation with ASLA and CSWE. The library contains 163,217 microform items and 8891 audio/video tapes/CDs/DVDs, and subscribes to 557 periodicals including electronic. Computerized library services include interlibrary loans, database searching, Internet access, and laptop Internet portals. Special learning facilities include a learning resource center, a demonstration school (early childhood to grade 8), and a communication/learning disorders center. The 52-acre campus is in an urban area about 4 miles west of downtown San Antonio. Including any residence halls, there are 23 buildings.

Student Life: 99% of undergraduates are from Texas. Others are from 17 states and 7 foreign countries. 61% are Hispanic; 19% white. 62% claim no religious affiliation; 24% are Catholic; 12% Protestant. The average age of freshmen is 18; all undergraduates, 27. 38% do not continue beyond their first year; 35% remain to graduate.

Housing: 639 students can be accommodated in college housing, which includes coed dorms. In addition, there are honors houses, and there is quiet and alsohol-drug-and smoke-free housing. On-campus housing is guaranteed for all 4 years. 73% of students commute. All students may keep cars.

Activities: There are no fraternities or sororities. There are 35 groups on campus, including art, cheerleading, choir, chorale, chorus, computers, dance, drama, ethnic, honors, newspaper, orchestra, political, professional, radio and TV, religious, social, social service, student government, and symphony. Popular campus events include Spirit Week.

Sports: There are 9 intramural sports for men and 9 for women. Facilities include playing fields, tennis courts, indoor and outdoor pools, and a gym equipped for weight lifting, aerobics, and other indoor sports.

Disabled Students: 90% of the campus is accessible. Wheelchair ramps, elevators, special parking, specially equipped rest rooms, special class scheduling, lowered drinking fountains, lowered telephones, and special housing are available.

Services: Counseling and information services are available, as is tutoring in some subjects. There is a reader service for the blind, and remedial math, reading, and writing.

Campus Safety and Security: Measures include 24-hour foot and vehicle patrol, pamphlets/posters/films, and lighted pathways/sidewalks.

Programs of Study: The Lake confers B.A., B.S., B.A.S., B.B.A., and B.S.W. degrees. Master's and doctoral degrees are also awarded. Bachelor's degrees are awarded in BIOLOGICAL SCIENCE (biology/biological science), BUSINESS (accounting, business administration and management, human resources, management information systems, marketing management, and personnel management), COMMUNICATIONS AND THE ARTS (art, communications, dramatic arts, English, fine arts, music, and Spanish), COMPUTER AND PHYSICAL SCIENCE (chemistry, information sciences and systems, mathematics, and natural sciences), EDUCATION (art, early childhood, and special), HEALTH PROFESSIONS (speech pathology/audiology), SOCIAL SCIENCE (behavioral science, history, liberal arts/general studies, Mexican-American/Chicano studies, philosophy, political science/government, psychology, religion, social studies, social work, and sociology). Biology and chemistry are the strongest academically. Business is the largest.

Required: A general education requirement includes competencies in English, math, the natural, social, and behavioral sciences, religion, philosophy, literature, art, history, and phys ed. Other graduation requirements are a minimum 2.0 GPA, 128 credit hours, requirements specific to the major, and satisfactory scores on the COMP/ACT.

Special: There is cross-registration through the United Colleges of San Antonio. Dual majors are possible in the B.A.-B.B.A. programs. A 3-2 engineering degree is offered with Washington University. Credit by exam and for life/work/military experience is available, as is a special degree program for working adults/nontraditional students through the Weekend College.

Admissions: The SAT scores for the 2005-2006 freshman class were: Verbal--66% below 500, 29% between 500 and 599, and 5% between 600 and 700; Math--67% below 500, 29% between 500 and 599, and 4% between 600 and 700. The ACT scores were 68% below 21, 23% between 21 and 23, 6% between 24 and 26, and 2% between 27 and 28. 34% of the current freshmen were in the top fifth of their class; 57% were in the top two fifths.

Requirements: The SAT or ACT is required. In addition, applicants should graduate from an accredited secondary school with 16 academic credits, including 4 in English, 3 in social studies, and 2 each in math and lab science. A combination of SAT or ACT scores and high school GPA or class rank determines admission. A GED with an average minimum score of 45 on each of the 5 tests and a satisfactory SAT or ACT score are also acceptable. Mature students returning to school may waive the SAT/ACT requirement for the college's own testing. AP and CLEP credits are accepted.

Procedure: Freshmen are admitted to all sessions. Entrance exams should be taken prior to December of the senior year. There is a deferred admissions plan and a rolling admissions plan. Application deadlines are open. Application fee is $25.

Transfer: Transfer applicants with 30 or more credit hours and a minimum 2.0 GPA are accepted. Others are evaluated by the same criteria as freshmen applicants. 30 of 128 credits required for the bachelor's degree must be completed at The Lake.

Visiting: There are regularly scheduled orientations for prospective students. There are guides for informal visits and visitors may sit in on classes and stay overnight. To schedule a visit, contact the Admissions Office.

Financial Aid: In 2005-2006, 99% of all full-time freshmen received some form of financial aid. 93% of full-time freshmen received need-based aid. Average annual earnings from campus work are $2000. The average financial indebtedness of the 2005 graduate was $26,000. The FAFSA or FFS is required.

International Students: There are 10 international students enrolled. The school actively recruits these students. They must score satisfactorily on the written TOEFL or on the electronic version.

Computers: All students may access the system. There are no time limits and no fees.

Graduates: The most popular majors were psychology (16%), business/marketing (13%), and social work (8%). In an average class, 14% graduate in 4 years or less, 30% graduate in 5 years or less, and 35% graduate in 6 years or less.

Admissions Contact: Dr. Mary Kay Cooper, Dean of Enrollment Management. E-mail: *admission@lake.ollusa.edu* Web: *www.ollusa.edu*

PAUL QUINN COLLEGE   D-3

Dallas, TX 75241-4398

(214) 302-3575 or 302-3520
237-2648; Fax: (214) 302-3559

Full-time: 300 men, 460 women	**Faculty:** n/av
Part-time: 10 men, 20 women	**Ph.D.s:** n/av
Graduate: none	**Student/Faculty:** n/av
Year: n/av	**Tuition:** $4700
Application Deadline: see profile	**Room & Board:** $3600
Freshman Class: n/av	
SAT or ACT: required	**LESS COMPETITIVE**

Paul Quinn College, founded in 1872, is a coeducational liberal arts college affiliated with the African Methodist Episcopal Church. Figures in the above capsule and in this profile are approximate. In addition to regional accreditation, PQC has baccalaureate program accreditation with CSWE. The library contains 88,187 volumes and 30,550 microform items, and subscribes to 131 periodicals including electronic. Special learning facilities include a learning resource center. The 130-acre campus is in an urban area 12 miles from downtown Dallas. Including any residence halls, there are 8 buildings.

Student Life: 61% of undergraduates are from Texas. Others are from 7 states. 89% are from public schools. 90% are African American; 10% Hispanic. The average age of freshmen is 18; all undergraduates, 20. 20% do not continue beyond their first year; 65% remain to graduate.

Housing: 700 students can be accommodated in college housing, which includes coed dormitories. On-campus housing is guaranteed for all 4 years. 51% of students commute. Alcohol is not permitted. All students may keep cars.

Activities: 40% of men belong to 4 national fraternities; 30% of women belong to 3 national sororities. There are 20 groups on campus, including cheerleading, choir, chorale, computers, dance, ethnic, newspaper, religious, social service, student government, and yearbook. Popular campus events include Honors Day and Founders Day.

Sports: There are 3 intercollegiate sports for men and 3 for women, and 5 intramural sports for men and 5 for women.

Services: There is remedial math, reading, and writing. Tutoring is available.

Campus Safety and Security: Measures include 24-hour foot and vehicle patrol.

Programs of Study: Bachelor's degrees are awarded in BIOLOGICAL SCIENCE (biology/biological science), BUSINESS (accounting, and business administration and management), COMMUNICATIONS AND THE ARTS (English and music), COMPUTER AND PHYSICAL SCIENCE (computer science and mathematics), EDUCATION (physical and secondary), SOCIAL SCIENCE (history, religion, and sociology).

Requirements: The SAT or ACT is required. In addition, and high school transcripts must be submitted. A GPA of 2.0 is required. CLEP credit is accepted. Important factors in the admissions decision are leadership record, advanced placement or honor courses, and recommendations by school officials.

Transfer: Applicants must meet the basic admissions requirements. 30 of 128 credits required for the bachelor's degree must be completed at PQC.

Visiting: There are regularly scheduled orientations for prospective students. There are guides for informal visits and visitors may sit in on classes and stay overnight. To schedule a visit, contact the Director of Admissions.

Financial Aid: PQC is a member of CSS. The FAFSA and the previous year's student's/parents' tax forms are required. Check with the school for current deadlines.

International Students: Satisfactory scores are required on the written TOEFL and the SAT or the ACT.

Computers: All students may access the system. There are no time limits and no fees.

Admissions Contact: Ralph Spencer, Jr., Admissions Officer.

PRAIRIE VIEW A&M UNIVERSITY   E-3

Prairie View, TX 77446

(936) 857-2618; Fax: (936) 857-2699

Full-time: 2265 men, 2886 women	**Faculty:** n/av
Part-time: 165 men, 386 women	**Ph.D.s:** n/av
Graduate: 599 men, 1611 women	**Student/Faculty:** n/av
Year: semesters, summer session	**Tuition:** $4906 ($13,186)
Application Deadline: July 1	**Room & Board:** $6204
Freshman Class: n/av	
SAT or ACT: required	**LESS COMPETITIVE**

Prairie View A&M University, established in 1878, is a comprehensive unit of the Texas A&M University System, offering undergraduate and graduate degree programs in applied sciences and engineering technology, business, engineering, nursing, arts and sciences, education, agriculture and human sciences, architecture, juvenile justice, and psychology. There are 8 undergraduate and 6 graduate schools. In addition to regional accreditation, PVAMU has baccalaureate program accreditation with ABET, CSWE, NAAB, NCATE, and NLN. The library contains 356,611 volumes, 699,675 microform items, and 6043 audio/video tapes/CDs/DVDs, and subscribes to 25,000 periodicals including electronic. Computerized library services include the card catalog, interlibrary loans, database searching, Internet access, and laptop Internet portals. Special learning facilities include a learning resource center, art gallery, radio station, and solar observatory. The 1440-acre campus is in a small town 40 miles northwest of Houston. Including any residence halls, there are 153 buildings.

Student Life: 93% of undergraduates are from Texas. Others are from 38 states and 34 foreign countries. 90% are from public schools. 90% are African American. The average age of freshmen is 19; all undergraduates, 22. 36% do not continue beyond their first year; 35% remain to graduate.

Housing: 3084 students can be accommodated in college housing, which includes coed dorms and on-campus apartments. In addition, there are special-interest houses and intensive learning community housing for 600 upperclass students. On-campus housing is guaranteed for the freshman year only and is available on a first-come, first-served basis. 58% of students commute. Alcohol is not permitted. All students may keep cars.

Activities: 5% of men belong to 4 national fraternities; 5% of women belong to 4 national sororities. There are 30 groups on campus, including band, cheerleading, choir, chorus, dance, drama, drill team, ethnic, honors, international, jazz band, marching band, newspaper, orchestra, photography, political, professional, radio and TV, religious, social, social service, student government and yearbook. Popular campus events include Honors Week, Family Day, and trail rides.

Sports: There are 8 intercollegiate sports for men and 10 for women, and 6 intramural sports for men and 6 for women. Facilities include a 5000-seat stadium and a large athletic and recreation complex.

Disabled Students: 5% of the campus is accessible. Wheelchair ramps, elevators, special parking, and specially equipped rest rooms are available.

Services: Counseling and information services are available, as is tutoring in some subjects. There is a reader service for the blind, and remedial math, reading, and writing.

Campus Safety and Security: Measures include 24-hour foot and vehicle patrol, informal discussions, pamphlets/posters/films, and emergency telephones. There are lighted pathways/sidewalks and a 24-hour department of traffic and security.

Programs of Study: PVAMU confers B.A., B.S., B.Arch., B.A.S.W., B.B.A., B.S.Ag., B.S.C.E., B.S.C.E.T., B.S.C.H.E., B.S.C.J., B.S.Diet., B.S.E.E., B.S.E.E.T., B.S.H.S., B.S.I.S., B.S.I.T., B.S.M.E., B.S.N., and B.S.T.C.H. degrees. Master's and doctoral degrees are also awarded. Bachelor's degrees are awarded in AGRICULTURE (agricultural business management, agricultural economics, agronomy, and animal science), BIOLOGICAL SCIENCE (biology/biological science), BUSINESS (accounting, banking and finance, business administration and management, and marketing/retailing/merchandising), COMMUNICATIONS AND THE ARTS (art, broadcasting, communications, dramatic arts, English, journalism, music, Spanish, and speech/debate/rhetoric), COMPUTER AND PHYSICAL SCIENCE (chemistry, computer science, mathematics, and physics), EDUCATION (physical), ENGINEERING AND ENVIRONMENTAL DESIGN (architecture, chemical engineering, civil engineering, computer engineering, electrical/electronics engineering, engineering technology, industrial engineering technology, and mechanical engineering), HEALTH PROFESSIONS (health, medical technology, and nursing), SOCIAL SCIENCE (criminal justice, dietetics, family and community services, geography, history, interdisciplinary studies, political science/government, psychology, social work, and sociology). Engineering, nursing and business are the strongest academically. Education, juvenile justice, and business are the largest.

Required: All students must complete at least 120 semester hours, with a minimum GPA of 2.5 or higher, depending on the major. Completion of a 42-hour core curriculum is required. Some majors require a comprehensive exam or thesis.

Special: Cooperative programs and internships in various majors, work-study programs, and combined B.A.-B.S. degrees in chemistry, biology, math, and computer science are offered. There are 24 national honor societies, including Phi Beta Kappa, and a freshman honors program.

Faculty/Classroom: 61% of faculty are male; 39%, female.

Admissions: 14% of the current freshmen were in the top fifth of their class; 37% were in the top two fifths.

Requirements: The SAT or ACT is required. In addition, a GPA of at least 2.0 is necessary for financial aid eligibility. Applicants should be graduates of accredited high schools or have earned the GED. Secondary school preparation should include 4 years each of English and academic electives, 3 years each of math and social studies, and 2 years of science. PVAMU requires applicants to be in the upper 50% of their class. A GPA of 2.5 is required. AP and CLEP credits are accepted. Important factors in the admissions decision are leadership record, advanced placement or honor courses, and recommendations by school officials.

Procedure: Freshmen are admitted to all sessions. Entrance exams should be taken during the junior or senior year of high school. There is a deferred admissions plan. Applications should be filed by July 1 for fall entry, November 1 for spring entry, and April 1 for summer entry, along with a $25 fee. Notification is sent on a rolling basis. Applications are accepted on-line.

Transfer: 247 transfer students enrolled in 2004-2005. Transfer applicants must present at least a 2.0 GPA from the last college attended. 30 of at least 120 credits required for the bachelor's degree must be completed at PVAMU.

Visiting: There are regularly scheduled orientations for prospective students, consisting of an orientation held 2 days prior to registration. There are guides for informal visits and visitors may sit in on classes and stay overnight. To schedule a visit, contact the Office of Records at (936) 857-2626 or *recruitment@pvamu.edu*.

Financial Aid: 64% of full-time freshmen received need-based aid. The CSS/Profile or FAFSA and the college's own financial statement are required.

International Students: There are 159 international students enrolled. They must score satisfactorily on the TOEFL and also take the SAT or the ACT.

Computers: All students may access the system after they receive security checks and training. PCs are available for use in courses. The fee is $12 per credit hour. It is strongly recommended that all students have a personal computer.

Graduates: From July 1, 2004 to June 30, 2005, 792 bachelor's degrees were awarded. The most popular majors were nursing (7%), interdisciplinary studies education (7%), and biology (6%). In an average class, 11% graduate in 4 years or less, 17% graduate in 5 years or less, and 35% graduate in 6 years or less.

Admissions Contact: Mary Gooch, Director of Admissions. A video is available. E-mail: *admissions@pvamu.edu* Web: *www.pvamu.edu*

RICE UNIVERSITY   E-3
Houston, TX 77251-1892   (713) 348-7423
(800) 527-OWLS; Fax: (713) 348-5952

Full-time: 1483 men, 1403 women	**Faculty:** 530; I, +$
Part-time: 30 men, 50 women	**Ph.D.s:** 96%
Graduate: 1246 men, 676 women	**Student/Faculty:** 5 to 1
Year: semesters	**Tuition:** $23,310
Application Deadline: see profile	**Room & Board:** $8980
Freshman Class: 8106 applied, 1802 accepted, 727 enrolled	
SAT or ACT: required	**MOST COMPETITIVE**

Rice University, founded in 1912, is a private institution offering undergraduate and graduate programs through the divisions of Engineering, Natural Sciences, Humanities, Social Sciences, Music and Architecture. There are 6 undergraduate and 7 graduate schools. Some figures in the above capsule and in this profile are approximate. In addition to regional accreditation, Rice has baccalaureate program accreditation with ABET, AACSB and NAAB. The library contains 2,314,820 volumes, 3,074,402 microform items, and 46,070 audio/video tapes/CDs/DVDs, and subscribes to 36,889 periodicals including electronic. Computerized library services include the card catalog, database searching, and Internet access. Special learning facilities include an art gallery, radio station, TV station, and media center. The 300-acre campus is in an urban area 3 miles southwest of downtown Houston. Including any residence halls, there are 71 buildings.

Student Life: 52% of undergraduates are from Texas. Students are from 50 states, 82 foreign countries, and Canada. 57% are white; 16% Asian American; 12% Hispanic. The average age of freshmen is 18; all undergraduates, 20. 4% do not continue beyond their first year; 92% remain to graduate.

Housing: Students can be accommodated in college housing, which includes coed dormitories. On-campus housing is available on a lottery system for upperclassmen. 76% of students live on campus; of those, 95% remain on campus on weekends. All students may keep cars.

Activities: There are no fraternities or sororities. There are 204 groups on campus, including art, band, cheerleading, chess, choir, chorale, chorus, computers, dance, debate, drama, ethnic, film, gay, honors, international, jazz band, literary magazine, marching band, musical theater, newspaper, orchestra, pep band, photography, political, professional, radio and TV, religious, social, social service, student government, symphony, and yearbook. Popular campus events include Baker Shakespeare Festival, an annual biking relay race, and Archi Arts, a costume ball.

Sports: There are 19 intercollegiate sports for men and 18 for women, and 14 intramural sports for men and 13 for women. Facilities include a 5000-seat gym, a pool, a track stadium, fields for soccer, lacrosse, and rugby, courts for tennis, squash, racquetball, volleyball, and basketball, and a 70,000-seat stadium.

Disabled Students: 90% of the campus is accessible. Wheelchair ramps, elevators, special parking, specially equipped rest rooms, special

class scheduling, lowered drinking fountains, lowered telephones, special housing, and a stair lift are available.

Services: Counseling and information services are available, as is tutoring in every subject.

Campus Safety and Security: Measures include 24-hour foot and vehicle patrol, self-defense education, security escort services, and shuttle buses. There are informal discussions, pamphlets/posters/films, emergency telephones, lighted pathways/sidewalks, and a campus police department with a variety of outreach programs.

Programs of Study: Rice confers B.A., B.S., B.Arch., B.F.A., B.Mus., and B.S.E degrees. Master's and doctoral degrees are also awarded. Bachelor's degrees are awarded in BIOLOGICAL SCIENCE (biology/biological science), BUSINESS (management science), COMMUNICATIONS AND THE ARTS (art history and appreciation, classics, English, linguistics, music, music history and appreciation, music performance, music theory and composition, and visual and performing arts), COMPUTER AND PHYSICAL SCIENCE (applied mathematics, chemistry, computer science, earth science, geology, geophysics and seismology, mathematics, physics, and statistics), ENGINEERING AND ENVIRONMENTAL DESIGN (architectural engineering, architecture, bioengineering, chemical engineering, civil engineering, electrical/electronics engineering, environmental engineering, and mechanical engineering), HEALTH PROFESSIONS (exercise science), SOCIAL SCIENCE (anthropology, Asian/Oriental studies, classical/ancient civilization, cognitive science, economics, French studies, German area studies, Hispanic American studies, history, medieval studies, philosophy, political science/government, psychology, public affairs, religion, Russian and Slavic studies, sociology, and women's studies).

Required: All students must complete at least 120 credits, with a 1.67 overall GPA and a 2.0 GPA in the major field. Distribution requirements include 12 credit/semester hours in natural sciences, social sciences, or humanities, depending on the major, and additional courses in these fields to meet distribution requirements. All students take 2 semesters of phys ed. At least 48 semester hours in upper-level courses are required.

Special: An 8-year guaranteed medical school program with the Baylor College of Medicine; a 5-year joint degree program for BSE/MSE in engineering; a 5-year joint degree for BSE/MBA in engineering and business, and a 3-2 engineering degree are possible, as are cross-registration, internships, study abroad, work-study, dual majors, and student-designed majors. There are 10 national honor societies, including Phi Beta Kappa, and 9 departmental honors programs.

Faculty/Classroom: 77% of faculty are male; 23%, female. 100% both teach and do research. The average class size in a regular course is 11.

Requirements: The SAT or ACT is required. In addition, official high school transcript(s), 1 counselor recommendation, 1 teacher recommendation, and 3 SAT: Subject tests (writing plus 2 others in fields related to the candidate's proposed field of study are required). Music students must arrange an audition. Architecture students must submit a portfolio. An interview is recommended but not required. Candidates should have completed 16 college-prep units, including 4 years in English, 3 in math, and 2 each in social studies, foreign language, and lab science. AP credits are accepted.

Procedure: Freshmen are admitted in the fall. Entrance exams should be taken between October and January of the senior year, depending on the decision plan. There are early decision and early admissions plans. Early decision applications should be filed by November 1; regular applications, by January 10 for fall entry, along with a $50 fee. Notification of early decision is sent December 15; regular decision, April 1. 125 early decision candidates were accepted in a recent year; 121 were admitted. Applications are accepted on-line.

Transfer: 63 transfer students enrolled in a recent year. Transfer applicants should present at least a 3.2 GPA in previous college work, SAT scores, 2 college teacher recommendations, high school and college transcripts, and a letter from the dean of current college. 60 of 120 credits required for the bachelor's degree must be completed at Rice.

Visiting: There are regularly scheduled orientations for prospective students, consisting of information sessions and tours available year-round. There are guides for informal visits and visitors may sit in on classes and stay overnight. To schedule a visit, contact the Office of Admissions at (800) 527-6957.

Financial Aid: In a recent year, 62% of all full-time freshmen and 67% of continuing full-time students received some form of financial aid. 34% of full-time freshmen and 37% of continuing full-time students received need-based aid. Need-based scholarships or need-based grants averaged $12,226; need-based self-help aid (loans and jobs) averaged $3386; non-need-based athletic scholarships averaged $23,239; and other non-need-based awards and non-need-based scholarships averaged $4999. The average financial indebtedness of the recent year's graduate was $12,942. Rice is a member of CSS. The CSS/Profile, FAFSA and the parents' and student's tax returns are required. Check with school for current deadlines.

International Students: In a recent year, there were 91 international students enrolled. Satisfactory scores are required on the written TOEFL the SAT or the ACT and SAT: Subject tests (writing and 2 others).

Computers: All students may access the system. There are no time limits and no fees. It is strongly recommended that all students have a personal computer.

Graduates: In recent year,, 977 bachelor's degrees were awarded. The most popular majors were economics (7%), psychology (7%), and electrical and computer engineering (7%). In an average class, 75% graduate in 4 years or less, 89% graduate in 5 years or less, and 92% graduate in 6 years or less. 137 companies recruited on campus in a recent year. Of the 2004 graduating class, 43% were enrolled in graduate school within 6 months of graduation and 49% were employed.

Admissions Contact: Julie M. Browning, Dean for Undergraduate Enrollment. Web: *www.rice.edu*

SAINT EDWARD'S UNIVERSITY   D-3
Austin, TX 78704

(512) 448-8500
(800) 555-0164; Fax: (512) 464-8877

Full-time: 1254 men, 1743 women	**Faculty:** 142; IIA, -$
Part-time: 404 men, 563 women	**Ph.D.s:** 83%
Graduate: 400 men, 583 women	**Student/Faculty:** 21 to 1
Year: semesters, summer session	**Tuition:** $17,320
Application Deadline: May 1	**Room & Board:** $6240
Freshman Class: 2217 applied, 1530 accepted, 650 enrolled	
SAT Verbal/Math: 560/545*	**ACT:** 23 COMPETITIVE

Saint Edward's University, founded in 1885, is an independent Catholic institution offering undergraduate courses in business, behavioral and social sciences, humanitites, education, and natural sciences, and graduate courses in human service, business administration, counseling, liberal arts, and computer science. There are 6 undergraduate and 7 graduate schools. In addition to regional accreditation, SEU has baccalaureate program accreditation with CSWE. The library contains 150,935 volumes, 6436 microform items, and 3001 audio/video tapes/CDs/DVDs, and subscribes to 659 periodicals including electronic. Computerized library services include the card catalog, interlibrary loans, database searching, Internet access, and laptop Internet portals. Special learning facilities include a learning resource center, art gallery, and a photography lab. The 160-acre campus is in an urban area in Austin. Including any residence halls, there are 48 buildings.

Student Life: 91% of undergraduates are from Texas. Others are from 37 states, 37 foreign countries, and Canada. 74% are from public schools. 55% are white; 31% Hispanic. The average age of freshmen is 18; all undergraduates, 21. 16% do not continue beyond their first year; 53% remain to graduate.

Housing: 1155 students can be accommodated in college housing, which includes single-sex and coed dorms and on-campus apartments. On-campus housing is guaranteed for the freshman year only and is available on a first-come, first-served basis. 63% of students commute. All students may keep cars.

Activities: There are no fraternities or sororities. There are 60 groups on campus, including art, cheerleading, choir, chorale, chorus, computers, dance, drama, ethnic, film, forensics, gay, honors, international, literary magazine, musical theater, newspaper, photography, political, professional, religious, social service, sports clubs, student government, and yearbook. Popular campus events include Festival of Lights, Multicultural Spring Fest, and Hillfest.

Sports: There are 6 intercollegiate sports for men and 7 for women, and 8 intramural sports for men and 8 for women. Facilities include 2 gyms, baseball and softball fields, 2 soccer fields, tennis, basketball, racquetball/handball, and volleyball courts, an indoor/outdoor pool, and a fitness center.

Disabled Students: 95% of the campus is accessible. Wheelchair ramps, elevators, special parking, specially equipped rest rooms, special class scheduling, lowered drinking fountains, lowered telephones, and special housing are available.

Services: Counseling and information services are available, as is tutoring in most subjects. There is remedial math, reading, and writing. There is also a learning strategies course.

Campus Safety and Security: Measures include 24-hour foot and vehicle patrol, self-defense education, security escort services, and informal discussions. There are pamphlets/posters/films, emergency telephones, and lighted pathways/sidewalks. The outside doors of residence halls are locked at all times. Residents swipe their student ID for access.

Programs of Study: SEU confers B.A., B.S., B.A.A.S., B.B.A., and B.L.S. degrees. Master's degrees are also awarded. Bachelor's degrees are awarded in BIOLOGICAL SCIENCE (biochemistry, bioinformatics, and biology/biological science), BUSINESS (accounting, banking and finance, business administration and management, entrepreneurial studies, international business management, and marketing management), COMMUNICATIONS AND THE ARTS (art, communications, creative writing, dramatic arts, English literature, graphic design, photography, and Spanish), COMPUTER AND PHYSICAL SCIENCE (chemistry, computer science, information sciences and systems, and mathematics), EDUCATION (art, drama, English, foreign languages, mathematics, physical, science, and social studies), ENGINEERING AND ENVIRON-

MENTAL DESIGN (preengineering), HEALTH PROFESSIONS (predentistry and premedicine), SOCIAL SCIENCE (criminal justice, criminology, economics, forensic studies, history, interdisciplinary studies, international relations, Latin American studies, liberal arts/general studies, philosophy, physical fitness/movement, political science/government, prelaw, psychology, religion, religious education, social work, and sociology). Communication, psychology, and business administration are the largest.

Required: All students must maintain a minimum GPA of 2.0 while taking 120 semester hours, including 36 to 75 in the major. The core curriculum includes courses from Foundational Skills, Cultural Foundations, and Foundations for Values and Decisions. In the required capstone class, seniors identify a problem in society, research it, and present their solutions in an extensive final paper.

Special: Internships and study abroad in a variety of countries through the ISEP, SEU and other university programs are available. A dual major in Spanish and international business credit for life experience, nondegree study, and pass/fail options also are possible. A flexible program for working adults is offered through New College. There are 8 national honor societies, and a freshman honors program.

Faculty/Classroom: 55% of faculty are male; 45%, female. 70% teach undergraduates. No introductory courses are taught by graduate students. The average class size in a laboratory is 14 and in a regular course, 20.

Admissions: 69% of the 2005-2006 applicants were accepted. The SAT scores for the 2005-2006 freshman class were: Verbal--17% below 500, 48% between 500 and 599, 30% between 600 and 700, and 5% above 700; Math--21% below 500, 55% between 500 and 599, 22% between 600 and 700, and 2% above 700. The ACT scores were 24% below 21, 32% between 21 and 23, 23% between 24 and 26, 17% between 27 and 28, and 4% above 28. 37% of the current freshmen were in the top fifth of their class; 67% were in the top two fifths. 4 freshmen graduated first in their class.

Requirements: The SAT or ACT is required. The ACT Optional Writing test is also required.The GED is accepted. An interview is recommended. An essay is required. SEU requires applicants to be in the upper 50% of their class. AP and CLEP credits are accepted. Important factors in the admissions decision are advanced placement or honor courses, extracurricular activities record, and leadership record.

Procedure: Freshmen are admitted fall and spring. Entrance exams should be taken in spring of the junior year or in summer or fall of the senior year. There is a deferred admissions plan. Early decision applications should be filed by February 1; regular applications, by May 1 for fall entry, November 15 for spring entry, and May 1 for summer entry, along with a $45 fee. Notification of early decision and regular decision is set on a rolling basis. 258 applicants were on the 2005 waiting list; 49 were admitted. Applications are accepted on-line.

Transfer: 313 transfer students enrolled in 2004-2005. Transfer applicants must have a minimum GPA of 2.25. Transfers with less than 30 hours must submit high school transcripts. 30 of 120 credits required for the bachelor's degree must be completed at SEU.

Visiting: There are regularly scheduled orientations for prospective students, including a tour, financial aid session, academic session, class visits, entertainment, and an overnight stay in a residence hall. There are guides for informal visits and visitors may sit in on classes.To schedule a visit, contact the Admissions Office.

Financial Aid: In 2005-2006, 88% of all full-time freshmen and 82% of continuing full-time students received some form of financial aid. 72% of full-time freshmen and 65% of continuing full-time students received need-based aid. The average freshman award was $15,519. Need-based scholarships or need-based grants averaged $10,640 ($19,390 maximum); need-based self-help aid (loans and jobs) averaged $2800 ($8625 maximum); non-need-based athletic scholarships averaged $8107 ($23,232 maximum); other non-need-based awards and non-need-based scholarships averaged $8619 ($15,315 maximum); and non-need-based loans and community scholarships. averaged $7730 ($25,116 maximum). 25% of undergraduates work part time. Average annual earnings from campus work are $2000. The average financial indebtedness of the 2005 graduate was $22,331. SEU is a member of CSS. The FAFSA is required. The priority date for freshman financial aid applications for fall entry is March 1. The deadline for filing freshman financial aid applications for fall entry is April 15.

International Students: There are 78 international students enrolled. The school actively recruits these students. They must score satisfactorily on the TOEFL and also take the SAT or ACT and the ACT Optional Writing.

Computers: Wireless access is available. Students have access to 502 computers on campus. There are labs staffed by lab assistants, labs in every residence hall, and specialized labs and classrooms for education, arts, and computer science. Every residence hall room has one Ethernet network connection per bed. All students may access the system. Dial-up is available 24 hours every day, although dial-in time is limited to 4 hours at a time, and 2 computer labs are open 24 hours every day. There are no time limits and no fees.

Graduates: From July 1, 2004 to June 30, 2005, 758 bachelor's degrees were awarded. The most popular majors were business and management (16%), communication (8%), and psychology (7%). In an average class, 2% graduate in 3 years or less, 31% graduate in 4 years or less, 50% graduate in 5 years or less, and 53% graduate in 6 years or less. 101 companies recruited on campus in 2004-2005.

Admissions Contact: Tracy Manier, Dean of Undergraduate Admission. E-mail: *seu.admit@admin.stedwards.edu*
Web: *http://www.stedwards.edu*

SAINT MARY'S UNIVERSITY OF SAN ANTONIO   D-4

San Antonio, TX 78228-8503   (210) 436-3126
                                  (800) FOR-STMU; Fax: (210) 431-6742

Full-time: 980 men, 1400 women	**Faculty:** 146; IIA, +$
Part-time: 90 men, 130 women	**Ph.Ds:** 85%
Graduate: 790 men, 760 women	**Student/Faculty:** 16 to 1
Year: semesters, summer session	**Tuition:** $16,600
Application Deadline: open	**Room & Board:** $6000
Freshman Class: n/av	
SAT or ACT required	**COMPETITIVE**

Saint Mary's University, established in 1852, is a private Roman Catholic institution in the Marianist tradition, offering undergraduate programs in humanities and social sciences, business and administration, and science, engineering, and technology. There are 3 undergraduate and 2 graduate schools. Figures in the above capsule and in this profile are approximate. In addition to regional accreditation, St. Mary's has baccalaureate program accreditation with ABET and NASM. The 2 libraries contain 481,137 volumes, 131,324 microform items, and 3104 audio/video tapes/CDs/DVDs, and subscribe to 1320 periodicals including electronic. Computerized library services include the card catalog, interlibrary loans, database searching, and Internet access. Special learning facilities include a learning resource center and the Learning Assistance Center. The 135-acre campus is in a suburban area 5 miles northwest of San Antonio. Including any residence halls, there are 32 buildings.

Student Life: 92% of undergraduates are from Texas. Others are from 32 states, 36 foreign countries, and Canada. 74% are from public schools. 69% are Hispanic; 21% white. 66% are Catholic; 17% Baptist, Buddhist, Christian, Eastern Orthodox, Episcopal, Hindu; 14% Protestant. The average age of freshmen is 18; all undergraduates, 22. 7% do not continue beyond their first year; 64% remain to graduate.

Housing: 1262 students can be accommodated in college housing, which includes single-sex and coed dormitories. On-campus housing is guaranteed for the freshman year only and is available on a first-come, first-served basis. Priority is given to out-of-town students. 58% of students commute. Alcohol is not permitted. All students may keep cars.

Activities: 15% of men belong to 1 local and 4 national fraternities; 13% of women belong to 1 local and 3 national sororities. There are 55 groups on campus, including art, band, cheerleading, choir, chorale, dance, drama, ethnic, honors, international, jazz band, newspaper, pep band, photography, political, professional, religious, social, social service, and student government. Popular campus events include Campus Ministry Retreat, Hunger Awareness Week, and Fiesta Oyster Bake.

Sports: There are 5 intercollegiate sports for men and 5 for women, and 28 intramural sports for men and 28 for women. Facilities include a gym, a weight room, tennis, handball, and basketball courts, and various playing fields.

Disabled Students: 80% of the campus is accessible. Wheelchair ramps, elevators, special parking, specially equipped rest rooms, special class scheduling, lowered drinking fountains, and special housing are available.

Services: Counseling and information services are available, as is tutoring in every subject. There is remedial math, reading, and writing.

Campus Safety and Security: Measures include 24-hour foot and vehicle patrol, security escort services, informal discussions, and pamphlets/posters/films. There are emergency telephones, lighted pathways/sidewalks, and and a crime prevention awareness program each semester.

Programs of Study: St. Mary's confers B.A., B.S., B.A.S., B.A.T., and B.B.A. degrees. Master's and doctoral degrees are also awarded. Bachelor's degrees are awarded in BIOLOGICAL SCIENCE (biochemistry and biology/biological science), BUSINESS (accounting, banking and finance, business administration and management, human resources, international business management, and marketing/retailing/merchandising), COMMUNICATIONS AND THE ARTS (communications, English, French, German, music, Spanish, and speech/debate/rhetoric), COMPUTER AND PHYSICAL SCIENCE (chemistry, computer science, earth science, mathematics, and physics), EDUCATION (business, elementary, science, and secondary), ENGINEERING AND ENVIRONMENTAL DESIGN (computer engineering, electrical/electronics engineering, engineering, and industrial engineering), HEALTH PROFESSIONS (predentistry and premedicine), SOCIAL SCIENCE (criminal justice, economics, history, international relations, international studies, Latin American studies, philosophy, political science/

government, prelaw, psychology, sociology, and theological studies). Biology, accounting, and political science are the strongest academically. Biology, business, and political science are the largest.

Required: All students must complete at least 129 semester hours, 24 to 30 in the major, with a minimum 2.5 GPA. Core curriculum requirements include courses in fine arts, English, foreign language, speech, natural science, math, social science, philosophy, and theology. Students must also take computer science, demonstrate computer literacy, and take interdisciplinary electives.

Special: St. Mary's offers cooperative programs and internships in all majors, depending on the student's needs. Students may cross-register at any of the United Colleges of San Antonio, spend a semester in Washington, D.C., or study in England, Austria, or Mexico. Dual majors are possible in computer science and engineering and public justice and sociology, political science, or psychology. Accelerated degree programs are offered in law, (J.D./M.B.A.) and dentistry (B.A. in combined science and dentistry). Required theology courses may be taken on a pass/fail basis. There are 3 national honor societies, a freshman honors program.

Faculty/Classroom: 67% of faculty are male; 33%, female. 72% teach undergraduates. No introductory courses are taught by graduate students. The average class size in an introductory lecture is 30; in a laboratory, 60; and in a regular course, 25.

Requirements: The SAT or ACT is required. In addition, all applicants must be high school graduates or have the GED, rank in the upper half of their graduating classes, and score in the 50th percentile on the SAT or the ACT. Secondary school preparation should include 4 units of English, 3 each of math and academic electives, and 2 each of social science, natural science, and foreign language. Potential science and engineering majors should have 4 units of math and 3 of lab science, including chemistry or physics. St. Mary's requires applicants to be in the upper 50% of their class. AP and CLEP credits are accepted. Important factors in the admissions decision are leadership record, advanced placement or honor courses, and personality/intangible qualities.

Procedure: Freshmen are admitted fall and spring. Entrance exams should be taken by the fall of the senior year. There are early admissions and deferred admissions plans. Check with the school for current applications and fee. Applications are accepted on-line.

Transfer: 129 transfer students enrolled in a recent year. Transfer applicants must present at least a 2.0 GPA in previous college work, which should include 3 hours of English composition. St. Mary's also recommends that applicants submit SAT or ACT scores and schedule an interview. 30 of 129 credits required for the bachelor's degree must be completed at St. Mary's.

Visiting: There are regularly scheduled orientations for prospective students, including a tour, an admissions/financial aid session, an overnight stay, and class visits. There are guides for informal visits and visitors may sit in on classes and stay overnight. To schedule a visit, contact the Undergraduate Admissions Office.

Financial Aid: In a recent year, 80% of all full-time freshmen and 78% of continuing full-time students received some form of financial aid. 74% of full-time freshmen and 69% of continuing full-time students received need-based aid. The average freshman award was $14,481. Need-based scholarships or need-based grants averaged $6965; need-based self-help aid (loans and jobs) averaged $5025; non-need-based athletic scholarships averaged $7152; and other non-need-based awards and non-need-based scholarships averaged $8479. 30% of undergraduates work part time. Average annual earnings from campus work are $2000. The average financial indebtedness of the recent graduate was $23,406. St. Mary's is a member of CSS. The CSS/Profile is required. Check with the school for current deadlines.

International Students: In a recent year, there were 107 international students enrolled. The school actively recruits these students. A satisfactory score is required on the written TOEFL.

Computers: All students may access the system. There are no time limits and no fees.

Graduates: In a recent year, 464 bachelor's degrees were awarded. The most popular majors were biology (13%), English communication arts (7%), and political science (6%). In an average class, 32% graduate in 4 years or less, 58% graduate in 5 years or less, and 62% graduate in 6 years or less. 30 companies recruited on campus in a recent year.

Admissions Contact: Richard Castillo, Director of Undergraduate Admissions. E-mail: *uadm@stmarytx.edu* Web: *www.stmarytx.edu*

SAM HOUSTON STATE UNIVERSITY   E-3
Huntsville, TX 77341   (936) 294-1845
                              (866) 232-7528; Fax: (936) 294-3758

Full-time: 4770 men, 6494 women	**Faculty:** 719; IIA, av$
Part-time: 789 men, 1140 women	**Ph.D.s:** 94%
Graduate: 696 men, 1468 women	**Student/Faculty:** 16 to 1
Year: semesters, summer session	**Tuition:** $3500 ($8500)
Application Deadline: open	**Room & Board:** $4500
Freshman Class: 9666 applied, 7988 accepted, 2208 enrolled	
SAT Verbal/Math: 500/510*	**ACT:** 20 **COMPETITIVE**

Sam Houston University, founded in 1879, is a public institution offering programs in arts and sciences, business administration, criminal justice, education, and applied science. Some information in this capsule is approximate There are 5 undergraduate and 5 graduate schools. In addition to regional accreditation, Sam Houston State has baccalaureate program accreditation with NASM and NCATE. The library contains 1.2 million volumes, 1.5 million microform items, and 20,000 audio/video tapes/CDs/DVDs, and subscribes to 3500 periodicals including electronic. Computerized library services include the card catalog, interlibrary loans, database searching, Internet access, and laptop Internet portals. Special learning facilities include a learning resource center, planetarium, radio station, TV station, and the Sam Houston Museum. The 1256-acre campus is in a small town 70 miles north of Houston. Including any residence halls, there are 228 buildings.

Student Life: 97% of undergraduates are from Texas. Others are from 33 states, 46 foreign countries, and Canada. 74% are white; 13% African American; 10% Hispanic. The average age of freshmen is 18; all undergraduates, 22. 30% do not continue beyond their first year; 39% remain to graduate.

Housing: 3431 students can be accommodated in college housing, which includes single-sex and coed dorms, on-campus apartments, off-campus apartments, married-student housing, fraternity houses, and sorority houses. In addition, there are honors houses and special-interest houses. On-campus housing is guaranteed for all 4 years. 73% of students commute. All students may keep cars.

Activities: There are 14 local fraternities and 13 local sororities. There are many groups and organizations on campus, including art, band, cheerleading, choir, chorale, chorus, computers, dance, drama, drill team, ethnic, film, gay, honors, international, jazz band, marching band, musical theater, newspaper, orchestra, pep band, photography, political, professional, radio and TV, religious, social, social service, student government, symphony, and yearbook. Popular campus events include Organization Fair, Greek Week, and Spring Fling.

Sports: There are 7 intercollegiate sports for men and 7 for women, and 13 intramural sports for men and 13 for women. Facilities include a 14,000-seat stadium, a 5200-seat gym, 4 basketball courts, 10 racquetball courts, 3 swimming pools, and 2 weight rooms.

Disabled Students: 90% of the campus is accessible. Wheelchair ramps, elevators, special parking, specially equipped rest rooms, lowered drinking fountains, closed-circuit television (CCTV), computer workstations with large print and speech output capabilities, and telecommunication devices for the deaf (TDD) are available.

Services: Counseling and information services are available, as is tutoring in every subject. There is a reader service for the blind, and remedial math, reading, and writing.

Campus Safety and Security: Measures include 24-hour foot and vehicle patrol, security escort services, informal discussions, and pamphlets/posters/films. There are emergency telephones and lighted pathways/sidewalks.

Programs of Study: Sam Houston State confers B.A., B.S., B.A.A.S., B.B.A., B.F.A., and B.M. degrees. Master's and doctoral degrees are also awarded. Bachelor's degrees are awarded in AGRICULTURE (agriculture, animal science, and horticulture), BIOLOGICAL SCIENCE (biology/biological science), BUSINESS (accounting, banking and finance, business administration and management, and marketing/retailing/merchandising), COMMUNICATIONS AND THE ARTS (art, dance, dramatic arts, English, French, German, graphic design, journalism, music, music performance, music theory and composition, musical theater, photography, Spanish, and speech/debate/rhetoric), COMPUTER AND PHYSICAL SCIENCE (chemistry, computer science, geology, mathematics, and physics), EDUCATION (physical), ENGINEERING AND ENVIRONMENTAL DESIGN (environmental science), HEALTH PROFESSIONS (health, medical technology, and music therapy), SOCIAL SCIENCE (criminal justice, economics, geography, history, law enforcement and corrections, philosophy, physical fitness/movement, political science/government, psychology, and sociology). Psychology and general business are the largest.

Required: All students must maintain a GPA of 2.0 while taking 128 semester hours, including 30 in the major. The core curriculum includes 15 hours of social and behavioral sciences, 9 hours of humanities and visual and performing arts, 8 hours of natural sciences, 6 hours of communication, 4 hours of an institutionally designated option, and 3 hours of math.

Special: Work-study programs with the university, study abroad in 6 countries, second degrees, and B.A.-B.S. degrees are available. There is 1 national honor society, and a freshman honors program.

Faculty/Classroom: 54% of faculty are male; 46%, female. All both teach and do research. Graduate students teach 6% of introductory courses.

Admissions: 83% of the 2005-2006 applicants were accepted. The SAT scores for the 2005-2006 freshman class were: Verbal--54% below 500, 37% between 500 and 599, 8% between 600 and 700, and 1% above 700; Math--44% below 500, 43% between 500 and 599, 12% between 600 and 700, and 1% above 700. The ACT scores were 53% below 21, 28% between 21 and 23, 13% between 24 and 26, 4% between 27 and 28, and 2% above 28. 33% of the current freshmen were in the top fifth of their class; 67% were in the top two fifths. 10 freshmen graduated first in their class.

Requirements: The SAT or ACT is required. In addition, applicants must have secondary school credits as follows: 4 of English, 2 each of math, history, and science, 1 1/2 of phys ed, and a half credit each of social studies and health education. The GED is accepted. A GPA of 2.0 is required. AP and CLEP credits are accepted.

Procedure: Freshmen are admitted fall, spring, and summer. There is an early admissions and a rolling admissions plan. Application deadlines are open. Application fee is $35. Notification is sent on a rolling basis.

Transfer: 1645 transfer students enrolled in 2004-2005. Transfer applicants must present a 2.0 GPA on all previous college work. 42 of 128 credits required for the bachelor's degree must be completed at Sam Houston State.

Visiting: There are regularly scheduled orientations for prospective students, including a tour of the campus, dorms, and departments. There are guides for informal visits. To schedule a visit, contact the Visitor Center at (936) 294-1844 or *visitsam@shsu.edu.*

Financial Aid: In 2005-2006, 59% of all full-time freshmen and 57% of continuing full-time students received some form of financial aid. 15% of undergraduates work part time. Average annual earnings from campus work are $2000. The FAFSA is required. The priority date for freshman financial aid applications for fall entry is March 31. The deadline for filing freshman financial aid applications for fall entry is May 31.

International Students: There are 112 international students enrolled. The school actively recruits these students. Satisfactory scores are required on the written TOEFL. and the SAT or the ACT.

Computers: All students may access the system. There are no time limits. The fee is $50 per semester.

Graduates: From July 1, 2004 to June 30, 2005, 2254 bachelor's degrees were awarded. The most popular majors were criminal justice (12%) and business administration (8%). In an average class, 17% graduate in 4 years or less, and 41% graduate in 6 years or less.

Admissions Contact: Trevor Thorn, Director Undergraduate Admissions. A video is available. E-mail: *admissions@shsu.edu*
Web: *www.shsu.edu*

SCHREINER UNIVERSITY   D-4
Kerrville, TX 78028-5697

	(830) 792-7217
	(800) 343-4919; Fax: (830) 792-7226
Full-time: 300 men, 380 women	Faculty: 49; IIB, --$
Part-time: 20 men, 60 women	Ph.D.s: 63%
Graduate: 10 men, 40 women	Student/Faculty: 14 to 1
Year: semesters, summer session	Tuition: $13,700
Application Deadline: see profile	Room & Board: $6900
Freshman Class: n/av	
SAT or ACT: required	COMPETITIVE

Schreiner University, founded in 1917, is an independent liberal arts institution affiliated with the Presbyterian Church (U.S.A.). There are 3 undergraduate schools and 1 graduate school. Figures in the above capsule and in this profile are approximate. The library contains 69,873 volumes, 593 microform items, and 477 audio/video tapes/CDs/DVDs, and subscribes to 225 periodicals including electronic. Computerized library services include the card catalog, interlibrary loans, database searching, and Internet access. Special learning facilities include a learning resource center. The 175-acre campus is in a small town 60 miles northwest of San Antonio. Including any residence halls, there are 43 buildings.

Student Life: 95% of undergraduates are from Texas. Others are from 9 states, 11 foreign countries, and Canada. 79% are white; 16% Hispanic. 59% are Protestant; 19% Catholic; 17% claim no religious affiliation. The average age of freshmen is 19; all undergraduates, 24. 37% do not continue beyond their first year; 38% remain to graduate.

Housing: 483 students can be accommodated in college housing, which includes coed dormitories and on-campus apartments. On-campus housing is guaranteed for all 4 years. 51% of students commute. All students may keep cars.

Activities: 10% of men belong to 2 national fraternities; 13% of women belong to 2 national sororities. There are 35 groups on campus, including art, cheerleading, choir, chorale, drama, honors, international, literary magazine, newspaper, pep band, photography, political, profession-

al, religious, social, student government, and yearbook. Popular campus events include Schreiner Speaker Series, Trull Casino Night, and Toga Party.

Sports: There are 5 intercollegiate sports for men and 7 for women, and 8 intramural sports for men and 8 for women. Facilities include basketball and volleyball courts, baseball and softball diamonds, 3 handball/racquetball courts, a track, 8 tennis courts, a swimming pool, soccer and intramural fields, a golf driving range, and a recreation room.

Disabled Students: 95% of the campus is accessible. Wheelchair ramps, elevators, special parking, specially equipped rest rooms, special class scheduling, lowered drinking fountains, and lowered telephones are available.

Services: Counseling and information services are available, as is tutoring in every subject, including introductory-level courses. There is remedial math, reading, and writing. There also are workshops, a certified peer-tutoring program, a math lab, a self-management orientation course, and computer-assisted instruction for learning skills.

Campus Safety and Security: Measures include informal discussions, pamphlets/posters/films, emergency telephones, and and a night vehicle patrol.

Programs of Study: Schreiner confers B.A., B.S., B.B.A., and B.G.S. degrees. Associate and master's degrees are also awarded. Bachelor's degrees are awarded in BIOLOGICAL SCIENCE (biochemistry and biology/biological science), BUSINESS (accounting, business administration and management, and management information systems), COMMUNICATIONS AND THE ARTS (art, dramatic arts, English, graphic design, music, and visual and performing arts), COMPUTER AND PHYSICAL SCIENCE (chemistry and mathematics), EDUCATION (art, early childhood, education, elementary, English, mathematics, middle school, music, physical, science, secondary, and social science), HEALTH PROFESSIONS (exercise science), SOCIAL SCIENCE (history, humanities, liberal arts/general studies, philosophy, political science/government, prelaw, psychology, and religion). History, English, and exercise science are the strongest academically. Business administration, exercise science, and psychology are the largest.

Required: To graduate, all students must have a minimum GPA of 2.0 for 120 semester hours, including 24 hours in the major. The core curriculum includes courses from English composition, oral communication, foreign language, history, natural science, math, philosophy or religion, computer studies, government, business administration, literature and fine arts, social science, and fitness. B.A. candidates must complete a senior capstone project, thesis, or course; B.B.A. candidates may substitute an internship.

Special: Schreiner offers study abroad in Japan and England, work-study with the university, second majors, a general studies degree, non-degree study, and a 3-2 engineering degree with the University of Texas, Texas Tech University, and Texas A&M University. There are 5 national honor societies, a freshman honors program, and 100 departmental honors programs.

Faculty/Classroom: 60% of faculty are male; 40%, female. All teach undergraduates. No introductory courses are taught by graduate students. The average class size in an introductory lecture is 18; in a laboratory, 17; and in a regular course, 13.

Requirements: The SAT or ACT is required. Applicants need 20 secondary-school academic credits, including 4 each of English and math, 2 each of social science, foreign language, and lab science, and 1 of history. An interview is advised. The GED is accepted; applicants with a GED are not required to take the SAT or ACT but are encouraged to do so. Schreiner requires applicants to be in the upper 50% of their class. A GPA of 2.0 is required. AP and CLEP credits are accepted.

Procedure: Freshmen are admitted to all sessions. Entrance exams should be taken in the spring of the junior year. There are early admissions and deferred admissions plans. Check with the school for current application deadlines and fee. Notification is sent on a rolling basis. Applications are accepted on-line.

Transfer: 87 transfer students enrolled in a recent year. Applicants with fewer than 15 transferable credit hours must meet freshman admissions requirements. For those with more, the SAT or ACT is not required. A 2.0 minimum GPA is necessary. 30 of 120 credits required for the bachelor's degree must be completed at Schreiner.

Visiting: There are regularly scheduled orientations for prospective students, including guided tours, financial aid information, and faculty and student discussions. There are guides for informal visits and visitors may sit in on classes and stay overnight. To schedule a visit, contact the Admission Office.

Financial Aid: In a recent year, 78% of all full-time freshmen and 87% of continuing full-time students received some form of financial aid. 65% of full-time freshmen and 73% of continuing full-time students received need-based aid. The average freshman award was $11,222. Need-based scholarships or need-based grants averaged $11,373; need-based self-help aid (loans and jobs) averaged $2588; and other non-need-based awards and non-need-based scholarships averaged $9483. 25% of undergraduates work part time. Average annual earnings from campus work are $995. The average financial indebtedness of the recent year's graduate was $19,208. The FAFSA and are required. Check with the school for current deadlines.

International Students: In a recent year, there were 7 international students enrolled. The school actively recruits these students. Satisfactory scores are required on the written TOEFL and the MELAB, the Comprehensive English Language Test, or the college's own test.

Computers: All students may access the system. There are no time limits and no fees.

Graduates: In a recent year, 113 bachelor's degrees were awarded. The most popular majors were business and marketing (32%), education (12%), and exercise science (12%). In an average class, 38% graduate in 6 years or less.

Admissions Contact: Peg Layton, Acting Dean of Admission and Financial Aid. A video is available. E-mail: *admissions@schreiner.edu* Web: *www.schreiner.edu*

SOUTHERN METHODIST UNIVERSITY   D-2

Dallas, TX 75275-0181   (214) 768-4223
                                      (800) 323-0672; Fax: (214) 768-0202

Full-time: 2801 men, 3328 women	**Faculty:** 511; I, -$
Part-time: 136 men, 229 women	**Ph.D.s:** 84%
Graduate: 2736 men, 1922 women	**Student/Faculty:** 12 to 1
Year: semesters, summer session	**Tuition:** $26,880
Application Deadline: January 15	**Room & Board:** $9208
Freshman Class: 6980 applied, 4076 accepted, 1402 enrolled	
SAT Verbal/Math: 610/620*	**ACT:** 26 **VERY COMPETITIVE+**

Southern Methodist University, founded in 1911, is a private nonsectarian institution affiliated with the United Methodist Church. SMU offers undergraduate and graduate programs in humanities and sciences, business, arts, and engineering and applied sciences. There are 5 undergraduate and 7 graduate schools. In addition to regional accreditation, SMU has baccalaureate program accreditation with AACSB, ABET, NASAD, and NASM. The 8 libraries contain 2,807,991 volumes, 826,398 microform items, and 43,620 audio/video tapes/CDs/DVDs, and subscribe to 11,800 periodicals including electronic. Computerized library services include the card catalog, interlibrary loans, database searching, Internet access, and laptop Internet portals. Special learning facilities include a learning resource center, art gallery, natural history museum, radio station, art museum, research labs, TV studio, and several performing arts theaters, including Classical Thrust Stage. The 175-acre campus is in a suburban area 5 miles north of downtown Dallas. Including any residence halls, there are 76 buildings.

Student Life: 62% of undergraduates are from Texas. Others are from 50 states, 66 foreign countries, and Canada. 65% are from public schools. 71% are white. 44% claim no religious affiliation; 39% Protestant; 13% Catholic; 13% Methodist. The average age of freshmen is 18; all undergraduates, 21. 13% do not continue beyond their first year; 73% remain to graduate.

Housing: 2100 students can be accommodated in college housing, which includes coed dorms, on-campus apartments, married-student housing, fraternity houses, and sorority houses. In addition, there are honors houses, Wellness Hall, Fine Arts Hall, FY Academic Focus Hall, Multicultural House, Transfer House, and Community Service House. On-campus housing is guaranteed for the freshman year only and is available on a first-come, first-served basis. Alcohol is not permitted. All students may keep cars.

Activities: 29% of men belong to 16 national fraternities; 35% of women belong to 14 national sororities. There are 200 groups on campus, including art, band, cheerleading, choir, chorale, chorus, computers, dance, debate, drama, drill team, ethnic, film, forensics, gay, honors, international, jazz band, literary magazine, marching band, musical theater, newspaper, opera, orchestra, pep band, photography, political, professional, radio and TV, religious, social, social service, student government, symphony, and yearbook. Popular campus events include Celebration of Lights, and Community Service Day.

Sports: There are 8 intercollegiate sports for men and 8 for women, and 16 intramural sports for men and 15 for women. Facilities include gymnastic and weight rooms, a dance studio, indoor and outdoor jogging tracks, indoor and outdoor pools, a 2400-seat outdoor stadium, a 6500-seat indoor stadium, and courts for basketball, volleyball, tennis, badminton, and racquetball.

Disabled Students: 95% of the campus is accessible. Wheelchair ramps, elevators, special parking, specially equipped rest rooms, special class scheduling, lowered drinking fountains, lowered telephones, and automatic doors are available.

Services: Counseling and information services are available, as is tutoring in most subjects. There is a reader service for the blind and remedial reading and writing. The Learning Enhancement Center provides study skills workshops, note-taking techniques, and time management skills seminars.

Campus Safety and Security: Measures include 24-hour foot and vehicle patrol, self-defense education, security escort services, and shuttle buses. There are informal discussions, pamphlets/posters/films, emergen-

cy telephones, and lighted pathways/sidewalks. Cardkey devices, issued to all students living in residence halls, must be used to enter these buildings.

Programs of Study: SMU confers B.A., B.S., B.B.A., B.F.A., B.Hum., B.M., B.S.Comp.Eng., B.S.E.E., B.S.Env.E., B.S.M.E., and B.Soc.Sci. degrees. Master's and doctoral degrees are also awarded. Bachelor's degrees are awarded in BIOLOGICAL SCIENCE (biochemistry and biology/biological science), BUSINESS (accounting, banking and finance, business administration and management, management information systems, management science, marketing/retailing/merchandising, organizational behavior, and real estate), COMMUNICATIONS AND THE ARTS (advertising, art history and appreciation, broadcasting, communications, communications technology, creative writing, dance, dramatic arts, English, film arts, French, German, journalism, languages, media arts, music performance, music theory and composition, performing arts, piano/organ, public relations, Russian, Spanish, studio art, telecommunications, and video), COMPUTER AND PHYSICAL SCIENCE (chemistry, computer science, environmental geology, geology, geophysics and seismology, mathematics, physics, and statistics), EDUCATION (art, dance, elementary, health, music, and physical), ENGINEERING AND ENVIRONMENTAL DESIGN (civil engineering, computer engineering, electrical/electronics engineering, engineering management, environmental engineering, environmental science, and mechanical engineering), HEALTH PROFESSIONS (music therapy and speech pathology/audiology), SOCIAL SCIENCE (African American studies, anthropology, criminal justice, economics, German area studies, history, humanities, international studies, Italian studies, Latin American studies, liberal arts/general studies, medieval studies, Mexican-American/Chicano studies, philosophy, physical fitness/movement, political science/government, psychology, public affairs, religion, Russian and Slavic studies, social science, sociology, and Southwest American studies). Performing arts, life sciences, and history are the strongest academically. Business, communications, and psychology are the largest.

Required: Basic requirements consist of 122 semester hours, including a general education requirement of 41 hours distributed across Fundamentals (writing, math, and information technology), Science and Technology, Perspectives (arts, literature, religious and philosophical thought, history, politics and economics, and behavioral sciences), Cultural Formations (interdisciplinary courses), and a corequirement in Human Diversity (race, ethnicity, and gender). There is also a 2-credit education requirement. Students must maintain a GPA of 2.0.

Special: SMU offers a co-op program in engineering, work-study programs, B.A.-B.S. degrees, study abroad in 12 countries, dual majors in any combination, student-designed majors, numerous internships, and interdisciplinary majors, including economics with finance applications and economics with systems analysis. A 3-2 advanced degree in business is available, as are evening degree programs in humanities and social sciences, and teacher certification programs. There are 14 national honor societies, including Phi Beta Kappa, and a freshman honors program.

Faculty/Classroom: 67% of faculty are male; 33%, female. 89% teach undergraduates and 89% both teach and do research.

Admissions: 58% of the 2005-2006 applicants were accepted. The SAT scores for the 2005-2006 freshman class were: Verbal--7% below 500, 39% between 500 and 599, 43% between 600 and 700, and 11% above 700; Math--5% below 500, 32% between 500 and 599, 47% between 600 and 700, and 16% above 700. The ACT scores were 1% below 18, 23% between 18 and 23, 61% between 24 and 29, and 15% between 30 and 28. 36% of the current freshmen were in the top fifth of their class; 85% were in the top two fifths.

Requirements: The SAT or ACT is recommended. In addition, applicants should graduate from an accredited high school with a minimum of 15 academic credits: 4 in English, 3 in higher math, including algebra I, II, and plane geometry, 3 each in natural science and social science, and 2 in a foreign language. Home School Certificate applicants may qualify with the SAT or ACT and 3 SAT Subject tests, including writing and math. Performing arts majors must audition. AP and CLEP credits are accepted. Important factors in the admissions decision are advanced placement or honor courses, leadership record, and recommendations by school officials.

Procedure: Freshmen are admitted to all sessions. Entrance exams should be taken by December of the senior year. There are early admissions, early action, and deferred admissions plans. Early action applications should be filed by November 1; regular applications, by January 15 for fall entry and March 15 for spring entry. Notification of early action is sent December 31; regular decision, on a rolling basis. 715 applicants were on the 2005 waiting list; 76 were admitted. Applications are accepted on-line.

Transfer: 303 transfer students enrolled in 2004-2005. A minimum 2.5 GPA is generally required for transfer, but specific requirements vary according to the program of study. Candidates must demonstrate math proficiency. A foreign language requirement may be met through high school or college work. 60 of 122 credits required for the bachelor's degree must be completed at SMU.

Visiting: There are regularly scheduled orientations for prospective students, including information about academic studies, financial-aid sessions, discussions with current students, lunch with faculty and students, and a tour of the campus. There is also a Spring Fest visitation in April for high school juniors. There are guides for informal visits and visitors may sit in on classes and stay overnight. To schedule a visit, contact the Undergraduate Admissions Office.

Financial Aid: In 2005-2006, 76% of all full-time freshmen and 65% of continuing full-time students received some form of financial aid. 32% of full-time freshmen and 35% of continuing full-time students received need-based aid. The average freshman award was $23,506. Need-based scholarships or need-based grants averaged $11,918; need-based self-help aid (loans and jobs) averaged $4547; and non-need-based athletic scholarships averaged $30,274. The average financial indebtedness of the 2005 graduate was $18,571. SMU is a member of CSS. The FAFSA is required.

International Students: There are 841 international students enrolled. The school actively recruits these students. They must take the TOEFL and also take the SAT or the ACT.

Computers: Wireless access is available. All students may access the system 24 hours a day. There are no time limits and no fees.

Graduates: From July 1, 2004 to June 30, 2005, 1492 bachelor's degrees were awarded. The most popular majors were business/marketing (27%), social sciences and history (15%), and communications (12%). In an average class, 1% graduate in 3 years or less, 56% graduate in 4 years or less, 72% graduate in 5 years or less, and 72% graduate in 6 years or less.

Admissions Contact: Nancy Peterson, Associate Director, Admissions. A video is available. E-mail: *enrol_serv@mail.smu.edu*
Web: *www.smu.edu*

SOUTHWEST TEXAS STATE UNIVERSITY
(See Texas State University - San Marcos)

SOUTHWESTERN ADVENTIST UNIVERSITY   D-2
Keene, TX 76059   (817) 202-6408
(800) 433-2240; Fax: (817) 556-4744

Full-time: 336 men, 399 women	**Faculty:** 50
Part-time: 54 men, 91 women	**Ph.D.s:** 63%
Graduate: 16 men, 7 women	**Student/Faculty:** 15 to 1
Year: semesters, summer session	**Tuition:** $12,484
Application Deadline: September 5	**Room & Board:** $5806
Freshman Class: n/av	
SAT: required	**LESS COMPETITIVE**

Southwestern Adventist College, founded in 1893, is a small Seventh-day Adventist institution offering liberal arts and professional degree programs. In addition to regional accreditation, SWAU has baccalaureate program accreditation with NLN. The library contains 110,261 volumes, 7031 microform items, and 1741 audio/video tapes/CDs/DVDs, and subscribes to 439 periodicals including electronic. Computerized library services include the card catalog, interlibrary loans, database searching, Internet access, and laptop Internet portals. Special learning facilities include a learning resource center, natural history museum, radio station, TV station, and observatory. The 150-acre campus is in a rural area 35 miles south of Fort Worth. Including any residence halls, there are 24 buildings.

Student Life: 25% of undergraduates are from Texas. Students are from 28 states, 67 foreign countries, and Canada. 44% are from public schools. 38% are white; 22% Hispanic; 15% foreign nationals; 13% African American. 77% are claim no religious affiliation; 23% Protestant. The average age of all undergraduates is 26. 23% do not continue beyond their first year; 33% remain to graduate.

Housing: 420 students can be accommodated in college housing, which includes single-sex dorms and married-student housing. On-campus housing is guaranteed for all 4 years. 56% of students commute. Alcohol is not permitted. All students may keep cars.

Activities: There are no fraternities or sororities. There are 22 groups on campus, including art, band, choir, chorale, computers, drama, ethnic, film, honors, international, newspaper, orchestra, pep band, photography, professional, radio and TV, religious, social, social service, student government, symphony, and yearbook. Popular campus events include Founders Day, Fall Holiday, and Memosa Memories.

Sports: There are 4 intramural sports for men and 4 for women. Facilities include jogging and fitness tracks, weight and aerobics rooms, courts for tennis, racquetball, and basketball, and fields for football and baseball.

Disabled Students: 78% of the campus is accessible. Wheelchair ramps, elevators, special parking, specially equipped rest rooms, and lowered drinking fountains are available.

Services: Counseling and information services are available, as is tutoring in some subjects, including accounting, biology, chemistry, English, Greek, math, nursing, and Spanish. There is remedial math and writing.

Campus Safety and Security: Measures include informal discussions, pamphlets/posters/films, lighted pathways/sidewalks, and a 12-hour night foot patrol.

Programs of Study: SWAU confers B.A., B.S., B.B.A., and B.S.W. degrees. Associate and master's degrees are also awarded. Bachelor's degrees are awarded in BIOLOGICAL SCIENCE (biology/biological science), BUSINESS (business administration and management, international economics, management science, and office supervision and management), COMMUNICATIONS AND THE ARTS (broadcasting, communications, English, journalism, music, and speech/debate/rhetoric), COMPUTER AND PHYSICAL SCIENCE (chemistry, computer science, information sciences and systems, mathematics, and physics), EDUCATION (business, elementary, physical, and secondary), HEALTH PROFESSIONS (exercise science, health, medical technology, and nursing), SOCIAL SCIENCE (criminal justice, history, international relations, psychology, religion, social science, social studies, social work, and theological studies). Nursing, biology, and religion are the strongest academically. Education, nursing, and business are the largest.

Required: To graduate, students must complete at least 128 hours, including 40 hours in upper-division courses and 27 to 48 in the major. An overall 2.0 GPA is required, with a 2.3 in upper-division courses in the major field. General education requirements include 62 hours of core courses in English, health and phys ed, math and science, religion, social science and humanities, and, in some cases, foreign language. Comprehensive and departmental exit exams are required.

Special: Cooperative programs in medical technology are available with several area hospitals. Internships are arranged on an individual basis. Students may study abroad in Germany, France, or Spain. Student-designed majors, interdisciplinary majors, including mathematical physics, a 3-2 engineering degree with Walla Walla College and Andrews University, and an adult degree program are offered. There is a freshman honors program, and 1 departmental honors program.

Faculty/Classroom: 63% of faculty are male; 37%, female. All teach undergraduates and 8% both teach and do research. No introductory courses are taught by graduate students. The average class size in an introductory lecture is 30; in a laboratory, 15; and in a regular course, 20.

Requirements: The SAT is required. In addition, applicants should be high school graduates or hold the GED. Secondary preparation is expected to include 12 academic credits in English, foreign language, math, natural or physical science, and social science. Potential nursing or education majors or Seventh-day Adventist ministers must meet additional requirements. AP and CLEP credits are accepted. Important factors in the admissions decision are recommendations by alumni, ability to finance college education, and leadership record.

Procedure: Freshmen are admitted fall, spring, and summer. Entrance exams should be taken before registration. There are early admissions, deferred admissions, and rolling admissions plans. Applications should be filed by September 5 for fall entry, January 16 for spring entry and May 6 for summer entry. Notification is sent on a rolling basis. Applications are accepted on-line.

Transfer: An official transcript from each college or university the student has attended must be mailed directly to SWAU's Admissions Office. Transfer students with less than a C average may be accepted on a probationary basis. Nursing, education, and theology majors have additional requirements. 30 of 128 credits required for the bachelor's degree must be completed at SWAU.

Visiting: There are regularly scheduled orientations for prospective students, including scheduled weekend visitation programs in February and the summer that consist of meeting the administration, touring the campus, and receiving financial and academic counseling; preregistration is available in summer. There are guides for informal visits and visitors may sit in on classes and stay overnight. To schedule a visit, contact the Enrollment Office at *tinabot@swau.edu*.

Financial Aid: The FAFSA and the college's own financial statement are required. Check with the school for current deadlines.

International Students: There are 139 international students enrolled. The school actively recruits these students. A satisfactory score is required on the written TOEFL or the MELAB. Students must also take the SAT or ACT. SAT/ACT scores are required of students from English-speaking countries.

Computers: Wireless access is available. The university provides 200 computers, with 24-hour access to the Internet, including from each dorm room. All students may access the system 24 hours per day. There are no time limits and no fees. It is strongly recommended that all students have a PC.

Graduates: From July 1, 2004 to June 30, 2005, 200 bachelor's degrees were awarded. The most popular majors were education (21%), business (15%), and nursing (15%). In an average class, 3% graduate in 3 years or less, 20% graduate in 4 years or less, 30% graduate in 5 years or less, and 33% graduate in 6 years or less.

Admissions Contact: Tina Bottsford, Director for Enrollment.
E-mail: *admissions@swau.edu* Web: *www.swau.edu*

SOUTHWESTERN UNIVERSITY
D-3
Georgetown, TX 78626
(512) 863-1200
(800) 252-3166; Fax: (512) 863-9601

Full-time: 532 men, 754 women	**Faculty:** 118; IIB, av$
Part-time: 7 men, 16 women	**Ph.D.s:** 99%
Graduate: none	**Student/Faculty:** 11 to 1
Year: semesters, summer session	**Tuition:** $20,220
Application Deadline: February 15	**Room & Board:** $6547
Freshman Class: 1760 applied, 1178 accepted, 329 enrolled	
SAT Verbal/Math: 620/610*	**ACT: 26 HIGHLY COMPETITIVE**

Southwestern University, founded in 1840, is a private liberal arts institution affiliated with the United Methodist Church. There are 2 undergraduate schools. In addition to regional accreditation, Southwestern has baccalaureate program accreditation with NASM. The library contains 312,490 volumes, 56,531 microform items, and 12,186 audio/video tapes/CDs/DVDs, and subscribes to 1372 periodicals including electronic. Computerized library services include the card catalog, interlibrary loans, and database searching. Special learning facilities include a learning resource center and art gallery. The 700-acre campus is in a suburban area 28 miles north of Austin. Including any residence halls, there are 31 buildings.

Student Life: 92% of undergraduates are from Texas. Others are from 33 states, 9 foreign countries, and Canada. 82% are from public schools. 76% are white; 14% Hispanic. 68% are Protestant; 20% Catholic; 14% claim no religious affiliation; 8% have no preference; 1% are Muslim, Buddhist, Mormon, or Hindu. The average age of freshmen is 18; all undergraduates, 20. 11% do not continue beyond their first year; 78% remain to graduate.

Housing: 1042 students can be accommodated in college housing, which includes single-sex and coed dormitories, on-campus apartments, and fraternity houses. In addition, there are special-interest houses. On-campus housing is guaranteed for the freshman year only, is available on a first-come, first-served basis, and is available on a lottery system for upperclassmen. 80% of students live on campus; of those, 55% remain on campus on weekends. All students may keep cars.

Activities: 29% of men belong to 3 national fraternities; 31% of women belong to 4 national sororities. There are 105 groups on campus, including art, band, cheerleading, choir, chorale, chorus, computers, dance, drama, ethnic, film, gay, honors, international, jazz band, literary magazine, musical theater, newspaper, opera, orchestra, pep band, political, professional, religious, social, social service, student government, and yearbook. Popular campus events include Homecoming Sing, Mall Ball, and Brown Symposium.

Sports: There are 7 intercollegiate sports for men and 7 for women, and 9 intramural sports for men and 9 for women. Facilities include a health and wellness center, a 2000-seat gym, a 9-hole golf course, tennis courts, a baseball field, soccer and lacrosse fields, and a recreation center that includes an indoor jogging track, large performance gym, weight training room, and indoor swimming pool.

Disabled Students: 90% of the campus is accessible. Wheelchair ramps, elevators, special parking, specially equipped rest rooms, lowered drinking fountains, and lowered telephones are available.

Services: Counseling and information services are available, as is tutoring in some subjects, including math, computer science, and sciences.

Campus Safety and Security: Measures include 24-hour foot and vehicle patrol, self-defense education, security escort services, and informal discussions. There are pamphlets/posters/films, emergency telephones, and lighted pathways/sidewalks.

Programs of Study: Southwestern confers B.A., B.S., B.F.A., and B.Mus. degrees. Bachelor's degrees are awarded in AGRICULTURE (animal science and environmental studies), BIOLOGICAL SCIENCE (biology/biological science), BUSINESS (accounting, and business administration and management), COMMUNICATIONS AND THE ARTS (art, classics, communications, dramatic arts, English, French, German, Latin, music, and Spanish), COMPUTER AND PHYSICAL SCIENCE (chemistry, computer science, mathematics, and physics), SOCIAL SCIENCE (American studies, early childhood studies, economics, history, international studies, philosophy, physical fitness/movement, political science/government, psychology, religion, sociology, and women's studies). Biology, sociology, and political science are the strongest academically. Psychology, biology, and business are the largest.

Required: To graduate, all students must complete at least 122 credits with a 2.0 GPA and satisfy distribution requirements in the arts, humanities, social science, and natural science. The total number of hours required in most majors in 30. A first-year seminar and math course are required. All students must take 1 semester of English composition and must demonstrate computer literacy. Seniors must complete a capstone requirement in the major.

Special: Students may study abroad in England, France, Mexico, Korea, and other countries. The university offers a Washington semester, dual, student-designed, and independent majors, and internships in government, fine arts, psychology, sociology, science, and other fields, within Texas or in New York or other states. A 3-2 engineering program may

be arranged with Washington, Texas A&M, and Arizona State Universities, and the University of Texas at Austin. Some pass/fail options are available, as are accelerated degrees in any field. There are 7 national honor societies, including Phi Beta Kappa, and 21 departmental honors programs.

Faculty/Classroom: 53% of faculty are male; 47%, female. All teach undergraduates. The average class size in an introductory lecture is 18; in a laboratory, 15; and in a regular course, 12.

Admissions: 67% of the 2005-2006 applicants were accepted. The SAT scores for the 2005-2006 freshman class were: Verbal--7% below 500, 31% between 500 and 599, 47% between 600 and 700, and 16% above 700; Math--6% below 500, 29% between 500 and 599, 51% between 600 and 700, and 14% above 700. The ACT scores were 3% below 21, 21% between 21 and 23, 28% between 24 and 26, 22% between 27 and 28, and 26% above 28. 73% of the current freshmen were in the top fifth of their class; 95% were in the top two fifths. There were 5 National Merit finalists and 7 semifinalists. 7 freshmen graduated first in their class.

Requirements: The SAT or ACT is required. In addition, the applicant should be a graduate of an accredited high school or have the GED. Secondary preparation should include 4 years each of English and math, 3 each of science and social science or history, 2 of a foreign language, and 1 of an academic elective. An essay is required, and an interview is recommended. AP and CLEP credits are accepted. Important factors in the admissions decision are advanced placement or honor courses, recommendations by school officials, and leadership record.

Procedure: Freshmen are admitted fall and spring. Entrance exams should be taken in the fall of the senior year. There are early admissions and deferred admissions plans. Early decision applications should be filed by November 1; regular applications, by February 15 for fall entry and December 1 for spring entry, along with a $40 fee. Notification of early decision is sent December 1; regular decision, March 3. 58 early decision candidates were accepted for the 2005-2006 class. 163 applicants were on the 2005 waiting list; 24 were admitted. Applications are accepted on-line.

Transfer: 38 transfer students enrolled in a recent year. Preference is given to students having a 3.0 in all college work. 31 of 122 credits required for the bachelor's degree must be completed at Southwestern.

Visiting: There are regularly scheduled orientations for prospective students, including 3 or 4 group overnight options and individually arranged visits throughout the year. All visits typically include tours, faculty appointments and interview, and may also include an overnight on campus and class visit. There are guides for informal visits and visitors may sit in on classes and stay overnight. To schedule a visit, contact the Admission Office.

Financial Aid: In 2005-2006, 84% of all full-time freshmen and 83% of continuing full-time students received some form of financial aid. 54% of full-time freshmen and 52% of continuing full-time students received need-based aid. The average freshman award was $18,807. Need-based scholarships or need-based grants averaged $14,602 ($19,638 maximum); need-based self-help aid (loans and jobs) averaged $4709 ($7625 maximum); and other non-need-based awards and non-need-based scholarships averaged $8121 ($29,100 maximum). 59% of undergraduates work part time. Average annual earnings from campus work are $1083. The average financial indebtedness of the 2005 graduate was $18,393. Southwestern is a member of CSS. The FAFSA is required. The deadline for filing freshman financial aid applications for fall entry is March 1.

International Students: In a recent year there are 4 international students enrolled. The school actively recruits these students. They must score satisfactorily on the written TOEFL or on the electronic version and also take the SAT or the ACT.

Computers: All students may access the system at any time. There are no time limits and no fees.

Graduates: From July 1, 2004 to June 30, 2005, 264 bachelor's degrees were awarded. The most popular majors were communications (14%), business (9%), and political science (9%). In an average class, 1% graduate in 3 years or less, 67% graduate in 4 years or less, 77% graduate in 5 years or less, and 78% graduate in 6 years or less. 26 companies recruited on campus in 2004-2005. Of the 2004 graduating class, 25% were enrolled in graduate school within 6 months of graduation and 65% were employed.

Admissions Contact: Tom Oliver, Vice President, Enrollment Services. E-mail: admission@southwestern.edu
Web: www.southwestern.edu

STEPHEN F. AUSTIN STATE UNIVERSITY   E-3
Nacogdoches, TX 75962

(936) 468-2504
(800) 731-2902; Fax: (936) 468-3849

Full-time: 3440 men, 4950 women	**Faculty:** 381; IIA, --$
Part-time: 540 men, 830 women	**Ph.D.s:** 75%
Graduate: 590 men, 1080 women	**Student/Faculty:** 22 to 1
Year: semesters, summer session	**Tuition:** $2752($8500)
Application Deadline: open	**Room & Board:** $5000
Freshman Class: 6506 applied, 4823 accepted, 1937 enrolled	
SAT or ACT: required	**COMPETITIVE**

Stephen F. Austin State University, founded in 1923, is a public regional university offering undergraduate and graduate degree programs through 7 colleges. Some information in this profile is approximate. There are 7 undergraduate schools and 1 graduate school. Figures in the above capsule and in this profile are approximate. In addition to regional accreditation, SFA has baccalaureate program accreditation with AACSB, ADA, CSWE, FIDER, NASM, NCATE, NLN, and SAF. The library contains 946,123 volumes, 832,219 microform items, and 23,739 audio/video tapes/CDs/DVDs, and subscribes to 2805 periodicals including electronic. Computerized library services include the card catalog, interlibrary loans, database searching, Internet access, and laptop Internet portals. Special learning facilities include a learning resource center, art gallery, planetarium, radio station, TV station, arboretum, beef and poultry research centers, experimental forest, and biotechnology and environmental science research centers. The 401-acre campus is in a small town 140 miles northeast of Houston. Including any residence halls, there are 90 buildings.

Student Life: 98% of undergraduate are from Texas. Students are from 38 states, 45 foreign countries, and Canada. 99% are from public schools. 76% are white; 15% African American. The average age of freshmen is 19; all undergraduates, 22. 40% do not continue beyond their first year; 35% remain to graduate.

Housing: 4308 students can be accommodated in college housing, which includes single-sex and coed dorms, on-campus apartments, and married-student housing. In addition, there are honors houses, special-interest houses, and an enrichment hall with required study hall hours. On-campus housing is guaranteed for all 4 years. 63% of students commute. Alcohol is not permitted. All students may keep cars.

Activities: 17% of men belong to 24 national fraternities; 12% of women belong to 15 national sororities. There are 224 groups on campus, including art, band, cheerleading, choir, chorale, chorus, computers, dance, debate, drama, drill team, ethnic, film, flag corps, gay, honors, international, jazz band, literary magazine, marching band, musical theater, newspaper, opera, orchestra, pep band, photography, political, professional, radio and TV, religious, social, social service, student government, symphony, and yearbook. Popular campus events include Parents Weekend, Watermelon Bash, and Howdy Week.

Sports: There are 6 intercollegiate sports for men and 8 for women, and 13 intramural sports for men and 9 for women. Facilities include 2 gyms, courts for handball, tennis, and racquetball, weight and gymnastics rooms, and various playing fields.

Disabled Students: All of the campus is accessible. Wheelchair ramps, elevators, special parking, specially equipped rest rooms, special class scheduling, lowered drinking fountains, and lowered telephones are available.

Services: Counseling and information services are available, as is tutoring in most subjects. There is a reader service for the blind, and remedial math, reading, and writing.

Campus Safety and Security: Measures include 24-hour foot and vehicle patrol, self-defense education, security escort services, and shuttle buses. There are informal discussions, pamphlets/posters/films, emergency telephones, and lighted pathways/sidewalks.

Programs of Study: SFA confers B.A., B.S., B.A.A.S., B.B.A., B.F.A., B.M., B.S.A.G., B.S.F., B.S.I.S., B.S.N., B.S.R.H.B., and B.S.W. degrees. Master's and doctoral degrees are also awarded. Bachelor's degrees are awarded in AGRICULTURE (agricultural business management, agricultural mechanics, agriculture, agronomy, animal science, fish and game management, forestry and related sciences, forestry production and processing, horticulture, poultry science, and range/farm management), BIOLOGICAL SCIENCE (biology/biological science and nutrition), BUSINESS (accounting, banking and finance, business administration and management, fashion merchandising, hospitality management services, international business management, management information systems, management science, marketing management, marketing/retailing/merchandising, and office supervision and management), COMMUNICATIONS AND THE ARTS (art, broadcasting, communications, dance, dramatic arts, English, fine arts, French, journalism, music, Spanish, and speech/debate/rhetoric), COMPUTER AND PHYSICAL SCIENCE (chemistry, computer programming, computer science, geology, information sciences and systems, mathematics, and physics), EDUCATION (agricultural), ENGINEERING AND ENVIRONMENTAL DESIGN (environmental science, interior design, and preengineering), HEALTH PROFESSIONS (health science, nursing, premedicine, preop-

tometry, prepharmacy, preveterinary science, rehabilitation therapy, and speech therapy), SOCIAL SCIENCE (child psychology/development, corrections, criminal justice, dietetics, economics, food production/management/services, food science, geography, gerontology, history, home economics, humanities, interdisciplinary studies, law enforcement and corrections, parks and recreation management, physical fitness/movement, political science/government, prelaw, psychology, public administration, social work, and sociology). Interdisciplinary studies, nursing, and kinesiology are the largest.

Required: All students must complete at least 130 hours with a minimum 2.0 GPA. The B.A. program requires courses in communication skills, math and natural science, humanities, social science, and physical activity.

Special: Internships, dual majors, and dual degrees are possible in some programs. Study abroad is available in more than 40 countries. Preengineering and 3-2 engineering programs with Texas A&M are offered, as are preprofessional programs and a general studies degree. There are 10 national honor societies, a freshman honors program, and 8 departmental honors programs.

Faculty/Classroom: 54% of faculty are male; 46%, female. 92% teach undergraduates. The average class size in an introductory lecture is 21 and in a laboratory, 30.

Requirements: The SAT or ACT is required. In addition, for clear admission, applicants must have been in the top 50% of their high school class or have a satisfactory SAT or ACT score. AP and CLEP credits are accepted.

Procedure: Freshmen are admitted to all sessions. Entrance exams should be taken during the junior year. Application deadlines are open. Check with the school ofr current application deadlines and fee. Notification is sent on a rolling basis. Applications are accepted on-line.

Transfer: 1339 transfer students enrolled in a recent year. Applicants with fewer than 15 hours of college work must meet freshman admission requirements. Those with more than 15 hours must have at least a 2.0 GPA. Those with GPAs lower than 2.0 may be admitted to the summer school on probation. 42 of 130 credits required for the bachelor's degree must be completed at SFA.

Visiting: There are regularly scheduled orientations for prospective students, including Showcase Saturdays, which are 1-day open house programs with faculty, staff, and current students. There are guides for informal visits and visitors may sit in on classes. To schedule a visit, contact the Admissions Office.

Financial Aid: In a recent year, 49% of all full-time freshmen and 42% of continuing full-time students received some form of financial aid. 50% of full-time freshmen and 64% of continuing full-time students received need-based aid. The average freshman award was $4394. Average annual earnings from campus work are $3500. The average financial indebtedness of a recent year's graduate was $9922. The FAFSA is required. Check with the school for current deadlines.

International Students: In a recent year, there were 69 international students enrolled in recent year. The school actively recruits these students. Satisfactory scores are required on the TOEFL and the SAT or the ACT.

Computers: All students may access the system at any time. Students are allowed 30 minutes of Internet access per 4 hours. There are no fees.

Graduates: In a recent year,1684 bachelor's degrees were awarded. The most popular majors were educational leadership (30%), general business (6%), and social work (6%). In an average class, 15% graduate in 4 years or less, 31% graduate in 5 years or less, and 35% graduate in 6 years or less. 72 companies recruited on campus in a recent year. Of a recent year graduating class, 10% were enrolled in graduate school within 6 months of graduation.

Admissions Contact: Monique Cossich, Executive Director of Enrollment Management. A video is available. E-mail: admissions@sfasu.edu Web: www.sfasu.edu

SUL ROSS STATE UNIVERSITY   B-3
Alpine, TX 79832

(915) 837-8050; Fax: (915) 837-8431

Full-time: 690 men, 580 women	**Faculty:** 95
Part-time: 100 men, 140 women	**Ph.D.s:** 69%
Graduate: 210 men, 300 women	**Student/Faculty:** 12 to 1
Year: semesters, summer session	**Tuition:** $2800 ($9200)
Application Deadline: open	**Room & Board:** $3800
Freshman Class: n/av	
SATor ACT: required	**LESS COMPETITIVE**

Sul Ross State University, founded in 1917, is a public institution offering programs in the liberal arts and broadcasting, fine arts and music, range animal science, business, and education. In addition, an upper-level and graduate center offers courses in Uralde, Del Rio, and Eagle Pass, Texas. There are 3 undergraduate schools and 1 graduate school. Figures in the above capsule and in this profile are approximate. The library contains 248,598 volumes, 444,950 microform items, and 13,011 audio/video tapes/CDs/DVDs, and subscribes to 1951 periodicals including electronic. Computerized library services include the card catalog, interlibrary loans, and database searching. Special learning facilities include a learning resource center, art gallery, natural history museum, planetarium, radio station, and extensive geology/chemistry lab equipment, including a scanning electron microscope. The 600-acre campus is in a rural area 165 miles from Odessa. Including any residence halls, there are 22 buildings.

Student Life: 97% of undergraduates are from Texas. Others are from 18 states and 7 foreign countries. 98% are from public schools. 55% are white; 41% Hispanic. 51% are Catholic; 48% Protestant. The average age of freshmen is 20; all undergraduates, 24. 55% do not continue beyond their first year; 20% remain to graduate.

Housing: 769 students can be accommodated in college housing, which includes single-sex and coed dormitories, on-campus apartments, and married-student housing. On-campus housing is guaranteed for the freshman year only and is available on a first-come, first-served basis. 67% of students commute. Alcohol is not permitted. All students may keep cars.

Activities: There are no fraternities or sororities. There are 41 groups on campus, including art, cheerleading, choir, drama, ethnic, honors, international, literary magazine, newspaper, pep band, political, professional, religious, student government, and yearbook. Popular campus events include cultural events, Fall on the Mall, and Honors Day.

Sports: There are 5 intercollegiate sports for men and 4 for women, and 4 intramural sports for men and 3 for women. Facilities include a gym and an undergraduate center.

Disabled Students: 90% of the campus is accessible. Wheelchair ramps, elevators, special parking, specially equipped rest rooms, special class scheduling, and lowered drinking fountains are available.

Services: Counseling and information services are available, as is tutoring in some subjects, including math, reading, and English. There is remedial math, reading, and writing.

Campus Safety and Security: Measures include 24-hour foot and vehicle patrol, informal discussions, pamphlets/posters/films, and lighted pathways/sidewalks.

Programs of Study: Sully confers B.A., B.S., B.B.A., and B.F.A. degrees. Associate and master's degrees are also awarded. Bachelor's degrees are awarded in AGRICULTURE (agricultural business management, animal science, equine science, natural resource management, and wildlife management), BIOLOGICAL SCIENCE (biology/biological science), BUSINESS (accounting, business administration and management, and office supervision and management), COMMUNICATIONS AND THE ARTS (applied music, communications, dramatic arts, English, fine arts, and Spanish), COMPUTER AND PHYSICAL SCIENCE (chemistry, computer science, geology, and mathematics), EDUCATION (art and elementary), ENGINEERING AND ENVIRONMENTAL DESIGN (environmental science and industrial engineering technology), SOCIAL SCIENCE (criminal justice, history, Mexican-American/Chicano studies, physical fitness/movement, political science/government, psychology, and social science). Behavioral and social sciences, education, and fine arts are the strongest academically. Phys ed, criminal justice, and education are the largest.

Required: All students must complete a general education requirement of 53 to 57 hours, including courses in English, history, foreign language, political science, math, the arts, social science, and natural science. A minimum 2.0 GPA and 130 credit hours are required to graduate. There are additional requirements for some degree programs. All students must take 2 courses in phys ed and 1 in computer science. The total number of hours required in the major varies.

Special: Sully offers unpaid internships in several departments, including psychology and criminal justice, as well as work-study programs, and nondegree study. There are 8 national honor societies, a freshman honors program.

Faculty/Classroom: 69% of faculty are male; 31%, female. 95% teach undergraduates and 85% both teach and do research. No introductory courses are taught by graduate students. The average class size in an introductory lecture is 42; in a laboratory, 15; and in a regular course, 21.

Requirements: The SAT or ACT is required. In addition, applicants should be graduates of an accredited secondary school and have a minimum of 14 credits, including 4 in English, 3 in math, 2 each in science, history, and phys ed/health, and 1 in government/economics. Applicants must meet 1 of the following criteria for full admission: present a satisfactory score on the ACT or on the SAT; or graduate in the upper half of their class. Probationary admission is possible for students who do not meet the admissions standards. AP and CLEP credits are accepted.

Procedure: Freshmen are admitted to all sessions. Entrance exams should be taken preferably early in the senior year. There is an early admissions plan. Check with the school for current application deadlines and fee.

Transfer: The GPA required for transfer students varies according to the number of college credits completed. 30 of 130 credits required for the bachelor's degree must be completed at Sully.

Visiting: There are regularly scheduled orientations for prospective students, consisting of 1 1/2-day programs in January, late August, June, and July. There are guides for informal visits and visitors may sit in on classes and stay overnight. To schedule a visit, contact the Office of Admissions at (915) 837-8059.

Financial Aid: In a recent year, 52% of full-time freshmen and 21% of continuing full-time students received need-based aid. The average freshman award was $5489. 7% of undergraduates work part time. Average annual earnings from campus work are $2000. Sully is a member of CSS. The CSS/Profile is required. Check with the school for current deadlines.

International Students: A satisfactory score is required on the written TOEFL and the SAT or the ACT.

Computers: All students may access the system. There are no time limits and no fees.

Admissions Contact: Robert C. Cullins, Dean of Admissions and Records. E-mail: rcullins@sul-ross-1.sulross.edu Web: www.sulross.edu

TARLETON STATE UNIVERSITY   D-2
Stephenville, TX 76402

(254) 968-9125
(800) 687-8236; Fax: (254) 968-9951

Full-time: 2689 men, 3391 women	Faculty: 278; IIA, --$
Part-time: 620 men, 914 women	Ph.D.s: 44%
Graduate: 507 men, 1024 women	Student/Faculty: 22 to 1
Year: semesters, summer session	Tuition: $3438 ($10,062)
Application Deadline: August 1	Room & Board: $5514
Freshman Class: 2478 applied, 1694 accepted, 1162 enrolled	
SAT Verbal/Math: 484/465*	ACT: 20	COMPETITIVE

Tarleton State University, founded in 1899 and a part of the Texas A&M University System, is a public institution offering undergraduate and graduate programs in agriculture and technology, arts and sciences, business, and education and fine arts. There are 5 undergraduate schools and 1 graduate school. In addition to regional accreditation, Tarleton has baccalaureate program accreditation with ACBSP, CSWE, NASM, and NCATE. The library contains 387,604 volumes, 915,492 microform items, and 9164 audio/video tapes/CDs/DVDs, and subscribes to 21,644 periodicals including electronic. Computerized library services include the card catalog, interlibrary loans, database searching, Internet access, and laptop Internet portals. Special learning facilities include a learning resource center, art gallery, planetarium, radio station, a 600-acre farm, a 1200-acre ranch, an equine center, and a center for industrial history of Texas. The 123-acre campus is in a small town 67 miles southwest of Fort Worth. Including any residence halls, there are 84 buildings.

Student Life: 95% of undergraduates are from Texas. Others are from 49 states, 33 foreign countries, and Canada. 91% are from public schools. 81% are white. Most are Protestant. The average age of freshmen is 19; all undergraduates, 24. 38% do not continue beyond their first year; 47% remain to graduate.

Housing: 1833 students can be accommodated in college housing, which includes single-sex and coed dorms, on-campus apartments, off-campus apartments, and married-student housing. On-campus housing is guaranteed for the freshman year only and is available on a first-come, first-served basis. 74% of students commute. Alcohol is not permitted. All students may keep cars.

Activities: 8% of men belong to 8 national fraternities; 7% of women belong to 6 national sororities. There are 113 groups on campus, including art, band, cheerleading, choir, computers, dance, debate, drama, drill team, ethnic, honors, international, jazz band, marching band, musical theater, newspaper, political, professional, religious, social, social service, student government, and yearbook. Popular campus events include Howdy Week, Spring Fest, and Tarleton Christmas.

Sports: There are 5 intercollegiate sports for men and 7 for women, and 16 intramural sports for men and 16 for women. Facilities include a fully equipped complex with a heated pool, track, courts for basketball, volleyball, tennis, and racquetball, and various playing fields. There is also a 7,000-seat stadium, a 3,300-seat gym, a fully lighted 550-seat baseball stadium, and a softball stadium.

Disabled Students: 90% of the campus is accessible. Wheelchair ramps, elevators, special parking, specially equipped rest rooms, special class scheduling, lowered drinking fountains, lowered telephones, and easy-access doors are available.

Services: Counseling and information services are available, as is tutoring in most subjects, including math, science, English, and social studies. The Teaching and Learning Center provides tutoring assistance in all academic areas.

Campus Safety and Security: Measures include 24-hour foot and vehicle patrol, self-defense education, security escort services, and shuttle buses. There are informal discussions, pamphlets/posters/films, emergency telephones, and lighted pathways/sidewalks.

Programs of Study: Tarleton confers B.A., B.S., B.A.A.S., B.B.A., B.F.A., B.M., B.S.N., and B.S.W. degrees. Master's and doctoral degrees are also awarded. Bachelor's degrees are awarded in AGRICULTURE (agricultural business management, agricultural economics, agricultural mechanics, agriculture, agronomy, animal science, horticulture, international agriculture, plant science, and range/farm management), BIO-

LOGICAL SCIENCE (biology/biological science and wildlife biology), BUSINESS (accounting, banking and finance, business administration and management, fashion merchandising, human resources, management science, marketing and distribution, marketing/retailing/merchandising, office supervision and management, and personnel management), COMMUNICATIONS AND THE ARTS (art, dramatic arts, English, fine arts, music, Spanish, and speech/debate/rhetoric), COMPUTER AND PHYSICAL SCIENCE (chemistry, computer programming, computer science, earth science, geology, information sciences and systems, mathematics, and physics), EDUCATION (agricultural, art, business, home economics, industrial arts, and physical), ENGINEERING AND ENVIRONMENTAL DESIGN (industrial engineering technology), HEALTH PROFESSIONS (medical laboratory technology, nursing, physical therapy, predentistry, premedicine, prepharmacy, and preveterinary science), SOCIAL SCIENCE (criminal justice, dietetics, economics, history, home economics, human development, interdisciplinary studies, law enforcement and corrections, physical fitness/movement, political science/government, prelaw, social work, sociology, and water resources). Science and business are the strongest academically. Business and education are the largest.

Required: All students must complete at least 128 hours, including 24 hours in the major, with a 2.0 GPA. The 47-hour required core curriculum includes courses in English, U.S. and Texas government, U.S. history, lab science, communications, computer information systems, and wellness. There are also distribution requirements that must be met in humanities and social sciences, and a writing proficiency exam.

Special: Tarleton offers work-study programs, internships, limited nondegree study, study abroad in 2 countries, and cross-registration with Texas A&M International University at Laredo. There is a 3-2 engineering degree available with Texas A&M University. Special degree programs may be designed to meet unusual requirements. There are 11 national honor societies, a freshman honors program, and 9 departmental honors programs.

Faculty/Classroom: 55% of faculty are male; 45%, female. 89% teach undergraduates and 13% both teach and do research. Graduate students teach 2% of introductory courses. The average class size in an introductory lecture is 29; in a laboratory, 19; and in a regular course, 22.

Admissions: 68% of the 2005-2006 applicants were accepted. The SAT scores for the 2005-2006 freshman class were: Verbal--58% below 500, 33% between 500 and 599, 8% between 600 and 700, and 1% above 700; Math--55% below 500, 35% between 500 and 599, 9% between 600 and 700, and 1% above 700. The ACT scores were 55% below 21, 25% between 21 and 23, 14% between 24 and 26, 4% between 27 and 28, and 2% above 28. 28% of the current freshmen were in the top fifth of their class; 63% were in the top two fifths. 22 freshmen graduated first in their class.

Requirements: Applicants must have a minimum composite score on the SAT or ACT, be graduates of an accredited Texas secondary school or advanced high school program, or rank in the top quarter of their graduating class. Secondary preparation should include 4 years of English and 3 years of college-preparatory math, including algebra I and II. A GED will be considered equivalent to a high school diploma, provided the average standard score is at least 55 or no subscore is less than 50. A GPA of 2.0 is required. AP and CLEP credits are accepted. Important factors in the admissions decision are advanced placement or honor courses, evidence of special talent, and extracurricular activities record.

Procedure: Freshmen are admitted to all sessions. Entrance exams should be taken in the junior year. There are early decision, early admissions, and deferred admissions plans There is a rolling admissions plan. Applications should be filed by August 1 for fall entry, January 7 for spring entry, and May 25 for summer entry, along with a $25 fee. Notification is sent on a rolling basis. 308 early decision candidates were accepted for the 2005-2006 class. Applications are accepted on-line.

Transfer: 1171 transfer students enrolled in 2004-2005. Applicants with 30 or more transferable credits must present a 2.0 GPA; those with fewer than 30 credits must present a 2.8 GPA. A GPA of 2.0 to 2.79 may be admitted provided transfers also meet regular admission standards of first-time freshman applicants. 32 of 128 credits required for the bachelor's degree must be completed at Tarleton.

Visiting: There are regularly scheduled orientations for prospective students, including a tour of the campus. There are guides for informal visits and visitors may sit in on classes. To schedule a visit, contact the Office of School Relations, Tarleton Center at (254) 968-9256 or (800) 687-4TSU or info@tarleton.edu.

Financial Aid: In 2005-2006, 67% of all full-time freshmen and 70% of continuing full-time students received some form of financial aid. 65% of full-time freshmen and 95% of continuing full-time students received need-based aid. The average freshman award was $7874. Need-based scholarships or need-based grants averaged $3811; need-based self-help aid (loans and jobs) averaged $3224; non-need-based athletic scholarships averaged $2343; other non-need-based awards and non-need-based scholarships averaged $3294; and private scholarships and grants averaged $1329. 18% of undergraduates work part time. Average annual earnings from campus work are $1642. The average financial indebtedness of the 2005 graduate was $16,776. Tarleton is a member of CSS.

The FAFSA or FFS is required. The priority date for freshman financial aid applications for fall entry is April 1. The deadline for filing freshman financial aid applications for fall entry is October 15.

International Students: There are 77 international students enrolled. The school actively recruits these students. They must achieve a satisfactory score on the TOEFL as well as on the SAT or the ACT.

Computers: Wireless access is available. The university provides various forms of information technology for use by its students, faculty, and staff to support its educational mission. Students should contact lab personnel to claim their free Tarleton e-mail account, which includes dial-up networking capabilities. All students may access the system. There are no time limits. The fee is $4 per hour.

Graduates: From July 1, 2004 to June 30, 2005, 1427 bachelor's degrees were awarded. The most popular majors were business administration/management (11%), interdisciplinary studies (8%), and educational administration (7%). In an average class, 18% graduate in 4 years, 20% graduate in 5 years, and 6% graduate in 6 years. 367 companies recruited on campus in 2004-2005. Of the 2004 graduating class, 5% were enrolled in graduate school within 6 months of graduation and 80% were employed.

Admissions Contact: Cindy Hess, Director of Admissions.
E-mail: *hess@tarleton.edu* Web: *www.tarleton.edu*

TEXAS A&M UNIVERSITY SYSTEM

The Texas A&M University System, established in 1876, is a public system in Texas. It is governed by a 9-member Board of Regents, whose chief administrator is the chancellor. The primary goal of the system is teaching, research, and service. The main priorities are to provide undergraduate and graduate students with a quality education, and to be a world leader in the development and dissemination of new knowledge. The total enrollment of all 9 campuses was more than 92,000; there were approximately 23,000 faculty and staff members. Altogether there are 500 baccalaureate, 400 master's, and 100 doctoral programs offered in Texas A&M University System. Profiles of the 4-year campuses are included in this section.

TEXAS A&M UNIVERSITY   D-3

College Station, TX 77843   **(979) 845-3741; Fax: (979) 847-8737**

Full-time: 16,787 men, 16,344 women	**Faculty:** 1898; I, -$
Part-time: 1760 men, 1477 women	**Ph.D.s:** 93%
Graduate: 4926 men, 3616 women	**Student/Faculty:** 17 to 1
Year: semesters, summer session	**Tuition:** $6399 ($14,679)
Application Deadline: February 15	**Room & Board:** $6952
Freshman Class: 17,250 applied, 11,630 accepted, 7079 enrolled	
SAT Verbal/Math: 587/616	**ACT:** 26 **HIGHLY COMPETITIVE**

Texas A&M University, founded in 1876, is part of the Texas A&M University system. Undergraduate degrees are offered in agriculture and life sciences, architecture, business administration, education, engineering, geosciences, liberal arts, science, and biomedical science. There are 9 undergraduate and 10 graduate schools. In addition to regional accreditation, Texas A&M has baccalaureate program accreditation with AACSB, ABET, ACCE, ACEJMC, ADA, ASLA, CSAB, NAAB, NCATE, and SAF. The 3 libraries contain 3,310,840 volumes, 5,433,728 microform items, and 782,081 audio/video tapes/CDs/DVDs, and subscribe to 49,197 periodicals including electronic. Computerized library services include the card catalog, interlibrary loans, database searching, Internet access, and laptop Internet portals. Special learning facilities include a learning resource center, art gallery, radio station, TV station, weather station, observatory, cyclotron, wind tunnel, visualization lab, nuclear reactor, ocean wave pool, and the Bush Museum and Library. The 8500-acre campus is in an urban area 90 miles northwest of Houston. Including any residence halls, there are 665 buildings.

Student Life: 95% of undergraduates are from Texas. Students are from 50 states, 115 foreign countries, and Canada. 75% are white; 10% Hispanic. The average age of freshmen is 18; all undergraduates, 20. 10% do not continue beyond their first year; 76% remain to graduate.

Housing: 9865 students can be accommodated in university housing, which includes single-sex and coed dorm s, on-campus apartments, and married-student housing. In addition, there are honors houses. On-campus housing is available on a first-come, first-served basis. 73% of students commute. All students may keep cars.

Activities: 6% of men belong to 19 national fraternities; 7% of women belong to 2 local and 19 national sororities. There are 700 groups on campus, including art, band, chess, choir, chorale, chorus, computers, dance, drama, drill team, drum and bugle corps, ethnic, film, gay, honors, international, jazz band, literary magazine, marching band, musical theater, newspaper, opera, orchestra, photography, political, professional, radio and TV, religious, social, social service, student government, symphony, and yearbook. Popular campus events include Midnight Yell Practice, Silver Taps, and Muster.

Sports: There are 9 intercollegiate sports for men and 12 for women, and 24 intramural sports for men and 23 for women. Facilities include

a coliseum, a natatorium, 11 basketball/volleyball courts, 27 handball/racquetball courts, badminton, weight and activity rooms, jogging trails, 14 tennis courts, a squash court, an 18-hole golf course, a 2500-seat auditorium/arena, a driving range, flag football fields, 4 soccer fields, 4 outdoor basketball courts, and 5 walking trails. Intercollegiate athletic facilities include a 70,210-seat football stadium, a 7200-seat indoor basketball and volleyball coliseum, a 7053-seat baseball stadium, a 1750-seat softball complex, a 1000-seat soccer complex, a 2000-seat natatorium, a 3000-seat track and field complex, a 1500-seat tennis center, and an 18,000-square-foot physical strength and conditioning lab.

Disabled Students: 85% of the campus is accessible. Wheelchair ramps, elevators, special parking, specially equipped rest rooms, special class scheduling, lowered drinking fountains, lowered telephones, and an office of support services for students with disabilities are available.

Services: Counseling and information services are available, as is tutoring in most subjects. There is a reader service for the blind, and remedial math, reading, and writing. Workshops in time management, basic study techniques, and test-taking skills are available.

Campus Safety and Security: Measures include 24-hour foot and vehicle patrol, self-defense education, security escort services, and shuttle buses. There are informal discussions, pamphlets/posters/films, emergency telephones, lighted pathways/sidewalks, a security awareness committee, and crime-watch and safety tip lines. Crime bulletins are aviable on the university police website.

Programs of Study: Texas A&M confers B.A., B.S., B.B.A., B.Ed., and B.L.A. degrees. Master's and doctoral degrees are also awarded. Bachelor's degrees are awarded in AGRICULTURE (agricultural business management, agricultural economics, animal science, dairy science, fish and game management, fishing and fisheries, forestry and related sciences, horticulture, poultry science, and range/farm management), BIOLOGICAL SCIENCE (biochemistry, biology/biological science, botany, entomology, genetics, microbiology, and zoology), BUSINESS (accounting, banking and finance, business systems analysis, management science, marketing/retailing/merchandising, and personnel management), COMMUNICATIONS AND THE ARTS (English, French, German, journalism, Russian, Spanish, and speech/debate/rhetoric), COMPUTER AND PHYSICAL SCIENCE (atmospheric sciences and meteorology, chemistry, computer science, geology, geophysics and seismology, mathematics, and physics), EDUCATION (elementary, health, physical, and secondary), ENGINEERING AND ENVIRONMENTAL DESIGN (aeronautical engineering, agricultural engineering, bioengineering, chemical engineering, civil engineering, computer engineering, construction engineering, electrical/electronics engineering, engineering technology, environmental design, environmental science, industrial engineering technology, landscape architecture/design, mechanical engineering, nuclear engineering, and petroleum/natural gas engineering), HEALTH PROFESSIONS (biomedical science), SOCIAL SCIENCE (anthropology, economics, history, international studies, parks and recreation management, philosophy, political science/government, psychology, and sociology). Engineering, business administration, and life sciences are the strongest academically. Psychology, accounting, and biomedical science are the largest.

Required: To graduate, students must complete at least 128 credit hours, including 30 to 33 in the major. A minimum 2.0 GPA is required. Students must complete a core curriculum of 48 hours in 8 subject areas, including courses in American history and government, phys ed, computers, foreign language, speech and writing skills, math/logical reasoning, science, humanities, and social science. Requirements in the major vary.

Special: The university offers extensive opportunities through the Career Center and Study Abroad Office. B.A.-B.S. degrees, study abroad in 12 countries, internships, a Washington semester, credit for military experience, nondegree study, co-op programs, dual majors, and pass/fail options are available. A 5-year graduate business/liberal arts program is offered, as well as a 3-2 engineering degree with Sam Houston State University. There are 41 national honor societies, including Phi Beta Kappa, and a freshman honors program.

Faculty/Classroom: 73% of faculty are male; 27%, female. 70% teach undergraduates, 72% do research, and 47% do both. Graduate students teach 10% of introductory courses. The average class size in an introductory lecture is 75; in a laboratory, 26; and in a regular course, 52.

Admissions: 67% of the 2005-2006 applicants were accepted. The SAT scores for the 2005-2006 freshman class were: Verbal--15% below 500, 40% between 500 and 599, 37% between 600 and 700, and 8% above 700; Math--9% below 500, 31% between 500 and 599, 45% between 600 and 700, and 15% above 700. The ACT scores were 10% below 21, 20% between 21 and 23, 30% between 24 and 26, 15% between 27 and 28, and 25% above 28. 80% of the current freshmen were in the top fifth of their class; 95% were in the top two fifths. There were 129 National Merit finalists. 232 freshmen graduated first in their class.

Requirements: The SAT or ACT is required. In addition, secondary school graduation is a condition of freshman admission. Required high school courses include 4 credits in English, 3 1/2 credits in math, 3 credits in science (2 from biology, chemistry, or physics), 2 credits of social studies and the same foreign language, and 1 of history. AP and CLEP

credits are accepted. Important factors in the admissions decision are leadership record, evidence of special talent, and extracurricular activities record.

Procedure: Freshmen are admitted fall, spring, and summer. Entrance exams should be taken during the spring of the junior year or by December of the senior year. Applications should be filed by February 15 for fall entry, October 15 for spring entry, and February 15 for summer entry, along with a $50 fee. Notification is sent on a rolling basis. A waiting list is an active part of the admissions procedure. Applications are accepted on-line.

Transfer: 1568 transfer students enrolled in 2004-2005. Applicants must submit transcripts from previously attended colleges. Requirements vary, depending on how many semester hours were attempted and the grades for those hours. Transfer applicants must submit high school transcripts and, if they have fewer than 12 graded semester hours, SAT or ACT scores. 30 of 128 credits required for the bachelor's degree must be completed at Texas A&M.

Visiting: There are regularly scheduled orientations for prospective students, Some 20 new-student conferences are held for students to meet with academic advisers to select courses, become acquainted with student life activities, and tour the campus. There are guides for informal visits and visitors may sit in on classes. To schedule a visit, contact the Aggieland Visitor Center at (979) 845-5851 or vis-ctr@tamu.edu.

Financial Aid: In 2005-2006, 73% of all full-time freshmen and 76% of continuing full-time students received some form of financial aid. 58% of full-time freshmen and 71% of continuing full-time students received need-based aid. The average freshman award was $7765. Need-based scholarships or need-based grants averaged $2936; need-based self-help aid (loans and jobs) averaged $6144; and other non-need-based awards and non-need-based scholarships averaged $3339. 41% of undergraduates work part time. Average annual earnings from campus work are $3824. The average financial indebtedness of the 2005 graduate was $15,490. The FAFSA is required. The deadline for filing freshman financial aid applications for fall entry is April 1.

International Students: There are 521 international students enrolled. They must take the written TOEFL. The SAT or ACT is required for graduates of U.S. high schools only.

Computers: Wireless access is available. All students may access the system at any time. There are no time limits. The fee is $17.30 per credit hour.

Graduates: From July 1, 2004 to June 30, 2005, 7711 bachelor's degrees were awarded. The most popular majors were interdisciplinary studies (6%), psychology (5%), and biomedical science (4%). In an average class, 1% graduate in 3 years or less, 32% graduate in 4 years or less, 69% graduate in 5 years or less, and 76% graduate in 6 years or less. 150 companies recruited on campus in 2004-2005. Of the 2004 graduating class, 12% were enrolled in graduate school within 6 months of graduation and 54% were employed.

Admissions Contact: Admissions Counseling.
E-mail: admissions@tamu.edu Web: www.tamu.edu/admissions

TEXAS A&M UNIVERSITY AT COMMERCE E-2
Commerce, TX 75429-3011 (903) 886-5106
(800) 331-3878; Fax: (903) 886-5888

Full-time: 1674 men, 2547 women	**Faculty:** 206; I, --$
Part-time: 753 men, 1340 women	**Ph.D.s:** 65%
Graduate: 782 men, 1528 women	**Student/Faculty:** 20 to 1
Year: semesters, summer session	**Tuition:** $3650 ($10,700)
Application Deadline: August 6	**Room & Board:** $5370
Freshman Class: 3589 applied, 2248 accepted, 1560 enrolled	
ACT: 20	**SAT:** 983 (compositte)*

COMPETITIVE

Texas A&M University at Commerce, founded in 1889, offers undergraduate and graduate programs in business and technology, arts and sciences, and education. Tuition figures in the above capsule are approximate. There are 3 undergraduate schools and 1 graduate school. In addition to regional accreditation, TAMU-C has baccalaureate program accreditation with AACSB, CSWE, NASM, and NCATE. The library contains 1,714,655 volumes and 131,926 microform items. Computerized library services include the card catalog, interlibrary loans, and database searching. Special learning facilities include a radio station, TV station, performing arts center, and farm. The 1883-acre campus is in a small town 65 miles northeast of Dallas. Including any residence halls, there are 121 buildings.

Student Life: 94% of undergraduates are from Texas. Students are from 33 states, 51 foreign countries, and Canada. 98% are from public schools. 69% are white; 18% African American. The average age of freshmen is 19; all undergraduates, 24. 36% do not continue beyond their first year; 66% remain to graduate.

Housing: 2750 students can be accommodated in college housing, which includes single-sex and coed dorms, on-campus apartments, married-student housing, fraternity houses, and sorority houses. In addition, there are honors houses and special-interest houses. On-campus housing is guaranteed for the freshman year only and is available on a first-come, first-served basis. 71% of students commute. Alcohol is not permitted. All students may keep cars.

Activities: 15% of men belong to 9 national fraternities; 12% of women belong to 7 national sororities. There are 96 groups on campus, including art, band, cheerleading, chess, choir, chorale, chorus, dance, drama, ethnic, film, gay, honors, international, jazz band, literary magazine, marching band, musical theater, newspaper, orchestra, pep band, photography, political, professional, radio and TV, religious, social, social service, and student government. Popular campus events include Sam Rayburn Symposium, Christmas Feast of Carols, and Spring fest.

Sports: There are 5 intercollegiate sports for men and 5 for women, and 7 intramural sports for men and 7 for women. Facilities include a 1700-seat auditorium, a 10,000-seat stadium, a gym, handball and racquetball courts, a bowling alley, a swimming pool, a weight room, tennis courts, a field house, and intramural fields.

Disabled Students: 85% of the campus is accessible. Wheelchair ramps, elevators, special parking, and specially equipped rest rooms are available.

Services: Counseling and information services are available, as is tutoring in some subjects, including math and writing. There is remedial math, reading, and writing.

Campus Safety and Security: Measures include 24-hour foot and vehicle patrol, self-defense education, security escort services, and informal discussions. There are pamphlets/posters/films, emergency telephones, lighted pathways/sidewalks, a victim assistance officer, a police service for special and social events, crime and date-rape prevention presentations, and motorist assistance.

Programs of Study: TAMU-C confers B.A., B.S., B.A.C.J., B.B.A., B.F.A., B.G.S., B.M., B.M.Ed., B.S.C.J., B.S.Lib.Sci., and B.S.W. degrees. Master's and doctoral degrees are also awarded. Bachelor's degrees are awarded in AGRICULTURE (agricultural economics, agriculture, animal science, and wildlife management), BIOLOGICAL SCIENCE (biology/biological science and botany), BUSINESS (accounting, banking and finance, business administration and management, and marketing/retailing/merchandising), COMMUNICATIONS AND THE ARTS (advertising, broadcasting, dramatic arts, English, fine arts, French, German, journalism, languages, music, photography, printmaking, and Spanish), COMPUTER AND PHYSICAL SCIENCE (chemistry, computer science, earth science, geology, mathematics, and physics), EDUCATION (agricultural, business, early childhood, elementary, guidance, health, industrial arts, music, science, and secondary), ENGINEERING AND ENVIRONMENTAL DESIGN (engineering technology and preengineering), HEALTH PROFESSIONS (predentistry, premedicine, and prepharmacy), SOCIAL SCIENCE (anthropology, criminal justice, economics, geography, history, political science/government, prelaw, psychology, religion, social work, and sociology). Education, computer science, and business administration are the strongest programs academically and the largest.

Required: To graduate, all students must earn a GPA of 2.0 while taking at least 126 semester hours, including 24 hours in the major. Distribution requirements include 24 in culture courses such as American history and foreign languages, 12 each in English composition, math, and speech skills, 8 in sciences, 6 in upper-division courses, and 4 in phys ed.

Special: TAMU-C offers co-op programs with E-Systems Inc. and numerous other firms, cross-registration by independent arrangement, study abroad in England, and work-study programs. B.A.-B.S. degrees, second degrees, dual majors, a general studies degree, credit for life experience, internships, nondegree study, and pass/fail options are also available. There are 18 national honor societies, a freshman honors program, and 26 departmental honors programs.

Faculty/Classroom: 53% of faculty are male; 47%, female. 77% teach undergraduates, 46% do research, and 37% do both. Graduate students teach 21% of introductory courses. The average class size in an introductory lecture is 30; in a laboratory, 20; and in a regular course, 25.

Admissions: 63% of recent applicants were accepted. 42% of recent freshmen were in the top fifth of their class; 72% were in the top two fifths.

Requirements: The SAT or ACT is required, with satisfactory SAT or ACT scores. Applicants need not be graduates of an accredited secondary school, although high school graduation is required. The GED is also accepted. A GPA of 2.0 is required. AP and CLEP credits are accepted.

Procedure: Freshmen are admitted to all sessions. Entrance exams should be taken prior to enrollment. There is a deferred admissions plan and a rolling admissions plan. Applications should be filed by August 6 for fall entry. Notification is sent on a rolling basis.

Transfer: 594 transfer students enrolled in 2004-2005. Applicants must have a college grade average of 2.0 with a minimum of 21 credit hours. The SAT or ACT is not required. College transcripts and a statement of good standing from the prior institution are required. 30 of 126 credits required for the bachelor's degree must be completed at TAMU-C.

Visiting: There are regularly scheduled orientations for prospective students. There are guides for informal visits and visitors may sit in on classes. To schedule a visit, contact the Admissions Office at (903) 886-5081 or *admissions@tamu-commerce.edu*.

Financial Aid: The average freshman award in a recent year was $3698. Need-based scholarships or need-based grants averaged $3285. The FAFSA and the college's own financial statement are required. The deadline for filing freshman financial aid applications for fall entry is October 1.

International Students: There are 61 international students enrolled. They must take the TOEFL and also take the SAT or the ACT, presenting satisfactory scores on the SAT or on the ACT.

Computers: All students may access the system 24 hours daily by modem, and most labs are open until 10 P.M. There are no time limits and no fees.

Graduates: From July 1, 2004 to June 30, 2005, 1080 bachelor's degrees were awarded. The most popular majors were interdisciplinary studies (22%), business/marketing (18%), and public administration (8%). 55 companies recruited on campus in 2004-2005.

Admissions Contact: Randy McDonald, Director of Admissions. A video is available. E-mail: *admissions@tamu-commerce.edu* Web: *www.tamu-commerce.edu*

TEXAS A&M UNIVERSITY AT CORPUS CHRISTI

Corpus Christi, TX 78412
(361) 825-2624
(800) 482-6822; Fax: (361) 825-5887

Full-time: 2040 men, 3215 women	**Faculty:** IIA, av$
Part-time: 544 men, 782 women	**Ph.D.s:** 74%
Graduate: 539 men, 1107 women	**Student/Faculty:** n/av
Year: semesters, summer session	**Tuition:** $3150 ($8810)
Application Deadline: July 1	**Room & Board:** $7130
Freshman Class: 3273 applied, 2792 accepted, 1155 enrolled	
SAT or ACT: required	**LESS COMPETITIVE**

Texas A&M University at Corpus Christi, part of the Texas A&M University System since 1989, is a public institution offering 34 undergraduate degree programs and 27 graduate degree programs. Tuition figures in the above capsule are approximate. The library contains 433,785 volumes, 654,518 microform items, and 6245 audio/video tapes/CDs/DVDs, and subscribes to 1706 periodicals including electronic. The university is located on its own 240-acre island approximately 10 miles from downtown Corpus Christi.

Student Life: 98% of undergraduates are from Texas. 57% are white; 37% Hispanic. The average age of freshmen is 19; all undergraduates, 23.

Housing: On campus housing includes single-sex and coed dorms and apartments for single students.

Activities: There are many groups and organizations on campus, including band, choir, dance, drama, film, jazz band, literary magazine, marching band, musical theater, newspaper, opera, pep band, student government, symphony, and yearbook.

Sports: There are 6 intercollegiate sports for men and 8 for women. Facilities include a field house with a full-size gym, a weight room, and 4 racquetball/handball courts. Adjacent to the gym are 6 lighted tennis courts, a practice court, a 25-meter swimming pool, and lighted playing fields. A wellness center offers a free-weight area, weight machines, cardiovascular equipment, a wellness resource area, 2 aerobic studios, and a game room.

Programs of Study: Texas A&M University at Corpus Christi confers B.A., B.S., B.B.A., B.F.A., B.M., B.S.H.S., B.S.I.S., and B.S.N. degrees. Master's and doctoral degrees are also awarded. Bachelor's degrees are awarded in BIOLOGICAL SCIENCE (biology/biological science), BUSINESS (accounting, banking and finance, business administration and management, management information systems, and marketing/retailing/merchandising), COMMUNICATIONS AND THE ARTS (art, communications, dramatic arts, English, music, Spanish, and speech/debate/rhetoric), COMPUTER AND PHYSICAL SCIENCE (chemistry, computer science, geology, and mathematics), EDUCATION (education), ENGINEERING AND ENVIRONMENTAL DESIGN (engineering technology, environmental science, and mechanical engineering technology), HEALTH PROFESSIONS (clinical science, health science, and nursing), SOCIAL SCIENCE (criminal justice, geography, history, political science/government, psychology, and sociology).

Required: To graduate, a minimum of 124 semester hours must be completed. A minimum of 45 semester hours of upper-division credit is required, as is a minimum GPA of 2.0 overall and in the major. In addition, all students must complete the core curriculum requirement, including 6 credit hours each of communication (English rhetoric/compstition), natural science, U.S. history, and political science and 3 each of math, visual and performing arts, humanities, and social/behavioral science. Students must also meet foreign language and computer literacy requirements and take a first-year seminar.

Special: Cooperative programs, internships, dual majors, and distance learning are available.

Faculty/Classroom: 57% of faculty are male; 43%, female.

Admissions: 85% of the 2005-2006 applicants were accepted. The SAT scores for the 2005-2006 freshman class were: Verbal--55% below 500, 35% between 500 and 599, 16% between 600 and 700, and 2%

above 700; Math--54% below 500, 36% between 500 and 599, and 10% between 600 and 700. The ACT scores were 84% below 21, and 16% between 21 and 23.

Requirements: The SAT or ACT is required. In addition, graduation from secondary school is required, with 4 units of English, 3 each of math, science, and social studies, and 2 of a foreign language. The GED is accepted. AP and CLEP credits are accepted. Advanced placement or honor courses is an important factor in the admission decision.

Procedure: Freshmen are admitted fall, spring, and summer. There is a rolling admissions plan. Applications should be filed by July 1 for fall entry, November 1 for spring entry, and April 1 for summer entry, along with a $20 fee. Notification is sent December 1. Applications are accepted on-line.

Transfer: 1412 transfer students enrolled in 2004-2005. College transcripts, a statement of good standing from prior institutions, and a GPA of 2.0 are required. 79 of 124 credits required for the bachelor's degree must be completed at Texas A&M University at Corpus Christi.

Visiting: There are regularly scheduled orientations for prospective students, including a tour of the campus and or introduction to various services on campus.

Financial Aid: In 2005-2006, 55% of all full-time students received some form of financial aid. 41% of full-time freshmen and 42% of continuing full-time students received need-based aid. The average freshman award was $6859. Need-based scholarships or need-based grants averaged $4145; need-based self-help aid (loans and jobs) averaged $2949; non-need-based athletic scholarships averaged $8395; and other non-need-based awards and non-need-based scholarships averaged $3453. The average financial indebtedness of a recent graduate was $16,886. The FAFSA is required. The priority date for freshman financial aid applications for fall entry is April 1.

International Students: They must score satisfactorily on the written TOEFL.

Graduates: In a recent year, 1085 bachelor's degrees were awarded. The most popular majors were business/marketing (24%), interdisciplinary studies (17%), and protective services/public administration (7%). In an average class, 15% graduate in 4 years or less, 29% graduate in 5 years or less, and 65% graduate in 6 years or less.

Admissions Contact: Mary Dechant, Director of Admissions. E-mail: *mary.dechant@mail.tamucc.edu* Web: *www.tamucc.edu*

TEXAS A&M UNIVERSITY AT GALVESTON   E-4

Galveston, TX 77553-1675   (409) 740-4414
                                   (877) 322-4443; Fax: (409) 740-4731

Full-time: 605 men, 640 women	**Faculty:** IIB, +$
Part-time: 70 men, 70 women	**Ph.D.s:** n/av
Graduate: 880 men, 750 women	**Student/Faculty:** n/av
Year: semesters, summer session	**Tuition:** $5100 ($11,000)
Application Deadline: open	**Room & Board:** $4900
Freshman Class: n/av	
SAT or ACT: required	**COMPETITIVE+**

Texas A&M University at Galveston, founded in 1962, is a public institution that offers marine and maritime-related programs. It is part of the Texas A&M University system. Figures in the above capsule and in this profile are approximate. In addition to regional accreditation, TAMUG has baccalaureate program accreditation with ABET. The library contains 43,000 volumes and 52,984 microform items, and subscribes to 970 periodicals including electronic. Computerized library services include the card catalog, interlibrary loans, and database searching. Special learning facilities include a learning resource center and a training ship, the T/S Texas Clipper, used for an annual summer training cruise. The 100-acre campus is in a suburban area 50 miles south of Houston. Including any residence halls, there are 11 buildings.

Student Life: 81% of undergraduates are from Texas. Students are from 43 states and 8 foreign countries. 94% are from public schools. 85% are white. The average age of freshmen is 18; all undergraduates, 20.

Housing: 650 students can be accommodated in college housing, which includes coed dormitories. On-campus housing is guaranteed for the freshman year only and is available on a first-come, first-served basis. 58% of students commute. Alcohol is not permitted. All students may keep cars.

Activities: There are no fraternities or sororities. There are 39 groups on campus, including chorale, drama, ethnic, international, literary magazine, newspaper, political, professional, religious, social, social service, student government, and yearbook. Popular campus events include Springfest, Mardi Grass, and Maritime Ball.

Sports: There are 2 intercollegiate sports for men and 1 for women, and 6 intramural sports for men and 5 for women. Facilities include tennis courts, a volleyball court, a swimming pool, and a basketball court.

Disabled Students: 80% of the campus is accessible. Wheelchair ramps, elevators, special parking, specially equipped rest rooms, special class scheduling, and lowered drinking fountains are available.

Services: Counseling and information services are available, as is tutoring in most subjects. There is a reader service for the blind, and remedial math, reading, and writing.

Campus Safety and Security: Measures include 24-hour foot and vehicle patrol, security escort services, shuttle buses, and lighted pathways/sidewalks.

Programs of Study: TAMUG confers the B.S. degree. Master's degrees are also awarded. Bachelor's degrees are awarded in AGRICULTURE (environmental studies, fishing and fisheries, and natural resource management), BIOLOGICAL SCIENCE (biology/biological science, environmental biology, marine biology, and marine science), BUSINESS (international business management, recreation and leisure services, and transportation management), COMPUTER AND PHYSICAL SCIENCE (earth science, geoscience, hydrology, natural sciences, oceanography, and science and management), ENGINEERING AND ENVIRONMENTAL DESIGN (civil engineering, electrical/electronics engineering technology, electromechanical technology, environmental science, land use management and reclamation, marine engineering, maritime science, mechanical engineering technology, naval architecture and marine engineering, ocean engineering, systems engineering, and transportation engineering), SOCIAL SCIENCE (archeology, geography, humanities and social science, liberal arts/general studies, and water resources). Marine sciences is the strongest academically. Marine biology is the largest.

Required: Depending on the major, students must complete 130 to 160 credit hours with a GPA of 2.0 overall as well as in the major. The required core curriculum includes courses in math, political science, American history, and macroeconomics. Distribution requirements include 6 credits each in English, calculus, humanities and social sciences; 8 credits in science; and 12 credits in citizenship. Students must also complete a 2-semester sequence of a foreign language and 1 computer language course.

Special: TAMUG offers dual majors, dual degrees, internships in marine biology and oceanography, a summer semester at sea, and credit for military service. Students may challenge any course for credit by exam. A pass/fail option is available for electives taken by juniors or seniors who have a minimum 2.5 GPA. Selected majors may earn a ship's officer license with a degree program.

Faculty/Classroom: All teach undergraduates. The average class size in an introductory lecture is 48; in a laboratory, 14; and in a regular course, 24.

Admissions: In a recent year, 95% of the 2005-2006 applicants were accepted.

Requirements: The SAT or ACT is required. Applicants must be graduates of an accredited high school or hold a GED. A minimum of 16 academic credits is required, including 4 units of English, 3.5 units of math, 2.5 units of either history or social studies, 2 units each of a foreign language and science, and the rest in electives. AP and CLEP credits are accepted. Important factors in the admissions decision are leadership record, extracurricular activities record, and recommendations by school officials.

Procedure: Freshmen are admitted to all sessions. Entrance exams should be taken late in the junior year or early in the senior year. There are early decision, early admissions, and deferred admissions plans. Check with the school for current application deadlines and fee. Applications are accepted on-line.

Transfer: 145 transfer students enrolled in 2004-2005. Applicants must have a cumulative 2.0 GPA in a minimum of 18 completed credit hours as well as a 2.0 GPA in each of the last 2 terms attended. 30 of 130 credits required for the bachelor's degree must be completed at TAMUG.

Visiting: There are regularly scheduled orientations for prospective students, including campus tours conducted Monday and Friday at 10 A.M. There are guides for informal visits and visitors may sit in on classes. To schedule a visit, contact the Student Relations Department at (409) 740-4422.

Financial Aid: In a recent year, 65% of undergraduates worked part time. Average annual earnings from campus work are $1200. The FAFSA is required. Check with the school for current deadlines.

International Students: There are 13 international students enrolled. Satisfactory scores are required on the written TOEFL the college's own test, and the SAT or the ACT.

Computers: All students may access the system. There are no time limits. Check with the school for current fee.

Graduates: In a recent year, 178 bachelor's degrees were awarded. 87 companies recruited on campus in a recent year.

Admissions Contact: Cheryl Moon, Director of Admissions. A video is available. E-mail: *seaaggie@tamug.edu* Web: *www.tamug.edu*

TEXAS A&M UNIVERSITY AT KINGSVILLE · D-5
Kingsville, TX 78363

(361) 593-2315
(800) 687-6000; Fax: (361) 595-2195

Full-time: 2130 men, 1950 women	**Faculty:** IIA, --$
Part-time: 600 men, 900 women	**Ph.D.s:** n/av
Graduate: 610 men, 700 women	**Student/Faculty:** n/av
Year: semesters, summer session	**Tuition:** $3200 ($8900)
Application Deadline: open	**Room & Board:** $3600
Freshman Class: n/av	
SAT or ACT: required	**LESS COMPETITIVE**

Texas A&M University at Kingsville, founded in 1925 as South Texas Teachers College, is a comprehensive university and part of the Texas A&M University System. Graduate and undergraduate programs are offered in agriculture and home economics, arts and sciences, business administration, education, and engineering. There are 5 undergraduate and 5 graduate schools. Figures in the above capsule and in this profile are approximate. In addition to regional accreditation, TAMUK has baccalaureate program accreditation with ABET, ADA, NASM, and NCATE. The library contains 358,466 volumes, 183,416 microform items, and 3224 audio/video tapes/CDs/DVDs, and subscribes to 2304 periodicals including electronic. Computerized library services include the card catalog, interlibrary loans, and database searching. Special learning facilities include a learning resource center, art gallery, natural history museum, planetarium, radio station, TV station, and wildlife and citrus research facilities. The 246-acre campus is in a small town 40 miles southwest of Corpus Christi. Including any residence halls, there are 82 buildings.

Student Life: 95% of undergraduates are from Texas. Students are from 35 states, 44 foreign countries, and Canada. 98% are from public schools. 62% are Hispanic; 29% white. The average age of freshmen is 19; all undergraduates, 23. 45% do not continue beyond their first year; 22% remain to graduate.

Housing: 1200 students can be accommodated in college housing, which includes single-sex and coed dormitories and married-student housing. On-campus housing is guaranteed for all 4 years. 70% of students commute. All students may keep cars.

Activities: 3% of men belong to 6 national fraternities; 3% of women belong to 3 national sororities. There are 106 groups on campus, including art, band, cheerleading, choir, chorale, chorus, computers, dance, debate, drama, drill team, ethnic, honors, international, jazz band, marching band, musical theater, newspaper, pep band, political, professional, radio and TV, religious, social, and student government. Popular campus events include Campus Capers, Fall Carnival, and Spring Block Party.

Sports: There are 3 intercollegiate sports for men and 3 for women, and 2 intramural sports for men and 2 for women. Facilities include 2 gyms, an Olympic-size swimming pool, courts for tennis and racquetball, an all-weather track, and various playing fields. There are facilities for archery, bowling, golf, fencing, weight training, and jogging.

Disabled Students: 90% of the campus is accessible. Wheelchair ramps, elevators, special parking, specially equipped rest rooms, lowered drinking fountains, and lowered telephones are available.

Services: Counseling and information services are available, as is tutoring in every subject. There is a reader service for the blind, and remedial math, reading, and writing.

Campus Safety and Security: Measures include 24-hour foot and vehicle patrol, self-defense education, security escort services, and informal discussions. There are pamphlets/posters/films, emergency telephones, and lighted pathways/sidewalks.

Programs of Study: TAMUK confers B.A., B.S., B.A.A.S., B.B.A., B.F.A., B.M., B.S.A., B.S.C.E., B.S.Ch.E., B.S.C.S., B.S.E.E., B.S.I.E., B.S. in Hum.Sci., B.S. in Nat. Gas Eng., B.S.I.T., and B.S.M.E. degrees. Master's and doctoral degrees are also awarded. Bachelor's degrees are awarded in AGRICULTURE (agricultural business management, animal science, plant science, range/farm management, and soil science), BIOLOGICAL SCIENCE (biology/biological science), BUSINESS (accounting, banking and finance, business administration and management, business economics, fashion merchandising, management science, marketing/retailing/merchandising, and real estate), COMMUNICATIONS AND THE ARTS (communications, dramatic arts, English, fine arts, music, and Spanish), COMPUTER AND PHYSICAL SCIENCE (chemistry, computer science, geology, mathematics, and physics), EDUCATION (agricultural, elementary, health, music, physical, and secondary), ENGINEERING AND ENVIRONMENTAL DESIGN (chemical engineering, civil engineering, electrical/electronics engineering, engineering management, industrial engineering technology, interior design, mechanical engineering, and petroleum/natural gas engineering), HEALTH PROFESSIONS (medical laboratory technology, nursing, predentistry, premedicine, prepharmacy, preveterinary science, and speech pathology/audiology), SOCIAL SCIENCE (anthropology, child care/child and family studies, food production/management/services, food science, geography, history, home economics, political science/government, prelaw,

psychology, public administration, and sociology). Engineering is the strongest academically. Education is the largest.

Required: All students must complete 124 to 135 semester hours, including a minimum of 24 in the major and 45 in advanced work, with at least a 2.0 GPA. General education requirements include courses in oral and written communication, math and reasoning, U.S. and Texas government, social sciences, American and world history, lab sciences, fine arts, and phys ed.

Special: There are co-op programs in engineering, business, and agriculture, and internships, B.A.-B.S. degrees and dual majors in most programs. A nontraditional Bachelor of Applied Arts and Sciences program is offered to students with vocational or technical training or experience. The Center for Continuing Education offers noncredit enrichment courses in a variety of subjects, a professional development program in organizational management, and a number of seminars and short courses that are held abroad. The university also offers a work-study program and the College I Freshman program. There are 10 national honor societies, a freshman honors program, and 20 departmental honors programs.

Faculty/Classroom: 66% of faculty are male; 34%, female. All teach undergraduates. The average class size in an introductory lecture is 30; in a laboratory, 20; and in a regular course, 25.

Requirements: The SAT or ACT is required. In addition, applicants should be high school graduates or have a GED. Secondary preparation must include 7 units of electives, no more than 4 of which may be in vocational subjects, 3 units of English, 2 units each of math (including algebra), foreign language, and natural science, and 1 unit each of history and another social science. The university sets minimum admissible scores each year. An interview is encouraged. AP and CLEP credits are accepted.

Procedure: Freshmen are admitted to all sessions. Entrance exams should be taken before graduation from high school. There is an early admissions plan. Check with the school for current application deadlines and fee.

Transfer: 427 transfer students enrolled in a recent year. All applicants must present a GPA of at least 2.0. 24 of 124 credits required for the bachelor's degree must be completed at TAMUK.

Visiting: There are regularly scheduled orientations for prospective students, including advisement, tours, stays in dorms, entertainment, registration, and financial information. There are guides for informal visits and visitors may sit in on classes and stay overnight. To schedule a visit, contact the Office of School Relations at (512) 593-3907.

Financial Aid: TAMUK is a member of CSS. The FAFSA is required. Check with the school for current deadlines.

International Students: In a recent year, there were 86 international students enrolled. Satisfactory scores are required on the written TOEFL the college's own test, and the SAT or the ACT.

Computers: All students may access the system. There are no time limits. Check with the school for current fee.

Graduates: In a recent year, 729 bachelor's degrees were awarded. The most popular majors were engineering (16%), business/marketing (13%), and interdisciplinary (11%). In an average class, 25% graduate in 5 years or less, and 30% graduate in 6 years or less.

Admissions Contact: Maggie Williams, Registrar and Director of Admissions. E-mail: *kgossrx@tamuk.edu* Web: *http://www.tamuk.edu*

TEXAS CHRISTIAN UNIVERSITY · D-2
Fort Worth, TX 76129

(817) 257-7490
(800) TCU-FROG; Fax: (817) 257-7268

Full-time: 2654 men, 4064 women	**Faculty:** 467; I, -$
Part-time: 199 men, 254 women	**Ph.D.s:** 91%
Graduate: 768 men, 810 women	**Student/Faculty:** 14 to 1
Year: semesters, summer session	**Tuition:** $17,630 ($21,320)
Application Deadline: February 15	**Room & Board:** $5780 ($6980)
Freshman Class: 8155 applied, 5471 accepted, 1610 enrolled	
SAT Verbal/Math: 570/590*	**ACT:** 26 **VERY COMPETITIVE+**

Texas Christian University, founded in 1873, is a private university affiliated with the Christian Church (Disciples of Christ). TCU is a teaching and research institution offering undergraduate programs in arts, sciences, business, education, fine arts, communications, nursing, and engineering. There are 7 undergraduate and 8 graduate schools. In addition to regional accreditation, TCU has baccalaureate program accreditation with AACSB, ABET, ACEJMC, ADA, ASLA, CAAHEP, CCNE, CSAB, CSWE, FIDER, and NASM. The library contains 2,073,391 volumes, 642,236 microform items, and 61,675 audio/video tapes/CDs/DVDs, and subscribes to 28,727 periodicals including electronic. Computerized library services include the card catalog, interlibrary loans, database searching, Internet access, and laptop Internet portals. Special learning facilities include a learning resource center, art gallery, natural history museum, radio station, TV station, an observatory, and a speech and hearing clinic. The 300-acre campus is in a suburban area 3 miles southwest of downtown Fort Worth. Including any residence halls, there are 99 buildings.

Student Life: 76% of undergraduates are from Texas. Others are from 48 states, 75 foreign countries, and Canada. 95% are from public schools. 76% are white. 51% are various religions; 30% claim no religious affiliation; 13% Catholic. The average age of freshmen is 18; all undergraduates, 21. 16% do not continue beyond their first year; 69% remain to graduate.

Housing: 3200 students can be accommodated in college housing, which includes single-sex and coed dorms, on-campus apartments, fraternity houses, and sorority houses. In addition, there are special-interest houses. On-campus housing is guaranteed for all 4 years. 54% of students commute. All students may keep cars.

Activities: 35% of men belong to 1 local and 12 national fraternities; 40% of women belong to 3 local and 13 national sororities. There are 200 groups on campus, including art, band, cheerleading, choir, chorale, chorus, computers, dance, drama, drill team, ethnic, film, gay, honors, international, jazz band, literary magazine, marching band, musical theater, newspaper, opera, orchestra, pep band, photography, political, professional, radio and TV, religious, social, social service, student government, symphony, and yearbook. Popular campus events include Parents Weekend, Howdy Rush Week, and Carols by Candlelight.

Sports: There are 8 intercollegiate sports for men and 9 for women. Facilities include a recreation center, a climbing wall and challenge course, fitness and wellness programs, and a pool.

Disabled Students: 89% of the campus is accessible. Wheelchair ramps, elevators, special parking, specially equipped rest rooms, lowered drinking fountains and lowered telephones are available. For visually-impaired and hearing-impaired students, there are flashing lights and vibrators on beds in case of fire. Hearing-assistance devices are also available.

Campus Safety and Security: Measures include 24-hour foot and vehicle patrol, self-defense education, security escort services, and shuttle buses. There are informal discussions, pamphlets/posters/films, emergency telephones, lighted pathways/sidewalks, bike patrol, and video monitoring of some parking lots.

Programs of Study: TCU confers B.A., B.S., B.B.A., B.F.A., B.G.S., B.Med., B.Mus., B.S.Ed., B.S.N., and B.S.S.W. degrees. Master's and doctoral degrees are also awarded. Bachelor's degrees are awarded in AGRICULTURE (range/farm management), BIOLOGICAL SCIENCE (biochemistry, biology/biological science, neurosciences, and nutrition), BUSINESS (accounting, banking and finance, business administration and management, electronic business, entrepreneurial studies, fashion merchandising, international business management, international economics, management science, marketing/retailing/merchandising, real estate, and supply chain management), COMMUNICATIONS AND THE ARTS (advertising, art history and appreciation, ballet, broadcasting, communications, dance, dramatic arts, English, film arts, graphic design, journalism, music, music performance, music theory and composition, piano/organ, public relations, publishing, radio/television technology, Spanish, speech/debate/rhetoric, and studio art), COMPUTER AND PHYSICAL SCIENCE (astrophysics, chemistry, computer science, geology, information sciences and systems, mathematics, and physics), EDUCATION (art, athletic training, bilingual/bicultural, early childhood, education of the deaf and hearing impaired, education of the exceptional child, elementary, English, mathematics, middle school, music, physical, science, secondary, and social studies), ENGINEERING AND ENVIRONMENTAL DESIGN (computer technology, engineering, environmental science, and interior design), HEALTH PROFESSIONS (exercise science, health, nursing, and speech pathology/audiology), SOCIAL SCIENCE (anthropology, criminal justice, dietetics, economics, food production/management/services, geography, history, international relations, Latin American studies, liberal arts/general studies, philosophy, physical fitness/movement, political science/government, psychology, religion, religious music, social work, and sociology). Nursing, biology, and advertising/public relations are the largest.

Required: The university requires completion of the 18-course university curriculum requirements, which are divided into foundations (reading, writing, and math) and explorations (physical, social, and life sciences, plus religion and history).

Special: A general studies degree and a combined B.A.-B.S. degree in numerous majors are offered. Student-designed majors, dual majors, nondegree study, and pass/no credit options are available. TCU also accepts credit by exam and credit for life, military, and work experience. 3-2 programs are available in business, education, and economics. Internships are available in almost all major areas. The university also offers a Washington semester, student exchange in Japan and Mexico, and study abroad in 28 countries. TCU also offers study at its London Center and study through the American Airlines Leadership for the Americas program. There are 4 national honor societies, including Phi Beta Kappa, a freshman honors program, and 29 departmental honors programs.

Faculty/Classroom: 63% of faculty are male; 37%, female. 96% teach undergraduates. The average class size in an introductory lecture is 36 and in a regular course, 28.

Admissions: 67% of the 2005-2006 applicants were accepted. 53% of the current freshmen were in the top fifth of their class.

Requirements: The SAT or ACT is recommended. In addition, candidates should be graduates of an accredited secondary school and have completed 15 Carnegie units, including 4 years of English, 3 years each of math, science, and social studies, and 2 each of the same foreign language and of academic electives. TCU also recommends an interview and requires an essay and counselor's recommendation. AP and CLEP credits are accepted. Important factors in the admissions decision are advanced placement or honor courses, leadership record, and evidence of special talent.

Procedure: Freshmen are admitted to all sessions. Entrance exams should be taken during or before the fall semester of the senior year. There is a deferred admissions plan. Applications should be filed by February 15 for fall entry and December 1 for spring entry. The fall 2005 application fee was $40. Notification is sent April 1. A waiting list is an active part of the admissions procedure. Applications are accepted on-line.

Transfer: 411 transfer students enrolled in 2004-2005. The recommended GPA is 2.5 and a minimum GPA of 2.0 is required. Applicants must complete an application form and submit official transcripts from each college attended as well as a secondary school transcript. If fewer than 24 semester hours of transferable work have been completed at the time of application, SAT or ACT scores are required and secondary school credentials are considered.

Visiting: There are regularly scheduled orientations for prospective students, including student-led campus tours, optional personal interviews, and departmental visits. There are guides for informal visits and visitors may sit in on classes and stay overnight. To schedule a visit, contact the Admissions Office.

Financial Aid: TCU is a member of CSS. The FAFSA is required. The deadline for filing freshman financial aid applications for fall entry is May 1.

International Students: There are 284 international students enrolled. The school actively recruits these students. They must take the TOEFL or either the SAT or ACT.

Computers: Wireless access is available. All students may access the system anytime. It is strongly recommended that all students have a personal computer.

Graduates: From July 1, 2004 to June 30, 2005, 1537 bachelor's degrees were awarded. In an average class, 69% graduate in 6 years or less. 135 companies recruited on campus in 2004-2005.

Admissions Contact: Ray Brown, Dean of Admissions.
E-mail: *frogmail@tcu.edu* Web: *tcu.edu*

TEXAS LUTHERAN UNIVERSITY   D-4
Seguin, TX 78155
(830) 372-8050
(800) 771-8521; Fax: (830) 372-8096

Full-time: 619 men, 709 women	**Faculty:** 75; IIB, --$
Part-time: 42 men, 60 women	**Ph.Ds:** 79%
Graduate: none	**Student/Faculty:** 18 to 1
Year: semesters, summer session	**Tuition:** $17,720
Application Deadline: June 1	**Room & Board:** $5810
Freshman Class: 1151 applied, 830 accepted, 380 enrolled	
SAT Math: 528*	**ACT:** 22 **COMPETITIVE**

Texas Lutheran University, founded in 1891, is a private liberal arts institution affiliated with the Evangelical Lutheran Church of America. There are 3 undergraduate schools. In addition to regional accreditation, TLU has baccalaureate program accreditation with ACBSP and CSWE. The library contains 171,134 volumes, 118,721 microform items, and 4241 audio/video tapes/CDs/DVDs, and subscribes to 565 periodicals including electronic. Computerized library services include the card catalog, interlibrary loans, database searching, Internet access, and laptop Internet portals. Special learning facilities include an art gallery, natural history museum, and a geological museum. The 196-acre campus is in a suburban area 37 miles east of San Antonio and 50 miles south of Austin. Including any residence halls, there are 36 buildings.

Student Life: 96% of undergraduates are from Texas. Others are from 23 states and 6 foreign countries. 88% are from public schools. 71% are white; 16% Hispanic. 22% are Protestant; 19% Catholic; 19% claim no religious affiliation. The average age of freshmen is 18; all undergraduates, 21. 33% do not continue beyond their first year; 51% remain to graduate.

Housing: 910 students can be accommodated in college housing, which includes single-sex and coed dorms, on-campus apartments, and married-student housing. On-campus housing is available on a first-come, first-served basis. 63% of students live on campus; of those, 50% remain on campus on weekends. All students may keep cars.

Activities: 5% of men belong to 5 local and 1 national fraternity; 9% of women belong to 3 local sororities. There are 65 groups on campus, including African American, art, band, cheerleading, choir, chorus, computers, dance, debate, drama, ethnic, forensics, gay, honors, international, intramural/athletic, jazz band, literary magazine, Mexican American, musical theater, newspaper, orchestra, pep band, political, professional, religious, science, social, social service, student government, symphony, and yearbook. Popular campus events include Christmas Vespers and Spring Fling.

Sports: There are 6 intercollegiate sports for men and 8 for women, and 14 intramural sports for men and 14 for women. Facilities include a 2200-seat gym, a fitness center, an 8-lane swimming pool, softball, baseball, and soccer fields, intramural/recreation fields, golf practice greens, and a lighted walking track.

Disabled Students: 90% of the campus is accessible. Wheelchair ramps, elevators, special parking, specially equipped rest rooms, special class scheduling, lowered drinking fountains, and special housing are available.

Services: Counseling and information services are available, as is tutoring in most subjects. Assistance with writing assignments is also available.

Campus Safety and Security: Measures include 24-hour foot and vehicle patrol, self-defense education, security escort services, and informal discussions. There are pamphlets/posters/films, lighted pathways/sidewalks, and coded locks in residence halls.

Programs of Study: TLU confers B.A., B.S., B.B.A., and B.M. degrees. Bachelor's degrees are awarded in BIOLOGICAL SCIENCE (biology/biological science), BUSINESS (accounting and business administration and management), COMMUNICATIONS AND THE ARTS (art, communications, dramatic arts, English, music, and Spanish), COMPUTER AND PHYSICAL SCIENCE (chemistry, computer science, information sciences and systems, mathematics, and physics), EDUCATION (athletic training and education), SOCIAL SCIENCE (economics, history, international studies, philosophy, political science/government, psychology, sociology, and theological studies). Business, biology, and psychology are the strongest academically. Business, kinesiology, and biology are the largest.

Required: All students must complete 124 semester hours, including 24 to 54 in their major, with a 2.0 GPA. Between 45 and 49 hours of distribution courses are required. A senior seminar, project, or concert is required in most majors.

Special: Internships are available in most majors. Study abroad in all countries affiliated with ISEP, a Washington semester with American University, and work-study programs are available. The college offers student-designed majors and dual majors. There is a 3-2 engineering program with Texas A&M, Baylor University, and Southern Methodist University. There are 11 national honor societies and a freshman honors program. All departments have honors programs.

Faculty/Classroom: 55% of faculty are male; 45%, female. All teach undergraduates. The average class size in an introductory lecture is 23; in a laboratory, 24; and in a regular course, 20.

Admissions: 72% of the 2005-2006 applicants were accepted. 42% of the current freshmen were in the top fifth of their class; 67% were in the top two fifths. There were 2 National Merit semifinalists. 5 freshmen graduated first in their class.

Requirements: The SAT or ACT is required. In addition, applicants must have 16 Carnegie units, including a recommended 4 years in English, 3 each of social studies, math, and science, and 2 in foreign language. The GED is accepted. A GPA of 2.5 is required. AP and CLEP credits are accepted. Important factors in the admissions decision are advanced placement or honor courses, recommendations by school officials, and extracurricular activities record.

Procedure: Freshmen are admitted fall and spring. Entrance exams should be taken in the spring of the junior year or the summer before the senior year. There is a rolling admissions plan. Applications should be filed by June 1 for fall entry and December 1 for spring entry, along with a $25 fee. Notification is sent on a rolling basis. A waiting list is an active part of the admissions procedure. Applications are accepted on-line.

Transfer: 69 transfer students enrolled in 2004-2005. Applicants for transfer must have a GPA of at least 2.25 and be in good academic standing. 33 of 124 credits required for the bachelor's degree must be completed at TLU.

Visiting: There are regularly scheduled orientations for prospective students, including a campus tour, classroom visits, a financial aid presentation, a study abroad session, an athlete session, and a student panel. There are guides for informal visits and visitors may sit in on classes and stay overnight. To schedule a visit, contact the Admissions Office.

Financial Aid: In 2005-2006, 95% of all full-time freshmen and 79% of continuing full-time students received some form of financial aid. 76% of full-time freshmen and 71% of continuing full-time students received need-based aid. The average freshman award was $13,500. 25% of undergraduates work part time. Average annual earnings from campus work are $554. The average financial indebtedness of the 2005 graduate was $26,800. The FAFSA is required. The priority date for freshman financial aid applications for fall entry is February 1. The deadline for filing freshman financial aid applications for fall entry is April 1.

International Students: In a recent year, there were 25 international students enrolled. The school actively recruits these students. Satisfactory scores are required on the written TOEFL and the SAT or the ACT.

Computers: Wireless access is available. There are computer labs in the student center, library, and various academic buildings. All students may access the system 24 hours a day, 7 days a week. There are no time limits and no fees.

Graduates: From July 1, 2004 to June 30, 2005, 263 bachelor's degrees were awarded. The most popular majors were natural science (23%), business administration (21%), and kinesiology (16%). In an average class, 36% graduate in 4 years, 51% graduate in 5 years, and 41% graduate in 6 years. 29 companies recruited on campus in 2004-2005. Of the 2004 graduating class, 33% were enrolled in graduate school within 6 months of graduation and 61% were employed.

Admissions Contact: E. Norman Jones, Vice President of Enrollment Services. A video is available. E-mail: *admissions@tlu.edu* Web: *www.tlu.edu*

TEXAS SOUTHERN UNIVERSITY   E-3

Houston, TX 77004   (713) 313-7472; Fax: (713) 313-1878

Full-time: 3243 men, 4496 women	Faculty: 409
Part-time: 821 men, 1200 women	Ph.D.s: 44%
Graduate: 785 men, 1358 women	Student/Faculty: 19 to 1
Year: semesters, summer session	Tuition: $3772 ($10,396)
Application Deadline: August 13	Room & Board: $6056
Freshman Class: 6602 applied, 3801 accepted, 3553 enrolled	
SATor ACT: recommended	COMPETITIVE

Texas Southern University, founded in 1947, is a state-supported institution offering undergraduate programs in the arts and sciences, education and behavioral sciences, pharmacy and health science, business, and technology. There are 7 undergraduate and 7 graduate schools. In addition to regional accreditation, TSU has baccalaureate program accreditation with AACSB, ABET, ACPE, CAAHEP, NAACLS, and NCATE.The 3 libraries contain 264,254 volumes, 464,308 microform items, and 4076 audio/video tapes/CDs/DVDs, and subscribe to 1750 periodicals including electronic. Computerized library services include the card catalog, interlibrary loans, database searching, and Internet access. Special learning facilities include an art gallery and radio station. The 150-acre campus is in an urban area 3 miles southeast of downtown Houston. Including any residence halls, there are 45 buildings.

Student Life: 85% of undergraduates are from Texas. Others are from 37 states, 40 foreign countries, and Canada. 97% are from public schools. 90% are African American. 90% are Protestant; 19% claim no religious affiliation. The average age of freshmen is 21; all undergraduates, 23. 35% do not continue beyond their first year; 17% remain to graduate.

Housing: 1182 students can be accommodated in college housing, which includes single-sex dormitories and off-campus apartments. On-campus housing is available on a first-come, first-served basis. Priority is given to out-of-town students. 96% of students commute. Alcohol is not permitted. All students may keep cars.

Activities: 1% of men and about 1% of women belong to 1 local and 7 national fraternities; 3% of women belong to 2 local and 7 national sororities. There are 58 groups on campus, including accounting, art, band, business, cheerleading, choir, chorus, computers, consumer services, dance, debate, drama, ethnic, film, health, honors, international, jazz band, marching band, newspaper, orchestra, pharmaceutical, photography, political, professional, radio and TV, religious, science, social, social service, student government, symphony, and yearbook. Popular campus events include Senior Day, Christmas Tree Lighting, and TSU Relays.

Sports: There are 7 intercollegiate sports for men and 9 for women, and 13 intramural sports for men and 13 for women. Facilities include a health and phys ed complex that seats 8100, a 7000-seat football stadium, 2 gyms (the larger seating 1000), and a recreational facility with a food court.

Disabled Students: 60% of the campus is accessible. Wheelchair ramps, elevators, special parking, specially equipped rest rooms, lowered drinking fountains, and lowered telephones are available.

Services: Counseling and information services are available, as is tutoring in most subjects. There is remedial math, reading, and writing.

Campus Safety and Security: Measures include 24-hour foot and vehicle patrol, self-defense education, security escort services, and shuttle buses. There are informal discussions, pamphlets/posters/films, emergency telephones, and lighted pathways/sidewalks.

Programs of Study: TSU confers B.A., B.S., B.B.A., B.S.Die, B.S.E.T., B.S.I.T., and B.S.P.A.F. degrees. Master's and doctoral degrees are also awarded. Bachelor's degrees are awarded in BIOLOGICAL SCIENCE (biology/biological science and nutrition), BUSINESS (accounting, banking and finance, business administration and management, and marketing/retailing/merchandising), COMMUNICATIONS AND THE ARTS (art, communications, dramatic arts, English, French, music, and Spanish), COMPUTER AND PHYSICAL SCIENCE (chemistry, computer science, mathematics, and physics), EDUCATION (bilingual/bicultural, early childhood, English, foreign languages, mathematics, and physical), ENGINEERING AND ENVIRONMENTAL DESIGN (aviation administration/management, civil engineering technology, drafting and design technology, electrical/electronics engineering technology, engineering technology, environmental engineering technology, and industrial engineering technology), HEALTH PROFESSIONS (environmental health science, health, health care administration, medical technology, and respiratory therapy), SOCIAL SCIENCE (criminal justice, dietetics, economics, history, human services, interdisciplinary studies, liberal arts/general studies, physical fitness/movement, political science/government, psychology, public affairs, social work, and sociology). Prepharmacy is the strongest academically. Biology and business are the largest.

Required: Students must complete between 136 and 148 semester hours, depending on the field of study, and maintain a minimum GPA of 2.0. The core curriculum is 44 hours. A minimum of 30 hours is required in the major. A course in phys ed is also required.

Special: Cross-registration is available with North Harris and Houston Community Colleges, as well as in military science with the University of Houston. Study abroad in Africa, internships, B.A.-B.S. degrees, and work-study programs are also available. There are 2 national honor societies, a freshman honors program, and 1 departmental honors program.

Faculty/Classroom: 54% of faculty are male; 46%, female. 76% teach undergraduates. Graduate students teach 2% of introductory courses. The average class size in an introductory lecture is 48; in a laboratory, 34; and in a regular course, 32.

Admissions: 58% of the 2005-2006 applicants were accepted.

Requirements: The SAT or ACT is recommended. In addition, candidates should be graduates of an accredited secondary school or have the GED. A GPA of 2.0 is required.

Procedure: Freshmen are admitted fall, spring, and summer. Entrance exams should be taken by the semester prior to enrollment. There is an early admissions plan and a rolling admissions plan. Applications should be filed by August 13 for fall entry, December 19 for spring entry, and May 21 for summer entry, along with a $42 fee. Notification is sent on a rolling basis. Applications are accepted on-line.

Transfer: 1951 transfer students enrolled in 2004-2005. The applicant must be a student in good standing and must submit an official transcripts. The SAT or ACT is required. 30 of 136 to 148 credits required for the bachelor's degree must be completed at TSU.

Visiting: There are regularly scheduled orientations for prospective students, including a required orientation for freshmen and transfer students. Orientation dates, including early registration, are posted in the orientation application. There are guides for informal visits and visitors may stay overnight. To schedule a visit, contact the Office of Recruitment at (713) 313-7951, (713) 313-7849, or em.tsu.edu.

Financial Aid: In 2005-2006, 74% of all full-time freshmen and 98% of continuing full-time students received some form of financial aid. 76% of full-time freshmen and all continuing full-time students received need-based aid. The FAFSA is required. The deadline for filing freshman financial aid applications for fall entry is April 15.

International Students: There are 88 international students enrolled. They must score satisfactorily on the written TOEFL.

Computers: Computer science students may access the system any time. There are no time limits. The fee is $83 per semester.

Graduates: From July 1, 2004 to June 30, 2005, 538 bachelor's degrees were awarded. The most popular majors were business (12%), biology (9%), and administration of justice (6%). In an average class, 2% graduate in 3 years or less, 5% graduate in 4 years or less, 6% graduate in 5 years or less, and 17% graduate in 6 years or less.

Admissions Contact: Joyce M. Waddell, Director of Admissions.
E-mail: waddell_jm@tsu.edu Web: www.tsu.edu

TEXAS STATE UNIVERSITY SYSTEM

The Texas State University System, established in 1911, is a public higher education system. It is governed by a 9-member Board of Regents, whose chief administrator is the chancellor. The primary mission of the system universities is the provision of a well-rounded education focusing on degree options ranging from educator preparation to chemical engineering. The total enrollment of the 9 campuses is approximately 70,000, with about 12,000 faculty and staff members. Altogether there are 416 baccalaureate, 250 master's, and 10 doctoral programs offered within the system. 4-year campuses are Angelo State University in San Angelo, Lamar University in Beaumont, Sam Houston State University in Huntsville, Texas State University-San Marcos, and Sul Ross State University in Alpine, with 2-year lower-division campuses in Beaumont, Orange, and Port Arthur, and 2-year upper-division campuses in Del Rio, Eagle Pass, and Uvalde. Profiles of the 4-year campuses are included in this section. For more information, visit www.tsus.edu.

TEXAS STATE UNIVERSITY - SAN MARCOS
(Formerly Southwest Texas State University)

D-4

San Marcos, TX 78666-4616

(512) 245-2364
Fax: (512) 245-8044

Full-time: 8320 men, 10,173 women	**Faculty:** 789; IIA, -$
Part-time: 1957 men, 2572 women	**Ph.D.s:** 76%
Graduate: 748 men, 2574 women	**Student/Faculty:** 23 to 1
Year: semesters, summer session	**Tuition:** $5252 ($15,532)
Application Deadline: June 1	**Room & Board:** $5610

Freshman Class: 9284 applied, 7095 accepted, 3076 enrolled
SAT Verbal/Math: 530/540*   **ACT:** 23   **COMPETITIVE**

Texas State University - San Marcos, formerly Southwest Texas State University, founded in 1899, is part of the Texas State University System and offers programs in general studies, applied arts and technology, business, education, fine arts, health professions, liberal arts, and science and engineering. There are 8 undergraduate schools and 1 graduate school. In addition to regional accreditation, Texas State has baccalaureate program accreditation with AACSB, ADA, AHEA, ASLA, CAAHEP, CSAB, CSWE, FIDER, NAACLS, NASM, and NRPA. The library contains 3,540,815 volumes, 1,873,257 microform items, and 275,855 audio/video tapes/CDs/DVDs, and subscribes to 8698 periodicals including electronic. Computerized library services include the card catalog, interlibrary loans, database searching, Internet access, and laptop Internet portals. Special learning facilities include a learning resource center, art gallery, planetarium, radio station, and a recording studio. The 456-acre campus is in a suburban area 30 miles south of Austin. Including any residence halls, there are 219 buildings.

Student Life: 98% of undergraduates are from Texas. Others are from 46 states, 50 foreign countries, and Canada. 98% are from public schools. 71% are white; 20% Hispanic. The average age of freshmen is 18; all undergraduates, 23. 26% do not continue beyond their first year; 52% remain to graduate.

Housing: 6075 students can be accommodated in university housing, which includes single-sex and coed dorms, on-campus apartments, and married-student housing. In addition, there are honors houses, special-interest houses, special residences for international students, single parents, upper division students, and freshmen experience. On-campus housing is guaranteed for the freshman year only and is available on a first-come, first-served basis. 77% of students commute. All students may keep cars.

Activities: 5% of men belong to 6 local and 15 national fraternities; 5% of women belong to 12 national sororities. There are 335 groups on campus, including art, band, cheerleading, chess, choir, chorale, chorus, computers, dance, debate, drama, drill team, ethnic, gay, honors, international, jazz band, literary magazine, marching band, musical theater, newspaper, nontraditional students, opera, orchestra, pep band, photography, political, professional, radio and TV, religious, social, social service, student government, symphony, and yearbook. Popular campus events include Welcome Week and Cricket Fest.

Sports: There are 6 intercollegiate sports for men and 8 for women, and 10 intramural sports for men and 10 for women. Facilities include a 14,104-seat stadium, a 7200-seat gym, tennis courts, a spring-fed pool, an aquatic sports center, basketball and volleyball courts, racquetball courts, an indoor jogging/walking track, weight-lifting equipment, and exercise machines.

Disabled Students: 85% of the campus is accessible. Wheelchair ramps, elevators, special parking, specially equipped rest rooms, special class scheduling, lowered drinking fountains, lowered telephones, special housing, curb cuts, pay TTY text telephones, adaptive computer technology, sign language interpreter, and reading recorder services for the visually impaired are available.

Services: Counseling and information services are available. There is a reader service for the blind, and remedial math, reading, and writing. Tutoring for all core curriculum classes is available.

Campus Safety and Security: Measures include 24-hour foot and vehicle patrol, self-defense education, security escort services, and shuttle buses. There are informal discussions, pamphlets/posters/films, emergency telephones, and lighted pathways/sidewalks.

Programs of Study: Texas State confers B.A., B.S., B.A.A.S., B.A.I.S., B.B.A., B.E.S.S., B.F.A., B.H.A., B.H.W.P., B.M., B.P.A., B.S.A.G., B.S.A.S.,B.S.C.D., B.S.C.J., B.S.C.L.S., B.S.F.C.S., B.S.H.I.M., B.S.H.P., B.S.R.A., B.S.R.C., B.S.R.T., B.S.T., and B.S.W. degrees. Master's and doctoral degrees are also awarded. Bachelor's degrees are awarded in AGRICULTURE (agricultural business management, agriculture, and animal science), BIOLOGICAL SCIENCE (biochemistry, biology/biological science, botany, marine biology, microbiology, nutrition, physiology, wildlife biology, and zoology), BUSINESS (accounting, banking and finance, business administration and management, business economics, fashion merchandising, marketing/retailing/merchandising, and recreational facilities management), COMMUNICATIONS AND THE ARTS (advertising, applied art, art, audio technology, broadcasting, communications, dance, dramatic arts, English, French,

German, jazz, journalism, music, music performance, public relations, Spanish, and studio art), COMPUTER AND PHYSICAL SCIENCE (chemistry, computer science, digital arts/technology, information sciences and systems, mathematics, and physics), EDUCATION (athletic training, early childhood, elementary, health, and special), ENGINEERING AND ENVIRONMENTAL DESIGN (cartography, city/community/regional planning, construction technology, engineering technology, environmental science, industrial engineering technology, interior design, manufacturing engineering, manufacturing technology, and water and wastewater technology), HEALTH PROFESSIONS (clinical science, community health work, exercise science, health care administration, medical records administration/services, radiation therapy, respiratory therapy, and speech pathology/audiology), SOCIAL SCIENCE (American studies, anthropology, Asian/Oriental studies, child care/child and family studies, corrections, criminal justice, economics, European studies, family/consumer studies, geography, history, interdisciplinary studies, international relations, international studies, law enforcement and corrections, Middle Eastern studies, philosophy, political science/government, psychology, public administration, Russian and Slavic studies, social work, and sociology). Geography and education are the strongest academically. Education, and business management, and marketing are the largest.

Required: All students must earn a minimum GPA of 2.0 while taking at least 128 semester hours, including 30 in the major. The core curriculum includes basic skills, history and politics, natural science, social science, philosophy, international perspectives, literature, fine arts, and physical fitness.

Special: Co-op programs in medicine, dentistry, engineering, architecture, law, pharmacy, nursing, occupational therapy, and veterinary medicine, internships in many departments, study abroad in 26 countries, and Washington semesters are available. Dual majors, credit for life experience, and nondegree study also are possible. 2 summer sessions are offered in most programs. A 3-2 engineering degree is possible with the University of Texas, Texas A&M, or Texas Tech Universities. There are 27 national honor societies, a freshman honors program, and 1 departmental honors program.

Faculty/Classroom: 54% of faculty are male; 46%, female. All teach undergraduates. Graduate students teach 13% of introductory courses. The average class size in an introductory lecture is 48; in a laboratory, 18; and in a regular course, 34.

Admissions: 76% of the 2005-2006 applicants were accepted. The SAT scores for the 2005-2006 freshman class were: Verbal--32% below 500, 50% between 500 and 599, 18% between 600 and 700, and 1% above 700; Math--25% below 500, 54% between 500 and 599, 21% between 600 and 700, and 1% above 700. The ACT scores were 29% below 21, 37% between 21 and 23, 26% between 24 and 26, 6% between 27 and 28, and 3% above 28. 38% of the current freshmen were in the top fifth of their class; 80% were in the top two fifths. 17 freshmen graduated first in their class.

Requirements: The SAT or ACT is required, with minimum scores determined by high school class rank. Applicants need 15 academic credits, including 4 units in English, 3 in math and social science, 3 in natural science, 2 in foreign language, and 1 in computer literacy. The GED is accepted; applicants with a GED are treated as though they were in the 4th quarter of their graduating class. AP and CLEP credits are accepted. Important factors in the admissions decision are advanced placement or honor courses, leadership record, and extracurricular activities record.

Procedure: Freshmen are admitted to all sessions. Entrance exams should be taken at the end of the junior year. There is an early admissions plan. Applications should be filed by June 1 for fall entry, December 1 for spring entry, and May 1 for summer entry, along with a $40 fee. Notification is sent on a rolling basis. Applications are accepted online.

Transfer: 2996 transfer students enrolled in 2004-2005. Transfer students with 29 or fewer credits must meet freshman requirements; those with 30 or more credits must submit official transcripts to verify a minimum 2.25 GPA. 30 of 128 credits required for the bachelor's degree must be completed at Texas State.

Visiting: There are regularly scheduled orientations for prospective students, consisting of a 2-day event, with registration required. First-time freshmen parents may attend. Students receive registration instructions, academic advising, and information concerning Texas State's academic policies, procedures, and student services. Time is allotted to register for classes. There are guides for informal visits and visitors may sit in on classes. To schedule a visit, contact the Admissions and Visitors Center at (512) 245-8871 or admissions@txstate.edu.

Financial Aid: In 2005-2006, 57% of all full-time freshmen and 55% of continuing full-time students received some form of financial aid. 45% of full-time freshmen and 46% of continuing full-time students received need-based aid. The average freshman award was $10,073. Need-based scholarships or need-based grants averaged $5139; need-based self-help aid (loans and jobs) averaged $2686; and non-need-based athletic scholarships averaged $3988. 4% of undergraduates work part time. Average annual earnings from campus work are $1981. The average financial indebtedness of the 2005 graduate was $16,826. The FAFSA is re-

quired. The priority date for freshman financial aid applications for fall entry is April 1.

International Students: There are 192 international students enrolled. They must take the TOEFL and also take the SAT or the ACT.

Computers: Wireless access is available. There are more than 1400 workstations with wireless access in the library, student center, and most academic buildings. All students may access the system 24 hours daily. There are no time limits. The fee is $10 per credit hour.

Graduates: From July 1, 2004 to June 30, 2005, 4314 bachelor's degrees were awarded. The most popular majors were interdisciplinary studies in education (8%), business administration and management (6%), and marketing (5%). In an average class, 1% graduate in 3 years or less, 17% graduate in 4 years or less, 38% graduate in 5 years or less, and 52% graduate in 6 years or less. 264 companies recruited on campus in 2004-2005.

Admissions Contact: Christie Kangas, Director of Admissions.
E-mail: admissions@txstate.edu Web: www.admissions.txstate.edu

TEXAS TECH UNIVERSITY   B-2

Lubbock, TX 79409-5005	(806) 742-1480; Fax: (806) 742-0062
Full-time: 11,405 men, 9416 women	Faculty: 1116; I, --$
Part-time: 1296 men, 885 women	Ph.D.s: 91%
Graduate: 2512 men, 2487 women	Student/Faculty: 19 to 1
Year: semesters, summer session	Tuition: $6151 ($14,431)
Application Deadline: May 1	Room & Board: $6875
Freshman Class: 12,583 applied, 8927 accepted, 3801 enrolled	
SAT Verbal/Math: 556/576*	ACT: 24 VERY COMPETITIVE

Texas Tech University, founded in 1923, is a large, comprehensive public university offering undergraduate and graduate programs in a variety of professional and vocational fields. There are 11 undergraduate and 2 graduate schools. In addition to regional accreditation, Texas Tech has baccalaureate program accreditation with AACSB, ABET, ACEJMC, CAHEA, CSWE, FIDER, NAAB, NASAD, NASM, NCATE, and NLN. The 4 libraries contain 4,853,033 volumes, 2,315,095 microform items, and 85,909 audio/video tapes/CDs/DVDs, and subscribe to 22,717 periodicals including electronic. Computerized library services include the card catalog, interlibrary loans, database searching, Internet access, and laptop Internet portals. Special learning facilities include a learning resource center, art gallery, natural history museum, planetarium, radio station, TV station, a ranching heritage center, international cultural center, international textile center, and Southwest collection. The 1839-acre campus is in an urban area in Lubbock. Including any residence halls, there are 134 buildings.

Student Life: 93% of undergraduates are from Texas. Others are from 49 states, 112 foreign countries, and Canada. 77% are white; 11% Hispanic. The average age of freshmen is 19; all undergraduates, 21. 16% do not continue beyond their first year; 56% remain to graduate.

Housing: 6762 students can be accommodated in college housing, which includes single-sex and coed dorms, on-campus apartments, and married-student housing. In addition, there are honors houses, living/learnig communities, intensive study floors, substance free floors, nonsmoking floors, upperclass graduate halls, and summer housing. On-campus housing is guaranteed for the freshman year only and is available on a first-come, first-served basis. 77% of students commute. Alcohol is not permitted. All students may keep cars.

Activities: 6% of men belong to 26 national fraternities; 8% of women belong to 1 local and 18 national sororities. There are 390 groups on campus, including art, band, cheerleading, chess, choir, chorale, chorus, computers, dance, drama, drill team, drum and bugle corps, ethnic, film, forensics, gay, honors, international, jazz band, literary magazine, marching band, musical theater, newspaper, opera, orchestra, pep band, photography, political, professional, radio and TV, religious, social, social service, student government, symphony, and yearbook. Popular campus events include Parents Day, Carol of the Lights, and Madrigal Dinner.

Sports: There are 6 intercollegiate sports for men and 7 for women, and 18 intramural sports for men and 18 for women. Facilities include an athletic training center, a student recreation center, an aquatic center, and an athletic study/learning center.

Disabled Students: 83% of the campus is accessible. Wheelchair ramps, elevators, special parking, specially equipped rest rooms, special class scheduling, lowered drinking fountains, lowered telephones, special housing, and kneel-down buses are available.

Services: Counseling and information services are available, as is tutoring in every subject. There is a reader service for the blind, and remedial math, reading, and writing. Books on tape, note taking services, tape recorders, and a learning center are available. An attorney is available for students to obtain legal advice and guidance.

Campus Safety and Security: Measures include 24-hour foot and vehicle patrol, shuttle buses, pamphlets/posters/films, and emergency telephones. There are lighted pathways/sidewalks and presentations on crime prevention.

Programs of Study: Texas Tech confers B.A., B.S., B.F.A., B.G.S., B.I.D., B.Land.Arch., B.M., B.S.Arch., B.S.C.E., B.S.Ch.E., B.S.E.E , B.S.Eng.Physics, B.S.Eng.Tech., B.S.Envir. Eng., B.S. in Family and Consumer Sciences, B.S.Home Eco., B.S. Indust.Eng., B.S.Int'l Eco., B.S.M.E., B.S.P.E., and B.S.R.H.I.M. degrees. Master's and doctoral degrees are also awarded. Bachelor's degrees are awarded in AGRICULTURE (agricultural business management, agricultural communications, agricultural economics, agronomy, animal science, conservation and regulation, fish and game management, horticulture, plant protection (pest management), range/farm management, and wildlife management), BIOLOGICAL SCIENCE (biochemistry, biology/biological science, cell biology, microbiology, molecular biology, and zoology), BUSINESS (accounting, banking and finance, business administration and management, business economics, hotel/motel and restaurant management, international business management, international economics, management information systems, marketing and distribution, and retailing), COMMUNICATIONS AND THE ARTS (advertising, apparel design, art history and appreciation, broadcasting, classics, communications, dance, design, dramatic arts, English, French, German, journalism, music, music performance, music theory and composition, performing arts, photography, public relations, publishing, Spanish, studio art, telecommunications, theater design, and visual and performing arts), COMPUTER AND PHYSICAL SCIENCE (chemistry, computer science, geology, geophysics and seismology, geoscience, mathematics, and physics), EDUCATION (early childhood, middle school, and science), ENGINEERING AND ENVIRONMENTAL DESIGN (architecture, chemical engineering, civil engineering, construction technology, electrical/electronics engineering, electrical/electronics engineering technology, engineering, engineering physics, engineering technology, environmental engineering, industrial engineering, interior design, landscape architecture/design, mechanical engineering, and mechanical engineering technology), HEALTH PROFESSIONS (exercise science and health), SOCIAL SCIENCE (anthropology, clothing and textiles management/production/services, dietetics, economics, family/consumer resource management, family/consumer studies, food production/management/services, food science, geography, history, home economics, human development, Latin American studies, liberal arts/general studies, parks and recreation management, philosophy, political science/government, psychology, Russian and Slavic studies, social work, and sociology). Business and human development and family studies are the largest.

Required: All students seeking a bachelor's degree must meet the requirements of the core curriculum. A minimum of 120 credit hours is required, depending on the degree program. A minimum GPA of 2.0 is required. The last 30 hours and 25% of all credit hours must be from Texas Tech.

Special: Texas Tech offers many bachelor-to-masters accelerated degree programs, internships, study abroad, dual degrees, dual majors, extended studies, and pass/fail options. There are 19 national honor societies, and a freshman honors program.

Faculty/Classroom: 60% of faculty are male; 40%, female. All teach undergraduates and 45% both teach and do research. The average class size in an introductory lecture is 45; in a laboratory, 21; and in a regular course, 36.

Admissions: 71% of the 2005-2006 applicants were accepted. The SAT scores for the 2005-2006 freshman class were: Verbal--20% below 500, 52% between 500 and 599, 25% between 600 and 700, and 3% above 700; Math--11% below 500, 51% between 500 and 599, 34% between 600 and 700, and 4% above 700. The ACT scores were 15% below 21, 32% between 21 and 23, 29% between 24 and 26, 12% between 27 and 28, and 12% above 28. 44% of the current freshmen were in the top fifth of their class; 76% were in the top two fifths. There were 13 National Merit finalists. 24 freshmen graduated first in their class.

Requirements: The SAT or ACT is required. In addition, applicants should be graduates of an accredited high school or have the GED. The university requires 11 credits of academic work in high school, including 4 credits in English, 3 in math, 2 in laboratory sciences, and 2 in foreign language. The university admits all students scoring 29 on the ACT or a comparable SAT score. Special circumstances may allow those not fulfilling the above requirements to be admitted. AP and CLEP credits are accepted.

Procedure: Freshmen are admitted fall, spring, and summer. Entrance exams should be taken before July 1. There is an early admissions plan. Applications should be filed by May 1 for fall entry, December 1 for spring entry, and May 1 for summer entry, along with a $50 fee. Notification is sent on a rolling basis. Applications are accepted on-line.

Transfer: 1968 transfer students enrolled in 2004-2005. To transfer 24 or more hours, the GPA must be a minimum of 2.25. To transfer 12 to 23 hours, applicants must have a 2.5 GPA. To transfer fewer than 12 hours, applicants must have a 2.0 GPA and meet freshman requirements for admission. 30 of 120 credits required for the bachelor's degree must be completed at Texas Tech.

Visiting: There are regularly scheduled orientations for prospective students. There are guides for informal visits. To schedule a visit, contact the Visitor Center at (806) 742-1299 or visitors@ttu.edu.

Financial Aid: 10% of undergraduates work part time. The FAFSA is required. Texas Tech is a member of CSS. The deadline for filing freshman financial aid applications for fall entry is April 15.

International Students: There are 199 international students enrolled. They must score satisfactorily on the written TOEFL or on the electronic version and also take the SAT or the ACT.

Computers: Wireless access is available. All students may access the system 24 hours per day. There are no time limits and no fees. It is strongly recommended that all students have a personal computer.

Graduates: From July 1, 2004 to June 30, 2005, 4264 bachelor's degrees were awarded. The most popular majors were human development and family studies (8%), marketing (6%), and management (5%). In an average class, 2% graduate in 3 years or less, 24% graduate in 4 years or less, 49% graduate in 5 years or less, and 56% graduate in 6 years or less. 392 companies recruited on campus in 2004-2005.

Admissions Contact: Djuana Young, Director. A video is available. E-mail: admissions@ttu.edu Web: http://www.admissions.ttu.edu

TEXAS WESLEYAN UNIVERSITY — D-2
Fort Worth, TX 76105-1536

(817) 531-4422
(800) 580-8980; Fax: (817) 531-4231

Full-time: 365 men, 620 women	**Faculty:** 84; IIA, av$
Part-time: 93 men, 270 women	**Ph.D.s:** 77%
Graduate: 602 men, 701 women	**Student/Faculty:** 12 to 1
Year: semesters, summer session	**Tuition:** $14,000
Application Deadline: open	**Room & Board:** $4700
Freshman Class: n/av	
SAT or ACT: required	**COMPETITIVE**

Texas Wesleyan University, founded in 1890, is a liberal arts institution affiliated with the United Methodist Church. There are 3 undergraduate and 4 graduate schools. In addition to regional accreditation, Texas Wesleyan has baccalaureate program accreditation with NASM. The 2 libraries contain 281,476 volumes, 827,410 microform items, and 5824 audio/video tapes/CDs/DVDs, and subscribe to 3452 periodicals including electronic. Computerized library services include the card catalog, interlibrary loans, and database searching. Special learning facilities include a learning resource center, art gallery, and a theater. The 79-acre campus is in an urban area 2 miles east of downtown Fort Worth. Including any residence halls, there are 30 buildings.

Student Life: 96% of undergraduates are from Texas. Others are from 23 states, 32 foreign countries, and Canada. 94% are from public schools. 60% are white; 17% African American; 17% Native American/Eskimo; 16% Hispanic. 58% are claim no religious affiliation; 32% Protestant; 10% Catholic. The average age of freshmen is 19; all undergraduates, 25.

Housing: 275 students can be accommodated in college housing, which includes single-sex and coed dormitories and on-campus apartments. On-campus housing is available on a first-come, first-served basis. 90% of students commute. Alcohol is not permitted. All students may keep cars.

Activities: 2% of men belong to 3 local and 1 national fraternity, 2% of women belong to 3 local and 2 national sororities. There are 55 groups on campus, including art, band, cheerleading, choir, computers, drama, ethnic, honors, international, jazz band, musical theater, opera, political, professional, radio and TV, religious, social, social service, and student government. Popular campus events include Oktoberfest and the Wilson lectures.

Sports: There are 5 intercollegiate sports for men and 5 for women, and 11 intramural sports for men and 11 for women. Facilities include a 1500-seat athletic center, 4 tennis courts, an off-campus baseball park, and softball and soccer fields.

Disabled Students: Wheelchair ramps, elevators, special parking, specially equipped rest rooms, special class scheduling, and lowered telephones are available.

Services: Counseling and information services are available, as is tutoring in most subjects. There is remedial math, reading, and writing.

Campus Safety and Security: Measures include 24-hour foot and vehicle patrol, self-defense education, security escort services, and pamphlets/posters/films. There are emergency telephones, lighted pathways/sidewalks, and residence hall programs.

Programs of Study: Texas Wesleyan confers B.A., B.S., B.B.A., B.F.A, and B.M.E. degrees. Master's degrees are also awarded. Bachelor's degrees are awarded in BIOLOGICAL SCIENCE (biochemistry, and biology/biological science), BUSINESS (accounting, business administration and management, business economics, international business management, management information systems, and marketing/retailing/merchandising), COMMUNICATIONS AND THE ARTS (art, communications, dramatic arts, English, fine arts, music, and Spanish), COMPUTER AND PHYSICAL SCIENCE (chemistry, computer science, earth science, information sciences and systems, mathematics, and physical sciences), EDUCATION (business, early childhood, elementary, middle school, music, physical, reading, secondary, and teaching English as a second/foreign language (TESOL/TEFOL)), SOCIAL SCIENCE (Christian studies, criminal justice, economics, history, human development, humanities, interdisciplinary studies, international studies, law, paralegal studies, political science/government, psychology, religion, and social science). Accounting and psychology are the strongest academically. Business administration is the largest.

Required: A minimum GPA of 2.0 and a minimum of 124 credit hours are required to graduate. All students must complete a general education requirement of 51 credits, including courses in writing, literature, religion, lab science, history, math, political or economic systems, fine arts, humanities, phys ed, and social science, philosophy, or psychology. The total number of hours in the major varies.

Special: Study abroad is offered in 5 countries. A 3-2 engineering degree is offered in conjunction with a number of universities. Pass/fail options are available, as are B.A.-B.S. degrees, and internships in sports management, business, psychology, and sociology. A predentistry program is available. There are 2 national honor societies, and 8 departmental honors programs.

Faculty/Classroom: 59% of faculty are male; 41%, female. No introductory courses are taught by graduate students.

Requirements: The SAT or ACT is required, with satisfactory scores. Applicants must be graduates of an accredited secondary school or have a GED equivalent. An interview is recommended. Texas Wesleyan requires applicants to be in the upper 50% of their class. A GPA of 2.0 is required. AP and CLEP credits are accepted. Important factors in the admissions decision are leadership record, extracurricular activities record, and recommendations by alumni.

Procedure: Freshmen are admitted to all sessions. Entrance exams should be taken as early as possible. There is a rolling admissions plan. Application deadlines are open. The fall 2005 application fee was $25. Applications are accepted on-line.

Transfer: Applicants with fewer than 30 credit hours must submit a high school transcript and the results of either the SAT or the ACT. A minimum GPA of 2.0 is required. 45 of 124 credits required for the bachelor's degree must be completed at Texas Wesleyan.

Visiting: There are regularly scheduled orientations for prospective students. There are guides for informal visits and visitors may sit in on classes and stay overnight. To schedule a visit, contact the Office of Admissions.

Financial Aid: The FAFSA and the college's own financial statement are required.

International Students: The school actively recruits these students. A satisfactory score is required on the written TOEFL.

Computers: All students may access the system 9 A.M. to 9 P.M. Monday through Thursday, 9 A.M. to 5 P.M. Friday, and 9 A.M. to 1 P.M. weekends. There are no time limits and no fees. It is strongly recommended that all students have a PC.

Admissions Contact: Carolyn Hall, Director, Freshman Admission. A video is available. E-mail: *freshman@txwesleyan.edu*
Web: *www.txwesleyan.edu*

TEXAS WOMAN'S UNIVERSITY   D-2

Denton, TX 76204-5765   (940) 898-3188
(866) 809-6130, ext. 3188; Fax: (940) 898-3081

Full-time: 200 men, 3630 women	**Faculty:** 381; I, --$
Part-time: 90 men, 1440 women	**Ph.D.s:** 70%
Graduate: 520 men, 3850 women	**Student/Faculty:** 10 to 1
Year: semesters, summer session	**Tuition:** $3100 ($8700)
Application Deadline: see profile	**Room & Board:** $4800
Freshman Class: n/av	
SAT or ACT: required	**LESS COMPETITIVE**

Texas Woman's University, founded in 1901, is a comprehensive public university primarily for women, offering degree programs in the liberal arts, education, music and fine arts, and the business and health professions. There are 7 undergraduate and 8 graduate schools. Figures ub the above capsule and in this profile are approximate. In addition to regional accreditation, TWU has baccalaureate program accreditation with ADA, APTA, CSWE, NASM, and NLN. The 2 libraries contain 549,116 volumes, 1,554,071 microform items, and 24,061 audio/video tapes/CDs/DVDs, and subscribe to 2445 periodicals including electronic. Computerized library services include the card catalog, interlibrary loans, database searching, and Internet access. Special learning facilities include a learning resource center, art gallery, medical centers and clinics, radio and TV studios, and a nursery school. The 270-acre campus is in an urban area 38 miles north of Dallas. Including any residence halls, there are 62 buildings.

Student Life: 93% of undergraduates are from Texas. Others are from 44 states, 72 foreign countries, and Canada. 62% are white; 18% African American; 11% Hispanic. The average age of freshmen is 21; all undergraduates, 26. 25% do not continue beyond their first year; 35% remain to graduate.

Housing: 1346 students can be accommodated in college housing, which includes single-sex and coed dormitories, on-campus apartments, and married-student housing. In addition, there are honors houses and

special-interest houses. On-campus housing is guaranteed for the freshman year only and is available on a first-come, first-served basis. 81% of students commute. All students may keep cars.

Activities: 66% of women belong to 2 local and 8 national sororities. There are no fraternities. There are 100 groups on campus, including art, band, choir, chorale, chorus, computers, dance, drama, ethnic, gay, honors, international, jazz band, musical theater, newspaper, opera, orchestra, political, professional, radio and TV, religious, social, social service, and student government. Popular campus events include Black Awareness Week, Mexican Festival, and Fall Festival.

Sports: There are 5 intercollegiate sports for women, and 11 intramural sports for men and 11 for women. Facilities include a gym, indoor and outdoor swimming pools, weight-training and fitness rooms, tennis and racquetball courts, a golf course, an indoor track, and aerobic exercise classrooms.

Disabled Students: 95% of the campus is accessible. Wheelchair ramps, elevators, special parking, specially equipped rest rooms, lowered drinking fountains, lowered telephones, and lowered library equipment, and an office to assist students with disabilities are available.

Services: Counseling and information services are available, as is tutoring in some subjects, including math, science, English (writing), and computer science. There is remedial math, reading, and writing.

Campus Safety and Security: Measures include 24-hour foot and vehicle patrol, self-defense education, security escort services, and informal discussions. There are pamphlets/posters/films, emergency telephones, and lighted pathways/sidewalks.

Programs of Study: TWU confers B.A., B.S., B.B.A., B.F.A., and B.S.W. degrees. Master's and doctoral degrees are also awarded. Bachelor's degrees are awarded in BIOLOGICAL SCIENCE (biology/biological science), BUSINESS (accounting, business administration and management, fashion merchandising, and marketing/retailing/merchandising), COMMUNICATIONS AND THE ARTS (art, communications, dance, dramatic arts, English, fine arts, and music), COMPUTER AND PHYSICAL SCIENCE (chemistry, computer science, and mathematics), HEALTH PROFESSIONS (dental hygiene, health science, medical technology, music therapy, and nursing), SOCIAL SCIENCE (child psychology/development, consumer services, criminal justice, dietetics, family/consumer studies, fashion design and technology, history, interdisciplinary studies, physical fitness/movement, political science/government, psychology, social work, and sociology). Nursing, interdisciplinary studies, and psychology are the largest.

Required: Core curriculum includes 6 units each of history, political science, composition, and science, 3 each of math, fine arts, multicultural studies, literature, and women's studies, plus 15 additional hours. General education requirements vary according to the degree. A 2.0 GPA, successful completion of the Texas-mandated examination in reading, writing, and math, and a minimum of 124 hours are needed to graduate.

Special: Co-op programs in most majors, study abroad, and internships are available. Cross-registration is possible with the University of North Texas and East Texas State University. A 3-2 engineering program exists with the University of Texas at Dallas and Texas A&M University. There are 14 national honor societies, a freshman honors program, and 15 departmental honors programs.

Faculty/Classroom: 20% of faculty are male; 80%, female.

Requirements: The SAT or ACT is required. Applicants should be graduates of an accredited secondary school or have a GED certificate and have completed 4 secondary school units in English, 3 each in math and social studies, and 2 in science, plus 3 in academic electives. A GPA of 2.0 is required. AP and CLEP credits are accepted.

Procedure: Freshmen are admitted to all sessions. Entrance exams should be taken during the junior or the senior year of high school. There are early admissions and deferred admissions plans. Check with the school for current application deadlines and fee. Notification is sent on a rolling basis.

Transfer: Transfer students must possess at least a 2.0 GPA and be in good standing at all previously attended institutions. Coursework must be from an accredited college or university. 30 of 124 credits required for the bachelor's degree must be completed at TWU.

Visiting: There are regularly scheduled orientations for prospective students, including admissions and financial aid sessions, and a campus tour. There are guides for informal visits and visitors may sit in on classes and stay overnight. To schedule a visit, contact the Office of Admissions at *admissions@twu.edu*.

Financial Aid: In a recent year, 272% of all full-time freshmen and 54% of continuing full-time students received some form of financial aid. 47% of full-time freshmen and 62% of continuing full-time students received need-based aid. The average freshman award was $6249. Need-based scholarships or need-based grants averaged $3924 ($8020 maximum); need-based self-help aid (loans and jobs) averaged $3090 ($7965 maximum); non-need-based athletic scholarships averaged $2990 ($8570 maximum); other non-need-based awards and non-need-based scholarships averaged $2543 ($3500 maximum); and non-need-based loans averaged $4684 ($11,157 maximum). 73% of undergraduates work part time. Average annual earnings from campus work are

$3090. The average financial indebtedness of the recent year's graduate was $11,076. TWU is a member of CSS. The FAFSA and the college's own financial statement are required. Check with the school for current deadlines.

International Students: In a recent year, there were 143 international students enrolled. The school actively recruits these students. A satisfactory score is required on the written TOEFL.

Computers: All students may access the system. There are no time limits. Check with the school for current fee. It is strongly recommended that all students have a personal computer.

Graduates: In a recent year, 824 bachelor's degrees were awarded. The most popular majors were nursing (36%), interdisciplinary studies (10%), and psychology (5%). In an average class, 18% graduate in 4 years or less, 31% graduate in 5 years or less, and 35% graduate in 6 years or less. 190 companies recruited on campus in a recent year.

Admissions Contact: Ms. Teresa Mauk, Director of Admissions.
E-mail: *admissions@twu.edu* Web: *www.twu.edu*

TRINITY UNIVERSITY   D-4

San Antonio, TX 78212-7200   (210) 999-7207
                                      (800) TRINITY; Fax: (210) 999-8164

Full-time: 1124 men, 1292 women	**Faculty:** IIA, +$
Part-time: 17 men, 20 women	**Ph.D.s:** 97%
Graduate: 91 men, 141 women	**Student/Faculty:** n/av
Year: semesters, summer session	**Tuition:** $22,277
Application Deadline: February 1	**Room & Board:** $7880
Freshman Class: 3864 applied, 2442 accepted, 651 enrolled	
SAT Verbal/Math: 649/648*	**ACT:** 29

HIGHLY COMPETITIVE+

Trinity University, founded in 1869, is a liberal arts and sciences institution affiliated with the Presbyterian Church (U.S.A.). In addition to regional accreditation, Trinity has baccalaureate program accreditation with AACSB, ABET, NASM, and NCATE. The library contains 927,349 volumes, 301,600 microform items, and 26,780 audio/video tapes/CDs/DVDs, and subscribes to 2135 periodicals including electronic. Computerized library services include the card catalog, interlibrary loans, and database searching. Special learning facilities include a radio station and TV station. The 117-acre campus is in a suburban area 3 miles north of downtown San Antonio. Including any residence halls, there are 45 buildings.

Student Life: 69% of undergraduates are from Texas. Others are from 44 states, 30 foreign countries, and Canada. 73% are from public schools. 64% are white; 11% Hispanic. 44% are Presbyterian, Methodist, Baptist, Episcopal, and Lutheran; 28% claim no religious affiliation; 21% Catholic. The average age of freshmen is 19; all undergraduates, 20. 11% do not continue beyond their first year; 74% remain to graduate.

Housing: 1900 students can be accommodated in college housing, which includes coed dorms. On-campus housing is available on a lottery system for upperclassmen. 73% of students live on campus. All students may keep cars.

Activities: 24% of men belong to 9 local fraternities; 29% of women belong to 6 local sororities. There are 100 groups on campus, including art, band, cheerleading, chess, choir, chorale, chorus, computers, dance, debate, drama, drill team, ethnic, film, forensics, gaming, gay, honors, international, jazz band, literary magazine, musical theater, newspaper, opera, orchestra, pep band, photography, political, professional, radio and TV, religious, social, social service, student government, symphony, wind ensemble and yearbook. Popular campus events include Tower Party and Trinity Night at the San Antonio Spurs game.

Sports: There are 9 intercollegiate sports for men and 9 for women, and 20 intramural sports for men and 17 for women. Facilities include an indoor Olympic pool and diving center, a 5000-seat stadium, and a 3000-seat auditorium/arena.

Disabled Students: 99% of the campus is accessible. Wheelchair ramps, elevators, special parking, specially equipped rest rooms, lowered drinking fountains, and lowered telephones are available. Learning disabled services are determined through Counseling and Career Services (one on one).

Services: Counseling and information services are available, as is tutoring in most subjects.

Campus Safety and Security: Measures include 24-hour foot and vehicle patrol, self-defense education, security escort services, and pamphlets/posters/films. There are emergency telephones, lighted pathways/sidewalks, and shuttle carts.

Programs of Study: Trinity confers B.A., B.S., and B.M. degrees. Master's degrees are also awarded. Bachelor's degrees are awarded in BIOLOGICAL SCIENCE (biochemistry and biology/biological science), BUSINESS (business administration and management), COMMUNICATIONS AND THE ARTS (communications, dramatic arts, English, French, German, music, Russian, Spanish, and speech/debate/rhetoric), COMPUTER AND PHYSICAL SCIENCE (chemistry, computer science, geoscience, mathematics, and physics), EDUCATION (art and foreign

languages), ENGINEERING AND ENVIRONMENTAL DESIGN (engineering and applied science), SOCIAL SCIENCE (anthropology, economics, history, international relations, philosophy, political science/government, psychology, religion, sociology, and urban studies). Business, modern languages and literature, and English are the largest.

Required: To graduate, students must satisfy the common curriculum and residency requirements and complete a minimum of 124 credit hours (129 for a B.S. in engineering science and 141 for a B.M. in performance and composition). Students must take at least 60 hours outside the major and 30 hours in upper-division courses. A minimum 2.0 GPA is required.

Special: The university offers study abroad in 35 countries. A Washington semester, accelerated programs, dual majors, student-designed majors, and pass/fail options are also available, as well as teacher certification and a liberal arts/career combination. There are 5 national honor societies, including Phi Beta Kappa, and 14 departmental honors programs.

Faculty/Classroom: 67% of faculty are male; 33%, female. No introductory courses are taught by graduate students.

Admissions: 63% of the 2005-2006 applicants were accepted. The SAT scores for the 2005-2006 freshman class were: Verbal--1% below 500, 21% between 500 and 599, 53% between 600 and 700, and 25% above 700; Math--20% between 500 and 599, 60% between 600 and 700, and 20% above 700. The ACT scores were 1% below 21, 3% between 21 and 23, 19% between 24 and 26, 26% between 27 and 28, and 51% above 28. 72% of the current freshmen were in the top fifth of their class. 212 freshmen graduated first in their class.

Requirements: The SAT or ACT is required. In addition, applicants should have completed 4 years of English, 3 1/2 of math, 3 each of lab science and social studies, and 2 of foreign language. A personal essay, an official high school transcript, a recommendation from a high school counselor, and a teacher's evaluation are also required. A campus visit and a visit with the university's counselor are also recommended. AP credits are accepted.

Procedure: Freshmen are admitted fall, spring, and summer. Entrance exams should be taken late in the junior year or early in the senior year. There are early decision, early admissions, and deferred admissions plans. Early decision applications should be filed by November 1; regular applications, by February 1 for fall entry and November 15 for spring entry. Notification of early decision is sent December 15; regular decision, April 1. 2 early decision candidates were accepted for the 2005-2006 class. 210 applicants were on the 2005 waiting list; 55 were admitted. The fall 2005 application fee was $50. Applications are accepted on-line. The application fee is waived for on-line applications.

Transfer: 23 transfer students were enrolled in a recent year. A 3.0 college GPA, high school and college transcripts, an essay, standardized test scores, and a statement of good standing from the prior institution are required. An interview is recommended. 60 of 124 credits required for the bachelor's degree must be completed at Trinity.

Visiting: There are regularly scheduled orientations for prospective students. There are guides for informal visits and visitors may sit in on classes and stay overnight. To schedule a visit, contact the Admissions Office.

Financial Aid: The FAFSA is required. The deadline for filing freshman financial aid applications for fall entry is February 1.

International Students: There are 60 international students enrolled. The school actively recruits these students. A satisfactory score is required on the written TOEFL.

Computers: All students may access the system 24 hours per day. There are no time limits and no fees. It is strongly recommended that all students have a personal computer.

Graduates: From July 1, 2004 to June 30, 2005, 528 bachelor's degrees were awarded. The most popular majors were business/marketing (21%), social sciences and history (20%), and foreign languages and literature (11%). In an average class, 1% graduate in 3 years, 67% graduate in 4 years, 75% graduate in 5 years, and 74% graduate in 6 years.

Admissions Contact: Chris Ellertson, Dean of Admissions.
E-mail: *admissions@trinity.edu* Web: *trinity.edu*

UNIVERSITY OF DALLAS   D-2

Irving, TX 75062-4736   (972) 721-5266
                                      (800) 628-6999; Fax: (972) 721-5017

Full-time: 454 men, 616 women	**Faculty:** 98; IIA, --$
Part-time: 58 men, 38 women	**Ph.D.s:** 92%
Graduate: 1091 men, 764 women	**Student/Faculty:** 11 to 1
Year: semesters, summer session	**Tuition:** $20,406
Application Deadline: August 1	**Room & Board:** $7026
Freshman Class: 817 applied, 662 accepted, 254 enrolled	
SAT Verbal/Math: 650/600*	**ACT:** 26 **VERY COMPETITIVE+**

The University of Dallas, founded in 1955, is a private liberal arts institution affiliated with the Roman Catholic Church. Undergraduate programs are offered through the Constantin College of Liberal Arts and the Braniff Graduate School has liberal arts and management divisions. In addition to regional accreditation, UD has baccalaureate program accreditation with AALE, ACBSP, and IACBE. The library contains 223,350 volumes, 75,554 microform items, and 1636 audio/video tapes/CDs/DVDs, and subscribes to 583 periodicals including electronic. Computerized library services include the card catalog, interlibrary loans, database searching, and Internet access. Special learning facilities include a learning resource center, art gallery, radio station, an 80-seat theater, and an observatory. The 750-acre campus is in an urban area 12 miles west of Dallas. Including any residence halls, there are 26 buildings.

Student Life: 57% of undergraduates are from Texas. Others are from 46 states, 19 foreign countries, and Canada. 58% are from public schools. 67% are white; 15% Hispanic. 67% are Catholic; 23% claim no religious affiliation; 7% Protestant. The average age of freshmen is 18; all undergraduates, 20. 15% do not continue beyond their first year; 64% remain to graduate.

Housing: 740 students can be accommodated in college housing, which includes single-sex and coed dormitories and on-campus apartments. On-campus housing is guaranteed for the freshman year only and is available on a first-come, first-served basis. 61% of students live on campus; of those, 95% remain on campus on weekends. All students may keep cars.

Activities: There are no fraternities or sororities. There are 42 groups on campus, including art, chamber ensemble, chess, choir, chorus, computers, dance, debate, drama, ethnic, film, honors, international, literary magazine, musical theater, newspaper, opera, photography, political, professional, radio and TV, religious, social, social service, student government, symphony, and yearbook. Popular campus events include Charity Week, Oktoberfest, and Alternative Springbreak to Ecuador.

Sports: There are 6 intercollegiate sports for men and 7 for women, and 6 intramural sports for men and 5 for women. Facilities include an athletic center with a gym, weight room, aerobics equipment and locker facilities, an outdoor pool, and 8 screened laykold tennis courts. A collegiate soccer field, a baseball field, a multipurpose field, and 5 miles of jogging trails are also available.

Disabled Students: 70% of the campus is accessible. Wheelchair ramps, elevators, special parking, specially equipped rest rooms, special class scheduling and lowered drinking fountains are available.

Services: Counseling and information services are available, as is tutoring in every subject. There is a reader service for the blind. There are writing and math labs and an ESL institute.

Campus Safety and Security: Measures include 24-hour foot and vehicle patrol, self-defense education, security escort services, and informal discussions. There are pamphlets/posters/films, emergency telephones, and lighted pathways/sidewalks.

Programs of Study: UD confers B.A. and B.S. degrees. Master's and doctoral degrees are also awarded. Bachelor's degrees are awarded in BIOLOGICAL SCIENCE (biochemistry and biology/biological science), BUSINESS (business administration and management), COMMUNICATIONS AND THE ARTS (art history and appreciation, ceramic art and design, classics, dramatic arts, English, French, German, painting, printmaking, sculpture, and Spanish), COMPUTER AND PHYSICAL SCIENCE (chemistry, mathematics, and physics), EDUCATION (art and elementary), SOCIAL SCIENCE (economics, history, philosophy, political science/government, psychology, and theological studies). Classics, English, and politics are the strongest academically. English, biology, and business leadership are the largest.

Required: To graduate with a B.A., students must complete at least 120 credits, including 38 in advanced credits, which included 12 in the major, with a 2.0 GPA. Completion of core curriculum requirements as well as major requirements is required. To graduate with a B.S degree, students must complete the above requirements for a B.A. plus 12 additional hours in the major. Seniors must pass a comprehensive exam in their major.

Special: UD offers internships in field experience or an off-campus research semester, summer study abroad, on-campus work-study programs, B.A.-B.S. degrees, and double majors. There are 4 national honor societies, including Phi Beta Kappa.

Faculty/Classroom: 77% of faculty are male; 23%, female. All teach undergraduates. No introductory courses are taught by graduate students. The average class size in an introductory lecture is 27; in a laboratory, 19; and in a regular course, 19.

Admissions: 81% of the 2005-2006 applicants were accepted. The SAT scores for the 2005-2006 freshman class were: Verbal--5% below 500, 24% between 500 and 599, 44% between 600 and 700, and 27% above 700; Math--9% below 500, 37% between 500 and 599, 44% between 600 and 700, and 10% above 700. The ACT scores were 9% below 21, 17% between 21 and 23, 24% between 24 and 26, 17% between 27 and 28, and 33% above 28. 49% of the current freshmen were in the top fifth of their class; 73% were in the top two fifths. There were 13 National Merit finalists. 8 freshmen graduated first in their class.

Requirements: The SAT or ACT is required. The ACT Optional Writing test is also required. In addition, the university seeks high school students who have pursued a curriculum of college preparatory courses including English, social science, math, science, and a foreign language.

Applicants pursuing a discipline in the sciences should have 4 years of math. Depth in a foreign language is advised. Although the university is flexible in its admission requests, applicants should be in the upper third of their graduating class and should present satisfactory SAT or ACT scores. AP and CLEP credits are accepted. Important factors in the admissions decision are advanced placement or honor courses, leadership record, and extracurricular activities record.

Procedure: Freshmen are admitted fall and spring. Entrance exams should be taken during the junior year or by the fall of the senior year. There are early admissions, deferred admissions and rolling admissions plans. Early decision applications should be filed by November 1; regular applications, by August 1 for fall entry and December 1 for spring entry. Notification of early decision is sent December 15; regular decision, on a rolling basis. Applications are accepted on-line. The fall 2005 application fee was $40.

Transfer: 44 transfer students enrolled in 2004-2005. Applicants must have a minimum 2.5 GPA from an accredited college or university. An associate degree and an interview are recommended. Official transcripts from all previoous colleges attended, a writing sample, a personal statement, and an academic letter of recommendation are required. Students with fewer than 30 transferable credits must also submit SAT or ACT scores and an official high school transcript. 30 of 120 credits required for the bachelor's degree must be completed at UD.

Visiting: There are regularly scheduled orientations for prospective students, including a campus tour, scholarship competition, visits to residence halls and classes, meetings with students, mass, parents' meetings, and departmental advising. There are guides for informal visits and visitors may sit in on classes and stay overnight. To schedule a visit, contact the Admission Office.

Financial Aid: In 2005-2006, 98% of all full-time freshmen and 95% of continuing full-time students received some form of financial aid. 58% of all full-time students received need-based aid. The average freshman award was $18,000. Need-based scholarships or need-based grants averaged $3460; need-based self-help aid (loans and jobs) averaged $4080; and other non-need-based awards and non-need-based scholarships averaged $8680. 37% of undergraduates work part time. Average annual earnings from campus work are $1200. The average financial indebtedness of the 2005 graduate was $21,700. The FAFSA is required. The deadline for filing freshman financial aid applications for fall entry is March 1.

International Students: There are 14 international students enrolled. The school actively recruits these students. They must score satisfactorily on the written TOEFL or on the electronic version. SAT or ACT scores may be submitted in place of the TOEFL.

Computers: Wireless access is available. There are 4 computer labs with an average of 25 PCs per lab. All students may access the system. There are no time limits and no fees. It is strongly recommended that all students have a personal computer.

Graduates: From July 1, 2004 to June 30, 2005, 244 bachelor's degrees were awarded. The most popular majors were English (14%), politics (12%), and biology (9%). In an average class, 57% graduate in 4 years or less, 63% graduate in 5 years or less, and 65% graduate in 6 years or less. 38 companies recruited on campus in 2004-2005.

Admissions Contact: Sr. Mary Brian Bole, SSND, Assistant Dean of Admission. A video is available. E-mail: *ugadmis@udallas.edu* Web: *www.udallas.edu*

UNIVERSITY OF HOUSTON SYSTEM

The University of Houston System, established in 1977, is a private system in Texas. It is governed by a 9-member board of regents, whose chief administrator is chancellor. The primary goal of the system is overall coordination of teaching, research, and service. The main priorities are long-range planning, governmental and private representation, and overall executive management. The total enrollment is usually about 49,000; with 3200 faculty members. Altogether there are some 180 baccalaureate, 160 master's, and 50 doctoral programs offered in University of Houston System. Profiles of the 4-year campuses are included in this section.

UNIVERSITY OF HOUSTON	E-3
Houston, TX 77204-2018	**(713) 743-1010**
	(800) 741-4449; Fax: (713) 743-9633

Full-time: 9100 men, 10,000 women	**Faculty:** 667; I, av$
Part-time: 3900 men, 4000 women	**Ph.D.s:** 83%
Graduate: 3700 men, 4300 women	**Student/Faculty:** 29 to 1
Year: semesters, summer session	**Tuition:** $4000 ($11,000)
Application Deadline: April 1	**Room & Board:** $6000
Freshman Class: n/av	
SAT or ACT: required	**COMPETITIVE**

The University of Houston, established in 1927, is a public institution with programs in arts and sciences, business, education, engineering, and health professions. There are 13 undergraduate schools and 1 graduate school. Figures in the above capsule and in this profile are approximate. In addition to regional accreditation, UH has baccalaureate program accreditation with AACSB, ABET, ACPE, ADA, CSWE, NAAB, NASM, and NCATE. The 6 libraries contain 2,173,342 volumes, 4,023,252 microform items, and 9359 audio/video tapes/CDs/DVDs, and subscribe to 20,276 periodicals including electronic. Computerized library services include the card catalog, interlibrary loans, database searching, and Internet access. Special learning facilities include a learning resource center, art gallery, radio station, TV station, and observatory. The 551-acre campus is in an urban area 3 miles from the Houston business district. Including any residence halls, there are 105 buildings.

Student Life: 94% of undergraduates are from Texas. Students are from 49 states, 135 foreign countries, and Canada. 40% are white; 19% Asian American; 18% Hispanic; 13% African American. The average age of freshmen is 19; all undergraduates, 23. 21% do not continue beyond their first year; 39% remain to graduate.

Housing: 3756 students can be accommodated in college housing, which includes coed dorms, on-campus apartments, off-campus apartments, married-student housing, fraternity houses, and sorority houses. In addition, there are honors houses, language houses, and special-interest houses. On-campus housing is available on a first-come, first-served basis. 90% of students commute. All students may keep cars.

Activities: 4% of men belong to 18 national fraternities; 3% of women belong to 18 national sororities. There are 300 groups on campus, including art, band, cheerleading, chess, choir, chorale, chorus, computers, dance, debate, drama, drill team, ethnic, film, forensics, gay, honors, international, jazz band, literary magazine, marching band, musical theater, newspaper, opera, orchestra, pep band, photography, political, professional, radio and TV, religious, social, social service, student government, symphony, and yearbook. Popular campus events include Greek Week, Diversity Week, and Frontier Fiesta.

Sports: There are 7 intercollegiate sports for men and 9 for women, and 25 intramural sports for men and 25 for women. Facilities include an athletics/alumni center for intercollegiate sports, a fast-pitch softball stadium, a football stadium, a 264,000 Square Foot recreation and wellness center that houses 5 basketball courts, 6 racquetball and 2 squash courts, a multi-activity court for soccer, roller hockey, tennis and special events, a 70-meter indoor pool with up to 10 meter platform diving, and an outdoor leisure pool with sand volleyball court, a 53-foot indoor climbing wall, a fitness area of over 24,000 square feet, 6 multipurpose group exercise rooms, and locker rooms.

Disabled Students: 98% of the campus is accessible. Wheelchair ramps, elevators, special parking, specially equipped rest rooms, special class scheduling, lowered drinking fountains, lowered telephones automatic doors, vehicle and handicap assists, an on-campus attendant-care program, registration assistance, counseling, and adaptive equipment are available.

Services: Counseling and information services are available, as is tutoring in most subjects, including core requirements. There is a reader service for the blind, and remedial math, reading, and writing. Accommodation assistance for students taking exams, tutors assisting with course work, and other accommodations are available.

Campus Safety and Security: Measures include 24-hour foot and vehicle patrol, security escort services, shuttle buses, and pamphlets/posters/films. There are emergency telephones, lighted pathways/sidewalks, community dialogues, and assistance with disabled vehicles.

Programs of Study: UH confers B.A., B.S., B.Acc., B.A.C.Y., B.Arch., B.B.A., B.F.A., B.I.S.C.I., B.M., B.S.C.E., B.S.C.P.E., B.S.Ch.E., B.S.E.E., B.S.I.E., and B.S.M.E. degrees. Master's and doctoral degrees are also awarded. Bachelor's degrees are awarded in BIOLOGICAL SCIENCE (biochemistry, biology/biological science, biophysics, and nutrition), BUSINESS (accounting, banking and finance, business administration and management, hotel/motel and restaurant management, management information systems, marketing and distribution, marketing/retailing/merchandising, operations research, personnel management, and sports management), COMMUNICATIONS AND THE ARTS (applied music, art, art history and appreciation, classical languages, classics, communications, creative writing, dramatic arts, English, fine arts, French, German, journalism, music, music theory and composition, painting, photography, printmaking, radio/television technology, sculpture, Spanish, speech/debate/rhetoric, and studio art), COMPUTER AND PHYSICAL SCIENCE (chemistry, computer science, earth science, geology, geophysics and seismology, information sciences and systems, mathematics, physics, quantitative methods, and statistics), EDUCATION (trade and industrial), ENGINEERING AND ENVIRONMENTAL DESIGN (architectural engineering, architecture, biomedical equipment technology, chemical engineering, civil engineering, civil engineering technology, computer engineering, computer technology, construction management, construction technology, drafting and design technology, electrical/electronics engineering, electrical/electronics engineering technology, electromechanical technology, environmental design, graphic arts technology, industrial administration/management, industrial engineering, industrial engineering technology, interior design, manufacturing technology, mechanical engineering, and mechanical engineering technology), HEALTH PROFESSIONS (health, optometry, pharmacy,

and prepharmacy), SOCIAL SCIENCE (anthropology, economics, family/consumer studies, German area studies, history, human development, interdisciplinary studies, Italian studies, philosophy, physical fitness/movement, political science/government, psychology, Russian and Slavic studies, social science, and sociology). Chemical engineering is the strongest academically. Business administration, engineering, and biological sciences are the largest.

Required: To graduate, students must complete 122 credits, including at least 36 in advanced-level courses, with a minimum GPA of 2.0. Core curriculum requirements include 6 hours each of English, math/math reasoning, history, American government, natural sciences, visual and performing arts, and social sciences (3 of which are writing intensive) and 3 hours of humanities.

Special: There is cross-registration with the University of Texas and Rice and Texas Wesleyan Universities. UH also offers internships and co-op programs in many majors, study abroad in 12 countries, work-study programs, and programs in Mexican American studies, Asian American studies, and inter-university African studies, as well as the Mickey Leland Internship in Washington, D.C. Also available are B.A.-B.S. degrees and dual majors in all areas of study, nondegree study, and pass/fail options. There are 8 national honor societies, a freshman honors program, and 13 departmental honors programs.

Faculty/Classroom: 61% of faculty are male; 39%, female. 73% teach undergraduates. Graduate students teach 21% of introductory courses. The average class size in an introductory lecture is 10; in a laboratory, 6; and in a regular course, 16.

Admissions: There were 26 National Merit finalists and 2 semifinalists in a recent year. 43 freshmen graduated first in their class.

Requirements: A satisfactory score on the SAT or ACT is required for consideration. Students in the top 10% of the high school class are automatically admitted. Lower ranks require higher scores. Applicants must be graduates of an accredited secondary school or have the GED. Students should complete 4 credits of English, 3 of math and social sciences, and 2 of lab science, with 2 of foreign language strongly recommended. There are special requirements for the College of Engineering, College of Business, College of Architecture, Department of Computer Science, and the School of Music, including an audition for music candidates. A GPA of 2.0 is required. AP and CLEP credits are accepted. Important factors in the admissions decision are evidence of special talent, advanced placement or honor courses, and recommendations by school officials.

Procedure: Freshmen are admitted to all sessions. Entrance exams should be taken no later than February of the senior year. Applications should be filed by April 1 for fall entry and December 1 for spring entry, along with a $50 fee. Notification is sent on a rolling basis. Applications are accepted on-line.

Transfer: 2614 transfer students enrolled in a recent year. Applicants must be eligible to return to their last college. A 2.0 GPA is required for students with 30 or more semester hours of college credit, a 2.5 GPA for those with 15 to 29. 30 of 122 credits required for the bachelor's degree must be completed at UH.

Visiting: There are regularly scheduled orientations for prospective students, including a campus tour, a meal in a residential dining hall, and a visit with an admissions counselor. Open houses are held in November and March. There are guides for informal visits and visitors may stay overnight. To schedule a visit, contact the Admissions Office, Visit Coordinator at (713) 743-9621.

Financial Aid: In a recent year, 62% of all full-time freshmen and 60% of continuing full-time students received some form of financial aid. 52% of full-time freshmen and 58% of continuing full-time students received need-based aid. The average freshman award was $9100. Need-based scholarships or need-based grants averaged $6378 ($8190 maximum); need-based self-help aid (loans and jobs) averaged $2730 ($5025 maximum); non-need-based athletic scholarships averaged $8668 ($15,276 maximum); and other non-need-based awards and non-need-based scholarships averaged $1500 ($22,200 maximum). 7% of undergraduates work part time. Average annual earnings from campus work are $3271. The average financial indebtedness of a recent year's graduate was $13,961. UH is a member of CSS. The FAFSA is required. The deadline for filing freshman financial aid applications for fall entry is April 1.

International Students: There were 963 international students enrolled in a recent year. A satisfactory score on the TOEFL is required.

Computers: All students may access the system. There are no time limits and no fees.

Graduates: In a recent year, 4116 bachelor's degrees were awarded. The most popular majors were business (35%), psychology (10%), and social sciences (6%). In an average class, 1% graduate in 3 years or less, 11% graduate in 4 years or less, 27% graduate in 5 years or less, and 39% graduate in 6 years or less. 284 companies recruited on campus in a recent year. Of a recent graduating class, 18% were enrolled in graduate school within 6 months of graduation and 87% were employed.

Admissions Contact: Admissions Director.
E-mail: *admissions@uh.edu* Web: *http://www.uh.edu*

UNIVERSITY OF HOUSTON-DOWNTOWN — E-3

Houston, TX 77002 — (713) 221-8423; Fax: (713) 221-5220

Full-time: 2397 men, 3507 women	Faculty: 277; IIB, av$
Part-time: 2250 men, 3205 women	Ph.D.s: 80%
Graduate: 42 men, 83 women	Student/Faculty: 21 to 1
Year: semesters, summer session	Tuition: $3326 ($9950)
Application Deadline: July 1	Room & Board: n/app
Freshman Class: 2044 applied, 2036 accepted, 1224 enrolled	
SAT or ACT: recommended	NONCOMPETITIVE

University of Houston-Downtown, founded in 1974, is part of the University of Houston System. The commuter university offers programs through the Colleges of Business, Science and Technology, Public Service, Humanities, and Social Sciences. There are 4 undergraduate and 2 graduate schools. In addition to regional accreditation, UHD has baccalaureate program accreditation with AACSB and ABET. The library contains 261,568 volumes, 20,290 microform items, and 3206 audio/video tapes/CDs/DVDs, and subscribes to 1048 periodicals including electronic. Computerized library services include the card catalog, interlibrary loans, database searching, Internet access, and laptop Internet portals. Special learning facilities include a learning resource center and art gallery. The 14-acre campus is in an urban area in the business district of Houston. There are 3 buildings.

Student Life: 96% of undergraduates are from Texas. Others are from 20 states, 76 foreign countries, and Canada. 38% are Hispanic; 26% African American; 24% white; 10% Asian American. The average age of all undergraduates is 26. 61% do not continue beyond their first year; 17% remain to graduate.

Housing: There are no residence halls. All students commute. Alcohol is not permitted. All students may keep cars.

Activities: 1% of men belong to 1 local and 3 national fraternities; 1% of women belong to 3 national sororities. There are 50 groups on campus, including computers, drama, ethnic, honors, international, jazz band, literary magazine, newspaper, political, professional, social, social service, and student government. Popular campus events include Crossroads Festival, Hispanic Heritage Month Films, and Poetry Recital and Music.

Sports: There are 13 intramural sports for men and 13 for women. Facilities include a three-level, 30,000-square-foot Student Life Center with 2 ball courts equipped for basketball, volleyball, and badminton, a multipurpose studio for aerobics and martial arts, and a fitness center with weight equipment and cardiovascular units.

Disabled Students: 95% of the campus is accessible. Wheelchair ramps, elevators, special parking, specially equipped rest rooms, lowered drinking fountains, lowered telephones, and braille materials are available.

Services: Counseling and information services are available, as is tutoring in some subjects, including science. There is a reader service for the blind, and remedial math, reading, and writing. Special labs for math and reading are available.

Campus Safety and Security: Measures include 24-hour foot and vehicle patrol, security escort services, shuttle buses, and informal discussions. There are pamphlets/posters/films, emergency telephones, and lighted pathways/sidewalks.

Programs of Study: UHD confers B.A., B.S., B.B.A., and B.S.E.T. degrees. Master's degrees are also awarded. Bachelor's degrees are awarded in BIOLOGICAL SCIENCE (microbiology), BUSINESS (accounting, banking and finance, business administration and management, marketing/retailing/merchandising, office supervision and management, and purchasing/inventory management), COMMUNICATIONS AND THE ARTS (English and technical and business writing), COMPUTER AND PHYSICAL SCIENCE (applied mathematics, computer science, information sciences and systems, natural sciences, physics, and quantitative methods), EDUCATION (bilingual/bicultural, elementary, and secondary), ENGINEERING AND ENVIRONMENTAL DESIGN (engineering technology), SOCIAL SCIENCE (criminal justice, humanities, interdisciplinary studies, and social science). General business, accounting, and criminal justice are the largest.

Required: To graduate, students must complete 42 to 43 core curriculum hours and a total of 120 to 136 hours. Courses in writing skills, math, and computers, enhancement courses, and a junior year writing proficiency exam are required. Students must maintain a minimum 2.0 GPA.

Special: The university offers co-op programs with Baylor College of Medicine and the University of Texas Health Science Center, cross-registration with the University of Houston System campuses, internships, and work-study programs. General studies degrees in applied math, natural sciences, arts and humanities, and social sciences, nondegree study in the language institute, and pass/fail options in selected courses are available. There are 3 national honor societies and 2 departmental honors programs.

Faculty/Classroom: 53% of faculty are male; 47%, female. All teach undergraduates.

Admissions: All of the 2005-2006 applicants were accepted.

Requirements: The SAT or ACT is recommended. In addition, applicants must be graduates of an accredited secondary school or have a GED certificate. High school courses must include English, math, science, and social studies. AP and CLEP credits are accepted.

Procedure: Freshmen are admitted fall, spring, and summer. Entrance exams should be taken during orientation. There is a deferred admissions plan and a rolling admissions plan. Applications should be filed by July 1 for fall entry and December 1 for spring entry. The fall 2005 application fee was $25. The college accepts all applicants. Applications are accepted on-line.

Transfer: Transfer students must have completed a minimum of 15 credit hours. 30 of 120 to 137 credits required for the bachelor's degree must be completed at UHD.

Visiting: There are regularly scheduled orientations for prospective students, including an information session, placement testing, advising, and registration. There are guides for informal visits and visitors may sit in on classes. To schedule a visit, contact the Office of Admissions at (713) 221-8522.

Financial Aid: The FAFSA and the college's own financial statement are required.

International Students: There are 323 international students enrolled. The school actively recruits these students. They must score satisfactorily on the written TOEFL.

Computers: All students may access the system 7 days a week.

Graduates: From July 1, 2004 to June 30, 2005, 1619 bachelor's degrees were awarded. The most popular majors were interdisciplinary studies (22%), computer information systems (9%), and accounting (8%).

Admissions Contact: Carmen Holland, Director of Admissions.
E-mail: *uhdadmit@dt.uh.edu* Web: *www.uhd.edu*

UNIVERSITY OF MARY HARDIN-BAYLOR — D-3

Belton, TX 76513 — (254) 295-4487
(800) 727-8642; Fax: (254) 295-5049

Full-time: 841 men, 1426 women	Faculty: 131; IIB, -$
Part-time: 102 men, 219 women	Ph.D.s: 72%
Graduate: 47 men, 90 women	Student/Faculty: 17 to 1
Year: semesters, summer session	Tuition: $13,700
Application Deadline: open	Room & Board: $5728
Freshman Class: 1138 applied, 981 accepted, 502 enrolled	
SAT Verbal/Math: 530/530*	ACT: 22 COMPETITIVE

The University of Mary Hardin-Baylor, founded in 1845, is a private facility affiliated with the Baptist General Convention of Texas. It offers undergraduate degrees in liberal arts, fine arts, music, business, education, nursing, and social work, as well as graduate degrees in business, information systems, education, psychology/counseling, and religion. There are 6 undergraduate and 5 graduate schools. In addition to regional accreditation, UMHB has baccalaureate program accreditation with CAAHEP and CSWE. The library contains 238,835 volumes, 48,106 microform items, and 5808 audio/video tapes/CDs/DVDs, and subscribes to 961 periodicals including electronic. Computerized library services include the card catalog, interlibrary loans, database searching, and Internet access. Special learning facilities include a learning resource center and nature walk. The 170-acre campus is in a small town in central Texas. Including any residence halls, there are 45 buildings.

Student Life: 95% of undergraduates are from Texas. Others are from 23 states, 10 foreign countries, and Canada. 92% are from public schools. 76% are white; 11% African American; 11% Hispanic. 78% are Protestant; 11% Catholic; 10% claim no religious affiliation. The average age of freshmen is 18; all undergraduates, 23. 29% do not continue beyond their first year; 43% remain to graduate.

Housing: 1215 students can be accommodated in college housing, which includes single-sex dorms and on-campus apartments. On-campus housing is guaranteed for all 4 years. 54% of students commute. Alcohol is not permitted. All students may keep cars.

Activities: There are no fraternities or sororities. There are 44 groups on campus, including art, band, cheerleading, chess, choir, chorale, chorus, computers, debate, drama, drill team, ethnic, forensics, honors, international, jazz band, literary magazine, marching band, musical theater, newspaper, opera, orchestra, pep band, photography, political, professional, religious, social service, student government, symphony, and yearbook. Popular campus events include Miss UMHB Pageants, Play Day, and Easter Pageant.

Sports: There are 6 intercollegiate sports for men and 6 for women, and 21 intramural sports for men and 21 for women. Facilities include the campus center, which houses a 2500-seat arena gym, a weight room/fitness center, a training room, dressing rooms, a recreational gym, and a pool. The Sports Plex contains a baseball stadium, a softball stadium, soccer practice and game fields, a tennis center, a field house (football locker room, weight room, training room), and 2.5 football practice fields.

Disabled Students: 85% of the campus is accessible. Wheelchair ramps, elevators, special parking, specially equipped rest rooms, special

class scheduling, lowered drinking fountains, lowered telephones, special housing, and automatic door openers are available.

Services: Counseling and information services are available, as is tutoring in most subjects. There is a reader service for the blind, and remedial math, reading, and writing. Academic counselors and Jaws (software for the blind) are also available.

Campus Safety and Security: Measures include 24-hour foot and vehicle patrol, self-defense education, security escort services, and informal discussions. There are pamphlets/posters/films, emergency telephones, lighted pathways/sidewalks, and a campus police force.

Programs of Study: UMHB confers B.A., B.S., B.A.S., B.B.A., B.C.M., B.F.A., B.M., B.P.S., B.S.N., and B.S.W. degrees. Master's degrees are also awarded. Bachelor's degrees are awarded in BIOLOGICAL SCIENCE (biology/biological science), BUSINESS (accounting, banking and finance, business administration and management, marketing/retailing/merchandising, and sports management), COMMUNICATIONS AND THE ARTS (art, communications, English, journalism, music, music performance, music theory and composition, performing arts, and Spanish), COMPUTER AND PHYSICAL SCIENCE (chemistry, computer science, information sciences and systems, and mathematics), EDUCATION (art, athletic training, business, drama, early childhood, elementary, English, foreign languages, mathematics, middle school, music, physical, reading, science, secondary, social studies, and special), ENGINEERING AND ENVIRONMENTAL DESIGN (computer graphics), HEALTH PROFESSIONS (exercise science, medical technology, and nursing), SOCIAL SCIENCE (biblical studies, Christian studies, criminal justice, economics, history, ministries, parks and recreation management, political science/government, psychology, religion, social work, and sociology). Education, business, and nursing are the strongest academically. Nursing is the largest.

Required: To graduate all students must complete at least 124 credits, including at least 24 in the major field and at least 36 upper-level credits, with a 2.0 GPA. Requirements include 6 credits each in English, social sciences, religion, and electives, 3 to 4 in math, lab science, or foreign language, 3 in speech communication and math, and 2 activity courses in phys ed. There is a chapel attendance requirement for full-time students and a residency requirement of 31 hours.

Special: Combined B.A.-B.S. degrees in most areas, study abroad in 4 countries, internships, a work-study program, dual majors, a professional studies degree, an applied science bachelor's degree, post-baccalaureate certification in education, and a 5-year B.B.A./M.B.A. accounting specialization are offered. There are 12 national honor societies and a freshman honors program.

Faculty/Classroom: 44% of faculty are male; 56%, female. 98% teach undergraduates, and 50% both teach and do research. No introductory courses are taught by graduate students. The average class size in an introductory lecture is 25; in a laboratory, 20; and in a regular course, 17.

Admissions: 86% of the 2005-2006 applicants were accepted. The SAT scores for the 2005-2006 freshman class were: Verbal--28% below 500, 57% between 500 and 599, 14% between 600 and 700, and 1% above 700; Math--26% below 500, 57% between 500 and 599, 16% between 600 and 700, and 1% above 700. The ACT scores were 29% below 21, 30% between 21 and 23, 28% between 24 and 26, 8% between 27 and 28, and 5% above 28. 37% of the current freshmen were in the top fifth of their class; 69% were in the top two fifths. 7 freshmen graduated first in their class.

Requirements: The SAT or ACT is required. There are minimum test scores for students who rank in the top half of their high school graduating class and those who graduate in the lower half of their class. There is no minimum test score for students who rank in the top 10% of their high school graduating class. All students should be graduates of an accredited high school and have 22 units of credit, including 4 in English, 3 in math, and 2 1/2 in social science. AP and CLEP credits are accepted. Important factors in the admissions decision are advanced placement or honor courses, recommendations by school officials, and extracurricular activities record.

Procedure: Freshmen are admitted fall, spring, and summer. Entrance exams should be taken by the fall of the senior year. There is a rolling admissions plan. Application deadlines are open. Application fee is $35. Notification is sent on a rolling basis. Applications are accepted on-line.

Transfer: 366 transfer students enrolled in 2004-2005. Applicants must present at least a 2.0 GPA, be in good standing at their previous institutions, and submit all college transcripts. Those with fewer than 12 transferable credits must also meet freshman requirements. 31 of 124 credits required for the bachelor's degree must be completed at UMHB.

Visiting: There are regularly scheduled orientations for prospective students, consisting of campus tours and visits with counselors to discuss admissions, financial aid, housing, and degree plans. There are guides for informal visits and visitors may sit in on classes and stay overnight. To schedule a visit, contact the Recruiting Office at (254) 295-4514 or admission@umhb.edu.

Financial Aid: In 2005-2006, 94% of all full-time freshmen and 89% of continuing full-time students received some form of financial aid. 65% of full-time freshmen and 69% of continuing full-time students received

need-based aid. The average freshman award was $7264. Need-based scholarships or need-based grants averaged $3102 ($11,946 maximum); need-based self-help aid (loans and jobs) averaged $1706 ($4000 maximum); and other non-need-based awards and non-need-based scholarships averaged $6777 ($21,140 maximum). 15% of undergraduates work part time. Average annual earnings from campus work are $2300. The average financial indebtedness of the 2005 graduate was $13,509. The FAFSA and the college's own financial statement are required. The priority date for freshman financial aid applications for fall entry is March 1. The deadline for filing freshman financial aid applications for fall entry is September 1.

International Students: There are 16 international students enrolled. The school actively recruits these students. They must take the TOEFL, the MELAB, the Comprehensive English Language Test, or the college's own test.

Computers: 16 computer labs on campus are equipped with PCs connected to the campuswide network. Software installed on these PCs includes Microsoft XP, Office 2003, and Internet Explorer. These labs have approximately 275 PCs available to students. All students may access the system any time. There are no time limits and no fees.

Graduates: From July 1, 2004 to June 30, 2005, 489 bachelor's degrees were awarded. The most popular majors were general studies (11%), nursing (10%), and elementary education (8%). In an average class, 1% graduate in 3 years or less, 23% graduate in 4 years or less, 38% graduate in 5 years or less, and 42% graduate in 6 years or less. 233 companies recruited on campus in 2004-2005.

Admissions Contact: Robbin Steen, Director of Admissions.
E-mail: *admissions@umhb.edu* Web: *www.umhb.edu*

UNIVERSITY OF NORTH TEXAS   D-2

Denton, TX 76203   (940) 565-2681
                              (800) UNT-8211; Fax: (940) 565-2408

Full-time: 7410 men, 9540 women	**Faculty:** 810; I, --$
Part-time: 2300 men, 2500 women	**Ph.D.s:** 87%
Graduate: 2400 men, 3800 women	**Student/Faculty:** 21 to 1
Year: semesters, summer session	**Tuition:** $3300 ($9700)
Application Deadline: see profile	**Room & Board:** $4500
Freshman Class: n/av	
SATor ACT: required	**COMPETITIVE**

The University of North Texas, founded in 1890, is a public institution offering programs through its colleges of arts and sciences, education, business administration, community services, library and information sciences, music, merchandising and hospitality management, and school of visual arts. There are 8 undergraduate schools and 1 graduate school.figures in the above capsule and in this profile are approximate. In addition to regional accreditation, UNT has baccalaureate program accreditation with AACSB, ACEJMC, CSAB, CSWE, FIDER, NASM, and NRPA. The 4 libraries contain 1,529,868 volumes, 3,166,145 microform items, and 75,169 audio/video tapes/CDs/DVDs, and subscribe to 20,157 periodicals including electronic. Computerized library services include the card catalog, interlibrary loans, and database searching. Special learning facilities include a learning resource center, art gallery, radio station, an observatory, and a TV and film production unit. The 500-acre campus is in an urban area 35 miles north of Dallas/Fort Worth. Including any residence halls, there are 151 buildings.

Student Life: 93% of undergraduates are from Texas. Students are from 49 states, 113 foreign countries, and Canada. 73% are white. The average age of freshmen is 19; all undergraduates, 23. 31% do not continue beyond their first year; 69% remain to graduate.

Housing: 4400 students can be accommodated in college housing, which includes single-sex and coed dormitories, on-campus apartments, and off-campus apartments. On-campus housing is available on a first-come, first-served basis. All students may keep cars.

Activities: 3% of men belong to 16 national fraternities; 3% of women belong to 11 national sororities. There are 250 groups on campus, including band, cheerleading, chess, choir, chorale, chorus, computers, dance, drama, ethnic, film, gay, honors, international, jazz band, literary magazine, marching band, musical theater, newspaper, opera, orchestra, pep band, photography, political, professional, radio and TV, religious, social, social service, student government, symphony, and yearbook. Popular campus events include Silver Christmas Ball, Howdy Week, and Taste of North Texas.

Sports: There are 6 intercollegiate sports for men and 9 for women, and 37 intramural sports for men and 37 for women. Facilities include a 30,000-seat stadium, an 18-hole golf course, a weight-training building, tennis courts, an indoor swimming pool, 3 gyms, 8 handball and racquetball courts, gymnastics equipment, intramural fields, and a recreational sports complex.

Disabled Students: 85% of the campus is accessible. Wheelchair ramps, elevators, special parking, specially equipped rest rooms, special class scheduling, lowered drinking fountains, lowered telephones, and 9 dorm rooms adapted for disabled students are available.

Services: Counseling and information services are available, as is tutoring in most subjects. There is a reader service for the blind, and remedial math, reading, and writing.

Campus Safety and Security: Measures include 24-hour foot and vehicle patrol, self-defense education, security escort services, and shuttle buses. There are informal discussions, pamphlets/posters/films, emergency telephones, and lighted pathways/sidewalks. In addition, there is a crime prevention program, sexual assault information services, and a full-time crime prevention officer on duty.

Programs of Study: UNT confers B.A., B.S., B.A.A.S., B.B.A., B.F.A., B.M., B.S.B.C., B.S.Bio, B.S.Chem., B.S.Eco., B.S.E.P., B.S.E.T., B.S.Math., B.S.M.T., B.S.Phy., and B.S.W. degrees. Master's and doctoral degrees are also awarded. Bachelor's degrees are awarded in BIOLOGICAL SCIENCE (biochemistry and biology/biological science), BUSINESS (accounting, banking and finance, business administration and management, business economics, entrepreneurial studies, hotel/motel and restaurant management, human resources, insurance, management information systems, management science, marketing/retailing/merchandising, operations research, organizational behavior, personnel management, real estate, recreation and leisure services, and small business management), COMMUNICATIONS AND THE ARTS (applied art, art, art history and appreciation, ceramic art and design, communications, dance, dramatic arts, drawing, English, fiber/textiles/weaving, film arts, French, German, jazz, journalism, metal/jewelry, music, music history and appreciation, music performance, music theory and composition, painting, photography, printmaking, radio/television technology, sculpture, Spanish, and visual and performing arts), COMPUTER AND PHYSICAL SCIENCE (chemistry, computer science, information sciences and systems, mathematics, and physics), EDUCATION (business, early childhood, elementary, health, physical, reading, and vocational), ENGINEERING AND ENVIRONMENTAL DESIGN (commercial art, emergency/disaster science, engineering technology, industrial administration/management, and interior design), HEALTH PROFESSIONS (cytotechnology, medical laboratory technology, rehabilitation therapy, and speech pathology/audiology), SOCIAL SCIENCE (anthropology, child psychology/development, clothing and textiles management/production/services, counseling/psychology, criminal justice, economics, fashion design and technology, geography, history, home furnishings and equipment management/production/services, interdisciplinary studies, liberal arts/general studies, philosophy, physical fitness/movement, political science/government, psychology, social science, social work, and sociology). Accounting, jazz studies, and city management are the strongest academically. Biology, psychology, and interdisciplinary studies (teacher education department) are the largest.

Required: All students must complete at least 124 semester hours, including a minimum of 24 hours in the major, with a 2.0 GPA. The 47 hours of core requirements include 12 hours of English, 6 hours each in science, American history, federal and state constitution, social sciences, and humanities, and 4 hours in phys ed. Proficiency in English composition must be demonstrated.

Special: UNT offers co-op programs in 34 majors, internships, and work-study programs with the university. Students may study abroad in the United Kingdom, France, Japan, Germany, Mexico, and Australia. An accelerated degree program in math and science allows Texas high school students to obtain 2 years of college credit during their last 2 years in high school. Dual degrees, a general studies degree, and pass/fail options are also offered. There are 3 national honor societies, a freshman honors program, and 1 departmental honors program.

Faculty/Classroom: 69% of faculty are male; 31%, female. 95% teach undergraduates. The average class size in a laboratory is 23 and in a regular course, 40.

Requirements: The SAT or ACT is required. In addition, applicants must be graduates of an accredited high school and submit a high school transcript. The required minimum score for entrance exams is determined by high school class rank. AP and CLEP credits are accepted. Important factors in the admissions decision are recommendations by school officials, advanced placement or honor courses, and evidence of special talent.

Procedure: Freshmen are admitted to all sessions. Entrance exams should be taken at least 2 months before admissions deadlines. There are early admissions and deferred admissions plans. Check with the school for current application deadlines and fee.

Transfer: Applicants with fewer than 30 hours from an accredited college must have a 2.5 GPA and meet freshman entrance requirements. Applicants with at least 30 but no more than 44 transferable hours must have a 2.3 GPA; those with more than 44 hours must have a 2.0 GPA. 30 of 124 credits required for the bachelor's degree must be completed at UNT.

Visiting: There are regularly scheduled orientations for prospective students, including UNT Previews held 1 Saturday in the fall and 1 in the spring. The agenda includes a campus tour, presentations by academic and student service offices, and question-and-answer sessions. There are guides for informal visits and visitors may sit in on classes and stay overnight. To schedule a visit, contact the information desk assistant at (940) 565-4104 or (940) 565-2000.

Financial Aid: In a recent year, 49% of all full-time freshmen received some form of financial aid. 39% of full-time freshmen received need-based aid. The average freshman award was $3800. 80% of undergraduates work part time. Average annual earnings from campus work are $2400. The average financial indebtedness of the recent year's graduate was $12,000. The FAFSA is required. Check with the school for current deadlines.

International Students: In a recent year there were 505 international students enrolled. The school actively recruits these students. Satisfactory scores are required on the written TOEFL and the MELAB, ECPE, FCE, CAE, CPE, IELTS, or ELPT.

Computers: All students may access the system. Students may access the system 1 hour if labs are busy. Check with the school for current fee.

Graduates: 315 companies recruited on campus in a recent year.

Admissions Contact: Marcilla Collinsworth, Director, Admissions and School Relations. A video is available.
E-mail: *undergrad@abn.unt.edu* Web: *www.unt.edu*

UNIVERSITY OF SAINT THOMAS

E-3

Houston, TX 77006-4696

(713) 525-3500
(800) 856-8565; Fax: (713) 525-3532

Full-time: 499 men, 866 women	**Faculty:** 112; IIA, av$
Part-time: 224 men, 295 women	**Ph.D.s:** 88%
Graduate: 540 men, 671 women	**Student/Faculty:** 12 to 1
Year: semesters, summer session	**Tuition:** $17,110
Application Deadline: open	**Room & Board:** $6700
Freshman Class: 807 applied, 744 accepted, 295 enrolled	
SAT Verbal/Math: 580/570*	**ACT:** 24 **VERY COMPETITIVE**

The University of St. Thomas is a private institution committed to the liberal arts and to the religious, ethical, and intellectual tradition of Catholic higher education. There are 3 undergraduate and 4 graduate schools. In addition to regional accreditation, UST has baccalaureate program accreditation with ACBSP. The 2 libraries contain 254,142 volumes, 578,469 microform items, and 1710 audio/video tapes/CDs/DVDs, and subscribe to 600 periodicals including electronic. Computerized library services include the card catalog, interlibrary loans, database searching, and Internet access. Special learning facilities include a learning resource center and archeology gallery. The 25-acre campus is in an urban area close to downtown Houston. Including any residence halls, there are 60 buildings.

Student Life: 96% of undergraduates are from Texas. Others are from 30 states and 32 foreign countries. 45% are white; 32% Hispanic; 13% Asian American. 66% are Catholic; 23% Protestant. The average age of freshmen is 18; all undergraduates, 25. 29% do not continue beyond their first year; 53% remain to graduate.

Housing: 500 students can be accommodated in college housing, which includes coed dorms and on-campus apartments. In addition, there is a living-learning center. On-campus housing is available on a first-come, first-served basis. Priority is given to out-of-town students. 85% of students commute. All students may keep cars.

Activities: There are no fraternities or sororities. There are 80 groups on campus, including choir, debate, drama, ethnic, forensics, honors, international, jazz band, literary magazine, musical theater, newspaper, political, professional, religious, social, social service, and student government. Popular campus events include spring formal and campus welcome-back-week activities.

Sports: There are 23 intramural sports for men and 23 for women. Facilities include an 800-seat gym, racquetball and tennis courts, a weight-training room, a cardiovascular room, a dance room, a bag/mat room, a swimming pool, and a multipurpose area.

Disabled Students: 44% of the campus is accessible. Wheelchair ramps, elevators, special parking, specially equipped rest rooms, special class scheduling, lowered drinking fountains, lowered telephones, and are available.

Services: Counseling and information services are available, as is tutoring in every subject. There is remedial math, reading, and writing. There are remedial classes, but if a student has special needs, the learning center will provide remedial tutoring.

Campus Safety and Security: Measures include 24-hour foot and vehicle patrol, security escort services, informal discussions, and pamphlets/posters/films. There are emergency telephones and lighted pathways/sidewalks.

Programs of Study: UST confers B.A., B.S., B.B.A., and B.Th. degrees. Master's and doctoral degrees are also awarded. Bachelor's degrees are awarded in BIOLOGICAL SCIENCE (biology/biological science), BUSINESS (accounting, banking and finance, business administration and management, management information systems, and marketing/retailing/merchandising), COMMUNICATIONS AND THE ARTS (communications, dramatic arts, English, fine arts, French, music, Spanish, and studio art), COMPUTER AND PHYSICAL SCIENCE (chemistry and mathematics), EDUCATION (education and music), ENGINEERING AND ENVIRONMENTAL DESIGN (environmental science), SOCIAL SCIENCE (economics, history, international studies, liberal arts/general studies, pastoral studies, philosophy, political science/government, psychology, and theological studies). Business administration, international studies, and biology are the largest.

Required: To graduate, students must complete the core curriculum in theology, philosophy, English, history, foreign language, natural and social science, math, fine arts, and oral communication and 30 to 48 hours in their selected majors. In some cases, students need to complete special projects according to the requirements of specific majors. Students must have a minimum 2.0 GPA in a total of 126 credit hours, including 36 hours of upper-division credits.

Special: UST offers cross-registration with the University of Houston and a 3-2 engineering program with the University of Houston, Texas A&M University, and University of Notre Dame. Internships in the major field of study and study abroad in 6 countries are also available. Dual and joint majors and 5 year joint bachelor's and master's degree programs, combining BBA/MBA or BBA/MIB, are available. There are 18 national honor societies and a freshman honors program.

Faculty/Classroom: 56% of faculty are male; 43%, female. All teach undergraduates. No introductory courses are taught by graduate students. The average class size in an introductory lecture is 24; in a laboratory, 17; and in a regular course, 20.

Admissions: 92% of the 2005-2006 applicants were accepted. The SAT scores for the 2005-2006 freshman class were: Verbal--14% below 500, 44% between 500 and 599, 35% between 600 and 700, and 8% above 700; Math--16% below 500, 42% between 500 and 599, 37% between 600 and 700, and 6% above 700. The ACT scores were 16% below 21, 28% between 21 and 23, 26% between 24 and 26, 12% between 27 and 28, and 19% above 28. 49% of the current freshmen were in the top fifth of their class; 71% were in the top two fifths. 4 freshmen graduated first in their class.

Requirements: A satisfactory score on the SAT or ACT is required. Applicants must have a GED certificate or be graduates of an accredited secondary school and have 18 academic credits, including: 4 years of English, 3 years of math, 3 years of science (2 of which must be lab sciences), 2 years of foreign language, 2 years of social studies, and 1 year of history. UST requires applicants to be in the upper 50% of their class. A GPA of 2.25 is required. AP and CLEP credits are accepted.

Procedure: Freshmen are admitted to all sessions. Entrance exams should be taken as early as possible. There are deferred admissions, and rolling admissions plans. Application deadlines are open. Notification is sent on a rolling basis. Applications are accepted on-line.

Transfer: 172 transfer students enrolled in 2004-2005. Transfer students must have a minimum 2.25 GPA, a high school diploma or GED, and be eligible to return to the last college of attendance. 36 of 126 credits required for the bachelor's degree must be completed at UST.

Visiting: There are regularly scheduled orientations for prospective students, including tours, class visitations, introductions to faculty, administrative members, and currently enrolled students, and financial aid sessions. There are guides for informal visits and visitors may sit in on classes and stay overnight. To schedule a visit, contact an admissions counselor at admissions@stthom.edu.

Financial Aid: In 2005-2006, 82% of all full-time freshmen and 77% of continuing full-time students received some form of financial aid. 59% of full-time freshmen and 56% of continuing full-time students received need-based aid. The average freshman award was $12,408. The average financial indebtedness of the 2005 graduate was $21,626. The FAFSA is required. The priority date for freshman financial aid applications for fall entry is March 1.

International Students: There are 42 international students enrolled. The school actively recruits these students. A satisfactory score is required on the written TOEFL.

Computers: Wireless access is available. The whole campus has wireless access. All students may access the system 9 A.M. to 10 P.M., 7 days a week; dial-up, 24 hours a day. There are no time limits and no fees.

Graduates: From July 1, 2004 to June 30, 2005, 350 bachelor's degrees were awarded. The most popular majors were business administration (49%), education (18%), and liberal arts (10%). In an average class, 2% graduate in 3 years or less, 24% graduate in 4 years or less, 43% graduate in 5 years or less, and 53% graduate in 6 years or less. 30 companies recruited on campus in 2004-2005.

Admissions Contact: Eduardo Prieto, Dean of Admissions. A video is available. E-mail: admissions@stthom.edu
Web: http://www.stthom.edu/admissions/index.html

UNIVERSITY OF TEXAS SYSTEM

The University of Texas System, established in 1950, is a public system in Texas. It is governed by a board of regents, whose chief administrator is the chancellor. The primary goal of the system is to provide instruction, research, and public service throughout the state. The main priorities are undergraduate education, social and economic development of Texas, and professional training in and effective management of healthcare. The total enrollment is usually about 145,000, with 9500 faculty members. Altogether there are some 390 baccalaureate, 300 master's, and 150 doctoral programs offered in University of Texas System. 4-year campuses are located in Arlington,, Austin,, El Paso, and, and San Antonio. Profiles of the 4-year campuses are included in this section.

UNIVERSITY OF TEXAS AT ARLINGTON   D-2

Arlington, TX 76019-   (817) 272-6287; Fax: (817) 272-3435

Full-time: 5250 men, 6000 women	Faculty: I, --$
Part-time: 2400 men, 2800women	Ph.D.s: 83%
Graduate: 2430men, 2425 women	Student/Faculty: n/av
Year: semesters, summer session	Tuition: $3070 ($8135)
Application Deadline: see profile	Room & Board: $4125
Freshman Class: n/av	
SAT or ACT: required	LESS COMPETITIVE

The University of Texas at Arlington, founded in 1895, is part of the University of Texas System and is organized into colleges and schools, including business administration, engineering, liberal arts, science, architecture, nursing, social work, graduate studies, urban and public affairs, and education. There are 9 undergraduate and 10 graduate schools. Figures in the above capsule and in this profile are approximate. In addition to regional accreditation, UTA has baccalaureate program accreditation with AACSB, ABET, ACS, ASLA, CSWE, FIDER, NAAB, NASM, NASPAA, and NLN. The 3 libraries contain 1,105,189 volumes, 1,518,208 microform items, and 3468 audio/video tapes/CDs/DVDs, and subscribe to 5073 periodicals including electronic. Computerized library services include the card catalog, interlibrary loans, and database searching. Special learning facilities include a learning resource center, art gallery, planetarium, cartographic history library, and nano lab. The 395-acre campus is in an urban area in the center of the Dallas/Fort Worth metroplex. Including any residence halls, there are 100 buildings.

Student Life: 92% of undergraduates are from Texas. Others are from 45 states, 88 foreign countries, and Canada. 56% are white; 12% African American; 11% foreign nationals; 10% Asian American; 10% Hispanic. The average age of freshmen is 18; all undergraduates, 24. 31% do not continue beyond their first year; 31% remain to graduate.

Housing: 3303 students can be accommodated in college housing, which includes single-sex and coed dormitories, on-campus apartments, off-campus apartments, married-student housing, fraternity houses, and sorority houses. In addition, there are honors houses. On-campus housing is available on a first-come, first-served basis. 86% of students commute. Alcohol is not permitted. All students may keep cars.

Activities: 6% of men belong to 12 national fraternities; 4% of women belong to 10 national sororities. There are 225 groups on campus, including art, band, cheerleading, chess, choir, chorale, chorus, computers, dance, drama, drill team, drum and bugle corps, ethnic, forensics, gay, honors, international, jazz band, marching band, opera, orchestra, photography, political, professional, religious, social, social service, student government, symphony, and yearbook. Popular campus events include Charity Week, The Big Event, and Last Day Blast.

Sports: There are 6 intercollegiate sports for men and 6 for women, and 10 intramural sports for men and 10 for women. Facilities include 12 racquetball, 4 basketball, and volleyball courts, 12 lighted tennis courts, an inside track, an Olympic-size pool, 3 weight rooms, a 12,000-seat stadium, and a 3000-seat gym.

Disabled Students: All of the campus is accessible. Wheelchair ramps, elevators, special parking, specially equipped rest rooms, special class scheduling, lowered drinking fountains, lowered telephones, and personal, academic, and career counseling, wheelchair repair, note copying, adaptive testing, adaptive exercise and sport activities, and wheelchair athletics are available.

Services: Counseling and information services are available, as is tutoring in most subjects, including English, math, computer science, and foreign languages. There is a reader service for the blind, and remedial math, reading, and writing. a math tutorial clinic, a nursing learning resource center, a reading lab, a science learning center, and a writing lab.

Campus Safety and Security: Measures include 24-hour foot and vehicle patrol, self-defense education, security escort services, and shuttle buses. There are informal discussions, pamphlets/posters/films, emergency telephones, lighted pathways/sidewalks, crime prevention programs, and an emergency on-campus phone number.

Programs of Study: UTA confers B.A., B.S., B.A.I.S., B.B.A., B.F.A., B.M., B.S.A.S.E., B.S.C.E., B.S.C.S., B.S.C.S.E., B.S.E.E., B.S.I.E., B.S.I.S., B.S.M.E., B.S.N., and B.S.W. degrees. Master's and doctoral degrees are also awarded. Bachelor's degrees are awarded in BIOLOGICAL SCIENCE (biochemistry, biology/biological science, and microbiology), BUSINESS (accounting, banking and finance, business administration and management, business economics, management science, marketing/retailing/merchandising, and real estate), COMMUNICATIONS AND THE ARTS (art history and appreciation, broadcasting, communications, dramatic arts, English, French, German, journalism, music, Russian, Spanish, speech/debate/rhetoric, and studio art), COMPUTER AND PHYSICAL SCIENCE (chemistry, computer science, geology, information sciences and systems, mathematics, and physics), EDUCATION (physical), ENGINEERING AND ENVIRONMENTAL DESIGN (architecture, civil engineering, computer engineering, electrical/electronics engineering, industrial engineering technology, interior design, landscape architecture/design, and mechanical engineering), HEALTH PROFESSIONS (medical technology and nursing), SOCIAL SCIENCE (anthropology, classical/ancient civilization, criminal justice, economics, history, interdisciplinary studies, philosophy, political science/government, psychology, social work, and sociology). Liberal arts, business, and engineering are the largest.

Required: All students must earn a GPA of 2.0 while taking at least 124 semester hours, including 30 in their major. The core curriculum requires 8 hours of science, 6 each of English composition, math, U.S. history, and U.S. political science, and 3 each of literature, liberal arts, social/cultural studies, and fine arts/philosophy. Students must demonstrate proficiency in oral presentations and computer use. Proficiency exams, or completion of a department-designated course, may be required by the major department. Theses are required of members of the Honors College.

Special: Cooperative education programs provide opportunities to gain experience in local business through the colleges of engineering and business. Cross-registration with the Summer Institute of Linguistics and the University of Texas Health Science Center, as well as with other members of the University of Texas System, is available. Study abroad in 10 countries, work-study at the university, B.A.-B.S. degrees, dual majors, student-designed interdisciplinary majors, credit for military experience, and pass/fail options are also offered. There are 2 national honor societies, a freshman honors program, and 10 departmental honors programs.

Faculty/Classroom: 60% of faculty are male; 40%, female. Graduate students teach 17% of introductory courses. The average class size in an introductory lecture is 47 and in a laboratory, 25.

Requirements: The SAT or ACT is required. In addition, students ranked in the top 10% of their high school class are admitted regardless of SAT/ACT. Those in the second, third, or fourth quarters of their class must submit a minimum score on the SAT or the ACT. The GED is accepted under certain circumstances. Applicants must have 20 academic credits, including 4 units of English, 3 each of math, social studies, and science, and 2 units of foreign language. AP and CLEP credits are accepted. Important factors in the admissions decision are advanced placement or honor courses, leadership record, and evidence of special talent.

Procedure: Freshmen are admitted to all sessions. Entrance exams should be taken during the fall of the senior year. There are early admissions and deferred admissions plans. Check with the school for current deadlines and fee. Notification is sent on a rolling basis. Applications are accepted on-line.

Transfer: 2897 transfer students enrolled in a recent year. Transfer students with 30 or more transferable semester hours need a 2.0 GPA or evidence of high school or GED completion and SAT or ACT scores comparable to the high school associated rank (varies by student) .Transfer students with fewer than 30 transferable semester hours must have a 2.0 GPA and also meet admission requirements for entering freshmen. 25 credits required for the bachelor's degree must be completed at UTA.

Visiting: There are regularly scheduled orientations for prospective students, including overnight summer orientations for freshmen and 1-day orientations for transfers and returning adult students. There are guides for informal visits and visitors may sit in on classes. To schedule a visit, contact the Admissions Office.

Financial Aid: Check with the school for current deadlines.

International Students: A satisfactory score is required on the written TOEFL and the SAT.

Computers: All students may access the system at all times. There are no time limits and no fees.

Admissions Contact: George Norton, Interim Director of Admissions. A video is available. E-mail: *admissions@uta.edu* Web: *www.uta.edu*

UNIVERSITY OF TEXAS AT AUSTIN D-3

Austin, TX 78712	(512) 475-7440; Fax: (512) 475-7473
Full-time: 15,973 men, 17,709 women	**Faculty:** 2482; I, av$
Part-time: 1721 men, 1475 women	**Ph.D.s:** 88%
Graduate: 6691 men, 6127 women	**Student/Faculty:** 14 to 1
Year: semesters, summer session	**Tuition:** $6972 ($16,310)
Application Deadline: February 1	**Room & Board:** $7638
Freshman Class: 23,925 applied, 12,207 accepted, 6836 enrolled
SAT Verbal/Math: 608/634*	**ACT: 26 HIGHLY COMPETITIVE**

University of Texas at Austin, founded in 1883, is a major research institution within the University of Texas System and provides a broad range of degree programs. There are 12 undergraduate and 15 graduate schools. In addition to regional accreditation, UT has baccalaureate program accreditation with AACSB, ABET, ACEJMC, ACPE, ADA, CSWE, FIDER, NAAB, NASAD, and NASM. The 17 libraries contain 8,229,689 volumes, 6,083,600 microform items, and 991,469 audio/video tapes/CDs/DVDs, and subscribe to 50,014 periodicals including electronic. Computerized library services include the card catalog, interlibrary loans, database searching, Internet access, and laptop Internet portals. Special learning facilities include a learning resource center, art gallery, natural history museum, radio station, TV station, observatory, marine science institute, fusion reactor, and Lyndon Baines Johnson Library and Museum. The 350-acre campus is in an urban area near downtown Austin, just off the interstate. Including any residence halls, there are 120 buildings.

Student Life: 92% of undergraduates are from Texas. Others are from 49 states, 125 foreign countries, and Canada. 57% are white; 14% Asian American; 14% Hispanic. The average age of freshmen is 18; all undergraduates, 21. 7% do not continue beyond their first year; 93% remain to graduate.

Housing: 6815 students can be accommodated in college housing, which includes single-sex and coed dormitories, off-campus apartments, and married-student housing. In addition, there are honors houses and living learning centers (for freshman). On-campus housing is available on a first-come, first-served basis. 81% of students commute. All students may keep cars.

Activities: 9% of men belong to 27 national fraternities; 13% of women belong to 23 national sororities. There are more than 1000 groups on campus, including art, band, cheerleading, chess, choir, chorale, chorus, computers, dance, drama, ethnic, film, forensics, gay, honors, international, jazz band, literary magazine, marching band, musical theater, newspaper, opera, orchestra, pep band, photography, political, professional, radio and TV, religious, social, social service, student government, symphony, and yearbook. Popular campus events include Gone to Texas (welcome for new students), Cinco de Mayo, and Texas Revue (talent show).

Sports: There are 8 intercollegiate sports for men and 10 for women, and 45 intramural sports for men and 45 for women. Facilities include an 80,106-seat football stadium, a 16,175-seat basketball center, a 4400-seat volleyball arena, a 6649-seat baseball stadium, a 2600-seat Olympic swimming facility, 6 multipurpose indoor recreational/athletic facilities of various sizes available for basketball, volleyball, racquetball, swimming, weight training, and related activities, and 3 outdoor facilities covering nearly 40 acres available for swimming, tennis, basketball, racquetball, and various field sports. There is also a 1252-seat softball stadium and a 20,000-seat track and soccer stadium.

Disabled Students: 98% of the campus is accessible. Wheelchair ramps, elevators, special parking, specially equipped rest rooms, lowered drinking fountains, lowered telephones, specially equipped reading rooms, a speech and hearing center, academic accommodations specific to the student's disability, and interpreters for the hearing impaired are available.

Services: Counseling and information services are available, as is tutoring in most subjects. There is a reader service for the blind, and remedial math, reading, and writing.

Campus Safety and Security: Measures include 24-hour foot and vehicle patrol, self-defense education, security escort services, and shuttle buses. There are informal discussions, pamphlets/posters/films, emergency telephones and lighted pathways/sidewalks. There is also a crime prevention unit and closed-circuit TV covering some parking areas and offices.

Programs of Study: UT confers B.A., B.S., B.Arch., B.B.A., B.F.A., B.M., B.J., and B.S.W. degrees. Master's and doctoral degrees are also awarded. Bachelor's degrees are awarded in BIOLOGICAL SCIENCE (biochemistry, biology/biological science, microbiology, molecular biology, and nutrition), BUSINESS (accounting, banking and finance, business administration and management, management information systems, management science, and marketing management), COMMUNICATIONS AND THE ARTS (advertising, applied music, Arabic, art history and appreciation, classics, dance, design, dramatic arts, English, film arts, French, German, Greek, Hebrew, Italian, journalism, Latin, linguistics, music, music theory and composition, Portuguese, public relations, Russian, Scandinavian languages, Slavic languages, Spanish, speech/debate/rhetoric, studio art, and visual and performing arts), COMPUTER AND PHYSICAL SCIENCE (astronomy, chemistry, computer science, geology, geophysics and seismology, mathematics, and physics), ENGINEERING AND ENVIRONMENTAL DESIGN (aerospace studies, architectural engineering, architecture, biomedical engineering, chemical engineering, civil engineering, electrical/electronics engineering, geophysical engineering, interior design, landscape architecture/design, mechanical engineering, and petroleum/natural gas engineering), HEALTH PROFESSIONS (medical technology, nursing, pharmacy, and speech pathology/audiology), SOCIAL SCIENCE (American studies, anthropology, archeology, Asian/Oriental studies, child care/child and family studies, classical/ancient civilization, dietetics, Eastern European studies, economics, ethnic studies, geography, history, human ecology, humanities, Islamic studies, Judaic studies, Latin American studies, liberal arts/general studies, Middle Eastern studies, philosophy, physical fitness/movement, political science/government, psychology, religion, Russian and Slavic studies, social work, sociology, textiles and clothing, and urban studies). Biological sciences, electrical and computer engineering, and government are the largest.

Required: All students must maintain a GPA of 2.0 while satisfactorily completing 120 to 167 semester hours. Distribution requirements include 6 hours each in American government, American history, natural science, and courses containing a substantial writing component (with at least 3 hours being upper-division); 3 hours each in math, social science, English composition, literature, and humanities/fine arts; plus 3 additional hours in either math, natural science, computer science, or social science; and a fourth semester proficiency in a single foreign language.

Special: Cooperative programs are available in most engineering courses, microbiology, chemistry, computer science, geology, and actuarial studies. Cross-registration is provided in pharmacy with the University of Texas at San Antonio. Internships, study abroad, B.A.-B.S. degrees, dual majors, student-designed majors for humanities students, and pass/fail options are offered. There are 45 national honor societies, including Phi Beta Kappa, a freshman honors program, and 50 departmental honors programs.

Faculty/Classroom: 64% of faculty are male; 36%, female. All both teach and do research.

Admissions: 51% of the 2005-2006 applicants were accepted. The SAT scores for the 2005-2006 freshman class were: Verbal--12% below 500, 31% between 500 and 599, 40% between 600 and 700, and 18% above 700; Math--7% below 500, 25% between 500 and 599, 43% between 600 and 700, and 26% above 700. The ACT scores were 10% below 21, 16% between 21 and 23, 26% between 24 and 26, 18% between 27 and 28, and 30% above 28. 88% of the current freshmen were in the top fifth of their class; 98% were in the top two fifths. There were 245 National Merit finalists.

Requirements: The SAT or ACT is required. The ACT Optional Writing test is also required. In addition, all students graduating in the top 10% of their class from an accredited Texas high school are eligible for admission. Applicants not meeting that requirement are reviewed based on SAT or ACT scores, class rank, writing samples, and related factors; consideration may be given to socioeconomic and geographic information. In addition, applicants need 15 1/2 academic credits, including 4 in English, 3 each in math and social studies, 2 each in science and foreign language, and 1 1/2 in electives. An audition is required for applied music majors. The GED is accepted, with supportive information. Home-schooled students are required to submit the results of either the SAT: Subject tests or AP exams in English, math, and a third subject of the student's choosing. AP and CLEP credits are accepted. Important factors in the admissions decision are leadership record, evidence of special talent, and extracurricular activities record.

Procedure: Freshmen are admitted fall, spring, and summer. Entrance exams should be taken in the junior year or early in the senior year. There are deferred admissions plans and rolling admissions. Applications should be filed by February 1 for fall entry, October 1 for spring entry, and February 1 for summer entry, along with a $60 fee. Notification is sent on a rolling basis. Applications are accepted on-line.

Transfer: 1981 transfer students enrolled in 2004-2005. Applicants must have at least 24 transferable hours (30 for business). 60 of 120 credits required for the bachelor's degree must be completed at UT.

Visiting: There are regularly scheduled orientations for prospective students. There are guides for informal visits and visitors may sit in on classes. To schedule a visit, contact the Office of Admissions, Freshman Admissions Center.

Financial Aid: In 2005-2006, 74% of all full-time freshmen and 77% of continuing full-time students received some form of financial aid. 57% of full-time freshmen and 44% of continuing full-time students received need-based aid. The average freshman award was $9100. Need-based scholarships or need-based grants averaged $6750; need-based self-help aid (loans and jobs) averaged $3650; and other non-need-based awards and non-need-based scholarships averaged $3500. The average financial indebtedness of the 2005 graduate was $16,850. UT is a member of CSS. The FAFSA is required. The priority date for freshman financial aid applications for fall entry is March 31.

International Students: There are 1189 international students enrolled. They must score satisfactorily on the written TOEFL or on the electronic version and also take the SAT or the ACT.

Computers: Wireless access is available. Complete Internet access is available in every dorm room, all libraries, and a multitude of departmental computer labs and classrooms. Several public wireless sites exist. All students may access the system 24 hours a day. There are no time limits and no fees. It is recommended that students in College of Education teacher preparation program have personal computers.

Graduates: From July 1, 2004 to June 30, 2005, 8836 bachelor's degrees were awarded. The most popular majors were social sciences (16%), business (13%), and communication (13%). In an average class, 4% graduate in 3 years or less, 47% graduate in 4 years or less, 71% graduate in 5 years or less, and 75% graduate in 6 years or less.

Admissions Contact: Freshman Admissions Center.
E-mail: *http://www.utexas.edu/student/admissions/about/email.htm*
Web: *http://bealonghorn.utexas.edu/freshmen*

UNIVERSITY OF TEXAS AT DALLAS — D-2

Richardson, TX 75083-0688 (972) 883-2346
(800) 889-2443; Fax: (972) 883-6803

Full-time: 3617 men, 2951 women	**Faculty:** 393; I, +$
Part-time: 1392 men, 1383 women	**Ph.D.s:** 93%
Graduate: 2772 men, 2282 women	**Student/Faculty:** 17 to 1
Year: semesters, summer session	**Tuition:** $6832 ($15,112)
Application Deadline: August 1	**Room & Board:** $6412
Freshman Class: 5584 applied, 2850 accepted, 1057 enrolled	
SAT Verbal/Math: 610/640*	**ACT:** 26 **HIGHLY COMPETITIVE**

The University of Texas at Dallas, founded in 1969 as part of the University of Texas system, offers undergraduate and graduate programs in the liberal arts and sciences, business, engineering, computer science, cognitive science, and neuroscience. There are 8 undergraduate and 8 graduate schools. In addition to regional accreditation, UTD has baccalaureate program accreditation with AACSB and ABET. The library contains 1,138,316 volumes, 1,878,345 microform items, and 5771 audio/video tapes/CDs/DVDs, and subscribes to 31,921 periodicals including electronic. Computerized library services include the card catalog, interlibrary loans, and database searching. Special learning facilities include a learning resource center, art gallery, radio station, a center for communications disorders, a rare books library, and special library collections on aviation history, geophysics, philatelic research, and botanicals. The 455-acre campus is in a suburban area 18 miles north of downtown Dallas. Including any residence halls, there are 119 buildings.

Student Life: 94% of undergraduates are from Texas. Others are from 48 states, 130 foreign countries, and Canada. 90% are from public schools. 53% are white; 18% Asian American; 13% foreign nationals. The average age of freshmen is 19; all undergraduates, 24. 18% do not continue beyond their first year; 56% remain to graduate.

Housing: 3950 students can be accommodated in college housing, which includes coed on-campus apartments, married-student housing, and privately-owned campus apartments. On-campus housing is available on a first-come, first-served basis. 60% of students commute. All students may keep cars.

Activities: 6% of men belong to 3 national fraternities; 3% of women belong to 4 national sororities. There are 120 groups on campus, including art, band, cheerleading, chess, choir, chorale, chorus, college bowl, computers, creative problem solving, dance, debate, drama, ethnic, film, forensics, gay, honors, international, jazz band, literary magazine, musical theater, opera, orchestra, political, professional, religious, social, social service, student government, and yearbook. Popular campus events include Messiah Sing, Jazz Concert, and Hispanic Month activities.

Sports: There are 6 intercollegiate sports for men and 7 for women, and 14 intramural sports for men and 14 for women. Facilities include 4 racquetball courts, 3 squash courts, saunas, 10 lighted tennis courts, indoor and outdoor basketball courts, a sand volleyball court, a 1-mile gravel track, 4 soccer fields, 4 softball fields, a junior Olympic pool/natatorium, and a 4000-seat gym.

Disabled Students: All of the campus is accessible. Wheelchair ramps, elevators, special parking, specially equipped rest rooms, lowered drinking fountains, lowered telephones, interpreters for the deaf, scribes, alternative testing, and a disability services coordinator are available.

Services: Counseling and information services are available, as is tutoring in most subjects. There is a reader service for the blind, and remedial math, reading, and writing.

Campus Safety and Security: Measures include 24-hour foot and vehicle patrol, self-defense education, security escort services, and informal discussions. There are pamphlets/posters/films, emergency telephones, and lighted pathways/sidewalks. There are campus crime watch bulletins for residents, bicycle patrols, crime prevention programs, Operation ID engraving, and a police liaison who works with students on any security or safety issue.

Programs of Study: UTD confers B.A., B.S., and B.S.E.E. degrees. Master's and doctoral degrees are also awarded. Bachelor's degrees are awarded in BIOLOGICAL SCIENCE (biochemistry, biology/biological science, molecular biology, and neurosciences), BUSINESS (accounting and business administration and management), COMMUNICATIONS AND THE ARTS (fine arts, literature, telecommunications, and visual and performing arts), COMPUTER AND PHYSICAL SCIENCE (applied mathematics, chemistry, computer science, geoscience, mathematics, physics, software engineering, and statistics), EDUCATION (education), ENGINEERING AND ENVIRONMENTAL DESIGN (airline piloting and navigation, aviation maintenance management, computer technology, and electrical/electronics engineering), HEALTH PROFESSIONS (speech pathology/audiology), SOCIAL SCIENCE (American studies, biopsychology, cognitive science, criminology, economics, gender studies, geography, history, humanities, interdisciplinary studies, political science/government, psychology, public administration, and sociology). Electrical engineering, biology, and biochemistry are the strongest academically. Business administration, computer science, and electrical engineering are the largest.

Required: To graduate, students must complete at least 120 credit hours, including 30 in the major and 51 in upper-division courses, with a minimum GPA of 2.0. Core courses include 15 credits in social science (with 6 each in U.S./Texas government and U.S./Texas history), 9 in natural science, and 6 each in communications, math, and humanities/fine arts. Magna and summa cum laude graduates must complete a thesis.

Special: Cross-registration is available with other University of Texas campuses and the Health Science Center at Dallas. Accelerated degree programs and B.A.-B.S. degrees are offered in several majors, as is a 3-2 engineering degree with Austin College, Texas Women's University, or Abilene Christian University. Co-op programs, internships, work-study programs with several major corporations, and dual and student-designed majors are possible. Students may study abroad in Europe, Asia, Mexico, and New Zealand. There are 4 national honor societies, a freshman honors program, and 1 departmental honors program.

Faculty/Classroom: 70% of faculty are male; 30%, female. 10% teach undergraduates, 4% do research, and 86% do both. Graduate students teach 1% of introductory courses. The average class size in an introductory lecture is 42; in a laboratory, 24; and in a regular course, 47.

Admissions: 51% of the 2005-2006 applicants were accepted. The SAT scores for the 2005-2006 freshman class were: Verbal--10% below 500, 34% between 500 and 599, 42% between 600 and 700, and 14% above 700; Math--4% below 500, 26% between 500 and 599, 49% between 600 and 700, and 21% above 700. The ACT scores were 8% below 21, 16% between 21 and 23, 30% between 24 and 26, 16% between 27 and 28, and 30% above 28. 65% of the current freshmen were in the top fifth of their class; 92% were in the top two fifths. There were 36 National Merit finalists and 20 semifinalists. 31 freshmen graduated first in their class.

Requirements: The SAT or ACT is required. In addition, applicants should be graduates of an accredited secondary school. In-state students who rank in the top 10% of their class gain automatic admission to UTD. Credentials for other students must include completion of 4 units of English, 3.5 of math, 3 each of social science and lab science, 2 of a foreign language, and course work in fine arts and electives, with health and phys ed courses recommended. An essay is required. A GPA of 3.0 is required. AP and CLEP credits are accepted. Important factors in the admissions decision are advanced placement or honor courses, leadership record, and evidence of special talent.

Procedure: Freshmen are admitted to all sessions. Entrance exams should be taken at the end of the junior year or beginning of the senior year. There are early decision and deferred admissions plans. There is a rolling admissions plan. Applications should be filed by August 1 for fall entry, December 1 for spring entry, and May 1 for summer entry, along with a $50 fee. Applications are accepted on-line.

Transfer: 2101 transfer students enrolled in 2004-2005. Sophomore applicants must present a GPA of 3.0 and 12 credits in the general education core. Upper-division applicants should have a GPA of 2.5 and be in good standing at the last school attended. 30 of 120 credits required for the bachelor's degree must be completed at UTD.

Visiting: There are regularly scheduled orientations for prospective students, including meetings with faculty and an admissions counselor, and a campus tour. There are guides for informal visits and visitors may sit in on classes. To schedule a visit, contact the Office of Enrollment Services at (972) 883-2270 or enrollment@utdallas.edu.

Financial Aid: In 2005-2006, 72% of all full-time freshmen and 61% of continuing full-time students received some form of financial aid. 31% of full-time freshmen and 37% of continuing full-time students received need-based aid. Need-based scholarships or need-based grants averaged $4111 and need-based self-help aid (loans and jobs) averaged $3408. 6% of undergraduates work part time. Average annual earnings from campus work are $6094. The CSS/Profile or FAFSA and the college's own financial statement are required. The deadline for filing freshman financial aid applications for fall entry is April 30.

International Students: There are 317 international students enrolled. They must score satisfactorily on the TOEFL and also take the SAT or the ACT.

Computers: Wireless access is available. There are several monitored computer labs for student use including PCs, Macs, PCs for visually impaired, scanners, and printers. There are approximately 240 computers for student use. Wireless LAN is part of UTD's network. Seven buildings and 24 nodes in 11 other buildings are covered by wireless. All students may access the system 8 A.M. to midnight in most labs, or 24 hours in specific labs and from remote locations. There are no time limits and no fees. It is strongly recommended that all students have a personal computer with wireless connection capability.

Graduates: From July 1, 2004 to June 30, 2005, 2019 bachelor's degrees were awarded. The most popular majors were business administration (23%), interdisciplinary studies (15%), and computer science (10%). In an average class, 3% graduate in 3 years or less, 32% graduate in 4 years or less, 51% graduate in 5 years or less, and 59% graduate in 6 years or less. 632 companies recruited on campus in a recent year. Of a recent graduating class, 15% were enrolled in graduate school within 6 months of graduation and 57% were employed.

Admissions Contact: Bryan J. Bradford, Director of Admissions. A video is available. E-mail: admissions-status@utdallas.edu
Web: www.utdallas.edu

UNIVERSITY OF TEXAS AT EL PASO   A-3

El Paso, TX 79968   (915) 747-5890; Fax: (915) 747-8893

Full-time: 4966 men, 5879 women   **Faculty:** 680
Part-time: 2162 men, 2799 women   **Ph.D.s:** n/av
Graduate: 1135 men, 1465 women   **Student/Faculty:** 16 to 1
Year: 4-1-4, summer session   **Tuition:** $4822 ($12,562)
Application Deadline: July 31   **Room & Board:** $8942
Freshman Class: 4012 applied, 3984 accepted, 2117 enrolled
SAT or ACT: required   NONCOMPETITIVE

The University of Texas at El Paso, founded in 1913 and the second oldest academic member of the University of Texas System, was originally called the Texas School of Mines and Metallurgy. It now offers a wide variety of classes through the schools and colleges of business, education, engineering, liberal arts, nursing and allied health, and science. There are 6 undergraduate schools and 1 graduate school. In addition to regional accreditation, UTEP has baccalaureate program accreditation with AACSB, ABET, and NLN. The library contains 1,080,588 volumes, 1,760,984 microform items, and 9995 audio/video tapes/CDs/DVDs, and subscribes to 3005 periodicals including electronic. Computerized library services include the card catalog, interlibrary loans, database searching, and Internet access. Special learning facilities include a learning resource center, art gallery, natural history museum, radio station, TV station, seismic observatory, and the El Paso Centennial Museum. The 366-acre campus is in an urban area. Including any residence halls, there are 87 buildings.

Student Life: 97% of undergraduates are from Texas. Students are from 49 states, 84 foreign countries, and Canada. 95% are from public schools. 75% are Hispanic; 10% foreign nationals; 10% white. The average age of freshmen is 19; all undergraduates, 22. 31% do not continue beyond their first year; 27% remain to graduate.

Housing: 443 students can be accommodated in college housing, which includes coed on-campus apartments, fraternity houses, and sorority houses. In addition, there are suites, private rooms, and 24-hour quiet floors. On-campus housing is available on a first-come, first-served basis. Alcohol is not permitted. All students may keep cars.

Activities: There are 100 groups on campus, including art, band, cheerleading, chess, choir, chorale, computers, dance, drama, drill team, drum and bugle corps, ethnic, film, honors, international, jazz band, literary magazine, marching band, musical theater, newspaper, opera, orchestra, pep band, photography, political, professional, radio and TV, religious, social, social service, student government, symphony, and yearbook. Popular campus events include Women's History and Hispanic Cultural weeks, and St. Patrick's Engineering Initiation.

Sports: There are 6 intercollegiate sports for men and 5 for women, and 1 intramural sport for men and 1 for women. Facilities include basketball, volleyball, badminton, racquetball, and tennis courts, grass fields for multiple use, an Outdoor Adventure Program with backpacking, bicycling, rafting, and ski trips, a 52,000-seat football stadium, a 12,222-seat basketball gym, a swimming pool, a bowling alley, and a weight room.

Disabled Students: Wheelchair ramps, elevators, special parking, specially equipped rest rooms, special class scheduling, lowered drinking fountains, and special housing are available.

Services: Counseling and information services are available, as is tutoring in every subject. There is a reader service for the blind, and remedial math, reading, and writing.

Campus Safety and Security: Measures include shuttle buses and lighted pathways/sidewalks.

Programs of Study: UTEP confers B.A., B.S., B.B.A., B.F.A., B.I.S., B.M., B.S.C.E., B.S.C.S., B.S.Ed., B.S.E.E., B.S.I.E., B.S.MeT.E., B.S.N., and B.S.W. degrees. Master's and doctoral degrees are also awarded. Bachelor's degrees are awarded in BIOLOGICAL SCIENCE (biology/biological science and microbiology), BUSINESS (accounting, banking and finance, business economics, management information systems, management science, and marketing/retailing/merchandising), COMMUNICATIONS AND THE ARTS (art, communications, dramatic arts, English, French, German, journalism, languages, linguistics, music, Spanish, speech/debate/rhetoric, and theater management), COMPUTER AND PHYSICAL SCIENCE (applied mathematics, chemistry, computer science, earth science, geology, geophysics and seismology, mathematics, physics, science, and statistics), ENGINEERING AND ENVIRONMENTAL DESIGN (civil engineering, electrical/electronics engineering, industrial engineering technology, mechanical engineering, and metallurgical engineering), HEALTH PROFESSIONS (allied health, clinical science, health science, medical laboratory technology, and nursing), SOCIAL SCIENCE (anthropology, criminal justice, economics, history, interdisciplinary studies, Latin American studies, Mexican-American/Chicano studies, philosophy, physical fitness/movement, political science/government, psychology, social work, and sociology). Business, nursing, and engineering are the strongest academically. Criminal justice, interdisciplinary, and kinesiology are the largest.

Required: All students must have a minimum GPA of 2.0 while taking 125 to 130 semester hours. Students also must complete a distribution of courses through the general foundation program. Course work is required in the areas of arts/fine arts, computer literacy, English, including composition, foreign languages, history, humanities, math, sciences, and social sciences.

Special: Cross-registration with the University of Texas and the University of Texas Health Science Center is available. Internships, mainly at the graduate level, study abroad in London and Hildesheim, Germany, work-study programs, nondegree study, and pass/fail options are available. There also is the Inter-American Sciences and Humanities Program for students from Spanish-speaking countries whose English is less than adequate for normal study in the United States. The Center for Inter-American and Border Studies also promotes teaching, research, and outreach programs to further the understanding of Latin America. Similar studies are offered through the Cross-Cultural Southwest Ethnic Study Center. An accelerated degree, co-op programs in information science, public health, nursing, pharmacy, and border studies, double majors, dual enrollment, distance learning, ESL, independent study, teacher certification, and weekend college programs are also offered. There is a freshman honors program.

Faculty/Classroom: 59% of faculty are male; 41%, female. The average class size in an introductory lecture is 25; in a laboratory, 15; and in a regular course, 22.

Admissions: 99% of the 2005-2006 applicants were accepted.

Requirements: The SAT or ACT is required. In addition, for citizens or permanent residents of the United States who have graduated within the past 5 years, satisfactory SAT or ACT scores are required. UTEP recommends high school preperation that includes of 4 years of English, 3 to 4 of math (more for science and engineering students), 3 of natural science, and 2 each of social studies, history, and foreign language. The GED is accepted. A GPA of 2.0 is required. AP and CLEP credits are accepted. Important factors in the admissions decision are extracurricular activities record, evidence of special talent, and recommendations by alumni.

Procedure: Freshmen are admitted to all sessions. There are early admissions, deferred admissions, and rolling admissiions plans. Applications should be filed by July 31 for fall entry. The college accepts all applicants. Notification is sent when admissions file is complete. Applications are accepted on-line.

Transfer: 1126 transfer students enrolled in 2004-2005. Transfer applicants must have at least a C average and must be eligible to return to all previous institutions attended. Transcripts must be provided. 30 of 125 credits required for the bachelor's degree must be completed at UTEP.

Visiting: There are regularly scheduled orientations for prospective students, including preenrollment counseling and campus tours. There are guides for informal visits and visitors may sit in on classes and stay overnight. To schedule a visit, contact Beto Lopez, Recruiting Office.

Financial Aid: In 2005-2006, 64% of all full-time students received some form of financial aid. At least 58% of all full-time students received need-based aid. The average freshman award was $7823. Need-based scholarships or need-based grants averaged $5068; need-based self-help aid (loans and jobs) averaged $2970; institutional non-need-based athletic scholarships averaged $7676; and other institutional non-need-based awards and non-need-based scholarships averaged $1208. The average financial indebtedness of the 2005 graduate was $6538. The FAFSA and the college's own financial statement are required. The deadline for filing freshman financial aid applications for fall entry is March 15.

International Students: There were 1559 international students enrolled in a recent year. The school actively recruits these students. A satisfactory score is required on the written TOEFL and the PAA. Students must also take the SAT or the ACT and achieve a required minimum score on the SAT and 20 (composite) on the ACT, with a 21 minimum on the English section.

Computers: Those students enrolled in computer courses or with department permission may access the system. There are no time limits. The fee is $10.

Graduates: From July 1, 2004 to June 30, 2005, 1646 bachelor's degrees were awarded. The most popular majors were business/marketing (21%), interdisciplinary studies (16%), and engineering or health (10%). In an average class, 4% graduate in 4 years or less, 16% graduate in 5 years or less, and 27% graduate in 6 years or less.

Admissions Contact: Irma Nu¹ez Rubio, Director of Admissions. A video is available. E-mail: *futureminer@utep.edu* Web: *www.utep.edu/enroll/*

UNIVERSITY OF TEXAS AT SAN ANTONIO   D-4

San Antonio, TX 78249   (210) 458-4536
                                    (800) 669-0919; Fax: (210) 458-7857

Full-time: 8470 men, 9152 women	**Faculty:** 512; IIA, av$
Part-time: 2664 men, 3398 women	**Ph.Ds:** 99%
Graduate: 1531 men, 2123 women	**Student/Faculty:** 34 to 1
Year: semesters, summer session	**Tuition:** $5520 ($13,800)
Application Deadline: July 1	**Room & Board:** $5805
Freshman Class: 9666 applied, 9081 accepted, 4472 enrolled	
SAT Verbal/Math: 500/520*	**ACT:** 20 **LESS COMPETITIVE**

The University of Texas at San Antonio was established as part of the state university system in 1969 and is now a large, comprehensive institution offering undergraduate and graduate programs in arts, business, engineering, music, health science, and education. There are 8 undergraduate schools. In addition to regional accreditation, UTSA has baccalaureate program accreditation with AACSB, ABET, CSWE, FIDER, NAAB, NASAD, and NASM. The 2 libraries contain 668,000 volumes, 3,200,000 microform items, and 41,000 audio/video tapes/CDs/DVDs, and subscribe to 35,000 periodicals including electronic. Computerized library services include the card catalog, interlibrary loans, database searching, Internet access, and laptop Internet portals. Special learning facilities include a learning resource center, art gallery, and Institute of Texan Cultures. The 600-acre campus is in a suburban area approximately 18 miles northwest of downtown San Antonio. Including any residence halls, there are 35 buildings.

Student Life: 96% of undergraduates are from Texas. Others are from 49 states, 85 foreign countries, and Canada. 91% are from public schools. 45% are Hispanic; 40% white. The average age of freshmen is 19; all undergraduates, 23. 35% do not continue beyond their first year; 27% remain to graduate.

Housing: 2965 students can be accommodated in college housing, which includes coed dormitories and on-campus apartments. In addition, there are special-interest houses. On-campus housing is available on a first-come, first-served basis. 89% of students commute. Alcohol is not permitted. All students may keep cars.

Activities: 4% of men belong to 11 national fraternities; 2% of women belong to 7 national sororities. There are 170 groups on campus, including art, band, cheerleading, chess, choir, chorale, chorus, computers, dance, debate, drama, ethnic, gay, honors, international, jazz band, musical theater, newspaper, orchestra, pep band, political, professional, radio and TV, religious, social, social service, student government, and symphony. Popular campus events include Fiesta UTSA, Best Fest, and Folk Life festival.

Sports: There are 7 intercollegiate sports for men and 9 for women, and 16 intramural sports for men and 16 for women. Facilities include gyms, weight machines, a cardio room, a climbing wall, a jogging path and a 400-meter track, a tennis center, an indoor pool, various playing fields, and courts for basketball, volleyball, badminton, shuffleboard, racquetball, and wallyball.

Disabled Students: All of the campus is accessible. Wheelchair ramps, elevators, special parking, specially equipped rest rooms, special class scheduling, lowered drinking fountains, and lowered telephones, are available.

Services: Counseling and information services are available, as is tutoring in every subject. There is a reader service for the blind, and remedial math, reading, and writing.

Campus Safety and Security: Measures include 24-hour foot and vehicle patrol, self-defense education, security escort services, and shuttle buses. There are informal discussions, pamphlets/posters/films, emergency telephones, and lighted pathways/sidewalks.

Programs of Study: UTSA confers B.A., B.S., B.B.A, B.F.A., B.M., B.S.C.E., B.S.E.E., and B.S.M.E. degrees. Master's and doctoral degrees are also awarded. Bachelor's degrees are awarded in BIOLOGICAL SCIENCE (biology/biological science), BUSINESS (accounting, banking and finance, business administration and management, business economics, business statistics, entrepreneurial studies, human resources, international business management, management information systems, management science, marketing/retailing/merchandising, personnel management, and tourism), COMMUNICATIONS AND THE ARTS (art, classics, communications, English, fine arts, French, German, music, music business management, music performance, music theory and composition, and Spanish), COMPUTER AND PHYSICAL SCIENCE (actuarial science, chemistry, computer science, geology, information sciences and systems, mathematics, and physics), ENGINEERING AND ENVIRONMENTAL DESIGN (architecture, civil engineering, construction management, electrical/electronics engineering, environmental science, interior design, and mechanical engineering), HEALTH PROFESSIONS (clinical science, health, and occupational therapy), SOCIAL SCIENCE (American studies, anthropology, criminal justice, economics, family and community services, geography, history, humanities, interdisciplinary studies, Mexican-American/Chicano studies, philosophy, physical fitness/movement, political science/government, psychology, and sociology).

Accounting, finance, and management are the strongest academically. Business, biology, and interdisciplinary studies are the largest.

Required: All students must complete at least 120 credit hours with a 2.0 GPA for graduation. Core curriculum requirements total 54 credits and include courses in fine arts, composition, computer science or logic, economics, foreign language, American and Texas history, social science, literacy studies, math, U.S. and Texas constitutions, natural science, and interdisciplinary studies.

Special: UTSA offers joint degrees in occupational therapy and clinical lab sciences with the University of Texas Health Science Center and study abroad in many countries. Internships, work-study, nondegree study, and pass/fail options are available. There are 36 national honor societies, a freshman honors program, and 17 departmental honors programs.

Faculty/Classroom: 57% of faculty are male; 41%, female. 84% teach undergraduates. Graduate students teach 14% of introductory courses. The average class size in an introductory lecture is 48; in a laboratory, 25; and in a regular course, 25.

Admissions: 94% of the 2005-2006 applicants were accepted. The SAT scores for the 2005-2006 freshman class were: Verbal--46% below 500, 40% between 500 and 599, 13% between 600 and 700, and 1% above 700; Math--39% below 500, 43% between 500 and 599, 17% between 600 and 700, and 1% above 700. The ACT scores were 53% below 21, 27% between 21 and 23, 14% between 24 and 26, 4% between 27 and 28, and 2% above 28. 21 freshmen graduated first in their class.

Requirements: The SAT or ACT is required. Admission is based on a formula derived from class rank and SAT or ACT scores. Applicants must be graduates of accredited high schools or have earned the GED. UTSA recommends that high school preparation include 4 units of English, at least 3 of math, at least 2 each of a foreign language, natural science, and social science, and at least 1 of fine arts. AP and CLEP credits are accepted.

Procedure: Freshmen are admitted to all sessions. Entrance exams should be taken in the spring of the junior year. There is a rolling admissions plan. Applications should be filed by July 1 for fall entry, December 1 for spring entry, and May 1 for summer entry. Notification is sent on a rolling basis. Applications are accepted on-line. The fall 2005 application fee was $30.

Transfer: 4118 transfer students enrolled in 2004-2005. Applicants with at least 30 hours of college credit must present a C average in all college work attempted and evidence of good standing. Those with fewer than 30 hours must meet freshman standards as well. 30 of 120 credits required for the bachelor's degree must be completed at UTSA.

Visiting: There are regularly scheduled orientations for prospective students. There are guides for informal visits. To schedule a visit, contact New Student Programs at (210) 458-4724.

Financial Aid: In 2005-2006, 54% of all full-time freshmen and 60% of continuing full-time students received some form of financial aid. 56% of full-time freshmen and 58% of continuing full-time students received need-based aid. The average freshman award was $5703. 15% of undergraduates work part time. Average annual earnings from campus work are $3500. The average financial indebtedness of the 2005 graduate was $18,000. The FAFSA and the college's own financial statement are required. The deadline for filing freshman financial aid applications for fall entry is March 31.

International Students: There are 246 international students enrolled. The school actively recruits these students. They must score satisfactorily on the written TOEFL or on the electronic version and also take the SAT or the ACT.

Computers: Wireless access is available. Students may use any of the 3 general access labs, which offer a total of about 550 computer systems. Any registered student who pays the automated services fee will be given a lab user account, which also allows access to the wireless network. Students may purchase PCs through Gateway that are preconfigured by UTSA and have on-campus support. All students may access the system 24 hours a day. There are no time limits and no fees. It is strongly recommended that all students have a personal computer. Certain capabilities are required for the computer. More information is available at *http://www.utsa.edu/infotech/laptop/*.

Graduates: From July 1, 2004 to June 30, 2005, 3257 bachelor's degrees were awarded. The most popular majors were multi/interdisciplinary studies, other (12%), biology/biological sciences, general (9%), and psychology, general (8%). In an average class, 6% graduate in 4 years or less, 20% graduate in 5 years or less, and 29% graduate in 6 years or less. 231 companies recruited on campus in 2004-2005.

Admissions Contact: Jennifer Ehlers, Director of Admissions. E-mail: *prospects@utsa.edu* Web: *www.utsa.edu*

UNIVERSITY OF TEXAS-PAN AMERICAN   D-5

Edinburg, TX 78541-2999   (956) 381-2482; Fax: (956) 381-2321

Full-time: 4511 men, 6106 women	**Faculty:** 525
Part-time: 1732 men, 2593 women	**Ph.D.s:** n/av
Graduate: 710 men, 1396 women	**Student/Faculty:** 20 to 1
Year: semesters, summer session	**Tuition:** $2957 ($9581)
Application Deadline: July	**Room & Board:** $4333
Freshman Class: 6988 applied, 3295 accepted, 2419 enrolled	
SAT Verbal/Math: 480/490*	**ACT:** 20 **COMPETITIVE+**

University of Texas-Pan American, founded in 1927, is a state-supported institution offering programs in the arts and sciences, education, business, and health-related professions. It is part of the University of Texas system. There are 6 undergraduate and 6 graduate schools. In addition to regional accreditation, UT Pan American has baccalaureate program accreditation with AACSB, ABET, ACOTE, ACS, ADA, AOTA, ASLA, CAHEA, CSWE, NAACLS, NCATE, and NLN. The library contains 573,803 volumes, 1,072,265 microform items, and 8838 audio/video tapes/CDs/DVDs, and subscribes to 30,013 periodicals including electronic. Computerized library services include interlibrary loans, database searching, and Internet access. Special learning facilities include a learning resource center, art gallery, planetarium, and a coastal studies lab. The 258-acre campus is in a small town close to the Mexican border and the Gulf of Mexico. Including any residence halls, there are 77 buildings.

Student Life: 97% of undergraduates are from Texas. Others are from 33 states, 25 foreign countries, and Canada. 88% are Hispanic. The average age of freshmen is 19; all undergraduates, 23. 34% do not continue beyond their first year; 66% remain to graduate.

Housing: 592 students can be accommodated in college housing, which includes single-sex and coed dorms and on-campus apartments. On-campus housing is available on a first-come, first-served basis. 90% of students commute. Alcohol is not permitted. All students may keep cars.

Activities: 1% of men belong to 7 national fraternities; 1% of women belong to 1 local and 6 national sororities. There are 102 groups on campus, including academic, art, cheerleading, choir, chorus, computers, dance, drama, ethnic, film, gay, honors, international, jazz band, literary magazine, musical theater, newspaper, opera, orchestra, photography, political, professional, radio and TV, religious, social, social service, student government, symphony, and yearbook. Popular campus events include Cinco de Mayo, Spirit Week, and Bronco Day.

Sports: There are 7 intercollegiate sports for men and 7 for women, and 33 intramural sports for men and 33 for women. Facilities include a 4000-seat field house, baseball and tennis stadiums, a track, and a soccer field.

Disabled Students: 95% of the campus is accessible. Wheelchair ramps, elevators, special parking, specially equipped rest rooms, special class scheduling, lowered drinking fountains, lowered telephones, special housing, TDD phones, readers, and note takers are available.

Services: Counseling and information services are available, as is tutoring in some subjects, including biology, chemistry, history, Spanish, math, philosophy, political science, French, English, physics, and physical sciences. There is a reader service for the blind, and remedial math, reading, and writing. The Learning Assistance Center provides small-group and individual tutoring and computer-aided instruction.

Campus Safety and Security: Measures include 24-hour foot and vehicle patrol, self-defense education, security escort services, and shuttle buses. There are pamphlets/posters/films, emergency telephones, lighted pathways/sidewalks, and a university police department.

Programs of Study: UT Pan American confers B.A., B.S., B.A.A.S., B.A.S.C., B.B.A., B.F.A., B.G.S., B.I.S., B.S.C.J., B.S.C.S., B.S.E.E., B.S.M.E., B.S.M.F., B.S.N., B.S.O.T., B.S.P.A., and B.S.W. degrees. Master's and doctoral degrees are also awarded. Bachelor's degrees are awarded in BIOLOGICAL SCIENCE (biology/biological science), BUSINESS (accounting, banking and finance, international business management, management science, and marketing/retailing/merchandising), COMMUNICATIONS AND THE ARTS (art, communications, dramatic arts, English, fine arts, journalism, music, and Spanish), COMPUTER AND PHYSICAL SCIENCE (chemistry, computer science, information sciences and systems, mathematics, and physics), EDUCATION (secondary), ENGINEERING AND ENVIRONMENTAL DESIGN (electrical/electronics engineering, manufacturing engineering, and mechanical engineering), HEALTH PROFESSIONS (health, medical technology, nursing, occupational therapy, physician's assistant, rehabilitation therapy, and speech pathology/audiology), SOCIAL SCIENCE (anthropology, corrections, criminal justice, dietetics, economics, history, interdisciplinary studies, Latin American studies, liberal arts/general studies, Mexican-American/Chicano studies, philosophy, physical fitness/movement, political science/government, psychology, social work, and sociology). Engineering and business are the strongest academically. Education, nursing, and engineering are the largest.

Required: To graduate, students must complete 124 to 137 semester hours with a 2.0 GPA. At least 30 hours are required in the major. Students must also fulfill a general education requirement of 48 hours by taking 18 hours in humanities (including English and a foreign language), 15 hours of social science (including U.S. history and Texas government), 11 hours of lab science and math, and 2 hours each of phys ed and computer science. Other requirements vary according to degree.

Special: Internships, co-op programs, study abroad, work-study programs, dual majors, and nondegree study are available. There are 9 national honor societies, a freshman honors program, and 6 departmental honors programs.

Faculty/Classroom: 59% of faculty are male; 41%, female. 65% teach undergraduates.

Admissions: 47% of the 2005-2006 applicants were accepted. The SAT scores for the 2005-2006 freshman class were: Verbal--59% below 500, 33% between 500 and 599, 7% between 600 and 700, and 1% above 700; Math--51% below 500, 37% between 500 and 599, 11% between 600 and 700, and 1% above 700. The ACT scores were 57% below 21, 28% between 21 and 23, 11% between 24 and 26, 3% between 27 and 28, and 1% above 28. 43% of the current freshmen were in the top fifth of their class; 72% were in the top two fifths.

Requirements: The SAT or ACT is required. The ACT is preferred. Applicants must be graduates of an accredited high school or have the GED. 21 academic units are required, including 4 units of English; 3 units of math, at least 1 of which must be algebra; 2 units of science; 1 unit each of world history and U.S. history; and 1/2 unit each of U.S. government, economics, phys ed, and health education. An additional 7 units may be taken in electives. A GPA of 2.0 is required. AP and CLEP credits are accepted.

Procedure: Freshmen are admitted to all sessions. The school prefers entrance exams be taken in the junior year of high school. Early decision applications should be filed by February; regular applications, by July for fall entry, November for spring entry, and April for summer entry. Notification is sent on a rolling basis. There is a rolling admissions plan. Applications are accepted on-line.

Transfer: 749 transfer students enrolled in 2004-2005. Transfer applicants must meet the same criteria as entering freshman. 30 of 124 to 137 credits required for the bachelor's degree must be completed at UT Pan American.

Visiting: There are regularly scheduled orientations for prospective students. There are guides for informal visits and visitors may sit in on classes. To schedule a visit, contact the Admissions Office: Recruitment and Orientation at (956) 381-3541.

Financial Aid: In 2005-2006, 79% of all full-time freshmen and 82% of continuing full-time students received some form of financial aid. 71% of full-time freshmen and 74% of continuing full-time students received need-based aid. Need-based scholarships or need-based grants averaged $5349 ($10,418 maximum); need-based self-help aid (loans and jobs) averaged $3176 ($8925 maximum); non-need-based athletic scholarships averaged $4887 ($9275 maximum); and other non-need-based awards and non-need-based scholarships averaged $2913 ($18,936 maximum). Average annual earnings from campus work are $2717. The average financial indebtedness of the 2005 graduate was $7467. The FAFSA is required. The priority date for freshman financial aid applications for fall entry is March 1. The deadline for filing freshman financial aid applications for fall entry is November 15.

International Students: There are 506 international students enrolled. The school actively recruits these students. They must score satisfactorily on the TOEFL and also take the SAT or the ACT.

Computers: Wireless access is available. All students have access to the Internet on university PCs by using their assigned login IDs. Access to the Internet outside the university is through the World Wide Web. PCs in the university for student access are located in the Academic Services Building. All students may access the system. There are no time limits. The fee is $61 semester.

Graduates: From July 1, 2004 to June 30, 2005, 1987 bachelor's degrees were awarded. The most popular majors were interdisciplinary studies (19%), biology (7%), and English (5%). In an average class, 10% graduate in 4 years or less, 20% graduate in 5 years or less, and 26% graduate in 6 years or less. 256 companies recruited on campus in 2004-2005.

Admissions Contact: Dr. Magdalena Williams, Dean of Admissions and Enrollment Services. A video is available.
E-mail: *admissions@panam.edu* Web: *http://www.panam.edu*

UNIVERSITY OF THE INCARNATE WORD   D-4
San Antonio, TX 78209-6397   (210) 829-6005
(800) 749-WORD; Fax: (210) 829-3921

Full-time: 833 men, 1764 women	**Faculty:** 160; IIA, --$
Part-time: 654 men, 1119 women	**Ph.D.s:** 69%
Graduate: 312 men, 535 women	**Student/Faculty:** 16 to 1
Year: semesters, summer session	**Tuition:** $17,072
Application Deadline: open	**Room & Board:** $6234
Freshman Class: 2040 applied, 1532 accepted, 578 enrolled	
SAT Verbal/Math: 480/470*	**ACT:** 20	**COMPETITIVE**

University of the Incarnate Word, founded in 1881, is a liberal arts institution affiliated with the Catholic Church that offers undergraduate programs in art, business, health science, education, music, religious studies, nursing, and fine arts. There are 6 undergraduate schools and 1 graduate school. In addition to regional accreditation, UIW has baccalaureate program accreditation with ACBSP, ADA, AHEA, CAHEA, NCATE, and NLN. The library contains 260,759 volumes, 273,017 microform items, and 13,000 audio/video tapes/CDs/DVDs, and subscribes to 19,100 periodicals including electronic. Computerized library services include the card catalog, interlibrary loans, database searching, Internet access, and laptop Internet portals. Special learning facilities include a learning resource center, art gallery, radio station, media service center, and teaching theater. The 100-acre campus is in an urban area about 3 miles north of downtown San Antonio. Including any residence halls, there are 20 buildings.

Student Life: 90% of undergraduates are from Texas. Others are from 27 states, 18 foreign countries, and Canada. 75% are from public schools. 59% are Hispanic; 26% white. 48% are Catholic; 28% claim no religious affiliation; 21% Protestant. The average age of freshmen is 18; all undergraduates, 22. 30% do not continue beyond their first year; 43% remain to graduate.

Housing: 800 students can be accommodated in college housing, which includes single-sex and coed dorms and on-campus apartments. On-campus housing is guaranteed for all 4 years. 81% of students commute. All students may keep cars.

Activities: 3% of men belong to 2 local fraternities; 1% of women belong to 2 local sororities. There are 40 groups on campus, including art, cheerleading, choir, chorale, chorus, dance, drama, drill team, ethnic, honors, international, jazz band, literary magazine, musical theater, newspaper, orchestra, pep band, political, professional, radio and TV, religious, social, social service, and student government. Popular campus events include Welcome Week, Light the Way, and Golden Harvest.

Sports: There are 6 intercollegiate sports for men and 9 for women, and 6 intramural sports for men and 6 for women. Facilities include a convocation center, a field house, 8 tennis courts, 2 soccer fields, softball and baseball fields, a 1/4-mile track, a 3/4-mile jogging trail, a gym, basketball courts, a natatorium, and weight and aerobics rooms.

Disabled Students: 88% of the campus is accessible. Wheelchair ramps, elevators, special parking, specially equipped rest rooms, special class scheduling, and special housing are available.

Services: Counseling and information services are available, as is tutoring in most subjects. There is remedial math, reading, and writing.

Campus Safety and Security: Measures include 24-hour foot and vehicle patrol, self-defense education, security escort services, and shuttle buses. There are informal discussions, pamphlets/posters/films, emergency telephones, lighted pathways/sidewalks, and a professional security force on campus.

Programs of Study: UIW confers B.A., B.S., B.B.A., and B.M. degrees. Master's and doctoral degrees are also awarded. Bachelor's degrees are awarded in BIOLOGICAL SCIENCE (biology/biological science and nutrition), BUSINESS (business administration and management, fashion merchandising, human resources, and sports management), COMMUNICATIONS AND THE ARTS (art, communications, dramatic arts, English, music, music business management, and Spanish), COMPUTER AND PHYSICAL SCIENCE (chemistry, information sciences and systems, and mathematics), EDUCATION (art, athletic training, elementary, music, physical, and secondary), ENGINEERING AND ENVIRONMENTAL DESIGN (engineering management, environmental science, and interior design), HEALTH PROFESSIONS (music therapy, nuclear medical technology, and nursing), SOCIAL SCIENCE (child care/child and family studies, fashion design and technology, history, Native American studies, philosophy, political science/government, prelaw, psychology, religion, and sociology). Nursing and business are the strongest academically. Business is the largest.

Required: To graduate, students must complete at least 128 credit hours, with a minimum GPA of 2.0. An extensive required core curriculum of 53 credit hours includes world literature, critical discourse, dimensions of wellness, computer literacy, and a capstone. A total of 45 hours of community service also is required.

Special: UIW offers cross-registration with Our Lady of the Lake and Saint Mary's Universities, internships, work-study programs, and study abroad, including programs in Japan, China, Brazil, Mexico, France, and Great Britain.

Faculty/Classroom: 43% of faculty are male; 57%, female. All teach undergraduates. No introductory courses are taught by graduate students.

Admissions: 75% of the 2005-2006 applicants were accepted. The SAT scores for the 2005-2006 freshman class were: Verbal--58% below 500, 32% between 500 and 599, 9% between 600 and 700, and 1% above 700; Math--58% below 500, 34% between 500 and 599, and 8% between 600 and 700. The ACT scores were 60% below 21, 24% between 21 and 23, 11% between 24 and 26, 3% between 27 and 28, and 2% above 28. 33% of the current freshmen were in the top fifth of their class; 62% were in the top two fifths.

Requirements: The SAT or ACT is required. In addition, students must have a minimum GPA of 2.0 wih satisfactory scores on the SAT or on the ACT. Applicants must be graduates of an accredited secondary school or have the GED, and have completed 16 Carnegie units, including at least 4 units of English, 3 of math, science, and social studies, 2 of foreign language, and 1 of fine arts. In some cases, applicants may be asked to take an assessment test and/or arrange for a personal interview to provide further information. A GPA of 2.0 is required. AP and CLEP credits are accepted. Important factors in the admissions decision are advanced placement or honor courses and recommendations by alumni.

Procedure: Freshmen are admitted to all sessions. Entrance exams should be taken in the junior or senior year of high school. There is a deferred admissions plan and a rolling admissions plan. Application deadlines are open. Notification is sent on a rolling basis. The fall 2005 application fee was $20. Applications are accepted on-line.

Transfer: 331 transfer students enrolled in 2004-2005. Applicants are advised to have at least a cumulative GPA of 2.5 or better for unconditional admission. Students may be admitted with less than a 2.5 GPA on the recommendation of the Admissions Committee. The Committee reserves the right to place conditions or requirements on the admittance of such a student. Applicants with fewer than 24 transferable hours must submit an official high school transcript with the scores of any SAT or ACT previously taken. Transfer applicants out of high school for more than 2 years, or who are GED recipients, are not required to submit SAT or ACT scores. 36 of 128 credits required for the bachelor's degree must be completed at UIW.

Visiting: There are regularly scheduled orientations for prospective students, consisting of an introduction to services, a campus tour, assessment testing, advisement, and registration. There are guides for informal visits and visitors may sit in on classes and stay overnight. To schedule a visit, contact the Office of Admissions at *admis@universe.uiwtx.edu.*

Financial Aid: In 2005-2006, 82% of all full-time freshmen and 71% of continuing full-time students received some form of financial aid. 74% of full-time freshmen and 66% of continuing full-time students received need-based aid. The average freshman award was $12,634. Need-based scholarships or need-based grants averaged $8274 ($14,800 maximum); need-based self-help aid (loans and jobs) averaged $3404 ($9330 maximum); non-need-based athletic scholarships averaged $12,533 ($22,000 maximum); and other non-need-based awards and non-need-based scholarships averaged $5869 ($16,500 maximum). 57% of undergraduates work part time. Average annual earnings from campus work are $2000. The average financial indebtedness of the 2005 graduate was $23,383. The FAFSA is required. The priority date for freshman financial aid applications for fall entry is January 1.

International Students: There are 89 international students enrolled. The school actively recruits these students. They must take the TOEFL.

Computers: Wireless access is available. Students may use the network for educational purposes and research, to access the library databases, and to access the university platform course management system. There are 161 PCs located in 9 computer labs in various locations on campus for student use. All students may access the system 24 hours a day, 7 days a week. There are no time limits and no fees. All students are required to have personal computers.

Graduates: From July 1, 2004 to June 30, 2005, 645 bachelor's degrees were awarded. The most popular majors were business administration (32%), nursing (8%), and liberal arts (7%). In an average class, 36% graduate in 5 years or less, and 43% graduate in 6 years or less. 52 companies recruited on campus in 2004-2005.

Admissions Contact: Andrea Cyterski-Acosta, Director of Admissions. A video is available. E-mail: *cyterski@universe.uiwtx.edu* Web: *www.uiw.edu*

WAYLAND BAPTIST UNIVERSITY	B-2
Plainview, TX 79072	**(806) 291-3500; (800) 588-1928**
Full-time: 370 men, 470 women	**Faculty:** 67
Part-time: 58 men, 106 women	**Ph.D.s:** 70%
Graduate: 40 men, 80 women	**Student/Faculty:** 12 to 1
Year: semesters, summer session	**Tuition:** $9900
Application Deadline: open	**Room & Board:** $3584
Freshman Class: n/av	
SAT or ACT: required	**COMPETITIVE**

Wayland Baptist University, founded in 1908, is a private liberal arts school affiliated with the Baptist General Convention of Texas (Southern Baptist). There are 8 undergraduate schools and 1 graduate school. In addition to regional accreditation, Wayland has baccalaureate program accreditation with NASM. The library contains 119,105 volumes, 279,301 microform items, and 11,475 audio/video tapes/CDs/DVDs, and subscribes to 540 periodicals including electronic. Computerized library services include the card catalog, interlibrary loans, database searching, and Internet access. Special learning facilities include a learning resource center, art gallery, natural history museum, radio station, and TV station. The 80-acre campus is in a small town 45 miles north of Lubbock. Including any residence halls, there are 41 buildings.

Student Life: 85% of undergraduates are from Texas. Others are from 17 states, 14 foreign countries, and Canada. 62% are white; 23% Hispanic. 56% are Protestant; 10% Catholic. The average age of freshmen is 19; all undergraduates, 22. 31% do not continue beyond their first year; 33% remain to graduate.

Housing: 535 students can be accommodated in college housing, which includes single-sex dorms and married-student housing. On-campus housing is guaranteed for all 4 years. 51% of students live on campus. Alcohol is not permitted. All students may keep cars.

Activities: 3% of men belong to 1 national fraternity; 4% of women belong to 1 local and 1 national sorority. There are 35 groups on campus, including art, band, cheerleading, choir, chorale, chorus, computers, drama, honors, international, marching band, musical theater, newspaper, photography, political, professional, radio and TV, religious, social, social service, student government, and yearbook. Popular campus events include Pride Week, Big Weekend, and Miss Wayland.

Sports: There are 5 intercollegiate sports for men and 4 for women, and 7 intramural sports for men and 7 for women. Facilities include a 2500-seat gym, basketball/volleyball, racquetball, and tennis courts, and an aerobics and weight training facility.

Disabled Students: All of the campus is accessible. Wheelchair ramps, elevators, special parking, specially equipped rest rooms, and special class scheduling are available.

Services: Counseling and information services are available, as is tutoring in every subject. There is a reader service for the blind, and remedial math, reading, and writing.

Campus Safety and Security: Measures include self-defense education, informal discussions, pamphlets/posters/films, and emergency telephones. There are lighted pathways/sidewalks and a security service on campus.

Programs of Study: Wayland confers B.A., B.S., B.B.A., B.C.M., B.M., B.S.I.S., and B.S.O.E. degrees. Associate and master's degrees are also awarded. Bachelor's degrees are awarded in BIOLOGICAL SCIENCE (biology/biological science), BUSINESS (business administration and management), COMMUNICATIONS AND THE ARTS (art, communications, dramatic arts, English, music, and Spanish), COMPUTER AND PHYSICAL SCIENCE (chemistry, mathematics, physical sciences, and science), EDUCATION (music, physical, and vocational), SOCIAL SCIENCE (criminal justice, history, human services, interdisciplinary studies, political science/government, psychology, religion, religious education, religious music, social science, and social studies). Religion, education, and social science are the strongest academically. Education, business, and religion are the largest.

Required: To graduate, all students must earn a GPA of at least 2.0 while taking 124 to 145 semester hours, with 30 to 42 in their major and 36 to 42 in upper-division hours. Distribution requirements include 12 hours of English; 8 to 16 in science; 6 each in Bible, history, and humanities; up to 6 in foreign language; 4 in phys ed; 3 to 6 in math; 3 in computer science; and 3 in philosophy, sociology, or psychology. Chapel attendance is also required. Honors students must complete a thesis.

Special: A cooperative education program with Texas Tech University, internships in social science, business administration, religion, education, and social work, and work-study plans through the Social Security Administration are available. In addition, credit for life and military experience is given in the individualized occupational education program. Nondegree study in the Community Classroom program is also offered. There are composite science, composite social science, all-level phys ed, and music programs available. There are 3 national honor societies and a freshman honors program.

Faculty/Classroom: 67% of faculty are male; 33%, female. All teach undergraduates. No introductory courses are taught by graduate stu-

dents. The average class size in an introductory lecture is 14; in a laboratory, 16; and in a regular course, 14.

Admissions: 44% of the current freshmen were in the top fifth of their class; 73% were in the top two fifths. 3 freshmen graduated first in their class.

Requirements: The SAT or ACT is required. In addition, Wayland requires graduation from an accredited secondary school with 3 years of English and 2 years each of science, math, and social science. The GED is accepted. Wayland requires applicants to be in the upper 50% of their class. AP and CLEP credits are accepted.

Procedure: Freshmen are admitted to all sessions. There is a rolling admissions plan Application deadlines are open. Applications are accepted on-line. The fall 2005 application fee was $35.

Transfer: 93 transfer students enrolled in 2004-2005. Applicants need a minimum GPA of 2.0 and must be able to reenter all colleges previously attended. 30 of 124 to 145 credits required for the bachelor's degree must be completed at Wayland.

Visiting: There are regularly scheduled orientations for prospective students. There are guides for informal visits and visitors may sit in on classes and stay overnight. To schedule a visit, contact Shawn Thomas, Director of Admissions at sthomas@wbu.edu.

Financial Aid: In 2005-2006, 84% of all full-time freshmen and 95% of continuing full-time students received some form of financial aid. 79% of full-time freshmen and 89% of continuing full-time students received need-based aid. The average freshman award was $9068. Need-based scholarships or need-based grants averaged $3768 ($9994 maximum); need-based self-help aid (loans and jobs) averaged $2151 ($9921 maximum); non-need-based athletic scholarships averaged $3928 ($14,500 maximum); and other non-need-based awards and non-need-based scholarships averaged $4096 ($16,400 maximum). 13% of undergraduates work part time. Average annual earnings from campus work are $2472. The average financial indebtedness of the 2005 graduate was $21,700. Wayland is a member of CSS. The FAFSA and the college's own financial statement are required. The deadline for filing freshman financial aid applications for fall entry is May 1.

International Students: There are 18 international students enrolled. The school actively recruits these students. They must score satisfactorily on the TOEFL and also take the SAT or the ACT.

Computers: There are 123 PCs available in division labs and at the LRC. Network is available on all university PCs and in dorm rooms. All students may access the system during posted lab hours. There are no time limits and no fees.

Graduates: From July 1, 2004 to June 30, 2005, 144 bachelor's degrees were awarded. The most popular majors were business administration (21%), religion (10%), and physical education (9%). In an average class, 1% graduate in 3 years or less, 18% graduate in 4 years or less, 28% graduate in 5 years or less, and 32% graduate in 6 years or less.

Admissions Contact: Shawn Thomas, Director of Admissions.
E-mail: admityou@wbu.edu Web: www.wbu.edu

WEST TEXAS A&M UNIVERSITY   B-1

Canyon, TX 79016   (806) 651-2020
                            (800) 99-WTAMU; Fax: (806) 651-5285

Full-time: 1891 men, 2442 women	**Faculty:** 210; IIA, --$
Part-time: 552 men, 703 women	**Ph.D.s:** 70%
Graduate: 548 men, 892 women	**Student/Faculty:** 21 to 1
Year: semesters, summer session	**Tuition:** $3756 ($12,036)
Application Deadline: open	**Room & Board:** $4696
Freshman Class: 1665 applied, 1204 accepted, 801 enrolled	
SAT Verbal/Math: 500/510*	**ACT:** 21 COMPETITIVE

West Texas A&M University, a member of the Texas A.M. University System, founded in 1910, is a public institution offering programs in the liberal arts and sciences, fine arts, agriculture, nursing, and education. There are 4 undergraduate schools and 1 graduate school. In addition to regional accreditation, WTAMU has baccalaureate program accreditation with ACBSP, CCNE, CSWE, and NASM. The 2 libraries contain 1,080,810 volumes, 1,266,671 microform items, and 1555 audio/video tapes/CDs/DVDs, and subscribe to 16,973 periodicals including electronic. Computerized library services include the card catalog, interlibrary loans, database searching, Internet access, and laptop Internet portals. Special learning facilities include a learning resource center, art gallery, natural history museum, radio station, an alternative energy institute, an electronic learning center, a communications disorders center, and a nursing learning center. The 135-acre campus is in a small town 17 miles south of Amarillo. Including any residence halls, there are 82 buildings.

Student Life: 90% of undergraduates are from Texas. Others are from 39 states, 26 foreign countries, and Canada. 93% are from public schools. 76% are white; 14% Hispanic. The average age of freshmen is 18; all undergraduates, 24. 36% do not continue beyond their first year; 66% remain to graduate.

Housing: 1520 students can be accommodated in college housing, which includes single-sex and coed dormitories. In addition, there are special-interest houses, sorority units within the residence halls, 24-hour

quiet areas, and an honors hall. On-campus housing is guaranteed for all 4 years. 82% of students commute. Alcohol is not permitted. All students may keep cars.

Activities: 4% of men belong to 1 local and 4 national fraternities; 4% of women belong to 2 local and 3 national sororities. There are 97 groups on campus, including academic, art, band, cheerleading, choir, chorale, chorus, computers, dance, debate, drama, ethnic, film, forensics, honors, international, jazz band, literary magazine, marching band, musical theater, newspaper, opera, orchestra, photography, political, professional, radio and TV, religious, social, social service, student government, and symphony. Popular campus events include Workathon, RHA Mud Pull, and Buffalo Branding.

Sports: There are 6 intercollegiate sports for men and 6 for women, and 39 intramural sports for men and 39 for women. Facilities include a swimming pool, an 8-lane bowling alley, weight-training rooms, a 20,000-seat stadium, an event center, handball, racquetball, tennis, badminton, basketball, and volleyball courts, a flag football field, and softball fields.

Disabled Students: All of the campus is accessible. Wheelchair ramps, elevators, special parking, specially equipped rest rooms, special class scheduling, lowered drinking fountains, lowered telephones, and special housing are available.

Services: Counseling and information services are available, as is tutoring in most subjects, including core curriculum courses. There is a reader service for the blind, and remedial math, reading, and writing.

Campus Safety and Security: Measures include 24-hour foot and vehicle patrol, self-defense education, security escort services, and shuttle buses. There are informal discussions, pamphlets/posters/films, emergency telephones, lighted pathways/sidewalks, and shuttle buses provided by city transport.

Programs of Study: WTAMU confers B.A., B.S., B.A.A.S., B.B.A., B.F.A., B.G.S., B.M., B.S.M.T., and B.S.N. degrees. Master's and doctoral degrees are also awarded. Bachelor's degrees are awarded in AGRICULTURE (agricultural business management, agricultural economics, agriculture, animal science, plant protection (pest management), plant science, and soil science), BIOLOGICAL SCIENCE (biology/biological science, biotechnology, and wildlife biology), BUSINESS (accounting, banking and finance, business administration and management, business economics, management science, and marketing/retailing/merchandising), COMMUNICATIONS AND THE ARTS (applied art, art, broadcasting, dance, dramatic arts, English, graphic design, music, music theory and composition, musical theater, performing arts, public relations, publishing, Spanish, speech/debate/rhetoric, and studio art), COMPUTER AND PHYSICAL SCIENCE (chemistry, computer science, geology, information sciences and systems, mathematics, and physics), EDUCATION (art, athletic training, business, drama, English, foreign languages, mathematics, music, physical, reading, science, social studies, and special), ENGINEERING AND ENVIRONMENTAL DESIGN (emergency/disaster science, engineering technology, environmental science, mechanical engineering, and preengineering), HEALTH PROFESSIONS (allied health, exercise science, medical technology, music therapy, nursing, predentistry, premedicine, prepharmacy, preveterinary science, and speech pathology/audiology), SOCIAL SCIENCE (criminal justice, economics, geography, history, interdisciplinary studies, liberal arts/general studies, political science/government, prelaw, psychology, public administration, social science, social work, and sociology). Education and music are the strongest academically. Education is the largest.

Required: A general education requirement of 46 hours includes courses in analytic reasoning and communication skills, cultural heritage, English, computer literacy, math, science, history, political science, humanities, and sports and exercise sciences. Additional core requirements vary according to major. A minimum 2.0 GPA and 127 credit hours, including at least 36 of advanced work, up to a maximum of 60, 30 of which must be at WTAMU, are required to graduate. At least 33 hours must be earned in residence at WTAMU, including at least 24 of the last 30 hours counted toward a degree.

Special: WTAMU offers work-study programs, a Washington semester, internships, co-op programs, credit by exam, B.A.-B.S. degrees, a general studies degree, interdisciplinary studies in elementary/secondary education fields, nondegree study, and pass/fail options. There are 12 national honor societies, a freshman honors program, and 14 departmental honors programs.

Faculty/Classroom: 56% of faculty are male; 44%, female. 95% teach undergraduates, 47% do research, and 44% do both. Graduate students teach 16% of introductory courses. The average class size in an introductory lecture is 28; in a laboratory, 23; and in a regular course, 26.

Admissions: 72% of the 2005-2006 applicants were accepted. The SAT scores for the 2005-2006 freshman class were: Verbal--50% below 500, 35% between 500 and 599, 14% between 600 and 700, and 2% above 700; Math--44% below 500, 42% between 500 and 599, and 14% between 600 and 700. The ACT scores were 49% below 21, 28% between 21 and 23, 15% between 24 and 26, 5% between 27 and 28, and 2% above 28. 44% of the current freshmen were in the top fifth of their class; 82% were in the top two fifths. There was 1 National Merit finalist. 27 freshmen graduated first in their class.

Requirements: The SAT or ACT is required. In addition, applicants should have graduated from an accredited secondary school or have a GED. Admission requires graduation in the top 50% of the student's high school class or a minimum composite score of 20 on the ACT or a comparable score on the SAT. WTAMU requires applicants to be in the upper 50% of their class. AP and CLEP credits are accepted.

Procedure: Freshmen are admitted to all sessions. Entrance exams should be taken in the fall of the senior year. There are deferred admissions and rolling admissions plans. Application deadlines are open. Application fee is $25. Applications are accepted on-line.

Transfer: 799 transfer students enrolled in 2004-2005. A 2.0 GPA is generally required for transfer students. 30 of 127 credits required for the bachelor's degree must be completed at WTAMU.

Visiting: There are regularly scheduled orientations for prospective students, including a tour of campus, admissions and financial services sessions, selection of a major, and a visit with faculty. There are guides for informal visits and visitors may sit in on classes and stay overnight. To schedule a visit, contact the Admissions Office at (806) 651-2833.

Financial Aid: In 2005-2006, 51% of all full-time freshmen and 47% of continuing full-time students received some form of financial aid. 39% of full-time freshmen and 45% of continuing full-time students received need-based aid. The average freshman award was $5958. Need-based scholarships or need-based grants averaged $3282 ($4562 maximum); need-based self-help aid (loans and jobs) averaged $1376 ($2160 maximum); and work contracts averaged $260. 4% of undergraduates work part time. Average annual earnings from campus work are $1405. The FAFSA is required. The priority date for freshman financial aid applications for fall entry is April 15. The deadline for filing freshman financial aid applications for fall entry is May 1.

International Students: The school actively recruits these students. They must score satisfactorily on the written TOEFL or on the electronic version and also take the SAT or the ACT.

Computers: All students may access the system. There is limited wireless access. There are no time limits. The fee is $7 per hour up to a maximum of $ 50.

Graduates: From July 1, 2004 to June 30, 2005, 980 bachelor's degrees were awarded. The most popular majors were general studies (23%), business (19%), and nursing/interdisciplinary studies (10%). In an average class, 1% graduate in 3 years or less, 14% graduate in 4 years or less, 28% graduate in 5 years or less, and 32% graduate in 6 years or less. 299 companies recruited on campus in 2004-2005. Of the 2004 graduating class, 40% were enrolled in graduate school within 6 months of graduation.

Admissions Contact: Lila Vars, Director of Admissions. A video is available. E-mail: *lvars@mail.wtamu.edu* Web: *http://www.wtamu.edu*

WILEY COLLEGE   E-2
Marshall, TX 75670   (903) 927-3311; Fax: (903) 938-8100

Full-time: none	**Faculty:** 35
Part-time: none	**Ph.D.s:** 63%
Graduate: none	**Student/Faculty:** 21 to 1
Year: semesters, summer session	**Tuition:** n/av
Application Deadline: open	**Room & Board:** n/av
Freshman Class: n/av	
SAT or ACT: required	**LESS COMPETITIVE**

Wiley College, founded in 1873 as an institution for black students, is affiliated with the United Methodist Church. The college offers programs in the liberal arts, sciences, and teacher training. Figures in the above capsule and in this profile are approximate. The library contains 80,000 volumes, and subscribes to 298 periodicals including electronic. The 58-acre campus is in a small town 35 miles west of Shreveport.

Programs of Study: Wiley confers B.A., B.S., and B.B.A. degrees. Bachelor's degrees are awarded in BIOLOGICAL SCIENCE (biology/biological science), BUSINESS (business administration and management, hotel/motel and restaurant management, and office supervision and management), COMMUNICATIONS AND THE ARTS (communications, English, music, and music performance), COMPUTER AND PHYSICAL SCIENCE (chemistry, computer science, mathematics, and physics), EDUCATION (business, elementary, English, mathematics, music, physical, secondary, social science, and special), SOCIAL SCIENCE (history, liberal arts/general studies, philosophy, religion, social science, and sociology).

Required: Core requirements include courses in education, English, humanities, history, religion, science, and math. 2 credits in phys ed and 3 in computer science are required. A 2.0 GPA and 124 semester hours are needed to graduate.

Faculty/Classroom: All teach undergraduates.

Requirements: The SAT or ACT is required. In addition, applicants must be graduates of an accredited secondary school or have scored at least 40 on the GED. A letter of recommendation from a high school counselor or teacher is required. Wiley requires applicants to be in the upper 50% of their class. A GPA of 2.0 is required.

Procedure: There are early decision and early admissions plans. Application deadlines are open. Check with the school for current deadlines and fee.

Transfer: Transfer applicants must be in good standing at their last college. 30 of 124 credits required for the bachelor's degree must be completed at Wiley.

International Students: A satisfactory score is required on the written TOEFL.

Computers: All students may access the system. There are no time limits and no fees.

Admissions Contact: Bishop B. Curry, Director of Admissions.

UTAH

POPULATION DENSITY
● 25,000 and over

Miles
0 20 40 60 80 100

BRIGHAM YOUNG UNIVERSITY

C-2

Provo, UT 84602 (801) 422-2500; Fax: (801) 422-0005

Full-time: 13,837 men, 13,623 women **Faculty:** n/av
Part-time: 1723 men, 1615 women **Ph.D.s:** 98%
Graduate: 1988 men, 1281 women **Student/Faculty:** n/av
Year: varies by program, summer **Tuition:** $3410 ($5116)
session **Room & Board:** $5790
Application Deadline: February 15
Freshman Class: 8696 applied, 6794 accepted, 5365 enrolled
ACT: required **VERY COMPETITIVE**

Brigham Young University, founded in 1875, is a private university affiliated with the Church of Jesus Christ of Latter-day Saints. The university follows a semester calendar with spring and summer terms. Tuition figures in the above capsule apply to members of the Latter-day Saints community; the parenthetical figure applies to nonmembers. There are 10 undergraduate schools and 1 graduate school. In addition to regional accreditation, BYU has baccalaureate program accreditation with AACSB, ABET, ACCE, ACEJMC, ADA, APA, ASHA, ASLA, CAAHEP, CCNE, CSAB, CSWE, NAACLS, NASAD, NASD, NASDTEC, NASM, NCATE, NLN, and NRPA. The 2 libraries contain 3,535,706 volumes, 3,251,198 microform items, and 195,431 audio/video tapes/CDs/DVDs, and subscribe to 198,871 periodicals including electronic. Computerized library services include the card catalog, interlibrary loans, database searching, Internet access, and laptop Internet portals. Special learning facilities include a learning resource center, art gallery, natural history museum, planetarium, radio station, TV station, an archeological museum, an earth science museum, reading and writing labs, and math, language, and computer labs. The 557-acre campus is in a suburban area 45 miles south of Salt Lake City. Including any residence halls, there are 330 buildings.

Student Life: 71% of undergraduates are from out of state, mostly the West. Students are from 50 states, 121 foreign countries, and Canada. 86% are white. The average age of freshmen is 19; all undergraduates, 21. 18% do not continue beyond their first year; 70% remain to graduate.

Housing: 8040 students can be accommodated in college housing, which includes single-sex dormitories, on-campus apartments, and married-student housing. In addition, there are honors houses, language houses, and 1324 student family residences. On-campus housing is

available on a first-come, first-served basis. 80% of students commute. Alcohol is not permitted. All students may keep cars.

Activities: There are no fraternities or sororities. There are 390 groups on campus, including art, band, cheerleading, chess, choir, chorale, chorus, computers, dance, debate, drama, drill team, ethnic, film, honors, international, jazz band, literary magazine, marching band, musical theater, newspaper, opera, orchestra, pep band, photography, political, professional, radio and TV, religious, social, social service, student government, symphony, and yearbook. Popular campus events include Fall Fling, Spring Fling, and Preference Dances.

Sports: There are 10 intercollegiate sports for men and 11 for women, and 34 intramural sports for men and 32 for women. Facilities include pools, tennis and racquetball courts, gyms, tracks, fields, and a strength and conditioning complex.

Disabled Students: 97% of the campus is accessible. Wheelchair ramps, elevators, special parking, specially equipped rest rooms, special class scheduling, lowered drinking fountains, lowered telephones, special housing, automatic door operators, and an access ramp to pools are available.

Services: Counseling and information services are available, as is tutoring in most subjects. There is a reader service for the blind, and remedial math, reading, and writing.

Campus Safety and Security: Measures include 24-hour foot and vehicle patrol, self-defense education, security escort services, and informal discussions. There are pamphlets/posters/films, emergency telephones, lighted pathways/sidewalks, a bicycle patrol, academic building security officers from 7 P.M. to 2 A.M., and nighttime limited access to dorms.

Programs of Study: BYU confers B.A., B.S., B.F.A., B.G.S., B.M., and B.Mus. degrees. Master's and doctoral degrees are also awarded. Bachelor's degrees are awarded in AGRICULTURE (agricultural business management, environmental studies, plant science, and wildlife management), BIOLOGICAL SCIENCE (biochemistry, bioinformatics, biology/ biological science, biophysics, biotechnology, botany, microbiology, molecular biology, neurosciences, nutrition, physiology, plant genetics, and plant physiology), BUSINESS (accounting, business administration and management, management information systems, management science, marketing management, recreation and leisure services, and tourism), COMMUNICATIONS AND THE ARTS (advertising, animation, art, art history and appreciation, audio technology, Chinese, classical languages, classics, communications, comparative literature, dance, dramatic arts, English, fine arts, French, German, graphic design, Greek, illustration, industrial design, Italian, Japanese, jazz, Korean, Latin, linguistics, literature, media arts, music, music performance, music technology, music theory and composition, musical theater, performing arts, photography, Portuguese, public relations, Russian, Spanish, studio art, and visual and performing arts), COMPUTER AND PHYSICAL SCIENCE (actuarial science, astronomy, chemistry, computer science, geology, information sciences and systems, mathematics, physics, and statistics), EDUCATION (art, dance, drama, early childhood, elementary, English, home economics, mathematics, music, science, social science, special, and technical), ENGINEERING AND ENVIRONMENTAL DESIGN (chemical engineering, city/community/regional planning, civil engineering, computer engineering, construction management, electrical/ electronics engineering, electrical/electronics engineering technology, environmental design, food services technology, landscape architecture/ design, manufacturing engineering, manufacturing technology, and mechanical engineering), HEALTH PROFESSIONS (clinical science, exercise science, health science, nursing, and speech pathology/audiology), SOCIAL SCIENCE (American studies, anthropology, archeology, Asian/ American studies, Asian/Oriental studies, classical/ancient civilization, dietetics, economics, family/consumer studies, food science, geography, history, human development, humanities, international relations, Latin American studies, Middle Eastern studies, Near Eastern studies, philosophy, political science/government, psychology, social work, and sociology). Engineering, accounting, and business are the strongest academically. Business, communications, and exercise science are the largest.

Required: To graduate, students must complete 120 semester hours with a minimum GPA of 2.0. All students must take a total of 14 semester hours of religion and 2 hours of phys ed. There are general education requirements in English, advanced writing, foreign language or math, arts and letters, natural sciences, social sciences, and American heritage.

Special: Brigham Young offers cooperative programs, national and international internships, study abroad in 55 countries, a Washington semester, dual majors, nondegree study, and credit for life and work experience. There are 22 national honor societies, including Phi Beta Kappa, a freshman honors program, and honors programs in all departments.

Faculty/Classroom: 72% of faculty are male; 28%, female.

Admissions: 78% of the 2005-2006 applicants were accepted. The SAT scores for the 2005-2006 freshman class were: Verbal--9% below 500, 35% between 500 and 599, 41% between 600 and 700, and 15% above 700; Math--6% below 500, 32% between 500 and 599, 4% be-

tween 600 and 700, and 18% above 700. The ACT scores were 1% below 18, 16% between 18 and 23, 61% between 24 and 29, and 23% between 30 and 36. 49% of the current freshmen were in the top tenth of their class; 99% were in the top half. There were 110 National Merit finalists. 2614 freshmen graduated first in their class.

Requirements: The ACT is required. In addition, applicants must be graduates of an accredited secondary school. The GED is accepted. The school recommends that applicants complete 4 years of English, 3 years of math, and 2 courses in foreign language, lab science, history, and literature or writing. Essays and letters of recommendation are required with the application. AP and CLEP credits are accepted. Important factors in the admissions decision are advanced placement or honor courses, recommendations by school officials, and evidence of special talent.

Procedure: Freshmen are admitted to all sessions. Entrance exams should be taken by December of the senior year. There are early admissions and deferred admissions plans. Applications should be filed by February 15 for fall entry, October 1 for winter entry, February 15 for spring entry, and February 15 for summer entry, along with a $25 fee. Notification is sent on a rolling basis. Applications are accepted on-line.

Transfer: 2145 transfer students enrolled in 2004-2005. For applicants, primary consideration is given to basic general education subjects (English, math, history, and foreign languages) and major subjects. The GPA from those subjects must be near 3.5 to be competitive for admission. 30 of 120 credits required for the bachelor's degree must be completed at BYU.

Visiting: There are regularly scheduled orientations for prospective students, including a campus tour, visits with the prospective major's department and advisement center, and an interview with a school relations counselor. There are guides for informal visits and visitors may sit in on classes. To schedule a visit, contact Derek Spriggs at (801) 422-4431.

Financial Aid: In 2005-2006, 20% of all full-time freshmen and 40% of continuing full-time students received some form of financial aid. 13% of full-time freshmen and 29% of continuing full-time students received need-based aid. The average freshman award for 2004-2005 was $2593. Need-based scholarships or need-based grants averaged $1756; need-based self-help aid (loans and jobs) averaged $837; and other non-need-based awards and non-need-based scholarships averaged $2762. 40% of undergraduates work part time. Average annual earnings from campus work were $4800. The average financial indebtedness of the 2005 graduate was $12,955. The FAFSA is required. The deadline for filing freshman financial aid applications for fall entry is June 30.

International Students: There are about 2000 international students enrolled. They must take the TOEFL and also take the ACT.

Computers: Wireless access is available. 4,658 computers are available for student use, 847 of which are universally available for student use; the rest are controlled by colleges or departments. Students also have access to 5 supercomputers (see http://marylou.byu.edu) for research purposes. All students may access the system any time. There are no time limits and no fees. It is recommended that students in accounting, business, and law school have personal computers.

Graduates: From July 1, 2004 to June 30, 2005, 8234 bachelor's degrees were awarded. The most popular majors were business marketing (16%), education (12%), and visual and performing arts (7%). In an average class, 22% graduate in 4 years or less, 38% graduate in 5 years or less, and 70% graduate in 6 years or less. 430 companies recruited on campus in 2004-2005.

Admissions Contact: Tom Gourley, Director, Admissions Office. A video is available. E-mail: *admissions@byu.edu* Web: *www.byu.edu*

SOUTHERN UTAH UNIVERSITY — B-4

Cedar City, UT 84720   (435) 586-7740; Fax: (435) 865-8223

Full-time: 1895 men, 2386 women	**Faculty:** 211; IIA, --$
Part-time: 313 men, 394 women	**Ph.D.s:** 99%
Graduate: 175 men, 200 women	**Student/Faculty:** 20 to 1
Year: semesters, summer session	**Tuition:** n/av
Application Deadline: August 1	**Room & Board:** n/app
Freshman Class: 2492 applied, 2001 accepted, 1014 enrolled	
SAT Verbal/Math: 512/510*	**ACT:** 22 **COMPETITIVE**

Southern Utah University, founded in 1897, is part of the Utah System of Higher Education and offers undergraduate degrees in arts and letters, science, education, and business. There are 6 undergraduate and 3 graduate schools. In addition to regional accreditation, SUU has baccalaureate program accreditation with AACSB, ACBSP, NASDTEC, NASM, and NLN. The library contains 202,784 volumes, 673,985 microform items, and 17,969 audio/video tapes/CDs/DVDs, and subscribes to 1100 periodicals including electronic. Computerized library services include the card catalog, interlibrary loans, and database searching. Special learning facilities include a learning resource center, art gallery, natural history museum, planetarium, radio station, and TV station. The 133-acre campus is in a small town 170 miles north of Las Vegas. Including any residence halls, there are 76 buildings.

Student Life: 86% of undergraduates are from Utah. Students are from 45 states, 32 foreign countries, and Canada. 98% are from public schools. Most claim no religious affiliation. The average age of freshmen is 18; all undergraduates, 23. 41% do not continue beyond their first year; 34% remain to graduate.

Housing: 395 students can be accommodated in college housing, which includes single-sex and coed dorms, on-campus apartments, fraternity houses, and sorority houses. On-campus housing is available on a first-come, first-served basis. Priority is given to out-of-town students. 87% of students commute. Alcohol is not permitted. All students may keep cars.

Activities: 4% of men belong to 2 national fraternities; 3% of women belong to 1 local and 2 national sororities. There are 48 groups on campus, including art, bagpipe band, band, cheerleading, choir, chorale, chorus, computers, dance, drama, drill team, ethnic, forensics, gay, honors, international, jazz band, literary magazine, marching band, musical theater, newspaper, opera, orchestra, pep band, political, professional, radio and TV, religious, social, social service, student government, symphony, and yearbook. Popular campus events include Founders Day, dances, and service programs.

Sports: There are 7 intercollegiate sports for men and 8 for women, and 13 intramural sports for men and 13 for women. Facilities include a 10,000-seat stadium for football and for track and field, a baseball field, recreation grounds, a 5300-seat special events facility for basketball, volleyball, and gymnastics, tennis and racquetball courts, and large, all-weather practice areas. SUU owns and operates a 1000-acre farm and a 3700-acre ranch.

Disabled Students: 95% of the campus is accessible. Wheelchair ramps, elevators, special parking, specially equipped rest rooms, special class scheduling, lowered drinking fountains, lowered telephones, and special housing are available.

Services: Counseling and information services are available, as is tutoring in most subjects. There is a reader service for the blind, and remedial math, reading, and writing.

Campus Safety and Security: Measures include self-defense education, security escort services, informal discussions, and pamphlets/posters/films. There are emergency telephones and lighted pathways/sidewalks.

Programs of Study: SUU confers B.A., B.S., and B.I.S. degrees. Associate and master's degrees are also awarded. Bachelor's degrees are awarded in AGRICULTURE (agriculture), BIOLOGICAL SCIENCE (biology/biological science), BUSINESS (accounting, banking and finance, business administration and management, marketing management, and marketing/retailing/merchandising), COMMUNICATIONS AND THE ARTS (art, communications, dance, dramatic arts, English, French, German, music, and Spanish), COMPUTER AND PHYSICAL SCIENCE (chemistry, computer science, geology, information sciences and systems, and mathematics), EDUCATION (art, athletic training, business, dance, drama, elementary, English, foreign languages, mathematics, music, physical, science, social science, social studies, and special), ENGINEERING AND ENVIRONMENTAL DESIGN (construction management, and engineering technology), SOCIAL SCIENCE (criminal justice, economics, family/consumer studies, history, interdisciplinary studies, political science/government, psychology, and sociology). Business, science, and education are the strongest academically. Business and education are the largest.

Required: To graduate, all students must complete at least 122 credit hours with a minimum 2.0 GPA. Students must satisfy general education, major, minor, and basic skills requirements, including 4 courses each in social and physical sciences, 2 each in English, fine arts, and humanities, 1 each in math, phys ed, and communications, and a course in either history, political science, or economics to fulfill the U.S. government requirement. Other courses required for graduation include computer literacy and philosophy.

Special: SUU offers co-op programs with Weber State University, work-study programs, study abroad, dual majors, student-designed majors leading to a B.I.S. degree, and internships with government officials in Washington, D.C. Other programs offered include distance learning, ESL, independent study, liberal arts/career combinations, a teacher certification program, and weekend college. There are 3 national honor societies and 3 departmental honors programs.

Faculty/Classroom: 66% of faculty are male; 34%, female. All teach undergraduates and 65% do research. No introductory courses are taught by graduate students. The average class size in an introductory lecture is 29 and in a laboratory, 14.

Admissions: 80% of the 2005-2006 applicants were accepted. 45% of the current freshmen were in the top fifth of their class.

Requirements: The SAT or ACT is required; the ACT is recommended. In addition, applicants should be graduates of an accredited secondary school or have a GED, and should have completed 4 years of English, (composition and literature emphasis), 3 of math, at least 2 of which are elementary algebra or beyond, 3 each of biological/physical sciences (1 with a lab) and social studies including U.S. history/government, and 2 years of a foreign language. A GPA of 2.0 is required. AP and CLEP credits are accepted.

Procedure: Freshmen are admitted to all sessions. There are early admissions, deferred admissions, and rolling admissions plans. Applications should be filed by August 1 for fall entry, along with a $35 fee. Notification is sent immediately after application is received. Applications are accepted on-line.

Transfer: 652 transfer students enrolled in 2004-2005. Applicants must submit transcripts from previously attended colleges and have a minimum 2.25 GPA in college courses and a 2.0 high school GPA. ACT scores as well as high school transcripts are required from students who have not completed English or math courses at another institution or who have not completed a minimum of 30 credit hours at an institution of higher education. 30 upper-division credits and 50% of 122 credits required for the bachelor's degree must be completed at SUU.

Visiting: There are regularly scheduled orientations for prospective students, including campus tours, which can be arranged by appointment. There are guides for informal visits and visitors may sit in on classes and stay overnight. To schedule a visit, contact the Director of School Relations at (435) 586-7741.

Financial Aid: In 2005-2006, 80% of all full-time freshmen and 84% of continuing full-time students received some form of financial aid. At least 37% of full-time freshmen and 52% of continuing full-time students received need-based aid. The average freshman award was $3611. Need-based scholarships or need-based grants averaged $2530; need-based self-help aid (loans and jobs) averaged $881; institutional non-need-based athletic scholarships averaged $3852; and other institutional non-need-based awards and non-need-based scholarships averaged $3941. The average financial indebtedness of the 2005 graduate was $11,239. The FAFSA and the college's own financial statement are required. The deadline for filing freshman financial aid applications for fall entry is rolling.

International Students: The school actively recruits these students. A satisfactory score is required on the written TOEFL. Students must also take the SAT or the ACT.

Computers: All students may access the system.

Graduates: From July 1, 2004 to June 30, 2005, 971 bachelor's degrees were awarded. The most popular majors were education (28%), business/marketing (13%), and commuications/journalism (9%). In an average class, 15% graduate in 4 years or less, 22% graduate in 5 years or less, and 27% graduate in 6 years or less.

Admissions Contact: Dale S. Orton, Director of Admissions.
E-mail: *adminfo@suu.edu* Web: *www.suu.edu*

UNIVERSITY OF UTAH C-2

Salt Lake City, UT 84112-9056   **(801) 581-7281**
(800) 685-8856; Fax: (801) 585-3257

Full-time: 8666 men, 6885 women	**Faculty:** 806; I, --$
Part-time: 3909 men, 3201 women	**Ph.D.s:** 86%
Graduate: 3450 men, 2901 women	**Student/Faculty:** 19 to 1
Year: semesters, summer session	**Tuition:** $4340 ($13,528)
Application Deadline: April 1	**Room & Board:** $5822
Freshman Class: 6450 applied, 5505 accepted, 2631 enrolled	
ACT: 24*	**VERY COMPETITIVE**

University of Utah, founded in 1850, is a part of the Utah System of Higher Education. The university offers undergraduate degrees through the colleges of architecture, business, education, engineering, fine arts, health, humanities, nursing, medicine, mines and earth sciences, pharmacy, science, and social and behavioral science. There are 14 undergraduate and 16 graduate schools. In addition to regional accreditation, U of U has baccalaureate program accreditation with AACSB, ABET, ACEJMC, ACPE, ADA, APTA, CSWE, NAAB, NASM, and NLN. The 3 libraries contain 3,152,586 volumes, 3,580,127 microform items, and 65,882 audio/video tapes/CDs/DVDs, and subscribe to 40,690 periodicals including electronic. Computerized library services include the card catalog, interlibrary loans, database searching, Internet access, and laptop Internet portals. Special learning facilities include a learning resource center, art gallery, natural history museum, radio station, TV station, and an arboretum. The 1535-acre campus is in an urban area in Salt Lake City. Including any residence halls, there are 335 buildings.

Student Life: 90% of undergraduates are from Utah. Others are from 50 states, 100 foreign countries, and Canada. 86% are white. The average age of freshmen is 22; all undergraduates, 25. 31% do not continue beyond their first year; 56% remain to graduate.

Housing: 2400 students can be accommodated in college housing, which includes single-sex and coed dormitories, on-campus apartments, off-campus apartments, married-student housing, fraternity houses, and sorority houses. In addition, there are honors houses and special-interest houses. On-campus housing is available on a first-come, first-served basis. 91% of students commute. Alcohol is not permitted. All students may keep cars.

Activities: 1% of men belong to 8 national fraternities; 1% of women belong to 7 national sororities. There are 300 groups on campus, including art, band, cheerleading, chess, choir, chorale, chorus, computers, dance, drama, drill team, drum and bugle corps, ethnic, film, gay, hon-

ors, international, jazz band, marching band, musical theater, opera, orchestra, pep band, photography, political, professional, radio and TV, religious, social, social service, student government, symphony, and yearbook. Popular campus events include Mayfest, Plazafest, and Autumn Openings.

Sports: There are 10 intercollegiate sports for men and 14 for women, and 68 intramural sports for men and 61 for women. Facilities include a 45635-seat stadium, a 15500-seat basketball arena, 6 indoor gyms, 13 indoor and 22 outdoor tennis courts, 3 indoor swimming pools, a gymnastics room, 5 weight rooms, 19 handball/racquetball/squash courts, a 200-meter indoor track, a 9-hole golf course, 3 outdoor playing fields, a 10-lane bowling alley, a movie theater, video games, and a big-screen TV.

Disabled Students: 93% of the campus is accessible. Wheelchair ramps, elevators, special parking, specially equipped rest rooms, special class scheduling, lowered drinking fountains, lowered telephones, and special housing are available.

Services: Counseling and information services are available, as is tutoring in most subjects. There is a reader service for the blind and remedial math and writing. There are also support services for the deaf, including readers, scribers, tutors, and interpreters.

Campus Safety and Security: Measures include 24-hour foot and vehicle patrol, self-defense education, security escort services, and shuttle buses. There are informal discussions, pamphlets/posters/films, emergency telephones, and lighted pathways/sidewalks.

Programs of Study: U of U confers B.A., B.S., B.F.A., B.Mus., B.S.W., and B.U.S. degrees. Master's and doctoral degrees are also awarded. Bachelor's degrees are awarded in AGRICULTURE (environmental studies), BIOLOGICAL SCIENCE (biology/biological science), BUSINESS (accounting, banking and finance, business administration and management, business economics, management information systems, and marketing/retailing/merchandising), COMMUNICATIONS AND THE ARTS (art, art history and appreciation, ballet, Chinese, classics, communications, dance, dramatic arts, English, film arts, French, German, Japanese, linguistics, media arts, music, Russian, Spanish, and visual and performing arts), COMPUTER AND PHYSICAL SCIENCE (atmospheric sciences and meteorology, chemistry, computer science, geology, geophysics and seismology, mathematics, and physics), EDUCATION (elementary, health, social science, special, and teaching English as a second/foreign language (TESOL/TEFOL)), ENGINEERING AND ENVIRONMENTAL DESIGN (architecture, bioengineering, biomedical engineering, chemical engineering, civil engineering, computer engineering, electrical/electronics engineering, engineering, environmental engineering, geological engineering, materials engineering, mechanical engineering, metallurgical engineering, mining and mineral engineering, and urban planning technology), HEALTH PROFESSIONS (exercise science, medical laboratory science, nursing, occupational therapy, physical therapy, public health, and speech pathology/audiology), SOCIAL SCIENCE (anthropology, Asian/Oriental studies, behavioral science, economics, family/consumer studies, geography, history, human development, humanities, international studies, Middle Eastern studies, parks and recreation management, philosophy, political science/government, psychology, social science, sociology, urban studies, and women's studies). Social and behavioral sciences and business are strongest academically and are the largest.

Required: To graduate, all students must satisfy requirements in the general education and intellectual exploration programs. The core curriculum consists of 1 course each in American institutions and lower division writing; 2 in quantitative reasoning and 2 each in fine arts, humanities, physical science, and social science, excluding their major area.Students must complete at least 183 credit hours, with 45 to 60 in the major. A minimum 2.0 GPA is required.

Special: The university offers numerous opportunities for cooperative programs, cross-registration through the Western Interstate Commission for Higher Education (WICHE), study abroad in 14 countries, internships, work-study and accelerated degree programs, and B.A.-B.S. degrees. Also available are the general studies degree, a Washington semester, student-designed and dual majors, credit for telecourses and military experience, nondegree study, and pass/fail options. There are 42 national honor societies, including Phi Beta Kappa, a freshman honors program, and 30 departmental honors programs.

Faculty/Classroom: 61% of faculty are male; 39%, female. 75% teach undergraduates. Graduate students teach 20% of introductory courses. The average class size in an introductory lecture is 40 and in a laboratory, 20.

Admissions: 85% of the 2005-2006 applicants were accepted. The ACT scores for the 2005-2006 freshman class were: 21% below 21, 28% between 21 and 23, 24% between 24 and 26, 12% between 27 and 28, and 15% above 28. 40% of the current freshmen were in the top fifth of their class; 70% were in the top two fifths. There were 21 National Merit finalists and 197 semifinalists. 55 freshmen graduated first in their class.

Requirements: The ACT is required. The SAT is accepted. In addition, applicants must be graduates of an accredited secondary school or have the GED. 15 academic credits are required, including 4 years each of

English and electives, 3 years of biological and /or physical science, 2 years each of foreign language, and math, 1 year of history. A GPA of 2.6 is required. AP and CLEP credits are accepted.

Procedure: Freshmen are admitted to all sessions. Entrance exams should be taken in the junior year of high school. There is an early admissions and a rolling admissions plan. Applications should be filed by April 1 for fall entry, November 1 for winter entry, November 1 for spring entry, and March 15 for summer entry, along with a $35 fee. Notification of early decision is sent rolling ; regular decision, on a rolling basis. Applications are accepted on-line.

Transfer: 2152 transfer students enrolled in 2004-2005. Transfer students must have completed at least 45 quarter (30 semester) hours with a minimum 2.6 GPA.

Visiting: There are regularly scheduled orientations for prospective students, including an information session with an admissions counselor to discuss academic and student involvement opportunities, scholarships, financial aid, admissions requirements, deadlines, along with a campus tour and tour of residence halls. If time permits, prospective students are encouraged to meet with academic advisors on various majors, visit classrooms and stay overnight in a residence hall. To schedule a visit, contact Connie Smith, Office of Student Recruitment.

Financial Aid: In 2005-2006, 42% of all full-time freshmen and 45% of continuing full-time students received some form of financial aid. 31% of full-time freshmen and 42% of continuing full-time students received need-based aid. The average freshman award was $7506. Need-based scholarships or need-based grants averaged $4414 ($26,764 maximum); need-based self-help aid (loans and jobs) averaged $3860 ($25,870 maximum); non-need-based athletic scholarships averaged $13,735 ($16,790 maximum); and other non-need-based awards and non-need-based scholarships averaged $2819 ($19,784 maximum). The average financial indebtedness of the 2005 graduate was $12,806. The FAFSA and the college's own financial statement are required. The priority date for freshman financial aid applications for fall entry is March 15.

International Students: There are 741 international students enrolled. They must score satisfactorily on the written TOEFL or on the electronic version. The ACT with a satisfactory score is required if the student graduated from a U.S. high school.

Computers: Wireless access is available. Numerous locations around campus are available for wireless access. All students may access the system 24 hours per day. There are no time limits. The fee is approximately $16 per credit.

Graduates: From July 1, 2004 to June 30, 2005, 5198 bachelor's degrees were awarded. The most popular majors were economics (6%), mass communications (5%), and political science (5%). In an average class, 24% graduate in 4 years or less, 45% graduate in 5 years or less, and 60% graduate in 6 years or less. 106 companies recruited on campus in 2004-2005.

Admissions Contact: John W. Boswell, Director of Admissions.
E-mail: *admissions@sa.utah.edu*
Web: *http://www.sa.utah.edu/admiss/index.htm*

UTAH STATE UNIVERSITY   C-1

Logan, UT 84322	**(435) 797-1129; Fax: (435) 797-3708**
Full-time: 5418 men, 5310 women	**Faculty:** 756; I, --$
Part-time: 1060 men, 949 women	**Ph.D.s:** 82%
Graduate: 1049 men, 672 women	**Student/Faculty:** 14 to 1
Year: semesters, summer session	**Tuition:** $3672 ($10,616)
Application Deadline: July 1	**Room & Board:** $4330
Freshman Class: 2054 enrolled	
SAT Verbal/Math: 540/570*	**ACT:** 24 **VERY COMPETITIVE**

Utah State University, founded in 1888, is a public institution that offers degree programs in the liberal arts and sciences, agriculture and natural resources, engineering, business, education, fine arts, music, family life, and the sciences. There are 7 undergraduate schools and 1 graduate school. In addition to regional accreditation, USU has baccalaureate program accreditation with AACSB, ABET, ADA, AHEA, ASLA, CSWE, FIDER, NASM, NCATE, NRPA, and SAF. The 3 libraries contain 1,377,026 volumes, 2,627,929 microform items, and 21,714 audio/video tapes/CDs/DVDs, and subscribe to 12,759 periodicals including electronic. Computerized library services include the card catalog, interlibrary loans, and database searching. Special learning facilities include a learning resource center, art gallery, radio station, TV station, laboratory school, historical farm, fine arts center, and developmental center for people who are handicapped. The 332-acre campus is in a small town 86 miles north of Salt Lake City. Including any residence halls, there are 104 buildings.

Student Life: 71% of undergraduates are from Utah. Others are from 49 states, 57 foreign countries, and Canada. 91% are white. The average age of freshmen is 20; all undergraduates, 23. 31% do not continue beyond their first year; 57% remain to graduate.

Housing: 3400 students can be accommodated in college housing, which includes single-sex dorms, on-campus apartments, married-student housing, fraternity houses, and sorority houses. In addition,

there are honors houses and special-interest houses. On-campus housing is available on a first-come, first-served basis. Alcohol is not permitted. All students may keep cars.

Activities: 2% of men belong to 1 local and 4 national fraternities; 2% of women belong to 1 local and 3 national sororities. There are 280 groups on campus, including art, band, cheerleading, choir, chorale, chorus, computers, dance, drama, drill team, ethnic, film, gay, honors, international, jazz band, literary magazine, marching band, musical theater, newspaper, opera, orchestra, pep band, photography, political, professional, radio and TV, religious, social, social service, student government, and symphony. Popular campus events include Festival of the American West, Founders Day, and Christmas Dinner at the Manor House.

Sports: There are 7 intercollegiate sports for men and 9 for women, and 23 intramural sports for men and 23 for women. Facilities include 5 gyms, indoor and outdoor tennis courts, 2 swimming pools, 40 acres of grass for outdoor sports, a field house, and golf and skiing areas. The campus stadium seats 30,257 and the largest auditorium seats 10,000.

Disabled Students: 95% of the campus is accessible. Wheelchair ramps, elevators, special parking, specially equipped rest rooms, special class scheduling, lowered drinking fountains, lowered telephones, special phones to receive calls from the deaf, and a disability resource center are available.

Services: Counseling and information services are available, as is tutoring in every subject. There is a reader service for the blind, and remedial math, reading, and writing. There is also a writing lab and a tutor room.

Campus Safety and Security: Measures include 24-hour foot and vehicle patrol, self-defense education, security escort services, and shuttle buses. There are informal discussions, pamphlets/posters/films, emergency telephones, lighted pathways/sidewalks, and and campus police.

Programs of Study: USU confers B.A., B.S., B.F.A., B.L.A., and B.M. degrees. Associate, master's, and doctoral degrees are also awarded. Bachelor's degrees are awarded in AGRICULTURE (agricultural business management, agricultural economics, animal science, dairy science, forestry and related sciences, international agriculture, natural resource management, plant science, range/farm management, soil science, and wildlife management), BIOLOGICAL SCIENCE (biochemistry, biology/biological science, and microbiology), BUSINESS (accounting, banking and finance, business administration and management, business economics, fashion merchandising, international business management, management information systems, marketing/retailing/merchandising, and personnel management), COMMUNICATIONS AND THE ARTS (dance, dramatic arts, English, fine arts, French, German, journalism, music, and Spanish), COMPUTER AND PHYSICAL SCIENCE (chemistry, computer science, earth science, geology, information sciences and systems, mathematics, physics, and statistics), EDUCATION (agricultural, art, business, early childhood, elementary, foreign languages, health, home economics, industrial arts, mathematics, music, physical, science, secondary, and special), ENGINEERING AND ENVIRONMENTAL DESIGN (agricultural engineering, civil engineering, electrical/electronics engineering, engineering, environmental science, industrial engineering, industrial engineering technology, interior design, landscape architecture/design, and mechanical engineering), HEALTH PROFESSIONS (medical laboratory technology, music therapy, predentistry, premedicine, public health, speech pathology/audiology, and veterinary science), SOCIAL SCIENCE (American studies, child care/child and family studies, economics, food science, geography, history, home economics, human development, international relations, liberal arts/general studies, parks and recreation management, philosophy, political science/government, prelaw, psychology, social work, and sociology). Natural resources, engineering, and special education are the strongest academically. Humanities, arts, and social science are the largest.

Required: The core curriculum of 30 semester credits includes at least 6 of writing; the total number of credits required for graduation is 120. Students must maintain a minimum GPA of 2.5. The number of credits required in the major varies, but there is a minimum of 40 in major classes.

Special: Internships are available in most departments through the Cooperative Education Program. The National Student Exchange Program allows students to cross-register in designated institutions and programs, and the International Student Exchange Program enables students to study abroad.There is also cross-registration with the University of Americas of Mexico. A general studies degree and student-designed majors are available. Nondegree study, work-study programs, co-op programs, B.A.-B.S. degrees, pass/fail options, and credit for military experience are offered. There are 11 national honor societies, a freshman honors program, and 35 departmental honors programs.

Faculty/Classroom: 65% of faculty are male; 35%, female. Graduate students teach 6% of introductory courses. The average class size in an introductory lecture is 35; in a laboratory, 20; and in a regular course, 25.

Admissions: The SAT scores for the 2005-2006 freshman class were: Verbal--33% below 500, 36% between 500 and 599, 25% between 600 and 700, and 6% above 700; Math--21% below 500, 43% between 500 and 599, 32% between 600 and 700, and 4% above 700. The ACT scores were 24% below 21, 25% between 21 and 23, 25% between 24 and 26, 14% between 27 and 28, and 12% above 28. 44% of the current freshmen were in the top fifth of their class; 71% were in the top two fifths. There were 25 National Merit finalists. 107 freshmen graduated first in their class.

Requirements: The SAT or ACT is required; the ACT is preferred. In addition, students should graduate from an accredited secondary school with 15 academic units, including 4 in English, 3 each in math and science, and 1 in social sciences. GED equivalency is accepted, provided ACT scores are satisfactory. Students not meeting entrance requirements may be considered for admission on a provisional basis. A GPA of 2.7 is required. AP and CLEP credits are accepted. Important factors in the admissions decision are evidence of special talent, parents or siblings attending the school, and recommendations by school officials.

Procedure: Freshmen are admitted to all sessions. Entrance exams should be taken in the spring of the junior year. There are early decision, early admissions, rolling admissions, and deferred admissions plans. Applications should be filed by July 1 for fall entry, November 1 for spring entry, and May 1 for summer entry, along with a $40 fee. Notification is sent on a rolling basis. Applications are accepted on-line.

Transfer: 968 transfer students enrolled in 2004-2005. A minimum 2.2 GPA, higher for some majors, is required for transfer students. Those applicants with fewer than 45 credits must also submit ACT scores. 30 of 120 credits required for the bachelor's degree must be completed at USU.

Visiting: There are regularly scheduled orientations for prospective students, a campus tour, including meeting with an academic adviser, lunch, and a housing tour, available at 10:30 A.M. and 1:30 P.M., September to May and 1:30 P.M., June to August. There are guides for informal visits and visitors may sit in on classes and stay overnight. To schedule a visit, contact Jimmy Moore at (435) 797-3963 or *jimmymo@cc.usu.edu.*

Financial Aid: 59% of undergraduates work part time. USU is a member of CSS. The FAFSA, the college's own financial statement, and student/parent tax forms are required.

International Students: There are 446 international students enrolled. They must score satisfactorily on the TOEFL or MELAB. The TOEFL is preferred.

Computers: Wireless access is available. All students may access the system 24 hours a day, 7 days a week. There are no time limits. The fee is $10 to $27.

Graduates: From July 1, 2004 to June 30, 2005, 2609 bachelor's degrees were awarded. The most popular majors were family and human development (5%), accounting (4%), and business information systems (4%). In an average class, 57% graduate in 6 years or less. 185 companies recruited on campus in 2004-2005. Of the 2004 graduating class, 20% were enrolled in graduate school within 6 months of graduation and 72% were employed.

Admissions Contact: Jimmy Moore, Director, Admissions Office. E-mail: *admit@cc.usu.edu* Web: *www.usu.edu*

UTAH SYSTEM OF HIGHER EDUCATION

The Utah System of Higher Education, established in 1969, is a public system. It is governed by a state Board of Regents whose chief administrator is commissioner of higher education. The primary goals of the system are teaching, research, and public service. The main priorities are to provide a high-quality, efficient, and economical public system of higher education; to coordinate, consolidate, and avoid unnecessary duplication; and to systematically develop the role of each institution within the system. The enrollment is approximately 144,000, with about 4,200 full-time faculty members. These numbers do not include the Utah College of Applied Technology, which serves secondary and post-secondary students in open-entry, open-exit, technical, and vocational training. 4-year campuses are located in Salt Lake City, Logan, Ogden, Cedar City, Orem, and St. George. Profiles of some campuses are included in this section. For more information, visit *www.utahsbr.edu.*

WEBER STATE UNIVERSITY   C-1

Ogden, UT 84408-	(801) 626-7670; Fax: (801) 626-6747
Full-time: 5324 men, 4926 women	Faculty: 452; IIA, --$
Part-time: 3443 men, 3935 women	Ph.D.s: 92%
Graduate: 188 men, 216 women	Student/Faculty: 23 to 1
Year: semesters, summer session	Tuition: $3164 ($9599)
Application Deadline: July 1	Room & Board: $6471
Freshman Class: 5196 applied, 5196 accepted, 2820 enrolled	
SAT Verbal/Math: 506/497*	ACT: 22 NONCOMPETITIVE

Weber State University, founded in 1889 and part of the Utah System of Higher Education, is a public, primarily commuter institution offering undergraduate degrees in health sciences, arts and humanities, business and economics, education, natural sciences, social sciences, and technology, and graduate degrees in education, professional accountancy, business management, and criminal justice. There are 7 undergraduate and 4 graduate schools. In addition to regional accreditation, WSU has baccalaureate program accreditation with AACSB, ADA, CAHEA, CSWE, FIDER, NASM, NCATE, and NLN. The library contains 520,530 volumes, 595,834 microform items, and 20,735 audio/video tapes/CDs/DVDs, and subscribes to 1711 periodicals including electronic. Computerized library services include the card catalog, interlibrary loans, database searching, and Internet access. Special learning facilities include a learning resource center, art gallery, natural history museum, planetarium, radio station, TV station, observatory, and a working crime lab. The 526-acre campus is in an urban area 35 miles north of Salt Lake City. Including any residence halls, there are 61 buildings.

Student Life: 93% of undergraduates are from Utah. Others are from 49 states, 40 foreign countries, and Canada. 99% are from public schools. 61% are white. 63% are Church of Jesus Christ of Latter-day Saints; 30% claim no religious affiliation; 6% Protestant. The average age of freshmen is 19; all undergraduates, 25. 33% do not continue beyond their first year; 45% remain to graduate.

Housing: 644 students can be accommodated in college housing, which includes single-sex and coed dorms and on-campus apartments. On-campus housing is guaranteed for all 4 years and is available on a first-come, first-served basis. 97% of students commute. Alcohol is not permitted. All students may keep cars.

Activities: 1% of men belong to 3 national fraternities; 1% of women belong to 3 local sororities. There are 100 groups on campus, including art, band, cheerleading, chess, choir, chorale, chorus, computers, dance, debate, drama, drill team, drum and bugle corps, ethnic, forensics, honors, international, jazz band, literary magazine, marching band, musical theater, newspaper, opera, orchestra, pep band, photography, political, professional, radio and TV, religious, social, social service, student government, and symphony. Popular campus events include SunFest, WinterFest, and Crystal Crest.

Sports: There are 5 intercollegiate sports for men and 5 for women, and 36 intramural sports for men and 36 for women. Facilities include an indoor track, a strength-training center, 3 indoor basketball courts, a swimming pool, racquetball and tennis courts, a 17,000-seat stadium, an 11,515-seat gym, a 7800-seat auditorium/arena, an events center, playing fields, an exercise/conditioning room, and a 1-mile jogging trail.

Disabled Students: 99% of the campus is accessible. Wheelchair ramps, elevators, special parking, specially equipped rest rooms, special class scheduling, lowered drinking fountains, lowered telephones, and special housing are available.

Services: Counseling and information services are available, as is tutoring in every subject. There is a reader service for the blind, and remedial math, reading, and writing. Translators are offered for the hearing impaired.

Campus Safety and Security: Measures include 24-hour foot and vehicle patrol, self-defense education, security escort services, and shuttle buses. There are informal discussions, pamphlets/posters/films, emergency telephones, and lighted pathways/sidewalks.

Programs of Study: WSU confers B.A., B.S., B.F.A., B.I.S., and B.M. degrees. Associate and master's degrees are also awarded. Bachelor's degrees are awarded in BIOLOGICAL SCIENCE (biology/biological science, botany, microbiology, and zoology), BUSINESS (accounting, banking and finance, business administration and management, business economics, human resources, management information systems, marketing management, personnel management, and purchasing/inventory management), COMMUNICATIONS AND THE ARTS (communications, dance, dramatic arts, English, fine arts, French, German, graphic design, journalism, media arts, music, music performance, musical theater, photography, piano/organ, public relations, Spanish, visual and performing arts, and voice), COMPUTER AND PHYSICAL SCIENCE (chemistry, computer programming, computer science, earth science, geology, information sciences and systems, mathematics, physical sciences, and physics), EDUCATION (art, athletic training, business, early childhood, educational media, elementary, foreign languages, health, music, physical, science, secondary, and social science), ENGINEERING AND ENVIRONMENTAL DESIGN (automotive technology, construction management, electrical/electronics engineering technology, environmental science, manufacturing technology, and mechanical engineering technology), HEALTH PROFESSIONS (clinical science, dental hygiene, health care administration, nursing, radiographic medical technology, and respiratory therapy), SOCIAL SCIENCE (criminal justice, early childhood studies, economics, family/consumer studies, geography, gerontology, history, interdisciplinary studies, political science/government, psychology, social work, and sociology). Dental hygiene is the strongest academically. Elementary education and nursing are the largest.

Required: To graduate, students must demonstrate math competency and complete courses in government/history, English, humanities, math, biological/physical sciences, and social sciences. At least 120 semester credit hours, with 45 at the upper-division level, and a minimum GPA of 2.0 are required. Hours in the major and distribution requirements vary with the degree.

Special: WSU offers co-op programs and internships in many majors, a Washington semester, study abroad in Mexico and England, work-study programs with community businesses, B.A.-B.S. degrees, dual majors in any combination, student-designed majors resulting in a B.I.S. degree, a general studies degree, credit for military experience, nondegree study, and pass/fail options. There is 1 national honor society, Phi Beta Kappa, and a freshman honors program.

Faculty/Classroom: 61% of faculty are male; 39%, female. All teach undergraduates. No introductory courses are taught by graduate students. The average class size in an introductory lecture is 37; in a laboratory, 16; and in a regular course, 26.

Admissions: All of the 2005-2006 applicants were accepted. The SAT scores for the 2005-2006 freshman class were: Verbal--45% below 500, 39% between 500 and 599, 13% between 600 and 700, and 3% above 700; Math--48% below 500, 34% between 500 and 599, 16% between 600 and 700, and 2% above 700. The ACT scores were 38% below 21, 24% between 21 and 23, 27% between 24 and 26, 7% between 27 and 28, and 4% above 28. 56% of the current freshmen were in the top fifth of their class; 89% were in the top two fifths.

Requirements: The ACT is recommended. In addition, applicants must be graduates of an accredited secondary school or have a GED. Other requirements vary by department. Out-of-state residents must have a minimum high school GPA of 2.0. AP and CLEP credits are accepted.

Procedure: Freshmen are admitted to all sessions. Entrance exams should be taken in the junior or senior year. There are early admissions, rolling admissions, and deferred admissions plans. Applications should be filed by July 1 for fall entry and January 8 for spring entry, along with a $30 fee. The college accepts all applicants. Notification is sent on a rolling basis. Applications are accepted on-line.

Transfer: 1879 transfer students enrolled in a recent year. Transfer students must submit official transcripts from previously attended colleges or universities and have a minimum GPA of 2.0. 30 of 120 credits required for the bachelor's degree must be completed at WSU.

Visiting: There are regularly scheduled orientations for prospective students. There are guides for informal visits and visitors may sit in on classes and stay overnight. To schedule a visit, contact John Allred at (801) 626-6049 or (800) 848-7770, ext. 6049 or jdallred@weber.edu.

Financial Aid: In 2005-2006, 66% of all full-time freshmen and 68% of continuing full-time students received some form of financial aid. 54% of full-time freshmen and 66% of continuing full-time students received need-based aid. The average freshman award was $5892. The average financial indebtedness of the 2005 graduate was $10,500. The FAFSA and the college's own financial statement are required. The deadline for filing freshman financial aid applications for fall entry is March 1.

International Students: There were 171 international students enrolled in a recent year. The school actively recruits these students. They must take the college's own test.

Computers: All students may access the system.

Graduates: From July 1, 2004 to June 30, 2005, 2069 bachelor's degrees were awarded. The most popular majors were sales and service technology (10%), psychology (5%), and nursing (3%). In an average class, 10% graduate in 3 years or less, 21% graduate in 4 years or less, 31% graduate in 5 years or less, and 39% graduate in 6 years or less. 563 companies recruited on campus in 2004-2005. Of the 2004 graduating class, 18% were enrolled in graduate school within 6 months of graduation and 44% were employed.

Admissions Contact: Christopher C. Rivera, Director of Admissions. A video is available. E-mail: crivera@weber.edu
Web: www.weber.edu/admissions

WESTMINSTER COLLEGE   C-2
Salt Lake City, UT 84105

	(801) 832-2200
	(800) 748-4753; Fax: (801) 832-3101

Full-time: 672 men, 959 women	**Faculty:** 121; IIB, av$
Part-time: 107 men, 104 women	**Ph.D.s:** 91%
Graduate: 311 men, 260 women	**Student/Faculty:** 13 to 1
Year: 4-1-4, summer session	**Tuition:** $19,724
Application Deadline: April 15	**Room & Board:** $5932
Freshman Class: 897 applied, 801 accepted, 350 enrolled	
SAT Verbal/Math: 550/540*	**ACT:** 23 **COMPETITIVE**

Westminster College, founded in 1875, is a private, comprehensive, liberal arts institution offering undergraduate programs through the Bill and Vieve Gore School of Business, the St. Marks Westminster School of Nursing and Health Sciences, the School of Arts and Sciences, and the School of Education. There are 4 undergraduate and 4 graduate schools. In addition to regional accreditation, Westminster College has baccalaureate program accreditation with ACBSP and NLN. The library contains 88,086 volumes, 114,183 microform items, and 3819 audio/video tapes/CDs/DVDs, and subscribes to 348 periodicals including electronic. Computerized library services include the card catalog, interlibrary loans, database searching, Internet access, and laptop Internet portals. Special learning facilities include a learning resource center, a multipurpose theater, networked classrooms, a flight simulation center, and a center for financial analysis. The 27-acre campus is in a suburban area 6 miles southeast of downtown Salt Lake City. Including any residence halls, there are 20 buildings.

Student Life: 90% of undergraduates are from Utah. Others are from 27 states, 21 foreign countries, and Canada. 75% are from public schools. 89% are white. 60% claim no religious affiliation; 33% Buddhist, Greek Orthodox, Christian, LDS, Presbyterian, Episcopalian; 6% Catholic. The average age of freshmen is 18; all undergraduates, 23. 26% do not continue beyond their first year; 57% remain to graduate.

Housing: 374 students can be accommodated in college housing, which includes single-sex and coed dorms and off-campus apartments. On-campus housing is guaranteed for all 4 years. 74% of students commute. All students may keep cars.

Activities: There are no fraternities or sororities. There are 41 groups on campus, including art, choir, chorale, chorus, computers, dance, drama, environmental, ethnic, film, gay, honors, international, jazz band, literary magazine, musical theater, newspaper, orchestra, outdoor, political, professional, religious, social service, student government, and symphony. Popular campus events include International Fest, Spring Fling, and Awards Day.

Sports: There are 2 intercollegiate sports for men and 2 for women, and 7 intramural sports for men and 7 for women. Facilities include a playing field, tennis courts, a gym, a weight room, a sand volleyball court, and an aerobics/yoga room.

Disabled Students: 85% of the campus is accessible. Wheelchair ramps, elevators, special parking, specially equipped rest rooms, special class scheduling, lowered drinking fountains, lowered telephones, and special housing are available.

Services: Counseling and information services are available, as is tutoring in most subjects. There is a reader service for the blind, and remedial math, reading, and writing.

Campus Safety and Security: Measures include 24-hour foot and vehicle patrol, self-defense education, security escort services, and informal discussions. There are pamphlets/posters/films, emergency telephones, lighted pathways/sidewalks, and separate dorm security.

Programs of Study: Westminster College confers B.A. and B.S. degrees. Master's degrees are also awarded. Bachelor's degrees are awarded in BIOLOGICAL SCIENCE (biology/biological science), BUSINESS (accounting, business administration and management, and marketing/retailing/merchandising), COMMUNICATIONS AND THE ARTS (communications, English, and fine arts), COMPUTER AND PHYSICAL SCIENCE (chemistry, computer science, mathematics, and physics), EDUCATION (early childhood, elementary, and secondary), ENGINEERING AND ENVIRONMENTAL DESIGN (aviation administration/management), HEALTH PROFESSIONS (nursing), SOCIAL SCIENCE (economics, history, human development, philosophy, psychology, social science, and sociology). Nursing, biology, and English are the strongest academically. Business, biology, and nursing are the largest.

Required: To graduate, all students must complete at least 124 credit hours, which include liberal education and major requirements, with a minimum 2.0 GPA and 40 to 80 hours in the major. Required courses in the core curriculum include arts/fine arts, computer literacy, English, foreign languages, history, public speaking, humanities, math, philosophy, sciences, and social science.

Special: The college offers internships in every major, study abroad in England, Spain, and Mexico, B.A.-B.S. degrees, dual and student-designed majors, an accelerated degree, co-op work-study, independent study, weekend college, a 3-2 engineering degree at USC at Los Angeles or Washington University in St. Louis, and freshman seminar courses. There is 1 national honor society, including Phi Beta Kappa, a freshman honors program, and 1 departmental honors program.

Faculty/Classroom: 49% of faculty are male; 51%, female. 89% teach undergraduates. No introductory courses are taught by graduate students. The average class size in an introductory lecture is 18; in a laboratory, 12; and in a regular course, 15.

Admissions: 89% of the 2005-2006 applicants were accepted. The SAT scores for the 2005-2006 freshman class were: Verbal--25% below 500, 34% between 500 and 599, 32% between 600 and 700, and 9% above 700; Math--34% below 500, 36% between 500 and 599, 22% between 600 and 700, and 8% above 700. The ACT scores were 22% below 21, 28% between 21 and 23, 28% between 24 and 26, 11% between 27 and 28, and 11% above 28. 49% of the current freshmen were in the top fifth of their class; 77% were in the top two fifths. There was 1 National Merit finalist. 6 freshmen graduated first in their class.

Requirements: The SAT or ACT is required. In addition, applicants must be graduates of an accredited secondary school or have a GED certificate. College preparatory work should include 4 units of English, 3 of science, 2 each of math, foreign language, social studies, and electives, and 1 of history. An interview is recommended. Applications are accepted on computer disk. AP and CLEP credits are accepted. Important factors in the admissions decision are evidence of special talent, extracurricular activities record, and advanced placement or honor courses.

Procedure: Freshmen are admitted to all sessions. Entrance exams should be taken in the junior or senior year of high school. There is a deferred admissions plan and a rolling admissions plan. Applications should be filed by April 15 for fall entry. The fall 2005 application fee was $40. Notification is sent on a rolling basis beginning October 10. Applications are accepted on-line.

Transfer: 222 transfer students enrolled in 2004-2005. Transfer students must have a minimum 2.5 GPA and be in good standing at all previously attended institutions. They must provide college transcripts and submit an essay. An interview is recommended. Some students may need to present standardized test scores and high school transcripts. 36 of 124 credits required for the bachelor's degree must be completed at Westminster College.

Visiting: There are regularly scheduled orientations for prospective students, including a welcome program, lunch, various workshops, a campus tour, and meetings with faculty. There are guides for informal visits and visitors may sit in on classes. To schedule a visit, contact Bonnie Sofarelli, Director of Admissions at *bsofarelli@westminstercollege.edu*.

Financial Aid: In 2005-2006, 65% of all full-time freshmen and 66% of continuing full-time students received some form of financial aid. Atleast 64% of full-time freshmen and 65% of continuing full-time students received need-based aid. The average freshman award was $17,204. Need-based scholarships or need-based grants averaged $11,241; need-based self-help aid (loans and jobs) averaged $5963; institutional non-need-based athletic scholarships averaged $4250; and other institutional non-need-based awards and non-need-based scholarships averaged $8946. 56% of undergraduates work part time. Average annual earnings from campus work are $2400. The average financial indebtedness of the 2005 graduate was $16,450. Westminster College is a member of CSS. The FAFSA is required. The priority date for freshman financial aid applications for fall entry is April 15. There is a rolling deadline for filing freshman financial aid applications for fall entry.

International Students: There are 29 international students enrolled. The school actively recruits these students. They must take the TOEFL and also take the MELAB.

Computers: All students may access the system 7 A.M. to 11 P.M. There are no time limits and no fees. It is strongly recommended that all students have a personal computer.

Graduates: From July 1, 2004 to June 30, 2005, 470 bachelor's degrees were awarded. The most popular majors were business (36%), health professions (11%), and psychology (8%). In an average class, 43% graduate in 4 years or less, 55% graduate in 5 years or less, and 57% graduate in 6 years or less. 106 companies recruited on campus in 2004-2005.

Admissions Contact: Bonnie Sofarelli, Director of Admissions.
E-mail: *admission@westminstercollege.edu*
Web: *www.westminstercollege.edu*

VERMONT

POPULATION
DENSITY

• 10,000 and over

0   10   20   30   40   50
Miles

BENNINGTON COLLEGE

A-6

Bennington, VT 05201

(802) 440-4312
(800) 833-6845; Fax: (802) 440-4320

Full-time: 192 men, 375 women	**Faculty:** 66
Part-time: 2 men, 2 women	**Ph.D.s:** 74%
Graduate: 52 men, 102 women	**Student/Faculty:** 9 to 1
Year: see profile	**Tuition:** $33,570
Application Deadline: January 1	**Room & Board:** $8320
Freshman Class: 723 applied, 445 accepted, 137 enrolled	
SAT Verbal/Math: 660/590*	**ACT:** 27 **HIGHLY COMPETITIVE**

Bennington College, founded in 1932, is a private liberal arts institution where students design their own programs in consultation with faculty, who are active practitioners of the disciplines they teach. The academic year consists of 3 terms: 2 15-week on-campus terms during fall and spring and a 7-week winter term of fieldwork off campus. The 2 libraries contain 122,950 volumes, 6117 microform items, and 11,909 audio/video tapes/CDs/DVDs, and subscribe to 11,891 periodicals including electronic. Computerized library services include the card catalog, interlibrary loans, database searching, Internet access, and laptop Internet portals. Special learning facilities include a learning resource center, art gallery, and Kaplan Center for Languages and Cultures, Center for Creative Teaching, early childhood center, computer center and media labs, digital arts lab, architecture, drawing, painting, printmaking, and sculpture studios, ceramics studio and kilns, color and black-and-white photography darkrooms, film and video editing studio, several fully equipped professional theaters, scripts library, dance studios and archives, electronic music and sound recording studios, music practice rooms and music library, radio station, observatory, greenhouse, and 550 acres of forest, ponds, wetlands, and fields for biological study. The 550-acre campus is in a small town 160 miles north of New York City. Including any residence halls, there are 64 buildings.

Student Life: 96% of undergraduates are from out of state, mostly the Northeast. Students are from 45 states, 8 foreign countries, and Canada. 85% are white. The average age of freshmen is 18; all undergraduates, 20. 13% do not continue beyond their first year; 60% remain to graduate.

Housing: 611 students can be accommodated in college housing, which includes coed dorms, on-campus apartments, and off-campus apartments. In addition, there are special-interest houses. On-campus housing is guaranteed for all 4 years. 98% of students live on campus. All students may keep cars.

Activities: There are no fraternities or sororities. There are 22 groups on campus, including art, band, campus activities board, chess, choir, chorus, dance, drama, film, international, literary magazine, maple sugaring, newspaper, outing, photography, political, radio and TV, religious, social service, student endownment for the arts, student government, and symphony. Popular campus events include Sunfest, faculty concerts, and student-work performances and exhibitions.

Sports: There is 1 intercollegiate sports for men and 1 for women, and 5 intramural sports for men and 5 for women. Facilities include soccer and other playing fields, a basketball court, a tennis court, a karate and aerobics studio, a weight room, hiking and biking areas, a climbing wall, and cardiovascular exercise equipment. Swimming, horseback riding, rock-climbing, canoeing, caving, snowshoeing, whitewater rafting, and skiing facilities are available in the surrounding area.

Disabled Students: 73% of the campus is accessible. Wheelchair ramps, elevators, special parking, specially equipped rest rooms, lowered drinking fountains, special housing, special fire alarms in houses, and amplifiers on phones are available.

Services: Counseling and information services are available, as is tutoring in some subjects. There is remedial writing. Tutoring for learning disabilities is available in the town of Bennington at a cost to the student.

Campus Safety and Security: Measures include 24-hour foot and vehicle patrol, security escort services, shuttle buses, and informal discussions. There are pamphlets/posters/films, emergency telephones, and lighted pathways/sidewalks.

Programs of Study: Bennington confers the B.A. degree. Master's degrees are also awarded. Bachelor's degrees are awarded in BIOLOGICAL SCIENCE (biology/biological science and ecology), COMMUNICATIONS AND THE ARTS (American literature, art, ceramic art and design, Chinese, comparative literature, creative writing, dance, dramatic arts, English, film arts, fine arts, French, illustration, Italian, Japanese, jazz, languages, literature, multimedia, music, music performance, music theory and composition, painting, performing arts, photography, playwriting/screenwriting, printmaking, sculpture, Spanish, studio art, theater design, video, visual and performing arts, and voice), COMPUTER AND PHYSICAL SCIENCE (astronomy, chemistry, computer science, digital arts/technology, mathematics, physics, and science), EDUCATION (drama, early childhood, education, and foreign languages), ENGINEERING AND ENVIRONMENTAL DESIGN (architecture), HEALTH PROFESSIONS (premedicine), SOCIAL SCIENCE (anthropology, history, humanities, humanities and social science, interdisciplinary studies, international relations, liberal arts/general studies, philosophy, political science/government, psychology, social psychology, social science, and sociology). Literature, languages, and visual and performing arts are the strongest academically. Literature, visual and performing arts, and interdisciplinary studies are the largest.

Required: A minimum of 128 credit hours is required to graduate. Students must also complete a Field Work Term (job/internship) for each term in residence. Students' programs must reflect breadth and depth in curricular choices, and their academic plan process must be approved by a faculty committee.

Special: 7-week work/internships (during January and February) are required each year in residence. Cross-registration with Southern Vermont and Williams Colleges and Massachusetts College of Liberal Arts is possible. In addition, study abroad and dual and student-designed majors are offered. Students receive narrative evaluations with the option of letter grades. A B.A./M.A.T. program is offered for teacher certification.

Faculty/Classroom: 62% of faculty are male; 38%, female. All both teach undergraduates and do research. The average class size in an introductory lecture is 12; in a laboratory, 12; and in a regular course, 12.

Admissions: 62% of the 2005-2006 applicants were accepted. The SAT scores for the 2005-2006 freshman class were: Verbal--15% between 500 and 599, 61% between 600 and 700, and 24% above 700; Math--11% below 500, 44% between 500 and 599, 40% between 600 and 700, and 5% above 700. The ACT scores were 4% below 21, 12% between 21 and 23, 24% between 24 and 26, 36% between 27 and 28, and 24% above 28. 63% of the current freshmen were in the top fifth of their class; 89% were in the top two fifths. 7 freshmen graduated first in their class.

Requirements: The SAT or ACT is required. In addition, applicants should have 16 credits, including 4 units in English, 3 each in math, science, and social studies, 2 or 3 in foreign language, and 2 in history; art and music courses are highly recommended. Bennington accepts the Common Application as well as the Bennington Supplement, which includes a separate essay question and the submission of a graded paper. Interviews are not required but are strongly encouraged. The GED is accepted. Applications may be downloaded from the college web site.

Procedure: Freshmen are admitted fall and spring. Entrance exams should be taken during the spring of the junior year or the fall of the senior year. There are early decision, early admissions, and deferred admissions plans. Early decision applications should be filed by November 15 and January 1; regular applications, by January 1 for fall entry and November 15 for spring entry, along with a $60 fee. Notification of early decision is sent December 15 and early February; regular decision, April 1. 29 early decision candidates were accepted for the 2005-2006 class. 14 applicants were on the 2005 waiting list; 4 were admitted. Applications are accepted on-line.

Transfer: 19 transfer students enrolled in 2004-2005. Applicants must submit the Common Application for transfer students, including essays, secondary school reports, college transcripts, and recommendations from 2 faculty members at the college from which they are transferring. They must also submit SAT or ACT scores and interview with a member of the admissions staff. 64 of 128 credits required for the bachelor's degree must be completed at Bennington.

Visiting: There are regularly scheduled orientations for prospective students, including a tour of campus, classes, lunch in the dining hall, and a meeting with an admissions counselor. Overnight visits are also possible during the term. There are guides for informal visits. To schedule a visit, contact the Admissions Office.

Financial Aid: In 2005-2006, 72% of all full-time freshmen and 80% of continuing full-time students received some form of financial aid. 66% of full-time freshmen and 68% of continuing full-time students received need-based aid. The average freshman award was $24,069. Need-based scholarships or need-based grants averaged $21,211; need-based self-help aid (loans and jobs) averaged $3233; and other non-need-based awards and non-need-based scholarships averaged $7325. The average financial indebtedness of the 2005 graduate was $20,340. Bennington is a member of CSS. The CSS/Profile or FAFSA, the college's own financial statement, and student and parent tax returns are required. The priority date for freshman financial aid applications for fall entry is January 1. The deadline for filing freshman financial aid applications for fall entry is March 1.

International Students: There are 12 international students enrolled. The school actively recruits these students. They must achieve a satisfactory score on the TOEFL and also take the SAT or the ACT.

Computers: Wireless access is available. About 75 computers are available in the computer center, Isabelle Kaplan Center for Languages and Culture, Commons, Visual and Performing Arts Center, and Crossett Library, with full access to the Internet and Web. Student housing on campus is fully networked, and students may access the network with their own computers. There is also wireless networking available in 5 main buildings. All students may access the system. There are no time limits and no fees. It is strongly recommended that all students have a personal computer.

Graduates: From July 1, 2004 to June 30, 2005, 138 bachelor's degrees were awarded. The most popular majors were visual and performing arts (53%), English (15%), and social sciences (12%). In an average class, 1% graduate in 3 years or less, 45% graduate in 4 years or less, 58% graduate in 5 years or less, and 60% graduate in 6 years or less. Of the 2004 graduating class, 11% were enrolled in graduate school within 6 months of graduation and 84% were employed.

Admissions Contact: Ken Himmelman, Dean of Admisisons and Financial Aid. E-mail: admissions@bennington.edu
Web: www.bennington.edu

BURLINGTON COLLEGE A-2
Burlington, VT 05401

	(802) 862-9616
	(800) 862-9616; Fax: (802) 660-4331
Full-time: 51 men, 50 women	**Faculty:** 6
Part-time: 32 men, 51 women	**Ph.D.s:** 67%
Graduate: none	**Student/Faculty:** 17 to 1
Year: semesters, summer session	**Tuition:** $14,670
Application Deadline: August	**Room & Board:** n/av
Freshman Class: 28 applied, 22 accepted, 11 enrolled	
SAT or ACT: not required	SPECIAL

Burlington College, founded in 1972, is an independent liberal arts college that offers a nontraditional, individualized approach in which classes are small and discussion based, narrative evaluations replace traditional grades, and students direct their own education. The library contains 12,000 volumes and 1000 audio/video tapes/CDs/DVDs, and subscribes to 60 periodicals including electronic. Computerized library services include interlibrary loans, database searching, and Internet access. Special learning facilities include a learning resource center, art gallery, digital video and audio editing suites, and a film-production studio. The 2-acre campus is in an urban area overlooking Lake Champlain. Including any residence halls, there are 4 buildings.

Student Life: 65% of undergraduates are from Vermont. Others are from 22 states, 3 foreign countries, and Canada. 74% are white. The average age of freshmen is 21; all undergraduates, 29. 43% do not continue beyond their first year; 20% remain to graduate.

Housing: 10 students can be accommodated in college housing, which includes single-sex and coed on-campus apartments. On-campus hous-

ing is available on a first-come, first-served basis. Priority is given to out-of-town students. 92% of students commute. Alcohol is not permitted. All students may keep cars.

Activities: There are no fraternities or sororities. There are many groups and organizations on campus, including art, ethnic, film, gay, international, literary magazine, newspaper, photography, political, social, social service, and student government. Popular campus events include coffeehouses, community service trips, and film society screenings.

Sports: There is no sports program at BC. Sailing, windsurfing, and a 9-mile bike path are available on or along nearby Lake Champlain. Bicycling, roller-blading, and walking trails are also available nearby, and students have access to the Burlington YMCA, which has a pool, basketball and squash courts, exercise rooms, and weight and aerobic conditioning.

Disabled Students: All of the campus is accessible. Wheelchair ramps, special parking, specially equipped rest rooms, special class scheduling, lowered drinking fountains, and lowered telephones are available.

Services: Counseling and information services are available, as is tutoring in most subjects. There is remedial math, reading, and writing.

Campus Safety and Security: Measures include informal discussions, lighted pathways/sidewalks, and distribution of campus safety and security policies and procedures.

Programs of Study: BC confers the B.A. degree. Associate degrees are also awarded. Bachelor's degrees are awarded in COMMUNICATIONS AND THE ARTS (creative writing, film arts, and fine arts), SOCIAL SCIENCE (Hispanic American studies, human ecology, human services, humanities, liberal arts/general studies, and psychology). Psychology, human services, and cinema studies and film production are the strongest academically. Individualized majors, cinema studies and film production, and writing and literature are the largest.

Required: All students are required to satisfactorily complete at least 120 semester credits, including an 18-credit interdisciplinary core curriculum, 40 credits in general education areas, and 36 to 45 upper-level credits in their major. Distribution requirements include 3 credits in each of the following areas: responsible action, creative expression, quantitative reasoning, media literacy, historical consciousness, cultural awareness, social awareness, written and oral communication, critical thinking, research methods, and scientific thought. Students are also required to take college-level math and 2 writing courses, demonstrate competency in the use of computers, and complete both a 6-credit capstone project and a 3-credit practicum.

Special: Cross-registration is available with the University of Vermont, St. Michael's College, Champlain College, and the Community College of Vermont. Internships through various organizations, study abroad, and work-study programs with nonprofit organizations are also available. The college offers dual majors, interdisciplinary majors, individualized majors, independent study, a nonresidential degree program, and credit for life experience. Professional certificates are offered in film studies and paralegal studies.

Faculty/Classroom: 55% of faculty are male; 45%, female. All teach undergraduates. The average class size in a regular course is 7.

Admissions: 79% of the 2005-2006 applicants were accepted.

Requirements: Burlington requires a high school diploma or the GED, and a successful interview with the Director of Admissions. AP and CLEP credits are accepted. Important factors in the admissions decision are personality/intangible qualities, extracurricular activities record, and recommendations by school officials.

Procedure: Freshmen are admitted fall, spring, and summer. There is a deferred admissions plan. There is a rolling admissions plan. Applications should be filed by August for fall entry, January for spring entry, and June for summer entry, along with a $50 fee. The college accepts all applicants. Notification is sent on a rolling basis. Applications are accepted on-line.

Transfer: 76 transfer students enrolled in 2004-2005. Transfer students must meet the same requirements as new students. High school transcripts precede acceptance. The Independent Degree Program requires 45 college credits prior to entrance. Transcripts precede acceptance. 30 of 120 credits required for the bachelor's degree must be completed at BC.

Visiting: There are guides for informal visits and visitors may sit in on classes. To schedule a visit, contact the Admissions Office at (802) 846-3057 or sullivan@burlcol.edu.

Financial Aid: In 2005-2006, 86% of all full-time freshmen and 75% of continuing full-time students received some form of financial aid. 86% of full-time freshmen and 71% of continuing full-time students received need-based aid. The average freshman award was $9708. Need-based scholarships or need-based grants averaged $4473 ($11,590 maximum); and need-based self-help aid (loans and jobs) averaged $7485 ($19,285 maximum). 38% of undergraduates work part time. The average financial indebtedness of the 2005 graduate was $22,498. The FAFSA, and the state aid form are required.

International Students: There is 1 international student enrolled. It is recommended that international students achieve a satisfactory score on the TOEFL.

Computers: There are 2 computer labs with a total of 12 PCs and 2 Macs and 2 digital editing labs with a total of 11 Macs. All students may access the system 80 hours per week. There are no time limits and no fees. It is strongly recommended that all students have a personal computer.

Graduates: From July 1, 2004 to June 30, 2005, 38 bachelor's degrees were awarded. The most popular majors were transpersonal psychology (29%), individualized majors (18%), and writing and literature (16%). In an average class, 20% graduate in 5 years, and 20% graduate in 6 years. Of the 2004 graduating class, 31% were enrolled in graduate school within 6 months of graduation.

Admissions Contact: Cathleen Sullivan, Director of Admissions. A video is available. E-mail: *admissions@burlcol.edu* Web: *www.burlingtoncollege.edu*

CASTLETON STATE COLLEGE   B-4
Castleton, VT 05735

(802) 468-1213
(800) 639-8521; Fax: (802) 468-1476

Full-time: 737 men, 947 women	**Faculty:** 89; IIB, --$
Part-time: 46 men, 161 women	**Ph.D.s:** 93%
Graduate: 83 men, 418 women	**Student/Faculty:** 19 to 1
Year: semesters, summer session	**Tuition:** $6484 ($13,804)
Application Deadline: open	**Room & Board:** $6674
Freshman Class: n/av	
SAT or ACT: required	**COMPETITIVE**

Castleton State College, founded in 1787, is the oldest institution of higher learning in Vermont. As part of the Vermont State Colleges system, it offers a state-supported undergraduate and graduate program in liberal arts, teacher preparation, and professional studies. In addition to regional accreditation, Castleton has baccalaureate program accreditation with CSWE and NLN. The library contains 166,011 volumes, 545,361 microform items, and 3420 audio/video tapes/CDs/DVDs, and subscribes to 739 periodicals including electronic. Computerized library services include the card catalog, interlibrary loans, and database searching. Special learning facilities include a learning resource center, art gallery, radio station, TV studio, observatory, and theater. The 165-acre campus is in a rural area 11 miles west of Rutland. Including any residence halls, there are 24 buildings.

Student Life: 66% of undergraduates are from Vermont. Others are from 18 states, 2 foreign countries, and Canada. 97% are white. The average age of freshmen is 18; all undergraduates, 22. 34% do not continue beyond their first year; 40% remain to graduate.

Housing: 880 students can be accommodated in college housing, which includes single-sex and coed dormitories and off-campus apartments. In addition, there are honors houses. On-campus housing is guaranteed for the freshman year only and is available on a lottery system for upperclassmen. 50% of students live on campus; of those, 50% remain on campus on weekends. All students may keep cars.

Activities: There are no fraternities or sororities. There are 40 groups on campus, including art, band, cheerleading, choir, chorale, chorus, computers, dance, drama, environmental, ethnic, film, gay, honors, international, jazz band, literary magazine, musical theater, newspaper, photography, political, professional, radio and TV, religious, social, social service, student government, and yearbook. Popular campus events include Spring, Winter, Alumni Weekends, and Martin Luther King Jr. Celebration.

Sports: There are 9 intercollegiate sports for men and 10 for women, and 9 intramural sports for men and 9 for women. Facilities include a 6-lane swimming pool, 2 racquetball courts, a fitness center, a recreation gym, and the nearby 2000-acre Pond Hill Ranch with more than 70 miles of trails, swimming, sailing, fishing, and golf facilities.

Disabled Students: 95% of the campus is accessible. Wheelchair ramps, elevators, special parking, specially equipped rest rooms, special class scheduling, lowered drinking fountains, and lowered telephones are available.

Services: Counseling and information services are available, as is tutoring in every subject. There is a reader service for the blind, and remedial math, reading, and writing.

Campus Safety and Security: Measures include 24-hour foot and vehicle patrol, self-defense education, security escort services, and informal discussions. There are pamphlets/posters/films, emergency telephones, and lighted pathways/sidewalks.

Programs of Study: Castleton confers B.A., B.S., and B.S.W. degrees. Associate and master's degrees are also awarded. Bachelor's degrees are awarded in BIOLOGICAL SCIENCE (biology/biological science), BUSINESS (business administration and management), COMMUNICATIONS AND THE ARTS (art, communications, dramatic arts, literature, music, and Spanish), COMPUTER AND PHYSICAL SCIENCE (computer science, geology, mathematics, and natural sciences), EDUCATION (athletic training and physical), ENGINEERING AND ENVIRONMENTAL DESIGN (environmental science), HEALTH PROFESSIONS (exercise science and health science), SOCIAL SCIENCE (criminal justice, history,

psychology, social science, social work, and sociology). Business and teacher preparation are the largest.

Required: All students must maintain a GPA of 2.0 while taking 122 semester hours, including 30 or more in their major. Distribution requirements include 3 courses each in literature and the arts, 2 each in math and natural sciences, and 1 each in foreign cultures, history, philosophy and psychology, and social analysis. Specific courses include computers, communication, and an introduction to liberal arts.

Special: Cross-registration with other Vermont State Colleges, co-op programs, internships, study abroad, and work-study programs are available. In addition, B.A.-B.S. degrees, dual majors, student-designed majors in history, math, and social sciences, credit for life experience, nondegree study, and pass/fail options are offered. There are 8 national honor societies, a freshman honors program, and 4 departmental honors programs.

Faculty/Classroom: 52% of faculty are male; 48%, female. All teach undergraduates and 50% both teach and do research. The average class size in an introductory lecture is 20; in a laboratory, 14; and in a regular course, 16.

Requirements: The SAT or ACT is required. In addition, the college recommends that candidates have 4 years of English, 3 each of math, and social studies or history, 2 each of foreign language and science, and 2 to 4 of electives. An essay is required, and an interview is recommended. The GED is accepted. A GPA of 2.5 is required. AP and CLEP credits are accepted. Important factors in the admissions decision are advanced placement or honor courses, leadership record, and recommendations by school officials.

Procedure: Freshmen are admitted fall and spring. Entrance exams should be taken during the spring of the junior year or fall of the senior year. There are early admissions, deferred admissions, and rolling admissions plans. Application deadlines are open. Application fee is $35. Applications are accepted on-line.

Transfer: 181 transfer students enrolled in 2004-2005. Transfer applicants must have a 2.0 GPA. An associate degree, 15 credit hours, and an interview are recommended. 30 of 122 credits required for the bachelor's degree must be completed at Castleton.

Visiting: There are regularly scheduled orientations for prospective students, including meetings with admissions counselors, faculty, and coaches as well as a campus tour. There are guides for informal visits and visitors may sit in on classes. To schedule a visit, contact the Admissions Office.

Financial Aid: Castleton is a member of CSS. The FAFSA is required. The deadline for filing freshman financial aid applications for fall entry is February 15.

International Students: They must score satisfactorily on the written TOEFL.

Computers: All students may access the system. There are no time limits and no fees.

Graduates: From July 1, 2004 to June 30, 2005, 261 bachelor's degrees were awarded. The most popular majors were business (18%), visual and performing arts (14%), and communicating (8%). In an average class, 4% graduate in 3 years or less, 29% graduate in 4 years or less, 40% graduate in 5 years or less, and 43% graduate in 6 years or less. 115 companies recruited on campus in 2004-2005.

Admissions Contact: Maurice Ouimet, Admissions Director. E-mail: *info@castleton.edu* Web: *www.castleton.edu*

CHAMPLAIN COLLEGE   A-2
Burlington, VT 05402-0670

(802) 860-2727
(800) 570-5858; Fax: (802) 860-2767

Full-time: 944 men, 813 women	**Faculty:** 74; IIB, -$
Part-time: 252 men, 287 women	**Ph.D.s:** 29%
Graduate: 38 men, 25 women	**Student/Faculty:** 24 to 1
Year: semesters, summer session	**Tuition:** $14,910
Application Deadline: open	**Room & Board:** $9695
Freshman Class: 2344 applied, 1420 accepted, 606 enrolled	
SAT Verbal/Math: 510/520*	**ACT:** 20 **COMPETITIVE**

Champlain College, founded in 1878, is a private school that offers professional training in a liberal arts setting. Students earn their bachelor's degree, with an embedded associate's degree, in one of 24 majors. Internship opportunities are built into the curriculum. Champlain also offers 2 on-line master's degrees. In addition to regional accreditation, Champlain has baccalaureate program accreditation with CAAHEP. The library contains 40,477 volumes, 3601 microform items, and 698 audio/video tapes/CDs/DVDs, and subscribes to 10,618 periodicals including electronic. Computerized library services include the card catalog, interlibrary loans, database searching, and Internet access. Special learning facilities include a learning resource center, a video production studio, and several multimedia and graphic design studios. The 21-acre campus is in a suburban area in the Hill Section of Burlington. Including any residence halls, there are 38 buildings.

Student Life: 70% of undergraduates are from out of state, mostly the Northeast. Students are from 26 states, 28 foreign countries, and Canada. 85% are from public schools. 95% are white. The average age of freshmen is 19; all undergraduates, 21. 18% do not continue beyond their first year; 71% remain to graduate.

Housing: 690 students can be accommodated in college housing, which includes single-sex and coed dorms. In addition, there are special-interest houses and performing arts, international, and wellness dorms. On-campus housing is guaranteed for all 4 years. 88% of students live on campus; of those, 90% remain on campus on weekends. Alcohol is not permitted. No one may keep cars.

Activities: There are no fraternities or sororities. There are 25 groups on campus, including art, chorale, chorus, computers, debate, drama, ethnic, flas animation, gay, honors, international, literary magazine, musical theater, newspaper, outing, photography, professional, religious, sailing, social, social service, and student government. Popular campus events include skiing/snowboarding trips, Spring Meltdown, and "Get Real" community service connection.

Sports: There are 6 intramural sports for men and 6 for women. Facilities include a fitness, activities, dining center and gym.

Disabled Students: 79% of the campus is accessible. Wheelchair ramps, elevators, special parking, specially equipped rest rooms, special class scheduling, lowered drinking fountains, and lowered telephones are available.

Services: Counseling and information services are available, as is tutoring in some subjects, including math, accounting, and writing. Peer tutoring is available.

Campus Safety and Security: Measures include 24-hour foot and vehicle patrol, self-defense education, security escort services, and shuttle buses. There are informal discussions, pamphlets/posters/films, emergency telephones, and lighted pathways/sidewalks.

Programs of Study: Champlain confers the B.S. degree. Associate and master's degrees are also awarded. Bachelor's degrees are awarded in BUSINESS (accounting, business administration and management, electronic business, hospitality management services, hotel/motel and restaurant management, international business management, management science, marketing management, and tourism), COMMUNICATIONS AND THE ARTS (advertising, broadcasting, communications technology, graphic design, journalism, media arts, multimedia, public relations, technical and business writing, and telecommunications), COMPUTER AND PHYSICAL SCIENCE (computer security and information assurance, information sciences and systems, radiological technology, software engineering, and web services), EDUCATION (early childhood, elementary, middle school, and secondary), SOCIAL SCIENCE (applied psychology, criminal justice, forensic studies, liberal arts/general studies, paralegal studies, psychology, and social work). Information security, software engineering, and electronic game and interactive development are the strongest academically. Business, multimedia/graphic design, and liberal studies are the largest.

Required: A GPA of 2.0 and 120 credits are required for the B.S. degree. Courses are required in professional writing, oral communication, global history, ethics, community service, and computer and quantitative proficiency. Distribution requirements include courses in literature, natural science with lab, philosophy, social science, and fine arts. Students must take between 30 and 60 hours in the major and a comprehensive exam and/or a thesis in some majors. The core curriculum is career-oriented by major.

Special: Cross-registration with St. Michael's College, co-op programs (with the Walt Disney World College Program, Federal Law Enforcement Training Center, the Vermont police academy, and student teaching), internships, and study abroad through school-sponsored programs in England, France, Sweden, and Switzerland are available. Study abroad in other countries is also available. Dual majors are possible throgh the professional studies and computer information systems programs. Accelerated degree programs, such as the 5-year B.S./M.B.A. with Clarkson and Southern New Hampshire Universities, and student-designed majors are also available. There is a freshman honors program. All departments have honors programs.

Faculty/Classroom: 59% of faculty are male; 41%, female. All teach undergraduates. No introductory courses are taught by graduate students. The average class size in an introductory lecture is 19; in a laboratory, 15; and in a regular course, 19.

Admissions: 61% of the 2005-2006 applicants were accepted. The SAT scores for the 2005-2006 freshman class were: Verbal--30% below 500, 58% between 500 and 599, 11% between 600 and 700, and 1% above 700; Math--30% below 500, 48% between 500 and 599, and 22% between 600 and 700. The ACT scores were 59% below 21, 26% between 21 and 23, 11% between 24 and 26, and 4% between 27 and 28. 25% of the current freshmen were in the top fifth of their class; 65% were in the top two fifths.

Requirements: The SAT or ACT is required. In addition, applicants must be graduates of an accredited high school or the equivalent. AP and CLEP credits are accepted. Important factors in the admissions decision are advanced placement or honor courses, recommendations by school officials, and leadership record.

Procedure: Freshmen are admitted fall and spring. Entrance exams should be taken prior to applying. There is a deferred admissions plan.

There is a rolling admissions plan. Application deadlines are open. The fall 2005 application fee was $50. Notification is sent on a rolling basis. Applications are accepted on-line.

Transfer: 109 transfer students enrolled in 2005-2006. High school and college transcripts are required. 45 of 120 credits required for the bachelor's degree must be completed at Champlain.

Visiting: There are regularly scheduled orientations for prospective students, including a group information session followed by a tour. Personal interviews are also available with an admissions counselor. There are guides for informal visits and visitors may sit in on classes. To schedule a visit, contact the Admissions Office.

Financial Aid: In 2005-2006, 60% of all full-time students received some form of financial aid, including need-based aid. The average freshman award was $10,544. 70% of undergraduates work part time. Average annual earnings from campus work are $1190. The FAFSA and the college's own financial statement are required. The priority date for freshman financial aid applications for fall entry is May 1.

International Students: There were 60 international students enrolled in a recent year. The school actively recruits these students. A satisfactory score on the TOEFL is required. Students whose high school was conducted in English must also take the SAT or ACT.

Computers: Wireless access is available. All students may access the system. There are no time limits and no fees. It is strongly recommended that all students have a personal computer. It is recommended that students in multimedia graphic design have personal computers. A Mac is recommended.

Graduates: From July 1, 2004 to June 30, 2005, 363 bachelor's degrees were awarded. The most popular majors were business (18%), elementary education (12%), and accounting (9%). In an average class, 71% graduate in 4 years or less, and 80% graduate in 6 years or less. 70 companies recruited on campus in 2004-2005. Of the 2004 graduating class, 3% were enrolled in graduate school within 6 months of graduation and 97% were employed.

Admissions Contact: Mary Kay Kennedy, Director of Admissions. A video is available. E-mail: *admission@champlain.edu* Web: *www.champlain.edu*

COLLEGE OF SAINT JOSEPH
B-4

Rutland, VT 05701-3899

(802) 773-5900, ext. 3205
(877) 270-9998; Fax: (802) 776-5258

Full-time: 76 men, 100 women	**Faculty:** 11
Part-time: 30 men, 65 women	**Ph.D.s:** 73%
Graduate: 56 men, 148 women	**Student/Faculty:** 16 to 1
Year: semesters, summer session	**Tuition:** $14,050
Application Deadline: open	**Room & Board:** $6850
Freshman Class: 141 applied, 114 accepted, 39 enrolled	
SAT: required	**ACT:** recommended
	NONCOMPETITIVE

The College of St. Joseph, founded in 1956, is a private Catholic institution offering undergraduate programs in the arts and sciences, business, computer information science, education, psychology, and human services, and graduate programs in business, education, and psychology. The college serves a primarily commuter student body. The library contains 53,300 volumes, 19,700 microform items, and 5250 audio/video tapes/CDs/DVDs, and subscribes to 84 periodicals including electronic. Computerized library services include the card catalog, interlibrary loans, database searching, Internet access, and laptop Internet portals. Special learning facilities include a learning resource center. The 90-acre campus is in a rural area 1 mile west of Rutland. Including any residence halls, there are 5 buildings.

Student Life: 63% of undergraduates are from Vermont. Students are from 13 states and 1 foreign country. 96% are white. 60% are Catholic; 22% Protestant. The average age of freshmen is 19; all undergraduates, 27. 19% do not continue beyond their first year; 56% remain to graduate.

Housing: 160 students can be accommodated in college housing, which includes single-sex dorms. On-campus housing is guaranteed for all 4 years. 55% of students live on campus; of those, 60% remain on campus on weekends. All students may keep cars.

Activities: There are no fraternities or sororities. There are 15 groups on campus, including chorus, drama, honors, literary magazine, musical theater, newspaper, political, professional, religious, social, social service, student government, and yearbook. Popular campus events include Spring Fling, cultural event series (year round), and Student Leadership-Academic Awards Dinner.

Sports: There are 3 intercollegiate sports for men and 4 for women, and 3 intramural sports for men and 3 for women. Facilities include a 1000-seat gym, a fitness center, racquetball courts, an aerobics studio, a cross-country skiing/running trail, a softball diamond, and a soccer field.

Disabled Students: All of the campus is accessible. Wheelchair ramps, special parking, specially equipped rest rooms, special class scheduling, lowered telephones, and special housing are available.

Services: Counseling and information services are available, as is tutoring in every subject. There is remedial math, reading, and writing. There is also personal growth counseling and spiritual counseling.

Campus Safety and Security: Measures include informal discussions, pamphlets/posters/films, emergency telephones, lighted pathways/sidewalks, and a nighttime security patrol.

Programs of Study: CSJ confers B.A. and B.S. degrees. Associate and master's degrees are also awarded. Bachelor's degrees are awarded in BUSINESS (accounting, business administration and management, marketing management, recreational facilities management, and sports management), COMMUNICATIONS AND THE ARTS (communications, English, and journalism), COMPUTER AND PHYSICAL SCIENCE (computer science and radiological technology), EDUCATION (computer, early childhood, elementary, secondary, and special), SOCIAL SCIENCE (history, human services, liberal arts/general studies, and psychology). Business is the strongest academically. Psychology and human services are the largest.

Required: To graduate, students must complete 127 credit hours with a minimum GPA of 2.0, (2.5 is required for acceptance to teacher certification program), including 12 credits in English/speech, 9 in social/behavioral sciences, 6 each in math/computer, philosophy/religious studies and natural sciences, and 3 in fine arts. Human services majors must complete 2 internships. The number of hours in the major varies, from 36 to 39 for arts and sciences, to 51 to 60 for business and education, to 40 to 58 for psychology and human services.

Special: The college offers internships in history, political science, business, human services, and psychology, and in Rutland County businesses, human service agencies, and elementary and secondary schools. In addition, dual majors, study abroad, and independent and directed study options are available. An accelerated degree program is available in organizational leadership. There are 5 national honor societies.

Faculty/Classroom: 56% of faculty are male; 44%, female. All teach undergraduates. No introductory courses are taught by graduate students. The average class size in an introductory lecture is 15; in a laboratory, 12; and in a regular course, 8.

Admissions: 81% of the 2005-2006 applicants were accepted. The SAT scores for the 2005-2006 freshman class were: Verbal--25% below 500, and 75% between 500 and 599; Math--25% below 500, and 75% between 500 and 599. The ACT scores were 100% between 21 and 23. 10% of the current freshmen were in the top fifth of their class; 60% were in the top two fifths.

Requirements: The SAT is required and the ACT is recommended. In addition, applicants should be graduates of accredited secondary schools or have earned a GED. College preparatory study must include 4 years of English, 3 of math, 2 each of science and social studies, and 5 other academic electives. The college prefers that students rank in the upper 70% of their graduating class. An essay is required and an interview is recommended. A GPA of 2.0 is required. AP and CLEP credits are accepted. Important factors in the admissions decision are advanced placement or honor courses, leadership record, and extracurricular activities record.

Procedure: Freshmen are admitted to all sessions. Entrance exams should be taken by December of the senior year. There are early admissions and deferred admissions plans. Application deadlines are open. Application fee is $25. Applications are accepted on-line.

Transfer: 47 transfer students enrolled in 2004-2005. Transfers must present a minimum GPA of 2.0. 30 of 127 credits required for the bachelor's degree must be completed at CSJ.

Visiting: There are regularly scheduled orientations for prospective students, including a campus tour, admissions interview, and visits to classes during fall and spring. There are guides for informal visits and visitors may sit in on classes and stay overnight. To schedule a visit, contact the Admissions Office at *admissions@csj.edu*.

Financial Aid: In 2005-2006, 83% of all full-time freshmen and 95% of continuing full-time students received some form of financial aid. 83% of full-time freshmen and 95% of continuing full-time students received need-based aid. Need-based scholarships or need-based grants averaged $11,488 ($21,550 maximum); need-based self-help aid (loans and jobs) averaged $5414 ($11,453 maximum); and other awards averaged $3472 ($7500 maximum). 40% of undergraduates work part time. Average annual earnings from campus work are $850. The average financial indebtedness of the 2005 graduate was $19,787. The FAFSA, the state aid form, and the college's own financial statement are required. The deadline for filing freshman financial aid applications for fall entry is March 1.

International Students: There were 4 international students enrolled in a recent year. They must score satisfactorily on the written TOEFL and also take the SAT or the ACT.

Computers: Library and teaching labs have computers for student use. Passwords are issued to students, who have Internet access in dorms. All students may access the system. There are no time limits and no fees.

Graduates: From July 1, 2004 to June 30, 2005, 61 bachelor's degrees were awarded. The most popular majors were business (39%), education (28%), and liberal studies (20%). In an average class, 28% graduate in 4 years or less, 37% graduate in 5 years or less, and 39% graduate in 6 years or less. 3 companies recruited on campus in 2004-2005. Of the 2004 graduating class, 35% were enrolled in graduate school within 6 months of graduation and 80% were employed.

Admissions Contact: Patricia Ryan, Director of Admissions and Marketing. E-mail: *admissions@csj.edu* Web: *www.csj.edu*

GODDARD COLLEGE   C-2
Plainfield, VT 05667   **(802) 454-8311, ext. 322**
(800) 468-4888; Fax: (802) 454-1029

Full-time: 130 men, 190 women	**Faculty:** 14
Part-time: none	**Ph.D.s:** 71%
Graduate: 100 men, 210 women	**Student/Faculty:** 23 to 1
Year: semesters	**Tuition:** $18,100
Application Deadline: open	**Room & Board:** $3000
Freshman Class: n/av	
SAT or ACT: not required	**COMPETITIVE**

Goddard College, founded in 1938, is a private college that stresses progressive, individualized education for personal and community transformation, based on John Dewey's learning-by-involvement theory. Figures in the above capsule and in this profile are approximate.The library contains 70,000 volumes and 1100 audio/video tapes/CDs/DVDs, and subscribes to 280 periodicals including electronic. Computerized library services include interlibrary loans and database searching. Special learning facilities include a learning resource center, radio station, a holograph lab, and a video/photo studio. The 200-acre campus is in a rural area 10 miles from Montpelier. Including any residence halls, there are 26 buildings.

Student Life: 87% of undergraduates are from out of state, mostly the Northeast. Others are from 49 states, 11 foreign countries, and Canada. 82% are white. The average age of freshmen is 21; all undergraduates, 26. 38% do not continue beyond their first year; 46% remain to graduate.

Housing: 225 students can be accommodated in college housing, which includes single-sex and coed dormitories and married-student housing. In addition, there are special-interest houses. On-campus housing is guaranteed for all 4 years. 70% of students live on campus; of those, 75% remain on campus on weekends. Alcohol is not permitted. All students may keep cars.

Activities: There are no fraternities or sororities. There are 9 groups on campus, including art, drama, gay, jazz band, literary magazine, newspaper, photography, radio and TV, and student government. Popular campus events include .

Sports: There is no sports program at Goddard. Facilities include tennis and volleyball courts and hiking and cross-country ski trails.

Disabled Students: Wheelchair ramps, elevators, special parking, and specially equipped rest rooms are available.

Services: There is remedial writing. An adviser system requires 1-hour weekly meetings with a faculty adviser.

Campus Safety and Security: Measures include 24-hour foot and vehicle patrol, self-defense education, shuttle buses, and informal discussions. There are pamphlets/posters/films and lighted pathways/sidewalks.

Programs of Study: Goddard confers the B.A. degree. Master's degrees are also awarded. Bachelor's degrees are awarded in COMMUNICATIONS AND THE ARTS (creative writing, media arts, and visual and performing arts), EDUCATION (education), ENGINEERING AND ENVIRONMENTAL DESIGN (environmental science), SOCIAL SCIENCE (counseling/psychology, crosscultural studies, human ecology, interdisciplinary studies, social science, and women's studies). Writing, literature, and education are the strongest academically. Women's studies is the largest.

Required: All degree programs are full-time only, provide individual faculty advisers for every semester (except study leaves), and require written study plans and narrative evaluations. Individual programs of study are student designed, although the program in general is course based. There are no declared majors, but in the last semester of enrollment, all students must complete an in-depth senior study or project that may be cross- or multidisciplinary and requires foundation work comparable to a major. A total of 120 credits is required to graduate.

Special: Students and faculty design all curricula; there are no prescribed courses. Learning takes the form of group or independent studies, workshops, action projects, research, field trips, seminars, and performances. There are a number of away-from-campus study options, including a field semester involving an internship, apprenticeship, or study-travel and a semester-abroad program offered in 20 countries.

Faculty/Classroom: 57% of faculty are male; 43%, female. All teach undergraduates. No introductory courses are taught by graduate students. The average class size in an introductory lecture is 8 and in a regular course, 10.

Requirements: Goddard admits students who can contribute to its learning community and who will thrive in a self-directed study program, and bases the admissions decision on the student's application, which includes several essays, letters of recommendation, and transcripts, and samples of the student's work. A personal interview, and SAT or ACT scores, when submitted, are also considered. AP and CLEP credits are accepted. Important factors in the admissions decision are personality/intangible qualities, advanced placement or honor courses, and evidence of special talent.

Procedure: Freshmen are admitted to all sessions. There are early decision and deferred admissions plans. Application deadlines are open. Applications are accepted on-line. Check with the school for current deadlines and fee.

Transfer: College transcripts must be submitted by transfer applicants. 30 of 120 credits required for the bachelor's degree must be completed at Goddard.

Visiting: There are regularly scheduled orientations for prospective students, including Discover Goddard Days held in fall and spring and individual tours and interviews. There are guides for informal visits and visitors may sit in on classes and stay overnight. To schedule a visit, contact the Admissions Office at (802) 454-8311, ext. 307 or (800) 468-4888, ext. or *admissions@goddard.edu.*

Financial Aid: The FAFSA is required. Check with the school for current deadlines.

International Students: A satisfactory score is required on the written TOEFL.

Computers: All students may access the system 24 hours a day, 7 days a week. There are no time limits and no fees.

Admissions Contact: Brenda Hawkins, Director of Admissions. E-mail: *admissions@.goddard.edu* Web: *http://www.goddard.edu*

GREEN MOUNTAIN COLLEGE A-4
Poultney, VT 05764

(802) 287-8000
(800) 776-6675; Fax: (802) 287-8099

Full-time: 345 men, 315 women	**Faculty:** 41
Part-time: 14 men, 10 women	**Ph.D.s:** 93%
Graduate: none	**Student/Faculty:** 16 to 1
Year: semesters	**Tuition:** $23,404
Application Deadline: open	**Room & Board:** $8760
Freshman Class: 925 applied, 839 accepted, 252 enrolled	
SAT Verbal/Math: 520/490*	**ACT:** 20	**COMPETITIVE**

Green Mountain College, established in 1834, is a private, nonprofit, environmental liberal arts institution. In addition to regional accreditation, GMC has baccalaureate program accreditation with NRPA. The library contains 60,000 volumes, 10,000 microform items, and 2000 audio/video tapes/CDs/DVDs, and subscribes to 300 periodicals including electronic. Computerized library services include the card catalog, interlibrary loans, database searching, Internet access, and laptop Internet portals. Special learning facilities include a learning resource center, art gallery, radio station, an organic farm, a rope course, an ice climbing wall, the Dean Nature Preserve, the Poultney River watershed, and the Welsh Heritage Center. The 155-acre campus is in a small town 20 miles southwest of Rutland. Including any residence halls, there are 26 buildings.

Student Life: 89% of undergraduates are from out of state, mostly the Northeast. Students are from 28 states, 10 foreign countries, and Canada. 83% are from public schools. 70% are white. The average age of freshmen is 18; all undergraduates, 21. 28% do not continue beyond their first year; 40% remain to graduate.

Housing: 575 students can be accommodated in college housing, which includes coed dorms. In addition, there are honors houses and special-interest houses. There are floors for adventure recreation, creative arts, quiet, substance free, and sustainable living. On-campus housing is guaranteed for all 4 years. 95% of students live on campus; of those, 80% remain on campus on weekends. All students may keep cars.

Activities: There are no fraternities or sororities. There are 30 groups on campus, including art, bagpipe band, band, big brothers/big sisters, cheerleading, choir, chorale, chorus, dance, drama, environmental, ethnic, gay, honors, international, jazz band, literary magazine, newspaper, orchestra, photography, professional, radio and TV, religious, rugby, social, social service, student government, ultimate frisbee, women's concerns, and yearbook. Popular campus events include family weekend, Honors Banquet, and Welsh Heritage Harvest Festival.

Sports: There are 7 intercollegiate sports for men and 7 for women, and 8 intramural sports for men and 7 for women. Facilities include a gym with an indoor pool, a weight room, playing fields, tennis courts, a par course, a fitness trail, and a ropes course.

Disabled Students: 70% of the campus is accessible. Wheelchair ramps, elevators, special parking, specially equipped rest rooms, special class scheduling, and lowered drinking fountains are available.

Services: Counseling and information services are available, as is tutoring in every subject. There is remedial math, reading, and writing. A transition to success program may be required or recommended to some applicants.

Campus Safety and Security: Measures include 24-hour foot and vehicle patrol, security escort services, shuttle buses, and lighted pathways/sidewalks.

Programs of Study: GMC confers B.A., B.S., and B.F.A. degrees. Bachelor's degrees are awarded in AGRICULTURE (environmental studies, and natural resource management), BIOLOGICAL SCIENCE (biology/biological science), BUSINESS (business administration and management, hospitality management services, hotel/motel and restaurant management, recreation and leisure services, and recreational facilities management), COMMUNICATIONS AND THE ARTS (art, arts administration/management, communications, creative writing, English, fine arts, and visual and performing arts), EDUCATION (art, elementary, English, secondary, social studies, and special), HEALTH PROFESSIONS (recreation therapy), SOCIAL SCIENCE (behavioral science, history, liberal arts/general studies, philosophy, psychology, and sociology). Recreation, environmental studies, and education have the largest enrollment and are the strongest academically.

Required: To graduate, students must complete 37 hours in Environmental Liberal Arts, including 4 core courses, a 1-credit orientation course, and 8 additional courses chosen from 4 distribution categories. A minimum GPA of 2.0 is required. Students must complete 120 to 125 credit hours, with 42 to 65 hours in the major. 33 credits must be completed in upper-division courses.

Special: Semester-long internships are required in all majors. Students may study abroad in Wales, Korea, England, Spain, Japan, France, and Italy. Work-study programs and a self-designed major are available. Co-op and accelerated degree programs are available in resort management and hospitality management. There is 1 national honor society, a freshman honors program, and 4 departmental honors programs.

Faculty/Classroom: 64% of faculty are male; 36%, female. 66% teach undergraduates and 34% both teach and do research. The average class size in an introductory lecture is 25; in a laboratory, 9; and in a regular course, 14.

Admissions: 91% of the 2005-2006 applicants were accepted. The SAT scores for the 2005-2006 freshman class were: Verbal--36% below 500, 39% between 500 and 599, 23% between 600 and 700, and 1% above 700; Math--51% below 500, 38% between 500 and 599, 10% between 600 and 700, and 1% above 700. The ACT scores were 41% below 21, 39% between 21 and 23, 11% between 24 and 26, 8% between 27 and 28, and 1% above 28. 13% of the current freshmen were in the top fifth of their class; 34% were in the top two fifths.

Requirements: The SAT is required and the ACT is recommended. In addition, applicants must graduate from an accredited secondary school or have a GED. 16 academic credits are required. Students must complete 4 years in English, 3 years in math, 2 to 3 years in science, and 2 years each in history and social studies. An essay is required. Interviews are recommended, along with portfolios where appropriate. A GPA of 2.4 is required. AP and CLEP credits are accepted. Important factors in the admissions decision are personality/intangible qualities, advanced placement or honor courses, and evidence of special talent.

Procedure: Freshmen are admitted fall and spring. Entrance exams should be taken in the fall of the senior year of high school. There are early admissions and deferred admissions plans. There is a rolling admissions plan. Application deadlines are open. Application fee is $30. Applications are accepted on-line.

Transfer: Transfer students need a GPA of 2.0. They must have earned a minimum of 12 credits and are required to submit an essay. The SAT or ACT is required, along with 2 letters of recommendation and a dean's statement from the last school attended. 30 of 120 to 125 credits required for the bachelor's degree must be completed at GMC.

Visiting: There are regularly scheduled orientations for prospective students, including a campus tour, presentations by administrators, a student panel, lunch in the dining hall, and academic offerings. There are guides for informal visits and visitors may sit in on classes and stay overnight. To schedule a visit, contact Tammy Dora, Campus Visit Coordinator at *visit@greenmtn.edu.*

Financial Aid: In a recent year, 80% of all full-time freshmen and 78% of continuing full-time students received some form of financial aid. 74% of full-time freshmen and 72% of continuing full-time students received need-based aid. The average freshman award was $10,983. Need-based scholarships or need-based grants averaged $8413; and need-based self-help aid (loans and jobs) averaged $2865. 45% of undergraduates work part time. Average annual earnings from campus work are $1500. The average financial indebtedness of the 2005 graduate was $19,000. The FAFSA is required.

International Students: There are 10 international students enrolled. The school actively recruits these students. They must take the TOEFL and also take the SAT or the ACT.

Computers: Wireless access is available. There are 80 PCs and Macs available for student use and 2 network jacks in each dorm room. Wireless access is available in the library. All students may access the system 24 hours/7 days a week. There are no time limits and no fees.

Graduates: From July 1, 2004 to June 30, 2005, 107 bachelor's degrees were awarded. The most popular majors were recreation (18%), environmental studies (14%), and education (12%). In an average class, 24% graduate in 4 years or less, 37% graduate in 5 years or less, and 40% graduate in 6 years or less. 21 companies recruited on campus in

2004-2005. Of the 2004 graduating class, 4% were enrolled in graduate school within 6 months of graduation and 75% were employed.

Admissions Contact: Joel R. Wincowski, Dean of Enrollment and Retention Management. A video is available.
E-mail: *admiss@greenmtn.edu* Web: *www.greenmtn.edu*

JOHNSON STATE COLLEGE
C-2
Johnson, VT 05656

(802) 635-1219
(800) 635-2356; Fax: (802) 635-1230

Full-time: 505 men, 610 women	**Faculty:** 62; IIB, -$
Part-time: 105 men, 320 women	**Ph.D.s:** 90%
Graduate: 60 men, 170 women	**Student/Faculty:** 18 to 1
Year: semesters, summer session	**Tuition:** $5810 ($12,400)
Application Deadline: see profile	**Room & Board:** $6020
Freshman Class: n/av	
SAT or ACT: required	**LESS COMPETITIVE**

Johnson State College, founded in 1828, is a public liberal arts and science college, offering more than 30 academic and professional degree programs. Figures in the above capsule and in this profile are approximate. The library contains 96,584 volumes, 180,158 microform items, and 7200 audio/video tapes/CDs/DVDs, and subscribes to 631 periodicals including electronic. Computerized library services include the card catalog, interlibrary loans, and database searching. Special learning facilities include a learning resource center, art gallery, radio station, and 24-hour study room. The 350-acre campus is in a small town 45 miles northeast of Burlington. Including any residence halls, there are 12 buildings.

Student Life: 63% of undergraduates are from Vermont. Others are from 23 states, 6 foreign countries, and Canada. 71% are white. The average age of freshmen is 19; all undergraduates, 21.

Housing: 549 students can be accommodated in college housing, which includes coed dormitories, on-campus apartments, and married-student housing. In addition, there are special-interest houses. On-campus housing is guaranteed for all 4 years. 57% of students live on campus. Alcohol is not permitted. All students may keep cars.

Activities: There are no fraternities or sororities. There are 35 groups on campus, including art, band, choir, chorus, dance, drama, gay, international, jazz band, literary magazine, musical theater, newspaper, photography, political, professional, radio and TV, religious, social, social service, student government, and yearbook. Popular campus events include Winter Carnival, Coffee House (weekly live entertainment), and Women's History Month Celebration.

Sports: There are 5 intercollegiate sports for men and 5 for women, and 20 intramural sports for men and 20 for women. Facilities include the athletic center which houses a 25-yard pool, a 700-seat varsity basketball court, 3 handball/racquetball courts, a weight training room, an aerobic fitness center, a 7000-square-foot multi-use gym, and a fully equipped training room.

Disabled Students: 60% of the campus is accessible. Wheelchair ramps, elevators, special parking, specially equipped rest rooms, special class scheduling, and lowered drinking fountains are available.

Services: Counseling and information services are available, as is tutoring in most subjects. There is a reader service for the blind, and remedial math, reading, and writing. The Academic Support Services Department provides accommodations for students with a documented learning disability.

Campus Safety and Security: Measures include 24-hour foot and vehicle patrol, self-defense education, security escort services, and shuttle buses. There are informal discussions, pamphlets/posters/films, emergency telephones, and lighted pathways/sidewalks.

Programs of Study: Johnson State confers B.A., B.S., and B.F.A. degrees. Associate and master's degrees are also awarded. Bachelor's degrees are awarded in AGRICULTURE (natural resource management), BIOLOGICAL SCIENCE (biology/biological science and cell biology), BUSINESS (accounting, business administration and management, business systems analysis, hospitality management services, management information systems, recreational facilities management, small business management, and tourism), COMMUNICATIONS AND THE ARTS (art, creative writing, English, fine arts, jazz, journalism, music, music business management, music history and appreciation, music performance, performing arts, studio art, theater design, theater management, and visual and performing arts), COMPUTER AND PHYSICAL SCIENCE (computer management, information sciences and systems, and mathematics), EDUCATION (art, athletic training, education, elementary, English, environmental, mathematics, middle school, music, physical, recreation, science, and secondary), ENGINEERING AND ENVIRONMENTAL DESIGN (environmental science), HEALTH PROFESSIONS (allied health, health science, premedicine, and sports medicine), SOCIAL SCIENCE (anthropology, behavioral science, history, humanities, liberal arts/general studies, physical fitness/movement, political science/government, prelaw, psychology, and sociology). Environmental science, sports medicine, and outdoor education are the largest.

Required: The bachelor's degree requires completion of at least 120 credit hours of course work (not including basic skills credits), with a

minimum cumulative GPA of 2.0. In addition, students must complete the general education core curriculum and an approved major as well as take a writing proficiency exam.

Special: All students are encouraged to complete an internship. Through the National Student Exchange Program, students may study at another institution or abroad in 51 countries for a semester or a year. Co-op programs are offered in business, tourism, hospitality management, and education, and cross-registration is available with other Vermont state colleges. There is 1 national honor society.

Faculty/Classroom: 58% of faculty are male; 42%, female. All teach undergraduates. No introductory courses are taught by graduate students.

Requirements: The SAT or ACT is required. In addition, successful candidates for admission have generally completed a college preparatory curriculum consisting of 4 years of English, 3 of math (2 of algebra, 1 of geometry), 3 of social sciences, and 2 of science (including 1 lab science). An official high school transcript or GED test score must be submitted with the application. In addition, 1 letter of recommendation, preferably from a guidance counselor, and SAT I or ACT scores should be sent with the application or under separate cover. A GPA of 2.0 is required. AP and CLEP credits are accepted. Important factors in the admissions decision are advanced placement or honor courses, recommendations by school officials, and extracurricular activities record.

Procedure: Freshmen are admitted fall and spring. There is a deferred admissions plan. Check with the schol for current deadlines and fee. Applications are accepted on-line.

Transfer: A GPA of at least 2.0 is required. 30 of 120 credits required for the bachelor's degree must be completed at Johnson State.

Visiting: There are regularly scheduled orientations for prospective students, including a campus tour and an admission interview. Students may request to meet with a faculty member. There are guides for informal visits and visitors may sit in on classes. To schedule a visit, contact Marie Burns, Admission Receptionist.

Financial Aid: Johnson State is a member of CSS. The FAFSA is required. Check with the school for current deadlines.

International Students: The school actively recruits these students. A satisfactory score is required on the written TOEFL.

Computers: All students may access the system. There are no time limits and no fees.

Admissions Contact: Penny P. Howrigan, Asociate Dean of Enrollment Services. E-mail: *jscappy@badger.jsc.vsc.edu*
Web: *www.jsc.vsc.edu*

LYNDON STATE COLLEGE
D-2
Lyndonville, VT 05851

(802) 626-6413
(800) 225-1998; Fax: (802) 626-6335

Full-time: 560 men, 570 women	**Faculty:** 56; IIB, --$
Part-time: 70 men, 230 women	**Ph.D.s:** 60%
Graduate: 1 man, 5 women	**Student/Faculty:** 20 to 1
Year: semesters, summer session	**Tuition:** $7549 ($14,869)
Application Deadline: open	**Room & Board:** $6674
Freshman Class: n/av	
SAT or ACT: required	**LESS COMPETITIVE**

Lyndon State College, founded in 1911 as a teachers' college, became a liberal arts school in 1962, offering undergraduate and graduate courses. There is 1 graduate school. Some figures in the above capsule and in this profile are approximate. In addition to regional accreditation, LSC has baccalaureate program accreditation with NRPA. The library contains 100,000 volumes, 10,000 microform items, and 3600 audio/video tapes/CDs/DVDs, and subscribes to 545 periodicals including electronic. Computerized library services include the card catalog, interlibrary loans, database searching, and Internet access. Special learning facilities include a learning resource center, art gallery, radio station, TV station, a founder's museum, and meteorology lab. The 175-acre campus is in a small town in northeastern Vermont, 184 miles north of Boston. Including any residence halls, there are 17 buildings.

Student Life: 60% of undergraduates are from Vermont. Others are from 24 states, 12 foreign countries, and Canada. 99% are white. The average age of freshmen is 18; all undergraduates, 24. 33% do not continue beyond their first year; 41% remain to graduate.

Housing: 600 students can be accommodated in college housing, which includes single-sex and coed dorms. In addition, there are special-interest houses. On-campus housing is available on a first-come, first-served basis. Priority is given to out-of-town students. 56% of students commute. All students may keep cars.

Activities: There are no fraternities or sororities. There are 22 groups on campus, including cheerleading, choir, chorale, chorus, dance, drama, film, gay, honors, international, jazz band, literary magazine, newspaper, photography, political, professional, radio and TV, religious, social, social service, student government, and yearbook. Popular campus events include Family Weekend, Alumni Weekend, and a concert series.

Sports: There are 5 intercollegiate sports for men and 5 for women, and 12 intramural sports for men and 12 for women. Facilities include

a fitness center, which includes a wide variety of cardiovascular, selectorized, and free-weight equipment, racquetball courts, an auxiliary gym, and an Olympic-size pool. Other facilities include outdoor tennis courts, cross-country ski trails and running trails, access to an ice rink, nearby mountains, and a ski resort, and softball, soccer, basketball, and rugby fields.

Disabled Students: 70% of the campus is accessible. Wheelchair ramps, elevators, special parking, specially equipped rest rooms, and lowered drinking fountains are available.

Services: Counseling and information services are available, as is tutoring in every subject. There is remedial math, reading, and writing. A math lab and a writing center are available for student use.

Campus Safety and Security: Measures include 24-hour foot and vehicle patrol, self-defense education, security escort services, and emergency telephones. There are lighted pathways/sidewalks and a security and safety service on campus as well as a 24-hour emergency rescue squad.

Programs of Study: LSC confers B.A. and B.S. degrees. Associate and master's degrees are also awarded. Bachelor's degrees are awarded in BUSINESS (accounting, business administration and management, recreation and leisure services, and sports management), COMMUNICATIONS AND THE ARTS (communications, English, graphic design, journalism, multimedia, and radio/television technology), COMPUTER AND PHYSICAL SCIENCE (atmospheric sciences and meteorology, mathematics, natural sciences, and science), EDUCATION (early childhood, elementary, English, physical, recreation, and science), SOCIAL SCIENCE (human services, interdisciplinary studies, psychology, and social science). Meteorology, natural science, and math are the strongest academically. Education, communications, and business are the largest.

Required: All students must maintain a minimum GPA of 2.0 while taking 122 semester hours, including 42 hours in liberal arts. Distribution requirements include 28 credits in arts, humanities, math and science, and social and behavioral sciences. Required courses include freshman English and college algebra.

Special: Cooperative programs in a variety of businesses, including local ski areas, social agencies, and radio and TV stations, internships in recreation programs and communications, and study abroad in Nova Scotia and England are available. B.A.-B.S. degrees, work-study, a general studies degree, dual and student-designed majors, a 3-2 engineering degree with Norwich University in Vermont, credit for life experience, nondegree study, cross-registration, accelerated degree programs, and pass/fail options also are offered. There is 1 national honor society, a freshman honors program, and 1 departmental honors program.

Faculty/Classroom: 66% of faculty are male; 34%, female. All teach undergraduates. The average class size in an introductory lecture is 20; in a laboratory, 16; and in a regular course, 16.

Admissions: 4 freshmen graduated first in their class, in a recent year.

Requirements: The SAT or ACT is required. In addition, LSC recommends that applicants have 4 years of English and 2 each of math, foreign language, history, and science. An essay is required, as is a recommendation from the high school principal or guidance counselor. An interview is recommended. The GED is accepted. A GPA of 2.0 is required. AP and CLEP credits are accepted. Important factors in the admissions decision are advanced placement or honor courses, recommendations by school officials, and leadership record.

Procedure: Freshmen are admitted fall and spring. There is a rolling admissions plan. There are early decision, early admissions, and deferred admissions plans. Application deadlines are open. Application fee is $34. Notification is sent on a rolling basis. Applications are accepted on-line.

Transfer: 115 transfer students enrolled in a recent year. Interviews are recommended for transfer students. An official transcript from each college attended is required. 30 of 122 credits required for the bachelor's degree must be completed at LSC.

Visiting: There are regularly scheduled orientations for prospective students, including a tour, an information session, and faculty presentations. There are guides for informal visits and visitors may sit in on classes and stay overnight. To schedule a visit, contact the Admissions Office.

Financial Aid: In a recent year, 87% of all full-time freshmen and 96% of continuing full-time students received some form of financial aid. 69% of full-time freshmen and 75% of continuing full-time students received need-based aid. The average freshman award was $8079. Need-based scholarships or need-based grants averaged $3879 ($5000 maximum); need-based self-help aid (loans and jobs) averaged $3817 ($4625 maximum); and other non-need-based awards and non-need-based scholarships averaged $3860 ($5646 maximum). Average annual earnings from campus work are $1262. The average financial indebtedness of the a recent year's graduate was $18,084. LSC is a member of CSS. The FAFSA is required. Parent and student income tax forms, may be requested. Check with the school for current deadlines.

International Students: There were 10 international students enrolled in a recent year. A satisfactory score on the TOEFL is required.

Computers: All students may access the system 24 hours a day, 7 days a week. There are no time limits and no fees. It is strongly recommended that all students have a personal computer.

Admissions Contact: Admissions.
E-mail: *admissions@lyndonstate.edu* Web: *www.lyndonstate.edu*

MARLBORO COLLEGE   B-6
Marlboro, VT 05344-0300   (802) 258-9261
                                    (800) 343-0049; Fax: (802) 258-9300

Full-time: 126 men, 201 women	Faculty: 35
Part-time: 4 men, 5 women	Ph.D.s: 77%
Graduate: none	Student/Faculty: 9 to 1
Year: semesters	Tuition: $27,790
Application Deadline: February 15	Room & Board: $8190
Freshman Class: 317 applied, 246 accepted, 69 enrolled	
SAT Verbal/Math: 660/580*	ACT: 25 VERY COMPETITIVE+

Marlboro College, established in 1946, is a small private institution offering degrees in the liberal and fine arts and humanities, and employing self-designed programs of study. The library contains 65,216 volumes, 5799 microform items, and 2990 audio/video tapes/CDs/DVDs, and subscribes to 188 periodicals and 20,000 electronic. Computerized library services include the card catalog, interlibrary loans, database searching, Internet access, and laptop Internet portals. Special learning facilities include a learning resource center, art gallery, planetarium, and observatory. The 366-acre campus is in a rural area 9 miles west of Brattleboro, 2 1/2 hours from Boston. Including any residence halls, there are 36 buildings.

Student Life: 89% of undergraduates are from out of state, mostly the Northeast. Students are from 36 states, 5 foreign countries, and Canada. 70% are from public schools. 83% are white. The average age of freshmen is 19; all undergraduates, 21. 28% do not continue beyond their first year; 48% remain to graduate.

Housing: 266 students can be accommodated in college housing, which includes single-sex and coed dormitories, on-campus apartments, and married-student housing.In addition, there are alcohol-free and smoke-free dorms. On-campus housing is guaranteed for the freshman year only and is available on a first-come, first-served basis. 84% of students live on campus; of those, 90% remain on campus on weekends. All students may keep cars.

Activities: There are no fraternities or sororities. There are 25 groups on campus, including art, chess, chorus, computers, dance, drama, film, gay, international, jazz band, literary magazine, musical theater, newspaper, photography, political, social, social service, and student government. Popular campus events include Green-up Day, Creativity Lecture Series, and Visiting Writers Series.

Sports: There is 1 intercollegiate sport for men and 1 for women, and 1 intramural sport for men and 1 for women. Facilities include a soccer field, a volleyball court, cross-country trails, a basketball court, a weight room, a climbing wall, and field trips for canoeing, white-water rafting, and skiing.

Disabled Students: 90% of the campus is accessible. Wheelchair ramps, special parking, specially equipped rest rooms, and special class scheduling are available.

Services: Counseling and information services are available, as is tutoring in some subjects, including writing and languages, math, and organic chemistry.

Campus Safety and Security: Measures include self-defense education, informal discussions and, pamphlets/posters/films.There is a buddy system.

Programs of Study: Marlboro confers B.A., B.S., B.A. in International Studies, B.S. in International Studies degrees. Master's degrees are also awarded. Bachelor's degrees are awarded in BIOLOGICAL SCIENCE (biochemistry, biology/biological science, botany, and microbiology), COMMUNICATIONS AND THE ARTS (creative writing, dance, dramatic arts, English, fine arts, French, German, Greek, Italian, Latin, linguistics, music, photography, Russian, and Spanish), COMPUTER AND PHYSICAL SCIENCE (chemistry, computer science, mathematics, and physics), HEALTH PROFESSIONS (premedicine), SOCIAL SCIENCE (anthropology, economics, history, interdisciplinary studies, international studies, philosophy, political science/government, prelaw, psychology, social science, and sociology). Sciences, humanities, and world studies are the strongest academically. Literature, biology, and sociology are the largest.

Required: To graduate, students must complete a plan of concentration, a writing requirement, and a freshman seminar. A minimum GPA of 2.0 is required. Students must earn 120 credits, with 50 credits in the major, and complete a thesis and an oral exam.

Special: Marlboro offers a variety of internships, cross-registration with Huron University in London, and study abroad in many countries. The World Studies Program combines liberal arts with international studies, including 5 to 8 months of internship work in another culture. Accelerated and B.A.-B.S. degree programs are available. Students may pursue dual majors. Majors reflect an integrated course of study designed by students and their faculty advisers during the junior year.

Faculty/Classroom: 62% of faculty are male; 38%, female. All teach undergraduates. The average class size in an introductory lecture is 10; in a laboratory, 8; and in a regular course, 8.

Admissions: 78% of the 2005-2006 applicants were accepted. The SAT scores for the 2005-2006 freshman class were: Verbal--4% below 500, 10% between 500 and 599, 57% between 600 and 700, and 29% above 700; Math--9% below 500, 51% between 500 and 599, 35% between 600 and 700, and 5% above 700. The ACT scores were 35% between 21 and 23, 29% between 24 and 26, 29% between 27 and 28, and 7% above 28. 46% of the current freshmen were in the top fifth of their class; 82% were in the top two fifths. 2 freshmen graduated first in their class in a recent year.

Requirements: The SAT or ACT is required. In addition, applicants typically graduate from an accredited secondary school or have a GED. They are encouraged to earn 16 Carnegie units and complete 4 years of English and 3 years each of math, science, history, and a foreign language. Essays and interviews are required. AP and CLEP credits are accepted. Important factors in the admissions decision are advanced placement or honor courses, evidence of special talent, and extracurricular activities record.

Procedure: Freshmen are admitted fall and spring. Entrance exams should be taken by October before entry. There are early decision, early admissions, and deferred admissions plans. Early decision applications should be filed by November 15; regular applications, by February 15 for fall entry and December 1 for spring entry. Notification of early decision is sent December 15; regular decision, April 1. Applications are accepted on-line. The fall 2005 application fee was $50.

Transfer: Transfers must have a minimum GPA of 2.0. 42 of 120 credits required for the bachelor's degree must be completed at Marlboro.

Visiting: There are regularly scheduled orientations for prospective students, including a tour, faculty interview, and discussions with admissions and financial aid. There are guides for informal visits and visitors may sit in on classes and stay overnight. To schedule a visit, contact the Office of Admissions.

Financial Aid: In a recent year, 85% of all full-time students received some form of financial aid. 68% of full-time freshmen and 80% of continuing full-time students received need-based aid. The average freshman award was $20,907. Need-based scholarships or need-based grants averaged $15,969 ($24,250 maximum); need-based self-help aid (loans and jobs) averaged $4289 ($4555 maximum); and other non-need-based awards and non-need-based scholarships averaged $11,723 ($20,950 maximum). 68% of undergraduates worked part time. Average annual earnings from campus work were $1118. Marlboro is a member of CSS. The CSS/Profile or FAFSA is required. The priority date for freshman financial aid applications for fall entry is February 15. The deadline for filing freshman financial aid applications for fall entry is March 1.

International Students: The school actively recruits these students. They must score satisfactorily on the written TOEFL or on the electronic version and also take the SAT or the ACT.

Computers: Wireless access is available. All students may access the system 24 hours a day. There are no time limits and no fees.

Admissions Contact: Alan E. Young, Dean of Enrollment and Financial Aid. A video is available. E-mail: *ayoung@marlboro.edu* Web: *www.marlboro.edu*

MIDDLEBURY COLLEGE   A-3

Middlebury, VT 05753   (802) 443-3000; Fax: (802) 443-2065

Full-time: 1186 men, 1234 women	Faculty: 254; IIB, ++$
Part-time: 8 men, 17 women	Ph.D.s: 94%
Graduate: none	Student/Faculty: 10 to 1
Year: 4-1-4	Tuition: $42,120
Application Deadline: December 15	Room & Board: n/app
Freshman Class: 5254 applied, 1241 accepted, 555 enrolled	
SAT Verbal/Math: 740/730*	ACT: 32 MOST COMPETITIVE

Middlebury College, founded in 1800, is a small, private liberal arts institution offering degree programs in languages, humanities, and social and natural sciences. The $42,120 comprehensive fee includes room and board. The 3 libraries contain 942,122 volumes, 378,902 microform items, and 32,365 audio/video tapes/CDs/DVDs, and subscribe to 2271 periodicals including electronic. Computerized library services include the card catalog, interlibrary loans, database searching, and Internet access. Special learning facilities include a learning resource center, art gallery, and radio station. The 355-acre campus is in a small town 35 miles south of Burlington. Including any residence halls, there are 96 buildings.

Student Life: 94% of undergraduates are from out of state, mostly the Northeast. Students are from 50 states, 64 foreign countries, and Canada. 54% are from public schools. 68% are white. The average age of freshmen is 18; all undergraduates, 20. 3% do not continue beyond their first year; 90% remain to graduate.

Housing: 2335 students can be accommodated in college housing, which includes single-sex and coed dorms, on-campus apartments, and married-student housing. In addition, there are language, coed social,

multicultural, special-interest, and environmental houses. On-campus housing is guaranteed for all 4 years. 94% of students live on campus; of those, 90% remain on campus on weekends. All students may keep cars.

Activities: There are no fraternities or sororities. There are 145 groups on campus, including art, band, cheerleading, chess, choir, chorus, computers, dance, debate, drama, ethnic, gay, honors, international, jazz band, literary magazine, MMC (Middlebury Mountain Club), musical theater, newspaper, orchestra, photography, political, professional, radio and TV, religious, social, social service, student government, and yearbook. Popular campus events include Winter Carnival, Student Concert Series, and Clifford Symposium.

Sports: There are 13 intercollegiate sports for men and 15 for women, and 16 intramural sports for men and 17 for women. Facilities include 2 field houses, gyms, a swimming pool, a fitness center, tennis courts, playing fields, an 18-hole golf course, alpine and nordic ski areas, a 3000-seat campus stadium, an 8-lane 400-meter outdoor track, and a 2600-seat ice hockey facility.

Disabled Students: 60% of the campus is accessible. Wheelchair ramps, elevators, special parking, specially equipped rest rooms, special class scheduling, lowered drinking fountains, lowered telephones, and special housing are available.

Services: Counseling and information services are available, as is tutoring in every subject. There is a reader service for the blind.

Campus Safety and Security: Measures include 24-hour foot and vehicle patrol, self-defense education, security escort services, and shuttle buses. There are informal discussions, pamphlets/posters/films, emergency telephones, lighted pathways/sidewalks, and paid student patrol, ski patrol at the Snow Bowl, and special events staff.

Programs of Study: Midd confers the A.B. degree. Master's and doctoral degrees are also awarded. Bachelor's degrees are awarded in BIOLOGICAL SCIENCE (biochemistry, biology/biological science, molecular biology, and neurosciences), BUSINESS (international economics), COMMUNICATIONS AND THE ARTS (American literature, Chinese, classics, dance, dramatic arts, English, film arts, French, German, Italian, Japanese, literature, music, Russian, Spanish, and studio art), COMPUTER AND PHYSICAL SCIENCE (chemistry, computer science, geology, mathematics, and physics), ENGINEERING AND ENVIRONMENTAL DESIGN (architectural history and environmental science), SOCIAL SCIENCE (American studies, anthropology, East Asian studies, economics, European studies, geography, history, international studies, Latin American studies, liberal arts/general studies, Middle Eastern studies, philosophy, political science/government, psychology, religion, Russian and Slavic studies, sociology, and women's studies). Foreign languages, international studies, and science are the strongest academically. Economics, psychology, and English are the largest.

Required: Students must complete 36 courses, including winter-term courses. Freshmen must take a freshman seminar and a writing course, and all students must take phys ed. A major normally requires 12 courses, and most students can fulfill the distribution requirement and the cultures and civilization requirement by taking 6 to 8 courses outside of their major. Students may also elect to complete a minor.

Special: Off-campus opportunities include an international major program at one of the Middlebury College schools abroad; exchange programs with Berea, St. Mary's, and Swarthmore; a junior year abroad; study through the American Collegiate Consortium for East-West Cultural and Academic Exchange; a 1-year program at Lincoln and Worcester Colleges, Oxford; a Washington, D.C., semester; and a maritime studies program with Williams College at Mystic Seaport. Middlebury also offers an independent scholar program, joint and double majors, various professional programs, dual degrees in business management, forestry/environmental studies, engineering, and nursing, and an early assurance premed program with Dartmouth, Rochester, Tufts, and the Medical College of Pennsylvania, which assures medical school acceptance by the end of the sophomore year. There is a chapter of Phi Beta Kappa.

Faculty/Classroom: 61% of faculty are male; 39%, female. All teach undergraduates. The average class size in a regular course is 19.

Admissions: 24% of the 2005-2006 applicants were accepted. The SAT scores for the 2005-2006 freshman class were: Verbal--1% below 500, 4% between 500 and 599, 22% between 600 and 700, and 73% above 700; Math--1% below 500, 3% between 500 and 599, 32% between 600 and 700, and 64% above 700. The ACT scores were 2% below 21, 4% between 21 and 23, 11% between 24 and 26, 20% between 27 and 28, and 63% above 28. 95% of the current freshmen were in the top fifth of their class; 99% were in the top two fifths. 33 freshmen graduated first in their class.

Requirements: The SAT or ACT is required. In addition, students should submit test scores as follows: the new ACT, SAT or, 3 SAT : Subject tests, AP tests, IB tests, or any combination thereof. Secondary school preparation should include 4 years each of English, math and/or computer science, and 1 foreign language, 3 or more years of lab science and history and social science, and some study of music, art, and/or drama. AP credits are accepted. Important factors in the admissions decision are advanced placement or honor courses, recommendations by school officials, and evidence of special talent.

Procedure: Freshmen are admitted fall and spring. Entrance exams should be taken by December of the senior year. There are early decision, early admissions, and deferred admissions plans. Early decision applications should be filed by November 15; regular applications, by December 15 for fall entry, along with a $55 fee. Notification of early decision is sent December 15; regular decision, April 1. 261 early decision candidates were accepted for the 2005-2006 class. 579 applicants were on the 2005 waiting list; 38 were admitted. Applications are accepted on-line.

Transfer: Transfer students must have the strongest academic record possible through high school and a minimum 3.0 average in college. 18 of 36 credits required for the bachelor's degree must be completed at Midd.

Visiting: There are regularly scheduled orientations for prospective students, including campus tours and a group or individual interview. There are guides for informal visits and visitors may sit in on classes.

Financial Aid: In 2005-2006, 48% of all full-time freshmen and 41% of continuing full-time students received some form of financial aid. 45% of full-time freshmen and 41% of continuing full-time students received need-based aid. The average freshman award was $30,828. Need-based scholarships or need-based grants averaged $25,834 ($42,120 maximum); and need-based self-help aid (loans and jobs) averaged $4682 ($5500 maximum). 60% of undergraduates work part time. Average annual earnings from campus work are $675. The average financial indebtedness of the 2005 graduate was $20,957. Midd is a member of CSS. The CSS/Profile or FAFSA, the college's own financial statement, and the federal tax form are required. The deadline for filing freshman financial aid applications for fall entry is January 15.

International Students: There are 222 international students enrolled. The school actively recruits these students. They must take the TOEFL and also take the SAT or ACT and fulfill the same requirements as first-year applicants.

Computers: Wireless access is available. All students may access the system 24 hours a day. There are no time limits and no fees.

Graduates: From July 1, 2004 to June 30, 2005, 610 bachelor's degrees were awarded. The most popular majors were economics (12%), psychology (8%), and English (7%). Of the 2004 graduating class, 12 to 15% were enrolled in graduate school within 6 months of graduation.

Admissions Contact: Robert S. Clagett, Dean of Admissions. A video is available. E-mail: *admissions@middlebury.edu* Web: *www.middlebury.edu*

NORWICH UNIVERSITY   C-3
Northfield, VT 05663

(802) 485-2001
(800) 468-6679; Fax: (802) 485-2032

Full-time: 1360 men, 502 women	**Faculty:** 117
Part-time: 34 men, 7 women	**Ph.D.s:** 85%
Graduate: 537 men, 211 women	**Student/Faculty:** 16 to 1
Year: semesters, summer session	**Tuition:** $20,838
Application Deadline: open	**Room & Board:** $7374
Freshman Class: 1899 applied, 1470 accepted, 578 enrolled	
SAT Verbal/Math: 532/540*	**ACT:** 22 **COMPETITIVE**

Norwich University, founded in 1819, offers programs in the arts and sciences, architecture, engineering, health and physical science, criminal justice, history, international studies, studies in war and peace, management and accounting. There are 6 undergraduate and 2 graduate schools. In addition to regional accreditation, Norwich has baccalaureate program accreditation with ABET, ACBSP, NLN, CAAHEP and NLN. The library contains 245,931 volumes, 90,435 microform items, and 2872 audio/video tapes/CDs/DVDs, and subscribes to 815 periodicals including electronic. Computerized library services include the card catalog, interlibrary loans, database searching, Internet access, and laptop Internet portals. Special learning facilities include a learning resource center, art gallery, natural history museum, radio station, a greenhouse, and 3 computer labs. The 1125-acre campus is in a rural area 11 miles south of Montpelier. Including any residence halls, there are 36 buildings.

Student Life: 80% of undergraduates are from out of state, mostly the Northeast. Students are from 39 states, 13 foreign countries, and Canada. 82% are white. The average age of freshmen is 18; all undergraduates, 21. 25% do not continue beyond their first year; 52% remain to graduate.

Housing: 1598 students can be accommodated in college housing, which includes single-sex and coed dormitories. On-campus housing is guaranteed for the freshman year only and is available on a lottery system for upperclassmen. Priority is given to out-of-town students. 83% of students live on campus; of those, 85% remain on campus on weekends. Alcohol is not permitted. Upperclassmen may keep cars.

Activities: There are no fraternities or sororities. There are 75 groups on campus, including band, cheerleading, chess, choir, chorus, computers, drama, drill team, ethnic, honors, international, jazz band, literary magazine, marching band, musical theater, newspaper, orchestra, pep band, photography, political, professional, radio and TV, religious, social

service, and student government. Popular campus events include Regimental Ball, Winter Carnival, and Junior Weekend.

Sports: There are 12 intercollegiate sports for men and 7 for women, and 8 intramural sports for men and 8 for women. Facilities include an ice hockey arena, field house with an indoor track, an indoor swimming pool, aerobics room, weight and wrestling rooms, playing fields and an outdoor track, a 1200-seat basketball arena, and a 1000-seat hockey arena.

Disabled Students: Wheelchair ramps, elevators, special parking, specially equipped rest rooms, and lowered drinking fountains are available.

Services: Counseling and information services are available, as is tutoring in most subjects. There is remedial math, reading, and writing.

Campus Safety and Security: Measures include 24-hour foot and vehicle patrol and lighted pathways/sidewalks.

Programs of Study: Norwich confers B.A., B.S., and B.Arch. degrees. Associate degrees are also awarded. Bachelor's degrees are awarded in BIOLOGICAL SCIENCE (biochemistry and biology/biological science), BUSINESS (accounting, business administration and management, and business economics), COMMUNICATIONS AND THE ARTS (communications and English), COMPUTER AND PHYSICAL SCIENCE (chemistry, computer science, computer security and information assurance, geology, information sciences and systems, mathematics, and physics), EDUCATION (physical), ENGINEERING AND ENVIRONMENTAL DESIGN (architecture, civil engineering, computer engineering, electrical/electronics engineering, environmental science, mechanical engineering, and military science), HEALTH PROFESSIONS (medical laboratory technology, nursing, and sports medicine), SOCIAL SCIENCE (criminal justice, history, international studies, liberal arts/general studies, peace studies, political science/government, and psychology). Engineering and architecture are the strongest academically. Criminal justice and nursing are the largest.

Required: The total number of required credits and courses vary by program. All students are required to complete 3 credit hours in history and English 101-102, and 2 semesters in phys ed. A 2.0 GPA is required to graduate.

Special: Norwich offers internships, a Washington semester, work-study on-and-off-campus for service organizations and criminal justice programs, a B.A.-B.S. degree in communiations, and study abroad in 15 countries through other schools and organizations and through the Vermont Overseas Studies Program. International studies majors must study abroad in a country whose language they are studying. There are 5 national honor societies, including Phi Beta Kappa and 5 departmental honors programs.

Faculty/Classroom: 74% of faculty are male; 26%, female. 82% teach undergraduates and 82% both teach and do research. The average class size in an introductory lecture is 20; in a laboratory, 13; and in a regular course, 18.

Admissions: 77% of the 2005-2006 applicants were accepted. The SAT scores for the 2005-2006 freshman class were: Verbal--36% below 500, 40% between 500 and 599, 22% between 600 and 700, and 3% above 700; Math--31% below 500, 42% between 500 and 599, 24% between 600 and 700, and 3% above 700. The ACT scores were 40% below 21, 28% between 21 and 23, 20% between 24 and 26, 7% between 27 and 28, and 5% above 28. 30% of the current freshmen were in the top fifth of their class; 58% were in the top two fifths. 3 freshmen graduated first in their class.

Requirements: The SAT or ACT is required. In addition, applicants should graduate from an accredited secondary school with 18 academic credits or achieve the GED equivalent. Applications are accepted on IBM/Windows formatted computer disks. AP and CLEP credits are accepted. Important factors in the admissions decision are leadership record, extracurricular activities record, and evidence of special talent.

Procedure: Freshmen are admitted fall and spring. Entrance exams should be taken starting with spring of the junior year. There is a rolling admissions plan. Application deadlines are open. Application fee is $35. 60 early decision candidates were accepted for the 2005-2006 class. Applications are accepted on-line.

Transfer: 91 transfer students enrolled in 2004-2005. Transfer students should present a 2.0 GPA and meet all standards for entering freshmen. 60 of 116 credits required for the bachelor's degree must be completed at Norwich.

Visiting: There are regularly scheduled orientations for prospective students, including meetings with representatives from admissions, financial aid, academic offices, including Dean of Students or Commandant's Office, athletics (if desired), and a campus tour. There are guides for informal visits and visitors may sit in on classes and stay overnight. To schedule a visit, contact Admissions, Main Office.

Financial Aid: In 2005-2006, 97% of all full-time freshmen and 96% of continuing full-time students received some form of financial aid. 90% of full-time freshmen and 89% of continuing full-time students received need-based aid. Need-based scholarships or need-based grants averaged $11,087 ($20,088 maximum); need-based self-help aid (loans and jobs) averaged $6620 ($22,000 maximum); other non-need-based awards and non-need-based scholarships averaged $2059 ($10,044 maximum); and other awards averaged $1329 ($21,338 maximum). 50% of undergraduates work part time. Average annual earnings from campus work are $990. The average financial indebtedness of the 2005 graduate was $26,072. Norwich is a member of CSS. The CSS/Profile or FAFSA is required. The priority date for freshman financial aid applications for fall entry is March 1.

International Students: There are 39 international students enrolled. They must score satisfactorily on the written TOEFL or on the electronic version.

Computers: Wireless access is available. There is open access. Dorms are wired and there is no limitation to Internet access or other use of the network. All students may access the system 24 hours per day. There are no time limits. The fee is $500/year. It is strongly recommended that all students have a personal computer. It is required that students in architecture have personal computers. Minimum specs are specified and the software that will be used is specified.

Graduates: From July 1, 2004 to June 30, 2005, 269 bachelor's degrees were awarded. The most popular majors were criminal justice (18%), management (12%), and nursing/civil engineering (7%). In an average class, 37% graduate in 4 years or less, 49% graduate in 5 years or less, and 52% graduate in 6 years or less. 25 companies recruited on campus in 2004-2005.

Admissions Contact: Karen McGarth, Dean of Enrollment Management. E-mail: nuadm@norwich.edu Web: www.norwich.edu

SAINT MICHAEL'S COLLEGE   A-2
Colchester, VT 05439

	(802) 654-3000
	(800) 762-8000; Fax: (802) 654-2906
Full-time: 894 men, 1051 women	Faculty: 150; IIB, +$
Part-time: 25 men, 36 women	Ph.D.s: 84%
Graduate: 114 men, 354 women	Student/Faculty: 13 to 1
Year: semesters, summer session	Tuition: $26,770
Application Deadline: February 1	Room & Board: $6560
Freshman Class: 2924 applied, 2119 accepted, 597 enrolled	
SAT Verbal/Math: 570/568*	**VERY COMPETITIVE**

Saint Michael's College, founded in 1904, is a private liberal arts college affiliated with the Roman Catholic Church. There is 1 undergraduate and 1 graduate school. The library contains 227,019 volumes, 130,709 microform items, and 7166 audio/video tapes/CDs/DVDs, and subscribes to 1209 periodicals including electronic. Computerized library services include the card catalog, interlibrary loans, database searching, Internet access, and laptop Internet portals. Special learning facilities include a learning resource center, art gallery, radio station, and observatory. The 440-acre campus is in a suburban area 2 miles east of Burlington. Including any residence halls, there are 50 buildings.

Student Life: 78% of undergraduates are from out of state, mostly the Northeast. Students are from 33 states, 12 foreign countries, and Canada. 70% are from public schools. 95% are white. 61% are Catholic; 18% Protestant; 16% claim no religious affiliation. The average age of freshmen is 18; all undergraduates, 20. 11% do not continue beyond their first year; 77% remain to graduate.

Housing: 1904 students can be accommodated in college housing, which includes single-sex and coed dorms and on-campus apartments. In addition, there are honors houses and special-interest houses. On-campus housing is guaranteed for all 4 years. 97% of students live on campus; of those, 85% remain on campus on weekends. All students may keep cars.

Activities: There are no fraternities or sororities. There are 50 groups on campus, including art, band, cheerleading, choir, chorale, chorus, computers, dance, drama, ethnic, fire and rescue, gay, honors, international, jazz band, literary magazine, musical theater, newspaper, pep band, photography, political, professional, radio and TV, religious, science, snowboarding, social, social service, student government, wilderness and yearbook. Popular campus events include Family Weekend, Chirstmas and spring semi-formals, and Spring Weekend.

Sports: There are 10 intercollegiate sports for men and 11 for women, and 22 intramural sports for men and 22 for women. Facilities include a 2,500-seat gym and field house with basketball, volleyball, tennis, and badminton courts, 4 multipurpose courts, a 6-lane swimming pool, a fitness center, a training room, a weight room, a climbing wall, pool, table tennis, a suspended track, racquetball and squash courts, and soccer, field hockey, lacrosse, baseball, and softball fields.

Disabled Students: 70% of the campus is accessible. Wheelchair ramps, elevators, special parking, specially equipped rest rooms, special class scheduling, lowered drinking fountains, lowered telephones, and special housing are available. Other accommodations are provided on an individual basis.

Services: Counseling and information services are available, as is tutoring in every subject. Tutoring can be arranged on an individual basis, through the Writing Center, the Tutoring Coordinator's Office, and departmental help sessions.

Campus Safety and Security: Measures include 24-hour foot and vehicle patrol, security escort services, shuttle buses, and informal discussions. There are pamphlets/posters/films, emergency telephones, lighted pathways/sidewalks, a campus fire and rescue squad, "Silent Witness" and "Tip Line".

Programs of Study: Saint Michael's confers B.A. and B.S. degrees. Master's degrees are also awarded. Bachelor's degrees are awarded in BIOLOGICAL SCIENCE (biochemistry and biology/biological science), BUSINESS (accounting and business administration and management), COMMUNICATIONS AND THE ARTS (dramatic arts, English, fine arts, French, journalism, music, and Spanish), COMPUTER AND PHYSICAL SCIENCE (chemistry, computer science, information sciences and systems, mathematics, physical sciences, and physics), EDUCATION (art, elementary, foreign languages, science, and secondary), ENGINEERING AND ENVIRONMENTAL DESIGN (environmental science and preengineering), HEALTH PROFESSIONS (predentistry), SOCIAL SCIENCE (American studies, anthropology, economics, history, philosophy, political science/government, prelaw, psychology, religion, and sociology). Biology, business administration, and education are the largest.

Required: To graduate, students must complete a minimum of 124 credit hours, with a minimum of 34 different courses, achieving a cumulative GPA of at least 2.0 and a minimum GPA of 2.0 in courses taken in the major. Students must also complete the liberal studies curriculum, which includes 3 courses in social sciences, organizational studies, and humanities (literary studies, historical studies, culture and civilization), 2 courses each in philosophy, religious studies, natural and mathematical sciences (with at least 1 lab course in natural science), 2 writing-intensive courses, and 2 credits in artistic expression. Students must also demonstrate writing and language proficiency and complete a first-year seminar.

Special: A variety of internships and on-campus work-study are available. There is a Washington semester with American University and study abroad in 35 countries. Student-designed majors may be pursued. The college offers a 3-2 engineering degree program in cooperation with Clarkson University and the University of Vermont, and a 4+1 graduate business program with Clarkson University. Nondegree study and pass/fail grading options are offered on a limited basis. Independent research opportunities are available through many departments. There are 11 national honor societies, including Phi Beta Kappa, a freshman honors program, and 1 departmental honors program.

Faculty/Classroom: 57% of faculty are male; 43%, female. All both teach and do research. No introductory courses are taught by graduate students. The average class size in an introductory lecture is 24; in a laboratory, 16; and in a regular course, 20.

Admissions: 72% of the 2005-2006 applicants were accepted. The SAT scores for the 2005-2006 freshman class were: Verbal--15% below 500, 50% between 500 and 599, 30% between 600 and 700, and 5% above 700; Math--14% below 500, 50% between 500 and 599, 32% between 600 and 700, and 4% above 700. 48% of the current freshmen were in the top fifth of their class; 78% were in the top two fifths. 4 freshmen graduated first in their class.

Requirements: The SAT or ACT is required. In addition, applicants must graduate from an accredited secondary school or have a GED. They must complete 16 Carnegie units. The college requires 4 credits in English, 3 to 4 credits in math and science, and 3 each in history (social studies) and a foreign language. An essay is required and an interview is recommended. AP and CLEP credits are accepted. Important factors in the admissions decision are advanced placement or honor courses, evidence of special talent, and recommendations by school officials.

Procedure: Freshmen are admitted fall and spring. Entrance exams should be taken in the fall of the senior year. There is a deferred admissions plan. Applications should be filed by February 1 for fall entry and November 1 for spring entry, along with a $45 fee. Notification is sent April 1. 130 applicants were on the 2005 waiting list; 2 were admitted. Applications are accepted on-line.

Transfer: 50 transfer students enrolled in 2004-2005. Transfer applicants must have a minimum GPA of 2.5; generally, those admitted have a GPA of at least 3.0. The SAT is required. An interview is recommended. 40 of 124 credits required for the bachelor's degree must be completed at Saint Michael's.

Visiting: There are regularly scheduled orientations for prospective students, including a group information session, a video about the school, a campus tour, and a meeting with a staff member to review admissions criteria. There are guides for informal visits and visitors may sit in on classes and stay overnight. To schedule a visit, contact the Admissions Office at (802) 654-3000.

Financial Aid: In 2005-2006, 83% of all full-time freshmen and 75% of continuing full-time students received some form of financial aid. 70% of full-time freshmen and 65% of continuing full-time students received need-based aid. The average freshman award was $19,222. Need-based scholarships or need-based grants averaged $19,222 ($32,100 maximum); need-based self-help aid (loans and jobs) averaged $5526 ($10,000 maximum); non-need-based athletic scholarships averaged $31,497 ($33,330 maximum); and other non-need-based awards and non-need-based scholarships averaged $7840 ($20,000 maximum). 52% of undergraduates work part time. Average annual earnings from campus work are $1402. The average financial indebtedness of the

2005 graduate was $20,706. Saint Michael's is a member of CSS. The FAFSA, federal tax forms from both student and parents, and W-2 forms are required. The deadline for filing freshman financial aid applications for fall entry is March 15.

International Students: There are 28 international students enrolled. The school actively recruits these students. They must score satisfactorily on the written TOEFL or on the electronic version. The SAT or ACT is recommended for international students, but the TOEFL may be used in place of the SAT.

Computers: All enrolled students have access to the campus network "Mikenet" which provides connectivity to network resources, including full Internet access, e-mail, and network printing. Computing resources include 345 computers in labs and classrooms, 6 public computing labs, 3 computing labs in residence halls, 11 specialized computer labs, and 31 electronic classrooms. There are some wireless labs. All students may access the system. There are no time limits and no fees. It is strongly recommended that all students have a personal computer. Recommended specifications are available on the school's web site.

Graduates: From July 1, 2004 to June 30, 2005, 494 bachelor's degrees were awarded. The most popular majors were business administration (19%), psychology (12%), and English literature (10%). In an average class, 71% graduate in 4 years or less, 75% graduate in 5 years or less, and 77% graduate in 6 years or less. 113 companies recruited on campus in 2004-2005. Of the 2004 graduating class, 12% were enrolled in graduate school within 6 months of graduation and 84% were employed.

Admissions Contact: Jerry E. Flanagan, Vice President, Admission and Enrollment. A video is available. E-mail: *admission@smcvt.edu* Web: *www.smcvt.edu*

SOUTHERN VERMONT COLLEGE
Bennington, VT 05201

A-6

(802) 447-6304
(800) 378-2782; Fax: (802) 447-4695

Full-time: 140 men, 210 women	Faculty: 21
Part-time: 35 men, 90 women	Ph.D.s: 19%
Graduate: none	Student/Faculty: 17 to 1
Year: semesters, summer session	Tuition: $14,374
Application Deadline: open	Room & Board: $6948
Freshman Class: 375 applied, 334 accepted, 143 enrolled	
SAT or ACT: required	LESS COMPETITIVE

Southern Vermont College, established in 1926, is a private institution offering a career-oriented, liberal arts education to a student body from diverse academic backgrounds. In addition to regional accreditation, SVC has baccalaureate program accreditation with NLN. The library contains 26,000 volumes, and subscribes to 1504 periodicals including electronic. Computerized library services include interlibrary loans, database searching, Internet access, and laptop Internet portals. Special learning facilities include a learning resource center, art gallery, and radio station. The 371-acre campus is in a small town 40 miles east of Albany, New York. Including any residence halls, there are 10 buildings.

Student Life: 59% of undergraduates are from out of state, mostly the Northeast. Students are from 22 states and 6 foreign countries. 81% are white.

Housing: 235 students can be accommodated in college housing, which includes coed dorms. On-campus housing is guaranteed for the freshman year only and is available on a lottery system for upperclassmen. 54% of students commute. All students may keep cars.

Activities: There are no fraternities or sororities. There are 17 groups on campus, including art, cheerleading, criminal justice, drama, environmental, ethnic, gay, honors, newspaper, nursing, photography, professional, radio and TV, social, social service, student government, and yearbook. Popular campus events include Family Weekend, Winter Formal, and Spring Dance.

Sports: There are 5 intercollegiate sports for men and 5 for women, and 4 intramural sports for men and 4 for women. Facilities include a multipurpose field for softball, baseball, soccer, and rugby, a volleyball court, and a field house, including gym and fitness center.

Disabled Students: 50% of the campus is accessible. Wheelchair ramps, special parking, and specially equipped rest rooms are available.

Services: Counseling and information services are available, as is tutoring in every subject. There is also a learning differences support program.

Campus Safety and Security: Measures include 24-hour foot and vehicle patrol, security escort services, informal discussions, and pamphlets/posters/films. There are lighted pathways/sidewalks.

Programs of Study: SVC confers B.A., B.S., and B.S.N. degrees. Associate degrees are also awarded. Bachelor's degrees are awarded in BUSINESS (business administration and management), COMMUNICATIONS AND THE ARTS (communications, creative writing, and English), HEALTH PROFESSIONS (nursing), SOCIAL SCIENCE (criminal justice, human services, liberal arts/general studies, and psychology). Nursing, criminal justice, and psychology are the largest.

Required: To graduate, students must complete a 42-credit core requirement consisting of course work in economics, English, environmental studies, government, history, cultural arts, math (including computer science), natural sciences, philosophy, psychology, and sociology. Minors are required in some programs. A minimum GPA of 2.0 is required. Students must earn a minimum of 120 credits, with 30 in the major.

Special: The individualized degree program allows students to formulate their own degree. Independent study, individualized study, internships, dual majors, student-designed majors, and cross-registration with Bennington College are available. There is 1 national honor society.

Faculty/Classroom: 52% of faculty are male; 48%, female. All teach undergraduates. The average class size in an introductory lecture is 18; in a laboratory, 13; and in a regular course, 12.

Admissions: 89% of the 2005-2006 applicants were accepted.

Requirements: The SAT or ACT is required. In addition, applicants must graduate from an accredited secondary school or have a GED. The college requires 4 years of English and 3 of math. SVC requires applicants to be in the upper 67% of their class. A GPA of 2.0 is required. AP and CLEP credits are accepted. Important factors in the admissions decision are leadership record, extracurricular activities record, and recommendations by school officials.

Procedure: Freshmen are admitted fall, spring, and summer. There are early admissions and deferred admissions plans. There is a rolling admissions plan. Application deadlines are open. Application fee is $30. There is a waiting list for the nursing and radiologic technology programs. Applications are accepted on-line.

Transfer: 45 transfer students enrolled in a recent year. Applicants must have a GPA of 2.0 and be in good standing. Interviews are recommended, and a dean's report is required. 30 of 120 credits required for the bachelor's degree must be completed at SVC.

Visiting: There are regularly scheduled orientations for prospective students. There are guides for informal visits and visitors may sit in on classes and stay overnight. To schedule a visit, contact Admissions.

Financial Aid: In a recent year, 90% of all full-time freshmen and 92% of continuing full-time students received some form of financial aid. 84% of full-time freshmen and 90% of continuing full-time students received need-based aid. The average freshman award was $11,200. The average financial indebtedness of a recent year's graduate was $13,500. SVC is a member of CSS. The FAFSA and the college's own financial statement are required. The priority date for freshman financial aid applications for fall entry is May 1.

International Students: There are 10 international students enrolled. A satisfactory score on the TOEFL is required.

Computers: Wireless access is available in the library. All students may access the system. There are no time limits and no fees.

Graduates: In a recent year,, 58 bachelor's degrees were awarded. The most popular majors were psychology (22%), business administration (16%), and criminal justice (14%).

Admissions Contact: Kathleen James, Director of Admissions. E-mail: *admis@svc.edu* Web: *www.svc.edu*

STERLING COLLEGE
Craftsbury Common, VT 05827

B-1

(802) 586-7711, ext. 135
(800) 648-3591; Fax: (802) 586-2596

Full-time: 61 men, 29 women	Faculty: 15
Part-time: 4 men, 4 women	Ph.D.s: 44%
Graduate: none	Student/Faculty: 6 to 1
Year: semesters, summer session	Tuition: $16,950
Application Deadline: open	Room & Board: $6336
Freshman Class: n/av	
SAT or ACT: recommended	VERY COMPETITIVE

Sterling College offers a liberal arts curriculum with an environmental focus. It combines traditional academics with experiential learning and offers internships and global field studies. The 2 libraries contain 13,630 volumes and 600 audio/video tapes/CDs/DVDs, and subscribe to 127 periodicals including electronic. Computerized library services include the card catalog, interlibrary loans, database searching, Internet access, and laptop Internet portals. Special learning facilities include a learning resource center, art gallery, woodshop, darkroom, managed woodlot, organic garden, working livestock farm, 30-foot-tall climbing tower, bouldering wall, greenhouse, sugar house, and a 300-acre boreal forest/wetland research area. The 430-acre campus is in a rural area 40 miles north of Montpelier and 60 miles from Burlington. Including any residence halls, there are 15 buildings.

Student Life: 86% of undergraduates are from out of state, mostly the Northeast. Students are from 24 states. 61% are white. The average age of freshmen is 20; all undergraduates, 22. 17% do not continue beyond their first year.

Housing: 90 students can be accommodated in college housing, which includes coed dorms. On-campus housing is guaranteed for all 4 years. 77% of students live on campus. All students may keep cars.

Activities: There are no fraternities or sororities. There are some groups and organizations on campus, including art, dance, newspaper, outing, photography, and yearbook. Popular campus events include All-College Work Days, Earth Day, and Annual Wood-Projects show.

Sports: There is no sports program at Sterling College. Facilities include a climbing tower, nature trails on campus, and nationally recognized cross-country ski trails managed by a nearby sports center.

Disabled Students: Wheelchair ramps and specially equipped rest rooms are available.

Services: Counseling and information services are available, as is tutoring in every subject. There is remedial math. Students seek assistance directly from faculty or teacher assistants. In addition, there is a learning support liaison and counselor.

Campus Safety and Security: Measures include informal discussions, pamphlets/posters/films, and lighted pathways/sidewalks. Weekly community meetings address personal safety and security when necessary.

Programs of Study: Sterling College confers the B.A. degree. Associate degrees are also awarded. Bachelor's degrees are awarded in AGRICULTURE (conservation and regulation, natural resource management, and wildlife management), EDUCATION (recreation), SOCIAL SCIENCE (area studies). Conservation ecology, northern studies, and sustainable agriculture are the strongest academically.

Required: Of the 120 total credit hours required, 28 must be taken in social sciences, 12.5 in arts and humanities, 19 in natural sciences, 6 in interdisciplinary studies, and 2 in applied sciences. 24 to 29 hours in the major are required. A minimum GPA of 2.0 must be maintained. A comprehensive math exam, an internship, and a senior applied research project are also required.

Special: Internships are required in the second year of study. Study abroad, work study, and student-designed majors are available.

Faculty/Classroom: 53% of faculty are male; 47%, female. All teach undergraduates, 25% do research, and 25% do both. The average class size in an introductory lecture is 15; in a laboratory, 10; and in a regular course, 12.

Requirements: The SAT or ACT is recommended. In addition, well-written essays, quality of the interview, and the comments provided by references are equal to the value of high school and college transcripts. Home-schooled students are strongly encouraged to contact the admissions office to discuss their particular needs and interests. AP credits are accepted. Important factors in the admissions decision are leadership record, recommendations by school officials, and personality/intangible qualities.

Procedure: Freshmen are admitted in the fall. There are early action and deferred admissions plans. Application deadlines are open. Notification is sent on a rolling basis. Application fee is $35. Applications are accepted on-line.

Transfer: 12 transfer students enrolled in 2004-2005. In addition to the standard application, transfer students must provide copies of college transcripts. They may begin in the spring semester. 30 of 120 credits required for the bachelor's degree must be completed at Sterling College.

Visiting: There are regularly scheduled orientations for prospective students, including a student-led campus tour, an interview with admissions, and a meal in the dining hall. Overnight visits are welcome Monday through Thursday nights; weekend and week day open houses offer a more comprehensive view of the college. There are 4 to 5 open houses per year. There are guides for informal visits and visitors may sit in on classes. To schedule a visit, contact the Admissions Office at 802-586-7711 or admissions@sterlingcollege.edu.

Financial Aid: In 2005-2006, 89% of all full-time freshmen and 75% of continuing full-time students received some form of financial aid. 78% of full-time freshmen and 69% of continuing full-time students received need-based aid. The average freshman award was $13,979. Need-based scholarships or need-based grants averaged $9255 ($14,100 maximum); and other non-need-based awards and non-need-based scholarships averaged $1000 ($4000 maximum). 90% of undergraduates work part time. Average annual earnings from campus work are $1400. The FAFSA and the college's own financial statement are required. The priority date for freshman financial aid applications for fall entry is March 1.

International Students: International students must take the TOEFL.

Computers: Wireless access is available. Students have access to PCs on campus in the library, the Career Resource Center, and the computer lab. These PCs are available for Internet access, student e-mailing, course work, searching library databases, access to the shared network, and laboratory related uses. All students may access the system. There are no time limits and no fees. It is strongly recommended that all students have a personal computer.

Graduates: From July 1, 2004 to June 30, 2005, 7 bachelor's degrees were awarded. The most popular majors were conservation ecology (72%), outdoor education and leardership (14%), and sustainable agriculture (14%). 28 companies recruited on campus in 2004-2005. Of the 2004 graduating class, 90% were employed within 6 months of graduation.

Admissions Contact: Gwyn Harris, Director of Admissions.
E-mail: admissions@sterlingcollege.edu Web: www.sterlingcollege.edu

UNIVERSITY OF VERMONT — A-2

Burlington, VT 05405 (802) 656-3370; Fax: (802) 656-8611

Full-time: 3400 men, 4400 women	Faculty: 578; I, --$
Part-time: 560 men, 900 women	Ph.D.s: 89%
Graduate: 700 men, 1000 women	Student/Faculty: 14 to 1
Year: semesters, summer session	Tuition: $10,748 ($24,934)
Application Deadline: January 15	Room & Board: $7332
Freshman Class: 10,456 applied, 7792 accepted, 1923 enrolled	
SAT or ACT: required	VERY COMPETITIVE

The University of Vermont, established in 1791, is a public, land-grant, comprehensive institution with a dual focus on teaching and research. Its undergraduate and graduate offerings include the liberal arts, business administration, engineering, math, natural resources, agricultural studies, fine arts, teacher preparation, social services, environmental studies, and health science, including nursing. There are 7 undergraduate and 2 graduate schools. In addition to regional accreditation, UVM has baccalaureate program accreditation with AACSB, ABET, APTA, ASLA, CAHEA, CSWE, NCATE, NLN, and SAF. The 3 libraries contain 2.5 million volumes, 1.75 million microform items, and 45,000 audio/video tapes/CDs/DVDs, and subscribe to 20,000 periodicals including electronic. Computerized library services include the card catalog, interlibrary loans, database searching, and Internet access. Special learning facilities include a learning resource center, art gallery, radio station, TV station, health care center, 4 research farms, the Fleming Museum, geology museum, 9 natural areas, lakeshore science center, and aquatic research vessel. The 450-acre campus is in a suburban area 90 miles south of Montreal and 200 miles north of Boston, on the shore of Lake Champlain. Including any residence halls, there are 118 buildings.

Student Life: 62% of undergraduates are from out of state, mostly the Northeast. Students are from 47 states, 24 foreign countries, and Canada. 93% are white. 40% claim no religious affiliation; 26% Catholic; 20% Protestant; 9% Jewish. The average age of freshmen is 18; all undergraduates, 20. 16% do not continue beyond their first year; 70% remain to graduate.

Housing: 3631 students can be accommodated in college housing, which includes coed dorms, on-campus apartments, off-campus apartments, married-student housing, fraternity houses, and sorority houses. In addition, there are honors houses, language houses, special-interest houses, and the living-learning center, which provides an integrated, theme-based academic and residential option. On-campus housing is available on a lottery system for upperclassmen. 50% of students live on campus; of those, 90% remain on campus on weekends. Upperclassmen may keep cars.

Activities: 7% of men belong to 2 local and 7 national fraternities; 6% of women belong to 5 national sororities. There are 100 groups on campus, including art, band, cheerleading, chess, choir, chorale, chorus, community service, computers, dance, debate, drama, environmental, ethnic, film, gay, honors, international, jazz band, literary magazine, musical theater, newspaper, orchestra, outing, pep band, photography, political, professional, radio and TV, religious, social, social service, student government, and yearbook. Popular campus events include National Coming Out Week, Winterfest, and Community Serve-a-thon.

Sports: There are 10 intercollegiate sports for men and 12 for women, and 24 intramural sports for men and 24 for women. Facilities include a 3228-seat gym, a 4000-seat ice hockey stadium, a field house, soccer and baseball fields, a fitness center, indoor and outdoor tracks, a natatorium, indoor tennis courts, a racquetball court, a climbing facility, a dance studio, and a gymnastics facility.

Disabled Students: 87% of the campus is accessible. Wheelchair ramps, elevators, special parking, specially equipped rest rooms, special class scheduling, lowered drinking fountains, lowered telephones, first-priority routes in poor weather, a TTY phone system for hearing-impaired students, and closed-caption video decoders are available.

Services: Counseling and information services are available, as is tutoring in most subjects. There is a reader service for the blind. There is also supplemental instruction, note-taking and test-taking seminars, time management instruction, outreach programs, exam proctoring, and writing tutors, as well as support for ESL students.

Campus Safety and Security: Measures include 24-hour foot and vehicle patrol, self-defense education, security escort services, and shuttle buses. There are informal discussions, pamphlets/posters/films, emergency telephones, lighted pathways/sidewalks, bike registration, identification of property, and 18 fully certified police officers.

Programs of Study: UVM confers B.A., B.S., B.M., B.S.A.E., B.S.B.A., B.S.C.E., B.S.C.S., B.S.Ed., B.S.E.E., B.S.E.M., B.S.M., B.S.M.E., and B.S.M.S. degrees. Associate, master's, and doctoral degrees are also awarded. Bachelor's degrees are awarded in AGRICULTURE (agriculture, animal science, environmental studies, fishing and fisheries, forestry and related sciences, horticulture, natural resource management and plant science), BIOLOGICAL SCIENCE (biochemistry, biology/biological science, botany, ecology, genetics, microbiology, nutrition, wildlife biology, and zoology), BUSINESS (business administration and management and entrepreneurial studies), COMMUNICATIONS AND

THE ARTS (art, art history and appreciation, classics, dramatic arts, English, French, German, Greek, Latin, music, Russian, and Spanish), COMPUTER AND PHYSICAL SCIENCE (chemistry, computer science, geology, information sciences and systems, mathematics, physics, and statistics), EDUCATION (art, early childhood, education, elementary, English, foreign languages, health, mathematics, middle school, music, nutrition, physical, science, secondary, and social studies), ENGINEERING AND ENVIRONMENTAL DESIGN (civil engineering, electrical/electronics engineering, engineering management, environmental engineering, environmental science, landscape architecture/design, and mechanical engineering), HEALTH PROFESSIONS (biomedical science, medical laboratory science, medical laboratory technology, nuclear medical technology, nursing, radiation therapy, and speech pathology/audiology), SOCIAL SCIENCE (anthropology, Asian/Oriental studies, Canadian studies, dietetics, economics, European studies, family/consumer studies, food science, geography, history, human development, Latin American studies, parks and recreation management, philosophy, political science/government, psychology, religion, Russian and Slavic studies, social work, sociology, and women's studies). Business administration, psychology, and English are the largest.

Required: Degree requirements vary among the individual colleges, but all require at least a 2.0 GPA and 122 credit hours to graduate. Most students must enroll in at least 30 distribution credits (approximately 10 courses) in the arts, humanities, social sciences, languages, literature, math, and the sciences. All academic units require a 3-credit course in Race and Culture or a course exploring race relations and ethnic diversity in the United States, and all students are expected to complete 2 credits of phys ed, unless granted an exemption.

Special: Special academic programs include co-op programs, internships in every discipline, study abroad in 60 countries, a Washington semester, work-study, an accelerated degree program in nursing, dual majors, and student-designed majors. In addition, a 3-4 veterinary medicine degree is offered with Tufts University, a 3-3 program with Vermont Law School, and a 3-3 physical therapy program at UVM. There are 25 national honor societies, including Phi Beta Kappa, a freshman honors program, and 14 departmental honors programs.

Faculty/Classroom: 61% of faculty are male; 39%, female. Graduate students teach 2% of introductory courses. The average class size in an introductory lecture is 38; in a laboratory, 16; and in a regular course, 20.

Admissions: 23 freshmen graduated first in their class.

Requirements: The SAT or ACT is required. Other admissions requirements include graduation from an accredited secondary school with 16 Carnegie units. Required high school course work includes 4 years of English, 3 years each of social science and math, including algebra I and II and geometry, and 2 years each of the same foreign language and science (one of which must be a lab science). An essay must be submitted. The GED is also accepted. AP and CLEP credits are accepted. Important factors in the admissions decision are advanced placement or honor courses, extracurricular activities record, and recommendations by school officials.

Procedure: Freshmen are admitted fall and spring. Entrance exams should be taken by November of the senior year. There are early action, early admissions, and deferred admissions plans. Early action applications should be filed by November 1; regular applications, by January 15 for fall entry and November 1 for spring entry, along with a $45 fee. Notification of early action is sent December 15; regular decision, March 20. 174 early decision candidates were accepted for a recent class. 359 applicants were on a recent waiting list. Applications are accepted on-line.

Transfer: 555 transfer students enrolled in a recent year. Transfer students generally must have a minimum GPA of 3.0 in credited courses and meet the same entrance requirements as freshmen. Considerations include the college and high school records, the major indicated, and availability of space at UVM. 30 of 122 credits required for the bachelor's degree must be completed at UVM.

Visiting: There are regularly scheduled orientations for prospective students, consisting of tours most weekdays during the academic year and information sessions on selected days in the fall and spring. Visitors may sit in on classes. To schedule a visit, contact the Admissions Office.

Financial Aid: In a recent year, 89% of all full-time freshmen and 71% of continuing full-time students received some form of financial aid. 54% of full-time freshmen and 53% of continuing full-time students received need-based aid. The average freshman award was $18,611. Need-based scholarships or need-based grants averaged $11,404 ($33,455 maximum); need-based self-help aid (loans and jobs) averaged $6067 ($13,325 maximum); non-need-based athletic scholarships averaged $21,009 ($35,061 maximum); and other non-need-based awards and non-need-based scholarships averaged $3534 ($36,524 maximum). The average financial indebtedness of a recent year's graduate was $24,799. The FAFSA is required. The priority date for freshman financial aid applications for fall entry is February 10.

International Students: There are 54 international students enrolled. They must take the TOEFL, achieving a satisfactory score, or the ELPT. They must also take the SAT or ACT.

Computers: All students may access the system at any time. There are no time limits and no fees. Business majors must provide a PC, An IBM, MAC, or Dell is recommended.

Graduates: From July 1, 2004 to June 30, 2005, 1795 bachelor's degrees were awarded. The most popular majors were business (10%), psychology (7%), and English (7%). In an average class, 49% graduate in 4 years or less, 63% graduate in 5 years or less, and 65% graduate in 6 years or less. 170 companies recruited on campus in a recent year. Of a recent graduating class, 17% were enrolled in graduate school within 6 months of graduation and 67% were employed.

Admissions Contact: Donald Honeman, Director of Admission.
E-mail: *admissions@uvm.edu* Web: *www.uvm.edu/admissions*

VERMONT STATE COLLEGES

The Vermont State Colleges, established in 1962, is a private system in Vermont. It is governed by a board of trustees, whose chief administrator is chancellor. The primary goal of the system is teaching. The main priorities are to insure that Vermonters and others have access to higher education; to provide educational programs that permit individuals to lead more productive and responsible lives; and to maintain the quality of cultural, social, and economic life in Vermont. The total enrollment is usually about 9000; with 250 faculty members. Altogether there are some 60 baccalaureate, and 5 master's programs offered in Vermont State Colleges. Profiles of the 4-year campuses are included in this section.

VERMONT TECHNICAL COLLEGE

Randolph Center, VT 05061	(802) 728-1000; (800) 442-8821
Full-time: 655 men, 378 women	Faculty: 71; III, --$
Part-time: 165 men, 158 women	Ph.D.s: 54%
Graduate: none	Student/Faculty: 15 to 1
Year: semesters	Tuition: $9077 ($16,037)
Application Deadline: open	Room & Board: $6674
Freshman Class: 757 applied, 528 accepted, 314 enrolled	
SAT Verbal/Math: 480/500*	COMPETITIVE

Vermont Technical College, founded in 1910, is one of the 5 institutions in the Vermont State Colleges System and is the state's only public technical college. In addition to regional accreditation, VTC has baccalaureate program accreditation with ABET. The library contains 59,480 volumes, 5920 microform items, and 4122 audio/video tapes/CDs/DVDs, and subscribes to 348 periodicals including electronic. Computerized library services include the card catalog, interlibrary loans, database searching, and Internet access. Special learning facilities include a learning resource center, radio station, and Vermont Interactive Television. The 544-acre campus is in a rural area. Including any residence halls, there are 19 buildings.

Student Life: 60% of undergraduates are from Vermont. Others are from 12 states and 2 foreign countries. 90% are from public schools. 94% are white. The average age of freshmen is 25; all undergraduates, 26. 25% do not continue beyond their first year; 55% remain to graduate.

Housing: 550 students can be accommodated in college housing, which includes single-sex and coed dorms. On-campus housing is guaranteed for all 4 years. 60% of students commute. All students may keep cars.

Activities: There are no fraternities or sororities. There are many groups and organizations on campus, including chess, computers, drama, ethnic, gay, international, photography, professional, radio and TV, religious, social, social service, and student government. Popular campus events include Harvest Days, Winter Carnival, and Spring Fling.

Sports: There are 6 intercollegiate sports for men and 5 for women, and 21 intramural sports for men and 21 for women. Facilities include a double-court gym, 2 racquetball courts, a 6-lane 25-yard pool, a fitness center, outdoor soccer, baseball, and softball fields, trails for cross-country skiing, and a downhill ski run.

Disabled Students: All of the campus is accessible. Wheelchair ramps, elevators, special parking, specially equipped rest rooms, special class scheduling, lowered drinking fountains, and lowered telephones are available.

Services: Counseling and information services are available, as is tutoring in every subject.

Campus Safety and Security: Measures include 24-hour foot and vehicle patrol, self-defense education, security escort services, and informal discussions. There are pamphlets/posters/films, emergency telephones, and lighted pathways/sidewalks.

Programs of Study: VTC confers the B.S. degree. Associate degrees are also awarded. Bachelor's degrees are awarded in COMPUTER AND PHYSICAL SCIENCE (information sciences and systems and software engineering), EDUCATION (business), ENGINEERING AND ENVIRONMENTAL DESIGN (architectural engineering, computer engineering, and electromechanical technology). Electromechanical engineering technology is the strongest academically. Architectural engineering technology and business are the largest.

Required: To graduate, students must complete 120 to 130 credit hours with a minimum GPA of 2.0. Required courses include those in English, technical communications, math, and computer.

Special: Cross-registration, internships, work-study programs, and dual majors are offered. There are 2 national honor societies, a freshman honors program, and 2 departmental honors programs.

Faculty/Classroom: 58% of faculty are male; 42%, female. All teach undergraduates. The average class size in an introductory lecture is 28; in a laboratory, 16; and in a regular course, 32.

Admissions: 70% of the 2005-2006 applicants were accepted. The SAT scores for the 2005-2006 freshman class were: Verbal--56% below 500, 30% between 500 and 599, 13% between 600 and 700, and 1% above 700; Math--45% below 500, 42% between 500 and 599, 12% between 600 and 700, and 1% above 700. 23% of the current freshmen were in the top fifth of their class; 70% were in the top two fifths.

Requirements: The SAT or ACT is required. AP and CLEP credits are accepted.

Procedure: Freshmen are admitted fall and spring. There is a rolling admissions plan. Application deadlines are open. Application fee is $32. A waiting list is an active part of the admissions procedure. Applications are accepted on-line.

Transfer: 251 transfer students enrolled in a recent year. Transcripts are required from all colleges attended. 50 of 120 to 130 credits required for the bachelor's degree must be completed at VTC.

Visiting: There are regularly scheduled orientations for prospective students. There are guides for informal visits and visitors may sit in on classes and stay overnight. To schedule a visit, contact Admissions.

Financial Aid: In 2005-2006, 77% of all full-time freshmen and 90% of continuing full-time students received some form of financial aid. 63% of full-time freshmen and 73% of continuing full-time students received need-based aid. The average freshman award was $12,400. Need-based scholarships or need-based grants averaged $4000 ($13,200 maximum); need-based self-help aid (loans and jobs) averaged $2750 ($5025 maximum); and other non-need-based awards and non-need-based scholarships averaged $5650 ($37,800 maximum). 26% of undergraduates work part time. Average annual earnings from campus work are $800. The average financial indebtedness of the 2005 graduate was $12,000. The FAFSA is required. The deadline for filing freshman financial aid applications for fall entry is March 1.

International Students: There are 2 international students enrolled. They must score satisfactorily on the written TOEFL or on the electronic version or take the MELAB, the Comprehensive English Language Test, or the college's own test and must also take the SAT, ACT, or the college's own entrance exam.

Computers: All students may access the system. There are no time limits and no fees. It is strongly recommended that all students have a personal computer.

Graduates: From July 1, 2004 to June 30, 2005, 64 bachelor's degrees were awarded. The most popular majors were business (37%) and electromechanical engineering (25%). In an average class, 50% graduate in 4 years or less, 55% graduate in 5 years or less, and 59% graduate in 6 years or less. 45 companies recruited on campus in 2004-2005. Of the 2004 graduating class, 97% were employed within 6 months of graduation.

Admissions Contact: Dwight Cross, Assistant Dean of Enrollment.
E-mail: *admissions@vtc.edu* Web: *www.vtc.edu*

WOODBURY COLLEGE

Montpelier, VT 05602　　　　　　　　　　　**(802) 229-0516**
　　　　　　　　　　　　　(800) 639-6039; Fax: (802) 229-2141

Full-time: 14 men, 79 women	**Faculty:** 6
Part-time: 8 men, 30 women	**Ph.D.s:** 75%
Graduate: 3 men, 10 women	**Student/Faculty:** 15 to 1
Year: trimesters	**Tuition:** $15,150
Application Deadline: open	**Room & Board:** n/app
Freshman Class: n/av	
SAT or ACT: not required	**LESS COMPETITIVE**

Woodbury College, established in 1975, offers adult-focused, career-oriented programs in Legal and Paralegal Studies, Mediation/Conflict Management, and Prevention and Community Development. There is 1 undergraduate school. The library contains 17,000 volumes, and subscribes to 20,000 periodicals including electronic. Computerized library services include the card catalog, interlibrary loans, and database searching. The 8-acre campus is in a small town 1.5 miles north of the Center of Montpelier and the Vermont state government district. There is one building.

Student Life: 97% of undergraduates are from Vermont. Students are from 3 states and 1 foreign country. 96% are white. The average age of freshmen is 35; all undergraduates, 35. 15% do not continue beyond their first year; 85% remain to graduate.

Housing: There are no residence halls. All students commute.

Activities: There are no fraternities or sororities. Popular campus events include town meetings and community luncheons.

Disabled Students: Wheelchair ramps, elevators, special parking, and specially equipped rest rooms are available.

Services: Counseling and information services are available, as is tutoring in most subjects.

Campus Safety and Security: Measures include informal discussions.

Programs of Study: Woodbury College confers the B.S. degree. Associate degrees are also awarded. Bachelor's degrees are awarded in SOCIAL SCIENCE (community services, human services, interdisciplinary studies, law, and paralegal studies). Paralegal Studies and mediation and applied conflict studies are the largest.

Required: Each student must demonstrate satisfactory competency in core courses and program requirements. A total of 120 credit hours must be completed, with 48 in the major.

Special: Internships are required for all undergraduate students. A student-designed major in interdisciplinary studies is possible. Certificate programs are offered.

Faculty/Classroom: 39% of faculty are male; 61%, female. All teach undergraduates. The average class size in an introductory lecture is 12; in a laboratory, 12; and in a regular course, 12.

Requirements: Students must submit a completed application, a high school diploma or GED, and an essay. An interview is optional. AP and CLEP credits are accepted. Important factors in the admissions decision are personality/intangible qualities, recommendations by alumni, and recommendations by school officials.

Procedure: Freshmen are admitted to all sessions. There are deferred admissions and rolling admissions plans. Application deadlines are open. Application fee is $30. Notification is sent on a rolling basis. Applications are accepted on-line.

Transfer: Requirements are the same as for incoming freshmen, including high school transcripts, and an essay. 45 of 120 credits required for the bachelor's degree must be completed at Woodbury College.

Visiting: There are regularly scheduled orientations for prospective students, including an introductory meeting, a school philosophy presentation, a financial aid discussion, a free class, a meal, and a Q&A session. There are guides for informal visits and visitors may stay overnight. To schedule a visit, contact Shannon Garrity at *shannon@woodbury-college.edu*.

Financial Aid: In 2005-2006, 83% of all full-time freshmen and 87% of continuing full-time students received some form of financial aid. 75% of full-time freshmen and 81% of continuing full-time students received need-based aid. The average freshman award was $10,110. The FAFSA and the college's own financial statement are required. Check with the school for current deadlines.

Computers: All students may access the system.

Admissions Contact: Kathleen Moore, Admissions Director.
E-mail: *admiss@woodbury-college.edu*
Web: *www.woodbury-college.edu*

VIRGINIA

POPULATION
DENSITY
• 50,000 and over

0 20 40 60 80 100
Miles

AVERETT UNIVERSITY

Danville, VA 24541

D-4

(434) 791-7301
(800) 283-7388; Fax: (434) 791-2784

Full-time: 560 men, 591 women
Part-time: 245 men, 392 women
Graduate: 231 men, 376 women
Year: varies by program, summer session
Application Deadline: July 15
Freshman Class: 1202 applied, 1006 accepted, 258 enrolled
SAT Verbal/Math: 480/500*

Faculty: 66; IIA, --$
Ph.D.s: 77%
Student/Faculty: 17 to 1
Tuition: $19,040
Room & Board: $5880

ACT: 19   **COMPETITIVE**

Founded in 1859, Averett University is a comprehensive university offering 32 undergraduate majors and 3 masters degree programs. The University offers classes on its main campus in Danville, Virginia and offers an adult degree program with satellite locations throughout the state. The library contains 151,753 volumes, 63,125 microform items, and 247 audio/video tapes/CDs/DVDs, and subscribes to 18,766 periodicals including electronic. Computerized library services include the card catalog, interlibrary loans, database searching, Internet access, and laptop Internet portals. Special learning facilities include a learning resource center and a performing arts center, regional archive collections, flight simulators, Averett-owned airplanes, and a flight center located at the Danville Regional Airport. The 19-acre campus is in a small town 45 miles from Greensboro, North Carolina. Including any residence halls, there are 26 buildings.

Student Life: 78% of undergraduates are from Virginia. Students are from 29 states, 14 foreign countries, and Canada. 94% are from public schools. 66% are white; 29% African American. 60% are Protestant; 32% claim no religious affiliation; 7% Catholic. The average age of freshmen is 18; all undergraduates, 21. 51% do not continue beyond their first year; 49% remain to graduate.

Housing: 526 students can be accommodated in college housing, which includes single-sex and coed dorms and on-campus apartments. On-campus housing is guaranteed for all 4 years. 53% of students live on campus; of those, 75% remain on campus on weekends. Alcohol is not permitted. All students may keep cars.

Activities: 2% of men belong to 1 national fraternity; 2% of women belong to 1 national sorority. There are 30 groups on campus, including art, cheerleading, choir, chorale, chorus, dance, drama, ethnic, gay, honors, international, literary magazine, musical theater, newspaper, photography, political, professional, radio and TV, religious, social, social service, student government, and yearbook. Popular campus events include campus movies, Family Weekend events, and Spring Formal.

Sports: There are 7 intercollegiate sports for men and 7 for women, and 5 intramural sports for men and 5 for women. Facilities include tennis courts, a 100-acre equestrian center, and a 70-acre athletic center.

Disabled Students: 58% of the campus is accessible. Wheelchair ramps, elevators, special parking, specially equipped rest rooms, lowered drinking fountains, lowered telephones, talking books and magnification devices for the visually challenged are available.

Services: Counseling and information services are available, as is tutoring in most subjects. There is a reader service for the blind, and remedial math, reading, and writing.

Campus Safety and Security: Measures include 24-hour foot and vehicle patrol, shuttle buses, informal discussions, and pamphlets/posters/films. There are emergency telephones and lighted pathways/sidewalks.

Programs of Study: Averett confers B.A., B.S., B.A.S., and B.B.A. degrees. Associate and master's degrees are also awarded. Bachelor's degrees are awarded in AGRICULTURE (equine science), BIOLOGICAL SCIENCE (biochemistry, biology/biological science, and environmental biology), BUSINESS (accounting, business administration and management, international business management, management science, marketing management, organizational behavior, and sports management), COMMUNICATIONS AND THE ARTS (art, dramatic arts, English, journalism, music, music performance, and performing arts), COMPUTER AND PHYSICAL SCIENCE (chemistry, computer science, information sciences and systems, mathematics, physical chemistry, and radiological technology), EDUCATION (art, athletic training, computer, drama, education, elementary, English, foreign languages, health, journalism, mathematics, middle school, physical, science, secondary, social science, and social studies), ENGINEERING AND ENVIRONMENTAL DESIGN (aircraft mechanics, airline piloting and navigation, aviation administration/management, aviation maintenance management, computer technology, and environmental science), HEALTH PROFESSIONS (biomedical science, health, medical technology, predentistry, premedicine, radiograph medical technology, and sports medicine), SOCIAL SCIENCE (biopsychology, clinical psychology, cognitive science, counseling/psychology, criminal justice, history, industrial and organizational psychology, interdisciplinary studies, law enforcement and corrections, liberal arts/general studies, political science/government, prelaw, psychobiology, psychology, religion, religious music, social science, and sociology). Business administration, education, and physical education are the largest.

Required: To graduate, all students must complete at least 123 hours with a minimum 2.0 GPA and attend commencement exercises. A minimum of 33 hours must be completed at Averett. Core requirements include 9 hours each of social science and English, and 6 hours each of history, fine arts, and religion, or philosophy. Students must pass 2 writing intensive and oral-intensive courses. B.A. students need an additional 6 to 8 hours of math or natural science and 6 to 14 hours in a foreign language, depending on proficiency; B.S. students need an additional 6 hours in math and 8 hours in natural science.

Special: Averett offers co-op programs and internships in several majors. Cross-registration is available through the Consortium for Global Education, and work-study is possible. Students may design their own majors with approval, or select dual majors or double majors. A general studies degree and nondegree study are offered, as are up to 5 pass/fail options, accelerated degrees, and a Washington semester in journalism or political science. Senior equestrian studies majors may spend a semester or summer in England preparing for the British Horse Society A.I. certificate. Study abroad is available in 9 countries. Students may graduate in 3 years by taking summer courses. There are 5 national honor societies and a freshman honors program. All departments have honors programs.

Faculty/Classroom: 67% of faculty are male; 33%, female. All teach undergraduates. No introductory courses are taught by graduate students. The average class size in an introductory lecture is 16; in a laboratory, 15; and in a regular course, 10.

Admissions: 84% of the 2005-2006 applicants were accepted. The SAT scores for the 2005-2006 freshman class were: Verbal--56% below 500, 35% between 500 and 599, 9% between 600 and 700, and 1% above 700; Math--47% below 500, 45% between 500 and 599, and 7% between 600 and 700. The ACT scores were 71% below 21, 13% between 21 and 23, 15% between 24 and 26, and 2% between 27 and 28. 29% of the current freshmen were in the top fifth of their class; 55% were in the top two fifths. 1 freshman graduated first in the class.

Requirements: The SAT or ACT is required. The ACT Optional Writing test is also recommended. In addition, applicants should have a high school diploma or its equivalent. 15 Carnegie units in college prep coursework should include a minimum of 5 in math and science (minimum 2 in math), 4 in English, 3 in social sciences, and 3 electives (foreign language recommended). Interviews are recommended with a campus visit. Auditions are required for music majors. Portfolios are recommended for art majors. GED are accepted. Recommendation letters are recommended but not required. A GPA of 2.2 is required. AP and CLEP credits are accepted. Important factors in the admissions decision are extracurricular activities record, leadership record, and advanced placement or honor courses.

Procedure: Freshmen are admitted to all sessions. Entrance exams should be taken in the junior year or the fall of the senior year. There is a deferred admissions plan. There is a rolling admissions plan. Applications should be filed by July 15 for fall entry and November 15 for spring entry. Notification is sent on a rolling basis. Applications are accepted on-line.

Transfer: 198 transfer students enrolled in 2004-2005. Applicants must present at least a 2.0 GPA on a 4.0 scale and be eligible to return to their previous college. 33 of 123 credits required for the bachelor's degree must be completed at Averett.

Visiting: There are regularly scheduled orientations for prospective students, including sessions with admissions, student life, financial aid, academics, athletics, campus tours, and lunch. There are guides for informal visits and visitors may sit in on classes and stay overnight. To schedule a visit, contact Teresa Hester at (434) 791-4996 or (800) 283-7388 ext. 4996 or teresa.hester@averett.edu.

Financial Aid: In 2005-2006, 95% of all full-time freshmen and 90% of continuing full-time students received some form of financial aid. 64% of full-time freshmen and 58% of continuing full-time students received need-based aid. The average freshman award was $14,984. Need-based scholarships or need-based grants averaged $11,097 ($11,097 maximum); need-based self-help aid (loans and jobs) averaged $4436 ($4843 maximum); and other non-need-based awards and non-need-based scholarships averaged $13,635. 100% of undergraduates work part time. Average annual earnings from campus work are $1200. The average financial indebtedness of the 2005 graduate was $16,398. The FAFSA and the college's own financial statement are required. The priority date for freshman financial aid applications for fall entry is April 1.

International Students: There are 20 international students enrolled. The school actively recruits these students. A satisfactory score on the written TOEFL is required. A satisfactory score on the SAT or ACT is also required for traditional first-time freshman only.

Computers: Wireless access is available. All students may access the system 24 hours a day. There are no time limits and no fees.

Graduates: From July 1, 2004 to June 30, 2005, 460 bachelor's degrees were awarded. The most popular majors were business/marketing (73%), education (5%), and physical education (4%). In an average class, 2% graduate in 3 years or less, 23% graduate in 4 years or less, 43% graduate in 5 years or less, and 46% graduate in 6 years or less.

Admissions Contact: Kathie Tune, Dean of Admissions. A video is available. E-mail: admit@averett.edu Web: www.averett.edu

BLUEFIELD COLLEGE · B-3
Bluefield, VA 24605

(276) 326-4339
(800) 872-0175; Fax: (276) 326-4288

Full-time: 287 men, 405 women	**Faculty:** 33
Part-time: 27 men, 57 women	**Ph.D.s:** 61%
Graduate: none	**Student/Faculty:** 21 to 1
Year: semesters, summer session	**Tuition:** $11,430
Application Deadline: open	**Room & Board:** $5800
Freshman Class: 731 applied, 358 accepted, 110 enrolled	
SAT Verbal/Math: 487/475*	**ACT:** 21 **COMPETITIVE+**

Bluefield College, founded in 1922, is a private, liberal arts institution affiliated with the Southern Baptist Church. The library contains 44,500 volumes and 2425 audio/video tapes/CDs/DVDs, and subscribes to 12,500 periodicals including electronic. Computerized library services include the card catalog, interlibrary loans, database searching, and Internet access. Special learning facilities include a learning resource center, a learning center, and a writing center. The 85-acre campus is in a small town 100 miles west of Roanoke on the Virginia-West Virginia state line. Including any residence halls, there are 9 buildings.

Student Life: 80% of undergraduates are from Virginia. Others are from 19 states and 2 foreign countries. 95% are from public schools. 79% are white; 18% African American. 77% are Protestant; 13% claim no religious affiliation; 9% Hindu and Muslim. The average age of freshmen is 18; all undergraduates, 28. 43% do not continue beyond their first year; 41% remain to graduate.

Housing: 243 students can be accommodated in college housing, which includes single-sex dorms and on-campus apartments. On-campus housing is guaranteed for all 4 years. 55% of students commute. Alcohol is not permitted. All students may keep cars.

Activities: 10% of men and about 11% of women belong to 3 local fraternities; 45% of women belong to 3 local sororities. There are 16 groups on campus, including cheerleading, choir, chorale, chorus, dance, drama, honors, literary magazine, musical theater, newspaper, pep band, political, professional, religious, social, and student government. Popular campus events include Spring Weekend and Christmas Banquet.

Sports: There are 4 intercollegiate sports for men and 4 for women, and 6 intramural sports for men and 6 for women. Facilities include a gym with game courts and weight rooms, a student activities center, a game room, tennis courts, and a sand volleyball court.

Disabled Students: 95% of the campus is accessible. Wheelchair ramps, elevators, special parking, specially equipped rest rooms, and lowered drinking fountains are available.

Services: Counseling and information services are available, as is tutoring in most subjects. There is a reader service for the blind, and remedial math, reading, and writing.

Campus Safety and Security: Measures include informal discussions, pamphlets/posters/films, lighted pathways/sidewalks, and foot and vehicle patrol from 11 P.M. to 6 A.M.

Programs of Study: BC confers B.A. and B.S. degrees. Bachelor's degrees are awarded in BIOLOGICAL SCIENCE (biology/biological science), BUSINESS (business administration and management), COMMUNICATIONS AND THE ARTS (communications, English, fine arts, and music), COMPUTER AND PHYSICAL SCIENCE (chemistry and mathematics), EDUCATION (middle school and secondary), HEALTH PROFESSIONS (exercise science), SOCIAL SCIENCE (Christian studies, criminal justice, history, interdisciplinary studies, psychology, religion, and social studies). Business, teacher education, and biology are the strongest academically. Business, organizational management and development, and criminal justice are the largest.

Required: To graduate, students must have completed a minimum of 126 semester hours, including a liberal arts requirement of 51 to 53 hours, with 30 to 45 hours in the major, and a minimum 2.0 GPA. Other requirements vary per program. All graduates must demonstrate computer proficiency by testing, passing computer courses, or having components in required courses.

Special: The college offers credit for life/military/work experience, nondegree study through the Fine Arts Community School, study abroad in England, an accelerated degree program in organizational management and development and in criminal justice, and internships in criminal justice, psychology, and recreation. There are 4 national honor societies, a freshman honors program, and 7 departmental honors programs.

Faculty/Classroom: 70% of faculty are male; 30%, female. All teach undergraduates, 30% do research, and 30% do both. The average class size in an introductory lecture is 17; in a laboratory, 12; and in a regular course, 10.

Admissions: 49% of the 2005-2006 applicants were accepted. The SAT scores for the 2005-2006 freshman class were: Verbal--65% below 500, 22% between 500 and 599, 12% between 600 and 700, and 1% above 700; Math--67% below 500, 26% between 500 and 599, and 7% between 600 and 700. The ACT scores were 57% below 21, 20% between 21 and 23, 13% between 24 and 26, 3% between 27 and 28, and 7% above 28. 38% of the current freshmen were in the top fifth of their class; 64% were in the top two fifths.

Requirements: The SAT or ACT is required. In addition, applicants must be graduates of an accredited secondary school or have a GED certificate, and have completed 4 years of English, 2 of social sciences, 1 of science, and 5 of electives. A GPA of 2.0 is required. AP and CLEP credits are accepted. Important factors in the admissions decision are leadership record, advanced placement or honor courses, and recommendations by school officials.

Procedure: Freshmen are admitted to all sessions. Entrance exams should be taken early in the senior year. There is a deferred admissions plan and a rolling admissions plan. Application deadlines are open. Notification is sent on a rolling basis. Application fee is $30. Applications are accepted on-line.

Transfer: 337 transfer students enrolled in 2004-2005. Prospective students must submit transcripts of all academic work, a financial aid transcript, and SAT or ACT scores if they have fewer than 30 hours of college-level work. 32 of 126 credits required for the bachelor's degree must be completed at BC.

Visiting: There are regularly scheduled orientations for prospective students, including campus tours, opportunities to develop class schedules, and financial aid workshops. Visitors may sit in on classes and stay overnight. To schedule a visit, contact the Admissions Office at (276) 326-4214.

Financial Aid: The FAFSA and the college's own financial statement are required. The deadline for filing freshman financial aid applications for fall entry is March 10.

International Students: There are 2 international students enrolled. The school actively recruits these students. They must take the TOEFL.

Computers: Wireless access is available. All students may access the system. There are no time limits and no fees. It is strongly recommended that all students have a personal computer. It is recommended that students in Organizational Management and leadership have personal computers.

Graduates: In a recent year, 246 bachelor's degrees were awarded. In an average class, 1% graduate in 3 years or less, 47% graduate in 4 years or less, 50% graduate in 5 years or less, and 55% graduate in 6 years or less. 4 companies recruited on campus in a recent year. Of a recent graduating class, 16% were enrolled in graduate school within 6 months of graduation.

Admissions Contact: Admissions Office. A video is available. Web: *www.bluefield.edu*

BRIDGEWATER COLLEGE D-2

Bridgewater, VA 22812-1599

(540) 828-5375
(800) 759-8328; Fax: (540) 828-5481

Full-time: 639 men, 856 women	Faculty: 96; IIB, --$
Part-time: 4 men, 7 women	Ph.D.s: 79%
Graduate: none	Student/Faculty: 16 to 1
Year: 4-1-4, summer session	Tuition: $18,990
Application Deadline: open	Room & Board: $8800
Freshman Class: 1502 applied, 1292 accepted, 394 enrolled	
SAT Verbal/Math: 520/530*	ACT: 22	COMPETITIVE

Bridgewater College, founded in 1880, is a private liberal arts institution affiliated with the Church of the Brethren. In addition to regional accreditation, Bridgewater has baccalaureate program accreditation with CAAHEP. The library contains 189,114 volumes, 412,055 microform items, and 9194 audio/video tapes/CDs/DVDs, and subscribes to 650 periodicals including electronic. Computerized library services include the card catalog, interlibrary loans, database searching, and Internet access. Special learning facilities include a learning resource center, art gallery, radio station, and museum of the Shenandoah Valley and Church of the Brethren. The 190-acre campus is in a small town 8 miles south of Harrisonburg. Including any residence halls, there are 30 buildings.

Student Life: 77% of undergraduates are from Virginia. Others are from 23 states, 11 foreign countries, and Canada. 88% are from public schools. 88% are white. 76% are Protestant; 12% Catholic; 8% claim no religious affiliation. The average age of freshmen is 18; all undergraduates, 20. 23% do not continue beyond their first year; 68% remain to graduate.

Housing: 1326 students can be accommodated in college housing, which includes single-sex and coed dormitories and on-campus apartments. In addition, there are honors houses. On-campus housing is guaranteed for all 4 years. 80% of students live on campus; of those, 60% remain on campus on weekends. Alcohol is not permitted. All students may keep cars.

Activities: There are no fraternities or sororities. There are 75 groups on campus, including art, band, cheerleading, choir, chorale, chorus, computers, dance, debate, drama, ethnic, forensics, honors, international, jazz band, literary magazine, musical theater, newspaper, pep band, political, professional, radio and TV, religious, social, social service, student government, and yearbook. Popular campus events include Parents Day, Messiah at Christmas, and May Day.

Sports: There are 10 intercollegiate sports for men and 11 for women, and 24 intramural sports for men and 24 for women. Facilities include a gym, a 2500-seat football stadium, a swimming pool, tennis courts, an all-weather track, playing fields for baseball, lacrosse, softball, football, field hockey, and soccer, and a 34,000-square-foot fitness center with basketball, volleyball, and racquetball courts, an indoor track, a cardiac and weight-training center, and aerobics/dance rooms.

Disabled Students: 90% of the campus is accessible. Wheelchair ramps, elevators, special parking, specially equipped rest rooms, lowered drinking fountains, lowered telephones, special housing, and accessible laundry facilities in 2 dorms are available.

Services: Counseling and information services are available, as is tutoring in every subject. There is a reader service for the blind and remedial writing. The academic support center provides workshops for all students and support for students with learning disabilities.

Campus Safety and Security: Measures include 24-hour foot and vehicle patrol, informal discussions, pamphlets/posters/films, and emergency telephones. There are lighted pathways/sidewalks.

Programs of Study: Bridgewater confers B.A., B.S., and B.G.S. degrees. Bachelor's degrees are awarded in BIOLOGICAL SCIENCE (biology/biological science and nutrition), BUSINESS (business administration and management), COMMUNICATIONS AND THE ARTS (art, communications, English, French, music, and Spanish), COMPUTER AND PHYSICAL SCIENCE (applied physics, chemistry, computer science, information sciences and systems, mathematics, and physics), EDUCATION (athletic training and physical), ENGINEERING AND ENVIRONMENTAL DESIGN (environmental science), HEALTH PROFESSIONS (allied health, exercise science, and medical technology), SOCIAL SCIENCE (economics, family/consumer studies, history, international studies, liberal arts/general studies, philosophy, political science/government, psychology, religion, and sociology). Biology,chemistry, and psychology are the strongest academically. Biology, business administration, and communication studies are the largest.

Required: To graduate, all students must complete a minimum of 123 credit hours, with 30 to 48 hours in the major. A minimum 2.0 GPA is required overall and in the major and all seniors must pass a comprehensive exam. In addition, PDP 150: Personal Development and the Liberal Arts must be completed by each entering student unless the student transfers 15 or more units to Bridgewater. Other general education requirements include courses in writing, oral communication, math, global perspectives, humanities, natural science, math, foreign language, and social science. A thesis is required for graduation with honors.

Special: Bridgewater offers internships to junior and seniors; study abroad in 16 countries; and a teacher certification program in elementary, secondary, and special education. Interdisciplinary majors include environmental science, history and political science, philosophy and religion, physics and math, and information systems management. Dual degree programs are offered in engineering with George Washington University and Virgina Tech (3-2), in forestry with Duke University (3-2), in veterinary science with Virginia Tech (3-4), in physical therapy with George Washington University (3-2) and Shenandoah University (3-4), and in nursing with Vanderbilt University (3-2). There are 8 national honor societies, a freshman honors program, and 17 departmental honors programs.

Faculty/Classroom: 56% of faculty are male; 44%, female. All teach undergraduates, 50% do research, and 50% do both. The average class size in an introductory lecture is 22; in a laboratory, 15; and in a regular course, 19.

Admissions: 86% of the 2005-2006 applicants were accepted. The SAT scores for the 2005-2006 freshman class were: Verbal--35% below 500, 46% between 500 and 599, 17% between 600 and 700, and 2% above 700; Math--31% below 500, 49% between 500 and 599, 17% between 600 and 700, and 3% above 700. The ACT scores were 37% below 21, 36% between 21 and 23, 11% between 24 and 26, 8% between 27 and 28, and 8% above 28. 39% of the current freshmen were in the top fifth of their class; 74% were in the top two fifths. There were 7 National Merit semifinalists. 7 freshmen graduated first in their class.

Requirements: The SAT or ACT is required; the SAT is preferred. An interview is recommended. Applicants must be graduates of an accredited secondary school or have a GED certificate, and have completed 15 units, including 4 in English, 3 in math, 2 each in foreign language, science, and history and social studies, and 4 in electives. Bridgewater requires applicants to be in the upper 50% of their class. A GPA of 2.0 is required. AP credits are accepted. Important factors in the admissions decision are advanced placement or honor courses, recommendations by school officials, and leadership record.

Procedure: Freshmen are admitted fall, spring, and summer. Entrance exams should be taken in spring of the junior year or fall of the senior year. There is a deferred admissions plan. Application deadlines are open. Application fee is $30. Applications are accepted on-line. There is no fee for on-line application.

Transfer: 68 transfer students enrolled in 2005-2006. A degree from an accredited high school and a 2.0 GPA in all undergraduate work are required. 27 of 123 credits required for the bachelor's degree must be completed at Bridgewater.

Visiting: There are regularly scheduled orientations for prospective students, including a meeting with a faculty adviser, course scheduling and registration, and social activities. There are guides for informal visits and visitors may sit in on classes and stay overnight. To schedule a visit, contact Linda F. Stout.

Financial Aid: In 2005-2006, 99% of all full-time students received some form of financial aid. 70% of full-time freshmen and 68% of continuing full-time students received need-based aid. The average freshman award was $18,376. Need-based scholarships or need-based grants averaged $3441 ($10,000 maximum); need-based self-help aid (loans and jobs) averaged $4067 ($6225 maximum); and other non-need-based awards and non-need-based scholarships averaged $10,868 ($21,490 maximum). 31% of undergraduates work part time. Average annual earnings from campus work are $1108. The average financial indebtedness of the 2005 graduate was $25,780. Bridgewater is a member of CSS. The FAFSA is required. The priority date for freshman financial aid applications for fall entry is March 1. The deadline for filing freshman financial aid applications for fall entry is August 15.

International Students: There are 13 international students enrolled. The school actively recruits these students. They must take the TOEFL and also take the SAT or the ACT.

Computers: Wireless access is available. All buildings are connected via a campus wide network. There are 176 PCs in classroom buildings and the library available for student use. Dorm rooms are wired for connection to the campus network. Access to e-mail and the Web is available in computer labs throughout the campus. Wireless networking is available in the library and campus center. All students may access the system 24 hours a day. There are no time limits and no fees.

Graduates: From July 1, 2004 to June 30, 2005, 277 bachelor's degrees were awarded. The most popular majors were business administration (17%), biology (13%), and communication studies (9%). In an average class, 68% graduate in 6 years or less. 3 companies recruited on campus in 2004-2005.

Admissions Contact: Linda F. Stout, Director of Enrollment Operations. A video is available. E-mail: *admissions@bridgewater.edu*
Web: *www.bridgewater.edu*

CHRISTENDOM COLLEGE

D-2

Front Royal, VA 22630

(540) 636-2900
(800) 877-5456; Fax: (540) 636-1655

Full-time: 159 men, 213 women	**Faculty:** n/av
Part-time: 3 men, 4 women	**Ph.D.s:** n/av
Graduate: 56 men and women	**Student/Faculty:** n/av
Year: semesters	**Tuition:** $15,818
Application Deadline: March 1	**Room & Board:** $5776
Freshman Class: 222 applied, 189 accepted, 105 enrolled	
SAT Verbal/Math: 659/581*	**ACT:** 25 **VERY COMPETITIVE+**

Christendom College, founded in 1977, is a private liberal arts institution affiliated with the Roman Catholic Church. The library contains 68,314 volumes, 860 microform items, and 1345 audio/video tapes/CDs/DVDs, and subscribes to 279 periodicals including electronic. Computerized library services include the card catalog, interlibrary loans, and database searching. Special learning facilities include a learning resource center and a writing center. The 100-acre campus is in a rural area 65 miles west of Washington, D.C. Including any residence halls, there are 19 buildings.

Student Life: 74% of undergraduates are from out of state, mostly the Middle Atlantic. Students are from 43 states, 1 foreign countries, and Canada. 91% are white. Most are Catholic. The average age of freshmen is 18; all undergraduates, 20. 13% do not continue beyond their first year; 69% remain to graduate.

Housing: Housing includes single-sex dorms and on-campus apartments. On-campus housing is guaranteed for all 4 years. 90% of students live on campus; of those, 100% remain on campus on weekends. Alcohol is not permitted. All students may keep cars.

Activities: There are no fraternities or sororities. There are 15 groups on campus, including chess, choir, chorale, debate, drama, literary magazine, musical theater, newspaper, photography, political, religious, social service, student government, and yearbook. Popular campus events include Octoberfest, Christmas Dinner Dance, and Medieval Fest.

Sports: There are 3 intercollegiate sports for men and 4 for women, and 7 intramural sports for men and 7 for women. Facilities include indoor basketball and volleyball courts, racquetball courts, playing fields, table games, a recreation center, and an outdoor swimming pool.

Disabled Students: 60% of the campus is accessible. Wheelchair ramps, elevators, special parking, and specially equipped rest rooms are available.

Campus Safety and Security: Measures include 24-hour foot and vehicle patrol, security escort services, emergency telephones, and lighted pathways/sidewalks.

Programs of Study: Christendom confers the B.A. degree. Associate and master's degrees are also awarded. Bachelor's degrees are awarded in COMMUNICATIONS AND THE ARTS (English and French), SOCIAL SCIENCE (classical/ancient civilization, history, philosophy, political science/government, and theological studies). Political science is the strongest academically. Philosophy is the largest.

Required: To graduate, all students must complete a total of 126 credit hours, including a 30-hour major and an 84-credit core curriculum, which includes 18 hours each in theology and philosophy. A minimum 2.0 GPA is required. All students must demonstrate proficiency in a foreign language and complete a thesis.

Special: Christendom offers summer internships in Washington, D.C. for political science students and also sponsors a semester in Rome during the junior year. Students may pursue dual majors. There is a work-study program with the college.

Faculty/Classroom: All teach undergraduates.

Admissions: 85% of the 2005-2006 applicants were accepted. The SAT scores for the 2005-2006 freshman class were: Verbal--2% below 500, 19% between 500 and 599, 47% between 600 and 700, and 32% above 700; Math--13% below 500, 48% between 500 and 599, 33% between 600 and 700, and 6% above 700. The ACT scores were 16% below 21, 16% between 21 and 23, 23% between 24 and 26, 16% between 27 and 28, and 29% above 28. 38% of the current freshmen were in the top fifth of their class; 84% were in the top two fifths.

Requirements: The SAT or ACT is required; the SAT is preferred. Applicants need not be graduates of an accredited secondary school. GED certificates are accepted. Essays and letters of recommendation are required. A campus visit and a meeting with the Admissions Director are highly recommended. Christendom requires applicants to be in the upper 50% of their class. A GPA of 3.0 is required. AP credits are accepted.

Procedure: Freshmen are admitted fall and spring. Entrance exams should be taken in the spring of the junior year or fall of the senior year. There is an early admissions and a rolling admissions plan. Early action applications should be filed by December 1; regular applications, by March 1 for fall entry and January 2 for spring entry, along with a $25 fee. Notification of early action is sent December 15; regular decision, April 1. 25 applicants were on the 2005 waiting list; 6 were admitted. Applications are accepted on-line.

Transfer: 17 transfer students enrolled in 2004-2005. Students must have a minimum 2.0 GPA and meet all other applicable standard admissions requirements. The SAT or ACT is recommended. 36 of 126 credits required for the bachelor's degree must be completed at Christendom.

Visiting: There are guides for informal visits and visitors may sit in on classes and stay overnight. To schedule a visit, contact an Admissions Counselor.

Financial Aid: In a recent year, 78% of all full-time freshmen and 66% of continuing full-time students received some form of financial aid. 53% of full-time freshmen and 52% of continuing full-time students received need-based aid. The average freshman award was $8665. Need-based scholarships or need-based grants averaged $3715 ($5580 maximum); need-based self-help aid (loans and jobs) averaged $4950 ($5580 maximum); and other non-need-based awards and non-need-based scholarships averaged $4035 ($5480 maximum). 40% of undergraduates work part time. Average annual earnings from campus work are $1750. The average financial indebtedness of a recent year's graduate was $7950. The college's own financial statement is required. Check with the school for current deadlines.

International Students: A satisfactory score is required on the written TOEFL.

Computers: All students may access the system. There are no time limits and no fees.

Graduates: From July 1, 2004 to June 30, 2005, 89 bachelor's degrees were awarded. In an average class, 2% graduate in 3 years or less, 70% graduate in 4 years or less, and 75% graduate in 5 years or less. 8 companies recruited on campus in 2004-2005. Of the 2004 graduating class, 25% were enrolled in graduate school within 6 months of graduation and 75% were employed.

Admissions Contact: Thomas L. McFadden, Jr., Director of Admissions. E-mail: *admissions@christendom.edu*
Web: *www.christendom.edu*

CHRISTOPHER NEWPORT UNIVERSITY

F-3

Newport News, VA 23606-2998

(757) 594-7015
(800) 333-4268; Fax: (757) 594-7333

Full-time: 1600 men, 2500 women	**Faculty:** 184; IIB, +$
Part-time: 440 men, 670 women	**Ph.D.s:** 87%
Graduate: 80 men, 160 women	**Student/Faculty:** 22 to 1
Year: semesters, summer session	**Tuition:** $5826 ($12,898)
Application Deadline: March 1	**Room & Board:** $7500
Freshman Class: n/av	
SAT or ACT: required	**VERY COMPETITIVE**

Christopher Newport University, founded in 1960, is a comprehensive public university offering undergraduate programs in business and economics, arts and humanities, social science and professional studies, and science and technology. There are 2 undergraduate schools and 1 graduate school. Some figures in the above capsule and in this profile are approximate. In addition to regional accreditation, CNU has baccalaureate program accreditation with AACSB, ABET, CSWE, and NASM. The library contains 330,014 volumes, 765,028 microform items, and 10,238 audio/video tapes/CDs/DVDs, and subscribes to 1600 periodicals including electronic. Computerized library services include the card catalog, interlibrary loans, and database searching. Special learning facilities include a learning resource center, art gallery, radio station, and greenhouse-herbarium, and Japanese teahouse. The 150-acre campus is in a suburban area 20 miles northwest of Norfolk and 20 miles southeast of Williamsburg. Including any residence halls, there are 19 buildings.

Student Life: 97% of undergraduates are from Virginia. Others are from 27 states and 15 foreign countries. 80% are white; 14% African American. The average age of freshmen is 18; all undergraduates, 23. 19% do not continue beyond their first year; 30% remain to graduate.

Housing: 1455 students can be accommodated in college housing, which includes coed dorms and on-campus apartments. On-campus housing is guaranteed for all 4 years. 70% of students commute. Alcohol is not permitted. All students may keep cars.

Activities: 5% of men belong to 5 national fraternities; 4% of women belong to 5 national sororities. There are 29 groups on campus, including art, band, cheerleading, chess, choir, chorale, chorus, computers, dance, drama, ethnic, gay, honors, international, jazz band, literary magazine, musical theater, newspaper, opera, orchestra, pep band, political, professional, radio and TV, religious, social, social service, student government, and symphony. Popular campus events include FallFest, Sand Jam, and Ella Fitzgerald Music Festival.

Sports: There are 11 intercollegiate sports for men and 11 for women, and 13 intramural sports for men and 13 for women. The sports and recreation center has a 200-meter indoor track, 3 basketball courts, and 10,000 square feet of recreation and fitness space with state-of-the-art equipment.

Disabled Students: 95% of the campus is accessible. Wheelchair ramps, elevators, special parking, specially equipped rest rooms, special class scheduling, and lowered drinking fountains are available. Services are available on an individual basis.

Services: Counseling and information services are available, as is tutoring in most subjects. There is remedial math, reading, and writing.

Campus Safety and Security: Measures include 24-hour foot and vehicle patrol, security escort services, pamphlets/posters/films, and emergency telephones. There are lighted pathways/sidewalks and a campus police department.

Programs of Study: CNU confers B.A., B.S., B.M., B.S.A., B.S.B.A., B.S.G.A., B.S.I.S., and B.S.N. degrees. Master's degrees are also awarded. Bachelor's degrees are awarded in AGRICULTURE (horticulture), BIOLOGICAL SCIENCE (biology/biological science), BUSINESS (accounting, banking and finance, business administration and management, business economics, international business management, marketing management, marketing/retailing/merchandising, real estate, and recreation and leisure services), COMMUNICATIONS AND THE ARTS (communications, creative writing, dramatic arts, English, English literature, fine arts, French, German, journalism, music, music performance, music theory and composition, performing arts, and Spanish), COMPUTER AND PHYSICAL SCIENCE (computer science, information sciences and systems, mathematics, and physics), EDUCATION (early childhood, foreign languages, middle school, music, science, and secondary), ENGINEERING AND ENVIRONMENTAL DESIGN (computer engineering and environmental science), HEALTH PROFESSIONS (nursing, predentistry, and premedicine), SOCIAL SCIENCE (criminal justice, criminology, economics, history, interdisciplinary studies, international public service, international relations, law, parks and recreation management, philosophy, political science/government, prelaw, psychology, public administration, religion, social work, and sociology). Business, psychology, and government administration are the largest.

Required: To graduate, all students must fulfill general education requirements in English, math, humanities, social science, lab science, communications, philosophy, foreign language, computer literacy, health, and phys ed. A minimum of 120 semester hours, with 58 to 66 hours in the major and in elective studies, is required. Students must have a minimum GPA of 2.0.

Special: CNU offers cross-registration with Thomas Nelson Community College and Hampton and Old Dominion Universities, dual majors, various B.A.-B.S. degrees, a student-designed interdisciplinary studies major, and internships in social service, communications, city government, computer science, and engineering. There are 9 national honor societies, a freshman honors program, and 9 departmental honors programs.

Faculty/Classroom: All teach undergraduates and 10% both teach and do research. No introductory courses are taught by graduate students. The average class size in an introductory lecture is 25; in a laboratory, 20; and in a regular course, 25.

Requirements: A satisfactory score on the SAT or ACT is required. Applicants must be graduates of an accredited secondary school or have a GED certificate. A total of 23 academic credits is recommended, including 4 units of English, 3 each of social science, math, and science, and either 3 units of 1 foreign language or 2 years of 2 foreign languages. An essay and interview are recommended. Applications are accepted online at *www.cnu.edu/admin/admit/*. CNU requires applicants to be in the upper 50% of their class. A GPA of 3.0 is required. AP and CLEP credits are accepted. Important factors in the admissions decision are recommendations by school officials, extracurricular activities record, and evidence of special talent.

Procedure: Freshmen are admitted fall and spring. Entrance exams should be taken in the junior year. There is a rolling admissions plan. There are early admissions and deferred admissions plans. Applications should be filed by March 1 for fall entry, along with a $35 fee. Applications are accepted on-line.

Transfer: Applicants must have at least 15 transferable semester hours with a minimum 3.0 GPA and be eligible to return to the most recently attended college or university. Students with fewer than 15 semester hours must submit SAT or ACT scores and official transcripts from their secondary school and all colleges attended. 30 of 120 credits required for the bachelor's degree must be completed at CNU.

Visiting: There are regularly scheduled orientations for prospective students, including information sessions and tours Monday through Friday at 10 A.M. and 2 P.M.; Saturday session and tour at 11 A.M. Tours run throughout the year. There are guides for informal visits and visitors may sit in on classes and stay overnight. To schedule a visit, contact the Admissions Office at *tourguide@cnu.edu*.

Financial Aid: CNU is a member of CSS. The FAFSA is required. Check with the school for current deadlines.

International Students: They must acheive satisfactory scores on the TOEFL as well as the SAT or ACT.

Computers: All students may access the system 24 hours a day, 7 days a week. There are no time limits and no fees.

Admissions Contact: Admissions Office. E-mail: *admit@cnu.edu* Web: *http://www.cnu.edu*

COLLEGE OF WILLIAM AND MARY
Williamsburg, VA 23187-8795

E-3

(757) 221-4223
Fax: (757) 221-1242

Full-time: 2500 men, 3200 women	**Faculty:** 446; I, av$
Part-time: 50 men, 40 women	**Ph.Ds:** 91%
Graduate: 1000 men, 980 women	**Student/Faculty:** 13 to 1
Year: semesters, summer session	**Tuition:** $7778 ($23,186)
Application Deadline: January 1	**Room & Board:** $6369
Freshman Class: n/av	
SAT or ACT: required	**MOST COMPETITIVE**

College of William and Mary, founded in 1693, is the second-oldest college in the United States. The public institution offers undergraduate degrees in the arts and sciences. Graduate programs are offered in arts and sciences, law, business, education, and marine science. Some of the figures in the above capsule and in this profile are approximate. There are 2 undergraduate and 5 graduate schools. In addition to regional accreditation, William and Mary has baccalaureate program accreditation with AACSB and NCATE. The 6 libraries contain 2,128,645 volumes, 2,346,524 microform items, and 29,977 audio/video tapes/CDs/DVDs, and subscribe to 11,313 periodicals including electronic. Computerized library services include the card catalog, interlibrary loans, and database searching. Special learning facilities include a learning resource center, art gallery, radio station, an anthropology museum, an art studio, a greenhouse, the Center for Archaeological Research, and the Omohundro Institute of Early American History and Culture. The 1200-acre campus is in a small town 50 miles southeast of Richmond. Including any residence halls, there are 166 buildings.

Student Life: 66% of undergraduates are from Virginia. Others are from 49 states, 52 foreign countries, and Canada. 74% are from public schools. 84% are white. The average age of freshmen is 18; all undergraduates, 20. 5% do not continue beyond their first year; 91% remain to graduate.

Housing: 4444 students can be accommodated in college housing, which includes single-sex and coed dorms, on-campus apartments, off-campus apartments, married-student housing, fraternity houses, and sorority houses. In addition, there are honors houses, language houses, special-interest houses, an international studies hall, and smoke-free housing. On-campus housing is guaranteed for the freshman year only and is available on a lottery system for upperclassmen. 75% of students live on campus; of those, All remain on campus on weekends. Upperclassmen may keep cars.

Activities: 33% of men belong to 15 national fraternities; 34% of women belong to 11 national sororities. There are 300 groups on campus, including art, band, cheerleading, chess, choir, chorale, chorus, computers, dance, drama, drill team, ethnic, film, gay, honors, international, jazz band, literary magazine, musical theater, newspaper, opera, orchestra, pep band, photography, political, professional, radio and TV, religious, social, social service, student government, symphony, and yearbook. Popular campus events include Yule Log Ceremony, King and Queen Ball, and Opening Convocation.

Sports: There are 11 intercollegiate sports for men and 12 for women, and 24 intramural sports for men and 24 for women. Facilities include an 8500-seat basketball arena, an indoor track, a strength training facility, a sports medicine/rehabilitation facility, a gym room, lighted tennis courts, a 2200-seat artificial turf stadium, a 14,500-seat football stadium, a 1000-seat baseball stadium, and a student recreation facility with a gym, swimming pool, weight room, and racquetball and squash courts.

Disabled Students: 80% of the campus is accessible. Wheelchair ramps, elevators, special parking, specially equipped rest rooms, special class scheduling, lowered drinking fountains, modified recreational facilities, TDD, braille signage, a Kurzweil reader, and a special learning lab for the visually impaired are available. Individual accommodations are made on a case-by-case basis.

Services: Counseling and information services are available, as is tutoring in most subjects. There is a reader service for the blind. There are reasonable in-class accommodations for learning-disabled students and hearing-impaired students and diagnostic services for learning disabilities.

Campus Safety and Security: Measures include 24-hour foot and vehicle patrol, self-defense education, security escort services, and shuttle buses. There are informal discussions, pamphlets/posters/films, emergency telephones, lighted pathways/sidewalks, and crime prevention programs.

Programs of Study: William and Mary confers B.A., B.S., A.B., and B.B.A. degrees. Master's and doctoral degrees are also awarded. Bachelor's degrees are awarded in BIOLOGICAL SCIENCE (biology/biological science), BUSINESS (business administration and management), COMMUNICATIONS AND THE ARTS (classics, English, fine arts, French, German, music, Spanish, and speech/debate/rhetoric), COMPUTER AND PHYSICAL SCIENCE (chemistry, computer science, geology, mathematics, and physics), SOCIAL SCIENCE (American studies, anthropology, economics, history, interdisciplinary studies, international relations, international studies, philosophy, political science/government, psychology, religion, and sociology). Business, psychology, and government are the largest.

Required: To graduate, students must demonstrate proficiencies in foreign language, writing, computing, and physical activity. Freshman seminars are required. Students must complete 120 credit hours, with 33 to 45 in the major and a minimum 2.0 GPA. Distribution requirements include courses in math and quantitative reasoning, natural sciences, social sciences, world cultures and history, literature and history of the arts, and philosophical, religious, and social thought.

Special: William and Mary offers a forestry/environmental science program with Duke University. Also available are departmental internships, study abroad in more than 40 countries, dual and student-designed majors, work-study programs, an accelerated degree in computer science, B.A.-B.S. degrees in math, psychology, computer science, and international studies, a Washington semester, nondegree study, and pass/fail options. There are 29 national honor societies, including Phi Beta Kappa, a freshman honors program, and 15 departmental honors programs.

Faculty/Classroom: 66% of faculty are male; 34%, female. 76% teach undergraduates and 69% do research. No introductory courses are taught by graduate students. The average class size in an introductory lecture is 43; in a laboratory, 26; and in a regular course, 26.

Admissions: 107 freshmen graduated first in their class, in a recent year.

Requirements: The SAT or ACT is required. In addition, an essay and 3 SAT Subject Tests, including the test in writing, are strongly recommended. AP credits are accepted. Important factors in the admissions decision are advanced placement or honor courses, evidence of special talent, and extracurricular activities record.

Procedure: Freshmen are admitted fall and spring. Entrance exams should be taken in spring of the junior year or fall of the senior year. There are early decision and deferred admissions plans. Early decision applications should be filed by November 1; regular applications, by January 1 for fall entry and November 1 for spring entry, along with a $60 fee. Notification of early decision is sent December 1; regular decision, early April . 497 early decision candidates were accepted for a recent class. 736 applicants were on a recent year's waiting list; 9 were admitted. Applications are accepted on-line.

Transfer: 181 transfer students enrolled in a recent year. Applicants must have at least 15 credit hours earned with a minimum 3.0 GPA recommended. Emphasis is placed on the individual's college records. The SAT or ACT is required if applicants have completed less than 1 full year of course work at their previous college. 60 of 120 credits required for the bachelor's degree must be completed at William and Mary.

Visiting: There are regularly scheduled orientations for prospective students, consisting of a group information session followed by a student-led tour. Visitors may sit in on classes and stay overnight. To schedule a visit, contact the Office of Admissions.

Financial Aid: William and Mary is a member of CSS. The CSS/Profile or FAFSA is required. The CSS Profile is required for early decision enrollees. Check with the school for current application deadlines.

International Students: There were 81 international students enrolled in a recent year. The school actively recruits these students. They must achieve a satisfactory score on the TOEFL and also take the ELPT (English Language Proficiency Test) and the SAT or ACT. SAT Subject Tests are considered if they are submitted.

Computers: All students may access the system. There are no time limits and no fees.

Graduates: In a recent year, 1354 bachelor's degrees were awarded. The most popular majors were business (14%), psychology (9%), and biology (9%). In an average class, 79% graduate in 4 years or less, 89% graduate in 5 years or less, and 91% graduate in 6 years or less. 422 companies recruited on campus in a recent year. Of a recent graduating class, 31% were enrolled in graduate school within 6 months of graduation and 48% were employed.

Admissions Contact: Office of Admission. A video is available. E-mail: *admiss@wm.edu* Web: *www.wm.edu*

DEVRY UNIVERSITY/CRYSTAL CITY   E-2
Arlington, VA 22202-3843

(703) 414-4100
(866) 338-7932; Fax: (703) 414-4040

Full-time: 300 men, 100 women	**Faculty:** n/av
Part-time: 150 men, 75 women	**Ph.D.s:** n/av
Graduate: none	**Student/Faculty:** n/av
Year: semesters, summer session	**Tuition:** $12,000
Application Deadline: open	**Room & Board:** n/app
Freshman Class: n/av	
SAT or ACT: n/av	**COMPETITIVE**

DeVry University/Crystal City, founded in 2001, is 1 of 67 DeVry University locations throughout the United States and Canada. The private institution offers career-oriented degree programs with hands-on training in various fields of business and technology. Figures in the above capsule and in this profile are approximate. Computerized library services include the card catalog, interlibrary loans, and database searching. Special learning facilities include a learning resource center and electronics and other labs. .

Student Life: 56% are African American; 19% white. The average age of all undergraduates is 24.

Housing: There are no residence halls. All of students commute. All students may keep cars.

Activities: There are no fraternities or sororities.

Sports: There is no sports program at DeVry.

Disabled Students: All of the campus is accessible. Wheelchair ramps, elevators, special parking, specially equipped rest rooms, lowered drinking fountains, and lowered telephones are available.

Services: Counseling and information services are available, as is tutoring in every subject.

Campus Safety and Security: Measures include security escort services and lighted pathways/sidewalks.

Programs of Study: DeVry confers the B.S. degree. Associate and master's degrees are also awarded. Bachelor's degrees are awarded in BUSINESS (business administration and management), COMMUNICATIONS AND THE ARTS (telecommunications), COMPUTER AND PHYSICAL SCIENCE (information sciences and systems), ENGINEERING AND ENVIRONMENTAL DESIGN (computer engineering, electrical/electronics engineering technology, and technological management). Business administration and computer information systems are the largest.

Required: To graduate, students must achieve a GPA of at least 2.0 and satisfactorily complete all curriculum requirements. Course requirements vary according to program. All first-year students take courses in business organization, computer applications, algebra, psychology, and student success strategies.

Special: An accelerated degree program in computer information systems, co-op programs, nondegree study, distance learning, and evening and weekend classes are possible.

Faculty/Classroom: All teach undergraduates.

Requirements: Admissions requirements include graduation from a secondary school; the GED is also accepted. Applicants must pass the DeVry entrance exam or present satisfactory ACT or SAT scores. An interview is required. CLEP credit is accepted.

Procedure: Freshmen are admitted to all sessions. There are early admissions and deferred admissions plans. Application deadlines are open. Check with the school for application fee. Applications are accepted on-line.

Transfer: Applicants must submit official transcripts from all previous colleges attended indicating passing grades in all completed course work, demonstrate language skills proficiency in at least 24 completed semester hours, and present evidence of math proficiency by appropriate college-level credits. A minimum GPA of 2.0 is required. 25 of 48 credits required for the bachelor's degree must be completed at DeVry.

Visiting: There are regularly scheduled orientations for prospective students. There are guides for informal visits and visitors may sit in on classes. To schedule a visit, contact Director of Admissions.

Financial Aid: In a recent year, 61% of all full-time freshmen and 68% of continuing full-time students received some form of financial aid. 60% of full-time freshmen and 68% of continuing full-time students received need-based aid. The average freshman award was $5819. Need-based scholarships or need-based grants averaged $3809; need-based self-help aid (loans and jobs) averaged $3987; and other non-need-based awards and non-need-based scholarships averaged $7601. The FAFSA is required.

International Students: International students must take the written TOEFL and also take the college's own entrance exam.

Admissions Contact: Charles Akinduro, Director of Admissions.
E-mail: *admissions@devry.edu* Web: *www.crys.devry.edu*

EASTERN MENNONITE UNIVERSITY   D-2

Harrisonburg, VA 22802-2462   (540) 432-4118
                                    (800) 368-2665; Fax: (540) 432-4444

Full-time: 345 men, 522 women	**Faculty:** 89; IIA, --$
Part-time: 15 men, 15 women	**Ph.D.s:** 71%
Graduate: 107 men, 307 women	**Student/Faculty:** 10 to 1
Year: semesters, summer session	**Tuition:** $19,500
Application Deadline: open	**Room & Board:** $5950
Freshman Class: 636 applied, 490 accepted, 206 enrolled	
SAT Verbal/Math: 545/550*	**ACT:** 25 **VERY COMPETITIVE**

Eastern Mennonite University, founded in 1917, is a private Christian liberal arts university affiliated with the Mennonite Church. The university offers programs in the arts and sciences, education, biology, and nursing. EMU also offers master's degrees in several areas. EMU's Lancaster site provides some programs in Lancaster, Pennsylvania. In addition to regional accreditation, EMU has baccalaureate program accreditation with ACPE, CSWE, NCATE, and NLN. The library contains 167,242 volumes, 92,096 microform items, and 3723 audio/video tapes/CDs/DVDs, and subscribes to 1056 periodicals including electronic. Computerized library services include the card catalog, interlibrary loans, database searching, Internet access, and laptop Internet portals. Special learning facilities include a learning resource center, art gallery, natural history museum, planetarium, radio station, arboretum and greenhouse, and nursing laboratory. The 93-acre campus is in a small town 110 miles southwest of Washington, D.C. Including any residence halls, there are 44 buildings.

Student Life: 57% of undergraduates are from out of state, mostly the Middle Atlantic. Students are from 32 states, 19 foreign countries, and Canada. 58% are from public schools. 81% are white. 91% are Protestant; 7% claim no religious affiliation. The average age of freshmen is 18; all undergraduates, 21. 23% do not continue beyond their first year; 62% remain to graduate.

Housing: 683 students can be accommodated in college housing, which includes single-sex and coed dorms, on-campus apartments, off-campus apartments, and married-student housing. On-campus housing is guaranteed for all 4 years. 57% of students live on campus; of those, 75% remain on campus on weekends. Alcohol is not permitted. All students may keep cars.

Activities: There are no fraternities or sororities. There are 51 groups on campus, including chess, choir, chorale, chorus, dance, drama, ethnic, film, honors, international, jazz band, literary magazine, musical theater, newspaper, orchestra, peace fellowship, pep band, political, professional, radio and TV, religious, social, social service, student government, student women's association, and yearbook. Popular campus events include Spring Fling, Fall Festival, and Multicultural Week.

Sports: There are 8 intercollegiate sports for men and 9 for women, and 15 intramural sports for men and 15 for women. Facilities include a fitness center, aerobics room, indoor track, and climbing wall. The gym includes 1 regular varsity court and 2 courts for team practice. Outside facilities include a lighted artificial turf playing field, lighted tennis courts, baseball, softball, and soccer fields, a rubberized outdoor track, as well as basketball and sand volleyball courts.

Disabled Students: 75% of the campus is accessible. Wheelchair ramps, elevators, special parking, specially equipped rest rooms, special class scheduling, lowered drinking fountains and special housing are available. Newer buildings on campus have accessible telephones.

Services: Counseling and information services are available, as is tutoring in most subjects, including core curriculum courses. There is a reader service for the blind and remedial reading and writing. EMU owns technology, such as the ability to burn textbooks onto CD's, for visually impaired students and those with other special learning needs. Technology for the hearing impaired will be provided as needed.

Campus Safety and Security: Measures include self-defense education, security escort services, informal discussions, and pamphlets/posters/films. There are emergency telephones, lighted pathways/sidewalks, and a 12-hour foot or vehicle watchman.

Programs of Study: EMU confers B.A. and B.S. degrees. Associate and master's degrees are also awarded. Bachelor's degrees are awarded in AGRICULTURE (international agriculture), BIOLOGICAL SCIENCE (biochemistry and biology/biological science), BUSINESS (accounting, business administration and management, international business management, and recreational facilities management), COMMUNICATIONS AND THE ARTS (art, communications, dramatic arts, English, French, German, music, and Spanish), COMPUTER AND PHYSICAL SCIENCE (chemistry, computer management, computer science, and mathematics), EDUCATION (early childhood, elementary, physical, secondary, and special), ENGINEERING AND ENVIRONMENTAL DESIGN (environmental science), HEALTH PROFESSIONS (medical laboratory technology and nursing), SOCIAL SCIENCE (biblical studies, development economics, economics, history, liberal arts/general studies, ministries, peace studies, philosophy, psychology, religion, social science, social work, sociology, and theological studies). Business, education, and nursing are the largest.

Required: To graduate, students must complete interdisciplinary core courses, courses in Bible and religion, cross-cultural study, writing, speech, and math, a major (minors are optional), and a variety of electives for a minimum of 128 semester hours. A minimum cumulative GPA of 2.0 is required while some majors require a higher GPA in the major or overall.

Special: EMU offers study-abroad programs each semester and during the summer at a variety of locations around the world. Students may also choose to study 1 or 2 semesters in Washington, D.C. There are internships in a variety of majors, dual majors, a student-designed major, and a 2 year general studies degree. There is 1 national honor society and a freshman honors program.

Faculty/Classroom: 58% of faculty are male; 42%, female. 75% teach undergraduates, 38% do research, and 35% do both. No introductory courses are taught by graduate students. The average class size in an introductory lecture is 40; in a laboratory, 17; and in a regular course, 18.

Admissions: 77% of the 2005-2006 applicants were accepted. The SAT scores for the 2005-2006 freshman class were: Verbal--32% below 500, 34% between 500 and 599, 24% between 600 and 700, and 10% above 700; Math--31% below 500, 35% between 500 and 599, 31% between 600 and 700, and 3% above 700. The ACT scores were 17% below 21, 21% between 21 and 23, 30% between 24 and 26, 9% between 27 and 28, and 23% above 28. 36% of the current freshmen were in the top fifth of their class; 65% were in the top two fifths. 7 freshmen graduated first in their class.

Requirements: A satisfactory score is required on the SAT or ACT is required. In addition, applicants must be graduates of an accredited secondary school or have a GED certificate. The university recommends that students have completed 4 credits of English, 3 each of math, science, and social studies, 2 or more of foreign language and chemistry for nursing majors. A personal reference is required and an interview is recommended. A GPA of 2.2 is required. AP and CLEP credits are accepted. Important factors in the admissions decision are leadership record, extracurricular activities record, and recommendations by school officials.

Procedure: Freshmen are admitted fall and spring. Entrance exams should be taken in the spring of the junior year or the fall of the senior year. There is a deferred admissions plan and a rolling admissions plan. Application deadlines are open. The fall 2005 application fee was $25. Applications are accepted on-line.

Transfer: 77 transfer students enrolled in 2004-2005. Transfer students must have a minimum college GPA of 2.0. 32 of 128 credits required for the bachelor's degree must be completed at EMU.

Visiting: There are regularly scheduled orientations for prospective students, including an address by the president, a financial aid seminar, a review of general education, and attendance at a chapel; the opportunity to sit in on classes, meet with professors and admissions representatives, sleep in residence halls, and eat in the cafeteria; and attendance at special campus events. There are guides for informal visits. To schedule a visit, contact the Admissions Office.

Financial Aid: In 2005-2006, 97% of all full-time freshmen and 96% of continuing full-time students received some form of financial aid. 89% of full-time freshmen and 87% of continuing full-time students received need-based aid. The average freshman award was $16,515. Need-based scholarships or need-based grants averaged $2700; need-based self-help aid (loans and jobs) averaged $6015; and other non-need-based awards and non-need-based scholarships averaged $7800. 35% of undergraduates work part time. Average annual earnings from campus work are $1300. The average financial indebtedness of the 2005 graduate was $18,208. EMU is a member of CSS. The FAFSA and the state aid form are required. The deadline for filing freshman financial aid applications for fall entry is April 15.

International Students: There are 40 international students enrolled. They must take the TOEFL and also take the SAT or the ACT, scoring satifactorily.

Computers: Wireless access is available. There are 2 public computer labs for student use. Residential students may connect their PC to the network in specified locations. There are several wireless locations for labtop users. All students may access the system day and evening. There are no time limits and no fees.

Graduates: From July 1, 2004 to June 30, 2005, 315 bachelor's degrees were awarded. The most popular majors were business (30%), nursing (16%), and education (9%). In an average class, 45% graduate in 4 years or less, 59% graduate in 5 years or less, and 62% graduate in 6 years or less. 15 companies recruited on campus in a recent year.

Of the 2004 graduating class, 8% were enrolled in graduate school within 6 months of graduation and 86% were employed.

Admissions Contact: Admissions Office. A video is available.
E-mail: *admiss@emu.edu* Web: *http://www.emu.edu*

EMORY & HENRY COLLEGE   B-4
Emory, VA 24327-0947

(276) 944-6133
(800) 848-5493; Fax: (276) 944-6935

Full-time: 502 men, 497 women	**Faculty:** 68; IIB, --$
Part-time: 17 men, 11 women	**Ph.D.s:** 88%
Graduate: 9 men, 65 women	**Student/Faculty:** 15 to 1
Year: semesters, summer session	**Tuition:** $19,530
Application Deadline: April 15	**Room & Board:** $7040
Freshman Class: 1329 applied, 1009 accepted, 338 enrolled	
SAT Verbal/Math: 1066 (total)*	**ACT:** 23 **COMPETITIVE**

Emory & Henry College, founded in 1836, is a private liberal arts institution affiliated with the United Methodist Church. In addition to regional accreditation, Emory & Henry College has baccalaureate program accreditation with CAAHEP. The library contains 179,315 volumes, 41,424 microform items, and 4119 audio/video tapes/CDs/DVDs, and subscribes to 650 periodicals including electronic. Computerized library services include the card catalog, interlibrary loans, database searching, and Internet access. Special learning facilities include a learning resource center, art gallery, and radio station. The 331-acre campus is in a rural area in southwest Virginia. Including any residence halls, there are 58 buildings.
Student Life: 71% of undergraduates are from Virginia. Others are from 23 states and 3 foreign countries. 99% are from public schools. 91% are white. The average age of freshmen is 18; all undergraduates, 20. 28% do not continue beyond their first year; 52% remain to graduate.
Housing: 723 students can be accommodated in college housing, which includes single-sex dorms. In addition, there are honors houses and special-interest houses. On-campus housing is guaranteed for all 4 years. 66% of students live on campus; of those, 50% remain on campus on weekends. Alcohol is not permitted. All students may keep cars.
Activities: 11% of men belong to 6 local fraternities; 26% of women belong to 6 local sororities. There are 50 groups on campus, including art, cheerleading, choir, chorus, dance, drama, ethnic, international, literary magazine, newspaper, opera, pep band, photography, political, professional, radio and TV, religious, social, social service, and student government. Popular campus events include Parents Day, Air Band, and the Literary Festival.
Sports: There are 7 intercollegiate sports for men and 6 for women, and 10 intramural sports for men and 10 for women. Facilities include a gym, a pool, a racquetball court, outdoor volleyball courts, tennis courts, a weight room, a dance room, a golf course, baseball and football fields, and a horseshoe area.
Disabled Students: 50% of the campus is accessible. Wheelchair ramps, elevators, special parking, specially equipped rest rooms, special class scheduling, lowered drinking fountains, and special housing are available.
Services: Counseling and information services are available, as is tutoring in most subjects. There is a reader service for the blind and remedial writing.
Campus Safety and Security: Measures include 24-hour foot and vehicle patrol, self-defense education, security escort services, and informal discussions. There are pamphlets/posters/films and lighted pathways/sidewalks.
Programs of Study: Emory & Henry College confers B.A. and B.S. degrees. Master's degrees are also awarded. Bachelor's degrees are awarded in BIOLOGICAL SCIENCE (biology/biological science), BUSINESS (business administration and management), COMMUNICATIONS AND THE ARTS (art, communications, creative writing, dramatic arts, English literature, journalism, literature, modern language, music performance, and music theory and composition), COMPUTER AND PHYSICAL SCIENCE (chemistry, computer management, computer science, mathematics, and physics), EDUCATION (English, mathematics, and physical), ENGINEERING AND ENVIRONMENTAL DESIGN (environmental science), SOCIAL SCIENCE (community services, East Asian studies, economics, European studies, geography, history, interdisciplinary studies, international studies, Middle Eastern studies, philosophy, political science/government, psychology, public affairs, religion, and sociology). Economics and business, interdisciplinary English, and mass communications are the largest.
Required: All students must complete a general studies curriculum covering Western traditions, great books, religion, ethical values inquiry, and global studies and must demonstrate proficiency in oral skills. Specific courses include a first-year writing course, 1 each from 3 disciplines, including social sciences, humanities and arts, and natural sciences, and according to major, either a foreign language or quantitative methods. A total of 116 semester hours for a B.A. or 124 for a B.S., with a GPA of 2.0, is required for graduation. The total number of hours in the major varies.

Special: A cooperative program in medical technology and 2-2, 4-1, and 3-2 engineering degrees are available. Dual and student-designed majors, an interdisciplinary English major, combined B.A.-B.S. degrees, internships, a Washington semester, work-study, nondegree study, and pass/fail options are also available. There are 10 national honor societies and 8 departmental honors programs.
Faculty/Classroom: 65% of faculty are male; 35%, female. All teach undergraduates. No introductory courses are taught by graduate students. The average class size in an introductory lecture is 25; in a laboratory, 13; and in a regular course, 22.
Admissions: 76% of the 2005-2006 applicants were accepted. The SAT scores for the 2005-2006 freshman class were: Verbal--33% below 500, 44% between 500 and 599, 19% between 600 and 700, and 4% above 700; Math--36% below 500, 43% between 500 and 599, 19% between 600 and 700, and 2% above 700. 88% of the current freshmen were in the top two fifths of their class. 4 freshmen graduated first in their class.
Requirements: The SAT or ACT is required. In addition, applicants should be high school graduates. High school courses required include 4 years of English, 3 or more units of math, including algebra I, algebra II, and geometry, 2 or more units of lab science, 2 units of a single foreign language, and 2 or more units of social studies and history. 1 additional unit in fine arts is strongly recommended. A personal essay is required. AP credits are accepted. Important factors in the admissions decision are advanced placement or honor courses, recommendations by school officials, and evidence of special talent.
Procedure: Freshmen are admitted fall, spring, and summer. Entrance exams should be taken in November of the senior year. There are early decision, early admissions, and deferred admissions plans. There is a rolling admissions plan. Early decision applications should be filed by November 1; regular applications, by April 15 for fall entry. Notification is sent on a rolling basis. 44 early decision candidates were accepted for the 2005-2006 class. The fall 2005 application fee was $30. Applications are accepted on-line.
Transfer: 64 transfer students enrolled in 2004-2005. Transfers must have at least a 2.5 GPA in previous college work. Those with at least 24 credits may be admitted without high school data; those with fewer than 24 credits must meet freshman admission standards. 33 of 120 credits required for the bachelor's degree must be completed at Emory & Henry College.
Visiting: There are regularly scheduled orientations for prospective students, including a program for students to meet faculty and staff and to attend education sessions on college life. There are guides for informal visits and visitors may sit in on classes and stay overnight. To schedule a visit, contact the Admissions Office at *ehadmiss@ehc.edu*.
Financial Aid: In 2005-2006, 99% of all full-time freshmen received some form of financial aid. 71% of full-time freshmen received need-based aid. The average freshman award was $14,955. Need-based scholarships or need-based grants averaged $11,711; and need-based self-help aid (loans and jobs) averaged $2543. 13% of undergraduates work part time. Average annual earnings from campus work are $1200. The average financial indebtedness of the 2005 graduate was $15,465. The FAFSA, the state aid form, and the college's own financial statement are required. The priority date for freshman financial aid applications for fall entry is April 1. The deadline for filing freshman financial aid applications for fall entry is August 1.
International Students: There are 2 international students enrolled. The school actively recruits these students. They must take the TOEFL.
Computers: Wireless access is available. All students may access the system. There are no time limits and no fees.
Graduates: From July 1, 2004 to June 30, 2005, 196 bachelor's degrees were awarded. The most popular majors were social science (16%), business management (13%), and English education (13%). In an average class, 43% graduate in 4 years or less, 51% graduate in 5 years or less, and 52% graduate in 6 years or less.
Admissions Contact: Liz Daniels, Director of Admissions and Financial Aid. A video is available. E-mail: *ehadmiss@ehc.edu*
Web: *www.ehc.edu*

FERRUM COLLEGE   C-3
Ferrum, VA 24088

(540) 365-4290
(800) 868-9797; Fax: (540) 365-4266

Full-time: 563 men, 399 women	**Faculty:** 62
Part-time: 7 men, 22 women	**Ph.D.s:** 77%
Graduate: none	**Student/Faculty:** 16 to 1
Year: semesters	**Tuition:** $17,990
Application Deadline: open	**Room & Board:** $6300
Freshman Class: n/av	
SAT or ACT: required	**LESS COMPETITIVE**

Ferrum College, founded in 1913, is a private, primarily residential, 4-year institution offering both professional and liberal arts majors. In addition to regional accreditation, Ferrum has baccalaureate program accreditation with CSWE and NRPA. The library contains 114,370 volumes and 2090 audio/video tapes/CDs/DVDs, and subscribes to 10,618 periodicals including electronic. Computerized library services include the card catalog, interlibrary loans, database searching, Internet access, and laptop Internet portals. Special learning facilities include a learning resource center, art gallery, radio station, a folklife museum, and a living history museum. The 720-acre campus is in a rural area 35 miles south of Roanoke. Including any residence halls, there are 54 buildings.

Student Life: 84% of undergraduates are from Virginia. Students are from 24 states and 9 foreign countries. 68% are white; 20% African American. 66% are Protestant; 34% claim no religious affiliation; 8% Catholic. The average age of freshmen is 18; all undergraduates, 21. 45% do not continue beyond their first year; 34% remain to graduate.

Housing: 1000 students can be accommodated in college housing, which includes single-sex and coed dorms, on-campus apartments, off-campus apartments, and married-student housing. On-campus housing is guaranteed for all 4 years. 74% of students live on campus; of those, 50% remain on campus on weekends. All students may keep cars.

Activities: There are no fraternities or sororities. There are 50 groups on campus, including art, cheerleading, choir, chorale, chorus, computers, dance, drama, ethnic, film, gay, honors, international, jazz band, literary magazine, musical theater, newspaper, photography, political, professional, radio and TV, religious, social, social service, and student government. Popular campus events include Spring Fling, Blue Ridge Folklife Festival, and Snow Ball.

Sports: There are 7 intercollegiate sports for men and 7 for women, and 13 intramural sports for men and 13 for women. Facilities include a gym, a field house, tennis courts, a weight room, an indoor pool, an outdoor volleyball court, a football stadium, a soccer field, a baseball field, a women's softball field, a recreation center (with indoor basketball courts, racquetball courts, and universal weights), and hiking/mountain biking trails.

Disabled Students: 75% of the campus is accessible. Wheelchair ramps, elevators, special parking, specially equipped rest rooms, special class scheduling, and lowered drinking fountains are available.

Services: Counseling and information services are available, as is tutoring in most subjects. There is remedial math, reading, and writing. College skills classes, individual assistance for study strategies, and subject-specific tutoring by professors and students are available.

Campus Safety and Security: Measures include 24-hour foot and vehicle patrol, self-defense education, security escort services, and informal discussions. There are pamphlets/posters/films, emergency telephones, and lighted pathways/sidewalks.

Programs of Study: Ferrum confers B.A., B.S., B.F.A., and B.S.W. degrees. Bachelor's degrees are awarded in AGRICULTURE (agriculture and horticulture), BIOLOGICAL SCIENCE (biology/biological science), BUSINESS (accounting, business administration and management, recreation and leisure services, and sports management), COMMUNICATIONS AND THE ARTS (art, dramatic arts, English, performing arts, Russian, and Spanish), COMPUTER AND PHYSICAL SCIENCE (chemistry, computer science, information sciences and systems, mathematics, and science), EDUCATION (physical), ENGINEERING AND ENVIRONMENTAL DESIGN (environmental science), HEALTH PROFESSIONS (health science and medical laboratory technology), SOCIAL SCIENCE (criminal justice, history, international studies, liberal arts/general studies, philosophy, political science/government, psychology, religion, social studies, and social work). Chemsitry, biology, and enviromental science are the strongest academically. Business administration, criminal justice, and liberal arts/teacher education are the largest.

Required: To graduate, students must complete at least 121 semester hours with a minimum GPA of 2.0. There are 37 hours of distribution requirements, including social sciences, natural sciences, English, religion/philosophy, math, literature, fine arts, and phys ed. A major may require up to 57 semester hours, and 30 hours of the total must be in upper-level courses.

Special: The college encourages internships, and some majors require internships. Study abroad, work-study programs, dual majors, an accelerated degree program in social work, and B.A.-B.S. degrees are offered. A liberal studies degree and nondegree study are available. There are 6 national honor societies, a freshman honors program, and 33 departmental honors programs.

Faculty/Classroom: 61% of faculty are male; 39%, female. 100% both teach and do research. The average class size in an introductory lecture is 17; in a laboratory, 15; and in a regular course, 11.

Admissions: 9% of the current freshmen were in the top fifth of their class; 24% were in the top two fifths.

Requirements: The SAT or ACT is required. In addition, applicants must be graduates of an accredited secondary school or receive a GED certificate. Applicants should complete 18 high school academic credits. The Admissions Committee considers courses taken, grades, extracurricular activities, SAT or ACT scores, and recommendations. Personal interviews may be required for students lacking appropriate GPA or standardized test scores. AP and CLEP credits are accepted. Important factors in the admissions decision are advanced placement or honor courses, leadership record, and evidence of special talent.

Procedure: Freshmen are admitted to all sessions. There is a deferred admissions plan and a rolling admissions plan. Application deadlines are open. Application fee is $25. Notification is sent on a rolling. Applications is sent on a rolling basis. Applications are accepted on-line.

Transfer: 99 transfer students enrolled in 2004-2005. Applicants for transfer must be in good academic standing at their current schools. 32 of 127 credits required for the bachelor's degree must be completed at Ferrum.

Visiting: There are regularly scheduled orientations for prospective students, including faculty information sessions, parent-to-parent and student-to-student sessions, and tours of the campus and residence halls. There are guides for informal visits, and visitors may sit in on classes and stay overnight. To schedule a visit, contact the Director of Admissions at *admissions@ferrum.edu.*

Financial Aid: In 2005-2006, 99% of all full-time freshmen and 97% of continuing full-time students received some form of financial aid. 80% of full-time freshmen and 74% of continuing full-time students received need-based aid. The average freshman award was $18,795. 37% of undergraduates work part time. Average annual earnings from campus work are $1400. The average financial indebtedness of the 2005 graduate was $16,300. The FAFSA and the state aid form are required. The deadline for filing freshman financial aid applications for fall entry is April 1.

International Students: There are 10 international students enrolled. The school actively recruits these students. A satisfactory score the written TOEFL is rquired TOEFL .Students must aslo take the Englisj Profivency

Computers: Wireless access is available. Ferrum College has over 500 PCs (including 1 in each residence hall room) on campus for student use. PC labs are also located in various buildings on campus. All students may access the system at all times. There are no time limits and no fees.

Graduates: From July 1, 2004 to June 30, 2005, 140 bachelor's degrees were awarded. The most popular majors were business administration (16%), psychology (9%), and liberal arts/teacher education (9%). In an average class, 18% graduate in 4 years or less, 31% graduate in 5 years or less, and 33% graduate in 6 years or less. 89 companies recruited on campus in 2004-2005. Of the 2004 graduating class, 9% were enrolled in graduate school within 6 months of graduation and 91% were employed.

Admissions Contact: Gilda Woods, Director of Admissions.
E-mail: *admissions@ferrum.edu* Web: *www.ferrum.edu*

GEORGE MASON UNIVERSITY   E-2
Fairfax, VA 22030-4444   (703) 993-2400; Fax: (703) 993-2392

Full-time: 6190 men, 7388 women	Faculty: 946; I, -$
Part-time: 2098 men, 2414 women	Ph.D.s: 86%
Graduate: 4436 men, 6460 women	Student/Faculty: 13 to 1
Year: semesters, summer session	Tuition: $5880 ($17,160)
Application Deadline: February 1	Room & Board: $4970
Freshman Class: 10,316 applied, 7101 accepted, 2540 enrolled	
SAT Verbal/Math: 547/560*	VERY COMPETITIVE

George Mason University, founded in 1972, offers undergraduate and graduate degrees in arts and sciences, business, information technology and engineering, fine arts, computational sciences and informatics, conflict analysis, nursing and health science, and education. A second campus in Arlington houses a professional school, the School of Law, and the International Institute. There are 6 undergraduate and 9 graduate schools. In addition to regional accreditation, GMU has baccalaureate program accreditation with AACSB, ABET, CSAB, CSWE, NASM, NCATE, and NLN. The 4 libraries contain 1,114,826 volumes, 2,942,692 microform items, and 32,014 audio/video tapes/CDs/DVDs, and subscribe to 11,565 periodicals including electronic. Computerized library services include the card catalog, interlibrary loans, and database searching. Special learning facilities include a learning resource center, art gallery, radio station, and TV station. The 806-acre campus is in a suburban area 18 miles southwest of Washington, D.C., in the Greater Washington Metropolitan area. Including any residence halls, there are 119 buildings.

Student Life: 88% of undergraduates are from Virginia. Others are from 47 states, 133 foreign countries, and Canada. 95% are from public schools. 63% are white; 14% Asian American. The average age of freshmen is 18; all undergraduates, 22. 21% do not continue beyond their first year.

Housing: 4000 students can be accommodated in college housing, which includes single-sex and coed dorms, on-campus apartments, and off-campus apartments. In addition, there are honors houses. On-campus housing is guaranteed for all 4 years. 79% of students commute. Alcohol is not permitted. All students may keep cars.

Activities: 5% of men belong to 15 national fraternities; 5% of women belong to 12 national sororities. There are 192 groups on campus, including band, cheerleading, chess, choir, chorale, chorus, computers, dance, drama, ethnic, film, forensics, gay, honors, international, jazz band, literary magazine, musical theater, newspaper, opera, orchestra, outing, pep band, photography, political, professional, radio and TV, religious, social, social service, student government, and symphony. Popular campus events include Mason Day, Patriot Day, and International Week.

Sports: There are 11 intercollegiate sports for men and 11 for women, and 11 intramural sports for men and 10 for women. Facilities include a 10,000-seat arena for basketball, indoor soccer, and concerts; a sports and recreation complex, which includes a 200-meter track, basketball, handball/racquetball, tennis, and volleyball courts, baseball and softball diamonds, batting cages, a weight room, saunas, and a golf and archery net; a 400-meter outdoor track; and playing fields.

Disabled Students: 99% of the campus is accessible. Wheelchair ramps, elevators, special parking, specially equipped rest rooms, special class scheduling, lowered drinking fountains, lowered telephones, and special housing are available. Special arrangements can be made for testing, readers, note takers, and interpreters.

Services: Counseling and information services are available, as is tutoring in most subjects. There is a reader service for the blind. A fee may apply.

Campus Safety and Security: Measures include 24-hour foot and vehicle patrol, self-defense education, security escort services, and shuttle buses. There are informal discussions, pamphlets/posters/films, emergency telephones, lighted pathways/sidewalks, and 33 security call boxes located throughout the campus.

Programs of Study: GMU confers B.A., B.S., B.A.I.N., B.A.I.S., B.F.A., B.I.S., B.M., B.S.E., B.S.E.D., and B.S.N. degrees. Master's and doctoral degrees are also awarded. Bachelor's degrees are awarded in BIOLOGICAL SCIENCE (biology/biological science), BUSINESS (accounting, banking and finance, business administration and management, management information systems, marketing/retailing/merchandising, and sports management), COMMUNICATIONS AND THE ARTS (art history and appreciation, communications, dance, dramatic arts, English, French, music, Spanish, and studio art), COMPUTER AND PHYSICAL SCIENCE (astronomy, chemistry, computer science, earth science, geology, information sciences and systems, mathematics, and physics), EDUCATION (athletic training, foreign languages, and physical), ENGINEERING AND ENVIRONMENTAL DESIGN (civil engineering, computer engineering, electrical/electronics engineering, and systems engineering), HEALTH PROFESSIONS (exercise science, health science, medical technology, and nursing), SOCIAL SCIENCE (anthropology, criminal justice, economics, geography, history, interdisciplinary studies, philosophy, political science/government, psychology, public administration, religion, Russian and Slavic studies, social work, and sociology). Psychology, communication, and government and international politics are the strongest academically.

Required: To graduate, all students must complete a core of study that includes 6 semester hours each of English composition, humanities, math/science, and social sciences, courses in communication, analytical reasoning, social science, natural science, and non-Western culture, and at least 45 hours of upper-division work. Hours in the major vary. A minimum 2.0 GPA is required and a total of 120 to 133 credit hours must be completed.

Special: GMU offers co-op programs in all majors with Shenandoah University, Virginia Polytechnic Institute and State University, Old Dominion University, and the University of Virginia, cross-registration with the Washington Consortium of Universities, internships through academic departments, study abroad in 13 countries, and on-campus work-study programs. Also available are dual and student-designed majors, nondegree study, and pass/fail options. The Program for Alternative General Education (PAGE) offers interdisciplinary studies for freshmen and sophomores. New Century College is an integrated program of study that emphasizes collaboration, experimental learning, and self-reflection. There are 3 national honor societies, a freshman honors program, and 8 departmental honors programs.

Faculty/Classroom: 45% of faculty are male; 55%, female. The average class size in an introductory lecture is 32; in a laboratory, 21; and in a regular course, 28.

Admissions: 69% of the 2005-2006 applicants were accepted. The SAT scores for the 2005-2006 freshman class were: Verbal--26% below 500, 48% between 500 and 599, 22% between 600 and 700, and 4% above 700; Math--21% below 500, 51% between 500 and 599, 25% between 600 and 700, and 3% above 700. 47% of the current freshmen were in the top fifth of their class; 86% were in the top two fifths.

Requirements: The SAT or ACT is required. In addition, applicants must be graduates of an accredited secondary school or have a GED certificate. A minimum of 18 credits is required, including 4 years of English, 3 each of math, science, social studies, and electives, and 2 of foreign language. An essay is recommended. A GPA of 2.0 is required. AP and CLEP credits are accepted. Important factors in the admissions decision are advanced placement or honor courses, evidence of special talent, and recommendations by school officials.

Procedure: Freshmen are admitted fall, spring, and summer. Entrance exams should be taken during the spring of the junior year. There are early admissions and deferred admissions plans. Applications should be filed by February 1 for fall entry and November 1 for spring entry, along with a $40 fee. Notification is sent April 1. A waiting list is an active part of the admissions procedure. Applications are accepted on-line.

Transfer: 2240 transfer students enrolled in 2004-2005. Applicants must have a minimum 2.0 GPA and at least 9 semester hours earned. College transcripts and an essay or personal statement are required. 30 of 120 to 133 credits required for the bachelor's degree must be completed at GMU.

Visiting: There are regularly scheduled orientations for prospective students. There are guides for informal visits and visitors may sit in on classes and stay overnight. To schedule a visit, contact the Admissions Office.

Financial Aid: In 2005-2006, 61% of all full-time freshmen and 54% of continuing full-time students received some form of financial aid. 35% of all full-time students received need-based aid. The average freshman award was $7518. Need-based scholarships or need-based grants averaged $4813 ($20,550 maximum); need-based self-help aid (loans and jobs) averaged $2808 ($6625 maximum); non-need-based athletic scholarships averaged $11,789 ($26,305 maximum); and other non-need-based awards and non-need-based scholarships averaged $5030 ($25,296 maximum). Average annual earnings from campus work are $2149. The average financial indebtedness of the 2005 graduate was $13,607. The FAFSA is required. The priority date for freshman financial aid applications for fall entry is March 1.

International Students: There are 575 international students enrolled. The school actively recruits these students. They must score satisfactorily on the TOEFL and also take the SAT.

Computers: All students may access the system 24 hours per day. There are no time limits and no fees.

Graduates: From July 1, 2004 to June 30, 2005, 3415 bachelor's degrees were awarded. The most popular majors were communication (12%), psychology (8%), and nursing (8%). In an average class, 33% graduate in 4 years or less, 48% graduate in 5 years or less, and 53% graduate in 6 years or less. 200 companies recruited on campus in 2004-2005.

Admissions Contact: Andrew Flagel, Dean of Undergraduate Admissions. E-mail: *admissions@gmu.edu* Web: *www.gmu.edu*

HAMPDEN-SYDNEY COLLEGE   D-3

Hampden-Sydney, VA 23943   (434) 223-6120
(800) 755-0733; Fax: (434) 223-6346

Full-time: 1050 men	**Faculty:** 87; IIB, +$
Part-time: none	**Ph.D.s:** 81%
Graduate: none	**Student/Faculty:** 12 to 1
Year: semesters, summer session	**Tuition:** $23,410
Application Deadline: see profile	**Room & Board:** $7738
Freshman Class: n/av	
SAT or ACT: required	**VERY COMPETITIVE**

Hampden-Sydney College, founded in 1775, is a private men's liberal arts institution affiliated with the Presbyterian Church (U.S.A.). Some figures in the above capsule and in this profile are approximate. The library contains 224,172 volumes, 45,312 microform items, and 4312 audio/video tapes/CDs/DVDs, and subscribes to 823 periodicals including electronic. Computerized library services include the card catalog, interlibrary loans, database searching, and Internet access. Special learning facilities include an art gallery, planetarium, radio station, international communications center, college history museum, and observatory. The 660-acre campus is in a rural area 60 miles southwest of Richmond. Including any residence halls, there are 76 buildings.

Student Life: 64% of undergraduates are from Virginia. Others are from 36 states, 9 foreign countries, and Canada. 65% are from public schools. 93% are white. 59% are Protestant; 25% claim no religious affiliation; 14% Catholic. The average age of freshmen is 19; all undergraduates, 20. 26% do not continue beyond their first year; 61% remain to graduate.

Housing: 1050 students can be accommodated in college housing, which includes single-sex dorms, on-campus apartments, married-student housing, a minority student house, and fraternity houses. On-campus housing is guaranteed for all 4 years. 97% of students live on campus; of those, 60% remain on campus on weekends. All students may keep cars.

Activities: 37% of men belong to 11 national fraternities. There are 36 groups on campus, including chorale, chorus, computers, debate, drama, ethnic, honors, international, literary magazine, newspaper, pep band, photography, political, professional, radio and TV, religious, social, social service, student government, and yearbook. Popular campus events include Greek Week, Macon Week, and Midwinters CAC events.

Sports: Facilities include a field house with 3 basketball courts, 5 racquetball/handball courts, an outdoor track, a pool, squash courts, a weight room, a gym, tennis courts, and many playing fields.

Disabled Students: 80% of the campus is accessible. Wheelchair ramps, elevators, special parking, specially equipped rest rooms, special class scheduling, and lowered telephones are available.

Services: Counseling and information services are available, as is tutoring in every subject.

Campus Safety and Security: Measures include 24-hour foot and vehicle patrol, informal discussions, pamphlets/posters/films, emergency telephones, and lighted pathways/sidewalks. There also is a fire department on campus and a first responder unit for emergency medical assistance. The dorm phone lines are hooked into 911.

Programs of Study: Hampden-Sydney confers B.A. and B.S. degrees. Bachelor's degrees are awarded in BIOLOGICAL SCIENCE (biology/biological science), BUSINESS (business economics), COMMUNICATIONS AND THE ARTS (classics, English, fine arts, French, German, Greek, Latin, and Spanish), COMPUTER AND PHYSICAL SCIENCE (applied mathematics, chemistry, computer science, mathematics, and physics), SOCIAL SCIENCE (economics, history, humanities, philosophy, political science/government, psychology, and religion). Science is the strongest academically. Economics, history, and political science are the largest.

Required: To graduate, students must complete 120 credit hours with a minimum GPA of 2.0. Distribution requirements include 7 courses in humanities, 4 in math and natural sciences, and 3 in social sciences. All students must also take rhetoric and foreign language and pass a rhetoric exam.

Special: The college offers co-op programs with Longwood, Randolph-Macon, Randolph-Macon Woman's, Sweet Briar, Hollins, and Mary Baldwin Colleges and Washington and Lee University. Cross-registration with Longwood College, internships, study abroad, a 3-2 engineering program with the University of Virginia, a Washington semester, work-study programs, B.A.-B.S. degrees, and dual majors are available. There is a public service concentration in all majors. There are 15 national honor societies, including Phi Beta Kappa, a freshman honors program, and 10 departmental honors programs.

Faculty/Classroom: 75% of faculty are male; 25%, female. All both teach and do research. The average class size in an introductory lecture is 18; in a laboratory, 15; and in a regular course, 15.

Admissions: There was 1 National Merit semifinalist in a recent year. 2 freshmen graduated first in their class.

Requirements: The SAT or ACT is required. In addition, the school recommends SAT Subject Tests in writing, math, and another subject of the student's choice. Applicants must be graduates of an accredited secondary school and have completed 16 high school academic credits, including 4 of English, 3 of math, 2 each of foreign language and science, and 1 of social studies. An essay is required, and an interview is recommended. The GED is accepted. A GPA of 2.5 is required. AP credits are accepted. Important factors in the admissions decision are advanced placement or honor courses, recommendations by school officials, and leadership record.

Procedure: Freshmen are admitted fall and spring. Entrance exams should be taken during the junior or senior year of high school. There is an early decision plan. Check with the school for current application deadlines and fee. 78 early decision candidates were accepted for a recent class. 38 applicants were on a recent year's waiting list; 25 were admitted. Applications are accepted on-line.

Transfer: 17 transfer students enrolled in a recent year. Applicants must have a minimum GPA of 2.5 and must take either the SAT or the ACT. An interview is recommended. 60 of 120 credits required for the bachelor's degree must be completed at Hampden-Sydney.

Visiting: There are regularly scheduled orientations for prospective students, consisting of lectures, information sessions, tours, lunch, and an athletic event. There are guides for informal visits and visitors may sit in on classes and stay overnight. To schedule a visit, contact the Admissions Office.

Financial Aid: In a recent year, 92% of all full-time students received some form of financial aid. 54% of full-time freshmen and 51% of continuing full-time students received need-based aid. The average freshman award was $16,791. 25% of undergraduates work part time. Average annual earnings from campus work are $900. The average financial indebtedness of a recent year's graduate was $7071. The CSS/Profile or FAFSA is required. The deadline for filing freshman financial aid applications for fall entry is March 1.

International Students: There are 16 international students enrolled. They must achieve a satisfactory score on the TOEFL and also take the SAT or the ACT.

Computers: All students may access the system. There are no time limits and no fees. It is strongly recommended that all students have a personal computer.

Graduates: In a recent year, 206 bachelor's degrees were awarded. The most popular majors were economics (49%), history (17%), and political science (15%). In an average class, 61% graduate in 4 years or less, 63% graduate in 5 years or less, and 64% graduate in 6 years or less. 30 companies recruited on campus in a recent year.

Admissions Contact: Anita H. Garland, Dean of Admissions.
E-mail: *admissions@hsc.edu* Web: *www.hsc.edu*

HAMPTON UNIVERSITY   F-3
Hampton, VA 23668   (757) 727-5328
(800) 624-3328; Fax: (757) 727-5095

Full-time: 1700 men, 2900 women	**Faculty:** 295
Part-time: 220 men, 150 women	**Ph.Ds:** 76%
Graduate: 290 men, 550 women	**Student/Faculty:** 16 to 1
Year: semesters, summer session	**Tuition:** $12,722
Application Deadline: April 15	**Room & Board:** $6746
Freshman Class: n/av	
SAT or ACT: required	**COMPETITIVE+**

Hampton University, founded in 1868, is a comprehensive institution of higher education. Its curriculum emphasis is scientific and professional, with a strong liberal arts undergirding. There are 8 undergraduate schools and 1 graduate school. Some figures in the above capsule and in this profile are approximate. In addition to regional accreditation, HU has baccalaureate program accreditation with ABET, ACEJMC, ACS, ASLA, CSAB, NAAB, NASM, NCATE, and NLN. The library contains 273,854 volumes, 711,759 microform items, and 1649 audio/video tapes/CDs/DVDs, and subscribes to 992 periodicals including electronic. Computerized library services include the card catalog, interlibrary loans, and database searching. Special learning facilities include a learning resource center, art gallery, natural history museum, radio station, TV station, and academic technology mall. The 204-acre campus is in an urban area 15 miles west of Norfolk. Including any residence halls, there are 125 buildings.

Student Life: 70% of undergraduates are from out of state, mostly the Middle Atlantic. Students are from 43 states, 33 foreign countries, and Canada. 90% are from public schools. 96% are African American. The average age of freshmen is 18; all undergraduates, 20. 15% do not continue beyond their first year; 75% remain to graduate.

Housing: 3000 students can be accommodated in college housing, which includes single-sex dorms. In addition, there are honors houses and student cottages. On-campus housing is available on a first-come, first-served basis and is available on a lottery system for upperclassmen. 59% of students live on campus; of those, 70% remain on campus on weekends. Alcohol is not permitted. Upperclassmen may keep cars.

Activities: 5% of men belong to 5 national fraternities; 4% of women belong to 4 national sororities. There are 80 groups on campus, including art, band, cheerleading, choir, chorale, chorus, dance, drama, drill team, ethnic, honors, international, jazz band, marching band, newspaper, orchestra, pep band, photography, political, radio and TV, religious, social service, student government, symphony, and yearbook. Popular campus events include Career Day, High School Day, and Black Family/Parents Weekend.

Sports: There are 5 intercollegiate sports for men and 4 for women, and 2 intramural sports for men and 1 for women. Facilities include a football stadium, a convocation center, 12 outdoor tennis courts, open fields for intramural sports, 2 basketball courts, 2 swimming pools, a volleyball court, an exercise and training room, a new student center with a health center, bowling alley, movie theater, indoor track, and restaurants.

Disabled Students: 90% of the campus is accessible. Wheelchair ramps, elevators, special parking, specially equipped rest rooms, lowered drinking fountains, and lowered telephones are available.

Services: Counseling and information services are available, as is tutoring in most subjects. There is remedial math, reading, and writing.

Campus Safety and Security: Measures include 24-hour foot and vehicle patrol, self-defense education, informal discussions, and pamphlets/posters/films. There are emergency telephones, lighted pathways/sidewalks, bike patrols, on-campus police officers, video cameras, gated campus, identification of valuables, limited access to campus, smoke detectors in residence halls, motorist assistance, and civilian support team.

Programs of Study: HU confers B.A., B.S., B.Arch., and B.S.Nurs. degrees. Associate and master's degrees are also awarded. Bachelor's degrees are awarded in BIOLOGICAL SCIENCE (biology/biological science), BUSINESS (accounting, banking and finance, business administration and management, marketing/retailing/merchandising, and sports management), COMMUNICATIONS AND THE ARTS (art, communications, dramatic arts, English, and music), COMPUTER AND PHYSICAL SCIENCE (chemistry, computer science, information sciences and systems, mathematics, and physics), EDUCATION (physical), ENGINEERING AND ENVIRONMENTAL DESIGN (architecture, chemical engineering, and electrical/electronics engineering), HEALTH PROFESSIONS (nursing, recreation therapy, and speech pathology/audiology), SOCIAL SCIENCE (economics, history, political science/government, psychology, and sociology). Architecture, biology, and physics are the strongest academically. Biology, psychology, and business management are the largest.

Required: To graduate, students must complete 120 credit hours, with 74 hours in the major, related subjects, and free electives, and a GPA of 2.0. There is a 44-to-48 hour distribution requirement in freshman studies, history, language, arts and humanities, English, social sciences, math, pure and applied sciences, speech, and health and phys ed.

Special: The college offers co-op programs in most majors, cross-registration with 6 schools, internships, and student-designed majors. Work-study, study abroad, and dual majors are also possible. Students may receive credit for life, military, and work experience. There are pass/fail options. There are 15 national honor societies and a freshman honors program.

Faculty/Classroom: 48% of faculty are male; 52%, female. 90% teach undergraduates and 10% do research. No introductory courses are taught by graduate students. The average class size in an introductory lecture is 50; in a laboratory, 20; and in a regular course, 25.

Requirements: The SAT or ACT is required. Applicants must be graduates of an accredited secondary school, or the GED is accepted. Students should complete 17 Carnegie units, including 4 units of English, 3 units of math (algebra I and II and geometry), 2 years of science (chemistry and biology), 2 years of social studies, and 6 academic electives. An interview is recommended. HU requires applicants to be in the upper 50% of their class. A GPA of 2.0 is required. AP and CLEP credits are accepted. Important factors in the admissions decision are advanced placement or honor courses, recommendations by school officials, and recommendations by alumni.

Procedure: Freshmen are admitted fall and spring. Entrance exams should be taken during the junior year or fall of the senior year. There is a rolling admissions plan. There are early admissions and deferred admissions plans. Applications should be filed by April 15 for fall entry and December 1 for spring entry, along with a $35 fee. Notification is sent on a rolling basis. A waiting list is an active part of the admissions procedure.

Transfer: Applicants for transfer must have a minimum GPA of 2.3 and 15 transferable hours. Students must have at least 60 semester or 90 quarter hours in order to be exempt from submitting their high school record and SAT or ACT scores. 30 of 120 credits required for the bachelor's degree must be completed at HU.

Visiting: There are regularly scheduled orientations for prospective students. There are guides for informal visits and visitors may sit in on classes. To schedule a visit, contact Office of Admissions at (757) 727-2051 or admissions@hamptonu.edu.

Financial Aid: The FAFSA is required. The priority deadline for filing freshman financial aid applications for fall entry is March 1.

International Students: Satisfactory scores are required on the TOEFL as well as the SAT or ACT.

Computers: All students may access the system 24 hours per day. There are no time limits and no fees. It is strongly recommended that all students have a personal computer. It is required that students in pharmacy have personal computers.

Admissions Contact: Director of Admissions.
E-mail: admissions@hamptonu.edu Web: www.hamptonu.edu

HOLLINS UNIVERSITY
C-3

Roanoke, VA 24020-1707

(540) 362-6214
(800) 456-9595; Fax: (540) 362-6218

Full-time: 790 women	**Faculty:** 68; IIB, av$
Part-time: 58 women	**Ph.D.s:** 98%
Graduate: 77 men, 198 women	**Student/Faculty:** 12 to 1
Year: 4-1-4	**Tuition:** $22,945
Application Deadline: February 15	**Room & Board:** $8160
Freshman Class: n/av	
SAT or ACT: required	**COMPETITIVE**

Founded in 1842 and Virginia's first chartered women's college, Hollins offers a broad liberal arts curriculum. In addition to regional accreditation, Hollins has baccalaureate program accreditation with SACS. The library contains 174,000 volumes, 110,050 microform items, and 5460 audio/video tapes/CDs/DVDs, and subscribes to 14,500 periodicals including electronic. Computerized library services include the card catalog, interlibrary loans, database searching, Internet access, and laptop Internet portals. Special learning facilities include a learning resource center, art gallery, and TV station. The 475-acre campus is in a suburban area in Roanoke. Including any residence halls, there are 73 buildings.

Student Life: 52% of undergraduates are from out of state, mostly the South. Students are from 45 states and 9 foreign countries. 75% are from public schools. 80% are white. The average age of freshmen is 19; all undergraduates, 22. 21% do not continue beyond their first year; 68% remain to graduate.

Housing: 1000 students can be accommodated in college housing, which includes single-sex dorms and on-campus apartments. In addition, there are language houses, special-interest houses, and a "global village" student residence. On-campus housing is guaranteed for all 4 years. 91% of students live on campus; of those, 60% remain on campus on weekends. All students may keep cars.

Activities: There are no fraternities or sororities. There are 45 groups on campus, including art, choir, chorale, computers, dance, drama, ethnic, film, gay, honors, international, literary magazine, newspaper, photography, political, professional, radio and TV, religious, social, social service, student government, and yearbook. Popular campus events in-

clude Literary Festival, French and German film festivals, and Classics Symposium.

Sports: There are 7 intercollegiate sports for women, and 2 intramural sports for men and 1 for women. Facilities include a swimming center, a fitness center and 2 weight rooms, a gym, an equestrian center, a ropes course, a jogging and exercise trail, tennis courts, 2 playing fields, an auxiliary gym, 2 training rooms, and a climbing wall.

Disabled Students: 40% of the campus is accessible. Wheelchair ramps, elevators, special parking, specially equipped rest rooms, special class scheduling, lowered drinking fountains, lowered telephones, and special housing are available.

Services: Counseling and information services are available, as is tutoring in most subjects. There is a reader service for the blind and a writing center.

Campus Safety and Security: Measures include 24-hour foot and vehicle patrol, self-defense education, security escort services, and informal discussions. There are pamphlets/posters/films, emergency telephones, lighted pathways/sidewalks, and emergency buttons located along walkways and in labs.

Programs of Study: Hollins confers the B.A. degree. Master's degrees are also awarded. Bachelor's degrees are awarded in AGRICULTURE (environmental studies), BIOLOGICAL SCIENCE (biology/biological science), BUSINESS (business administration and management), COMMUNICATIONS AND THE ARTS (art history and appreciation, communications, creative writing, dance, dramatic arts, English, French, German, media arts, music, Spanish, and studio art), COMPUTER AND PHYSICAL SCIENCE (chemistry, computer mathematics, computer science, mathematics, and physics), SOCIAL SCIENCE (classical/ancient civilization, economics, history, interdisciplinary studies, international studies, philosophy, political science/government, psychology, religion, sociology, and women's studies). English/creative writing and psychology are the strongest academically. English/creative writing, psychology, and communication studies are the largest.

Required: To graduate, students must complete 128 credits of academic work and 4 short terms. At least 32 hours in the major and a 2.0 GPA are required. Distribution requirements include 8 credits each in the humanities, social sciences, natural sciences and math, and fine arts. All students meet the following skills components: writing, oral communication, quantitative reasoning, and information technology. Students are also required to fulfill 2 semesters of phys ed or varsity sport participation. A thesis is required for some majors.

Special: Hollins offers internships during the January term, dual majors, student-designed majors, accelerated degrees, and study abroad in Greece, Italy, England, France, Ireland, Japan, Mexico, and Spain. A 3-2 engineering degree is possible with Washington University in St. Louis and Virginia Polytechnic Institute and State University. There is cross-registration with the Virginia Seven College Exchange and Roanoke College. There are 14 national honor societies, including Phi Beta Kappa, a freshman honors program, and 23 departmental honors programs.

Faculty/Classroom: 49% of faculty are male; 51%, female. All teach undergraduates. No introductory courses are taught by graduate students. The average class size in an introductory lecture is 18; in a laboratory, 9; and in a regular course, 14.

Admissions: There was 1 National Merit finalist in a recent year. 2 freshmen graduated first in their class.

Requirements: The SAT or ACT is required. In addition, applicants must be graduates of an accredited secondary school. The GED is accepted, as is home school. Applicants should complete 16 high school academic credits, including 4 credits of English and 3 credits each of foreign language, math, science, and social studies. SAT Subject Tests are recommended. An essay is required, and an interview is recommended. AP credits are accepted. Important factors in the admissions decision are advanced placement or honor courses, recommendations by school officials, and evidence of special talent.

Procedure: Freshmen are admitted fall and spring. Entrance exams should be taken by January of the senior year. There are early decision and deferred admissions plans. There is a rolling admissions plan. Early decision applications should be filed by November 15; regular applications, by February 15 for fall entry and December 1 for spring entry. The fall 2005 application fee was $35. Notification of early decision is sent December 15; regular decision, on a rolling basis. 39 early decision candidates were accepted for a recent class. 23 applicants were on a reent year's waiting list; 8 were admitted. Applications are accepted on-line.

Transfer: 34 transfer students enrolled in a recent year.. Applicants for transfer should have a minimum college GPA of 2.5. Other criteria are the same as for entering freshmen. 64 of 128 credits required for the bachelor's degree must be completed at Hollins.

Visiting: There are regularly scheduled orientations for prospective students, including 2 programs for high school seniors offered in October and November, 1 for admitted applicants in April, and 1 for juniors and sophomores in March. There are guides for informal visits and visitors may sit in on classes and stay overnight. To schedule a visit, contact the Admissions Office at (540) 362-6401 or huadm@hollins.edu.

Financial Aid: In 2005-2006, 98% of all full-time freshmen and 97% of continuing full-time students received some form of financial aid. 65% of full-time freshmen and 47% of continuing full-time students received need-based aid. The average freshman award was $18,826. 46% of undergraduates work part time. Average annual earnings from campus work are $1245. The average financial indebtedness of the 2005 graduate was $19,592. The FAFSA and parent and student tax returns are required. The deadline for filing freshman financial aid applications for fall entry is February 1.

International Students: There are 17 international students enrolled. The school actively recruits these students. Students whose native language is not English must achieve a satisfactory score on the TOEFL. For students whose native language is English, the SAT or ACT will be accepted in place of the TOEFL.

Computers: Wireless access is available. All students may access the system 24 hours a day, 7 days a week. There are no time limits. The fee is $100. It is strongly recommended that all students have a personal computer.

Graduates: From July 1, 2004 to June 30, 2005, 178 bachelor's degrees were awarded. The most popular majors were English/creative writing (21%), psychology (10%), and communication studies (10%). In an average class, 55% graduate in 4 years or less, 61% graduate in 5 years or less, and 64% graduate in 6 years or less. 14 companies recruited on campus in 2004-2005. Of the 2004 graduating class, 21% were enrolled in graduate school within 6 months of graduation and 77% were employed.

Admissions Contact: Rebecca Eckstein, Dean of Admissions. A video is available. E-mail: *huadm@hollins.edu* Web: *www.hollins.edu*

JAMES MADISON UNIVERSITY   D-2

Harrisonburg, VA 22807   (540) 568-5681; Fax: (540) 568-3332

Full-time: 5800 men, 9085 women	**Faculty:** 725; IIA, av$
Part-time: 371 men, 362 women	**Ph.D.s:** 80%
Graduate: 449 men, 871 women	**Student/Faculty:** 21 to 1
Year: semesters, summer session	**Tuition:** $5886 ($15,322)
Application Deadline: January 15	**Room & Board:** $6124
Freshman Class: 16,388 applied, 11,094 accepted, 3798 enrolled	
SAT Verbal/Math: 570/580*	**VERY COMPETITIVE**

James Madison University, founded in 1908, is a public institution with programs in science and math, business, education, arts and letters, visual and performing arts, and integrated science and technology. There are 6 undergraduate schools and 1 graduate school. In addition to regional accreditation, JMU has baccalaureate program accreditation with AACSB, ACS, ADA, AOTA, APA, CAAHEP, CACREP, CSWE, FIDER, NASAD, NASM, NAST, NCATE, and NLN. The 3 libraries contain 627,410 volumes, 1,053,570 microform items, and 35,444 audio/video tapes/CDs/DVDs, and subscribe to 7393 periodicals including electronic. Computerized library services include the card catalog, interlibrary loans, and database searching. Special learning facilities include a learning resource center, art gallery, planetarium, radio station, an arboretum, a music library, and CISAT Library Services. The 647-acre campus is in a small town 123 miles southwest of Washington, D.C. Including any residence halls, there are 105 buildings.

Student Life: 70% of undergraduates are from Virginia. Others are from 44 states, 52 foreign countries, and Canada. 95% are from public schools. 84% are white. 32% are Catholic; 30% Protestant; 21% claim no religious affiliation. The average age of freshmen is 18; all undergraduates, 20. 9% do not continue beyond their first year; 80% remain to graduate.

Housing: 5717 students can be accommodated in college housing, which includes coed dorms, off-campus apartments, and sorority houses. In addition, there are special-interest houses and 3 types of theme housing communities: Madison International Community, Learning Community, and a Substance Free Community. Students must apply. On-campus housing is guaranteed for the freshman year only. 62% of students commute. Upperclassmen may keep cars.

Activities: 9% of men belong to 13 national fraternities; 11% of women belong to 8 national sororities. There are 287 groups on campus, including art, band, cheerleading, chess, choir, chorale, chorus, computers, dance, drama, ethnic, gay, honors, international, jazz band, literary magazine, marching band, musical theater, newspaper, opera, orchestra, pep band, photography, political, professional, radio and TV, religious, social, social service, student government, symphony, and yearbook. Popular campus events include Madison Symposium, James Madison Week, and International Week.

Sports: There are 13 intercollegiate sports for men and 15 for women, and 18 intramural sports for men and 18 for women. Facilities include a 12,800-seat stadium, a convocation center, an all-weather track, a gym, a natatorium, tennis courts, a lighted Astroturf field, and baseball, soccer, and softball fields. A recreation center houses a fitness center, racquetball courts, basketball gyms, an indoor track, a pool, and a climbing wall.

Disabled Students: 85% of the campus is accessible. Wheelchair ramps, elevators, special parking, specially equipped rest rooms, special

class scheduling, lowered drinking fountains, lowered telephones, special housing, and automated doors in 52 buildings are available.

Services: Counseling and information services are available, as is tutoring in every subject. There is a reader service for the blind. There is a reading and writing resource center, a science and math resource center, and a communication resource center.

Campus Safety and Security: Measures include 24-hour foot and vehicle patrol, self-defense education, security escort services, and informal discussions. There are pamphlets/posters/films, emergency telephones, lighted pathways/sidewalks, and public bus transportation routes through the campus.

Programs of Study: JMU confers B.A., B.S., B.B.A., B.F.A., B.I.S., B.M., B.S.N., and B.S.W. degrees. Master's and doctoral degrees are also awarded. Bachelor's degrees are awarded in BIOLOGICAL SCIENCE (biology/biological science and biotechnology), BUSINESS (accounting, banking and finance, business administration and management, business economics, hospitality management services, international business management, marketing/retailing/merchandising, recreation and leisure services, and tourism), COMMUNICATIONS AND THE ARTS (art, art history and appreciation, communications, communications technology, dance, dramatic arts, English, fine arts, media arts, modern language, music, and speech/debate/rhetoric), COMPUTER AND PHYSICAL SCIENCE (chemistry, computer science, geology, information sciences and systems, mathematics, physics, quantitative methods, science technology, and statistics), EDUCATION (athletic training and business), HEALTH PROFESSIONS (health care administration, health science, nursing, and speech pathology/audiology), SOCIAL SCIENCE (anthropology, criminal justice, dietetics, economics, geography, history, international studies, liberal arts/general studies, philosophy, physical fitness/movement, political science/government, psychology, public administration, religion, social science, social work, and sociology). Biology, business, and communications are the strongest academically. Psychology, interdisciplinary liberal studies, and biology are the largest.

Required: To graduate, students must complete a minimum of 120 credit hours, with a GPA of at least 2.0, meet the general education requirements and the requirements of their major, have been enrolled at JMU a minimum of 2 regular semesters, and have earned a minimum of 30 credit hours at JMU during that period of enrollment.

Special: JMU offers internships, work-study programs, a Washington semester, and study abroad in London, Antwerp, Florence, and Salamanca. There are combined programs in physics and engineering with the University of Virginia and in forestry with Virginia Tech. An individualized study degree, nondegree study, pass/fail options, and credit for life, military, and work experience are available. There are 14 national honor societies, a freshman honors program, and 30 departmental honors programs.

Faculty/Classroom: 58% of faculty are male; 42%, female. 91% teach undergraduates. Graduate students teach 3% of introductory courses. The average class size in an introductory lecture is 38; in a laboratory, 22; and in a regular course, 31.

Admissions: 68% of the 2005-2006 applicants were accepted. The SAT scores for the 2005-2006 freshman class were: Verbal--15% below 500, 53% between 500 and 599, 29% between 600 and 700, and 3% above 700; Math--13% below 500, 50% between 500 and 599, 34% between 600 and 700, and 3% above 700.

Requirements: The SAT or ACT is required. In addition, applicants must be graduates of an accredited secondary school. They must show solid achievement in 4 or more academic courses each year of high school, including some honors or advanced course work. A personal statement is optional. Art students must present a portfolio. Theater, dance, and music students must audition. Nursing students must apply to the nursing department in addition to applying for undergraduate admission. AP credits are accepted. Important factors in the admissions decision are advanced placement or honor courses, recommendations by school officials, and extracurricular activities record.

Procedure: Freshmen are admitted in the fall. Entrance exams should be taken in the spring of the junior year or the fall of the senior year. There are early admissions and deferred admissions plans. Early decision applications should be filed by November 1; regular applications, by January 15 for fall entry. Notification of early decision is sent January 15; regular decision, April 1. 653 applicants were on the 2005 waiting list; 4 were admitted. Applications are accepted on-line.

Transfer: 602 transfer students enrolled in 2004-2005. Applicants must have a minimum GPA of 2.0 and must submit a complete application, official college transcripts, secondary school records or a copy of their GED. A one-page personal statement is optional. If applicants have fewer than 30 credit hours completed at the time of application, they must submit SAT scores unless they are 25 years old or older. 30 of 120 credits required for the bachelor's degree must be completed at JMU.

Visiting: There are regularly scheduled orientations for prospective students, including daily campus tours during the week and on Saturdays and tours following group conferences with an admissions counselor. There are guides for informal visits. To schedule a visit, contact the Admissions Office at (540) 568-5681 or *visit-jmu@jmu.edu*.

Financial Aid: In 2005-2006, 56% of all full-time freshmen and 39% of continuing full-time students received some form of financial aid. 36% of full-time freshmen and 28% of continuing full-time students received need-based aid. The average freshman award was $10,248. Need-based scholarships or need-based grants averaged $6035 ($12,260 maximum); need-based self-help aid (loans and jobs) averaged $2330 ($3500 maximum); non-need-based athletic scholarships averaged $11,734 ($21,694 maximum); and other non-need-based awards and non-need-based scholarships averaged $2747 ($4000 maximum). 19% of undergraduates work part time. Average annual earnings from campus work are $1920. The average financial indebtedness of the 2005 graduate was $10,642. The FAFSA is required. The deadline for filing freshman financial aid applications for fall entry is March 1.

International Students: There are 106 international students enrolled. The school actively recruits these students. A satisfactory score on the TOEFL is required.

Computers: Wireless access is available. Students have access from their residence hall rooms to the network from their own PC. All students may access the system 24 hours a day. There are no time limits and no fees. It is strongly recommended that all students have a personal computer, and students in the Colleges of Integrated Science and Technology are required to have them. Recommended configurations for use in specific departments and majors can be found on-line at www.jmu.edu/computing/computerpurchase/depreq.shtml.

Graduates: From July 1, 2004 to June 30, 2005, 3329 bachelor's degrees were awarded. The most popular majors were psychology (7%), marketing (6%), and media arts and design (5%). In an average class, 64% graduate in 4 years or less, 78% graduate in 5 years or less, and 80% graduate in 6 years or less. 162 companies recruited on campus in 2004-2005. Of the 2004 graduating class, 27% were enrolled in graduate school within 6 months of graduation and 62% were employed.

Admissions Contact: Michael D. Walsh, Director of Admissions.
E-mail: *admissions@jmu.edu* Web: *www.jmu.edu/admissions*

LIBERTY UNIVERSITY   D-3
Lynchburg, VA 24502

(434) 582-7307
(800) 543-5317; Fax: (434) 582-2421

Full-time: 2800 men, 3300 women	**Faculty:** 200; IIA, --$
Part-time: 110 men, 120 women	**Ph.D.s:** 67%
Graduate: 310 men, 140 women	**Student/Faculty:** 31 to 1
Year: semesters, summer session	**Tuition:** $13,700
Application Deadline: open	**Room & Board:** $5400
Freshman Class: n/av	
SAT or ACT: required	**COMPETITIVE**

Liberty University, founded in 1971, is a private liberal arts institution affiliated with the Baptist Church. There are 6 undergraduate and 5 graduate schools. Some figures in the above capsule and in this profile are approximate. In addition to regional accreditation, Liberty has baccalaureate program accreditation with NASM and NLN. The library contains 211,092 volumes, 95,329 microform items, and 7149 audio/video tapes/CDs/DVDs, and subscribes to 10,806 periodicals including electronic. Computerized library services include the card catalog, interlibrary loans, database searching, and Internet access. Special learning facilities include a learning resource center, radio station, and TV station. The 160-acre campus is in a suburban area 45 miles east of Roanoke. Including any residence halls, there are 73 buildings.

Student Life: 60% of undergraduates are from out of state, mostly the Middle Atlantic. Students are from 48 states, 76 foreign countries, and Canada. 78% are white; 11% African American. Most are Protestant. The average age of freshmen is 19; all undergraduates, 21.

Housing: 4303 students can be accommodated in college housing, which includes single-sex dorms and on-campus apartments. On-campus housing is guaranteed for all 4 years. 64% of students live on campus; of those, 90% remain on campus on weekends. Alcohol is not permitted. All students may keep cars.

Activities: There are no fraternities or sororities. There are 40 groups on campus, including band, cheerleading, choir, chorale, chorus, computers, debate, drama, drill team, ethnic, honors, international, marching band, musical theater, newspaper, opera, orchestra, pep band, political, professional, radio and TV, religious, social service, student government, and yearbook. Popular campus events include Super Conference and Missions Emphasis Week.

Sports: There are 9 intercollegiate sports for men and 8 for women, and 16 intramural sports for men and 16 for women. Facilities include an 11,000-seat football stadium, an 8000-seat basketball arena/convention center, baseball and soccer fields, a track complex, and a tennis center.

Disabled Students: 90% of the campus is accessible. Wheelchair ramps, elevators, special parking, specially equipped rest rooms, special class scheduling, lowered drinking fountains, lowered telephones, and special housing are available.

Services: Counseling and information services are available, as is tutoring in every subject. There is remedial math, reading, and writing.

Campus Safety and Security: Measures include 24-hour foot and vehicle patrol, self-defense education, security escort services, and shuttle buses. There are informal discussions, pamphlets/posters/films, and lighted pathways/sidewalks.

Programs of Study: Liberty confers B.A., B.S., B.M., and B.S.N. degrees. Associate, master's, and doctoral degrees are also awarded. Bachelor's degrees are awarded in BIOLOGICAL SCIENCE (biology/biological science), BUSINESS (accounting, business administration and management, management information systems, and sports management), COMMUNICATIONS AND THE ARTS (communications, English, English as a second/foreign language, music, and Spanish), COMPUTER AND PHYSICAL SCIENCE (computer science and mathematics), EDUCATION (athletic training, elementary, and physical), HEALTH PROFESSIONS (community health work, exercise science, and nursing), SOCIAL SCIENCE (family/consumer studies, history, interdisciplinary studies, international studies, liberal arts/general studies, political science/government, psychology, religion, and social science). Education, psychology, and business are the strongest academically and have the largest enrollments.

Required: Students must complete 120 to 123 credit hours to graduate, with a minimum GPA of 2.0. With few exceptions, by major, all must complete 18 hours of foundational studies in English, math, speech communications, and general education. An additional 42 credits of investigative studies are required; these vary according to the degree sought, either B.A. or B.S., but include English, natural sciences, history, arts, music, languages, government, social sciences, philosophy, theology, Bible studies, and integrated studies.

Special: Liberty offers internships, B.A.-B.S. degrees, and student-designed majors in interdisciplinary and general studies. There are 8 national honor societies, including Phi Beta Kappa, and a freshman honors program.

Faculty/Classroom: 67% of faculty are male; 33%, female. 90% teach undergraduates. No introductory courses are taught by graduate students. The average class size in an introductory lecture is 43; in a laboratory, 22; and in a regular course, 23.

Admissions: There were 5 National Merit finalists in a recent year.

Requirements: The SAT or ACT is required. In addition, applicants must have completed 16 high school academic credits. The GED is accepted. An essay is required. A GPA of 2.0 is required. AP and CLEP credits are accepted. Important factors in the admissions decision are ability to finance college education, recommendations by school officials, and advanced placement or honor courses.

Procedure: Freshmen are admitted to all sessions. Entrance exams should be taken during the junior year. There is a rolling admissions plan. There are early decision, early admissions, and deferred admissions plans. Application deadlines are open. Application fee is $40. Applications are accepted on-line.

Transfer: 743 transfer students enrolled in a recent year. Applicants for transfer must have a GPA of 2.0. If transferring fewer than 60 hours, a high school transcript and test scores are required. 30 of 120 credits required for the bachelor's degree must be completed at Liberty.

Visiting: There are regularly scheduled orientations for prospective students, including College for a Weekend, a 2-day program offering a chance to attend classes and special meetings. There are guides for informal visits and visitors may sit in on classes and stay overnight. To schedule a visit, contact the Visitor's Center at (434) 582-2064 or *visitorscenter@liberty.edu*.

Financial Aid: In a recent year, 98% of all full-time freshmen and 88% of continuing full-time students received some form of financial aid. 64% of all full-time students received need-based aid. The average freshman award was $8506. Need-based scholarships or need-based grants averaged $1800 ($4000 maximum); need-based self-help aid (loans and jobs) averaged $3725 ($3940 maximum); non-need-based athletic scholarships averaged $8172 ($18,850 maximum); and other non-need-based awards and non-need-based scholarships averaged $4667 ($15,220 maximum). 15% of undergraduates work part time. Average annual earnings from campus work are $2500. The average financial indebtedness of a recent year, graduate was $15,619. The FAFSA and Singlefile Form (preferred) are required. Check with the school for current deadlines.

International Students: There were 238 international students enrolled in a recent year. The school actively recruits these students. They must take the TOEFL or the MELAB.

Computers: All students may access the system 24 hours a day Sunday through Thursday and 7:30 A.M. to 9 P.M. Friday and Saturday. There are no time limits. The fee is $200 per semester.

Graduates: In a recent year, 945 bachelor's degrees were awarded. The most popular majors were psychology (17%), business (16%), and religion (14%).

Admissions Contact: Director of Admissions. A video is available.
E-mail: *admissions@liberty.edu* Web: *http://www.liberty.edu*

LONGWOOD UNIVERSITY — D-3
Farmville, VA 23909

(434) 395-2060
(800) 281-4677; Fax: (434) 395-2332

Full-time: 1211 men, 2388 women	Faculty: 201; IIA, --$
Part-time: 68 men, 84 women	Ph.D.s: 84%
Graduate: 86 men, 537 women	Student/Faculty: 18 to 1
Year: semesters, summer session	Tuition: $6840 ($10,270)
Application Deadline: March 1	Room & Board: $5586
Freshman Class: 3369 applied, 2574 accepted, 958 enrolled	
SAT Verbal/Math: 543/535*	COMPETITIVE

Longwood University, founded in 1839, is a state-supported institution with programs in liberal arts, business, and teacher preparation. There are 3 undergraduate and 2 graduate schools. In addition to regional accreditation, Longwood has baccalaureate program accreditation with AACSB, CSWE, NASM, NCATE, and NRPA. The library contains 1,060,855 volumes, 695,530 microform items, and 31,587 audio/video tapes/CDs/DVDs, and subscribes to 2503 periodicals including electronic. Computerized library services include the card catalog, interlibrary loans, database searching, and Internet access. Special learning facilities include a learning resource center, art gallery, radio station, a greenhouse, a language lab, 6 computer labs, and a psychology lab. The 160-acre campus is in a small town 60 miles west of Richmond and 60 miles south of Charlottesville. Including any residence halls, there are 53 buildings.

Student Life: 90% of undergraduates are from Virginia. Students are from 22 states, 19 foreign countries, and Canada. 93% are from public schools. 88% are white. The average age of freshmen is 18; all undergraduates, 21. 20% do not continue beyond their first year; 61% remain to graduate.

Housing: 2451 students can be accommodated in college housing, which includes single-sex and coed dorms and off-campus apartments. In addition, there are honors houses, language houses, special-interest houses, a substance-free dorm, and international, fraternity/sorority, and ecology floor. On-campus housing is guaranteed for the freshman year only, is available on a first-come, first-served basis, and is available on a lottery system for upperclassmen. 69% of students live on campus; of those, 70% remain on campus on weekends. Upperclassmen may keep cars.

Activities: 14% of men belong to 9 national fraternities; 19% of women belong to 13 national sororities. There are 125 groups on campus, including art, band, cheerleading, chess, choir, chorus, computers, dance, debate, drama, drill team, ethnic, forensics, gay, honors, international, jazz band, literary magazine, musical theater, newspaper, photography, political, professional, radio and TV, religious, social, social service, and student government. Popular campus events include Spring Weekend and Oktoberfest.

Sports: There are 6 intercollegiate sports for men and 8 for women, and 31 intramural sports for men and 31 for women. Facilities include a 9-hole golf course, a weight training facility, 2 gyms, racquetball courts, 11 lighted tennis courts, 2 pools, a bowling alley, 3 outdoor sand volleyball courts, a 10-station fitness trail, a Frisbee golf course, outdoor basketball courts, and soccer, baseball, and softball fields.

Disabled Students: 90% of the campus is accessible. Wheelchair ramps, elevators, special parking, special class scheduling, lowered drinking fountains, and lowered telephones are available. The campus is being made fully accessible. Until then, classes can be scheduled in accessible buildings.

Services: There is a reader service for the blind. Thee is also assistance in study skills, learning strategies, advocacy training, and compensatory strategy instruction.

Campus Safety and Security: Measures include 24-hour foot and vehicle patrol, self-defense education, security escort services, and shuttle buses. There are informal discussions, pamphlets/posters/films, emergency telephones, lighted pathways/sidewalks, electronic card key entry into dorms, and video cameras.

Programs of Study: Longwood confers B.A., B.S., B.F.A., B.M., B.S.B.A. degrees. Master's degrees are also awarded. Bachelor's degrees are awarded in BIOLOGICAL SCIENCE (biology/biological science), BUSINESS (business administration and management), COMMUNICATIONS AND THE ARTS (art, communications, English, modern language, music, and visual and performing arts), COMPUTER AND PHYSICAL SCIENCE (chemistry, computer science, mathematics, and physics), EDUCATION (art, athletic training, elementary, music, physical, and special), HEALTH PROFESSIONS (community health work and recreation therapy), SOCIAL SCIENCE (anthropology, criminal justice, criminology, economics, history, liberal arts/general studies, political science/government, psychology, social work, and sociology). Natural sciences and secondary education are the strongest academically. Business and elementary education are the largest.

Required: To graduate, students must complete 120 to 145 credits, including 36 to 77 in the major, with a minimum GPA of 2.0 overall. A 41-hour general education core curriculum, 4 intensive writing courses, a phys ed course, and 30 upper-level credit hours are also required.

Special: Longwood offers internships or directed research projects in all majors, study abroad in 12 countries, and B.A.-B.S. degrees in many majors. Cross-registration is possible with Hampden-Sydney College, as are 3-2 engineering degrees with several regional universities. Also, there is a 3-3 preprofessional program in physical therapy with University of Virginia, Old Dominion, and Virginia Commonwealth Universities. There are 21 national honor societies, a freshman honors program, and 21 departmental honors programs.

Faculty/Classroom: 58% of faculty are male; 42%, female. All teach undergraduates and 50% both teach and do research. No introductory courses are taught by graduate students. The average class size in an introductory lecture is 31; in a laboratory, 21; and in a regular course, 27.

Admissions: 76% of the 2005-2006 applicants were accepted. The SAT scores for the 2005-2006 freshman class were: Verbal--33% below 500, 51% between 500 and 599, 14% between 600 and 700, and 2% above 700; Math--37% below 500, 50% between 500 and 599, 13% between 600 and 700, and 1% above 700. 22% of the current freshmen were in the top fifth of their class; 58% were in the top two fifths. 9 freshmen graduated first in their class.

Requirements: The SAT or ACT is recommended. In addition, applicants must be graduates of an accredited secondary school; the GED is accepted. Students should complete 4 years of high school English, 3 years each of foreign language and science (including 2 lab courses), 2 years of history, and algebra I, II, and geometry. A personal statement is required. An audition is required for music students. Longwood requires applicants to be in the upper 50% of their class. A GPA of 2.6 is required. AP and CLEP credits are accepted. Important factors in the admissions decision are advanced placement or honor courses, leadership record, and evidence of special talent.

Procedure: Freshmen are admitted fall and spring. Entrance exams should be taken in the fall of the senior year. There are early decision, deferred admissions and rolling admissions plans. Early decision applications should be filed by December 1; regular applications, by March 1 for fall entry and November 15 for spring entry. Notification of early decision is sent January 1; regular decision, on a rolling basis. A waiting list is an active part of the admissions procedure. Applications are accepted on-line. The fall 2005 application fee was $40.

Transfer: 213 transfer students enrolled in 2004-2005. Applicants for transfer must have a GPA of at least 2.5 in all college course work attempted. Other criteria are the same as for entering freshmen. 30 of 120 to 145 credits required for the bachelor's degree must be completed at Longwood.

Visiting: There are regularly scheduled orientations for prospective students, including informational and tour programs, and open houses September- December, March and May. Visitors may sit in on classes and stay overnight. To schedule a visit, contact the Admissions Office at (800) 281-4677.

Financial Aid: In a recent year, need-based scholarships or need-based grants averaged $3606; need-based self-help aid (loans and jobs) averaged $4057; non-need-based athletic scholarships averaged $3740; and other non-need-based awards and non-need-based scholarships averaged $4304. 27% of undergraduates worked part time. Average annual earnings from campus work were $1344. The average financial indebtedness of a recent graduate was $14,889. The FAFSA is required.

International Students: In a recent year, there were 20 international students enrolled. The school actively recruits these students. They must score satisfactory on the written TOEFL or on the electronic version and also take the SAT or the ACT.

Computers: All students may access the system. There are no time limits and no fees. All students are required to have personal computers.

Graduates: In a recent year, 706 bachelor's degrees were awarded. The most popular majors were liberal studies (23%), business administration (23%), and visual and performing arts (7%). In an average class, 1% graduate in 3 years or less, 44% graduate in 4 years or less, 58% graduate in 5 years or less, and 57% graduate in 6 years or less. 167 companies recruited on campus in a recent year. Of a recent graduating class, 21% were enrolled in graduate school within 6 months of graduation and 91% were employed.

Admissions Contact: Robert J. Chonko, Dean of Enrollment.
E-mail: admissions@longwood.edu Web: www.whylongwood.com

LYNCHBURG COLLEGE — D-3
Lynchburg, VA 24501

(434) 544-8300
(800) 426-8101; Fax: (434) 544-8653

Full-time: 792 men, 1132 women	Faculty: 142; IIA, --$
Part-time: 47 men, 78 women	Ph.D.s: 76%
Graduate: 109 men, 270 women	Student/Faculty: 14 to 1
Year: semesters, summer session	Tuition: $24,245
Application Deadline: open	Room & Board: $6400
Freshman Class: 4009 applied, 2883 accepted, 554 enrolled	
SAT Verbal/Math: 515/510*	ACT: 20 COMPETITIVE

Lynchburg College, established in 1903, is a private, nonprofit institution affiliated with the Christian Church (Disciples of Christ), offering bachelor's degrees in liberal arts and sciences, and professional studies. There are 6 undergraduate and 2 graduate schools. In addition to regional accreditation, L.C. has baccalaureate program accreditation with NLN. The library contains 192,000 volumes, 437,000 microform items, and 5600 audio/video tapes/CDs/DVDs, and subscribes to 578 periodicals including electronic. Computerized library services include the card catalog, interlibrary loans, database searching, and Internet access. Special learning facilities include a learning resource center and art gallery. The 214-acre campus is in a suburban area 180 miles southwest of Washington, D.C. Including any residence halls, there are 42 buildings.

Student Life: 57% of undergraduates are from Virginia. Students are from 36 states and 17 foreign countries. 79% are from public schools. 81% are white. 76% are Protestant; 17% Catholic. The average age of freshmen is 19; all undergraduates, 22. 28% do not continue beyond their first year; 54% remain to graduate.

Housing: 1369 students can be accommodated in college housing, which includes single-sex and coed dorms, on-campus apartments, on-campus townhouses, fraternity houses, and sorority houses. In addition, there are honors houses, language houses, and special-interest houses. On-campus housing is guaranteed for all 4 years. 82% of students live on campus; of those, 80% remain on campus on weekends. Upperclassmen may keep cars.

Activities: 4% of men belong to 5 national fraternities; 8% of women belong to 5 national sororities. There are 70 groups on campus, including art, cheerleading, choir, computers, dance, drama, ethnic, gay, honors, international, jazz band, literary magazine, musical theater, newspaper, political, professional, religious, social, social service, student government, TV and yearbook. Popular campus events include a new student convocation and Academic Awards Banquet.

Sports: There are 10 intercollegiate sports for men and 11 for women, and 12 intramural sports for men and 12 for women. Facilities include a gym with a weight room and exercise physiology lab, a field house, athletic fields, and a ropes course.

Disabled Students: 78% of the campus is accessible. Wheelchair ramps, elevators, special parking, specially equipped rest rooms, special class scheduling, lowered drinking fountains, lowered telephones, and special housing are available.

Services: Counseling and information services are available, as is tutoring in most subjects. Tutoring is available in most freshman and sophomore subjects, some upperclass subjects, and in math and writing.

Campus Safety and Security: Measures include 24-hour foot and vehicle patrol, security escort services, informal discussions, and pamphlets/posters/films. There are emergency telephones and lighted pathways/sidewalks. All residence halls are locked 24 hours a day. Admission is only by scanning an ID card.

Programs of Study: L.C. confers B.A. and B.S. degrees. Master's degrees are also awarded. Bachelor's degrees are awarded in BIOLOGICAL SCIENCE (biology/biological science), BUSINESS (accounting, business administration and management, management science, marketing/retailing/merchandising, and sports management), COMMUNICATIONS AND THE ARTS (art, communications, dramatic arts, English, French, music, and Spanish), COMPUTER AND PHYSICAL SCIENCE (chemistry, computer science, mathematics, and physical sciences), EDUCATION (athletic training and education), ENGINEERING AND ENVIRONMENTAL DESIGN (engineering and environmental science), HEALTH PROFESSIONS (biomedical science, exercise science, nursing, and sports medicine), SOCIAL SCIENCE (economics, history, human development, international relations, philosophy, physical fitness/movement, political science/government, psychology, religion, and sociology). Communication studies, nursing, and human development and learning are the largest.

Required: To graduate, students must complete a 15- to 18-hour basic skills requirement. The 51 hour core includes foreign language, fine arts, written composition, history, lab science, literature, math, oral communication, philosophy, religious studies, social science, and wellness. A senior symposium is also required, as is a thesis in some programs. Students must also complete 124 credit hours to graduate, with a 2.0 GPA, and 30 to 69 hours in the major.

Special: Students may cross-register with Sweet Briar and Randolph-Macon Woman's Colleges, and they may study abroad in 20 countries. There is a Washington semester available, B.A.-B.S. degrees, internships, and a work-study program. Dual majors may be pursued in religious studies, philosophy, political science, sociology, business, and a foreign language. A 3-2 engineering degree is available in cooperation with Old Dominion University. Nondegree study and a pass/fail grading option are also available. There are 14 national honor societies and a freshman honors program.

Faculty/Classroom: 52% of faculty are male; 48%, female. All teach undergraduates and 25% both teach and do research. No introductory courses are taught by graduate students. The average class size in an introductory lecture is 25; in a laboratory, 16; and in a regular course, 25.

Admissions: 72% of the 2005-2006 applicants were accepted. The SAT scores for the 2005-2006 freshman class were: Verbal--44% below 500, 43% between 500 and 599, 11% between 600 and 700, and 2%

above 700; Math--43% below 500, 43% between 500 and 599, 13% between 600 and 700, and 1% above 700. The ACT scores were 53% below 21, 33% between 21 and 23, 8% between 24 and 26, 2% between 27 and 28, and 4% above 28. 24% of the current freshmen were in the top fifth of their class; 64% were in the top two fifths. 6 freshmen graduated first in their class.

Requirements: The SAT or ACT is required. In addition, SAT Subject Tests are recommended. Applicants must graduate from an accredited secondary school. They must have earned 16 to 20 academic high school credits in English, math and social science, lab science, and foreign language. AP and CLEP credits are accepted. Important factors in the admissions decision are advanced placement or honor courses, leadership record, and recommendations by school officials.

Procedure: Freshmen are admitted fall and spring. Entrance exams should be taken in the junior year and in the first semester of the senior year. There are early decision and early admissions plans. There is a rolling admissions plan. Early decision applications should be filed by November 15; the deadline for regular applications is open for fall entry. The fall 2005 application fee was $30. Notification of early decision is sent December 15; regular decision, on a rolling basis. 103 early decision candidates were accepted for the 2005-2006 class. Applications are accepted on-line.

Transfer: 69 transfer students enrolled in 2004-2005. Transfer students must have a minimum GPA of 2.0 to be considered and must be in good academic and social standing. The SAT or ACT is required. An interview is recommended. 62 of 124 credits required for the bachelor's degree must be completed at L.C.

Visiting: There are regularly scheduled orientations for prospective students, including individual appointments. There are guides for informal visits and visitors may sit in on classes and stay overnight. To schedule a visit, contact the Enrollment Services Office.

Financial Aid: In 2005-2006, 99% of all full-time students received some form of financial aid. 64% of all full-time students received need-based aid. The average freshman award was $18,519. Need-based scholarships or need-based grants averaged $15,060; need-based self-help aid (loans and jobs) averaged $3706; and other non-need-based awards and non-need-based scholarships averaged $8379. 37% of undergraduates work part time. Average annual earnings from campus work are $1250. The average financial indebtedness of a recent graduate was $18,698. L.C. is a member of CSS. The FAFSA and the state aid form are required. The deadline for filing freshman financial aid applications for fall entry is March 1.

International Students: There were 17 international students enrolled in a recent year. They must achieve a satisfactory score on the TOEFL and also take the SAT or the ACT.

Computers: All students may access the system 8 A.M. to 1 A.M. Monday through Thursday, 8 A.M. to 5 P.M. Friday and Saturday, and noon to 1 A.M. Sunday. There are no time limits and no fees. It is strongly recommended that all students have a personal computer.

Graduates: In a recent year, 350 bachelor's degrees were awarded. The most popular majors were human development and learning (11%), business administration (9%), and English (9%). In an average class, 1% graduate in 3 years or less, 50% graduate in 4 years or less, and 57% graduate in 5 or 6 years or less. 78 companies recruited on campus in 2004-2005. Of the 2004 graduating class, 22% were enrolled in graduate school within 6 months of graduation and 75% were employed.

Admissions Contact: Rita Detwiler, Vice President, Enrollment Management. A video is available. E-mail: admissions@lynchburg.edu Web: www.lynchburg.edu

MARY BALDWIN COLLEGE   D-2
Staunton, VA 24401
(540) 887-7260
(800) 468-2262; Fax: (540) 887-7292

Full-time: 36 men, 966 women	**Faculty:** 73; IIB, -$
Part-time: 90 men, 443 women	**Ph.D.s:** 93%
Graduate: 44 men, 161 women	**Student/Faculty:** 14 to 1
Year: semesters	**Tuition:** $20,605
Application Deadline: April 15	**Room & Board:** $5860
Freshman Class: 1273 applied, 985 accepted, 221 enrolled	
SAT Verbal/Math: 550/510*	**ACT:** 23 **COMPETITIVE**

Mary Baldwin College, established in 1842, is a private liberal arts college primarily for women. Its Residential College for Women offers several programs, among them the Program for the Exceptionally Gifted, which allows girls of extraordinary ability the opportunity to skip high school and enter college as young as 12 or 13; the Virginia Women's Institute for Leadership, the only all-female cadet corps in the country; and the Quest Interfaith Village, which fosters spiritual growth through academic study, community service, and extracurricular activities. MBC also offers an Adult Degree Program on the main campus and at 5 regional centers, as well as 2 graduate programs. The library contains 140,466 volumes, 69,644 microform items, and 6668 audio/video tapes/CDs/DVDs, and subscribes to 11,889 periodicals including electronic. Computerized library services include the card catalog, interlibrary loans, database searching, Internet access, and laptop Internet portals. Special learning facilities include a learning resource center, art gallery, radio station, TV station, language lab, and military/leadership museum. The 54-acre campus is in a small town 100 miles west of Richmond. Including any residence halls, there are 30 buildings.

Student Life: 62% of undergraduates are from Virginia. Others are from 39 states and 4 foreign countries. 80% are from public schools. 57% are white; 23% African American. 40% are Protestant; 15% Catholic. The average age of freshmen is 18; all undergraduates, 21. 31% do not continue beyond their first year; 52% remain to graduate.

Housing: 775 students can be accommodated in college housing, which includes single-sex dorms and on-campus apartments. In addition, there are honors houses, language houses, and special-interest houses. On-campus housing is guaranteed for all 4 years. 85% of students live on campus; of those, 65% remain on campus on weekends. All students may keep cars.

Activities: There are no fraternities or sororities. There are 48 groups on campus, including art, choir, chorale, chorus, computers, dance, drama, drill team, drum and bugle corps, Ethics Bowl team, ethnic, film, gay, honors, international, literary magazine, marching band, musical theater, newspaper, orchestra, photography, political, professional, radio and TV, religious, social, social service, student government, Student in free Enterprise and yearbook. Popular campus events include Apple Day, Junior Dads Weekend, and Signature Ball.

Sports: There are 8 intercollegiate sports for women and 4 intramural sports for women. Facilities include a gym, a Universal Gym room, a room for dance and fencing, tennis, basketball, and racquetball courts, cardio and muscle strength equipment, Nautilus equipment, and soccer, softball, and hockey fields.

Disabled Students: 30% of the campus is accessible. Wheelchair ramps, elevators, special parking, specially equipped rest rooms, and individual accommodations for those with physical challenges or visual and hearing impairments are available.

Services: Counseling and information services are available, as is tutoring in most subjects. There is a reader service for the blind and remedial math.

Campus Safety and Security: Measures include 24-hour foot and vehicle patrol, self-defense education, security escort services, and informal discussions. There are pamphlets/posters/films, emergency telephones, lighted pathways/sidewalks, and 24-hour locked residence halls.

Programs of Study: MBC confers B.A. and B.S. degrees. Master's degrees are also awarded. Bachelor's degrees are awarded in BIOLOGICAL SCIENCE (biochemistry and biology/biological science), BUSINESS (business administration and management and marketing management), COMMUNICATIONS AND THE ARTS (art, art history and appreciation, arts administration/management, communications, dramatic arts, English, French, German, music, Spanish, and studio art), COMPUTER AND PHYSICAL SCIENCE (applied mathematics, chemistry, computer mathematics, computer science, mathematics, and physics), EDUCATION (education and mathematics), HEALTH PROFESSIONS (health care administration, medical laboratory science, and medical laboratory technology), SOCIAL SCIENCE (Asian/Oriental studies, economics, history, international relations, philosophy, political science/government, psychology, religion, social work, and sociology). Psychology, political science, and history are the strongest academically. Psychology, sociology, and art are the largest.

Required: To graduate, students must complete 9 hours each in natural sciences, social sciences, and history, arts, and humanities; 6 hours each of writing courses and international education (foreign language, cross-cultural studies, and/or study abroad); 3 hours each of math, women's studies, and experiential education; and 2 hours of health and phys ed. A minimum GPA of 2.0 is required. Students must earn 132 credits, with at least 33 credits in the major. Most disciplines require upper-level seminars and significant projects consisting of some type of original research.

Special: MBC and 6 other colleges in Virginia (Hampden-Sydney College, Hollins University, Randolph-Macon College, Randolph-Macon Women's College, Sweet Briar College, and Washington and Lee University) form a consortium through with students may attend another of the participating colleged a semster or a year. Students in the Women's Institute for Leadership program may participate in an exchange program with Norwich University. Students may earn a bachelor's degree in physics by taking courses at Washington and Lee as well as MBC. MBC has articulation and transfer agreements with many colleges in the Virginia Community College System. MBS offers the minor in public history through a partnership with the Woodro Wilson Presidential Library. Internships, study abroad, B.A.-B.S. degrees in biology, biochemistry, chemistry, and psychology, and work-study programs are available. The college offers an accelerated degree program as well as dual and student-designed majors. There are 3-2 programs available in engineering with the University of Virginia and in nursing with Vanderbilt University. There is an advanced degree program in teaching with the University of Virginia. Credit for life, military, and work experience may be granted through the Adult Degree Program only. Nondegree study and a pass/fail grading option are also available. There are 11 national honor societies, including Phi Beta Kappa, a freshman honors program, and honors program in all departments.

Faculty/Classroom: 47% of faculty are male; 53%, female. 96% teach undergraduates. No introductory courses are taught by graduate students. The average class size in an introductory lecture is 21; in a laboratory, 12; and in a regular course, 18.

Admissions: 77% of the 2005-2006 applicants were accepted. The SAT scores for the 2005-2006 freshman class were: Verbal--33% below 500, 32% between 500 and 599, 26% between 600 and 700, and 9% above 700; Math--43% below 500, 41% between 500 and 599, 13% between 600 and 700, and 3% above 700. The ACT scores were 46% below 21, 11% between 21 and 23, 23% between 24 and 26, 17% between 27 and 28, and 3% above 28. 33% of the current freshmen were in the top fifth of their class; 59% were in the top two fifths.

Requirements: The SAT or ACT is required. In addition, SAT. Subject Tests are recommended. Applicants must graduate from an accredited secondary school, have a GED, or meet state equivalency requirements for homeschooling. A minimum of 16 academic units are required, including 4 in English, 3 in math, 2 to 3 in social studies, and 2 each in a foreign language and science. Essays and interviews are recommended. A GPA of 2.0 is required. AP and CLEP credits are accepted. Important factors in the admissions decision are advanced placement or honor courses, extracurricular activities record, and leadership record.

Procedure: Freshmen are admitted fall and spring. Entrance exams should be taken in the junior or senior year. There are early decision, early admissions, and deferred admissions plans. There is a rolling admissions plan. Early decision applications should be filed by November 15; regular applications, by April 15 for fall entry and December 15 for spring entry, along with a $35 fee. Notification of early decision is sent December 1; regular decision, within 2 weeks of receipt of application. 9 early decision candidates were accepted for the 2005-2006 class. Applications are accepted on-line.

Transfer: 40 transfer students enrolled in 2004-2005. Transfer applicants must have a 2.0 GPA from the institution where they are currently enrolled. 66 of 132 credits required for the bachelor's degree must be completed at MBC.

Visiting: There are regularly scheduled orientations for prospective students, consisting of a tour, an interview, scheduled classes upon request, as well as athletic tours and presentations. There are guides for informal visits and visitors may sit in on classes and stay overnight. To schedule a visit, contact the Admissions Office.

Financial Aid: In a recent year, 99% of all full-time freshmen and 95% of continuing full-time students received some form of financial aid. 78% of full-time freshmen and 60% of continuing full-time students received need-based aid. The average freshman award was $20,214. Need-based scholarships or need-based grants averaged $6500 ($11,850 maximum); need-based self-help aid (loans and jobs) averaged $2000 ($2000 maximum); and other non-need-based awards and non-need-based scholarships averaged $7000 ($9350 maximum). 69% of undergraduates work part time. Average annual earnings from campus work are $2000. The average financial indebtedness of a recent graduate was $18,625. The FAFSA and the state aid form are required. The deadline for filing freshman financial aid applications for fall entry is May 1.

International Students: There are 22 international students enrolled. The school actively recruits these students. They must take the written TOEFL and also take the SAT or the ACT, scoring satisfactorily.

Computers: Wireless access is available. There are 227 PCs located throughout academic buildings. All students may access the system. There are no time limits and no fees.

Graduates: From July 1, 2004 to June 30, 2005, 292 bachelor's degrees were awarded. The most popular majors were psychology (16%), business administration (13%), and sociology (11%). In an average class, 3% graduate in 3 years or less, 52% graduate in 4 years or less, and 57% graduate in 5 years or less. 12 companies recruited on campus in 2004-2005. Of the 2004 graduating class, 25% were enrolled in graduate school within 6 months of graduation and 86% were employed.

Admissions Contact: Lisa Branson, Dean of Admissions and Financial Aid. E-mail: *admit@mbc.edu* Web: *www.mbc.edu*

MARY WASHINGTON COLLEGE
(See University of Mary Washington)

MARYMOUNT UNIVERSITY

E-2

Arlington, VA 22207-4299

(703) 284-1500
(800) 548-7638; Fax: (703) 522-0349

Full-time: 483 men, 1388 women	**Faculty:** 104; IIA, av$
Part-time: 94 men, 362 women	**Ph.D.s:** 81%
Graduate: 331 men, 1026 women	**Student/Faculty:** 18 to 1
Year: semesters, summer session	**Tuition:** $18,114
Application Deadline: open	**Room & Board:** $7820
Freshman Class: 1802 applied, 1492 accepted, 426 enrolled	
SAT Verbal/Math: 510/490*	**ACT:** 20 COMPETITIVE

Marymount University, established in 1950, is a private, comprehensive Catholic university offering undergraduate and graduate programs through 4 schools: arts and sciences, business administration, education and human services, and health professions. There are 4 undergraduate and 4 graduate schools. In addition to regional accreditation, Marymount has baccalaureate program accreditation with ABA, ACBSP, APTA, CACREP, CAHMA, CAPTE, FIDER, NCATE, and NLN. The library contains 197,379 volumes, 336,578 microform items, and 1480 audio/video tapes/CDs/DVDs, and subscribes to 3054 periodicals including electronic. Computerized library services include the card catalog, interlibrary loans, database searching, Internet access, and laptop Internet portals. Special learning facilities include a learning resource center, art gallery, and an instructional media center. The 21-acre campus is in a suburban area 6 miles southwest of Washington, D.C. Including any residence halls, there are 13 buildings.

Student Life: 58% of undergraduates are from Virginia. Others are from 36 states, 68 foreign countries, and Canada. 68% are from public schools. 47% are white; 14% African American; 11% Hispanic. 38% are Catholic; 20% Protestant. The average age of freshmen is 18; all undergraduates, 23. 27% do not continue beyond their first year; 54% remain to graduate.

Housing: 695 students can be accommodated in college housing, which includes single-sex and coed dorms and off-campus apartments. On-campus housing is available on a lottery system for upperclassmen. 70% of students commute. Upperclassmen may keep cars.

Activities: There are no fraternities or sororities. There are 30 groups on campus, including art, cheerleading, choir, chorus, dance, drama, ethnic, honors, international, literary magazine, newspaper, political, professional, religious, social, social service, student government, and yearbook. Popular campus events include Portfolio in Motion (Fashion Show), Snowball (Winter Formal Dance), and International Week.

Sports: There are 6 intercollegiate sports for men and 6 for women, and 5 intramural sports for men and 5 for women. Facilities include a student center with a 1000-seat sports arena, pool, fitness center, and recreation gym.

Disabled Students: 75% of the campus is accessible. Wheelchair ramps, elevators, special parking, specially equipped rest rooms, special class scheduling, lowered drinking fountains, and lowered telephones are available.

Services: Counseling and information services are available, as is tutoring in most subjects. There is a reader service for the blind, and remedial math, reading, and writing.

Campus Safety and Security: Measures include 24-hour foot and vehicle patrol, security escort services, shuttle buses, and emergency telephones. There are lighted pathways/sidewalks.

Programs of Study: Marymount confers B.A., B.S., B.B.A., and B.S.N. degrees. Associate, master's, and doctoral degrees are also awarded. Bachelor's degrees are awarded in BIOLOGICAL SCIENCE (biology/biological science), BUSINESS (accounting, banking and finance, business administration and management, business economics, business law, fashion merchandising, international business management, and marketing/retailing/merchandising), COMMUNICATIONS AND THE ARTS (art, communications, English, and graphic design), COMPUTER AND PHYSICAL SCIENCE (computer science, information sciences and systems, and mathematics), EDUCATION (art, computer, English, mathematics, and psychology), ENGINEERING AND ENVIRONMENTAL DESIGN (environmental science and interior design), HEALTH PROFESSIONS (health science and nursing), SOCIAL SCIENCE (criminal justice, economics, fashion design and technology, history, liberal arts/general studies, paralegal studies, philosophy, political science/government, psychology, sociology, and theological studies). Interior design, fashion, merchandising, and biology are the largest.

Required: To graduate, students must complete all course requirements with a minimum cumulative grade point average of 2.0. Core curriculum requirements includes courses in writing, humanities, math, sciences, social science, and health and wellness. Students must earn 120 credits by completing all liberal arts, general education, and major requirements.

Special: Students are given the opportunity to cross-register with the Consortium of Universities of the Washington Metropolitan Area or study abroad in London, Limerick, Rome, or Florence. Marymount offers dual and student-designed majors, accelerated degrees in nursing, and interior design, and 4+1 programs in computer science and business administration. An internship and a clinical or student teaching ex-

perience is required in all majors except nursing. There are 9 national honor societies an a freshman honors program.

Faculty/Classroom: 37% of faculty are male; 63%, female. 77% teach undergraduates. Graduate students teach 1% of introductory courses. The average class size in an introductory lecture is 27; in a laboratory, 11; and in a regular course, 23.

Admissions: 83% of the 2005-2006 applicants were accepted. The SAT scores for the 2005-2006 freshman class were: Verbal--46% below 500, 36% between 500 and 599, 17% between 600 and 700, and 1% above 700; Math--51% below 500, 38% between 500 and 599, and 11% between 600 and 700. The ACT scores were 54% below 21, 32% between 21 and 23, 11% between 24 and 26, 1% between 27 and 28, and 1% above 28. 24% of the current freshmen were in the top fifth of their class; 55% were in the top two fifths.

Requirements: The SAT or ACT is required. The ACT Optional Writing test is also recommended. In addition, applicants must graduate from an accredited secondary school or have a GED. Marymount requires 15 academic credits in preparatory courses and strongly recommends biology and chemistry for nursing candidates. A letter of recommendation is also required. A GPA of 2.0 is required. AP and CLEP credits are accepted. Important factors in the admissions decision are advanced placement or honor courses, extracurricular activities record, and evidence of special talent.

Procedure: Freshmen are admitted to all sessions. There is a rolling admissions plan. Application deadlines are open. Application fee is $35. 1 applicant was on the 2005 waiting list. Applications are accepted on-line.

Transfer: 355 transfer students enrolled in 2004-2005. Applicants with 30 or more credits must have a minimum GPA of 2.0. Those with fewer than 30 must also meet freshman requirements. 36 of 120 credits required for the bachelor's degree must be completed at Marymount.

Visiting: There are regularly scheduled orientations for prospective students, including Campus Visit Days, Information Nights, and new student summer orientation. There are guides for informal visits and visitors may sit in on classes and stay overnight. To schedule a visit, contact Mary Kay Eldridge at (703) 284-1511 or admissions@marymount.edu.

Financial Aid: In 2005-2006, 87% of all full-time freshmen and 81% of continuing full-time students received some form of financial aid. 49% of full-time freshmen and 50% of continuing full-time students received need-based aid. The average freshman award was $16,720. Need-based scholarships or need-based grants averaged $7333 ($17,000 maximum); need-based self-help aid (loans and jobs) averaged $3406 ($6625 maximum); and other non-need-based awards and non-need-based scholarships averaged $11,922 ($28,468 maximum). Average annual earnings from campus work are $1800. The average financial indebtedness of the 2005 graduate was $25,008. The FAFSA is required. The deadline for filing freshman financial aid applications for fall entry is June 1.

International Students: There are 150 international students enrolled. The school actively recruits these students. They must take the TOEFL.

Computers: Wireless access is available. All residence halls have a PC connection in each room. Students have access to a wireless network in the student center and the library on the main campus. The 4 computer labs on campus offer Windows and Mac systems, laser printers, scanners, projectors, and a wide variety of software. All students may access the system. There are no time limits. The fee is $6 per credit hour.

Graduates: From July 1, 2004 to June 30, 2005, 348 bachelor's degrees were awarded. The most popular majors were interior design (11%), social psychology (8%), and computer information systems (7%). In an average class, 2% graduate in 3 years or less, 38% graduate in 4 years or less, 50% graduate in 5 years or less, and 54% graduate in 6 years or less.

Admissions Contact: Chris E. Domes, Vice President for Enrollment Management and Student Services. A video is available.
E-mail: admissions@marymount.edu Web: www.marymount.edu

NORFOLK STATE UNIVERSITY

F-4

Norfolk, VA 23504

(757) 823-8396
(800) 274-1821; Fax: (757) 823-2078

Full-time: 1732 men, 2688 women	**Faculty:** II A, -$
Part-time: 312 men, 605 women	**Ph.D.s:** 63%
Graduate: 178 men, 581 women	**Student/Faculty:** n/av
Year: semesters, summer session	**Tuition:** $4295 ($14,255)
Application Deadline: May 31	**Room & Board:** $6236
Freshman Class: 4651 applied, 3297 accepted, 1157 enrolled	
SAT Verbal/Math: 450/440*	**ACT:** 18 LESS COMPETITIVE

Norfolk State University, founded in 1935, is an independent institution offering undergraduate and graduate programs in the liberal arts and sciences, business education, health-related professions, and vocational, technical, and professional training. There are 5 undergraduate schools and 1 graduate school. In addition to regional accreditation, NSU has baccalaureate program accreditation with AACSB, ACEJMC, ACS, ADA, APA, CSAB, CSWE, NAIT, NASM, NCATE, and NLN. The library contains 341,068 volumes, 60,882 microform items, and 27 audio/video tapes/CDs/DVDs, and subscribes to 1186 periodicals including electronic. Computerized library services include the card catalog, interlibrary loans, database searching, and Internet access. Special learning facilities include a learning resource center, art gallery, planetarium, radio station, TV station, and musical theater. The 134-acre campus is in an urban area in the port city of Norfolk. Including any residence halls, there are 31 buildings.

Student Life: 87% of undergraduates are from Virginia. Others are from 40 states and 34 foreign countries. 87% are African American. The average age of freshmen is 18; all undergraduates, 23. 30% do not continue beyond their first year; 27% remain to graduate.

Housing: 2070 students can be accommodated in college housing, which includes single-sex dorms. On-campus housing is available on a first-come, first-served basis. 62% of students commute. Alcohol is not permitted. Upperclassmen may keep cars.

Activities: 10% of men belong to 12 national fraternities; 10% of women belong to 8 national sororities. There are 112 groups on campus, including art, band, cheerleading, choir, chorus, computers, dance, debate, drama, drill team, ethnic, honors, international, jazz band, literary magazine, marching band, newspaper, pep band, political, professional, radio and TV, religious, social, social service, student government, and yearbook. Popular campus events include Martin Luther King Commemorative Activity and Black History Month activities.

Sports: There are 6 intercollegiate sports for men and 7 for women, and 8 intramural sports for men and 7 for women. Facilities include a stadium and track seating 28,088, an arena seating 7,500, a baseball field, a softball field, a gym, a swimming pool, tennis courts, and a bowling alley.

Disabled Students: 80% of the campus is accessible. Wheelchair ramps, elevators, special parking, specially equipped rest rooms, special class scheduling, lowered telephones, and special housing are available.

Services: Counseling and information services are available, as is tutoring in most subjects. There is a reader service for the blind.

Campus Safety and Security: Measures include 24-hour foot and vehicle patrol, security escort services, shuttle buses, and informal discussions. There are pamphlets/posters/films, emergency telephones, lighted pathways/sidewalks, and town meetings.

Programs of Study: NSU confers B.A., B.S., B.Mus., and B.S.W. degrees. Associate, master's, and doctoral degrees are also awarded. Bachelor's degrees are awarded in BIOLOGICAL SCIENCE (biology/biological science and environmental biology), BUSINESS (accounting, banking and finance, and hospitality management services), COMMUNICATIONS AND THE ARTS (communications, English, fine arts, graphic design, and journalism), COMPUTER AND PHYSICAL SCIENCE (chemistry, computer science, mathematics, and physics), EDUCATION (business, early childhood, music, and technical), ENGINEERING AND ENVIRONMENTAL DESIGN (computer technology, construction technology, drafting and design technology, electrical/electronics engineering technology, and military science), HEALTH PROFESSIONS (exercise science, health care administration, health science, medical records administration/services, medical technology, and nursing), SOCIAL SCIENCE (history, interdisciplinary studies, political science/government, psychology, public administration, and sociology). Social work and computer science are the strongest academically. Business, computer science, and nursing are the largest.

Required: Students must complete at least 120 semester hours with a minimum 2.0 GPA, including general education courses such as communication, humanities, social science, natural science, health ed, phys ed, and computer literacy. They must also demonstrate writing competence.

Special: NSU offers cross-registration with other institutions in the Tidewater Consortium, a student-exchange program with Old Dominion University, co-op education, a second baccalaureate degree with a minimum of 30 additional semester hours earned, a B.A.-B.S. degree, and a general studies degree. Credit for military experience is possible. There are 14 national honor societies and a freshman honors program.

Faculty/Classroom: 55% of faculty are male; 45%, female. No introductory courses are taught by graduate students. The average class size in an introductory lecture is 20; in a laboratory, 16; and in a regular course, 17.

Admissions: 71% of the 2005-2006 applicants were accepted. The SAT scores for the 2005-2006 freshman class were: Verbal--79% below 500, 18% between 500 and 599, 2% between 600 and 700, and 1% above 700; Math--81% below 500, 17% between 500 and 599, and 2% between 600 and 700. The ACT scores were 81% below 21, 13% between 21 and 23, and 6% between 24 and 26. 16% of the current freshmen were in the top fifth of their class; 37% were in the top two fifths.

Requirements: The SAT or ACT is required. In addition, applicants should be graduates of an accredited secondary school or have the GED equivalent and have completed 22 academic units: 4 in English, 3 in history/social studies, 3 each in math and science, and 9 in electives. Nursing applicants must meet additional requirements. A GPA of 2.0 is required. AP and CLEP credits are accepted.

Procedure: Freshmen are admitted fall, spring, and summer. Entrance exams should be taken by March of the senior year. There is a deferred admissions plan. Applications should be filed by May 31 for fall entry. The fall 2005 application fee was $25. Notification is sent on a rolling basis. Applications are accepted on-line.

Transfer: 374 transfer students enrolled in 2004-2005. Transfers must meet freshman admissions criteria. 30 of 120 credits required for the bachelor's degree must be completed at NSU.

Visiting: There are regularly scheduled orientations for prospective students, including registration, a general information session, visits to academic departments, admissions, and a tour. There are guides for informal visits and visitors may sit in on classes and stay overnight. To schedule a visit, contact the Admissions Office.

Financial Aid: NSU is a member of CSS. The FAFSA and the SAR are required. The priority date for freshman financial aid applications for fall entry is March 15. The deadline for filing freshman financial aid applications for fall entry is April 15.

International Students: There are 37 international students enrolled. The school actively recruits these students. They must score satisfactorily on the written TOEFL and also take the SAT or the ACT.

Computers: All students may access the system any time. There are no time limits and no fees. It is strongly recommended that all students have a personal computer.

Graduates: In a recent year, 820 bachelor's degrees were awarded. The most popular majors were interdisciplinary studies (23%), business (11%), and psychology (8%). In an average class, 10% graduate in 4 years or less, 22% graduate in 5 years or less, and 28% graduate in 6 years or less. 172 companies recruited on campus in a recent year. Of a recent graduating class, 5% were enrolled in graduate school within 6 months of graduation.

Admissions Contact: Michelle Marable, Director of Admissions. A video is available. E-mail: *admissions@nsu.edu* Web: *www.nsu.edu*

OLD DOMINION UNIVERSITY F-4
Norfolk, VA 23529-0050 (757) 683-3648
(800) 348-7926; Fax: (757) 683-3255

Full-time: 4501 men, 6183 women	Faculty: 620; I, --$
Part-time: 1499 men, 2422 women	Ph.D.s: 81%
Graduate: 1592 men, 2151 women	Student/Faculty: 17 to 1
Year: semesters, summer session	Tuition: $5615 ($15,394)
Application Deadline: March 15	Room & Board: $6292
Freshman Class: 7067 applied, 4904 accepted, 2094 enrolled	
SAT Verbal/Math: 530/530*	ACT: 21 COMPETITIVE

Old Dominion University, founded in 1930, is a public institution with programs in arts and letters, business and public administration, engineering, education, sciences, and health sciences. There are 6 undergraduate and 6 graduate schools. In addition to regional accreditation, ODU has baccalaureate program accreditation with AACSB, ABET, ADA, APTA ASHA, CAHEA, CCNE, JRCMT, NAACLS, NASAD, NASM, NASPE, NAST, NCATE, NEHS, NLN, and NRPA. The 3 libraries contain 1,110,719 volumes, 2,057,443 microform items, and 51,459 audio/video tapes/CDs/DVDs, and subscribe to 14,607 periodicals including electronic. Computerized library services include the card catalog, interlibrary loans, database searching, and Internet access. Special learning facilities include an art gallery, planetarium, radio station, music library, art library, and digital library. The 188-acre campus is in an urban area in the Norfolk/Hampton Roads Metropolitan region. Including any residence halls, there are 110 buildings.

Student Life: 91% of undergraduates are from Virginia. Others are from 41 states, 74 foreign countries, and Canada. 90% are from public schools. 55% are white; 24% African American. The average age of freshmen is 19; all undergraduates, 22. 23% do not continue beyond their first year; 77% remain to graduate.

Housing: 3372 students can be accommodated in college housing, which includes coed dorms, on-campus apartments, and off-campus apartments. In addition, there are honors houses, and honors, international, coed, and quiet-study floors. On-campus housing is available on a first-come, first-served basis and is available on a lottery system for upperclassmen. 77% of students commute. All students may keep cars.

Activities: 5% of men belong to 13 national fraternities; 4% of women belong to 10 national sororities. There are 220 groups on campus, including cheerleading, chess, choir, chorale, computers, dance, debate, drama, ethnic, forensics, gay, honors, international, jazz band, literary magazine, musical theater, newspaper, pep band, political, professional, radio and TV, religious, social, and student government. Popular campus events include concerts, fashion shows/pageants, and movies.

Sports: There are 8 intercollegiate sports for men and 8 for women, and 15 intramural sports for men and 15 for women. Facilities include an arena, a playing field, a baseball complex, 2 pools, intramural fields, a soccer stadium, a sailing center, and a convocation center.

Disabled Students: 95% of the campus is accessible. Wheelchair ramps, elevators, special parking, specially equipped rest rooms, special class scheduling, lowered drinking fountains, special housing, and automatic doors are available.

Services: Counseling and information services are available, as is tutoring in some subjects, including English and sciences. There is a reader service for the blind and remedial math and writing.

Campus Safety and Security: Measures include 24-hour foot and vehicle patrol, security escort services, shuttle buses, and emergency telephones. There are lighted pathways/sidewalks and a bicycle patrol.

Programs of Study: ODU confers B.A., B.S., B.F.A., B.M., B.S.B.A., B.S.C.E., B.S.C.O.M.E., B.S.C.S., B.S.D.H., B.S.E.E., B.S.E.H., B.S.E.N.V.E., B.S.E.T., B.S.H.S., B.S.M.E., B.S.M.T., B.S.N., and B.S.N.M.T. degrees. Master's and doctoral degrees are also awarded. Bachelor's degrees are awarded in BIOLOGICAL SCIENCE (biochemistry, biology/biological science, marine biology, and marine science), BUSINESS (accounting, banking and finance, business administration and management, business economics, electronic business, fashion merchandising, international business management, management information systems, management science, marketing management, recreation and leisure services, and sports management), COMMUNICATIONS AND THE ARTS (art history and appreciation, communications, creative writing, dance, dramatic arts, English, film arts, fine arts, French, German, graphic design, journalism, linguistics, literature, music, music performance, music theory and composition, performing arts, Spanish, and studio art), COMPUTER AND PHYSICAL SCIENCE (chemistry, computer science, earth science, geology, information sciences and systems, mathematics, oceanography, and physics), EDUCATION (art, dance, drama, early childhood, elementary, English, foreign languages, industrial arts, marketing and distribution, mathematics, music, physical, science, secondary, and social studies), ENGINEERING AND ENVIRONMENTAL DESIGN (civil engineering, civil engineering technology, computer engineering, electrical/electronics engineering, electrical/electronics engineering technology, engineering technology, environmental engineering, mechanical engineering, mechanical engineering technology, nuclear engineering technology, and optical engineering), HEALTH PROFESSIONS (cytotechnology, dental hygiene, environmental health science, exercise science, health science, medical technology, nuclear medical technology, nursing, and speech pathology/audiology), SOCIAL SCIENCE (anthropology, Asian/Oriental studies, criminal justice, economics, geography, history, human services, interdisciplinary studies, international studies, philosophy, political science/government, psychology, sociology, and women's studies). Criminal justice, accounting, speech pathology, nursing, finance, exercise science, and mechanical engineering technology are the strongest academically. Psychology, biology, phys ed, criminal justice, and communication are the largest.

Required: At least 120 credits, with a minimum GPA of 2.0, are required to graduate. Students must complete the university's general education program, consisting of specific skills and perspectives courses outside the student's major. English composition is a required course, and students must pass a writing proficiency exam.

Special: Old Dominion offers cross-registration with schools in the Tidewater Consortium program. There are co-op programs, guaranteed internships, study abroad in 40 countries, and a work-study program. Students may take a B.A.-B.S. degree in engineering and liberal arts. An interdisciplinary program, student-designed and dual majors, accelerated degrees, 3-2 engineering degrees in business and engineering, nondegree study, pass/fail options, and credit for military and life experience are available. There are 19 national honor societies, including Phi Beta Kappa, and a freshman honors program. All departments have honors programs.

Faculty/Classroom: 57% of faculty are male; 43%, female. 68% teach undergraduates. The average class size in an introductory lecture is 36; in a laboratory, 22; and in a regular course, 24.

Admissions: 69% of the 2005-2006 applicants were accepted. The SAT scores for the 2005-2006 freshman class were: Verbal--32% below 500, 50% between 500 and 599, 17% between 600 and 700, and 1% above 700; Math--33% below 500, 48% between 500 and 700, 17% between 600 and 700, and 1% above 700. The ACT scores were 47% below 21, 32% between 21 and 23, 14% between 24 and 26, 4% between 27 and 28, and 3% above 28. 34% of the current freshmen were in the top fifth of their class; 74% were in the top two fifths. 13 freshmen graduated first in their class.

Requirements: The SAT or ACT is required. The ACT Optional Writing test is also required. In addition, applicants must be graduates of an accredited secondary school. The GED is accepted. Applicants should have completed 4 years of math, and 3 years each of English, foreign languages, science, and social science. An essay and an interview are recommended. A list of extracurricular activities is required. A GPA of 2.7 is required. AP and CLEP credits are accepted. Important factors in the admissions decision are advanced placement or honor courses, recommendations by school officials, and extracurricular activities record.

Procedure: Freshmen are admitted fall and spring. Entrance exams should be taken in May of the junior year or November/December of the senior year. There are early admissions and deferred admissions plans. There is a rolling admissions plan. Applications should be filed by March 15 for fall entry, October 1 for spring entry, and March 1 for summer entry, along with a $40 fee. Notification is sent on a rolling basis. Applications are accepted on-line.

Transfer: 1766 transfer students enrolled in 2004-2005. Applicants must have a minimum GPA of 2.2 and must have at least 24 semester hour credits. Applicants with fewer semester hours must meet the same requirements as freshmen. 30 of 120 credits required for the bachelor's degree must be completed at ODU.

Visiting: There are regularly scheduled orientations for prospective students, consisting of campus tours, available Monday through Friday at 10 A.M., Monday and Friday at 2 P.M., and Saturday at 11 A.M. Special tours can be arranged with the Office of Admissions. There are guides for informal visits and visitors may sit in on classes. To schedule a visit, contact the Admissions Office at (757) 683-3685 or *admit@odu.edu.*

Financial Aid: In 2005-2006, 75% of all full-time freshmen and 77% of continuing full-time students received some form of financial aid. 65% of full-time freshmen and 68% of continuing full-time students received need-based aid. The average freshman award was $7231. Need-based scholarships or need-based grants averaged $4723 ($15,163 maximum); need-based self-help aid (loans and jobs) averaged $3083 ($15,163 maximum); non-need-based athletic scholarships averaged $9886 ($15,163 maximum); and other non-need-based awards and non-need-based scholarships averaged $3025 ($15,163 maximum). Average annual earnings from campus work are $1854. The average financial indebtedness of the 2005 graduate was $16,775. The FAFSA is required. The priority date for freshman financial aid applications for fall entry is February 15. The deadline for filing freshman financial aid applications for fall entry is March 15.

International Students: There are 230 international students enrolled. The school actively recruits these students. They must take the TOEFL and also take the college's own test. Student with satisfactory SAT scores or completed the ELC Bridge Program don't have to take either proficiency exam.

Computers: There are computer labs at various locations on campus. The system also may be acessed via modem from home or dorm rooms. All students may access the system 24 hours a day. There are no time limits and no fees.

Graduates: From July 1, 2004 to June 30, 2005, 2411 bachelor's degrees were awarded. The most popular majors were human services counseling (7%), interdisciplinary studies (6%), and communication (6%). In an average class, 22% graduate in 4 years or less, 42% graduate in 5 years or less, and 48% graduate in 6 years or less. 336 companies recruited on campus in 2004-2005. Of the 2004 graduating class, 21% were enrolled in graduate school within 6 months of graduation and 65% were employed.

Admissions Contact: Alice McAdory, Director of Admissions. A video is available. E-mail: *admit@odu.edu* Web: *www.admissions.odu.edu*

RADFORD UNIVERSITY

C-3

Radford, VA 24141-6972

(540) 831-5371
(800) 890-4265; Fax: (540) 831-5038

Full-time: 3352 men, 4676 women	**Faculty:** 377; IIA, --$
Part-time: 175 men, 279 women	**Ph.D.s:** 83%
Graduate: 242 men, 828 women	**Student/Faculty:** 21 to 1
Year: semesters, summer session	**Tuition:** $7025 ($14,263)
Application Deadline: February 1	**Room & Board:** $6120
Freshman Class: 5793 applied, 4726 accepted, 1896 enrolled	
SAT Verbal/Math: 500/500*	**COMPETITIVE**

Radford University, founded in 1910, is a public comprehensive institution with a diverse curricula in arts and sciences, business and economics, education and human development, nursing and health services, and visual and performing arts. There are 6 undergraduate schools and 1 graduate school. In addition to regional accreditation, RU has baccalaureate program accreditation with AACSB, ABET, ADA, APA, ASHLA, CACREP, CSAB, CSWE, NASM, NAST NCATE, NLN, and NRPA. The library contains 367,893 volumes, 1,473,288 microform items, and 16,374 audio/video tapes/CDs/DVDs, and subscribes to 8633 periodicals including electronic. Computerized library services include the card catalog, interlibrary loans, database searching, Internet access, and laptop Internet portals. Special learning facilities include a learning resource center, art gallery, planetarium, radio station, TV station, and a 376-acre conservancy used for studies in ecology, botany, mapping geological features as a model in resource management and maintenance formation on actual building techniques, and cultural and oral history. The 177-acre campus is in a small town 36 miles southwest of Roanoke. Including any residence halls, there are 75 buildings.

Student Life: 92% of undergraduates are from Virginia. Others are from 41 states, 56 foreign countries, and Canada. 96% are from public schools. 89% are white. The average age of freshmen is 18; all undergraduates, 21. 22% do not continue beyond their first year; 57% remain to graduate.

Housing: 3331 students can be accommodated in college housing, which includes coed dorms and off-campus apartments. In addition, there are honors houses and special-interest houses. On-campus housing is guaranteed for all 4 years. 61% of students commute. All students may keep cars.

Activities: 6% of men belong to 16 national fraternities; 10% of women belong to 12 national sororities. There are 159 groups on campus, including art, band, cheerleading, chess, choir, chorale, computers, dance, drama, ethnic, gay, honors, international, jazz band, literary magazine, musical theater, newspaper, political, professional, radio and TV, religious, social, social service, student government, and yearbook. Popular campus events include Club Fair, Family Weekend, and Annual Highlander Picnic.

Sports: There are 7 intercollegiate sports for men and 10 for women, and 10 intramural sports for men and 9 for women. Facilities include a 5000-seat recreation and convocation complex housing a natatorium with an 8-lane swimming pool, areas for free exercise, a weight room, steam rooms, a 1/6-mile jogging track, and basketball, volleyball, handball, and racquetball courts. Outdoor facilities include a jogging trail, 12 tennis courts, and areas for baseball, soccer, lacrosse, softball, and intramural football.

Disabled Students: 85% of the campus is accessible. Wheelchair ramps, elevators, special parking, specially equipped rest rooms, special class scheduling, lowered drinking fountains, lowered telephones, and special housing are available.

Services: Counseling and information services are available, as is tutoring in most subjects. There are writing and reading centers, math workshops, and a center to teach students study and time-management skills. Tutors trained in teaching English as a second language are available to help international students.

Campus Safety and Security: Measures include 24-hour foot and vehicle patrol, self-defense education, security escort services, and shuttle buses. There are informal discussions, pamphlets/posters/films, emergency telephones, and lighted pathways/sidewalks.

Programs of Study: RU confers B.A., B.S., B.B.A., B.F.A., B.G.S., B.M., B.S.N., and B.S.W. degrees. Master's degrees are also awarded. Bachelor's degrees are awarded in BIOLOGICAL SCIENCE (biology/biological science and nutrition), BUSINESS (accounting, banking and finance, business administration and management, marketing/retailing/merchandising, and recreation and leisure services), COMMUNICATIONS AND THE ARTS (art, broadcasting, communications, dance, design, English, fine arts, media arts, music, and speech/debate/rhetoric), COMPUTER AND PHYSICAL SCIENCE (chemistry, computer science, geology, information sciences and systems, mathematics, and physical sciences), EDUCATION (art, foreign languages, and physical), HEALTH PROFESSIONS (medical technology, nursing, and speech pathology/audiology), SOCIAL SCIENCE (anthropology, criminal justice, economics, food science, geography, history, interdisciplinary studies, liberal arts/general studies, philosophy, political science/government, psychology, religion, social science, social work, and sociology). Nursing, education, and psychology are the strongest academically. Interdisciplinary studies, criminal justice, and psychology are the largest.

Required: To graduate, students must complete at least 120 credit hours, including 30 to 90 in the major, with a 2.0 GPA. There are general education requirements in English, foreign language, speech, fine arts, philosophy/religion, lab science, math/statistics/computer science, history, psychology, social science, health, and international studies.

Special: RU offers internships, dual majors in any subject, study abroad in 16 countries, a general studies degree, and pass/fail options. On-campus work-study is available. There are 23 national honor societies and a freshman honors program. All departments have honors programs.

Faculty/Classroom: 49% of faculty are male; 51%, female. All teach undergraduates. Graduate students teach 1% of introductory courses. The average class size in an introductory lecture is 34; in a laboratory, 26; and in a regular course, 26.

Admissions: 82% of the 2005-2006 applicants were accepted. The SAT scores for the 2005-2006 freshman class were: Verbal--47% below 500, 41% between 500 and 599, 11% between 600 and 700, and 1% above 700; Math--47% below 500, 42% between 500 and 599, 10% between 600 and 700, and 1% above 700. The ACT scores were 57% below 21, 28% between 21 and 23, 11% between 24 and 26, and 4% between 27 and 28. 15% of the current freshmen were in the top fifth of their class; 50% were in the top two fifths.

Requirements: The SAT or ACT is required. In addition, most successful applicants have taken 4 units each of English, preparatory math, and social sciences, including American history, and 3 or 4 units each in laboratory sciences and foreign language. The GED is accepted. A GPA of 2.0 is required. AP and CLEP credits are accepted. Important factors in the admissions decision are extracurricular activities record, evidence of special talent, and advanced placement or honor courses.

Procedure: Freshmen are admitted fall, spring, and summer. Entrance exams should be taken between April of the junior year and December of the senior year. There are early action and deferred admissions plans. Early action applications should be filed by December 15; regular applications, by February 1 for fall entry, along with a $35 fee. Notification of early action is sent in early January; regular decision, in mid-March. Applications are accepted on-line.

Transfer: 746 transfer students enrolled in 2004-2005. Applicants must have a minimum GPA of 2.0 for consideration. Those with fewer than 30 semester hours of college work must submit their high school record. 30 of 120 credits required for the bachelor's degree must be completed at RU.

Visiting: There are regularly scheduled orientations for prospective students, consisting of open houses in the fall, information sessions and tours Monday through Friday, and Admitted Student Days in the spring. There are guides for informal visits and visitors may sit in on classes. To schedule a visit, contact the Office of Admissions.

Financial Aid: In 2005-2006, 64% of all full-time freshmen and 61% of continuing full-time students received some form of financial aid. 34% of full-time freshmen and 37% of continuing full-time students received need-based aid. The average freshman award was $8215. Need-based scholarships or need-based grants averaged $4869 ($10,350 maximum); need-based self-help aid (loans and jobs) averaged $2918; non-need-based athletic scholarships averaged $5795 ($18,908 maximum); and other non-need-based awards and non-need-based scholarships averaged $5108. 15% of undergraduates work part time. Average annual earnings from campus work are $1441. The average financial indebtedness of the 2005 graduate was $14,702. The FAFSA is required. The deadline for filing freshman financial aid applications for fall entry is March 1.

International Students: There are 82 international students enrolled. The school actively recruits these students. They must achieve a satisfactory score on the TOEFL.

Computers: RU has a ubiquitous wireless network allowing users with mobile computers to establish wireless connections from anywhere on campus. Each residence hall room includes 2 Ethernet connects for high-speed access. In addition to wireless and network connections, RU maintains 550 PCs in labs and public areas across campus for student use. All students may access the system. There are no time limits and no fees.

Graduates: From July 1, 2004 to June 30, 2005, 1795 bachelor's degrees were awarded. The most popular majors were interdisciplinary studies (11%), criminal justice (8%), and marketing management (7%). In an average class, 37% graduate in 4 years or less, 54% graduate in 5 years or less, and 57% graduate in 6 years or less. 500 companies recruited on campus in 2004-2005.

Admissions Contact: David W. Kraus, Director of Admissions. A video is available. E-mail: *ruadmiss@radford.edu* Web: *www.radford.edu*

RANDOLPH-MACON COLLEGE   D-3
Ashland, VA 23005

(804) 752-7305
(800) 888-1762; Fax: (804) 752-4707

Full-time: 541 men, 561 women	**Faculty:** 88; IIB, av$
Part-time: 9 men, 14 women	**Ph.D.s:** 93%
Graduate: none	**Student/Faculty:** 13 to 1
Year: 4-1-4, summer session	**Tuition:** $23,945
Application Deadline: March 1	**Room & Board:** $7305
Freshman Class: 1727 applied, 1357 accepted, 305 enrolled	
SAT Verbal/Math: 560/550*	**COMPETITIVE**

Randolph-Macon College, established in 1830, is a private liberal arts college historically affiliated with the United Methodist Church. In addition to regional accreditation, Randolph-Macon has baccalaureate program accreditation with ACS. The library contains 182,368 volumes, 209,300 microform items, and 5116 audio/video tapes/CDs/DVDs, and subscribes to 1455 periodicals including electronic. Computerized library services include the card catalog, interlibrary loans, database searching, and Internet access. Special learning facilities include a learning resource center, art gallery, radio station, TV station, an observatory, a radio telescope, a darkroom, and a greenhouse. The 115-acre campus is in a suburban area 15 miles north of Richmond. Including any residence halls, there are 65 buildings.

Student Life: 68% of undergraduates are from Virginia. Others are from 32 states, 19 foreign countries, and Canada. 70% are from public schools. 89% are white. 54% are Protestant; 17% Catholic; 7% claim no religious affiliation. The average age of freshmen is 18; all undergraduates, 20. 22% do not continue beyond their first year; 70% remain to graduate.

Housing: 1005 students can be accommodated in college housing, which includes single-sex and coed dorms, on-campus apartments, fraternity houses, and sorority houses. In addition, there are honors houses, language houses, special-interest houses, senior apartments, and several college-owned houses. On-campus housing is guaranteed for all 4 years. 89% of students live on campus; of those, 75% remain on campus on weekends. All students may keep cars.

Activities: 33% of men belong to 6 national fraternities; 33% of women belong to 4 national sororities. There are 104 groups on campus, including art, cheerleading, chess, choir, chorale, chorus, computers, dance, debate, drama, environmental, ethnic, film, honors, international, jazz band, literary magazine, musical theater, newspaper, outdoors, pep band, photography, political, professional, radio and TV, religious, social, social service, student government, and yearbook. Popular campus events include Springfest, cultural arts series, and Dance Marathon.

Sports: There are 7 intercollegiate sports for men and 8 for women, and 12 intramural sports for men and 12 for women. Facilities include 10 tennis courts, several playing fields for men's and women's sports, 2 gyms, an indoor track, an indoor pool, a football field, a weight room, and an exercise room. A sports and recreation center includes racquetball and squash courts, a 25-meter pool, a weight room, an aerobics room, a 3-lane track, a multipurpose gym, and a climbing wall.

Disabled Students: 50% of the campus is accessible. Wheelchair ramps, elevators, special parking, specially equipped rest rooms, special class scheduling, and advisers for learning-disabled students are available.

Services: Counseling and information services are available, as is tutoring in every subject. There is a reader service for the blind, and remedial math, reading, and writing.

Campus Safety and Security: Measures include 24-hour foot and vehicle patrol, self-defense education, security escort services, and informal discussions. There are pamphlets/posters/films, emergency telephones, and lighted pathways/sidewalks.

Programs of Study: Randolph-Macon confers B.A. and B.S. degrees. Bachelor's degrees are awarded in AGRICULTURE (environmental studies), BIOLOGICAL SCIENCE (biology/biological science), BUSINESS (accounting and business economics), COMMUNICATIONS AND THE ARTS (art history and appreciation, arts administration/management, classics, dramatic arts, English, French, German, Greek, Latin, music, Spanish, and studio art), COMPUTER AND PHYSICAL SCIENCE (chemistry, computer science, mathematics, and physics), SOCIAL SCIENCE (economics, history, international relations, international studies, philosophy, political science/government, psychology, religion, sociology, and women's studies). Biological and physical sciences, psychology, and political science are the strongest academically. Economics/business, psychology, and sociology are the largest.

Required: To graduate, students must complete 112 credit hours, with 30 to 42 hours in the major and a minimum GPA of 2.0. All students must take 2 courses each in math, social science, lab science, literature, philosophy/theology, and phys ed, 1 course in fine arts, and enough foreign language to demonstrate proficiency. Specific courses required are English composition and European history. There is also a computer proficiency and oral communication requirement. All first-year students must complete the First-Year Experience a year-long course team-taught by two professors in different disciplines and a one-semester companion intensive writing course.

Special: The college offers cooperative programs in engineering with Columbia University and the University of Virginia, in forestry with Duke University, and in accounting with Virginia Commonwealth University. There is cross-registration with Hollins, Sweet Briar, Randolph-Macon Woman's College, Hampden-Sydney, Washington and Lee, and Mary Baldwin. Internships, dual majors, and a Washington semester are available. Students in all majors may take part in an accelerated degree program. Study-abroad programs are offered in 12 countries. There are 19 national honor societies, including Phi Beta Kappa, and a freshman honors program.

Faculty/Classroom: 59% of faculty are male; 41%, female. 100% both teach and do research. The average class size in an introductory lecture is 20; in a laboratory, 15; and in a regular course, 15.

Admissions: 79% of the 2005-2006 applicants were accepted. The SAT scores for the 2005-2006 freshman class were: Verbal--20% below 500, 54% between 500 and 599, 23% between 600 and 700, and 3% above 700; Math--21% below 500, 59% between 500 and 599, 18% between 600 and 700, and 2% above 700. 34% of the current freshmen were in the top fifth of their class; 67% were in the top two fifths. There was 1 National Merit semifinalist.

Requirements: The SAT is required. The ACT Optional Writing test is also recommended. In addition, SAT Subject tests are recommended in math and foreign language. Applicants must be graduates of an accredited secondary school. The GED is accepted. Applicants should complete a minimum of 16 high school academic credits, including 4 years of English, 3 to 4 years each of math and science, and 2 to 3 years of foreign language, history, and social studies. An essay is required; an interview is recommended. A GPA of 2.0 is required. AP and CLEP credits are accepted. Important factors in the admissions decision are advanced placement or honor courses, recommendations by school officials, and extracurricular activities record.

Procedure: Freshmen are admitted fall and spring. Entrance exams should be taken by January of the senior year. There are early decision, early action, and deferred admissions plans. Early decision applications should be filed by November 15; early action, by December 1; regular applications, by March 1 for fall entry and January 1 for spring entry. Notification of early decision is sent December 1; early action, January 1; regular decision, April 1. 36 early decision candidates were accepted for the 2005-2006 class. 49 applicants were on the 2005 waiting list; 9 were admitted. Applications are accepted on-line.

Transfer: 28 transfer students enrolled in 2004-2005. Applicants must have a minimum GPA of 2.0 and must be eligible to return to their previous institution. They must submit high school and college transcripts

and SAT scores. At least half of credits for the major must be completed at Randolph-Macon.

Visiting: There are regularly scheduled orientations for prospective students, including interviews, information sessions, tours, open houses, and visitation days. There are guides for informal visits and visitors may sit in on classes and stay overnight. To schedule a visit, contact the Office of Admissions at *admissions@rmc.edu*.

Financial Aid: In 2005-2006, 99% of all full-time freshmen and 93% of continuing full-time students received some form of financial aid. 54% of full-time freshmen and 48% of continuing full-time students received need-based aid. The average freshman award was $20,966. 22% of undergraduates work part time. Average annual earnings from campus work are $1100. The average financial indebtedness of the 2005 graduate was $15,130. The FAFSA is required. The priority date for freshman financial aid applications for fall entry is February 1. The deadline for filing freshman financial aid applications for fall entry is March 1.

International Students: There are 19 international students enrolled. The school actively recruits these students. They must take the TOEFL, the SAT or ACT is recommended but not required.

Computers: There are 350 workstations available to students. Wireless access is available in the library and adjoining quad. All students are connected to the network when they arrive on campus. There are 2 high-speed Internet connections in every dorm room. All students may access the system. Computer labs are open from 8 A.M. to 1 A.M. Wireless access and access in dorm rooms are available at all times. There are no time limits and no fees. It is strongly recommended that all students have a personal computer.

Graduates: From July 1, 2004 to June 30, 2005, 196 bachelor's degrees were awarded. The most popular majors were economics/business (16%), sociology (13%), and psychology (12%). In an average class, 1% graduate in 3 years or less, 65% graduate in 4 years or less, 70% graduate in 5 years or less, and 70% graduate in 6 years or less. 40 companies recruited on campus in 2004-2005. Of the 2004 graduating class, 27% were enrolled in graduate school within 6 months of graduation, and 85% were employed.

Admissions Contact: John C. Conkright, Dean of Admissions and Financial Aid. A video is available. E-mail: *admissions@rmc.edu* Web: *www.rmc.edu*

RANDOLPH-MACON WOMAN'S COLLEGE   D-3
Lynchburg, VA 24503

(434) 947-8100
(800) 745-7692; Fax: (434) 947-8996

Full-time: 700 women	**Faculty:** 77; IIB, +$
Part-time: 5 men, 30 women	**Ph.Ds:** 92%
Graduate: none	**Student/Faculty:** 9 to 1
Year: semesters, summer session	**Tuition:** $22,550
Application Deadline: March 1	**Room & Board:** $8610
Freshman Class: n/av	
SAT or ACT: required	**VERY COMPETITIVE+**

Randolph-Macon Woman's College, founded in 1891, is an independent, liberal arts institution affiliated with the United Methodist Church. Some figures in the above capsule and in this profile are approximate. In addition to regional accreditation, R-MWC has baccalaureate program accreditation with NASDTEC. The library contains 197,332 volumes, 187,000 microform items, and 3600 audio/video tapes/CDs/DVDs, and subscribes to 618 periodicals including electronic. Computerized library services include the card catalog, interlibrary loans, and database searching. Special learning facilities include a learning resource center, art gallery, radio station, an observatory, an art museum, 2 theaters, a 100-acre equestrian center, and 3 nature preserves. The 100-acre campus is in a suburban area in the foothills of the Blue Ridge Mountains, 1 hour south of Charlottesville. Including any residence halls, there are 18 buildings.

Student Life: 59% of undergraduates are from out of state, mostly the South. Students are from 42 states, 46 foreign countries, and Canada. 80% are from public schools. 74% are white; 12% foreign nationals. 69% are Protestant; 19% Catholic; 9% predominantly Muslim, Hindu, Buddhist, and Orthodox. The average age of freshmen is 18; all undergraduates, 20. 20% do not continue beyond their first year; 65% remain to graduate.

Housing: 675 students can be accommodated in college housing, which includes single-sex dorms, a special senior residence hall, and shared housing for Prime Time Students. On-campus housing is guaranteed for all 4 years. 87% of students live on campus; of those, 75% remain on campus on weekends. All students may keep cars.

Activities: There are no sororities. There are 35 groups on campus, including art, chorale, chorus, dance, debate, drama, enviromental, equestrian, ethnic, film, foreign language, gay, honors, international, literary magazine, newspaper, outdoor, pep band, political, professional, radio and TV, religious, social, social service, student government, and yearbook. Popular campus events include Tacky Party and Never-Ending Weekend, Senior Dinner Dance, and Pumpkin Parade.

Sports: Facilities include a gym, an indoor heated swimming pool, dance studios, aerobic and weight rooms, 8 tennis courts, 2 athletic fields, a 100-acre riding center with teaching and amphitheater show rings and indoor and outdoor arenas, and a 900-seat auditorium.

Disabled Students: 50% of the campus is accessible. Wheelchair ramps, elevators, special parking, specially equipped rest rooms, special class scheduling, special housing, a wheelchair lift, and TDY telephone for hearing impaired are available.

Services: Counseling and information services are available, as is tutoring in every subject. There are computing and study skills resources, a writing lab, and a science and math center.

Campus Safety and Security: Measures include 24-hour foot and vehicle patrol, self-defense education, security escort services, and informal discussions. There are pamphlets/posters/films, emergency telephones, and lighted pathways/sidewalks.

Programs of Study: R-MWC confers B.A. and B.S. degrees. Bachelor's degrees are awarded in AGRICULTURE (environmental studies), BIOLOGICAL SCIENCE (biology/biological science), COMMUNICATIONS AND THE ARTS (art, classics, communications, dance, dramatic arts, English, French, German, music, and Spanish), COMPUTER AND PHYSICAL SCIENCE (chemistry, mathematics, and physics), HEALTH PROFESSIONS (health science), SOCIAL SCIENCE (American studies, economics, history, international relations, philosophy, political science/government, psychology, religion, Russian and Slavic studies, and sociology). Psychology, biology, and English are the largest.

Required: To graduate, all students must complete at least 124 credit hours with a minimum GPA of 2.0. Students must satisfy the requirements for the general education and major programs and must have a minimum GPA of 2.0 in the major.

Special: R-MWC offers a junior year spring semester American Culture Program, as well as study abroad in 11 countries. A Washington semester at American University is available, as is the Tri-College Consortium with Sweet Briar and Lynchburg Colleges, and the Seven-College Exchange Program with Hampden-Sydney, Hollins, Mary Baldwin, Randolph-Macon, and Sweet Briar Colleges, and Washington and Lee University. There is a 3-2 nursing program with Johns Hopkins University and a 3-2 engineering degree with several institutions. There are 9 national honor societies, including Phi Beta Kappa.

Faculty/Classroom: 47% of faculty are male; 53%, female. All teach undergraduates and 58% both teach and do research. The average class size in an introductory lecture is 18; in a laboratory, 13; and in a regular course, 13.

Admissions: There was 1 National Merit semifinalist in a recent year. 4 freshmen graduated first in their class.

Requirements: The SAT or ACT is required. In addition, applicants must be graduates of an accredited secondary school with at least 16 academic credits, including 4 units in English, 3 to 4 in a foreign language, 3 in math, 2 in biology, chemistry, or physics with lab work, and 1 to 2 in electives from other academic study. An interview is strongly recommended. AP and CLEP credits are accepted. Important factors in the admissions decision are advanced placement or honor courses, recommendations by school officials, and leadership record.

Procedure: Freshmen are admitted fall and spring. Entrance exams should be taken in the junior or senior year. There is a rolling admissions plan. There are early decision and deferred admissions plans. Early decision applications should be filed by November 15; regular applications, by March 1 for fall entry and December 1 for spring entry, along with a $35 fee. Notification of early decision is sent December 15; regular decision, on a rolling basis. 16 early decision candidates were accepted for a recent class. Applications are accepted on-line.

Transfer: 41 transfer students enrolled in a recent year. Transfer students must submit college and high school transcripts, 2 letters of recommendation, a copy of their current college's catalog, and SAT or ACT scores. An interview is recommended. Seniors may not transfer in. Courses within a liberal arts curriculum will be considered for transfer credit if grades are at least in the C range. 62 of 124 credits required for the bachelor's degree must be completed at R-MWC.

Visiting: There are regularly scheduled orientations for prospective students, including a campus tour, student panels, faculty panels, class visits, and individual sessions with admissions and financial planning counselors. There are guides for informal visits and visitors may sit in on classes and stay overnight. To schedule a visit, contact the Admissions Office.

Financial Aid: In a recent year, 99% of all full-time students received some form of financial aid. 70% of full-time freshmen and 66% of continuing full-time students received need-based aid. The average freshman award was $19,845. Need-based scholarships or need-based grants averaged $15,490 ($20,690 maximum); need-based self-help aid (loans and jobs) averaged $4118 ($9860 maximum); and other non-need-based awards and non-need-based scholarships averaged $14,470 ($15,710 maximum). 64% of undergraduates work part time. Average annual earnings from campus work are $981. The average financial indebtedness of a recent year's graduate was $21,992. The FAFSA and the state aid form are required. The priority date for freshman financial aid applications for fall entry is March 1.

International Students: There were 84 international students enrolled in a recent year. The school actively recruits these students. A satisfactory score on the TOEFL is required.

Computers: All students may access the system. There are no time limits and no fees.

Graduates: In a recent year, 159 bachelor's degrees were awarded. The most popular majors were biology (15%), psychology (12%), and English (11%). In an average class, 2% graduate in 3 years or less, 61% graduate in 4 years or less, 63% graduate in 5 years or less, and 63% graduate in 6 years or less. 102 companies recruited on campus in a recent year. Of a recent graduating class, 35% were enrolled in graduate school within 6 months of graduation and 60% were employed.

Admissions Contact: Patricia N. LeDonne, Director of Admissions. A video is available. E-mail: *admissions@rmwc.edu* Web: *www.rmwc.edu*

ROANOKE COLLEGE   C-3

Salem, VA 24153   (540) 375-2270
(800) 388-2276; Fax: (540) 375-2267

Full-time: 798 men, 1035 women	Faculty: 133; IIB, av$
Part-time: 51 men, 52 women	Ph.D.s: 87%
Graduate: none	Student/Faculty: 14 to 1
Year: semesters, summer session	Tuition: $23,453
Application Deadline: March 15	Room & Board: $7295
Freshman Class: 3016 applied, 2220 accepted, 534 enrolled	
SAT Verbal/Math: 560/550*	VERY COMPETITIVE

Roanoke College, founded in 1842, is a private institution affiliated with the Evangelical Lutheran Church in America. The college offers undergraduate programs in the arts and sciences and business administration. In addition to regional accreditation, Roanoke has baccalaureate program accreditation with ACBSP. The library contains 215,021 volumes, 336,765 microform items, and 5373 audio/video tapes/CDs/DVDs, and subscribes to 3791 periodicals including electronic. Computerized library services include the card catalog, interlibrary loans, database searching, Internet access, and laptop Internet portals. Special learning facilities include a learning resource center, art gallery, radio station, media classrooms, TV production facility, and multimedia computer labs. The 70-acre campus is in a suburban area 5 miles west of Roanoke. Including any residence halls, there are 40 buildings.

Student Life: 59% of undergraduates are from Virginia. Students are from 38 states, 26 foreign countries, and Canada. 79% are from public schools. 91% are white. 61% are Protestant; 18% Catholic; 9% claim no religious affiliation. The average age of freshmen is 18; all undergraduates, 20. 15% do not continue beyond their first year; 65% remain to graduate.

Housing: 1314 students can be accommodated in college housing, which includes single-sex and coed dorms, on-campus apartments, off-campus apartments, fraternity houses, and sorority houses. In addition, there are honors houses, special-interest houses and freshman residence halls. On-campus housing is guaranteed for all 4 years. 65% of students live on campus. All students may keep cars.

Activities: 15% of men belong to 4 national fraternities; 22% of women belong to 4 national sororities. There are 84 groups on campus, including art, cheerleading, chess, choir, chorale, chorus, computers, dance, debate, drama, ethnic, gay, honors, international, jazz band, literary magazine, musical theater, newspaper, pep band, photography, political, professional, radio and TV, religious, social, social service, and student government. Popular campus events include Family Weekend, Alumni Weekend, and WinterFest.

Sports: There are 9 intercollegiate sports for men and 10 for women, and 9 intramural sports for men and 9 for women. Facilities include a 2400-seat gym, a 400-seat arena, athletic fields, an all-weather track, practice and playing fields, tennis and racquetball courts, a swimming pool, and a fitness center with weight training and physical conditioning equipment.

Disabled Students: 80% of the campus is accessible. Wheelchair ramps, elevators, special parking, specially equipped rest rooms, special class scheduling, and lowered drinking fountains are available.

Services: Counseling and information services are available, as is tutoring in every subject. A supervised peer tutoring program is available at no charge to students.

Campus Safety and Security: Measures include 24-hour foot and vehicle patrol, self-defense education, security escort services, and informal discussions. There are pamphlets/posters/films, emergency telephones, and lighted pathways/sidewalks.

Programs of Study: Roanoke confers B.A., B.S., and B.B.A. degrees. Bachelor's degrees are awarded in AGRICULTURE (environmental studies), BIOLOGICAL SCIENCE (biochemistry and biology/biological science), BUSINESS (business administration and management), COMMUNICATIONS AND THE ARTS (art, dramatic arts, English, French, music, and Spanish), COMPUTER AND PHYSICAL SCIENCE (chemistry, computer science, information sciences and systems, mathematics, and physics), EDUCATION (athletic training and physical), ENGINEER-

ING AND ENVIRONMENTAL DESIGN (environmental science), HEALTH PROFESSIONS (medical technology), SOCIAL SCIENCE (criminal justice, economics, history, international relations, philosophy, political science/government, psychology, religion, sociology, and theological studies). Computer science, biology, and chemistry are the strongest academically. Business, psychology, and English are the largest.

Required: Requirements for graduation include completion of 34 courses, including about 12 in the major. Specific course requirements include 2 courses each in math, lab science, social science, and phys ed, as well as a 2-course sequence in humanities, a freshman-year writing course, a values course, and a senior symposium. All students must attain a 2.0 GPA and be able to demonstrate competency in a foreign language. An intensive learning course and a cocurricular learning and service experience are also required.

Special: There is cross-registration with Hollins University and study abroad in more than 100 countries. Roanoke also offers internships, a Washington semester, the Virginia at Oxford Program, a 3-2 engineering degree with Virginia Polytechnic Institute and State University, Washington University in St. Louis, and University of Tennessee at Knoxville, credit by exam, and pass/fail options. Nondegree study is available to those students admitted with special status. There are 20 national honor societies, including Phi Beta Kappa, a freshman honors program, and 13 departmental honors programs.

Faculty/Classroom: 53% of faculty are male; 47%, female. All teach undergraduates and 60% both teach and do research. The average class size in an introductory lecture is 22; in a laboratory, 18; and in a regular course, 18.

Admissions: 74% of the 2005-2006 applicants were accepted. The SAT scores for the 2005-2006 freshman class were: Verbal--15% below 500, 54% between 500 and 599, 27% between 600 and 700, and 4% above 700; Math--20% below 500, 51% between 500 and 599, 27% between 600 and 700, and 2% above 700. 43% of the current freshmen were in the top fifth of their class; 66% were in the top two fifths. 14 freshmen graduated first in their class.

Requirements: The SAT or ACT is required, but the SAT is preferred. SAT Subject tests, an essay, and an interview are recommended. Applicants must be graduates of accredited secondary schools or have earned a GED. The college requires 18 academic units, based on 4 years of English, 4 courses in foreign language, 3 courses in math, and 2 courses each in lab science and social studies. An audition is also recommended for performing arts majors. AP and CLEP credits are accepted. Important factors in the admissions decision are advanced placement or honor courses, evidence of special talent, and leadership record.

Procedure: Freshmen are admitted fall and spring. Entrance exams should be taken by January of the senior year. There is a deferred admissions plan. Applications should be filed by March 15 for fall entry, along with a $30 fee. Notification is sent April 1. 114 early decision candidates were accepted for the 2005-2006 class. 172 applicants were on the 2005 waiting list; 3 were admitted. Applications are accepted on-line.

Transfer: 80 transfer students enrolled in 2004-2005. Transfers must have a minimum GPA of 2.2. SAT scores and an interview are recommended. 16 of 34 courses required for the bachelor's degree must be completed at Roanoke.

Visiting: There are regularly scheduled orientations for prospective students, consisting of open houses that provide a sampling of college life at Roanoke. There are guides for informal visits and visitors may sit in on classes and stay overnight. To schedule a visit, contact the Admissions Office at admissions@roanoke.edu.

Financial Aid: In 2005-2006, 95% of all full-time freshmen and 96% of continuing full-time students received some form of financial aid. 74% of full-time freshmen and 73% of continuing full-time students received need-based aid. The average freshman award was $17,375. Need-based scholarships or need-based grants averaged $16,416 ($26,460 maximum); need-based self-help aid (loans and jobs) averaged $4133 ($5625 maximum); and other non-need-based awards and non-need-based scholarships averaged $9150 ($30,143 maximum). 30% of undergraduates work part time. Average annual earnings from campus work are $1300. The average financial indebtedness of the 2005 graduate was $18,543. The FAFSA is required. The deadline for filing freshman financial aid applications for fall entry is March 1.

International Students: There are 34 international students enrolled. The school actively recruits these students. They must take the TOEFL.

Computers: Wireless access is available. Students may access the network from PCs in dorm rooms, from about 175 PCs in labs around campus, and via wireless locations in classrooms and numerous other locations. All students may access the system any time. There are no time limits and no fees.

Graduates: From July 1, 2004 to June 30, 2005, 402 bachelor's degrees were awarded. The most popular majors were business administration (22%), English (12%), and history (11%). In an average class, 2% graduate in 3 years or less, 55% graduate in 4 years or less, 60% graduate in 5 years or less, and 65% graduate in 6 years or less. 70 companies recruited on campus in 2004-2005. Of the 2004 graduating class, 20%

were enrolled in graduate school within 6 months of graduation and 96% were employed.

Admissions Contact: Michael Maxey, Vice President of Admissions. A video is available. E-mail: admissions@roanoke.edu Web: www.roanoke.edu

SAINT PAUL'S COLLEGE
E-4

Lawrenceville, VA 23868
(434) 848-6492
(800) 678-7071; Fax: (434) 848-1862

Full-time: 330 men, 310 women	**Faculty:** 33; IIB, --$
Part-time: 10 men, 40 women	**Ph.D.s:** 59%
Graduate: none	**Student/Faculty:** 20 to 1
Year: semesters, summer session	**Tuition:** $10,500
Application Deadline: open	**Room & Board:** $5530
Freshman Class: n/av	
SAT: required	**NONCOMPETITIVE**

Saint Paul's College, founded in 1888, is a small, private liberal arts college affiliated with the Protestant Episcopal Church, offering undergraduate programs in arts and sciences, business, and teacher education. Some figures in the above capsule and in this profile are approximate. The library contains 41,500 volumes, 29,000 microform items, and 914 audio/video tapes/CDs/DVDs, and subscribes to 167 periodicals including electronic. Computerized library services include the card catalog, interlibrary loans, database searching, and Internet access. Special learning facilities include a learning resource center. The 180-acre campus is in a small town 55 miles south of Petersburg and 80 miles South of Richmond. Including any residence halls, there are 34 buildings.

Student Life: 67% of undergraduates are from Virginia. Students are from 19 states and 6 foreign countries. 99% are from public schools. 96% are African American. 90% are Protestant; 6% claim no religious affiliation. The average age of freshmen is 19; all undergraduates, 21. 45% do not continue beyond their first year; 55% remain to graduate.

Housing: 431 students can be accommodated in college housing, which includes single-sex dorms. In addition, there are special-interest houses and single-parent housing. On-campus housing is guaranteed for the freshman year only and is available on a lottery system for upperclassmen. 62% of students live on campus; of those, 52% remain on campus on weekends. Alcohol is not permitted. All students may keep cars.

Activities: 7% of men belong to 5 national fraternities; 5% of women belong to 3 national sororities. There are 22 groups on campus, including art, cheerleading, chess, choir, dance, drama, ethnic, honors, pep band, political, religious, social service, student government, Students in Free Enterprise, and Virginia Highway Safety Project. Popular campus events include a lecture and concert series, College for a Day, and Founders Day.

Sports: There are 7 intercollegiate sports for men and 7 for women, and 2 intramural sports for men and 2 for women. Facilities include a gym, baseball and football fields, practice fields, and tennis courts.

Disabled Students: 30% of the campus is accessible. Wheelchair ramps, elevators, special parking, specially equipped rest rooms, and lowered drinking fountains are available.

Services: Counseling and information services are available, as is tutoring in most subjects. There is remedial math, reading, and writing.

Campus Safety and Security: Measures include 24-hour foot and vehicle patrol, self-defense education, security escort services, and shuttle buses. There are informal discussions, pamphlets/posters/films, emergency telephones, and lighted pathways/sidewalks.

Programs of Study: SPC confers B.A., B.S., and B.S.Ed. degrees. Bachelor's degrees are awarded in BIOLOGICAL SCIENCE (biology/biological science, marine biology, and marine science), BUSINESS (business administration and management), COMMUNICATIONS AND THE ARTS (English), COMPUTER AND PHYSICAL SCIENCE (mathematics), EDUCATION (business, elementary, and secondary), ENGINEERING AND ENVIRONMENTAL DESIGN (environmental science), SOCIAL SCIENCE (law enforcement and corrections, political science/government, social science, and sociology). Organizational management is the strongest academically. Business administration is the largest.

Required: All students must complete 42 semester hours of general education requirements, including courses in humanities, natural science and math, social sciences, health and phys ed, and computer information systems. A minimum of 120 hours, including at least 30 in the major, with at least a 2.0 GPA is required to graduate. Students in the Organizational Management Program (OMP) are required to write a thesis. All students must take PRAXIS for teacher certification.

Special: Cross-registration is possible with members of the Southside Higher Education Consortium and with Richard Bland College and Parkland College. Minors and the B.A.-B.S. degree are offered in most disciplines. Nonmajor preprofessional programs are available in the health professions. Endorsements in early childhood, middle, and secondary education are available in appropriate majors. Co-op programs in aquatic science and environmentive science, a general studies degree, and work-study programs are available. Nondegree study is possible.

There are 2 national honor societies, a freshman honors program, and 3 departmental honors programs.

Faculty/Classroom: 62% of faculty are male; 38%, female. All teach undergraduates and 6% both teach and do research. The average class size in an introductory lecture is 15; in a laboratory, 8; and in a regular course, 10.

Requirements: The SAT is required. In addition, applicants should be graduates of an accredited secondary school and have completed 16 academic units, including English, math, science, and social sciences. A GPA of 2.0 is required. AP and CLEP credits are accepted. Important factors in the admissions decision are recommendations by school officials, leadership record, and evidence of special talent.

Procedure: Freshmen are admitted fall and spring. Entrance exams should be taken during the senior year of high school. There is a rolling admissions plan. There are early decision and early admissions plans. Application deadlines are open. The application Fee is $20.

Transfer: Transfer applicants must supply all former official high school and college transcripts as well as a background form completed by the former college. 30 of 120 credits required for the bachelor's degree must be completed at SPC.

Visiting: There are regularly scheduled orientations for prospective students, including Homecoming, Open House, College for a Day, Honors Convocation, and Pre-Orientation. There are guides for informal visits and visitors may sit in on classes and stay overnight. To schedule a visit, contact the Vice President for Student Affairs at (434) 848-6456 or *admissions@saintpauls.edu.*

Financial Aid: In a recent year, 98% of all full-time freshmen and 93% of continuing full-time students received some form of financial aid. 80% of full-time freshmen and 75% of continuing full-time students received need-based aid. The average freshman award was $8386. 45% of undergraduates work part time. Average annual earnings from campus work are $2000. The average financial indebtedness of a recent year's graduate was $12,695. SPC is a member of CSS. The FAFSA and the state aid form are required. Check with the school for current deadlines.

International Students: There were 10 international students enrolled in a recent year. They must take the TOEFL as well as the SAT or ACT.

Computers: All students may access the system Monday through Friday from 3 A.M. to 6 P.M. There are no time limits. The fee is $140. It is strongly recommended that all students have a personal computer.

Graduates: In a recent year, 102 bachelor's degrees were awarded. The most popular majors were business administration (67%), criminal justice (11%), and sociology and social sciences (9%). In an average class, 13% graduate in 4 years or less, 25% graduate in 5 years or less, and 28% graduate in 6 years or less. 26 companies recruited on campus in a recent year. Of a recent graduating class, 14% were enrolled in graduate school within 6 months of graduation.

Admissions Contact: Director of Admissions.
E-mail: *admissions@saintpauls.edu* Web: *www.saintpauls.edu*

SHENANDOAH UNIVERSITY — D-1
Winchester, VA 22601
(540) 665-4581
(800) 432-2266; Fax: (540) 665-4627

Full-time: 616 men, 914 women	Faculty: 124
Part-time: 29 men, 47 women	Ph.D.s: 80%
Graduate: 448 men, 944 women	Student/Faculty: 12 to 1
Year: semesters, summer session	Tuition: $20,050
Application Deadline: open	Room & Board: $7550
Freshman Class: 1480 applied, 1037 accepted, 372 enrolled	
SAT Verbal/Math: 515/513*	ACT: 20 COMPETITIVE

Shenandoah University, founded in 1875, is a private university, affiliated with the United Methodist Church and offering programs in arts and sciences, nursing and health professions, business, music, theater, and dance. There are 4 undergraduate and 6 graduate schools. In addition to regional accreditation, Shenandoah, SU has baccalaureate program accreditation with ACPE, APTA, NASM, and NLN. The 2 libraries contain 127,164 volumes, 134,649 microform items, and 18,513 audio/video tapes/CDs/DVDs, and subscribe to 16,508 periodicals including electronic. Computerized library services include the card catalog, interlibrary loans, database searching, and Internet access. Special learning facilities include a learning resource center, radio station, and TV station. The 100-acre campus is in a small town 72 miles west of Washington, D.C. Including any residence halls, there are 23 buildings.

Student Life: 57% of undergraduates are from Virginia. Others are from 47 states, 45 foreign countries, and Canada. 91% are white. 42% claim no religious affiliation; 35% Protestant; 16% Catholic. The average age of freshmen is 21; all undergraduates, 23. 25% do not continue beyond their first year; 42% remain to graduate.

Housing: 795 students can be accommodated in college housing, which includes coed dormitories. In addition, there are honors houses, special-interest houses and a nonalcohol residence hall. On-campus housing is guaranteed for all 4 years. 55% of students commute. All students may keep cars.

Activities: 2% of men and about 1% of women belong to 7 national fraternities; 1% of women belong to 1 national sorority. There are 49 groups on campus, including band, cheerleading, chess, choir, chorale, chorus, dance, drama, drum and bugle corps, ethnic, gay, honors, international, jazz band, musical theater, newspaper, opera, orchestra, political, professional, radio and TV, religious, social service, student government, and symphony. Popular campus events include conservatory productions, International Days, and Sun Block Party.

Sports: There are 8 intercollegiate sports for men and 8 for women, and 12 intramural sports for men and 12 for women. Facilities include a soccer field, a gym with basketball and volleyball courts, 2 weight rooms, a fitness room, a track, lacrosse, field hockey and softball fields, and a football stadium.

Disabled Students: 91% of the campus is accessible. Wheelchair ramps, elevators, special parking, specially equipped rest rooms, special class scheduling, lowered drinking fountains, and electric doors are available.

Services: Counseling and information services are available, as is tutoring in every subject. There is a reader service for the blind and remedial math.

Campus Safety and Security: Measures include 24-hour foot and vehicle patrol, security escort services, informal discussions, and pamphlets/posters/films. There are emergency telephones and lighted pathways/sidewalks.

Programs of Study: Shenandoah, SU confers B.A., B.S., B.B.A., B.F.A, B.M., and B.M.T. degrees. Associate, master's, and doctoral degrees are also awarded. Bachelor's degrees are awarded in BIOLOGICAL SCIENCE (biology/biological science), BUSINESS (business administration and management), COMMUNICATIONS AND THE ARTS (applied art, arts administration/management, communications, dance, design, dramatic arts, English, jazz, music, music performance, music theory and composition, musical theater, performing arts, piano/organ, Spanish, and theater design), COMPUTER AND PHYSICAL SCIENCE (chemistry and mathematics), EDUCATION (dance, music, and psychology), ENGINEERING AND ENVIRONMENTAL DESIGN (environmental science), HEALTH PROFESSIONS (music therapy, nursing, and respiratory therapy), SOCIAL SCIENCE (history, liberal arts/general studies, physical fitness/movement, political science/government, psychology, public administration, religion, religious music, and sociology). Psychology, and history are the strongest academically. Phramacy, nursing, and music are the largest.

Required: To graduate, all students must have taken the required core curriculum including 1 religion/philosophy course, 2 phys ed courses and 1 computer literacy course. Students must complete at least 120 credit hours with a minimum 2.0 GPA. Other requirements vary depending on the program of study.

Special: Internships, dual majors, a B.A./B.S. in university studies, and work-study programs are available. Nondegree study is possible. There are 2 national honor societies, a freshman honors program, and 1 departmental honors program.

Faculty/Classroom: 45% of faculty are male; 55%, female. 79% teach undergraduates. Graduate students teach 1% of introductory courses. The average class size in an introductory lecture is 18; in a laboratory, 12; and in a regular course, 13.

Admissions: 70% of the 2005-2006 applicants were accepted. The SAT scores for the 2005-2006 freshman class were: Verbal--46% below 500, 31% between 500 and 599, 20% between 600 and 700, above 700; Math--45% below 500, 35% between 500 and 599, between 600 and 700, and 1% above 700. The ACT scores were low 21, 17% between 21 and 23, 20% between 24 and 26, 27 and 28, and 2% above 28.

Requirements: The SAT or ACT is required. Applicants ates of an accredited secondary school. The GED is ac should complete 15 high school academic credits, in English, 3 years of math, and 2 years each of foreign and social studies. A minimum GPA of 2.5 is required for music, theater, and dance. A GPA of 2 CLEP credits are accepted. Important factors in the de are evidence of special talent, advanced place and personality/intangible qualities.

Procedure: Freshmen are admitted fall an should be taken by junior year or early in th ferred admissions and a rolling admission are open. Application fee is $30. 3 applic list. Applications are accepted on-line.

Transfer: 188 transfer students enroll cants must have a GPA of 2.0. An au and theater. Official transcripts from work must be submitted in addition applicant has been out of school required for the bachelor's degre SU.

Visiting: There are regularly s dents, including information sess guided campus tours. There are guides for informal visits and visitors may sit in on classes and stay overnight. To schedule a visit, contact the Admissions Office at 800-432-2266 or admit@su.edu.

Financial Aid: In a recent year 91% of all full-time freshmen and 80% of continuing full-time students received some form of financial aid. 61% of full-time freshmen and 60% of continuing full-time students received need-based aid. The average freshman award for 2005-2006 was $13,500. Need-based scholarships or need-based grants averaged $3311 ($7956 maximum); need-based self-help aid (loans and jobs) averaged $5089 ($7410 maximum); and other non-need-based awards and non-need-based scholarships averaged $5349 ($16,000 maximum). 36% of undergraduates work part time. Average annual earnings from campus work are $841. The average financial indebtedness of the 2005 graduate was $18,588. Shenandoah, SU is a member of CSS. The FAFSA and the state aid form are required. The priority date for freshman financial aid applications for fall entry is March 1. The deadline for filing freshman financial aid applications for fall entry is June 30.

International Students: There are 75 international students enrolled. The school actively recruits these students. They must score satisfactorily on the written TOEFL.

Computers: Wireless access is available. All students may access the system during scheduled hours. There are no time limits and no fees. It is recommended that students in nursing and pharmacy have personal computers. An IBM is recommended.

Graduates: From July 1, 2004 to June 30, 2005, 268 bachelor's degrees were awarded. The most popular majors were music (25%), business administration (16%), and music theater (theater arts) (13%). In an average class, 28% graduate in 4 years or less, 41% graduate in 5 years or less, and 46% graduate in 6 years or less. 100 companies recruited on campus in 2004-2005. Of the 2004 graduating class, 33% were enrolled in graduate school within 6 months of graduation and 71% were employed.

Admissions Contact: David Anthony, Dean of Admissions.
E-mail: admit@su.edu Web: http://www.su.edu

SWEET BRIAR COLLEGE   D-3
Sweet Briar, VA 24595

(434) 381-6142
(800) 381-6142; Fax: (434) 381-6152

Full-time: 29 men, 674 women	Faculty: 67; IIB, av$
Part-time: 4 men, 32 women	Ph.D.s: 100%
Graduate: 3 men, 10 women	Student/Faculty: 10 to 1
Year: semesters	Tuition: $22,430
Application Deadline: February 1	Room & Board: $9030
Freshman Class: 623 applied, 495 accepted, 182 enrolled	
SAT Verbal/Math: 570/550*	ACT: 24 VERY COMPETITIVE

Sweet Briar College, founded in 1901, is a private women's liberal arts institution. The 3 libraries contain 284,748 volumes, more than 451,000 microform items, and 11,716 audio/video tapes/CDs/DVDs, and subscribe to 28,787 periodicals including electronic. Computerized library services include the card catalog, interlibrary loans, database searching, Internet access, and laptop Internet portals. Special learning facilities include a learning resource center, art gallery, radio station, TV station, college museum, observatory, Center for Civic Renewal, and environmental education/nature center. The 3250-acre campus is in a rural area 165 miles southwest of Washington, D.C., 120 miles west of Richmond, 12 miles north of Lynchburg. Including any residence halls, there are 34 buildings.

Student Life: 62% of undergraduates are from out of state, mostly the South. Students are from 42 states, 16 foreign countries, and Canada. 3% are from public schools. 83% are white. 25% do not continue beyond their first year; 67% remain to graduate.

Housing: 551 students can be accommodated in college housing, includes single-sex dormitories, substance-free, and first-year [housing]. On-campus housing is guaranteed for all 4 years. 90% of students live on campus; of those, 75% remain on campus on weekends. Students may keep cars.

There are no fraternities. There are 51 groups on campus, cheerleading, chemistry, choir, chorus, computers, dance, environmental, ethnic, film, gay, health-related, honors, international, magazine, musical theater, National Organization for Women, newspaper, orchestra, outdoor, photography, political, professional, radio, TV, religious, riding clubs, social, social service, student symphony, and yearbook. Popular campus events include parties, and Founders Day.

Disabled facilities include a natatorium, a gym, a Nautilus center, a rampway and trail system for walking, biking, and a riding, drinking center, soccer/lacrosse/field hockey fields, campgrounds, and 2 lakes.

Services: ing in m% of the campus is accessible. Wheelchair parking, specially equipped rest rooms, lowered red telephones are available.

formation services are available, as is tutor-

Campus Safety and Security: Measures include 24-hour foot and vehicle patrol, self-defense education, security escort services, and shuttle buses. There are informal discussions, pamphlets/posters/films, emergency telephones, lighted pathways/sidewalks, gates manned by security personnel from 6 P.M. to 6 A.M., and locked dorms with student key access.

Programs of Study: Sweet Briar confers B.A., B.S., and B.F.A. degrees. Master's degrees are also awarded. Bachelor's degrees are awarded in AGRICULTURE (environmental studies), BIOLOGICAL SCIENCE (biochemistry, biology/biological science, and molecular biology), BUSINESS (business administration and management), COMMUNICATIONS AND THE ARTS (art history and appreciation, creative writing, dance, dramatic arts, English, French, German, modern language, music, Spanish, and studio art), COMPUTER AND PHYSICAL SCIENCE (chemistry, computer science, mathematics, and physics), ENGINEERING AND ENVIRONMENTAL DESIGN (engineering and applied science, engineering management, and environmental science), SOCIAL SCIENCE (anthropology, classical/ancient civilization, economics, German area studies, history, interdisciplinary studies, international relations, Italian studies, liberal arts/general studies, philosophy, political science/government, psychology, religion, sociology, and Spanish studies). Government, English and history are the strongest academically. Business, biology, and psychology are the largest.

Required: To graduate, students must complete 120 credits, of which 60 must be earned at Sweet Briar, with a minimum GPA of 2.0. 30 to 36 must be in the major. In addition to major requirements, specific degree requirements include English: Thought and Expression. Students must take 7 hours in scientific theory and experiment; 6 in global cultures; 4 in study or practice of the arts; 3 each in Western culture, social science, literature, and economic, political, or legal systems; and 2 in physical activity. Students must demonstrate proficiency in oral and written communication, quantitative reasoning, and a foreign language. A senior capstone course/experience is also required.

Special: The college offers a coordinate program in general business management and arts management, as well as internships to explore career opportunities and gain work experience. Study abroad, a Washington semester with American University, student-designed and interdisciplinary majors, accelerated degree programs, and 3-2 engineering degrees with Columbia University, Washington University in St. Louis, Virginia Polytechnic Institute, and University of Virginia are available. Cross-registration with Lynchburg and Randolph-Macon Woman's Colleges (the Tri-College Consortium) and the Seven College Exchange is also possible. There are 9 national honor societies, including Phi Beta Kappa, a freshman honors program, and all departments have honors programs.

Faculty/Classroom: 47% of faculty are male; 53%, female. All both teach and do research. The average class size in an introductory lecture is 14; in a laboratory, 8; and in a regular course, 10.

Admissions: 79% of the 2005-2006 applicants were accepted. The SAT scores for the 2005-2006 freshman class were: Verbal--15% below 500, 45% between 500 and 599, 33% between 600 and 700, and 7% above 700; Math--23% below 500, 53% between 500 and 599, 22% between 600 and 700, and 2% above 700. The ACT scores were 14% below 21, 29% between 21 and 23, 32% between 24 and 26, 16% between 27 and 28, and 9% above 28. 52% of the current freshmen were in the top fifth of their class; 82% were in the top two fifths. 2 freshmen graduated first in their class.

Requirements: The SAT or ACT is required. The ACT Optional Writing test is also required. The Admissions Committee looks for qualities such as independent thinking, ethical principles, assertiveness, and appreciation of diversity. Requirements normally include a minimum of 4 units in English, 3 in math, 3 in social studies, 2 sequential years in a foreign language, and 3 units in science, as well as additional units in these subjects to total 16. Most candidates have 20 such academic units. An interview is strongly encouraged but not required. AP credits are accepted. Important factors in the admissions decision are recommendations by school officials, leadership record, and advanced placement or honor courses.

Procedure: Freshmen are admitted fall and spring. Entrance exams should be taken by spring of the junior year and/or fall of the senior year. There are early decision, early admissions, and deferred admissions plans. Early decision applications should be filed by December 1; regular applications, by February 1 for fall entry and November 1 for spring entry, along with a $40 fee. Notification of early decision is sent December 15; regular decision, March 15. 63 early decision candidates were accepted for the 2005-2006 class. Applications are accepted on-line.

Transfer: 15 transfer students enrolled in 2004-2005. Transfer applicants must submit official transcripts from high school and college, test scores, a college catalog, recommendations from a previous dean and professor, and a statement explaining why the applicant wishes to transfer and why the applicant is interested in Sweet Briar. 60 of 120 credits required for the bachelor's degree must be completed at Sweet Briar.

Visiting: There are regularly scheduled orientations for prospective students, consisting of attendance at classes and campus events, meetings with faculty and coaches, an overnight stay in a dorm, a campus tour, and an interview. There are guides for informal visits and visitors may sit in on classes and stay overnight. To schedule a visit, contact Ken Huus, Dean of Admissions.

Financial Aid: In 2005-2006, 88% of all full-time freshmen and 92% of continuing full-time students received some form of financial aid. 46% of full-time freshmen and 48% of continuing full-time students received need-based aid. The average freshman award was $21,430. Need-based scholarships or need-based grants averaged $17,143; need-based self-help aid (loans and jobs) averaged $5657; and other non-need-based awards and non-need-based scholarships averaged $2243. 66% of undergraduates work part time. Average annual earnings from campus work are $980. The average financial indebtedness of the 2005 graduate was $17,807. Sweet Briar is a member of CSS. The FAFSA, the college's own financial statement, the Business/Farm Supplement, and noncustodial parents statement are required. The deadline for filing freshman financial aid applications for fall entry is March 1.

International Students: There are 23 international students enrolled. The school actively recruits these students. They must score satisfactorily on the written TOEFL or on the electronic version and also take the SAT or the ACT.

Computers: Wireless access is available. All students may access the system 24 hours a day. There are no time limits and no fees. It is strongly recommended that all students have a personal computer.

Graduates: From July 1, 2004 to June 30, 2005, 126 bachelor's degrees were awarded. The most popular majors were psychology (11%), international affairs (8%), and government (8%). In an average class, 6% graduate in 3 years or less, 63% graduate in 4 years or less, 66% graduate in 5 years or less, and 66% graduate in 6 years or less. 62 companies recruited on campus in 2004-2005. Of the 2004 graduating class, 25% were enrolled in graduate school within 6 months of graduation and 56% were employed.

Admissions Contact: Ken Huus, Dean of Admissions. A video is available. E-mail: *admissions@sbc.edu* Web: *www.admissions.sbc.edu*

UNIVERSITY OF MARY WASHINGTON   E-2
(Formerly Mary Washington College)

Fredericksburg, VA 22401-5300　　　(540) 654-2000
(800) 468-5614; Fax: (540) 654-1857

Full-time: 1205 men, 2323 women	Faculty: 210; IIB, av$
Part-time: 109 men, 245 women	Ph.D.s: 83%
Graduate: 1 man, 25 women	Student/Faculty: 17 to 1
Year: semesters, summer session	Tuition: $5634 ($14,776)
Application Deadline: February 1	Room & Board: $6002
Freshman Class: 4635 applied, 2979 accepted, 914 enrolled	
SAT Verbal/Math: 617/606*	ACT: 27 HIGHLY COMPETITIVE

Mary Washington University, formerly Mary Washington College, founded in 1908, is a public liberal arts and sciences institution. In addition to regional accreditation, University of Mary Washington has baccalaureate program accreditation with NASM. The library contains 366,938 volumes, 631,701 microform items, and 1206 audio/video tapes/CDs/DVDs, and subscribes to 5782 periodicals including electronic. Computerized library services include the card catalog, interlibrary loans, database searching, Internet access, and laptop Internet portals. Special learning facilities include an art gallery, radio station, the Center for Historic Preservation, Leidecker Center for Asian Studies, and James Farmer Multicultural Center. The 176-acre campus is in a small town 50 miles south of Washington, D.C. and 50 miles north of Richmond. Including any residence halls, there are 42 buildings.

Student Life: 73% of undergraduates are from Virginia. Students are from 42 states, 18 foreign countries, and Canada. 9% are from public schools. 88% are white. The average age of freshmen is 18; all undergraduates, 21. 15% do not continue beyond their first year; 78% remain to graduate.

Housing: 2575 students can be accommodated in college housing, which includes single-sex and coed dorms and on-campus apartments. In addition, there are special-interest houses, a foreign language floor of a hall, an international house, and a community service area. On-campus housing is available on a lottery system for upperclassmen. 71% of students live on campus; of those, 80% remain on campus on weekends. Upperclassmen may keep cars.

Activities: There are no fraternities or sororities. There are 90 groups on campus, including art, bagpipe band, cheerleading, choir, chorale, chorus, computers, dance, debate, drama, ethnic, film, gay, honors, international, jazz band, literary magazine, musical theater, newspaper, opera, orchestra, photography, political, professional, radio and TV, religious, social, social service, student government, and yearbook. Popular campus events include Grill on the Hill, Junior Ring Dance, and a Multicultural Fair.

Sports: There are 10 intercollegiate sports for men and 12 for women, and 15 intramural sports for men and 15 for women. Facilities include a 6-lane, 25-yard indoor pool, regulation basketball and volleyball courts, a weight room, batting cages, training rooms, playing fields for all outdoor sports, a running course, handball/racquetball courts, an 8-lane,

400-meter track, a 20,000-square-foot fitness and recreation facility, and an indoor tennis center.

Disabled Students: 65% of the campus is accessible. Wheelchair ramps, elevators, special parking, specially equipped rest rooms, lowered drinking fountains, lowered telephones, and special housing are available.

Services: Counseling and information services are available, as is tutoring in most subjects. There is a reader service for the blind, a writing center, a center for the visually impaired, and a speaking center.

Campus Safety and Security: Measures include 24-hour foot and vehicle patrol, self-defense education, security escort services, and informal discussions. There are pamphlets/posters/films, emergency telephones, and lighted pathways/sidewalks.

Programs of Study: University of Mary Washington confers B.A., B.S. degrees. Master's degrees are also awarded. Bachelor's degrees are awarded in BIOLOGICAL SCIENCE (biology/biological science), BUSINESS (business administration and management), COMMUNICATIONS AND THE ARTS (art history and appreciation, classics, dramatic arts, English, French, German, historic preservation, languages, music, Spanish, and studio art), COMPUTER AND PHYSICAL SCIENCE (chemistry, computer science, mathematics, and physics), ENGINEERING AND ENVIRONMENTAL DESIGN (environmental science), SOCIAL SCIENCE (American studies, anthropology, economics, geography, history, international relations, philosophy, political science/government, psychology, religion, and sociology). Historic preservation is the strongest academically. Business administration, psychology, and biology are the largest.

Required: To graduate, students must complete 122 credit hours with a minimum GPA of 2.0. Hours required in the major vary. General education curriculum includes courses in composition, math, lab science, arts/literature, Western civilization, social science, foreign language, phys ed, and computer technology. Additionally, students take thematic courses across the curriculum, with requirements including writing intensive, speaking intensive, global awareness, environmental awareness, and race/gender intensive courses. A thesis is required in some majors and programs of study.

Special: Study abroad anywhere in the world, a Washington semester, and credit for off-campus work experience are available. The university offers dual majors, work-study programs, student-designed majors, and pass/fail options. More than 500 internships for credit are also available. Teacher licensure preparation is offered for elementary and secondary education. Elementary education is a 5-year masters degree program. There are 25 national honor societies, including Phi Beta Kappa.

Faculty/Classroom: 61% of faculty are male; 39%, female. All teach undergraduates. No introductory courses are taught by graduate students. The average class size in an introductory lecture is 27; in a laboratory, 20; and in a regular course, 21.

Admissions: 64% of the 2005-2006 applicants were accepted. The SAT scores for the 2005-2006 freshman class were: Verbal--3% below 500, 28% between 500 and 599, 52% between 600 and 700, and 17% above 700; Math--5% below 500, 41% between 500 and 599, 47% between 600 and 700, and 7% above 700. 65% of the current freshmen were in the top fifth of their class; 91% were in the top two fifths. 7 freshmen graduated first in their class.

Requirements: The SAT or ACT is recommended. The ACT Optional Writing test is also recommended. In addition, applicants must be graduates of an accredited secondary school or hold the GED. The Admissions Committee recommends that applicants complete 4 years of each of math, English, foreign language, science, and social studies. A SAT: Subject Test is strongly recommended. Application essays are required. AP and CLEP credits are accepted. Important factors in the admissions decision are recommendations by school officials, evidence of special talent, and advanced placement or honor courses.

Procedure: Freshmen are admitted fall and spring. Entrance exams should be taken by January of the senior year. There is a deferred admissions plan. Applications should be filed by February 1 for fall entry and November 1 for spring entry. UMW offers an early notification plan called Honors Admissions; applications must be received by January 15 to be considered. The fall 2005 application fee was $45. Notification is sent April 1. 127 early decision candidates were accepted for the 2005-2006 class. 300 applicants were on the 2005 waiting list; 150 were admitted. Applications are accepted on-line.

Transfer: 176 transfer students enrolled in 2004-2005. The college recommends that applicants for transfer have a minimum GPA of 3.0 and a recommended 30 college credits. The SAT and high school transcripts are required. Graduates from the Virginia community colleges are given preference for admission. 30 of 122 credits required for the bachelor's degree must be completed at University of Mary Washington.

Visiting: There are regularly scheduled orientations for prospective students, including information sessions, available Monday through Friday at 10:30 A.M. and 2 P.M., followed by a student-guided tour, and 2 Saturday open houses each semester. Visitors may sit in on classes and stay overnight. To schedule a visit, contact the Office of Admissions.

Financial Aid: In a recent year, 65% of all full-time freshmen and 63% of continuing full-time students received some form of financial aid. 40%

of full-time freshmen and 45% of continuing full-time students received need-based aid. The average freshman award was $4500. Need-based scholarships or need-based grants averaged $2245 ($15,600 maximum); need-based self-help aid (loans and jobs) averaged $2400 ($4170 maximum); and other non-need-based awards and non-need-based private scholarships averaged $1550 ($12,000 maximum). 25% of undergraduates work part time. Average annual earnings from campus work are $1600. The average financial indebtedness of the recent year's graduate was $13,100. The FAFSA is required. The deadline for filing freshman financial aid applications for fall entry is March 1.

International Students: There are 20 international students enrolled. Students must take the SAT or the ACT. In addition, it is recommended that students take the SAT Subject Tests in writing and 2 other subjects.

Computers: Wireless access is available. Students at UMW may use either our wired or wireless system to connect to the World Wide Web. They can use our networks to collaborate on course work, to access documents and other information from their classes, and to connect to proprietary databases and information services such as Lexis-Nexis, Project MUSE, and ARTstor. UMW provides general-access and program-specific labs on both campuses, and data ports on a "one per pillow" basis in the residence halls. All students may access the system. There are no time limits and no fees.

Graduates: The most popular majors were business administration (14%), English (10%), and biology (8%). In an average class, 64% graduate in 4 years or less, 72% graduate in 5 years, and 72% graduate in 6 years. 87 companies recruited on campus in 2004-2005. Of the 2004 graduating class, 30% were enrolled in graduate school within 6 months of graduation and 88% were employed.

Admissions Contact: Dr. Martin A. Wilder, Vice President for Enrollment. E-mail: admit@umw.edu Web: www.umw.edu

UNIVERSITY OF RICHMOND   E-3

University of Richmond, VA 23173   (804) 289-8640
(800) 700-1662; Fax: (804) 287-6003

Full-time: 1422 men, 1459 women	**Faculty:** 262; IIA, +$
Part-time: 23 men, 16 women	**Ph.D.s:** 98%
Graduate: 140 men, 126 women	**Student/Faculty:** 11 to 1
Year: semesters, summer session	**Tuition:** $34,850
Application Deadline: January 15	**Room & Board:** $5660

Freshman Class: 5778 applied, 2743 accepted, 772 enrolled
SAT or ACT: required   **MOST COMPETITIVE**

The University of Richmond, founded in 1830, is a private independent institution offering programs in arts and sciences, business, and leadership studies. There are 3 undergraduate and 3 graduate schools. In addition to regional accreditation, UR has baccalaureate program accreditation with AACSB, ACS, and NASM. The 4 libraries contain 805,520 volumes, 87,148 microform items, and 30,174 audio/video tapes/CDs/DVDs, and subscribe to 43,747 periodicals including electronic. Computerized library services include the card catalog, interlibrary loans, database searching, Internet access, and laptop Internet portals. Special learning facilities include a learning resource center, art gallery, radio station, TV station, and the Lora Robins Gallery of Design from Nature. The 350-acre campus is in a suburban area 6 miles west of Richmond. Including any residence halls, there are 90 buildings.

Student Life: 85% of undergraduates are from out of state, mostly the Middle Atlantic. Others are from 45 states, 75 foreign countries, and Canada. 62% are from public schools. 85% are white. The average age of freshmen is 18; all undergraduates, 20. 7% do not continue beyond their first year; 93% remain to graduate.

Housing: 2686 students can be accommodated in college housing, which includes single-sex and coed dorms and on-campus apartments. In addition, there are special-interest houses and 1 international house. On-campus housing is available on a first-come, first-served basis and is available on a lottery system for upperclassmen. 92% of students live on campus; of those, 90% remain on campus on weekends. All students may keep cars.

Activities: 29% of men belong to 8 national fraternities; 5% of women belong to 8 national sororities. There are 250 groups on campus, including art, band, cheerleading, choir, chorale, chorus, computers, dance, debate, drama, drill team, ethnic, forensics, gay, honors, international, jazz band, literary magazine, musical theater, newspaper, orchestra, pep band, political, professional, radio and TV, religious, social, social service, student government, and yearbook. Popular campus events include Ring Dance.

Sports: There are 9 intercollegiate sports for men and 10 for women, and 24 intramural sports for men and 23 for women. Facilities include a 10,000-seat gym, a stadium, a soccer/track complex, lighted intramural fields, an intramural gym, aerobics and weight rooms, a swimming pool, and tennis, racquetball, and squash courts.

Disabled Students: 85% of the campus is accessible. Wheelchair ramps, elevators, special parking, specially equipped rest rooms, lowered drinking fountains, and special housing are available.

Services: Counseling and information services are available, as is tutoring in most subjects. There are support centers for help with academic skills, writing, and speech.

Campus Safety and Security: Measures include 24-hour foot and vehicle patrol, self-defense education, security escort services, and shuttle buses. There are informal discussions, pamphlets/posters/films, emergency telephones, lighted pathways/sidewalks, and a card-access system in all residence halls, vehicle assistance, emergency first aid service, fingerprinting, firearms storage, and personal property engraving and identification.

Programs of Study: UR confers B.A., B.S., B.A.S., B.L.A., and B.S.B.A. degrees. Associate and master's degrees are also awarded. Bachelor's degrees are awarded in BIOLOGICAL SCIENCE (biochemistry, biology/biological science, and molecular biology), BUSINESS (accounting, business administration and management, and business economics), COMMUNICATIONS AND THE ARTS (art history and appreciation, dramatic arts, English, French, German, Greek, journalism, Latin, music, Spanish, speech/debate/rhetoric, and studio art), COMPUTER AND PHYSICAL SCIENCE (chemistry, computer science, mathematics, and physics), SOCIAL SCIENCE (American studies, classical/ancient civilization, criminal justice, economics, history, interdisciplinary studies, international studies, philosophy, political science/government, psychology, religion, sociology, urban studies, and women's studies). Business, biology, and political science are the largest.

Required: To graduate, students must complete 120 credits with a minimum GPA of 2.0. In addition to the first-year core course, there are specific requirements in English composition, foreign language, natural science, phys ed, social analysis, literary studies, historical studies, symbolic reasoning, visual and performing arts, and wellness.

Special: Internships in nearly every major, study abroad in 30 countries, and a Washington semester with American University are available. UR also offers work-study programs, B.A.-B.S. and B.S.B.A. degrees, dual majors, student-designed majors, and a general studies degree through the School of Continuing Studies. There is a marine biology study option with the Marine Sciences Laboratory at Duke University. Also available are a 3-2 engineering degree with George Washington University, Virginia Tech, and Columbia University, a 3-1-1 degree with the University of Virginia, and a 4-1 degree with Virginia Commonwealth. There are 31 national honor societies, including Phi Beta Kappa, and 7 departmental honors programs.

Faculty/Classroom: 60% of faculty are male; 40%, female. 100% both teach and do research. No introductory courses are taught by graduate students. The average class size in an introductory lecture is 23 and in a regular course, 18.

Admissions: 47% of the 2005-2006 applicants were accepted. The SAT scores for the 2005-2006 freshman class were: Verbal--4% below 500, 19% between 500 and 599, 56% between 600 and 700, and 21% above 700; Math--3% below 500, 14% between 500 and 599, 57% between 600 and 700, and 26% above 700. The ACT scores were 6% below 21, 8% between 21 and 23, 13% between 24 and 26, 25% between 27 and 28, and 48% above 28. 81% of the current freshmen were in the top fifth of their class; 97% were in the top two fifths. There were 27 National Merit finalists and 35 semifinalists. 58 freshmen graduated first in their class.

Requirements: The SAT or ACT is required. In addition, in addition, SAT Subject tests are required in writing and math I or II if the student is taking the SAT. Applicants must be graduates of an accredited secondary school. The GED is accepted. Applicants must complete 16 high school academic credits, including 4 years of English, 3 of math, and at least 2 each of history, foreign language, and lab science. An essay, counselor recommendation, and auditions for music scholarships are required. AP and CLEP credits are accepted. Important factors in the admissions decision are advanced placement or honor courses, leadership record, and evidence of special talent.

Procedure: Freshmen are admitted in the fall. Entrance exams should be taken by February 1 of the senior year. There are early decision, early admissions, and deferred admissions plans. Early decision applications should be filed by November 15; regular applications, by January 15 for fall entry, along with a $50 fee. Notification of early decision is sent December 15; regular decision, April 1. 160 early decision candidates were accepted for the 2005-2006 class. 1092 applicants were on the 2005 waiting list; 267 were admitted. Applications are accepted on-line.

Transfer: 41 transfer students enrolled in 2004-2005. Applicants must have earned a minimum of 24 credit hours in transferable courses. A minimum GPA of 2.0 is required; however, to be competitive an applicant needs about a 3.3 GPA. 60 of 120 credits required for the bachelor's degree must be completed at UR.

Visiting: There are regularly scheduled orientations for prospective students, Conferences and tours are offered Monday through Friday with Saturday tours available on select dates from September through November, as well as Junior Preview Days in early spring. There are guides for informal visits and visitors may sit in on classes and stay overnight. To schedule a visit, contact the Admissions Office at (800) 700-1662 or (804) 289-8640 or admissions@richmond.edu.

Financial Aid: In 2005-2006, 65% of all full-time freshmen and 68% of continuing full-time students received some form of financial aid. 36% of full-time freshmen and 32% of continuing full-time students received need-based aid. The average freshman award was $26,400. Need-based scholarships or need-based grants averaged $22,300 ($38,690 maximum); need-based self-help aid (loans and jobs) averaged $3500 ($4000 maximum); non-need-based athletic scholarships averaged $27,770 ($40,510 maximum); and other non-need-based awards and non-need-based scholarships averaged $20,000 ($40,510 maximum). 42% of undergraduates work part time. Average annual earnings from campus work are $1042. The average financial indebtedness of the 2005 graduate was $18,500. The FAFSA, the college's own financial statement and the are required. The deadline for filing freshman financial aid applications for fall entry is February 25.

International Students: There are 165 international students enrolled. The school actively recruits these students. Satisfactory scores are required on the written TOEFL and the SAT or the ACT.

Computers: Wireless access is available. UR's high-speed wireless network allows students to register for classes, check their e-mail, access library databases, view their class web sites, and access the Internet from nearly anywhere on campus. The wireless neetwork, with approximately 560 wireless access points, allows access from all buuildings on campus and many outdoor areas. In addition, UR, provides approximately 700 public computers spread across 14 computer labs, classrooms, and other public areas. All students may access the system.

Graduates: From July 1, 2004 to June 30, 2005, 757 bachelor's degrees were awarded. The most popular majors were business (24%), social sciences (19%), and English (8%). In an average class, 76% graduate in 4 years, 72% graduate in 5 years, and 85% graduate in 6 years. 325 companies recruited on campus in 2004-2005. Of the 2004 graduating class, 23% were enrolled in graduate school within 6 months of graduation and 69% were employed.

Admissions Contact: Pamela W. Spence, Dean of Admission. A video is available. E-mail: *admissions@richmond.edu* Web: *www.richmond.edu*

UNIVERSITY OF VIRGINIA   D-3
Charlottesville, VA 22904-4160

(434) 982-3200
Fax: (434) 924-3587

Full-time: 6137 men, 7258 women	Faculty: 1012; I, +$
Part-time: 375 men, 443 women	Ph.D.s: 91%
Graduate: 4129 men, 5423 women	Student/Faculty: 13 to 1
Year: semesters, summer session	Tuition: $7370 ($24,114)
Application Deadline: January 2	Room & Board: $6389
Freshman Class: 15,657 applied, 5898 accepted, 3112 enrolled	
SAT Verbal/Math: 660/670*	ACT: 28 MOST COMPETITIVE

The University of Virginia, founded in 1819, is a public institution with undergraduate programs in architecture, arts and sciences, commerce, education, engineering and applied science, and nursing. There are 6 undergraduate and 9 graduate schools. In addition to regional accreditation, UVA has baccalaureate program accreditation with AACSB, ABET, ACS, APA, ASLA, ASLHA, NAAB, NAST, NATA, NLN, and TEAC. The 19 libraries contain 4,987,437 volumes, 5,505,799 microform items, and 91,529 audio/video tapes/CDs/DVDs, and subscribe to 52,192 periodicals including electronic. Computerized library services include the card catalog, interlibrary loans, database searching, Internet access, and laptop Internet portals. Special learning facilities include a learning resource center, art gallery, radio station, TV station, art museum, and observatory. The 1160-acre campus is in a suburban area 70 miles northwest of Richmond/ Virginia. Including any residence halls, there are 530 buildings.

Student Life: 69% of undergraduates are from Virginia. Others are from 49 states, 110 foreign countries, and Canada. 77% are from public schools. 63% are white. 47% are Protestant; 22% Catholic; 19% claim no religious affiliation. The average age of freshmen is 18; all undergraduates, 20. 3% do not continue beyond their first year; 91% remain to graduate.

Housing: 6779 students can be accommodated in college housing, which includes coed dormitories, on-campus apartments, and married-student housing. In addition, there are honors houses, language houses, special-interest houses and 3 residential colleges. On-campus housing is guaranteed for the freshman year only, is available on a first-come, first-served basis, and is available on a lottery system for upperclassmen. 54% of students commute. Upperclassmen may keep cars.

Activities: 28% of men belong to 1 local and 37 national fraternities; 28% of women belong to 1 local and 23 national sororities. There are 561 groups on campus, including art, band, cheerleading, chess, choir, chorale, chorus, computers, dance, debate, drama, ethnic, film, forensics, gay, honors, international, jazz band, judiciary, literary magazine, marching band, musical theater, newspaper, orchestra, pep band, photography, political, professional, radio and TV, religious, social, social service, student government, symphony, tour guides, and yearbook. Popular campus events include Culturefest and Family Weekend.

Sports: There are 11 intercollegiate sports for men and 12 for women, and 18 intramural sports for men and 18 for women. Facilities include a 61,500-seat stadium, an 8500-seat gym, and 4 recreation centers including an aquatics and fitness center.

Disabled Students: All of the campus is accessible. Wheelchair ramps, elevators, special parking, specially equipped rest rooms, special class scheduling, lowered drinking fountains, lowered telephones, curb cuts, voice synthesizers, braille printers, and large-screen monitors are available.

Services: Counseling and information services are available, as is tutoring in every subject. There is a reader service for the blind. There are transcribers, note takers, and taped readings for disabled students.

Campus Safety and Security: Measures include 24-hour foot and vehicle patrol, self-defense education, security escort services, and shuttle buses. There are informal discussions, pamphlets/posters/films, emergency telephones, lighted pathways/sidewalks, and bicycle registration.

Programs of Study: UVA confers B.A., B.S., B.A.R.H., B.C.P., B.I.S., B.S.C., B.S.Ed., and B.S.N. degrees. Master's and doctoral degrees are also awarded. Bachelor's degrees are awarded in BIOLOGICAL SCIENCE (biology/biological science), BUSINESS (business administration and management), COMMUNICATIONS AND THE ARTS (art, classics, comparative literature, dramatic arts, English, French, German, Italian, music, Slavic languages, and Spanish), COMPUTER AND PHYSICAL SCIENCE (astronomy, chemistry, computer science, mathematics, physics, and statistics), EDUCATION (health and physical), ENGINEERING AND ENVIRONMENTAL DESIGN (architecture, biomedical engineering, chemical engineering, city/community/regional planning, civil engineering, electrical/electronics engineering, engineering and applied science, environmental science, mechanical engineering, and systems engineering), HEALTH PROFESSIONS (nursing and speech pathology/audiology), SOCIAL SCIENCE (African American studies, anthropology, area studies, economics, history, interdisciplinary studies, international relations, philosophy, political science/government, psychology, religion, and sociology). English, history, and biology are the strongest academically. Psychology, commerce, and economics are the largest.

Required: To graduate, students must complete 120 credit hours, with 18 to 42 hours in the major and a minimum GPA of 2.0. Distribution requirements include 12 hours of math and science, 6 hours each of humanities, composition, and social sciences, 4 semesters of foreign languages, 3 hours of historical studies, and 3 hours of non-Western perspectives.

Special: The college offers internships, study abroad, accelerated degree programs, B.A.-B.S. degrees in biology, environmental sciences, chemistry and physics, co-op programs in engineering, and nondegree study. Dual majors in most arts and sciences programs, student-designed majors, an interdisciplinary major and Echols Scholars program, and pass/fail options are available. There is a chapter of Phi Beta Kappa and a freshman honors program.

Faculty/Classroom: 63% of faculty are male; 37%, female. 39% teach undergraduates, 76% do research, and 39% do both. Graduate students teach 32% of introductory courses. The average class size in an introductory lecture is 50; in a laboratory, 20; and in a regular course, 34.

Admissions: 38% of the 2005-2006 applicants were accepted. The SAT scores for the 2005-2006 freshman class were: Verbal--4% below 500, 18% between 500 and 599, 45% between 600 and 700, and 32% above 700; Math--3% below 500, 14% between 500 and 599, 44% between 600 and 700, and 39% above 700. The ACT scores were 7% below 21, 8% between 21 and 23, 20% between 24 and 26, 21% between 27 and 28, and 43% above 28. 95% of the current freshmen were in the top fifth of their class; 99% were in the top two fifths. 188 freshmen graduated first in their class.

Requirements: The SAT or ACT is required. In addition, two SAT subject tests in writing, math IC or IIC, and a third test of the students choice, are required. With few exceptions, candidates graduate from accredited secondary schools. While the GED is accepted, it is rare for candidates for first-year admission who have this credential to be competitive in the admissions process. Applicants should complete 16 high school academic courses, including 4 courses of English, 4 courses of math, beginning with algebra I, 2 courses of physics, biology, or chemistry (3 if applying to engineering), 2 years of foreign language, and 1 course of social science. An essay is also required. AP credits are accepted. Important factors in the admissions decision are advanced placement or honor courses and evidence of special talent.

Procedure: Freshmen are admitted in the fall. Entrance exams should be taken by December of the senior year. There are early decision and deferred admissions plans. Early decision applications should be filed by November 1; regular applications, by January 2 for fall entry, along with a $60 fee. Notification of early decision is sent December 1; regular decision, April 1. 977 early decision candidates were accepted for the 2005-2006 class. 1848 applicants were on the 2005 waiting list; 83 were admitted. Applications are accepted on-line.

Transfer: 532 transfer students enrolled in 2004-2005. Applicants for transfer must have a minimum GPA of 3.0, submit SAT or ACT scores, and meet prerequisite courses. 60 of 120 credits required for the bachelor's degree must be completed at UVA.

Visiting: There are regularly scheduled orientations for prospective students, consisting of comprehensive information sessions and campus tours. Visitors may sit in on classes and stay overnight. To schedule a visit, contact the Monroe Society at (434) 924-3321.

Financial Aid: In 2005-2006, 53% of all full-time freshmen and 43% of continuing full-time students received some form of financial aid. 23% of full-time freshmen and 22% of continuing full-time students received need-based aid. The average freshman award was $10,299. 25% of undergraduates work part time. The average financial indebtedness of the 2005 graduate was $15,176. The FAFSA and the college's own financial statement are required. The deadline for filing freshman financial aid applications for fall entry is March 1.

International Students: There are 1059 international students enrolled. The school actively recruits these students. They must take the TOEFL, and the International English Language Testing System (IELTS), and also take the SAT or the ACT as well as the same tests as all other entering students. Students must take SAT: Subject tests in, math (either level) and another of the student's choice.

Computers: Wireless access is available. Dormitories, libraries, and student centers have both wired and wireless access. Wireless access is available at about 75% of all buildings on campus. All students may access the system 24 hours a day, 7 days a week. There are no time limits and no fees. It is strongly recommended that all students have a personal computer.

Graduates: From July 1, 2004 to June 30, 2005, 3353 bachelor's degrees were awarded. The most popular majors were economics (10%), commerce (10%), and psychology (9%). In an average class, 1% graduate in 3 years or less, 83% graduate in 4 years or less, 92% graduate in 5 years or less, and 92% graduate in 6 years or less. 504 companies recruited on campus in 2004-2005.

Admissions Contact: John A. Blackburn, Dean of Admission.
E-mail: *undergradadmission@virginia.edu*
Web: *www.virginia.edu/undergradadmission*

UNIVERSITY OF VIRGINIA'S COLLEGE AT WISE A-4

Wise, VA 24293 (276) 328-0322
(888) 282-9324; Fax: (276) 328-0251

Full-time: 708 men, 731 women	**Faculty:** 89; IIB, -$
Part-time: 121 men, 332 women	**Ph.D.s:** 70%
Graduate: none	**Student/Faculty:** 16 to 1
Year: semesters, summer session	**Tuition:** $5081 ($15,153)
Application Deadline: August 1	**Room & Board:** $5995
Freshman Class: 1085 applied, 824 accepted, 366 enrolled	
SAT Verbal/Math: 496/485*	**ACT:** 20 COMPETITIVE

The University of Virginia's College at Wise, founded in 1954, offers undergraduate programs through the departments of business studies, education, languages and literature, behavioral and social sciences, natural sciences, math and computer science, history and philosophy, visual and performing arts, and nursing. In addition to regional accreditation, UVA's College at Wise has baccalaureate program accreditation with NLN. The library contains 143,265 volumes, 66,230 microform items, and 4786 audio/video tapes/CDs/DVDs, and subscribes to 2265 periodicals including electronic. Computerized library services include the card catalog, interlibrary loans, database searching, and Internet access. Special learning facilities include an observatory. The 396-acre campus is in a small town 60 miles northwest of Bristol. Including any residence halls, there are 42 buildings.

Student Life: 95% of undergraduates are from Virginia. Students are from 11 states and 7 foreign countries. 99% are from public schools. 89% are white. The average age of freshmen is 18; all undergraduates, 24. 35% do not continue beyond their first year; 29% remain to graduate.

Housing: 575 students can be accommodated in college housing, which includes single-sex and coed dorms, on-campus apartments, and off-campus apartments. In addition, there are special-interest houses. On-campus housing is available on a first-come, first-served basis and is available on a lottery system for upperclassmen. 75% of students commute. All students may keep cars.

Activities: 7% of men belong to 1 local and 3 national fraternities; 7% of women belong to 3 local and 1 national sorority. There are 53 groups on campus, including art, band, cheerleading, chess, choir, chorale, chorus, dance, drama, ethnic, film, gay, Honor court, honors, inter-Greek council, international, jazz band, literary magazine, multicultural alliance, musical theater, newspaper, pep band, political, professional, radio and TV, religious, residence hall association, social, social service, student activities board, and student government. Popular campus events include The Holly Ball, Jam for Man, and Extramural Flag Football Scramble.

Sports: There are 6 intercollegiate sports for men and 5 for women, and 56 intramural sports for men and 56 for women. Facilities include baseball and softball fields, a gym, tennis courts, a swimming pool, 3 practice football fields, a football stadium, racquetball court, fitness center, and a dance practice room.

Disabled Students: All of the campus is accessible. Wheelchair ramps, elevators, special parking, specially equipped rest rooms, special class scheduling, lowered drinking fountains, and special housing are available.

Services: Counseling and information services are available, as is tutoring in every subject. There is a reader service for the blind and remedial math and writing. Tutoring is free to all registered students.

Campus Safety and Security: Measures include 24-hour foot and vehicle patrol, self-defense education, security escort services, and informal discussions. There are pamphlets/posters/films, emergency telephones, lighted pathways/sidewalks, and a crime prevention office.

Programs of Study: UVA's College at Wise confers B.A., B.S., and B.S.N. degrees. Bachelor's degrees are awarded in BIOLOGICAL SCIENCE (biology/biological science), BUSINESS (accounting and business administration and management), COMMUNICATIONS AND THE ARTS (art, communications, dramatic arts, English, French, and Spanish), COMPUTER AND PHYSICAL SCIENCE (chemistry, information sciences and systems, and mathematics), ENGINEERING AND ENVIRONMENTAL DESIGN (environmental science), HEALTH PROFESSIONS (medical laboratory technology and nursing), SOCIAL SCIENCE (criminal justice, economics, history, international studies, law enforcement and corrections, liberal arts/general studies, political science/government, psychology, and social science). Natural science, accounting, and math are the strongest academically. Business administration, history, and education are the largest.

Required: To graduate, all students must complete 52 hours of general education requirements including a liberal arts course, arts, humanities, social sciences, natural sciences, English composition, literature, math, foreign language, phys ed, and Western heritage. At least 120 credit hours are required, with a minimum 2.0 GPA overall and in the major area.

Special: The college offers co-op programs in all majors, internships in education, social sciences, and communication, on-campus work-study programs, B.A.-B.S. degrees in most majors, dual and student-designed majors, and pass/fail options for classes not required for the major. There are 4 national honor societies, a freshman honors program, and 9 departmental honors programs.

Faculty/Classroom: 60% of faculty are male; 40%, female. All teach undergraduates, 50% do research, and 50% do both. The average class size in an introductory lecture is 20; in a laboratory, 17; and in a regular course, 18.

Admissions: 76% of the 2005-2006 applicants were accepted. The SAT scores for the 2005-2006 freshman class were: Verbal--52% below 500, 38% between 500 and 599, 9% between 600 and 700, and 2% above 700; Math--57% below 500, 37% between 500 and 599, and 6% between 600 and 700. The ACT scores were 58% below 21, 24% between 21 and 23, 11% between 24 and 26, 4% between 27 and 28, and 3% above 28. 49% of the current freshmen were in the top fifth of their class; 86% were in the top two fifths. 10 freshmen graduated first in their class.

Requirements: The SAT or ACT is required. The ACT Optional Writing test is also recommended. In addition, all applicants must be graduates of approved secondary schools or hold a GED. Preference is given to students who earn an Advanced Studies Diploma or its equivalent, rank in the top half of their graduating class, have a satisfactory minimum score on the SAT (ACT 18), and complete 4 years of English; 3 or more courses in math, including algebra 1 and 2 and a course selected from among geometry, trigonometry, advanced math, or calculus; 2 or more years of natural science beyond general science; 2 or more years of a foreign language; and 1 year each of American history and world history. A GPA of 2.4 is required. AP credits are accepted. Important factors in the admissions decision are advanced placement or honor courses, recommendations by school officials, and leadership record.

Procedure: Freshmen are admitted to all sessions. Entrance exams should be taken by January 1 of the application year. There are early admissions deferred admissions, and rolling admissions plans. Applications should be filed by August 1 for fall entry and January 5 for spring entry, along with a $25 fee. Notification is sent on a rolling basis. Applications are accepted on-line.

Transfer: 160 transfer students enrolled in 2004-2005. Transfer students must meet all general admissions requirements and submit secondary school transcripts or GED results and transcripts of all previous college work. A minimum 2.2 GPA is required. Students with either a minimum of 30 semester hours of college work, an associate degree, or who are at least 25 years old, need not submit the SAT or ACT scores. For others, a minimum composite score on the SAT or 18 on the ACT is recommended. 58 of 120 credits required for the bachelor's degree must be completed at UVA's College at Wise.

Visiting: There are regularly scheduled orientations for prospective students, including an interview, a campus tour, a meal, and class visitation. There are guides for informal visits and visitors may sit in on classes. To schedule a visit, contact the Admissions Office.

Financial Aid: In 2005-2006, 70% of all full-time students received some form of financial aid. 63% of all full-time students received need-based aid. The average freshman award was $6125. Need-based scholarships or need-based grants averaged $3953 ($9132 maximum); need-based self-help aid (loans and jobs) averaged $2233 ($4625 maximum); non-need-based athletic scholarships averaged $2201; and other non-need-based awards and non-need-based scholarships averaged $2034. 12% of undergraduates work part time. Average annual earnings from campus work are $1275. The average financial indebtedness of the 2005 graduate was $9175. The FAFSA and the college's own financial statement are required. The priority date for freshman financial aid applications for fall entry is February 1.

International Students: There are 12 international students enrolled. The school actively recruits these students. Satisfactory scores are required on the written TOEFL and the SAT or the ACT.

Computers: All students may access the system 24 hours per day. There are no time limits and no fees.

Graduates: From July 1, 2004 to June 30, 2005, 287 bachelor's degrees were awarded. The most popular majors were business administration (17%), history (12%), and liberal arts and sciences (12%). In an average class, 23% graduate in 4 years or less, 28% graduate in 5 years or less, and 29% graduate in 6 years or less. 3 companies recruited on campus in 2004-2005.

Admissions Contact: Russell Necessary, Vice Chancellor for Enrollment Management. A video is available.
E-mail: *admissions@uvawise.edu or rdn2f@wvawise.edu*
Web: *www.uvawise.edu*

VIRGINIA COMMONWEALTH UNIVERSITY E-3
Richmond, VA 23284-2527

(804) 828-1222
(800) 841-3638; Fax: (804) 828-1899

Full-time: 6461 men, 9648 women	**Faculty:** n/av
Part-time: 1786 men, 2613 women	**Ph.D.s:** 80%
Graduate: 3200 men, 5641 women	**Student/Faculty:** n/av
Year: semesters, summer session	**Tuition:** $5385 ($17,440)
Application Deadline: February 1	**Room & Board:** $7602
Freshman Class: 11,766 applied, 8021 accepted, 3540 enrolled	
SAT Verbal/Math: 540/530*	**ACT:** 21 **COMPETITIVE**

Virginia Commonwealth University, founded in 1838, is a public research university. There are 13 undergraduate and 15 graduate schools. In addition to regional accreditation, VCU has baccalaureate program accreditation with AACSB, ABET, ACPE, ADA, APTA, CSAB, CSWE, FIDER, NASAD, NASDTEC, NASM, NCATE, NLN, and NRPA. The 7 libraries contain 1,813,234 volumes, 3,121,479 microform items, and 48,006 audio/video tapes/CDs/DVDs, and subscribe to 22,340 periodicals including electronic. Computerized library services include the card catalog, interlibrary loans, database searching, Internet access, and laptop Internet portals. Special learning facilities include a learning resource center, art gallery, radio station, and TV station. The 131-acre campus is in an urban area 2 miles west of downtown Richmond. Including any residence halls, there are 170 buildings.

Student Life: 92% of undergraduates are from Virginia. Others are from 42 states, 70 foreign countries, and Canada. 59% are white; 20% African American; 10% Asian American. The average age of freshmen is 18; all undergraduates, 21. 20% do not continue beyond their first year.

Housing: 4705 students can be accommodated in college housing, which includes coed dorms and on-campus apartments. In addition, there are honors houses. On-campus housing is guaranteed for the freshman year only and is available on a first-come, first-served basis. All students may keep cars.

Activities: There are 10 national fraternities and 9 national sororities. There are 280 groups on campus, including art, athletic training, band, cheerleading, chess, choir, chorale, chorus, computers, dance, debate, drama, ethnic, gay, honors, international, jazz band, literary magazine, marching band, newspaper, opera, orchestra, pep band, photography, political, professional, radio and TV, religious, social, social service, student government, symphony and yearbook. Popular campus events include First Fridays, Annual Fall Block Show, and Career Fair.

Sports: There are 8 intercollegiate sports for men and 8 for women, and 28 intramural sports for men and 28 for women. Facilities include a multi-purpose indoor facility for intercollegiate athletics and recreational sports; a 24,495-square-foot recreation space with a fitness center, an activity center, and a wellness resource center; a 3,250-seat stadium for soccer and track and field events; a 250-seat tennis center open year-round; and a 25,990-square-foot recreation complex containing a gym, handball/racquetball courts, a weight room, and a cardiovascular fitness space; a 1,200-seat field and jogging track with artificial turf; a baseball field; and a 42,989-square-foot aquatic and recreational facility with a 6-lane pool and spa, handball/racquetball and squash courts, and gyms.

Disabled Students: 79% of the campus is accessible. Wheelchair ramps, elevators, special parking, specially equipped rest rooms, special class scheduling, lowered drinking fountains, and lowered telephones are available.

Services: Counseling and information services are available, as is tutoring in some subjects, including biology, math, chemistry, physics, mass communications, political science, some foreign languages, psychology, sociology, history, art history, and engineering. These are mostly 100 to 200 level classes. There is a reader service for the blind, and remedial math, reading, and writing. One-on-one tutoring in specific subjects is available. For undergraduates, tutoring is available by department.

Campus Safety and Security: Measures include 24-hour foot and vehicle patrol, self-defense education, security escort services, and shuttle buses. There are informal discussions, pamphlets/posters/films, emergency telephones, lighted pathways/sidewalks, and formal presentations, on-line crime prevention information @ www.vcu.edu and police, an annual security report, crime prevention through environmental design, community police officers/certified prevention specialists, security inspections of facilities, operation ID bike and computer registration, and a victim/witness assistance program.

Programs of Study: VCU confers B.A., B.S., B.F.A., B.I.S., B.Mus., B.Mus.Ed., B.S.N., and B.S.W. degrees. Master's and doctoral degrees are also awarded. Bachelor's degrees are awarded in AGRICULTURE (environmental studies), BIOLOGICAL SCIENCE (biology/biological science), BUSINESS (accounting, business administration and management, marketing/retailing/merchandising, recreation and leisure services, and sports management), COMMUNICATIONS AND THE ARTS (art history and appreciation, communications, dance, design, dramatic arts, English, languages, music, painting, photography, and sculpture), COMPUTER AND PHYSICAL SCIENCE (chemistry, computer science, information sciences and systems, mathematics, physics, and science), EDUCATION (art, foreign languages, and health), ENGINEERING AND ENVIRONMENTAL DESIGN (biomedical engineering, chemical engineering, computer engineering, electrical/electronics engineering, interior design, and mechanical engineering), HEALTH PROFESSIONS (dental hygiene, and nursing), SOCIAL SCIENCE (African American studies, anthropology, criminal justice, economics, fashion design and technology, forensic studies, geography, history, interdisciplinary studies, international studies, philosophy, political science/government, psychology, religion, safety science, social work, sociology, and urban studies). Psychology, biology, and mass communications are the largest.

Required: The total number of credit hours required for graduation varies with the major. Students must achieve a minimum GPA of 2.0.

Special: The college offers co-op programs in all majors, and internships with private industry, government agencies, banking and finance centers, media, and community service organizations. VCU also offers study abroad in more than 100 countries, work-study programs, and dual and student-designed majors. There is a freshman honors program.

Faculty/Classroom: The average class size in an introductory lecture is 37; in a laboratory, 20; and in a regular course, 31.

Admissions: 68% of the 2005-2006 applicants were accepted. The SAT scores for the 2005-2006 freshman class were: Verbal--30% below 500, 44% between 500 and 599, 23% between 600 and 700, and 3% above 700; Math--32% below 500, 46% between 500 and 599, 20% between 600 and 700, and 2% above 700. The ACT scores were 49% below 21, 27% between 21 and 23, 16% between 24 and 26, 4% between 27 and 28, and 4% above 28. 25% of the current freshmen were in the top fifth of their class; 49% were in the top two fifths. 15 freshmen graduated first in their class.

Requirements: The SAT is required. In addition, a minimum of 20 Carnegie credits is required to be considered for admission. Students may submit either SAT or ACT scores, and the highest critical reading or verbal score and the highest math score on the SAT will be considered for admission. An essay may be required for some programs. A portfolio and audition are required for the visual arts programs. Applicants will be considered for admission with a GED, and applicants over the age of 22 are not required to submit a SAT or ACT score. A GPA of 2.0 is required. AP and CLEP credits are accepted. Important factors in the admissions decision are ability to finance college education, recommendations by school officials, and leadership record.

Procedure: Freshmen are admitted fall and spring. Entrance exams should be taken by February 1. There is a deferred admissions plan. Applications should be filed by February 1 for fall entry and December 1 for spring entry. The fall 2005 application fee was $30. Notification is sent April 1. Applications are accepted on-line.

Transfer: 1789 transfer students enrolled in 2004-2005. Transfer students with 30 semester hours or more or who are 22 or older are not required to submit SAT or ACT test scores. Transcripts from all previous colleges must be submitted. Requirements vary by program. 30 of 120 credits required for the bachelor's degree must be completed at VCU.

Visiting: Information sessions and campus tours are offered Monday through Saturday at 10:30 A.M., except holiday weekends. The information session is conducted by an admissions counselor and the campus tour is led by a current VCU student. Visitors may sit in on classes. To schedule a visit, contact the Office of Admissions at (800) 841-3638 or ugrad@vcu.edu.

Financial Aid: In 2005-2006, 79% of all full-time freshmen and 59% of continuing full-time students received some form of financial aid. 53% of full-time freshmen and 40% of continuing full-time students received

need-based aid. Need-based scholarships or need-based grants averaged $4122 ($8650 maximum); need-based self-help aid (loans and jobs) averaged $4789 ($9625 maximum); non-need-based athletic scholarships averaged $1000 ($26,704 maximum); and other non-need-based awards and non-need-based scholarships averaged $100 ($14,098 maximum). The average financial indebtedness of the 2005 graduate was $19,912. VCU is a member of CSS. The FAFSA is required. The priority date for freshman financial aid applications for fall entry is March 1.

International Students: There are 331 international students enrolled. The school actively recruits these students. They must score satisfactorily on the written TOEFL or on the electronic version or on the IELTS or the college's own test or the SAT.

Computers: Students may access the university's wired and wireless networks through university-owned or the students' personal computers. There are numerous public access computers located throughout campus. Network access is generally not restricted for students, although some activities may be blocked or limited. Internet access is unrestricted as far as sites and content. All students may access the system. There are no time limits and no fees. All students are required to have personal computers. Computer specifications are issued each year.

Graduates: From July 1, 2004 to June 30, 2005, 2684 bachelor's degrees were awarded. The most popular majors were psychology (10%), business administration (6%), and mass communication (5%). In an average class, 18% graduate in 4 years or less, and 41% graduate in 6 years or less.

Admissions Contact: Delores T. Taylor, Director, Admissions. A video is available. E-mail: ugrad@vcu.edu Web: www.vcu.edu

VIRGINIA INTERMONT COLLEGE   B-4
Bristol, VA 24201-4298

	(276) 466-7851
	(800) 451-1842; Fax: (276) 466-7855
Full-time: 286 men, 700 women	**Faculty:** 45
Part-time: 57 men, 95 women	**Ph.D.s:** 52%
Graduate: none	**Student/Faculty:** 22 to 1
Year: semesters, summer session	**Tuition:** $16,450
Application Deadline: open	**Room & Board:** $5750
Freshman Class: n/av	
SAT Verbal/Math: 490/480*	**ACT:** 20 LESS COMPETITIVE

Virginia Intermont College, founded in 1884, is a private institution affiliated with the Baptist General Association of Virginia. In addition to regional accreditation, V.I. College has baccalaureate program accreditation with ABA and CSWE. The library contains 54,735 volumes, 9205 microform items, and 2275 audio/video tapes/CDs/DVDs, and subscribes to 15,004 periodicals including electronic. Computerized library services include the card catalog, interlibrary loans, database searching, and Internet access. Special learning facilities include a learning resource center, art gallery, an equestrian center, a ballet center, and a film lab. The 13-acre campus is in an urban area 144 miles southwest of Roanoke and 114 miles northeast of Knoxville, Tennessee. Including any residence halls, there are 18 buildings.

Student Life: 55% of undergraduates are from Virginia. Others are from 38 states, 30 foreign countries, and Canada. 85% are from public schools. 89% are white. 44% are Protestant; 40% claim no religious affiliation; 11% Catholic. The average age of freshmen is 18; all undergraduates, 27. 40% do not continue beyond their first year; 40% remain to graduate.

Housing: 470 students can be accommodated in college housing, which includes single-sex and coed dormitories, off-campus apartments, and married-student housing. On-campus housing is guaranteed for all 4 years. 65% of students live on campus; of those, 50% remain on campus on weekends. Alcohol is not permitted. All students may keep cars.

Activities: There are no fraternities or sororities. There are 21 groups on campus, including art, cheerleading, choir, computers, dance, drama, honors, international, literary magazine, musical theater, newspaper, photography, political, professional, religious, social service, and student government. Popular campus events include May Day, Family Weekend, and Spring Fling.

Sports: There are 8 intercollegiate sports for men and 8 for women, and 12 intramural sports for men and 12 for women. Facilities include a gym, a 1,200-seat amphitheater, a 900-seat auditorium, lighted tennis courts, a swimming pool, a fitness center, and an equine center.

Disabled Students: 35% of the campus is accessible. Wheelchair ramps, elevators, special parking, specially equipped rest rooms, special class scheduling, and special housing are available.

Services: Counseling and information services are available, as is tutoring in every subject. There is a reader service for the blind and remedial math and reading.

Campus Safety and Security: Measures include 24-hour foot and vehicle patrol, self-defense education, security escort services, and informal discussions. There are pamphlets/posters/films and lighted pathways/sidewalks.

Programs of Study: V.I. College confers B.A., B.S., B.F.A., and B.S.W. degrees. Associate degrees are also awarded. Bachelor's degrees are awarded in AGRICULTURE (equine science), BIOLOGICAL SCIENCE (biology/biological science), BUSINESS (business administration and management and sports management), COMMUNICATIONS AND THE ARTS (art, dance, dramatic arts, English, fine arts, performing arts, and photography), COMPUTER AND PHYSICAL SCIENCE (information sciences and systems), EDUCATION (education and secondary), HEALTH PROFESSIONS (premedicine and preveterinary science), SOCIAL SCIENCE (criminal justice, culinary arts, history, interdisciplinary studies, liberal arts/general studies, paralegal studies, political science/government, psychology, public administration, religion, and social work). Equine studies, business, and photography are the largest.

Required: To graduate, students must complete 124 credits with a minimum GPA of 2.0. Required courses are English compostition, English literature, world history, computer fundamentals, college math, natural science, performing arts, visual arts, psychology or sociology, economics or political science, philosophy or religion, speech, and phys ed.

Special: V.I. College offers cross-registration with King College and internships in paralegal studies, social work, business, art, dance, photography, sports management, political science, psychology, and theater. Dual majors, study abroad, a general studies degree, and nondegree study are available. Evening degree programs in management and leadership, interdisciplinary studies, computer information management, graphic design, and social work are designed for working adults. There are 4 national honor societies and a freshman honors program.

Faculty/Classroom: 57% of faculty are male; 43%, female. All teach undergraduates. The average class size in an introductory lecture is 19; in a laboratory, 10; and in a regular course, 12.

Admissions: The SAT scores for the 2005-2006 freshman class were: Verbal--63% below 500, 24% between 500 and 599, 12% between 600 and 700, and 1% above 700; Math--69% below 500, 23% between 500 and 599, 6% between 600 and 700, and 2% above 700. The ACT scores were 60% below 21, 21% between 21 and 23, 16% between 24 and 26, 2% between 27 and 28, and 1% above 28. 24% of the current freshmen were in the top fifth of their class; 35% were in the top two fifths. 7 freshmen graduated first in their class.

Requirements: The SAT or ACT is required. Applicants must be graduates of an accredited secondary school or home school. The GED is accepted. Applicants should complete 15 academic credits, including 4 credits of English, 2 each of social science and math, 1 of a lab science, and 6 electives. An essay is required of students not meeting the normal admissions requirements. A GPA of 2.0 is required. AP and CLEP credits are accepted. Important factors in the admissions decision are advanced placement or honor courses, evidence of special talent, and ability to finance college education.

Procedure: Freshmen are admitted to all sessions. Entrance exams should be taken late in the junior year or early in the senior year. There are early admissions, deferred admissions and rolling admissions plans. Application deadlines are open. Applications are accepted on-line. The fall 200 application fee was $15.

Transfer: 106 transfer students enrolled in 2004-2005. Applicants for transfer should have a minimum GPA of 2.0. An interview is recommended. 30 of 124 credits required for the bachelor's degree must be completed at V.I. College.

Visiting: There are regularly scheduled orientations for prospective students, consisting of a campus tour, an admissions interview, meetings with faculty, auditions for performance scholarships, and planning sessions with financial aid staff. There are guides for informal visits and visitors may sit in on classes and stay overnight. To schedule a visit, contact the Admissions Office at (276) 466-7856.

Financial Aid: In 2005-2006, 67% of all full-time freshmen and 78% of continuing full-time students received some form of financial aid. 65% of full-time freshmen and 73% of continuing full-time students received need-based aid. The average freshman award was $12,445. Need-based scholarships or need-based grants averaged $1000 ($2000 maximum); need-based self-help aid (loans and jobs) averaged $4125 ($4125 maximum); and other non-need-based awards and non-need-based scholarships averaged $5000 ($13,900 maximum). 60% of undergraduates work part time. Average annual earnings from campus work are $1500. The average financial indebtedness of the 2005 graduate was $17,125. V.I. College is a member of CSS. The FAFSA is required. The deadline for filing freshman financial aid applications for fall entry is April 15.

International Students: In a recent year there were 63 international students enrolled. The school actively recruits these students. They must score satisfactorily on the written TOEFL.

Computers: Wireless access is available. All students may access the system. There are no time limits and no fees.

Graduates: From July 1, 2004 to June 30, 2005, 224 bachelor's degrees were awarded. The most popular majors were interdisciplinary sturdies (32%), business administration (23%), and visual and performing arts (13%). In an average class, 20% graduate in 4 years or less, 29% graduate in 5 years or less, and 29% graduate in 6 years or less. 22 companies recruited on campus in 2004-2005. Of the 2004 graduating class,

15% were enrolled in graduate school within 6 months of graduation and 92% were employed.

Admissions Contact: Roger Lowe, Director of Admissions. A video is available. E-mail: *viadmit@vic.edu* Web: *www.vic.edu*

VIRGINIA MILITARY INSTITUTE D-3
Lexington, VA 24450

(540) 464-7211
(800) 767-4207; Fax: (540) 464-7746

Full-time: 1265 men, 104 women	**Faculty:** 110; IIB, +$
Part-time: none	**Ph.D.s:** 96%
Graduate: none	**Student/Faculty:** 12 to 1
Year: semesters, summer session	**Tuition:** $6988 ($21,188)
Application Deadline: April 1	**Room & Board:** $5666
Freshman Class: 1811 applied, 913 accepted, 391 enrolled	
SAT or ACT: required	**VERY COMPETITIVE**

Virginia Military Institute, established in 1839, is the nation's first state-supported military college. It offers academic programs in engineering, sciences, and liberal arts. All students are members of the Corps of Cadets, live in barracks, eat together in the mess hall, wear uniforms, and adhere to the Honor System. In addition to regional accreditation, VMI has baccalaureate program accreditation with ABET and ACS. The 2 libraries contain 240,000 volumes, 18,000 microform items, and 4540 audio/video tapes/CDs/DVDs, and subscribe to 800 periodicals including electronic. Computerized library services include the card catalog, interlibrary loans, and database searching. Special learning facilities include a learning resource center, an observatory, a research library, and 2 history museums. The 134-acre campus is in a small town 50 miles north of Roanoke. Including any residence halls, there are 68 buildings.

Student Life: 55% of undergraduates are from Virginia. Students are from 37 states, 9 foreign countries, and Canada. 78% are from public schools. 86% are white. 56% are Protestant; 30% Catholic. The average age of freshmen is 18; all undergraduates, 20. 23% do not continue beyond their first year; 67% remain to graduate.

Housing: 1370 students can be accommodated in college housing, which includes coed dorms. On-campus housing is guaranteed for all 4 years. All students live on campus; of those, 60% remain on campus on weekends. Alcohol is not permitted. Upperclassmen may keep cars.

Activities: There are no fraternities or sororities. There are 50 groups on campus, including bagpipe band, band, cheerleading, choir, chorus, dance, drama, drill team, ethnic, honors, international, jazz band, literary magazine, marching band, musical theater, newspaper, orchestra, pep band, photography, political, professional, religious, social, social service, student government, and yearbook. Popular campus events include Ring Figure, Virginia Transportation Conference, and dance and concert weekends.

Sports: There are 10 intercollegiate sports for men and 5 for women, and 4 intramural sports for men and 4 for women. Facilities include basketball, racquetball, and tennis courts, fields for lacrosse, football, baseball, and soccer, a swimming pool, a rifle range, indoor and outdoor running tracks, a wrestling facility, access to a golf course, a weight training and aerobic facility, and auxiliary indoor and outdoor basketball courts.

Disabled Students: 50% of the campus is accessible. Wheelchair ramps, elevators, special parking, and specially equipped rest rooms are available.

Services: Counseling and information services are available, as is tutoring in some subjects, including French, Spanish, German, Arabic, chemistry, math, physics, economics, and business. Tutoring for intercollegiate athletes, paid for by NCAA, also is available.

Campus Safety and Security: Measures include 24-hour foot and vehicle patrol, informal discussions, pamphlets/posters/films, and emergency telephones. There are lighted pathways/sidewalks and a 24-hour student guard team.

Programs of Study: VMI confers B.A. and B.S. degrees. Bachelor's degrees are awarded in BIOLOGICAL SCIENCE (biology/biological science), BUSINESS (business economics), COMMUNICATIONS AND THE ARTS (English), COMPUTER AND PHYSICAL SCIENCE (chemistry, computer science, mathematics, and physics), ENGINEERING AND ENVIRONMENTAL DESIGN (civil engineering, electrical/electronics engineering, and mechanical engineering), SOCIAL SCIENCE (history, international studies, and psychology). Engineering (civil, electrical, and mechanical) and sciences are the strongest academically. History, business/economics, and civil and mechanical engineering are the largest.

Required: To graduate, students must complete 136 to 144 semester hours, with a GPA of 2.0. All students must pass chemistry, English, history, math, phys ed, ROTC, and public speaking. In addition, all cadets must pass swimming, boxing, and wrestling.

Special: Study abroad in 14 countries and work-study programs are available, as are for-credit internships in English and international studies and summer internships in foreign countries. VMI offers dual majors in any combination and B.A.-B.S. degrees in liberal arts, physical sciences, and engineering. Minors are offered in each field of study. There are 11 national honor societies, a freshman honors program, and 3 departmental honors programs.

Faculty/Classroom: 81% of faculty are male; 19%, female. All teach undergraduates, 67% do research, and 67% do both. The average class size in an introductory lecture is 19; in a laboratory, 14; and in a regular course, 15.

Admissions: 50% of the 2005-2006 applicants were accepted. The SAT scores for the 2005-2006 freshman class were: Verbal--17% below 500, 43% between 500 and 599, 36% between 600 and 700, and 5% above 700; Math--12% below 500, 50% between 500 and 599, 35% between 600 and 700, and 4% above 700. 44% of the current freshmen were in the top fifth of their class; 85% were in the top two fifths. 3 freshmen graduated first in their class.

Requirements: The SAT or ACT is required. In addition, applicants must be graduates of an accredited secondary school. Applicants should complete 19 to 20 high school academic units, including 4 years of English and math, 3 of science, history, and foreign language, and 2 of social studies. An essay is encouraged and an interview is recommended. AP credits are accepted. Important factors in the admissions decision are advanced placement or honor courses, extracurricular activities record, and leadership record.

Procedure: Freshmen are admitted in the fall. Entrance exams should be taken during the second semester of the junior year. There are early decision and early admissions plans. There is a rolling admissions plan. Early decision applications should be filed by November 15; regular applications, by April 1 for fall entry. Notification of early decision is sent December 15; regular decision, on a rolling basis. The fall 2005 application fee was $35. 46 applicants were on the 2005 waiting list; 31 were admitted.

Transfer: 43 transfer students enrolled in 2004-2005. Applicants for transfer must have a minimum GPA of 2.0, 24 transferable credit hours, and a satisfactory high school record. Either the SAT or the ACT is required. 67 of 136 to 144 semester hours required for the bachelor's degree must be completed at VMI.

Visiting: There are regularly scheduled orientations for prospective students, consisting of tours, conferences with academic and ROTC instructors, interaction with current freshmen, and overnight stays. There are guides for informal visits and visitors may sit in on classes and stay overnight. To schedule a visit, contact Admissions.

Financial Aid: In 2005-2006, 59% of all full-time freshmen and 81% of continuing full-time students received some form of financial aid. 37% of full-time freshmen and 34% of continuing full-time students received need-based aid. The average freshman award was $11,613. 9% of undergraduates work part time. Average annual earnings from campus work are $800. The average financial indebtedness of the 2005 graduate was $13,000. VMI is a member of CSS. The FAFSA and the college's own financial statement are required. The deadline for filing freshman financial aid applications for fall entry is April 1.

International Students: There are 51 international students enrolled. The school actively recruits these students. They must take the written TOEFL. International students who will play intercollegiate athletics must take the SAT or ACT.

Computers: Wireless access is available. There are 200 common PCs available in locations across campus. All students may access the system. There are no time limits and no fees. It is strongly recommended that all students have a personal computer. A PC, IBM, ThinkPad, or Toshiba laptop are recommended.

Graduates: From July 1, 2004 to June 30, 2005, 299 bachelor's degrees were awarded. The most popular majors were history (22%), economics (20%), and international studies (12%). In an average class, 54% graduate in 4 years or less, 65% graduate in 5 years or less, and 67% graduate in 6 years or less. 45 companies recruited on campus in 2004-2005. Of the 2004 graduating class, 18% were enrolled in graduate school within 6 months of graduation and 99% were employed.

Admissions Contact: Col. Vernon L. Beitzel, Director, Admissions. A video is available. E-mail: *admissions@vmi.edu* Web: *www.vmi.edu*

VIRGINIA POLYTECHNIC INSTITUTE AND STATE C-3
UNIVERSITY
Blacksburg, VA 24061

(540) 231-6267; Fax: (540) 231-3242

Full-time: 12,384 men, 8701 women	**Faculty:** 1265; I, -$
Part-time: 339 men, 201 women	**Ph.D.s:** 87%
Graduate: 3562 men, 2421 women	**Student/Faculty:** 17 to 1
Year: semesters, summer session	**Tuition:** $6378 ($17,837)
Application Deadline: January 15	**Room & Board:** $4456
Freshman Class: 17,637 applied, 12,411 accepted, 4993 enrolled	
SAT Verbal/Math: 590/620*	**ACT:** 24 **VERY COMPETITIVE**

Virginia Polytechnic Institute and State University, founded in 1872, is a public land-grant institution. It offers a cadet program within the larger, nonmilitary student body. There are 7 undergraduate and 2 graduate schools. In addition to regional accreditation, Virginia Tech has baccalaureate program accreditation with AACSB, ABET, ACCE, ADA, AHEA, ASLA, FIDER, NAAB, NCATE, and SAF. The 4 libraries contain 2.1 million volumes, 6.2 million microform items, and 17,510 audio/video tapes/CDs/DVDs, and subscribe to 18,737 periodicals including electronic. Computerized library services include the card catalog, interlibrary loans, and database searching. Special learning facilities include a learning resource center, art gallery, natural history museum, radio station, TV station, airport, wind tunnels, agricultural stations, radio/visual observatories, satellite up-link station, multimedia, digital music, writing, and CAD/CAM labs, math emporium, and CAVE (cave automatic virtual environment). The 2600-acre campus is in a rural area 40 miles southwest of Roanoke. Including any residence halls, there are 110 buildings.

Student Life: 72% of undergraduates are from Virginia. Others are from 49 states, 69 foreign countries, and Canada. 74% are white. The average age of freshmen is 18; all undergraduates, 22. 12% do not continue beyond their first year; 74% remain to graduate.

Housing: 9113 students can be accommodated in college housing, which includes single-sex and coed dorms, fraternity houses, and sorority houses. In addition, there are honors houses and special-interest houses. On-campus housing is guaranteed for the freshman year only and is available on a lottery system for upperclassmen. 59% of students commute. Upperclassmen may keep cars.

Activities: 13% of men belong to 34 national fraternities; 15% of women belong to 16 national sororities. There are 600 groups on campus, including art, band, cheerleading, chess, choir, chorale, chorus, computers, dance, drama, drill team, drum and bugle corps, ethnic, film, gay, honors, international, jazz band, literary magazine, marching band, musical theater, newspaper, orchestra, pep band, photography, political, professional, radio and TV, religious, social, social service, student government, symphony, and yearbook. Popular campus events include Quad Jams, Ring Dance, and German's Mid-Winter Dance.

Sports: There are 11 intercollegiate sports for men and 10 for women, and 19 intramural sports for men and 19 for women. Facilities include a football stadium, a basketball coliseum, a field house, an indoor tennis pavilion, a 9-hole golf course, soccer and baseball fields, a swimming pool, a diving well, basketball, volleyball, racquetball, handball, squash, and tennis courts, a gymnastics room, a weight-lifting room, lighted multipurpose recreation fields, and a pond for ice skating. Residential quads are also equipped with weight-room and exercise facilities; there are also 2 gyms.

Disabled Students: 60% of the campus is accessible. Wheelchair ramps, elevators, special parking, specially equipped rest rooms, special class scheduling, lowered drinking fountains, lowered telephones, and a special services library room for the visually impaired are available.

Services: Counseling and information services are available, as is tutoring in most subjects. There is a reader service for the blind and remedial reading.

Campus Safety and Security: Measures include 24-hour foot and vehicle patrol, self-defense education, security escort services, and shuttle buses. There are informal discussions, pamphlets/posters/films, emergency telephones, and lighted pathways/sidewalks.

Programs of Study: Virginia Tech confers B.A., B.S., B.Arch., B.F.A., B.Land.Arch., B.S.Bus., B.S.E., and B.S.Ed. degrees. Master's and doctoral degrees are also awarded. Bachelor's degrees are awarded in AGRICULTURE (agricultural economics, animal science, dairy science, forestry and related sciences, horticulture, poultry science, and soil science), BIOLOGICAL SCIENCE (biochemistry, biology/biological science, and nutrition), BUSINESS (accounting, apparel and accessories marketing, banking and finance, business economics, entrepreneurial studies, hotel/motel and restaurant management, management science, marketing management, and tourism), COMMUNICATIONS AND THE ARTS (art, communications, dramatic arts, English, French, German, industrial design, music, and Spanish), COMPUTER AND PHYSICAL SCIENCE (chemistry, computer science, geology, mathematics, physics, planetary and space science, and statistics), EDUCATION (agricultural, business, environmental, foreign languages, science, and secondary), ENGINEERING AND ENVIRONMENTAL DESIGN (aerospace studies, agricultural engineering, architecture, chemical engineering, civil engineering, computer engineering, construction engineering, construction management, electrical/electronics engineering, engineering mechanics, environmental science, industrial engineering, interior design, landscape architecture/design, materials engineering, mechanical engineering, mining and mineral engineering, and ocean engineering), HEALTH PROFESSIONS (physical therapy, predentistry, and premedicine), SOCIAL SCIENCE (dietetics, economics, food science, geography, history, human development, interdisciplinary studies, international studies, interpreter for the deaf, parks and recreation management, philosophy, physical fitness/movement, political science/government, prelaw, psychology, public affairs, sociology, and urban studies). Engineering, architecture, and business are the strongest academically. Engineering, computer science, and biology are the largest.

Required: To graduate, students must complete between 120 and 156 credit hours (depending on the major), with a minimum GPA of 2.0. There is a required core curriculum that includes 8 hours of science and 6 hours each of humanities, social science, math, and writing and discourse. Students must also meet a foreign language requirement.

Special: Students may cross-register with Miami University in Ohio, Oxford Polytechnic Institute, California Polytechnic Institute, and Florida A

& M. Study abroad in 36 countries, internships in nearly every major, a Washington semester, and a wide range of work-study programs are available, as well as co-ops in 48 majors. There are honors options for most majors, B.A.-B.S. degrees, dual and student-designed majors, credit for independent study or research, nondegree study, and pass/fail options. The Corps of Cadets, a militarily structured organization, is open to men and women. Undergraduate advising programs are available to students wishing to prepare for professional school in law, dentistry, medicine, pharmacy, physical therapy, or veterinary medicine. There are 13 national honor societies, including Phi Beta Kappa, and a freshman honors program.

Faculty/Classroom: 71% of faculty are male; 29%, female. 74% teach undergraduates and all do research. Graduate students teach 12% of introductory courses. The average class size in an introductory lecture is 46 and in a laboratory, 30.

Admissions: 70% of the 2005-2006 applicants were accepted. The SAT scores for the 2005-2006 freshman class were: Verbal--8% below 500, 46% between 500 and 599, 41% between 600 and 700, and 5% above 700; Math--3% below 500, 36% between 500 and 599, 50% between 600 and 700, and 11% above 700. The ACT scores were 9% below 21, 28% between 21 and 23, 33% between 24 and 26, 16% between 27 and 28, and 14% above 28. 68% of the current freshmen were in the top fifth of their class; 94% were in the top two fifths. There were 36 National Merit finalists. 74 freshmen graduated first in their class.

Requirements: The SAT or ACT is required. In addition, applicants must be graduates of an accredited secondary school, or the GED is accepted. Applicants should complete 18 high school academic credits, including 4 years of English, 3 of math, including algebra II and geometry, 2 of lab science, to be chosen from biology, chemistry, or physics, and 1 each of history and social studies. An additional 3 years from college preparatory courses and 4 from any credit course offerings are required. AP and CLEP credits are accepted. Important factors in the admissions decision are advanced placement or honor courses, evidence of special talent, and extracurricular activities record.

Procedure: Freshmen are admitted to all sessions. Entrance exams should be taken by January 1 of the senior year. There are early decision and deferred admissions plans. Early decision applications should be filed by November 1; regular applications, by January 15 for fall entry, October 1 for spring entry, and April 22 for summer entry, along with a $40 fee. Notification of early decision is sent December 15; regular decision, April 1. 1134 early decision candidates were accepted for the 2005-2006 class. 1150 applicants were on the 2005 waiting list. Applications are accepted on-line.

Transfer: 711 transfer students enrolled in 2004-2005. Applicants must have a minimum GPA of 2.0 and must specify a major. Competitive GPA is 3.0. 30 of 120 to 156 credits required for the bachelor's degree must be completed at Virginia Tech.

Visiting: There are regularly scheduled orientations for prospective students, consisting of a Fall Open House Series: half-day on-campus programs that include presentations, tours, and question-and-answer sessions. There are guides for informal visits and visitors may sit in on classes. To schedule a visit, contact the Office of Undergraduate Admissions.

Financial Aid: The FAFSA is required. The deadline for filing freshman financial aid applications for fall entry is March 11.

International Students: There are 498 international students enrolled. The school actively recruits these students. They must achieve a satisfactory score on the TOEFL and also take the SAT or the ACT.

Computers: Each student brings a personal computer and has access to high-speed Ethernet connections in all residence halls, labs, and lecture rooms, as well as wireless access in all academic buildings. There are 912 university-owned workstations available for general student use. All students may access the system any time. All students are required to have personal computers.

Graduates: From July 1, 2004 to June 30, 2005, 4835 bachelor's degrees were awarded. The most popular majors were biological science (6%), finance (5%), and psychology (5%). In an average class, 44% graduate in 4 years or less, 70% graduate in 5 years or less, and 74% graduate in 6 years or less. More than 250 companies recruited on campus in 2004-2005. Of the 2004 graduating class, 13% were enrolled in graduate school within 6 months of graduation and 52% were employed.

Admissions Contact: Office of Undergraduate Admissions. A video is available. E-mail: *vtadmiss@vt.edu* Web: *www.vt.edu*

VIRGINIA STATE UNIVERSITY   E-3
Petersburg, VA 23806

(804) 524-5902
(800) 871-7611; Fax: (804) 524-5055

Full-time: 1350 men, 1800 women	**Faculty:** 168
Part-time: 200 men, 200 women	**Ph.Ds:** 74%
Graduate: 220 men, 580 women	**Student/Faculty:** 19 to 1
Year: semesters, summer session	**Tuition:** $4834 ($12,046)
Application Deadline: see profile	**Room & Board:** $6484
Freshman Class: n/av	
SAT or ACT: required	**COMPETITIVE**

Virginia State University is a historically black public land-grant institution of higher education providing academic programs that integrate instruction, research, and extension/public service. Some information in this capsule and profile is approximate. There are 4 undergraduate schools and 1 graduate school. In addition to regional accreditation, VSU has baccalaureate program accreditation with ABET, ADA, CSWE, NASM, and NCATE. The library contains 280,599 volumes, 662,075 microform items, and 3939 audio/video tapes/CDs/DVDs, and subscribes to 1198 periodicals including electronic. Computerized library services include the card catalog, interlibrary loans, and database searching. Special learning facilities include a learning resource center, art gallery, radio station, and TV station. The 652-acre campus is in a suburban area 25 miles south of Richmond. Including any residence halls, there are 52 buildings.

Student Life: 65% of undergraduates are from Virginia. Others are from 35 states and 1 foreign country. 96% are from public schools. 90% are African American. The average age of freshmen is 18; all undergraduates, 21. 40% do not continue beyond their first year; 18% remain to graduate.

Housing: 2050 students can be accommodated in college housing, which includes single-sex dorms. In addition, there are honors houses. On-campus housing is guaranteed for the freshman year only and is available on a first-come, first-served basis. 52% of students live on campus; of those, 20% remain on campus on weekends. Alcohol is not permitted. Upperclassmen may keep cars.

Activities: 10% of men belong to 4 national fraternities; 10% of women belong to 4 national sororities. There are 44 groups on campus, including band, cheerleading, chess, choir, chorus, computers, dance, drama, drill team, ethnic, honors, international, jazz band, marching band, musical theater, newspaper, orchestra, pep band, photography, political, professional, radio and TV, religious, social, student government, symphony, and yearbook. Popular campus events include High School Day, VSU Day, and Commencement.

Sports: There are 7 intercollegiate sports for men and 6 for women, and 5 intramural sports for men and 6 for women. Facilities include a gym, an Olympic-size pool, a dance studio, tennis courts, track, football and baseball fields, and indoor and outdoor basketball courts.

Disabled Students: 75% of the campus is accessible. Wheelchair ramps, elevators, special parking, and specially equipped rest rooms are available.

Services: Counseling and information services are available, as is tutoring in most subjects. There is a reader service for the blind.

Campus Safety and Security: Measures include 24-hour foot and vehicle patrol, informal discussions, emergency telephones, and lighted pathways/sidewalks.

Programs of Study: VSU confers B.A., B.S., B.F.A., B.I.S., and B.Mus. degrees. Master's degrees are also awarded. Bachelor's degrees are awarded in AGRICULTURE (agriculture), BIOLOGICAL SCIENCE (biology/biological science), BUSINESS (accounting, business administration and management, hotel/motel and restaurant management, management information systems, and marketing management), COMMUNICATIONS AND THE ARTS (English literature, music performance, and visual and performing arts), COMPUTER AND PHYSICAL SCIENCE (chemistry, mathematics, and physics), EDUCATION (athletic training, business, physical, and trade and industrial), ENGINEERING AND ENVIRONMENTAL DESIGN (engineering technology), SOCIAL SCIENCE (economics, history, home economics, interdisciplinary studies, political science/government, psychology, public administration, social work, and sociology). Business administration, accounting, and business information systems are the largest.

Required: To graduate, students must have a minimum GPA of 2.0. They must earn at least 120 credits, with the last 27 semester hours in residence. Requirements include those in phys ed, freshman writing, math, biology, social or physical science, history, and psychology. Freshman orientation must also be completed.

Special: VSU offers dual majors, a general studies degree, a 3-2 engineering degree program, nondegree study, and a pass/fail grading option. There are 10 national honor societies, including Phi Beta Kappa, a freshman honors program, and 7 departmental honors programs.

Faculty/Classroom: 67% of faculty are male; 33%, female. Graduate students teach 2% of introductory courses.

Requirements: The SAT or ACT is required. In addition, applicants must graduate from an accredited secondary school with 16 academic credits and 12 Carnegie units, or have a GED. Students must take 4 years of English, 2 each of a foreign language, math, and science, and 1 each of history and social studies. Essays, 2 letters of recommendation, evidence of physical condition, interviews, and, if appropriate, auditions are required. A GPA of 2.2 is required. AP and CLEP credits are accepted. Important factors in the admissions decision are advanced placement or honor courses, recommendations by school officials, and leadership record.

Procedure: Freshmen are admitted fall and spring. There is a rolling admissions plan and a deferred admissions plan. Check with the school for current application deadlines. Application frr is $25. Notification is sent on a rolling basis. Applications are accepted on-line.

Transfer: Applicants must have a minimum GPA of 2.0. Those transferring fewer than 25 semester hours must meet freshman standards. 30 of 120 credits required for the bachelor's degree must be completed at VSU.

Visiting: There are regularly scheduled orientations for prospective students. There are guides for informal visits and visitors may sit in on classes. To schedule a visit, contact Admissions.

Financial Aid: In a recent year, 95% of all full-time freshmen received some form of financial aid. Average annual earnings from campus work are $2000. VSU is a member of CSS. The CSS/Profile and the college's own financial statement are required. Check with the school for current application deadlines.

International Students: Students must achieve a satisfactory score on theTOEFL and also take the SAT or the ACT.

Computers: All students may access the system 8 A.M. to 10 P.M. Monday through Friday and 8 A.M. to 4 P.M. Saturdays. There are no time limits and no fees. It is strongly recommended that all students have a personal computer.

Admissions Contact: Irene Logan, Director of Admissions. A video is available. E-mail: *ilogan@vsu.edu* Web: *www.vsu.edu*

VIRGINIA UNION UNIVERSITY   E-3
Richmond, VA 23220

(804) 329-8456
(800) 368-3227; Fax: (804) 329-8477

Full-time: 540 men, 780 women	**Faculty:** 82; IIB, --$
Part-time: 30 men, 30 women	**Ph.Ds:** 55%
Graduate: 200 men, 120 women	**Student/Faculty:** 16 to 1
Year: semesters, summer session	**Tuition:** $12,770
Application Deadline: see profile	**Room & Board:** $5662
Freshman Class: n/av	
SAT: required	**LESS COMPETITIVE**

Virginia Union University, established in 1865 and affiliated with the Baptist Church, is a private institution offering undergraduate programs in education and psychology, business, humanities, natural science and math, and social sciences. There are 2 undergraduate schools and 1 graduate school. Some figures in the above capsule and in this profile are approximate. In addition to regional accreditation, VUU has baccalaureate program accreditation with ACBSP and CSWE. The library contains 145,305 volumes, 62,079 microform items, and 1523 audio/video tapes/CDs/DVDs, and subscribes to 308 periodicals including electronic. Computerized library services include database searching. Special learning facilities include a learning resource center and art gallery. The 72-acre campus is in an urban area in the city of Richmond. Including any residence halls, there are 18 buildings.

Student Life: 52% of undergraduates are from Virginia. Others are from 27 states and 4 foreign countries. 85% are from public schools. 98% are African American. The average age of freshmen is 18. 31% do not continue beyond their first year; 55% remain to graduate.

Housing: 700 students can be accommodated in college housing, which includes single-sex dorms. In addition, there are honors houses. On-campus housing is available on a first-come, first-served basis. Priority is given to out-of-town students. 50% of students live on campus. Alcohol is not permitted. All students may keep cars.

Activities: There are 2 national fraternities and 4 national sororities. There are 32 groups on campus, including cheerleading, drama, international, newspaper, religious, student government, and yearbook. Popular campus events include films, lectures, and concerts.

Sports: There are 6 intercollegiate sports for men and 6 for women, and 3 intramural sports for men and 2 for women. Facilities include a gym-auditorium and a 10,000-seat stadium.

Disabled Students: 90% of the campus is accessible. Wheelchair ramps, elevators, and special parking are available.

Services: Counseling and information services are available, as is tutoring in every subject. There is remedial math, reading, and writing.

Campus Safety and Security: Measures include 24-hour foot and vehicle patrol, security escort services, informal discussions, and pamphlets/posters/films. There are emergency telephones and lighted pathways/sidewalks.

Programs of Study: VUU confers B.A., B.S., and B.S.W. degrees. Master's and doctoral degrees are also awarded. Bachelor's degrees are awarded in BIOLOGICAL SCIENCE (biology/biological science), BUSINESS (accounting, banking and finance, and business administration and management), COMMUNICATIONS AND THE ARTS (English, journalism, and music), COMPUTER AND PHYSICAL SCIENCE (chemistry and mathematics), EDUCATION (art, business, early childhood, elementary, music, secondary, and special), SOCIAL SCIENCE (criminology, history, political science/government, psychology, religion, social work, and sociology). Teacher education, accounting, and history/political science are the strongest academically. Teacher education, criminology, and business administration are the largest.

Required: To graduate, all students must complete at least 124 credit hours with a GPA of at least 2.0. Courses in religion, English, math, science, social science, a foreign language, and phys ed are required. There are also chapel and VUU events attendance requirements. All students must successfully complete a computer science course and must take an English essay exam, usually by the end of the junior year, as well as a comprehensive exam in their major.

Special: The university offers cross-registration with Virginia Commonwealth and Virginia State Universities, and the University of Richmond. Internships, co-op programs, federal work-study programs, a general studies degree, a joint law degree with St. John's University School of Law in New York, a 3-2 degree in engineering with the Universities of Michigan and Iowa and Howard University, and exchange programs are also offered. There are 2 national honor societies and a freshman honors program.

Faculty/Classroom: 55% of faculty are male; 45%, female. 86% teach undergraduates. No introductory courses are taught by graduate students. The average class size in an introductory lecture is 28; in a laboratory, 20; and in a regular course, 22.

Requirements: The SAT is required. In addition, in addition, graduation from an accredited secondary school is required; the GED is accepted. 16 academic units are required, including 4 of English, 3 each of math and academic electives, and 2 each of foreign language, social science, and natural science. Special consideration is given to disadvantaged students. Children of alumni are given some preference. A GPA of 2.0 is required. AP and CLEP credits are accepted. Important factors in the admissions decision are extracurricular activities record, advanced placement or honor courses, and leadership record.

Procedure: Freshmen are admitted fall and spring. Entrance exams should be taken between March of the junior year and March of the senior year. There are rolling admissions, early admissions, and deferred admissions plans. Check with the school for current application deadlines. The application fee is $25. Notification is sent on a rolling basis.

Transfer: Transfer students must be in good standing at their previous institutions and must submit all college transcripts. 30 of 124 credits required for the bachelor's degree must be completed at VUU.

Visiting: There are guides for informal visits and visitors may sit in on classes. To schedule a visit, contact the Admissions Office at (804) 257-5600.

Financial Aid: VUU is a member of CSS. The CSS/Profile is required. Check with the school for current application deadlines.

International Students: They must achieve satisfactory scores on the TOEFL and the SAT or ACT.

Computers: All students may access the system. There are no time limits and no fees. It is strongly recommended that all students have a personal computer.

Admissions Contact: Gil Powell, Director of Admissions. E-mail: *admissions@vuu.edu* Web: *vuu.edu*

VIRGINIA WESLEYAN COLLEGE
F-4

Norfolk, VA 23502-5599

(757) 455-3208
(800) 737-8684; Fax: (757) 461-5238

Full-time: 438 men, 683 women	**Faculty:** 80; IIB, -$
Part-time: 62 men, 209 women	**Ph.D.s:** 85%
Graduate: none	**Student/Faculty:** 14 to 1
Year: 4-1-4, summer session	**Tuition:** $21,733
Application Deadline: open	**Room & Board:** $6700
Freshman Class: n/av	
SAT or ACT: required	**COMPETITIVE**

Virginia Wesleyan College, established in 1961, is a private institution affiliated with the United Methodist Church, offering undergraduate degrees in the humanities, the social sciences, the natural sciences, and math. In addition to regional accreditation, Virginia Wesleyan has baccalaureate program accreditation with NRPA. The library contains 121,373 volumes, 15,869 microform items, and 3813 audio/video tapes/CDs/DVDs, and subscribes to 800 periodicals including electronic. Computerized library services include the card catalog, interlibrary loans, database searching, and Internet access. Special learning facilities include a learning resource center, art gallery, radio station, a greenhouse, the Center for the Study of Religious Freedom, 142 acres of woodland used as a lab for biological and environmental sciences, a social sciences lab, the Center for Sacred Music, and an apiary. The 300-acre campus is in a suburban area 8 miles east of downtown Norfolk and 10 miles west of the Virginia Beach oceanfront. Including any residence halls, there are 31 buildings.

Student Life: 79% of undergraduates are from Virginia. Others are from 33 states, 7 foreign countries, and Canada. 82% are from public schools. 77% are white; 15% African American. 46% are Protestant; 22% Catholic; 22% claim no religious affiliation; 9% Eastern Orthodox, nondenominational, Mennonite, and others. The average age of freshmen is 18; all undergraduates, 24. 34% do not continue beyond their first year; 42% remain to graduate.

Housing: 696 students can be accommodated in college housing, which includes single-sex and coed dorms and on-campus apartments. In addition, there are honors houses, special-interest houses, and fraternity, sorority, and international residence halls. On-campus housing is guaranteed for all 4 years. 58% of students commute. All students may keep cars.

Activities: 10% of men belong to 2 national fraternities; 15% of women belong to 4 national sororities. There are 62 groups on campus, including cheerleading, chorus, commuter, dance, departmental, drama, ethnic, gay, honors, international, literary magazine, model UN, musical theater, newspaper, political, professional, radio and TV, religious, social, social service, student government, womens's and yearbook. Popular campus events include TGIF Series and seafood party in the Dell.

Sports: There are 8 intercollegiate sports for men and 9 for women, and 5 intramural sports for men and 5 for women. Facilities include the student center, which includes a multiactivity athletic center, a 36-foot-high climbing wall, NCAA regulation swimming pool, indoor running track, and racquetball and basketball courts. Also baseball, softball, lacrosse, field hockey, and soccer fields, and tennis courts are available.

Disabled Students: 90% of the campus is accessible. Wheelchair ramps, elevators, special parking, specially equipped rest rooms, special class scheduling, lowered drinking fountains, lowered telephones, special desks, and preferential seating and registration are available.

Services: Counseling and information services are available, as is tutoring in most subjects. There is a reader service for the blind, and remedial math, reading, and writing. Note takers, special co-advising, test proctoring, and Learning Plus for Praxis are available.

Campus Safety and Security: Measures include 24-hour foot and vehicle patrol, self-defense education, security escort services, and shuttle buses. There are informal discussions, pamphlets/posters/films, emergency telephones, lighted pathways/sidewalks, and a bicycle patrol.

Programs of Study: Virginia Wesleyan confers B.A., B.S. degrees. Bachelor's degrees are awarded in AGRICULTURE (environmental studies), BIOLOGICAL SCIENCE (biology/biological science), BUSINESS (business administration and management), COMMUNICATIONS AND THE ARTS (art, classics, communications, dramatic arts, English, French, German, journalism, languages, music, and Spanish), COMPUTER AND PHYSICAL SCIENCE (chemistry, computer science, earth science, mathematics, and natural sciences), EDUCATION (art, elementary, secondary, and social studies), SOCIAL SCIENCE (American studies, criminal justice, history, human ecology, humanities, interdisciplinary studies, international relations, liberal arts/general studies, parks and recreation management, philosophy, political science/government, psychology, religion, social science, social studies, social work, sociology, and women's studies). Art, history, and math are the strongest academically. Biology, education, and liberal arts management program are the largest.

Required: To graduate, students must complete general studies requirements, which include English, math, a foreign language, and Frames of Reference courses. These include: Empirical Knowledge; Aesthetic Understanding and Activity; Ethical Values, World Views, Faith Perspectives; Historical Perspective; Communications; and Institutional and Cultural Systems. Students must earn 120 credits, including 40 in the major, with a minimum 2.0 GPA. Students must complete 3 credits designated to fulfill a Senior Integrative Experience requirement. Students must complete at least one-fifth of their Virginia Wesleyan work courses designated as writing courses for transfer students; the required number of writing courses depends upon hours of credit upon admission. A First Year Seminar Introduction to Inquiry is also required for first-time college students. All graduates must demonstrate computer literacy in a manner related to their field and designated by their major program. Oral communications proficiency also must be demonstrated in a manner prescribed by the major program. The number of hours required for the major varies; the maximum is 50.

Special: Students may cross-register with Old Dominion University, the College of William and Mary, or Norfolk State University through the Virginia Tidewater Consortium. Internships are available and are usually completed during the senior year. The college offers study-abroad programs and international internships through partnerships and exchange programs in several countries; additional arrangements for study abroad can be made in almost any country. Dual majors, individualized and interdivisional majors, and interdisciplinary majors are available. Work-study programs with Virginia Wesleyan are offered. Credit may be granted for life, military, and work experience. Nondegree study and pass/fail options are also available. There are 16 national honor societies and a freshman honors program.

Faculty/Classroom: 55% of faculty are male; 45%, female. All teach undergraduates. The average class size in a regular course is 12.

Admissions: The SAT scores for the 2005-2006 freshman class were: Verbal--42% below 500, 40% between 500 and 599, 16% between 600 and 700, and 2% above 700; Math--38% below 500, 43% between 500 and 599, 17% between 600 and 700, and 2% above 700. The ACT scores were 55% below 21, 23% between 21 and 23, 19% between 24 and 26, 2% between 27 and 28, and 2% above 28. 25% of the current freshmen were in the top fifth of their class; 53% were in the top two fifths.

Requirements: The SAT or ACT is required. In addition, applicants must graduate from an accredited secondary school or have a GED. The college recommends 15 academic credits. Students should complete 4 years of English, 3 of social studies/history, math, and science, and 2 of foreign language. Essays are required and interviews are recommended. Home-schooled graduates are reviewed individually. A GPA of 2.0 is required. AP and CLEP credits are accepted. Important factors in the admissions decision are advanced placement or honor courses, extracurricular activities record, and leadership record.

Procedure: Freshmen are admitted fall and spring. Entrance exams should be taken in the spring of the junior year and the fall of the senior year. There are non-binding early admissions, deferred admissions, and rolling admissions plans. Application deadlines are open. Application fee is $40. Notification is sent on a rolling basis. Applications are accepted on-line.

Transfer: 143 transfer students enrolled in 2004-2005. Applicants must have a minimum GPA of 2.0 in courses to be transferred. For applicants who have not completed 12 semester hours of college work, official transcripts of college and high school records (including SAT or ACT scores) are required. All others must submit a high school diploma or GED in addition to official college transcripts. 30 of 120 credits required for the bachelor's degree must be completed at Virginia Wesleyan.

Visiting: There are regularly scheduled orientations for prospective students, consisting of 3 Open House Days on Saturdays for prospective students to meet faculty and current students, and to tour the campus. There are guides for informal visits and visitors may sit in on classes and stay overnight. To schedule a visit, contact the Admissions Office at *admissions@vwc.edu.*

Financial Aid: In 2005-2006, 68% of all full-time freshmen and 63% of continuing full-time students received some form of financial aid. 87% of full-time freshmen and 84% of continuing full-time students received need-based aid. The average freshman award was $14,326. Need-based scholarships or need-based grants averaged $3091; need-based self-help aid (loans and jobs) averaged $3424; and other non-need-based awards and non-need-based scholarships averaged $4594. The average financial indebtedness of the 2005 graduate was $16,029. The FAFSA is required. The deadline for filing freshman financial aid applications for fall entry is March 1.

International Students: There are 8 international students enrolled. The school actively recruits these students. Satisfactory scores are required on the written TOEFL and also take and the SAT or the ACT.

Computers: Wireless access is available. Approximately 100 classrooms and labs are linked to the college's network. Wireless access is available at the student center and the library. Residential rooms are equipped with Internet access. All students may access the system 5:30 A.M. to 1 A.M. There are no time limits and no fees. It is strongly recommended that all students have a PC. The Dell OptiPlex or Latitude is recommended.

Graduates: From July 1, 2004 to June 30, 2005, 287 bachelor's degrees were awarded. The most popular majors were business (20%), communications (11%), and criminal justice (9%). In an average class, 1% graduate in 3 years, 30% graduate in 4 years, 30% graduate in 5 years, and 42% graduate in 6 years. 86 companies recruited on campus in 2004-2005. Of the 2004 graduating class, 18% were enrolled in graduate school within 6 months of graduation and 77% were employed.

Admissions Contact: Richard T. Hinshaw, Vice President for Enrollment Management. E-mail: *admissions@vwc.edu* Web: *www.vwc.edu*

WASHINGTON AND LEE UNIVERSITY — D-3

Lexington, VA 24450-0303   (540) 458-8710; Fax: (540) 458-8062

Full-time: 889 men, 877 women	**Faculty:** 206; IIB, +$
Part-time: 3 men, 1 woman	**Ph.D.s:** 94%
Graduate: 239 men, 170 women	**Student/Faculty:** 9 to 1
Year: n/app	**Tuition:** $28,655
Application Deadline: January 15	**Room & Board:** $7225
Freshman Class: 3948 applied, 1136 accepted, 467 enrolled	
SAT Verbal/Math: 690/690*	**ACT:** 29 **MOST COMPETITIVE**

Washington and Lee University, established in 1749, is a private institution offering undergraduate liberal arts and sciences and preprofessional programs. There are 2 undergraduate schools and 1 graduate school. In addition to regional accreditation, Washington and Lee has baccalaureate program accreditation with AACSB, ACEJMC, and ACS. The 3 libraries contain 907,325 volumes, 1,024,212 microform items, and

16,079 audio/video tapes/CDs/DVDs, and subscribe to 8027 periodicals including electronic. Computerized library services include the card catalog, interlibrary loans, database searching, Internet access, and laptop Internet portals. Special learning facilities include an art gallery, radio station, TV station, and performing arts center, multimedia center, history, fine arts, and archeological museums, and special collections. The 322-acre campus is in a small town 50 miles northeast of Roanoke. Including any residence halls, there are 100 buildings.

Student Life: 85% of undergraduates are from out of state, mostly the Middle Atlantic. Others are from 49 states and 36 foreign countries. 60% are from public schools. 87% are white. 48% are claim no religious affiliation; 38% Protestant; 15% Catholic. The average age of freshmen is 18; all undergraduates, 20. 5% do not continue beyond their first year; 87% remain to graduate.

Housing: 1284 students can be accommodated in college housing, which includes coed dorms, on-campus apartments, fraternity houses, and sorority houses. In addition, there are language houses and special-interest houses. On-campus housing is available on a lottery system for upperclassmen. 61% of students live on campus. All students may keep cars.

Activities: 83% of men belong to 14 national fraternities; 77% of women belong to 6 national sororities. There are 124 groups on campus, including cheerleading, choir, chorale, chorus, dance, debate, drama, ethnic, film, forensics, gay, honors, international, jazz band, leadership, literary magazine, musical theater, newspaper, orchestra, outing, photography, political, radio and TV, religious, social, social service, Spanish, sports, student government, symphony, volunteer, and yearbook. Popular campus events include the Presidential Mock Convention, a fancy-dress ball, and NABORS Service Day.

Sports: There are 12 intercollegiate sports for men and 11 for women, and 15 intramural sports for men and 7 for women. Facilities include a gym, a 2400-seat arena, a 7000-seat stadium, a pool with a 500-seat gallery, a fitness center, weight training and exercise rooms, handball, racquetball, squash, and tennis courts, an outdoor track, baseball and practice fields, an indoor tennis facility, a 1000-seat soccer/lacrosse stadium, and a 1000-seat turf field for field hockey and lacrosse.

Disabled Students: 55% of the campus is accessible. Wheelchair ramps, elevators, special parking, specially equipped rest rooms, special class scheduling, and lowered drinking fountains are available.

Services: Counseling and information services are available, as is tutoring in every subject. There is a reader service for the blind.

Campus Safety and Security: Measures include 24-hour foot and vehicle patrol, self-defense education, security escort services, and shuttle buses. There are informal discussions, pamphlets/posters/films, emergency telephones, lighted pathways/sidewalks, and required safety programs for freshmen.

Programs of Study: Washington and Lee confers B.A. and B.S. degrees. Doctoral degrees are also awarded. Bachelor's degrees are awarded in BIOLOGICAL SCIENCE (biochemistry, biology/biological science, and neurosciences), BUSINESS (accounting and business administration and management), COMMUNICATIONS AND THE ARTS (art history and appreciation, classics, dramatic arts, English, French, German, Germanic languages and literature, journalism, music, romance languages and literature, Russian languages and literature, Spanish, and studio art), COMPUTER AND PHYSICAL SCIENCE (chemistry, computer science, geology, mathematics, natural sciences, and physics), ENGINEERING AND ENVIRONMENTAL DESIGN (chemical engineering, engineering physics, and environmental science), SOCIAL SCIENCE (anthropology, archeology, East Asian studies, economics, history, interdisciplinary studies, medieval studies, philosophy, political science/government, psychology, public affairs, religion, and sociology). Business administration, economics, and politics are the largest.

Required: To graduate, students must achieve proficiency in a foreign language and English composition, and complete 12 credits in fine arts and humanities, 10 in lab science and math, 9 in social sciences, and 6 in literature. A total of 121 credits, with a minimum GPA of 1.9 overall and 2.0 in the major, is required. All students must take 5 courses in phys ed and a swim test.

Special: There is cross-registration with area colleges, including VMI, and colleges in Georgia and Maine, and various internships, including commerce, government, and journalism are available. Study-abroad programs are offered in several countries. There is a 3-3 law program and a 3-2 engineering degree with Rensselaer Polytechnic Institute and Washington and Columbia Universities. Washington and Lee also offers B.A.-B.S. degrees and dual, interdisciplinary, and student-designed majors. There are 12 national honor societies, including Phi Beta Kappa, and 29 departmental honors programs.

Faculty/Classroom: 70% of faculty are male; 30%, female. 100% both teach and do research. No introductory courses are taught by graduate students. The average class size in an introductory lecture is 16 and in a regular course, 16.

Admissions: 29% of the 2005-2006 applicants were accepted. The SAT scores for the 2005-2006 freshman class were: Verbal--4% between 500 and 599, 55% between 600 and 700, and 40% above 700; Math--

-3% between 500 and 599, 58% between 600 and 700, and 39% above 700. The ACT scores were 2% between 21 and 23, 12% between 27 and 28, and 85% above 28. 91% of the current freshmen were in the top fifth of their class; 100% were in the top two fifths. There were 27 National Merit finalists. 28 freshmen graduated first in their class.

Requirements: The SAT or ACT is required. In addition, 2 unrelated SAT Subject Tests are required. A high school diploma is not required. Applicants must earn 16 units, including 4 units in English, 3 in math, 2 in a foreign language, and 1 each in history and natural science. Course work in social sciences is also required. Essays, test scores, school transcript, and recommendation letters are needed to apply. An interview is recommended. AP credits are accepted. Important factors in the admissions decision are advanced placement or honor courses, leadership record, and recommendations by school officials.

Procedure: Freshmen are admitted in the fall. Entrance exams should be taken between March of the junior year and January of the senior year. There are early decision and deferred admissions plans. Early decision applications should be filed by November 15; regular applications, by January 15 for fall entry. Notification of early decision is sent December 22; regular decision, April 1. 230 early decision candidates were accepted for the 2005-2006 class. 912 applicants were on the 2005 waiting list; 69 were admitted. Applications are accepted on-line.

Transfer: 4 transfer students enrolled in 2004-2005. Transfer applicants must have a GPA of at least 2.0 (at least 3.5 to be competitive); no more than 87 credits will transfer. There is a 2-year residency requirement. 60 of 121 credits required for the bachelor's degree must be completed at Washington and Lee.

Visiting: There are regularly scheduled orientations for prospective students, consisting of hourly interview slots and campus tours, 2 group information sessions daily, and seasonal Saturday tours and interviews. There are guides for informal visits and visitors may sit in on classes. To schedule a visit, contact the Admissions Office at 540-458-8710 or *admissions@wlu.edu.*

Financial Aid: In 2005-2006, 36% of all full-time freshmen and 31% of continuing full-time students received some form of financial aid. 27% of full-time freshmen and 24% of continuing full-time students received need-based aid. The average freshman award was $22,468. Need-based scholarships or need-based grants averaged $19,728; need-based self-help aid (loans and jobs) averaged $3874; and other non-need-based awards and non-need-based scholarships averaged $12,091. The average financial indebtedness of the 2005 graduate was $17,374. Washington and Lee is a member of CSS. The CSS/ Profile, FAFSA, the noncustodial parent's statement, and the business/farm supplement are required. The priority date for freshman financial aid applications for fall entry is April 1. The deadline for filing freshman financial aid applications for fall entry is February 1.

International Students: There are 73 international students enrolled. The school actively recruits these students. A satisfactory score is required on the written TOEFL. Applicants must also take APIEL or ELPT and the SAT or the ACT.

Computers: Wireless access is available. All students have Internet access and e-mail accounts. Computer and network access are available in computer labs, residence halls, libraries, and the student center. There are 320 PCs and over 1500 network connections available. It is recommended that students have a personal laptop. All students may access the system 24 hours a day, 7 days a week while classes are in session. There are no time limits. The fee is $200 per year.

Graduates: From July 1, 2004 to June 30, 2005, 461 bachelor's degrees were awarded. The most popular majors were business administration (11%), economics (10%), and politics (9%). In an average class, 84% graduate in 4 years or less, and 87% graduate in 6 years or less. 31 companies recruited on campus in 2004-2005. Of the 2004 graduating class, 24% were enrolled in graduate school within 6 months of graduation and 63% were employed.

Admissions Contact: William M. Hartog, Dean of Admissions and Financial Aid. A video is available. E-mail: *admissions@wlu.edu* Web: *www.wlu.edu*

A B C D E F

1 • Bellingham
5
Everett
Seattle
• Bellevue
Bremerton • Reunion
90
Lakes District • Spokane
2
Tacoma
Fort Lewis

Yakima
3 5 Richland •
Longview

Vancouver

4

WASHINGTON

0 20 40 60 80 100
Miles

POPULATION DENSITY
• 25,000 and over

CENTRAL WASHINGTON UNIVERSITY D-2
Ellensburg, WA 98926-7512 (509) 963-1211
(866) 298-4968; Fax: (509) 963-3022

Full-time: 4068 men, 4462 women	**Faculty:** 338; IIA, --$
Part-time: 477 men, 610 women	**Ph.D.s:** 90%
Graduate: 216 men, 355 women	**Student/Faculty:** 24 to 1
Year: quarters, summer session	**Tuition:** $4806 ($13,101)
Application Deadline: April 1	**Room & Board:** $6924
Freshman Class: 4656 applied, 3554 accepted, 1435 enrolled	
SAT Verbal/Math: 490/490*	**ACT:** 20 COMPETITIVE

Central Washington University is a public institution offering undergraduate programs in the arts and sciences, business administration, and education. There are 4 undergraduate schools and 1 graduate school. In addition to regional accreditation, CWU has baccalaureate program accreditation with ABET, ACCE, ADA, NASM, NCATE, and NRPA. The library contains 546,025 volumes, 1,165,466 microform items, and 9500 audio/video tapes/CDs/DVDs. Computerized library services include the card catalog, interlibrary loans, and database searching. Special learning facilities include a learning resource center, art gallery, natural history museum, planetarium, radio station, an anthropology museum, a botanical greenhouse, and a primate research lab. The 380-acre campus is in a rural area 100 miles east of Seattle. Including any residence halls, there are 74 buildings.

Student Life: 97% of undergraduates are from Washington. Students are from 35 states, 32 foreign countries, and Canada. 95% are from public schools. 78% are white. The average age of freshmen is 19; all undergraduates, 23. 24% do not continue beyond their first year; 52% remain to graduate.

Housing: 2525 students can be accommodated in college housing, which includes coed dorms, on-campus apartments, off-campus apartments, and married-student housing. In addition, there are special-interest houses, a freshman-only enrichment hall, and a residence hall for transfers and upper-classmen only. On-campus housing is guaranteed for the freshman year only and is available on a first-come, first-served basis. All students may keep cars.

Activities: There are no fraternities or sororities. There are 80 groups on campus, including art, band, cheerleading, chess, choir, chorale, chorus, computers, dance, drama, ethnic, film, gay, honors, international, jazz band, literary magazine, marching band, musical theater, newspaper, opera, orchestra, pep band, photography, political, professional, ra-

dio and TV, religious, social, social service, student government, and symphony. Popular campus events include Tower Theater productions and Jazz Night.

Sports: There are 8 intercollegiate sports for men and 8 for women, and 9 intramural sports for men and 9 for women. Facilities include a 3500-seat stadium, a swimming pool, an arena, a weight training room, an athletic field, and 3 gyms.

Disabled Students: All of the campus is accessible. Wheelchair ramps, elevators, special parking, specially equipped rest rooms, special class scheduling, lowered drinking fountains, and lowered telephones are available.

Services: Counseling and information services are available, as is tutoring in most subjects. There is a reader service for the blind, and remedial math, reading, and writing.

Campus Safety and Security: Measures include 24-hour foot and vehicle patrol, self-defense education, security escort services, and shuttle buses. There are informal discussions, pamphlets/posters/films, emergency telephones, lighted pathways/sidewalks, and controlled-entry residence halls.

Programs of Study: CWU confers B.A., B.S., B.A.Ed., B.F.A., and B.M. degrees. Master's degrees are also awarded. Bachelor's degrees are awarded in BIOLOGICAL SCIENCE (biology/biological science), BUSINESS (accounting, banking and finance, business administration and management, business economics, fashion merchandising, international business management, marketing/retailing/merchandising, recreation and leisure services, and tourism), COMMUNICATIONS AND THE ARTS (art, broadcasting, Chinese, communications, dramatic arts, English, fine arts, French, German, guitar, Japanese, journalism, language arts, music, music business management, music theory and composition, percussion, piano/organ, public relations, Russian, Spanish, speech/debate/rhetoric, strings, studio art, visual and performing arts, and voice), COMPUTER AND PHYSICAL SCIENCE (actuarial science, chemistry, computer programming, computer science, earth science, geology, information sciences and systems, mathematics, physics, and software engineering), EDUCATION (art, business, early childhood, elementary, English, foreign languages, health, home economics, industrial arts, marketing and distribution, mathematics, middle school, music, physical, science, secondary, social studies, and special), ENGINEERING AND ENVIRONMENTAL DESIGN (aeronautical technology, aviation administration/management, aviation maintenance management, construction management, electrical/electronics engineering, engineering technology, industrial engineering technology, and mechanical engineering),

HEALTH PROFESSIONS (community health work, emergency medical technologies, exercise science, and public health), SOCIAL SCIENCE (anthropology, Asian/Oriental studies, criminal justice, economics, family and community services, family/consumer studies, food science, geography, gerontology, history, liberal arts/general studies, paralegal studies, parks and recreation management, philosophy, political science/government, prelaw, psychology, public administration, safety science, social science, social work, and sociology). Accounting, music, and geology are the strongest academically. Business and education are the largest.

Required: Students must complete a minimum of 180 quarter credits, including 60 in upper-division courses and a minimum of 45 in the major plus a minor or 60 in the major. Core curriculum requirements include 61 credits of Basic and Breadth courses, including 15 credits each in arts and humanities, social and behavioral sciences, and natural science, 6 credits of English composition, and a philosophy logic or finite math course. Students must maintain a 2.3 GPA in the major and 2.0 GPA overall. A comprehensive exam in reading comprehension, sentence skills, and math is required.

Special: Students may study abroad; there is a formal exchange program with Japanese universities. There are 3-2 engineering degree programs in conjunction with the University of Puget Sound, the University of Washington, and Washington State University. CWU also offers co-op programs, cross-registration, internships, work-study programs, an accelerated degree program, credit/no credit options, dual and student-designed majors, and credit for military experience. Nondegree study is offered through adult/continuing education programs. There are 11 national honor societies, a freshman honors program, and 12 departmental honors programs.

Faculty/Classroom: 58% of faculty are male; 42%, female. All both teach and do research. Graduate students teach 7% of introductory courses. The average class size in an introductory lecture is 45; in a laboratory, 20; and in a regular course, 40.

Admissions: 76% of the 2005-2006 applicants were accepted. The SAT scores for the 2005-2006 freshman class were: Verbal--44% below 500, 40% between 500 and 599, 15% between 600 and 700, and 2% above 700; Math--44% below 500, 40% between 500 and 599, 15% between 600 and 700, and 1% above 700. The ACT scores were 51% below 21, 23% between 21 and 23, 12% between 24 and 26, 12% between 27 and 28, and 2% above 28.

Requirements: The SAT or ACT is required. In addition, test scores and GPA are considered in combination according to a sliding scale. Applicants must be graduates of accredited secondary schools or have earned a GED. The university requires 15 academic credits or Carnegie units: 4 years of English, 3 each of math and social studies, 2 of the same foreign language, 2 of science, and 1 of performing arts or an academic elective. A GPA of 2.0 is required. AP and CLEP credits are accepted. Important factors in the admissions decision are leadership record, personality/intangible qualities, and recommendations by school officials.

Procedure: Freshmen are admitted to all sessions. Entrance exams should be taken before the fall of the senior year. There is a rolling admissions plan. Applications should be filed by April 1 for fall entry, November 1 for winter entry, February 1 for spring entry, and June 1 for summer entry. The fall application fee was $50. Notification is sent on a rolling basis. Applications are accepted on-line.

Transfer: 1203 transfer students enrolled in 2004-2005. Students presenting an associate degree need a minimum GPA of 2.5 for automatic offer of admission; 2.5 to 2.0 will be asked to provide additional information for review. 45 of 180 credits required for the bachelor's degree must be completed at CWU.

Visiting: There are regularly scheduled orientations for prospective students, consisting of an information session, a tour of residence halls, a tour of the campus, prearranged appointments with faculty, and a financial aid presentation. There are guides for informal visits and visitors may sit in on classes and stay overnight. To schedule a visit, contact the Admissions Office.

Financial Aid: In 2005-2006, 45% of all full-time freshmen and 50% of continuing full-time students received some form of financial aid. 36% of full-time freshmen and 43% of continuing full-time students received need-based aid. The average freshman award was $7020. 41% of undergraduates work part time. Average annual earnings from campus work are $3000. The average financial indebtedness of the 2005 graduate was $27,024. The FAFSA is required. The deadline for filing freshman financial aid applications for fall entry is March 1.

International Students: There are 93 international students enrolled in a recent year. The school actively recruits these students. A satisfactory score is required on the written TOEFL. Students must also take the SAT or the ACT.

Computers: All students may access the system 24 hours a day. There are no time limits. The fee is $25 per quarter.

Graduates: From July 1, 2004 to June 30, 2005, 2296 bachelor's degrees were awarded. The most popular majors were business administration/marketing (25%), education (25%), and law and justice (9%). In an

average class, 1% graduate in 3 years or less, 23% graduate in 4 years or less, 46% graduate in 5 years or less, and 52% graduate in 6 years or less. 124 companies recruited on campus in 2004-2005.

Admissions Contact: Lisa Garcia-Hanson, Director of Admissions.
E-mail: *cwuadmis@cwu.edu* Web: *cwu@cwu.edu*

CITY UNIVERSITY	C-2
Renton, WA 98055	**(425) 637-1010**
	(800) 426-5596; Fax: (425) 277-2437

Full-time: 1100 men, 1000 women	**Faculty:** 14
Part-time: 520 men, 460 women	**Ph.D.s:** n/av
Graduate: 1600 men, 1600 women	**Student/Faculty:** n/av
Year: quarters, summer session	**Tuition:** $7500
Application Deadline: open	**Room & Board:** n/app
Freshman Class: n/av	
ACT: n/av	**NONCOMPETITIVE**

City University, established in 1973, is a private nonresidential institution offering undergraduate and graduate programs at a variety of instructional sites in addition to the Renton campus, including locations in Washington, California, British Columbia, Europe, Asia, and Slovakia. There are 2 undergraduate and 3 graduate schools. Figures in the above capsule and in this profile are approximate. The library contains 33,000 volumes, 415,000 microform items, and 1100 audio/video tapes/CDs/DVDs, and subscribes to 650 periodicals including electronic. Computerized library services include the card catalog, interlibrary loans, and database searching. Special learning facilities include a learning resource center. The 2-acre campus is in a suburban area a few miles southeast of Seattle. There are 2 buildings.

Student Life: 51% of undergraduates are from out of state, mostly the West. Students are from 45 states, 30 foreign countries, and Canada. 58% are white. The average age of all undergraduates is 33.

Housing: There are no residence halls. Alcohol is not permitted.

Activities: There are no fraternities or sororities.

Sports: There is no sports program at City University.

Disabled Students: 90% of the campus is accessible. Wheelchair ramps, elevators, special parking, and specially equipped rest rooms are available.

Services: Tutoring is available.

Programs of Study: City University confers B.A. and B.S. degrees. Associate and master's degrees are also awarded. Bachelor's degrees are awarded in BUSINESS (accounting, business administration and management, and marketing/retailing/merchandising), COMPUTER AND PHYSICAL SCIENCE (computer programming), EDUCATION (elementary and middle school), SOCIAL SCIENCE (liberal arts/general studies). Business administration is the largest.

Required: Students are required to complete 180 quarter credits, with a minimum of 45 of these credits taken at City University, and maintain a minimum GPA of 2.0. A minimum of 30 credits are required in the major. All students must complete 55 general education credits, which include courses in the humanities, social sciences, natural sciences, and math.

Special: Opportunities are provided for cooperative programs with other schools, internships, study abroad, work-study programs, dual majors, and student-designed majors. A general studies degree, pass/fail options, independent study, weekend programs, and credit for military service are offered.

Faculty/Classroom: The average class size in an introductory lecture is 25.

Requirements: Graduation from an accredited secondary school is not required; a GED will be accepted. An interview is recommended. AP and CLEP credits are accepted.

Procedure: Freshmen are admitted to all sessions. There is a rolling admissions plan. Application deadlines are open. The application fee is $80.

Transfer: Students applying for transfer must submit official transcripts from all colleges previously attended. Applicants may transfer up to 135 quarter credits from accredited 4-year colleges, with at least 45 of these credits in upper-level courses. Up to 90 quarter credits may be transferred from 2-year colleges. 45 of 180 credits required for the bachelor's degree must be completed at City University.

Visiting: To schedule a visit, contact the Student Affairs Office.

Financial Aid: The FAFSA, the college's own financial statement are required. Check with the school for current deadlines.

International Students: The school actively recruits these students. They must achieve a satisfactory score on the TOEFL and also take the college's own English placement exam to determine placement in ESL classes if necessary.

Computers: All students may access the system. There are no time limits and no fees. It is strongly recommended that all students have a personal computer.

Admissions Contact: Student Affairs/Admissions.
E-mail: *info@cityu.edu* Web: *www.cityu.edu*

CORNISH COLLEGE OF THE ARTS

C-2

Seattle, WA 98121

(206) 726-5016
(800) 726-ARTS; Fax: (206) 720-1011

Full-time: 250 men, 430 women	Faculty: 51
Part-time: 10 men, 20 women	Ph.D.s: 59%
Graduate: none	Student/Faculty: 13 to 1
Year: semesters, summer session	Tuition: $21,200
Application Deadline: August 15	Room & Board: n/app
Freshman Class: n/av	
SAT or ACT: recommended	SPECIAL

Cornish College of the Arts, founded in 1914, is an independent commuter institution offering undergraduate programs in the fine arts, dance, design, music, theater, and performance production. There are 6 undergraduate schools. Some figures in the above capsule and this profile are approximate. In addition to regional accreditation, Cornish has baccalaureate program accreditation with NASAD and NASC. The library contains 17,914 volumes and 4570 audio/video tapes/CDs/DVDs, and subscribes to 104 periodicals including electronic. Computerized library services include the card catalog, database searching, and Internet access. Special learning facilities include a learning resource center, art gallery, dance studios, large black box theater, studio theater, concert hall, rehearsal facilities, photography, printmaking, painting, sculpture studios, and digital labs. The 4-acre campus is in an urban area in the Capitol Hill and downtown neighborhoods of Seattle. There are 5 buildings.

Student Life: 55% of undergraduates are from Washington. Others are from 28 states, 10 foreign countries, and Canada. 67% are white. The average age of freshmen is 23; all undergraduates, 23. 20% do not continue beyond their first year; 50% remain to graduate.

Housing: There are no residence halls. Alcohol is not permitted. All students may keep cars.

Activities: There are no fraternities or sororities. There are more than 20 groups on campus, including art, band, chess, choir, chorus, computers, dance, drama, ethnic, film, gay, international, jazz band, literary magazine, musical theater, newspaper, opera, orchestra, photography, political, professional, religious, social, and student government. Popular campus events include Theater Seniors Productions, Costume Design Tea and Fashion Show, and Dance Theater Performances.

Sports: There is no sports program at Cornish.

Disabled Students: 50% of the campus is accessible. Wheelchair ramps, elevators, special parking, specially equipped rest rooms, lowered drinking fountains, and lowered telephones are available.

Services: Counseling and information services are available, as is tutoring in every subject. There is a reader service for the blind and remedial writing. There is a staffed writing center with computers.

Campus Safety and Security: Measures include 24-hour foot and vehicle patrol, self-defense education, security escort services, and shuttle buses. There are pamphlets/posters/films, emergency telephones, lighted pathways/sidewalks, and card-key access during nonbusiness hours.

Programs of Study: Cornish confers B.F.A. and B.M. degrees. Bachelor's degrees are awarded in COMMUNICATIONS AND THE ARTS (dance, design, dramatic arts, fine arts, music, and theater design). Design and dance are the strongest academically. Fine arts and theater are the largest.

Required: General education requirements include 30 semester hours in the humanities and sciences, as well as 6 to 8 in arts electives. To graduate, students must complete at least 127 semester hours, including 94 in their specific discipline, and maintain a minimum GPA of 2.0 during their senior year.

Special: Cornish offers a premajor first year of study to those music students who initially need more fundamental training. Internships are available to upperclassmen in all majors. Students may earn credit by exam in humanities and science courses, as well as credit for life experience in all majors where appropriate. Work-study programs and nondegree study are also offered.

Faculty/Classroom: 49% of faculty are male; 51%, female. All teach undergraduates. The average class size in an introductory lecture is 18; in a laboratory, 15; and in a regular course, 15.

Requirements: The SAT or ACT is recommended. In addition, the required audition or portfolio review is the single most important criterion in the admissions decision. Applicants should be graduates of accredited secondary schools or have earned a GED. In addition to providing evidence of their artistic talent, students must submit 2 essays and arrange for an interview. AP and CLEP credits are accepted. Important factors in the admissions decision are evidence of special talent, personality/intangible qualities, and recommendations by school officials.

Procedure: Freshmen are admitted in the fall. There is a rolling admissions plan. There is a deferred admissions plan. Applications should be filed by August 15 for fall entry and December 15 for spring entry, along with a $35 fee. Notification is sent on a rolling basis. Applications are accepted on-line.

Transfer: 38 transfer students enrolled in a recent year. Applicants must meet the same requirements as freshmen. 60 of 127 credits required for the bachelor's degree must be completed at Cornish.

Visiting: There are regularly scheduled orientations for prospective students, consisting of Preview Days during which applicants can attend classes, interact with students and faculty, and experience campus life. There are guides for informal visits and visitors may sit in on classes. To schedule a visit, contact the Admissions Office.

Financial Aid: Cornish is a member of CSS. The FAFSA and the college's own financial statement are required. Check with the school for current deadlines.

International Students: There are 21 international students enrolled. A satisfactory score on the TOEFL is required.

Computers: All students may access the system. There are no time limits. The fee is $50. It is recommended that students in design have personal computers. An Apple G4 iBook is recommended.

Graduates: In a recent year, 119 bachelor's degrees were awarded. The most popular majors were design (26%), art (21%), and theater (21%). In an average class, 50% graduate in 4 years or less.

Admissions Contact: Director of Admissions.
E-mail: admissions@cornish.edu Web: www.cornish.edu

DEVRY UNIVERSITY/SEATTLE

C-2

Federal Way, WA 98001-9558

(253) 943-2810
(877) 923-3879; Fax: (253) 943-3291

Full-time: 610 men, 170 women	Faculty: n/av
Part-time: 200 men, 100 women	Ph.D.s: n/av
Graduate: none	Student/Faculty: n/av
Year: semesters, summer session	Tuition: $12,000
Application Deadline: open	Room & Board: n/app
Freshman Class: n/av	
SAT or ACT: n/av	LESS COMPETITIVE

DeVry University/Seattle, founded in 2001, is a private institution offering hands-on programs in electronics, business administration, computer information systems, telecommunications management, and information technology and computer engineering technology. The school is 1 of 67 DeVry University locations the United States and Canada. Figures in the above capsule and in this profile are approximate. The library contains 6000 volumes and 170 audio/video tapes/CDs/DVDs, and subscribes to 70 periodicals including electronic. Computerized library services include the card catalog, interlibrary loans, and database searching. Special learning facilities include a learning resource center and electronics and other labs.

Student Life: 64% are white; 13% Asian American; 12% African American. The average age of all undergraduates is 25.

Housing: All students commute. Alcohol is not permitted. All students may keep cars.

Activities: There are no fraternities or sororities. There are 4 groups on campus, including computers, professional, social, and yearbook. Popular campus events include Summer BBQ, Holiday Banquet, and Stress Breaks.

Sports: There is no sports program at DeVry.

Disabled Students: All of the campus is accessible. Wheelchair ramps, elevators, special parking, specially equipped rest rooms, lowered drinking fountains, and lowered telephones are available.

Services: Counseling and information services are available, as is tutoring in every subject.

Campus Safety and Security: Measures include informal discussions, emergency telephones, lighted pathways/sidewalks, and 17-hour patrols by trained security personnel and Emergency Response Team.

Programs of Study: DeVry confers the B.S. degree. Associate and master's degrees are also awarded. Bachelor's degrees are awarded in BUSINESS (business administration and management), COMMUNICATIONS AND THE ARTS (telecommunications), COMPUTER AND PHYSICAL SCIENCE (information sciences and systems), ENGINEERING AND ENVIRONMENTAL DESIGN (computer engineering, electrical/electronics engineering technology, and technological management). Computer information systems and telecommunications are the largest.

Required: To graduate, students must achieve a GPA of at least 2.0 and satisfactorily complete all curriculum requirements, including 48 to 154 credits. Course requirements vary according to program. All first-semester students take courses in business organization, computer applications, algebra, psychology, and student success strategies.

Special: Accelerated degrees, co-op programs, nondegree study, and evening and weekend classes are possible.

Faculty/Classroom: All teach undergraduates.

Requirements: Admissions requirements include graduation from a secondary school; the GED is also accepted. Applicants must pass the DeVry entrance exam or present satisfactory ACT or SAT scores. An interview is required. CLEP credit is accepted.

Procedure: Freshmen are admitted fall, spring, and summer. There are early admissions and deferred admissions plans. Application deadlines are open. Check with the school for application fee. Applications are accepted on-line.

Transfer: Applicants must present passing grades in all completed college course work, demonstrate language skills proficiency in at least 24 completed semester hours, and present evidence of math proficiency by appropriate college-level credits. A minimum GPA of 2.0 is required. 25 of 48 credits required for the bachelor's degree must be completed at DeVry.

Visiting: There are guides for informal visits and visitors may sit in on classes. To schedule a visit, contact the New Student Coordinator.

Financial Aid: In a recent year, 68% of all full-time freshmen and 80% of continuing full-time students received some form of financial aid. 66% of full-time freshmen and 78% of continuing full-time students received need-based aid. The average freshman award was $5285. Need-based scholarships or need-based grants averaged $3739; need-based self-help aid (loans and jobs) averaged $3538; and other non-need-based awards and non-need-based scholarships averaged $9284. The FAFSA is required.

International Students: International students must take the TOEFL and also take the college's own entrance exam.

Admissions Contact: Director of Admissions.
E-mail: admissions@sea.devry.edu Web: www.sea.devry.edu

EASTERN WASHINGTON UNIVERSITY   E-2
Cheney, WA 99004-2496

(509) 359-2397
(888) 740-1914; Fax: (509) 359-6692

Full-time: 3300 men, 4400 women	**Faculty:** 352; IIA, --$
Part-time: 580 men, 810 women	**Ph.D.s:** 52%
Graduate: 400 men, 870 women	**Student/Faculty:** 22 to 1
Year: quarters, summer session	**Tuition:** $4374 ($14,325)
Application Deadline: see profile	**Room & Board:** $6234
Freshman Class: n/av	
SAT or ACT: required	**COMPETITIVE**

Eastern Washington University, founded in 1882, is a comprehensive public university that provides programs in the arts and sciences, business, health sciences and nursing, and technology.There are 4 undergraduate schools and 1 graduate school. Some figures in the above capsule and in this profile are approximate. In addition to regional accreditation, EWU has baccalaureate program accreditation with AACSB, ABET, ADA, APTA, ASLA, CSAB, CSWE, NASM, NCATE, NLN, and NRPA. The library contains 759,977 volumes, 608,400 microform items, and 27,595 audio/video tapes/CDs/DVDs, and subscribes to 4717 periodicals including electronic. Computerized library services include the card catalog, interlibrary loans, and database searching. Special learning facilities include a learning resource center, art gallery, natural history museum, planetarium, radio station, TV station, and Reid Laboratory Elementary School. The 35-acre campus is in a small town 18 miles southwest of Spokane. Including any residence halls, there are 32 buildings.

Student Life: 91% of undergraduates are from Washington. Others are from 31 states, 30 foreign countries, and Canada. 98% are from public schools. 77% are white. The average age of freshmen is 19; all undergraduates, 25. 19% do not continue beyond their first year; 88% remain to graduate.

Housing: 2066 students can be accommodated in college housing, which includes coed dorms, on-campus apartments, and married-student housing. In addition, there are all-male, all-female, academic, music, and drama floors and floors for older students. On-campus housing is guaranteed for all 4 years. 80% of students commute. All students may keep cars.

Activities: 8% of men belong to 5 national fraternities; 6% of women belong to 1 local sorority and 4 national sororities. There are 99 groups on campus, including art, band, cheerleading, chess, choir, chorale, chorus, computers, dance, drama, ethnic, film, gay, honors, international, jazz band, literary magazine, marching band, musical theater, opera, orchestra, outdoor, pep band, photography, political, professional, radio and TV, religious, social, social service, student government, symphony, and yearbook. Popular campus events include Club Vegas, Holiday in the Pub, and Spring Fling.

Sports: There are 6 intercollegiate sports for men and 7 for women, and 16 intramural sports for men and 14 for women. Facilities include a 200-meter indoor track, 12 racquetball courts, an indoor swimming pool, wrestling rooms, a dance studio, a 7000-seat stadium, a 5800-seat indoor gym, a fitness studio, and volleyball, baseball, and basketball courts.

Disabled Students: 93% of the campus is accessible. Wheelchair ramps, elevators, special parking, specially equipped rest rooms, special class scheduling, lowered drinking fountains, lowered telephones, and special housing are available.

Services: Counseling and information services are available, as is tutoring in every subject. There is a reader service for the blind, and remedial math, reading, and writing.

Campus Safety and Security: Measures include 24-hour foot and vehicle patrol, security escort services, informal discussions, and pamphlets/posters/films. There are emergency telephones, lighted pathways/sidewalks, crisis lines, and emergency contact light standards.

Programs of Study: EWU confers B.A., B.S., B.A.B., B.A.E., B.D.H., B.F.A., B.Mus., and B.S.N. degrees. Master's degrees are also awarded. Bachelor's degrees are awarded in BIOLOGICAL SCIENCE (biochemistry, biology/biological science, botany, microbiology, and zoology), BUSINESS (accounting, banking and finance, business administration and management, management science, marketing/retailing/merchandising, personnel management, and recreation and leisure services), COMMUNICATIONS AND THE ARTS (art, art history and appreciation, broadcasting, communications, creative writing, dance, dramatic arts, English, French, German, graphic design, journalism, literature, music, music performance, Spanish, speech/debate/rhetoric, and studio art), COMPUTER AND PHYSICAL SCIENCE (chemistry, computer science, geology, information sciences and systems, mathematics, and physics), EDUCATION (art, computer, elementary, foreign languages, guidance, health, marketing and distribution, mathematics, middle school, music, physical, recreation, science, secondary, and social science), ENGINEERING AND ENVIRONMENTAL DESIGN (computer technology, mechanical engineering technology, and military science), HEALTH PROFESSIONS (dental hygiene, health care administration, medical laboratory technology, nursing, predentistry, premedicine, preveterinary science, recreation therapy, and speech pathology/audiology), SOCIAL SCIENCE (anthropology, criminal justice, economics, geography, history, humanities, international relations, parks and recreation management, philosophy, political science/government, prelaw, psychology, social science, social work, sociology, and urban studies). Health sciences, biology, and computer science are the strongest academically. Business, education, and social science and history are the largest.

Required: All students must complete 180 quarter credits, including 60 to 110 in their major, while earning a minimum GPA of 2.0. Specific requirements include English composition and math courses to demonstrate competency. Distribution requirements include 11 total courses from 3 breadth areas: humanities, natural sciences and math, and social sciences. Seniors must complete a capstone course.

Special: Cooperative programs in nursing, cross-registration with the Intercollegiate School of Nursing, internships with area businesses, and work-study based on federal financial aid are available. B.A.-B.S. degrees, dual majors in any subject, study abroad in 12 countries, 3 types of general studies degrees, student-designed majors, and a 3-2 engineering degree with Washington State University are offered. Credit for military experience, nondegree study, and pass/fail options for nonmajor or nonminor courses also are possible. There are 14 national honor societies, a freshman honors program, and 39 departmental honors programs.

Faculty/Classroom: 47% of faculty are male; 53%, female. 98% teach undergraduates.

Requirements: The SAT or ACT is required. Admission is determined by an index coordinating the GPA with entrance exam scores. The GED is accepted. EWU requires 4 years of English, 3 each of math and social science, 2 each of science (including a lab science) and a single foreign language (ASL accepted), and 1 of fine arts or academic electives. A GPA of 2.0 is required. AP and CLEP credits are accepted. Important factors in the admissions decision are recommendations by school officials, advanced placement or honor courses, and evidence of special talent.

Procedure: Freshmen are admitted to all sessions. Entrance exams should be taken during the spring of the junior year or fall of the senior year. There is a rolling admissions plan. There is a deferred admissions plan. Check with the school for current application deadlines and fee. Notification is sent on a rolling basis. A waiting list is an active part of the admissions procedure. Applications are accepted on-line.

Transfer: Applicants with fewer than 40 credits must submit high school and college transcripts and test scores; those with more than 40 credits acceptable by Eastern or who have earned an associate degree from a Washington community college must submit a college transcript. 45 of 180 credits required for the bachelor's degree must be completed at EWU.

Visiting: There are regularly scheduled orientations for prospective students, consisting of overnight programs for students and parents that present informational sessions on campus life and academic survival skills, academic advising, course registration, and social functions. There are guides for informal visits and visitors may sit in on classes and stay overnight. To schedule a visit, contact the Admissions Office at (509) 359-6555.

Financial Aid: The FAFSA is required. Check with the school for current deadlines.

International Students: The school actively recruits these students. A satisfactory score on the TOEFL is required.

Computers: All students may access the system throughout the workday, plus evenings and weekends. There are no time limits. The fee is $7 per term.

Admissions Contact: Shannon Carr, Director of Admissions. A video is available. E-mail: admissions@mail.ewu.edu Web: www.ewu.edu

EVERGREEN STATE COLLEGE   B-3

Olympia, WA 98505   (360) 867-6170; Fax: (360) 867-6576

Full-time: 1663 men, 1992 women	**Faculty:** 160
Part-time: 211 men, 305 women	**Ph.D.s:** 73%
Graduate: 119 men, 180 women	**Student/Faculty:** 23 to 1
Year: quarters, summer session	**Tuition:** $4337 ($14,747)
Application Deadline: March 1	**Room & Board:** $6924
Freshman Class: 1657 applied, 1611 accepted, 605 enrolled	
SAT Verbal/Math: 600/530*	**ACT:** 24 COMPETITIVE+

The Evergreen State College, founded in 1967 is a public liberal arts and sciences college offering interdisciplinary, collaborative, and team-taught academic programs. The library contains 471,105 volumes, 492,853 microform items, and 89,050 audio/video tapes/CDs/DVDs, and subscribes to 2731 periodicals including electronic. Computerized library services include the card catalog, interlibrary loans, database searching, Internet access, and laptop Internet portals. Special learning facilities include a learning resource center, art gallery, radio station, TV station, communications lab, Longhouse Cultural Center, and Art Annex. The 1000-acre campus is in a small town 7 miles west of Olympia. Including any residence halls, there are 76 buildings.

Student Life: 79% of undergraduates are from Washington. Others are from 49 states and 14 foreign countries. 70% are white. The average age of freshmen is 19; all undergraduates, 26. 31% do not continue beyond their first year; 52% remain to graduate.

Housing: 900 students can be accommodated in college housing, which includes coed dormitories, on-campus apartments, and married-student housing. In addition, there is drug-and alcohol-free housing, first-year experience, quiet housing a Community Actin House, and a sustainability house. On-campus housing is guaranteed for the freshman year only and is available on a first-come, first-served basis. 79% of students commute. Alcohol is not permitted. All students may keep cars.

Activities: There are no fraternities or sororities. There are 68 groups on campus, including art, chorale, dance, drama, ethnic, film, gay, international, literary magazine, newspaper, photography, political, professional, radio and TV, religious, social, social service, and student government. Popular campus events include Super Saturday, Evergreen Expressions Series (Performance/Media Art), and Olympia Film Society festivals.

Sports: There are 3 intercollegiate sports for men and 4 for women, and 10 intramural sports for men and 10 for women. Facilities include a recreation center, which houses an 11-lane swimming pool, a diving well, exercise and weight training rooms, 5 racquetball courts, and indoor climbing walls. There is a 3100-seat gym, a covered pavilion, 4 tennis courts, and 5 playing fields.

Disabled Students: All of the campus is accessible. Wheelchair ramps, elevators, special parking, specially equipped rest rooms, lowered drinking fountains, and lowered telephones are available.

Services: Counseling and information services are available, as is tutoring in some subjects. The Writing Center offers assistance in writing; the Quantitive and Symbolic Reasoning Center offers assistance with all levels of math, economics, statistics, chemistry, biology, physics, and so on. There is a reader service for the blind.

Campus Safety and Security: Measures include 24-hour foot and vehicle patrol, self-defense education, security escort services, and informal discussions. There are pamphlets/posters/films, emergency telephones, and lighted pathways/sidewalks.

Programs of Study: Evergreen confers B.A. and B.S. degrees. Master's degrees are also awarded. Bachelor's degrees are awarded in SOCIAL SCIENCE (liberal arts/general studies). All bachelor's degrees are awarded in liberal arts and sciences. Students can design their own paths, focusing on their own interest areas.

Required: Students must earn a minimum of 180 quarter hours of credit to receive a B.A. or B.S. degree. For a B.A., 45 of the last 90 credits must be earned at Evergreen (for transfer students). For a B.S. students must have completed 72 credits of science, math, or computer science, 48 of which must be upper division. For a B.A.S. dual degree, 225 credits are required and students must meet the requirements of a B.A. and B.S.

Special: All work at the college is interdisciplinary, and the programs of study change annually. The college's credit-generating options include the comprehensive Coordinated Study Program, which allows students and faculty to work together intensively. Credits may be earned through cooperative programs, work-study programs, internships, or from prior learning and military experience. All majors are awarded in Liberal Arts and Sciences. A B.A.S. dual degree is possible in liberal arts. Study abroad is possible all over the world. Evergreen participates in numerous consortium programs for international study.

Faculty/Classroom: 51% of faculty are male; 49%, female. All teach undergraduates. No introductory courses are taught by graduate students. The average class size in an introductory lecture is 52; in a laboratory, 25; and in a regular course, 25.

Admissions: 97% of the 2005-2006 applicants were accepted. The SAT scores for the 2005-2006 freshman class were: Verbal--15% below 500, 32% between 500 and 599, 42% between 600 and 700, and 11% above 700; Math--32% below 500, 42% between 500 and 599, 24% between 600 and 700, and 2% above 700. The ACT scores were 22% below 21, 24% between 21 and 23, 27% between 24 and 26, 14% between 27 and 28, and 14% above 28. 16% of the current freshmen were in the top fifth of their class; 47% were in the top two fifths.

Requirements: The SAT or ACT is required. In addition, candidates should be graduates of an accredited secondary school and have completed 15 academic credits, consisting of 4 in English, 3 each in math and social studies, 2 each in foreign language and science, and 1 in fine or performing arts. A GED certificate is acceptable. A GPA of 2.0 is required. AP and CLEP credits are accepted.

Procedure: Freshmen are admitted fall, winter, and spring. Entrance exams should be taken during spring of the junior year or fall of the senior year. Applications should be filed by March 1 for fall entry, October 1 for winter entry, and December 1 for spring entry, along with a $50 fee. Notification is sent April 1. Applications are accepted on-line.

Transfer: 932 transfer students enrolled in 2004-2005. Applicants with fewer than 40 credits must submit SAT or ACT scores and a high school transcript. A 2.0 minimum GPA is required. An associate degree is recommended. All applicants must submit all college transcripts. 45 of 180 credits required for the B.A. or B.S. degree and 45 of 225 for the B.A.S. duel degree must be completed at Evergreen.

Visiting: There are regularly scheduled orientations for prospective students, including an admissions session, a class visit, and a campus tour. There are guides for informal visits and visitors may sit in on classes and stay overnight. To schedule a visit, contact the Student Visitor Program at (360) 867-6172.

Financial Aid: In 2004-2005, 50% of all full-time freshmen and 58% of continuing full-time students received some form of financial aid. 28% of full-time freshmen and 45% of continuing full-time students received need-based aid. The average freshman award was $9824. Need-based scholarships or need-based grants averaged $4635; need-based self-help aid (loans and jobs) averaged $3315; and non-need-based athletic scholarships averaged $833. 63% of undergraduates work part time. Average annual earnings from campus work are $2625. The average financial indebtedness of the 2005 graduate was $13,000. Evergreen is a member of CSS. The FAFSA and the college's own financial statement are required. The priority date for freshman financial aid applications for fall entry is February 15. The deadline for filing freshman financial aid applications for fall entry is March 15.

International Students: There are 18 international students enrolled. They must score satisfactorily on the written TOEFL or on the electronic version and also take the SAT or the ACT.

Computers: Wireless access is available. There are 12 computer labs and classrooms accessible to students. All classrooms used for undergraduate instruction allow wire connectivity between labtops and the Internet and 15% of classrooms allo wireless connectivity. Network access is available in dorm rooms. All students may access the system 18 hours per day. There are no time limits and no fees.

Graduates: From July 1, 2004 to June 30, 2005, 1260 bachelor's degrees were awarded. The most popular major was liberal arts and sciences (100%). In an average class, 5% graduate in 3 years or less, 39% graduate in 4 years or less, 49% graduate in 5 years or less, and 52% graduate in 6 years or less. 57 companies recruited on campus in 2004-2005. Of the 2004 graduating class, 29% were enrolled in graduate school within 6 months of graduation and 80% were employed.

Admissions Contact: Doug Scrima, Director of Admissions.
E-mail: *admissions@evergreen.edu* Web: *www.evergreen.edu*

GONZAGA UNIVERSITY   E-2

Spokane, WA 99258-0001   (509) 323-6591
(800) 322-2584; Fax: (509) 324-5780

Full-time: 1866 men, 2140 women	**Faculty:** 281
Part-time: 70 men, 95 women	**Ph.D.s:** 86%
Graduate: 646 men, 871 women	**Student/Faculty:** 14 to 1
Year: semesters, summer session	**Tuition:** $23,518
Application Deadline: February 1	**Room & Board:** $6700
Freshman Class: 3190 accepted, 986 enrolled	
SAT Verbal/Math: 593/598*	**ACT:** 26 HIGHLY COMPETITIVE

Gonzaga University, founded in 1887, is a private, liberal arts institution affiliated with the Roman Catholic Church and the Society of Jesus (Jesuits). The university offers undergraduate and graduate degrees in arts and sciences, business, education, engineering, and professional studies. There are 5 undergraduate and 5 graduate schools. In addition to regional accreditation, Gonzaga has baccalaureate program accreditation with AACSB, ABET, NCATE, and NLN. The 2 libraries contain 459,393 volumes, 49,577 microform items, and 7460 audio/video tapes/CDs/DVDs, and subscribe to 4612 periodicals including electronic. Computerized library services include the card catalog, interlibrary loans, database searching, Internet access, and laptop Internet portals (wireless and 10/100). Special learning facilities include a learning resource center, art gallery, radio station, and TV station. The 108-acre campus is in an urban area near downtown Spokane. Including any residence halls, there are 87 buildings.

Student Life: 51% of undergraduates are from mostly the West. Students are from 47 states, 21 foreign countries, and Canada. 65% are from public schools. 77% are white. 47% are Catholic; 30% claim no religious affiliation; 22% Protestant. The average age of freshmen is 18; all undergraduates, 21. 10% do not continue beyond their first year; 76% remain to graduate.

Housing: 2300 students can be accommodated in college housing, which includes single-sex and coed dormitories, on-campus apartments, off-campus apartments, and married-student housing. In addition, there are honors houses, special-interest houses, and a first-year experience hall. On-campus housing is guaranteed for the freshman year only, is available on a first-come, first-served basis, and is available on a lottery system for upperclassmen. Priority is given to out-of-town students. 51% of students live on campus; of those, 88% remain on campus on weekends. Alcohol is not permitted. All students may keep cars.

Activities: There are no fraternities or sororities. There are 88 groups on campus, including art, band, cheerleading, chess, choir, chorale, chorus, computers, dance, debate, drama, drill team, ethnic, gay, honors, international, jazz band, literary magazine, musical theater, newspaper, orchestra, pep band, photography, political, professional, radio and TV, religious, social, social service, student government, symphony, and yearbook. Popular campus events include Search, Charity Ball, and Fall Family Weekend.

Sports: There are 7 intercollegiate sports for men and 7 for women, and 12 intramural sports for men and 12 for women. Facilities include 3 basketball/volleyball courts, an indoor golf practice area, an athletic training room, an indoor crew practice room, an athletic weight room, 3 outdoor grass athletic fields, and a student fitness center with cardiovascular and weight areas, 3 multipurpose courts, 4 racquetball courts, 2 aerobics rooms, an indoor running track, and a 6-lane, 25-yard swimming pool.

Disabled Students: 90% of the campus is accessible. Wheelchair ramps, elevators, special parking, specially equipped rest rooms, special class scheduling, lowered drinking fountains, lowered telephones and special housing are available. Academic adjustments are provided for students with disabilities who provide appropriate documentation and request services from Disabilities, Resources, Education, and Access Management (DREAM).

Services: There is a reader service for the blind. Informal peer tutoring in English and math is available.

Campus Safety and Security: Measures include 24-hour foot and vehicle patrol, security escort services, informal discussions, and pamphlets/posters/films. There are emergency telephones and lighted pathways/sidewalks.

Programs of Study: Gonzaga confers B.A., B.S., B.B.A., B.Ed., B.G.S., and B.S.N. degrees. Master's and doctoral degrees are also awarded. Bachelor's degrees are awarded in BIOLOGICAL SCIENCE (biochemistry and biology/biological science), BUSINESS (accounting, business administration and management, and business economics), COMMUNICATIONS AND THE ARTS (art, broadcasting, communications, dramatic arts, English, French, German, journalism, literature, music, public relations, Spanish, and speech/debate/rhetoric), COMPUTER AND PHYSICAL SCIENCE (chemistry, computer science, mathematics, and physics), EDUCATION (music, physical, and special), ENGINEERING AND ENVIRONMENTAL DESIGN (civil engineering, computer engineering, electrical/electronics engineering, and mechanical engineering), HEALTH PROFESSIONS (exercise science and nursing), SOCIAL SCIENCE (classical/ancient civilization, criminal justice, economics, history, interdisciplinary studies, international studies, Italian studies, liberal arts/general studies, philosophy, political science/government, psychology, religion, and sociology). Engineering and business administration are the strongest academically. Business, engineering, and liberal arts are the largest.

Required: All students must complete 128 credit hours with a minimum 2.0 GPA. The major requirements are 18 hours in upper-division courses and supporting courses required by the major department. Students must complete 9 credits each of philosophy and religious studies, 7 credits in English, speech, and critical thinking, and 3 credits each in math and English literature.

Special: Cross-registration with Whitworth College and the Intercollegiate Consortium for Nursing Education, internships, study abroad in 9 countries, a Washington semester, and on- and off-campus work-study programs are offered. High school juniors and seniors may take 6 credits per semester. There is a limited pass/fail option, and an accelerated general studies degree and dual majors are possible. There are 12 national honor societies and a freshman honors program.

Faculty/Classroom: 63% of faculty are male; 37%, female. 91% teach undergraduates. No introductory courses are taught by graduate students. The average class size in an introductory lecture is 23; in a laboratory, 13; and in a regular course, 23.

Admissions: The SAT scores for the 2005-2006 freshman class were: Verbal--9% below 500, 45% between 500 and 599, 36% between 600 and 700, and 10% above 700; Math--8% below 500, 40% between 500 and 599, 43% between 600 and 700, and 10% above 700. The ACT scores were 4% below 21, 18% between 21 and 23, 30% between 24 and 26, 19% between 27 and 28, and 29% above 28. 65% of the current freshmen were in the top fifth of their class; 97% were in the top two fifths. There were 13 National Merit finalists and 4 semifinalists. 67 freshmen graduated first in their class.

Requirements: The SAT or ACT is required. In addition, applicants should be graduates of an accredited secondary school or hold a GED certificate. They must have completed 17 academic credits consisting of 4 years of English, 3 of math, 2 of a foreign language, 1 each of history and science, and 6 years of electives, 4 of which must be from the above subjects and the arts. An essay and letters of recommendation are required. An interview is optional but recommended for students with a GPA lower than 3.1 or an unsatisfactory SAT score for Verbal/Critical Reading and Math. AP and CLEP credits are accepted. Important factors in the admissions decision are advanced placement or honor courses, leadership record, and extracurricular activities record.

Procedure: Freshmen are admitted fall and spring. Entrance exams should be taken by May of the junior year. There are early action, early admissions, and deferred admissions plans. Early action applications should be filed by November 15; regular applications, by February 1 for fall entry and November 1 for spring entry, along with a $45 fee. Notification of early action is sent by January 15; regular decision, by April 1. 252 applicants were on the 2005 waiting list; 58 were admitted. Applications are accepted on-line.

Transfer: 203 transfer students enrolled in 2004-2005. A minimum GPA of 2.7 is required. Students younger than 21 must submit test scores for the SAT or ACT. An interview is recommended. 30 of 128 credits required for the bachelor's degree must be completed at Gonzaga.

Visiting: There are regularly scheduled orientations for prospective students. Day visits are permitted Monday through Friday; overnight visits, Sunday through Thursday (except for holiday periods). There are guides for informal visits and visitors may sit in on classes and stay overnight. To schedule a visit, contact the Admissions Office Visitation Coordinator at (800) 322-2584, ext. 6531.

Financial Aid: In 2005-2006, 95% of all full-time freshmen and 93% of continuing full-time students received some form of financial aid. 60% of full-time freshmen and 62% of continuing full-time students received need-based aid. The average freshman award was $17,176. Need-based scholarships or need-based grants averaged $5291 ($11,894 maximum); need-based self-help aid (loans and jobs) averaged $6156 ($12,383 maximum); non-need-based athletic scholarships averaged $16,793 ($31,173 maximum); and other non-need-based awards and non-need-based scholarships averaged $6226 ($34,164 maximum). 41% of undergraduates work part time. Average annual earnings from campus work are $1773. The average financial indebtedness of the 2005 graduate was $23,140. The FAFSA is required. The deadline for filing freshman financial aid applications for fall entry is February 1.

International Students: There are 48 international students enrolled. The school actively recruits these students. They must score satisfactorily on the written TOEFL or on the electronic version or take the ESL Exit Exam, which includes a writing test.

Computers: All students may access the system 24 hours per day. There are no time limits and no fees. It is strongly recommended that all students have a personal computer.

Graduates: From July 1, 2004 to June 30, 2005, 932 bachelor's degrees were awarded. The most popular majors were business and management (24%), social studies (23%), and engineering (8%). In an average class, 1% graduate in 3 years or less, 63% graduate in 4 years or less, 77% graduate in 5 years or less, and 78% graduate in 6 years or less. 100 companies recruited on campus in 2004-2005.

Admissions Contact: Julie McCullon, Dean of Admission. A video is available. E-mail: *mcculloh@gu.gonzaga.edu* Web: *www.gonzaga.edu*

HENRY COGSWELL COLLEGE C-2
Everett, WA 98201 (425) 258-3351, ext. 116
(866) 411-HCC1; Fax: (425) 257-0405

Full-time: 84 men, 34 women	Faculty: 14
Part-time: 65 men, 17 women	Ph.D.s: 43%
Graduate: none	Student/Faculty: 8 to 1
Year: trimesters, summer session	Tuition: $16,680
Application Deadline: open	Room & Board: n/app
Freshman Class: 86 applied, 72 accepted, 56 enrolled	
SAT Verbal/Math: 540/580*	ACT: 20 SPECIAL

Henry Cogswell College, established in 1979, is a private institution specializing in business, engineering, computer science, and digital arts. There are 3 undergraduate schools. In addition to regional accreditation, Cogswell has baccalaureate program accreditation with ABET and IACBE. The library contains 9252 volumes and 262 audio/video tapes/CDs/DVDs, and subscribes to 5212 periodicals including electronic. Computerized library services include the card catalog, interlibrary loans, database searching, and Internet access. Special learning facilities include a learning resource center. The 1-acre campus is in a suburban area 30 miles north of Seattle. There are 2 buildings.

Student Life: 98% of undergraduates are from Washington. Others are from 3 states. 96% are from public schools. 72% are white. The average age of freshmen is 22; all undergraduates, 29. 25% do not continue beyond their first year; 66% remain to graduate.

Housing: There are no residence halls. All students commute. Alcohol is not permitted.

Activities: There are no fraternities or sororities. There are 6 groups on campus, includingACM, ASME, IEFE, professional, Professional gamer's club, and student government. Popular campus events include Winter Holiday Party and Summer Barbecue.

Sports: There is no sports program at Cogswell.

Disabled Students: 95% of the campus is accessible. Wheelchair ramps, elevators, special parking, specially equipped rest rooms, lowered drinking fountains, and lowered telephones are available.

Services: Counseling and information services are available, as is tutoring in most subjects. There is remedial math and writing.

Campus Safety and Security: Measures include informal discussions, pamphlets/posters/films, and lighted pathways/sidewalks.

Programs of Study: Cogswell confers B.A., B.S., B.S.E.E., and B.S.M.E. degrees. Bachelor's degrees are awarded in BUSINESS (business administration and management), COMPUTER AND PHYSICAL SCIENCE (computer science and digital arts/technology), ENGINEERING AND ENVIRONMENTAL DESIGN (electrical/electronics engineering and mechanical engineering). Electrical engineering is the strongest academically. Mechanical engineering and digital arts are the largest.

Required: Students must complete a minimum of 121 trimester hours, including 51 in the major, and maintain a minimum 2.0 GPA. The core curriculum includes a minimum of 20 credits in humanities and social sciences, 3 classes each in written and oral communication, and classes in math, lab sciences, and moral and ethical problems. A senior thesis or project is required.

Special: Internships and accelerated degree programs are available in all majors. There are also work-study programs.

Faculty/Classroom: 75% of faculty are male; 25%, female. All teach undergraduates. The average class size in an introductory lecture is 11; in a laboratory, 11; and in a regular course, 10.

Admissions: 84% of the 2005-2006 applicants were accepted. The SAT scores for the 2005-2006 freshman class were: Verbal--100% between 500 and 599; Math--60% between 500 and 599, and 40% between 600 and 700. The ACT scores were 100% between 21 and 23.

Requirements: The SAT is required; the ACT is accepted. A high school diploma or GED is required. A portfolio is required of all art students. A GPA of 2.5 is required. AP and CLEP credits are accepted. Important factors in the admissions decision are evidence of special talent, personality/intangible qualities, and ability to finance college education.

Procedure: Freshmen are admitted in the fall. Entrance exams should be taken prior to registration. There is a rolling admissions plan. Application deadlines are open. Notification is sent September 1. Application fee is $50. Applications are accepted on-line.

Transfer: 16 transfer students enrolled in 2004-2005. Transferring students must forward all transcripts from previously attended schools and may be required to take placement exams. 30 of 121 credits required for the bachelor's degree must be completed at Cogswell.

Visiting: There are regularly scheduled orientations for prospective students each month from 10 A.M. to 2 P.M. 2 open houses are held each year in the fall. There are guides for informal visits and visitors may sit in on classes. To schedule a visit, contact Jane Buckman, Dean of Enrollment at *j.buckman@henrycogswell.edu.*

Financial Aid: In a recent year, 92% of all full-time freshmen and 38% of continuing full-time students received some form of financial aid. 40% of full-time freshmen and 30% of continuing full-time students received need-based aid. The average freshman award was $9556. Need-based scholarships or need-based grants averaged $3866; need-based self-help aid (loans and jobs) averaged $2344; and other non-need-based awards and non-need-based scholarships averaged $2969. 8% of undergraduates work part time. Average annual earnings from campus work are $978. The average financial indebtedness of a recent graduate was $23,658. The CSS Profile, FAFSA, FFS, or SFS, and the college's own financial statement are required. The deadline for filing freshman financial aid applications for fall entry is September 1.

International Students: The school actively recruits these students. They must take the TOEFL.

Computers: Students have full access to the Internet at 150 workstations in basic, intermediate, and advanced labs throughout the campus. There is a basic computer usage policy that must be followed to safeguard both the student and the college. Strict adherence to copyright laws are expected of all computer users on campus. All students may access the system. There are no time limits and no fees.

Graduates: From July 1, 2004 to June 30, 2005, 63 bachelor's degrees were awarded. The most popular majors were digital arts (48%), business (15%), and electrical engineering (13%). In an average class, 70%

graduate in 3 years or less, and 30% graduate in 6 years or less. 10 companies recruited on campus in a recent year. Of a recent graduating class, 12% were enrolled in graduate school within 6 months of graduation and 65% were employed.

Admissions Contact: Jane Buckman, Dean of Enrollment.
E-mail: *j.buckman@henrycogswell.edu* Web: *www.henrycogswell.edu*

HERITAGE UNIVERSITY   D-3
Toppenish, WA 98948   **(509) 865-8500**
                                          (888) 272-6190; Fax: (509) 865-4469

Full-time: 110 men, 330 women	**Faculty:** 38
Part-time: 80 men, 230 women	**Ph.D.s:** 40%
Graduate: 180 men, 350 women	**Student/Faculty:** 12 to 1
Year: semesters, summer session	**Tuition:** $6800 ($8300)
Application Deadline: open	**Room & Board:** n/app
Freshman Class: n/av	
SAT or ACT: recommended	**NONCOMPETITIVE**

Heritage University, formerly Heritage College and founded in 1982, is a private, nonprofit commuter college offering undergraduate and graduate programs in liberal arts and teacher education, half of which are given on evenings and weekends. Figures in the above capsule and in this profile are approximate. The library contains 40,000 volumes, 151,960 microform items, and 208 audio/video tapes/CDs/DVDs, and subscribes to 265 periodicals including electronic. Computerized library services include database searching. Special learning facilities include a learning resource center and , K-20 network, and geographic information systems (GIS) lab. The 19-acre campus is in a rural area 20 miles south of Yakima. There are 15 buildings.

Student Life: 99% of undergraduates are from Washington. Students are from 2 states and 2 foreign countries. 48% are white; 41% Hispanic. The average age of freshmen is 25; all undergraduates, 31. 23% do not continue beyond their first year; 56% remain to graduate.

Housing: There are no residence halls. All of students commute. Alcohol is not permitted. All students may keep cars.

Activities: There are no fraternities or sororities. There are 10 groups on campus, including art, computers, dance, ethnic, honors, literary magazine, newspaper, professional, social service, and student government. Popular campus events include Spring Faire, Academic Convocation, and Founders Day.

Sports: Facilities include a basketball court and a track and field used for soccer, flag football, and softball.

Disabled Students: 95% of the campus is accessible. Wheelchair ramps, special parking, specially equipped rest rooms, special class scheduling, and lowered drinking fountains are available.

Services: Counseling and information services are available, as is tutoring in most subjects. There is remedial math, reading, and writing.

Campus Safety and Security: Measures include security escort services, emergency telephones, and lighted pathways/sidewalks.

Programs of Study: Heritage confers B.A., B.S., B.A.Ed., and B.S.W. degrees. Associate and master's degrees are also awarded. Bachelor's degrees are awarded in BUSINESS (business administration and management), COMMUNICATIONS AND THE ARTS (English and Spanish), COMPUTER AND PHYSICAL SCIENCE (computer science, mathematics, and science), EDUCATION (elementary, science, secondary, and social studies), ENGINEERING AND ENVIRONMENTAL DESIGN (environmental science), SOCIAL SCIENCE (interdisciplinary studies, psychology, public administration, social work, and sociology). Education is the largest.

Required: All students must complete 44 to 45 credits of general college requirements, which include 12 credits each in arts and letters, 10 credits in science and math, 9 credits in social sciences, 1 year of English, a computer course, a math course above the 100 level, and a world civilization course. At least 126 semester credit hours must be completed, with at least 48 upper-division credits. Education majors must have a minimum GPA of 2.5; others must have a 2.0.

Special: Heritage provides individualized assistance. Credit by exam available in many courses, and credit may be given for work experience. The college also has cooperative programs with 3 school districts, internships in local businesses, social service agencies, and cross-registration with Northwest Indian College. Pass/fail options are possible for some courses. An accelerated degree program is available in business administration. There is a freshman honors program.

Faculty/Classroom: 51% of faculty are male; 49%, female. 40% teach undergraduates and 40% both teach and do research. No introductory courses are taught by graduate students. The average class size in an introductory lecture is 20; in a laboratory, 16; and in a regular course, 20.

Requirements: The SAT or ACT is recommended, but entrance exams are not required. Applicants must have graduated from an accredited secondary school or hold a GED certificate. An interview is recommended. Assessment for placement in English and math courses is required. AP and CLEP credits are accepted.

Procedure: Freshmen are admitted to all sessions. Entrance exams should be taken before registering. There is a rolling admissions plan. Application deadlines are open.

Transfer: 104 transfer students enrolled in a recent year. Students must have completed 30 credits. 32 of 126 credits required for the bachelor's degree must be completed at Heritage.

Visiting: There are regularly scheduled orientations for prospective students, consisting of a day and an evening fall orientation. There are guides for informal visits and visitors may sit in on classes. To schedule a visit, contact the Director of Admissions.

Financial Aid: In a recent year, 93% of all full-time freshmen received some form of financial aid. 55% of full-time freshmen received need-based aid. Need-based scholarships or need-based grants averaged $8608 ($18,465 maximum); need-based self-help aid (loans and jobs) averaged $3338 ($10,225 maximum); and other non-need-based awards and non-need-based scholarships averaged $339 ($8233 maximum). 13% of undergraduates work part time. Average annual earnings from campus work are $3600. The average financial indebtedness of the 2005 graduate was $5000. Heritage is a member of CSS. The CSS/Profile or FAFSA and the college's own financial statement are required. Check with the school for current application deadlines.

International Students: A satisfactory score on the TOEFL is required.

Computers: All students may access the system. There are no time limits and no fees.

Graduates: In a recent year, 78 bachelor's degrees were awarded. The most popular majors were education (30%), social science/social work (24%), and business (11%). In an average class, 17% graduate in 4 years or less, 44% graduate in 5 years or less, and 56% graduate in 6 years or less.

Admissions Contact: Director of Admissions.
E-mail: *ward_c@heritage.edu* Web: *www.heritage.edu*

NORTHWEST UNIVERSITY   C-2
Kirkland, WA 98033

	(425) 889-5231
	(800) 669-3781; Fax: (425) 889-5224
Full-time: 360 men, 610 women	**Faculty:** 49
Part-time: 40 men, 50 women	**Ph.D.s:** 41%
Graduate: 30 men, 50 women	**Student/Faculty:** 20 to 1
Year: semesters, summer session	**Tuition:** $17,920
Application Deadline: August 1	**Room & Board:** $6450
Freshman Class: n/av	
SAT or ACT: required	**COMPETITIVE**

Northwest University, formerly Northwest College and founded in 1934, is a private institution offering programs in ministry, business, nursing, and education. Some figures in the above capsule and in this profile are approximate. There are 2 graduate schools. In addition to regional accreditation, NC has baccalaureate program accreditation with AACTE. The library contains 174,100 volumes, 40,800 microform items, and 5000 audio/video tapes/CDs/DVDs, and subscribes to 900 periodicals including electronic. Computerized library services include the card catalog, interlibrary loans, database searching, and Internet access. Special learning facilities include a radio station. The 56-acre campus is in a suburban area in Kirkland, 10 miles east of Seattle and overlooking Lake Washington. Including any residence halls, there are 27 buildings.

Student Life: 79% of undergraduates are from Washington. Students are from 23 states, 15 foreign countries, and Canada. 60% are white. Most are Protestant. The average age of freshmen is 19; all undergraduates, 25. 34% do not continue beyond their first year; 34% remain to graduate.

Housing: 544 students can be accommodated in college housing, which includes single-sex dorms, on-campus apartments, and married-student housing. On-campus housing is guaranteed for all 4 years. 63% of students live on campus; of those, 80% remain on campus on weekends. Alcohol is not permitted. All students may keep cars.

Activities: There are no fraternities or sororities. There are 20 groups on campus, including band, choir, chorale, chorus, debate, drama, forensics, international, jazz band, literary magazine, musical theater, newspaper, orchestra, photography, professional, radio religious, social, social service, student government, and yearbook. Popular campus events include Christmas Holiday Social, All-School Banquet, and Roomies Night-out.

Sports: There are 4 intercollegiate sports for men and 4 for women, and 2 intramural sports for men and 2 for women. Facilities include a gym pavilion, outdoor tennis courts, a practice field for soccer and intramural football, access to the Seattle Seahawks' fields, outdoor basketball, and sand volleyball.

Disabled Students: 75% of the campus is accessible. Wheelchair ramps, elevators, special parking, specially equipped rest rooms, and special residence hall rest rooms and shower facilities are available.

Services: There is a reader service for the blind and remedial writing. The Student Success Office provides assistance in most areas, including study skills.

Campus Safety and Security: Measures include 24-hour foot and vehicle patrol, security escort services, shuttle buses, and informal discussions. There are pamphlets/posters/films, emergency telephones, and lighted pathways/sidewalks.

Programs of Study: NC confers the B.A. degree. Associate and master's degrees are also awarded. Bachelor's degrees are awarded in BIOLOGICAL SCIENCE (life science), BUSINESS (business administration and management), COMMUNICATIONS AND THE ARTS (communications, English, journalism, music, and music business management), COMPUTER AND PHYSICAL SCIENCE (computer management), EDUCATION (education, elementary, middle school, physical, secondary, and special), ENGINEERING AND ENVIRONMENTAL DESIGN (environmental science), HEALTH PROFESSIONS (nursing), SOCIAL SCIENCE (behavioral science, biblical studies, counseling/psychology, history, interdisciplinary studies, liberal arts/general studies, ministries, missions, pastoral studies, philosophy, psychology, religion, religious education, religious music, theological studies, and youth ministry). Teacher education, business, and psychology are the strongest academically. Teacher education, church ministries, and business are the largest.

Required: Students must complete 18 credits in humanities, 16 in religion, 12 in social science, and 10 each in science and math. At least 125 semester credits (up to 139 for teacher education), with a minimum GPA of 2.0, are required. The number of semester credits needed in the major varies from 36 to 50.

Special: Northwest offers study in several locations in the United States and foreign countries through the Council for Christian Colleges and Universities. Dual majors are available. There are 2 national honor societies and 1 departmental honors program.

Faculty/Classroom: 65% of faculty are male; 35%, female. All teach undergraduates. The average class size in an introductory lecture is 30; in a laboratory, 20; and in a regular course, 24.

Requirements: The SAT or ACT is required. A GPA of 2.3 is required. AP and CLEP credits are accepted. Important factors in the admissions decision are personality/intangible qualities, recommendations by alumni, and leadership record.

Procedure: Freshmen are admitted to all sessions. Entrance exams should be taken in the spring of the junior year. There is a rolling admissions plan. There are early decision and deferred admissions plans. Applications should be filed by August 1 for fall entry, and December 15 for spring entry. The application fee is $30. Notification is sent on a rolling basis. 56 early decision candidates were accepted for a recent class.

Transfer: Transfers must have a minimum 2.3 GPA from high school and college and must submit SAT or ACT scores, an essay, and 2 letters of reference. 30 of 125 credits required for the bachelor's degree must be completed at NC.

Visiting: There are regularly scheduled orientations for prospective students, including Northwest Fridays. There are guides for informal visits and visitors may sit in on classes and stay overnight.

Financial Aid: In a recent year, 77% of all full-time freshmen and 66% of continuing full-time students received some form of financial aid. 72% of full-time freshmen and 61% of continuing full-time students received need-based aid. The average freshman award was $7974. 82% of undergraduates work part time. Average annual earnings from campus work are $2050. The average financial indebtedness of a recent year's graduate was $20,374. The FAFSA and the college's own financial statement are required. Check with the school for current deadlines.

International Students: There were 19 international students enrolled in a recent year. A satisfactory score on the TOEFL is required.

Computers: All students may access the system. There are set hours for labs; residence halls are always connected. There are no time limits. The fee is $50 per semester. It is strongly recommended that all students have a personal computer.

Graduates: In a recent year, 252 bachelor's degrees were awarded.

Admissions Contact: Ben Thomas, Enrollment Services. A video is available. E-mail: *admissions@northwestu.edu*
Web: *www.northwestu.edu*

PACIFIC LUTHERAN UNIVERSITY   C-2
Tacoma, WA 98447

	(253) 535-7151
	(800) 274-6758; Fax: (253) 536-5136
Full-time: 1100 men, 1900 women	**Faculty:** 216; IIA, -$
Part-time: 120 men, 150 women	**Ph.D.s:** 90%
Graduate: 110 men, 170 women	**Student/Faculty:** 14 to 1
Year: 4-1-4, summer session	**Tuition:** $22,040
Application Deadline: open	**Room & Board:** $6765
Freshman Class: n/av	
SAT or ACT: required	**VERY COMPETITIVE**

Pacific Lutheran University, founded in 1890, is an independent, non-profit institution affiliated with the Evangelical Lutheran Church in America. PLU offers programs in arts and sciences, business, education, nursing, fine arts, and phys ed. There are 6 undergraduate and 3 graduate schools. Some figures in the above capsule and in this profile are approximate. In addition to regional accreditation, PLU has baccalaureate program accreditation with AACSB, ABET, CSAB, CSWE, NASM, NCATE, and NLN. The library contains 597,094 volumes, 234,764 microform items, and 11,884 audio/video tapes/CDs/DVDs, and subscribes to 4732 periodicals including electronic. Computerized library services include the card catalog, interlibrary loans, database searching, and Internet access. Special learning facilities include a learning resource center, art gallery, radio station, TV station, an herbarium, invertebrate and vertebrate museums, a biology field station, Northwest history collections, a Scandinavian history collection, and a language resource center. The 126-acre campus is in a suburban area 7 miles south of Tacoma. Including any residence halls, there are 40 buildings.

Student Life: 73% of undergraduates are from Washington. Others are from 38 states, 24 foreign countries, and Canada. 97% are from public schools. 77% are white. 67% are Protestant; 10% Catholic; 6% claim no religious affiliation. The average age of freshmen is 18; all undergraduates, 22. 17% do not continue beyond their first year; 65% remain to graduate.

Housing: 1650 students can be accommodated in college housing, which includes single-sex and coed dorms, on-campus apartments, and married-student housing. On-campus housing is guaranteed for the freshman year only. 50% of students live on campus; of those, 75% remain on campus on weekends. Alcohol is not permitted. All students may keep cars.

Activities: There are no fraternities or sororities. There are 46 groups on campus, including adult student, advertising, art, band, cheerleading, choir, chorale, chorus, comedy, commuter, computers, dance, debate, drama, ethnic, film, gay, honors, international, jazz band, literary magazine, musical theater, newspaper, opera, orchestra, pep band, photography, political, professional, radio and TV, religious, social, social service, student government, symphony, and yearbook. Popular campus events include Lucia Bride Festival, Songfest, and Family Weekend.

Sports: There are 11 intercollegiate sports for men and 10 for women, and 12 intramural sports for men and 12 for women. Facilities include a 4000-seat gym, a 4000-seat auditorium, a fitness center with an all-weather track, a 9-hole golf course, a swimming pool, and racquetball, squash, and tennis courts.

Disabled Students: 90% of the campus is accessible. Wheelchair ramps, elevators, special parking, specially equipped rest rooms, special class scheduling, lowered drinking fountains, and lowered telephones are available.

Services: Counseling and information services are available, as is tutoring in most subjects. Study groups and pretest and posttest reviews are also available.

Campus Safety and Security: Measures include 24-hour foot and vehicle patrol, self-defense education, security escort services, and informal discussions. There are pamphlets/posters/films, emergency telephones, and lighted pathways/sidewalks.

Programs of Study: PLU confers B.A., B.S., B.A.E., B.A.P.E., B.A.Rec., B.B.A., B.F.A., B.M., B.M.A., B.M.Ed., B.S.N., and B.S.P.E. degrees. Master's degrees are also awarded. Bachelor's degrees are awarded in BIOLOGICAL SCIENCE (biology/biological science), BUSINESS (business administration and management and recreation and leisure services), COMMUNICATIONS AND THE ARTS (art, classics, communications, English, fine arts, French, German, music, music performance, music theory and composition, piano/organ, Scandinavian languages, Spanish, and voice), COMPUTER AND PHYSICAL SCIENCE (applied physics, chemistry, computer programming, computer science, geoscience, mathematics, and physics), EDUCATION (education, music, and physical), ENGINEERING AND ENVIRONMENTAL DESIGN (computer engineering, engineering and applied science, and environmental science), HEALTH PROFESSIONS (nursing), SOCIAL SCIENCE (anthropology, Asian/Oriental studies, economics, history, international studies, philosophy, political science/government, psychology, religion, Scandinavian studies, social work, sociology, and women's studies). Business administration, education, and nursing are the largest.

Required: All students must complete 128 credit hours, with a maximum of 40 in the major. Candidates for degrees in nursing, business administration, and education need a cumulative 2.5 GPA; all others must have a 2.0 GPA. The required curriculum is 36 credit hours of distributive core courses in arts/literature, natural sciences/math, philosophy, religious studies, and social sciences; writing and critical conversation courses; and diversity classes.

Special: PLU offers 2 different bachelor's degrees simultaneously, 3-2 engineering degrees with Washington University in St. Louis and Columbia University, and accelerated degree programs in most majors. Dual majors and student-designed majors can be arranged. Extensive internships with local businesses and nonprofit organizations, work-study programs, nondegree study, and pass/fail options are also available. The Wang Center for International Programs supports the university's internationally focused academic programs. There are study-abroad programs in 28 countries. There are 7 national honor societies.

Faculty/Classroom: 54% of faculty are male; 46%, female. 98% teach undergraduates, and 90% both teach and do research, and 90% do both. No introductory courses are taught by graduate students. The average class size in an introductory lecture is 23; in a laboratory, 16; and in a regular course, 17.

Admissions: There were 5 National Merit finalists in a recent year. 28 freshmen graduated first in their class.

Requirements: The SAT or ACT is required. In addition, applicants should be graduates of accredited secondary schools, although GED certificates are accepted. PLU requires 2 years each of college preparatory math and a foreign language and recommends 4 years of English, 2 each of social studies and lab science, 1 of fine or performing arts, and 3 of electives. An essay is required. PLU requires applicants to be in the upper 50% of their class. A GPA of 2.5 is required. AP and CLEP credits are accepted. Important factors in the admissions decision are advanced placement or honor courses, leadership record, and evidence of special talent.

Procedure: Freshmen are admitted fall and spring. Entrance exams should be taken by January of the senior year. There is a rolling admissions plan. There is a deferred admissions plan. Application deadlines are open. Application fee is $35. Applications are accepted on-line.

Transfer: 290 transfer students enrolled in a recent year. Candidates must be in good academic and personal standing at the institutions last attended full time. Although it does not guarantee admission, a 2.5 GPA in all college work is usually required. For applicants with fewer than 30 semester hours or 45 quarter hours, secondary school records and standardized test scores must be submitted. All students must meet the foreign language and math entrance requirements. 32 of 128 credits required for the bachelor's degree must be completed at PLU.

Visiting: There are regularly scheduled orientations for prospective students, consisting of activities based on the students' individual interests. There are guides for informal visits and visitors may sit in on classes and stay overnight. To schedule a visit, contact the Office of Admissions.

Financial Aid: In a recent year, 95% of all full-time freshmen and 93% of continuing full-time students received some form of financial aid. 69% of full-time freshmen and 72% of continuing full-time students received need-based aid. The average freshman award was $17,193. Need-based scholarships or need-based grants averaged $6966 ($18,597 maximum); need-based self-help aid (loans and jobs) averaged $5821 ($12,125 maximum); and other non-need-based awards and non-need-based scholarships averaged $5502 ($19,610 maximum). 51% of undergraduates work part time. Average annual earnings from campus work are $2145. The average financial indebtedness of a recent year's graduate was $22,190. The FAFSA is required. The deadline for filing freshman financial aid applications for fall entry is February 15.

International Students: There were 136 international students enrolled in a recent year. The school actively recruits these students. A satisfactoy score on the TOEFL is required.

Computers: All students may access the system 18 hours per day, or 24 hours with a modem. There are no time limits and no fees.

Graduates: In a recent year, 796 bachelor's degrees were awarded. The most popular majors were business (16%), education (13%), and nursing (7%). In an average class, 2% graduate in 3 years or less, 45% graduate in 4 years or less, 65% graduate in 5 years or less, and 68% graduate in 6 years or less. 53 companies recruited on campus in a recent year. Of a recent graduating class, 11% were enrolled in graduate school within 6 months of graduation and 85% were employed.

Admissions Contact: Director of Admissions.
E-mail: *admissions@plu.edu* Web: *www.plu.edu*

SAINT MARTIN'S UNIVERSITY (Formerly Saint Martin's College) B-3

Lacey, WA 98503

(360) 438-4311
(800) 368-8803; Fax: (360) 412-6189

Full-time: 397 men, 539 women	**Faculty:** 56; IIB, --$
Part-time: 109 men, 133 women	**Ph.D.s:** 80%
Graduate: 106 men, 167 women	**Student/Faculty:** 13 to 1
Year: semesters, summer session	**Tuition:** $21,155
Application Deadline: March 1	**Room & Board:** $6400
Freshman Class: 522 applied, 382 accepted, 169 enrolled	
SAT or ACT: required	**COMPETITIVE**

Saint Martin's University, formerly Saint Martin's College and founded in 1895, is a small, private (not for profit) Roman Catholic institution conducted by the Benedictine order, offering undergraduate and graduate programs in liberal arts and sciences, business, engineering, and pre-professional areas. There are 6 undergraduate and 6 graduate schools. In addition to regional accreditation, Saint Martin's University has baccalaureate program accreditation with ABET. The library contains 100,540 volumes, 132,768 microform items, and 1403 audio/video tapes/CDs/DVDs, and subscribes to 811 periodicals including electronic. Computerized library services include the card catalog, interlibrary loans, and database searching. Special learning facilities include a learning resource center, art gallery, and natural history museum. The 303-acre campus is in a suburban area 3 miles from Olympia and 60 miles south of Seattle. Including any residence halls, there are 14 buildings.

Student Life: 88% of undergraduates are from Washington. Others are from 17 states, 13 foreign countries, and Canada. 85% are from public schools. 64% are white; 10% African American. 39% claim no religious affiliation; 36% Catholic; 15% Protestant. The average age of freshmen is 18; all undergraduates, 30. 20% do not continue beyond their first year; 69% remain to graduate.

Housing: 282 students can be accommodated in college housing, which includes coed dorms. On-campus housing is guaranteed for the freshman year only and is available on a first-come, first-served basis. 71% of students commute. Alcohol is not permitted. All students may keep cars.

Activities: There are no fraternities or sororities. There are 30 groups on campus, including band, cheerleading, choir, computers, drama, ethnic, honors, international, newspaper, pep band, professional, religious, social, social service, student government, and yearbook. Popular campus events include Career Fair, International Day, and Capital Food and Wine Festival.

Sports: There are 5 intercollegiate sports for men and 6 for women, and 9 intramural sports for men and 9 for women. Facilities include a 5300-seat multipurpose pavilion, athletic fields, tennis courts, and nearby golf courses, lakes, and mountains.

Disabled Students: 90% of the campus is accessible. Wheelchair ramps, elevators, special parking, specially equipped rest rooms, lowered drinking fountains, and lowered telephones are available. Access services provide assistance to students with disabilities.

Services: Counseling and information services are available, as is tutoring in some subjects, including writing. There is a reader service for the blind and remedial writing.

Campus Safety and Security: Measures include 24-hour foot and vehicle patrol, security escort services, pamphlets/posters/films, and lighted pathways/sidewalks.There is a security patrol from dark to dawn.

Programs of Study: Saint Martin's University confers B.A., B.S., B.S.C.E., and B.S.M.E. degrees. Master's degrees are also awarded. Bachelor's degrees are awarded in BIOLOGICAL SCIENCE (biology/biological science), BUSINESS (accounting, banking and finance, management science, and marketing/retailing/merchandising), COMMUNICATIONS AND THE ARTS (English and music), COMPUTER AND PHYSICAL SCIENCE (chemistry, computer science, and mathematics), EDUCATION (computer, elementary, social studies, and special), ENGINEERING AND ENVIRONMENTAL DESIGN (civil engineering and mechanical engineering), HEALTH PROFESSIONS (predentistry, premedicine, prepharmacy, and preveterinary science), SOCIAL SCIENCE (community services, criminal justice, economics, history, humanities, political science/government, prelaw, psychology, and religion). Education and engineering are the strongest academically. Education, business, and science/math are the largest.

Required: All students must complete freshman composition and general education requirements, including 2 courses in social sciences, 1 course each in literature, philosophy, the arts, religious studies, natural science with lab, math (precalculus), computer science, U.S. history, and non-U.S. history, as well as 2 credits of phys ed. Students must pass an English proficiency exam. A total of 128 semester credits with a 2.0 GPA is required. 1 year of foreign language is required if the student did not take 2 years of a single foreign language in high school.

Special: Double majors, work-study with the state of Washington, nonprofit organizations, and Saint Martin's, internships in all disciplines, a Washington semester with American University, and pass/fail options are offered. The FOCUS program offers credit for job experience. Nondegree study and study abroad is possible. There are 2 national honor societies.

Faculty/Classroom: 61% of faculty are male; 39%, female. All teach undergraduates and 70% both teach and do research. No introductory courses are taught by graduate students. The average class size in an introductory lecture is 20; in a laboratory, 12; and in a regular course, 12.

Admissions: 73% of the 2005-2006 applicants were accepted.

Requirements: The SAT or ACT is required. In addition, applicants must be graduates of an accredited secondary school or have a GED, with a minimum of 16 academic units, including 4 in English, 2 or 3 in math, 2 in history/social science, 1 or 2 each in foreign language and lab science, and 7 in electives. Class standing also is considered. An essay and recommendation from a teacher or counselor are required. Students should have a score of 800 on the SAT I and a 2.5 GPA. A GPA of 2.5 is required. AP and CLEP credits are accepted. Important factors in the admissions decision are advanced placement or honor courses, recommendations by school officials, and personality/intangible qualities.

Procedure: Freshmen are admitted to all sessions. There is a rolling admissions plan. The priority deadline for applications for Fall entry is March 1. The application fee is $35. Notification is sent on a rolling basis. Applications are accepted on-line.

Transfer: 165 transfer students enrolled in 2004-2005. Transfer applicants must submit transcripts from all colleges previously attended and have a 2.0 GPA. 32 of 128 credits required for the bachelor's degree must be completed at Saint Martin's University.

Visiting: There are regularly scheduled orientations for prospective students, including a campus tour and faculty, student service, and financial

aid presentations. There are guides for informal visits and visitors may sit in on classes and stay overnight. To schedule a visit, contact the Admissions Office.

Financial Aid: In a recent year, 98% of all full-time freshmen and 65% of continuing full-time students received some form of financial aid. 94% of full-time freshmen and 63% of continuing full-time students received need-based aid. The average freshman award was $20,003. Need-based scholarships or need-based grants averaged $6404; need-based self-help aid (loans and jobs) averaged $6349; non-need-based athletic scholarships averaged $3615; and other non-need-based awards and non-need-based scholarships averaged $3635. 34% of undergraduates work part time. Average annual earnings from campus work are $1587. The average financial indebtedness of a recent year's graduate was $29,866. Saint Martin's University is a member of CSS. The FAFSA and the college's own financial statement are required. The priority deadline for filing freshman financial aid applications for fall entry is March 1.

International Students: There are 81 international students enrolled. The school actively recruits these students. A satisfactory score on the TOEFL is required.

Computers: All students may access the system. There are no time limits. The fee is $50 per semester.

Graduates: From July 1, 2004 to June 30, 2005, 268 bachelor's degrees were awarded. The most popular majors were business/marketing (26%), social science (20%), and psychology (14%). In an average class, 1% graduate in 3 years or less, 43% graduate in 4 years or less, 60% graduate in 5 years or less, and 69% graduate in 6 years or less. 160 companies recruited on campus in a recent year. Of a recent graduating class, 8% were enrolled in graduate school within 6 months of graduation and 97% were employed.

Admissions Contact: Director of Admissions.
E-mail: *admissions@stmartin.edu* Web: *www.stmartin.edu*

SEATTLE PACIFIC UNIVERSITY
C-2
Seattle, WA 98119-1997
(206) 281-2021
(800) 366-3344; Fax: (206) 281-2669

Full-time: 944 men, 1926 women	**Faculty:** IIA, -$
Part-time: 37 men, 71 women	**Ph.D.s:** 85%
Graduate: 235 men, 509 women	**Student/Faculty:** n/av
Year: quarters, summer session	**Tuition:** $21,783
Application Deadline: March 1	**Room & Board:** $7572
Freshman Class: 1858 applied, 1576 accepted, 710 enrolled	
SAT or ACT: required	**COMPETITIVE**

Seattle Pacific University, founded in 1891, is a private, nonprofit institution affiliated with the Free Methodist Church. It offers programs in business and economics, education, fine and performing arts, health science, humanities, natural and mathematical sciences, phys ed and athletics, religion, and social and behavioral sciences. There are 9 undergraduate and 6 graduate schools. In addition to regional accreditation, SPU has baccalaureate program accreditation with ABET, ADA, NASM, NCATE, and NLN. The library contains 189,371 volumes, 500,296 microform items, and 3303 audio/video tapes/CDs/DVDs, and subscribes to 1219 periodicals including electronic. Computerized library services include the card catalog and database searching. Special learning facilities include a learning resource center, art gallery, a science center, a performing arts theater, a writing lab, and a media center. The 35-acre campus is in an urban area on the north slope of Queen Anne Hill, 7 minutes from downtown Seattle. Including any residence halls, there are 94 buildings.

Student Life: 68% of undergraduates are from out of state, mostly the Northwest. Students are from 45 states, 31 foreign countries, and Canada. 80% are white. 75% are Protestant; 17% claim no religious affiliation; 7% Catholic. The average age of freshmen is 18; all undergraduates, 20. 15% do not continue beyond their first year; 67% remain to graduate.

Housing: 1284 students can be accommodated in college housing, which includes single-sex and coed dorms, on-campus apartments, off-campus apartments, and married-student housing. In addition, there are theme houses. On-campus housing is guaranteed for all 4 years. 59% of students live on campus; of those, 80% remain on campus on weekends. Alcohol is not permitted. All students may keep cars.

Activities: There are no fraternities or sororities. There are 50 groups on campus, including art, cheerleading, chess, choir, chorale, drama, ethnic, honors, international, jazz band, literary magazine, newspaper, orchestra, pep band, political, professional, radio, religious, social, social service, student government, symphony, and yearbook. Popular campus events include Family Weekend, Talent Show, and Ivy Cutting at Graduation.

Sports: There are 5 intercollegiate sports for men and 6 for women, and 19 intramural sports for men and 18 for women. Facilities include a soccer field, an oval track, tennis and basketball courts, a gym and crew house, a crew dock, a 2600-seat indoor gym, an 800-seat campus auditorium, and a community swimming pool available to students with free passes.

Disabled Students: 70% of the campus is accessible. Wheelchair ramps, elevators, special parking, specially equipped rest rooms, and special class scheduling are available.

Services: Counseling and information services are available, as is tutoring in most subjects. There is a reader service for the blind and remedial math and writing. In addition, there is priority registration for disabled students.

Campus Safety and Security: Measures include 24-hour foot and vehicle patrol, security escort services, pamphlets/posters/films, and emergency telephones. There are lighted pathways/sidewalks and closed-circuit TV monitors.

Programs of Study: SPU confers B.A. and B.S. degrees. Master's and doctoral degrees are also awarded. Bachelor's degrees are awarded in BIOLOGICAL SCIENCE (biochemistry and biology/biological science), BUSINESS (accounting and business administration and management), COMMUNICATIONS AND THE ARTS (art, classics, communications, dramatic arts, English, French, German, Latin, music, Russian, Spanish, and visual and performing arts), COMPUTER AND PHYSICAL SCIENCE (chemistry, computer science, mathematics, and physics), EDUCATION (art, Christian, English, home economics, mathematics, music, science, social science, and special), ENGINEERING AND ENVIRONMENTAL DESIGN (electrical/electronics engineering and engineering and applied science), HEALTH PROFESSIONS (exercise science and nursing), SOCIAL SCIENCE (clothing and textiles management/production/services, economics, European studies, family/consumer studies, food science, history, Latin American studies, liberal arts/general studies, philosophy, physical fitness/movement, political science/government, psychology, religion, religious education, sociology, and theological studies). Education, nursing, and business administration are the largest.

Required: All students must demonstrate competency in math and English. Students must complete 15 quarter credits in Christian heritage and values, 56 in general education, plus up to 15 credits of foreign language competency, and at least 45 to 60 in the major, depending on the program. A minimum of 180 credits is needed for the bachelor's degree, with a 2.0 GPA overall. At least 60 credits must be earned in 3000-level courses or higher.

Special: There is a cooperative program with Fashion Institute of Technology in New York City, Fashion Institute of Design and Merchandising in Los Angeles, and Han Nam University in Korea, cross-registration with the Christian College Consortium and Christian College Coalition, and a Washington semester in American studies through the Christian College Coalition. SPU offers internships, study abroad in more than 5 countries, work-study programs, dual and student-designed majors, interdisciplinary majors such as language arts, and a liberal studies major for associate degree graduates. A general studies degree, pass/no credit options, and nondegree study are available. There are 5 national honor societies, a freshman honors program, and 10 departmental honors programs.

Faculty/Classroom: 62% of faculty are male; 38%, female. No introductory courses are taught by graduate students. The average class size in a regular course is 18.

Admissions: 85% of the 2005-2006 applicants were accepted. 24 freshmen graduated first in their class in a recent year.

Requirements: The SAT or ACT is required; The SAT is preferred with a required minimum composite score. Candidates should be graduates of an accredited secondary school with a minimum high school GPA of 2.5 or hold a GED certificate. A strong college preparatory program in high school is recommended, including 4 years of English, 3 each of math, science, and foreign language, 2 of history, and 1 of social studies. An essay and 2 letters of recommendation are required, and an interview is recommended. AP and CLEP credits are accepted. Important factors in the admissions decision are advanced placement or honor courses, leadership record, and extracurricular activities record.

Procedure: Freshmen are admitted to all sessions. Entrance exams should be taken before January of the senior year. There are early action and early admissions plans. There is a rolling admissions plan. Early action applications should be filed by November 15; regular applications, by March 1 for fall entry, along with a $45 fee. Notification of early decision is sent February 15; regular decision, on a rolling basis. 519 applicants were on the 2005 waiting list; 346 were admitted. Applications are accepted on-line.

Transfer: 224 transfer students enrolled in 2004-2005. A minimum 2.5 GPA is required, and an interview is recommended. Transcripts from all previous colleges attended and from high school are required, along with 2 letters of recommendation and an essay or personal statement. Evidence of honorable dismissal from the previous school is also required. Students with at least 30 credits earned are not required to take the SAT or ACT. 45 of 180 credits required for the bachelor's degree must be completed at SPU.

Visiting: There are regularly scheduled orientations for prospective students. There are guides for informal visits and visitors may sit in on classes and stay overnight. To schedule a visit, contact the Admissions Office.

Financial Aid: In 2005-2006, 66% of all full-time freshmen and 60% of continuing full-time students received some form of financial aid. At least 65% of full-time freshmen and 58% of continuing full-time students received need-based aid. The average freshman award was $18,573. Need-based scholarships or need-based grants averaged $15,431; need-based self-help aid (loans and jobs) averaged $6905; institutional non-need-based athletic scholarships averaged $11,317; and other institutional non-need-based awards and non-need-based scholarships averaged $11,096. The average financial indebtedness of the 2005 graduate was $22,569. The FAFSA is required. The priority date for freshman financial aid applications for fall entry is April 1.

International Students: The school actively recruits these students. They must take the TOEFL, achieving a satisfactory score, or take the MELAB. The Michigan Test must be administered through SPU.

Computers: All students may access the system during lab hours, Monday through Saturday during the academic year. There are no time limits and no fees. It is strongly recommended that all students have a personal computer.

Graduates: From July 1, 2004 to June 30, 2005, 673 bachelor's degrees were awarded. The most popular majors were business/marketing (16%), health professions and related sciences (11%), family and consumer sciences (9%) social sciences (9%). In an average class, 48% graduate in 4 years or less, 64% graduate in 5 years or less, and 66% graduate in 6 years or less.

Admissions Contact: Jennifer Kenney, Director of Undergraduate Admissions. E-mail: *admissions@spu.edu* Web: *www.spu.edu*

SEATTLE UNIVERSITY C-2

Seattle, WA 98122

(206) 296-2000
(800) 426-7123; Fax: (206) 296-5656

Full-time: 1507 men, 2324 women	**Faculty:** IIA, +$
Part-time: 108 men, 171 women	**Ph.D.s:** 85%
Graduate: 651 men, 1065 women	**Student/Faculty:** n/av
Year: quarters, summer session	**Tuition:** $22,905
Application Deadline: February 1	**Room & Board:** $7158
Freshman Class: 4339 applied, 2935 accepted, 761 enrolled	
SAT or ACT: required	**VERY COMPETITIVE**

Seattle University, founded in 1891, is a private, comprehensive institution affiliated with the Roman Catholic Church and operated by the Jesuit Fathers. The emphasis of the undergraduate and graduate programs is on the liberal arts and sciences, business, engineering, health science, teacher preparation, theological studies, and law. There are 5 undergraduate and 7 graduate schools. In addition to regional accreditation, Seattle U has baccalaureate program accreditation with AACSB, ABET, CAHEA, NCATE, and NLN. The 2 libraries contain 234,978 volumes, 570,839 microform items, and 5608 audio/video tapes/CDs/DVDs, and subscribe to 2709 periodicals including electronic. Computerized library services include the card catalog, interlibrary loans, database searching, Internet access, and laptop Internet portals. Special learning facilities include a learning resource center, art gallery, planetarium, radio station, electron microscope, recording studio, and MRI. The 46-acre campus is in an urban area just east of downtown Seattle. Including any residence halls, there are 27 buildings.

Student Life: 60% of undergraduates are from Washington. Others are from 49 states, 69 foreign countries, and Canada. 53% are white; 20% Asian American. 40% claim no religious affiliation; 39% Catholic; 18% Protestant. The average age of freshmen is 18; all undergraduates, 22. 13% do not continue beyond their first year; 63% remain to graduate.

Housing: 1600 students can be accommodated in college housing, which includes single-sex and coed dorms and on-campus apartments. In addition, there are language houses., 24-hour quiet houses, and single-sex floors. On-campus housing is guaranteed for the freshman year only and is available on a lottery system for upperclassmen. Priority is given to out-of-town students. 63% of students commute. All students may keep cars.

Activities: There are no fraternities or sororities. There are 61 groups on campus, including art, cheerleading, choir, chorale, dance, debate, drama, ethnic, forensics, gay, honors, international, jazz band, literary magazine, musical theater, newspaper, photography, political, professional, radio and TV, religious, social, social service, and student government. Popular campus events include Hawaiian Luau, Quad Stock, and International Student Dinner.

Sports: There are 12 intercollegiate sports for men and 13 for women, and 7 intramural sports for men and 7 for women. Facilities include a center with 2 swimming pools, a fitness/weight room, and 5 racquetball, 2 squash, and 3 basketball courts, and an Astroturf gym for indoor soccer/tennis.

Disabled Students: 95% of the campus is accessible. Wheelchair ramps, elevators, special parking, specially equipped rest rooms, special class scheduling, lowered drinking fountains, and lowered telephones are available.

Services: Counseling and information services are available, as is tutoring in most subjects, including math, English, accounting, language, and science. There is a reader service for the blind and a writing center.

Campus Safety and Security: Measures include 24-hour foot and vehicle patrol, self-defense education, security escort services, and shuttle buses. There are informal discussions, pamphlets/posters/films, emergency telephones, and lighted pathways/sidewalks.

Programs of Study: Seattle U confers B.A., B.S., B.A.B.A., B.A.E., B.A.H., B.C.J., B.P.A., B.S.B., B.S.B.C., B.S.C., B.S.C.E., B.S.C.S., B.S.D.U., B.S.E.E., B.S.G.S., B.S.M., B.S.M.E., B.S.M.T., B.S.N., and B.S.P. degrees. Master's and doctoral degrees are also awarded. Bachelor's degrees are awarded in BIOLOGICAL SCIENCE (biochemistry, biology/biological science, and ecology), BUSINESS (accounting, banking and finance, business administration and management, business economics, international business management, marketing/retailing/merchandising, and operations research), COMMUNICATIONS AND THE ARTS (communications, creative writing, dramatic arts, English, fine arts, French, German, journalism, and Spanish), COMPUTER AND PHYSICAL SCIENCE (chemistry, computer science, mathematics, physics, and science), ENGINEERING AND ENVIRONMENTAL DESIGN (civil engineering, electrical/electronics engineering, environmental engineering, manufacturing engineering, and mechanical engineering), HEALTH PROFESSIONS (medical technology, nursing, and ultrasound technology), SOCIAL SCIENCE (criminal justice, economics, history, humanities, international studies, liberal arts/general studies, philosophy, political science/government, psychology, public administration, religion, social work, and sociology). Engineering, accounting, and nursing are the strongest academically and have the largest enrollments.

Required: Students must complete 180 to 192 quarter hours, depending on the degree, with 70 to 90 in the major, and maintain a minimum GPA of 2.25 to 2.5. Core curriculum requirements total 73 quarter hours, of which 10 quarter hours in religious studies must be taken. All students must take courses in English, math, science, philosophy, social studies, and fine arts.

Special: Special academic programs include internships in numerous disciplines, study abroad in 5 countries, and both on- and off-campus work-study through the Washington State Work-Study Program. A liberal studies degree and an accelerated degree program in business are offered. Pass/fail options, dual majors, and student-designed majors are possible. There is a freshman honors program.

Faculty/Classroom: 51% of faculty are male; 49%, female. No introductory courses are taught by graduate students. The average class size in a regular course is 22.

Admissions: 68% of the 2005-2006 applicants were accepted. 18 freshmen graduated first in their class.

Requirements: The SAT or ACT is required. In addition, admissions requirements include graduation from an accredited secondary school, with 16 academic credits, including 4 years of English, 3 each of math and social studies, 2 of foreign language, 2 of lab science, and 2 academic electives; 4 years of math and lab physics and chemistry are required of science and engineering students; lab biology and chemistry are needed by nursing students. The GED is also accepted. A GPA of 2.75 is required. AP and CLEP credits are accepted. Important factors in the admissions decision are advanced placement or honor courses, recommendations by school officials, and extracurricular activities record.

Procedure: Freshmen are admitted to all sessions. Entrance exams should be taken during the fall of the senior year. There are early admissions, and deferred admissions and rolling admissions plans. Applications should be filed by February 1 for fall entry, November 1 for winter entry, February 1 for spring entry, and May 1 for summer entry, along with a $45 fee. Notification is sent on a rolling basis.

Transfer: 439 transfer students enrolled in 2004-2005. Generally, transfer students should have a GPA of at least 2.5. An associate degree is recommended; a 2.75 GPA is required for nursing and business administration students. 45 of 180 credits required for the bachelor's degree must be completed at Seattle U.

Visiting: There are regularly scheduled orientations for prospective students. There are guides for informal visits and visitors may sit in on classes and stay overnight. To schedule a visit, contact the Admissions Office.

Financial Aid: In 2005-2006, 67% of all full-time students received some form of financial aid. 64% of full-time freshmen and 65% of continuing full-time students received need-based aid. The average freshman award was $21,431. Need-based scholarships or need-based grants averaged $19,528; need-based self-help aid (loans and jobs) averaged $5554; non-need-based athletic scholarships averaged $4625; and institutional non-need-based awards and non-need-based scholarships averaged $6510. The average financial indebtedness of the 2005 graduate was $25,311. The FAFSA is required. The priority date for freshman financial aid applications for fall entry is February 1.

International Students: The school actively recruits these students. They must score satisfactorily on the written TOEFL.

Computers: All students may access the system during posted hours or any time from networked residence hall rooms. There are no time limits and no fees.

Graduates: From July 1, 2004 to June 30, 2005, 986 bachelor's degrees were awarded. The most popular majors were business/marketing

(27%), health professions and related sciences (11%), and psychology (7%). In an average class, 49% graduate in 4 years or less, 68% graduate in 5 years or less, and 63% graduate in 6 years or less. 175 companies recruited on campus in 2004-2005.

Admissions Contact: Michael K. McKeon, Dean of Admissions. E-mail: *admissions@seattleu.edu* Web: *www.seattleu.edu*

UNIVERSITY OF PUGET SOUND C-2
Tacoma, WA 98416
(253) 879-3211
(800) 396-7191; Fax: (253) 879-3993

Full-time: 1069 men, 1496 women	**Faculty:** 225; IIB, +$
Part-time: 16 men, 8 women	**Ph.D.s:** 86%
Graduate: 53 men, 210 women	**Student/Faculty:** 11 to 1
Year: semesters, summer session	**Tuition:** $28,460
Application Deadline: February 1	**Room & Board:** $7140
Freshman Class: 4711 applied, 3343 accepted, 670 enrolled	
SAT Verbal/Math: 635/615*	**ACT:** 27 **HIGHLY COMPETITIVE**

The University of Puget Sound, founded in 1888, is an independent, residential, undergraduate liberal arts and sciences college with selected graduate programs building effectively on a liberal arts foundation. In addition to regional accreditation, Puget Sound has baccalaureate program accreditation with ACS and NASM. The library contains 549,571 volumes, 354,420 microform items, and 16,044 audio/video tapes/CDs/DVDs, and subscribes to 23,798 periodicals including electronic. Computerized library services include the card catalog, interlibrary loans, database searching, and Internet access. Special learning facilities include a learning resource center, radio station, and student science labs, an observatory, computer labs, seminar rooms, turnaround computer classrooms, a media center, language houses, theater workshops, a newspaper, a concert hall, a center for writing and learning, a bibliographic instruction room, a natural history museum, an electron microscopy facility, and a student theater. The 97-acre campus is in a suburban area 35 miles south of Seattle and 1 mile from Commencement Bay on Puget Sound. Including any residence halls, there are 38 buildings.

Student Life: 70% of undergraduates are from out of state, mostly the West. Students are from 44 states, 12 foreign countries, and Canada. 77% are from public schools. 75% are white. 68% claim no religious affiliation; 22% Protestant; 6% Catholic. The average age of freshmen is 18; all undergraduates, 20. 13% do not continue beyond their first year; 73% remain to graduate.

Housing: 1651 students can be accommodated in college housing, which includes single-sex and coed dormitories, on-campus apartments, fraternity houses, and sorority houses. In addition, there are honors houses, language houses, special-interest houses, and theme houses and halls. On-campus housing is guaranteed for the freshman year only, is available on a first-come, first-served basis, and is available on a lottery system for upperclassmen. 62% of students live on campus; of those, 80% remain on campus on weekends. All students may keep cars.

Activities: 22% of men belong to 4 national fraternities; 22% of women belong to 4 national sororities. There are 102 groups on campus, including art, band, cheerleading, choir, chorale, chorus, computers, dance, debate, diversity awareness, drama, environmental, ethnic, film, forensics, gay, gender, health and wellness, honors, international, jazz band, literary magazine, musical theater, newspaper, opera, orchestra, pep band, photography, political, professional, radio and TV, religious, social, social service, student government, symphony, and yearbook. Popular campus events include Foolish Pleasures (student film festival), Mistletoast Holiday, and Hawaiian Luau.

Sports: There are 11 intercollegiate sports for men and 12 for women, and 7 intramural sports for men and 6 for women. Facilities include a 3000-seat basketball and volleyball gym, a 6-lane pool, a 2488-seat football, soccer, lacrosse, and track stadium, 6 indoor tennis courts, a fitness room, an aerobics exercise area and dance studio, a track, baseball, softball, and intramural fields, 2 outdoor sand volleyball courts, an indoor climbing wall, and an auxiliary gym for intramurals and recreation.

Disabled Students: 80% of the campus is accessible. Wheelchair ramps, elevators, special parking, specially equipped rest rooms, special class scheduling, lowered drinking fountains, lowered telephones, TDDs, and adaptive computer equipment are available.

Services: Counseling and information services are available, as is tutoring in most subjects. There is a reader service for the blind and remedial reading.

Campus Safety and Security: Measures include 24-hour foot and vehicle patrol, security escort services, informal discussions, and pamphlets/posters/films. There are emergency telephones and lighted pathways/sidewalks.

Programs of Study: Puget Sound confers B.A., B.S., and B.M. degrees. Master's degrees are also awarded. Bachelor's degrees are awarded in BIOLOGICAL SCIENCE (biology/biological science), BUSINESS (business administration and management and international economics), COMMUNICATIONS AND THE ARTS (art, classics, communications, dramatic arts, English, French, German, music, music performance, and Spanish), COMPUTER AND PHYSICAL SCIENCE (chemistry, computer science, geology, mathematics, natural sciences, and physics), EDUCATION (music), HEALTH PROFESSIONS (exercise science), SOCIAL SCIENCE (economics, history, philosophy, political science/government, psychology, religion, and sociology). Physics, chemistry, and exercise science are the strongest academically. Business, psychology, and English are the largest.

Required: Core requirements include writing and rhetoric, scholarly and creative inquiry, and courses in fine arts, humanities, math, natural science, and social science.

Special: Special academic programs include on- and off-campus work-study, paid and unpaid internships in the community in conjunction with an internship seminar, and study abroad in 50 countries. There are 3-2 engineering degrees with Washington University at St. Louis, Columbia, and Duke Universities, and the University of Southern California. B.A.-B.S. degrees in chemistry, physics, economics, and a special interdisciplinary major, and a B.A.-B.M. degree. Dual majors in foreign language and international affairs, music and business, and computer science and business, as well as pass/fail options are possible. 2 special features of the curriculum are the intensive 4-year study of the classics of Western civilization and the Business Leadership Program, combining traditional business and liberal arts study. There are 15 national honor societies, including Phi Beta Kappa, a freshman honors program, and 13 departmental honors programs.

Faculty/Classroom: 55% of faculty are male; 45%, female. 96% teach undergraduates. No introductory courses are taught by graduate students. The average class size in an introductory lecture is 21; in a laboratory, 13; and in a regular course, 19.

Admissions: 71% of the 2005-2006 applicants were accepted. The SAT scores for the 2005-2006 freshman class were: Verbal--4% below 500, 27% between 500 and 599, 50% between 600 and 700, and 19% above 700; Math--6% below 500, 35% between 500 and 599, 48% between 600 and 700, and 11% above 700. The ACT scores were 3% below 21, 14% between 21 and 23, 31% between 24 and 26, 20% between 27 and 28, and 32% above 28. 59% of the current freshmen were in the top fifth of their class; 85% were in the top two fifths. There were 12 National Merit finalists. 31 freshmen graduated first in their class.

Requirements: The SAT or ACT is required. The SAT is preferred. Other admission requirements include graduation from an accredited secondary school, with a recommended 4 years of English, 3 to 4 of math and natural or physical lab science, 3 of social studies or history, 2 to 3 of foreign language, and 1 of fine, visual, or performing arts. Also required are letters of personal recommendation from a teacher and counselor; 2 are preferred. An essay must be submitted, and an interview is recommended. It is recommended that art students present a portfolio and that music students audition. The GED is also accepted. AP credits are accepted. Important factors in the admissions decision are advanced placement or honor courses, evidence of special talent, and extracurricular activities record.

Procedure: Freshmen are admitted to all sessions. Entrance exams should be taken during the fall of the senior year. There are early decision, early admissions, and deferred admissions plans. Early decision applications should be filed by December 15; regular applications, by February 1 for fall entry and March 1 for summer entry, along with a $40 fee. Notification of early decision is sent January 15; regular decision, April 1. 132 early decision candidates were accepted for the 2005-2006 class. 359 applicants were on the 2005 waiting list; 32 were admitted. Applications are accepted on-line.

Transfer: 90 transfer students enrolled in 2004-2005. Applicants must have an honorable dismissal from the institution(s) previously attended and good academic standing, with a minimum GPA of 2.0. All college transcripts and the rigor of prior course work and resulting grades are evaluated. High school transcripts and SAT or ACT scores are required if less than 1 year of college has been completed. An interview is recommended. An essay or a copy of a graded paper is required of all undergraduate transfers. 64 of 128 credits required for the bachelor's degree must be completed at Puget Sound.

Visiting: There are regularly scheduled orientations for prospective students, including meetings with counselors, faculty, and coaches, tours of campus, and classroom experiences. There are guides for informal visits and visitors may sit in on classes and stay overnight. To schedule a visit, contact the Campus Visit Coordinator, Office of Admission.

Financial Aid: In 2005-2006, 87% of all full-time freshmen and 85% of continuing full-time students received some form of financial aid. 59% of full-time freshmen and 55% of continuing full-time students received need-based aid. The average freshman award was $22,032. Need-based scholarships or need-based grants averaged $11,000 ($32,400 maximum); need-based self-help aid (loans and jobs) averaged $5665 ($8925 maximum); and other awards averaged $7649 ($30,020 maximum). 42% of undergraduates work part time. Average annual earnings from campus work are $2000. The average financial indebtedness of the 2005 graduate was $25,842. Puget Sound is a member of CSS. The CSS/Profile or FAFSA is required. The CSS/Profile is required of early decision candidates. The deadline for filing freshman financial aid applications for fall entry is February 1.

International Students: There are 11 international students enrolled. The school actively recruits these students. They must score satisfactorily on the written TOEFL or on the electronic version and also take the SAT or ACT. All freshman applicants and transfers with less than one full year of college work must take the SAT or ACT.

Computers: There are more than 400 wired computers placed across campus for general access in academic buildings, computer labs, classrooms, residence halls, and other spaces. Wireless access is available in the library, the student building, residence halls, science labs, and some classrooms. There is an aggressive plan to make wireless access available across the entire campus. All students may access the system. There are no time limits and no fees. It is strongly recommended that all students have a personal computer.

Graduates: From July 1, 2004 to June 30, 2005, 619 bachelor's degrees were awarded. The most popular majors were business (11%), English (8%), and biology (8%). In an average class, 1% graduate in 3 years or less, 65% graduate in 4 years or less, 72% graduate in 5 years or less, and 73% graduate in 6 years or less. 126 companies recruited on campus in 2004-2005. Of the 2004 graduating class, 30% were enrolled in graduate school within 6 months of graduation and 52% were employed.

Admissions Contact: George H. Mills, Jr., Vice President for Enrollment. E-mail: *admission@ups.edu* Web: *www.ups.edu*

UNIVERSITY OF WASHINGTON   C-2

Seattle, WA 98195   **(206) 543-9686**

Full-time: 10,400 men, 11,260 women	**Faculty:** 3015; I, av$
Part-time: 1900 men, 2100 women	**Ph.D.s:** 99%
Graduate: 4990 men, 4960 women	**Student/Faculty:** 7 to 1
Year: quarters, summer session	**Tuition:** $4000 ($13,300)
Application Deadline: see profile	**Room & Board:** $6400
Freshman Class: n/av	
SAT or ACT: required	**VERY COMPETITIVE**

The University of Washington, founded in 1861, is a public institution offering a broad range of degree programs. Figures in the above capsule and in this profile are approximate. There are 13 undergraduate schools and 1 graduate school. In addition to regional accreditation, UW has baccalaureate program accreditation with AACSB, ABET, NCATE, and NLN. The 19 libraries contain 5,601,263 volumes, 6,432,950 microform items, and 56,295 audio/video tapes/CDs/DVDs. Computerized library services include the card catalog, interlibrary loans, and database searching. Special learning facilities include a learning resource center, art gallery, natural history museum, planetarium, radio station, TV station, state museum, full teaching hospital, marine science lab, 200-acre arboretum, and field research forest. The 703-acre campus is in an urban area 5 miles from downtown Seattle. Including any residence halls, there are 213 buildings.

Student Life: 88% of undergraduates are from Washington. Others are from 44 states, 68 foreign countries, and Canada. 57% are white; 24% Asian American. The average age of freshmen is 18; all undergraduates, 21. 10% do not continue beyond their first year; 71% remain to graduate.

Housing: 5200 students can be accommodated in college housing, which includes coed dorms, on-campus apartments, married-student housing, fraternity houses, and sorority houses. In addition, there are language houses, special-interest houses, and a freshman house. On-campus housing is guaranteed for all 4 years. Alcohol is not permitted. All students may keep cars.

Activities: 17% of men belong to 29 national fraternities; 16% of women belong to 16 national sororities. There are 450 groups on campus, including band, cheerleading, choir, chorale, chorus, computers, dance, drama, ethnic, film, gay, honors, international, jazz band, literary magazine, marching band, musical theater, newspaper, opera, orchestra, pep band, political, professional, radio and TV, religious, social, social service, student government, symphony, and yearbook. Popular campus events include Four Bands for 4 Bucks concert, Opening Day (of boating/crew season), and Convocation.

Sports: There are 10 intercollegiate sports for men and 11 for women, and 20 intramural sports for men and 18 for women. Facilities include a 72,500-seat football stadium, a baseball field, a track and field complex, lakeside facilities, tennis courts, the intramurals building, a golf driving range, and a swimming pool.

Disabled Students: 85% of the campus is accessible. Wheelchair ramps, elevators, special parking, specially equipped rest rooms, special class scheduling, lowered drinking fountains, and lowered telephones are available.

Services: Counseling and information services are available, as is tutoring in every subject. There is a reader service for the blind, and remedial math, reading, and writing.

Campus Safety and Security: Measures include 24-hour foot and vehicle patrol, self-defense education, security escort services, and shuttle buses. There are informal discussions, pamphlets/posters/films, emergency telephones, lighted pathways/sidewalks, and and emergency telephone numbers.

Programs of Study: UW confers B.A., B.S., B.A.B.A., B.C.H.S., B.L.Arch., B.Mus., B.S.A.&A., B.S.B.C., B.S.Cer.E., B.S.Comp.E., B.S.F., B.S.Fish., B.S.I.E., B.S.M.E., B.S.Med.Tech., B.S.Met.E., and B.S.Nur. degrees. Master's and doctoral degrees are also awarded. Bachelor's degrees are awarded in AGRICULTURE (fishing and fisheries, forest engineering, forestry production and processing, and wood science), BIOLOGICAL SCIENCE (biochemistry, biology/biological science, botany, microbiology, neurosciences, and zoology), BUSINESS (accounting, banking and finance, business administration and management, business economics, international business management, marketing/retailing/merchandising, and personnel management), COMMUNICATIONS AND THE ARTS (art history and appreciation, classics, communications, comparative literature, dance, dramatic arts, English, fiber/textiles/weaving, French, Germanic languages and literature, graphic design, Italian, Japanese, jazz, metal/jewelry, music history and appreciation, music performance, painting, photography, printmaking, Scandinavian languages, sculpture, Slavic languages, Spanish, speech/debate/rhetoric, studio art, and technical and business writing), COMPUTER AND PHYSICAL SCIENCE (astronomy, atmospheric sciences and meteorology, computer science, geology, information sciences and systems, mathematics, oceanography, physics, quantitative methods, and statistics), EDUCATION (music), ENGINEERING AND ENVIRONMENTAL DESIGN (aeronautical engineering, ceramic engineering, chemical engineering, civil engineering, computer engineering, construction engineering, electrical/electronics engineering, engineering, landscape architecture/design, materials science, ocean engineering, and paper and pulp science), HEALTH PROFESSIONS (dental hygiene, environmental health science, health care administration, medical laboratory technology, nursing, and speech pathology/audiology), SOCIAL SCIENCE (African American studies, anthropology, Asian/American studies, Asian/Oriental studies, Canadian studies, economics, ethnic studies, food science, geography, history, international relations, Judaic studies, liberal arts/general studies, Near Eastern studies, peace studies, philosophy, political science/government, psychology, religion, Russian and Slavic studies, social work, sociology, South Asian studies, and women's studies). Biological and life sciences, computer science and engineering, and physics are the strongest academically. Business, political science, and art are the largest.

Required: All students must maintain a GPA of 2.0 while taking 180 quarter credits, with 45 in the major. Distribution requirements include 40 credits from the humanities, social sciences, and math/natural sciences, with 12 credits in English composition/writing and a course in quantitative/symbolic reasoning.

Special: A wide variety of internships, including those for minority students in engineering, concurrent dual majors, study abroad in 21 countries, a Washington semester, a general studies degree, and co-op programs are available. Work-study programs, cross-registration with the National Student Exchange, credit/no credit options, student-designed majors, accelerated degree programs, nondegree study, and a 5-year B.A.-B.S. degree also are offered. There are 20 national honor societies, including Phi Beta Kappa, a freshman honors program, and 36 departmental honors programs.

Faculty/Classroom: 66% of faculty are male; 34%, female. 85% both teach and do research. Graduate students teach 40% of introductory courses. The average class size in an introductory lecture is 54; in a laboratory, 24; and in a regular course, 40.

Requirements: The SAT or ACT is required. In addition, applicants must have completed 15 academic units, including 4 years of English, 3 each of math and social sciences, 2 each of foreign language and science, and 1/2 year each in fine/visual performing arts and electives. Admission is based on an indexing system. A GPA of 2.0 is required. AP credits are accepted. Important factors in the admissions decision are advanced placement or honor courses and evidence of special talent.

Procedure: Freshmen are admitted to all sessions. Entrance exams should be taken by December of the senior year. Check with the school for current application deadlines and fee. Applications are accepted online.

Transfer: The school has a special direct transfer agreement with Washington community colleges. Admission is based on an indexing system. 45 of 180 credits required for the bachelor's degree must be completed at UW.

Visiting: There are regularly scheduled orientations for prospective students, including attendance at class, a meeting with an admissions counselor, a campus tour, and information sessions. There are guides for informal visits and visitors may sit in on classes. To schedule a visit, contact the Student Visitation Program at (206) 543-5429 or *visituw@u.washington.edu.*

Financial Aid: The CSS/Profile is required. Check with the school for current deadlines.

International Students: They must take the TOEFL, achieving a satisfactory score, or take the MELAB or the APIEL..

Computers: All students may access the system 24 hours daily. There are no time limits and no fees.

Admissions Contact: Office of Admissions.
E-mail: askuwadm@u.washington.edu
Web: *www.washington.edu/students/uga*

WALLA WALLA COLLEGE — E-3

College Place, WA 99324-1198
(509) 527-2327
(800) 541-8900; Fax: (509) 527-2397

Full-time: 794 men, 734 women	**Faculty:** 122; IIB, --$
Part-time: 74 men, 68 women	**Ph.D.s:** 48%
Graduate: 57 men, 215 women	**Student/Faculty:** 13 to 1
Year: quarters, summer session	**Tuition:** $19,917
Application Deadline: open	**Room & Board:** $4572
Freshman Class: 452 applied, 351 accepted, 292 enrolled	
SAT Verbal/Math: 490/490*	**ACT:** 22 **NONCOMPETITIVE**

Walla Walla College, founded in 1892, is a private comprehensive institution affiliated with the Seventh-day Adventist Church. There are 6 undergraduate and 4 graduate schools. In addition to regional accreditation, WWC has baccalaureate program accreditation with ABET, ACBSP, CSWE, NASM, and NLN. The 3 libraries contain 281,170 volumes, 19,781 microform items, and 3483 audio/video tapes/CDs/DVDs, and subscribe to 1317 periodicals including electronic. Computerized library services include the card catalog, interlibrary loans, and database searching. Special learning facilities include a learning resource center, art gallery, radio station, audio listening/music library, and observatory. The 77-acre campus is in a small town 120 miles southwest of Spokane. Including any residence halls, there are 28 buildings.

Student Life: 60% of undergraduates are from out of state, mostly the West. Students are from 39 states, 32 foreign countries, and Canada. 17% are from public schools. 82% are white. Most are Protestant. The average age of freshmen is 19; all undergraduates, 21. 24% do not continue beyond their first year; 54% remain to graduate.

Housing: 1500 students can be accommodated in college housing, which includes single-sex dorms, on-campus apartments, off-campus apartments, married-student housing, and off-campus houses. On-campus housing is guaranteed for all 4 years. 54% of students live on campus; of those, 90% remain on campus on weekends. Alcohol is not permitted. All students may keep cars.

Activities: There are no fraternities or sororities. There are 50 groups on campus, including art, band, choir, chorale, chorus, drama, ethnic, honors, international, literary magazine, newspaper, orchestra, photography, professional, radio and TV, religious, social service, student government, and symphony. Popular campus events include the Mud Bowl football game and the Sonneberg Series basketball tournament.

Sports: There are 5 intercollegiate sports for men and 3 for women, and 9 intramural sports for men and 7 for women. Facilities include an Olympic-size pool, track, tennis and racquetball courts, a gymnastics sports gym, a gym, weight rooms, and residence hall health spas.

Disabled Students: 90% of the campus is accessible. Wheelchair ramps, elevators, special parking, special class scheduling, and special housing are available.

Services: Counseling and information services are available, as is tutoring in most subjects, including math, languages, sciences, and engineering. There is remedial math, reading, and writing.

Campus Safety and Security: Measures include 24-hour foot and vehicle patrol, self-defense education, security escort services, and informal discussions. There are pamphlets/posters/films, emergency telephones, and lighted pathways/sidewalks.

Programs of Study: WWC confers B.A., B.S., B.B.A., B.Mus., B.S.E., and B.S.W. degrees. Associate and master's degrees are also awarded. Bachelor's degrees are awarded in BIOLOGICAL SCIENCE (biochemistry, biology/biological science, and biophysics), BUSINESS (business administration and management), COMMUNICATIONS AND THE ARTS (art, communications, English, French, German, graphic design, music, music performance, Spanish, and speech/debate/rhetoric), COMPUTER AND PHYSICAL SCIENCE (chemistry, computer science, digital arts/technology, information sciences and systems, mathematics, and physics), EDUCATION (business, elementary, music, physical, and special), ENGINEERING AND ENVIRONMENTAL DESIGN (automotive technology, aviation computer technology, bioengineering, engineering, and environmental science), HEALTH PROFESSIONS (health and nursing), SOCIAL SCIENCE (biblical languages, history, humanities, psychology, religion, social work, sociology, and theological studies). Social Work, engineering, and nursing are the strongest academically.

Required: To graduate, students must successfully complete 192 quarter hours, including at least 45 in the major and at least 60 in upper-level work, with a minimum GPA of 2.0. Grades below C- will not apply toward the major. Students must also meet a general studies requirement that includes 16 to 20 quarter hours in religion and theology, 13 to 21 in language arts, 12 to 20 in history and social science, 12 to 16 in humanities and math/natural science, and 2 to 6 in health and phys ed. A comprehensive exam is required, as is attendance at chapel and assemblies.

Special: Opportunities are provided for internships, co-op programs, cross-registration with Whitman College, study abroad in 6 countries, work-study programs, a B.A.-B.S. degree, dual majors, credit by exam, and nondegree study. There is a freshman honors program.

Faculty/Classroom: 54% of faculty are male; 46%, female. All teach undergraduates. No introductory courses are taught by graduate students. The average class size in an introductory lecture is 24 and in a regular course, 13.

Admissions: 78% of the 2005-2006 applicants were accepted. The SAT scores for the 2005-2006 freshman class were: Verbal--31% below 500, 38% between 500 and 599, 29% between 600 and 700, and 2% above 700; Math--36% below 500, 36% between 500 and 599, 24% between 600 and 700, and 4% above 700. The ACT scores were 40% below 21, 21% between 21 and 23, 24% between 24 and 26, 8% between 27 and 28, and 7% above 28.

Requirements: The ACT is required. Scores are used for placement and academic advisement. Graduation from an accredited secondary school is required; a GED will be accepted. Applicants should submit an academic record containing a minimum 4 years of English, and 2 each of history, science, and math, including algebra and geometry, along with a letter of recommendation from a teacher or school official. A GPA of 2.0 is required. AP and CLEP credits are accepted. Important factors in the admissions decision are advanced placement or honor courses, recommendations by school officials, and leadership record.

Procedure: Freshmen are admitted to all sessions. Entrance exams should be taken during the junior or senior year. There are early decision, early admissions, deferred admissions and rolling admissions plans. Application deadlines are open. Application fee is $30. Applications are accepted on-line.

Transfer: Applicants should have a 2.0 minimum GPA and must submit all college transcripts and a letter of recommendation (3 for nursing majors) from a former teacher or school official. 36 of 192 quarter hours required for the bachelor's degree must be completed at WWC.

Visiting: Visitors may sit in on classes and stay overnight. To schedule a visit, contact the Admissions and Marketing Office.

Financial Aid: The FAFSA and the college's own financial statement are required. The deadline for filing freshman financial aid applications for fall entry is April 30.

International Students: The school actively recruits these students. A satisfactory score is required on the written TOEFL.

Computers: All students may access the system 6:30 A.M. to 11 P.M. Sunday through Thursday and 6:30 A.M. to 3:30 P.M. Fridays. There are no time limits and no fees.

Admissions Contact: Dallas Weis, Director of Admissions. A video is available. E-mail: *weisda@wwc.edu* Web: *www.wwc.edu*

WASHINGTON STATE UNIVERSITY E-3
Pullman, WA 99164-1067

(509) 335-5586
(888) 468-6978; Fax: (509) 335-4902

Full-time: 8253 men, 8533 women	**Faculty:** 1102; I, --$
Part-time: 1096 men, 1703 women	**Ph.D.s:** 89%
Graduate: 1747 men, 2212 women	**Student/Faculty:** 15 to 1
Year: semesters, summer session	**Tuition:** $5980 ($14,988)
Application Deadline: January 31	**Room & Board:** $6280
Freshman Class: 9193 applied, 6793 accepted, 2878 enrolled	
SAT or ACT: required	**COMPETITIVE**

Washington State University, founded in 1890, is a public, land-grant, research institution. Its undergraduate and graduate programs stress the liberal arts, business, economics, art and fine arts, engineering, architecture, agricultural and technical studies, home economics, music, teacher preparation, and health sciences, including nursing, pharmacy, and veterinary medicine. There are 10 undergraduate schools and 1 graduate school. In addition to regional accreditation, Washington State has baccalaureate program accreditation with AACSB, AACTE, ABET, ACCE, ACPE, ACS, ADA, APA, ASLA, AVMA, FIDER, NAAB, NASM, NCATE, NLN, NRPA, SAF, and many others. The 11 libraries contain 2,193,803 volumes, 4,662,429 microform items, and 46,540 audio/video tapes/CDs/DVDs, and subscribe to 31,718 periodicals including electronic. Computerized library services include the card catalog, interlibrary loans, database searching, Internet access, and laptop Internet portals. Special learning facilities include a learning resource center, art gallery, natural history museum, planetarium, radio station, TV station, an observatory, an electron microscopy center, a nuclear radiation center, a vet anatomy teaching museum, a vet teaching hospital, an agricultural research center, a cancer prevention and research center, and many other facilities. The 1875-acre campus is in a small town 80 miles south of Spokane and 285 miles east of Seattle. Including any residence halls, there are 456 buildings.

Student Life: 83% of undergraduates are from Washington. Others are from 49 states, 91 foreign countries, and Canada. 72% are white. The average age of freshmen is 18; all undergraduates, 23. 15% do not continue beyond their first year; 85% remain to graduate.

Housing: 6613 students can be accommodated in college housing, which includes single-sex and coed dorms, on-campus apartments, married-student housing, fraternity houses, and sorority houses. In addition, there are honors houses, language houses, and special-interest houses. On-campus housing is guaranteed for the freshman year only. 65% of students commute. All students may keep cars.

Activities: 12% of men belong to 24 national fraternities; 15% of women belong to 15 national sororities. There are more than 225 groups on campus, including academic, art, band, cheerleading, chess, choir, chorale, chorus, computers, dance, debate, drama, drill team, ethnic, film, gay, honors, international, jazz band, literary magazine, marching band, musical theater, newspaper, opera, orchestra, pep band, photography, political, professional, radio and TV, religious, social, social service, student government, symphony, and yearbook. Popular campus events include Dad's/Mom's Weekend, Land Grant Days, and Up All Night.

Sports: There are 6 intercollegiate sports for men and 9 for women, and 45 intramural sports for men and 45 for women. Facilities include a 40,000-seat stadium, a 12,000-seat coliseum, an indoor and outdoor track, tennis courts, a 160,000-square-foot student recreation center, a golf course, bowling lanes, baseball and soccer fields, swimming pools, lockers, racquetball and squash courts, a climbing wall, ballrooms, riding stables, gyms, crew rowing facilities, an outdoor recreation center, basketball courts, sand volleyball courts, and an outdoor recreation center.

Disabled Students: 90% of the campus is accessible. Wheelchair ramps, elevators, special parking, specially equipped rest rooms, special class scheduling, lowered drinking fountains, lowered telephones, and a van to provide transportation to and from classes are available.

Services: Counseling and information services are available, as is tutoring in most subjects. There is a reader service for the blind. There is also a reading and study skills course. There are many free Learning Strategy Workshops available, including Time Management, Active Textbook Reading, Writing, Text Anxiety, Skills for Science, Winning at Math, and others.

Campus Safety and Security: Measures include 24-hour foot and vehicle patrol, self-defense education, security escort services, and informal discussions. There are pamphlets/posters/films, emergency telephones, lighted pathways/sidewalks, monitored lighting levels on campus, a women's transit service, resident hall security hours, a police intern program, and housing patrols.

Programs of Study: Washington State confers B.A., B.S., B.Arch., B.F.A., B.L.A., and B.M. degrees. Master's and doctoral degrees are also awarded. Bachelor's degrees are awarded in AGRICULTURE (agricultural business management, agricultural economics, agricultural mechanics, agriculture, agronomy, animal science, forestry and related sciences, horticulture, natural resource management, plant protection (pest management), range/farm management, soil science, and wildlife management), BIOLOGICAL SCIENCE (biochemistry, biology/biological science, cell biology, entomology, genetics, microbiology, neurosciences, nutrition, plant genetics, plant pathology, wildlife biology, and zoology), BUSINESS (accounting, banking and finance, business administration and management, business economics, business law, business statistics, entrepreneurial studies, hotel/motel and restaurant management, insurance and risk management, international business management, management information systems, management science, marketing management, personnel management, real estate, sports management, and trade and industrial supervision and management), COMMUNICATIONS AND THE ARTS (advertising, broadcasting, classics, communications, digital communications, English, fine arts, French, German, journalism, linguistics, multimedia, music, music performance, music theory and composition, public relations, Russian, Spanish, and visual and performing arts), COMPUTER AND PHYSICAL SCIENCE (chemistry, computer science, geology, mathematics, physical sciences, physics, and science), EDUCATION (agricultural, athletic training, bilingual/bicultural, early childhood, education, English, foreign languages, physical, recreation, science, secondary, and social studies), ENGINEERING AND ENVIRONMENTAL DESIGN (agricultural engineering, architecture, chemical engineering, civil engineering, computer engineering, construction management, electrical/electronics engineering, environmental science, interior design, landscape architecture/design, manufacturing engineering, and materials engineering), HEALTH PROFESSIONS (exercise science, nursing, predentistry, premedicine, speech pathology/audiology, and veterinary science), SOCIAL SCIENCE (American studies, anthropology, area studies, Asian/Oriental studies, clothing and textiles management/production/services, criminal justice, crosscultural studies, economics, family/consumer studies, food science, French studies, history, home economics, human development, humanities, liberal arts/general studies, philosophy, political science/government, psychology, public administration, public affairs, religion, social science, social studies, social work, sociology, Spanish studies, women's studies, and youth ministry). Engineering, sciences and health sciences are the strongest academically. Business administration, communication, and engineering are the largest.

Required: Students must complete 120 semester hours, with fulfillment of a major and 40 hours of upper-division work, and maintain a minimum GPA of 2.0. Specific disciplines to be taken vary within majors.

General university requirements include 10 hours of science, 9 of arts and humanities and social science, 6 of world civilization, and 3 each of intercultural studies and communications proficiency. Students must complete a writing portfolio and pass a writing qualifying exam prior to graduation.

Special: Special academic programs include internships through the Professional Experience Program, study abroad in 25 countries, and work-study with numerous employers. There are co-op programs in numerous majors and cross-registration with the University of Idaho, University of Washington, Eastern Washington University, Yakima Valley Community College, and Northwest Indian College. Students may attend the Intercollegiate Center for Nursing Education, which is a consortium of Washington State, Eastern Washington and Gonzaga Universities, and Whitworth College. Dual majors are available, as is a general studies degree. Credit may be granted for military service, and nondegree and pass/fail options are possible. Special features of the school include the opportunity for undergraduates to become involved in research and its honors programs. There are 23 national honor societies, including Phi Beta Kappa, a freshman honors program, and 1 departmental honors program.

Faculty/Classroom: 60% of faculty are male; 40%, female. The average class size in a regular course is 46.

Admissions: 74% of the 2005-2006 applicants were accepted.

Requirements: The SAT or ACT is required. The ACT Optional Writing test is also required. In addition, other admissions requirements include graduation from an accredited secondary school with 4 years of English, 3 each of math (1 year each of algebra, geometry, and advanced algebra) and social studies/history, and 2 each of a foreign language (includes Native American languages and American Sign Language) and science. A combination of the high school GPA and test scores is considered. The GED is accepted. A GPA of 2.0 is required. AP and CLEP credits are accepted. Important factors in the admissions decision are recommendations by school officials, extracurricular activities record, and leadership record.

Procedure: Freshmen are admitted fall and spring. Entrance exams should be taken during spring of the junior year or fall of the senior year. There is a rolling admissions plan. Applications should be filed by January 31 for fall entry. The application fee is $50. Notification is sent on a rolling basis. 549 applicants were on the 2005 waiting list; 174 were admitted. Applications are accepted on-line.

Transfer: 3271 transfer students enrolled in 2004-2005. Applicants must have at least 27 semester hours, or 40 quarter hours, with a GPA of at least 2.0. If they have fewer hours, the criteria are the same as for freshmen. 30 of 120 credits required for the bachelor's degree must be completed at Washington State.

Visiting: There are regularly scheduled orientations for prospective students, consisting of a campus tour and presentation. There are guides for informal visits and visitors may sit in on classes. To schedule a visit, contact the campus visit web site at *www.wsu.edu/future-students/visiting.*

Financial Aid: In 2005-2006, 78% of all full-time freshmen and 72% of continuing full-time students received some form of financial aid. 36% of full-time freshmen and 48% of continuing full-time students received need-based aid. The average freshman award was $13,031. Need-based scholarships or need-based grants averaged $5379 ($11,424 maximum); need-based self-help aid (loans and jobs) averaged $3810 ($8282 maximum); non-need-based athletic scholarships averaged $12,852 ($25,714 maximum); and other non-need-based awards and non-need-based scholarships averaged $4051 ($29,460 maximum). 18% of undergraduates work part time. Average annual earnings from campus work are $3000. The average financial indebtedness of the 2005 graduate was $20,494. Washington State is a member of CSS. The FAFSA is required. The priority date for freshman financial aid applications for fall entry is March 1. The deadline for filing freshman financial aid applications for fall entry is June 1.

International Students: There are 578 international students enrolled. A satisfactory score on the TOEFL is required.

Computers: Wireless access is available. There are 250 computer labs and classrooms. All classrooms used for undergraduate instruction allow wire connectivity, and 70% allow wireless connectivity. Network access is available in dorms and lounges. All students may access the system 24 hours a day. There are no time limits. The fee is $120. It is strongly recommended that all students have a personal computer.

Graduates: From July 1, 2004 to June 30, 2005, 4133 bachelor's degrees were awarded. The most popular majors were communication (8%), nursing (6%), and psychology (5%). In an average class, 32% graduate in 4 years or less, 58% graduate in 5 years or less, and 63% graduate in 6 years or less. 510 companies recruited on campus in 2004-2005.

Admissions Contact: Wendy Peterson, Director of Admissions.
E-mail: *admiss@wsu.edu* Web: *wsu.edu/admissions*

WESTERN WASHINGTON UNIVERSITY   C-1

Bellingham, WA 98225-5996

(360) 650-3440
Fax: (360) 650-7369

Full-time: 5277 men, 6666 women	**Faculty:** 455; IIA, av$
Part-time: 474 men, 585 women	**Ph.Ds:** 86%
Graduate: 470 men, 775 women	**Student/Faculty:** 25 to 1
Year: quarters, summer session	**Tuition:** $4738 ($14,688)
Application Deadline: March 1	**Room & Board:** $6524
Freshman Class: 8645 applied, 5778 accepted, 2381 enrolled	
SAT Verbal/Math: 569/567*	**ACT:** 24 **VERY COMPETITIVE**

Western Washington University, founded in 1893, is a public, comprehensive institution whose emphasis is on the liberal arts and sciences, business and business administration and economics, art, fine arts, and performing arts, music, teacher preparation, interdisciplinary learning, and environmental studies. There are 7 undergraduate schools and 1 graduate school. In addition to regional accreditation, WWU has baccalaureate program accreditation with AACSB, ABET, ASLA, NASM, NCATE, and NRPA. The 2 libraries contain 1,400,000 volumes, 200,000,000 microform items, and 30,000 audio/video tapes/CDs/DVDs, and subscribe to 5000 periodicals including electronic. Computerized library services include the card catalog, interlibrary loans, database searching, Internet access, and laptop Internet portals. Special learning facilities include a learning resource center, art gallery, planetarium, radio station, marine lab, neutron generator lab, motor vehicle research lab, wind tunnel, air pollution lab, electronic music studio, and performing arts center. The 195-acre campus is in a small town 60 miles south of Vancouver, British Columbia, and 90 miles north of Seattle. Including any residence halls, there are 80 buildings.

Student Life: 92% of undergraduates are from Washington. Students are from 47 states, 34 foreign countries, and Canada. 90% are from public schools. 80% are white. The average age of freshmen is 18; all undergraduates, 22. 16% do not continue beyond their first year; 62% remain to graduate.

Housing: 3700 students can be accommodated in college housing, which includes coed dorms, on-campus apartments, off-campus apartments, and married-student housing. On-campus housing is available on a first-come, first-served basis. 68% of students commute. All students may keep cars.

Activities: There are no fraternities or sororities. There are 125 groups on campus, including art, band, cheerleading, chess, choir, chorale, chorus, computers, dance, debate, drama, ethnic, film, forensics, gay, honors, international, jazz band, literary magazine, musical theater, newspaper, opera, orchestra, pep band, photography, political, professional, radio and TV, religious, social, social service, student government, and symphony. Popular campus events include the Western Jam Talent Show, Casino Night, and Cinco de Mayo.

Sports: There are 7 intercollegiate sports for men and 8 for women, and 34 intramural sports for men and 34 for women. Facilities include a 3000-seat gym, playing fields, 8 tennis courts, a 6000-seat stadium, a golf course, salt/freshwater recreational facilities and equipment, an artificial-surface football field/track, a pool, a fitness center, and a student-run outdoor center (equipment and excursions).

Disabled Students: All of the campus is accessible. Wheelchair ramps, elevators, special parking, specially equipped rest rooms, special class scheduling, lowered drinking fountains, lowered telephones, and transcription services are available.

Services: Counseling and information services are available, as is tutoring in most subjects, including English, humanities, social sciences, and math and natural sciences. There is a reader service for the blind.

Campus Safety and Security: Measures include 24-hour foot and vehicle patrol, self-defense education, security escort services, and shuttle buses. There are informal discussions, pamphlets/posters/films, emergency telephones, and lighted pathways/sidewalks.

Programs of Study: WWU confers B.A., B.S., B.A.E., B.F.A., and B.Mus. degrees. Master's degrees are also awarded. Bachelor's degrees are awarded in BIOLOGICAL SCIENCE (biochemistry and biology/biological science), BUSINESS (accounting, business administration and management, international business management, management science, and marketing/retailing/merchandising), COMMUNICATIONS AND THE ARTS (art, communications, dramatic arts, English, fine arts, French, German, journalism, linguistics, music, and Spanish), COMPUTER AND PHYSICAL SCIENCE (chemistry, computer science, geology, mathematics, and physics), EDUCATION (art, early childhood, elementary, foreign languages, health, music, science, and secondary), ENGINEERING AND ENVIRONMENTAL DESIGN (electrical/electronics engineering technology, engineering technology, environmental science, and manufacturing technology), HEALTH PROFESSIONS (speech pathology/audiology), SOCIAL SCIENCE (anthropology, Canadian studies, East Asian studies, economics, geography, history, human services, parks and recreation management, philosophy, political science/government, psychology, and sociology). Computer science, business, and technology are the strongest academically. Psychology, environmental studies, and education are the largest.

Required: Students must complete at least 180 quarter hours, with fulfillment of a major and at least 60 credits in upper-division study, and maintain at least a 2.0 GPA or that prescribed by departments/divisions. General university requirements include 70 to 75 credits, and students must satisfy writing proficiency requirements as well. Fairhaven College has a separate interdisciplinary core program.

Special: Special academic programs include internships through various academic departments and study abroad in 75 countries. Dual majors are available through various departments, and there is a general studies degree, a B.A. in humanities. A 3-2 engineering degree is possible with the University of Washington. Student-designed majors are offered through the liberal studies department in the College of Arts and Sciences and through Fairhaven College, which affords an unusual degree of student involvement in the structure and content of their own programs and which uses faculty narrative for students' academic evaluations. In addition, Huxley College of Environmental Studies provides specialized education and research. Up to 30 credits of electives may be granted for military service, and nondegree study and pass/fail options are possible. There are 13 national honor societies, a freshman honors program, and 3 departmental honors programs.

Faculty/Classroom: 60% of faculty are male; 40%, female. All teach undergraduates, 90% do research, and 90% do both. Graduate students teach 4% of introductory courses. The average class size in an introductory lecture is 80; in a laboratory, 20; and in a regular course, 27.

Admissions: 67% of the 2005-2006 applicants were accepted. The SAT scores for the 2005-2006 freshman class were: Verbal--20% below 500, 43% between 500 and 599, 30% between 600 and 700, and 7% above 700; Math--16% below 500, 48% between 500 and 599, 32% between 600 and 700, and 4% above 700.

Requirements: The SAT or ACT is required. In addition, other admissions requirements include completion of 15 academic units, comprised of 4 years of college preparatory English composition and literature courses; 3 years of college preparatory math, including 2 years of algebra; 3 years of social studies/history; 2 years of science, including 1 year of a chemistry or physics with an algebra prerequisite; 2 years of the same foreign language; 1 semester of fine and performing arts; and 1 semester in another academic field. Freshman applicants meeting minimum GPA and subject requirements are ranked by an index combining the GPA and a standardized test score. The GED is also accepted. Other factors taken into consideration include curricular rigor (level of difficulty of courses), grade trends, leadership, community involvement, special talent, multicultural experience, and personal hardship or circumstances. A GPA of 2.5 is required. AP credits are accepted. Important factors in the admissions decision are advanced placement or honor courses, leadership record, and personality/intangible qualities.

Procedure: Freshmen are admitted to all sessions. Entrance exams should be taken by fall of the senior year. Applications should be filed by March 1 for fall entry, October 15 for winter entry, January 15 for spring entry, and March 1 for summer entry, along with a $50 fee. Notification is sent March 15. 227 applicants were on the 2005 waiting list; 116 were admitted. Applications are accepted on-line.

Transfer: 996 transfer students enrolled in 2004-2005. Applicants with fewer than 40 quarter credits are eligible for consideration if they have completed the last term before transferring with a GPA of at least 2.0 and if they satisfy the requirements for freshman admission. Those with 40 or more transferable quarter credits are eligible if they have achieved a cumulative GPA of at least 2.0. Admission is selective. 45 of 180 credits required for the bachelor's degree must be completed at WWU.

Visiting: There are regularly scheduled orientations for prospective students, including tours, class visits, and advisement. There are guides for informal visits and visitors may sit in on classes and stay overnight. To schedule a visit, contact the STARS Program - Student Admissions Representatives at (360) 650-3861 or *campusvisit@wwu.edu.*

Financial Aid: In 2005-2006, 68% of all full-time freshmen and 59% of continuing full-time students received some form of financial aid. 28% of full-time freshmen and 31% of continuing full-time students received need-based aid. The average freshman award was $8542. Need-based scholarships or need-based grants averaged $5608 ($10,337 maximum); need-based self-help aid (loans and jobs) averaged $3365 ($9625 maximum); non-need-based athletic scholarships averaged $4273 ($5639 maximum); and alternative bank loans, PLUS loans, and unsubsidized loans. averaged $13,246 ($23,220 maximum). The FAFSA is required. Check with the school for current deadlines.

International Students: A satisfactory score is required on the written TOEFL. Students must also take the SAT or the ACT.

Computers: All students may access the system. There are no time limits and no fees.

Graduates: In a recent year, 2651 bachelor's degrees were awarded. The most popular majors were business administration and management (7%), psychology (6%), and English (6%). In an average class, 28% graduate in 4 years or less, 58% graduate in 5 years or less, and 65% graduate in 6 years or less. 64 companies recruited on campus in a recent year. Of the recent year's graduating class, 13% were enrolled in graduate school within 6 months of graduation and 93% were employed.

Admissions Contact: Karen Copetas, Director.
E-mail: *admit@cc.wwu.edu* Web: *www.wwu.edu/~admit*

WHITMAN COLLEGE   E-3
Walla Walla, WA 99362-2083

(509) 527-5176
(877) 462-9448; Fax: (509) 527-4967

Full-time: 682 men, 798 women	**Faculty:** 115; IIB, +$
Part-time: 13 men, 19 women	**Ph.D.s:** 84%
Graduate: none	**Student/Faculty:** 13 to 1
Year: semesters	**Tuition:** $28,640
Application Deadline: January 15	**Room & Board:** $7470
Freshman Class: 2544 applied, 1251 accepted, 361 enrolled	
SAT Verbal/Math: 670/660*	**HIGHLY COMPETITIVE+**

Whitman College, founded in 1883, is a nonprofit, private, independent residential liberal arts and sciences college. In addition to regional accreditation, Whitman College has baccalaureate program accreditation with ACS. The library contains 374,131 volumes, 260,000 microform items, and 6548 audio/video tapes/CDs/DVDs, and subscribes to 2200 periodicals including electronic. Computerized library services include the card catalog, interlibrary loans, database searching, and Internet access. Special learning facilities include a learning resource center, art gallery, natural history museum, planetarium, radio station, electron microscope lab, an indoor planetarium, an off-campus observatory and on-campus astronomical telescopes, an Asian art collection, a video-conferencing center, an outdoor sculpture walk, an organic garden, and indoor and outdoor rock climbing walls. The 117-acre campus is in a small town 150 miles south of Spokane, 260 miles southeast of Seattle, and 235 miles east of Portland. Including any residence halls, there are 41 buildings.

Student Life: 58% of undergraduates are from out of state, mostly the Northwest. Others are from 50 states, 31 foreign countries, and Canada. 75% are from public schools. 66% are white. The average age of freshmen is 18; all undergraduates, 20. 5% do not continue beyond their first year; 95% remain to graduate.

Housing: 882 students can be accommodated in college housing, which includes single-sex and coed dorms, off-campus apartments, and fraternity houses. In addition, there are language houses and special-interest houses. On-campus housing is guaranteed for the freshman year only and is available on a lottery system for upperclassmen. 63% of students live on campus; of those, 95% remain on campus on weekends. All students may keep cars.

Activities: 34% of men belong to 4 national fraternities; 26% of women belong to 4 national sororities. There are 60 groups on campus, including art, choir, chorale, chorus, dance, debate, drama, ethnic, film, forensics, gay, honors, international, jazz band, literary magazine, musical theater, newspaper, opera, orchestra, photography, political, professional, radio and TV, religious, social service, student government, and symphony. Popular campus events include Renaissance Fair, Choral Contest, and Interest House Block Party.

Sports: There are 8 intercollegiate sports for men and 8 for women, and 4 intramural sports for men and 4 for women. Facilities include a stadium, a center with a 3000-seat gym, squash and handball courts, saunas, a pool, indoor and outdoor climbing walls, a small gym, a weights/Nautilus room, aerobic/dance room, cardiovascular room, 4 outdoor tennis courts, a soccer field, an indoor tennis facility, a dance studio, and an off-campus playing field complex.

Disabled Students: 96% of the campus is accessible. Wheelchair ramps, elevators, special parking, specially equipped rest rooms, lowered drinking fountains, and lowered telephonesare available. Any modifications necessary for specific cases will be made.

Services: Counseling and information services are available, as is tutoring in most subjects. There is a reader service for the blind. There are also centers for study skills and writing.

Campus Safety and Security: Measures include self-defense education, security escort services, informal discussions, and pamphlets/posters/films. There are emergency telephones, lighted pathways/sidewalks, and 24-hour foot patrol.

Programs of Study: Whitman College confers the B.A. degree. Bachelor's degrees are awarded in BIOLOGICAL SCIENCE (biology/biological science), COMMUNICATIONS AND THE ARTS (art history and appreciation, classics, dramatic arts, English, film arts, fine arts, French, German, music, Spanish, and speech/debate/rhetoric), COMPUTER AND PHYSICAL SCIENCE (chemistry, geology, mathematics, and physics), ENGINEERING AND ENVIRONMENTAL DESIGN (environmental science), SOCIAL SCIENCE (anthropology, Asian/Oriental studies, economics, history, philosophy, political science/government, psychology, religion, and sociology). Biology, psychology and politics are the strongest academically and have the largest enrollments.

Required: Students must complete 124 credits, with 32 to 36 in the major, and maintain a minimum GPA of 2.0. Distribution requirements include a minimum of 6 credits in social sciences, humanities, fine arts, and science (including one course with a lab); 1 course of 3 or more credits in quantitative analysis; and 2 courses that fulfill the alternative voices requirement. Freshman core must be taken, and written and oral tests are also required.

Special: Special academic programs include more than 500 internships, study abroad in 43 countries, a Washington semester, and study programs in Chicago and Philadelphia. Dual majors are available in any area, and student-designed majors are offered. There is a 3-2 environmental management and forestry program with Duke University, and a 3-2 engineering program with Washington University in St. Louis, California Institute of Technology and Applied Science, Columbia and Duke Universities, and University of Washington. A 3-3 law program is offered through Columbia University. A 4-1 education program is available through Bank Street College of Education and University of Puget Sound Cooperative. Certification is offered for elementary and secondary education. A pass-D-fail option is available. A special feature of the curriculum is the integrated general studies program for freshmen. A 3-2 program is available with the Monterey Institute of International Studies. There are 3 national honor societies, including Phi Beta Kappa, a freshman honors program, and 41 departmental honors programs.

Faculty/Classroom: 60% of faculty are male; 40%, female. 100% both teach and do research. The average class size in an introductory lecture is 21; in a laboratory, 18; and in a regular course, 14.

Admissions: 49% of the 2005-2006 applicants were accepted. The SAT scores for the 2005-2006 freshman class were: Verbal--2% below 500, 15% between 500 and 599, 46% between 600 and 700, and 37% above 700; Math--1% below 500, 12% between 500 and 599, 56% between 600 and 700, and 31% above 700. The ACT scores were 1% below 21, 8% between 21 and 23, 11% between 24 and 26, 20% between 27 and 28, and 60% above 28. 91% of the current freshmen were in the top fifth of their class. There were 17 National Merit finalists. 54 freshmen graduated first in their class.

Requirements: The SAT or ACT is required. In addition, the GED is accepted. 3 essays must be submitted, and an interview is recommended. Credit by challenge examination is accepted. AP credits are accepted. Important factors in the admissions decision are advanced placement or honor courses, evidence of special talent, and extracurricular activities record.

Procedure: Freshmen are admitted fall and spring. Entrance exams should be taken by February of the senior year. There are early decision and deferred admissions plans. Early decision applications should be filed by November 15; regular applications, by January 15 for fall entry and December 1 for spring entry. Notification of early decision is sent December 15; regular decision, April 1. 140 early decision candidates were accepted for the 2005-2006 class. 343 applicants were on the 2005 waiting list; 47 were admitted. Applications are accepted on-line.

Transfer: 29 transfer students enrolled in 2004-2005. Transfer applicants must submit the common application, a transfer supplement, a teacher/counselor recommendation, a statement of good standing from prior institutions, their high school and college transcripts, SAT or ACT scores (required for some), and the application fee. 54 of 124 credits required for the bachelor's degree must be completed at Whitman College.

Visiting: There are regularly scheduled orientations for prospective students, including Fall and Spring Visitors' Days. There are guides for informal visits and visitors may sit in on classes and stay overnight. To schedule a visit, contact the Admission Office at *admission@whitman.edu.*

Financial Aid: In 2005-2006, 47% of all full-time freshmen and 35% of continuing full-time students received some form of financial aid. The average freshman award was $30,000. Need-based scholarships or need-based grants averaged $16,850; need-based self-help aid (loans and jobs) averaged $5975; and other non-need-based awards and non-need-based scholarships averaged $4250. 99% of undergraduates work part time. Average annual earnings from campus work are $1126. The average financial indebtedness of the 2005 graduate was $16,200. Whitman College is a member of CSS. The CSS/Profile or FAFSA is required. The priority date for freshman financial aid applications for fall entry is January 5. The deadline for filing freshman financial aid applications for fall entry is February 1.

International Students: There are 570 international students enrolled. The school actively recruits these students. They must take the TOEFL APIEL or ELPT and also take the SAT or the ACT.

Computers: All students may access the system 24 hours a day. There are no time limits and no fees.

Graduates: From July 1, 2004 to June 30, 2005, 359 bachelor's degrees were awarded. The most popular majors were biology (11%), psychology (11%), and politics (10%). In an average class, 83% graduate in 5 years or less, and 86% graduate in 6 years or less. 112 companies recruited on campus in 2004-2005.

Admissions Contact: Tony Cabasco, Dean of Admission and Financial Aid. A video is available. E-mail: *admission@whitman.edu* Web: *http://www.whitman.edu*

WHITWORTH COLLEGE   C-2
Spokane, WA 99251

(509) 777-4348
(800) 533-4668; Fax: (509) 777-3758

Full-time: 837 men, 1229 women	**Faculty:** 120; IIB, -$
Part-time: 51 men, 109 women	**Ph.D.s:** 86%
Graduate: 61 men, 154 women	**Student/Faculty:** 17 to 1
Year: 4-1-4, summer session	**Tuition:** $22,678
Application Deadline: March 1	**Room & Board:** $675
Freshman Class: 2147 applied, 1369 accepted, 451 enrolled	
SAT Verbal/Math: 595/610*	**ACT:** 26 **VERY COMPETITIVE+**

Whitworth College, founded in 1890, is an independent, comprehensive institution affiliated with the Presbyterian Church (U.S.A.). The emphasis of its undergraduate and graduate programs is on the liberal arts, business, art and fine arts, music, religious studies, and teacher preparation. In addition to regional accreditation, Whitworth has baccalaureate program accreditation with NASM, NCATE, and NLN. The 2 libraries contain 141,000 volumes, 54,250 microform items, and 1528 audio/video tapes/CDs/DVDs, and subscribe to 810 periodicals including electronic. Computerized library services include the card catalog, interlibrary loans, database searching, Internet access, and laptop Internet portals. Special learning facilities include a learning resource center, art gallery, radio station, and a writing center. The 200-acre campus is in a suburban area 7 miles north of Spokane. Including any residence halls, there are 40 buildings.

Student Life: 55% of undergraduates are from Washington. Students are from 29 states, 16 foreign countries, and Canada. 88% are from public schools. 86% are white. 76% are Protestant; 10% claim no religious affiliation; 7% Catholic. The average age of freshmen is 18; all undergraduates, 21. 13% do not continue beyond their first year; 77% remain to graduate.

Housing: 1200 students can be accommodated in college housing, which includes single-sex and coed dorms, on-campus apartments, and off-campus apartments. In addition, there are language houses and special-interest houses. On-campus housing is guaranteed for all 4 years. 66% of students live on campus; of those, 90% remain on campus on weekends. Alcohol is not permitted. All students may keep cars.

Activities: There are no fraternities or sororities. There are 45 groups on campus, including art, band, cheerleading, choir, chorale, chorus, computers, dance, drama, ethnic, honors, international, jazz band, literary magazine, musical theater, newspaper, orchestra, photography, political, radio and TV, religious, social, social service, and student government. Popular campus events include guest speakers, student research conference, and community building day.

Sports: There are 10 intercollegiate sports for men and 10 for women, and 10 intramural sports for men and 8 for women. Facilities include a 2000-seat stadium, a 1200-seat gym, a field house, an aquatic center, and playing fields.

Disabled Students: 70% of the campus is accessible. Wheelchair ramps, elevators, special parking, specially equipped rest rooms, special class scheduling, lowered drinking fountains, and lowered telephones are available.

Services: Counseling and information services are available, as is tutoring in most subjects, including biology, chemistry, computer science, French, German, Spanish, math, physics, and writing.

Campus Safety and Security: Measures include 24-hour foot and vehicle patrol, security escort services, informal discussions, and pamphlets/posters/films. There are emergency telephones and lighted pathways/sidewalks.

Programs of Study: Whitworth confers B.A. and B.S. degrees. Master's degrees are also awarded. Bachelor's degrees are awarded in BIOLOGICAL SCIENCE (biology/biological science), BUSINESS (accounting, business administration and management, and international business management), COMMUNICATIONS AND THE ARTS (art, communications, dramatic arts, English, French, journalism, music, Spanish, and speech/debate/rhetoric), COMPUTER AND PHYSICAL SCIENCE (applied physics, chemistry, computer science, mathematics, physics, and quantitative methods), EDUCATION (athletic training, elementary, English, foreign languages, mathematics, music, science, secondary, and social studies), ENGINEERING AND ENVIRONMENTAL DESIGN (environmental science), HEALTH PROFESSIONS (nursing, predentistry, and premedicine), SOCIAL SCIENCE (American studies, crosscultural studies, economics, history, international studies, peace studies, philosophy, political science/government, prelaw, psychology, religion, sociology, and women's studies). English, history, and chemistry are the strongest academically. Biology, education, and business management are the largest.

Required: Students must complete 126 credit hours, with about 42-54 in the major, and maintain a GPA of at least 2.0. The curriculum includes 3 core courses on religious, rationalist, and scientific traditions; distribution requirements are comprised of 4 phys ed activity courses, 2 each in a foreign language and science/math, and 1 course each in biblical literature, oral communication, fine arts, social science, and humanities. Additionally, an other-culture course or experience must be fulfilled.

Special: Special academic programs include many work-study opportunities, 1 to 3 internship course credits that may be earned by juniors and seniors, and a January Washington term. Study abroad is available in 15 countries. There is cross-registration with the Intercollegiate Language Study Consortium and Gonzaga University. Accelerated degree programs are possible as is a 3-2 engineering degree, and students may choose to specialize in an area of concentration in lieu of a major. Credit may be granted for life, military, or work experience. Nondegree study is possible for those auditing or in seminars, and there is 1 pass/fail option allowed per year. A special feature of the school is the modified semester calendar, which affords unusual opportunities for internships, study tours, and other activities. There is a freshman honors program.

Faculty/Classroom: 70% of faculty are male; 30%, female. All teach undergraduates. No introductory courses are taught by graduate students. The average class size in an introductory lecture is 30; in a laboratory, 15; and in a regular course, 19.

Admissions: 64% of the 2005-2006 applicants were accepted. The SAT scores for the 2005-2006 freshman class were: Verbal--9% below 500, 46% between 500 and 599, 38% between 600 and 700, and 7% above 700; Math--10% below 500, 48% between 500 and 599, 37% between 600 and 700, and 6% above 700. 40% of the current freshmen were in the top fifth of their class; 75% were in the top two fifths. There were 6 National Merit semifinalists. In a recent year, 42 freshmen graduated first in their class.

Requirements: The SAT or ACT is required. In addition, other admissions criteria include 4 high school credits in English, 3 each in math, science, and history/social studies, and 2 of a foreign language. An essay must be submitted, and an interview is recommended. Music students are advised to audition. AP and CLEP credits are accepted. Important factors in the admissions decision are advanced placement or honor courses, extracurricular activities record, and leadership record.

Procedure: Freshmen are admitted fall, winter, and spring. Entrance exams should be taken by the fall of the senior year, though the spring of the junior year is preferred. There are deferred admissions and rolling admissions plans. Early decision applications should be filed by November 30; regular applications, by March 1 for fall entry. Notification of early decision is sent December 15; regular decision, March 15. 150 applicants were on the 2005 waiting list; 60 were admitted. Applications are accepted on-line.

Transfer: 102 transfer students enrolled in a recent year. Transfer students must have a GPA of at least 2.25 and a recommended 45 quarter credits earned. The SAT or ACT is recommended. 32 of 126 credits required for the bachelor's degree must be completed at Whitworth.

Visiting: There are regularly scheduled orientations for prospective students, including a class visit, a tour, and an overnight stay, if desired. There are guides for informal visits and visitors may sit in on classes and stay overnight. To schedule a visit, contact Carrie Streepy, Associate Director of Admission at (509) 777-4330 or *cstreepy@whitworth.edu*.

Financial Aid: All undergraduates work part time. Average annual earnings from campus work are $1402. The average financial indebtedness of the 2005 graduate was $18,000. The CSS/Profile, FAFSA, FFS or SFS are required; FAFSA is preferred. The deadline for filing freshman financial aid applications for fall entry is March 1.

International Students: There were 65 international students enrolled in a recent year. The school actively recruits these students. A satisfactory score is required on the written TOEFL.

Computers: Wireless access is available. All students may access the system any time during library hours. There are no time limits and no fees. It is strongly recommended that all students have a PC.

Graduates: From July 1, 2004 to June 30, 2005, 466 bachelor's degrees were awarded. The most popular majors were business management (9%), English (8%), and psychology (8%). In an average class, 3% graduate in 3 years or less, 58% graduate in 4 years or less, 73% graduate in 5 years or less, and 76% graduate in 6 years or less. 60 companies recruited on campus in 2004-2005. Of the 2004 graduating class, 30% were enrolled in graduate school within 6 months of graduation and 66% were employed.

Admissions Contact: Fred Pfursich, Dean of Enrollment.
E-mail: *admission@whitworth.edu* Web: *www.whitworth.edu*

WEST VIRGINIA

ALDERSON-BROADDUS COLLEGE   C-3
Philippi, WV 26416

(304) 457-6310
(800) 263-1549; Fax: (304) 457-6239

Full-time: 260 men, 420 women	**Faculty:** 61
Part-time: 15 men, 50 women	**Ph.D.s:** 45%
Graduate: 30 men, 30 women	**Student/Faculty:** 11 to 1
Year: semesters, summer session	**Tuition:** $18,136
Application Deadline: August 1	**Room & Board:** $5870
Freshman Class: n/av	
SAT or ACT: required	**COMPETITIVE**

Alderson-Broaddus College is a private institution, founded in 1871 and affiliated with American Baptist Churches USA. It offers a liberal arts program along with teacher preparation and professional, music, business, religion, and science studies. Some figures in the above capsule and in this profile are approximate. In addition to regional accreditation, Alderson-Broaddus; has baccalaureate program accreditation with CAHEA, NCATE, and NLN. The library contains 100,000 volumes, 8000 microform items, and 5000 audio/video tapes/CDs/DVDs, and subscribes to 670 periodicals including electronic. Computerized library services include the card catalog, interlibrary loans, and database searching. Special learning facilities include a learning resource center, art gallery, radio station, and TV station. The 170-acre campus is in a small town 100 miles south of Pittsburgh and 100 miles north of Charleston. Including any residence halls, there are 19 buildings.

Student Life: 67% of undergraduates are from West Virginia. Others are from 26 states, 5 foreign countries, and Canada. 90% are from public schools. 91% are white. 75% are Protestant; 14% Catholic; 11% claim no religious affiliation. The average age of freshmen is 21. 31% do not continue beyond their first year; 44% remain to graduate.

Housing: 700 students can be accommodated in college housing, which includes single-sex and coed dorms, on-campus apartments, off-campus apartments, and married-student housing. On-campus housing is guaranteed for all 4 years. 60% of students live on campus; of those, 40% remain on campus on weekends. Alcohol is not permitted. All students may keep cars.

Activities: 8% of men belong to 3 local fraternities; 10% of women belong to 3 local sororities. There are 40 groups on campus, including art, band, choir, chorale, chorus, computers, dance, debate, drama, ethnic, forensics, honors, jazz band, musical theater, newspaper, pep band, photography, political, professional, radio and TV, religious, social, social service, student government, and yearbook. Popular campus events include Spring Weekend, Christmas programs, and Homeless Weekend.

Sports: There are 10 intramural sports for men and 10 for women. Facilities include several playing fields near the main campus, a swimming pool, a weight room, handball courts, auxiliary gyms, an archery range, a batting cage, and a tennis court.

Disabled Students: 75% of the campus is accessible. Wheelchair ramps, elevators, special parking, specially equipped rest rooms, and special class scheduling are available.

Services: Counseling and information services are available, as is tutoring in every subject. There is remedial math, reading, and writing. There is also an Academic Support Network.

Campus Safety and Security: Measures include 24-hour foot and vehicle patrol, informal discussions, pamphlets/posters/films, and lighted pathways/sidewalks.

Programs of Study: Alderson-Broaddus; confers B.A. and B.S. degrees. Associate and master's degrees are also awarded. Bachelor's degrees are awarded in BIOLOGICAL SCIENCE (biology/biological science), BUSINESS (accounting, business administration and management, and management information systems), COMMUNICATIONS AND THE ARTS (communications, creative writing, literature, and music), COMPUTER AND PHYSICAL SCIENCE (chemistry, computer science, and mathematics), EDUCATION (athletic training, elementary, music, recreation, and secondary), HEALTH PROFESSIONS (cytotechnology, medical science, medical technology, nursing, ophthalmic technology, and radiograph medical technology), SOCIAL SCIENCE (Christian studies, history, liberal arts/general studies, political science/government, psychology, and religious music). Health sciences, business, and education are the strongest academically. Nursing and health sciences are the largest.

Required: Each graduate is required to complete at least 1 major and Liberal Studies Program requirements amounting to 51 to 55 semester hours plus electives for a minimum of 128 semester hours. The Liberal Studies requirements include courses in English, literature, math, computer literacy, physical and biological science, philosophy/religion, social science, history, global concerns, aesthetic expression, and health. All graduates must have attained a GPA of 2.0 overall and in the major. Certain disciplines may require a GPA higher than the minimum to continue in the major and to graduate.

Special: Internships in numerous majors, student-designed majors in liberal arts, cross-registration with the Mountain State Association of Colleges, study abroad through the college's programs in Austria or through the Junior Year Abroad program in conjunction with other schools, and work scholarships at the college are available. In addition, the college offers dual majors, a general studies degree, the B.A.-B.S. degree, nondegree study, and pass/fail grading in certain courses. There is a freshman honors program.

Faculty/Classroom: 57% of faculty are male; 43%, female. 97% teach undergraduates and 10% both teach and do research. No introductory courses are taught by graduate students. The average class size in an introductory lecture is 40; in a laboratory, 30; and in a regular course, 20.

Requirements: The SAT or ACT is required. Applicants who are graduates of secondary schools or have passed the GED are considered for admission. An audition for certain majors and an interview are recommended. Applications are accepted on-line. A GPA of 2.5 is required. AP and CLEP credits are accepted. Important factors in the admissions decision are advanced placement or honor courses, leadership record, and recommendations by school officials.

Procedure: Freshmen are admitted to all sessions. Entrance exams should be taken in spring of the junior year. There is a rolling admissions plan. There is a deferred admissions plan. Applications should be filed by August 1 for fall entry and December 15 for spring entry. The application fee is $25. Notification is sent on a rolling basis. Applications are accepted on-line.

Transfer: Transfer applicants must have a minimum 2.0 GPA. If they have fewer than 29 transfer credit hours, ACT or SAT results and a high school diploma are required. 60 of 128 credits required for the bachelor's degree must be completed at Alderson-Broaddus.

Visiting: There are regularly scheduled orientations for prospective students, including placement tests and social programs. There are guides for informal visits and visitors may sit in on classes and stay overnight. To schedule a visit, contact the Admissions Office.

Financial Aid: The FAFSA and the college's own financial statement are required. Check with the school for current deadlines.

International Students: The school actively recruits these students. They must achieve a satisfactory score on the TOEFL and also take the SAT or the ACT.

Computers: All students may access the system. There are no time limits and no fees. It is recommended that students in computer science have personal computers. A PC or Mac is recommended.

Admissions Contact: Kim Klaus, Director of Admissions. A video is available. E-mail: *admissions@ab.edu* Web: *www.ab.edu*

BETHANY COLLEGE
C-1

Bethany, WV 26032
(304) 829-7611
(800) 922-7611; Fax: (304) 829-7142

Full-time: 408 men, 487 women	Faculty: 63; IIB, --$
Part-time: 2 men, 5 women	Ph.D.s: 59%
Graduate: none	Student/Faculty: 14 to 1
Year: semesters	Tuition: $14,370
Application Deadline: open	Room & Board: $7025
Freshman Class: 1009 applied, 739 accepted, 272 enrolled	
SAT Verbal/Math: 510/500*	ACT: 22	COMPETITIVE

Bethany College, founded in 1840, is a liberal arts institution affiliated with the Christian Church (Disciples of Christ). In addition to regional accreditation, Bethany has baccalaureate program accreditation with CSWE and NCATE. The library contains 116,601 volumes, 116,065 microform items, and 1658 audio/video tapes/CDs/DVDs, and subscribes to 302 periodicals including electronic. Computerized library services include the card catalog, interlibrary loans, database searching, Internet access, and laptop Internet portals. Special learning facilities include a learning resource center, art gallery, radio station, and TV station. The 300-acre campus is in a small town 14 miles north of Wheeling and 48 miles southwest of Pittsburgh. Including any residence halls, there are 33 buildings.

Student Life: 76% of undergraduates are from out of state, mostly the Middle Atlantic. Students are from 23 states, 15 foreign countries, and Canada. 70% are from public schools. 94% are white. 44% are Protestant; 36% Catholic; 18% claim no religious affiliation. The average age of freshmen is 18; all undergraduates, 20. 12% do not continue beyond their first year; 60% remain to graduate.

Housing: 880 students can be accommodated in college housing, which includes single-sex and coed dormitories, on-campus apartments, off-campus apartments, fraternity houses, and sorority houses. In addition, there are special-interest houses. On-campus housing is guaranteed for all 4 years. 97% of students live on campus; of those, 87% remain on campus on weekends. All students may keep cars.

Activities: 44% of men belong to 5 national fraternities; 53% of women belong to 3 national sororities. There are 38 groups on campus, including art, athletic clubs, band, cheerleading, choir, chorale, chorus, computers, dance, drama, ethnic, gay, honors, international, jazz band, literary magazine, musical theater, newspaper, orchestra, outdoor club, pep band, photography, political, professional, radio and TV, religious, social, social service, student government, and yearbook. Popular campus events include Spring Weekend, Mid-Term Break, and Snow Carnival.

Sports: There are 9 intercollegiate sports for men and 9 for women, and 7 intramural sports for men and 7 for women. Facilities include a 2000-seat stadium, a 1000-seat gym, a natatorium, and football, soccer, baseball, and softball fields.

Disabled Students: 20% of the campus is accessible. Wheelchair ramps, elevators, special parking, and specially equipped rest rooms are available.

Services: Counseling and information services are available, as is tutoring in every subject. There is also a center for academic success, which provides guidance for students needing special assistance.

Campus Safety and Security: Measures include 24-hour foot and vehicle patrol, informal discussions, pamphlets/posters/films, and lighted pathways/sidewalks.

Programs of Study: Bethany confers B.A. and B.S. degrees. Bachelor's degrees are awarded in AGRICULTURE (equine science), BIOLOGICAL SCIENCE (biochemistry and biology/biological science), BUSINESS (accounting and business economics), COMMUNICATIONS AND THE ARTS (communications, English, fine arts, French, German, journalism, languages, and Spanish), COMPUTER AND PHYSICAL SCIENCE (chemistry, computer science, mathematics, and physics), EDUCATION (early childhood, elementary, English, foreign languages, physical, science, secondary, and special), HEALTH PROFESSIONS (predentistry and premedicine), SOCIAL SCIENCE (economics, history, international studies, philosophy, political science/government, prelaw, psychology, religion, and social work). Chemistry, economics, and political science are the strongest academically. Communication, economics, and education are the largest.

Required: All students must earn 128 semester hours, including 24 to 48 in the major, while maintaining a 2.0 GPA. A freshman seminar is required. Distribution credits must be earned in contemporary society and institutions, creative arts, cultural awareness, human behavior, international understanding, life science, literature, mathematical understanding, physical science, and the Western tradition. Students must complete a writing proficiency requirement, a senior project thesis, and a senior comprehensive exam (oral and written) to graduate.

Special: Bethany offers a 3-2 engineering degree with Columbia, Washington at St. Louis, and Case Western Reserve Universities, internships (required with many majors), study abroad in France, Spain, England, Germany, Canada, Japan, Puerto Rico, Argentina, and Sweden, a Washington semester, and work-study programs. B.A.-B.S. degrees and dual majors in all majors, a general studies degree, student-designed

majors in interdisciplinary studies, and pass/fail options in nonmajor courses also are offered. There is also a voluntary January term. There are 16 national honor societies.

Faculty/Classroom: 67% of faculty are male; 33%, female. All teach undergraduates, 35% do research, and 35% do both. The average class size in an introductory lecture is 30; in a laboratory, 18; and in a regular course, 20.

Admissions: 73% of the 2005-2006 applicants were accepted. The SAT scores for the 2005-2006 freshman class were: Verbal--48% below 500, 37% between 500 and 599, 11% between 600 and 700, and 4% above 700; Math--43% below 500, 42% between 500 and 599, 10% between 600 and 700, and 4% above 700. The ACT scores were 30% below 21, 41% between 21 and 23, 21% between 24 and 26, 6% between 27 and 28, and 3% above 28. 29% of the current freshmen were in the top fifth of their class; 55% were in the top two fifths. 6 freshmen graduated first in their class in a recent year.

Requirements: The SAT or ACT is required. In addition, applicants must have 15 Carnegie units, which should include 4 years of English, 3 each in math and science, and 2 each in foreign language, history, and social studies. An essay, an interview, a portfolio, and an audition are recommended, depending on the major. The GED is accepted. A GPA of 2.5 is required. AP and CLEP credits are accepted. Important factors in the admissions decision are advanced placement or honor courses, recommendations by school officials, and leadership record.

Procedure: Freshmen are admitted fall and spring. Entrance exams should be taken during the junior year. There are deferred admissions and rolling admissions plans. Application deadlines are open. Application fee is $25. A waiting list is an active part of the admissions procedure. Applications are accepted on-line.

Transfer: 26 transfer students enrolled in 2004-2005. Transfer students must have a minimum GPA of 2.0. 32 of 128 credits required for the bachelor's degree must be completed at Bethany.

Visiting: There are regularly scheduled orientations for prospective students, including a tour and meetings with faculty, coaches, and financial aid and admission personnel. There are guides for informal visits and visitors may sit in on classes and stay overnight. To schedule a visit, contact the Office of Admission.

Financial Aid: In 2005-2006, 97% of all full-time freshmen and 96% of continuing full-time students received some form of financial aid. 68% of full-time freshmen and 64% of continuing full-time students received need-based aid. The average freshman award was $13,292. Need-based scholarships or need-based grants averaged $5900 ($9000 maximum); need-based self-help aid (loans and jobs) averaged $6135 ($7000 maximum); and other non-need-based awards and non-need-based scholarships averaged $6200 ($9000 maximum). 79% of undergraduates work part time. Average annual earnings from campus work are $820. The average financial indebtedness of the 2005 graduate was $18,000. The FAFSA and the college's own financial statement are required. The priority date for freshman financial aid applications for fall entry is April 1. The deadline for filing freshman financial aid applications for fall entry is May 1.

International Students: In a recent year, there were 45 international students enrolled. The school actively recruits these students. A satisfactory score is required on the written TOEFL or the electronic version and also take the SAT or the ACT.

Computers: All students may access the system 24 hours daily. It is strongly recommended that all students have a personal computer.

Graduates: In a recent year, 140 bachelor's degrees were awarded. The most popular majors were communications (18%), psychology (16%), and biology (9%). In an average class, 3% graduate in 3 years or less, 56% graduate in 4 years or less, 58% graduate in 5 years or less, and 1% graduate in 6 years or less. Of a recent graduating class, 35% were enrolled in graduate school within 6 months of graduation and 85% were employed.

Admissions Contact: Wray Blair, Director of Admission.
E-mail: *admission@mail.bethanywv.edu* Web: *www.bethanywv.edu*

BLUEFIELD STATE COLLEGE
B-5

Bluefield, WV 24701
(304) 327-4068
(800) 654-7798; Fax: (304) 325-7747

Full-time: 573 men, 827 women	Faculty: 79; IIB, av$
Part-time: 116 men, 192 women	Ph.D.s: 52%
Graduate: none	Student/Faculty: 30 to 1
Year: semesters, summer session	Tuition: $3140 ($7014)
Application Deadline: open	Room & Board: n/app
Freshman Class: 615 applied, 591 accepted, 254 enrolled	
ACT: 18		LESS COMPETITIVE

Bluefield State College, founded in 1895, is a state-supported commuter college offering programs in engineering technologies, business, teacher education, arts and sciences, health science professions, and a variety of career fields. The college also offers a wide variety of off-campus courses. In addition to regional accreditation, Bluefield State has baccalaureate program accreditation with ABET and NCATE. The library contains 75,803 volumes, 5195 microform items, and 7500 audio/video tapes/CDs/DVDs, and subscribes to 6258 periodicals including electronic. Computerized library services include the card catalog, interlibrary loans, database searching, and Internet access. Special learning facilities include a learning resource center and art gallery. The 40-acre campus is in a small town 90 miles south of Charleston. There are 9 buildings.

Student Life: 95% of undergraduates are from West Virginia. Others are from 12 states, 10 foreign countries, and Canada. 99% are from public schools. 90% are white. The average age of freshmen is 21; all undergraduates, 27. 34% do not continue beyond their first year; 52% remain to graduate.

Housing: There are no residence halls. All of students commute. Alcohol is not permitted. All students may keep cars.

Activities: 3% of men belong to 3 local and 3 national fraternities; 1% of women belong to 1 national and 3 local sororities. There are 42 groups on campus, including cheerleading, choir, ethnic, honors, international, jazz band, newspaper, student government, and yearbook. Popular campus events include dances and sports events.

Sports: There are 5 intercollegiate sports for men and 5 for women, and 20 intramural sports for men and 15 for women. Facilities include a gym, a pool, tennis courts, an athletic field, and physical fitness and aerobics rooms.

Disabled Students: All of the campus is accessible. Wheelchair ramps, elevators, special parking, specially equipped rest rooms, and lowered drinking fountains are available.

Services: Counseling and information services are available, as is tutoring in most subjects. There is a reader service for the blind, and remedial math, reading, and writing.

Campus Safety and Security: Measures include 24-hour foot and vehicle patrol, self-defense education, pamphlets/posters/films, and emergency telephones. There are lighted pathways/sidewalks.

Programs of Study: Bluefield State confers B.A., B.S., B.S.E.T., and B.S.N. degrees. Associate degrees are also awarded. Bachelor's degrees are awarded in BIOLOGICAL SCIENCE (biology/biological science), BUSINESS (accounting and business administration and management), COMPUTER AND PHYSICAL SCIENCE (computer science), EDUCATION (elementary and middle school), ENGINEERING AND ENVIRONMENTAL DESIGN (engineering technology), HEALTH PROFESSIONS (nursing), SOCIAL SCIENCE (criminal justice, humanities, and social science). Engineering, technology, and health science are the strongest academically. Business is the largest.

Required: The minimum requirement for graduation is a 2.0 GPA overall and in the student's major and minor, and 128 semester hours. All graduating students must have completed the general program specific to their degree and a core curriculum of 40 hours among humanities, social science, lab science, basic skills, and computer science.

Special: A general studies degree and life experience credentials are offered through the Regents Bachelor of Arts Degree Program, designed for adults. Nondegree study is offered. There are 2 national honor societies, a freshman honors program, and 1 departmental honors program.

Faculty/Classroom: 62% of faculty are male; 38%, female. All teach undergraduates and 10% do research. The average class size in an introductory lecture is 40; in a laboratory, 25; and in a regular course, 25.

Admissions: 96% of the 2005-2006 applicants were accepted. The ACT scores for the 2005-2006 freshman class were: 73% below 21, 17% between 21 and 23, 8% between 24 and 26, 1% between 27 and 28, and 1% above 28. 27% of the current freshmen were in the top fifth of their class; 46% were in the top two fifths.

Requirements: The ACT is required and the SAT is accepted. In addition, regular admission is granted to students meeting GED requirements or having a high school diploma, with an overall 2.0 GPA or a composite score of at least 17 on the ACT or a comparable SAT score. They also must have successfully completed minimum high school curricular unit requirements consisting of 4 units in English, 3 in social studies, 2 in math (algebra I and higher), and 2 in lab science. Other students not meeting these requirements may be admitted on a conditional basis. AP and CLEP credits are accepted.

Procedure: Freshmen are admitted to all sessions. Entrance exams should be taken before enrolling. There are early admissions and deferred admissions plans. There is rolling admissions plan Application deadlines are open. Applications are accepted on-line.

Transfer: 146 transfer students enrolled in 2004-2005. Applicants must be in good standing at the institution from which they are transferring. 32 of 128 credits required for the bachelor's degree must be completed at Bluefield State.

Visiting: There are regularly scheduled orientations for prospective students. There are guides for informal visits and visitors may sit in on classes. To schedule a visit, contact the Admissions Office at (304) 327-4065.

Financial Aid: In a recent year, 70% of all full-time students received some form of financial aid. 60% of all full-time students received need-based aid. The average freshman award was $4200. Need-based scholarships or need-based grants averaged $500 ($2000 maximum); need-based self-help aid (loans and jobs) averaged $4000 ($10,500 maximum); and non-need-based athletic scholarships averaged $2000

($3200 maximum). 75% of undergraduates work part time. Average annual earnings from campus work are $1600. The average financial indebtedness of a recent graduate was $7500. The FAFSA and the college's own financial statement are required. The deadline for filing freshman financial aid applications for fall entry is March 15.

International Students: There are 27 international students enrolled. They must score satisfactorily on the written TOEFL and also take the ACT.

Computers: All students may access the system during class and lab hours. There are no time limits and no fees.

Graduates: From July 1, 2004 to June 30, 2005, 196 bachelor's degrees were awarded. The most popular majors were education (18%), nursing (14%), and business administration (13%). In an average class, 15% graduate in 4 years or less, 23% graduate in 5 years or less, and 35% graduate in 6 years or less. 60 companies recruited on campus in 2004-2005. Of the 2004 graduating class, 7% were enrolled in graduate school within 6 months of graduation and 95% were employed.

Admissions Contact: John C. Cardwell, Vice President for Enrollment Management. E-mail: bscadmit@bluefieldstate.edu Web: www.bluefieldstate.edu

CONCORD COLLEGE   B-5

Athens, WV 24712   (304) 384-5248
(888) 384-5249; Fax: (304) 384-9044

Full-time: 1100 men, 1400 women	**Faculty:** 84; IIB, -$
Part-time: 200 men, 400 women	**Ph.D.s:** n/av
Graduate: none	**Student/Faculty:** 29 to 1
Year: semesters, summer session	**Tuition:** $3912 ($8686)
Application Deadline: open	**Room & Board:** $5796
Freshman Class: n/av	
SAT or ACT: required	**COMPETITIVE**

Concord College, founded in 1872, is a public institution with undergraduate programs in liberal arts and professional training. Some information in this capsule and profile is approximate. In addition to regional accreditation, Concord has baccalaureate program accreditation with CSWE and NCATE. The library contains 96,787 volumes, 268,451 microform items, and 1077 audio/video tapes/CDs/DVDs, and subscribes to 552 periodicals including electronic. Computerized library services include the card catalog, interlibrary loans, and database searching. Special learning facilities include a learning resource center, art gallery, radio station, and TV station. The 123-acre campus is in a small town 85 miles south of Charleston. Including any residence halls, there are 19 buildings.

Student Life: 84% of undergraduates are from West Virginia. Students are from 25 states, 27 foreign countries, and Canada. 97% are from public schools. 92% are white. 40% claim no religious affiliation; 40% Protestant; 15% Catholic. The average age of freshmen is 19; all undergraduates, 23. 33% do not continue beyond their first year; 41% remain to graduate.

Housing: 1078 students can be accommodated in college housing, which includes single-sex dorms and married-student housing. In addition, there are honors floors in residence halls and housing for international students. On-campus housing is guaranteed for all 4 years. Alcohol is not permitted. All students may keep cars.

Activities: 20% of men belong to 2 local and 4 national fraternities; 20% of women belong to 4 national sororities. There are 52 groups on campus, including art, bagpipe band, band, cheerleading, choir, chorale, computers, drama, film, honors, international, jazz band, literary magazine, newspaper, pep band, political, professional, radio and TV, religious, social, social service, student government, and yearbook. Popular campus events include big-name concerts, Alumni Day, and faculty and student plays.

Sports: There are 8 intercollegiate sports for men and 7 for women, and 15 intramural sports for men and 15 for women. Facilities include 5 tennis courts, 4 racquetball courts, 2 gyms, a Nautilus fitness room, a pool, a dance studio, and various outdoor fields. The campus stadium seats 4000, the larger gym 2700, and the largest auditorium 900.

Disabled Students: 90% of the campus is accessible. Wheelchair ramps, elevators, special parking, special class scheduling, and special housing are available.

Services: Counseling and information services are available, as is tutoring in every subject. There is a reader service for the blind, and remedial math, reading, and writing.

Campus Safety and Security: Measures include security escort services, informal discussions, pamphlets/posters/films, and emergency telephones. There are lighted pathways/sidewalks. A foot and vehicle patrol is available 24 hours Monday through Friday and is on call Saturday and Sunday.

Programs of Study: Concord confers B.A., B.S., B.B.A., B.S.C.I.S., B.S.Ed., B.S.Med.Tech., and B.S.W. degrees. Associate degrees are also awarded. Bachelor's degrees are awarded in BIOLOGICAL SCIENCE (biology/biological science), BUSINESS (accounting, banking and finance, business administration and management, hotel/motel and restaurant management, marketing/retailing/merchandising, office supervision and management, and small business management), COMMUNICATIONS AND THE ARTS (broadcasting, communications, and English), COMPUTER AND PHYSICAL SCIENCE (chemistry, computer programming, computer science, information sciences and systems, and mathematics), EDUCATION (art, business, early childhood, elementary, middle school, music, science, secondary, and special), HEALTH PROFESSIONS (medical laboratory technology, predentistry, premedicine, and prepharmacy), SOCIAL SCIENCE (geography, history, parks and recreation management, political science/government, prelaw, psychology, social science, social work, and sociology). Teacher education, business, and preprofessional biology and chemistry are the strongest academically. Teacher education, business, and travel industry management are the largest.

Required: To graduate, students must earn 128 credit hours, including 36 to 50 in the major, with a minimum GPA of 2.0 (2.5 in many departments). All students must complete the college's general studies curriculum. Required courses include 14 to 15 semester hours of math and science, 12 of English and literature, 12 of social studies, 6 of fine arts, 3 of speech, and 2 of phys ed.

Special: Students may serve internships in medical technology, social work, travel industry management, commercial art/advertising, and communications arts. Concord offers a Washington semester, cross-registration with Bluefield State College, dual majors, interdisciplinary student-designed majors, and nondegree study. Credit for life, military, and work experience is granted to adult students through the Regents Bachelor of Arts Degree Program. There are 4 national honor societies and a freshman honors program.

Faculty/Classroom: All teach undergraduates. The average class size in an introductory lecture is 45; in a laboratory, 20; and in a regular course, 45.

Requirements: The SAT or ACT is required; the ACT is preferred. Applicants must be high school graduates or hold a GED. Students should present 17 academic credits, including 4 in English, 3 each in social studies, math, and science, and 1 each in history and health/phys ed. An interview is recommended and, where appropriate, a portfolio or an audition. A GPA of 2.0 is required. AP and CLEP credits are accepted.

Procedure: Freshmen are admitted to all sessions. Entrance exams should be taken in the junior year or preferably early in the senior year. There is a rolling admissions plan and a deferred admissions plan. Notification is sent on a rolling basis. Application deadlines are open. Applications are accepted on-line.

Transfer: Applicants must have a GPA of at least 2.0. Concord recommends a minimum of 15 credit hours of college work completed and an interview. 36 of 128 credits required for the bachelor's degree must be completed at Concord.

Visiting: There are regularly scheduled orientations for prospective students. There are guides for informal visits and visitors may sit in on classes and stay overnight. To schedule a visit, contact the Admissions Office.

Financial Aid: In a recent year, 91% of all full-time freshmen and 76% of continuing full-time students received some form of financial aid. 80% of full-time freshmen and 65% of continuing full-time students received need-based aid. The average freshman award was $7135. 23% of undergraduates work part time. Average annual earnings from campus work are $1800. The average financial indebtedness of the a recent year's graduate was $10,000. The FAFSA and the college's own financial statement are required. Check with the school for current deadlines.

International Students: The school actively recruits these students. They must achieve a satisfactory score on the TOEFL and also take the SAT or the ACT.

Computers: All students may access the system. There are no time limits and no fees.

Admissions Contact: Michael Curry, Vice President for Admissions and Financial Aid. E-mail: *admissions@concord.edu* Web: *http://www.concord.edu*

DAVIS AND ELKINS COLLEGE   C-3
Elkins, WV 26241
(304) 637-1326
(800) 624-3157; Fax: (304) 637-1800

Full-time: 240 men, 350 women	Faculty: 66
Part-time: 20 men, 50 women	Ph.Ds: 73%
Graduate: none	Student/Faculty: 9 to 1
Year: semesters, summer session	Tuition: $16,312
Application Deadline: open	Room & Board: $6104
Freshman Class: n/av	
SAT or ACT: required	COMPETITIVE

Davis and Elkins College, founded in 1904 and affiliated with the Presbyterian Church (U.S.A.), offers programs in the liberal arts, business, professional training, teacher preparation, nursing, and recreation management. Some information in this capsule and profile is approximate. The library contains 225,000 volumes, 300,000 microform items, and 14,000 audio/video tapes/CDs/DVDs, and subscribes to 410 periodicals including electronic. Computerized library services include the card cata-

log and interlibrary loans. Special learning facilities include a learning resource center, art gallery, planetarium, and radio station. The 170-acre campus is in a small town 200 miles west of Washington, D.C. Including any residence halls, there are 21 buildings.

Student Life: 55% of undergraduates are from West Virginia. Students are from 26 states, 12 foreign countries, and Canada. 95% are from public schools. 90% are white. 38% claim no religious affiliation; 24% Protestant; 7% Catholic. The average age of freshmen is 18; all undergraduates, 20. 30% do not continue beyond their first year; 70% remain to graduate.

Housing: 572 students can be accommodated in college housing, which includes single-sex and coed dorms. On-campus housing is guaranteed for all 4 years. 50% of students live on campus; of those, 75% remain on campus on weekends. All students may keep cars.

Activities: 15% of men belong to 2 national fraternities; 15% of women belong to 2 national sororities. There are 42 groups on campus, including art, bagpipe band, cheerleading, choir, computers, drama, environmental, honors, international, jazz band, leadership, literary magazine, musical theater, newspaper, pep band, photography, political, professional, radio and TV, religious, social, social service, student government, and yearbook. Popular campus events include Parents Weekend, Deja Vu, and International Week.

Sports: There are 6 intercollegiate sports for men and 6 for women, and 10 intramural sports for men and 10 for women. Facilities include a 2000-seat gym, 1300-seat arena, fields, fitness center and fitness trails, a tennis court, and a pool. A national forest is nearby.

Disabled Students: 80% of the campus is accessible. Wheelchair ramps, elevators, special parking, specially equipped rest rooms, special class scheduling, lowered drinking fountains, and lowered telephones are available.

Services: Counseling and information services are available, as is tutoring in every subject. There is remedial math, reading, and writing. Learning disabilities services also are available.

Campus Safety and Security: Measures include self-defense education, security escort services, informal discussions, and pamphlets/posters/films. There are lighted pathways/sidewalks. The campus security service is on duty from 6 P.M. to 5 A.M.

Programs of Study: D&E confers B.A. and B.S. degrees. Associate degrees are also awarded. Bachelor's degrees are awarded in BIOLOGICAL SCIENCE (biology/biological science), BUSINESS (accounting, business administration and management, hospitality management services, management science, and marketing/retailing/merchandising), COMMUNICATIONS AND THE ARTS (art, communications, dramatic arts, English, languages, and music), COMPUTER AND PHYSICAL SCIENCE (chemistry, computer science, and mathematics), EDUCATION (elementary, physical, and secondary), ENGINEERING AND ENVIRONMENTAL DESIGN (environmental science), HEALTH PROFESSIONS (predentistry and premedicine), SOCIAL SCIENCE (economics, history, political science/government, prelaw, psychology, religion, and sociology). Business, psychology, and biology are the strongest academically. Business, nursing, and hospitality management are the largest.

Required: To graduate, students must complete 124 credit hours, including 30 to 40 in the major, with a GPA of 2.0. General education requirements include 7 hours of natural science, 6 each of history, social science, English composition, philosophy, religion, literature, and math, 5 of fine arts, and 2 of phys ed, as well as a course in computer literacy. A freshman experience class and a public speaking course are also required.

Special: Students may study abroad or take a Washington semester. The college offers co-op programs with Syracuse University and SUNY, as well as internships. Students may take dual majors in psychology/human services, biology/environmental sciences, and history/political science, and student-designed majors are permitted through a contract degree program. The college awards credit for life, military, and work experience. Nondegree study is allowed, and pass/fail options are offered. The college's mentor-assisted degree-completion program allows adults to earn degrees through credit for life experience and off-campus study. There are 6 national honor societies, a freshman honors program, and 100 departmental honors programs.

Faculty/Classroom: 61% of faculty are male; 39%, female. All teach undergraduates. The average class size in an introductory lecture is 15; in a laboratory, 11; and in a regular course, 11.

Requirements: A satisfactory score on the SAT or ACT is required. Applicants should be high school graduates or hold a GED. Students should have earned 16 academic credits, including 4 in English and 3 each in social studies, math (including a minimum of algebra I and geometry), and natural science (including a lab course). 2 years of foreign language is recommended. D&E requires applicants to be in the upper 50% of their class. A GPA of 2.0 is required. AP and CLEP credits are accepted. Important factors in the admissions decision are advanced placement or honor courses, recommendations by school officials, and leadership record.

Procedure: Freshmen are admitted to all sessions. Entrance exams should be taken during the fall of the senior year. There is a rolling admissions plan. There are early decision and deferred admissions plans. Application deadlines are open. Application fee is $35. Notification is sent on a rolling basis. Applications are accepted on-line.

Transfer: Transfer applicants should have earned 62 credit hours, with a GPA of 2.0. An associate degree is recommended. 15 of 124 credits required for the bachelor's degree must be completed at D&E.

Visiting: There are regularly scheduled orientations for prospective students, including meals, a tour of campus, and panel discussions. There are guides for informal visits and visitors may sit in on classes and stay overnight. To schedule a visit, contact the Admissions Office at (304) 637-1230.

Financial Aid: In a recent year, 89% of all full-time students received some form of financial aid. 69% of full-time freshmen and 70% of continuing full-time students received need-based aid. The average freshman award was $16,512. Need-based scholarships or need-based grants averaged $2807 ($5550 maximum); need-based self-help aid (loans and jobs) averaged $2587 ($6125 maximum); non-need-based athletic scholarships averaged $3402 ($8000 maximum); and other non-need-based awards and non-need-based scholarships averaged $7716 ($10,000 maximum). 40% of undergraduates work part time. Average annual earnings from campus work are $1200. The FAFSA is required, and the CSS Profile Application is optional. Check with the school for current deadlines.

International Students: The school actively recruits these sutdents. They must take the TOEFL, achieving a satisfactory score, or take the MELAB. They must also take the SAT or the ACT.

Computers: All students may access the system. There are no time limits and no fees.

Admissions Contact: Renee Heckel, Director of Admissions. E-mail: *admiss@davisandelkins.edu* Web: *www.davisandelkins.edu*

FAIRMONT STATE
Fairmont, WV 26554

C-2

(304) 367-4062
(800) 641-5678; Fax: (304) 367-4584

Full-time: 2450 men, 2700 women	**Faculty:** IIB, -$
Part-time: 850 men, 1450 women	**Ph.D.s:** n/av
Graduate: 25 men, 40 women	**Student/Faculty:** n/av
Year: semesters, summer session	**Tuition:** $3200 ($7100)
Application Deadline: see profile	**Room & Board:** $5200
Freshman Class: n/av	
SAT or ACT: required	**LESS COMPETITIVE**

Fairmont State, founded in 1865, is a public institution offering programs in business, education, engineering technology, and health careers. Figures in the above capsule and in this profile are approximate. In addition to regional accreditation, Fairmont State has baccalaureate program accreditation with ABET, NCATE, and NLN. The library contains 256,991 volumes, 54,241 microform items, and 7298 audio/video tapes/CDs/DVDs, and subscribes to 1175 periodicals including electronic. Computerized library services include the card catalog, interlibrary loans, and database searching. Special learning facilities include a learning resource center. The 89-acre campus is in a small town 75 miles south of Pittsburgh, Pennsylvania. Including any residence halls, there are 12 buildings.

Student Life: 94% of undergraduates are from West Virginia. Others are from 23 states and 17 foreign countries. 98% are from public schools. 94% are white. The average age of freshmen is 21; all undergraduates, 24. 26% do not continue beyond their first year; 37% remain to graduate.

Housing: 437 students can be accommodated in college housing, which includes single-sex dorms. On-campus housing is available on a first-come, first-served basis. 94% of students commute. Alcohol is not permitted. All students may keep cars.

Activities: 4% of men belong to 3 national fraternities; 4% of women belong to 3 national sororities. There are 80 groups on campus, including art, band, cheerleading, choir, chorus, computers, debate, drama, gay, honors, jazz band, literary magazine, marching band, musical theater, newspaper, pep band, photography, political, professional, religious, service, social, student government, symphony, and yearbook. Popular campus events include multicultural events.

Sports: There are 7 intercollegiate sports for men and 6 for women, and 24 intramural sports for men and 24 for women. Facilities include a phys ed center, a 5000-seat stadium, a 4000-seat basketball arena, and playing fields.

Disabled Students: All of the campus is accessible. Wheelchair ramps, elevators, special parking, specially equipped rest rooms, special class scheduling, lowered drinking fountains, and lowered telephones are available.

Services: Counseling and information services are available, as is tutoring in most subjects. There is a reader service for the blind, and remedial math, reading, and writing.

Campus Safety and Security: Measures include 24-hour foot and vehicle patrol, pamphlets/posters/films, emergency telephones, and lighted pathways/sidewalks.

Programs of Study: Fairmont State confers B.A., B.S., B.A.E., B.E.T., and B.S.N. degrees. Associate and master's degrees are also awarded. Bachelor's degrees are awarded in BIOLOGICAL SCIENCE (biology/biological science), BUSINESS (accounting, banking and finance, business administration and management, business economics, and marketing/retailing/merchandising), COMMUNICATIONS AND THE ARTS (communications, English, French, and speech/debate/rhetoric), COMPUTER AND PHYSICAL SCIENCE (chemistry, computer science, and mathematics), EDUCATION (art, business, early childhood, elementary, foreign languages, health, middle school, music, science, and secondary), ENGINEERING AND ENVIRONMENTAL DESIGN (architectural technology, civil engineering technology, electrical/electronics engineering technology, engineering technology, manufacturing technology, and mechanical engineering technology), SOCIAL SCIENCE (criminal justice, family/consumer studies, history, political science/government, psychology, and sociology). Engineering technology, education, and business are the strongest academically. Business, health careers, and criminal justice are the largest.

Required: To graduate, students must complete 128 hours with a GPA of 2.0. (2.5 in education specializations). Students must complete 50 core curriculum hours for the B.S. or B.A. degree. All students must take 2 hours of phys ed. Course and distribution requirements vary according to the program.

Special: The college offers internships in teacher education, retailing, and psychology and awards a B.S. degree in chemistry/math. There is a freshman honors program.

Faculty/Classroom: All teach undergraduates. The average class size in an introductory lecture is 106; in a laboratory, 20; and in a regular course, 30.

Requirements: A satisfactory score on the SAT or ACT is required for students who have graduated from high school or completed GED requirements fewer than 5 years prior to seeking admission. Applicants must be high school graduates or hold a GED. The college requires 4 credits in English, and 3 each in social studies (1 in U.S. history), math (algebra I and at least 1 higher), and lab science. A foreign language is recommended. A GPA of 2.5 is required. AP and CLEP credits are accepted.

Procedure: Freshmen are admitted to all sessions. Entrance exams should be taken during the fall of the senior year. Check with the school for current application deadlines. The college accepts all applicants. Notification is sent on a rolling basis. Applications are accepted on-line.

Transfer: Applicants must have a GPA of 2.0. The ACT is required for applicants with fewer than 30 college credits. 32 of 128 credits required for the bachelor's degree must be completed at Fairmont State.

Visiting: There are guides for informal visits and visitors may sit in on classes. To schedule a visit, contact the Student Affairs Office at (304) 367-4216.

Financial Aid: In a recent year, 81% of all full-time freshmen and 77% of continuing full-time students received some form of financial aid. 65% of full-time freshmen and 64% of continuing full-time students received need-based aid. The average freshman award was $1914. Need-based scholarships or need-based grants averaged $2167 ($6242 maximum); need-based self-help aid (loans and jobs) averaged $1831 ($5418 maximum); non-need-based athletic scholarships averaged $1542 ($7300 maximum); other non-need-based awards and non-need-based scholarships averaged $2756 ($11,199 maximum); and WIA, vocational rehabilitation, National Guard, veterans benefits, and so on averaged $5160 ($9175 maximum). Fairmont State is a member of CSS. The FAFSA is required. Check with the school for current deadlines.

International Students: They must achieve a satisfactory score on the TOEFL. If ACT or SAT scores are not supplied, the ACT must be taken upon arrival on campus.

Computers: Those students with accounts may access the system 8 A.M. to 11 P.M., 4 days per week. There are no time limits and no fees.

Admissions Contact: Director of Enrollment Services. A video is available. E-mail: *admit@fairmontstate.edu* Web: *www.fscwv.edu*

GLENVILLE STATE COLLEGE
Glenville, WV 26351

C-3

(304) 462-4128
(800) 924-2010; Fax: (304) 462-8619

Full-time: 614 men, 579 women	**Faculty:** 53; IIB, --$
Part-time: 11 men, 84 women	**Ph.D.s:** 49%
Graduate: none	**Student/Faculty:** 23 to 1
Year: semesters, summer session	**Tuition:** $3628 ($8640)
Application Deadline: open	**Room & Board:** $5150
Freshman Class: 875 applied, 875 accepted, 290 enrolled	
SAT Verbal/Math: 452/461*	**ACT:** 19 **NONCOMPETITIVE**

Glenville State College, founded in 1872, is a public college offering programs in education, the arts and sciences, and business. In addition to regional accreditation, GSC has baccalaureate program accreditation with CCNE and NCATE. The library contains 114,924 volumes, 607,791 microform items, 18883 e-books, and 2713 audio/video tapes/CDs/DVDs, and subscribes to 137 periodicals including electronic. Computerized library services include the card catalog, interlibrary loans, database searching, Internet access, and laptop Internet portals. Special learning facilities include a learning resource center and art gallery. The 360-acre campus is in a rural area 100 miles northeast of Charleston. Including any residence halls, there are 28 buildings.

Student Life: 90% of undergraduates are from West Virginia. Others are from 22 states, 4 foreign countries, and Canada. 92% are white. 39% do not continue beyond their first year.

Housing: 596 students can be accommodated in college housing, which includes single-sex dorms, on-campus apartments, and married-student housing. On-campus housing is guaranteed for all 4 years. 66% of students commute. Alcohol is not permitted. All students may keep cars.

Activities: 2% of men belong to 2 local fraternities; 2% of women belong to 3 local sororities. There are 25 groups on campus, including art, band, cheerleading, chess, choir, chorus, drama, drill team, gay, honors, international, jazz band, literary magazine, marching band, musical theater, newspaper, pep band, political, professional, religious, social, and student government. Popular campus events include GSC Week (a campus celebration) in April, comedians, and bands.

Sports: There are 5 intercollegiate sports for men and 6 for women, and 10 intramural sports for men and 7 for women. Facilities include a field house, a 5000-seat football stadium, a running track, tennis courts, a softball field, a 700-seat gym, a swimming pool, a fitness center, and a weight room.

Disabled Students: 95% of the campus is accessible. Wheelchair ramps, elevators, special parking, specially equipped rest rooms, lowered drinking fountains, and lowered telephones are available. Adaptations are made to class delivery locations to accommodate student needs.

Services: Counseling and information services are available, as is tutoring in most subjects. There is remedial math, reading, and writing.

Campus Safety and Security: Measures include security escort services, shuttle buses, informal discussions, and emergency telephones. There are lighted pathways/sidewalks and electronically operated dorm entrances.

Programs of Study: GSC confers B.A. and B.S. degrees. Associate degrees are also awarded. Bachelor's degrees are awarded in BIOLOGICAL SCIENCE (biology/biological science), BUSINESS (accounting, banking and finance, business administration and management, and marketing/retailing/merchandising), COMMUNICATIONS AND THE ARTS (English), COMPUTER AND PHYSICAL SCIENCE (chemistry, computer science, and information sciences and systems), EDUCATION (business, early childhood, elementary, middle school, music, physical, science, secondary, and special), HEALTH PROFESSIONS (nursing), SOCIAL SCIENCE (behavioral science, history, and liberal arts/general studies). Teacher education is the strongest academically. Behavioral science is the largest.

Required: All students must take the general studies programs, consisting of 43 hours in English, math, science, the social sciences, humanities, and phys ed. Computer science is also required. To graduate, students must complete 128 credit hours, with 42 in the major. Non-education majors must maintain a 2.0 GPA; education majors, a 2.5.

Special: The college offers B.A.-B.S. degrees in numerous majors, credit by exam, student-designed majors in interdisciplinary studies, and pass/fail options. Some programs of study require internships. There are 4 national honor societies.

Faculty/Classroom: 57% of faculty are male; 43%, female. All teach undergraduates.

Admissions: All of the 2005-2006 applicants were accepted. The SAT scores for the 2005-2006 freshman class were: Verbal--72% below 500, 23% between 500 and 599, and 5% between 600 and 700; Math--78% below 500 and 22% between 500 and 599. The ACT scores were 68% below 21, 19% between 21 and 23, 11% between 24 and 26, and 2% between 27 and 28. 17% of the current freshmen were in the top fifth of their class; 43% were in the top two fifths.

Requirements: The SAT or ACT is required. Applicants should be graduates of an accredited secondary school and have taken 4 courses in English, 3 in social studies, and 3 each in higher math and lab sciences. GED admission is also possible. A GPA of 2.0 is required. AP and CLEP credits are accepted.

Procedure: Freshmen are admitted to all sessions. Entrance exams should be taken at the end of the junior year. There is an early admissions plan. Application deadlines are open. Notification is sent on a rolling basis.

Transfer: 57 transfer students enrolled in 2004-2005. Applicants must be in good standing at their previous institution. 32 of 128 credits required for the bachelor's degree must be completed at GSC.

Visiting: There are regularly scheduled orientations for prospective students, including meetings with an admissions officer and a division officer and a campus tour. There are guides for informal visits and visitors may sit in on classes and stay overnight. To schedule a visit, contact the Office of Admissions at admissions@glenville.edu.

Financial Aid: In 2005-2006, 77% of all full-time freshmen and 73% of continuing full-time students received some form of financial aid. 66% of full-time freshmen and 90% of continuing full-time students received need-based aid. Need-based scholarships or need-based grants averaged $4484; need-based self-help aid (loans and jobs) averaged $2604; and non-need-based athletic scholarships averaged $2359. 11% of undergraduates work part time. Average annual earnings from campus work are $885. The average financial indebtedness of the 2005 graduate was $16,029. The FAFSA for first-time students and the state aid form are required. The priority date for freshman financial aid applications for fall entry is March 1.

International Students: There are 21 international students enrolled. The school actively recruits these students. They must score satisfactorily on the written TOEFL and also take the ACT.

Computers: Wireless access is available. PCs are available in the student union, the library, residence halls, some classroom buildings, and the center court of campus. All students may access the system. There are no time limits and no fees.

Graduates: From July 1, 2004 to June 30, 2005, 182 bachelor's degrees were awarded. The most popular majors were business (27%), teacher education (27%), and behavioral science (24%).

Admissions Contact: Michelle Wicks, Director of Admissions and Marketing. E-mail: michellewicks@glenville.edu
Web: http://www.glenville.edu

MARSHALL UNIVERSITY
A-4
Huntington, WV 25755
(304) 696-3160
(800) 642-3499; Fax: (304) 696-3135

Full-time: 3800 men, 4700 women	**Faculty:** 411; IIA, -$
Part-time: 560 men, 970 women	**Ph.Ds:** 79%
Graduate: 1200 men, 2600 women	**Student/Faculty:** 20 to 1
Year: semesters, summer session	**Tuition:** $3300 ($9000)
Application Deadline: see profile	**Room & Board:** $5900
Freshman Class: n/av	
SAT or ACT: required	**COMPETITIVE**

Marshall University, founded in 1837 and part of the University of West Virginia system, is a comprehensive public institution offering programs in liberal arts and sciences, business, education, fine arts, and nursing. There are 10 undergraduate and 2 graduate schools. Figures in the above capsule and in this profile are approximate. In addition to regional accreditation, Marshall has baccalaureate program accreditation with AACSB, ABET, ACEJMC, CSWE, NASM, NCATE, NLN, and NRPA. The 3 libraries contain 415,910 volumes, 966,733 microform items, and 20,785 audio/video tapes/CDs/DVDs, and subscribe to 4138 periodicals including electronic. Computerized library services include the card catalog, interlibrary loans, database searching, and Internet access. Special learning facilities include a learning resource center, art gallery, natural history museum, radio station, TV station, and a greenhouse. The 70-acre campus is in an urban area 126 miles east of Lexington, Kentucky, and 50 miles west of Charleston, West Virginia. Including any residence halls, there are 35 buildings.

Student Life: 83% of undergraduates are from West Virginia. Students are from 37 states, 44 foreign countries, and Canada. 86% are white. The average age of freshmen is 19; all undergraduates, 22. 25% do not continue beyond their first year; 36% remain to graduate.

Housing: 2315 students can be accommodated in college housing, which includes single-sex and coed dorms, on-campus apartments, and married-student housing. In addition, there are honors and quiet study floors. On-campus housing is available on a first-come, first-served basis. Alcohol is not permitted. All students may keep cars.

Activities: 7% of men belong to 11 national fraternities; 4% of women belong to 8 national sororities. There are 94 groups on campus, including art, band, cheerleading, choir, chorale, chorus, computers, dance, debate, drama, ethnic, gay, honors, international, jazz band, literary magazine, marching band, musical theater, newspaper, opera, orchestra, pep band, political, professional, radio and TV, religious, social, social service, student government, symphony, and yearbook. Popular campus events include Parents Day, Springfest, and International Festival.

Sports: There are 8 intercollegiate sports for men and 10 for women, and 9 intramural sports for men and 9 for women. Facilities include a 10,500-seat basketball arena, a 30,000-seat football stadium, tennis courts, a baseball field, an Olympic-size pool, an auxiliary gym, a health and fitness center, racquetball courts, a human performance enhancement lab, and a track and field.

Disabled Students: All of the campus is accessible. Wheelchair ramps, elevators, special parking, specially equipped rest rooms, special class scheduling, lowered drinking fountains, lowered telephones, special housing, and an attendant care program are available.

Services: Counseling and information services are available, as is tutoring in most subjects, including all lower-division courses. There is a reader service for the blind, remedial math, reading, and writing, study skills courses, and other services for all students with disabilities.

Campus Safety and Security: Measures include 24-hour foot and vehicle patrol, self-defense education, security escort services, and informal

discussions. There are pamphlets/posters/films, emergency telephones, and lighted pathways/sidewalks.

Programs of Study: Marshall confers B.A., B.S., B.B.A., B.F.A., B.S. Cyotech, B.S.M.T., B.S.N., and B.S.W. degrees. Associate, master's, and doctoral degrees are also awarded. Bachelor's degrees are awarded in BIOLOGICAL SCIENCE (biology/biological science), BUSINESS (accounting, banking and finance, business economics, management science, and marketing/retailing/merchandising), COMMUNICATIONS AND THE ARTS (communications, English, fine arts, journalism, and music), COMPUTER AND PHYSICAL SCIENCE (chemistry, geology, information sciences and systems, mathematics, physics, and science technology), EDUCATION (elementary, foreign languages, home economics, and middle school), ENGINEERING AND ENVIRONMENTAL DESIGN (environmental science), HEALTH PROFESSIONS (cytotechnology, medical laboratory technology, and nursing), SOCIAL SCIENCE (criminal justice, dietetics, economics, geography, history, humanities, international relations, parks and recreation management, physical fitness/movement, political science/government, psychology, safety and security technology, social work, and sociology). Biological science, elementary education, and secondary education are the largest.

Required: The Marshall Plan, including a capstone experience, is key to each student's studies at Marshall University. Generally speaking, a 2.0 GPA (2.5 in education, 2.25 in journalism) and 128 credit hours, as well as other specific criteria, are required for graduation.

Special: Many programs require or offer internships. Work-study opportunities are available on campus. Students study abroad in 10 countries. B.A.-B.S. degrees, dual and student-designed majors, nondegree study, credit for life experience, and credit/no-credit options are available. There are 13 national honor societies, including Phi Beta Kappa, and a freshman honors program.

Faculty/Classroom: 54% of faculty are male; 46%, female. The average class size in an introductory lecture is 27; in a laboratory, 23; and in a regular course, 24.

Requirements: The SAT or ACT is required. In addition, regular admission is open to all students who have graduated from a secondary school with the required units of study and a 2.0 GPA or with a satisfactory score on the ACT or SAT. Required study is 4 years in English, 3 in social studies, and 2 each in higher math and lab science. 2 years of a foreign language is strongly recommended. The GED is also accepted. Students not meeting university requirements are admitted to the University College, through which students must successfully complete developmental courses with 3 semesters. AP and CLEP credits are accepted. Important factors in the admissions decision are advanced placement or honor courses, evidence of special talent, and recommendations by school officials.

Procedure: Freshmen are admitted to all sessions. Entrance exams should be taken during the junior year or early in the senior year. There is a rolling admissions plan. There are early admissions and deferred admissions plans. Check with the school for current application deadlines and fee. Notification is sent on a rolling basis. Applications are accepted on-line.

Transfer: 535 transfer students enrolled in a recent year. A 2.0 GPA on all previous college work is generally required of transfer applicants. 36 of 128 credits required for the bachelor's degree must be completed at Marshall.

Visiting: There are regularly scheduled orientations for prospective students. There are guides for informal visits and visitors may sit in on classes and stay overnight. To schedule a visit, contact the Orientation Office at (304) 696-2354.

Financial Aid: In a recent year, 87% of all full-time freshmen and 78% of continuing full-time students received some form of financial aid. 62% of full-time freshmen and 52% of continuing full-time students received need-based aid. The average freshman award was $5710. Need-based scholarships or need-based grants averaged $4034 ($9832 maximum); need-based self-help aid (loans and jobs) averaged $3085 ($11,925 maximum); non-need-based athletic scholarships averaged $7799 ($15,852 maximum); and other non-need-based awards and non-need-based scholarships averaged $4423 ($22,189 maximum). 4% of undergraduates work part time. Average annual earnings from campus work are $2212. The average financial indebtedness of a recent year's graduate was $15,652. Marshall is a member of CSS. The FAFSA is required. Check with the school for current deadlines.

International Students: There were 113 international students enrolled in a recent year. The school actively recruits these students. They must take the TOEFL, achieving a satisfactory score, or take the MELAB, or pass level 9 ELS at the university. They must also take the SAT or the ACT.

Computers: All students may access the system during scheduled hours, 7 days a week. There are no time limits and no fees. It is strongly recommended that all students have a personal computer.

Graduates: In a recent year, 1447 bachelor's degrees were awarded. The most popular majors were elementary education (10%), management (7%), and biological science (6%). In an average class, 36% graduate in 6 years or less.

Admissions Contact: Director of Admissions.
E-mail: *admissions@marshall.edu* Web: *www.marshall.edu/admissions*

MOUNTAIN STATE UNIVERSITY   B-4
Beckley, WV 25802-9003

(304) 929-1334
(800) 766-6067; Fax: (304) 253-5072

Full-time: 1062 men, 1182 women	**Faculty:** 79
Part-time: 302 men, 722 women	**Ph.D.s:** 34%
Graduate: 194 men, 232 women	**Student/Faculty:** 28 to 1
Year: semesters, summer session	**Tuition:** $5880
Application Deadline: open	**Room & Board:** $5526
Freshman Class: 1224 accepted, 365 enrolled	
SAT Verbal/Math: 475/495*	**ACT:** 19 **NONCOMPETITIVE**

Mountain State University, founded in 1933, is a private institution offering more than 40 professionally oriented degree programs in health and human services, business and technology, and arts and sciences, along with such specialized fields as culinary arts and legal studies. There are 4 undergraduate schools and 1 graduate school. In addition to regional accreditation, MSU has baccalaureate program accreditation with APTA, CAAHEP, CAHEA, CSWE, IACBE, and NLN. The library contains 95,656 volumes, 1460 microform items, and 5766 audio/video tapes/CDs/DVDs, and subscribes to 152 periodicals including electronic. Computerized library services include the card catalog, interlibrary loans, database searching, and Internet access. Special learning facilities include a learning resource center, a greenhouse, medicinal-botanical gardens, and a gross anatomy (cadaver) lab. The 24-acre campus is in a small town about 50 miles south of Charleston. Including any residence halls, there are 31 buildings.

Student Life: 75% of undergraduates are from West Virginia. Others are from 44 states, 42 foreign countries, and Canada. 83% are white; 10% African American. The average age of freshmen is 23; all undergraduates, 31. 45% do not continue beyond their first year; 26% remain to graduate.

Housing: 192 students can be accommodated in college housing, which includes coed dorms and off-campus apartments. In addition, there is housing for athletes. On-campus housing is guaranteed for the freshman year only and is available on a first-come, first-served basis. 99% of students commute. Alcohol is not permitted. All students may keep cars.

Activities: There are no fraternities or sororities. There are 17 groups on campus, including cheerleading, ethnic, gay, honors, international, literary magazine, professional, religious, SGA Newsletter, social, social service, and student government. Popular campus events include Appalachian Vision series, Business and Technology show, and Performing Arts Series.

Sports: There is 1 intercollegiate sport for men and 2 for women, and 7 intramural sports for men and 4 for women. Facilities include a pool, a track, racquetball courts, exercise equipment, and an aerobics area. All MSU students receive a membership in the local YMCA.

Disabled Students: 75% of the campus is accessible. Wheelchair ramps, elevators, special parking, specially equipped rest rooms, special class scheduling, lowered drinking fountains, lowered telephones, and electronic door-opening mechanisms are available.

Services: Counseling and information services are available, as is tutoring in most subjects. There is a reader service for the blind and remedial math and writing.

Campus Safety and Security: Measures include 24-hour foot and vehicle patrol, security escort services, informal discussions, and pamphlets/posters/films. There are emergency telephones and lighted pathways/sidewalks.

Programs of Study: MSU confers B.A., B.S., B.S.N., and B.S.W. degrees. Associate and master's degrees are also awarded. Bachelor's degrees are awarded in AGRICULTURE (environmental studies), BIOLOGICAL SCIENCE (biology/biological science and ecology), BUSINESS (accounting, banking and finance, business administration and management, business law, electronic business, entrepreneurial studies, hotel/motel and restaurant management, marketing and distribution, organizational behavior, recreation and leisure services, and sports management), COMMUNICATIONS AND THE ARTS (communications and English literature), COMPUTER AND PHYSICAL SCIENCE (computer science), EDUCATION (health), ENGINEERING AND ENVIRONMENTAL DESIGN (aviation administration/management, computer technology, and engineering), HEALTH PROFESSIONS (biomedical science, emergency medical technologies, health care administration, nursing, physician's assistant, respiratory therapy, and ultrasound technology), SOCIAL SCIENCE (criminal justice, culinary arts, forensic studies, humanities, interdisciplinary studies, law, psychology, public administration, and social work). Nursing, physician assistant, and diagnostic medical sonography are the strongest academically. Organizational leadership, strategic leadership, and nursing are the largest.

Required: Requirements for graduation are a 2.0 GPA overall and 128 or 129 semester hours. All students must complete 36 hours of general studies and a minimum of 93 in the major.

Special: Internships and a degree completion program are available. B.A.-B.S. degrees and student-designed majors are offered in interdisciplinary studies. There are 5 national honor societies.

Faculty/Classroom: 35% of faculty are male; 65%, female. All teach undergraduates, and 15% both teach and do research. The average class size in an introductory lecture is 15; in a laboratory, 16; and in a regular course, 15.

Admissions: The SAT scores for the 2005-2006 freshman class were: Verbal--70% below 500, and 30% between 500 and 599; Math--50% below 500, 30% between 500 and 599, 10% between 600 and 700, and 10% above 700. The ACT scores were 70% below 21, 20% between 21 and 23, 6% between 24 and 26, and 3% between 27 and 28. 9% of the current freshmen were in the top fifth of their class; 28% were in the top two fifths.

Requirements: The SAT or ACT is recommended for placement only. The ACT Optional Writing test is also recommended. The GED is accepted. AP and CLEP credits are accepted. Important factors in the admissions decision are recommendations by school officials, parents or siblings attending the school, and ability to finance college education.

Procedure: Freshmen are admitted to all sessions. Entrance exams should be taken any time prior to application. There are early admissions and deferred admissions plans. There is a rolling admissions plan. Application deadlines are open. Application fee is $25. Notification is sent on a rolling basis. Applications are accepted on-line.

Transfer: 781 transfer students enrolled in 2004-2005. Applicants must submit official transcripts from all colleges attended. 24 of 128 credits required for the bachelor's degree must be completed at MSU.

Visiting: There are regularly scheduled orientations for prospective students, including a campus tour, registration, financial aid information, and housing and meal plan sign-ups. There are guides for informal visits and visitors may sit in on classes and stay overnight. To schedule a visit, contact the Admissions Department at (304) 253-7351, ext. 1433 or dbrown@mountainstate.edu.

Financial Aid: In 2005-2006, 83% of all full-time freshmen received some form of financial aid. 53% of full-time freshmen received need-based aid. The average freshman award was $2437. Need-based scholarships or need-based grants averaged $1774 ($3450 maximum); need-based self-help aid (loans and jobs) averaged $1285 ($2626 maximum); non-need-based athletic scholarships averaged $5124 ($7223 maximum); and other non-need-based awards and non-need-based scholarships averaged $1652 ($3943 maximum). 3% of undergraduates work part time. Average annual earnings from campus work are $489. The average financial indebtedness of the 2005 graduate was $23,570. The FAFSA and the college's own financial statement are required. The deadline for filing freshman financial aid applications for fall entry is May 1.

International Students: There are 90 international students enrolled. The school actively recruits these students. A satisfactory score is required on the TOEFL. The ACT is recommended for placement.

Computers: Wireless access is available at some locations on campus. Students have access to the campus network for research. MSU provides 4 computer labs for classroom use and 1 lab located in the library for further studies. There are 4 computer labs with hard-wired connection to the network. Approximately 120 computers are used for academic advancement on the main campus. All students may access the system when school is in session. There are no time limits and no fees.

Graduates: From July 1, 2004 to June 30, 2005, 410 bachelor's degrees were awarded. The most popular majors were business (33%), interdisciplinary studies (14%), and nursing (13%). In an average class, 1% graduate in 3 years, 13% graduate in 4 years, 9% graduate in 5 years, and 5% graduate in 6 years. 63 companies recruited on campus in 2004-2005. Of the 2004 graduating class, 12% were enrolled in graduate school within 6 months of graduation.

Admissions Contact: Tammy Toney, Director of Admissions. A video is available. E-mail: ttoney@mountainstate.edu
Web: http://mountainstate.edu

OHIO VALLEY UNIVERSITY
(Formerly Ohio Valley College)
B-3

Vienna, WV 26105

(304) 865-6202
(877) 446-8668; Fax: (304) 865-6175

Full-time: 242 men, 266 women	Faculty: 25; IIB, --$
Part-time: 12 men, 22 women	Ph.Ds: 75%
Graduate: none	Student/Faculty: 20 to 1
Year: semesters, summer session	Tuition: $13,092
Application Deadline: open	Room & Board: $5660
Freshman Class: 304 applied, 170 accepted, 85 enrolled	
SAT Verbal/Math: 510/460*	ACT: 23	COMPETITIVE

Ohio Valley University, Formerly Ohio Valley College and founded in 1960, is a liberal arts institution affiliated with the Church of Christ. There are 4 undergraduate schools and 1 graduate school. The library contains 31,750 volumes, 51,530 microform items, and 2946 audio/video tapes/CDs/DVDs, and subscribes to 165 periodicals including electronic. Computerized library services include the card catalog, interlibrary loans, and database searching. Special learning facilities include a learning resource center. The 270-acre campus is in a suburban area 120 miles southwest of Pittsburgh, Pennsylvania. Including any residence halls, there are 9 buildings.

Student Life: 65% of undergraduates are from out of state, mostly the Midwest. Students are from 28 states, 13 foreign countries, and Canada. 97% are from public schools. 88% are white. Most are Protestant. The average age of freshmen is 18; all undergraduates, 22. 26% do not continue beyond their first year; 35% remain to graduate.

Housing: 500 students can be accommodated in college housing, which includes single-sex dorms, on-campus apartments, and married-student housing. On-campus housing is guaranteed for all 4 years. 55% of students live on campus; of those, 30% remain on campus on weekends. Alcohol is not permitted. All students may keep cars.

Activities: There are no fraternities or sororities. There are 16 groups on campus, including band, cheerleading, choir, chorale, chorus, drama, jazz band, newspaper, pep band, religious, social, and student government. Popular campus events include Expressions, a schoolwide musical review.

Sports: There are 5 intercollegiate sports for men and 4 for women, and 11 intramural sports for men and 10 for women. Facilities include a weight room, a student union with recreation facilities, an activity center, and 2 gyms.

Disabled Students: 30% of the campus is accessible. Wheelchair ramps, elevators, special parking, specially equipped rest rooms, special class scheduling, and lowered telephones are available.

Services: Counseling and information services are available, as is tutoring in most subjects. There is remedial math, reading, and writing.

Campus Safety and Security: Measures include 24-hour foot and vehicle patrol.

Programs of Study: Ohio Valley confers B.A. and B.S. degrees. Associate degrees are also awarded. Bachelor's degrees are awarded in BUSINESS (accounting, business administration and management, and human resources), EDUCATION (elementary and secondary), SOCIAL SCIENCE (biblical studies, liberal arts/general studies, psychology, and religion). Business is the strongest academically. Elementary education is the largest.

Required: To graduate, students must complete 128 credit hours, including 53 to 60 in the major, with a minimum GPA of 2.0. General requirements include 4 courses of Bible studies, 2 of English composition, 1 to 2 of history, and 1 each of speech, computer literacy, math, and social science. There is also a phys ed requirement. Students must attend chapel daily and take 1 Bible class each semester.

Special: Ohio Valley offers internships with churches for student ministers. Summer study in London or Italy is possible.

Faculty/Classroom: 68% of faculty are male; 32%, female. All teach undergraduates. The average class size in an introductory lecture is 30; in a laboratory, 20; and in a regular course, 15.

Admissions: 56% of the 2005-2006 applicants were accepted. 10% of the current freshmen were in the top fifth of their class; 32% were in the top two fifths. 10 freshmen graduated first in their class.

Requirements: The ACT is required. In addition, applicants should be graduates of an accredited secondary school or have earned a GED. Ohio Valley requires applicants to be in the upper 50% of their class. A GPA of 2.0 is required. AP and CLEP credits are accepted. Important factors in the admissions decision are recommendations by school officials, personality/intangible qualities, and leadership record.

Procedure: Freshmen are admitted fall and spring. Entrance exams should be taken during the senior year. There is an early admissions plan and a rolling admissions plan. Application fee is $20. Notification is sent on a rolling basis.

Transfer: Transfer applicants must provide high school, college, and financial aid transcripts, and test scores. 32 of 128 credits required for the bachelor's degree must be completed at Ohio Valley.

Visiting: There are guides for informal visits and visitors may sit in on classes and stay overnight. To schedule a visit, contact the Office of Admissions.

Financial Aid: In 2005-2006, 95% of all full-time freshmen and 98% of continuing full-time students received some form of financial aid. 70% of full-time freshmen and 65% of continuing full-time students received need-based aid. The average freshman award was $9768. Need-based scholarships or need-based grants averaged $7219; need-based self-help aid (loans and jobs) averaged $3248 ($5500 maximum); non-need-based athletic scholarships averaged $5442 ($16,796 maximum); and other non-need-based awards and non-need-based scholarships averaged $7732 ($15,000 maximum). 44% of undergraduates work part time. Average annual earnings from campus work are $800. The average financial indebtedness of the 2005 graduate was $9035. Ohio Valley is a member of CSS. The FAFSA is required. The priority date for freshman financial aid applications for fall entry is February 14.

International Students: There are 33 international students enrolled. The school actively recruits these students. They must achieve a satisfactory score on the TOEFL and also take the ACT, scoring 16.

Computers: All students may access the system. There are no time limits and no fees.

Graduates: From July 1, 2004 to June 30, 2005, 101 bachelor's degrees were awarded. The most popular majors were business (46%), education (25%), and psychology (16%). In an average class, 18% graduate in 4 years, 35% graduate in 5 years, and 27% graduate in 6 years.

Admissions Contact: Rob E. Dudley, Director of Admissions.
E-mail: *admissions@ovc.edu* Web: *ovc.edu*

SALEM INTERNATIONAL UNIVERSITY	C-3
Salem, WV 26426	**(304) 782-5336**
	(800) 283-4562; Fax: (304) 782-5592
Full-time: 160 men, 170 women	**Faculty:** 26; IIB, --$
Part-time: 5 men, 5 women	**Ph.D.s:** 88%
Graduate: 50 men, 90 women	**Student/Faculty:** 13 to 1
Year: multimodular terms, summer session	**Tuition:** $12,660
	Room & Board: $5360
Application Deadline: open	
Freshman Class: n/av	
SAT or ACT: required	**COMPETITIVE**

Salem International University, founded in 1888, is a private institution offering both liberal arts and career-oriented degree programs, including international business, biotechnology, Japanese studies, equine careers, and industry management. Figures in the above capsule and profile are approximate. In addition to regional accreditation, SIU has baccalaureate program accreditation with ACBSP. The library contains 105,437 volumes, 284,302 microform items, and 974 audio/video tapes/CDs/DVDs, and subscribes to 94 periodicals including electronic. Computerized library services include the card catalog, interlibrary loans, and database searching. Special learning facilities include a learning resource center, art gallery, radio station, TV station, Fort New Salem (an 1800s settlement), an equestrian center, and a greenhouse. The 300-acre campus is in a rural area 120 miles south of Pittsburgh, Pennsylvania. Including any residence halls, there are 19 buildings.

Student Life: 69% of undergraduates are from out of state, mostly the Middle Atlantic. Students are from 34 states, 26 foreign countries, and Canada. 53% are white; 22% foreign nationals. The average age of freshmen is 19; all undergraduates, 21. 37% do not continue beyond their first year; 51% remain to graduate.

Housing: 550 students can be accommodated in college housing, which includes single-sex and coed dorms. In addition, there are honors houses and special-interest houses. On-campus housing is guaranteed for all 4 years. 90% of students live on campus; of those, 75% remain on campus on weekends. All students may keep cars.

Activities: 10% of men belong to 2 local fraternities; 12% of women belong to 3 local sororities. There are 25 groups on campus, including cheerleading, ethnic, gay, honors, international, newspaper, professional, radio and TV, religious, social, social service, student government, and yearbook. Popular campus events include Winterfest, Spring Arts Series, and Spring Fling.

Sports: There are 6 intercollegiate sports for men and 6 for women, and 12 intramural sports for men and 12 for women. Facilities include a gym, a pool, a weight room, tennis courts, a soccer stadium, a fitness trail, racquetball courts, and horseback-riding trails.

Disabled Students: 90% of the campus is accessible. Wheelchair ramps, elevators, special parking, specially equipped rest rooms, special class scheduling, and special wheelchair lifting equipment are available.

Services: Counseling and information services are available, as is tutoring in most subjects. Most classes have a tutoring option. There is a reader service for the blind, and remedial math, reading, and writing.

Campus Safety and Security: Measures include 24-hour foot and vehicle patrol, security escort services, informal discussions, and pamphlets/posters/films. There are emergency telephones, lighted pathways/sidewalks, and Dial-a-Ride on weekends.

Programs of Study: SIU confers B.A. and B.S. degrees. Associate and master's degrees are also awarded. Bachelor's degrees are awarded in AGRICULTURE (equine science), BIOLOGICAL SCIENCE (biology/biological science and molecular biology), BUSINESS (business administration and management and sports management), COMMUNICATIONS AND THE ARTS (communications and English as a second/foreign language), COMPUTER AND PHYSICAL SCIENCE (computer mathematics and information sciences and systems), EDUCATION (athletic training, elementary, and secondary), ENGINEERING AND ENVIRONMENTAL DESIGN (aviation administration/management and environmental science), SOCIAL SCIENCE (criminal justice, human services, Japanese studies, and liberal arts/general studies). Molecular biology and Japanese studies are the strongest academically. Management studies, equine, and criminal justice are the largest.

Required: All students must take 57 hours in the core curriculum, including courses in communication skills, humanities, science/math, social studies, psychology, and health and phys ed. A minimum 2.0 GPA overall, with a minimum 2.25 GPA in the major, and 128 credit hours are required to graduate.

Special: A student may cross-register with another college within the Mountain State Association of Colleges. Many internships are available. Study abroad is offered. Dual majors, credit by exam, and credit for life experience may be arranged. There are 2 national honor societies.

Faculty/Classroom: 54% of faculty are male; 46%, female. All both teach and do research. No introductory courses are taught by graduate students. The average class size in an introductory lecture is 25; in a laboratory, 10; and in a regular course, 14.

Requirements: The SAT or ACT is required. In addition, applicants should be graduates of an accredited secondary school with 15 academic courses, including 4 in English, 3 each in math, science, and social studies, and 2 in a foreign language. A GPA of 2.0 is required. AP and CLEP credits are accepted. Important factors in the admissions decision are advanced placement or honor courses, evidence of special talent, and extracurricular activities record.

Procedure: Freshmen are admitted to all sessions. Entrance exams should be taken in the junior year or fall of the senior year. There is a deferred admissions plan. There is a rolling admissions plan. Application deadlines are open. Application fee is $25. Applications are accepted on-line.

Transfer: 43 transfer students enrolled in a recent year. A minimum GPA of 2.0 is required for acceptance as a transfer student. 32 of 128 credits required for the bachelor's degree must be completed at SIU.

Visiting: There are regularly scheduled orientations for prospective students, consisting of meetings with academic and administrative department heads, tours, question-and-answer sessions, and a reception. There are guides for informal visits and visitors may sit in on classes and stay overnight. To schedule a visit, contact the Admissions Office at (800) 283-4562, ext. 336.

Financial Aid: In a recent year, 97% of all full-time freshmen and 99% of continuing full-time students received some form of financial aid. 79% of full-time freshmen and 74% of continuing full-time students received need-based aid. The average freshman award was $17,579. Need-based scholarships or need-based grants averaged $6912 ($12,662 maximum); need-based self-help aid (loans and jobs) averaged $5430 ($11,290 maximum); non-need-based athletic scholarships averaged $5213 ($10,085 maximum); and other non-need-based awards and non-need-based scholarships averaged $8815 ($19,219 maximum). 34% of undergraduates work part time. Average annual earnings from campus work are $1450. The average financial indebtedness of a recent year's graduate was $18,228. SIU is a member of CSS. The FAFSA is required. Check with the school for current deadlines.

International Students: There were 77 international students enrolled in a recent year. The school actively recruits these students. .

Computers: All students may access the system. There are no time limits. The fee is $40. It is strongly recommended that all students have a personal computer.

Graduates: In a recent year, 93 bachelor's degrees were awarded. The most popular majors were criminal justice (14%), equine (9%), and molecular bio/biotechnology (6%). In an average class, 47% graduate in 6 years or less.

Admissions Contact: Director of Admissions.
E-mail: *admissions@salemiu.edu* Web: *www.salemiu.edu*

SHEPHERD UNIVERSITY (Formerly Shepherd College)	E-2
Shepherdstown, WV 25443-3210	**(304) 876-5212**
	(800) 344-5231; Fax: (304) 876-5165
Full-time: 1294 men, 1655 women	**Faculty:** 103; IIB, --$
Part-time: 338 men, 522 women	**Ph.D.s:** 88%
Graduate: 33 men, 59 women	**Student/Faculty:** 29 to 1
Year: semesters, summer session	**Tuition:** $4046 ($10,618)
Application Deadline: see profile	**Room & Board:** $6020
Freshman Class: 1593 applied, 1485 accepted, 675 enrolled	
SAT Verbal/Math: 516/506*	**ACT:** 22 **COMPETITIVE**

Shepherd University, formerly Shepherd College, founded in 1871, is a state-supported institution offering programs in the liberal and creative arts, business administration, teacher education, social and natural sciences, health fields, and other career-oriented areas. There are 4 undergraduate schools and 1 graduate school. In addition to regional accreditation, Shepherd has baccalaureate program accreditation with CSWE, IACBE, NASM, NCATE, and NLN. The library contains 189,025 volumes, 373,100 microform items, and 7632 audio/video tapes/CDs/DVDs, and subscribes to 539 periodicals including electronic. Computerized library services include the card catalog, interlibrary loans, database searching, Internet access, and laptop Internet portals. Special learning facilities include an art gallery, radio station, a nursery school, and 3 theaters. The 323-acre campus is in a small town 70 miles northwest of Washington, D.C. and Baltimore. Including any residence halls, there are 47 buildings.

Student Life: 60% of undergraduates are from West Virginia. Others are from 47 states, 22 foreign countries, and Canada. 94% are from public schools. 90% are white. The average age of freshmen is 19; all undergraduates, 23. 31% do not continue beyond their first year; 40% remain to graduate.

Housing: 1000 students can be accommodated in college housing, which includes coed dorms and on-campus apartments. In addition, there are honors houses and special-interest houses. On-campus housing is guaranteed for all 4 years, is available on a first-come, first-served basis, and is available on a lottery system for upperclassmen. 75% of students commute. All students may keep cars.

Activities: 6% of men belong to 4 national fraternities; 5% of women belong to 3 national sororities. There are 59 groups on campus, including art, band, cheerleading, choir, chorale, chorus, computers, debate, drama, drill team, ethnic, forensics, gay, honors, international, jazz band, literary magazine, marching band, musical theater, newspaper, orchestra, pep band, political, professional, radio and TV, religious, social, social service, and student government. Popular campus events include Family Day, Shepfest, and Midnight Breakfast.

Sports: There are 6 intercollegiate sports for men and 5 for women, and 12 intramural sports for men and 12 for women. Facilities include a 5000-seat football and soccer field, baseball and softball fields, a 3000-seat gym, 3 outdoor and 2 indoor tennis courts, 2 outdoor sand volleyball courts, a fitness/wellness center, and a swimming pool.

Disabled Students: 95% of the campus is accessible. Wheelchair ramps, elevators, special parking, specially equipped rest rooms, special class scheduling, lowered drinking fountains, lowered telephones, and automatic door openers are available.

Services: Counseling and information services are available, as is tutoring in most subjects. There is remedial math, reading, and writing. There also is tutorial assistance for learning-disabled students.

Campus Safety and Security: Measures include 24-hour foot and vehicle patrol, self-defense education, security escort services, and shuttle buses. There are informal discussions, pamphlets/posters/films, emergency telephones, and lighted pathways/sidewalks.

Programs of Study: Shepherd confers B.A., B.S., B.F.A, B.S.N., and B.S.W. degrees. Master's degrees are also awarded. Bachelor's degrees are awarded in BIOLOGICAL SCIENCE (biology/biological science), BUSINESS (accounting, business administration and management, hospitality management services, recreation and leisure services, and sports management), COMMUNICATIONS AND THE ARTS (art, communications, English, graphic design, music, music performance, music theory and composition, painting, photography, printmaking, and sculpture), COMPUTER AND PHYSICAL SCIENCE (chemistry, computer science, information sciences and systems, and mathematics), EDUCATION (art, elementary, English, health, home economics, mathematics, music, physical, science, secondary, and social studies), ENGINEERING AND ENVIRONMENTAL DESIGN (environmental science), HEALTH PROFESSIONS (nursing and recreation therapy), SOCIAL SCIENCE (economics, family/consumer studies, history, physical fitness/movement, political science/government, psychology, social work, and sociology). Business, science, and art are the strongest academically. Education, business, and recreation are the largest.

Required: To graduate, students must complete a minimum of 128 semester hours with a 2.0 GPA overall institutionally and in the major and minor fields. The general studies core totals 47 hours, including 19 of humanities, 15 of social sciences, 8 of life or physical science, 3 of math, and 2 of phys ed. There is also a computer literacy requirement. B.A. candidates (except for education majors) must demonstrate foreign language proficiency through course work or exams.

Special: Shepherd offers study abroad, a B.A.-B.S. degree in mass communications, and internships and co-op programs in most majors. There is a Washington semester, and dual majors are possible in any 2 majors. Credit by exam, life experience, credentialing through the Regents degree, nondegree study, and pass/fail options for electives are offered. There are 9 national honor societies, a freshman honors program, and 20 departmental honors programs.

Faculty/Classroom: 58% of faculty are male; 42%, female. All teach undergraduates, 70% do research, and 70% do both. No introductory courses are taught by graduate students. The average class size in an introductory lecture is 26; in a laboratory, 20; and in a regular course, 19.

Admissions: 93% of the 2005-2006 applicants were accepted. The SAT scores for the 2005-2006 freshman class were: Verbal--41% below 500, 47% between 500 and 599, 10% between 600 and 700, and 2% above 700; Math--44% below 500, 48% between 500 and 599, and 8% between 600 and 700. The ACT scores were 37% below 21, 33% between 21 and 23, 21% between 24 and 26, 6% between 27 and 28, and 3% above 28.

Requirements: Satisfactory scores are required on the SAT or ACT. Applicants should be graduates of an accredited secondary school and have earned academic credits, including 4 in English, 3 in social science (1 in American history), 3 each in lab science and math, 1 in phys ed, and the rest in computer, foreign language, and other academic electives. The GED is accepted. A GPA of 2.0 is required. AP and CLEP credits are accepted. Important factors in the admissions decision are advanced placement or honor courses, leadership record, and extracurricular activities record.

Procedure: Freshmen are admitted fall, spring, and summer. Entrance exams should be taken during the junior year. There are early decision, early admissions, and deferred admissions, and rolling admissions plans. Early decision applications should be filed by November 15, along with a $35 fee. Notification of early decision is sent in December ; regular decision, on a rolling basis.

Transfer: 362 transfer students enrolled in 2004-2005. Applicants must have a 2.0 cumulative GPA in a minimum of 15 semester hours completed and must submit a transcripts from each college attended. 32 of 128 credits required for the bachelor's degree must be completed at Shepherd.

Visiting: There are regularly scheduled orientations for prospective students, consisting of 3 fall open houses and 2 spring open houses, and weekday campus tours. There are guides for informal visits and visitors may sit in on classes and stay overnight. To schedule a visit, contact the Admissions Office at *admissions@shepherd.edu.*

Financial Aid: In 2005-2006, 77% of all full-time freshmen and 67% of continuing full-time students received some form of financial aid. 48% of full-time freshmen and 46% of continuing full-time students received need-based aid. The average freshman award was $7677. Need-based scholarships or need-based grants averaged $3627 ($15,000 maximum); need-based self-help aid (loans and jobs) averaged $2530 ($12,000 maximum); and non-need-based athletic scholarships averaged $4465 ($10,600 maximum). 91% of undergraduates work part time. Average annual earnings from campus work are $1225. The average financial indebtedness of the 2005 graduate was $14,887. The FAFSA and the state aid form are required. The priority date for freshman financial aid applications for fall entry is March 1.

International Students: There are 30 international students enrolled. The school actively recruits these students. Satisfactory scores are required on the written TOEFL and the SAT or the ACT.

Computers: Residence halls are wired for Internet access. The university maintains more than 300 computers in labs and public areas. All students may access the system weekdays from 8 A.M. to 11 P.M. There are no time limits and no fees.

Graduates: From July 1, 2004 to June 30, 2005, 537 bachelor's degrees were awarded. The most popular majors were business administration (11%), secondary education (9%), and recreation and leisure studies (8%). In an average class, 1% graduate in 3 years or less, 12% graduate in 4 years or less, 35% graduate in 5 years or less, and 40% graduate in 6 years or less. 140 companies recruited on campus in 2004-2005. Of the 2004 graduating class, 14% were enrolled in graduate school within 6 months of graduation and 83% were employed.

Admissions Contact: Kimberly Scranage, Director of Admissions. E-mail: *kscranag@shepherd.edu* Web: *www.shepherd.edu*

UNIVERSITY OF CHARLESTON   B-4

Charleston, WV 25304

(304) 357-4750

(800) 995-4682; Fax: (304) 357-4781

Full-time: 346 men, 506 women	**Faculty:** 60; IIB, --$
Part-time: 47 men, 88 women	**Ph.D.s:** 43%
Graduate: 10 men, 9 women	**Student/Faculty:** 14 to 1
Year: semesters, summer session	**Tuition:** $20,200
Application Deadline: open	**Room & Board:** $7400
Freshman Class: 1112 applied, 811 accepted, 286 enrolled	
SAT Verbal/Math: 478/488*	**ACT:** 22 **COMPETITIVE**

The University of Charleston, founded in 1888, is a private liberal arts institution offering programs in business and the health sciences, as well as traditional arts and sciences. In addition to regional accreditation, UC has baccalaureate program accreditation with AHEA, CAHEA, NCATE, and NLN. The library contains 118,779 volumes, 217,778 microform items, and 3387 audio/video tapes/CDs/DVDs, and subscribes to 7000 periodicals including electronic. Computerized library services include the card catalog, interlibrary loans, database searching, Internet access, and laptop Internet portals. Special learning facilities include a learning resource center and art gallery. The 40-acre campus is in an urban area in Charleston. Including any residence halls, there are 11 buildings.

Student Life: 66% of undergraduates are from West Virginia. Students are from 33 states, 10 foreign countries, and Canada. 85% are white; 10% African American. The average age of freshmen is 20; all undergraduates, 22.

Housing: 547 students can be accommodated in college housing, which includes coed dorms. In addition, there are living/learning communities (freshman are housed based on their courses).On-campus housing is guaranteed for all 4 years. 52% of students commute. All students may keep cars.

Activities: 6% of men belong to 2 national fraternities; 8% of women belong to 2 national sororities. There are 42 groups on campus, including art, cheerleading, chess, choir, chorale, chorus, computers, dance, debate, drama, ethnic, film, honors, international, musical theater, newspaper, photography, political, professional, radio and TV, religious, social, social service, and student government. Popular campus events include the Holiday Dinner served by faculty, the Governor's Cup Regatta, and World Fest.

Sports: There are 10 intercollegiate sports for men and 9 for women, and 6 intramural sports for men and 7 for women. Facilities include a gym, a game room, a Nautilus center, an indoor pool, soccer, softball, and baseball fields, and racquetball, volleyball, and tennis courts.

Disabled Students: 85% of the campus is accessible. Wheelchair ramps, elevators, special parking, specially equipped rest rooms, lowered drinking fountains, lowered telephones, and special housing are available.

Services: Counseling and information services are available, as is tutoring in some subjects, including math, English, and sciences. There is remedial math, reading, and writing.

Campus Safety and Security: Measures include 24-hour foot and vehicle patrol, self-defense education, security escort services, and shuttle buses. There are informal discussions, pamphlets/posters/films, emergency telephones, and lighted pathways/sidewalks. There are burglar alarms in dorms, safety and date-rape seminars, drug awareness programs, surveillance cameras at dorms (used in conjunction with card access), and emergency radio communications.

Programs of Study: UC confers B.A., B.S., and B.S.N. degrees. Associate and master's degrees are also awarded. Bachelor's degrees are awarded in BIOLOGICAL SCIENCE (biology/biological science), BUSINESS (accounting, banking and finance, business administration and management, and sports management), COMMUNICATIONS AND THE ARTS (art and communications), COMPUTER AND PHYSICAL SCIENCE (chemistry and information sciences and systems), EDUCATION (physical, science, and social studies), ENGINEERING AND ENVIRONMENTAL DESIGN (interior design), HEALTH PROFESSIONS (nursing, radiological science, and sports medicine), SOCIAL SCIENCE (liberal arts/general studies, political science/government, and psychology). Education and business are the strongest academically. Business and health sciences are the largest.

Required: All students must fulfill the general education program requirements, which include 48 hours of courses in English, computer systems, social sciences, humanities, natural science, health or phys ed, and elective options. A total of 120 to 128 credit hours and a GPA of 2.0 are required for graduation. A comprehensive exam also is required.

Special: The university offers credit by exam and credit for prior learning. A general studies degree, student-designed majors, nondegree study, an accelerated degree program in business administration, and pass-fail options are available. Internships, on-campus work-study, hospital clinical experience in qualified programs, a dual major in biology/chemistry, and a Washington semester are offered. There are 6 national honor societies.

Faculty/Classroom: 53% of faculty are male; 47%, female. All teach undergraduates, and 20% both teach and do research. No introductory courses are taught by graduate students. The average class size in an introductory lecture is 17; in a laboratory, 23; and in a regular course, 15.

Admissions: 73% of the 2005-2006 applicants were accepted. The SAT scores for the 2005-2006 freshman class were: Verbal--67% below 500, 25% between 500 and 599, and 8% between 600 and 700; Math--56% below 500, 33% between 500 and 599, 10% between 600 and 700, and 1% above 700. The ACT scores were 42% below 21, 23% between 21 and 23, 20% between 24 and 26, 9% between 27 and 28, and 6% above 28. 42% of the current freshmen were in the top fifth of their class; 63% were in the top two fifths.

Requirements: The SAT or ACT is required. Applicants should have a minimum academic GPA of 2.25 on a 4.0 scale and be in the upper 50% of their class, with a minimum composite score on the SAT or ACT for automatic admission. Applicants should be graduates of an accredited secondary school or have the GED and have taken 15 academic courses. AP and CLEP credits are accepted. Important factors in the admissions decision are advanced placement or honor courses, leadership record, and extracurricular activities record.

Procedure: Freshmen are admitted to all sessions. Entrance exams should be taken by December of the senior year. There is a rolling admissions plan. Application deadlines are open. Application fee is $25. Notification is sent on a rolling basis. Applications are accepted on-line.

Transfer: 109 transfer students enrolled in 2004-2005. Applicants should have a minimum GPA of 2.25. 30 of 120 credits required for the bachelor's degree must be completed at UC.

Visiting: There are regularly scheduled orientations for prospective students, including meetings with faculty, financial aid and student life information sessions, a campus tour, and lunch. There are guides for informal visits and visitors may sit in on classes and stay overnight. To schedule a visit, contact the Admissions Office.

Financial Aid: In 2005-2006, 90% of all full-time freshmen and 85% of continuing full-time students received some form of financial aid. 72% of full-time freshmen and 75% of continuing full-time students received need-based aid. The average freshman award was $20,760. Need-based scholarships or need-based grants averaged $10,000 ($15,000 maximum); need-based self-help aid (loans and jobs) averaged $6600 ($8500 maximum); non-need-based athletic scholarships averaged $3500 ($23,500 maximum); and other non-need-based awards and non-need-based scholarships averaged $4500 ($24,500 maximum).

25% of undergraduates work part time. Average annual earnings from campus work are $975. The average financial indebtedness of the 2005 graduate was $23,500. UC is a member of CSS. The FAFSA is required. The priority date for freshman financial aid applications for fall entry is March 1. The deadline for filing freshman financial aid applications for fall entry is September 15.

International Students: There are 78 international students enrolled. The school actively recruits these students. They must take the TOEFL, achieving a satisfactory score, or take the MELAB. The SAT or ACT is required of students from English-speaking countries, with a minimum composite score on the ACT.

Computers: Wireless access is available. All students may access the system. There is 24-hour dial-in availability. There are no time limits and no fees. It is strongly recommended that all students have a personal computer.

Graduates: From July 1, 2004 to June 30, 2005, 123 bachelor's degrees were awarded. The most popular majors were nursing (26%), business (18%), and radiologic science (11%). In an average class, 3% graduate in 3 years or less, 33% graduate in 4 years or less, 39% graduate in 5 years or less, and 41% graduate in 6 years or less. 63 companies recruited on campus in 2004-2005.

Admissions Contact: Brad Parrish, Associate Vice President for Enrollment. E-mail: *admissions@ucwv.edu* Web: *www.ucwv.edu*

WEST LIBERTY STATE COLLEGE C-1

West Liberty, WV 26074

(304) 336-8076
(800) 732-6204; Fax: (304) 336-8403

Full-time: 935 men, 1111 women	**Faculty:** 107; IIB, --$
Part-time: 136 men, 192 women	**Ph.D.s:** 46%
Graduate: none	**Student/Faculty:** 20 to 1
Year: semesters, summer session	**Tuition:** $3686 ($9054)
Application Deadline: see profile	**Room & Board:** $5456
Freshman Class: n/av	
SAT or ACT: required	**LESS COMPETITIVE**

West Liberty State College, founded in 1837, is a state-assisted college offering programs in teacher education, liberal and fine arts, sciences, business, and preprofessional and technical fields. There are 4 undergraduate schools. Figures in the above capsule and in this profile are approximate. In addition to regional accreditation, West Liberty has baccalaureate program accreditation with ADA, CAHEA, NASM, NCATE, and NLN. The library contains 196,338 volumes and 131,000 microform items, and subscribes to 485 periodicals including electronic. Computerized library services include the card catalog, interlibrary loans, and database searching. Special learning facilities include a learning resource center, art gallery, radio station, TV station, and a publication area. The 290-acre campus is in a rural area 10 miles north of Wheeling and 56 miles southwest of Pittsburgh. Including any residence halls, there are 22 buildings.

Student Life: 72% of undergraduates are from West Virginia. Others are from 21 states, 9 foreign countries, and Canada. 90% are from public schools. 95% are white. The average age of freshmen is 18; all undergraduates, 22. 30% do not continue beyond their first year; 43% remain to graduate.

Housing: College housing includes single-sex and coed dorms, on-campus apartments, and married-student housing. In addition, there are honors houses and an honors dorm. On-campus housing is available on a first-come, first-served basis. 55% of students commute. Alcohol is not permitted. All students may keep cars.

Activities: 6% of men belong to 4 local fraternities; 10% of women belong to 1 local sorority and 3 national sororities. There are 48 groups on campus, including art, cheerleading, choir, chorus, drama, ethnic, honors, hospitality and tourism, jazz band, literary magazine, marching band, musical theater, newspaper, pep band, photography, professional, radio and TV, religious, social, social service, steel drum band, and student government. Popular campus events include Multi-Cultural Day, Greek Week, and Spring Fling.

Sports: There are 8 intercollegiate sports for men and 7 for women, and 8 intramural sports for men and 7 for women. Facilities include handball and racquetball courts, training rooms, 3 gyms, an indoor track, a wellness center, and an indoor swimming pool. There is also a game area with pool tables and table tennis, 8 all-weather-surface tennis courts, and football and softball/baseball fields.

Disabled Students: 90% of the campus is accessible. Wheelchair ramps, elevators, special parking, specially equipped rest rooms, lowered drinking fountains, and lowered telephones are available.

Services: Counseling and information services are available, as is tutoring in every subject. There is a reader service for the blind and remedial math and writing.

Campus Safety and Security: Measures include 24-hour foot and vehicle patrol, self-defense education, security escort services, and informal discussions. There are pamphlets/posters/films, emergency telephones, lighted pathways/sidewalks, and late night transport.

Programs of Study: West Liberty confers B.A., B.S., and B.S.N. degrees. Associate degrees are also awarded. Bachelor's degrees are awarded in BIOLOGICAL SCIENCE (biology/biological science), BUSINESS (accounting, banking and finance, business administration and management, business economics, management science, marketing/retailing/merchandising, and tourism), COMMUNICATIONS AND THE ARTS (communications, English, fine arts, graphic design, and music), COMPUTER AND PHYSICAL SCIENCE (chemistry, information sciences and systems, and mathematics), EDUCATION (art, early childhood, elementary, health, middle school, music, physical, science, secondary, and special), ENGINEERING AND ENVIRONMENTAL DESIGN (preengineering), HEALTH PROFESSIONS (clinical science, dental hygiene, nursing, predentistry, premedicine, prepharmacy, and speech pathology/audiology), SOCIAL SCIENCE (criminal justice, economics, history, interdisciplinary studies, physical fitness/movement, political science/government, prelaw, psychology, social science, and sociology). Business, natural sciences, and health sciences are the strongest academically. Business, elementary education, and criminal justice are the largest.

Required: The required core curriculum varies for B.A. and B.S. candidates, but both include courses in communications, fine arts and humanities, natural science and math, social science and history, and phys ed and health. A minimum GPA of 2.0 and 128 credit hours are required to graduate.

Special: Communications, exercise physiology, criminal justice, hospitality, tourism management, sports management, and golf management require an on-campus internship. The Washington Center Program, an internship, is also offered. However, students may also choose to complete an internship in the areas of business, clinical lab science, phys ed, or nursing. Interdisciplinary studies is a student-designed degree taken as either a B.A. or B.S. Biology, chemistry, and math are offered as a B.S. degree but may also be taken as a B.A. degree in education. Work and life experience credit is accepted in the Regents B.A. degree program. There are 10 national honor societies, a freshman honors program, and 6 departmental honors programs.

Faculty/Classroom: 59% of faculty are male; 41%, female. All teach undergraduates. The average class size in an introductory lecture is 25; in a laboratory, 20; and in a regular course, 20.

Requirements: The SAT or ACT is required. In addition, applicants must graduate from an accredited secondary school with a minimum GPA of 2.0, or have a minimum score on the ACT or SAT. Students must have completed 4 years of English, 3 of social sciences, including U.S. history, 2 of math (algebra I and higher), and 2 of lab science. The GED is accepted. A GPA of 2.0 is required. AP and CLEP credits are accepted.

Procedure: Freshmen are admitted to all sessions. Entrance exams should be taken in time so that all admissions credentials, including test scores, are received 2 weeks prior to the beginning of the term. There is a deferred admissions plan and a rolling admissions plan. Check with the school for current application deadlines. Notification is sent on a rolling basis. Applications are accepted on-line.

Transfer: Students must be eligible to return to the institution from which they wish to transfer. An official college transcript and a minimum GPA of 2.0 overall are required. Admissions criteria are the same as for freshmen if the student has completed fewer than 28 hours of college-level course work. 36 of 128 credits required for the bachelor's degree must be completed at West Liberty.

Visiting: There are guides for informal visits and visitors may sit in on classes and stay overnight. To schedule a visit, contact the Office of Admissions.

Financial Aid: The FAFSA is required. Check with the school for current deadlines.

International Students: There were 13 international students enrolled in a recent year. They must achieve a satisfactory score on the TOEFL and also take the SAT or the ACT.

Computers: All students may access the system. There are no time limits and no fees. It is strongly recommended that all students have a personal computer.

Graduates: In a recent year, 427 bachelor's degrees were awarded. The most popular majors were education (33%), business administration (21%), and criminal justice (11%). In an average class, 19% graduate in 4 years or less, 37% graduate in 5 years or less, and 41% graduate in 6 years or less. 8 companies recruited on campus in a recent year.

Admissions Contact: Brenda King, Director of Admissions.
E-mail: *kingbren@wlsc.edu* Web: *www.wlsc.edu*

West Virginia State University, formerly West Virginia State College, founded in 1891, is a state-supported institution offering broad programs in the arts and sciences and in preprofessional studies, including business and education. It also offers a comprehensive evening class schedule. Figures in the above capsule and in this profile are approximate. In addition to regional accreditation, State University has baccalaureate program accreditation with ABET, CSWE, NCATE, and NRPA. The library contains 30,000 volumes, 500,000 microform items, and 6000 audio/video tapes/CDs/DVDs, and subscribes to 700 periodicals including electronic. Computerized library services include the card catalog, interlibrary loans, and database searching. Special learning facilities include a learning resource center, art gallery, and TV station. The 91-acre campus is in a suburban area 8 miles west of Charleston. Including any residence halls, there are 40 buildings.

Student Life: 94% of undergraduates are from West Virginia. Students are from 34 states and 8 foreign countries. 99% are from public schools. 84% are white; 14% African American. The average age of freshmen is 26; all undergraduates, 27. 30% do not continue beyond their first year; 64% remain to graduate.

Housing: 794 students can be accommodated in college housing, which includes single-sex dorms, on-campus apartments, and married-student housing. 93% of students commute. Alcohol is not permitted. All students may keep cars.

Activities: 1% of men belong to 1 local and 4 national fraternities; 1% of women belong to 3 national sororities. There are 42 groups on campus, including art, band, cheerleading, choir, chorale, chorus, drama, drill team, ethnic, film, honors, international, jazz band, literary magazine, newspaper, orchestra, pep band, photography, political, radio and TV, religious, social, social service, student government, and yearbook. Popular campus events include movies, comedy shows, and plays.

Sports: There are 5 intercollegiate sports for men and 4 for women, and 8 intramural sports for men and 7 for women. Facilities include a 6000-seat stadium, a swimming pool, a sports center, a 1500-seat gym, the student union, and a student mall/plaza.

Disabled Students: Wheelchair ramps, elevators, special parking, specially equipped rest rooms, special class scheduling, and lowered drinking fountains are available.

Services: Counseling and information services are available, as is tutoring in most subjects, including economics, political science, upper-division math, and accounting. There is remedial math, reading, and writing.

Campus Safety and Security: Measures include 24-hour foot and vehicle patrol, informal discussions, pamphlets/posters/films, and lighted pathways/sidewalks. Formal educational sessions are held in the dormitories each semester.

Programs of Study: State University confers B.A., B.S., and B.S.Ed. degrees. Associate degrees are also awarded. Bachelor's degrees are awarded in BIOLOGICAL SCIENCE (biology/biological science), BUSINESS (accounting, banking and finance, business administration and management, and marketing/retailing/merchandising), COMMUNICATIONS AND THE ARTS (communications, English, and fine arts), COMPUTER AND PHYSICAL SCIENCE (applied mathematics, chemistry, and mathematics), EDUCATION (art, early childhood, elementary, and secondary), HEALTH PROFESSIONS (recreation therapy), SOCIAL SCIENCE (criminal justice, economics, history, political science/government, psychology, social work, and sociology). Biology is the strongest academically. Education and business are the largest.

Required: Bachelor's degree candidates must take 52 to 53 semester credits of general studies courses, including freshman seminar, English, math, natural science, literature, fine arts, history, and cultural studies. To graduate, students must complete 121 to 128 credits with a minimum 2.0 GPA overall and in the major.

Special: State University offers internships, a Washington semester, work-study programs, and B.A.-B.S. degrees in communications, psychology, and biology. Credit by exam and for life/military/work experience is available. Nondegree study and pass/fail options are possible. There are 7 national honor societies, a freshman honors program, and 7 departmental honors programs.

Faculty/Classroom: 49% of faculty are male; 51%, female. All teach undergraduates. The average class size in a regular course is 25.

Requirements: The ACT is required and the SAT is recommended. In addition, a minimum ACT composite score of 14 or a 2.0 GPA is required for regular admission. Applicants should be graduates of an accredited secondary school and have completed a minimum of 4 years each in English and academic electives, 3 in social studies, and 2 each in math and science. The GED is accepted. Applications are accepted on-line. A GPA of 2.0 is required. AP and CLEP credits are accepted. Important factors in the admissions decision are evidence of special talent, leadership record, and advanced placement or honor courses.

Procedure: Freshmen are admitted to all sessions. Entrance exams should be taken 6 months prior to entry. There are early decision and rolling admissions plans. The college accepts all in-state residents. Notification is sent on a rolling basis. Applications are accepted on-line. Check with the school for current deadlines and fee.

Transfer: 186 transfer students enrolled in 2004-2005. Applicants must submit ACT scores and high school and college transcripts, and must have a 2.0 GPA. 30 of 121 credits required for the bachelor's degree must be completed at State University.

Visiting: There are regularly scheduled orientations for prospective students, including both academic and social activities. There are guides for informal visits and visitors may sit in on classes and stay overnight. To schedule a visit, contact the Office of Admissions.

Financial Aid: The CSS/Profile is required. Check with the school for current deadlines.

International Students: A satisfactory score is required on the written TOEFL. Students must also take the ACT, scoring 14.

Computers: All students may access the system Monday through Thursday, 9 A.M. to 10 P.M., Friday, 9 A.M. to 7 P.M., and Saturday, 9 A.M. to 2 P.M. Each student is allocated $200 of use per semester.

Admissions Contact: Tryreno Sowell, Director of Admissions and Recruitment. E-mail: *sowell@wvstateu.edu* Web: *wvstateu.edu*

WEST VIRGINIA UNIVERSITY · C-2
Morgantown, WV 26506-6009 (304) 293-2121
(800) 344-9881; Fax: (304) 293-3080

Full-time: 9985 men, 8464 women	**Faculty:** 712; I, --$
Part-time: 78 men, 583 women	**Ph.D.s:** 85%
Graduate: 2872 men, 3669 women	**Student/Faculty:** 26 to 1
Year: semesters, summer session	**Tuition:** $4164 ($12,874)
Application Deadline: August 1	**Room & Board:** $6342
Freshman Class: 10,957 applied, 10,110 accepted, 4574 enrolled	
SAT Verbal/Math: 510/520*	**ACT:** 23 **COMPETITIVE**

West Virginia University, founded in 1867, is a comprehensive, public land-grant research university offering more than 100 undergraduate degrees in liberal arts and sciences, health science, and professional training. There are 13 undergraduate and 14 graduate schools. In addition to regional accreditation, WVU has baccalaureate program accreditation with AACSB, ABET, ACEJMC, ACPE, ADA, APTA, ASLA, CAHEA, CSWE, FIDER, NASAD, NASM, NCATE, NLN, NRPA, and SAF. The 10 libraries contain 1,538,497 volumes, 2,344,404 microform items, and 46,031 audio/video tapes/CDs/DVDs, and subscribe to 23,581 periodicals including electronic. Computerized library services include the card catalog, interlibrary loans, database searching, and Internet access. Special learning facilities include a learning resource center, art gallery, planetarium, radio station, TV station, and a discovery lab for inventors, a coal, mining, and minerals history museum, a pharmacy museum, and an arboretum. The 913-acre campus is in a small town 75 miles south of Pittsburgh and 200 miles west of Baltimore. Including any residence halls, there are 160 buildings.

Student Life: 58% of undergraduates are from West Virginia. Others are from 49 states, 67 foreign countries, and Canada. 90% are white; 44% African American. The average age of freshmen is 19; all undergraduates, 21. 22% do not continue beyond their first year; 57% remain to graduate.

Housing: 4250 students can be accommodated in college housing, which includes single-sex and coed dormitories, on-campus apartments, off-campus apartments, married-student housing, fraternity houses, and sorority houses. In addition, there are honors houses, language houses, special-interest houses, and sections within residence halls designated for special programming. On-campus housing is available on a first-come, first-served basis and is available on a lottery system for upperclassmen. 79% of students live on campus. Alcohol is not permitted. All students may keep cars.

Activities: 9% of men belong to 14 national fraternities; 10% of women belong to 1 local sorority and 11 national sororities. There are 300 groups on campus, including art, band, cheerleading, chess, choir, chorale, chorus, computers, debate, drama, environmental, ethnic, film, gay, honors, international, jazz band, literary magazine, marching band, newspaper, opera, orchestra, pep band, photography, political, professional, radio and TV, religious, social, social service, student government, symphony, and yearbook. Popular campus events include Mountaineer Week, Parents Weekend, and Greek Week.

Sports: There are 7 intercollegiate sports for men and 11 for women, and 14 intramural sports for men and 14 for women. Facilities include a natatorium with swimming and diving pools, and rifle facilities, tennis

courts, a weight room, indoor/outdoor tracks, a bowling alley, lacrosse, baseball, football, and soccer fields, a 63,500-seat stadium, and a 14,000-seat gym, a student recreation center with weight/fitness equipment; courts for basketball, volleyball, badminton, squash and racquetball; a 6-lane fitness and leisure pool, a coliseum offering basketball, wrestling, volleyball, and gymnastics, and a soccer stadium.

Disabled Students: 90% of the campus is accessible. Wheelchair ramps, elevators, special parking, specially equipped rest rooms, special class scheduling, lowered drinking fountains, and lowered telephones are available. Academic programs are made accessible by transferring class to an architecturally accessible facility. Other facilities include tactile signage, specially designed lab facilities, portable lab stations, a Kurzweil reading machine, special apartments for hearing-and-mobility impaired students, and a specially equipped van for inner-city transportation. All coordination is done through the ADA coordinator.

Services: Counseling and information services are available, as is tutoring in most subjects. There is a reader service for the blind, and remedial math, reading, and writing.

Campus Safety and Security: Measures include 24-hour foot and vehicle patrol, self-defense education, security escort services, and shuttle buses. There are informal discussions, pamphlets/posters/films, emergency telephones, lighted pathways/sidewalks, neighborhood watch programs, and sexual assault prevention booths staffed by city and university police.

Programs of Study: WVU confers B.A., B.S., B.F.A., B.M., B.S.A.E., B.S.Agr., B.S.B.Ad., B.S.B.S., B.S.C.E., B.S.Ch.E., B.S.Cp.E., B.S.E.E., B.S.F., B.S.F. & C.S., B.S.I.E., B.S.J., B.S.L.A., B.S.M.E., B.S.Min.E., B.S.N., B.S.P.Ed., B.S.P.N.G.E., B.S.R., and B.S.W. degrees. Master's and doctoral degrees are also awarded. Bachelor's degrees are awarded in AGRICULTURE (agricultural business management, agriculture, agronomy, animal science, fish and game management, fishing and fisheries, forestry and related sciences, horticulture, natural resource management, and plant science), BIOLOGICAL SCIENCE (biology/biological science and nutrition), BUSINESS (accounting, banking and finance, business administration and management, fashion merchandising, marketing and distribution, recreation and leisure services, sports management, and tourism), COMMUNICATIONS AND THE ARTS (advertising, art, broadcasting, communications, dramatic arts, English, journalism, music, public relations, speech/debate/rhetoric, and visual and performing arts), COMPUTER AND PHYSICAL SCIENCE (chemistry, computer science, geology, geoscience, mathematics, physics, and science), EDUCATION (agricultural, athletic training, English, environmental, foreign languages, mathematics, and physical), ENGINEERING AND ENVIRONMENTAL DESIGN (aeronautical engineering, aerospace studies, chemical engineering, civil engineering, computer engineering, electrical/electronics engineering, engineering, environmental science, interior design, landscape architecture/design, mechanical engineering, mining and mineral engineering, petroleum/natural gas engineering, and systems engineering), HEALTH PROFESSIONS (dental hygiene, medical technology, nursing, occupational therapy, pharmacy, physical therapy, speech pathology/audiology, and veterinary science), SOCIAL SCIENCE (anthropology, child care/child and family studies, economics, family/consumer resource management, geography, history, interdisciplinary studies, international studies, liberal arts/general studies, parks and recreation management, philosophy, political science/government, psychology, social work, and sociology). Engineering and mineral resources, psychology, and political science are the strongest academically. Business and economics, engineering and mineral resources, and health sciences are the largest.

Required: All students are required to take 12 credit hours in each of 3 areas: humanities and fine arts, social and behavioral sciences, and natural sciences and math. The 36 credit hours must include international/minority/gender studies, math, composition, and an advanced course emphasizing writing skills. A minimum 2.0 GPA and at least 128 credit hours are required to graduate.

Special: A co-op program in engineering and cross-registration with schools in the Southern Regional Education Board through the Academic Common Market are possible. Internships, study abroad in 23 countries, a Washington semester, student-designed majors, dual majors in business and foreign languages, and B.A.-B.S. degrees in economics, chemistry, physics, biology, math, psychology, and geology are available. A liberal studies degree, credit by exam, credit for life experience, nondegree study, and pass/fail options are also offered. There are 27 national honor societies, including Phi Beta Kappa, and a freshman honors program.

Faculty/Classroom: 63% of faculty are male; 37%, female. Graduate students teach 4% of introductory courses. The average class size in a regular course is 34.

Admissions: 92% of the 2005-2006 applicants were accepted. The SAT scores for the 2005-2006 freshman class were: Verbal--41% below 500, 45% between 500 and 599, 12% between 600 and 700, and 2% above 700; Math--33% below 500, 46% between 500 and 599, 18% between 600 and 700, and 3% above 700. The ACT scores were 26% below 21, 30% between 21 and 23, 25% between 24 and 26, 10% between 27 and 28, and 9% above 28.

Requirements: A satisfactory score on the SAT or ACT is required. In addition, in-state students need a minimum high school GPA of 2.0. Out-of-state students need a minimum high school GPA of 2.25. Applicants should graduate from an accredited school no sooner than their junior year, after completing 4 years of English, 3 of social studies including U.S. history, 3 of math, and 2 each of lab sciences and foreign language. 1 year of typing is recommended. Music students must audition, and art applicants must submit a portfolio. AP and CLEP credits are accepted. Important factors in the admissions decision are leadership record, evidence of special talent, and advanced placement or honor courses.

Procedure: Freshmen are admitted fall, spring, and summer. Entrance exams should be taken by spring of the junior year. There are early admissions and deferred admissions plans. Applications should be filed by August 1 for fall entry, along with a $25 fee. Notification is sent on a rolling basis. Applications are accepted on-line.

Transfer: 897 transfer students enrolled in 2004-2005. A minimum college GPA of 2.0 is required of transfers; all applicants must submit college transcripts. Students having fewer than 29 transferable credit hours are subject to freshman admission criteria and must submit SAT or ACT scores and high school transcripts. 30 of 128 credits required for the bachelor's degree must be completed at WVU.

Visiting: There are regularly scheduled orientations for prospective students, including 2-day sessions with campus tours, placement testing, academic and advisement meetings, parent/student orientation discussions, and transitional meetings. There are guides for informal visits and visitors may sit in on classes. To schedule a visit, contact the Visitors Resource Center at (304) 293-3489 or visitwvu@mail.wvu.edu.

Financial Aid: WVU is a member of CSS. The FAFSA is required. The deadline for filing freshman financial aid applications for fall entry is March 1.

International Students: There are 292 international students enrolled. They must take the written TOEFL. International students serving as graduate teaching assistants must also demonstrate mastery of spoken English.

Computers: All students may access the system 24 hours a day, 7 days a week. There are no time limits and no fees. It is strongly recommended that all students have a personal computer.

Graduates: From July 1, 2004 to June 30, 2005, 3157 bachelor's degrees were awarded. The most popular majors were business/marketing (12%), liberal arts (11%), and communication/journalism (10%). In an average class, 27% graduate in 4 years or less, 49% graduate in 5 years or less, and 56% graduate in 6 years or less.

Admissions Contact: Chen Khoo, Director of Admissions and Records. E-mail: wvuadmissions@arc.wvu.edu Web: www.arc.wvu.edu

WEST VIRGINIA UNIVERSITY INSTITUTE OF TECHNOLOGY

B-4

Montgomery, WV 25136

(304) 442-3167
(888) 554-TECH; Fax: (304) 442-3097

Full-time: 1100 men, 590 women	Faculty: 120; IIB, --$
Part-time: 400 men, 310 women	Ph.D.s: 52%
Graduate: 20 men, 5 women	Student/Faculty: 14 to 1
Year: semesters, summer session	Tuition: $4078 ($10416)
Application Deadline: see profile	Room & Board: $4710
Freshman Class: n/av	
SAT or ACT: required	NONCOMPETITIVE

West Virginia University Institute of Technology, part of the Western Virginia University system and founded in 1895, is a public institution offering programs in business and economics, arts and sciences, community and technical fields, and engineering. There are 3 undergraduate schools and 1 graduate school. Figures in the above capsule and in this profile are approximate. In addition to regional accreditation, West Virginia Tech has baccalaureate program accreditation with ABET, ADA, and NLN. The library contains 166,967 volumes and 438,232 microform items, and subscribes to 510 periodicals including electronic. Computerized library services include the card catalog, interlibrary loans, and database searching. Special learning facilities include a learning resource center and art gallery. The 112-acre campus is in a small town 28 miles southeast of Charleston. Including any residence halls, there are 15 buildings.

Student Life: 91% of undergraduates are from West Virginia. Others are from 25 states, 24 foreign countries, and Canada. 95% are from public schools. 87% are white. The average age of freshmen is 19; all undergraduates, 24. 35% do not continue beyond their first year; 40% remain to graduate.

Housing: 776 students can be accommodated in college housing, which includes single-sex and coed dorms. On-campus housing is guaranteed for all 4 years. 69% of students commute. All students may keep cars.

Activities: 10% of men belong to 5 national fraternities; 8% of women belong to 2 national sororities. There are 42 groups on campus, including art, band, cheerleading, choir, chorus, computers, drama, drill team, ethnic, international, jazz band, marching band, newspaper, pep band, photography, political, professional, religious, social, student government, and yearbook. Popular campus events include comedy and film series, Black History Month, and Greek Week.

Sports: There are 5 intercollegiate sports for men and 4 for women, and 8 intramural sports for men and 8 for women. Facilities include 2 gyms, a weight room, tennis and handball courts, a student union, a football field and 3000-seat stadium, an Olympic-size swimming pool, game rooms, and a fitness center.

Disabled Students: 60% of the campus is accessible. Wheelchair ramps, elevators, special parking, specially equipped rest rooms, special class scheduling, and lowered drinking fountains are available.

Services: Counseling and information services are available, as is tutoring in most subjects. There is remedial math, reading, and writing and a math learning center.

Campus Safety and Security: Measures include 24-hour foot and vehicle patrol, self-defense education, security escort services, and informal discussions. There are pamphlets/posters/films and lighted pathways/sidewalks.

Programs of Study: West Virginia Tech confers B.A., B.S., B.E.T., B.M.E.T., B.S.C.E., B.S.E., and B.S.E.E. degrees. Associate and master's degrees are also awarded. Bachelor's degrees are awarded in BIOLOGICAL SCIENCE (biology/biological science), BUSINESS (accounting and business administration and management), COMPUTER AND PHYSICAL SCIENCE (chemistry, computer programming, computer science, and physics), ENGINEERING AND ENVIRONMENTAL DESIGN (chemical engineering, civil engineering, electrical/electronics engineering, electrical/electronics engineering technology, engineering technology, industrial administration/management, industrial engineering technology, and mechanical engineering), HEALTH PROFESSIONS (health care administration and nursing), SOCIAL SCIENCE (history and public administration). Engineering is the strongest academically. Nursing is the largest.

Required: Core curriculum requirements include 8 hours of lab science, 6 to 12 each of humanities and social science, 6 each of English and math/computer science, and 2 of phys ed and health. Other requirements vary according to the degree sought. To graduate, students must complete 128 semester hours with a minimum 2.0 GPA overall and in the major.

Special: An extensive co-op program is offered in all areas as well as a number of internships in public service and industrial relations. Credit for armed service experience and credit by departmental exam are available.

Faculty/Classroom: 70% of faculty are male; 30%, female. All teach undergraduates and 10% do research. No introductory courses are taught by graduate students. The average class size in an introductory lecture is 30; in a laboratory, 15; and in a regular course, 20.

Requirements: A satisfactory score on the SAT or ACT is required . Higher minimum composite scores are required for engineering and health majors. Applicants should be graduates from an accredited secondary school or have qualifying scores on the GED. Students must have completed 4 units of English, 3 of social studies, and 2 each of math (4 for engineering majors) and lab science. A GPA of 2.0 is required. AP and CLEP credits are accepted.

Procedure: Freshmen are admitted to all sessions. Entrance exams should be taken in sufficient time for the scores to reach the Institute by the application deadline. There is an early admissions plan and rolling admissions plan. Applications are accepted on-line. Check with the school for current application deadlines. The college accepts all in-state residents. Notification is sent on a rolling basis.

Transfer: Criteria for transfer admission vary according to the college. 30 of 128 credits required for the bachelor's degree must be completed at West Virginia Tech.

Visiting: There are regularly scheduled orientations for prospective students. There are guides for informal visits and visitors may sit in on classes and stay overnight. To schedule a visit, contact the Admissions Office.

Financial Aid: West Virginia Tech is a member of CSS. The FAFSA and the college's own financial statement are required. Check with the school for current deadlines.

International Students: The school actively recruits these students. They must achieve a satisfactory score on the TOEFL and also take the SAT or the ACT.

Computers: All students may access the system 24 hours a day. There are no time limits and no fees. It is strongly recommended that all students have a personal computer.

Admissions Contact: Director of Admissions. A video is available. E-mail: admissions@wvutech.edu Web: www.wvutech.edu

WEST VIRGINIA WESLEYAN COLLEGE   C-3
Buckhannon, WV 26201   (304) 473-8510
                                          (800) 722-9933; Fax: (304) 473-8108

Full-time: 595 men, 702 women	**Faculty:** 78; IIB, --$
Part-time: 13 men, 14 women	**Ph.D.s:** 77%
Graduate: 16 men, 26 women	**Student/Faculty:** 17 to 1
Year: semesters, summer session	**Tuition:** $21,330
Application Deadline: August 1	**Room & Board:** $5550
Freshman Class: 1272 applied, 984 accepted, 369 enrolled	
SAT Verbal/Math: 512/510*	**ACT:** 23 COMPETITIVE

West Virginia Wesleyan College, founded in 1890, is an independent liberal and applied arts college affiliated with the United Methodist Church. In addition to regional accreditation, WVWC has baccalaureate program accreditation with CAAHEP, IACBE, NCATE, and NLN. The library contains 116,240 volumes, 39,119 microform items, and 6322 audio/video tapes/CDs/DVDs, and subscribes to 14,126 periodicals including electronic. Computerized library services include the card catalog, interlibrary loans, database searching, Internet access, and laptop Internet portals. Special learning facilities include a learning resource center, art gallery, planetarium, and radio station. The 80-acre campus is in a small town in the Appalachian foothills, 135 miles south of Pittsburgh, Pennsylvania. Including any residence halls, there are 23 buildings.

Student Life: 53% of undergraduates are from West Virginia. Students are from 37 states, 12 foreign countries, and Canada. 85% are from public schools. 88% are white. 53% are Protestant; 20% Catholic. The average age of freshmen is 18; all undergraduates, 21.

Housing: 1275 students can be accommodated in college housing, which includes single-sex and coed dorms and on-campus apartments. In addition, there are honors houses, quiet study living areas, and substance-free small group living units. On-campus housing is guaranteed for all 4 years. 83% of students live on campus; of those, 65% remain on campus on weekends. Alcohol is not permitted. All students may keep cars.

Activities: 25% of men belong to 5 national fraternities; 25% of women belong to 5 national sororities. There are 75 groups on campus, including art, band, cheerleading, choir, chorale, chorus, computers, dance, drama, ethnic, forensics, honors, international, jazz band, literary magazine, musical theater, newspaper, political, professional, radio and TV, religious, social, social service, student government, and yearbook. Popular campus events include Founders Day, Festivals of Lessons and Carols, and Spring Sing.

Sports: There are 9 intercollegiate sports for men and 8 for women, and 9 intramural sports for men and 8 for women. Facilities include baseball and football fields with seating for 3500, as well as a phys ed center with a 3800-seat intercollegiate basketball court, 2 intramural practice courts, 4 handball courts, an auxiliary gym, indoor tennis courts, volleyball courts, golf and wrestling practice areas, sauna baths, a dance studio, and gymnastics and weight rooms. A state park is near the campus.

Disabled Students: 75% of the campus is accessible. Wheelchair ramps, elevators, special parking, specially equipped rest rooms, special class scheduling, and lowered drinking fountains are available.

Services: Counseling and information services are available, as is tutoring in every subject. There is a reader service for the blind, and remedial math, reading, and writing.

Campus Safety and Security: Measures include 24-hour foot and vehicle patrol, self-defense education, security escort services, and informal discussions. There are pamphlets/posters/films, emergency telephones, lighted pathways/sidewalks, rape awareness educational programs, and appropriate training for residence hall staff.

Programs of Study: WVWC confers B.A., B.S., B.M.E., and B.S.N. degrees. Master's degrees are also awarded. Bachelor's degrees are awarded in BIOLOGICAL SCIENCE (biology/biological science and nutrition), BUSINESS (accounting, business administration and management, and marketing/retailing/merchandising), COMMUNICATIONS AND THE ARTS (dramatic arts, English, music, public relations, and speech/debate/rhetoric), COMPUTER AND PHYSICAL SCIENCE (chemistry, computer science, mathematics, and physics), EDUCATION (art, elementary, music, physical, and secondary), ENGINEERING AND ENVIRONMENTAL DESIGN (engineering physics), HEALTH PROFESSIONS (nursing), SOCIAL SCIENCE (economics, history, international studies, philosophy, political science/government, psychology, religion, religious education, social science, and sociology). Physical and natural sciences and accounting are the strongest academically. Business, biology, and education are the largest.

Required: To graduate, students must earn 120 semester hours with a minimum GPA of 2.0; 24 to 51 hours must be in the major, 48 to 53 in general studies. Required disciplines are cultural studies, natural science and math, social sciences, health and phys ed, religion, philosophy, humanities and fine arts, and communications.

Special: WVWC offers cross-registration with the Mountain State Association of Colleges. Students may participate in a wide variety of internships, including a Washington center internship and work-study and

study-abroad programs; there are exchange agreements in Korea, the People's Republic of China, Norway, and Bulgaria. Nondegree and pass/fail study, dual, student-designed, and contract majors, and credit for life, military, and work experience are available. A 3-2 engineering degree is offered with West Virginia University and the University of Virginia. There is 1 national honor society and a freshman honors program.

Faculty/Classroom: 79% of faculty are male; 21%, female. All teach undergraduates. No introductory courses are taught by graduate students. The average class size in an introductory lecture is 24; in a laboratory, 12; and in a regular course, 21.

Admissions: 77% of the 2005-2006 applicants were accepted. The SAT scores for the 2005-2006 freshman class were: Verbal--26% below 500, 26% between 500 and 599, and 10% between 600 and 700; Math--25% below 500, 25% between 500 and 599, and 11% between 600 and 700. The ACT scores were 18% below 21, 19% between 21 and 23, 16% between 24 and 26, 6% between 27 and 28, and 4% above 28. 10 freshmen graduated first in their class.

Requirements: The SAT or ACT is required, a satisfactory score is needed on the SAT or on the ACT. In addition, applicants must be high school graduates, or hold a GED. Students should have earned 26 academic credits, consisting of 4 in English, 3 each in math, science, and academic electives, and 2 each in foreign language, lab science, and social studies, as well as a total of 7 academic credits in fine arts, technology education, health, and phys ed. An essay and an interview are recommended. A GPA of 2.2 is required. AP and CLEP credits are accepted. Important factors in the admissions decision are extracurricular activities record, recommendations by school officials, and leadership record.

Procedure: Freshmen are admitted fall and spring. Entrance exams should be taken in fall of the senior year or spring/summer of the junior year. There are early decision, deferred admissions, and rolling admissions plans. Early decision applications should be filed by December 1; regular applications, by August 1 for fall entry and January 10 for spring entry, along with a $35 fee. Notification is sent on a rolling basis. Applications are accepted on-line.

Transfer: 34 transfer students enrolled in 2004-2005. Transfer applicants must supply a high school transcript if their GPA for college work is less than 2.5. An associate degree and an interview are recommended. 30 of 120 credits required for the bachelor's degree must be completed at WVWC.

Visiting: There are regularly scheduled orientations for prospective students. There are guides for informal visits and visitors may sit in on classes and stay overnight. To schedule a visit, contact Director of Admission at 304-473-8510.

Financial Aid: In 2005-2006, 98% of all full-time students received some form of financial aid. 77% of full-time freshmen and 75% of continuing full-time students received need-based aid. The average freshman award was $21,700. 41% of undergraduates work part time. Average annual earnings from campus work are $1000. The average financial indebtedness of the 2005 graduate was $18,000. The FAFSA is required. The deadline for filing freshman financial aid applications for fall entry is March 1.

International Students: The school actively recruits these students. They must score satisfactorily on the written TOEFL.

Computers: Wireless access is available. All students may access the system. There are no time limits and no fees. All students are required to have personal computers; using Windows 2000 and a Pentium processor.

Graduates: From July 1, 2004 to June 30, 2005, 303 bachelor's degrees were awarded. The most popular majors were business (14%), elementary education (12%), and biology (8%). In an average class, 1% graduate in 3 years or less, 44% graduate in 4 years or less, 52% graduate in 5 years or less, and 55% graduate in 6 years or less.

Admissions Contact: Director of Admission. A video is available.
E-mail: *admissions@wvwc.edu* Web: *www.wvwc.edu*

WHEELING JESUIT UNIVERSITY   C-2
Wheeling, WV 26003   (304) 243-2359
                                          (800) 624-6992; Fax: (304) 243-2397

Full-time: 446 men, 602 women	**Faculty:** 75; IIB, --$
Part-time: 53 men, 117 women	**Ph.D.s:** 74%
Graduate: 70 men, 178 women	**Student/Faculty:** 14 to 1
Year: semesters, summer session	**Tuition:** $21,000
Application Deadline: open	**Room & Board:** $5910
Freshman Class: 853 accepted, 285 enrolled	
SAT Verbal/Math: 520/500*	**ACT:** 21 COMPETITIVE

Wheeling Jesuit College, founded in 1954, is an independent college affiliated with the Society of Jesus, offering undergraduate programs in the liberal arts and sciences, nursing, allied health, and business, and graduate programs in business administration and applied theology. Some information in this profile is approximate. In addition to regional accreditation, Wheeling Jesuit has baccalaureate program accreditation with CAHEA and NLN. The library contains 155,953 volumes, 120,278 microform items, and 1200 audio/video tapes/CDs/DVDs, and subscribes to 504 periodicals including electronic. Computerized library services include the card catalog and database searching. Special learning facilities include a learning resource center. The 70-acre campus is in a suburban area 60 miles southwest of Pittsburgh. Including any residence halls, there are 15 buildings.

Student Life: 66% of undergraduates are from out of state, mostly the Middle Atlantic. Students are from 31 states, 28 foreign countries, and Canada. 90% are white. 57% are Catholic; 33% Protestant. The average age of freshmen is 18; all undergraduates, 24. 28% do not continue beyond their first year; 62% remain to graduate.

Housing: 764 students can be accommodated in college housing, which includes single-sex dorms. On-campus housing is guaranteed for all 4 years. 78% of students live on campus; of those, 75% remain on campus on weekends. All students may keep cars.

Activities: There are no fraternities or sororities. There are 20 groups on campus, including cheerleading, choir, chorus, drama, honors, international, literary magazine, newspaper, pep band, professional, religious, social, social service, student government, and yearbook. Popular campus events include Week of the Person, Day of Diversity, and Coffee House.

Sports: There are 8 intercollegiate sports for men and 8 for women, and 7 intramural sports for men and 7 for women. Facilities include a recreation center with a swimming pool, 2 gyms, 2 racquetball courts, complete Nautilus equipment, an indoor jogging track, 3 fields, and game rooms.

Disabled Students: 80% of the campus is accessible. Wheelchair ramps, elevators, special parking, specially equipped rest rooms, lowered drinking fountains, and lowered telephones are available.

Services: Counseling and information services are available, as is tutoring in most subjects. There is a reader service for the blind, and remedial math, reading, and writing.

Campus Safety and Security: Measures include 24-hour foot and vehicle patrol, self-defense education, informal discussions, and pamphlets/posters/films. There are lighted pathways/sidewalks and a student intern campus patrol.

Programs of Study: Wheeling Jesuit confers B.A., B.S., and B.S.N. degrees. Master's degrees are also awarded. Bachelor's degrees are awarded in BIOLOGICAL SCIENCE (biology/biological science), BUSINESS (accounting, international business management, management science, and marketing/retailing/merchandising), COMMUNICATIONS AND THE ARTS (English, French, romance languages and literature, Spanish, and technical and business writing), COMPUTER AND PHYSICAL SCIENCE (chemistry, computer science, mathematics, physics, and science), HEALTH PROFESSIONS (nuclear medical technology, nursing, and respiratory therapy), SOCIAL SCIENCE (criminal justice, ethics, politics, and social policy, history, international studies, philosophy, political science/government, psychology, and religion). Psychology, nursing, and biology are the largest.

Required: To graduate, students must complete 120 credit hours, with a GPA of 2.0. The core curriculum consists of 58 credits in English composition, math, modern languages, literature, history, social science, natural science, philosophy, theology, and 1 course in either ethics or Christian morality, as well as 1 additional math or science course. Students are also required to complete 2 units of each of the dimensions of the school's Wellness Program.

Special: The university offers internships with many businesses and institutions, as well as a Washington semester and study abroad. Students may obtain an advanced degree in business administration, as well as a 3-2 engineering degree with Case Western Reserve University. The school permits dual and student-designed majors. Credit for life, military, and work experience may be granted to adult students. Pass/fail options are open in some courses. There are 17 national honor societies, a freshman honors program, and 12 departmental honors programs.

Faculty/Classroom: 53% of faculty are male; 47%, female. All both teach and do research. The average class size in an introductory lecture is 21; in a laboratory, 12; and in a regular course, 14.

Admissions: The SAT scores for the 2005-2006 freshman class were: Verbal--41% below 500, 41% between 500 and 599, 14% between 600 and 700, and 4% above 700; Math--46% below 500, 34% between 500 and 599, 19% between 600 and 700, and 1% above 700. The ACT scores were 41% below 21, 27% between 21 and 23, 22% between 24 and 26, 5% between 27 and 28, and 5% above 28. 41% of the current freshmen were in the top fifth of their class; 73% were in the top two fifths.

Requirements: The SAT or ACT is required, with a satisfactory composite score on the SAT or on the ACT. In addition, applicants must be high school graduates or hold a GED. Students should have earned 15 academic credits, consisting of 4 in English, 2 each in math and history or social science, 1 in lab science (2 are recommended for science majors), and 6 in academic electives, with a foreign language recommended. Students entering programs in the natural sciences should have taken 1 course each of chemistry and biology. Exceptions are made, especially if the high school GPA is 3.0 or better. An interview is recommended. Wheeling Jesuit requires applicants to be in the upper 90% of their class. A GPA of 2.0 is required. AP and CLEP credits are accepted. Important factors in the admissions decision are leadership record, recommendations by school officials, and extracurricular activities record.

Procedure: Freshmen are admitted to all sessions. There are early admissions, deferred admissions and rolling admissions plans. Application deadlines are open. Application fee is $25. Applications are accepted on-line.

Transfer: 51 transfer students enrolled in 2004-2005. Applicants must have a GPA of 2.0 for college work, or supply high school transcripts if entering at the freshman level. The SAT or ACT is required if the student has less than 1 year of college work; otherwise, it is still recommended, as is an interview. Transfer students must take placement tests given by the university. 30 of 120 credits required for the bachelor's degree must be completed at Wheeling Jesuit.

Visiting: There are regularly scheduled orientations for prospective students, including meetings with faculty, discussions by students and parents, meals, and campus tours. There are guides for informal visits and visitors may sit in on classes and stay overnight. To schedule a visit, contact the Campus Visit Coordinator.

Financial Aid: In 2005-2006, 83% of all full-time freshmen and 78% of continuing full-time students received some form of financial aid. 72% of full-time freshmen and 58% of continuing full-time students received need-based aid. The average freshman award was $19,947. Need-based scholarships or need-based grants averaged $7200 ($14,483 maximum); need-based self-help aid (loans and jobs) averaged $3208 ($6175 maximum); and non-need-based athletic scholarships averaged $2222 ($12,060 maximum). The FAFSA is required. Check with the school for current application deadlines.

International Students: The school actively recruits these students. They must score satisfactorily on the written TOEFL.

Computers: All students may access the system every day, for a total 85 hours per week and in 1 lab 24 hours a day, 7 days a week.

Admissions Contact: Carol Descak, Dean of Admissions. A video is available. E-mail: *admiss@wju.edu* Web: *www.wju.edu*

WISCONSIN

POPULATION
DENSITY
● 25,000 and over

0 20 40 60 80 100
Miles

ALVERNO COLLEGE

E-4

Milwaukee, WI 53234-3922

(414) 382-6100
(800) 933-3401; Fax: (414) 382-6354

Full-time: 1515 women	**Faculty:** 104; IIB, --$
Part-time: 12 men, 649 women	**Ph.D.s:** 89%
Graduate: 30 men, 166 women	**Student/Faculty:** 23 to 1
Year: semesters, summer session	**Tuition:** $15,418
Application Deadline: open	**Room & Board:** $5670

Freshman Class: 789 applied, 438 accepted, 255 enrolled

SAT or ACT: required

COMPETITIVE

Alverno College is an independent, four-year liberal arts college for women affiliated with the Roman Catholic Church . Alverno is dedicated to the personal and professional development of women through a practical, interactive learning environment. There are 7 undergraduate and 2 graduate schools. In addition to regional accreditation, Alverno has baccalaureate program accreditation with CCNE, NASM, and NCATE. The library contains 91,723 volumes, 261,484 microform items, and 14,413 audio/video tapes/CDs/DVDs, and subscribes to 2487 periodicals including electronic. Computerized library services include the card catalog, interlibrary loans, database searching, Internet access, and laptop Internet portals. Special learning facilities include a learning resource center and TV studio, art and culture gallery, nursing skills lab, student-centered multimedia production facility, computer center, science labs, theater venue, and conferencing center. The 46-acre campus is in an urban area on the southwest edge of Milwaukee. Including any residence halls, there are 10 buildings.

Student Life: 97% of undergraduates are from Wisconsin. Others are from 10 states and 12 foreign countries. 63% are white; 20% African American; 11% Hispanic. 33% are Catholic; 32% Protestant; 24% claim no religious affiliation. The average age of freshmen is 19; all undergraduates, 26. 24% do not continue beyond their first year; 63% remain to graduate.

Housing: 220 students can be accommodated in college housing, which includes dorms. On-campus housing is guaranteed for all 4 years. 87% of students commute. All students may keep cars.

Activities: 11% of women belong to 3 local sororities. There are 35 groups on campus, including art, choir, chorus, Circle K, dance, drama, ethnic, honors, international, literary magazine, newspaper, orchestra,

political, professional, PSE, religious, SIFE, social, and social service. Popular campus events include Career Day, fine arts performances, and interdenominational religious services.

Sports: Facilities include a gym with regulation intercollegiate volleyball and basketball courts, a fitness center with state-of-the-art free motion fitness and cardio equipment, an outdoor volleyball court, and a multipurpose room for dancing, aerobics, and cardio kickboxing.

Disabled Students: 95% of the campus is accessible. Wheelchair ramps, elevators, special parking, specially equipped rest rooms, lowered drinking fountains, lowered telephones, and pushbuttons to open exterior doors are available.

Services: Counseling and information services are available, as is tutoring in most subjects. There is remedial math, reading, and writing. There are selected workshops for such issues as writing anxiety, time management, note taking, speaking anxiety, documenting work, stategies for doing research papers, Internet introduction, and math EXCEL.

Campus Safety and Security: Measures include 24-hour foot and vehicle patrol, security escort services, informal discussions, and pamphlets/posters/films. There are emergency telephones, lighted pathways/sidewalks, electronically operated and video-surveillanced dorm entrances, walkways, and buildings, a security staff equipped with 2-way radios, pagers, and cell phones, and motion detector and audible alarms in buildings.

Programs of Study: Alverno confers B.A., B.S., B.M., B.S.Ed., and B.S.N. degrees. Associate and master's degrees are also awarded. Bachelor's degrees are awarded in BIOLOGICAL SCIENCE (biology/biological science and molecular biology), BUSINESS (business administration and management and international business management), COMMUNICATIONS AND THE ARTS (art, communications, communications technology, English, music, and visual and performing arts), COMPUTER AND PHYSICAL SCIENCE (chemistry, computer science, information sciences and systems, mathematics, physical sciences, and science), EDUCATION (art, elementary, middle school, science, and secondary), ENGINEERING AND ENVIRONMENTAL DESIGN (environmental science), HEALTH PROFESSIONS (art therapy, music therapy, and nursing), SOCIAL SCIENCE (child psychology/development, community services, history, international relations, philosophy, psychology, religion, and social science). Nursing, elementary education, and psychology are the largest.

Required: Students must complete a learning program that integrates accomplishment in required areas of knowledge, with the achievement of required competence levels in the following 8 core abilities: communication, analysis, problem solving, valuing in decision making, social interaction, developing a global perspective, effective citizenship, and aesthetic engagement. This is accomplished through general education courses in history, English, philosophy, religious studies, arts, sciences, math, psychology, and social science; through completion of a major and minor area of study; and completion of at least 1 required internship or practice.

Special: Alverno offers internships, dual majors, nondegree study, and pre professional programs in dentistry, law, medicine, pharmacy, physician's assistant, and veterinary medicine. Alverno offers study abroad in 16 countries and also offers courses that include an international travel component. Alverno can arrange other programs through a worldwide consortium of facilities. The school's interactive curriculum is outcome oriented and performance based; letter grades are not assigned. There are 3 national honor societies.

Faculty/Classroom: 25% of faculty are male; 75%, female. All both teach and do research. No introductory courses are taught by graduate students. The average class size in a regular course is 25.

Admissions: 56% of the 2005-2006 applicants were accepted. The ACT scores for the 2005-2006 freshman class were: 62% below 21, 22% between 21 and 23, 10% between 24 and 26, 5% between 27 and 28, and 1% above 28.

Requirements: The ACT or SAT is required. In addition, applicants must be graduates of an accredited secondary school, having completed 17 academic credits with college preparatory courses. The GED is accepted. A GPA of 2.5 is required. AP and CLEP credits are accepted.

Procedure: Freshmen are admitted fall and spring. Entrance exams should be taken as early as possible. There is a deferred admissions plan. Applications should be filed by August 1 for fall entry. December 1 for spring. Application fee is $20. Notification is sent on a rolling basis. Applications are accepted on-line.

Transfer: 157 transfer students enrolled in 2004-2005. Applicants should have a minimum college GPA of 2.0 and must submit transcripts from all schools previously attended. The number of credits that must be completed at Alverno varies by program.

Visiting: There are regularly scheduled orientations for prospective students, consisting of open houses and overnight events that include tours of the campus, classroom visits, and meetings with faculty and current students. There are guides for informal visits. To schedule a visit, contact the Admissions Office at *admissions@alverno.edu*.

Financial Aid: In 2005-2006, 83% of continuing full-time students received some form of financial aid. 87% of full-time freshmen and 81% of continuing full-time students received need-based aid. The average freshman award was $14,333. 38% of undergraduates work part time. Average annual earnings from campus work are $2500. Alverno is a member of CSS. The FAFSA and the college's own financial statement are required. The priority date for freshman financial aid applications for fall entry is April 15.

International Students: There were 13 international students enrolled in a recent year. The school actively recruits these students. They must score satisfactorily on the written TOEFL or on the electronic version or take the IELTS.

Computers: The college has more than 450 desktop and notebook computers available for student use in a variety of locations (computer labs, computer classrooms, discipline-specific labs, and residence hall labs). The entire campus is networked and Internet access is available in all locations. Wireless access is available in the library, the student cafeteria/commons, and the student coffeehouse. All students may access the system. There are no time limits and no fees.

Graduates: From July 1, 2004 to June 30, 2005, 234 bachelor's degrees were awarded. The most popular majors were nursing (23%), elementary education (13%), and psychology (10%). In an average class, 35% graduate in 4 years or less, 42% graduate in 5 years or less, and 47% graduate in 6 years or less. 48 companies recruited on campus in 2004-2005. Of the 2004 graduating class, 17% were enrolled in graduate school within 6 months of graduation and 90% were employed.

Admissions Contact: Mary Kay Farrell, Director of Admissions. A video is available. E-mail: *admissions@alverno.edu*
Web: *www.alverno.edu*

BELOIT COLLEGE
D-5

Beloit, WI 53511-5595

(608) 363-2500
(800) 9-BELOIT; Fax: (608) 363-2075

Full-time: 551 men, 779 women	Faculty: 103; IIB, av$
Part-time: 20 men, 35 women	Ph.D.s: 95%
Graduate: none	Student/Faculty: 13 to 1
Year: semesters	Tuition: $26,884
Application Deadline: January 15	Room & Board: $5924
Freshman Class: 2054 applied, 1324 accepted, 326 enrolled	
SAT Verbal/Math: 640/620*	ACT: 27 HIGHLY COMPETITIVE

Beloit College, founded in 1846, is a private liberal arts institution. The library contains 253,279 volumes, 140,965 microform items, and 7315 audio/video tapes/CDs/DVDs, and subscribes to 1666 periodicals including electronic. Computerized library services include the card catalog, interlibrary loans, database searching, and Internet access. Special learning facilities include a learning resource center, art gallery, natural history museum, planetarium, radio station, TV station, and , comprehensive language lab, observatory, and theater complex. The 40-acre campus is in a small town 50 miles south of Madison, Wisconsin. Including any residence halls, there are 54 buildings.

Student Life: 83% of undergraduates are from out of state, mostly the Midwest. Others are from 48 states, 41 foreign countries, and Canada. 78% are from public schools. 84% are white. The average age of freshmen is 18; all undergraduates, 20. 11% do not continue beyond their first year; 72% remain to graduate.

Housing: 1180 students can be accommodated in college housing, which includes single-sex and coed dorms on-campus apartments, fraternity houses, and sorority houses. In addition, there are language houses and special-interest houses. On-campus housing is guaranteed for all 4 years. 93% of students live on campus; of those, 95% remain on campus on weekends. All students may keep cars.

Activities: 15% of men belong to 3 national fraternities; 5% of women belong to 2 local and 1 national sorority. There are 90 groups on campus, including art, band, cheerleading, chess, choir, chorus, computers, dance, drama, ethnic, film, gay, honors, international, jazz band, literary magazine, musical theater, newspaper, orchestra, pep band, photography, political, professional, radio and TV, religious, science fiction, social, social service, student government, symphony, women's and yearbook. Popular campus events include Great Lecture Series, Folk and Blues Weekend, and Spring Day.

Sports: There are 10 intercollegiate sports for men and 10 for women, and 15 intramural sports for men and 13 for women. Facilities include a sports center, that houses a 2250-seat arena for basketball and volleyball, racquetball/handball courts, a dance studio, a fitness center, and a natatorium; a field house that contains a running track, an indoor soccer area, batting/pitching cage, and space for indoor tennis; a 3500-seat football stadium; outdoor playing fields; 6 all-weather tennis court and a stadium that hosts football, soccer, track and field. There are facilities nearby for sailing, ice skating, and other recreation.

Disabled Students: 35% of the campus is accessible. Wheelchair ramps, elevators, special parking, specially equipped rest rooms, special

class scheduling, lowered drinking fountains, and lowered telephones are available.

Services: Counseling and information services are available, as is tutoring in most subjects, including most introductory and some advanced courses.

Campus Safety and Security: Measures include 24-hour foot and vehicle patrol, security escort services, informal discussions, and pamphlets/posters/films. There are emergency telephones and lighted pathways/sidewalks.

Programs of Study: Beloit confers B.A. and B.S. degrees. Bachelor's degrees are awarded in BIOLOGICAL SCIENCE (biochemistry, biology/ biological science, cell biology, ecology, and environmental biology), BUSINESS (business administration and management), COMMUNICATIONS AND THE ARTS (art history and appreciation, classical languages, comparative literature, creative writing, dramatic arts, East Asian languages and literature, English, French, German, literature, modern language, music, Russian, Spanish, speech/debate/rhetoric, and studio art), COMPUTER AND PHYSICAL SCIENCE (applied physics, chemistry, computer science, geology, mathematics, and physics), EDUCATION (art, and education), ENGINEERING AND ENVIRONMENTAL DESIGN (environmental science), HEALTH PROFESSIONS (predentistry, premedicine, and preveterinary science), SOCIAL SCIENCE (anthropology, classical/ancient civilization, economics, history, interdisciplinary studies, international relations, philosophy, political science/ government, prelaw, psychology, religion, sociology, and women's studies). Anthropology, English, and geology are the strongest academically. Anthropology, biology, and English are the largest.

Required: To graduate, students must complete 31 units, including 8 to 15 in the major, with a minimum GPA of 2.0. Distribution requirements include 2 courses each from natural sciences and math, social sciences, and arts and humanities. Writing and interdisciplinary course work is also required. Degree expectations include international and experiential learning components, as well as a comprehensive academic plan.

Special: Beloit offers cross-registration with the University of Wisconsin/ Madison, internships, study abroad in more than 29 countries, and a Washington semester. Dual majors, student-designed and interdisciplinary majors, and nondegree study are available. Students may take a 2-2 nursing program and a 3-2 medical technology program with Rush University. A 3-2 engineering degree is offered with 9 institutions, and co-op programs are available in social services, forestry and environmental management, engineering, nursing, medical technology, and business administration. An intensive summer language program is offered in Chinese, Japanese, Hungarian, and Russian. There are 6 national honor societies, including Phi Beta Kappa.

Faculty/Classroom: 57% of faculty are male; 43%, female. All both teach and do research. The average class size in an introductory lecture is 15; in a laboratory, 15; and in a regular course, 15.

Admissions: 64% of the 2005-2006 applicants were accepted. The SAT scores for the 2005-2006 freshman class were: Verbal--6% below 500, 23% between 500 and 599, 43% between 600 and 700, and 28% above 700; Math--7% below 500, 32% between 500 and 599, 51% between 600 and 700, and 10% above 700. The ACT scores were 3% below 21, 11% between 21 and 23, 24% between 24 and 26, 23% between 27 and 28, and 39% above 28. 60% of the current freshmen were in the top fifth of their class; 89% were in the top two fifths. There were 6 National Merit semifinalists. 8 freshmen graduated first in their class.

Requirements: The SAT or ACT is required. In addition, and SAT Subject tests are recommended. In addition, applicants must be graduates of an accredited secondary school, with 4 years of English, 3 each of math, science, and history/social sciences, and 2 of foreign language. The GED is accepted. An essay and a letter of recommendation are required, and an interview is recommended. AP and CLEP credits are accepted. Important factors in the admissions decision are extracurricular activities record, leadership record, and personality/intangible qualities.

Procedure: Freshmen are admitted fall and spring. Entrance exams should be taken before the end of the first semester of the senior year. There are early admissions deferred admissions, and rolling sdmissions plans. Early action applications should be filed by November 15; regular applications, by January 15 for fall entry, along with a $35 fee. Notification of early action is sent January 15; regular decision, March 15. Applications are accepted on-line. 99 applicants were on the 2005 waiting list; 7 were admitted. Applications are accepted on-line.

Transfer: 28 transfer students enrolled in 2004-2005. Applicants must have a minimum GPA of 2.5 and submit official transcripts of all college work completed. The SAT or the ACT is required, and an interview is recommended. Also, a letter of recommendation from a professor at a current/previous institution is required. 16 of 31 credits required for the bachelor's degree must be completed at Beloit.

Visiting: There are regularly scheduled orientations for prospective students, including a tour, class visits, and meeting with professors, including an interview. Enrolled students are the hosts. There are guides for informal visits and visitors may sit in on classes and stay overnight. To schedule a visit, contact the Admissions Office at *visit@beloit.edu*.

Financial Aid: In 2005-2006, 80% of all full-time freshmen and 77% of continuing full-time students received some form of financial aid. The average freshman award was $18,219. Need-based scholarships or need-based grants averaged $15,676 ($23,000 maximum); need-based self-help aid (loans and jobs) averaged $3482 ($8000 maximum); and other non-need-based awards and non-need-based scholarships averaged $14,025 ($17,500 maximum). 87% of undergraduates work part time. Average annual earnings from campus work are $1300. The average financial indebtedness of the 2005 graduate was $18,783. Beloit is a member of CSS. The FAFSA and the college's own financial statement are required. The deadline for filing freshman financial aid applications for fall entry is March 1.

International Students: There were 107 international students enrolled in a recent year. The school actively recruits these students. Satisfactory scores are required on the written TOEFL, the MELAB, the Comprehensive English Language Test, or the college's own test. Applicants must also take the SAT, or the ACT. Applicants from selected countries must also supply a school-leaving exam/certificate.

Computers: Wireless access is available. Most academic and cultural buildings on campus feature wireless access. The wired campus network is accessible from every campus building. Terminal access is available at the library (250 computers, PC and Mac), a dozen departmental labs, and 24-hour labs in academic and residential buildings. Every residence hall room includes data ports. All students may access the system at any time. There are no time limits and no fees.

Graduates: From July 1, 2004 to June 30, 2005, 291 bachelor's degrees were awarded. The most popular majors were psychology (11%), anthropology (10%), and economics (8%). In an average class, 62% graduate in 4 years or less, 70% graduate in 5 years or less, and 72% graduate in 6 years or less. 62 companies recruited on campus in 2004-2005. Of the 2004 graduating class, 20% were enrolled in graduate school within 6 months of graduation and 74% were employed.

Admissions Contact: James Zielinski, Director of Admissions. A video is available. E-mail: *admiss@beloit.edu* Web: *www.beloit.edu*

CARDINAL STRITCH UNIVERSITY   E-4

Milwaukee, WI 53217-7516   (414) 410-4040
                                    (800) 347-8822; Fax: (414) 410-4049

Full-time: 910 men, 2000 women	**Faculty:** 98; IIA, --$
Part-time: 50 men, 170 women	**Ph.D.s:** 54%
Graduate: 820 men, 1900 women	**Student/Faculty:** 30 to 1
Year: semesters, summer session	**Tuition:** $16,480
Application Deadline: see profile	**Room & Board:** $5430
Freshman Class: n/av	
SAT or ACT: required	**COMPETITIVE**

Cardinal Stritch University, founded in 1937 as a college, is a private, Catholic institution sponsored by the Sisters of St. Francis. There are 4 undergraduate schools and 1 graduate school. Figures in the above capsule and in this profile are approximate. In addition to regional accreditation, Stritch has baccalaureate program accreditation with NCATE and NLN. The library contains 132,293 volumes, 173,216 microform items, and 6310 audio/video tapes/CDs/DVDs, and subscribes to 1309 periodicals including electronic. Computerized library services include the card catalog, interlibrary loans, and database searching. Special learning facilities include a learning resource center, art gallery, and radio station. The 40-acre campus is in a suburban area 10 miles north of Milwaukee. Including any residence halls, there are 9 buildings.

Student Life: 89% of undergraduates are from Wisconsin. Others are from 16 states, 27 foreign countries, and Canada. 60% are from public schools. 72% are white; 16% African American. Most are Catholic. The average age of freshmen is 19; all undergraduates, 32. 27% do not continue beyond their first year; 43% remain to graduate.

Housing: 278 students can be accommodated in college housing, which includes coed dorms. On-campus housing is available on a first-come, first-served basis. 95% of students commute. All students may keep cars.

Activities: There are no fraternities or sororities. There are 50 groups on campus, including art, band, cheerleading, choir, chorus, computers, dance, drama, ethnic, film, honors, international, jazz band, musical theater, newspaper, orchestra, photography, political, professional, radio and TV, religious, social, social service, student government, and yearbook. Popular campus events include Thursday night events and weekly activities, such as sporting events or plays.

Sports: There are 5 intercollegiate sports for men and 5 for women, and 2 intramural sports for men and 2 for women. Facilities include basketball and volleyball courts, an indoor track, a weight and exercise room, an area for table tennis and billiards, and a soccer field.

Disabled Students: 80% of the campus is accessible. Wheelchair ramps, special parking, specially equipped rest rooms, special class scheduling, and lowered telephones are available.

Services: Counseling and information services are available, as is tutoring in every subject. There is remedial math, reading, and writing.

Campus Safety and Security: Measures include 24-hour foot and vehicle patrol, informal discussions, pamphlets/posters/films, and lighted pathways/sidewalks.

Programs of Study: Stritch confers B.A., B.S., and B.F.A. degrees. Associate, master's, and doctoral degrees are also awarded. Bachelor's degrees are awarded in BIOLOGICAL SCIENCE (biology/biological science), BUSINESS (accounting, business administration and management, and international business management), COMMUNICATIONS AND THE ARTS (art, communications, creative writing, dramatic arts, English, fine arts, French, music, public relations, and Spanish), COMPUTER AND PHYSICAL SCIENCE (chemistry, computer science, and mathematics), EDUCATION (early childhood, elementary, middle school, secondary, and special), HEALTH PROFESSIONS (nursing, predentistry, premedicine, preoptometry, and preveterinary science), SOCIAL SCIENCE (history, prelaw, psychology, religion, social science, and sociology). Education in general and special education in particular are the strongest academically. Business, education, and nursing are the largest.

Required: To graduate, students must complete 128 credits, 34 to 72 in the major, with a GPA of at least 2.0. Required disciplines include history, foreign language, literature, written communication, and communication arts. 5 courses are required in humanities, 3 in social/behavioral sciences, 2 each in communication arts and written communication, and 1 each in math and natural science. An English proficiency exam must be taken.

Special: Students may participate in a variety of internships with Milwaukee businesses and organizations. Stritch offers an accelerated degree program and a B.A.-B.S. degree in business, dual majors, a general studies degree, and nondegree study. There is study abroad, work-study programs, pass/fail options, and credit for life, military, and work experience. An accelerated evening program and a management program are offered for working adults. There are 9 national honor societies and a freshman honors program.

Faculty/Classroom: 49% of faculty are male; 51%, female. All teach undergraduates. No introductory courses are taught by graduate students. The average class size in a laboratory is 12 and in a regular course, 11.

Requirements: The SAT or ACT is required. Applicants must be graduates of an accredited secondary school, with 16 academic credits, including 4 years of English and 2 years each of math (algebra required), science, and social studies. The GED is accepted. Stritch requires an essay and recommends an interview. Stritch requires applicants to be in the upper 50% of their class. A GPA of 2.0 is required. AP and CLEP credits are accepted. Important factors in the admissions decision are leadership record, evidence of special talent, and advanced placement or honor courses.

Procedure: Freshmen are admitted to all sessions. Entrance exams should be taken as early as possible. There is a deferred admissions plan and a rolling admissions plan. Check with the school for current application deadlines. Application fee is $25. Notification is sent on a rolling basis. Applications are accepted on-line.

Transfer: Applicants for transfer should have a minimum GPA of 2.0, and be eligible for return to the previous institution. 32 of 128 credits required for the bachelor's degree must be completed at Stritch.

Visiting: There are regularly scheduled orientations for prospective students, including a campus tour, meetings with admissions and financial aid counselors, and possible meetings with department chairs. There are guides for informal visits and visitors may sit in on classes and stay overnight. To schedule a visit, contact the Admissions Office.

Financial Aid: The FAFSA and the college's own financial statement are required. The deadline for filing freshman financial aid applications for fall entry is open.

International Students: A satisfactory score on the TOEFL is required.

Computers: All students may access the system. There are no time limits and no fees.

Admissions Contact: Kristine Bueno, Director of Admissions. E-mail: *admityou@stritch.edu* Web: *www.stritch.edu*

CARROLL COLLEGE   D-5

Waukesha, WI 53186   (262) 524-7220
                                    (800) CARROLL; Fax: (262) 524-7139

Full-time: 771 men, 1522 women	**Faculty:** 101; IIB, --$
Part-time: 193 men, 375 women	**Ph.D.s:** 71%
Graduate: 62 men, 177 women	**Student/Faculty:** 23 to 1
Year: semesters, summer session	**Tuition:** $19,050
Application Deadline: open	**Room & Board:** $5810
Freshman Class: 2429 applied, 1912 accepted, 598 enrolled	
ACT: 23	**COMPETITIVE**

Carroll College, founded in 1846, is an independent, co-educational comprehensive college grounded in the liberal arts tradition. There are 3 undergraduate and 3 graduate schools. In addition to regional accreditation, Carroll has baccalaureate program accreditation with APTA and NLN. The library contains 150,000 volumes, 21,637 microform items, and 1400 audio/video tapes/CDs/DVDs, and subscribes to 14,000 periodicals including electronic. Computerized library services include the card catalog, interlibrary loans, database searching, Internet access, and laptop Internet portals. Special learning facilities include a learning resource center, art gallery, radio station, and a studio theater and recital hall. The 52-acre campus is in a suburban area 15 miles west of Milwaukee. Including any residence halls, there are 31 buildings.

Student Life: 77% of undergraduates are from Wisconsin. Others are from 25 states, 31 foreign countries, and Canada. 85% are from public schools. 91% are white. The average age of freshmen is 19; all undergraduates, 22. 23% do not continue beyond their first year; 58% remain to graduate.

Housing: 1289 students can be accommodated in college housing, which includes single-sex and coed dorms and on-campus apartments. 50% of students live on campus. All students may keep cars.

Activities: 3% of men belong to 2 local fraternities; 8% of women belong to 4 national sororities. There are 40 groups on campus, including activities board, art, band, cheerleading, choir, chorale, chorus, computers, dance, diversity, drama, ethnic, film, gay, greek life, honors, international, jazz band, literary magazine, musical theater, newspaper, orchestra, photography, political, professional, radio and TV, religious, social, social service, student government, symphony, and yearbook. Popular campus events include International Folk Fair, Madrigal Dinner, and Spring Fling.

Sports: There are 10 intercollegiate sports for men and 10 for women, and 5 intramural sports for men and 5 for women. Facilities include an all-purpose field house, gym including volleyball court, 2 basketball courts, and an indoor track, 6 tennis courts, 6-lane pool, 2 sand volleyball courts, football/soccer field, practice field, softball diamond, batting cages, athletic training rooms, exercise/physiology laboratory, weight room, fitness weight room, dance studio, and a campus center which houses ping pong tables, pool tables, dart machine and video games.

Disabled Students: 20% of the campus is accessible. Wheelchair ramps, elevators, special parking, specially equipped rest rooms, and special class scheduling are available.

Services: Counseling and information services are available, as is tutoring in most subjects. There is a reader service for the blind. Academic coaching is available.

Campus Safety and Security: Measures include 24-hour foot and vehicle patrol, self-defense education, security escort services, and shuttle buses. There are informal discussions, pamphlets/posters/films, emergency telephones, and lighted pathways/sidewalks.

Programs of Study: Carroll confers B.A., B.S., and B.S.N. degrees. Master's degrees are also awarded. Bachelor's degrees are awarded in BIOLOGICAL SCIENCE (biochemistry, biology/biological science, and marine biology), BUSINESS (accounting, business administration and management, organizational behavior, recreational facilities management, and small business management), COMMUNICATIONS AND THE ARTS (art, communications, dramatic arts, English, music, and Spanish), COMPUTER AND PHYSICAL SCIENCE (actuarial science, chemistry, computer science, information sciences and systems, and mathematics), EDUCATION (art, athletic training, early childhood, elementary, foreign languages, music, physical, and science), ENGINEERING AND ENVIRONMENTAL DESIGN (environmental science and graphic arts technology), HEALTH PROFESSIONS (clinical science, exercise science, and nursing), SOCIAL SCIENCE (criminal justice, history, international relations, political science/government, psychology, religion, and sociology). Computer science, education, and business are the strongest academically. Nursing, communication, and criminal justice are the largest.

Required: To graduate, students must complete 128 credit hours, 32 to 88 in the major, with a minimum GPA of 2.0. Students must take 7 courses from the Liberal Studies Progarm and a first-year seminar and writing seminar. 1 computer science course and a math course are needed for the B.S.; 12 credits of modern language or the humanities and math competency is needed for the B.A.

Special: A Washington semester at American University and a United Nations semester are offered, as are internships and individually designed majors. Under the International and Off-Campus Program, short and long-term study abroad programs are offered to sophomores, juniors and seniors so that they may travel to places that are culturally different from their own. IOP offers programs in such areas as Western and Eastern Europe, Latin America, Africa, or Asia. A capstone experience bridges the student's college work to employment or graduate school. There are 5 national honor societies and a freshman honors program.

Faculty/Classroom: 45% of faculty are male; 55%, female. All teach undergraduates, 41% do research, and 41% do both. No introductory courses are taught by graduate students. The average class size in a laboratory is 18 and in a regular course, 23.

Admissions: 79% of the 2005-2006 applicants were accepted. The ACT scores for the 2005-2006 freshman class were: 31% below 21, 34% between 21 and 23, 22% between 24 and 26, 9% between 27 and 28, and 4% above 28. 34% of the current freshmen were in the top fifth of their class; 65% were in the top two fifths. There was 1 National Merit finalist and 3 semifinalists. 18 freshmen graduated first in their class.

Requirements: The SAT or ACT is required. In addition, applicants must be graduates of an accredited secondary school. The GED is ac-

cepted. An essay and interview are recommended for all students, and a portfolio or audition is advised for art and music students, respectively. Carroll requires applicants to be in the upper 50% of their class. A GPA of 2.0 is required. AP and CLEP credits are accepted. Important factors in the admissions decision are advanced placement or honor courses, recommendations by school officials, and evidence of special talent.

Procedure: Freshmen are admitted fall and spring. Entrance exams should be taken during the junior year. There are deferred admissions and rollingadmissions plans. Application deadlines are open. Applications are accepted on-line.

Transfer: 197 transfer students enrolled in 2004-2005. Applicants for transfer must have a minimum GPA of 2.0. An interview is required. 32 of 128 credits required for the bachelor's degree must be completed at Carroll.

Visiting: There are regularly scheduled orientations for prospective students, consisting of a campus tour, financial aid/admissions counseling, academic department meetings, and extracurricular activities meetings. There are guides for informal visits and visitors may sit in on classes and stay overnight. To schedule a visit, contact the Office of Admissions.

Financial Aid: In 2005-2006, 98% of all full-time students received some form of financial aid. 63% of full-time freshmen and 70% of continuing full-time students received need-based aid. The average freshman award was $15,039. Need-based scholarships or need-based grants averaged $11,100; need-based self-help aid (loans and jobs) averaged $3607; and tuition remission averaged $360. 59% of undergraduates work part time. Average annual earnings from campus work are $850. The average financial indebtedness of the 2005 graduate was $15,195. Carroll is a member of CSS. The FAFSA is required. The deadline for filing freshman financial aid applications for fall entry is September 1.

International Students: There are 40 international students enrolled. The school actively recruits these students. A satisfactory score is required on the written TOEFL.

Computers: Wireless access is available. Wired Internet and LAN access is available from each dorm room. Computer labs and classrooms include approximately 200 Windows desktop systems. Wireless Internet and LAN access is available in select academic buildings. All students may access the system 24 hours every day. There are no time limits and no fees.

Graduates: From July 1, 2004 to June 30, 2005, 487 bachelor's degrees were awarded. The most popular majors were education (19%), business (13%), and nursing (11%). In an average class, 39% graduate in 4 years or less, 54% graduate in 5 years or less, and 58% graduate in 6 years or less. 5 companies recruited on campus in 2004-2005. Of the 2004 graduating class, 33% were enrolled in graduate school within 6 months of graduation and 97% were employed.

Admissions Contact: James V. Wiseman, Vice President, Enrollment. E-mail: *cc.info@ccadmin.cc.edu* Web: *www.cc.edu*

CARTHAGE COLLEGE
Kenosha, WI 53140

E-5

(262) 551-6000
(800) 351-4058; Fax: (262) 551-5762

Full-time: 850 men, 875 women	**Faculty:** 102; IIB, av$
Part-time: 160 men, 380 women	**Ph.D.s:** 85%
Graduate: 20 men	**Student/Faculty:** 17 to 1
Year: 4-1-4, summer session	**Tuition:** $19,500
Application Deadline: open	**Room & Board:** $6500
Freshman Class: n/av	
SAT or ACT: required	**COMPETITIVE**

Carthage College, founded in 1847, is an independent liberal arts institution affiliated with the Evangelical Lutheran Church in America. Figures in the above capsule and in this profile are approximate. In addition to regional accreditation, Carthage has baccalaureate program accreditation with CSWE and NASM. The library contains 130,000 volumes, 9000 microform items, and 1300 audio/video tapes/CDs/DVDs, and subscribes to 450 periodicals including electronic. Computerized library services include the card catalog, interlibrary loans, and database searching. Special learning facilities include a learning resource center, art gallery, and radio station. The 75-acre campus is in a suburban area 30 miles south of Milwaukee and 60 miles north of Chicago, on the shore of Lake Michigan. Including any residence halls, there are 16 buildings.

Student Life: 52% of undergraduates are from out of state, mostly the Midwest. Students are from 23 states, 14 foreign countries, and Canada. 88% are from public schools. 89% are white. 31% are Catholic; 26% claim no religious affiliation; 13% Protestant; 7% Orthodox, Muslim. The average age of freshmen is 18; all undergraduates, 20. 24% do not continue beyond their first year; 50% remain to graduate.

Housing: 1250 students can be accommodated in college housing, which includes single-sex and coed dormitories. In addition, there are study-intensive floors and a health and wellness floor. On-campus housing is guaranteed for all 4 years. 70% of students live on campus; of those, 75% remain on campus on weekends. Alcohol is not permitted. All students may keep cars.

Activities: 28% of men belong to 5 local and 3 national fraternities; 22% of women belong to 4 local and 2 national sororities. There are 85 groups on campus, including art, band, cheerleading, choir, chorus, computers, debate, drama, ethnic, film, forensics, gay, Habitat for Humanity, honors, international, jazz band, literary magazine, musical theater, newspaper, orchestra, pep band, photography, political, professional, radio and TV, religious, social, social service, student government, and yearbook. Popular campus events include May Madness, Little Sibling Weekend, and Casino Night.

Sports: There are 10 intercollegiate sports for men and 10 for women, and 10 intramural sports for men and 5 for women. Facilities include a phys ed center, a 3000-seat stadium, a 3500-seat gym, tennis courts, baseball, soccer, and softball fields, and a natatorium.

Disabled Students: 90% of the campus is accessible. Wheelchair ramps, elevators, special parking, specially equipped rest rooms, special class scheduling, lowered drinking fountains, lowered telephones, and TDD phones are available.

Services: Counseling and information services are available, as is tutoring in most subjects.

Campus Safety and Security: Measures include 24-hour foot and vehicle patrol, self-defense education, security escort services, and informal discussions. There are pamphlets/posters/films, emergency telephones, lighted pathways/sidewalks, and electronic exit locks on residence halls.

Programs of Study: Carthage confers the B.A. degree. Master's degrees are also awarded. Bachelor's degrees are awarded in BIOLOGICAL SCIENCE (biology/biological science), BUSINESS (accounting, business administration and management, international economics, and marketing management), COMMUNICATIONS AND THE ARTS (art, English, fine arts, French, German, graphic design, languages, music, performing arts, Spanish, and studio art), COMPUTER AND PHYSICAL SCIENCE (chemistry, mathematics, natural sciences, and physics), EDUCATION (elementary, English, foreign languages, mathematics, middle school, music, physical, and secondary), SOCIAL SCIENCE (criminal justice, economics, geography, history, philosophy, political science/government, psychology, religion, social science, social work, and sociology). Education, business, and sciences are the strongest academically. Business and education are the largest.

Required: To graduate, students must complete 138 credits, with up to 56 in the major, and a minimum GPA of 2.0 (education requires 2.75). Students must complete 50 credits in liberal arts studies, including the Heritage Seminar Series, which includes 3 courses that help develop competencies in cultural studies, writing, thinking, reading, speaking, and listening. 2 courses each are required in religion and foreign language, and 1 in math. There is also a phys ed requirement. Each student must complete one of the junior symposia, a series of 3 interdependent courses, and a senior project in the major.

Special: Internships are available during the January term or, in some cases, for a semester. Carthage offers study abroad in 5 countries, cross-registration with the University of Wisconsin, a Washington semester, a general studies degree, an accelerated degree program in business administration, work-study programs, and dual and student-designed majors. Students may take a 3-2 engineering degree with Case Western Reserve or Washington Universities, and the University of Minnesota-Twin Cities or the University of Wisconsin/Madison, or a 3-2 occupational therapy degree with Washington University. There are pass/fail options and credit for military and work experience. There are 3 national honor societies, and a freshman honors program.

Faculty/Classroom: 68% of faculty are male; 33%, female. All teach undergraduates. No introductory courses are taught by graduate students. The average class size in an introductory lecture is 19; in a laboratory, 19; and in a regular course, 19.

Requirements: The SAT or ACT is required. In addition, applicants should be graduates of an accredited secondary school, having earned 16 academic credits, including English, foreign language, math, science, and social studies. The GED is accepted. An interview is recommended. A GPA of 2.0 is required. AP and CLEP credits are accepted. Important factors in the admissions decision are advanced placement or honor courses, leadership record, and extracurricular activities record.

Procedure: Freshmen are admitted to all sessions. Entrance exams should be taken in spring of the junior year or fall of the senior year. There are deferred admissions and rolling admissions plans. Application deadlines are open. Application fee is $25. Applications are accepted on-line.

Transfer: Transfer students are accepted based on academic performance at their previous school; they should have a GPA greater than 2.0. If they have fewer than 12 credits, the high school record is considered. Either the SAT or ACT and an interview are recommended. 32 of 138 credits required for the bachelor's degree must be completed at Carthage.

Visiting: There are regularly scheduled orientations for prospective students, including small group meetings with first year adviser and faculty members, class selection, and curriculum overview. Informational sessions for parents are offered. There are guides for informal visits and visitors may sit in on classes and stay overnight. To schedule a visit, contact the Office of Admissions, Mary Schuch, Visit Coordinator.

Financial Aid: Check with the school for current application deadlines.

International Students: The school actively recruits these students. They must score satisfactorily on the written TOEFL.

Computers: All students may access the system 24 hours on weekdays, 8 A.M. to 8 P.M. on weekends. There are no time limits and no fees.

Admissions Contact: Thomas J. Augustine, Director of Admissions and Financial Aid. E-mail: *admissions@carthage.edu*
Web: *www.carthage.edu*

CONCORDIA UNIVERSITY WISCONSIN E-4

Mequon, WI 53097 (414) 243-4305; Fax: (414) 243-4545

Full-time: 776 men, 1231 women	Faculty: 96
Part-time: 717 men, 1258 women	Ph.D.s: 60%
Graduate: 478 men, 958 women	Student/Faculty: 21 to 1
Year: 4-1-4, summer session	Tuition: $16,430
Application Deadline: August 1	Room & Board: $6230
Freshman Class: 1224 accepted, 373 enrolled	
ACT: 22	VERY COMPETITIVE

Concordia University Wisconsin, established in 1881, is a private institution affiliated with the Lutheran Church-Missouri Synod. There are 4 undergraduate schools and 1 graduate school. In addition to regional accreditation, CUW has baccalaureate program accreditation with NLN. The library contains 110,929 volumes, 270,602 microform items, and 4645 audio/video tapes/CDs/DVDs, and subscribes to 1411 periodicals including electronic. Computerized library services include the card catalog, interlibrary loans, and database searching. Special learning facilities include a learning resource center, art gallery, radio station, and a curriculum library for education students. The 155-acre campus is in a suburban area 15 miles north of Milwaukee. Including any residence halls, there are 17 buildings.

Student Life: 60% of undergraduates are from Wisconsin. Others are from 19 states and 25 foreign countries. 83% are white; 12% African American. 80% are Protestant; 13% Catholic; 7% claim no religious affiliation. The average age of freshmen is 18; all undergraduates, 21. 25% do not continue beyond their first year; 42% remain to graduate.

Housing: 916 students can be accommodated in college housing, which includes single-sex dorms. On-campus housing is guaranteed for all 4 years. 69% of students live on campus; of those, 50% remain on campus on weekends. Alcohol is not permitted. All students may keep cars.

Activities: There are no fraternities or sororities. There are 20 groups on campus, including art, band, cheerleading, choir, chorale, drama, drill team, ethnic, honors, international, jazz band, literary magazine, musical theater, newspaper, pep band, political, professional, radio and TV, religious, and student government. Popular campus events include Winterfest and Springfest.

Sports: There are 9 intercollegiate sports for men and 7 for women, and 10 intramural sports for men and 9 for women. Facilities include a field house, a stadium, a gym, a weight room, and a fitness center.

Disabled Students: 80% of the campus is accessible. Wheelchair ramps, elevators, special parking, and specially equipped rest rooms are available.

Services: Counseling and information services are available, as is tutoring in every subject. There is a reader service for the blind, and remedial math, reading, and writing.

Campus Safety and Security: Security guards are on staff from 4 P.M. to 8 A.M. on weekdays and 24 hours a day on weekends.

Programs of Study: CUW confers B.A., B.S., and B.S.N. degrees. Associate and master's degrees are also awarded. Bachelor's degrees are awarded in BIOLOGICAL SCIENCE (biology/biological science), BUSINESS (accounting, banking and finance, business administration and management, management science, and marketing/retailing/merchandising), COMMUNICATIONS AND THE ARTS (art, communications, English, graphic design, music, Spanish, speech/debate/rhetoric, and telecommunications), COMPUTER AND PHYSICAL SCIENCE (mathematics and radiological technology), EDUCATION (athletic training, early childhood, elementary, physical, and secondary), ENGINEERING AND ENVIRONMENTAL DESIGN (interior design), HEALTH PROFESSIONS (nursing, occupational therapy, and sports medicine), SOCIAL SCIENCE (biblical languages, criminal justice, history, humanities, ministries, paralegal studies, pastoral studies, psychology, religion, religious music, social science, social work, and theological studies). Education, business, and health sciences are the strongest academically.

Required: To graduate, students must complete 126 credits, including at least 30 in the major, with a minimum GPA of 2.0. The 47 1/2-credit core curriculum includes theology/philosophy, humanities, cross culture, social science, natural science, communication, math, and phys ed.

Special: Internships, study abroad, pass/fail options, and credit for life, military, and work experience are available. Concordia offers a general studies degree, dual, student-designed, and interdisciplinary majors, including justice and public policy, and nondegree study. Accelerated degree programs are available in several fields. There is 1 national honor society.

Faculty/Classroom: 50% of faculty are male; 50%, female. All teach undergraduates. No introductory courses are taught by graduate students. The average class size in a regular course is 17.

Requirements: A satisfactory score on the SAT or ACT is required. Applicants must be graduates of an accredited secondary school, having completed 16 academic credits, including 3 of English and 2 each of math, science, and social studies. The GED is accepted. A GPA of 2.5 is required. AP and CLEP credits are accepted. Important factors in the admissions decision are leadership record, recommendations by school officials, and personality/intangible qualities.

Procedure: Freshmen are admitted to all sessions. Entrance exams should be taken in the junior year. There is a rolling admissions plan. Applications should be filed by August 1 for fall entry. The fall 2005 application fee was $25. Notification is sent on a rolling basis.

Transfer: 97 transfer students enrolled in 2004-2005. Applicants for transfer must have a minimum GPA of 2.0 and meet the same entrance exam criteria as entering freshmen. 36 of 126 credits required for the bachelor's degree must be completed at CUW.

Visiting: There are regularly scheduled orientations for prospective students, including a tour and financial aid and academic information sessions. There are guides for informal visits and visitors may sit in on classes and stay overnight. To schedule a visit, contact the Admission Office at (262) 243-5700 or *admission@cuw.edu.*

Financial Aid: The CSS/Profile or FAFSA, the college's own financial statement, and income tax forms are required. The deadline for filing freshman financial aid applications for fall entry is April 30.

International Students: There were 49 international students enrolled in a recent year. The school actively recruits these students. They must achieve a satisfactory score on the TOEFL and also take the college's own test. If the student's TOEFL score is not satisfactory, the student must take an English proficiency exam for placement.

Computers: All students may access the system. There are no time limits and no fees.

Graduates: In an average class, 52% graduate in 6 years or less.

Admissions Contact: Kenneth Gaschk, Vice President of Enrollment. E-mail: *admission@cuw.edu* Web: *www.cuw.edu*

EDGEWOOD COLLEGE   C-4

Madison, WI 53711-1997   (608) 663-2294
(800) 444-4861 ext. 2294; Fax: (608) 663-2214

Full-time: 401 men, 1116 women	**Faculty:** 86
Part-time: 145 men, 361 women	**Ph.D.s:** 80%
Graduate: 219 men, 404 women	**Student/Faculty:** 18 to 1
Year: 4-1-4, summer session	**Tuition:** $17,000
Application Deadline: August 25	**Room & Board:** $5862
Freshman Class: 1035 applied, 835 accepted, 309 enrolled	
ACT: 22	**COMPETITIVE**

Edgewood College, established in 1927, is a private Catholic institution sponsored by the Sinsinawa Dominican Sisters. Some information in this capsule and profile is approximate. In addition to regional accreditation, Edgewood has baccalaureate program accreditation with NCATE. The library contains 88,329 volumes, 94,050 microform items, and 3946 audio/video tapes/CDs/DVDs, and subscribes to 494 periodicals including electronic. Computerized library services include the card catalog, interlibrary loans, and database searching. Special learning facilities include a learning resource center and art gallery. The 55-acre campus is in a suburban area 5 miles southwest of Madison. Including any residence halls, there are 10 buildings.

Student Life: 98% of undergraduates are from Wisconsin. Others are from 11 states and 10 foreign countries. 75% are from public schools. 52% are white. 39% are Catholic; 24% Protestant. The average age of freshmen is 20; all undergraduates, 25. 32% do not continue beyond their first year; 39% remain to graduate.

Housing: 325 students can be accommodated in college housing, which includes single-sex and coed dormitories and on-campus apartments. On-campus housing is guaranteed for all 4 years. 80% of students commute. Alcohol is not permitted. All students may keep cars.

Activities: There are no fraternities or sororities. There are 30 groups on campus, including art, band, choir, chorale, chorus, drama, ethnic, gay, honors, international, literary magazine, musical theater, newspaper, orchestra, pep band, political, religious, social, social service, student government, and symphony. Popular campus events include Springfest, Mazzuchelli Fest, and Winter Frost.

Sports: There are 5 intercollegiate sports for men and 7 for women, and 9 intramural sports for men and 9 for women. Facilities include a 1000-seat gym, soccer, baseball, and softball fields, a fitness center, and access to tennis courts.

Disabled Students: 85% of the campus is accessible. Wheelchair ramps, elevators, special parking, specially equipped rest rooms, special class scheduling, lowered drinking fountains, lowered telephones, automated doors in the library, science center, activities center, and residence halls, and a chairlift are available.

Services: Counseling and information services are available, as is tutoring in some subjects, including most sciences, introductory math courses, and Spanish. There is a reader service for the blind, and remedial math, reading, and writing.

Campus Safety and Security: Measures include self-defense education, security escort services, informal discussions, and pamphlets/posters/films. There are emergency telephones and lighted pathways/sidewalks. Residence halls have alarms, a security card system, and capus security guards. RAs are on duty 24 hours a day weekends and 7 A.M. to 3 P.M. and 8 P.M. to 4 A.M. weekdays.

Programs of Study: Edgewood confers B.A. and B.S. degrees. Associate and master's degrees are also awarded. Bachelor's degrees are awarded in BIOLOGICAL SCIENCE (biology/biological science), BUSINESS (accounting and business administration and management), COMMUNICATIONS AND THE ARTS (art, English, French, graphic design, music, performing arts, and Spanish), COMPUTER AND PHYSICAL SCIENCE (chemistry, information sciences and systems, mathematics, and natural sciences), EDUCATION (early childhood, education of the exceptional child, elementary, science, and social studies), ENGINEERING AND ENVIRONMENTAL DESIGN (preengineering), HEALTH PROFESSIONS (art therapy, cytotechnology, medical technology, and nursing), SOCIAL SCIENCE (child care/child and family studies, criminal justice, economics, history, international relations, political science/government, prelaw, psychology, public administration, religion, and sociology). Liberal arts is the strongest academically. Business, education, and nursing are the largest.

Required: To graduate, students must complete a minimum of 120 credit hours with a minimum cumulative GPA of 2.0. There are general education requirements, and each student must complete a major field of study and a human issues study.

Special: Students may cross-register with the University of Wisconsin/Madison. Internships, study abroad, dual and student-designed majors, nondegree study, pass/fail options, and credit for prior learning experience are available. There is a weekend degree program. There is an accelerated undergraduate degree program for working adults. There are 5 national honor societies and a freshman honors program.

Faculty/Classroom: All teach undergraduates. No introductory courses are taught by graduate students. The average class size in a regular course is 18.

Admissions: 81% of the 2005-2006 applicants were accepted. The ACT scores for the 2005-2006 freshman class were: 38% below 21, 31% between 21 and 23, 22% between 24 and 26, 7% between 27 and 28, and 3% above 28. 25% of the current freshmen were in the top fifth of their class; 59% were in the top two fifths. 1 freshman graduated first in the class.

Requirements: The ACT is recommended. In addition, candidates for admission to Edgewood are expected to present a 2.5 cumulative high school GPA, rank in the upper half of their class, and have a composite score of 18 on the ACT or a satisfactory score on the SAT. The GED is accepted. Applicants should complete 16 Carnegie units, 12 of which should be chosen from the following fields: natural science, speech, social science, English, foreign language, history, religious studies, and mathematics. 2 years of the same foreign language in grades 9-12 with grades of C or better are also recommended. Edgewood requires applicants to be in the upper 50% of their class. A GPA of 2.5 is required. AP and CLEP credits are accepted.

Procedure: Freshmen are admitted fall and spring. Entrance exams should be taken by the senior year. There is a rolling admissions plan. Applications should be filed by August 25 for fall entry and January 12 for spring entry, along with a $25 fee. Notification is sent on a rolling basis. Applications are accepted on-line.

Transfer: Transfer students must complete an application for undergraduate admission and have official transcripts from each high school, college and university attended sent directly to the Office of Admissions. High school transcripts should include class rank and cumulative GPA. GEDs are accepted. Students are expected to present a minimum of 12 academic-level credits and a cumulative college grade point average of 2.0 (on a 4.0 scale) from an accredited institution. Students dismissed from a previous college must wait one full year prior to applying to Edgewood and supply additional information. 32 of 120 credits required for the bachelor's degree must be completed at Edgewood.

Visiting: There are regularly scheduled orientations for prospective students, including Experience Edgewood Days, a program where admitted freshmen spend a day on campus as if they were Edgewood College students. They choose their own schedule for the day, which may include sitting in on classes, attending athletics presentations, and learning about study abroad opportunities, residence life and student activities. Students also have the opportunity to take campus tours and exclusive tours of the residence halls. Complimentary lunch is included. There are guides for informal visits and visitors may sit in on classes and stay overnight. To schedule a visit, contact the Admissions Office.

Financial Aid: In a recent year, 85% of undergraduates worked part time. Average annual earnings from campus work were $1360. Edgewood is a member of CSS. The FAFSA, the college's own financial statement and, a tax return are required.

International Students: The school actively recruits these students. They must score satisfactorily on the written TOEFL or take the MELAB.

Computers: All students may access the system The labs are open 7:30 A.M. to midnight Monday through Friday, and 8 A.M. to 5 P.M. on weekends. There are no time limits and no fees. It is strongly recommended that all students have a personal computer. Students in the computer science class CS 180 must lease an IBM ThinkPad. have personal computers.

Admissions Contact: Christine Benedict, Director of Undergraduate Admissions. E-mail: *admissions@edgewood.edu*
Web: *www.edgewood.edu*

LAKELAND COLLEGE   E-4

Sheboygan, WI 53082-0359   (920) 565-1588
                                   (800) 242-3347; Fax: (920) 565-1206

Full-time: 390 men, 400 women	**Faculty:** 41; IIB, --$
Part-time: 20 men, 30 women	**Ph.D.s:** 59%
Graduate: 50 men, 130 women	**Student/Faculty:** 19 to 1
Year: semesters, summer session	**Tuition:** $16,795
Application Deadline: see profile	**Room & Board:** $6195
Freshman Class: n/av	
SAT or ACT: required	**COMPETITIVE**

Lakeland College, established in 1862, is a private institution affiliated with the United Church of Christ. The 4-4-1 academic calendar consists of 4-month fall and spring terms, and an optional 3 1/2 week May term. Figures in the above capsule and in this profile are approximate. The library contains 57,447 volumes, 33,169 microform items, and 2099 audio/video tapes/CDs/DVDs, and subscribes to 322 periodicals including electronic. Computerized library services include the card catalog, interlibrary loans, and database searching. Special learning facilities include a learning resource center, art gallery, and a college history museum. The 240-acre campus is in a rural area 10 miles northwest of Sheboygan. Including any residence halls, there are 24 buildings.

Student Life: 79% of undergraduates are from Wisconsin. Others are from 16 states, 31 foreign countries, and Canada. 90% are from public schools. 76% are white. 32% are Protestant; 29% Catholic; 25% claim no religious affiliation. The average age of all undergraduates is 22. 32% do not continue beyond their first year; 43% remain to graduate.

Housing: 488 students can be accommodated in college housing, which includes single-sex and coed dorms and on-campus apartments. In addition, there are honors houses and housing for students with senior standing. On-campus housing is guaranteed for all 4 years. 57% of students live on campus; of those, 60% remain on campus on weekends. All students may keep cars.

Activities: 17% of men belong to 3 local fraternities; 11% of women belong to 3 local sororities. There are 27 groups on campus, including band, choir, chorus, dance team, drama, ethnic, honors, international, literary magazine, newspaper, pep band, professional, radio and TV, religious, social, student government, and yearbook. Popular campus events include Winter Carnival and Spring Celebration.

Sports: There are 8 intercollegiate sports for men and 7 for women, and 2 intramural sports for men and 2 for women. Facilities include a sports complex, a fitness lab, 3 full-size basketball courts, a weight room, indoor and outdoor tennis courts, indoor pitching and batting facilities, and softball, baseball, football, soccer, and practice fields.

Disabled Students: 83% of the campus is accessible. Wheelchair ramps, elevators, special parking, specially equipped rest rooms, and lowered drinking fountains are available though not at every building.

Services: Counseling and information services are available, as is tutoring in every subject. There is a reader service for the blind, and remedial math, reading, and writing.

Campus Safety and Security: Measures include security escort services, informal discussions, pamphlets/posters/films, and emergency telephones. There are lighted pathways/sidewalks and foot patrol on weekends and evenings.

Programs of Study: Lakeland confers the B.A. degree. Master's degrees are also awarded. Bachelor's degrees are awarded in BIOLOGICAL SCIENCE (biology/biological science), BUSINESS (accounting, business administration and management, business economics, hospitality management services, international business management, and marketing management), COMMUNICATIONS AND THE ARTS (art, creative writing, dramatic arts, English, German, music, and Spanish), COMPUTER AND PHYSICAL SCIENCE (chemistry, computer science, and mathematics), EDUCATION (business, early childhood, elementary, music, and secondary), SOCIAL SCIENCE (behavioral science, criminal justice, economics, history, philosophy, physical fitness/movement, psychology, public administration, religion, and sociology). Business, education, and accounting are the strongest academically. Education, business, and computer science are the largest.

Required: To graduate, students must complete 128 semester hours, with at least 32 in the major and a minimum 2.0 GPA. There are requirements in history, humanities, natural sciences, social sciences, and religion.

Special: Internships in all majors, study abroad in Germany and Japan, a Washington semester, and work-study programs are available. There are some dual majors, a general studies degree, a 3-2 engineering degree with the University of Wisconsin/Madison, a 2-2 1/2 nursing program with Bellin College of Nursing, and nondegree study. There is a freshman honors program.

Faculty/Classroom: 51% of faculty are male; 49%, female. All both teach and do research. No introductory courses are taught by graduate students. The average class size in an introductory lecture is 20; in a laboratory, 15; and in a regular course, 16.

Requirements: A satisfactory score on the SAT or ACT is required. Applicants must be graduates of an accredited secondary school or have the GED. An interview is recommended. Lakeland requires applicants to be in the upper 50% of their class. A GPA of 2.0 is required. AP and CLEP credits are accepted. Important factors in the admissions decision are advanced placement or honor courses, leadership record, and evidence of special talent.

Procedure: Freshmen are admitted fall, spring, and summer. Entrance exams should be taken after the enrollment commitment is made. Check with school for current application deadlines and fee. Notification is sent on a rolling basis. Applications are accepted on-line.

Transfer: Applicants should have a GPA of at least 2.0. Lakeland recommends an interview. 36 of 128 credits required for the bachelor's degree must be completed at Lakeland.

Visiting: There are regularly scheduled orientations for prospective students, consisting of meetings with faculty and financial aid personnel, activities meetings, and a campus tour. There are guides for informal visits and visitors may sit in on classes and stay overnight. To schedule a visit, contact the Admissions Office.

Financial Aid: Lakeland is a member of CSS. The FAFSA and the college's own financial statement are required. Check with the school for current deadlines.

International Students: There are 100 international students enrolled. The school actively recruits these students. A satisfactory score onn the TOEFL is required.

Computers: All students may access the system 7 A.M. to 2 A.M.

Admissions Contact: Nathan Dehne, Director of Admissions.
E-mail: *admissions@lakeland.edu* Web: *www.lakeland.edu*

LAWRENCE UNIVERSITY   D-3

Appleton, WI 54912   (920) 832-6500
                                   (800) 227-0982; Fax: (920) 832-6782

Full-time: 620 men, 736 women	**Faculty:** 144; IIB, av$
Part-time: 29 men, 20 women	**Ph.D.s:** 99%
Graduate: none	**Student/Faculty:** 9 to 1
Year: trimesters	**Tuition:** $27,924
Application Deadline: January 15	**Room & Board:** $6034
Freshman Class: 2060 applied, 1407 accepted, 401 enrolled	
SAT Verbal/Math: 650/640*	**ACT:** 28
	HIGHLY COMPETITIVE+

Lawrence University, founded in 1847, is an independent liberal arts institution with a conservatory of music. In addition to regional accreditation, Lawrence has baccalaureate program accreditation with NASM. The library contains 389,000 volumes, 104,000 microform items, and 20,000 audio/video tapes/CDs/DVDs, and subscribes to 1800 periodicals including electronic. Computerized library services include the card catalog, interlibrary loans, database searching, and Internet access. Special learning facilities include a learning resource center, art gallery, natural history museum, and radio station. The 84-acre campus is in an urban area 100 miles north of Milwaukee. Including any residence halls, there are 60 buildings.

Student Life: 61% of undergraduates are from out of state, mostly the Midwest. Students are from 48 states, 50 foreign countries, and Canada. 76% are from public schools. 82% are white. 49% claim no religious affiliation; 21% Protestant; 16% Catholic; 13% Buddhist, Hindu, Muslim, other. The average age of freshmen is 18; all undergraduates, 20. 13% do not continue beyond their first year; 76% remain to graduate.

Housing: Housing includes single-sex and coed dormitories, on-campus apartments, married-student housing, and fraternity houses. In addition, there are language houses and special-interest houses. On-campus housing is guaranteed for all 4 years. All of students live on campus; of those, 80% remain on campus on weekends. All students may keep cars.

Activities: 23% of men belong to 5 national fraternities; 10% of women belong to 3 national sororities. There are 90 groups on campus, including art, band, cheerleading, chess, choir, chorale, chorus, computers, dance, drama, ethnic, film, gay, honors, international, jazz band, literary magazine, musical theater, newspaper, opera, orchestra, pep band, political, professional, radio and TV, religious, social, social service, student government, symphony, and yearbook. Popular campus events include Octoberfest and Annual Midwest Trivia Contest.

Sports: There are 14 intercollegiate sports for men and 11 for women, and 22 intramural sports for men and 22 for women. Facilities include a 5255-seat lighted football stadium; 8-lane all-weather and 4-lane indoor tracks; baseball, soccer, practice fields; 6 tennis, 1 squash, and 7 racquetball/handball courts; 2 gyms for basketball, volleyball, and badminton; 3 batting cages; an 8-lane swimming pool with diving well; weight, exercise, and sauna rooms; and a dance studio.

Disabled Students: 80% of the campus is accessible. Wheelchair ramps, elevators, special parking, specially equipped rest rooms, special class scheduling, lowered drinking fountains, and special housing are available.

Services: Counseling and information services are available, as is tutoring in every subject. There is a reader service for the blind and remedial math and writing. The writing lab focuses on enhancing writing skills, as well as remedial writing.

Campus Safety and Security: Measures include 24-hour foot and vehicle patrol, self-defense education, security escort services, and informal discussions. There are pamphlets/posters/films, emergency telephones, lighted pathways/sidewalks, and the Whistle Stop Program.

Programs of Study: Lawrence confers B.A. and B.Mus. degrees. Bachelor's degrees are awarded in BIOLOGICAL SCIENCE (biology/ biological science and neurosciences), COMMUNICATIONS AND THE ARTS (art history and appreciation, classics, dramatic arts, English, French, German, linguistics, music performance, music theory and composition, Russian, Spanish, and studio art), COMPUTER AND PHYSICAL SCIENCE (chemistry, computer science, geology, mathematics, and physics), EDUCATION (art, music, and secondary), ENGINEERING AND ENVIRONMENTAL DESIGN (environmental science), SOCIAL SCIENCE (anthropology, East Asian studies, economics, gender studies, history, international relations, philosophy, political science/government, psychology, and religion). Biology, music, and physics are the strongest academically. Biology, music, and psychology are the largest.

Required: Students must complete 216 units (270 units for a double-degree program), including 48 to 72 in the major, with a minimum GPA of 2.0. All students must take Freshmen Studies. Distribution requirements include 12 units each in humanities, social sciences, and natural sciences, including a lab course, and 6 units in fine arts. Competency requirements must also be met in writing, speaking, foreign language, and quantitative analysis. Some majors require a comprehensive exam or a thesis. The B.Mus. requires that two thirds of courses are in the conservatory and one third are in subjects other than music.

Special: Lawrence offers Chicago-based programs in urban studies, urban education, and the arts, a humanities program at the Newberry Library, and a science internship at Oak Ridge National Laboratory. There are study-abroad programs in 26 countries, a Washington semester, limited pass/fail options, student-designed majors, and nondegree study. Students may take a 3-2 engineering degree with Columbia or Washington Universities, or Rensselaer Polytechnic Institute. Also available are 3-2 programs in forestry and environmental studies with Duke University, in occupational therapy with Washington University in St. Louis and in allied health sciences (nursing/medical technology) with Rush-Presbyterian-St. Luke's Medical Center in Chicago. A 5-year B.A.-B.Mus. degree is offered. There are 8 national honor societies, including Phi Beta Kappa.

Faculty/Classroom: 67% of faculty are male; 33%, female. All both teach and do research. The average class size in an introductory lecture is 29; in a laboratory, 14; and in a regular course, 16.

Admissions: 68% of the 2005-2006 applicants were accepted. The SAT scores for the 2005-2006 freshman class were: Verbal--5% below 500, 25% between 500 and 599, 46% between 600 and 700, and 24% above 700; Math--2% below 500, 27% between 500 and 599, 50% between 600 and 700, and 21% above 700. The ACT scores were 4% below 21, 10% between 21 and 23, 22% between 24 and 26, 21% between 27 and 28, and 43% above 28. 65% of the current freshmen were in the top fifth of their class; 93% were in the top two fifths. There were 20 National Merit finalists and 8 semifinalists. 20 freshmen graduated first in their class.

Requirements: The SAT or ACT is required. In addition, applicants should complete 16 high school academic credits. Lawrence requires an essay, reports from a teacher and counselor, and, for music majors, an audition. The school recommends an interview, and, for art majors, a portfolio. AP credits are accepted. Important factors in the admissions decision are advanced placement or honor courses, evidence of special talent, and extracurricular activities record.

Procedure: Freshmen are admitted in the fall. Entrance exams should be taken in the spring of the junior year or fall of the senior year. There are early decision and deferred admissions plans. Early decision applications should be filed by November 15; regular applications, by January 15 for fall entry, along with a $40 fee. Notification of early decision is sent December 1; regular decision, April 1. 18 early decision candidates were accepted for the 2005-2006 class. 60 applicants were on the 2005 waiting list; 2 were admitted. Applications are accepted on-line.

Transfer: 27 transfer students enrolled in 2004-2005. Applicants must present official transcripts of their college and secondary school work, and the recommendation of a college professor. Typically, candidates with a college GPA of 2.75 or higher will receive serious consideration. 108 of 216 units required for the bachelor's degree must be completed at Lawrence.

Visiting: There are regularly scheduled orientations for prospective students, including an extensive day-long program with many choices of classes and presentations. There are guides for informal visits and visitors may sit in on classes and stay overnight. To schedule a visit, contact the Office of Admissions at (800) 448-3072.

Financial Aid: In 2005-2006, 90% of all full-time students received some form of financial aid. 73% of full-time freshmen and 72% of continuing full-time students received need-based aid. The average freshman award was $22,764. Need-based scholarships or need-based grants averaged $16,694 ($30,800 maximum); need-based self-help aid (loans and jobs) averaged $5838 ($8625 maximum); and other non-need-based awards and non-need-based scholarships averaged $8212 ($20,000 maximum). 70% of undergraduates work part time. Average annual earnings from campus work are $1500. The average financial indebtedness of the 2005 graduate was $19,294. Lawrence is a member of CSS. The FAFSA and the college's own financial statement are required. The priority date for freshman financial aid applications for fall entry is March 15.

International Students: There are 114 international students enrolled. The school actively recruits these students. They must score satisfactorily on the written TOEFL or on the electronic version.

Computers: The campus network provides high-speed access to various servers as well as the Internet. Besides access to shared resources, students can have their own work space on the network as well as an area for web development. All students receive an e-mail account. There are wired residence halls as well as computer labs in all major residence halls and academic facilties. Limited wireless access is available. All students may access the system 24 hours a day. There are no time limits and no fees. It is strongly recommended that all students have a personal computer.

Graduates: From July 1, 2004 to June 30, 2005, 294 bachelor's degrees were awarded. The most popular majors were music performance (9%), English (8%), and government (8%). In an average class, 1% graduate in 3 years or less, 59% graduate in 4 years or less, 75% graduate in 5 years or less, and 76% graduate in 6 years or less. 40 companies recruited on campus in 2004-2005. Of the 2004 graduating class, 23% were enrolled in graduate school within 6 months of graduation and 52% were employed.

Admissions Contact: Steven Syverson, Dean of Admissions. E-mail: *excel@lawrence.edu* Web: *www.lawrence.edu*

MARIAN COLLEGE OF FOND DU LAC   D-4
Fond du Lac, WI 54935

(920) 923-7650
(800) 2-MARIAN; Fax: (920) 923-8755

Full-time: 355 men, 1006 women	**Faculty:** 64; IIB, --$
Part-time: 209 men, 507 women	**Ph.D.s:** 57%
Graduate: 326 men, 572 women	**Student/Faculty:** 21 to 1
Year: varies by program, summer session	**Tuition:** $16,705
	Room & Board: $5070

Application Deadline: open
Freshman Class: 766 applied, 661 accepted, 262 enrolled
ACT: 20   **LESS COMPETITIVE**

Marian College, founded in 1936, is a private, Catholic, liberal arts based institution offering degree programs in the arts and sciences, business, education, and health fields. There is 1 undergraduate school and 3 graduate schools. In addition to regional accreditation, Marian has baccalaureate program accreditation with CSWE, IACBE, NCATE, and NLN. The library contains 90,327 volumes, 14,978 microform items, and 913 audio/video tapes/CDs/DVDs, and subscribes to 737 periodicals including electronic. Computerized library services include the card catalog, interlibrary loans, database searching, and Internet access. Special learning facilities include a learning resource center. The 77-acre campus is in a small town 60 miles north of Milwaukee. Including any residence halls, there are 27 buildings.

Student Life: 95% of undergraduates are from Wisconsin. Others are from 10 states, 3 foreign countries, and Canada. 70% are from public schools. 89% are white. 41% are Catholic; 30% Protestant. The average age of freshmen is 19; all undergraduates, 24. 28% do not continue beyond their first year; 50% remain to graduate.

Housing: 440 students can be accommodated in college housing, which includes single-sex and coed dorms, on-campus apartments, fraternity houses, sorority houses, and a chemical-free wellness residence hall. On-campus housing is guaranteed for all 4 years. 64% of students commute. All students may keep cars.

Activities: 15% of men belong to 2 national fraternities; 9% of women belong to 1 local and 2 national sororities. There are 36 groups on campus, including band, campus ministry, cheerleading, choir, chorus, dance, drama, ethnic, gay, honors, international, jazz band, literary magazine, multicultural, newspaper, orchestra, photography, political, professional, radio and TV, religious, social, social service, student government, symphony, and yearbook. Popular campus events include Heritage Festival of Arts, Fine Arts Series, and Sabre Show.

Sports: There are 6 intercollegiate sports for men and 6 for women, and 8 intramural sports for men and 6 for women. Facilities include a soccer field, a softball field, a gym, tennis courts, a game room, a hockey rink, and a weight room.

Disabled Students: All of the campus is accessible. Wheelchair ramps, elevators, special parking, specially equipped rest rooms, special class scheduling, lowered drinking fountains, and lowered telephones are available.

Services: Counseling and information services are available, as is tutoring in most subjects. There is a reader service for the blind, and remedial math, reading, and writing.

Campus Safety and Security: Measures include self-defense education, security escort services, shuttle buses, and informal discussions. There are pamphlets/posters/films, emergency telephones, lighted pathways/sidewalks, and evening foot and vehicle patrol.

Programs of Study: Marian confers B.A., B.S., B.A.J., B.B.A., B.I.S., B.O.C., B.S.B.A., B.S.Ed., B.S.I.S., B.S.M.T., B.S.N., B.S.R.T., and B.S.W. degrees. Master's and doctoral degrees are also awarded. Bachelor's degrees are awarded in BIOLOGICAL SCIENCE (biology/biological science), BUSINESS (accounting, business administration and management, management science, marketing/retailing/merchandising, and sports management), COMMUNICATIONS AND THE ARTS (art, communications, English, music, music business management, and Spanish), COMPUTER AND PHYSICAL SCIENCE (chemistry, information sciences and systems, mathematics, and radiological technology), EDUCATION (art, early childhood, elementary, English, foreign languages, mathematics, middle school, music, science, secondary, and social science), HEALTH PROFESSIONS (art therapy, cytotechnology, medical laboratory technology, and nursing), SOCIAL SCIENCE (criminal justice, economics, history, interdisciplinary studies, psychology, social work, and sociology). Nursing, education, and business are the strongest academically and have the largest enrollments.

Required: To graduate, students must complete 128 credits with a minimum GPA of 2.0 (nursing and social work, 2.75; education, 3.0). Core requirements include 25 credits in arts and humanities, 12 to 13 in social and behavioral science, and 12 in math and natural science, as well as a freshman seminar.

Special: Internships are offered in most areas of study, cooperative education programs in all majors, and accelerated-degree programs in nursing, business administration, and operation management. Student-designed and dual majors, credit for prior learning, work-study, nondegree study, and cooperative education (paid work experience) are available. Study abroad at Harlaxton College, England, and Spain is possible. There are evening degree completion programs for working adults. There are 7 national honor societies, and a freshman honors program.

Faculty/Classroom: 59% of faculty are male; 41%, female. 84% teach undergraduates. No introductory courses are taught by graduate students. The average class size in an introductory lecture is 18; in a laboratory, 10; and in a regular course, 13.

Admissions: 86% of the 2005-2006 applicants were accepted. The ACT scores for the 2005-2006 freshman class were: 56% below 21, 26% between 21 and 23, 13% between 24 and 26, 5% between 27 and 28, and 1% above 28. 23% of the current freshmen were in the top fifth of their class; 48% were in the top two fifths. 2 freshmen graduated first in their class.

Requirements: The ACT is required. Applicants must be graduates of an accredited secondary school or have earned a GED. An interview is recommended. Marian requires applicants to be in the upper 50% of their class. A GPA of 2.0 is required. AP and CLEP credits are accepted. Important factors in the admissions decision are advanced placement or honor courses, leadership record, and evidence of special talent.

Procedure: Freshmen are admitted to all sessions. Entrance exams should be taken in the junior year. There are early admissions and deferred admissions plans. Application deadlines are open. Applications are accepted on-line.

Transfer: 140 transfer students enrolled in 2004-2005. The school recommends a minimum GPA of 2.0, the SAT or ACT, and an interview. 32 of 128 credits required for the bachelor's degree must be completed at Marian.

Visiting: There are regularly scheduled orientations for prospective students, consisting of sessions in April, May, June, and July for course selection and meeting with advisors. There are guides for informal visits and visitors may sit in on classes and stay overnight. To schedule a visit, contact the Admissions Office at (800) 2-MARIAN ext.7650 or admissions@mariancollege.edu.

Financial Aid: In 2004-2005, 96% of all full-time freshmen and 91% of continuing full-time students received some form of financial aid. 86% of full-time freshmen and 81% of continuing full-time students received need-based aid. The average freshman award was $13,981. Need-based scholarships or need-based grants averaged $9650 ($22,000 maximum); need-based self-help aid (loans and jobs) averaged $4066 ($13,125 maximum); and other non-need-based awards and non-need-based scholarships averaged $4186 ($11,200 maximum). 38% of undergradu-

ates work part time. Average annual earnings from campus work are $809. The average financial indebtedness of the 2005 graduate was $19,500. The FAFSA and the college's own financial statement are required. The deadline for filing freshman financial aid applications for fall entry is March 15.

International Students: There are 16 international students enrolled. The school actively recruits these students. They must score satisfactory on the written TOEFL or on the electronic version.

Computers: Each student is assigned an e-mail account, and each resident student has a hookup. More than 250 computers are available for general access and there are several computer classrooms. All students may access the system. There are no time limits and no fees. It is strongly recommended that all students have a personal computer.

Graduates: From July 1, 2004 to June 30, 2005, 335 bachelor's degrees were awarded. The most popular majors were business administration (40%), nursing (16%), and education (14%). In an average class, 32% graduate in 4 years or less, 47% graduate in 5 years or less, and 50% graduate in 6 years or less. 27 companies recruited on campus in 2004-2005. Of the 2004 graduating class, 9% were enrolled in graduate school within 6 months of graduation and 84% were employed.

Admissions Contact: Eric Peterson, Dean of Admissions. A video is available. E-mail: admissions@mariancollege.edu
Web: www.mariancollege.edu

MARQUETTE UNIVERSITY   E-4
Milwaukee, WI 53201-1881   **(414) 288-7302**
                                          (800) 222-6544; Fax: (414) 288-3764

Full-time: 3423 men, 4107 women	**Faculty:** 512; I, --$
Part-time: 221 men, 259 women	**Ph.D.s:** 88%
Graduate: 1783 men, 1801 women	**Student/Faculty:** 15 to 1
Year: semesters, summer session	**Tuition:** $23,346
Application Deadline: December 1	**Room & Board:** $7720
Freshman Class: 10,348 applied, 7257 accepted, 1784 enrolled	
SAT Verbal/Math: 600/600*	**ACT:** 27 **HIGHLY COMPETITIVE**

Marquette University, established in 1881, is a private Roman Catholic Jesuit institution. There are 7 undergraduate and 4 graduate schools. In addition to regional accreditation, Marquette has baccalaureate program accreditation with AACSB, ABET, ACEJMC, ADA, APTA, ASLA, CSWE, NCATE, and NLN. The 2 libraries contain 1,319,451 volumes, 1,454,579 microform items, and 12,059 audio/video tapes/CDs/DVDs, and subscribe to 15,868 periodicals including electronic. Computerized library services include the card catalog, interlibrary loans, database searching, Internet access, and laptop Internet portals. Special learning facilities include a learning resource center, art gallery, radio station, and TV station. The 80-acre campus is in an urban area in the heart of Milwaukee. Including any residence halls, there are 60 buildings.

Student Life: 52% of undergraduates are from out of state, mostly the Midwest. Others are from 50 states, 77 foreign countries, and Canada. 55% are from public schools. 84% are white. 63% are Catholic; 19% claim no religious affiliation; 17% Protestant. The average age of freshmen is 18; all undergraduates, 21. 10% do not continue beyond their first year; 90% remain to graduate.

Housing: 3330 students can be accommodated in college housing, which includes single-sex and coed dormitories, on-campus apartments, and married-student housing. In addition, there are honors houses, specified majors, quiet/study, and multicultural floors. On-campus housing is guaranteed for the freshman year only and is available on a lottery system for upperclassmen. 55% of students live on campus; of those, 80% remain on campus on weekends. All students may keep cars.

Activities: 5% of men belong to 11 national fraternities; 7% of women belong to 11 national sororities. There are 180 groups on campus, including band, cheerleading, choir, chorale, chorus, community awareness, dance, drama, ethnic, gay, honors, international, jazz band, literary magazine, musical theater, newspaper, orchestra, pep band, photography, political, professional, radio and TV, recreational, religious, social, social service, and student government. Popular campus events include Student Organizational Fest, Winter Flurry, and Hunger Clean Up.

Sports: There are 7 intercollegiate sports for men and 7 for women, and 39 intramural sports for men and 39 for women. Facilities include 2 recreation centers and Valley Fields, an outdoor soccer, track, and football facility.

Disabled Students: 90% of the campus is accessible. Wheelchair ramps, elevators, special parking, specially equipped rest rooms, special class scheduling, lowered drinking fountains, lowered telephones, and special housing are available.

Services: Counseling and information services are available, as is tutoring in some subjects, including many lower-division classes taken by freshmen and sophomores. There is a reader service for the blind. Book taping and note taking are available for the physically disabled.

Campus Safety and Security: Measures include 24-hour foot and vehicle patrol, self-defense education, security escort services, and shuttle buses. There are informal discussions, pamphlets/posters/films, emergency telephones, lighted pathways/sidewalks, and and closed-circuit cameras in selected parking lots and buildings throughout the campus. Public Safety has bicycle patrols and the Milwaukee Police conduct patrols on horseback.

Programs of Study: Marquette confers B.A., B.S., and B.S.N. degrees. Associate, master's, and doctoral degrees are also awarded. Bachelor's degrees are awarded in BIOLOGICAL SCIENCE (biochemistry, biology/ biological science, molecular biology, and physiology), BUSINESS (accounting, banking and finance, business administration and management, business economics, human resources, international business management, management information systems, and marketing/ retailing/merchandising), COMMUNICATIONS AND THE ARTS (advertising, broadcasting, classical languages, classics, communications, dramatic arts, English, French, German, journalism, public relations, and Spanish), COMPUTER AND PHYSICAL SCIENCE (chemistry, computer science, information sciences and systems, mathematics, physics, and statistics), EDUCATION (secondary), ENGINEERING AND ENVIRONMENTAL DESIGN (biomedical engineering, civil engineering, computer engineering, electrical/electronics engineering, engineering, environmental engineering, industrial engineering technology, and mechanical engineering), HEALTH PROFESSIONS (biomedical science, exercise science, medical laboratory science, nursing, premedicine, and speech pathology/audiology), SOCIAL SCIENCE (anthropology, criminology, economics, history, interdisciplinary studies, international relations, philosophy, political science/government, psychology, sociology, and theological studies). Biomedical engineering, nursing, and premedicine are the strongest academically. Business administration, nursing, and engineering are the largest.

Required: To graduate, students must complete a total of 126 to 135 credit hours and maintain a minimum GPA of 2.0, or 2.5 in accounting. The 36-credit-hour core of common studies includes 6 credit hours each of rhetoric, human nature and ethics, and theology, and 3 each of mathematical reasoning, individual and social behavior, science and nature, histories of cultures and societies, literature and performing arts, and diverse cultures. The total number of hours in the major varies.

Special: Marquette offers co-op programs in engineering, internships, study abroad in 16 countries, a Washington summer term, and work-study programs. Dual and student-designed majors, nondegree study, an accelerated degree program for predental and prelaw students, and pass/ fail options are available. Cross-registration is possible with Milwaukee Institute of Art and Design, and there is a 2-2 engineering program with Waukesha County Technical College. The Freshman Frontier Program offers academic support for selected freshmen who do not meet regular admission requirements but show potential for success. The Educational Opportunity Program affords students from minority groups and low-income families the opportunity to attend the school. There are 8 national honor societies, including Phi Beta Kappa, a freshman honors program, and 100 departmental honors programs.

Faculty/Classroom: 62% of faculty are male; 38%, female. 77% teach undergraduates, 65% do research, and 60% do both. No introductory courses are taught by graduate students.

Admissions: 70% of the 2005-2006 applicants were accepted. The SAT scores for the 2005-2006 freshman class were: Verbal--9% below 500, 40% between 500 and 599, 40% between 600 and 700, and 11% above 700; Math--8% below 500, 39% between 500 and 599, 38% between 600 and 700, and 15% above 700. The ACT scores were 8% below 21, 12% between 21 and 23, 29% between 24 and 26, 23% between 27 and 28, and 28% above 28. 56% of the current freshmen were in the top fifth of their class; 86% were in the top two fifths.

Requirements: The SAT or ACT is required. In addition, applicants must be graduates of an accredited secondary school with a recommended 18 credits, including 4 years of English, 3 each of social studies and math, 2 each of sciences and foreign language, and 4 of additional academic subjects. Most students rank in the upper quarter of their high school class. The GED is accepted, with a minimum score of 225. Applicants must demonstrate ability, preparation, and motivation. An interview is recommended. AP and CLEP credits are accepted. Important factors in the admissions decision are advanced placement or honor courses, recommendations by school officials, and leadership record.

Procedure: Freshmen are admitted to all sessions. Entrance exams should be taken in the junior year and repeated early in the senior year if necessary. Applications should be filed by December 1 for fall entry. Notification is sent January 31. 1516 applicants were on the 2005 waiting list; 334 were admitted. Applications are accepted on-line.

Transfer: 176 transfer students enrolled in 2004-2005. Applicants for transfer must have a minimum GPA of 2.0; some programs require a higher average. The SAT or ACT is required if the applicant has completed fewer than 12 hours of college-level work. 30 of 126 to 135 credits required for the bachelor's degree must be completed at Marquette.

Visiting: There are regularly scheduled orientations for prospective students, including an agenda for visits that varies according to the specific program; open houses are available on scheduled weekends throughout the academic year. There are guides for informal visits and visitors may sit in on classes and stay overnight. To schedule a visit, contact the Admissions Office.

Financial Aid: In 2005-2006, 90% of all full-time freshmen and 86% of continuing full-time students received some form of financial aid. 54% of full-time freshmen and 51% of continuing full-time students received need-based aid. The average freshman award was $17,835. Need-based scholarships or need-based grants averaged $8449 ($22,950 maximum); need-based self-help aid (loans and jobs) averaged $5762 ($7125 maximum); non-need-based athletic scholarships averaged $19,129 ($22,950 maximum); and other non-need-based awards and non-need-based scholarships averaged $8828. In a recent year, 44% of undergraduates worked part time. Average annual earnings from campus work are $2000. The average financial indebtedness of the 2005 graduate was $26,345. The FAFSA is required. The priority date for freshman financial aid applications for fall entry is February 1.

International Students: There are 181 international students enrolled. The school actively recruits these students. A satisfactory score is required on the written TOEFL. Students must also take the MELAB, the Comprehensive English Language Test, the college's own test or IELTS. Marquette requires success in final external secondary exams according to the student's country of education.

Computers: Wireless access is available. All rooms in university housing have high speed Internet access. Selected buildings (including the library) have wireless access, up to 3000 connections. The library also has wired connections and laptops available for 4-hour checkout. There are 1200 university-owned computers available for general student use all over campus including dorms, the student center, and the library. All students may access the system 24 hours a day. There are no time limits and no fees. Marquette has specially priced and configured laptops available through MPC, registered for campus wireless access. This is made available to help students select a PC with adequate capability for school use.

Graduates: From July 1, 2004 to June 30, 2005, 1685 bachelor's degrees were awarded. The most popular majors were business and marketing (22%), communications (14%), and engineering (10%). In an average class, 62% graduate in 4 years or less, 78% graduate in 5 years or less, and 80% graduate in 6 years or less. 320 companies recruited on campus in 2004-2005. Of the 2004 graduating class, 29% were enrolled in graduate school within 6 months of graduation and 67% were employed.

Admissions Contact: Robert Blust, Dean of Admissions.
E-mail: *admissions@marquette.edu* Web: *www.marquette.edu*

MILWAUKEE INSTITUTE OF ART AND DESIGN E-4
Milwaukee, WI 53202-6003
(414) 291-8070
(888) 749-MIAD; Fax: (414) 291-8077

Full-time: 300 men, 300 women	**Faculty:** 26
Part-time: 30 men, 40 women	**Ph.D.s:** 85%
Graduate: none	**Student/Faculty:** 23 to 1
Year: semesters, summer session	**Tuition:** $22,200
Application Deadline: see profile	**Room & Board:** $6500
Freshman Class: n/av	
SAT or ACT: recommended	**SPECIAL**

Milwaukee Institute of Art and Design, founded in 1974, is a private, 4-year professional college of art and design. Figures in the above capsule and in this profile are approximate. In addition to regional accreditation, MIAD has baccalaureate program accreditation with NASAD. The library contains 29,000 volumes and 380 audio/video tapes/CDs/DVDs, and subscribes to 85 periodicals including electronic. Computerized library services include the card catalog, interlibrary loans, and database searching. Special learning facilities include a learning resource center, art gallery, and museum. The campus is in an urban area in downtown Milwaukee. Including any residence halls, there are 4 buildings.

Student Life: 72% of undergraduates are from Wisconsin. Others are from 20 states. 80% are from public schools. 88% are white. The average age of freshmen is 19; all undergraduates, 23. 21% do not continue beyond their first year; 73% remain to graduate.

Housing: 144 students can be accommodated in college housing, which includes coed dorms. On-campus housing is available on a first-come, first-served basis. 77% of students commute. Alcohol is not permitted. All students may keep cars.

Activities: There are no fraternities or sororities. There are 8 groups on campus, including art, ethnic, literary magazine, photography, professional, religious, student government, and yearbook. Popular campus events include visiting artist lectures and workshops, student and faculty exhibitions, and a scholarship show.

Sports: There is no sports program at MIAD.

Disabled Students: All of the campus is accessible. Wheelchair ramps, elevators, specially equipped rest rooms, lowered drinking fountains, and lowered telephones are available.

Services: Counseling and information services are available, as is tutoring in some subjects, including liberal studies. There is remedial writing. There is a program in developmental freshman English as well as student tutoring, and a writing center.

Campus Safety and Security: Measures include security escort services, informal discussions, pamphlets/posters/films, and emergency telephones. There are lighted pathways/sidewalks.

Programs of Study: MIAD confers the B.F.A. degree. Bachelor's degrees are awarded in COMMUNICATIONS AND THE ARTS (drawing, fine arts, graphic design, illustration, industrial design, painting, photography, printmaking, and sculpture), ENGINEERING AND ENVIRONMENTAL DESIGN (interior design). Graphic design, illustration, and industrial design are the largest.

Required: About 66% of the graduation credits are in studio courses. Students must complete 124 credits, with 81 studio credits, 43 in liberal studies, and a minimum GPA of 2.0. MIAD requires 12 credits in art history and at least 12 credits in English/writing and 19 credits in the humanities and sciences.

Special: Students may cross-register with Marquette University and 29 other nationally accredited art colleges. Study abroad in Japan, Germany, Poland, and France, a semester at New York Artists Studio, and internships in all design fields and photography are available. Nondegree study and credit for life, military, and work experience are possible.

Faculty/Classroom: 64% of faculty are male; 36%, female. All teach undergraduates. The average class size in a regular course is 16.

Requirements: The SAT or ACT is recommended. In addition, applicants must be graduates of an accredited secondary school. 4 years of art are recommended. A portfolio review and an interview are required. A GPA of 2.0 is required. AP and CLEP credits are accepted. Important factors in the admissions decision are evidence of special talent, advanced placement or honor courses, and personality/intangible qualities.

Procedure: Freshmen are admitted fall and spring. There is a deferred admissions plan. There is a rolling admissions plan. Check with the school for current application deadlines. Application fee is $25. Notification is sent on a rolling basis.

Transfer: A transfer portfolio evaluation is done. Transcripts are reviewed for courses comparable to MIAD's programs. A grade of C or better is required for transfer. 30 of 124 credits required for the bachelor's degree must be completed at MIAD.

Visiting: There are guides for informal visits and visitors may sit in on classes. To schedule a visit, contact the Admissions Office.

Financial Aid: The FAFSA is required. The deadline for filing freshman financial aid applications for fall entry is March 1.

International Students: The school actively recruits these students. A satisfactory score on the TOEFL is required.

Computers: All students may access the system more than 80 hours a week.

Admissions Contact: Director of Admissions. A video is available. E-mail: *admissions@miad.edu* Web: *www.miad.edu*

MILWAUKEE SCHOOL OF ENGINEERING   E-4

Milwaukee, WI 53202-3109

(414) 277-7481
(800) 332-6763; Fax: (414) 277-7475

Full-time: 1494 men, 325 women	Faculty: 118; IIB, +$
Part-time: 232 men, 41 women	Ph.D.s: 64%
Graduate: 171 men, 52 women	Student/Faculty: 15 to 1
Year: quarters, summer session	Tuition: $23,955
Application Deadline: open	Room & Board: $5892
Freshman Class: 1742 applied, 1203 accepted, 456 enrolled	
SAT Verbal/Math: 580/610*	ACT: 26 VERY COMPETITIVE+

Milwaukee School of Engineering, established in 1903, is a private institution with programs in engineering, engineering technology, business, communication, and nursing. There are 5 undergraduate and 3 graduate schools. In addition to regional accreditation, MSOE has baccalaureate program accreditation with ABET, ACCE, and CCNE. The library contains 48,164 volumes, 79,054 microform items, and 1423 audio/video tapes/CDs/DVDs, and subscribes to 481 periodicals including electronic. Computerized library services include the card catalog, interlibrary loans, database searching, Internet access, and laptop Internet portals. Special learning facilities include a learning resource center and radio station. The 15-acre campus is in an urban area in Milwaukee. Including any residence halls, there are 14 buildings.

Student Life: 70% of undergraduates are from Wisconsin. Others are from 32 states, 20 foreign countries, and Canada. 78% are white. The average age of freshmen is 18; all undergraduates, 21. 19% do not continue beyond their first year; 58% remain to graduate.

Housing: 889 students can be accommodated in college housing, which includes coed dorms and on-campus apartments. In addition, there are special-interest houses. On-campus housing is guaranteed for all 4 years. 51% of students commute. All students may keep cars.

Activities: 8% of men and about 1% of women belong to 3 national fraternities; 12% of women belong to 1 local and 1 national sorority. There are 72 groups on campus, including bowling, cheerleading, chess, choir, cycling, drama, ecology, ethnic, fencing, gay, honors, international, literary magazine, paintball, pep band, political, professional, radio and TV, religious, rugby, social, social service, student government, sym-

---

phony, tae kwondo and yearbook. Popular campus events include St. Patrick's Week, Greek Week, and Sub-zero Days.

Sports: There are 11 intercollegiate sports for men and 9 for women, and 9 intramural sports for men and 9 for women. Facilities include a 210,000-square-foot recreation athletic, health and wellness center. It contains an ice arena, fitness center, wrestling room, field house, counseling center, health services, campus ministry, basketball arena, and an indoor track facility.

Disabled Students: 75% of the campus is accessible. Wheelchair ramps, elevators, special parking, specially equipped rest rooms, special class scheduling, lowered drinking fountains, lowered telephones, and special housing are available.

Services: Counseling and information services are available, as is tutoring in every subject. There is a reader service for the blind, and remedial math, reading, and writing.

Campus Safety and Security: Measures include 24-hour foot and vehicle patrol, security escort services, shuttle buses, and informal discussions. There are pamphlets/posters/films, emergency telephones, lighted pathways/sidewalks, and 24-hour security in residence halls.

Programs of Study: MSOE confers B.A. and B.S. degrees. Master's degrees are also awarded. Bachelor's degrees are awarded in BUSINESS (business administration and management, international business management, management information systems, and management science), COMMUNICATIONS AND THE ARTS (technical and business writing), COMPUTER AND PHYSICAL SCIENCE (software engineering), ENGINEERING AND ENVIRONMENTAL DESIGN (architectural engineering, biomedical engineering, computer engineering, construction management, electrical/electronics engineering, engineering technology, industrial engineering, and mechanical engineering), HEALTH PROFESSIONS (nursing). Biomedical engineering and computer engineering are the strongest academically. Architectural, mechanical, and electrical engineering programs are the largest.

Required: To graduate, students must complete approximately 197 quarter credits with a minimum GPA of 2.0 and also a minumum GPA of 2.0 in their major area of study. There are requirements in speech, composition, computer programming, ethics, and business.

Special: MSOE offers internships in the student's discipline, study-abroad in Germany, India, and Czech Republic, on-campus work-study programs, and nondegree study. A number of dual degrees along with a 5-year dual degree with a bachelor's in engineering and a master's in environmental engineering are available. There are 2 national honor societies.

Faculty/Classroom: 79% of faculty are male; 21%, female. 98% teach undergraduates, 2% do research, and 25% do both. No introductory courses are taught by graduate students. The average class size in an introductory lecture is 21; in a laboratory, 12; and in a regular course, 20.

Admissions: 69% of the 2005-2006 applicants were accepted. The SAT scores for the 2005-2006 freshman class were: Verbal--17% below 500, 43% between 500 and 599, 34% between 600 and 700, and 6% above 700; Math--6% below 500, 30% between 500 and 599, 60% between 600 and 700, and 4% above 700. The ACT scores were 1% below 21, 21% between 21 and 23, 29% between 24 and 26, 33% between 27 and 28, and 16% above 28.

Requirements: The ACT is required though the SAT is acceptable. In addition, applicants must be graduates of an accredited secondary school, having completed 15 academic credits, including 4 units of English, 2 units each of science and math, and 1 unit each of social studies and history. More units in math, science, and English are strongly advised; 1 unit in computer science is helpful. The GED is accepted. An essay is required, and an interview is recommended. A GPA of 2.5 is required. AP and CLEP credits are accepted. Important factors in the admissions decision are advanced placement or honor courses, leadership record, and personality/intangible qualities.

Procedure: Freshmen are admitted to all sessions. There is a deferred admissions and a rolling admissions plan. The application deadlines are open. Application fee is $25. Applications are accepted on-line.

Transfer: 156 transfer students enrolled in 2004-2005. Applicants for transfer should have a minimum GPA of 2.5 and must have completed 24 semester or 36 quarter credits. 100 of 200 credits required for the bachelor's degree must be completed at MSOE.

Visiting: There are regularly scheduled orientations for prospective students, consisting of personal visits, Spring and Fall Open Houses, and the Shadow Program. There are guides for informal visits and visitors may sit in on classes and stay overnight. To schedule a visit, contact the Admission Office at *explore@msoe.edu*.

Financial Aid: In 2005-2006, 97% of all full-time freshmen and 96% of continuing full-time students received some form of financial aid. 74% of full-time freshmen and 78% of continuing full-time students received need-based aid. The average freshman award was $22,637. Need-based scholarships or need-based grants averaged $3626 ($10,015 maximum); need-based self-help aid (loans and jobs) averaged $2684 ($5082 maximum); other non-need-based awards and non-need-based scholarships averaged $6745; and private loans, Plus loans, and unsubsidized Stafford loans averaged $8958 ($25,955 maximum). 50% of undergraduates work part time. Average annual earnings from campus work are $1450. The average financial indebtedness of the 2005 graduate was $31,808. The FAFSA is required. The priority date for freshman financial aid applications for fall entry is March 15.

International Students: There are 40 international students enrolled. The school actively recruits these students. They must score satisfactorily on the TOEFL and also take IELTS.

Computers: Wireless access is available. Students lease a laptop until graduation and after that, they own it. There are wireless networks or hard-line connections in every building. All students may access the system. There are no time limits and no fees. All students are required to have personal computers.

Graduates: From July 1, 2004 to June 30, 2005, 361 bachelor's degrees were awarded. The most popular majors were mechanical engineering (17%), architectural engineering (14%), and electrical engineering (13%). In an average class, 30% graduate in 4 years or less, and 60% graduate in 5 years or less. 158 companies recruited on campus in 2004-2005. Of the 2004 graduating class, 3% were enrolled in graduate school within 6 months of graduation and 93% were employed.

Admissions Contact: Paul Borens, Director of Admission.
E-mail: *borens@msoe.edu* Web: *www.msoe.edu\admiss*

MOUNT MARY COLLEGE   E-4
Milwaukee, WI 53222

(414) 256-1219
(800) 321-6265; Fax: (414) 256-0180

Full-time: 14 men, 907 women	**Faculty:** 55; IIB, --$
Part-time: 24 men, 507 women	**Ph.D.s:** 63%
Graduate: 13 men, 257 women	**Student/Faculty:** 17 to 1
Year: semesters, summer session	**Tuition:** $17,105
Application Deadline: August	**Room & Board:** $5790
Freshman Class: 319 applied, 288 accepted, 160 enrolled	
ACT: required	**COMPETITIVE**

Mount Mary College, founded in 1913, is a private women's liberal arts institution sponsored by the School Sisters of Notre Dame, and affiliated with the Roman Catholic Church. In addition to regional accreditation, Mount Mary has baccalaureate program accreditation with ADA, AOTA, CSWE, FIDER, and NLN. The library contains 104,606 volumes, 1615 microform items, and 7238 audio/video tapes/CDs/DVDs, and subscribes to 19,385 periodicals including electronic. Computerized library services include the card catalog, interlibrary loans, database searching, and Internet access. Special learning facilities include a learning resource center, art gallery, and computer centers, CAD labs, S.M.A.R.T. classrooms, and a historic costume collection. The 80-acre campus is in an urban area 7 miles west of downtown Milwaukee. Including any residence halls, there are 8 buildings.

Student Life: 96% of undergraduates are from Wisconsin. Others are from 9 states and 14 foreign countries. 90% are from public schools. 69% are white; 16% African American. 35% are claim no religious affiliation; 34% Catholic; 20% Protestant. The average age of freshmen is 19; all undergraduates, 26. 35% do not continue beyond their first year; 51% remain to graduate.

Housing: 200 students can be accommodated in college housing, which includes single-sex dorms. On-campus housing is available on a first-come, first-served basis and is available on a lottery system for upperclassmen. Priority is given to out-of-town students. 88% of students commute. All students may keep cars.

Activities: There are no fraternities or sororities. There are 42 groups on campus, including art, choir, chorale, chorus, computers, dance, department affiliated clubs, drama, ethnic, honors, international, literary magazine, newspaper, political, professional, religious, social, social service, and student government. Popular campus events include Freshman Investiture, Madrigal Dinner, and All-School Christmas Dinner.

Sports: There are 5 intercollegiate sports for women and 5 intramural sports for women. Facilities include a gym, a swimming pool, an exercise room, a weight room, and a soccer field.

Disabled Students: 98% of the campus is accessible. Wheelchair ramps, elevators, special parking, specially equipped rest rooms, lowered drinking fountains, and lowered telephones are available.

Services: Counseling and information services are available, as is tutoring in most subjects. There is a reader service for the blind, and remedial math, reading, and writing. A tutoring language lab is also available.

Campus Safety and Security: Measures include 24-hour foot and vehicle patrol, self-defense education, security escort services, and informal discussions. There are pamphlets/posters/films, emergency telephones, and lighted pathways/sidewalks.

Programs of Study: Mount Mary confers B.A., B.S., and B.S.N. degrees. Master's degrees are also awarded. Bachelor's degrees are awarded in BIOLOGICAL SCIENCE (biology/biological science), BUSINESS (accounting, business administration and management, fashion merchandising, and marketing/retailing/merchandising), COMMUNICATIONS AND THE ARTS (communications, English, fine arts, French, graphic design, public relations, Spanish, and technical and business writing), COMPUTER AND PHYSICAL SCIENCE (chemistry and math-

ematics), EDUCATION (art, bilingual/bicultural, business, early childhood, elementary, English, foreign languages, music, science, and secondary), ENGINEERING AND ENVIRONMENTAL DESIGN (interior design), HEALTH PROFESSIONS (art therapy, nursing, occupational therapy, predentistry, and premedicine), SOCIAL SCIENCE (behavioral science, criminal justice, dietetics, fashion design and technology, history, international studies, philosophy, prelaw, psychology, social work, and theological studies). Business administration, nursing and teacher education are the largest.

Required: To graduate, students must complete 128 credit hours, including at least 24 (but as many as 74) in the major, while maintaining a GPA of at least 2.0, with many majors requiring a higher GPA. A 48-credit liberal arts core curriculum and demonstrated math competency are required.

Special: Mount Mary College offers internships, accelerated degree programs in business administration, business/professional communication, and marketing, and study abroad in Japan and other countries. Student-designed majors, a joint degree with Columbia College of Nursing, pass/fail options, and credit for life, military, and work experience are available. There are 10 national honor societies and a freshman honors program.

Faculty/Classroom: 22% of faculty are male; 78%, female. 94% teach undergraduates. No introductory courses are taught by graduate students. The average class size in an introductory lecture is 17; in a laboratory, 12; and in a regular course, 15.

Admissions: 90% of the 2005-2006 applicants were accepted. The ACT scores for the 2005-2006 freshman class were: 61% below 21, 23% between 21 and 23, 10% between 24 and 26, 3% between 27 and 28, and 3% above 28. 46% of the current freshmen were in the top fifth of their class; 73% were in the top two fifths.

Requirements: The ACT is required. In addition, applicants must be graduates of an accredited secondary school. The GED is accepted. Students should have completed 16 credits, including 4 each in English, history, social sciences, and foreign language, and 2 each in math and science. An interview is recommended. Mount Mary requires applicants to be in the upper 40% of their class. A GPA of 2.5 is required. AP and CLEP credits are accepted. Important factors in the admissions decision are advanced placement or honor courses, recommendations by school officials, and leadership record.

Procedure: Freshmen are admitted fall and spring. Entrance exams should be taken in the junior year or fall of the senior year. There are deferred admissions and rolling admissions plans. Applications should be filed by August for fall entry and December for spring entry, along with a $25 fee. Notification is sent on a rolling basis. Applications are accepted on-line.

Transfer: 173 transfer students enrolled in a recent year. Applicants should have a minimum GPA of 2.0, though each department has its own admission requirements. The school recommends either the SAT or ACT and an interview. 32 of 128 credits required for the bachelor's degree must be completed at Mount Mary.

Visiting: There are regularly scheduled orientations for prospective students, including tours, meetings with faculty and staff, and information sessions. There are guides for informal visits and visitors may sit in on classes and stay overnight. To schedule a visit, contact the Enrollment Office.

Financial Aid: 75% of full-time freshmen and 76% of continuing full-time students received need-based aid. The average freshman award was $12,944. 12% of undergraduates work part time. The average financial indebtedness of the 2005 graduate was $19,040. The FAFSA is required. The priority date for freshman financial aid applications for fall entry is March 1.

International Students: There are 16 international students enrolled. The school actively recruits these students. A satisfactory score is required on the written TOEFL.

Computers: Mount Mary College provides 336 networked computers for student use in the residence hall common areas and dorm rooms, classrooms, computer labs, library, and cyber café. Windows 2000 and Macintosh operating systems are supported. All students may access the system 7 days a week, 24 hours a day. There are no time limits and no fees.

Graduates: In a recent year, 174 bachelor's degrees were awarded. The most popular majors were nursing (15%), business adminstration (7%), and interior design (6%). In an average class, 1% graduate in 3 years or less, 37% graduate in 4 years or less, 43% graduate in 5 years or less, and 47% graduate in 6 years or less. 3 companies recruited on campus in a recent year. In a recent graduating class, 19% were enrolled in graduate school within 6 months of graduation and 87% were employed.

Admissions Contact: Brooke Konopacki, Dean of Enrollment. A video is available. E-mail: *admiss@mtmary.edu* Web: *www.mtmary.edu*

NORTHLAND COLLEGE   B-1

Ashland, WI 54806   **(715) 682-1224**

(800) 753-1840; Fax: (715) 682-1258

Full-time: 285 men, 364 women	**Faculty:** 41; IIB, --$
Part-time: 27 men, 63 women	**Ph.D.s:** 85%
Graduate: none	**Student/Faculty:** 16 to 1
Year: 4-4-1, summer session	**Tuition:** $20,188
Application Deadline: Open	**Room & Board:** $5891
Freshman Class: 804 applied, 605 accepted, 181 enrolled	
SAT Verbal/Math: 576/561*	**ACT:** 23 COMPETITIVE+

Northland College, founded in 1892, is a private liberal arts institution affiliated with the United Church of Christ and offers undergraduate programs in the arts and sciences, business, education, health professions, and social sciences. There are 3 undergraduate schools. The library contains 77,700 volumes and 9300 microform items, and subscribes to 350 periodicals including electronic. Computerized library services include the card catalog, interlibrary loans, and database searching. Special learning facilities include a learning resource center, art gallery, natural history museum, environmental research acreage, community garden, and wind tower. The 80-acre campus is in a small town 70 miles east of Duluth, Minnesota. Including any residence halls, there are 20 buildings.
Student Life: 65% of undergraduates are from out of state, mostly the Midwest. Students are from 43 states, 7 foreign countries, and Canada. 90% are from public schools. 84% are white. The average age of freshmen is 20; all undergraduates, 21. 20% do not continue beyond their first year; 44% remain to graduate.
Housing: 530 students can be accommodated in college housing, which includes single-sex and coed dorms and on-campus apartments. In addition, there are special-interest houses and a farm house. On-campus housing is guaranteed for all 4 years. 60% of students live on campus; of those, 80% remain on campus on weekends. Alcohol is not permitted. All students may keep cars.
Activities: 2% of men belong to 1 local and 1 national fraternity; 2% of women belong to 2 local sororities. There are 25 groups on campus, including art, band, cheerleading, choir, chorale, chorus, computers, drama, ethnic, gay, honors, international, jazz band, literary magazine, newspaper, orchestra, photography, political, professional, religious, social, social service, student government, symphony, and yearbook. Popular campus events include Snow Festival and Spring Fling.
Sports: There are 4 intercollegiate sports for men and 4 for women, and 11 intramural sports for men and 11 for women. Facilities include an Olympic-size pool, a weight-lifting room, tennis and racquetball courts, a ropes course, and an outdoor recreation program.
Disabled Students: 90% of the campus is accessible. Wheelchair ramps, elevators, special parking, specially equipped rest rooms, and special class scheduling are available.
Services: Counseling and information services are available, as is tutoring in every subject. There is a reader service for the blind, and remedial math, reading, and writing.
Campus Safety and Security: Measures include security escort services, informal discussions, pamphlets/posters/films, and emergency telephones. There are lighted pathways/sidewalks.
Programs of Study: Northland confers B.A. and B.S. degrees. Bachelor's degrees are awarded in AGRICULTURE (natural resource management), BIOLOGICAL SCIENCE (biology/biological science), BUSINESS (business administration and management and business economics), COMMUNICATIONS AND THE ARTS (creative writing, English, and fine arts), COMPUTER AND PHYSICAL SCIENCE (atmospheric sciences and meteorology, chemistry, earth science, information sciences and systems, and mathematics), EDUCATION (elementary, middle school, music, and secondary), ENGINEERING AND ENVIRONMENTAL DESIGN (environmental science), SOCIAL SCIENCE (history, parks and recreation management, peace studies, psychology, public administration, religion, and sociology). Biology, natural resources, and meteorology are the strongest academically. Biology, natural resources, and outdoor education are the largest.
Required: Students must complete 124 credits, including 35 to 60 in the major, with a minimum GPA of 2.0. All students must meet requirements that include courses in English composition, literature, history, philosophy, social and natural sciences, physical science, fine arts, phys ed, and studies of other cultures.
Special: Opportunities are provided for cooperative programs in many majors and with other schools, internships, work-study programs with state and federal agencies, student-designed majors, credit for life experience, pass/fail options, and study abroad in 7 countries. Cross-registration is offered with Spring Term Consortium Schools, Allegheny and Beloit Colleges, and Kansai Gaidai University in Japan. 3-2 engineering degrees are available in conjunction with Michigan Technological University and Washington University in St. Louis. A 3-2 degree program in forestry is also available. There are 2 national honor societies.
Faculty/Classroom: 81% of faculty are male; 19%, female. All teach undergraduates. The average class size in an introductory lecture is 30; in a laboratory, 30; and in a regular course, 22.

Admissions: 75% of the 2005-2006 applicants were accepted. The SAT scores for the 2005-2006 freshman class were: Verbal--20% below 500, 55% between 500 and 599, 20% between 600 and 700, and 5% above 700; Math--22% below 500, 58% between 500 and 599, 15% between 600 and 700, and 5% above 700. The ACT scores were 27% below 21, 20% between 21 and 23, 28% between 24 and 26, 10% between 27 and 28, and 15% above 28. 46% of the current freshmen were in the top fifth of their class; 74% were in the top two fifths.
Requirements: The SAT or ACT is required. In addition, graduation from an accredited secondary school is required; the GED is accepted. An essay and interview are recommended. A GPA of 2.0 is required. AP and CLEP credits are accepted. Important factors in the admissions decision are advanced placement or honor courses, extracurricular activities record, and recommendations by school officials.
Procedure: Freshmen are admitted fall and winter. Entrance exams should be taken in the fall. There are early decision, early admissions, deferred admissions, and rolling admisions plans. Early decision applications should be filed by November 22; regular applications are open. Notification of early decision is sent December 22; regular decision, on a rolling basis. Applications are accepted on-line.
Transfer: Applicants must have maintained a minimum GPA of 2.0 in previously attended colleges. 30 of 124 credits required for the bachelor's degree must be completed at Northland.
Visiting: There are regularly scheduled orientations for prospective students, including an interview, a tour, class visits, and an overnight stay in a dorm. There are guides for informal visits and visitors may sit in on classes and stay overnight. To schedule a visit, contact the Admissions Office.
Financial Aid: In 2005-2006, 89% of all full-time freshmen and 92% of continuing full-time students received some form of financial aid. 83% of all full-time students received need-based aid. The average freshman award was $15,708. 90% of undergraduates work part time. Average annual earnings from campus work are $1200. The average financial indebtedness of the 2005 graduate was $17,765. Northland is a member of CSS. The FAFSA and the college's own financial statement are required. The deadline for filing freshman financial aid applications for fall entry is April 15.
International Students: There were 21 international students enrolled in a recent year. The school actively recruits these students. A satisfactory score is required on the written TOEFL or the MELAB.
Computers: All students may access the system. There are no time limits and no fees.
Graduates: In a recent year, 109 bachelor's degrees were awarded. The most popular majors were natural resources (15%), outdoor education (15%), and biology (15%). In an average class, 2% graduate in 3 years or less, and 80% graduate in 4 years or less. Of the recent year's graduating class, 15% were enrolled in graduate school within 6 months of graduation and 95% were employed.
Admissions Contact: Jaso Turley, Director of Admissions. A video is available. E-mail: *admit@northland.edu* Web: *www.northland.edu*

RIPON COLLEGE   D-4

Ripon, WI 54971   **(920) 748-8185**

(800) 94-RIPON; Fax: (920) 748-8335

Full-time: 477 men, 476 women	**Faculty:** 52; IIB, --$
Part-time: 9 men, 17 women	**Ph.D.s:** 92%
Graduate: none	**Student/Faculty:** 18 to 1
Year: semesters	**Tuition:** $21,550
Application Deadline: August 1	**Room & Board:** $5610
Freshman Class: 976 applied, 791 accepted, 262 enrolled	
SAT Verbal/Math: 579/570*	**ACT:** 24 COMPETITIVE+

Ripon College, established in 1851, is a private, residential, liberal arts institution. The library contains 161,000 volumes, 25,000 microform items, and 600 audio/video tapes/CDs/DVDs, and subscribes to 800 periodicals including electronic. Computerized library services include the card catalog, interlibrary loans, and database searching. Special learning facilities include a learning resource center, art gallery, radio station, a music library, an art slide library, and college archives. The 250-acre campus is in a small town 80 miles north of Milwaukee in the east-central part of the state. Including any residence halls, there are 26 buildings.
Student Life: 74% of undergraduates are from Wisconsin. Others are from 35 states, 13 foreign countries, and Canada. 57% are from public schools. 85% are white. The average age of freshmen is 18; all undergraduates, 20. 15% do not continue beyond their first year; 74% remain to graduate.
Housing: 940 students can be accommodated in college housing, which includes single-sex and coed dorms, fraternity houses, and sorority houses. Theme and interest groups may form living areas in the residence halls. On-campus housing is guaranteed for all 4 years. 82% of students live on campus; of those, 80% remain on campus on weekends. All students may keep cars.
Activities: 28% of men belong to 2 local and 3 national fraternities; 14% of women belong to 1 local sorority and 2 national sororities. There

are 80 groups on campus, including art, band, cheerleading, choir, chorale, chorus, dance, drama, ethnic, film, forensics, gay, honors, international, jazz band, literary magazine, musical theater, newspaper, orchestra, pep band, photography, political, professional, radio and TV, religious, social, social service, student government, symphony, and yearbook. Popular campus events include Spring and Winter Festivals, Milwaukee Symphony concerts, and theater events.

Sports: There are 9 intercollegiate sports for men and 9 for women, and 15 intramural sports for men and 15 for women. Facilities include a phys ed center, 2 fields, tennis courts, a recreation center, and an exercise room and a fitness center in the residence halls. The campus is within 5 miles of lakes and cross-country skiing opportunities.

Disabled Students: 50% of the campus is accessible. Wheelchair ramps, elevators, special parking, specially equipped rest rooms, special class scheduling, and lowered drinking fountains are available.

Services: Counseling and information services are available, as is tutoring in every subject. Tutoring and services are also available for learning-disabled students.

Campus Safety and Security: Measures include 24-hour foot and vehicle patrol, security escort services, informal discussions, and pamphlets/posters/films. There are emergency telephones, lighted pathways/sidewalks, and a paging system.

Programs of Study: Ripon College confers the A.B. degree. Bachelor's degrees are awarded in BIOLOGICAL SCIENCE (biochemistry and biology/biological science), BUSINESS (business administration and management), COMMUNICATIONS AND THE ARTS (art, art history and appreciation, communications, dramatic arts, English, French, German, music, and Spanish), COMPUTER AND PHYSICAL SCIENCE (chemistry, computer science, mathematics, physical sciences, and physics), EDUCATION (early childhood, elementary, middle school, and secondary), ENGINEERING AND ENVIRONMENTAL DESIGN (environmental science), HEALTH PROFESSIONS (exercise science), SOCIAL SCIENCE (anthropology, economics, history, international studies, Latin American studies, philosophy, political science/government, psychobiology, psychology, religion, and sociology). Biology and chemistry are the strongest academically. Economics, education, and business administration are the largest.

Required: To graduate, students must complete 124 credit hours, including usually 24 in the major, with a minimum GPA of 2.0. Required courses include 1 course each in fine arts, humanities, natural sciences, and social and behavioral sciences, a first-year seminar, a first-year writing course, 1 phys ed course, and a capstone experience.

Special: Students may cross-register with the Associated Colleges of the Midwest. Internships, study abroad in 13 countries and study through 7 domestic programs, and a Washington semester are available. The college offers 3-year degrees in all areas, dual and student-designed majors, and pass/fail options. A 3-2 engineering degree is available with Rensselaer Polytechnic Institute, Washington University, and the University of Minnesota; other 3-2 programs are in environmental studies and in forestry with Duke University and in social welfare with the University of Chicago. A 2-2 nursing program is possible with Rush University. There are 12 national honor societies, including Phi Beta Kappa, and a freshman honors program.

Faculty/Classroom: 61% of faculty are male; 39%, female. All both teach and do research. The average class size in an introductory lecture is 24; in a laboratory, 16; and in a regular course, 17.

Admissions: 81% of the 2005-2006 applicants were accepted. The SAT scores for the 2005-2006 freshman class were: Verbal--27% below 500, 18% between 500 and 599, 41% between 600 and 700, and 14% above 700; Math--20% below 500, 36% between 500 and 599, 36% between 600 and 700, and 8% above 700. The ACT scores were 21% below 21, 23% between 21 and 23, 26% between 24 and 26, 13% between 27 and 28, and 17% above 28. 41% of the current freshmen were in the top fifth of their class; 76% were in the top two fifths. 7 freshmen graduated first in their class.

Requirements: The SAT or ACT is required. In addition, applicants must be graduates of an accredited secondary school. The GED is accepted. Applicants should complete at least 17 Carnegie units, including 4 of English, 2 to 4 each of math, social studies, and natural sciences, and up to 7 of other college-preparatory electives. An essay may be required, and an interview is recommended. Ripon College requires applicants to be in the upper 50% of their class. A GPA of 2.0 is required. AP and CLEP credits are accepted. Important factors in the admissions decision are leadership record, recommendations by school officials, and advanced placement or honor courses.

Procedure: Freshmen are admitted fall and spring. Entrance exams should be taken in the junior year or the fall of the senior year. There is a deferred admissions plan. There is a rolling admissions plan. Applications should be filed by August 1 for fall entry and December 15 for spring entry, along with a $30 fee. Notification is sent on a rolling basis. Applications are accepted on-line.

Transfer: 27 transfer students enrolled in 2004-2005. Applicants must have a minimum 2.0 GPA and be in good standing at their previous college. The SAT or ACT, a personal statement, and an interview are rec-

ommended. 32 of 124 credits required for the bachelor's degree must be completed at Ripon College.

Visiting: There are regularly scheduled orientations for prospective students, including a tour, an interview, and meetings with professors and coaches. There are guides for informal visits and visitors may sit in on classes and stay overnight. To schedule a visit, contact the Admission Office at (800) 947-4766 or (920) 748-8337 or *adminfo@ripon.edu*.

Financial Aid: In 2005-2006, 99% of all full-time freshmen and 88% of continuing full-time students received some form of financial aid. 78% of full-time freshmen and 71% of continuing full-time students received need-based aid. The average freshman award was $21,953. Need-based scholarships or need-based grants averaged $15,713; need-based self-help aid (loans and jobs) averaged $5255; and other non-need-based awards and non-need-based scholarships averaged $10,465. 38% of undergraduates work part time. Average annual earnings from campus work are $766. The average financial indebtedness of the 2005 graduate was $16,210. The FAFSA is required. The priority date for freshman financial aid applications for fall entry is March 15.

International Students: There are 17 international students enrolled. The school actively recruits these students. They must achieve a satisfactory score on the TOEFL and also take the SAT if available.

Computers: All students may access the system. There are no time limits and no fees.

Graduates: From July 1, 2004 to June 30, 2005, 178 bachelor's degrees were awarded. The most popular majors were history (10%), biology (10%), and psychology (9%). In an average class, 2% graduate in 3 years or less, 61% graduate in 4 years or less, 71% graduate in 5 years or less, and 74% graduate in 6 years or less. 15 companies recruited on campus in 2004-2005. Of the 2004 graduating class, 22% were enrolled in graduate school within 6 months of graduation and 75% were employed.

Admissions Contact: Steven M. Schuetz, Dean of Admission and Financial Aid. E-mail: *schuetzs@ripon.edu* Web: *www.ripon.edu*

SAINT NORBERT COLLEGE   D-3
De Pere, WI 54115

	(920) 403-3005
	(800) 236-4878; Fax: (920) 403-4072
Full-time: 829 men, 1093 women	**Faculty:** 109; IIB, -$
Part-time: 30 men, 35 women	**Ph.D.s:** 92%
Graduate: 19 men, 44 women	**Student/Faculty:** 18 to 1
Year: semesters, summer session	**Tuition:** $22,509
Application Deadline: open	**Room & Board:** $6068
Freshman Class: 1683 applied, 1453 accepted, 511 enrolled	
ACT: 24	**COMPETITIVE+**

Saint Norbert College, founded in 1898, is a Catholic college in the Norbertine tradition of community, offering bachelor's degrees in the arts, the sciences, and business administration. The library contains 220,030 volumes, 30,016 microform items, and 6629 audio/video tapes/CDs/DVDs, and subscribes to 652 periodicals including electronic. Computerized library services include the card catalog, database searching, and Internet access. Special learning facilities include a learning resource center, art gallery, radio station, TV station, language labs, media center with satellite hookup, observatory, 3 theaters, environmental sciences research craft, and international center. The 93-acre campus is in a suburban area 5 miles south of Green Bay. Including any residence halls, there are 37 buildings.

Student Life: 71% of undergraduates are from Wisconsin. Others are from 22 states, 13 foreign countries, and Canada. 70% are from public schools. 92% are white. 51% are Catholic; 13% Protestant. The average age of freshmen is 19; all undergraduates, 20. 12% do not continue beyond their first year; 71% remain to graduate.

Housing: 1546 students can be accommodated in college housing, which includes single-sex and coed dormitories and on-campus apartments. In addition, there are special-interest houses a town house complex, a living center, and off campus housing. On-campus housing is guaranteed for all 4 years. 77% of students live on campus; of those, 80% remain on campus on weekends. All students may keep cars.

Activities: 6% of men belong to 1 local and 3 national fraternities; 8% of women belong to 2 local and 3 national sororities. There are 65 groups on campus, including band, cheerleading, choir, chorale, chorus, computers, dance, drama, environmental, ethnic, faith and service, film, gay, honors, international, jazz band, literary magazine, musical theater, newspaper, political, professional, radio and TV, religious, social, social service, student government, and Y.E.S entertainment service. Popular campus events include "taste of SNC (involvement fair), Heritage Week, and Make a Difference Day.

Sports: There are 10 intercollegiate sports for men and 10 for women, and 7 intramural sports for men and 7 for women. Facilities include a 3100-seat stadium, a sports complex, a 1800-seat sports center, and an activity center.

Disabled Students: 68% of the campus is accessible. Wheelchair ramps, elevators, special parking, specially equipped rest rooms, special

class scheduling, lowered drinking fountains, lowered telephones, and special housing are available.

Services: Counseling and information services are available, as is tutoring in most subjects. There is a reader service for the blind, and remedial math, reading, and writing.

Campus Safety and Security: Measures include self-defense education, security escort services, informal discussions, and pamphlets/posters/films. There are emergency telephones, lighted pathways/sidewalks, motorist assistance, and a crime prevention program.

Programs of Study: St. Norbert confers B.A., B.S., B.B.A., and B.Mus. degrees. Master's degrees are also awarded. Bachelor's degrees are awarded in AGRICULTURE (environmental studies), BIOLOGICAL SCIENCE (biology/biological science), BUSINESS (accounting, business administration and management, and international business management), COMMUNICATIONS AND THE ARTS (art, communications, English, fine arts, French, German, music, Spanish, and speech/debate/rhetoric), COMPUTER AND PHYSICAL SCIENCE (chemistry, computer science, geology, mathematics, natural sciences, and physics), EDUCATION (elementary and music), ENGINEERING AND ENVIRONMENTAL DESIGN (commercial art and environmental science), SOCIAL SCIENCE (economics, history, humanities, international relations, philosophy, political science/government, psychology, religion, and sociology). Business administration, communications, and elementary education are the largest.

Required: To graduate, students must complete 128 credits with at least a 2.0 GPA, and a minimum of 40 semester credits in a particular major. There are general education requirements in the areas of religious studies, human nature, human relationships, natural science, creative expression, United States heritage, foreign heritages, quantitative skills, Western tradition, global society, a writing-intensive course, and Senior Colloquium.

Special: Cross-registration with the University of Wisconsin-Green Bay for German courses, internships, study abroad in more than 20 countries, a Washington semester, and work-study programs are available. The college offers dual and student-designed majors, B.A.-B.S. degrees, nondegree study, and limited credit for military experience and work training. The Leadership and Service Program and leadership minor help students improve their leadership abilities through courses and activities. There are 8 national honor societies, and a freshman honors program.

Faculty/Classroom: 63% of faculty are male; 37%, female. All both teach and do research. No introductory courses are taught by graduate students.

Admissions: 86% of the 2005-2006 applicants were accepted. The ACT scores for the 2005-2006 freshman class were: 19% below 21, 30% between 21 and 23, 29% between 24 and 26, 10% between 27 and 28, and 12% above 28. 50% of the current freshmen were in the top fourth of their class; 80% were in the top half. In a recent year there was 1 National Merit finalist. 17 freshmen graduated first in their class.

Requirements: The SAT or ACT is required. In addition, admissions requirements ar either graduation from accredited secondary school with 16 units, including 4 English, 3 math, 3 lab sciences, 2 foreign langauge, 2 social studies, 2 history; or GED score in the 55% range; minimum G.P.A. of 2.5 and either a SAT or ACT entrance exam. AP and CLEP credits are accepted. Important factors in the admissions decision are advanced placement or honor courses, extracurricular activities record, and recommendations by school officials.

Procedure: Freshmen are admitted to all sessions. Entrance exams should be taken by the end of the junior year. There are early decision, early admissions, deferred admissions and rolling admissions plans. Application deadlines are open. Application fee is $25. 26 early decision candidates were accepted for the 2005-2006 class. Applications are accepted on-line.

Transfer: 46 transfer students enrolled in 2004-2005. Applicants should have a minimum GPA of 2.5 and at least their senior year at St. Norbert and 25% of their major credits must be taken st St. Norbert. 32 of 128 credits required for the bachelor's degree must be completed at St. Norbert.

Visiting: There are regularly scheduled orientations for prospective students, including preregistrations, meetings with advisers, and meetings regarding programming and activities, housing, and student life. There are guides for informal visits and visitors may sit in on classes and stay overnight. To schedule a visit, contact the Office of Admissions.

Financial Aid: In 2004-2005, 98% of all full-time freshmen and 96% of continuing full-time students received some form of financial aid. 68% of full-time freshmen and 70% of continuing full-time students received need-based aid. The average freshman award was $17,585. Need-based scholarships or need-based grants averaged $11,136; need-based self-help aid (loans and jobs) averaged $4583; and other non-need-based awards and non-need-based scholarships averaged $1866. 54% of undergraduates work part time. Average annual earnings from campus work are $1150. The average financial indebtedness of the 2004 graduate was $20,770. The FAFSA is required. The priority date for freshman financial aid applications for fall entry is March 1.

International Students: In a recent year there were 56 international students enrolled. The school actively recruits these students. They must score satisfactorily on the written TOEFL.

Computers: Wireless access is available. St. Norbert provides access to the Internet from all residence hall rooms, classrooms, offices, and labs. The College has 220 PCs in public labs for student use, as well as the library and campus center. Wireless computing is available in the library and campus center, as well as several instructional areas. All students may access the system during the semester as needed or as required by the instructor. There are no time limits and no fees.

Graduates: From July 1, 2004 to June 30, 2005, 462 bachelor's degrees were awarded. The most popular majors were business administration (28%), communication/media/theater (12%), and elementary education (12%). In an average class, 64% graduate in 4 years or less, 70% graduate in 5 years or less, and 71% graduate in 6 years or less. 63 companies recruited on campus in 2004-2005. Of the 2004 graduating class, 16% were enrolled in graduate school within 6 months of graduation and 71% were employed.

Admissions Contact: Bridget K. O'Connor, Interim Associate V.P. for Enrollment Mangement. A video is available. E-mail: *admit@snc.edu* Web: *www.snc.edu*

SILVER LAKE COLLEGE OF THE HOLY FAMILY   E-3
Manitowoc, WI 54220
(920) 686-6187
(800) 236-4752, ext. 1; Fax: (920) 684-7082

Full-time: 60 men, 190 women	**Faculty:** 35
Part-time: 200 men, 340 women	**Ph.Ds:** 49%
Graduate: 100 men, 230 women	**Student/Faculty:** 7 to 1
Year: semesters, summer session	**Tuition:** $14,400
Application Deadline: open	**Room & Board:** $4100
Freshman Class: 84 applied, 75 accepted, 34 enrolled	
ACT: required	**LESS COMPETITIVE**

Silver Lake College of the Holy Family, founded in 1935, is a private Catholic liberal arts institution offering undergraduate and graduate programs. Figures in the above capsule and in this profile are approximate. In addition to regional accreditation, Silver Lake College has baccalaureate program accreditation with NASM. The library contains 60,466 volumes, 2154 microform items, and 12,593 audio/video tapes/CDs/DVDs, and subscribes to 300 periodicals including electronic. Computerized library services include the card catalog, interlibrary loans, and database searching. Special learning facilities include a learning resource center and a special education clinic used for the training of special education teachers. The 30-acre campus is in a rural area 4 miles west of Manitowoc. Including any residence halls, there are 2 buildings.

Student Life: 99% of undergraduates are from Wisconsin. Others are from 4 states and 1 foreign country. 89% are from public schools. 94% are white. The average age of freshmen is 19; all undergraduates, 27. 18% do not continue beyond their first year; 50% remain to graduate.

Housing: 30 students can be accommodated in college housing, which includes coed off-campus apartments. On-campus housing is guaranteed for the freshman year only. 95% of students commute. Alcohol is not permitted. All students may keep cars.

Activities: There are no fraternities or sororities. There are 18 groups on campus, including art, band, choir, chorus, computers, dance, honors, jazz band, literary magazine, newspaper, orchestra, professional, religious, and student government. Popular campus events include Fine Arts Series, campus ministry programs, and Parents Day.

Sports: There is 1 intercollegiate sports for women, and 2 intramural sports for men and 2 for women. Facilities include a YMCA and the Two Rivers and Manitowoc Recreation Department.

Disabled Students: 95% of the campus is accessible. Wheelchair ramps, elevators, special parking, specially equipped rest rooms, and special class scheduling are available.

Services: Counseling and information services are available, as is tutoring in most subjects, including study groups as needed. There is a reader service for the blind, and remedial math, reading, and writing.

Campus Safety and Security: Measures include informal discussions, pamphlets/posters/films, emergency telephones, and lighted pathways/sidewalks.

Programs of Study: Silver Lake College confers B.A., B.S., B.B.A., and B.M. degrees. Associate and master's degrees are also awarded. Bachelor's degrees are awarded in BIOLOGICAL SCIENCE (biology/biological science), BUSINESS (accounting, business administration and management, human resources, and personnel management), COMMUNICATIONS AND THE ARTS (English, fine arts, music, and studio art), COMPUTER AND PHYSICAL SCIENCE (computer science, information sciences and systems, and mathematics), EDUCATION (art, early childhood, elementary, music, secondary, and special), SOCIAL SCIENCE (history, psychology, public administration, religion, and social science). Elementary education and special education are the strongest academically. Business administration and management are the largest.

Required: To graduate, students must complete at least 120 credit hours with a minimum GPA of 2.0. 45 to 50 credits of liberal arts studies must be taken.

Special: Silver Lake offers cross-registration with several Wisconsin technical colleges, internships, B.A.-B.S. degrees, dual majors, work-study programs, and student-designed majors. Nondegree study, pass/fail options, and credit for life, military, and work experience are available. An accelerated degree program in business management, accounting, human resources, and public administration is offered. There are 4 national honor societies and 4 departmental honors programs.

Faculty/Classroom: 37% of faculty are male; 63%, female. 85% teach undergraduates and 1% both teach and do research. No introductory courses are taught by graduate students. The average class size in an introductory lecture is 19; in a laboratory, 7; and in a regular course, 10.

Requirements: The SAT or ACT is required. In addition, applicants must be graduates of an accredited secondary school. The GED is accepted. Applicants should complete 3 units of high school English, 2 each of math and history or social studies, and 1 of lab science. A GPA of 2.0 is required. AP and CLEP credits are accepted. Important factors in the admissions decision are recommendations by school officials, evidence of special talent, and advanced placement or honor courses.

Procedure: Freshmen are admitted fall and spring. Entrance exams should be taken in the spring of the junior year. Application deadlines are open. Application fee is $35. Applications are accepted on-line.

Transfer: 89 transfer students enrolled in a recent year. Applicants who have 30 acceptable credits must have a minimum GPA of 2.0; those with fewer credits must meet the requirements for entering freshmen, except that the SAT or ACT is not required. 30 of 120 credits required for the bachelor's degree must be completed at Silver Lake College.

Visiting: There are regularly scheduled orientations for prospective students, including a tour and meetings with an admissions counselor, an adviser, the financial aid department, and the housing director. There are guides for informal visits and visitors may sit in on classes. To schedule a visit, contact the Admissions Office at (920) 686-6175 or *admslc@silver.sl.edu.*

Financial Aid: In 2005-2006, 75% of all full-time freshmen and 65% of continuing full-time students received some form of financial aid. 75% of full-time freshmen and 60% of continuing full-time students received need-based aid. The average freshman award was $10,625. Need-based scholarships or need-based grants averaged $8181; need-based self-help aid (loans and jobs) averaged $2443; non-need-based athletic scholarships averaged $2000; and other non-need-based awards and non-need-based scholarships averaged $750. 25% of undergraduates work part time. Average annual earnings from campus work are $1268. The FAFSA, the college's own financial statement, and tax returns are required. Check with the school for current deadlines.

International Students: A satisfactory score on the TOEFL is required.

Computers: All students may access the system. There are no time limits and no fees.

Graduates: In a recent year, 106 bachelor's degrees were awarded. The most popular majors were management (33%), education (13%), and psychology (9%). In an average class, 1% graduate in 4 years or less, 31% graduate in 5 years or less, and 8% graduate in 6 years or less. 10 companies recruited on campus in a recent year. Of a recent graduating class, 6% were enrolled in graduate school within 6 months of graduation and 96% were employed.

Admissions Contact: Admissions Office.
E-mail: *admslc@silver.sl.edu* Web: *www.sl.edu*

UNIVERSITY OF WISCONSIN SYSTEM

The University of Wisconsin System, established in 1971, is a private system in Wisconsin. It is governed by a 17-member appointed board of regents, whose chief administrator is president. The primary goal of the system is teaching, research, and public service. The main priorities are to develop human resources; to discover and disseminate knowledge; and to extend kwowledge and its application. The total enrollment is usually about 165,000; with 7200 faculty members. Altogether there are some 400 baccalaureate, 300 master's, and 137 doctoral programs offered in University of Wisconsin System. Profiles of the 4-year campuses are included in this section.

UNIVERSITY OF WISCONSIN/EAU CLAIRE B-3

Eau Claire, WI 54701 (715) 836-5415
(888) INFO-UWE; Fax: (715) 836-2409

Full-time: 3829 men, 5545 women	**Faculty:** 401; IIA, -$
Part-time: 262 men, 427 women	**Ph.D.s:** 86%
Graduate: 165 men, 338 women	**Student/Faculty:** 23 to 1
Year: semesters, summer session	**Tuition:** $5178 ($15,224)
Application Deadline: open	**Room & Board:** $4737
Freshman Class: 7134 applied, 5007 accepted, 2068 enrolled	
SAT: recommended	**ACT:** required

VERY COMPETITIVE

The University of Wisconsin/Eau Claire, founded in 1916, is a public institution offering programs in the liberal arts and sciences, business, teacher education, nursing, music, and the fine arts. There are 4 undergraduate schools. In addition to regional accreditation, UW-Eau Claire has baccalaureate program accreditation with AACSB, ACEJMC, CSWE, and NASM. The library contains 764,275 volumes, 1,366,298 microform items, and 17,676 audio/video tapes/CDs/DVDs, and subscribes to 2448 periodicals including electronic. Computerized library services include the card catalog, interlibrary loans, database searching, Internet access, and laptop Internet portals. Special learning facilities include a learning resource center, art gallery, planetarium, radio station, TV station, a geographic research center, a bird museum, and an observatory. The 333-acre campus is in an urban area 95 miles east of Minneapolis, Minnesota. Including any residence halls, there are 28 buildings.

Student Life: 78% of undergraduates are from Wisconsin. Others are from 28 states, 43 foreign countries, and Canada. 94% are from public schools. 93% are white. The average age of freshmen is 18; all undergraduates, 21. 17% do not continue beyond their first year; 59% remain to graduate.

Housing: 3754 students can be accommodated in college housing, which includes single-sex and coed dormitories and on-campus apartments. On-campus housing is guaranteed for the freshman year only and is available on a first-come, first-served basis. 60% of students commute. All students may keep cars.

Activities: 1% of men belong to 4 national fraternities; 1% of women belong to 4 national sororities. There are 150 groups on campus, including art, band, cheerleading, choir, chorale, chorus, computers, dance, drama, ethnic, forensics, gay, honors, international, jazz band, literary magazine, marching band, musical theater, newspaper, orchestra, political, professional, radio and TV, religious, social, social service, student government, and symphony. Popular campus events include Viennese Ball, Artsfest, and Winter Carnival.

Sports: There are 9 intercollegiate sports for men and 11 for women, and 40 intramural sports for men and 40 for women. Facilities include a gym, a pool, 30 acres of intramural and recreation fields, a game room, bowling and billiards, a Nautilus fitness center, racquetball courts, a weight room, a ropes course, a 3212-seat stadium, tennis courts, and a climbing wall.

Disabled Students: 80% of the campus is accessible. Wheelchair ramps, elevators, special parking, specially equipped rest rooms, special class scheduling, lowered drinking fountains, and lowered telephones are available.

Services: Counseling and information services are available, as is tutoring in some subjects, including writing, math/problem solving, and reading/study skills. There is a reader service for the blind, and remedial math, reading, and writing. Entry-level courses in foreign languages, humanities, and social and physical sciences are available.

Campus Safety and Security: Measures include 24-hour foot and vehicle patrol, self-defense education, security escort services, and informal discussions. There are pamphlets/posters/films and lighted pathways/sidewalks.

Programs of Study: UW-Eau Claire confers B.A., B.S., B.B.A., B.F.A., B.M., B.M.E., B.M.T., B.S.E.Ph., B.S.H.C.A., B.S.N., and B.S.W. degrees. Associate and master's degrees are also awarded. Bachelor's degrees are awarded in BIOLOGICAL SCIENCE (biochemistry and biology/biological science), BUSINESS (accounting, banking and finance, business administration and management, business economics, and marketing/retailing/merchandising), COMMUNICATIONS AND THE ARTS (advertising, art, broadcasting, communications, dramatic arts, English, fine arts, French, German, journalism, music, photography, and Spanish), COMPUTER AND PHYSICAL SCIENCE (chemistry, computer programming, computer science, geology, information sciences and systems, mathematics, physical sciences, physics, and statistics), EDUCATION (art, athletic training, elementary, foreign languages, music, science, secondary, and special), HEALTH PROFESSIONS (health care administration, music therapy, nursing, public health, and speech pathology/audiology), SOCIAL SCIENCE (American Indian studies, criminal justice, economics, geography, history, Latin American studies, philosophy, physical fitness/movement, political science/government, psychology, religion, social science, social work, and sociology). Elementary education, nursing, and biology are the largest.

Required: All students must complete 39 hours in general education, including 11 each in social sciences, humanities, and natural sciences, and 6 in communications. All students must also take 4 to 5 credits in English, and 2 in wellness, and complete a minimum of 3 credits that contain significant content dealing with race and ethnicity, and must complete 30 or more hours of service-learning. A minimum 2.0 GPA and 120 credit hours, including 60 in the major, are required to graduate.

Special: Numerous internships, work-study programs, and study abroad in 15 countries are offered. Dual majors and interdisciplinary majors are possible. Credit by examination, nondegree study, and pass/fail options are offered. There are 32 national honor societies, a freshman honors program, and 17 departmental honors programs.

Faculty/Classroom: 53% of faculty are male; 47%, female. 68% teach undergraduates, 33% do research, and 33% do both. No introductory courses are taught by graduate students. The average class size in an introductory lecture is 31 and in a laboratory, 17.

Admissions: 70% of the 2005-2006 applicants were accepted. The SAT scores for the 2005-2006 freshman class were: Verbal--16% below 500, 44% between 500 and 599, 30% between 600 and 700, and 10% above 700; Math--12% below 500, 47% between 500 and 599, 32% between 600 and 700, and 9% above 700. The ACT scores were 6% below 21, 36% between 21 and 23, 36% between 24 and 26, 13% between 27 and 28, and 9% above 28. 48% of the current freshmen were in the top fifth of their class; 87% were in the top two fifths. There were 4 National Merit finalists. 69 freshmen graduated first in their class.

Requirements: The ACT is required and the SAT is recommended. In addition, applicants should graduate from an accredited secondary school or present its equivalent, with 17 academic credits, including 4 in English, 3 each in social studies, college preparatory math, and science and 2 years of a single foreign language. Students must graduate in the upper 50% of their class or present a satisfactory score on the SAT or on the ACT. Probationary admission is sometimes offered for the spring semester. Music majors or minors must audition. UW-Eau Claire requires applicants to be in the upper 50% of their class. AP and CLEP credits are accepted. Important factors in the admissions decision are advanced placement or honor courses, recommendations by school officials, and leadership record.

Procedure: Freshmen are admitted to all sessions. Entrance exams should be taken by December of the senior year. There is an early admissions and a rolling admissions plan. Application deadlines are open. 103 applicants were on the 2005 waiting list; 54 were admitted. Applications are accepted on-line. The fall 2005 application fee was $35.

Transfer: 497 transfer students enrolled in 2004-2005. Transfer applicants must be in good standing at their previous schools and carry a minimum 2.0 GPA. Preference is given to transfers who have completed the equivalent of freshman composition and college algebra. Students with less than 30 semester credits must meet the freshman admissions requirements. 30 of 120 credits required for the bachelor's degree must be completed at UW-Eau Claire.

Visiting: There are regularly scheduled orientations for prospective students, during which students meet with academic advisers, develop a class schedule, register for classes, and tour the campus. There are guides for informal visits and visitors may sit in on classes. To schedule a visit, contact the Admissions Office.

Financial Aid: In 2005-2006, 70% of all full-time freshmen and 67% of continuing full-time students received some form of financial aid. 42% of full-time freshmen and 44% of continuing full-time students received need-based aid. The average freshman award was $6522. Need-based scholarships or need-based grants averaged $3446 ($12,196 maximum); need-based self-help aid (loans and jobs) averaged $4028 ($12,254 maximum); and other non-need-based awards and non-need-based scholarships averaged $4456 ($12,525 maximum). 98% of undergraduates work part time. Average annual earnings from campus work are $1292. The average financial indebtedness of the 2005 graduate was $16,953. The FAFSA is required. The deadline for filing freshman financial aid applications for fall entry is April 15.

International Students: There are 112 international students enrolled. The school actively recruits these students. They must score satisfactorily on the written TOEFL and also take the ACT.

Computers: Wireless access is available. Students may use computer facilities for classroom assignments, research, network access to other resources, and mail. Terminals and PCs are located across campus. There are 17 supported labs plus labs in housing and the library. Dial-in access is offered. All students may access the system 24 hours a day, 7 days per week. There are no time limits and no fees.

Graduates: From July 1, 2004 to June 30, 2005, 1849 bachelor's degrees were awarded. The most popular majors were management (7%), marketing (6%), and elementary education (6%). In an average class, 19% graduate in 4 years or less, 51% graduate in 5 years or less, and 59% graduate in 6 years or less. 255 companies recruited on campus in a recent year.

Admissions Contact: Kristina Anderson, Director of Admissions. E-mail: *admissions@uwec.edu* Web: *www.uwec.edu/Admissions/*

UNIVERSITY OF WISCONSIN/GREEN BAY · D-3

Green Bay, WI 54311 (920) 465-2111; Fax: (920) 465-2765

Full-time: 1589 men, 2930 women	Faculty: 179; IIA, --$
Part-time: 329 men, 774 women	Ph.D.s: 87%
Graduate: 62 men, 142 women	Student/Faculty: 25 to 1
Year: semesters, summer session	Tuition: $5425 ($15,471)
Application Deadline: February 1	Room & Board: $3990
Freshman Class: 3349 applied, 2224 accepted, 908 enrolled	
SAT Verbal/Math: 520/560*	ACT: 23 VERY COMPETITIVE

The University of Wisconsin/Green Bay, founded in 1968, is a public institution offering programs in humanities and fine arts, natural sciences, social sciences, business, education, health, and preprofessional areas. In addition to regional accreditation, UW-Green Bay has baccalaureate program accreditation with ADA, CSWE, NASM, and NLN. The library contains 339,013 volumes, 733,713 microform items, and 47,593 audio/video tapes/CDs/DVDs, and subscribes to 5299 periodicals including electronic. Computerized library services include the card catalog, interlibrary loans, database searching, Internet access, and laptop Internet portals. Special learning facilities include a learning resource center, art gallery, natural history museum, radio station, TV station, a 270-acre arboretum, and a regional performing arts center. The 700-acre campus is in a suburban area 111 miles north of Milwaukee. Including any residence halls, there are 43 buildings.

Student Life: 95% of undergraduates are from Wisconsin. Others are from 31 states, 25 foreign countries, and Canada. 97% are from public schools. 91% are white. The average age of freshmen is 18; all undergraduates, 23. 24% do not continue beyond their first year; 45% remain to graduate.

Housing: 1844 students can be accommodated in college housing, which includes coed dorms and on-campus apartments. In addition, there are special-interest houses. On-campus housing is available on a first-come, first-served basis and is available on a lottery system for upperclassmen. 65% of students commute. All students may keep cars.

Activities: 1% of men belong to 1 national fraternity; 1% of women belong to 2 national sororities. There are 90 groups on campus, including art, band, cheerleading, choir, chorale, chorus, computers, dance, drama, drill team, environmental, ethnic, gay, honors, international, jazz band, literary magazine, musical theater, newspaper, orchestra, pep band, photography, political, professional, radio and TV, religious, social, social service, and student government. Popular campus events include Fall Fest, Spring Screamer, and Pow Wow.

Sports: There are 7 intercollegiate sports for men and 8 for women, and 7 intramural sports for men and 7 for women. Facilities include a sports center housing a swimming pool, racquetball courts, a weight room, and a 2000-seat gym, intramural fields, a soccer field, a golf course, tennis courts, an outing center, a 2500-seat stadium, and student recreation facilities in the student union.

Disabled Students: All of the campus is accessible. Wheelchair ramps, elevators, special parking, specially equipped rest rooms, lowered drinking fountains, lowered telephones, and automatic door openers are available.

Services: Counseling and information services are available, as is tutoring in most subjects. There is a reader service for the blind, and remedial math, reading, and writing. There is an academic support office, language and writing centers, student health services, and individual counseling. Available equipment includes a visual enlarger, an automatic page turner, an accessible computer station with attached voice synthesizer, slow speed cassette recorders, taped texts, and a printing Telecommunications Device for the Deaf (TDD). Note takers, typists, readers, and aides are also available to students.

Campus Safety and Security: Measures include 24-hour foot and vehicle patrol, security escort services, informal discussions, and pamphlets/posters/films. There are emergency telephones and lighted pathways/sidewalks.

Programs of Study: UW-Green Bay confers B.A., B.S., B.B.A., B.M., B.S.N., and B.S.W. degrees. Associate and master's degrees are also awarded. Bachelor's degrees are awarded in BIOLOGICAL SCIENCE (biology/biological science), BUSINESS (accounting and business administration and management), COMMUNICATIONS AND THE ARTS (communications, dramatic arts, English, fine arts, French, German, music, and Spanish), COMPUTER AND PHYSICAL SCIENCE (chemistry, computer science, earth science, information sciences and systems, and mathematics), EDUCATION (education), ENGINEERING AND ENVIRONMENTAL DESIGN (environmental science), HEALTH PROFESSIONS (nursing), SOCIAL SCIENCE (economics, history, human development, humanities, liberal arts/general studies, philosophy, political science/government, psychology, public administration, social work, and urban studies). Education, accounting, and human biology are the strongest academically. Business, human biology, and human development are the largest.

Required: All students must complete at least 120 semester hours, including an average of 36 in the major, with a minimum GPA of 2.0, depending on the major. A 31-credit requirement in general education consists of 10 credits in natural sciences, 9 each in humanities, and social sciences, and 3 in fine arts. Students must declare an interdisciplinary minor or major and must complete at least 30 credits in the discipline. Courses in Other Culture Studies and Ethnic Studies are required; other course requirements vary by major.

Special: UW-Green Bay offers cross-registration with Bellin College of Nursing and the University of Wisconsin at Milwaukee or Oshkosh. There are study-abroad programs and travel courses in numerous countries. Students can receive credit by exam or for life, military, or work experience. There are internships in almost all fields, interdisciplinary majors, including communication and the arts, human biology, and regional planning, dual and student-designed majors, work-study, B.A.-B.S. degrees in most areas, nondegree study, a general studies degree, and pass/fail options. A 3-2 engineering degree with the University of Wisconsin/Milwaukee is offered. There are 3 national honor societies and 34 departmental honors programs.

Faculty/Classroom: 60% of faculty are male; 40%, female. 99% teach undergraduates, 85% both teach and do research. No introductory courses are taught by graduate students. The average class size in an introductory lecture is 40; in a laboratory, 20; and in a regular course, 25.

Admissions: 66% of the 2005-2006 applicants were accepted. The SAT scores for the 2005-2006 freshman class were: Verbal--23% below 500, 71% between 500 and 599, and 6% between 600 and 700; Math--18% below 500, 53% between 500 and 599, and 29% between 600 and 700. The ACT scores were 24% below 21, 40% between 21 and 23, 22% between 24 and 26, 8% between 27 and 28, and 6% above 28.

Requirements: The ACT is required. In addition, candidates must be graduates of an accredited secondary school or hold a GED certificate. They must have completed 17 academic credits consisting of 4 in English, 3 each in social sciences, in science, and math, 2 in any of the above areas or a foreign language, and 2 other electives. A GPA of 2.25 is required. AP and CLEP credits are accepted. Important factors in the admissions decision are advanced placement or honor courses, extracurricular activities record, and leadership record.

Procedure: Freshmen are admitted to all sessions. Entrance exams should be taken between the junior and senior years. There is a deferred admissions plan. There is a rolling admissions plan. Applications should be filed by February 1 for fall entry and November 1 for spring entry, along with a $35 fee. Notification is sent on a rolling basis. 209 applicants were on the 2005 waiting list; 25 were admitted. Applications are accepted on-line.

Transfer: 495 transfer students enrolled in 2004-2005. Transfer students must have a minimum GPA of 2.0 based on at least 15 transferable credits; priority for admission is given to students with 24 credits and a minimum GPA of 2.5. 31 of 120 credits required for the bachelor's degree must be completed at UW-Green Bay.

Visiting: There are regularly scheduled orientations for prospective students, including Campus Preview Days, which consist of information sessions, academic area workshops, and campus tours. There are guides for informal visits and visitors may sit in on classes. To schedule a visit, contact Pam Harvey-Jacobs, Director of Admissions.

Financial Aid: In 2005-2006, 51% of all full-time freshmen and 55% of continuing full-time students received some form of financial aid, including need-based aid. The average freshman award was $7334. Need-based scholarships or need-based grants averaged $4135 ($15,000 maximum); need-based self-help aid (loans and jobs) averaged $3232 ($10,000 maximum); non-need-based athletic scholarships averaged $5928 ($25,000 maximum); and other non-need-based awards and non-need-based scholarships averaged $2399 ($10,000 maximum). 80% of undergraduates work part time. Average annual earnings from campus work are $1500. The average financial indebtedness of the 2005 graduate was $15,448. The CSS/Profile, FAFSA, or FFS is required. The deadline for filing freshman financial aid applications for fall entry is April 15.

International Students: There are 56 international students enrolled. The school actively recruits these students. A satisfactory score on the TOEFL is required.

Computers: Wireless access is available. Students may use over 600 computers spread across campus in labs, housing, the library, and the union. All dorms are wired for access to the university network, with Internet access. Many classrooms have desk network portals for laptop connections. Many locations now have WAN access. All students may access the system 7 A.M. to 12 P.M. or 24 hours a day through network or modem. There are no time limits and no fees.

Graduates: From July 1, 2004 to June 30, 2005, 928 bachelor's degrees were awarded. The most popular majors were business administration (20%), psychology (11%), and human development (11%). In an average class, 2% graduate in 3 years or less, 22% graduate in 4 years or less, 44% graduate in 5 years or less, and 47% graduate in 6 years or less. 60 companies recruited on campus in 2004-2005. Of the 2004 graduating class, 15% were enrolled in graduate school within 6 months of graduation and 95% were employed.

Admissions Contact: Pam Harvey-Jacobs, Director of Admissions. A video is available. E-mail: *admissions@uwgb.edu* Web: *http://www.uwgb.edu/admissions*

UNIVERSITY OF WISCONSIN/LA CROSSE   B-4

La Crosse, WI 54601	(608) 785-8067; Fax: (608) 785-8940
Full-time: 3092 men, 4535 women	Faculty: 310; IIA, -$
Part-time: 129 men, 152 women	Ph.D.s: 79%
Graduate: 302 men, 768 women	Student/Faculty: 24 to 1
Year: semesters, summer session	Tuition: $5225 ($15,271)
Application Deadline: open	Room & Board: $4820
Freshman Class: 6347 applied, 4282 accepted, 1764 enrolled	
SAT Verbal/Math: 570/590*	ACT: 25 VERY COMPETITIVE

The University of Wisconsin/La Crosse, founded in 1909, is a public institution offering undergraduate and graduate studies in arts and sciences, health and human services, business administration, education, phys ed and recreation, professional development, and educational administration. There are 6 undergraduate schools and 1 graduate school. In addition to regional accreditation, UW-L has baccalaureate program accreditation with AACSB, ACOTE, ACS, APTA, CAPTE, NAACLS, NASM and NCATE. The library contains 666,883 volumes, 1,222,613 microform items, and 2027 audio/video tapes/CDs/DVDs, and subscribes to 1603 periodicals including electronic. Computerized library services include the card catalog, interlibrary loans, and database searching. Special learning facilities include a learning resource center, art gallery, planetarium, radio station, TV station, the River Studies Center, and the Allied Health Center. The 121-acre campus is in a small town 140 miles west of Madison and 150 miles southeast of Minneapolis/St. Paul. Including any residence halls, there are 32 buildings.

Student Life: 84% of undergraduates are from Wisconsin. Others are from 38 states, 48 foreign countries, and Canada. 90% are from public schools. 93% are white. The average age of freshmen is 18; all undergraduates, 20. 10% do not continue beyond their first year; 61% remain to graduate.

Housing: 2823 students can be accommodated in college housing, which includes single-sex and coed dorms, fraternity houses, and sorority houses. In addition, there are special-interest houses, a residence hall for international students and students 21 years or older and substance free, first year experience housing. On-campus housing is available on a first-come, first-served basis and is available on a lottery system for upperclassmen. 64% of students commute. All students may keep cars.

Activities: 1% of men and about 1% of women belong to 3 national fraternities; 1% of women belong to 2 national sororities. There are 140 groups on campus, including art, band, cheerleading, chess, choir, chorale, chorus, computers, dance, drama, ethnic, gay, honors, international, jazz band, literary magazine, marching band, musical theater, newspaper, orchestra, pep band, photography, political, professional, radio and TV, religious, social, social service, student government, and symphony. Popular campus events include Parents Weekend, a community-sponsored Oktoberfest, and various cultural events.

Sports: There are 9 intercollegiate sports for men and 10 for women, and 11 intramural sports for men and 11 for women. Facilities include 3 regulation basketball courts, a wrestling room, an indoor track, 6 indoor tennis courts, 16 outdoor tennis courts, an Olympic-size swimming pool, 2 strength-training centers, a dance studio, racquetball courts, a 4363-seat stadium, a 2880-seat gym, and an 880-seat auditorium.

Disabled Students: 98% of the campus is accessible. Wheelchair ramps, elevators, special parking, specially equipped rest rooms, special class scheduling, lowered drinking fountains, lowered telephones, special housing, and specialized computer equipment are available.

Services: Counseling and information services are available, as is tutoring in most subjects. There is a reader service for the blind and remedial math and writing. There is also a counseling and testing center and a writing lab.

Campus Safety and Security: Measures include 24-hour foot and vehicle patrol, self-defense education, security escort services, and informal discussions. There are pamphlets/posters/films, emergency telephones, and lighted pathways/sidewalks.

Programs of Study: UW-L confers B.A. and B.S. degrees. Associate and master's degrees are also awarded. Bachelor's degrees are awarded in BIOLOGICAL SCIENCE (biology/biological science and microbiology), BUSINESS (accounting, banking and finance, business administration and management, international business management, and marketing/retailing/merchandising), COMMUNICATIONS AND THE ARTS (art, communications, dramatic arts, English, fine arts, French, music, Spanish, and speech/debate/rhetoric), COMPUTER AND PHYSICAL SCIENCE (chemistry, computer science, information sciences and systems, mathematics, and physics), EDUCATION (athletic training, elementary, health, physical, science, secondary, and social studies), HEALTH PROFESSIONS (community health work, exercise science, medical laboratory technology, nuclear medical technology, occupational therapy, physician's assistant, radiation therapy, and recreation therapy), SOCIAL SCIENCE (archeology, economics, geography, German area studies, history, parks and recreation management, philosophy, political science/government, psychology, public administration, and sociology). Microbiology, nuclear medicine technology, and physics are the strongest academically. Business administration, elementary education, and biology are the largest.

Required: To graduate, students must earn 120 semester credits, including 68 in subjects outside the major and at least 40 in 300- or 400-level courses. The minimum GPA is 2.0, though it is considerably higher for some programs. Distribution requirements include 30 to 40 credits in liberal studies and 13 to 19 credits in skill courses.

Special: Cooperative programs and cross-registration are available with Viterbo College. There are study-abroad programs in 14 countries and an international student exchange program. UW-L also offers a 3-2 engineering degree with the University of Wisconsin/Madison, the University of Wisconsin/Milwaukee, Platteville, and the University of Minnesota, work-study programs, internships, nondegree study, credit by exam, and pass/fail options. There are 10 national honor societies, a freshman honors program, and 11 departmental honors programs.

Faculty/Classroom: 59% of faculty are male; 41%, female. 95% teach undergraduates, 5% do research, and 80% do both. No introductory courses are taught by graduate students. The average class size in an introductory lecture is 37; in a laboratory, 20; and in a regular course, 30.

Admissions: 67% of the 2005-2006 applicants were accepted. The SAT scores for the 2005-2006 freshman class were: Verbal--23% below 500, 32% between 500 and 599, and 45% between 600 and 700; Math--21% below 500, 30% between 500 and 599, 40% between 600 and 700, and 9% above 700. The ACT scores were 5% below 21, 28% between 21 and 23, 41% between 24 and 26, 17% between 27 and 28, and 9% above 28. 65% of the current freshmen were in the top fifth of their class; 94% were in the top two fifths. 49 freshmen graduated first in their class.

Requirements: The SAT or ACT is required. In addition, candidates must be graduates of an accredited secondary school or hold a GED certificate. They must have completed 17 academic credits, including 4 courses in English, 3 each in social studies and science, 2 in algebra and 1 in geometry, and 4 other academic courses. Students completing rigorous courses, including in the senior year, will be stronger candidates for admission. Students must rank in the top 35% of their high school graduating class and score at least 22 on the ACT or the top 40% and score 25 on the ACT. UW-L requires applicants to be in the upper 40% of their class. A GPA of 2.0 is required. AP and CLEP credits are accepted. Important factors in the admissions decision are advanced placement or honor courses, leadership record, and recommendations by school officials.

Procedure: Freshmen are admitted to all sessions. Entrance exams should be taken at the end of the junior year or at the beginning of the senior year. There are early admissions and rolling admissions plans. Application deadlines are open. Application fee is $35. Notification is sent on a rolling basis. 385 applicants were on the 2005 waiting list; 330 were admitted.

Transfer: 409 transfer students enrolled in 2004-2005. Transfer admission is likely with a GPA of 3.2; with a GPA of 2.0 to 2.74, admission is on a space-available basis. College transcripts are required, along with a statement of good standing from prior institutions. 30 of 120 credits required for the bachelor's degree must be completed at UW-L.

Visiting: There are regularly scheduled orientations for prospective students, including 2 academic sessions, a parent panel, a UW-L student panel, and a tour of the campus. There are guides for informal visits and visitors may sit in on classes. To schedule a visit, contact the Admissions Office at (608) 785-8939.

Financial Aid: In 2005-2006, 56% of all full-time freshmen and 60% of continuing full-time students received some form of financial aid. At least 26% of full-time freshmen and 28% of continuing full-time students received need-based aid. The average freshman award was $4874. Need-based scholarships or need-based grants averaged $1609; need-based self-help aid (loans and jobs) averaged $3265; and other institutional non-need-based awards and non-need-based scholarships averaged $447. 79% of undergraduates work part time. Average annual earnings from campus work are $900. The average financial indebtedness of the 2005 graduate was $13,948. The FAFSA and the college's own financial statement are required. The priority date for freshman financial aid applications for fall entry is March 15.

International Students: There are 106 international students enrolled. The school actively recruits these students. Satisfactory scores are required on the written TOEFL, the college's own test, and the La Crosse Battery (based on MELAB). Applicants must also write a 30-minute composition.

Computers: All students may access the system 7 A.M. to midnight. There are no time limits and no fees.

Graduates: From July 1, 2004 to June 30, 2005, 1524 bachelor's degrees were awarded. The most popular majors were business/marketing (21%), parks and recreation (13%), and social sciences (10%). In an average class, 21% graduate in 4 years or less, 55% graduate in 5 years or less, and 64% graduate in 6 years or less. 96 companies recruited on campus in 2004-2005. Of the 2004 graduating class, 24% were enrolled in graduate school within 6 months of graduation and 98% were employed.

Admissions Contact: Timothy R. Lewis, Director of Admissions. E-mail: *admissions@uwlax.edu* Web: *www.uwlax.edu*

UNIVERSITY OF WISCONSIN/MADISON — C-4

Madison, WI 53706-1481   (608) 262-3961; Fax: (608) 262-7706

Full-time: 12,728 men, 14,713 women	**Faculty:** 2167; I, av$
Part-time: 1240 men, 1425 women	**Ph.D.s:** 92%
Graduate: 5542 men, 5832 women	**Student/Faculty:** 13 to 1
Year: semesters, summer session	**Tuition:** $6617 ($20,617)
Application Deadline: February 1	**Room & Board:** $6500
Freshman Class: 21,682 applied, 14,718 accepted, 6141 enrolled	
ACT: 28 (mean)	**HIGHLY COMPETITIVE**

The University of Wisconsin/Madison, founded in 1849, is a public, land-grant institution offering undergraduate and graduate study in almost every major field. There are 8 undergraduate and 12 graduate schools. In addition to regional accreditation, Wisconsin has baccalaureate program accreditation with AACSB, ABET, ACEJMC, ADA, AHEA, ASLA, CSWE, FIDER, NASAD, NASM, NCATE, and NLN. The 43 libraries contain 7,230,000 volumes. Computerized library services include the card catalog, interlibrary loans, database searching, Internet access, and laptop Internet portals. Special learning facilities include a learning resource center, art gallery, natural history museum, planetarium, radio station, and TV station. The 933-acre campus is in an urban area 75 miles west of Milwaukee and 150 miles northwest of Chicago. Including any residence halls, there are 192 buildings.

Student Life: 70% of undergraduates are from Wisconsin. Students are from 50 states, 110 foreign countries, and Canada. 83% are white. The average age of freshmen is 18; all undergraduates, 20. 6% do not continue beyond their first year; 78% remain to graduate.

Housing: 6662 students can be accommodated in college housing, which includes single-sex and coed dorms, on-campus apartments, and married-student housing. In addition, there are honors houses, language houses, and special-interest houses. No one may keep cars.

Activities: 9% of men belong to 26 national fraternities; 8% of women belong to 11 national sororities. There are 617 groups on campus, including art, band, cheerleading, chess, choir, chorale, chorus, computers, dance, drama, ethnic, film, gay, honors, international, jazz band, literary magazine, marching band, musical theater, newspaper, opera, orchestra, pep band, photography, political, professional, radio and TV, religious, social, social service, student government, and symphony.

Sports: There are 12 intercollegiate sports for men and 12 for women, and 14 intramural sports for men and 14 for women.

Disabled Students: 90% of the campus is accessible. Wheelchair ramps, elevators, special parking, specially equipped rest rooms, special class scheduling, lowered drinking fountains, and lowered telephones are available.

Services: Counseling and information services are available, as is tutoring in most subjects. There is a reader service for the blind.

Campus Safety and Security: Measures include 24-hour foot and vehicle patrol, self-defense education, security escort services, and shuttle buses. There are informal discussions, pamphlets/posters/films, emergency telephones, and lighted pathways/sidewalks.

Programs of Study: Wisconsin confers B.A., B.S., B.B.A., B.F.A., B.M., and B.N.S. degrees. Master's and doctoral degrees are also awarded. Bachelor's degrees are awarded in AGRICULTURE (agricultural business management, agricultural economics, animal science, conservation and regulation, dairy science, forestry and related sciences, horticulture, poultry science, and soil science), BIOLOGICAL SCIENCE (bacteriology, biochemistry, biology/biological science, botany, entomology, genetics, microbiology, molecular biology, nutrition, plant pathology, toxicology, wildlife biology, and zoology), BUSINESS (accounting, banking and finance, insurance and risk management, marketing/retailing/merchandising, operations management, real estate, and retailing), COMMUNICATIONS AND THE ARTS (African languages, art, art history and appreciation, Chinese, classics, communications, comparative literature, dance, dramatic arts, English, French, German, Hebrew, Italian, Japanese, journalism, Latin, linguistics, music, Polish, Portuguese, Russian, and Spanish), COMPUTER AND PHYSICAL SCIENCE (actuarial science, applied mathematics, astronomy, atmospheric sciences and meteorology, chemistry, computer science, geology, information sciences and systems, mathematics, physics, and statistics), EDUCATION (agricultural, art, elementary, physical, and secondary), ENGINEERING AND ENVIRONMENTAL DESIGN (bioengineering, biomedical engineering, cartography, chemical engineering, civil engineering, computer engineering, electrical/electronics engineering, engineering mechanics, engineering physics, geological engineering, industrial engineering, interior design, landscape architecture/design, materials science, mechanical engineering, naval architecture and marine engineering, nuclear engineering, and textile technology), HEALTH PROFESSIONS (medical laboratory technology, medical science, nursing, physician's assistant, and speech pathology/audiology), SOCIAL SCIENCE (African American studies, anthropology, Asian/Oriental studies, child care/child and family studies, consumer services, economics, family/consumer studies, food science, geography, history, history of science, human ecology, international relations, Judaic studies, Latin American studies, law, philosophy, political science/government, psychology, religion, rural sociology, Scandinavian studies, social work, sociology, textiles and clothing, and women's studies). Political science, psychology, and English are the largest.

Required: Required courses vary with individual programs. A total of 120 to 136 credit hours, with at least 30 in the major, and a cumulative GPA of 2.0 are minimum requirements for graduation. In addition to courses required for each major, all students must complete general education in communication, quantitative reasoning, breadth (science, math, humanities, and social science), and ethnic studies.

Special: C-op programs, internships, study abroad, work-study programs and accelerated degrees in any major are available. B.A.-B.S. degrees and dual and student-designed majors also are available. There are 24 national honor societies, including Phi Beta Kappa, and a freshman honors program.

Faculty/Classroom: 67% of faculty are male; 33%, female. 95% teach undergraduates, and all do research. The average class size in a regular course is 29.

Admissions: 68% of the 2005-2006 applicants were accepted. The SAT scores for the 2005-2006 freshman class were: Verbal--10% below 500, 30% between 500 and 599, 44% between 600 and 700, and 16% above 700; Math--2% below 500, 19% between 500 and 599, 50% between 600 and 700, and 29% above 700. 91% of the current freshmen were in the top fifth of their class; 99% were in the top two fifths.

Requirements: The SAT or ACT is required. The ACT Optional Writing test is also required. In addition, applicants must have completed the following number of units in high school (these are minimums; the number of units recommended is higher): 17 total units, including 4 English, 3 math, 3 science, 2 foreign language, 3 social studies, and 2 electives. Wisconsin requires applicants to be in the upper 50% of their class. AP and CLEP credits are accepted.

Procedure: Freshmen are admitted fall, spring, and summer. Entrance exams should be taken in the junior year. There is a deferred admissions plan. There is a rolling admissions plan. Applications should be filed by February 1 for fall entry, November 15 for spring entry, and February 1 for summer entry, along with a $35 fee. Notification is sent on a rolling basis. Applications are accepted on-line.

Transfer: 1169 transfer students enrolled in 2004-2005. Admission is competitive and vaires by program. Generally, applicants must have at least sophomore standing. 30 of 120 to 136 credits required for the bachelor's degree must be completed at Wisconsin.

Visiting: There are regularly scheduled orientations for prospective students, including an admission information session, a tour, and class visits. There are guides for informal visits and visitors may sit in on classes and stay overnight. To schedule a visit, contact the Tour Coordinator, Office of Admissions, at (608) 262-3318.

Financial Aid: In 2005-2006, 52% of all full-time freshmen received some form of financial aid. 25% of full-time freshmen received need-based aid. The average financial indebtedness of the 2005 graduate was $18,630. Wisconsin is a member of CSS. The FAFSA, the college's own financial statement, and a federal income tax return are required.

International Students: There are 923 international students enrolled. They must achieve a satisfactory score on the TOEFL and also take the SAT or ACT.

Computers: Wireless access is available. All students may access the system. There are no time limits and no fees.

Graduates: From July 1, 2004 to June 30, 2005, 6303 bachelor's degrees were awarded. The most popular majors were political science (6%), psychology (5%), and English (4%). In an average class, 46% graduate in 4 years or less, 75% graduate in 5 years or less, and 78% graduate in 6 years or less.

Admissions Contact: Undergraduate Admissions Office.
E-mail: *onwisconsin@admissions.wisc.edu* Web: *www.wisc.edu*

UNIVERSITY OF WISCONSIN/MILWAUKEE   E-4

Milwaukee, WI 53201	(414) 229-3800; Fax: (414) 229-6940
Full-time: 7500 men, 9100 women	Faculty: 824; I, -$
Part-time: 1500 men, 1800 women	Ph.D.s: 90%
Graduate: 1500 men, 2300 women	Student/Faculty: 20 to 1
Year: semesters, summer session	Tuition: $5200 ($18,000)
Application Deadline: see profile	Room & Board: $4400
Freshman Class: 9918 applied, 7881 accepted, 3635 enrolled	
SAT or ACT: required	LESS COMPETITIVE

The University of Wisconsin/Milwaukee, founded in 1885, offers undergraduate and graduate degrees in arts and sciences, fine arts, business, education, engineering and applied sciences, architecture and urban planning, social welfare, and health fields. Figures in the above capsule and in this profileare approximate. There are 10 undergraduate schools and 1 graduate school. In addition to regional accreditation, UWM has baccalaureate program accreditation with AACSB, ABET, ACEJMC, CAHEA, CSWE, NAAB, NASAD, NASM, NCATE, and NLN. The library contains 2,141,859 volumes, 1,717,205 microform items, and 38,716 audio/video tapes/CDs/DVDs, and subscribes to 8757 periodicals including electronic. Computerized library services include the card catalog, interlibrary loans, database searching, and Internet access. Special learning facilities include a learning resource center, art gallery, planetarium, radio station, TV station, and the American Geographical Society Library. The 93-acre campus is in an urban area in Milwaukee. Including any residence halls, there are 42 buildings.

Student Life: 99% of undergraduates are from Wisconsin. Students are from 49 states, 59 foreign countries, and Canada. 83% are white. The average age of freshmen is 19; all undergraduates, 22.

Housing: 1904 students can be accommodated in college housing, which includes coed dorms and married-student housing. On-campus housing is available on a first-come, first-served basis. 87% of students commute. All students may keep cars.

Activities: 3% of men belong to 1 local and 6 national fraternities; 3% of women belong to 6 national sororities. There are 250 groups on campus, including art, band, cheerleading, chorale, computers, dance, drama, ethnic, film, gay, honors, international, jazz band, literary magazine, musical theater, newspaper, orchestra, pep band, photography, political, professional, radio and TV, religious, social, social service, student government, and symphony. Popular campus events include concerts, art exhibitions, and dance performances.

Sports: There are 9 intercollegiate sports for men and 8 for women, and 15 intramural sports for men and 13 for women. Facilities include a center for phys ed, a gym, a field, courts, and a 3000-seat auditorium.

Disabled Students: 90% of the campus is accessible. Wheelchair ramps, elevators, special parking, specially equipped rest rooms, special class scheduling, lowered drinking fountains, lowered telephones, and special library facilities are available.

Services: Counseling and information services are available, as is tutoring in some subjects, including English composition, math, science, business, reading, and study skills. There is a reader service for the blind, and remedial math, reading, and writing.

Campus Safety and Security: Measures include 24-hour foot and vehicle patrol, self-defense education, security escort services, and shuttle buses. There are pamphlets/posters/films, emergency telephones, and lighted pathways/sidewalks.

Programs of Study: UWM confers B.A., B.S., B.B.A., B.F.A., B.S.Applied S., and B.S.E. degrees. Master's and doctoral degrees are also awarded. Bachelor's degrees are awarded in AGRICULTURE (conservation and regulation), BIOLOGICAL SCIENCE (biochemistry, biology/biological science, botany, microbiology, and zoology), BUSINESS (accounting, banking and finance, business administration and management, management information systems, marketing/retailing/merchandising, real estate, and recreation and leisure services), COMMUNICATIONS AND THE ARTS (art history and appreciation, classics, communications, comparative literature, dance, dramatic arts, English, film arts, fine arts, French, German, Hebrew, Italian, linguistics, music, Russian, and Spanish), COMPUTER AND PHYSICAL SCIENCE (applied mathematics, chemistry, computer science, geology, geoscience, mathematics, and physics), EDUCATION (art, education, music, and social science), ENGINEERING AND ENVIRONMENTAL DESIGN (architecture, civil engineering, electrical/electronics engineering, engineering, industrial administration/management, industrial engineering, materials engineering, and mechanical engineering), HEALTH PROFESSIONS (clinical science, health care administration, health science, medical science, nursing, occupational therapy, predentistry, premedicine, and speech pathology/audiology), SOCIAL SCIENCE (African American studies, anthropology, criminal justice, economics, geography, history, law, philosophy, political science/government, prelaw, psychology, religion, social work, and sociology). Architecture and engineering are the strongest academically.

Required: English composition and math proficiency exams must be passed with satisfactory scores. Distribution requirements include 6 credits each in humanities, natural sciences, and social sciences and 3 credits each in the arts and cultural diversity. All students must complete a minimum of 120 credits.

Special: UWM offers cooperative programs in engineering, cross-registration with UW/Parkside, study abroad in Europe and Asia, internships, a Washington semester, and work-study programs. Students may select an accelerated degree program, dual majors, a general studies degree, and student-designed majors. Credit/no credit options, nondegree study, credit by exam, and credit for life, military, and work experience are also available. There is 1 national honor society, including Phi Beta Kappa, a freshman honors program, and 1 departmental honors program.

Faculty/Classroom: 70% of faculty are male; 30%, female. All teach undergraduates. The average class size in an introductory lecture is 48; in a laboratory, 15; and in a regular course, 27.

Admissions: In a recent year 79% of the applicants were accepted.

Requirements: The SAT or ACT is required; the ACT is preferred, with a minimum score of 21 on the ACT required of all Wisconsin residents. Out-of-state students may substitute the SAT with a minimum required composite score. Candidates must have graduated from an accredited secondary school with 17 Carnegie units, including at least 4 in English, 3 in history/social science, and 3 each in math and the natural sciences. A GED certificate is accepted. Music and theater majors must audition. For the School of Architecture and Urban Planning, higher rank and ACT requirements apply. UWM requires applicants to be in the upper 50% of their class. AP and CLEP credits are accepted. Important factors in the admissions decision are advanced placement or honor courses, evidence of special talent, and leadership record.

Procedure: Freshmen are admitted to all sessions. Entrance exams should be taken in the spring of the junior year. There are deferred admissions and rolling admissions plans. Check with the school for current application deadlines and fee. Notification is sent on a rolling basis. Applications are accepted on-line.

Transfer: 1509 transfer students enrolled in a recent year. Transfer applicants must have earned a minimum of 12 credit hours and have at least a 2.0 GPA. 30 of 120 credits required for the bachelor's degree must be completed at UWM.

Visiting: There are regularly scheduled orientations for prospective students. There are guides for informal visits and visitors may sit in on classes and stay overnight. To schedule a visit, contact the Student Visitor Center at (414) 229-4397.

Financial Aid: Check with the school for current deadlines.

International Students: A satisfactory score is required on the written TOEFL.

Computers: All students may access the system any time. There are no time limits and no fees.

Graduates: In a recent year, 2298 bachelor's degrees were awarded. The most popular majors were business/marketing (25%), visual and performing arts (8%), and social sciences and history (8%). 166 companies recruited on campus in a recent year.

Admissions Contact: Director of Admissions.
E-mail: *uwmlook@uwm.edu* Web: *www.uwm.edu*

UNIVERSITY OF WISCONSIN/OSHKOSH   D-4

Oshkosh, WI 54901	(920) 424-0202; Fax: (920) 424-1098
Full-time: 3400 men, 4600 women	Faculty: 407; IIA, -$
Part-time: 450 men, 840 women	Ph.D.s: 81%
Graduate: 570 men, 933 women	Student/Faculty: 19 to 1
Year: semesters, summer session	Tuition: $4982 ($15,028)
Application Deadline: see profile	Room & Board: $5444
Freshman Class: n/av	
ACT: required	LESS COMPETITIVE

The University of Wisconsin/Oshkosh, founded in 1871, is a public institution offering undergraduate and graduate programs in education, business, the arts and sciences, and health fields. There are 4 undergraduate schools and 1 graduate school. Figures in the above capsule and in this profile are approximate. In addition to regional accreditation, UW/Oshkosh has baccalaureate program accreditation with AACSB, ACEJMC, CSWE, NASM, NCATE, and NLN. The library contains 487,000 volumes, 1,275,000 microform items, and 7000 audio/video tapes/CDs/DVDs, and subscribes to 1850 periodicals including electronic. Computerized library services include the card catalog, interlibrary loans, and database searching. Special learning facilities include a learning resource center, art gallery, planetarium, radio station, TV station, and a speech and hearing clinic. The 192-acre campus is in an urban area 90 miles north of Milwaukee. Including any residence halls, there are 36 buildings.

Student Life: 96% of undergraduates are from Wisconsin. Others are from 30 states, 32 foreign countries, and Canada. 94% are white. The average age of freshmen is 18; all undergraduates, 22. 29% do not continue beyond their first year; 55% remain to graduate.

Housing: 3667 students can be accommodated in college housing, which includes single-sex and coed dorms. On-campus housing is guaranteed for all 4 years. 66% of students commute. All students may keep cars.

Activities: 5% of men belong to 8 national fraternities; 5% of women belong to 5 national sororities. There are 175 groups on campus, including art, band, cheerleading, chess, choir, computers, dance, debate, ethnic, film, forensics, gay, honors, international, jazz band, literary magazine, musical theater, newspaper, opera, pep band, political, professional, radio and TV, religious, social, social service, student government, and symphony. Popular campus events include Winter Carnival, Taste of UW Oshkosh, and Celebration of Racial Inclusiveness.

Sports: There are 10 intercollegiate sports for men and 11 for women, and 15 intramural sports for men and 15 for women. Facilities include a hall for basketball, swimming, and volleyball, a sports center for basketball, tennis, and indoor track, a pool, a 10400-seat stadium for football and outdoor track, a 2500-seat indoor gym, and a 5808-seat arena.

Disabled Students: Wheelchair ramps, elevators, special parking, specially equipped rest rooms, special class scheduling, lowered drinking fountains, and lowered telephones are available.

Services: Counseling and information services are available, as is tutoring in most subjects. There is a reader service for the blind, and remedial math, reading, and writing.

Campus Safety and Security: Measures include 24-hour foot and vehicle patrol, self-defense education, security escort services, and informal discussions. There are pamphlets/posters/films, emergency telephones, and lighted pathways/sidewalks.

Programs of Study: UW/Oshkosh confers B.A., B.S., B.Art Ed., B.B.A., B.F.A., B.L.S., B.M., B.M.E., B.S.N., and B.S.W. degrees. Associate and master's degrees are also awarded. Bachelor's degrees are awarded in BIOLOGICAL SCIENCE (biology/biological science and microbiology), BUSINESS (accounting, banking and finance, business administration and management, human resources, management information systems, and marketing/retailing/merchandising), COMMUNICATIONS AND THE ARTS (art, English, fine arts, French, German, journalism, music, Spanish, and speech/debate/rhetoric), COMPUTER AND PHYSICAL SCIENCE (chemistry, computer science, geology, mathematics, and physics), EDUCATION (art, elementary, music, physical, science, secondary, social science, and special), HEALTH PROFESSIONS (medical laboratory technology, music therapy, nursing, and speech pathology/audiology), SOCIAL SCIENCE (anthropology, criminal justice, economics, geography, history, human services, international studies, liberal arts/general studies, philosophy, political science/government, psychology, religion, social work, sociology, and urban studies). Business, education, and nursing are the largest.

Required: All students must complete a minimum of 120 credit hours with at least a 2.0 GPA. A minimum of 42 credits in general education requirements includes 9 credits each in humanities and social science, 8 in natural science, 6 in English composition, 3 in math or logic, 3 in non-Western culture, 3 in speech, and 2 in phys ed.

Special: UW/Oshkosh offers internships and study abroad. There are 15 national honor societies and a freshman honors program.

Faculty/Classroom: 56% of faculty are male; 44%, female. No introductory courses are taught by graduate students. The average class size in an introductory lecture is 31 and in a laboratory, 21.

Requirements: The ACT is required. In addition, students must graduate in the upper 50% of their class from an accredited secondary school or score a 22 on the enhanced ACT if ranked in the third quartile. They should have completed 17 academic credits, including 4 in English, 3 each in math, social sciences, and natural sciences, and 4 in electives, preferably in a foreign language or fine arts/humanities. AP and CLEP credits are accepted.

Procedure: Freshmen are admitted to all sessions. Entrance exams should be taken in spring of the junior year or early fall of the senior year. There is a deferred admissions plan. There is a rolling admissions plan. Check with the school for current application deadlines. Appication fee is $35. Notification is sent on a rolling basis. Applications are accepted on-line.

Transfer: Candidates should have completed 30 or more semester credits; if not, high school transcripts are reviewed. Students must have at least a 2.0 cumulative GPA. 30 of 120 credits required for the bachelor's degree must be completed at UW/Oshkosh.

Visiting: There are regularly scheduled orientations for prospective students, including preview days, campus tours, and an individual appointment with an admissions counselor. There are guides for informal visits and visitors may sit in on classes and stay overnight. To schedule a visit, contact the Admissions Office and Gruenhagen Conference Center at (920) 424-0202 or (920) 424-1107.

Financial Aid: UW/Oshkosh is a member of CSS. The FAFSA is required. The deadline for filing freshman financial aid applications for fall entry is March 15.

International Students: A satisfactory score on the TOEFL is required.

Computers: All students may access the system 24 hours, 7 days a week. There are no time limits and no fees.

Admissions Contact: Jill Endries, Director of Admissions. A video is available. E-mail: *oshadmuw@uwosh.edu* Web: *http://www.uwosh.edu*

UNIVERSITY OF WISCONSIN/PARKSIDE   E-5

Kenosha, WI 53141-2000	(414) 595-2355; Fax: (414) 595-2202
Full-time: 1160 men, 1570 women	Faculty: 144; IIA, av$
Part-time: 680 men, 960 women	Ph.D.s: 93%
Graduate: 70 men, 110 women	Student/Faculty: 19 to 1
Year: semesters, summer session	Tuition: $5001 ($15,047)
Application Deadline: August 1	Room & Board: $5180
Freshman Class: n/av	
SAT or ACT: required	LESS COMPETITIVE

The University of Wisconsin/Parkside, founded in 1968, offers undergraduate programs in liberal arts, business, education, and science and technology. Some figures in the above capsule and in this profile are approximate. There are 4 undergraduate and 3 graduate schools. The library contains 350,000 volumes, 150,000 microform items, and 10,200 audio/video tapes/CDs/DVDs, and subscribes to 1500 periodicals including electronic. Computerized library services include the card catalog. Special learning facilities include a learning resource center, art gallery, and radio station. The 700-acre campus is in a suburban area 30 miles south of Milwaukee. Including any residence halls, there are 11 buildings.

Student Life: 91% are white. 22% do not continue beyond their first year; 60% remain to graduate.

Housing: 400 students can be accommodated in college housing, which includes coed on-campus apartments and off-campus apartments. In addition, there are special-interest houses. On-campus housing is guaranteed for all 4 years. 52% of students commute. All students may keep cars.

Activities: There are no fraternities or sororities. There are 60 groups on campus, including art, band, cheerleading, choir, chorale, chorus, computers, drama, ethnic, gay, honors, international, jazz band, literary magazine, musical theater, newspaper, orchestra, political, professional, religious, social, social service, student government, and yearbook. Popular campus events include Cinco de Mayo, Winter Carnival, and Black History Month.

Sports: There are 8 intercollegiate sports for men and 6 for women. Facilities include a cross-country course, tennis courts, playing fields, and an all-purpose phys ed building with a 3000-seat auditorium for athletic events and concerts.

Disabled Students: All of the campus is accessible. Wheelchair ramps, elevators, special parking, specially equipped rest rooms, lowered drinking fountains, and lowered telephones are available.

Services: Counseling and information services are available, as is tutoring in every subject. There is a reader service for the blind, and remedial math, reading, and writing.

Campus Safety and Security: Measures include shuttle buses, pamphlets/posters/films, emergency telephones, and lighted pathways/sidewalks.

Programs of Study: UW/Parkside confers B.A. and B.S. degrees. Master's degrees are also awarded. Bachelor's degrees are awarded in BIOLOGICAL SCIENCE (biology/biological science), BUSINESS (business administration and management), COMMUNICATIONS AND THE ARTS (communications, dramatic arts, English, fine arts, French, German, music, and Spanish), COMPUTER AND PHYSICAL SCIENCE (chemistry, computer science, geology, mathematics, physics, and science), EDUCATION (education), ENGINEERING AND ENVIRONMENTAL DESIGN (industrial administration/management), SOCIAL SCIENCE (economics, geography, history, humanities, international studies, philosophy, political science/government, psychology, and sociology). Social sciences and physical sciences are the strongest academically. Business is the largest.

Required: A total of 120 credits with at least 30 in the major and a GPA of 2.0 are required for graduation. Students must complete a minimum of 12 credits in humanities and the arts, 12 in social and behavioral sciences, and 9 in natural sciences. Nonengineering majors with fewer than 2 units of foreign language in high school must also fulfill a foreign language requirement.

Special: UW/Parkside offers on-campus work-study programs, internships, study abroad, student-designed majors, and an accelerated premedicine program. Nondegree study and credit by exam are possible. There is a freshman honors program.

Faculty/Classroom: No introductory courses are taught by graduate students. The average class size in an introductory lecture is 150; in a laboratory, 50; and in a regular class, 30.

Requirements: The ACT is required for in-state students; either the ACT or the SAT for out-of-state students. A minimum score of 21 is required on the ACT. Students may use a lower ACT score in combination with class rank to gain admission. Candidates must be graduates of an accredited secondary school or hold a GED diploma. At least 16 academic credits are required, including 4 in English, 3 in social sciences, 2 in natural sciences, and 1 each in algebra and plane geometry. UW/Parkside requires applicants to be in the upper 50% of their class. AP and CLEP credits are accepted. Important factors in the admissions decision are geographic diversity, extracurricular activities record, and ability to finance college education.

Procedure: Freshmen are admitted fall and spring. Entrance exams should be taken by the fall of the senior year. There are early admissions and deferred admissions plans. There is a rolling admissions plan. Applications should be filed by August 1 for fall entry. Notification is sent on a rolling basis.

Transfer: Students must have a GPA of 2.0 and be in good standing with the previous institution attended. 30 of 120 credits required for the bachelor's degree must be completed at UW/Parkside.

Visiting: There are regularly scheduled orientations for prospective students, including open houses and campus tours. There are guides for informal visits and visitors may sit in on classes. To schedule a visit, contact Student Enrollment Services.

Financial Aid: The FAFSA and the college's own financial statement are required. Check with the school for current deadlines.

International Students: A satisfactory score on the TOEFL is required.

Computers: 2 general-purpose labs are available to all students. There are no time limits and no fees.

Admissions Contact: Matthew Jensen, Director of Admissions.
E-mail: *admissions@uwp.edu* Web: *www.uwp.edu*

UNIVERSITY OF WISCONSIN/PLATTEVILLE   C-5
Platteville, WI 53818-3099   (608) 342-1125
                                          (800) 362-5515; Fax: (608) 342-1122

Full-time: 3264 men, 1916 women	**Faculty:** 249; IIA, -$
Part-time: 312 men, 283 women	**Ph.D.s:** 83%
Graduate: 316 men, 340 women	**Student/Faculty:** 21 to 1
Year: semesters, summer session	**Tuition:** $5125 ($15,171)
Application Deadline: open	**Room & Board:** $4654
Freshman Class: 3074 applied, 2620 accepted, 1218 enrolled	
ACT: 22	**NONCOMPETITIVE**

The University of Wisconsin/Platteville, founded in 1866, offers undergraduate programs in arts, social sciences, humanities, sciences, agriculture, education, engineering, communication, business, and industry, as well as graduate programs in computer science, education, engineering, criminal justice, and project management. There are 3 undergraduate schools and 1 graduate school. In addition to regional accreditation, UWP has baccalaureate program accreditation with ABET, ABFSE, and NASM. The library contains 223,730 volumes, 1 million microform items, and 11,000 audio/video tapes/CDs/DVDs. Computerized library services include interlibrary loans, database searching, Internet access, and laptop Internet portals. Special learning facilities include a learning resource center, art gallery, radio station, and TV station. The 820-acre campus is in a small town 20 miles northeast of Dubuque, Iowa, and 75 miles southwest of Madison. Including any residence halls, there are 65 buildings.

Student Life: 89% of undergraduates are from Wisconsin. Others are from 43 states, 20 foreign countries, and Canada. 90% are from public schools. 93% are white. The average age of freshmen is 18; all undergraduates, 21. 23% do not continue beyond their first year; 55% remain to graduate.

Housing: 2329 students can be accommodated in college housing, which includes single-sex and coed dorms. There are intensive-study quiet floors, alcohol-free floors, and an engineering hall. All students may keep cars.

Activities: 3% of men belong to 2 local and 7 national fraternities; 2% of women belong to 2 local and 3 national sororities. There are 160 groups on campus, including art, band, cheerleading, choir, chorale, chorus, computers, debate, drama, drill team, ethnic, film, forensics, gay, honors, international, jazz band, literary magazine, marching band, musical theater, newspaper, opera, orchestra, pep band, photography, political, professional, radio and TV, religious, social, social service, student government, symphony, and yearbook. Popular campus events include Heartland Festival, international student dinners, and Ebony Weekend.

Sports: There are 7 intercollegiate sports for men and 7 for women, and 12 intramural sports for men and 12 for women. Facilities include a 2000-seat gym, a 10,000-seat stadium, a 200-meter indoor track, a 400-meter outdoor track, 7 basketball and 7 volleyball courts, 6 tennis and 4 racquetball courts, a weight room, a swimming pool, a baseball diamond, and soccer fields.

Disabled Students: 95% of the campus is accessible. Wheelchair ramps, elevators, special parking, specially equipped rest rooms, special class scheduling, lowered drinking fountains, lowered telephones, and special housing are available.

Services: Counseling and information services are available, as is tutoring in most subjects. There is a reader service for the blind, and remedial math, reading, and writing as well as university counseling services.

Campus Safety and Security: Measures include 24-hour foot and vehicle patrol, security escort services, informal discussions, and pamphlets/posters/films. There are emergency telephones, lighted pathways/sidewalks, and locked residence halls.

Programs of Study: UWP confers B.A. and B.S. degrees. Associate and master's degrees are also awarded. Bachelor's degrees are awarded in AGRICULTURE (agricultural business management, animal science, horticulture, and soil science), BIOLOGICAL SCIENCE (biology/biological science), BUSINESS (accounting, business administration and management, and business economics), COMMUNICATIONS AND THE ARTS (communications, English, fine arts, German, music, Spanish, speech/debate/rhetoric, and visual and performing arts), COMPUTER AND PHYSICAL SCIENCE (chemistry, computer science, mathematics, physical sciences, physics, and software engineering), EDUCATION (agricultural, art, elementary, middle school, physical, secondary, and technical), ENGINEERING AND ENVIRONMENTAL DESIGN (civil engineering, electrical/electronics engineering, engineering, environmental engineering, industrial engineering, industrial engineering technology, land use management and reclamation, and mechanical engineering), SOCIAL SCIENCE (criminal justice, economics, geography, history, international studies, philosophy, political science/government, psychology, and social science). Engineering, middle school education, and technology management are the strongest academically. Engineering is the largest.

Required: To graduate, students must complete a minimum of 120 credit hours, with a minimum GPA of 2.0 overall and within the major. Course requirements include 12 credits in humanities and fine arts, 9 each in social sciences and natural sciences, 4 in ethnic and gender studies, and 3 in international education. Other competency requirements include 6 credits in English composition, 3 in math, and 2 each in speech and phys ed.

Special: UWP offers internships in business, industry, and communication, a co-op program in engineering, and study abroad in 13 countries. Credit by exam, credit for life, military, and work experience, work-study programs, dual majors, student-designed majors, nondegree study, and pass/fail options are also available. There are 12 national honor societies, a freshman honors program, and 4 departmental honors programs.

Faculty/Classroom: 67% of faculty are male; 33%, female. All teach undergraduates. The average class size in an introductory lecture is 30; in a laboratory, 20; and in a regular course, 22.

Admissions: 85% of the 2005-2006 applicants were accepted. The ACT scores for the 2005-2006 freshman class were: 29% below 21, 33% between 21 and 23, 26% between 24 and 26, 8% between 27 and 28, and 4% above 28. 27% of the current freshmen were in the top fifth of their class; 61% were in the top two fifths. 20 freshmen graduated first in their class.

Requirements: The SAT or ACT is required; the ACT is preferred. Applicants must have successfully completed 17 college preparatory units, including 4 units of English, 3 of math (algebra and higher), 3 of social science, 3 of natural science, or courses in vocational areas. Standard admission will be given to those students who are in the top 50% of their graduating class or have a satisfactory score. AP and CLEP credits are accepted. Important factors in the admissions decision are leadership record, recommendations by school officials, and advanced placement or honor courses.

Procedure: Freshmen are admitted to all sessions. Entrance exams should be taken in April or June of the junior year. There is a deferred admissions plan. There is a rolling admissions plan. Application deadlines are open. Application fee is $35. Applications are accepted on-line.

Transfer: 402 transfer students enrolled in 2004-2005. Applicants must have a cumulative GPA of at least 2.0 and be eligible to return to the institution last attended or currently attending. 32 of 120 credits required for the bachelor's degree must be completed at UWP.

Visiting: There are regularly scheduled orientations for prospective students, The Pioneer Previews, held on 6 dates each year, include group tours, an admissions briefing, and visits to specific colleges and departments. Daily visits (Monday through Friday) are also available. There are guides for informal visits and visitors may sit in on classes and stay overnight. To schedule a visit, contact UWP Visitor's Center at (877) 897-5288 or admit@uwplatt.edu.

Financial Aid: In 2005-2006, 47% of all full-time freshmen and 64% of continuing full-time students received some form of financial aid. 38% of full-time freshmen and 47% of continuing full-time students received need-based aid. The average freshman award was $6105. Need-based scholarships or need-based grants averaged $3809; need-based self-help aid (loans and jobs) averaged $4128; and other non-need-based awards and non-need-based scholarships averaged $1507. 56% of undergraduates work part time. Average annual earnings from campus work are $1528. The average financial indebtedness of the 2005 graduate was $17,348. The FAFSA is required. The priority date for freshman financial aid applications for fall entry is March 15.

International Students: There are 96 international students enrolled. The school actively recruits these students. They must score satisfactorily on the TOEFL and also take Wisconsin English and math placement exam.

Computers: Wireless access is available. UWP has 2600 computer workstations in 40 labs across campus. There are also 60 laptop computers for student checkout and wireless Internet installed in all the major meeting places and large classrooms, including the library and the student center. All students may access the system. There are no time limits and no fees.

Graduates: From July 1, 2004 to June 30, 2005, 920 bachelor's degrees were awarded. The most popular majors were engineering (23%), trade and industry (8%), and education (7%). In an average class, 1% graduate in 3 years or less, 13% graduate in 4 years or less, 39% graduate in 5 years or less, and 51% graduate in 6 years or less. 210 companies recruited on campus in 2004-2005. Of the 2004 graduating class, 10% were enrolled in graduate school within 6 months of graduation and 88% were employed.

Admissions Contact: Angela Udelhofen, Director of Admissions and Enrollment Services. A video is available. E-mail: admit@uwplatt.edu Web: www.uwplatt.edu/admission

UNIVERSITY OF WISCONSIN/RIVER FALLS   A-3

River Falls, WI 54022	(715) 425-3500; Fax: (715) 425-0676
Full-time: 2000 men, 3100 women	**Faculty:** 221; IIA, av$
Part-time: 160 men, 230 women	**Ph.D.s:** 85%
Graduate: 160 men, 330 women	**Student/Faculty:** 23 to 1
Year: semesters, summer session	**Tuition:** $5322 ($15,368)
Application Deadline: open	**Room & Board:** $4400
Freshman Class: n/av	
ACT: required	**LESS COMPETITIVE**

The University of Wisconsin/River Falls, founded in 1874, is a public institution offering undergraduate programs in arts and sciences, education, agriculture, and food and environmental sciences. There are 4 undergraduate schools and 1 graduate school. Figures in the above capsule and in this profile are approximate. In addition to regional accreditation, UW/River Falls has baccalaureate program accreditation with ACEJMC, ASLA, CSWE, NASM, and NCATE. The library contains 221,453 volumes, 726,035 microform items, and 8455 audio/video tapes/CDs/DVDs, and subscribes to 1322 periodicals including electronic. Computerized library services include the card catalog, interlibrary loans, database searching, and Internet access. Special learning facilities include a learning resource center, art gallery, planetarium, radio station, TV station, and greenhouse, climbing wall, communicative disorders lab, educational technology center, food science and meat facilities, 2 campus lab farms, and sundial. The 225-acre campus is in a suburban area 29 miles east of Minneapolis-St. Paul, Minnesota. Including any residence halls, there are 28 buildings.

Student Life: 52% of undergraduates are from Wisconsin. Others are from 25 states, 13 foreign countries, and Canada. 95% are from public schools. 95% are white. The average age of freshmen is 18; all undergraduates, 21. 25% do not continue beyond their first year; 54% remain to graduate.

Housing: 2172 students can be accommodated in college housing, which includes single-sex and coed dorms. On-campus housing is guaranteed for all 4 years. 59% of students commute. All students may keep cars.

Activities: 5% of men belong to 5 national fraternities; 5% of women belong to 4 national sororities. There are 120 groups on campus, including art, band, cheerleading, choir, chorus, computers, dance, debate, drama, ethnic, forensics, gay, honors, international, jazz band, literary magazine, musical theater, newspaper, orchestra, pep band, political, professional, radio and TV, religious, social, student government, and symphony. Popular campus events include Winter Carnival, Annual Rodeo, and Unity in the Community.

Sports: There are 7 intercollegiate sports for men and 11 for women, and 11 intramural sports for men and 12 for women. Facilities include an ice arena, a 4550-seat stadium, 2 multipurpose phys ed centers, a swimming pool, a 2600-seat gym and a smaller gym, handball courts, a field house, an indoor track, an indoor rock-climbing wall, and basketball, tennis, and volleyball courts.

Disabled Students: 95% of the campus is accessible. Wheelchair ramps, elevators, special parking, specially equipped rest rooms, special class scheduling, lowered drinking fountains, and lowered telephones are available.

Services: Counseling and information services are available, as is tutoring in every subject. There is a reader service for the blind, and remedial math, reading, and writing.

Campus Safety and Security: Measures include 24-hour foot and vehicle patrol, self-defense education, security escort services, and informal discussions. There are pamphlets/posters/films, emergency telephones, and lighted pathways/sidewalks.

Programs of Study: UW/River Falls confers B.A., B.S., B.F.A, B.M.E., and B.S.W. degrees. Master's degrees are also awarded. Bachelor's degrees are awarded in AGRICULTURE (agricultural business management, agronomy, animal science, conservation and regulation, horticulture, and soil science), BIOLOGICAL SCIENCE (biology/biological science and biotechnology), BUSINESS (accounting and business administration and management), COMMUNICATIONS AND THE ARTS (art, communications, English, fine arts, journalism, modern language, music, and speech/debate/rhetoric), COMPUTER AND PHYSICAL SCIENCE (chemistry, computer programming, geology, mathematics, physics, and science), EDUCATION (agricultural, art, elementary, foreign languages, music, physical, and secondary), ENGINEERING AND ENVIRONMENTAL DESIGN (agricultural engineering and land use management and reclamation), HEALTH PROFESSIONS (premedicine, prepharmacy, and speech pathology/audiology), SOCIAL SCIENCE (economics, food science, geography, history, political science/government, prelaw, psychology, social studies, social work, and sociology). Physics, chemistry, and elementary education are the strongest academically. Business, elementary education, and animal science are the largest.

Required: To graduate, students must complete at least 120 semester hours, with a GPA of 2.0 overall and 2.25 in the major field. General education requirements include 39 semester hours in English composition, speech and humanities, natural and social sciences, math, and phys ed.

Special: Co-op programs in food science and environmental science, on-campus work-study, and accelerated degree programs in several pre-professional areas are available. UW/River Falls also offers internships, student-designed majors, credit by exam, nondegree study, and pass/fail options. Study abroad is available through the National Student Exchange and the International Student Exchange Program in some 15 countries. There are 11 national honor societies and a freshman honors program.

Faculty/Classroom: 70% of faculty are male; 30%, female. All teach undergraduates. No introductory courses are taught by graduate students. The average class size in an introductory lecture is 30; in a laboratory, 24; and in a regular course, 20.

Requirements: The ACT is required, with a minimum composite score of or 18 if in upper 40% of high school class. Candidates must be graduates of an accredited secondary school and have completed at least 17 academic credits, including 4 in English, 3 in social sciences, and 3 each in math and science, with 4 college prep courses. A GED certificate is accepted. UW/River Falls requires applicants to be in the upper 40% of their class. AP and CLEP credits are accepted.

Procedure: Freshmen are admitted to all sessions. Entrance exams should be taken in the spring of the junior year. There are early admissions and deferred admissions plans. There is a rolling admissions plan. Application deadlines are open. Application fee is $35. A waiting list is an active part of the admissions procedure. Applications are accepted on-line.

Transfer: Priority admission is given to students with a college GPA of 2.6 or higher. Students with a GPA of 2.0 to 2.6 are placed on a waiting list. Transfers in elementary education must have a GPA of 3.0. 30 of 120 credits required for the bachelor's degree must be completed at UW/River Falls.

Visiting: There are regularly scheduled orientations for prospective students, including College Visit Days and tours. There are guides for informal visits and visitors may sit in on classes. To schedule a visit, contact the Admissions Office.

Financial Aid: UW/River Falls is a member of CSS. The FAFSA is required. Check with the school for current deadlines.

International Students: There were 47 international students enrolled in a recent year. They must take TOEFL, achieving a satisfactory score, and also take the ACT.

Computers: All students may access the system more than 80 hours per week, and by telephone request when labs are closed. There are no time limits and no fees.

Graduates: In a recent year, 1045 bachelor's degrees were awarded. The most popular majors were education (18%), agriculture (15%), and business (15%). In an average class, 25% graduate in 4 years or less, 35% graduate in 5 years or less, and 54% graduate in 6 years or less.

Admissions Contact: Alan J. Tuchtenhagen, Admissions Director. E-mail: admit@uwrf.edu Web: http://www.uwrf.edu

---

UNIVERSITY OF WISCONSIN/STEVENS POINT   C-3

Stevens Point, WI 54481-3897   (715) 346-2441
                                          Fax: (715) 346-2441

Full-time: 3587 men, 4159 women	Faculty: 357; IIA, -$
Part-time: 271 men, 336 women	Ph.D.s: 87%
Graduate: 53 men, 171 women	Student/Faculty: 22 to 1
Year: semesters, summer session	Tuition: $5062 ($15,109)
Application Deadline: open	Room & Board: $4322
Freshman Class: 4583 applied, 3681 accepted, 1523 enrolled	
SAT Verbal/Math: 505/520*	ACT: 22 VERY COMPETITIVE

The University of Wisconsin/Stevens Point, founded in 1894, offers undergraduate programs in natural resources, education, business, arts and sciences, and professional areas. There are 4 undergraduate schools and 1 graduate school. In addition to regional accreditation, UWSP has baccalaureate program accreditation with ADA, ASLA, FIDER, NASAD, NASM, and SAF. The library contains 996,623 volumes, 910,300 microform items, and 4104 audio/video tapes/CDs/DVDs, and subscribes to 3861 periodicals including electronic. Computerized library services include the card catalog, interlibrary loans, database searching, Internet access, and laptop Internet portals. Special learning facilities include a learning resource center, art gallery, natural history museum, planetarium, radio station, TV station, and an observatory, map center, 275-acre nature preserve, groundwater center, and wellness institute. The 335-acre campus is in a small town 110 miles north of Madison. Including any residence halls, there are 35 buildings.

Student Life: 93% of undergraduates are from Wisconsin. Others are from 32 states, 28 foreign countries, and Canada. 93% are white. The average age of freshmen is 18; all undergraduates, 22. 24% do not continue beyond their first year; 58% remain to graduate.

Housing: 3316 students can be accommodated in college housing, which includes single-sex and coed dorms. In addition, there are special-interest houses, privately owned offcampus apartments, and off-campus

---

fraternity and soroty houses. 63% of students commute. All students may keep cars.

Activities: 1% of men belong to 4 national fraternities; 1% of women belong to 3 national sororities. There are 180 groups on campus, including art, band, cheerleading, choir, chorale, chorus, computers, dance, drama, ethnic, film, gay, honors, international, jazz band, literary magazine, musical theater, newspaper, orchestra, pep band, photography, political, professional, radio and TV, religious, social, social service, student government, symphony, and yearbook. Popular campus events include Trivia Contest, International Club dinner, and Spud Bowl.

Sports: There are 10 intercollegiate sports for men and 12 for women, and 14 intramural sports for men and 12 for women. Facilities include 2 gyms, a health enhancement center, a cardio center, and the university center. The campus stadium seats 5500; the indoor gym, 3500. There is also a 391-seat auditorium.

Disabled Students: All of the campus is accessible. Wheelchair ramps, elevators, special parking, specially equipped rest rooms, special class scheduling, lowered drinking fountains, lowered telephones, note-taking services, and talking books are available.

Services: Counseling and information services are available, as is tutoring in most subjects. There is a reader service for the blind, and remedial math, reading, and writing.

Campus Safety and Security: Measures include 24-hour foot and vehicle patrol, informal discussions, emergency telephones, and lighted pathways/sidewalks. There are and an evening van service.

Programs of Study: UWSP confers B.A., B.S., B.F.A., and B.M. degrees. Associate and master's degrees are also awarded. Bachelor's degrees are awarded in AGRICULTURE (forestry and related sciences, natural resource management, and soil science), BIOLOGICAL SCIENCE (biology/biological science and wildlife biology), BUSINESS (accounting, business administration and management, and management science), COMMUNICATIONS AND THE ARTS (arts administration/management, communications, dance, dramatic arts, English, fine arts, French, German, music, and Spanish), COMPUTER AND PHYSICAL SCIENCE (chemistry, information sciences and systems, mathematics, natural sciences, physics, and web services), EDUCATION (athletic training, early childhood, education of the exceptional child, elementary, health, home economics, music, and physical), ENGINEERING AND ENVIRONMENTAL DESIGN (interior design and paper and pulp science), HEALTH PROFESSIONS (clinical science, nursing, and speech pathology/audiology), SOCIAL SCIENCE (dietetics, economics, family/consumer studies, geography, history, international studies, liberal arts/general studies, philosophy, physical fitness/movement, political science/government, psychology, public administration, social science, sociology, and water resources). Business administration, elementary education, and biology are the largest.

Required: To graduate, students must complete 120 credit hours, with a minimum GPA of 2.0. Core curriculum requirements must also be fulfilled, along with courses in writing, natural science, non-Western culture, minorities studies, social science, humanities, and wellness, and 3 credits in phys ed. Some majors require additional credits and higher minimum GPAs.

Special: A co-op program in nursing is offered with UW/Eau Claire and St. Joseph's Hospital. Internships, study abroad in 9 countries, work-study programs, dual and student-designed majors, independent study, and pass/fail options are also available. Credit is given for military, life, and work experience. There are 10 national honor societies.

Faculty/Classroom: 60% of faculty are male; 40%, female. All teach undergraduates and all do research. No introductory courses are taught by graduate students. The average class size in an introductory lecture is 43; in a laboratory, 21; and in a regular course, 34.

Admissions: 80% of the 2005-2006 applicants were accepted. The SAT scores for the 2005-2006 freshman class were: Verbal--50% below 500, 32% between 500 and 599, and 18% between 600 and 700; Math--32% below 500, 46% between 500 and 599, 5% between 600 and 700, and 18% above 700. The ACT scores were 26% below 21, 36% between 21 and 23, 25% between 24 and 26, 8% between 27 and 28, and 5% above 28. 32% of the current freshmen were in the top fifth of their class; 76% were in the top two fifths. 23 freshmen graduated first in their class.

Requirements: The SAT or ACT is required, with the ACT prefered. In addition, applicants should rank in the top 25% of their high school class, or have a cumulative high school GPA of 3.25 or higher with a minimum ACT composite score of 21 or the SAT equivalent or rank in the top 50% of their high school class with an ACT composite score of 21 or above. The GED is accepted. Required academic preparation includes 4 units of English, 3 of social studies, and 2 each of math and lab science, along with 5 electives; 2 units of foreign language are recommended. An interview is suggested. AP and CLEP credits are accepted.

Procedure: Freshmen are admitted fall and spring. Entrance exams should be taken by February of the senior year. There is a rolling admission plan. Application deadlines are open. Application fee is $35. 370 applicants were on the 2005 waiting list; 120 were admitted. Applications are accepted on-line.

Transfer: 712 transfer students enrolled in 2004-2005. Applicants must submit high school and college transcripts. A college minimum GPA of 2.75 is required. 30 of 120 credits required for the bachelor's degree must be completed at UWSP.

Visiting: There are regularly scheduled orientations for prospective students, consisting of a 2-day program that includes a meeting with an academic adviser as well as with upperclass students and other new students. There are guides for informal visits. To schedule a visit, contact the Office of Admissions at *admiss@uwsp.edu*.

Financial Aid: In 2005-2006, 52% of all full-time freshmen and 54% of continuing full-time students received some form of financial aid. 47% of full-time freshmen and 49% of continuing full-time students received need-based aid. The average freshman award was $5301. Need-based scholarships or need-based grants averaged $4078; need-based self-help aid (loans and jobs) averaged $3639; and other non-need-based awards and non-need-based scholarships averaged $2072. 26% of undergraduates work part time. The average financial indebtedness of the 2005 graduate was $14,975. The FAFSA is required. The deadline for filing freshman financial aid applications for fall entry is June 15.

International Students: There are 117 international students enrolled. The school actively recruits these students. They must score satisfactorily on the written TOEFL or on the electronic version.

Computers: Wireless access is available. All students may access the system. There are no time limits and no fees. It is recommended that students in interior architecture have personal computers.

Graduates: From July 1, 2004 to June 30, 2005, 1536 bachelor's degrees were awarded. The most popular majors were business administration (9%), communication (8%), and education (7%). In an average class, 1% graduate in 3 years or less, 20% graduate in 4 years or less, 52% graduate in 5 years or less, and 58% graduate in 6 years or less. 100 companies recruited on campus in 2004-2005. Of the 2004 graduating class, 16% were enrolled in graduate school within 6 months of graduation and 98% were employed.

Admissions Contact: Catherine Glennon, Director of Admissions. E-mail: *admiss@uwsp.edu* Web: *http://www.uwsp.edu/admissions*

UNIVERSITY OF WISCONSIN/STOUT | B-3

Menomonie, WI 54751

(715) 232-1411
(800) HI-STOUT; Fax: (715) 232-1667

Full-time: 3292 men, 3298 women	Faculty: 289; IIA, -$
Part-time: 386 men, 272 women	Ph.D.s: 78%
Graduate: 160 men, 357 women	Student/Faculty: 23 to 1
Year: 4-1-4, summer session	Tuition: $6592 ($16,925)
Application Deadline: open	Room & Board: $4572
Freshman Class: 3953 applied, 3205 accepted, 1694 enrolled	
ACT: 21	COMPETITIVE

The University of Wisconsin/Stout, founded in 1891, offers undergraduate programs in liberal studies, human environmental sciences, industry and technology, education, and human services. There are 4 undergraduate schools and 1 graduate school. In addition to regional accreditation, UW-Stout has baccalaureate program accreditation with AAMET, ABET, ACCE, ADA, FIDER, IACBE and NASAD. The library contains 225,672 volumes, 1,213,627 microform items, and 14,254 audio/video tapes/CDs/DVDs, and subscribes to 1012 periodicals including electronic. Computerized library services include the card catalog, interlibrary loans, database searching, Internet access, and laptop Internet portals. Special learning facilities include a learning resource center, art gallery, radio station, and TV station. The 110-acre campus is in a rural area 60 miles east of Minneapolis/St. Paul. Including any residence halls, there are 33 buildings.

Student Life: 69% of undergraduates are from Wisconsin. Others are from 26 states, 28 foreign countries, and Canada. 93% are white. The average age of freshmen is 18; all undergraduates, 22. 27% do not continue beyond their first year.

Housing: 2936 students can be accommodated in college housing, which includes coed dormitories, smoke-free, alcohol-free, upperclassmen-only, and freshman student housing. On-campus housing is guaranteed for all 4 years. 60% of students commute. All students may keep cars.

Activities: 2% of men belong to 3 local and 2 national fraternities; 3% of women belong to 3 national sororities. There are 117 groups on campus, including art, band, cheerleading, choir, chorale, chorus, computers, dance, debate, drama, ethnic, film, forensics, gay, honors, international, jazz band, literary magazine, marching band, musical theater, newspaper, pep band, photography, political, professional, religious, social, social service, and student government. Popular campus events include Family Weekend, Cheese Week, and Biggest House Party.

Sports: There are 6 intercollegiate sports for men and 8 for women, and 20 intramural sports for men and 19 for women. Facilities include baseball, soccer, and football fields, indoor and outdoor tracks, and a field house with basketball, racquetball, and volleyball courts, a pool, weight and gymnastics rooms, and indoor and outdoor tennis courts.

Disabled Students: All of the campus is accessible. Wheelchair ramps, elevators, special parking, specially equipped rest rooms, special class scheduling, lowered drinking fountains, lowered telephones, and special housing are available.

Services: Counseling and information services are available, as is tutoring in most subjects. There is a reader service for the blind, and remedial math, reading, and writing.

Campus Safety and Security: Measures include 24-hour foot and vehicle patrol, informal discussions, pamphlets/posters/films, lighted pathways/sidewalks, and training sessions.

Programs of Study: UW-Stout confers B.A., B.S., and B.F.A. degrees. Master's degrees are also awarded. Bachelor's degrees are awarded in BUSINESS (business administration and management, hospitality management services, management science, marketing/retailing/merchandising, and retailing), COMMUNICATIONS AND THE ARTS (apparel design, art, communications, fine arts, and telecommunications), COMPUTER AND PHYSICAL SCIENCE (applied mathematics, applied science, and science), EDUCATION (art, early childhood, home economics, marketing and distribution, technical, and vocational), ENGINEERING AND ENVIRONMENTAL DESIGN (construction technology, engineering technology, graphic and printing production, graphic arts technology, industrial administration/management, industrial engineering technology, and manufacturing engineering), HEALTH PROFESSIONS (rehabilitation therapy), SOCIAL SCIENCE (child care/child and family studies, dietetics, family/consumer studies, food production/management/services, and psychology). General business administration, art, and hotel restaurant and tourism management are the largest.

Required: Students must complete a minimum of 124 credits, including a general education component. Some degree programs have specific general education courses that must be taken in order to satisfy certification, accreditation, or prerequisite standards. Students must also fulfill an ethnic studies requirement.

Special: UW-Stout offers business and industry internships, cooperative programs, work-study programs, and study abroad in London. Dual majors, credit by examination, credit for life, military, and work experience, nondegree study, and pass/fail options are also available. There is 1 national honor society, a freshman honors program, and 3 departmental honors program.

Faculty/Classroom: 58% of faculty are male; 42%, female. All both teach and do research. The average class size in an introductory lecture is 31 and in a laboratory, 21.

Admissions: 81% of the 2005-2006 applicants were accepted. The ACT scores for the 2005-2006 freshman class were: 42% below 21, 35% between 21 and 23, 17% between 24 and 26, 5% between 27 and 28, and 2% above 28. 18% of the current freshmen were in the top fifth of their class; 50% were in the top two fifths. 10 freshmen graduated first in their class.

Requirements: The SAT or ACT is required; the ACT is preferred, with a satisfactory on the SAT. Minimum test scores are waived if students rank in the upper 50% of their class. Applicants should graduate from an accredited secondary school. The GED is accepted if applicants are over 21, or if their graduating class has been out for at least 2 years. Secondary school preparation should include 4 academic credits in English, 3 each in social studies, math, and science, and 4 in electives. UW-Stout requires applicants to be in the upper 50% of their class. A GPA of 2.75 is required. AP and CLEP credits are accepted.

Procedure: Freshmen are admitted fall, spring, and summer. There is a rolling admission plan. Entrance exams should be taken in June of the junior year. Application deadlines are open. Application fee is $35. A waiting list is an active part of the admissions procedure. Applications are accepted on-line.

Transfer: 581 transfer students enrolled in 2004-2005. A minimum college GPA of 2.0 is required for student transfers from VW system institutions. A 2.2 GPA is required for those transferring from outside the VW system. A high school transcript and a statement of good standing from prior institutions are required. 32 of 124 credits required for the bachelor's degree must be completed at UW-Stout.

Visiting: There are regularly scheduled orientations for prospective students, including an interview with an admissions counselor and a campus tour. There are also campus preview days throughout the academic year. There are guides for informal visits and visitors may sit in on classes and stay overnight. To schedule a visit, contact Dawn Steinmeyer at (800) 447-8688 or (715) 232-1232.

Financial Aid: In 2005-2006, 48% of all full-time freshmen and 51% of continuing full-time students received some form of financial aid. At least 24% of full-time freshmen and at least 26% of continuing full-time students received need-based aid. The average freshman award was $6893. Need-based scholarships or need-based grants averaged $3811; need-based self-help aid (loans and jobs) averaged $4153; and other institutional scholarships averaged $8887. 69% of undergraduates work part time. Average annual earnings from campus work are $1351. The average financial indebtedness of the 2005 graduate was $18,496. UW-Stout is a member of CSS. The FAFSA is required. The priority date for freshman financial aid applications for fall entry is March 1.

International Students: In a recent year there were 39 international students enrolled. The school actively recruits these students. They must score satisfactorily on the written TOEFL.

Computers: All students may access the system 24 hours a day, 7 days a week. There are no time limits and no fees. All students are required to have personal computers.

Graduates: From July 1, 2004 to June 30, 2005, 1239 bachelor's degrees were awarded. The most popular majors were business marketing (38%), education (17%), and visual and performing arts (9%). In an average class, 14% graduate in 4 years or less, and 41% graduate in 5 years or less. 306 companies recruited on campus in a recent year.

Admissions Contact: Cindy Jenkins, Director of Admissions. A video is available. E-mail: *admissions@uwstout.edu* Web: *www.uwstout.edu*

UNIVERSITY OF WISCONSIN/SUPERIOR A-1

Superior, WI 54880 — (715) 394-8230; Fax: (715) 394-8407

Full-time: 810 men, 1200 women	**Faculty:** 115; IIA, -$
Part-time: 140 men, 300 women	**Ph.D.s:** 75%
Graduate: 140 men, 270 women	**Student/Faculty:** 17 to 1
Year: semesters, summer session	**Tuition:** $5188 ($15,234)
Application Deadline: April 1	**Room & Board:** $4422
Freshman Class: n/av	
ACT: required	**COMPETITIVE+**

The University of Wisconsin/Superior, founded in 1893, offers undergraduate programs in the liberal arts and sciences, business, education, fine arts, applied arts, and social sciences. There are 5 undergraduate schools and 1 graduate school. Figures in the above capsule and in this profile are approximate. The library contains 455,313 volumes, 105,398 microform items, and 5467 audio/video tapes/CDs/DVDs, and subscribes to 753 periodicals including electronic. Computerized library services include the card catalog, interlibrary loans, and database searching. Special learning facilities include a learning resource center, art gallery, planetarium, TV station, an aquatic lab, color television studio, and an FM radio station. The 230-acre campus is in an urban area 150 miles north of Minneapolis/St. Paul. Including any residence halls, there are 17 buildings.

Student Life: 58% of undergraduates are from Wisconsin. Others are from 21 states, 18 foreign countries, and Canada. 90% are from public schools. 95% are white. The average age of freshmen is 17; all undergraduates, 21. 15% do not continue beyond their first year; 40% remain to graduate.

Housing: 650 students can be accommodated in college housing, which includes single-sex and coed dorms. On-campus housing is guaranteed for all 4 years. 76% of students commute. All students may keep cars.

Activities: There are no fraternities or sororities. There are 48 groups on campus, including art, band, cheerleading, choir, chorale, chorus, computers, dance, drama, ethnic, gay, honors, international, jazz band, newspaper, orchestra, photography, political, professional, radio and TV, religious, social, social service, student government, and symphony. Popular campus events include Snow Week, sports events, and Fall Fest.

Sports: There are 5 intercollegiate sports for men and 7 for women, and 5 intramural sports for men and 5 for women. Facilities include a 4000-seat stadium, a 3000-seat gym, an ice arena, a swimming pool, a weight-training room, a dance studio, an all-weather track, and softball and baseball fields.

Disabled Students: 95% of the campus is accessible. Wheelchair ramps, elevators, special parking, specially equipped rest rooms, special class scheduling, lowered drinking fountains, and lowered telephones are available.

Services: Counseling and information services are available, as is tutoring in every subject. There is remedial math and writing.

Campus Safety and Security: Measures include 24-hour foot and vehicle patrol, self-defense education, security escort services, and informal discussions. There are pamphlets/posters/films, emergency telephones, and lighted pathways/sidewalks.

Programs of Study: UW/Superior confers B.A., B.S., B.F.A., B.M., and B.M.E. degrees. Associate and master's degrees are also awarded. Bachelor's degrees are awarded in BIOLOGICAL SCIENCE (biology/biological science), BUSINESS (accounting and business administration and management), COMMUNICATIONS AND THE ARTS (art history and appreciation, communications, dramatic arts, English, fine arts, music, music performance, speech/debate/rhetoric, and studio art), COMPUTER AND PHYSICAL SCIENCE (chemistry, computer science, information sciences and systems, and mathematics), EDUCATION (art, elementary, mathematics, music, physical, science, and secondary), HEALTH PROFESSIONS (art therapy and community health work), SOCIAL SCIENCE (criminal justice, history, international studies, law, political science/government, psychology, public administration, social studies, social work, and sociology). Business, education, and aquatic biology are the strongest academically. Business is the largest.

Required: To graduate, students must complete 120 credit hours, with a GPA of 2.0. A minimum of 54 hours must be credited toward comple-

tion of 1 comprehensive major, 2 majors, or 1 major and 1 minor. The required core curriculum includes 55 credits in communications, English, math, phys ed, world culture, contemporary society, aesthetic experience, natural science, and human behavior. A comprehensive exam and a senior project are required.

Special: UW/Superior offers co-op programs in business and internships in social work, business, mass communication, and criminal justice. There is a comprehensive program of student-designed majors, along with a cooperative program in marine studies with Texas A&M University, and 3-2 engineering and forestry programs with Michigan Technological University. Students may cross-register for 2 classes per semester at the University of Minnesota/Duluth, the College of St. Scholastica, or Northland College. An extended degree is offered. Credit for life experience and pass/fail options are available. There is a chapter of Phi Beta Kappa and a freshman honors program.

Faculty/Classroom: 60% of faculty are male; 40%, female. All both teach and do research. No introductory courses are taught by graduate students. The average class size in an introductory lecture is 40; in a laboratory, 20; and in a regular course, 23.

Requirements: The ACT is required. Out-of-state residents may submit SAT scores instead. Applicants must graduate from an accredited secondary school or the equivalent. They must rank in the upper 50% of their graduating class or achieve a minimum composite score of 20 on the ACT. AP and CLEP credits are accepted. Important factors in the admissions decision are parents or siblings attending the school and recommendations by school officials.

Procedure: Freshmen are admitted fall, spring, and summer. Entrance exams should be taken before admission in spring of the junior year. There are early admissions and deferred admissions plans. There is a rolling admissions plan. Applications should be filed by April 1 for fall entry, along with a $35 fee. Notification is sent on a rolling basis.

Transfer: A college GPA of 2.0 is required. 30 of 120 credits required for the bachelor's degree must be completed at UW/Superior.

Visiting: There are regularly scheduled orientations for prospective students, consisting of a day and a half of social and educational programs. There are guides for informal visits and visitors may sit in on classes and stay overnight. To schedule a visit, contact the Admissions Office.

Financial Aid: UW/Superior is a member of CSS. The FAFSA is required. The priority date for filing freshman financial aid applications for fall entry is March 15.

International Students: The school actively recruits these students. They must take the TOEFL, achieving a satisfactory score, or take the MELAB or the college's own test or complete on ELS language center program.

Computers: All students may access the system 24 hours a day. There are no time limits and no fees.

Admissions Contact: Admissions Counselor.
E-mail: *admissions@uwsuper.edu* Web: *www.uwsuper.edu*

UNIVERSITY OF WISCONSIN/WHITEWATER D-5

Whitewater, WI 53190 — (262) 472-1440; Fax: (262) 472-1515

Full-time: 4000 men, 4400 women	**Faculty:** 384; IIA, av$
Part-time: 400 men, 550 women	**Ph.D.s:** 73%
Graduate: 450 men, 900 women	**Student/Faculty:** 22 to 1
Year: semesters, summer session	**Tuition:** $5254 ($15,652)
Application Deadline: open	**Room & Board:** $4020
Freshman Class: n/av	
SAT or ACT: recommended	**COMPETITIVE**

The University of Wisconsin/Whitewater, founded in 1868, offers programs in teacher education, business, liberal arts, preprofessional studies, fine arts, and music. Some information in this capsule and profile is approximate. There are 4 undergraduate schools and 1 graduate school. In addition to regional accreditation, UW/Whitewater has baccalaureate program accreditation with AACSB, ASLA, CSWE, NASM, and NCATE. The library contains 356,000 volumes, 993,000 microform items, and 7300 audio/video tapes/CDs/DVDs, and subscribes to 5000 periodicals including electronic. Computerized library services include the card catalog, interlibrary loans, and database searching. Special learning facilities include a learning resource center, art gallery, radio station, TV station, observatory, and weather station. The 385-acre campus is in a small town 50 miles southwest of Milwaukee. Including any residence halls, there are 45 buildings.

Student Life: 94% of undergraduates are from Wisconsin. Others are from 26 states, 38 foreign countries, and Canada. 85% are from public schools. 93% are white. The average age of freshmen is 19; all undergraduates, 22. 22% do not continue beyond their first year; 61% remain to graduate.

Housing: 4000 students can be accommodated in college housing, which includes single-sex and coed dorms. 50% of students live on campus; of those, 35% remain on campus on weekends. All students may keep cars.

Activities: 5% of men belong to 1 local fraternity and 6 national fraternities; 5% of women belong to 1 local sorority and 4 national sororities.

There are 130 groups on campus, including art, band, cheerleading, choir, chorus, computers, dance, drama, drill team, ethnic, film, gay, honors, international, marching band, musical theater, newspaper, orchestra, pep band, photography, political, professional, radio and TV, religious, social, social service, student government, symphony, and yearbook. Popular campus events include Job Fair, Performing Arts Series, and athletic contests.

Sports: There are 9 intercollegiate sports for men and 8 for women, and 12 intramural sports for men and 12 for women. Facilities include tennis courts, pools, playing fields, a 13,000-seat stadium, and a 3500-seat gym.

Disabled Students: 75% of the campus is accessible. Wheelchair ramps, elevators, special parking, specially equipped rest rooms, special class scheduling, lowered drinking fountains, lowered telephones, and vans for mobility are available.

Services: Counseling and information services are available, as is tutoring in most subjects and in study skills. There is a reader service for the blind, and remedial math, reading, and writing.

Campus Safety and Security: Measures include 24-hour foot and vehicle patrol, self-defense education, security escort services, and shuttle buses. There are informal discussions, pamphlets/posters/films, emergency telephones, and lighted pathways/sidewalks.

Programs of Study: UW/Whitewater confers B.A., B.S., B.B.A., B.F.A., B.M., and B.S.Ed. degrees. Associate and master's degrees are also awarded. Bachelor's degrees are awarded in BIOLOGICAL SCIENCE (biology/biological science), BUSINESS (accounting, banking and finance, business administration and management, business economics, marketing/retailing/merchandising, office supervision and management, and personnel management), COMMUNICATIONS AND THE ARTS (art history and appreciation, communications, dramatic arts, English, French, German, journalism, music, public relations, Spanish, and speech/debate/rhetoric), COMPUTER AND PHYSICAL SCIENCE (chemistry, computer programming, mathematics, and physics), EDUCATION (art, business, early childhood, elementary, foreign languages, middle school, music, physical, science, secondary, social studies, and special), SOCIAL SCIENCE (economics, geography, history, international studies, political science/government, prelaw, psychology, public administration, safety and security technology, social work, sociology, and women's studies). Accounting, computer science, and education are the strongest academically. Business/accounting and education are the largest.

Required: Students must complete 50 credits of general studies, a writing competency requirement, and 3 credits in minority issues. A GPA of 2.0 and 120 hours are required to graduate.

Special: Internships, study abroad in 9 nations, accelerated degree programs in safety studies and speech communication, student-designed majors, and a general studies degree are available. Credit by exam, non-degree study, and pass/fail options are also offered. There are 14 national honor societies, a freshman honors program, and 7 departmental honors programs.

Faculty/Classroom: 57% of faculty are male; 43%, female. All teach undergraduates and 78% do research. No introductory courses are taught by graduate students. The average class size in a regular course is 26.

Requirements: The SAT or ACT is recommended. In addition, applicants should graduate from an accredited secondary school or with 17 academic units, including 4 in English and 3 each in social studies, math, and science. The GED may be accepted. Applicants should rank in the upper 40% of their graduating class or achieve a combined high school and ACT/SAT percentile rank of 100% or above. A GPA of 2.8 is required. AP and CLEP credits are accepted. Important factors in the admissions decision are evidence of special talent, advanced placement or honor courses, and recommendations by school officials.

Procedure: Freshmen are admitted to all sessions. There is an early admissions plan and a rolling admissions plan. Application deadlines are open. Application fee is $35. Notification is sent on a rolling basis. A waiting list is an active part of the admissions procedure.

Transfer: Applicants should have a minimum college GPA of 2.0. 30 of 120 credits required for the bachelor's degree must be completed at UW/Whitewater.

Visiting: There are regularly scheduled orientations for prospective students. There are guides for informal visits and visitors may sit in on classes. To schedule a visit, contact the Admissions Office.

Financial Aid: In a recent year, 67% of all full-time students received some form of financial aid. 42% of full-time freshmen and 43% of continuing full-time students received need-based aid. The average freshman award was $5692. UW/Whitewater is a member of CSS. The FAFSA is required. Check with the school for current deadlines.

International Students: The school actively recruits these students. They must take the TOEFL, achieving a satisfactory score, or take the MELAB.

Computers: All students may access the system 24 hours if they have their own terminal or 8 A.M. to 11 P.M. Monday through Thursday and varied weekend hours in the general lab. There are no time limits and no fees.

Admissions Contact: Director of Admissions. A video is available.
E-mail: *uwwadmit@uww.edu* Web: *www.uww.edu*

VITERBO UNIVERSITY
(Formerly Viterbo College)
B-4

LaCrosse, WI 54601

(608) 796-3010
(800) 848-3726; Fax: (608) 796-3020

Full-time: 390 men, 1100 women	**Faculty:** 103; IIA, --$
Part-time: 70 men, 290 women	**Ph.D.s:** 63%
Graduate: 150 men, 540 women	**Student/Faculty:** 15 to 1
Year: semesters, summer session	**Tuition:** $16,240
Application Deadline: open	**Room & Board:** $5430
Freshman Class: n/av	
ACT: required	**COMPETITIVE**

Viterbo University, founded in 1890, is a private, Catholic, Franciscan liberal arts university. Viterbo offers undergraduate programs in liberal arts, sciences, fine arts, business, education, and health sciences. Master's degrees are offered in education, business, servant leadership, and nursing. Viterbo University embraces persons of all faiths and prepares students for leadership and service. There are 6 undergraduate and 4 graduate schools. Figures in the above capsule and in this profile are approximate. In addition to regional accreditation, Viterbo has baccalaureate program accreditation with ACS, CCNE, CSWE, NASM, NCATE, and NLN. The library contains 108,672 volumes, 233,392 microform items, and 6002 audio/video tapes/CDs/DVDs, and subscribes to 9838 periodicals including electronic. Computerized library services include the card catalog, interlibrary loans, database searching, and Internet access. Special learning facilities include a learning resource center, art gallery, and music resource center. The 26-acre campus is in a suburban area 145 miles west of Madison and 270 miles Northwest of Chicago. Including any residence halls, there are 13 buildings.

Student Life: 80% of undergraduates are from Wisconsin. Others are from 21 states and 12 foreign countries. 88% are from public schools. 89% are white. 40% are Catholic; 39% Protestant; 10% claim no religious affiliation. The average age of freshmen is 18; all undergraduates, 25. 34% do not continue beyond their first year; 53% remain to graduate.

Housing: 572 students can be accommodated in college housing, which includes single-sex and coed dorms and on-campus apartments. In addition, there are special-interest houses, on-campus houses, and special-interest floors. On-campus housing is guaranteed for the freshman year only and is available on a first-come, first-served basis. 63% of students commute. Alcohol is not permitted. Upperclassmen may keep cars.

Activities: There are no fraternities or sororities. There are 22 groups on campus, including art, choir, chorale, chorus, dance, drama, drill team, ethnic, international, literary magazine, musical theater, opera, pep band, professional, religious, social, social service, student government, and yearbook. Popular campus events include Orientation Weekend, St. Francis Day Celebration, and Hog Wild.

Sports: There are 3 intercollegiate sports for men and 4 for women, and 14 intramural sports for men and 14 for women. Facilities include a student activity center with weight-training and fitness rooms and courts for basketball, volleyball, and racquetball. A 12.5-acre outdoor athletic complex has facilities for soccer, baseball, and softball, located 2 1/2 miles from campus. There also are on-campus sand volleyball and paved basketball outdoor courts. The nearby Mississippi River and Mt. LaCrosse provide opportunities for canoeing and skiing.

Disabled Students: 90% of the campus is accessible. Wheelchair ramps, elevators, special parking, specially equipped rest rooms, special class scheduling, lowered drinking fountains, and lowered telephones are available.

Services: Counseling and information services are available, as is tutoring in every subject. There is a reader service for the blind, and remedial math, reading, and writing.

Campus Safety and Security: Measures include self-defense education, security escort services, informal discussions, and pamphlets/posters/films. There are emergency telephones, lighted pathways/sidewalks, an emergency evacuation plan, 24-hour, phone access to security personnel, a security patrol from 5 P.M. to 7 A.M., ID check-in in dorms after 10 P.M., card access to all campus buildings after regular hours, and 6 emergency blue lights.

Programs of Study: Viterbo confers B.A., B.S., B.Art.Ed., B.B.A., B.F.A., B.I.L., B.L.S., B.M.T., B.S. Community-Medical Dietetics, B.S.Ed., B.S.N., and B.T.A. degrees. Master's degrees are also awarded. Bachelor's degrees are awarded in BIOLOGICAL SCIENCE (biology/biological science and nutrition), BUSINESS (accounting, business administration and management, institutional management, management information systems, management science, marketing/retailing/merchandising, and organizational behavior), COMMUNICATIONS AND THE ARTS (applied music, arts administration/management, dramatic arts, English, fine arts, graphic design, music, music performance, musical theater, Spanish, studio art, and theater management), COMPUTER AND PHYSICAL SCIENCE (chemistry, digital arts/technology, information sciences and systems, and mathematics), EDUCATION (art, business, computer, drama, elementary, music, and science), HEALTH PROFESSIONS (health care administration and nursing), SOCIAL SCIENCE (criminal justice, dietetics, liberal arts/general studies, ministries, psychology, religion, social studies, social work, and sociology). Nutrition/dietetics, natural sciences, and English are the strongest academically. Nursing, business, and education are the largest.

Required: Students must complete a minimum of 128 semester hours of credit. A minimum of 43 of these must be upper-division level. All students must complete the general education requirements (45 credit hours from various disciplines) and competencies, as well as all of the specified requirements for their major. Also, students must complete a service component designed by their major program. All students must have a GPA of at least 2.0 and must take as a minimum the last 30 consecutive semester hours at Viterbo University or complete 45 of the last 60 semester hours from Viterbo. Students seeking a B.S. must complete 7 credits of natural science and/or math in addition to the 4 credits of natural science in the general education requirements. Students seeking a B.A. must complete the equivalent of 14 semester hours of the same modern foreign language.

Special: Students may cross-register at the University of Wisconsin/LaCrosse, enroll for independent study, or earn a dual degree. Co-op programs, study abroad in 7 countries, double majors, student-designed majors, accelerated degree programs, work-study, internships in many areas, credit by exam, and credit/no credit options are available. There are 2 national honor societies.

Faculty/Classroom: 42% of faculty are male; 58%, female. 99% teach undergraduates, 8% both teach and do research. No introductory courses are taught by graduate students. The average class size in an introductory lecture is 21; in a laboratory, 14; and in a regular course, 15.

Admissions: 8 freshmen graduated first in their class in a recent year.

Requirements: The ACT is required. In addition, graduation from an accredited secondary school is required; the GED is accepted. Secondary preparation should include 16 credits, with 3 or 4 in English and 2 each in math, natural science, and social science or history. Fine arts students may be required to audition or submit a portfolio. Nursing, dietetics, and premedical students must have high school chemistry. A GPA of 2.0 is required. AP and CLEP credits are accepted.

Procedure: Freshmen are admitted to all sessions. Entrance exams should be taken at placement listing at registration. There is a rolling admission plan. Application deadlines are open. Application fee is $25. Notification is sent on a rolling basis. Applications are accepted on-line.

Transfer: 251 transfer students enrolled in a recent year. Transfer students must have a cumulative GPA of at least 2.0, be free to return to their previous school, and be considered to be in good academic standing both at their previous school and at Viterbo. They must submit an application, the $25 fee, official transcripts of course work in high school, official transcripts from all postsecondary institutions, and ACT/SAT results, if already taken. 30 of 128 credits required for the bachelor's degree must be completed at Viterbo.

Visiting: There are regularly scheduled orientations for prospective students, including a meeting with an admissions staff member, a tour of the campus, and optional meetings with a financial aid officer and faculty members. There are guides for informal visits and visitors may sit in on classes. To schedule a visit, contact Tessica Ray at jeray@viterbo.edu.

Financial Aid: In a recent year, 99% of all full-time freshmen and 97% of continuing full-time students received some form of financial aid. 84% of full-time freshmen and 80% of continuing full-time students received need-based aid. The average freshman award was $13,683. Need-based scholarships or need-based grants averaged $8317 ($14,900 maximum); need-based self-help aid (loans and jobs) averaged $3423; non-need-based athletic scholarships averaged $501 ($3000 maximum); and other non-need-based awards and non-need-based scholarships averaged $1875 ($14,900 maximum). 43% of undergraduates work part time. Average annual earnings from campus work are $911. The average financial indebtedness of a recent year's graduate was $15,678. The FAFSA and the college's own financial statement are required. Check with the school for current deadlines.

International Students: There were 17 international students enrolled in a recent year. The school actively recruits these students. They must take the TOEFL, achieving a satisfactory score, and also take the college's own test.

Computers: All students may access the system 6 A.M. to 1 A.M. daily. There are no time limits and no fees. It is strongly recommended that all students have a personal computer.

Graduates: In a recent year, 352 bachelor's degrees were awarded. The most popular majors were nursing (25%), business/organizational management (9%), and education (9%). In an average class, 32% graduate in 4 years or less, 51% graduate in 5 years or less, and 53% graduate in 6 years or less. 80 companies recruited on campus in a recent

year. Of a recent year's graduating class, 10% were enrolled in graduate school within 6 months of graduation and 88% were employed.

Admissions Contact: Roland W. Nelson, Vice President for Enrollment. A video is available. E-mail: admission@viterbo.edu Web: www.viterbo.edu

WISCONSIN LUTHERAN COLLEGE   E-4
Milwaukee, WI 53226
(414) 443-8811
(888) 947-5884; Fax: (414) 443-8514

Full-time: 270 men, 400 women	**Faculty:** 47
Part-time: 20 men, 20 women	**Ph.D.s:** 65%
Graduate: none	**Student/Faculty:** 14 to 1
Year: semesters, summer session	**Tuition:** $17,470
Application Deadline: see profile	**Room & Board:** $6040
Freshman Class: n/av	
ACT: required	**VERY COMPETITIVE**

Wisconsin Lutheran College, founded in 1973 in affiliation with the Wisconsin Evangelical Lutheran Synod, offers higher education in the arts and sciences within a conservative Christian environment. Some figures in the above capsule and in this profile are approximate. The library contains 72,621 volumes, 9211 microform items, and 4634 audio/video tapes/CDs/DVDs, and subscribes to 998 periodicals including electronic. Computerized library services include the card catalog, interlibrary loans, database searching, and Internet access. Special learning facilities include a learning resource center, art gallery, sound studio, electronic music lab, and language lab. The 21-acre campus is in a suburban area on the western edge of Milwaukee. Including any residence halls, there are 27 buildings.

Student Life: 80% of undergraduates are from Wisconsin. Others are from 27 states and 6 foreign countries. 41% are from public schools. 95% are white. Most are Protestant. The average age of freshmen is 18; all undergraduates, 20. 20% do not continue beyond their first year; 74% remain to graduate.

Housing: 600 students can be accommodated in college housing, which includes single-sex dorms and on-campus apartments. On-campus housing is guaranteed for all 4 years. 78% of students live on campus. Alcohol is not permitted. All students may keep cars.

Activities: There are no fraternities or sororities. There are 31 groups on campus, including Ambassador Club (admissions), art, band, cheerleading, choir, dance, drama, ethnic, international, jazz band, musical theater, newspaper, pep band, photography, political, professional, religious, social, social service, student government, and yearbook. Popular campus events include musical and theater events, Winterfest, and Commencement weekend.

Sports: There are 7 intercollegiate sports for men and 8 for women, and 5 intramural sports for men and 5 for women. Facilities include 3 full basketball courts, a 2500-seat gym, a weight room, a fitness center, a dance/aerobics room, training and therapy rooms, and a walking/running track.

Disabled Students: 90% of the campus is accessible. Wheelchair ramps, elevators, special parking, specially equipped rest rooms, lowered drinking fountains, and lowered telephones are available.

Services: Counseling and information services are available, as is tutoring in some subjects, including math, writing, and foreign language.

Campus Safety and Security: Measures include 24-hour foot and vehicle patrol, self-defense education, security escort services, and shuttle buses. There are informal discussions, pamphlets/posters/films, lighted pathways/sidewalks, a security service, and electronically operated dorm entrances.

Programs of Study: Wisconsin Lutheran confers B.A. and B.S. degrees. Bachelor's degrees are awarded in BIOLOGICAL SCIENCE (biology/biological science), BUSINESS (business economics), COMMUNICATIONS AND THE ARTS (art, communications, dramatic arts, English, music, and Spanish), COMPUTER AND PHYSICAL SCIENCE (chemistry and mathematics), EDUCATION (elementary), SOCIAL SCIENCE (history, interdisciplinary studies, political science/government, psychology, social science, and theological studies). Chemistry, education, and biology are the strongest academically. Music, theology, and education are the largest.

Required: Composition, speech, math, and foreign language competencies are required. All students must complete a core curriculum that includes courses in theology, aesthetics, literature, natural science, history, social science, and intellectual diversity, plus 1 credit in phys ed/lifetime sport and 2 freshman seminars. A minimum overall GPA of 2.0 and 2.5 in the major (some require a higher GPA) plus 128 credit hours are required to graduate.

Special: Student-designed majors and study abroad are offered. Internships are available in most departments.

Faculty/Classroom: 70% of faculty are male; 30%, female. All both teach and do research. The average class size in an introductory lecture is 20; in a laboratory, 10; and in a regular course, 16.

Admissions: 10 freshmen graduated first in their class in a recent year.

Requirements: The ACT is required, with a minimum composite score. Students should be graduates of an accredited high school or its equivalent with a minimum of 16 high school units, including 4 in English, 3 each in academic electives and math, and 2 each in science, foreign language, and social studies/history. The Academic Recommendation Form must be submitted. A portfolio for art grants and an audition for music and drama grants are required. Wisconsin Lutheran requires applicants to be in the upper 50% of their class. A GPA of 2.7 is required. AP and CLEP credits are accepted. Important factors in the admissions decision are leadership record and personality/intangible qualities.

Procedure: Freshmen are admitted fall and spring. Entrance exams should be taken in the spring of the junior year. There is a rolling admissions plan. Check with the school for current application deadlines. Application fee is $20. Notification is sent on a rolling basis. Applications are accepted on-line.

Transfer: 16 transfer students enrolled in a recent year. Students should have a GPA of at least 2.5 for transfer credit. The Transfer Recommendation Form is required. 30 of 128 credits required for the bachelor's degree must be completed at Wisconsin Lutheran.

Visiting: There are regularly scheduled orientations for prospective students, including a tour of the campus, a meal, and meetings with admissions, financial aid, cocurriculars, and faculty in academic areas of interest. There are guides for informal visits and visitors may sit in on classes and stay overnight. To schedule a visit, contact the Admissions Office.

Financial Aid: In a recent year, all full-time freshmen received some form of financial aid. 77% of full-time freshmen and 76% of continuing full-time students received need-based aid. The average freshman award was $14,526. The average financial indebtedness of a recent year's graduate was $13,707. The FAFSA and the college's own financial statement are required. Check with the school for current deadlines.

International Students: There were 10 international students enrolled in a recent year. They must achieve a satisfactory score on the TOEFL or the SAT or ACT.

Computers: All students may access the system. There are no time limits and no fees. It is strongly recommended that all students have a personal computer.

Graduates: In a recent year, 121 bachelor's degrees were awarded. The most popular majors were communication (17%), psychology (11%), and biology (11%). In an average class, 47% graduate in 4 years or less, 62% graduate in 5 years or less, and 74% graduate in 6 years or less.

Admissions Contact: Craig Swiontek, Director of Admissions. E-mail: *admissions@wlc.edu* Web: *www.wlc.edu/admissions/*

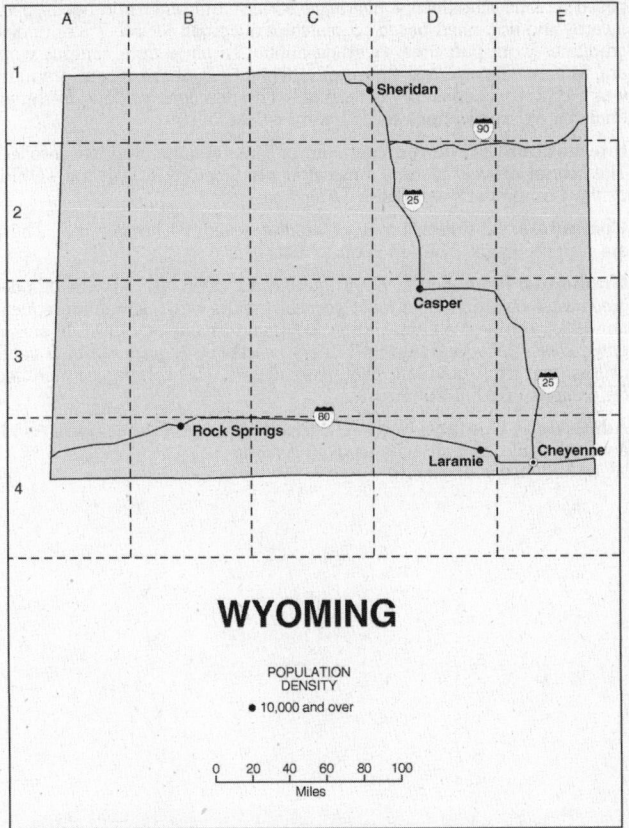

WYOMING

POPULATION
DENSITY
● 10,000 and over

0   20   40   60   80   100
Miles

UNIVERSITY OF WYOMING   D-4
Laramie, WY 82071

(307) 766-5160
(800) 342-5996; Fax: (307) 766-4042

Full-time: 3921 men, 3841 women	**Faculty:** 630; I, --$
Part-time: 561 men, 1260 women	**Ph.D.s:** 82%
Graduate: 1269 men, 2349 women	**Student/Faculty:** 12 to 1
Year: semesters, summer session	**Tuition:** $3426 ($9816)
Application Deadline: August 10	**Room & Board:** $6240

Freshman Class: 3211 applied, 3065 accepted, 1518 enrolled
SAT Verbal/Math: 530/540*   **ACT:** 23   **COMPETITIVE**

The University of Wyoming, founded in 1886, is a public institution offering programs in agriculture, arts and sciences, business, education, engineering, health science, and law. There are 6 undergraduate schools and 1 graduate school. In addition to regional accreditation, UW has baccalaureate program accreditation with AACSB, ABA, ABET, ACPE, ACS, ADA, APA, CACREP, CCNE, CSWE, IAME, NASM, NCATE, and NLN. The 9 libraries contain 1,366,000 volumes, 2,932,429 microform items, and 4919 audio/video tapes/CDs/DVDs, and subscribe to 11,642 periodicals including electronic. Computerized library services include the card catalog, interlibrary loans, database searching, and Internet access. Special learning facilities include a learning resource center, art gallery, natural history museum, planetarium, radio station, TV station, and the American Heritage Center. The 785-acre campus is in a small town 128 miles north of Denver, Colorado, and 45 miles west of Cheyenne, Wyoming's capital. Including any residence halls, there are 223 buildings.

Student Life: 73% of undergraduates are from Wyoming. Others are from 50 states, 71 foreign countries, and Canada. 83% are white. The average age of freshmen is 18; all undergraduates, 24. 24% do not continue beyond their first year; 56% remain to graduate.

Housing: 2198 students can be accommodated in college housing, which includes single-sex and coed dorms, on-campus apartments, off-campus apartments, married-student housing, fraternity houses, and sorority houses. In addition, there are honors houses. On-campus housing is guaranteed for all 4 years. 80% of students commute. All students may keep cars.

Activities: 7% of men belong to 9 national fraternities; 5% of women belong to 4 national sororities. There are 203 groups on campus, including art, band, cheerleading, chess, choir, chorale, chorus, computers, dance, debate, drama, drill team, ethnic, film, forensics, gay, honors, international, jazz band, literary magazine, marching band, musical theater, newspaper, opera, orchestra, pep band, photography, political, professional, radio and TV, religious, social, social service, student government, and symphony. Popular campus events include President's Welcome, Parents Weekend, and Weeks of Welcome.

Sports: There are 7 intercollegiate sports for men and 8 for women, and 45 intramural sports for men and 45 for women. Facilities include a 33,000-seat stadium, a 15,000-seat indoor gym and arena, basketball, volleyball, and racquetball courts, running tracks, 2 pools, weight rooms, an indoor tennis complex, a baseball and track stadium, a football training center, a 6,855-yard golf course, and a sports complex.

Disabled Students: 95% of the campus is accessible. Wheelchair ramps, elevators, special parking, specially equipped rest rooms, special class scheduling, lowered drinking fountains, lowered telephones, and braille signs are available.

Services: Counseling and information services are available, as is tutoring in most subjects. There is a reader service for the blind. note-taking services, tape recorders, and interpreters for the hearing impaired.

Campus Safety and Security: Measures include 24-hour foot and vehicle patrol, self-defense education, security escort services, and shuttle buses. There are informal discussions, pamphlets/posters/films, emergency telephones, and lighted pathways/sidewalks.

Programs of Study: UW confers B.A., B.S., B.F.A., B.M., B.S.Arch.Eng., B.S.C.E., B.S.Ch.E., B.S.Comp.Eng., B.S.C.S., B.S.D.H., B.S.E.E., B.S.F.C., B.S.M.E., B.S.M.I., B.S.N., and B.S.W. degrees. Master's and doctoral degrees are also awarded. Bachelor's degrees are awarded in AGRICULTURE (agricultural business management, agricultural communications, agriculture, agronomy, animal science, natural resource management, range/farm management, and wildlife management), BIOLOGICAL SCIENCE (biology/biological science, botany, microbiology, molecular biology, and zoology), BUSINESS (accounting, banking and finance, business administration and management, business economics, management information systems, and marketing/retailing/merchandising), COMMUNICATIONS AND THE ARTS (art, communications, dance, dramatic arts, English, French, German, journalism, music, music performance, music theory and composition, Russian, and Spanish), COMPUTER AND PHYSICAL SCIENCE (astronomy, chemistry, computer science, earth science, environmental geology, geology, mathematics, physics, science, and statistics), EDUCATION (agricultural, elementary, health, industrial arts, music, physical, secondary, special, and trade and industrial), ENGINEERING AND ENVIRONMENTAL DESIGN (architectural engineering, chemical engineering, civil engineering, computer engineering, electrical/electronics engineering, and industrial administration/management), HEALTH PROFESSIONS (dental hygiene, exercise science, health science, nursing, speech pathology/audiology, and veterinary science), SOCIAL SCIENCE (American studies, anthropology, criminal justice, economics, family/consumer studies, geography, history, humanities, international studies, parks and recreation management, philosophy, political science/government, psychology, social science, social work, sociology, water resources, and women's studies). Elementary education, business administration, and nursing are the largest.

Required: To graduate, students must complete 120 to 157 credit hours, depending on the major, with a minimum GPA of 2.0. The core curriculum includes 12 credit hours of cultural context, 9 of math, 6 to 8 of science, 3 of writing, 3 of constitution studies, 3 of oral communications, 1 of phys ed, and 1 to 3 of intellectual community.

Special: UW offers co-op programs in health sciences, internships, study abroad in many countries, Washington and U.N. semesters, work-study programs, dual and interdisciplinary majors, pass/fail options, student-designed majors, credit by exam, accelerated degree programs, and credit for life, military, and work experience. There are 21 national honor societies, including Phi Beta Kappa, a freshman honors program, and 11 departmental honors programs.

Faculty/Classroom: 67% of faculty are male; 33%, female. 97% teach undergraduates and 82% do research. Graduate students teach 10% of introductory courses. The average class size in an introductory lecture is 41; in a laboratory, 20; and in a regular course, 40.

Admissions: 95% of the 2005-2006 applicants were accepted. The SAT scores for the 2005-2006 freshman class were: Verbal--32% below 500, 43% between 500 and 599, 23% between 600 and 700, and 3% above 700; Math--29% below 500, 42% between 500 and 599, 26% between 600 and 700, and 3% above 700. The ACT scores were 29% below 21, 27% between 21 and 23, 23% between 24 and 26, 10% between 27 and 28, and 10% above 28. 39% of the current freshmen were in the top fifth of their class; 65% were in the top two fifths. 100 freshmen graduated first in their class.

Requirements: The SAT or ACT is required for students under 21; the ACT is preferred. Applicants must be graduates of an accredited secondary school or hold a GED certificate. Secondary preparation should include at least 13 academic credits consisting of 4 years of English (or 3 of English and 2 of a single foreign language) and 3 each of math, science, and cultural context electives. A visit is suggested. A GPA of 2.75 is required. AP and CLEP credits are accepted. Important factors in the admissions decision are recommendations by school officials, personality/intangible qualities, and extracurricular activities record.

Procedure: Freshmen are admitted fall, spring, and summer. Entrance exams should be taken in the spring of the junior year or fall of the senior year. There is a deferred admissions plan. Applications should be filed by August 10 for fall entry and December 10 for spring entry. Notification is sent on a rolling basis. Applications are accepted on-line.

Transfer: 1050 transfer students enrolled in 2004-2005. Applicants with 30 or more transferable college-level credits must have a minimum GPA of 2.0. All applicants with fewer credits must submit a high school transcript, and those students under age 21 must also present SAT or ACT scores. 30 of 120 to 157 credits required for the bachelor's degree must be completed at UW.

Visiting: There are regularly scheduled orientations for prospective students, including campus tours and meetings with academic advisers. There are guides for informal visits and visitors may sit in on classes and stay overnight. To schedule a visit, contact the Admissions Office at *why_wy@uwyo.edu.*

Financial Aid: In 2005-2006, 61% of all full-time freshmen and 48% of continuing full-time students received some form of financial aid. 47% of full-time freshmen received need-based aid. The average freshman award in a recent year was $7698. Need-based scholarships or need-based grants averaged $3823 ($4050 maximum); need-based self-help aid (loans and jobs) averaged $3875 ($5525 maximum); non-need-based athletic scholarships averaged $3428; and other non-need-based awards and non-need-based scholarships averaged $1955. 7% of undergraduates work part time. Average annual earnings from campus work are $1175. The average financial indebtedness of the recent graduate was $15,250. The FAFSA is required. The deadline for filing freshman financial aid applications for fall entry is March 1.

International Students: There are 131 international students enrolled. The school actively recruits these students. They must take the TOEFL or the Comprehensive English Language Test, .

Computers: All students may access the system 24 hours a day. There are no time limits. The fee is up to $35.

Graduates: From July 1, 2004 to June 30, 2005, 1695 bachelor's degrees were awarded. The most popular majors were elementary education (9%), business administration (6%), and psychology (5%). In an average class, 26% graduate in 4 years or less, 50% graduate in 5 years or less, and 56% graduate in 6 years or less. 153 companies recruited on campus in 2004-2005.

Admissions Contact: Noah A. Buckley, Director of Admissions. A video is available. E-mail: *why-wyo@uwyo.edu* Web: *http://www.uwyo.edu*

ARIZONA

SOUTHWESTERN COLLEGE   C-4

Phoenix, AZ 85032   (602) 992-6101; (800) 247-2697, ext. 100
                              Fax: (602) 404-2159

Full-time: 110 men, 120 women   **Faculty:** 32
Part-time: 15 men, 15 women   **Tuition:** $11,130
Application Deadline: August 1   **Room & Board:** $4040
SAT: required   **ACT:** required

Southwestern College, founded in 1960, is affiliated with Southwest Conservative Baptist Association. Its mission is to prepare students for vocational and lay ministries as educators in public, private, or Christian schools. Enrollment figures in the above capsule are approxiamate. In addition to regional accreditation, the college is accredited by AABC. Southwestern College awards the B.A. and B.S. in elementary education, biblical studies, Christian ministries, secondary education, business administration, counseling, and music education. The school also awards associate degree. Web: *http://www.swcaz.edu*

ARKANSAS

CENTRAL BAPTIST COLLEGE   C-3

Conway, AR 72032   (501) 329-6872; Fax: (501) 329-6872

Full-time: 181 men, 147 women   **Faculty:** 41
Part-time: 37 men, 30 women   **Tuition:** $6860
Application Deadline: August 15   **Room & Board:** $4660
ACT: 20

Central Baptist College, founded in 1952, is affiliated with the Baptist Missionary Association of Arkansas. Its mission is to train Christian men and women for lay and professional ministry and church-related vocations. Central Baptist College awards the B.A., B.S., and B.B.A. in Bible studies, church music, youth ministry, organizational management, management information systems, social service, music and general studies. The school also awards associate degrees. Web: *www.cbc.edu*

CALIFORNIA

BETHANY UNIVERSITY   B-3

Scotts Valley, CA 95066   (831) 438-3800 (800) 843-9410
                                    Fax: (831) 438-6104

Full-time: 141 men, 241 women   **Faculty:** 86
Part-time: 67 men, 82 women   **Tuition:** $15,315
Graduate: 18 men, 44 women   **Room & Board:** $6320
Application Deadline: July 31
SAT Verbal/Math: 505/488*   **ACT:** 21

Bethany University, formerly Bethany College and founded in 1919, is affiliated with Assemblies of God. Its mission is to provide a biblically centered education, anchored in Pentecostal doctrine, preparing excellently trained leaders for the Church and society. Bethany University awards the B.A. in addiction studies, applied professional studies, biblical and theological studies, business, church leadership and children's ministries, church leadership and urban ministries, church leadership and world missions, church music, early child development, English, general ministries, intercultural child development, liberal studies, missions, multicultural studies, music, psychology, social science, teacher education program, liberal arts, music (emphasis in teaching), music leadership, youth ministries leadership, and social science (emphasis in teaching). The school also awards associate, and master's degrees. Web: *http://www.bethany.edu*

PATTEN UNIVERSITY   B-3
(Formerly Patten College)

Oakland, CA 94601   (510) 261-8500, ext. 765; Fax: (510) 534-4344

Full-time: 70 men, 140 women   **Faculty:** 45
Part-time: 300 men, 140 women   **Tuition:** $11,520
Graduate: 5 men, 140 women   **Room & Board:** $5800
Application Deadline: March 31
SAT Verbal: 950   **ACT:** 20

Patten University, founded in 1944, is affiliated with Christian Evangelical Churches of America/ Church of God. Its mission is to offer a balanced liberal arts education with a strong biblical studies emphasis and to help students prepare for a life of Christian service. Enrollment figures in the above capsule are approximate. Patten University awards the B.A. and B.S. in biblical studies, Christian ministries, liberal studies, pastoral studies, preseminary studies, sacred music, liberal arts, organizational management, early childhood development, English, art, social science, and sports management. The school also awards associate and master's degrees. Web: *www.patten.edu*

SAINT JOHN'S SEMINARY COLLEGE   C-4

Camarillo, CA 93012   (805) 482-2755, ext. 2006
                                Fax: (805) 987-5097

Full-time: 85 men   **Faculty:** 35
Application Deadline: June 20   **Tuition:** $10,750
                                     Room & Board: $7750
SAT Verbal/Math: 410/420*   **ACT:** 17

Saint John's Seminary College, founded in 1927, is affiliated with Roman Catholic. Its mission is to provide a liberal arts education for young men interested in becoming priests for the Archdiocese of Los Angeles and for other sponsoring dioceses and religious communities. The enrollment figure in the above capsule is approximate. Saint John's Seminary College awards the B.A. in philosophy, English, Spanish, and theology. Web: *www.stjohnsem.edu*

WILLIAM JESSUP UNIVERSITY   B-3
(Formerly San Jose Christian College)

Rocklin, CA 95678   (916) 577-2222; Fax: (916) 577-2220

Full-time: 168 men, 220 women   **Faculty:** 74
Part-time: 63 men, 70 women   **Tuition:** $15,814
Application Deadline: June 1   **Room & Board:** $6360
SAT Verbal/Math: 520/520*   **ACT:** 20

William Jessup University, founded in 1939, is nondenominational. Its mission is to prepare Christians for leadership and service in church and society through Christian higher education, spiritual formation, and directed experiences. The college is accredited by AABC. William Jessup University awards the B.A. and B.S. in Bible and theology, pastoral ministry, youth ministry, Christian education, intercultural studies, counseling, music and worship, business management, liberal arts ed. and Christian leadership. The school also awards associate degrees and a post-baccalaureate certificate. Web: *www.jessup.edu*

CONNECTICUT

HOLY APOSTLES COLLEGE AND SEMINARY   C-2

Cromwell, CT 06416   (860) 632-3033; Fax: (860) 632-3075

Full-time: 6 men, 3 women   **Faculty:** 25
Part-time: 23 men, 8 women   **Tuition:** $9175
Graduate: 152 men, 61 women   **Room & Board:** $7200
Application Deadline: open

Holy Apostles College and Seminary, founded in 1956, is affiliated with the Roman Catholic Church. Its mission is to provide adult men who have a calling to the Catholic priesthood with an academic and seminary environment suited to their age and background and to provide lay students with training for personal interest, and various certificates and degrees. Holy Apostles College and Seminary awards the B.A. in humanities, philosophy, religious studies, and social sciences. The school also awards associate, and master's degrees. Web: *www.holyapostles.edu*

FLORIDA

BAPTIST COLLEGE OF FLORIDA — B-1

Graceville, FL 32440 (800) 328-2660, ext. 460
Fax: (850) 263-9026

Full-time: 253 men, 176 women	**Faculty:** 65
Part-time: 150 men, 44 women	**Tuition:** $7250
Application Deadline: August 1	**Room & Board:** $3570

Baptist College of Florida, founded in 1943, is affiliated with Florida Baptist Convention. Its mission is to promote, provide for, operate, and control a program of education and training for ministers and other religious workers. Baptist College of Florida awards the B.A., B.S., and B.M. in music ministry, teacher education, Christian education, Christian counseling, ministry, leadership, and biblical studies. The school also awards associate degrees. Web: www.baptistcollege.edu

FLORIDA CHRISTIAN COLLEGE — D-3

Kissimmee, FL 34744 (407) 569-1172; Fax: (407) 847-3925

Full-time: 105 men, 110 women	**Faculty:** 24
Part-time: 30 men, 30 women	**Tuition:** $9910
Application Deadline: July 15	**Room & Board:** $2200
ACT: 24	

Florida Christian College, founded in 1976, is affiliated with Christian Churches/Churches of Christ/Independent. Its mission is to conduct a course of study educating men and women for Christian service, to provide a program of instruction on the college level, to grant appropriate degrees, and to serve as a resource to churches, especially in Florida. In addition to regional accreditation, the college is accredited by ABHE. Florida Christian College awards the B.A., B.S., and B.Th. in Bible, Christian education ministries, and Christian ministries. The school also awards associate degrees. Web: www.fcc.edu

SAINT JOHN VIANNEY COLLEGE SEMINARY — E-5

Miami, FL 33165 (305) 223-4561, ext. 15; Fax: (305) 223-0650

Full-time: 49 men	**Faculty:** 21
Part-time: 1 man	**Tuition:** $11,000
Application Deadline: open	**Room & Board:** $6500

Saint John Vianney College Seminary, founded in 1959, is affiliated with the Roman Catholic Church. Its mission is to provide an undergraduate education preparatory for students whose stated objective is to serve the Catholic Church in the priesthood, and to provide spiritual and intellectual formation within an Anglo-Hispanic bilingual, bicultural setting. Saint John Vianney College Seminary awards the B.A. in philosophy and theology. Web: www.sjvcs.edu

GEORGIA

ATLANTA CHRISTIAN COLLEGE — B-2

East Point, GA 30344 (404) 669-2088; Fax: 404-460-2451

Full-time: 165 men, 185 women	**Faculty:** 33
Part-time: 25 men, 30 women	**Tuition:** $12,380
Application Deadline: open	**Room & Board:** $4800

Atlanta Christian College, founded in 1937, is affiliated with Christian Churches and Churches of Christ. Its mission is to provide education in biblical studies, the arts and sciences, and professional studies to equip men and women for Christian service. Atlanta Christian College awards the B.A., B.S., and B.Th. in Christian education in the church, Christian education in the school, missions, music, preaching ministry, human relations, early childhood education, youth ministry, business administration, the humanities, and English. The school also awards associate degrees. Web: acc.edu

ILLINOIS

LINCOLN CHRISTIAN COLLEGE AND SEMINARY — D3

Lincoln, IL 62656-2111 (217) 732-3168, ext. 2251
Fax: (217) 732-5914

Full-time: 300 men, 300 women	**Faculty:** 88
Part-time: 75 men, 85 women	**Tuition:** $10,000
Graduate: 220 men, 90 women	**Room & Board:** $5000
Application Deadline: open	
ACT: required	

Lincoln Christian College and Seminary, founded in 1944, is affiliated with the Christian Church/Church of Christ. Its mission is to educate and train preachers, Christian teachers, and other Christian workers. Figures in the above capsule are approximate. In addition to regional accreditation, the college is accredited by AABC. Lincoln Christian College and Seminary awards the B.A. and B.S. in Bible, Christian business administration, Christian education ministry, Christian leadership and management, discipleship and small group ministry, early childhood ministry, family life ministry, general ministry, intercultural studies, music ministry, preaching ministry, and youth ministry. The school also awards associate, and master's degrees. Web: www.lccs.edu

MOODY BIBLE INSTITUTE — E-2

Chicago, IL 60610 (312) 329-4400; Fax: (312) 329-8955

Full-time: 873 men, 739 women	**Faculty:** 92
Part-time: 807 men, 490 women	**Tuition:** $1400
Graduate: 230 men, 137 women	**Room & Board:** $7000
Application Deadline: March 1 or December 1	
ACT: 25	

Moody Bible Institute, founded in 1886, is affiliated with the Evangelical Protestant Church. Its mission is to educate and train individuals to proclaim the gospel of the Lord Jesus Christ, to promote evangelism, and to serve the Evangelical Christian Church vocationally and/or avocationally in its worldwide ministry. In addition to regional accreditation, the college is accredited by AABC. Moody Bible Institute awards the B.A., B.S., and B.Mus. in missionary aviation technology, biblical studies, evangelism/discipleship, communication, educational ministries, world missions, pastoral studies, religious education, church music, sacred music, Bible-theology, applied linguistics, youth ministry, urban ministry, Jewish and modern Israel studies, family ministries, women's ministries, and teaching English to speakers of other languages. The school also awards associate and master's degrees. Web: http://www.moody.edu

IOWA

DIVINE WORD COLLEGE — E-2

Epworth, IA 52045-0380 (800) 553-3321; Fax: (563) 876-3407

Full-time: 68 men	**Faculty:** 25
Application Deadline: July 15	**Tuition:** $9600
	Room & Board: $2300
SAT Verbal/Math: 570/545*	

Divine Word College, founded in 1912, is affiliated with the Roman Catholic Church. Its mission is to offer excellence in combining a liberal arts education with a cross-cultural program of missionary formation for Divine Word missionaries and other leaders in the Roman Catholic Church. Divine Word College awards the B.A. in philosophy and cross-cultural studies. The school also awards associate degrees. Web: www.dwci.edu

FAITH BAPTIST BIBLE COLLEGE AND THEOLOGICAL SEMINARY — C-3

Ankeny, IA 50023 (888) FAITH 4 U; Fax: (515) 964-1638
Full-time: 136 men, 153 women **Faculty:** 37
Part-time: 16 men, 25 women **Tuition:** $11,204
Graduate: 111 men, 49 women **Room & Board:** $4316
Application Deadline: August 1
SAT Verbal/Math: 520/500* **ACT:** 21

Faith Baptist Bible College and Theological Seminary, founded in 1921, is affiliated with General Association of Regular Baptist Churches. Its mission is to provide an intensive biblical and vocational education on the college level with the goal of preparing students to minister effectively in Christian service through leadership positions in fundamental Baptist churches and other organizations of like convictions. In addition to regional accreditation, the college is accredited by AABC. Faith Baptist Bible College and Theological Seminary awards the B.A. and B.S. in Bible and theology, assistant pastor, Christian education, Christian school, missions, music ministries, and pastoral training. The school also awards associate, and master's degrees. Web: www.faith.edu

KENTUCKY

CLEAR CREEK BAPTIST BIBLE COLLEGE — F-3

Pineville, KY 40977-9752 (606) 337-3196; Fax: (606) 337-2372
Full-time: 147 men, 14 women **Faculty:** 22
Part-time: 38 men, 9 women **Tuition:** $4870
Application Deadline: July 15 **Room & Board:** $3380

Clear Creek Baptist Bible College, founded in 1926, is affiliated with the Southern Baptist Church. Its mission is providing theological education for adults called to Christian service. In addition to regional accreditation, the college is accredited by AABC. Clear Creek Baptist Bible College awards the B.A. in Bible. The school also awards associate and bachelor's degrees. Web: www.ccbbc.edu

MID-CONTINENT UNIVERSITY (Formerly Mid-Continent College) — A-4

Mayfield, KY 42066-0357 (502) 247-8521, ext. 311
Fax: (502) 247-3115
Full-time: 309 men, 294 women **Faculty:** 63
Part-time: 47 men, 33 women **Tuition:** $10,000
Application Deadline: see profile **Room & Board:** $3500
ACT: 19

Mid-Continent University, founded in 1949, is affiliated with the Baptist Church. Its mission is to educate students for Christian leadership and service throughout the world. Figures in the above capsule are approximate. Mid-Continent University awards the B.A., B.S., and B.Min. in biblical languages, biblical studies, Christian education, and leadership, Christian ministry, evangelism, missions, psychology and counseling, behavioral studies, communication arts, English, general studies, social studies, elementary teacher education, organizational leadership, and business administration (management emphasis). The school also awards associate degrees. Check with the school for application deadlines. Web: www.midcontinent.edu

LOUISIANA

SAINT JOSEPH SEMINARY COLLEGE — D-3

St. Benedict, LA 70457 (504) 867-2248; Fax: (504) 867-2270
Full-time: 64 men **Faculty:** 43
Application Deadline: open **Tuition:** $10,445
Room & Board: $7414
ACT: 21

Saint Joseph Seminary College, founded in 1891, is affiliated with the Roman Catholic Church. Its mission is to provide the education and training of men for the priesthood in the Roman Catholic Church and to support preparation for lay ministry. Saint Joseph Seminary College awards the B.A. in philosophy and the liberal arts, and philosophy and theological studies. Web: www.sjasc.edu

MICHIGAN

SACRED HEART MAJOR SEMINARY — E-5

Detroit, MI 48206-1799 (313) 883-8512; Fax: (313) 883-8682
Full-time: 42 men, 1 woman **Faculty:** 52
Part-time: 130 men, 122 women **Tuition:** $10,421
Graduate: 98 men, 48 women **Room & Board:** $6250
Application Deadline: August 1

Sacred Heart Major Seminary, founded in 1919, is affiliated with the Roman Catholic Church. Its mission is to provide spiritual formation and a liberal arts education for candidates preparing for the Roman Catholic priesthood in Detroit and for students preparing for other ministries within the church. Sacred Heart Major Seminary awards the A.B. and B.Phil. in philosophy. The school also awards associate, bachelor's and master's degrees.

MINNESOTA

CROWN COLLEGE — C-4

Saint Bonifacius, MN 55375 (612) 446-4142
Fax: (952) 446-4149
Full-time: 369 men, 481 women **Faculty:** 63
Part-time: 111 men, 228 women **Tuition:** $15,646
Graduate: 80 men, 35 women **Room & Board:** $6558
Application Deadline: open
SAT Verbal/Math: 551/536* **ACT:** 22

Crown College, founded in 1916, is affiliated with the Christian and Missionary Alliance. Its mission is to provide a biblically based education for Christian leadership in the Christian and Missionary Alliance, the church at large, and the world. In addition to regional accreditation, the college is accredited by AABC. Crown College awards the B.A., B.S., and B.Mus.Ed. in biblical and theological studies, biology, business administration, child and family ministries, communication, discipleship ministries, elementary education, English, English education, general studies, history, history education, intercultural studies, liberal arts, linguistics, management, music, music education, network administration, New Testament, Pastoral leadership, physical education, prelaw, psychology, social studies education, sports management, workshop arts, youth ministry, and youth social ministry. The school also awards associate and master's degrees. Web: www.crown.edu

MARTIN LUTHER COLLEGE — C-4

New Ulm, MN 56073-3965 (507) 354-8221; Fax: (507) 354-8225
Full-time: 515 men, 525 women **Faculty:** 98
Part-time: 10 men, 10 women **Tuition:** $6000
Application Deadline: see profile **Room & Board:** $2500
ACT: required

Martin Luther College, founded in 1995, is affiliated with the Wisconsin Evangelical Lutheran Synod. Its mission is to provide training for elementary and secondary teaching, preseminary training for pastoral students, and training for other church vocations through the Staff Ministry Program. Figures in the above capsule are approximate. Martin Luther College awards the B.A. and B.S.Ed. in education and preseminary studies. Check with the school for current application deadlines. Web: www.mlc-wels.edu

OAK HILLS CHRISTIAN COLLEGE — B-2

Bemidji, MN 56601 (218) 751-8670; Fax: (218) 751-8825
Full-time: 87 men, 64 women **Faculty:** 16
Part-time: 9 men, 7 women **Tuition:** $11,590
Application Deadline: open **Room & Board:** $4320
ACT: 21

Oak Hills Christian College, founded in 1946, is interdenominational. The college is accredited by AABC. Oak Hills Christian College awards the B.A. in biblical studies, biblical studies and applied psychology, applied studies, campus ministry, contemporary worship, contemporary Christian ministry, intercultural studies, pastoral ministry, and youth ministry. The school also awards associate degrees. Web: www.oakhills.edu

MISSISSIPPI

MAGNOLIA BIBLE COLLEGE — D-3

Kosciusko, MS 39090   (662) 289-2896; Fax: (662) 289-1850
Application Deadline: open   **Faculty:** 11
        Tuition: $5000
        Room & Board: $700
ACT: required

Magnolia Bible College, founded in 1976, is affiliated with Churches of Christ. Its mission is to enable students to acquire a college-level education in general and biblical studies that will enable them to serve as preachers of the gospel. Figures in the above capsule are approximate. In addition to regional accreditation, the college is accredited by AABC. Magnolia Bible College awards the B.A. in Bible and theology. Web: *www.magnolia.edu*

MISSOURI

CONCEPTION SEMINARY COLLEGE — A-1

Conception, MO 64433   (660) 944-2886; Fax: (660) 944-2829
Full-time: 85 men   **Faculty:** 30
Part-time: 2 men, 50 women   **Tuition:** $10,000
Application Deadline: see profile   **Room & Board:** $6000
ACT: required

Conception Seminary College, founded in 1886, is affiliated with the Roman Catholic Church. Its mission is to prepare men for the Roman Catholic priesthood. Conception Seminary College places emphasis on spiritual, personal, and academic formation. Figures in the above capsule are approximate. Conception Seminary College awards the B.A. in liberal arts. Check with the school for application deadlines. Web: *www.conceptionabbey.org*

NORTH CAROLINA

ROANOKE BIBLE COLLEGE — F-2

Elizabeth City, NC 27909-4054   (800) RBC-8980
        Fax: (252) 334-2071
Full-time: 80 men, 78 women   **Faculty:** 19
Part-time: 12 men, 12 women   **Tuition:** $8459
Application Deadline: open   **Room & Board:** $4760
SAT Verbal/Math: 510/490   **ACT:** 19

Roanoke Bible College, founded in 1948, is affiliated with the Christian Church/Church of Christ. Its mission is to prepare men and women for career and volunteer Christian service. In addition to regional accreditation, the college is accredited by AABC. Roanoke Bible College awards the B.A. and B.S. in biblical and theological studies. The school also awards associate degrees. Web: *www.roanokebible.edu*

NORTH DAKOTA

TRINITY BIBLE COLLEGE — E-4

Ellendale, ND 58436   (888) TBC-2DAY; Fax: (701) 349-5443
Full-time: 130 men, 145women   **Faculty:** 30
Part-time: 8 men, 25 women   **Tuition:** $10,500
Application Deadline: see profile   **Room & Board:** $5000

Trinity Bible College, founded in 1948, is affiliated with the Assemblies of God. Its mission is to prepare pastors, church leaders, and Christian professionals in various fields in a Bible-based Pentecostal environment of academic excellence. Figures in the above capsule are approximate. In addition to regional accreditation, the college is accredited by AABC. Trinity Bible College awards the B.A. in biblical studies, business administration, elementary education, ministerial studies, and missions. The school also awards associate degrees. Check with the school for application deadlines. Web: *www.trinitybiblecollege.edu*

OHIO

CINCINNATI CHRISTIAN UNIVERSITY (Formerly Cincinnati Blible College and Seminary) — A-5

Cincinnati, OH 45204-3200   (513) 244-8116; Fax: (513) 244-8111
Full-time: 270 men, 236 women   **Faculty:** 85
Part-time: 85 men, 44 women   **Tuition:** $9820
Graduate: 169 men, 86 women   **Room & Board:** $5390
Application Deadline: August 10

Cincinnati Christian University, formerly Cincinnati Bible College and Seminary and founded in 1924, is affiliated with Christian Churches/Churches of Christ. Its mission is to teach men and women to live by biblical principles and to equip and empower them with skills, insight, and vision both to lead the church and to impact society for Christ. In addition to regional accreditation, the university is accredited by AABC. Cincinnati Christian University awards the B.A., B.S., and B.Mus. in biblical studies (primary major), education, ministries (second major), signing interpreter's training program, psychology, preaching, youth ministry, worship, music, children's ministry, urban/intercultural ministry, music education, and history. The school also awards associate, and master's degrees. Web: *www.ccuniversity.edu*

CIRCLEVILLE BIBLE COLLEGE

Circleville, OH 43113   (740) 477-7701 or (800) 701-0222
        Fax: (740) 477-7755
Full-time: 198 men, 232 women   **Faculty:** 44
Part-time: 22 men, 18 women   **Tuition:** $10,552
Application Deadline: open   **Room & Board:** $5884
SAT Verbal/Math: 460/480*   **ACT:** 20

Circleville Bible College, founded in 1948, is affiliated with Churches of Christ in Christian Union (CCCU). Its mission is The mission of Circleville Bible College is to provide a holistic Bible college education in the Wesleyan tradition that equips students to grow spiritually and intellectually and to serve effectively in society and the church. The college is accredited by AABC. Circleville Bible College awards the B.A. in religion. The school also awards associate degrees. Web: *www.biblecollege.edu*

PONTIFICAL COLLEGE JOSEPHINUM — C-3

Columbus, OH 43235   (888) 252-5812; Fax: (614) 885-2307
Full-time: 76 men   **Faculty:** 45
Part-time: 1 woman   **Tuition:** $14,635
Graduate: 56 men, 3 women   **Room & Board:** $7000
Application Deadline: open

Pontifical College Josephinum, founded in 1888, is affiliated with the Roman Catholic Church. Its mission is to prepare young men for the priesthood. Pontifical College Josephinum awards the B.A. in philosophy and the humanities English literature, Hispanic studies, history, and classical studies). The school also awards master's degrees. Web: *pcj.edu*

OKLAHOMA

MID-AMERICA CHRISTIAN UNIVERSITY — D-3

Oklahoma City, OK 73170   (405) 691-3800; (405) 692-3241
        Fax: (405) 692-3165
Full-time: 310 men, 226 women   **Faculty:** 45
Part-time: 79 men, 57 women   **Tuition:** $3646 ($7292)
Application Deadline: open   **Room & Board:** $2000

Mid-America Christian University, founded in 1953, is affiliated with Church of God in Anderson, Indiana. Its mission is to train and prepare men and women for the Christian ministry. Mid-America Christian University awards the B.A. and B.S. in behavioral science, elementary education, English, music, music performance, pastoral ministry, worship and music ministries, secondary education, specialized ministries, management and ethics, English/business, and business administration. The school also awards associate degrees. Web: *www.macu.edu*

SOUTHWESTERN CHRISTIAN UNIVERSITY
(Formerly Southwestern College of Christian Ministries)
D-3

Bethany, OK 73008 (405) 789-7661, ext. 3436
Fax: (405) 495-0078

Full-time: 91 men, 92 women	**Faculty:** 35
Part-time: 11 men, 15 women	**Tuition:** $8250
Graduate: 58 men, 20 women	**Room & Board:** $2100
Application Deadline: open	
ACT: 18	

Southwestern Christian University, founded in 1946, is affiliated with Pentecostal Holiness. Its mission is the education and training for Christian service leading toward professional competence in the practice of various ministry forms. Southwestern Christian University awards the B.A. and B.S. and B.B.A. in Biblical studies, church growth, church music, music performance, missions, Christian education, Christian elementary education, pastoral ministry, youth ministry, religion, Biblical leadership, human and family services, business leadership, nonprofit organizational leadership, and business administration. The school also awards associate and master's degrees. Web: www.swcu.edu

OREGON

MOUNT ANGEL SEMINARY
B-2

St. Benedict, OR 97373 (503) 845-3951; Fax: (503) 845-3126

Full-time: 80 men	**Faculty:** 40
Graduate: 65 men, 50 women	**Tuition:** $8850
Application Deadline: July 15	**Room & Board:** $6300

Mount Angel Seminary, founded in 1889, is affiliated with the Roman Catholic Church. Its mission is to prepare students of the Roman Catholic priesthood for religious orders and dioceses. Figures in the above capsule are approximate. Mount Angel Seminary awards the B.A. in philosophy and literature. The school also awards master's degrees. Check with the school for application deadlines.

PENNSYLVANIA

BAPTIST BIBLE COLLEGE OF PENNSYLVANIA
E-2

Clarks Summit, PA 18411 (570) 586-2400; Fax: (570) 585-9400

Full-time: 290 men, 410 women	**Faculty:** 30
Part-time: 25 men, 25 women	**Tuition:** $12,000
Graduate: 10 men, 30 women	**Room & Board:** $5000
Application Deadline: see profile	
SAT Verbal/Math: required	**ACT:** required

Baptist Bible College of Pennsylvania, founded in 1932, is affiliated with the Baptist Church. Its mission is to prepare men and women for service in selected Christian ministries as pastors, missionaries, Christian education workers, teachers for Christian schools, counselors, church musicians, and secretaries for Christian organizations. Figures in the above capsule are approximate. In addition to regional accreditation, the college is accredited by AABC. Baptist Bible College of Pennsylvania awards the B.S. in Bible and B.S.M. in church music, communications, elementary education, general missions, local church ministries, music education, outreach and evangelism pastor, pastoral ministry, pastor of Christian education, preseminary, secondary education, secretarial ministries, sports ministries, youth pastor, precounseling, general ministries, and women's ministries. The school also awards associate, master's, and doctorate degrees. Check with the school for application deadlines. Web: http://www.bbc.edu

LANCASTER BIBLE COLLEGE
E-3

Lancaster, PA 17601 (717) 560-8271; Fax: (717) 560-8213

Full-time: 277 men, 312 women	**Faculty:** 86
Part-time: 118 men, 122 women	**Tuition:** $13,020
Graduate: 80 men, 74 women	**Room & Board:** $5700
Application Deadline: open	
SAT Verbal/Math: 510/490*	**ACT:** 20

Lancaster Bible College, founded in 1933, is nondenominational. Its mission is to educate Christian men and women to live according to a biblical world view and to serve through professional Christian ministries. In addition to regional accreditation, the college is accredited by AABC. Lancaster Bible College awards the B.S. in Bible and B.S.Ed. in Bible education K-l2, Christian education, biblical counseling, early childhood education, elementary education, guidance counselor/Bible education, health and physical education, intercultural studies, pastoral church planning, pastoral studies, music, music education/Bible education, preseminary pastoral studies, physical education/Bible education, TESOL, women's ministry, and youth ministry. The school also awards associate, and master's degrees. Web: www.lbc.edu

SAINT CHARLES BORROMEO SEMINARY
F-3

Wynnewood, PA 19096 (610) 785-6271; Fax: (610) 617-9267

Full-time: 83 men	**Faculty:** 64
Part-time: 23 men, 93 women	**Tuition:** $11,175
Graduate: 100 men, 37 women	**Room & Board:** $7500
Application Deadline: July 1	

Saint Charles Borromeo Seminary, founded in 1832, is affiliated with the Roman Catholic Church. Its mission is to prepare and educate men for the Roman Catholic priesthood and to provide undergraduate and graduate programs for men and women pursuing theological studies. Saint Charles Borromeo Seminary awards the B.A. in philosophy. The school also awards master's degrees. Web: www.scs.edu

SOUTH CAROLINA

COLUMBIA INTERNATIONAL UNIVERSITY
C-3

Columbia, SC 29230 (803) 754-4100; Fax: (803) 786-4041

Full-time: 235 men, 330 women	**Faculty:** 49
Part-time: 25 men, 35 women	**Tuition:** $12,000
Graduate: 190 men, 150 women	**Room & Board:** $5000
Application Deadline: open	
SAT: required	

Columbia International University, founded in 1923, is a multidenominational Christian school. Its mission is to prepare students to grow in spiritual maturity, Bible knowledge, and ministry skills in preparation for vocational or lay Christian ministry. Figures in the above capsule are approximate. In addition to regional accreditation, the college is accredited by AABC. Columbia International University awards the B.A. and B.S. in Bible, general studies, intercultural studies, psychology, biblical languages, music, Bible teaching, youth ministry, middle eastern studies, family and church education, teacher education, humanities, pastoral ministries, and communications. The school also awards associate, master's, and doctorate degrees. Web: www.ciu.edu

TENNESSEE

FREE WILL BAPTIST BIBLE COLLEGE
C-2

Nashville, TN 37205 (615) 383-1340, ext. 5233
Fax: (615) 269-6028

Full-time: 130 men, 145 women	**Faculty:** 25
Part-time: 30 men, 25 women	**Tuition:** $7500
Application Deadline: open	**Room & Board:** $4000

Free Will Baptist Bible College, founded in 1942, is affiliated with National Association of Free Will Baptists. Its mission is to equip men and women, through Bible-based education, to serve Christ and His church. Figures in the above capsule are approximate. In addition to regional accreditation, the college is accredited by AABC. Free Will Baptist Bible College awards the B.A. and B.S. in biblical studies, biblical and ministry studies, business administration, church music, church music and youth ministry, English, elementary education, music education, music performance, sports medicine, physical education, secondary English education, and psychology and learning. The school also awards associate and bachelor's degrees.

JOHNSON BIBLE COLLEGE — E-3

Knoxville, TN 37998   (865) 251-3403; Fax: (865) 251-2337

Full-time: 374 men, 393 women	**Faculty:** 61
Part-time: 11 men, 5 women	**Tuition:** $6490
Graduate: 93 men, 46 women	**Room & Board:** $4090
Application Deadline: June 1	
SAT Verbal/Math: 540/520*	**ACT:** 22

Johnson Bible College, founded in 1893, is Christian-centered. Its mission is to educate students for specialized Christian ministries. In addition to regional accreditation, the college is accredited by AABC. Johnson Bible College awards the B.A. and B.S. degrees. All students who graduate from Johnson Bible College with a Bachelor of Arts or a Bachelor of Science degree major in Bible. In addition, five professional programs require a second major. They are: counseling, preaching, interdisciplinary major with focus on teacher education, music, and youth ministry/preaching. The school also awards associate, and master's degrees. Web: *jbc.edu*

TEXAS

AUSTIN GRADUATE SCHOOL OF THEOLOGY — D-3
(Formerly Institute for Christian Studies)

Austin, TX 78705   (512) 476-2772; Fax: (512) 476-3919

Full-time: 3 men, 1 woman	**Faculty:** 10
Part-time: 15 men, 10 women	**Tuition:** $200
Graduate: 25 men, 10 women	**Room & Board:** n/app
Application Deadline: see profile	

Austin Graduate School of Theology, founded in 1917, is affiliated with the Church of Christ. Its mission is to equip ministers and other Christians for service in the kingdom of God. Figures in the above capsule are approximate. Austin Graduate School of Theology awards the B.A. in Ministry and Christian Studies. The school also awards master's degrees. Check with the school for application deadlines. Web: *http://www.austingrad.edu*

BAPTIST MISSIONARY ASSOCIATION THEOLOGICAL SEMINARY — E-2

Jacksonville, TX 75766   (903) 586-2501; Fax: (903) 586-0378

Full-time: 10 men	**Faculty:** 13
Part-time: 20 men, 2 women	**Tuition:** $2500
Graduate: 40 men, 6 women	**Room & Board:** $4000
Application Deadline: open	

Baptist Missionary Association Theological Seminary, founded in 1955, is affiliated with the Baptist Missionary Association. Its mission is to train individuals for Christian ministry. Figures in the above capsule are approximate. Baptist Missionary Association Theological Seminary awards the B.A.R. in religion. The school also awards associate, and master's degrees. Web: *http://www.bmats.edu*

CRISWELL COLLEGE — D-2

Dallas, TX 75246   (214) 821-5433; Fax: (214) 818-1310

Full-time: 140 men, 30 women	**Faculty:** 27
Part-time: 160 men, 50 women	**Tuition:** $4000
Graduate: 100 men, 20 women	**Room & Board:** n/app
Application Deadline: see profile	

Criswell College, founded in 1970, is affiliated with the Southern Baptist Church. Its mission is to educate and train laymen and full-time Christian workers in biblical, theological, and professional studies so they can serve effectively in evangelistic, educational, pastoral, and missionary vocations of the Christian church. Figurs in the above capsule are approximate. Criswell College awards the B.A. in biblical studies, counseling, missions, evangelism, pastoral, and urban ministries. The school also awards associate, and master's degrees. Check with the school for application deadlines. Web: *http://www.criswell.edu*

SOUTHWESTERN ASSEMBLIES OF GOD UNIVERSITY — D-2

Waxahachie, TX 75165   1.888.YES.SAGU; Fax: (972) 923-0006

Full-time: 531 men, 579 women	**Faculty:** 109
Part-time: 165 men, 131 women	**Tuition:** $10,110
Graduate: 117 men, 96 women	**Room & Board:** $2160
Application Deadline: open	
SAT Verbal/Math: 463/480*	**ACT:** 19

Southwestern Assemblies of God University, founded in 1927, is affiliated with Assemblies of God. Its mission is to provide the training of Christian individuals to carry the gospel to the ends of the earth or to fill any other divinely approved place in the Kingdom of God. In addition to regional accreditation, the college is accredited by AABC. Southwestern Assemblies of God University awards the B.A. and B.S. in accounting, Bible, biblical studies, broadcasting, business administration, children's ministries, Christian education, church, church ministries, church music, church planting and revitalization, contemporary worship, counseling psychology, criminial justice, cross-cultural missions, education, elementary education, English, general business, general ministries, general studies, history, instrumental performance, management, marketing, media ministries, music education - Instrumental, music education - keyboard, music education - vocal, music ministries, pastoral ministries, piano performance, pre-professional counseling, pre-professional psychology, professional development, secondary education - English language arts & reading, secondary education - social studies, social science - social studies, social work, sports management, theological studies, vocal performance, and youth ministries. The school also awards associate and master's degrees. Web: *www.sagu.edu*

WASHINGTON

TRINITY LUTHERAN COLLEGE — C-2

Issaquah, WA 98029-9299   (425) 392-0400; Fax: (425) 392-0404

Full-time: 30 men, 60 women	**Faculty:** 26
Part-time: 7 men, 15 women	**Tuition:** $9140
Application Deadline: open	**Room & Board:** $5100
ACT: 21	

Trinity Lutheran College, founded in 1944, is affiliated with the Lutheran Church. Its mission is to train students for professional ministry and service careers. Figures in the above capsule are approximate. Trinity Lutheran awards the B.A. in biblical studies, Christian education, youth and family ministry, urban missions, global missions, music and worship, and early childhood education. The school also awards associate degrees. Web: *www.tlc.edu*

WISCONSIN

MARANATHA BAPTIST BIBLE COLLEGE — D-4

Watertown, WI 53094   (920) 261-9300; Fax: (920) 261-9109

Full-time: 350 men, 400 women	**Faculty:** 57
Part-time: 30 men, 45 women	**Tuition:** $8000
Graduate: 30 men, 3 women	**Room & Board:** $4500
Application Deadline: open	
ACT: 21	

Maranatha Baptist Bible College, founded in 1968, is affiliated with the Baptist Church. Its mission is to train men and women for effective professional or lay gospel ministry in the local church through a postsecondary program of biblical, general, and professional studies. Figures in the above capsule are approximate. Maranatha Baptist Bible College awards the B.A. and B.S. in Bible, church ministries, education, general studies, fine arts, business, nursing, and office administration. The school also awards associate and master's degrees. Web: *www.mbbc.edu*

AIR FORCE

In the Air Force ROTC program, young men and women may earn commissions while attending college. The amount of academic credit given for Air Force ROTC varies from school to school.

Most new Air Force officers come through the Air Force ROTC program. It offers students the opportunity to attend a civilian college while studying officership as part of their undergraduate curriculum.

The AFROTC program begins with the General Military Course. Freshmen or sophomores attend one hour of ROTC classes and one to two hours of leadership laboratory weekly. During these first two years, study is focused on the history of the Air Force and the part it plays in the world today. During the summer between sophomore and junior years, students attend a four-week basic training course located at an Air Force base.

The Professional Officer Course is completed during the junior and senior years. Study includes management principles and defense policy and offers the opportunity for managing, organizing, directing, and evaluating the cadet corps activities. Cadets who are medically qualified will have the opportunity to compete for pilot or navigator positions. Upon graduation, students are commissioned as Second Lieutenants.

For academically qualified students in selected majors, the AFROTC offers scholarships, including tuition, fees and books, and a monthly nontaxable allowance during the school year.

The majority of scholarships are awarded in the technical degree areas of engineering and computer science, but there are opportunities in nontechnical areas as well. Scholarships are based on individual merit, not financial need. Those who receive a scholarship must still apply and be accepted by the school they wish to attend and notify the AFROTC headquarters of their selection.

The scholarship program is broken down into different types and durations. All scholarships include full or partial tuition, fees, textbook allowance, and $250–$400 per month tax-free allowance during the academic year. Type 1 pays full tuition at any school offering AFROTC. Type 2 pays tuition and fees up to a maximum of $15,000 per year. There are two variations of the Type 7 scholarship. A Type 7 scholarship winner can attend any post-secondary institution (public or private) where tuition does not exceed $9,000 per year, or he/she can attend any public post-secondary institution where the student qualifies for in-state tuition rates.

The application deadline is December 1 of the senior year, but priority consideration is given to those who get the application in early. AFROTC only accepts on-line applications and they are available during the spring prior to the senior year of high school.

Further information can be obtained from the professor of aerospace studies at any of the host campuses where Air Force ROTC is offered. The listing that follows represents the host schools that offer these programs. Hundreds more schools have crosstown agreements with these institutions to make AFROTC more accessible to students. Please be sure to contact the school directly for more details. You may also find useful and current information at the Air Force Reserve Officer Training Corps web site, *www.afrotc.com*.

ALABAMA

- Alabama State University
- Auburn University
- Samford University
- Troy University
- Tuskegee University
- University of Alabama
- University of South Alabama

ARIZONA

- Arizona State University
- Embry-Riddle Aeronautical University
- Northern Arizona University
- University of Arizona

ARKANSAS

- University of Arkansas at Fayetteville

CALIFORNIA

- California State University, Fresno
- California State University, Sacramento
- California State University, San Bernadino
- Loyola Marymount University
- San Diego State University
- San Jose State University
- University of California at Berkeley
- University of California at Los Angeles
- University of Southern California

COLORADO

- Colorado State University
- University of Colorado at Boulder

CONNECTICUT

- University of Connecticut

DELAWARE

- University of Delaware

DISTRICT OF COLUMBIA

- Howard University

FLORIDA

- Embry-Riddle Aeronautical University
- Florida State University
- University of Central Florida
- University of Florida
- University of Miami
- University of South Florida

GEORGIA

- Georgia Institute of Technology
- University of Georgia
- Valdosta State University

HAWAII

- University of Hawaii at Manoa

ILLINOIS

- Illinois Institute of Technology
- Southern Illinois University at Carbondale
- University of Illinois at Urbana-Champaign

INDIANA

- Indiana State University
- Indiana University at Bloomington
- Purdue University
- University of Notre Dame

IOWA

- Iowa State University
- University of Iowa

KANSAS

- Kansas State University
- University of Kansas

KENTUCKY

- University of Kentucky
- University of Louisville

LOUISIANA

- Louisiana State University and Agricultural and Mechanical College
- Louisiana Tech University
- Tulane University

MARYLAND
- University of Maryland

MASSACHUSETTS
- Boston University
- Massachusetts Institute of Technology
- University of Massachusetts
- University of Massachusetts, Lowell
- Worcester Polytechnic Institute

MICHIGAN
- Michigan State University
- Michigan Technological University
- University of Michigan

MINNESOTA
- University of Minnesota/Duluth
- University of Minnesota/Twin Cities
- University of Saint Thomas

MISSISSIPPI
- Jackson State University
- Mississippi State University
- University of Mississippi
- University of Southern Mississippi

MISSOURI
- St. Louis University
- Southeast Missouri State University
- University of Missouri/Columbia
- University of Missouri/Rolla

MONTANA
- Montana State University

NEBRASKA
- University of Nebraska at Lincoln
- University of Nebraska at Omaha

NEVADA
- University of Nevada—Las Vegas

NEW HAMPSHIRE
- University of New Hampshire

NEW JERSEY
- New Jersey Institute of Technology
- Rutgers, the State University of New Jersey/University College—New Brunswick

NEW MEXICO
- New Mexico State University
- University of New Mexico

NEW YORK
- Clarkson University
- Cornell University
- Manhattan College
- Rensselaer Polytechnic Institute
- Rochester Institute of Technology
- Syracuse University

NORTH CAROLINA
- Duke University
- East Carolina University
- Fayetteville State University
- North Carolina State University
- University of North Carolina at Chapel Hill
- University of North Carolina at Charlotte

NORTH DAKOTA
- North Dakota State University

OHIO
- Bowling Green State University
- Kent State University
- Miami University
- Ohio State University
- Ohio University
- University of Cincinnati
- Wright State University

OKLAHOMA
- Oklahoma State University
- University of Oklahoma

OREGON
- Oregon State University
- University of Portland

PENNSYLVANIA
- Pennsylvania State University/University Park Campus
- Saint Joseph's University
- University of Pittsburgh
- Wilkes University

PUERTO RICO
- University of Puerto Rico/Mayaguez
- University of Puerto Rico/Río Piedras

SOUTH CAROLINA
- Charleston Southern University
- The Citadel
- Clemson University
- University of South Carolina

SOUTH DAKOTA
- South Dakota State University

TENNESSEE
- Tennessee State University
- University of Memphis
- University of Tennessee at Knoxville

TEXAS
- Angelo State University
- Baylor University
- Southwest Texas State University
- Texas A & M University
- Texas Christian University
- Texas Tech University
- University of Houston
- University of North Texas
- University of Texas at Austin
- University of Texas at San Antonio

UTAH
- Brigham Young University
- University of Utah
- Utah State University

VERMONT
- Norwich University

VIRGINIA
- University of Virginia
- Virginia Military Institute
- Virginia Polytechnic Institute and State University

WASHINGTON
- Central Washington University
- University of Washington
- Washington State University

WEST VIRGINIA
- West Virginia University

WISCONSIN
- Marquette University
- University of Wisconsin/Madison

WYOMING
- University of Wyoming

ARMY

The Army Reserve Officers' Training Corps (ROTC) provides college students with the opportunity to combine leadership and management training with their other academic studies. The curriculum, which consists of a series of classroom and hands-on leadership training experiences, provides students with the necessary foundation to serve successfully in positions of responsibility in either the U.S. Army or the corporate world.

Those with a strong academic background, an active mindset, and the ability to rapidly assimilate information thrive in the program. These scholar-athlete-leaders note that the lead ership skills developed through their participation in the program are further honed during their period of service as Army officers. After service as an Army lieutenant, many graduates elect to continue their service in uniform. Others elect to enter the corporate world where their leadership skills and experience as ROTC-trained Army officers allow them to advance rapidly.

Although the program is designed to be completed in four years, students may complete all requirements within a two-year period through participation in a summer training session called the Leaders' Training Course, normally held during the summer between the sophomore and junior years. A generous series of merit-based scholarships that cover tuition, fees, textbooks, and supplies exist to help students and their families defray the cost of college. Applications for four-year scholarships must be postmarked by November 13 to be considered for the following school year. Tax-free stipends of up to $5000 per academic year are also available to those meeting course requirements. For more information on the program, call (800) USA-ROTC, or contact the professor of military science at a college that offers Army ROTC. Detailed information about the program is also available on the Internet at *www.armyrotc.com*.

ALABAMA

- Alabama Agricultural and Mechanical University
- Auburn University
- Auburn University at Montgomery
- Jacksonville State University
- Marion Military Institute
- Tuskegee University
- University of Alabama
- University of Alabama at Birmingham
- University of North Alabama
- University of South Alabama

ALASKA

- University of Alaska/Fairbanks

ARIZONA

- Arizona State University
- Northern Arizona University
- University of Arizona

ARKANSAS

- Arkansas State University
- University of Arkansas at Fayetteville
- University of Arkansas at Pine Bluff
- University of Central Arkansas

CALIFORNIA

- California Polytechnic State University at San Luis Obispo
- California State University at Fresno
- California State University at Fullerton
- Claremont McKenna College
- San Diego State University
- Santa Clara University
- University of California at Berkeley
- University of California at Davis
- University of California at Los Angeles
- University of California at Santa Barbara
- University of San Francisco
- University of Southern California

COLORADO

- Colorado State University
- University of Colorado at Boulder
- University of Colorado at Colorado Springs

CONNECTICUT

- University of Connecticut

DELAWARE

- University of Delaware

DISTRICT OF COLUMBIA

- Georgetown University
- Howard University

FLORIDA

- Embry-Riddle Aeronautical University
- Florida A & M University
- Florida Institute of Technology
- Florida International University
- Florida Southern College
- Florida State University
- University of Central Florida
- University of Florida
- University of South Florida
- University of Tampa
- University of West Florida

GEORGIA

- Augusta State University
- Columbus State University
- Fort Valley State University
- Georgia Institute of Technology
- Georgia Military College
- Georgia Southern University
- Georgia State University
- North Georgia College
- University of Georgia

GUAM

- University of Guam

HAWAII

- University of Hawaii at Manoa

IDAHO

- Boise State University
- University of Idaho

ILLINOIS

- Eastern Illinois University
- Illinois State University
- Northern Illinois University
- Southern Illinois University at Carbondale
- Southern Illinois University at Edwardsville
- University of Illinois at Chicago
- University of Illinois at Urbana-Champaign
- Western Illinois University
- Wheaton College

INDIANA

- Ball State University
- Indiana University at Bloomington
- Indiana University/Purdue University Indianapolis
- Purdue University/West Lafayette
- Rose-Hulman Institute of Technology
- University of Notre Dame

IOWA

- Iowa State University
- University of Iowa
- University of Northern Iowa

KANSAS

- Kansas State University
- Pittsburg State University
- University of Kansas

KENTUCKY

- Eastern Kentucky University
- Morehead State University
- University of Kentucky
- University of Louisville
- Western Kentucky University

LOUISIANA

- Grambling State University
- Louisiana State University
- Northwestern State University
- Southern University and A & M College
- Tulane University

MAINE

- University of Maine

MARYLAND

- Bowie State University
- Johns Hopkins University
- Loyola College
- McDaniel College
- Morgan State University
- University of Maryland at College Park

MASSACHUSETTS

- Boston University
- Massachusetts Institute of Technology
- Northeastern University
- University of Massachusetts
- Worcester Polytechnic Institute

MICHIGAN

- Central Michigan University
- Eastern Michigan University
- Michigan State University
- Michigan Technological University
- Northern Michigan University
- University of Michigan
- Western Michigan University

MINNESOTA

- Minnesota State University, Mankato
- Saint John's University Minnesota
- University of Minnesota/Twin Cities

MISSISSIPPI

- Alcorn State University
- Jackson State University
- Mississippi State University
- University of Mississippi
- University of Southern Mississippi

MISSOURI

- Central Missouri State University
- Lincoln University

- Missouri Western State University
- Southwest Missouri State University
- Truman State University
- University of Missouri/Columbia
- University of Missouri/Rolla
- Washington University
- Wentworth Military Academy & Junior College

MONTANA

- Montana State University
- University of Montana

NEBRASKA

- Creighton University
- University of Nebraska at Lincoln

NEVADA

- University of Nevada/Reno

NEW HAMPSHIRE

- University of New Hampshire

NEW JERSEY

- Princeton University
- Rutgers University
- Seton Hall University

NEW MEXICO

- New Mexico Military Institute
- New Mexico State University
- University of New Mexico

NEW YORK

- Canisius College
- Clarkson University
- Cornell University
- Fordham University
- Hofstra University
- Niagara University
- Rochester Institute of Technology
- Saint Bonaventure University
- Saint John's University New York
- State University of New York/Brockport
- Syracuse University

NORTH CAROLINA

- Appalachian State University
- Campbell University
- Duke University
- East Carolina University
- Elizabeth City State University
- North Carolina Agricultural and Technical State University
- North Carolina State University
- Saint Augustine's College
- University of North Carolina at Chapel Hill
- University of North Carolina at Charlotte
- Wake Forest University

NORTH DAKOTA

- North Dakota State University
- University of North Dakota

OHIO

- Bowling Green State University
- Capital University
- Central State University
- John Carroll University

- Kent State University
- Ohio State University
- Ohio University
- University of Akron
- University of Cincinnati
- University of Dayton
- University of Toledo
- Wright State University
- Xavier University

OKLAHOMA

- Cameron University
- Oklahoma State University
- University of Central Oklahoma
- University of Oklahoma

OREGON

- Oregon State University
- University of Oregon
- University of Portland

PENNSYLVANIA

- Bucknell University
- Dickinson College
- Drexel University
- Edinboro University of Pennsylvania
- Gannon University
- Indiana University of Pennsylvania
- Lehigh University
- Lock Haven University of Pennsylvania
- Pennsylvania State University
- Shippensburg University of Pennsylvania
- Slippery Rock University
- Temple University
- University of Pittsburgh
- University of Scranton
- Valley Forge Military Academy & College
- Widener University

PUERTO RICO

- University of Puerto Rico/Mayaguez
- University of Puerto Rico/Río Piedras

RHODE ISLAND

- Providence College
- University of Rhode Island

SOUTH CAROLINA

- The Citadel
- Clemson University
- Furman University
- Presbyterian College
- South Carolina State University
- University of South Carolina
- Wofford College

SOUTH DAKOTA

- South Dakota School of Mines and Technology
- South Dakota State University
- University of South Dakota

TENNESSEE

- Austin Peay State University
- Carson-Newman College
- East Tennessee State University
- Middle Tennessee State University
- Tennessee Technological University
- University of Memphis

- University of Tennessee at Knoxville
- University of Tennessee at Martin
- Vanderbilt University

TEXAS

- Prairie View A & M University
- Saint Mary's University
- Sam Houston State University
- Stephen F. Austin State University
- Tarleton State University
- Texas A & M University
- Texas A & M University at Kingsville
- Texas Christian University
- Texas State University
- Texas Tech University
- University of Houston
- University of Texas at Arlington
- University of Texas at Austin
- University of Texas at El Paso
- University of Texas at San Antonio
- University of Texas-Pan American

UTAH

- Brigham Young University
- University of Utah
- Weber State University

VERMONT

- Norwich University
- University of Vermont

VIRGINIA

- College of William and Mary
- George Mason University
- Hampton University
- James Madison University
- Norfolk State University
- Old Dominion University
- University of Richmond
- University of Virginia
- Virginia Military Institute
- Virginia Polytechnic Institute and State University
- Virginia State University

WASHINGTON

- Central Washington University
- Eastern Washington University
- Gonzaga University
- Pacific Lutheran University
- Seattle University
- University of Washington
- Washington State University

WEST VIRGINIA

- Marshall University
- West Virginia State College
- West Virginia University

WISCONSIN

- Marquette University
- University of Wisconsin/La Crosse
- University of Wisconsin/Madison
- University of Wisconsin/Oshkosh
- University of Wisconsin/Stevens Point

WYOMING

- University of Wyoming

NAVY

The NROTC Program educates and trains qualified young men and women for service as commissioned officers in the unrestricted line Naval Reserve or Marine Corps Reserve. Two programs are available: the NROTC Scholarship Program and the NROTC College Program.

The NROTC Scholarship Program plays an important role in preparing young men and women for leadership and management positions in an increasingly technical Navy and Marine Corps. The four-year NROTC Scholarship Program is available to qualified students who graduate from high school before August 1 of the year they intend to start college. The two-year NROTC Scholarship Program is available to qualified college sophomores who have completed one year of differential and integral calculus with a grade of C or better and maintain a minimum GPA of 2.5.

Selected applicants for NROTC Scholarship Programs (four-year and two-year) are awarded scholarships through a highly competitive national selection process, and receive full tuition, fees, book stipend, and other financial benefits at many of the country's leading colleges and universities. Upon graduation, midshipmen are commissioned as officers in the unrestricted line Navy or Marine Corps.

Students selected for the NROTC Scholarship Program make their own arrangements for college enrollment and room and board, and take the normal course load required by the college or university for degree completion. Additionally, scholarship midshipmen are required to follow specific academic guidelines. Full information concerning the NROTC Scholarship Program is available from any of the colleges and universities with NROTC units or from Navy and Marine Corps recruiters.

For information on the NROTC scholarship programs, call 1-800-USA-NAVY or 1-800-NAV-ROTC, e-mail *PNSC_NROTC.scholarship@navy.mil*; or visit *https://www.nrotc.navy.mil*. Electronic application for the four-year scholarship program must be submitted by January 20.

The NROTC College Program may be either two or four years. Additional points include:

- Applicants are selected from students already attending or accepted by colleges with the NROTC program.
- Students selected for "advance standing" receive a stipend for a maximum of 20 months. Advance standing is only available starting in the junior year of college. Stipend per academic month is $350 in junior year and $400 in senior year.
- Students will complete naval science and other university courses, a few specific university courses, and attend one summer training session, normally at sea for Navy Officers, and in Quantico, VA for Marine Corps-option midshipmen.

The following list shows the colleges and universities that have an NROTC unit on campus. Many more institutions offer the program through cross-town arrangements. We recommend that you visit *https://www.nrotc.navy.mil* for a listing of participating colleges and universities. Contact the schools directly for the most current and accurate information.

ALABAMA
- Auburn University

ARIZONA
- University of Arizona

CALIFORNIA
- San Diego State University
- University of California/Berkeley
- University of California/Los Angeles
- University of San Diego
- University of Southern California

COLORADO
- University of Colorado at Boulder

DISTRICT OF COLUMBIA
- George Washington University

FLORIDA
- Embry Riddle Aeronautical University
- Florida A & M University
- Jacksonville University
- University of Florida
- University of South Florida

GEORGIA
- Georgia Institute of Technology
- Morehouse College
- Savannah State College

IDAHO
- University of Idaho.

ILLINOIS
- Illinois Institute of Technology
- Northwestern University
- University of Illinois at Urbana-Champaign

INDIANA
- Purdue University/West Lafayette
- University of Notre Dame

IOWA
- Iowa State University

KANSAS
- University of Kansas

LOUISIANA
- Southern University and A & M College
- Tulane University

MAINE
- Maine Maritime Academy

MASSACHUSETTS
- Boston University
- College of the Holy Cross
- Massachusetts Institute of Technology

MICHIGAN
- University of Michigan/Ann Arbor

MINNESOTA
- University of Minnesota

MISSISSIPPI
- University of Mississippi

MISSOURI
- University of Missouri

NEBRASKA
- University of Nebraska at Lincoln

NEW MEXICO
- University of New Mexico

NEW YORK
- Cornell University
- Rensselaer Polytechnic Institute
- State University of New York/Maritime College
- University of Rochester

NORTH CAROLINA
- Duke University
- North Carolina State University
- University of North Carolina at Chapel Hill

OHIO
- Miami University
- Ohio State University

OKLAHOMA

- University of Oklahoma

OREGON

- Oregon State University

PENNSYLVANIA

- Carnegie Mellon University
- Pennsylvania State University Park Campus
- University of Pennsylvania
- Villanova University

SOUTH CAROLINA

- The Citadel
- University of South Carolina

TENNESSEE

- University of Memphis
- Vanderbilt University

TEXAS

- Prairie View A & M University
- Rice University
- Texas A & M University
- University of Texas at Austin

UTAH

- University of Utah

VERMONT

- Norwich University

VIRGINIA

- Hampton University
- Norfolk State University
- Old Dominion University
- University of Virginia
- Virginia Military Institute
- Virginia Polytechnic Institute and State University

WASHINGTON

- University of Washington

WISCONSIN

- Marquette University
- University of Wisconsin/Madison

ENROLLMENT IN CANADIAN SCHOOLS

In 2003, Canadian universities hosted a record 58,600 full-time international students, up by more than 37 percent in just two years. The fall 2005 number is estimated to be about 70,000. International students account for 6 percent of full-time undergraduate students and 18 percent at the graduate level. Most Canadian universities admit international students—although some have a quota on the number they will accept—and will give interested students information on how their academic qualifications are equated with Canadian requirements.

The Association of Universities and Colleges of Canada (AUCC) represents 90 universities and university-level colleges. These institutions account for almost 99 percent of the total university enrollment in Canada. Almost all Canadian colleges are coeducational. Of the 90, 19 use French as the language of instruction, six use both French and English, and the rest primarily use English. This section contains individual profiles for those English-language universities that enroll more than 10,000 students.

Affiliated with each of these universities are a number of general, theological, or residential colleges, which also have been listed here. The names and addresses of the three French-speaking colleges with enrollments of more than 10,000 may be found at the end of this introduction.

Admissions Requirements

Each university has its own entrance requirements and will assess you on an individual basis. The university will determine the equivalency of your academic credentials. There is no nationwide set of entrance exams. For more details about this or any other part of the application process, contact the registrar at the university you wish to attend.

Admissions Procedure

Once you have determined which universities meet your needs, contact the registrar's office at each institution to obtain an application for a bachelor's program or a professional degree. If you anticipate pursuing postgraduate studies in Canada, you may obtain more information by contacting the dean of graduate studies at the universities that interest you. It is important to apply early. Remember that the Canadian academic year usually starts in September. Some programs, however, do admit students to courses that start in January and May.

The AUCC's web site *www.aucc.ca* has links to the web pages of all Canadian universities, the majority of which accept applications via e-mail.

To study at a Canadian university, you will need a study permit. You may also need a visitor's visa, which will be issued to you at the same time as your study permit. To apply for a study permit, please contact your nearest Canadian diplomatic post.

You will have to arrange for medical coverage before you arrive in Canada. Medical coverage varies from province to province and sometimes from university to university within each province. Please ask an official at the nearest Canadian diplomatic post for detailed information. Also, check whether the universities you are applying to have any medical insurance plans for international students.

Degrees Offered

Canadian universities, like those in the United States, grant three levels of degrees: bachelor's and first professional, master's, and doctoral as well as undergraduate certificates and diplomas and graduate diploma programs.

Earning the first degree can take three to five years. A general, or unspecialized, program leading to a Bachelor of Arts or Bachelor of Science usually can be completed in three years. An honors degree, earned in a specialized program, usually requires four years. Students must meet more rigorous requirements to enter an honors-degree program and must maintain high grades to remain in it. First professional degrees in some fields may take more than four years to earn, and students may be required to undertake two or three years of university study before enrolling in the professional program. Students who enter graduate programs with a general degree usually must study a year longer than those with honors degrees. Undergraduate diplomas and certificates may be from one to three years' duration and may (although not necessarily) be used as a basis for entry to a degree program. A graduate diploma may be considered as conferring a qualification that is intermediate between the bachelor's (or first professional degree) and master's degree. It may be completed in as little as two or as long as three academic years.

Organizations

Virtually all universities have organizations for international students, and sponsor international student centers and advisers. There also are national organizations that aid international students, including the World University Service of Canada and the Canadian Bureau for International Education, which arranges for representatives to meet international students arriving at Canadian airports.

Tuition, Fees, and Aid

Universities and colleges are heavily subsidized by provincial and federal governments, and tuition fees actually cover one third of university operating costs. Canadian institutions charge different fees for different programs, unlike American institutions, which charge the same tuition regardless of the program of study. Each profile in this book lists the range of tuitions, which may or may not include student fees. Some universities have higher fees for international students, and where that is the case, the profile includes just the international fees. All costs are given in Canadian (CDN) dollars. In all cases, you should check with the university in which you are interested to obtain the most up-to-date information about tuition and room-and-board charges.

Most awards available to international students through Canadian universities or from the Canadian government are restricted to graduate and post graduate studies. Some of the scholarship programs for international students to study in Canada include the Commonwealth Scholarship and Fellowship Plan, the Canadian International Development Agency awards, the Government of Canada awards program of cultural exchanges and the Programme canadien de bourses de la Francophonie. Students interested in applying for aid should contact a Canadian diplomatic mission in their home countries and, for information on cultural exchange programs, their own nation's education department or ministry.

Additional Information

Association of Universities and Colleges of Canada
600-350 Albert Street
Ottawa, ON, Canada K1R 1B1
(613) 563-3961
Fax: (613) 563-9745
www.aucc.ca
(publications include *Notes for International Students, The Directory of Canadian Universities*)

Canadian Bureau for International Education
220 Laurier Avenue W., Ste. 1100
Ottawa, ON Canada K1P 5Z9
(613) 237-4820
Fax: (613) 237-1073
www.cbie.ca
(publications include *The National Report on International Students in Canada*) (2000–01)

Canadian International Development Agency
200 promenade du Portage
Gatineau, QC Canada K1A 0G4
(819) 997-5006
(800) 230-6349
Fax: (819) 953-6088
www.acdi-cida.gc.ca

Citizenship and Immigration Canada
Ottawa, ON Canada K1A 0J9
www.cic.gc.ca
(publications include *Studying in Canada: A Guide to Foreign Students*) (July 2002)

Consulate General of Canada
1251 Avenue of the Americas
New York, NY 10020-1175
(212) 596-1628
Fax: (212) 596-1790
www.dfait-maeci.ca/can-am/new_york/

Social Sciences and Humanities Research Council of Canada
350 Albert Street, P.O. Box 1610
Ottawa, ON Canada K1P 6G4
(613) 992-0691
Fax: (613) 992-1787
www.sshrc-crsh.ge.ca

Statistics Canada
National Contact Centre
Advisory Services Division
Lobby, R.H. Coats Building, West
120 Parkdale Avenue
Ottawa, Ontario K1A 0T6
(800) 263-1136 or (613) 951-8116 (outside Canada & USA)
Fax: (877) 287-4369 (toll free)
www.statcan.ca
(publications include *Education Quarterly Review* and *Education in Canada*)

World University Service of Canada
1404 Scott Street
Ottawa, ON Canada K1Y 4M8
(613) 798-7477
Fax: (613) 798-0990
www.wusc.ca

CANADA

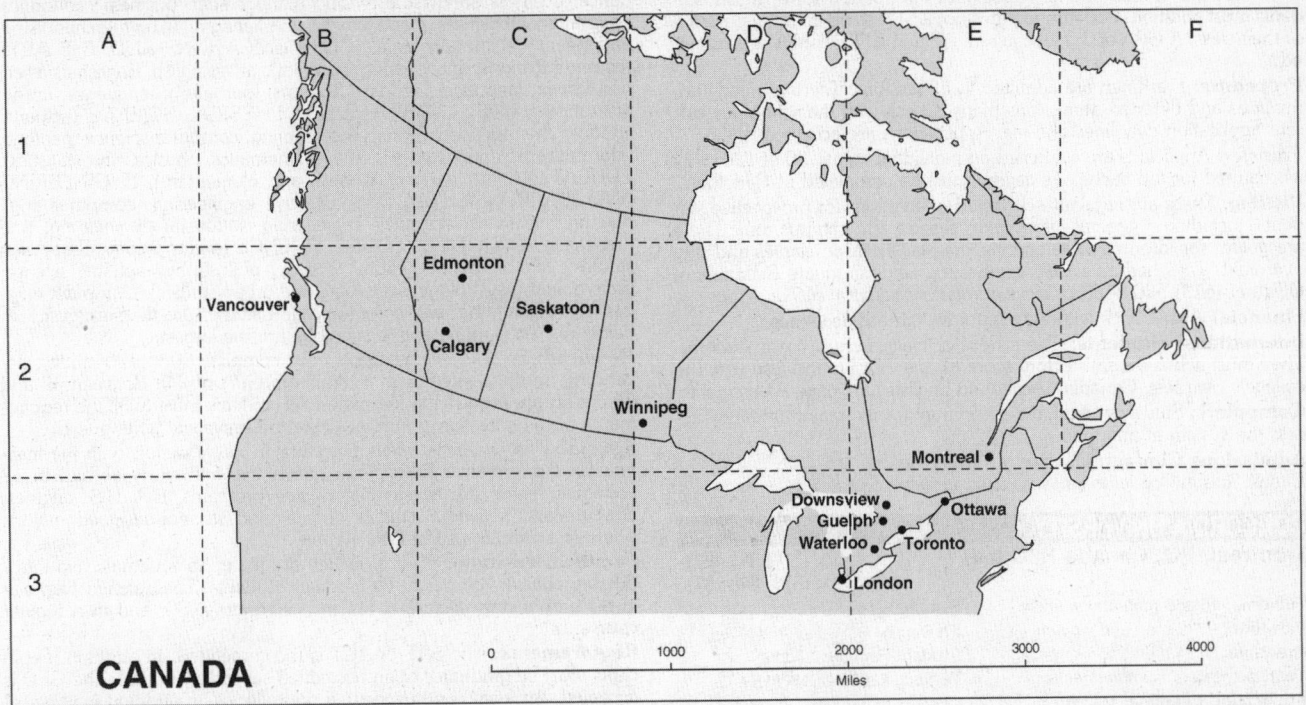

CANADA

CARLETON UNIVERSITY

E-3

Ottawa, ON, Canada K1S 5B6

(613) 520-3609
Fax: (613) 520-3517

Full-time: 16,508 men and women
Part-time: 4074 men and women
Graduate: 3001 men and women
Year: semesters, summer session
Application Deadline: see profile

Freshman Class: n/av
SAT: required

Faculty: 676
Ph.D.s: 80%
Student/Faculty: 16 to 1
Tuition: $4691 CDN ($12,426 CDN)
Room & Board: $6696 CDN

Carleton University, founded in 1942, is a public institution operated by the province of Ontario. There are 14 undergraduate and 14 graduate degree programs offered. There are 8 undergraduate schools and 1 graduate school. Some figures in the above capsule and in this profile are approximate. The library contains 1.7 million volumes, 1.3 million microform items, and 20,000 audio/video tapes/CDs/DVDs, and subscribes to 9000 periodicals including electronic. Computerized library services include the card catalog, interlibrary loans, and database searching. Special learning facilities include a learning resource center, art gallery, radio station, and an environmental biology laboratories annex. The 152-acre campus is in an urban area in Ottawa. Including any residence halls, there are 29 buildings.

Student Life: 85% of undergraduates are from Ontario. The average age of freshmen is 20.

Housing: 2180 students can be accommodated in college housing, which includes single-sex and coed dorms. On-campus housing is available on a lottery system for upperclassmen. Priority is given to out-of-town students. 89% of students commute. All students may keep cars.

Activities: There are no fraternities or sororities. There are 80 groups on campus, including chess, computers, drama, ethnic, gay, international, newspaper, pep band, photography, political, radio and TV, religious, and student government. Popular campus events include Orientation.

Sports: There are 9 intercollegiate sports for men and 9 for women, and 4 intramural sports for men and 3 for women. Facilities include a physical recreation center with an Olympic-size pool, squash courts, Nautilus and fitness centers, and a double gym. Outdoor tennis courts and playing fields are also available.

Disabled Students: 98% of the campus is accessible. Wheelchair ramps, elevators, special parking, specially equipped rest rooms, lowered drinking fountains, and lowered telephones are available. There are also automatic doors in some buildings, tactile control panels in elevators, tunnels connecting buildings, specially equipped residence rooms, and attendant services.

Services: Counseling and information services are available, as is tutoring in most subjects. There is a reader service for the blind. Study skills workshops are available in essay writing and preparation and writing of exams. There is special exam scheduling and a study center for disabled students.

Campus Safety and Security: Measures include 24-hour foot and vehicle patrol, security escort services, pamphlets/posters/films, and emergency telephones. There are lighted pathways/sidewalks and electronic access to residences.

Programs of Study: Carleton confers B.A., B.Sc., B.Arch., B.Comm., B.C.S., B.Eng., B.Hum., B.I.B., B.I.D., B.J., B.Math., B.Mus., B.P.A.P.H., and B.S.W. degrees. Master's and doctoral degrees are also awarded. Bachelor's degrees are awarded in BIOLOGICAL SCIENCE (biochemistry, biology/biological science, biometrics and biostatistics, biotechnology, and neurosciences), BUSINESS (accounting, business economics, business systems analysis, human resources, international business management, management information systems, marketing and distribution, marketing/retailing/merchandising, and operations research), COMMUNICATIONS AND THE ARTS (art history and appreciation, classics, communications, communications technology, English, English literature, film arts, French, German, industrial design, Italian, journalism, linguistics, music, Russian, and Spanish), COMPUTER AND PHYSICAL SCIENCE (chemistry, computer mathematics, computer programming, computer science, earth science, geology, information sciences and systems, mathematics, physical sciences, physics, and statistics), EDUCATION (teaching English as a second/foreign language (TESOL/TEFOL)), ENGINEERING AND ENVIRONMENTAL DESIGN (aeronautical engineering, architecture, civil engineering, computer engineering, electrical/electronics engineering, engineering, engineering physics, environmental engineering, environmental science, mechanical engineering, and systems engineering), SOCIAL SCIENCE (anthropology, Canadian studies, child care/child, and family studies, classical/ancient civilization, cognitive science, criminology, Eastern European studies, economics, European studies, geography, German area studies, history, human ecology, interdisciplinary studies, law, liberal arts/general studies, philosophy, political science/government, psychology, public administration, religion, social work, sociology, and women's studies). Arts, engineering, and science are the largest.

Required: Requirements for graduation vary according to programs.

Special: Carleton offers co-op programs in many majors and an exchange program with the University of Ottawa. Study abroad, internships in industrial design, dual and student-designed majors, accelerated degree programs, and interdisciplinary programs are available. The university also utilizes instructional television.

Faculty/Classroom: 69% of faculty are male; 31%, female. The average class size in an introductory lecture is 107 and in a regular course, 58.

Requirements: A satisfactory score on the SAT is required. Applicants must be graduates of an accredited secondary school. Architecture, humanities, and industrial design students must present a portfolio; social work students should submit a personal information form; music students must audition. Carleton requires applicants to be in the upper 25% of their class. A GPA of 3.0 is required. AP and CLEP credits are accepted.

Procedure: Freshmen are admitted to all sessions. There are early admissions and deferred admissions plans. Check with the school for current application deadlines and fee. Applications are accepted on-line.

Transfer: Applicants are evaluated on individual merits. 30 of 120 credits required for the bachelor's degree must be completed at Carleton.

Visiting: There are regularly scheduled orientations for prospective students, including a general information session and campus tour. There are guides for informal visits and visitors may sit in on classes and stay overnight. To schedule a visit, contact the Undergraduate Recruitment Office at (613) 520-3663 or www.admissions.carleton.ca/Tours/tour.

Financial Aid: Check with the school for current deadlines.

International Students: The school actively recruits these students. They must achieve a satisfactory score on the TOEFL and also take the college's own test, Canadian Academic English Language Assessment.

Computers: Students who have an account for the mainframe may access the system at any time.

Admissions Contact: Director of Admissions.
E-mail: liaison@carleton.ca Web: www.carleton.ca

CONCORDIA UNIVERSITY E-2
Montreal, PQ, Canada H3G IM8

(514) 848-4971
Fax: (514) 848-2837

Full-time: 16,365 men and women	**Faculty:** 714
Part-time: 9772 men and women	**Ph.D.s:** 84%
Graduate: 4794 men and women	**Student/Faculty:** 17 to 1
Year: semesters, summer session	**Tuition:** $2800 CDN ($15,400 CDN)
Application Deadline: March 1	
Freshman Class: n/av	**Room & Board:** $5000 CDN
SAT or ACT: recommended	

Concordia University, established in 1974, is a public institution operated by the province of Quebec. There are 5 undergraduate schools and 1 graduate school. Some figures in the above capsule and in this profile are approximate. In addition to regional accreditation, Concordia University has baccalaureate program accreditation with AACSB. The 2 libraries contain 3 million volumes, 75,000 microform items, and 2000 audio/video tapes/CDs/DVDs, and subscribe to 5500 periodicals including electronic. Computerized library services include the card catalog, interlibrary loans, and database searching. Special learning facilities include a learning resource center, art gallery, radio station, TV station, and greenhouse, audiovisual instruction service, and specialized research center. The 1555-acre campus is in an urban area in downtown Montreal and in suburban Loyola. Including any residence halls, there are 80 buildings.

Student Life: 90% of undergraduates are from Quebec. The average age of freshmen is 21; all undergraduates, 25. 11% do not continue beyond their first year; 52% remain to graduate.

Housing: 144 students can be accommodated in college housing, which includes single-sex and coed dorms, off-campus apartments, fraternity houses, and sorority houses. On-campus housing is available on a first-come, first-served basis. Priority is given to out-of-town students. 98% of students commute. All students may keep cars.

Activities: 1% of men belong to 3 national fraternities; 1% of women belong to 3 national sororities. There are 125 groups on campus, including art, choir, chorale, chorus, computers, dance, drama, ethnic, film, gay, honors, international, jazz band, literary magazine, musical theater, newspaper, orchestra, photography, political, professional, radio and TV, religious, social, social service, student government, symphony, and yearbook.

Sports: There are 9 intercollegiate sports for men and 7 for women, and 16 intramural sports for men and 12 for women. Facilities include an arena, a gym, and a football stadium.

Disabled Students: 75% of the campus is accessible. Wheelchair ramps, elevators, special parking, specially equipped rest rooms, special class scheduling, lowered drinking fountains, lowered telephones, and assistance for hearing/visual/mobility impaired are available.

Services: Counseling and information services are available, as is tutoring in most subjects. There is a reader service for the blind, and remedial math, reading, and writing.

Campus Safety and Security: Measures include 24-hour foot and vehicle patrol, self-defense education, security escort services, and shuttle buses. There are informal discussions, pamphlets/posters/films, emergency telephones, and lighted pathways/sidewalks.

Programs of Study: Concordia University confers B.A., B.Admin., B.Comm., B.Comp.Sci., B.Ed., B.Eng., B.F.A., and B.S.C. degrees.

Master's and doctoral degrees are also awarded. Bachelor's degrees are awarded in BIOLOGICAL SCIENCE (biochemistry, biology/biological science, and microbiology), BUSINESS (accounting, banking and finance, business administration and management, business economics, international business management, marketing/retailing/merchandising, and personnel management), COMMUNICATIONS AND THE ARTS (communications, dance, design, dramatic arts, English, English as a second/foreign language, film arts, fine arts, journalism, languages, music, and photography), COMPUTER AND PHYSICAL SCIENCE (actuarial science, chemistry, computer programming, computer science, geology, information sciences and systems, mathematics, physics, and statistics), EDUCATION (art, early childhood, and elementary), ENGINEERING AND ENVIRONMENTAL DESIGN (civil engineering, computer engineering, electrical/electronics engineering, industrial engineering, and mechanical engineering), SOCIAL SCIENCE (anthropology, East Asian studies, economics, geography, history, philosophy, political science/government, psychology, sociology, and urban studies). Computer engineering, accounting, and communication studies are the strongest academically. Accounting and psychology are the largest.

Required: To graduate, students must complete 90 to 120 credits, depending on the degree, with a minimum GPA of 2.0. Between 42 and 54 credits are required in the major. All students must fulfill the requirements of the core curriculum and take the university writing test.

Special: The university offers programs in many majors with the Institute for Co-operative Education, internships, and study abroad in 12 countries. There are accelerated degree programs, B.A.-B.S. degrees, dual majors, a general studies degree, and student-designed majors. There is a chapter of Phi Beta Kappa.

Faculty/Classroom: 65% of faculty are male; 35%, female. No introductory courses are taught by graduate students. The average class size in an introductory lecture is 50; in a laboratory, 50; and in a regular course, 50.

Requirements: The SAT or ACT is recommended. In addition, applicants must be graduates of an accredited secondary school. The GED is accepted. An essay, an interview, a portfolio, or an audition may be required for some programs. Concordia University requires applicants to be in the upper 30% of their class. A GPA of 2.5 is required. AP and CLEP credits are accepted. Important factors in the admissions decision are advanced placement or honor courses and recommendations by school officials.

Procedure: Freshmen are admitted to all sessions. There are early decision and early admissions plans. Early decision applications should be filed by February 1; regular applications, by March 1 for fall entry, November 1 for winter entry, and April 15 for summer entry, along with a $50 fee. The college accepts all in-state residents. Notification is sent on a rolling basis. A waiting list is an active part of the admissions procedure.

Transfer: Applicants must have a minimum GPA of 2.2. 45 of 90 credits required for the bachelor's degree must be completed at Concordia.

Visiting: There are regularly scheduled orientations for prospective students. There are guides for informal visits and visitors may sit in on classes. To schedule a visit, contact the Office of Student Recruitment at (514) 848-4779 or tours@vaxz.concordia.ca.

Financial Aid: Check with the school for current deadlines.

International Students: The school actively recruits these students. They must take the TOEFL, achieving a satisfactory score, or take the MELAB or the college's own test.

Computers: All students may access the system from 8:30 A.M. to 11:30 P.M. There are no time limits and no fees.

Admissions Contact: Assistant Registrar.
E-mail: admreg@alcor.concordia.ca Web: www.concordia.ca

DALHOUSIE UNIVERSITY E-2
Halifax, NS, Canada B3H 4H6

(902) 494-2148
Fax: (902) 494-1630

Total Enrollment: more than 15,800 men and women	**Faculty:** 1113
	Ph.D.s: 90%
Year: semesters, summer session	**Student/Faculty:** n/av
Application Deadline: June 1	**Tuition:** $6452 CDN ($12,697 CDN)
Freshman Class: n/av	**Room & Board:** $7500 CDN
SAT: required	

Dalhousie University, founded in 1818, is a public, nonsectarian institution offering undergraduate, graduate, and professional programs. There are 11 undergraduate schools and 1 graduate school. Some figures in the above capsule and in this profile are approximate. The 4 libraries contain 1,270,000 volumes, 340,000 microform items, and 13,800 audio/video tapes/CDs/DVDs, and subscribe to 8182 periodicals including electronic. Computerized library services include the card catalog, interlibrary loans, database searching, and Internet access. Special learning facilities include a learning resource center, art gallery, natural history museum, planetarium, radio station, a science museum, an aquatron, a slowpoke nuclear reactor, and a supercomputer. The 80-acre campus is in an urban area in Halifax. Including any residence halls, there are 102 buildings.

Student Life: 60% of undergraduates are from Nova Scotia. The average age of freshmen is 19. 14% do not continue beyond their first year.

Housing: 2200 students can be accommodated in college housing, which includes single-sex and coed dorms, on-campus apartments, off-campus apartments, and married-student housing. In addition, there are language houses and special-interest houses. On-campus housing is available on a first-come, first-served basis and is available on a lottery system for upperclassmen. Priority is given to out-of-town students. 80% of students commute. All students may keep cars.

Activities: There are 8 national fraternities and 1 national sorority. There are 200 groups on campus, including cheerleading, chess, chorale, computers, dance, debate, drama, ethnic, gay, international, musical theater, newspaper, photography, political, professional, radio and TV, religious, social, student government, and yearbook. Popular campus events include Frosh Week and Winter Carnival.

Sports: There are 8 intercollegiate sports for men and 8 for women, and 30 intramural sports for men and 30 for women. Facilities include an athletic center, an arena, indoor and outdoor tennis courts, a track, a playing field, an Olympic-size swimming pool, squash and volleyball courts, a climbing wall, a soccer field, a hockey rink, a dance studio, and weight rooms.

Disabled Students: 70% of the campus is accessible. Wheelchair ramps, elevators, special parking, specially equipped rest rooms, special class scheduling, lowered drinking fountains, and lowered telephones are available. The Office of the Vice President of Student Services is also available to provide assistance on an individual basis.

Services: Counseling and information services are available, as is tutoring in most subjects. There is a reader service for the blind and remedial math and writing.

Campus Safety and Security: Measures include 24-hour foot and vehicle patrol, self-defense education, security escort services, and shuttle buses. There are informal discussions, pamphlets/posters/films, and lighted pathways/sidewalks. The university also offers a student-organized campus patrol program.

Programs of Study: Dalhousie confers B.A., B.Sc., B.C.D., B.Comm., B.C.S., B.Eng., B.Hsc., B.Laws, B.Mgmt, B.Mus., B.Recreation and Health Ed., B.S.C.Kinesiology, B.S.N., B.S.O.T., B.S.Pharm., B.S.Physiotherapy, and B.S.W. degrees. Master's and doctoral degrees are also awarded. Bachelor's degrees are awarded in BIOLOGICAL SCIENCE (biochemistry, biology/biological science, marine biology, microbiology, and neurosciences), BUSINESS (business economics and recreation and leisure services), COMMUNICATIONS AND THE ARTS (classics, dramatic arts, English, French, German, music, Russian, and Spanish), COMPUTER AND PHYSICAL SCIENCE (chemistry, computer science, earth science, mathematics, physics, and statistics), EDUCATION (health), ENGINEERING AND ENVIRONMENTAL DESIGN (engineering), HEALTH PROFESSIONS (dental hygiene, nursing, occupational therapy, pharmacy, physical therapy, predentistry, and premedicine), SOCIAL SCIENCE (economics, history, international studies, law, philosophy, physical fitness/movement, political science/government, psychology, religion, social work, sociology, and women's studies). Science, health science, and engineering are the strongest academically. Arts, science, and commerce are the largest.

Required: To graduate, most students must complete a minimum of 15 full-year courses, including at least 5 in the major. Most students are required to take some classes outside their area of study. Programs vary in requirements.

Special: Co-op programs may be arranged in many majors. The university offers cross-registration, study abroad in 28 countries, and accelerated degree programs. Student-designed majors are available. The honors programs provide an extra year of advanced study to qualified students. A 4-year engineering degree is offered. The Science Foundation Year uses an integrated approach to teach a variety of first-year sciences. B.A.-B.S. degrees and dual majors are possible. There is a freshman honors program.

Faculty/Classroom: 60% of faculty are male; 40%, female. The average class size in an introductory lecture is 65; in a laboratory, 30; and in a regular course, 40.

Requirements: A satisfactory score on the SAT is required. Grade 12 credit in English is also required. Students are expected to have at least a B average. An audition is necessary for music and theater students. AP credits are accepted. Important factors in the admissions decision are advanced placement or honor courses, leadership record, and recommendations by school officials.

Procedure: Freshmen are admitted to all sessions. There are early decision, early admissions, and deferred admissions plans. There is a rolling admissions plan. Check with the school for current deadlines and fee.

Transfer: Applicants are assessed on an individual basis. They should have grades of C or 65% and higher from a recognized university.

Visiting: There are regularly scheduled orientations for prospective students, including a 1-hour walking tour of campus and a meeting with an admissions officer. There are guides for informal visits and visitors may sit in on classes. To schedule a visit, contact the campus tour coordinator at (902) 494-2587 or *campus.tours@dal.ca*.

International Students: The school actively recruits these students. Students applying on a visa from outside Canada or the United States must achieve a satisfactory score on the TOEFL if English is not their first language of communication or education. A satisfactory score on the SAT is also required.

Computers: All students may access the system at any time. There are no time limits and no fees.

Admissions Contact: Associate Registrar Admissions and Awards. E-mail: *admissions@dal.ca* Web: *www.dal.ca*

LAVAL UNIVERSITY E-2

Quebec, PQ, Canada G1K 7P4 (418) 656-2764
(877) 785-2825; Fax: (418) 656-5216

Full-time: 8297 men, 11,667 women	Faculty: n/av
Part-time: 3226 men, 5130 women	Ph.D.s: 90%
Graduate: 4492 men, 5632 women	Student/Faculty: n/av
Year: semesters, summer session	Tuition: $2052 CDN ($10,709
Application Deadline: see profile	CDN)
	Room & Board: $9000 CDN

Freshman Class: 28,717 applied, 20,234 accepted, 10,726 enrolled
SAT or ACT: not required

Laval University, founded in 1852, is the oldest French-language university in North America. It offers undergraduate and graduate programs through 17 faculties and 9 institutes. There are 16 undergraduate and 17 graduate schools. In addition to regional accreditation, Laval University has baccalaureate program accreditation with AACSB, ACU, AUCC, and Group of Ten. The 2 libraries contain 3.4 million volumes, 1.3 million microform items, and 37,832 audio/video tapes/CDs/DVDs, and subscribe to 17,625 periodicals including electronic. Computerized library services include the card catalog, interlibrary loans, database searching, and Internet access. Special learning facilities include a learning resource center, art gallery, natural history museum, radio station, language lab, and business simulations. The 465-acre campus is in an urban area 2 miles west of old Quebec City. Including any residence halls, there are 35 buildings.

Student Life: 94% of undergraduates are from Quebec. Students are from 105 foreign countries. The average age of all undergraduates is 26.

Housing: 2400 students can be accommodated in college housing, which includes single-sex and coed on-campus apartments. On-campus housing is available on a first-come, first-served basis. All students may keep cars.

Activities: There are no fraternities or sororities. There are 150 groups on campus, including art, band, chess, choir, chorale, computers, dance, drama, ethnic, film, forensics, gay, international, jazz band, literary magazine, musical theater, newspaper, opera, orchestra, photography, political, radio and TV, religious, social, social service, student government, and symphony. Popular campus events include Thematic Weeks, Rendez-vous Laval, and Student Festivals.

Sports: There are 13 intercollegiate sports for men and 10 for women, and 7 intramural sports for men and 7 for women. Facilities include a covered stadium with a 200-meter running track and 4 tennis courts; a 50-meter swimming pool with a 10-meter diving tower; a double ice arena; 1 triple and 2 single gyms; 4 squash courts; 4 handball and racquetball courts; judo, karate, and self-defense rooms; a dance studio; an open-air stadium with a 400-meter running track; softball, football, and soccer fields; 6 outdoor tennis courts; 3 physical training rooms; a golf driving range; an indoor golf practice room; 2 outdoor basketball courts; a 1-kilometer hiking trail; and a jogging track.

Disabled Students: 95% of the campus is accessible. Wheelchair ramps, elevators, special parking, specially equipped rest rooms, special class scheduling, lowered drinking fountains, lowered telephones, teletype machines for the deaf, computerized classrooms for the visually disabled, electric doors, sidewalks adjusted for physically disabled students, elevators equipped with speaking devices, and a campus plan in braille are available.

Services: There is a reader service for the blind and remedial math and writing. Tutoring in French grammar is available.

Campus Safety and Security: Measures include 24-hour foot and vehicle patrol, security escort services, informal discussions, and pamphlets/posters/films. There are emergency telephones, and lighted pathways/sidewalks, and Other services include 24-hour camera surveillance in pedestrian tunnels and trained evacuating teams in all buildings. Security training for social events is offered to all student associations.

Programs of Study: Laval University confers B.A., B.A.A., B.A.V., B.Ed., B.Ens., B.Ing., B.Mus., B.Pharm., B.Sc., B.Sc.A., B.Sc.Arch., B.Serv.Soc., B.Th., and LL.B. degrees. Master's and doctoral degrees are also awarded. Bachelor's degrees are awarded in AGRICULTURE (agricultural business management, agricultural economics, agronomy, forest engineering, forestry and related sciences, and wood science), BIOLOGICAL SCIENCE (biochemistry, biology/biological science, microbiology, and nutrition), BUSINESS (business administration and management), COMMUNICATIONS AND THE ARTS (art, art history and appreciation, communications, dramatic arts, English, English as a second/foreign language, French, languages, linguistics, literature, music, and visual and performing arts), COMPUTER AND PHYSICAL SCIENCE (actuarial science, chemistry, computer science, geology, geoscience, mathematics, physics, software engineering, and statistics), EDUCATION (art, athletic training, early childhood, education, elementary, music, physical, secondary, and technical), ENGINEERING AND ENVIRONMENTAL DESIGN (agricultural engineering, architecture, chemical engineering, civil engineering, computer engineering, electrical/electronics engineering, engineering and applied science, engineering physics, geological engineering, graphic arts technology, industrial administration/management, mechanical engineering, metallurgical engineering, and mining and mineral engineering), HEALTH PROFESSIONS (nursing, occupational therapy, pharmacy, physical therapy, predentistry, and premedicine), SOCIAL SCIENCE (anthropology, classical/ancient civilization, consumer services, counseling/psychology, economics, food science, French studies, geography, history, interdisciplinary studies, international studies, Judaic studies, law, philosophy, physical fitness/movement, political science/government, psychology, social work, sociology, Spanish studies, and theological studies). Business administration, sciences, and education are the largest.

Required: Requirements for graduation vary according to the program. A minimum GPA of 2.0 out of 4.33 is required per 30 credits.

Special: Laval offers co-op programs in forest operation, mining, metallurgical engineering, mineral engineering, and wood processing engineering, and study abroad in 65 countries. Dual majors are possible in anthropology and ethnology, economics and politics, international studies and modern languages, historical sciences and patrimonial studies, French language and professional writing, and math and computer science. Intensive French courses are offered during the summer.

Faculty/Classroom: All teach undergraduates.

Admissions: 70% of the 2005-2006 applicants were accepted.

Requirements: The only general requirement is the D.E.C. (Diploma of Collegial Studies—13 years of scholarity) or the equivalent. Some programs have specific requirements. All undergraduate students (except those who are nonfrancophones) must show a sufficient knowledge of the French language to obtain their bachelor's degree.

Procedure: Freshmen are admitted to all sessions. A waiting list is an active part of the admissions procedure. Applications are accepted online. Check with the school for current application deadlines and fee.

Transfer: 1662 transfer students enrolled in 2004-2005. Applicants must have the D.E.C. or the equivalent.

Visiting: There are regularly scheduled orientations for prospective students. There are guides for informal visits and visitors may stay overnight. To schedule a visit, contact the Public Affairs Office at *accveil@dap.ulaval.ca*.

Financial Aid: The deadline for filing freshman financial aid applications for fall entry is June 30.

International Students: There are 1013 international students enrolled. The school actively recruits these students. A French proficiency test is required.

Computers: All students may access the system 24 hours a day. There are no time limits and no fees. It is recommended that students in business administration and architecture have PCs. An IBM ThinkPad is recommended.

Graduates: From July 1, 2004 to June 30, 2005, 6734 bachelor's degrees were awarded. The most popular majors were administration (18%), science and engineering (14%), and letters (13%). 14000 companies recruited on campus in 2004-2005. Of the 2004 graduating class, 83% were employed within 6 months of graduation.

Admissions Contact: Public Affairs Office.
E-mail: *accveil@dap.vlaval.ca* Web: *http://www.ulaval.ca/bip*

MCGILL UNIVERSITY
E-2

Montreal, PQ, Canada H3A 2T5

(514) 398-3910
Fax: (514) 398-4193

Full-time: 7171 men, 10,801 women	**Faculty:** n/av
Part-time: 1290 men, 2073 women	**Ph.D.s:** 95%
Graduate: 3574 men, 3972 women	**Student/Faculty:** n/av
Year: semesters, summer session	**Tuition:** $2786 CDN ($14,222 CDN)
Application Deadline: March 1	
	Room & Board: $7964 CDN
Freshman Class: 18,963 applied, 10,689 accepted, 4834 enrolled	
SAT Verbal/Math: 680/680*	**ACT:** 29

McGill University, founded in 1821, is a publicly funded private institution that grants undergraduate, graduate, and professional degrees. Tuition fees may vary depending on program. There are 11 undergraduate and 79 graduate schools. In addition to regional accreditation, McGill has baccalaureate program accreditation with APTA. The 14 libraries contain 3,338,367 volumes, 1,623,988 microform items, and 71,765 audio/video tapes/CDs/DVDs, and subscribe to 22,513 periodicals including electronic. Computerized library services include the card catalog, interlibrary loans, and database searching. Special learning facilities include a learning resource center, natural history museum, radio station, McCord Museum of Canadian History, Mont St. Hilaire Nature Conservation Center, an herbarium, an arboretum, a subarctic research station, the Institute of Air and Space Law, the Institute of Islamic Studies, the Redpath Museum of Natural History, the Lyman Entomological Museum, the Ecomuseum, the Osler Library of the History of Medicine, and the Lande Canadiana Collection. The 80-acre campus is in an urban area in downtown Montreal, with the MacDonald campus located on the far west end of the island. Including any residence halls, there are 150 buildings.

Student Life: 53% of undergraduates are from Quebec. Students are from 140 foreign countries. The average age of freshmen is 19; all undergraduates, 21.

Housing: 2080 students can be accommodated in college housing, which includes single-sex and coed dorms, off-campus apartments, and married-student housing. On-campus housing is available on a lottery system for upperclassmen. Priority is given to out-of-town students. 83% of students commute.

Activities: 4% of men belong to 1 local fraternity and 12 national fraternities; 2% of women belong to 4 national sororities. There are 180 groups on campus, including band, cheerleading, chess, choir, chorale, chorus, computers, dance, debate, drama, ethnic, film, gay, honors, international, jazz band, literary magazine, model UN, musical theater, newspaper, opera, orchestra, photography, political, professional, radio and TV, religious, social, social service, student government, symphony, walksafe, and yearbook. Popular campus events include multicultural festivals, 4-floor parties, and music, film, and theatrical productions.

Sports: There are 23 intercollegiate sports for men and 24 for women, and 23 intramural sports for men and 15 for women. Facilities include a 20,000-seat stadium; a 1,000-seat competition hall; 2 double gyms for basketball, volleyball, and badminton; 8 outdoor tennis courts; 4 indoor tennis courts; a 400-meter outdoor track and a banked 6-lane 200-meter indoor track; 2 weight-training rooms; dance, aerobics, and martial arts rooms; 1 pool; a gymnastics facility; 3 sports fields; a fitness center; a sport medicine center; and a hyperbaric chamber.

Disabled Students: 80% of the campus is accessible. Wheelchair ramps, elevators, special parking, specially equipped rest rooms, special class scheduling, lowered telephones, braille, variable-speed tape recorders, talking calculators, books on tape, exam accommodations, adapted computers (voice synthesis and voice recognition), sign language interpreters, computerized note taking, note takers, print enlargement, readers, and adapted transport are available.

Services: Counseling and information services are available, as is tutoring in every subject. There is a reader service for the blind, and remedial math, reading, and writing.

Campus Safety and Security: Measures include 24-hour foot and vehicle patrol, security escort services, informal discussions, and pamphlets/posters/films. There are emergency telephones, lighted pathways/sidewalks, and Drivesafe.

Programs of Study: McGill confers B.A., B.Sc., B.C.L., B.Com., B.Ed., B.Eng., B.Mus., B.Sc., B.Sc.Agr., B.Sc.Agr.Eng., B.Sc.Arch., B.Sc.F.Sc., B.Sc.N., B.Sc.Nutr.Sc., B.Sc.Occ.Ther., B.Sc.Phys.Ther., B.S.W., B.Th., and LL.B. degrees. Master's and doctoral degrees are also awarded. Bachelor's degrees are awarded in AGRICULTURE (agricultural economics, agriculture, animal science, conservation and regulation, plant science, and soil science), BIOLOGICAL SCIENCE (anatomy, biochemistry, biology/biological science, botany, cell biology, environmental biology, microbiology, molecular biology, nutrition, physiology, wildlife biology, and zoology), BUSINESS (accounting, banking and finance, entrepreneurial studies, human resources, institutional management, insurance and risk management, international business management, labor studies, management information systems, management science, marketing management, and organizational behavior), COMMUNICATIONS AND THE ARTS (art history and appreciation, classics, English, French, jazz, linguistics, modern language, music history and appreciation, music performance, music technology, music theory and composition, Russian, and Spanish), COMPUTER AND PHYSICAL SCIENCE (applied mathematics, atmospheric sciences and meteorology, chemistry, computer science, earth science, geology, geophysics and seismology, information sciences and systems, mathematics, physics, planetary and space science, and software engineering), EDUCATION (elementary, foreign languages, music, physical, secondary, special, teaching English as a second/foreign language (TESOL/TEFOL), and vocational), ENGINEERING AND ENVIRONMENTAL DESIGN (agricultural engineering, architecture, chemical engineering, civil engineering, computer engineering, electrical/electronics engineering, environmental engineering, mechanical engineering, metallurgical engineering, and mining and mineral engineering), HEALTH PROFESSIONS (clinical science, exercise science, nursing, occupational therapy, and physical therapy), SOCIAL SCIENCE (African studies, American studies, anthropology, Canadian studies, Caribbean studies, dietetics, East Asian studies, economics, food science, French studies, geography, German area studies, Hispanic American studies, history, humanities, international studies, Italian studies, Judaic studies, Latin American studies, law, Middle Eastern studies, philosophy, political science/government, psychology, religion, social work, sociology, Western civilization/culture, and women's studies).

Required: To graduate, students must successfully complete a required number of approved credits, usually between 90 and 120. Students must also be in satisfactory standing, with a minimum cumulative GPA of 2.0.

Special: There is cross-registration with area universities. Study abroad, work-study within the university, co-op programs in mining and metallurgical engineering, dual majors, internships, and student-designed majors are available.

Faculty/Classroom: 67% of faculty are male; 33%, female. No introductory courses are taught by graduate students. The average class size in an introductory lecture is 30; in a laboratory, 25; and in a regular course, 45.

Admissions: 56% of the 2005-2006 applicants were accepted. The SAT scores for the 2005-2006 freshman class were: Math--1% below 500, 11% between 500 and 599, 51% between 600 and 700, and 38% above 700.

Requirements: The SAT is required; the ACT may be submitted instead of the SAT. McGill requires applicants to be in the upper 25% of their class. A GPA of 3.3 is required. AP credits are accepted. Important factors in the admissions decision are advanced placement or honor courses, recommendations by school officials, and evidence of special talent.

Procedure: Freshmen are admitted in the fall. Entrance exams should be taken during the spring of the junior year and/or fall of the senior year. There is a deferred admissions plan and a rolling admissions plan. Applications should be filed by March 1 for fall entry, along with a fee of $60 CDN. Notification is sent on a rolling basis. Applications are accepted on-line.

Transfer: 528 transfer students enrolled in 2004-2005. Requirements vary with the program. Standard admission requirements must also be met. Students must submit high school and college transcripts and have a 3.0 GPA in college course work. 60 of 90 credits required for the bachelor's degree must be completed at McGill.

Visiting: There are regularly scheduled orientations for prospective students, with a varying agenda (including campus tours and student for a day programs). There are guides for informal visits and visitors may sit in on classes and stay overnight. To schedule a visit, contact the Welcome Center at (514) 398-6555 (tours) or *welcome@mcgill.ca*.

Financial Aid: In 2005-2006, 30% of all students received some form of financial aid. 17% of all students received need-based aid. The average freshman award was $5855 CDN. Need-based scholarships or need-based grants averaged $3022 CDN; and need-based self-help aid (loans and jobs) averaged $6146 CDN. McGill is a member of CSS. The FAFSA and the college's own financial statement are required. The deadline for filing freshman financial aid applications for fall entry is June 1.

International Students: There are 3732 international students enrolled. The school actively recruits these students. They must take the TOEFL, achieving a satisfactory score, or the MELAB. A McGill Certificate of Proficiency in English must be earned. SAT and/or ACT tests are required for U.S. applicants and recommended for other international applicants. Students must take program-specific SAT Subject Tests.

Computers: All students may access the system any time. There is a time limit depending on the application. There are no fees. It is strongly recommended that all students have a personal computer.

Graduates: From July 1, 2004 to June 30, 2005, 4277 bachelor's degrees were awarded. The most popular majors were social sciences (18%), health professions (11%), and biological/life sciences (10%). In an average class, 65% graduate in 4 years or less; 81% graduate in 5 years or less, and 83% graduate in 6 years or less.

Admissions Contact: Admissions, Recruitment, and Registrar's Office. A video is available. E-mail: *admissions@mcgill.ca*
Web: *www.mcgill.ca*

MCMASTER UNIVERSITY
E-3

Hamilton, ON, Canada L8S 4L8
(905) 525-4600
Fax: (905) 527-1105

Full-time: 5160 men, 6790 women	**Faculty:** 927
Part-time: 870 men, 1750 women	**Ph.D.s:** n/av
Graduate: 1190 men, 930 women	**Student/Faculty:** 13 to 1
Year: terms, summer session	**Tuition:** $4600 CDN ($14,000 CND)
Application Deadline: see profile	
	Room & Board: $6700 CND
Freshman Class: n/av	
SAT or ACT: not required	

McMaster University is a public nonsectarian institution, offering programs in the arts and sciences, business, engineering, health sciences, kinesiology, and social work. Figures given in the above capsule and in this profile are approximate. There are 2 graduate schools. The 4 libraries contain 1.8 million volumes, 1.4 million microform items, and 20,000 audio/video tapes/CDs/DVDs, and subscribe to 12,000 periodi-

cals including electronic. Computerized library services include the card catalog, interlibrary loans, and database searching. Special learning facilities include a learning resource center, art gallery, planetarium, radio station, nuclear reactor, tandem accelerator, greenhouses, the Chedoke-McMaster Hospital, communication research lab, the Bertrand Russell archives, the Humanities Communication Centre, and computing labs. The 300-acre campus is in an urban area 60 miles southwest of Toronto. Including any residence halls, there are 44 buildings.

Student Life: 95% of undergraduates are from Ontario. The average age of freshmen is 20; all undergraduates, 22. 1% do not continue beyond their first year.

Housing: 2765 students can be accommodated in college housing, which includes single-sex and coed dorms and on-campus apartments. In addition, there are language houses. On-campus housing is guaranteed for the freshman year only and is available on a lottery system for upperclassmen. Priority is given to out-of-town students. 77% of students commute. All students may keep cars.

Activities: There are no fraternities or sororities. There are 100 groups on campus, including art, band, cheerleading, chess, choir, chorale, chorus, computers, debate, drama, ethnic, gay, international, jazz band, musical theater, newspaper, orchestra, photography, political, radio and TV, religious, social, student government, and yearbook. Popular campus events include Marauder Weekend.

Sports: There are 16 intercollegiate sports for men and 14 for women, and 16 intramural sports for men and 14 for women. Facilities include 2 multipurpose gyms, an outdoor track and field, a mini-weight room, a swimming pool, cross-country trails, rugby, soccer, and football fields, tennis, squash, and handball courts, and a state-of-the-art fitness facility.

Disabled Students: 60% of the campus is accessible. Wheelchair ramps, elevators, special parking, specially equipped rest rooms, special class scheduling, lowered telephones, and basement-level and aboveground tunnels with connecting walkways are available.

Services: Counseling and information services are available, as is tutoring in some subjects. There is a reader service for the blind.

Campus Safety and Security: Measures include 24-hour foot and vehicle patrol, security escort services, shuttle buses, and informal discussions. There are pamphlets/posters/films, emergency telephones, and lighted pathways/sidewalks. Additional services include the Emergency First-Response Team, Mac Alert bulletins, a campus watch program, a prevention programs officer, and video monitoring in some parking areas.

Programs of Study: Mac confers B.A., B.S., B.A.S., B.A./B.S.W., B.C., B.Eng., B.Eng. and Management, B.Eng. and Society, B.H.S., B.Kinesiology, B.Mus., and B.S.N. degrees. Master's and doctoral degrees are also awarded. Bachelor's degrees are awarded in BIOLOGICAL SCIENCE (biochemistry, biology/biological science, and life science), BUSINESS (business administration and management and labor studies), COMMUNICATIONS AND THE ARTS (art, art history and appreciation, classics, comparative literature, dramatic arts, English, French, linguistics, modern language, music, and Russian), COMPUTER AND PHYSICAL SCIENCE (chemistry, computer science, earth science, geology, mathematics, physical sciences, physics, science, and statistics), ENGINEERING AND ENVIRONMENTAL DESIGN (chemical engineering, civil engineering, computer engineering, electrical/electronics engineering, engineering physics, environmental science, manufacturing engineering, materials engineering, materials science, and mechanical engineering), HEALTH PROFESSIONS (medical science, nursing, occupational therapy, and physical therapy), SOCIAL SCIENCE (anthropology, economics, geography, German area studies, gerontology, history, interdisciplinary studies, Japanese studies, Latin American studies, liberal arts/general studies, philosophy, physical fitness/movement, political science/government, psychology, religion, social work, sociology, and women's studies).

Required: Requirements for graduation vary according to the program of study. A minimum 3.5 GPA in 90 to 150 units is required for most programs.

Special: Many opportunities exist to combine 2 subjects of study within 1 faculty, or between 2 faculties. All honors students have the option of taking a minor in a second subject area. Nondegree study is possible through the Center for Continuing Education. Internships and study abroad are offered. Students may repeat failed courses provided they are eligible to continue in the program.

Faculty/Classroom: 71% of faculty are male; 29%, female. All both teach and do research.

Requirements: U.S. applicants must have a high school grade average of 80. Applicants must be graduates of an accredited secondary school. The required high school courses should include 5 years each of English and math. A portfolio is required for art students and an audition for music students. A supplementary application form is required for some programs. Offers of admission are made based on academic standing and audition/portfolio/supplementary application requirements where necessary. Important factors in the admissions decision are evidence of special talent, extracurricular activities record, and leadership record.

Procedure: Freshmen are admitted to all sessions. There is an early decision plan. Check with the school for current application deadlines and fee. A waiting list is an active part of the admissions procedure.

Transfer: Applicants are considered on an individual basis. Review of high school, college, and/or university work determines admission status.

Visiting: There are regularly scheduled orientations for prospective students, including campus tours, information sessions, and panel discussions. There are guides for informal visits and visitors may sit in on classes. To schedule a visit, contact the Tour Coordinator, Division of Student Liaison at (905) 525-9140, ext. 24796.

Financial Aid: Check with the school for current deadlines.

International Students: The school actively recruits these students. They must take the TOEFL, achieving a satisfactory score, or take the MELAB, or the IELTS.

Computers: All students may access the system any time. There are no time limits and no fees.

Admissions Contact: Registrar, Admissions.
E-mail: *macadmit@mcmail.mcmaster.ca* Web: *www.mcmaster.ca*

MEMORIAL UNIVERSITY OF NEWFOUNDLAND F-2

St. John's, NF, Canada A1C 5S7 (709) 737-3705
Fax: (709) 737-2337

Full-time: 4800 men, 6300 women	**Faculty:** 932
Part-time: 680 men, 1370 women	**Ph.D.s:** 50%
Graduate: 840 men, 760 women	**Student/Faculty:** 12 to 1
Year: trimesters, summer session	**Tuition:** $2842 CDN ($9410 CDN)
Application Deadline: March 1	**Room & Board:** $4686 CDN
Freshman Class: n/av	
SAT or ACT: not required	

Memorial University of Newfoundland, founded in 1925, is a public liberal arts institution. There are 13 undergraduate and 12 graduate schools. Some figures in the above capsule and in this profile are approximate. The 3 libraries contain 2.5 million volumes, and subscribe to 700 periodicals including electronic. Computerized library services include the card catalog, interlibrary loans, and database searching. Special learning facilities include a learning resource center, art gallery, natural history museum, planetarium, radio station, TV station, and language labs. The 220-acre campus is in an urban area within St. John's. Including any residence halls, there are 40 buildings.

Student Life: 98% of undergraduates are from Newfoundland.

Housing: 1750 students can be accommodated in college housing, which includes single-sex and coed dorms, on-campus apartments, off-campus apartments, and married-student housing. On-campus housing is available on a first-come, first-served basis. Priority is given to out-of-town students. 89% of students commute. All students may keep cars.

Activities: There are no fraternities or sororities. There are 100 groups on campus, including band, cheerleading, chess, choir, chorale, computers, dance, debate, drama, ethnic, gay, international, jazz band, literary magazine, musical theater, newspaper, orchestra, photography, political, professional, radio and TV, religious, social, social service, student government, symphony, and yearbook. Popular campus events include Winter Carnival and Orientation.

Sports: There are 6 intercollegiate sports for men and 6 for women, and 6 intramural sports for men and 6 for women. Facilities include a gym, squash courts, a rifle range, a weight room, a soccer field, and swimming facilities.

Disabled Students: 85% of the campus is accessible. Wheelchair ramps, elevators, special parking, specially equipped rest rooms, special class scheduling, lowered drinking fountains, lowered telephones, classroom aids, note-taking volunteers, and other facilities based on individual needs are available.

Services: Counseling and information services are available. There is a reader service for the blind, and remedial math, reading, and writing. Students staying in residence have access to tutoring in every subject. In addition, lectures are offered on topics such as public speaking, speed reading, and time management.

Campus Safety and Security: Measures include 24-hour foot and vehicle patrol, self-defense education, security escort services, and informal discussions. There are pamphlets/posters/films, emergency telephones, and lighted pathways/sidewalks.

Programs of Study: MUN confers B.A., B.Sc., B.Comm.(Co-op.), B.Comm.(Gen.), B.Ed., B.Eng., B.F.A., B.Kin., B.M.S., B.Mus., B.Mus.Ed., B.Med.Sc., B.N., B.P.E., B.Rec., B.Sc.(Pharm.), B.Spec.Ed., B.S.W., B.Tech., and B.Voc.Ed. degrees. Master's and doctoral degrees are also awarded. Bachelor's degrees are awarded in AGRICULTURE (forestry and related sciences), BIOLOGICAL SCIENCE (biochemistry, biology/biological science, cell biology, ecology, entomology, environmental biology, evolutionary biology, marine biology, marine science, microbiology, and neurosciences), BUSINESS (entrepreneurial studies, human resources, labor studies, management science, marketing/retailing/merchandising, organizational behavior, and small business management), COMMUNICATIONS AND THE ARTS (dramatic arts,

English, English literature, fine arts, folklore and mythology, French, German, linguistics, literature, music, music history and appreciation, music performance, music theory and composition, Russian, Spanish, and visual and performing arts), COMPUTER AND PHYSICAL SCIENCE (applied mathematics, applied physics, chemistry, computer science, earth science, information sciences and systems, mathematics, oceanography, and statistics), EDUCATION (athletic training, education, elementary, guidance, middle school, music, physical, recreation, secondary, and special), ENGINEERING AND ENVIRONMENTAL DESIGN (civil engineering, electrical/electronics engineering, engineering technology, maritime science, mechanical engineering, naval architecture and marine engineering, and ocean engineering), HEALTH PROFESSIONS (medical science, nursing, and pharmacy), SOCIAL SCIENCE (anthropology, archeology, Canadian studies, criminology, dietetics, economics, French studies, geography, German area studies, history, humanities, medieval studies, philosophy, physical fitness/movement, political science/government, psychology, religion, social studies, social work, sociology, Spanish studies, and women's studies). Marine Biology, naval architecture, and business are the strongest academically. Arts, science, business, and engineering are the largest.

Required: Students must complete 40 to 50 credits to graduate. Each discipline has different requirements for graduation.

Special: The university offers co-op programs in commerce, phys ed, recreation, kinesiology, and engineering. Internships are available in education and nursing. Study abroad may be arranged in at least 20 countries. Work-study programs, dual majors, and B.A.-B.S. degrees are available.

Faculty/Classroom: 80% of faculty are male; 20%, female. All both teach and do research. Graduate students teach 71% of introductory courses. The average class size in an introductory lecture is 40.

Requirements: Admission is based on a high school grade average of 70 as computed from university preparatory courses required for admission. AP credits are accepted.

Procedure: Freshmen are admitted to all sessions. Applications should be filed by March 1 for fall entry, October 1 for winter entry, February 1 for spring entry, and February 1 for summer entry. Application fee is $80 CDN. Notification is sent on a rolling basis. Application are accepted on-line.

Transfer: Applicants must be in good academic standing at the previous institution. 10 of 40 credits required for the bachelor's degree must be completed at MUN.

Visiting: There are regularly scheduled orientations for prospective students, including various student activities, mock lectures, campus tours, and educational sessions. There are guides for informal visits and visitors may sit in on classes. To schedule a visit, contact Student Development at (709) 737-2192.

Financial Aid: Check with the school for current deadlines.

International Students: The school actively recruits these students. They must take the TOEFL, achieving a satisfactory score, or take the MELAB.

Computers: All students may access the system. There are no time limits and no fees.

Admissions Contact: Registrar's Office. A video is available.
E-mail: *www.mun.ca/reg.off* Web: *www.mun.ca*

QUEEN'S UNIVERSITY E-3

Kingston, ON, Canada K7L 3N6 (613) 533-2218
Fax: (613) 533-6810

Full-time: 12,300 men and women	**Faculty:** 973
Part-time: 2300 men and women	**Ph.D.s:** n/av
Graduate: 2600 men and women	**Student/Faculty:** 13 to 1
Year: semesters, summer session	**Tuition:** $5000 ($12,000)
Application Deadline: see profile	**Room & Board:** $8561
Freshman Class: n/av	
SAT: required	

Queen's University, founded in 1841, is a public institution offering undergraduate and graduate programs in the arts and sciences, business, engineering, health sciences, and teacher education. There are 10 undergraduate and 5 graduate schools. Some figures in the above capsule and in this profile are approximate. The 8 libraries contain 1.8 million volumes, 2 million microform items, and 7000 audio/video tapes/CDs/DVDs, and subscribe to 15,000 periodicals including electronic. Computerized library services include the card catalog, interlibrary loans, and database searching. Special learning facilities include a learning resource center, art gallery, radio station, TV station, geology museum, and observatory. The 160-acre campus is in an urban area 150 miles east of Toronto. Including any residence halls, there are 100 buildings.

Student Life: 85% of undergraduates are from Ontario. 89% are from public schools. 5% do not continue beyond their first year; 90% remain to graduate.

Housing: 3071 students can be accommodated in college housing, which includes single-sex and coed dorms, on-campus apartments, off-campus apartments, and married-student housing. In addition, there are language houses and special-interest houses. On-campus housing is guaranteed for the freshman year only. 80% of students commute. All students may keep cars.

Activities: There are no fraternities or sororities. There are 220 groups on campus, including art, bagpipe band, band, cheerleading, chess, choir, chorale, chorus, computers, dance, debate, drama, ethnic, film, gay, international, jazz band, literary magazine, marching band, musical theater, newspaper, orchestra, photography, political, professional, radio and TV, religious, social, social service, student government, symphony, and yearbook. Popular campus events include Orientation Week, Alumni Weekend, and Applied Science Formal.

Sports: There are 19 intercollegiate sports for men and 21 for women, and 39 intramural sports for men and 39 for women. Facilities include a pool, an indoor track, a hockey arena, tennis, squash, and racquetball courts, a weight room, a dance studio, and a projectile range. There is also a 5000-seat indoor gym and a 12000-seat football stadium.

Disabled Students: 80% of the campus is accessible. Wheelchair ramps, elevators, special parking, specially equipped rest rooms, special class scheduling, lowered drinking fountains, and lowered telephones are available.

Services: Counseling and information services are available, as is tutoring in most subjects. There is a reader service for the blind, and remedial math, reading, and writing.

Campus Safety and Security: Measures include 24-hour foot and vehicle patrol, self-defense education, security escort services, and shuttle buses. There are informal discussions, pamphlets/posters/films, emergency telephones, and lighted pathways/sidewalks.

Programs of Study: Queen's confers B.A., B.Sc., B.A./B.Ed., B.A./B.Phe., B.Comm., B.F.A., B.Mus., B.N.Sc., B.Sc./B.Ed., B.Sc./B.Phe., B.S.C.E., B.Sc.O.T., and B.Sc.P.T. degrees. Master's and doctoral degrees are also awarded. Bachelor's degrees are awarded in BIOLOGICAL SCIENCE (biochemistry, biology/biological science, and life science), COMMUNICATIONS AND THE ARTS (art history and appreciation, classics, dramatic arts, English, film arts, fine arts, French, German, Greek, Italian, Latin, music, and Spanish), COMPUTER AND PHYSICAL SCIENCE (chemistry, computer science, geology, mathematics, physics, and statistics), EDUCATION (elementary, middle school, and secondary), ENGINEERING AND ENVIRONMENTAL DESIGN (chemical engineering, civil engineering, electrical/electronics engineering, engineering physics, geological engineering, and mechanical engineering), HEALTH PROFESSIONS (health, nursing, occupational therapy, and physical therapy), SOCIAL SCIENCE (economics, geography, history, Judaic studies, philosophy, political science/government, psychology, religion, sociology, and women's studies). Arts, science, and engineering are the largest.

Required: Each faculty and school establishes the academic requirements for the graduation of its students.

Special: Internships are available in life science, commerce, and engineering. Students may study abroad in 25 countries. Dual majors are available. Cross-registration with St. Lawrence College for the B.S.N. is possible. There is a freshman honors program.

Faculty/Classroom: 72% of faculty are male; 27%, female. All teach undergraduates. The average class size in a laboratory is 40.

Requirements: The SAT is required. In addition, candidates for admission are required to submit a school profile. A high school grade average of 70 is required. Important factors in the admissions decision are evidence of special talent, leadership record, and extracurricular activities record.

Procedure: Freshmen are admitted in the fall. There is a deferred admissions plan and rolling admissions plan. Check with school for current application deadlines and fee. Notification is sent on a rolling basis. A waiting list is an active part of the admissions procedure. Applications are accepted on-line.

Transfer: Admission requirements for transfer applicants vary by program. 10 of 19 credits required for the bachelor's degree must be completed at Queen's.

Visiting: There are regularly scheduled orientations for prospective students, consisting of a short briefing session and a walking tour. There are guides for informal visits and visitors may sit in on classes and stay overnight. To schedule a visit, contact Student Recruitment at (613) 533-2217 or *tours@post.queensu.ca*.

Financial Aid: Check with the school for current deadlines.

International Students: The school actively recruits these students. They must achieve a satisfactory score on the TOEFL or take the MELAB. Applicants from American Schools must achieve a satisfactory score on the SAT.

Computers: All students may access the system 24 hours. It is strongly recommended that all students have a personal computer. An IBM ThinkPad is recommended.

Admissions Contact: Associate University Registrar (Admissions Services). A video is available. E-mail: *admissn@post.queensu.ca* Web: *www.queensu.ca*

RYERSON UNIVERSITY E-3
Toronto, ON, Canada M5B 2K3
(416) 979-5000
Fax: (416) 979-5341

Full-time: 21,000 men and women	**Faculty:** 547
Part-time: none	**Ph.D.s:** n/av
Graduate: 700 men and women	**Student/Faculty:** 23 to 1
Year: semesters	**Tuition:** $5000 CDN ($12,000 CDN)
Application Deadline: see profile	
	Room & Board: $8000 CDN
Freshman Class: n/av	
SAT or ACT: required	

Ryerson University, founded in 1948, is a public institution offering undergraduate programs in arts, applied arts, business, community services, and engineering and applied science. Figures given in the above capsule and this profile are approximate. There are 29 undergraduate schools. In addition to regional accreditation, Ryerson has baccalaureate program accreditation with FIDER. The library contains 320,898 volumes, 400 microform items, and 6283 audio/video tapes/CDs/DVDs, and subscribes to 3239 periodicals including electronic. Computerized library services include the card catalog, interlibrary loans, and database searching. Special learning facilities include a learning resource center, radio station, and a film and photography gallery. The 20-acre campus is in an urban area in downtown Toronto. Including any residence halls, there are 22 buildings.

Student Life: 94% of undergraduates are from Ontario. 21% do not continue beyond their first year.

Housing: 858 students can be accommodated in college housing, which includes coed dorms. In addition, there are language houses and special-interest houses. On-campus housing is available on a first-come, first-served basis. Priority is given to out-of-town students. 94% of students commute. All students may keep cars.

Activities: There are no fraternities or sororities. There are 55 groups on campus, including choir, chorale, ethnic, film, gay, international, literary magazine, newspaper, political, professional, radio and TV, religious, social, student government, and yearbook. Popular campus events include Orientation, Island Picnic, and Winter Carnival.

Sports: There are 8 intercollegiate sports for men and 7 for women, and 7 intramural sports for men and 6 for women. Facilities include a recreation and athletic center, 7 squash courts, a fitness training center that includes an indoor running track and weight-training equipment, a rehabilitation center, a 25-yard pool, saunas, 3 studios, and 6 gyms.

Disabled Students: Wheelchair ramps, elevators, special parking, specially equipped rest rooms, special class scheduling, and lowered telephones are available. The Access Center on campus offers information, seminars, and workshops; test and exam adaptations; computer-equipped exam and study rooms; assistive listening devices for personal use and for use in auditorium settings; advocacy services; individual needs assessment; and access to a wide range of technical devices.

Services: There is a reader service for the blind, remedial math, reading, and writing and study skills development.

Campus Safety and Security: Measures include 24-hour foot and vehicle patrol, self-defense education, security escort services, and informal discussions. There are pamphlets/posters/films, emergency telephones, lighted pathways/sidewalks, sexual assault training, harassment prevention and crime prevention programs, and community policing programs.

Programs of Study: Ryerson confers B.A.A., B.B.M., B.Eng., B.H.Sc., B.S.N., B.S.W., and B.Tech. degrees. Bachelor's degrees are awarded in BUSINESS (business administration and management, hospitality management services, and management information systems), COMMUNICATIONS AND THE ARTS (broadcasting, journalism, and photography), COMPUTER AND PHYSICAL SCIENCE (chemical technology and computer programming), EDUCATION (early childhood), ENGINEERING AND ENVIRONMENTAL DESIGN (aeronautical engineering, architecture, chemical engineering, civil engineering, electrical/electronics engineering, graphic and printing production, industrial engineering, interior design, mechanical engineering, and urban planning technology), HEALTH PROFESSIONS (environmental health science and nursing), SOCIAL SCIENCE (child care/child and family studies, family/consumer studies, fashion design and technology, geography, public administration, and social work). Business management, electrical engineering, and administration and information management are the largest.

Required: To graduate, students must have a 2.0 GPA and complete the requirements of their program of study.

Special: The university offers co-op programs in applied chemistry and biology, chemical engineering, and midwifery. Accelerated degree programs are available in journalism, radio and television arts, nurse practitioner, and nursing, and many programs have a work-study component.

Faculty/Classroom: All teach undergraduates. The average class size in a regular course is 30.

Requirements: The SAT or ACT is required for U.S. students. Students should be high school graduates with a minimum B overall average.

Procedure: Freshmen are admitted in the fall. Check with the school for current application deadlines and fee. A waiting list is an active part of the admissions procedure.

Transfer: Transfer applicants must have completed 1 year at the college level. Acceptance of transfer credits is at the discretion of the Office of Admissions/Liaison/Curriculum Advising. Half of the required credits for a particular degree program must be completed at Ryerson.

Visiting: There are regularly scheduled orientations for prospective students, including a half-day tour and discussion session featuring campus tours and visits to specific schools and departments. There are guides for informal visits and visitors may sit in on classes. To schedule a visit, contact the Liaison Office at (416) 979-5030.

Financial Aid: Ryerson is a member of CSS. The financial statements applicable to Ontario government requirements are needed. Check with the school for current deadlines.

International Students: They must take the TOEFL, achieving a satisfactory score, or take the MELAB or the college's own test.

Computers: All students may access the system. There are no fees.

Admissions Contact: Director of Admissions.
E-mail: *inquire@acs.ryerson.ca* Web: *http://www.ryerson.ca*

SIMON FRASER UNIVERSITY   B-2
Burnaby, BC, Canada V5A 1S6   (604) 291-3211
    Fax: (604) 291-4969

Undergraduate 23,480 men and women	**Faculty:** n/av
	Ph.Ds: 88%
Graduate: 3190 men and women	**Student/Faculty:** n/av
Year: trimesters, summer session	**Tuition:** $4365 CDN ($13,080 CDN)
Application Deadline: May 1	
	Room & Board: $4100 CDN
Freshman Class: n/av	
SAT: required	**ACT:** recommended

Simon Fraser University, established in 1965, is a public institution offering undergraduate and graduate programs in the arts, sciences, business, education, and applied sciences. In addition to its main campus, the university maintains the Harbour Centre campus in downtown Vancouver to provide midcareer education to the urban population and the new SFU Surrey campus offering programs in information technology and interactive arts. There are 5 undergraduate and 35 graduate schools. Figures in the above capsule and in this profile are approximate. The library contains 1,397,816 volumes, 1,136,745 microform items, and 10,213 audio/video tapes/CDs/DVDs, and subscribes to 15,513 periodicals including electronic. Computerized library services include the card catalog, interlibrary loans, database searching, and Internet access. Special learning facilities include a learning resource center, art gallery, radio station, archeology museum, special literature and map collections, fine and performing arts theater, hypo/hyperbaric chamber, back test unit, rock-climbing wall, apiary, underwater lab, television and photography studios, and dance floors. The 400-acre campus is in a suburban area 9 miles east of Vancouver. Including any residence halls, there are 51 buildings.

Student Life: 89% of undergraduates are from British Columbia. Students are from 90 foreign countries. 92% are from public schools. The average age of freshmen is 19; all undergraduates, 23.

Housing: 1117 students can be accommodated in college housing, which includes single-sex and coed dorms, on-campus apartments, and married-student housing. Priority for on-campus housing is given to out-of-town students. 96% of students commute. All students may keep cars.

Activities: There are no fraternities or sororities. There are 35 groups on campus, including bagpipe band, chess, choir, computers, ethnic, gay, international, newspaper, political, professional, religious, social, social service, and student government. Popular campus events include Convocation, Clubs Day, and various orientation activities.

Sports: There are 9 intercollegiate sports for men and 9 for women, and 7 intramural sports for men and 7 for women. Facilities include 2 gyms, swimming and diving pools, a running track, weight rooms, saunas, playing fields, a combative room, tennis, squash, and racquetball courts, and a fitness center.

Disabled Students: 95% of the campus is accessible. Wheelchair ramps, elevators, special parking, specially equipped rest rooms, lowered drinking fountains, lowered telephones, and special housing are available. There are computers with software such as large text and voice output features, a scanner, a braille printer, a Visualtek machine, closed-circuit TV for text or graphic enlargement, note-taking tutor support, adaptive technology, exam modifications, sign language interpreters, closed captioning in lectures, and alternate format texts.

Services: There is a reader service for the blind and taped library books. Some lectures are taped.

Campus Safety and Security: Measures include 24-hour foot and vehicle patrol, security escort services, pamphlets/posters/films, and emergency telephones. There are lighted pathways/sidewalks, safe-walk stations, and student patrols.

Programs of Study: SFU confers B.A., B.Sc., B.A.Sc., B.B.A., B.Ed., B.F.A., and B.G.S. degrees. Master's and doctoral degrees are also awarded. Bachelor's degrees are awarded in BIOLOGICAL SCIENCE (biology/biological science, molecular biology, and physiology), BUSINESS (business administration and management and management science), COMMUNICATIONS AND THE ARTS (art, communications, dance, dramatic arts, English, film arts, French, linguistics, music, and visual and performing arts), COMPUTER AND PHYSICAL SCIENCE (actuarial science, applied mathematics, applied physics, chemistry, computer science, earth science, mathematics, physics, science, and statistics), EDUCATION (education), ENGINEERING AND ENVIRONMENTAL DESIGN (engineering and applied science and environmental science), SOCIAL SCIENCE (anthropology, archeology, Canadian studies, cognitive science, criminology, economics, geography, history, humanities, liberal arts/general studies, philosophy, physical fitness/movement, political science/government, psychology, sociology, and women's studies). Engineering science is the strongest academically. Business administration, economics, and psychology are the largest.

Required: General bachelor's degrees require completion of 120 semester hours with a 2.0 cumulative GPA; honors degrees, 132 hours. Some programs require a thesis.

Special: Simon Fraser offers cooperative education in most areas of study, study abroad in 28 countries, many opportunities for joint majors, a general studies degree, work-study programs, dual majors, student-designed majors, and a variety of certificate and diploma programs, as well as nondegree and evening study. Interdisciplinary majors are offered in such areas as chemical physics, management and systems science, mathematical physics, and physics and physiology. There is a freshman honors program.

Faculty/Classroom: 71% of faculty are male; 29%, female.

Requirements: The SAT or ACT is required for U.S. applicants. In addition, applicants must be graduates of an accredited secondary school and have a minimum grade average of 70. A GPA of 3.2 is required. AP credits are accepted.

Procedure: Freshmen are admitted to all sessions. There are early decision and early admissions plans. Early decision applications should be filed by February 28; regular applications, by May 1 for fall entry, September 30 for spring entry, and January 31 for summer entry. Check with the school for the current application fee. Notification of early decision is sent April 15; regular decision, June 30. 1300 early decision candidates were accepted for a recent class. Applications are accepted online.

Transfer: 1560 transfer students enrolled in a recent year. Applicants must have a minimum GPA of 2.0 and be in good standing at their previous school. 60 of 120 credits required for the bachelor's degree must be completed at SFU.

Visiting: There are regularly scheduled orientations for prospective students, consisting of regularly scheduled 1-day campus orientations. There are guides for informal visits and visitors may stay overnight. To schedule a visit, contact the Residence and Housing Office at (604) 291-4330.

Financial Aid: The average financial indebtedness of a recent year's graduate was $20,000. The FAFSA is required. Check with the school for current deadlines.

International Students: There were 672 international students enrolled in a recent year. The school actively recruits these students. They must achieve a satisfactory score on the TOEFL and also take IELTS (minimum score 6.5 on academic modules).

Computers: All students may access the system any time. There are no time limits and no fees.

Graduates: In a recent year, 3168 bachelor's degrees were awarded. The most popular majors were business (14%), economics (9%), and communication (8%).

Admissions Contact: Director of Admissions.
E-mail: *undergraduate-admissions@sfu.ca* Web: *http://www.sfu.ca*

UNIVERSITÉ DE MONTRÉAL   E-2
Montreal, PQ, Canada H3C 3J7   (514) 343-7076
    Fax: (514) 343-5788

Full-time: 11,227 men, 15,530 women	**Faculty:** n/av
Part-time: 5182 men, 9423 women	**Ph.Ds:** 96%
Graduate: 6354 men, 7434 women	**Student/Faculty:** n/av
Year: trimesters, summer session	**Tuition:** $1685 CDN ($11,255 CDN)
Application Deadline: March 1	
	Room & Board: $678 CDN
Freshman Class: 25,593 applied, 13,584 accepted, 11,039 enrolled	
SAT or ACT: not required	

Université de Montréal, founded in 1878, is the largest French-language university in North America, with 13 faculties, 2 affiliated schools, 62 teaching departments, and more than 170 research units. Cost figures above are for 8 months. There are 16 undergraduate schools and 1 graduate school. The 19 libraries contain 3 million volumes, 1,604,798 microform items, and 2 million audio/video tapes/CDs/DVDs, and subscribe to 50,000 periodicals including electronic. Computerized library services include the card catalog, interlibrary loans, database searching, Internet access, and laptop Internet portals. Special learning facilities include a learning resource center, art gallery, natural history museum, radio station, and concert hall. The 145-acre campus is in an urban area in Montreal. Including any residence halls, there are 38 buildings.

Student Life: 88% of students from public schools. The average age of freshmen is 24; all undergraduates, 26. 16% do not continue beyond their first year; 84% remain to graduate.

Housing: 1164 students can be accommodated in college housing, which includes coed off-campus apartments. On-campus housing is available on a first-come, first-served basis. 98% of students commute. All students may keep cars.

Activities: There are no fraternities or sororities. There are up to 100 groups on campus, including art, choir, chorale, computers, dance, drama, ethnic, film, international, jazz band, literary magazine, newspaper, orchestra, photography, radio and TV, religious, social, social service, student government, and yearbook. Popular campus events include Multicultural Week and Welcoming Week.

Sports: There are 8 intercollegiate sports for men and 6 for women, and 12 intramural sports for men and 12 for women. Facilities include a skating rink, a football field, a gym, squash and racquetball courts, an Olympic-size pool, a diving pool, a running field with tennis courts, and aerobic and muscular exercise equipment.

Disabled Students: 95% of the campus is accessible. Wheelchair ramps, elevators, special parking, specially equipped rest rooms, lowered drinking fountains, lowered telephones, and special housing are available. There is also a specialized equipment center for students with disabilities.

Services: Counseling and information services are available, as is tutoring in some subjects, including math and French. There is a reader service for the blind, and remedial math, reading, and writing.

Campus Safety and Security: Measures include 24-hour foot and vehicle patrol, security escort services, informal discussions, and pamphlets/posters/films. There are emergency telephones and lighted pathways/sidewalks.

Programs of Study: UdeM confers B.A., B.Sc., B.A.A., B.A.P., B.D.I., B.Ed., B.Gest, B.Ing., B.Int., B.Mus., B. Pharm., and B.Th. degrees. Associate, master's, and doctoral degrees are also awarded. Bachelor's degrees are awarded in BIOLOGICAL SCIENCE (biochemistry, biology/biological science, biometrics and biostatistics, and nutrition), BUSINESS (business administration and management), COMMUNICATIONS AND THE ARTS (art history and appreciation, classics, English, film arts, French, German, industrial design, linguistics, and music), COMPUTER AND PHYSICAL SCIENCE (chemistry, computer science, mathematics, and physics), EDUCATION (education, physical, and psychology), ENGINEERING AND ENVIRONMENTAL DESIGN (architectural engineering, architecture, engineering, industrial administration/management, and landscape architecture/design), HEALTH PROFESSIONS (health science, nursing, occupational therapy, pharmacy, physical therapy, predentistry, premedicine, preveterinary science, speech pathology/audiology, and veterinary science), SOCIAL SCIENCE (anthropology, Asian/Oriental studies, criminology, economics, geography, history, law, philosophy, political science/government, psychology, social work, sociology, Spanish studies, theological studies, and urban studies). Medicine is the strongest academically. Arts and science are the largest.

Required: To graduate, students must have a GPA of 2.0 on a 4.3 scale. The total number of credit hours required in most programs is 90, although it can range up to 187. Professional programs, particularly those in health-related fields, require more hours.

Special: The university offers co-op programs in math, translation, mining, and civil, chemical, and software material engineering, and work-study programs in hospitals and businesses in Quebec. Dual majors in math and economics, math and physics, math and computer science, communication and politics, economics and politics, and 3-2 engineering degrees may also be arranged. Study abroad is available in 31 countries. There is a freshman honors program.

Faculty/Classroom: 71% of faculty are male; 29%, female. All teach undergraduates. The average class size in an introductory lecture is 48; in a laboratory, 19; and in a regular course, 40.

Admissions: 53% of recent applicants were accepted.

Requirements: Applicants in certain programs must take the university's admissions tests. An interview is also required in some programs.

Procedure: Freshmen are admitted fall and winter. Applications should be filed by March 1 for fall, spring, or summer entry, and November 1 for winter entry. The fall 2005 application fee was $50 CDN. Notification is sent March 15. A waiting list is an active part of the admissions procedure. Applications are accepted on-line.

Transfer: Transfers are considered if there are openings in the second or third year of the university's programs. 90 credits required for the bachelor's degree in most of the programs, must be completed at UdeM.

Visiting: There are regularly scheduled orientations for prospective students, including Orientation and Employment Week in November, guided tours February through May, and open house in January and August. There are guides for informal visits. To schedule a visit, contact Direction des communications et du recrutement at (514) 343-6032 or *umontreal.ca/portesouvertes/.*

Financial Aid: In a recent year, 42% of all full-time freshmen and 50% of continuing full-time students received some form of financial aid, including need-based aid. The average freshman award was $6000. 57% of undergraduates work part time. Average annual earnings from campus work are $4500. The deadline for filing freshman financial aid applications for fall entry is March 31.

International Students: The school actively recruits these students. A French proficiency test is required upon admission.

Computers: Wireless access is available. There are many computers in the libraries and in public rooms; there is access to the Internet from housing services room. All students may access the system 24 hours per day. There are no time limits and no fees. It is strongly recommended that all students have a personal computer, especially students in management programs. An IBM ThinkPad is recommended.

Admissions Contact: Jacinthe Gauthier, Responsable admissions.
E-mail: *admissions@regis.umontreal.ca*
Web: *http://www.etudes.umontreal.ca*

UNIVERSITY OF ALBERTA C-2
Edmonton, AB, Canada T6G 2M7

(780) 492-3113
Fax: (780) 492-7172

Full-time: 11,452 men, 15,089 women	**Faculty:** 1659
Part-time: 837 men, 1359 women	**Ph.Ds:** 92%
Graduate: 2875 men, 3005 women	**Student/Faculty:** 16 to 1
Year: semesters, summer session	**Tuition:** $5295 CDN ($15,849 CDN)
Application Deadline: May 1	
	Room & Board: $4700 CDN
Freshman Class: n/av	
SAT or ACT: not required	

The University of Alberta, founded in 1908, is a publicly supported institution offering undergraduate and graduate programs in arts and science, agricultural sciences, business, education, engineering, nursing, phys ed, native studies, and professional studies. There are 17 undergraduate schools and 1 graduate school. The 13 libraries contain 3.4 million volumes and 2.8 million microform items, and subscribe to 18,900 periodicals including electronic. Computerized library services include the card catalog, interlibrary loans, database searching, and Internet access. Special learning facilities include a learning resource center, art gallery, radio station, an agricultural meteorological research station, an ecological sanctuary, a botanical garden, and the Kurimoto Japanese Garden farm. The 155-acre campus is in an urban area 2 miles southwest of downtown Edmonton. Including any residence halls, there are 90 buildings.

Student Life: Students are from 10 states and 121 foreign countries. The average age of freshmen is 18; all undergraduates, 21.

Housing: 4900 students can be accommodated in college housing, which includes single-sex and coed dorms, on-campus apartments, off-campus apartments, and married-student housing. In addition, there are honors houses and special-interest houses. On-campus housing is guaranteed for all 4 years. 88% of students commute. All students may keep cars.

Activities: There are 12 national fraternities and 8 national sororities. There are more than 300 groups on campus, including art, band, cheerleading, chess, choir, chorale, chorus, computers, dance, debate, drama, ethnic, forensics, gay, honors, international, jazz band, musical theater, newspaper, opera, orchestra, pep band, photography, political, radio and TV, religious, social, social service, student government, and symphony. Popular campus events include WOW (Week of Welcome) and AntiFreeze (winter activity).

Sports: There are 10 intercollegiate sports for men and 11 for women, and 60 intramural sports for men and 45 for women. Facilities include a stadium, swimming pools, gyms, combatives and weight rooms, ballet/fencing and aerobics studios, a 400-meter outdoor track, an ice arena, racquetball and squash courts, a wrestling gym, an indoor field house, a sports medicine clinic, a training center for disabled athletes, curling rinks, and tennis courts.

Disabled Students: 98% of the campus is accessible. Wheelchair ramps, elevators, special parking, specially equipped rest rooms, special class scheduling, lowered drinking fountains, lowered telephones, and automatic doors are available.

Services: Counseling and information services are available, as is tutoring in most subjects. There is a reader service for the blind, and remedial math, reading, and writing.

Campus Safety and Security: Measures include 24-hour foot and vehicle patrol, security escort services, pamphlets/posters/films, and emergency telephones. There are lighted pathways/sidewalks.

Programs of Study: U of A confers B.A., B.Comm., B.Des., B.Ed., B.F.A., B.Mus., and B.P.E.,B.Sc., and B.ScN., degrees. Master's and doctoral degrees are also awarded. Bachelor's degrees are awarded in AGRICULTURE (agricultural economics, agriculture, animal science, and soil science), BIOLOGICAL SCIENCE (biochemistry, biology/ biological science, botany, cell biology, entomology, genetics, microbiology, physiology, and zoology), BUSINESS (accounting, management science, and marketing/retailing/merchandising), COMMUNICATIONS AND THE ARTS (classics, comparative literature, dance, dramatic arts, English, film arts, French, Germanic languages and literature, linguistics, music, romance languages and literature, and Slavic languages), COMPUTER AND PHYSICAL SCIENCE (applied mathematics, chemistry, computer science, earth science, geology, geophysics and seismology, mathematics, physical sciences, physics, and statistics), EDUCATION (education of the deaf and hearing impaired, education of the multiply handicapped, elementary, physical, secondary, special, and vocational), ENGINEERING AND ENVIRONMENTAL DESIGN (chemical engineering technology, civil engineering, computer engineering, electrical/ electronics engineering, engineering physics, mechanical engineering, metallurgical engineering, mining and mineral engineering, and petroleum/natural gas engineering), HEALTH PROFESSIONS (medical laboratory science, nursing, occupational therapy, pharmacy, and physical therapy), SOCIAL SCIENCE (anthropology, Canadian studies, clothing and textiles management/production/services, criminology, East Asian studies, Eastern European studies, economics, geography, history, law, philosophy, political science/government, psychology, sociology, and women's studies). Arts, science, and education are the largest.

Required: The requirements for graduation vary according to the program. A minimum GPA of 2.0 and at least 120 credit hours are required for graduation.

Special: The university offers co-op programs in business and engineering. Opportunities for study abroad, internships, dual majors, bilingual classes in French and English, credit by exam (special assessment), and pass/fail options are also available. There is 1 national honor society, and a freshman honors program.

Faculty/Classroom: 83% of faculty are male; 17%, female. All both teach and do research. The average class size in an introductory lecture is 90; in a laboratory, 20; and in a regular course, 35.

Requirements: Graduation from an accredited secondary school is required. A minimum grade average of 70 is required in all courses submitted for academic credit. Depending on the program selected by the student, an essay, portfolio, audition, or interview may be required. AP credits are accepted.

Procedure: Freshmen are admitted to all sessions. There is an early admissions plan. Applications should be filed by May 1 for fall entry, November 15 for winter entry, and March 1 for spring entry, along with a $100 CDN fee. The university accepts all applicants. Notification of early decision is sent January 2; regular decision, August 1. Applications are accepted on-line.

Transfer: 2689 transfer students enrolled in 2004-2005. Applicants must meet minimum matriculation requirements or complete 24 credits of transferable work with satisfactory standing. 60 of 120 credits required for the bachelor's degree must be completed at U of A.

Visiting: There are regularly scheduled orientations for prospective students, including University Open House on the first weekend in October. There are guides for informal visits and visitors may sit in on classes. To schedule a visit, contact the Office of the Registrar and Student Awards.

International Students: There are 2186 international students enrolled. The school actively recruits these students. They must take the TOEFL or the MELAB as well as the IELTS, the CAEL, or the university's own test.

Computers: Wireless access is available. All students may access the system 24 hours a day. There are no time limits. The fee varies by amount of CPU usage.

Graduates: From July 1, 2004 to June 30, 2005, 6210 bachelor's degrees were awarded.

Admissions Contact: Office of the Registrar and Student Awards. A video is available. E-mail: *www.registrar.ualberta.ca/contact* Web: *www.ualberta.ca*

UNIVERSITY OF BRITISH COLUMBIA   B-2

Vancouver, BC, Canada V6T 1Z1

(604) 822-3014
(877) 272-1422; Fax: (604) 822-3599

Full-time: 9028 men, 10,933 women	**Faculty:** n/av
Part-time: 4134 men, 5816 women	**Ph.D.s:** 98%
Graduate: 3639 men, 4239 women	**Student/Faculty:** 10 to 1
Year: terms, summer session	**Tuition:** $4160 CDN($14,880 CDN)
Application Deadline: February 28	
	Room & Board: $5400 CDN
Freshman Class: 23,165 applied, 14,819 accepted, 8152 enrolled	
SAT: recommended	

The University of British Columbia, established in 1908, is a publicly supported institution offering a wide range of undergraduate, graduate, and professional programs in the arts, sciences, and other fields of study. The winter session lasts from early September through April; some courses extend into May. Summer session begins in May and goes to mid-August, consisting of 2 terms. There are 16 undergraduate schools

and 1 graduate school. The 22 libraries contain 4 million volumes, 5 million microform items, and 33,647 audio/video tapes/CDs/DVDs, and subscribe to 44,722 periodicals including electronic. Computerized library services include the card catalog, interlibrary loans, database searching, Internet access, and laptop Internet portals. Special learning facilities include a learning resource center, art gallery, natural history museum, radio station, and a learning center, an anthropology museum, Canada's largest accelerator for subatomic physics, a space observatory, a center for integated computer systems research, a center for the study of global issues, and a center for the performing arts. The 1000-acre campus is in an urban area 6 miles from the center of Vancouver. Including any residence halls, there are 500 buildings.

Student Life: 88% of undergraduates are from British Columbia. Others are from 138 foreign countries. 98% are from public schools. The average age of all undergraduates is 21. 9% do not continue beyond their first year; 91% remain to graduate.

Housing: 7500 students can be accommodated in college housing, which includes single-sex and coed dormitories, on-campus apartments, and married-student housing. In addition, there are special-interest houses and international houses. On-campus housing is available on a first-come, first-served basis. Priority is given to out-of-town students. 80% of students commute. All students may keep cars.

Activities: 6% of men belong to 7 national fraternities; 2% of women belong to 7 national sororities. There are 250 groups on campus, including art, band, cheerleading, chess, choir, chorale, chorus, computers, dance, debate, drama, ethnic, film, gay, international, jazz band, literary magazine, musical theater, newspaper, opera, orchestra, photography, political, professional, radio and TV, religious, ski and snowboard, social, social service, student government, symphony, varsity outdoors and yearbook. Popular campus events include Storm the Wall, Day of the Longboat, and Great Trek Run.

Sports: There are 15 intercollegiate sports for men and 13 for women, and 18 intramural sports for men and 18 for women. Facilities include a winter sports center, a 3500-seat stadium, a gym, an aquatic center, playing fields, a recreation center, and a tennis center.

Disabled Students: 95% of the campus is accessible. Wheelchair ramps, elevators, special parking, specially equipped rest rooms, special class scheduling, lowered drinking fountains, lowered telephones, special housing, accessible shower stalls in fitness facilities, tactile maps, TTY pay phones, an accessible security bus, and audible street crossing signals are available.

Services: Counseling and information services are available, as is tutoring in most subjects. There is a reader service for the blind, and remedial math, reading, and writing.

Campus Safety and Security: Measures include 24-hour foot and vehicle patrol, security escort services, shuttle buses, and informal discussions. There are pamphlets/posters/films, emergency telephones, and lighted pathways/sidewalks. A Royal Canadian Mounted Police detachment is on campus, and campus security provides awareness programs on theft and personal safety lectures for women.

Programs of Study: UBC confers B.A., B.A.Sc., B.B.R.E., B.Com., B.C.S., B.D.Sc., B.Ed., B.End., B.F.A., B.H.E., B.H.K., B.M., B.M.l.Sc., B.Mus., B.Sc., B.Sc.Die., B.Sc.F., B.Sc.Pharm., B.S.F., B.S.N., B.S.W., and L.L.B degrees. Master's and doctoral degrees are also awarded. Bachelor's degrees are awarded in AGRICULTURE (agricultural economics, animal science, forestry and related sciences, forestry production and processing, horticulture, natural resource management, and soil science), BIOLOGICAL SCIENCE (biochemistry, biology/biological science, biophysics, biotechnology, microbiology, nutrition, and physiology), BUSINESS (accounting, banking and finance, business administration and management, business economics, human resources, international business management, management information systems, marketing/retailing/merchandising, real estate, recreational facilities management, and transportation management), COMMUNICATIONS AND THE ARTS (art history and appreciation, Chinese, classics, creative writing, dramatic arts, English, film arts, fine arts, French, German, Italian, Japanese, linguistics, music, music history and appreciation, music performance, music theory and composition, romance languages and literature, and Spanish), COMPUTER AND PHYSICAL SCIENCE (astronomy, atmospheric sciences and meteorology, chemistry, computer science, earth science, geophysics and seismology, mathematics, oceanography, physics, science, and statistics), EDUCATION (elementary, museum studies, and physical), ENGINEERING AND ENVIRONMENTAL DESIGN (chemical engineering, civil engineering, computer engineering, electrical/electronics engineering, engineering, engineering physics, environmental design, environmental engineering, environmental science, geological engineering, mechanical engineering, metallurgical engineering, and mining and mineral engineering), HEALTH PROFESSIONS (exercise science, health, nursing, pharmacology, preveterinary science, and speech pathology/audiology), SOCIAL SCIENCE (anthropology, archeology, Asian/Oriental studies, Canadian studies, classical/ancient civilization, cognitive science, dietetics, economics, European studies, family/consumer studies, food production/management/services, food science, geography, Hispanic American studies, history, home economics, human ecology, international relations, Latin American studies, medieval studies, Native American studies, philosophy, political science/ government, psychology, religion, sociology, South Asian studies, and women's studies). Applied sciences and commerce are the strongest academically. Education and psychology are the largest.

Required: Graduation requirements vary according to the degree sought. B.A. candidates must complete course work in English composition, science, literature, and a foreign language.

Special: UBC offers co-op programs in science, applied science, commerce, arts, and forestry, and study abroad through 150 student exchange opportunities in 40 countries. Nondegree study is possible. A B.A.-B.A.Sc. degree, student-designed majors, and dual majors in most faculties are available. There is 1 national honor society and 10 departmental honors programs.

Faculty/Classroom: 62% of faculty are male; 38%, female.

Admissions: 64% of the 2005-2006 applicants were accepted. 96% of the current freshmen were in the top fifth of their class.

Requirements: The SAT is recommended. In addition, graduation from an accredited secondary school is required. General admission for students following a U.S. system is based on 4 years of English and 3 of math. There are also specific program requirements in math, chemistry, physics, and biology for students applying to science-based programs. A GPA of 2.6 is required. AP credits are accepted.

Procedure: Freshmen are admitted fall and spring. There are early decision, early admissions, and deferred admissions plans. There is a rolling admissions plan. Applications should be filed by February 28 along with a $100 CDN fee. Notification of early decision is sent May 1; regular decision, on a rolling basis. Applications are accepted on-line.

Transfer: 968 transfer students enrolled in 2004-2005. Official transcripts, completion of the equivalent of 24 course credits, and no failures are required. A competitive GPA is required to get into the program at the second or third year. Applicants must have attended an accredited postsecondary institution. 60 of 120 credits required for the bachelor's degree must be completed at UBC.

Visiting: There are regularly scheduled orientations for prospective students, consisting of a campus tour from 9:30 A.M. to 11 A.M. every Friday and from 1 P.M. to 2:30 P.M. on Tuesdays; some Saturday sessions are available. There are guides for informal visits and visitors may sit in on classes and stay overnight. To schedule a visit, contact the Student Information Center at (604) 822-9836 or *student.information@ubc.ca.*

Financial Aid: The FAFSA and the college's own financial statement are required. Need-based aid is principally limited to Canadian citizens and permanent residents.

International Students: There are 3421 international students enrolled. The school actively recruits these students. They must take the TOEFL or the MELAB, and also take the comprehensive English Language Test, the college's own test the IELTS, the CAEL, the CAE, or the CPE.

Computers: Wireless access is available. PCs and wireless access are available across the campus. All students may access the system 24 hours per day. There are no time limits and no fees. It is strongly recommended that all students have a personal computer.

Graduates: From July 1, 2004 to June 30, 2005, 5125 bachelor's degrees were awarded. The most popular majors were psychology (9%), biology (7%), and English (6%). In an average class, 62% graduate in 4 years or less, and 78% graduate in 6 years or less.

Admissions Contact: Office of the Registrar. A video is available. E-mail: *international.reception@ubc.ca* Web: *www.ubc.ca/okanagan*

UNIVERSITY OF CALGARY C-2
Calgary, AB, Canada T2N 1N4

(403) 220-6645
Fax: (403) 220-0762

Full-time: 8994 men, 10,606 women
Part-time: 1293 men, 1901 women
Graduate: 2578 men, 2556 women
Year: semesters, summer session
Application Deadline: April 1

Faculty: n/av
Ph.D.s: n/av
Student/Faculty: 13 to 1
Tuition: $5170 CDN ($9760 CDN)
Room & Board: $5475 CDN

Freshman Class: 6928 applied, 3992 accepted, 2744 enrolled
SAT: required

The University of Calgary, founded in 1945, is a public institution offering undergraduate programs in numerous liberal arts and professional fields. There are 13 undergraduate and 2 graduate schools. Enrollment figures above are from a recent year. The 5 libraries contain 2,481,808 volumes, 3,564,512 microform items, and 36,920 audio/video tapes/CDs/DVDs, and subscribe to 20,237 periodicals including electronic. Computerized library services include the card catalog, interlibrary loans, database searching, Internet access, and laptop Internet portals. Special learning facilities include a learning resource center, art gallery, radio station, TV station, environmental research center, observatory, and human performance and theater labs. The 526-acre campus is in an urban area in northwest Calgary. Including any residence halls, there are 33 buildings.

Housing: 1500 students can be accommodated in college housing, which includes coed dorms, on-campus apartments, and married-student housing. On-campus housing is available on a first-come, first-served basis. Priority is given to out-of-town students. All students may keep cars.

Activities: There are no fraternities or sororities. There are some groups and organizations on campus, including band, choir, drama, newspaper, orchestra, political, radio and TV, religious, social, and student government. Popular campus events include Bermuda Shorts Day (last day of classes in April).

Sports: There are 9 intercollegiate sports for men and 9 for women, and 20 intramural sports for men and 18 for women. Facilities include 3 gyms, a 50-meter swimming pool, a 200-meter indoor track, a 3-story climbing wall, an indoor speed-skating arena, an outdoor stadium, rooms for weight training, aerobics, and combatives, and squash, tennis, and racquetball courts. There is also a 200-seat lecture theater, a games area, and an outdoor recreation center.

Disabled Students: All of the campus is accessible. Wheelchair ramps, elevators, special parking, specially equipped rest rooms, lowered drinking fountains, lowered telephones, and special housing are available.

Services: Counseling and information services are available, as is tutoring in most subjects. There is a reader service for the blind and remedial writing.

Campus Safety and Security: Measures include security escort services, informal discussions, emergency telephones, and lighted pathways/sidewalks.

Programs of Study: U of C confers B.A., B.Sc., B.Comm., B.C.R., B.C.S., B.Ed., B.F.A., B.G.S., B.H.R.M., B.H.Sc., B.Kin., B.Mus., B.N., B.Sc.Eng., B.S.W., and LL.B. degrees. Master's and doctoral degrees are also awarded. Bachelor's degrees are awarded in BIOLOGICAL SCIENCE (biochemistry, bioinformatics, biology/biological science, botany, cell biology, ecology and zoology), BUSINESS (accounting, business administration and management, hotel/motel and restaurant management and marketing/retailing/merchandising), COMMUNICATIONS AND THE ARTS (art history and appreciation, communications, dance, dramatic arts, English, fine arts, French, German, linguistics, music, music history and appreciation, music performance, music theory and composition, Russian, and Spanish), COMPUTER AND PHYSICAL SCIENCE (actuarial science, applied mathematics, astrophysics, chemical physics, chemistry, computer science, earth science, geology, geophysics and seismology, mathematics, natural sciences, physics, and statistics), EDUCATION (education, elementary, and secondary), ENGINEERING AND ENVIRONMENTAL DESIGN (chemical engineering, civil engineering, computer engineering, electrical/electronics engineering, environmental science, manufacturing engineering, mechanical engineering, petroleum/natural gas engineering, surveying engineering, systems engineering, and technology and public affairs), HEALTH PROFESSIONS (biomedical science, exercise science, nursing, public health, and sports medicine), SOCIAL SCIENCE (anthropology, archeology, Asian/Oriental studies, Canadian studies, classical/ancient civilization, community services, economics, geography, history, international relations, Latin American studies, law, liberal arts/general studies, philosophy, physical fitness/movement, political science/government, psychology, religion, social work, sociology, urban studies and women's studies). Engineering and medicine are the strongest academically. Education, management and engineering are the largest.

Required: To graduate, all students must satisfy the required courses, course sequences, and credit distribution in their particular program. Students must maintain a minimum 2.0 GPA and complete 7 to 10 full-course equivalents in the major field.

Special: The university offers co-op programs in applied chemistry, management, and many other fields. Dual majors, work-study programs, internships in engineering and computer science, combined degrees in many disciplines, and study abroad in 28 countries are also available. Students may cross-register with any of 8 member colleges in the Big Country Education Consortium. U of C sponsors or is affiliated with 20 research institutes and groups.

Faculty/Classroom: The average class size in an introductory lecture is 60 and in a laboratory, 24.

Admissions: 58% of the 2005-2006 applicants were accepted.

Requirements: The SAT is required. In addition, U.S. applicants must be graduates of a secondary school and submit SAT scores, as required by the individual faculties. AP credits are accepted.

Procedure: Freshmen are admitted in the fall. There is an early admissions plan. Applications should be filed by April 1 for fall entry. The fall 2005 application fee was $100 (CDN). Applications are accepted on-line.

Transfer: Applicants must have a cumulative GPA of 2.0 or above on all transfer courses. 5 credits required for the bachelor's degree must be completed at U of C.

Visiting: There are regularly scheduled orientations for prospective students. There are guides for informal visits. To schedule a visit, contact the Prospective Student Office at (403) 220-6920.

International Students: There are 928 international students enrolled. The school actively recruits these students. They must take the TOEFL or take the IELTS, the CAEL, or the university's English program.

Computers: Wireless access is available. All students may access the system. 800 terminals are available 24 hours per day. There are no time limits and no fees. It is strongly recommended that all students have a personal computer.

Graduates: From January 1, 2004 to December 31, 2004, 5102 bachelor's degrees were awarded.

Admissions Contact: Kathleen Massey, Assistant Vice-President Enrollment. A video is available. E-mail: *askus@ucalgary.ca* Web: *www.ucalgary.ca*

UNIVERSITY OF GUELPH — E-3
Guelph, ON, Canada N1G 2W1

(519) 824-4120
Fax: (519) 766-9481

Full-time: 15,041 men and women	**Faculty:** 800
Part-time: 1454 men and women	**Ph.D.s:** 98%
Graduate: 2055 men and women	**Student/Faculty:** 19 to 1
Year: trimesters, summer session	**Tuition:** $4904 CDN
Application Deadline: April 1	($11,063CDN)
	Room & Board: $6644 CDN

Freshman Class: 18,852 applied, 13,765 accepted, 3479 enrolled

SAT or ACT: required

The University of Guelph, founded in 1964, is a public institution offering programs in arts and sciences, agriculture, engineering, commerce, landscape architecture, veterinary medicine, applied science, and technology. There are 6 undergraduate and 45 graduate schools. Enrollment Figures in the above capsule are for fall 2004.The 2 libraries contain 2 million volumes, 1.5 million microform items, and 17,000 audio/video tapes/CDs/DVDs, and subscribe to 7600 periodicals including electronic. Computerized library services include interlibrary loans, database searching, Internet access, and laptop Internet portals. Special learning facilities include a learning resource center, art gallery, radio station, observatory, learning commons, research park, and arboretum. The 1017-acre campus is in a suburban area 2 miles south of the center of Guelph. Including any residence halls, there are 80 buildings.

Student Life: 93% of undergradutes are from Canada. Students are from 100 Foreign countries.The average age of freshmen is 18; all undergraduates, 21. 9% do not continue beyond their first year; 89% remain to graduate.

Housing: 5500 students can be accommodated in college housing, which includes single-sex and coed dorms, on-campus apartments, and married-student housing. In addition, there are language houses and special-interest houses. On-campus housing is guaranteed for the freshman year only, is available on a first-come, first-served basis, and is available on a lottery system for upperclassmen. 67% of students commute. All students may keep cars.

Activities: There are no fraternities or sororities. There are 100 groups on campus, including art, cheerleading, chess, choir, chorale, computers, dance, debate, drama, ethnic, gay, international, jazz band, newspaper, photography, political, professional, radio and TV, religious, social, social service, student government, and yearbook. Popular campus events include College Royal open house weekend in March and Community Bar-B-Que in July.

Sports: There are 15 intercollegiate sports for men and 15 for women, and 17 intramural sports for men and 17 for women. Facilities include a twin-pad arena with an Olympic-size ice surface, 5 squash courts, a fitness gym, weight-training rooms, a 6-lane swimming pool and an Olympic-size pool, a fitness circuit, and 3 gyms. Outdoor facilities include 4 tennis courts, a running track, lighted football, field hockey, soccer, rugby, and fastball fields, jogging trails, and multipurpose fields. There are also 2 dance studios, a climbing wall, a wrestling/combatives room, a covered field with artificial turf, and a 200-meter track.

Disabled Students: 90% of the campus is accessible. Wheelchair ramps, elevators, special parking, specially equipped rest rooms, special class scheduling, lowered drinking fountains, lowered telephones, and special library services, equipment, and software are available.

Services: Counseling and information services are available, as is tutoring in most subjects. There is a reader service for the blind. ESL, learning, studying, and writing resources are available.

Campus Safety and Security: Measures include 24-hour foot and vehicle patrol, self-defense education, security escort services, and pamphlets/posters/films. There are emergency telephones, lighted pathways/sidewalks, a campus safe walk, and a campus police patrol.

Programs of Study: U of G confers B.A., B.Sc., B.A.S., B.A.Sc., B.B.R.M., B.Comm., B.Comp., B.L.A., B.Sc.Agr., B.Sc.Eng., B.Sc.Env., and B.Sc.(Tech); degrees. Master's and doctoral degrees are also awarded. Bachelor's degrees are awarded in AGRICULTURE (agricultural business management, agricultural economics, agriculture, agronomy, animal science, horticulture, natural resource management, and plant science), BIOLOGICAL SCIENCE (biochemistry, biology/biological science, biophysics, ecology, environmental biology, marine science, mi-

crobiology, molecular biology, nutrition, wildlife biology, and zoology), BUSINESS (hotel/motel and restaurant management, human resources, marketing management, real estate, and tourism), COMMUNICATIONS AND THE ARTS (art history and appreciation, classical languages, classics, English, music, Spanish, and studio art), COMPUTER AND PHYSICAL SCIENCE (chemical physics, chemistry, computer science, earth science, information sciences and systems, physical sciences, physics, and statistics), ENGINEERING AND ENVIRONMENTAL DESIGN (biomedical engineering, engineering technology, environmental engineering, and landscape architecture/design), SOCIAL SCIENCE (anthropology, child care/child and family studies, classical/ancient civilization, criminal justice, economics, food science, French studies, geography, gerontology, history, interdisciplinary studies, philosophy, political science/government, psychology, public administration, rural sociology, sociology, water resources, and women's studies). Biological and physical sciences and veterinary medicine are the strongest academically. Biological and physical sciences, arts, and social sciences are the largest.

Required: To graduate, students must complete 30 credits (half courses) for a general degree and 40 credits (half courses) for an honors degree. U of G requires a minimum of 10 credits in the major.

Special: U of G offers co-op programs in 34 majors, study abroad in 29 countries, and work-study programs. Accelerated degree programs, dual majors, a general studies degree, and nondegree study are available. There is a freshman honors program.

Faculty/Classroom: The average class size in an introductory lecture is 300 and in a laboratory, 25.

Admissions: 73% of the 2005-2006 applicants were accepted.

Requirements: The SAT or ACT is required for U.S. applicants; The ACT Optional Writing test is also required. Standardized test scores are not considered in the admissions decision for Ontario applicants. Applicants must have a minimum overall average of 75% on 6 Ontario Academic Course (Grade 13) credits. Higher averages may be required for admission to individual programs. U.S. applicants should rank in the upper quarter of their high school class and have a B average for admission consideration. Some programs require an interview, background information, or a portfolio. AP credits are accepted. Important factors in the admissions decision are advanced placement or honor courses, extracurricular activities record, and leadership record.

Procedure: Freshmen are admitted in the fall. There are early decision and deferred admissions plans. Early decision applications should be filed by March 1; regular applications, by April 1 for fall entry. Application fee is $115 CDN. Notification of early decision is sent April; regular decision, May. 5000 early decision candidates were accepted for the 2005-2006 class. Applications are accepted on-line.

Transfer: Applicants must meet general admissions requirements and have a B average in all college-level courses. 10 of 20 credits required for the bachelor's degree must be completed at U of G.

Visiting: There are regularly scheduled orientations for prospective students, including daily tours of the campus, Fall Preview Day, and Campus Days and Connection Conference in the spring. There are guides for informal visits and visitors may sit in on classes. To schedule a visit, contact the tour coordinator at (519) 824-4120, ext. 58712.

Financial Aid: The FAFSA, the college's own financial statement, and the Federal and Provincial Government Canadian Form are required. Check with the school for current deadlines.

International Students: There are 700 international students enrolled. The school actively recruits these students. They must achieve a satisfactory score on the TOEFL and also take the TWE and TSE. The IELTS or MELAB may be substituted for these tests. U.S. students are required to submit SAT or ACT scores, with minimum acceptable scores.

Computers: Wireless access is available. All residence rooms have high-speed network access. More than 1000 PCs are available to students, in the main library. Students can use their own laptops on a wireless system, or borrow from 100 available for use in the library. All students may access the system at any time. There are no time limits and no fees.

Admissions Contact: Ray Darling, Director of Admission Services. Web: *www.uoguelph.ca/admissions*

UNIVERSITY OF OTTAWA — E-3
Ottawa, ON, Canada K1N 6N5

(613) 562-5847
Fax: (613) 562-5100

Full-time: 9223 men, 13,108 women	**Faculty:** n/av
Part-time: 2177 men, 3095 women	**Ph.D.s:** 96%
Graduate: 1584 men, 2252 women	**Student/Faculty:** 22 to 1
Year: semesters, summer session	**Tuition:** $4600 CDN ($13,030
Application Deadline: see profile	CDN)
	Room & Board: $5360 CDN

Freshman Class: n/av

SAT: required

The University of Ottawa, founded in 1848, is a bilingual (French/English) institution offering undergraduate and graduate degrees through the faculties of Arts, Law, Health Sciences, Medicine, Science, Engineering, Management, Social Sciences, and Education. There are 9 undergraduate and 9 graduate schools. Enrollment Figures in the above capsule are for fall 2004. In addition to regional accreditation, UO has baccalaureate program accreditation with AACSB. The 8 libraries contain 1,862,999 volumes, 1,890,046 microform items, and 10,800 audio/video tapes/CDs/DVDs, and subscribe to 10,563 periodicals electronic. Computerized library services include the card catalog, interlibrary loans, database searching, Internet access, and laptop Internet portals. Special learning facilities include a learning resource center, art gallery, radio station, TV station, and Museum of Classical Antiquities. The 70-acre campus is in an urban area. Including any residence halls, there are 33 buildings.

Student Life: 80% of undergraduates are from Ontario.

Housing: 2880 students can be accommodated in college housing, which includes single-sex and coed dorms, on-campus apartments, and married-student housing. On-campus housing is available on a lottery system for upperclassmen. All students may keep cars.

Activities: There are no fraternities or sororities. There are more than 100 groups on campus, including art, band, cheerleading, chess, choir, chorale, computers, debate, drama, ethnic, gay, honors, international, jazz band, newspaper, orchestra, photography, political, professional, radio and TV, religious, social, social service, student government, and symphony. Popular campus events include University of Ottawa Day, Gee-gees football games, and Winter Challenge.

Sports: There are 5 intercollegiate sports for men and 7 for women, and 13 intramural sports for men and 11 for women. Facilities include weight-training and combat rooms, a 50-meter swimming pool, gyms, racquetball and squash courts, billiards and Ping=Pong tables, an indoor arena, and a multipurpose sports field.

Disabled Students: 75% of the campus is accessible. Wheelchair ramps, elevators, special parking, specially equipped rest rooms, special class scheduling, lowered drinking fountains, lowered telephones, special housing, automatic doors, and specialized equipment are available.

Services: Counseling and information services are available, as is tutoring in most subjects. There is a reader service for the blind, and remedial math, reading, and writing.

Campus Safety and Security: Measures include 24-hour foot and vehicle patrol, self-defense education, security escort services, and shuttle buses. There are informal discussions, pamphlets/posters/films, emergency telephones, and lighted pathways/sidewalks. The university participates in a community crime-stoppers program.

Programs of Study: UO confers B.A., B.Sc., B.Ad., B.A.Sc., B.Com., B.Ed., B.F.A., B.H.Sc., B.Mus., B.Sc.N., and B.Soc.Sc., degrees. Master's and doctoral degrees are also awarded. Bachelor's degrees are awarded in AGRICULTURE (environmental studies), BIOLOGICAL SCIENCE (biochemistry, biology/biological science, biotechnology, and life science), BUSINESS (accounting, banking and finance, electronic business, human resources, management information systems, management science, and marketing/retailing/merchandising), COMMUNICATIONS AND THE ARTS (Arabic, art history and appreciation, arts administration/management, classics, communications, English, English as a second/foreign language, French, German, Italian, journalism, Latin, linguistics, modern language, music, Spanish, and visual and performing arts), COMPUTER AND PHYSICAL SCIENCE (chemistry, computer science, geology, mathematics, physics, and software engineering), EDUCATION (education and foreign languages), ENGINEERING AND ENVIRONMENTAL DESIGN (chemical engineering, civil engineering, computer engineering, electrical/electronics engineering, environmental engineering, and mechanical engineering), HEALTH PROFESSIONS (biomedical science, health science, and nursing), SOCIAL SCIENCE (Canadian studies, criminology, economics, ethics, politics, and social policy, geography, gerontology, history, international studies, law, medieval studies, philosophy, political science/government, psychology, public administration, religion, Russian and Slavic studies, sociology, and women's studies). Law, medicine, and education are the strongest academically. Arts, social sciences, and science are the largest.

Required: Students must maintain a GPA of 3.5 out of 10 for all courses, including those in the major. Students must also complete a second language requirement: French for English students, and English for French students.

Special: Opportunities are provided for cooperative programs, study abroad in 50 countries, a general studies degree in arts and in sciences, and combined programs in all fields in arts and in social sciences.

Faculty/Classroom: 67% of faculty are male; 33%, female. All both teach and do research. The average class size in an introductory lecture is 60; in a laboratory, 30; and in a regular course, 30.

Requirements: The SAT is required, with a minimum acceptable score required. Graduation from an accredited secondary school is required. Those students planning to major in occupational or physical therapy must speak French. A portfolio is required for fine arts students and an audition for music students. AP credits are accepted.

Procedure: Freshmen are admitted fall and winter. There is a rolling admissions plan. Check with the school for current application deadlines and fee. Notification is sent on a rolling basis.

Transfer: Admissions requirements vary according to program. 60 of 90 to 120 credits required for the bachelor's degree must be completed at UO.

Visiting: There are regularly scheduled orientations for prospective students, including open houses and campus visits. There are guides for informal visits and visitors may sit in on classes. To schedule a visit, contact the Liaison Office at (613) 562-5800, ext. 1000 or liaison@uottawa.ca.

Financial Aid: Average annual earnings from campus work are $3000. Check with the school for current deadlines.

International Students: There are 1716 international students enrolled. The school actively recruits these students. They must take the TOEFL, achieving a satisfactory score, or take the MELAB, the college's own test, or the Can Test.

Computers: Wireless access is available. PCs are available in campus labs, in the wireless zone through out the campus, and in all residence rooms (all have access to the Internet). All students may access the system 24 hours a day. There are no time limits and no fees.

Admissions Contact: Andre-Pierre Lepage.
E-mail: eureka@uottawa.ca Web: www.admission.uottawa.ca

UNIVERSITY OF SASKATCHEWAN C-2
Saskatoon, SK, Canada S7N 5A2

(306) 966-5788
Fax: (306) 966-2115

Full-time: 5780 men, 7610 women
Part-time: 830 men, 1390 women
Graduate: 970 men, 790 women
Year: semesters, summer session
Application Deadline: February 15

Faculty: n/av
Ph.D.s: n/av
Student/Faculty: n/av
Tuition: $4828 CDN ($7288 CDN)
Room & Board: $3426 CDN ($5872 CDN)

Freshman Class: n/av
SAT or ACT: not required

The University of Saskatchewan, founded in 1907, is a public institution offering programs in business, agriculture, arts and sciences, education, engineering, and health professions. Enrollment figures given in above capsule are approximate. Cost figures in parentheses are for Out-of-Province students. International students pay 2.6 times this amount. There are 14 undergraduate schools and 1 graduate school. The 7 libraries contain 1,896,000 volumes, 3,068,000 microform items, and 33,764 audio/video tapes/CDs/DVDs, and subscribe to 10,311 periodicals including electronic. Computerized library services include the card catalog, interlibrary loans, database searching, Internet access, and laptop Internet portals. Special learning facilities include a learning resource center, art gallery, natural history museum, planetarium, and museum of antiquities. The 363-acre campus is in an urban area in Saskatoon. Including any residence halls, there are 55 buildings.

Student Life: The average age of all undergraduates is 21. 7% do not continue beyond their first year.

Housing: 2072 students can be accommodated in college housing, which includes single-sex and coed dorms, off-campus apartments, and married-student housing. On-campus housing is available on a first-come, first-served basis. 88% of students commute. All students may keep cars.

Activities: There are no fraternities or sororities. There are more than 100 groups and organizations on campus, including band, cheerleading, chess, choir, chorale, chorus, computers, drama, ethnic, gay, international, jazz band, newspaper, orchestra, political, professional, religious, social, social service, and student government. Popular campus events include Powwow in the Bowl, Experience US!, and Greystone Scholar Spend a Day.

Sports: There are 8 intercollegiate sports for men and 7 for women, and 17 intramural sports for men and 17 for women. Facilities include the PAC, a Physical Activity Complex that houses a 40-foot climbing wall, gym, fitness center and weight room, walk/jog track, squash and racquetball courts, dance studio, gymnastics areas and swimming pool. There also is a football stadium, hockey rink, curling rink, track and field area, and outdoor soccer field.

Disabled Students: 99% of the campus is accessible. Wheelchair ramps, elevators, special parking, specially equipped rest rooms, special class scheduling, lowered drinking fountains, and lowered telephones are availabale. There is also a coordinator of services for students with disabilities, special funding application assistance, and special exam scheduling and accommodations. Adaptive computerized equipment is located in the main library building.

Services: Counseling and information services are available, as is tutoring in most subjects.

Campus Safety and Security: Measures include 24-hour foot and vehicle patrol, self-defense education, security escort services, and pamphlets/posters/films. There are emergency telephones and lighted pathways/sidewalks.

Programs of Study: U of S confers B.A., B.Comm., B.E., B.Ed., B.F.A., B.Mus., B.Mus/Mus.Ed., B.S.A., B. Sc., B.Sc.(Nutr.), B.Sc.(P.T.),

B.S.N., and B.S.P. degrees. Master's and doctoral degrees are also awarded. Bachelor's degrees are awarded in AGRICULTURE (agronomy, animal science, horticulture, plant science, range/farm management, and soil science), BIOLOGICAL SCIENCE (anatomy, biochemistry, biology/biological science, microbiology, nutrition, and physiology), BUSINESS (accounting, business administration and management, business economics, human resources, and marketing/retailing/merchandising), COMMUNICATIONS AND THE ARTS (art, classics, English, French, German, Greek, Hebrew, Latin, linguistics, music, Russian, and Spanish), COMPUTER AND PHYSICAL SCIENCE (chemistry, computer science, geology, geophysics and seismology, mathematics, paleontology, and physics), EDUCATION (elementary, home economics, and physical), ENGINEERING AND ENVIRONMENTAL DESIGN (chemical engineering, civil engineering, electrical/electronics engineering, engineering physics, geological engineering, land use management and reclamation, and mechanical engineering), HEALTH PROFESSIONS (nursing, pharmacy, physical therapy, and veterinary science), SOCIAL SCIENCE (economics, food science, geography, history, international studies, law, Native American studies, Near Eastern studies, philosophy, political science/government, psychology, public administration, sociology, and urban studies).

Required: Requirements for graduation vary according to the program of study.

Special: The University of Saskatchewan offers interdisciplinary majors, including agricultural biology, agricultural chemistry, agricultural and bioresource engineering, agricultural extension, and anthropology and archeology. Co-op programs are offered through the Program for Agricultural Cooperative Education. There are computer science internships, as well as internships offered through the Engineering Professional Internship program. The university has exchange agreements with 41 countries.

Requirements: Applicants must be graduates of an accredited secondary school. In direct-entry programs, priority is given to Saskatchewan residents, with the exception being the College of Arts and Sciences. A grade average of 70.0 is required. AP credits are accepted.

Procedure: Freshmen are admitted in the fall. There are early decision and early admissions plans. Applications should be filed by February 15 for fall entry, along with a $75 CDN fee. Applications are accepted online.

Transfer: Applicants must meet promotion levels for the college to which transfer is sought; in most cases they should be Saskatchewan residents.

Visiting: There are regularly scheduled orientations for prospective students. To schedule a visit, contact Recruitment and Admissions *uofs_tours@usask.ca*.

International Students: The school actively recruits these students. They must take the written TOEFL or the MELAB, and also take IELTS, CanTEST, CAEL, or iBT.

Computers: Wireless access is available. Computer labs are open 7 days a week, 365 days a year. All have access to the Internet/University newtork/personal account. All students may access the system 24/7. There are no time limits and no fees.

Graduates: From July 1, 2004 to June 30, 2005, 3029 bachelor's degrees were awarded.

Admissions Contact: Chelsea Jukes, Recruitment Officer.
E-mail: *admissions@usask.ca* Web: *explore.usask.ca*

UNIVERSITY OF TORONTO

E-3

Toronto, ON, Canada M5S 1A1

(416) 978-2190
Fax: (416) 978-6089

Full-time: 21,463 men, 28,391 women	**Faculty:** 1300
Part-time: 2746 men, 3566 women	**Ph.D.s:** n/av
Graduate: 5640 men, 6834 women	**Student/Faculty:** 18 to 1
Year: terms or trimesters, summer session	**Tuition:** $4400 CDN ($14,228 CDN)
Application Deadline: see profile	**Room & Board:** $9797 CDN
Freshman Class: n/av	
SAT: required	

The University of Toronto, founded in 1827, is a public institution offering undergraduate programs in applied science and engineering, arts and science, education, dentistry, law, medicine, music, nursing, pharmacy, physical and health education, and radiation sciences. Degrees are also offered at the graduate level in a wide range of programs. There are 19 undergraduate schools and 1 graduate school. The 32 libraries contain 10,161,812 volumes, 299,721 microform items, and 1,131,557 audio/video tapes/CDs/DVDs, and subscribe to 61,256 periodicals including electronic. Computerized library services include the card catalog, interlibrary loans, database searching, Internet access, and laptop Internet portals. Special learning facilities include a learning resource center, art gallery, radio station, and observatory. The 1797-acre campus is in an urban area including 3 campuses in downtown and suburban Toronto. Including any residence halls, there are 249 buildings.

Student Life: 88% of undergraduates are from Ontario. The average age of freshmen is 18; all undergraduates, 21. 5% do not continue beyond their first year; 83% remain to graduate.

Housing: 8310 students can be accommodated in college housing, which includes single-sex and coed dorms, on-campus apartments, off-campus apartments, and married-student housing. On-campus housing is guaranteed for the freshman year only and is available on a first-come, first-served basis. Priority is given to out-of-town students. 80% of students commute. All students may keep cars.

Activities: There are no fraternities or sororities. There are 200 groups on campus, including art, band, cheerleading, chess, choir, chorus, computers, dance, debate, drama, ethnic, film, gay, international, jazz band, literary magazine, musical theater, newspaper, opera, orchestra, photography, political, radio and TV, religious, social, student government, symphony, and yearbook. Popular campus events include U of T Day, concerts, and theater productions.

Sports: There are 27 intercollegiate sports for men and 26 for women, and 29 intramural sports for men and 29 for women. Facilities include swimming pools, an outdoor hockey rink, weight and exercise rooms, gyms, squash and multipurpose courts, a rifle range, dance studios, playing fields, a stadium, an arena, and a 200-meter indoor running track.

Disabled Students: Wheelchair ramps, elevators, special parking, specially equipped rest rooms, lowered drinking fountains, and lowered telephones are available.

Services: Counseling and information services are available, as is tutoring in every subject. There is a reader service for the blind.

Campus Safety and Security: Measures include 24-hour foot and vehicle patrol, self-defense education, security escort services, and shuttle buses. There are informal discussions, pamphlets/posters/films, emergency telephones, and lighted pathways/sidewalks.

Programs of Study: U of T confers B.A., B.Sc., B.A.Sc., B.B.A., B.Com., B.Ed., B.Sc.Med.Rad.Sc., B.Sc.N., B.Sc.O.T., B.Sc.Phm., B.Sc.P.T., B.S.P.H.E., and Mus.Bac. degrees. Master's and doctoral degrees are also awarded. Bachelor's degrees are awarded in AGRICULTURE (environmental studies, forestry and related sciences, and natural resource management), BIOLOGICAL SCIENCE (biochemistry, biology/biological science, biophysics, biotechnology, botany, cell biology, ecology, evolutionary biology, life science, microbiology, molecular biology, neurosciences, nutrition, physiology, toxicology, and zoology), BUSINESS (banking and finance, business administration and management, business economics, electronic business, and human resources), COMMUNICATIONS AND THE ARTS (art history and appreciation, arts administration/management, classics, communications, communications technology, comparative literature, dramatic arts, English, film arts, French, German, Greek, Italian, journalism, Latin, linguistics, media arts, modern language, music, music history and appreciation, music theory and composition, musicology/ethnomusicology, Polish, Portuguese, Russian languages and literature, Slavic languages, Spanish, technical and business writing, and visual and performing arts), COMPUTER AND PHYSICAL SCIENCE (actuarial science, applied mathematics, applied physics, astronomy, astrophysics, chemical physics, chemistry, computer science, digital arts/technology, earth science, geology, mathematics, paleontology, physical sciences, physics, planetary and space science, statistics, and systems analysis), EDUCATION (education, education of the exceptional child, foreign languages, music, and physical), ENGINEERING AND ENVIRONMENTAL DESIGN (architecture, chemical engineering, civil engineering, computer engineering, electrical/electronics engineering, engineering and applied science, environmental science, industrial engineering, materials engineering, materials science, mechanical engineering, mining and mineral engineering, and water and wastewater technology), HEALTH PROFESSIONS (environmental health science, health, nursing, occupational therapy, pharmacology, pharmacy, physical therapy, physician's assistant, and radiological science), SOCIAL SCIENCE (African studies, American studies, anthropology, applied psychology, archeology, behavioral science, Canadian studies, Caribbean studies, Celtic studies, Christian studies, classical/ancient civilization, cognitive science, criminology, East Asian studies, economics, ethics, politics, and social policy, European studies, forensic studies, geography, German area studies, Hispanic American studies, history, history of science, human ecology, humanities, international relations, international studies, Judaic studies, medieval studies, Middle Eastern studies, Native American studies, Pacific area studies, peace studies, philosophy, political science/government, psychology, public affairs, religion, Russian and Slavic studies, Scandinavian studies, sociology, South Asian studies, urban studies, and women's studies). Arts and science, applied science, and engineering are the largest.

Required: Arts and science students must satisfy a breadth requirement, which includes 3 courses from outside the major. Students must complete 20 credits for a 4-year degree, plus prerequisite subjects.

Special: The university offers co-op programs in management, arts management, cell and molecular biology, computer science, mathematical and physical sciences, sociology, applied psychology, public policy, humanities, and international development studies. Study abroad, interdisciplinary programs, and various work-study programs are also available.

Faculty/Classroom: 69% of faculty are male; 31%, female.

Requirements: The SAT is required. In addition, the Faculties of Arts and Science, of Music, and of Physical Education and Health will consider Grade 12 applicants from an accredited U.S. high school with a high GPA and good scores on the SAT. The ACT will also be considered. Engineering will consider excellent grade 12 students with high SAT scores who also are completing at least 2 AP courses. The SAT: Subject Tests and AP courses and exams must include math, physics, and chemistry. Other requirements may apply. Architecture students must submit a questionnaire and a portfolio. Music students must audition. A GPA of 3.0 is required. AP credits are accepted.

Procedure: Freshmen are admitted in the fall. There are early decision, early admissions, and deferred admissions plans. There is a rolling admissions plan. Notification is sent on a rolling basis. Check with the school for current appication deadlines and fee.

Transfer: For the Arts and Science divisions, normally a B average is required. 5 of 20 credits required for the bachelor's degree must be completed at U of T.

Visiting: There are regularly scheduled orientations for prospective students. There are guides for informal visits. To schedule a visit, contact Student Recruitment at (416) 978-5000.

International Students: There were 3023 international students enrolled in a recent year. The school actively recruits these students. They must take the TOEFL and also take the TWE.MELAB, IELTS, or COPE scores may also be submitted.

Computers: All students may access the system. There are no time limits and no fees.

Graduates: In a recent year, 8680 bachelor's degrees were awarded. In an average class, 83% graduate in 4 years or less.

Admissions Contact: Admissions Counselor. A video is available. E-mail: *admissions.help@utoronto.ca* Web: *www.utoronto.ca*

UNIVERSITY OF VICTORIA   B-2
Victoria, BC, Canada V8W 3P2
                                                     (250) 721-8121
                                                 Fax: (250) 721-6225

Full-time: 11,000 men and women	**Faculty:** 640
Part-time: 5500 men and women	**Ph.Ds:** 93%
Graduate: 2400men and women	**Student/Faculty:** 14 to 1
Year: terms, summer session	**Tuition:** $5020 CDN ($14,890 CDN)
Application Deadline: see profile	**Room & Board:** $5000

Freshman Class: n/av
SAT or ACT: not required

The University of Victoria, founded in 1903 as Victoria College, is a public institution operated by the province of British Columbia. It offers undergraduate and graduate programs in the arts and sciences, business, education, engineering, fine arts, human and social development, and law. There are 8 undergraduate schools and 1 graduate school. Some figures in the above capsule and in this profile are approximate.The 4 libraries contain 1.6 million volumes, 1.7 million microform items, and 177,000 audio/video tapes/CDs/DVDs, and subscribe to 8000 periodicals including electronic. Computerized library services include the card catalog, interlibrary loans, and database searching. Special learning facilities include a learning resource center, art gallery, radio station, and language labs. The 385-acre campus is in an urban area in Victoria. Including any residence halls, there are 107 buildings.

Student Life: 86% of undergraduates are from British Columbia.

Housing: 1700 students can be accommodated in college housing, which includes single-sex and coed dorms, on-campus apartments, and married-student housing. On-campus housing is available on a first-come, first-served basis and is available on a lottery system for upperclassmen. Priority is given to out-of-town students. Alcohol is not permitted. All students may keep cars.

Activities: There are no fraternities or sororities. There are many groups and organizations on campus, including chess, choir, chorus, computers, dance, debate, ethnic, gay, international, jazz band, musical theater, newspaper, orchestra, photography, political, radio and TV, religious, social service, student government, symphony, and yearbook. Popular campus events include Week of Welcome and the President's BBQ.

Sports: There are 7 intercollegiate sports for men and 7 for women, and 12 intramural sports for men and 12 for women. Facilities include 3 gyms, a dance studio, 2 weight and fitness training rooms, racquetball and squash courts, playing fields, an outdoor stadium, tennis courts, 2 swimming pools, a sailing compound, and jogging trails.

Disabled Students: Wheelchair ramps, elevators, special parking, specially equipped rest rooms, lowered drinking fountains, lowered telephones, speech synthesizers, and Arkenstone reading computers are available.

Services: There is remedial reading and writing.

Campus Safety and Security: Measures include 24-hour foot and vehicle patrol, self-defense education, security escort services, and pamphlets/posters/films. There are emergency telephones and lighted pathways/sidewalks.

Programs of Study: UVic confers B.A., B.S., B.Com., B.Ed., B.Eng., B.F.A., B.Mus., B.Sc., B.S.N., B.S.W., and L.L.B. degrees. Master's and doctoral degrees are also awarded. Bachelor's degrees are awarded in BIOLOGICAL SCIENCE (biochemistry, biology/biological science, and microbiology), BUSINESS (business administration and management and recreation and leisure services), COMMUNICATIONS AND THE ARTS (art history and appreciation, classics, creative writing, dramatic arts, English, French, Germanic languages and literature, linguistics, music, and visual and performing arts), COMPUTER AND PHYSICAL SCIENCE (astronomy, chemistry, computer science, earth science, mathematics, and physics), EDUCATION (elementary, physical, and secondary), ENGINEERING AND ENVIRONMENTAL DESIGN (computer engineering, electrical/electronics engineering, and mechanical engineering), HEALTH PROFESSIONS (health science and nursing), SOCIAL SCIENCE (anthropology, child care/child and family studies, economics, geography, history, Italian studies, medieval studies, Pacific area studies, philosophy, political science/government, psychology, Russian and Slavic studies, social work, sociology, and women's studies).

Required: To graduate, students must complete the university English requirement, a minimum of 60 units above the 100 level, at least 21 of which must be upper level, and have a 2.0 GPA.

Special: A number of co-op and internship programs are available in specific disciplines as are many dual majors, including biochemistry/microbiology and Hispanic/Italian studies. Work-study is possible on a limited basis for Canadian students only.

Faculty/Classroom: 68% of faculty are male; 32%, female. All teach undergraduates and do research. No introductory courses are taught by graduate students. The average class size in an introductory lecture is 53 and in a regular course, 30.

Requirements: Application requires high school graduation with a 2.5 GPA or higher, 4 semesters of English, 2 each of social science, math, science, and language, and 6 semesters of 2.5 work at grade 12 level. AP credits are accepted.

Procedure: Freshmen are admitted to all sessions. Check with the school for current application deadlines and fee. Applications are accepted on-line.

Transfer: Requirements vary with the program and the individual. 30 of 60 credits required for the bachelor's degree must be completed at UVic.

Visiting: There are guides for informal visits and visitors may sit in on classes and stay overnight. To schedule a visit, contact Public Relations at (250) 721-7645.

Financial Aid: Check with the school for current deadlines.

International Students: The school actively recruits these students. They must take the TOEFL, achieving a satisfactory score, or take the MELAB or the I.E.L.T.S.

Computers: All students may access the system at any time. There are no time limits and no fees.

Admissions Contact: Admissions Officer. A video is available. E-mail: *srsad13@uvvm.uvic.ca* Web: *www.uvic.ca*

UNIVERSITY OF WATERLOO   E-3
Waterloo, ON, Canada N2L 3G1
                                              (519) 888-4567, ext. 3777
                                                 Fax: (519) 746-8088

Full-time: 11,469 men, 9555 women	**Faculty:** 787
Part-time: 688 men, 1323 women	**Ph.Ds:** 96%
Graduate: 1771 men, 1094 women	**Student/Faculty:** 25 to 1
Year: trimesters, summer session	**Tuition:** $4994 CDN ($16,715 CDN)
Application Deadline: March 31	**Room & Board:** $7500 CDN

Freshman Class: 23,500 applied, 19,700 accepted, 5065 enrolled
SAT or ACT: required for some programs

The University of Waterloo, founded in 1957, is a public institution that offers undergraduate and graduate programs in applied health sciences, arts, engineering, environmental studies, independent studies, math, and science. Students have a home base in 1 of 6 faculties or 4 affiliated institutions. Most programs are offered in either the traditional or the cooperative system of study. There are 10 undergraduate and 6 graduate schools. The 9 libraries contain 2,006,887 volumes, 1,707,697 microform items, and 1179 audio/video tapes/CDs/DVDs, and subscribe to 20,028 periodicals including electronic. Computerized library services include the card catalog, interlibrary loans, database searching, Internet access, and laptop Internet portals. Special learning facilities include a learning resource center, art gallery, radio station, 4 museums, 2 theaters, and an observatory. The 1000-acre campus is in a suburban area 60 miles southwest of Toronto. Including any residence halls, there are 59 buildings.

Student Life: 95% of undergraduates are from Ontario. Students are from 13 provinces.

Housing: 6100 students can be accommodated in college housing, which includes single-sex and coed dorms and on-campus apartments.

In addition, there are special-interest houses, language floors, and off-campus housing services. On-campus housing is guaranteed for the freshman year only. Priority is given to out-of-town students. All students may keep cars.

Activities: 1% of men belong to 1 national fraternity; 1% of women belong to 1 national sorority. There are many groups and organizations on campus, including band, bridge, cheerleading, chess, choir, computers, dance, debate, drama, ethnic, film, gay, honors, international, juggling, literary magazine, marching band, material arts, musical theater, newspaper, photography, political, professional, radio and TV, religious, social, social dance, social service, student government, and yearbook. Popular campus events include Oktoberfest and Canada Day.

Sports: There are 16 intercollegiate sports for men and 15 for women, and 14 intramural sports for men and 14 for women. Facilities include outdoor playing fields, an ice arena, a swimming pool, a diving tank, squash courts, weight rooms, 2 gyms, a dance studio, tennis courts, and activity areas.

Disabled Students: All of the campus is accessible. Wheelchair ramps, elevators, special parking, specially equipped rest rooms, special class scheduling, lowered drinking fountains, lowered telephones, and up-to-date technical equipment for the visually disabled and the hearing impaired are available.

Services: Counseling and information services are available, as is tutoring in most subjects. There is a reader service for the blind, and remedial math, reading, and writing.

Campus Safety and Security: Measures include 24-hour foot and vehicle patrol, self-defense education, security escort services, and shuttle buses. There are informal discussions, pamphlets/posters/films, emergency telephones, and lighted pathways/sidewalks.

Programs of Study: UW confers B.A., B.Sc., B.A.Sc., B.A.F.M., B.Arch., B.C.S., B.E.S., B.I.S., B.Math., B.S.E., and B.S.W., degrees. Master's and doctoral degrees are also awarded. Bachelor's degrees are awarded in AGRICULTURE (environmental studies), BIOLOGICAL SCIENCE (biochemistry, bioinformatics, biology/biological science, and biotechnology), BUSINESS (accounting, business administration and management, human resources, management science, operations research, and recreation and leisure services), COMMUNICATIONS AND THE ARTS (art history and appreciation, arts administration/management, classics, dramatic arts, English, English literature, film arts, fine arts, French, German, music, Russian, Spanish, speech/debate/rhetoric, and studio art), COMPUTER AND PHYSICAL SCIENCE (actuarial science, applied mathematics, chemistry, computer mathematics, computer science, digital arts/technology, earth science, information sciences and systems, mathematics, physics, science, science and management, software engineering, and statistics), EDUCATION (foreign languages, mathematics, and science), ENGINEERING AND ENVIRONMENTAL DESIGN (architecture, chemical engineering, city/community/regional planning, civil engineering, computational sciences, computer engineering, electrical/electronics engineering, engineering, environmental engineering, environmental science, geological engineering, mechanical engineering, and systems engineering), HEALTH PROFESSIONS (health, health science, optometry, preallied health, preoptometry, and respiratory therapy), SOCIAL SCIENCE (anthropology, economics, French studies, geography, history, international studies, medieval studies, philosophy, physical fitness/movement, political science/government, psychology, religion, Russian and Slavic studies, social work, sociology, and women's studies). Engineering, accounting, and math are the strongest academically. The arts program is the largest.

Required: To graduate, all students must satisfy specific program requirements, including a writing skills requirement. The total number of credits and minimum grade average vary.

Special: Cross-registration with Wilfrid Laurier University, study abroad in 27 countries, dual, student-designed, and interdisciplinary majors, a combined bachelor's-master's degree in accounting and engineering, and noncredit courses are available. Students may study under the regular or cooperative system, which allows off-campus work terms in education, professional organizations and agencies, business, industry, or government. There are concurrent education programs in conjunction with the faculties of education at Brock and Queen's Universities.

Faculty/Classroom: All both teach and do research.

Admissions: 84% of the 2005-2006 applicants were accepted.

Requirements: The SAT or ACT is required for some programs, as is the ACT Optional Writing Test. In addition, candidates from the United States must have a high school diploma with exceptionally high standing and AP exams in prerequisite subjects or first-year university standing in acceptable subjects from an accredited university. An audition, portfolio, and/or interview may be required for certain programs. A GPA of 3.0 is required. Important factors in the admissions decision are advanced placement or honor courses, extracurricular activities record, and leadership record.

Procedure: Freshmen are admitted fall, winter, and spring. Entrance exams should be taken in time to meet deadlines for completion of files. There is an early admissions plan. Applications should be filed by March 31 for fall entry, October 31 for winter entry, and March 1 for spring entry, along with a $160 CDN fee. Notification is sent June 2. Applications are accepted on-line.

Transfer: Applicants are considered on an individual basis. 10 of 20 credits required for the bachelor's degree must be completed at UW.

Visiting: There are regularly scheduled orientations for prospective students, including tours and individual and group information sessions. There are guides for informal visits and visitors may sit in on classes. To schedule a visit, contact the Visitors Reception Center at (519) 888-4567, ext. 3614 or *www.findoutmore.uwaterloo.ca/visitus.*

Financial Aid: The FAFSA is required.

International Students: There are 1525 international students enrolled. The school actively recruits these students. They must take the TOEFL and also take the TWE and the TSE. The MELAB or the IELTS may also be submitted.

Computers: All students may access the system, but some restrictions may apply in some faculties. There are no time limits and no fees.

Graduates: From July 1, 2004 to June 30, 2005, 4000 bachelor's degrees were awarded. The most popular majors were arts (32%), mathematics (21%), and engineering (18%).

Admissions Contact: Undergraduate Recruitment.
Web: *www.findoutmore.uwaterloo.ca*

UNIVERSITY OF WESTERN ONTARIO D-3
London, ON, Canada N6A 5B8
(519) 661-2100
Fax: (519) 661-3710

Full-time: 9325 men, 13,291 women	Faculty: 1249
Part-time: 1011 men, 1660 women	Ph.D.s: n/av
Graduate: 2040 men, 1979 women	Student/Faculty: 18 to 1
Year: semesters, summer session	Tuition: $13,129 CDN
Application Deadline: May 15	Room & Board: $6738 CDN
Freshman Class: 40,319 applied, 21,772 accepted, 4350 enrolled	
SAT: required	

The University of Western Ontario, chartered in 1878, is a public institution offering daytime, evening, and correspondence programs in the liberal arts and sciences, fine arts, engineering, education, health services, and business. There are 12 undergraduate and 4 graduate schools. The 7 libraries contain 3,085,319 volumes, 3,883,392 microform items, and 52,133 audio/video tapes/CDs/DVDs, and subscribe to 45,424 periodicals including electronic. Computerized library services include the card catalog, interlibrary loans, database searching, Internet access, and laptop Internet portals. Special learning facilities include a learning resource center, art gallery, radio station, TV station, wind tunnel, observatory, and Centre for Olympic Studies. The 402-acre campus is in an urban area 120 miles northwest of Detroit, Michigan. Including any residence halls, there are 72 buildings.

Student Life: 95% of undergraduates are from Ontario. Students are from 80 foreign countries. The average age of freshmen is 19; all undergraduates, 21. 8% do not continue beyond their first year; 76% remain to graduate.

Housing: 5350 students can be accommodated in college housing, which includes single-sex and coed dorms, on-campus apartments, and married-student housing. In addition, there are special-interest houses, an international floor, quiet floors, a volunteer services flloor, faculty-based floors, a leadership development floor, and a global cillage floor. On-campus housing is guaranteed for the freshman year only and is available on a lottery system for upperclassmen. Priority is given to out-of-town students. 77% of students commute. All students may keep cars.

Activities: There are no fraternities or sororities. There are 161 groups on campus, including art, cheerleading, chess, choir, computers, drama, ethnic, gay, international, jazz band, marching band, musical theater, newspaper, political, professional, radio and TV, religious, social, social service, student government, and yearbook. Popular campus events include Orientation Week.

Sports: There are 19 intercollegiate sports for men and 19 for women, and 17 intramural sports for men and 13 for women. Facilities include skating rinks, weight rooms, pools, gyms, and numerous outdoor facilities.

Disabled Students: 92% of the campus is accessible. Wheelchair ramps, elevators, special parking, specially equipped rest rooms, special class scheduling, lowered drinking fountains, lowered telephones, and special housing are available.

Services: Counseling and information services are available, as is tutoring in most subjects. There is a reader service for the blind, and remedial math, reading, and writing.

Campus Safety and Security: Measures include security escort services, emergency telephones, and lighted pathways/sidewalks.

Programs of Study: UWO confers B.A., B.Sc., B.A.C.S., B.Ed., B.E.Sc., B.F.A., B.H.Sc., B.M.O.S., B.M.Sc., B.Mus., B.Mus.A., B.Sc.H.Ec., B.S.N., and B.S.W.Hons. degrees. Master's and doctoral degrees are also awarded. Bachelor's degrees are awarded in AGRICULTURE (natural resource management and plant science), BIOLOGICAL SCIENCE (anatomy, biochemistry, bioinformatics, biology/biological science, biophysics, cell biology, ecology, genetics, microbiology, nutrition, physiology, toxicology, and zoology), BUSINESS (accounting, business administration and management, business communications, and human resources), COMMUNICATIONS AND THE ARTS (applied music, art, art history and appreciation, arts administration/management, Chinese, classical languages, classics, communications, communications technology, comparative literature, creative writing, digital communications, English, English literature, film arts, fine arts, French, German, Germanic languages and literature, Greek, Italian, Japanese, Latin, linguistics, media arts, modern language, music, music business management, music history and appreciation, music performance, music theory and composition, musicology/ethnomusicology, opera, piano/organ, public relations, radio/television technology, Russian, Spanish, strings, studio art, and visual and performing arts), COMPUTER AND PHYSICAL SCIENCE (actuarial science, applied mathematics, astronomy, astrophysics, chemistry, computer mathematics, computer programming, computer science, cybernetics, earth science, geology, geophysics and seismology, information sciences and systems, mathematics, medical physics, physics, planetary and space science, science, software engineering, and statistics), EDUCATION (elementary, middle school, museum studies, music, physical, and secondary), ENGINEERING AND ENVIRONMENTAL DESIGN (aviation administration/management, biomedical engineering, chemical engineering, civil engineering, computer engineering, computer technology, electrical/electronics engineering, engineering, engineering management, environmental engineering, environmental science, materials engineering, materials science, and mechanical engineering), HEALTH PROFESSIONS (health science, medical science, nursing, and pharmacology), SOCIAL SCIENCE (American studies, anthropology, Asian/American studies, Asian/Oriental studies, biblical studies, Canadian studies, child psychology/development, classical/ancient civilization, clinical psychology, criminology, East Asian studies, economics, family/consumer studies, food science, French studies, gender studies, geography, gerontology, history, home economics, human ecology, humanities, humanities and social science, interdisciplinary studies, international relations, Italian studies, Japanese studies, Latin American studies, law, liberal arts/general studies, Native American studies, peace studies, philosophy, philosophy and religion, physical fitness/movement, political science/government, psychology, public administration, religion, social science, social work, sociology, Spanish studies, theological studies, urban studies, Western civilization/culture, and women's studies).

Required: All students are required to take 2 essay courses and courses in the arts and humanities, science, and social science; other distribution and course requirements vary by major. A 60% overall average and 15 courses are the minimum requirements for a 3-year bachelor's degree. Many have additional requirements.

Special: There is cross-registration with Fanshawe College. Internships in engineering, computer science, physics, statistics, and acturial science, study abroad in 40 countries, dual majors, and student-designed majors are available. There are many 3-year bachelor's degree programs. Pass/fail options are possible. All departments have honors programs.

Faculty/Classroom: 73% of faculty are male; 27%, female.

Admissions: 54% of the 2005-2006 applicants were accepted.

Requirements: The SAT is required. In addition, U.S. applicants must be graduates of an accredited secondary school with 4 academic course credits in their senior year, and in the top 15% of their class in order to be eligible to apply for admission their first year. First-year admissions are limited. Admission to the music program requires an audition. A GPA of 3.0 is required. AP credits are accepted. Important factors in the admissions decision are advanced placement or honor courses, recommendations by school officials, and leadership record.

Procedure: Freshmen are admitted in the fall. There are early decision and deferred admissions plans There is a rolling admissions plan. Early decision applications should be filed by May 15; regular applications, by May 15 for fall entry. Application fee is $115 CDN. Notification of early decision is sent April ; regular decision is sent in July. Applications are accepted on-line.

Transfer: A minimum overall average of 70% is required to transfer. 5 of 15 credits required for the bachelor's degree must be completed at UWO.

Visiting: There are regularly scheduled orientations for prospective students, including academic counseling appointments and campus tours. Visitors may sit in on classes. To schedule a visit, contact Undergraduate Recruitment, Office of the Registrar at (519) 661-2150 or welcome.uwo.ca.

Financial Aid: UWO is a member of CSS.

International Students: The school actively recruits these students. They must take the TOEFL, the MELAB, or the IELTS.

Computers: See http://wireless.uwo.caital/coverage.html and www.uwo.caital/its/genlabs/locations.html. All students may access the system. There are no time limits and no fees.

Graduates: From July 1, 2004 to June 30, 2005, 6206 bachelor's degrees were awarded. 1000 companies recruited on campus in 2004-2005.

Admissions Contact: Lori Gribbon, Manager, Admissions and Liaison. E-mail: reg-admissions@uwo.ca Web: http://www.uwo.ca

UNIVERSITY OF WINDSOR   E-2

Windsor, ON, Canada N9B 3P4   (519) 973-7014, ext. 3315
864-2860 (in Canada); Fax: (519) 971-3653

Full-time: 4400 men, 5200 women	**Faculty:** 500
Part-time: 1300 men, 1900 women	**Ph.D.s:** 90%
Graduate: 510 men, 410 women	**Student/Faculty:** 19 to 1
Year: trimesters, summer session	**Tuition:** $4900 CDN ($11,400
Application Deadline: see profile	CDN)
	Room & Board: $6100

Freshman Class: n/av
SAT or ACT: required

The University of Windsor, founded in 1857, is a public liberal arts institution offering undergraduate and graduate programs through 8 faculties and 6 schools. There is 1 graduate school. Figures given in the above capsule and in this profile are approximate. The 2 libraries contain 1,600,000 volumes, 160,000 microform items, and 2000 audio/video tapes/CDs/DVDs, and subscribe to 15,000 periodicals including electronic. Computerized library services include the card catalog, interlibrary loans, and database searching. Special learning facilities include a learning resource center, art gallery, natural history museum, radio station, TV station, a videoconferencing center, a computing services theater, the Chrysler Canada/University of Windsor Research Center, and the Great Lakes Institute. The 200-acre campus is in an urban area 2 kilometers from downtown Windsor and 3 kilometers from downtown Detroit, Michigan. Including any residence halls, there are 50 buildings.

Student Life: 90% of undergraduates are from Canada. Students are from 41 foreign countries. 95% are from public schools. The average age of freshmen is 19; all undergraduates, 22. 10% do not continue beyond their first year.

Housing: 1800 students can be accommodated in college housing, which includes coed dorms, on-campus apartments, and married-student housing. On-campus housing is guaranteed for the freshman year only and is available on a lottery system for upperclassmen. 80% of students commute. All students may keep cars.

Activities: 2% of men belong to 4 national fraternities; 1% of women belong to 1 national sorority. There are 75 groups on campus, including cheerleading, chess, choir, chorale, drama, ethnic, gay, honors, international, jazz band, literary magazine, musical theater, newspaper, orchestra, political, professional, radio and TV, religious, social, and student government. Popular campus events include Campus Week in September.

Sports: There are 7 intercollegiate sports for men and 5 for women, and 11 intramural sports for men and 9 for women. Facilities include a 6-lane 200-meter track, a multiuse gym, a field house, a stadium, an indoor pool, weight rooms, and a sports therapy clinic.

Disabled Students: 90% of the campus is accessible. Wheelchair ramps, elevators, special parking, specially equipped rest rooms, special class scheduling, lowered drinking fountains, lowered telephones, and specially equipped residence rooms are available.

Services: Counseling and information services are available, as is tutoring in some subjects, including math and physical sciences. There is a reader service for the blind, remedial math, reading, and writing, exam accommodations, special needs counselors, and recreation buddies for assistance at the athletic complex.

Campus Safety and Security: Measures include 24-hour foot and vehicle patrol, self-defense education, security escort services, and informal discussions. There are pamphlets/posters/films, emergency telephones, and lighted pathways/sidewalks.

Programs of Study: U of W confers B.A., B.Sc., B.A.Sc., B.Comm., B.C.S., B.Ed., B.F.A., B.H.K., B.Mus., B.Mus.Th., B.P.A., B.Sc.N., B.S.W., and L.L.B. degrees. Master's and doctoral degrees are also awarded. Bachelor's degrees are awarded in BIOLOGICAL SCIENCE (biochemistry and biology/biological science), BUSINESS (business administration and management), COMMUNICATIONS AND THE ARTS (art history and appreciation, classics, communications, comparative literature, creative writing, dramatic arts, English, French, languages, modern language, music, musical theater, and visual and performing arts), COMPUTER AND PHYSICAL SCIENCE (chemistry, computer science, geology, mathematics, physics, science, and statistics), EDUCATION (drama, education, and science), ENGINEERING AND ENVIRONMENTAL DESIGN (civil engineering, electrical/electronics engineering, engineering, environmental engineering, industrial engineering, land use management and reclamation, and mechanical engineering), HEALTH PROFESSIONS (music therapy and nursing), SOCIAL SCIENCE (anthropology, Asian/Oriental studies, Canadian studies, criminology, crosscultural studies, economics, family/consumer studies, geography, history, international relations, law, philosophy, physical fitness/movement, political science/government, psychology, public administration, religion, social work, sociology, urban studies, and women's studies). Social science, engineering, and education are the largest.

Required: To graduate, students must complete a total of 90 credit hours, including 30 in the major, with a C average. Honors students must complete 120 hours, including 60 in the major, with a B average. All students must fulfill the requirements of the core curriculum.

Special: The college offers a variety of co-op programs and internships. Cross-registration may be arranged with the University of Detroit Mercy, Wayne State University, the University of Central Florida, and the University of Darby (England). Students may study abroad in the United States, France, Japan, and England.

Faculty/Classroom: 78% of faculty are male; 22%, female. All both teach and do research. The average class size in an introductory lecture is 100; in a laboratory, 25; and in a regular course, 50.

Requirements: The SAT or ACT is required for U.S. students. AP credits are accepted.

Procedure: Freshmen are admitted to all sessions. Entrance exams should be taken as early as possible. There are early decision and early admissions plans. There is a rolling admissions plan. Check with the school for current application deadlines and fee. Notification is sent on a rolling basis. A waiting list is an active part of the admissions procedure.

Transfer: Applicants must present an official transcript and be in good academic standing.

Visiting: There are regularly scheduled orientations for prospective students, including a tour, counseling, and classes. There are guides for informal visits and visitors may sit in on classes. To schedule a visit, contact the Liaison Office.

International Students: They must take the TOEFL, achieving a satisfactory score, or take the MELAB.

Computers: All students may access the system. There are no time limits. The fee is minimal.

Admissions Contact: Assistant Registrar, Liaison and Applicant Services. E-mail: *liaison@uwindsor.ca* Web: *www.uwindsor.ca*

YORK UNIVERSITY   E-3
Toronto (North York), ON, Canada M3J 1P3

(416) 736-5825
Fax: (416) 650-8195

Full-time: 13,300 men, 21,700 women	**Faculty:** 1357
Part-time: 2800 men, 4200 women	**Ph.D.s:** 98%
Graduate: 2300 men, 2500 women	**Student/Faculty:** n/av
Year: semesters, summer session	**Tuition:** $4987 CDN($15,520 CDN)
Application Deadline: February 1	**Room & Board:** $5119 CDN
Freshman Class: n/av	
SAT or ACT: required	

York University, founded in 1959, is a public institution offering programs in computer science, design, education, environmental studies, fine arts, business, social science, law, engineering, health, humanities, human resources, pure and applied sciences, and social work. Enrollment figures in the above capsule are approximate. There are 10 undergraduate and 43 graduate schools. The 5 libraries contain 2.5 million volumes, 3,963,000 microform items, and 54,184 audio/video tapes/CDs/DVDs, and subscribe to 24,576 periodicals including electronic. Computerized library services include the card catalog, interlibrary loans, database searching, Internet access, and laptop Internet portals. Special learning facilities include a learning resource center, art gallery, radio station, TV station, observatory, language labs, writing center, geographical information systems lab, computer science labs, science-related labs, and fine arts studios and labs (editing studios). The 635-acre campus is in an urban area. The university has 2 campuses, totaling 635 acres, in northwest and midtown Toronto. Including any residence halls, there are 96 buildings.

Student Life: 91% of undergraduates are from Ontario. Others are from 159 foreign countries. The average age of freshmen is 18; all undergraduates, 22. 97% of freshmen remain to graduate.

Housing: 4000 students can be accommodated in college housing, which includes single-sex and coed dorms, on-campus apartments, and married-student housing. In addition, there are language houses, special-interest houses, and co-op housing. On-campus housing is available on a first-come, first-served basis and is available on a lottery system for upperclassmen. Priority is given to out-of-town students. 93% of students commute. All students may keep cars.

Activities: There are no fraternities or sororities. There are 249 groups on campus, including art, band, cheerleading, chess, choir, computers, dance, debate, drama, ethnic, film, gay, international, jazz band, literary magazine, musical theater, newspaper, orchestra, photography, political, professional, radio and TV, religious, social, social service, student government, and yearbook. Popular campus events include The Blue Bowl (football), Orientation Week, and Multicultural Week.

Sports: There are 11 intercollegiate sports for men and 12 for women, and 17 intramural sports for men and 17 for women. Facilities include a stadium, a 6-rink ice arena, 5-sport playing fields, 4 softball diamonds, a cricket pitch, an indoor and outdoor track and field center, and 26 indoor and outdoor tennis courts. There is a fitness center with 29 cardio

machines and free weights, a 25-meter swimming pool, 4 gyms, 7 squash courts, 3 dance/aerobic studios, a spinning studio, and a sports therapy clinic. There is a combative room, 3 teaching labs, and an outdoor events facility.

Disabled Students: 65% of the campus is accessible. Wheelchair ramps, elevators, special parking, specially equipped rest rooms, special class scheduling, lowered drinking fountains, and lowered telephones, are available. The Office for Persons with Disabilities offers a variety of additional services.

Services: Counseling and information services are available, as is tutoring in most subjects. There is a reader service for the blind, a writing support center, and a multimedia language center. The Counseling and Development Center offers a variety of services and workshops.

Campus Safety and Security: Measures include 24-hour foot and vehicle patrol, self-defense education, security escort services, and shuttle buses. There are informal discussions, pamphlets/posters/films, emergency telephones, and lighted pathways/sidewalks. There is also a bicycle patrol team monitoring the campuses.

Programs of Study: York confers B.A., B.Sc., B.A.S., B.B.A., B.Des., B.Ed., B.E.S., B.F.A., B.H.R.M., B.H.S., B.Sc.N., B.S.W., I.B.B.A., and L.L.B. degrees. Master's and doctoral degrees are also awarded. Bachelor's degrees are awarded in AGRICULTURE (conservation and regulation and environmental studies), BIOLOGICAL SCIENCE (biochemistry, biology/biological science, biotechnology, and ecology), BUSINESS (accounting, banking and finance, business administration and management, business economics, business statistics, entrepreneurial studies, human resources, international business management, international economics, labor studies, management science, marketing and distribution, and organizational behavior), COMMUNICATIONS AND THE ARTS (art history and appreciation, classics, communications, creative writing, dance, design, dramatic arts, English, film arts, fine arts, French, German, Greek, Italian, linguistics, music, photography, Russian, Spanish, video, and visual and performing arts), COMPUTER AND PHYSICAL SCIENCE (applied mathematics, astronomy, atmospheric sciences and meteorology, chemistry, computer science, earth science, information sciences and systems, mathematics, physics, science, science technology, and statistics), EDUCATION (education, education of the deaf and hearing impaired, elementary, middle school, and secondary), ENGINEERING AND ENVIRONMENTAL DESIGN (computer engineering, engineering, environmental science, and industrial administration/management), HEALTH PROFESSIONS (community health work, environmental health science, exercise science, health, health care administration, health science, nursing, and rehabilitation therapy), SOCIAL SCIENCE (African studies, anthropology, Canadian studies, Caribbean studies, cognitive science, criminal justice, criminology, East Asian studies, economics, European studies, French studies, geography, German area studies, gerontology, Hispanic American studies, history, humanities, international studies, Judaic studies, Latin American studies, law, liberal arts/general studies, peace studies, philosophy, physical fitness/movement, political science/government, psychology, public administration, religion, Russian and Slavic studies, science and society, social science, social work, sociology, South Asian studies, Third World studies, urban studies, and women's studies). Business, science, and some fine arts and liberal arts programs are the strongest academically. Psychology, administrative studies, and sociology are the largest.

Required: Students must maintain at least a C average in 90 credits to receive an ordinary degree and a C+ in 120 credits to receive an honors degree. Requirements for graduation vary according to the program.

Special: Co-op programs and cross-registration with Seneca, Centennial, Sheridan, and Humber Colleges, internships, study abroad in more than 100 countries, and work-study are available. York offers dual, student-designed, multi-, and interdisciplinary majors, including atmospheric chemistry, physics and astronomy, science, technology, culture, and society, social and political thought, space and communication sciences, and translation. Independent study and nondegree study are also possible. There is a freshman honors program.

Faculty/Classroom: 59% of faculty are male; 41%, female. All both teach and do research. No introductory courses are taught by graduate students. The average class size in an introductory lecture is 72 and in a laboratory, 25.

Requirements: The SAT or ACT is required. In addition, U.S. applicants must present evidence of superior academic achievement. Secondary school record, SAT or ACT scores, and teacher or counselor recommendation will be taken into consideration. Applicants to a fine arts program are required to successfully pass an audition or evaluation, and business administration applicants are required to submit a supplementary application. Admission averages and course prerequisites vary by faculty. York requires applicants to be in the upper 25% of their class. A GPA of 3.0 is required. AP credits are accepted.

Procedure: Freshmen are admitted to all sessions. Entrance exams should be taken in the fall of the senior year. There is an early admissions plan and a rolling admissions plan. Applications should be filed by February 1 for fall entry, November 1 for winter entry, and March 1 for spring entry, along with a fee of $60 CDN. Notification is sent on a rolling basis. Applications are accepted on-line.

Transfer: 954 transfer students enrolled in 2004-2005. Requirements vary depending on the program. Postsecondary transcripts are required.

Visiting: There are regularly scheduled orientations for prospective students, consisting of a general information session and campus tour and 1 week of orientation prior to the start of classes. There are guides for informal visits and visitors may sit in on classes and stay overnight. To schedule a visit, contact the International Admissions Office at (416) 736-5000 or *www.yorku.ca/futurestudents/events*.

Financial Aid: The FAFSA is required. Check with the school for current deadlines.

International Students: There are 2708 international students enrolled. The school actively recruits these students. They must take the TOEFL, achieving a satisfactory score, or take the MELAB, the Compre-hensive English Language Test, the college's own test, the York English Language Test (YELT), or the IELTS. They must also take the SAT or the ACT achieving a minimum score (24on the ACT).

Computers: Wireless access is available. All students may access the system 24 hours per day. There are no time limits and no fees.

Graduates: In a recent year, 6803 bachelor's degrees were awarded. The most popular majors were psychology (12%), computer science and information technology (9%), and administration (7%). 152 companies recruited on campus in 2004-2005. Of the 2004 graduating class, 94% were employed within 6 months of graduation.

Admissions Contact: Office of International Admissions.
E-mail: *vgrafi@yorku.ca* Web: *http://www.yorku.ca/futurestudents*

STUDY ABROAD

Study abroad programs are now available in more than 60 countries in fields that range from Costa Rican tropical biology to Finnish architecture. Program directors have responded to the vocational interests of the student of the 21st century by organizing programs in international management, health care administration, and other career-oriented fields.

In fact, study in both traditional and nontraditional fields is enriched by overseas experience. An international perspective can benefit study of environmental sciences, anthropology, political science, urban planning, oceanography, hotel administration, psychology, social work, journalism, marketing and law, as well as film, art history, theater, music and dance.

The vast majority of U.S. students enter European schools through organized, ongoing programs sponsored and managed by the colleges and universities in which they are already enrolled. In this way, they automatically earn U.S. academic credit from their home institution for their overseas course work. Academic credit *directly* earned at a foreign institution is often not acceptable toward a U.S. degree. Applying directly to a foreign school is not difficult but unusual.

There are colleges and universities located in foreign nations that are organized on the U.S. system and accredited by U.S. accrediting agencies, e.g. American University of Paris. A list of accredited U.S. institutions overseas is provided in the annual *Accredited Institutions of Postsecondary Education*, published for the Commission on Recognition of Postsecondary Accreditation by the American Council on Education, and is available from Praeger Publishers, Greenwood Publishing Group, Inc., 88 Post Road West, Westport, CT 00881, (800) 225-5800 or (203) 236-3571; *www.greenwood.com*.

According to the Institute of International Education, in their *Open Doors 2005 Report on International Educational Exchange*, based on a recent academic year, 61% of U.S. students who study abroad for credit do so in Western Europe. The four leading destinations—the United Kingdom, Italy, Spain, and France—hosted nearly 88,000 or 46 percent of U.S. students who study abroad. Of those U.S. students who study abroad, nearly 66 percent are women. The largest proportion of U.S. students abroad major in the social sciences (23 percent), and other traditional study abroad majors such as humanities (13 percent) and foreign languages (8 percent), but more varied majors are also study abroad. Business and management majors are the second largest proportion of U.S. students abroad (18 percent).

The report also indicated that during a recent academic year, 565,039 international students were studying in the United States. Their largest fields of study were business and management (18 percent) and engineering (17 percent).

A Productive Experience

If you are interested in study abroad, plan ahead by taking the following steps to ensure that the experience is productive:

- **Assess the ways in which study abroad will benefit your educational and career plans.** Study abroad can be a casual choice or a pleasant way to spend a semester but you will derive the greatest benefit if you bring more thought to it: How will the overseas experience complement your other courses or your educational major? Can you maximize its value by seeking language as well as academic study or by combining independent study or an internship with traditional course work?
- **Consult your campus study-abroad adviser.** Most colleges and universities have a person or an office charged with the responsibility of counseling students on overseas study. The study-abroad adviser is best qualified to help you make the right choices.
- **Make sure your college will accept credit earned at the study-abroad program you have chosen.** Speak with both your academic adviser and your study-abroad adviser and resolve any issues before you leave. Many students have assumed incorrectly that credit is granted automatically for another institution's program. You cannot take this for granted.

- **Be realistic about your foreign language proficiency.** It is one thing to be able to order a meal or buy a train ticket in a foreign language. It is quite another to follow a professor lecturing on a complex subject. If you discover that your linguistic ability is inadequate, it is quite possible that you can find abroad the subject matter you want taught in English. You will get more out of the overseas experience however, if you make the effort to function in the language of the chosen country.
- **Look carefully at costs.** If you are dealing with a program sponsor that is not your home institution, it is wise to read program literature carefully. Ask questions before you go if you have any qualms! Are charges clearly specified? Does the literature specify what services *are* covered and more important, what services are *not* covered? What is the refund policy, if any? Is there a clearly identified organization with an official base in the United States which would be legally responsible in the event of disaster?

   While drawing up your budget, think about the extras. You will want to make the small side trips to new places that help to make overseas living rewarding. Try to give yourself some financial flexibility in working out your budget.
- **Think about what it means to live abroad.** Be sure to arrange for substitutes for the support systems you take for granted at home. Will your medical insurance cover you? Do you need vaccinations or a doctor who can manage your specific health problems while you are living abroad? What about visas?

   It is critically important to find out about housing before you leave. Student housing is difficult to find almost everywhere. Be sure to find out whether securing housing abroad is your responsibility and what the alternatives are in the country in which you plan to live.
- **Don't assume that you can work abroad.** Because of foreign labor laws, students should not plan to seek paid employment. The practice of working one's way through college is not common abroad, nor are the relatively high-paying part-time jobs that make it possible in the United States. However, increasing numbers of students are looking to combine practical work experience with study abroad. There are many work exchanges, volunteer opportunities, and internships available. Contact the Council on International Exchange, 7 Custom House Street, 3rd Floor, Portland, ME 04101, (207) 553-7600, Fax: (207) 553-7699 for further information.
- **Find out what you can about the sponsoring agency, especially if it is not an accredited U.S. college or university.** Talk to your study-abroad adviser if you have any doubts. Most private agencies engaged in study abroad are legitimate organizations but their basic purposes may not match yours. Does the organization have experience in placing students in an academic environment, not just in arranging travel? Are descriptions of its study program specific or vague? Does it make unverifiable claims about the academic reputation of its programs, or their recognition by U.S. higher educational institutions?

For further information, consult:
Institute of International Education
809 United Nations Plaza
New York, NY 10017
(212) 883-8200   Fax: (212) 984-5358
(For further information, consult the following IIE publications: *IIE Passport: Academic Year Abroad*, (annual), *IIE Passport: Short-Term Study Abroad* (annual), *Financial Resources for International Study 1996*. See the IIE web site *www.iiebooks.org* for more information.

Council on International Educational Exchange
7 Custom House Street, 3rd Floor
Portland, ME 04101
(207) 553-7600   Fax: (207) 553-7699

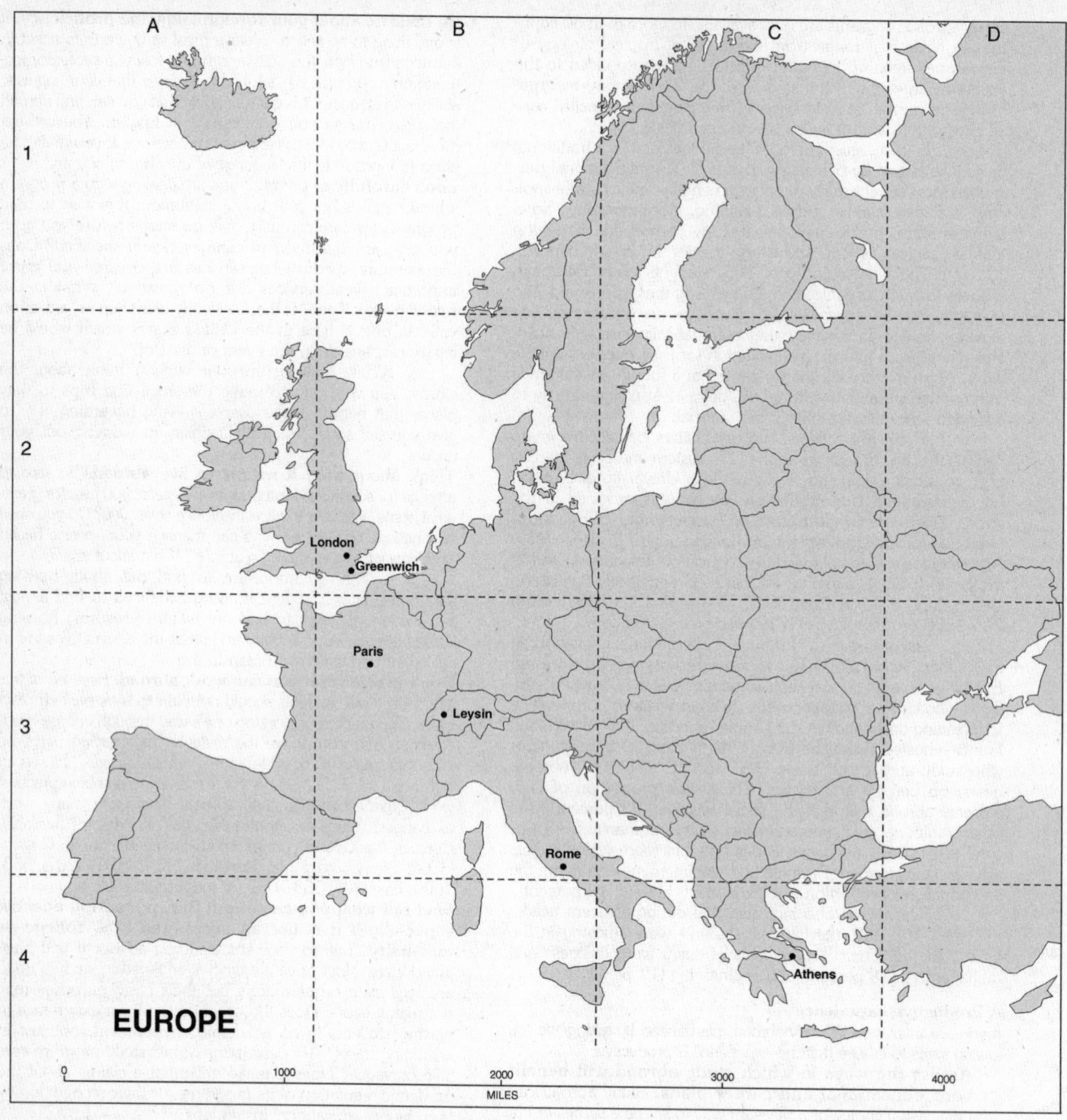

EUROPE

AMERICAN COLLEGE OF GREECE
Athens, Greece   +30210 600-9800, ext. 1254; Fax: +30210 600-9811   C-4

Full-time: 912 men, 1186 women	**Faculty:** 78
Part-time: 829 men, 946 women	**Ph.D.s:** 51%
Graduate: none	**Student/Faculty:** 27 to 1
Year: semesters, summer session	**Tuition:** $5990
Application Deadline: July 25	**Room & Board:** n/app
Freshman Class: n/av	
SAT or ACT: not required	

Deree College is the undergraduate division of the American College of Greece, which was founded in 1875 as the American School for Girls. ACG has 5 divisions and 2 campuses in Athens. Deree offers bachelor's degrees in 15 areas of the liberal arts and business. The 3 libraries contain 117,400 volumes, 4000 microform items, and 1332 audio/video tapes/CDs/DVDs, and subscribe to 950 periodicals including electronic. Computerized library services include the card catalog, interlibrary loans, database searching, Internet access, and laptop Internet portals. Special learning facilities include a museum of the history of the college and writing centers. The 60-acre campus is in a suburban area 6 miles northeast of Athens. There are 7 buildings.

Student Life: 90% of undergraduates are from Greece. Students are from 51 foreign countries and Canada. 52% are from public schools. The average age of freshmen is 21; all undergraduates, 24. 5% do not continue beyond their first year; 88% remain to graduate.

Housing: There are no residence halls. All of students commute. No one may keep cars.

Activities: There are no fraternities or sororities. There are 44 groups on campus, including chess, choir, coin/stamp, computers, dance, debate, drama, drill team, environmental, ethnic, film, international, newspaper, orchestra, photography, radio, social service, sociology, student government, and yearbook. Popular campus health events include career forum, film previews, and May Fest.

Sports: There are 4 intercollegiate sports for men and 3 for women, and 9 intramural sports for men and 7 for women. Facilities include a gym, a fitness center, 2 dance studios, aerobic rooms, 4 outdoor tennis courts, a 50-meter swimming pool, a 400-meter track, and a soccer field.

Disabled Students: 90% of the campus is accessible. Wheelchair ramps, elevators, special parking, specially equipped rest rooms, and special class scheduling are available.

Services: There is remedial writing.

Campus Safety and Security: Measures include 24-hour foot and vehicle patrol, security escort services, shuttle buses, and pamphlets/posters/films. There are lighted pathways/sidewalks.

Programs of Study: Deree College confers B.A. and B.S. degrees. Associate and master's degrees are also awarded. Bachelor's degrees are awarded in BUSINESS (accounting, business administration and management, management information systems, and marketing/retailing/merchandising), COMMUNICATIONS AND THE ARTS (art history and appreciation, English, and music), SOCIAL SCIENCE (economics, history, philosophy, psychology, and sociology). English, psychology, and marketing are the strongest academically. Marketing, management, and accounting and finance are the largest.

Required: All students must maintain a minimum CI (cumulative index) of 2.0 and complete 128 semester hours, including 47 hours in general education, at least 30 in the major, and the last 30 in residence. Distribution requirements vary with the major but include composition, literature, public speaking, humanities, ethics, history, computer, music, and political science.

Special: Study abroad, work-study programs, and dual degrees are offered. Nondegree study and pass/fail options are available.

Faculty/Classroom: 47% of faculty are male; 53%, female. All teach undergraduates. The average class size in an introductory lecture is 40; in a laboratory, 20; and in a regular course, 23.

Requirements: Applicants must be graduates of an accredited secondary school. The GED is accepted. English speakers are required to pass an English language proficiency test. A GPA of 2.0 is required. AP and CLEP credits are accepted. Important factors in the admissions decision are recommendations by school officials, recommendations by alumni, and personality/intangible qualities.

Procedure: Freshmen are admitted to all sessions. There is a deferred admissions plan and a rolling admissions plan. Applications should be filed by July 25 for fall entry, December 15 for winter entry, January 25 for spring entry, and June 1 for summer entry. Notification is sent on a rolling basis.

Transfer: 554 transfer students enrolled in 2004-2005. Applicants must have a minimum GPA of 2.0 and submit high school transcripts, an official catalog, and a diploma. English proficiency also must be demonstrated, if students are not native speakers of English. All credits required for the bachelor's degree must be completed at Deree College.

Visiting: There are regularly scheduled orientations for prospective students, consisting of information sessions and campus tours. There are guides for informal visits and visitors may sit in on classes. To schedule a visit, contact the Admissions Vistor Center at 0030-210 600-9800 ext.1254 or *visitorcenter@acgmail.gr*.

Financial Aid: In a recent year, 5% of all full-time freshmen received some form of financial aid. 2% of full-time freshmen received need-based aid. The average freshman award was $1872. 3% of undergraduates work part time. Average annual earnings from campus work are $769. Deree College is a member of CSS. The college's own financial statement and an Internal Revenue statement are required. The deadline for filing freshman financial aid applications for fall entry is September 1.

International Students: There are 434 international students enrolled. They must take the TOEFL or the MELAB, and also take the Comprehensive English Language Test, the college's own test GCE "O" levels, or Cambridge Proficiency.

Computers: All students may access the system 8 A.M. to 10 P.M. daily. There are no time limits. The fee is $50. It is strongly recommended that all students have a personal computer.

Graduates: From July 1, 2004 to June 30, 2005, 1163 bachelor's degrees were awarded. The most popular majors were marketing (22%), management (20%), and accounting and finance (16%). In an average class, 1% graduate in 3 years or less, 17% graduate in 4 years, 48% graduate in 5 years, and 17% graduate in 6 years. 150 companies recruited on campus in 2004-2005. Of the 2004 graduating class, 75% were enrolled in graduate school within 6 months of graduation and 85% were employed.

Admissions Contact: Kastalia Samoili, Director Office of Admissions. A video is available. E-mail: *visitorcenter@acgmail.gr*

AMERICAN UNIVERSITY IN CAIRO

Cairo, Egypt — (212) 730-8800; Fax: (212) 730-1600

Full-time: 1885 men, 2004 women	Faculty: 310
Part-time: 195 men, 217 women	Ph.D.s: 95%
Graduate: 480 men, 587 women	Student/Faculty: 10 to 1
Year: semesters, summer session	Tuition: $13,618
Application Deadline: June 1	Room & Board: $2900
Freshman Class: 2058 applied, 1265 accepted, 888 enrolled	
SAT Verbal/Math: 440/550*	

The American University in Cairo, founded in 1919, is a private liberal arts institution offering accredited American undergraduate and graduate programs in Egypt. There are 3 undergraduate and 3 graduate schools. In addition to regional accreditation, AUC has baccalaureate program accreditation with ABET and CSAB. The 4 libraries contain 359,811 volumes, 163,563 microform items, and 1428 audio/video tapes/CDs/DVDs, and subscribe to 1732 periodicals including electronic. Computerized library services include the card catalog, interlibrary loans, database searching, Internet access, and laptop Internet portals. Special learning facilities include a learning resource center, art gallery, radio station, and a theater. The 26-acre campus is in an urban area in central Cairo. Including any residence halls, there are 12 buildings.

Student Life: 91% of undergraduates are from in state. Others are from 91 foreign countries and Canada. The average age of freshmen is 18; all undergraduates, 20. 88% of freshmen remain to graduate.

Housing: 435 students can be accommodated in college housing, which includes single-sex dormitories and off-campus apartments. On-campus housing is available on a first-come, first-served basis. 95% of students commute. Alcohol is not permitted. No one may keep cars.

Activities: There are no fraternities or sororities. There are 25 groups on campus, including art, chess, choir, chorus, dance, drama, ethnic, international, literary magazine, musical theater, newspaper, photography, professional, radio and TV, social, social service, student government, and yearbook. Popular campus events include International Day, National University Cultural Activities Competition, and Model United Nations.

Sports: There are 17 intercollegiate sports for men and 13 for women, and 10 intramural sports for men and 8 for women. Facilities include tennis courts, multipurpose courts, an exercise gym, a weight room, and a 400-seat stadium. There are also private clubs in the area and other provisions for horseback riding, rowing, swimming and scuba diving, track and field, water polo, squash, and soccer.

Disabled Students: Wheelchair ramps, elevators, and specially equipped rest rooms are available.

Services: There is remedial reading and writing.

Campus Safety and Security: Measures include 24-hour foot and vehicle patrol, shuttle buses, lighted pathways/sidewalks, and security personnel at all open entrances 24 hours a day.

Programs of Study: AUC confers B.A. and B.S. degrees. Master's degrees are also awarded. Bachelor's degrees are awarded in BIOLOGICAL SCIENCE (biology/biological science), BUSINESS (accounting and business administration and management), COMMUNICATIONS AND THE ARTS (Arabic, art, communications, comparative literature, dramatic arts, English, and journalism), COMPUTER AND PHYSICAL SCIENCE (chemistry, computer science, mathematics, and physics), ENGINEERING AND ENVIRONMENTAL DESIGN (construction engineering, electrical/electronics engineering, and mechanical engineering), SOCIAL SCIENCE (anthropology, archeology, economics, history, Islamic studies, Middle Eastern studies, philosophy, political science/government, psychology, and sociology). Journalism and mass communications, business admiistration, and mechanical engineering are the largest.

Required: All students must maintain a C average and must complete from 120 to 162 semester credits, depending on the major. Core courses include a writing program, an interdisciplinary seminar in humanities, natural science, social science, a scientific-thinking course, and Arab literature, history, and society.

Special: Study abroad through a consortium of U.S. schools, work-study programs with the university, and nondegree study are available.

Faculty/Classroom: 52% of faculty are male; 48%, female. No introductory courses are taught by graduate students. The average class size in an introductory lecture is 39; in a laboratory, 13; and in a regular course, 40.

Admissions: 61% of the 2005-2006 applicants were accepted. The SAT scores for the 2005-2006 freshman class were: Verbal--74% below 500, 18% between 500 and 599, 7% between 600 and 700, and 1% above 700; Math--20% below 500, 51% between 500 and 599, 24% between 600 and 700, and 5% above 700.

Requirements: The SAT or ACT is required of U.S. applicants, who must also be graduates of an accredited secondary school and submit complete transcripts and a copy of their diploma. The ACT Optional Writing test is also required. Others must submit the Egyptian Thanawiya Amma certificate or other national high school certificate recognized by the university as equivalent to it, or the GCE, GCSE, or IGCSE. A minimum high school GPA of 2.0 is required. Students should have taken courses in 3 of the following subjects: languages and humanities, math, social studies, and biological and physical sciences. AP credits are accepted. Important factors in the admissions decision are ability to finance college education, evidence of special talent, and extracurricular activities record.

Procedure: Freshmen are admitted fall and spring. There is a rolling admissions plan. Entrance exams should be taken in July for fall admission. Early decision applications should be filed by April 1; regular applications, by June 1 for fall entry and November 1 for spring entry. Notification is sent on a rolling basis. Applications are accepted on-line. The fall 2005 application fee was $50.

Transfer: 12 transfer students enrolled in 2004-2005. Transfer students must have a C average on secondary school and college transcripts. 45 of 120 credits required for the bachelor's degree must be completed at AUC.

Visiting: There are guides for informal visits and visitors may sit in on classes and stay overnight. To schedule a visit, contact the General Director of Admission in Egypt at 20-2 797-5551.

Financial Aid: In 2005-2006, 65% of all full-time students received some form of financial aid. 40% of full-time freshmen and 45% of continuing full-time students received need-based aid. The average freshman award was $4280. Need-based scholarships or need-based grants averaged $2200; non-need-based athletic scholarships averaged $100; and other non-need-based awards and non-need-based scholarships averaged $1000. 5% of undergraduates work part time. The college's own financial statement is required. The deadline for filing freshman financial aid applications for fall entry is September 15.

International Students: There are 351 international students enrolled. The school actively recruits these students. They must score satisfactorily on the written TOEFL.

Computers: There are no time limits and no fees.

Graduates: From July 1, 2004 to June 30, 2005, 889 bachelor's degrees were awarded. The most popular majors were business administration (17%), journalism and mass communication (16%), and political science (13%). In an average class, 5% graduate in 3 years or less, 21% graduate in 4 years or less, 71% graduate in 5 years or less, and 85% graduate in 6 years or less. 424 companies recruited on campus in 2004-2005.

Admissions Contact: American University in Cairo's, New York Office. E-mail: *aucegypt@aucnyo.edu* Web: *http://www.aucegypt.edu*

AMERICAN UNIVERSITY OF PARIS — B-3

Paris, France 75007	(212) 983-1414; Fax: (212) 983-0444
Total Enrollment: 900 men and women	**Faculty:** n/av
	Ph.D.s: 67%
Year: semesters, summer session	**Student/Faculty:** n/av
Application Deadline: see profile	**Tuition:** $20,940 euros
	Room & Board: n/app
Freshman Class: n/av	
SAT: required	**ACT:** recommended

The American University of Paris, founded in 1962, is a private, institution providing a liberal arts program in an international context. It has regional U.S. accreditation and is recognized by the French government as an institute of higher learning. Classes are in English except for foreign language and literature courses. Figures in the above capsule and in this profile are approximate. The library contains 65,000 volumes and 1000 microform items. Computerized library services include the card catalog, interlibrary loans, and database searching. Special learning facilities include a learning resource center. The campus is in an urban area in Paris. There are 6 buildings.

Programs of Study: AUP confers B.A. and B.S. degrees. Bachelor's degrees are awarded in BUSINESS (international business management and international economics), COMMUNICATIONS AND THE ARTS (art history and appreciation and comparative literature), COMPUTER AND PHYSICAL SCIENCE (computer science), ENGINEERING AND ENVIRONMENTAL DESIGN (engineering), SOCIAL SCIENCE (economics, European studies, French studies, history, and international relations). Art history, international affairs, and international economics are the strongest academically. International business administration, international affairs, and international communications are the largest.

Required: Students must maintain a minimum GPA of 2.0 while taking at least 120 semester credits, including an average of 50 in the major. Distribution requirements include 16 semester hours of French, 8 of lab science or math, and 6 each if English composition, humanities, and social sciences.

Special: There are co-op programs with Tulane, Northeastern, and Boston Universities, Monmouth, Mills, New England, Notre Dame, and St. Mary's (CA) Colleges, Universite de Paris-Sorbonne, and Kansai Gaidai in Japan. Cross-registration is available in foreign language programs at 3 other French colleges. Juniors and seniors with good academic standing are encouraged to undertake internships. Study abroad, second

degrees, nondegree study, and pass/fail options also are offered. There are 4 national honor societies and 3 departmental honors programs.

Faculty/Classroom: 52% of faculty are male; 48%, female. The average class size in an introductory lecture is 18; in a laboratory, 12; and in a regular course, 16.

Requirements: The SAT is required, and the ACT is recommended. In addition, candidates must be graduates of an accredited secondary school. An essay and 2 letters of recommendation are also needed. Knowledge of French is not required. A GPA of 2.8 is required. AP and CLEP credits are accepted. Important factors in the admissions decision are advanced placement or honor courses, personality/intangible qualities, and recommendations by school officials.

Procedure: Freshmen are admitted fall and spring. Entrance exams should be taken by April 1. There is a deferred admissions plan. There is a rolling admissions plan. Check with the school for current application deadlines and fee. Notification is sent on a rolling basis.

Transfer: Transfer applicants must submit college and high school transcripts, and SAT or ACT scores if they have fewer than 45 credits. An interview, 2 letters of recommendation, and an essay are required. 30 of 120 credits required for the bachelor's degree must be completed at AUP.

Visiting: There are guides for informal visits and visitors may sit in on classes. To schedule a visit, contact the Admissions Office.

Financial Aid: AUP is a member of CSS. The FAFSA is required. Check with the school for current deadlines.

International Students: The school actively recruits these students. They must take the TOEFL, achieving a satisfactory score, or take the MELAB, and the college's own test and the SAT or the ACT.

Computers: All students may access the system. There are no time limits and no fees. It is strongly recommended that all students have a personal computer.

Admissions Contact: Admissions Office. E-mail: *usoffice@aup.edu or admissions@aup.edu (Paris)* Web: www.aup.fr

AMERICAN UNIVERSITY OF ROME — B-3

Rome, Italy 00153	011 39 6 58330919; Fax: 011 396 58330992
Full-time and part-time: 515 men and women	**Faculty:** n/av
	Ph.D.s: 67%
Graduate: none	**Student/Faculty:** n/av
Year: semesters, summer session	**Tuition:** $13,600
Application Deadline: May 15	**Room & Board:** $8500
Freshman Class: n/av	
SAT or ACT: required	

American University of Rome, founded in 1969, is a private institution offering programs in liberal arts, international business, international relations, Italian studies, and communications. The library contains 5000 volumes and 30 audio/video tapes/CDs/DVDs, and subscribes to 15 periodicals including electronic. Computerized library services include the card catalog, interlibrary loans, and database searching. The campus is in a suburban area on the Janiculum Hill 2 miles from downtown. Including any residence halls, there are 2 buildings.

Student Life: 65% of undergraduates are from Italy. Students are from 25 foreign countries and Canada. 20% are from public schools. 83% are white. The average age of freshmen is 18; all undergraduates, 20. 20% do not continue beyond their first year; 26% remain to graduate.

Housing: 160 students can be accommodated in college housing, which includes single-sex off-campus apartments. On-campus housing is available on a first-come, first-served basis. 55% of students commute. Alcohol is not permitted. No one may keep cars.

Activities: There are no fraternities or sororities. There are some groups and organizations on campus, including art, drama, film, honors, international, literary magazine, newspaper, and student government. Popular campus events include the Distinguished Lecture Series, liberal arts and business excursions, and international relations debates.

Sports: There is 1 intercollegiate sport for men. There are 3 intramural sports for men and 3 for women. Facilities include off-campus access to soccer, tennis, and swimming facilities.

Disabled Students: 30% of the campus is accessible.

Services: There is remedial writing.

Campus Safety and Security: Measures include informal discussions.

Programs of Study: AUR confers B.A. and B.S. degrees. Associate degrees are also awarded. Bachelor's degrees are awarded in BUSINESS (business administration and management), COMMUNICATIONS AND THE ARTS (communications), SOCIAL SCIENCE (international relations, international studies, and Italian studies). Business administration and international relations are the largest.

Required: To graduate, students must complete 120 credits, including 45 to 66 in the major, with a minimum GPA of 2.0. Distribution requirements include English composition and courses in humanities, social sciences, and science/math.

Special: Internships in business, international relations, communications, and Italian studies are available. Study abroad is possible by special arrangement, and work-study is available with AUR. Cross-registration with the College of Staten Island in New York is possible. There is 1 national honor society.

Faculty/Classroom: 58% of faculty are male; 42%, female. All teach undergraduates. The average class size in an introductory lecture is 18 and in a regular course, 13.

Requirements: The SAT or ACT is required. In addition, a high school diploma and transcript or the non-American equivalent is required, as are a letter of recommendation and an essay. The GED is accepted. A GPA of 2.5 is required. AP and CLEP credits are accepted. Important factors in the admissions decision are recommendations by school officials, advanced placement or honor courses, and personality/intangible qualities.

Procedure: Freshmen are admitted to all sessions. There is a deferred admissions plan. Applications should be filed by May 15 for fall entry, October 10 for spring entry, and March 30 for summer entry, along with a $60 fee.

Transfer: Applicants must submit a high school transcript, a diploma, all transcripts of universities attended, a letter of recommendation, and an essay. 45 of 120 credits required for the bachelor's degree must be completed at AUR.

Visiting: There are regularly scheduled orientations for prospective students, which AUR organizes directly and through its agents in many U.S. states and in other countries. Orientation is assisted by use of audiovisual materials. There are guides for informal visits and visitors may sit in on classes. To schedule a visit, contact the Director of Admissions.

Financial Aid: 1% of undergraduates work part time. The FAFSA is required. Check with the school for current application deadlines.

International Students: The school actively recruits these students. A satisfactory score is required on the written TOEFL, the MELAB, or the college's own test.

Computers: All students may access the system 8:30 A.M. to 8:30 P.M. Monday through Friday; 10 A.M. to 6 P.M. Saturday. Students may access the system 12 hours per day Monday through Friday and 8 hours Saturday. There are no fees. It is strongly recommended that all students have a PC.

Admissions Contact: Mara Nisdeo, Dean of Administration. A video is available. E-mail: *admissions@aur.edu* Web: *www.aur.edu*

FRANKLIN COLLEGE SWITZERLAND   B-3

Sorengo, Switzerland 6924

(718) 335-6800, (011-41-91-985-2260)
Fax: (718) 335-6733, (011-41-91-994-4117)

Full-time: 110 men, 160 women	**Faculty:** 17
Part-time: 1 woman	**Ph.D.s:** 82%
Graduate: none	**Student/Faculty:** 16 to 1
Year: semesters, summer session	**Tuition:** $26,620
Application Deadline: March 15	**Room & Board:** $8580
Freshman Class: n/av	
SAT: required	

Franklin College Switzerland, founded in 1969, is a private institution providing a liberal education through courses that are international in perspective and cross-cultural in content. The baccalaureate degree offers concentrations in international management, art history, modern languages (French, Italian, German), international relations, history/literature, and visual and communiction arts. Some figures in the above capsule and in this profile are approximate. The library contains 33,500 volumes, 15 microform items, and 1620 audio/video tapes/CDs/DVDs, and subscribes to 174 periodicals including electronic. Computerized library services include the card catalog, interlibrary loans, and database searching. Special learning facilities include a radio station. The 4-acre campus is in a suburban area on a hillside above Lugano in the southern region of Switzerland called the Ticino. Including any residence halls, there are 8 buildings.

Student Life: Students are from 23 states, 62 foreign countries, and Canada. The average age of freshmen is 18; all undergraduates, 19. 48% do not continue beyond their first year.

Housing: Housing includes single-sex dorms, on-campus apartments, and off-campus apartments. 76% of students live on campus; of those, 60% remain on campus on weekends. All students may keep cars.

Activities: There are no fraternities or sororities. There are some groups and organizations on campus, including art, drama, international, literary magazine, newspaper, photography, social, student government, and yearbook.

Sports: There are 3 intramural sports for men and 2 for women.

Services: Counseling and information services are available, as is tutoring in most subjects.

Campus Safety and Security: Measures include emergency telephones and lighted pathways/sidewalks.

Programs of Study: Franklin College Switzerland confers the B.A. degree. Associate degrees are also awarded. Bachelor's degrees are awarded in BUSINESS (international business management and international

economics), COMMUNICATIONS AND THE ARTS (art history and appreciation, literature, media arts, and modern language), SOCIAL SCIENCE (European studies, history, and international relations). International management/international relations is the strongest academically.

Required: All students must complete 126 credit hours. A general core requirement of 48 credit hours includes 12 credit hours in foreign languages, 9 in humanities, 6 in math/science and history, and 3 in English. Academic travel is required each year (each travel program is 1 academic credit). A minimum GPA of 2.0 overall and 42 credits or more in the major, with a C or better, are also required. Some majors require a thesis.

Special: Cross-registration with most U.S. colleges having an international management major, internships, study abroad as part of the academic travel requirement, accelerated degree programs in any major, and dual majors are offered.

Faculty/Classroom: 61% of faculty are male; 39%, female. All teach undergraduates. The average class size in an introductory lecture is 13; in a laboratory, 10; and in a regular course, 10.

Requirements: The SAT is required. In addition, the college recommends that applicants have completed 4 years of English, 3 years each of history and a foreign language, and 2 years each of science and math. Electives in art, music, and computers are recommended. An essay, a personal statement, and academic references are required. An interview is strongly encouraged. A GPA of 2.0 is required. AP credits are accepted. Important factors in the admissions decision are leadership record, personality/intangible qualities, and extracurricular activities record.

Procedure: Freshmen are admitted to all sessions. Entrance exams should be taken in the fall prior to the desired entrance. There are early decision, early admissions, and deferred admissions plans. There is a rolling admissions plan. Early decision applications should be filed by December 1; regular applications, by March 15 for fall entry, October 1 for spring entry, and May 1 for summer entry, along with a $50 fee. Notification of early decision is sent December 15; regular decision, on a rolling basis.

Transfer: Applicants must have a C average and provide 1 recommendation. 60 of 126 credits required for the bachelor's degree must be completed at Franklin College Switzerland.

Visiting: There are guides for informal visits and visitors may sit in on classes. To schedule a visit, contact the New York Admissions Office.

Financial Aid: Franklin College Switzerland is a member of CSS. The FAFSA and the college's own financial statement are required. Check with the school for current deadlines.

International Students: The school actively recruits these students. They must achieve a satisfactory score on the TOEFL and also take the SAT or the ACT.

Computers: All students may access the system. There are no time limits and no fees. It is strongly recommended that all students have a personal computer.

Admissions Contact: U.S. Admissions Office. E-mail: *info@fc.edu* Web: *www.fc.edu*

JOHN CABOT UNIVERSITY   B-3

Rome, Italy 00165   011-39-06-681-9121; Fax: 011-39-06-5897429

Full-time: 280 men, 360 women	**Faculty:** 20
Part-time: 22 men, 18 women	**Ph.D.s:** 80%
Graduate: none	**Student/Faculty:** 32 to 1
Year: semesters, summer session	**Tuition:** ($14,500)
Application Deadline: July 15	**Room & Board:** n/app
Freshman Class: n/av	
SAT or ACT: recommended	

John Cabot University, founded in 1972, is an independent institution of liberal arts and sciences offering an American university education in Rome. Besides degree seeking students, the university accepts study-abroad or visiting students from a number of U.S. colleges and universities. In addition to regional accreditation, JCU has baccalaureate program accreditation with U.K. validation of Business Administration, Political Science, and International Affairs. The library contains 21,000 volumes and 1000 audio/video tapes/CDs/DVDs, and subscribes to 40 periodicals including electronic. Computerized library services include the card catalog, database searching, Internet access, and laptop Internet portals. Special learning facilities include a center for public affairs and communications, and art studios for painting, drawing, and photography. The campus is in an urban area in Trastevere, the historic center of Rome. Including any residence halls, there are 2 buildings.

Student Life: Students are from 47 states, 60 foreign countries, and Canada. The average age of freshmen is 18; all undergraduates, 22. 13% do not continue beyond their first year; 87% remain to graduate.

Housing: 400 students can be accommodated in college housing, which includes single-sex off-campus apartments. In addition, there are special-interest houses. No one may keep cars.

Activities: There are many groups and organizations on campus, including art, chess, debate, drama, film, international, jazz band, musical theater, newspaper, opera, photography, political, social, social service, student government, and yearbook. Popular campus events include, trips to Florence, Capri, and Venice, 2 musical theater productions per year, and Presidental Lecture Series.

Sports: There are 8 intramural sports for men and 10 for women. Facilities include leased sports facilities provided by the athletics department.

Disabled Students: Specially equipped rest rooms are available.

Services: There is remedial math and writing.

Campus Safety and Security: Measures include security escort services, informal discussions, emergency telephones, and guards on duty Monday through Friday 8:30 A.M. to 9:30 P.M.

Programs of Study: JCU confers B.A. and B.B.A. degrees. Associate degrees are also awarded. Bachelor's degrees are awarded in BUSINESS (business administration and management), COMMUNICATIONS AND THE ARTS (art history and appreciation and English literature), SOCIAL SCIENCE (economics, humanities, international studies, Italian studies, and political science/government). Business administration and international affairs are the largest.

Required: To graduate, students must complete 120 semester hours with a GPA of 2.0, including required courses in writing, math, and foreign language.

Special: Internships are available with multinational and Italian businesses, governmental organizations, and embassies. There is study abroad in the United States, Europe, and Australia, and a work-study program.

Faculty/Classroom: 60% of faculty are male; 40%, female. All teach undergraduates and 40% do research. The average class size in an introductory lecture is 40 and in a regular course, 25.

Admissions: 66% of the 2005-2006 applicants were accepted.

Requirements: The SAT or ACT is recommended. The ACT Optional Writing Test is also recommended. SAT or ACT tests are required of U.S. high school graduates and are recommended for students graduating from other educational systems. Also required are a personal essay and 2 letters of academic recommendation. An interview is recommended; the GED diploma may be recognized for admission. A GPA of 2.75 is required. AP and CLEP credits are accepted. Important factors in the admissions decision are advanced placement or honor courses, recommendations by school officials, and extracurricular activities record.

Procedure: Freshmen are admitted to all sessions. Entrance exams should be taken at the orientation session. There are early decision, early admissions, and deferred admissions plans. There is a rolling admissions plan. Applications should be filed by July 15 for fall entry and November 15 for spring entry, along with a $50 fee. Notification is sent on a rolling basis. 20 early decision candidates were accepted for the 2005-2006 class. Applications are accepted on-line.

Transfer: 80 transfer students enrolled in 2004-2005. Transfer applicants must be in good academic standing at the previous institution. 60 of 120 credits required for the bachelor's degree must be completed at JCU.

Visiting: There are regularly scheduled orientations for prospective students, consisting of sessions set up a week before every term for incoming students, parents, or family. Orientation includes academic and extra-academic events to assist students in adjusting to a new city and in many cases to a new academic system. There are guides for informal visits and visitors may sit in on classes. To schedule a visit, contact Admissions Office at +39-06-6819121 or admissions@johncabot.edu.

Financial Aid: In 2005-2006, 18% of all full-time freshmen and 12% of continuing full-time students received some form of financial aid, including need-based aid. The average freshman award was $5000. 10% of undergraduates work part time. The FAFSA and the college's own financial statement are required.

International Students: There are 300 international students enrolled. The school actively recruits these students. They must take the TOEFL and also take the college's own test and the SAT or the ACT.

Computers: Wireless access is available. All students may access the system. There are no time limits and no fees.

Graduates: In a recent year, 59 bachelor's degrees were awarded. The most popular majors were business administration (50%), international affairs (25%), and art history (10%). 32 companies recruited on campus in a recent year.

Admissions Contact: Ricarda Van De Sandt, Assistant Director. A video is available. E-mail: admissions@johncabot.edu Web: http://www.johncabot.edu

RICHMOND, THE AMERICAN INTERNATIONAL UNIVERSITY IN LONDON   B-2

Richmond, Surrey, UK TW10 6JP   +44 (0) 20 8332 9000
                                         Fax: +44 (0) 20 8832 1596

Full-time: 550 men, 550 women	**Faculty:** 50
Part-time: 5 men, 50 women	**Ph.D.s:** 72%
Graduate: 50 men, 50 women	**Student/Faculty:** 22 to 1
Year: semesters, summer session	**Tuition:** $21,020
Application Deadline: March 1	**Room & Board:** $10,970
Freshman Class: n/av	
SAT or ACT: required	

Richmond College, The American University in London, established in 1972, is an independent, international, liberal arts and professional studies university. It occupies the campus of the original Richmond College, founded in 1843 and part of the University of London, and is incorporated as a not-for-profit educational institution in the state of Delaware. Some figures in the above capsule and in this profile are approximate. There are 2 graduate schools. The 2 libraries contain 60,000 volumes, and subscribe to 300 periodicals including electronic. Computerized library services include database searching. Special learning facilities include a learning resource center. The 5-acre campus is in a suburban area 8 miles southwest of London. There are 3 buildings.

Programs of Study: Richmond confers B.A. and B.S. degrees. Associate and master's degrees are also awarded. Bachelor's degrees are awarded in BUSINESS (business administration and management and international business management), COMMUNICATIONS AND THE ARTS (art history and appreciation, communications, literature, performing arts, and studio art), COMPUTER AND PHYSICAL SCIENCE (computer programming and mathematics), ENGINEERING AND ENVIRONMENTAL DESIGN (environmental science and systems engineering), SOCIAL SCIENCE (anthropology, economics, history, international relations, political science/government, psychology, and sociology). Business and economics are the largest.

Required: Students must complete 12 courses in 7 fields: English, humanities, social science, intercultural studies, math, science, and the creative arts. Proficiency in English composition, math, and computer skills is required. A 2.0 GPA and 120 credit hours are needed to graduate.

Special: The International Internship Program utilizes London-based businesses and institutions. Study abroad is offered at the university's study centers in Florence, Italy, and Shizuoka, Japan. A field study project in a developing country may be arranged during the summer. A limited number of students can be placed in family helper/au pair positions with British families. Joint degrees are offered in engineering with George Washington University. There is a freshman honors program.

Faculty/Classroom: 65% of faculty are male; 35%, female. 97% teach undergraduates. The average class size in an introductory lecture is 22; in a laboratory, 12; and in a regular course, 17.

Requirements: The SAT or ACT is required, for American students. U.S. applicants should have completed secondary school with a 2.5 GPA. A GED equivalent is acceptable. An autobiographical essay is an important part of the application. AP and CLEP credits are accepted. Important factors in the admissions decision are advanced placement or honor courses, geographic diversity, and recommendations by school officials.

Procedure: Freshmen are admitted to all sessions. There is a deferred admissions plan. There is a rolling admissions plan. Applications should be filed by March 1 for fall entry and November 1 for spring entry, along with a $50 fee.

Transfer: A 2.0 GPA, official transcripts from all previous institutions, and 2 references are required for admission. 45 of 120 credits required for the bachelor's degree must be completed at Richmond.

Visiting: There are regularly scheduled orientations for prospective students. There are guides for informal visits and visitors may sit in on classes and stay overnight. To schedule a visit, contact an admissions counselor in the U.K.

Financial Aid: The FAFSA and the college's own financial statement are required. Check with the school for current deadlines.

International Students: The school actively recruits these students. .

Computers: All students may access the system daily from 8:30 A.M. to 10 P.M. There are no time limits and no fees.

Admissions Contact: Director of Undergraduate Admissions. E-mail: enroll@richmond.ac.uk Web: www.richmond.ac.uk

More and more American colleges and universities are welcoming students from foreign countries. Did you know that there are nearly 600,000 international students enrolled in U.S. institutions of higher learning, and that number continues to increase?

Why Colleges and Universities Seek International Students

There are several reasons why American colleges and universities seek international students. First, they recognize that international students help educate the American students on campus by introducing them to different ideas and cultures. Second, the number of college-age American students is declining, and international students can fill places that otherwise would go unfilled. Third, the money that international students spend on tuition and other expenses helps the U.S. economy; education is a valuable export for the United States. And fourth, education has long been an important part of America's foreign aid program, providing foreign nationals with skills that they can use to improve life in their homelands.

Why International Students Seek to Study in the United States

There are also a number of reasons why international students seek to study in the United States. For some students, colleges and universities in the United States offer opportunities to study major fields that are not available in their own countries. For other students, American colleges and universities offer an alternative to colleges and universities in their own countries where places may not be available for all of the qualified students who wish to attend. For still other students, study in the United States provides them not only with an education but also with experiences in living in another culture and in exchanging ideas with students from many nations.

Whatever *your* reason may be for studying in the United States, this book will help you make decisions and plans.

Investigating a College or University

Although most of the colleges and universities in the United States are very honest about their programs and services, a few have been known to misrepresent themselves. When choosing a college or university, as when making any other major purchase, you should investigate carefully. In addition to checking whether your exact major field is offered, you should compare the special services for international students offered by the schools that you are considering. You will want to know whether a representative of the school will pick you up at the airport when you arrive, whether dormitories or other housing is available, and whether there is a foreign student adviser to help you with decisions that you will have to make and problems that you may have to solve after you arrive.

The Difference Between a College and a University

Most international students want to know the difference between a college and a university. This is a difficult question because there is more than one correct answer. In fact, there are three definitions for the word *college* (as it refers to a college in the United States) listed in the *American Heritage Dictionary of the English Language*.

According to the dictionary, a *college* is (1) a school of higher learning that grants a bachelor's degree (undergraduate degree) in arts or sciences or both; (2) an undergraduate division of a university that offers courses and grants undergraduate degrees in a particular field of study; or (3) a technical or professional school, often affiliated with a university, that grants a bachelor's or master's degree in that field.

A *university* is a school of higher learning that grants a bachelor's degree (undergraduate degree), master's degree, and doctorate (Ph.D.) through various colleges within the university.

The Comparison of a College and a University

Many international students ask whether a university is better than a college. The answer is that a university has advantages and disadvantages for an international student, and a college has advantages and disadvantages.

The advantages of a university are that there are usually more research and recreational facilities, and more different kinds of courses offered. The disadvantages of a university are that courses taught to first-year students are often taught by teaching assistants who are graduate students themselves, and that the classes can be very large. The advantages of a college are that the courses are almost always taught by professors, and that the classes are usually small. The disadvantages of a college are that there are usually fewer research and recreational facilities.

Remember, as you decide what is best for you, that there are excellent colleges and there are excellent universities.

Accreditation

Unlike most countries, the United States does not have a national ministry of education that approves the programs at colleges and universities throughout the country. Instead, programs are approved by professional organizations and regional associations. This approval is called accreditation.

All of the schools listed in this book are accredited or are in the process of being accredited.

Requirements for Admission
Academic Preparation

To study in the United States, an international student should begin preparing in secondary school. A good secondary school report is one of the most important requirements for admission to a college or university. When applying to a college or university, you must submit an English translation of your grades with a seal and signature on it. This grade report is called a transcript. In addition, most colleges and universities require undergraduate students to submit standardized test scores. Some of the most common tests are the ACT (American College Test), the SAT (Scholastic Aptitude Test), and the SAT Subject Tests. Each test is described below.

ACT Achievement Test	A test of general academic preparation
SAT Reasoning Test	An aptitude test for college
SAT Subject Tests	Skill tests in academic subjects

The ACT is a national college admission examination that measures your general educational development in English, mathematics, reading, and science, as well as your writing ability in a thirty-minute essay. The SAT is a test that measures your general skills in critical reading, mathematics, and writing. In addition, the SAT Subject Tests measure your knowledge in key academic areas such as languages, social sciences, natural sciences, and mathematics. Some highly selective schools require applicants to take several SAT Subject Tests in addition to the SAT Reasoning Test. Both the SAT and the ACT are administered by Educational Testing Service for the College Board. For more information, visit *www.ets.org* or *www.collegeboard.com*.

The following books are available from Barron's Educational Series, Inc., 250 Wireless Boulevard, Hauppauge, New York 11788, USA, to help you prepare for the ACT and the SAT:

Barron's ACT
Pass Key to the ACT
Barron's SAT 2400
Barron's New SAT
Pass Key to the SAT
Math Workbook for the New SAT
Critical Reading Workbook for the SAT
Writing Workbook for the New SAT
Hot Words for the SAT

1648 STUDY IN THE UNITED STATES

Barron's also has a series of study guides for the SAT Subject Tests in the following areas: Biology, Physics, Chemistry, Math, U.S. History, World History, Literature, French, and Spanish.

Barron's books are available worldwide at major bookstores or directly from the publisher at *www.barronseduc.com*. Click on Test Preparation for further information.

English Language Proficiency

In addition, if your native language is not English, you will probably have to take a test of your ability to use English. The most widely used of these tests is the TOEFL (Test of English as a Foreign Language), given at official test centers throughout the world. Three TOEFL® formats are being used in different parts of the world while the new TOEFL® iBT is being phased in: The new Internet-Based TOEFL (iBT), the Computer-Based TOEFL (CBT), and the Supplemental Paper-Based TOEFL (PBT). The Michigan English Language Assessment Battery (MELAB) is sometimes accepted as proof of English language proficiency also. These tests are described as follows:

TOEFL® iBT	An Internet-based test. The newest TOEFL format, being phased in throughout the world. A test of listening, speaking, reading, and writing.
Supplemental PBT	A pencil and paper alternative to the iBT available in remote locations or by special arrangement with the test administrator. A test of listening, structure, and reading, with a separate essay. A speaking part is being developed for the PBT.
TOEFL CBT	A computer-based test that is being replaced by the iBT. In some areas this test is still used while the iBT is being phased in throughout the world.
MELAB	The Michigan English Language Assessment Battery, which is sometimes accepted as evidence of English language proficiency instead of the TOEFL. A test of listening, writing, and multiple-choice items in grammar, vocabulary, and reading.

You can take the TOEFL at an official test center. To register, visit *www.ets.org* or register by mail or fax, using the form in the *TOEFL Bulletin of Information*, which can be downloaded from the web site or obtained in print at one of the regional registration sites or counseling centers around the world. For more information about the test, visit *www.ets.org/toefl*. For information about preparing for the test, visit *www.teflprep.com*.

To download a bulletin or to register for the MELAB, visit the official web site at *www.lsa.umich.edu/eli/melab.hlm* or write to the MELAB Office at the following address: English Language Institute, TCF Building, University of Michigan, 401 E. Liberty, Suite 350, Ann Arbor, MI 48104-2298.

Barron's TOEFL books are available worldwide at major bookstores or directly from the publisher at *www.barronseduc. com*. Click on Test Preparation, and then click on TOEFL.

Barron's How to Prepare for the TOEFL® iBT, 12th Edition
Barron's Practice Exercises for the TOEFL, 5th Edition
Barron's Pass Key to the TOEFL, 6th Edition
Barron's How to Prepare for the TOEFL Essay, 3rd Edition
Barron's How to Prepare for the Michigan Test Battery

Financial Guarantees

All schools require that international students show proof of their ability to pay tuition, fees, and living expenses. Most schools require a statement from a bank that shows adequate finances for one year's study. If the name on the account is not the same as the name of the student, a signed letter from the person who has the account must accompany the bank statement. In the letter this person promises to support the international student while the student is in the United States. This person is called the student's sponsor.

Application Procedures

Select a few schools and write for information

When you are ready to apply—usually about a year before the date on which you hope to enter college—write to the schools that interest you for application materials. You should include the field you wish to study, a brief outline of your previous education, the number of years you have studied English, the amount of money you can spend, and the proposed date of enrollment. The college admissions officers will review this information and should let you know if the college cannot meet your needs. You should also ask the schools for information about special programs and organizations for international students.

Remember, this book provides general information about the requirements for admission to colleges and universities, but each school has the authority to set its own standards for admission. For the specific requirements for admission, you must write directly to the schools that most interest you. Some schools will be glad to send you a catalog free of charge; most schools will charge you a fee for the catalog.

Libraries of college catalogs also can be found at the offices of the Institute of International Education, a private, non-profit, international educational exchange agency administered in 13 international locations. To find an office near you, visit *www.iie.org*. Counseling centers, generally located at U.S. embassies and the offices of binational and Fulbright commissions also have collections of college catalogs. The Department of State supports a network of advising centers around the world. To find a center near you, visit *www.educationusa. state.gov/centers.htm*. Another web site that offers limited free access to college catalogs is *www.collegesource.org*. After a search for three catalogs and a time limit of ten days, a subscription is required to continue looking through their database.

Apply to more than one school

Remember, most American students apply to more than one college or university, and you should, too, especially if you are interested in competitive schools with very high admissions standards. By using this book and by reviewing catalogs from the schools that interest you, you can select several colleges and universities to which you can apply. Because the application fees are almost always nonrefundable, you should truly be serious about the schools where you make application.

Be sure that you have selected some schools where you are likely to be accepted. If you were an average student in high school and your standardized test scores are average, you have little chance of being accepted by a highly competitive school. Evaluate yourself realistically.

Remember, too, that the rating of colleges and universities in this book is based upon information about American students only. Although it is usually accurate for international students as well, some large state universities that are listed as noncompetitive have open admission for state residents. This means that anyone with a high school diploma who is a resident of that state may attend the state school. These schools, listed as noncompetitive, may actually be very competitive for students from other states and for international students. Nevertheless, the rating scale will be useful to you, especially for schools that are not large state universities.

Be sure that you submit all of the documents that the schools require along with application fees. The most common reason for delays in admission to American colleges and universities is because international students do not send everything that is required along with their application forms.

When you are ready to apply to the schools of your choice, consider the following points:

1. Be sure that the schools offer your major field of study.
2. Be sure that the schools are accredited.
3. Be sure that you apply to more than one school.
4. Be sure that you apply to schools where you meet the requirements for admission.

5. Be sure that you submit all of the documents and fees with your application to avoid delays.

Make a Decision

Some international students choose a school in the United States because their friends are going there. It is nice to have friends on campus, but the right school for your friend may not be the right school for you. There is no list of the best schools in the United States. A school may be the best in one major field and only average in another major field. It may have famous professors who only do research and do not teach. It may be well known but not academically excellent.

Consider the following points in making a decision where you will go to school.

1. Be sure that the school offers your major field of study or a premajor for your major field of study.
2. Be sure that the school is accredited.
3. Be sure that the school offers an English program if you need one.
4. Be sure that you understand how much credit you will receive if you are transferring from another school.
5. Be sure that the school has a foreign-student adviser or someone assigned to help international students.
6. Be sure that the expenses for the school are within your budget.

Going to the United States

You should start investigating requirements for visas from the United States and from your home country (if applicable) as soon as you decide to study overseas. You cannot apply for an American visa, however, until you have been accepted by a school in the United States. You must apply for the visa at a U.S. embassy or consulate. You probably will need the following items.

1. A passport (except for Canadians) from your own country.
2. A passport-sized photograph.
3. A Form I-20 (Certificate of Eligibility for Non-Immigrant Student Status) from the school that has accepted you.
4. A notarized bank statement or other proof that you have enough money available and/or financial aid promised to cover your expenses for the entire term of your program. (If you have been accepted to a bachelor's degree program, for instance, the term is four years.)
5. Evidence that you are in good health, including a recent chest X-ray and, in some countries, proof that you have been vaccinated against smallpox within the past three years.
6. A supplemental visa application, and a fee for the Student and Exchange Visitor Information Service, or other security information.

Most students are admitted to the United States under an F-1 (foreign student) visa. Those who come under certain grant or scholarship programs may qualify for a J-1 (exchange visitor) visa. After you have qualified for your visa, any spouse and children of yours may be admitted under F-2 or J-2 visas. You must provide evidence that there is enough money to support them while you are studying.

You may want to consider participating in predeparture orientation programs offered by education services abroad and by the U.S. Information Service. Information about these programs is available from the agency or from any U.S. embassy or consulate.

Many schools send representatives to meet students at local airports and bus and train stations, if they have correct arrival information. If your school offers this service, take advantage of it. Send your travel plans to the foreign-student adviser on your campus.

Arriving on Campus

As soon as you arrive on campus, you should visit the foreign-student adviser, an official who is responsible for the welfare of students from other countries. If your college has no such official, you should see the dean of students. Bring your passport and immigration documents.

Your university will also assign a faculty member to advise you on your academic program. Other services available through the school may include psychological counseling and health-care services. Although some schools provide limited health care to students at no charge, you should keep in mind that, in the United States, medical care is the responsibility of the individual, not the government. You would be wise to obtain health insurance. Many colleges offer such plans (some *require* foreign students to have health insurance) and your foreign-student adviser can provide information on them.

Most colleges and universities offer campus orientation programs for all new students; some also hold special orientations for foreign students. The latter are generally held during the summer and may continue on after the academic year has begun. On- and off-campus tours and placement exams may be included.

English Language and Cultural Orientation Programs

Many American colleges and universities provide English language instruction often in conjunction with courses and activities that orient foreign students to the various phases of life in the United States. Full-time English language programs generally involve at least 15 hours of intensive instruction per week and usually include orientation activities. Single courses involve fewer hours and are generally taken to help students engaged in academic courses.

You should know that your ability to speak and write English will affect your admission to most American colleges and universities. If your ability falls below that required for admission, you may be accepted conditionally, with the understanding that you will participate in an intensive English course or program. Some schools require that all foreign students enroll in such a course or program.

For more information, you should refer to the booklet *Intensive English Program in the USA*, published by the Institute of International Education, 809 United Nations Plaza, 7th Floor, New York, New York 10017 and available in their overseas offices and many U.S. embassy libraries as well as their web site, *www.iiebooks.org*. This publication gives detailed information on the intensive English-language courses and programs at many of the institutions in this book.

Expenses

Most colleges will expect you to pay all fixed costs—tuition, room-and-board, if you live and eat in college facilities and student fees—in U.S dollars at the beginning of each academic term. Some colleges provide installment plans, under which these costs may be paid monthly over the course of the term.

Keep in mind when determining your probable expenses that personal expenses, including travel, entertainment, and textbooks may be considerable and generally are not listed as part of a college's tuition schedule. While some colleges will provide an estimate of a typical student's personal expenses, you should generally expect to spend considerably more.

International students generally are not permitted to hold jobs in the United States. Work permits are issued only when there is unexpected economic need. Part-time jobs on campus, however, are permitted and do not require government approval.

Financial aid may be available from your government, the U.S. government cultural exchange programs, corporations, the college you attend, or religious, fraternal, or special-interest groups. For information, contact a U.S. embassy or consulate and your government's ministry or department of education. If you are already in the United States, see your foreign-student adviser.

Pamela J. Sharpe, Ph.D.
Author, *Barron's How to Prepare for the TOEFL® iBT, 12th Edition*

INDEX

NOTES

NOTES

NOTES

NOTES

Profiles of American Colleges, 27ᵗʰ Edition
CD-ROM
You should read the following documentation before you begin to use the CD-ROM

Installation Instructions:
The CD-ROM includes an "autorun" feature that automatically launches the application when the CD-ROM is inserted into the CD-ROM drive. In the unlikely event that the autorun features are disabled, alternate launching instructions ar provided below.

Windows 98/NT/2000/ME/XP:
1. Put the Barron's **PAC27ᵗʰEdition** CD-ROM into the CD-ROM drive.
2. Click on the Start button and choose Run.
3. Type D:\ **PAC27ᵗʰEdition** (assuming the CD is in drive D), then click OK.

Macintosh:
1. Put the Barron's **PAC27ᵗʰEdition** CD-ROM into the CD-ROM drive.
2. Double-click the **PAC27ᵗʰEdition** Installer icon.
3. Follow the onscreen instruction.

The program will run optimally on a PC with

1. Intel Pentium® II 450MHZ or equivalent processor
2. 128 MB RAM
3. MS Windows 2000/ME/XP
4. SVGA (256 Colors) Monitor
5. 16X CD-ROM drive
6. Keyboard, Mouse

The program will run optimally on a Macintosh with

1. 500 MHz Power PC G3 or later
2. Operating System 9.0 (or higher)
3. 128 MB RAM
4. SVGA (256 Colors) Monitor
5. 16X CD-ROM drive
6. Keyboard, Mouse